Funk & Wagnalls

NEW INTERNATIONAL DICTIONARY

OF THE

ENGLISH LANGUAGE

Comprehensive Edition

PUBLISHERS INTERNATIONAL PRESS
NEWARK, NEW JERSEY

FUNK & WAGNALLS
NEW INTERNATIONAL DICTIONARY
OF THE ENGLISH LANGUAGE
Comprehensive Edition

Funk & Wagnalls New International Dictionary of the English Language
was previously published as
Funk & Wagnalls New Comprehensive International Dictionary of the English Language

Funk & Wagnalls New International Dictionary of the English Language
also published as
Webster Comprehensive Dictionary

Funk & Wagnalls New Comprehensive International Dictionary, Encyclopedic Edition,
includes the *Funk & Wagnalls Standard Dictionary, International Edition.*

Acknowledgement is made of the courtesy of Holt, Rinehart and Winston, Inc.,
New York, New York, for permission to reprint art and caption material from
Field & Stream Guide to Physical Fitness, with illustrations by Alex Orr.

ISBN: 0-89434-044-1

H-5

TABLE OF CONTENTS

pleu·ron (ploor′on) *n. pl.* **pleu·ra** (ploor′ə) **1** *Entomol.* The lateral wall of a thoracic segment in insects. **2** *Zool.* In crustaceans, the lateral process of an abdominal segment. [< NL <Gk., a rib]

pleu·ro·pneu·mo·ni·a (ploor′ō·noo·mō′nē·ə, -mōn′yə, -nyōō-), *n. Pathol.* Pleurisy combined with pneumonia.

pleu·rot·o·my (plōōr·ot′ə·mē) *n. Surg.* The operation of making an incision into the pleural cavity, for drawing off effused liquids.

pleus·ton (plōōs′tən) *n. Bot.* That type of vegetation which consists of large aquatic plants floating on the water. [<NL <Gk. *pleus-*, stem of *pleein* swim]

Plev·en (plev′ən) A city in northern Bulgaria; surrendered by the Turks after a siege, 1877. Also **Plev·na** (plev′nä).

plex·i·form (plek′sə·fôrm) *adj.* Having the form of a plexus; complicated.

Plex·i·glas (plek′si·glas, gläs) *n.* A thermoplastic acrylic resin used in the fabrication of transparent objects, as windows for airplane gun turrets, gages, etc.: a trade name.

plex·im·e·ter (plek·sim′ə·tər) *n.* A plate to be placed against the body to receive the blows in percussion. [<Gk. *plēxis* a stroke + -METER] **—plex·i·met·ric** (plek′si·met′rik) *adj.* **—plex·im′e·try** *n.*

plex·or (plek′sər) *n. Med.* An instrument used like a hammer in percussion of the chest: also called *plessor.* [<Gk. *plēssein* strike, on analogy with *flexor*]

plex·us (plek′səs) *n. pl.* **·us·es** or **·us** **1** A network or interlacement; a complication of structures, such as nerves. [<L, braid]

pli·a·ble (plī′ə·bəl) *adj.* **1** Easily bent or twisted; flexible. **2** Easily persuaded or controlled. See synonyms under DOCILE, SUPPLE. **—pli′a·bil′i·ty, pli′a·ble·ness** *n.* **—pli′a·bly** *adv.*

pli·an·cy (plī′ən·sē) *n.* The state or quality of being pliant; pliability: opposed to *rigidity.*

pli·ant (plī′ənt) *adj.* **1** Capable of being bent or twisted with ease; supple; lithe. **2** Easily yielding to influence; tractable. [<OF, ppr. of *plier.* See PLY.] **—pli′ant·ly** *adv.*

pil·ca (plī′kə) *n. pl.* **·cae** (-sē) **1** A fold of membrane, skin, or the like, as between the fingers. **2** *Zool.* A ridge, as on the outer wall of the body whorl in a shell, or on the wing covers of some beetles. **3** *Pathol.* A disease affecting the hair, causing it to become matted and agglutinated. [<Med. <L *plicare* fold]

pli·cate (plī′kāt) *adj.* Plaited; folded in plaits like a fan, as a leaf. Also **pli′cat·ed. —pli′cate·ness** *n.* **—pli′cate·ly** *adv.*

pli·ca·tion (plī·kā′shən) *n.* A folding, or that which is folded; a fold. Also **plic·a·ture** (plik′·ə·chōōr).

pli·er (plī′ər) *n.* **1** One who or that which plies. **2** *pl.* Small pincers for bending, holding, or cutting.

VARIOUS TYPES OF PLIERS
a. Round-nose.
b. Flat-nose, showing wire running through.
c. Flat-nose, with wire-cutting attachment.
d. Gas fitter's.

plight[1] (plīt) *n.* A condition, state, or case: usually distressed or complicated. [<OF *ploit,* var. of *pleit.* See PLAIT.]

plight[2] (plīt) *n.* A solemn engagement; betrothal; a pledge subject to forfeiture. *—v.t.* **1** To pledge (one's word, faith, etc.). **2** To promise, as in marriage; betroth: She is *plighted* to a judge. **—to plight one's troth 1** To pledge one's solemn word. **2** To promise oneself in marriage. [OE *pliht* peril] **—plight′er** *n.*

Plim·soll (plim′sol, -səl), **Samuel,** 1824–98, English statesman; secured Parliamentary reforms, 1876, against overloading of ships.

Plimsoll line A mark painted on the outside of a British vessel's hull to show how deeply she may be loaded; load line. Also called **Plimsoll mark.** [after Samuel *Plimsoll*]

plinth (plinth) *n. Archit.* **1** The slab, block, or stone on which a column, pedestal, or statue rests. **2** A thin course, as of slabs, usually projecting: also **plinth course.** [<L *plinthus* < Gk. *plinthos* a brick]

Plin·y (plin′ē) Anglicized name of two Roman authors; **Pliny the Elder,** 23–79, Gaius Plinius Secundus, naturalist, and his nephew, **Pliny the Younger,** 62–113, Galus Plinius Caecilius Secundus, statesman.

Pli·o·cene (plī′ə·sēn) *Geol. adj.* Of or pertaining to the latest epoch of the Tertiary period, following the Miocene and succeeded by the Pleistocene. *—n.* The Pliocene epoch or rock series. Also *Pleiocene.* [<Gk. *pleiōn* more + *kainos* new] **—Pli′o·cen′ic** (-sen′ik) *adj.*

Pli·o·film (plī′ə·film′) *n.* A flexible, transparent rubber sheeting, used for raincoats, umbrellas, etc.: a trade name.

plod (plod) *v.* **plod·ded, plod·ding** *v.t.* **1** To walk heavily or laboriously; trudge. **2** To work in a steady, laborious manner; drudge. *—v.t.* **3** To walk along heavily or laboriously. *—n.* **1** A tiring walk; tramp; act or duration of plodding. **2** The sound of a heavy step, as of a horse. [Imit.] **—plod′ding** *adj.* **—plod′ding·ly** *adv.*

plod·der (plod′ər) *n.* One who plods; a drudge; also, a slow but perserving person.

Plo·es·ti (plō·yesh′tē) A city of south central Rumania; chief center of the Rumanian petroleum industry. Also **Plo·esh′ti.**

–ploid *combining form Biol.* In cytology and genetics, having a (specified) number of chromosomes: *diploid.* Corresponding nouns end in **–ploidy.** [<Gk. *-ploos,* as in *diploos* twofold]

plonk (plonk) *n. Austral. Slang* Cheap wine.

plop (plop) *v.t. & v.i.* **plopped, plop·ping** To drop with a sound like that of a pebble striking the water without making a splash. *—n.* The act or sound of plopping. *—adv.* Suddenly with the sound of plop: They fell *plop* into the river. [Imit.]

plo·sion (plō′zhən) *n. Phonet.* The sudden release of breath after closure of the oral passage in the articulation of a stop consonant, as after the *p* in *pat:* also *explosion.* [<EXPLOSION]

plo·sive (plō′siv) *Phonet. adj.* Designating a speech sound produced by a total blockage of the breath stream followed by an explosive release, as (p) and (t) before vowels. *—n.* A consonant so produced; a stop. Also *explosive.*

plot (plot) *n.* **1** A piece or patch of ground set apart; also called *plat.* **2** A chart or diagram, as of a building, for showing certain data; also, a surveyor's map. **3** A secret plan to accomplish some questionable purpose; conspiracy. **4** The series of incidents forming the plan of action of a story, play, or poem. *—v.* **plot·ted, plot·ting** *v.t.* **1** To make a map, chart, or plan of, as a ship's course, a building, etc. **2** To plan for secretly: to *plot* an enemy's ruin. **3** To arrange the plot of (a novel, etc.) **4** *Math.* **a** To represent graphically the position of (a measured value) by a point located with reference to its coordinates on plotting paper. **b** To draw (a curve) through a series of such points. *—v.i.* **5** To form a plot; conspire. [OE]

Plo·ti·nus (plō·tī′nəs), 205?–270?, Roman philosopher born in Egypt.

plot·ter (plot′ər) *n.* **1** One who plots or contrives; a conspirator. **2** A maker of a plot or map. **3** A contrivance, as for plotting coordinates.

plotting paper Paper which has been ruled into small squares for plotting curves, and making diagrams.

plot·ty (plot′ē) *n. Scot.* A hot, spiced beverage.

plough (plou) See PLOW.

Plov·div (plôv′dēf) The second largest city of Bulgaria, in the south central part: ancient *Philippopolis.*

plov·er (pluv′ər, plō′vər) *n.* **1** A shore bird (family *Charadriidae*), especially of *Charadrius* or related genus, with long, pointed wings and a short tail, especially the **American golden plover** *(Pluvialis dominica).* **2** Any of certain related shore birds, as the ruddy turnstone and the **upland plover** *(Bartramia longicauda).* [<AF, ult. <L *pluvia* rain]

plow (plou) *n.* **1** An implement (usually drawn by horses, or oxen, or by mechanical power) for cutting, turning over, stirring, or breaking up the soil. **2** Any implement that operates like a plow: often in combination: a *snowplow;* also, any one of various furrowing or grooving tools. **3** Figuratively, agriculture. *—v.t.* **1** To turn up the surface of (land) with a plow. **2** To make or form (a furrow, ridge, etc.) by means of a plow. **3** To furrow or score the surface of: Shot *plowed* the field. **4** To dig out or remove with a plow: with *up* or *out.* **5** To move out or cut through (water): to *plow* the waves. **6** To pluck (def. 7). *—v.i.* **7** To turn up soil with a plow. **8** To undergo plowing in a specified way, as land. **9** To move or proceed as a plow does: usually with *through* or *into.* **10** To advance laboriously; plod. **—to plow under** *U.S.* To put from sight by or as by plowing in such a way as to cover with soil; obliterate. Also spelled *plough.* [OE *ploh*] **—plow′a·ble** *adj.* **—plow′er** *n.*

Plow The group of seven stars commonly called *Charles's Wain* or *the Dipper,* sometimes also *Ursa Major.* Also **Plough.**

plow beam The horizontal projecting part of a plow frame, whose front end is attached to the swingletree. See illustration under SWINGLETREE.

plow·boy (plou′boi′) *n.* A boy who drives or guides a team in plowing; hence, a young rustic. Also **plough′boy′.**

plow·man (plou′mən) *n. pl.* **·men** (-mən) One who plows; a cultivator; hence, a rustic. Also **plough′man.**

plow·share (plou′shâr′) *n.* The blade of a plow. Also **plough′share′.**

plow·staff (plou′staf′, -stäf′) *n.* The handle of a plow. Also **plough′staff′.**

ploy[1] (ploi) *v.i. Mil.* To diminish front; maneuver from line into column: opposite of *deploy.* [<DEPLOY] **—poly′ment** *n.*

ploy[2] (ploi) *n. Scot.* Sport; merrymaking.

pluck (pluk) *v.t.* **1** To pull out or off; pick: to *pluck* a flower. **2** To pull with force; snatch or drag: with *off, away,* etc. **3** To pull out the feathers, hair, etc., of: to *pluck* a chicken. **4** To give a twitch or pull to, as a sleeve. **5** To cause the strings of (a musical instrument) to sound by such action. **6** To rob; swindle. **7** *Brit. Slang* To reject (a candidate) for failure to pass an examination. *—v.i.* **8** To give a sudden pull; tug: with *at.* **—to pluck up** To rouse or summon (one's courage). *—n.* **1** Confidence and spirit in the face of difficulty or danger; courage. **2** The heart, liver, windpipe, and lungs of an animal. **3** A sudden pull; twitch. **4** The act of plucking or state of being plucked; also, the person plucked. See synonyms under COURAGE. [OE *pluccian*] **—pluck′er** *n.*

pluck·y (pluk′ē) *adj.* **pluck·i·er, pluck·i·est** Brave and spirited; courageous. **—pluck′i·ly** *adv.* **—pluck′i·ness** *n.*

plug (plug) *n.* **1** Anything, as a piece of wood or a cork, used to stop a hole; a wedge or peg driven into anything. **2** A spark plug. **3** *Electr.* A device containing conducting material, as projecting prongs, for inserting in an outlet, etc., so as to complete a circuit or make contact. **4** A flat cake of pressed or twisted tobacco. **5** Any worn-out or useless thing, particularly a horse past its prime: often with *old.* **6** *U.S. Slang* A man's high silk hat; also **plug hat.** **7** *Slang* Mention of a product, song, etc., as on a radio or television program, to give it publicity; an advertisement. **8** *Geol.* The hard core of igneous rock which fills the neck of a volcano. **9** The discharge outlet from a water main: also called *hydrant.* **10** *Mech.* The cylindrical part of a cylinder lock which contains the keyhole and is turned by the key. **11** In angling, a type of lure, usually cylindrical and with several hooks attached, similar to a spoon. *—v.* **plugged, plug·ging** *v.t.* **1** To stop or close, as a hole, by inserting a plug: often with *up.* **2** To insert as a plug. **3** *Slang* To shoot a bullet into. **4** *U.S. Slang* To advertise frequently or insistently; publicize. *—v.i.* **5** *Colloq.* To work doggedly; persevere. **—to plug in** To insert the plug of (a lamp, etc.) in an electrical outlet. [<MDu. *plugge*] **—plug′ger** *n.*

plug-ug·ly (plug′ug′lē) *n. pl.* **·lies** *U.S. Slang* A city ruffian; gangster; a street rowdy.

plum (plum) *n.* **1** The edible drupaceous fruit of any one of various trees of the genus *Prunus,* especially *P. domestica,* the **European** or **garden plum. 2** The tree. **3** The plumlike fruit of any one of various other trees having an edible drupe; also, the tree bearing such fruit. **4** A raisin, especially as used in cooking: *plum* pudding. **5** The best part of anything; a choice piece or portion; a desirable post or appointment. **6** *Brit. Slang* A sum of £100,000 sterling; a handsome fortune, or the possessor of it. **7** Any of various shades of dull reddish purple or purplish red. **8** A sugarplum; anything resembling a plum, as in shape or flavor. ◆ Homophone: *plumb.* [OE *plume* <LL *pruna.* Doublet of PRUNE[1].]

plum·age (plōō′mij) *n.* **1** The feathers that cover a bird, collectively. **2** Gaudy costume; adornment. [<F < *plume* plume]

plu·mate (plōō′māt) *adj.* Resembling plumage or feathers. [<L *plumatus* feathered]

plumb (plum) *n.* **1** A lead weight on the end of a line used by masons, carpenters, etc., to find the exact perpendicular; a plumb bob; a plummet. **2** A plummet or nautical sounding lead; a sinker on a fishing line, etc. **— off** (or **out of**) **plumb** Not exactly vertical; not in alinement. *— adj.* **1** True, accurate, and upright; vertical or perpendicular; hence, figuratively, upright in principle. **2** *Colloq.* Sheer; complete: also **plum.** *— adv.* **1** In a line perpendicular to the plane of the horizon; vertically. **2** *Colloq.* With exactness; correctly; exactly; completely; entirely: also **plum.** *— v.t.* **1** To test the perpendicularity of with a plumb. **2** To make vertical; straighten: usually with *up.* **3** To test the depth of; sound. **4** To reach the lowest level or extent of; fathom: to *plumb* the depths of despair. **5** To seal with lead. ◆ Homophone: *plum.* [<F *plomb* <L *plumbum* lead]

plumb- Var. of PLUMBO-.

plum·ba·go (plum·bā′gō) *n. pl.* **·gos 1** Graphite: used for pencils, crucibles, lubricating, and in electroplating to coat non-conducting surfaces, as gutta-percha. **2** A drawing made with a lead-pointed instrument. **3** Any of a genus *(Plumbago)* of hardy, shrubby plants cultivated for their showy blue, white, or purplish flowers: also called *leadwort.* [<L *plumbum* lead] **— plum·bag′i·nous** (-baj′ə·nəs) *adj.*

plumb bob The weight used at the end of a plumb line.

plum·be·ous (plum′bē·əs) *adj.* **1** Resembling lead; heavy. **2** Lead-colored. [<L *plumbeus* < *plumbum* lead]

plumbeous vireo A blue-headed vireo *(Vireo solitarius plumbeus),* of northern Nevada to Mexico.

plumb·er (plum′ər) *n.* One who makes a business of plumbing.

plumb·er's friend (plum′ərz) A plunger (def. 3).

plumb·er·y (plum′ər·ē) *n. pl.* **·er·ies 1** The business of plumbing. **2** A plumber's place of business. **3** Leadwork.

PLUMB BOB
a. Plumb line.
b. Bob.
c. Wall.

plum·bic (plum′bik) *adj. Chem.* Of or pertaining to lead, especially in its higher valence.

plum·bif·er·ous (plum·bif′ər·əs) *adj.* Containing or yielding lead.

plumb·ing (plum′ing) *n.* **1** The art or trade of putting into buildings the tanks, pipes, etc., for water, gas, and sewage. **2** The pipe system of a building. **3** The act of sounding for depth, etc., with a plumb line.

plum·bism (plum′biz·əm) *n. Pathol.* Chronic lead poisoning.

plumb line 1 A cord by which a weight is suspended to test the perpendicularity or depth of something. **2** A plumb bob and its cord together. **3** A sounding line.

plumbo- *combining form* Lead; of or containing lead. Also, before vowels, *plumb-,* as in *plumbiferous.* [<L *plumbum* lead]

plum·bous (plum′bəs) *adj. Chem.* Of, pertaining to, or containing lead, especially in its lower valence.

plumb rule A narrow rule furnished with a plumb line or a cross level, with which masons and carpenters test the verticality of their work.

plum·bum (plum′bəm) *n.* Lead: so called in pharmacy and old chemistry. [<L]

plum duff A suet and flour pudding with raisins, currants, etc., boiled in a cloth bag.

plume (plōōm) *n.* **1** A feather, especially when long and ornamental. **2** A large feather or tuft of feathers worn as an ornament, especially on a helmet; a panache. **3** *Her.* Three feathers, unless more are specified. **4** A featherlike form or part; the plumose appendage of a seed. **5** Plumage. **6** A decoration of honor; a prize. *— v.t.* **plumed, plum·ing 1** To adorn, dress, or furnish with or as with plumes. **2** To smooth or dress (itself or its feathers); preen. **3** To congratulate or pride (oneself): with *on* or *upon.* [<F <L *pluma* small soft feather]

PLUME *(def. 3)* Prince of Wales.

plumed partridge The mountain quail *(Oreortyx picta)* of the western United States.

plume·let (plōōm′lit) *n.* **1** A plumule. **2** A little plume.

plu·mi·ped (plōō′mə·ped) *adj.* Having feathered feet. *— n.* A plumiped bird, as an owl. Also **plu′mi·pede** (-pēd). [<L *pluma* feather + -PED]

plum·met (plum′it) *n.* **1** A piece of lead or heavy substance, attachable to a line for making soundings, adjusting walls to the vertical, etc.; a plumb bob; hence, a standard of truth or rectitude. **2** A plumb rule. **3** A weight; especially an oppressive weight. *— v.i.* To drop straight down; plunge. [<OF *plommet,* dim. of *plom* lead]

plum·my (plum′ē) *adj.* **·mi·er, ·mi·est 1** Full of plums. **2** *Colloq.* Full of desirable things; profitable.

plu·mose (plōō′mōs) *adj.* **1** Bearing feathers or plumes. **2** Having fine processes on opposite sides, like the vane of a feather. **3** Resembling plumes. [<L *plumosus* < *pluma* feather] **— plu′mose·ly** *adv.* **— plu·mos·i·ty** (plōō·mos′ə·tē) *n.*

plump[1] (plump) *adj.* Swelled out or enlarged to the full; somewhat fat. See synonyms under ROUND[1]. *— v.t. & v.i.* To make or become plump: often with *up* or *out. — n. Archaic* A closely united group; a cluster or clump. [<MDu. *plomp*] **— plump′ly** *adv.* **— plump′·ness** *n.*

plump[2] (plump) *v.i.* **1** To fall suddenly or heavily; drop with full impact. **2** To give one's complete support: with *for. — v.t.* **3** To drop or throw down heavily or all at once. **4** To utter bluntly or abruptly: often with *out. — n.* The act of plumping or falling; the sound made by the impact of a falling object. *— adj.* Containing no reservation or qualification; blunt; downright. *— adv.* **1** With a sudden impact or fall into or as into water; in a sudden or forcible manner; also, unexpectedly. **2** Directly; without hesitation, circumlocution, or qualification; bluntly. [< MDu. *plompen*] **— plump′ly** *adv.*

plump·er[1] (plum′pər) *n.* **1** A heavy fall or drop. **2** Votes cast all for one candidate instead of for several; also, a person so voting. **3** *Brit. Slang* An unqualified lie.

plump·er[2] (plum′pər) *n.* A disk or padding placed in the mouth, as by persons who have lost their teeth, to distend the cheek and give it an appearance of plumpness.

plum pudding A boiled pudding made with flour, raisins, suet, currants, spices, etc.

plu·mule (plōō′myōōl) *n.* **1** *Ornithol.* A feather having the barbs soft and free; a downy feather. **2** *Bot.* The rudimentary or first bud of a plant embryo; the first bud of a germinating plant above the cotyledons. [<L *plumula,* dim. of *pluma* feather]

plum·y (plōō′mē) *adj.* **plum·i·er, plum·i·est 1** Covered with feathers. **2** Adorned with plumes.

plun·der (plun′dər) *v.t.* **1** To rob of goods or property by open violence, as in war; pillage; loot. **2** To despoil by robbery or fraud. **3** To take as plunder. *— v.i.* **4** To take plunder; steal. See synonyms under STEAL. *— n.* **1** That which is taken by plundering; booty. **2** The act of plundering or robbing. **3** *U.S. Colloq.* Personal belongings or goods, etc. **4** Political booty. [<G *plündern*] **— plun′der·er** *n.*

Synonyms (noun): booty, pillage, prey, rapine, robbery, spoil.

plun·der·age (plun′dər·ij) *n.* Pillage.

plunge (plunj) *v.* **plunged, plung·ing** *v.t.* **1** To thrust or force suddenly into a fluid, penetrable substance, hole, etc. **2** To force into some condition or state: to *plunge* a nation into debt. *— v.i.* **3** To dive, jump, or fall into a fluid, chasm, etc. **4** To move suddenly or with a rush: to *plunge* through a door. **5** To move violently forward and downward, as a horse or ship. **6** To descend abruptly or steeply, as a road or cliff. **7** *Colloq.* To gamble or speculate heavily and recklessly. See synonyms under IMMERSE. *— n.* **1** The act of plunging; a leap; dive. **2** A sudden and violent motion, as of a breaking wave. **3** A place, tank, or pool for diving or swimming. **4** An extravagant or reckless bet or speculation. [<OF *plunjer,* ult. <L *plumbum* lead]

plung·er (plun′jər) *n.* **1** One who or that which plunges; a heavy or reckless speculator. **2** *Mech.* Any appliance having or adapted for a plunging motion, as the piston of a pump. **3** A cuplike device made of rubber and attached to a stick, used to clean out clogged drains, etc.: also called *plumber's friend.*

plunk (plungk) *Colloq. v.t.* **1** To pluck, as a banjo or its strings; strum. **2** To place or throw heavily and suddenly: with *down. — v.i.* **3** To emit a twanging sound. **4** To fall heavily or suddenly; plump. *— n.* **1** A heavy blow, or its sound. **2** *Slang* A dollar. [Imit.]

plu·per·fect (plōō·pûr′fikt) See PAST PERFECT.

plu·ral (plŏŏr′əl) *adj.* **1** Containing, consisting of or designating more than one. **2** *Gram.* Denoting more than one (in languages that have dual number, such as Sanskrit and Greek, more than two): opposed to *singular. — n. Gram.* The plural number, or a word in this number. [<L *pluralis* < *plus* more] **— plu′·ral·ly** *adv.*

◆ English nouns regularly form their plurals by adding *s* or *es* to the singular; most nouns ending in *f* change the *f* to *v* and add *es*; as wol*f,* wol*ves*; hal*f,* hal*ves.* Nouns ending in *y* change it to *ies* if it is preceded by a consonant: bod*y,* bod*ies*; or merely add an *s* if it is preceded by a vowel; as donke*y,* donke*ys.* Some nouns of Old English origin have an irregular plural in *en,* as, child, childr*en*; or by a vowel change; as, mouse, *mice*; goose, *geese*; man, *men*; tooth, *teeth.* A few nouns retain the singular form unchanged in the plural; as, *deer, hose, moose, series, sheep, species, vermin.* Some such nouns, especially the names of animals, have also an alternative plural regularly formed: as, fish, *fish* or *fishes. Fish* is the usual collective plural; *fishes* is used to indicate more than one genus, variety, species, etc. Many words of foreign derivation retain the plural form peculiar to the languages from which they are severally derived; as, addendum, *addenda*; antithesis, *antitheses*; crisis, *crises*; datum, *data,* etc. Many nouns of this class have also a plural of the regular English form; as, appendix, *appendixes* or *appendices*; beau, *beaus* or *beaux*; cherub, *cherubs* or *cherubim*; focus, *focuses* or *foci*; index, *indexes* or *indices,* etc. Compounds commonly form the plural regularly by adding *s* or *es* to the complete word; as, armful, *armfuls*; cut-throat, *cut-throats*; football, *footballs*; teaspoonful, *teaspoonfuls.* If the last element of the compound forms its plural irregularly, the same form usually appears in the plural of the compound; as, footman, *footmen.* Nouns that end in *-man,* but are not compounds, form the plural regularly by adding *s,* as Mussulman, *Mussulmans.* Hyphenated compounds in which the principal word forms the first element change that element to form the plural; as, father-in-law, *fathers-in-law.*

plu·ral·ism (plŏŏr′əl·iz′əm) *n.* **1** The condition of being plural. **2** *Eccl.* The holding of more than one office, or, in the Anglican church, of more than one ecclesiastical living, at one time. **3** *Philos.* The doctrine that there is a plurality of ultimate substances, as spirit and matter: opposed to *monism.* **4** The existence within a society of diverse groups, as in religion, race, or ethnic origin, which contribute to the cultural matrix of the society while retaining their distinctive characters; also, a doctrine advocating this. **— plu′ral·is′tic** *adj.*

plu·ral·ist (plŏŏr′əl·ist) *n.* **1** One who holds more than one ecclesiastical benefice at the same time. **2** Anyone who holds a plurality of offices. 3 One who believes in or advocates pluralism.

plu·ral·i·ty (ploo͞·ral′ə·tē) *n. pl.* **·ties** 1 The state of being plural. 2 The larger portion or greater number; majority. 3 In U.S. politics, the greatest of more than two numbers, whether it is or is not a majority of the whole; also, the excess of the highest number of votes cast for any one candidate over the next highest number. 4 *Eccl.* Pluralism; also, one of the livings held by a pluralist. 5 Polygamy.

plu·ral·ize (plo͝or′əl·īz) *v.t.* **·ized, ·iz·ing** 1 To make plural. 2 To express in the plural.

pluri– *combining form* More; many; several: *pluriaxial.* [<L *plus, pluris* more]

plu·ri·ax·i·al (plo͝or′ē·ak′sē·əl) *adj.* 1 Having more than one axis. 2 *Bot.* Denoting plants whose flowers grow on secondary shoots.

plus (plus) *prep.* 1 Added to or to be added to: Three *plus* two equals five: opposed to *minus.* 2 Increased by: salary *plus* commission. — *adj.* 1 Being or indicating more than nothing; above zero; positive. 2 Electrified positively. 3 *Colloq.* Possessing (something) in addition: used predicatively: He was *plus* a new hat. 4 Extra; supplemental: *plus* value. 5 *Colloq.* Denoting a value higher than ordinary in a specified grade: B *plus.* 6 *Bot.* Designating a form of sexual differentiation in certain plants: the *plus* strain of heterothallic fungi. — *n. pl.* **plus·es** 1 The plus sign. 2 An addition; an extra quantity. 3 A positive quantity. 4 *Colloq.* Something considered advantageous or desirable: a definite *plus* for the business. — *adv. Electr.* Positively. [<L, more]

plus–fours (plus′fôrz′, -fōrz′) *n.* Knickerbockers, cut very full and bagging below the knees. [Orig. tailor's cant; because they were four inches longer than ordinary knickerbockers]

plush (plush) *n.* A pile fabric of silk, rayon, or mohair having a deeper pile than velvet. — *adj.* 1 Of or made of plush. 2 *Slang* Luxurious. [<F *pluche, peluche* <L *pilus* hair] — **plush′y** *adj.*

plus sign The symbol (+) signifying addition or a positive quantity: opposed to *minus sign.*

Plu·tarch (ploo͞′tärk), A.D. 46?–120?, Greek moralist and biographer.

plu·tar·chy (ploo͞′tär·kē) *n. pl.* **·chies** Government by the rich. [<Gk. *ploutos* wealth + *archein* rule]

Plu·to (ploo͞′tō) 1 In Greek and Roman mythology, the god of the dead: identified with the Greek *Hades* and the Roman *Dis.* 2 *Astron.* The ninth planet of the solar system in order of distance from the sun, invisible to the naked eye: discovered 1930. See PLANET. [<L <Gk. *Ploutōn*]

plu·toc·ra·cy (ploo͞·tok′rə·sē) *n. pl.* **·cies** 1 A class in a community that controls the government by its wealth; the wealthy classes. 2 Plutarchy. [<Gk. *ploutokratia* <*ploutos* wealth + *kratein* rule]

plu·to·crat (ploo͞′tə·krat) *n.* One who has or exercises power by virtue of his wealth; one of a plutocracy. — **plu′to·crat′ic** or **·i·cal** *adj.* — **plu′to·crat′i·cal·ly** *adv.*

plu·to·ma·ni·a (ploo͞′tə·mā′nē·ə, -mān′yə) *n.* An excessive desire for great wealth. [<Gk. *ploutos* wealth + -MANIA]

Plu·to·ni·an (ploo͞·tō′nē·ən) *adj.* 1 Pertaining to Pluto and the lower world; hence, subterranean. 2 *Geol.* Of or pertaining to the Plutonic theory of rock formation. Also **Plu·ton′ic** (-ton′ik). [<L *Plutonius* <Gk. *Ploutonios* like Pluto]

plu·ton·ic (ploo͞·ton′ik) *adj. Geol.* Deeply subterranean in original position; crystallized, probably from a fused condition: said of igneous rocks: distinguished from *volcanic.* [<L *Pluto, -onis*]

Plutonic theory *Geol.* The doctrine that the principal phenomena of rock structure are chiefly due to igneous agency: distinguished from *Neptunian theory.*

plu·to·ni·um (ploo͞·tō′nē·əm) *n.* A radioactive element (symbol Pu), of atomic number 94, occurring in several isotopes, of which Pu–239, formed as a decay product of neptunium, was produced by fission during research on the atomic bomb: an important source of atomic energy. [<NL <*Pluto* (the planet)]

Plu·tus (ploo͞′təs) In Greek mythology, the god of riches, blinded by Zeus so that his gifts should be distributed without discrimination.

plu·vi·al (ploo͞′vē·əl) *adj.* 1 Pertaining to rain; rainy. 2 Arising from the action of rain. [<L *pluvialis* <*pluvia* rain]

pluvio– *combining form* Rain; pertaining to rain: *pluviometer.* Also, before vowels, **pluvi–.** [<L *pluvia* rain]

plu·vi·om·e·ter (ploo͞′vē·om′ə·tər) *n.* An instrument for measuring the depth of rainfall. [<PLUVIO- + -METER] — **plu′vi·o·met′ric** (-ə·met′rik) or **·ri·cal** *adj.* — **plu′vi·o·met′ri·cal·ly** *adv.* — **plu′vi·om′e·try** *n.*

Plu·vi·ôse (ploo͞′vē·ōs, *Fr.* plü·vyôs′) See under CALENDAR (Republican).

plu·vi·ous (ploo͞′vē·əs) *adj.* Pertaining to rain; rainy. Also **plu′vi·ose** (-ōs). [<L *pluviosus*]

ply[1] (plī) *v.* **plied, ply·ing** *v.t.* To bend; mold; shape. — *v.i. Obs.* To bend or yield. — *n. pl.* **plies** 1 A web, layer, fold, or thickness, as in a carpet, cloth, etc. 2 A strand, turn, or twist of rope, yarn, thread, etc.: used in combination to mean (a certain) number of folds, twists, or strands: three-*ply* yarn. 3 A bent or bias; inclination to one side, as of the mind. [<F *plier* <L *plicare*]

ply[2] (plī) *v.* **plied, ply·ing** *v.t.* 1 To use in working, fighting, etc.; wield; employ. 2 To work at; be engaged in: He *plies* the trade of shoemaker. 3 To subject to repeated action, as by offering unwanted gifts, asking questions insistently, etc.: to *ply* a person with drink; to *ply* one with requests. 4 To strike or assail persistently: He *plied* the donkey with a whip. 5 To traverse regularly: ferryboats that *ply* the river. — *v.i.* 6 To make regular trips; sail: usually with *between.* 7 To work steadily; do one's or its work. 8 *Poetic* To proceed; steer. 9 *Naut.* To beat; tack. [Aphetic var. of APPLY]

ply·er (plī′ər) *n.* 1 A plier. 2 *pl.* A balance of crossed timbers used in raising and lowering a drawbridge.

Plym·outh (plim′əth) 1 A city of eastern Massachusetts; first settlement (*Plymouth Colony*) in New England; site of Plymouth Rock. 2 A port on **Plymouth Sound,** an inlet of the English Channel between Cornwall and Devon in SW England.

Plymouth Colony The colony on the shore of Massachusetts Bay founded by the Pilgrim Fathers who sailed from Plymouth, England, in 1620.

Plymouth Rock 1 The rock at Plymouth, Massachusetts, on which the Pilgrim Fathers are said to have stepped when landing from the *Mayflower* in 1620. 2 One of a breed of domestic fowls of large size, with small single comb and buff, white, black, or gray barred plumage.

ply·wood (plī′wo͝od′) *n.* Laminated wood consisting of an odd number of sheets or plies tightly glued together, the grains of adjoining layers usually being at right angles to each other: widely used as a structural and building material.

Pl·zeň (pul′zen′y′) The Czech name for PILSEN.

pne·o·ste·no·sis (nē′ō·stə·nō′sis) *n. Pathol.* A condition marked by any obstruction of air entering or leaving the respiratory tract. [< Gk. *pneein* breathe + STENOSIS]

pneu·ma (noo͞′mə, nyoo͞′-) *n.* The breath of life; the soul or spirit. [<Gk.]

pneu·mat·ic (noo͞·mat′ik, nyoo͞-) *adj.* 1 Pertaining to the science of pneumatics. 2 Describing machines or devices that make use of compressed air: a *pneumatic* engine. 3 Pertaining to or containing air or gas, especially compressed air: a *pneumatic* tire. Also **pneu·mat′i·cal.** — *n.* A pneumatic tire. [<L *pneumaticus* <Gk. *pneumatikos* <*pneuma* breath <*pneein* breathe] — **pneu·mat′i·cal·ly** *adv.*

pneu·ma·tics (noo͞·mat′iks, nyoo͞-) *n.* The branch of physics that treats of the mechanical properties of air and other gases, such as their pressure, elasticity, and density, and also of pneumatic mechanisms.

pneumato– *combining form* 1 Air: *pneumatophore.* 2 Breath; breathing: *pneumatometer.* 3 Spirit; spirits: *pneumatology.* Also, before vowels, **pneumat–.** [<Gk. *pneuma, pneumatos* air, spirit, breath]

pneu·ma·tog·ra·phy (noo͞′mə·tog′rə·fē, nyoo͞′-) *n.* Spirit writing. [<PNEUMATO- + -GRAPHY]

pneu·ma·tol·o·gy (noo͞′mə·tol′ə·jē, nyoo͞′-) *n.* 1 The doctrine of the nature and operation of spirit, or a treatise on that science; the science of spiritual beings or existence. 2 The science of the beliefs of men touching a world of spirits. 3 The science dealing with the physiology of air or gases. 4 *Obs.* Pneumatics. — **pneu′ma·to·log′ic** (-tə·loj′ik) or **·i·cal** *adj.* — **pneu′ma·tol′o·gist** *n.*

pneu·ma·tol·y·sis (noo͞′mə·tol′ə·sis, nyoo͞′-) *n. Geol.* The process of forming minerals during the later stages in the consolidation of molten rock–magmas under the influence of the gases which are then present.

pneu·ma·to·lyt·ic (noo͞′mə·tō·lit′ik, nyoo͞′-) *adj.* Of, pertaining to, formed by, or characteristic of pneumatolysis.

pneu·ma·tom·e·ter (noo͞′mə·tom′ə·tər, nyoo͞′-) *n.* An instrument for measuring the volume of air exhaled or inhaled at one breath; a spirometer. — **pneu′ma·tom′e·try** *n.*

pneu·ma·to·phore (noo͞′mə·tə·fôr′, -fōr′, nyoo͞′-) *n.* 1 *Zool.* The air-containing sac of a siphonophore. 2 *Bot.* A root structure found on certain tropical swamp trees: it contains lenticels and is supposed to act as a respiratory organ. — **pneu′ma·toph′o·rous** (-tof′ər·əs) *adj.*

pneu·ma·to·ther·a·py (noo͞′mə·tō·ther′ə·pē, nyoo͞′-) *n. Med.* The treatment of disease by rarefied or condensed air; also, the use of gases for the relief of pain, asphyxiation, etc.

pneu·mec·to·my (noo͞·mek′tə·mē, nyoo͞-) *n. Surg.* The operation of removing lung tissue or a part of the lung. [<PNEUM(O)- + -ECTOMY]

pneumo– *combining form* Lung; related to the lungs; respiratory: *pneumobacillus*: also *pneumono–.* Also, before vowels, **pneum–.** [<Gk. *pneumon, pneumonos* a lung]

pneu·mo·ba·cil·lus (noo͞′mō·bə·sil′əs, nyoo͞′-) *n. pl.* **·cil·li** (-sil′ī) A bacillus (*Klebsiella pneumoniae*) found in infections of the respiratory tract.

pneu·mo·coc·cus (noo͞′mə·kok′əs, nyoo͞′-) *n. pl.* **·coc·ci** (-kok′sī) Any of a group of bacteria (genus *Diplococcus*) which inhabit the respiratory tract of man and animals, especially *D. pneumoniae,* the causative agent of lobar pneumonia. — **pneu′mo·coc′cal, pneu′mo·coc′cous, pneu′mo·coc′cic** (-kok′sik) *adj.*

pneu·mo·con·i·o·sis (noo͞′mō·kon′ē·ō′sis, nyoo͞′-) *n. Pathol.* Any of various lung disorders resulting from the inhalation of dust or other minute particles. Also **pneu′mo·no·con′i·o′sis** (noo͞′mə·nō-, nyoo͞′-). [<PNEUMO- + Gk. *konia* dust + -OSIS]

pneu·mo·dy·nam·ics (noo͞′mō·dī·nam′iks, nyoo͞′-) *n.* The dynamics of gases; pneumatics.

pneu·mo·ec·ta·sis (noo͞′mō·ek′tə·sis, nyoo͞′-) *n. Pathol.* Emphysema of the lungs. [<PNEUMO- + Gk. *ektasis* extension, swelling <*ekteinein* stretch out <*ek-* out + *teinein* stretch]

pneu·mo·e·de·ma (noo͞′mō·i·dē′mə, nyoo͞′-) *n. Pathol.* An abnormal accumulation of fluid in the intercellular cavities of the lungs. [<PNEUMO- + EDEMA]

pneu·mo·gas·tric (noo͞′mō·gas′trik, nyoo͞′-) *adj.* 1 Of or pertaining to the lungs and the stomach. 2 Of or pertaining to the vagus. — *n.* The vagus.

pneu·mo·graph (noo͞′mə·graf, -gräf, nyoo͞′-) *n.* An instrument which records movements of the chest in breathing.

pneu·mo·nec·to·my (noo͞′mə·nek′tə·mē, nyoo͞′-) *n. Surg.* The total removal of a lung. [<PNEUMON(O)- + -ECTOMY]

pneu·mon·ia (noo͞·mōn′yə, nyoo͞-) *n. Pathol.* An infectious disease characterized by inflammation of the lung tissue. The two principal types are *bronchopneumonia,* involving the bronchi and parenchyma of the lungs; and *lobar* or *croupous pneumonia,* affecting one or more lobes of the lungs. [<NL <Gk. *pneumonia* <*pneumōn* lung <*pneein* breathe]

pneu·mon·ic (noo͞·mon′ik, nyoo͞-) *adj.* 1 Affected with pneumonia; pertaining to pneumonia. 2 Pulmonary. [<NL *pneumonicus* <Gk. *pneumonikos*]

pneumono– *combining form* Pneumo–.

pneu·mo·tho·rax (noo͞′mō·thôr′aks, -thō′raks,

nyōō′-) *n.* An accumulation of air or gas within the pleural cavity: sometimes artificially induced to collapse the lung in tuberculosis.

Pnom-Penh (nom′pen′, pnōōm-pen′y′) A city on the Mekong, capital of Cambodia; also *Phnompenh.* Also **Pnom Penh.**

Pnyx (niks) The place in ancient Athens where the people met to deliberate and vote upon public affairs.

Po (pō) The largest river in Italy, flowing 405 miles from the Alps to the Adriatic: ancient *Padus.*

po·a·ceous (pō·ā′shəs) *adj. Bot.* Of or pertaining to a large, widely distributed family *(Poaceae)* of annual or perennial herbs, the grasses. The inflorescence is spicate, racemose, or paniculate, with very small flowers, generally perfect or staminate. The fruit is a seedlike grain *(caryopsis),* having a starchy endosperm. The grasses producing food grains are known as cereals. Formerly called *Gramineae* or *Graminaceae.* [<Gk. *poa* grass + -ACEOUS]

poach[1] (pōch) *v.t.* To cook (eggs without their shells, fish, etc.) in boiling water, milk, or other liquid until coated. [<OF *pochier* put in a pocket < *poche* pocket; from the "pocketed" position of the egg yolk]

poach[2] (pōch) *v.i.* **1** To trespass on another's property, etc., especially for the purpose of taking game or fish. **2** To take game or fish unlawfully. **3** To become soft and muddy by being trampled: said of land. **4** To sink into mud or soft earth while walking. — *v.t.* **5** To trespass on, as for taking game or fish. **6** To take (game or fish) unlawfully. **7** To make muddy or tear up (land, etc.) by trampling. **8** To reduce to a uniform consistency by mixing with water, as clay. [<OF *pochier* thrust one's fingers into <LG *poken* poke] — **poach′er** *n.*

poach·y (pō′chē) *adj.* Easily trodden into holes by cattle; soft and miry. [<POACH[2] (def. 3)] — **poach′i·ness** *n.*

Po·ca·hon·tas (pō′kə·hon′təs), 1595?–1617, American Indian princess; daughter of Powhatan, a Virginian chief; she reputedly saved the life of Captain John Smith.

po·chard (pō′chərd, -kərd) *n.* A sea duck (genus *Aythya*) having the head and neck reddish, found in America, Europe, and South Africa. *A. ferina* is the **common pochard** of the Old World; *A. americana,* the **American pochard** or redhead. [Origin uncertain]

pock[1] (pok) *n.* **1** A pustule in an eruptive disease, as in smallpox; a pockmark. **2** *Obs.* Smallpox. [OE *poc*]

pock[2] (pok) *n. Scot.* A bag; pouch: also spelled *poke.*

pock·et (pok′it) *n.* **1** A small bag or pouch; especially, a pouch attached to a garment, as for carrying money. **2** Hence, money; pecuniary means or interests. **3** A cavity, opening, or receptacle. **4** *Mining* A cavity containing gold or other ore; also, an accumulation of alluvial gold in one spot. **5** One of the pouches in a billiard or pool table, into which the balls are driven. **6** A bin for holding grain, coal, etc., for storage. **7** A glen among mountains. **8** In horse-racing, a position in which a horse is behind the leading horse or horses, and is kept from going past by others at the side. **9** An air pocket. — **in one's pocket 1** On terms of intimacy as close to one as one's pocket. **2** Under one's influence or control. — *adj.* **1** Diminutive, as if pocketable. **2** Pertaining to, for, or carried in a pocket: *pocket* lining, *pocket* knife. — *v.t.* **1** To put into or confine in a pocket. **2** To appropriate as one's own, especially dishonestly, as profits or funds. **3** To enclose as if in a pocket. **4** To accept or endure without open resentment or reply, as an insult. **5** To conceal or suppress: *Pocket* your pride. **6** To retain without signing. See POCKET VETO. **7** In billiards, etc., to drive (a ball) into a pocket. [<AF *pokette, poquette,* dim. of OF *poque, poche* bag, pouch] — **pock′et·a·ble** *adj.* — **pock′et·er** *n.*

pock·et·book (pok′it·bŏŏk′) *n.* **1** A small book or case for carrying money and papers in the pocket; wallet. **2** A woman's purse or handbag. **3** A notebook or other book for the pocket. **4** Money or pecuniary resources.

pocket borough In England before the Reform Bill of 1832, a Parliamentary borough owned or controlled by a single individual or family; hence, any constituency controlled by a boss.

pocket edition An edition or copy of a book small enough to be carried in the pocket.

pock·et·ful (pok′it·fŏŏl′) *n. pl.* **·fuls** As much as a pocket will hold.

pocket knife A knife, having one or more blades which fold into the handle, for carrying in the pocket; a penknife.

pocket money Money for occasional expenses; spending money.

pocket veto *U.S.* The act of a chief executive who, where the legislative session will end within the period allowed for returning a measure with his signature or veto, simply retains ("pockets") it until the session adjourns and thus achieves an indirect veto.

pock·et·y (pok′it·ē) *adj.* **1** Characterized by pockets: said of a lode or a placer. **2** Characterized by air pockets.

pock·mark (pok′märk′) *n.* A pit or scar left on the skin by smallpox or similar diseases. — **pock′marked′** *adj.*

pock·y (pok′ē) *adj.* **pock·i·er, pock·i·est 1** Pertaining to, resembling, or affected with smallpox; pockmarked. **2** Syphilitic.

po·co (pō′kō) *adv. Music* Slightly; a little. [<Ital.]

po·co a po·co (pō′kō ä pō′kō) *Music* Little by little; gradually. [<Ital.]

po·co·cu·ran·te (pō′kō·kōō·ran′tē, *Ital.* pō′kō·kōō·rän′tā) *adj.* Indifferent; not caring. — *n.* An indifferent person. [<Ital. *poco curante* caring (but) little < *poco* (<L *paucus*) little + *curante,* ppr. of *curare* care <L] — **po′co·cu·ran′te·ism** or **·ran′tism** *n.*

pod[1] (pod) *n.* **1** A seed vessel or capsule of a plant; a legume. **2** Any dry and many-seeded dehiscent fruit. — *v.i.* **pod·ded, pod·ding 1** To fill out like a pod. **2** To produce pods. [Origin uncertain]

pod[2] (pod) *n.* A flock or collection of animals, especially of seals, whales, or walruses. [Origin unknown]

pod[3] (pod) *n. Mech.* **1** The lengthwise groove in certain augers, bits, and gimlets. **2** An auger so grooved. [Origin unknown]

-pod *combining form* **1** One who or that which has (a specified number or kind of) feet: *arthropod.* **2** A (specified kind of) foot: *pleopod.* Also **-pode.** [<Gk. *pous, podos* a foot]

-poda *combining form Zool.* Plural of -POD: used in names of phyla, orders, classes, etc.: *Arthropoda.* [<NL <Gk. *pous, podos* a foot]

po·dag·ra (pō·dag′rə, pod′ə·grə) *n. Pathol.* Gout in the foot. [<L <Gk. < *pous, podos* foot + *agra* seizure] — **po·dag′ral, po·dag′ric** *adj.*

pod·dy (pod′ē) *Austral. n.* A handfed calf, lamb, or foal. — *v.i.* **·died, ·dy·ing** To rear by hand feeding.

po·des·ta (pō·des′tə, *Ital.* pō′des·tä′) *n.* **1** A chief magistrate in the medieval Italian republics. **2** One of the governors of the Lombard cities appointed by Frederick I. **3** A subordinate municipal judge in Fascist Italy. [<Ital. *podestà* <L *potestas* power]

podg·y (poj′ē) *adj.* **podg·i·er, podg·i·est** Dumpy and fat. [Var. of PUDGY] — **podg′i·ness** *n.*

po·di·a·try (pə·dī′ə·trē, pō-) *n.* The study and treatment of diseases of the feet. [<Gk. *pous, podos* foot + -IATRY] — **po·di′a·trist** *n.*

po·dis·mos (pō·dis′məs) *n.* In ancient Greece, a dance performed in full battle dress, simulating pursuit and victory. [<Gk.]

po·di·um (pō′dē·əm) *n. pl.* **·di·a** (-dē·ə) **1** *Archit.* **a** A solid basement or pedestal supporting a structure, as a Roman temple. **b** The parapet surrounding the arena of an ancient amphitheater or circus, and hence also the platform or path behind or above it. **2** A dais, platform, or stage; especially, the platform for the conductor of an orchestra. **3** *Zool.* A foot, or any footlike structure. [<L <Gk. *podion,* dim. of *pous, podos* foot]

-podium *combining form* A footlike part: *pseudopodium.*

Po·do·li·a (pō·dō′lē·ə) A region of SW Ukrainian S.S.R.

Po·dolsk (po·dôlsk′) A city 23 miles south of Moscow in Russian S.F.S.R.

pod·o·phyl·lin (pod′ə·fil′in) *n.* A bitter, resinous substance obtained from the dried root of *Podophyllum,* the May apple, used in medicine as a purgative. [<NL *Podophyllum,* generic name of the May apple <Gk. *pous, podos* foot + *phyllon* leaf]

-podous *combining form* -footed: used in adjectives corresponding to nouns in *-pod* and *-poda: arthropodous.* [<-POD + -OUS]

Po·dunk (pō′dungk) *n.* One of a tribe of North American Indians of Algonquian stock, formerly inhabiting parts of Connecticut and Massachusetts.

Po·dunk (pō′dungk) *n.* Any small town regarded as typically dull and non-progressive. [? from *Podunk,* Massachusetts <N. Am. Ind.]

po·du·rid (pō·dŏŏr′id, -dyŏŏr′-) *n.* Any of a widely distributed family *(Poduridae)* of primitive insects which includes the springtails. [<NL *Podura* <Gk. *pous, podos* foot + *oura* tail; from their ability to leap by sudden extensions of their infolded tails]

pod·zol (pod′zol) *adj.* Of, pertaining to, or designating a major soil type of northern regions developed principally under forest conditions and characterized by a strongly acid, infertile humus underlying a thin mat of leaves and decayed vegetation. Also **pod·zol′ic.** — *n.* Podzol soil. Also **pod′sol** (-sol). [<Russian, ashlike, salty < *sol′* salt]

pod·zol·i·za·tion (pod′zol·ə·zā′shən, -ī·zā′-) *n.* The process or processes by which a soil develops podzol characteristics.

Poe (pō), **Edgar Allan,** 1809–49, U.S. poet, critic, and short story writer.

po·e·chore (pō′ə·kôr, -kōr) *n. Ecol.* The semi-arid regions of the steppes. [<Gk. *poa* grass + *chōra* region] — **po′e·chor′ic** (-kôr′ik, -kor′·ik) *adj.*

po·em (pō′əm) *n.* **1** A composition in verse, either in meter or in free verse, characterized by the imaginative treatment of experience and a heightened use of language more intensive than ordinary speech. **2** Any composition in verse. **3** Any composition characterized by intensity and beauty of language or thought: a prose *poem.* **4** Any experience which produces an effect upon the mind similar or likened to that of a poem: a *poem* in stone. See synonyms under POETRY, SONG. [<F *poème* <L *poema* <Gk. *poiēma,* lit., anything made < *poieein* make]

poe·nol·o·gy (pē·nol′ə·jē) See PENOLOGY.

po·e·sy (pō′ə·sē, -zē) *n. pl.* **·sies 1** *Poetic* Poetry taken collectively. **2** *Poetic* The art or faculty of writing poetry. **3** *Obs.* A poem. **4** *Obs.* A motto or conceit, as one engraved on jewelry. See synonyms under POETRY, SONG. [<OF *poesie* <L *poesia* <Gk. *poiēsis* < *poieein*]

po·et (pō′it) *n.* **1** One who writes poems. **2** One especially endowed with imagination, the power of rhythmical expression, and the creative faculty or power of artistic construction. [<OF *poete* <L *poeta* <Gk. *poiētēs* < *poieein* make] — **po′et·ess** *n. fem.*

Synonyms: bard, minnesinger, minstrel, rimer, rimester, singer, troubadour. Compare synonyms for POETRY.

po·et·as·ter (pō′it·as′tər) *n.* An inferior poet; a mere rimer or writer of mediocre verse. [<NL]

po·et·ic (pō·et′ik) *adj.* **1** Pertaining to poetry; having the nature or quality of or expressed in poetry: a *poetic* theme. **2** Pertaining to, befitting, or characteristic of a poet: *poetic* fire. **3** Fit to be described in poetry; of a nature to evoke poetic expression: a *poetic* incident or scene. **4** Having or showing the sensibility, feelings, faculty, etc., of a poet. **5** Celebrated or recounted in poetry or verse. Also **po·et′i·cal.** — *n.* Poetics. [<F *poétique* <L *poeticus* <Gk. *poiētikos*]

poetic justice The distribution of rewards to the good and punishment to the evil as often represented in literature; ideal justice.

poetic license The departure from the rules of diction, pronunciation, or from what is generally regarded as fact, for the sake of rime, meter, or an over-all enhancement of effect.

po·et·ics (pō·et′iks) *n. pl. (construed as singular)* **1** The principles and nature of poetry or, by extension, of any art: the *poetics* of music. **2** A treatise on poetry. Also *poetic.*

po·et·ize (pō′it·īz) *v.* **·ized, ·iz·ing** *v.i.* **1** To write poetry. — *v.t.* **2** To turn into or describe by means of poetry; express in poetic form. **3** To make poetic. — **po′et·iz′er** *n.*

poet laureate *pl.* **poets laureate 1** The poet officially invested with the title of laureate by the crown of England, an officer of the royal household receiving a salary and formerly expected to write for public occasions. **2** In former times, a poet publicly crowned with laurel in recognition of his merits, usually by a sovereign. **3** A poet acclaimed as the most eminent in a locality.

po·et·ry (pō′it·rē) *n.* **1** The writing of poems; the art by which the poet projects feeling and experience onto an imaginative plane, in rhythmical words, to stir the imagination and the emotions. **2** The quality or effect of a poem manifested in any work of literature. **3** That which resembles poetry: Dancing is the *poetry* of motion. **4** A work or works metrically composed; verse or poems collectively; also, metrical composition in general: a book of *poetry.* [<OF *poetrie* <LL *poetria* <L *poeta* poet]

Synonyms: meter, numbers, poem, poesy, rime, song, verse. In ordinary usage, *poetry* is both imaginative and metrical. *Poetry* often exists without *rime*; it may exist without regular *meter,* as in free verse; substitution may be made for *meter,* as in the Hebrew parallelism; *poetry* may be expressed in a way beautiful, lyrically comic, or sharply satiric, but it must involve, besides the artistic form, the exercise of the fancy or imagination to heighten, intensify, and integrate feeling or experience. Failing this, there may be *verse, rime,* and *meter,* but not *poetry.* In a very wide sense *poetry* may be anything rhythmical; as, the *poetry* of motion. There is much in literature that is beautiful and sublime in thought and artistic in construction, which is yet not *poetry,* in the strict sense, because quite devoid of the rhythmical element, and the patterned arrangement and economy of words; the dividing line between poetry and "the other music of prose" is hard to draw. Compare METER², SONG. *Antonym*: prose.

pog·a·mog·gan (pog′ə·mog′ən) *n.* A war club consisting of a stone or antler secured to the end of a wooden handle, used as a weapon and as a ceremonial symbol by the Plains Indians and also by the Algonquians around the Great Lakes. [<Algonquian]

Po·ga·ny (pō·gä′nē, *Hungarian* pō′gän·y′), **Willy,** 1882–1955, U.S. illustrator, mural painter, and designer, born in Hungary.

po·gey bait (pō′gē) *U.S. Slang* Any confection, as candy bars, etc.

po·go·ni·a (pə·gō′nē·ə, -gōn′yə) *n.* One of a genus *(Pogonia)* of widely distributed terrestrial orchids, especially an American species, *P. ophioglossoides,* having fragrant, rose-pink flowers. [<NL <Gk. *pōgōn* a beard]

pog·o·nip (pog′ə·nip) *n. Meteorol.* A cold fog containing particles of ice, characteristic of the Sierra Nevada mountains and valleys; a frost fog. [<Shoshonean (Paiute)]

po·go stick (pō′gō) A stiltlike toy, with a spring at the base and fitted with two projections for the feet, on which a person may stand and propel himself in a series of hops.

po·grom (pō′grəm, pō·grom′) *n.* An officially instigated local massacre, especially one directed against the Jews. [<Russian, destruction]

po·gy (pō′gē, pog′ē) *n. pl.* **·gies** or **·gy** The menhaden. [<N. Am. Ind. *pauhagen*]

poh (pô) *interj.* Pshaw! bah! an expletive signifying disgust or contempt. [Imit.]

Po·hai (bō′hī′), **Strait of** See CHIHLI, STRAIT OF.

Po·hang (pō·häng) A town in southern Korea on the Sea of Japan. *Japanese* **Ho·ko** (hō·kō).

poi (poi, pō′ē) *n.* A native Hawaiian food made from the ground root of the taro. [<Hawaiian]

-poietic *combining form* Making; producing; creating: *hemapoietic.* [<Gk. *poiētikos* forming <*poieein* make]

poign·ant (poin′yənt, poi′nənt) *adj.* **1** Severely painful or acute to the spirit; keenly piercing; bitter; severe: *poignant* grief; a *poignant* retort. **2** Sharp or stimulating to the taste; pungent; biting. See synonyms under VIOLENT. [<OF, ppr. of *poindre* prick <L *pungere*] **—poign′·an·cy** *n.* **—poign′ant·ly** *adv.*

poi·ki·lo·ther·mal (poi′kə·lō·thûr′məl) *adj. Zool.* Variable in body temperature, as cold-blooded animals: distinguished from *homothermal.* [<Gk. *poikilos* variegated + THERMAL]

poi·lu (pwȧ·lü′) *French adj.* Hairy; bearded. **—** *n.* A French soldier; originally, an experienced French soldier of World War I.

Poin·ca·ré (pwaṅ·kȧ·rā′), **Jules Henri,** 1854–1912, French mathematician and author. **— Raymond,** 1860–1934, French statesman.

poin·ci·a·na (poin′sē·ā′nə, -an′ə) *n.* **1** One of a small genus of tropical trees or shrubs *(Poinciana,* family *Leguminosae),* especially the flower-fence. **2** The royal poinciana *(Delonix regia),* a tropical tree with bright orange and scarlet flowers and large flat pods. [<NL, after M. de *Poinci,* a 17th century governor of the West Indies]

poind (poind) *v.t. Scot.* **1 a** To seize and sell (the property of a debtor) to satisfy a debt. **b** To distrain the property of. **2** To impound.

poin·set·ti·a (poin·set′ē·ə) *n.* Any of a genus *(Euphorbia)* of American plants of the spurge family, with large showy bracts and inconspicuous flowers, especially an ornamental evergreen hothouse shrub *(E. pulcherrima)* from Mexico, with richly colored, red, leaflike bracts. [after J. R. *Poinsett,* 1779–1851, U. S. statesman]

POINSETTIA
Flower in bracts.

point (point) *n.* **1** The sharp end of a thing, particularly of anything that tapers so as to be very small and keen at the extremity: the *point* of a needle or a thorn. **2** *pl.* The extremities of a horse. **3** An object, as a tool or instrument, having a sharp or tapering end, as a needle, etching tool, etc. **4** A tapering tract of land extending into water; a promontory; cape: *Point* Judith. **5** A prominent feature or peculiarity; typical attribute; salient quality; essential physical characteristic: the *points* of a thoroughbred horse. **6** That to which effort is directed, on which attention is fixed, or to which especial importance is attached; the precise subject of discussion; aim; gist; purport: the *point* of a story. **7** A particular place, location, or position. **8** A position considered as one of a series; a unit of fluctuation, as of count in a game: to gain a *point.* **9** A precise grade, limit, or degree attained or determined, especially in temperature. **10** A particular juncture in the course of events. **11** Any single item or particular; detail. **12** A vital step or division of an argument or discourse; a proposition; head: to note every *point*; to contest *point* by *point.* **13** In schools and colleges, a unit of credit equal to a certain number of hours of academic work. **14** An indivisible portion of time; a particular moment. **15** The moment when something is about or likely to be done or to take place; verge: on the *point* of starting; at the *point* of death. **16** Point lace. **17** A cord or strap by which a thing is fastened, as a rope for reefing sails. **18** In 16th and 17th century costume, a ribbon or string with an aglet on one end, used to fasten together two pieces of clothing. **19** A mark made by or as by the end of a pointed instrument or tool; a prick; puncture; dot. **20** Any mark of punctuation; especially, among printers, a period; stop; end. **21** *Ling.* A vowel point as used in Hebrew. **22** *Music* A dot or other mark to designate time, or formerly tone; also, a short tune or strain; also, such tune when played on an instrument as a signal. **23** A decimal point. **24** Point system (def. 5). **25** The attitude of a pointer or setter when it finds game: The dog came to a *point.* **26** In fencing, a thrust; also, in dancing, the act of pointing the foot downward. **27** A trifle; punctilio: a mere *point.* **28** In cricket, a fielder stationed the nearest to the right of the wicket and slightly in advance of it; also, the position thus occupied. **29** *pl.* In baseball, the positions occupied by the pitcher and catcher. **30** The leading group of an advanced guard. **31** One of the 32 divisions of the compass. See POINT OF THE COMPASS. **32** That which is conceived to have position, but not parts or dimensions, as the extremity of a line. **33** A unit of variation in price of shares, stocks, etc., in the stock market; also, a rumor on which speculation is made; a tip. **34** A fixed place from which position and distance are reckoned. **35** A spot or place which is regarded as having position only, without extent, as a locality. **36** The tail of an animal: used in the phrase *heads and points.* **37** *Electr.* Any of a set of contacts determining the direction of current flow in a circuit. See synonyms under CIRCUMSTANCE, END, TOPIC. **—at** (or **on, upon**) **the point of** On the verge of. **—beside the point** Irrelevant. **—in point** Pertinent. **—in point of** In the matter of; as regards. **—to make a point of** To treat as vital or essential. **—to see the point** To understand the purpose of a course of action; get the important meaning of a story, joke, etc. **—to stretch a point** To make an exception. **—to the point** Relevant. **—** *v.t.* **1** To direct or aim, as a finger or weapon. **2** To indicate; direct attention to: often with *out*: to *point* the way; to *point* out errors. **3** To give force or point to, as a meaning or remark: often with *up.* **4** To shape or sharpen to a point. **5** To punctuate, as writing. **6** To mark or separate with points, as decimal fractions: with *off.* **7** In hunting, to indicate the presence or location of (game) by standing rigid and directing the muzzle toward it: said of dogs. **8** In masonry, to fill and finish the joints of (brickwork) with mortar. **9** *Ling.* To mark with a vowel point. **—** *v.i.* **10** To call attention or indicate direction by or as by extending the finger: usually with *at* or *to.* **11** To direct the mind: Everything *points* to your being wrong. **12** To be directed; have a specified direction; tend; face: with *to* or *toward.* **13** To point game: said of hunting dogs. **14** *Med.* To come to a head, as an abscess. **15** *Naut.* To sail close to the wind. See synonyms under ALLUDE. [Fusion of OF *pointe* a sharp point (<Med. L *puncta* <L *punctus*) + OF *point* prick, dot, moment <L *punctum,* neut. of *punctus,* pp. of *pungere* prick]

point alphabet The alphabet of the point system for the blind.

Point Bar·row (bar′ō) See BARROW, POINT.

point-blank (point′blangk′) *adj.* **1** Aimed directly at the mark; in gunnery, fired horizontally without allowing for dropping. **2** Hence, direct; plain: a *pointblank* question. **—** *n.* A shot with direct aim. **—** *adv.* In a horizontal line; hence, directly; without circumlocution.

point d'ap·pui (pwaṅ dȧ·pwē′) *French* Point of support; base.

Point de Galle (pwaṅ də gäl) A former name for GALLE.

point d'es·prit (pwaṅ des·prē′) *French* **1** Net or tulle with dots. **2** Lace with the small oval or square dots first used in Normandy lace.

point-de·vice (point′di·vīs′) *adj.* Scrupulously neat; precise; finical. **—** *adv.* Precisely; exactly. Also **point′-de·vise′.** [ME *(at point) devis,* i.e., (at an) exact (point) <OF *devis* exact]

Pointe-à-Pi·tre (pwaṅ·tȧ·pē′tr′) A city on Grande-Terre, principal port and commercial center of Guadeloupe.

point·ed (poin′tid) *adj.* **1** Having a point. **2** Piquant; pungent; epigrammatic; to the point. **3** Aimed at a particular person; emphasized; conspicuous. See synonyms under ACUTE, SHARP. **—point′ed·ly** *adv.* **—point′ed·ness** *n.*

pointed arch A narrow, pointed arch used in medieval architecture in Europe, characteristic of the Gothic style: also called *Gothic arch.*

pointed architecture The European architecture of the Middle Ages characterized by its consistent use of the pointed arch, with details to correspond.

Pointe-Noire (pwaṅt·nwȧr′) The capital of Middle Congo since 1950.

point·er (poin′tər) *n.* **1** One who or that which points. **2** A hand or index finger, as on a clock or scale. **3** A long tapering rod used in class rooms to point out things on wall maps, charts, diagrams, etc. **4** One of a breed of dogs trained to scent and point out game. **5** A useful bit of information; hint. **6** *Nav.*

One whose business is to bring the gun or turret to its proper elevation. Compare TRAINER. 7 The cowboy who rides at the head of the herd in a cattle drive.

Point·ers (poin′tərz) *n. pl. Astron.* Two stars, Alpha and Beta in the constellation Ursa Major, whose connecting line points nearly to the North Star: called *Dubhe* and *Merak.*

pointes (points) *n. pl.* In ballet, dancing on tiptoe. [<F]

Point Four The fourth point in President Truman's Inaugural Address, January 20, 1949, in which he recommended "a bold new program for making the benefits of our scientific advances and industrial progress available for the improvement and growth of underdeveloped areas."

poin·til·lism (pwan′tə·liz′əm) *n.* A French neoimpressionist method of producing effects of light by placing small spots of varying hues on a surface in close proximity, the eye blending them together. [<F *pointillisme* < *pointiller* mark with dots] — **point′til·list** *n.*

point·ing (poin′ting) *n.* **1** The act of sharpening or bringing to a point. **2** *Punctuation.* See under PUNCTUATION. **3** In sculpture, the making of a plaster or clay model with points or marks at intervals and the transferring of these points to the surface of a stone block as an aid in reproducing the model accurately. **4** *Archit.* **a** The process of treating joints in masonry, slating, or tiling, by filling interstices, smoothing out, etc., to finish or repair and to weatherproof. **b** The removal of the thin top layer of mortar between courses of brick and masonry, to replace it with a more moisture-resistant compound. **5** In milling, the rubbing off of the points of grain.

Point Judith A promontory and lighthouse at the western entrance of Narragansett Bay, Rhode Island.

point lace Needlepoint (def. 2). — **point-laced** (point′lāst′) *adj.*

point·less (point′lis) *adj.* Without a point; dull; also, having no significance: a *pointless* remark. See synonyms under BLUNT, FLAT[1]. — **point′less·ly** *adv.* — **point′less·ness** *n.*

point of honor Something that vitally affects one's honor.

point of order In parliamentary language, a question of procedure under the rules.

point of the compass One of the 32 equidistant directions or division points marked on the card of the mariners' compass, or a corresponding point in the horizon, or a vertical plane passing through the horizon and one of such points. See COMPASS CARD.

point of view The relative position from which one sees an object, a proposition, or the like. Compare STANDPOINT.

point system **1** *Printing* A standard system of sizes for type bodies, 996 points of which are equal to 35 centimeters, one point being .0138 inch (or approximately 1/72 inch), as adopted by the Typefounders' Association of the United States. **2** Any system of raised letters for the blind, as braille, in which the alphabet is formed of groups of raised dots or points. **3** An academic system of allowing students to progress according to points or credits earned in individual subjects. **4** Any method of rating based on the accumulation of points.

point target A particular structure, object, or installation selected for direct gunfire or bombing. Compare AREA TARGET.

poise[1] (poiz) *v.* **poised, pois·ing** *v.t.* **1** To bring into or hold in balance; maintain in equilibrium. **2** To hold; support, as in readiness. **3** *Rare* To weigh. — *v.i.* **4** To be balanced or suspended; hover. — *n.* **1** The state or quality of being balanced; equilibrium; equipoise; also, indecision; suspense. **2** Equanimity; repose; dignity, as in bearing or carriage. **3** A balance weight or counterpoise. **4** Any position that indicates suspended motion. [<OF *il poise, peise,* 3rd person sing. of *peser* <L *pensare,* intens. of *pendere* weigh] — **pois′er** *n.*

poise[2] (poiz) *n. pl.* **poise** The unit of viscosity in the cgs system, equal to 1 dyne-second per square centimeter. [after Jean Marie *Poiseuille,* 1797?–1869, French physiologist]

poi·son (poi′zən) *n.* **1** Any substance which, introduced into an organism in relatively small amounts, acts chemically upon the tissues to produce serious injury or death. **2** *Physics* Any substance or material which, by absorbing neutrons, prevents fission in an atomic reactor. **3** Anything that tends to taint or destroy character or to mislead, corrupt, or pervert. — *v.t.* **1** To administer poison to; kill or injure with poison. **2** To put poison into or on. **3** To affect wrongfully; corrupt; pervert: to *poison* one's mind. — *adj.* Killing; venomous; corrupting. [<OF <L *potio, -onis* a drink, poisonous draft. Doublet of POTION.] — **poi′son·er** *n.*

poison dogwood, poison elder Poison sumac.

poison gas Any of a class of toxic chemical agents, usually a liquid under high vapor pressure, employed in warfare for the purpose of disabling or killing enemy personnel.

poison hemlock See under HEMLOCK.

poison ivy A climbing shrub (*Toxicodendron radicans* or *Rhus toxicodendron*), a species of sumac with three broadly ovate, variously notched, sinuate or cut-lobed leaflets and whitish berries: poisonous to many persons by touch.

poison oak **1** A species of poison sumac, especially *Toxicodendron quercifolium.* **2** A species of poison ivy (*T. rydlergii*) common in the western United States.

poi·son·ous (poi′zən·əs) *adj.* **1** Containing or being a poison. **2** Having the effect of a poison; toxic; vitiating. See synonyms under NOISOME. — **poi′son·ous·ly** *adv.* — **poi′son·ous·ness** *n.*

poison sumac **1** A handsome shrub or small tree (*Toxicodendron vernix* or *Rhus vernix*), growing in swamps in the United States and Canada. It has smooth, entire leaflets, and loose panicles of smooth greenish-yellow drupes. The whole plant is poisonous to taste or touch. **2** Poison ivy.

Poi·tiers (pwà·tyā′) A city of west central France; formerly, capital of Poitou.

Poi·tou (pwà·to͞o′) A region and former province of west central France.

poi·trel (poi′trəl) *n.* The armor formerly used to protect the breast of a war horse. [<OF *poitral* <L *pectorale* breastplate < *pectus* breast]

poke[1] (pōk) *v.* **poked, pok·ing** *v.t.* **1** To push or prod, as with the elbow; jab: to *poke* a person in the ribs. **2** To make by or as by thrusting: to *poke* a hole. **3** To thrust or push in, out, through, from, etc.: to *poke* one's head from a window. **4** To stir (a fire, etc.) by prodding: often with *up.* — *v.i.* **5** To make thrusts, as with a stick or weapon: often with *at.* **6** To intrude or meddle. **7** To go or look curiously; pry. **8** To appear or show: logs *poking* above the surface. **9** To proceed slowly; dawdle; putter. — **to poke one's nose into** To meddle in. — **to poke fun at** To ridicule, especially slily. — *n.* **1** A push; prod. **2** A yokelike collar with long projections to prevent animals from passing through fences. **3** One who moves sluggishly; a dawdler. **4** *Colloq.* A punch. [ME *poken.* Cf. LG, Du. *poken* push.]

poke[2] (pōk) *n.* A pocket, or small bag. See POCK[2]. [<OF <Gmc. Cf. ON *poki* and MDu. *poke.*]

poke[3] (pōk) *n.* The pokeweed. [< earlier *pocan* <Algonquian (Virginian) *pakon* weed used for staining < *pak* blood. Akin to PUCCOON.]

poke[4] (pōk) *n.* A large bonnet with projecting front. Also **poke bonnet.**

poke·ber·ry (pōk′ber′ē) *n. pl.* **·ries** **1** A berry of the pokeweed. **2** The plant.

pok·er[1] (pō′kər) *n.* **1** One who or that which pokes. **2** An iron rod for poking a fire.

pok·er[2] (pō′kər) *n.* Any of several games of cards in which the players bet on the value of the cards, usually five, dealt to them, and he whose hand contains the group of highest value wins the entire sum wagered, provided he has not dropped out of the betting. The groups usually recognized, in the ascending order of value, are the *pair, two pairs, three of a kind, straight, flush, full hand* or *house, four of a kind, straight flush.* [Origin uncertain. Cf. G *pochspiel,* lit., bragging game < *pochen* brag.]

pok·er·face (pō′kər·fās′) *n.* A face that reveals nothing: so called from the controlled and inscrutable faces of professional poker-players.

pok·er·ish (pō′kər·ish) *adj.* **1** Stiff or unbending, as a poker. **2** Ghastly; unearthly. — **pok′·er·ish·ly** *adv.*

poke·weed (pōk′wēd′) *n.* A stout perennial herb of the United States (*Phytolacca americana*), having dark-purple berries and a root used in medicine: often called *inkberry.* Also **poke′root′** (-ro͞ot′, -ro͝ot′). [See POKE[3]]

pok·ing (pō′king) *adj.* **1** Drudging; servile; mean. **2** Projecting.

pok·y (pō′kē) *adj.* **pok·i·er, pok·i·est** **1** Lacking life or spirit; dull; slow. **2** Shabby. **3** Cramped; stuffy. Also **poke′y.**

Po·la (pō′lä) The Italian name for PULA.

po·lac·ca (pō·lak′ə) *n.* A two- or three-masted Mediterranean vessel. Also **po·la·cre** (pō·lä′·kər). [<Ital.]

Po·lack (pō′lok, -lak) *n. Slang* A Pole; especially, an immigrant from Poland: a contemptuous term. — *adj.* Polish. [<Polish *polak*]

Po·land (pō′lənd) A republic of north central Europe; 120,359 square miles; capital, Warsaw: Polish *Polska.*

Poland China An American mixed breed of large pigs, similar to Berkshires.

Po·land·er (pō′lən·dər) *n.* A Pole.

po·lar (pō′lər) *adj.* **1** Pertaining to the poles of a sphere, as of the earth. **2** Coming from or found near the North or South Pole. **3** Pertaining to the poles of a magnet or other center of attraction or repulsion. **4** Exhibiting ionization. **5** Having or proceeding from a point of radiation. **6** Attracting; guiding. **7** *Math.* **a** Of or pertaining to a coordinate system of representing equations graphically whereby a point is located by its linear distance from the pole and by the angle subtended by a line from the point to the pole and the polar axis. **b** Of or pertaining to a curve or an equation traced or traceable by means of such coordinates. [<Med. L *polaris* < *polus* pole]

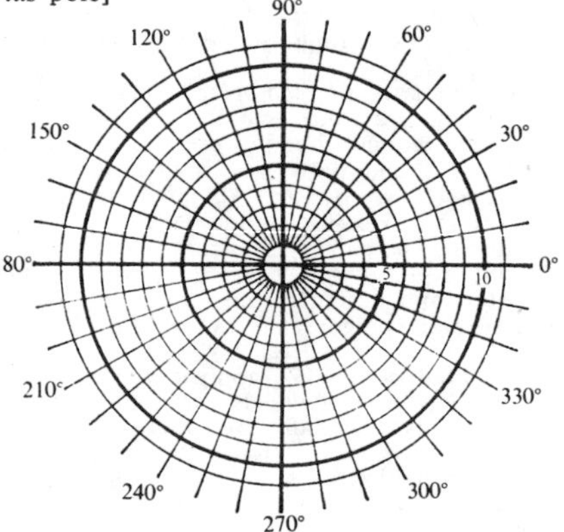

POLAR COORDINATE SYSTEM
The polar axis is the horizontal axis.

polar angle *Math.* In a polar coordinate system, the angle subtended between the polar axis and a line drawn from a point to the pole.

polar axis *Math.* A fixed line directed from the pole in the polar coordinate system from which angles are measured in a counterclockwise direction.

polar bear A large, amphibious, white bear of arctic regions (*Thalarctus maritimus*).

polar body *Biol.* One of the two spherical bodies that separate from the ovum at the time of its maturation.

polar circles The Arctic and Antarctic circles.

polar compound *Chem.* Any of a class of compounds which will conduct an electric current when either fused or in solution, as most inorganic acids, bases, and salts.

polar distance Codeclination.

polar front *Meteorol.* The line or surface of discontinuity separating an air mass originating in polar regions from one of tropical origin.

po·lar·im·e·ter (pō′lə·rim′ə·tər) *n.* **1** An instrument for measuring the rotation of the plane of polarization or the proportion of polarized light in a beam. **2** A form of polariscope. [<L *polaris* polar + -METER]

Po·lar·is (pō·lar′is) **1** The polestar or North Star: Alpha in the constellation Ursa Minor. See under STAR. **2** An intermediate range ballistic missile of the U.S. Navy designed to be launched from a submerged submarine. [<L]

po·lar·i·scope (pō·lar′ə·skōp) *n.* An optical instrument for exhibiting or measuring the polarization of light. [<L *polaris* polar + -SCOPE]

po·lar·i·ty (pō·lar′ə·tē) *n.* **1** The quality of having opposite poles. **2** *Physics* That quality of a body by which it exhibits certain properties related to a line of direction through its mass, the properties at one end of this line being of opposite or contrasting nature to the properties at the other end, as in a magnet. **3** The quality of being attracted to one pole and repelled from the other.

po·lar·i·za·tion (pō′lər·ə·zā′shən, -ī·zā′-) *n.* **1** The act of polarizing, or state of being polarized; bestowal or gaining of polarity. **2** *Physics* A condition of radiant energy, most noticeable in light, in which its vibrations assume a definite form or direction when subjected to special influences. Light may be polarized by reflection, at an angle which differs for different substances, or by transmission, as through most crystals or solutions. If light thus treated be examined by subjecting it to such reflection or transmission a second time, it is found that in certain positions of the reflector or crystal it will pass most easily, while in the positions at right angles to these it will be totally quenched, and in intermediate positions it will pass partially. The plane of polarization is altered or rotated by the passage of light through suitable media; this is called **rotary polarization,** which takes two directions, right-handed and left-handed. **3** *Electr.* A change in the potential of the electrode of a cell due to the accumulation upon it of dissociation products liberated by the current. **— angle of polarization** or **polarizing angle** That angle of reflection from a plane surface at which light is polarized. **— plane of polarization** The plane in which the light vibrations occur when polarized.

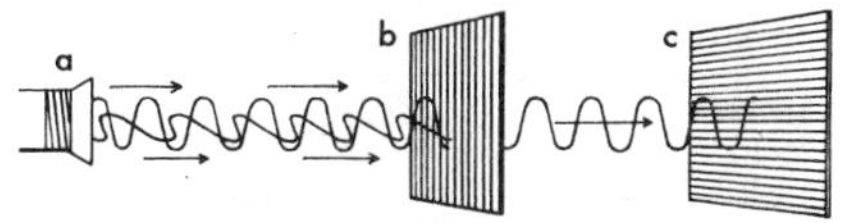

POLARIZATION
Of the light emitted at *a*, only the part whose electric oscillations are parallel to the axis of polarizing medium *b* can pass through it. This is blocked at polarizing medium *c*, whose axis is at right angles to that of *b*.

po·lar·ize (pō′lə·rīz) *v.t.* **·ized, ·iz·ing** **1** To develop polarization in; give polarity to. **2** To give a special meaning or direction to. Also *Brit.* **po′lar·ise.** **— po′lar·iz′a·ble** *adj.* **— po′lar·iz′er** *n.*

polar lights The aurora borealis or the aurora australis.

Po·lar·oid (pō′lə·roid) *n.* A material composed of a sheet of specially prepared plastic between layers of glass and having the property of polarizing and thus reducing the intensity of the light passing through it: a trade name.

Polar Regions The areas within the Arctic and Antarctic circles.

polar star The polestar.

pol·der (pōl′dər) *n.* A tract of marshy land, lower than the sea, which has been diked and reclaimed to cultivation. Also **pol′der·land′.** [<Du.]

pole[1] (pōl) *n.* **1** Either of the extremities of an axis or sphere. **2** One of two points where the axis of rotation, as of the earth, meets the surface. **3** Either of the Polar Regions of the earth; also, either of the two extremities of the earth's axis, called the North *Pole* and the South *Pole.* See CELESTIAL POLE. **4** *Physics* One of the two points at which opposite physical qualities are concentrated; especially, a point (usually one of two) of maximum intensity of electric or magnetic force. **5** The polestar. **6** *Biol.* The differentiated extremities of an ovum or other cell. **7** *Physiol.* The point of a nerve cell where a process has its origin. **8** *Math.* In polar coordinate and spherical coordinate systems, that point where all radius vectors equal zero. ◆ Homophone: *poll.* [<L *polus* <Gk. *polos* pivot, pole <*pelein* be in motion]

pole[2] (pōl) *n.* **1** A long slender piece of wood or metal, commonly tapering and more or less rounded; a Maypole, beanpole, the mast of a vessel, etc. **2** The tongue of a vehicle. **3** In linear and surface measure, a perch or rod. **4** A fishing rod. **—** *v.* **poled, pol·ing** *v.t.* **1** To propel, push, or strike with a pole. **2** To support on poles, as growing beans. **—** *v.i.* **3** To push a boat, raft, etc., with a pole. ◆ Homophone: *poll.* [OE *pal* <L *palus* stake]

Pole (pōl) *n.* A native or inhabitant of Poland.

Pole (pōl), **Reginald,** 1500–58, English statesman; archbishop of Canterbury.

pole–ax (pōl′aks′) *n.* A medieval weapon consisting of an ax, or a combined ax and pick, set on a long pole; a battle–ax. **—** *v.t.* To strike or fell with a pole–ax. Also **pole′–axe′.** [ME *pollax* <*pol* poll[1] + AX]

pole bean Any variety of climbing bean supported by poles.

pole·cat (pōl′kat′) *n.* **1** One of certain European carnivores (genus *Mustela*) of the weasel family, noted for a fetid odor when irritated or alarmed. **2** *U.S.* A skunk. [<F *poule* pullet + CAT; from its predacity]

pole fence A fence made of horizontal unsplit poles.

pole horse A horse hitched beside the pole, as distinguished from a leader.

pole jump See POLE VAULT.

pole line A line of telephone or telegraph poles.

po·lem·ic (pō·lem′ik) *adj.* Pertaining to controversy; disputatious. Also **po·lem′i·cal.** **—** *n.* **1** A controversy; also, the speeches, papers, etc., comprising this. **2** One who engages in controversy. [<Gk. *polemikos* warlike < *polemos* war]

po·lem·i·cist (pō·lem′ə·sist) *n.* One skilled or engaged in polemics. Also **pol·e·mist** (pol′ə·mist).

po·lem·ics (pō·lem′iks) *n.* The art or practice of disputation; especially, the use of aggressive argument to refute errors of doctrine.

pol·e·mo·ni·a·ceous (pol′ə·mō′nē·ā′shəs) *adj. Bot.* Designating or belonging to a family *(Polemoniaceae)* of herbs (rarely shrubs or small trees) including many ornamental garden species; the phlox family. [<Gk. *polemōnion* kind of plant]

pol·er (pō′lər) *n.* **1** The draft animal harnessed nearest the pole of a cart or wagon; a wheeler. **2** One who poles a boat.

pole·star (pōl′stär′) *n.* **1** *Astron.* The North Star; Polaris; Alpha in Ursa Minor. **2** That which governs, guides, or directs; an attracting or controlling principle.

pole–vault (pōl′vôlt′) *v.i.* To perform a pole vault. **— pole′–vault′er** *n.*

pole vault A vault or jump with a long pole, usually over a light horizontal bar: an athletic field event.

po·lice (pə·lēs′) *n.* **1** A body of civil officers, especially in a city, organized under authority to maintain order and enforce law; constabulary. **2** The whole system of internal regulation of a state, or the local government of a city or town; that department of government that maintains and enforces law and order, and prevents, detects, or deals with crime. **3** The cleansing or keeping clean of a camp or garrison; also, the soldiers detailed for the duties of policing in camp. **—** *v.t.* **·liced, ·lic·ing** **1** To protect, regulate, or maintain order in (a city, country, etc.) with or as with police. **2** *U.S.* To make clean or orderly, as a military camp. [<F <LL *politia* governmental administration <Gk. *politeia* polity <*politēs* citizen <*polis* city]

police court A municipal court where minor criminal cases are tried. Its jurisdiction corresponds with that of a justice of the peace.

police dog See GERMAN SHEPHERD DOG.

po·lice·man (pə·lēs′mən) *n. pl.* **·men** (-mən) A member of a police force.

police power The broad authority of a state to limit private rights to the extent necessary to promote the peace, good order, morals, health, and safety of the general community.

police state A country whose citizens are rigidly supervised by a national police, often working secretly.

police station The headquarters of a community police force, to which arrested persons are taken and from which policemen operate.

po·lice·wom·an (pə·lēs′wo͝om′ən) *n. pl.* **·wom·en** (-wim′in) A woman member of a police force.

pol·i·clin·ic (pol′i·klin′ik) *n.* The dispensary of a hospital, or that part of it in which outpatients are treated. Compare POLYCLINIC. [<G *poliklinik* <Gk. *polis* city + G *klinik* clinic]

pol·i·cy[1] (pol′ə·sē) *n. pl.* **·cies** **1** Prudence or sagacity in the conduct of affairs. **2** A course or plan of action, especially of administrative action. **3** Any system of management based on self-interest as opposed to equity; finesse in general; artifice. **4** *Obs.* Political science; government. See synonyms under POLITY. [<OF *policie* <L *politia* <Gk. *politeia.* See POLICE.]

pol·i·cy[2] (pol′ə·sē) *n. pl.* **·cies** **1** A written contract of insurance. **2** A gambling game in which certain numbers (12 or 13) are drawn from a possible 78, bets being made as to what combinations will appear; also, any variation of this game. [<F *police* <Ital. *polizza,* aphetic alter. of Med. L *apodixa, apodissa* receipt <Gk. *apodeixis* proof <*apodeiknynai* make known]

pol·i·cy·hol·der (pol′ə·sē·hōl′dər) *n.* One who holds a policy of insurance.

policy racket Numbers pool.

Po·lil·lo Islands (pō·lē′yō) A Philippine island group off the eastern coast of central Luzon; approximately 295 square miles.

po·li·o (pō′lē·ō) *n. Colloq.* Poliomyelitis.

polio– *combining form Med.* Of or pertaining to the gray matter of the brain, or the spinal cord: *polioencephalitis.* [<Gk. *polios* gray]

pol·i·o·en·ceph·a·li·tis (pol′ē·ō·en·sef′ə·lī′tis) *n. Pathol.* Inflammation of the gray matter of the brain. Also **pol′i·en·ceph′a·li′tis.** [< POLIO- + ENCEPHALITIS]

pol·i·o·my·e·li·tis (pol′ē·ō·mī′ə·lī′tis, pō′lē-) *n.*

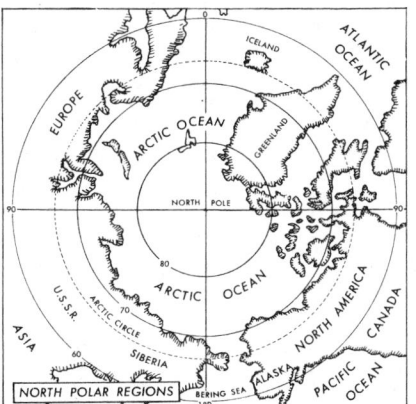

NORTH POLAR REGIONS

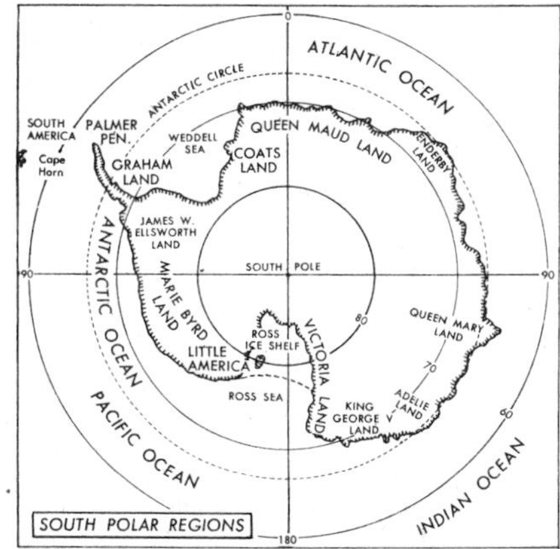

Pathol. An acute, communicable disease caused by infection with a virus, occurring especially in children, and characterized by inflammation of the gray matter of the spinal cord, followed by paralysis and atrophy of various muscle groups: also called *infantile paralysis.* [<NL <POLIO- + Gk. *myelos* marrow + -ITIS]

pol·ish (pol′ish) *n.* **1** Smoothness or glossiness of surface; finish. **2** A substance used to produce a bright, smooth, or glossy surface; a varnish. **3** Refinement of manner or style. **4** The process of polishing. — *v.t.* **1** To make smooth or lustrous, as by rubbing. **2** To make complete; finish; perfect. **3** To free from crudeness; make refined or elegant: to *polish* the mind. — *v.i.* **4** To take a gloss; shine. **5** To become elegant or refined. — **to polish off 1** To do or finish completely or quickly. **2** To dispose of; overwhelm. — **to polish up** To make better; improve. [<OF *poliss-*, stem of *polir* <L *polire* make smooth] — **pol′ish·er** *n.*

Po·lish (pō′lish) *adj.* Pertaining to Poland, its inhabitants, or their language. — *n.* The West Slavic language of the Poles.

Polish Corridor A strip of land in NW Poland, extending to the Baltic between Germany and East Prussia 1919–1939; part of Germany prior to 1919, and from 1939 to 1945; now a part of Poland.

pol·ished (pol′isht) *adj.* **1** Made smooth by polishing. **2** Naturally smooth and glossy. **3** Refined and polite. See synonyms under FINE[1], POLITE, SMOOTH.

Po·lit·bu·ro (po·lit′byŏŏr′ō) *n.* The leading policy-forming committee of the Communist party in the U. S. S. R. until 1952, when it was replaced by the Presidium. [<Russian *polit(icheskoe) buro*]

po·lite (pə·līt′) *adj.* **1** Exhibiting in manner or speech a considerate regard for others; courteous; also, cultivated: *polite* society. **2** Finished and elegant in style. [<L *politus,* pp. of *polire* polish] — **po·lite′ly** *adv.* — **po·lite′ness** *n.*

Synonyms: accomplished, civil, complaisant, courteous, courtly, cultivated, cultured, elegant, genteel, gracious, obliging, polished, urbane, well-behaved, well-bred, well-mannered. A man may be *civil* with no consideration for others, simply because self-respect forbids him to be rude; but one who is *polite* has at least some care for the opinions of others, and if *polite* in the highest and truest sense, he cares for the comfort and happiness of others in the smallest matters. *Civil* is a colder and more distant word than *polite*; *courteous* is fuller and richer, dealing often with greater matters, and is used only in the good sense. *Courtly* suggests that which befits a royal court, and is used of external grace and stateliness without reference to the prompting feeling. *Genteel* refers to an external elegance, which may be showy and superficial, and the word is thus inferior to *polite* or *courteous. Urbane* refers to a politeness that is genial and successful in giving others a sense of ease and cheer. *Polished* refers to external elegancies of speech and manner without reference to spirit or purpose; as, a *polished* gentleman or a *polished* scoundrel; *cultured* refers to a real and high development of mind and soul, of which the external manifestation is the smallest part. *Complaisant* denotes a disposition to please or favor. *Antonyms*: awkward, bluff, blunt, boorish, brusk, clownish, coarse, discourteous, ill-behaved, ill-bred, ill-mannered, impertinent, impolite, impudent, insolent, insulting, raw, rude, rustic, uncivil, uncouth, unpolished, untaught, untutored.

po·li·tesse (pô·lē·tes′) *n. French* Politeness; civility.

pol·i·tic (pol′ə·tik) *adj.* **1** Sagacious and wary in planning; artful; crafty; shrewd, especially in statesmanship. **2** Wisely adapted to an end; specious. **3** *Rare* Pertaining to public polity, or to the state or its government; political. See BODY POLITIC. [<OF *politique* <L *politicus* <Gk. *politikos* civic <*politēs* citizen] — **pol′i·tic·ly** *adv.*

Synonyms: artful, crafty, cunning, diplomatic, discreet, judicious, prudent, sagacious, shrewd, wary, wily, wise.

po·lit·i·cal (pə·lit′i·kəl) *adj.* **1** Pertaining to public policy; concerned in the administration of government: a *political* system: distinguished from *civil.* **2** Belonging to the science of government; treating of polity or politics: *political* principles. **3** Having an organized system of government; administering a polity. **4** Pertaining to or connected with a party or parties controlling or seeking to control government in a state: *political* methods. [<L *politicus*] — **po·lit′i·cal·ly** *adv.*

political economist A person skilled in political economy.

political economy Economics.

political science The science of the form and principles of civil government, and the extent and manner of its intervention in public and private affairs; politics.

pol·i·ti·cian (pol′ə·tish′ən) *n.* **1** One engaged in politics, especially professionally. **2** *U.S.* One who engages in politics for personal or partisan aims rather than for reasons of principle; also, a political schemer or opportunist. **3** *Brit.* One skilled in the science of government or politics; a statesman. **4** The white-eyed vireo: so called because it feathers its nest with bits of newspaper or whatever comes easily. [<F *politicien*]

po·lit·i·cize (pə·lit′ə·sīz) *v.t.* **·cized, ·ciz·ing 1** To make politically active or aware. **2** To make into a political issue. Also **po·lit′i·cal·ize′** (-kəl·īz′). — **po·lit′i·ci·za′tion** *n.*

pol·i·tick·ing (pol′ə·tik·ing) *n.* Involvement in politics. — **pol′i·tick·er** *n.*

po·lit·i·co (pə·lit′i·kō) *n. pl.* **·cos** A politician. [<Sp. *político*]

pol·i·tics (pol′ə·tiks) *n.* **1** The science of civil government. **2** Political affairs in a party sense; party intrigues, etc. **3** One's political sentiments: construed as plural. — **to play politics** To speak or act for political reasons; hence, to scheme for an advantage.

pol·i·ty (pol′ə·tē) *n. pl.* **·ties 1** The form or method of government of a nation, state, church, etc. **2** Any community living under some definite form of government. [<OF *politie,* var. of *policie.* See POLICY[1].]

Synonym: policy. *Polity* is the permanent system of government of a state, a church, or a society; *policy* is the method of management with reference to the attainment of certain ends; the national *polity* of the United States is republican; each administration has a *policy* of its own. *Policy* is often used as equivalent to expediency; as, Many think honesty to be good *policy. Polity* in ecclesiastical use serves a valuable purpose in distinguishing that which relates to administration and government from that which relates to faith and doctrine. See LEGISLATION.

Polk (pōk), **James Knox,** 1795–1849, president of the United States 1845–49.

pol·ka (pōl′kə, pō′-) *n.* **1** A round dance of Bohemian origin in common time, with three steps to every second measure. **2** Music for such a dance: a lively Bohemian or Polish tune in 2/4 time. — *v.i.* **·kaed, ·ka·ing** To dance the polka. [<F <Czech *pulka* half (step)]

polka dot 1 One of a series of spots of various sizes and spacing on a textile fabric. **2** A pattern made up of such spots.

poll[1] (pōl) *n.* **1** The head; hence, a person; also, the top or back of the head; crown. **2** A list of persons. **3** The voting at an election; the votes thus registered or voted; also, the place where they are registered or voted: used in the United States in the plural. **4** A poll tax. **5** The blunt or round end of a hammer or ax. **6** A survey of public opinion on a given subject, usually obtained from a sample group. — *v.t.* **1** To receive (a specified number of votes). **2** To enrol, as for taxation or voting; register. **3** To cast at the polls. **4** To canvass in a poll (def. 6). **5** To cut off or trim, as hair, horns, etc.; clip; shear. **6** To cut off or trim the hair, horns, top, etc., of: to *poll* cattle; to *poll* a tree. — *v.i.* **7** To vote at the polls; cast one's vote. ◆ Homophone: *pole.* [<MDu. *polle* top of the head] — **poll′er** *n.*

poll[2] (pol) *n.* In Cambridge University, England, a student who contents himself with a degree, without trying for honors. Such students are called collectively *the poll.* [<Gk. *(hoi) polloi* (the) many]

Poll (pol) *n.* A parrot. Also **Poll parrot, Pol′ly.**

pol·lack (pol′ək) *n.* A gadoid food fish (genera *Pollachius* and *Theragra*), resembling the true cod, but with the lower jaw projecting and barbel obsolete. *P. pollachius* is the common **European pollack,** *P. virens,* the **green pollack** or coalfish of the North Atlantic, and *T. chalcogramma,* of the North Pacific. Also spelled *pollock.* [Origin uncertain]

pol·lard (pol′ərd) *n.* **1** A tree shorn of its top so that it puts out a dense head of slender shoots. **2** An animal that has lost its horns. — *v.t.* To convert into a pollard. [<POLL[1]]

polled (pōld) *adj.* **1** Shorn of the head or top. **2** Shorn of the hair; bald.

poll·ee (pōl·ē′) *n.* A person whose opinion is polled.

pol·len (pol′ən) *n.* The fine yellowish powder formed within the anther of the flowering plant; the fecundating element in seed plants. [<L, fine flour]

pollen count A measure of the relative concentration of pollen grains in the atmosphere at a given locality and date: usually expressed in the number of grains of a specified variety of pollen per cubic yard.

poll evil An ulcerous abscess on a horse's poll, usually resulting from a bruise.

pol·lex (pol′eks) *n. pl.* **pol·li·ces** (pol′ə·sēz) The first or radial digit of the hand or forelimb of a vertebrate; the thumb. [<L] — **pol′li·cal** *adj.*

pol·li·ce ver·so (pol′ə·sē vûr′sō) *Latin* With thumbs reversed or extended downward: used among the Romans to denote that a defeated gladiator be killed. (The exact signals of mercy and punishment are matters of dispute.)

pol·li·nate (pol′ə·nāt) *v.t.* **·nat·ed, ·nat·ing** To supply or convey pollen to. Also **pol′len·ate.**

pol·li·na·tion (pol′ə·nā′shən) *n.* The transfer of pollen from anthers to stigmas. Also **pol′len·a′tion.**

pol·li·nif·er·ous (pol′ə·nif′ər·əs) *adj.* **1** Producing pollen. **2** Bearing or carrying pollen. Also **pol′len·if′er·ous.**

pol·lin·i·um (pə·lin′ē·əm) *n. pl.* **·i·a** (-ē·ə) A mass or body of pollen grains more or less coherent; a pollen mass. [<NL <L *pollen, pollinis* fine flour]

pol·li·no·sis (pol′ə·nō′sis) *n. Pathol.* Hay fever. [<NL <L *pollen, pollinis* dust + -OSIS]

Pol·li·o (pol′ē·ō), **Gaius Asinius,** 75 B.C.–A.D. 5, Roman orator and politician.

pol·li·wog (pol′ē·wog) *n.* A tadpole. Also **pol′ly·wog.** [ME *polwygle.* Cf. POLL[1], WIGGLE.]

pol·lock (pol′ək) See POLLACK.

Pol·lock (pol′ək), **Channing,** 1880–1946, U.S. dramatist, novelist, and lecturer. — **Sir Frederick,** 1845–1937, English jurist. — **Jackson,** 1912–1956, U.S. painter.

poll·ster (pōl′stər) *n.* One who takes public opinion polls. Also **poll′ist.**

poll tax A tax on a person, as distinguished from that on property, especially as a prerequisite for voting.

pol·lut·ant (pə·lōō′tənt) *n.* **1** That which pollutes. **2** Any of various noxious chemicals and refuse materials which impair the purity of water, soil, or the atmosphere.

pol·lute (pə·lōōt′) *v.t.* **·lut·ed, ·lut·ing** To make unclean or impure; dirty; corrupt; profane. [<L *pollutus,* pp. of *polluere* make unclean] — **pol·lut′ed** *adj.* — **pol·lut′ed·ly** *adv.* — **pol·lut′ed·ness** *n.* — **pol·lut′er** *n.* — **pol·lu′tion** *n.*

Synonyms: abuse, contaminate, corrupt, debauch, defile, degrade, deprave, dishonor, infect, ravish, soil, stain, taint, violate, vitiate. See CORRUPT, DEFILE[1], VIOLATE. *Antonyms*: clarify, clean, cleanse, clear, filter, fine, purge, purify, redeem, refine, renew, restore.

Pol·lux (pol′əks) See CASTOR AND POLLUX.

Pol·ly (pol′ē) **1** Mary; a familiar nickname used instead of *Molly.* **2** A parrot.

Pol·ly·an·na (pol′ē·an′ə) *n.* A person who always finds good in everything: so called from the heroine of stories by Eleanor H. Porter, 1868–1920.

po·lo (pō′lō) *n.* **1** A game played on horseback, usually with a light wooden ball and long-handled mallets. **2** A similar game played on ice or roller skates. [Cf. Tibetan *pulu* ball] — **po′lo·ist** *n.*

Po·lo (pō′lō), **Marco,** 1254?–1324?, Venetian traveler and author.

polo coat A tailored coat of camel's hair or material imitating camel's hair.

pol·o·naise (pol′ə·nāz′, pō′lə-) *n.* **1** A garment

for women, consisting of a waist and an overskirt in one piece. 2 A stately marchlike Polish dance, or the music for it. 3 A kind of antique Oriental carpet with a silk pile. [<F]

po·lo·ni·um (pə·lō′nē·əm) *n.* A radioactive element (symbol Po) produced by the disintegration of various uranium minerals: discovered in 1898 by Pierre and Marie Curie. See ELEMENT. [<NL <Med. L *Polonia* Poland]

Po·lo·ni·us (pə·lō′nē·əs) In Shakespeare's *Hamlet,* the chamberlain to the king and father of Ophelia and Laertes.

Pol·ska (pôl′skä) The Polish name for POLAND.

Pol·ta·va (pol·tä′və) A city of NE Ukrainian S.S.R.; scene of Peter the Great's victory over the Swedes under Charles XII, 1709.

pol·ter·geist (pōl′tər·gīst) *n.* A ghost or spirit reputed to make its presence known by any kind of clatter, as knockings and the noises of moving objects. [<G <*poltern* make a noise + *geist* spirit]

pol·troon (pol·trōōn′) *n.* 1 A mean-spirited coward; dastard. 2 A lazy idler; sluggard. — *adj.* Cowardly; contemptible. [<F *poltron* <Ital. *poltrone* cowardly, sluggish <*poltro* bed] — **pol·troon′er·y** *n.*

poly– *combining form* 1 Many; several; much: *polygamy, polygon.* 2 Excessive; abnormal: *polydactylism.* [<Gk. *polys* much, many]

pol·y·am·ide (pol′ē·am′īd) *n. Chem.* A polymer derived from compounds containing amine and carboxyl groups: used in the making of various synthetic fibers.

pol·y·an·dry (pol′ē·an′drē) *n.* 1 The civil condition of having more than one husband. 2 A social order that includes a plurality of husbands. 3 *Bot.* Having 20 or more stamens. [<POLY- + Gk. *anēr, andros* a man] — **pol′y·an′drous** *adj.*

pol·y·an·thus (pol′ē·an′thəs) *n.* 1 A variety of primrose (*Primula polyantha*), with many-flowered umbels. 2 A widely distributed, fragrant-flowered narcissus (*Narcissus tazetta*). [<POLY- + Gk. *anthos* flower]

pol·y·ar·chy (pol′ē·är′kē) *n. pl.* **·chies** Government by several persons of whatever class. — **pol′y·ar′chic** or **·chi·cal** *adj.*

pol·y·a·tom·ic (pol′ē·ə·tom′ik) *adj. Chem.* 1 Having more than one atom in the molecule. 2 Containing or capable of combining with several replaceable atoms.

po·ly·ba·sic (pol′ē·bā′sik) *adj. Chem.* Containing two or more atoms of hydrogen replaceable by a base or basic radicals: said of certain acids.

pol·y·ba·site (pol′ē·bā′sīt) *n.* A metallic, iron-black ore of silver crystallizing in the monoclinic system. [<G *polybasit*]

Po·lyb·i·us (pə·lib′ē·əs), 205?–120? B.C., Greek historian.

pol·y·brid (pol′i·brid) *n. Bot.* A hybrid plant derived from the crossing of two particular genera, species, or varieties. [<POLY- + (HY)BRID]

Pol·y·carp (pol′i·kärp), **Saint,** 69?–155?, bishop of Smyrna; martyred.

pol·y·car·pel·lar·y (pol′i·kär′pə·ler′ē) *adj. Bot.* Made up of many carpels.

pol·y·car·pous (pol′i·kär′pəs) *adj. Bot.* 1 Having the fruit composed of two or more distinct carpels. 2 Fruiting many times. Also **pol′y·car′pic.**

pol·y·cen·trism (pol′i·sen′triz·əm) *n.* The existence of several centers of power within an organization or political system, especially in the Communist world. — **pol′y·cen′trist** *n. & adj.*

pol·y·chae·tous (pol′i·kē′təs) *adj. Zool.* 1 Having several setae. 2 Of or pertaining to a class (*Polychaeta*) of annelids, including most marine worms. Also **pol′y·chae′tal, pol′y·chae′tan.** [<POLY- + Gk. *chaitē* hair] — **pol′y·chaete** *adj. & n.*

pol·y·cha·si·um (pol′i·kā′zē·əm, -zhē·əm) *n. pl.* **·si·a** (-zē·ə, -zhē·ə) *Bot.* A form of cymose inflorescence in which, below each flower, more than two secondary branches are given off from the main axis. [<NL <POLY- + Gk. *chasis* division]

pol·y·chrome (pol′i·krōm) *adj.* Done in several or many colors. — *n.* An association of several colors, as in decoration.

pol·y·chro·mic (pol′i·krō′mik) *adj.* Exhibiting many colors or changes of color. Also **pol′y·chro·mat′ic** (-krō·mat′ik) **pol′y·chro′mous.**

pol·y·chro·my (pol′i·krō′mē) *n.* The art of decorating or executing in several or many colors, as in ancient statuary and architecture.

pol·y·clin·ic (pol′i·klin′ik) *n.* 1 An institution furnishing clinical instruction in all kinds of diseases. 2 A general hospital in which many diseases are treated. Compare POLICLINIC.

Pol·y·cli·tus (pol′i·klī′təs) A Greek sculptor of the fifth century B.C. Also **Pol′y·cle′tus** (-klē′təs). — **Pol′y·cli′tan** or **·cle′tan** *adj.*

pol·y·con·ic (pol′i·kon′ik) *adj.* Of, relating to, or based on many cones.

polyconic projection A type of map projection in which the parallels of latitude are arcs of circles which are not concentric and the meridians, except the central one, are curved lines.

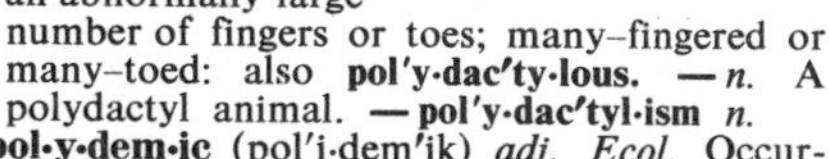

POLYCONIC PROJECTION

Po·lyc·ra·tes (pə·lik′rə·tēz), died 522 B.C., tyrant of Samos; crucified.

pol·y·dac·tyl (pol′i·dak′til) *adj.* Having an abnormally large number of fingers or toes; many-fingered or many-toed: also **pol′y·dac′ty·lous.** — *n.* A polydactyl animal. — **pol′y·dac′tyl·ism** *n.*

pol·y·dem·ic (pol′i·dem′ik) *adj. Ecol.* Occurring or dwelling in two or more regions: said of plants and animals. [<POLY- + Gk. *dēmos* region]

Pol·y·deu·ces (pol′i·dōō′sēz, -dyōō′-) Pollux. See CASTOR AND POLLUX.

Pol·y·do·rus (pol′i·dôr′əs, -dō′rəs) Greek sculptor of the first century B.C.

pol·y·em·bry·o·ny (pol′ē·em′brē·ō′nē, -brē·ə·nē) *n.* 1 *Bot.* The production of two or more viable embryos in a seed. 2 *Zool.* The production of two or more offspring from a single fertilized ovum, as identical twins in man.

pol·y·er·gic (pol′ē·ûr′jik) *adj.* Capable of accomplishing many tasks; energetically versatile. [<POLY- + Gk. *ergon* work]

pol·y·es·ter fiber (pol′ē·es′tər) *Chem.* A synthetic fiber of high tensile strength made by the esterification of ethylene glycol and other organic compounds.

pol·y·eth·y·lene (pol′ē·eth′ə·lēn) *n. Chem.* A tough, flexible thermoplastic resin, C_2H_4, made by the polymerization of ethylene: used in the making of moistureproof plastics having high electrical resistance.

Pol·y·euc·tus (pol′ē·yōōk′təs) Greek sculptor of the third century B.C.

po·lyg·a·la (pə·lig′ə·lə) *n.* 1 Any of a large genus (*Polygala*) of herbs and shrubs, natives of temperate and subtropical regions, and distinguished by simple, entire leaves, sometimes dotted, and showy magenta, purple, or white flowers; especially, the North American fringed polygala (*P. paucifolia*). 2 The milkwort. [<POLY- + Gk. *gala* milk]

po·lyg·a·mous (pə·lig′ə·məs) *adj.* 1 Of, pertaining to, or characterized by polygamy. 2 Mating with more than one of the opposite sex. 3 *Bot.* Bearing male, female, and bisexual or hermaphrodite flowers on the same plant. [<POLY- + -GAMOUS] — **po·lyg′a·mous·ly** *adv.*

po·lyg·a·my (pə·lig′ə·mē) *n.* 1 The condition of having more than one wife or husband at the same time. 2 The state of having more than one mate. Compare MONOGAMY. — **po·lyg′a·mist** *n.*

pol·y·gen·e·sis (pol′i·jen′ə·sis) *n. Biol.* The doctrine that organisms originate from cells of different kinds. Compare MONOGENESIS. — **pol′y·ge·net′ic** (-jə·net′ik), **pol′y·gen′ic** *adj.*

pol·y·glot (pol′i·glot) *adj.* 1 Expressed in several tongues. 2 Speaking several languages. — *n.* 1 A book giving versions of the same text, as of the Scriptures, in several languages. 2 One who speaks or writes several languages. [<Gk. *polyglōttos*]

pol·y·gon (pol′i·gon) *n. Geom.* A closed, usually plane, figure bounded by straight lines or arcs, especially more than four; a figure having many sides and angles. [<LL *polygonum* <Gk. *polygōnon*]

po·ly·go·na·ceous (pol′i·gə·nā′shəs) *adj. Bot.* Designating a family (*Polygonaceae*) of apetalous, widely distributed herbs, vines, shrubs, and trees; the buckwheat family, including the sorrels. [<POLYGONUM]

po·lyg·o·nal (pə·lig′ə·nəl) *adj.* Constituting or having the form of a polygon; having many angles: a *polygonal* figure. Also **po·lyg′o·nous.** — **po·lyg′o·nal·ly** *adv.*

polygonal number See under NUMBER.

po·lyg·o·num (pə·lig′ə·nəm) *n.* Any of a large and widely distributed genus (*Polygonum*) of annual or perennial herbs. The common smartweed, the prince's-feather, and the bistort are among the best-known species. Also **po·lyg′o·ny.** [<NL <L *polygonos* <Gk. *polygonon* knotgrass <*poly-* many + *gony* knee; from its many joints]

pol·y·graph (pol′i·graf, -gräf) *n.* 1 A device for reproducing a drawing or writing many times; a copy pad. 2 A mechanism for multiplying a drawing or writing. 3 A versatile or prolific author. 4 A collection of different treatises or books. 5 *Med.* A device for recording variations in the heartbeat and in respiratory movements: used as a lie detector. Compare PSYCHOGALVANOMETER. [<Gk. *polygraphos*] — **pol′y·graph′ic** or **·i·cal** *adj.*

po·lyg·ra·phy (pə·lig′rə·fē) *n.* 1 The use of a polygraph. 2 The art of writing in or of interpreting various ciphers.

po·lyg·y·nous (pə·lij′ə·nəs) *adj.* 1 Of, pertaining to, or practicing polygyny. 2 *Bot.* Having many styles.

po·lyg·y·ny (pə·lij′ə·nē) *n.* The marriage, mating, or cohabitation of one male with more than one female. [<POLY- + Gk. *gynē* woman]

pol·y·he·dral (pol′i·hē′drəl) *adj.* Of or pertaining to a polyhedron.

polyhedral angle *Geom.* The angle formed by three or more planes passing through a point; an angle at a vertex of a solid.

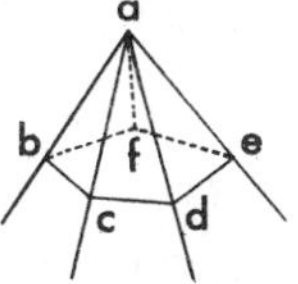

POLYHEDRAL ANGLE
Lateral angles *bac, bad,* etc., form angle at vertex *a.*

pol·y·he·dron (pol′i·hē′drən) *n. pl.* **·dra** (-drə) or **·drons** *Geom.* A solid bounded by plane faces, especially by more than four. [<NL <Gk. *polyedros* many-sided <*polys* many + *hedra* side]

Pol·y·hym·ni·a (pol′i·him′nē·ə) The Muse of sacred song. Also **Po·lym·ni·a** (pə·lim′nē·ə).

pol·y·math (pol′ə·math) *n.* One who is learned in many different fields or disciplines. [<POLY- + Gk. *mathanein* learn] — **pol′y·math′ic** *adj.*

pol·y·mer (pol′i·mər) *n. Chem.* 1 Any of two or more polymeric compounds. 2 Any compound formed by polymerization, especially one of higher molecular weight than the parent substance. [<POLY- + Gk. *meros* part]

pol·y·mer·ic (pol′i·mer′ik) *adj. Chem.* 1 Of, pertaining to, or manifesting polymerism. 2 Having the same chemical composition but different molecular weights and different properties, as acetylene and benzene.

po·lym·er·ism (pə·lim′ə·riz′əm, pol′i·mə-) *n. Chem.* The property possessed by several compounds of having identical percentage composition but different molecular weights.

po·lym·er·i·za·tion (pə·lim′ər·ə·zā′shən, pol′·i·mər·ə-) *n. Chem.* The process of changing the molecular arrangement of a compound so as to form new compounds having the same percentage composition as the original, but of different (usually greater) molecular weight and different properties. The method may be *linear,* by the successive addition of small structural units to form a chain; *cyclic,* by the formation of rings; or *cross-linked,* by a three-dimensional fusion of either linear or cyclic elements.

po·lym·er·ize (pə·lim′ə·rīz, pol′i·mə·rīz′) *v.t. & v.i.* **·ized, ·iz·ing** To subject to or undergo polymerization. Also *Brit.* **po·lym′er·ise.**

po·lym·er·ous (pə·lim′ər·əs) *adj.* 1 *Biol.* Consisting of many parts. 2 *Bot.* Having many parts or members in each whorl or series.

pol·y·morph (pol′i·môrf) *n.* A substance or organism that exhibits polymorphism. [<Gk. *polymorphos* <*poly-* many + *morphē* form]

pol•y•morph•ism (pol′i·môr′fiz·əm) *n.* **1** *Zool.* The property of assuming or passing through several forms, as an animal exhibiting seasonal changes in coloration. **2** *Mineral.* The occurrence in a mineral of two or more distinct crystal forms of identical chemical composition.

pol•y•mor•phous–per–verse (pol′i·môr′fəs·pər·vûrs′) *adj. Psychoanal.* Designating the generalized sexual potentialities of an individual, especially of a young child.

Pol•y•ne•sia (pol′i·nē′zhə, -shə) The islands of Oceania in the central and SE Pacific, extending east of Melanesia and Micronesia from the Hawaiian Islands to New Zealand; total, about 10,000 square miles.

Pol•y•ne•sian (pol′i·nē′zhən, -shən) *n.* **1** One of the native brown–skinned people of Polynesia: believed to be either of Malay stock originally stemming from a Caucasian strain of Asia, or of mixed Melanesian, Malay, and Caucasian stock. **2** A subfamily of the Austronesian family of languages spoken by these people. —*adj.* Of or pertaining to Polynesia, its people, or their languages.

pol•y•neu•ri•tis (pol′i·nōō·rī′tis, -nyōō-) *n. Pathol.* Simultaneous inflammation of many peripheral nerves.

pol•y•neu•rop•a•thy (pol′i·nōō·rop′ə·thē, -nyōō-) *n. Pathol.* Any morbid condition which affects several nerves at once, as alcoholism or vitamin deficiency. [<POLY- + NEURO- + -PATHY] —**pol′y•neu′ro•path′ic** (-nŏŏr′ə·path′·ik, -nyŏŏr′-) *adj.*

Pol•y•ni•ces (pol′i·nī′sēz) In Greek legend, a son of Oedipus and Jocasta. See SEVEN AGAINST THEBES.

pol•y•no•mi•al (pol′i·nō′mē·əl) *adj.* Of, pertaining to, or consisting of many names or terms. —*n.* **1**. *Math.* An expression, as in algebra, containing two or more terms. **2** *Biol.* A scientific name consisting of more than two terms. [<POLY- + (BI)NOMIAL]

pol•y•nu•cle•ar (pol′i·nōō′klē·ər, -nyōō′-) *adj.* Having many nuclei. Also **pol′y•nu′cle•ate** (-klē·it).

pol•y•ose (pol′ē·ōs) *n.* Polysaccharide. [< POLY- + -OSE[2]]

pol•yp (pol′ip) *n.* **1** *Zool.* **a** A many–tentacled, sessile aquatic coelenterate having a radially symmetrical body typically cylindrical or cup–shaped, as a sea anemone or coral. **b** A single unit of a colonial organism. **2** *Pathol.* A polypus. [<MF *polype* <L *polypus* a cuttlefish, a polypus <Gk. *polypous* <*poly-* many + *pous* a foot]

pol•y•par•y (pol′i·per′ē) *n. pl.* **•par•ies** *Zool.* The solid calcareous or chitinous stock of a colony of polyps, especially of coral. Also called *polypidom.* [<NL *polyparium* <L *polypus* a polypus]

pol•y•pep•tide (pol′i·pep′tīd) *n. Chem.* A compound formed by the union of two or more amino acids.

pol•y•pet•al•ous (pol′i·pet′əl·əs) *adj. Bot.* Having the petals free and distinct. [<NL *polypetalus* <Gk. *poly-* many + *petalon* a leaf, a petal]

pol•y•pha•gi•a (pol′i·fā′jē·ə) *n.* **1** Excessive craving for food; voracity. **2** *Zool.* The practice of eating many kinds of food. [<NL <Gk. <*polyphagos* eating to excess <*poly-* much + *phagein* eat] —**pol′y•pha′gi•an** *n.* & *adj.*

pol•y•phag•ic (pol′i·faj′ik) *adj.* Eating many things; subsisting on various kinds of food. Also **po•lyph•a•gous** (pə·lif′ə·gəs).

pol•y•phase (pol′i·fāz) *adj. Electr.* Having or producing several phases, as an alternating current.

pol•y•phe•mus (pol′i·fē′məs) *n.* **1** An animal, or sometimes a person, having but one eye. **2** A large American silkworm moth *(Telea polyphemus)* having a conspicuous ocellus on each hind wing. [<NL <L, POLYPHEMUS]

Pol•y•phe•mus (pol′i·fē′məs) In Homer's *Odyssey,* the Cyclops who imprisoned Odysseus and his companions in a cave, from which they escaped after blinding him in his sleep. [<L <Gk. *Polyphēmos,* a Cyclops, lit., many–voiced <*poly-* many + *phēmē* a voice]

pol•y•phon•ic (pol′i·fon′ik) *adj.* **1** *Phonet.* Representing more than one sound or combination of sounds, as some written characters. **2** Consisting of many sounds or voices. **3** *Music* **a** Designating or involving the simultaneous and harmonious combination of two or more independent parts or melodies. **b** Denoting an instrument, as a piano, by which two or more sounds may be produced simultaneously. Also **po•lyph•o•nous** (pə·lif′ə·nəs). [<Gk. *polyphōnos* having many tones < *poly-* many + *phōnē* a voice, sound]

polyphonic prose A poem set down on the page as prose: closer to the rhythms of prose than to those of verse and employing such devices as rime, assonance, and alliteration to produce poetic effects.

po•lyph•o•ny (pə·lif′ə·nē, pol′i·fō′nē) *n.* **1** Multiplicity of sounds, as in an echo. **2** *Phonet.* The representation by one written character or sign of more than one sound. **3** Counterpoint. [<Gk. *polyphōnia* a variety of tones or speech <*polyphōnos.* See POLYPHONIC.]

pol•y•phy•le•sis (pol′i·fī·lē′sis) *n. Biol.* The separate and distinct origin of a species of plants or animals from more than one line of descent. Also **pol•y•phy•ly** (pol′i·fī′lē). [<NL <Gk. *polyphylos* of many tribes <*poly-* many + *phylē* a clan] —**pol′y•phy•let′ic** (-let′ik) *adj.*

po•lyp•i•dom (pə·lip′ə·dəm) *n.* A polypary. [< L *polypus* a polypus + *domus* house <Gk. *domos*]

pol•y•ploid (pol′i·ploid) *adj. Genetics* Having more than two basic chromosome sets in the body cells. —*n.* A polyploid cell. [<POLY- + -PLOID]

pol•y•pod (pol′i·pod) *adj.* **1** Having many feet. **2** *Zool.* Pertaining to many–footed organisms. —*n.* A myriapod. [<POLY- + -POD]

pol•y•po•dy (pol′i·pō′dē) *n. pl.* **•dies** **1** Any one of a genus *(Polypodium)* of widely distributed ferns, typically epiphytic, and having naked sori. **2** The possession of many legs or abdominal attachments. [<NL <L <Gk. *polypodion* a kind of fern, dim. of *polypous, -podos* many–footed; so called from its many root branches]

pol•y•pous (pol′i·pəs) *adj.* **1** Having many feet or roots. **2** Pertaining to or resembling a polyp. **3** *Pathol.* Pertaining to, afflicted with, or resembling polypi.

pol•yp•tych (pol′ip·tik) *n.* An altarpiece or panel having more than three folds or leaves. [< Gk. *polyptychos* having many folds <*poly-* many + *ptyx, ptychos* a fold]

POLYPTYCH

pol•y•pus (pol′i·pəs) *n. pl.* **•pi** (-pī) *Pathol.* **1** A smooth growth of hypertrophied mucus found in mucous membrane, as in the nasal passages, bladder, rectum, etc. **2** A tumor. [<NL <L, a polypus]

pol•y•sac•cha•rid (pol′i·sak′ə·rīd, -rid) *n. Chem.* Any of a class of carbohydrates of high molecular weight, formed by the union of three or more monosaccharide molecules: they include starch, dextrin, inulin, cellulose, mucilage, and glycogen. Also **pol′y•sac′cha•rose** (-rōs).

pol•y•sep•al•ous (pol′i·sep′əl·əs) *adj. Bot.* Having sepals free and unconnected.

pol•y•sperm (pol′i·spûrm) *n. Bot.* A tree bearing a many–seeded fruit. [<Gk. *polyspermos* abounding in seed <*poly-* many + *sperma* a seed]

pol•y•sper•my (pol′i·spûr′mē) *n. Bot.* The condition of having numerous seeds in the fruit. Also **pol′y•sper′mi•a.** [<Gk. *polyspermia* < *polyspermos.* See POLYSPERM.] —**pol′y•sper′•mal** or **•sper′mic** or **•sper′mous** *adj.*

pol•y•ste•lic (pol′i·stē′lik) *adj. Bot.* Consisting of more than one stele or internal vascular cylinder. [<POLY- + STELE[2]]

pol•y•sty•rene (pol′i·stī′rēn) *n. Chem.* A thermoplastic polymer of styrene, C_8H_8; a clear, colorless, water–resistant resin: much used in the making of plastics, housewares, light fixtures, electrical components, surface coatings, etc. [<POLY(MER) + STYRENE]

pol•y•sul•fide (pol′i·sul′fīd, -fid) *n. Chem.* A binary compound containing more than one atom of sulfur in the molecule.

pol•y•syl•la•ble (pol′i·sil′ə·bəl) *n.* A word of several syllables, especially of more than three. [<Med. L *(vox) polysyllaba* (a) many–syllabled (word), fem. of *polysyllabus* polysyllabic <Gk. *polysyllabos* <*poly-* many + *syllabē* a syllable] —**pol′y•syl•lab′ic** (-si·lab′·ik) or **•i•cal** *adj.* —**pol′y•syl′la•bism** *n.*

pol•y•syn•de•ton (pol′i·sin′də·ton) *n.* Repetition of connectives or conjunctions for rhetorical effect, as, "east and west and south and north": distinguished from *asyndeton.* [<NL <Gk. *poly-* much + *syndetos* bound together <*syndeein* <*syn-* together + *deein* bind]

pol•y•syn•thet•ic (pol′i·sin·thet′ik) *adj. Ling.* Describing a language, such as Eskimo, or certain of the American Indian languages, in which the subject, object, verb, etc., of a sentence are combined into a single word and have no existence as separate elements. [<Gk. *polysynthetos* much compounded < *poly-* much + *syntithenai* <*syn-* together + *tithenai* put]

pol•y•tech•nic (pol′i·tek′nik) *adj.* Embracing many arts: also **pol′y•tech′ni•cal.** —*n.* A school of applied science and the industrial arts. [<F *polytechnique* <Gk. *polytechnos* skilled in many arts <*poly-* many + *technē* an art]

pol•y•the•ism (pol′i·thē·iz′əm) *n.* The belief in and worship of more gods than one. [<F *polythéisme* <Gk. *polytheos* of many gods <*poly-* many + *theos* a god] —**pol′y•the′ist** *n.* —**pol′y•the•is′tic** or **•is′ti•cal** *adj.*

Pol•y•thene (pol′ə·thēn) *n.* Polyethylene: a trade name. [Contraction of POLYETHYLENE]

pol•y•troph•ic (pol′i·trof′ik, -trō′fik) *adj.* Obtaining nourishment from several sources, as certain pathogenic bacteria. [<Gk. *polytrophos* highly nourished <*poly-* much + *trephein* feed]

pol•y•typ•ic (pol′i·tip′ik) *adj.* Existing in many types or forms. Also **pol′y•typ′i•cal.** [<POLY- + Gk. *typikos* <*typos* a type]

pol•y•un•sat•u•rat•ed (pol′ē·un′sach′ə·rā′tid) *adj. Chem.* Pertaining to or designating an aliphatic compound having many pairs of adjacent carbon atoms linked by two or more pairs of shared valence electrons: used especially of edible oils and fats.

pol•y•u•re•thane (pol′ē·yŏŏr′ə·thān′) *n. Chem.* Any of a group of synthetic, nitrogen–containing polymers with diverse properties, widely used in the manufacture of rigid or flexible solid foams for insulation and upholstery, resins for waterproofing, etc.

pol•y•u•ri•a (pol′i·yŏŏr′ē·ə) *n. Pathol.* Excessive urination. [<NL <Gk. *poly-* much + *ouron* urine] —**pol′y•u′ric** *adj.*

pol•y•va•lent (pol′i·vā′lənt) *adj.* **1** *Bacteriol.* Designating a type of vaccine containing antigens derived from two or more different strains of micro–organisms. **2** *Chem.* Multivalent. —**pol′y•va′lence** *n.*

pol•y•vi•nyl (pol′i·vī′nil) *adj. Chem.* Designating any of a group of polymerized vinyl derivatives extensively used in the production of high–quality resins: *polyvinyl* acetate.

Po•lyx•e•na (pə·lik′sə·nə) In Greek legend, a daughter of Priam, betrothed to Achilles and after his death sacrificed to appease his shade by Neoptolemus.

pol•y•zo•ar•i•um (pol′i·zō·âr′ē·əm) *n. pl.* **•ar•i•a** (-âr′ē·ə) *Zool.* The entire colony of a compound bryozoan, or its supporting skeleton. [<NL <*polyzoa* a bryozoan <Gk. *poly-* many + *zōion* an animal]

pol•y•zo•ic (pol′i·zō′ik) *adj. Zool.* **1** Of or pertaining to the *Bryozoa.* **2** Denoting a spore which produces many sporozoites. [< NL *polyzoa.* See POLYZOARIUM.]

pom•ace (pum′is) *n.* **1** The substance of apples or like fruit crushed by grinding. **2** Fish scrap. **3** The cake left after the expression of oil from castor beans. [<Med. L *pomacium* cider <L *pomum* an apple]

pomace fly A fruit fly.

po•ma•ceous (pō·mā′shəs) *adj.* **1** Relating to or made of apples. **2** Of or pertaining to a pome, or to trees of the rose family that produce pomes. [<NL *pomaceus* <L *pomum* an apple]

po•made (pō·mād′, -mäd′) *n.* A perfumed dressing for the hair or an ointment for the scalp. —*v.t.* **•mad•ed, •mad•ing** To anoint with pomade. [<MF *pommade* <Ital. *pomata* <*pomo* an apple, fruit <L *pomum*]

po•man•der (pō′man·dər, pō·man′dər) *n.* A perfume ball, or perfumed powder, formerly worn as an amulet; also, a box for carrying such perfume. [Earlier *pomamber* <OF *pomme*

d'ambre apple of amber < *pomme* an apple (<L *pomum*) + *ambre* amber]

pome (pōm) *n. Bot.* A fleshy, many-celled fruit with a core, as an apple, quince, pear, or the like. [<OF, an apple <L *pomum*, orig. a fruit]

pome·gran·ate (pom′gran·it, pum′-, pəm·gran′·it) *n.* **1** The fruit of a tropical Asian and African tree *(Punica granatum)*, about the size of an orange and having a hard rind and subacid red pulp with many seeds. **2** The tree. [<OF *pome grenate* < *pome* an apple (<L *pomum*) + *grenate* <LL *granata* <L *granatum*, orig. neut. of *granatus* very seedy < *granum* a grain, a seed]

pom·e·lo (pom′ə·lō) *n. pl.* **·los** A small variety of the shaddock; grapefruit. [Prob. <POME; infl. in form by Du. *pompelmoes* a pompelmous]

Pom·e·ra·ni·a (pom′ə·rā′nē·ə) A region of north central Europe along the Baltic, extending from Stralsund to the Vistula and including a former Prussian province with its capital at Stettin and the former Free City of Danzig; now a part of Poland except for a small area in NE East Germany: German *Pommern.*

Pom·e·ra·ni·an (pom′ə·rā′nē·ən) *adj.* Relating to Pomerania or its inhabitants. —*n.* **1** A native or inhabitant of Pomerania. **2** A small dog with pointed ears and muzzle, a bushy tail turned over the back, and long, straight, silky coat varying in color: believed to have originated in Pomerania.

POMERANIAN
(From 7 to 10 inches high; weight, 3 to 7 pounds)

Pom·er·el·ia (pom′ə·rēl′yə) A region of northern Poland on the Baltic and the Gulf of Danzig. *German* **Pom·mer·el·len** (pôm′ə·rel′·ən), *Polish* **Po·mo·rze** (pô·mô′zhe).

po·mi·cul·ture (pō′mi·kul′chər) *n.* Fruit culture. [< *pomi-* (<L *pomum* an apple, fruit) + CULTURE]

po·mif·er·ous (pō·mif′ər·əs) *adj.* Pome-bearing. [<L *pomifer* < *pomum* an apple, fruit + *ferre* bear]

pom·mel (pum′əl, pom′-) *v.t.* **·meled** or **·melled, ·mel·ing** or **·mel·ling** To beat with or as if with the pommel of a sword or with the fists. See synonyms under BEAT. —*n.* **1** A knob at the front of a saddle or on the hilt of a sword. **2** The butt of a firearm. Also spelled *pummel.* [<OF *pomel* a rounded knob, dim. of *pome.* See POME.]

Pom·mern (pôm′ərn) The German name for POMERANIA.

po·mol·o·gy (pō·mol′ə·jē) *n.* The science of fruits and the art of fruit culture. [<NL *pomologia* <L *pomum* an apple, fruit + *-logia* -LOGY] —**po·mo·log·i·cal** (pō′mə·loj′i·kəl) *adj.* —**po′mo·log′i·cal·ly** *adv.* —**po·mol′o·gist** *n.*

Po·mo·na (pə·mō′nə) In Roman mythology, the goddess of fruit and fruit trees.

Po·mo·na Island (pə·mō′nə) Largest of the Orkney Islands, Scotland; about 189 square miles: also *Mainland.*

pomp (pomp) *n.* **1** Magnificent or ostentatious display, especially in costume, equipage, etc. **2** *Obs.* A grand procession; pageant. See synonyms under OSTENTATION. [<OF *pompe* <L *pompa* <Gk. *pompē* a sending, pomp < *pempein* send]

pom·pa·dour (pom′pə·dôr, -dŏŏr, -dōr) *n.* **1** A style of arranging the hair by brushing it up from the forehead in a manner reminiscent of an 18th century style. **2** A style of bodice with low, square neck. —*adj.* Characterizing anything made fashionable by the Marquise de Pompadour: *pompadour* silk. [after Marquise de *Pompadour*]

Pom·pa·dour (pôn·pȧ·dŏŏr′), **Marquise de,** 1721–64, Jeanne Antoinette Poisson, mistress of Louis XV of France.

pom·pa·no (pom′pə·nō) *n. pl.* **·nos 1** A highly prized carangoid food fish (genus *Trachinotus*) of warm seas, especially *T. carolinus*, found off the coasts of the South Atlantic States. **2** A food fish of the American Pacific coast *(Rhombus simillimus).* [<Sp. *pámpano*]

Pom·pe·ii (pom·pā′ē) An ancient city of southern Italy SE of Naples; destroyed by an eruption of Vesuvius, A.D. 79. —**Pom·pe·ian** (pom·pā′ən, -pē′ən) *adj.* & *n.*

pom·pel·mous (pom′pəl·mōōs) *n.* An East Indian variety of shaddock. [<Du. *pompelmoes,* ? <Du. *pompoen* a pumpkin + older Malay *limoes* a shaddock <Pg., pl. of *limão* a lemon, citron]

Pom·pey (pom′pē) Anglicized name of Gnaeus Pompeius Magnus, 106–48 B.C., Roman general, statesman, and triumvir; rival of Julius Caesar: known as *Pompey the Great.*

pom·pho·ly·he·mi·a (pom′fə·li·hē′mē·ə) *n. Pathol.* An abnormal accumulation of gas bubbles in the blood, as in caisson disease. [<NL <Gk. *pompholyx* a bubble (< *pomphos* a blister) + *haima* blood]

pom-pom (pom′pom′) *n.* A rapid-fire, automatic cannon used especially as an anti-aircraft weapon. [From the sound made by the charge when fired]

pom·pon (pom′pon, *Fr.* pôn·pôn′) *n.* **1** In millinery, a tuft or ball, as of feathers or ribbon. **2** The colored ball of wool on the front of a shako, or on top of a sailor's cap. **3** A variety of chrysanthemum or dahlia having a small, compact, globe-shaped flower head. [<F <MF *pomper* exhibit pomp <OF *pompe* pomp]

pom·pous (pom′pəs) *adj.* **1** Marked by assumed stateliness; overbearing; ostentatious. **2** Magnificent; marked by ceremonious or impressive display. —**pom·pos·i·ty** (pom·pos′ə·tē), **pom′pous·ness** *n.* —**pom′pous·ly** *adv.*

Po·na·pe (pō′nə·pā) One of the most important of the eastern Caroline Islands; 129 square miles: formerly *Ascension.*

Pon·ce (pôn′sā) A port in southern Puerto Rico.

Ponce de Le·ón (pons′ də lē′ən, *Sp.* pôn′·thā thā lā·ôn′), **Juan,** 1460–1521, Spanish discoverer of Florida.

pon·cho (pon′chō) *n. pl.* **·chos 1** A South American cloak like a blanket with a hole in the middle for the head. **2** A similar garment, waterproofed or rubberized, and used as a raincoat. [<Sp. <Araucan *poncho, pontho*]

pond (pond) *n.* A body of still water, smaller than a lake. [ME *ponde,* var. of POUND[2]]

pon·der (pon′dər) *v.t.* To weigh in the mind; consider carefully. —*v.i.* To meditate; reflect. See synonyms under CONSIDER, DELIBERATE, EXAMINE, MUSE. [<OF *ponderer* <L *ponderare* < *pondus, ponderis* a weight] —**pon′der·a·ble** *adj.* —**pon′der·a·bil′i·ty** *n.* —**pon′der·er** *n.*

pon·der·ous (pon′dər·əs) *adj.* **1** Having great weight; also, huge; bulky. **2** Heavy to the extent of dulness; lumbering; labored. See synonyms under HEAVY. [<OF *pondereux* <L *ponderosus* < *pondus, ponderis* a weight] —**pon′der·os′i·ty** (-də·ros′ə·tē), **pon′der·ous·ness** *n.* —**pon′der·ous·ly** *adv.*

Pon·di·cher·ry (pon′di·cher′ē, -sher′ē) A former French settlement in SE Madras, India; a free city 1947–54; incorporated into India, November 1, 1954; 112 square miles. *French* **Pon·di·ché·ry** (pôn·dē·shā·rē′).

pond·lil·y (pond′lil′ē) *n. pl.* **·lil·ies** The water-lily.

Pon·do·land (pon′dō·land′) A district of eastern Cape of Good Hope Province, Union of South Africa; 4,000 square miles.

pond scum Any of a group of free-floating, fresh-water, green algae (*Spirogyra* and related genera).

pond·weed (pond′wēd′) *n.* Any of various submersed or partially floating perennial aquatic plants (genus *Potamogeton*) common in the Old and the New World.

pone[1] (pōn) *n.* **1** Bread made of cornmeal, sometimes with milk and eggs: also *corn pone.* **2** A small cake or patty of cornbread. [< Algonquian (Virginian), bread < *äpân* something baked]

pone[2] (pōn) *n.* In card games, the player at the dealer's right. [<L, imperative sing. of *ponere* place]

po·nent (pō′nənt) *adj.* Affirmative; constructive; positing: term used in logic. [<L *ponens, -entis,* ppr. of *ponere* place]

pon·gee (pon·jē′) *n.* A thin, natural, unbleached silk with a knotty, rough weave, originally made in China from the product of wild silkworms. [? Alter. of dial. Chinese *pen chi* home loom <Chinese *pun ki*]

pon·iard (pon′yərd) *n.* A small dagger, especially one with a slender triangular or square blade. —*v.t.* To stab with a poniard. [<MF *poignard* < *poing* a fist <L *pugnus*]

a b c

PONIARDS
a. Knife.
b. Japanese.
c. Senegalese.

pons (ponz) *n. pl.* **pon·tes** (pon′tēz) *Latin* A bridge: in Latin phrases.

pons as·i·no·rum (ponz as′·i·nôr′əm, -nō′rəm) *Latin* Asses' bridge.

pons Va·ro·li·i (ponz və·rō′·lē·ī) *Anat.* The organ containing the commissural fibers which connect the cerebrum, cerebellum, and medulla oblongata. Also **pons.** [<NL, bridge of Varoli; after Costanzo *Varoli,* 1542–75, Italian anatomist]

Pon·selle (pon·sel′), **Rosa,** born 1897, U.S. soprano.

Pon·ta Del·ga·da (pon′tə del·gä′də) **1** Easternmost of the three districts of the Azores; 326 square miles. **2** Its capital, a port and chief city of the Azores, on São Miguel.

Pont·char·train (pon′chər·trān), **Lake** A shallow lake in SE Louisiana, joining with the Mississippi at New Orleans by a canal; about 40 by 25 miles.

Pon·te·fract (pom′frit, pum′-, pon′ti·frakt) A municipal borough of West Riding, Yorkshire; site of an 11th century castle where Richard II died. Also **Pom·fret** (pom′frit).

Pon·te·ve·dra (pōn′tā·vā′thrä) An Atlantic province of NW Spain; 1,427 square miles; capital, Pontevedra.

Pon·ti·ac (pon′tē·ak), died 1769, Ottawa Indian chief who made war on the British.

Pon·ti·ac (pon′tē·ak) An industrial city in SE Michigan, 24 miles NW of Detroit.

pon·ti·a·nak (pon′tē·ä′näk) *n.* **1** A grayish-white gum resin obtained from the jelutong tree of Borneo: used as a friction compound on belting, etc. **2** A variety of copal from various species of dammar pine (genus *Agathis*): used in varnishes. [after *Pontianak*]

Pon·ti·a·nak (pon′tē·ä′näk) An Indonesian port on the west coast of Borneo.

Pon·tic (pon′tik) *adj.* Of or pertaining to the Black Sea or adjacent regions. [<L *Ponticus* <Gk. *Pontikos* <*Pontos* the Black Sea, Pontus < *pontos* open sea]

pon·ti·fex (pon′tə·feks) *n. pl.* **pon·tif·i·ces** (pon·tif′ə·sēz) A member of the highest priestly college of ancient Rome, the Pontifical College, which had supreme jurisdiction in religious matters. [<L *pontifex, -ficis* <Osco-Umbrian *puntis* a sacrificial offering + L *facere* make; infl. in form by L *pons, pontis* a bridge]

pon·tiff (pon′tif) *n.* **1** The pope; also, any bishop. **2** A pontifex of ancient Rome. [<F *pontife* <L *pontifex* a pontifex] —**pon·tif′ic** *adj.*

pon·tif·i·cal (pon·tif′i·kəl) *adj.* **1** Of, pertaining to or appropriate for a pontiff. **2** Having the pomp or dogmatism sometimes ascribed to a pontiff; hence, haughty; pompous; dogmatic. [<L *pontificalis* < *pontifex* a pontifex]

pon·tif·i·cate (pon·tif′ə·kit, -kāt) *n.* **1** The office of a pontiff. **2** A pope's term of office. —*v.i.* (-kāt) **·cat·ed, ·cat·ing 1** To perform the offices of a pontiff. **2** To act or speak pompously or dogmatically.

pon·til (pon′til) *n.* An iron rod used in glass-making to shape hot glass; a punty. [<F, appar. <Ital. *pontello, puntello,* dim. of *punto* a point <L *punctus*]

pontil mark The slight excrescence or scar left on a finished glass article after detaching it from the pontil: also spelled *punty mark.*

pon·tine (pon′tīn) *adj.* Of or pertaining to a bridge or bridges. [<L *pons, pontis* a bridge + -INE[1]]

Pon·tine Marshes (pon′tin, -tīn) A plain SE of Rome in west central Italy; about 300 square miles; formerly a swamp.

Pon·tius (pon′shəs, -tē·əs) See PILATE.

pon·ton (pon′tən) *n.* A pontoon. [<OF. See PONTOON.]

pon·to·nier (pon′tə·nir′) *n.* **1** A soldier in charge of pontoons. **2** A builder of pontoon bridges. [<OF *pontonnier* <Med. L *pontonarius* <L, *ponto, -onis* a pontoon]

pon·toon (pon·to͞on′) *n.* **1** A flat-bottomed boat, an air-tight cylinder, or the like, used in the construction of floating bridges, to support the roadway. **2** A bridge so supported: in the United States Army, usually *ponton.* **3** A float or a raft to ferry goods across water. **4** A float on the landing gear of a hydroplane. [<OF *ponton* <L *ponto, pontonis* < *pons, pontis* a bridge]

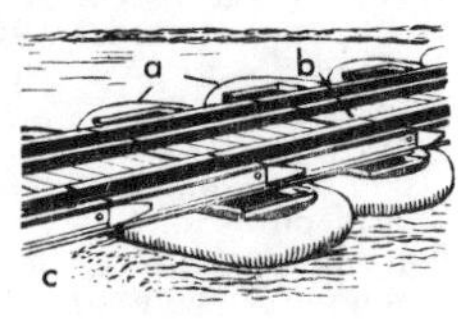

PONTOON BRIDGE
a. Pontoons.
b. Locking bridge sections.
c. Shore.

pontoon bridge A bridge supported on pontoons: distinguished from *fixed bridge.* Also **ponton bridge.**

Pon·top·pi·dan (pôn·tôp′i·dän), **Henrik,** 1857–1943, Danish novelist.

Pon·tus (pon′təs) An ancient country, later a Roman province, on the Black Sea in NE Asia Minor.

po·ny (pō′nē) *n. pl.* **·nies 1** A very small horse, especially one of a small breed; specifically, an Indian pony. **2** Anything small of its kind; specifically, a pony engine. **3** *U. S. Slang* A translation used in the preparation of foreign language lessons; a crib; trot. **4** In British racing slang, the sum of 25 pounds. **5** *Colloq.* A very small glass, for spirits, beer, etc. — *v.t.* & *v.i.* **·nied, ·ny·ing** *U. S. Slang* **1** To translate (lessons) with the aid of a pony or trot. **2** To pay (money) that is due: with *up.* [Var. of dial. E (Scottish) *powney,* prob. <OF *poulenet,* dim. of *poulain* a foal, colt <LL *pullanus* <L *pullus* a young animal]

pony engine *U. S.* A small locomotive for use in railroad yards.

pony express In 1860–61, a postal system by which mail was relayed from Missouri to California by riders mounted on swift ponies; also, the rider. See HORSE-POST.

po·ny·tail (pō′nē·tāl′) *n.* **1** A style of arranging long hair by gathering it tightly at the back of the head and letting it hang down like a pony's tail. **2** Hair so worn.

poo (po͞o) *v.t. Scot.* To pull.

pooch (po͞och) *n. Slang* A dog, especially a small mongrel. [? < dial. E and obs. *pooch,* var. of POUCH; ? with ref. to appetite]

pood (po͞od) *n.* A Russian weight equivalent to 36.1 pounds avoirdupois. [<Russian *pud* < LG *pund* ult. <L *pondo* a pound]

poo·dle (po͞od′l) *n.* One of a breed of dogs of high intelligence, with long, curly, usually white or black hair. [<G *pudel* <LG, short for *pudelhund* < *pudeln* splash in water; with ref. to its being a water dog]

pooh (po͞o) *interj.* Bah! foh!: an exclamation of disdain: also spelled *poh.*

Pooh-Bah (po͞o′bä′) *n. Colloq.* One who fills many offices inefficiently: from a character in Gilbert and Sullivan's *The Mikado.*

pooh-pooh (po͞o′po͞o′) *v.t.* To reject or speak of disdainfully. — **pooh′-pooh′er** *n.*

pook (po͝ok) *v.t. Scot.* To pluck; pick.

pool[1] (po͞ol) *n.* **1** A small body, usually of fresh water, as a spring. **2** A deep place in a stream. **3** Any small, isolated body of liquid: a *pool* of blood; a puddle. [OE *pōl*]

pool[2] (po͞ol) *n.* **1** A collective stake in a gambling game. **2** A combination, generally formed to overcome the effects of excessive competition, whereby companies or corporations agree to fix rates or prices and divide the collective profits pro rata; also, any combination formed for a speculative operation, as in stocks or the like, or the common fund raised for that purpose. **3** Any of various games played on a six-pocket billiard table, in which the object is to drive balls numbered from 1 to 15 into the pockets. **4** A combining of efforts or resources, as for a purpose or the benefit of the contributors. — *v.t.* To combine in a mutual fund or pool, as to satisfy a mutual need, finance an enterprise, etc. — *v.i.* To form a pool. [<F *poule* a stake, orig. a hen <L *pulla;* infl. in form by POOL[1]]

Poole (po͞ol) A municipal borough of SE Dorset, England, on the English Channel.

pool·room (po͞ol′ro͞om′, -ro͝om′) *n.* A place equipped for playing pool, billiards, etc.

pool table A billiard table with six pockets, one at each corner and one in the middle of each long side.

pool train *Canadian* A train operated by more than one railroad. Also **pooled train.**

poon (po͞on) *n.* Any of various East Indian trees (genus *Calophyllum*): also spelled *puna.* [<Singhalese *pūna*]

Poo·na (po͞o′nə) A city of central Bombay State, India.

poop[1] (po͞op) *Naut. n.* **1** A short deck built over the after part of the spar deck of a vessel of war; hence, generally, the stern of a vessel: also **poop deck. 2** A cabin covered by the poop deck: also **poop cabin.** — *v.t.* **1** To break over the stern or poop of: said of a wave. **2** To take (a wave) over the stern. [<OF *pupe, pope* <Ital. *poppa* <L *puppis*]

poop[2] (po͞op) *U.S. Slang v.t.* To bring to exhaustion; weary: usually used passively: He was *pooped* by the long climb. — *v.i.* To stop; cease or withdraw. [Origin uncertain]

Po·o·pó (pō′ō·pō′), **Lake** A lake in west central Bolivia; 12,106 feet above sea level; 60 miles long, 20 to 30 miles wide; about 8 feet deep.

poo·quaw (po͞o′kwä) *n.* A quahaug. [<Algonquian *poquau hock* a tightly closed shell]

poor (po͝or) *adj.* **1** Lacking means of comfortable subsistence; indigent; needy. **2** Lacking in good qualities, or the qualities that render a thing valuable; specifically, lacking in abundance or quality; scanty: a *poor* crop; of inferior workmanship or quality: a *poor* watch; deficient in vigor; feeble: *poor* health; lean; thin; feeble from ill feeding: That animal is *poor;* lacking in fertility; sterile: *poor* soil. **3** Wanting in strength or spirit; cowardly. **4** Devoid of elegance or refinements; uncomfortable: *poor* surroundings. **5** Deserving of pity; unhappy; wretched: the *poor* dog. **6** Devoid of merit; unsatisfactory: a very *poor* speaker. See synonyms under BAD[1], BASE[2], HUMBLE, MEAGER, SCANTY. [<OF *povre* <L *pauper.* Doublet of PAUPER.] — **poor′ness** *n.*

Poor Clare A member of a religious order founded in 1212 by St. Clare of Assisi and following a rule prescribed by St. Francis of Assisi; a Franciscan nun.

poor farm A farm where paupers are cared for at public expense.

poor·house (po͝or′hous′) *n.* A public establishment maintained as a dwelling for paupers.

poor·ly (po͝or′lē) *adv.* **1** With poor results. **2** Imperfectly; badly. **3** In the manner of the poor. **4** In a spiritless manner. — *adj. Colloq.* Poor in health; somewhat ailing.

poor-mouth (po͝or′mouth′) *v.i. Colloq.* To exaggerate one's financial difficulties. — **poor mouth**

Poor Richard Richard Saunders, the imaginary author of wise precepts in almanacs issued by Benjamin Franklin from 1732 to 1757.

poor-spir·it·ed (po͝or′spir′it·id) *adj.* Having little spirit or courage; cowardly. See synonyms under BASE[2]. — **poor′-spir′it·ed·ness** *n.*

poor white In the southern United States, one of a class of poverty-stricken white farmers or laborers, contemptuously called **poor white trash.**

pop[1] (pop) *v.* **popped, pop·ping** *v.i.* **1** To make a sharp, explosive sound. **2** To burst open or explode with such a sound. **3** To move or go suddenly or quickly: with *in, out,* etc. **4** To protrude; bulge: His eyes *popped.* **5** In baseball, to bat the ball into the air so that an opposing player can catch it, thus retiring the batter: with *up* or *out.* — *v.t.* **6** To cause to burst or explode, as corn by heating. **7** To thrust or put suddenly: with *in, out,* etc.: He *popped* his head out of the window. **8** To fire (a gun, etc.). **9** To shoot; also, to hit. **10** In baseball, to bat (the ball) into the air. **11** *Slang* To take (habit-forming or harmful drugs) by mouth or injection: to *pop* pills. — **to pop the question** *Colloq.* To make a proposal of marriage. — *n.* **1** A sharp explosive noise; a small report: the *pop* of a pistol. **2** The shot of a firearm. **3** A flavored soft drink containing carbon dioxide. **4** A shot, as in basketball. — *adv.* Like, or with the sound of, a pop; suddenly. [Imit.]

pop[2] (pop) *n. Slang* Papa. [Short for *poppa,* var. of PAPA]

pop[3] (pop) *adj. Colloq.* **1** Of or pertaining to a pervasive mass culture, especially that of young people. **2** Of or characteristic of the music favored by this group. **3** Of or suggesting pop art. [Short for POPULAR]

pop art *U. S.* A style of painting the subjects and manner of which resemble those of comic strips and advertising posters.

pop·corn (pop′kôrn′) *n.* A variety of maize, the kernels of which explode when heated, forming large white balls; also, the corn after popping.

pope (pōp) *n.* **1** *Often cap.* The bishop of Rome, the visible head of the Roman Catholic Church, accounted by that church the vicar of Christ and successor of St. Peter. He is elected by the college of cardinals, usually from their own number. **2** Any person having, or thought to have, similar great authority. **3** In the Greek Church, a parish priest. [OE *papa* <LL <LGk. *papas* a bishop, father <Gk. *pappas* father]

Pope (pōp), **Alexander,** 1688–1744, English poet and satirist. — **John,** 1822–92, U.S. general in the Civil War.

pope·dom (pōp′dəm) *n.* The office or dominion of a pope; papacy.

Pope Joan An old card game, a variety of newmarket. [after an alleged female pope, central figure of a 9th c. legend]

pop·er·y (pō′pər·ē) *n.* The religion of the Roman Catholic Church with all its doctrines and practices: an opprobrious term.

pope's-nose (pōps′nōz′) See PARSON'S-NOSE.

pop-eyed (pop′īd′) *adj.* Having bulging or protruding eyes; hence, amazed.

pop·gun (pop′gun′) *n.* A tube with a piston that expels a pellet with a pop.

pop·in·jay (pop′in·jā) *n.* **1** A coxcomb. **2** The figure of a bird, formerly used as a mark in archery, and later for firearms. **3** *Archaic* A parrot. [<OF *papegai* <Med. Gk. *papagas* a parrot <Arabic *babhagā;* infl. in form by AF *gai,* OF *geai* a jay]

pop·ish (pō′pish) *adj.* Pertaining to popes or popery: used opprobriously. — **pop′ish·ly** *adv.* — **pop′ish·ness** *n.*

pop·lar (pop′lər) *n.* **1** Any of a genus (*Populus*) of dioecious trees and bushes of the willow family, widely distributed in the northern hemisphere; especially, the **white** or **silver poplar** (*P. alba*) or the **Lombardy poplar** (*P. nigra*). **2** The wood of any of these trees. **3** Any one of several trees in some way resembling a poplar: the **Queensland poplar** (*Homalanthus populifolius*) of tropical Australia, and the **western, white,** or **yellow poplar** of the United States, more properly called *tuliptree.* [<OF *poplier* <L *populus*]

pop·lin (pop′lin) *n.* A durable plain-weave silk, cotton, rayon, or wool fabric, having cross ribs made of warp threads finer than the woof or filling threads: used for dresses, upholstery, etc. [<F *popeline, papeline* <Ital. *papalina* papal; with ref. to Avignon, a papal residence where the fabric was originally made]

pop·lit·e·al (pop·lit′ē·əl, pop′li·tē′əl) *adj.* Of or pertaining to the back part of the leg behind the knee. Also **pop·li·tae·al** (pop′li·tē′əl), **pop·lit′ic.** [<NL (*musculus*) *popliteus* popliteal (muscle) <L *poples, poplitis* ham]

Po·po·cat·e·pet·l (pō′pə·kat′ə·pet′l, pō·pō′·kä·tā′pet′l) A dormant volcano in central Mexico 45 miles SE of Mexico City in Puebla state; crater 250 feet deep, 2,000 feet across, and over a mile in circumference; 17,887 feet high.

pop·o·ver (pop′ō′vər) *n.* A very light egg muffin: so named from its rising over the dish in which it is baked.

Pop·pae·a Sa·bi·na (po·pē′ə sə·bī′nə), died A.D. 65?, wife of Nero.

pop·per (pop′ər) *n.* **1** Anything that pops or makes an explosive noise, as a popgun, firecracker, etc. **2** A container or device for popping corn.

pop·pet (pop′it) *n.* **1** *Mech.* A poppet head or a poppet valve. **2** A dainty little person; darling: a pet name. **3** One of several small bits of wood on a boat's gunwale to support the rowlocks. [Earlier form of PUPPET]

poppet head A pulley frame over a mine shaft, bearing the hoisting gear.

poppet valve *Mech.* A disk valve mounted on a stem and having a reciprocating motion in the direction of the longitudinal axis of the stem.

pop·pied (pop′ēd) *adj.* 1 Abounding in or adorned with poppies. 2 Caused by or as by the poppy; causing sleep: a *poppied* drink. 3 Drowsy as with opium.

pop·ple[1] (pop′əl) *v.i.* **·pled, ·pling** To have a heaving motion; ripple; bubble, as agitated water. — *n.* Rippling or bubbling water; bubbling, or its sound. [Prob. imit.]

pop·ple[2] (pop′əl) *n. Dial.* Poplar. [<L *populus*]

pop·py (pop′ē) *n. pl.* **·pies** 1 Any plant of the genus *Papaver,* typical of a widely distributed family (*Papaveraceae*) having lobed or toothed leaves and vivid red, violet, orange, or white flowers; especially, the **opium poppy** (*P. somniferum*), the **oriental poppy** (*P. orientale*), the **Iceland poppy** (*P. nudicaule*), the **mission poppy** (*P. californicum*), etc. ◆ Collateral adjective: *papaverous.* 2 The medicinal extract from such a plant. 3 The bright scarlet color of certain poppy blossoms: also **poppy red.** See CALIFORNIA POPPY. [OE *popæg, papoeg* <L *papaver*]

pop·py·cock (pop′ē·kok) *n. Colloq.* Pretentious talk; humbug; nonsense. [<colloq. Du. *pappekak,* lit., soft dung]

pop·py·head (pop′ē·hed′) *n.* A small, carved wooden finial, particularly at the end of a church pew.

Pop·si·cle (pop′sik·əl) *n.* A slab of frozen colored and flavored water at the end of two flat sticks: a trade name. Also **pop′si·cle.**

pop·u·lace (pop′yə·lis) *n.* The body of the common people; the masses. See synonyms under MOB[1]. [<MF <Ital. *popolaccio, popolazzo* <L *populus*]

pop·u·lar (pop′yə·lər) *adj.* 1 Pertaining to the people at large: *popular* demonstrations or government. 2 Widely approved or admired: a *popular* officer. 3 Suitable for the common people; easily comprehended: *popular* lectures. 4 Prevalent among the people: *popular* errors. 5 Suited to the means of the people: *popular* prices. 6 Of folk origin: the *popular* ballad. 7 Used by the people; current; colloquial: said also of many words on the borderline between slang and reputable usage. 8 Plebeian; vulgar; common. See synonyms under COMMON, GENERAL. [<L *popularis* <*populus* the people] — **pop′u·lar·ly** *adv.*

popular etymology A folk etymology.

pop·u·lar·i·ty (pop′yə·lar′ə·tē) *n.* The condition of being popular, especially of possessing the confidence and favor of the people or of a set of people.

pop·u·lar·ize (pop′yə·lə·rīz′) *v.t.* **·ized, ·iz·ing** To make popular. Also *Brit.* **pop′u·lar·ise′.** — **pop′u·lar·i·za′tion** *n.* — **pop′u·lar·iz′er** *n.*

pop·u·late (pop′yə·lāt) *v.t.* **·lat·ed, ·lat·ing** 1 To furnish with inhabitants; people. 2 To inhabit. [<Med. L *populatus,* pp. of *populare* <L *populus* the people]

pop·u·la·tion (pop′yə·lā′shən) *n.* 1 The whole number of people in a place or given area; also, any specific portion of that number: the foreign *population* of New York. 2 The act or process of populating or furnishing with inhabitants; the multiplying of inhabitants. 3 *Biol.* The total number of individual organisms being studied by statistical or biometric methods. See synonyms under PEOPLE. [<LL *populatio, -onis* <L *populus* the people]

Pop·u·list (pop′yə·list) *adj.* Of or pertaining to the Populist or People's party. — *n.* A member of the People's party. [<L *populus* the people] — **Pop′u·lism** *n.* — **Pop′u·lis′tic** *adj.*

Populist party See PEOPLE'S PARTY.

pop·u·lous (pop′yə·ləs) *adj.* Containing many inhabitants; thickly settled. [<L *populosus* <*populus* the people] — **pop′u·lous·ly** *adv.* — **pop′u·lous·ness** *n.*

por·bea·gle (pôr′bē·gəl) *n.* A large voracious shark (*Lamna nasus*) of northern waters, sometimes 10 feet long. [<dial. E (Cornish); ult. origin unknown]

porce·lain (pôrs′lin, pōrs′-, pôr′sə-, pōr′-) *n.* A white, hard, translucent ceramic ware, usually glazed, existing in many varieties, according to its composition and method of manufacture; china; chinaware. It is made from pure clay to which a little of the more fusible feldspar is added. [<OF *porcelaine* <Ital. *porcellana,* orig. a cowry] — **por·ce·la·ne·ous** (pôr′sə·lā′nē·əs, pōr′-) or **por′cel·la′ne·ous** *adj.*

porch (pôrch, pōrch) *n.* 1 A covered structure forming an entrance to a building, outside and with a separate roof, or as a recess in the interior as a kind of vestibule; a veranda. 2 An ancient covered walk or portico. Compare LOGGIA. — **the Porch** The Stoic school of philosophy in ancient Athens, named from the Stoa Poecile, or Painted Porch. See STOIC. [<OF *porche* <L *porticus* a colonnade <*porta* a gate. Doublet of PORTICO.]

por·cine (pôr′sīn, -sin) *adj.* Pertaining to, like, or characteristic of swine. [<F, fem. of *porcin* <L *porcinus* <*porcus* a hog]

por·cu·pine (pôr′kyə·pīn) *n.* A large, hystricomorphic rodent, having coarse hair thickly interspersed with erectile quill-like spines used for defense. *Hystrix cristata* is the common porcupine of the Mediterranean region; *Erethizon dorsatum* is the common Canada porcupine of eastern North America: also called *hedgehog.* [<OF *porc espin,* lit., a spiny hog <*porc* a hog (<L *porcus*) + *espin* a thorn <L *spina*]

CANADA PORCUPINE
(From 30 to 35 inches long in body length)

porcupine ant-eater An echidna.

porcupine fish A globefish.

porcupine grass A tall grass (*Stipa spartea*) of the western United States, yielding good forage and hay, but having long, stiff, sharp awns which twist through the wool into the flesh of sheep.

Porcupine River A river in northern Yukon and NE Alaska, flowing 525 miles north to the Yukon River.

pore[1] (pôr, pōr) *v.i.* **pored, por·ing** 1 To gaze steadily or intently. 2 To study or read with care and application: with *over:* to *pore* over one's accounts. 3 To meditate; ponder. [ME *pouren;* origin unknown]

pore[2] (pôr, pōr) *n.* 1 A small orifice or opening, especially a minute perforation in a membrane or tissue, as in the skin. 2 A minute interstice between the molecules of a body. 3 Any inlet or means of absorption or communication. [<OF *pore, porre* <L *porus* <Gk. *poros*]

por·gy (pôr′gē) *n. pl.* **·gies** 1 A sparoid, perchlike, salt-water food fish (*Pagrus pagrus*) of the Mediterranean and North Atlantic: often called **red porgy.** 2 Any of various other fishes, as the scup, sailor's-choice, or pinfish. [? Var. of PARGO; infl. by *pogy*]

po·rif·er·ous (pō·rif′ər·əs, pō-) *adj.* 1 Bearing or having pores. 2 Of or pertaining to a phylum (*Porifera*) of primitive, aquatic, chiefly marine animals, having bodies perforated by pores which lead to an internal cavity, and living attached to rocks, shells, and other supports; the sponges. [<NL *porifer* <L *porus* a pore + *ferre* bear]

po·rism (pôr′iz·əm, pō′riz-) *n. Math.* One of an ancient class of geometrical propositions intermediate between theorems and problems that asserted a relation between variables or affirmed the possibility of finding conditions under which a problem would become indeterminate. [<L *porisma* a corollary, a problem <Gk. <*porizein* carry, deduce <*poros* a way, a voyage]

pork (pôrk, pōrk) *n.* 1 The flesh of swine used as food. 2 A swine or swine collectively. 3 *U.S. Slang* Government money, distinctions, favors, etc., obtained by a representative for his constituency: a form of political patronage. [<OF *porc* <L *porcus* a hog]

pork barrel 1 A barrel in which pork is pickled and kept. 2 *U.S. Slang* A Federal appropriation for some local enterprise that will favorably impress a representative's constituents.

pork·er (pôr′kər, pōr′-) *n.* A pig or hog, especially regarded as a source of pork.

pork·pie (pôrk′pī, pōrk′-) *n.* 1 A thick-crusted pie with pork filling. 2 A man's hat with a low, flat crown.

pork·wood (pôrk′wo͝od′, pōrk′-) *n.* 1 The brown, coarse-grained wood of a small tree (*Torrubia longifolia*) with small flowers in cymes, found in southeastern Florida and tropical America. 2 The tree.

pork·y (pôr′kē, pōr′-) *adj.* **pork·i·er, pork·i·est** 1 Of or like pork. 2 Obese; fat.

porn (pôrn) *Slang adj.* Pornographic. — *n.* Pornography. Also **por·no** (pôr′nō).

por·no·graph·ic (pôr·nə·graf′ik) *adj.* Of or having the nature of pornography. — **por′no·graph′i·cal·ly** *adv.*

por·nog·ra·phy (pôr·nog′rə·fē) *n.* 1 Depictions of sexual acts or behavior, as in writing, photographs, motion pictures, etc., to stimulate erotic feelings. 2 The material containing such descriptions. [<Gk. *pornographos* writing of harlots <*pornē* a harlot + *graphein* write] — **por·nog′ra·pher** *n.*

po·ros·co·py (pō·ros′kə·pē, pō-) *n.* The study of the character and arrangement of the sweat pores, especially as shown on fingerprints: used in identification. [<*poro-* (<Gk. *poros* a pore) + -SCOPY] — **po·ro·scop·ic** (pôr′ə·skop′ik, pō′rə-) or **·i·cal** *adj.*

po·ros·i·ty (pō·ros′ə·tē, pō-) *n.* 1 The property of being porous; porousness. 2 A porous part or structure. [<Med. L *porositas, -tatis* <*porosus* <L *porus* a pore]

po·rous (pôr′əs, pō′rəs) *adj.* Having pores. — **po′rous·ly** *adv.* — **po′rous·ness** *n.*

por·phy·rin (pôr′fə·rin) *n. Biochem.* Any of a class of organic pigments derived from the breakdown of hemoglobin and chlorophyll, and consisting of four pyrrole nuclei. [Short for (*hemato*)*porphyrin* <HEMATO- + Gk. *porphyra* the purple whelk and its dye + -IN]

por·phy·rit·ic (pôr′fə·rit′ik) *adj.* 1 Pertaining or relating to porphyry. 2 *Mineral.* Containing well-defined, relatively large crystals in a fine-grained, glassy base or groundmass. Also **por′phy·rit′i·cal.** [<Med. L *porphyriticus* <L *porphyrites* porphyry <Gk. *porphyritēs* (*lithos*), lit., (a) purplelike (stone) <*porphyros* purple]

Por·phy·ro·gen·i·tus (pôr′fə·rō·jen′i·təs) See CONSTANTINE VII.

por·phy·roid (pôr′fə·roid) *n.* A greenish, grayish, or reddish crystalline and perfectly schistose rock, containing porphyritic crystals.

por·phy·ry (pôr′fə·rē) *n. pl.* **·ries** An igneous rock that has a groundmass enclosing crystals of feldspar or quartz. [<OF *porfire* <Med. L *porphyreus* <Gk. *porphyros* purple <*porphyra* the purple whelk and its dye]

Por·phy·ry (pôr′fə·rē) Anglicized name of Malchus Porphyrius, 233-304?, Neo-Platonic philosopher of Syrian origin; a disciple of Plotinus; opposed Christianity.

por·poise (pôr′pəs) *n. pl.* **·poises** or **·poise** 1 A gregarious cetacean, of the genus *Phocaena,* without a distinct beak; especially, *P. phocaena* of the North Atlantic and Pacific, from 5 to 6 feet long, blackish above and white below. 2 Any small cetacean; popularly, the common dolphin or the bottlenose. [<OF *porpeis, porpois,* lit., hog fish <L *porcus* a hog + *piscis* a fish]

COMMON PORPOISE
(Smaller than the 7 to 8 foot common dolphin)

por·ridge (pôr′ij, por′-) *n.* 1 A soft food made by boiling meal or flour in water or milk until it becomes thick. 2 A broth or stew of vegetables, sometimes containing meat. [Alter. of POTTAGE; infl. in form by OF *poree* vegetable soup]

por·rin·ger (pôr′in·jər, por′-) *n.* A small, shallow dish, having straight sides and sometimes ears. [Earlier *pottanger* <MF *potager* a soup bowl; infl. in form by PORRIDGE]

Por·se·na (pôr′sə·nə), **Lars** A semilegendary Etruscan king of the sixth century B.C. who marched against Rome to restore the Tarquins. Also **Por·sen·na** (pôr·sen′ə).

port[1] (pôrt, pōrt) *n.* 1 A harbor or haven; hence, a place of customary entry and exit for vessels, as for commerce. 2 *Law* Any place designated as a point at which persons or merchandise may enter or pass out of a country, under specified supervision: also *port of entry.*

[Fusion of OE and OF, both <L *portus* a harbor]

port[2] (pôrt, pōrt) *n.* **1** An opening in the side of a ship, as for a gun, light and air, or for the passage of cargo. **2** A gate, portal, door, or other entrance. **3** An orifice for the passage of a motive fluid, as air, gas, etc.: a steam *port*; exhaust *port.* [Prob. fusion of OE and OF, both <L *porta* a gate, door]

port[3] (pôrt, pōrt) *n.* **1** The way in which one bears or carries himself; mien; external manner: a majestic *port.* **2** The position of a rifle when ported. See synonyms under AIR[1]. — **high port** *Mil.* The position in which a soldier carries his rifle, diagonally across his body, while running or jumping. — *v.t.* **1** *Mil.* To carry, as a rifle, saber, or other weapon, diagonally across the body and sloping to the left shoulder. **2** To carry. [<OF *porte* < *porter* carry <L *portare*]

port[4] (pôrt, pōrt) *Naut. n.* The left side of a vessel as one looks from stern to bow: formerly called *larboard*: opposed to *starboard.* — *v.t.* To put or turn to the port or larboard side: to *port* the helm. — *adj.* Left; larboard: *port* side. [Prob. <PORT[1]]

port[5] (pôrt, pōrt) *n.* A sweet variety of wine, usually of a dark-red color. [Short for *Oporto wine,* from *Oporto,* Portugal; so called because orig. shipped from there]

port·a·ble (pôr'tə·bəl, pōr'-) *adj.* **1** That can be readily carried or moved. **2** *Obs.* Endurable; supportable. [<LL *portabilis* <L *portare* carry] — **port'a·ble·ness, port'a·bil'i·ty** *n.* — **port'a·bly** *adv.*

port·age (pôr'tij, pōr'-) *n.* **1** The act of transporting, especially canoes, boats, and goods, from one navigable water to another. **2** The route over which such transportation is made, or that which is transported. **3** The charge for transportation. [<F <OF <Med. L *portaticum* <L *portare* carry]

Por·ta (pôr'tä), **Giacomo della,** 1541–1604, Italian architect and sculptor. — **Giambattista della,** 1538?–1577, Italian physicist.

por·tal (pôr'təl, pōr'-) *n.* **1** A passage for gaining entrance; door; gate; especially, one that is grand and imposing. **2** The architectural composition that includes the entrances and porches of a large church or similar building. **3** Any opening or entrance resembling or suggesting the portal of an edifice: often in the plural. See synonyms under ENTRANCE[1]. — *adj.* **1** Pertaining to or entering at a port or gate. **2** *Anat.* Pertaining to or arranged like the **portal vein,** which conveys blood from the intestines and other abdominal viscera to the liver, there subdividing into capillaries. [<OF, a gate <Med. L *portale* a city gate, a porch, orig. neut. of *portalis* <L *porta* a gate]

Por·tal (pôr·tàl'), **Baron Antoine,** 1742–1832, French anatomist.

por·tal-to-por·tal pay (pôr'təl·tə·pôr'təl, pōr'-) A wage computed on the full time spent on mine or factory property from arrival to departure, not on actual working time.

por·ta·men·to (pôr'tə·men'tō, pōr'-; *Ital.* pôr'·tä·men'tō) *n. pl.* **·ti** (-tē) *Music* **1** A slur or glide from one note to another, sounding all the intervening tones. **2** Loosely, à legato passage or effect. [<Ital., lit., a carrying < *portare* carry <L]

port·ance (pôr'təns, pōr'-) *n. Archaic* Personal carriage; deportment; mien. [<MF, a carrying, support < *porter* carry <L *portare*]

Port A·pra (ä'prä) See APRA HARBOR.

port arms *Mil.* **1** A command to carry a rifle, saber, or other weapon at the port. **2** The position of the weapon when so carried. [< PORT[3], *v.* + ARMS]

Port Arthur A city of southern Manchuria at the tip of Liaotung Peninsula; site of a major naval base, operated jointly by the Soviet Union and the Chinese People's Republic after 1945: Chinese *Lüshun,* Japanese *Ryojun.*

por·ta·tive (pôr'tə·tiv, pōr'-) *adj.* **1** Of or pertaining to carrying; capable of carrying. **2** Portable. [<OF, fem. of *portatif,* lit., portable <L *portatus,* pp. of *portare* carry]

Port-au-Prince (pôrt'ō·prins', pōrt'-; *Fr.* pôr·tō·prañs') A port, capital of Haiti.

port authority Any official body having charge of the coordination of all rail and water traffic of a port.

Port Blair The capital of the Andaman and Nicobar Islands, a port on SE South Andaman Island.

Port Castries See CASTRIES.

port·cul·lis (pôrt·kul'is, pōrt-) *n.* A grating made of strong bars of wood or iron that can be let down suddenly to close the portal of a fortified place. [<OF *porte coleïce* < *porte* a gate (<L *porta*) + fem. of *coleis* sliding <L *colare* strain, filter]

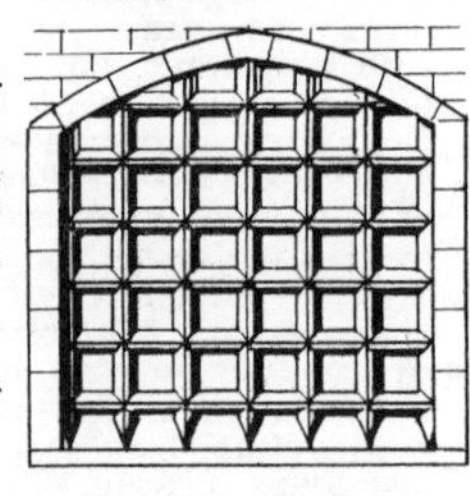

MEDIEVAL PORTCULLIS

Port du Sa·lut (pôrt də sə·lōōt', sə·lōō') A creamy, compact cheese with a flavor similar to that of Gouda.

Porte (pôrt, pōrt) *n.* The former Turkish government: with *the*: officially called **the Sublime Porte.** [<F *(la Sublime) Porte* (the High) Gate, trans. of Turkish *Babi Ali,* the chief office of the Ottoman Empire]

porte-co·chère (pôrt'kō·shâr', pōrt'-; *Fr.* pôrt·kô·shâr') *n.* **1** A large gateway for vehicles, leading into a courtyard. **2** A porch at the door of a building for sheltering persons entering or leaving carriages. [<F < *porte* a gate (<L *porta*) + *cochère,* fem. adj. < *coche* a coach]

por·tée (pôr·tē', -tā', pōr-) *adj.* Towed, carried, or transported by vehicles: said of artillery, cavalry units, etc. Also **por·té'** (-tē', -tā'). [<F, pp. fem. of *porter* carry <L *portare*]

Port Elizabeth A port of SE Cape of Good Hope Province, Union of South Africa.

porte-mon·naie (pôrt'mun'ē, pōrt'-; *Fr.* pôrt·mô·ne') *n. French* A pocketbook for money; especially, a small purse with clasps.

por·tend (pôr·tend', pōr-) *v.t.* **1** To warn of as an omen; presage; forebode. **2** *Obs.* To mean; signify. See synonyms under AUGUR. [<OF *portendre* stretch forth <L *portendere,* var. of *protendere* < *pro-* forth + *tendere* stretch]

Por·te·ño (pôr·tā'nyō) *n.* A native or inhabitant of Buenos Aires.

por·tent (pôr'tent, pōr'-) *n.* **1** Anything that portends what is to happen, especially a momentous or calamitous event. **2** The quality of portending; ominous significance. **3** A prodigy; marvel. [<L *portentum* < *portendere.* See PORTEND.]

por·ten·tous (pôr·ten'təs, pōr-) *adj.* **1** Full of portents of ill; ominous. **2** Of strange and ill-boding character, as if supernatural; monstrous; prodigious. See synonyms under AWFUL, FRIGHTFUL. — **por·ten'tous·ly** *adv.* — **por·ten'tous·ness** *n.*

por·ter[1] (pôr'tər, pōr'-) *n.* **1** One who carries things; especially, a man who carries travelers' luggage, etc., for hire, as in a hotel or at a railroad station. **2** *U.S.* An attendant in a Pullman car. [<OF *porteour* <L *portator* < *portatus,* pp. of *portare* carry]

por·ter[2] (pôr'tər, pōr'-) *n.* **1** A keeper of a door or gate. **2** One who waits at a door to carry messages. [<AF, OF *portier* <LL *portarius* <L *porta* a gate, a door]

por·ter[3] (pôr'tər, pōr'-) *n.* A dark-brown, heavy, English malt liquor resembling ale. [Short for *porter's beer* <PORTER[1]; so called because formerly drunk chiefly by porters]

Por·ter (pôr'tər, pōr'-), **Cole,** born 1893, U.S. composer and lyricist. — **David,** 1780–1843, U. S. commodore. — **David Dixon,** 1813–91, U. S. admiral; son of David Porter. — **Jane,** 1776–1850, English novelist. — **Noah,** 1811–1892, U. S. educator and editor. — **William Sydney** See O. HENRY.

por·ter·age (pôr'tər·ij, pōr'-) *n.* **1** The business of a porter. **2** The cost of carriage by a porter.

por·ter·house (pôr'tər·hous', pōr'-) *n.* **1** A place where porter, ale, etc., are retailed. **2** A restaurant; chophouse. **3** A choice cut of beefsteak including a part of the tenderloin, usually next to the sirloin: also **porterhouse steak.** [<PORTER[3] + HOUSE]

port·fo·li·o (pôrt·fō'lē·ō, pōrt-) *n. pl.* **·li·os** **1** A portable case for holding drawings, writing materials, documents, etc. **2** The position or office of a minister of state or member of a government. **3** A list of investments. [Earlier *porto folio* <Ital. *portafoglio* < *portare* carry (<L) + *foglio* a leaf <L *folium*]

port·hole (pôrt'hōl', pōrt'-) *n.* **1** A small opening in a ship's side. **2** Hence, an embrasure; loophole for shooting through. **3** The entrance to a port in an engine. See PORT[2].

Port Hudson A village on the east bank of the Mississippi in Louisiana; scene of a Union victory in the Civil War, 1863.

Port Huron A city on the St. Clair River and Lake Huron, SE Michigan.

Por·tia (pôr'shə, -shē·ə, pōr'-) The heroine of Shakespeare's *The Merchant of Venice.* She acts the part of a lawyer and defeats Shylock's claim for a pound of Antonio's flesh.

por·ti·co (pôr'ti·kō, pōr'-) *n. pl.* **·coes** or **·cos** An open space or ambulatory with roof upheld by columns; a porch. [<Ital. <L *porticus.* Doublet of PORCH.] — **por'ti·coed** *adj.*

por·tière (pôr·tyâr', pōr-; *Fr.* pôr·tyâr') *n.* A curtain for a doorway, used either instead of a door or as an ornament. Also **por·tiere'.** [<F < *porte* a door <L *porta*]

por·tion (pôr'shən, pōr'-) *n.* **1** A part of a whole, whether separated from it or not. **2** An allotment; share; especially, the quantity of any kind of food usually served to one person. **3** The part of an estate coming to an heir. **4** A dowry (def. 1). **5** One's fortune or destiny. — *v.t.* **1** To divide into shares for distribution; parcel: often with *out.* **2** To give a dowry to; dower. **3** To assign; allot. [<OF *porcion* <L *portio, -onis*] — **por'tion·a·ble** *adj.* — **por'tion·less** *adj.*

Synonyms (noun): part, proportion. When any whole is divided into *parts,* any *part* that is allotted to some person, subject, or purpose is called a *portion,* whether or not the division may be by some fixed rule or relation. But when we speak of a *part* as a *proportion,* we think of the whole as divided according to some rule or scale, so that the different *parts* bear a contemplated and intended relation or ratio to one another; thus, the *portion* allotted to a child by will may not be a fair *proportion* of the estate. See PART.

por·tion·er (pôr'shən·ər, pōr'-) *n.* One who divides in shares or holds a share or shares.

Port Jackson An inlet on the southern shore of New South Wales, Australia, forming the harbor of Sydney.

Port Jin·nah (jin'ə) A port of SW East Bengal, East Pakistan: also *Chalna Anchorage.*

Port·land (pôrt'lənd, pōrt'-) **1** A port on Casco Bay, SW Maine. **2** A port of entry on the Willamette River, NW Oregon.

Portland Bight See OLD HARBOR BAY.

Portland cement See under CEMENT.

Portland Race A dangerous, swift current off the coast of Dorset, SW England.

Port Lou·is (lōō'is, lōō'ē) A port, capital of Mauritius.

port·ly (pôrt'lē, pōrt'-) *adj.* **·li·er, ·li·est** **1** Somewhat corpulent; stout. **2** Of a stately appearance and carriage; impressive, especially on account of size. See synonyms under CORPULENT. [<PORT[3] + -LY] — **port'li·ness** *n.*

Port-Ly·au·tey (pôrt'lē·ō·tā', *Fr.* pôr·lyō·tā') A river port of NW French Morocco ten miles from the Atlantic: formerly *Kénitra.*

Port Ma·hón (mə·hōn', *Sp.* mä·ōn') A former name for MAHÓN.

port·man·teau (pôrt·man'tō, pōrt-) *n. pl.* **·teaus** or **·teaux** (-tōz) **1** Originally, a case for carrying clothing, etc., behind a saddle. **2** An oblong leather suitcase, hinged at the back, and fitted with catches, straps, and a lock, and with handles by which it can be carried. [<MF < *porter* carry (<L *portare*) + *manteau* a coat <OF *mantel* a mantle]

portmanteau word A word arbitrarily formed of two distinct words, as *chortle,* from *chuckle* and *snort; cyclotron,* from *cycle* and *electron*; a telescope word; a blend. [Coined by Lewis Carroll]

Port Mores·by (môrz'bē, mōrz'-) A port on the SE coast of New Guinea; administrative center of the Territory of Papua and New Guinea.

Pôr·to (pôr'tōō) The Portuguese name for OPORTO.

Pôr·to A·le·gre (pôr'tōō ä·le'grə) A port of southern Brazil, capital of Río Grande do Sul state.

Por·to Bel·lo (pôr'tō bel'ō) A port NE of

Colón on the Caribbean coast of Panama. Also **Por·to·be·lo** (pôr′tō·bā′lō).

port of call A port where vessels put in for supplies, repairs, discharge or taking on of cargo, etc.

port of entry A place, whether on the coast or inland, designated as a point at which persons or merchandise may enter or pass out of a country under the supervision of customs and other proper authorities.

Port–of–Spain (pôrt′əv·spān′, pōrt′-) A port of NW Trinidad, capital of Trinidad and Tobago colony. Also **Port of Spain.**

Por·to–No·vo (pôr′tō·nō′vō, pōr′-) A port in western Africa, capital of Benin.

Porto No·vo (nō′vō) A port in SE Madras State, India.

Porto Ri·co (rē′kō) The former official name of PUERTO RICO.

Porto San·to (sän′tō) Northernmost island of Madeira; 16 square miles.

Pôr·to Vê·lho (pôr′tŏŏ ve′lyŏŏ) Capital of Guaporé territory, western Brazil.

Port Philip Bay A bay on the southern coast of Victoria, Australia, forming the harbor of Melbourne.

por·trait (pôr′trit, pōr′-, -trāt) *n.* **1** A likeness of an individual, especially of the face, produced by an artist in oils, water color, etc., or by photography. **2** Hence, a vivid description of something or someone having existence. [<MF, orig. pp. of *portraire* <OF *pourtraire* PORTRAY]

por·trait·ist (pôr′trā·tist, pōr′-) *n.* One who makes portraits; a portrait painter or photographer.

por·trai·ture (pôr′tri·chər, pōr′-) *n.* **1** A representation of an object. **2** The act or art of portraying; especially, the art or practice of making portraits. **3** Portraits or pictures collectively. [<OF <*pourtrait,* pp. of *pourtraire* PORTRAY]

por·tray (pôr·trā′, pōr-) *v.t.* **1** To represent by drawing, painting, etc.; delineate. **2** To describe in words; depict verbally. **3** To represent, as in a play; act. See synonyms under IMITATE. [<OF *pourtraire* <Med. L *protrahere* <L, draw forth <*pro-* forth + *trahere* draw] **— por·tray′a·ble** *adj.* **— por·tray′er** *n.*

por·tray·al (pôr·trā′əl, pōr-) *n.* **1** The act of portraying by any method of depiction or delineation: the *portrayal* of a character on the stage. **2** The making of a likeness of persons, places, or things; picturing. **3** A portrait.

por·tress (pôr′tris, pōr′-) *n.* A woman porter or doorkeeper. Also **por′ter·ess.**

Port–Roy·al (pôrt′roi′əl, pōrt′-; *Fr.* pôr·rwȧ·yȧl′) A Cistercian abbey SW of Paris, France; noted as a Jansenist center in the 17th century; suppressed, 1709. Also **Port–Royal–des–Champs** (-dā·shäṅ′).

Port Royal **1** A town and naval station in Jamaica, British West Indies; destroyed by earthquake, 1692. **2** A town in southern South Carolina on **Port Royal Island,** one of the Sea Islands. **3** The former name for Annapolis Royal.

Port Sa·id (sä·ēd′) A port on the Mediterranean end of the Suez Canal, Egypt.

Ports·mouth (pôrts′məth, pōrts′-) **1** A port and the chief naval station of Great Britain, in Hampshire, England. **2** A port and naval station in New Hampshire; site of the signing of the **Treaty of Portsmouth,** ending the Russo-Japanese war, Sept. 5, 1905. **3** A port in SE Virginia, site of a U. S. naval base.

Por·tu·gal (pôr′chə·gəl, pōr′-; *Pg.* pôr′tŏŏ·gäl′) A republic of SW Europe in the western Iberian Peninsula; 34,222 square miles; including the Azores and Madeira islands, 35,419 square miles; capital Lisbon: ancient *Lusitania.*

Por·tu·guese (pôr′chə·gēz′, -gēs′, pōr′-) *adj.* Pertaining to Portugal, its inhabitants, or their language. **—** *n.* **1** A native or inhabitant of Portugal. **2** The people of Portugal collectively: with *the.* **3** The Romance language of Portugal and Brazil. [<Pg. *Portuguez* <*Portugal* <*Portucal* <Med. L *Portus Cale* Oporto]

Portuguese East Africa A former name of MOZAMBIQUE.

Portuguese Guin·ea (gin′ē) A Portuguese overseas province on the coast of western Africa; 13,944 square miles; capital, Bissau.

Portuguese India A former Portuguese overseas province on the west coast of India, comprising the territories of Goa, Damão, and Diu; annexed by India in 1961.

Portuguese man–of–war A pelagic siphonophore (genus *Physalia*) of warm seas, having long, stinging tentacles hanging down from a bladderlike float: also *man-of-war.*

Portuguese Timor See TIMOR.

Portuguese West Africa See ANGOLA.

por·tu·lac·a (pôr′chə·lak′ə, pōr′-) *n.* Any plant of a genus *(Portulaca)* of low, fleshy herbs of the purslane family, with scattered leaves, ephemeral flowers which open only in sunshine, and a globular pod. [<L, purslane] **— por′tu·la·ca′ceous** (-lə·kā′shəs) *adj.*

po·sa·da (pō·sä′thä) *n. Spanish* An inn.

pose[1] (pōz) *n.* **1** The position of the whole or part of the body, especially such a position assumed for or represented by an artist, photographer, etc.: the *pose* of the head. **2** Hence, a mental attitude; attitudinizing for effect. See synonyms under ATTITUDE. **—** *v.* **posed, pos·ing** *v.i.* **1** To assume or hold an attitude or position, as for a portrait. **2** To affect poses; attitudinize. **3** To represent oneself: to *pose* as an expert. **—** *v.t.* **4** To cause to assume an attitude or position, as an artist's model. **5** To state or propound; put forward, as a theory or problem. [<F <*poser* put down, rest; fusion of L *pausare* lie down and *pos-,* stem of *ponere* lay down, put]

pose[2] (pōz) *v.t.* **posed, pos·ing** **1** To puzzle or confuse by asking a difficult question. **2** *Obs.* To question closely. [Aphetic var. of obs. *appose,* var. of OPPOSE]

Po·sei·don (pō·sī′dən) In Greek mythology, brother of Zeus and husband of Amphitrite, god of the sea and of horses: identified with the Roman *Neptune.* **— Po′sei·do′ni·an** (-dō′nē·ən) *adj.*

Po·sen (pō′zən) The German name for POZNAŃ.

pos·er[1] (pō′zər) *n.* One who poses; one who strikes affected attitudes. [<POSE[1], *v.*]

pos·er[2] (pō′zər) *n.* A question or problem that baffles. [<POSE[2], *v.*]

po·seur (pō·zœr′) *n.* One who assumes or affects a particular attitude to make an impression on others. [<F <*poser* POSE[1], *v.*]

posh (posh) *adj. Slang* Very luxurious or elegant. [Origin unknown] **— posh′ly** *adv.* **— posh′ness** *n.*

po·sied (pō′zēd) *adj.* **1** Inscribed with a posy, as a ring. **2** With many posies or bunches of flowers.

pos·it (poz′it) *v.t.* To lay down or assume as a fact; affirm; postulate. Compare INFER. **—** *n.* That which is posited. [<L *positus,* pp. of *ponere* place]

po·si·tion (pə·zish′ən) *n.* **1** The manner in which a thing is placed; also, the place of its location. **2** Disposition of the parts of the body, especially with reference to therapeutic, surgical, or obstetric procedures; posture. **3** Relative social standing; high rank: Wealth commands *position.* **4** Employment or job: He lost his *position.* **5** The act of positing a principle or proposition, or the proposition posited; also, ground of argument; hence, the attitude assumed with reference to a subject; point of view: my *position* on the labor question. **6** *Music* The arrangement of the notes of a chord, as in voice parts. **7** In ancient prosody, the situation of a short vowel before two consonants or their equivalent, causing prolonged utterance: In "texunt," the vowels are long by *position.* See synonyms under ATTITUDE, CIRCUMSTANCE, PLACE. **—** *v.t.* To place in a particular or appropriate position. [<OF <L *positio, -onis* <*positus,* pp. of *ponere* place] **— po·si′tion·al** *adj.*

position light *Aeron.* Any of several variously colored lights used on an aircraft to indicate its position and path of motion.

position paper A report from a person or group setting forth a set of principles, a description of policy, or recommendations for action on a specific issue.

pos·i·tive (poz′ə·tiv) *adj.* **1** That is or may be directly affirmed; real; actual; existing: opposed to *negative.* **2** Inherent in a thing by and of itself, regardless of its relations to other things; absolute: opposed to *relative.* **3** Openly and plainly expressed; explicit; express; emphatic: opposed to *implied* or *inferred*: a *positive* denial. **4** Imperative: opposed to *discretionary.* **5** Dependent on authority, agreement, or convention: opposed to *natural*: *positive* law. **6** Not admitting of doubt or denial; incontestable: *positive* proof. **7** Free from doubt or hesitation; confident; certain; also, overconfident; dictatorial. **8** *Philos.* Pertaining to positivism (def. 2). **9** Noting one of two opposite directions, qualities, properties, etc., which is taken as primary, or as indicating increase or progression. **10** *Math.* Greater than zero; plus: said of quantities. **11** *Electr.* Having a relatively high potential: the *positive* electrode of a cell; specifically, designating the kind of electricity exhibited by a glass object when rubbed with silk. **12** *Physics* Having a deficiency of electrons: said of atoms which yield electrons. **13** *Biol.* Noting the response of an organism toward a stimulus: a *positive* tropism. **14** *Bacteriol.* Noting the presence of a specified condition or organism: a *positive* bacterial culture. **15** *Mech.* Operated by mechanical power, not by springs or gravity; operated or communicating power through intermediate inelastic parts that are under exact control. **16** Noting the north-seeking pole of a magnet and the corresponding (south) pole of the earth. **17** *Phot.* Having the lights and shades in their natural relation, as in a photograph. **18** *Gram.* Denoting the simple, uncompared degree of the adjective or adverb. See synonyms under DOGMATIC, RADICAL, SURE. **—** *n.* **1** That which is capable of being directly and certainly affirmed. **2** *Philos.* In positivism, that which is cognizable by the senses. **3** *Phot.* A picture giving the lights and shades as in nature; a print from a negative. **4** *Gram.* The positive degree of an adjective or adverb; also, a word in this degree, as *good, glad.* **5** *Electr.* A positive plate, pole, etc. See synonyms under CERTAINTY. [<OF, fem. of *positif* <L *positivus* <*positus.* See POSITION.] **— pos′i·tive·ly** *adv.* **— pos′i·tive·ness** *n.*

positive rays *Physics* Canal rays.

pos·i·tiv·ism (poz′ə·tiv·iz′əm) *n.* **1** A way of thinking that regards nothing as ascertained or ascertainable beyond the facts of physical science or of sense. **2** A system of philosophy elaborated by Auguste Comte, holding that man can have no knowledge of anything but actual phenomena and facts and their interrelations, rejecting all speculation concerning ultimate origins or causes. Compare HUMANITARIANISM. **3** Certitude, or the claim of certitude, in knowledge. **— pos′i·tiv·ist** *n.* **— pos′i·tiv·is′tic** *adj.*

pos·i·tron (poz′ə·tron) *n. Physics* A positively charged particle of an atom, with a mass equal to that of the electron. [<POSI(TIVE) + (ELEC)TRON]

pos·i·tron·i·um (poz′ə·trō′nē·əm) *n. Physics* An unstable, short-lived atomic entity consisting of a positron and an electron subject to mutual annihilation, with conversion of mass into energy. [<NL <POSITRON + *-ium,* suffix of names of elements]

po·sol·o·gy (pō·sol′ə·jē) *n.* The branch of medicine that treats of the dosages of drugs. [<F *posologie* <Gk. *posos* how much + *logos* word, study] **— pos·o·log·ic** (pos′ə·loj′ik) or **·i·cal** *adj.*

pos·se (pos′ē) *n.* **1** A posse comitatus. **2** A force of men; squad. **3** *Law* Possibility: chiefly in the phrase *in posse* (capable of being): distinguished from *in esse.* [<Med. L, power, armed force <L, be able]

pos·se com·i·ta·tus (pos′ē kom′ə·tā′təs) The body of men that a sheriff or other peace officer calls or may call to his assistance in the discharge of his official duty, as to quell a riot or make an arrest. [<Med. L, power of the county <*posse* a posse + *comitatus* a county <*comes, -itis* a count]

pos·sess (pə·zes′) *v.t.* **1** To have as property; own. **2** To have as a quality, attribute, etc.: to *possess* a conscience. **3** To enter and exert control over; dominate: often used passively: He was *possessed* by a devil; The idea *possessed* him. **4** To maintain control over (oneself, one's mind, etc.): *Possess* yourself in patience. **5** To put in possession, as of property, news, etc.: with *of.* **6** To have knowledge of, as a language. **7** To imbue or impress, as with an idea: with *with.* **8** *Obs.* To seize; gain. See synonyms under HAVE, OCCUPY. [<OF *possessier* <L *possessus,* pp. of *possidere* possess] — **pos·ses'sor** *n.*

pos·sessed (pə·zest') *adj.* **1** Having; owning: *possessed* of a ready tongue. **2** Calm; cool: to be *possessed* in time of danger. **3** Controlled by or as if by evil spirits; beyond self–control; frenzied. — **like all possessed** *U.S. Colloq.* As if driven by the devil; frenziedly.

pos·ses·sion (pə·zesh'ən) *n.* **1** The act or state of possessing. **2** A thing possessed or owned. **3** *pl.* Property; wealth. **4** The state of being possessed, as by evil spirits. **5** Self–possession. See synonyms under OCCUPATION, PROPERTY, WEALTH. Compare POSSESS.

pos·ses·sive (pə·zes'iv) *adj.* **1** Pertaining to or expressive of possession. **2** *Gram.* Designating a case of the noun or pronoun that denotes possession, origin, or the like. In English, this is formed in nouns by adding *'s* to the singular and to irregular plurals: *John's* book; *men's* souls; the *boss's* office; and a simple apostrophe to the regular plural and sometimes to singulars and proper names ending in a sibilant: *boys'* shoes; *Dickens'* (or *Dickens's*) writings; *James'* (or *James's*) brother. See also –'s[1]. Pronouns in the possessive case have special forms, as *my, mine, his, her, hers, its, our, ours, your, yours, their, theirs, whose.* By some grammarians possessive nouns and pronouns are called *possessive adjectives.* — *n. Gram.* **1** The possessive case. **2** A possessive form or construction. — **double possessive** A redundant possessive. Example: a book *of Mike's.*

pos·ses·sive·ness (pə·zes'iv·nis) *n.* Strong or excessive concern with one's own possessions.

pos·ses·so·ry (pə·zes'ər·ē) *adj.* **1** Pertaining to or having possession. **2** *Law* Proceeding from or depending upon possession.

pos·set (pos'it) *n.* A drink of hot milk curdled with liquor, sweetened and spiced. [ME *poshote, possot;* origin unknown]

pos·si·bil·i·ty (pos'ə·bil'ə·tē) *n. pl.* **·ties** **1** The fact or state of being possible. **2** A possible thing. See synonyms under ACCIDENT, EVENT.

pos·si·ble (pos'ə·bəl) *adj.* **1** That may be or may become true: opposed to *actual*: said of a thing, an event, or a statement. **2** That may be true in some contingency; imaginably true: sometimes used to denote extreme improbability: opposed to *certain, necessary, impossible.* [<OF <L *possibilis* <*posse* be able <*potis* able + *esse* be] — **pos'si·bly** *adv.*

pos·sum (pos'əm) *n.* **1** *Colloq.* An opossum. **2** *Austral.* A phalanger. — **to play possum** To pretend; deceive; feign ignorance or inattention; dissemble: from the fact that the opossum feigns death when threatened. [Short for OPOSSUM]

possum glider *Austral.* A flying phalanger.

pos·sum·haw (pos'əm·hô') *n.* The bearberry. [<POSSUM + HAW[2]]

post[1] (pōst) *n.* **1** An upright piece of timber or other material used as a support, a point of attachment, etc., as in a building. **2** A central projection in a lock for receiving the tube of a key. **3** A line or post serving to mark the starting or finishing point of a racecourse. — *v.t.* **1** To put up (a poster, etc.) in some public place. **2** To fasten posters upon; placard. **3** To announce by or as by a poster: to *post* a reward. **4** To denounce thus: to *post* one as a coward. **5** To publish the name of on a list. **6** To publish the name of (a ship) as lost or overdue. See synonyms under SET. [OE <L *postis* a door post]

post[2] (pōst) *n.* **1** Any fixed place or station, occupied or for occupation; especially, a place occupied by a detachment of troops; also, the garrison of such a station; the limits of a sentry's beat; the beat or position to which a policeman is assigned. **2** *U.S.* A local unit of a veterans' organization. **3** An office or employment; a position, as of trust or emolument; situation; especially, a public office. **4** A trading post or settlement. **5** *Brit.* One of the two bugle calls known respectively as **first post** and **last post.** The latter corresponds to *taps* in the army of the United States. See synonyms under PLACE. — *v.t.* **1** To assign to a particular position or post; station, as a sentry. **2** To appoint to a military or naval command. [<MF *poste* a post, a station < Ital. *posto* <LL *postum,* contraction of L *positum,* pp. neut. of *ponere* place]

post[3] (pōst) *n.* **1** **a** A rider or courier who travels over a fixed route or between stations on such a route carrying letters, dispatches, etc. **b** Any of the series of stations furnishing relays of men and horses on such a route. **2** An established system, especially a government system, for transporting the mails; also, the aggregate of mail matter transported from one place to another at one time; the mail; by extension, a post office: Has the *post* come in? Put your letter in the *post.* **3** A size of writing paper, 16 by 20 inches: so called because it bore a postman's horn for watermark. — *v.t.* **1** *Brit.* To place in a mailbox or post office; mail. **2** To inform: He *posted* us on the latest news. **3** In bookkeeping: **a** To transfer (items or accounts) to the ledger. **b** To make the proper entries in (a ledger). — *v.i.* **4** To travel with post horses. **5** To travel with speed; hasten. **6** In horseback riding, to rise from the saddle in rhythm with a horse's gait when trotting. — *adv.* By post horses; hence, rapidly. [<MF *poste* <Ital. *posta,* orig. a station <LL, contraction of L *posita,* pp. fem. of *ponere* place]

post– *prefix* **1** After in time or order; following: *postdate, postwar.* **2** Chiefly in scientific terms, after in position; behind: *postorbital.* [<L *post-* <*post* behind, after]

Post (pōst), **Emily,** 1873–1960, *née* Price, U. S. columnist and writer on social etiquette.

post·age (pōs'tij) *n.* **1** The charge levied on mail matter. **2** The act of going by post. [< POST[3] (def. 2) + -AGE]

postage stamp A small, printed label issued and sold by a government to be affixed to letters, parcels, etc., in payment of postage.

pos·tal (pōs'təl) *adj.* Pertaining to the mails or to mail service. — *n.* A postal card.

postal card A card, issued officially, for carrying a written or printed message through the mails under government stamp: also *postal.* Compare POSTCARD.

postal currency An emergency stamp money, used during the Civil War in the United States (1862–65). Also **postage currency.**

Postal Union An aggregation of countries, organized in 1874, agreeing to deliver foreign mail: officially designated *Universal Postal Union.*

post–bel·lum (pōst'bel'əm) *adj.* Coming or occurring after the war, especially the Civil War. [<L, after the war <*post* after + *bellum* a war]

post box A mailbox.

post·ca·non·i·cal (pōst'kə·non'i·kəl) *adj.* Occurring later than the writing of the Scripture canon.

post captain **1** Formerly, in the British Navy, a captain of three years' standing. **2** Formerly, in the U.S. Navy, a senior captain.

post·card (pōst'kärd') *n.* **1** A postal card. **2** An unofficial card of any regulation size transmissible under postal regulations through the mails on prepayment of the same postage as a postal card.

post–chaise (pōst'shāz') *n.* A traveling carriage.

post·clas·si·cal (pōst'klas'i·kəl) *adj.* Being or occurring between the Greek and Latin classical and the medieval writers. Also **post'·clas'sic.**

post·com·mun·ion (pōst'kə·myōōn'yən) *adj.* Coming after communion: a *postcommunion* prayer. — *n.* The part of the Eucharist which follows the distribution of the elements.

post·date (pōst'dāt') *v.t.* **·dat·ed, ·dat·ing** **1** To assign or affix a date later than the actual date to (a check, document, etc.). **2** To follow in time.

post·di·lu·vi·al (pōst'di·lōō'vē·əl) *adj.* Coming after the deluge.

post·di·lu·vi·an (pōst'di·lōō'vē·ən) *n.* One living after the deluge. — *adj.* Postdiluvial.

post·ed (pōs'tid) *adj.* Possessed of the latest information or news: Keep me *posted.* [< POST[3], *v.* (def. 2)]

pos·teen (pos·tēn') *n.* An Indian garment made of sheepskin with the fleece left on: also *postin.* [<Persian *pōstīn* of leather < *pōst* a skin]

post·er[1] (pōs'tər) *n.* **1** A placard or bill used for advertising, public information, etc., to be posted on a wall or other surface. **2** A billposter. [< *post*[1], *v.*]

post·er[2] (pōs'tər) *n.* **1** One who travels post. **2** A post horse. [<POST[3], *v.*]

poste res·tante (pōst res·tänt', *Fr.* pôst res·tänt') *French* The department of a post office that has charge of mail matter to be held until called for.

pos·te·ri·or (pos·tir'ē·ər) *adj.* **1** Situated behind or toward the hinder part: opposed to *anterior.* **2** Coming after another in a series; especially, subsequent in point of time; later: in this sense opposed to *prior.* **3** *Bot.* Situated or growing on the side next the parent axis: the *posterior* side of an axillary flower. **4** *Zool.* In the direction of the tail; caudal. **5** *Anat.* Dorsal. — *n. Often pl.* The buttocks. [<L *posterior,* comp. of *posterus* following < *post* after]

pos·te·ri·or·i·ty (pos·tir'ē·ôr'ə·tē, -or'ə-) *n.* The state of being posterior or later in point of time: opposed to *priority.*

pos·te·ri·or·ly (pos·tir'ē·ər·lē) *adv.* **1** Subsequently. **2** Behind.

pos·ter·i·ty (pos·ter'ə·tē) *n.* **1** The stock that proceeds from a progenitor; a person's descendants; also, succeeding generations, taken collectively: the *posterity* of Adam. **2** Posteriority. [<OF *posterite* <L *posteritas* < *posterus.* See POSTERIOR.]

pos·tern (pōs'tərn, pos'-) *n.* **1** A back gate or door; a private entrance, especially a small gate beside a large one in a fortified place. **2** A covered passage closed by a gate and leading from a bastion to the ditch. — *adj.* Situated at the back; private: a *postern* gate. [<OF *posterne, posterle* <L *posterus.* See POSTERIOR.]

Post Exchange An establishment for the sale of merchandise and services to military personnel: abbr. *PX.*

post·ex·il·i·an (pōst'eg·zil'ē·ən) *adj.* Pertaining to that period of Jewish history subsequent to the Babylonian exile (605 to 536 B.C.). Also **post'ex·il'ic.**

post·fix (pōst'fiks') *v.t.* To add at the end of a word, as a letter, syllable, etc.: opposed to *prefix.* — *n.* (pōst'fiks') That which is so added; a suffix. [<POST- + (AF)FIX]

post·gla·cial (pōst'glā'shəl) *Geol. adj.* Later than the glacial epoch; specifically, formed since the disappearance of the Pleistocene continental glaciers. — *n.* A sedimentary deposit resulting from the retreat of a continental glacier.

post·grad·u·ate (pōst'graj'ōō·it, -āt) *adj.* Of or pertaining to studies pursued after receiving a first degree; graduate. — *n.* One who pursues or has completed a postgraduate course.

post·haste (pōst'hāst') *adj.* Done with speed; instant. — *n.* Great haste or speed like that of the post. — *adv.* With utmost speed; hurriedly. [Appar. < *Haste, post, haste,* an old direction written on letters]

post horse A horse kept at a post–house for postriders or for hire to travelers.

post–house (pōst'hous') *n.* A house where post horses were kept for relay; also, formerly, a post office.

post·hu·mous (pos'chōō·məs) *adj.* **1** Born after the father's death: said of a child. **2** Published after the author's death, as a book. **3** Arising or continuing after a person's death: a *posthumous* reputation. [<LL *posthumus* <L *postumus* latest, last, superl. of *posterus.* See POSTERIOR.] — **post'hu·mous·ly** *adv.*

pos·tiche (pôs·tēsh') *adj.* **1** Added after the completion of the work: said especially of a superadded and inappropriate architectural ornament. **2** Spurious; artificial. — *n.* **1** Pretense; sham. **2** An imitation; artificial substitute. Also **pos·tique'** (-tēk'). [<F <Ital. *posticcio* counterfeit <LL *appositicius* <L *appositus.* See APPOSITE.]

pos·ti·cous (pos·tī'kəs) *adj. Bot.* Hinder; posterior. [<L *posticus* < *post* after]

pos·til (pos'til) *n.* A marginal note; especially, one written on the margin of the Scriptures; also, a series of Scriptural comments. [<OF *postille* <Med. L *postilla* a gloss on the gospel, ? <L *post illa (verba textus)* after those (words of the text) < *post* after + *illa* those]

pos·til·ion (pōs·til'yən, pos-) *n.* A rider of one of the near horses of a team drawing a vehicle, with or without a coachman. Also **pos·til'lion.** [<MF *postillon* <Ital. *postiglione* < *posta* a post, station]

post·im·pres·sion·ism (pōst′im·presh′ən·iz′əm) *n.* The methods, theories, or practice of a group of painters of the late 19th century who emphasized the subjective prerogatives of the artist as opposed to the literal or idealistic representation of academic painting and the supposed objectivity of impressionism. Cézanne, Van Gogh, and Gauguin are considered its chief exponents. — **post′im·pres′sion·ist** *n.* & *adj.* — **post′im·pres′sion·is′·tic** *adj.*

pos·tin (pos·tēn′, -tin′) See POSTEEN.

post·li·min·i·um (pōst′li·min′ē·əm) *n.* In international law, a right (*Latin* **jus postliminii**), derived from Roman law, whereby persons or things taken in war by the enemy are restored to their former civil condition or previous ownership upon their coming again under the power of the nation to which they belonged. Also **post·lim·i·ny** (pōst·lim′ə·nē). [<L <*post* after, behind + *limen, liminis* a threshold]

post·lude (pōst′lo͞od) *n.* An organ voluntary concluding a church service. See PRELUDE. [<POST- + (PRE)LUDE]

post·man (post′mən) *n.* *pl.* **·men** (-mən) A letter-carrier; mail-carrier; formerly, a courier.

post·mark (pōst′märk′) *n.* The stamp of a post office on mail matter handled there, sometimes also serving to cancel stamps, and giving the name of the office and the day (in large cities also the hour) of mailing or arrival. — *v.t.* To stamp with a postmark.

post·mas·ter (pōst′mas′tər, -mäs′-) *n.* **1** An official having charge of a post office. **2** One who provides horses for posting. — **post′·mis′tress** (-mis′tris) *n. fem.*

postmaster general *pl.* **postmasters general** The executive head of the postal service of a government.

post·me·rid·i·an (pōst′mə·rid′ē·ən) *adj.* Pertaining to the afternoon. Also **post′me·rid′i·o·nal.** [<L *postmeridianus* <*post-* after + *meridianus* MERIDIAN]

post me·rid·i·em (pōst mə·rid′ē·əm) After midday: abbr. *p.m.* or *P.M.* [<L]

post·mil·len·ni·al (pōst′mi·len′ē·əl) *adj.* Of or pertaining to a period after the millennium. Also **post′mil·len′ni·an.**

post·mil·len·ni·al·ism (pōst′mi·len′ē·əl·iz′əm) *n.* *Theol.* The tenet that Christ's second coming will follow the millennium: opposed to *premillennialism.* Also **post·mil·le·nar·i·an·ism** (pōst·mil′ə·nâr′ē·ən·iz′əm). — **post′mil·len′ni·al·ist** *n.*

post-mor·tem (pōst·môr′təm) *n.* Expert examination of a human body after death for pathological or judicial purposes; an autopsy. [<L, after death <*post* after + *mors, mortis* death]

post mor·tem (môr′təm) *Latin* After death.

post·na·tal (pōst·nāt′l) *adj.* Occurring after birth.

post note A promissory note issued by a bank and payable at a fixed time after its date.

post·nup·tial (pōst·nup′chəl) *adj.* Happening or occurring after marriage; made after marriage: a *postnuptial* settlement.

post-o·bit (pōst·ō′bit) *adj.* Made or done after death; taking effect after death: also **post′-o·bit′u·ar′y** (-ō·bich′o͞o·er′ē). — *n.* A bond given to secure payment by the obligor of a sum of money on the death of a designated person, generally one from whose estate he has expectations: also **post-obit bond.** [Contraction of POST OBITUM]

post ob·i·tum (ob′i·təm) *Latin* After death.

post office **1** That branch of the civil service of a government charged with carrying and delivering the mails. **2** An office for the receipt, transmission, and delivery of mails, and for the transaction of business connected with the same. **3** Any town or place having a post office. **4** A kissing game. — **post-of·fice** (pōst′ôf′is, -of′-) *adj.*

Post Office Department An executive department of the U.S. government since 1872 (originally established in 1789), headed by the Postmaster General, which maintains and operates the postal system.

post·op·er·a·tive (pōst·op′ər·ə·tiv, -ə·rā′-) *adj.* *Surg.* Occurring after an operation.

post·or·bi·tal (pōst·ôr′bi·təl) *adj.* *Anat.* Situated behind the orbit or socket of the eye. — *n.* **1** A bone of some reptiles at the posterior part of the orbit. **2** A scale behind the orbit, as in snakes.

post-paid (pōst′pād′) *adj.* Having postage prepaid.

post·par·tum (pōst′pär′təm) *adj.* *Med.* After childbirth: a *postpartum* fever. [<POST- + L *partus* childbirth <*parere* bear]

post·pone (pōst·pōn′) *v.t.* **·poned, ·pon·ing** **1** To put off to a future time; defer; delay. **2** To subordinate. [<L *postponere* <*post-* after + *ponere* put] — **post·pon′a·ble** *adj.* — **post·pone′ment** *n.* — **post·pon′er** *n.*

Synonyms: adjourn, defer, delay, procrastinate. *Adjourn* signifies literally to put off to another day, and, hence, to any future time. A deliberative assembly may *adjourn* to another day or to another hour of the same day, and resume business, where it left off, as if there had been no interval; or it may *adjourn* to a definite later date or, when no day can be fixed, to meet at the call of the president or other officer. In common usage, to *adjourn* a matter is to hold it in abeyance until it may be more conveniently or suitably attended to; in such use *defer* and *postpone* are close synonyms of *adjourn*; *defer* is simply to lay or put aside temporarily; to *postpone* is strictly to lay or put aside until after something else occurs, or is done, known, obtained, or the like; but *postpone* is often used without such limitation. *Adjourn, defer,* and *postpone* all imply definite expectation of later consideration or action; *delay* is much less definite, while *procrastinate* is hopelessly vague. One who *procrastinates* gives no assurance that he will ever act. Compare HINDER, PROCRASTINATE. *Antonyms*: act, complete, consummate, dispatch, do, expedite, hasten, hurry, quicken.

post·po·si·tion (pōst′pə·zish′ən) *n.* **1** The act of placing after or state of being placed behind. **2** *Gram.* A word placed after another word, as an enclitic; especially, a suffixed element which functions as a preposition, as *-de* in Greek *oikade* homeward. [<L *postpositus,* pp. of *postponere.* See POSTPONE.]

post position The place, in relation to the inner rail, occupied by a horse at the start of a race.

post·pos·i·tive (pōst·poz′ə·tiv) *Gram.* *adj.* Appended to something; suffixed; enclitic. — *n.* An appended word; a postposition. [<L *postpositus.* See POSTPOSITION.]

post·pran·di·al (pōst·pran′dē·əl) *adj.* After-dinner.

post·rid·er (pōst′rī′dər) *n.* A person who journeys by relays of horses.

post road A road built and maintained for the transportation of mail, formerly having post-houses at specified distances.

post·script (pōst′skript′) *n.* **1** A supplemental addition to a written or printed document. **2** Something added to a letter after the writer's signature: abbr. *P.S.* [<L *postscriptum,* pp. of *postscribere* write after]

post terminal A point or port of destination to which goods are transshipped after being delivered by an oceanic carrier: usually applied to additional rates for extra haulage.

post town **1** A town furnishing relays of post horses. **2** A town containing a post office.

pos·tu·lant (pos′chə·lənt) *n.* **1** One who or that which presents a request. **2** *Eccl.* An applicant for admission into a religious order or the sacred ministry. Compare NOVICE. [<F <L *postulans, -antis,* ppr. of *postulare* demand] — **pos′tu·lant·ship** *n.*

pos·tu·late (pos′chə·lit) *n.* **1** A position claimed or basis of argument laid down as well known or too plain to require proof; a self-evident truth. **2** *Geom.* A self-evident statement regarding the possibility of a geometrical construction: distinguished from *axiom.* **3** A condition precedent that must be assumed to explain or account for a thing: Peace is a *postulate* of prosperity. **4** A hypothesis; an unproved assumption. — *v.t.* (pos′chə·lāt) **·lat·ed, ·lat·ing** **1** To claim; demand; require. **2** To set forth as self-evident or already known: to *postulate* the existence of matter. **3** To assume the truth or reality of, especially as a basis for discussion: His theory *postulates* the validity of an older theory. See synonyms under ASSUME. [<L *postulatus,* pp. of *postulare* demand] — **pos′tu·la′tor** *n.*

pos·tu·la·tion (pos′chə·lā′shən) *n.* **1** The act of postulating or supposing something as not needing proof; the assumption of a thing as a fact or truth. **2** *Eccl.* The election or presentation of a person to an office notwithstanding some disqualification.

pos·tu·la·tum (pos′chə·lā′təm) *n.* *pl.* **·ta** (-tə) A postulate. [<L]

pos·ture (pos′chər) *n.* **1** The visible disposition, either natural or assumed, of the several parts of a material thing, and especially of a living thing, with reference to each other; attitude; pose; in art, the position of a figure with regard to its members. **2** Situation as connected with or resulting from a relation of parts; state: the *posture* of national affairs. **3** Mental or spiritual attitude or condition. See synonyms under ATTITUDE. — *v.t.* & *v.i.* **·tured, ·tur·ing** To place in or assume a posture; pose. [<F <L *positura* <*positus,* pp. of *ponere* place] — **pos′tur·al** *adj.* — **pos′tur·er, pos′tur·ist** *n.*

pos·tur·ize (pos′chə·rīz) *v.t.* & *v.i.* **·ized, ·iz·ing** To posture.

post·war (pōst′wôr′) *adj.* After a war.

po·sy (pō′zē) *n.* *pl.* **·sies** **1** A bunch of flowers, or a single flower; a bouquet; nosegay. **2** Generally, a brief inscription or motto, originally one in verse; especially, one inscribed on a ring or other trinket. [Contraction of POESY]

pot (pot) *n.* **1** A round earthen, metal, or glass vessel for culinary and other domestic purposes. **2** A metal drinking cup; mug. **3** The contents of a pot; hence, liquor; drink. **4** The amount of stakes wagered or played for; the pool, as in poker. **5** *Colloq.* A large sum of money. **6** A chimney pot. **7** *Scot.* A deep pit. **8** In fishing, the circular part of a net; also, a basketlike trap for catching lobsters, eels, fish, etc. **9** *Colloq.* A pot shot. **10** *Slang* A potbelly. **11** *Slang* Marihuana. — *v.* **pot·ted, pot·ting** *v.t.* **1** To put into a pot. **2** To preserve, as meat, in pots or jars. **3** To cook in a pot; stew. **4** To shoot (game) for food rather than for sport. **5** To shoot or kill with a pot shot. **6** *Colloq.* To secure, capture, or win; bag. — *v.i.* **7** To take a pot shot. [OE *pott*]

po·ta·ble (pō′tə·bəl) *adj.* Suitable for drinking: said of water. — *n.* Something drinkable; a drink. [<F <L *potabilis* <*potare* drink]

po·tage (pō·täzh′) *n.* *French* Any thick soup.

pot·ash (pot′ash′) *n.* **1** Potassium hydroxide: also called *caustic potash* or *potassa.* **2** The crude potassium carbonate obtained by leaching the ashes of plants: when purified it is called *pearl ash.* **3** The oxide of potassium, K_2O. **4** Potash water. Also, in pharmaceutical use, **po·tass** (pə·tas′). [Earlier *potashes,* pl., after Du. *potasschen*; from being prepared in iron pots]

potash feldspar Orthoclase.

potash water An artificial mineral water containing potassium bicarbonate and charged with carbon dioxide. Also **potassic water.**

po·tas·sa (pə·tas′ə) *n.* Potassium hydroxide.

po·tas·si·um (pə·tas′ē·əm) *n.* A bluish-white, highly reactive, metallic element (symbol K). It is never found free in nature, but its many salts are of great practical value, as in fertilizers, gunpowder, dyeing, and medicine. See ELEMENT. [<NL <POTASSA] — **po·tas′sic** *adj.*

potassium arsenite *Chem.* A white, hygroscopic, very poisonous mixture of potassium, arsenic, hydrogen, and oxygen, used mostly in solution, as in Fowler's mixture.

potassium carbonate *Chem.* A white, strongly alkaline compound, K_2CO_3, prepared from wood ashes and also from potassium sulfate obtained from salt beds: used in the manufacture of soft soap and glass. Also called *potash.*

potassium chlorate *Chem.* A colorless crystalline salt, $KClO_3$, used in the manufacture of matches, explosives, etc.

potassium chloride *Chem.* A colorless crystalline salt, KCl, occurring naturally in large mineral deposits in Germany, and also in certain giant kelps of the Pacific coast; sylvite.

potassium cyanide *Chem.* An intensely poisonous, white, crystalline compound, KCN, used in photography, in electrometallurgy, and as a reagent.
potassium dichromate *Chem.* A reddish crystalline salt, $K_2Cr_2O_7$, used in the arts as an oxidizing agent and in making sensitive coatings for photographs.
potassium hydroxide *Chem.* A whitish deliquescent solid, KOH, yielding a strong caustic solution: used in saltmaking, electroplating, as a chemical reagent, etc. Also called *potash.*
potassium nitrate Niter.
potassium permanganate *Chem.* A purple-red crystalline salt, $KMnO_4$, used as an oxidizing agent in antiseptics and deodorizing substances.
potassium sulfate *Chem.* A salt, K_2SO_4, used in the manufacture of glass and alum, and in the crude state as a component of fertilizers: derived from kainite.
po·ta·tion (pō·tā′shən) *n.* **1** The act of drinking; a drink. **2** A drinking bout. [<OF <L *potatio, -onis* <*potatus,* pp. of *potare* drink]
po·ta·to (pə·tā′tō) *n. pl.* **·toes 1** One of the edible, farinaceous tubers of a plant *(Solanum tuberosum)* of the nightshade family. **2** The plant. **3** The sweet potato. [<Sp. *patata* < Arawakan (Taino) *batata* sweet potato]
potato beetle 1 The Colorado beetle *(Leptinotarsa decemlineata),* yellowish, with ten longitudinal black stripes on the wing covers. Both the adult and the larva feed on the leaves of the potato, tomato, and similar plants, and are among the world's greatest agricultural pests: also **potato bug.** For illustration see also INSECTS (injurious). **2** Any of several beetles feeding on the foliage of the potato, especially *Lema trilineata,* with three longitudinal black stripes on the wing covers.

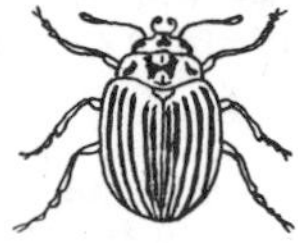

POTATO BEETLE
First described in 1824; widespread by 1874. (About 3/8 inch long; 1/4 inch wide)

potato chip A very thin slice of potato fried crisp and salted.
potato rot A disease of the potato caused by a mildew (genus *Phytophthora*).
po·ta·to·ry (pō′tə·tôr′ē, -tō′rē) *adj.* Pertaining to potation; given or addicted to drinking: a *potatory* club. [<L *potatorius* <*potator* drinker <*potare* drink]
potato stone A quartz geode resembling a potato.
pot-au-feu (pô·tō·fœ′) *n. French* A variety of beef stew.
Pot·a·wat·o·mi (pot′ə·wot′ə·mē) *n.* One of a tribe of North American Indians of Algonquian stock, formerly inhabiting the western shores of Lake Michigan.
pot·bel·ly (pot′bel′ē) *n. pl.* **·lies** A protuberant belly. **— pot′bel′lied** *adj.*
pot·boil·er (pot′boi′lər) *n. Colloq.* A literary or artistic work produced simply to obtain the means of subsistence. **— pot′boil′ing** *n.*
pot·boy (pot′boi′) *n.* In a public house, a boy or young man who cleans the pots, serves customers, etc.
pot cheese Cottage cheese.
pot companion A boon companion; fellow toper.
po·teen (pō·tēn′) *n.* In Ireland, illicitly manufactured whisky: also spelled *potheen, potteen.* [<Irish *poitīn,* dim. of *poite* pot]
Po·tem·kin (pō·tem′kin, *Russian* pô·tyôm′kin), **Prince Grigory Alexandrovich,** 1739–91, Russian field marshal and favorite of Catherine the Great.
po·ten·cy (pōt′n·sē) *n. pl.* **·cies 1** The quality of being potent; inherent ability; mental, moral, or physical power. **2** The power of effecting particular results: the *potency* of a drug or liquor. **3** In homeopathy, the efficacy of a drug as increased by dilution or attenuation; also, the degree to which such attenuation has been carried. **4** Power arising from external circumstances; authority: the *potency* of the prime minister; hence, power to move or influence. **5** Capacity to respond to certain influences; latent power. Also **po′tence.** [<L *potentia*]
po·tent (pōt′nt) *adj.* **1** Physically powerful; able to accomplish material results; efficacious: a *potent* drug. **2** Morally powerful; of a character to influence; convincing: a *potent* argument. **3** Having great authority: a *potent* prince. **4** Sexually competent; able to procreate. See synonyms under POWERFUL. [<L *potens, -entis,* ppr. of *posse* be able, have power <*potis* able + *esse* be] **— po′tent·ly** *adv.* **— po′tent·ness** *n.*
po·ten·tate (pōt′n·tāt) *n.* One having great power or sway; a sovereign. [<LL *potentatus*]
po·ten·tial (pə·ten′shəl) *adj.* **1** Possible but not actual. **2** Having capacity for existence, but not yet existing. **3** *Physics* Existing by virtue of position: said of energy: distinguished from *kinetic.* **4** *Gram.* Indicating possibility or power. See POTENTIAL MOOD. **5** Having force or power. **—** *n.* **1** Anything that may be possible; a possible development. **2** *Gram.* The potential mood. **3** *Physics* A condition at a point in space, due to local attraction or repulsion, such that a mass, electric charge, etc., at that point becomes capable of doing work. **4** *Electr.* The ratio of the potential energy possessed by an electrically charged body because of its position in an electric field to the charge carried by the body. [<LL *potentialis*] **— po·ten′tial·ly** *adv.*
potential energy Energy stored in any of numerous forms, as chemical energy in coal, mechanical energy in a coiled spring, etc.
po·ten·ti·al·i·ty (pə·ten′shē·al′ə·tē) *n. pl.* **·ties 1** Inherent capacity for development or accomplishment; capability; power; efficiency. **2** Potential quality or being; possibility. [< Med. L *potentialitas, -tatis*]
potential mood *Gram.* The verb phrase made up by means of the auxiliaries *may, can, could, must, should,* or *would,* with an infinitive, and expressing power, liberty, or possibility: I *could* go; it *may* be.
po·ten·til·la (pō′tən·til′ə) *n.* Any plant of a large genus *(Potentilla)* of herbs or, rarely, of shrubs of the rose family, the cinquefoils or five-fingers, having compound leaves and solitary or cymose flowers with a many-bracted calyx. Many are in cultivation for their profuse, showy flowers. [<NL <L *potens, -entis,* ppr. of *posse* be able + *-illa,* dim. suffix]
po·ten·ti·om·e·ter (pə·ten′shē·om′ə·tər) *n.* An apparatus for measuring electromotive force or difference of potential. [<L *potenti(a)* potency + -METER]
po·tent·ize (pōt′n·tīz) *v.t.* **·ized, ·iz·ing** In homeopathy, to render potent, as drugs, by attenuation. **— po′tent·iz′er** *n.*
pot·head (pot′hed′) *n. U.S. Slang* A person who habitually smokes marihuana.
poth·e·car·y (poth′ə·ker′ē) *n. Scot. & Brit. Dial.* Apothecary.
po·theen (pō·thēn′) See POTEEN.
poth·er (poth′ər) *n.* Excitement mingled with confusion; bustle; fuss. **—** *v.t. & v.i.* To worry; bother. [Origin uncertain]
pot herb Any plant, especially greens, cooked by boiling, or used to flavor boiled foods.
pot·hold·er (pot′hōl′dər) *n.* A padded cloth or mitten used for handling hot cooking pots and pans.
pot·hole (pot′hōl′) *n.* **1** A pot-shaped cavity in a rock, as that worn by loose stone gyrated in an eddy. **2** A deep hole, as in a road.
pot·hook (pot′ho͝ok′) *n.* **1** A curved or hooked piece of iron for lifting or hanging pots. **2** A curved mark or elementary stroke used in teaching penmanship; also, a scrawl, or, popularly, any curved stroke in stenography.
pot·house (pot′hous′) *n.* An alehouse; saloon.
pot·hunt·er (pot′hun′tər) *n.* **1** One who kills game for food rather than for sport: usually a contemptuous use. **2** One who engages in a competition simply to win the prizes offered. **— pot′hunt′ing** *adj. & n.*
po·tiche (pô·tēsh′) *n.* A vase having an elongated round body, a cylindrical neck, and a detached cover. [<F]
Pot·i·dae·a (pot′ə·dē′ə) An ancient Macedonian city on the Chalcidice peninsula, near the Aegean Sea. Also **Pot′i·dæ′a.**
po·tion (pō′shən) *n.* A draft, as a large dose of liquid medicine: often used of a magic or poisonous draft. [<F <L *potio, -onis* <*potare* drink. Doublet of POISON.]
Pot·i·phar (pot′i·fär, -fər) An officer of Pharaoh, who bought Joseph as a slave. *Gen.* xxxix 1.
pot·latch (pot′lach) *n.* **1** Among American Indians of the northern Pacific coast: **a** A gift. **b** *Often cap.* A winter festival. **2** A ceremonial feast in which gifts are exchanged and property destroyed in a competitive show of wealth. Also **pot′lach, pot′lache.** [< Chinook *patshatl* gift]
pot·lead (pot′led′) *n.* Graphite, especially as used on the bottoms of racing vessels to reduce friction.
pot-lead (pot′led′) *v.t.* To coat with potlead.
pot liquor The liquid left in a pot after cooking greens and meat (usually pork or bacon) together.
pot luck Whatever may chance to be in the pot; hence, a meal or food not prepared for guests: usually in the phrase **to take pot luck.**
pot marigold The calendula.
pot metal 1 Cast iron suitable for making pots. **2** A copper-and-lead alloy formerly used for large pots. **3** A kind of glass colored throughout while still in a molten state.
Po·to·mac River (pə·tō′mək) A river forming the boundaries between Maryland, West Virginia, and Virginia, and flowing 287 miles from the Allegheny Mountains near Cumberland, Md., to Chesapeake Bay about 70 miles SE of Washington, D.C.
po·to·ma·ni·a (pō′tə·mā′nē·ə, -mān′yə) *n.* Delirium tremens; dipsomania. [<Gk. *potos* drunk + -MANIA]
po·tom·e·ter (pō·tom′ə·tər) *n.* An instrument for measuring the amount of moisture absorbed by a plant, as determined by the amount lost in transpiration. [<Gk. *poton* drink + -METER]
Po·to·sí (pō′tō·sē′) A city of south central Bolivia; 13,255 feet above sea level.
pot·pie (pot′pī′) *n.* A pie, baked in a deep dish, containing meat and vegetables and having only a top crust; also, meat stewed with dumplings.
pot·pour·ri (pot·po͝or′ē, *Fr.* pō·po͞o·rē′) *n.* **1** A ragout of meats and vegetables; a stew. **2** A mixture of dried sweet-smelling flower petals used to perfume a room; also, a small covered jar for containing such a mixture. **3** A collection of various things; miscellany. [<F, lit., rotten pot. See OLLA PODRIDA.]
pot roast Meat braised and cooked in a pot until tender, often with vegetables.
Pots·dam (pots′dam, *Ger.* pôts′däm) A city in East Germany, capital of the former state of Brandenburg; scene of a United Nations conference, July–August, 1945.
pot·sherd (pot′shûrd) *n.* A bit of broken crockery. Also **pot′shard** (-shärd). [<POT + SHARD]
pot shot 1 A shot fired to kill, without regard to the rules of sports. **2** A shot fired, as from ambush, at a person or animal within easy range. **3** A random shot.
pot·stone (pot′stōn′) *n.* Steatite.
pott (pot) *n.* A size of paper, varying in size according to use, but generally about 15 1/2 × 12 1/2 inches. [Var. of POT; so named from having once borne the watermark of a pot]
pot·tage (pot′ij) *n.* **1** A thick broth or stew. **2** A porridge. [<F *potage* <*pot* pot]
pot·ted (pot′id) *adj.* **1** Placed or kept in a pot. **2** Cooked or preserved in a pot. **3** *Slang* Drunk.
pot·teen (pō·tēn′) See POTEEN.
pot·ter[1] (pot′ər) *v.t. & v.i., n. Brit.* Putter.
pot·ter[2] (pot′ər) *n.* **1** One who makes earthenware or porcelain. **2** One who pots meats, vegetables, etc. [OE *potere*]
Pot·ter (pot′ər), **Paul,** 1625–54, Dutch painter.
potter's field A piece of ground appropriated as a burial ground for the destitute and the unknown. *Matt.* xxvii 7.
potter's flint Finely pulverized quartz mixed with porcelain to impart strength and rigidity and to reduce shrinkage: used also in enamel mixtures.
potter's wheel A horizontal rotating disk used by potters for holding and manipulating prepared clay.
potter wasp A digger wasp (genus *Eumenes*) which constructs vaselike cells of mud as a nest, especially the North

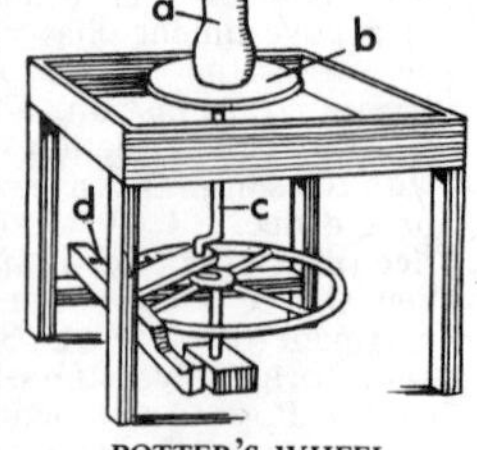

POTTER'S WHEEL
a. Molding clay.
b. Rotating wheel.
c. Shaft.
d. Treadle.

American potter wasp, *E. fraterna.* For illustration see INSECTS (beneficial).

pot·ter·y (pot′ər·ē) *n. pl.* **·ter·ies** 1 A factory where potters' ware is made. 2 The manufacture of earthenware or porcelain. 3 Clay ware molded and hardened. ◆ Collateral adjective: *fictile.* [<F *poterie* <*potier* a potter <*pot* a pot]

pot·ting (pot′ing) *n.* 1 The preserving of articles of food in pots for future use. 2 The placing of buds, bulbs, or plants in pots.

pot·tin·ger (pot′in·jər) *n.* 1 *Obs.* A maker of pottage; a cook. 2 *Scot. & Brit. Dial.* A porridge dish. [See PORRINGER]

pot·tle (pot′l) *n.* 1 A drinking vessel, pot, or tankard holding about half a gallon. 2 An old liquid measure of half a gallon. 3 A small vessel or basket for holding fruit. [<OF *potel,* dim. of *pot* pot]

pot·to (pot′ō) *n. pl.* **·tos** 1 A small, slow-moving lemur (genus *Perodicticus*) of tropical Africa, having a rudimentary tail and large hands and feet. 2 The kinkajou. [<West African native name]

Pott's disease *Pathol.* Caries or tuberculosis of the vertebrae, causing angular curvature of the spine: first described scientifically by Percival Pott, 1714–88, English surgeon.

pot·ty (pot′ē) *adj. Brit. Colloq.* 1 Insignificant. 2 Slightly drunk; hence, a little silly. [Prob. <POT, in the phrase *go to pot* deteriorate]

pot-val·iant (pot′val′yənt) *adj.* Courageous from drink. — **pot′-val′ian·cy, pot′-val′ian·try, pot′-val′or** (-val′ər) *n.*

pot·wal·lo·per (pot′wol′ə·pər, pot′wol′-) *n.* 1 *Slang* One employed to clean or wash pots, etc.; a scullion. 2 *Brit.* Formerly, by the requirements of some boroughs before 1832, a parliamentary voter who was a householder (not a tenant), having his own fireplace as a qualification for suffrage. [<POT + WALLOP (def. 5)]

pouch (pouch) *n.* 1 A small bag or sack, or something serving a similar purpose, as a pocket or a purse. 2 *Zool.* A saclike part for temporarily containing food, as in gophers and pelicans; also, a marsupium. 3 *Bot.* Any pouchlike cavity, as the silique of the mustard plant. 4 A leather receptacle for carrying small-arms ammunition; also, a wooden cartridge box. 5 An inner mailbag. — *v.t.* 1 To put in or as in a pouch; pocket. 2 To fashion or arrange in pouchlike form. 3 To swallow. — *v.i.* 4 To take on a pouchlike shape; form a pouchlike cavity. [<OF *poche,* var. of *poke, poque* bag] — **pouch′y** *adj.*

pouched (poucht) *adj.* Having pouches or sacs; characterized by pouches.

pouched rat 1 A rodent with cheek pouches; especially, a pocket gopher. 2 A kangaroo rat. 3 Any of certain ratlike rodents of Africa having large cheek pouches (genera *Cricetomys* and *Saccostomus*).

pouf (po͞of) *n.* 1 A hair arrangement in high rolled puffs, popular in the 18th century. 2 Any puffed part of a dress. 3 An upholstered tabouret for one or more persons. [<F, a puff]

Pough·keep·sie (pə·kip′sē) A city on the Hudson River in SE New York.

pou·laine (po͞o·lān′) *n.* 1 The long pointed toe of a medieval shoe. 2 A shoe with such a toe. [<OF *(soulier à la) poulaine* (shoe in the) Polish (fashion)]

pou·lard[1] (po͞o·lärd′) *n.* A pullet having the ovaries removed to produce abnormal growth and fattening and superior quality; hence, a fat pullet. Compare CAPON. [<F *poularde* <*poule* pullet]

pou·lard[2] (po͞o·lärd′) *n.* A variety of spring or winter wheat closely related to durum, having broad leaves, thick culms, and hard, starchy kernels. Also **poulard wheat.** [<POULARD[1]; so named because suitable only for stock feed]

Poul·sen (poul′sən), **Valdemar,** 1869–1942, Danish electrical engineer and inventor.

poult (pōlt) *n.* A young turkey, chicken, etc. [Contraction of ME *pulet* pullet]

poul·ter (pōl′tər) *n. Obs.* A poulterer. [<OF *pouletier* <*poulet* pullet]

poul·ter·er (pōl′tər·ər) *n.* A dealer in poultry. [<POULTER + -ER[2]]

poulter's measure A verse form consisting of alternating lines of twelve and fourteen syllables: so called from the poulterer's custom of sometimes giving fourteen eggs to the dozen.

poul·tice (pōl′tis) *n.* A mollifying remedy of a moist, mealy nature, applied to inflamed surfaces. — *v.t.* **·ticed, ·tic·ing** To cover or treat with a poultice. [<L *pultes,* pl. of *puls* porridge]

poul·try (pōl′trē) *n.* Domestic fowls, generally or collectively, as hens, ducks, etc. [<OF *pouleterie* <*poulet* fowl]

pounce[1] (pouns) *v.i.* **pounced, pounc·ing** To swoop or spring in or as in seizing prey: with *on, upon,* or *at.* — *n.* 1 A talon or claw. 2 The act of pouncing; a sudden leap, swoop, spring, or seizure. [Origin uncertain] — **pounc′er** *n.*

pounce[2] (pouns) *v.t.* 1 To perforate with holes in decorative patterns; scallop; pink. 2 To emboss (metalwork) with a design hammered on the reverse side. [<OF *poinçonnier, ponchonner* <*poinçon, poinchon* a puncheon]

pounce[3] (pouns) *n.* 1 A powder formerly used to absorb excess of ink, as on a manuscript. 2 A finely pulverized substance used in transferring designs. — *v.t.* **pounced, pounc·ing** To sprinkle, smooth, or rub with pounce. [<F *ponce* <L *pumex, pumicis* pumice]

pounce box 1 A box with perforated lid formerly used for dusting out pounce as a perfume; a perfume box. 2 A box formerly used for dusting powder or sand on freshly written paper. Also **poun·cet** (poun′sit) **box.**

pound[1] (pound) *n.* 1 A variable unit of weight (symbol lb.): the avoirdupois pound is 16 ounces, 7,000 grains, or 453.59 grams; the troy pound, 12 ounces, 5,760 grains, or 373.24 grams. 2 An English money of account, equal to 20 shillings; specifically, a pound sterling (symbol £). See SOVEREIGN. [OE *pund* <L *pondus* weight]

pound[2] (pound) *n.* 1 A place, enclosed by authority, in which stray or trespassing cattle and distrained cattle or goods are left till redeemed; also, a similar enclosure for stray dogs. 2 An enclosed shelter for cattle or sheep. 3 A trap for wild animals. 4 An area or place in which to catch or stow fish; a poundnet. — *v.t.* To confine in or as in a pound; impound; restrain. [OE *pund(fald)* pinfold] — **pound′keep′er** (-kē′pər) *n.*

pound[3] (pound) *v.t.* 1 To strike heavily and repeatedly, as with a hammer; beat. 2 To reduce to a pulp or powder by beating; pulverize; triturate. 3 To teach or impress by constant repetition: to *pound* facts into someone's head. 4 To walk tediously or heavily: to *pound* a beat. — *v.i.* 5 To strike heavy, repeated blows: with *on, at,* etc. 6 To move or proceed heavily or vigorously. 7 To rise and fall heavily, as a ship in rough water. 8 To throb heavily or resoundingly: Her heart was *pounding* from fear and excitement. — *n.* 1 A heavy blow; thump; thud. 2 The act of pounding. See synonyms under BEAT. [OE *punian*] — **pound′er** *n.*

Pound (pound), **Sir Dudley,** 1877–1943, English admiral in World War II. — **Ezra Loomis,** 1885–1972, U.S. poet. — **Louise,** 1872–1958, U.S. linguist. — **Roscoe,** 1870–1964, U.S. jurist; brother of Louise.

pound·age[1] (poun′dij) *n.* 1 A rate on the pound sterling. 2 Formerly, in England, a subsidy to the crown on each pound of merchandise exported or imported.

pound·age[2] (poun′dij) *n.* 1 The charges for the redemption of impounded cattle. 2 The act of impounding cattle.

pound·al (poun′dəl) *n. Physics* The unit of force in the foot-pound-second system, which, acting on the mass of a pound, imparts to it an acceleration of one foot per second per second.

pound cake A rich cake having ingredients equal in weight, as a pound each of flour, butter, and sugar, with eggs added.

pound·er (poun′dər) *n.* 1 Anything weighing a pound: The trout's a *pounder.* 2 A person or thing weighing, having, or having a certain relation to, a given number of pounds: used only in compounds: The baby is an eight-*pounder.*

pound-fool·ish (pound′fo͞o′lish) *adj.* 1 Extravagant with large sums, but watching small sums closely: penny-wise and *pound-foolish.* 2 Having little capacity for business.

pound·net (pound′net′) *n.* A weir or arrangement of nets supported upon stakes to form a trap for fish.

pound party *U. S.* A social gathering to which each guest brings a pound of something, usually food, to be given to an individual or a charitable cause.

pour (pôr, pōr) *v.t.* 1 To cause to flow in a continuous stream, as water, sand, etc. 2 To send forth, emit, or utter profusely or continuously: The radio *poured* forth music. — *v.i.* 3 To flow in a continuous stream; gush. 4 To rain heavily. 5 To move in great numbers; swarm: The northern hordes *poured* over Italy. 6 To serve as a hostess at a social tea. — *n.* A pouring, flow, or downfall. [Origin unknown] — **pour′er** *n.*

pour·boire (po͝or·bwär′) *n. French* A gratuitous gift of money as a tip; literally, for drink.

pour le mé·rite (po͝or lə mā·rēt′) *French* For merit.

pour·par·ler (po͝or·pȧr·lā′) *n. French* A preliminary or informal conference or consultation.

pour·point (po͝or′point′, *Fr.* po͝or·pwaṅ′) *n.* A quilted cloth doublet worn in the 14th and 15th centuries. [<F, prob. orig. pp. of *pourpoindre* perforate]

pour point 1 *Physics* The lowest temperature at which a liquid, especially a fuel oil, will flow under prescribed conditions. 2 *Metall.* The temperature at which molten metal is cast.

pousse-ca·fé (po͞os·kȧ·fā′) *n. French* A drink, commonly a mixture of cordials and brandy in successive layers, served after the coffee at dinner.

pous·sette (po͞o·set′) *n.* A dance figure in which a couple or couples swing round and round while holding hands. — *v.i.* **·set·ted, ·set·ting** To perform a poussette. [<F, dim. of *pousse* a push <*pousser* push]

pous·sie (po͞o′sē) *n. Scot.* Pussy; also, a hare.

Pous·sin (po͞o·saṅ′), **Nicolas,** 1594–1665, French painter.

pou sto (po͞o′ stō′, pou′) A place to stand on; hence, a foundation for operations in any line of endeavor. [<Gk. *pou stō* where I may stand: from the alleged saying of Archimedes on his discovery of the lever, "Give me a place where I may stand and I will move the earth."]

pout[1] (pout) *v.i.* 1 To thrust out the lips, especially in ill humor. 2 To be sullen; sulk. 3 To swell out; protrude. — *v.t.* 4 To thrust out (the lips, etc.). 5 To utter with a pout. — *n.* A pushing out of the lips as in pouting; hence, a fit of ill humor. [Cf. Sw. *puta* be swollen]

pout[2] (pout) *n.* 1 One of various fresh-water catfishes having a pouting appearance. 2 The eelpout. [OE *(ǣle)pūte* eelpout]

pout·er[1] (pou′tər) *n.* 1 One who or that which pouts. 2 A breed of pigeon having the habit of puffing out the crop.

pout·er[2] (pou′tər) *v.t. & v.i. Scot.* To poke; stir.

pou·ther (po͞o′thər) *v. & n. Scot.* Powder. Also spelled *powther.*

pou·try (po͞o′trē) *n. Scot.* Poultry.

pov·er·ty (pov′ər·tē) *n.* 1 The state of being poor or without competent subsistence; need; penury. 2 The condition that relates to the absence or scarcity of requisite substance or elements. 3 A lack or meagerness of supply; dearth. [<OF *povreté* <L *paupertas* <*pauper* poor]

Synonyms: beggary, destitution, distress, indigence, mendicancy, need, pauperism, penury, privation, want. *Poverty* denotes a condition below that of easy, comfortable living; *privation* denotes a condition of painful lack of what is useful or desirable; *indigence* is lack of ordinary means of subsistence; *destitution* is lack of the comforts, and even of the necessaries of life; *penury* is cramping *poverty*; *pauperism* is such *destitution* as throws one upon public charity for support; *beggary* and *mendicancy* denote *poverty* that appeals for indiscriminate private charity.

poverty grass Any of certain grasses, especially *Aristida divaricata,* having little or no nutriment and found growing in old fields too poor for cultivation.

pov·er·ty-strick·en (pov′ər·tē·strik′ən) *adj.* Suffering from poverty; destitute.

pow (pou) *n. Scot.* The poll; head.

pow·der (pou′dər) *n.* **1** A finely ground or comminuted mass of free particles formed from a solid substance in the dry state; dust. **2** A pulverized cosmetic preparation for toilet use. **3** A medicine in the form of powder. **4** An explosive dry powder, as gunpowder. — *v.t.* **1** To reduce to powder; pulverize. **2** To sprinkle or cover with or as with powder. **3** To sprinkle with small objects or ornaments. — *v.i.* **4** To be reduced to powder. **5** To use powder as a cosmetic. [<OF *poudre* <L *pulvis, pulveris* dust] — **pow′der·er** *n.*

powder blue **1** Pulverized smalt having a deep-blue color: used as laundry bluing. **2** Its deep-blue color. **3** A valuable porcelain glaze. **4** The color of this glaze, a soft medium blue.

powder flask A metallic or other flask for carrying gunpowder.

powder horn The hollow horn of an ox or cow, formerly fitted with a cover and used by hunters or soldiers for holding gunpowder.

powder metallurgy The science and technique of manufacturing objects from finely powdered metals and alloys.

powder puff A soft pad used to apply powder to the skin.

Powder River **1** A river in NE Oregon, flowing 110 miles NE to the Snake River. **2** A river in Wyoming and Montana, flowing 486 miles north to the Yellowstone River.

powder room **1** A women's rest-room. **2** A small room or bathroom decorated daintily for use as a woman's dressing-room.

pow·der·y (pou′dər·ē) *adj.* **1** Consisting of or like fine powder or dust. **2** Covered with or as with powder; mealy; dusty. **3** Capable of being easily powdered or crumbled; friable.

Pow·ell (pou′əl), **Lewis F., Jr.,** born 1907, U.S. jurist, associate Supreme Court justice 1972–.

pow·er (pou′ər) *n.* **1** Ability to act; potency; specifically, the property of a substance or being that is manifested in effort or action, and by virtue of which that substance or being produces change, moral or physical. **2** Potential capacity. **3** Strength or force actually put forth. **4** The right, ability, or capacity to exercise control; legal authority, capacity, or competency, particularly, authority to do some act in relation to lands, as to create estates therein or charges thereon; also, a legal instrument or document conferring it. See POWER OF APPOINTMENT. **5** Any agent that exercises power, as in control or dominion; a military or naval force; an important and influential sovereign nation. **6** Great or telling force or effect. **7** *Colloq.* A great number or quantity. **8** Religious frenzy, especially as exemplified in exhortation: believed to be by possession of the Holy Spirit. **9** Any form of energy available for doing work; specifically, energy developed by mechanical or electrical means. **10** *Physics* The time rate at which energy is transferred, or converted into work. **11** *Math.* **a** The product of a number multiplied by itself a given number of times. **b** An exponent. **12** *Optics* Magnifying capacity, as of a lens. **13** *pl.* The sixth of the nine grades or orders of angels. — *v.t.* **1** To provide with means of propulsion. **2** *Colloq.* To force or push in the act of overcoming resistance: *powered* his way through for a touchdown. — *v.i.* **3** *Colloq.* To move forcefully: to *power* through mud. [<OF *poeir,* ult. <L *posse* be able]

Synonyms: ability, capacity, efficacy, efficiency, energy, force, might, potency, puissance, strength. *Power* is the most general term of this group of words, including every quality, property, or faculty by which any change, effect, or result is, or may be, produced, as, the *power* of the legislature to enact laws, or of the executive to enforce them; the *power* of an acid to corrode a metal; the *power* of a polished surface to reflect light. *Ability* is nearly coextensive with *power,* but does not reach its positiveness and vigor, *ability* often implying latent, as distinguished from active, *power. Power* and *ability* include *capacity,* which is *power* to receive; but *ability* is often distinguished from *capacity,* as *power* that may be manifested in doing, as *capacity* is in receiving. *Efficacy* is *power* to produce effects; *efficiency* is effectual agency, competent *power. Energy* is *power* both actual and potential; *force* is *power* enough to overcome resistance. *Puissance* is a poetic or literary synonym. See ABILITY, CAUSE, GENIUS, WEIGHT.

power- *combining form* Powered by a motor or by electricity: *power drill, power mower.*

power boat A motorboat.

power dive *Aeron.* A descent in which the engine increases the acceleration due to gravity.

power drill A motor-operated drill.

pow·er·ful (pou′ər·fəl) *adj.* **1** Possessing great force; very efficient; strong. **2** Having great intensity or energy. **3** Exercising great authority, or manifesting high qualities; mighty. **4** Having great effect on the mind; convincing. — *adv. Colloq.* Very; exceedingly. — **pow′er·ful·ly** *adv.*

Synonyms (adj.): able, cogent, commanding, controlling, effective, effectual, efficacious, efficient, forceful, influential, mighty, potent, puissant, robust, strong, sturdy, vigorous.

pow·er·house (pou′ər·hous′) *n.* **1** *Electr.* A station where electricity is generated. **2** *Slang* A person or thing of great might or force.

pow·er·less (pou′ər·lis) *adj.* **1** Destitute of power; unable to accomplish an effect; impotent. **2** Without authority. — **pow′er·less·ly** *adv.* — **pow′er·less·ness** *n.*

power loading *Aeron.* The gross weight of an aircraft divided by its rated engine power.

power of appointment *Law* Authority conferred, as by power of attorney, deed, or will, to appoint or designate a person or persons to make disposition of an estate or interest in the property of another.

power of attorney *Law* **1** The authority or power to act conferred upon an agent. **2** The instrument or document by which that power or authority is conferred or guaranteed. See under ATTORNEY.

power pack A compact assemblage of electrical units to provide requisite steady power, as in radio communication from an airplane.

power plant Any source of power, together with its housing, installations and accessory equipment: the *power plant* of an airplane.

power politics The use or threatened use of force to exact international concessions.

power train Drive train.

Pow·ha·tan (pou′hə·tan′) *n.* **1** A confederacy of Algonquian Indian tribes of Virginia (1607–1705) comprising about thirty tribes. **2** One of a tribe of North American Indians of Algonquian stock, formerly inhabiting a part of eastern Virginia.

pow·ney (pou′nē) *n. Scot.* A pony.

pow·ter (pou′tər) *n.* The pouter pigeon.

pow·ther (po͞o′thər) See POUTHER.

pow·wow (pou′wou′) *U.S. n.* **1** A North American Indian medicine man, priest, or magician. **2** The ceremony of a medicine man involving a dance, feast, or other demonstration, to cure the sick or effect success in hunting, war, etc. **3** Hence, magic; witchcraft. **4** An Indian council. **5** *Colloq.* Any meeting for conference. — *v.i.* To hold a deliberative council. [<Algonquian (Massachuset) *pauwaw,* lit., he dreams]

Pow·ys (pō′is) Name of three English authors, brothers: **John Cowper,** 1872–1963; **Llewelyn,** 1884–1939; **Theodore Francis,** 1875–1953.

pox (poks) *n.* **1** Any disease characterized by eruptions of a purulent nature: chicken *pox.* **2** Syphilis. [Var. of *pocks,* pl. of POCK]

Po·yang (pō′yäng′) A lake in northern Kiangsi province, eastern China; about 1,070 square miles at low water, 3,600 square miles when flooded in summer by waters of the Yangtze.

poy·ou (poi′o͞o) *n.* The six-banded armadillo *(Dasypus sexcinctus)* of Argentina and Brazil. [<Guarani *(tatu)-po-yu* (armadillo) with a yellow band <*po* band + *yu* yellow]

Poz·nań (pôz′nän·y′) A city of western Poland: German *Posen.*

Po·zsony (pô′zhōn′y′) The Hungarian name for BRATISLAVA.

poz·zuo·la·na (pot′swə·lä′nə, *Ital.* pōt′tswô·lä′nä) *n.* A volcanic ash, first collected at Pozzuoli, used in making hydraulic cement: also made artificially. Also **poz′zo·la′na** (pot′sə-). [<Ital., from *Pozzuoli*] — **poz′zuo·lan′ic** (-lan′ik) *adj.*

Poz·zuo·li (pōt·tswô′lē) A town on the site of an ancient city SW of Naples, Italy. Ancient **Pu·te·o·li** (pyo͞o·tē′ə·lī).

P-P factor *Biochem.* The pellagra-preventive factor of the vitamin B complex; nicotinic acid.

praam (präm) *n.* A Baltic flat-bottomed barge. Also spelled *pram.* [<Du. <Slavic. Cf. Polish *pram* boat.]

prac·tic (prak′tik) *adj. Obs.* Practical.

prac·ti·ca·ble (prak′tə·kə·bəl) *adj.* **1** That can be put into practice; feasible. **2** That can be used for an intended purpose; usable. — **prac′ti·ca·bil′i·ty, prac′ti·ca·ble·ness** *n.* — **prac′ti·ca·bly** *adv.*

prac·ti·cal (prak′ti·kəl) *adj.* **1** Pertaining to or governed by actual use and experience or action, as contrasted with ideals and speculations. **2** Trained by or derived from practice or experience. **3** Having reference to useful ends to be attained; applicable to use. **4** Manifested in practice. **5** Being such to all intents and purposes; virtual. [< obs. *practic* < obs. F *practique* <LL *practicus* <Gk. *praktikos* fit for doing <*prassein* do] — **prac′ti·cal′i·ty** (-kal′ə·tē), **prac′ti·cal·ness** *n.*

Practical Christianity New Thought.

practical joke A joke involving action instead of wit or words; a prank or trick.

prac·ti·cal·ly (prak′tik·lē) *adv.* **1** In a practical manner. **2** To all intents and purposes; in fact or effect; virtually.

practical nurse A nurse with practical experience in the care of the sick, but who is not a registered nurse.

prac·tice (prak′tis) *v.* **·ticed, ·tic·ing** *v.t.* **1** To make use of habitually or often: to *practice* economy. **2** To apply in action; make a practice of: *Practice* what you preach. **3** To work at or pursue as a profession: to *practice* law. **4** To do or perform repeatedly in order to acquire skill or training; rehearse. **5** To instruct, as pupils, by repeated exercise or lessons. — *v.i.* **6** To repeat or rehearse something in order to acquire skill or proficiency: to *practice* for a concert. **7** To work at or pursue a profession: He *practiced* for twenty years. **8** *Rare* To conspire; scheme. — *n.* **1** Any customary action or proceeding regarded as individual; habit. **2** An established custom or usage. **3** The act or process of executing or accomplishing; doing or performance: distinguished from *theory.* **4** The regular prosecution of a business pursuit requiring education; professional business. **5** Frequent and repeated exercise in any matter. **6** *pl.* Stratagems or schemes for bad purposes; tricks. **7** A rule or method in arithmetic to facilitate multiplying quantities in different denominations. **8** The rules by which legal proceedings are governed. Also **prac′tise.** [< OF *practiser* < *practiquer* <Med. L *practicare* <LL *practicus.* See PRACTICAL.] — **prac′tic·er** *n.*

◆ In Britain, *practice* is almost invariably the spelling used for the noun, *practise* for the verb. In the U.S., the noun form is more commonly *practice,* although *practise* is also used; both spellings are widely used as verbs.

Synonyms (noun): drill, exercise. *Exercise* is action with a view to employing, maintaining, or increasing power, or merely for enjoyment; *practice* is systematic *exercise* with a view to the acquirement of facility and skill; a person takes a walk for *exercise,* or takes time for *practice* on the piano. *Practice* is also used of putting into action and effect what one has learned or holds as a theory; as, the *practice* of law or medicine. Educationally, *practice* is the voluntary and persistent attempt to make skill a *habit*; as, *practice* in penmanship. *Drill* is systematic, rigorous, and commonly enforced *practice* under a teacher or commander. See CUSTOM, EXERCISE, HABIT, MANNER.

prac·ticed (prak′tist) *adj.* **1** Expert by practice; skilled by use or habit; experienced. **2** Acquired by practice. Also **prac′tised.**

prac·ti·tion·er (prak·tish′ən·ər) *n.* **1** One who practices an art or profession. **2** A Christian Science healer. [< earlier *practician* <OF *practicien,* ult. <L *practica* practice]

prae- See PRE-.

prae·ci·pe (pres′i·pē, prē′si-) See PRECIPE.

prae·di·al (prē′dē·əl), **prae·fect** (prē′fekt), etc. See PREDIAL, PREFECT, etc.

prae·mu·ni·re (prē′myo͞o·nī′rē) *n.* In English law, the offense of introducing an alien power within the realm; specifically, the offense of maintaining the papal power in England. [<Med. L *praemunire (facias)* (see that you)

warn, a legal phrase; from a confusion of L *praemunire* protect with *praemonere* warn]

prae·no·men (prē·nō′mən) *n.* *pl.* **·nom·i·na** (-nom′ə·nə) The name prefixed to an ancient Roman family name to mark the individual, corresponding to the modern Christian name: also spelled *prenomen.* [<PRAE- + L *nomen* name]

prae·pos·tor (prē·pos′tər) *n.* A prepositor: also spelled *prepostor.* Also **prae·pos′i·tor.** [< Med. L *praepositor* one who puts another in charge <L *praepositus,* pp. of *praeponere.* See PREPOSITION.]

praeter– See PRETER–.

prae·tex·ta (prē·teks′tə) *n.* *pl.* **·tae** (-tē) An ordinary white toga with a purple border or stripe, worn by free-born Roman boys until they assumed the toga virilis at 14–16 years, and by girls until they were married. It was also the distinctive mark of the Roman curule magistrates, censors, state priests (when performing their functions), and emperors. [<L, lit., woven before, fringed, fem. of *praetextus,* pp. of *praetexere*]

prae·tor (prē′tər), **prae·to·ri·al** (prē·tôr′ē·əl, -tō′rē-), **prae·to·ri·an** (prē·tôr′ē·ən, -tō′rē-), etc. See PRETOR, etc.

Pra·ga (prä′gä) A suburb of Warsaw, Poland, on the east bank of the Vistula.

prag·mat·ic (prag·mat′ik) *adj.* **1** Pertaining to the accomplishment of duty or of business; specifically, relating to the civil affairs of a sovereign state. **2** Pertaining to or occupied with the scientific evolution of causes and effects; philosophical: said especially of history: the *pragmatic* method. **3** Pragmatical; practical. **4** Of or pertaining to the philosophy of pragmatism. [<L *pragmaticus* active or skilled in practical affairs <Gk. *pragmatikos* < *pragma, pragmatos* a thing done, an affair < *prassein* do, perform]

prag·mat·i·cal (prag·mat′i·kəl) *adj.* **1** Inclined to be officious or meddlesome; self-important; busy. **2** Relating to or engrossed with everyday business; practical; hence, commonplace. **— prag·mat′i·cal·ly** *adv.* **— prag·mat′i·cal·ness** *n.*

prag·mat·i·cism (prag·mat′ə·siz′əm) *n.* *Philos.* The pragmatism of C. S. Peirce, renamed by him to distinguish it from the teachings of William James and others, and referring to his philosophy that concepts are predictions of facts to be found and consequences to result should specified action be taken.

pragmatic sanction An imperial or royal edict or decree operating as a fundamental law. The most famous of these edicts was that of Charles VI of Austria in 1724, which admitted heirs in the female line to the Austrian succession.

prag·ma·tism (prag′mə·tiz′əm) *n.* *Philos.* The doctrine that thought or ideas have value only in terms of their practical consequences, and that results are the sole test of the validity or truth of one's beliefs. **— prag′ma·tist** *n.*

Prague (präg) The capital of Czechoslovakia, on the Vltava, in central Bohemia. *German* **Prag** (präkh), *Czech* **Pra·ha** (prä′hä).

pra·hu (prä·hōō′) *n.* A proa. [<Malay *práu*]

Prai·ri·al (pre·rē·äl′) See under CALENDAR (Republican).

prai·rie (prâr′ē) *n.* A level or rolling tract of treeless land covered with coarse grass and generally of rich soil, especially as in parts of the western United States. [<F, a large meadow <Med. L *prataria* <L *pratum* meadow]

prairie chicken See under GROUSE. Also **prairie hen.**

prairie cock The cock of the plains.

prairie dog A burrowing rodent (genus *Cynomys*) of the plains of North America; specifically, *C. ludovicianus,* which lives in large communities and is very destructive to vegetation. Also **prairie squirrel.**

PRAIRIE DOG
(Body from 12 to 15 inches long; tail, 3 to 4 inches)

prairie owl **1** The burrowing owl. **2** The short-eared owl.

Prairie Provinces The provinces of Manitoba, Saskatchewan, and Alberta, in western Canada.

prairie schooner A covered wagon.

prairie state One of the States of the prairie regions of the Western and Middle Western United States.

Prairie State Nickname of ILLINOIS.

prairie wolf A coyote: distinguished from *timber wolf.*

praise (prāz) *v.t.* **praised, prais·ing** **1** To express approval and commendation of; applaud; eulogize. **2** To express adoration of; glorify (God, etc.). *— n.* **1** Commendation expressed, as of a person for his virtues, or concerning meritorious actions; utterance of approval; honor given; also, applause. **2** Thanksgiving for blessings conferred; laudation to God; worship expressed in song. **3** The object, ground, reason, or subject of praise. ◆ Homophone: *prase.* [<OF *preisier* <LL *pretiare* prize <L *pretium* price. See PRICE.] **— prais′er** *n.*

Synonyms (verb): adore, applaud, approve, bless, celebrate, commend, eulogize, extol, flatter, glorify, honor, laud, magnify, worship. See PUFF. *Antonyms*: see synonyms for ASPERSE, BLAME.

Synonyms (noun): acclaim, acclamation, adulation, applause, approbation, approval, commendation, compliment, encomium, eulogy, flattery, laudation, panegyric, plaudit, sycophancy. *Praise* is the hearty approval of an individual, or of a multitude considered individually, and is expressed by spoken or written words; *applause,* the spontaneous outburst of many at once. *Applause* is expressed by stamping of feet, clapping of hands, waving of handkerchiefs, etc., as well as by the voice; *acclamation* is the spontaneous and hearty approval of many at once, and strictly by the voice alone. One is chosen moderator by *acclamation* when he receives a practically unanimous viva voce vote; he could not be nominated by *applause. Acclaim* is the more poetic term for *acclamation*; as, a nation's *acclaim. Plaudit* is a shout of *applause,* and is commonly used in the plural; as, the *plaudits* of a throng. *Applause* is also used in the general sense of *praise. Approbation* is a milder and more qualified word than *praise*; *praise* is always uttered, *approbation* may be silent. The industry and intelligence of a clerk win his employer's *approbation*; his decision in a special instance receives his *approval. Praise* is always understood as genuine and sincere, unless the contrary is expressly stated; *compliment* is a light form of *praise* that may or may not be sincere; *flattery* is often insincere. Compare APPLAUSE, EULOGY. *Antonyms*: abuse, animadversion, blame, censure, condemnation, contempt, denunciation, disapprobation, disapproval, disparagement, obloquy, reproach, reproof, repudiation, scorn, slander, vilification, vituperation.

praise·wor·thy (prāz′wûr′thē) *adj.* Worthy of praise; commendable. **— praise′wor′thi·ly** *adv.* **— praise′wor′thi·ness** *n.*

Pra·ja·dhi·pok (prä·jä′di·pôk), 1893–1941, king of Siam 1925–35; abdicated.

Pra·krit (prä′krit) *n.* The popular dialects or any one of the vernaculars of northern and central India, arising from or connected with Sanskrit, and forming a link between Sanskrit and the modern Indic languages. [<Skt. *prakṛtā* natural, common, lit., created before < *pra-* before + *kṛ* do. Cf. SANSKRIT.]

pra·line (prä′lēn, prā′-) *n.* A crisp confection made of pecans or other nuts browned in boiling sugar. [<F, after Marshal Duplessis-*Praslin,* 1598–1675, whose cook invented it]

prall·tril·ler (präl′tril·ər) *n.* *Music* An inverted mordent. [<G, lit., elastic trill]

pram[1] (pram) *n.* *Brit. Colloq.* A baby carriage. [Short for PERAMBULATOR]

pram[2] (präm) See PRAAM.

prance (prans, präns) *v.* **pranced, pranc·ing** *v.i.* **1** To move proudly with high steps, as a spirited horse; spring from the hind legs. **2** To ride gaily, proudly, or insolently, as on a prancing horse. **3** To move in an arrogant or elated manner; swagger. **4** To gambol; caper. *— v.i.* **5** To cause to prance. *— n.* The act of prancing; a high step; a caper. [ME *prauncen,* ? <Scand. Cf. dial. Dan. *pranse* walk proudly.] **— pranc′er** *n.*

pran·di·al (pran′dē·əl) *adj.* Of or pertaining to a meal, especially a dinner. [<L *prandium* breakfast or lunch]

prank[1] (prangk) *v.t.* To decorate gaudily; deck with showy ornaments. *— v.i.* To make an ostentatious show. [Cf. Du. *pronken,* G *prunken* make a show of]

prank[2] (prangk) *n.* A mischievous or frolicsome act. See synonyms under FROLIC, SPORT. *— v.i.* To play pranks or tricks. [Origin uncertain] **— prank′ish** *adj.*

pranked (prangkt) *adj.* Decorated; dressed up: often with *out* or *up.*

prase (prāz) *n.* An olive-green, translucent quartz, usually cryptocrystalline. ◆ Homophone: *praise.* [<F <L *prasius* light green <Gk. *prason* leek; with ref. to its color]

pra·se·o·dym·i·um (prā′zē·ō·dim′ē·əm, prā′sē-) *n.* A yellowish-white metallic element (symbol Pr) of the lanthanide series, having olive-green salts. See ELEMENT. [<NL <Gk. *prasios* light green + (DI)DYMIUM]

prate (prāt) *v.* **prat·ed, prat·ing** *v.i.* To talk idly and at length; chatter. *— v.t.* To utter idly or emptily. See synonyms under BABBLE. *— n.* Idle talk; prattle. [<Cf. MDu. & MLG *praten* chatter, ON *prata* talk] **— prat′er** *n.* **— prat′ing·ly** *adv.*

prat·fall (prat′fôl′) *n.* *Slang* A fall on the buttocks.

prat·in·cole (prat′ing·kōl, prā′tin-) *n.* Any one of a genus *(Glareola)* of Old World shore birds having long, pointed wings and deeply forked tail. [<L *pratum* meadow + *incola* inhabitant]

pra·tique (pra·tēk′, prat′ik; *Fr.* prà·tēk′) *n.* Intercourse or correspondence; especially, privilege granted to the master of a vessel to land passengers after compliance with sanitary inspection or quarantine. [<F]

prat·tle (prat′l) *v.* **·tled, ·tling** *v.i.* To talk foolishly or like a child; prate. *— v.t.* To utter in a foolish or childish way: to *prattle* secrets. See synonyms under BABBLE. *— n.* **1** Childish speech; babble. **2** Idle or foolish talk. [Freq. of PRATE] **— prat′tler** *n.*

Prav·dinsk (präv′dēnsk) **1** A town on the Volga in Russian S.F.S.R. **2** A city in the former German province of East Prussia, now in Russian S.F.S.R.: formerly *Friedland.*

prawn (prôn) *n.* An edible shrimplike decapod (suborder *Natantia*) occurring in a variety of genera and species, especially numerous in tropical and temperate waters, principally marine. [ME *prane*; origin unknown]

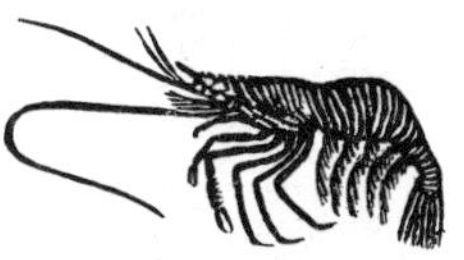

PRAWN
(Up to 6 inches in length)

prax·is (prak′sis) *n.* Exercise or discipline for a specific purpose; practical application of rules as distinguished from theory. [<NL <Gk. < *prassein* accomplish, do]

Prax·it·e·les (prak·sit′ə·lēz) Greek sculptor of the fourth century B.C.

pray (prā) *v.i.* **1** To address prayers to a deity, idol, etc.; say prayers. **2** To make entreaty; beg. *— v.t.* **3** To address by means of prayers; say prayers to. **4** To ask (someone) earnestly; entreat. **5** To ask for by prayers or entreaty. **6** To effect by prayer. ◆ Homophone: *prey.* [<OF *preier* <LL *precare* <L *precari* ask, pray < *prex, precis* prayer]

Synonyms: ask, beg, beseech, bid, conjure, entreat, implore, importune, invoke, petition, request, supplicate. See ASK.

prayer (prâr) *n.* **1** The act of offering reverent petitions, especially to God. **2** The act of beseeching earnestly; entreaty. **3** *Often pl.* A religious service of which prayer is the most prominent part: evening *prayers.* **4** Communion with God and recognition of His presence, as in praise, thanksgiving, intercession, etc. **5** A form of words appropriate to prayer. **6** A memorial or petition. **7** *Law* The request in a bill in equity for the specific relief sought by the complainant; also, the part of the bill

in which the request is made. **—common prayer** The prescribed form of public worship of the Anglican Church as contained in the *Book of Common Prayer.* [<OF *preiere* < Med. L *precaria* <L *precarius* obtained by prayer <*precari.* See PRAY.]
Synonyms: adoration, devotion, invocation, litany, orison, petition, request, suit, supplication. See PETITION.

prayer book A book of ritual prescribed for conducting divine service.

prayer·ful (prâr′fəl) *adj.* Inclined or given to prayer; devotional. **—prayer′ful·ly** *adv.* **—prayer′ful·ness** *n.*

prayer wheel A wheel, cylinder, or vertical drum containing written prayers, which is revolved to make the prayers efficacious: used by the Buddhists of Tibet. Also **praying wheel.**

praying mantis The mantis.

pre– *prefix* **1** Before in time or order; prior to; preceding; as in:

preaccusation	**preconfiguration**
preacquaint	**preconfirm**
preacquaintance	**preconnection**
preacquire	**preconnubial**
preact	**preconsent**
preaction	**preconsideration**
preadapt	**preconsign**
preadaptation	**preconstitute**
preadjust	**preconstruction**
preadjustment	**preconsult**
preadministration	**preconsultation**
preadmit	**preconsume**
preadmonish	**precontract**
preadmonition	**precontrive**
preadvertise	**preconviction**
preadvertiser	**pre–cool**
preadvise	**precorrupt**
preadviser	**precounsel**
preaestival	**pre–Darwinian**
preallege	**predecision**
preannounce	**prededication**
preannouncement	**predeliberation**
preannouncer	**predemand**
preantiquity	**predescribe**
preapperception	**predesign**
preappoint	**predeterminable**
preappointment	**predevised**
preapproval	**predirect**
prearm	**prediscipline**
prearrange	**prediscovery**
prearrangement	**preelect**
pre–Aryan	**preelection**
preassemble	**preembodiment**
preassigned	**preembody**
preassume	**preemploy**
preassurance	**preenact**
preassure	**preengage**
preattachment	**preengagement**
preattune	**pre–epic**
preavowal	**preestablish**
prebaptize	**preestablishment**
prebasal	**preexamination**
prebasilar	**preexamine**
preboding	**preexist**
preboil	**preexistence**
prebranchial	**preexistent**
pre–British	**preexpose**
prebronchial	**preform**
prebuccal	**preglacial**
precalculable	**preheat**
precalculate	**preheater**
precalculation	**preinhabitation**
precancerous	**preinstruct**
pre–Carboniferous	**preintimation**
pre–Centennial	**preknowledge**
precerebellar	**prepaid**
pre–Christian	**pre–Paleozoic**
pre–Christianize	**pre–Reformation**
precited	**pre–Renaissance**
preclassical	**prerequire**
precogitate	**prerevolutionary**
precogitation	**pre–Roman**
precognition	**preselect**
precognizable	**preshadow**
precognizant	**pre–Shakespearian**
precollection	**preshow**
pre–Columbian	**presuccess**
precompose	**pre–Tertiary**
precomputation	**pretribal**
precompute	**pretypify**
preconcession	**preunite**
preconclusion	**pre–Victorian**
precondemn	**prewarm**
precondemnation	**prewarn**

2 Before in position; anterior: chiefly in scientific terms; as in:

preabdomen	**precardiac**	**prerectal**
preanal	**precerebral**	**prerenal**
preaortic	**precostal**	**preretinal**
preauricular	**prepatellar**	**prevertebral**

3 Preliminary to; preparing for; as in:

precollege	**prelegal**	**premedical**
preflight	**prelexical**	**pre–military**

[<L *prae-* <*prae* before]

preach (prēch) *v.i.* **1** To deliver a sermon, as on a religious topic or a text of Scripture. **2** To give advice or instruction, especially persistently and intrusively. **—** *v.t.* **3** To advocate or recommend urgently: to *preach* temperance. **4** To proclaim; expound upon: to *preach* the gospel. **5** To deliver (a sermon, etc.). [<OF *prechier* <L *praedicare* proclaim <*prae-* before + *dicare* make known]

preach·er (prē′chər) *n.* One who preaches; specifically, a clergyman. [<OF *prechor*]

preach·i·fy (prē′chə·fī) *v.i.* **·fied, ·fy·ing** *Colloq.* To preach or discourse tediously. **—preach′i·fi·ca′tion** *n.*

preach·ing (prē′ching) *n.* **1** The act or practice of delivering sermons. **2** The style of a preacher. **3** The doctrine preached.

Preaching Friars See DOMINICAN.

preach·ment (prēch′mənt) *n.* A preaching or moral lecture; especially, a wearisome exhortation. [<OF *prechement*]

preach·y (prē′chē) *adj.* **preach·i·er, preach·i·est** Given to or resembling preachments; marked by sanctimony or cant: not a complimentary term.

pre·ad·am·ite (prē·ad′əm·īt) *adj.* Existing before Adam; relating to the preadamites. Also **pre·a·dam·ic** (prē′ə·dam′ik), **pre·ad′am·it′ic** (-it′ik). **—** *n.* **1** One who or that which existed before Adam or before man. **2** One holding that there were men on the earth before Adam.

pre·ag·o·nal (prē·ag′ə·nəl) *adj.* Immediately preceding the death agony. [<PRE- + AGON(Y) + -AL[1]]

pre·am·ble (prē′am·bəl) *n.* **1** A statement introductory to and explanatory of what follows; the introductory portion of a writing or speech: used chiefly of formal resolutions. **2** *Law* An introductory clause in a constitution, contract, or other instrument. [<F *préamble* <Med. L *praeambulum,* orig. neut. of L *praeambulus* walking before <L *praeambulare* precede <*prae-* before + *ambulare* walk] **—pre·am′bu·lar′y** *adj.*

pre·ax·i·al (prē·ak′sē·əl) *adj. Biol.* Situated on that side of the axis of a limb or body that is in front.

preb·end (preb′ənd) *n.* **1** A stipend allotted to an ecclesiastic from the revenues of a cathedral or conventual church in consideration of his officiating and serving therein; also, the land or tithe yielding the stipend, the tenure of which is a benefice. **2** A prebendary. [<OF *prebende* <Med. L *praebenda,* lit., things to be furnished, neut. pl. of L *praebendus,* gerundive of *praebere* supply <*prae-* in front of, before + *habere* have] **—preb′·en·dal** *adj.*

preb·en·dar·y (preb′ən·der′ē) *n. pl.* **·dar·ies** A person, as a canon, who receives a stated income from the revenues of a cathedral. [<Med. L *prebendarius*]

Preb·le (preb′əl), **Edward,** 1761–1807, U.S. naval officer; captain of the *Constitution.*

Pre–Cam·bri·an (prē·kam′brē·ən) *adj. Geol.* Of or pertaining to all geological time and rock formations preceding the Cambrian. **—** *n.* Pre-Cambrian rocks.

pre·can·cel (prē·kan′səl) *v.t.* **·celed** or **·celled, ·cel·ing** or **·cel·ling** To cancel (stamps) before use on mail. **—** *n.* A stamp so canceled.

pre·car·i·ous (pri·kâr′ē·əs) *adj.* **1** Subject to continued risk; that may be taken away at another's pleasure or by accident; uncertain. **2** Subject or leading to danger; hazardous. **3** Not firmly established; untrustworthy; without foundation. [<L *precarius.* See PRAYER.] **—pre·car′i·ous·ly** *adv.* **—pre·car′i·ous·ness** *n.*
Synonyms: doubtful, dubious, equivocal, hazardous, insecure, perilous, risky, unassured, uncertain, unsettled, unstable, unsteady. *Uncertain* is applied to things that human knowledge cannot certainly determine or that human power cannot certainly control; *precarious* originally meant dependent on the will or pleasure of another; now it also means dependent on chance or hazard; one holds office by a *precarious* tenure, or land by a *precarious* title; the strong man's hold on life is *uncertain,* the invalid's is *precarious. Antonyms*: assured, certain, firm, immutable, incontestable, settled, stable, steady, strong, sure, undoubted, unquestionable.

pre–cast (prē′kast′, -käst′) *adj.* Receiving a finished shape before being put to final use: *pre–cast* concrete blocks.

prec·a·tive (prek′ə·tiv) *adj.* Expressing entreaty; supplicatory. Also **prec′a·to′ry.** [<L *precativus*]

pre·cau·tion (pri·kô′shən) *n.* **1** Prudent forethought, as against danger, etc. **2** A provision made for some emergency. See synonyms under CARE. [<F *précaution* <LL *praecautio, -onis* <L *praecautus,* pp. of *praecavere* guard against beforehand <*prae-* before + *cavere* take care]

pre·cau·tion·ar·y (pri·kô′shən·er′ē) *adj.* **1** Of or pertaining to precaution. **2** Expressing, advising, or using precaution. Also **pre·cau′·tion·al.**

pre·cau·tious (pri·kô′shəs) *adj.* Exercising care; precautional. **—pre·cau′tious·ly** *adv.* **—pre·cau′tious·ness** *n.*

pre·cede (pri·sēd′) *v.* **·ced·ed, ·ced·ing** *v.t.* **1** To go before in order, place, rank, time, etc. **2** To preface; introduce. **—** *v.i.* **3** To have or take precedence. [<F *précéder* <L *praecedere* go before <*prae-* before + *cedere* go]
Synonyms: head, herald, lead. See LEAD[1]. *Antonyms*: see synonyms for FOLLOW.

pre·ce·dence (pri·sēd′ns, pres′ə·dəns) *n.* The act or right of preceding, or the state of being precedent; priority in place, time, or rank. Also **pre·ce′den·cy.**
Synonyms: antecedence, ascendency, lead, leadership, preeminence, preference, priority, superiority, supremacy. *Antonyms*: inferiority, subjection, subjugation, subordination.

prec·e·dent (pres′ə·dənt) *n.* **1** Previous usage or established mode of precedure. **2** An antecedent. **3** A judicial decision taken as furnishing a rule for subsequent decisions. **—pre·ce·dent** (pri·sēd′nt) *adj.* Former; previous; preceding. [<F *précédent* <L *praecedens, -entis,* ppr. of *praecedere.* See PRECEDE.]
Synonyms (noun): antecedent, case, example, instance, pattern, warrant. A *precedent* is an authoritative *case, example,* or *instance. Cases* decided by irregular or unauthorized tribunals are not *precedents* for the regular administration of law. See ANTECEDENT, CAUSE, EXAMPLE.

prec·e·den·tial (pres′ə·den′shəl) *adj.* Of the nature of a precedent; preliminary; having social priority.

pre·ced·ing (pri·sē′ding) *adj.* Going before, as in time, place, or rank; earlier; foregoing; immediately antecedent: The citation was on the *preceding* page.

pre·cent (pri·sent′) *v.i.* To act as precentor. [Back formation <PRECENTOR]

pre·cen·tor (pri·sen′tər) *n.* The leader of the musical part of a church service. [<LL *praecentor* <L *praecinere* sing before <*prae-* before + *canere* sing] **—pre·cen·to·ri·al** (prē′sen·tôr′ē·əl, -tō′rē-) *adj.* **—pre·cen′tor·ship** *n.*

pre·cept (prē′sept) *n.* **1** A prescribed rule of conduct or action; instruction or direction regarding a given course or action; especially, a maxim in morals: distinguished from *counsel.* **2** *Law* A judicial command in writing; writ; process. See synonyms under ADAGE. [<OF <L *praeceptum,* pp. of *praecipere* give rules, instruct <*prae-* before + *capere* receive, take]

pre·cep·tive (pri·sep′tiv) *adj.* Consisting of precepts; didactic.

pre·cep·tor (pri·sep′tər) *n.* A teacher; instructor; specifically, the principal of a school. [<L *praeceptor*] **—pre·cep·to·ri·al** (prē′sep·tôr′ē·əl, -tō′rē-) *adj.*

pre·cep·to·ry (pri·sep′tər·ē) *adj.* Preceptive; mandatory. **—** *n. pl.* **·ries** A place of instruction; specifically, a religious house of the Knights Templars. [<Med. L *praeceptoria*]

pre·cep·tress (pri·sep′tris) *n.* A woman preceptor; governess.

pre·ces·sion (pri·sesh′ən) *n.* The act of preceding or coming in advance of time or of other persons or things. [<LL *praecessio, -onis* < *praecessus,* pp. of *praecedere.* See PRECEDE.]

pre·ces·sion·al (pri·sesh′ən·əl) *adj.* Pertaining to or of the nature of precession.

precession of the equinoxes *Astron.* A slow rotary motion of the equinoctial points on the ecliptic from east to west, causing the time between successive equinoxes to be appreciably shorter than it would otherwise be: caused by the combined attractive forces of the moon, sun, and planets upon the equatorial protuberance of the earth and completing a full cycle in about 26,000 years, a period known as the *Platonic* or *great year.*

pre·cinct (prē′singkt) *n.* 1 A place definitely marked off by fixed lines; also, the boundary of a designated place. 2 A minor territorial or jurisdictional district. 3 An election district of a town, township, county, etc. 4 A police subdivision of a city or town, or its police station. 5 *Brit.* The immediate neighborhood of a church or temple. 6 *pl.* Neighborhood; environs. [<LL *praecinctum* boundary, orig. neut. of *praecinctus,* pp. of *praecingere* gird about <*prae-* before + *cingere* gird]

pre·ci·os·i·ty (presh′ē·os′ə·tē) *n.* Extreme fastidiousness or affected refinement, as in speech, style, or taste. [<OF *preciosité* <L *pretiositas* <*pretiosus.* See PRECIOUS.]

pre·cious (presh′əs) *adj.* 1 Highly priced or prized, as for rarity, or for intrinsic, exchangeable, or other value; valuable. 2 Beloved; dear. 3 Good-for-nothing; undeserving: used ironically. 4 *Colloq.* Very considerable; surpassing: a *precious* scoundrel. 5 Overnice; fastidious: a *precious* writer. See synonyms under CHOICE, EXCELLENT, GOOD, RARE[1]. [<OF *precios* <L *pretiosus* <*pretium* price] — **pre′cious·ly** *adv.* — **pre′cious·ness** *n.*

precious garnet Pyrope.

prec·i·pe (pres′i·pē, prē′si-) *n. Law* 1 A written order directing the issuance of a specified writ. 2 *Brit.* Formerly, a writ commanding a defendant, in the alternative, to do some particular thing, or to show cause for not doing it. Also spelled *praecipe.* [<L *praecipe,* lit., admonish, imperative of *praecipere* admonish, instruct. See PRECEPT.]

prec·i·pice (pres′i·pis) *n.* 1 A high, steep place; the brink of a cliff. 2 A perilous situation. [<F *précipice* <L *praecipitium* <*praeceps* headlong <*prae-* before + *caput* head]

pre·cip·i·ta·ble (pri·sip′ə·tə·bəl) *adj.* Capable or susceptible of being precipitated: a *precipitable* salt.

pre·cip·i·tance (pri·sip′ə·təns) *n.* 1 The quality of being precipitant; rashness. 2 An instance of this. Also **pre·cip′i·tan·cy.**

pre·cip·i·tant (pri·sip′ə·tənt) *adj.* 1 Rushing or falling headlong; moving onward quickly and heedlessly: *precipitant* speed. 2 Rash in thought or action; overhasty; impulsive; precipitate; sudden; abrupt. — *n. Chem.* Any substance, as a reagent, that when added or applied to a solution results in the formation of a precipitate. [<L *praecipitans, -antis,* ppr. of *praecipitare.* See PRECIPITATE.] — **pre·cip′i·tant·ly** *adv.*

pre·cip·i·tate (pri·sip′ə·tāt, -tit) *adj.* 1 Rushing down headlong; moving or moved speedily or hurriedly. 2 Wanting due deliberation; hasty; rash. 3 Done prematurely; hurried; undeliberated. 4 Sudden and brief, as a disease. See synonyms under IMPETUOUS. — *v.* (pri·sip′ə·tāt) **·tat·ed, ·tat·ing** *v.t.* 1 To bring about before expected or needed; hasten the occurrence of: to *precipitate* a quarrel. 2 To throw headlong; hurl from or as from a height. 3 *Meteorol.* To cause (vapor, etc.) to condense and fall as dew, rain, etc. 4 *Chem.* To separate (a constituent) in solid form, as from a solution. — *v.i.* 5 *Meteorol.* To fall as condensed vapor. 6 *Chem.* To separate and settle, as a substance held in solution. 7 To fall headlong; rush. — *n.* (pri·sip′ə·tāt, -tit) *Physics* A deposit of solid matter formed in a solution by the action of chemical reagents or by certain physical forces, as low temperature. [<L *praecipitatus,* pp. of *praecipitare* <*praeceps.* See PRECIPICE.] — **pre·cip′i·tate·ly** *adv.* — **pre·cip′i·tate·ness** *n.* — **pre·cip′i·ta′tive** *adj.* — **pre·cip′i·ta′tor** *n.*

pre·cip·i·ta·tion (pri·sip′ə·tā′shən) *n.* 1 The act of casting down; the state of being thrown downward. 2 Headlong or rash haste or hurry; precipitancy; hastening; acceleration. 3 A falling, flowing, or rushing down with violence or rapidity. 4 *Chem.* The process of rendering insoluble and so separating any of the constituents of a solution, as by reagents; also, the precipitate. 5 *Meteorol.* The deposition of moisture from the atmosphere upon the general surface of the earth. 6 Materialization, as of spirits. [<F *précipitation*]

pre·cip·i·tin (pri·sip′ə·tin) *n. Biochem.* An antibody produced in the blood serum by inoculation with foreign protein and capable of providing immunity against specific bacteria; coagulin. [<PRECIPIT(ATE) + -IN]

pre·cip·i·tin·o·gen (pri·sip′ə·tin′ə·jen) *n. Biochem.* The antigen which reacts with the blood to form precipitin. [<PRECIPITIN + -(O)GEN]

pre·cip·i·tous (pri·sip′ə·təs) *adj.* 1 As steep as or consisting of a precipice; very steep. 2 Headlong and downward in motion. 3 Headlong in disposition; precipitate; hasty. See synonyms under STEEP[1]. [<MF *précipiteux*] — **pre·cip′i·tous·ly** *adv.* — **pre·cip′i·tous·ness** *n.*

pré·cis (prā·sē′, prā′sē) *n. pl.* **·cis** (-sēz′, -sēz) A concise, brief summary of the ideas and point of view of a book, article, or document. [<F]

pre·cise (pri·sīs′) *adj.* 1 Sharply or clearly determined; strictly accurate; exact. 2 No more and no less than. 3 Noting or confined to a certain thing; particular; identical. 4 Scrupulously observant of rule; punctilious. [<F *précis* <L *praecisus,* pp. of *praecidere* cut off short <*prae-* before + *caedere* cut] — **pre·cise′ly** *adv.* — **pre·cise′ness** *n.*

Synonyms: accurate, careful, correct, definite, distinct, exact, explicit, faultless, flawless, minute, nice, particular, perfect, rigid, right, scrupulous, strict. *Accurate, correct, definite, exact, precise, nice,* all denote absolute conformity to some standard or truth. *Accurate* indicates conformity secured by *scrupulous* care. An *accurate* measurement or account can be verified and found true in all particulars. *Careful* carries less sharp certainty. *Exact* indicates that which is worked out to the utmost limit of requirement in every respect; *precise* refers to a like conformity or to an excessive *exactness. Exact* and *precise* are often interchangeable; but *precise* has often an invidious meaning, denoting excessive care of petty details; we speak of the martinet as insufferably *precise,* not insufferably *exact. Correct* applies to a required or enforced correspondence with a standard. This is especially seen in the use of the verb; the printer *corrects* the proof. That is *correct* which is free from fault or mistake. *Nice* denotes a very fine and discriminating exactness, and refers to intellectual distinctions oftener than to material measurements. Compare CORRECT, MINUTE[2]. *Antonyms*: careless, doubtful, erroneous, false, faulty, inaccurate, inexact, loose, mistaken, misty, nebulous, untrue, vague, wrong.

pre·ci·sian (pri·sizh′ən) *n.* One who adheres punctiliously to rules and forms: a term especially applied in a religious sense to the Puritans.

pre·ci·sion (pri·sizh′ən) *n.* The quality of being precise; accuracy of limitation, definition, or adjustment. [<F *précision* <L *praecisio, -onis*] — **pre·ci′sion·ist** *n.*

pre·clin·i·cal (prē·klin′i·kəl) *adj.* 1 *Med.* In the period of disease before the appearance of symptoms sufficient for diagnosis. 2 Pertaining to medical studies which precede practical study of patients.

pre·clude (pri·klōōd′) *v.t.* **·clud·ed, ·clud·ing** 1 To render impossible or ineffectual by antecedent action; prevent. 2 To shut out; exclude. [<L *praecludere* <*prae-* before + *cludere* shut] — **pre·clu′sion** (-klōō′zhən) *n.* — **pre·clu′sive** (-klōō′siv) *adj.* — **pre·clu′sive·ly** *adv.*

Synonyms: obviate, prevent. To *obviate* is to *prevent* by interception and making unnecessary; to *preclude,* to close or shut in advance, is to *prevent* by anticipation or by logical necessity; walls and bars *precluded* the possibility of escape; a supposition is *precluded*; a necessity or difficulty is *obviated.* Compare PROHIBIT, SHUT.

pre·co·cial (pri·kō′shəl) *adj. Ornithol.* Of or pertaining to birds whose young are able to run about as soon as they are hatched. [See PRECOCIOUS]

pre·co·cious (pri·kō′shəs) *adj.* 1 Developing before the natural season. 2 Unusually forward or advanced, especially mentally. 3 *Bot.* Flowering or ripening early, as certain plants. [<OF *precoce* <L *praecox, praecocis* <*praecoquere* cook or ripen beforehand <*prae-* before + *coquere* cook] — **pre·co′cious·ly** *adv.* — **pre·co′cious·ness, pre·coc′i·ty** (-kos′ə·tē) *n.*

pre·con·ceive (prē′kən·sēv′) *v.t.* **·ceived, ·ceiv·ing** To conceive in advance; form an idea or opinion of beforehand.

pre·con·cep·tion (prē′kən·sep′shən) *n.* 1 An idea or opinion formed or conceived in advance. 2 A prejudice or misconception; bias. — **pre′con·cep′tion·al** *adj.*

pre·con·cert (prē′kən·sûrt′) *v.t.* To arrange in advance, as by agreement. — *n.* (prē·kon′sûrt) Previous arrangement.

pre·co·nize (prē′kə·nīz) *v.t.* **·nized, ·niz·ing** 1 To announce the appointment of (a new bishop) in public consistory: said of the pope. 2 To proclaim or extol publicly. [<LL *praeconizare* proclaim <L *praeco, praeconis* crier, herald]

pre·con·scious (prē·kon′shəs) *n. Psychoanal.* That area of the psyche containing mental processes of which the individual is unaware at any given time but which are more or less readily available to consciousness: formerly called *foreconscious.*

pre·crit·i·cal (prē·krit′i·kəl) *adj. Med.* Preceding the crisis (of a disease).

pre·cur·sive (pri·kûr′siv) *adj.* Going before as a precursor or harbinger; premonitory; preliminary. Also **pre·cur′so·ry** (-sər·ē).

pre·cur·sor (pri·kûr′sər) *n.* One who or that which precedes and gives intimation of a coming event. See synonyms under HERALD. [<L *praecursor* <*praecursus,* pp. of *praecurrere* run before <*prae-* before + *currere* run]

pre·da·cious (pri·dā′shəs) *adj.* Predatory. Also **pre·da′ceous.** [<L *praeda* prey] — **pre·da′cious·ness, pre·dac′i·ty** (-das′ə·tē) *n.*

pre·date (prē·dāt′) *v.t.* **·dat·ed, ·dat·ing** 1 To date before the actual time. 2 To precede in time.

pred·a·to·ry (pred′ə·tôr′ē, -tō′rē) *adj.* 1 Characterized by or undertaken for plundering. 2 Addicted to pillaging. 3 Constituted for living by preying upon others, as a beast or bird; raptorial. [<L *predatorius* <*praeda* prey] — **pred′a·to′ri·ly** *adv.* — **pred′a·to′ri·ness** *n.*

pre·de·cease (prē′di·sēs′) *v.t.* **·ceased, ·ceas·ing** To die before: She *predeceased* her husband by five years.

pred·e·ces·sor (pred′ə·ses′ər) *n.* 1 One who goes or has gone before another in point of time, as an early settler, a previous incumbent of an office, etc. 2 An ancestor. [<OF *predecesseur* <LL *praedecessor* <*prae-* before + *decessor* retiring official <*decessus* pp. of *decedere* go away. See DECEASE.]

pre·des·ig·nate (prē·dez′ig·nāt) *v.t.* **·nat·ed, ·nat·ing** 1 To designate beforehand. 2 *Logic* To begin (a proposition) with a designation of quantity, as *some, many,* etc. — **pre·des′ig·na′tion** *n.*

pre·des·ti·nar·i·an (prē·des′tə·nâr′ē·ən) *adj.* 1 Pertaining to predestination. 2 Holding the doctrine of predestination. — *n.* A believer in theological predestination; also, a fatalist. — **pre·des′ti·nar′i·an·ism** *n.*

pre·des·ti·nate (prē·des′tə·nit, -nāt) *adj.* 1 Designed for some special fate. 2 Foreordained by divine decree, as to salvation. — *n.* One who is predestined, as to salvation. — *v.t.* (-nāt) **·nat·ed, ·nat·ing** 1 To destine or decree beforehand; foreordain. 2 *Theol.* To foreordain by divine decree or purpose. [<L *praedestinatus,* pp. of *praedestinare* <*prae-* before + *destinare* destine]

pre·des·ti·na·tion (prē·des′tə·nā′shən) *n.* 1 The act of predestinating, or the state of being predestinated; destiny; fate. 2 *Theol.* The foreordination of all things by God, including the future bliss or sorrow of men. See CALVINISM. [<LL *predestinatio, -onis*]

pre·des·tine (prē·des′tin) *v.t.* **·tined, ·tin·ing** To predestinate.

pre·de·ter·mi·nate (prē′di·tûr′mə·nit, -nāt) *adj.* Decided or decreed beforehand.

pre·de·ter·mine (prē′di·tûr′min) *v.t.* **·mined, ·min·ing 1** To determine beforehand; decide in advance. **2** To foreordain. **3** To imbue with an antecedent tendency. — **pre′de·ter′mi·na′tion** *n.*

pre·di·al (prē′dē·əl) *adj.* Of, pertaining to, or attached to the land. Also spelled *praedial.* [<OF <Med. L *praedialis* <L *praedium*]

pred·i·ca·ble (pred′i·kə·bəl) *adj.* That may be predicated or affirmed. —*n.* **1** Anything ascribable. **2** *Logic* A property or attribute affirmable of a class. [<F *prédicable* <L *praedicabilis* <*praedicare.* See PREACH.] — **pred′i·ca·bil′i·ty, pred′i·ca·ble·ness** *n.*

pre·dic·a·ment (pri·dik′ə·mənt) *n.* **1** A trying, embarrassing, puzzling, or amusing situation or plight. **2** A specific state, position, or situation. **3** *Logic* A class or kind distinguished by definite marks; a category. [<LL *praedicamentum* that which is predicated < *praedicare.* See PREACH.]

pred·i·cate (pred′i·kāt) *v.* **·cat·ed, ·cat·ing** *v.t.* **1** To declare; affirm; proclaim. **2** To state or affirm concerning the subject of a proposition. **3** To affirm as a quality or attribute of something. **4** To imply or connote. **5** *U.S.* To found or base (an argument, proposition, etc.): with *on* or *upon.* —*v.i.* **6** To make a statement or affirmation. See synonyms under AFFIRM. —*adj.* (-kit) **1** Predicated. **2** *Gram.* Belonging, relating to, or of the nature of a predicate: a *predicate* adjective. —*n.* (-kit) **1** *Gram.* The word or words in a sentence that express what is affirmed or denied of a subject, as, in the sentence, "Life is short," "is short" is the *predicate.* **2** A quality or property inherent in or asserted to belong to a thing. **3** *Logic* In a proposition, that which is stated about a subject. [<L *praedicatus,* pp. of *praedicare* make known] — **pred′i·ca′tive** *adj.* — **pred′i·ca′·tive·ly** *adv.*

predicate adjective *Gram.* An adjective which describes the subject of a copulative verb, as, He is *sad*; The water turned *green,* etc.

predicate noun *Gram.* A noun which designates or identifies the subject of a copulative verb, as, He was *king*; The water became *ice.*

pred·i·ca·tion (pred′i·kā′shən) *n.* **1** The act of publicly setting forth or proclaiming. **2** The act of predicating or asserting. **3** *Logic* The assertion of something of or concerning a subject; assertion. **4** Something predicated; a predicate. [<L *praedicatio, -onis*] — **pred′i·ca′tion·al** *adj.*

pred·i·ca·to·ry (pred′i·kə·tôr′ē, -tō′rē) *adj.* **1** Of or pertaining to a preacher or preaching. **2** Proclaimed. [<LL *praedicatorius*]

pre·dict (pri·dikt′) *v.t.* **1** To make known beforehand; prophesy; foretell. **2** To assert on the basis of theory, data, or experience but in advance of proof: Einstein *predicted* that space was curved; The computer *predicted* the winning candidate based on a sample poll of voters. —*v.i.* **3** To make a prediction. See synonyms under AUGUR, PROPHESY. [<L *praedictus,* pp. of *praedicere* speak beforehand < *prae-* before + *dicere* say] — **pre·dict′a·ble** *adj.* — **pre·dict′a·bly** *adv.*

pre·dic·tion (pri·dik′shən) *n.* **1** The act of predicting. **2** The thing predicted; forecast: an accurate *prediction.* [<L *praedictio, -onis*] — **pre·dic′tive** *adj.* — **pre·dic′tive·ly** *adv.*

pre·dic·tor (pri·dik′tər) *n.* **1** One who or that which predicts. **2** *Mil.* A mechanism used in connection with anti-aircraft guns for automatically determining the position, speed, and course of approaching aircraft.

pre·di·gest (prē′di·jest′, -dī-) *v.t.* To treat (food) by a process of partial digestion before introduction into the stomach; peptonize. — **pre′di·ges′tion** *n.*

pre·di·lec·tion (prē′də·lek′shən, pred′ə-) *n.* A favorable prepossession or predisposition; partiality; preference: with *for.* See synonyms under FANCY, INCLINATION, RELISH. [<F *prédilection* <Med. L *praedilectio, -onis* < *praedilectus,* pp. of *praedilegere* prefer <L *prae-* before + *diligere* love, choose]

pre·dis·pose (prē′dis·pōz′) *v.t.* **·posed, ·pos·ing 1** To give a tendency or inclination to; make susceptible or liable: Exhaustion *predisposes* one to sickness. **2** To dispose beforehand. **3** To dispose of beforehand; bequeath. — **pre·dis·po·si·tion** (prē′dis·pə·zish′ən) *n.*

pre·dom·i·nance (pri·dom′ə·nəns) *n.* **1** The state or quality of being predominant. **2** Superiority; ascendance; preponderance. Also **pre·dom′i·nan·cy.**

pre·dom·i·nant (pri·dom′ə·nənt) *adj.* Superior in power, influence, effectiveness, number, or degree; prevailing over others. [<F *prédominant*] — **pre·dom′i·nant·ly** *adv.*

Synonyms: ascendent, chief, commanding, controlling, dominant, prevailing, prevalent, regnant, sovereign, superior, supreme. *Antonyms*: accessory, complementary, contributory, inferior, subordinate, subsidiary, unimportant.

pre·dom·i·nate (pri·dom′ə·nāt) *v.i.* **·nat·ed, ·nat·ing 1** To have governing influence or control; be in control: often with *over.* **2** To be superior to all others, as in power, height, number, etc.; prevail; preponderate. [<Med. L *predominatus*] — **pre·dom′i·nat′ing·ly** *adv.* — **pre·dom′i·na′tion** *n.*

pree (prē) *v.t. Scot.* To test, especially by tasting; also, to kiss.

preef (prēf) *n. Scot.* Proof.

pre·em·i·nent (prē·em′ə·nənt) *adj.* **1** Supremely eminent; distinguished above all others; transcendent; supreme. **2** Extraordinary in degree; outstanding; conspicuous; superlative. See synonyms under PARAMOUNT. [<L *praeëminens, -entis,* ppr. of *praeëminere* be prominent < *prae-* before + *eminere* stand out, project] — **pre·em·i·nent·ly** *adv.* — **pre·em′i·nence** *n.*

pre·empt (prē·empt′) *v.t.* **1** To acquire or appropriate beforehand. **2** To secure by preemption; occupy (public land) so as to acquire by preemption. [Back formation < PREEMPTION] — **pre·emp′tor** *n.* — **pre·emp′to·ry** (-tər·ē) *adj.*

pre·emp·tion (prē·emp′shən) *n.* **1** The right or act of purchasing before others. **2** Public land obtained by exercising this right. [< Med. L *praeëmptio, -onis* <L *prae-* before + *emptus,* pp. of *emere* buy]

pre·emp·tive (prē·emp′tiv) *adj.* Pertaining to or capable of preemption.

preemptive bid In auction or contract bridge, a bid of a high number of tricks in order to shut out probable bids of an opponent.

preen[1] (prēn) *v.t.* **1** To trim and dress with the beak, as birds their feathers. **2** To dress or adorn (oneself) carefully; primp; prink. —*v.i.* **3** To primp; prink. [Prob. var. of PRUNE[3]]

preen[2] (prēn) *n. Scot.* A pin; a brooch. —*v.t.* To sew; pin.

pre·ex·il·i·an (prē′eg·zil′ē·ən) *adj.* In Jewish history, pertaining to or denoting a period prior to the Babylonian exile (sixth century B.C.). Also **pre′ex·il′ic.**

pre·fab (prē′fab′) *n.* A prefabricated structure or part: also used attributively.

pre·fab·ri·cate (prē·fab′rə·kāt) *v.t.* **·cat·ed, ·cat·ing 1** To fabricate or build beforehand. **2** To manufacture in standard sections that can be rapidly assembled. — **pre·fab′ri·ca′·tion** *n.*

pref·ace (pref′is) *n.* **1** A brief explanation or address to the reader at the beginning of a book or other publication. **2** Any introductory speech, writing, etc. —*v.t.* **·aced, ·ac·ing 1** To introduce or furnish with a preface. **2** To serve as a preface for. [<OF <L *praefatio* < *praefatus,* pp. of *praefari* utter beforehand, premise < *prae-* before + *fari* speak]

Pref·ace (pref′is) *n. Eccl.* **1** The prayer of thanksgiving, ending with the Sanctus, which introduces the canon of the mass. **2** The corresponding section in other eucharistic liturgies.

pref·a·to·ry (pref′ə·tôr′ē, -tō′rē) *adj.* Of the nature of a preface; introductory. Also **pref′a·to′ri·al.** — **pref′a·to′ri·ly** *adv.*

pre·fect (prē′fekt) *n.* **1** In ancient Rome, any of various civil and military officials, as certain magistrates, governors, and commanders. **2** Any magistrate, chief official, etc.; specifically, in France, the chief administrator of a department, or the head of the Paris police. **3** In Roman Catholic schools, the dean. **4** *Brit.* A senior pupil charged with maintaining order and discipline among other pupils. Also spelled *praefect.* [<OF <L *praefectus,* orig. pp. of *praeficere* set over <L *prae-* before + *facere* make, do]

pre·fec·ture (prē′fek·chər) *n.* **1** The office, jurisdiction, or province of a prefect. **2** The official building for his use. [<L *praefectura*] — **pre·fec′tur·al** *adj.*

pre·fer (pri·fûr′) *v.t.* **·ferred, ·fer·ring 1** To hold in higher regard or esteem; like better. **2** To give priority to, as one creditor or form of securities over others. **3** To advance or promote, as in status or rank. **4** To offer, as a suit or charge, for consideration or decision. See synonyms under CHOOSE, PROMOTE. [<F *préferer* <L *praeferre* carry, set in front < *prae-* before + *ferre* bear] — **pre·fer′rer** *n.*

pref·er·a·ble (pref′ər·ə·bəl) *adj.* To be preferred; more desirable; worthy of choice. — **pref′er·a·ble·ness, pref′er·a·bil′i·ty** *n.* — **pref′·er·a·bly** *adv.*

pref·er·ence (pref′ər·əns) *n.* **1** The act of preferring; estimation or choice of one thing or person over another; also, the privilege of making such choice. **2** The state of being preferred. **3** That which is preferred; an object of favor or choice. **4** A priority of payment given by an insolvent debtor to one or to a certain class of his creditors over others; also, priority of payment by operation of law. **5** Promotion; preferment. **6** The granting of special advantage over others to one country or group of countries in international trade. See synonyms under ALTERNATIVE, PRECEDENCE. [<F *préférence* <L *praeferentia,* orig. neut. pl. of *praeferens, -entis,* ppr. of *praeferre.* See PREFER.]

pref·er·en·tial (pref′ə·ren′shəl) *adj.* **1** Indicating or arising from preference or partiality. **2** Possessing or giving priority or preference, as in tariffs or railroad charges. — **pref′er·en′tial·ism** *n.* — **pref′er·en′tial·ly** *adv.*

preferential shop A shop that gives precedence to union members when hiring employees, usually by agreement with a union.

preferential voting A form of voting in which an order of choice of candidates may be signified by a voter on his ballot.

pre·fer·ment (pri·fûr′mənt) *n.* **1** The act of preferring. **2** The state of being preferred. **3** The act of promoting or appointing to higher office; advancement; promotion. **4** A superior post or dignity: said especially of ecclesiastical rank.

pre·ferred (pri·fûrd′) *adj.* **1** Having the first claim: *preferred* bonds or stock. **2** Having gained promotion. **3** Chosen by preference.

pre·fig·ur·a·tion (prē·fig′yə·rā′shən) *n.* **1** Antecedent representation by types, figures, etc. **2** A prototype. — **pre·fig·ur·a·tive** (prē·fig′yər·ə·tiv) *adj.* — **pre·fig′ur·a·tive·ly** *adv.* — **pre·fig′ur·a·tive·ness** *n.*

pre·fig·ure (prē·fig′yər) *v.t.* **·ured, ·ur·ing 1** To represent in advance; serve as an indication or suggestion of; foreshadow. **2** To imagine or picture to oneself beforehand. [<LL *praefigurare*]

pre·fix (prē′fiks) *n.* **1** *Gram.* A non-separable syllable, or syllables, affixed to the beginning of a word to modify or alter the meaning, as *pre-* in prefix, *be-* in behead, *dis-* in disagree, *re-* in renew, *post-* in postwar, *un-* in unhorse, etc. **2** Something placed before, as a title before a noun. Compare SUFFIX. —*v.t.* (prē·fiks′) **1** To put or attach before or at the beginning; add as a prefix: opposed to *postfix.* **2** *Obs.* To arrange or settle beforehand. [< OF *prefixer* <L *praefixus,* pp. of *praefigere* < *prae-* before + *figere* fix] — **pre′fix·al** *adj.* — **pre′fix·al·ly** *adv.* — **pre·fix·ion** (prē·fik′shən) *n.*

pre·flight training (prē′flīt) *Aeron.* Preliminary ground instruction in aviation.

pre·flo·ra·tion (prē′flə·rā′shən) *n. Bot.* The disposition of flowers within the flower bud; estivation. [<PRE- + L *flos, floris* flower + -ATION]

pre·fo·li·a·tion (prē·fō′lē·ā′shən) *n. Bot.* The disposition of leaves within a bud; vernation.

pre·for·ma·tion (prē′fôr·mā′shən) *n.* **1** The act of preforming; the state of being formed in advance. **2** *Biol.* An early theory of generation according to which an organism exists fully preformed in the germ, developing only by increase in size. Compare EPIGENESIS.

Pre·gel (prā′gəl) A river in the former German province of East Prussia, now in Russian

S.F.S.R., flowing 78 miles west to the Vistula Lagoon below Kaliningrad.

Pre·gl (prā′gəl), **Fritz,** 1869–1930, Austrian chemist.

preg·na·ble (preg′nə·bəl) *adj.* Weak enough to be conquered; likely to yield when attacked, as a fort. [<OF *prenable* <*prendre* take <L *prehendere* seize] — **preg′na·bil′i·ty** *n.*

preg·nan·cy (preg′nən·sē) *n.* **1** The state of being with young or with child. **2** *Obs.* Quickness of intelligence.

preg·nan·di·ol (preg·nan′dē·ôl, -ol) *n. Biochem.* A complex organic compound of the sterol group, found in the urine of pregnant women and chemically related to progesterone. [< *pregnane,* a sterol from the urine of pregnant women + *diol,* a glycol]

preg·nant (preg′nənt) *adj.* **1** Carrying a growing fetus in the uterus; with child; impregnated; gestating. **2** Carrying great weight or significance; full of meaning or contents; leading to important results. **3** Fruitful; prolific; teeming with ideas; imaginative; inventive. **4** In rhetoric and logic, implying more than is expressed. [<L *praegnans, -antis,* ult. < *prae-* before + *gnasci* be born] — **preg′nant·ly** *adv.*

pre·hen·si·ble (pri·hen′sə·bəl) *adj.* Capable of being apprehended or grasped. [<L *prehensus,* pp. of *prehendere* seize]

pre·hen·sile ◆ (pri·hen′sil) *adj.* Adapted for grasping or holding; formed to grasp or coil around and cling to objects, as the tail of a monkey. [<F *préhensile*] — **pre·hen·sil·i·ty** (prē′hen·sil′ə·tē) *n.*

pre·hen·sion (pri·hen′shən) *n.* The act of grasping, physically or mentally. [<L *prehensio, -onis*]

pre·his·tor·ic (prē′his·tôr′ik, -tor′-) *adj.* Of or belonging to a period before that covered by written history. Also **pre′his·tor′i·cal.** — **pre′·his·tor′i·cal·ly** *adv.*

pre·his·to·ry (prē·his′tə·rē) *n.* The history of the development of mankind based on archeological and ethnological findings; the period of history preceding written records.

prehn·ite (pren′īt) *n.* A light-green, gray, or white hydrous silicate of calcium and aluminum: similar in composition and occurrence to zeolite. [after Col. van *Prehn,* 18th century Dutch colonist]

pre·ig·ni·tion (prē′ig·nish′ən) *n.* Ignition of the charge in the cylinder of an internal-combustion engine previous to the completion of the compression stroke, often the result of faulty ignition timing.

pre·judge (prē·juj′) *v.t.* **·judged, ·judg·ing** To judge before or without proper inquiry; pass judgment on hastily or beforehand. [<F *préjuger* <*praejudicare* <*prae-* before + *judicare* judge] — **pre·judg′er** *n.* — **pre·judg′·ment,** *Brit.* **pre·judge′ment** *n.*

prej·u·dice (prej′ōō·dis) *n.* **1** A judgment or opinion, favorable or unfavorable, formed beforehand or without due examination; a mental decision based on other grounds than reason or justice; especially, a premature or adversely biased opinion. **2** Detriment arising from a hasty and unfair judgment; injury; harm. — **in** (or **to**) **the prejudice of** To the injury or detriment of. — **without prejudice** *Law* Without detriment to any right that previously existed: usually applied to the dismissal of a bill in equity without consideration of the merits; or to the reservation, express or implied, of all rights in favor of one who offers to compromise a claim or litigation, in case his offer is rejected. — *v.t.* **·diced, ·dic·ing 1** To affect or influence with a prejudice; bias. **2** To affect injuriously or detrimentally; damage; impair. [<OF <L *praejudicium* <*prae-* before + *judicium* judgment]

Synonyms (noun): bias, preconception, predilection, prepossession, unfairness. A *prejudice* or *prepossession* is grounded often on feeling, fancy, associations, etc. A *prepossession* is always favorable, a *prejudice* usually unfavorable, unless the contrary is expressly stated. See INJURY. *Antonyms*: certainty, conclusion, conviction, demonstration, evidence, reason, reasoning.

prej·u·di·cial(prej′ōō·dish′əl) *adj.* Having power or tendency to prejudice or injure; injurious; detrimental. — **prej′u·di′cial·ly** *adv.*

prel·a·cy (prel′ə·sē) *n. pl.* **·cies 1** The system of church government by prelates: often a hostile term for episcopacy. **2** The dignity or function of a prelate. **3** Prelates collectively. [<AF *prelacie* <Med. L *praelatia* <*praelatus.* See PRELATE.]

prel·ate (prel′it) *n.* One of a higher order of clergy, as a bishop or abbot. [<OF *prelat* <L *praelatus,* pp. to *praeferre* set over. See PREFER.] — **prel′ate·ship** *n.* — **pre·lat·ic** (pri·lat′ik) or **·i·cal** *adj.*

prel·a·tism (prel′ə·tiz′əm) *n.* **1** Prelacy; episcopacy. **2** Prelatic partisanship.

prel·a·tist (prel′ə·tist) *n.* One who supports the prelacy; an advocate of High Church government: sometimes used contemptuously.

prel·a·ture (prel′ə·chər) *n.* Prelacy (defs. 2 and 3).

pre·lect (pri·lekt′) *v.i.* To lecture; discourse. [<L *praelectus,* pp. of *praelegere* read before <*prae-* before + *legere* read] — **pre·lec′tion** *n.* — **pre·lec′tor** *n.*

pre·li·ba·tion (prē′lī·bā′shən) *n.* **1** A preliminary offering. **2** A tasting beforehand or by anticipation; anticipation. [<LL *praelibatio, -onis* <*prae-* before + *libatio* a libation]

pre·lim·i·nar·y (pri·lim′ə·ner′ē) *adj.* Antecedent or introductory to the main discourse, proceedings, or business; prefatory; preparatory. — *n. pl.* **·ries 1** An initiatory step; a preparatory act. **2** A preliminary examination. See synonyms under ANTECEDENT. [<PRE- + L *liminaris* pertaining to a threshold < *limen, liminis* threshold] — **pre·lim′i·nar′i·ly** *adv.*

pre·lit·er·ate (prē·lit′ər·it) *adj.* Without written records; prehistoric: said especially of the earliest human cultures.

prel·ude (prel′yōōd, prē′lōōd) *n.* **1** *Music* **a** An independent instrumental composition of moderate length, in a free style suggesting improvisation. **b** An opening piece at the start of a church service; a voluntary. **c** The overture of an opera. **d** An opening strain or movement at the beginning of a musical composition, usually introducing the theme of the whole work. **2** Any introductory or opening performance or event, or that which foreshadows a coming event. — *v.* **·ud·ed, ·ud·ing** *v.t.* **1** To introduce with a prelude. **2** To serve as a prelude to. — *v.i.* **3** To serve as a prelude. **4** To provide or play a prelude. [<F *prélude* <Med. L *praeludium* <L *praeludere* play before <*prae-* before + *ludere* play] — **pre·lud·er** (pri·lōō′dər, prel′yə·dər) *n.* — **pre·lu·di·al** (pri·lōō′dē·əl) *adj.*

pre·lu·sion (pri·lōō′zhən) *n.* That which serves as a prelude. [<L *praelusio, -onis* <*praelusus,* pp. of *praeludere.* See PRELUDE.]

pre·lu·sive (pri·lōō′siv) *adj.* Having the character of a prelude; indicating beforehand. Also **pre·lu′so·ry** (-sər·ē). [<L *praelusus.* See PRELUSION.] — **pre·lu′sive·ly, pre·lu′so·ri·ly** *adv.*

pre·ma·ture (prē′mə·chŏŏr′, -tŏŏr′, -tyŏŏr′) *adj.* Existing, happening, matured or developed before the natural period; done before the proper time; untimely. [<L *praematurus* <*prae-* before + *maturus* ripe, seasonable] — **pre′ma·ture′ly** *adv.* — **pre′ma·tu′ri·ty, pre′·ma·ture′ness** *n.*

pre·max·il·la (prē′mak·sil′ə) *n. pl.* **·max·il·lae** (-mak·sil′ē) *Anat.* One of the two bones set between the maxillae in front of the vertebrate jaw. [<NL] — **pre·max·il·lar·y** (prē·mak′sə·ler′ē) *adj.*

pre·med·i·tate (prē·med′ə·tāt) *v.t.* & *v.i.* **·tat·ed, ·tat·ing** To plan or consider beforehand. [<L *praemeditatus,* pp. of *praemeditari* think over <*prae-* before + *meditari.* See MEDITATE.] — **pre·med′i·tat′ed·ly** *adv.* — **pre·med′i·ta′tive** *adj.* — **pre·med′i·ta′tor** *n.*

pre·med·i·ta·tion (prē·med′ə·tā′shən) *n.* The considering and planning of a subsequent act; deliberate intention and plan to do a certain thing, especially to commit a crime.

pre·mi·er (prē′mē·ər, *esp. Brit.* prem′yər) *adj.* **1** First in rank or position; principal: the *premier* place, *premier* officer. **2** First in order of occurrence; earliest; specifically, first in order of creation; senior: the *premier* duke of England. — *n.* (prē′mē·ər, pri·mir′; *Brit.* prem′yər) The head of government; the prime minister of England, France, etc. [<F <L *primarius* <L *primus* first] — **pre′mi·er·ship′** *n.*

pre·mière (pri·mir′, *Fr.* prə·myâr′) *adj.* First. — *n.* **1** The leading lady in a theatrical company. **2** The first public presentation of a play, etc. [<F]

pre·mil·le·nar·i·an (prē′mil·ə·nâr′ē·ən) *adj.* Existing or occurring before the millennium: also **pre′mil·len′ni·al** (-mi·len′ē·əl). — *n.* One who believes in premillennialism: also **pre′·mil·len′ni·al·ist.**

pre·mil·len·ni·al·ism (prē′mi·len′ē·əl·iz′əm) *n.* The doctrine that the millennium is to be introduced by the personal return of Christ: opposed to *postmillennialism.*

prem·ise (prem′is) *n.* **1** A proposition laid down, proved, supposed, or assumed, that serves as a ground for argument or for a conclusion; a judgment leading to another judgment as a conclusion. **2** *Logic* Either of the two propositions in a syllogism from which, their truth being granted, the conclusion necessarily follows. **3** *pl. Law* **a** Foregoing statements; facts previously stated. **b** That part in a deed that sets forth the date, names of parties, the land or thing conveyed or granted, the consideration, and all other matters down to the phrase "to have and to hold." **4** *pl.* A distinct portion of real estate; land or lands; land with its appurtenances, as buildings: He lingered about the *premises.* Also **prem′iss.** — **major premise** *Logic* The premise in which the predicate of the conclusion of a syllogism, called the **major term,** is contained; the first proposition of a syllogism. — **minor premise** *Logic* The premise in which the subject of the conclusion of a syllogism, called the **minor term,** is contained; the second proposition of a syllogism.

— **pre·mise** (pri·mīz′, prem′is) *v.* **·mised, ·mis·ing** *v.t.* **1** To stay or state beforehand, as by way of introduction or explanation. **2** To state or assume as a premise or basis of argument. **3** *Obs.* To send in advance. — *v.i.* **4** To make a premise. [<OF *premisse* <Med. L *praemissa,* orig. fem. of L *praemissus,* pp. of *praemittere* send before <*prae-* before + *mittere* send]

pre·mi·um (prē′mē·əm) *n.* **1** A reward or prize for a superior performance or production in competition. **2** A price paid for a loan; a sum offered or given to secure a loan, either a sum in addition to interest, a bonus, or the interest itself. **3** The rate or price at which stocks, shares, or money are valued in excess of their nominal or par value: bank shares at a *premium* of five percent. **4** The amount paid for insurance, as admission fees, annual dues, periodical payments, etc., according to the kind of insurance secured. **5** Any object offered free to those who purchase goods to a certain value, as a set of books given free as an inducement to subscribe to a magazine. **6** A fee for instruction in a trade or a profession. See synonyms under SUBSIDY. — **at a premium** Above par; hence, valuable and in demand. [<L *praemium,* ult. <*prae-* before + *emere* buy]

pre·mo·lar (prē·mō′lər) *n. Anat.* One of the teeth situated before the molars and behind the canines. Compare BICUSPID. — *adj.* Situated in front of or appearing before the molar teeth.

pre·mon·ish (pri·mon′ish) *v.t.* To admonish in advance; forewarn. [<PRE- + MONISH]

pre·mo·ni·tion (prē′mə·nish′ən, prem′ə-) *n.* **1** An actual warning of something yet to occur. **2** A presentiment not based on information received; an instinctive foreboding. [<OF *premonicion* <LL *praemonitio, -onis* <*praemonitus,* pp. of *praemonere* premonish <*prae-* before + *monere* warn] — **pre·mon·i·to·ry** (pri·mon′ə·tôr′ē, -tō′rē) *adj.* — **pre·mon′i·to′·ri·ly** *adv.*

pre·morse (pri·môrs′) *adj. Biol.* Terminating abruptly, as if bitten or broken off: a *premorse* root. [<L *praemorsus,* pp. of *praemordere* bite off <*prae-* before + *mordere* bite]

pre·mun·dane (prē·mun′dān) *adj.* Antemundane.

pre·name (prē′nām′) *n.* A forename; Christian name. [Trans. of L *praenomen*]

pre·na·tal (prē·nāt′l) *adj.* Before birth: *prenatal* care or health. — **pre·na′tal·ly** *adv.*

pre·no·men (prē·nō′mən) See PRAENOMEN.

pre·nom·i·nate (prē·nom′ə·nāt) *Obs. v.t.* To mention or name beforehand. — *adj.* Named beforehand.

pre·no·tion (prē·nō′shən) *n.* A preconception; a generalization with slight basis of fact or experience.

prent (prent) *v.* & *n. Scot.* Print.

pren·tice (pren′tis) *n.* An apprentice. Also **'pren'tice.** [Aphetic var. of APPRENTICE]

pre·oc·cu·pa·tion (prē·ok′yə·pā′shən) *n.* **1** The act of occupying before others, or the state of being or having a prior occupant: also **pre·oc′cu·pan·cy.** **2** The state of being preoccupied, as in mind, attention, or inclination; prepossession. **3** Something that preoccupies. [<L *praeoccupatio, -onis*] — **pre·oc′cu·pant** *n.*

pre·oc·cu·pied (prē·ok′yə·pīd) *adj.* **1** Engrossed in thought or business; abstracted. **2** Previously occupied. **3** Already in use, as a scientific name. See synonyms under ABSTRACTED.

pre·oc·cu·py (prē·ok′yə·pī) *v.t.* **·pied, ·py·ing** **1** To engage fully; engross, as the mind. **2** To occupy or take possession of in advance of another or others. See synonyms under OCCUPY. [<L *praeoccupare*]

pre·or·dain (prē′ôr·dān′) *v.t.* To foreordain. — **pre·or·di·na·tion** (prē′ôr·də·nā′shən) *n.*

prep (prep) *adj. Colloq.* Preparatory: a *prep* school, student, etc.

prep·a·ra·tion (prep′ə·rā′shən) *n.* **1** The act, process, or operation of preparing. **2** An act or proceeding designed to bring about some event; a precaution; provision: *preparations* for war or for a journey. **3** The fact or state of being prepared; readiness. **4** Something made or prepared, as a compound, composition, etc.: medicinal or chemical *preparations.* **5** Preliminary study; training, as for college or business. **6** *Music* The previous introduction, as an integral part of a chord, of a note which is then continued into a following dissonance; also, the note so treated. **7** *Eccl.* Devotional exercises introducing an office, as that of the Eucharist. [<OF <L *praeparatio, -onis*]

pre·par·a·tive (pri·par′ə·tiv) *adj.* Serving or tending to prepare. — *n.* **1** That which is preparatory. **2** An act of preparation. — **pre·par′a·tive·ly** *adv.*

pre·par·a·tor (pri·par′ə·tər) *n.* One who prepares subjects for scientific purposes, as specimens for dissection or objects for preservation in collections. [<LL *praeparator*]

pre·par·a·to·ry (pri·par′ə·tôr′ē, -tō′rē) *adj.* **1** Serving as a preparation. **2** Occupied in preparation: a *preparatory* scholar. — *adv.* As a preparation: *Preparatory* to writing, I will consider this: also **pre·par′a·to′ri·ly.**

preparatory school A school in which students are prepared for admission to a college or university.

pre·pare (pri·pâr′) *v.* **·pared, ·par·ing** *v.t.* **1** To make ready, fit, or qualified; put in readiness. **2** To provide with what is needed; outfit; equip: to *prepare* an expedition. **3** To bring to a state of completeness, as a meal, lesson, or prescription. **4** *Music* To introduce by a preliminary note or notes. — *v.i.* **5** To make preparations; get ready. [<F *préparer* <L *praeparare* <*prae-* before + *parare* make ready] — **pre·par·ed·ly** (pri·pâr′id·lē) *adv.* — **pre·par′er** *n.*

pre·par·ed·ness (pri·pâr′id·nis, -pârd′-) *n.* Readiness; especially, a condition of military readiness for war.

pre·pay (prē·pā′) *v.t.* **·paid, ·pay·ing** To pay or pay for in advance. — **pre·pay′ment** *n.*

pre·pense (pri·pens′) *adj.* Premeditated; considered beforehand: chiefly in the phrase malice *prepense.* [<OF *purpensé,* pp. of *purpenser* < *pur-* (<L *pro-*) ahead + *penser* think <L *pensare*] — **pre·pense′ly** *adv.*

pre·pon·der·ance (pri·pon′dər·əns) *n.* Superiority in weight, influence, force, quantity, etc. Also **pre·pon′der·an·cy.**

pre·pon·der·ant (pri·pon′dər·ənt) *adj.* Having such superior force, weight, importance, efficacy, quantity, or number as to overbalance something else or all other things of a class; predominant. — **pre·pon′der·ant·ly** *adv.*

pre·pon·der·ate (pri·pon′də·rāt) *v.i.* **·at·ed, ·at·ing** **1** To be of greater weight. **2** To incline downward or descend, as the scale of a balance. **3** To be of greater power, importance, quantity, etc.; predominate; prevail. [<L *praeponderatus,* pp. of *praeponderare* <*prae-* before + *ponderare* weigh <*pondus, ponderis* weight] — **pre·pon′der·a′tion** *n.*

prep·o·si·tion (prep′ə·zish′ən) *n. Gram.* **1** In some languages, a word functioning to indicate the relation of a substantive (the object of the preposition) to another substantive, a verb, or an adjective: one of the eight traditional parts of speech. Some English prepositions are *by, for, from, in, to, with.* A preposition is usually placed before its object (whence its name), and together they constitute a prepositional phrase which serves as an adjectival or an adverbial modifier: He sat *beside* the fire; sick *at* heart; a man *of* honor. There is a close relationship between certain prepositions and adverbs, and the same word may have either function, depending on the context: We saw it *through* (adverb); It sailed out *through* the window (preposition). **2** Any word or construction that functions in a similar manner: He telephoned *in reference to* (equals *about*) your letter. — **inseparable preposition** A preposition so closely connected with a verb as to have all the force of a compound: to *laugh at.* — **participal preposition** A participle used without direct connection with a subject, so that it has the force of a preposition: They spoke to him *concerning* that affair. — **postpositive preposition** A preposition in postposition; also, a suffix added to a noun and serving as a preposition: Hope soars heaven*ward.* [<L *praepositio, -onis* <*praepositus,* pp. of *praeponere* place before <*prae-* before + *ponere* place]

prep·o·si·tion·al (prep′ə·zish′ən·əl) *adj.* Pertaining to, formed with, or having the character or force of prepositions. — **prep′o·si′tion·al·ly** *adv.*

pre·pos·i·tive (prē·poz′ə·tiv) *adj.* **1** Prefixed. **2** *Gram.* Placed before the word governed or qualified. — *n. Gram.* A prepositive word or particle. [<L *praepositivus* <*praepositus.* See PREPOSITION.]

pre·pos·i·tor (prē·poz′ə·tər) *n. Brit.* A pupil or student in a school or college who directs or oversees others; monitor. [Alter. of L *praepositus.* See PREPOSITION.] — **pre·pos·i·to·ri·al** (prē·poz′ə·tôr′ē·əl, -tō′rē-) *adj.*

pre·pos·sess (prē′pə·zes′) *v.t.* **1** To preoccupy to the exclusion of other ideas, beliefs, etc.; prejudice; bias. **2** To impress or influence beforehand or at once, especially favorably. **3** *Rare* To take possession of in advance of others, as land.

pre·pos·sess·ing (prē′pə·zes′ing) *adj.* Inspiring a favorable opinion from the beginning. — **pre′pos·sess′ing·ly** *adv.*

pre·pos·ses·sion (prē′pə·zesh′ən) *n.* **1** The state of being prepossessed; a previous impression of a particular person or thing; a preconceived liking; bias. **2** Prior possession. See synonyms under INCLINATION, PREJUDICE.

pre·pos·ter·ous (pri·pos′tər·əs) *adj.* Contrary to nature, reason, or common sense; strikingly or utterly absurd or impracticable. See synonyms under ABSURD, EXTRAORDINARY, RIDICULOUS. [<L *praeposterus* the last first, inverted <*prae-* before + *posterus* last] — **pre·pos′ter·ous·ly** *adv.* — **pre·pos′ter·ous·ness** *n.*

pre·pos·tor (prē·pos′tər) *n.* A prepositor. [Alter. of PREPOSITOR]

pre·po·ten·cy (pri·pō′tən·sē) *n.* **1** The quality of superior potency; preponderance of influence or efficiency. **2** *Biol.* The pronounced capacity of one parent, strain, or breed to transmit its own characteristics to the offspring. Also **pre·po′tence.** [<PREPOTENT]

pre·po·tent (pri·pō′tənt) *adj.* **1** Endowed with prevailing potency; predominant. **2** Having potential power or efficacy; possessing power to shape or influence what comes after. **3** Pertaining to or exhibiting prepotency. Also **pre·po·ten·tial** (prē′pə·ten′shəl). [<L *praepotens, -entis* very powerful] — **pre·po′tent·ly** *adv.*

pre·puce (prē′pyōōs) *n. Anat.* The loose skin that covers the glans of the penis; the foreskin. [<F *prépuce* <L *praeputium*] — **pre·pu·tial** (pri·pyōō′shəl) *adj.*

Pre–Raph·a·el·ite (prē·raf′ē·ə·līt, -rā′fē-) *n.* **1** A follower or adherent of the Pre–Raphaelite Brotherhood, a society of artists, formed in England, 1847–49, by D. G. Rossetti, W. Holman–Hunt, John Millais, and others, stressing the truth to nature and delicacy of poetic sentiment that supposedly characterized Italian art before the time of Raphael. **2** Any modern artist with similar or related aims. **3** Any Italian painter before the time of Raphael. — *adj.* **1** Before the time of Raphael. **2** Of or pertaining to the Pre–Raphaelite Brotherhood or its followers. — **Pre–Raph′a·el·it′ism** *n.*

pre·req·ui·site (prē·rek′wə·zit) *adj.* Required as an antecedent condition; necessary to something that follows. — *n.* A necessary antecedent condition.

pre·rog·a·tive (pri·rog′ə·tiv) *n.* **1** An indefeasible and unquestionable right belonging to a person or body of persons by virtue of position or relation, and exercised without control or accountability; specifically, a hereditary or official right: the royal *prerogative.* **2** Hence, any characteristic and generally recognized privilege peculiar to a person or class: It is a woman's *prerogative* to change her mind. **3** Precedence; preeminence. See synonyms under RIGHT. — *adj.* Of or pertaining to a prerogative; possessing or held by prerogative. [<OF <L *praerogativa* right of voting first <*praerogatus,* pp. of *praerogare* ask before another <*prae-* before + *rogare* ask]

prerogative court **1** *Brit.* Formerly, a court having jurisdiction of testamentary matters, as an archbishop's court in which were involved effects up to five pounds in each of two or more dioceses of the archiepiscopal province. **2** *U.S.* A court held in New Jersey by the chancellor sitting as ordinary in probate matters, and for the determination of appeals from the Orphan's Court.

pre·sa (prā′sä) *n. Music* A sign :S:, +, or ✻ in fugues or canons, where the voices are successively to take up the theme. [<Ital., lit., a taking, orig. fem. of *preso,* pp. of *prendere* take <L *prehendere*]

pres·age (pres′ij) *n.* **1** An indication of something to come; prophetic token; portent; omen. **2** A prophetic impression; presentiment; foreboding. **3** Prophetic meaning or import; prediction; foresight. See synonyms under SIGN.

— **pre·sage** (pri·sāj′) *v.* **·saged, ·sag·ing** *v.t.* **1** To give a presage or portent of; betoken; foreshadow. **2** To have a presentiment of. **3** To predict; foretell. — *v.i.* **4** To make a prediction; prophesy. See synonyms under AUGUR. [<F *présage* <L *presagium* omen <*praesagire* perceive beforehand <*prae-* before + *sagire* be aware of. Akin to SAGACIOUS.] — **pre·sage′ment** *n.* — **pre·sag′er** *n.*

pres·by·cu·sis (prez′bi·kyōō′sis, pres′-) *n. Pathol.* Impairment of hearing due to advancing years or old age. Also **pres·by·a·cu·sis** (prez′bē·ə·kyōō′sis, pres′-). [<NL <Gk. *presbys* old + *akousis* hearing]

pres·by·o·phre·ni·a (prez′bē·ə·frē′nē·ə, pres′-) *n. Psychiatry* Failure of mental powers due to old age, characterized by confabulation and loss of memory. [<NL <Gk. *presbys* old + *phrēn* mind] — **pres′by·o·phren′ic** (-fren′ik) *adj.*

pres·by·o·pi·a (prez′bē·ō′pē·ə, pres′-) *n. Pathol.* Long-sightedness, especially that incident to old age and due to rigidity of the crystalline lens, which renders accommodation difficult for near objects. [<NL <Gk. *presbys* old + -OPIA] — **pres′by·op′ic** (-op′ik) *adj.*

pres·by·ter (prez′bə·tər, pres′-) *n.* **1** In the early church, one of the elders of a church. **2** *Eccl.* **a** In hierarchical churches, a priest. **b** In Presbyterian churches, an ordained clergyman (a **teaching elder**); also, a layman who is a member of the governing body of a congregation (a **ruling elder**). [<LL <Gk. *presbyteros* an elder. Doublet of PRIEST.]

pres·byt·er·ate (prez·bit′ər·it, -ə·rāt, pres-) *n.* **1** The office or dignity of a presbyter or elder. **2** The order or the body of presbyters.

pres·by·te·ri·al (prez′bə·tir′ē·əl, pres′-) *adj.* Pertaining to a presbytery or a presbyter. Also **pres·byt′er·al.** — **pres·byt′er·al·ly** *adv.*

Pres·by·te·ri·an (prez′bə·tir′ē·ən, pres′-) *n.* **1** One who believes in the government of the church by presbyters. **2** A member of any of various Protestant churches, mostly Calvinist in doctrine, and holding to the government of the church by presbyters. — *adj.* Of or pertaining to the Presbyterian Church, its form of government, or its doctrines. [<LL *presbyterium* presbytery + -IAN] — **Pres′by·te′ri·an·ism** *n.*

pres·by·ter·y (prez′bə·ter′ē, pres′-) *n.* *pl.* **·ter·ies** 1 In the Presbyterian Church, a court having the ecclesiastical and spiritual rule and oversight of a given district; the district so represented; also, presbyters collectively. 2 The system of church government by presbyters: distinguished from the *Independent* system and *prelacy.* 3 That part of a church set apart for the clergy. 4 In the Roman Catholic Church, the residence of the priest. [<OF *presbiterie* <LL *presbyterium* assembly of elders <Gk. *presbyterion* < *presbyteros* elder]

pre-school (prē·sko͞ol′) *adj.* For or designating a child past infancy but under school age.

pre·sci·ence (prē′shē·əns, presh′ē-) *n.* Knowledge of events before they take place. See synonyms under WISDOM. [<OF <L *praescientia,* orig. neut. pl. of *praesciens, -entis,* ppr. of *praescire* know beforehand < *prae-* before + *scire* know]

pre·sci·ent (prē′shē·ənt, presh′ē-) *adj.* Having prescience; foreknowing; also, far-seeing. [<F <L *presciens, -entis.* See PRESCIENCE.] — **pre′sci·ent·ly** *adv.*

pre·scind (pri·sind′) *v.t.* 1 To set apart in thought; consider separately. 2 To cut off; remove. — *v.i.* 3 To withdraw the attention: with *from.* [<L *praescindere* cut off in front < *prae-* before + *scindere* cut]

Pres·cott (pres′kət), **William,** 1726–95, American officer; commanded at Bunker Hill in the Revolutionary War. — **William Hickling,** 1796–1859, U.S. historian.

pre·scribe (pri·skrīb′) *v.* **·scribed, ·scrib·ing** *v.t.* 1 To set down as a direction or rule to be followed; ordain; enjoin. 2 *Med.* To order the use of (a medicine, treatment, etc.) as a remedy. 3 *Law* To render invalid by lapse of time. — *v.i.* 4 To lay down laws or rules; give directions. 5 *Law* **a** To assert a title to something on the basis of prescription: with *for* or *to.* **b** To become invalid or unenforceable by lapse of time. See synonyms under DICTATE, SET. [<L *praescribere* write beforehand < *prae-* before + *scribere* write] — **pre·scrib′er** *n.*

pre·script (prē′skript) *n.* A prescription or direction, as a rule of conduct. — *adj.* (pri·skript′, prē′skript) Prescribed as a rule or model; laid down. [<L *praescriptus,* pp. of *praescribere.* See PRESCRIBE.]

pre·scrip·ti·ble (pri·skrip′tə·bəl) *adj.* Derived from or acquirable by prescription; depending on prescriptive right. — **pre·scrip′ti·bil′i·ty** *n.*

pre·scrip·tion (pri·skrip′shən) *n.* 1 The act of prescribing, directing, or dictating. 2 That which is prescribed or appointed, as a rule or precept; a prescript. 3 *Med.* **a** A physician's formula for compounding and administering a medicine. **b** The remedy so prescribed. **c** A formula issued by a licensed oculist or optometrist giving directions for the grinding of eyeglass lenses. 4 *Law* A title to property, or a mode of acquiring title to property, founded on uninterrupted possession; a mode of losing a right or title by failure to assert it within a given time; the period after which a neglected right or title cannot be asserted; also, the period, if any, after which prosecution for a crime is barred. 5 Old or continued custom, particularly when considered authoritative. 6 A claim based on long usage. [<L *praescriptio, -onis*]

pre·scrip·tive (pri·skrip′tiv) *adj.* 1 Making strict requirements or rules: *prescriptive* grammar. 2 Sanctioned by custom or long use: a *prescriptive* right to grumble. 3 *Law* Acquired by immemorial use; based on prescription: a *prescriptive* title. [<LL *praescriptivus*] — **pre·scrip′tive·ly** *adv.*

preselector gearbox An automobile transmission which allows the manual selection of a gear ratio in advance of its actual use, the gear being automatically engaged by the actuation of the clutch.

pres·ence (prez′əns) *n.* 1 The state or fact of being present: opposed to *absence.* 2 Situation face to face; close approach or vicinity within view or access. 3 Something invisible but near and sensible, as a spiritual being. 4 Personal appearance; bearing. 5 Personal qualities collectively; self; personality: used also absolutely of a sovereign. 6 *Obs.* A distinguished assembly, as before a prince or exalted personage. 7 Formerly, the room or apartment in which a high dignitary or ruler received assemblies: also **presence chamber.** [<OF <L *praesentia,* orig. neut. pl of *praesens, -entis,* ppr. of *praeesse.* See PRESENT.]

presence of mind Full command of one's faculties; coolness, alertness, and readiness of resource in a situation of sudden danger, embarrassment, etc.

pres·ent[1] (prez′ənt) *adj.* 1 Being in a place or company referred to or contemplated; being at hand: opposed to *absent.* 2 Now going on; current; not past or future. 3 Actually in mind. 4 Immediately impending or actually coming on; not delayed; instant. 5 *Gram.* Relating to or signifying what is going on at the time being: the *present* tense, *present* participle. 6 Ready at hand; prompt in emergency: a *present* wit, a *present* aid. See synonyms under IMMEDIATE. — *n.* 1 Present time; now; the time being. 2 *Gram.* The present tense; also, a verbal form denoting it. 3 A present matter or affair; a question under consideration. 4 *pl. Law* Present writings: term for the document in which the word occurs: Know all men by these *presents.* — **at present** Now. — **for the present** For the time being. [<OF <L *praesens, -entis* being in front of or at hand, ppr. of *praeesse* < *prae-* before + *esse* be]

pre·sent[2] (pri·zent′) *v.t.* 1 To bring into the presence or acquaintance of another; introduce, especially to a superior: The ambassador was *presented* to the king. 2 To exhibit to view or notice; display. 3 To suggest to the mind: This *presents* a problem. 4 To put forward for consideration or action; submit, as a petition. 5 To make a gift or presentation of or to, usually formally. 6 *Archaic* To represent on the stage; act. 7 *Law* **a** To offer, as a charge, for judicial action or inquiry. **b** To bring a charge or indictment against.
— **pres·ent** (prez′ənt) *n.* That which is presented or given; a gift; donation. [<OF *presenter* <L *praesentare* set before < *praesens, -entis* present. See PRESENT[1].] — **pre·sent′er** *n.*

pre·sent·a·ble (pri·zen′tə·bəl) *adj.* 1 Fit to be presented; in suitable condition or attire for company. 2 Capable of being offered, exhibited, or bestowed. — **pre·sent′a·bil′i·ty, pre·sent′a·ble·ness** *n.* — **pre·sent′a·bly** *adv.*

present arms A command requiring a soldier to salute by holding his gun or other weapon vertically, in front of and close to his body. Correct position for the gun is muzzle up and trigger facing forward.

pres·en·ta·tion (prez′ən·tā′shən, prē′zən-) *n.* 1 The act of presenting or proffering for acceptance, approval, etc.; especially, the formal offering of a complimentary gift. 2 *Rare* That which is bestowed; a present. 3 The act of introducing or bringing to notice; formal introduction, especially to a superior: *presentation* at court. 4 *Eccl.* The nomination of a clergyman to a living; also, the right of such nomination. 5 The manner of bringing into view, as a play, thought, or case; way of putting; exhibition; representation; also, that which is represented. 6 The fact or process of being present in consciousness; also, the object of consciousness, without added reference. 7 *Med.* The position of the fetus at birth: designated by the part that is first presented to the touch at the mouth of the womb: breech *presentation,* etc. 8 The condition of being placed in a certain position or direction, with regard to something else, or to an observer. 9 Presentment; the offering of a negotiable instrument for payment. [<OF *presentacion* <L *praesentatio, -onis*]

pres·en·ta·tion·al (prez′ən·tā′shən·əl, prē′zən-) *adj.* Relating to or composed of presentations.

pres·en·ta·tion·al·ism (prez′ən·tā′shən·əl·iz′·əm, prē′zən-) *n. Philos.* The doctrine that man has an immediate perception of all the elemental forms of entity, as space, time, substance, and power; natural realism. Also **pres′·en·ta′tion·ism.** — **pres′en·ta′tion·ist** *adj.* & *n.*

pre·sen·ta·tive (pri·zen′tə·tiv) *adv.* 1 Having to do with the mental awareness or knowledge of an activity, power, or object: distinguished from *representative*: a *presentative* judgment. 2 Having the right to present to a benefice; also, admitting of the presentation of a clergyman. — **pre·sen′ta·tive·ness** *n.*

pres·ent-day (prez′ənt·dā′) *adj.* Of the present time; current.

pres·en·tee (prez′ən·tē′) *n.* 1 One who is presented, as to a benefice or at court. 2 The recipient of a gift.

pre·sen·ti·ment (pri·zen′tə·mənt) *n.* A prophetic sense of something to come; a foreboding. See synonyms under ANTICIPATION. [<MF <L *praesentire* perceive beforehand < *prae-* before + *sentire* feel]

pre·sen·tive (pri·zen′tiv) *adj.* Conveying or embodying (as nouns, adjectives, and most verbs) a distinct and complete conception, whether of an object, act, or quality: distinguished from *symbolic.* — *n.* A presentive word. — **pre·sen′tive·ly** *adv.* — **pre·sen′tive·ness** *n.*

pres·ent·ly (prez′ənt·lē) *adv.* 1 After a little time; shortly. 2 *Archaic & Dial.* At once; immediately. See synonyms under IMMEDIATELY. ◆ *Presently* in the sense "at once" has not been in use in literary English since the 17th century, though it has persisted in dialectal use in both England and the United States.

pre·sent·ment (pri·zent′mənt) *n.* 1 The act of presenting; also, the state or manner of being presented; presentation. 2 That which is represented or exhibited; a representation or picture; semblance. 3 *Law* A report made by a grand jury, concerning some wrongdoing, and presented to the court; also, the finding and setting forth of charges in an indictment by a grand jury; an indictment. 4 The presentation of a negotiable instrument for payment. 5 *Philos.* The mental images of a perception or idea.

present participle See under PARTICIPLE.

present perfect *Gram.* The verb tense expressing an action completed by the present time: By now he *has finished* the task.

present tense The tense marking present time: I *go, do go, am going.*

pre·ser·va·tive (pri·zûr′və·tiv) *adj.* Serving or tending to preserve. — *n.* That which serves or tends to preserve; a substance that preserves; a safeguard. [<F *préservatif, -ive* <Med. L *praeservativus*]

pre·serve (pri·zûrv′) *v.* **·served, ·serv·ing** *v.t.* 1 To keep in safety; protect from destruction, loss, death, or detriment; guard: May the gods *preserve* you. 2 To keep intact or unimpaired; maintain: to *preserve* appearances. 3 To prepare (food) for future consumption, as by boiling with sugar or salting. 4 To keep from decomposition or change, as by chemical treatment: to *preserve* a specimen in alcohol. 5 To keep for one's private hunting or fishing: to *preserve* foxes; to *preserve* a wood. — *v.i.* 6 To make preserves, as of fruit. 7 To maintain a game preserve. — *n.* 1 *Usually pl.* Fruit which has been cooked, usually with sugar, to prevent its fermenting. 2 Something preserved or which preserves. 3 A place set apart for one's own private use, or in which game or fish are protected for purposes of sport. [<OF *preserver* <LL *praeservare* <L *prae-* before + *servare* keep] — **pre·serv′a·bil′i·ty** *n.* — **pre·serv′a·ble** *adj.* — **pres·er·va·tion** (prez′ər·vā′shən) *n.* — **pre·serv′er** *n.*

Synonyms (verb): conserve, defend, guard, keep, maintain, protect, save, secure, sustain, uphold. See KEEP, RETAIN. *Antonyms*: abandon, lavish, lose, neglect, scatter, spend, spoil, waste.

pre-shrunk (prē′shrungk′) *adj.* Shrunk during manufacture to minimize later shrinkage: *pre-shrunk* cotton.

pre·side (pri·zīd′) *v.i.* **·sid·ed, ·sid·ing** 1 To sit in authority, as over a meeting; be in charge of an assembly, government, etc.; act as chairman or president. 2 To exercise direction or control. [<F *présider* <L *praesidere* sit in front of, protect, guard < *prae-* before + *sedere* sit] — **pre·sid′er** *n.*

pres·i·den·cy (prez′ə·dən·sē) *n. pl.* **·cies** 1 The office, function, or term of office of a president. 2 *Often cap.* The office of president of the United States. 3 *Often cap.* Formerly, any of the three original provinces of British India: Bengal, Madras, and Bombay. 4 *Brit.* An administrative subdivision. 5 In the Mormon

Church, a local administrative council of three men; also, the highest governing body of the church (**First Presidency**), consisting of the president and his two counselors. [<Med. L *praesidentia*]

pres·i·dent (prez′ə·dənt) *n.* **1** One who is chosen to preside over an organized body; specifically, the chief executive of a republic. **2** The chairman of the meetings and chief executive officer of a department of the government, a corporation, society, etc. **3** The chief officer of a college or university. **4** The chairman of a meeting conducted under parliamentary rules. [<F *président* <L *praesidens, -entis,* ppr. of *praesidere.* See PRESIDE.] — **pres·i·den·tial** (prez′ə·den′shəl) *adj.*

THE PRESIDENTS OF THE UNITED STATES

Number — Name	*Birthplace—Inaugurated: year*		*Age*
1 George Washington	Westmoreland Co., Va.	1789	57
2 John Adams	Quincy, Mass.	1797	61
3 Thomas Jefferson	Shadwell, Va.	1801	57
4 James Madison	Port Conway, Va.	1809	57
5 James Monroe	Westmoreland Co., Va.	1817	58
6 John Quincy Adams	Quincy, Mass.	1825	57
7 Andrew Jackson	Union Co., N.C.	1829	61
8 Martin Van Buren	Kinderhook, N.Y.	1837	54
9 William H. Harrison	Berkeley, Va.	1841	68
10 John Tyler	Greenway, Va.	1841	51
11 James K. Polk	Little Sugar Creek, N.C.	1845	49
12 Zachary Taylor	Orange Co., Va.	1849	64
13 Millard Fillmore	Summerhill, N.Y.	1850	50
14 Franklin Pierce	Hillsboro, N.H.	1853	48
15 James Buchanan	Cove Gap, Pa.	1857	65
16 Abraham Lincoln	Hardin Co., Ky.	1861	52
17 Andrew Johnson	Raleigh, N.C.	1865	56
18 Ulysses S. Grant	Point Pleasant, O.	1869	46
19 Rutherford B. Hayes	Delaware, O.	1877	54
20 James A. Garfield	Cuyahoga Co., O.	1881	49
21 Chester A. Arthur	Fairfield, Vt.	1881	50
22 Grover Cleveland	Caldwell, N.J.	1885	47
23 Benjamin Harrison	North Bend, O.	1889	55
24 Grover Cleveland	Caldwell, N. J.	1893	55
25 William McKinley	Niles, O.	1897	54
26 Theodore Roosevelt	New York, N.Y.	1901	42
27 William H. Taft	Cincinnati, O.	1909	51
28 Woodrow Wilson	Staunton, Va.	1913	56
29 Warren G. Harding	Corsica, O.	1921	55
30 Calvin Coolidge	Plymouth, Vt.	1923	51
31 Herbert C. Hoover	West Branch, Ia.	1929	55
32 Franklin D. Roosevelt	Hyde Park, N.Y.	1933	51
33 Harry S Truman	Lamar, Mo.	1945	60
34 Dwight D. Eisenhower	Denison, Tex.	1953	62
35 John F. Kennedy	Brookline, Mass.	1961	43
36 Lyndon B. Johnson	Gillespie County, Tex.	1963	55
37 Richard M. Nixon	Yorba Linda, Calif.	1969	56
38 Gerald R. Ford	Omaha, Nebr.	1974	61

pre·sid·i·al (pri·sid′ē·əl) *adj.* Of or having a garrison or a garrisoned post. [<F *présidial* <LL *praesidium* a garrison, fort]

pre·sid·i·o (pri·sid′ē·ō) *n. pl.* **·sid·i·os** **1** A garrisoned post; fort; fortified settlement. **2** A Spanish penal settlement in a foreign country. — **the Presidio** A U. S. military reservation in San Francisco. [<Am. Sp.]

pre·sid·i·um (pri·sid′ē·əm) *n.* Any of several executive committees in the U.S.S.R. serving as the permanent organ of a larger governmental body. [<L *praesidium*]

Pre·sid·i·um (pri·sid′ē·əm) *n.* **1** A governmental body of the Soviet Union that exercises the powers of the Supreme Soviet between plenary sessions. **2** The supreme policy-making committee of the Communist party of the Soviet Union, headed by the party secretary. See POLITBURO.

pre·sig·ni·fy (prē·sig′nə·fī) *v.t.* **·fied, ·fy·ing** To signify in advance; presage.

press[1] (pres) *v.t.* **1** To act upon by weight or pressure: to *press* a button. **2** To compress so as to extract the juice: to *press* grapes. **3** To extract by pressure, as juice. **4** To exert pressure upon so as to smooth, shape, make compact, etc. **5** To smooth or shape by heat and pressure, as clothes; iron. **6** To embrace closely; hug. **7** To force or impel; drive. **8** To distress or harass; place in difficulty: I am *pressed* for time. **9** To urge persistently; importune; entreat: They *pressed* me for an answer. **10** To advocate persistently; insist on; emphasize. **11** To put forward insistently: to *press* a gift on a friend. **12** To urge onward; hasten. **13** *Obs.* To crowd. — *v.i.* **14** To exert pressure; bear heavily. **15** To advance forcibly or with speed: *Press* on! **16** To press clothes, etc. **17** To crowd; cram. **18** To be urgent or importunate. See synonyms under IMPRESS[1], JAM, PLEAD, PUSH. — *n.* **1** A dense throng. **2** The act of crowding together or of straining forward. **3** Hurry or pressure of affairs; urgency: the *press* of business. **4** A movable upright closet or case in which clothes, books, etc., are kept: a linen *press.* **5** An apparatus or machine by which pressure is applied, as for making wine, compressing bulky substances for packing, etc.; a printing press. **6** Newspapers or periodical literature collectively, or the body of persons collectively, as editors, reporters, etc., engaged upon such publications; also, printed literature in the abstract. **7** The art, process, or business of printing. **8** The place of business in which a printing press is set up and where printing is carried on: the Clarendon *Press;* to go to *press.* **9** Criticism, comments, news, etc., in newspapers and periodicals. See synonyms under THRONG. [<OF *presser* <L *pressare,* freq. of *premere* (pp. *pressus*) press]

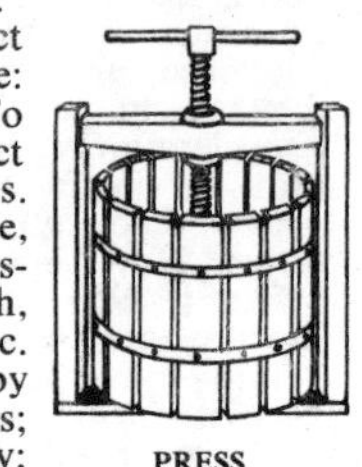

PRESS
Cider, wine, and fruit press.

press[2] (pres) *v.t.* **1** To force into military or naval service; impress. **2** To put to use in a manner not intended or desired. — *n.* A commission to impress men into the public service; also, the impressment of men. [< obs. *prest* engage for military service by payment of earnest money <OF *prester* lend <L *praestare* guarantee, furnish money for < *prae-* before + *stare* stand; influenced in form and meaning by *press*[1]]

press agent A person employed to advance the interests of his client by advertisements and other notices; a publicity agent for any person or business. — **press-a·gen·try** (pres′·ā′jən·trē) *n.*

press·board (pres′bôrd′, -bōrd′) *n.* **1** A wooden board placed between sheets in a standing press. **2** An ironing board. — **imitation pressboard** Millboard. — **electrical pressboard** Fullerboard.

Press·burg (pres′bŏŏrkh) The German name for BRATISLAVA.

press conference An interview granted by a celebrity, government official, etc., to a number of journalists at the same time.

press·er (pres′ər) *n.* **1** One who or that which presses. **2** *Mech.* Any machine or apparatus exerting pressure, as by a spring; a presser foot. **3** One who cleans and presses clothes. **4** One who operates a press: a cotton *presser.*

presser foot A footpiece in a sewing machine to hold the fabric down to the feed plate.

press·gang (pres′gang′) *n.* A detachment of men detailed to press men into naval or military service. Also **press gang.**

press·ing (pres′ing) *adj.* **1** Demanding immediate attention; urgent; important. **2** Importunate. — **press′ing·ly** *adv.*

press·man[1] (pres′mən) *n. pl.* **·men** (-mən) **1** A man who has charge of a press, as a printing press. **2** A man who presses clothes. **3** *Brit.* A member of the press; journalist.

press·man[2] (pres′mən) *n. pl.* **·men** (-mən) *Obs.* A member of a pressgang.

press·mark (pres′märk′) *n.* **1** A mark in a book to point out its particular place in a book press or bookcase of a library. **2** A mark, as a number or letter on the margin of a newspaper, showing on which press it was printed.

press money The king's shilling. See under SHILLING.

press of canvas or **sail** *Naut.* The maximum spread of sail that can be carried with safety under wind pressure.

press·or (pres′ər) *adj. Physiol.* Increasing the functional activities of an organ: a *pressor* nerve, the stimulating of which raises the arterial blood pressure: opposed to *depressor.* [<PRESS[1]]

press·pahn (pres′pän) *n.* Fullerboard. [<G]

press proof **1** The last proof taken before printing. **2** A proof taken on a press.

press release A bulletin, prepared by a press agent, public relations department, or other official representative, announcing an event, development in a business, newsworthy decision, etc.

press·room (pres′rōōm′, -rŏŏm′) *n.* A room containing the presses of a printing concern.

pres·sure (presh′ər) *n.* **1** The act of pressing, or the state of being pressed. **2** *Physics* Any force which acts against an opposing force; a thrust, stress, or strain between opposed masses, uniformly distributed over the surfaces in contact: steam *pressure;* the *pressure* of gas in a confined space. **3** An impelling or constraining moral force; compulsory motive: bringing *pressure* to bear. **4** Exigent demand on one's time or strength; urgency: the *pressure* of business. **5** The oppressive influence or depressing effect of something hard to bear; weight, as of grief or trouble; onerousness: *pressure* of taxation; *pressure* of calamity. **6** A printed character; stamp; an impression. — **fluid pressure** Pressure of a fluid or resembling that of a fluid, being invariable and uniform in all directions. — *v.t.* **·sured, ·sur·ing** *Colloq.* To compel, as by forceful persuasion or influence: He was *pressured* to accept the job. [<OF <L *pressura* < *pressus,* pp. of *premere* press]

pressure cabin *Aeron.* An enclosed compartment in an airplane, supplied with air maintained at or near sea-level pressure to provide sufficient oxygen for crew and passengers at high altitudes.

pressure cooker An airtight receptacle for the cooking of food at high temperature under pressure; an autoclave.

pressure gage An instrument for measuring the pressure of a gas or liquid, and for indicating it by a pointer on a graduated dial; a manometer. Also **pressure gauge.**

pressure gradient *Meteorol.* The decrease in barometric pressure per unit of horizontal distance along the course in which the pressure decreases most rapidly.

pressure group An organized minority group which seeks, through propaganda and lobbying, to influence legislators and public opinion in behalf of its own special interests, or to defeat restrictive legislation.

pres·sur·ize (presh′ə·rīz) *v.t.* **·ized, ·iz·ing** **1** To subject to high pressure. **2** *Aeron.* To maintain normal atmospheric pressure in (the cabin or cockpit of an airplane) at high altitudes. — **pres′sur·i·za′tion** *n.*

press·work (pres′wûrk′) *n.* **1** The operating, adjustment, or management of a printing press. **2** The work done by the press. **3** Cabinetwork made up of cross veneers glued together and pressed while hot.

prest[1] (prest) *adj. Obs.* Ready; prepared at hand; daring; also, tidy; neat. [<OF <L *praesto,* dative of *praestus* ready, at hand]

prest[2] (prest) *n.* **1** An advance or loan; also,

ready money. 2 Press money: also **prest money.** [<OF <*prester* lend <L *praestare.* See PRESS².]

Pres·teigne (pres·tēn′) The county town of Radnorshire, Wales.

pres·ti·dig·i·ta·tion (pres′tə·dij′ə·tā′shən) *n.* The practice of sleight of hand; jugglery; legerdemain. [<F <*preste* (<Ital. *presto* <LL *praestus*) nimble + L *digitus* finger] —**pres′·ti·dig′i·ta′tor** *n.*

pres·tige (pres·tēzh′, pres′tij) *n.* Authority or importance based on past achievements or reputation; ascendency based on recognition of power; renown. [<F <L *praestigium* illusion, juggler's trick, spell <*praestringere* bind fast <*prae-* before + *stringere* bind]

pres·ti·gious (pres·tij′əs, -tē′jəs) *adj.* Having or bestowing prestige. —**pres·ti′gious·ly** *adv.* —**pres·ti′gious·ness** *n.*

pres·tis·si·mo (pres·tis′i·mō, *Ital.* pres·tēs′sē·mō) *adj.* & *adv.* *Music* As fast as possible; in very quick time. [<Ital., superlative of *presto.* See PRESTO.]

pres·to (pres′tō) *adv.* & *adj.* 1 *Music* In fast time. 2 At once; speedily. —*n.* *Music* A movement, passage, or phrase performed in fast tempo. [<Ital. <L *praesto.* See PREST¹.]

Pres·ton (pres′tən) A county borough and river port in central Lancashire, England.

Pres·tone (pres′tōn) *n.* Ethylene glycol, used as an anti-freeze mixture: a trade name.

Pres·ton·pans (pres′tən·panz′) A burgh in East Lothian, Scotland, east of Edinburgh on the Firth of Forth; scene of a Scottish victory over the English, 1745.

pre·stressed concrete (prē′strest′) Concrete cast over taut steel cables, etc., to increase its tensile strength.

pre·sum·able (pri·zōō′mə·bəl) *adj.* That may be assumed or presumed; reasonable. See synonyms under APPARENT, LIKELY, PROBABLE. —**pre·sum′a·bly** *adv.*

pre·sume (pri·zōōm′) *v.* **·sumed, ·sum·ing** *v.t.* 1 To take upon oneself without warrant or permission; dare; venture: usually with the infinitive: Do you *presume* to address me? 2 To take for granted; assume to be true until disproved: I *presume* you are right. 3 To indicate the probability of; seem to prove: The receipt for this month *presumes* preceding payments. —*v.i.* 4 To act or proceed presumptuously or overconfidently. 5 To make excessive demands; rely too heavily: with *on* or *upon*: He *presumes* on my good nature. See synonyms under ASSUME. [<OF *presumer* <L *praesumere* take first <*prae-* before + *sumere* take] —**pre·sum·ed·ly** (pri·zōō′mid·lē) *adv.* —**pre·sum′er** *n.*

pre·sump·tion (pri·zump′shən) *n.* 1 Blind or overweening confidence or self-assertion. 2 A passing beyond the ordinary bounds of good breeding, respect, or reverence; offensively forward or arrogant conduct or expression; effrontery. 3 The act of forming a judgment on probable grounds, awaiting further evidence; also, the judgment so formed, or a ground or reason for it. 4 That which may be logically or legally assumed to be true until disproved: the *presumption* of guilt. 5 *Law* The inference of a fact on proof of circumstances that usually or necessarily attend such a fact. See synonyms under ARROGANCE, ASSURANCE, IMPUDENCE, PROBABILITY, TEMERITY. [<OF *presomption* <L *praesumtio, -onis* <*praesumptus,* pp. of *praesumere.* See PRESUME.]

pre·sump·tive (pri·zump′tiv) *adj.* Creating or resting upon a presumption; affording reasonable grounds for belief. [<F *présomptif*] —**pre·sump′tive·ly** *adv.*

presumptive heir See HEIR PRESUMPTIVE.

pre·sump·tu·ous (pri·zump′chōō·əs) *adj.* 1 Unduly confident or bold; audacious; arrogant; insolent. 2 Exhibiting, characterized by, or founded on presumption; presuming unduly, as upon success or the forbearance of others; foolhardy. [<OF *presumptuoux* <LL *praesumptiosus*] —**pre·sump′tu·ous·ly** *adv.* —**pre·sump′tu·ous·ness** *n.*

pre·sup·pose (prē′sə·pōz′) *v.t.* **·posed, ·pos·ing** 1 To imply or involve as a necessary antecedent condition. 2 To take for granted; assume to start with. [<F *présupposer*] —**pre·sup·po·si·tion** (prē′sup·ə·zish′ən) *n.*

pre·tend (pri·tend′) *v.t.* 1 To assume or display a false appearance of; feign: to *pretend* friendship for an enemy. 2 To claim or assert falsely: He *pretended* that there was gold on his property. 3 To feign in play; make believe. —*v.i.* 4 To make believe, as in play or for the purpose of deception: She is only *pretending* when she says that. 5 To put forward a claim: with *to.* [<OF *pretendre* <L *praetendere* spread out before <*prae-* before + *tendere* spread out]

Synonyms: affect, assume, counterfeit, feign, profess, sham, simulate. See ASSUME, MASK¹.

pre·tend·ed (pri·ten′did) *adj.* Alleged; asserted; professed. —**pre·tend′ed·ly** *adv.*

pre·tend·er (pri·ten′dər) *n.* 1 One who advances a claim or title; a claimant; specifically, a claimant of a throne who is an heir of a deposed dynasty. 2 In English history, the son and grandson of James II, the former being known in literature as the **Pretender** or the **Old Pretender,** and the latter as the **Young Pretender.** 3 A hypocrite. See synonyms under HYPOCRITE.

pre·tense (pri·tens′, prē′tens) *n.* 1 That which is pretended; a pretext; a ruse or wile. 2 The act or state of pretending, or of being a pretender or claimant; specifically, a false assumption of a character or condition; hence, affectation; ostentation. 3 Any act of simulation. 4 A right or title asserted. 5 An intention, aim, or effort. Also *Brit.* **pre·tence′.** [<AF *pretensse* <Med. L *praetensus,* alter. of L *praetentus,* pp. of *praetendere.* See PRETEND.]

Synonyms: affectation, air, assumption, cloak, color, disguise, dissimulation, excuse, mask, pretension, pretext, ruse, seeming, semblance, show, simulation. A *pretense,* in the unfavorable and usual sense, is something advanced or displayed for the purpose of concealing the reality. A person makes a *pretense* of something for the credit or advantage to be gained by it; he makes what is allowed or approved a *pretext* for doing what would be opposed or condemned; a tricky schoolboy makes a *pretense* of doing an errand which he does not do, or he makes the actual doing of an errand a *pretext* for playing truant. A *ruse* is something employed to blind or deceive so as to mask an ulterior design, and enable a person to gain some end that he would not be allowed to approach directly. A *pretension* is a claim that is or may be contested; the word is now commonly used in an unfavorable sense. See DISGUISE, HYPOCRISY. *Antonyms*: actuality, candor, fact, guilelessness, honesty, ingenuousness, openness, reality, simplicity, sincerity, truth.

pre·ten·sion (pri·ten′shən) *n.* 1 A claim put forward, whether true or false. 2 Affectation; display. 3 A bold or presumptuous assertion. See synonyms under PRETENSE.

pre·ten·tious (pri·ten′shəs) *adj.* Characterized by pretension; making an ambitious outward show; ostentatious. [<F *prétentieux*] —**pre·ten′tious·ly** *adv.* —**pre·ten′tious·ness** *n.*

preter- *prefix* Beyond; past; more than: *preternatural.* [<L *praeter* beyond <*prae* before]

pret·er·hu·man (prē′tər·hyōō′mən) *adj.* Beyond what is human.

pret·er·it (pret′ər·it) *adj.* 1 *Gram.* Signifying past time or completed past action. 2 *Rare* Belonging to the past; bygone. —*n.* *Gram.* The tense that expresses absolute past time; the past tense. Also **pret′er·ite.** [<OF *preterit* <L *praeteritus* past, pp. of *praeterire* go past <*praeter-* beyond + *ire* go]

pret·er·i·tion (pret′ə·rish′ən) *n.* 1 The act of passing over or omitting. 2 The omission or passing by of a natural heir without mention by a testator in his will. 3 In the doctrine of predestination, the passing-by of the non-elect. [<LL *praeteritio, -onis* <L *praeteritus.* See PRETERIT.]

pre·ter·i·tive (pri·ter′ə·tiv) *adj.* *Gram.* 1 Used to indicate past actions or states: said of tenses of verbs. 2 Employed only in a past tense or past tenses: said of certain verbs.

pre·ter·mit (prē′tər·mit′) *v.t.* **·mit·ted, ·mit·ting** 1 To fail or cease to do; neglect; omit. 2 To let pass without noticing; overlook; disregard. [<L *praetermittere* let go by <*praeter-* beyond + *mittere* send] —**pre′ter·mis′sion** (-mish′ən) *n.*

pre·ter·nat·u·ral (prē′tər·nach′ər·əl) *adj.* Diverging from or exceeding the common order of nature; inexplicable in terms of the known facts and laws of science, but not outside the universal natural order: distinguished from *supernatural.* See synonyms under SUPERNATURAL. —**pre′ter·nat′u·ral·ism** *n.* —**pre′ter·nat′·u·ral·ly** *adv.*

pre·text (prē′tekst) *n.* 1 A fictitious reason or motive advanced to conceal a real one. 2 A specious excuse or explanation. See synonyms under PRETENSE. [<F *prétexte* <L *praetextus.* See PRAETEXTA.]

pre·tor (prē′tər) *n.* An ancient Roman city magistrate having charge of the administration of justice: also spelled *praetor.* [<L *praetor* <*praeire* go before. See PRETERITE.] —**pre·to·ri·al** (pri·tôr′ē·əl, -tō′rē-) *adj.* —**pre′·tor·ship** *n.*

Pre·to·ri·a (pri·tôr′ē·ə, -tō′rē·ə) Capital of Transvaal province and administrative capital of the Republic of South Africa, in south central Transvaal.

pre·to·ri·an (pri·tôr′ē·ən, -tō′rē-) *adj.* Of or pertaining to a pretor; pretorial. —*n.* A pretor or ex-pretor. Also spelled *praetorian.*

Pre·to·ri·an (pri·tôr′ē·ən, -tō′rē-) *adj.* Denoting the imperial bodyguard of the Caesars. —*n.* A soldier of the imperial bodyguard of the Caesars. Also spelled *Praetorian.*

Pretorian Guard 1 The bodyguard of the Roman emperors, organized by Augustus to take the place of the old *cohors praetoria,* or bodyguard of the general, and disbanded by Constantine the Great. 2 A member of the Pretorian Guard.

Pre·to·ri·us (prə·tōō′rē·ōōs), **Andries Wilhelmus,** 1799–1853, and his son **Marthinus,** 1819–1901, South African Dutch colonizers.

pret·ti·fy (prit′i·fī) *v.t.* **·fied, ·fy·ing** To make pretty; embellish overmuch. [<PRETTY + -FY]

pret·ty (prit′ē) *adj.* **·ti·er, ·ti·est** 1 Characterized by delicacy, gracefulness, or proportion rather than by striking beauty; pleasing; attractive. 2 Decent; good; sufficient: often used ironically as a term of deprecation: A *pretty* mess you've made of it! 3 *Colloq.* Considerable; rather large in size or degree. 4 Sweet; precious: a diminutive of endearment: *pretty* girl. 5 Characterized by effeminacy; affected; foppish. 6 *Scot.* Bold; vigorous; athletic. 7 *Obs.* Strong; able; cunning. See synonyms under BEAUTIFUL. —*adv.* 1 Moderately; somewhat; to a fair extent: He looked *pretty* well. 2 Very; quite: He's grown *pretty* fast. 3 *Dial.* Prettily; finely. —**sitting pretty** *Colloq.* In good circumstances. —*n.* A pretty thing or person. [OE *prættig* tricky, cunning] —**pret′ti·ly** *adv.* —**pret′ti·ness** *n.*

pret·zel (pret′səl) *n.* A glazed salted biscuit baked in the form of a loose knot. [<G *brezel*]

Preus·sen (proi′sən) The German name for PRUSSIA.

pre·vail (pri·vāl′) *v.i.* 1 To gain mastery; be victorious; triumph: with *over* or *against.* 2 To be effective or efficacious; succeed. 3 To use persuasion or influence successfully: with *on, upon,* or *with.* 4 To be or become a predominant feature or quality; be prevalent. 5 To have general or wide-spread use or acceptance; be in force. See synonyms under SUCCEED. [<OF *prevaloir* <L *prevalere* <*prae-* before + *valere* be strong]

pre·vail·ing (pri·vā′ling) *adj.* 1 Current; prevalent. 2 Having effective power or influence; efficacious. See synonyms under PREDOMINANT, USUAL. —**pre·vail′ing·ly** *adv.* —**pre·vail′ing·ness** *n.*

prev·a·lent (prev′ə·lənt) *adj.* 1 Predominant. 2 Of wide extent or frequent occurrence; common. 3 Efficacious; effective. See synonyms under GENERAL, PREDOMINANT, USUAL. [<L *praevalens, -entis,* ppr. of *praevalere* PREVAIL] —**prev′a·lence** *n.* —**prev′a·lent·ly** *adv.*

pre·var·i·cate (pri·var′ə·kāt) *v.i.* **·cat·ed, ·cat·ing** To speak or act in a deceptive, ambiguous, or evasive manner; quibble; lie. [<L *praevaricatus,* pp. of *praevaricare,* lit., walk crookedly <*prae-* before + *varicare* straddle <*varicus* straddling <*varus* crooked] —**pre·var′i·ca′·tor** *n.*

add, āce, câre, pälm; end, ēven; it, īce; odd, ōpen, ôrder; tŏŏk, pōōl; up, bûrn; ə = a in *above,* e in *sicken,* i in *clarity,* o in *melon,* u in *focus*; yōō = u in *fuse*; oi, oil; ou, pout; ch, check; g, go; ng, ring; th, thin; th, this; zh, vision. Foreign sounds à, œ, ü, kh, ṅ; and ◆: see page xx. <from; + plus; ? possibly.

pre•var•i•ca•tion (pri·var′ə·kā′shən) *n.* **1** The act of prevaricating. **2** Misleading or equivocal statement. **3** A trick. See synonyms under DECEPTION, SOPHISTRY.

pré•ve•nance (prā·və·näṅs′) *n. French* Prevenience.

pre•ven•ience (pri·vēn′yəns) *n.* The act or state of going before; anticipation.

pre•ven•ient (pri·vēn′yənt) *adj.* **1** Preceding or preventing. **2** Anticipatory; expectant. [<L *praeveniens, -entis,* ppr. of *praevenire.* See PREVENT.]

pre•vent (pri·vent′) *v.t.* **1** To keep from happening, as by previous measures or preparations; preclude; thwart. **2** To keep from doing something; forestall; hinder. **3** *Obs.* To anticipate; precede. [<L *praeventus;* pp. of *praevenire* precede, come before, anticipate <*prae-* before + *venire* come] —**pre•vent′a•ble** or **pre•vent′i•ble** *adj.* —**pre•vent′a•bil′i•ty** or **pre•vent′i•bil′i•ty** *n.* —**pre•vent′er** *n.*

Synonyms: anticipate, forestall. The original sense of *prevent,* to go or come before, act in advance of, now practically obsolete, was still in good use when the authorized version of the Bible was made, as appears in such passages as "Thou *preventest* him with the blessings of goodness" (that is, by sending the blessings before the desire is formulated or expressed), *Ps.* xxi 3. *Anticipate* is now the only single word usable in this sense; to *forestall* is to take or act in advance in one's own behalf and to the prejudice or hindrance of another. But to *anticipate* is very frequently used in the favorable sense; as, his thoughtful kindness *anticipated* my wish (that is, met the wish before it was expressed); or one *anticipates* a payment (by making it before the time). For the present use of *prevent,* see synonyms for HINDER[1], PRECLUDE, PROHIBIT.

pre•ven•tion (pri·ven′shən) *n.* **1** The act of preventing. **2** A hindrance; obstruction. **3** A preventive.

pre•ven•tive (pri·ven′tiv) *adj.* Intended or serving to ward off harm, diseases, etc.: *preventive* medicine. —*n.* That which prevents or hinders, as a medicine to ward off disease; a precautionary measure. Also **pre•vent•a•tive** (pri·ven′tə·tiv). —**pre•ven′tive•ly** *adv.* —**pre•ven′tive•ness** *n.*

pre•verb (prē′vûrb′) *n.* A verbal prefix, as *be-* in *behave.*

pre•ver•nal (pri·vûr′nəl) *adj.* **1** Prior to spring. **2** *Bot.* Flowering in the early spring, as certain trees and plants.

pre•view (prē′vyōō′) *n.* **1** An advance showing, as of a motion picture, a fashion show, etc., to invited guests before it is presented publicly. **2** In motion pictures, the showing of scenes or parts of scenes to advertise a coming picture.

pre•vi•ous (prē′vē·əs) *adj.* **1** Being or taking place before something else in time or order; antecedent; prior to. **2** *Colloq.* Acting, occurring, or speaking too soon; premature. [<L *praevius* going before <*prae-* before + *via* way, road] —**pre′vi•ous•ly** *adv.* —**pre′vi•ous•ness** *n.*

Synonyms: antecedent, anterior, earlier, foregoing, former, precedent, preceding, preliminary, prior. *Antecedent* may denote simple priority in time, implying no direct connection between that which goes before and that which follows; as, the striking of one clock may be always *antecedent* to the striking of another with no causal connection between them. *Antecedent* and *previous* may refer to that which goes or happens at any distance in advance, *preceding* is limited to that which is immediately or next before; an *antecedent* event may have happened at any time before; the *preceding* transaction is the one completed just before the one with which it is compared; a *previous* statement or chapter may be in any part of the book that has gone before; the *preceding* statement or chapter comes next before without an interval. *Foregoing* is used only of that which is spoken or written; as, the *foregoing* statements. *Anterior,* while it can be used of time, is coming to be employed chiefly with reference to place; as, the *anterior* lobes of the brain. *Prior* bears exclusive reference to time, and commonly where that which is first in time is first also in right; as, a *prior* demand. *Former* is used of time, or of position in written or printed matter, not of space in general. We say *former* times, a *former* chapter, etc. *Former* has a close relation, or sharp contrast, with something following; the *former* always implies the latter, even when not fully expressed. Compare ANTECEDENT. *Antonyms:* after, concluding, consequent, following, hind, hinder, hindmost, later, latter, posterior, subsequent, succeeding.

Previous Examination See LITTLE GO.

previous question In parliamentary practice, a motion to avoid or secure a vote at once. In the British Parliament, the motion is put to prevent a speedy vote on a measure. In the United States House of Representatives it is used to end debate and secure an immediate vote. Compare CLOSURE.

previous to **1** Antecedent to; being before. **2** Before: *previous* being loosely used for *previously.*

pre•vise (prē·vīz′) *v.t.* **•vised, •vis•ing** **1** To see beforehand; foresee. **2** To notify beforehand; forewarn. [<L *praevisus,* pp. of *praevidere* foresee <*prae-* before + *videre* see]

pre•vi•sion (prē·vizh′ən) *n.* **1** The act or power of foreseeing; prescience; foresight. **2** A prophetic or anticipatory vision. See synonyms under ANTICIPATION. [<F *prévision*]

pre•vo•ca•tion•al (prē′vō·kā′shən·əl) *adj.* Of or pertaining to the training given or requisite in schools of a lower grade than the vocational schools.

Pré•vost (prā·vō′), **Marcel,** 1862–1941, French novelist.

Pré•vost d'Ex•iles (prā·vō′ deg·zēl′), **Antoine François,** 1679–1763, French novelist: known as *Abbé Prévost.*

pre•vue (prē′vyōō′) *n.* A preview. [<F *prévue,* fem. pp. of *prévoir* foresee]

pre•war (prē′wôr′) *adj.* Of or pertaining to a condition, arrangement, time, etc., before a war.

prex•y (prek′sē) *n. Slang* A college president. Also **prex.**

prey (prā) *n.* **1** Any animal seized by another for food. **2** Booty; plunder; pillage. **3** Anything made the victim of that which is hostile or evil. **4** The act of preying; depredation; robbery. See synonyms under PLUNDER. —*v.i.* **1** To seek or take prey for food: Cats *prey* on birds. **2** To take booty; plunder. **3** To make a victim of someone, as by cheating. **4** To exert a wearing or harmful influence: His losses *preyed* on his mind. ◆ Homophone: *pray.* [<OF *preie* <L *praeda* booty] —**prey′er** *n.*

Pri•am (prī′əm) In Greek legend, the son of Laomedon, husband of Hecuba, and father of fifty sons including Hector and Paris; he was the last king of Troy and was killed during its capture at the end of the Trojan War.

Pri•a•pe•an (prī′ə·pē′ən) *adj.* Of or pertaining to Priapus; phallic.

pri•a•pus (prī·ā′pəs) *n.* A phallus. [<PRIAPUS]

Pri•a•pus (prī·ā′pəs) In Greek and Roman mythology, the god of male procreative power, son of Dionysos and Aphrodite. [<L <Gk. *Priapos*]

Prib•i•lof Islands (prib′i·lof) A group of four Alaskan islands in the SE Bering Sea; major breeding ground of the Alaska fur seal.

price (prīs) *n.* **1** An equivalent given or asked in exchange; valuation; cost (to the buyer). **2** Anything given or done to obtain something: Death is the *price* of glory. **3** The quality of possessing value; worth; especially, high value. **4** A bribe or anything used for a bribe. **5** A reward for the capture or death of. —**beyond price** **1** So valuable that no adequate price can be set; priceless. **2** Unbribable. —**market price** The price that something will bring in the open market. —**to set a price on one's head** To offer a reward for the capture of a person, dead or alive. —*v.t.* **priced, pric•ing** **1** To ask the price of. **2** To set a price on; value; appraise. [<OF *pris* <L *pretium.* Related to PRAISE.]

Synonyms (noun): charge, cost, expenditure, expense, outlay, value, worth. The *cost* of a thing is all that has been expended upon it, whether in discovery, production, refinement, decoration, transportation, or otherwise, to bring it to its present condition in the hands of its present possessor; the *price* of a thing is what the seller asks for it. *Price* always implies that an article is for sale; what a man will not sell he declines to put a *price* on. *Value* is the estimated equivalent for an article, whether the article is for sale or not; the market *value* is what something would bring if it were for sale in the open market; the intrinsic *value* is the inherent *worth* of the article considered by itself alone; the market *value* of an old and rare volume may be very great, while its intrinsic *value* may be practically nothing. *Value* has always more reference to others' estimation (literally, what the thing will avail with others) than *worth,* which regards the thing in and by itself; thus, intrinsic *value* is a weaker expression than intrinsic *worth. Charge* has especial reference to services, *expense* to outlays; as, the *charges* of a lawyer or physician; traveling *expenses,* etc.

Price may appear as a combining form in hyphemes or solidemes, or as the first element in two-word phrases:

price adjustment
price administration
price boom
price–control
price cut
price–fixer
price freeze
price history
price–level
price–maintenance
price–making
price–manipulation
price notice
price reduction
price–ruling
price–stabilizer
price–stabilizing
price–support
price–supporting
price tag

price cutting The act of reducing the price of an article to one below the figure at which it is usually advertised or sold.

price–fix•ing (prīs′fik′sing) *n.* **1** The establishment and maintenance of a scale of prices agreed upon within specified groups of producers or distributors. **2** The establishing by government action of maximum or minimum or fixed prices for certain goods and services. **3** The fixing by a manufacturer or producer of the price at which retailers must sell his product. —*adj.* Of or pertaining to price–fixing.

price•less (prīs′lis) *adj.* **1** Beyond price or valuation; invaluable. **2** *Colloq.* Wonderfully amusing or absurd.

price•list (prīs′list′) *n.* A catalog of goods in which the prices are named.

prick (prik) *v.t.* **1** To pierce slightly, as with a sharp point; puncture. **2** To affect with sharp mental pain; sting; spur. **3** To mark, outline, or indicate by or as by punctures. **4** *Obs.* To urge on with or as with a spur; goad. **5** In farriery: **a** To drive a nail into the quick of (a horse's hoof), causing lameness. **b** To nick (a horse's tail). **6** To transplant, as young plants, preparatory to later planting. —*v.i.* **7** To have or cause a stinging or piercing sensation. **8** *Archaic* To ride at full speed; go at a gallop. —**to prick up one's** (or **its**) **ears** **1** To raise the ears erect. **2** To listen attentively. —*n.* **1** The act of pricking; the state or sensation of being pricked. **2** A mental sting or spur: the *prick* of conscience. **3** That which pricks; a slender, sharp-pointed thing, as a thorn or pointed weapon. **4** A mark made by a sharp, pointed instrument; puncture; dot. **5** The footprint of an animal, as a rabbit or deer. **6** *Archaic* A goad or spur. [OE *prica* sharp point] —**prick′er** *n.*

prick•et (prik′it) *n.* **1** A buck of the second year. **2** A sharp point upon which to stick a candle; hence, a candlestick. [Dim. of PRICK]

prick•ing (prik′ing) *n.* **1** The act of puncturing with a sharp point, or the resulting sensation. **2** The laming of a horse by improper shoeing. **3** The nicking of a horse's tail.

pricking wheel A toothed wheel mounted on a handle, used by saddlers to mark equidistant places for stitch holes, or by dressmakers in copying patterns. Also **prick wheel.**

prick•le (prik′əl) *n.* **1** A small, sharp point, as on the bark of a plant. **2** A prickling or stinging sensation. —*v.* **•led, •ling** *v.t.* **1** To prick; pierce. **2** To cause a prickling or stinging sensation in. —*v.i.* **3** To have a prickling or stinging sensation; tingle. [OE *pricel*]

prick•ly (prik′lē) *adj.* **1** Furnished with prickles. **2** Stinging, as if from a prick or sting: a *prickly* sensation.

prickly ash A prickly shrub or tree (*Zanthoxylum americanum*) of the rue family, with pungent and aromatic bark.

prickly heat *Pathol.* A summer rash of bright red pimples, with heat, itching, and prickling as if by needles; miliaria.

prickly pear 1 A flat-stemmed cactus (genus *Opuntia*) bearing a pear-shaped and often prickly fruit. 2 The fruit itself.

prickly poppy A weedlike annual *(Argemone mexicana)* of the poppy family, with prickly stem and leaves, showy yellow flowers, and yellow juice.

prick punch A pointed steel punch for marking reference points on metal.

prick-song (prik′sông′, -song′) *n. Archaic* 1 Music pricked down or written. 2 Counterpoint.

pride (prīd) *n.* 1 An undue sense of one's own superiority; inordinate self-esteem; arrogance or superciliousness; conceit. 2 A proper sense of personal dignity and worth; honorable self-respect. 3 That of which one is justly proud; a cause of exultation. 4 The acme of excellence. 5 Consciousness of youth or power; high spirits; mettle. 6 *Obs.* Sexual desire. 7 *Archaic* Ostentatious splendor; display. 8 A group or company: said only of lions. — *v.t.* **prid·ed, prid·ing** To take pride in (oneself) for something: with *on* or *upon.* [OE *prȳte* < *prūt* proud]
Synonyms (noun): conceit, ostentation, self-complacency, self-conceit, self-esteem, self-exaltation, self-respect, vainglory, vanity. *Conceit* and *vanity* are associated with weakness, *pride* with strength. *Conceit* may be founded upon nothing, *pride* is founded upon something that one is, or has, or has done; *vanity,* too, is commonly founded on something real, but far slighter than would afford foundation for *pride. Vanity* is eager for admiration and praise and seeks them; *pride* could never solicit admiration or praise. *Conceit* is stronger than *self-conceit. Self-conceit* is ridiculous; *conceit* is offensive. *Self-respect* is a thoroughly worthy feeling; *self-esteem* is a more generous estimate of one's own character and abilities than the rest of the world is ready to allow. *Vainglory* is more pompous and boastful than *vanity.* Compare synonyms for ARROGANCE, EGOTISM, OSTENTATION, RESERVE. *Antonyms*: humility, lowliness, meekness, modesty, self-abasement.

Pride (prīd), **Thomas,** died 1658, English general; one of the judges who condemned Charles I.

pride·ful (prīd′fəl) *adj.* Full of pride; haughty; disdainful.

pride of China The azedarach tree.

Pride's Purge The expulsion of Royalist and Presbyterian members from the House of Commons in 1648, conducted by Thomas Pride.

Prid·win (prid′win) King Arthur's shield.

prie-dieu (prē·dyœ′) *n.* A small desk arranged to support a book or books and with a footpiece on which to kneel; a praying desk. [<F, pray God]

PRIE–DIEU

pri·er (prī′ər) *n.* One who pries.

priest (prēst) *n.* 1 One especially consecrated to the service of a divinity, and serving as mediator between the divinity and his worshipers in sacrifice, worship, prayer, teaching, etc. 2 In the Anglican, Greek, and Roman Catholic churches, a clergyman in the second order of the ministry, ranking next below a bishop, and having authority to administer the sacraments. 3. Any ordained clergyman or pastor; an official minister of any religious system: distinguished from *layman.* 4 In the early Christian church, an elder or presbyter. 5 One who performs functions or duties similar to those of a priest. — **parish priest** The priest in charge of a parish; specifically, in the Roman Catholic Church, a priest exercising personal jurisdiction in a parish, all members of which are obliged to apply to him for the ministrations of the church: distinguished from *rector* and *curate.* [OE *prēost,* ult. <L *presbyter.* Doublet of PRESBYTER.]

priest·craft (prēst′kraft′, -kräft′) *n.* 1 Priestly arts and wiles: an invidious term. 2 The knowledge and skill of priests.

priest·ess (prēs′tis) *n.* A woman or girl who exercises priestly functions or who performs sacred rites.

priest·hood (prēst′ho͝od) *n.* 1 The priestly office or character. 2 The priestly order; priests collectively. [OE *prēosthad*]

Priest·ley (prēst′lē), **J(ohn) B(oynton),** born 1894, English author. — **Joseph,** 1733–1804, English philosopher and chemist; discoverer of oxygen.

priest·ly (prēst′lē) *adj.* 1 Of or pertaining to a priest or the priesthood; sacerdotal. 2 Suitable to or befitting a priest. — **priest′li·ness** *n.*

priest-rid·den (prēst′rid′n) *adj.* Completely under the influence or domination of priests.

prig[1] (prig) *n.* A formal and narrow-minded person who assumes superior virtue, wisdom, or learning; pedant. [Origin unknown]

prig[2] (prig) *v.* **prigged, prig·ging** *v.t. Brit. Slang* To steal. — *v.i. Scot & Brit. Dial.* To bargain haggle.

prig·gish (prig′ish) *adj.* Like a prig; conceited. — **prig′gish·ly** *adv.* — **prig′gish·ness** *n.*

prig·gism (prig′iz·əm) *n.* The characteristics or manners of a prig.

prill (pril) *n.* 1 A small metal particle formed in assay work. 2 A spherical pellet about the size of buckshot. — *v.t.* To convert into prills for some purpose or use. [? <Cornish]

prim (prim) *adj.* Minutely or affectedly precise and formal; stiffly proper and neat. See synonyms under NEAT[1]. — *v.* **primmed, prim·ming** *v.i.* To fix the face or mouth in a precise or prim expression; be prim. — *v.t.* To fix in a precise or prim manner. [Prob. <OF *prim* first, prime, fine, delicate <L *primus* first] — **prim′ly** *adv.* — **prim′ness** *n.*

Pri·ma·cord (prī′mə·kôrd) *n.* A flexible tube of fabric or lead, filled with high explosive and used as a primer or bursting charge: a trade name.

pri·ma·cy (prī′mə·sē) *n. pl.* **·cies** 1 The state of being first, as in rank or excellence. 2 The office or province of a primate; archbishopric: also **pri′mate·ship** (-mit·ship). [<OF *primacie* <Med. L *primatia* <LL *primas, primatis* one of the first. See PRIMATE.]

pri·ma don·na (prē′mə don′ə) 1 A leading female singer, as in an opera company. 2 *Colloq.* A temperamental or vain person. [<Ital., lit., first lady]

pri·ma fa·ci·e (prī′mə fā′shi·ē, fā′shē) *Latin* At first view; so far as at first appears.

prima-facie evidence Evidence which, if unexplained or uncontradicted, would establish the fact alleged.

pri·mage (prī′mij) *n.* An allowance in addition to wages, formerly paid by a shipper to the master of a vessel, now paid to the owner of the vessel as an addition to freight charges, for care in loading or unloading goods in port. [<PRIME + -AGE; after Med. L *primagium*]

pri·mal (prī′məl) *adj.* 1 Being at the beginning or foundation; first; original. 2 Most important; chief. See synonyms under PRIMEVAL. [<Med. L *primalis*]

primal cut Any one of the cuts into which a side of beef may be divided for sale at wholesale. These cuts are: hindquarter, trimmed full loin, round sirloin, short loin, flank, flank steak, kidney, hanging tender, forequarter, cross-cut chuck, triangle, arm chuck, rib, short plate, brisket, fore shank, back, regular chuck.

pri·ma·quine (prī′mə·kwīn) *n.* An antimalarial drug synthesized from chemicals derived from corn and coal tar. [<PRIM(E) + A(MINO)-QUIN(OLIN)E]

pri·ma·ri·ly (prī′mer·ə·lē, -mər·ə·lē, *emphatic* prī·mâr′ə·lē) *adv.* In the first place; originally; essentially.

pri·ma·ry (prī′mer·ē, -mər·ē) *adj.* 1 First in time or origin; primitive; original. 2 First in a series or sequence. 3 First in degree, rank, or importance; chief. 4 Constituting the fundamental or original elements of which a whole is comprised; basic; elemental: the *primary* forces of life. 5 Of the first stage of development; elementary; lowest: *primary* school. 6 *Ornithol.* Of or pertaining to the principal flight feathers of a bird's wing. 7 *Geol.* Paleozoic. 8 *Electr.* Of, pertaining to, or noting an inducing current or its circuit: a *primary* coil. 9 *Chem.* **a** Having some characteristic in the first degree, as an initial replacement, substitution, etc. **b** In organic compounds, denoting a radical in which a carbon atom is directly joined to only one other carbon atom. **c** Denoting a compound containing such a radical. — *n. pl.* **·ries** 1 That which is first in rank, dignity, or importance, as a primary planet in distinction from a satellite. 2 A primary meeting or balloting of the voters belonging to one political party in an election district to nominate candidates. 3 *Ornithol.* One of the large flight feathers of the pinion or hand bones of a bird's wings. See synonyms under FIRST, PRIMEVAL. — **direct primary election** A primary election in which candidates for office are nominated directly by the voters and not by a convention or by a body of delegates. [<L *primarius* < *primus* first]

primary cell *Electr.* A cell which cannot be efficiently recharged after use owing to an irreversible electrochemical reaction.

primary colors See under COLOR.

pri·mate (prī′mit, -māt) *n.* 1 The prelate highest in rank in a nation or province. 2 Any of an order *(Primates)* of mammals, including the tarsiers, lemurs, marmosets, monkeys, apes, and man. [<OF *primat* <LL *primas, primatis* of the first <L *primus*] — **pri·ma·tial** (prī·mā′shəl) *adj.*

pri·ma·tol·o·gy (prī′mə·tol′ə·jē) *n.* The branch of zoology which treats of the origin, structure, evolution, and development of primates. — **pri′ma·tol′o·gist** *n.*

pri·ma·ve·ra (prē′mä·vā′rä) *n.* A tropical American tree *(Cybistax donnell-smithi)* of the bignonia family, yielding a creamy-white or yellowish wood resembling satinwood: erroneously called *white mahogany.* [<Sp., lit., spring <L *prima vera,* pl. of *primum ver* earliest spring]

prime[1] (prīm) *adj.* 1 First in rank, dignity, or importance; chief. 2 First in value or excellence; of excellent quality; first-rate. 3 First in time or order; original; primitive; primeval. 4 *Math.* Divisible by no whole number except itself and unity: said of a number. Two or more numbers are said to be *prime* to each other when they have no common factor but unity. 5 Having or pertaining to the strength and vigor of fresh maturity; blooming. 6 Original; not derived; first: opposed to *secondary.* 7 Marked with the sign (′). See synonyms under EXCELLENT, PRIMEVAL. — *n.* 1 The period of fresh, full vigor, beauty, and power succeeding youth and preceding age; formerly, youth. 2 The period of full perfection in anything. 3 The beginning of anything, as of the day; dawn; spring. 4 The best of anything; a prime grade. 5 A prime number. 6 A mark or accent (′) written above and to the right of a letter or figure; also, an inch, a minute, etc., as indicated by that sign, used in indicating and measuring degrees. 7 *Music* The tonic; the interval of unison; also, a note in unison with another. — *v.* **primed, prim·ing** *v.t.* 1 To prepare; make ready for some purpose. 2 To put a primer into (a gun, mine, etc.) preparatory to firing. 3 To pour water into (a pump) so as to displace air and promote suction. 4 To cover (a surface) with sizing, a first coat of paint, etc. 5 To supply beforehand with facts, information, etc.: to *prime* a witness. — *v.i.* 6 To carry water along with the steam into the cylinder: said of a steam boiler or engine. 7 To make something ready, as for firing, pumping, etc. [<OF <L *primus*] — **prime′ly** *adv.* — **prime′ness** *n.*

prime[2] (prīm) *n.* 1 The first canonical hour succeeding lauds; first of the day hours. 2 The office recited at this time. [OE *prīm* <LL *prima (hora)* first (hour)]

prime conductor *Electr.* The conductor of a frictional machine which collects and retains the positive electricity.

prime cost The direct cost of obtaining or producing something; the cost of labor and material, exclusive of capital and management expenses.

prime meridian A meridian from which longitude is reckoned: now, generally, the one that passes through Greenwich, England, but formerly that of the local capital, as, in the United States, Washington, D.C.: in France, Paris; etc.

prime minister The chief of the cabinet or ministry; in Great Britain, the principal minister of the sovereign. Compare PREMIER.

prime ministry The office of a prime minister.

prime mover **1** An original or chief force in an undertaking. **2** That which is regarded as an original or natural source of the energy required to perform work or develop power, as muscular force, wind, the motion of water, etc. **3** An object or machine used to convert natural forces to productive power, as a turbine, water wheel, windmill, or the like. **4** In Aristotelian philosophy, the first cause of all movement, which does not itself move.

prime number See under NUMBER.

prim·er[1] (prim′ər) *n.* **1** An elementary textbook; especially, a beginning reading book. **2** Originally, a small prayer book or the like. **3** *Printing* Either of two sizes of type, **great primer** (18-point) and **long primer** (10-point). [<Med. L *primarius*]

prim·er[2] (prī′mər) *n.* **1** Any device, as a cap, tube, etc., used to detonate the main charge of a gun, mine, etc. **2** One who or that which primes.

prim·er[3] (prim′ər, prī′mər) *adj. Obs.* First; original; primary. [<OF <L *primarius* <*primus* prime]

pri·me·ro (pri·mâr′ō) *n.* An old gambling card game. [<Sp.]

pri·me·val (prī·mē′vəl) *adj.* Belonging to the first ages; primitive in time; primary. [<L *primaevus* youthful <*primus* first + *aevum* age] — **pri·me′val·ly** *adv.*

Synonyms: aboriginal, ancient, autochthonic, immemorial, indigenous, native, old, original, primal, primary, prime, primitive, primordial, pristine. *Aboriginal* signifies pertaining to the earliest known inhabitants of a country in the widest sense, including not merely human beings, but animals and plants. *Primeval* signifies strictly belonging to the first ages, earliest in time, but often only the earliest of which man knows or conceives. *Prime* and *primary* may signify either first in time, or first in importance; *primary* has also the sense of elementary or preparatory; we speak of a *prime* minister, a *primary* school. *Primal* is chiefly poetic, in the sense of *prime*; as, the *primal* curse. *Primordial* is first in an order of existence or development; as, a *primordial* leaf. *Primitive* frequently signifies having the original characteristics of that which it represents, as well as standing first in time; as, the *primitive* church, or early characteristics without remoteness in time. *Primeval* simplicity is the simplicity of the earliest ages; *primitive* simplicity may be found in retired villages now. *Pristine* is used almost exclusively in a good sense of that which is *original* and perhaps *ancient*; as, *pristine* purity, innocence, vigor. *Immemorial* refers solely to time, independently of quality, denoting, in legal phrase, that "whereof the memory of man runneth not to the contrary." Compare synonyms for ANCIENT, FIRST, OLD. *Antonyms*: adventitious, exotic, foreign, fresh, late, modern, new, novel, recent.

pri·mi·ge·ni·al (prī′mə·jē′nē·əl) *adj.* Being the first or first-born; primal; primitive; original. [<L *primigenius* first, original]

pri·mine (prī′min) *n. Bot.* The outermost and last-developed integument of an ovule; also, the inner integument as being formed first. Compare SECUNDINE. [<L *primus* first]

prim·ing (prī′ming) *n.* **1** That with which anything is primed. **2** A combustible composition used to ignite an explosive charge. **3** The ground or first layer of paint laid on a surface that is to be painted.

pri·mip·a·ra (prī·mip′ər·ə) *n. pl.* **·a·rae** (-ər·ē) A woman pregnant for the first time or one who has borne just one child. [<L <*primus* first + *parere* give birth to] — **pri·mi·par·i·ty** (prī′mi·par′ə·tē) *n.* — **pri·mip′a·rous** *adj.*

prim·i·tive (prim′ə·tiv) *adj.* **1** Pertaining to the beginning or origin; first; earliest; primary. **2** Resembling the manners or style of long ago; old-fashioned; simple; plain. **3** *Geol.* Of, belonging to, or characterized by the earliest geological period: said especially of the crystalline, unstratified, and massive rocks, the oldest known. **4** *Anthropol.* Of or pertaining to the beginning or earliest anthropological forms or civilizations: *primitive* man, *primitive* weapons. **5** *Biol.* **a** Being or occurring at an early stage of development or growth; first-formed; rudimentary. **b** Not much changed by evolution: a *primitive* species. **6** *Ling.* Standing in original relation, as a word from which a derivative is made; radical: opposed to *derived.* **7** *Theol.* Adhering to strictly traditional interpretation of doctrine and Scripture: the *primitive* church. —*n.* **1** *Ling.* A primary or radical word; also, a word from which another is derived. **2** *Math.* A form in algebra or geometry from which another is derived. **3** An artist, or a work of art, belonging to a very early period of art, or to the earliest phase of an art development or movement; also, a work of any period resembling or imitating such art, or an artist producing it: often characterized by simplicity or a childlike quality. See synonyms under FIRST, PRIMEVAL, RADICAL. [<L *primitivus* <*primus* first] — **prim′i·tive·ly** *adv.* — **prim′i·tive·ness, prim′i·tiv′i·ty** *n.*

Primitive Baptist A member of a branch of the Baptist church (separate since 1835) holding to Calvinistic and antimission doctrines: also called *Hardshell Baptist.*

prim·i·tiv·ism (prim′ə·tiv·iz′əm) *n.* Belief in or adherence to primitive forms and customs.

pri·mo·gen·i·tor (prī′mə·jen′ə·tər) *n.* An earliest ancestor; a forefather. [<Med. L <L *primus* first + *genitor* a father]

pri·mo·gen·i·ture (prī′mə·jen′ə·chər) *n.* **1** The state of being the first-born child of the same parents. **2** The right of the eldest son to inherit the property, title, etc., of a parent, to the exclusion of all other children. See ULTIMOGENITURE. [<Med. L *primogenitura* <L *primus* first + *genitura* birth <*genitus*, pp. of *gignere* beget]

prim′·o·mo (prē·mô′mō) *Italian* First man; leading actor or singer.

pri·mor·di·al (prī·môr′dē·əl) *adj.* **1** First in order or time; original; elemental. **2** *Biol.* First in order of appearance in the growth or development of an organism. —*n.* An elementary principle. See synonyms under FIRST, PRIMEVAL, TRANSCENDENTAL. [<LL *primordialis* <*primordius* original <*primordium* beginning <*primus* first + *ordiri* begin a web] — **pri·mor′di·al·ly** *adv.*

pri·mor·di·al·ism (prī·môr′dē·əl·iz′əm) *n.* The survival or persistence of primitive arts and customs.

primp (primp) *v.t.* & *v.i.* To prink; dress up, especially with superfluous attention to detail. [Akin to PRIM]

prim·rose (prim′rōz) *n.* **1** An early-blossoming perennial herb (genus *Primula*) with tufted basal leaves and variously colored flowers. **2** The flower. **3** The evening primrose. **4** A pale-yellow color, named for the common English primrose: a term indiscriminately applied to various yellow pigments. —*adj.* **1** Pertaining to a primrose; of primrose color. **2** Flowery; gay. [Alter. of ME *primerole* <OF <Med. L *primula*, fem. dim. of L *primus* first; infl. by *rose*]

PRIMROSE
(*def. 1*)
(The wild species from 1 to 18 inches tall)

primrose path The life of worldly or sensual pleasures.

prim·sie (prim′zē) *adj. Scot.* Demure; prim.

prim·u·la·ceous (prim′yə·lā′shəs) *adj. Bot.* Designating or belonging to a family (*Primulaceae*) of herbs widely distributed in the northern hemisphere, including the pimpernel, cyclamen, and loosestrife. [<NL <Med. L *primula* a primrose]

pri·mum mo·bi·le (prī′məm mō′bi·lē) **1** A prime mover. **2** *Astron.* In the Ptolemaic cosmology, the tenth and outermost of the concentric spheres of the universe, regarded as causing all the other spheres to repeat its own revolution around the earth once in 24 hours. [<L, first moving thing]

pri·mus in·ter pa·res (prī′məs in′tər pâr′ēz) *Latin* First among equals.

prince (prins) *n.* **1** A non-reigning male member of a royal family. **2** A male monarch or sovereign. **3** *Brit.* The son of a sovereign or of a son of the sovereign. **4** One of a high order of nobility. **5** The ruler of a small state; head of a principality. **6** A chief or leader, or one of the highest rank of the class to which he belongs: a merchant *prince.* See synonyms under MASTER. [<OF <L *princeps* first, principal <*primus* first + stem of *capere* take]

Prince Albert A long, double-breasted frock coat.

Prince Albert National Park A park in central Saskatchewan, Canada; 1,496 square miles; established 1927.

prince consort The husband of a reigning female sovereign.

Prince Edward Island An island in the Gulf of St. Lawrence off eastern New Brunswick, comprising a maritime province of Canada; 2,184 square miles; capital, Charlottetown.

Prince Island The English name for PRINCIPE. See SÃO TOMÉ E PRINCIPE.

prince·kin (prins′kin) *n.* A little or inferior prince.

prince·ling (prins′ling) *n.* **1** A young prince. **2** A subordinate prince. Also **prince′let** (-lit).

prince·ly (prins′lē) *adj.* **·li·er, ·li·est** **1** Like or characteristic of a prince; liberal; generous. **2** Belonging to, ruled by, or suitable for a prince. **3** Having the rank of a prince. See synonyms under KINGLY. —*adv.* In a princely manner. — **prince′li·ness** *n.*

Prince of Darkness Satan.

Prince of Peace Jesus Christ.

Prince of Wales The eldest son or male heir apparent of the British sovereign: he is born Duke of Cornwall, and becomes Prince of Wales only by creation.

Prince of Wales, Cape The westernmost point of the American continent, at the tip of Seward Peninsula, Alaska, on the Bering Strait 100 miles NW of Nome.

Prince of Wales Island **1** A former name for PENANG ISLAND. **2** An island in the Arctic Ocean, in south central Franklin district of Northwest Territories, Canada; 13,736 square miles; the north magnetic pole was located on it in 1948. **3** The largest island of the Alexander Archipelago, SE Alaska, in the North Pacific west of Ketchikan; 2,231 square miles; 135 miles long, 45 miles wide.

Prince of Wales plumes In furniture and decoration, a motif of three ostrich feathers tied with a bowknot.

Prince Rupert A port in western British Columbia, Canada.

prin·ce's-feath·er (prin′siz-feth′ər) *n.* A tall, hardy plant (*Polygonum orientale*) with plumelike inflorescences and dark-crimson flowers, growing wild in eastern North America.

prin·cess (prin′sis) *n.* **1** A non-reigning female member of a royal family. **2** The consort of a prince. **3** A female sovereign. **4** *Brit.* The daughter of a sovereign or of a son of the sovereign. [<F *princesse*]

prin·cesse (prin·ses′, prin′sis) *adj.* Designating a woman's close-fitting garment cut in a single piece from shoulder to flared hem. Also **prin′cess.** [<F, princess]

princess feather A tall, graceful plant (*Amaranthus hybridus hypochondriacus*) with many-branched panicles of showy flowers.

princess royal The eldest daughter of a sovereign.

Prince·ton (prins′tən) A borough of central New Jersey; scene of an American victory in the Revolutionary War (1777) and seat of Princeton University, founded 1746.

Prince William Sound An inlet of the Gulf of Alaska in southern Alaska; 100 miles across.

prin·ci·pal (prin′sə·pəl) *adj.* First in rank, character, or importance; chief. See synonyms under FIRST, PARAMOUNT. —*n.* **1** One who takes a leading part; one concerned directly and not as an auxiliary; one who is a leader or chief in some action. **2** *Law* **a** The actor in a crime, or one present aiding and abetting. **b** The employer of one who acts as an agent. **c** One primarily liable for whom another has become surety. **d** The most important thing, or part of a given property, to which other things or parts are incidental. **e** The capital or body of an estate. **3** One who is at the head of some body; a chief; one in authority; a presiding officer, as of a society. **4** The head teacher or master in a public or private school. **5** The chief executive of some colleges and universities in Great Britain. 6 Property or capital, as opposed to interest or income. 7 A rafter extending to the ridge pole; a principal rafter. 8 *Music* **a** The chief metal organ stop, an octave higher in pitch than the other diapasons. **b** The subject of a fugue: distinguished from *answer.* See synonyms under CHIEF, MASTER. ◆ Homophone: *principle.* [< F < L *principalis* < *princeps* chief] —**prin'ci·pal·ly** *adv.* —**prin'ci·pal·ship'** *n.*

prin·ci·pal·i·ty (prin'sə·pal'ə·tē) *n. pl.* **·ties 1** The territory of a reigning prince, or one that gives to a prince a title of courtesy. 2 *pl.* Powers or powerful influences, as celestial or demoniacal powers; in the celestial hierarchy of Dionysius, the seventh of the nine emanations from the Divine. 3 *Obs.* Sovereignty.

principal part See under PART.

Prin·ci·pe (prin'si·pē, *Pg.* prēn'sē·pə) See under SÃO TOMÉ E PRINCIPE.

prin·cip·i·um (prin·sip'ē·əm) *n. pl.* **·cip·i·a** (-sip'ē·ə) **1** Beginning; origin; first principle. 2 *pl.* Fundamentals. [< L]

prin·ci·ple (prin'sə·pəl) *n.* **1** A general truth or law, basic to other truths: the *principle* of self-government. 2 A settled law or rule of personal conduct: He followed the *principle* of the Golden Rule. 3 That which is inherent in anything, determining its nature; essential character; essence. 4 A source or cause from which a thing proceeds; fundamental cause. 5 An established mode of action or operation in natural phenomena: the *principle* of Archimedes. 6 *Chem.* An essential constituent of a compound or substance that gives character to it. 7 Moral standards collectively. See synonyms under DOCTRINE, LAW[1], REASON. ◆ Homophone: *principal.* [< L *principium* a beginning]

prin·cock (prin'kok) *n. Obs.* A coxcomb. Also **prin'cox** (-koks). [Prob. < PRIM + COCK[1]]

prink (pringk) To dress or (oneself) for show. —*v.i.* To dress oneself showily or fussily. [Prob. alter. of PRANK[1] under infl. of PREEN] —**prink'er** *n.*

print (print) *n.* **1** An impression with ink from type, plates, etc.; printed characters collectively; printed matter. 2 Anything printed from an engraved plate or lithographic stone; a proof; a printed picture or design. 3 A newspaper, pamphlet, or the like. 4 An impression or mark made upon or sunk into a substance by pressure; imprint. 5 A reproduction from such an impression. 6 Any fabric stamped with a design by means of dyes used on engraved rollers, wood blocks, or screens. 7 Any tool or device bearing a pattern or design, or that upon which it is impressed. 8 *Phot.* A positive picture made from a negative. 9 Newsprint. —**in print 1** Printed; also, for sale in printed form: opposed to *out of print.* 2 *Obs.* In an exact or formal manner. —**India print** Muslin printed, specifically hand blocked, with the native patterns and glowing colors of India. —**out of print** No longer on sale, the edition being exhausted. See synonyms under MARK[1], PICTURE. —*v.t.* **1** To mark, as with inked type, a stamp, die, etc. 2 To stamp or impress (a mark, seal, etc.) on or into a surface. 3 To fix as if by impressing: The scene is *printed* on my memory. 4 To produce (a book, newspaper, etc.) by the application of inked type, plates, etc., to paper or similar material. 5 To cause to be put in print; publish: The newspaper *printed* the story. 6 To write in letters similar to those used in print: Please *print* your name and address. 7 *Phot.* To produce (a positive picture) by transmitting light through a negative onto a sensitized surface. —*v.i.* 8 To be a printer. 9 To take or give an impression in printing. 10 To form letters similar to printed ones. —**to print out** To deliver (information) automatically in printed form, as a computer. See synonyms under IMPRESS[1]. [< OF *preinte, priente,* fem. of pp. of *preindre* < L *premere* press] —**print'a·ble** *adj.*

printed circuit A circuit in various electronic devices, the paths and connections for which are printed or otherwise deposited on an insulating surface.

print·er (prin'tər) *n.* **1** One engaged in the trade of typographical printing; one who sets type or runs a printing press; specifically, a compositor. 2 One who owns a printing establishment and employs printers. 3 One who prints, stamps, impresses, or transfers copies of anything as a business.

printer's devil A printer's apprentice. See under DEVIL.

print·er·y (prin'tər·ē) *n. pl.* **·er·ies 1** A place where cotton goods, as calico, are printed. 2 A printing office.

print·ing (prin'ting) *n.* **1** The making and issuing of matter for reading by means of type and the printing press. 2 Presswork. 3 The act of reproducing a design upon a surface by any process. 4 That which is printed.

printing press A mechanism for printing from an inked surface as of type, plates, woodblocks, etc., operating by pressure, either against a flat bed, as in the platen press, or against a series of revolving cylinders, as in the rotary press.

print·less (print'lis) *adj.* Making, bearing, or retaining no print or impression.

print·out (print'out') *n.* Material printed automatically, as by a computer.

pri·or (prī'ər) *adj.* Preceding in time, order, or importance. See synonyms under ANTECEDENT, ANTERIOR. —**prior to** Before: The theater closed *prior to* our arrival. —*n.* **1** A monastic officer next in rank below an abbot. 2 Formerly, an Italian magistrate. [< L, earlier, superior] —**pri'or·ate** (-it), **pri'or·ship** *n.*

Pri·or (prī'ər), **Matthew,** 1664–1721, English poet and diplomat.

pri·or·ess (prī'ər·is) *n.* A woman holding a position corresponding to that of a prior; a nun next in rank below an abbess.

pri·or·i·ty (prī·ôr'ə·tē, -or'-) *n. pl.* **·ties 1** Antecedence; precedence: opposed to *posteriority.* 2 A first right established on emergency or need: Defense plants have *priority* on steel in time of war. 3 A certificate giving this right to a manufacturer or contractor; hence, a restriction on the use of a commodity or service.

pri·or·y (prī'ər·ē) *n. pl.* **·or·ies** A monastic house presided over by a prior or prioress. See synonyms under CLOISTER. [< OF *priorie*]

Pri·pet (prē'pet) A river in NE Ukrainian S.S.R. and southern Belorussian S.S.R., flowing about 500 miles east through the **Pripet Marshes,** a swampy region of 33,500 square miles, to the Dnieper, 50 miles north of Kiev. *Russian* **Pri·pyat** (pryē'pyət·y'), *Polish* **Pry·peć** (prē'pech).

Pris·cian (prish'ən) Latin grammarian of the fifth century A.D.: full name *Priscianus Caesariensis.*

Pris·cil·la (pri·sil'ə; *Du.* pri·sil'ä, *Ital.* prē·sil'·lä) A feminine personal name. Also *Fr.* **Pris·cille** (prē·sēl'). [< L, somewhat ancient] —**Priscilla** In Longfellow's poem *The Courtship of Miles Standish,* the Puritan maiden, Priscilla Mullens, courted by John Alden as proxy for Standish. Later she married Alden.

Pris·cil·li·an (pri·sil'ē·ən, -sil'yən), died 385, bishop of Avila, Spain; burned at the stake for sorcery. —**Pris·cil'li·an·ist, Pris·cil'li·an·ite'** *n.*

prise (prīz) *n. & v.t.* Prize[2]; lever.

prism (priz'əm) *n.* **1** *Geom.* A solid whose bases or ends are any similar equal and parallel plane figures, and whose lateral faces are parallelograms. 2 *Optics* An instrument consisting of such a solid, usually having triangular ends and made of glass or other translucent substance, its refracting surfaces making an angle with each other. 3 Any medium that resolves a seemingly simple matter into its elements. 4 The spectrum. 5 *Mineral.* A crystal form consisting of three or more intersecting planes whose intersections are parallel and vertical. —**Nicol prism** A prism of calcite (Iceland spar) so cut that light emerging from it is polarized in a definite plane: used in polarizing microscopes, etc. [< LL *prisma* < Gk., something sawed < *prixein* saw]

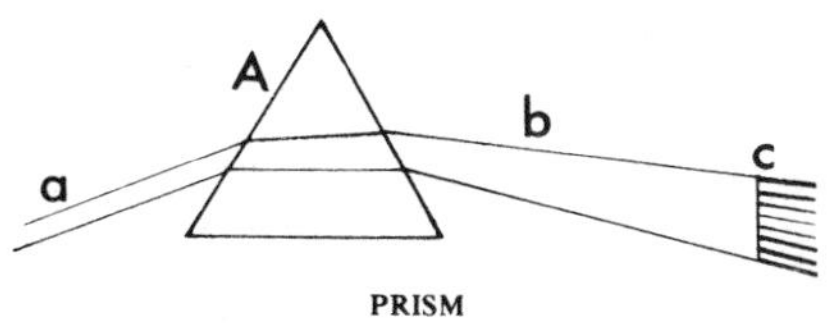

PRISM

pris·mat·ic (priz·mat'ik) *adj.* **1** Refracted or formed by a prism. 2 Resembling the spectrum; exhibiting rainbow tints. 3 Pertaining to or shaped like a prism. 4 Orthorhombic. Also **pris·mat'i·cal.** [< Gk. *prisma, prismatos*] —**pris·mat'i·cal·ly** *adv.*

pris·moid (priz'moid) *n.* A body resembling a prism in form. —**pris·moi·dal** (priz·moid'l) *adj.*

pris·on (priz'ən) *n.* A place of confinement; specifically, a public building for the safekeeping of persons in legal custody; a penitentiary. —*v.t.* To imprison. [< F *prisoun* < L *praehensio, -onis* seizure < *praehensus,* pp. of *praehendere*]

pris·on–breach (priz'ən·brēch') *n.* The escape of a prisoner, against the will of his custodian, from the place where he is held in lawful custody. Also **pris'on–break'ing** (-brā'king).

pris·on·er (priz'ən·ər, -nər) *n.* **1** One who is confined in a prison or whose liberty is forcibly restrained; one held in custody; a captive; specifically, in law, a person confined in a prison by virtue of an order of arrest or of a legal committal. 2 A person confined to a place or position through some cause over which he has not control: A sick man is a *prisoner* to his bed. [< OF *prisonier*]

prisoner of war A combatant or person in arms taken by the enemy either by capture or surrender during war.

prisoner's base A game played in various forms and popular in England as early as the 14th century. Opposing players occupy opposite bases, the object being to touch a player of the opposite side while he is away from his base, when he either joins his captor's side or is confined at another goal called a prison.

prison fever Malignant typhus: so called from its former prevalence in prisons: also called *ship fever.*

pris·sy (pris'ē) *adj.* **·si·er, ·si·est** Effeminate; over precise; prim. —*n.* A person who acts, dresses, or speaks very meticulously. [Blend of PRIM or PRECISE + SISSY]

Priš·ti·na (prēsh'ti·na) A city of south central Yugoslavia, capital of an autonomous region included in Serbia as its SW part; a 12th century capital of Serbia; included in Albania 1941–44.

pris·tine (pris'tēn, -tin; *Brit.* pris'tīn) *adj.* Of or pertaining to the earliest state or time; primitive; untouched. See synonyms under FIRST. [< L *pristinus* primitive]

prith·ee (prith'ē) *interj. Archaic* I pray thee.

pri·va·cy (prī'və·sē) *n. pl.* **·cies 1** The condition of being private; seclusion; retirement. 2 A matter that is or should be private. 3 The state of being secret; avoidance of display or publicity; secrecy. 4 A place of seclusion; retreat. See synonyms under RETIREMENT, SECLUSION, SOLITUDE.

Pri·vat·do·zent (prē·vät'dō·tsent') *n. German* A lecturer or tutor recognized by a university but unsalaried and dependent on his student fees. Also **Pri·vat'do·cent'.**

pri·vate (prī'vit) *adj.* **1** Removed from public view; retired; secluded; confidential; secret: a *private* parlor, a *private* agreement. 2 Personal or unofficial, as opposed to public; hence, without rank: a *private* citizen, *private* property, a *private* soldier. 3 Not common or general; special: a *private* interpretation. 4 *Obs.* Privy. See synonyms under SECRET. —*n.* **1** A soldier in the ranks. See table under GRADE. 2 *pl.* The private parts; genitals. 3 Privacy. —**in private** In secret; privately. See synonyms under SECRET. [< L *privatus* apart from the state, orig. pp. of *privare* set apart < *privus* single, one's own. Doublet of PRIVY.] —**pri'vate·ly** *adv.* —**pri'vate·ness** *n.*

private enterprise 1 Business owned and operated by private individuals, as opposed to government-owned operations. 2 An economic system based upon private ownership and operation of business. Also called *free enterprise.*

pri·va·teer (prī'və·tir') *n.* **1** A vessel owned and officered by private persons, but carrying on maritime war under letters of marque. 2 The commander or one of the crew of a privateer: also **pri′va·teers′man.** — *v.i.* To cruise in or as a privateer. — **pri′va·teer′ing** *n.*

private first class A soldier ranking next above a private and below a corporal. See table under GRADE.

private nurse A nurse in exclusive attendance on one patient, whether in a hospital or at home.

private school See under SCHOOL.

pri·va·tion (prī·vā′shən) *n.* 1 The state of lacking something necessary or desirable; especially, want of the common comforts of life. 2 Deprivation. 3 *Logic* The absence from an object of what ordinarily or naturally belongs to objects of that kind. 4 *Eccl.* Suspension or degradation from office, as of a priest. See synonyms under LOSS, POVERTY, WANT. [<OF <L *privatio, -onis* <*privare.* See PRIVATE.]

priv·a·tive (priv′ə·tiv) *adj.* 1 Causing privation, want, or destitution; depriving. 2 *Gram.* Altering a word so as to express a negative instead of a positive meaning; also, denoting negation: *privative* particles (such prefixes and suffixes as *a–, an–, in–, –less*). 3 *Logic* Noting or denoting negation or privation. — *n.* 1 That which has its only reality in the absence of something; a negative conception. 2 *Gram.* A prefix indicating negation; an adjective indicating the absence of that which is ordinarily or naturally inherent. [<L *privativus*] — **priv′a·tive·ly** *adv.* — **priv′a·tive·ness** *n.*

priv·et (priv′it) *n.* 1 An ornamental, bushy European shrub *(Ligustrum vulgare)* with white flowers and black berries, used for hedges: naturalized in the United States. 2 Any other plants of the same genus. 3 The swamp privet, an oleaceous tree *(Forestiera acuminata)* of the southern United States. [Earlier *primet*; prob. infl. by *private* because of its screening effect]

priv·i·lege (priv′ə·lij) *n.* 1 A special or peculiar benefit, favor, or advantage; a right or immunity enjoyed only under special conditions; a prerogative, franchise, or permission: the *privileges* of the rich. 2 A special right or power conferred on or possessed by one or more individuals, in derogation of the general right; also, the law or grant conferring it. 3 An exemption, by virtue of one's office or station, from burdens or liabilities to which others are subject: the *privilege* of a member of Congress. 4 A fundamental or specially important legal or political right: the *privilege* of voting. 5 A form of contract used by speculators, but not recognized by the exchanges, giving the holder the privilege of putting (tendering to) or calling for, or either (in which latter case the privilege is called a *straddle*), a certain number of shares of a certain stock, or a specified quantity, as of grain or provisions, under specified conditions as to time and price. Compare OPTION. 6 An advantage. See synonyms under RIGHT. — *v.t.* **·leged, ·leg·ing** 1 To grant a privilege to. 2 To exempt or free: with *from.* [<OF <L *privilegium* a piece of special legislation < *privus* one's own + *lex, legis* law]

priv·i·leged (priv′ə·lijd) *adj.* Having or invested with a privilege; enjoying a peculiar right or immunity.

priv·i·ly (priv′ə·lē) *adv.* Privately; secretly.

priv·i·ty (priv′ə·tē) *n. pl.* **·ties** 1 Knowledge shared with another or others regarding a private matter: usually implying consent or concurrence. 2 *Law* **a** A mutual or successive relationship to the same rights of property. **b** A participation in interest. **c** A relation to another founded on common knowledge. 3 *Obs.* Privacy; secrecy; a secret. [<OF *privité* <L *privus* one's own]

priv·y (priv′ē) *adj.* 1 Participating with another or others in the knowledge of a secret transaction: with *to*: *privy* to the plot. 2 *Archaic* Removed from publicity; clandestine; secret: a *privy* meeting. 3 Designed for individual or private use; personal: a *privy* purse, *privy* chamber. — *n. pl.* **priv·ies** 1 One who is concerned with another in a matter affecting the interests of both: *privies* in contract, *privies* in estate. 2 A small room or outhouse for evacuation and disposal of feces. See WATERCLOSET. [<F *privé* <L *privatus.* Doublet of PRIVATE.]

Privy Council In Great Britain, the sovereign's ordinary council. Since the duties of government were assumed by the cabinet, the political importance of the Privy Council has largely disappeared.

privy council 1 A body similar to the Privy Council in some British colonies and dominions. 2 A term used by British writers for an analogous body in other countries.

privy councilor 1 A member of a privy council. Also **privy councillor** or **counsellor.**

privy seal In Great Britain, the seal used by the king on papers which later pass under the great seal: also affixed to such documents as do not demand the great seal.

prix fixe (prē fēks′) *French* Table d'hôte: literally, fixed price.

prize[1] (prīz) *n.* 1 That which is offered or won as an honor and reward for superiority or success, as in a contest; an award. 2 Anything to be striven for; a desirable acquisition; also, anything offered or won in a scheme of chance. — *adj.* 1 Offered or awarded as a prize: a *prize* medal. 2 Having drawn a prize; entitled to a prize. 3 Highly valued or esteemed. — *v.t.* **prized, priz·ing** 1 To value highly; regard as very valuable. 2 To estimate the value of; appraise. See synonyms under APPRECIATE, ESTEEM. [Var. of PRICE]

prize[2] (prīz) *n.* 1 In international law, property, as a vessel and cargo, captured by a belligerent at sea in conformity with the laws of war. 2 The act of capturing; also, the person or thing captured. 3 A lever or pry; also, the hold or purchase of a lever: also spelled *prise.* — *v.t.* **prized, priz·ing** 1 To seize as a prize, as a ship. 2 To raise or force with a lever; pry: also spelled *prise.* [<F *prise* something taken, booty, orig. fem. of pp. of *prendre* take <L *praehendere* seize]

prize court A court sitting for the adjudication of prize causes. In the United States the federal courts have exclusive jurisdiction as prize courts.

prize crew A crew put on board a captured vessel by the captor, to navigate and carry her into port.

prize fight A fight between pugilists for a wager or prize, generally limited to a specified number of rounds. — **prize fighter** — **prize fighting**

prize money The proceeds of the sale of a maritime prize, distributable among the officers and crew of the vessel making the capture: abolished in the United States in 1899.

priz·er (prī′zər) *n.* 1 An appraiser. 2 *Archaic* A contestant for a prize, as in athletics.

prize ring A roped enclosure, 16 or 24 feet square, within which pugilists fight; also, with the definite article, professional pugilism.

pro[1] (prō) *n. pl.* **pros** 1 An argument or vote in favor of something: in the phrase *pros and cons.* 2 One who votes for or favors a proposal: usually in the plural. — *adv.* In behalf of; in favor of; for: to argue *pro* and con. [<L *pro* for]

pro[2] (prō) *n. pl.* **pros** *Colloq.* 1 A professional athlete. 2 An expert in any field.

pro–[1] *prefix* 1 Forward; to or toward the front from a position behind; forth: *produce,* to lead forth; *project,* to throw forth. 2 Forth from its place; away: *profugate,* to flee away. 3 To the front of; forward and down: *prolapse,* to slip forward and down. 4 Forward in time or direction: *proceed,* to go forward. 5 In front of: *prohibit,* to hold in front of. 6 In behalf of: *prolocutor.* 7 In place of; substituted for: *procathedral, proconsul.* 8 In favor of: *pro-Russian.* [<L *pro-* <*pro* before, forward, for]

pro–[2] *prefix* 1 Prior; occurring earlier in time: *prognosis.* 2 Situated in front; forward; before: *prognathous.* [<Gk. *pro-* <*pro* before, in front]

pro·a (prō′ə) *n.* A swift Malaysian vessel, sailing equally well in either direction, having a sharp stem and stern, a flat lee side, a single outrigger, and a lateen sail. Also *prahu.* [<Malay *prāu*]

prob·a·bil·ism (prob′ə·bəl·iz′əm) *n. Philos.* 1 The doctrine that certainty is unattainable, but that belief and action must be governed by probability. 2 The doctrine that, as long as the existence, interpretation, or application of a law remains truly doubtful, one may follow his own inclination, on the ground that a doubtful law cannot impose a certain obligation. [<L *probabilis*] — **prob′a·bil·ist** *n.* — **prob′a·bil·is′tic** *adj.*

prob·a·bil·i·ty (prob′ə·bil′ə·tē) *n. pl.* **·ties** 1 The state or quality of being probable; likelihood; also, a probable event or statement. 2 *Stat.* The ratio of the chances favoring an event to the total number of chances for and against it. [<F *probabilité* <L *probabilitas, -tatis* <*probabilis.* See PROBABLE.]

Synonyms: chance, credibility, likelihood, likeliness, presumption, verisimilitude. *Antonyms*: doubt, dubiousness, impossibility, improbability, inconceivability, inconceivableness, unlikelihood.

prob·a·ble (prob′ə·bəl) *adj.* 1 Having more evidence than the contrary, but not proof; likely to be true or to happen, but leaving room for doubt. 2 That renders something worthy of belief, but falls short of demonstration: *probable* evidence. [<OF <L *probabilis* <*probare* prove, test]

Synonyms: credible, likely, presumable, reasonable. See APPARENT, LIKELY. *Antonyms*: doubtful, dubious, improbable, incredible, questionable, unlikely.

probable cause A state of facts to warrant the belief that an accused person committed the crime charged.

prob·a·bly (prob′ə·blē) *adv.* In all probability; so far as the evidence shows; presumably.

pro·bands (prō′bandz) *n. Genetics* The original cases constituting the starting point of studies of a specific tainted family. [<L *probandus* to be proved, gerundive of *probare*]

pro·bang (prō′bang) *n. Med.* A slender, flexible rod, tipped with sponge, ball, button, or other attachment, especially used for the insertion of remedies into, or the removal of an obstruction from, the esophagus or larynx; also, a larger form for the relief of choking cattle. [Earlier *provang,* ? blend of obs. *provet* a probe + *fang* catch; infl. in form by *probe*]

pro·bate (prō′bāt) *adj.* 1 Of or pertaining to a probate court. 2 Pertaining to making proof: *probate* proceedings. — *n.* 1 Formal, legal proof, as of a will. 2 The right or jurisdiction of proving wills. Compare PROBATE COURT under COURT. — *v.t.* **·bat·ed, ·bat·ing** To secure probate of, as a will. [<L *probatus,* pp. of *probare* prove]

pro·ba·tion (prō·bā′shən) *n.* 1 A proceeding designed to test character, qualifications, etc., as of candidates for holy orders; examination; trial; novitiate. 2 In criminal administration, a method of allowing a person convicted of a minor offense to go at large under suspension of sentence, but usually under the supervision of a probation officer. 3 The period throughout which a trial or examination extends. 4 The act of proving; also, proof. [<L *probatio, -onis*] — **pro·ba′tion·al, pro·ba′tion·ar′y** *adj.*

pro·ba·tion·er (prō·bā′shən·ər) *n.* 1 One on probation or trial; a novice. 2 A candidate for membership in a church. 3 A convicted criminal or delinquent allowed to be at large but under the supervision of the convicting court and its probation officer.

probation officer A person delegated by the magistrate of a municipal criminal court to supervise an offender on suspended sentence.

pro·ba·tive (prō′bə·tiv) *adj.* 1 Serving to prove or test. 2 Pertaining to probation; proving. Also **pro·ba·to·ry** (prō′bə·tôr′ē, -tō′rē). [<L *probativus*]

probe (prōb) *v.* **probed, prob·ing** *v.t.* 1 To explore with a probe. 2 To investigate or examine thoroughly. — *v.i.* 3 To penetrate; search. — *n.* 1 *Med.* An instrument for exploring cavities, the course of wounds, etc. 2 That which proves or tests. 3 *U.S.* An examination; a searching investigation or inquiry, especially into crime. 4 A space probe. [<L *probare* <*probus* good, proper. Doublet of PROVE.] — **prob′er** *n.*

pro·bi·ty (prō′bə·tē, prob′ə-) *n.* Virtue or integrity tested and confirmed; strict honesty. See synonyms under VIRTUE. [<F *probité* <L *probitas* <*probus* good, honest]

prob·lem (prob′ləm) *n.* 1 A perplexing question demanding settlement, especially when difficult or uncertain of solution; also, any puzzling circumstance or person. 2 *Math.* A proposition in which some operation or construction is required, as to bisect an angle; anything proposed to be worked out. See synonyms under RIDDLE[2]. — *adj.* 1 Presenting and dealing with a problem, especially a moral, sociological, or emotional problem: *problem* drama. **2** Being a problem, especially in point of behavior, maladjustment, etc.: a *problem* child. [<L *problema* <Gk. *problēma* something thrown forward (for discussion) <*pro-* forward + *ballein* throw]

prob·lem·at·ic (prob′ləm·at′ik) *adj.* Constituting or involving a problem; questionable; contingent. Also **prob′lem·at′i·cal.** [<Gk. *problēmatikos*] **— prob′lem·at′i·cal·ly** *adv.*

pro bo·no pub·li·co (prō bō′nō pub′li·kō) *Latin* For the public good; for the benefit of the public.

pro·bos·cid·i·an (prō′bə·sid′ē·ən) *n.* Any of an order (*Proboscidea*) of ungulates with columnar legs and a snout bearing a proboscis, consisting of the elephants and certain extinct related mammals, as the mammoth, mastodon, etc. *— adj.* **1** Pertaining or belonging to the *Proboscidea.* **2** Of, having, or pertaining to a proboscis.

pro·bos·cis (prō·bos′is) *n.* *pl.* **·bos·cis·es** or **·bos·ci·des** (-bos′ə·dēz) **1** *Zool.* A long flexible snout, as in the tapir; specifically, the trunk of an elephant. **2** *Entomol.* One of various tubular structures protruding or capable of being protruded from the front of the head of certain insects, as the combined mouth parts adapted for sucking in bees, or in certain dipterous insects, as the mosquito, the sheath and needlelike organs for piercing. **3** A human nose, especially when unusually large or prominent: a humorous use. [<L <Gk. *proboskis* <*pro-* before + *boskein* feed]

pro·caine (prō·kān′, prō′kān) *n.* A white crystalline compound, $C_{13}H_{20}O_2N_2$, used in its hydrochloride form as a local anesthetic. [<PRO-[1] + (CO)CAINE]

pro·cam·bi·um (prō·kam′bē·əm) *n.* *Bot.* The nascent tissue giving rise to the vascular bundle of plants. [<NL <PRO-[1] + CAMBIUM] **— pro·cam′bi·al** *adj.*

pro·carp (prō′kärp) *n.* *Bot.* A one– or several–celled female sexual organ in certain algae, which on fertilization becomes a sporocarp. [<PRO-[1] + -CARP]

pro·ca·the·dral (prō′kə·thē′drəl) *n.* A church or edifice used temporarily as a cathedral.

pro·ce·den·do (prō′sə·den′dō) *n.* *pl.* **·dos** *Law* A writ issued by a superior court to an inferior, remitting a cause that had been brought up on insufficient grounds, and commanding the inferior court to proceed to its determination. [<L, oblique case of *procedendum,* gerundive of *procedere* proceed]

pro·ce·dure (prə·sē′jər) *n.* **1** A manner of proceeding or acting; also, an act or a special course of action. **2** The methods or forms of conducting a business, collectively. **3** *Law* The methods of conducting judicial proceedings as distinguished from the legal definition and recognition of rights. **4** A course of action; a proceeding. **5** The manner of carrying on parliamentary affairs. See synonyms under OPERATION. [<F *procédure*] **— pro·ce′du·ral** *adj.*

pro·ceed (prə·sēd′) *v.i.* **1** To go on or forward, especially after a stop or interruption. **2** To begin and carry on an action or process: He *proceeded* to strike her about the head. **3** To issue or come, as from some cause, source, or origin: with *from.* **4** *Law* To institute and carry on legal proceedings. [<OF *proceder* <L *procedere* go forward <*pro-* forward + *cedere* go] **— pro·ceed′er** *n.*

pro·ceed·ing (prə·sē′ding) *n.* **1** An act or course of action; a transaction or procedure: an outrageous *proceeding.* **2** The action of issuing forth; emanation. **3** *pl.* The records or minutes of the meetings of a society, etc. **4** *Law* **a** Any action instituted in a court: a judicial *proceeding.* **b** Any of the various steps taken in a cause by either party: a *proceeding* by writ of error. See synonyms under ACT, TRANSACTION.

pro·ceeds (prō′sēdz) *n. pl.* The useful or material results of an action or course; also, that which accrues therefrom; the amount derived from the disposal of goods, work, or the use of capital; return; yield. See synonyms under HARVEST, PRODUCT, PROFIT.

proc·e·leus·mat·ic (pros′ə·lo͞os·mat′ik) *adj.* **1** In prosody, composed of four short syllables, or pertaining to feet so composed. **2** Animating or inciting, as a song. *— n.* A metrical foot of four short syllables. [<Gk. *prokeleusmatikos* <*prokeleusma* incitement <*prokeleuein* incite <*pro-* before + *keleuein* rouse]

pro·ce·phal·ic (prō′sə·fal′ik) *adj.* *Anat.* Of or pertaining to the anterior part of the head: a *procephalic* lobe of an invertebrate.

proc·ess (pros′es, *esp. Brit.* prō′ses) *n.* **1** A course or method of operations in the production of something: a metallurgical *process.* **2** A forward movement; progressive or continuous proceeding; passage; advance; course. **3** Any judicial writ or order issued at the commencement or during the progress of an action, as summons, citation, subpoena, or execution; especially, a writ issued to bring a defendant into court; also, the whole course of proceedings in a cause, civil or criminal, from beginning to end. **4** *Biol.* An accessory outgrowth or prominence of an organism. **5** *Physiol.* The fibrous prolongation from the body of the nerve cell (neuron) that carries the outgoing nervous impulse. **6** In patent law, a means of effecting a result otherwise than by mechanism, as by chemical action. **7** *Phot.* Any of the modern methods of producing relief printing surfaces by photography and mechanical or chemical means. *— adj.* **1** Produced by a special method: *process* butter; *process* cheese. **2** Pertaining to, for, or made by, a mechanical or chemical photographic process: a *process* illustration. *— v.t.* **1** To treat or prepare by a special method. **2** *Law* **a** To issue or serve a process on. **b** To proceed against. [<L *processus* progress, orig. pp. of *procedere.* See PROCEED.]

processing tax A tax imposed by the government on the processing of various farm products.

pro·ces·sion (prə·sesh′ən) *n.* **1** An array, as of persons or vehicles, arranged in succession and moving in a formal manner; a parade: a funeral *procession;* also, any continuous course: the *procession* of the stars. **2** The act of proceeding or issuing forth: the *procession* of the Holy Ghost from the Father. **3** A litany or hymn sung by persons moving in orderly array; a processional. *— v.i.* To march in procession. [<OF]

Synonyms: cavalcade, column, cortège, train. *Antonyms*: herd, mob, rabble, rout.

pro·ces·sion·al (prə·sesh′ən·əl) *adj.* Of or pertaining to or moving in a procession. *— n.* **1** A book containing the services in a religious procession. **2** A hymn sung during a religious procession. **— pro·ces′sion·al·ly** *adv.*

process printing Color printing from halftone plates each of which carries one of the primary colors, red, yellow, and blue, with sometimes a fourth plate for black.

process server A person, as a deputy sheriff, who serves summonses or processes.

pro·cès–ver·bal (prô·se′ver·bàl′) *n.* *pl.* **·baux** (-bō′) In French law, a detailed statement in writing made by an official relating to the commission of a crime within his jurisdiction; hence, any official report. [<F, lit., verbal process]

pro·chein (prō′shen) *adj.* *Law* Nearest in time, relation, or degree. Also **pro·chain** (prō′shān, *Fr.* prô·shaṅ′). [<F *prochain* <L *proximus* next]

pro·claim (prō·klām′) *v.t.* **1** To announce or make known publicly or officially; declare. **2** To make plain; manifest: His manner *proclaimed* his innocence. **3** To outlaw, prohibit, or restrict by proclamation. See synonyms under ANNOUNCE, AVOW, PUBLISH. [<OF *proclamer* <L *proclamare* <*pro-* before + *clamare* call] **— pro·claim′er** *n.*

proc·la·ma·tion (prok′lə·mā′shən) *n.* **1** The act of proclaiming. **2** That which is proclaimed; a public authoritative announcement. [<OF *proclamacion*]

pro·clit·ic (prō·klit′ik) *adj.* Attached to or dependent on a following word: said of monosyllables attached so closely as to have no separate accent. Compare ENCLITIC, ATONIC. *— n.* A proclitic word. [<NL *procliticus* <Gk. *proklinein* lean forward; formed on analogy of ENCLITIC]

pro·cliv·i·ty (prō·kliv′ə·tē) *n.* *pl.* **·ties** Natural disposition or tendency; propensity: usually with *to*: a *proclivity* to grumble. See synonyms under APPETITE, DESIRE, INCLINATION. [<L *proclivitas* <*proclivus* downward <*pro-* before + *clivus* slope]

Proc·ne (prok′nē) In Greek mythology, an Athenian princess whom the gods transformed into a swallow after she killed her son. Compare PHILOMELA.

pro·con·sul (prō·kon′səl) *n.* **1** In ancient Rome, an official, usually an ex–consul, who exercised consular authority over a province or an army. **2** A governor of a dependency, especially a British one; a viceroy. [<L] **— pro·con′su·lar** (-sə·lər) *adj.* **— pro·con′su·late** (-sə·lit), **pro·con′sul·ship** *n.*

Pro·con·sul (prō·kon′səl) *n.* *Paleontol.* An extinct ape related to Dryopithecus. [<NL]

Pro·co·pi·us (prō·kō′pē·əs), 500?–565?, Byzantine historian.

pro·cras·ti·nate (prō·kras′tə·nāt) *v.* **·nat·ed, ·nat·ing** *v.i.* To put off taking action until a future time; be dilatory. *— v.t.* To defer or postpone. [<L *procrastinatus,* pp. of *procrastinare* <*pro-* forward + *crastinus* pertaining to the morrow <*cras* tomorrow] **— pro·cras′ti·na′tor** *n.*

Synonyms: adjourn, defer, delay, postpone. See POSTPONE. *Antonyms*: accelerate, dispatch, drive, expedite, hasten, hurry, press, quicken, urge.

pro·cras·ti·na·tion (prō·kras′tə·nā′shən) *n.* The act, tendency, or habit of procrastinating; dilatoriness; delay.

pro·cre·ant (prō′krē·ənt) *adj.* Effecting, conducive to, or connected with procreation or reproduction; generating; fruitful. [<L *procreans, -antis*]

pro·cre·ate (prō′krē·āt) *v.t.* **·at·ed, ·at·ing** **1** To engender or beget (offspring). **2** To originate; produce. See synonyms under PROPAGATE. [<L *procreatus,* pp. of *procreare* <*pro-* before + *creare* create] **— pro′cre·a′tion** *n.* **— pro′cre·a′tor** *n.*

pro·cre·a·tive (prō′krē·ā′tiv) *adj.* Possessed of generative power; reproductive; pertaining to procreation.

Pro·crus·te·an (prō·krus′tē·ən) *adj.* **1** Pertaining to or characteristic of Procrustes. **2** Hence, ruthlessly or violently forcing to conform.

Pro·crus·tes (prō·krus′tēz) In Greek mythology, an Attic giant, killed by Theseus, who tied travelers to an iron bed and amputated or stretched their limbs until they fitted it. [<L <Gk. *Prokroustēs* <*prokrouein* stretch out <*pro-* thoroughly + *krouein* beat]

pro·cryp·tic (prō·krip′tik) *adj.* *Biol.* **1** Having protective or imitative coloration: said of certain animals, insects, etc. **2** Having the power to adapt coloration to environment, as chameleons. [<PRO-[1] + CRYPTIC]

procto– *combining form Med.* Related to or affecting the rectum or anus: *proctology.* Also, before vowels, **proct–.** [<Gk. *proktos* the anus]

proc·tol·o·gy (prok·tol′ə·jē) *n.* The branch of medicine which treats of the anatomy, physiology, and diseases of the rectum. [<PROCTO- + -LOGY] **— proc·to·log·i·cal** (prok′tə·loj′i·kəl) *adj.* **— proc·tol′o·gist** *n.*

proc·to·plas·ty (prok′tə·plas′tē) *n.* Plastic surgery of the rectum and anus. [<PROCTO- + -PLASTY]

proc·tor (prok′tər) *n.* **1** An agent acting for another; attorney; proxy; specifically, a practitioner in an admiralty, ecclesiastical, or probate court. **2** A university or college official charged with maintaining order, supervising examinations, etc. *— v.t.* & *v.i.* To supervise (an examination). [ME *proketour, procutour,* contraction of L *procurator* PROCURATOR] **— proc·to·ri·al** (prok·tôr′ē·əl, -tō′rē-) *adj.* **— proc′tor·ship** *n.*

proc·to·scope (prok′tə·skōp) *n.* A surgical instrument for examining the interior of the rectum. **— proc·tos·co·py** (prok·tos′kə·pē) *n.*

Proc·u·lus (prok′yə·ləs), 412?–485, Greek Neo–Platonist and religious commentator. Also **Pro·clos** (prō′kləs, prok′ləs).

pro·cum·bent (prō·kum′bənt) *adj.* **1** *Bot.* Lying on the ground; trailing: said of certain vines and trailing plants. **2** Leaning forward or lying down or on the face; prone; prostrate. [<L *procumbens, -entis,* ppr. of *procumbere* lean forward <*pro-* forward + *cubare* lie down]

pro·cur·a·ble (prō·kyŏŏr′ə·bəl) *adj.* That can be procured.

proc·u·ra·cy (prok′yər·ə·sē) *n. pl.* **·cies** The management of another's affairs; the office or service of a procurator or proctor.

pro·cur·ance (prō·kyŏŏr′əns) *n.* The process of procuring. Also **pro·cur′al.**

proc·u·ra·tion (prok′yə·rā′shən) *n.* **1** The act of procuring. **2** *Law* **a** The function of an attorney; an agency; a proxy. **b** A power of attorney. [<F <L *procuratio, -onis*] — **proc′u·ra·to′ry** (-rə·tôr′ē, -tō′rē) *adj.*

proc·u·ra·tor (prok′yə·rā′tər) *n.* **1** A person authorized and employed to act for and manage the affairs of another. **2** In ancient Rome, one who had charge of the imperial revenues; an imperial collector, especially in a province; a provincial administrator; a viceroy. **3** The public magistrate of some Italian cities. [<L <*procurare.* See PROCURE.] — **proc′u·ra·to′ri·al** (-rə·tôr′ē·əl, -tō′rē-) *adj.* — **proc′u·ra′tor·ship** *n.*

pro·cure (prō·kyŏŏr′) *v.* **·cured, ·cur·ing** *v.t.* **1** To obtain by some effort or means; acquire. **2** To bring about; cause. **3** To obtain (women) for the gratification of the lust of others. — *v.i.* **4** To be a procurer or procuress. See synonyms under GAIN, GET, OBTAIN, PROVIDE, PURCHASE. [<F <L *procurare* look after <*pro-* on behalf of + *curare* attend to <*cura* care]

pro·cure·ment (prō·kyŏŏr′mənt) *n.* **1** The act of procuring; obtainment; attainment. **2** The act of effecting or causing to be effected.

pro·cur·er (prō·kyŏŏr′ər) *n.* One who procures for another, as to gratify lust; a pander. [<AF *procurour* <L *procurator*] — **pro·cur′ess** *n. fem.*

Pro·cy·on (prō′sē·on) *n.* The most conspicuous star in the constellation Canis Minor; magnitude, 0.5. See STAR. [<L <Gk. *Prokyōn* <*pro-* before + *kyōn* dog]

prod (prod) *v.t.* **prod·ded, prod·ding** **1** To punch or poke with or as with a pointed instrument. **2** To arouse mentally; urge; goad. — *n.* **1** Any pointed instrument used for prodding; a goad. **2** A thrust or punch with or as with a prod; a poke. **3** Hence, a reminder. [Origin unknown] — **prod′der** *n.*

prod·i·gal (prod′ə·gəl) *adj.* **1** Addicted to wasteful expenditure, as of money, time, or strength; extravagant. **2** Yielding in profusion; bountiful. **3** Lavish; profuse. — *n.* One who is wasteful or profligate; a spendthrift. See synonyms under IMPROVIDENT. [<OF <Med. L *prodigalis* <L *prodigus* wasteful <*prodigere* drive forth, get rid of <*pro-* forward + *agere* drive] — **prod′i·gal·ly** *adv.*

prod·i·gal·i·ty (prod′ə·gal′ə·tē) *n. pl.* **·ties** Extravagance; wastefulness; lavishness; also, bounteousness. See synonyms under EXCESS. [<OF *prodigalité*]

pro·dig·ious (prə·dij′əs) *adj.* **1** Enormous or extraordinary in size, quantity, or degree; vast; excessive. **2** Marvelous; amazing. **3** *Obs.* Of the nature of a prodigy. See synonyms under IMMENSE. [<L *prodigiosus*] — **pro·dig′ious·ly** *adv.* — **pro·dig′ious·ness** *n.*

prod·i·gy (prod′ə·jē) *n. pl.* **·gies** **1** Something so extraordinary as to excite wonder and admiration. **2** A person or thing of remarkable qualities or powers: an infant *prodigy.* **3** Something out of the ordinary course of nature; a monstrosity. **4** *Archaic* A portent. [<L *prodigium*]

Synonyms: marvel, monster, miracle, portent, wonder.

pro·drome (prō′drōm) *n. Pathol.* A sign of approaching disease; a premonitory symptom. [<F <L *prodromus* <Gk. *prodromos* forerunner <*pro-* before + *dromos* a running] — **prod·ro·mal** (prod′rə·məl) *adj.*

pro·duce (prə·dōōs′, -dyōōs′) *v.* **·duced, ·duc·ing** *v.t.* **1** To bring forth or bear; yield, as young or a natural product. **2** To bring forth by mental effort; compose, write, etc.: to *produce* a book. **3** To bring about; cause to happen or be: His words *produced* a violent reaction. **4** To bring to view; exhibit; show: to *produce* evidence. **5** To manufacture; make. **6** To bring to performance before the public, as a play. **7** To extend or lengthen, as a line. **8** *Econ.* To create (anything with exchangeable value). — *v.i.* **9** To yield or generate an appropriate product or result. — **prod·uce** (prod′ōōs, -yōōs, prō′dōōs, -dyōōs) *n.* That which is produced; a product; specifically, farm products collectively. See synonyms under HARVEST, PRODUCT, WEALTH. [<L *producere* lead forward <*pro-* forward + *ducere* lead] — **pro·duc′i·ble** *adj.*

Synonyms (verb): bear, breed, cause, create, effect, engender, furnish, generate, make, manufacture, occasion, originate, propagate, yield. See ALLEGE, EFFECT, PROVIDE.

pro·duc·er (prə·dōō′sər, -dyōō′-) *n.* **1** One who produces. **2** One who cultivates or makes things for sale and use in distinction from the user or consumer. **3** That which produces or generates. **4** An apparatus for manufacturing producer gas.

producer gas A combustible gas formed by driving air and steam over burning coke: used for heating and to drive engines for power.

producers' goods *Econ.* Goods having indirect use, as tools or raw materials used in making other goods: opposed to *consumers' goods.*

prod·uct (prod′əkt, -ukt) *n.* **1** Anything produced or obtained as a result of some operation or work, as by generation, growth, labor, study, or skill. **2** *Math.* The result obtained by multiplication. **3** *Chem.* Any substance resulting from chemical change. Compare EDUCT. [<L *productus,* pp. of *producere.* See PRODUCE.]

Synonyms: crop, effect, fruit, harvest, outcome, output, proceeds, produce, production, result, return, yield. See HARVEST, WORK.

pro·duc·tile (prə·duk′til) *adj.* Capable of being extended or drawn out. [<PRO-[1] + DUCTILE]

pro·duc·tion (prə·duk′shən) *n.* **1** The act or process of producing. **2** In political economy, a producing for use, involving the creating or increasing of economic wealth: in contradistinction to *consumption* (by use). **3** That which is produced or made; any tangible result of industrial, artistic, or literary labor. [<F <L *productio, -onis* a prolongation]

Synonyms: composition, performance, work. See PRODUCT, WORK.

pro·duc·tive (prə·duk′tiv) *adj.* **1** Producing or tending to produce; fertile; creative, as of artistic things. **2** Producing or tending to produce profits or increase in quantity, quality, or value: *productive* labor. **3** Causing; resulting in: with *of.* See synonyms under FERTILE, PROFITABLE. [<Med. L *productivus* <LL, fit for production] — **pro·duc′tive·ly** *adv.* — **pro·duc·tiv·i·ty** (prō′·duk·tiv′ə·tē), **pro·duc′·tive·ness** *n.*

pro·em (prō′əm) *n.* An introductory statement; preface; prelude. [<OF *proeme* <L *prooemium* <Gk. *prooimion* an overture <*pro-* before + *oimē* way of a song, lay] — **pro·e·mi·al** (prō·ē′mē·əl) *adj.*

pro et con (prō′ et kon′) *Latin* For and against.

prof·a·na·tion (prof′ə·nā′shən) *n.* **1** The act of profaning; abuse or dishonoring of sacred things; desecration. **2** Abusive or improper treatment of anything; misuse. [<F <LL *profanatio, -onis*]

pro·fane (prə·fān′) *v.t.* **·faned, ·fan·ing** **1** To treat (something sacred) with irreverence or abuse; desecrate; pollute. **2** To put to an unworthy or degrading use; debase. See synonyms under VIOLATE. — *adj.* **1** Manifesting irreverence, disrespect, or undue familiarity toward the Deity or sacred things; blasphemous. **2** Secular: opposed to *sacred.* **3** Not initiated into the inner mysteries; hence, vulgar; common. [<F *profaner* <L *profanare* <*profanus* before or outside the temple, hence, unsacred <*pro-* before + *fanum* temple] — **pro·fan·a·to·ry** (prə·fan′ə·tôr′ē, -tō′rē) *adj.* — **pro·fane′ly** *adv.* — **pro·fan′er** *n.*

Synonyms (adj.): blasphemous, godless, impious, irreligious, sacrilegious, secular, temporal, unconsecrated, ungodly, unhallowed, unholy, unsanctified, wicked, worldly. *Antonyms*: consecrated, devout, godly, holy, pious, religious, reverent, sacred, sanctified, spiritual.

pro·fan·i·ty (prə·fan′ə·tē) *n. pl.* **·ties** **1** The state of being profane. **2** Profane speech or action. Also **pro·fane′ness** (-fān′nis). See synonyms under OATH.

pro·fa·num vul·gus (prō·fā′nəm vul′gəs) *Latin* The common herd.

pro·fert (prō′fərt) *n. Law* The formal allegation in a pleading or on the record that the pleader produces in court an instrument on which an action or defense is founded. [<L, he brings forward]

pro·fess (prə·fes′) *v.t.* **1** To declare openly; avow; affirm. **2** To assert, usually insincerely; make a pretense of: to *profess* remorse. **3** To declare or affirm faith in: to *profess* Taoism. **4** To claim skill or learning in; have as one's profession: to *profess* the law. **5** To receive into a religious order. — *v.i.* **6** To make open declaration; avow; offer public affirmation. **7** To take the vows of a religious order. See synonyms under ACKNOWLEDGE, AVOW, PRETEND. [<OF *professe,* fem. of *profes* bound by a vow <L *professus,* pp. of *profiteri* avow, confess <*pro-* before + *fateri* confess]

pro·fess·ed·ly (prə·fes′id·lē) *adv.* **1** By open profession; avowedly. **2** Pretendedly.

pro·fes·sion (prə·fesh′ən) *n.* **1** An occupation that properly involves a liberal education or its equivalent, and mental rather than manual labor; especially, one of **the three learned professions,** law, medicine, or theology. **2** Hence, any calling or occupation other than commercial, manual, etc., involving special attainments or discipline, as editing, music, teaching, etc.; also, the collective body of those following such vocation. **3** The act of professing or declaring; declaration; avowal: *professions* of good will. **4** That which is avowed or professed; a declaration; a faith; also, a pretense: His *professions* are not trustworthy. See synonyms under BUSINESS. [<F]

pro·fes·sion·al (prə·fesh′ən·əl) *adj.* **1** Connected with, preparing for, engaged in, appropriate, or conforming to a profession: *professional* courtesy, a *professional* soldier, a *professional* job. **2** Of or pertaining to a special occupation, often for gain: opposed to *amateur*: a *professional* ball game or player. — *n.* **1** One who pursues as a business some vocation or occupation. **2** A person who engages for money to compete in sports: opposed to *amateur.* **3** One skilled in a profession. — **pro·fes′sion·al·ly** *adv.*

pro·fes·sion·al·ism (prə·fesh′ən·əl·iz′əm) *n.* **1** The methods, manner, or spirit of a profession; also, its practitioners. **2** The practice of some profession as a business: opposed to *amateurism.*

pro·fes·sor (prə·fes′ər) *n.* **1** A teacher of the highest grade in a university or college, or in an institution where professional or technical studies are pursued; usually, an officer holding a chair in some particular branch of higher instruction. **2** One who professes skill and offers instruction in some sport or art: a *professor* of gymnastics. **3** One who makes open declaration of his opinions or sentiments; specifically, one who avows a religious faith. [<L, a public teacher <*professus.* See PROFESS.]

pro·fes·sor·ate (prə·fes′ər·it) *n.* The position of a professor.

pro·fes·so·ri·al (prō′fə·sôr′ē·əl, -sō′rē-, prof′ə-) *adj.* Of or pertaining to a professor; pedagogic; academic. — **pro′fes·so′ri·al·ly** *adv.*

pro·fes·so·ri·ate (prō′fə·sôr′ē·it, -sō′rē-, prof′·ə-) *n.* Professors collectively, as in a college; professorship.

pro·fes·sor·ship (prə·fes′ər·ship) *n.* The office and duties of a professor; the state of being a professor.

prof·fer (prof′ər) *v.t.* To offer for acceptance. — *n.* The act of proffering, or that which is proffered; a tender; offer. [<AF *proffrir,* OF *poroffrir* <*por-* (<L *pro-*) in behalf of + L *offerre.* See OFFER.] — **prof′fer·er** *n.*

pro·fi·cien·cy (prə·fish′ən·sē) *n. pl.* **·cies** An advanced state of attainment in some knowledge, art, or skill; expertness.

pro·fi·cient (prə·fish′ənt) *adj.* Thoroughly versed, as in an art or science; skilled; expert. — *n.* An expert in any branch of skill or knowledge; an adept. See synonyms under SKILFUL. [<L *proficiens, -entis,* ppr. of *proficere* make progress, go forward <*pro-* forward + *facere* do] — **pro·fi′cient·ly** *adv.*

pro·file (prō′fīl, *esp. Brit.* prō′fēl) *n.* **1** An outline, or contour; a drawing in outline. **2** *Archit.* The outline of a perpendicular section of a building, fort, etc., or the contour of an architectural member, as a base or cornice. **3** A drawing showing the outline of a human face or figure as seen from the side. **4** A short biographical sketch vividly presenting the most striking characteristics of a personality. **5** Degree of exposure to public attention; public image: The army generals who seized control maintained a very low *profile.* **6** A vertical section of soil extending from the surface through all its levels to the underlying parent material. —*v.t.* **·filed, ·fil·ing 1** To draw a profile of; outline. **2** To write a profile of. [<Ital. *profilo, proffilo* outline <*proffilare* draw in outline <L *pro-* forward + *filum* thread, line]

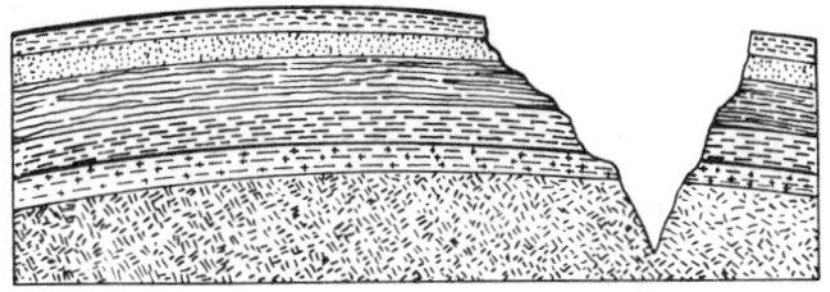

PROFILE OF GRAND CANYON AND KAIBAB PLATEAU

profile drag *Aeron.* The difference between the total wing drag of an airplane and the induced drag.

prof·it (prof′it) *n.* **1** Any accession of good—physical, mental, or moral—from labor or exertion; benefit; return. **2** *Often pl.* Excess of returns over outlay or expenditure: a business yielding fair *profits.* **3** The return from the employment of capital after deducting the amount paid for raw material and for wages, real or estimated rent, interest, insurance, etc. **4** That part of the amount received for goods which exceeds the sum originally paid for them with or without all secondary expenses involved. **5** The income of invested property without counting its increased value by any actual rise in the market. **6** In invested capital, the ratio of the increment to the actual amount of capital for a given year. —**gross profit** The profit apparent on the face of a transaction or business; the excess of receipts from sales over expenditures for purchase: opposed to **net profit,** the surplus remaining after all necessary deductions, as for interest, transportation, bad debts, etc. —*v.i.* **1** To be of advantage or benefit. **2** To derive gain or benefit. —*v.t.* **3** To be of profit or advantage to. ◆ Homophone: *prophet.* [<OF <L *profectus,* pp. of *proficere* go forward. See PROFICIENT.]

Synonyms (noun): advantage, avail, benefit, emolument, expediency, gain, good, improvement, proceeds, receipts, return, returns, service, utility, value. The *returns* or *receipts* include all that is received from any outlay or investment; the *profit* is the excess (if any) of the *receipts* over the outlay; hence, in government, morals, etc., the *profit* is what is really good, helpful, useful, valuable. *Utility* is chiefly used in the sense of some immediate or personal and generally some material *good. Advantage* is that which gives one a vantage ground, either for coping with competitors or with difficulties, needs, or demands; as, to have the *advantage* of a good education; it is frequently used of what one has beyond another or secures at the expense of another; as, to have the *advantage* in argument, or to take *advantage* in a bargain. *Gain* is what one secures beyond what he previously possessed. *Benefit* is anything that does one good. *Emolument* is *profit, return,* or *value* accruing through official position. *Expediency* has respect to *profit* or *advantage,* real or supposed, considered apart from or perhaps in opposition to right, in actions having a moral character. See UTILITY. *Antonyms*: damage, detriment, disadvantage, harm, hurt, injury, loss, ruin, waste.

prof·it·a·ble (prof′it·ə·bəl) *adj.* Bringing profit or gain; remunerative; advantageous. —**prof′·it·a·ble·ness** *n.* —**prof′it·a·bly** *adv.*

Synonyms: advantageous, beneficial, desirable, expedient, gainful, lucrative, productive, remunerative, useful. See EXPEDIENT, GOOD, USEFUL. Compare synonyms for PROFIT. *Antonyms*: detrimental, disadvantageous, disastrous, fruitless, harmful, hurtful, undesirable, unproductive, unprofitable, worthless.

profit and loss In bookkeeping, an account in the ledger in which profits are entered on the creditor side and losses on the debtor side. —**prof′it-and-loss′** (prof′it·ənd·lôs′, -los′) *adj.*

prof·i·teer (prof′ə·tir′) *v.i.* To seek or obtain excessive profits. —*n.* One who is given to making excessive profits, especially to the detriment of others. —**prof′i·teer′ing** *n.*

prof·it·less (prof′it·lis) *adj.* Resulting in no gain or benefit; unprofitable.

prof·it–shar·ing (prof′it·shâr′ing) *n.* A system of remuneration by which workmen are given a percentage, according to wages, of the net profits of a business. —*adj.* Of or related to profit-sharing.

prof·li·ga·cy (prof′lə·gə·sē) *n.* **1** Corruptness of morals; viciousness of character or conduct. **2** Great extravagance; wastefulness; overabundance. Also **prof′li·gate·ness** (-git·nis, -gāt′nis).

prof·li·gate (prof′lə·git, -gāt) *adj.* **1** Lost or insensible to principle, virtue, or decency; abandoned to vice. **2** Recklessly extravagant; in great profusion. —*n.* **1** A depraved or dissolute person. **2** A reckless spendthrift. See synonyms under IMMORAL. [<L *profligatus,* pp. of *profligare* strike to the ground, destroy <*pro-* forward + *fligere* dash] —**prof′li·gate·ly** *adv.*

prof·lu·ent (prof′lo͞o·ənt) *adj.* Fluent. [<L *profluens, -entis,* ppr. of *profluere* flow along <*pro-* before + *fluere* flow] —**prof′lu·ence** *n.*

pro for·ma (prō fôr′mə) *Latin* As a matter of form.

pro·found (prə·found′) *adj.* **1** Intellectually deep; thorough; exhaustive: *profound* learning. **2** Reaching to, arising from, or affecting the depth of one's nature or of any matter: *profound* respect. **3** Situated far below the surface; deep; unfathomable. **4** Bent low: said of a bow. —*n.* **1** A fathomless depth; an abyss. **2** The ocean; the deep. See synonyms under OBSCURE, WISE. [<OF *profond* <L *profundus* <*pro-* very + *fundus* deep] —**pro·found′ly** *adv.* —**pro·found′ness** *n.*

pro·fun·di·ty (prə·fun′də·tē) *n. pl.* **·ties 1** The state or quality of being profound, in any sense; depth. **2** A deep place or thing. **3** A profound or abstruse statement, theory, or the like. See synonyms under WISDOM. [<OF *profundité* <LL *profunditas*]

pro·fuse (prə·fyo͞os′) *adj.* **1** Giving or given forth lavishly; liberal; extravagant; prodigal. **2** Copious; overflowing: *profuse* vegetation. [<L *profusus,* pp. of *profundere* pour forth <*pro-* forward + *fundere* pour] —**pro·fuse′ly** *adv.* —**pro·fuse′ness** *n.*

pro·fu·sion (prə·fyo͞o′zhən) *n.* **1** A lavish supply or condition; plenty: a *profusion* of ornaments. **2** The act of pouring forth or supplying in great abundance; prodigality: *profusion* in giving. See synonyms under EXCESS. [<F]

pro·gen·i·tor (prō·jen′ə·tər) *n.* A forefather or parent. [<L <*progenitus,* pp. of *progignere* beget <*pro-* forth + *gignere* beget] —**pro·gen′i·tor·ship′** *n.*

prog·e·ny (proj′ə·nē) *n. pl.* **·nies** Offspring. [<L *progenies* <*progignere.* See PROGENITOR.]

pro·ge·ri·a (prō·jir′ē·ə) *n. Pathol.* Retarded development with premature senility. [<NL <PRO-[1] + Gk. *gēras* old age]

pro·ges·ta·tion·al (prō′jes·tā′shən·əl) *adj. Med.* **1** Promoting gestation. **2** Designating those substances and processes which are active in the menstrual cycle or during pregnancy.

pro·ges·ter·one (prō·jes′tə·rōn) *n. Biochem.* A hormone from the corpus luteum: isolated as a white, crystalline compound, $C_{21}H_{30}O_2$, and also made synthetically. It is active in preparing the uterus for reception of the fertilized ovum. [<PRO-[1] + GE(STATION) + STER(OL) + -ONE]

pro·ges·tin (prō·jes′tin) *n. Biochem.* **1** Any substance which promotes the gestational activity of the corpus luteum and uterus after fertilization of the ovum. **2** Progesterone.

pro·glot·tid (prō·glot′id) *n. pl.* **·glot·ti·des** (-glot′ə·dēz) *Zool.* One of the segments or joints of a tapeworm, in which the reproductive organs develop. Also **pro·glot′tis.** [<NL *proglottis, proglottidis* <Gk. *proglossis* tip of the tongue; from its shape] —**pro·glot′tic** *adj.*

prog·na·thous (prog′nə·thəs, prog·nā′-) *adj.* Having projecting jaws: opposed to *opisthognathous.* Also **prog·nath·ic** (prog·nath′ik). [<PRO-[2] + -GNATHOUS] —**prog·na·thism** (prog′nə·thiz′əm), **prog·na·thy** (prog′nə·thē) *n.*

prog·no·sis (prog·nō′sis) *n. pl.* **·ses** (-sēz) **1** *Med.* A prediction or conclusion in regard to the course and termination of a disease. **2** Any prediction or forecast; foreknowledge. [<NL <Gk. *prognōsis* <*pro-* before + *gignōskein* know]

prog·nos·tic (prog·nos′tik) *adj.* Relating to prognosis. —*n.* **1** A sign of some future occurrence; an omen. **2** *Med.* A symptom indicative of the course of a disease. [<Med. L *prognosticum* omen <Gk. *prognōstikon* <*prognōsis.* See PROGNOSIS.]

prog·nos·ti·cate (prog·nos′tə·kāt) *v.t.* **·cat·ed, ·cat·ing 1** To foretell (future events, etc.) by present indications. **2** To indicate beforehand; foreshadow. See synonyms under AUGUR, PROPHESY. [<Med. L *prognosticatus,* pp. of *prognosticare* <L *prognosticum.* See PROGNOSTIC.] —**prog·nos′ti·ca′tor** *n.*

prog·nos·ti·ca·tion (prog·nos′tə·kā′shən) *n.* **1** The act of prognosticating; prediction. **2** That which foretokens.

pro·gram (prō′gram, -grəm) *n.* **1** A list giving in order the items, turns, selections, etc., making up an entertainment; also, the selections, etc., collectively. **2** Any prearranged plan or course of proceedings; a prospectus. **3** *Electronics* A sequence of instructions set up on the control panels of an electronic computer as guides in the performance of a desired operation or group of operations. **4** A preface, or prefatory statement. **5** *Obs.* A public proclamation; official edict or decree. Also *Brit.* **pro′gramme.** —*v.t.* **·gramed** or **·grammed, ·gram·ing** or **·gram·ming 1** To arrange in an appropriate sequence the separate items of (a program, set of instructions, etc.). **2** To schedule (an act, performer, etc.) for a program. **3** To furnish a program for (a computer). **4** To feed (information, instructions, etc.) into a computer. [<F *programme* <LL *programma* public announcement <Gk. <*prographein* write in public <*pro-* before + *graphein* write] —**pro′gram·er** or **pro′gram·mer** *n.* —**pro·gram·mat·ic** (prō′·grə·mat′ik) *adj.*

programed instruction Instruction in which the learner responds to a prearranged series of questions, items, or statements, using various printed texts, audio-visual means, or a teaching machine. Also **programmed instruction.**

program music Descriptive music; music intended to suggest moods, scenes, or incidents: distinguished from *absolute music.*

Pro·gre·so (prō·grā′sō) A port of entry in Yucatán state, SE Mexico.

prog·ress (prog′res, *esp. Brit.* prō′gres) *n.* **1** A moving forward in space; movement forward nearer a goal. **2** Advancement toward maturity or completion; gradual development, as of mankind or civilization; improvement. **3** A journey of state, as of a monarch.

—**pro·gress** (prə·gres′) *v.i.* **1** To move forward or onward. **2** To advance toward completion or fuller development. [<OF *progres* <L *progressus,* pp. of *progredi* go forward <*pro-* forward + *gradi* walk]

Synonyms (noun): advance, advancement, attainment, development, growth, improvement, increase, proficiency, progression. *Attainment, development,* and *proficiency* are more absolute than the other words of the group, denoting some point of advantage or of comparative perfection reached by forward or onward movement; we speak of *attainments* in scholarship, *proficiency* in music or languages, the *development* of new powers or organs; *proficiency* includes the idea of skill. *Advance* denotes a forward movement or the point gained by forward movement; *progress* (Latin *progredior,* walk forward) is steady and constant forward movement, admitting of pause, but not of retreat. Compare ATTAIN. *Antonyms*: check, decline, delay, retreat, recession, retrogression, stay, stop, stoppage.

pro·gres·sion (prə·gresh′ən) *n.* **1** The act of progressing; advancement. **2** *Math.* A sequence of numbers or quantities each of which is derived from the preceding by a constant law. See ARITHMETIC PROGRESSION, GEOMETRIC PROGRESSION, SERIES (def. 2). **3** *Music* a An advance from one tone or chord to another. b A sequence or succession of tones or chords. 4 Course or lapse of time; passage. See synonyms under PROGRESS. [<L *progressio, -onis*] — **pro·gres'sion·al** *adj.* — **pro·gres'sion·ism** *n.*

pro·gres·sion·ist (prə·gresh'ən·ist) *n.* 1 One who believes that society is progressing toward perfection. 2 An evolutionist.

prog·ress·ist (prog'res·ist, prō'gres-) *n.* 1 A progressionist. 2 A member of any party devoted to some scheme of progress.

pro·gres·sive (prə·gres'iv) *adj.* 1 Moving forward; advancing: *progressive* movement; also, moving forward gradually or step by step. 2 Aiming at or characterized by progress. 3 Spreading from one part to others; increasing: said of a disease: *progressive* paralysis. 4 Striving for or favoring progress or reform, especially social, political, educational or religious: a *progressive* party, *progressive* schools. 5 *Gram.* Designating an aspect of the verb which expresses the action as being in progress at some time in the past, present, or future: formed with any tense of the auxiliary *be* and the present participle; as, He *is speaking*; he *had been speaking*; he *was to have been speaking*; he *will be speaking*. See synonyms under GRADUAL. — *n.* 1 One who believes in progress or progressive methods; especially, one who favors or promotes reforms or changes, as in politics or religion; a radical: opposed to *conservative* or *reactionary*. 2 *Gram.* A progressive verb form. — **pro·gres'sive·ly** *adv.* — **pro·gres'sive·ness** *n.* — **pro·gres'siv·ism** *n.* — **pro·gres'siv·ist** *n.*

Progressive party 1 A political party formed under the leadership of Theodore Roosevelt in 1912, which sought political and labor reforms and social security legislation. 2 A political party seeking labor and agricultural reforms, formed in 1924 under the leadership of Robert M. LaFollette. 3 A political party formed in 1948, which nominated Henry A. Wallace for president on a platform advocating full employment and a modification of the then current U.S. foreign policy, particularly in respect to the U.S.S.R.

pro·hib·it (prō·hib'it) *v.t.* 1 To forbid, especially by authority or law; interdict. 2 To prevent or hinder. [<L *prohibitus*, pp. of *prohibere* < *pro-* before + *habere* have] — **pro·hib'it·er** *n.*

Synonyms: debar, disallow, forbid, hinder, inhibit, interdict, preclude, prevent. *Debar* is said of persons, *disallow* of acts; one is *debarred* from anything when shut off by authority or necessity; an act is *disallowed* by the authority that might have allowed it. *Forbid* is less formal and more personal, *prohibit* more official and judicial, with the implication of readiness to use force; a parent *forbids* a child to take part in some game or to associate with certain companions; the opium trade is now *prohibited* by the leading nations of the world. Many things are *prohibited* by law which cannot be wholly *prevented*, as gambling and prostitution; on the other hand, things may be *prevented* which are not *prohibited*, as the services of religion, the payment of bets or military conquest. Compare ABOLISH, HINDER, PREVENT, SHUT. *Antonyms*: allow, authorize, command, direct, empower, enjoin, let, license, order, permit, require, sanction, suffer, tolerate, vouchsafe, warrant.

pro·hi·bi·tion (prō'ə·bish'ən) *n.* 1 The act of prohibiting, preventing, or stopping; also, a decree or order forbidding anything; an interdiction. 2 The forbidding of the manufacture, transportation, and sale of alcoholic liquors as beverages: instituted in the United States effective January 16, 1920. See synonyms under BARRIER, ORDER. [<L *prohibitio, -onis*]

Prohibition Amendment The Eighteenth Amendment to the Constitution of the United States, ratified January 1919, prohibiting the manufacture, sale, or transportation of intoxicating liquors for beverage purposes: repealed in 1933. Compare VOLSTEAD ACT.

Pro·hi·bi·tion·ist (prō'ə·bish'ən·ist) *n.* 1 One who believes in prohibition. 2 One who favors the prohibition by law of the manufacture and sale of alcoholic liquors as beverages.

Prohibition party A political party advocating the prohibition by law of the manufacture and sale of alcoholic liquors as beverages.

pro·hib·i·tive (prō·hib'ə·tiv) *adj.* Prohibiting or tending to prohibit. Also **pro·hib'i·to'ry** (-tôr'ē, -tō'rē). — **pro·hib'i·tive·ly** *adv.*

proj·ect (proj'ekt) *n.* 1 Something proposed or mapped out in the mind, as a course of action; a plan. 2 In schools, a problem involving the theory of the subject matter, given to a student or group of students to be worked out in practice.
— **pro·ject** (prə·jekt') *v.t.* 1 To cause to extend forward or out. 2 To throw forth or forward, as missiles. 3 To visualize as an external reality: to *project* an image of one's destiny. 4 To cause (an image, shadow, etc.) to fall on a surface. 5 To propose or plan. 6 *Math.* a To make a projection of (a solid, etc.) on a plane. b To reproduce (a figure) by drawing lines from a vertex through every point (of the figure) to the corresponding point of the reproduction. — *v.i.* 7 To extend forward or out; protrude. See synonyms under PLAN, THROW. [<L *projectus*, pp. of *projicere* throw out, cause to protrude < *pro-* before + *jacere* throw]

Synonyms (noun): contrivance, design, device, invention, plan, purpose, scheme.

pro·jec·tile (prə·jek'təl) *adj.* 1 Projecting, or impelling forward. 2 Capable of being or intended to be projected or shot forth. 3 Protrusile. — *n.* 1 A body projected or thrown forth by force. 2 *Mil.* A missile for discharge from a gun or cannon. [<F]

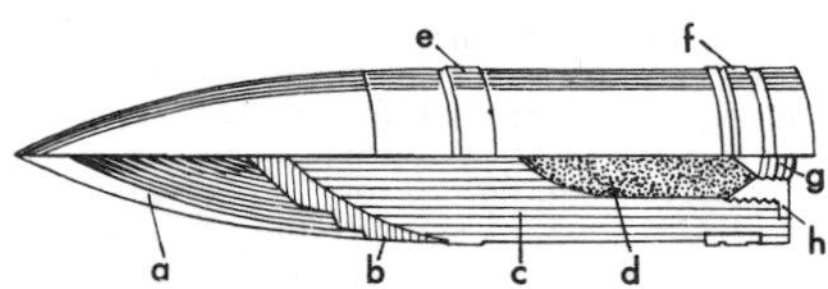

ARMOR–PIERCING PROJECTILE
a. Windshield. *b.* Armor–piercing cap. *c.* Body. *d.* Bursting charge. *e.* Bourrelet. *f.* Copper rotating band. *g.* Fuze. *h.* Plug.

pro·jec·tion (prə·jek'shən) *n.* 1 The act of projecting; a jutting, throwing, or shooting out or forth. 2 That which projects; a prominence; projecting part or subject. 3 A scheme; project. 4 A system of lines drawn on a given fixed plane, as in a map, which represents, point for point, a corresponding system of imaginary lines on a given terrestrial or celestial datum surface: when used in delineating part of the earth's surface, called a *map projection*. 5 *Psychol.* The process or result of externalizing or objectifying a perception or mental image: compare INTROJECTION. 6 The exhibiting of motion pictures or lantern slides upon a screen. [<F <L *projectio, -onis*] — **pro·jec'tion·al** *adj.*

pro·jec·tion·ist (prə·jek'shən·ist) *n.* 1 One who projects. 2 The operator of motion–picture and sound–reproducing equipment.

projection printing *Phot.* The process of enlarging a photograph by projecting the original negative onto sensitized paper by appropriate adjustment of light source and lens.

projection test *Psychol.* Any of various tests for the determination of personality traits and concealed motivations, as by theatrical performances, the completion of sentences or designs, the interpretation of ink blots, and the like.

pro·jec·tive (prə·jek'tiv) *adj.* 1 Pertaining to, treating of, or derived by projection: *projective* geometry, a *projective* figure. 2 *Geom.* Such as may be derived from one another by projection, as two plane figures. — **pro·jec'tive·ly** *adv.*

projective geometry A branch of geometry which investigates the properties of figures by means of projections in two or three dimensions, including the study of corresponding forms of various dimensions.

pro·jec·tor (prə·jek'tər) *n.* 1 One who devises projects; a schemer; a promoter. 2 That which projects something. 3 A mirror or combination of lenses for projecting a beam of light. 4 An apparatus for throwing illuminated images or motion pictures upon a screen. 5 A device for throwing grenades, bombs, etc.

pro·jet (prô·zhe') *n. French* A plan or outline; specifically, a draft of a proposed treaty or law.

Pro·kof·iev (prô·kôf'yəf), **Sergei**, 1891–1953, Russian composer. Also **Pro·kof'ieff.**

Pro·ko·pyevsk (prô·kô'pyifsk) A city in the Kuznetsk Basin of Russian S.F.S.R.

pro·lac·tin (prō·lak'tin) *n. Biochem.* A hormone from the anterior lobe of the pituitary gland, believed to be active in initiating lactation. [<PRO-[1] + LACT- + -IN]

pro·la·mine (prō'lə·mēn, -min) *n. Biochem.* Any of a group of simple proteins that are insoluble in pure water or absolute alcohol, as gliadin from wheat. Also **pro'la·min** (-min). [<PROL(INE) + AM(MONIA) + -INE[2]]

pro·lapse (prō·laps') *v.i.* **·lapsed, ·laps·ing** *Pathol.* To fall out of place, as an organ or part. — *n.* Prolapsus. [<L *prolapsus*, pp. of *prolabi* fall forward < *pro-* forward + *labi* glide, fall]

pro·lap·sus (prō·lap'səs) *n. Pathol.* The falling down of an organ, as the womb, from its normal position. [<L]

pro·late (prō'lāt) *adj.* 1 Extended lengthwise. 2 Lengthened toward the poles, as a spheroid generated by the revolution of an ellipse around its long axis: opposed to *oblate*. [<L *prolatus*, pp. to *proferre* extend, carry forward < *pro-* forward + *ferre* carry]

pro·leg (prō'leg) *n. Entomol.* One of the abdominal legs of insect larvae, as of caterpillars. [<PRO-[1] + LEG]

pro·le·gom·e·non (prō'lə·gom'ə·non) *n. pl.* **·na** (-nə) *Often pl.* An introductory remark or remarks; a preface. [<Gk., neut. passive ppr. of *prolegein* say beforehand < *pro-* before + *legein* say] — **pro'le·gom'e·nous** *adj.*

pro·lep·sis (prō·lep'sis) *n. pl.* **·ses** (-sēz) 1 Anticipation. 2 A rhetorical figure consisting in the anticipation, and answering or nullifying beforehand, of objections or opposing arguments. 3 The use of an adjective or a noun as an objective predicate in anticipation of the result of the verbal action: to shoot a person *dead*. 4 An error by which a date earlier than the true date is assigned to an event. [<L <Gk. *prolēpsis* anticipation < *prolambanein* take beforehand < *pro-* before + *lambanein* seize, take] — **pro·lep'tic** (-tik) or **·ti·cal** *adj.*

pro·le·tar·i·an (prō'lə·târ'ē·ən) *adj.* 1 Formerly, of or pertaining to the lower classes of society. 2 Of or pertaining to proletarians or the proletariat. — *n.* 1 Formerly, a person of the lowest or poorest class. 2 A laborer; a wageworker. [<L *proletarius* < *proles* offspring; so called because, being propertyless, they served the state only by having children] — **pro'le·tar'i·an·ism** *n.*

pro·le·tar·i·at (prō'lə·târ'ē·ət) *n.* 1 Formerly, the indigent classes collectively of a community; the lower classes. 2 Wageworkers collectively, regarded as the creators of wealth; workingmen. 3 *Bot.* Self–pollinated plants having a small or limited reserve of food materials. [<F *prolétariat*. See PROLETARIAN.]

pro·le·tar·y (prō'lə·ter'ē) *n. pl.* **·tar·ies** In ancient Rome, one of the lowest or poorest class, regarded as contributing to the state nothing but offspring. [See PROLETARIAN]

pro·let·cult (prō·let'kōōlt) *n.* A group formed in Russia at the time of the 1917 revolution, originally to develop a proletarian culture as an educational instrument; later transformed into a literary movement. [< Russian *Prolet(arskaya) Kult(ura)* proletarian culture]

pro·li·cide (prō'lə·sīd) *n.* The crime of killing one's own child, before or after birth; infanticide. [<L *proles* offspring + -CIDE]

pro·lif·er·ate (prō·lif'ə·rāt) *v.t.* & *v.i.* **·at·ed, ·at·ing** To produce, reproduce, or grow, especially with rapidity, as cells in tissue formation. [<PROLIFER(OUS) + -ATE[1]] — **pro·lif'er·a'tion** *n.* — **pro·lif'er·a'tive** *adj.*

pro·lif·er·ous (prō·lif'ər·əs) *adj.* 1 Producing offspring freely. 2 Producing branchlets; as a coral. 3 *Bot.* Having an excessive development of parts; developing buds, branches, and flowers from unusual places; bearing progeny in the way of offshoots, buds, etc. [<Med. L *prolifer* <L *proles, prolis* offspring + *ferre* bear]

pro·lif·ic (prō·lif'ik) *adj.* 1 Producing abundantly, as offspring or fruit; fertile. 2 Producing results abundantly; creative: a *prolific* writer. See synonyms under FERTILE. [<F

prolifique <Med. L *prolificus* <L *proles, prolis* offspring + stem of *facere* make] —**pro·lif′·i·ca·cy** (-i·kə·sē), **pro·lif′ic·ness** *n.* —**pro·lif′·i·cal·ly** *adv.*

pro·line (prō′lēn, -lin) *n. Biochem.* An amino acid, $C_5H_9O_2N$, found in proteins. [Contraction of *pyrroline* <PYRROLE + -INE[2]]

pro·lix (prō′liks, prō·liks′) *adj.* **1** Unduly long and verbose, as an address. **2** Indulging in long and wordy discourse; tedious: a *prolix* orator. [<F *prolixe* <L *prolixus* extended <*pro-* before + stem of *liquere* flow] —**pro·lix·i·ty** (prō·lik′sə·tē), **pro′lix·ness** *n.* —**pro′·lix·ly** *adv.*

pro·loc·u·tor (prō·lok′yə·tər) *n.* **1** One who speaks for another; a spokesman or advocate. **2** The presiding officer of a convocation; specifically, the speaker or chairman of the lower house of convocation in the Church of England. [<L <*prolocutus,* pp. of *proloqui* declare, speak for <*pro-* in behalf of + *loqui* talk]

Pro·loc·u·tor (prō·lok′yə·tər) *n. Brit.* In the House of Lords, the lord chancellor. [See PROLOCUTOR]

pro·log (prō′lôg, -log) *n.* A prefatory statement to a poem, discourse, or performance; specifically, an introduction, often in verse, spoken or sung by an actor before a play or opera; hence, any anticipatory act or event. —*v.t.* To introduce with a prolog or preface. Also **pro′logue.** [<OF *prologue* <L *prologus* <Gk. *prologos* <*pro-* before + *logos* discourse]

pro·log·ize (prō′lôg·īz, -log-) *v.i.* **·ized, ·iz·ing** To make or utter a prolog. Also **pro′logu·ize.** —**pro′log·iz′er** or **pro′logu·iz′er** *n.*

pro·long (prə·lông′, -long′) *v.t.* To extend in time or space; continue; lengthen. See synonyms under INCREASE, PROTRACT. Also **pro·lon′gate** (-lông′gāt, -long′-). [<OF *prolonguer* <L *prolongare* <*pro-* forth + *longus* long] —**pro·long′er** *n.* —**pro·long′ment** *n.*

pro·lon·ga·tion (prō′lông·gā′shən, -long-) *n.* **1** The act of prolonging. **2** That by which anything is increased; an extension. [<F]

pro·longe (prō·lonj′, *Fr.* prô·lônzh′) *n. Mil.* A rope having a hook at one end and a toggle at the other: used for drawing a gun carriage. [<F <*prolonger* <OF *prolonguer.* See PROLONG.]

pro·lu·sion (prō·lo͞o′zhən) *n.* **1** That which is introductory to the principal effort or performance; a preliminary attempt; a prolog; prelude. **2** An essay written as a test of the writer's powers, or as preliminary to a more elaborate treatise. [<L *prolusio, -onis* prelude <*prolusus,* pp. of *proludere* play beforehand <*pro-* before + *ludere* play]

prom (prom) *n. U.S. Colloq.* A formal college or school dance or ball: short for *promenade.*

prom·e·nade (prom′ə·nād′, -näd′) *n.* **1** A walk for amusement or exercise, or as part of a formal or social entertainment. **2** A ceremonious parade on horseback or in a vehicle. **3** A place for promenading. **4** A concert or ball opened with a formal march; also, the march. —*v.* **·nad·ed, ·nad·ing** *v.i.* **1** To take a promenade. —*v.t.* **2** To take a promenade through or along. **3** To take or exhibit on or as on a promenade; parade. [<F <*promener* take for a walk <L *prominare* drive forward <*pro-* before + *minare* drive (cattle)] —**prom′·e·nad′er** *n.*

promenade deck The deck above the shelter deck in merchant vessels.

Pro·me·the·an (prə·mē′thē·ən) *adj.* **1** Of, pertaining to, or like Prometheus. **2** Creative or life-bringing.

Pro·me·theus (prə·mē′thē·əs) In Greek mythology, a Titan who stole fire from heaven for mankind and as a punishment was chained to a rock, where an eagle daily devoured his liver, which was made whole again at night: he was released by Hercules.

pro·me·thi·um (prə·mē′thē·əm) *n.* The rare radioactive element of atomic number 61, separated from uranium fission products and belonging to the lanthanide series: new name for the element formerly known as *illinium.* [<NL <PROMETHEUS]

prom·i·nence (prom′ə·nəns) *n.* **1** The state of being prominent; conspicuousness; fame. **2** That which is prominent; a protuberance. **3** *Astron.* One of the great tongues of flame shooting out from the sun's surface, seen during total eclipses: also **solar prominence.** Also **prom′i·nen·cy.**

prom·i·nent (prom′ə·nənt) *adj.* **1** Jutting out; projecting; protuberant. **2** Conspicuous in position, character, or importance. **3** Eminent. See synonyms under EMINENT, IMPORTANT. [<L *prominens, -entis,* ppr. of *prominere* project] —**prom′i·nent·ly** *adv.*

pro·mis·cu·i·ty (prō′mis·kyo͞o′ə·tē, prom′is-) *n.* **1** Condition or state of being promiscuous; indiscriminate or confused mixture. **2** Promiscuous sexual union.

pro·mis·cu·ous (prə·mis′kyo͞o·əs) *adj.* **1** Composed of individuals or things confusedly mingled. **2** Unrestricted in distribution or application; exercised or shared without discrimination. **3** Indiscriminate; not fastidious, especially in sexual relations. **4** *Colloq.* Lacking plan or purpose; casual; irregular. [<L *promiscuus* mixed <*pro-* thoroughly + stem of *miscere* mix] —**pro·mis′cu·ous·ly** *adv.* —**pro·mis′cu·ous·ness** *n.*

prom·ise (prom′is) *n.* **1** An assurance given by one person to another that the former will or will not do a specified act. **2** Reasonable ground for hope or expectation, especially of future excellence or satisfaction: a youth of great *promise.* **3** Something promised; the fulfilment or obtainment of that which is promised. See synonyms under CONTRACT. —*v.* **·ised, ·is·ing** *v.t.* **1** To engage or pledge by a promise: used with the infinitive or a clause: He *promised* that he would do it. **2** To make a promise of (something) to someone. **3** To give reason for expecting: The sky *promised* rain. **4** *Colloq.* To assure (someone). —*v.i.* **5** To make a promise. **6** To give reason for expectation: often with *well* or *fair.* [<F *promesse* <L *promissum,* pp. of *promittere* send forward <*pro-* forth + *mittere* send] —**prom′is·er** *n.*

Promised Land See LAND OF PROMISE.

prom·is·ee (prom′is·ē′) *n. Law* One to whom a promise is made.

prom·is·ing (prom′is·ing) *adj.* Giving promise of good results or development. See synonyms under AUSPICIOUS. —**prom′is·ing·ly** *adv.*

prom·is·or (prom′is·ôr) *n. Law* One who makes a promise.

prom·is·so·ry (prom′ə·sôr′ē, -sō′rē) *adj.* **1** Containing or of the nature of a promise; expressing an engagement to pay: a *promissory* note. **2** Indicating what is to be required or to take place after the signing of an insurance contract. Compare WARRANTY. [<Med. L *promissorius*]

promissory note A written promise by one person to pay another unconditionally a certain sum of money at a specified time: also called *note of hand.*

prom·on·to·ry (prom′ən·tôr′ē, -tō′rē) *n. pl.* **·ries** **1** A high point of land extending into the sea; headland. **2** *Anat.* A rounded projection or part. [<LL *promontorium* <L *promunturium,* ? <*prominere.* See PROMINENT.]

Promontory Point A peninsula extending 20 miles south into Great Salt Lake, NW Utah.

pro·mote (prə·mōt′) *v.t.* **·mot·ed, ·mot·ing** **1** To contribute to the progress, development, or growth of; further; encourage. **2** To advance to a higher position, grade, or honor. **3** To work in behalf of; advocate actively: to *promote* social reforms. **4** In education, to advance (a pupil) to the next higher school grade. [<L *promotus,* pp. of *promovere* move forward <*pro-* forward + *movere* move]

Synonyms: advance, aid, assist, elevate, encourage, exalt, excite, foment, forward, foster, further, help, prefer, raise. We *promote* a person by *advancing, elevating,* or *exalting* him to a higher position or dignity. A person *promotes* a scheme or an enterprise which others have projected or begun, and which he *encourages, forwards, furthers,* especially when he acts as the agent of the prime movers of the enterprise. One who *excites* a quarrel originates it; to *promote* a quarrel is strictly to *foment* it, the one who *promotes* keeping himself in the background. See ABET, ENCOURAGE, QUICKEN, SERVE. *Antonyms*: see synonyms for ABASE, ALLAY.

pro·mot·er (prə·mō′tər) *n.* **1** One who or that which promotes. **2** One who assists (by securing capital, etc.) in promoting a financial or commercial enterprise, or who makes this his regular business. **3** *Chem.* A substance used to increase the action of a catalyst. See synonyms under AGENT, AUXILIARY.

pro·mo·tion (prə·mō′shən) *n.* **1** Advancement or preferment in honor, dignity, rank, or grade. **2** Furtherance; encouragement. **3** The act of promoting. **4** The state of being promoted. —**pro·mo′tion·al** *adj.*

pro·mo·tive (prə·mō′tiv) *adj.* Tending to promote.

prompt (prompt) *v.t.* **1** To incite to action; instigate. **2** To suggest or inspire (an act, thought, etc.). **3** To remind of what has been forgotten or of what comes next; give a cue to. —*v.i.* **4** To give help or suggestions. See synonyms under ACTUATE, ENCOURAGE, INFLUENCE, STIR[1]. —*adj.* **1** Acting, or ready to act, at the moment; quick to respond or decide; punctual. **2** Done or rendered with readiness or alacrity; taking place at the appointed time. See synonyms under ACTIVE, ALERT, NIMBLE. —*n.* **1** A term of credit allowed for the payment of a debt as stated in a prompt-note. **2** An act of prompting; also, the information imparted by prompting; a reminder. [<OF <L *promptus* brought forth, hence, at hand, pp. of *promere* <*pro-* forth + *emere* take] —**prompt′ly** *adv.* —**prompt′ness** *n.*

prompt·book (prompt′bo͝ok′) *n.* An annotated script of a play used by a prompter or director.

prompt·er (promp′tər) **1** In a theater, one who follows the lines and prompts the actors. **2** One who or that which prompts.

promp·ti·tude (promp′tə·to͞od, -tyo͞od) *n.* The quality, habit, or fact of being prompt; promptness. [<F]

prompt–note (prompt′nōt′) *n.* In commerce, a note or memorandum delivered to a purchaser of merchandise as a reminder, and containing a statement of the sum due, day of payment, etc.

pro·mul·gate (prō·mul′gāt, prom′əl·gāt) *v.t.* **·gat·ed, ·gat·ing** To make known or announce officially and formally; put into effect by public proclamation, as a law or dogma. See synonyms under ANNOUNCE, PUBLISH, SPREAD. [<L *promulgatus,* pp. of *promulgare* make known, prob. alter. of *provulgare* <*pro-* forth + *vulgus* the people] —**pro·mul·ga·tion** (prō′mul·gā′shən, prom′əl-) *n.* —**pro·mul·ga·tor** (prō·mul′gā·tər, prom′əl-) *n.*

pro·mulge (prō·mulj′) *v.t.* **·mulged, ·mulg·ing** *Archaic* To promulgate. [<L *promulgare*]

pro·my·ce·li·um (prō′mī·sē′lē·əm) *n. pl.* **·li·a** (-lē·ə) *Bot.* A short-jointed filament, developed on the germination of certain smut or rust spores, and which gives rise to sporidia. —**pro′my·ce′li·al** *adj.*

pro·na·os (prō·nā′os) *n.* In ancient Greece, a portico or vestibule of a temple. [<Gk. <*pro-* before + *naos* temple]

pro·nate (prō′nāt) *v.t.* **·nat·ed, ·nat·ing** To place in a position of pronation. [<L *pronatus,* pp. of *pronare* bow <*pronus* prone]

pro·na·tion (prō·nā′shən) *n. Physiol.* **1** The act or movement of turning the palm of the hand, or the corresponding surface of the forelimb, downward or backward. **2** The position of a limb so turned: opposed to *supination.*

pro·na·tor (prō·nā′tər) *n. pl.* **pro·na·to·res** (prō′nə·tôr′ēz, -tō′rēz) *Anat.* A muscle of the forearm by which pronation is effected.

prone (prōn) *adj.* **1** Lying flat, especially with the face, front, or palm downward; prostrate: opposed to *supine.* **2** Leaning forward or downward; also, moving or sloping sharply downward. **3** Mentally inclined or predisposed: with *to.* See synonyms under ADDICTED, SUBJECT. [<L *pronus* prostrate <*pro-* before] —**prone′ly** *adv.* —**prone′ness** *n.*

pro·neph·ros (prō·nef′ros) *n. Anat.* The primordial kidney, the anterior of three similar tubular organs found in connection with the genitourinary apparatus of typical vertebrates. [<NL <Gk. *pro-* before + *nephros* kidney] —**pro·neph′ric** *adj.*

prong (prông, prong) *n.* **1** A pointed end of an instrument; a tine of a fork. **2** Any pointed and projecting part, as the end of an antler, etc. — *v.t.* To prick or stab with or as with a prong. [Cf. LG *prange* a pointed stick, Du. *prangen* pinch.]

prong·buck (prông′buk, prong′-) *n.* The male of the pronghorn.

prong·horn (prông′hôrn′, prong′-) *n.* *pl.* **·horns** or **·horn** A ruminant (*Antilocapra americana*) of western North America, having deciduous branched horns; the Rocky Mountain antelope: not a true antelope.

PRONGHORN
(About 3 feet high at the shoulder)

pro·nom·i·nal (prō·nom′ə·nəl) *adj.* Of, pertaining to, like, or having the nature of a pronoun. [<LL *pronominalis* <L *pronomen.* See PRONOUN.] — **pro·nom′i·nal·ly** *adv.*

pronominal adjective The possessive case of a personal pronoun used attributively: *my, your, his, her, its, our, their, whose,* and, poetically, *mine* and *thine.*

pro·noun (prō′noun) *n.* A word used as a substitute for a noun, as *he, she, that.* [<OF *pronom* <L *pronomen* <*pro-* in place of + *nomen* name, noun]

— **adjective pronoun** Any pronoun used like an adjective; as, *that* boy, *this* house, *which* man. Any demonstrative pronoun, any indefinite pronoun (except *none*), and any interrogative and relative pronoun (except *who*) may be used as an adjective pronoun.

— **demonstrative pronoun** A pronoun that directly points out its antecedents.

Singular	*Plural*
this	these
that	those

The same forms are used for all genders, persons, and cases.

— **indefinite pronoun** A pronoun that represents an object indefinitely or generally. The principal indefinite pronouns are *another, any, both, each, either, neither, none, one, other, some, such. None* and *any* are both singular and plural.

— **interrogative pronoun** A pronoun that is used to ask a question.

	Subjective	*Possessive*	*Objective*
Singular	who	whose	whom
and	which	whose, of which	which
Plural	what	of what	what

Of what occurs in such sentences as *Of what* are you speaking? *What* are you speaking *of*?

— **personal pronoun** A pronoun that shows by its form the person speaking, the person spoken to, or the person or thing spoken of.

Singular	*Subjective*	*Possessive*	*Objective*
1st person	I	my *or* mine	me
2nd person	you (thou)	your *or* yours (thy *or* thine)	you (thee)
3rd person			
masculine	he	his	him
feminine	she	her *or* hers	her
neuter	it	its	it
Plural:			
1st person	we	our *or* ours	us
2nd person	you (ye)	your *or* yours	you
3rd person	they	their *or* theirs	them

— **reflexive pronoun** A pronoun formed by adding *-self* or *-selves* to the oblique cases of the personal pronoun. They serve as an intensive: I, *myself,* was there; or a reference back to a personal pronoun where the same person is both subject and object: He hit *himself.*

	Singular	*Plural*
1st person	myself	ourselves
2nd person	yourself	yourselves
3rd person	himself, herself, itself	themselves

— **relative pronoun** A pronoun that relates to an antecedent and introduces a qualifying clause: We found a boatman *who* ferried us.

Subjective	*Possessive*	*Objective*
who	whose	whom
which	of which	which
what	of what	what
that		that

Sometimes *as* and *but* are regarded as relative pronouns: Such men *as* survived the accident; There is not a man *but* remembers that day. ◆ The relative pronouns *who* (with its inflected forms *whose* and *whom*), *which,* and *what,* are identical in form with the interrogative pronouns but they undergo shifts of meaning in interrogative use, often being indefinite and general in reference: *What* (if anything or of all possible things) is he talking about? But: He is talking about *what* (specifically) he knows best. These pronouns, when used to introduce an indirect question, are by nature both relative and interrogative: They asked *what* he wanted; *whom* he preferred as a colleague; *which* party he belonged to. Similarly, *that* is not only a demonstrative but a relative pronoun and it makes a specific and limiting reference in either use.

pro·nounce (prə·nouns′) *v.* **·nounced, ·nounc·ing** *v.t.* **1** To utter or deliver officially or solemnly; proclaim. **2** To assert; declare, especially as one's judgment: The judge *pronounced* her insane. **3** To give utterance to; articulate (words, etc.). **4** To articulate in a prescribed manner. **5** To indicate the sound of (a word) by phonetic symbols. — *v.i.* **6** To make a pronouncement or assertion. **7** To articulate words; speak. See synonyms under ASSERT, SPEAK. [<OF *pronuncier* <LL *pronunciare* <L *pronuntiare* proclaim <*pro-* forth + *nuntiare* announce] — **pro·nounce′a·ble** *adj.* — **pro·nounc′er** *n.*

pro·nounced (prə·nounst′) *adj.* Of marked character; decided.

pro·nounce·ment (prə·nouns′mənt) *n.* The act of pronouncing; a formal declaration or announcement.

pro·nounc·ing (prə·noun′sing) *adj.* Pertaining to or serving as a guide in pronunciation.

pron·to (pron′tō) *adv. U.S. Slang* Quickly; promptly; instantly. [<Sp. <L *promptus.* See PROMPT.]

pro·nu·cle·us (prō·no͞o′klē·əs, -nyo͞o′-) *n.* *pl.* **·cle·i** (-klē·ī) *Biol.* The nucleus of either the spermatozoon or ovum, the union of which forms the nucleus of the fertilized ovum. [<NL <Gk. *pro-* before + L *nucleus* a kernel]

pro·nu·mer·al (prō·no͞o′mər·əl, -nyo͞o′-) *n.* *Math.* A letter or symbol that stands for a number, as *x, y,* and *z* in the equation $3x + 2y - z = 13$.

pro·nun·ci·a·men·to (prə·nun′sē·ə·men′tō, -shē·ə-) *n.* *pl.* **·tos** A public announcement; proclamation; manifesto. [<Sp. *pronunciamiento,* lit., a pronouncement <L *pronuntiare.* See PRONOUNCE.]

pro·nun·ci·a·tion (prə·nun′sē·ā′shən) *n.* The act or manner of pronouncing words; articulation. [<L *pronunciatio, -onis* <*pronuntiatus,* pp. of *pronuntiare.* See PRONOUNCE.]

proof (pro͞of) *n.* **1** The act or process of proving, in any sense; specifically, the establishment of a fact by evidence or a truth by other truths. **2** A trial of strength, truth, fact, or excellence, etc.; a test. **3** Evidence and argument sufficient to induce belief. **4** *Law* Anything that serves to convince the mind of the truth or falsity of a fact or proposition, including facts and admissions of parties, which are properly called *evidence,* and presumptions either of fact or of law, and citations of law. **5** The state or quality of having successfully undergone a proof or test; impenetrability; also, impenetrable armor. **6** The standard of strength of alcoholic liquors: see PROOF SPIRIT. **7** *Printing* A printed trial sheet showing the contents or condition of matter in type or of a plate, or the like, either with or without marked corrections. **8** In engraving and etching, a trial impression taken from an engraved plate, stone, or block; also, a perfect impression from such a plate, etc., when finished, and usually before the title or inscription has been added. **9** *Phot.* A trial print from a negative. **10** *Math.* A process to check a computation by using its result; also, a demonstration. **11** Anything proved true; experience. **12** In philately, an experimental printing of a stamp. — *adj.* **1** Employed in or connected with proving or correcting. **2** Capable of resisting successfully; firm; impenetrable: with *against*: *proof* against bribes. **3** Of standard alcoholic strength, as liquors. [<OF *prueve* <LL *proba* <*probare* PROVE]

Synonyms (noun): attestation, certification, confirmation, demonstration, essay, evidence, fact, ordeal, test, testimony, trial. See CERTAINTY, DEMONSTRATION, TESTIMONY. *Antonyms*: assertion, conjecture, disproof, failure, fallacy, fancy, hypothesis, imagination, likelihood, possibility, presumption, probability, refutation.

-proof *combining form* **1** Impervious to; able to withstand; not damaged by: *waterproof, bombproof.* **2** Protected against: *mothproof, stormproof.* **3** As strong as: *armorproof.* **4** Resisting; showing no effects of: *joyproof, panicproof.* Adjectives formed with *-proof* may also be used as verbs. [<PROOF, *adj.*]

proof·read (pro͞of′rēd′) *v.t. & v.i.* **·read** (-red′) **·read·ing** (-rē′ding) To read and correct (printers' proofs).

proof·read·er (pro͞of′rē′dər) *n.* One whose business is to read and mark the errors in printers' proofs. — **proof′read′ing** *n.*

proof spirit An alcoholic liquor that contains

PROOFREADER'S MARKS

Symbols in the column headed MARGIN are used only in the outer margins of the proof: the symbols used within the body of the text are given in the TEXT column.

MARGIN		TEXT
l.c.	Set in lower-case type	circled or /
Cap.	Set in capitals	underscored
S.C.	Set in small capitals	underscored
C+S.C.	Set in caps and small caps	
l.f.	Set in lightface type	circled
b.f.	Set in boldface type	underscored
Rom.	Set in roman type	circled
Ital.	Set in italic type	underscored
⊙	Insert period	^
:/ ;/	Insert colon; semicolon	^ ^
,	Insert comma	^
’	Insert apostrophe	^
/?/	Insert interrogation mark	^
/!/	Insert exclamation mark	^
/=/	Insert hyphen	^
“ ”	Insert quotation marks	^
	Insert superior figure or letter	^
	Insert inferior figure or letter	^
1/m	Insert one em-dash	^
	Take out (delete matter marked)	/
wf.	Wrong font	circled or /

MARGIN		TEXT
×	Broken letter: examine	circled
tr.	Transpose matter marked	
eq.#	Equalize spacing	^^^^
[	Move to left to point marked	[
]	Move to right to point marked	]
	Raise to point marked	
	Lower to point marked	
	Push down space	/
⁐	Close up	⁐
¶	Begin new paragraph	
No ¶	Run matter on, not a paragraph	~
=	Aline type	=
Stet.	Retain words crossed out	......
	Take out and close up	
‖	Line up matter	‖
Out	Omission here; see copy	^
[	Move this to left	
]	Move this to right	
Qu.?	Query: is this right?	^
Sp.	Spell out	circled
#	Insert space	^

a standard amount of alcohol: in the United States, half its volume of alcohol, with a specific gravity of 0.7939 at 60° F., which is rated *100-proof.*

prop[1] (prop) *v.t.* **propped, prop·ping** 1 To support or keep from falling by or as by means of a prop. 2 To lean or place: usually with *against.* 3 To support; sustain. —*n.* That which sustains an incumbent weight; a buttress; stay. [<MDu. *proppe* a vine prop, a support]
Synonyms: bolster, brace, buttress, shore, stay, support, sustain. See SUPPORT.

prop[2] (prop) *n. Colloq.* On a theater stage, any adjunct except the scenery or the costumes of the actors; a property. [Short for PROPERTY]

prop[3] (prop) *n. Colloq.* A propeller.

pro·pae·deu·tic (prō′pə·do͞o′tik, -dyo͞o′-) *adj.* Pertaining to or of the nature of preliminary instruction; relating to or introductory to an art or science: also **pro′pae·deu′ti·cal.** —*n.* A preparatory or introductory subject or course. [<Gk. *propaideuein* teach beforehand <*pro-* before + *paideuein* teach <*pais, paidos* a child]

pro·pae·deu·tics (prō′pə·do͞o′tiks, -dyo͞o′-) *n.* The body of principles or rules introductory to an art or science.

prop·a·ga·ble (prop′ə·gə·bəl) *adj.* That can be propagated; capable of being disseminated or spread abroad, as principles, etc. [<L *propagare* PROPAGATE + -ABLE]

prop·a·gan·da (prop′ə·gan′də) *n.* 1 Any institution or scheme for propagating a doctrine, or system. 2 Effort directed systematically toward the gaining of public support for an opinion or course of action. 3 The tenets, views, etc., put forward by propaganda. [<PROPAGANDA]

Prop·a·gan·da (prop′ə·gan′də) *n.* A society of cardinals, the overseers of foreign missions; also, the College for the Propagation of the Faith, founded by Pope Urban VIII, in 1627, for the education of missionary priests; Sacred Congregation *de Propaganda Fide.* Also **College of Propaganda.** [<Ital. <NL *(congregatio de) propaganda (fide)* (the congregation for) propagating (the faith) <L, gerund of *propagare.* See PROPAGATE.]

prop·a·gan·dism (prop′ə·gan′diz·əm) *n.* The art, practice, or system of using propaganda. —**prop′a·gan′dist** *n.*

prop·a·gan·dize (prop′ə·gan′dīz) *v.* **·dized, ·diz·ing** *v.t.* 1 To subject to propaganda. 2 To spread by means of propaganda. —*v.i.* 3 To carry on or spread propaganda.

prop·a·gate (prop′ə·gāt) *v.* **·gat·ed, ·gat·ing** *v.t.* 1 To cause (animals, plants, etc.) to multiply by natural reproduction; breed. 2 To reproduce (itself). 3 To spread abroad or from person to person; diffuse; disseminate. 4 To transmit through a medium; extend the action of: to *propagate* heat. 5 *Obs.* To increase. —*v.i.* 6 To multiply by natural reproduction; have offspring; breed. [<L *propagatus,* pp. of *propagare* slip or layer a plant, multiply <*propago* a slip for transplanting <*pro-* forth + *pag-,* root of *pangere* fasten] —**prop′a·ga′tive** *adj.* —**prop′a·ga′tor** *n.*
Synonyms: beget, breed, engender, generate, increase, multiply, originate, procreate. See PRODUCE, SPREAD. *Antonyms*: annihilate, destroy, eradicate, exterminate, extirpate.

prop·a·ga·tion (prop′ə·gā′shən) *n.* 1 The act of propagating; reproduction. 2 Dissemination; diffusion.

prop·a·gule (prop′ə·gyo͞ol) *n. Bot.* A bud, shoot, or other plant part which vegetatively propagates the species. Also **pro·pag·u·lum** (prō·pag′yə·ləm). [<NL *propagulum,* dim. of L *propago.* See PROPAGATE.]

pro·pane (prō′pān) *n. Chem.* A gaseous hydrocarbon of the methane series, C_3H_8, obtained from petroleum and also made synthetically. [<PROP(YL) + (METH)ANE]

pro·par·ox·y·tone (prō′pə·rok′sə·tōn) *adj.* Having an acute accent on the antepenult. —*n.* A word with an acute accent on the antepenult. [<Gk. *proparoxytonos* <*pro-* before + *paroxytonos* paroxytone]

pro pa·tri·a (prō pä′trē·ə) *Latin* For one's country.

pro·pel (prə·pel′) *v.t.* **·pelled, ·pel·ling** To cause to move forward or ahead; drive or urge forward. See synonyms under DRIVE, PUSH, SEND. [<L *propellere* drive before one <*pro-* forward + *pellere* drive]

pro·pel·lant (prə·pel′ənt) *n.* 1 That which propels. 2 *Mil.* An explosive which, upon ignition, propels a projectile from a gun. 3 A solid or liquid fuel which serves to propel a rocket, guided missile, or the like.

pro·pel·lent (prə·pel′ənt) *adj.* Propelling; able to propel. [<L *propellens, -entis,* ppr. of *propellere.* See PROPEL.]

pro·pel·ler (prə·pel′ər) *n.* 1 One who or that which propels. 2 Any device for propelling a craft through water or air; especially, one having blades mounted at an angle on a power-driven shaft and producing a thrust by their rotary action on the fluid.

pro·pend (prō·pend′) *v.i. Obs.* To be disposed in favor; tend. [<L *propendere* hang forward, be inclined or favorable <*pro-* forward + *pendere* hang]

pro·pene (prō′pēn) *n.* Propylene. [<PROP(YL) + -ENE]

pro·pe·no·ic acid (prō′pə·nō′ik) See under ACRYLIC. [<PROPEN(E) + (BENZ)OIC]

pro·pense (prō·pens′) *adj. Obs.* Having a propensity; prone. [<L *propensus,* pp. of *propendere.* See PROPEND.] —**pro·pense′ly** *adv.*

pro·pen·si·ty (prə·pen′sə·tē) *n. pl.* **·ties** 1 Natural disposition to or for; tendency. 2 *Obs.* A liking for; partiality. See synonyms under APPETITE, DESIRE, INCLINATION. [<L *propensus.* See PROPENSE.]

prop·er (prop′ər) *adj.* 1 Having special adaptation or fitness; specially suited; applicable; appropriate. 2 Conforming to a standard; becoming; seemly; correct. 3 Naturally belonging to a person or thing; particular; peculiar. 4 Understood in the most correct sense; strictly so called: commonly following the noun modified. 5 *Gram.* Belonging to an individual person, family, place, or the like: a *proper* noun: opposed to *common.* 6 *Archaic* Belonging to or affecting oneself; own. 7 *Her.* Represented in the natural color. 8 *Eccl.* Appointed for special use: the *proper* psalms for Christmas. 9 *Archaic* Of becoming form or appearance. 10 *Archaic* Good; excellent; pleasant. 11 *Obs.* Respectable; worthy; honest. See synonyms under APPROPRIATE, BECOMING, CONVENIENT, CORRECT, GOOD, MODEST. —*n.* A collection of prayers; specifically, that portion of the breviary or missal containing the prayers and collects suitable to special occasions. [<OF *propre* <L *proprius* one's own] —**prop′er·ness** *n.*

proper fraction See under FRACTION.

prop·er·ly (prop′ər·lē) *adv.* In a proper manner; suitably; rightly.

proper noun See under NOUN.

prop·er·tied (prop′ər·tēd) *adj.* Owning property.

Pro·per·tius (prō·pûr′shəs), **Sextus,** 50?–14? B.C., Roman poet.

prop·er·ty (prop′ər·tē) *n. pl.* **·ties** 1 Any object of value that a person may lawfully acquire and hold; anything that may be owned; stocks, land, etc.; any possession. 2 Ownership or dominion; the legal right to the possession, use, enjoyment, and disposal of a thing; a valuable legal right or interest in or to particular things. 3 Whatever belongs or pertains to any object, as a distinguishing quality or characteristic; a peculiarity. 4 In the theater, any portable article, except scenery, which is not personally owned by the actors, but which is used by them in the performance, as flowers, books, dishes, etc. 5 A characteristic attribute of a body or substance under stated conditions, especially in relation to the senses, as color, odor, hardness, density, etc. 6 Any typical mode of action or behavior observed in natural phenomena: a *property* of radiation. [<OF *proprieté* <L *proprietas, -tatis* <*proprius* one's own. Doublet of PROPRIETY.]
Synonyms: chattels, estate, goods, means, money, ownership, possessions, resources, right, wealth. See ATTRIBUTE, CHARACTERISTIC, MONEY, WEALTH.

pro·phase (prō′fāz) *n. Biol.* One of the preparatory changes in the mitosis of the cell, during which the chromatin of the nucleus is formed into longitudinally split chromosomes. [<PRO-[2] before + PHASE]

proph·e·cy (prof′ə·sē) *n. pl.* **·cies** 1 A prediction made under divine influence and direction; loosely, any prediction. 2 Discourse delivered by a prophet under divine inspiration: the common Biblical sense. 3 A book of prophecies. 4 *Obs.* Public interpretation of Scripture; preaching. [<OF *profecie* <LL *prophetia* <Gk. *prophēteia* <*prophētēs* <*pro-* before + *phanai* speak]

proph·e·sy (prof′ə·sī) *v.* **·sied, ·sy·ing** *v.t.* 1 To utter or foretell with or as with divine inspiration. 2 To predict (a future event). 3 To point out beforehand. —*v.i.* 4 To speak by divine influence, or as a medium between God and man. 5 To foretell the future; make predictions. 6 To explain or teach religious subjects; preach. [<OF *prophecier* <*profecie* PROPHECY] —**proph′e·si′er** *n.*
Synonyms: augur, divine, foretell, predict, prognosticate. *Prophesy* differs from *predict* by assuming a claim to supernatural or divine inspiration. To *prognosticate* is to *predict* from observed signs, indications, or conditions. To *prophesy* in the Scriptural sense is to utter religious truth under divine inspiration, not necessarily to *foretell* future events, but to warn, exhort, comfort, etc. See AUGUR. *Antonyms*: chronicle, recall, recite, recollect, record, remember.

proph·et (prof′it) *n.* 1 One who delivers divine messages or interprets the divine will. 2 One who foretells the future; especially, an inspired predictor. 3 A religious leader. 4 An interpreter or spokesman for any cause. 5 A mantis. —**the Prophet** According to Islam, Mohammed. —**the Prophets** The Old Testament books written by the prophets. ◆ Homophone: *profit.* [<Gk. *prophētēs* <*pro-* before + *phanai* speak] —**proph′et·ess** *n. fem.* —**proph′et·hood** (-ho͝od) *n.*

pro·phet·ic (prə·fet′ik) *adj.* 1 Of or pertaining to a prophet or prophecy; vatic. 2 Pertaining to or involving prediction or presentiment; predictive. Also **pro·phet′i·cal.** —**pro·phet′i·cal·ly** *adv.* —**pro·phet′i·cal·ness** *n.*

pro·phy·lac·tic (prō′fə·lak′tik, prof′ə-) *adj.* Operating to ward off something, especially disease; preventive. —*n.* A prophylactic medicine or appliance. [<Gk. *prophylaktikos* <*prophylassein* be on guard <*pro-* before + *phylassein* guard]

pro·phy·lax·is (prō′fə·lak′sis, prof′ə-) *n.* Preventive treatment for disease. [<NL <Gk. *pro-* before + *phylaxis* a guarding]

pro·pine (prō·pīn′) *Scot. v.t.* To offer, as a gift; propose. —*n.* An offering; pledge.

pro·pin·qui·ty (prō·ping′kwə·tē) *n.* 1 Nearness in place or time. 2 Kinship. See synonyms under APPROXIMATION. [<OF *propinquité* <L *propinquitas, -tatis* <*propinquus* near]

pro·pi·o·nate (prō′pē·ə·nāt′) *n. Chem.* An organic compound containing the radical CH_3-CH_2COO. [<PRO(TO)- + Gk. *piōn* fat + -ATE[3]]

pro·pi·on·ic (prō′pē·on′ik, -ō′nik) *adj. Chem.* Designating a colorless, liquid acid, $C_3H_6O_2$, occurring in nature, as in beet root molasses, and also produced variously by synthesis. It is the first member in the series of fatty acids.

pro·pi·theque (prō′pə·thēk′) *n.* Sifaka. [<F <NL *Propithecus* <Gk. *pro-* before + *pithēkos* an ape]

pro·pi·ti·ate (prō·pish′ē·āt) *v.t.* **·at·ed, ·at·ing** To cause to be favorably disposed; appease; conciliate. [<L *propitiatus,* pp. of *propitiare* render favorable, appease <*propitius* PROPITIOUS] —**pro·pi·ti·a·ble** (prō·pish′ē·ə·bəl) *adj.* —**pro·pi′ti·at′ing·ly** *adv.* —**pro·pi′ti·a′tive** *adj.* —**pro·pi′ti·a′tor** *n.*

pro·pi·ti·a·tion (prō·pish′ē·ā′shən) *n.* 1 The act of propitiating. 2 That which propitiates.
Synonyms: atonement, expiation, reconciliation, satisfaction. *Atonement* (at-one-ment), originally denoting *reconciliation,* or the bringing into agreement of those who have been estranged, is now chiefly used, as in theology, in the sense of some offering, sacrifice, or suffering sufficient to win forgiveness or make up for an offense. *Expiation* is the enduring of the full penalty of a wrong or crime. *Propitiation* is an offering, action, or sacrifice that makes the governing power propitious toward the offender. *Satisfaction*

denotes the rendering a full legal equivalent for the wrong done. *Propitiation* appeases the lawgiver; *satisfaction* meets the requirements of the law. *Antonyms*: alienation, condemnation, estrangement, offense, penalty, punishment, reprobation.

pro·pi·ti·a·to·ry (prō·pish′ē·ə·tôr′ē, -tō′rē) *adj.* Pertaining to or causing propitiation. —*n. pl.* **·ries 1** A propitiation. **2** In Jewish antiquity, the mercy seat regarded as symbolizing the merciful presence of Jehovah.

pro·pi·tious (prō·pish′əs) *adj.* **1** Kindly disposed; gracious. **2** Attended by favorable circumstances; auspicious. [<OF *propicius* <L *propitius* favorable, prob. <*pro-* before, forward + *petere* seek] —**pro·pi′tious·ly** *adv.* —**pro·pi′tious·ness** *n.*

Synonyms: auspicious, benign, benignant, clement, favorable, friendly, gracious, kind, kindly, merciful. That which is *auspicious* is of *favorable* omen; that which is *propitious* is of favoring influence or tendency; as, an *auspicious* morning; a *propitious* breeze. *Propitious* applies to persons, implying *kind* disposition and *favorable* inclinations, especially toward the suppliant; *auspicious* is not used of persons. See AUSPICIOUS. *Antonyms*: adverse, antagonistic, ill–disposed, inauspicious, repellent, unfavorable, unfriendly, unpropitious.

prop·jet (prop′jet′) *n.* Turboprop.

prop·o·lis (prop′ə·lis) *n.* A resinous, adhesive substance elaborated by bees to serve as a cementing material. [<L <Gk. <*pro-* before + *polis* a city]

pro·pone (prə·pōn′) *v.t.* **·poned, ·pon·ing** *Scot.* To propose or propound; put forward.

pro·po·nent (prə·pō′nənt) *n.* **1** One who makes a proposal or puts forward a proposition; one who propounds a thing. **2** *Law* One who presents a will for probate. **3** One who advocates or supports a cause or doctrine. [<L *proponens, -entis,* ppr. of *proponere* set forth <*pro-* forth + *ponere* put]

Pro·pon·tis (prə·pon′tis) The ancient name for the SEA OF MARMARA.

pro·por·tion (prə·pôr′shən, -pōr′-) *n.* **1** Relative magnitude, number, or degree, as existing between parts, a part and a whole, or different things. **2** Fitness and harmony; symmetry. **3** A proportionate or proper share; any share or part. **4** An equality or identity between ratios. **5** *Math.* That rule by which, when three numbers are given, a fourth can be found having the same ratio to the third as the second has to the first: also called *the rule of three,* three of the four terms being always given. **6** *pl.* Size; dimensions: a picture of large *proportions.* See synonyms under ANALOGY, PORTION, SYMMETRY. —*v.t.* **1** To adjust properly as to relative magnitude, amount, or degree: to *proportion* one's expenses to one's means. **2** To form with a harmonious relation of parts. [<OF *proporcion* <L *proportio, -onis* <*pro* before + *portio, -onis* a share] —**pro·por′tion·a·ble** *adj.* —**pro·por′tion·a·bly** *adv.* —**pro·por′tion·er** *n.*

pro·por·tion·al (prə·pôr′shən·əl, -pōr′-) *adj.* **1** Of, pertaining to, or being in proportion. **2** *Math.* **a** Constituting the terms of a proportion: said of four quantities: The numbers 2, 3, and 8, 12 are *proportional.* **b** Varying so that corresponding values form a proportion. —*n.* Any quantity or number in proportion to another or others. —**pro·por′tion·al·ly** *adv.* —**pro·por′tion·al′i·ty** (-al′ə·tē) *n.*

proportional representation A system of election by which political parties secure legislative representation in a government in proportion to voting strength.

pro·por·tion·ate (prə·pôr′shən·it, -pōr′-) *adj.* Being in due proportion; proportional. —*v.t.* (-āt) **·at·ed, ·at·ing** To make proportionate. —**pro·por′tion·ate·ly** *adv.* —**pro·por′tion·ate·ness** *n.*

pro·por·tion·ment (prə·pôr′shən·mənt, -pōr′-) *n.* The act of placing or putting things in proportion; arrangement; distribution.

pro·po·sal (prə·pō′zəl) *n.* **1** An offer proposing something to be accepted or adopted. **2** An offer of marriage. **3** Something proposed, as a scheme or plan.

Synonyms: bid, offer, overture, proposition. An *offer* or *proposal* puts something before one for acceptance or rejection, *proposal* being the more formal word; a *proposition* sets forth truth (or what is claimed to be truth) in formal statement. The *proposition* is for consideration, the *proposal* for action; as, a *proposition* in geometry, a *proposal* of marriage; but *proposition* is often used nearly in the sense of *proposal* when it is a matter for deliberation; as, a *proposition* for the surrender of a fort. A *bid* is commercial and often verbal; as, a *bid* at an auction. An *overture* opens negotiation or conference, and the word is especially used of some movement toward reconciliation; as, *overtures* of peace. See synonyms under DESIGN. *Antonyms*: acceptance, decision, denial, refusal, rejection, repulse.

pro·pose (prə·pōz′) *v.* **·posed, ·pos·ing** *v.t.* **1** To put forward for acceptance or consideration. **2** To nominate, as for admission or appointment. **3** To intend; purpose. **4** To suggest the drinking of (a toast or health). —*v.i.* **5** To form or announce a plan or design. **6** To make an offer, as of marriage. [<OF *proposer* <*pro-* forth (<L) + *poser.* See POSE[1].] —**pro·pos′er** *n.*

Synonym: purpose. In its most frequent use, *propose* differs from *purpose* in that what we *purpose* lies in our own mind as a decisive act of will, a determination; what we *propose* is offered or stated to others. In this use of the word, what we *propose* is open to deliberation, as what we *purpose* is not. In another use of the word one *proposes* something to or by himself which may or may not be stated to others. In this latter sense *propose* is nearly identical with *purpose.* See PLAN, PURPOSE.

prop·o·si·tion (prop′ə·zish′ən) *n.* **1** A scheme or proposal offered for consideration or acceptance. **2** *U.S. Colloq.* Any matter or person to be dealt with: a tough *proposition.* **3** *Colloq.* An indecent or immodest proposal. **4** A subject or statement presented for discussion. **5** *Logic* A statement in which something (the *subject*) is affirmed or denied in terms of something else (the *predicate*), the two being related usually by a copula. In the propositions, *Grass is green* and *Grass is not red,* grass in each case is the subject and green and red are the predicates respectively. **6** *Math.* A statement of a truth to be demonstrated (a *theorem*) or of an operation to be performed (a *problem*). See synonyms under PROPOSAL. —*v.t. Colloq.* To make an improper suggestion to. [<OF <L *propositio, -onis* a setting forth <*propositus,* pp. of *proponere.* See PROPONENT.] —**prop′o·si′tion·al** *adj.* —**prop′o·si′tion·al·ly** *adv.*

pro·pos·i·tus (prō·poz′i·təs) *n. pl.* **·ti** (-tī) *Law* The person from whom a line of descent is reckoned. [<L. See PROPOSITION.]

pro·pound (prō·pound′) *v.t.* To put forward for consideration, solution, etc. See synonyms under AFFIRM, ANNOUNCE. [Earlier *propone* <L *proponere* set forth. See PROPONENT.] —**pro·pound′er** *n.*

pro·pre·tor (prō·prē′tər) *n.* In ancient Rome, an officer, especially a governor of a province, having the authority of a pretor without pretorian rank. Also **pro·prae′tor.** [<L *propraetor* <*pro praetore* (one acting) for the pretor < *pro-* for + *praetor* a pretor]

pro·pri·e·tar·y (prə·prī′ə·ter′ē) *adj.* **1** Pertaining to a proprietor; subject to exclusive ownership. **2** Designating an article, as a therapeutic device or medicine, protected as to name, composition, or process of manufacture by copyright, patent, secrecy, or other means. —*n. pl.* **·tar·ies 1** A proprietor or proprietors collectively. **2** Proprietorship. [<LL *proprietarius* <*proprietas* PROPERTY]

proprietary colony A colony organized under a royal grant of territory with full administrative powers to a private person or persons. Maryland, Pennsylvania, and Delaware remained proprietary colonies until the Revolution.

pro·pri·e·tor (prə·prī′ə·tər) *n.* A person having the exclusive title to anything. —**pro·pri′e·tor·ship′** *n.* —**pro·pri′e·tress** *n. fem.*

pro·pri·e·ty (prə·prī′ə·tē) *n. pl.* **·ties 1** The character or quality of being proper; especially, accordance with recognized usage, custom, or principles; becomingness; fitness; correctness. **2** *Obs.* An exclusive right of possession; also, a possession or property owned. —**the proprieties** The methods or standards of good society. [<OF *proprieté.* Doublet of PROPERTY.]

pro·pri·o·cep·tor (prō′prē·ə·sep′tər) *n. Physiol.* One of the sensory receptors situated within the body which are responsive to internal stimuli, as the muscles, joints, and tendons. [<NL <L *proprius* one's own + (RE)CEPTOR] —**pro′pri·o·cep′tive** *adj.*

prop root *Bot.* The supporting root of a plant, growing into the soil from above ground, as in corn.

prop·to·sis (prop·tō′sis) *n. Med.* A forward displacement; bulging, as of the eyeball. [< LL <Gk. *proptōsis* a falling forward < *propiptein* fall forwards <*pro-* forward + *piptein* fall]

pro·pul·sion (prə·pul′shən) *n.* **1** The act or operation of propelling. **2** An impulse given or received. [<F <L *propulsus,* pp. of *propellere* PROPEL] —**pro·pul′sive** (-siv) *adj.*

pro·pyl (prō′pil) *n. Chem.* The univalent radical, C_3H_7, derived from propane. [<PROP(ION-IC) + -YL]

prop·y·lae·um (prop′ə·lē′əm) *n. pl.* **·lae·a** (-lē′ə) *Usually pl.* A structure forming an imposing entrance or gateway before an ancient temple; more widely, a porch or vestibule. [<L <Gk. *propylaion* <*pro-* before +*pylē* a gate]

pro·pyl·ene (prō′pə·lēn) *n. Chem.* A gaseous hydrocarbon, C_3H_6, obtained from propane and as a by–product in petroleum refining. Also called *propene.* [<PROPYL +-ENE]

prop·y·lite (prop′ə·līt) *n.* A variety of andesite which has been altered by the action of hot water. [<Gk. *propylon* PROPYLON + -ITE[1]; so called because thought of as opening the Tertiary epoch]

prop·y·lon (prop′ə·lon) *n. pl.* **·la** (-lə) A monumental gateway placed before the principal entrance of an important building of ancient Egypt, as a temple. [<L <Gk. <*pro-* before + *pylē* a gate]

pro ra·ta (prō rā′tə, rat′ə, rä′tə) In proportion: The loss was shared *pro rata.* [<L *pro rata (parte)* according to the calculated (share)]

pro·rate (prō·rāt′, prō′rāt′) *v.t.* & *v.i.* **·rat·ed, ·rat·ing** To distribute or divide proportionately. [<PRO RATA] —**pro·rat′a·ble** *adj.* —**pro·ra′tion** *n.*

prore (prôr) *n. Obs.* A prow. [<MF <L *prora* a prow]

pro·ro·ga·tion (prō′rə·gā′shən) *n.* **1** The act of proroguing, as a session of the British Parliament. **2** The act of prolonging or extending in time; also, continuance; prolongation. [< OF *prorogacion* <L *prorogatio, -onis* < *prorogatus,* pp. of *progrogare* PROROGUE]

pro·rogue (prō·rōg′) *v.t.* **·rogued, ·ro·guing 1** To discontinue a session of (an assembly, especially the British Parliament). **2** *Obs.* To put off or postpone. **3** *Obs.* To protract or prolong. [<MF *proroguer* <L *prorogare* prolong <*pro-* forth + *rogare* ask]

pro·sa·ic (prō·zā′ik) *adj.* **1** Lacking in those qualities that impart animation or interest; unimaginative; commonplace; dull. **2** Pertaining to or having the form of prose. Also **pro·sa′i·cal.** [<LL*prosaicus* <L *prosa* prose] —**pro·sa′ic·ness** *n.*

pro·sa·ism (prō′zā·iz′əm) *n.* A prosaic expression, phrase or style. [<F *prosaïsme* <L *prosa* prose]

pro·sce·ni·um (prō·sē′nē·əm) *n. pl.* **·ni·a** (-nē·ə) **1** In a modern theater or similar building, that part of the stage between the curtain or drop scene and the orchestra, sometimes including the curtain and its arch. **2** In the ancient theater, the wall that formed a background for the actors. [<L <Gk. *proskēnion* <*pro-* before + *skēnē* a stage, orig. a tent]

pro·sciut·to (prō·shōō′tō) *n.* A spicy, cured ham. [<Ital.]

pro·scribe (prō·skrīb′) *v.t.* **·scribed, ·scrib·ing 1** To denounce or condemn; prohibit; interdict. **2** To outlaw or banish. **3** In ancient Rome, to publish the name of (one condemned or exiled). [<L *proscribere* <*pro-* before + *scribere* write] —**pro·scrib′er** *n.*

pro·scrip·tion (prō·skrip′shən) *n.* The act of proscribing, or state of being proscribed; interdiction; ostracism; outlawry. [<L *proscriptio, -onis* <*proscriptus,* pp. of *proscribere* PROSCRIBE] —**pro·scrip′tive** *adj.* —**pro·scrip′tive·ly** *adv.* —**pro·scrip′tive·ness** *n.*

prose (prōz) *n.* **1** Speech or writing without metrical structure: opposed to *verse* or *poetry.* **2** Common place or tedious discourse. **3** *Eccl.* A hymn of irregular meter sometimes sung in the eucharistic liturgy after the gradual; a sequence. 4 A proser. —*adj.* Pertaining to prose; not poetic; hence, tedious. —*v.t.* & *v.i.* **prosed, pros·ing** To write or speak in prose. [<OF <L *prosa (oratio)* straightforward (discourse) <*prorsus* <*pro-* forward + *versus,* pp. of *vertere* turn]

pro·se·cre·tin (prō′si·krē′tin) *n. Biochem.* The inactive form of secretin converted into the active form by stomach acids. [<PRO-[2] before + SECRETIN]

pro·sect (prō·sekt′) *v.t.* To dissect for purposes of anatomical demonstration and instruction. [Back formation <*prosector* an anatomist <LL <L *prosectus,* pp. of *prosecare* cut up <*pro-* before + *secare* cut] —**pro·sec′tion** (-sek′shən) *n.* —**pro·sec′tor** *n.*

pros·e·cute (pros′ə·kyōōt) *v.* **·cut·ed, ·cut·ing** *v.t.* 1 To go on with so as to complete; pursue to the end: to *prosecute* an inquiry. 2 To carry on or engage in, as a trade or profession. 3 *Law* a To bring suit against for redress of wrong or punishment of crime. b To seek to enforce or obtain, as a claim or right, by legal process. —*v.i.* 4 To begin and carry on a legal proceeding. See synonyms under PUSH. [<L *prosecutus,* pp. of *prosequi* pursue <*pro-* before + *sequi* follow]

prosecuting attorney The attorney empowered to act in behalf of the government, whether state, county, or national, in prosecuting for penal offenses.

pros·e·cu·tion (pros′ə·kyōō′shən) *n.* 1 The act or process of prosecuting. 2 *Law* a The instituting and carrying forward of a judicial proceeding to obtain some right or to redress and punish some wrong. b The institution and continuance of a criminal proceeding. c The party instituting and conducting it.

pros·e·cu·tor (pros′ə·kyōō′tər) *n.* 1 One who prosecutes, in any sense. 2 *Law* a One who institutes and carries on a suit, especially a criminal suit. b A prosecuting attorney.

pros·e·lyte (pros′ə·līt) *n.* One brought over to any opinion, belief, sect, or party, especially from one religious belief to another. See synonyms under CONVERT. —*v.* **·lyt·ed, ·lyt·ing** *v.i.* To make proselytes. —*v.t.* To make a convert of. [<LL *proselytus* <Gk. *prosēlytos* a convert to Judaism, orig. a newcomer <*prosēlyth-,* stem of *proserchesthai* approach]

pros·e·lyt·ism (pros′ə·līt′iz·əm, -li·tiz′əm) *n.* The making of converts to a religion, sect, or party, or the state of being thus converted. —**pros′e·lyt·ist** *n.*

pros·e·lyt·ize (pros′ə·lit·īz′) *v.t.* & *v.i.* **·ized, ·iz·ing** To proselyte. Also *Brit.* **pros′e·lyt·ise′.**

pros·en·ceph·a·lon (pros′en·sef′ə·lon) *n. Anat.* The forebrain. [<NL <Gk. *pros-* near, before + *encephalon* the brain. See ENCEPHALON.] —**pros′en·ce·phal′ic** (-sə·fal′ik) *adj.*

pros·en·chy·ma (pros·eng′ki·mə) *n. Bot.* Plant tissue composed of elongated, pointed, typically thick-walled cells, as distinguished from the parenchyma. [<NL <Gk. *pros-* toward, near + *enchyma* an infusion. See ENCHYMA.] —**pros·en·chym·a·tous** (pros′eng·kim′ə·təs) *adj.*

prose poem A prose work which resembles poetry either in style, structure, or emotional content.

pros·er (prō′zər) *n.* A dull or tedious writer or talker; a bore.

Pros·er·pine (pros′ər·pīn, prō·sûr′·pə·nē) In Roman mythology, the daughter of Ceres and wife of Pluto: identified with the Greek *Persephone.* Also **Pro·ser·pi·na** (prō·sûr′pə·nə).

pro·sim·i·an (prō·sim′ē·ən) *adj. Zool.* Designating any member of a suborder or group *(Prosimii)* of widely distributed early primates, as lemurs, indris, lorises, and tarsiers, characterized by small size, primitive brain development, and extensive adaptive radiation. —*n.* Any primate of this group. [<NL <Gk. *pro-* before + L *simia* an ape]

pro·sit (prō′sit) *Latin* Literally, may it benefit (you): a toast used in drinking health.

pro·slav·er·y (prō·slā′vər·ē, -slāv′rē) *adj.* In United States history, advocating Negro slavery or the policy of non-interference with it. —*n.* The advocacy of slavery.

pros·o·dem·ic (pros′ə·dem′ik) *adj. Med.* Transmitted from one person to another: said of diseases which spread by contact with affected individuals. [<*proso-* forward (<Gk. *prosō*) + (EPI)DEMIC]

pros·o·dist (pros′ə·dist) *n.* One versed in prosody.

pros·o·dy (pros′ə·dē) *n.* The science of poetical forms, including quantity and accent of syllables, meter, and versification and metrical composition. [<L *prosodia* the accent of a syllable <Gk. *prosōidia* a song sung to music <*pros-* to + *ōidē* a song] —**pro·sod·ic** (prō·sod′ik) or **·i·cal, pro·so·di·ac** (prō·sō′·dē·ak). **pro·so·di·al** (prō·sō′dē·əl) *adj.*

pro·so·po·pe·ia (prō·sō′pə·pē′ə) *n.* 1 A rhetorical figure in which the speaker impersonates another. 2 Personification. Also **pro·so′po·poe′ia.** [<L <Gk. *prosōpopoiia* <*prosōpon* a face, person + *poieein* make]

pros·pect (pros′pekt) *n.* 1 A future probability based on present indications. 2 A scene spread out before one's eyes; an extended view. 3 The direction in which anything faces; an exposure; outlook. 4 A prospective buyer. 5 The act of observing; sight; survey. 6 *Mining* a An indication of the presence of mineral ore. b A place having promising signs of the presence of mineral ore. c The sample or specimen of mineral obtained by washing a small portion of ore or dirt. 7 A consideration of the future; foresight. See synonyms under SCENE. —*v.t.* & *v.i.* To explore (a region) for gold, oil, etc. [<L *prospectus* a look-out, view <*prospicere* look forward <*pro-* forward + *specere* look]

pro·spec·tive (prə·spek′tiv) *adj.* 1 Being still in the future; anticipated; expected. 2 Looking toward or concerned with the future; anticipatory. —**pro·spec′tive·ly** *adv.*

pros·pec·tor (pros′pek·tər) *n.* One who searches or examines a region for mineral deposits or precious stones.

pro·spec·tus (prə·spek′təs) *n.* 1 A paper containing information of a proposed literary, commercial, or industrial undertaking. 2 A summary; outline. [<L. See PROSPECT.]

pros·per (pros′pər) *v.i.* To be prosperous; thrive; flourish. —*v.t.* To render prosperous: God *prospers* the Republic. See synonyms under FLOURISH, SUCCEED. [<OF *prosperer* <L *prosperare* cause to succeed or prosper <*prosper, prosperus* favorable, prosperous]

pros·per·i·ty (pros·per′ə·tē) *n.* The state of being prosperous; attainment of the object desired; material well-being; success.

Pros·per·o (pros′pər·ō) In Shakespeare's *Tempest,* the banished Duke of Milan.

pros·per·ous (pros′pər·əs) *adj.* 1 Successful; flourishing. 2 Favoring or tending to success; auspicious. 3 Promising; favorable. See synonyms under AUSPICIOUS, FORTUNATE, HAPPY, WELL. [<MF *prospereus* <OF *prospere* <L *prosper, prosperus* favorable] —**pros′per·ous·ly** *adv.* —**pros′per·ous·ness** *n.*

pros·tate (pros′tāt) *adj.* 1 *Anat.* Designating a partly muscular gland at the base of the bladder around the urethra in male mammals. 2 Standing in front. —*n.* The prostate gland. [<Med. L *prostata* <Gk. *prostatēs* one who stands before <*proïstania* <*pro-* before + *histanai* set] —**pro·stat·ic** (prō·stat′ik) *adj.*

pros·ta·tec·to·my (pros′tə·tek′tə·mē) *n. Surg.* Excision of the prostate gland.

prostato- *combining form Med.* The prostate gland; of or related to the prostate: *prostatotomy.* Also, before vowels, **prostat-.** [<Gk. *prostatēs.* See PROSTATE.]

pros·ta·tot·o·my (pros′tə·tot′ə·mē) *n. Surg.* An incision into the prostate gland. [<PROSTATO- + -TOMY]

pros·the·sis (pros′thə·sis) *n.* 1 The addition of a letter or syllable to a word, especially at the beginning, as *yclept, bewail:* also spelled *prothesis.* 2 *Surg.* The fitting of artificial parts to the body, as a glass eye, a false tooth, etc. 3 Replacement or substitution of parts. [<L <Gk., addition <*prostithenai* add <*pros-* toward, besides + *tithenai* place, put] —**pros·thet·ic** (pros·thet′ik) *adj.*

pros·thet·ics (pros·thet′iks) *n.* The branch of surgery or dentistry which specializes in artificial parts and organs. [<Gk. *prosthetikos* additional <*prosthetos* added, put on < *prostithenai.* See PROSTHESIS.] —**pros·the·tist** (pros′thə·tist) *n.*

pros·tho·don·ti·a (pros′thə·don′shē·ə, -shə) *n.* Dental prosthetics. [<NL <Gk. *prosthesis* addition + *odous, odontos* tooth]

pros·tho·don·tist (pros′thə·don′tist) *n.* A dentist who specializes in dental prosthetics.

pros·ti·tute (pros′tə·tōōt, -tyōōt) *n.* 1 A woman who practices prostitution; a harlot; whore. 2 Any base hireling; a corrupt person. —*v.t.* **·tut·ed, ·tut·ing** 1 To apply to base or unworthy purposes: to *prostitute* one's talent. 2 To offer (oneself or another) for lewd purposes, especially for hire. See synonyms under ABUSE. —*adj.* 1 Openly devoted to lewdness or promiscuity, as a woman. 2 Surrendered to base purposes. [<L *prostitutus,* pp. of *prostituere* expose publicly, prostitute <*pro-* before + *statuere* cause to stand] —**pros′ti·tu′tor** *n.*

pros·ti·tu·tion (pros′tə·tōō′shən, -tyōō′-) *n.* 1 The act or business of prostituting; the offering, by a woman, of her body for purposes of intercourse with men for hire. 2 The act of hiring or devoting to base purposes, as one's honor, talents, resources, etc.

pros·trate (pros′trāt) *adj.* 1 Lying prone, or with the face to the ground; hence, figuratively, brought low in mind or spirit. 2 Lying at the mercy of another; defenseless. 3 *Bot.* Trailing along the ground; procumbent. —*v.t.* **·trat·ed, ·trat·ing** 1 To bow or cast (oneself) down, as in adoration or pleading. 2 To throw flat; lay on the ground. 3 To overthrow or overcome; reduce to weakness or helplessness. [<L *prostratus,* pp. of *prosternere* lay flat <*pro-* before + *sternere* stretch out] —**pros′tra·tor** *n.*

pros·tra·tion (pros·trā′shən) *n.* 1 The act of prostrating in any sense. 2 Exhaustion of body or mind; great dejection or depression.

pro·style (prō′stīl) *adj. Archit.* Having a range of detached columns in front, but no columns on the sides or back of the building; also, constituting such a portico: a *prostyle* temple. [<L *prostylus* <Gk. *prostylos* <*pro-* before + *stylos* a pillar]

pros·y (prō′zē) *adj.* **pros·i·er, pros·i·est** 1 Like mere prose; prosaic. 2 Dull; tedious; commonplace. —**pros′i·ly** *adv.* —**pros′i·ness** *n.*

prot- Var. of PROTO-.

pro·tac·tin·i·um (prō′tak·tin′ē·əm) *n.* A radioactive element (symbol Pa) intermediate between thorium and uranium: its disintegration by the loss of an alpha particle gives rise to actinium. [<PROT- + ACTINIUM]

pro·tag·o·nist (prō·tag′ə·nist) *n.* The actor who played the chief part in a Greek drama; hence, a leader in any enterprise or contest. [<Gk. *prōtagōnistēs* <*prōtos* first + *agōnistēs* a contestant, an actor]

Pro·tag·o·ras (prō·tag′ər·əs), 481?–411 B.C., Greek philosopher.

pro·ta·mine (prō′tə·mēn, -min) *n. Biochem.* One of a class of strongly basic simple proteins, uncoagulable by heat, soluble in ammonia, and yielding a few amino acids when hydrolyzed. Also **pro′ta·min** (-min). [<PROT- + -AMINE]

pro·ta·no·pi·a (prō′tə·nō′pē·ə) *n. Pathol.* Color blindness marked by inability to distinguish between red and green; red blindness. [<NL <Gk. *prōtos* first + *an-* not + *ōps, ōpos* an eye] —**pro·ta·nope** (prō′tə·nōp) *n.*

prot·a·sis (prot′ə·sis) *n.* 1 In a conditional sentence, the clause (usually introductory) that contains the condition or antecedent: distinguished from *apodosis.* 2 The introductory or subordinate clause in a sentence not conditional. 3 In classical drama, the introductory part of a play. [<LL <Gk., a hypothesis <*pro-* before + *teinein* stretch]

pro·te·an (prō′tē·ən, prō·tē′an) *adj.* Readily assuming different forms or various aspects; changeable. —*n. Biochem.* Any of a group of derived proteins which are the first product of protein hydrolysis. [<PROTEUS]

pro·te·ase (prō′tē·ās) *n. Biochem.* An enzyme that digests proteins. [<PROTE(OLYSIS) + -ASE]

pro·tect (prə·tekt′) *v.t.* 1 To shield or defend from attack, harm, or injury; guard; defend. 2 *Econ.* To assist (domestic industry) by means of protective tariffs. 3 In commerce, to provide funds to guarantee payment of (a draft, etc.). See synonyms under CHERISH,

KEEP, PRESERVE, SHELTER. [<L *protectus*, pp. of *protegere* protect <*pro-* before + *tegere* cover] — **pro·tect′ing** *adj.* — **pro·tect′ing·ly** *adv.*

pro·tec·tant (prə·tek′tənt) *n.* That which protects from or guards against damage, disease, or injury; especially, a germicide, insecticide, fungicide, or the like.

pro·tect·ed (prə·tek′tid) *adj.* Shielded from harm; cared for; guarded.

pro·tec·tion (prə·tek′shən) *n.* **1** The act of protecting; a protected condition; that which protects. **2** Specifically, a system aiming to protect the industries of a country by governmental action, as by imposing duties. See PROTECTIVE TARIFF. **3** A safe-conduct; passport. **4** *U.S. Slang* Security purchased under threat of violence from racketeers; also, the money so paid. See synonyms under DEFENSE, REFUGE, SHELTER.

pro·tec·tion·ism (prə·tek′shən·iz′əm) *n.* The economic doctrine or system of protection. — **pro·tec′tion·ist** *n.*

pro·tec·tive (prə·tek′tiv) *adj.* **1** Affording or suitable for protection; sheltering; defensive; specifically, in political economy, insuring or intended to insure protection to home industries: a *protective* tariff. **2** Providing or alleging to provide protection: *protective* custody. — *n.* Something that protects; specifically, an aseptic covering for a wound. — **pro·tec′tive·ly** *adv.* — **pro·tec′tive·ness** *n.*

protective coloration *Biol.* Any coloration of a plant or animal that makes it almost indistinguishable from its natural or habitual environment, and thus safe from detection by its enemies.

protective tariff *Econ.* A tariff that is intended to insure protection of domestic industries against foreign competition: opposed to *free trade.*

pro·tec·tor (prə·tek′tər) *n.* **1** One who protects; a defender. **2** In English history, one appointed as a regent of the kingdom during minority or incapacity of the sovereign. Also **pro·tect′er.** — **pro·tec′tress** *n. fem.*

Pro·tec·tor (prə·tek′tər) *n.* The official title of the chief ruler during the Commonwealth: in full, **Lord Protector.** The title was borne by Oliver Cromwell, 1653–58, and by Richard Cromwell, 1658–59.

pro·tec·tor·ate (prə·tek′tər·it) *n.* **1** A relation of protection and partial control by a strong nation over a weaker power. **2** A country or region under the protection of another. **3** The office, or period of office, of a protector of a kingdom. Also **pro·tec′tor·ship.**

Pro·tec·tor·ate (prə·tek′tər·it) *n.* The English government during the time of the Cromwells, 1653–59.

pro·tec·to·ry (prə·tek′tər·ē) *n. pl.* **·to·ries** An institution for the care and education of homeless or destitute children.

pro·tect·o·scope (prə·tek′tə·skōp) *n. Mil.* A device resembling the periscope, to permit tank gunners to observe around their protective shields without exposing themselves to gunfire. [<PROTECT + -(O)SCOPE]

pro·té·gé (prō′tə·zhā, *Fr.* prô·tā·zhā′) *n.* One specially cared for by another who is older or more powerful. [<F pp. of *protéger* <L *protegere* PROTECT] — **pro′té·gée** *n. fem.*

pro·te·in (prō′tē·in, -tēn) *n. Biochem.* Any of a class of highly complex nitrogenous organic compounds occurring naturally in all living matter, and forming an essential part of animal food requirements. They are composed principally of amino acids in varying combinations, and are usually classified as: *simple* (hydrolyzed only by enzymes or acids into alpha-amino acids or their derivatives); *conjugated* (simple proteins combined with non-proteins in a form other than a salt); *derived* (obtained by the action of heat, enzymes, or reagents upon naturally occurring proteins). Also **pro′te·id** (-id). [<G <Gk. *prōteios* chief <*prōtos* first; so called because the chief constituent of living matter]

pro tem·po·re (prō tem′pə·rē) *Latin* For the time being; temporary: abbr. *pro tem.*

pro·tend (prō·tend′) *v.i. Psychol.* To exhibit protensity. [<L *protendere* stretch forth < *pro-* forth + *tendere* stretch]

pro·ten·si·ty (prō·ten′sə·tē) *n. Psychol.* The temporal attribute of a sensation or other mental phenomenon: the psychic analog of duration. [<L *protensus*, pp. of *protendere.* See PROTEND.] — **pro·ten′sive** *adj.*

pro·te·ol·y·sis (prō′tē·ol′ə·sis) *n. Biochem.* The change or splitting up of proteins into simpler products during digestion. [<NL <*proteo-* (<PROTEIN) + Gk. *lysis* a loosening <*lyein* loosen] — **pro′te·o·lyt′ic** (-ə·lit′ik) *adj.*

pro·te·ose (prō′tē·ōs) *n. Biochem.* Any of a group of derived proteins formed naturally in the process of digestion and produced artificially, as by treating the corresponding proteins with dilute mineral acids. [<PROTE(IN) + -OSE[2]]

Prot·er·o·zo·ic (prot′ər·ə·zō′ik) *Geol. adj.* Pertaining to or designating the geological era following the Archeozoic and succeeded by the Paleozoic. — *n.* The Proterozoic era. [<*protero-* (<Gk. *proteros* former) + -ZOIC]

Pro·tes·i·la·us (prō·tes′ə·lā′əs) In the *Iliad,* the husband of Laodamia and first of the Greeks killed at Troy.

pro·test (prō′test) *n.* **1** The act of protesting; a solemn or formal objection or declaration. **2** A public expression of dissent, especially if organized. **3** A formal notarial certificate attesting the fact that a note or bill of exchange has been presented for acceptance or payment and that it has been refused. **4** In maritime law, a written declaration by the master of a vessel stating that an injury to the vessel or the cargo was not owing to the neglect or misconduct of the master. **5** A formal statement in writing made by a person called upon by public authority to pay a sum of money, as an import duty or a tax, in which he declares that he does not concede the legality of the claim. — *adj.* Of or relating to public protest: *protest* demonstrations. — *v.* (prə·test′) *v.t.* **1** To assert earnestly or positively; state formally, especially against opposition or doubt. **2** To make a protest against; object to: I *protested* his actions. **3** To declare formally that payment of (a promissory note, etc.) has been duly submitted and refused. — *v.i.* **4** To make solemn affirmation. **5** To make a protest; object. See synonyms under AFFIRM, ASSERT, AVOW. [<OF *protester* <L *protestari* <*pro-* forth + *testari* affirm, give evidence <*testis* a witness] — **pro·test′er** *n.*

prot·es·tant (prot′is·tənt, prə·tes′-) *n.* One who makes a protest. [<MF <L *protestans, -antis,* ppr. of *protestari* PROTEST]

Prot·es·tant (prot′is·tənt) *n.* **1** A member of one of those bodies of Christians that adhere to Protestantism, as opposed to Roman Catholicism: a use opposed by some Anglicans. **2** In the 17th century, a Lutheran or Anglican. **3** Originally, one of those German princes who, at the second Council of Spires, April 19, 1529, protested against the decree of the majority representing the Roman Catholic states which involved a virtual submission to the authority of the Roman Catholic Church. — *adj.* Pertaining to Protestants or Protestantism.

Protestant Episcopal Church A religious body in the United States which is descended from the Church of England, but has been organized as a separate and independent body since 1789.

Prot·es·tant·ism (prot′is·tənt·iz′əm) *n.* **1** The principles and common system of doctrines taught by Luther, and by the evangelical churches since. Its positive and formal principle is that nothing that is not taught in the Holy Scriptures, the authoritative rule of faith and practice in the church, enters as an essential element into the Christian system. **2** The ecclesiastical system founded upon this faith; also, Protestants, collectively. **3** The state of being a Protestant.

prot·es·ta·tion (prot′is·tā′shən) *n.* **1** The act of protesting; also, that which is protested. **2** A formal declaration of dissent. **3** Any solemn or urgent avowal.

Pro·test·er (prə·tes′tər) *n.* A Scotsman who protested against the union of the Presbyterians and the Royalists in 1650. Also **Pro·tes′tor.**

pro·test·ing·ly (prə·tes′ting·lē) *adv.* In such a manner as to protest.

Pro·te·us (prō′tē·əs, -tyōōs) In Greek mythology, a sea god who had the power of assuming different forms. — **Pro′te·an** *adj.*

pro·tha·la·mi·on (prō′thə·lā′mē·on, -ən) *n. pl.* **·mi·a** (-mē·ə) A song celebrating a marriage. Also **pro′tha·la′mi·um** (-me·əm). [<NL <Gk. *pro-* before + *thalamos* a bridal chamber; coined by Spenser on analogy with *epithalamion*]

pro·thal·li·um (prō·thal′ē·əm) *n. pl.* **·li·a** (-ē·ə) *Bot.* The first or false thallus formed on the germination of the asexually produced spores in pteridophytes; a delicate, evanescent cellular structure bearing the sexual organs. Also **pro·thal′lus.** [<NL <Gk. *pro-* before + *thallion*, dim. of *thallos* a shoot] — **pro·thal′li·al** *adj.* — **pro·thal′line** (-thal′in, -in) *adj.*

proth·e·sis (proth′ə·sis) *n.* **1** Prosthesis (def. 1). **2** In the Greek Orthodox Church, a service by which the elements are prepared for consecration in the Eucharist. [<LL <Gk., a placing before, or in public <*protithenai* set before <*pro-* before + *tithenai* place] — **pro·thet·ic** (prō·thet′ik) *adj.* — **pro·thet′i·cal·ly** *adv.*

pro·thon·o·tar·y (prō·thon′ə·ter′ē, prō′thə·nō′·tər·ē) *n. pl.* **·tar·ies** **1** A chief clerk; specifically, in the Roman Catholic Church, one of the seven (formerly twelve) ecclesiastics at Rome who keep the registry of important pontifical proceedings, or one having the title and some of the associated privileges. **2** In some States of the United States, a probate officer. Also spelled *protonotary.* [<LL *protonotarius* <LGk. *prōtonotarios* <Gk. *prōtos* first + L *notarius.* See NOTARY.] — **pro·thon′o·tar′i·al** (-târ′ē·əl) *adj.*

prothonotary warbler A North American warbler (*Protonotaria citrea*) the male of which is noted for the brilliant yellow to orange coloring of its head and under parts, with bluish-gray wings and tail.

pro·tho·rax (prō·thôr′aks, -thō′raks) *n. pl.* **·rax·es** or **·tho·ra·ces** (-thôr′ə·sēz, -thō′rə-) *Entomol.* The anterior segment of the thorax of an insect. [<NL <Gk. *pro-* in front + *thorax* thorax] — **pro·tho·rac·ic** (prō′thô·ras′·ik, -thō-) *adj.*

pro·throm·bin (prō·throm′bin) *n. Biochem.* The inactive precursor of thrombin: it is converted into thrombin by the action of calcium and thromboplastin, and is essential to the process of blood-clotting: also called *thrombogen.* [<NL <Gk. *pro-* before + *thrombos* a clot]

pro·tist (prō′tist) *n. Biol.* **1** Any unicellular organism, whether animal or plant. **2** Formerly, any member of a large division (*Protista*) including all single-celled organisms. [<NL <Gk. *prōtista*, neut. pl. of *prōtistos* the very first, superl. of *prōtos* first] — **pro·tis′tan** *adj.* & *n.* — **pro·tis′tic** *adj.*

pro·ti·um (prō′tē·əm) *n. Chem.* The hydrogen isotope of atomic mass 1 (symbol, H^1): sometimes so called in distinction from deuterium and tritium. [<NL <Gk. *prōtos* first. Cf. PROTO- (def. 3).]

proto- *combining form* **1** First in rank or time; chief; typical: *protomartyr.* **2** Primitive; original: *prototype.* **3** *Chem.* **a** Designating the first or lowest member of a series; having the least amount (of an element or radical): *protoxide.* **b** Denoting the parent form or source of: *protoactinium.* Also, before vowels, *prot-.* [<Gk. *prōto-* <*prōtos* first]

pro·to·ac·tin·i·um (prō′tō·ak·tin′ē·əm) *n.* Protactinium.

Pro·to·coc·cus (prō′tə·kok′əs) *n.* The typical genus of a family (*Chlorophyceae*) of green algae, growing on damp walls, rocks, and trunks of trees. [<PROTO- + COCCUS]

pro·to·col (prō′tə·kol) *n.* **1** The preliminary draft of an official document, as a treaty; specifically, the preliminary draft or report of the negotiations and conclusions arrived at by a diplomatic conference, having the force of a treaty when ratified. **2** The rules of diplomatic and state etiquette and ceremony. — *v.i.* To write or form protocols. [<OF *prothocole* <Med. L *protocollum* <LGk. *prōtokollon* the first glued sheet of a papyrus roll <*prōtos* first + *kolla* glue]

pro·to·derm (prō′tə·dûrm) *n.* Dermatogen.

pro·to·gene (prō′tə·jēn) *n.* The hypothetical prototype of the gene, assumed to have been formed from complex carbon compounds at the time when life evolved from inorganic matter.

pro·to·gram (prō′tə·gram) *n.* An acronym.

Pro·to·hip·pus (prō′tō·hip′əs) *n. Paleontol.* A genus of extinct, three-toed horses of the Miocene period. [<NL <Gk. *prōtos* first + *hippos* a horse]

pro·to·hu·man (prō′tō·hyōō′mən) *adj.* **1** Anterior to or more primitive than man. **2** *Paleontol.* Of, pertaining to, or describing any of several hominoid primates regarded as being at an earlier stage of development than *Homo sapiens.* —*n.* Any primate antedating modern man in evolutionary characteristics. Principal types are:

Africanthropus	Meganthropus
Australopithecus	Oreopithecus
Dryopithecus	Pithecanthropus
Gigantopithecus	Sinanthropus

pro·to·lith·ic (prō′tō·lith′ik) *adj.* Pertaining to the earliest period of the stone age; eolithic.
pro·to·mar·tyr (prō′tō·mär′tər) *n.* The first martyr or victim in any cause. [<OF *prothomartir* <Med. L *protomartyr* <Gk. *prōtomartyr* <*prōtos* first + *martyr* a witness]
pro·to·mor·phic (prō′tō·môr′fik) *adj. Biol.* Of or pertaining to, or having the most primitive or elementary form or structure. —**pro′to·morph** *n.*
pro·ton (prō′ton) *n. Physics* **1** The positively charged nucleus of the atom of the light isotope of hydrogen (symbol, H^1), constituting its principal mass. **2** One of the elementary particles in the nucleus of an atom, having a unitary positive charge and a mass of approximately 1.672×10^{-24} gram. The atomic number of an element is equivalent to the number of protons in its nucleus. [<NL <Gk. *prōton,* neut. of *prōtos* first]
pro·to·ne·ma (prō′tə·nē′mə) *n. pl.* **·ne·ma·ta** (-nē′mə·tə) *Bot.* An early stage in the development of the prothallium of ferns; a green confervoid or filamentous structure developed from the spore in mosses, on which the leafy plant arises as a lateral or terminal shoot. Also **pro′to·neme** (-nēm). [<NL <Gk. *prōtos* first + *nēma* a thread]
pro·ton·o·tar·y (prō·ton′ə·ter′ē, prō′tə·nō′tər·ē) See PROTHONOTARY.
pro·ton–pro·ton reaction (prō′ton·prō′ton) A thermonuclear chain reaction which is assumed to provide stellar energy by means of the fusion of 4 protons to make a helium nucleus, with a residue of 2 protons returned to the cycle. Compare CARBON CYCLE.
proton synchrotron *Physics* A bevatron.
pro·to·path·ic (prō′tə·path′ik) *adj. Physiol.* Pertaining to or designating primary sensibility, responsive only to gross, typically painful stimuli: distinguished from *epicritic.* [<PROTO- + -PATHIC]
pro·to·phyte (prō′tə·fīt) *n. Bot.* **1** Any single-celled plant. **2** A member of a former division (*Protophyta*) embracing only the lowest and simplest plants. [<NL <Gk. *prōtos* first + *phyton* a plant]
pro·to·plasm (prō′tə·plaz′əm) *n. Biol.* **1** The physicochemical basis of living matter, a viscid, grayish, translucent, colloidal substance of granular structure and complex composition that forms the essential part of plant and animal cells. **2** The cytoplasm of the cell, as distinguished from the nuclear material. [<G *protoplasma* <Gk. *prōtos* first + *plasma.* See PLASMA.] —**pro′to·plas′mic** or **·plas′mal** or **·plas·mat′ic** *adj.*
pro·to·plast (prō′tə·plast) *n. Biol.* **1** That which is first formed; the original or primordial cell. **2** The parent pair or one of the parent pair of the first-formed individuals of a species. **3** The protoplasmic contents of a cell. **4** A plastid. [<F *protoplaste* <LL *protoplastus* <Gk. *protoplastos* formed first < *prōtos* first + *plastos* formed <*plassein* form] —**pro′to·plas′tic** *adj.*
pro·to·ste·le (prō′tə·stē′lē, -stēl) *n. Bot.* The dense central cylinder of roots and young stems, and, in various pteridophytes, the axes. [<PROTO- + STELE²] —**pro′to·ste′lic** *adj.*
Pro·to·the·ri·a (prō′tə·thir′ē·ə) *n. pl.* A subclass of primitive, egg-laying mammals; the monotremes, as the duckbill. [<NL <Gk. *prōtos* first + *thēria,* pl. of *thērion,* dim. of *thēr* a beast]
pro·to·troph·ic (prō′tə·trof′ik, -trō′fik) *adj. Biol.* Capable of assimilating only simple inorganic substances: said of the earliest forms of life.
pro·to·type (prō′tə·tīp) *n.* **1** *Biol.* A primitive or ancestral organism; an archetype: opposed to *ectype.* **2** A first or original model on which subsequent forms are to be based. **3** An accepted standard to which all others must conform. See synonyms under EXAMPLE, IDEAL, MODEL. [<MF <NL *prototypon* <Gk. *prōtotypon,* orig. neut. sing. of *prōtotypos* original <*prōtos* first + *typos* a model] —**pro′to·typ′al** (-tī′pəl), **pro′to·typ′ic** (-tip′ik), **pro′to·typ′i·cal** *adj.*
pro·tox·ide (prō·tok′sīd, -sid) *n. Chem.* An oxide containing the lowest proportion of oxygen for a given series: contrasted with *peroxide*: iron *protoxide* (ferrous oxide). Also **pro·tox′id** (-sid). [<PROT- + OXIDE]
Pro·to·zo·a (prō′tə·zō′ə) *n. pl.* A phylum of the animal kingdom embracing microscopic organisms consisting of a single cell, and reproducing typically by binary fission. They are largely aquatic, and include many parasitic forms. [<NL <Gk. *prōtos* first + *zōia,* pl. of *zōion* an animal] —**pro′to·zo′an** *adj.* & *n.* —**pro′to·zo′ic** *adj.* —**pro′to·zo′on** *n.*
pro·to·zo·ol·o·gy (prō′tō·zō·ol′ə·jē) *n.* The study or science of unicellular organisms. —**pro′to·zo′o·log′i·cal** (-zō′ə·loj′i·kəl) *adj.* —**pro′to·zo·ol′o·gist** *n.*
pro·tract (prō·trakt′) *v.t.* **1** To extend in time; prolong. **2** In surveying, to draw or map by means of a scale and protractor; plot. **3** *Zool.* To protrude or extend: opposed to *retract.* [<L *protractus,* pp. of *protrahere* extend <*pro-* forward + *trahere* draw] —**pro·trac′tive** *adj.*
Synonyms: continue, delay, elongate, extend, lengthen, prolong. To *protract* is to cause to occupy a longer time than is usual, expected, or desirable. We *protract* a negotiation which we are slow to conclude; *delay* may be used either of the beginning or of any stage in the proceedings; we may *delay* a person as well as an action, but *protract* is not used of persons. *Elongate* is used only of material objects or extension in space; *protract* is rarely, except in mathematics, used of concrete objects or extension in space; we *elongate* a line, *protract* a discussion. *Protract* has usually an unfavorable sense; *continue* is neutral, applying equally to the desirable or the undesirable. Compare HINDER. *Antonyms*: abbreviate, abridge, conclude, contract, curtail, hasten, hurry, limit, reduce, shorten.
pro·tract·ed (prō·trak′tid) *adj.* Unduly or unusually extended or prolonged.
protracted meeting A series of religious, usually revival, meetings, held morning, afternoon, and evening, and sometimes continued for several days.
pro·tract·er (prō·trak′tər) *n.* **1** One who or that which protracts. **2** A protractor.
pro·trac·tile (prō·trak′til) *adj.* Capable of being protracted or protruded; protrusile.
pro·trac·tion (prō·trak′shən) *n.* **1** The act of drawing out or lengthening in time; the act of delaying the termination of anything. **2** In prosody, the irregular lengthening of a syllable ordinarily short. **3** The making of a surveyor's plot on paper.
pro·trac·tor (prō·trak′tər) *n.* **1** An instrument for measuring and laying off angles. **2** A tailor's adjustable pattern. **3** *Anat.* A muscle that extends a limb or moves it forward. **4** *Surg.* An instrument for extracting foreign bodies from a wound.
pro·trude (prō·trōōd′) *v.t.* & *v.i.* **·trud·ed, ·trud·ing** To push or thrust out; project outward. [<L *protrudere* <*pro-* forward + *trudere* thrust]
pro·tru·sile (prō·trōō′sil) *adj.* Adapted to being thrust out, often rapidly, as the tongue of an ant-eater. Also **pro·tru′si·ble.** [<L *protrusus,* pp. of *protrudere* PROTRUDE + -ILE]
pro·tru·sion (prō·trōō′zhən) *n.* **1** The act of protruding, or the state of being protruded. **2** The part or object protruded. [<F <L *protrusus.* See PROTRUSILE.]
pro·tru·sive (prō·trōō′siv) *adj.* **1** Tending to protrude; protruding. **2** Pushing or driving forward. —**pro·tru′sive·ly** *adv.* —**pro·tru′sive·ness** *n.*
pro·tu·ber·ance (prō·tōō′bər·əns, -tyōō′-) *n.* **1** Something that protrudes; a knob; prominence. **2** The state of being protuberant. Also **pro·tu′ber·an·cy, pro·tu′ber·a′tion.**
pro·tu·ber·ant (prō·tōō′bər·ənt, -tyōō′-) *adj.* Swelling out beyond the surrounding surface; bulging. [LL *protuberans, -antis,* ppr. of *protuberare* bulge out <L *pro-* forth + *tuber* a swelling] —**pro·tu′ber·ant·ly** *adv.*
pro·tu·ber·ate (prō·tōō′bə·rāt, -tyōō′-) *v.i.* **·at·ed, ·at·ing** To be protuberant; bulge out. [<LL *protuberatus,* pp. of *protuberare.* See PROTUBERANT.]
pro·tyle (prō′tīl, -til) *n.* The hypothetical primitive material of the universe; a substance of which all existing elements have been supposed to be modifications. Also **pro′tyl** (-til). [<Gk. *prōtos* first + *hylē* timber, matter]
proud (proud) *adj.* **1** Actuated by, possessing, or manifesting pride; arrogant; haughty; also, self-respecting. **2** Sensible of honor and personal elation: generally followed by *of* or by a verb in the infinitive. **3** High-mettled, as a horse; spirited. **4** Proceeding from or inspired by pride. **5** Being a cause of honorable pride, as a distinction or achievement. **6** *Obs.* Bold; fearless; daring. See synonyms under HAUGHTY, HIGH. [OE *prūt, prūd* <OF *prud, prod,* prob. ult. <L *prodesse* be of value] —**proud′ly** *adv.*
proud flesh *Pathol.* A granulated growth resembling flesh in a wound or sore. [So called because of its swelling up]
Prou·dhon (prōō·dôṅ′), **Pierre Joseph,** 1809–1865, French socialist, philosophical anarchist, and writer on politics and economics.
Proust (prōōst), **Joseph Louis,** 1754–1826, French chemist. —**Marcel,** 1871–1922, French novelist.
proust·ite (prōōs′tīt) *n.* An adamantine ruby-red sulfide of silver and arsenic, crystallizing in the rhombohedral system. [<F, after J. L. *Proust,* its discoverer]
Prout's hypothesis (prouts) *Chem.* A hypothesis that all atomic weights are simple multiples of the atomic weight of hydrogen. [after William *Prout,* 1785–1850, English chemist]
prove (prōōv) *v.* **proved, proved** or **prov·en, prov·ing** *v.t.* **1** To show to be true or genuine, as by evidence or argument. **2** To determine the quality or genuineness of; test: to *prove* a gun. **3** To establish the authenticity or validity of, as a will. **4** *Math.* To verify the accuracy of (a calculation or demonstration) by an independent process. **5** *Printing* To take a proof of or from. **6** *Archaic* To learn by experience; undergo. —*v.i.* **7** To be shown to be by the result or outcome; turn out to be: His hopes *proved* vain. **8** *Archaic* To make trial. See synonyms under CONFIRM. [OF *prouver* <L *probare* test, try. Doublet of PROBE.] —**prov′a·ble** *adj.* —**prov′er** *n.*
pro·vec·tion (prō·vek′shən) *n. Ling.* A transfer of the final consonant of one word to the beginning of the next word, as in *a newt,* the old form of which was *an ewt.* [<LL *provectio, -onis* <*provectus,* pp. of *provehere* advance <*pro-* forward + *vehere* carry]
prov·en (prōō′vən) Alternative past participle of PROVE: the less common form. —*adj.* Proved; established; verified.
prov·e·nance (prov′ə·nəns) *n.* Provenience; origin. [<F <*provenant,* ppr. of *provenir* come forth <L *provenire* <*pro-* forth + *venire* come]
Pro·ven·çal (prō′vən·säl′, *Fr.* prō·väṅ·säl′) *n.* **1** A native or resident of Provence, France. **2** The Romance language of Provence: developed from *langue d'oc,* and used especially in the 12th and 13th centuries in the lyric literature of the troubadours. —*adj.* Of or pertaining to Provence, its inhabitants, or their language. [<MF, of Provence <L *provincialis* <(*nostra*) *provincia* (our) province, i.e., Provence]
Pro·vence (prô·väṅs′) A region and former province of SE France.
prov·en·der (prov′ən·dər) *n.* Food for cattle; especially, dry food, as hay; rarely, provisions generally. See synonyms under FOOD. —*v.t.* To provide with food, as cattle. [<OF *provendre, provende* an allowance of food <L *praebenda.* See PREBEND.]
pro·ve·ni·ence (prō·vē′nē·əns, -vēn′yəns) *n.* The origin or source of a thing: used especially in the fine arts and archeology. [<L *proveniens, -entis,* ppr. of *provenire.* See PROVENANCE.]
prov·erb (prov′ərb) *n.* **1** A pithy saying, especially one condensing the wisdom of experience; adage; saw; maxim. **2** An enigmatical saying: to speak in a *proverb.* **3** Something

proverbial; a typical example; byword. [<OF *proverbe* <L *proverbium* < *pro-* before + *verbum* a word]

Synonyms: adage, aphorism, apothegm, axiom, byword, dictum, maxim, motto, precept, saw, saying, truism. The *proverb* or *adage* gives homely truth in condensed, practical form; the latter especially gains authority by long usage. An *aphorism* is a summary statement of a general truth. An *apothegm* is a sententious statement. A *dictum* is a statement of some person or school, on whom it depends for authority. A *saying* is impersonal, current among the people. A *saw* is a *saying* that is old, but somewhat worn and tiresome. *Precept* is a command or a rule for behavior; a *motto* or *maxim* is a brief statement of cherished truth, the *maxim* being more uniformly and directly practical. A *byword* is a *saying* used reproachfully or contemptuously. Compare ADAGE, AXIOM.

pro·ver·bi·al (prə·vûr′bē·əl) *adj.* 1 Of the nature of, pertaining to, or like a proverb: *proverbial* brevity. 2 Supplying the subject for a proverb; being the object of general remark, especially as a typical case; well-known; notorious. — **pro·ver′bi·al·ly** *adv.*

Prov·erbs (prov′ərbz) An Old Testament didactic poetical book of moral sayings and instructions.

pro·vide (prə·vīd′) *v.* **·vid·ed, ·vid·ing** *v.t.* 1 To supply or furnish. 2 To afford; yield. 3 To prepare, make ready, or procure beforehand. 4 To set down as a condition; stipulate. — *v.i.* 5 To take measures in advance: with *for* or *against.* 6 To furnish means of subsistence: usually with *for.* 7 To make a stipulation. [<L *providere* foresee < *pro-* before + *videre* see. Doublet of PURVEY.]

Synonyms: arrange, cater, furnish, prepare, procure, produce, supply. *Antonyms*: alienate, divert, lose, misemploy, mismanage, neglect, overlook, scatter, squander, waste.

pro·vid·ed (prə·vī′did) *conj.* On condition: with *that* expressed or understood: He will get the loan *provided* he offers good security. See synonyms under BUT. [Orig. pp. of PROVIDE]

prov·i·dence (prov′ə·dəns) *n.* 1 The care exercised by the Supreme Being over the universe. 2 An event or circumstances ascribable to divine interposition. 3 The exercise of foresight and care for the future; prudent economy. See synonyms under FRUGALITY, PRUDENCE. [<OF <L *providentia* < *providens, -entis,* ppr. of *providere.* See PROVIDE.]

Prov·i·dence (prov′ə·dəns) God; the Deity.

Prov·i·dence (prov′ə·dəns) The capital of Rhode Island, a port of entry on Narragansett Bay.

Providence Plantations Original name of the colony established by Roger Williams (1636) in Rhode Island.

prov·i·dent (prov′ə·dənt) *adj.* Exercising foresight; economical; anticipating and making ready for future wants or emergencies. See synonyms under THOUGHTFUL. —**prov′i·dent·ly** *adv.*

prov·i·den·tial (prov′ə·den′shəl) *adj.* Resulting from or exhibiting the action of God's providence. — **prov′i·den′tial·ly** *adv.*

pro·vid·er (prə·vī′dər) *n.* One whose income supports a family: He's a good *provider.*

pro·vid·ing (prə·vī′ding) *conj.* Provided; in case that.

prov·ince (prov′ins) *n.* 1 A considerable country incorporated with a kingdom or empire and subject to the central administration without having itself any voice in that administration. 2 Any large administrative division of a country with a permanent local government: the *provinces* of the Roman Empire, the *Provinces* of the Dominion of Canada or of the Union of South Africa, the United *Provinces* of Agra and Oudh. The word is often loosely used in the plural to denote those regions that lie at a distance from the capital; specifically, in Great Britain, the whole country except London. 3 A comprehensive department or sphere of knowledge or activity: the *province* of chemistry. 4 A definite sphere of action, especially one authoritatively assigned or properly belonging to a person: The *province* of the judge is to apply the laws. 5 *Ecol.* A zoogeographical area less than a region, having its own special flora, fauna, and types of mankind. [<OF <L *provincia* an official duty or charge, a province]

Province Welles·ley (welz′lē) See PENANG, SETTLEMENT OF.

pro·vin·cial (prə·vin′shəl) *adj.* 1 Pertaining to or characteristic of a province. 2 Confined to a province; rustic; hence, local, as a word or idiom; also, narrow; uncultured; illiberal: said of people. — *n.* A native or inhabitant of a province; one who is provincial, in any sense. — **pro·vin′ci·al′i·ty** (-shē·al′ə·tē) *n.* — **pro·vin′cial·ly** *adv.*

pro·vin·cial·ism (prə·vin′shəl·iz′əm) *n.* The quality of being provincial; a provincial custom or peculiarity, especially of speech.

proving ground A site used for testing new weapons, equipment, scientific theories, etc.

pro·vi·sion (prə·vizh′ən) *n.* 1 Measures taken or means made ready in advance; the act of taking such measures. 2 *pl.* Food or a supply of food; victuals. 3 Something provided or prepared, as against future need. 4 A stipulation or requirement; the part of an agreement, instrument, etc., referring to one specific thing. 5 Appointment to a see or benefice not yet vacant, including designation, institution, and installation; especially, such appointment when made by the pope, before a vacancy, so as to set aside nomination by the ordinary patron. 6 *pl.* Medieval English statutes by which certain important matters were provided for: the *provisions* of Oxford. See synonyms under NUTRIMENT, STOCK. — *v.t.* To provide with food or provisions. [<OF <L *provisio, -onis* a foreseeing < *provisus,* pp. of *providere.* See PROVIDE.] — **pro·vi′sion·er** *n.*

pro·vi·sion·al (prə·vizh′ən·əl) *adj.* Provided for a present service or temporary necessity: a *provisional* army; adopted tentatively or for lack of something better. — **pro·vi′sion·al·ly** *adv.*

provisional government A temporary government established to provide for a present situation or emergency, to be superseded later by a permanent government.

pro·vi·sion·ar·y (prə·vizh′ən·er′ē) *adj.* 1 Providing or intended to provide for some future occasion or want; provident; also, containing the statement of a provision. 2 Provisional.

pro·vi·so (prə·vī′zō) *n. pl.* **·sos** or **·soes** A conditional stipulation; a clause, as in a contract or statute, limiting, modifying, or rendering conditional its operation. [<Med. L *proviso (quod)* it being provided (that), ablative neut. sing. pp. of L *providere.* See PROVIDE.]

pro·vi·so·ry (prə·vī′zər·ē) *adj.* 1 Containing or made dependent on a proviso; conditional. 2 Provisional. — **pro·vi′so·ri·ly** *adv.*

pro·vi·ta·min (prō·vī′tə·min) *n. Biochem.* Any of various substances believed to promote the formation of vitamins, as carotene (**provitamin A**) or ergosterol. [< *pro-* undeveloped (<L, before) + VITAMIN]

prov·o·ca·tion (prov′ə·kā′shən) *n.* 1 The act of provoking. 2 An incitement to action; stimulus; something that stirs to anger. [<OF <L *provocatio, -onis* < *provocatus,* pp. of *provocare* PROVOKE]

pro·voc·a·tive (prə·vok′ə·tiv) *adj.* Serving to provoke; stimulating. — *n.* That which provokes or tends to provoke. — **pro·voc′a·tive·ly** *adv.* — **pro·voc′a·tive·ness** *n.*

pro·voke (prə·vōk′) *v.t.* **·voked, ·vok·ing** 1 To stir to anger or resentment; irritate; vex. 2 To arouse or stimulate to some action. 3 To stir up or bring about: to *provoke* a quarrel. 4 To induce or cause; elicit: to *provoke* a smile. 5 *Obs.* To call forth; summon. [<OF *provoker* <L *provocare* challenge < *pro-* forth + *vocare* call] — **pro·vok′ing** *adj.* — **pro·vok′ing·ly** *adv.* — **pro·vok′ing·ness** *n.*

prov·ost (prov′əst) *n.* 1 A person having charge or authority over others. 2 The chief magistrate of a Scottish city, corresponding to the English mayor: in Edinburgh, Dundee, Glasgow, and Aberdeen called **Lord Provost.** 3 In some English and American colleges, the head of the faculty. 4 The head of a collegiate chapter or a cathedral; a dean. 5 (prō′vō) Provost marshal. [Fusion of OE *profost, prafost* and AF, OF *provost,* both <LL *propositus* <L *praepositus* a prefect, orig. pp. of *praeponere* < *prae-* before + *ponere* place] — **prov′ost·ship** *n.*

pro·vost court (prō′vō) A summary military court for trying those (especially civilians in a theater of war) charged with minor offenses committed within areas controlled by the army. They are usually guided by the rules of evidence. Their jurisdiction is concurrent with that of courts martial. The military commission is resorted to in like situations for graver offenses such as espionage.

pro·vost guard (prō′vō) A company of soldiers detailed for police duty under the provost marshal.

pro·vost marshal (prō′vō) A military or naval officer exercising police functions.

pro·vost sergeant (prō′vō) A non-commissioned officer who supervises the work and duties of the military police.

prow[1] (prou) *n.* 1 The fore part of a vessel's hull or of an airship; the bow. 2 Any pointed projection. 3 *Poetic* A ship. [<MF *prove* <Provençal *proa* <L *prora* <Gk. *prōira*]

prow[2] (prou) *adj. Archaic* Brave; valiant: a *prow* knight. [<OF *prou* brave <LL *prode,* back formation <L *prodesse* be of use < *pro-, prod-* for + *esse* be]

prow·ess (prou′is) *n.* 1 Strength, skill, and courage in battle. 2 A daring and valiant deed. [<OF *prouesse, proece* < *prou* PROW[2]]

Synonyms: bravery, courage, gallantry, heroism, intrepidity, strength, valor. *Bravery, courage, heroism,* and *intrepidity* may be silent, spiritual, or passive; they may be exhibited by a martyr at the stake. *Courage* is a nobler word than *bravery,* involving more of the deep, spiritual, and enduring elements of character; it applies to matters to which *valor* and *prowess* cannot, as submission to a surgical operation, or the facing of censure or detraction for conscience' sake. *Prowess* and *valor* imply both daring and doing. *Valor* meets odds or perils with courageous action, doing its utmost to conquer at any risk or cost; *prowess* has power and ability adapted to the need; dauntless *valor* is often vain against superior *prowess.* Compare synonyms for BRAVE, COURAGE, FORTITUDE. *Antonyms*: cowardice, cowardliness, effeminacy, fear, timidity.

prowl (proul) *v.t.* & *v.i.* To roam about stealthily, as in search of prey or plunder. — *n.* A roaming about for prey. [ME *prollen* search; ult. origin uncertain] — **prowl′er** *n.*

prowl car *U.S.* A police patrol car.

prox·i·mal (prok′sə·məl) *adj.* 1 *Anat.* Relatively nearer the central portion of the body or point of origin: opposed to *distal.* 2 Proximate. — **prox′i·mal·ly** *adv.*

prox·i·mate (prok′sə·mit) *adj.* Being in immediate relation with something else; next. See synonyms under IMMEDIATE. [<LL *proximatus,* pp. of *proximare* come near <L *proximus* nearest, superl. of *prope* near] — **prox′i·mate·ly** *adv.*

prox·im·i·ty (prok·sim′ə·tē) *n.* The state or fact of being near or next; nearness. [<MF *proximité* <L *proximitas, -tatis* < *proximus.* See PROXIMATE.]

proximity fuze A complete miniature radio set placed in the nose of a projectile or bomb, capable of detonating the charge by simple proximity to the target: also called *VT fuze.*

prox·i·mo (prok′sə·mō) *adv.* In or of the next or coming month: opposed to *ultimo.* Abbr. *prox.* [<L *proximo (mense)* in the next (month), ablative of *proximus.* See PROXIMATE.]

prox·y (prok′sē) *n. pl.* **prox·ies** A person empowered by another to act for him, the office or right so to act, or the instrument conferring it. [Contraction of PROCURACY]

prude (pro͞od) *n.* A person who makes an affected display of modesty and propriety, especially in matters relating to sex. [<F, prob. back formation < *prudefemme* an excellent woman <OF *prou, prode* honest, upright + *feme* a woman]

pru·dence (pro͞od′ns) *n.* The quality of being prudent; sagacity; economy; discretion.

Synonyms: care, carefulness, caution, circumspection, consideration, discretion, forecast, foresight, forethought, frugality, judgment, judiciousness, providence, wisdom. *Care* may respect only the present; *prudence* and *providence* look far ahead and sacrifice the present to the future, *prudence* watching, saving, guarding, *providence* planning, doing, preparing, and perhaps expending largely to meet the future demand. *Frugality* is in many cases one form of *prudence*. *Foresight* merely sees the future, and may even lead to the recklessness and desperation to which *prudence* and *providence* are strongly opposed. *Forethought* is thinking of the future, a *consideration* of what might arise. See CARE, FRUGALITY, WISDOM. *Antonyms*: folly, heedlessness, improvidence, imprudence, indiscretion, rashness, recklessness, thoughtlessness.

pru·dent (pro͞od′nt) *adj.* **1** Habitually careful to avoid errors and in following the most politic and profitable course; cautious; worldly-wise. **2** Exercising sound judgment; sagacious; judicious. **3** Characterized by practical wisdom or discretion; not extravagant. **4** Decorously discreet: a *prudent* maiden. [<OF <L *prudens, -entis* knowing, skilled, contraction of *providens*. See PROVIDENCE.] **—pru′·dent·ly** *adv.*

Synonyms: careful, cautious, circumspect, considerate, discreet, economical, frugal, judicious, politic, provident, sagacious, thoughtful, thrifty, wary, wise. See POLITIC. Compare synonyms for PRUDENCE. *Antonyms*: audacious, daring, desperate, foolhardy, foolish, imprudent, indiscreet, rash, reckless, spendthrift, thoughtless, unwary.

pru·den·tial (pro͞o·den′shəl) *adj.* **1** Proceeding from or marked by prudence. **2** Exercising prudence and wisdom officially. **—pru·den′tial·ly** *adv.*

prud·er·y (pro͞o′dər·ē) *n. pl.* **·er·ies** Primness; extreme priggishness; also, prudish action or language.

prud·ish (pro͞o′dish) *adj.* Showing prudery; prim. **—prud′ish·ly** *adv.* **—prud′ish·ness** *n.*

pru·i·nose (pro͞o′i·nōs) *adj. Biol.* Having the surface characterized by a secretion or outgrowth so as to appear frosted; powdery, as the bloom on a cabbage leaf, or the floury appearance of some cicadas and beetles. [<L *pruinosus* frosty <*pruina* hoarfrost]

prune[1] (pro͞on) *n.* **1** The dried fruit of any of several varieties of plum. **2** Any of various plums that may be dried without spoiling. **3** *Slang* A stupid or uninteresting person. [<OF <LL *pruna* <L *prunum* <Gk. *proumnon, prounon* a plum. Doublet of PLUM.]

prune[2] (pro͞on) *v.t.* & *v.i.* **pruned, prun·ing 1** To trim or cut superfluous branches or parts (from) so as to improve growth, appearance, etc. **2** To cut off (superfluous branches or parts). See synonyms under ABBREVIATE. [<OF *proöignier, proignier,* ? <*provaignier* cut <*provain* a slip <L *propago*; prob. infl. in form by *rooignier* cut off, ult. <L *rotundus* round] **—prun′er** *n.*

prune[3] (pro͞on) *v.t.* & *v.i.* **pruned, prun·ing** *Archaic* To dress up; preen. [<OF *poroindre* anoint <*por-* (<L *pro* before) + *oindre* anoint <L *ungere*]

pru·nel·la (pro͞o·nel′ə) *n.* **1** A strong woolen cloth used for the uppers of shoes. **2** A similar twilled heavy dress fabric. **3** *pl.* Shoes made partly of prunella. Also **pru·nel′lo** (-nel′ō). [<F *prunelle* a sloe, dim. of *prune* plum, prune; prob. so called from its dark color]

pru·nelle (pro͞o·nel′) *n.* **1** A small yellow prune, usually packed with the stone and skin removed. **2** A plum-flavored liqueur. [<F, dim. of *prune*. See PRUNE[1].]

pru·nif·er·ous (pro͞o·nif′ər·əs) *adj.* Plum-bearing. [<*pruni-* plum (<L *prunum*) + -FEROUS]

pru·ri·ent (pro͝or′ē·ənt) *adj.* **1** Impure in thought and desire; lewd. **2** Having lustful cravings or desires. **3** Longing; desirous. [<L *pruriens, -entis,* ppr. of *prurire* itch, long for] **—pru′ri·ence, pru′ri·en·cy** *n.* **—pru′·ri·ent·ly** *adv.*

pru·ri·go (pro͞o·rī′gō) *n. Pathol.* A chronic inflammatory skin disease marked by eruption and severe itching. [<L, an itching, lasciviousness <*prurire* itch] **—pru·rig′i·nous** (-rij′ə·nəs) *adj.*

pru·ri·tus (pro͞o·rī′təs) *n. Pathol.* Itching. [<L <*prurire* itch] **—pru·rit·ic** (-rit′ik) *adj.*

pruritus hi·e·ma·lis (hī′ə·mā′lis) Frost itch.

Pru·sa (pro͞o′sä) An ancient name for BRUSA.

Prus·sia (prush′ə) A former state, the largest and most important, of northern Germany; 113,410 square miles; capital, Berlin; formally dissolved, Feb. 1947; territory divided between East and West Germany, Poland, and Russian S.F.S.R.: German *Preussen*.

Prus·sian (prush′ən) *adj.* **1** Of or pertaining to Prussia, its inhabitants, or their language. **2** Characteristic of the Junkers of Prussia; militaristic; overbearing. **—*n.*** **1** A native or naturalized inhabitant of Prussia. **2** The old language of Prussia, belonging to the Baltic branch of the Balto-Slavic subfamily of Indo-European languages: extinct since the 17th century, and often called *Borussian*: also **Old Prussian.**

Prussian blue 1 *Chem.* Any one of a group of cyanogen compounds formed from ferrous sulfate and potassium ferrocyanide: formerly much used in dyeing. **2** A deep, strong, blue pigment with a coppery sheen, obtained from these compounds: used in oil painting but impermanent on alkali surfaces, as fresco: also called *Paris blue* (formerly called *Berlin blue*). Heat changes it to **Prussian brown.** [So called because discovered accidentally in Berlin, 1704, by H. de Diesbach, a colormaker]

Prus·sian·ism (prush′ən·iz′əm) *n.* The practices or policies of the Prussian ruling class during its leadership of Germany, characterized by militarism and *esprit de corps*.

prus·si·ate (prush′ē·āt, -it, prus′-) *n. Chem.* **1** A salt of prussic acid; also, a cyanide. **2** A ferrocyanide or a ferricyanide.

prus·sic (prus′ik) *Chem. adj.* Hydrocyanic. **—*n.*** Prussic acid. [<F *prussique* <*Prusse* Prussia + *-ique* -IC; so called because derived from *Prussian blue*]

prussic acid Hydrocyanic acid.

Prut (pro͞ot) A river forming the boundary between SW U.S.S.R. and Rumania and flowing 530 miles from the Carpathians in SW Ukrainian S.S.R. to the Danube. Formerly **Pruth.**

pry[1] (prī) *v.i.* **pried, pry·ing** To look or peer carefully, curiously, or slyly; snoop. **—*n.*** *pl.* **pries 1** A sly and searching inspection. **2** One who pries; an inquisitive, prying person. [ME *prien*; ult. origin unknown] **—pry′·ing** *adj.* & *n.* **—pry′ing·ly** *adv.*

pry[2] (prī) *v.t.* **pried, pry·ing 1** To raise, move, or open by means of a lever; prize. **2** To obtain by effort. **—*n.*** A lever, as a bar, stick, or beam; also, leverage. [Back formation <PRIZE[2], *v.*, mistaken as a 3rd person sing.]

pry·er (prī′ər) See PRIER.

Prynne (prin), **William,** 1600–69, English Presbyterian lawyer, pamphleteer, and statesman.

Prze·myśl (pshe′mish·əl) A city in SE Poland near the Ukrainian S.S.R. border; scene of several battles in World War I, 1915.

psalm (säm) *n.* A sacred song or lyric, especially one of those contained in the Old Testament Book of Psalms; a hymn. See synonyms under SONG. **—*v.t.*** To celebrate or praise in psalms; hymn. [Fusion of OE *sealm, psalm* and OF *salme, psaume,* both <LL *psalmus* <Gk. *psalmos* a song sung to the harp, lit., a twanging <*psallein* twitch]

psalm·ist (sä′mist) *n.* **1** A maker or composer of psalms. **2** In the early Christian church, one of the minor clergy who led the singing; a precentor. **—the Psalmist** King David, as the traditional author of many of the Scriptural psalms.

psalm·o·dy (sä′mə·dē, sal′-) *n. pl.* **·dies 1** The use of psalms in divine worship; psalm-singing. **2** A collection of psalms. [<LL *psalmodia* <Gk. *psalmōidia* singing to the harp <*psalmōidos* a psalmist <*psalmos* a psalm + *ōidē* a song] **—psalm′o·dist** *n.*

Psalms (sämz) A lyrical book of the Old Testament, containing 150 hymns, many ascribed to David. Also **Book of Psalms.**

psal·ter (sôl′tər) *n.* **1** The psalms appointed to be read or sung at any given service. **2** In the Roman Catholic Church, a rosary of 150 beads, equaling the number of the Psalms. [OE *psaltere, saltere* <L *psalterium* a psaltery] **—psal·te·ri·an** (sôl·tir′ē·ən, sal-) *adj.*

Psal·ter (sôl′tər) *n.* **1** The Book of Psalms; specifically, the version of Psalms in the Book of Common Prayer. **2** The Latin version of Psalms used in the Roman Catholic breviary. Also **Psal′ter·y.**

psal·te·ri·um (sôl·tir′ē·əm, sal-) *n. pl.* **·te·ri·a** (-tir′ē·ə) The manyplies, or third stomach of a ruminant. [<L, a psaltery; so called because its many folds make it resemble the instrument] **—psal·te′ri·al** *adj.*

psal·ter·y (sôl′tər·ē) *n. pl.* **·ter·ies** An ancient stringed musical instrument, similar to a dulcimer but played by plucking with the fingers or a plectrum. [<OF *sautere, psalterie* <L *psalterium* <Gk. *psaltērion* <*psallein* twitch, twang]

PSALTERY
Twelfth century.

psam·mite (sam′īt) *n.* Fine-grained sandstone. [<F <Gk. *psammos* sand + *-ite* -ITE[1]]

psam·mit·ic (sa·mit′ik) *adj. Geol.* **1** Composed of material in the form of rounded grains of sand: contrasted with *gritty*. **2** Specifically, having the texture of fine sand: said of detrital deposits or fragmental rocks: contrasted with *psephitic*.

psel·lism (sel′iz·əm) *n.* Imperfect articulation; stammering. [<Gk. *psellismos* stammering <*psellizein* stammer]

pse·phite (sē′fīt) *n.* A conglomeration of small pebbles; fragmental rock. [<Gk. *psēphos* a pebble + -ITE[1]]

pse·phit·ic (sē·fit′ik) *adj. Geol.* Having the texture of coarse sand: said of detrital deposits or fragmental rocks: contrasted with *psammitic*.

pseph·ol·o·gy (sef·ol′ə·jē) *n.* The study and statistical analysis of the elective process and its results. [<Gk. *psēphos* pebble used in voting, the vote itself + -LOGY; coined by R. B. McCallum of Oxford University in 1952] **—pseph·ol′o·gist** *n.*

pseu·dax·is (so͞o·dak′sis) *n.* A sympodium. [<PSEUD(O)- + AXIS]

pseu·de·pig·ra·pha (so͞o′də·pig′rə·fə) *n. pl.* Spurious writing; especially, spurious religious writings, falsely ascribed to Scriptural characters or times and not considered as canonical by any branch of the Christian church. [<Gk., neut. pl. of *pseudepigraphos* with a false title <*pseudēs* false + *epigraphein*. See EPIGRAPH.] **—pseu·dep·i·graph·ic** (so͞o′dep·i·graf′ik) or **·i·cal, pseu′de·pig′ra·phous** *adj.*

pseu·do (so͞o′dō) *adj.* Pretended; sham.

pseudo- *combining form* **1** False; pretended: *pseudonym*. **2** Counterfeit; not genuine: *pseudepigrapha*. **3** Closely resembling; serving or functioning as: *pseudopodium*. **4** Illusory; apparent: *pseudoaquatic*. **5** Abnormal; erratic: *pseudocarp*. Also, before vowels, **pseud-**. [<Gk. <*pseudēs* false]

pseu·do·a·quat·ic (so͞o′dō·ə·kwat′ik, -kwot′-) *adj.* Not really aquatic, but native to or found in wet places.

pseu·do·bulb (so͞o′dō·bulb′) *n. Bot.* A swollen, bulblike internode at the base of the stem in many orchids.

pseu·do·carp (so͞o′dō·kärp) *n. Bot.* A false fruit; an often conspicuous portion of a fructification which consists of other parts besides the pericarp and seeds, as the apple, checkerberry, and mulberry. [<PSEUDO- + -CARP] **—pseu′do·car′pous** *adj.*

pseu·do·clas·sic (so͞o′dō·klas′ik) *adj.* Emulating classic style; pretending to be classic; wrongly classed as classic.

pseu·do-Is·i·dore (so͞o′dō·iz′ə·dôr, -dōr) The unknown author or compiler of the "False Decretals." See DECRETALS. **—pseu′do-Is·i·do′ri·an** *adj.*

pseu·do·morph (so͞o′dō·môrf) *n.* **1** An irregular or false form. **2** *Mineral.* A mineral having the external crystalline form of another mineral. [<PSEUDO- + -MORPH] **—pseu′do·mor′phic** *adj.* **—pseu′do·mor′phism** *n.* **—pseu′·do·mor′phous** *adj.*

pseu·do·nym (so͞o′də·nim) *n.* A fictitious name; pen name. [<F <Gk. *pseudonymon,* orig. neut. of *pseudonymos* having a false name <*pseudēs* false + *onoma, onyma* a name] **—pseu·don·y·mous** (so͞o·don′ə·məs) *adj.* **—pseu·don′y·mous·ly** *adv.* **—pseu·don′y·mous·ness, pseu′do·nym′i·ty** *n.*

pseu·do·pod (so͞o′də·pod) *n.* **1** A pseudopodium. **2** An organism with pseudopodia;

a rhizopod. — **pseu·dop·o·dal** (so͞o·dop′ə·dəl) *adj.*

pseu·do·po·di·um (so͞o′də·pō′dē·əm) *n. pl.* **·di·a** (-dē·ə) **1** *Zool.* A process formed by the temporary extension of the protoplasm of a cell or of a unicellular animal, serving for taking in food, for locomotion, etc. **2** *Bot.* A false pedicel in certain mosses. Also **pseu′do·pode** (-pōd). [<NL <Gk. *pseudēs* false + *podion.* See PODIUM.]

pshaw (shô) *interj. & n.* An exclamation of annoyance, disapproval, disgust, or impatience. — *v.t. & v.i.* To exclaim *pshaw* at (a person or thing).

psi[1] (sī, psī, psē) *n.* The twenty-third letter in the Greek alphabet (Ψ, ψ): equivalent to English *ps.*

psi[2] (sī) *n.* Pounds per square inch: a unit of pressure.

psi·lo·cy·bin (sī′lə·sī′bin) *n.* A hallucinogenic drug derived from a Mexican mushroom, used in Indian religious rites. [< *Psilocybe (mexicana),* the mushroom from which it is obtained + -IN]

Psi·lo·ri·ti (psē′lô·rē′tē) See IDA.

psi·lo·sis (sī·lō′sis) *n.* **1** Sprue. **2** Alopecia. [<NL <Gk. *psilōsis* a stripping bare < *psiloein* strip bare] — **psi·lot′ic** (-lot′ik) *adj.*

Psit·ta·ci·for·mes (sit′ə·si·fôr′mēz) *n. pl.* An order of climbing, arboreal birds, including the parrots, macaws, and cockatoos. [<NL <Gk. *psittakos* a parrot + L *forma* form]

psit·ta·cine (sit′ə·sin, -sin) *adj.* Of or pertaining to parrots. [<L *psittacinus* < *psittacus* a parrot <Gk. *psittakos*]

psit·ta·co·sis (sit′ə·kō′sis) *n.* An acute, infectious, wasting disease of parrots and related birds, caused by a filtrable virus: transmitted to man, it causes fever and nausea, with complications resembling influenza and typhoid fever: also called *parrot fever.* [<NL <Gk. *psittakos* a parrot + *-osis* -OSIS]

Pskov (pskôf) A city of NW European Russian S.F.S.R. near the border of the Estonian S.S.R. on the southern end of **Lake Pskov.**

pso·as (sō′əs) *n. Anat.* Either of two muscles of the interior of the pelvis, arising from the spine and constituting the loins. [<NL <Gk., acc. pl. of *psoa* the muscle of the loins]

Pso·cop·ter·a (sō·kop′tər·ə) See CORRODENTIA.

pso·ra (sôr′ə, sō′rə) *n. Pathol.* **1** Scabies. **2** Psoriasis. [<L <Gk. *psōra* an itch] — **pso′ric** *adj. & n.*

pso·ra·le·a (sə·rā′lē·ə) *n.* A scented herb or shrub (genus *Psoralea*) of the bean family, especially the common breadroot. [<NL <Gk. *psōraleos* scabby]

pso·ri·a·sis (sə·rī′ə·sis) *n. Pathol.* A noncontagious, inflammatory skin disease, chronic or acute, characterized by reddish patches and white scales. [<NL <Gk. *psōriaein* have an itch < *psōra* an itch] — **pso·ri·at·ic** (sôr′ē·at′ik, sō′rē-) *adj.*

psych (sīk) *v.t. Slang* **1** To make mentally ready, as by inducing alertness or tension; key up: often with *up.* **2** To cause to lose self-assurance, especially in order to place at a competitive disadvantage; demoralize: often with *out*: to *psych* rivals. **3** To manipulate by the use of psychology; especially, to outwit: often with *out*: *psyched* him into giving me a loan. **4** To understand: with *out*: couldn't *psych* it out. Also **psyche.**

psych– See PSYCHO–.

psy·chal·gi·a (sī·kal′jē·ə) *n. Psychiatry* Mental suffering; morbid depression: distinguished from *somatalgia.* [<NL <Gk. *psychē* mind + *algos* a pain, an affliction]

psy·chas·the·ni·a (sī′kas·thē′nē·ə) *n. Psychiatry* A morbid mental state characterized by mental fatigue, obsessive anxiety, phobias, tics, etc. [<NL <Gk. *psychē* mind + *astheneia* debility, weakness] — **psy′chas·then′ic** (-then′ik) *adj. & n.*

psy·che (sī′kē) *n.* **1** The human soul; the mind; the intelligence. **2** *Psychoanal.* The aggregate of all the psychic components constituting a human individual, sometimes considered as an entity functioning apart from or independently of the body. **3** A knot of hair coiled at the back of the head by women in imitation of an ancient Greek style of hairdressing: also **Psyche knot.** [<Gk. *psychē* < *psychein* breathe, blow]

Psy·che (sī′kē) In Greek and Roman mythology, a maiden beloved by Eros, who, after many tribulations caused by the jealousy of Venus, is united with her lover and accorded a place among the gods as a personification of the soul.

psy·che·de·li·a (sī′kə·dē′lē·ə, -dēl′yə) *n.* Psychedelic drugs and accessories, or things associated with them.

psy·che·del·ic (sī′kə·del′ik) *adj.* Causing or having to do with an abnormal stimulation of consciousness or perception: *psychedelic* drugs; a *psychedelic* experience. [<Gk. *psychē* + *del(os)* manifest + -IC]

psy·chi·a·trist (sī·kī′ə·trist) *n.* A medical doctor specializing in the practice of psychiatry.

psy·chi·a·try (sī·kī′ə·trē) *n.* The branch of medicine that treats disorders of the mind or psyche, especially psychoses, but also neuroses. [<PSYCH- + -IATRY] — **psy·chi·at·ric** (sī′kē·at′rik) or **·ri·cal** *adj.*

psy·chic (sī′kik) *adj.* **1** Pertaining to the mind or soul; mental, as distinguished from physical and physiological. **2** *Psychol.* Pertaining to or designating those mental phenomena which are, or appear to be, independent of normal sensory stimuli and which cannot be fully explained in terms of the known data of experimental science, as clairvoyance, telepathy, and extrasensory perception. Compare PARAPSYCHOLOGY. **3** Caused by, proceeding from, associated with, or attributed to a nonmaterial or occult agency. **4** Sensitive to mental or occult phenomena. Also **psy′chi·cal.** — *n.* **1** A person sensitive to mental or extrasensory phenomena; especially, a spiritualistic medium. **2** The field of extrasensory phenomena: with *the.* [<Gk. *psychikos* < *psychē* soul] — **psy′chi·cal·ly** *adv.*

psy·cho (sī′kō) *n. pl.* **·chos** *Slang* A mentally disturbed person; a neurotic or psychopath. — *adj.* **1** Psychologically disturbed. **2** Psychological or psychiatric. [<PSYCHO(NEUROTIC)]

psycho– *combining form* Mind; soul; spirit: *psychosomatic.* Also, before vowels, *psych–.* [<Gk. *psychē* spirit, soul]

psy·cho·a·nal·y·sis (sī′kō·ə·nal′ə·sis) *n.* **1** The doctrine that mental life and all forms of behavior may be interpreted in terms of reciprocally acting forces largely governed by the dynamic interplay of conflicting drives and processes originating in the unconscious. **2** A system of psychotherapy originated and developed by Freud which seeks to alleviate mental and nervous disorders by the technical analysis of controlling factors persistently repressed in, and manifested through, the unconscious. — **psy′cho·an′a·lyt′ic** (-an′ə·lit′ik) or **·i·cal** *adj.* — **psy′cho·an′a·lyt′i·cal·ly** *adv.*

psy·cho·an·a·lyst (sī′kō·an′ə·list) *n.* One who practices psychoanalysis.

psy·cho·an·a·lyze (sī′kō·an′ə·līz) *v.t.* **·lyzed, ·lyz·ing** To treat by psychoanalysis. Also *Brit.* **psy′cho·an′a·lyse.**

psy·cho·bi·ol·o·gy (sī′kō·bī·ol′ə·jē) *n.* **1** The study of the mind and of mental processes in relation to anatomy, physiology, and the nervous system, with special reference to the influence of the environment. **2** Psychology in its biological aspects. Also called *biopsychology.* — **psy′cho·bi′o·log′i·cal** (-bī′ə·loj′i·kəl) *adj.* — **psy′cho·bi·ol′o·gist** *n.*

psy·cho·dra·ma (sī′kō·drä′mə, -dram′ə) *n.* A form of psychotherapy in which the patient acts out situations involving his problems. — **psy′cho·dra·mat′ic** *adj.*

psy·cho·dy·nam·ics (sī′kō·dī·nam′iks) *n.* The study of mental processes in action. — **psy′·cho·dy·nam′ic** *adj.*

psy·cho·gen·e·sis (sī′kō·jen′ə·sis) *n.* **1** The development of the individual soul; the science of the origin of psychic life. **2** Genesis or specific change due to vitality of the organism, as opposed to external influences. Also **psy·chog·e·ny** (sī·koj′ə·nē). — **psy′cho·ge·net′ic** (-jə·net′ik) *adj.* — **psy′cho·ge·net′i·cal·ly** *adv.*

psy·cho·gen·ic (sī′kō·jen′ik) *adj.* Having mental origin, or being affected by mental actions and states.

psy·chog·no·sis (sī′kog·nō′sis) *n.* The close study and diagnosis of mental states. [< PSYCHO- + -GNOSIS] — **psy′chog·nos′tic** (-nos′·tik) *adj.*

psy·cho·graph (sī′kə·graf, -gräf) *n.* **1** A chart graphically representing the personality traits of an individual: also **psy′cho·gram** (-gram). **2** A description of the personality traits of an individual, especially in literary form. — **psy′·cho·graph′ic** *adj.*

psy·chog·ra·phy (sī·kog′rə·fē) *n.* **1** Involuntary or unconscious writing, as by a medium. **2** The making of a psychograph.

psy·cho·his·to·ry (sī′kō·his′tə·rē, -his′trē) *n.* History or a work of history in which major emphasis is given the psychological states or dispositions of important participants as contributing causes of certain actions, decisions, or developments. — **psy′·cho·his′tor′i·an** (-his′tôr′ē·ən, -tō′rē-) *n.* — **psy′cho·his′tor′i·cal** *adj.* — **psy′cho·his′tor′i·cal·ly** *adv.*

psy·cho·ki·ne·sis (sī′kō·ki·nē′sis) *n.* The alleged power of controlling the chance behavior of physical objects, as cards, dice, etc., by the direct influence upon them of emotional states, strong desire, or other psychic factors.

psy·cho·log·i·cal (sī′kə·loj′i·kəl) *adj.* **1** Of or pertaining to psychology. **2** Of or in the mind. **3** Suitable for affecting the mind: the *psychological* moment. Also **psy′cho·log′ic.** — **psy′cho·log′i·cal·ly** *adv.*

psy·chol·o·gism (sī·kol′ə·jiz′əm) *n.* Idealistic philosophy as opposed to sensationalism. Compare ONTOLOGISM.

psy·chol·o·gist (sī·kol′ə·jist) *n.* A student of or a specialist in psychology.

psy·chol·o·gize (sī·kol′ə·jīz) *v.i.* **·gized, ·giz·ing** **1** To study psychology. **2** To theorize psychologically.

psy·chol·o·gy (sī·kol′ə·jē) *n.* **1** The science of the human mind in any of its aspects, operations, powers, or functions. **2** The systematic investigation of mental phenomena, especially those associated with consciousness, behavior, and the problems of adjustment to the environment. **3** The aggregate of the emotions, traits, and behavior patterns regarded as characteristic of an individual or type: the *psychology* of a fanatic. [<NL *psychologia* <Gk. *psychē* soul + -LOGY]

psy·chom·e·try (sī·kom′ə·trē) *n.* **1** The science of the measurement of psychophysical processes, especially of their accuracy or duration in time; mental testing: also **psy·cho·met·rics** (sī·kō·met′riks). **2** Divination by physical contact or proximity of the properties of things touched or approached. — **psy·chom′e·trist** *n.*

psy·cho·mo·tor (sī′kō·mō′tər) *adj. Physiol.* Of or pertaining to muscular movements resulting from or caused by compulsive mental processes.

psy·cho·neu·ro·sis (sī′kō·no͞o·rō′sis, -nyo͞o-) *n. pl.* **·ses** (-sēz) *Psychiatry* A nervous disorder originating in disturbed psychic or mental functions, usually without or independent of organic symptoms: characterized by anxiety, phobias, compulsions, obsessions, etc. — **psy′·cho·neu·rot′ic** (-rot′ik) *adj. & n.*

psy·cho·path (sī′kō·path) *n.* One subject to or afflicted by mental instability.

psy·cho·path·ic (sī′kō·path′ik) *n.* A psychopath. — *adj.* Of or marked by psychopathy.

psy·cho·pa·thol·o·gy (sī′kō·pə·thol′ə·jē) *n.* The pathology of the mind. — **psy′cho·path′o·log′i·cal** (-path′ə·loj′i·kəl) *adj.* — **psy′cho·pa·thol′o·gist** *n.*

psy·chop·a·thy (sī·kop′ə·thē) *n.* **1** Mental disorder, especially as apart from disease of the brain, and typified by emotional immaturity and instability, moral deficiency, and perversions. **2** Psychotherapy.

psy·cho·phar·ma·col·o·gy (sī′kō·fär′mə·kol′ə·jē) *n.* The branch of pharmacology which investigates the properties and uses of drugs acting primarily on the nervous system and serving to modify human behavior.

psy·cho·phys·ics (sī′kō·fiz′iks) *n.* The science of the relations between mental and physical phenomena. — **psy′cho·phys′i·cal** *adj.* — **psy′·cho·phys′i·cist** *n.*

psy·cho·phys·i·ol·o·gy (sī′kō·fiz′ē·ol′ə·jē) *n.* The physiology of mental processes.

psy·cho·sex·u·al (sī′kō·sek′sho͞o·əl) *adj.* Of or pertaining to the psychological aspects of sexuality or sexual development. — **psy′cho·sex′u·al′i·ty** (-sek′sho͞o·al′ə·tē) *n.* — **psy′cho·sex′u·al·ly** *adv.*

psy·cho·sis (sī·kō′sis) *n. pl.* **·ses** (-sēz) *Psychiatry* A mental disorder, severe in character, often involving disorganization of the total personality, with or without organic disease. ◆ Homophone: *sycosis.* [<NL <Gk. *psychōsis* a giving of life < *psychoein* animate < *psychē* a soul]

psy·cho·so·mat·ic (sī′kō·sō·mat′ik) *adj.* **1** Of

or pertaining to the interrelationships of mind and body, with especial reference to disease. 2 Designating a branch of medicine which investigates the reciprocal influences of body and mind in the cause, prevention, treatment, and cure of disease.

psy·cho·sur·ger·y (sī′kō·sûr′jər·ē) *n.* Brain surgery performed to treat a mental disorder or alter behavior. —**psy′cho·sur′geon** (-sûr′jən) *n.* —**psy′cho·sur′gi·cal** *adj.*

psy·cho·tech·ni·cian (sī′kō·tek·nish′ən) *n.* One skilled in psychotechnics.

psy·cho·tech·nics (sī′kō·tek′niks) *n.* The direct application of psychological principles and methods to practical ends, especially in the management of large industrial and business enterprises. —**psy′cho·tech′ni·cal** *adj.*

psy·cho·ther·a·py (sī′kō·ther′ə·pē) *n.* The treatment of nervous and mental disorders, especially by psychological methods, as hypnosis, re–education, psychoanalysis, etc. Also **psy′·cho·ther′a·peu′tics** (-ther′ə·pyōō′tiks). —**psy′·cho·ther′a·peu′tic** *adj.* —**psy′cho·ther′a·pist** *n.*

psy·chot·ic (sī·kot′ik) *n.* One suffering from a psychosis. —*adj.* Of or characterized by a psychosis.

psy·chot·o·mi·met·ic (sī·kot′ō·mə·met′ik) *adj.* Pertaining to or productive of psychotic behavior: *psychotomimetic drugs.* —**psy·chot′o·mi·met′i·cal·ly** *adv.*

psy·cho·trop·ic (sī′kō·trop′ik) *adj.* Acting on or affecting the mind, as certain drugs. —*n.* A psychotropic drug. [<PSYCHO– + –TROPIC]

psychro– *combining form* Cold: *psychrophobia.* [<Gk. *psychros* cold]

psy·chrom·e·ter (sī·krom′ə·tər) *n.* An instrument for measuring the vapor tension and relative humidity of the air, consisting of two thermometers, the bulb of one being kept moist. [<PSYCHRO- + -METER]

psy·chro·ther·a·py (sī′krō·ther′ə·pē) *n.* Medical treatment by the use of cold.

psyl·li·um (sil′ē·əm) *n.* 1 A plantain of Asia Minor *(Plantago psyllium).* 2 Its small, reddish–brown seeds, resembling flaxseed in medicinal properties, used as a mild laxative. [<L <Gk. *psyllion* <*psylla* a flea; so called because supposed to destroy fleas]

Ptah (ptä, ptäkh) In ancient Egyptian religion, the chief divinity of ancient Memphis, the creator of gods and men.

ptar·mi·gan (tär′mə·gən) *n. pl.* **·gans** or **·gan** A grouse (genus *Lagopus*) of the northern hemisphere, with the winter plumage chiefly pure white, and with feathered toes. [<Scottish Gaelic *tarmachan*; excrescent *p* prob. due to false analogy with Gk. *pteron* wing]

PT boat A patrol torpedo boat.

pter·i·dol·o·gy (ter′i·dol′ə·jē) *n.* The department of botany that treats of ferns. [<Gk. *pteris, pteridos* a fern + -LOGY] —**pter′i·do·log′i·cal** (-dō·loj′i·kəl) *adj.* —**pter′i·dol′o·gist** *n.*

pter·i·do·phyte (ter′i·dō·fīt′) *n.* Any of a phylum *(Pteridophyta)* of flowerless plants comprising the ferns, clubmosses, and their allies. [<NL <Gk. *pteris, pteridos* a fern + *phyton* a plant] —**pter′i·do·phyt′ic** (-fit′ik), **pter′i·doph′y·tous** (-dof′ə·təs) *adj.*

ptero– *combining form* Wing; feather; plume; resembling wings: *pterodactyl.* Also, before vowels, **pter–.** [<Gk.*pteron* wing]

pter·o·dac·tyl (ter′ə·dak′til) *n. Paleontol.* 1 Any of a genus *(Pterodactylus)* of extinct flying reptiles which flourished in the Jurassic period, characterized by a large, birdlike skull, long jaws, and flying membrane somewhat like that of a bat. 2 A pterosaurian. [<NL < Gk. *pteron* a wing + *daktylos* a finger]

PTERODACTYL
(American Cretaceous: wing span about 6 feet)

pter·o·pod (ter′ə·pod) *n.* One of a subclass or order *(Pteropoda)* of gastropods with the middle region of the foot expanded into winglike lobes or fins; a sea butterfly. —*adj.* 1 Having the foot expanded into swimming lobes. 2 Of or pertaining to the *Pteropoda*: also **pte·rop·o·dan** (tə·rop′ə·dən). [<NL <Gk. *pteron* a wing + *pous, podos* a foot]

pter·o·sau·ri·an (ter′ə·sôr′ē·ən) *n. Paleontol.* One of an extinct order *(Pterosauria)* of flying reptiles, including pterodactyls, of the Mesozoic, with external digits long and developed to support a flying membrane. Also **pter′o·saur.** —*adj.* Of or pertaining to the *Pterosauria.* [<NL <Gk. *pteron* a wing + *sauros* a lizard]

pter·y·goid (ter′ə·goid) *adj.* 1 Having the form of a wing; winglike. 2 *Anat.* Pertaining to, or situated near the winglike processes of the sphenoid. Also **pter′y·goi′dal, pter′y·goi′·de·an.** —*n. Anat.* A pterygoid bone, plate, process, or muscle. [<Gk. *pteryx, pterygos* a wing + -OID]

ptis·an (tiz′ən) *n.* 1 A slightly medicinal decoction or tea of herbs: also spelled *tisane.* 2 The juice of grapes drained off without pressure. 3 A decoction of barley water. [<OF *ptisane, tisane* <L *ptisana* barley groats, a drink made from them <Gk. *ptisanē* peeled barley <*ptissein* peel]

Ptol·e·ma·ic (tol′ə·mā′ik) *adj.* Of or pertaining to Ptolemy, the astronomer, or to the Ptolemies, the Egyptian kings.

Ptolemaic system The ancient astronomical system of Ptolemy, which assumed that the earth was the central body around which the sun, planets, and celestial bodies revolved: this system was accepted till replaced in the 16th century by the Copernican system.

Ptol·e·ma·is (tol′ə·mā′is) The New Testament name for ACRE.

Ptol·e·ma·ist (tol′ə·mā′ist) *n.* A believer in or adherent of the Ptolemaic system.

Ptol·e·my (tol′ə·mē) Second century A.D. astronomer, mathematician, and geographer of Alexandria: full name *Claudius Ptolomaeus.*

Ptol·e·my (tol′ə·mē) Name of 14 kings of Egypt, of whom the most noted are:

—**Ptolemy I,** 367?–283? B.C., king 323–285; a general of Alexander the Great; founded the dynasty: called "Soter."

—**Ptolemy II,** 309–246 B.C., king 285–46; patron of literature and the arts: called "Philadelphus."

—**Ptolemy III,** 282?–221 B.C., king 246–21; conquered much of the Seleucid dominions; built many temples: called "Euergetes."

pto·maine (tō′mān, tō·mān′) *n. Biochem.* Any of a class of basic organic chemical compounds derived from decomposing or putrefying animal or vegetable protein. They bear some resemblance to the alkaloids, and some of them are poisonous. Also **pto′main.** [<Ital. *ptomaina* <Gk. *ptōma* a corpse]

ptomaine poisoning Botulism.

pto·sis (tō′sis) *n. Pathol.* The permanent drooping of the upper eyelid, due to paralysis of the lifting muscle of the lid. [<NL <Gk. *ptōsis* a falling <*piptein* fall] —**pto·tic** (tō′·tik) *adj.*

pty·a·lin (tī′ə·lin) *n. Biochem.* An amylase contained in the saliva of man and other mammals; the enzyme of saliva which converts starch into dextrin and maltose. [<Gk. *ptyalon* saliva + -IN]

pty·a·lism (tī′ə·liz′əm) *n.* Abnormal flow of saliva. [<Gk. *ptyalon* saliva + -ISM]

pub (pub) *n. Brit. Slang* A public house; an inn; tavern. [Short for *public house*]

pu·ber·ty (pyōō′bər·tē) *n.* The period in life at which a person of either sex becomes functionally capable of reproduction: in civil law, usually the age of 14 years in males and 12 in females. [<OF *puberte* <L *pubertas* <*pubes, puberis* an adult]

pu·bes (pyōō′bēz) *n.* 1 *Anat.* The part of the lower central hypogastric region covered with hair in the adult; the pubic region. 2 The hair that appears on the body at puberty; specifically, the hair on the pubic region. 3 *Biol.* Pubescence. [<L, pubic hair, groin]

pu·bes·cence (pyōō·bes′əns) *n.* 1 The state or quality of being pubescent (def. 1). 2 *Biol.* A covering or growth of soft, fine hairs or down, especially that upon certain plants.

pu·bes·cent (pyōō·bes′ənt) *adj.* 1 Arriving or having arrived at puberty. 2 *Biol.* Covered with hairs, especially fine, soft, short hairs; hairy or downy, as leaves, etc. [<MF <L *pubescens, -entis,* ppr. of *pubescere* become downy, attain puberty <*pubes.* See PUBES.]

pu·bic (pyōō′bik) *adj.* Of or pertaining to the region in the lower part of the abdomen: the *pubic* bones.

pu·bis (pyōō′bis) *n. pl.* **·bes** (-bēz) *Anat.* Either of the two bones which join with a third to form an arch on either ventral side of the pelvis. [<NL, short for L *os pubis* pubic bone < *pubes.* See PUBES.]

pub·lic (pub′lik) *adj.* 1 Of, pertaining to, or affecting the people at large or the community: distinguished from *private* or *personal.* 2 Open to all; maintained by or for the public: *public* parks; participated in by the people: a *public* demonstration. 3 For the use of the public; specifically, for hire: a *public* cab, hall, etc. 4 Done or made in public or without concealment; well–known; open; notorious: a *public* scandal. 5 Occupying an official or professional position; acting before or for the community: a *public* speaker. See synonyms under COMMON, GENERAL. —*n.* The people collectively, or in general, of a particular locality or nation; also, all those persons who may be grouped together for any given purpose: the church–going *public.* [<OF <L *publicus,* alter. of *poplicus* (through infl. of *pubes* an adult) <*poplus, populus* people]

pub·lic–ad·dress system (pub′lik·ə·dres′) A complete assembly of sound–reproducing apparatus for broadcasting messages, etc., in public places.

pub·li·can (pub′lə·kən) *n.* 1 In England, the keeper of a public house. 2 In ancient Rome, one who farmed or collected the public revenues. [<OF *publicain* <L *publicanus* a tax farmer, tax gatherer <*publicum* public revenue, orig. neut. of *publicus* PUBLIC]

pub·li·ca·tion (pub′lə·kā′shən) *n.* 1 The act of publishing or offering to public notice; notification to people at large orally or by writing or print; promulgation; proclamation. 2 In the law of libel and slander, the communication of a defamation to a third person. 3 That which is published; any printed work placed on sale or otherwise distributed or offered for distribution. See PUBLISH. [<OF *publicacion* <L *publicatio, -onis* <*publicatus,* pp. of *publicare* PUBLISH]

public debt The national debt.

public domain Lands owned by a state or national government; public lands. —**in the public domain** Available for unrestricted use: said of material on which copyright or patent right has expired.

public enemy 1 Any government with which a nation is at open war. 2 A person, especially a criminal, regarded as a menace to the public.

Public Health Service *U.S.* A Federal agency under the Surgeon General, which, as a constituent organization of the Department of Health, Education, and Welfare, is responsible for protecting and improving the health of the nation.

public house 1 An inn, tavern, or hotel. 2 In England, a place licensed to sell intoxicating liquors; a saloon.

pub·li·cist (pub′lə·sist) *n.* 1 A writer on international law or on topics of public interest. 2 A public–relations man or publicity agent. [<F *publiciste* <L *(jus) publicum* public (law), neut. of *publicus* PUBLIC]

pub·lic·i·ty (pub·lis′ə·tē) *n.* 1 The state of being public, or the act or fact of making or becoming public; exposure; notoriety: opposed to *secrecy.* 2 Advertising; advance information, or personal news intended to promote the interests of individuals, institutions, causes, etc., especially that appearing in print. 3 The attention or interest of the public gained by any method.

pub·li·cize (pub′lə·sīz) *v.t.* **·cized, ·ciz·ing** To give publicity to; advertise.

public library 1 A library maintained for the use of the public. 2 The building in which it is contained.

pub·lic·ly (pub′lik·lē) *adv.* 1 In an open or public manner; openly. 2 In the name or with the consent and concurrence of the public.

pub·lic·ness (pub′lik·nis) *n.* 1 The state or quality of being public or of belonging to the public. 2 Publicity.

public opinion The prevailing ideas, beliefs, and aims of the people, collectively: in politics, considered as a massed power or entity.

public relations 1 The activities and techniques utilized by public and private organizations and enterprises to establish favorable attitudes and responses in their behalf on the part of the general public or of special groups: included are analysis of attitudes, appraisal of procedures and policies, recommendations for internal change, and effective presentation of the organization's purposes and objectives. 2 The public conduct of the affairs of an organization with regard to its reputation and standing and to public opinion. 3 The relationship between the general public and an institution of any kind.

public school See under SCHOOL.

public servant A government official.

public service 1 Official employment under the government, especially in the civil departments. 2 The radio or television broadcasting of announcements of civic interest.

pub·lic–ser·vice corporation (pub′lik·sûr′vis) Any corporation operating a public utility, as a railroad, gas, electric, or water company.

public spirit Active, enlightened interest in and concern for matters that affect the welfare of the community. —**pub·lic–spir·it·ed** (pub′lik·spir′it·id) *adj.*

public utility A business organization or industry which performs some public service, as the supplying of water or electric power, and is subject to particular governmental regulations; a public–service corporation.

public works Permanent architectural or engineering works or improvements built with public money, as post offices, museums, canals, harbors, parks, playgrounds, roads, bridges, etc.

pub·lish (pub′lish) *v.t.* 1 To make known or announce publicly; promulgate; proclaim. 2 To print and issue (a book, magazine, map, etc.) to the public. 3 *Law* To communicate (a defamation) to a third person. 4 To print and issue the work of: to *publish* Hemingway. —*v.i.* 5 To engage in the business of publishing books, magazines, newspapers, etc. 6 To have one's work printed and issued. [<OF *publier, puplier* <L *publicare* make public <*publicus* PUBLIC] —**pub′lish·a·ble** *adj.*
Synonyms: advertise, announce, blazon, bruit, communicate, declare, disclose, divulge, impart, proclaim, promulgate, reveal, spread, tell. See ANNOUNCE, SPREAD. *Antonyms*: conceal, cover, hide, hush, suppress, withhold.

pub·lish·er (pub′lish·ər) *n.* One who publishes; especially, one who makes a business of publishing books or periodicals.

Puc·ci·ni (po͞ot·chē′nē), **Giacomo,** 1858–1924, Italian operatic composer.

puc·coon (pə·ko͞on′) *n.* 1 Any of several North American herbs (genus *Lithospermum*) of the borage family, yielding a red or yellow dye; especially, the **hoary puccoon** *(L. canescens)*, with orange–yellow flowers, of which the root yields a red dye. 2 The pigment or dye made from these plants. 3 The bloodroot. [<Algonquian (Virginian) *puccoon, pakon* <*pak* blood]

puce (pyo͞os) *adj.* Of a dark–brown or purplish–brown. [<F, flea color, a flea <L *pulex, -icis* a flea]

pu·celle (pyo͞o·sel′, *Fr.* pü·sel′) *n.* A virgin; maid: obsolete except in the phrase **La Pucelle,** Joan of Arc, the Maid of Orleans. [< OF *pucele, pulcella* <LL *pulicella* a young girl; ult. origin uncertain]

puck[1] (puk) *n.* 1 An evil sprite or hobgoblin. 2 In English folklore, **Puck,** a mischievous elf or goblin: also called *Robin Goodfellow*; specifically, in Shakespeare's *A Midsummer Night's Dream,* a mischievous fairy servant of Oberon. [OE *pūca* a goblin] —**puck′ish** *adj.*

puck[2] (puk) *n.* The hard rubber disk used in playing hockey. [<dial. E, strike. Akin to POKE[1].]

puck·a (puk′ə) *adj. Anglo–Indian* Made of good materials; substantial; hence, genuine; superior: also spelled *pukka.* [<Hind. *pakkā* substantial, lit., cooked, ripe]

puck·er (puk′ər) *v.t. & v.i.* To gather or draw up into small folds or wrinkles. —*n.* 1 A wrinkle, or group of wrinkles. 2 *Colloq.* Agitation; perplexity; confusion. [Appar. freq. of POKE[2]] —**puck′er·y** *adj.*

pud·ding (po͝od′ing) *n.* 1 A sweetened and flavored dessert of soft food, usually farinaceous. 2 A skin or gut filled with seasoned minced meat, blood, or the like, and usually boiled or broiled. [ME *poding,* orig. sausage, black pudding, prob. <OF *bodin, boudin*]

pud·dle (pud′l) *n.* 1 A small pool of dirty water. 2 Pudding (def. 2). —*v.t.* **·dled, ·dling** 1 *Metall.* To convert (molten pig iron) into wrought iron by melting and stirring in the presence of oxidizing substances. 2 To mix (clay, etc.) with water so as to obtain a watertight paste. 3 To line, as canal banks, with such a mixture. 4 To make muddy; stir up. [ME *podel,* appar. dim. of OE *pudd* a ditch] —**pud′dly** *adj.*

pud·dle·ball (pud′l·bôl′) *n.* A ball of heated iron fresh from the puddling furnace.

pud·dle·bar (pud′l·bär′) *n.* A bar into which a puddleball is rolled or hammered.

pud·dler (pud′lər) *n.* 1 One who puddles. 2 A device for stirring fused metal. 3 A puddling furnace.

pud·dling (pud′ling) *n.* 1 *Metall.* The operation or business of making wrought iron from pig iron in a puddling furnace. 2 Puddled clay for lining the banks of canals, etc.; puddle. 3 The operation of lining a canal with such clay.

puddling furnace A reverberatory furnace for puddling pig iron.

pu·den·cy (pyo͞o′dən·sē) *n.* Shame; modesty; also, prudishness. [<LL *pudentia* <L *pudens, -entis,* ppr. of *pudere* be ashamed]

pu·den·dum (pyo͞o·den′dəm) *n. pl.* **·da** (-də) 1 The vulva. 2 *pl.* The external genitals of either sex. [<L, neut. of *pudendus* (something) to be ashamed of, gerundive of *pudere* be ashamed] —**pu′dic, pu·den′dal** *adj.*

pudg·y (puj′ē) *adj.* **pudg·i·er, pudg·i·est** Short and thick; fat. [? <dial. E (Scottish) <*pud* belly] —**pudg′i·ly** *adv.* —**pudg′i·ness** *n.*

Pue·bla (pwā′blä) A state in SE Mexico; 13,124 square miles; capital, Puebla.

pueb·lo (pweb′lō *for def. 1,* pwā′blō *for defs. 2 and 3*) *n. pl.* **·los** 1 A communal adobe or stone building or group of buildings of the Indians of the SW United States. 2 A town or village of Indians or Spanish Americans, as in Mexico. 3 In the Philippines, a municipality: originally the civilian quarter of a Spanish community. [<Sp., a town, people <L *populus*]

HOPI INDIAN PUEBLO

Pueb·lo (pweb′lō) *n.* A member of one of the Indian tribes of Mexico and the SW United States, representing several linguistic stocks, as Zuñi, Uto–Aztecan, etc., but having in common the pueblo culture.

pu·er·ile (pyo͞o′ər·il, *Brit.* pyo͞o′ə·rīl) *adj.* Pertaining to or characteristic of childhood; juvenile; hence, immature; weak; silly: a *puerile* suggestion. See synonyms under CHILDISH, YOUTHFUL. [<MF *puéril* <L *puerilis* <*puer, pueri* a boy] —**pu′er·ile·ly** *adv.* —**pu′er·ile·ness** *n.*

pu·er·il·ism (pyo͞o′ər·il·iz′əm) *n.* Childishness, especially as indicative of mental disorder.

pu·er·il·i·ty (pyo͞o′ə·ril′ə·tē) *n. pl.* **·ties** 1 Puerile state; childishness. 2 A childish act or expression.

pu·er·per·al (pyo͞o·ûr′pər·əl) *adj. Med.* Pertaining to, resulting from, or following childbirth: *puerperal* fever. [<L *puerperus* parturient < *puer* a boy + *parere* bring forth]

Puer·to A·ya·cu·cho (pwer′tō ä′yä·ko͞o′chō) Capital of Amazonas territory, on the Orinoco in southern Venezuela.

Puerto Bar·rios (bär′ryōs) A port of eastern Guatemala.

Puerto Ca·bel·lo (kä·bā′yō) A port on the Caribbean in northern Venezuela.

Puerto Li·món (lē·mōn′) See LIMÓN.

Puerto Me·xi·co (mā′hē·kō) A former name of COATZACOALCOS.

Puerto Montt (mōnt) A port of south central Chile.

Puerto Ri·co (rē′kō) The easternmost island of the Greater Antilles, ceded to the United States by Spain in 1898; since 1952 a commonwealth; 3,423 square miles; capital, San Juan: former official name, *Porto Rico.* Abbr. PR —**Puer′to–Ri′can** *adj. & n.*

puff (puf) *n.* 1 A breath emitted suddenly and with force; a sudden emission, as of air, smoke, or steam; a whiff. 2 A light, air–filled piece of pastry: a cream *puff.* 3 A light ball, tuft, wad, or pad for dusting powder on the hair or skin; a powder puff. 4 A loose roll of hair in a coiffure, or a light cushion over which it is rolled. 5 A quilted bed coverlet, usually filled with cotton, wool, or down; a comforter. 6 In dressmaking, a part of a fabric so gathered as to produce a loose, fluffy distention. 7 A public expression of fulsome praise, as in a newspaper or advertisement. 8 A puffball. —*v.i.* 1 To blow in puffs, as the wind. 2 To breathe hard, as after violent exertion. 3 To emit smoke, steam, etc., in puffs. 4 To smoke a cigar, etc., with puffs. 5 To move, act, or exert oneself while emitting puffs: with *away, up,* etc. 6 To swell as with air or pride; dilate: often with *up* or *out.* —*v.t.* 7 To send forth or emit with short puffs or breaths. 8 To move, impel, or stir up with or in puffs. 9 To smoke, as a pipe or cigar, with puffs. 10 To swell or distend: He *puffed* his cheeks with pride. 11 To praise fulsomely; advertise in a puff (def. 7). 12 To arrange (the hair) in a puff. [ME *puf* <*puffen, pyffan*]
Synonyms (verb): blow, compliment, flatter, inflate, pant, praise, swell. Compare SWELL. *Antonyms*: belittle, contract, disparage, shrink, shrivel.

puff adder 1 A large, sluggish, venomous African viper *(Bitis arietans),* with variously colored chevron–and–crescent markings and a habit of violently puffing out its breath. 2 The American hognose snake.

puff·ball (puf′bôl′) *n.* A globular fungus (genus *Lycoperdon*) that puffs out its dustlike spores when broken open. Some species are edible.

puff·er (puf′ər) *n.* 1 One who puffs. 2 A plectognath fish that inflates its body with air; a globefish. 3 The little harbor porpoise *(Phocaena phocaena)* of the North Atlantic and Pacific oceans.

puff·er·y (puf′ər·ē) *n.* **·er·ies** 1 The act or practice of puffing. 2 Fulsome public praise or commendation.

puf·fin (puf′in) *n.* 1 A sea bird allied to the auk and murre (family *Alcidae*), with deep compressed bill and thick naked skin at the corner of the mouth; especially, the common puffin *(Fratercula arctica)* of the North Atlantic; the Labrador auk. 2 The Pacific coast sea parrot *(Lunda cirrhata).* [Prob. <PUFF; with ref. to its puffed–out beak or the plumpness of its young]

PUFFIN
(Body from 12 to 15 inches long)

puff paste A short flaky paste for fine pastry.

puff·y (puf′ē) *adj.* **puff·i·er, puff·i·est** 1 Swollen with air or any soft matter; soft; bloated. 2 Inflated in manner; bombastic. 3 Blowing in puffs. —**puff′i·ly** *adv.* —**puff′i·ness** *n.*

pug[1] (pug) *n.* 1 Clay ground and worked with water, for molding pottery or bricks. 2 A machine in which clay is ground and mixed or tempered: also **pug mill.** —*v.t.* **pugged, pug·ging** 1 To knead or work (clay) with water, as in brickmaking. 2 To fill in with clay, etc. 3 To fill in or cover with mortar, felt, etc., to deaden sound. [<dial. E, ? < *pug* punch]

pug[2] (pug) *n.* 1 A breed of dog characterized by a short, square body, upturned nose, curled tail, and short, smooth coat. 2 A pug nose. [Prob. alter. of PUCK]

pug[3] (pug) *n. Anglo–Indian* An animal's footprint; trail. —*v.t.* **pugged, pug·ging** To track,

as game, by pugs; trail. [<Hind. *pag* a foot]
pug[4] (pug) *n. Slang* A professional pugilist. [Short for PUGILIST]
Pu·get Sound (pyōō′jit) An inlet of the Pacific in NW Washington, extending 100 miles south from Juan del Fuca Strait to Olympia.
pugh (pyōō, pōō) *interj.* An exclamation of contempt or disgust.
pu·gi·lism (pyōō′jə·liz′əm) *n.* The art or practice of boxing or fighting with the fists, as in the prize ring. [<L *pugil* a boxer]
pu·gi·list (pyōō′jə·list) *n.* One who fights with his fists; a boxer; specifically, a prize fighter. —**pu′gi·lis′tic** *adj.*
pug·na·cious (pug·nā′shəs) *adj.* Disposed or inclined to fight; quarrelsome. [<L *pugnax, -acis* <*pugnare* fight <*pugnus* a fist] —**pug·na′cious·ly** *adv.*
pug·nac·i·ty (pug·nas′ə·tē) *n.* The quality of being pugnacious; quarrelsome disposition; combativeness. Also **pug·na′cious·ness** (-nā′·shəs·nis).
pug nose A thick, short nose, tilted upward at the end. [<PUG[2] + NOSE] —**pug–nosed** (pug′nōzd′) *adj.*
pug·ree (pug′rē) *n. Anglo–Indian* A light scarf wound round a hat to keep off the sun; also, a turban worn by natives of India. Also **pug′·gree, pug′gry.** [<Hind. *pagri* a turban]
puir (pür) *adj. Scot.* Poor.
puis·ne (pyōō′nē) *adj. Law* Junior as to rank; younger; inferior: a *puisne* judge. —*n.* One who is of inferior rank or younger; a junior associate. ◆ Homophone: *puny.* [<OF *puisne* <*puis* afterwards (<L *postea* <*post* after) + *ne* born <L *natus*]
pu·is·sance (pyōō′ə·səns, pyōō·is′əns, pwis′·əns) *n.* The power to accomplish or achieve, especially against resistance; potency. [<OF]
pu·is·sant (pyōō′ə·sənt, pyōō·is′ənt, pwis′ənt) *adj.* Powerful; mighty. See synonyms under POWERFUL. [<OF <L *posse* be able] —**pu′is·sant·ly** *adv.*
puke (pyōōk) *v.t.* & *v.i.* **puked, puk·ing** To vomit or cause to vomit. —*n.* Vomit, or the act of vomiting. [Cf. LG *spucken* spew, spit <L *spuere*]
puk·ka (puk′ə) See PUCKA.
Pu·la (pōō′lä) A port of NW Croatia, Yugoslavia; formerly in Italy: Italian *Pola.*
Pu·las·ki (pŏŏ·las′kē, pə-; *Polish* pōō·läs′kē), **Count Casimir,** 1748?–79, Polish soldier and American Revolutionary general; killed at Savannah.
pu·lay (pə·lī′) See PALAY.
pul·chri·tude (pul′krə·tōōd, -tyōōd) *n.* Beauty; grace; physical charm. [<L *pulchritudo, -inis* <*pulcher* beautiful]
pul·chri·tu·di·nous (pul′krə·tōō′də·nəs, -tyōō′-) *adj.* Beautiful; lovely; especially, having physical beauty.
pule (pyōōl) *v.i.* **puled, pul·ing** To cry plaintively, as a child; whimper; whine. [Cf. F *piauler* <MF *pioler* chirp] —**pul′er** *n.*
pu·lex (pyōō′leks) *n.* **1** One of a genus (*Pulex*) of fleas, including the human flea (*P. irritans*). **2** Any flea. [<L, a flea]
pu·li (pōō′lē) *n. pl.* **pu·lik** (pōō′lik) A breed of working dog, of medium height, white, gray, or black in color, with a long, wavy coat: used in Hungary for sheepherding. [Hungarian]
pu·li·cene (pyōō′lə·sēn) *adj.* Of, pertaining to, or abounding with fleas. [<L *pulex, -icis* a flea]
pul·ing (pyōō′ling) *n.* A plaintive cry; whining. —*adj.* Whimpering; whining. —**pul′ing·ly** *adv.*
Pul·itz·er (pyōō′lit·sər, pōōl′it-), **Joseph,** 1847–1911, U.S. journalist and publisher, born in Hungary.
Pulitzer Prize One of several annual awards for outstanding work in American journalism and literature: established by Joseph Pulitzer.
pul·kha (pul′kə) *n.* A canoe–shaped traveling sledge, drawn by one reindeer: used in Lapland. [<Lapp *pulkke*]
pull (pŏŏl) *v.t.* **1** To apply force to so as to cause motion toward or after the person or thing exerting force; drag; tug. **2** To draw or remove from a natural or fixed place: to *pull* a tooth or plug. **3** To give a pull or tug to. **4** To pluck, as a fowl. **5** To draw asunder; tear; rend: with *to pieces, apart,* etc. **6** To strain so as to cause injury: to *pull* a ligament. **7** In sports, to strike (the ball) so as to cause it to curve obliquely from the direction in which the striker faces. **8** *Slang* To put into effect; carry out: often with *off:* to *pull* off a prank. **9** *Slang* To make a raid on; arrest. **10** *Slang* To draw out so as to use: to *pull* a knife. **11** *Printing* To make or obtain by impression from type: to *pull* a proof. **12** In boxing, to deliver (a punch, etc.) with less than one's full strength. **13** In horse–racing, to rein in or otherwise restrain (a horse) so as to prevent its winning. **14** In rowing: **a** To operate (an oar) by drawing toward one. **b** To propel or transport by rowing. **c** To be propelled by: The gig *pulls* four oars. —*v.i.* **15** To use force in hauling, dragging, moving, etc. **16** To move: with *out, in, away, ahead,* etc. **17** To drink deeply: to *pull* at a bottle. **18** To inhale deeply: to *pull* at a cigar. **19** To row. See synonyms under DRAW. —**to pull for 1** To strive in behalf of. **2** *Colloq.* To declare one's allegiance to. —**to pull oneself together** To regain one's composure. —**to pull out** *Aeron.* To return to level flight after a dive, as an airplane. —**to pull through 1** Succeed. **2** To survive. —**to pull up** To come to a halt. —**to pull up with** To advance to a position even with. —*n.* **1** The act of pulling; the exertion of force to draw something toward one. **2** Something that is pulled; specifically, the handle of a doorbell, drawer, cabinet, or the like. **3** An impression made by pulling the lever of a hand press. **4** A long swallow, or a deep puff, as on a pipe or cigar. **5** Exercise in rowing: a *pull* on the river. **6** The exertion expended in climbing a mountain; hence, any steady, continuous effort. **7** *Slang* A means of influencing those in power: political *pull;* influence to one's advantage. **8** Attraction: These ads have *pull.* **9** The action of restraining a horse by pulling on the reins; specifically, in horse–racing, the dishonest checking of a horse so that he may be defeated. **10** In sports, the act of pulling the ball. [OE *pullian* pluck] —**pull′er** *n.*
pull·back (pŏŏl′bak′) *n.* The act of pulling back; a withdrawal, as of troops.
pull·doo (pŏŏl′dōō) *n.* The coot. [<F *poule d'eau* a water hen]
pul·let (pŏŏl′it) *n.* A young hen, or one not fully grown. [<OF *polete, poulet,* dim. of *poule* a hen <L *pullus* a chicken, young animal]
pul·ley (pŏŏl′ē) *n.* **1** A wheel grooved to receive a rope, and usually mounted in a block, used to increase the mechanical advantage of an applied force and to transmit or change the direction of power by means of a flexible belt or rope; a sheave. **2** A block with its pulleys or tackle. **3** *Mech.* A flat or flanged wheel driving, carrying, or being driven by a flat belt, used in a system for transmitting power. [<OF *polie* <Med. L *poleia,* prob. ult <Gk. *polos* a pivot, axis]

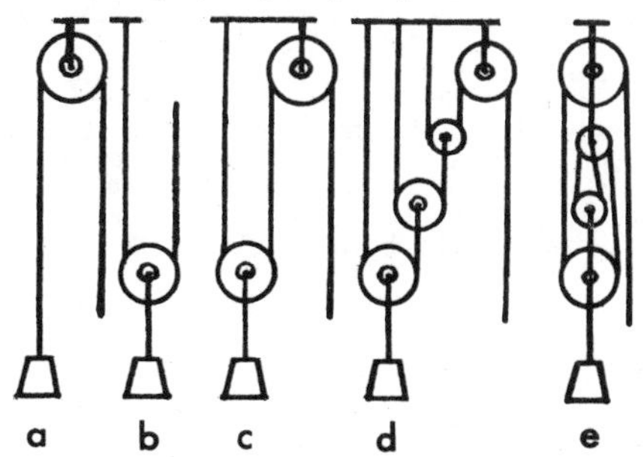

PULLEYS
a. Single fixed. *c.* Fixed and runner.
b. Single runner. *d.* First system.
e. Second system.

Pull·man (pŏŏl′mən) *n.* A sleeping–car or chair car on a passenger train: a trade name. Also **Pullman car.** [after George M. *Pullman,* 1831–97, U.S. inventor]
pull·out (pŏŏl′out′) *n.* **1** A withdrawal or removal, as of troops. **2** Something to be pulled out, as an oversize leaf folded into a magazine. **3** *Aeron.* The maneuver of an airplane in passing from a dive to horizontal flight.
pull–o·ver (pŏŏl′ō′vər) *adj.* Donned by being drawn over the head. —*n.* A garment so donned, as a sweater or shirt.
pull toy A toy designed to be pulled by a string, often producing a noise as it moves.
pul·lu·late (pul′yə·lāt) *v.i.* **·lat·ed, ·lat·ing 1** To germinate; bud. **2** To breed in abundance; swarm; teem. [<L *pullulatus,* pp. of *pullulare* sprout <*pullulus,* dim. of *pullus* a young animal] —**pul′lu·la′tion** *n.* —**pul′lu·la′·tive** *adj.* —**pul′lu·la′tive·ly** *adv.*
pul·mom·e·ter (pul·mom′ə·tər) *n.* An instrument for determining lung capacity by measuring the quantity of air in a single respiration; a spirometer. [<L *pulma* lung + -METER] —**pul·mom′e·try** *n.*
pul·mo·nar·y (pul′mə·ner′ē) *adj.* **1** Pertaining to or affecting the lungs. **2** Having lunglike organs. [<L *pulmonarius* <*pulmo, -onis* lung]
pulmonary artery *Anat.* An artery which conveys (venous) blood from the right ventricle of the heart to the lungs. In man it divides into the right and left pulmonary arteries, leading respectively to the right and left lungs.
pulmonary vein *Anat.* One of four veins which return arterial blood from the lungs to the left side of the heart.
pul·mo·nate (pul′mə·nāt, -nit) *adj.* **1** Having lunglike organs. **2** Of or pertaining to an order of gastropods (*Pulmonata*), including most land snails, slugs, and fresh–water snails, which have lunglike organs. —*n.* One of the *Pulmonata.* [<NL *pulmonatus* <L *pulmo, -onis* lung]
pul·mon·ic (pul·mon′ik) *adj.* **1** Pertaining to or affecting the lungs; pulmonary. **2** Pertaining to pneumonia. —*n.* **1** A medicine for lung disease. **2** One affected by lung disease. [<MF *pulmonique* <L *pulmo, -onis* lung]
Pul·mo·tor (pul′mō′tər, pŏŏl′-) *n.* An apparatus for producing artificial respiration by forcing oxygen into the lungs: a trade name. [<L *pul(mo)* lung + MOTOR]
pulp (pulp) *n.* **1** A moist, soft, slightly cohering mass of matter, usually organic, as chyme, or the soft, succulent part of fruit. **2** A mixture of wood fibers or rags, reduced to a pulpy consistency, and forming the basis from which paper is made. **3** *pl.* Magazines printed on rough, unglazed, wood–pulp paper, and usually having contents of a cheap, sensational nature: distinguished from *slicks.* **4** Powdered ore mixed with water; slime. **5** A pulplike organ or part. **6** *Dent.* The soft tissue of vessels and nerves that fills the central cavity of a tooth. —*v.t.* **1** To reduce to pulp. **2** To remove the pulp or envelope from. —*v.i.* **3** To be or become of a pulpy consistency. [<MF *pulpe* <L *pulpa* flesh, pulp of fruit, pith] —**pulp′less** *adj.*
pulp·ous (pul′pəs) *adj.* Resembling pulp; pulpy.
pul·pit (pŏŏl′pit) *n.* **1** An elevated stand or desk for a preacher in a church. **2** The office or work of preaching; hence, the clergy as a class. **3** An elevated platform usually boxed in and variously used: the harpooner's *pulpit* on a whaling vessel. —*adj.* Of or pertaining to the pulpit: *pulpit* oratory. [<L *pulpitum* a scaffold, stage, platform]
pulp·wood (pulp′wŏŏd′) *n.* The soft wood of certain trees, as the spruce, used in the manufacture of paper.
pulp·y (pul′pē) *adj.* **pulp·i·er, pulp·i·est 1** Consisting of or resembling pulp. **2** Of a soft, juicy consistency; succulent. —**pulp′i·ly** *adv.* —**pulp′i·ness** *n.*
pul·que (pul′kē, pŏŏl′-; *Sp.* pōōl′kā) *n.* A fermented drink made from various species of agave, especially from the juice of the maguey. [<Sp., prob. <Nahuatl]
pul·sar (pul′sär) *n.* An astronomical object that emits radio waves in pulses whose repetition rate is extremely uniform. [<*puls(ating)* + *(st)ar*]
pul·sate (pul′sāt) *v.i.* **·sat·ed, ·sat·ing 1** To move or throb with rhythmical impulses, as the pulse or heart. **2** To vibrate; quiver. [<L *pulsatus,* pp. of *pulsare,* freq. of *pellere* (pp. *pulsus*) beat]
pul·sa·tile (pul′sə·til) *adj.* **1** Pulsatory. **2** That must be struck in order to produce sound; specifically, in music, percussive.
pul·sa·til·la (pul′sə·til′ə) *n.* The dried herb of

the pasqueflower, used as a sedative and alterative; also, the plant itself. [<Med. L, dim. of L *pulsata,* pp. fem. of *pulsare* beat, strike; with ref. to the beating of the flower by the wind]

pul·sa·tion (pul·sā′shən) *n.* **1** A throbbing or vibrating. **2** A single throb or heartbeat.

pul·sa·tive (pul′sə·tiv) *adj.* Pulsating; throbbing; pulsatile. **— pul′sa·tive·ly** *adv.*

pul·sa·tor (pul·sā′tər) *n.* A machine which operates by pulsation, as a pneumatic rock drill operated by puffs of air.

pul·sa·to·ry (pul′sə·tôr′ē, -tō′rē) *adj.* Of or pertaining to pulsation; having rhythmical movement; throbbing; beating; pulsatile.

pulse[1] (puls) *n.* **1** *Physiol.* The rhythmic beating of the arteries due to the successive contractions of the heart, especially as felt in pressing upon the radial artery at the wrist. ◆ Collateral adjectives: *sphygmic, sphygmoid.* **2** Any throbbing characterized by a short, quick, regular stroke or motion; pulsation. **3** *Telecom.* A brief surge of electrical or electromagnetic energy, usually transmitted as a signal in communication. **4** Any movement, drift, or tendency indicative of general opinion, feeling, or sentiment. **—** *v.i.* **pulsed, puls·ing** To manifest a pulse; pulsate; throb. [< OF *pous* <L *pulsus (venarum)* the beating (of the veins), orig. pp. of *pellere* beat] **— pulse′less** *adj.*

pulse[2] (puls) *n.* Leguminous plants collectively, as peas, beans, etc., or their edible seeds. [< OF *pols* <L *puls* pottage of meal or pulse]

pulse·jet (puls′jet′) *adj. Aeron.* Designating a type of jet engine equipped in front with movable vanes which intermittently take in air to develop power in rapid bursts rather than continuously. Also **pul′so·jet′.**

pulse repeater *Electronics* A transponder.

pul·sim·e·ter (pul·sim′ə·tər) *n.* An instrument for indicating and registering the frequency, force, and variations of the pulse; a sphygmograph. [< *pulsi-* (<PULSE[1]) + -METER]

pul·som·e·ter (pul·som′ə·tər) *n.* **1** A device for pumping liquids by steam pressure, operating without pistons and consisting of two pear-shaped chambers connected by valves; a vacuum pump. **2** A pulsimeter.

Pul·tusk (pōō·ōō·tōōsk′) A town in east central Poland, north of Warsaw.

pul·ver·a·ble (pul′vər·ə·bəl) *adj.* Pulverizable.

pul·ver·a·ceous (pul′və·rā′shəs) *adj.* Having a powdery surface; pulverulent. [<L *pulvis, pulveris* a powder + -ACEOUS]

pul·ver·ize (pul′və·rīz) *v.* **·ized, ·iz·ing** *v.t.* **1** To reduce to powder or dust, as by grinding or crushing. **2** To demolish; annihilate. **—** *v.i.* **3** To become reduced to powder or dust. Also *Brit.* **pul′ver·ise.** [<MF *pulveriser* <LL *pulverizare* <L *pulvis, pulveris* a powder, dust] **— pul′ver·iz′a·ble** *adj.* **— pul′ver·i·za′tion** *n.* **— pul′ver·iz′er** *n.*

pul·ver·u·lent (pul·ver′yə·lənt) *adj.* **1** Consisting of, reducible or reduced to, fine powder or dust. **2** Dusty; powdery. [<L *pulverulentus* dusty < *pulvis, pulveris* a powder, dust] **— pul·ver′u·lence** *n.*

pul·vil·lus (pul·vil′əs) *n. pl.* **·vil·li** (-vil′ī) *Entomol.* One of a pair of adhesive pads between the claws of an insect's foot, as the paired cushions of a fly's foot. [<L, contraction of *pulvinulus,* dim. of *pulvinus* a cushion]

pul·vi·nate (pul′və·nāt) *adj.* **1** Cushion- or pillow-shaped. **2** Having a pulvinus. **3** Swelling out like a pillow: said of a convex frieze. Also **pul′vi·nat′ed.** [<L *pulvinatus* < *pulvinus* a cushion] **— pul′vi·nar** *adj.*

pul·vi·nus (pul·vī′nəs) *n. pl.* **·ni** (-nī) *Bot.* The enlargement or swelling at the base of the leaves and leaflets of many leguminous and other plants, through which the sensitive movements are rendered possible. [<L, a cushion]

pu·ma (pyōō′mə) *n.* An American carnivore *(Felis cougar)* ranging from Canada to Patagonia, of a reddish-tawny color, about 4 feet in length, exclusive of the tail; the cougar: also called *mountain lion.* [<Sp. <Quechua]

PUMA
(From 2 to 2 1/2 feet at the shoulder)

pum·ice (pum′is) *n.* Spongy or cellular volcanic lava, used as an abrasive and polishing material, especially when powdered: also **pumice stone.** **—** *v.t.* **·iced, ·ic·ing** To smooth, polish, or clean with pumice. [<OF *pomis, pumis* <L *pumex, pumicis*] **— pu·mi·ceous** (pyōō·mish′əs) *adj.*

pum·mel (pum′əl) See POMMEL.

pump[1] (pump) *n.* A mechanical device for raising, circulating, exhausting, or compressing a liquid or gas by drawing or pressing it through apertures and pipes. **—** *v.t.* **1** To raise with a pump, as water or other liquid. **2** To remove the water, etc., from. **3** To inflate with air by means of a pump. **4** To propel, discharge, force, etc., from or as if from a pump: The heart *pumps* blood. **5** To cause to operate in the manner of a pump or pump handle. **6** To question or obtain information from persistently or subtly: to *pump* a witness. **7** To obtain (information) in such a manner. **—** *v.i.* **8** To work a pump; raise water or other liquid with a pump. **9** To move up and down like a pump or pump handle. [<MDu. *pompe,* prob. <Sp. *bomba;* prob. ult. imit.] **— pump′er** *n.*

pump[2] (pump) *n.* A low-cut slipper without a fastening, having either a high or a low heel. [? <F *pompe* pomp]

pum·per·nick·el (pum′pər·nik′əl) *n.* A coarse, dark, sour bread made from unsifted rye. [<G, Westphalian rye bread, orig. a lout, a peasant]

pump gun A repeating shotgun operated by a sliding handle.

pump·kin (pump′kin, pung′-) *n.* **1** A large trailing vine *(Cucurbita pepo)* with heart-shaped leaves. **2** Its large, round, edible, yellow fruit. **3** In Europe, the winter squash *(C. maxima)* or any of its varieties. [Earlier *pompion* <MF *pompon, popon* <L *pepo, peponis* <Gk. *pepōn* a melon, lit., ripe, cooked by the sun]

pump·kin·seed (pump′kin·sēd′, pung′-) *n.* **1** The seed of a pumpkin. **2** A small fresh-water sunfish, especially the common North American sunfish (*Lepomis gibbosus*). **3** The butterfish.

pump-prim·ing (pump′prī′ming) *n.* **1** Any device or method for priming a pump, usually the application of a little water to wet the valve. **2** Government spending for the purpose of stimulating business.

pun (pun) *n.* The witty use of two words having the same or similar sounds but different meanings, or of two different, more or less incongruous meanings of the same word. **—** *v.* **punned, pun·ning** *v.i.* **1** To make a pun or puns. **—** *v.t.* **2** To treat as a pun. **3** To affect in a specified manner by puns. [? <Ital. *puntiglio* a fine point, a verbal quibble. See PUNCTILIO.] **— pun′ning·ly** *adv.*

pu·na[1] (pōō′nä) See POON.

pu·na[2] (pōō′nä) *n.* **1** A cold, arid region at high altitudes, as in the Andes. **2** Mountain sickness; illness caused by rarefaction of the air; soroche. [<Sp. <Quechua]

punch[1] (punch) *n.* **1** A tool for perforating or indenting, or for driving out or in an object inserted in a hole: frequently tapered at one end. The working end may have a cutting edge enclosing an area or a pattern: often used in connection with a die or counter having a hole in which the punch fits with slight clearance. **2** A machine for impressing a design or stamping a die. **—** *v.t.* To perforate, shape, indent, etc., with a punch. [Short for ME *punchon* a puncheon[1]]

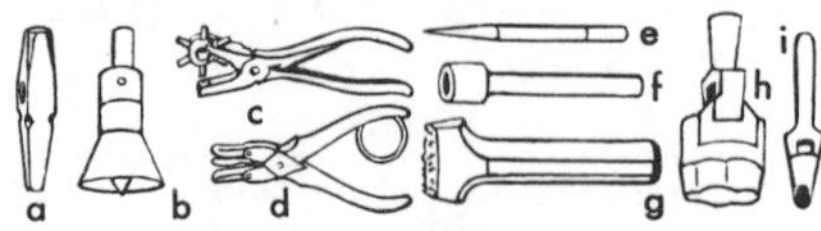

PUNCHES
a. Blacksmith's square. *b.* Center. *c.* Revolving belt. *d.* Ticket. *e, g.* Stamping. *f, h, i.* Cutting.

punch[2] (punch) *v.t.* **1** To strike sharply, especially with the fist. **2** To poke with a stick; prod. **3** *Western U.S.* To drive (cattle). **—** *n.* **1** A swift blow with the fist; also, a thrust or nudge. **2** *Slang* Hence, vitality; effectiveness; force; directness: an editorial with *punch.* [Prob. var. of POUNCE[2]]

punch[3] (punch) *n.* A beverage having wine or spirits, milk, tea, or fruit juices as a basic ingredient, sweetened, sometimes spiced, and diluted with water. [<Hind. *pānch* <Skt. *pañchan* five; from the five original ingredients: arrack, tea, sugar, water, and lemon]

Punch (punch) The quarrelsome, grotesque hero of a comic puppet show, **Punch and Judy.** **— pleased as Punch** Extremely pleased; highly gratified. [Short for PUNCHINELLO]

Punch (punch) An English illustrated humorous weekly journal, founded in 1841.

punch card In data processing, a card having a well-defined arrangement of positions by means of which information can be stored by the presence or absence of punched holes. Also **punched card** (puncht).

punch-drunk (punch′drungk′) *adj.* **1** Suffering from the effects of repeated blows so as to be groggy, slow in movement, etc.: said usually of prize fighters. **2** Confused; dazed. Also *Slang* **punch·y** (punch′ē).

pun·cheon[1] (pun′chən) *n.* **1** An upright supporting timber. **2** A punch or perforating tool, especially one for chipping stone or for stamping figures. **3** A broad, heavy piece of roughly dressed timber, having one flat, hewed side. [<OF *poinçon, poinchon* a punch, ult. <L *punctus,* pp. of *pungere* prick]

pun·cheon[2] (pun′chən) *n.* **1** A liquor cask of variable capacity, from 72 to 120 gallons. **2** A liquor measure of varying amount: mostly of wine, 84 gallons. [<OF *ponçon, poinchon;* ult. same as PUNCHEON[1]]

punch·er (pun′chər) *n.* **1** One who or that which punches. **2** A cowboy; cowpuncher.

Pun·chi·nel·lo (pun′chə·nel′ō) *n. pl.* **·los** or **·loes** **1** A character in an Italian burlesque or puppet show, the original of the English Punch. **2** Hence, **punchinello,** any comic or grotesque character; buffoon. [Earlier *polichinello* < dial. Ital. (Neapolitan) *Polcenella*]

punching bag An inflated or stuffed ball, usually suspended, that is punched with the fists for exercise.

punch press A machine equipped with dies for cutting or forming metal.

punc·tate (pungk′tāt) *adj.* **1** Covered or studded with dots, points, or minute depressions. **2** Pointed. Also **punc′tat·ed.** [<NL *punctatus* <L *punctum* a point] **— punc·ta′tion** *n.*

punc·til·i·o (pungk·til′ē·ō) *n. pl.* **·til·i·os** **1** A nice point of etiquette. **2** Preciseness in the observance of etiquette or ceremony. [<Sp. *puntillo* <Ital. *puntiglio,* dim. of *punto* a point <L *punctum*]

punc·til·i·ous (pungk·til′ē·əs) *adj.* **1** Very nice or exact in the observance of forms of etiquette, etc. **2** Of or pertaining to precise etiquette. [<F *pointelleux* < *pointille* <Ital. *puntiglio* small point] **— punc·til′i·ous·ly** *adv.* **— punc·til′i·ous·ness** *n.*

punc·tu·al (pungk′chōō·əl) *adj.* **1** Exact as to appointed time; acting or arriving promptly; prompt. **2** Done or made precisely at an appointed time. **3** Punctilious; exact. **4** Consisting of or confined to a point as related to space. [<Med. L *punctualis* <L *punctus* a pricking, a point] **— punc′tu·al·ly** *adv.*

punc·tu·al·i·ty (pungk′chōō·al′ə·tē) *n. pl.* **·ties** The quality, characteristic, or habit of being punctual, in any sense.

punc·tu·ate (pungk′chōō·āt) *v.* **·at·ed, ·at·ing** *v.t.* **1** To divide or mark with punctuation. **2** To interrupt at intervals. **3** To emphasize. **—** *v.i.* **4** To use punctuation. [<Med. L *punctuatus,* pp. of *punctuare* <L *punctus* a point] **— punc′tu·a′tor** *n.*

punc·tu·a·tion (pungk′chōō·ā′shən) *n.* The use of points or marks in written or printed matter, to indicate the separation of the words into sentences, clauses, and phrases, and to aid in the better comprehension of the meaning and grammatical relation of the words; also, the marks so used. See also under PRINTING. **— punc′tu·a′tive** *adj.* The chief punctuation points are:

period	.	parentheses	()
colon	:	brackets	[]
semicolon	;	dash (em-dash)	—
comma	,	(en-dash)	–
interrogation point (question mark)	?	hyphen	-
exclamation point	!	quotation marks	" "
		virgule (virgil)	/

punc·ture (pungk′chər) *v.* **·tured, ·tur·ing** *v.t.* **1** To pierce with a sharp point. **2** To make by pricking, as a hole. 3 To cause to collapse: to *puncture* a reputation. —*v.i.* 4 To be pierced or punctured. See synonyms under PIERCE. —*n.* 1 A small hole, as in a pneumatic tire, made by piercing with something sharp-pointed. 2 A minute depression; pit. 3 The act of puncturing. [<LL *punctura* a prick, puncture <L *punctus*, pp. of *pungere* prick] —**punc'tur·a·ble** *adj.*

punc·ture·vine (pungk'chər·vīn') *n.* A low-growing weed (*Tribulus terrestris*) of the caltrop family, having sharp divergent spines which often damage automobile tires: common in the western United States.

pun·dit (pun'dit) *n.* A learned Brahman, especially one versed in Sanskrit lore and in the science, laws, and religion of the Hindus; hence, any learned man. [<Hind. *paṇḍit* <Skt. *paṇḍita*, lit., learned, skilled]

pung (pung) *n.* *U.S. Dial.* A low box sled for one horse. [Short for *tom pung*, prob. alter. of TOBOGGAN]

pun·gent (pun'jənt) *adj.* 1 Having or causing sharp pricking, stinging, piercing, or acrid effects upon the senses. 2 Affecting the mind or feelings, as by sharp points, so as to cause pain; piercing; sharp. 3 Caustic; keen; racy: *pungent* sarcasm. 4 Terminating in a hard sharp point, as a pine needle. See synonyms under BITTER, HOT, RACY. [<L *pungens*, *-entis*, ppr. of *pungere* prick] —**pun'gence** or **pun'gen·cy** *n.* —**pun'gent·ly** *adv.*

Pu·nic (pyōō'nik) *adj.* Of or pertaining to ancient Carthage or the Carthaginians, who were regarded by the Romans as treacherous; hence, faithless; untrustworthy. —*n.* The Northwest Semitic language of the Carthaginians, a dialect of Phoenician. [<L *punicus* <*poenicus* <*Poenus* a Carthaginian, a Phoenician <Gk. *Phoinix*, *-ikos*]

Punic Wars See table under WAR.

pun·ish (pun'ish) *v.t.* 1 To subject (a person) to pain, confinement, or other penalty for a crime or fault. 2 To subject the perpetrator of (an offense) to a penalty: to *punish* forgery. 3 To use roughly; injure; hurt. 4 To make heavy inroads upon; deplete, as a stock of food. See synonyms under AVENGE, CHASTEN, REQUITE. [<OF *puniss-*, stem of *punir* <L *punire* punish <*poenire* <*poena* a punishment, penalty, fine] —**pun'ish·er** *n.*

pun·ish·a·ble (pun'ish·ə·bəl) *adj.* Deserving of or liable to punishment: said of offenders or offenses. —**pun'ish·a·bil'i·ty** *n.*

pun·ish·ment (pun'ish·mənt) *n.* 1 Penalty imposed, as for transgression of law. ◆ Collateral adjective: *penal*. 2 Any ill suffered in consequence of wrongdoing. 3 The act of punishing. 4 *Colloq.* Rough handling, as in a pugilistic encounter, a naval engagement, etc.

pu·ni·tive (pyōō'nə·tiv) *adj.* 1 Pertaining to or inflicting punishment. 2 *Law* Of a character to punish or vindicate. Also **pu'ni·to'ry** (-tôr'ē, -tō'rē). [<Med. L *punitivus* <L *punitus*, pp. of *punire* PUNISH] —**pu'ni·tive·ly** *adv.* —**pu'ni·tive·ness** *n.*

Pun·jab (pun'jäb, pun·jäb') 1 A region of NW India and West Pakistan; 148,610 square miles. 2 A former province of British India in this region, divided in 1947 between Punjab State, India, and West Pakistan; 99,089 square miles; former capital, Lahore. 3 A State of India in this region; 47,456 square miles; capital, Chandigarh. 4 A former province of West Pakistan in this region, a part of West Pakistan province since October, 1955; 63,134 square miles; former capital, Lahore.

Punjab Hill States A former political agency in NW India, under British rule, consisting of 22 princely states which came to be part of India: one in Uttar Pradesh, two in Punjab, and the rest in Himachal Pradesh; from 1936 to 1947–48 included in Punjab States; 11,375 square miles; headquarters, Simla.

Pun·ja·bi (pun·jä'bē) *n.* 1 A native of the Punjab. 2 The Sanskritic language of the Punjab, belonging to the Indic branch of the Indo-Iranian languages: also spelled *Panjabi*.

Punjab States A former political agency in NW India, under British rule, consisting of 14 princely states (of which two were included in West Pakistan, three in Himachal Pradesh, India, and the rest in Punjab, India) and also, after 1936, the Punjab Hill States; 38,146 square miles; headquarters, Lahore.

punk[1] (pungk) *n.* 1 Wood decayed through the action of some fungus, and useful as tinder; touchwood. 2 An artificial preparation that will smolder without flame. [<Algonquian (Lenape) *punk*, *ponk* fine ashes]

punk[2] (pungk) *n.* 1 *U.S. Slang* Rubbish; nonsense; anything worthless. 2 *U.S. Slang* A petty hoodlum. 3 *Obs.* A prostitute. —*adj.* *U.S. Slang* Worthless; useless. [Origin uncertain]

pun·ka (pung'kə) *n.* A fan; especially, a rectangular strip of cloth, etc., swung from the ceiling and moved by a servant or by machinery. Also **pun'kah.** [<Hind. *pankhā* a fan <Skt. *pakshaka* <*paksha* a wing]

pun·ky (pung'kē) *n.* *pl.* **·kies** A minute, annoying, bloodsucking gnat or midge (genus *Culicoides*): also called *sand fly*. Also **pun'key, pun'kie.** [<Du. *punki* <Algonquian (Lenape) *punk*, *ponk*, orig. fine ashes]

pun·ster (pun'stər) *n.* One who puns; one addicted to punning. Also **pun'ner.**

punt[1] (punt) *n.* A flat-bottomed, square-ended boat, usually with a seat in the middle and a well or seat at one or each end, for use in shallow waters, and propelled with a pole. —*v.t.* 1 To propel (a boat) by pushing with a pole against the bottom of a shallow stream, lake, etc. 2 To convey in a punt. —*v.i.* 3 To go or hunt in a punt. [OE <L *ponto*, *-onis* a punt, a pontoon <*pons*, *pontis* a bridge] —**punt'er** *n.*

PUNT

punt[2] (punt) *v.i.* To gamble or bet, especially against a bank, as at faro, roulette, or baccarat. [<F *ponter* <*ponte* a point <L *punctum*] —**punt'er** *n.*

punt[3] (punt) *n.* In football, a kick made by dropping the ball from the hands and kicking it before it strikes the ground. —*v.t.* In football, to propel (the ball) with a punt. —*v.i.* In football, to make a punt. [Prob. var. of BUNT] —**punt'er** *n.*

Pun·ta A·re·nas (pōōn'tä ä·rā'näs) A port of southern Chile, on the Strait of Magellan.

pun·til·la (pun·til'ə) *n.* Lacework, lace edging, or lace design with points. [<Sp., dim. of *punto* a point <L *punctum*]

pun·to (pun'tō) *n.* A hit or thrust in fencing. [<Ital., a point <L *punctum*]

pun·ty (pun'tē) See PONTIL.

pu·ny (pyōō'nē) *adj.* **·ni·er, ·ni·est** 1 Weak and insignificant; of small and feeble development or importance; petty. 2 *Obs.* Puisne; born later; younger. See synonyms under SMALL. ◆ Homophone: *puisne*. [<OF *puisne*. See PUISNE.] —**pu'ni·ly** *adv.* —**pu'ni·ness** *n.*

pup (pup) *n.* 1 A puppy (def. 1). 2 A young seal. —*v.i.* **pupped, pup·ping** To bring forth pups. [Short for PUPPY]

pu·pa (pyōō'pə) *n.* *pl.* **·pae** (-pē) 1 *Entomol.* The quiescent stage in the development of an insect that undergoes a complete metamorphosis, following the larval and preceding the adult stage; also, an insect in such a stage. 2 *Zool.* A similar developmental state in some echinoderms, as holothurians. [<NL <L, a girl, doll, puppet] —**pu'pal** *adj.*

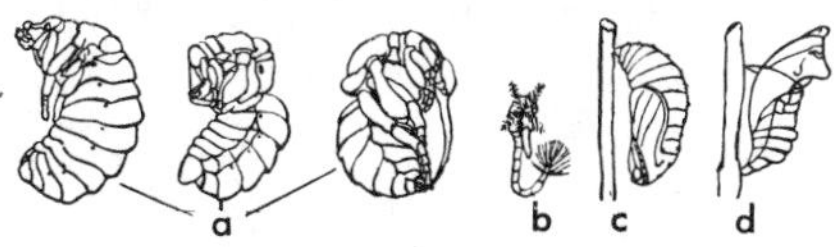

PUPAE

a. Three pupal stages of a bumblebee.
b. Aquatic pupa of a gnat.
c. Suspended pupa of a butterfly.
d. Girdled pupa of a butterfly.

pu·pate (pyōō'pāt) *v.i.* **·pat·ed, ·pat·ing** To enter upon or undergo the pupal condition. —**pu·pa'tion** *n.*

pu·pil[1] (pyōō'pəl) *n.* 1 A person of either sex or of any age under the care of a teacher; scholar; learner. 2 In civil law, a minor who is under the age of puberty and has a guardian. See synonyms under SCHOLAR. [<OF *pupille*, orig. an orphan, ward <L *pupillus*, dim. of *pupus* a boy and *pupilla*, dim. of *pupa* a girl]

pu·pil[2] (pyōō'pəl) *n.* *Anat.* The contractile opening in the iris of the eye, through which light reaches the retina. [<L *pupilla* a figure reflected in the eye, the pupil of the eye, dim. of *pupa*. See PUPA.]

pu·pil·age (pyōō'pəl·ij) *n.* The state or period of being a pupil. Also **pu'pil·lage.**

pu·pi·lar·i·ty (pyōō'pə·lar'ə·tē) *n.* In Scots law, the interval between birth and the age of 14 in males and 12 in females. Also **pu'pil·lar'i·ty.** [<OF *pupillarité* <L *pupillaris* pertaining to an orphan <*pupillus*, *pupilla*. See PUPIL[1].]

pu·pi·lar·y (pyōō'pə·ler'ē) *adj.* Of or pertaining to a pupil or a ward. Also **pu'pil·lar'y.**

Pu·pin (pyōō·pēn', *Hungarian* pōō·pēn'), **Michael Idvorsky,** 1858–1935, U. S. physicist and inventor born in Hungary.

pu·pip·a·rous (pyōō·pip'ər·əs) *adj.* Of or pertaining to a division (*Pupipara*) of dipterous insects in which the young are born ready to pupate, as bat ticks, sheep ticks, etc. [<NL <PUPA + L *parere* bring forth]

pup·pet (pup'it) *n.* 1 A small figure of a human being, that by means of strings or wires is made to perform mock drama; a marionette. 2 A person slavishly subject to the will of another; a tool. 3 A doll. —*adj.* 1 Of or pertaining to puppets or mummery. 2 Performing the will of an unseen power; not autonomous: a *puppet* state or government. [<OF *poupette* <L *pupa* a girl, doll, puppet]

pup·pet·eer (pup'i·tir') *n.* A person who manipulates puppets.

pup·pet·ry (pup'it·rē) *n.* The performances of puppets or the manipulation of puppets; mummery.

puppet show A mock drama, with puppets for the actors.

pup·py (pup'ē) *n.* *pl.* **·pies** 1 The young of a canine mammal, as of a dog; a pup. 2 A conceited and forward young man; a silly fop. [<OF *poupee*, *popee* <L *pupa* a girl, doll] —**pup'py·ish** *adj.*

puppy love Adolescent love; sentimental, temporary infatuation.

pup tent A shelter tent.

pur (pûr) See PURR.

Pu·ra·cé (pōō'rä·sā') An active volcano in SW Colombia; 15,420 feet; last major eruption, 1869.

Pu·ra·na (pōō·rä'nə) *n.* Any of a number of Hindu scriptures in the form of verse dialogs, coming next in order after the Vedas, dealing mainly with theogony and cosmogony, especially with the god Vishnu and his incarnations. There are 18 Puranas and 18 Upa Puranas or subordinate works. [<Skt. *purāna*, lit., ancient <*purā* of old]

pur·blind (pûr'blīnd') *adj.* 1 Afflicted with dimness of vision; near-sighted. 2 Having little or no insight or understanding. 3 *Obs.* Totally blind. [ME *pur blind* <*pur* (<OF, plain) + *blind* blind] —**pur'blind'ly** *adv.* —**pur'blind'ness** *n.*

Pur·cell (pûr'səl), **Henry,** 1658?–95, English composer.

Pur·chas (pûr'chəs), **Samuel,** 1575?–1626, English author and compiler.

pur·chas·a·ble (pûr'chəs·ə·bəl) *adj.* That can be purchased; hence, venal; corrupt. —**pur'chas·a·bil'i·ty** *n.*

pur·chase (pûr'chəs) *v.t.* **·chased, ·chas·ing** 1 To acquire by paying money or its equivalent; buy. 2 To obtain by exertion, sacrifice, flattery, etc. 3 *Law* To acquire (property) by means other than descent or inheritance. 4 To move, hoist, or hold by a mechanical purchase. —*n.* 1 The act of purchasing; acquisition by giving an equivalent in money or other exchange, or by exertion, risk, etc. 2 That which is purchased; especially, that which is bought with money. 3 A mechanical hold or grip. 4 A device that gives a mechanical advantage, as a tackle or lever. 5 Leverage. 6 Any means of increasing influence or advantage. 7 *Law* The act of acquiring property by payment of a price or value; hence, any lawful mode of acquiring property other than by inheritance or descent or by the mere operation of law. 8 Value; worth, especially as measured by the annual income, expressed in terms of years to indicate the period at the end of which the income received from a property will have covered the price paid for it: to buy at ten years' *purchase.* **9** A small territorial division in New Hampshire, originally made when the land was sold in lots to individuals by the State. **10** *Obs.* A seeking; also, attempt; endeavor. [<AF *purchacer,* OF *porchacier* seek for < *pur-, por-* for (<L *pro-*) + *chacier* CHASE] — **pur'chas·er** *n.*

Synonyms (verb): acquire, buy, get, obtain, procure, secure. *Buy* and *purchase* are close synonyms, in numerous cases freely interchangeable, but with the difference usually found between words of Anglo-Saxon and French or Latin origin. The Anglo-Saxon *buy* is used for all the concerns of common life, the French *purchase* is often restricted to transactions of more dignity; yet *buy* is commonly more emphatic, and also appeals more strongly to the feelings. One may either *buy* or *purchase* fame, favor, honor, pleasure, etc., but we speak of victory or freedom as dearly *bought. Antonyms*: barter, exchange, sell.

pur·dah (pûr'də) *n. Anglo-Indian* **1** A curtain or screen, especially one used to seclude women; also, the state of seclusion so secured. **2** The material of which a curtain is made. [<Urdu *pardah* <Persian]

pure (pyŏŏr) *adj.* **1** Free from mixture or contact with that which weakens, impairs, or pollutes; containing no foreign or vitiating material. **2** Free from adulteration; clear; clean; hence, genuine; stainless: *pure* food, *pure* motives. **3** Free from moral defilement; innocent; chaste; unsullied; also, free from coarseness; refined: a *pure* life, *pure* language. **4** Free from foreign or imported elements: said especially of language and works of art. **5** *Music* Mathematically correct as to intervals; free from harsh quality in tone; also, correct in form or style; finished. **6** *Philos.* Considered apart from its attributes or from concrete experience; abstract; also, a priori. **7** *Phonet.* Having a single, unvarying tone or sound: said of vowels. **8** Theoretical; concerned with fundamental research, as distinguished from practical application: said of sciences. **9** *Genetics* Breeding true with respect to one or more characters; homozygous. **10** Nothing but; real; sheer: *pure* mischief, *pure* luck. [<OF *pur* <L *purus* clean, pure] — **pure'ness** *n.*

Synonyms: absolute, chaste, classic, classical, clean, clear, continent, fair, genuine, guileless, guiltless, holy, immaculate, incorrupt, innocent, mere, perfect, real, sheer, simple, spotless, stainless, true, unadulterated, unblemished, uncorrupted, undefiled, unmingled, unmixed, unpolluted, unspotted, unstained, unsullied, untainted, untarnished, upright, virtuous. Material substances are called *pure* in the strict sense when free from foreign admixture of any kind; as, *pure* oxygen; the word is often used to signify free from any defiling or objectionable admixture (the original sense); we speak of water as *pure* when it is bright, clear, and refreshing, even if it contains mineral salts in solution; in the medical and chemical sense, only distilled water *(aqua distillata)* is *pure.* In moral and religious use *pure* denotes positive excellence of a high order; one is *innocent* who knows nothing of evil and has experienced no touch of temptation; one is *pure* who, with knowledge of evil and exposure to temptation, keeps heart and soul *unstained. Virtuous* refers primarily to right action, *pure* to right feeling; as, "Blessed are the *pure* in heart: for they shall see God." *Matt.* v 8. See FINE[1], INNOCENT, MODEST, VIRTUOUS. *Antonyms*: adulterated, defiled, dirty, filthy, gross, impure, indecent, indelicate, lewd, mixed, obscene, polluted, stained, sullied, tainted, tarnished, unchaste, unclean; see also synonyms for FOUL, IMMODEST.

pure·blood (pyŏŏr'blud) *n.* **1** An individual descended from a long line of ancestors of the same ethnic or racial stock: said especially of American Indians. **2** A purebred animal. — **pure'-blood'ed** *adj.*

pure·bred (pyŏŏr'bred') *adj.* Bred from stock having had no admixture for many generations: said especially of livestock. — *n.* (pyŏŏr'-bred') A purebred animal.

pure culture *Bacteriol.* A culture or medium for the isolation and cultivation of microorganisms of a particular kind, as those of anthrax, diphtheria, etc.

pu·rée (pyōō·rā', pyŏŏr'ā; *Fr.* pü·rā') *n.* A thick pulp, usually of vegetables, boiled and strained. — *v.t.* **·réed, ·rée·ing** To put (cooked or soft food) through a sieve, blender, etc.: to *purée* vegetables. [<F <OF, pp. fem. of *purer* strain <L *purare* purify < *purus* pure]

pure line *Genetics* A strain of plants or animals which through self-fertilization, continued inbreeding, or other means, exhibit a high degree of stability in one or more genetic characteristics.

pure·ly (pyŏŏr'lē) *adv.* **1** So as to be free from admixture, taint, or any harmful substance. **2** Chastely; innocently. **3** Merely.

pur·fle (pûr'fəl) *v.t.* **·fled, ·fling** To decorate, as with a wrought or flowered border; border. — *n.* A richly ornamented border: also **pur'·fling.** [<OF *porfiler, pourfiler* < *por-, pour-* for (<L *pro-*) + *fil* a thread <L *filum*]

pur·ga·tion (pûr·gā'shən) *n.* A purging; catharsis. [<OF *purgacion* <L *purgatio, -onis* < *purgatus,* pp. of *purgare* PURGE]

pur·ga·tive (pûr'gə·tiv) *adj.* Efficacious in purging; cathartic. — *n.* A cathartic.

pur·ga·to·ry (pûr'gə·tôr'ē, -tō'rē) *n. pl.* **·ries** **1** In Roman Catholic theology, a state or place where the souls of those who have died penitent are made fit for paradise by expiating venial sins and undergoing any punishment remaining for previously forgiven sins. **2** Any place or state of temporary banishment, suffering, or punishment. [<AF *purgatorie,* OF *purgatoire* <Med. L *purgatorium* <L *purgatorius* cleansing < *purgare* PURGE] — **pur'ga·to'ri·al** *adj.*

purge (pûrj) *v.* **purged, purg·ing** *v.t.* **1** To cleanse of what is impure or extraneous; purify. **2** To remove (impurities, etc.) in cleansing: with *away, off,* or *out.* **3** To rid (a group, nation, etc.) of elements regarded as undesirable or inimical, especially by killing. **4** To remove or kill (a person or persons) in such a manner. **5** To cleanse or rid of sin, fault, or defilement. **6** *Med.* **a** To cause evacuation of (the bowels, etc.). **b** To induce evacuation of the bowels of. **7** *Law* To clear of accusation, suspicion, or guilt. — *v.i.* **8** To become clean or pure. **9** *Med.* To have or induce evacuation. — *n.* **1** The act or operation of purging, in any sense. **2** That which purges; specifically, a medicine causing active evacuation of the bowels; a cathartic; also, its administration or operation. [<OF *purgier* <L *purgare* cleanse < *purigare* < *purus* pure] — **purg'er** *n.* — **purg'ing** *n.*

Pu·ri (pōō'rē) A port and Hindu pilgrimage center on the Bay of Bengal in SW Orissa, India: also *Jaganath.*

pu·ri·fi·ca·tion (pyŏŏr'ə·fə·kā'shən) *n.* **1** The act or operation of purifying: said of things physical or spiritual. **2** The act or observance of formal cleansing from ceremonial defilement. ◆ Collateral adjective: *lustral.*

pu·ri·fy (pyŏŏr'ə·fī) *v.* **·fied, ·fy·ing** *v.t.* **1** To make pure or clean; rid of extraneous or noxious matter. **2** To free from sin or defilement. **3** To free of foreign or debasing elements, as a language. — *v.i.* **4** To become pure or clean. [<OF *purifier* <L *purificare* < *purus* pure + *facere* make] — **pu·rif·i·ca·to·ry** (pyōō·rif'ə·kə·tôr'ē, -tō'rē-) *adj.* — **pu'·ri·fi'er** *n.*

Synonyms: clarify, clean, cleanse, filter, refine, wash. See AMEND, CHASTEN, CLEANSE. *Antonyms*: contaminate, corrupt, debase, defile, deprave, infect, poison, taint, vitiate.

Pu·rim (pŏŏr'im, pyŏŏr'im; *Hebrew* pōō·rēm') A Jewish festival commemorating the defeat of Haman's plot to massacre the Jews (*Esth.* ix 26), observed about the first of March. [<Hebrew *pūrīm,* pl. of *pūr* a lot]

pu·rine (pyŏŏr'ēn, -in) *n. Biochem.* A white, crystalline compound, $C_5H_4N_4$, which is closely related to uric acid in structure. Also **pu·rin** (pyŏŏr'in). [<G *purin* <L *purus* pure + NL *uricum* uric acid + *-in* -INE[2]]

purine group *Biochem.* An important group of organic compounds widely distributed in nature and related to purine, as caffeine, xanthine, uric acid, etc.

pur·ism (pyŏŏr'iz·əm) *n.* Extreme strictness in regard to the use of words, or an instance of it. — **pur'ist** *n.* — **pu·ris'tic** *adj.*

Pu·ri·tan (pyŏŏr'ə·tən) *n.* **1** One of a group or party of English Protestants (1599) who advocated simpler forms of creed and ritual in the established church, freedom of conscience and worship, and condemned all laxity of morals. Many of them emigrated to the American colonies in the 17th century, especially to the Massachusetts Bay colony. **2** One who is scrupulously strict, or censorious and exacting in his religious life: often not capitalized. — *adj.* Of or pertaining to the Puritans or their beliefs or customs. [<LL *puritas* purity <L *purus* pure + -AN; orig. used by opponents to suggest a resemblance to the *Cathari* (lit., purists)] — **Pu'ri·tan'ic** *adj.*

pu·ri·tan·i·cal (pyŏŏr'ə·tan'i·kəl) *adj.* Governed by the Puritan code; rigidly scrupulous in religious observance and morals; strict. — **pu'·ri·tan'i·cal·ly** *adv.* — **pu'ri·tan'i·cal·ness** *n.*

Pu·ri·tan·ism (pyŏŏr'ə·tən·iz'əm) *n.* **1** The spirit, doctrines, and practices of the Puritans. **2** Religious and moral scrupulousness and austerity. **3** The New England character and spirit.

pu·ri·ty (pyŏŏr'ə·tē) *n.* **1** The character or state of being pure, in any sense, as freedom from dirt or foreign or adulterating matter; cleanness; moral cleanness; innocence; freedom from sinister or improper design; absence of admixture. **2** Saturation: said of a color. **3** The use of no foreign words, phrases, or idioms; use of words with only the precise form, connection, and meaning assigned to them by good usage. See synonyms under INNOCENCE, VIRTUE.

Pur·kin·je (pŏŏr'kin·ye), **Johannes Evangelista,** 1787–1869, Czech physiologist.

Purkinje cell *Physiol.* One of the large, flask-shaped ganglion cells interposed as a single layer between the two layers of gray matter in the cerebellar cortex of the brain. [after J. E. *Purkinje*]

purl[1] (pûrl) *v.i.* **1** To whirl; turn. **2** To flow with a bubbling sound; ripple. **3** To move in eddies. — *n.* **1** A circling movement of water; an eddy. **2** A gentle, continued murmur, as of a rippling stream. ◆ Homophone: *pearl.* [Cf. Norw. *purla* gush out, bubble up]

purl[2] (pûrl) *v.t.* **1** To purfle. **2** In knitting, to make (a stitch) backward. **3** To edge with lace, embroidery, etc. — *v.i.* **4** To do edging with lace, etc. [< *n.*] — *n.* **1** An edge of lace, embroidery, etc.; in lacework, a spiral of gold or silver wire. **2** In knitting, the inversion of the knit stitch giving a horizontal rib effect. ◆ Homophone: *pearl.* [Earlier *pyrle,* orig. twisted gold or silver thread < *pyrl* twist; ult. origin unknown]

pur·lieu (pûr'lōō) *n.* **1** *pl.* The outlying districts or outskirts of any place. **2** A place in which one is free to come and go; a haunt. **3** Formerly, ground unlawfully taken for a royal forest, but afterward disafforested and restored to its rightful owners. [<AF *puralee* <OF < *puraler* go through < *pur-* through (<L *per-*) + *aler* go; infl. in form by MF *lieu* a place]

pur·lin (pûr'lin) *n.* One of several horizontal timbers supporting rafters. Also **pur'line** (-lin). [ME *purlyn,* prob. <OF]

pur·loin (pûr·loin') *v.t.* & *v.i.* To steal; filch. See synonyms under ABSTRACT, STEAL. [<AF *purloignier,* OF *porloignier* remove, put far off < *pur-, por-* for (<L *pro-*) + *loing, loin* far <L *longe*] — **pur·loin'er** *n.*

pur·ple (pûr'pəl) *n.* **1** A color of mingled red and blue, between crimson and violet; in ancient times, the color obtained from the murex, properly a crimson. **2** Cloth or a garment of this color, worn formerly by sovereigns, especially the emperors of Rome; hence, royal power or dignity; preeminence in rank or wealth. **3** The office of a cardinal: from the official red hat and robes; also, the episcopal dignity: from its purple insignia. — *v.t.* & *v.i.* **·pled, ·pling** To make or become purple. — *adj.* **1** Of the color of purple. **2** Hence, imperial; regal. **3** Conspicuously brilliant or ornate: said of language. [Alter. of ME *purpre,* OE *purpure,* the color purple <L *purpura,* orig. the shellfish yielding Tyrian purple dye, the dye, or cloth dyed with it <Gk. *porphyra*]

purple finch The rose-breasted American finch *(Carpodacus purpureus).*

pur·ple-fringed orchid (pûr'pəl·frinjd') A terrestrial orchid of North America (genus

Habenaria) with fragrant, purple, lilac, or, rarely, white flowers.

Purple Heart A decoration of honor of the **Order of the Purple Heart** in the form of a purple enameled heart surrounded by a gold-colored border and bearing the head of George Washington in gold-colored relief: established by George Washington in 1782, revived 1932: awarded to members of the armed forces or to citizens of the United States honorably wounded in action, or as a result of enemy action.

PURPLE HEART

purple medic Lucerne.

purple of Cassius A rich and powerful pigment obtained from a mixture of stannic, stannous, and gold chlorides: used chiefly in miniature painting and enamel painting.

purple osier Red osier.

pur·plish (pûr′plish) *adj.* Somewhat purple.

pur·port (pər·pôrt′, -pōrt′, pûr′pôrt, -pōrt) *v.t.* **1** To have or bear as its meaning; signify; imply. **2** To claim or profess (to be), especially falsely. See synonyms under IMPORT. —*n.* (pûr′pôrt, -pōrt) **1** That which is conveyed or suggested to the mind as the meaning or intention; import; significance. **2** The substance of a statement, etc., given in other than the exact words. See synonyms under PURPOSE. [<AF, OF *purporter* extend <*pur-* forth (<L *pro-*) + *porter* carry <L *portare*] —**pur·port′ed·ly** *adv.*

pur·pose (pûr′pəs) *v.t.* & *v.i.* **·posed, ·pos·ing** To have the intention of doing or accomplishing (something); intend; aim; design. —*n.* **1** The idea or ideal kept before the mind as an end of effort or action; plan; design; aim. **2** The particular thing to be effected or attained; practical advantage or result; consequence; use: words to little *purpose.* **3** Settled resolution; determination; constancy. **4** Purport; intent, as of spoken or written language. **5** A proposition; proposal; question at issue. —**on purpose** With previous design; intentionally. [<OF *porposer,* var. of *proposer. See* PROPOSE.]

Synonyms (noun): aim, design, determination, drift, end, intent, intention, meaning, motive, object, plan, project, purport, resolution, resolve, view. Compare AIM, CAUSE, DESIGN, END, IDEA, PLAN, PROJECT, REASON, SERVICE. *Antonyms*: See synonyms for ACT.

Synonyms (verb): design, determine, intend, mean, propose, resolve. See PROPOSE.

pur·pose·ful (pûr′pəs·fəl) *adj.* Having, or marked by, purpose; intentional; important; significant. —**pur′pose·ful·ly** *adv.* —**pur′pose·ful·ness** *n.*

pur·pose·less (pûr′pəs·lis) *adj.* Having no definite design or use; aimless. See synonyms under FAINT. —**pur′pose·less·ly** *adv.*

pur·pose·ly (pûr′pəs·lē) *adv.* For a purpose; intentionally; deliberately; on purpose.

pur·po·sive (pûr′pə·siv) *adj.* **1** Pertaining to, having, or indicating purpose. **2** Functional. —**pur′po·sive·ly** *adv.* —**pur′po·sive·ness** *n.*

pur·pu·ra (pûr′pyŏŏ·rə) *n. Pathol.* A disease characterized by especially livid spots on the skin caused by extravasated blood. [<L. See PURPLE.]

pur·pure (pûr′pyŏŏr) *n.* Purple: one of the colors or tinctures used in heraldic description. [OE]

pur·pu·ric (pûr·pyŏŏr′ik) *adj.* **1** Of or pertaining to a purple tint. **2** Relating to or resembling purpura.

pur·pu·rin (pûr′pyŏŏ·rin) *n. Chem.* A red crystalline compound, $C_{14}H_8O_5$, contained in madder, largely used in dyeing: also prepared synthetically. Also **pur′pu·rine** (-rin). [<L *purpura* purple + -IN]

purr (pûr) *n.* An intermittent murmuring sound, such as a cat makes when pleased. —*v.i.* To make such a sound. —*v.t.* To express by or as by purring. Also spelled *pur.* [Imit.]

purse (pûrs) *n.* **1** A small bag or pouch of leather or the like, often having the mouth drawn together with a drawstring; especially, one for carrying money; hence, anything for carrying money on the person. **2** Available resources or means; a treasury: the public *purse.* **3** A sum of money offered as a prize or tendered as a gift, as for a contest or charitable collection. —*v.t.* **pursed, purs·ing** **1** To contract into wrinkles or folds like the mouth of a purse; pucker: to *purse* the lips. **2** *Rare* To place in a purse. [OE *purs* <LL *bursa* <Gk. *byrsa* a skin, a hide]

purse-pride (pûrs′prīd′) *n.* Arrogance due to the possession of wealth. —**purse′proud′** (-proud′) *adj.*

purs·er (pûr′sər) *n.* An officer having charge of the accounts, etc., of a vessel; formerly, a naval paymaster. —**purs′er·ship** *n.*

purs·lane (pûrs′lin, -lān) *n.* A procumbent fleshy annual plant (*Portulaca oleracea*) of gardens and waste places, with reddish-green stem and leaves and small yellow flowers: used in Europe as a salad, but regarded as a weed in the United States. Also spelled *pussley.* [<OF *porcelaine* <L *porcilaca* < *portulaca*]

PURSLANE

pur·su·ance (pər·sōō′əns) *n.* The act of pursuing; a following after or following out; prosecution: usually in the phrase *in pursuance of.*

pur·su·ant (pər·sōō′ənt) *adj.* Done in accordance with or by reason of something; conformable. —*adv.* In accordance; agreeably; conformably: usually with *to*: also **pur·su′ant·ly.**

pur·sue (pər·sōō′) *v.* **·sued, ·su·ing** *v.t.* **1** To follow in an attempt to overtake or capture; chase. **2** To seek or attain or gain: to *pursue* fame. **3** To advance along the course of; keep to the direction or provisions of, as a path, plan, or system. **4** To apply one's energies to or have as one's profession or chief interest: to *pursue* one's studies. **5** To follow persistently; harass; worry. —*v.i.* **6** To follow. **7** To continue. See synonyms under FOLLOW. [<AF *pursuer,* OF *porsievre* <LL *prosequere* <L *prosequi* <*pro-* forth + *sequi* follow] —**pur·su′a·ble** *adj.* —**pur·su′er** *n.*

pur·suit (pər·sōōt′) *n.* **1** The act of pursuing; a chase. **2** That which is followed as a continued employment; a business; vocation. See synonyms under HUNT. [<AF *purseute,* OF *porsieute, poursuite* <*porsievre* PURSUE]

pursuit plane *Mil.* A powerful, speedy, highly maneuverable airplane, heavily armed, but with short range, designed to intercept, pursue, and attack enemy aircraft: also called *fighter plane.*

pur·sui·vant (pûr′swi·vənt) *n.* **1** An attendant upon a herald; an officer of the third and lowest rank in the College of Heralds, performing similar duties to a herald. **2** *Obs.* A follower; especially, a military attendant of the king. [<OF *porsivant,* ppr. of *porsievre* pursue]

purs·y (pûr′sē) *adj.* **purs·i·er, purs·i·est** Short-breathed; asthmatic; hence, fat. See synonyms under CORPULENT. [Earlier *pursive* <AF *pursif,* OF *polsif* <*polser* pant, gasp] —**purs′i·ness** *n.*

pur·te·nance (pûr′tə·nəns) *n. Obs.* Appurtenance; specifically, the inwards of an animal. [<AF *purtinaunt,* OF *partenant.* See PERTINENT.]

pu·ru·lent (pyŏŏr′ə·lənt, -yə·lənt) *adj.* Consisting of or secreting pus; suppurating. [<L *purulentus* <*pus, puris* pus] —**pu′ru·lence** or **·len·cy** *n.* —**pu′ru·lent·ly** *adv.*

Pu·rus (pōō·rōōs′) A river in SE Peru and western Brazil, flowing 2,100 miles NE to the Amazon.

pur·vey (pər·vā′) *v.t.* & *v.i.* To furnish or provide (provisions, etc.). [<AF *purveier,* OF *porveier* <L *providere.* Doublet of PROVIDE.]

pur·vey·ance (pər·vā′əns) *n.* **1** The act of purveying. **2** That which is purveyed or supplied; provisions. **3** A former prerogative of royalty, abolished in 1660, enabling a monarch to buy goods at an appraised value, and also to enforce personal service.

pur·vey·or (pər·vā′ər) *n.* **1** One who furnishes supplies for living, especially for the table; a caterer. **2** Formerly, an officer who, by exaction or otherwise, made provision for the king's household.

pur·view (pûr′vyōō) *n.* **1** Extent, sphere, or scope of anything, as of official authority. **2** Range of view, experience, or understanding; outlook. **3** *Law* The body or the scope or limit of a statute. [<AF *purveu* provided, OF *porveu,* pp. of *porveier* PURVEY; orig. in AF legal phrases *purveu est* it is provided and *purveu que* provided that]

pus (pus) *n. Med.* A secretion from inflamed tissues, as in healing wounds, usually viscid or creamy, and consisting of modified leucocytes and other cells in a liquid plasma: the result of suppuration. [<L. Akin to PUTRID.]

Pu·san (pōō·sän) A port on Korea Strait in SE Korea: Japanese *Fusan.*

Pu·sey (pyōō′zē), **Edward Bouverie,** 1800–82, English theologian.

Pu·sey·ism (pyōō′zē·iz′əm) *n.* Tractarianism. [after E. B. *Pusey*] —**Pu′sey·ite** *n.*

push (pŏŏsh) *v.t.* **1** To exert force upon or against (an object) for the purpose of moving. **2** To force (one's way), as through a crowd, jungle, etc. **3** To press forward, prosecute, or develop with vigor and persistence: to *push* trade with South America. **4** To urge, advocate, or promote vigorously and persistently: to *push* a new product. **5** To bear hard upon; distress; harass: I am *pushed* for time. **6** *Slang* To sell (narcotic drugs) illegally. —*v.i.* **7** To exert steady pressure against something so as to move it. **8** To move or advance vigorously or persistently. **9** To exert great effort. **10** To project; extend; reach: The island *pushed* out far into the sea. —*n.* **1** A propelling or thrusting pressure; repulsion as opposed to attraction or pull; a shove. **2** *Colloq.* An extremity; exigency: at a *push* for money. **3** Determined activity; energy. **4** Anything pushed to cause action; a pushbutton. **5** *Slang* The crowd; a number of friends or associates: He fooled the whole *push*; also, an influential clique. **6** *Austral. Slang* A body of larrikins. [<OF *pousser, polser* <L *pulsare.* See PULSATE.]

Synonyms: crowd, drive, expedite, force, hasten, impel, importune, press, propel, prosecute, shove, thrust, urge. See DRIVE, HUSTLE, JAM[1]. *Antonyms*: see DRAW.

push·ball (pŏŏsh′bôl′) *n.* A game, played with a ball 6 feet in diameter and weighing 48 pounds, in which each of two sides tries to push the ball across the opponent's goal.

push·but·ton (pŏŏsh′but′n) *n.* A button or knob which, on being pushed, opens or closes a circuit in an electric system, thereby turning on or off a light, ringing a bell, etc.

push·cart (pŏŏsh′kärt′) *n.* A two- or four-wheeled cart pushed by hand: used by fruit venders, peddlers, hawkers, etc.

push·er (pŏŏsh′ər) *n.* **1** One who or that which pushes; especially, an active, energetic person. **2** *Aeron.* An airplane with the propeller in the rear of the wings. **3** *U.S. Slang* One who sells illegally, especially one who sells narcotics to addicts.

push·ing (pŏŏsh′ing) *adj.* **1** Possessing business enterprise and energy. **2** Possessing aggressiveness; impertinent. —**push′ing·ly** *adv.*

Push·kin (pŏŏsh′kin) A city south of Leningrad in Russian S.F.S.R.: formerly *Tsarskoe Selo.*

Push·kin (pŏŏsh′kin), **Alexander Sergeyevich,** 1799–1837, Russian poet.

push-o·ver (pŏŏsh′ō′vər) *n. Slang* A susceptible person; an easy mark; also, anything done or that can be done with little or no effort

push·pin (pŏŏsh′pin′) *n.* A sharp pin with a large head, inserted by thumb pressure into a bulletin board, drawing board, etc., for mounting and holding in place papers, drawings, etc.

Push·tu (push′tōō) *n.* The Iranian language of the dominant peoples of Afghanistan; Afghan: also spelled *Pashto.* Also **Push′to** (-tō).

pu·sil·la·nim·i·ty (pyōō′səl·ə·nim′ə·tē) *n.* Faint-heartedness; indecision; cowardice. Also **pu′·sil·lan′i·mous·ness.**

pu·sil·lan·i·mous (pyōō′sə·lan′ə·məs) *adj.* **1** Lacking strength of mind, courage, or spirit; mean-spirited; cowardly. **2** Characterized by weakness of purpose or lack of courage.

[<LL *pusillanimis* <L *pusillus* very little + *animus* mind] — **pu′sil·lan′i·mous·ly** *adv.*
Synonyms: cowardly, dastardly, faint-hearted, feeble, mean-spirited, recreant, spiritless, timid, timorous, weak. *Antonyms*: see synonyms for BRAVE.

puss[1] (pŏŏs) *n.* **1** A cat. **2** A child or young woman: a term of affection. [Cf. Du. *poes,* LG *puus,* a name for a cat]

puss[2] (pŏŏs) *n. Slang* The mouth; face. [<Irish *pus* mouth, lips]

puss·ley (pus′lē) *n.* Purslane. Also **puss′ly.** [Alter. of PURSLANE]

puss moth A common European moth *(Cerura vinula)* with grayish wings and two rows of black spots on the abdomen.

pus·sy[1] (pŏŏs′ē) *n. pl.* **·sies 1** Puss; a cat: a diminutive. **2** A fuzzy catkin, as of a willow, a birch, etc. [Dim. of PUSS[1]]

pus·sy[2] (pus′ē) *adj.* Full of pus.

pus·sy·foot (pŏŏs′ē·fŏŏt′) *v.i.* **1** To move softly and stealthily, as a cat does. **2** To act or proceed without committing oneself or revealing one's intentions.

pus·sy willow (pŏŏs′ē) **1** A small American willow *(Salix discolor)* with silky catkins in early spring: also called *glaucous willow.* **2** One of various other willows bearing catkins in early spring.

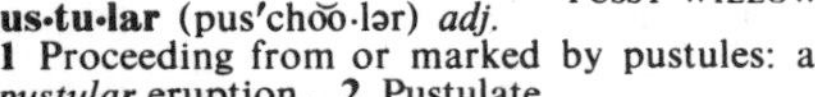
PUSSY WILLOW

pus·tu·lant (pus′chŏŏ·lənt) *adj.* Causing pustules. —*n.* A medicine that causes pustules.

pus·tu·lar (pus′chŏŏ·lər) *adj.* **1** Proceeding from or marked by pustules: a *pustular* eruption. **2** Pustulate.

pus·tu·late (pus′chŏŏ·lāt) *v.t.* & *v.i.* **·lat·ed, ·lat·ing** To form into or become pustules. —*adj.* (-lāt, -lit) Covered with pustules or pustule-like elevations. [<L *pustulatus,* pp. of *pustulare* blister <*pustula* a pustule]

pus·tu·la·tion (pus′chŏŏ·lā′shən) *n.* **1** The formation of pustules; a pustular eruption. **2** A pustule.

pus·tule (pus′chŏŏl) *n.* **1** *Pathol.* A small, circumscribed elevation of the skin with an inflamed base containing pus. **2** Any elevation resembling a pimple or a blister. [<L *pustula*]

put (pŏŏt) *v.* **put, put·ting** *v.t.* **1** To bring into or set in a specified or implied place or position; lay: *Put* the book on the table. **2** To bring into a specified state, condition, or relation: to *put* a prisoner to death. **3** To apply; bring to bear: *Put* your back into it! **4** To impose: to *put* a tariff on bicycles. **5** To ascribe or attribute, as the wrong interpretation on a remark. **6** To place according to one's estimation: I *put* the time at five o'clock. **7** To throw with a pushing motion of the arm: to *put* the shot. **8** To incite; prompt. Who *put* him up to it? **9** To bring forward for debate, answer, consideration, etc.: to *put* a question. **10** To subject: Let's *put* it to a vote. **11** To express in words; state: That's *putting* it mildly. **12** To risk; bet: I'll *put* six dollars on that horse. —*v.i.* **13** To go; proceed: to *put* to sea. —**to put about** *Naut.* To change to the opposite tack; change direction. —**to put aside** (or **away** or **by**) **1** To place in reserve; save. **2** To thrust aside; discard. —**to put down 1** To repress; crush. **2** To degrade; demote. **3** To write. —**to put forth 1** To extend, as the arm or hand. **2** To grow, as shoots or buds. **3** To exert. **4** To set out; leave port. —**to put forward** To advance; urge, as a claim. —**to put in 1** *Naut.* To enter a harbor or place of shelter. **2** To interpolate; interpose. **3** *Colloq.* To devote; expend, as time. **4** To advance (a claim, etc.). **5** To submit, as an application. —**to put off 1** To delay; postpone. **2** To discard. **3** To make uneasy or uncomfortable; disconcert. —**to put on 1** To don. **2** To bring into action; turn on. **3** To simulate; pretend. **4** To give a representation of; stage. —**to put out 1** To extinguish. **2** To expel; eject. **3** To disconcert; embarrass. **4** To inconvenience. **5** To put forth. **6** In baseball, to retire (a batter or base runner). —**to put over 1** To place in command or charge. **2** *Colloq.* To accomplish successfully. —**to put one** (or **something**) **over on** *Colloq.* To deceive or dupe. —**to put through 1** To bring to successful completion. **2** To cause to perform. —**to put up 1** To erect; build. **2** To preserve or can. **3** To wager. **4** To provide (money, capital, etc.). **5** To sheathe, as a weapon. —**to put upon** To deceive; cheat. —**to put up with** To endure; tolerate. —*n.* **1** The act of putting, as a cast or throw. **2** A contract by which one person, in consideration of money paid to another, acquires the privilege of selling or delivering to the latter within a certain time some article named, as wheat or cotton, or shares at a stipulated price: opposed to *call.* —*adj. Colloq.* Fixed; settled as fixed: My hat won't stay *put.* [Fusion of OE *putian* place, *potian* thrust, and *pӯtan* push, prob. all <Scand. Cf. Dan. *putte.*]
Synonyms (verb): deposit, lay, place, set. *Put* is the most general term for bringing an object to some point or within some space, however exactly or loosely; we may *put* a horse in a pasture, or *put* a bullet in a rifle or into an enemy. *Place* denotes more careful movement and more exact location; as, to *place* a crown on one's head, or a garrison in a city. To *lay* is to *place* in a horizontal or recumbent position; to *set* is to *place* or adjust in a certain place or position; we *lay* a cloth, and *set* a dish upon a table. To *deposit* is to *put* in a place of security for future use; as, to *deposit* money in a bank; the original sense, to *lay* down is also common; as, the stream *deposits* sediment; insects *deposit* eggs. Compare SET.

pu·ta·men (pyōō·tā′min) *n. pl.* **·tam·i·na** (-tam′ə·nə) *Bot.* The hard bony stone of certain fruits, as the cherry. [<L, waste, a husk <*putare* cleanse, prune] —**pu·tam′i·nous** *adj.*

put and take A game of chance in which the players add to or take from a pool.

pu·ta·tive (pyōō′tə·tiv) *adj.* Supposed; reported; reputed. [<MF *putatif* <LL *putativus* <L *putatus,* pp. of *putare* think] —**pu′ta·tive·ly** *adv.*

put-down (pŏŏt′doun′) *n. Slang* Something that humbles or deflates, as a cutting remark, a snub, or the like.

Put-in-Bay (pŏŏt′in·bā′) A harbor on South Bass Island in Lake Erie near the Canadian border in northern Ohio; site of Perry's defeat of the British in a naval battle (1813) in the War of 1812.

put·log (pŏŏt′lôg, -log, put′-) *n.* A crosspiece in a scaffolding, its inner end resting in a hole in the wall and its outer on a ledger. [Earlier *putlock* <*put,* pp. of PUT[1]]

Put·nam (put′nəm), **Israel,** 1718–90, American Revolutionary general.

put-off (pŏŏt′ôf′, -of′) *n.* An evasion; excuse.

put-on (pŏŏt′on′) *n. Slang* A hoax; deception.

put-out (pŏŏt′out′) *n.* The act of causing an out, as of batter or base runner in baseball.

put-put (put′put′) *n. Slang* A gasoline engine; especially, one used in propelling a small boat. [Imit.]

pu·tre·fac·tion (pyōō′trə·fak′shən) *n.* **1** The progressive chemical decomposition of organic matter, as by the agency of anaerobic bacteria, with the production of evil-smelling compounds. **2** The state of being putrefied. **3** Putrescent or putrefied matter. [<OF <L *putrefactio, -onis* <*putrefacere* PUTREFY]

pu·tre·fac·tive (pyōō′trə·fak′tiv) *adj.* **1** Of or pertaining to putrefaction. **2** Producing putrefaction.

pu·tre·fy (pyōō′trə·fī) *v.t.* & *v.i.* **·fied, ·fy·ing 1** To decay or cause to decay with fetid odor; rot; decompose. **2** To make or become gangrenous. [<L *putrefacere* <*putrere* decay (<*puter* rotten) + *facere* make] —**pu′tre·fi′er** *n.*
Synonyms: corrupt, decay, decompose, rot. See CORRUPT, DECAY. *Antonyms*: disinfect, embalm, freshen, preserve, purify, vitalize.

pu·tres·cence (pyōō·tres′əns) *n.* **1** The state of undergoing putrefaction. **2** Something that is putrescent.

pu·tres·cent (pyōō·tres′ənt) *adj.* **1** Becoming putrid; undergoing putrefaction. **2** Pertaining to putrefaction. [<L *putrescens, -entis,* ppr. of *putrescere* grow rotten, inceptive of *putrere.* See PUTREFY.]

pu·tres·ci·ble (pyōō·tres′ə·bəl) *adj.* Liable to putrefy. —*n.* A substance that decomposes at a certain temperature in contact with air and moisture: generally containing nitrogen. —**pu·tres′ci·bil′i·ty** *n.*

pu·tres·cine (pyōō·tres′ēn, -in) *n. Biochem.* A colorless, ill-smelling ptomaine, $C_4H_{12}N_2$, resulting from the bacterial decomposition of animal tissues.

pu·trid (pyōō′trid) *adj.* **1** Being in a state of putrefaction; decomposed or decomposing; rotten: *putrid* meat. **2** Indicating or produced by putrefaction: a *putrid* smell. **3** Rotten; corrupt. See synonyms under BAD[1], ROTTEN. [<L *putridus* <*putrere.* See PUTREFY.] —**pu·trid′i·ty** *n.* —**pu′trid·ness** *n.*

Putsch (pŏŏch) *n.* An outbreak or rebellion; an attempted coup d'état. [<G <dial. G (Swiss), lit., a push, blow]

putt (put) *n.* In golf, a light stroke made on a putting green to place the ball in or near the hole. [<*v.*] —*v.t.* & *v.i.* To strike (the ball) with such a stroke. [Var. of PUT[1]]

put·tee (put′ē, pu·tē′) *n.* A strip of cloth wound spirally about the leg from knee to ankle, as used by soldiers, sportsmen, etc.; also, a leather gaiter strapped around the leg. Also **put′ty.** [<Hind. *paṭṭī* a bandage <Skt. *paṭṭa* a strip of cloth]

put·ter[1] (put′ər) *n.* **1** One who putts: He is a poor *putter.* **2** An upright, stiff-shafted golf club used on the putting green. [<PUTT]

put·ter[2] (put′ər) *v.i.* To act, work, or proceed in a dawdling or ineffective manner; trifle. —*v.t.* To waste or spend (time, etc.) in dawdling or puttering. [Var. of POTTER[1]]

put·ti·er (put′ē·ər) *n.* One who putties; a glazier. [<PUTTY]

put·ting (pŏŏt′ing) *n.* The action of the verb *to put,* as *putting* the shot.

put·ting green (put′ing) In golf, the smooth ground within twenty yards of the hole; also, a place set aside for putting practice. [<PUTT]

put·ty (put′ē) *n.* **1** Whiting mixed with linseed oil to the consistency of dough: used for filling holes or cracks in wood surfaces, securing panes of glass in the sash, making relief ornaments, etc. **2** Fine lime mortar for filling cracks, finishing, etc. —**iron putty** Ferric oxide mixed with boiled linseed oil: used in making pipe-joint connections. —**red-lead putty** Red and white lead mixed with boiled linseed oil, used mainly for cementing pipe joints. —*v.t.* **·tied, ·ty·ing** To fill, stop, fasten, etc., with putty. [<OF *potee* calcined tin, lit., a potful <*pot* a pot]

putty knife A knife with a spatulalike blade, used by glaziers in puttying window glass, etc.

putty powder Tin oxide, or tin and lead oxide, used for polishing glass, metals, etc.

put·ty·root (put′ē·rōōt′, -rŏŏt′) *n.* An American orchid *(Aplectrum hyemale)* with a scape bearing a loose raceme of brownish flowers produced yearly. [So called from a sticky substance found in its bulbs]

Pu·tu·ma·yo (pōō′tōō·mä′yō) A river in Ecuador, Colombia, and Peru, flowing about 1,000 miles SE to the Amazon, forming the greater part of the boundary between Colombia and Peru: called *Içá* in its lower courses in Brazil.

put-up (pŏŏt′up′) *adj. Colloq.* Prearranged or contrived in an artful manner: a *put-up* job.

Pu·vis de Cha·vannes (pü·vē′ də shà·vàn′), **Pierre,** 1824–98, French painter.

puy (pwē) *n.* A conical hill of volcanic origin. [<F <OF *pui, poi* a hill <L *podium* a height]

Puy-de-Dôme (pwē·də·dōm′) An extinct volcano of the Massif Central in central France; site of an observatory and a ruined temple of Mercury; 4,806 feet.

Pu-yi (pōō′yē′), **Henry,** 1906–1967, last Manchu emperor of China 1908–12; abdicated; puppet emperor of Manchukuo 1934–45, under name *Kang Te*; abdicated.

puz·zle (puz′əl) *v.* **·zled, ·zling** *v.t.* **1** To confuse or perplex; mystify. **2** To solve by investigation and study, as something perplexing: with *out.* —*v.i.* **3** To be perplexed or confused. See synonyms under PERPLEX. —**to puzzle over** To attempt to understand or solve. —*n.* **1** A thing difficult to understand or explain; perplexing problem; an enigma or problem. **2** Something, as a toy, purposely arranged so as to require time, patience, and ingenuity to solve its intricacies. **3** The state of being puzzled; a quandary; perplexity. See synonyms under RIDDLE[2]. —**cross-word puzzle** A pattern of white and black spaces, of which the white spaces are to be filled with letters that form words, vertically, horizontally, or diagonally, to agree with accompanying definitions. [Related to ME *poselet* confused; ult. origin unknown]

puz·zle·ment (puz′əl·mənt) *n.* State of being nonplused; perplexity.
puz·zler (puz′lər) *n.* One who or that which puzzles; a knotty question.
PX A military post exchange or general store. [<P(OST) (E)X(CHANGE)]
py– Var. of PYO–.
Pya·ti·gorsk (pyä′ti·gôrsk′) A city in the northern Caucasus, Russian S.F.S.R.
pyc·nid·i·um (pik·nid′ē·əm) *n.* *pl.* **·nid·i·a** (-nid′ē·ə) *Bot.* A spore–bearing receptacle found in certain fungi. [<NL <Gk. *pyknos* thick + *-idion*, dim. suffix] — **pyc·nid′i·al** *adj.*
pyc·nom·e·ter (pik·nom′ə·tər) *n.* A specific–gravity bottle or flask. [<Gk. *pyknos* dense, thick + -METER]
pyc·no·spore (pik′nə·spôr, -spōr) *n.* *Bot.* A conidium developed within a pycnidium. [Contraction of *pycnidiospore* <PYCNIDIUM + SPORE]
Pyd·na (pid′nə) An ancient city in south central Macedonia, Greece; scene of the final Roman victory over Macedonia, 168 B.C.
pye (pī) See PIE[4].
py·e·li·tis (pī′ə·lī′tis) *n.* *Pathol.* Inflammation of the pelvis and calices of the kidneys. [<NL <Gk. *pyelos* the pelvis, orig. a trough + *-itis* -ITIS] — **py′e·lit′ic** (-lit′ik) *adj.*
py·e·lo·gram (pī′ə·lō·gram′) *n.* A picture taken by pyelography. [<*pyelo-* <Gk. *pyelos* a trough, pelvis + -GRAM]
py·e·log·ra·phy (pī′ə·log′rə·fē) *n.* The technique of making X–rays of the ureter and the kidney by the use of a radiopaque dye. [<*pyelo-* <Gk. *pyelos* a trough, pelvis + -GRAPHY] — **py′e·lo·graph′ic** (-lō·graf′ik) *adj.*
py·e·mi·a (pī·ē′mē·ə) *n.* *Pathol.* A poisonous infection of the blood, due to the absorption of vitiated pus or pyogenic micro–organisms into the circulation: it causes suppuration marked by multiple abscesses, phlebitis, high fever, etc. Also **py·ae′mi·a.** [<NL <Gk. *pyon* pus + *haima* blood] — **py·e′mic** *adj.*
py·et (pī′it) *n.* *Scot.* The magpie.
py·gid·i·um (pī·jid′ē·əm) *n.* *pl.* **·gid·i·a** (-jid′ē·ə) *Entomol.* The terminal or posterior segment, as of an insect; a caudal shield. [<NL <Gk. *pygidion*, dim. of *pygē* rump] — **py·gid′i·al** *adj.*
Pyg·ma·li·on (pig·mā′lē·ən, -māl′yən) In Greek mythology, a sculptor of Cyprus, who fell in love with his statue, Galatea, which Aphrodite later brought to life.
pyg·my (pig′mē) See PIGMY.
Pyg·my (pig′mē) *n.* *pl.* **·mies 1** A member of a Negroid people of equatorial Africa, ranging in height from four to five feet. **2** Any of the Negrito peoples of the Philippines, Andaman Islands, and Malaya. **3** In the *Iliad*, one of a race of dwarfs. [<L *pygmaeus*. See PIGMY.]
py·ic (pī′ik) *adj.* Of or pertaining to pus; purulent. [<PY- + -IC]
py·in (pī′in) *n.* *Biochem.* A protein compound contained in pus. [<PY- + -IN]
py·ja·mas (pə·jä′məz, -jam′əz) See PAJAMAS.
pyke (pīk) *v.t.* *Scot.* To pick.
pyk·nic (pik′nik) *adj.* Characterized by plump contours and a broad, stocky build; fat; squat. — *n.* A person of this physical type. [<Gk. *pyknos* thick, compact]
pyk·no·phra·si·a (pik′nə·frā′zhē·ə, -zhə) *n.* *Pathol.* A thickening of speech. [<NL <Gk. *pyknos* thick + *phrasis* speech]
Pyl·a·des (pil′ə·dēz) In Greek legend, a nephew of Agamemnon and friend of Orestes, whose sister Electra he married.
pyle (pīl) *n.* *Scot.* A grain.
Pyle (pīl), **Howard,** 1853–1911, U. S. illustrator, painter, and writer.
py·lon (pī′lon) *n.* **1** *Archit.* A monumental structure constituting an entrance to an Egyptian temple or other large edifice, consisting of a central gateway, flanked on each side by a truncated pyramidal tower. **2** A stake marking the course in an airdrome or turning point in an aerial race. **3** One of the tall, mastlike metal structures from whose summits high–tension wires are carried across open country. **4** *Surg.* An artificial leg, usually temporary. [<Gk. *pylōn* a gateway <*pylē* a gate]
py·lo·rec·to·my (pī′lə·rek′tə·mē) *n.* *Surg.* Excision of the pylorus. [<PYLOR(US) + -ECTOMY]
py·lo·rus (pī·lôr′əs, -lō′rəs, pi-) *n.* *pl.* **·ri** (-rī) *Anat.* The opening between the stomach and the duodenum, surrounded by circular muscle fibers; also, the adjoining portion of the stomach. [<LL <Gk. *pylōros* a gatekeeper <*pylē* a gate + *ouros* a watcher] — **py·lor′ic** (-lôr′ik, -lor′ik) *adj.*
Py·los (pī′los) **1** A port of SW Peloponnesus, Greece, at the southern entrance to **Pylos Bay. 2** An ancient city, 4 miles NW of modern Pylos; said to be the seat of Nestor. Medieval *Navarino*: also *Pilos. Latin* **Py·lus** (pī′ləs).
Pym (pim), **John,** 1584–1643, English statesman and orator.
pyo– *combining form* Pus; of or related to pus: *pyorrhea*. Also, before vowels, *py–*. [<Gk. *pyon* pus]
py·o·gen·e·sis (pī′ō·jen′ə·sis) *n.* **1** *Pathol.* The formation or secretion of pus; suppuration. **2** The doctrine or theory of the origin, source, and process of the generation of pus. — **py′o·gen′ic** *adj.*
py·oid (pī′oid) *adj.* Resembling pus; purulent. [<PY- + -OID]
Pyong·yang (pyông·yäng) A city in northern Korea, capital of the Democratic People's Republic of Korea: *Japanese* **Hei·jo** (hā·jō).
py·or·rhe·a (pī′ə·rē′ə) *n.* *Pathol.* A discharge of pus with a continuous flow; especially, **pyorrhea al·ve·o·la·ris** (al·vē′ō·lā′ris), a loosening of the teeth accompanied by progressive inflammation of their lining membrane; Riggs's disease. Also **py′or·rhoe′a.** [<NL <Gk. *pys, pyos* pus + *rheein* flow] — **py′or·rhe′al** *adj.*
py·o·sis (pī·ō′sis) *n.* Suppuration. [<NL <Gk. *pyōsis* <*pys, pyos* pus]
pyr– Var. of PYRO–.
py·ra·can·tha (pī′rə·kan′thə, pir′ə-) *n.* The firethorn. [<L <Gk. *pyrakantha* <*pyr, pyros* fire + *akantha, -ēs* a thorn]
py·ral·i·did (pi·ral′ə·did) *adj.* Of or pertaining to a family *(Pyralididae)* of small or medium–sized moths of slender build and broad hind wings, including many groups sometimes classified as separate families. — *n.* A moth belonging to this family. Also **pyr·a·lid** (pir′ə·lid). [<NL <L *pyralis, -idis* a winged insect supposed to live in fire <Gk. <*pyr, pyros* a fire] — **py·ral′i·dan** *adj.* & *n.*
pyr·a·mid (pir′ə·mid) *n.* **1** *Archit.* A solid structure of masonry with a square base and triangular sides meeting in an apex. Such structures were used as tombs or temples. The pyramids of Egypt, raised over the sepulchral chambers of kings, are the best examples. The most interesting group is at Giza, near Cairo. The pyramids of Mexico

THE PYRAMIDS AT GIZA

served as temples. The largest is the pyramid near Cholula on the Pueblo plateau, in central Mexico. **2** Something in pyramidal form. **3** *Geom.* A solid consisting of a polygonal base and triangular sides, the apices of the triangles coming together at the vertex. **4** *Mineral.* A crystal form consisting of three or more similar planes having a common point of intersection. **5** *Physiol.* One of various pyramidal or conical structures found in animal organisms. **6** *Anat.* A small bony projection in the cavity of the tympanum. **7** Any tree trained in pyramidal form. **8** The operations involved in pyramiding. — *v.t.* & *v.i.* **1** To arrange or form in the shape of a pyramid. **2** To buy or sell (stock) with paper profits shown by the change in price of stock already purchased or sold, without any additional deposit of money being made, and to continue so buying or selling on each movement in price. [<F *pyramide* <L *pyramis, -idis* <Gk. *pyramis, -idos*, prob. <Egyptian *pi-mar* a pyramid]
py·ram·i·dal (pi·ram′ə·dəl) *adj.* Of or shaped like a pyramid. Also **pyr·a·mid·ic** (pir′ə·mid′ik), **pyr′a·mid′i·cal.** — **py·ram′i·dal·ly** *adv.*
py·ram·i·da·lis (pi·ram′i·dā′lis) *n.* *pl.* **·les** (-lēz) *Anat.* Any one of several conical or triangular muscles; especially, the flat triangular muscle arising from the pubis and inserted into the linea alba. [<NL <LL, pyramidal; with ref. to its shape]
Pyr·a·mus and This·be (pir′ə·məs, thiz′bē) In classical legend, two Babylonian lovers: believing Thisbe slain by a lion, Pyramus killed himself, and Thisbe, finding his body, took her own life.
py·ran (pī′ran, pī·ran′) *n.* *Chem.* Either of two isomeric cyclic compounds, C_5H_6O, each having in its ring 5 carbon atoms: the parent forms of certain carbohydrates, alkaloids, and other physiologically active compounds. [<PYRONE]
py·ra·nom·e·ter (pī′rə·nom′ə·tər) *n.* An instrument for measuring sky radiation or radiation from the earth, especially at night. [<PYR- + ANO- + -METER]
py·rar·gy·rite (pī·rär′jə·rīt) *n.* A metallic, black sulfide of antimony and silver, Ag_3SbS_3, crystallizing in the rhombohedral system. [<PYR- + Gk. *argyros* silver + -ITE[1]]
pyre (pīr) *n.* **1** A heap of combustibles arranged for burning a dead body. **2** Any pile or heap of combustible material. [<L *pyra* a hearth, funeral pile <Gk. <*pyr* a fire]
py·rene[1] (pī′rēn) *n.* *Chem.* A tetracyclic hydrocarbon, $C_{16}H_{10}$, contained in that portion of coal–tar oil boiling above 360° C. [<PYR- + -ENE]
py·rene[2] (pī′rēn) *n.* *Bot.* The stone of a drupe; also, any nutlet; putamen. [<NL *pyrena* <Gk. *pyrēn* fruit stone]
Py·rene (pī′rēn) *n.* Carbon tetrachloride, prepared for use as a chemical fire extinguisher: a trade name.
Pyr·e·nees (pir′ə·nēz) A mountain chain between France and Spain, extending about 270 miles from the Bay of Biscay to the Mediterranean; highest point, Pico de Aneto, 11,168 feet. — **Pyr′e·ne′an** *adj.*
py·re·noid (pī·rē′noid) *adj.* Having the form of a fruit stone. — *n.* **1** *Bot.* A small, colorless mass of protein substance of a crystalline form, appearing in the chloroplasts of green algae. **2** *Zool.* A transparent body in the chromatophores of certain protozoa. [<Gk. *pyrēnoeidēs* <*pyrēn* a fruit stone + *eidos* a form, shape] — **py·re·no·de·an** (pī′ri·nō′dē·ən) *adj.*
Py·re·no·my·ce·tes (pī·rē′nō·mī·sē′tēz) *n. pl.* A large class of fungi characterized by the forcible expulsion of ascospores from the perithecium, including many parasitic species, as ergot. [<NL <Gk. *pyrēn* a fruit stone + *mykēs, mykētis* a mushroom]
py·reth·rum (pī·reth′rəm, -rē′thrəm) *n.* **1** The dried and powdered roots of the pellitory used in medicine as a sialogog and rubefacient. **2** The powdered flowers of a chrysanthemum *(Chrysanthemum cinerariaefolium)*, used medically as an ointment, and as an insecticide. [<L, feverfew <Gk. *pyrethron* <*pyr* fire]
py·ret·ic (pī·ret′ik) *adj.* **1** Affected with or relating to fever; febrile. **2** Remedial in fevers. — *n.* A febrifuge. [<NL *pyreticus* <Gk. *pyretos* a fever <*pyr* fire]
pyr·e·tol·o·gy (pir′ə·tol′ə·jē, pī′rə-) *n.* The department of medical science that treats of fevers. [<Gk. *pyretos* a fever + -LOGY] — **pyr′e·tol′o·gist** *n.*
pyr·e·to·ther·a·py (pir′ə·tō·ther′ə·pē, pī′rə-) *n.* Medical treatment by the artificial induction of fever by electricity, bacterial infection, etc.; fever therapy. [<Gk. *pyretos* (a fever) + THERAPY]
Py·rex (pī′reks) *n.* A type of heat–resisting glass having a high silica content, with additions of soda, aluminum, and boron: a trade name.
py·rex·i·a (pī·rek′sē·ə) *n.* *Pathol.* An abnormal elevation of bodily temperature; fever. [<NL <Gk. *pyrexis* <*pyressein* be feverish

< *pyretos.* See PYRETIC.] **—py·rex′i·al** *adj.* **—py·rex′ic** *adj.*

pyr·ge·om·e·ter (pīr′jē·om′ə·tər, pir′-) *n.* A pyranometer. [<PYR- + GEO- + -METER]

pyr·he·li·om·e·ter (pīr·hē′lē·om′ə·tər, ′pir-) *n. Astron.* An instrument for measuring the quantity and rate of solar radiation by its thermal effects on a silvered disk or other sensitive surface. [<PYR- + HELIO- + -METER]

Pyr·i·ben·za·mine (pir′ə·ben′zə·mēn, -min) *n.* Proprietary name of an antihistamine drug, $C_{16}H_{21}N_3HC$, used in the treatment of certain allergies.

pyr·i·dine (pir′ə·dēn, -din) *n. Chem.* A colorless, liquid, nitrogenous compound, C_5H_5N, with a pungent, noxious odor, obtained by the distillation of coal tar and bone oil and also made synthetically: used in organic syntheses, as a disinfectant, antiseptic, alcohol denaturant, and asthma remedy. [< PYR(ROLE) + -ID(E) + -INE[2]] **—py·rid·ic** (pī·rid′ik) *adj.*

pyr·i·dox·ine (pir′ə·dok′sēn, -sin) *n. Biochem.* A factor of the vitamin B complex known to prevent dermatitis in rats, vitamin B_6, a water-soluble compound, $C_8H_{10}NO_3$, occurring in cereal grains, vegetable oils, legumes, yeast, meats, and fish: also made synthetically. [PYRID(INE) + OX(Y)-[2] + -INE[2]]

pyr·i·form (pir′ə·fôrm) *adj.* Pear-shaped. [< NL *pyriformis* <Med. L *pyrum* a pear (<L *pirum*) + L *forma* form]

py·rim·i·dine (pī·rim′ə·dēn, -din, pir′ə·mə·dēn′, -din′) *n. Chem.* An organic compound, $C_4H_4N_2$, resulting from the acid hydrolysis of a nucleic acid; a constituent of thiamine. Also **py·rim′i·din** (-din). [<G *pyrimidin* <*pyridin* pyridine]

py·rite (pī′rīt) *n. pl.* **py·ri·tes** (pī·rī′tēz) A metallic, pale brass-yellow, opaque, isometric iron disulfide, FeS_2; fool's gold; iron pyrites. [<L *pyrites* <Gk. *pyritēs* flint <*pyritēs (lithos)* fire (stone) <*pyr* fire] **—py·rit′ic** (-rit′ik) or **·i·cal** *adj.*

py·ri·tes (pī·rī′tēz) *n. pl.* The common name for various metallic sulfides: copper *pyrites.* Compare CHALCOPYRITE, PYRITE.

py·ro (pī′rō) *n.* Pyrogallol: so called in photography. [Short for PYROGALLOL]

pyro- *combining form* **1** Fire; heat: *pyromania.* **2** *Chem.* Denoting actual or hypothetical derivation by the action of heat; specifically, in certain inorganic acids, indicating derivation from two molecules of an ordinary acid by the elimination of one molecule of water: $2H_3AsO_4$ (arsenic acid) — H_2O = $H_4As_2O_7$ (*pyroarsenic* acid). **3** *Geol.* Resulting from the action of fire or heat: *pyrolusite.* Also, before vowels, *pyr-.* [<Gk. *pyr, pyros* fire]

py·ro·cat·e·chol (pī′rə·kat′ə·kōl, -chōl, -kol, pir′ə-) *n. Chem.* A white crystalline phenol compound, $C_6H_6O_2$, contained in various barks, originally obtained when catechin was subjected to dry distillation: used in photography as a developer and in medicine. Also **py′ro·cat′e·chin** (-kin, -chin). [<PYRO- + CATECH(U) + (PHEN)OL]

py·ro·cel·lu·lose (pī′rə·sel′yə·lōs) *n.* A form of guncotton used as a propellant in smokeless powder. Also **py′ro·cot′ton** (-kot′n).

Py·ro·ce·ram (pī′rō·sə·ram′) *n.* A strongly heat-resistant, crystalline ceramic material formed from glass and characterized by extreme hardness, great tensile strength, and high dielectric properties: a trade name.

py·ro·chem·i·cal (pī′rə·kem′i·kəl) *adj.* Pertaining to chemical changes induced or effected by high temperature.

py·ro·clas·tic (pī′rə·klas′tik) *adj. Geol.* Formed from or consisting of the fragmentary or comminuted ejecta of volcanic or igneous eruptions: said of rocks or their composition. [<PYRO- + CLASTIC]

py·ro·con·duc·tiv·i·ty (pī′rə·kon′duk·tiv′ə·tē) *n.* Conductivity of an electric current dependent upon or improved by the application of heat. **—py′ro·con·duc′tive** (-kən·duk′tiv) *adj.*

py·ro·crys·tal·line (pī′rə·kris′tə·lin, -līn, pir′ə-) *adj.* Crystallized from materials in a state of fusion: *pyrocrystalline* masses.

py·ro·e·lec·tric (pī′rō·i·lek′trik, pir′ō-) *adj.* **1** Of or pertaining to pyroelectricity. **2** Manifesting pyroelectricity; developing poles when heated. **—*n.*** A substance that becomes polar when heated.

py·ro·e·lec·tric·i·ty (pī′rō·i·lek′tris′ə·tē, -ē′lek-, pir′ō-) *n.* **1** Electrification or electric polarity developed in certain minerals by a change in temperature. **2** The branch of science treating of this phenomenon.

py·ro·gal·late (pī′rə·gal′āt, pir′ə-) *n.* A salt of pyrogallol.

py·ro·gal·lic (pī′rə·gal′ik, pir′ə-) *adj. Chem.* **1** Of, pertaining to, or derived by heat from gallic acid. **2** Pertaining to or designating pyrogallol.

py·ro·gal·lol (pī′rə·gal′ōl, -ol, -gə·lōl′, pir′ə-) *n. Chem.* A white, crystalline, poisonous compound, $C_6H_3(OH)_3$, obtained by heating gallic acid: used to reduce silver and mercury salts to a metallic state, as a photographic developer, as a dye, and in certain medical preparations. Also **pyrogallic acid.** [<PYRO- + GALL(IC) + (PHEN)OL]

py·ro·gen·ic (pī′rə·jen′ik, pir′ə-) *adj.* **1** Causing or produced by heat. **2** Caused by or inducing fever. **3** Igneous. Also **py·rog·e·nous** (pī·roj′ə·nəs, pi-).

py·rog·nos·tics (pī′rog·nos′tiks, pir′əg-) *n. pl.* The characteristics of a mineral as shown by heat of varying intensity produced with a blowpipe. [<PYRO- + Gk. *gnostikos* knowing]

py·rog·ra·phy (pī·rog′rə·fē, pi-) *n.* The art or process of producing a design, as on wood or leather, by a red-hot point or fine flame. **—py·ro·graph** (pī′rə·graf, -gräf, pir′ə-) *n.* **—py·rog′ra·pher** *n.* **—py′ro·graph′ic** *adj.*

py·ro·gra·vure (pī′rō·grə·vyŏŏr′, pir′ō-) *n.* **1** The art or process of producing a design on wood by pyrography. **2** A picture thus made.

py·ro·lig·ne·ous (pī′rə·lig′nē·əs, pir′ə-) *adj.* Pertaining to that which is derived from wood by heat, specifically by dry distillation. [<PYRO- + LIGNEOUS]

pyroligneous acid Crude acetic acid as derived from wood by distillation; wood vinegar.

py·rol·o·gy (pī·rol′ə·jē, pi-) *n.* **1** The scientific examination of materials by heat; blowpipe analysis. **2** The branch of physics that treats of heat. [<PYRO- + -LOGY] **—py·ro·log·i·cal** (pī′rə·loj′i·kəl, pir′ə·loj′i·kəl) *adj.*

py·ro·lu·site (pī′rə·lōō′sīt, pī·rol′yə·sīt) *n.* A soft, metallic, iron-black or steel-gray manganese dioxide, MnO_2, of great value in the arts, and used in the manufacture of oxygen, chlorine, etc. [<G *pyrolusit* <Gk. *pyr, pyros* a fire + *lousis* a washing (<*louein* wash) + G *-it* -ITE[1]]

py·rol·y·sis (pī·rol′ə·sis) *n. Chem.* Decomposition by the application of or as a result of heat. [<NL <Gk. *pyr, pyros* a fire + *lysis* a loosing <*lyein* loosen] **—py·ro·lit·ic** (pī′rə·lit′ik, pir′ə-) *adj.*

py·ro·mag·net·ic (pī′rō·mag·net′ik, pir′ō-) *adj.* Of, pertaining to, or produced by the changes in magnetic intensity caused by change of temperature.

py·ro·man·cy (pī′rə·man′sē, pir′ə-) *n.* Divination by fire. [<PYRO- + -MANCY]

py·ro·ma·ni·a (pī′rə·mā′nē·ə, -mān′yə, pir′ə-) *n.* A morbid propensity to set things on fire. **—py′ro·ma′ni·ac** (-ak) *adj.* & *n.* **—py·ro·ma·ni·a·cal** (pī′rō·mə·nī′ə·kəl, pir′ō-) *adj.*

py·ro·man·tic (pī′rə·man′tik, pir′ə-) *adj.* Of or pertaining to pyromancy. **—*n.*** One who professes to divine by means of fire.

py·rom·e·ter (pī·rom′ə·tər) *n.* An instrument for measuring high degrees of heat, as caused by electrical resistance, degree of incandescence, expansion, radiation, etc. **—py·ro·met·ric** (pī′rə·met′rik, pir′ə-) or **·ri·cal** *adj.* **—py·rom′e·try** *n.*

py·ro·mor·phite (pī′rə·môr′fīt, pir′ə-) *n.* A resinous, variously colored phosphate and chloride of lead, found in masses or crystals; green lead ore. [<G *pyromorphit* <Gk. *pyr, pyros* a fire + *morphos* form]

py·rone (pī′rōn, pī·rōn′) *n. Chem.* A cyclic compound, $C_5H_4O_2$, existing in two isomeric forms: it yields yellow dyestuffs. [<G *pyron*]

py·rope (pī′rōp) *n.* A variety of deep-red garnet: also called *precious garnet.* [<OF *pirope* <L *pyropus* gold-bronze <Gk. *pyrōpos,* lit., fiery-eyed <*pyr, pyros* a fire + *ōps, ōpos* eye, face]

py·ro·phor·ic (pī′rə·fôr′ik, -for′ik) *adj.* **1** Fire-bearing; spontaneously combustible. **2** Designating materials which are easily and quickly inflammable, as finely divided metals on exposure to air. [<Gk. *pyrophoros* <*pyr, pyros* a fire + *pherein* carry] **—py′ro·phore** (-fôr, -fōr) *n.*

py·ro·phos·phate (pī′rə·fos′fāt, pir′ə-) *n.* A salt of pyrophosphoric acid.

py·ro·phos·phor·ic acid (pī′rō·fos·fôr′ik, -for′ik, pir′ō-) *Chem.* An acid, $H_4P_2O_7$, obtained by heating orthophosphoric acid to about 255° C.

py·ro·pho·tom·e·ter (pī′rō·fō·tom′ə·tər, pir′ō-) *n.* A pyrometer used to determine high temperatures by means of the luminosity of a substance.

py·ro·phyl·lite (pī′rə·fil′īt, pir′ə-) *n.* A compact, soft, variously colored, hydrous aluminum silicate, $HAlSi_2O_6$, used in making slate pencils. [<PYRO- + PHYLL(O)- + -ITE[1]]

py·ro·sis (pī·rō′sis) *n. Pathol.* Heartburn; acid dyspepsia, accompanied by a burning sensation and belching of an acrid fluid. [<NL <Gk. *pyrōsis* a burning <*pyroein* burn < *pyr* fire]

py·ro·stat (pī′rə·stat, pir′ə-) *n.* A thermostat; specifically, one for the higher temperatures. [<PYRO- + -STAT]

py·ro·sul·fate (pī′rə·sul′fāt, pir′ə-) *n.* A salt of pyrosulfuric acid; a disulfate.

py·ro·sul·fu·ric acid (pī′rō·sul·fyŏŏr′ik, pir′ō-) *Chem.* A brown, fuming liquid, $H_2SO_4SO_3$, obtained by adding liquid sulfuric oxide to strong sulfuric acid: also called *disulfuric acid.*

py·ro·tech·nic (pī′rə·tek′nik, pir′ə-) *adj.* Pertaining to fireworks or their manufacture. Also **py′ro·tech′ni·cal.**

py·ro·tech·nics (pī′rə·tek′niks, pir′ə-) *n.* **1** The art of making or using fireworks: also **py′ro·tech′ny.** **2** A display of fireworks. **3** An ostentatious display, as of oratory. [Earlier *pyrotechny* <F *pyrotechnie* <Gk. *pyr, pyros* fire + *technē* an art; infl. in form by *pyrotechnic*] **—py′ro·tech′nist** *n.*

py·rot·ic (pī·rot′ik, pi-) *adj.* Caustic. **—*n.*** A caustic substance or remedy. [<NL *pyroticus* <Gk. *pyrōtikos* <*pyroein* burn <*pyr* fire]

py·ro·tox·in (pī′rə·tok′sin, pir′ə-) *n. Biochem.* Any one of a number of toxic substances found in the body as a result of bacterial action and inducing a rise of bodily temperature, or symptoms of fever.

py·rox·ene (pī′rok·sēn) *n.* **1** A monoclinic mineral, usually in short, prismatic crystals, composed principally of calcium and magnesium: next to feldspar, the most frequent component of igneous rocks. **2** Any member of the pyroxene group, as diopside and augite: they are essentially metasilicates. [<F *pyroxène* <Gk. *pyr, pyros* fire + *xenos* a stranger; because at first considered alien to igneous rocks] **—py·rox·en·ic** (pī′rok·sen′ik) *adj.*

py·rox·e·nite (pī·rok′sə·nīt) *n.* A granitoid igneous rock composed mostly of pyroxene, but without olivine. [<PYROXENE + -ITE[1]]

py·rox·y·lin (pī·rok′sə·lin) *n. Chem.* A cellulose nitrate mixture soluble in ether, alcohol, and organic solvents, less explosive than guncotton, and widely used in making Celluloid, lacquers, adhesives, etc. Also **py·rox′y·line** (-lēn, -lin). [<F *pyroxyline* <Gk. *pyr, pyros* fire + *xylon* wood + -INE[2]]

Pyr·rha (pir′ə) In Greek mythology, the daughter of Epimetheus and wife of Deucalion.

pyr·rhic[1] (pir′ik) *n.* A foot in ancient prosody composed of two short syllables. **—*adj.*** Of, pertaining to, or composed of pyrrhics. [<L *(pes) pyrrhicius* a pyrrhic (foot) <Gk. *(pous) pyrrichios* warlike, martial]

pyr·rhic[2] (pir′ik) *adj.* In Greek antiquity, pertaining to a martial dance in which the movements necessary to assail and avoid an enemy were imitated. **—*n.*** The pyrrhic dance. [<L *pyrrhicius* <Gk. *pyrrhichios* <*pyrrhichē* a war-dance <*Pyrrhichos* Pyrrhichus, a Greek said to have invented it]

Pyrrhic victory A victory gained at a ruinous loss, such as that of Pyrrhus over the Romans at Heracles Asculum, 279 B.C. [after *Pyrrhus*]

Pyr·rho·nism (pir′ə·niz′əm) *n.* A system of philosophy taught by Pyrrho of Elis, 365?–275? B.C., founder of the first and inspirer of subsequent skeptical schools of Greek philosophy; skepticism. [<L *Pyrrhoneus* pertaining to Pyrrho <Gk. *Pyrrhōn* Pyrrho]

pyr·rho·tite (pir′ə·tīt) *n.* A metallic, bronze-colored, magnetic iron sulfide, FeS; magnetic pyrites. Also **pyr′rho·lite** (-līt), **pyr′rho·tine** (-tīn). [<Gk. *pyrrhotēs* redness (<*pyrrhos* flame-colored <*pyr* a fire) + -ITE[1]]

pyr·rhu·lox·i·a (pir′ə·lok′sē·ə) *n.* A grosbeak of the western United States *(Pyrrhuloxia* *sinuata)* with a slender, gray-and-red body and parrotlike bill. [<NL <*Pyrrhula,* a genus of Fringillidae (dim. <Gk. *pyrrhos* fiery < *pyr* fire) + *Loxia,* genus of the crossbills < Gk. *loxos* oblique]

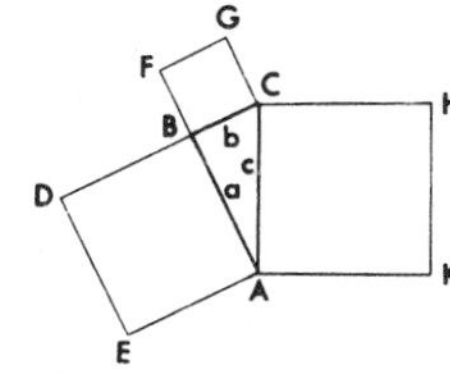

PYTHAGOREAN THEOREM

Sum of squares ABDE and BCGF equals square ACHK ($a^2 + b^2 = c^2$)

Pyr·rhus (pir′əs), 318?–272 B.C., king of Epirus; aided Tarentum against the Romans.
Pyr·rhus (pir′əs) In Greek legend, Neoptolemus.
pyr·role (pi·rōl′, pir′ōl) *n. Chem.* A colorless, poisonous, weakly basic, liquid compound, C_4H_4NH, having an odor of chloroform, obtained from bone oil, coal tar, and by synthesis, and occurring in many natural substances, as chlorophyll and hemoglobin. Also **pyr·rol′.** [<G *pyrrol* (<Gk. *pyrros* reddish < *pyr* fire) + *-ol* -OLE[1]]
pyr·rol·i·dine (pi·rol′ə·dēn, -din) *n. Chem.* A colorless nitrogenous compound, C_4H_9N, with a mild ammonia odor, found in tobacco and carrot leaves. [<PYRROL(E) + -ID(E) + -INE[2]]
py·ru·vic acid (pī·ro͞o′vik, pi-) *Chem.* A colorless to pale-yellow ketone compound, $C_3H_4O_3$, obtained by the distillation of a mixture of racemic acid and potassium bisulfate. [<PYR- + L *uva* grape + -IC]
Py·thag·o·ras (pi·thag′ər·əs) Greek philosopher of the sixth century B.C. — **Py·thag′o·re′an** *adj.* & *n.*
Py·thag·o·re·an·ism (pi·thag′ə·rē′ən·iz′əm) *n.* The mystical philosophy taught by Pythagoras, its central idea being that number is the essence of all things and the metaphysical principle of rational order in the universe. The leading theological doctrine was metempsychosis. [<L *Pythagoreus* <Gk. *Pythagoreios* <*Pythagoras* Pythagoras]
Pythagorean numbers See under NUMBER.
Pythagorean theorem *Math.* The theorem that the sum of the squares of the legs of a right triangle is equal to the square of the hypotenuse.
Pyth·i·a (pith′ē·ə) In ancient Greece, the priestess of the Pythian Apollo at Delphi, who was believed to be inspired by the god when seated on a tripod over the rock sacred to him, and to utter his oracles. — **Pyth′ic** *adj.*
Pyth·i·ad (pith′ē·ad) *n.* The period from one celebration of the ancient Greek Pythian games to another. [<Gk. *Pythias, -ados* <*(hiera) Pythia* the Pythian (games), neut. pl. of *Pythios* Pythian]
Pyth·i·an (pith′ē·ən) *adj.* **1** Relating to Delphi, to Apollo's temple there, its oracle, or priestess. **2** Relating to the Pythian games. — *n.* **1** A native or inhabitant of Delphi; specifically, the priestess of Apollo. **2** An epithet of the Delphic Apollo. [<L *Pythius* <Gk. *Pythios* <*Pytho,* older name for Delphi]
Pythian games Games held every four years in ancient Greece, of which musical contests were a feature.
Pyth·i·as (pith′ē·əs) See DAMON AND PYTHIAS. Also *Phintias.*
py·tho·gen·e·sis (pī′thō·jen′ə·sis, pith′ō-) *n.* Generation from or because of filth. [<Gk. *pythein* rot + GENESIS] — **py′tho·gen′ic, py′tho·ge·net′ic** (-jə·net′ik) *adj.*
pythogenic fever *Pathol.* **1** Typhoid fever. **2** Any fever due to filth. Also **pythogenetic fever.**
py·thon (pī′thon, -thən) *n.* **1** A large, non-venomous serpent (genus *Python*) that crushes its prey in its folds. **2** Any non-venomous serpent related to the boas. **3** A soothsayer or soothsaying spirit: from the tradition that the Python delivered oracles at Delphi; also, a ventriloquist. [<L <Gk. *Pythōn* Python <*Pytho.* See PYTHIAN.]

PYTHON
(From 3 to 32 feet in length)

Py·thon (pī′thon, -thən) In Greek mythology, a monstrous serpent which haunted the caves of Parnassus and was killed by Apollo near Delphi.
py·tho·ness (pī′thə·nis, pith′ə-) *n.* **1** The priestess of the Delphic oracle. **2** Any woman supposed to be possessed of the spirit of prophecy; a witch. [<OF *phitonise* <Med. L *phitonissa* <LL *pythonissa* <Gk. *Pytho* a familiar spirit, orig. Delphi]
py·thon·ic (pī·thon′ik, pi-) *adj.* **1** Of, pertaining to, or resembling pythons or a python. **2** Inspired; prophetic.
py·u·ri·a (pī·yo͝or′ē·ə) *n. Pathol.* The presence of pus in the urine. [<NL <Gk. *pyon* pus + *ouron* urine]
pyx (piks) *n.* **1** A vessel or casket, usually of precious metal, in which the Host is preserved. **2** A receptacle for coins selected for trial at the British mint: short for **pyx chest.** [<L *pyxis* a box <Gk. < *pyxos* a box tree. Doublet of BOX.]
pyx·ie[1] (pik′sē) See PIXY.
pyx·ie[2] (pik′sē) *n.* A creeping shrub *(Pyxidanthera barbulata)* with numerous solitary white or rose-colored flowers: it is the flowering moss or pixie of the pine barrens of New Jersey and North Carolina. [Prob. short for NL *Pyxidanthera,* the genus name <Gk. *pyxos* the box tree + *antheros* flowery]
pyx·is (pik′sis) *n. pl.* **pyx·i·des** (pik′sə·dēz) **1** A box or pyx; especially, an ancient form of ornamental jewel case or toilet box. **2** An emollient ointment. **3** *Bot.* A capsule or seed vessel with transverse dehiscence, the upper portion separating as a lid, as in the common purslane: also **pyx·id·i·um** (pik·sid′ē·əm). [<L. See PYX.]

Q

q, Q (kyo͞o) *n. pl.* **q's, Q's** or **qs, Qs, ques** (kyo͞oz) **1** The 17th letter of the English alphabet, from Phoenician *Q'oph* and Greek *koppa,* which was present in five eastern Greek alphabets, obsolete in the late alphabets of Elis and Athens, but survived in the Chalcidian and Boeotian, whence it passed into the Italian, to Roman *Q.* **2** The sound of the letter *q.* In English *q* is always followed by *u* and is pronounced *kw,* as in quack, queen, quest, quote, conquest, equal, etc. In some words borrowed from French, however, it retains its French pronunciation of *k,* as in appliqué, conquer, coquette, pique, piquant, toque. Final *-que* is always pronounced as *k,* as in antique, oblique, physique, unique, etc. See ALPHABET.
Qair·wan (kīr·wän′) See KAIROUAN.
Qan·da·har (kän′dä·här′) See KANDAHAR.
Qaz·vin (kȧz·vēn′) See KAZVIN.
Qa·tar (kä′tär) An independent Arab sheikdom under British protection, containing the whole **Qatar Peninsula** on the Persian Gulf coast of the Arabian Peninsula; about 8,000 miles; capital, Doha.
Qat·ta·ra Depression (kä·tä′rä) A desert basin in the Libyan Desert of northern Egypt; 7,500 square miles. Also **Qat·ta′rah.**
Q-boat (kyo͞o′bōt′) *n.* A merchant vessel having masked guns: used in World War I as a decoy for submarines. Also **Q′-ship′.**
Qe·na (kä′nə) A city on the east bank of the Nile, Upper Egypt. Also **Qi·na** (kē′nə).
Qishm (kish′əm) The largest island in the Persian Gulf, at the entrance of the Strait of Hormuz, southern Iran; 70 by 7 to 20 miles. Also **Qeshm** (kesh′əm).
Qi·shon (kī′shon, kish′on) A river in NW Israel, flowing 45 miles NW to the Bay of Acre.
qua (kwā, kwä) *adv.* In the capacity of; by virtue of being; in so far as. [<L, ablative sing. fem. of *qui* who]
quack[1] (kwak) *v.i.* To utter a harsh, croaking cry, as a duck. — *n.* The sound made by a duck, or a similar croaking noise. [Imit.]
quack[2] (kwak) *n.* **1** A pretender to medical knowledge or skill. **2** A charlatan. — *adj.* Of or pertaining to quacks or quackery; ignorantly or falsely pretending to cure. — *v.i.* To play the quack. [Short for QUACKSALVER] — **quack′ish** *adj.* — **quack′ish·ly** *adv.*
Synonyms (noun): charlatan, empiric, humbug, impostor, mountebank. *Antonyms*: adept, expert, master.
quack·er·y (kwak′ər·ē) *n. pl.* **·er·ies** Ignorant or fraudulent practice.
quack·grass (kwak′gras′, -gräs′) *n.* Couchgrass.
quack·sal·ver (kwak′sal′vər) *n.* A quack. [< MDu. < *quacken* quack[1] + *salf* a salve]
quad[1] (kwod) *n. Colloq.* A quadrangle of a college or prison. [Short for QUADRANGLE]
quad[2] (kwod) *n. Printing* A quadrat. [Short for QUADRAT]
quad[3] (kwod) See QUOD.
quad[4] (kwod) *adj.* Quadraphonic.
quad·ra·ge·nar·i·an (kwod′rə·jə·nâr′ē·ən) *adj.* Forty years old or relating to this age. — *n.* A person forty years old. [<L *quadragenarius* < *quadrageni* forty each < *quadraginta* forty]
Quad·ra·ges·i·ma (kwod′rə·jes′ə·mə) *n. Obs.* The forty fast days before Easter; Lent. [<L, fortieth]
quad·ra·ges·i·mal (kwod′rə·jes′ə·məl) *adj.* **1** Of or pertaining to the number forty, especially to the forty days of Lent. **2** Used during or appropriate to Lent; Lenten.
Quadragesima Sunday The first Sunday in Lent.
quad·ran·gle (kwod′rang·gəl) *n.* **1** *Geom.* A plane figure having four sides and four angles. **2** A court, square or oblong, as within a public building. **3** A tract of land as represented by the United States Geological Survey on one of its atlas sheets. [<L *quadrangulum* < *quattuor* four + *angulus* angle] — **quad·ran′gu·lar** *adj.*
quad·rant (kwod′rənt) *n.* **1** The quarter of a circle, or of its circumference. **2** An instrument having a graduated arc of 90°, with a movable radius for measuring angles on it; especially, a nautical instrument for measuring the altitude of the sun. **3** *Geom.* In a Cartesian coordinate system, any of the four sections formed by the intersection of the axes: beginning with the upper right-hand quadrant where the ordinate and abscissa are positive, they are called the **first, second, third,** and **fourth quadrants,** in counterclockwise order. See illustration on page 1030. **4** A device or machine-part having the shape of, or suggest-

ing the quadrant of a circle. [<L *quadrans, -antis* a fourth part <*quattuor* four] — **quad·ran·tal** (kwod·ran′təl) *adj.*

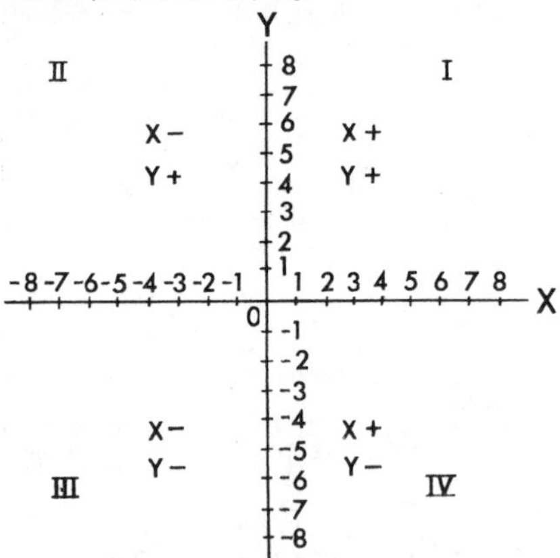

CARTESIAN QUADRANT

quad·ra·phon·ic (kwod′rə·fon′ik) *adj.* Of, pertaining to, or employing a system of sound reproduction that uses four transmission channels and loudspeakers.
quad·rat (kwod′rət) *n.* **1** *Printing* A piece of type metal lower than the letters, used for spacing: abbreviated *quad.* **2** *Ecol.* A square area of varying size laid down in a plant association or formation to estimate the number of plants enclosed, or to determine the character of successional changes. [See QUADRATE]
quad·rate (kwod′rāt, -rit) *n.* **1** *Zool.* A bone or cartilaginous element suspending the lower jaw in certain vertebrates below the mammals. **2** In astrology, an aspect of two heavenly bodies in which they are distant from each other 90°. **3** A cubical or square object, or an object resembling a cube. — *adj.* **1** Square; four-sided, as a muscle. **2** Distant from each other 90°: said of two heavenly bodies. **3** Of or pertaining to the quadrate bone or cartilage. — *v.* (-rāt) **·rat·ed, ·rat·ing** *v.i.* To correspond or agree: with *with.* — *v.t.* To cause to conform; bring in accordance with. [<L *quadratus,* pp. of *quadrare* square <*quattuor* four]
quad·rat·ic (kwod·rat′ik) *adj.* **1** Pertaining to or resembling a square. **2** Relating to a quadratic equation. — *n. Math.* **1** An equation of the second degree. It is a **pure, simple,** or **incomplete quadratic** when it contains only the second power of the variable, as $ax^2+c=0$; a **complete** or **adfected quadratic** when it contains also the first power, as $ax^2 + bx + c = 0$. **2** A formula, $x=\frac{-b \pm \sqrt{b^2-4ac}}{2a}$, for computing the roots of the standard quadratic equation, $ax^2 + bx + c = 0$. **3** *pl.* The part of algebra that treats of quadratic equations.
quad·ra·ture (kwod′rə·chər) *n.* **1** The act or process of squaring. **2** The finding in square measure of the area of any surface, especially one bounded by a curve. **3** *Astron.* **a** The relative position of two heavenly bodies that are 90° apart as viewed from the center of a third body. **b** Either intersection of an orbit with a line whose ends terminate in the curve drawn perpendicular to the major axis through the focus.
quad·ren·ni·al (kwod·ren′ē·əl) *adj.* **1** Occurring once in four years. **2** Comprising four years. — **quad·ren′ni·al·ly** *adv.*
quad·ren·ni·um (kwod·ren′ē·əm) *n. pl.* **·ren·ni·a** (-ren′ē·ə) A space or period of four years. Also **quad·ri·en·ni·um** (kwod′rē·en′ē·əm). [<L]
quadri– *combining form* Four: *quadrinomial.* Also, before vowels, **quadr–**: also *quadru–.* [<L *quattuor* four]
quad·ric (kwod′rik) *adj. Math.* Of the second degree: applied especially where there are more than two variables. — *n.* A quantic of the second degree. [<L *quadra* square]
quadric curve *Math.* A curve with an algebraic Cartesian equation of the second degree.
quad·ri·cen·ten·ni·al (kwod′ri·sen·ten′ē·əl) *n.* A four-hundredth anniversary. — *adj.* Of or pertaining to such an anniversary.
quad·ri·ceps (kwod′rə·seps) *n. Anat.* The extensor of the leg. [<QUADRI- + L *caput* head] — **quad′ri·cip′i·tal** (-sip′ə·təl) *adj.*
quad·ri·fid (kwod′rə·fid) *adj. Bot.* Four-cleft; divided into four segments, as a flower petal.
quad·ri·ga (kwod·rī′gə) *n. pl.* **·gae** (-jē) In ancient Rome, a two-wheeled chariot to which four horses were harnessed abreast. [<L <*quattuor* four + *jugum* yoke]
quad·ri·lat·er·al (kwod′rə·lat′ər·əl) *adj.* Formed or bounded by four lines; four-sided. — *n.* **1** *Geom.* **a** A figure bounded by four straight lines terminated at four angles. **b** A figure formed of four infinite straight lines, having six intersections. **2** A space or area defended by four enclosing fortresses. [<L *quadrilaterus* <*quattuor* four + *latus, lateris* side]

QUADRILATERAL
abdc. Quadrilateral.
ad., bc. Diagonals.
ebfc. Quadrilateral.
a., b., c., d., f. Vertices.
ai., bh., ei. Diagonals.
g., hh., i. Centers.

quad·ri·lin·gual (kwod′rə·ling′gwəl) *adj.* **1** Consisting of, or knowing, four languages. **2** Written in four languages.
qua·drille[1] (kwə·dril′) *n.* **1** A square dance for four couples and having five figures. **2** Music for such a dance. [<F <Sp. *cuadrilla* little square <L *quadrum* <*quattuor* four]
qua·drille[2] (kwə·dril′) *n.* A card game for four persons, played with a deck of 40 cards and popular in the 18th century. [<F <Sp. *cuartillo* <*cuarto* fourth <L *quartus*]
quadrille paper See GRAPH PAPER.
quad·ril·lion (kwod·ril′yən) *n.* **1** In the French and United States system of numeration, a thousand trillions, or 1 followed by 15 ciphers. **2** In the English system, a million trillions, or 1 followed by 24 ciphers. [<F <*quatre* four + *(m)illion*]
quad·ri·mes·ter (kwod′rə·mes′tər) *n.* A period of four months; one third of a year. [<L *quadrimestris* of four months] — **quad′ri·mes′·tral** *adj.*
quad·ri·no·mi·al (kwod′rə·nō′mē·əl) *n. Math.* An algebraic expression having four terms.
quad·ri·par·tite (kwod′rə·pär′tīt) *adj.* **1** Consisting of or embracing four parts. **2** Having four parties, as an agreement or contract. [<L *quadripartitus* <*quattuor* four + *partitus* divided] — **quad′ri·par·ti′tion** (-tish′ən) *n.*
quad·ri·syl·la·ble (kwod′rə·sil′ə·bəl) *n.* A word of four syllables. — **quad′ri·syl·lab′ic** (-si·lab′·ik) *adj.*
quad·ri·va·lent (kwod′rə·vā′lənt) *adj. Chem.* Having a valence of four, as carbon; tetravalent. [<QUADRI- + L *valens, -entis,* ppr. of *valere* be worth] — **quad′ri·va′lence** or **·len·cy** *n.*
quad·riv·i·al (kwod·riv′ē·əl) *adj.* **1** Having four radiating ways. **2** Leading to or going in four directions: *quadrivial* streets. [<L *quadrivius* <*quattuor* four + *via* way]
quad·riv·i·um (kwod·riv′ē·əm) *n. pl.* **·i·a** (-ē·ə) In the Pythagorean system, the four sciences, geometry, astronomy, arithmetic, and music, making up with the trivium the seven liberal arts. Compare TRIVIUM. [<L, a place where four roads meet]
quad·roon (kwod·rōōn′) *n.* A person having one-fourth Negro and three-fourths white blood. [<Sp. *cuarteron* <*cuarto* fourth]
quadru– Var. of QUADRI–.
quad·ru·ma·nous (kwod·rōō′mə·nəs) *adj.* **1** Four-handed; having four feet resembling hands. **2** Of or pertaining to a former order *(Quadrumana)* of mammals now classed with man under the primates. [<QUADRU- + L *manus* hand] — **quad·ru·mane** (kwod′rōō·mān) *n.*
quad·ru·ped (kwod′rōō·ped) *n.* An animal having four feet; especially, a four-footed mammal. — *adj.* Having four feet. [<L *quadrupes, -pedis* <*quattuor* four + *pes* foot] — **quad·ru·pe·dal** (kwod·rōō′pə·dəl, kwod′rōō·ped′l) *adj.*
quad·ru·ple (kwod′rōō·pəl, kwod·rōō′pəl) *adj.* Consisting of four; having four parts or members; fourfold; also, taken by fours. — *n.* A number or sum four times as great as another. — *v.t.* & *v.i.* **·pled, ·pling** To multiply by four; make or become four times larger. — *adv.* Fourfold. [<L *quadruplus*]
quad·ru·plet (kwod′rōō·plit, kwod·rōō′-) *n.* **1** A compound or combination of four things or objects. **2** One of four offspring born of the same mother at one birth.
quadruple time *Music* Measure or time having four beats; four-two, four-four, or four-eight time.
quad·ru·plex (kwod′rōō·pleks, kwod·rōō′-) *adj.* **1** Fourfold. **2** Pertaining to or designating a telegraph system such that four messages, two in each direction, may be sent simultaneously over one wire. — *n.* A sending instrument used in quadruplex telegraphy. [<L <*quattuor* four + stem of *plicare* fold]
quad·ru·pli·cate (kwod·rōō′plə·kit, -kāt) *adj.* **1** Fourfold. **2** Raised to the fourth power. — *v.t.* (-kāt) **·cat·ed, ·cat·ing** To multiply by four; quadruple. — *n.* One of four like things. — **quad·ru′pli·ca′tion** *n.* — **quad·ru′pli·cate·ly** *adv.*
quae·re (kwē′rē) *n.* Literally, seek; inquire: an annotation inserted, as in law reports. [<L. See QUERY.]
quaes·tor (kwes′tər, kwēs′-) *n.* Any of a number of public officials in ancient Rome; originally, one of two magistrates who inquired into and punished capital crimes; later, one who took charge of the public treasury and expenditure: also spelled *questor.* [<L <*quaerere* seek, inquire] — **quaes·to·ri·al** (kwes·tôr′·ē·əl, -tō′rē-, kwēs-) *adj.* — **quaes′tor·ship** *n.*
quaff (kwaf, kwof, kwôf) *v.t.* & *v.i.* To drink, especially copiously or with relish. — *n.* A drink; swallow. [<earlier *quaft,* ? blend of QUENCH and DRAUGHT] — **quaff′er** *n.*
quag (kwag, kwog) *n.* A quagmire. [<obs. *quag, v.,* blend of QUAKE and SAG]
quag·ga (kwag′ə) *n.* **1** A South African equine mammal *(Equus quagga)* intermediate between the ass and the zebra and resembling the latter: now extinct. **2** A zebra: an erroneous use. [<native Hottentot name]

QUAGGA
(About 11 hands high at the withers)

quag·gy (kwag′ē, kwog′ē) *adj.* Yielding to or quaking under the foot, as soft, wet earth; boggy.
quag·mire (kwag′mīr′, kwog′-) *n.* **1** Marshy ground that gives way under the foot; bog. **2** A difficult situation. [<QUAG + MIRE] — **quag′mired′, quag′mir′y** *adj.*
qua·haug (kwô′hôg, -hog, kwə·hôg′, -hog′) *n.* The round, thick-shelled clam *(Venus mercenaria)* of the Atlantic coast of North America. The young are called cherrystone clams. Also **qua′hog**: sometimes spelled *cohog, quohog.* [<Algonquian (Narraganset) *poquauhock*]
Quai d'Or·say (kā dôr·sā′) **1** A quay on the left bank of the Seine in Paris, toward which the French Foreign Office faces. **2** The French Foreign Office.
quaigh (kwākh) *n. Scot.* A small cup or drinking vessel. Also **quaich.**
quail[1] (kwāl) *n.* **1** An Old World migratory game bird *(Coturnix coturnix)* similar to the partridge, having a very short tail. **2** Any of various small American game birds related to the partridge (family *Perdicadae*), especially the bobwhite and the California quail *(Lophortyx californica).* See BOBWHITE. **3** *Obs.* A prostitute. [<OF *quaille,* prob. <Gmc.]
quail[2] (kwāl) *v.i.* To shrink with fear; lose heart or courage. [ME *quailen;* origin uncertain]
quaint (kwānt) *adj.* **1** Combining an antique appearance with a pleasing oddity, fancifulness, or whimsicalness. **2** Hence, pleasingly odd or old-fashioned; fanciful. **3** *Obs.* Curiously wrought; hence, ornamental. **4** *Obs.* Crafty. See synonyms under ANTIQUE, ODD, QUEER. [<OF *cointe* <L *cognitus* known] — **quaint′ly** *adv.* — **quaint′ness** *n.*
quake (kwāk) *v.i.* **quaked, quak·ing** **1** To shake, as with violent emotion or cold; quiver. **2** To shake or tremble, as earth during an earthquake. — *n.* A shaking, tremulous motion, quickly repeated; a shaking or shuddering. [OE *cwacian* shake]
Synonyms (verb): quaver, quiver, shake, shiver, shudder, tremble, vibrate, waver. See SHAKE.

Quak·er (kwā′kər) *n.* A member of the Society of Friends: originally a term of derision, and still not used within the society. See SOCIETY OF FRIENDS. [<QUAKE, *v.*; with ref. to their founder's admonition to them to tremble at the word of the Lord] — **Quak′er·ess** *n. fem.* — **Quak′er·ish** *adj.* — **Quak′er·ish·ly** *adv.*

quaker buttons The dried, ripe seeds of nux vomica.

Quaker City A nickname of PHILADELPHIA.

Quaker gun A dummy gun, as one made of wood: from the Friends' doctrine of non-resistance.

Quak·er·ism (kwā′kə·riz′əm) *n.* The beliefs or practices of the Quakers.

quaker ladies Bluets.

Quak·er·ly (kwā′kər·lē) *adj.* Like the Quakers. — *adv.* After the manner of the Quakers.

Quaker meeting 1 Any meeting of the Society of Friends for worship, in which, following their usage, they remain silent until the Spirit moves some member to speak or pray aloud. 2 Any silent gathering.

Quaker State Nickname of PENNSYLVANIA.

quak·y (kwā′kē) *adj.* **quak·i·er, quak·i·est** Shaky; tremulous. — **quak′i·ly** *adv.* — **quak′i·ness** *n.*

qual·i·fi·ca·tion (kwol′ə·fə·kā′shən) *n.* 1 The act of qualifying, or the state of being qualified. 2 That which fits a person or thing for something. 3 A restriction; mitigation. See synonyms under ABILITY.

qual·i·fied (kwol′ə·fīd) *adj.* 1 Competent or fit, as for public office. 2 Restricted or modified in some way. See synonyms under COMPETENT. — **qual′i·fied′ly** *adv.*

qual·i·fy (kwol′ə·fī) *v.* **·fied, ·fy·ing** *v.t.* 1 To make fit or capable, as for an office, occupation, or privilege. 2 To make legally capable, as by the administration of an oath. 3 To limit or restrict, as by conditions or exceptions. 4 To attribute a quality to; describe; characterize or name. 5 To make less strong or extreme; soften; moderate. 6 To change the strength or flavor of. 7 *Gram.* To modify. — *v.i.* 8 To be or become qualified or fit; meet the requirements, as for entering a race. See synonyms under CHANGE. [<MF *qualifier* <Med. L *qualificare* <L *qualis* of such a kind + *facere* make] — **qual′i·fi′a·ble** *adj.* — **qual′i·fi′er** *n.*

qual·i·ta·tive (kwol′ə·tā′tiv) *adj.* Of or pertaining to quality: distinguished from *quantitative.* [<LL *qualitativus* <L *qualitas* quality] — **qual′i·ta′tive·ly** *adv.*

qualitative analysis *Chem.* The process of finding how many and what elements or ingredients are present in a substance or compound.

qual·i·ty (kwol′ə·tē) *n. pl.* **·ties** 1 That which makes a being or thing such as it is; a distinguishing element or characteristic. 2 The characteristics of anything regarded as determining its value, place, worth, rank, position, etc., or the condition of a thing as so determined; character; kind; when unqualified, peculiar excellence. 3 A moral trait or characteristic. 4 Degree of excellence; relative goodness; grade: high *quality* of fabric. 5 Capability of producing specific effects. 6 Particular character or part; capacity; function. 7 *Archaic* Social rank; persons of rank, collectively. 8 *Music* That which distinguishes sounds of the same pitch and intensity from different sources, as from different instruments; timbre. 9 *Logic* The character of a proposition or judgment as asserting or denying. 10 *Philos.* An essential property or attribute. 11 *Phonet.* The character of a vowel sound as determined by the resonance of the oral cavity. See synonyms under ATTRIBUTE, CHARACTERISTIC. — *adj.* Characterized by high quality: a *quality* product. [<L *qualitas, -tatis* < *qualis* of such a kind]

qualm (kwäm, kwôm) *n.* 1 A feeling of sickness. 2 A twinge of conscience; moral scruple. 3 A sensation of fear or misgiving. [OE *cwealm* death]

qualm·ish (kwä′mish, kwô′-) *adj.* 1 Feeling or affected with qualms. 2 Likely to produce qualms. See synonyms under SQUEAMISH. Also **qualm′y.** — **qualm′ish·ly** *adv.* — **qualm′ish·ness** *n.*

quam·ash (kwom′ash, kwə·mash′) *n.* Camas.

quan·da·ry (kwon′dər·ē, -drē) *n. pl.* **·da·ries** A state of hesitation or perplexity; predicament. [Origin uncertain]

quand même (käṅ mem′) *French* Notwithstanding; even though; nevertheless.

quan·dong (kwon′dong) *n.* 1 A small Australian tree of the sandalwood family (*Fusanus acuminatus*). 2 Its edible drupaceous fruit, used as a preserve. Also **quan′dang.** [< native Australian name]

quant (kwant, kwont) *n. Brit.* A punting pole with a flange at the end to prevent its sinking in the mud. — *v.t.* & *v.i.* To propel or be propelled with a quant. [? <L *contus* a boat pole]

quan·ta (kwon′tə) Plural of QUANTUM.

quan·tic (kwon′tik) *n. Math.* A rational homogeneous function of two or more variables, usually containing only positive integers.

Quan·ti·co (kwon′ti·kō) A town on the Potomac in northern Virginia; site of a United States Marine Corps base.

quan·ti·fy (kwon′tə·fī) *v.t.* **·fied, ·fy·ing** 1 To determine the quantity of. 2 *Logic* To express the quantity of explicitly, as by using *all, some,* or *none.* [<Med. L *quantificare* <L *quantus* how great + *facere* make] — **quan′ti·fi·ca′tion** *n.* — **quan′ti·fi′er** *n.*

quan·tim·e·ter (kwon·tim′ə·tər) *n. Med.* A dosimeter.

quan·ti·ta·tive (kwon′tə·tā′tiv) *adj.* 1 Of or pertaining to quantity. 2 Having to do with quantities only: distinguished from *qualitative.* [<LL *quantitativus* <L *quantitas* quantity] — **quan′ti·ta′tive·ly** *adv.* — **quan′ti·ta′tive·ness** *n.*

quantitative analysis *Chem.* The process of finding the amount or percentage of each element or ingredient present, as in a compound.

quan·ti·ty (kwon′tə·tē) *n. pl.* **·ties** 1 The condition of being much. 2 That property of a thing which admits of exact measurement and numerical statement. 3 An object regarded as possessing a certain determinable magnitude, as of length, size, mass, volume, or number. 4 *Electr.* The strength of a current, as opposed to intensity or potential. 5 In prosody, the relative period of time, regarded as short or long, required to pronounce a syllable. 6 *Music* The duration of a musical note. 7 A specified, or indefinite, number of persons or things. 8 *Logic* The extent of a general term or proposition as applying to the whole or to a part of a class. Considered with reference to quantity, propositions are *universal,* as "all men are mortal," and *particular,* as "some men are honest," while with reference to conceptions quantity relates either to their extension, or to their intension or comprehension. 9 Considerable bulk or amount. [<OF *quantité* <L *quantitas, -tatis* < *quantus* how much, how large]

quan·tize (kwon′tīz) *v.t.* **·tized, ·tiz·ing** *Physics* To express (an energy relationship) in terms of quanta or in accordance with the quantum theory. — **quan′ti·za′tion** *n.*

quan·tum (kwon′təm) *n. pl.* **·ta** (-tə) 1 An object that has quantity or is concrete. 2 A certain amount; also, a prescribed or a sufficient quantity. 3 *Physics* A fundamental unit of energy or action as provided for in the quantum theory. [<L, neuter of *quantus* how much]

quantum liquid *Physics* Helium in the superfluid condition: so called because it confirms the quantum theory that even at temperature of absolute zero molecular motion does not completely cease.

quantum number *Physics* A number indicating any of the energy levels possible in an atom under specified conditions.

quantum state Energy level.

quantum theory *Physics* The theory that energy is not a smoothly flowing continuum but is manifested by the emission from radiating bodies of discrete particles or *quanta,* the values of which are expressed as the product of Planck's constant, *h,* and the frequency, *v,* of the given radiation.

Qua·paw (kwä′pô) *n.* One of a tribe of North American Indians of Siouan stock, formerly living in Arkansas, now in Oklahoma: also called *Arkansas.*

quar·an·tine (kwôr′ən·tēn, kwor′-) *n.* 1 The enforced isolation for a fixed period of persons, ships, or goods arriving from places infected with contagious disease, or of any persons who have been exposed to such infection. 2 A place designated for the enforcement of such interdiction. 3 The enforced isolation of any person or place infected with contagious disease; loosely, any enforced isolation. 4 A period of forty days. — *v.t.* **·tined, ·tin·ing** To subject to or retain in quarantine; isolate by or as by quarantine. [<Ital. *quarantina* <L *quadraginta* forty]

quark (kwärk) *n. Physics* Any of a group of three types of hypothetical fundamental particles proposed as the entities of which all other strongly interacting particles are composed. [Coined by Murray Gell-Mann, born 1929, U.S. physicist, appar. after use by James Joyce in *Finnegans Wake*]

Quarles (kwôrlz, kworlz), **Francis,** 1592–1644, English poet.

Quar·ne·ro (kwär·ne′rō), **Gulf of** See VELIKI KVARNER.

quar·rel[1] (kwôr′əl, kwor′-) *n.* 1 An unfriendly, angry, or violent dispute. 2 A falling out or contention; breach of amity: a lover's *quarrel.* 3 The cause for dispute. — *v.i.* **·reled** or **·relled, ·rel·ing** or **·rel·ling** 1 To engage in a quarrel; dispute; contend; fight: to *quarrel* about money. 2 To break off a mutual friendship; fall out; disagree. 3 To find fault; cavil. [<F *querelle* <L *querela* complaint] — **quar′rel·er** or **quar′rel·ler** *n.*

Synonyms (noun): affray, altercation, bickering, brawl, breach, broil, contention, contest, controversy, disagreement, discussion, dispute, dissension, feud, fracas, fray, fuss, jangle, jar, misunderstanding, quarreling, rupture, scene, squabble, strife, wrangle. A *quarrel* is in word or act, or both, and is often slight and transient, as we speak of childish *quarrels*; but *quarrel* may denote the cause or ground of *contention* or *strife,* and so be deep and enduring. *Contention* and *strife* may be in word or deed; *contest* ordinarily involves some form of action. *Controversy* is commonly in words; *strife* extends from verbal *controversy* to the *contests* of armies. See ALTERCATION, FEUD[1]. *Antonyms*: accord, amity, acquiescence, concord, harmony, peace, reconciliation.

quar·rel[2] (kwôr′əl, kwor′-) *n.* 1 A dart or arrow with a four-edged head, formerly used with a crossbow. 2 A graver, stonemason's chisel, glazier's diamond, or other tool having a several-edged point. [<OF <LL *quadrellus,* dim. of L *quadrum* a square < *quattuor* four]

quar·rel·some (kwôr′əl·səm, kwor′-) *adj.* Inclined to quarrel; contentious. — **quar′rel·some·ly** *adv.* — **quar′rel·some·ness** *n.*

quar·ri·er (kwôr′ē·ər, kwor′-) *n.* A workman in a stone quarry.

quar·ry[1] (kwôr′ē, kwor′ē) *n. pl.* **·ries** 1 A beast or bird hunted, seized, or killed, as in the chase; game; prey: now chiefly poetical. 2 Anything hunted, slaughtered, or eagerly pursued. 3 *Obs.* A heap of slaughtered game. [<OF *cuirée* <L *corium* hide]

quar·ry[2] (kwôr′ē, kwor′ē) *n. pl.* **·ries** An excavation from which stone is taken by cutting, blasting, or the like. — *v.t.* **·ried, ·ry·ing** 1 To cut, dig, or take from or as from a quarry. 2 To establish a quarry in. [<Med. L *quareia, quareria* <LL *quadraria* place for squaring stone < *quadrare.* See QUADRATE.]

quar·ry[3] (kwôr′ē, kwor′ē) *n. pl.* **·ries** 1 A square or lozenge. 2 A small square or lozenge-shaped pane of glass, tile, etc. 3 In archery, a quarrel. [<OF *quarré* <L *quadratus.* See QUADRATE.]

quart[1] (kwôrt) *n.* 1 A measure of capacity; the fourth part of a gallon, or two pints. In the United States, the dry quart is equal to 1.10 liters and the liquid quart is equal to 0.946 liter. 2 A vessel of such capacity. [<F *quarte* <L *quartus* fourth]

quart[2] (kärt) *n.* 1 In fencing, a quarte. 2 In piquet, a sequence of four cards of the same suit: called **quart major** if they are the highest four. [<F *quarte.* See QUART[1]]

quar·tan (kwôr′tən) *adj.* Pertaining to the fourth in a series; especially, occurring every fourth day. — *n. Pathol.* A malarial fever caused by the parasite *Plasmodium malariae,* in which the paroxysms recur every fourth

add, āce, câre, pälm; end, ēven; it, īce; odd, ōpen, ôrder; to͝ok, po͞ol; up, bûrn; ə = a in *above,* e in *sicken,* i in *clarity,* o in *melon,* u in *focus;* yo͞o = u in *fuse*; oi, oil; ou, pout; ch, check; g, go; ng, ring; th, thin; th, this; zh, vision. Foreign sounds à, œ, ü, kh, ṅ; and ◆: see page xx. < from; + plus; ? possibly.

day, or 72 hours, reckoning inclusively. [<F *quartaine* <L *quartanus* < *quartus* fourth]

quarte (kärt, *Fr.* kȧrt) *n.* In fencing, a thrust or parry: the fourth regular position: also spelled *carte.* [<F]

quar·ter (kwôr′tər) *n.* **1** One of four equal parts into which anything is or may be divided; a fourth part; specifically, the fourth of a hundredweight; eight bushels; a fourth of a ton (of grain); the fourth of a yard, or a span; a fourth of a pound; a fourth of a mile; fifteen minutes or the fourth of an hour, or the moment with which it begins or ends. **2** A fourth of a year or three months; hence, a term of school. **3** A limb of a quadruped with the adjacent parts; also, a haunch of venison. **4** In the United States and Canada, a coin of the value of 25 cents. **5** *Astron.* Either of two phases of the moon: the first quarter, between the new and full moon; or the last quarter, between the full moon and the new. **6** *Music* A quarter note. **7** *Nav.* One of the four principal points of the compass or divisions of the horizon; also, a point or direction of the compass. **8** The place, origin, or source from which anything comes. **9** A particular division or district; a locality. **10** *Usually pl.* Proper or assigned station, position, or place, as of officers and crew on a warship. **11** *pl.* A place of lodging or residence, especially temporary shelter; specifically, a group of cabins provided for the Negroes on a Southern plantation. **12** A region embracing one fourth, or about one fourth, of a space; one of four corresponding localities or parts. **13** The side of a horse's hoof, just in front of the heel; also that part of a boot or shoe from the middle of the heel to the line of the ankle bone. **14** *Naut.* **a** The upper part of a vessel's side from the after part of the main chains to the stern. **b** That part of a yard outside the slings. **15** *Her.* Any of four equal divisions into which a shield is divided, or an ordinary occupying such a division. **16** Mercy shown to a vanquished foeman by sparing his life; clemency. **17** One of the four periods into which a game, as football, is divided. — **at close quarters** Close by; at close range. — *adj.* **1** Being one of four equal parts. **2** Having one fourth of a standard value. — *v.t.* **1** To divide into four equal parts. **2** To divide into a number of parts or pieces. **3** To cut the body of (an executed person) into four parts: He was hanged, drawn, and *quartered.* **4** To range from one side to the other of (a field, etc.) while advancing: The dogs *quartered* the field. **5** To furnish with quarters or shelter; lodge, station, or billet. **6** *Her.* **a** To divide (a shield) into quarters by vertical and horizontal lines. **b** To bear or arrange (different coats of arms) quarterly upon a shield or escutcheon. **7** *Mech.* To mark or place at intervals of a quarter, especially of a quarter of a circle. — *v.i.* **8** To be stationed or lodged. **9** To range from side to side of an area, as dogs in hunting. **10** *Naut.* To blow on a ship's quarter: said of the wind. [<OF <L *quartarius* < *quartus* fourth]

quar·ter·age (kwôr′tər·ij) *n.* **1** A quarterly allowance or payment. **2** Board and lodging; quarters, especially for troops, a work gang, etc.; also, the cost of lodging or shelter.

quar·ter·back (kwôr′tər·bak′) *n.* In American football, one of the backfield, who often calls the signals.

quar·ter-crack (kwôr′tər·krak′) *n.* A crack on the inner quarter of a horse's forehoof. Compare SANDCRACK.

quar·ter-day (kwôr′tər·dā′) *n.* One fourth of a day.

quarter day Any of the days of the year when quarterly payments are due. Quarter days for the U.S. government are the first days of January, April, July, and October; for England, Lady Day (March 25), Midsummer Day (June 24), Michaelmas (September 29), and Christmas (December 25).

quar·ter-deck (kwôr′tər·dek′) *n. Naut.* The rear part of a ship's upper deck, reserved for officers.

quar·tered (kwôr′tərd) *adj.* **1** Divided into four quarters. **2** *Her.* Divided into quarterings. **3** Quarter-sawed: *quartered* oak. **4** Lodged; stationed; also, having quarters.

quar·ter·fi·nal (kwôr′tər·fī′nəl) *n.* A competition immediately preceding the semifinal in sporting events; also, one of four competitions in a tournament, the winners of which play in the two semifinals. — *adj.* Next to the semifinal. — **quar′ter·fi′nal·ist** *n.*

quar·ter·foil (kwôr′tər·foil′) See QUATREFOIL.

Quarter horse A breed of horse descendent from the thoroughbred stallion *Janus* imported from England in 1756: first known as a racing breed, now widely popular as a ranch horse and cow pony. [From the quarter-of-a-mile path over which it was raced by the early settlers of Virginia]

quar·ter-hour (kwôr′tər·our′) *n.* Fifteen minutes. — **quar′ter-hour′ly** *adj.*

quar·ter·ing (kwôr′·tər·ing) *adj.* **1** *Naut.* **a** Blowing against or being on the quarter. **b** Blowing from any point between beam and stern: a *quartering* wind. **c** Sailing so as to have the wind on the quarter. **2** Set or being at right angles. — *n.* **1** A dividing or marking off into quarters. **2** *Her.* **a** The grouping of two or more coats of arms in compartments on one shield, to indicate family alliances, etc. **b** Any of the coats which are quartered on the shield, or the quarter containing it. **3** Quarters, or the assigning of quarters, as for soldiers.

QUARTERING

quar·ter·ly (kwôr′tər·lē) *adj.* **1** Containing or being a fourth part. **2** Occurring at intervals of three months. — *n. pl.* **·lies** A publication issued once every three months. — *adv.* **1** Once in a quarter of a year. **2** In or by quarters.

quar·ter·mas·ter (kwôr′tər·mas′tər, -mäs′-) *n.* **1** *Usually cap.* The officer on an Army post who is responsible for carrying out the functions required of the Quartermaster Corps. **2** On shipboard, a petty officer who assists the navigator.

Quartermaster Corps A branch of the U. S. Army which is responsible for the supply of food, fuel, clothing, and other equipment.

Quartermaster General In the U. S. Army, the major general who is at the head of the Quartermaster Corps.

quar·tern (kwôr′tərn) *n.* **1** A fourth part of certain measures or weights, as of a peck or pound; a gill. **2** A four-pound loaf of bread. [<OF *quarteron* < *quarte* a fourth part <L *quartus* fourth]

quar·ter·ni·on (kwôr·tûr′nē·ən) *n. Printing* A gathering of four sheets, each folded into pages, usually four to a sheet, to make a section of a book, pamphlet, etc.

quarter note *Music* A note having one fourth the value of a semibreve. See illustration under NOTE.

quar·ter-phase (kwôr′tər·fāz′) *adj. Electr.* Diphase.

quar·ter-sawed (kwôr′tər·sôd′) *adj.* Sawed lengthwise into quarters, as a log, or sawed from quartered timber.

quar·ter-sec·tion (kwôr′tər·sek′shən) *n.* A tract of land half a mile square, containing one fourth of a square mile; 160 acres.

quar·ter-ses·sions (kwôr′tər·sesh′ənz) *n.* A court held quarterly. In England and Scotland it tries many indictable offenses, hears appeals from the petty sessions, and exercises a minor civil jurisdiction.

quar·ter·staff (kwôr′tər·staf′, -stäf′) *n. pl.* **·staves** (-stāvz′) A stout, iron-tipped staff about 6 1/2 feet long, formerly used in England as a weapon; also, the use of, or exercise with, the quarterstaff.

quar·ter·tone (kwôr′tər·tōn′) *n.* **1** In photoengraving, a coarse zinc halftone plate having 65 lines or less to the inch. **2** *Music* Half of a semitone: **quarter tone.**

quar·tet (kwôr·tet′) *n.* **1** A composition for four voices or instruments. **2** The set of four persons who render such compositions. **3** A stanza of four lines. **4** Any group or set of four things of a kind. Also **quar·tette′.** [< Ital. *quartetto* < *quarto* fourth]

quar·tic (kwôr′tik) *Math. adj.* Denoting a quantic function of the fourth degree. — *n.* Such a function.

quar·tile (kwôr′tīl, -til) *n.* **1** In astrology, a quadrate. **2** *Stat.* That portion of a frequency distribution which comprises an exact fourth of the total observed cases. — *adj.* Of or pertaining to a quartile. [<LL *quartilis* <L *quartus* fourth]

quar·to (kwôr′tō) *adj.* Having four leaves or eight pages to the sheet: a *quarto* book. — *n. pl.* **·tos** A book or pamphlet whose pages are of the size of the fourth of a sheet: often written *4to* or *4°.* [<L *(in) quarto* (in) fourth]

quartz (kwôrts) *n.* Silicon dioxide, SiO_2, a hard, vitreous, widely distributed mineral occurring in many varieties, sometimes massive, as jasper and chalcedony: sometimes in colorless and transparent or diversely colored forms crystallizing in the hexagonal system. [<G *quarz*]

quartz crystal A thin section of pure quartz, accurately ground so as to vibrate at the required frequency in radio transmission; a piezoelectric oscillator. Also **quartz plate.**

quartz·if·er·ous (kwôrt·sif′ər·əs) *adj.* Consisting of or containing quartz.

quartz·ite (kwôrt′sīt) *n.* A massive or schistose metamorphic rock formed by the induration of sandstone through the deposition of secondary quartz about each grain.

quartz lamp A mercury-vapor lamp enclosed in a quartz tube, which transmits ultraviolet wavelengths.

qua·sar (kwā′zär, -sär) *n. Astron.* Any of a class of very distant, celestial objects that are strong radio sources, have unusual light spectra, show large red shifts, and have a vast, unexplained energy output. [<QUAS(I) + (STELL)AR]

quash[1] (kwosh) *v.t. Law* To make void or set aside, as an indictment; annul. See synonyms under ANNUL, CANCEL. [<OF *quasser* <LL *cassare* < *cassus* empty]

quash[2] (kwosh) *v.t.* To put down or suppress forcibly or summarily. [<OF *quasser* <L *quassare,* freq. of *quatere* shake]

quasi- *prefix* **1** (With nouns) Resembling; not genuine, as in:

quasi-accident
quasi-adult
quasi-approval
quasi-artist
quasi-attack
quasi-authority
quasi-bargain
quasi-blunder
quasi-certificate
quasi-characteristic
quasi-comprehension
quasi-conquest
quasi-conservative
quasi-consultation
quasi-dependence
quasi-despair
quasi-development
quasi-difference
quasi-distress
quasi-endorsement
quasi-escape
quasi-faith
quasi-farmer
quasi-friend
quasi-guarantee
quasi-handicap
quasi-illness
quasi-injury
quasi-insight
quasi-integrity
quasi-invasion
quasi-kindred
quasi-lament
quasi-luxury
quasi-market
quasi-method
quasi-miracle
quasi-neutrality
quasi-owner
quasi-pleasure
quasi-poem
quasi-protection
quasi-purity
quasi-reality
quasi-recreation
quasi-refusal
quasi-remedy
quasi-repair
quasi-scholar
quasi-tradition
quasi-triumph
quasi-victory
quasi-worship
quasi-zeal

2 (With adjectives) Nearly; almost, as in:

quasi-absolute
quasi-amiable
quasi-beneficial
quasi-classic
quasi-colloquial
quasi-comic
quasi-complex
quasi-conservative
quasi-continuous
quasi-converted
quasi-devoted
quasi-eligible
quasi-equal
quasi-evil
quasi-exempt
quasi-explicit
quasi-financial
quasi-forgotten
quasi-formidable
quasi-genteel
quasi-grateful
quasi-hereditary
quasi-human
quasi-humorous
quasi-important
quasi-infinite
quasi-internal
quasi-jocose
quasi-medical
quasi-natural
quasi-normal
quasi-official
quasi-practical
quasi-private
quasi-probable
quasi-righteous
quasi-similar
quasi-spiritual
quasi-stylish
quasi-sufficient

quasi-tangible
quasi-theatrical
quasi-typical
quasi-valid
quasi-vital
quasi-willing

3 *Law* Superficially resembling but intrinsically different, as in:

quasi-corporation
quasi-delict
quasi-deposit
quasi-entail
quasi-legislative
quasi-partner

[<L, as if]

qua·si-con·tract (kwā′sī·kon′trakt, -zī-, kwä′·sē-) *n.* An obligation to do something, enforceable by a contract remedy, but imposed by operation of law regardless of the consent of the defendant.

qua·si-ju·di·cial (kwā′sī·jōō·dish′əl, -zī-, kwä′·sē-) *adj.* Exercising functions of a judicial nature as a guide for official action, as a committee investigating facts and drawing conclusions from them.

quas·qui·cen·ten·ni·al (kwäs′kwi·sen·ten′ē·əl) *adj.* Of or pertaining to a century and a quarter. — *n.* A 125th anniversary, or its celebration. [coined <L *quadrans que* plus a fourth + CENTENNIAL, for Delavan, Illinois (1962).]

quas·si·a (kwosh′ē·ə, kwosh′ə) *n.* **1** The wood of either of two tropical American trees (*Picrasma excelsa* or *Quassia amara*). **2** The bitter principle of this wood, used in medicine as a tonic and anthelmintic. **3** The tree itself. [<NL, after Graman *Quassi*, a Surinam Negro who discovered its use in 1730]

quas·sin (kwos′in, kwas′-) *n. Chem.* A white, crystalline, intensely bitter amaroid, $C_{22}H_{30}O_6$, contained in quassia wood.

quatch·grass (kwoch′gras′, -gräs′) *n.* Couchgrass.

qua·ter·na·ry (kwə·tûr′nə·rē) *adj.* **1** Consisting of four things. **2** Fourth in order. — *n. pl.* **·ries** **1** The number four; a group of four things. **2** *Math.* A quantic function having four variables. [<L *quaternarius* < *quaterni* by fours]

Qua·ter·na·ry (kwə·tûr′nə·rē) *adj. Geol.* Of, pertaining to, or designating a geological period and system of the Cenozoic era, following the Tertiary and still continuing. — *n.* The Quaternary system or period.

qua·ter·ni·on (kwə·tûr′nē·ən) *n.* **1** A set, system, or file of four. **2** *Math.* **a** An operator or factor that changes one vector into another: so called because expressible as the sum of four quantities. **b** The form of the calculus of vectors based on and making use of the quaternion operator. [<LL *quaternio, -onis* < *quattuor* four]

Quath·lam·ba (kwät·läm′bä) See DRAKENSBERG.

quat·rain (kwot′rān) *n.* A stanza of four lines. [<F < *quatre* four]

qua·tre (kä′tər, *Fr.* kà′tr′) *n. French* **1** Anything, as a card or a domino, marked with four spots or pips. **2** The number four; four.

Qua·tre-Bras (kà′tr′·brä′) A village in Belgium, SE of Brussels; scene of an English victory by Wellington over French forces under Marshal Ney in the Waterloo campaign of the Napoleonic Wars, 1815.

quat·re·foil (kat′ər·foil′, kat′·rə-) *n.* **1** *Bot.* A leaf or flower with four leaflets or petals. **2** *Archit.* An ornament with four foils or lobes. Sometimes spelled *quarterfoil.* [<OF *quatre* four + *foil* leaf]

QUATREFOILS

quat·tro·cen·to (kwät′trō·chen′tō) *n.* The 15th century as connected with the revival of art and literature (especially in Italy). — *adj.* Of or pertaining to the quattrocento. [<Ital., four hundred < *quattro* four + *cento* hundred]

qua·ver (kwā′vər) *v.i.* **1** To tremble or shake: said usually of the voice. **2** To produce trills or quavers in singing or in playing a musical instrument. — *v.t.* **3** To utter or sing in a tremulous voice. See synonyms under QUAKE, SHAKE. — *n.* **1** A quivering or tremulous motion. **2** A shake or trill, as in singing. **3** An eighth note. [Freq. of obs. *quave*, ME *cwafian* tremble] — **qua′·ver·y** *adj.*

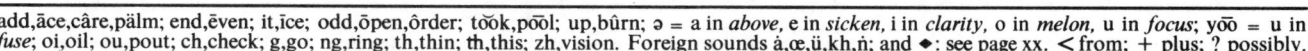

quay (kē) *n.* A wharf or artificial landing place where vessels unload. ◆ Homophone: *key.* [<F]

quay·age (kē′ij) *n.* **1** Wharfage; quay dues. **2** Space for quays; quays collectively.

quean (kwēn) *n.* **1** A brazen or ill-behaved woman; harlot; prostitute. **2** *Scot.* A young or unmarried woman; a girl. [OE *cwene* prostitute]

quea·sy (kwē′zē) *adj.* **·si·er, ·si·est** **1** Sick at the stomach. **2** Nauseating; also, caused by nausea. **3** Easily nauseated; hence, fastidious; squeamish. **4** Requiring to be carefully treated; delicate; ticklish. **5** Uncertain; hazardous. [Cf. Norw. *kveis* nausea] — **quea′·si·ly** *adv.* — **quea′si·ness** *n.*

Que·bec (kwi·bek′) **1** A province in eastern Canada; 523,860 square miles: formerly *Lower Canada*: abbr. *Que.* or *P.Q.* **2** Its capital, a port on the St. Lawrence River; captured from the French under Montcalm by Wolfe, Sept. 13, 1759.

que·bra·cho (kā·brä′chō) *n. pl.* **·chos** **1** Any of several tropical American trees producing a medicinal bark, especially the **white quebracho** (*Aspidosperma quebracho-blanco*), a Chilean tree whose bark is used as a febrifuge and for diseases of the respiratory organs; also, **red quebracho** (*Schinopsis lorentzii*), a tree whose heartwood is rich in tannin. **2** The wood or bark of any of these trees. [<Sp., var. of *quiebrahacha*, lit., ax-breaker < *quebrar* break + *hacha* ax]

Quech·ua (kech′wä) *n.* **1** One of a tribe of South American Indians which dominated the Inca empire prior to the Spanish conquest. **2** The language of the Quechuas, still spoken as a mother tongue in parts of Peru and Ecuador: also called *Incan.* Also spelled *Kechua.*

Quech·uan (kech′wən) *adj.* Of or pertaining to the Quechua or their language. — *n.* Quechua. Also spelled *Kechuan.*

queen (kwēn) *n.* **1** The wife of a king. **2** A female sovereign or monarch. **3** A woman preeminent in a given sphere. **4** The most powerful piece in chess, capable of moving any number of squares in a straight line. **5** A playing card bearing a conventional picture of a queen in her robes. **6** *Entomol.* The single fully developed female in a colony of social insects, as bees, ants, etc.: distinguished from workers, soldiers, and unproductive females. — *v.t.* **1** To make a queen of. **2** In chess, to make a queen of (a pawn) by moving it to the eighth row. — *v.i.* **3** To reign as or play the part of a queen: usually with *it.* [OE *cwēn* woman, queen]

Queen Anne's lace The wild carrot (*Daucus carota*), having filmy white flowers in umbels.

Queen Anne style **1** *Archit.* A style prevalent in England in the early 18th century, or a style similar to it used in the United States in the latter part of the 19th century, characterized by the use of red brickwork on which relief ornaments are carved, and by plain, unpretentious design. **2** A type of furniture characterized by much upholstery and marquetry.

Queen Anne's War See WAR OF THE SPANISH SUCCESSION in table under WAR.

Queen Charlotte Sound A bay of the Pacific in British Columbia between Vancouver Island and **Queen Charlotte Islands,** an archipelago (3,970 square miles) of western British Columbia; narrowing to **Queen Charlotte Strait,** 60 miles long and 16 miles wide, the northern end of the channel separating Vancouver Island from the mainland.

queen consort The wife of a reigning king, who does not share his sovereignty.

queen dowager The widow of a king who has reigned in his own right.

queen·ly (kwēn′lē) *adj.* & *adv.* Like a queen; stately; regional. See synonyms under IMPERIAL. — **queen′li·ness** *n.*

Queen Mary Coast Part of Antarctica on the Indian Ocean, west of Wilkes Land.

Queen Maud Land Part of Antarctica south of Africa, claimed by Norway, 1939; made a dependency of Norway, 1949.

Queen Maud Mountains A range extending south of the Ross Shelf Ice, Antarctica; rising over 13,000 feet.

queen mother A queen dowager who is mother of a reigning sovereign.

queen of the meadows An Old World meadowsweet (*Filipendula ulmaria*), naturalized in the United States.

queen of the prairie A tall perennial herb (*Filipendula rubra*) common to American meadows and prairies.

queen olive A large variety of Spanish olive.

queen·post (kwēn′pōst′) *n.* One of two upright suspending or sustaining posts or compression members in a truss.

queen regent **1** A queen who rules in behalf of another. **2** A queen who rules in her own right: also **queen regnant.**

Queens (kwēnz) The easternmost borough of New York City, located on Long Island; 108 square miles.

Queen's Bench See under COURT.

Queens·ber·ry Rules (kwēnz′ber·ē) See MARQUIS OF QUEENSBERRY RULES.

queen's counsel See KING'S COUNSEL.

queen's-de·light (kwēnz′di·līt′) *n.* A smooth, erect perennial (*Stillingia sylvatica*) of the spurge family, with alternate leaves and a medicinal root.

queen's English See KING'S ENGLISH under ENGLISH.

queen's evidence See STATE'S EVIDENCE.

Queens·land (kwēnz′lənd) The second largest state of the Commonwealth of Australia, in the NE part; 670,500 square miles; capital, Brisbane.

queen's metal An alloy of tin, antimony, bismuth, and lead, used for ornamental purposes.

queen snake A water snake (*Natrix lebris*) of the central and eastern United States.

Queens·town (kwēnz′toun) A former name for COBH.

queen's ware Fine, glazed, cream-colored English earthenware; specifically, cream-colored Wedgwood: named for Queen Charlotte by Josiah Wedgwood, 1761.

queer (kwir) *adj.* **1** Being out of the usual course of events in minor respects; singular; odd. **2** Of questionable character; open to suspicion; mysterious. **3** *Slang* Counterfeit. — *n. Slang* **1** Counterfeit money. **2** A homosexual, especially a male homosexual: a contemptuous term. — *v.t. U.S. Slang* To jeopardize or spoil. [<G *quer* oblique] — **queer′ly** *adv.* — **queer′ness** *n.*

Synonyms (adj.): anomalous, bizarre, crotchety, curious, droll, eccentric, erratic, fantastic, funny, grotesque, laughable, ludicrous, mysterious, odd, peculiar, quaint, ridiculous, singular, strange, unique, unusual, whimsical. *Odd* is unmated, as an *odd* shoe, and so uneven, as an *odd* number. *Singular* is alone of its kind; as, the *singular* number. What is *singular* is *odd,* but what is *odd* may not be *singular,* as, a drawerful of *odd* gloves. A *strange* thing is something either unnatural or extraordinary. A *singular* coincidence is one the happening of which is unusual; a *strange* coincidence is one the cause of which is hard to explain. That which is *peculiar* belongs especially to a person as his own; in its ordinary use there is the implication that the thing *peculiar* to one is not common to the majority. *Eccentric* is off center, and so off or aside from the ordinary and normal course; as, genius is commonly *eccentric. Eccentric* is a higher and more respectful word than *odd* or *queer. Erratic* signifies wandering, a stronger and more censorious term than *eccentric. Queer* is aside from the common in a way that is comical or perhaps slightly *ridiculous* or *mysterious. Quaint* denotes that which is pleasingly *odd* and fanciful, often with something of the antique; as, the *quaint* architecture of medieval towns. That which is *funny* is calculated to provoke laughter; that which is *droll* is more quietly amusing. That which is *grotesque* in the material sense is irregular or misshapen in form or outline or ill-proportioned so as to be somewhat *ridiculous*; the French *bizarre* is practically equivalent to *grotesque.* See ODD. *Antonyms*: common, customary, familiar, natural, normal, ordinary, regular, usual.

quell (kwel) *v.t.* **1** To put down or suppress

by force; extinguish. 2 To quiet; allay, as pain. [OE *cwellan* kill] —**quell′er** *n.*
Quel·part (kwel′pärt) A former name for CHEJU.
quel·que chose (kel′kə shōz′) *French* A trifle; something.
quench (kwench) *v.t.* 1 To put out or extinguish, as a fire. 2 To put an end to; cause to cease. 3 To slake or satisfy (thirst). 4 To suppress or repress, as emotions. 5 To cool, as heated iron or steel, by thrusting into water or other liquid. [ME *cwenken*] —**quench′a·ble** *adj.* —**quench′er** *n.*
quench·less (kwench′lis) *adj.* Incapable of being quenched; insatiable; irrepressible. —**quench′less·ly** *adv.* —**quench′less·ness** *n.*
que·nelle (kə·nel′) *n. French* A ball of savory paste made of minced meat, as chicken, veal, or fish, with bread crumbs and egg, usually poached.
Quen·tin (kwen′tin) A masculine personal name. [<L, fifth]
quer·ce·tin (kwûr′sə·tin) *n. Biochem.* A yellow crystalline compound, $C_{15}H_{10}O_7 \cdot H_2O$, found in the bark of the American oak and in the rind of certain fruits: used as a base for dyestuffs. [Prob. <L *quercus* oak + -IN] —**quer·cet·ic** (kwər·set′ik, -sē′tik) *adj.*
quer·cine (kwûr′sin, -sīn) *adj.* Of or pertaining to oaks. [<LL *quercinus* <L *quercus* oak]
quer·cit·rin (kwûr′sit′rin) *n. Biochem.* A yellow crystalline glycoside, $C_{21}H_{20}O_{11} \cdot 2H_2O$, contained in quercitron bark. Also **quer′cit·rine.**
quer·cit·ron (kwûr′sit·ron) *n.* 1 The crushed and powdered inner bark of the American black oak *(Quercus velutina),* used in dyeing and tanning. 2 The yellow dye made therefrom. 3 The dyer's oak *(Q. coccinea).* [<L *quercus* oak + CITRON]
Quer·cus (kwûr′kəs) *n.* A genus of hardwood trees and shrubs of the beech family, widely distributed in north temperate regions; the oaks. [<NL <L, an oak]
Que·ré·ta·ro (kā·rā′tä·rō) A state in central Mexico; 4,432 square miles; capital, Querétaro.
que·ri·da (kā·rē′dä) *n. fem. SW U.S.* A beloved; a darling. [<Sp.]
que·rist (kwir′ist) *n.* An inquirer; questioner.
querl (kwûrl) *v.t.* & *n. U.S. Dial.* Curl; twist: also spelled *quirl.* [? <G]
quern (kwûrn) *n.* 1 An old form of hand mill for grinding grain. 2 A small hand mill for grinding spices. [OE *cweorn*]
quer·u·lous (kwer′ə·ləs, -yə·ləs) *adj.* 1 Disposed to complain or be fretful; faultfinding. 2 Indicating or expressing a complaining or whining disposition. 3 Quarrelsome. [<LL *querulosus* <L *querulus* <*queri* complain] —**quer′u·lous·ly** *adv.* —**quer′u·lous·ness** *n.*
que·ry (kwir′ē) *v.* **·ried, ·ry·ing** *v.t.* 1 To inquire into; ask about. 2 To ask questions of; interrogate. 3 To express doubt concerning the correctness or truth of, especially, as in printing, by marking with a query. —*v.i.* 4 To have or express doubt; question. See synonyms under INQUIRE, QUESTION. [<*n.*] —*n. pl.* **·ries** 1 An inquiry, or a memorandum of an inquiry, to be answered; a question. 2 A doubt; interrogation: often indicated, as in printing, by the interrogation point (?). See synonyms under INQUIRY, QUESTION. [<L *quaere,* imperative sing. of *quaerere* ask]
Ques·nay (ke·nā′), **François,** 1694–1774, French physician and economist.
quest (kwest) *n.* 1 The act of seeking; a looking for something; a search, as an adventure or expedition in medieval romance; also, the person or persons making the search. 2 *Rare* An inquest. —*v.i.* 1 To go on a quest. 2 To make a search. 3 To search for game; also, to bay on the trail of game: said of hunting dogs. —*v.t.* 4 To search for; seek. [<OF *queste* <L *quaesitus,* pp. of *quaerere* ask, seek] —**quest′er** *n.*
ques·tion (kwes′chən) *n.* 1 An interrogative sentence calling for an answer; an inquiry. 2 A subject of inquiry or debate; a matter to be decided; a point at issue; problem. 3 A subject of dispute; a controversy; difference: A *question* rose about it. 4 A proposition under discussion in a deliberative assembly. 5 Objection raised or entertained; doubt: a statement accepted without *question.* 6 Interrogation: the act of asking or inquiring. —*v.t.* 1 To put a question or questions to; interrogate. 2 To be uncertain of; doubt. 3 To make objection to; challenge; dispute. —*v.i.* 4 To ask a question or questions. [<AF *questiun* <L *quaestio, -onis* <*quaerere* ask] —**ques′tion·er** *n.*

Synonyms (noun): doubt, inquiry, inquisition, interrogation, interrogatory, investigation, query. An *inquiry* seeks information for the benefit of the inquirer; a *question* may do the same, or may have the intent to perplex, confuse, or entrap the one of whom it is asked; one makes *inquiry* as to his way; we speak of idle or frivolous *questions* rather than of idle or frivolous *inquiries.* A *query* is a *question* more or less vaguely formulated and indefinite in purpose, often amounting to no more than a suspense of judgment. An *interrogation* or *interrogatory* is a formal *inquiry. Interrogatory* has a special legal use, denoting an *inquiry* in writing by order of a court, to be answered under oath. An *investigation* is an elaborate search for truth or fact, not only by *questions,* but by every other means of procuring information; an *inquisition* is an *investigation* which is either unwarranted, unduly minute, or in some other way offensive. See DOUBT, INQUIRY, TOPIC.

Synonyms (verb): ask, challenge, dispute, doubt, inquire, interrogate, investigate, query, quiz. To *ask* is to seek information, favor, or aid; *inquire, question, interrogate,* respect only the obtaining of information. To *interrogate* is to *examine* formally or officially, commonly by a series of questions. One may *inquire* casually and indifferently; he *questions* intently and resolutely. *Question* also has nearly the meaning of *challenge*; as, "I *question* that statement." See INQUIRE.

ques·tion·a·ble (kwes′chən·ə·bəl) *adj.* 1 Liable to be called in question; debatable; open to question or to suspicions; dubious; suspicious: *questionable* motives. 2 Of doubtful meaning; difficult to decide. 3 *Obs.* Capable of being questioned or inquired of. See synonyms under EQUIVOCAL. —**ques′tion·a·ble·ness, ques′tion·a·bil′i·ty** *n.* —**ques′tion·a·bly** *adv.*
ques·tion·ar·y (kwes′chən·er′ē) *adj.* Of the nature of an examination; interrogatory. —*n. pl.* **·ar·ies** A questionnaire.
ques·tion·less (kwes′chən·lis) *adj.* Unquestionable; indubitable; also, unquestioning. —**ques′tion·less·ly** *adv.*
question mark 1 An interrogation point (?). 2 Something open to question; an unknown.
ques·tion·naire (kwes′chə·nâr′) *n.* A written or printed form comprising a series of questions submitted to a number of persons in order to obtain data for a survey or report. [<F]
ques·tor (kwes′tər) See QUAESTOR.
Quet·ta (kwet′ə) 1 A commissioners' division of west central West Pakistan, near the border of Afghanistan; 35,027 square miles. 2 The leading city of this division, formerly capital of the former province of Baluchistan, included, October, 1955, in the province of West Pakistan.
quet·zal (ket·säl′) *n. pl.* **·zal·es** (-sä′lās) 1 A trogon *(Pharomacrus mocinno)* of brilliant plumage, the national symbol of Guatemala, and anciently regarded as a deity by the Mayas, whose chiefs alone were permitted to wear its plumes. 2 A silver coin, the monetary unit of Guatemala. Also **que·zal** (kā·säl′). [<Sp. <Nahuatl]

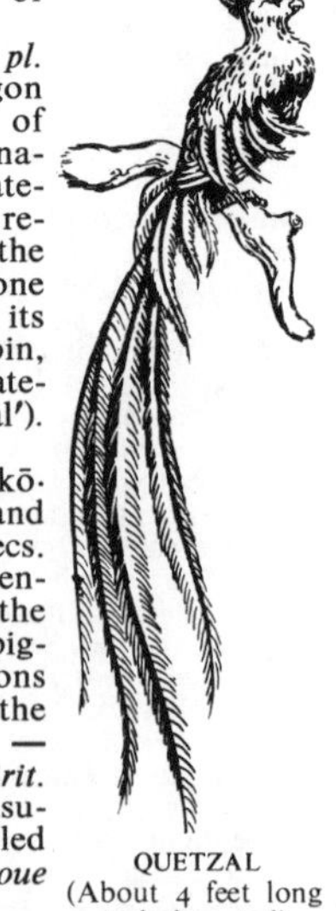
QUETZAL
(About 4 feet long including tail)

Quet·zal·co·a·tl (ket·säl′kō·at′l) A traditional god and heroic figure of the Aztecs.
queue (kyōō) *n.* 1 A pendent braid of hair on the back of the head; a pigtail. 2 A line of persons or vehicles waiting in the order of their arrival. —*v.i.* **queued, queu·ing** *Brit.* To form such a line: usually with *up.* Also spelled *cue.* [<F <OF *coe, coue* <L *cauda* a tail]
que vou·lez–vous (kə vōō·lā·vōō′) *French* What do you want? What can you expect?: an expression of indifference or cynicism.
Que·zal·te·nan·go (kā·säl′tā·näng′gō) The second largest city of Guatemala, in the SW part of the western highlands.
Que·zon (kā′zon, *Sp.* kā′sôn, -thôn), **Manuel Luis,** 1878–1944, Filipino statesman; first president of the Philippines, 1935–1944. Also **Que·zon y Mo·li·na** (kā′sôn ē mō·lē′nä).
Que·zon City (kā′sôn, -thôn) The capital (since 1948) of the Philippines, in southern Luzon, NE of Manila.
quib·ble (kwib′əl) *n.* 1 An evasion of a point or question; an equivocation. 2 *Rare* A pun. —*v.i.* **·bled, ·bling** To use quibbles; evade the truth or the point in question. [<obs. *quib* <L *quibus,* ablative pl. of *qui* who, which; with ref. to its use in legal documents] —**quib′bler** *n.*
Qui·be·ron (kēb·rôn′) A town at the southern end of **Quiberon Peninsula,** which projects seven miles into the Bay of Biscay from Brittany, France, nearly enclosing **Quiberon Bay.**
quiche (kēsh) *n.* Any of various non–dessert, custardlike pies, having meat, cheese, vegetables, etc., as principal ingredients. [<F]
Qui·ché (kē·chā′) *n.* 1 An Indian of a tribe of Mayan linguistic stock inhabiting Guatemala. 2 The Mayan language of this tribe.
quick (kwik) *adj.* 1 Done or occurring in a short time; expeditious; brisk; rapid; swift; speedy. 2 Characterized by rapidity or readiness of movement or action; nimble; prompt. 3 Sharp; steep, as a curve. 4 Alert; sensitive; perceptive: a *quick* ear; *quick* wit. 5 Responding readily to impressions; excitable; hasty. 6 Having life; living: opposed to *dead*: an archaic use. 7 Pregnant; with child. 8 Burning briskly; fiery. 9 Shifting; moving: said of soil or sand. 10 Refreshing; bracing. See synonyms under ACTIVE, ALIVE, CLEVER, IMPETUOUS, NIMBLE, SWIFT[1], VIVID. —*n.* 1 That which has life; those who are alive: chiefly in the phrase **the quick and the dead.** 2 The living flesh; any vital or tender part; especially, the tender flesh under a nail; hence, the feelings: cut to the *quick.* 3 A hedge plant; quickset. —*adv.* Quickly; rapidly. [OE *cwic* alive]
quick assets Assets which are readily convertible into cash; liquid assets.
quick bread Any bread, biscuits, etc., whose leavening agent makes immediate baking possible.
quick–break (kwik′brāk′) *n. Electr.* A current switch equipped with a spring or other device to permit rapid contact–opening independent of the operator.
quick·en (kwik′ən) *v.t.* 1 To cause to move more rapidly; hasten or accelerate. 2 To make alive or quick; give or restore life to. 3 To excite or arouse; stimulate: to *quicken* the appetite. —*v.i.* 4 To move or act more quickly; become more rapid. 5 To come or return to life; revive. 6 To reach the stage of pregnancy at which the motions of the fetus first become perceptible: said of the mother. 7 To begin to manifest signs of life: said of the fetus. —**quick′en·er** *n.*

Synonyms: accelerate, advance, dispatch, drive, expedite, facilitate, further, hasten, hurry, promote, speed, urge. To *quicken* is to increase speed, move or cause to move more rapidly, as through more space or with a greater number of motions in the same time. To *accelerate* is to increase the speed of action or of motion. A motion whose speed increases upon itself is said to be *accelerated,* as the motion of a falling body, which becomes swifter with every second of time. To *accelerate* any work is to *hasten* it toward a finish. To *dispatch* is to do and be done with, to get a thing off one's hands. To *dispatch* an enemy is to kill him outright and quickly; to *dispatch* a messenger is to send him in haste; to *dispatch* a business is to bring it quickly to an end. To *promote* a cause is in any way to bring it forward, *advance* it in power, prominence, etc. To *speed* is really to secure swiftness; to *hasten* is to attempt it, whether successfully or unsuccessfully. *Hurry* always indicates something of confusion. To *facilitate* is to *quicken* by making easy; to *expedite* is to *quicken* by removing hindrances. *Antonyms*: check, clog, delay, drag, hinder, impede, obstruct, retard.
quick fire The firing of quick successive shots:

faster than *rapid fire*, and used chiefly against moving or bobbing targets. **—quick-fire** (kwik′fīr′) *adj.*

quick-fir·ing (kwik′fīr′ing) *adj.* Able to fire shots rapidly and continuously.

quick-freeze (kwik′frēz′) *v.t.* **-froze, -fro·zen, -freez·ing** To subject (food) to rapid refrigeration for storing at or below freezing temperatures. **—quick′-fro′zen** *adj.*

quick·grass (kwik′gras′, -gräs′) *n.* Couchgrass.

quick·ie (kwik′ē) *n. U.S. Slang* Anything done hastily, as by short cuts or makeshift methods.

quick·lime (kwik′līm′) *n.* Unslaked lime. See LIME[1].

quick·ly (kwik′lē) *adv.* In a quick manner; rapidly; soon.

quick march A march in quick time; quickstep.

quick·match (kwik′mach′) *n.* A cord impregnated with black powder and used as a fast-burning fuse for flares, fireworks, etc.

quick·ness (kwik′nis) *n.* **1** The state or quality of being quick; speed; celerity; liveliness; readiness. **2** Acuteness of perception or sensibility; sharpness; keenness.

quick·sand (kwik′sand′) *n.* A bed of sand so water-soaked as readily to engulf any person or animal that attempts to move or rest upon it.

quick·set (kwik′set′) *n.* **1** A hedge plant, especially hawthorn. **2** A hedge made of it. *—adj.* Composed of quickset.

quick·sil·ver (kwik′sil′vər) *n.* **1** Metallic mercury: widely used in metallurgy, industry, and the arts. All of its compounds are poisonous. **2** An amalgam of tin, used for the backs of mirrors. [Trans. of L *argentum vivum*]

quick·step (kwik′step′) *n.* A march or dance written in a rapid tempo; also, a quick march.

quick-tem·pered (kwik′tem′pərd) *adj.* Easily angered.

quick time A marching step of 120 paces a minute, each pace of 30 inches: used in military drills and ceremonies.

quick·wa·ter (kwik′wô′tər, -wot′ər) *n.* A stream or that part of a stream having a decided current.

quick-wit·ted (kwik′wit′id) *adj.* Having a ready wit or quick discernment; keen; alert. See synonyms under CLEVER, SAGACIOUS. **—quick′-wit′ted·ly** *adv.* **—quick′-wit′ted·ness** *n.*

qui·cun·que vult (kwī·kung′kwē vult) *Latin* Whosoever will. See ATHANASIAN CREED.

quid[1] (kwid) *n.* **1** A small portion of chewing tobacco. **2** A cud, as of a cow. [Var. of CUD]

quid[2] (kwid) *n. Brit. Slang* In England, a pound sterling, or a sovereign. [Origin uncertain]

Quid·de (kvid′ə), **Ludwig,** 1858–1941, German historian and pacifist.

quid·di·ty (kwid′ə·tē) *n. pl.* **·ties 1** The essence of a thing. **2** A subtle or trifling distinction or objection; cavil. [<LL *quidditas, -tatis* <L *quid* which, what]

quid·nunc (kwid′nungk′) *n.* One who seeks or affects to know all that is going on; an inquisitive busybody. [<L *quid nunc* what now]

quid pro quo (kwid′ prō kwō′) *Latin* **1** Something for something; an equivalent in return. **2** Formerly, one medicine used in place of another; hence, a substitution.

quién sa·be (kyen sä′vā) *Spanish* Literally, "who knows?": used to mean, in reply to a question, "I do not know," or "I do not care to say."

qui·es·cent (kwī·es′ənt, kwē-) *adj.* **1** Being in a state of repose or inaction; quiet; still. **2** Resting free from anxiety, emotion, or agitation. **3** *Phonet.* In Semitic languages, having no sound; silent. See synonyms under PASSIVE. [<L *quiescens, -entis,* ppr. of *quiescere* be quiet] **—qui·es′cence** *n.* **—qui·es′cent·ly** *adv.*

qui·et (kwī′ət) *adj.* **1** Being in a state of repose; still; calm; motionless. **2** Free from turmoil, strife, or alarm; tranquil; peaceful. **3** Silent. **4** Gentle or mild of disposition. **5** Undisturbed by din or bustle; retired; secluded: a *quiet* nook. **6** Restful to the eye; soft in hue; hence, not showy or obtrusive, as dress. See synonyms under CALM, PACIFIC, SEDATE, SOBER. *—n.* The condition or quality of being free from motion, disturbance, noise, etc.; peace; calm. See synonyms under REST[1]. *—v.t. & v.i.* To make or become quiet: often with *down.* See synonyms under ALLAY, REPRESS, SETTLE, TRANQUILIZE. *—adv.* In a quiet or peaceful manner. [<OF *quiete* <L *quietus* < *quies* rest, repose. Doublet of COY.] **—qui′et·ly** *adv.* **—qui′et·ness** *n.*

qui·et·en (kwī′ə·tən) *v.t. & v.i. Brit. or Dial.* To make or become quiet: often with *down.*

qui·et·ism (kwī′ə·tiz′əm) *n.* **1** The doctrine that spiritual exaltation is attained by self-abnegation and passive religious contemplation; especially, mystic meditation or introspection, as cultivated by certain devotees in the 17th century. **2** A state of quiet; quietude.

qui·et·ist (kwī′ə·tist) *n.* **1** An advocate or practicer of quietism. **2** One who seeks or enjoys quiet.

qui·e·tude (kwī′ə·tōōd, -tyōōd) *n.* A state or condition of calm or tranquillity; repose; rest.

qui·e·tus (kwī·ē′təs) *n.* **1** A silencing or suppressing; death; repose. **2** A final discharge or quittance; a settlement. **3** A killing blow. [<L *quietus est* he is quiet]

quill[1] (kwil) *n.* **1** *Ornithol.* One of the large, strong flight feathers or tail feathers of a bird. **2** A pen made from a feather; hence, any pen. **3** The hollow, horny stem of a feather; a calamus. **4** Such a stem used for a receptacle or measure, as for a drug, or as a plectrum for playing a stringed instrument. **5** *Zool.* One of the large, sharp spines of a porcupine or hedgehog. **6** A piece of cane or reed used as a musical pipe. **7** A slow-burning fuse made formerly of the quill of a feather filled with powder. **8** A piece of bark rolled into cylindrical form: a cinnamon *quill.* **9** A quill toothpick. **10** *Mech.* A hollow shaft, with or without openings, designed to revolve on a solid shaft when the clutches are engaged. **11** In weaving, a spindle or bobbin; pirn. **12** A fluted, rounded ridge, or cylindrical fold, as in a ruff or ruffle. *—v.t.* **1** To make or iron (a garment or fabric) with rounded plaits or ridges. **2** To wind (thread or yarn) on a quill or quills. *—v.i.* **3** To wind thread or yarn on a quill or quills. [Cf. LG *quiele* a quill of a feather]

quil·lai (ki·lī′) *n.* A large Chilean evergreen tree, the soapbark tree, whose alkaline inner bark (**quillai bark**) is used as medicine and as a substitute for soap: also spelled *cullay.* [<Sp. <Araucanian]

quill·back (kwil′bak′) *n.* A carplike fish *(Carpiodes velifer)* common in the Mississippi Valley.

quill·driv·er (kwil′drī′vər) *n. Colloq.* **1** One who writes; a literary hack. **2** Formerly, a clerk; copyist.

Quil·ler-Couch (kwil′ər·kōōch′), **Sir Arthur Thomas,** 1863–1944, English author and editor.

quil·let (kwil′it) *n. Obs.* A quibble; subtlety; nice distinction. [?Alter. of L *quidlibet* what you please < *quid* what + *libet* it pleases]

quill·pig (kwil′pig′) *n. U.S. Colloq.* A porcupine.

quill·wort (kwil′wûrt′) *n.* A small plant (genus *Isoetes*), found in marshes, pond edges, etc., consisting of a cormlike stem sending up a tuft of quill-like leaves.

Quil·mes (kēl′mās) A city on the Río de la Plata SE of Buenos Aires, Argentina.

quilt (kwilt) *n.* **1** A bedcover made by stitching together firmly two layers of cloth or patchwork with some soft and warm substance (as wool or cotton) between them. **2** Any bedcover, especially if thick. **3** A quilted skirt or other quilted article. **4** *Obs.* A mattress. *—v.t.* **1** To stitch together (two pieces of material) with a soft substance between. **2** To stitch in ornamental patterns or crossing lines. **3** To sew up or secure between two layers. **4** To pad or line with something soft. *—v.i.* **5** To make a quilt or quilted work. [<OF *cuilte* <L *culcita*]

quilt·ing (kwil′ting) *n.* **1** The act or process of making a quilt, or of stitching as in making a quilt. **2** Material for quiltwork. **3** A quilting bee or party.

quilting bee A social gathering of the women of a community for working on a quilt or quilts. Also **quilting frolic, quilting party.**

quin·a·crine (kwin′ə·krēn) *n.* Atabrine.

qui·na·ry (kwī′nər·ē) *adj.* Consisting of or containing five parts or elements; arranged by fives, or in sets or groups of five. *—n. pl.* **·ries** A number, body, group, or system of five; something composed of five like parts. [<L *quinarius* < *quini* five each]

qui·nate (kwī′nāt, kwin′āt) *adj.* **1** Arranged in five. **2** *Bot.* Having five similar parts together, as the five leaflets of the Virginia creeper. [<L *quini* five each < *quinque* five]

quince (kwins) *n.* **1** The hard, acid, applelike, yellowish fruit, used for preserves, of a small deciduous Asian tree *(Cydonia oblonga)* of the rose family. **2** The tree. [Orig. pl. of obs. *coyn* <OF *cooin* <L *cotoneum,* var. of *(malum) cydonium* (apple) of Cydonia <Gk. *Kydōnia,* a town in Crete]

quin·cun·cial (kwin·kun′shəl) *adj.* **1** Arranged in the form of a quincunx. **2** *Bot.* Arranged in a set of five, as leaves. Also **quin·cunx′ial** (-kungk′shəl). **—quin·cun′cial·ly** *adv.*

quin·cunx (kwin′kungks) *n.* **1** An arrangement of five things, as trees, in a square having one in each corner and one in the center. **2** A disposition of such squares repeated indefinitely. **3** A quincuncial arrangement, as of flower parts. [<L *quincunx* five twelfths < *quinque* five + *uncia* twelfth part]

Quin·cy (kwin′sē), **Josiah,** 1744–75, American statesman and Revolutionary leader.

Quin·cy (kwin′sē) A city in eastern Massachusetts south of Boston.

quin·dec·a·gon (kwin·dek′ə·gon) *n. Geom.* A figure, especially a plane figure, with fifteen sides and fifteen angles. [<L *quindecim* fifteen + Gk. *gōnia* angle]

quin·de·cen·ni·al (kwin′di·sen′ē·əl) *n.* A fifteenth anniversary. *—adj.* Of or pertaining to the fifteenth anniversary. [<L *quindecim* fifteen + *annus* year]

quin·dec·i·mal (kwin·des′ə·məl) *adj.* Fifteen. [<L *quindecim* fifteen]

quin·ic (kwin′ik) *adj.* Of, pertaining to, or derived from quinine.

quinic acid *Chem.* A white crystalline compound, $C_7H_{12}O_6$, contained in cinchona bark, coffee beans, etc.

quin·i·dine (kwin′ə·dēn, -din) *n. Chem.* A white crystalline alkaloid, $C_{20}H_{24}N_2O_2$, isomeric with quinine, contained in certain cinchona barks. It is used in medicine to regulate the heartbeat, and its sulfate is officinal.

qui·nine (kwī′nīn, *esp. Brit.* kwi·nēn′) *n. Chem.* A white, amorphous or slightly crystalline, very bitter alkaloid, $C_{20}H_{24}N_2O_2$, contained in cinchona barks. Its salts, as the hydrochlorate, sulfate, and others, are largely used in medicine on account of their tonic and antipyretic qualities, especially in malarial affections of all kinds. Also **quin·in** (kwin′in). [< earlier *quina* (<Sp. <Quechua *kina* bark) + -INE[2]]

quin·nat (kwin′at) *n.* A salmon *(Oncorhynchus tschawytscha)* of the coasts of the North Pacific: also called *Chinook salmon.* [<Chinook *ikwána*]

quin·oid (kwin′oid) *adj.* Having a quinone nucleus.

qui·noi·dine (kwi·noi′dēn, -din) *n. Chem.* A brown, resinous, amorphous compound, consisting chiefly of uncrystallizable products of cinchona bark: a cheap substitute for real quinine. Also **qui·noi′din** (-din).

quin·o·line (kwin′ə·lēn, -lin) *n. Chem.* **1** A colorless liquid compound, C_9H_7N, with a tarry odor, obtained variously, as by distilling quinine, cinchonine, or by the destructive distillation of coal and bones. **2** Any of a class of quinoline derivatives, among which are many dyes and medicinal compounds. Also **quin′o·lin** (-lin).

qui·none (kwi·nōn′, kwin′ōn) *n. Chem.* Either of two isomeric compounds obtained from benzene and its homologs; especially, a golden-yellow crystalline compound, $C_6H_4O_2$, with pungent odor, formed variously, as by the oxidation of quinic acid, aniline, etc.: also called *paraquinone.*

qui·non·i·mine (kwi·non′ə·mēn, -min) *n. Chem.* A crystalline organic compound, C_5H_5NO, derived from a quinone through replacement of an oxygen atom by an imine. See INDOPHENOL.

quin·o·noid (kwin′ə·noid) *adj.* Resembling or like quinone.

quin·ox·a·line (kwin·ok′sə·lēn, -lin) *n. Chem.*

A fully basic, white, crystalline compound, $C_8H_6N_2$, used in organic synthesis.

quin·qua·ge·nar·i·an (kwin′kwə·jə·nâr′ē·ən) *adj.* Being fifty years old; relating to this age. —*n.* A person fifty years old.

quin·qua·gen·a·ry (kwin′kwə·jen′ər·ē) *adj.* **1** Consisting of or containing fifty. **2** Denoting a group or set of fifty. [<L *quinquagenarius* < *quinquageni* fifty each]

quin·qua·ges·i·ma (kwin′kwə·jes′ə·mə) *adj.* Fiftieth. —*n.* A period of fifty days. [<L *quinquagesima (dies)* fiftieth (day)]

quin·qua·ges·i·mal (kwin′kwə·jes′ə·məl) *adj.* Of, pertaining to, comprising, or containing fifty.

Quinquagesima Sunday The fiftieth day before Easter; the Sunday before Lent; Shrove Sunday.

quinque– *combining form* Five: *quinquefoliate.* Also, before vowels, **quinqu–.** [<L *quinque* five]

quin·que·fo·li·ate (kwin′kwə·fō′lē·it, -āt) *adj. Bot.* Five–leaved. Also **quin′que·fo′li·o·late′** (-fō′lē·ə·lāt′). [<QUINQUE- + L *foliatus* < *folium* leaf]

quin·quen·ni·al (kwin·kwen′ē·əl) *adj.* Occurring every five years, or once in five years; also, lasting five years. —*n.* **1** A fifth anniversary or its celebration. **2** A quinquennium. [<L *quinque* five + *annus* year]

quin·quen·ni·um (kwin·kwen′ē·əm) *n.* A period of five years. [<L]

quin·que·va·lent (kwin′kwə·vā′lənt) *adj. Chem.* Having a valence or combining value of five; pentavalent. See VALENCE. —**quin′que·va′·lence** *n.*

quin·sy (kwin′zē) *n. Pathol.* Inflammation of the tonsils and the adjoining tissues, especially when suppurative. [<Med. L *quinancia* <Gk. *kynanchē* a dog's collar < *kyōn* dog + *anchein* choke]

quint (kwint) *n.* **1** A fifth. **2** A set of five. **3** The E string of a violin. **4** *Colloq.* A quintuplet. **5** In piquet, a sequence of five of the same suit: if of the five highest cards, called a **quint major.** **6** An organ stop giving tones a fifth above those of the keys that are pressed. [<L *quintus* < *quinque* five]

quin·tain (kwin′tin) *n. Obs.* An object set up to be tilted at; also, the place for the sport. [OF *quintaine* <L *quintana* street in a camp < *quintus* fifth]

quin·tal (kwin′təl) *n.* A measure of weight, a hundredweight; in the metric system, 100 kilograms: also called *metric centner.* See METRIC SYSTEM. [<OF <Arabic *qinṭar*]

quin·tan (kwin′tən) *adj.* Recurring on every fifth day, reckoning inclusively: a *quintan* fever. —*n.* A quintan fever. [<L *quintanus* < *quintus* fifth]

Quin·ta·na Ro·o (kēn·tä′nä rō′ō) A territory in the eastern part of the Yucatán peninsula, Mexico; 19,625 square miles; capital, Chetumal.

Quin·te·ro (kēn·tā′rō), **Alvarez** See ALVAREZ QUINTERO.

quin·tes·sence (kwin·tes′əns) *n.* **1** An extract from anything, containing in concentrated form its most essential principle. **2** The purest and most essential part, manifestation, or embodiment of anything. **3** *Philos.* In the doctrine of the Pythagoreans, the fifth or celestial essence, ether, above the four elements of earth, air, fire, and water. [<F <L *quinta essentia* fifth essence] —**quin′tes·sen′tial** *adj.*

quin·tet (kwin·tet′) *n.* **1** A musical composition arranged for five voices or instruments; also, the five persons performing it. **2** Any group of five; anything arranged for a set of five performers, as in a game. Also **quin·tette′.** [<Ital. *quintetto* < *quinto* fifth]

quin·tic (kwin′tik) *Math. adj.* Denoting a quantic function of the fifth degree. —*n.* Such a function.

quin·tile (kwin′til) *n.* **1** In astrology, the aspect of planets separated by 72°, or the fifth part of the zodiac. **2** *Stat.* **a** That part of a frequency distribution containing one fifth of the total observations or cases. **b** The point marking such a part. [<L *quintus* fifth, on analogy with *quartile*]

Quin·til·i·an (kwin·til′ē·ən, -til′yən), A.D. 35?–95?, Roman rhetorician: full name *Marcus Fabius Quintilianus.*

quin·til·lion (kwin·til′yən) *n.* In the French system of numeration, almost universally followed in the United States, 1 followed by 18 ciphers; in the English system, 1 followed by 30 ciphers. [<L *quintus* fifth + MILLION] —**quin·til′lionth** (-yənth) *adj.* & *n.*

quin·tin (kwin′tin) *n. Rare* A fine linen fabric. Also **quin′tain** (-tin). [from *Quintin,* a town in Brittany]

quin·tu·ple (kwin′tŏŏ·pəl, -tyŏŏ-, kwin·tŏŏ′pəl, -tyŏŏ′-) *v.t.* & *v.i.* **·pled, ·pling** To multiply by five; make or become five times as large. [< *adj.*] —*adj.* **1** Consisting of five united or of five parts. **2** Multiplied by five. —*n.* A number or a sum five times as great as another. [<F <L *quintuplex* < *quintus* fifth + *plic-,* stem of *plicare* fold]

quin·tu·plet (kwin′tŏŏ·plit, -tyŏŏ-, kwin·tŏŏ′·plit, -tyŏŏ′-) *n.* **1** Five things of a kind used or occurring together. **2** One of five born of the same mother at one birth.

quin·tu·pli·cate (kwin·tŏŏ′plə·kit, -tyŏŏ′-) *adj.* **1** Fivefold. **2** Raised to the fifth power. —*v.t.* & *v.i.* (-kāt) **·cat·ed, ·cat·ing** To multiply by five; quintuple. —*n.* (-kit) One of five identical things. [<L *quintuplex, -icis* + -ATE[1]] —**quin·tu′pli·cate·ly** *adv.* —**quin·tu′·pli·ca′tion** *n.*

quip (kwip) *n.* **1** A sarcastic or sharp jest, remark, or retort; gibe; also, a clever or witty sally without sarcasm. **2** A quibble. **3** An odd, fantastic action or object. —*v.i.* **quipped, quip·ping** To make a witty remark; jest. [Earlier *quippy* <L *quippe* indeed] —**quip′pish** *adj.*

quip·ster (kwip′stər) *n.* One who makes quips.

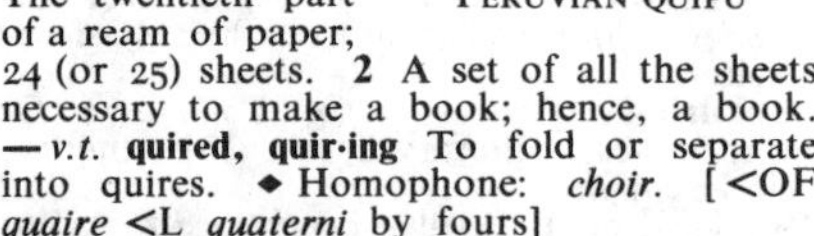

PERUVIAN QUIPU

qui·pu (kē′pōō, kwip′·ōō) *n.* An aboriginal Peruvian device for recording and conveying information, consisting of a series of varicolored and knotted strings tied at one end to a thicker cord. The order, color, and knots of the strings were used like elements of a written language. Also **quip′pu.** [<Quechua *quipu* knot]

quire[1] (kwīr) *n.* **1** The twentieth part of a ream of paper; 24 (or 25) sheets. **2** A set of all the sheets necessary to make a book; hence, a book. —*v.t.* **quired, quir·ing** To fold or separate into quires. ◆ Homophone: *choir.* [<OF *quaire* <L *quaterni* by fours]

quire[2] (kwīr) See CHOIR.

Quir·i·nal (kwir′ə·nəl) **1** One of the seven hills on which Rome stands, containing the **Quirinal palace,** formerly a papal residence; after 1870 the official residence of the kings of Italy. **2** Figuratively, the monarchical regime of Italy, as distinguished from the *Vatican,* or papal government. —*adj.* Pertaining to or situated on the Quirinal.

Qui·ri·no (kē·rē′nō), **Elpidio,** 1890–1956, president of the Philippines 1948–54.

Qui·ri·nus (kwi·rī′nəs) An ancient Italic god of war: ultimately identified with the deified *Romulus.*

Qui·ri·tes (kwi·rī′tēz) *n. pl.* The citizens of ancient Rome in their civil as distinguished from their military or political capacity. [<L]

quirk (kwûrk) *n.* **1** A short or sharp turn; twist. **2** A quaint turn of the fancy; bright retort; hence, a personal peculiarity; caprice. **3** An artful turn for evasion or subterfuge; quibble. **4** A sudden curve or flourish, especially in drawing or writing. **5** *Archit.* **a** A small groove in, beside, or between moldings or beads. **b** A molding or bead having a groove on one or both edges. See synonyms under WHIM. [Origin uncertain]

quirk·y (kwûrk′ē) *adj.* **quirk·i·er, quirk·i·est** Peculiar, unpredictable, and idiosyncratic: a *quirky* individual. —**quirk′i·ly** *adv.* —**quirk′·i·ness** *n.*

quirl (kwûrl) See QUERL.

quirt (kwûrt) *n.* A short–handled riding whip with a braided rawhide lash. —*v.t.* To strike with a quirt. [<Mexican Sp. *cuarta*]

quish (kwish) See CUISH.

quis·ling (kwiz′ling) *n.* One who betrays his country to the enemy and is then given political power by the conquerors. [after Vidkun *Quisling,* 1887–1945, Norwegian Nazi party leader and traitor] —**quis′ling·ism** *n.*

quit (kwit) *v.* **quit** or **quit·ted, quit·ting** *v.t.* **1** To cease or desist from; discontinue. **2** To give up; renounce; relinquish. **3** To go away from; leave. **4** To let go of (something held). **5** *Archaic* To acquit (oneself). —*v.i.* **6** To stop; cease; discontinue. **7** To leave; depart. **8** *Colloq.* To resign from a position, etc. See synonyms under ABANDON, CEASE, END, REQUITE. —*adj.* Released, relieved, or absolved from something, as a duty, obligation, encumbrance, or debt; clear; free; rid. —*n.* The act of quitting. —**to be quits** To be even (with another). —**to cry quits** To declare to be even, or that neither has the advantage; declare (oneself) willing to stop competing. [<OF *quiter* <LL *quietare* set free <L *quies* rest, repose]

quitch·grass (kwich′gras′, -gräs′) *n.* Couch-grass. Also **quitch.**

quit·claim (kwit′klām′) *n. Law* A full release and acquittance given by one to another in regard to a certain demand, suit, or right of action: also **quit′claim′ance.** —*v.t.* To relinquish or give up claim or title to; release from a claim. [<QUIT + CLAIM]

quitclaim deed A conveyance, in the nature of a release, of all the maker's interest in the land in question, but not professing that the title is valid, nor containing any warranty or covenants for title.

quite (kwīt) *adv.* **1** To the fullest extent; without limitation or reservation; fully; totally: *quite* dead. **2** *Colloq.* To a great or considerable extent; noticeably; very: *quite* ill. [ME; var. of QUIT, *adj.*]

Qui·to (kē′tō) The capital of Ecuador; 9,343 feet above sea level in the Andes of north central Ecuador.

quit–quit (kwit′kwit′) *n.* The honey creeper.

quit–rent (kwit′rent′) *n.* A fixed rent formerly paid by a freeholder, whereby he was released from feudal services.

quit·tance (kwit′ns) *n.* **1** Discharge or release, as from a debt or obligation; acquittance. **2** Something given or tendered by way of requital; repayment. [<F < *quiter* QUIT]

quit·ter[1] (kwit′ər) *n.* One who quits needlessly; a shirker; slacker; coward.

quit·ter[2] (kwit′ər) *n.* **1** A fistulous sore on the hoof of a horse or any solid–hoofed animal: also **quit′ter·bone′** (-bōn′), **quit′tor.** **2** Purulent matter. [? <OF *quiture* a cooking]

qui va là? (kē vȧ lȧ′) *French* Who goes there?: a watchword.

quiv·er[1] (kwiv′ər) *v.i.* To shake with a slight, tremulous motion; vibrate; tremble. See synonyms under QUAKE, SHAKE. —*n.* The act or fact of quivering; a trembling or shaking. [Prob. related to QUAVER]

quiv·er[2] (kwiv′ər) *n.* A portable case or sheath for arrows; also, its contents. [<AF *quiveir,* OF *coivre* <Gmc.]

quiv·er[3] (kwiv′ər) *adj. Obs.* Brisk; active; nimble. [OE *cwifer-,* found in *cwiferlice* zealously]

Qui·vi·ra (kē·vē′rä) A land in the central United States, sought and found by Coronado in 1541: often identified with Kansas.

qui vive? (kē vēv′) *French* Literally, who lives?: as used by French sentinels, "Who goes there?" —**to be on the qui vive** To be on the look–out; be wide–awake.

quix·ot·ic (kwik·sot′ik) *adj.* Pertaining to or like Don Quixote, the hero of a Spanish romance ridiculing knight–errantry; hence, ridiculously chivalrous or romantic; having high but impractical sentiments, aims, etc.; extravagant; visionary. See synonyms under IMAGINARY. —**quix·ot′i·cal·ly** *adv.* —**quix·ot·ism** (kwik′sə·tiz′əm) *n.*

quiz (kwiz) *n. pl.* **quiz·zes** **1** The act of questioning; specifically, an oral or written examination of a class or individual. **2** Something or someone odd or ridiculous; an eccentric. **3** A hoax; practical joke. —*v.t.* **quizzed, quiz·zing** **1** To examine by asking questions; question. **2** *Brit.* To make fun of; ridicule. See synonyms under QUESTION. [Origin unknown] —**quiz′zer** *n.*

quiz program A television or radio program in which selected contestants or a panel of experts try to answer questions presented by the master of ceremonies.

quiz·zi·cal (kwiz′i·kəl) *adj.* **1** Addicted to quizzing or chaffing; bantering. **2** Queer; odd. —**quiz′zi·cal·ly** *adv.*

quizzing glass A monocle or single eyeglass.
Qum (ko͝om) A city in north central Iran. Also **Qom** (kōm).
quo' (kwō) *v. Scot.* Quoth.
quod (kwod) *n. Brit. Slang* A prison. Also spelled *quad.*
quod e·rat de·mon·stran·dum (kwod er′at dem′ən·stran′dəm) *Latin* Which was to be demonstrated: abbreviated *Q.E.D.*
quod·li·bet (kwod′li·bet) *n.* **1** A debatable or nice point; subtlety; especially, a scholarly dissertation on such a subject. **2** *Music* A fantasia or medley, usually humorous. [<L, anything at all] **—quod·li·bet·ic** (kwod′li·bet′ik) or **·i·cal** *adj.*
quod vi·de (kwod vī′dē) *Latin* Which see: usually abbreviated to *q.v.* and used in parentheses after a word by way of reference.
quo·hog (kwô′hôg, -hog, kwə·hôg′, -hog′) *n.* A quahaug.
quoin (koin, kwoin) *n.* **1** A large square ashlar or stone at the angle of a wall. **2** An external angle of a building. **3** A vertical, angular, ornamental projection from a wall face. **4** A wedge-shaped stone of an arch. **5** A block cut obliquely at the bottom to support a vertical column or pilaster on an inclined plane. **6** An internal angle, as of a room; a corner. **7** A wedge, or wedgelike piece. **8** *Printing* A wedge, or pair of wedges, by which to lock up type in a chase or galley. **—*v.t.*** To fasten or provide with a quoin or quoins. [Var. of COIN]

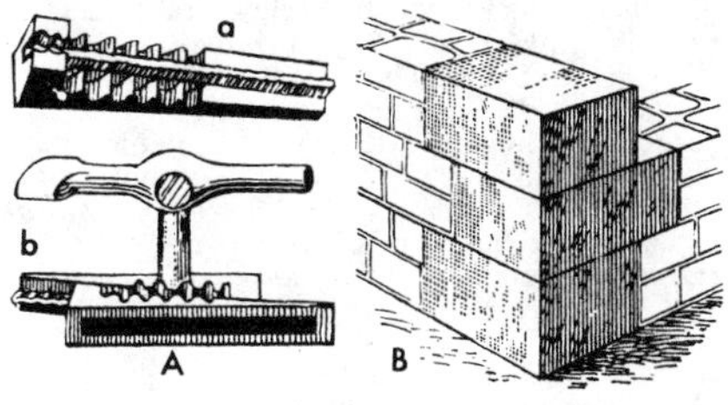

QUOINS

A. Printer's metal quoins.
a. Single quoin.
b. Pair of quoins ready for locking with key.
B. Quoins of dressed stone.

quoit (kwoit, *esp. Brit.* koit) *n.* **1** A disk of iron or other material with a round hole in the center to be thrown over a stake: used in the game of quoits. **2** *pl.* A game played by throwing these disks at a short stake. **—*v.t.*** To pitch as a quoit. [ME *coyte*; origin unknown]
quo ju·re (kwō jo͝or′ē) *Latin* By what right? By what law?
quoll (kwōl) *n.* Any of several carnivorous marsupials of Australia, as the **northern quoll** (*Satanellus hallucatus*).
quo·mo·do (kwō·mō′dō) *Latin adv.* In what manner? How? **—*n.*** The means; manner.
quon·dam (kwon′dəm) *adj.* Having been formerly; former. [<L]
Quon·set hut (kwon′·sit) A portable structure resembling the Nissen hut, designed for use by the U. S. armed services: a trade name. [from *Quonset,* a town in Rhode Island where first made]

QUONSET HUT

quo·rum (kwôr′əm, kwō′rəm) *n.* **1** Such a number of members of any deliberative or corporate body as is necessary for the legal transaction of business: commonly, a majority. **2** Formerly, in England, certain designated justices of the peace without the presence of some one of whom the others could not act: now applied loosely to all justices. **3** A select or chosen body. [<L, of whom < *qui* who]
quo·ta (kwō′tə) *n.* A proportional part or share required for making up a certain number or quantity; proportionate contribution. [<Med. L *quota (pars)* how great (a part) <L *quotus* how great]
quot·a·ble (kwō′tə·bəl) *adj.* Suitable for quotation. **—quot′a·bil′i·ty** *n.*
quo·ta·tion (kwō·tā′shən) *n.* **1** The act of quoting. **2** The words quoted or cited; a passage from a book or writing, cited or adduced. **3** A price quoted or current, as of securities, etc. [<Med. L *quotatio, -onis* < *quotare.* See QUOTE.] **—quo·ta′tion·al** *adj.* **—quo·ta′tion·al·ly** *adv.* **—quo·ta′tion·ist** *n.*
quotation mark One of the marks placed at the beginning and end of a quoted word or passage. In English usage, one or two inverted commas (‘,“) mark the beginning of a quotation, and, correspondingly, one or two apostrophes (’,”) the close, the single marks usually being used to set off a quotation within a quotation.
quote (kwōt) *v.* **quot·ed, quot·ing** *v.t.* **1** To repeat or reproduce the words of. **2** To repeat or cite (a rule, author, etc.), as for authority or illustration. **3** In commerce: **a** To state (a price). **b** To give the current or market price of. **4** *Printing* To enclose within quotation marks. **—*v.i.*** **5** To make a quotation, as from a book. **—*n.*** A quotation; also, a quotation mark. [<Med. L *quotare* distinguish by number <L *quot* how many] **—quot′a·ble** *adj.* **—quot′er** *n.* **—quote′·wor′thy** (-wûr′thē) *adj.* **—quot′ing·ly** *adv.*
Synonyms (verb): cite, excerpt, extract, paraphrase, plagiarize, recite, repeat. To *quote* is to give an author's words, either exactly, as in direct quotation, or in substance, as in indirect quotation; to *cite* is, etymologically, to call up a passage, as a witness is summoned. In *citing* a passage its exact location by chapter, page, or otherwise must be given, so that it can be promptly called into evidence; in *quoting,* the location may or may not be given, but the words or substance of the passage must be given. To *paraphrase* is to state an author's thought more freely than in indirect quotation, keeping the substance of his thought and his order of statement, but changing the language and style, and perhaps expanding by explanation, inference, etc. To *plagiarize* is to *quote* without credit, appropriating another's words or thought as one's own. To *recite* or *repeat* is usually to *quote* orally, but *recite* is applied in legal phrase to a particular statement of facts which is not a quotation.
quoth (kwōth) *v.t.* Said or spoke; uttered: the imperfect tense of the obsolete verb *queth,* used only in the first and third persons, the nominative always following the verb, as *quoth* he. [OE *cwæth,* pt. of *cwethan* say]
quo·tha (kwō′thə) *interj. Archaic* Indeed! forsooth!: usually in slight contempt. [<*quoth he*]
quo·tid·i·an (kwō·tid′ē·ən) *adj.* Recurring or occurring every day. **—*n.*** A fever whose paroxysms return every day. [<L *quotidianus* daily]
quo·tient (kwō′shənt) *n. Math.* The result obtained by division; a number indicating how many times one number or quantity is contained in another. [<L *quotiens* how often < *quot* how many]
quo war·ran·to (kwō wô·ran′tō, wo-) *Latin* Literally, by what warrant; a judicial writ commanding a person to show by what authority he exercises an office or franchise never granted or forfeited by some fault. In England, and generally in the United States, this writ has given way to an **information in the nature of a quo warranto,** criminal in form, but in substance civil.

R

r, R (är) *n. pl.* **r's, R's** or **rs, Rs, ars** (ärz) **1** The 18th letter of the English alphabet: from Phoenician *resh,* Greek *rho,* Roman *R.* **2** The sound of the letter *r.* See ALPHABET. **—*symbol*** **1** *Chem.* An organic radical. **2** *Math.* Ratio. **3** *Electr.* Resistance. **—the three R's** Reading, writing, and arithmetic (regarded humorously as spelled *reading, 'riting,* and *'rithmetic*); hence, the essential elements of a primary education.
Ra (rä) The supreme Egyptian deity, the sun-god, usually represented as a hawk-headed man crowned with the solar disk and uraeus: also spelled *Re.* [<Egyptian *Rā* the sun]

RA

Raab (räb) The German name for GYŐR, Hungary.
ra·ban·na (rə·ban′ə) *n.* A textile fabric of raffia, made in Madagascar and used for draperies, curtains, and the like. [<Malagasy *rebana*]
Ra·bat (rä·bät′) A port on the Atlantic, capital of Morocco.
ra·ba·to (rə·bā′tō, -bä′-) See REBATO.
Ra·baul (rə·boul′, rä′boul) The chief city of New Britain; formerly the administrative center of the Territory of New Guinea.
Rab·bath Am·mon (rab′əth am′ən) The Old Testament name for AMMAN.
rab·bet (rab′it) *n.* **1** A recess or groove in or near the edge of one piece of wood or other material to receive the edge of another piece. **2** A joint so made. **3** A rabbet plane. **—*v.*** **·bet·ed, ·bet·ing** *v.t.* **1** To cut a rectangular groove in. **2** To unite in a rabbet. **—*v.i.*** **3** To be jointed by a rabbet. Also spelled *rebate.* ◆ Homophone: *rabbit.* [<OF *rabat* < *rabattre* beat down. See REBATE.]

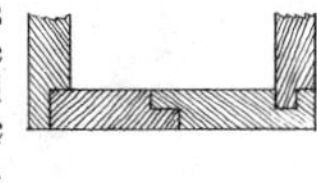

RABBET JOINTS

rabbet joint A joint between two edges, as of timbers, each of which is partly cut away so that their faces are flush.
rabbet plane A plane for cutting a rectangular groove, as in or near the edge of a plank.
rab·bi (rab′ī) *n. pl.* **·bis** Master, teacher: a Jewish title for those distinguished for learning, authoritative teachers of the Law, and appointed spiritual heads of a community. Also **rab′bin** (-in). [OE <L <Gk. *rhabbi* <Hebrew *rabbī* my master < *rab* great, master + *-i* my (pronominal suffix)]
rab·bin·ate (rab′in·āt) *n.* **1** The office or term of office of a rabbi. **2** Rabbis collectively. [<Med. L *rabbinus* rabbi]
Rab·bin·ic (rə·bin′ik) *n.* The language or dialect of the rabbis; especially, the Hebrew language as used in Biblical and Talmudic exegesis by Jewish scholars of the late ancient and early medieval periods.
rab·bin·i·cal (rə·bin′i·kəl) *adj.* Pertaining to the rabbis or to their opinions, languages, or writings. Also **rab·bin′ic.** **—rab·bin′i·cal·ly** *adv.*
rab·bin·ism (rab′in·iz′əm) *n.* **1** The teachings or doctrines of the rabbis. **2** A rabbinical phrase, expression, or idiom.
rab·bin·ist (rab′in·ist) *n.* One among the Jews who adhered to the Talmud and the

traditions of the rabbis, in opposition to those who rejected the traditions. Also **rab′bin·ite** (-īt). [<Med. L *rabbinus*] — **rab′bin·is′tic, rab′bin·is′ti·cal, rab′bin·it′ic** (-it′ik) *adj.* — **rab′bin·is′ti·cal·ly** *adv.*

rab·bit (rab′it) *n.* **1** Any of various small burrowing rodents (family *Leporidae*), resembling but smaller than the hare, as the common American cottontail (*Sylvilagus floridanus*). **2** A hare. **3** The pelt of a rabbit or hare. **4** Welsh rabbit. — *v.i.* To hunt rabbits. ◆ Homophone: *rabbet.* [ME *rabette.* Akin to Walloon *robbett,* Flemish *robbe.*] — **rab′bit·er** *n.*

rabbit fever Tularemia.

rab·bit–foot (rab′it·fo͝ot′) *n.* **1** A common clover (*Trifolium arvense*) having soft, hairy flower heads supposed to resemble rabbits' paws: also **rabbit's–foot clover.** **2** The left hind foot of a rabbit carried as a good–luck charm.

rabbit hawk The red–tailed hawk (*Buteo borealis*).

rabbit hutch A coop in which domestic rabbits are bred.

rabbit punch In boxing, a short chopping blow at the base of the skull or back of the neck.

rab·bit·ry (rab′it·rē) *n. pl.* **·ries** A place where rabbits are kept; also, a group of rabbit hutches.

rab·ble[1] (rab′əl) *n.* A rude crowd; mob. — **the rabble** The populace; hoi polloi: used contemptuously. — *adj.* Of or pertaining to, suited to, or characteristic of a rabble; noisy; disorderly. — *v.t.* **·bled, ·bling** To mob. [? <RABBLE[3]]

rab·ble[2] (rab′əl) *n. Metall.* An iron implement, usually bent at one end, for stirring or skimming melted iron in puddling: also **rab′bler.** — *v.t.* **·bled, ·bling** To stir or skim with a rabble. [<F *râble* <L *rutabulum* poker]

rab·ble[3] (rab′əl) *v.t.* & *v.i.* **·bled, ·bling** *Scot.* & *Brit. Dial.* To speak or utter in an incoherent or disconnected manner; gabble. [Cf. Du. *rabbelen* speak indistinctly]

rab·ble·ment (rab′əl·mənt) *n.* **1** An uproar; disturbance. **2** A rabble; crowd.

rab·ble–rous·er (rab′əl·rou′zər) *n.* One who tries to incite mobs by arousing prejudices and passions; a demagog.

rab·bo·ni (ra·bō′nē) *n.* My great master: a term of address. [<Hebrew, aug. of RABBI]

rab·do·man·cy (rab′də·man′sē) See RHABDOMANCY.

Rab·e·lais (rab′ə·lā, *Fr.* rȧ·ble′), **François,** 1494?–1553, French humorist and satirist.

Rab·e·lai·si·an (rab′ə·lā′zē·ən, -zhən) *adj.* Characteristic of or like Rabelais or his works, especially with regard to his boisterous, coarse humor and his extravagance of satire and caricature. — *n.* A student or imitator of Rabelais. — **Rab′e·lai′si·an·ism, Rab′e·la′ism** *n.*

Ra·bi (rä′bē), **Isadore Isaac,** born 1898, U.S. physicist born in Austria.

Ra·bi·a (rə·bē′ə) *n.* Either of two Mohammedan months. See under CALENDAR (Mohammedan). [<Arabic *Rabi,* lit., spring]

rab·id (rab′id) *adj.* **1** Affected with, arising from, or pertaining to rabies; mad. **2** Unreasonably zealous; fanatical; violent. **3** Furious; raging. Also **rab′ic.** [<L *rabidus* < *rabere* be mad. Akin to RAGE.] — **rab′id·ly** *adv.* — **rab′id·ness** *n.*

ra·bies (rā′bēz, -bi·ēz) *n.* An acute infectious disease of animals, especially of dogs, caused by a virus and affecting the central nervous system; hydrophobia: readily transmissible to man by the bite of an affected animal. [<L < *rabere* rave] — **ra′bi·et′ic** (-et′ik) *adj.*

ra·ca (rā′kə, rə·kä′) *adj.* Worthless; contemptible. *Matt.* v 22. [<LL <Gk. *rhakē* <Aramaic *rēqā*]

rac·coon (ra·ko͞on′) *n.* **1** An American nocturnal plantigrade carnivore (genus *Procyon*): the common North American raccoon (*P. lotor*) is gray-ish–brown, with a black cheek patch, and black–and–white–ringed bushy tail. **2** The fur of this animal. Also spelled *racoon.* [Alter. of Algonquian *arakunem* hand–scratcher]

RACCOON
(Body from 20 to 30 inches long; tail, 10 to 12 inches)

raccoon dog A wild dog (*Nyctereutes procyonoides*) of Japan and northeastern Asia, with long, loose fur, short ears, and a long bushy tail.

race[1] (rās) *n.* **1** One of the major subdivisions of mankind, regarded as having a common origin and exhibiting a relatively constant set of physical traits. On the basis of the more commonly used criteria such as stature, the cephalic index, the nasal index, prognathism, skull capacity, texture of the hair, degree of pilosity, color of the skin, and hair and eye color, mankind has been divided into primary stocks or races, each of which is regarded as including a varying number of ethnic groups. According to some, the primary stocks are: the Caucasoid, the Mongoloid, and the Negroid. A number of races, such as the Australian and Polynesian, are of doubtful classification. **2** Any group of people or any grouping of peoples having, or assumed to have, common characteristics. **3** A nation: the German *race.* **4** A genealogical or family stock; clan: the *race* of MacGregor. **5** Pedigree; lineage: a noble *race.* **6** Any class of beings having characteristics uniting them, or differentiating them from others: the *race* of lawyers. **7** *Biol.* A group of plants or animals, having characteristics clearly differentiating it from other groups within the same species, which breeds true except for minor variations; a variety: a *race* of wheat. **8** A stock, breed, or strain of domestic animals or plants. **9** A quality or aggregate of qualities by which origin is determined; especially, the characteristic flavor or taste of wine. See synonyms under AFFINITY, KIN, PEOPLE, SORT. [<F <Ital. *razza* <L (*gene*)*ratio* lineage, breed]

race[2] (rās) *n.* **1** A contest to determine the relative speed of the contestants. **2** Any contest. **3** Movement or progression; swift movement. **4** Duration of life; course; career. **5** A swift current of water or its channel. **6** A swift current or heavy sea resulting from the meeting of two tides: the Portland *Race.* **7** A sluice or channel by which to conduct water to or from a waterwheel or around a dam. See HEADRACE, MILLRACE, TAILRACE. **8** Any groove or channel along which some part of a machine slides or is guided. **9** Slipstream. — *v.* **raced, rac·ing** *v.i.* **1** To take part in a contest of speed. **2** To move at great or top speed. **3** To move at an accelerated or too great speed, usually because of decreased resistance: said of machinery. — *v.t.* **4** To contend against in a race. **5** To cause to take part in a race. **6** To cause to move at an accelerated or too great speed: to *race* an engine. [<ON *rās.* Akin to OE *rǣs* a rushing.]

race[3] (rās) *n.* A root; specifically, a root of ginger. [<OF *rais* <L *radix* root]

Race (rās), **Cape** The southeasternmost point of Newfoundland.

race–a·bout (rās′ə·bout′) *n. Naut.* A sloop–rigged racing boat having a short bowsprit. Compare KNOCK–ABOUT.

race·course (rās′kôrs′, -kōrs′) *n.* The track over which a horse race, dog race, or the like is run. Also *racetrack.*

race horse A horse bred and trained for contests of speed; a racer.

race knife A tool having a very narrow U–shaped blade, used for tracing or outlining on metal or glass or for scribing on wood.

ra·ceme (rā·sēm′, rə-) *n. Bot.* A centripetal or indeterminate flower cluster in which the flowers are arranged singly on distinct, nearly equal pedicels at intervals on an elongated common axis. [<L *racemus* cluster] — **rac·e·mif·er·ous** (ras′ə·mif′ər·əs) *adj.*

ra·ce·mic (rā·sē′mik, -sem′ik, rə-) *adj.* **1** *Bot.* Of, pertaining to, or contained in racemes or in grapes. **2** *Chem.* Indicating or relating to any chemical compound that is optically inactive. Also **rac·e·moid** (ras′ə·moid).

racemic acid *Chem.* A white, crystalline, optically inactive compound, $C_4H_6O_6$, contained with tartartic acid in certain grapes and extracts from tartar: it is separable into dextrorotatory and levorotatory forms.

rac·e·mism (ras′ə·miz′əm, rā·sē′miz·əm) *n. Chem.* The quality or condition of being racemic.

rac·e·mize (ras′ə·mīz, rā·sē′mīz) *v.t.* **·mized, ·miz·ing** *Chem.* To change (an optically active compound) into an optically inactive compound. — **rac′e·mi·za′tion** *n.*

rac·e·mose (ras′ə·mōs) *adj.* Arranged in or as in clusters or racemes: a *racemose* gland. Also **rac′e·mous.** [<L *racemosus*] — **rac′e·mose·ly** *adv.*

race psychology A division of psychology which investigates human traits and behavior in relation to racial factors, actual or assumed.

rac·er (rā′sər) *n.* **1** One who races, or one who contends in a race. **2** Anything having unusually rapid speed, as a race horse, steamer, or yacht; also, an automobile designed for racing. **3** A turntable on which a heavy gun is turned to left or right. **4** One of various colubrine snakes, as the blacksnake.

race riot A violent conflict between groups in the same community, based on differences of color, creed, etc.

race suicide The slow reduction in numbers of a people through voluntary failure on the part of individuals to maintain the birth rate at or above the level of the death rate.

race·track (rās′trak′) *n.* A racecourse.

race·way (rās′wā′) *n.* **1** A channel for conducting water. **2** A tube for protecting wires, as in a subway. **3** *U.S.* A racecourse for trotting horses.

Ra·chel (rā′chəl; *Fr.* rȧ·shel′, *Pg.* rä·kel′, *Sw.* rä′kel) A feminine personal name. Also *Ital.* **Ra·che·le** (rä·kā′lā). [<Hebrew, ewe] — **Rachel** The wife of Jacob; mother of Joseph and Benjamin. *Gen.* xxix 6.
— **Rachel** (rȧ·shel′) Stage name of Elisabeth Rachel–Félix, 1821–58, French tragic actress.

ra·chis (rā′kis) *n. pl.* **ra·chi·des** (rā′kə·dēz) or **·chis·es** **1** *Bot.* The axis of an inflorescence; a raceme. **2** *Ornithol.* The shaft of a feather, especially the part filled with pith, which bears the barbs. **3** *Anat.* The spinal column. Sometimes spelled *rhachis.* [<NL <Gk. *rhachis* spine] — **ra·chi·al** (rā′kē·əl) *adj.*

ra·chi·tis (rə·kī′tis) *n. Pathol.* Rickets. [<NL <Gk. *rhachitis* spinal inflammation] — **ra·chit′ic** (-kit′ik) *adj.*

Rach·ma·ni·nov (räkh·mä′ni·nôf), **Sergei Vassilievich,** 1873–1943, Russian pianist and composer. Also **Rach·ma′ni·noff.**

ra·cial (rā′shəl) *adj.* Pertaining to or characteristic of a race, races, or descent. — **ra′cial·ly** *adv.*

ra·cial·ism (rā′shəl·iz′əm) *n.* **1** The doctrine of the preponderant influence of actual or assumed racial factors in the origin, development, and rank of various human societies; race prejudice. **2** Racism. — **ra′cial·ist** *n.*

Ra·ci·bórz (rä·chē′bo͞osh) See RATIBOR.

Ra·cine (rə·sēn′) A city on Lake Michigan in SE Wisconsin.

Ra·cine (rȧ·sēn′), **Jean,** 1639–99, French dramatist.

ra·cism (rā′siz·əm) *n.* An excessive and irrational belief in or advocacy of the superiority of a given group, people, or nation, on racial grounds alone; race hatred. — **ra′cist** *n.*

rack[1] (rak) *n.* **1** An open grating, framework, or the like, in or on which articles may be placed, as a frame to hold dishes, a tier or row of pigeonholes, or a framework to hold fodder for horses, cattle, or sheep. **2** A triangular frame for arranging the balls on a billiard table. **3** A device in an airplane for carrying bombs: also **bomb rack.** **4** *Mech.* A bar or the like having teeth that engage with those of a gearwheel, pinion, or worm gear. **5** A machine for stretching or making tense; especially, an intrument of torture which stretches the limbs of victims. **6** Torture or punishment as by the rack; hence, intense mental or physical suffering. **7** A wrenching or straining, as from a storm. — *v.t.* **1** To place or arrange in or on a rack. **2** To torture on the rack. **3** To cause suffering to; torment. **4** To strain, as with the effort of thinking: to *rack* one's brains. **5** To raise (rents) excessively: see RACK–RENT. ◆ Homophone: *wrack.* [ME *rekke,* prob. <MDu. *rec, recke* < *recken* stretch] — **rack′er** *n.*

rack[2] (rak) *n.* The single–foot. — *v.i.* To proceed or move with this gait. ◆ Homophone: *wrack.* [? Var. of ROCK[2]]

rack[3] (rak) *n.* **1** Thin, flying, or broken clouds. **2** Any floating vapor. — *v.i.* To move rapidly; send, as clouds before the wind. Also spelled *wrack.* [<Scand. Cf. ON *rek* drifting wreckage, *reka* drive, drift.]

rack[4] (rak) *n.* Wrack; wreck; demolition: obsolete except in the phrase "to go to rack and ruin." [Var. of WRACK[2]]

rack[5] *v.t.* To draw off from the lees, as liquor. ◆ Homophone: *wrack.* [<Provençal *arracar* <*raca* refuse of grapes]

rack and pinion *Mech.* A machine movement in which a toothed rack and a pinion mesh together for converting rotary motion into reciprocating motion or vice versa.

RACK AND PINION

rack·et[1] (rak′it) *n.* **1** An implement for striking a ball, as in the game of tennis. It is a nearly elliptical hoop of bent wood, usually strung with catgut, and has a handle. **2** A large wooden sole or shoe to support the weight of a man or horse on swampy ground. **3** A snowshoe. **4** A ratchet: a misnomer. **5** An organ stop. **6** *sing. & pl.* A game resembling court tennis, played in a court with four walls. Often spelled *racquet.* [<F *raquette* < Arabic *rāha* palm of the hand]

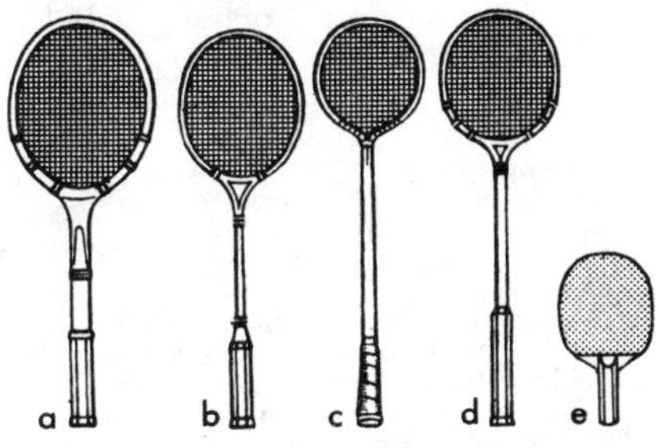

TYPES OF RACKETS
a. Tennis. *c, d.* Squash.
b. Badminton. *e.* Table tennis.

rack·et[2] (rak′it) *n.* **1** A clattering, vociferous, or confused noise; fuss; commotion. **2** *Colloq.* **a** A scheme for getting money or other benefits by fraud, intimidation, or other illegitimate means. **b** Any business or occupation: the retailing *racket.* **3** Social activity or excitement. —*v.i.* **1** To make a loud, clattering noise. **2** To indulge in noisy sport or diversion; carouse. [? Metathetic var. of dial. *rattick* make a din, clatter]

rack·et·eer (rak′ə·tir′) *n.* **1** One who extorts money from, or seeks to gain control over, a person or organization by intimidation, fraud, violence, or other criminal means; one engaged in a racket. **2** Formerly, a bootlegger or rum–runner. —**rack′et·eer′ing** *n.*

rack·et·y (rak′it·ē) *adj.* Making a racket; noisy.

Rack·ham (rak′əm), **Arthur,** 1867–1939, English artist and illustrator.

rack railway An inclined railway having a rack or toothed rail **(rack rail)** placed between the regular rails, in the cogs of which open pinions on the driving axle of the locomotive engage: also called *cogway.*

rack–rent (rak′rent′) *n.* An exorbitant rent (equal or nearly equal to the full annual value of the property). —*v.t.* To exact rack–rent from or for. [<RACK[1] (stretch) +RENT[1]]

rack·work (rak′wûrk′) *n.* A mechanism with a rack, or rack and pinion, as the leading characteristic.

ra·con (rā′kon) *n.* A device for the immediate identification of friendly or hostile aircraft by means of radar signals automatically transmitted in code: adapted also as an aid in navigation. [<RA(DAR) (BEA)CON]

rac·on·teur (rak′on·tûr′, *Fr.* rà·kôṅ·tœr′) *n.* A skilled story teller. [<F <*raconter* recount] —**ra′con·teuse′** (-tōōs′, -tōōz′; *Fr.* -tœz′) *n. fem.*

ra·coon (ra·kōōn′) See RACCOON.

rac·quet (rak′it) See RACKET[1].

rac·quet·ball (rak′it·bôl′) *n.* **1** An indoor walled–court game played with a hollow rubber ball and a short–handled racquet. **2** The ball used in this game, somewhat larger and softer than a handball.

rac·y (rā′sē) *adj.* **rac·i·er, rac·i·est 1** Having a spirited or pungent interest; spicy; piquant: a *racy* style. **2** Having a characteristic flavor assumed to be indicative of origin, as wine; rich, fresh, or fragrant. **3** Suggestive; slightly immodest: a *racy* story. [<RACE[1]] —**rac′i·ly** *adv.* —**rac′i·ness** *n.*

Synonyms: flavorous, forcible, high–flavored, lively, piquant, pungent, rich, spicy, spirited. *Racy* applies (def. 2) to the pleasing flavor characteristic of certain wines. *Pungent* denotes something sharply stimulating to the organs of taste or smell, as vinegar, ammonia; *piquant* denotes a quality similar in kind to *pungent* but less in degree, alluring and agreeable; *pungent* spices may be deftly compounded in a *piquant* sauce. *Antonyms*: dull, flat, flavorless, insipid, tasteless, vapid.

rad (rad) *n. Physics* A unit of absorbed nuclear radiation equivalent to 100 ergs of absorbed energy per gram of absorbing material. Compare REM, REP. [<R(ADIATION) + A(BSORBED) + D(OSE)]

ra·dar (rā′där) *n. Electronics* A locating device which instantaneously detects the presence and indicates the position of aircraft, ships, etc., by measuring the interval between the emission and return of high–frequency radio waves effective under varied conditions. [< RA(DIO) D(ETECTING) A(ND) R(ANGING)]

ra·dar·scope (rā′där·skōp) *n. Electronics* The oscilloscope of a radar set.

Rad·cliffe (rad′klif), **Ann,** 1764–1823, *née* Ward, English novelist.

rad·dle[1] (rad′l) See REDDLE, RUDDLE.

rad·dle[2] (rad′l) *v.t.* **·dled, ·dling** To intertwine or weave together. [<obs. *raddle* a wattle < AF *reidele,* OF *reddale* stout stick]

ra·deau (rà·dō′) *n. French* A raft; float.

Ra·dek (rä′dek), **Karl,** 1885–1959, U.S.S.R. revolutionist and journalist.

Ra·detz·ky (rä·dets′kē), **Count Joseph Wenzel,** 1766–1858, Austrian field marshal.

Rad·ford (rad′fərd), **Arthur William,** born 1896, U.S. admiral; chairman, joint chiefs of staff 1953–57.

ra·di·ac (rā′dē·ak) *n. Physics* A Geiger counter. [<RA(DIOACTIVITY) D(ETECTION), I(DENTIFICATION), A(ND) C(OMPUTATION)]

ra·di·al (rā′dē·əl) *adj.* **1** Pertaining to, consisting of, or resembling a ray or radius. **2** Extending from a center in the manner of rays. **3** Of or pertaining to the radius or a radiating part. **4** Developing uniformly on all sides. —*n.* **1** A radiating part. **2** A radial tire. —**ra′di·al·ly** *adv.*

radial engine A multicylinder internal–combustion engine having its cylinders arranged like the spokes in a wheel.

radial tire A pneumatic tire constructed with plies of fabric that are laid at right angles to the circumference of the tread and extend to the beads, sometimes reinforced with other plies, as of steel, laid at right angles to the radial plies under the tread. Also **ra·di·al–ply tire** (rā′dē·əl·plī′).

ra·di·an (rā′dē·ən) *n. Math.* **1** An arc equal in length to the radius of the circle of which it is a part. **2** The angle subtended by such an arc: 2π radians = 360°, π radians = 180° or 1 radian = $(180/\pi)°$ or 57° 17′ 44.80625″ +. [<RADIUS]

ra·di·ance (rā′dē·əns) *n.* The quality or state of being radiant; brilliant or sparkling luster; lightness; effulgence. Also **ra′di·an·cy, ra′di·ant·ness.**

ra·di·ant (rā′dē·ənt) *adj.* **1** Emitting rays of light or heat. **2** Beaming with light or brightness, kindness, or love: a *radiant* smile. **3** Resembling rays; consisting of or transmitted by radiations: *radiant* heat. See synonyms under BRIGHT. —*n.* **1** A straight line proceeding from and conceived as revolving around a given point. **2** *Astron.* That point in the heavens from the direction of which, during a meteoric shower, the meteors seem to shoot. **3** The luminous point from which light proceeds or is made to radiate. **4** That which radiates. [< L *radians, -antis,* ppr. of *radiare* emit rays < *radius* ray] —**ra′di·ant·ly** *adv.*

radiant energy *Physics* **1** The energy associated with and transmitted by waves emanating from some specified source, as of light, heat, or sound. **2** The energy of radium, atomic disintegration, X–rays, electromagnetic radiation, or the like.

ra·di·ate (rā′dē·āt) *v.* **·at·ed, ·at·ing** *v.i.* **1** To emit rays or radiation; be diant. **2** To issue forth in rays, as light from the sun. **3** To spread out from a center, as the spokes of a wheel. —*v.t.* **4** To send out or emit in rays. **5** To cause to spread as if from a center; diffuse; disseminate. —*adj.* (-dē·it) **1** Divided or separated into rays; having rays; radiating. **2** *Bot.* Bearing rays or ray flowers. **3** *Zool.* Characterized by radial symmetry, as echinoderms and coelenterates. **4** Adorned with rays, as a head on a coin; radiated. —*n.* (-dē·it) **1** An organism having radial symmetry. **2** A ray or raylike projection. [<L *radiatus,* pp. of *radiare* emit rays. See RADIANT.] —**ra′·di·a′tive** *adj.*

ra·di·a·tion (rā′dē·ā′shən) *n.* **1** The act of radiating or the state of being radiated. **2** *Physics* **a** The emission and propagation of radiant energy or of alpha or beta rays. **b** The energy so propagated. **c** The stages of emission, absorption, and transmission involved in such propagation: distinguished from *conduction.* **3** *Biol.* Adaptive radiation.

radiation pressure *Physics* The force exerted upon an exposed surface by radiant energy, as from light or electromagnetic waves.

radiation sickness *Pathol.* A morbid condition due to the body's absorption of excess radiation and marked by fatigue, nausea, vomiting, internal hemorrhage, and progressive tissue breakdown.

ra·di·a·tor (rā′dē·ā′tər) *n.* **1** That which radiates. **2** A chamber, coil, or flat hollow vessel, through which is passed steam or hot water for warming a building or apartment. **3** In engines, a nest of tubes for cooling water flowing through them. —**ra′di·a·to′ry** (-ə·tôr′·ē, -tō′rē) *adj.*

rad·i·cal (rad′i·kəl) *adj.* **1** Of, proceeding from, or pertaining to the root or foundation; essential; fundamental; inherent; basic. **2** Thoroughgoing; unsparing; extreme: a *radical* operation; *radical* measures. **3** *Math.* Pertaining to the root or roots of a number. **4** In philology, belonging or referring to a root or a root syllable; underived. **5** *Bot.* Springing from or belonging or relating to the root: *radical* leaves. **6** *Chem.* Pertaining to a radical. **7** Of or pertaining to political radicals. —*n.* **1** One who carries his theories or convictions to their furthest application; an extremist. **2** In politics, one who advocates wide–spread governmental changes and reforms at the earliest opportunity. **3** The primitive or underived part of a word; a primitive word or syllable; a root; radicle. **4** *Math.* **a** A quantity of which the root is to be extracted or used in calculation; a radical expression. **b** The radical sign. **5** *Chem.* A fundamental constituent or part of a compound; specifically, a group of atoms which acts as a unit in a compound and may either pass unchanged through a series of reactions or be replaced as though it were a single atom. ◆ Homophone: *radicle.* [<LL *radicalis* having roots <L *radix, radicis* root] —**rad′i·cal·ness** *n.*

Synonyms (adj.): basic, complete, constitutional, entire, essential, extreme, fundamental, ingrained, inherent, innate, native, natural, organic, original, perfect, positive, primary, primitive, thorough, thoroughgoing, total. The widely divergent senses in which the word *radical* is used, by which it can be at sometime interchanged with any word in the above list, are all formed upon the one primary sense of that which is connected with the root (Latin *radix*). A *radical* difference is one that springs from the root, and is thus *constitutional, essential, fundamental, organic, original*; a *radical* change is one that does not stop at the surface, but reaches down to the very root, and is *entire, thorough, total*; since the majority find superficial treatment of any matter the easiest and most comfortable, *radical* measures, which strike at the root of evil or need, are apt to be looked upon as *extreme.* See NATURAL. *Antonyms*: compromising, conciliatory, conservative, half–way, inadequate, incomplete, moderate, palliative, partial, superficial.

radical expression *Math.* A surd, or an algebraic expression involving a surd.

rad·i·cal·ism (rad′i·kəl·iz′əm) *n.* **1** The state of being radical. **2** Advocacy of thoroughgoing or extreme measures.

rad·i·cal·ize (rad′i·kə·līz′) *v.t.* **·ized, ·iz·ing** To make radical, especially in politics. **—rad·i·cal·i·za·tion** (rad′i·kə·lə·zā′shən), **rad′i·cal·iz′·er** *n.*

rad·i·cal·ly (rad′ik·lē) *adv.* **1** Completely; thoroughly; fundamentally. **2** With reference to root or origin; originally; primitively.

radical sign *Math.* The symbol $\sqrt{}$ placed before a quantity to indicate that its root is to be taken: a modification of the letter *r* (Latin *radix* root). A number written above it (called its *index*) shows what root is to be taken; thus $\sqrt[4]{a}$ stands for the fourth root of *a*; when used without a superior number, the symbol means square root of.

rad·i·cand (rad′i·kand′) *n. Math.* The quantity under the radical sign: $x + 1$ is the *radicand* of $\sqrt{x+1}$. [<RADIC(AL) + *-and,* as in *multiplicand*]

rad·i·cel (rad′i·sel) *n.* A rootlet. [<NL *radicella,* dim. of L *radix, radicis* root]

rad·i·cle (rad′i·kəl) *n.* **1** *Bot.* **a** The embryonic root below the cotyledon of a plant. **b** A diminutive root or rootlet. **2** *Anat.* A rootlike part, as the stem of an embryo, the initial fiber of a nerve, the beginning of a vein, etc. **3** *Chem.* A radical. ◆ Homophone: *radical.* [< L *radicula,* dim. of *radix, radicis* root]

ra·di·i (rā′dē·ī) Plural of RADIUS.

ra·di·o (rā′dē·ō) *n. pl.* **·os** **1** The science, art, and process of communicating by means of radiant energy transmitted directly through space in waves. **2** The wireless transmission of radio waves within assigned frequencies and their reception by devices adapted for reconverting the frequencies into their corresponding original signals. **3** A radio program or broadcast; also, the combined operations for its production. **4** A radio receiving set and its accessories. **5** A radio message or radiogram. **6** The exploitation and development of radio as a commercial enterprise; the radio business and industry. — *adj.* **1** Of, pertaining to, designating, employing, or produced by radiant energy, especially in the form of electromagnetic waves: a *radio* beam. **2** Wireless. —*v.t. & v.i.* To transmit (a message, etc.) or communicate with (someone) by radiotelegraphy or radiotelephony. [<RADIO(TELEGRAPHY)]

radio– *combining form* **1** *Anat.* Radial; pertaining to the radius: *radiodigital,* of the fingers on the radial edge of the hand. **2** Radio; produced by or related to radio: *radiogram.* **3** *Chem.* Radioactive; of, produced by, or causing radioactivity: *radioscope, radiothorium.* **4** *Med.* Radiant energy; using radiant energy: *radiotherapy.* [<L *radius* a ray]

ra·di·o·ac·tive (rā′dē·ō·ak′tiv) *adj.* Pertaining to, exhibiting, caused by, or characteristic of radioactivity: a *radioactive* isotope.

radioactive series *Physics* The sequence of products formed in the disintegration of a heavy radioactive element. The disintegration of any member of the series produces each of the following members in turn. The three naturally occurring series are those of uranium, thorium, and actinium, each terminating with a stable isotope of lead.

ra·di·o·ac·tiv·i·ty (rā′dē·ō·ak·tiv′ə·tē) *n. Physics* **1** The propagation of radiant energy. **2** The spontaneous nuclear disintegration of certain elements and isotopes, with the emission of alpha particles, electrons, positrons, or electromagnetic radiation. **3** A particular form of such disintegration: gamma *radioactivity.*

radio astronomy That branch of astronomy and astrophysics which studies celestial phenomena by the interception and analysis of radio waves emitted by stars and other objects in interstellar space.

ra·di·o·au·tog·ra·phy (rā′dē·ō·ô·tog′rə·fē) *n.* Autoradiography. [<RADIO- + AUTOGRAPH + -Y]

ra·di·o·au·to·gram (rā′dē·ō·ô′tə·gram) *n.* Autoradiograph. Also **ra′di·o·au′to·graph** (-graf, -gräf).

radio beacon A stationary radio transmitter which sends out characteristic signals for the guidance of ships and aircraft.

radio beam **1** A steady flow of radio signals concentrated along a given course or direction. **2** The narrow zone marked out for the guidance of aircraft by the overlapping of recurrent signals transmitted from ground radio stations on either side of an assigned flight course.

ra·di·o·broad·cast (rā′dē·ō·brôd′kast′, -käst′) *v.t. & v.i.* **·cast** or **·cast·ed, ·cast·ing** To broadcast by radio. —*n.* Broadcast (def. 1). **—ra′di·o·broad′cast′er** *n.*

ra·di·o·car·bon (rā′dē·ō·kär′bən) *n. Physics* The radioactive isotope of carbon of mass 14, with a half–life of about 5,700 years: it is much used in the dating of fossils, artifacts, and certain kinds of geological formations. Also called *carbon 14.*

ra·di·o·car·di·o·gram (rā′dē·ō·kär′dē·ə·gram) *n.* The record made in radiocardiography.

ra·di·o·car·di·og·ra·phy (rā′dē·ō·kär′dē·og′rə·fē) *n. Med.* A method for studying the blood flow through the heart by recording the passage of injected radioisotopes with the aid of a specially constructed Geiger counter.

ra·di·o·chem·is·try (rā′dē·ō·kem′is·trē) *n.* That branch of chemistry dealing with the properties and reactions of radioactive substances, as radium and thorium.

radio circuit A radio system consisting of two stations in direct communication with each other.

radio compass *Aeron.* A direction–finder serving to determine the position of a radio transmitting station.

radio conductor Any material or apparatus that indicates, by some alteration of its conductivity, the presence and strength of electric waves, such as the coherer of a wireless telegraph.

ra·di·o·dat·ing (rā′dē·ō·dā′ting) *n.* The technique of dating objects by measuring their radioactivity.

ra·di·ode (rā′dē·ōd) *n.* **1** A radium container, built to prevent any dangerous leakage of radioactivity. **2** *Med.* An apparatus used in some forms of radiotherapy. [<RADIO- + -ODE[1]]

ra·di·o·dust (rā′dē·ō·dust′) *n.* Radioactive dust particles precipitated from the atmosphere, especially in the fall–out from an atomic or thermonuclear bomb.

ra·di·o·el·e·ment (rā′dē·ō·el′ə·mənt) *n. Physics* **1** An element exhibiting radioactivity. **2** Any of the disintegration products of such elements, as radon, thoron, etc., which are themselves radioactive.

radio fix The position of an aircraft, ship, or radio transmitter, as determined with reference to radio signals from two or more stations, or by similar means.

radio frequency Any wave frequency, or set of frequencies, adapted for the transmission of radio signals. The range is roughly from the upper limit of normal audibility to the lower limit of heat and light waves, or upwards from about 10 kilocycles per second.

ra·di·o–ge·net·ics (rā′dē·ō·jə·net′iks) *n.* The study of genetics in relation to the effects of radioactivity upon the processes of inheritance and the nature of hereditary changes. **—ra′di·o–ge·net′ic** *adj.*

ra·di·o·ge·nic (rā′dē·ō·jē′nik, -jen′ik) *adj.* Resulting from or developed by radioactivity.

ra·di·o·gram (rā′dē·ō·gram′) *n.* **1** A message sent by wireless telegraphy. **2** A radiographic negative or print.

ra·di·o·graph (rā′dē·ō·graf′, -gräf′) *n.* A negative or picture made by means of radioactivity; an X–ray photograph. —*v.t.* To make a radiograph of. **—ra′di·og′ra·pher** (-og′rə·fər) *n.* **—ra′di·o·graph′ic** or **·ic** *adj.* **—ra′di·og′ra·phy** *n.*

ra·di·o·im·mu·no·as·say (rā′dē·ō·im′yə·nō·ə·sā′, -im·yōō′-) *n.* A method of assaying the amount or other characteristics of a substance by labeling it with a radioactive chemical and combining it with an antibody to induce an immunological reaction.

ra·di·o·i·so·tope (rā′dē·ō·ī′sə·tōp) *n. Physics* A radioactive isotope, usually one produced artificially from a normally stable element: extensively used in biological and physical research and used in medicine for diagnostic and therapeutic purposes.

ra·di·o·lar·i·an (rā′dē·ō·lâr′ē·ən) *n.* Any member of an order *(Radiolaria,* class *Sarcodina)* of marine protozoans having typically a siliceous skeleton enclosing a perforated membrane. —*adj.* Of or pertaining to the *Radiolaria* [<NL *Radiolaria,* name of the order <*radiolus,* dim. of L *radius* ray]

ra·di·o·lo·ca·tion (rā′dē·ō·lō·kā′shən) *n.* Radar.

ra·di·ol·o·gy (rā′dē·ol′ə·jē) *n.* That branch of science that relates to radiant energy and its applications, especially in the diagnosis and treatment of disease. [<RADIO- + -LOGY] **—ra·di·o·log·i·cal** (rā′dē·ə·loj′i·kəl) or **ra′di·o·log′ic** *adj.* **—ra′di·ol′o·gist** *n.*

ra·di·o·lu·cent (rā′dē·ō·lōō′sənt) *adj.* Permeable to X–rays and other forms of electromagnetic radiation. See RADIOPAQUE.

ra·di·o·lu·mi·nes·cence (rā′dē·ō·lōō′mə·nes′·əns) *n.* Luminescence produced by, or resulting from, any form of radiant energy, as X–rays, radioactivity, etc. **—ra′di·o·lu′mi·nes′·cent** *adj.*

ra·di·o·ma·te·ri·al (rā′dē·ō·mə·tir′ē·əl) *n.* Any material that is, or has been made, radioactive.

ra·di·om·e·ter (rā′dē·om′ə·tər) *n.* An instrument for detecting and measuring radiant energy by converting it into mechanical energy, as by the rotation of blackened disks suspended in a vacuum and exposed to sunlight. [< RADIO- + METER[1]] **—ra′di·o·met′ric** (-ō·met′rik) *adj.* **—ra′di·om′e·try** *n.*

RADIOMETER

ra·di·o·mi·crom·e·ter (rā′dē·ō·mī·krom′ə·tər) *n.* An instrument, consisting primarily of an extremely sensitive thermoelectric couple suspended in a magnetic field, for measuring minute variations of heat.

ra·di·o·mi·met·ic (rā′dē·ō·mi·met′ik) *adj. Physics* Pertaining to or designating any of a class of chemicals, as mustard gas, which produce biological effects similar to and sometimes indistinguishable from those produced by radioactive substances.

ra·di·o·nu·clide (rā′dē·ō·nōō′klīd, -nyōō′-) *n. Physics* A radioactive nuclide.

ra·di·o·paque (rā′dē·ō·pāk′) *adj.* Impermeable to X–rays or other forms of electromagnetic radiation. [<RADIO + OPAQUE]

ra·di·o·phone (rā′dē·ō·fōn′) *n.* **1** Any device for the production or transmission of sound by radiant energy. **2** A radiotelephone. — **ra′di·o·phon′ic** (-fon′ik) *adj.* **—ra′di·oph′o·ny** (-of′ə·nē) *n.*

ra·di·o·pho·tog·ra·phy (rā′dē·ō·fə·tog′rə·fē) *n.* The transmission of a photograph by radio in such a way that each spot on the picture is reproduced by an electric impulse. **—ra′di·o·pho′to·graph** (-fō′tə·graf, -gräf) *n.*

ra·di·o·prax·is (rā′dē·ō·prak′sis) *n.* Radiotherapy.

ra·di·o·scope (rā′dē·ō·skōp′) *n.* An apparatus for detecting radioactivity or X–rays.

ra·di·os·co·py (rā′dē·os′kə·pē) *n.* Examination of opaque bodies with the aid of X–rays or some other form of radiant energy. [<RADIO- + -SCOPY] **—ra′di·o·scop′ic** (-skop′ik) or **·i·cal** *adj.*

ra·di·o·sen·si·tive (rā′dē·ō·sen′sə·tiv) *adj.* **1** Sensitive to X–rays and ultraviolet rays. **2** *Med.* Reducible or destructible by X–rays. as certain tumors.

radio shielding *Aeron.* Metallic covering on the electric wiring and ignition apparatus of an aircraft, intermittently grounded to the frame in order to eliminate disturbances in radio communication.

ra·di·o·sonde (rā′dē·ō·sond′) *n. Meteorol.* A device, attached to a small balloon sent aloft, which measures the pressure, temperature, and humidity of the upper air and radios the data to the ground. Also **ra′di·o·me′te·or·o·graph′** (-mē′tē·ər·ə·graf′, -gräf′). [<RADIO- + F *sonde* sounding]

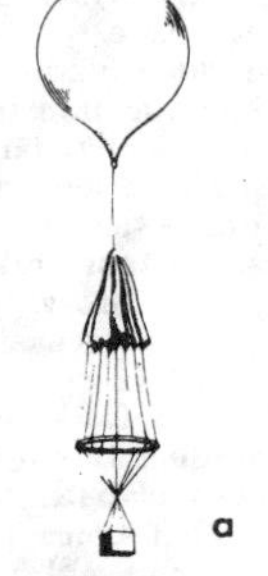

RADIOSONDE
a. Instrument box.

radio spectrum The full range of frequencies pertaining to and associated with radiant energy; specifically, those frequencies employed in radio and television.

radio star Any of a large number of stars which may be identified and studied by means of the characteristic electromagnetic impulses which they emit.

radio station An installation of all the equipment and apparatus necessary for effective radio communication.

ra·di·o·stron·tium (rā′dē·ō·stron′shəm, -tē·əm) *n. Physics* Strontium 90.

ra·di·o·tel·e·gram (rā′dē·ō·tel′ə·gram) *n.* A message sent by radiotelegraphy.

ra·di·o·te·leg·ra·phy (rā′dē·ō·tə·leg′rə·fē) *n.* Telegraphic communication by means of radio waves. **— ra′di·o·tel′e·graph′ic** (-tel′ə·graf′ik) *adj.* **— ra′di·o·tel′e·graph** (-graf, -gräf) *n.*

ra·di·o·tel·e·phone (rā′dē·ō·tel′ə·fōn) *n.* A telephone set that, without the agency of connecting wires, transmits a verbal message to a similar set by means of radio waves. **— ra′di·o·tel′e·phon′ic** (-tel′ə·fon′ik) *adj.* **— ra′di·o·te·leph′o·ny** (-tə·lef′ə·nē) *n.*

radio telescope A sensitive astronomical instrument designed on the principle of a radio receiver, but adapted to intercept and amplify electromagnetic waves in the megacycle range emanating from interstellar space.

ra·di·o·ther·a·py (rā′dē·ō·ther′ə·pē) *n.* The use of X-rays and other forms of radioactivity in the treatment of disease.

ra·di·o·tho·ri·um (rā′dē·ō·thôr′ē·əm, -thō′·rē·əm) *n.* A radioactive product of the thorium series, with a half-life of 1.9 years.

ra·di·o·tox·ic (rā′dē·ō·tok′sik) *adj. Med.* Of or pertaining to the toxic effect of radioactive materials, especially radioisotopes. **— ra′di·o·tox·ic′i·ty** (-tok·sis′ə·tē) *n.*

radio transcription An electrically recorded radio program, speech, musical selection, or the like, intended for subsequent broadcasting.

radio tube A vacuum tube for radio.

radio wave Any of a class of electromagnetic waves propagated at frequencies intermediate between those of audible sound and infrared.

rad·ish (rad′ish) *n.* **1** A tall, branching herb *(Raphanus sativus)* of the mustard family. **2** Its pungent, edible root, commonly eaten raw. [<F *radis* <Ital. *radice* <L *radix, radicis* root. Doublet of RADIX.]

ra·di·um (rā′dē·əm) *n.* A powerfully radioactive metallic element (symbol Ra) chemically related to barium, obtained principally as a disintegration product of uranium but found also in minute quantities in sea water and in certain plants and animals. It has a half-life of about 1,600 years and its atoms undergo spontaneous disintegration associated with a wide range of properties and effects, emitting alpha and beta particles and gamma rays in a succession of stages terminating in radium G, a stable isotope of lead. See ELEMENT. [<NL <L *radius* ray]

radium F Polonium of mass 210.

radium therapy The treatment of skin diseases and of cancer by means of radium.

ra·di·us (rā′dē·əs) *n. pl.* **·di·i** (-dē·ī) **1** A straight line from the center of a circle or sphere to its periphery. **2** *Anat.* The thicker and shorter bone of the forearm, on the same side as the thumb. **3** *Bot.* A ray floret of a composite flower; also, a branch of an umbel. **4** *Zool.* **a** In radiolarians and similar organisms, the imaginary line or plane dividing the body into two theoretically equal parts. **b** A ray or radiating part, as, the barb of a feather. **c** A lateral part of a cirriped shell when overlapping others. **5** *Entomol.* One of the main longitudinal veins of an insect's wings. **6** In a sextant, quadrant, etc., a pivoted arm, mounted so as to move radially, as on a graduated arc or circle. **7** *Mech.* A wheel spoke; a rod or bar which with others extends from a common point. **8** A circular area or boundary measured by the length of its radius. **9** Sphere, scope, or limit, as of activity. **10** A fixed limit of travel beyond which higher fares are charged. [<L, orig., rod, spoke of a wheel, hence radius, ray of light. Doublet of RAY]

radius vector *pl.* **radius vectors** or **ra·di·i vec·to·res** (rā′dē·ī vek·tôr′ēz, -tō′rēz) **1** *Math.* **a** The distance from a fixed origin to any point of a curve. **b** The distance from a point to the pole in the polar coordinate or spherical coordinate system. **2** *Astron.* A line from a center of attraction to a body describing an orbit about it.

ra·dix (rā′diks) *n. pl.* **rad·i·ces** (rad′ə·sēz, rā′·də-) or **ra·dix·es** **1** *Rare* The origin or source. **2** *Math.* A number or symbol used as the basis of a scale of enumeration: 10 is the *radix* of the common system of logarithms. **3** *Bot.* The root of a plant. **4** An original word from which others are derived; radical; root; etymon. [<L, root. Doublet of RADISH.]

Rad·nor·shire (rad′nər·shir) A county of eastern Wales; 471 square miles; county town, Presteigne. Also **Rad′nor.**

Ra·dom (rä′dôm) A city in east central Poland.

ra·dome (rā′dōm) *n. Electronics* A protective housing, radiolucent to radar waves, for the antenna and other equipment of a radar assembly. [<RA(DAR) + DOME]

ra·don (rā′don) *n.* A heavy, gaseous, radioactive element (symbol Rn), an emanation of radium with a half-life of about 4 days: formerly called *niton.* [<RAD(IUM) + -ON, as in *neon*]

rad·u·la (raj′o͞o·lə) *n. pl.* **·lae** (-lē) *Zool.* A rasplike organ, the odontophore or lingual ribbon of a mollusk. [<L, scraper < *radere* scrape] **— rad′u·lar** *adj.*

Rae·burn (rā′bərn), **Sir Henry,** 1756–1823, Scottish painter.

Rae·der (rā′dər), **Erich,** 1876–1960, German admiral in World War II.

Ra·fa·el (rä′fä·el′) Spanish form of RAPHAEL. Also *Ital.* **Raf·fa·e·le** (räf′fä·ā′lā) or **Raf·fa·el·lo** (räf′fä·el′lō).

raff (raf) *n.* **1** The rabble; riff-raff. **2** *Scot. & Brit. Dial.* A disorderly collection. [<RIFF-RAFF]

raf·fer·ty rules (raf′ər·tē) *Austral.* No rules at all; rough-and-ready.

raf·fi·a (raf′ē·ə) *n.* **1** A cultivated palm *(Raphia pedunculata)* of Madagascar, the leafstalks of which furnish fiber for making hats, mats, baskets, etc. **2** Its fiber. Also spelled *raphia.* [<Malagasy *rafia*]

raf·fi·nose (raf′ə·nōs) *n. Chem.* A colorless crystalline carbohydrate, $C_{18}H_{32}O_{16}$, having a mildly sweetish taste, found in cottonseed and in the molasses of the sugar beet: it hydrolyzes into fructose, galactose, and glucose. [<F *raffiner* refine + -OSE[2]]

raff·ish (raf′ish) *adj.* **1** Tawdry; gaudy; flashy. **2** Disreputable. [<RAFF + -ISH[1]]

raf·fle[1] (raf′əl) *n.* A form of lottery in which a number of people buy chances on an object. **—** *v.* **·fled ·fling** *v.t.* To dispose of by a raffle: often with *off.* **—** *v.i.* To take part in a raffle. [<OF *rafle* a clean sweep at dice < *rafler* snatch, prob. <Gmc. Cf. G *rafflen* snatch, freq. of *raffen* seize.] **— raf′fler** *n.*

raf·fle[2] (raf′əl) *n.* A jumble of rubbish; tangle: a nautical term. [Prob. <RAFF]

raf·fle·si·a (ra·flē′zhē·ə, -zē·ə) *n.* Any plant of the genus *Rafflesia* (family *Rafflesiaceae*), parasitic on the stems of the Malayan grape, and having huge, stemless, malodorous flowers and no leaves. [<NL, after Sir T. S. *Raffles,* 1781–1826, British governor in Sumatra, who discovered it] **— raf·fle′si·a′·ceous** (-zē·ā′shəs) *adj.*

raft[1] (raft, räft) *n.* A float of logs, planks, etc., fastened together for transportation by water. **—** *v.t.* **1** To transport on a raft. **2** To form into a raft. **—** *v.i.* **3** To travel by, be employed on, or manage a raft. [<ON *raptr* log]

raft[2] (raft, räft) *n. Colloq.* A large number or an indiscriminate collection of any kind. [<RAFF]

raft·er (raf′tər, räf′-) *n.* A timber or beam giving form, slope, and support to a roof. [OE *ræfter*]

rafts·man (rafts′mən, räfts′-) *n. pl.* **·men** (-mən) One who manages or works on a raft.

rag[1] (rag) *v.t.* **ragged, rag·ging** *Slang* **1** To tease or irritate. **2** To scold. **3** *Brit.* To play a practical joke on. **—** *n. Brit.* A ragging. [? <ON *ragna* curse, swear]

rag[2] (rag) *n.* **1** A torn piece of cloth; a fragment or semblance of anything. **2** *pl.* Cotton or linen textile remnants used in the making of rag paper. **3** *pl.* Tattered or shabby clothing; hence, any clothing: a jocular use. **4** A cloth of any kind, or something resembling one or characterized as such: used humorously or in disparagement. **5** In citrus fruits, the axis and carpellary walls. **— glad rags** *Slang* One's best clothes. **— to chew the rag** *Slang* To talk or argue at great length. [<ON *rögg* tuft or strip of fur]

rag[3] (rag) *n.* **1** A roofing slate rough on one side, and measuring 2 x 3 feet. **2** *Brit.* Any hard rock of cellular or coarsely granular texture. [Origin uncertain]

rag[4] (rag) *v.t.* **ragged, rag·ging** To compose or play in ragtime. **—** *n.* Ragtime.

rag·a·muf·fin (rag′ə·muf′in) *n.* Anyone, especially a boy, wearing very ragged clothes; a vagabond. [after *Ragamoffyn,* demon in a 15th century mystery play <RAG[2] + fanciful ending]

rag-bag (rag′bag′) *n.* A bag in which rags or scraps of unused cloth are kept.

rag carpet A carpet made from rags woven together by hand.

rag doll A cloth doll stuffed with rags.

rage (rāj) *n.* **1** Violent anger; wrath; fury. **2** Any great violence or intensity, as of a fever or a storm. **3** Extreme eagerness or emotion; ardent desire; great enthusiasm. **4** Any object eagerly sought after; a fad; fashion: Crossword puzzles are all the *rage.* See synonyms under ANGER, VIOLENCE. **—** *v.i.* **raged, rag·ing** **1** To speak, act, or move with unrestrained anger; feel or show violent anger. **2** To act or proceed with great violence: The storm *raged* for three days. **3** To spread or prevail uncontrolled, as an epidemic. [<OF <LL *rabia* <L *rabies* madness] **— rag′ing** *adj.* **— rag′ing·ly** *adv.*

rag·ged (rag′id) *adj.* **1** Rent or worn into rags; frayed: a *ragged* coat. **2** Wearing worn, frayed, or shabby garments; ill-dressed. **3** Of rough, broken or uneven character or aspect; harsh; dissonant: *ragged* rocks, *ragged* sounds. **4** Naturally of a rough or shaggy appearance (the original meaning): a *ragged* horse or sheep. See synonyms under ROUGH. **— rag′·ged·ly** *adv.* **— rag′ged·ness** *n.*

ragged edge *Colloq.* The extreme or precarious edge; the verge: the *ragged edge* of starvation; *ragged edge* of insanity. **— on the ragged edge** Dangerously near to losing one's self-control, sanity, etc.

ragged lady Fennelflower.

ragged robin A slender perennial European herb *(Lychnis floscuculi)* having red or pink flowers in panicles; the cuckoo flower.

rag·i (rag′ē, rä′gē) *n.* A cereal grass *(Eleusine coracona)* of the East Indies. Also **rag′ee, rag′·gy.** [<Hind. *rāgī*]

rag·lan (rag′lən) *n.* An overcoat or topcoat, the sleeves of which extend in one piece up to the collar. **—** *adj.* Denoting a garment with such sleeves. [after Lord Fitzroy *Raglan*]

Rag·lan (rag′lən), **Lord Fitzroy,** 1788–1855, English field marshal.

rag·man (rag′man′, -mən) *n. pl.* **·men** (-men′, -mən) One who buys and sells old rags and other waste; a ragpicker.

Rag·na·rök (räg′nä·rœk) In Norse mythology, the twilight of the gods, and the doomsday of the world, preceding its regeneration. Also **Rag′na·rok** (-rok). [<ON < *ragna* of the gods (genitive pl. of *regin*) + *rök* judgment]

ra·gout (ra·go͞o′) *n.* A highly seasoned dish of meat and vegetables stewed; hence, something spicy or piquant. **—** *v.t.* **ra·gouted** (-go͞od′), **ra·gout·ing** (-go͞o′ing) To make into a ragout. [<F < *ragouter* revive the appetite < *re-* anew + *à* (<L *ad*) to + *goût* (<L *gustus*) taste]

rag·pick·er (rag′pik′ər) *n.* One who picks up rags and other junk for a livelihood.

rag rug A rug made of rags.

rag·stone (rag′stōn′) *n.* **1** Rag; a rough, sandy, fossiliferous limestone: also **ragg.** **2** Stone quarried in thin slabs, as for pavements. Also **ragg′stone′.**

rag-tag (rag′tag′) *n.* Ragged people; the rabble. Also **rag-tag and bobtail.**

rag·time (rag′tīm′) *n.* **1** A kind of American dance music, developed from about 1890 to 1920, achieving its effects by highly syncopated rhythm in fast time. **2** The rhythm of this dance. [< *ragged time*]

Ra·gu·el (rə·gyo͞o′el) One of the seven archangels of Hebrew and Christian legend.

Ra·gu·sa (rä·go͞o′sä) **1** Italian name for DUBROVNIK. **2** A city in SE Sicily.

rag·weed (rag′wēd′) *n.* **1** A coarse, very common, annual or perennial herb (genus *Ambrosia*), especially the common ragweed *(A. artemisiifolia),* which induces hay fever, and the **great ragweed** *(A. trifida),* a tall species with stout hairy stem 5 to 15 feet high: also called *hogweed.* 2 *Brit.* The ragwort.

rag·wort (rag'wûrt') *n.* Any one of several herbs of the genus *Senecio,* as the European ragwort *(S. jacoboea),* a tall, smooth, cottony plant, with bright-yellow flowers.

rah (rä) *interj.* Hurrah! a cheer used chiefly in college yells. [<HURRAH]

Ra·hab (rā'hab) A harlot of Jericho who sheltered two Israelite spies. *Josh.* ii 1.

Ra·hab (rā'hab) In the Old Testament, a symbolical name for Egypt. *Isaiah* li 9.

Ra·hel (rä'həl) German form of RACHEL.

ra·ia (rä'yə, rī'ə) See RAYAH.

Ra·ia·te·a (rä'yä·tā'ä) The largest of the Society Islands in the Leeward group; 92 square miles.

rai·ble (rā'bəl) *v.t. & v.i. Scot.* To gabble.

raid (rād) *n.* 1 A hostile or predatory incursion by a rapidly moving body of troops or an armed vessel; a foray. 2 An attack by military aircraft; an air raid. 3 Any sudden invasion, capture, or irruption, as by the police. 4 An attempt to lower stock prices. See synonyms under INVASION —*v.t.* To make a raid on. —*v.i.* To participate in a raid. [Scottish var. of ROAD] —**raid'er** *n.*

raiding party A body of troops assigned to make a sudden raid in enemy territory.

rail[1] (rāl) *n.* 1 A bar, usually of wood or iron, resting on supports, as in a fence, at the side of a stairway, or capping the bulwarks of a ship; a horizontal wooden piece between panels, joining the stiles; also, a railing. 2 One of a series of parallel bars, of iron or steel, resting upon cross-ties, forming a support and guide for wheels, as of a railway. 3 A railway track considered as a means of transportation: to ship by *rail.* —**to go by rail** To travel by train. —**to ride (someone) on a rail** To put (a person) astride a rail and carry around or beyond the limits of a community, as a punishment. —*v.t.* To furnish or shut in with rails; fence. [<OF *reille* <L *regula.* Doublet of RULE.]

RAIL FENCE

rail[2] (rāl) *n.* 1 Any of numerous marsh-haunting, wading birds (family *Rallidae,* subfamily *Rallinae*) having very short wings, moderately long legs and toes, a short turned-up tail, long compressed bill, and soft, dun-colored plumage; specifically, in North America, the **king rail** *(Rallus elegans),* the **clapper rail** or mud hen *(R. longirostris),* and the sora or **Carolina rail.** They are esteemed as game birds. ◆ Collateral adjective: *ralline.* 2 Any of various other birds of northern Europe, as the corn crake. Also **rail'bird'.** [<OF *raale, ralle,* prob. ult. <L *radere* scratch]

rail[3] (rāl) *v.i.* To use scornful, insolent, or abusive language: with *at* or *against.* —*v.t.* To drive or force by railing. [<F *railler* <Pg. *ralhar* chatter, prob. <L *ragere* shriek. Doublet of RALLY[2].] —**rail'er** *n.*

rail·head (rāl'hed') *n.* 1 On an incompleted railroad, the farthest point to which rails have been laid. 2 That point on a railroad from which a military unit draws its supplies, ammunition, etc.

rail·ing (rā'ling) *n.* 1 A series of rails; a balustrade. 2 Rails, or material from which rails are made.

rail·ler·y (rā'lər·ē) *n. pl.* **·ler·ies** Merry jesting or teasing; a merry jest or bantering speech. [<F *raillerie* jesting]

rail·road (rāl'rōd') *n.* 1 A graded road, having metal rails supported by ties or sleepers, for the passage of rolling stock drawn by locomotives. 2 The system of tracks, stations, rolling stock, etc., used in transportation by rail. 3 The corporation or persons owning or operating such a system. —*v.t.* 1 To transport by railroad. 2 *U.S. Colloq.* To rush or force with great speed or without deliberation: to *railroad* a bill through Congress. 3 *U.S. Slang* To cause to be imprisoned on false charges or without fair trial. —*v.i.* 4 To work on a railroad.

rail·road·er (rāl'rō'dər) *n.* One who works on a railroad.

rail·road·ing (rāl'rō'ding) *n.* The construction, operation, or business of a railroad.

rail-split·ter (rāl'split'ər) *n.* One who splits logs into fence rails. —**the Rail-Splitter** Abraham Lincoln.

rail·way (rāl'wā') *n.* 1 A railroad: the common British term. 2 A trackway or set of rails, as in a warehouse or factory, for convenience in handling heavy articles, etc.: a parcel *railway* in a store.

railway post office Formerly, a government post office in a railroad car, sometimes occupying a whole car.

rai·ment (rā'mənt) *n. Archaic* Wearing apparel; clothing; garb. See synonyms under DRESS. [Aphetic var. of *arrayment* <ARRAY + -MENT]

Rai·mon·do (rī·mōn'dō) Italian form of RAYMOND. Also *Sp.* **Rai·mun·do** (rī·mo͞on'dō).

rain (rān) *n.* 1 The condensed vapor of the atmosphere falling in drops. ◆ Collateral adjective: *hyetal.* 2 The fall of such drops. 3 A fall or shower of anything in the manner of rain, or the substance poured down: a *rain* of bombs. 4 A rainstorm; shower; in the plural, the rainy season in a tropical country; also, a rainy region of the Atlantic Ocean. —*v.i.* 1 To fall from the clouds in drops of water: usually with *it* as the subject. 2 To fall like rain, as tears. 3 To send or pour down rain: said of clouds, God, etc. —*v.t.* 4 To send down like rain; shower. ◆ Homophones: *reign, rein.* [OE *regn*]

rain·band (rān'band') *n. Astron.* A dark band in the solar spectrum, caused by the presence of water vapor in the atmosphere.

rain·bow (rān'bō') *n.* 1 An arch of light formed opposite the sun during or after the close of a shower, exhibiting the colors of the spectrum, and caused by refraction, reflection, and dispersion of light in drops of water falling through the air. 2 Hence, any brilliant display of color. [OE *regnboga*]

Rainbow Bridge National Monument A region in southern Utah, site of a natural bridge; 160 acres; established, 1910.

rainbow cactus A cactus *(Echinocereus rigidissimus)* of the SW United States having red and white spines and red flowers.

rain·bow-chas·er (rān'bō'chā'sər) *n.* One who seeks the legendary pot of gold at the foot of the rainbow; a visionary.

rainbow trout See under TROUT.

rain check The stub of a ticket to an outdoor event, as a baseball game, entitling the holder to free admission at a future date if for any reason the event is called off: used figuratively of any postponed invitation.

rain·coat (rān'kōt') *n.* A cloak or coat intended to be worn in rainy weather.

rain crow The yellow-billed or the black-billed cuckoo (genus *Coccyzus*), so called from the belief among farmers that its cry is a sign of rain.

rain·drop (rān'drop') *n.* A drop of rain.

rain·fall (rān'fôl') *n.* 1 A fall of rain. 2 *Meteorol.* The amount of water precipitated in a given region over a stated time, as rain, hail, snow, or the like: measured in inches.

rain gage An instrument for measuring rainfall at a given place or during a given time; a pluviometer. Also **rain gauge.**

Rai·nier (rā·nir', rā'nir), **Mount** An extinct volcano in the Cascade Range, SW Washington; 14,408 feet; in Mount Rainier National Park.

rain-mak·er (rān'mā'kər) *n.* One reputedly able to cause rain; specifically, among certain American Indians, one who brings rain by incantation.

rain·out (rān'out') *n.* 1 *Physics* Precipitation of radioactive water droplets from cloud masses resulting from an underwater nuclear explosion. 2 A baseball game postponed because of rain. 3 Postponement of an outdoor event, esp. a baseball game.

rain·proof (rān'pro͞of') *adj.* Impervious to or shedding rain: said of garments. —*n. Brit.* A raincoat.

rain shadow *Meteorol.* An area of relatively small average rainfall on the leeward side of mountain barriers which serve to break the prevailing rain-bearing winds.

rain·spout (rān'spout') *n.* A waterspout (def. 2).

rain·storm (rān'stôrm') *n.* A storm accompanied by rain.

rain water Water that falls or has fallen directly from the clouds in the form of rain.

rain·wear (rān'wâr') *n.* Clothing for rainy weather, esp. raincoats, rubbers, galoshes, ponchos, etc.

rain·y (rā'nē) *adj.* **rain·i·er, rain·i·est** Characterized by, abounding in, or bringing rain. —**rain'i·ly** *adv.* —**rain'i·ness** *n.*

rainy day A time of need; hard times.

Rain·y Lake (rā'nē) A lake in northern Minnesota and SW Ontario; 50 miles long; 350 square miles.

raise (rāz) *v.* **raised, rais·ing** *v.t.* 1 To cause to move upward or to a higher level; lift; elevate. 2 To place erect; set up. 3 To construct or build; erect. 4 To make greater in amount, size, or value: to *raise* the price of corn. 5 To advance or elevate in rank, estimation, etc. 6 To increase the strength, intensity, or degree of. 7 To breed; grow: to *raise* chickens or tomatoes. 8 *U.S.* To rear (children, a family, etc.). 9 To give utterance to; cause to be heard: to *raise* a hue and cry. 10 To cause; occasion, as a smile or laugh. 11 To stir to action or emotion; arouse. 12 To waken; animate or reanimate: to *raise* the dead. 13 To gather together; obtain or collect, as an army, capital, etc. 14 To bring up for consideration, as a question. 15 To cause to swell or become lighter; leaven. 16 To put an end to, as a siege. 17 In poker, to bet more than. 18 *Naut.* To cause to appear above the horizon, as land or a ship, by approaching nearer. 19 *Scot.* To madden; enrage. —*v.i.* 20 *Colloq.* To cough up phlegm. 21 *Dial.* To rise or arise. 22 In poker, to make a raise. —**to raise Cain** (or **the devil, the dickens, a rumpus,** etc.) *Colloq.* To make a great disturbance; stir up confusion. —**to raise steam** To get or produce steam, as in a boiler, for the purpose of starting up a steam engine. —*n.* 1 The act of raising, in any sense; specifically, an increase, as of wages or a bet. 2 *Brit. Dial.* Something raised; an ascent; mound. ◆ Homophone: *raze.* [<ON *reisa* lift, set up. Akin to OE *rǣran* rear.] ◆ In British usage, *rise* is used for an increase in wages. —**rais'er** *n.*

Synonyms (verb): aggrandize, elevate, erect, exalt, lift, rear, uplift. See HEIGHTEN, INCREASE, PROMOTE. *Antonyms:* degrade, depress, humble, lower, reduce, sink.

raised (rāzd) *adj.* 1 Elevated in low relief. 2 Made with yeast or leaven.

rai·sin (rā'zən) *n.* A grape of a special sort dried in the sun or in an oven, and used for a dessert or in cookery. [<OF <L *racemus* bunch of grapes]

rais·ing (rā'zing) *n.* 1 The act or process of causing to rise, in any sense. 2 A gathering of persons for the purpose of erecting the frame of a building: also **raising bee.**

Rai·sin River (rā'zən) A river in SE Michigan, flowing 115 miles SE to Lake Erie.

rai·son d'ê·tre (re·zôn' de'tr') *French* Literally, a reason for being; a reason or excuse for existing.

rai·son·né (re·zô·nā') *adj. French* Arranged analytically or systematically; logical: a catalog *raisonné.*

Rai·su·li (ra·so͞o'lē), **Ahmed ibn-Muhammed,** 1875?–1925, Berber brigand in Morocco.

raj (räj) *n.* In India, sovereignty; rule. [<Hind. *rāj*]

ra·ja (rä'jə) *n.* A Hindu prince or chief of a tribal state in India; also, a Malay or Javanese ruler: often a mere title of distinction. Also **ra'jah.** [<Hind. *rājā* <Skt. *rājan* king]

Ra·ja·go·pa·la·cha·ria (rä'jə·gō·pä'lä·chä'ryə) **Chakravarti,** 1879–1972, governor general of India 1948–50.

Raj·ab (ruj'əb) See under CALENDAR (Mohammedan). [<Arabic]

Ra·ja·sthan (rä'jə·stän) A constituent State of NW India, formed by the merger of most of the Rajputana States (1948–50) and the former state of Ajmer (1956); 132,077 square miles; capital, Jaipur. Also **Ra'ja·stan.**

Raj·kot (räj'kōt) The capital city of the former state of Saurashtra, western India, in NW Bombay State after 1956.

Raj·put (räj'po͝ot) *n.* One of a powerful and warlike Hinducaste, said to be a branch of the Kshatriyas, which gives its name to Rajputana. Also **Raj'poot.** [<Hind. *rājpūt* prince <Skt. *rājaputra* <*rājan* a king, ruler + *putra* son]

Raj·pu·ta·na (räj'poo·tä'nə) A region in NW India, land of the Rajput princes; 134,959 square miles; roughly equivalent to the constituent State of Rajasthan.

Rajputana States The former princely states in Rajputana, merged 1948–50, to form Rajasthan, except for four included in Bombay State; 132,559 square miles.

rake[1] (rāk) *n.* A toothed implement for drawing together loose material, or making a surface loose. —*v.* **raked, rak·ing** *v.t.* **1** To scrape or gather together with or as with a rake. **2** To smooth, clean, or prepare with a rake: to *rake* a lawn. **3** To gather by diligent effort; scrape together. **4** To search or examine carefully. **5** To direct heavy gunfire along the length of, as a ship or column of troops; enfilade. —*v.i.* **6** To use a rake. **7** To scrape or pass roughly or violently: with *across, over,* etc. **8** To make a search. —**to rake in** *Colloq.* To earn or acquire (money, etc.) in large quantities. [OE *raca*] —**rak'er** *n.*

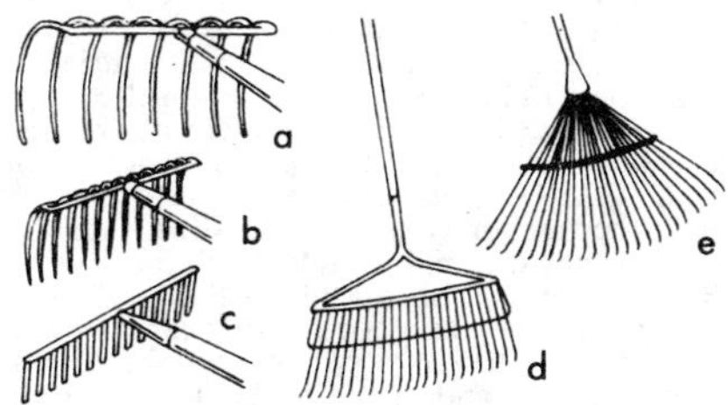

TYPES OF RAKES
a. Refuse. *b.* Clam. *c.* Garden.
d Steel lawn *e* Broom lawn

rake[2] (rāk) *v.* **raked, rak·ing** *v.i.* To lean from the perpendicular, as a ship's masts. —*v.t.* To cause to lean; incline. —*n.* Inclination from the perpendicular or horizontal, as of the sustaining surfaces of an airplane, or the edge of a cutting tool. [Origin uncertain. Cf. G *ragen* project.] —**raked** *adj.*

rake[3] (rāk) *n.* A dissolute, lewd person; debauchee. —*v.i.* **raked, rak·ing** To play the rake; live a lewd, dissolute life: with *it.* [Short for RAKEHELL]

rake[4] (rāk) *v.i.* **raked, rak·ing 1** To hunt with the nose to the ground, thus following by track rather than by wind: said of hunting dogs. **2** To fly after game: said of hawks; also, to fly wide of the game. [OE *racian* go forward, proceed]

rake·hell (rāk'hel') *adj. Archaic* Recklessly abandoned and dissolute: also **rake'hell'y.** —*n.* A rake; a profligate debauchee. [ME *rakel* rash, wild; refashioned after RAKE[1] + HELL. Cf. ON *reikal* reckless.]

rake–off (rāk'ôf', -of') *n. U.S. Slang* A share, as of profits; commission; rebate, usually illegitimate.

rak·i (rak'ē, rä'kē) *n. Turkish* An aromatic liquor flavored with mastic; mastic brandy; also, a coarse liquor made from grain spirit. Compare ARRACK. Also **rak'ee.** [<Turkish *rāqi* <Arabic *'araq.* Akin to ARRACK.]

rak·ish[1] (rā'kish) *adj.* **1** *Naut.* Having the masts unusually inclined: usually connoting a suggestion of speed. **2** Dashing; jaunty. [< RAKE[2]; def. 2 infl. by *rakish*[2]] —**rak'ish·ly** *adv.* —**rak'ish·ness** *n.*

rak·ish[2] (rā'kish) *adj.* Like or behaving like a rake; dissolute; profligate. —**rak'ish·ly** *adv.* —**rak'ish·ness** *n.*

Rá·kó·czy March (rä'kō·tsē) A national patriotic song of Hungary. [after Francis *Rákóczy,* 1676–1735, Hungarian patriot]

râle (räl) *n. Pathol.* A sound additional to that of normal respiration, heard on auscultation of the chest and indicative of the presence, nature, or stage of a disease. [<F, rattle]

Ra·leigh (rô'lē) The capital of North Carolina.

Ra·leigh (rô'lē), **Sir Walter,** 1552–1618, English courtier, colonizer of Roanoke, soldier, and author; beheaded. Also spelled **Ra'legh.**

Ra·lik Chain (rä'lik) The western group of the Marshall Islands, including Kwajalein, Eniwetok, Bikini, Rongelap, Rongerik and others.

ral·len·tan·do (ral'ən·tan'dō, *Ital.* räl'len·tän'·dō) *adv. Music* Gradually slower. [<Ital., ppr. of *rallentare* slow down <*lento* slow <L *lentus*]

ral·li·form (ral'ə·fôrm) *adj.* Pertaining to or like the rails. See RAIL[2]. [<NL *rallus* (<OF *ralle* rail[2]) + -FORM]

ral·line (ral'in, -in) *adj.* Of, pertaining, or belonging to the rail subfamily of birds *(Rallinae).* [<NL *rallus* rail[2]]

ral·ly[1] (ral'ē) *n. pl.* **·lies 1** An assembling or reassembling, as of scattered troops. **2** A rapid recovery of a normal condition after exhaustion or depression: a *rally* from sickness, a *rally* in stocks. **3** A mass meeting to arouse enthusiasm. **4** In tennis, the interchange of several strokes before one side wins the point. —*v.* **·lied, ·ly·ing** *v.t.* **1** To bring together and restore to effective discipline: to *rally* fleeing troops. **2** To summon up or revive: to *rally* one's spirits. **3** To bring together for common action. —*v.i.* **4** To return to effective discipline or action: The enemy *rallied.* **5** To unite for common action. **6** To make a partial or complete return to a normal condition. **7** In tennis, to engage in a rally. See synonyms under ENCOURAGE. [<F *rallier* <*re-* again + *allier* join. See ALLY.] —**ral'li·er** *n.*

ral·ly[2] (ral'ē) *v.t. & v.i.* To attack with raillery; joke; tease; banter. See synonyms under RIDICULE. [<F *railler* rail. Doublet of RAIL[3].] —**ral'li·er** *n.*

Ralph (ralf, *Brit.* räf) A masculine personal name. Also *Lat.* **Ra·dul·phus** (ra·dul'fəs). [< Gmc, house wolf]

ram (ram) *n.* **1** A male sheep. **2** An instrument or device for driving, forcing, or crushing by heavy blows or thrusts; specifically, a battering–ram, the striking weight of a pile driver or steamhammer, or the plunger of a force pump. **3** Formerly, a projection or beak on the bow of a warship, for crushing or cutting into an opposing vessel; also, a warship constructed with such a beak. **4** An instrument for raising water by pressure of condensed air; a hydraulic ram. —*v.t.* **rammed, ram·ming 1** To strike with or as with a ram; dash against. **2** To drive or force down or into something. **3** To cram; stuff. [OE] —**ram'mer** *n.*

Ram (ram) *Astron.* The zodiacal constellation Aries.

Ra·ma (rä'mə) In Hindu mythology, the name of three heroes, especially that of Ramachandra.

Ra·ma·chan·dra (rä'mə·chun'drə) The hero of the *Ramayana,* called the seventh avatar of Vishnu.

Ram·a·dan (ram'ə·dän') *n.* The Mohammedan ninth month, the time of the annual fast of thirty days; also, the fast. See under CALENDAR (Mohammedan). Also **Ram'a·dhan', Ram'a·zan'** (-zän'). [<Arabic *ramaḍan,* lit., the hot month]

Ra·ma·krish·na (rä'mä·krish'nə), 1834–86, religious name of Gadadhar Chatterji, a Hindu mystic and religious teacher, regarded as a divine incarnation by his disciples.

Ra·man (rä'mən), **Sir Chandrasekhara Venkata,** 1888–1970, Indian physicist.

Ra·man effect (rä'mən) *Physics* The scattering of monochromatic light by a medium, in frequencies both equal to and other than the frequency of the incident light, because of a gain or loss in quanta during transmission. [after Sir Chandrasekhara Venkata *Raman*]

Ra·ma·pi·the·cus (rä'mə·pith'ə·kəs) *n.* a manlike primate, originally discovered in the Siwalik Range of NW India. [<RAMA + Gk *pithēkos* ape]

Ra·ma·ya·na (rä·mä'yə·nə) A Hindu epic poem in seven books, of about 400 B.C. Compare MAHABHARATA. [<Skt. *Rāmāyana* < *Rāma* Rama + *-ayana* relating to]

ram·ble (ram'bəl) *v.i.* **·bled, ·bling 1** To walk about freely and aimlessly; roam. **2** To write or talk aimlessly or without sequence of ideas. **3** To proceed with turns and twists; meander. —*n.* **1** The act of rambling; an aimless movement with change of direction; a leisurely stroll. **2** A meandering path; maze. [Origin unknown]

Synonyms (verb): range, roam, rove, stray, stroll, wander. See WANDER.

ram·bler (ram'blər) *n.* **1** One who or that which rambles. **2** Any of several varieties of roses, as the crimson rambler *(Rosa bierana),* with climbing stems and huge clusters of small or medium–sized flowers.

Rambler, The A semiweekly publication, 1750–52, published and written for the most part by Dr. Samuel Johnson.

ram·bling (ram'bling) *adj.* Showing absence of plan or system; aimless; wandering. —**ram'·bling·ly** *adv.*

Ram·bouil·let (ram'bo͝o·lā, *Fr.* räṅ·bo͞o·ye') *n.* A variety of merino sheep bred in France for meat and wool. [from *Rambouillet,* a town in northern France]

ram·bunc·tious (ram·bungk'shəs) *adj. U.S. Colloq.* Rude and boisterous; rough and uncontrollable. [Prob. <RAM + alter. of BUMPTIOUS]

ram·bu·tan (ram·bo͞o'tən) *n.* **1** The spiny, bright–red, pleasantly acid fruit of an East Indian and Malaysian tree *(Nephelium lappaceum).* **2** The tree that bears it. [< Malay <*rambut* hair]

Ra·mée (rə·mā'), **Louise de la** See OUIDA.

ram·e·kin (ram'ə·kin) *n.* **1** A seasoned dish of bread crumbs baked with eggs and cheese. **2** A dish in which ramekins are baked. **3** Any dish used both for baking and serving. Also **ram'e·quin.** [<F *ramequin*]

ra·men·tum (rə·men'təm) *n. pl.* **·ta** (-tə) **1** A part of something scraped off; a minute part. **2** *Bot.* A thin, membranous, chaffy scale, formed on the surface of leaves, the stems of ferns, etc.: an outgrowth from the epidermis. [<L, scraping <*radere* scrape] —**ram·en·ta·ceous** (ram'ən·tā'shəs) *adj.*

Ram·e·ses (ram'ə·sēz) Name of 12 Egyptian monarchs: also spelled *Ramses.*

—**Rameses II,** 1292–25 B.C., built many temples; sometimes said to be the pharaoh who oppressed the Israelites.

ra·met (rā'mit) *n. Bot.* Any individual member of a clon. [<L *ramus* branch]

Ram·gan·ga (räm·gung'gə) A river in northern Uttar Pradesh, India, flowing about 350 miles SW and SE to the Ganges.

ram·ie (ram'ē) *n.* **1** A shrubby Chinese and East Indian perennial *(Boehmeria nivea)* of the nettle family, with numerous rodlike stems and large heart–shaped leaves. **2** The fine, glossy bast fiber yielded by its stem, used for cordage and certain coarse textile fabrics. Also **ram'ee.** [<Malay *rami*]

ram·i·fi·ca·tion (ram'ə·fə·kā'shən) *n.* **1** The act or process of ramifying. **2** *Bot.* The arrangement of branches or parts, as on a plant; also, one of the parts. **3** An offshoot or subdivision.

ram·i·form (ram'ə·fôrm) *adj.* **1** Branch–shaped. **2** Branched. [<L *ramus* branch + -FORM]

ram·i·fy (ram'ə·fī) *v.t. & v.i.* **·fied, ·fy·ing** To divide or spread out into or as to branches; branch out. [<F *ramifier* <Med. L *ramificare* <L *ramus* branch + *facere* make]

ram·il·lie (ram'ə·lē) *n.* A type of wig with a plaited tail, worn in 18th century England: named in honor of the British victory at Ramillies. Also **ram'i·lie, ram'i·lies, ram'il·lies.**

Ram·il·lies (ram'ə·lēz, *Fr.* rà·mē·yē') A village in central Belgium; scene of Marlborough's victory over French forces, 1706. Also **Ra·mil·lies–Of·fus** (rà·mē·yē'ô·fü').

ram·mish (ram'ish) *adj.* **1** Like a ram; strong–scented. **2** Lustful. Also **ram'my.** —**ram'·mish·ness** *n.*

ram·jet (ram'jet') *n.* A type of jet engine which provides continuous jet propulsion on the principle of the athodyd.

Ra·món (rä·mōn') Spanish form of RAYMOND.

Ra·món y Ca·jal (rä·mōn' ē kä·häl'), **Santiago,** 1852–1934, Spanish histologist.

ra·mose (rā'mōs, rə·mōs') *adj.* **1** Branching. **2** Consisting of or having branches. [<L *ramosus* <*ramus* branch]

ra·mous (rā'məs) *adj.* **1** Of, pertaining to, or like branches. **2** Ramose. [See RAMOSE]

ramp[1] (ramp) *n.* **1** An inclined passageway or roadway, as between floors or different levels of a building. **2** In building, a concave part at the top or cap of a railing, wall, or coping. [<F *rampe* <*ramper* climb]

ramp[2] (ramp) *v.i.* **1** To rear up on the hind legs and stretch out the forepaws. **2** *Her.* To be in a rampant or threatening position.

3 To act in a violent or threatening manner; storm; rampage. —*n.* The act of ramping. [<OF *ramper* climb]

ram·page (ram′pāj) *n.* Boisterous agitation or excitement; a dashing about with anger or violence. —*v.i.* (ram·pāj′) **·paged, ·pag·ing 1** To rush or act violently. **2** To storm; rage. [Prob. <RAMP²] —**ram·pag′er** *n.*

ram·pa·geous (ram·pā′jəs) *adj.* Violent; boisterous. —**ram·pa′geous·ly** *adv.* —**ram·pa′geous·ness** *n.*

ram·pan·cy (ram′pən·sē) *n.* The condition or quality of being rampant.

ram·pant (ram′pənt) *adj.* **1** Exceeding all bounds; unrestrained; wild. **2** Widespread; unchecked, as an erroneous belief or superstition. **3** Standing on the hind legs; rearing; leaping: said of a quadruped. **4** *Her.* Standing on the sinister hind leg, with both forelegs elevated, the dexter above the sinister, and the head in profile: said of a beast of prey. **5** *Archit.* Springing from points on an inclined plane. [<OF, ppr. of *ramper* climb] —**ram′pant·ly** *adv.*

RAMPANT

ram·part (ram′pärt, -pərt) *n.* **1** The embankment surrounding a fort, on which the parapet is raised: sometimes including the parapet. **2** A bulwark or defense. —*v.t.* To supply with or as with ramparts; fortify. [<F *rempart* < *remparer* fortify < *re-* again + *emparer* prepare <L *ante* before + *parare* prepare]
Synonyms (noun): barbican, barricade, barrier, breastwork, bulwark, defense, embankment, fence, fortification, guard, mole, mound, outwork, security, wall.

ram·pike (ram′pīk′) *n. Canadian* The bleached skeleton of a tree killed by fire: also *ranpike.* Also **ram′pole′** (-pōl′).

ram·pi·on (ram′pē·ən) *n.* **1** A European perennial *(Campanula rapunculus)* cultivated in gardens for its root, which is eaten as a salad. **2** One of various similar plants, as the horned rampion (genus *Phyteuma*), bearing spikes of blue flowers. [<Ital. *ra(m)ponzolo* <L *rapum* turnip]

Ram·pur (räm′po͝or) A former princely state in north central India, included (1949) in Uttar Pradesh State; 894 square miles; also, a city, its capital.

ram·rod (ram′rod′) *n.* **1** A rod used to drive home the charge of a muzzleloading gun or pistol. **2** A similar rod used for cleaning the barrel of a rifle, etc.

Ram·say (ram′zē), **Allan,** 1686–1758, Scottish poet. —**James Andrew** See DALHOUSIE, MARQUIS OF. —**Sir William,** 1852–1916, Scottish chemist. —**Sir William Mitchell,** 1851–1939, Scottish classicist and geologist.

Ram·ses (ram′sēz) See RAMESES.

Rams·gate (ramz′gāt, *Brit.* -git) A port on the North Sea in eastern Kent, England; a seaside resort.

ram·shack·le (ram′shak′əl) *adj.* About to go to pieces from age and neglect; shaky; unsteady. [Origin uncertain]

ram·son (ram′zən, -sən) *n.* **1** A species of garlic *(Allium ursinum)*; broad-leaved garlic. **2** Its root, used for salads. [OE *hrameson,* pl. of *hramsa*]

ram-stam (ram′stam′, räm′stäm′) *Brit. Dial. & Scot. adj.* Rash; thoughtless; precipitate. —*n.* **1** A hasty and venturesome person. **2** Recklessness. —*adv.* With rashness; heedlessly.

ram·til (ram′til) *n.* An annual herb *(Guizotia abyssinica)* cultivated in Abyssinia and India for its oil-producing seeds, **ramtil seeds.** Also called *Niger seed.* [<Hind.]

ram·u·lose (ram′yə·lōs) *adj. Bot.* Bearing many small branches. [<L *ramulosus* < *ramulus,* dim. of *ramus* branch]

ra·mus (rā′məs) *n. pl.* **·mi** (-mī) **1** A branch. **2** *Biol.* One division of a forked structure, as the branch of a nerve, etc. [<L, branch]

ran (ran) Past tense of RUN.

Ran (rän) In Norse mythology, the wife of Ægir and goddess of the sea.

Ra·na (rä′nä) *n.* Prince: formerly the title of a ruling chief in various parts of India. [< Hind.]

ra·nar·i·um (rə·nâr′ē·əm) *n. pl.* **·nar·i·a** (-nâr′ē·ə) A place where frogs are raised or kept. [<L *rana* frog]

rance (rans) *n.* A fine hard stone, dull red in color, with blue and white markings; Belgian marble. [<F]

ranch (ranch) *n.* **1** An establishment for rearing or grazing cattle, sheep, horses, etc., in large herds. **2** The buildings, personnel, and lands connected with it. **3** A large farm: a fruit *ranch.* Also **ranche.** —*v.i.* To manage or work on a ranch. [<Sp. *rancho* mess]

ranch·er (ran′chər) *n.* **1** The owner of a ranch. **2** One who works on a ranch; a cowboy.

ran·che·ro (ran·châr′ō) *n. pl.* **·ros** *SW U.S.* A rancher. [<Sp.]

ranch·ing (ran′ching) *n.* **1** The operation of a ranch. **2** Work on a ranch.

ranch·man (ranch′mən) *n. pl.* **·men** (-mən) **1** A herdsman on a ranch. **2** The owner of a ranch; a rancher.

ran·cho (ran′chō, rän′-) *n. pl.* **·chos** *SW U.S.* **1** A hut or group of huts, in which ranchmen lodge. **2** A stock farm; ranch. [<Sp.]

ran·cid (ran′sid) *adj.* Having the peculiar tainted smell of oily substances that have begun to spoil owing to oxidation or hydrolysis; rank; sour. Compare SWEET. [<L *rancidus* < *rancere* be rancid]

ran·cid·i·ty (ran·sid′ə·tē) *n.* **1** The quality or state of being rancid. **2** A rancid smell or taste. Also **ran′cid·ness.**

ran·cor (rang′kər) *n.* Bitter and vindictive enmity; malice; spitefulness. Also *Brit.* **ran′·cour.** See synonyms under ENMITY, HATRED. [<OF <L < *rancere* be rank] —**ran′cor·ous** *adj.* —**ran′cor·ous·ly** *adv.* —**ran′cor·ous·ness** *n.*

rand¹ (rand) *n.* **1** In shoe manufacturing, a strip of leather at the heel of a shoe to which the lifts are attached. **2** *Brit. Dial. & Scot.* A river border overgrown with reeds, or the unplowed border round a field; margin; strip. [OE, border, edge]

rand² (rand, ränd) *n.* The standard monetary unit of South Africa, worth in 1964 about $1.40. [< THE RAND]

Rand (rand), **The** See WITWATERSRAND.

ran·dan (ran′dan, ran·dan′) *n.* **1** A boat rowed by three persons, the one amidships having two oars and the others one each. **2** This style of rowing. [Origin uncertain]

ran·dem (ran′dəm) *adv.* With three horses harnessed one in front of the other. —*n.* A team or vehicle driven randem. Also **ran′dem-tan′·dem.** [<RANDOM, on analogy with *tandem*]

RANDEM

Ran·dolph (ran′dolf), **A(sa) Philip,** born 1889, U.S. labor leader. —**John,** 1773–1833, U. S. statesman: known as *Randolph of Roanoke.* —**Peyton,** 1723?–75, American patriot; first president, Continental Congress, 1774–75.

ran·dom (ran′dəm) *n.* **1** Want of definite aim or intention. **2** Something done, made, or chosen without method or purpose. **3** *Printing* A sloping board for holding galleys of type matter intended for making up forms. —**at random** Without definite purpose or aim; haphazardly. —*adj.* **1** Done or chosen without definite aim or deliberate purpose; chance; casual. **2** In statistics, erratic. [<OF *randon* force, violence < *randonner, rander* move rapidly, gallop] —**ran′dom·ly** *adv.*

random sample *Stat.* A limited group of individuals, cases, or observations, so assembled from the total array as to be truly representative of its characteristics, properties, trends, and the like. Also **random selection.**

ran·dy (ran′dē) *Scot. adj.* **1** Disorderly; riotous; also, coarse. **2** Lewd; lustful. —*n.* **1** An impudent beggar. **2** A boisterous, coarse, or loose woman; also, a virago.

ra·nee (rä′nē) See RANI.

rang (rang) Past tense of RING².

range (rānj) *n.* **1** The area over which anything moves, operates, or is distributed. **2** *U.S.* An extensive tract of land over which cattle, sheep, etc., roam and graze. **3** *U.S.* Pasturage; grazing ground. **4** *Bot. & Zool.* The geographical area throughout which a specific plant or animal exists. **5** The extent or scope of something: the whole *range* of politics. **6** The extent to which any power can be made effective: *range* of vision; *range* of influence. **7** The extent of variation of anything: the temperature *range.* **8** The extent of possible variation in pitch: said of musical instruments or the voice. **9** A line, row, or series, as of mountains. **10** *U.S.* A row of townships, each six miles square, numbered east or west from a base meridian. **11** *Rare* Rank; order. **12** The horizontal distance between a gun and its target. **13** The horizontal distance covered by a projectile. **14** A place for shooting at a mark: a rifle *range.* **15** In archery, the number of ends shot at each given distance: compare ROUND. **16** A large cooking stove for conducting several cooking operations at one time. **17** *Stat.* The inclusive difference between the extreme values in any series of variable data: a *range* of 20 from a value of 0 to a value of 19. —*adj.* Of or pertaining to a range. —*v.* **ranged, rang·ing** *v.t.* **1** To place or arrange in definite order, as in rows or lines. **2** To assign to a class, division, or category; classify; rank. **3** To move about or over (a region, etc.), as in exploration. **4** To put (cattle) to graze on a range. **5** *Mil.* To obtain the range of (a target) by firing alternately above and below it. **6** To place in position; adjust or train, as a telescope or gun. **7** *Naut.* To lay out (the anchor cable) on deck so that the anchor may descend without hindrance. —*v.i.* **8** To move over an area in a thorough, systematic manner, as a dog hunting game. **9** To rove; roam. **10** To occur; extend; be found: said of plants and animals. **11** To extend or proceed: The shot *ranged* to the right. **12** To exhibit variation within specified limits: weights *ranging* from 20 to 50 pounds. **13** To lie in the same direction, line, etc. **14** *Mil.* To be capable of achieving a specified range (def. 12): That old cannon *ranged* about one mile. See synonyms under RAMBLE, WANDER. [<OF < *ranger, rengier* arrange < *renc* row <Gmc. Doublet of RANK¹.]

range finder An instrument with which to determine the distance of an object or target from a given point, as from a gun.

Range·ley Lakes (rānj′lē) A chain of lakes in western Maine.

rang·er (rān′jər) *n.* **1** One who or that which ranges; a rover. **2** One of an armed band, usually mounted, designed to protect large tracts of country. **3** One of a herd of cattle that feeds on a range. **4** *Brit.* A government official in charge of a royal forest or park: formerly a gamekeeper. **5** *U.S.* A warden employed in patrolling forest tracts. —**rang′·er·ship** *n.*

Rang·er (rān′jər) *n.* One of a select group of U. S. soldiers who were trained for raiding action on enemy territory: the equivalent of the English *Commando.*

range rake A T-shaped instrument for obtaining quick angular measurements in correcting deviations in the range of a gun.

Ran·gi·ro·a (rän′gi·rō′ä) Largest of the Tuamotu islands, consisting of 20 islets around a lagoon 45 miles long and 15 miles wide.

Rang·i·tik·ei (räng′gi·tik′ē) A river in southern North Island, New Zealand, flowing 115 miles SW to Cook Strait.

Ran·goon (rang·go͞on′) The capital of Burma, a port of Lower Burma on the **Rangoon River,** a marine estuary formed at Rangoon by the junction of two inland rivers, flowing 25 miles SE to the Andaman Sea.

rang·y (rān′jē) *adj.* **rang·i·er, rang·i·est 1** Disposed to roam, or adapted for roving, as cattle. **2** Having long legs adapted to a long, limber gait. **3** Having long thin arms and legs: said of a person. **4** Affording wide range; roomy. **5** Resembling a mountain range.

ra·ni (rä′nē) *n.* **1** The wife of a raja or prince. **2** A reigning Hindu queen or princess. Also spelled *ranee.* [<Hind.]

Ran·jit Singh (run′jēt siṅ′hə), 1780–1839, maharajah of the Punjab; founded Sikh empire. Also *Runjeet Singh.*

rank¹ (rangk) *n.* **1** A series of objects ranged in a line or row; a range. **2** Degree of official standing, especially in the army and navy. See table under GRADE. **3** A line of soldiers drawn up side by side in close order: distinguished from *file.* **4** *pl.* An army; also, the mass of soldiery; the order of private soldiers: The colonel rose from the *ranks.* **5** A row of eight squares on a chessboard extending from the left of the player to the right. 6 Relative position in a scale of dignity or of life; degree; grade: the *rank* of baronet; the *rank* of a plant or animal organism. 7 High degree or position; especially, the state of being a member of a titled nobility: a lady of *rank*. 8 Degree of worth or excellence; relative status. See synonyms under CLASS, SORT. — *v.t.* 1 To place or arrange in a rank or ranks. 2 To place in a class, order, etc.; assign to a position or classification. 3 To take precedence of; outrank: Sergeants *rank* corporals. — *v.i.* 4 To hold a specified place or rank: His poetry *ranks* with the best. 5 To have the highest rank or grade. [<OF *ranc, renc* <Gmc. Doublet of RANGE.]

rank[2] (rangk) *adj.* 1 Very vigorous and flourishing in growth as from fertilization or moisture. 2 Strong and disagreeable to the taste or smell. 3 Excessive or immoderate, in unfavorable sense: *rank* injustice. 4 Producing a luxuriant growth; fertile. 5 *Law* Inequitable; excessive. 6 Strong or deep: said of a cut or the adjustment of the tool making a cut. 7 *Obs.* In heat; lustful. [OE *ranc* strong] — **rank'ly** *adv.* — **rank'ness** *n.*

rank and file 1 The common soldiers of an army, including all from the corporals downward. 2 Those who form the bulk of any organization, as distinct from officers or leaders.

Ran·ke (räng'kə), **Leopold von,** 1795–1886, German historian.

rank·er (rangk'ər) *n.* 1 One who has served in the ranks. 2 A commissioned officer who has risen from the ranks.

rank·ing (rangk'ing) *adj.* Superior in rank; taking precedence (over others in the grade): a *ranking* senator, officer, etc.

ran·kle (rang'kəl) *v.* **·kled, ·kling** *v.i.* 1 To cause continued resentment, sense of injury, etc.: The defeat *rankles* in his breast. 2 To become irritated or inflamed; fester. — *v.t.* 3 To irritate; embitter. [<OF *rancler,* alter. of *draoncler* fester <Med. L *dracunculus,* dim. of *draco* dragon]

Ran·noch (ran'əkh), **Loch** A lake in NW Perth, central Scotland; 9 miles by 1 mile.

ran·oid (ran'oid) *adj. Zool.* Of, pertaining, or belonging to a family *(Ranidae)* of frogs, especially as distinguished from the toads. [<L *rana* a frog + -OID]

ran·pike (ran'pīk') *n.* A rampike.

ran·sack (ran'sak) *v.t.* 1 To search through every part of. 2 To search throughout for plunder; pillage. See synonyms under EXAMINE. [<ON *rannsaka* search a house < *rann* house + *sœkja* seek] — **ran'sack·er** *n.*

ran·som (ran'səm) *v.t.* 1 To secure the release of (a person, property, etc.) for a required price, as from captivity or detention. 2 To set free on payment of ransom. 3 To redeem from sin or its consequences. See synonyms under DELIVER. — *n.* 1 The consideration paid for the release of a person or property captured or detained. 2 Release purchased, as from captivity. [<OF *rançon, raençon* <L *redemptio, -onis* redemption < *redimere* redeem. Doublet of REDEMPTION.] — **ran'som·er** *n.* — **ran'som·less** *adj.*

Ran·som (ran'səm), **John Crowe,** U.S. poet, 1888–1974.

rant (rant) *v.i.* 1 To speak in loud, violent, or extravagant language; declaim vehemently; rave. 2 *Scot. & Brit. Dial.* To frolic noisily; be uproariously jolly. — *v.t.* 3 To exclaim or utter in a ranting manner. — *n.* 1 Declamatory and bombastic talk. 2 *Scot. & Brit. Dial.* Wild gaiety; a boisterous revel. [<MDu. *ranten* rave] — **rant'ing** *adj.* — **rant'ing·ly** *adv.*

rant·er (ran'tər) *n.* One who rants; a noisy, boisterous speaker or declaimer: applied opprobriously to various religious speakers.

ra·nun·cu·la·ceous (rə·nung'kyə·lā'shəs) *adj. Bot.* Belonging or pertaining to a family *(Ranunculaceae)* of plants, the crowfoot or buttercup family, including larkspur, aconite, peony, and hellebore.

ra·nun·cu·lus (rə·nung'kyə·ləs) *n. pl.* **·lus·es** or **·li** (-lī) Any of a genus *(Ranunculus)* of herbaceous annuals or perennials, the buttercups or crowfoots, typical of the family *Ranunculaceae.* [<L *ranunculus,* a medicinal plant, orig. dim. of *rana* frog]

Ra·oul (rä·o͞ol') French form of RALPH.

rap[1] (rap) *v.* **rapped, rap·ping** *v.t.* 1 To strike sharply and quickly; hit. 2 To utter in a sharp manner: with *out*: to *rap* out an oath. 3 *Slang* To criticize severely. — *v.i.* 4 To strike sharp, quick blows. 5 *Slang* To have a frank discussion; talk. — *n.* 1 A sharp blow. 2 A sound caused by or as by knocking; specifically, such a sound ascribed to the agency of spirits. 3 *Slang* A reprimand; blame; also, consequences: to take the *rap.* 4 *Slang* A prison sentence. 5 *Slang* A severe criticism. 6 *Slang* A talk; discussion. See synonyms under BLOW[2]. — *adj. Slang* Marked by frank discussion: a *rap* session. [Imit. Cf. Dan. *rap,* Sw. *rapp.*] — **rap'per** *n.*

rap[2] (rap) *v.t.* **rapt** or **rapped, rap·ping** 1 *Obs.* To snatch. 2 *Archaic* To seize or transport as with ecstasy; carry away: now current only in the past participle *rapt* (sometimes erroneously spelled *wrapt*). [Back formation <RAPT]

rap[3] (rap) *n.* A counterfeit coin used as a halfpenny in Ireland in the 18th century; hence, anything worthless: I don't care a *rap.* [Origin uncertain. Cf. G. *rappe,* a small coin.]

rap[4] (rap) *n.* A skein of yarn containing 120 yards. [Origin unknown]

ra·pa·cious (rə·pā'shəs) *adj.* 1 Given to plunder or rapine. 2 Extortionate; grasping. 3 Predaceous; subsisting on prey seized alive: said of hawks, etc. [<L *rapax, -acis* < *rapere* seize] — **ra·pa'cious·ly** *adv.*

ra·pac·i·ty (rə·pas'ə·tē) *n.* The quality or character of being rapacious. Also **ra·pa'cious·ness.** [<L *rapacitas, -tatis*]

Ra·pal·lo (rä·päl'lō) A port in NW Italy, at the head of the **Gulf of Rapallo,** an inlet on the Gulf of Genoa.

Ra·pa Nu·i (rä'pä no͞o'ē) The native name for EASTER ISLAND.

rape[1] (rāp) *v.* **raped, rap·ing** *v.t.* 1 To commit rape upon; ravish. 2 To plunder or sack (a city, etc.). 3 *Archaic* To carry off by force. — *v.i.* 4 To commit rape. See synonyms under VIOLATE. — *n.* 1 The act of a man who has sexual intercourse with a woman against her will or (called **statutory rape**) with a girl below the age of consent. 2 Any unlawful sexual intercourse or sexual connection by force or threat: homosexual *rape* in prison. 3 The plundering or sacking of a city, etc. 4 Any gross violation, assault, or abuse: the *rape* of our natural resources. [<AF <L *rapere* seize]

rape[2] (rāp) *n.* An Old World annual *(Brassica napus)* grown as a forage crop for sheep and hogs, and having seeds which yield rape oil. [<L *rapum* turnip]

rape[3] (rāp) *n.* 1 *pl.* In winemaking, refuse stalks and skins of grapes. 2 A filter used in vinegarmaking. [<F *râpe* <Med. L *raspa* < *raspare* grate <Gmc. Cf. OHG *raspon.*]

rape oil A yellowish to brown oil obtained from rapeseed: used as a lubricant and in the manufacture of rubber substitutes, soft soaps, etc. Also called *colza oil.*

rape·seed (rāp'sēd') *n.* 1 The seed of the rape. 2 The plant.

Raph·a·el (raf'ē·əl, rā'fē-; *Fr.* rà·fà·el', *Du.* rä'fel, *Ger.* rä'fä·el) A masculine personal name. [<Hebrew, God hath healed]

— **Raphael** One of the seven archangels of Christian legend.

— **Raphael,** 1483–1520, Italian painter: full name Raffaello Sanzio.

Raph·a·el·esque (raf'ē·əl·esk') *adj.* Characteristic of, or in the style of Raphael.

ra·phe (rā'fē) *n. pl.* **·phae** (-fē) 1 *Anat.* A seamlike appearance often seen in organs, especially at the median line of the body. 2 *Bot.* The fibrovascular cord that connects the hilum of plant ovules with the chalaza. 3 A line or rib connecting the nodules on a diatom valve. Also spelled *rhaphe.* [<NL <Gk. *rhaphē* seam < *rhaptein* stitch together]

ra·phi·a (rā'fē·ə) See RAFFIA.

ra·phide (rā'fid) *n. pl.* **raph·i·des** (raf'ə·dēz) *Bot.* A needle-shaped crystal of oxalate of lime found in many plant cells. Also **ra'phis.** [<Gk. *rhaphis, rhaphidos* needle]

rap·id (rap'id) *adj.* 1 Having great speed. 2 Bearing the marks of or characterized by rapidity. 3 Done or completed in a short time; advancing speedily to a termination: *rapid* growth. See synonyms under SWIFT[1]. — *n.* *Usually pl.* A descent in a river less abrupt than a waterfall. [<L *rapidus* < *rapere* seize, rush] — **rap'id·ly** *adv.* — **rap'id·ness** *n.*

Rap·i·dan River (rap'ə·dan') A river of northern Virginia, flowing 90 miles east to the Rappahannock; scene of severe fighting in the Civil War.

rap·id-fire (rap'id·fīr') *adj.* 1 Firing shots rapidly. 2 Characterized by speed: *rapid-fire* repartee. Also **rap'id-fir'ing.**

rapid fire A rate of gunfire lower than that of quick fire.

ra·pid·i·ty (rə·pid'ə·te) *n.* The quality or state of being rapid; swiftness.

rapid transit The local transportation of passengers by means faster than surface vehicles; specifically, elevated or subway passenger transportation.

ra·pi·er (rā'pē·ər, rāp'yər) *n.* 1 In the 16th and 17th centuries, a long, straight, two-edged sword with a large cup hilt, used in dueling, chiefly for thrusting. 2 The French small sword of the 18th century, a shorter straight sword without cutting edge and therefore used for thrusting only. [<F *rapière,* prob. < *raspière* poker, rasper; appar. first used derisively]

RAPIER

rap·ine (rap'in) *n.* The taking of property by force, as in war; spoliation; pillage. See synonyms under PLUNDER. [<F <L *rapina* < *rapere* seize. Doublet of RAVEN[2], *n.,* RAVINE.]

rap·ist (rā'pist) *n.* One who commits rape.

rap·loch (rap'ləkh) *Scot. & Brit. Dial. adj.* Unkempt; coarse. — *n.* Coarse homespun cloth made of inferior undyed wool.

Rap·pa·han·nock (rap'ə·han'ək) A river in northern Virginia, flowing 212 miles SE to Chesapeake Bay.

rap·pa·ree (rap'ə·rē') *n.* 1 An Irish guerrilla of the 17th century. 2 A freebooter or bandit. [<Irish *rapaire* short pike]

rap·pee (ra·pē') *n.* A dark, coarse, strong-flavored snuff. [<F *(tabac) râpé* grated (tobacco), pp. of *râper* scrape]

rap·pel (ra·pel') *v.i.* **·pelled, ·pel·ling** In mountaineering, to descend from a precipitous height by letting oneself down on a rope. — *n.* Descent by means of a rope. [<F]

rap·per (rap'ər) *n.* 1 One who raps. 2 A spiritualist medium. 3 A knocker, as on a door or at the mouth of a mining shaft.

rap·port (ra·pôrt', -pōrt'; *Fr.* rà·pôr') *n.* Harmony of relation; accordance; sympathetic relation: commonly with *in.* — **en rapport** *French* In close accord. [<F < *rapporter* refer, bring back < *re-* again + *apporter* bring <L *apportare* < *ad-* to + *portare* bring]

rap·proche·ment (rà·prôsh·män') *n. French* The act of coming or of being brought together; a state of harmony or reconciliation; restoration of cordial relations, as between nations.

rap·scal·lion (rap·skal'yən) *n.* A rogue; scamp; rascal. [< earlier *rascallion* <RASCAL + fanciful ending]

rapt (rapt) *adj.* 1 Carried away with lofty emotion; enraptured; transported. 2 Engrossed; intent; deeply engaged. Sometimes erroneously spelled *wrapt.* [<L *raptus,* pp. of *rapere* seize]

Rap·ti (räp'tē) A river in Nepal and northern India, flowing 400 miles SE to the Gogra river in Uttar Pradesh State.

rap·to·ri·al (rap·tôr'ē·əl, -tō'rē-) *adj.* 1 Seizing and devouring living prey; predatory. 2 *Ornithol.* Having talons adapted for seizing and holding prey: said especially of hawks, vultures, eagles, owls, and other carnivorous birds. [<L *raptor* snatcher < *raptus,* pp. of *rapere* seize]

rap·ture (rap'chər) *n.* 1 The state of being rapt or transported; ecstatic joy; ecstasy. 2 The act of transferring a person from one place to another: Elijah's *rapture* to heaven. 3 An act or expression of excessive delight. 4 *Obs.* A snatching away; violent seizure. — *v.t.* **·tured, ·tur·ing** To enrapture. [<RAPT]

add,āce,câre,pälm; end,ēven; it,īce; odd,ōpen,ôrder; to͝ok,po͞ol; up,bûrn; ə = a in *above,* e in *sicken,* i in *clarity,* o in *melon,* u in *focus;* yo͞o = u in *fuse;* oi,oil; ou,pout; ch,check; g,go; ng,ring; th,thin; t͟h,this; zh,vision. Foreign sounds à,œ,ü,kh,ṅ; and ◆: see page xx. < from; + plus; ? possibly.

Synonyms (noun): bliss, delight, ecstasy, exultation, happiness, joy, rejoicing, transport, triumph. *Rejoicing* is *happiness* or *joy* that finds utterance in word, song, festivity, etc. *Delight* is vivid, overflowing *happiness* of a somewhat transient kind; *ecstasy* is a state of extreme or extravagant *delight*; *rapture* is closely allied to *ecstasy*, but is more serene, exalted, and enduring. *Transport* is the condition of one carried away out of himself by some powerful passion or emotion, whether joyous or the reverse. *Triumph* is such *joy* as results from victory, success, achievement. See ENTHUSIASM, HAPPINESS. *Antonyms*: agony, apathy, dejection, despair, distress, ennui, horror, misery, pain, tedium, torture, woe, wretchedness.

rap·tur·ous (rap′chər·əs) *adj.* Being in a state of, exhibiting, or characterized by rapture. See synonyms under HAPPY. **— rap′tur·ous·ly** *adv.* **— rap′tur·ous·ness** *n.*

Ra·quel (rä·kel′) Spanish form of RACHEL.

ra·ra a·vis (râr′ə ā′vis) *pl.* **ra·rae aves** (râr′ē ā′vēz) *Latin* Literally, a rare bird; any uncommon or peculiar person or thing.

rare[1] (râr) *adj.* **1** Of infrequent occurrence. **2** Highly esteemed because of infrequency or uncommonness; valuable; choice. **3** Rarefied: now chiefly of the atmosphere. **4** *Obs.* Dispersed. [<F <L *rarus* rare]

Synonyms: curious, extraordinary, incomparable, infrequent, odd, peculiar, precious, remarkable, scarce, singular, strange, uncommon, unique, unusual. *Extraordinary*, signifying greatly beyond the ordinary, is a neutral word, capable of a high and good sense or of an invidious, opprobrious, or contemptuous signification. *Unique* is alone of its kind; *rare* is *infrequent* of its kind; great poems are *rare*. To say of a thing that it is *rare* is simply to affirm that it is now seldom found, whether previously common or not; as, a *rare* old book; a *rare* word; to call a thing *scarce* implies that it was at some time more plentiful, as when we say money is *scarce*. A particular coin may be *rare*; *scarce* applies to demand and use, and almost always to concrete things; to speak of virtue, genius, or heroism as *scarce* would be somewhat ludicrous. See CHOICE, EXTRAORDINARY, OBSOLETE, ODD. *Antonyms*: see synonyms for COMMON.

rare[2] (râr) *adj.* Not thoroughly cooked: applied to roasted or broiled meat retaining its redness and juices: in England commonly termed *underdone*. [OE *hrēre* lightly boiled]

rare·bit (râr′bit) *n.* Welsh rabbit. [Alter. of (WELSH) RABBIT]

rare earth *Chem.* Any of the metallic oxides of the rare-earth elements.

rare-earth elements (râr′ûrth′) *Chem.* A group of metallic elements comprising the lanthanide series. Also **rare-earth metals.**

rar·ee show (râr′ē) **1** A show carried or contained in a box; a peepshow. **2** A cheap street show or any street show or spectacle. [Alter. of *rare show*; after the mispronunciation characteristic of the Savoyard promoters of these shows]

rar·e·fac·tion (râr′ə·fak′shən) *n.* The process or act of making rare or less dense. Also **rar′e·fi·ca′tion.** [<L *rarefactus*, pp. of *rarefacere*] **— rar′e·fac′tive** *adj.*

rar·e·fy (râr′ə·fī) *v.* **·fied, ·fy·ing** *v.t.* **1** To make rare, thin, less solid, or less dense; expand by dispersion of the particles. **2** To refine or purify. **—** *v.i.* **3** To become rare, thin, or less solid. **4** To become more pure. [<F *raréfier* <L *rarefacere* < *rarus* rare + *facere* make] **— rar′e·fi′a·ble** *adj.*

rare·ly (râr′lē) *adv.* **1** Not often; infrequently. **2** With unusual excellence or effect; finely: The breeze blows *rarely*. **3** Exceptionally; extremely; in an unusual degree: She dressed in raiment *rarely* rich.

rare·ness (râr′nis) *n.* The condition or quality of being rare in any sense.

rare·ripe (râr′rīp′) *adj.* Ripening early. **—** *n.* A fruit that ripens early: applied especially to many varieties of peaches, and to a variety of onion. [OE *hrathe* early, soon + RIPE]

Rar·i·tan River (rar′ə·tən) A river of NE New Jersey, flowing 25 miles south to **Raritan Bay,** a western arm of Lower New York Bay.

rar·i·ty (râr′ə·tē) *n. pl.* **·ties 1** The quality or state of being rare, uncommon, or infrequent; infrequency. **2** That which is exceptionally valued from scarceness. **3** The state of being rare, thin, or tenuous; tenuity: opposed to *density*. [<L *raritas, -tatis*]

Ra·ro·ton·ga (rä′rô·tông′gə) The largest and southwesternmost of the Cook Islands, capital of the group; 26 square miles.

ras (räs) *n.* In Ethiopia, a prince. [<Arabic *ra's* the head]

ras·cal (ras′kəl) *n.* **1** An unprincipled fellow; a rogue; knave: sometimes used playfully. **2** *Obs.* One of the common herd; a man of low birth or station. **—** *adj.* Pertaining to the rabble; contemptible; base; mean. [<OF *rascaille* < *rasque* filth, shavings, ult. <L *radere* shave, scrape]

ras·cal·i·ty (ras·kal′ə·tē) *n. pl.* **·ties 1** The quality of being rascally. **2** A rascally act.

ras·cal·ly (ras′kəl·ē) *adj.* Worthy of a rascal; knavish; base. See synonyms under BAD[1]. **—** *adv.* After the manner of a rascal.

Ras Da·shan (räs dä·shän′) The highest peak in Ethiopia; 15,157 feet.

rase (rāz) *v.t.* **rased, ras·ing** To raze. [Var. of RAZE]

rash[1] (rash) *adj.* **1** Acting without due caution or regard of consequences; reckless; precipitate. **2** Exhibiting recklessness or precipitancy. **3** *Obs.* Quick; speedy. See synonyms under IMPETUOUS, IMPRUDENT. [ME *rasch*. Akin to Du. & G *rasch* quick.] **— rash′ly** *adv.* **— rash′ness** *n.*

rash[2] (rash) *n.* A superficial eruption of the skin, often localized. [? <F *rache* <OF *rasque*. See RASCAL.]

rash[3] (rash) *n. Scot.* A rush; bulrush.

rash·er[1] (rash′ər) *n.* A thin slice of meat: used especially of bacon. [Prob. < obs. *rash* cut, slash]

rash·er[2] (rash′ər) *n.* A vermilion-colored California rockfish (*Sebastodes miniatus*). [<Sp. *rascacio*, kind of fish]

Rask (räsk), **Rasmus Christian,** 1787–1832, Danish philologist and writer.

Ras·kol·nik (räs·kôl′nik) *n. pl.* **·ni·ki** (-nē·kē) or **·niks** A Russian dissenter; a member of one of the sects that split off from the Orthodox Church in the 17th century. [<Russian *raskolenik* dissenter < *raskole* schism]

Ras·mus·sen (räs′mo͝os·ən), **Knud Johan Victor,** 1879–1933, Danish Arctic explorer.

ra·son (rā′son) *n. Meteorol.* A method of obtaining and recording weather information at high altitudes by combining a radiosonde with automatic signal-recording devices and radio direction-finders. [<RA(DIO)SON(DE)]

ra·so·ri·al (rə·sôr′ē·əl, -sō′rē-) *adj.* In the habit of scratching the ground for food, as domestic fowl and other gallinaceous birds. [<NL *Rasores*, lit., scratchers <L *rasum*, pp. of *radere* scrape]

rasp (rasp, räsp) *n.* **1** A filelike tool having coarse pyramidal projections for abrasion. **2** A machine containing a large cylindrical grater. **3** The act or sound of rasping. **—** *v.t.* **1** To scrape with or as with a rasp. **2** To scrape or rub roughly. **3** To affect unpleasantly; irritate. **4** To utter in a rough voice. **—** *v.i.* **5** To grate; scrape [<OF *raspe* < *rasper* scrape, prob. <Gmc.] **— rasp′er** *n.*

rasp·ber·ry (raz′ber′ē, -bər·ē, räz′-) *n. pl.* **·ries 1** The round fruit of certain brambles (genus *Rubus*) of the rose family, composed of drupes clustered around a fleshy receptacle. **2** The plant yielding this fruit. **3** *Slang* A vulgar sound indicating contempt and produced by vibrating the tongue between the lips [< earlier *rasp* raspberry (? <OF (*vin*) *raspé* thin wine < *râpe* RAPE[3]) + BERRY]

rasped (raspt, räspt) *adj.* Rough or roughened, with or as with a coarse file: said of uncut book edges.

rasp·ing (ras′ping, räs′-) *adj.* Making a harsh sound; hence, irritating.

Ras·pu·tin (ras·pyo͞o′tin, *Russian* räs·po͞o′tin), **Grigori,** 1871–1916, Russian monk, favorite of Czar Nicholas II and his wife; assassinated: real name Novikh.

rasp·y (ras′pē, räs′-) *adj.* **rasp·i·er, rasp·i·est 1** Inclined to rasp; rough; grating. **2** Irritable.

Ras·se·las (ras′ə·ləs) The hero of a philosophical romance of this name by Samuel Johnson.

ra·sure (rā′zhər) *n.* Erasure.

rat (rat) *n.* **1** A destructive and injurious rodent (family *Muridae*) of world-wide distribution, larger and more aggressive than the mouse; especially, the **Norway rat** (*Rattus norvegicus*) and the smaller **roof** or **black rat** (*R. rattus*): both are carriers of the plague bacillus transmitted by the rat flea. **2** Some other mammal like or likened to the rat. **3** *Slang* A cowardly or selfish person who deserts or betrays his associates. **4** A slender cushion of curled hair or the like, worn by women, with the natural hair rolled over it. **—** *v.i.* **rat·ted, rat·ting 1** To hunt rats. **2** *Slang* To desert one's party, companions, etc., especially for one's own safety or advantage. **3** *Slang* To inform; act the betrayer. [OE *ræt*]

rat·a·ble (rā′tə·bəl) *adj.* **1** *Brit.* Subject to assessment; legally liable to taxation. **2** Estimated proportionally; pro rata: a *ratable* distribution. **3** That may be rated or valued. Also **rate′a·ble.** **— rat′a·bil′i·ty, rat′a·ble·ness** *n.* **— rat′a·bly** *adv.*

rat·a·fi·a (rat′ə·fē′ə) *n.* **1** A cordial flavored with fruits. **2** A flavoring essence based on the essential oil of bitter almonds. **3** A sweet biscuit. Also **rat′a·fee′** (-fē′). [<F]

Ra·tak (rä′täk) The eastern chain of the Marshall Islands.

ra·tal (rāt′l) *n.* An amount on which rates are assessed. [<RATE + -AL[1]]

ra·tan (ra·tan′) See RATTAN.

rat·a·ny (rat′ə·nē) See RHATANY.

rat·a·plan (rat′ə·plan′) *n.* A rapidly repeated sound, as of the beating of a drum. **—** *v.t.* & *v.i.* **·planned, ·plan·ning** To sound a rataplan (on). [<F; imit. of drumming]

rat·a·tat·tat (rat′ə·tat′tat′) *n.* A quick, sharp rapping sound, as a knock at a door. [Imit.]

rat·bag (rat′bag′) *n. Austral. Slang* An eccentric person: a derogatory term.

rat·bag·ger·y (rat′bag′ər·ē) *n. Austral. Slang* Eccentric behavior.

rat·bite fever (rat′bīt′) *Pathol.* An infectious disease caused by the bite of a rat infested with certain bacteria: characterized by local ulcerations, rash, severe muscular pains, and relapsing fever. Also **ratbite disease.**

ratch[1] (rach) *n.* **1** A ratchet or ratchet wheel. **2** A spot on a horse's face. [Short for RATCHET]

ratch[2] (rach) *v.i. Naut.* To sail by the wind on any tack. [Back formation < obs. *raught*, pp. of REACH, on analogy with *caught, catch*]

ratch·et (rach′it) *n.* **1** A mechanism consisting of a notched wheel, the teeth of which engage with a pawl, permitting motion of the wheel in one direction only. **2** The pawl or the wheel thus used. Also **ratchet wheel.** [<F *rochet* spool <Ital. *rochetto* bobbin, dim. of *rocca* distaff <Gmc. Cf. OHG *roccho* spindle.]

rate[1] (rāt) *n.* **1** The measure of a thing by its relation to a standard; proportional or comparative amount or degree: a high *rate* of interest. **2** Degree of value; price: railway *rates*; also, the unit cost of a commodity or service: the *rate* for electricity, gas, water, and the like. **3** Comparative rank or class; condition. **4** The amount of variation of a timepiece; gain or loss in seconds. **5** A ratio for the assessment of property taxes: a *rate* of 40 mills per thousand dollars. **6** *Brit.* A local tax on property. **7** The proportion which a given fact or event bears to the total of relevant cases involved: a death *rate*, marriage *rate*. **8** A fixed allowance or amount. **9** *Obs.* Degree; estimation. See synonyms under TAX. **— at any rate** In any case; under any circumstances; anyhow. **— differential rate** The lower of two rates given usually by two competing railroad lines to one of two places in the same territory in order to make profits even: in England called **preferential rate. —** *v.* **rat·ed, rat·ing** *v.t.* **1** To estimate the value or worth of; appraise. **2** To place in a certain rank or grade. **3** To fix the amount of tax or liability on. **4** To consider; regard: He is *rated* as a great statesman. **5** To fix the rate for the transportation of (goods), as by rail, water, or air. **—** *v.i.* **6** To have rank, rating, or value. See synonyms under CALCULATE. [<OF <L *rata (pars)* reckoned (part), fem. of *ratus*, pp. of *reri* reckon]

rate[2] (rāt) *v.t* & *v.i.* **rat·ed, rat·ing** To reprove with vehemence; rail at; scold. [Origin uncertain. Cf. OF *rater* scold and Sw. *rata* find fault.]

ra·tel (rā′təl, rä′-) *n.* A nocturnal carnivore (genus *Mellivora*) resembling the badger, ashy-gray above and black below, of South and West Africa and India. [<Afrikaans *rateldas* <Du. *raat* honeycomb + *das* badger]

rate·pay·er (rāt′pā′ər) *n. Brit.* One who pays local property taxes or rates.
rat·er[1] (rā′tər) *n.* One who or that which rates or estimates.
rat·er[2] (rā′tər) *n.* One who scolds or berates.
rat-foot dots In Chinese painting, a method of representing pine boughs or branches by brush strokes that resemble the print of a rat's foot: four or five slightly curved strokes radiating from a white center dot.
rath (rath) *adj. Obs.* **1** Unusually early; vehement. **2** Swift; quick; soon. **3** Relating to the forenoon, or to the early part of a period of time. Also **rathe** (rāth). [OE *hrathe* early]
Rat·haus (rät′hous′) *n. German* A government or municipal building; a town hall.
rathe (rāth) *adv. Obs.* Early; betimes; promptly. [OE *hrathe* soon]
Ra·the·nau (rä′tə·nou), **Walther,** 1867–1922, German statesman and industrialist.
rath·er (rath′ər, rä′thər) *adv.* **1** With preference for one of two things or courses; more willingly. **2** With more reason; more wisely; more strictly or accurately. **3** Somewhat; in a greater or less degree; to a certain extent. **4** Very much; exceedingly. **5** *Obs.* Sooner; earlier; more quickly. [OE *hrathor* sooner, compar. of *hrathe* soon, quick]
rath·er·est (rath′ər·ist, rä′thər-) *adv. Brit. Dial.* Most especially; most of all.
raths·kel·ler (rath′skel·ər, räts′kel·ər) *n.* **1** In Germany, the cellar of a city hall, often used as a beer hall or restaurant. **2** Any beer hall or restaurant patterned after the German type, but not necessarily located below the street level. [<G < *rat* town hall + *keller* cellar]
Ra·ti·bor (rä′tē·bôr) A port on the Oder in southern Poland: Polish *Racibórz.*
rat·i·fi·ca·tion (rat′ə·fə·kā′shən) *n.* The act of ratifying, or the state of being ratified.
rat·i·fy (rat′ə·fī) *v.t.* **·fied, ·fy·ing** To give sanction to, especially official or authoritative sanction; make valid by approving, especially the work of an agent or representative; confirm. [<F *ratifier* <Med. L *ratificare* <L *ratus* fixed, reckoned + *facere* make] —**rat′i·fi′er** *n.*
Synonyms: accept, approve, confirm, corroborate, endorse, establish, justify, sanction, seal, settle, substantiate, validate. See ASSENT, CONFIRM, JUSTIFY. *Antonyms*: abolish, abrogate, annul, cancel, deny, disavow, disown, extinguish, nullify, repeal, rescind, revoke.
rat·ing[1] (rā′ting) *n.* **1** Classification according to a standard; grade; rank. **2** The classification of a vessel. **3** An evaluation of the financial standing of a business firm or an individual. **4** The designation of the operating capacity of a piece of machinery, as expressed in horsepower, kilowatts, etc. **5** Any specialist grade held by an enlisted man or officer: the *rating* of a pilot, gunner, parachutist, etc., in the U.S. Army, or of boatswain's mate in the Navy. **6** *Brit.* An enlisted man in the Royal Navy. See synonyms under TAX.
rat·ing[2] (rā′ting) *n.* A harsh rebuke; scolding. [<RATE[2]]
ra·tio (rā′shō, -shē·ō) *n. pl.* **·tios** **1** Relation of degree, number, etc.; relative amount; proportion; rate: There has always been a *ratio* between demand and supply. **2** The relation between two numbers or two magnitudes of the same kind; especially, the quotient of one magnitude divided by the other, or the factor that, multiplied into one, will produce the other. **3** Formerly, the relation expressed by subtracting one quantity from the other; the difference. **4** *Obs.* A portion; ration. [<L. Doublet of RATION, REASON.]
ra·ti·oc·i·nant (rash′ē·os′ə·nənt) *adj.* Reasoning, as contrasted with *ratiocinate.* [See RATIOCINATE]
ra·ti·oc·i·nate (rash′ē·os′ə·nāt) *v.i.* **·nat·ed, ·nat·ing** To make a deduction from premises; reason. —*adj.* Reasoned about. [<L *ratiocinatus,* pp. of *ratiocinari* calculate, deliberate < *ratio* reckoning. See REASON.] —**ra′ti·oc′i·na′tor** *n.*
ra·ti·oc·i·na·tion (rash′ē·os′ə·nā′shən) *n.* The deduction of conclusions from premises; reasoning. See synonyms under REASONING. [<L *ratiocinatio, -onis*]
ra·ti·oc·i·na·tive (rash′ē·os′ə·nā′tiv) *adj.* **1** Of or pertaining to the act or process of reasoning. **2** Given to ratiocination; argumentative. [<L *ratiocinativus*]
ra·tio·ing (rā′shō·ing) *n.* The reduction or enlargement of a series of aerial photographs so that all are on one scale for use in a mosaic map. [<RATIO + -ING]
ra·tion (rash′ən, rā′shən) *n.* **1** A portion; share. **2** A fixed allowance or portion of food, etc., allotted in time of scarcity. —**emergency ration** Portions of canned beef, hardtack, milk chocolate, etc., for use in the field by soldiers. —*v.t.* **1** To provide with rations; issue rations to, as an army. **2** To give out or allot in rations, as gasoline, rubber, butter, etc. [<F <L *ratio, -onis.* Doublet of RATIO, REASON.] —**ra′tion·ing** *n.*
ra·tion·al (rash′ən·əl) *adj.* **1** Possessing the faculty of reasoning. **2** Conformable to reason; judicious; sensible. **3** Pertaining to reason; attained by reasoning. **4** Pertaining to rationalism. **5** *Math.* **a** Pertaining to a rational number. **b** Denoting an algebraic expression containing variables within radicals, as $\sqrt{x^2-y^2}$, $\sqrt{4x-1}$. Compare IRRATIONAL. **6** In Greek and Latin prosody, denoting the measurement of metrical units; capable of being measured in metrical units. —*n.* That which is rational. [<L *rationalis* < *ratio, -onis*] —**ra′tion·al·ly** *adv.* —**ra′tion·al·ness** *n.*
Synonym (adj.): reasonable. A *rational* mind is one that is capable of the ordinary and normal processes of thought; a *reasonable* mood is one at the time susceptible to the influence of reasons. A *rational* man is capable of using his reasoning powers; a *reasonable* man has them habitually in exercise. *Rational* is opposed to *insane, reasonable* to *fanatical, misguided, obstinate, unreasonable, visionary.* See SAGACIOUS, SANE[1], WISE[1].
ra·tion·ale (rash′ən·al′, -ä′lē, -ā′lē) *n.* **1** A rational exposition of principles. **2** The logical basis of a fact; the reason or reasons collectively. [<L, neut. of *rationalis*]
ra·tion·al·ism (rash′ən·əl·iz′əm) *n.* **1** The formation of opinions by relying upon reason alone, independently of authority or of revelation: opposed to *supernaturalism.* **2** *Philos.* **a** The theory of a priori ideas, that truth and knowledge are attainable through reason rather than through experience: opposed to *empiricism.* **b** The theory that reason itself is a source of knowledge independent of sense perception: opposed to *sensationalism.* —**ra′tion·al·ist** *n.* —**ra′tion·al·is′tic** or **·ti·cal** *adj.* —**ra′tion·al·is′ti·cal·ly** *adv.*
ra·tion·al·i·ty (rash′ən·al′ə·tē) *n. pl.* **·ties** **1** Sanity; reasonableness; naturalness. **2** The cause or reason; rationale. [<LL *rationalitas*]
ra·tion·al·i·za·tion (rash′ən·əl·ə·zā′shən, -ī·zā′·shən) *n.* **1** The act or process of rationalizing. **2** *Psychol.* The process of devising acceptable reasons for desires, emotions, acts, beliefs, or opinions which cannot be creditably justified to oneself or to others in terms of their actual motives. **3** *Brit.* The act of bringing an industry into accord with up-to-date methods of organization and operation.
ra·tion·al·ize (rash′ən·əl·īz′) *v.* **·ized, ·iz·ing** *v.t.* **1** *Psychol.* To explain (one's behavior) on grounds ostensibly rational but not in accord with the actual or unconscious motives. **2** To explain or treat from a rationalistic point of view. **3** To make rational or reasonable; render conformable to reason. **4** *Math.* To remove the radicals containing variables from (an expression or equation); also, to alter the radicals so as to change (the expression) into more workable form: thus, if $\sqrt{x^2+2x} = 3$, then, by squaring, $x^2 + 2x = 9$, and $x^2 + 2x - 9 = 0$. —*v.i.* **5** To think in a rational or rationalistic manner. **6** *Psychol.* To rationalize one's behavior. —**ra′tion·al·iz′er** *n.*
rational number See under NUMBER.
Rat·is·bon (rat′is·bon, -iz-) An English name for REGENSBURG.
Rat Islands (rat) A group in the Aleutian Islands, extending 110 miles west of the Andreanof Islands.
rat·ite (rat′īt) *adj.* Designating a division of flightless birds *(Ratitae),* including ostriches, cassowaries, kiwis, emus, etc., which have aborted wings and a breastbone without a keel. —*n.* One of the *Ratitae.* [<L *ratis* raft]
rat kangaroo Any of several tiny kangaroos, as the **rufous rat kangaroo** *(Aepyprymnus rufescens).*
rat·line (rat′lin) *n. Naut.* **1** One of the small ropes fastened across the shrouds of a ship, used as the rounds of a ladder for going aloft or descending. **2** The material so used. See SHROUD[2]. Also **rat′lin** (-lin), **rat′·ling** (-ling). [Origin unknown]

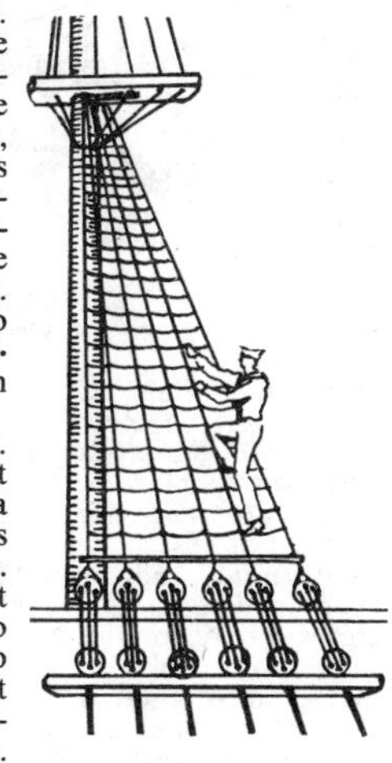
RATLINES

ra·toon (ra·tōōn′) *n.* **1** A new shoot from the root of a cropped plant, as from a sugarcane. **2** One of the heart leaves in a tobacco plant. —*v.i.* To sprout from a root planted the previous year. [<Sp. *retoño* <Hind. *ratun*]
rat race *Slang* A frantic, usually fruitless, struggle; a wearisome hustle or strife.
rats·bane (rats′bān′) *n.* Rat poison.
rat-tail (rat′tāl′) *adj.* Resembling a rat's tail in form. Also **rat′-tailed′.**
rat·tan (ra·tan′) *n.* **1** The long, tough, flexible stem of a palm (genera *Calamus* and *Daemonorops*) growing in East India, Africa, and Australia. **2** The palm itself. **3** A cane or switch of rattan. Also spelled *ratan.* [<Malay *rotan*]
rat·teen (ra·tēn′) *n. Obs.* A thick woolen twilled cloth. [<F *ratine*]
rat·ten[1] (rat′n) *v.t. Brit. Slang* To persecute or harass (an employer or employee) because of refusal to join or obey a trade union. [<RATTEN[2]] —**rat′ten·er** *n.* —**rat′ten·ing** *n.*
rat·ten[2] (rat′n) *n. Scot. & Brit. Dial.* A rat.
rat·ter (rat′ər) *n.* **1** A dog or cat that catches rats. **2** *Slang* A deserter or traitor.
rat·tish (rat′ish) *adj.* Belonging to or resembling a rat.
rat·tle[1] (rat′l) *v.* **·tled, ·tling** *v.i.* **1** To make a series of sharp noises in rapid succession, as by striking together: dead limbs *rattling* in the wind. **2** To move or act with such noises. **3** To talk rapidly and foolishly; chatter. —*v.t.* **4** To cause to rattle: to *rattle* pennies in a tin cup. **5** To utter or perform rapidly or noisily. **6** *Colloq.* To confuse; disconcert: Her reaction *rattled* me. See synonyms under SHAKE. —*n.* **1** A series of short, sharp sounds in rapid succession, as from the collision of small, hard objects. **2** A plaything, implement, etc., adapted to produce a rattling noise: a watchman's *rattle.* **3** The series of jointed horny rings in the tail of a rattlesnake, or one of these; also, the noise produced by the vibration of this organ. **4** Rapid and noisy talk; chatter. **5** One who talks fast and foolishly. **6** A râle; the death rattle, caused by the passage of air through mucus. See synonyms under NOISE. [Imit.]
rat·tle[2] (rat′l) *v.t.* **·tled, ·tling** *Naut.* To fit with ratlines: used in the phrase **to rattle down the rigging.** [<RATLINE]
rat·tle·box (rat′l·boks′) *n.* **1** A toy or the like having a chamber to contain something, as a ball, that will rattle. **2** A low hairy North American annual (genus *Crotalaria*) having seeds which rattle in the inflated pod. **3** The bladder campion.
rat·tle·brain (rat′l·brān′) *n.* A talkative, flighty person; foolish chatterer. Also **rat′tle·head′** (-hed′), **rat′tle·pate′** (-pāt′). —**rat′tle-brained′** *adj.*
rat·tler (rat′lər) *n.* **1** One who or that which rattles. **2** A rattlesnake.
rat·tle·snake (rat′l·snāk′) *n.* Any of various venomous, thick-bodied American snakes (genera *Crotalus* and *Sistrurus,* family *Viperidae*) with a tail ending in a series of

horny, loosely connected, modified joints, which clash together with a rattling noise when the tail is vibrated.

RATTLESNAKE
(From 2 to 8 feet in length)

rattlesnake flag One of the early flags of the American Revolution, bearing a rattlesnake and the motto "Don't Tread On Me."

rattlesnake plantain A small orchid *(Goodyera pubescens)* of Canada and the eastern United States.

rattlesnake root 1 Any of several erect perennial herbs (genus *Prenanthes*) considered to be a cure for the bite of a rattlesnake. 2 The root or tuber. 3 Senega.

rattlesnake weed 1 A species of hawkweed *(Hieracium venosum)* of the northern United States. 2 Rattlebox. 3 Button snakeroot (genus *Eryngium*).

rat·tle·trap (rat′l·trap′) *n.* 1 Any rickety, clattering, or worn-out vehicle or article. 2 *Slang* A loquacious or gossipy person. —*adj.* Shaky; dilapidated.

rat·tling (rat′ling) *adj.* 1 Making a clatter. 2 Garrulous; sprightly. 3 *Colloq.* Very; extraordinary; good. —*adv. Colloq.* Extraordinarily; very: a *rattling* good time.

rat·tly (rat′lē) *adj.* 1 Inclined to rattle. 2 Clattering.

rat·ton (rat′n) *n. Scot. & Brit. Dial.* A small rat.

rat·trap (rat′trap′) *n.* 1 A trap foı catching rats. 2 A situation from which escape is impossible; any hopeless or fatal predicament.

rat·ty (rat′ē) *adj.* **·ti·er, ·ti·est** 1 Ratlike, or abounding in rats. 2 *Slang* Disreputable; shabby.

rau·cle (rô′kəl) *adj. Scot.* Rough; harsh; strong; fearless.

rau·cous (rô′kəs) *adj.* Rough in sound; hoarse; harsh. [<L *raucus*] —**rau′cit·y** (-sə·tē), **rau′·cous·ness** *n.* —**rau′cous·ly** *adv.*

raunch·y (rôn′chē, rän′-) *adj. Slang* **raunch·i·er, raunch·i·est** 1 Sloppy; inept; slovenly. 2 Sexually vulgar; lewd; a *raunchy* joke. 3 Lustful. [?Alter. of Scot. *randy* disorderly, lewd; ult. origin unknown] —**raunch′i·ly** *adv.* —**raunch′i·ness** *n.*

Rau·wol·fi·a (rô·wol′fē·ə, -wōōl′-) *n.* A genus of tropical trees or shrubs of the dogbane family, several of which contain alkaloids having valuable medicinal properties; especially, *R. serpentina,* an Indian species from which the alkaloid reserpine was first isolated. [after Leonard *Rauwolf,* 17th century German botanist]

rav·age (rav′ij) *v.* **·aged, ·ag·ing** *v.t.* To lay waste, as by pillaging or burning; despoil; ruin. —*v.i.* To wreak havoc; be destructive. —*n.* Violent and destructive action, or its result; ruin; desolation. [<F <*ravir.* See RAVISH.] —**rav′ag·er** *n.*

rave[1] (rāv) *v.* **raved, rav·ing** *v.i.* 1 To speak wildly or incoherently. 2 To speak with extravagant enthusiasm. 3 To make a wild, roaring sound; rage: The wind *raved* through the trees. —*v.t.* 4 To utter wildly or incoherently. —*n.* 1 The act or state of raving; a frenzy. 2 *Colloq.* A highly favorable critical comment: The play drew *raves.* —*adj. Colloq.* Extravagantly enthusiastic: *rave* reviews. [<OF *raver, rever* <L *rabere* rage]

rave[2] (rāv) *n.* 1 A vertical sidepiece in a wagon body, or in a hand car or sleigh. 2 The wooden or iron piece that fastens the beam to the runners of a logging sled. [Origin unknown]

rav·el (rav′əl) *v.* **·eled** or **·elled, ·el·ing** or **·el·ling** *v.t.* 1 To separate the threads or fibers of; unravel. 2 To make clear or plain; explain: often with *out.* 3 *Archaic* To tangle; confuse. —*v.i.* 4 To become separated thread from thread or fiber from fiber; unravel; fray. 5 *Archaic* To become tangled or confused. —*n.* 1 A broken or rejected thread. 2 A raveling. [? <MDu. *ravelen* tangle] —**rav′·el·er** or **rav′el·ler** *n.*

Ra·vel (rà·vel′), **Maurice Joseph,** 1875–1937, French composer.

rave·lin (rav′lin) *n. Mil.* An outwork with two faces forming a salient angle at the front. [<F <Ital. *ravellino.* Origin uncertain.]

rav·el·ing (rav′əl·ing) *n.* 1 A thread or threads raveled from a fabric. 2 The act of raveling. 3 The process of being raveled. Also **rav′·el·ling.**

rav·el·ment (rav′əl·mənt) *n.* A ravel, or the act of raveling; confusion.

ra·ven[1] (rā′vən) *n.* A large, omnivorous, crowlike bird *(Corvus corax)* of North America, Europe, and Asia, having lustrous black plumage, with the feathers of the throat elongated and lanceolate. —*adj.* Black and shining, like the plumage of a raven. [OE *hræfn*]

rav·en[2] (rav′ən) *v.t.* 1 To devour hungrily or greedily. 2 To take by force; ravage. —*v.i.* 3 To search for or take prey or plunder. 4 To eat voraciously; be ravenous. —*n.* The act of plundering; spoliation; pillage. [<OF *raviner* <*ravine* rapine <L *rapina*; *n.* doublet of RAPINE, RAVINE] —**rav′en·er** *n.*

Ra·ven (rā′vən) The southern constellation, Corvus. See CONSTELLATION.

Rav·e·na·la (rav′i·nā′lə) *n.* A genus of palmlike trees of the banana family, having a fan-shaped group of elongated flat leaves arranged around the trunk, especially the traveler's tree *(R. madagascariensis).* [<Malagasy]

rav·en·ing (rav′ən·ing) *adj.* 1 Seeking eagerly for prey; rapacious. 2 Mad; rabid. —*n.* 1 Propensity for prey or booty; rapacity. 2 The prey seized. [ppr. of RAVEN[2]] —**rav′en·ing·ly** *adv.*

Ra·ven·na (rä·ven′nä) A city in north central Italy, 6 miles west of the Adriatic, formerly on it; capital of the Western Roman Empire 402–476.

rav·en·ous (rav′ən·əs) *adj.* 1 Violently voracious or hungry. 2 Extremely eager for gratification. See synonyms under GREEDY. [<OF *ravinos.* See RAVEN[2].] —**rav′en·ous·ly** *adv.* —**rav′en·ous·ness** *n.*

Ra·vi (rä′vē) A river in NW India and West Pakistan, flowing SW 474 miles from northern Punjab State, India to the Chenab river above Multan, West Pakistan: ancient *Hydraotes.*

rav·in (rav′in) *n.* 1 The act of plundering or ravaging. 2 That which is obtained by violence or robbery. —*v.t. & v.i.* To raven. [<OF *ravine.* See RAPINE.]

ra·vine (rə·vēn′) *n.* 1 A deep gorge or gully, especially one worn by a stream or flow of water. 2 A long, narrow cleft between heights. See synonyms under VALLEY. [<F. Doublet of RAVEN[2], *n.,* RAPINE.]

rav·ing (rā′ving) *adj.* 1 Furious; delirious; frenzied. 2 *Colloq.* Excessive; extraordinary: a *raving* beauty. —*n.* Furious, incoherent, or irrational utterance. See synonyms under FRENZY. Compare INSANITY.

ra·vio·li (rä·vyō′lē, rä′vē·ō′lē, rav′ē-) *n. pl.* Balls of forcemeat, encased in little envelopes of dough and boiled in broth or water: commonly construed in the singular. [<Ital., dim. pl. of dial. *rava* <L *rapa* turnip, beet]

rav·ish (rav′ish) *v.t.* 1 To fill with strong emotion, especially delight; enrapture. 2 To commit a rape upon. 3 To carry off (a woman) by force. 4 To seize and carry off by violence. [<OF *raviss-,* stem of *ravir* carry off <L *rapere* seize. Related to RAPE, RAPTURE.] —**rav′ish·er** *n.* —**rav′ish·ing·ly** *adv.*

Synonyms: capitivate, charm, delight, enchant, enrapture, entrance, overjoy, transport. See ABUSE, CHARM[1], POLLUTE, REJOICE. *Antonyms*: disenchant, disgust, nauseate, repel.

rav·ish·ing (rav′ish·ing) *adj.* Filling with transports of delight; enchanting.

rav·ish·ment (rav′ish·mənt) *n.* The act of ravishing or the state of being ravished; especially, ecstasy; delight. [<OF *ravissement*]

raw (rô) *adj.* 1 Not changed or prepared by cooking; in its natural state; uncooked. 2 Not covered with whole skin; abraded. 3 Bleak; chilling: a *raw* wind. 4 In a natural state; crude; unprepared, as wool, drugs, etc.; also, untempered or without tone, as colors; unrefined; unfinished. 5 Newly done; fresh: *raw* paint, *raw* work. 6 Inexperienced; undisciplined: a *raw* recruit. 7 Unrefined; crude; off-color: a *raw* joke. 8 Unexposed: said of photographic film. —*n.* 1 A sore or abraded spot; a sensitive point. 2 The state of being raw, untamed, or unspoiled: nature in the *raw.* [OE *hrēaw*] —**raw′ly** *adv.* —**raw′ness** *n.*

Ra·wal·pin·di (rä′wəl·pin′dē, rôl·pin′dē) A city in the northern Punjab region of Pakistan, near the border of Jammu and Kashmir state.

raw-boned (rô′bōnd′) *adj.* Having large bones and little flesh; bony; gaunt.

Raw·bones (rô′bōnz′) Death.

raw deal *Slang* Harsh or unfair treatment in a transaction.

raw fibers Textile fibers in their natural state, as silk in the gum or cotton as it comes from the bale.

raw·hide (rô′hīd′) *n.* 1 A hide dressed without tanning. 2 A whip made of such hide.

raw·ish (rô′ish) *adj.* Somewhat raw.

Raw·lin·son (rô′lin·sən), **George,** 1812–1902, English Orientalist and historian. —**Sir Henry,** 1810–95, English soldier and Assyriologist; brother of the preceding.

raw material Unprocessed material (animal, vegetable, or mineral) needed and used in manufacturing, as contrasted with finished products.

raw milk Unpasteurized milk.

rax (raks) *v.t. & v.i. Scot.* To stretch out; reach.

ray[1] (rā) *n.* 1 A narrow beam of light or other line of propagation of any form of radiant energy; line of radiating force; radiation. 2 A manifestation of intellectual light. 3 One of several lines radiating from an object. 4 *Geom.* A straight line emerging from a center and unlimited in one direction only. 5 A streak or line; a straight row. 6 *Zool.* **a** One of the rods supporting the membrane of a fish's fin. **b** One of the radiating parts of a radiate animal, as a starfish. 7 *Bot.* **a** A ray-like flower. **b** One of the pedicels or flower stalks of an umbel. 8 *Physics* A stream of particles spontaneously emitted by a radioactive substance. 9 A trace or minute particle: Not a *ray* of life was present. —*v.i.* 1 To emit rays; shine. 2 To issue forth as rays; radiate. —*v.t.* 3 To send forth as rays. 4 To mark with rays or radiating lines. 5 To irradiate. 6 To treat with or expose to X-rays, etc. [<OF *rai* <L *radius.* Doublet of RADIUS.]

ray[2] (rā) *n.* An elasmobranch fish (order *Selachii*) having a cartilaginous skeleton and a flattened body, with expanded pectoral fins, dorsally placed eyes, and a long caudal appendage; especially, the sting ray or torpedo. [<F *raie* <L *raia*]

Ray (rā), **Cape** A promontory at the SW extremity of Newfoundland at the entrance to the Gulf of Saint Lawrence.

ra·yah (rä′yə, rī′ə) *n.* A non-Moslem inhabitant of Turkey: sometimes spelled *raia.* Also **ra′ya.** [<Arabic *ra'īyah* flock, herd]

ray flower *Bot.* Any of the flat marginal flowers of an inflorescence when distinct from the disk, as in the daisy or sunflower. Also **ray floret.**

ray·grass (rā′gras′, -gräs′) *n.* Ryegrass.

Ray·leigh (rā′lē), **Lord,** 1842–1919, John William Strutt, third baron, English physicist.

ray·less (rā′lis) *adj.* 1 Having no light rays. 2 Extremely dark. 3 Having no rays, as certain composite plants. —**ray′less·ly** *adv.* —**ray′less·ness** *n.*

Ray·mond (rā′mənd, *Fr.* rā·môn′) A masculine personal name. Also **Ray′mund.** Also *Lat.* **Ray·mun·dus** (rā·mun′dəs). [<Gmc., wise protection]

ray·on (rā′on) *n.* A lustrous synthetic fiber variously made by chemical means from cellulose or with cellulose as a base, the viscous material being forced through fine spinnerets to produce filaments suitable for textiles and fabrics. [<F, ray; from its sheen]

raze (rāz) *v.t.* **razed, raz·ing** 1 To level to the ground; tear down; demolish. 2 *Rare* To scrape or shave off. 3 *Obs.* To wound slightly; graze. See synonyms under DEMOLISH. Also spelled *rase.* ◆ Homophone: *raise.* [<F *raser* <L *rasum,* pp. of *radere* scrape]

ra·zee (rā·zē′) *v.t.* To make lower by cutting down, as a ship of war by removing the upper deck or decks; reduce; abridge. —*n.* A vessel that has been reduced by cutting away the upper deck or decks. [<F *rasé,* pp. of *raser* shave, raze]

ra·zor (rā′zər) *n.* A sharp cutting implement

used for shaving off the beard or hair. —**safety razor** A razor provided with a guard or guards for the blade to prevent accidental gashing of the skin. [<OF *rasor* <*raser* scrape]

ra·zor·back (rā′zər·bak′) *n.* **1** A rorqual. **2** A lean-bodied, half-wild hog with long legs, common in the southeastern United States. **3** A hill with a sharp narrow ridge. —**ra′zor-backed′** *adj.*

ra·zor-billed auk (rā′zər·bild′) A small auk *(Alca torda)* of the North Atlantic, having a compressed and deeply furrowed bill. Also **ra′zor·bill′.**

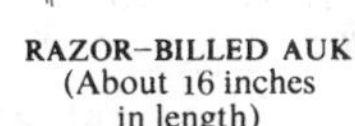

RAZOR-BILLED AUK
(About 16 inches in length)

razor clam A clam (genus *Ensis*) having a long, narrow, slightly curved shell resembling a razor. Also **ra′zor-shell′ clam.**

razor grinder One who sharpens or grinds razors or razor blades.

razor strop A strip, of specially prepared leather, canvas, or other material, upon which the blade of a razor is stroked to give it a fine edge.

razz (raz) *n. Slang* Raspberry (def. 3). —*v.t.* To heckle; deride. [<RASPBERRY]

raz·zi·a (raz′ē·ə) *n.* A foray or armed expedition, as for plunder or conquest, or for the capture of cattle or slaves. [<F <Arabic *ghāzīah* <*ghasw* war, battle]

raz·zle-daz·zle (raz′əl·daz′əl) *n. U.S. Slang* Anything bewildering and exciting; dazzling activity or performance. [Varied reduplication of DAZZLE]

razz·ma·tazz (raz′mə·taz′) *n. U.S. Slang* **1** Razzle-dazzle. **2** Skill.

re[1] (rā) *n. Music* The second note of any major scale in solmization. [<L *re(sonare)* resound. See GAMUT.]

re[2] (rē) *prep.* Concerning; about; in the matter of: used in business letters: *re* your letter of the 6th instant. [<L, ablative of *res* thing]

Re (rā) See RA.

re- *prefix* **1** Back: *reduce* to lead back, *remit* to send back. **2** Again; anew; again and again: *regenerate. Re-* in this second sense is freely used in Modern English, as in the list of words below. It is hyphenated, in certain cases, to prevent confusion with a similarly spelled word having a different meaning (*re-treat* to treat again, *retreat* to go back), to prevent mispronunciation *(re-argue, re-urge)*, and also in the coining of new words. Also, before vowels, sometimes *red-*, as in *redeem.* [<L *re-, red-* back, again]

reach (rēch) *v.t.* **1** To stretch out or forth, as the hand or foot. **2** To present by means of or as by means of the outstretched hand; deliver; hand over. **3** To extend as far as; touch or grasp, as with the hand: Can you *reach* the top shelf? **4** To arrive at or come to by motion or progress; attain: When do we *reach* Miami? **5** To achieve communication with; gain access to. **6** To amount to; total. **7** To strike or hit, as with a blow or missile. —*v.i.* **8** To stretch the hand, foot, etc., out or forth. **9** To attempt to touch or grasp something: He *reached* for his wallet. **10** To have extent in space, time, amount, or influence: The ladder *reached* to the ceiling. **11** *Naut.* To sail on a tack with the wind on or forward of the beam. —*n.* **1** The act or power of reaching; also, the distance one is able to reach, as with the hand, an instrument, or missile, or by thought, influence, etc.; scope; range. **2** A point, position, or result attained or attainable. **3** An unbroken stretch, as of a stream; a vista or expanse. **4** A pole or bar connecting the rear axle, truck, or runners of a vehicle with some part at the forward end. **5** *Naut.* The sailing, or the distance sailed, by a vessel on one tack. [OE *rǣcan.* Akin to G *reichen* reach]

Synonyms (verb): attain, gain, hit, land, make, strike, touch. To *reach,* in the sense here considered, is to come to by motion or progress. *Attain* is now oftenest used of abstract relations; as, to *attain* success. To *gain* is to *reach* or *attain* a thing eagerly sought; the wearied swimmer *reaches* or *gains* the shore. See ARRIVE, GET, MAKE[1], STRETCH.

reach·less (rēch′lis) *adj.* That cannot be reached; unattainable; lofty.

reach-me-down (rēch′mē·doun′) *Slang adj.* Ready-made, as a garment; also, second-hand. —*n. Usually pl.* Ready-made or second-hand clothing.

re·act (rē·akt′) *v.i.* **1** To act in response, as to a stimulus. **2** To act in a manner contrary to some preceding act; come into or tend toward a former state or an opposite state. **3** *Physics* To exert an opposite and equal force on an acting or impinging body: said of the body acted upon. **4** *Chem.* To exert mutual action, as substances undergoing chemical change. Compare RE-ACT.

re-act (rē·akt′) *v.t.* To act again.

re·ac·tance (rē·ak′təns) *n. Electr.* In an alternating-current circuit, that component of the impedance that does not oppose the current, but tends to cause a difference of phase between it and the electromotive force: measured in ohms.

re·ac·tion (rē·ak′shən) *n.* **1** Reverse or return action; tendency toward a former or reversed state of things; especially, a trend toward an earlier social, political, or economic policy or condition. **2** *Physiol.* Contrary action or reversed effects following a stimulus; a reflex action. **3** *Psychol.* The partial or total response made to any kind or degree of stimulation. **4** *Physics* In the second law of motion, the equal and opposite force exerted on an agent by the body acted upon. **5** *Chem.* The mutual action of substances subjected to chemical change, or some distinctive result of such action. **6** *Biol.* The effect upon any organism or any of its parts made by the introduction of any foreign substance for diagnostic or therapeutic purposes, or for testing, immunizing, etc. —**re·ac′tive** *adj.*

re·ac·tion·ar·y (rē·ak′shən·er′ē) *adj.* Of, relating to, favoring, or characterized by reaction. —*n. pl.* **·ar·ies** One who favors political or social reaction; a conservative. Also **re·ac′·tion·ist.**

reaction engine An engine which obtains thrust by the expulsion of the hot gases of combustion to the rear; a jet engine.

reaction formation *Psychoanal.* The conscious development of character traits, attitudes, and forms of behavior in contrast with and opposition to original trends of the ego, for which they serve as deceptive and relatively unstable concealment. Compare SUBLIMATION.

reaction time *Physiol.* **1** The time required for a response to a sensory stimulus. **2** The time required for an electric current to acton a muscle.

re·ac·ti·vate (rē·ak′tə·vāt) *v.t.* **·vat·ed, ·vat·ing** To make active or effective again. —**re·ac′ti·va′tion** *n.*

re·ac·tive (rē·ak′tiv) *adj.* **1** Reacting, tending to react, or resulting from reaction. **2** Responsive to a stimulus.

reactive factor *Electr.* In a circuit, the ratio of the reactive volt-amperes to the total volt-amperes.

reactive volt-ampere *Electr.* That component of the volt-amperes in an alternating-current circuit not representing the work done in watts. Also **reactive power.** See VAR.

re·ac·tor (rē·ak′tər) *n.* **1** One who or that which reacts. **2** *Electr.* A device for introducing reactance into a circuit, as for starting motors, controlling current, and the like. **3** *Biol.* An animal or person giving a positive reaction to a specified bacteriological or medical test. **4** *Physics* Any of variously designed assemblies for the initiation and control of nuclear fission, consisting essentially of reserves of fissionable material used as fuel, moderators to check the rate of nuclear reactions, reflectors, and auxiliary structures, equipment, shielding, etc.: also called *pile.*

read (rēd) *v.* **read** (red), **read·ing** (rē′ding) *v.t.* **1** To apprehend the meaning of (a book, writing, etc.) by perceiving the form and relation of the printed or written characters. **2** To utter aloud (something printed or written). **3** To understand the significance of as if by reading: to *read* the sky. **4** To apprehend the meaning of something printed or written in (a foreign language). **5** To make a study of; also, to obtain knowledge of: to *read* law. **6** To discover the true nature of (a person, character, etc.) by observation or scrutiny. **7** To interpret (something read) in a specified manner. **8** To take as the meaning of something read. **9** To have or exhibit as the wording: The passage *reads* "principal," not "principle." **10** To indicate or register: The meter *reads* zero. **11** To bring into a specified condition by reading: I *read* her to sleep. —*v.i.* **12** To apprehend the characters of a book, musical score, etc. **13** To utter aloud the words or contents of a book, etc. **14** To gain information by reading: with *of* or *about.* **15** To learn by means of books; study. **16** To have a specified wording: The contract *reads* as follows. **17** To admit of being read in a specified manner. **18** To give a public reading or recital. —**to read between the lines** To perceive or infer what is not expressed or obvious, as a hidden or true meaning, implication, or motive. —**to read into** To discern (implicit meanings or implications) in a statement or position: Don't *read* anything *into* my decision not to run for office. —**to read out** To expel from a religious body, political party, etc., by proclamation or concerted action. —**to read up** (or **up on**) To learn by reading. —*adj.* (red) Informed by books or reading; acquainted with books or literature: well *read.* —*n.* (rēd) *Colloq.* A reading; a period spent in reading. [OE *rædan* advise, read]

read·a·ble (rē′də·bəl) *adj.* **1** Legible. **2** Easy and pleasant to read. —**read′a·bil′i·ty, read′·a·ble·ness** *n.* —**read′a·bly** *adv.*

Reade (rēd), **Charles,** 1814–84, English novelist.

read·er (rē′dər) *n.* **1** One who reads; specifically, a professional reciter or elocutionist. **2** One who reads and criticizes manuscripts offered to publishers. **3** A proofreader. **4** A layman authorized to read the lesson in church services. **5** A textbook containing matter for exercises in reading. **6** *Brit.* A university or college lecturer.

read·i·ly (red′ə·lē) *adv.* **1** In a ready manner; promptly; easily. **2** Willingly.

read·i·ness (red′i·nis) *n.* **1** The quality or state of being ready. **2** The quality of being quick or prompt; facility; aptitude. **3** A disposition for prompt compliance; willingness. See synonyms under ABILITY, ADDRESS, DEXTERITY, EASE, INGENUITY.

read·ing (rē′ding) *n.* **1** The act, practice, or art of reading, in any sense of the verb; a public recital; the act of reading formally to a legislative body a bill, etc., proposed for adoption. **2** Literary research; study; scholarship. **3** Matter which is read or is designed to be read. **4** The indication of a graduated instrument, as a thermometer. **5** The form in which any passage or word appears in any copy of a work. **6** An interpretation, as of a riddle, or of any latent and hidden meaning; delineation; rendering. See synonyms under EDUCATION. —*adj.* Pertaining to or suitable for reading.

Read·ing (red′ing) **1** A county borough and

reabsorb	**readdress**	**readvance**	**reallege**	**reanimation**	**reappear**	**reapportion**
reabsorption	**readjourn**	**reafforest**	**re-alliance**	**reannex**	**reappearance**	**reapportionment**
reaccess	**readjournment**	**reafforestation**	**re-ally**	**reannexation**	**reapply**	**re-argue**
reaccommodate	**readopt**	**reagree**	**realphabet**	**reanoint**	**reappoint**	**re-argument**
reaccuse	**readorn**	**re-alinement**	**reamputate**	**reapparel**	**reappointment**	**reascend**

county town of Berkshire, England. **2** A city on the Schuylkill River in SE Pennsylvania.

reading desk A desk adapted to hold books, manuscripts, etc., for a speaker or reader, as in church services.

READING DESK

reading room A room provided with periodicals, books, etc., in which the public, or certain classes of readers, may read.

re·ad·just (rē′ə·just′) *v.t.* & *v.i.* To adjust again or anew; rearrange. **—re′ad·just′er** *n.*

re·ad·just·ment (rē′ə·just′mənt) *n.* **1** The act or process of readjusting, or the state of being readjusted. **2** The reorganization of a company or corporation, usually voluntary.

re·ad·mit (rē′əd·mit′) *v.t.* **·mit·ted, ·mit·ting** To admit again; allow to enter again. **—re′·ad·mis′sion, re′ad·mit′tance** *n.*

read·y (red′ē) *adj.* **read·i·er, read·i·est** **1** Prepared for use or action. **2** Prepared in mind; willing. **3** Likely or liable: with *to*: *ready* to sink. **4** Quick to act, follow, occur, or appear; prompt. **5** At hand; immediately available; convenient; handy. **6** Designating the standard position in which a rifle is held just before aiming. **7** Quick to understand; alert; quick; facile: a *ready* wit. **8** *Obs.* Here; present: used in answering a roll call. See synonyms under ACTIVE, ALERT, GOOD, RIPE[1]. **—*n.*** **1** In the manual of arms, the position in which a rifle is held before aiming, the left hand at the balance, the right hand at the small of the stock. **2** *Slang* Cash: with *the.* **—*v.t.*** **read·ied, read·y·ing** To make ready; prepare. [OE *rǣde, gerǣde*]

read·y-made (red′ē·mād′) *adj.* **1** Not made to order; prepared or kept on hand for general demand: said especially of clothing. **2** Prepared beforehand; not impromptu. **3** Prepared by someone else. **4** Borrowed; lacking in originality; inferior.

ready money Money in hand; cash.

read·y-to-wear (red′ē·tə·wâr′) *adj.* Ready-made: said of clothing.

read·y-wit·ted (red′ē·wit′id) *adj.* Quick to apprehend or learn; alert.

re·af·firm (rē′ə·fûrm′) *v.t.* To affirm again, as for emphasis. **—re′af·firm′ance, re·af·fir·ma·tion** (rē′af·ər·mā′shən) *n.*

re·a·gent (rē·ā′jənt) *n.* **1** One who or that which reacts; a source of reflex action. **2** *Chem.* Any substance used to ascertain the nature or composition of another by means of their mutual chemical action. **3** *Psychol.* The subject of an experiment; particularly, one who or that which reacts to a stimulus. [<RE- + AGENT]

re·al[1] (rē′əl, rēl) *adj.* **1** Having existence or actuality as a thing or state; not imaginary: a *real* event. **2** Being in accordance with appearance or claim; genuine; not artificial or counterfeit. **3** Representing the true or actual, as opposed to the apparent or ostensible: the *real* reason. **4** Unaffected; unpretentious: a *real* person. **5** *Philos.* Having actual existence, and not merely possible, apparent, or imaginary. **6** *Law* **a** Of, pertaining to, or consisting of land and tenements: *real* property, as contrasted with personal property. **b** Pertaining to things, as distinguished from persons. **—*n.*** That which is real; a real thing. **—*adv. Colloq.*** Very; extremely: to be *real* glad. [<OF <Med. L *realis* <L *res* thing] **—re′al·ness** *n.*

re·al[2] (rē′əl, *Sp.* rä·äl′) *n.* **1** *pl.* **re·als** or **re·a·les** (rä·ä′läs) A small silver coin of several Spanish countries, including Mexico, and formerly current in the United States, where it was called a *bit,* and had the value of 12 1/2 cents. **2** *pl.* **reis** (räs) A former Portuguese and Brazilian coin; one thousandth of a milreis. [<Sp., lit., royal <L *regalis*]

real estate Land, including whatever is made part of or attached to it by man or nature, as trees, houses, etc. Also **real property.**

re·al·gar (rē·al′gər) *n.* A resinous, orange-red arsenic sulfide, As_2S_2, formerly extensively used as a pigment and still employed in pyrotechnics. [<OF <Med. L <Arabic *rahj al-ghār* powder of the cave. Cf. Sp. *rejalgar.*]

real image See under IMAGE.

re·al·ism (rē′əl·iz′əm) *n.* **1** In literature and art, the principle of depicting persons and scenes as they exist, without any attempt at idealization. **2** The tendency to be concerned solely with reality, as opposed to ideals; specifically, the tendency to think and act in the light of actuality, disregarding idealistic motives. **3** *Philos.* **a** The doctrine that universals (abstract concepts) have objective existence and are more real than things: opposed to *nominalism.* Compare CONCEPTUALISM. **b** The doctrine that things have reality apart from the conscious perception of them: opposed to *idealism.* **—re′al·is′tic** *adj.* **—re′·al·is′ti·cal·ly** *adv.*

re·al·ist (rē′əl·ist) *n.* **1** An adherent of the doctrine of realism in any of its forms, as applied in literature, art, or philosophy. **2** One who is devoted to what is real rather than imaginary or ideal.

re·al·i·ty (rē·al′ə·tē) *n.* *pl.* **·ties** **1** The fact, state, condition, or quality of being real or genuine. **2** That which is real; an actual person, thing, situation, or event; in the aggregate, the sum of real things; also, the substance that lies back of form and external appearances. **3** That which exists, as contrasted with what is fictitious; that which is objective, not merely an idea. **4** *Philos.* The absolute; that which is self-existent; the ultimate, as contrasted with phenomena or the apparent. See synonyms under VERACITY. [<Med. L *realitas, -tatis* <*realis* real]

reality principle *Psychoanal.* The adjustment of the ego to meet the requirements of the external world. Compare PLEASURE PRINCIPLE.

re·al·i·za·tion (rē′əl·i·zā′shən) *n.* **1** The act of realizing. **2** The state of being realized. **3** A product or instance of realizing. **4** The conversion into fact or action (of plans, ambitions, fears, etc.).

re·al·ize (rē′əl·īz) *v.* **·ized, ·iz·ing** *v.t.* **1** To understand or appreciate fully. **2** To make real or concrete. **3** To cause to appear real. **4** To obtain as a profit or return. **5** To obtain money in return for: He *realized* his holdings for a profit. **6** To bring as a profit or return: said of property. **—*v.i.*** **7** To sell property for cash. See synonyms under ACCOMPLISH, EFFECT, GAIN[1], KNOW. **—re′al·iz′·a·ble** *adj.* **—re′al·iz′er** *n.*

re·al·iz·ing (rē′əl·īz′ing) *adj.* **1** Conceiving of as real; comprehending. **2** Able to visualize vividly. **3** Converting (hopes, plans, etc.) into fact, or (assets) into money.

re·al·ly (rē′ə·lē, rē′lē) *adv.* In reality; in point of fact; as a matter of fact; actually; indeed: also used without precise meaning, for emphasis.

realm (relm) *n.* **1** A kingdom. **2** The domain or jurisdiction of any power or influence: the *realm* of imagination. **3** A primary division of the globe with reference to its fauna; a zoogeographical area larger than a region; also, as used by some authors, a division equivalent to a region. [<OF *realme* <L *regalis* royal. See REGAL.]

real number See under NUMBER.

Re·al·po·li·tik (rā·äl′pō·li·tēk′) *n.* *German* Literally, practical or realistic politics: a term often used cynically to mean the attainment of political ends by the use or threatened use of armed force.

Real Presence *Theol.* The actual presence of the body and blood of Christ in the Eucharist.

Re·al·schu·le (rā·äl′shōō′lə) *n.* *pl.* **·len** (-lən) *German* A modern non-classical German secondary school preparing students for commercial or technical occupations that do not require a university education.

Re·al·tor (rē′əl·tər, -tôr) *n.* A person engaged in the real estate business, as a broker, appraiser, manager, etc., who is a member of the National Association of Real Estate Boards: a trade name.

re·al·ty[1] (rē′əl·tē) *n.* *pl.* **·ties** *Law* Real estate or real property in any form. [<REAL[1] (def. 6) + -TY[1]]

re·al·ty[2] (rē′əl·tē) *n. Obs.* **1** Fealty. **2** Royalty. [<OF *realté* <L *regalis* regal]

real wages Wages evaluated in terms of purchasing power, as contrasted with *nominal wages,* evaluated in money.

ream[1] (rēm) *n.* **1** Twenty quires of paper; properly, 480 sheets (a **short ream**), but often 500 sheets (a **long ream**) or, in a **printer's** or **perfect ream,** 516 sheets. **2** *pl. Colloq.* A prodigious amount of printed, written, or spoken material: *reams* of footnotes. [<OF *reyme* <Sp. *resma* <Arabic *rizmah* packet <*razama* pack together]

ream[2] (rēm) *v.t.* **1** To increase the size of (a hole). **2** To enlarge or taper (a hole) with a rotating cutter or reamer. **3** To turn or roll over the edge of: to *ream* a cartridge shell. **4** To get rid of (a defect) by reaming. [OE *rēman* enlarge, make room. Akin to ROOM.]

ream[3] (rēm) *n. Scot.* & *Brit. Dial.* Cream; froth; foam. **—*v.t. Scot.*** To skim, as cream. **—ream′y** *adj.*

ream·er (rē′mər) *n.* **1** One who or that which reams. **2** A finishing tool with a rotating cutting edge for reaming: sometimes spelled *rimmer.* **3** A device with a ridged cone for extracting juice from citrus fruits.

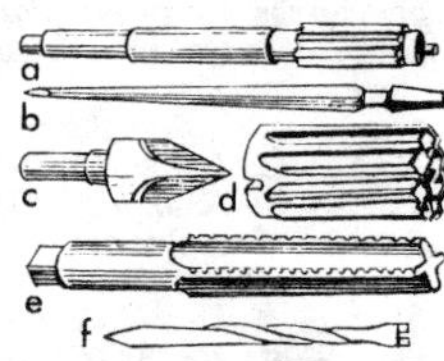

REAMERS
a. Adjustable.
b. Square.
c. Center.
d. Rose-shell.
e. Roughening taper.
f. Root reamer.

re·an·i·mate (rē·an′ə·māt) *v.t.* **·mat·ed, ·mat·ing** **1** To bring back to life; resuscitate. **2** To revive; encourage. **—re′an·i·ma′tion** *n.*

reap (rēp) *v.t.* **1** To cut and gather (grain); harvest or gather (a fruit or product) with a scythe, reaper, or the like. **2** To cut the growth from or gather the fruit of, as a field. **3** To obtain as the result of action or effort; receive as a return or result. **—*v.i.*** **4** To harvest grain, etc. **5** To receive a return or result. See synonyms under GAIN[1] [OE *repan*] **—reap′a·ble** *adj.* **—reap′ing** *n.*

reap-dole (rēp′dōl′) *n. Brit.* A gratuity for reapers after harvesting: a relic of feudalism.

reap·er (rē′pər) *n.* **1** One who reaps. **2** A machine for harvesting standing grain; a reaping machine.

reaper and binder A reaping machine having a device that binds the grain as it cuts it.

reaping machine A machine for harvesting standing grain. It usually consists of a reciprocating cutter resembling that of a mowing machine, a platform or table on which the cut grain falls, and a dropper which is dropped to deposit the bundles of grain. In addition, it often has a reel for bending the grain toward the cutter, or a raking mechanism for pressing the grain down on the table and sweeping it off in bundles, and a binding mechanism. Also called *harvester.*

rear[1] (rir) *n.* **1** The hinder or hindmost part. **2** A place or position at the back of or behind any person or thing. **3** That division of a military force which is last or farthest from the front: opposed to *van.* **—*adj.*** Being in the rear; last; hindmost. [Aphetic form of ARREAR]

rear[2] (rir) *v.t.* **1** To place upright; raise; elevate. **2** To build; erect. **3** To care for and bring to maturity. **4** To breed or grow. **—*v.i.*** **5** To rise upon its hind legs, as a horse. **6** To rise high; tower: The mountain *rears* above the forest. See synonyms under RAISE. [OE *rǣran* set upright, causative of *rīsan* rise. Akin to ON *reisa* raise.] **—rear′er** *n.*

rear admiral See under ADMIRAL.

reascension	**reassertion**	**reassume**	**reattempt**	**rebind**	**rebury**	**rechange**
reascent	**reassign**	**reattach**	**reavow**	**rebloom**	**recarriage**	**recharge**
reassemblage	**reassimilate**	**reattachment**	**reawake**	**reblossom**	**recarry**	**recharter**
reassemble	**reassimilation**	**reattain**	**rebaptism**	**reboil**	**recelebrate**	**rechoose**
reassert	**reassociate**	**reattainment**	**rebaptize**	**rebuild**	**recelebration**	**rechristen**

rear–end (rir′end′) *n.* In automobiles, the after part of the drive train, consisting of the differential gears and rear axles with their housings and the driving wheels. — *adj.* Of or pertaining to the rear–end of an automobile.

rear guard A body of troops to protect the rear of an army. [<AF *reregard,* OF *rereguarde.* Doublet of REARWARD[2].]

rear·horse (rir′hôrs′) *n.* A mantis. [From its habit of rearing when touched]

re·arm (rē·ärm′) *v.t.* & *v.i.* **1** To arm again. **2** To arm with more modern weapons. — **re·ar′ma·ment** *n.*

rear·most (rir′mōst′) *adj.* Coming or stationed last.

rear·mouse (rir′mous′) See REREMOUSE.

re·ar·range (rē′ə·rānj′) *v.t.* & *v.i.* **·ranged, ·rang·ing** To arrange again or in some new way. — **re′ar·range′ment** *n.*

rear sight The sight of a gun which is nearest the breech.

rear–view mirror (rir′vyōō′) In motor vehicles, a mirror so placed in front of the driver that he can see the reflection of the road and vehicles behind. Also **rear′–vi′sion mirror.**

rear·ward[1] (rir′wərd) *adj.* Coming last or toward the rear; hindward. — *adv.* Toward or at the rear; backward. Also **rear′wards.** — *n.* Hindward position; the rear; end.

rear·ward[2] (rir′wôrd′) *n. Obs.* A rear guard. [<AF *rerewarde.* Doublet of REAR GUARD.]

rea·son (rē′zən) *n.* **1** That which is thought or alleged as the basis or ground for any opinion, determination, or action; something adduced or adapted to influence the mind in determining or acting; proof; argument; motive; principle. **2** That which explains or accounts for any fact, act, proceeding, or event; loosely, an efficient or final cause, or a condition. **3** The entire mental or rational nature of man, as distinguished from the intelligence of the brute; the mind; in a more limited sense, the purely intellectual faculties. **4** Specifically, the normal exercise of the rational faculties. **5** That which is in conformity to general opinion; common sense: The anarchist was brought to *reason.* **6** A logical ground for thinking; an antecedent; also, the premise or premises of an argument, generally the minor premise. **7** That which is right or befitting; just procedure; a reasonable act or proposition. **8** Intuition. — *v.i.* **1** To think logically; obtain inferences or conclusions from known or presumed facts. **2** To talk or argue logically. — *v.t.* **3** To think out carefully and logically; analyze: with *out.* **4** To influence by means of reason; persuade or dissuade. **5** To argue; debate. See synonyms under ARGUE, DISPUTE. [<OF *raison* <L *ratio, -onis* < *ratus,* pp. of *reri* reckon. Doublet of RATION, RATIO.]

Synonyms (noun): account, aim, argument, cause, consideration, design, end, ground, motive, object, principle, purpose. While the *cause* of any event, act, or fact, as commonly understood, is the power that makes it to be, the *reason* of or for it is the explanation given by the human mind; but *reason* is often used as equivalent to *cause,* especially in the sense of *final cause.* In the statement of any reasoning, the *argument* may be an entire syllogism, or the premises considered together apart from the conclusion, or in logical strictness the middle term only by which the particular conclusion is connected with the general statement. But when the reasoning is not in strict logical form, the middle term following the conclusion is called the *reason*; thus in the statement "All tyrants deserve death; Caesar was a tyrant; therefore Caesar deserved death," "Caesar was a tyrant" would in the strictest sense be called the *argument*; but if we say "Caesar deserved death because he was a tyrant," the latter clause would be termed the *reason.* See CAUSE, INTELLECT, MIND, REASONING, UNDERSTANDING, WISDOM. Compare BECAUSE.

rea·son·a·ble (rē′zən·ə·bəl) *adj.* **1** Conformable to reason; sensible. **2** Having the faculty of reason; rational. **3** Governed by reason in acting or thinking. **4** Moderate, as in price; fair. See synonyms under JUST, LIKELY, PROBABLE, RATIONAL, WISE[1]. [<OF *raisonable*; after L *rationabilis*] — **rea′son·a·bil′i·ty, rea′·son·a·ble·ness** *n.* — **rea′son·a·bly** *adv.*

rea·soned (rē′zənd) *adj.* Founded upon or characterized by reason; premeditated or studied.

rea·son·er (rē′zən·ər) *n.* One who reasons or argues.

rea·son·ing (rē′zən·ing) *n.* The act or process of the mind by which from propositions known or assumed new propositions are reached; argumentation; also, the reasons, proofs, or arguments employed in such process.

Synonyms: argument, argumentation, debate, ratiocination. *Argumentation* and *debate* always suppose two parties alleging reasons for and against a proposition. *Reasoning* may be the act of one alone, as it is simply the orderly setting forth of reasons, whether for the instruction of inquirers, the confuting of opponents, or the clear establishment of truth for oneself. *Reasoning* may be either deductive or inductive. *Argument* or *argumentation* was formerly used of deductive *reasoning* only. With the rise of the inductive philosophy these words have come to be applied to inductive processes also; but while *reasoning* may be informal or even unconscious, *argument* and *argumentation* strictly imply logical form. Compare INTELLECT, REASON.

rea·son·less (rē′zən·lis) *adj.* Devoid of the faculty of reason; also, not conformable to reason.

re·as·sur·ance (rē′ə·shōōr′əns) *n.* **1** The act of reassuring; repeated assurance. **2** Restored confidence. **3** Reinsurance.

re·as·sure (rē′ə·shōōr′) *v.t.* **·sured, ·sur·ing** **1** To restore to courage or confidence. **2** To assure again. **3** To reinsure. See synonyms under ENCOURAGE. — **re′as·sur′ing** *adj.* — **re′·as·sur′ing·ly** *adv.*

Re·au·mur (rā′ə·myōōr′, rā′ə·myōōr; *Fr.* rā·ō·mür′) *adj.* Relating to or designating the thermometric scale devised by de Réaumur, in which the zero point corresponds to the temperature of melting ice, and 80° to the temperature of boiling water. Also **Ré′au·mur′.** Abbr. *R.*

Ré·au·mur (rā′ə·myōōr′, rā′ə·myōōr; *Fr.* rā·ō·mür′), **René Antoine de,** 1683–1757, French physicist and naturalist.

reave (rēv) *v.t.* **reaved** or **reft, reav·ing** *Obs.* **1** To carry off as spoil or booty; rape; rob; plunder. **2** To deprive of something; bereave. **3** To tear up or apart; unravel; pull down; strip. [OE *rēafian* rob]

re·bate[1] (rē′bāt, ri·bāt′) *v.t.* **·bat·ed, ·bat·ing** **1** To allow as a deduction. **2** To make a deduction from. **3** *Obs.* To blunt, as a sharp edge. — *n.* A deduction from a gross amount; discount: also **re·bate′ment.** [<OF *rabattre* beat down < *re-* again + *abattre.* See ABATE.] — **re′bat·er** *n.*

re·bate[2] (rē′bāt, rab′it) See RABBET.

re·ba·to (re·bä′tō) *n. pl.* **·tos** A collar turned down and falling over the shoulders: worn by both sexes in the 15th and 16th centuries. Also spelled *rabato.* [<MF *rabat* < *rabattre* beat down. See REBATE.]

re·bec (rē′bek) *n.* The earliest form of the violin. Also **re′beck.** [<F alter. of OF *rebebe* <Arabic *rabāb*]

MEDIEVAL THREE–STRING REBEC

Re·bec·ca (ri·bek′ə, *Ital.* rā·bek′kä) A feminine personal name. Also *Fr.* **Ré·bec·ca** (rā·be·kȧ′), *Sp.* **Re·be·ca** (rā·bā′kä), *Ger.* **Re·bek·ka** (rā·bek′ə). [<Hebrew, ensnarer]

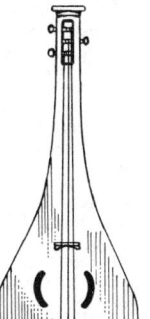

— **Rebecca** Wife of Isaac; mother of Esau and Jacob. *Gen.* xxiv 15.

re·bel (ri·bel′) *v.i.* **·belled, ·bel·ling** **1** To rise in armed resistance against the established government or ruler of one's land. **2** To resist any authority or established usage. **3** To react with violent aversion: usually with *at.*

— **reb·el** (reb′əl) *n.* One who rebels; specifically, one who espoused the American Revolution, or the cause of the South during the Civil War. — *adj.* Rebellious; refractory. [<OF *rebeller* <L *rebellare* make war again < *re-* again + *bellare* make war < *bellum* war. Doublet of REVEL.]

reb·el·dom (reb′əl·dəm) *n.* **1** The domain of rebels; specifically, the Confederate States during the Civil War; also, rebels collectively. **2** Rebellious behavior.

re·bel·lion (ri·bel′yən) *n.* **1** The act of rebelling. **2** Organized resistance to a government or to any lawful authority. See synonyms under REVOLUTION. — **the Rebellion** The American Civil War. [<OF <L *rebellio, -onis*]

re·bel·lious (ri·bel′yəs) *adj.* **1** Being in a state of rebellion; insubordinate. **2** Of or pertaining to a rebel or rebellion. **3** Resisting control; refractory: *rebellious* curls. — **re·bel′lious·ly** *adv.* — **re·bel′lious·ness** *n.*

Synonyms: contumacious, disobedient, insubordinate, intractable, mutinous, refractory, seditious, uncontrollable, ungovernable, unmanageable. *Ungovernable* applies to that which successfully defies authority and power; *unmanageable* to that which resists the utmost exercise of skill or of skill and power combined; *rebellious* to that which is defiant of authority, whether successfully or unsuccessfully; *seditious* to that which partakes of or tends to excite a *rebellious* spirit, *seditious* suggesting more of covert plan, scheming, or conspiracy, *rebellious* more of overt act or open violence. While the *unmanageable* or *ungovernable* defies control, the *rebellious* or *seditious* may be forced to submission. *Insubordinate* applies to the disposition to resist and resent control as such; *mutinous,* to open defiance of authority, especially in the army, navy, or merchant marine. A *contumacious* act or spirit is contemptuous as well as defiant. See RESTIVE, TURBULENT. Compare OBSTINATE, REVOLUTION. *Antonyms*: compliant, controllable, deferential, docile, dutiful, manageable, obedient, submissive, subservient, tractable, yielding.

re·bill (rē·bil′) *v.t.* To render another bill to; bill again.

re·birth (rē·bûrth′, rē′bûrth′) *n.* **1** A new birth. **2** A revival or renaissance.

reb·o·ant (reb′ō·ənt) *adj.* Bellowing back; resounding loudly. [<L *reboans, -antis,* ppr. of *reboare* resound < *re-* again + *boare* bellow. Ult. imit.]

re·born (rē·bôrn′) *adj.* Born again; having undergone emotional or mental regeneration; renascent.

re·bound (ri·bound′) *v.i.* To bound back; recoil. — *v.t.* To cause to rebound. — *n.* (rē′bound′, ri·bound′) **1** Recoil; elasticity. **2** Something which rebounds or resounds; an echo. **3** Reaction of feeling or emotion after a disappointment: to fall in love on the *rebound.* [<F *rebondir* < *re-* back + *bondir* bound]

re·bo·zo (rā·bō′sō) *n. Spanish* A long scarf of cotton or silk, often embroidered, worn wrapped about the head and shoulders, and sometimes over the face, by women in Spain and Spanish America.

re·broad·cast (rē·brôd′kast′, -käst′) *v.t.* **·cast** or **·cast·ed, ·cast·ing** **1** To broadcast (the same program) more than once from the same station. **2** To broadcast (a program received from another station). — *n.* A program so transmitted.

re·buff (ri·buf′) *v.t.* **1** To reject or refuse abruptly or rudely. **2** To drive or beat back; repel; repulse. — *n.* **1** A sudden repulse; curt

reclasp	**recolonize**	**recommission**	**recondense**	**reconquest**	**reconstitute**	**recopy**
reclose	**recolor**	**recommittal**	**reconduct**	**reconsecrate**	**reconstitution**	**recross**
reclothe	**recombine**	**recompact**	**reconfirm**	**reconsecration**	**reconvene**	**recrucify**
recoin	**recomfort**	**reconceive**	**reconjoin**	**reconsolidate**	**reconversion**	**recrystallization**
recoinage	**recommence**	**recondensation**	**reconquer**	**reconsolidation**	**reconvert**	**recrystallize**

denial. 2 A sudden check; defeat. 3 A beating back. [<MF *rebuffer* <Ital. *ribuffare,* metathetic alter. of *baruffare* <OHG *biroufan* scuffle]

re-buff (rē·buf′) *v.t.* To buff again.

re·buke (ri·byo͞ok′) *v.t.* **·buked, ·buk·ing 1** To reprove sharply; reprimand. 2 *Obs.* To check or restrain by a command. See synonyms under ADMONISH, BLAME, REPROVE. — *n.* A strong and authoritative expression of disapproval. See synonyms under ANIMADVERSION, REPROOF. [<AF *rebuker,* OF *rebuchier* < *re-* back + *bucher* beat] — **re·buk′a·ble** *adj.*

re·buk·er (ri·byo͞o′kər) *n.* One who rebukes.

re·bus (rē′bəs) *n.* A puzzle representing a word, phrase, or sentence by letters, numerals, pictures, etc., often with pictures of objects whose names have the same sounds as the words represented. [<L, ablative pl. of *res* thing]

re·but (ri·but′) *v.t.* **·but·ted, ·but·ting 1** *Law* To overthrow by contrary evidence; contradict by countervailing proof; disprove; refute. 2 *Obs.* To push or drive back. [<OF *rebouter* push back < *re-* back + *bouter, boter.* See BUTT[1].]

re·but·ta·ble (ri·but′ə·bəl) *adj.* Capable of being rebutted.

re·but·tal (ri·but′l) *n.* The act of rebutting; refutation.

re·but·ter (ri·but′ər) *n.* **1** One who or that which rebuts. **2** In common-law pleading, a defendant's answer to the plaintiff's surrejoinder.

re·cal·ci·trant (ri·kal′sə·trənt) *adj.* Not complying; obstinate; rebellious; refractory. — *n.* One who is recalcitrant. [<L *recalcitrans, -antis,* ppr. of *recalcitrare* kick back < *re-* back + *calcitrare* kick < *calx, calcis* heel] — **re·cal′ci·trance, re·cal′ci·tran·cy** *n.*

re·cal·ci·trate (ri·kal′sə·trāt) *v.i.* **·trat·ed, ·trat·ing** To refuse compliance or submission; be recalcitrant. [<L *recalcitratus,* pp. of *recalcitrare.* See RECALCITRANT.] — **re·cal′ci·tra′tion** *n.*

re·ca·lesce (rē′kə·les′) *v.i.* **·lesced, ·lesc·ing** To grow hot again; specifically, in physics, to exhibit recalescence. [<L *recalescere* < *re-* again + *calescere* grow warm, inceptive of *calere* be warm]

re·ca·les·cence (rē′kə·les′əns) *n.* **1** A glowing again. **2** *Physics* A phenomenon peculiar to heated iron or steel of glowing more brightly when certain temperatures are reached in the process of gradual cooling from a state of high incandescence. [<L *recalescens,* ppr. of *recalescere.* See RECALESCE.] — **re′ca·les′cent** *adj.*

re·call (ri·kôl′) *v.t.* **1** To call back; order or summon to return. **2** To summon back in awareness or attention. **3** To recollect; remember. **4** To take back; revoke; countermand. **5** *Poetic* To revive; restore. See synonyms under REMEMBER, RENOUNCE. — *n.* (ri·kôl′, rē′kôl′) **1** A calling back or to mind. **2** A signal to call back soldiers, etc., as by a bugle call, the display of a flag, etc. **3** Revocation, as of an order. **4** In certain States, a system whereby public officials may be removed from office by popular vote.

Ré·ca·mier (rā·kȧ·myā′), **Jeanne Françoise Julie Adélaide,** 1777–1849, *née* Bernard, French social leader and patroness of literature: commonly known as *Madame Récamier.*

re·cant (ri·kant′) *v.t.* To withdraw formally one's belief in (something previously believed or maintained). — *v.i.* To disavow an opinion or belief previously held. [<L *recantare* < *re-* again + *cantare* sing, freq. of *canere* sing] — **re·can·ta·tion** (rē′kan·tā′shən) *n.* — **re·cant′er** *n.*

Synonyms: abandon, abjure, deny, disavow, discard, disclaim, disown, forswear, recall, renounce, repudiate, retract, revoke. To *recant* is to *deny* formally and publicly some opinion or statement, especially in religion, that one has held or advocated. *Abjure* is etymologically the exact equivalent of the Saxon *forswear,* signifying to put away formally and under oath, as an error, heresy, or evil practice, or a condemned and detested person. A man *recants* his belief, *abjures* or *renounces* his allegiance, *repudiates* another's claim, *renounces* his own, *retracts* a false statement. A person may *deny, disavow, disclaim, disown* what has been truly or falsely imputed to him or supposed to be his. He may *deny* his signature, *disavow* the act of his agent, *disown* his child; he may *repudiate* either a just claim or a base suggestion. Compare ABANDON, RENOUNCE.

re·cap (rē′kap′, rē·kap′) *v.t.* **·capped, ·cap·ping** To reprocess (an automobile tire) by vulcanizing new rubber onto the surface which comes into contact with the road. — *n.* (rē′kap′) A tire which has been so treated. Also *retread.* [RE- + CAP]

re·cap·i·tal·ize (rē·kap′ə·təl·īz′) *v.t.* **·ized, ·iz·ing** To capitalize again or differently. — **re·cap′i·tal·i·za′tion** *n.*

re·ca·pit·u·late (rē′kə·pich′o͝o·lāt) *v.t.* & *v.i.* **·lat·ed, ·lat·ing** To review briefly; sum up. [<LL *recapitulare* < *re-* again + *capitulare.* See CAPITULATE.]

re·ca·pit·u·la·tion (rē′kə·pich′o͝o·lā′shən) *n.* **1** The act of recapitulating; a summing up. **2** *Biol.* The process in which a developing embryo reproduces many of the typical forms of the organisms that precede it in the line of evolution. [<L *recapitulatio, -onis*]

re·ca·pit·u·la·to·ry (rē′kə·pich′o͝o·lə·tôr′ē, -tō′rē) *adj.* Containing or of the nature of recapitulation. Also **re′ca·pit′u·la′tive** (-lā′tiv).

re·cap·tion (rē·kap′shən) *n. Law* **1** The rearrest of one who has escaped custody. **2** The retaking by peaceable means of one's goods, wife, child, or chattel from one who wrongfully detains them. [<RE- + CAPTION (def. 5)]

re·cap·ture (rē·kap′chər) *v.t.* **·tured, ·tur·ing 1** To capture again; obtain by recapture. **2** To recall; remember. — *n.* **1** The act of retaking; especially, in war, the forcible recovery of booty or goods. **2** A prize retaken; anything recaptured. **3** The taking by the public of the earnings of a public service corporation over and above a stated profit.

re·cast (rē·kast′, -käst′) *v.t.* **·cast, ·cast·ing 1** To form anew; cast again. **2** To fashion anew by changing style, arrangement, etc., as a discourse. **3** To calculate anew. — *n.* (rē′kast′, -käst′) Something which has been recast.

re·cede (ri·sēd′) *v.i.* **·ced·ed, ·ced·ing 1** To move back; withdraw, as flood waters. **2** To withdraw, as from an assertion, position, agreement, etc. **3** To slope backward: a *receding* forehead. **4** To become more distant; incline away. [<L *recedere* < *re-* back + *cedere* go]

re-cede (rē·sēd′) *v.t.* **–ced·ed, –ced·ing** To cede back; grant or yield to a former owner. [<RE- + CEDE]

re·ceipt (ri·sēt′) *n.* **1** The act or state of receiving anything: to be in *receipt* of good news. **2** That which is received: usually in the plural: cash *receipts.* **3** A written acknowledgment of the payment of money, of the delivery of goods, etc. **4** A recipe. — *v.t.* **1** To give a receipt for the payment of. **2** To write acknowledgment of payment on, as a bill. — *v.i.* **3** To give a receipt, as for money paid. [<OF *recete* <L *recepta,* fem. of *receptus,* pp. of *recipere* RECEIVE; refashioned after Latin]

re·ceipt·or (ri·sē′tər) *n. Law* One who gives a receipt; specifically, one who gives a receipt for goods that have been attached.

re·ceiv·a·ble (ri·sē′və·bəl) *adj.* **1** Capable of being received; fit to be received, as legal tender. **2** Maturing for payment: said of a bill.

re·ceiv·a·bles (ri·sē′və·bəlz) *n. pl.* Outstanding accounts listed among the assets of a business.

re·ceive (ri·sēv′) *v.* **·ceived, ·ceiv·ing** *v.t.* **1** To take into one's hand or possession (something given, offered, delivered, etc.); acquire; accept. **2** To gain knowledge or information of: He *received* the news at breakfast. **3** To take from another by hearing or listening: The king *received* his oath of fealty. **4** To bear; support: These columns *receive* the weight of the building. **5** To experience; meet with: to *receive* abuse. **6** To undergo; suffer: He *received* a wound in his arm. **7** To intercept or encounter the force of (a blow, etc.). **8** To contain; hold. **9** To allow entrance to; admit to one's presence; greet. **10** To perceive mentally; understand. **11** To accept as true, proven, authoritative, etc. — *v.i.* **12** To be a recipient; get, obtain, or acquire something from some other person or source. **13** To welcome visitors or callers. **14** To partake of the Eucharist. **15** *Telecom.* To convert incoming radio waves into intelligible sounds or shapes, as a radio or television receiving set. See synonyms under ACCOMMODATE, GET, OBTAIN. [<OF *receivre* <L *recipere* < *re-* back + *capere* take]

re·ceived (ri·sēvd′) *adj. Chiefly Brit.* Accepted by established opinion or authority; standard: *received* ways of thinking.

Received Standard The form of educated English identified with that spoken at the English public schools and the universities of Oxford and Cambridge.

re·ceiv·er (rĭ·sē′vər) *n.* **1** One who receives; a recipient. **2** An official assigned to receive money due. **3** *Law* A person appointed by a court to take into his custody, control, and management the property or funds of another pending judicial action concerning them. **4** One who buys or receives stolen or embezzled goods, knowing them to be stolen. **5** Something which receives; a receptacle. **6** A vessel considered as a receptacle for a gas or fluid, as a jar for receiving and condensing a fluid that has been distilled. **7** A bolthead. **8** *Telecom.* An instrument in an electric circuit serving to receive and reproduce signals transmitted from another part of the circuit: a telephone *receiver.* **9** A radio or television receiving set.

re·ceiv·er·ship (ri·sē′vər·ship) *n.* **1** The office and functions pertaining to a receiver under appointment of a court. **2** *Law* The state of being in the hands of a receiver.

receiving set An apparatus for the reception of radio or television signals.

receiving ship A vessel stationed in a harbor to receive and provide for naval recruits, or for men awaiting transfer to new assignments.

re·cense (ri·sens′) *v.t.* **·censed, ·cens·ing** *Obs.* To revise or review, as a book; make a recension of. [<L *recensere.* See RECENSION.]

re·cen·sion (ri·sen′shən) *n.* **1** A critical revision of the text of a book; also, the edition so revised. **2** A review; critique. [<L *recensio, -onis* enumeration < *recensere* examine, survey < *re-* thoroughly + *censere* estimate, value]

re·cent (rē′sənt) *adj.* Pertaining to, or formed, developed, or created in time not long past; modern; fresh; new. See synonyms under FRESH, MODERN, NEW. [<OF <L *recens, -entis*] — **re′cent·ly** *adv.* — **re′cen·cy, re′cent·ness** *n.*

Re·cent (rē′sənt) *adj. Geol.* Pertaining to or designating the present or Holocene geological epoch, succeeding the Pleistocene.

re·cept (rē′sept) *n. Psychol.* A mental image of an external object, formed by the repetition of the same percept, with reinforcing of common characteristics. [<L *receptum,* neut. pp. of *recipere* receive; on analogy with *concept*]

re·cep·ta·cle (ri·sep′tə·kəl) *n.* **1** Anything that serves to contain or hold other things. **2** *Bot.* The base to which the parts of the flower, fruit, or seeds are fixed. **3** An outlet (def. 3). [<OF <L *receptaculum* < *receptare,* freq. of *recipere* RECEIVE]

re·cep·tion (ri·sep′shən) *n.* **1** The act of receiving, or the state of being received; receipt. **2** A formal social entertainment of guests: a wedding *reception*; also, the manner of receiving a person or persons: a warm *reception.* **3** Mental acceptance, as of a proposition. **4** In radio and television, the act or process of receiving or, especially, the quality of reproduction achieved: This radio gives very poor *reception.* [<OF <L *receptio, -onis* < *receptus,* pp. of *recipere* RECEIVE]

reception center A central receiving point; specifically, the point at which newly inducted military personnel are received and examined, and from which they are sent to their assigned units.

re·cep·tion·ist (ri·sep′shən·ist) *n.* A person employed to receive callers, provide information, and the like, at the entrance to an office.

reception room 1 A room for callers in a private house. **2** A waiting room in a hospital, or adjoining a doctor's, dentist's, or

recultivate
recultivation
redecorate
rededicate
rededication
redeliberate
redemonstrate
redeposit
redescend
redescent
redescribe
redetermine
redigest
rediminish
rediscover
rediscovery
redispose
redissolution
redissolve
redistil
redistrainer
redistribute
redistribution
redivide
redo
redraw
redrawer
redrive
re-echo
re-edify
reelaborate
reelect
reelection
re-elevate
reembark

lawyer's office. 3 A large room for a formal reception.

re·cep·tive (ri·sep′tiv) *adj.* Able or inclined to receive, as truths or impressions; able to take in or hold. [<OF *receptif* <Med. L *receptivus* <L *recipere* RECEIVE] —**re·cep′tive·ly** *adv.* —**re·cep·tiv·i·ty** (rē′sep·tiv′ə·tē), **re·cep′tive·ness** *n.*

re·cep·tor (ri·sep′tər) *n.* 1 *Bacteriol.* A combination of atoms in a cell that, by combining with extraneous substances, as drugs or toxins, may be thrown off from the cell and circulate in the blood, thus conferring immunity. 2 *Physiol.* The terminal structure, or free nerve ending, which is specialized to receive various forms of external and internal stimuli, transmitting them to the brain nerve centers: also called *sense organ.* Compare EFFECTOR. [<L, receiver]

re·cess (ri·ses′, rē′ses; *for def. 2, usually* rē′ses) *n.* 1 A depression or indentation in any otherwise continuous line, especially in a wall; niche; alcove. 2 A time of cessation from employment or occupation: The school took a *recess.* 3 *Usually pl.* A quiet and secluded spot; withdrawn or inner place: the *recesses* of the mind. 4 *Anat. & Bot.* A depression or cavity. —*v.* (ri·ses′) *v.t.* 1 To place in or as in a recess. 2 To make a recess in, as a wall. 3 To interrupt for a recess: to *recess* a court. —*v.i.* 4 To take a recess. [<L *recessus,* pp. of *recedere.* See RECEDE[1].]

re·ces·sion (ri·sesh′ən) *n.* 1 The act of receding; a withdrawal. 2 The procession of the clergy, choir, etc., as they leave the chancel after a church service. 3 An economic setback in commercial and industrial activity; especially, one occurring as a downward turn during a period of generally rising prosperity; a slight depression. [<L *recessio, -onis* < *recedere.* See RECEDE[1].]

re–ces·sion (rē·sesh′ən) *n.* The act of ceding again; a giving back.

re·ces·sion·al (ri·sesh′ən·əl) *adj.* Of or pertaining to recession. —*n.* A hymn sung as the choir or clergy leave the chancel after service: also **recessional hymn.**

re·ces·sive (ri·ses′iv) *adj.* 1 Having a tendency to recede or go back; receding. 2 Failing to come into expression. 3 *Genetics* Designating that one of a pair of contrasted allelomorphic characters which is suppressed in a hybrid offspring when both are present: opposed to *dominant.* —*n. Genetics* 1 A hybrid which carries and transmits a character suppressed by the corresponding dominant character. 2 The suppressed character. —**re·ces′sive·ly** *adv.*

Rech·a·bite (rek′ə·bīt) *n.* 1 One of a Jewish family descended from Jonadab, son of Rechab, who abstained from wine and the planting of vineyards. *Jer.* xxxv 3. 2 Hence, a total abstainer from intoxicants; a teetotaler. 3 A member of a society of teetotalers called the Independent Order of Rechabites, founded in England in 1835 and in the United States in 1842. —**Rech′a·bit′ism** *n.*

ré·chauf·fé (rā·shō·fā′) *n. French* 1 Food warmed over. 2 Reworked or "warmed over" literary work; rehash.

re·cheat (ri·chēt′) *n. Archaic* A strain sounded on a huntsman's horn to recall the hounds from a wrong course or at the end of the hunt; also, the act of sounding this signal. —*v.i. Obs.* To sound the recheat. [<OF *rachater* rally, reassemble]

re·cher·ché (rə·sher·shā′) *adj. French* 1 Much sought after; hence, choice; rare. 2 Far-fetched.

re·cid·i·vist (rə·sid′ə·vist) *n.* 1 Anyone who relapses into a former state or condition. 2 A confirmed criminal; in the United States, one committed to prison for a second term. [<F *récidiviste* <L *recidivus* relapsing < *recidere* < *re-* back + *cadere* fall] —**re·cid′i·vism, rec·i·div·i·ty** (res′ə·div′ə·tē) *n.* —**re·cid′i·vis′tic** *adj.*

re·cid·i·vous (rə·sid′ə·vəs) *adj.* Liable to backslide.

Re·ci·fe (re·sē′fə) A port of NE Brazil; capital of Pernambuco state: also *Pernambuco.*

rec·i·pe (res′ə·pē) *n.* 1 A formula or list of ingredients of a mixture, giving the exact proportions together with proper directions for compounding, cooking, etc. 2 A medical prescription: so called from its opening word: usually abbreviated to ℞. 3 A method prescribed for attaining a desired result. [<L, take, imperative of *recipere.* See RECEIVE.]

re·cip·i·ence (ri·sip′ē·əns) *n.* 1 The process or act of receiving. 2 Receptivity. Also **re·cip′i·en·cy.**

re·cip·i·ent (ri·sip′ē·ənt) *adj.* Receiving or ready to receive; receptive. —*n.* One who or that which receives; one who accepts a gift or favor. [<L *recipiens, -entis,* ppr. of *recipere* RECEIVE]

re·cip·ro·cal (ri·sip′rə·kəl) *adj.* 1 Done or given by each of two to the other; mutual. 2 Mutually interchangeable. 3 Alternating; moving to and fro. 4 So related, as two concepts, that if the first determines the second, then the second determines the first. 5 Expressive of mutual relationship or action: used in connection with certain pronouns and verbs or their meaning. 6 *Math.* Of or pertaining to a fraction the numerator and denominator of which have been reversed. —*n.* 1 That which is reciprocal. 2 *Math.* The quotient obtained by dividing unity by a number or expression, as $\frac{1}{x}$ is the reciprocal of *x.* In a fraction, this reverses the numerator and denominator, as $\frac{3}{2}$ is the reciprocal of $\frac{2}{3}$. See synonyms under MUTUAL. [<L *reciprocus*] —**re·cip′ro·cal′i·ty** (-kal′ə·tē), **re·cip′ro·cal·ness** *n.* —**re·cip′ro·cal·ly** *adv.*

reciprocal pronouns *Gram.* Pronouns or pronominal phrases denoting reciprocal action or relation, as *each other, one another.*

re·cip·ro·cate (ri·sip′rə·kāt) *v.* **·cat·ed, ·cat·ing** *v.t.* 1 To cause to move backward and forward alternately. 2 To give and receive mutually, as favors or gifts; interchange. 3 To give, feel, do, etc., in return; requite, as an emotion. —*v.i.* 4 To move backward and forward. 5 To make a return in kind. 6 To give and receive favors, gifts, etc., mutually. 7 To correspond; be equivalent. See synonyms under REQUITE. [<L *reciprocatus,* pp. of *reciprocare* move to and fro < *reciprocus* returning] —**re·cip′ro·ca′tive** *adj.* —**re·cip′ro·ca′tor** *n.*

reciprocating engine An engine having a piston or pistons which move to and fro: distinguished from *rotary engine.*

re·cip·ro·ca·tion (ri·sip′rə·kā′shən) *n.* The act of reciprocating; a mutual giving and returning; alternation; alternate motion. See synonyms under INTERCOURSE. [<L *reciprocatio, -onis* < *reciprocus* returning]

re·cip·ro·ca·to·ry (ri·sip′rə·kə·tôr′ē, -tō′rē) *adj.* Alternating in direction or movement; reciprocating: opposed to *rotary.*

rec·i·proc·i·ty (res′ə·pros′ə·tē) *n.* 1 Reciprocal obligation, action, or relation. 2 That trade relation or policy between two countries by which each makes concessions favoring the importation of the products of the other. See synonyms under INTERCOURSE. [<F *réciprocité*]

re·ci·sion (ri·sizh′ən) *n.* 1 The act of rescinding. 2 The act of pruning. [<OF <L *recisio, -onis* < *recisum,* pp. of *recidere* cut off < *re-* back + *caedere* cut]

re·cit·al (ri·sīt′l) *n.* 1 A telling over in detail, or that which is thus told; a narration. 2 A public delivery of something previously memorized. 3 A musical program performed by one person, or consisting of works by one person. 4 A detailed statement. See synonyms under HISTORY, REPORT, STORY[1].

rec·i·ta·tion (res′ə·tā′shən) *n.* 1 The act of repeating from memory; the reciting of a lesson, or the meeting of a class for that purpose. 2 That which is allotted for recital or actually recited. [<L *recitatio, -onis* < *recitare.* See RECITE.]

rec·i·ta·tive[1] (res′ə·tā′tiv, ri·sī′tə·tiv) *adj.* Of the nature of a recital as of facts or details; narrative.

rec·i·ta·tive[2] (res′ə·tə·tēv′, rə·sit′ə·tiv) *n. Music* Language uttered as in ordinary speech, but in musical tones; that style of singing or a vocal passage so rendered. Also *Italian* **re·ci·ta·ti·vo** (rā′chē·tä·tē′vō). —*adj.* Having the character of a recitative. [<Ital. *recitativo,* ult. <L *recitare*]

re·cite (ri·sīt′) *v.* **·cit·ed, ·cit·ing** *v.t.* 1 To declaim or say from memory, especially formally, as a lesson in class. 2 To tell in particular detail; relate. 3 To enumerate. —*v.i.* 4 To declaim or speak something from memory. 5 To repeat or be examined in a lesson or part of a lesson in class. See synonyms under RELATE. [<F *réciter* <L *recitare* < *re-* again + *citare.* See CITE.] —**re·cit′er** *n.*

re–cite (rē·sīt′) *v.t. & v.i.* **–cit·ed, –cit·ing** To cite again. [<RE- + CITE]

reck (rek) *v.t. & v.i. Obs.* 1 To have a care or thought (for); heed; mind. 2 To be of concern or interest (to): It *recks* me not. ◆ Homophone: *wreck.* [OE *rēccan*]

reck·less (rek′lis) *adj.* 1 Foolishly heedless of danger; rash. 2 Indifferent; neglectful. See synonyms under IMPROVIDENT, IMPRUDENT, WANTON. [OE *recceléas*] —**reck′less·ly** *adv.* —**reck′less·ness** *n.*

Reck·ling·hau·sen (rek′ling·hou′zən) A city in the Ruhr in NW North Rhine-Westphalia, West Germany.

reck·on (rek′ən) *v.t.* 1 To count; compute; calculate. 2 To look upon as being; regard: They *reckon* him a fool. 3 *Dial.* To suppose or guess; expect. —*v.i.* 4 To make computation; count up. 5 To rely or depend: with *on* or *upon*: to *reckon* on help. See synonyms under CALCULATE. —**to reckon for** To pay for; receive the penalty of. —**to reckon with** 1 To settle accounts with. 2 To take into consideration; bear in mind; consider. —**to reckon without one's host** To reckon a bill without consulting the landlord; hence, to neglect important facts in reaching a conclusion. [OE *recenian* explain. Akin to G *rechnen* count.]

reck·on·er (rek′ən·ər) *n.* 1 One who reckons. 2 A book or device for aiding one to compute: often called **ready reckoner.**

reck·on·ing (rek′ən·ing) *n.* 1 The act of counting; computation; a settlement of accounts. 2 Account; score; bill, as at a hotel. 3 *Naut.* The calculation of a ship's position, especially when made only by log and compass; dead reckoning. 4 An accounting to God.

re·claim (ri·klām′) *v.t.* 1 To bring (swamp, desert, etc.) into a condition to support cultivation or life, as by draining or irrigating. 2 To obtain (a substance) from used or waste products: to *reclaim* rubber. 3 To cause to return from wrong or sinful ways of life; reform. 4 *Obs.* To tame, as a hawk. —*n.* 1 The act of reclaiming or state of being reclaimed; also, that which is reclaimed. 2 A fresh claim. [<OF *reclamer* call back <L *reclamare* < *re-* against + *clamare* cry out] —**re·claim′a·ble** *adj.* —**re·claim′er, re·claim′ant** *n.*

Synonyms (verb): amend, convert, correct, recover, redeem, reform, renew, rescue, restore, subdue, tame. *Antonyms*: corrupt, degrade, deprave, destroy, seduce, vitiate.

re–claim (rē·klām′) *v.t.* To claim again.

rec·la·ma·tion (rek′lə·mā′shən) *n.* 1 The act or process of reclaiming, in any sense. 2 Restoration, as to ownership, cultivation, usefulness, or a moral life. —**Bureau of Reclamation** A branch of the U. S. Department of the Interior which constructs and operates Federal water-power plants and irrigation projects. [<F *réclamation* <L *reclamatio, -onis* a cry of disapproval < *reclamare.* See RECLAIM.]

ré·clame (rā·klàm′) *n. French* 1 Publicity. 2 A striving after publicity.

re·cline (ri·klīn′) *v.* **·clined, ·clin·ing** *v.i.* To assume a recumbent position; lie down or back. —*v.t.* To cause to assume a recumbent position; lay down or back. See synonyms under

reembarkation	**re–emit**	**reencouragement**	**reenjoy**	**reenslave**	**reerect**	**reexamine**
reembody	**reenact**	**reendow**	**reenjoyment**	**reenslavement**	**reestablish**	**reexhibit**
reembrace	**reenaction**	**reengage**	**reenkindle**	**reenstamp**	**reestablishment**	**reexpel**
reemerge	**reenactment**	**reengagement**	**reenlist**	**reenthrone**	**re–evaluate**	**reexperience**
reemergence	**reencourage**	**reengrave**	**reenlistment**	**reenthronement**	**reexamination**	**reexport**

LEAN[1], REST[1]. [<L *reclinare* <*re-* back + *clinare* lean] —**rec·li·na·tion** (rek′lə·nā′shən) *n.* —**re·clin′er** *n.*

rec·luse (rek′lōōs, ri·klōōs′) *n.* **1** One who lives in retirement or seclusion. **2** One who retires from intercourse with the world, as a religious devotee; specifically, one who lives shut up in a cell and practices exceptional austerities. —**re·cluse** (ri·klōōs′) *adj.* Secluded or retired from the world; solitary. [<OF *reclus* <LL *reclusus,* pp. of L *recludere* shut off <*re-* again + *claudere* close] —**re·clu′sive** *adj.*

re·clu·sion (ri·klōō′zhən) *n.* **1** The state of being a recluse; retirement from the world. **2** Rigorous immurement as practiced by certain ascetics in the Middle Ages. **3** Imprisonment; especially, solitary confinement.

re·clu·sive (ri·klōō′siv) *adj.* Affording or living in seclusion; recluse.

rec·og·ni·tion (rek′əg·nish′ən) *n.* **1** The act of recognizing; the process of memory that identifies an object, person, etc., as already known or experienced. **2** Acknowledgment of a fact or claim. **3** Friendly notice; salutation; attention: *recognition* of a speaker by the chair. **4** Acknowledgment and acceptance on the part of one government of the independence and validity of another. See synonyms under KNOWLEDGE. [<L *recognitio, -onis* <*recognitus,* pp. of *recognoscere.* See RECOGNIZANCE.] —**re·cog·ni·to·ry** (ri·kog′nə·tôr′ē, -tō′rē), **re·cog′ni·tive** *adj.*

re·cog·ni·zance (ri·kog′nə·zəns, -kon′ə-) *n.* **1** *Law* **a** An acknowledgment or obligation of record, with condition to do some particular act, as to appear and answer, or to keep the peace. **b** A sum of money deposited as surety for fulfilment of such act or obligation, and forfeited by its non-performance. **2** *Obs.* A badge or token to aid in recognition. [<OF *recognoissance* <*reconoissant,* ppr. of *reconoistre* <L *recognoscere* call to mind <*re-* again + *cognoscere* know. See COGNITION.] —**re·cog′ni·zant** *adj.*

rec·og·nize (rek′əg·nīz) *v.t.* **·nized, ·niz·ing 1** To know again; perceive as identical with someone or something previously known. **2** To identify or know, as by previous experience or knowledge: I *recognize* poor poetry when I see it. **3** To perceive as true; realize: to *recognize* the facts in a case. **4** To acknowledge the independence and validity of, as a newly constituted government. **5** To indicate appreciation or approval of: to *recognize* merit. **6** To approve formally; regard as valid or genuine: to *recognize* a claim. **7** To give (someone) permission to speak, as in a legislative body. **8** To admit the acquaintance of; greet. **9** *Law* To bind by a recognizance. See synonyms under ACKNOWLEDGE, CONFESS, DISCERN. [Back formation <RECOGNIZANCE] —**rec′og·niz′a·ble** *adj.* —**rec′og·niz′a·bly** *adv.* —**rec′og·niz′er** *n.*

re·cog·ni·zee (ri·kog′nə·zē′, -kon′ə-) *n. Law* One in whose favor a recognizance is made.

re·cog·ni·zor (ri·kog′nə·zər, -kon′ə-) *n. Law* One who enters into a recognizance.

re·coil (ri·koil′) *v.i.* **1** To start back, as in fear or loathing; shrink: He *recoiled* at the sight. **2** To spring back, as from force of discharge or force of impact. **3** To return to the source; react: with *on* or *upon*: Crime *recoils* upon its perpetrator. **4** To move or draw back; retreat. —*n.* (rē′koil′) **1** A backward movement or impulse, as of a gun at the moment of firing; rebound; also, a shrinking. **2** The condition existing as the result of a recoil. [<OF *reculer* <L *re-* again + *culus* buttocks] —**re·coil′er** *n.*

re·coil-op·er·at·ed (rē′koil·op′ə·rā′tid) *adj.* Operated or working by the energy generated in recoil, as certain automatic weapons.

rec·ol·lect (rek′ə·lekt′) *v.t.* To call back to the mind; revive in the memory; remember. —*v.i.* To have a recollection of something. See synonyms under REMEMBER. [<L *recollectus,* pp. of *recolligere* gather together again <*re-* again + *colligere.* See COLLECT.]

re-col·lect (rē′kə·lekt′) *v.t.* **1** to collect again, as things scattered. **2** To collect or compose (one's thoughts or nerves); compose or recover (oneself). [<RE- + COLLECT]

rec·ol·lect·ed (rek′ə·lek′tid) *adj.* Recalled to mind; remembered.

re-col·lect·ed (rē′kə·lek′tid) *adj.* Calm; composed; collected.

rec·ol·lec·tion (rek′ə·lek′shən) *n.* **1** The act or power of recollecting or remembering; remembrance. **2** Something remembered; a reminiscence; a memory. See synonyms under MEMORY. —**rec′ol·lec′tive** *adj.* —**rec′ol·lec′tive·ly** *adv.*

re-col·lec·tion (rē′kə·lek′shən) *n.* The act of re-collecting, or the state of being re-collected.

re·com·bi·na·tion (rē′kom·bə·nā′shən) *n. Genetics* **1** A cross-over. **2** An offspring exhibiting characters caused by such a rearrangement.

rec·om·mend (rek′ə·mend′) *v.t.* **1** To commend with favorable representations; praise as desirable, worthy, etc. **2** To make attractive or acceptable: His sagacity *recommends* him. **3** To advise; urge. **4** To give in charge; commend. [<Med. L *recommendare* <*re-* again + *commendare.* See COMMEND.] —**rec′om·mend′er** *n.*

rec·om·men·da·tion (rek′ə·men·dā′shən) *n.* **1** The act of recommending, or that which recommends. **2** A note commending a person to confidence or favor. See synonyms under COUNSEL.

rec·om·mend·a·to·ry (rek′ə·men′də·tôr′ē, -tō′rē) *adj.* **1** Serving to recommend. **2** Advisory but not imperative, as applied to certain official appointments.

re·com·mit (rē′kə·mit′) *v.t.* **·mit·ted, ·mit·ting 1** To commit again. **2** To refer back to a committee, as a bill.

rec·om·pense (rek′əm·pens) *v.t.* **·pensed, ·pens·ing 1** To give compensation to; pay or repay; reward; requite. **2** To give compensation for; make up for, as a loss. See synonyms under PAY[1], REQUITE. —*n.* An equivalent for anything given, done, or suffered; payment or repayment; compensation; reward. [<OF *recompenser* <LL *recompensare* <L *re-* again + *compensare.* See COMPENSATE.]

Synonyms (noun): amends, compensation, indemnification, indemnity, remuneration, repayment, requital, retribution, reward, satisfaction. See RESTITUTION, SALARY.

re·com·pose (rē′kəm·pōz′) *v.t.* **·posed, ·pos·ing 1** To restore the composure of; tranquilize. **2** To compose or form anew; rearrange; reconstitute; recombine. —**re·com·po·si·tion** (rē′kom·pə·zish′ən) *n.*

re·con·cen·tra·do (rā·kōn′sen·trä′dō) *n. pl.* **·dos** In Cuba and the Philippine Islands, during and before the Spanish-American War, a dweller in the country who was forced by decree of the Spanish authorities to move within the city limits. [<Sp., pp. of *reconcentrar* move to the center again; so called because the authorities had previously ordered the country population to move within a certain radius of the town]

re·con·cen·trate (rē·kon′sən·trāt) *v.t.* **·at·ed, ·at·ing** To concentrate again; specifically, to treat as reconcentrados. —**re·con′cen·tra′tion** *n.*

rec·on·cil·a·ble (rek′ən·sī′lə·bəl) *adj.* **1** Capable of being reconciled or of renewing friendship. **2** Capable of being adjusted or harmonized. —**rec′on·cil′a·bil′i·ty, rec′on·cil′a·ble·ness** *n.* —**rec′on·cil′a·bly** *adv.*

rec·on·cile (rek′ən·sīl) *v.t.* **·ciled, ·cil·ing 1** To bring back to friendship after estrangement; also, to make friendly; win the good will of. **2** To settle or adjust, as a quarrel. **3** To bring to acquiescence, content, or submission: to *reconcile* one to his lot. **4** To make or show to be consistent or congruous; harmonize: often with *to* or *with*: Can he *reconcile* his statement with his conduct? See synonyms under ACCOMMODATE. [<OF *reconciler* <L *reconciliare* <*re-* again + *conciliare* unite. See CONCILIATE.] —**rec′on·cile′ment** *n.* —**rec′on·cil′er** *n.*

rec·on·cil·i·a·tion (rek′ən·sil′ē·ā′shən) *n.* **1** The act of reconciling, or the state of being reconciled; atonement. **2** The effecting or showing of agreement between things; explanation of differences. See synonyms under PROPITIATION. —**rec′on·cil′i·a·to′ry** (-sil′ē·ə·tôr′ē, -tō′rē) *adj.*

rec·on·dite (rek′ən·dīt, ri·kon′dīt) *adj.* **1** Remote from ordinary or easy perception; abstruse; secret. **2** Dealing in abstruse matters; profound. **3** Hidden; not readily observed. See synonyms under MYSTERIOUS, SECRET. [<L *reconditus,* pp. of *recondere* put away, hide <*re-* back + *condere* construct, hide] —**rec′on·dite′ly** *adv.* —**rec′on·dite′ness** *n.*

re·con·di·tion (rē′kən·di′shən) *v.t.* To put into good or working condition, as by making repairs; overhaul.

re·con·nais·sance (ri·kon′ə·səns, -säns) *n.* **1** A reconnoitering; a preliminary examination or survey, as of the territory and resources of a country. **2** The act of obtaining information of military value, especially regarding the position, strength, and movement of enemy forces. Also **re·con′nois·sance.** [<F]

re·con·noi·ter (rē′kə·noi′tər, rek′ə-) *v.t.* To examine by the eye; survey, as for military, engineering, or geological purposes. —*v.i.* To make a reconnaissance. Also **re′con·noi′tre.** [<OF *reconoistre.* See RECOGNIZANCE.] —**re′con·noi′ter·er, re′con·noi′trer** *n.*

re·con·sid·er (rē′kən·sid′ər) *v.t.* **1** To consider again, especially with a view to a reversal of previous action. **2** In parliamentary usage, to bring before the house for renewed action (a matter previously decided). —*v.i.* **3** To reconsider a matter or decision. —**re′con·sid′er·a′tion** *n.*

re·con·sign (rē′kən·sīn′) *v.t.* To consign again; specifically, to consign (goods) to a different place or person while still in transit. —**re′·con·sign′ment** *n.*

re·con·sti·tute (rē·kon′stə·tōōt, -tyōōt) *v.t.* **·tut·ed, ·tut·ing** To constitute again; make over: to *reconstitute* dehydrated fruits by adding water. —**re·con′sti·tu′tion** *n.*

re·con·struct (rē′kən·strukt′) *v.t.* To construct again; rebuild.

re·con·struct·ed (rē′kən·struk′tid) *adj.* Rebuilt or made anew: said especially of gems artificially made: a *reconstructed* ruby.

re·con·struc·tion (rē′kən·struk′shən) *n.* **1** The act of reconstructing, or the state of being reconstructed; specifically, the restoration of the seceded States as members of the Union under the **Reconstruction Acts** of March 2 and 23, 1867. **2** The repair of mutilated limbs, as of soldiers, by means of mechanical appliances. —**re′con·struc′tive** *adj.*

Reconstruction Finance Corporation A former (1932–54) branch of the Federal Loan Agency of the U.S. Department of the Interior, authorized to extend financial assistance to agriculture, industry, and commerce.

Reconstruction period *U.S.* The period following the Civil War during which the seceded Southern States were reorganized in accordance with the Congressional program.

re·con·vey (rē′kən·vā′) *v.t.* To convey back to an original owner or place. —**re′con·vey′·ance** *n.*

rec·ord (rek′ərd) *n.* **1** An account in written or other permanent form serving as a memorial or authentic evidence of a fact or event. **2** Something on which such an account is made, as a document or monument. **3** Information on facts or events, preserved and handed down: the heaviest rainfall on *record.* **4** The known career or performance of a person, animal, organization, etc., regarded as a series of things done or achieved: a good *record* in politics. **5** The best listed achievement, as in a competitive sport: to beat the world *record.* **6** *Law* **a** A written account of an act, statement, or transaction made by an officer acting under authority of law, and intended as permanent evidence thereon. **b** An official written account of a judicial or legislative proceeding, including the judgments or enactments and an official copy of all related documents. **7** A cylinder, disk, roll, or other article perforated, indented, or otherwise prepared so as to reproduce sounds. —**off the record 1** Unofficial or unofficially. **2** Not for quotation or publication, or not from a source to be identified. —*adj.* Surpassing any previously recorded achievement or performance of its kind: a *record* vote. —**re·cord** (ri·kôrd′) *v.t.* **1** To write down or otherwise inscribe, as for preserving an

reexportation
reexpulsion
reface
refashion
refasten
refertilize
reflorescence
reflourish
reflow
reflower
refluctuation
refold
reforge
reforger
refortification
refortify
refreeze
refurbish
refurnish
regather
regerminate
regermination
regild
regraft
regrant
regreet
rehandle
rehearing
reheel
rehire
rehybridize
rehypothecate
reillume
reimplant
reimport

authentic account, evidence, etc. **2** To indicate; register, especially in permanent form, as a cardiograph does. **3** To make a phonograph record of. —*v.i.* **4** To record something. [<OF <*recorder* <L *recordari* call to mind <*re-* again + *cor, cordis* heart, mind]

Synonyms (noun): account, archives, catalog, chronicle, document, enrolment, entry, enumeration, history, inscription, instrument, inventory, memorandum, memorial, muniment, register, roll, scroll. *Record* is a word of wide signification, applying to any writing, mark, or trace that serves as a *memorial* giving enduring attestation of an event or fact; an extended *account, chronicle,* or *history* is a *record*; so, too, may be a brief *inventory* or *memorandum.* A *memorial* is any object, whether a writing, a monument, or other permanent thing that is designed or adapted to keep something in remembrance. A *register* is a formal or official written *record,* especially a series of entries made for preservation or reference; as, a *register* of births and deaths. *Archives,* in the sense here considered, are *documents* or *records,* often legal *records,* preserved in a public or official depository; the word *archives* is also applied to the place where such *documents* are regularly deposited and preserved. *Muniments* are *records* that enable one to defend his title. See CHARACTER, HISTORY, REPORT, STORY[1].

re·cord·er (ri·kôr′dər) *n.* **1** One who records. **2** A magistrate having criminal jurisdiction in a city or borough. **3** A registering apparatus. **4** A fipple flute, having eight holes and any one of four ranges: treble, alto, tenor, or bass. **5** A tape recorder or wire recorder. —**re·cord′er·ship** *n.*

TREBLE RECORDER

re·count (ri·kount′) *v.t.* **1** To relate the particulars of; narrate in detail. **2** To enumerate; recite. See synonyms under RELATE. [< AF, OF *reconter* relate]

re–count (rē·kount′) *v.t.* To count again. —*n.* (rē′kount′, rē·kount′) A repetition of a count; specifically, a second count of votes cast.

re·count·al (ri·koun′təl) *n.* A thing told, or the act of telling; a detailed narration. Also **re·count′ment.**

re·coup (ri·kōōp′) *v.t.* **1** To recover or obtain an equivalent for; make up, as a loss. **2** To reimburse for a loss; indemnify. **3** *Law* To keep back (something due) in order to make good a counterclaim. —*n.* The act or process of recouping. [<F *recouper* <*re-* again + *couper* cut. See COUP.] —**re·coup′a·ble** *adj.* —**re·coup′ment** *n.*

re·course (rē′kôrs, -kōrs, ri·kôrs′, -kōrs′) *n.* **1** Resort to or application for help or security in trouble. **2** *Law* The right to exact payment from a party secondarily liable, where the first party liable has failed to pay. **3** A source of help or supply; the person or thing resorted to. **4** *Obs.* Admission; entrance. —**without recourse** A restricted or qualified endorsement of a promissory note or transfer thereof, which signifies that the endorser merely transfers the title to the instrument, but disclaims liability for non–payment. —**to have recourse to** To go to for advice or help. [<OF *recours* <L *recursus* a running back < *recurrere.* See RECUR.]

re·cov·er (ri·kuv′ər) *v.t.* **1** To obtain again after losing; regain, as property, self–control, health, etc. **2** To make up for; retrieve, as a loss. **3** To restore (oneself) to natural balance, health, etc. **4** In sports, to regain (one's normal position of guard, balance, etc.). **5** To reclaim, as land, **6** *Law* **a** To gain in judicial proceedings: to *recover* judgment. **b** To gain or regain by legal process. —*v.i.* **7** To regain health, composure, etc. **8** *Law* To succeed in a lawsuit. **9** In sports, to regain one's balance or position of guard. [<OF *recovrer* <L *recuperare.* See RECUPERATE.] —**re·cov′er·a·ble** *adj.* —**re·cov′er·er** *n.*

Synonyms: cure, heal, reanimate, recruit, recuperate, regain, repossess, restore, resume, retrieve. See RECLAIM. *Antonyms*: die, fail, lapse, sink.

re–cov·er (rē·kuv′ər) *v.t.* To cover again. —**re–cov′er·er** *n.*

re·cov·er·y (ri·kuv′ər·ē) *n. pl.* **·er·ies** **1** The act of recovering. **2** The state of being or having recovered. **3** Restoration from sickness or from any undesirable or abnormal condition. **4** In boating, the forward movement of an oarsman, after having finished one stroke, to take the next. **5** In fencing and sparring, the act of regaining a defensive position after attack. **6** The extraction of valuable substances and materials from original sources, by–products, waste, etc. **7** The retrieval of a flying object, as a balloon, space vehicle, meteorite, etc., after it has fallen to earth. [<AF *recoverie*]

recovery room A room in a hospital for the treatment of patients recovering immediately after an operation or childbirth.

rec·re·ant (rek′rē·ənt) *adj.* **1** Unfaithful to a cause or pledge; apostate; false. **2** Crying for mercy, as in the old trial by combat; hence, craven; cowardly. See synonyms under PUSILLANIMOUS. —*n.* A cowardly or faithless person; also, a deserter; an apostate. [<OF, ppr. of *recreire* surrender allegiance <Med. L *recredere* <L *re-* back + *credere* believe] —**rec′re·an·cy, rec′re·ance** *n.* —**rec′re·ant·ly** *adv.*

rec·re·ate (rek′rē·āt) *v.* **·at·ed, ·at·ing** *v.t.* To impart fresh vigor to; refresh, especially after toil, by some form of relaxation or entertainment. —*v.i.* To take recreation. See synonyms under ENTERTAIN, RELAX. [<L *recreatus,* pp. of *recreare* create anew <*re-* again + *creare* create] —**rec′re·a′tive** *adj.*

re–cre·ate (rē′krē·āt′) *v.t.* **·at·ed, ·at·ing** To create anew. —**re′–cre·a′tion** *n.*

rec·re·a·tion (rek′rē·ā′shən) *n.* **1** Refreshment of body or mind, but generally of both; diversion; amusement. **2** Any pleasurable exercise or occupation. See synonyms under ENTERTAINMENT, REST[1], SPORT. —**rec′re·a′tion·al** *adj.*

rec·re·ment (rek′rə·mənt) *n.* **1** *Physiol.* A secretion reabsorbed by the body after having performed its function, as gastric juice, saliva, etc. **2** Waste material; dross; scoria; spume. [<F *récrément* <L *recrementum* dross <*re-* back + *cretum,* pp. of *cernere* sift] —**rec′re·men′tal** (-men′təl) *adj.* —**rec′re·men·ti′tial** (-men·tish′əl), **rec′re·men·ti′tious** *adj.*

re·crim·i·nate (ri·krim′ə·nāt) *v.* **·nat·ed, ·nat·ing** *v.t.* To accuse in return. —*v.i.* To repel one accusation by making another in return. [<Med. L *recriminatus,* pp. of *recriminare* < L *re-* again + *criminare.* See CRIMINATE.] —**re·crim′i·na′tive, re·crim·i·na·to·ry** (ri·krim′ə·nə·tôr′ē, -tō′rē) *adj.* —**re·crim′i·na′tor** *n.*

re·crim·i·na·tion (ri·krim′ə·nā′shən) *n.* **1** The act of recriminating. **2** An accusation made in return; a countercharge.

re·cru·desce (rē′krōō·des′) *v.i.* **·desced, ·desc·ing** To break out or become active again. [<L *recrudescere* <*re-* again + *crudescere* become harsh, break out <*crudus* raw, harsh]

re·cru·des·cence (rē′krōō·des′əns) *n.* **1** A breaking out afresh, as of a disease or wound. **2** A reappearance; return. [<L *recrudescens, -entis* ppr. of *recrudescere.* See RECRUDESCE.] —**re′cru·des′cent** *adj.*

re·cruit (ri·krōōt′) *v.t.* **1** To enlist (men) for military or naval service. **2** To muster; raise, as an army, by enlistment. **3** To supply with recruits. **4** To regain or revive (lost health, strength, etc.). **5** *Rare* To replenish. —*v.i.* **6** To enlist new men for military or naval service. **7** To regain lost health or strength. **8** To gain or raise new supplies of anything lost or needed. —*n.* **1** A newly enlisted soldier, sailor, or marine; loosely, any new adherent of a cause, organization, or the like. **2** *Obs.* A new supply of something necessary or useful. [<F *recruter* <*recrute* a recruit <*recrû* grown again, pp. of *recroître* <L *re-* again + *crescere* grow, increase] —**re·cruit′er** *n.* —**re·cruit′ment** *n.*

Synonyms (verb): enlist, reinforce, repair, replenish. See RECOVER. *Antonyms*: decimate, disperse, lose, reduce, scatter.

rec·tal (rek′təl) *adj. Anat.* Relating to, involving, or in the region of the rectum.

rec·tan·gle (rek′tang′gəl) *n.* A right–angled parallelogram. [<F <LL *rectiangulum* <L *rectus* straight + *angulus* angle]

rec·tan·gu·lar (rek·tang′gyə·lər) *adj.* **1** Having one or more right angles. **2** Resembling a rectangle in shape or appearance. —**rec·tan′gu·lar′i·ty** (-lar′ə·tē) *n.* —**rec·tan′gu·lar·ly** *adv.*

rectangular coordinate system See CARTESIAN COORDINATE SYSTEM.

rectangular hyperbola *Math.* A hyperbola with axes of equal length and perpendicular asymptotes.

recti– *combining form* Straight: *rectilinear.* Also, before vowels, **rect–.** [<L *rectus* right]

rec·ti·fi·ca·tion (rek′tə·fə·kā′shən) *n.* **1** The act or process of rectifying. **2** A setting right of what is wrong. **3** Refining by fractional or renewed distillation. [<F]

rec·ti·fi·er (rek′tə·fī′ər) *n.* **1** On who or that which rectifies. **2** *Electr.* A device used to convert an alternating current into a direct or unidirectional current. **3** A refiner or compounder of spirituous liquors.

rec·ti·fy (rek′tə·fī) *v.t.* **·fied, ·fy·ing** **1** To make right; correct; amend. **2** *Chem.* To refine, as a liquid, by repeated distillations until a desired degree of purity is obtained. **3** *Electr.* To change (an alternating current) into a direct current by reversing the direction of alternate impulses. **4** *Math.* To determine the length of (a curve or arc). **5** To allow for errors or inaccuracies in, as a compass reading. **6** To adjust for accurate calculations: to *rectify* a globe. See synonyms under AMEND. [< OF *rectifier* <LL *rectificare* <L *rectus* right + *facere* make] —**rec′ti·fi′a·ble** *adj.*

rec·ti·graph (rek′tə·graf, -gräf) *n. Optics* A separable part which may be inserted into the tube of an optical instrument in order to reinvert an inverted image. [<RECTI- + -GRAPH] —**rec′ti·graph′ic** *adj.*

rec·ti·lin·e·ar (rek′tə·lin′ē·ər) *adj.* Pertaining to, consisting of, moving in, or bounded by a right line or lines; straight. Also **rec′ti·lin′e·al.** —**rec′ti·lin′e·ar·ly** *adv.*

rec·ti·tude (rek′tə·tōōd, -tyōōd) *n.* **1** Upright in principles and conduct. **2** Freedom from error; correctness of judgment, method, or application; accuracy. **3** *Obs.* Straightness. See synonyms under JUSTICE, VIRTUE. [<F <LL *rectitudo* <L *rectus* right]

rec·to (rek′tō) *n. pl.* **·tos** A right–hand page, as of a book: opposed to *verso* (or *reverso*). [< L *recto (folio)* on the right (page)]

recto– *combining form* Rectal; pertaining to the rectum: *rectocele,* hernia of the rectum. Also, before vowels, **rect–.** [See RECTUM]

rec·tor (rek′tər) *n.* **1** In the Church of England, a priest who has full charge of a parish, and receives the parochial tithes: distinguished from *vicar.* **2** In the Protestant Episcopal Church, a priest in charge of a parish. **3** In the Roman Catholic Church: **a** A priest in charge of a congregation or church, especially one not having parochial status: distinguished from *parish priest.* **b** The head of a seminary or religious house. **4** In certain universities, colleges, and schools, the head or chief officer. [<L *rectus,* pp. of *regere* rule] —**rec′tor·ate** (-it) *n.* —**rec·to·ri·al** (rek·tôr′ē·əl, -tō′rē-) *adj.*

rec·to·ry (rek′tər·ē) *n. pl.* **·ries** **1** A rector's dwelling. **2** In England, a parish domain with its buildings, revenue, etc.

reimportation	**reimpress**	**reincrease**	**reinflame**	**reinoculation**	**reinspection**	**reinter**
reimportune	**reimprison**	**reincur**	**reinform**	**reinscribe**	**reinspire**	**reinterment**
reimpose	**reinaugurate**	**reinduce**	**reinfuse**	**reinsert**	**reinstruct**	**reinterrogate**
reimposition	**reincite**	**reinfect**	**reingratiate**	**reinsertion**	**reintegrate**	**reintrench**
reimpregnate	**reincorporate**	**reinfection**	**reinhabit**	**reinspect**	**reintegration**	**reintroduce**

rec·tum (rek′təm) *n. pl.* **·ta** (-tə) *Anat.* The terminal portion of the large intestine, extending from the sigmoid bend of the colon to the anus. [<NL *rectum (intestinum)* straight (intestine)]

rec·tus (rek′təs) *n. pl.* **·ti** (-tī) *Anat.* A straight muscle, as of the eye, the abdomen, the femur, etc. [<NL <L, straight]

rec·u·ba·tion (rek′yə·bā′shən) *n. Obs.* A lying down; specifically, in Roman antiquity, a reclining at table. [<L *recubare* recline]

Re·cu·let (rə·kü·le′) The highest peak of the Jura mountains, in eastern France.

re·cum·ben·cy (ri·kum′bən·sē) *n. pl.* **·cies** 1 The state of being recumbent. 2 The act of reclining. 3 A recumbent attitude. Also **re·cum′bence.**

re·cum·bent (ri·kum′bənt) *adj.* 1 Lying down, wholly or partly; reclining; leaning. 2 *Biol.* Tending to rest upon a surface from which they extend: said of certain structures. [<L *recumbens, -entis,* ppr. of *recumbere* < *re-* back + *cumbere* lie, nasalized var. of *cubare* lie down] — **re·cum′bent·ly** *adv.*

re·cu·per·ate (ri·ko͞o′pə·rāt, -kyo͞o′-) *v.* **·at·ed, ·at·ing** *v.i.* 1 To regain health or strength. 2 To recover from loss, as of money. — *v.t.* 3 To obtain again after loss; recover. 4 To restore to vigor and health. See synonyms under RECOVER. [<L *recuperatus,* pp. of *recuperare*]

re·cu·per·a·tion (ri·ko͞o′pə·rā′shən, -kyo͞o′-) *n.* The recovery of lost power or excellence, especially of health or strength.

re·cu·per·a·tive (ri·ko͞o′pə·rā′tiv, -pər·ə·tiv, -kyo͞o′-) *adj.* Tending, assisting, or pertaining to recovery; restorative. Also **re·cu′per·a·to′ry** (-pər·ə·tôr′ē, -tō′rē).

re·cu·per·a·tor (ri·ko͞o′pə·rā′tər, -kyo͞o′-) *n.* 1 One who or that which recuperates. 2 A mechanism, operated by springs or compressed air, for restoring a gun to firing position after the recoil. 3 *Chem.* An apparatus for the recovery of heat from hot gases.

re·cur (ri·kûr′) *v.i.* **·curred, ·cur·ring** 1 To happen again or repeatedly, especially at regular intervals: a paroxysm that *recurs.* 2 To come back or return; especially, to return to the mind or in recollection. 3 *Rare* To turn for aid; have recourse. [<L *recurrere* < *re-* back + *currere* run]

re·cur·rence (ri·kûr′əns) *n.* The act or fact of recurring; recourse. Also **re·cur′ren·cy.**

re·cur·rent (ri·kûr′ənt) *adj.* 1 Happening or appearing again or repeatedly; recurring. 2 Running back: said of arteries and nerves. See synonyms under FREQUENT. [<L *recurrens, -entis,* ppr. of *recurrere.* See RECUR.] — **re·cur′rent·ly** *adv.*

recurrent fever Relapsing fever.

recurring decimal A circulating decimal.

re·cur·vant (ri·kûr′vənt) *adj. Her.* Coiled with the head raised to strike: said of a serpent. [<L *recurvans, -antis,* ppr. of *recurvare* bend back]

re·cur·vate (ri·kûr′vit, -vāt) *adj.* Bent back. [<L *recurvatus,* pp. of *recurvare.* See RECURVE.] — **re·cur′va·ture** (-və·chər) *n.*

re·curve (ri·kûrv′) *v.t.* & *v.i.* **·curved, ·curv·ing** To curve or bend back or down. [<L *recurvare* < *re-* back + *curvus* curved] — **re·cur·va·tion** (rē′kûr·vā′shən) *n.*

rec·u·sant (rek′yə·zənt, ri·kyo͞o′zənt) *adj.* Persistently refusing to conform; specifically, in English history, refusing to attend services of the Anglican Church. — *n.* One of a recusant character, position, or party; a non-comformist. [<L *recusans, -antis,* ppr. of *recusare.* See RECUSE.] — **rec′u·san·cy** *n.*

rec·u·sa·tion (rek′yə·zā′shən) *n. Law* An exception by which a defendant challenges the judge on grounds of interest or prejudice as to his right to sit. [<L *recusatio, -onis* < *recusatus,* pp. of *recusare* < *re-* against + *causa* cause, case]

re·cy·cle (rē·sī′kəl) *v.t.* **·cy·cled, ·cy·cling** To reclaim (waste materials, as newsprint, bottles, etc.) by using in the manufacture of new products. — **re·cy′cla·ble** *adj.*

red[1] (red) *adj.* **red·der, red·dest** 1 Of a bright color resembling blood; of the same hue as that color of the spectrum farthest from the violet; also, of a hue approximating red: *red* gold. 2 Ultra-radical in politics; especially, communistic. 3 Pertaining to the pole of a magnet which points to the north. Compare BLUE. — *n.* 1 One of the primary colors, occurring at the opposite end of the spectrum from violet; the color of fresh human blood. 2 Any pigment or dye having or giving this color. 3 An ultra-radical in political views, especially a communist. 4 A red object considered with special reference to its color: the *red* (color) in roulette, the *red* (ball) in billiards. — **in the red** *Colloq.* Operating at a loss; owing money: from the practice of making entries in the debit column of an account book in red ink. — **to see red** To be very angry. [OE *rēad*] — **red′ly** *adv.* — **red′ness** *n.*

red[2] (red) See REDD.

Red (red) *n.* 1 A member of the Communist party of Russia; hence, often, any Russian. 2 A member of the Communist party of any country. 3 Any person who supports or approves of the aims of the Communist party. 4 An ultra-radical; anarchist. [<RED; from the color of their flags and banners]

re·dact (ri·dakt′) *v.t.* 1 To prepare, as for publication; edit; revise. 2 To draw up or frame, as a message or edict. [<L *redactus,* pp. of *redigere* reduce to order < *re-* back + *agere* drive] — **re·dac′tor** *n.*

re·dac·tion (ri·dak′shən) *n.* 1 The act of reducing or shaping, as literary matter, into proper form and condition for publication; editing. 2 Literary matter so edited or revised. [<F *rédaction* <LL *redactio, -onis* < *redactus.* See REDACT.]

red algae See RHODOPHYCEAE.

re·dan (ri·dan′) *n.* A fortification with two parapets meeting at a salient angle. See also illustration under BASTION. [<F *redan* <OF *redent* < *re-* back + *dent* tooth; from its appearance]

Red Army The army of the U.S.S.R.: now officially the Soviet Army.

red astrachan A large roundish variety of apple, yellow with red stripes or slashes.

red·bay (red′bā′) *n.* A tree of the laurel family *(Persea borbonia)* of eastern North America, yielding a bluish-black fruit sometimes called alligator pear.

red·bird (red′bûrd′) *n.* 1 The cardinal bird. 2 The scarlet tanager.

red-blood·ed (red′blud′id) *adj.* Having vitality and vigor; hence, manly.

Red Book *Brit.* 1 A book containing a list of all persons in state offices. 2 An official list of the peerage; specifically, a *Royal Kalendar* or *Complete . . . Annual Register* published from 1767 to 1893; also, a similar later publication.

red·breast (red′brest′) *n.* 1 A bird having a red breast, as the American or European robin. 2 The long-eared sunfish *(Lepomis auritus)* of the Atlantic coast of the United States: also **red-breasted bream.** 3 An American sandpiper, the knot *(Calidris canutus rufus)*: also **red-breasted sandpiper.**

red·bud (red′bud′) *n.* The Judas tree.

red·bug (red′bug′) *n.* 1 Any of several red insects; especially, the chigger of the southern United States. 2 The cotton stainer *(Dysdercus suturellus),* that stains growing cotton an indelible red.

red·cap (red′kap′) *n.* 1 *U.S.* A railroad porter: so called from his red-colored cap. 2 The European goldfinch.

red cedar 1 An American juniper tree (genus *Juniperus*) of the cypress family, having a fine-grained, durable wood of a bright- or dark-red color resembling cedar; especially, the **eastern** *(J. virginiana)* and the **western** *(J. scopulorum)* **red cedar.** 2 The giant arborvitae *(Thuja plicata)* of the western United States, having a light, brittle but durable heartwood: known in the lumber trade and popularly as **western red cedar.** 3 The wood of any of these trees.

red cent A United States copper one-cent piece. — **not worth a red cent** *U.S. Colloq.* Worthless.

red·coat (red′kōt′) *n.* 1 A person wearing a red coat. 2 A British soldier of the period when a red coat was part of the uniform worn by the British Army, during the American Revolution and the War of 1812.

red corpuscle An erythrocyte.

red cross 1 The cross of St. George, the emblem of the English. 2 A Greek cross, red on a white ground.

Red Cross Convention See GENEVA CONVENTION.

Red Cross Society A society for the succor of the sick and wounded in war, formed in accordance with the international convention signed at Geneva in 1864, the members wearing a red Geneva cross as a badge of neutrality. These societies are now national organizations, as the **American Red Cross,** and continue their beneficent activities in times of peace, as in fighting disease, etc.

redd (red) *v.t. Dial.* 1 To put in order, as a room; make ready: usually with *up.* 2 To make clear or empty. 3 To adjust, as a quarrel. Also spelled *red.* [OE *hreddan* rescue] — **redd′er** *n.*

red deer 1 The common European and Asian stag *(Cervus elaphus).* 2 The common Virginia white-tailed deer in its rufous summer coat.

red·den (red′n) *v.t.* To make red. — *v.i.* To grow red; flush.

red·den·dum (ri·den′dəm) *n. pl.* **·da** (-də) *Law* A clause in a deed whereby the grantor reserves to himself some new thing, such as rent, out of what he has granted. [<L, neut. of *reddendus,* gerundive of *reddere* give in return. See RENDER.]

red·dish (red′ish) *adj.* Mixed with or somewhat red. — **red′dish·ness** *n.*

red·dle (red′l) *n.* Red ocher or red chalk, used for marking sheep. — *v.t.* **·dled, ·dling** To mark or stain with reddle. Also spelled *raddle.* [Var. of RUDDLE]

red·dle·man (red′l·mən) *n. pl.* **·men** (-mən) One who deals in reddle.

red drum A large drumfish *(Sciaenops ocellatus)* of the Atlantic coast, esteemed as a food fish. Also **red drumfish.**

rede[1] (rēd) *Scot.* or *Obs. v.t.* 1 To advise; counsel. 2 To explain; interpret. — *n.* 1 Advice; counsel. 2 A plan or scheme; decision. 3 A story or narrative; also, interpretation.

rede[2] (rēd) *adj. Scot.* 1 Fierce; impetuous. 2 Drunk.

re·deem (ri·dēm′) *v.t.* 1 To regain possession of by paying a price; specifically, to recover, as mortgaged property. 2 To pay off; receive back and satisfy, as a promissory note. 3 To set free; rescue; ransom. 4 *Theol.* To rescue from sin and its penalties. 5 To fulfil, as an oath or promise. 6 To make amends for; compensate for: The play was *redeemed* by its acting. See synonyms under DELIVER, RECLAIM. [<F *rédimer* <L *redimere* < *re-* back + *emere* buy] — **re·deem′a·ble** *adj.*

re·deem·er (ri·dē′mər) *n.* One who redeems. — **The Redeemer** Jesus Christ.

re-de·fec·tor (rē′di·fek′tər) *n.* One who returns to his native country after having previously fled because of real or imagined injustice.

re·de·liv·er (rē′di·liv′ər) *v.t.* 1 To deliver again, as a message or a speech. 2 To give back; return; restore. — **re′de·liv′er·ance, re′de·liv′er·y** *n.*

re·de·mand (rē′di·mand′, -mänd′) *v.t.* 1 To demand again. 2 To demand or ask the return of.

re·demp·ti·ble (ri·demp′tə·bəl) *adj.* Redeemable. [<L *redemptus* + -IBLE]

re·demp·tion (ri·demp′shən) *n.* 1 The act of redeeming, or the state of being redeemed. 2 The recovery of what is mortgaged or pledged. 3 The payment of a debt or obligation; specifically, the paying of the value of its notes, warrants, etc., by a government. 4 *Theol.* Salvation from sin through the atonement of Christ. [<OF <L *redemptio, -onis* < *redemptus,* pp. of *redimere* redeem. Doublet of RANSOM.]

re·demp·tion·er (ri·demp′shən·ər) *n.* One who redeems himself, as an emigrant by service in payment of passage money.

reintroduction	**reinvigorate**	**rejolt**	**relet**	**reload**	**remake**	**remerge**
reinundate	**reinvigoration**	**rejudge**	**reliquidate**	**reloan**	**remast**	**remigrate**
reinvent	**reinvite**	**rekindle**	**reliquidation**	**relocate**	**remasticate**	**remigration**
reinvestigate	**reinvolve**	**relade**	**relisten**	**relocation**	**remeasure**	**remix**
reinvestment	**rejoint**	**reland**	**relive**	**relodge**	**remelt**	**remodification**

re·demp·tive (ri·demp′tiv) *adj.* Serving to redeem, or connected with redemption. Also **re·demp′to·ry** (-tər·ē). [<L *redemptus,* pp. of *redimere.* See REDEEM.]

Re·demp·tor·ist (ri·demp′tər·ist) *n.* A member of a religious order, the Congregation of the Most Holy Redeemer, founded in 1732 by St. Alphonso de Liguori.

re·des·ig·nate (rē·dez′ig·nāt) *v.t.* **·nat·ed, ·nat·ing** To designate again.

re·de·vel·op (rē′di·vel′əp) *v.t.* **1** To develop again. **2** *Phot.* To intensify with chemicals and put through a second developing process. —*v.i.* **3** To develop again. —**re′de·vel′op·er** *n.* —**re′de·vel′op·ment** *n.*

red eye 1 *U.S. Colloq.* The danger signal in a railroad semaphore system. **2** *U.S. Slang* Poor–quality whisky. **3** The American rock bass. **4** The red–eyed vireo. **5** The rudd.

red–eyed vireo (red′īd′) See under VIREO.

red–fig·ured (red′fig′yərd) *adj.* Having red figures or markings; specifically, denoting an ancient Greek ceramic ware in which a black glaze was painted over the surface so as to leave the design in the red of the body: a style developed early in the fifth century B.C.

red·fin (red′fin′) *n. pl.* **·fins** or **·fin** One of various cyprinoid fishes, especially the common shiner or red dace *(Notropis cornutus)* of eastern North America.

red fir 1 Any of several varieties of fir, as the **California red fir** *(Abies magnifica),* the largest of the genus. **2** The wood of any of these trees. **3** Douglas fir.

red fire A mixture of easily combustible ingredients, especially strontium salts, that burns with a red light.

red fox The common American fox. See under FOX.

red grouper A grouper *(Epinephelus morio)* of the southern Atlantic and Gulf coasts.

red gum Strophulus.

red–hand·ed (red′han′did) *adj.* **1** Having hands red with blood, as a murderer caught in the act; hence, having just committed any crime. **2** Caught in the act of doing some particular thing: not always in a bad sense. —**red′–hand′ed·ly** *adv.* —**red′–hand′ed·ness** *n.*

red·head (red′hed′) *n.* **1** A person with red hair. **2** An American duck *(Aythya americana)*; the pochard. **3** The red–headed woodpecker.

red–head·ed woodpecker (red′hed′id) See under WOODPECKER.

red heat 1 The state of being red–hot. **2** The temperature at which a metal is red–hot.

red herring 1 Herring dried and smoked to a reddish brown color. **2** An irrelevant topic introduced in order to divert attention from the main point under discussion: from the use of a red herring to distract a hunting dog from the scent being followed (used to train hounds to ignore such distractions).

red hind A serranoid fish *(Epinephelus maculosus)* of the West Indies and southward: one of the groupers. See CABRILLA.

red–hot (red′hot′) *adj.* **1** Heated to redness. **2** New, as if just from the fire. **3** Heated; excited: *red–hot* argument. **4** Extreme.

red Indian 1 A North American Indian: also **Red Indian. 2** The painted cup.

red·in·gote (red′ing·gōt) *n.* An outer coat with long full skirts. [<F *rédingote,* alter. of E *riding coat*]

red·in·te·grate (ri·din′tə·grāt) *v.t.* **·grat·ed, ·grat·ing** To restore to a perfect state; make complete; renew. —*adj.* Restored to a whole or perfect state; renewed. [<L *redintegratus,* pp. of *redintegrare* <*red-,* var. of *re-* again + *integrare.* See INTEGRATE.]

re·din·te·gra·tion (ri·din′tə·grā′shən) *n.* **1** The act or process of restoration to a whole or sound state. **2** *Psychol.* The act or tendency of the mind to complete again a complex mental state previously experienced, upon the renewal of any part of it.

re·di·rect[1] (rē′di·rekt′) *v.t.* To direct again or anew: to *redirect* a letter. —**re′di·rec′tion** *n.*

re·di·rect[2] (rē·di·rekt′) *adj. Law* Designating the examination of a witness, after cross–examination, by the party who first examined him.

re·dis·count (rē·dis′kount) *n.* **1** A second (or any subsequent) discount on a sum. **2** *Usually pl.* Commercial paper which has been rediscounted. —*v.t.* To discount again.

re·dis·trict (rē·dis′trikt) *v.t.* To district again; especially, to redraw the boundaries of the election districts of.

red·i·vi·vus (red′ə·vī′vəs) *adj.* Come or brought into existence again; revived; restored. [<LL <*redivivus* renewed]

Red Jacket, 1751–1830, a chief of the Senecas, ally of the United States in the War of 1812: real name *Sagoyewatha.*

red lead (led) A lead preparation having a fine red color, used chiefly as a pigment; minium.

red–lead ore (red′led′) Crocoite.

red–let·ter (red′let′ər) *adj.* Happy, fortunate, or memorable: from the use on calendars of red letters to indicate holidays.

red light 1 A traffic signal light meaning stop: opposed to *green light.* **2** Any similar light used to warn of danger or an emergency.

red–light district (red′līt′) That part of a city or town in which brothels, sometimes marked by a red light, are numerous.

red·line (red′līn′) *v.t.* **·lined, ·lin·ing.** *U.S.* **1** To cross out with, or as with, a red line; cancel. **2** To discriminate against economically, esp. by refusing to grant mortgages or by charging unreasonably high mortgage.

red lobelia The cardinal flower.

red man An American Indian.

red maple The swamp maple.

Red·mond (red′mənd), **John Edward,** 1851–1918, Irish statesman.

red·neck (red′nek′) *n. U.S.* In the rural South, a poor, uneducated, white person, especially one having violently anti–Negro sentiments: a disparaging term. Also **red′–neck′.**

red oak 1 One of several oaks having a dense, cross–grained wood, as the northern red oak *(Quercus borealis).* **2** The wood of these oaks.

red ocher Ocher.

red·o·lent (red′ə·lənt) *adj.* Full of or diffusing a pleasant fragrance; odorous: often figuratively: *redolent* of the past. [<OF <L *redolens, -entis,* ppr. of *redolere* emit a smell <*red-* thoroughly + *olere* smell] —**red′o·lence, red′o·len·cy** *n.* —**red′o·lent·ly** *adv.*

Re·don (rə·dôn′), **Odilon,** 1840–1916, French painter.

Re·don·da (rə·don′də) See ANTIGUA.

red osier 1 A willow *(Salix purpurea)* whose red–tinted twigs are used in making baskets: also called *purple osier.* **2** The red–osier dogwood *(Cornus stolonifera),* with dark–reddish branches and bluish or white fruit.

re·doub·le (rē·dub′əl) *v.t.* & *v.i.* **·led, ·ling 1** To make or become double. **2** To increase greatly. **3** To echo or re–echo. **4** To fold or turn back. **5** In bridge, to double (an opponent's double).

re·doubt (ri·dout′) *n.* **1** An enclosed fortification, especially a temporary one of any form, employed to defend a pass, a hilltop, etc. **2** An earthwork or simple fortification placed within the main rampart line of a permanent fortification. [<F *redoute* <Ital. *ridotto* < Med. L *reductus,* lit., a refuge, orig. pp. of *reducere* lead back]

re·doubt·a·ble (ri·dou′tə·bəl) *adj.* **1** Inspiring fear; formidable. **2** Deserving respect or deference. Also **re·doubt′ed.** See synonyms under FORMIDABLE. [<F *redoubtable* <*redouter* fear, dread <L *re-* thoroughly + *dubitare* doubt] —**re·doubt′a·ble·ness** *n.* —**re·doubt′a·bly** *adv.*

re·dound (ri·dound′) *v.i.* **1** To have an effect, as by reaction, to the credit, discredit, advantage, etc., of the original agent; return; react; accrue. **2** *Obs.* To surge or flow back. **3** *Obs.* To overflow. —*n.* A return by way of consequence; result; requital. [<F *redonder* < L *redundare* overflow <*red-* back + *undare* surge <*unda* wave]

red·o·wa (red′ə·wə, -və) *n.* Either of two Bohemian dances, one in 3/4 time, resembling a mazurka, the other in 2/4 time. [<F <Czech *rejdovák* <*rejdovati* steer, whirl, carouse]

red pepper See PEPPER (def. 3).

red·poll (red′pōl′) *n.* A small finch (genus *Acanthis*) of northern regions, having a reddish crown.

Red Poll One of an English breed of hornless, reddish dairy cattle.

re·draft (rē′draft′, -dräft′) *n.* **1** A second draft or copy. **2** A bill of exchange drawn by the holder of a protested bill on the drawer or endorsers for the reimbursement of the amount of the original bill with costs and charges.

re·dress (ri·dres′) *v.t.* **1** To set right, as a wrong, by compensation or by punishment of the wrongdoer; make reparation for. **2** To make reparation to; compensate: to *redress* the victims of injustice. **3** To remedy; correct. **4** To adjust, as balances. —*n.* (rē′dres, ri·dres′) **1** Satisfaction for wrong done; reparation; amends. **2** A restoration; reformation; correction. [<F *redresser* straighten <*re-* again (<L) +*dresser.* See DRESS.] —**re·dress′·er** or **re·dres′sor** *n.*

re–dress (rē·dres′) *v.t.* & *v.i.* To dress again.

Red River 1 A river in Texas, Arkansas, and Louisiana, flowing 1,018 miles east to the Mississippi. **2** A river in the United States and Canada, flowing 545 miles north from NW Minnesota through Manitoba to Lake Winnipeg: also **Red River of the North. 3** The longest river of Northern Vietnam, flowing 730 miles SE from Yünnan province, China, to the Gulf of Tonkin: Annamese *Song Coi. Chinese* **Yü·an Chiang** (yü·än′ jyäng′) or **Hung Ho** (hōōng′ hu′).

red·root (red′rōōt′, -root′) *n.* **1** An herb *(Lachnanthes tinctoria)* with sword–shaped, fleshy leaves and fibrous red root, found in swamps along the Atlantic coast of the United States. **2** Any of certain other American plants, as bloodroot, alkanet, bittersweet, etc.

Red Sea An elongated sea between Egypt and Arabia; 1,450 miles long; 170,000 square miles; joined to the Mediterranean by the Suez Canal and connected with the Indian Ocean by the Gulf of Aden.

red·sear (red′sir′) *v.i. Metall.* To break or crack when red–hot, as iron when hammered.

red·shank (red′shangk′) *n.* **1** A Scottish Highlander: so called in allusion to the national costume of Scotland, which leaves the legs bare. **2** A common Old World shore bird *(Totanus totanus)*; a tattler.

red shift *Physics* Displacement toward the red end of the spectrum of light from a nebula, star, or other luminous celestial body: caused by an apparent increase in the wavelength of the emitted light. See DOPPLER EFFECT.

red·shirt (red′shûrt′) *n.* A member of Garibaldi's brigade in the struggle for Italian independence.

red–short (red′shôrt′) *adj. Metall.* Weak or brittle while red–hot, as iron or steel. [<Sw. *rödskört* <*röd* red + *skör* brittle] —**red′–short′ness** *n.*

red·skin (red′skin′) *n.* A North American Indian. —*adj.* Pertaining to or characteristic of the North American Indians.

red squirrel The chickaree.

red·start (red′stärt′) *n.* **1** A small singing bird (genus *Phoenicura*) allied to the warblers; especially, the common **Old World redstart** *(P. phoenicura),* dark–gray, with a black throat, white forehead, and rust–red breast, sides, and tail: also called *brantail.* **2** A small fly–catching warbler (genus *Setophaga*), especially *S. ruticilla,* with bright orange–red patches, common in eastern North America. [<RED[1] + START[2]]

red–tailed buzzard (red′tāld′) See under BUZZARD.

red tape Rigid official procedure involving delay or inaction: from the tying of public

remodify	**renerve**	**reobtain**	**reordain**	**repack**	**reperuse**	**replume**
remold	**renominate**	**reobtainable**	**reorder**	**repaint**	**rephrase**	**replunge**
remolten	**renomination**	**reoccupation**	**reordination**	**repass**	**replant**	**repolarization**
rename	**renumber**	**reoccupy**	**reossify**	**repassage**	**replantation**	**repolish**
renavigate	**renumerate**	**reoppose**	**repacify**	**reperusal**	**repledge**	**repopulate**

documents with red tape. —**red-tape** (red′·tāp′) *adj.* —**red′-tap′ism** *n.*

red·top (red′top′) *n.* Any of certain grasses valuable for hay and pasturage; specifically, herd's-grass *(Agrostis alba)*. [From the reddish panicle of some varieties]

re·duce (ri·do͞os′, -dyo͞os′) *v.* **·duced, ·duc·ing** *v.t.* **1** To make less in size, amount, number, intensity, etc.; diminish. **2** To bring from a higher to a lower condition; lower; degrade. **3** To bring to submission; subdue; conquer. **4** To bring to a specified condition or state: with *to*: to *reduce* rock to powder; to *reduce* a person to desperation. **5** To thin (paint, etc.) with oil or turpentine. **6** *Math.* To change (an expression) to a more elementary form. **7** *Surg.* To restore (displaced parts) to normal position. **8** *Chem.* **a** To decrease the positive valence of (an element) by the addition of electrons. **b** To deprive wholly or partially of oxygen; deoxidize. **9** *Phot.* To diminish the density of (a photographic negative). —*v.i.* **10** To become less in any way. **11** To decrease one's weight, as by dieting. [<L *reducere* <*re-* back + *ducere* lead] —**re·duc′i·bil′i·ty** *n.* —**re·duc′i·ble** *adj.* —**re·duc′i·bly** *adv.*

Synonyms: compress, concentrate, condense, consolidate, contract, diminish, solidify, thicken. See ABASE, ABATE, ABBREVIATE, ALLAY, ALLEVIATE, CONQUER, IMPAIR, RELAX, RETRENCH, SCRIMP, SUBDUE, WEAKEN.

re·duc·er (ri·do͞o′sər, -dyo͞o′-) *n.* **1** One who or that which reduces. **2** *Phot.* A chemical solution for reducing the density of negatives.

reducing agent *Chem.* A substance used to effect a chemical reduction; more specifically, any element which gives up a valence electron to another.

reducing glass A concave lens of considerable diameter used to produce a minified view of drawings, to see how they will appear when they are reduced in size.

reducing valve A valve for maintaining uniform reduced pressure of a fluid, as steam or gas, above or below the valve.

re·duc·tase (ri·duk′tās) *n. Biochem.* Any of a class of enzymes which promote the reduction of compounds to simpler forms. [<REDUCT(ION) + -ASE]

re·duc·ti·o ad ab·sur·dum (ri·duk′shē·ō ad ab·sûr′dəm) *Latin* Literally, reduction to an absurdity; disposal of a proposition by showing that its logical conclusion is absurd; also, proof of a proposition by showing its contradictory to be absurd.

re·duc·tion (ri·duk′shən) *n.* **1** The act or process of reducing, or its results. **2** *Biol.* The halving of the total number of chromosomes during meiotic cell division. **3** *Chem.* **a** The process of depriving a compound of oxygen. **b** The process of decreasing the positive valence of an element by the addition of electrons: distinguished from *oxidation.* **4** *Math.* **a** One of those formulas by means of which trigonometric functions of angles greater than 90° can be reduced to functions of angles less than 90°. **b** The process of expressing a fraction in decimal terms. See synonyms under ABBREVIATION. [<F *réduction* <L *reductio, -onis* <*reductus,* pp. of *reducere.* See REDUCE.] —**re·duc′tion·al** *adj.* —**re·duc′tive** *adj.*

re·dun·dance (ri·dun′dəns) *n.* **1** The condition or quality of being redundant. **2** That which is redundant. **3** Excess; surplus. See synonyms under CIRCUMLOCUTION, EXCESS.

re·dun·dan·cy (ri·dun′dən·sē) *n. pl.* **·cies** **1** Redundance. **2** In information theory, deliberate repetition in a message, in whatever medium expressed, in order to lessen the possibility of error.

re·dun·dant (ri·dun′dənt) *adj.* **1** Being more than is required; constituting an excess. **2** Unnecessarily verbose; tautological. [<L *redundans, -antis,* ppr. of *redundare.* See REDOUND.] —**re·dun′dant·ly** *adv.*

Synonyms: excessive, exuberant, overflowing, superabundant, superfluous. *Antonyms*: insufficient, limited, little, scant, scanty, scarce, short, wanting.

re·du·pli·cate (ri·do͞o′plə·kāt, -dyo͞o′-) *v.* **·cat·ed, ·cat·ing** *v.t.* **1** To repeat again and again; redouble; iterate. **2** *Ling.* To affix a reduplication to. —*v.i.* **3** To undergo reduplication. —*adj.* (-kit) **1** Repeated again and again; duplicated; doubled. **2** *Bot.* Valvate with the margins reflexed. [<L *reduplicatus,* pp. of *reduplicare* <*re-* again + *duplicare.* See DUPLICATE.]

re·du·pli·ca·tion (ri·do͞o′plə·kā′shən, -dyo͞o′-) *n.* **1** The act of reduplicating, or the state of being reduplicated; a redoubling. **2** A rhetorical figure in which the ending of a sentence, line, or clause is repeated and emphasized at the beginning of the next. **3** *Ling.* **a** The repetition of an initial element or elements in a word; especially, in the verbs of some Indo-European languages, repetition of some part of the root, usually with vowel modification, serving as a mark of the perfect, as in Greek *bebeka* I have walked, Latin *dedidi* I have given. **b** The doubling of all or part of a word, often with vowel or consonant change, as in *fiddle-faddle, razzle-dazzle.* **c** The sound or syllable thus repeated.

re·du·pli·ca·tive (ri·do͞o′plə·kā′tiv, -dyo͞o′-) *adj.* **1** Tending to reduplicate. **2** Of or formed by reduplication. **3** *Bot.* Reduplicate.

red·vein maple (red′vān′) The flowering maple.

red·ware (red′wâr′) *n.* A large brown seaweed *(Laminaria digitata)* of the New England coast, sometimes used for food.

red-wat (red′wot′) *adj. Scot.* Made wet by something red, as blood.

red·wing (red′wing′) *n.* **1** An American blackbird *(Agelaius phoeniceus)* with bright scarlet patches on the wings of the male: commonly **red-winged blackbird. 2** An Old World red-winged thrush *(Turdus musicus)*, bright reddish-orange on the sides of the body and the under-wing coverts.

red·wood (red′wo͝od′) *n.* **1** An immense California tree *(Sequoia sempervirens,* family *Taxodiaceae).* See SEQUOIA. **2** Its durable reddish wood. **3** Any one of various other trees yielding a reddish wood, or the wood itself, which yields a red dye.

REDWOOD (From 200 to 240 feet high)

red-wud (red′wud′) *adj. Scot.* Raging mad; furious; insane.

red-yel·low (red′yel′ō) *n.* One of the range of colors situated between the red and yellow portions of the visible spectrum, sharing the hue of each but identical with neither.

ree¹ (rē) *adj. Scot.* Wild; tipsy; delirious.

ree² (rē) See REEVE³.

reed (rēd) *n.* **1** The slender, frequently jointed stem of certain tall grasses growing in wet places, or the grasses themselves. **2** A thin, elastic plate of reed, wood, or metal nearly closing an opening, as in a pipe: used in reed organs, the reed pipes of pipe organs, and instruments of the bassoon and clarinet order, to produce a musical tone either by itself or when reinforced by the vibration of air in a pipe. **3** A musical pipe made of the hollow stem of a plant; a shepherd's pipe. **4** *Archit.* A semicylindrical ornamental molding or bead. **5** That part of a loom that drives the filling against the woven fabric, consisting of two horizontal parallel bars near together and connected by numerous thin parallel slips. See illustration under LOOM. **6** An arrow. **7** An ancient Hebrew measure of length; six cubits. **8** The abomasum. —*v.t.* **1** To fashion into or decorate with reeds. **2** To thatch with reeds. [OE *hrēod*]

Reed (rēd), **John,** 1887–1920, U. S. journalist and poet. —**Walter,** 1851–1902, U. S. army surgeon; demonstrated the transmission of yellow fever by mosquitos.

reed·bird (rēd′bûrd′) *n.* The bobolink: so called chiefly in the southern United States.

reed·buck (rēd′buk′) *n.* An antelope *(Redunca arundineum)* of southern Africa that frequents reedy places; the reitbok.

reed bunting The European black-headed bunting (genus *Emberiza*), with a white collar, common in marshy places.

reed·ing (rē′ding) *n.* **1** Beading or semicylindrical moldings collectively. **2** Ornamentation by such moldings. **3** A molding of this kind: the reverse of *fluting.* **4** The knurling on the edge of a coin, as distinguished from *milling.*

reed·ling (rēd′ling) *n.* The European bearded titmouse *(Panurus biarmicus),* common in reedy places. The male has a black tuft of feathers on each side of the chin.

reed·mace (rēd′mās′) *n.* A cat-tail; any plant of the genus *Typha,* especially *T. latifolia* and *T. angustifolia.*

reed organ A keyboard musical instrument sounding by means of free reeds.

reed pipe An organ pipe having a reed whose vibrations set in motion the air column: distinguished from *flue pipe.*

reed-stop (rēd′stop′) *n.* An organ stop controlling a set of reed pipes.

re-ed·u·cate (rē·ej′o͞o·kāt) *v.t.* **·cat·ed, ·cat·ing** **1** To educate again. **2** To rehabilitate, as a criminal, by education. —**re′-ed·u·ca′·tion** *n.*

reed warbler A bird (genus *Acrocephalus*) with moderately rounded tail, found in most parts of the Old World.

reed·y (rē′dē) *adj.* **reed·i·er, reed·i·est** **1** Full of reeds. **2** Like a reed. **3** Having a thin, sharp tone, like a reed instrument. —**reed′i·ness** *n.*

reef¹ (rēf) *n.* **1** A ridge of sand or rocks, or especially of coral, at or near the surface of the water. **2** A lode, vein, or ledge. **3** A shoal. [<ON *rif* rib, reef] —**reef′y** *adj.*

reef² (rēf) *Naut. n.* **1** The part of a sail that is folded and secured or untied and let out in regulating its size on the mast. **2** The tuck taken in a sail when reefed. —*v.t.* **1** To reduce (a sail) by folding a part and tying it round, and usually fastening it to, a yard or boom. **2** To shorten or lower, as a topmast by taking part of it in. [ME *riff,* prob. <ON *rif* rib]

reef-band (rēf′band′) *n. Naut.* A strip of canvas used to give additional strength to sails along the lines where the reef-points are attached.

reef·er¹ (rē′fər) *n.* **1** One who reefs. **2** A short double-breasted coat or jacket of heavy material.

reef·er² (rē′fər) *n. U.S. Slang* A marihuana cigarette. [? from its resemblance to the reef of a sail]

reef knot A square knot. See illustration under KNOT.

reef-point (rēf′point′) *n. Naut.* One of a series of short lines attached by their centers to the eyelets of a reef-band, and used to fasten the sail in reefing.

reek (rēk) *v.i.* **1** To give off smoke, vapor, etc. **2** To give off a strong, offensive smell. **3** To be pervaded with anything offensive. —*v.t.* **4** To expose to smoke or its action. **5** To give off; emit. —*n. Scot.* Smoke; vapor; steam. ◆ Homophone: *wreak.* [OE *rēc*] —**reek′er** *n.*

reek·y (rē′kē) *adj.* **reek·i·er, reek·i·est** Having been smoked; smoky; soiled by or emitting smoke. Also **reek′ie.**

reel¹ (rēl) *n.* **1** A rotatory device or frame for winding rope, cord, photographic film, or other flexible substance. **2** In cinematography, the film wound on one reel: used as a unit of length, usually from 1,000 to 2,000 feet. **3** A wooden spool for wire, thread, etc. **4** Material, such as thread, paper, and the like, when wound on a reel. —*v.t.* **1** To wind on a reel or bobbin, as a line. **2** To draw in by reeling a line: with *in*: to *reel* a fish in. **3** To say, do, etc., easily and fluently: with *off.* [OE *hrēol*] —**reel′a·ble** *adj.* —**reel′er** *n.*

reel² (rēl) *v.i.* **1** To stagger, sway, or lurch, as when giddy or drunk. **2** To whirl round and round. **3** To have a sensation of giddiness or whirling: My head *reels.* **4** To waver or fall back, as attacking troops. —*v.t.* **5** To cause to reel. See synonyms under SHAKE. —*n.* **1** A

repopulation	**re-prove**	**requicken**	**rerestitution**	**reseek**	**resettle**	**resolder**
repour	**reprune**	**reread**	**rerise**	**reseize**	**resettlement**	**re-solve**
re-press	**repurchase**	**re-record**	**resail**	**reseizure**	**reshape**	**resow**
repromulgate	**repurge**	**re-refer**	**resale**	**resend**	**resharpen**	**restipulate**
repromulgation	**repurify**	**rereign**	**resalute**	**re-serve**	**resmooth**	**restipulation**

staggering motion; giddiness. 2 A lively Scottish dance, or its music; also, the Virginia reel. [<REEL[1]] — **reel′er** *n.*

re·em·pha·size (rē·em′fə·sīz) *v.t.* **·sized, ·siz·ing** To stress or emphasize again.

re·en·force (rē′en·fôrs′, -fōrs′), **re·en·force·ment** (rē′en·fôrs′mənt, -fōrs′-), etc. See REINFORCE, etc.

re·en·ter (rē·en′tər) *v.t.* & *v.i.* To enter again. — **re·en′trance** *n.*

re·en·ter·ing (rē·en′tər·ing) *adj.* 1 Entering again. 2 Extending inward, as an angle.

reentering angle An angle which is turned inward, as in a figure or structure.

re·en·trant (rē·en′trənt) *adj.* Reentering; extending inward. — *n.* 1 One who or that which reenters. 2 A reentering angle, as in a fortification wall.

re·en·try (rē·en′trē) *n.* 1 The act of entering again. 2 *Law* The act of resuming possession of lands or tenements. 3 In whist and bridge, a card by which a player gains or can gain the lead. 4 *Aerospace* The return into the atmosphere of an object launched into space from the earth.

reest[1] (rēst) *v.t.* & *v.i. Scot.* & *Brit. Dial.* To check; balk. — **reest′y** *adj.*

reest[2] (rēst) *v.t.* & *v.i. Scot.* To dry or cure, as by smoking.

reeve[1] (rēv) *v.t.* **reeved** or **rove** (*for pp. also* **rov·en**), **reev·ing** *Naut.* 1 To pass, as a rope or rod, through a hole, block, or aperture. 2 To fasten in such manner. 3 To pass a rope, etc., through (a block or pulley). [<Du. *reven* reef a sail]

reeve[2] (rēv) *n.* In medieval England, a high administrative officer formerly holding authority over landed areas; bailiff; overseer; steward. [OE *gerēfa* steward]

reeve[3] (rēv) *n.* The female of the ruff: also called *ree.* [Origin unknown]

re·ex·change (rē′iks·chānj′) *v.t.* **·changed, ·chang·ing** To exchange again. — *n.* 1 A second or renewed exchange. 2 The sum that the holder of a bill of exchange may demand of the drawer or indorser as indemnity for the loss incurred by its dishonor in a foreign country, where it was payable.

re·fect (ri·fekt′) *v.t. Obs.* To refresh after weariness or hunger; restore; repair. [<L *refectus* refreshed. See REFECTION.]

re·fec·tion (ri·fek′shən) *n.* 1 Refreshment by food; a light meal. 2 In civil law, repair of property. 3 *Med.* Spontaneous recovery, as from an ailment or the effects of a vitamin deficiency. [<OF <L *refectio, -onis* < *refectus,* pp. of *reficere* remake, refresh < *re-* again + *facere* make] — **re·fec′tion·er** *n.* — **re·fec′tive** *adj.*

re·fec·to·ry (ri·fek′tər·ē) *n. pl.* **·ries** A room for eating; usually, in a religious house or college, a hall set apart for meals. [<Med. L *refectorium* <L *refectus.* See REFECTION.]

re·fer (ri·fûr′) *v.* **·ferred, ·fer·ring** *v.t.* 1 To direct or send for information or other purpose: I *refer* you to another department. 2 To hand over or submit for consideration, settlement, etc.: They *referred* the bill to a special committee. 3 To attribute the cause or source of; assign; relate: He *refers* his success to unceasing application. 4 To assign or attribute to a group, class, period, etc. — *v.i.* 5 To make reference; allude. 6 To turn, as for information, help, or authority; have recourse: to *refer* to the dictionary. See synonyms under ALLUDE, ATTRIBUTE. [<OF *referer* <L *referre* < *re-* back + *ferre* bear, carry] — **ref·er·a·ble** (ref′ər·ə·bəl), **re·fer′ra·ble** or **re·fer′ri·ble** *adj.* — **re·fer′rer** *n.*

ref·e·ree (ref′ə·rē′) *n.* 1 A person to whom a thing is referred. 2 In certain games, as football, an official who has general control of the game. 3 *Law* A person to whom a case is sent by order of court for investigation and report; an arbitrator. See synonyms under JUDGE. — *v.t.* & *v.i.* To judge as a referee.

ref·er·ence (ref′ər·əns, ref′rəns) *n.* 1 The act of referring. 2 An incidental allusion or direction of the attention: *reference* to a recent event. 3 A note or other indication in a book, referring to some other book or passage: compare CROSS-REFERENCE. 4 One who or that which is or may be referred to. 5 The state of being referred or related: used in the phrases *with* or *in reference to.* 6 *Law* The act or process of submitting a matter to a referee; also, the proceedings of and before a referee. 7 The person or persons to whom one seeking employment may refer for recommendation; also, a written statement or testimonial, as of character or dependability. — **ref′er·enc·er** *n.*

ref·er·end (ref′ə·rend) *n.* The instrument, vehicle, or means by which an act of reference is made. [<REFERENDUM]

ref·er·en·dum (ref′ə·ren′dəm) *n. pl.* **·dums** or **·da** (-də) 1 The submission, by a diplomatic representative to his government, of a proposition not covered by his original instructions. 2 The submission of a proposed public measure or law, which has been passed upon by a legislature or convention, to a vote of the people for ratification or rejection. [<L, gerund of *referre.* See REFER.]

ref·er·ent (ref′ər·ənt) *n.* The particular object, concept, class, event, or the like to which reference is made in any verbal statement or its symbolic equivalent. [<L *referens, -entis,* ppr. of *referre.* See REFER.]

re·fer·ral (ri·fûr′əl) *n.* 1 The act of referring, or the condition of being referred. 2 One who has been referred.

re·fill (rē·fil′) *v.t.* To fill again. — *n.* (rē′fil′) Any commodity packaged to fit and fill a container originally containing that commodity: a *refill* for a lipstick case.

re·fine (ri·fīn′) *v.* **·fined, ·fin·ing** *v.t.* 1 To make fine or pure; free from impurities or extraneous matter. 2 To make polished or cultured; free from coarseness or vulgarity. — *v.i.* 3 To become fine or pure. 4 To become more polished or cultured. 5 To make fine distinctions; use subtlety. See synonyms under CHASTEN, PURIFY. — **re·fin′er** *n.*

re·fined (ri·fīnd′) *adj.* 1 Characterized by refinement or polish. 2 Free from impurity; purified; clarified. 3 Exceedingly precise or exact; subtle: *refined* tortures. See synonyms under FINE.

re·fine·ment (ri·fīn′mənt) *n.* 1 Fineness of thought, taste, language, etc.; freedom from coarseness or vulgarity; delicacy; culture. 2 The act, effect, or process of refining; purification. 3 A nice distinction; subtlety; also, fastidiousness. [<REFINE]

Synonyms: civilization, cultivation, culture. *Civilization* applies to nations, denoting the sum of those civil, social, economic, and political attainments by which a community is removed from barbarism; a people may be civilized while still far from *refinement* or *culture,* but *civilization* is susceptible of various degrees and of continued progress. *Refinement* applies either to nations or individuals, denoting the removal of what is coarse and rude, and a corresponding attainment of what is delicate, elegant, and beautiful. *Culture* in the fullest sense, as distinct from *cultivation,* denotes that degree of *refinement* and development which results from continued *cultivation* through successive generations; a man's faculties may be brought to a high degree of *cultivation* in some specialty, while he himself remains uncultured even to the extent of coarseness and rudeness. See HUMANITY. *Antonyms*: barbarism, boorishness, brutality, clownishness, coarseness, grossness, rudeness, rusticity, vulgarity.

re·fin·er·y (ri·fī′nər·ē) *n. pl.* **·er·ies** A place where some crude material, as sugar or petroleum, is purified.

re·fit (rē·fit′) *v.t.* & *v.i.* **·fit·ted, ·fit·ting** To make or be made fit or ready again; return to serviceable condition, as by making repairs, replacing equipment, etc. — *n.* The repair of damages or wear, as of a ship.

re·flate (rē·flāt′) *v.t.* **·flat·ed, ·flat·ing** To inflate again. [<RE- + (IN)FLATE]

re·flect (ri·flekt′) *v.t.* 1 To turn or throw back, as rays of light, heat, or sound. 2 To give back an image of; mirror. 3 To cause to rebound or return; cast: He *reflects* credit on his teacher. 4 *Obs.* To bend or fold back. — *v.i.* 5 To send back rays, as of light or heat. 6 To return in rays: The light *reflects* into my eyes. 7 To give back an image; also, to be mirrored. 8 To think carefully; ponder. 9 To bring blame, discredit, etc.: with *on* or *upon.* See synonyms under CONSIDER, DELIBERATE, MUSE. [<OF *reflecter* <L *reflectere* < *re-* back + *flectere* bend]

re·flec·tance (ri·flek′təns) *n. Physics* The ratio of the radiant or luminous flux reflected from a given surface to the total light falling upon it.

reflecting telescope See under TELESCOPE.

re·flec·tion (ri·flek′shən) *n.* 1 The act of reflecting, or the state of being reflected. 2 *Physics* The throwing off or back (from a surface) of impinging light, heat, sound, or any form of radiant energy. 3 The result of reflecting; reflected rays or an image thrown by reflection. 4 Consideration of or meditation upon past knowledge or experience; thought: *Reflection* increases wisdom; also, its result: a wise *reflection.* 5 The casting of blame; censure. 6 *Anat.* The folding of a part upon itself; a fold, as in a membrane. 7 Reflex action, as of the nerves. Also spelled *reflexion.* [<OF *reflexion* <L *reflexio, -onis*] — **re·flec′tion·al** or **re·flex′ion·al** *adj.*

Synonyms: cogitation, consideration, contemplation, deliberation, meditation, musing, rumination, study, thinking, thought. See ANIMADVERSION, THOUGHT[1]. *Antonyms*: carelessness, heedlessness, imprudence, inconsiderateness, negligence, thoughtlessness.

re·flec·tive (ri·flek′tiv) *adj.* 1 Given to reflection or thought; meditative: a *reflective* person. 2 Used in or capable of consideration or reflection. 3 Having the quality of throwing back light, heat, sound, etc. — **re·flec′tive·ly** *adv.* — **re·flec′tive·ness** *n.*

re·flec·tiv·i·ty (rē′flek·tiv′ə·tē) *n.* 1 The state or quality of being reflective. 2 *Physics* That portion of light or other forms of radiant energy which is reflected by a surface exposed to uniform radiation.

re·flec·tor (ri·flek′tər) *n.* 1 That which reflects. 2 A polished surface, of glass or metal (usually concave), for reflecting light, heat, or sound, and also pictures or slides in a particular direction. 3 A telescope which transmits an image from a reflecting surface to the eyepiece. 4 *Physics* A substance placed around the core of a nuclear reactor for the purpose of reducing neutron leakage and maintaining the level of the chain reaction: sometimes called a *tamper.* 5 *Telecom.* The rear portion of an antenna, serving to increase its directional characteristics.

re·flet (rə·fle′) *n.* 1 Iridescence of surface; especially, the metallic glaze on pottery. 2 Pottery having metallic or iridescent luster. [<F, reflection]

re·flex (rē′fleks) *adj.* 1 Turned or thrown backward; reflected, as light. 2 *Physiol.* Of, pertaining to, or produced by a reflex. 3 Turned back upon itself or in the direction whence it came: *reflex* motion. 4 Bent back; reflexed. 5 *Telecom.* Designating a radio receiving circuit in which a single vacuum tube serves for the simultaneous amplification of two different frequencies. — *n.* 1 Reflection, or an image produced by reflection, as from a mirror or like surface. 2 An image or copy; also, an adaptation from another language or dialect, as of a word. 3 Light reflected from an illuminated surface to a shady one. 4 *Physiol.* An involuntary movement or action produced by the transmission of an afferent impulse to a nerve center and its reflection thence as an efferent impulse, as in winking when the eye is threatened: also **reflex action.** — *v.t.* (ri·fleks′) To bend back; turn back or reflect. [<L *reflexus* reflected, pp. of *reflectere.* See REFLECT.]

restrengthen
restrike
restrive
resubject
resubjection
resummon
resummons
resupply
resurprise
resurvey
retraverse
retrial
retrim
re-urge
re-use
re-utilize
re-utter
revaluation
revalue
revarnish
revegetate
revictual
revictualment
revindicate
revindication
reweigh
rewin
rework

reflex angle See under ANGLE.
reflex arc *Physiol.* The entire path covered by a nerve impulse from the point of origin in the receptors to the nerve center, and thence outwards to the effectors.
re·flex·ive (ri·flek′siv) *adj.* **1** Reflex. **2** *Gram.* Reflected upon or referring to itself or its subject: in the sentence "He dresses himself," "dresses" is a *reflexive* verb, "himself" is a *reflexive* pronoun. —*n.* A reflexive verb or pronoun. —**re·flex′ive·ly** *adv.* —**re·flex′ive·ness, re·flex·iv·i·ty** (rē′flek·siv′ə·tē) *n.*
re·flight (rē′flīt′) *n. Aeron.* A subsequent flight made over a given area to obtain supplementary photographs or to obtain other necessary details of information.
ref·lu·ent (ref′lōō·ənt) *adj.* Flowing back; ebbing, as the tide. [<L *refluens, -entis,* ppr. of *refluere* flow back < *re-* back + *fluere* flow] —**ref′lu·ence, ref′lu·en·cy** *n.*
re·flux (rē′fluks′) *n.* A flowing back; ebb; return: the flux and *reflux* of fortune. [<L *refluxus,* pp. of *refluere.* See REFLUENT.]
re·for·est (rē·fôr′ist, -for′-) *v.t.* & *v.i.* To replant (an area) with trees. —**re′for·es·ta′tion** *n.*
re·form (ri·fôrm′) *v.t.* **1** To make better by removing abuses, altering, etc.; restore to a better condition: to *reform* a corrupt city government; to *reform* inefficient business procedures. **2** To make better morally; persuade or educate from a sinful to a moral life: to *reform* a prostitute. **3** To put an end to; stop (an abuse, malpractice, etc.). —*v.i.* **4** To give up sin or error; become better. See synonyms under AMEND, RECLAIM. —*n.* An act or result of reformation; change for the better, especially in administration; correction of evils or abuses; abandonment of vicious habits. [<OF *reformer* <L *reformare* < *re-* again + *formare* form] —**re·form′a·tive** *adj.* —**re·form′er, re·form′ist** *n.*
Reform Judaism Judaism as practiced by those who emphasize the historical continuity of the Jewish community and the ethical and prophetic content of the Scriptures and the oral laws, and reject or modify much of the traditional ritual. Compare CONSERVATIVE JUDAISM, ORTHODOX JUDAISM.
re-form (rē·fôrm′) *v.t.* & *v.i.* To form again. [<RE- + FORM] —**re′-for·ma′tion** *n.*
ref·or·ma·tion (ref′ər·mā′shən) *n.* **1** The act of reforming. **2** The state of being reformed. **3** Moral or religious restoration or revival.
Ref·or·ma·tion (ref′ər·mā′shən) *n.* The religious revolution of the 16th century in Europe which began as a movement to reform Catholicism and ended with the establishment of Protestantism in many parts of northern and western Europe.
re·form·a·to·ry (ri·fôr′mə·tôr′ē, -tō′rē) *adj.* Having a tendency or aiming to produce reformation. —*n. pl.* **·ries** An institution for the reformation and instruction of juvenile offenders.
Reform Bill The electoral reform bill passed by the British Parliament in 1832 for the correction and extension of the suffrage.
re·formed (ri·fôrmd′) *adj.* Restored to a better state; corrected or amended; delivered from vicious habits.
Re·formed (ri·fôrmd′) *adj.* Designating those Protestant churches which separated from the Lutherans in the 16th century on questions of doctrine; specifically, those churches which follow the teachings of Calvin and Zwingli. See CALVINISM, ZWINGLIAN.
reform school A reformatory.
re·fract (ri·frakt′) *v.t.* **1** To deflect (a ray) by refraction. **2** *Optics* To determine the degree of refraction of (an eye or lens). [<L *refractus,* pp. of *refringere* turn aside < *re-* back + *frangere* break]
refracting telescope See under TELESCOPE.
re·frac·tion (ri·frak′shən) *n. Physics* The change of direction of a ray, as of light or heat, in oblique passage from one medium to another of different density, or in traversing a medium whose density is not uniform. —**double refraction** The property possessed by certain types of crystals of breaking up a beam of light into two differently refracted and polarized rays. —**re·frac′tive** *adj.* —**re·frac′tive·ness, re·frac·tiv·i·ty** (rē′frak·tiv′ə·tē) *n.* —**re·frac′tor** *n.*

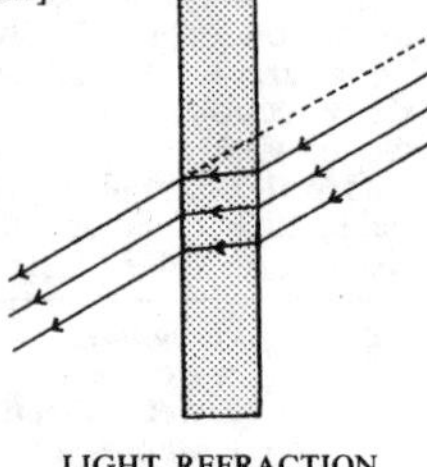
LIGHT REFRACTION

re·frac·tom·e·ter (rē′frak·tom′ə·tər) *n.* Any instrument for measuring indices of refraction. [<REFRACT + -(O)METER]
re·frac·to·ry (ri·frak′tər·ē) *adj.* **1** Not amenable to control; disobedient; unmanageable; obstinate. **2** Resisting ordinary methods of reduction: said of an ore. See synonyms under OBSTINATE, REBELLIOUS, RESTIVE, TURBULENT. —*n. pl.* **·ries** **1** A refractory or obstinate person or thing. **2** Any of various materials highly resistant to the action of great heat, as fireclay, graphite, magnesite, etc. [<L *refractarius*] —**re·frac′to·ri·ly** *adv.* —**re·frac′to·ri·ness** *n.*
ref·ra·ga·ble (ref′rə·gə·bəl) *adj.* Capable of being refuted. [<Med. L *refragabilis* <L *refragari* oppose]
re·frain[1] (ri·frān′) *v.i.* To keep oneself back; abstain from action; forbear. —*v.t.* To restrain; curb. [<OF *refrener* <L *refrenare* curb < *re-* back + *frenum* a bridle] —**re·frain′er** *n.*
Synonyms: abstain, forbear, restrain. See CEASE, KEEP. *Antonyms*: begin, continue, persevere, persist.
re·frain[2] (ri·frān′) *n.* **1** A phrase or strain repeated at intervals, generally regular, in a poem or a song; the burden. It generally recurs at the end of a stanza or strophe, and is common in old ballads and in Provençal poetry. **2** Any saying that is repeated over and over. [<OF < *refraindre* check, repeat <L *refringere* break off. See REFRACT.]
re·fran·gi·ble (ri·fran′jə·bəl) *adj.* Capable of being refracted, as light. [<RE- + L *frangere* break + -IBLE] —**re·fran′gi·bil′i·ty, re·fran′gi·ble·ness** *n.*
re·fresh (ri·fresh′) *v.t.* **1** To make (a person) fresh or vigorous again, as by food or rest; reinvigorate; revive. **2** To make fresh, clean, cool, etc. **3** To stimulate, as the memory. **4** To renew or replenish with or as with new supplies. —*v.i.* **5** To become fresh again; revive. **6** To take refreshment. **7** To lay in provisions. [<OF *refreschier* < *re-* again (<L) + *fres* fresh. See FRESH.]
re·fresh·er (ri·fresh′ər) *n.* **1** One who or that which refreshes. **2** A refresher course. —*adj.* Designating something that reacquaints one with the material of subjects previously studied and forgotten: a *refresher* course.
re·fresh·ing (ri·fresh′ing) *adj.* Serving to refresh: often used sarcastically: *refreshing* impudence. See synonyms under DELIGHTFUL. —**re·fresh′ing·ly** *adv.*
re·fresh·ment (ri·fresh′mənt) *n.* **1** The act of refreshing, or the state of being refreshed; restoration of vigor or liveliness. **2** That which refreshes, as food or drink. **3** *pl.* Food, or food and drink, served as a light meal.
re·frig·er·ant (ri·frij′ər·ənt) *adj.* Cooling or freezing; allaying heat or fever. —*n.* **1** Any medicine or material, as ice, which reduces abnormal heat of the body. **2** A substance used for obtaining and maintaining a low temperature, as carbon dioxide, ammonia, or methyl chloride; a freezing mixture; a freezing agent. [<L *refrigerans, -antis,* ppr. of *refrigerare.* See REFRIGERATE.]
re·frig·er·ate (ri·frij′ə·rāt) *v.t.* **·at·ed, ·at·ing** **1** To keep or cause to become cold; cool. **2** To freeze or chill (foodstuffs) for preservative purposes. [<L *refrigeratus,* pp. of *refrigerare* < *re-* thoroughly + *frigerare* cool < *frigus, frigoris* cold] —**re·frig′er·a′tion** *n.* —**re·frig′er·a′tive** *adj.* & *n.*
re·frig·er·a·tor (ri·frij′ə·rā′tər) *n.* **1** That which makes or keeps cold. **2** A box, cabinet, room, railroad car, etc., equipped with apparatus for preserving the freshness of perishable foods, etc., by means of ice or other refrigerant.
re·frig·er·a·to·ry (ri·frij′ər·ə·tôr′ē, -tō′rē) *adj.* Reducing heat. —*n. pl.* **·ries** That which cools or refrigerates. [<L *refrigeratorius*]
re·frin·gen·cy (ri·frin′jən·sē) *n.* Power to refract. Also **re·frin′gence.** [< obs. *refringe* <L *refringere.* See REFRACT.] —**re·frin′gent** *adj.*
reft (reft) Past tense and past participle of REAVE.
re·fu·el (rē·fyōō′əl, -fyōōl′) *v.* **·eled** or **·elled, ·el·ing** or **·el·ling** *v.t.* To replenish with fuel. —*v.i.* To take on a fresh supply of fuel.
ref·uge (ref′yōōj) *n.* **1** Shelter or protection, as from danger or distress. **2** One who or that which shelters or protects. **3** A safe place; asylum. **4** *Brit.* A raised or enclosed safety area for the use of pedestrians at busy street crossings. —*v.t.* & *v.i. Obs.* To give or take refuge. [<OF <L *refugium* < *refugere* retreat < *re-* back + *fugere* flee]
Synonyms (noun): asylum, cover, covert, harbor, hiding-place, protection, retreat, sanctuary, stronghold. See SHELTER.
ref·u·gee (ref′yŏŏ·jē′) *n.* **1** One who flees to a refuge. **2** One who flees from invasion, persecution, or political danger. [<F *réfugié,* pp. of *réfugier* <L *refugere.* See REFUGE.]
re·ful·gence (ri·ful′jəns) *n.* Splendor; brilliant radiance. Also **re·ful′gen·cy.**
re·ful·gent (ri·ful′jənt) *adj.* Shining with a bright light; brilliant; splendid. See synonyms under BRIGHT. [<L *refulgens, -entis,* ppr. of *refulgere* reflect light < *re-* back + *fulgere* shine] —**re·ful′gent·ly** *adv.*
re·fund (ri·fund′) *v.t.* **1** To give or pay back (money, etc.). **2** *Obs.* To pour back. —*v.i.* **3** To make repayment. —*n.* (rē′fund) A repayment; refunding; also, the amount repaid. [<L *refundere* pour back < *re-* back + *fundere* pour out, discharge] —**re·fund′er** *n.* —**re·fund′ment** *n.*
re-fund (rē·fund′) *v.t.* To fund anew; replace (an old loan) by issuing new securities.
re·fus·al (ri·fyōō′zəl) *n.* **1** The act of refusing; denial of what is asked. **2** The privilege of accepting or rejecting; an option.
re·fuse[1] (ri·fyōōz′) *v.* **·fused, ·fus·ing** *v.t.* **1** To decline to do, permit, take, or yield. **2** *Mil.* To turn back (the wing of a line of troops), so that it stands at an angle with the main body. **3** To decline to jump over: said of a horse at a ditch, hedge, etc. **4** *Obs.* To disown; renounce; resign. —*v.i.* **5** To decline to do, permit, take, or yield something. [<OF *refuser* <L *refusus,* pp. of *refundere.* See REFUND.] —**re·fus′er** *n.*
ref·use[2] (ref′yōōs) *adj.* Rejected as worthless. —*n.* Anything worthless; rubbish. See synonyms under WASTE. [<OF *refus,* pp. of *refuser.* See REFUSE[1].]
re-fuse (rē·fyōōz′) *v.t.* & *v.i.* **-fused, -fus·ing** To fuse again.
re-fu·sion (rē·fyōō′zhən) *n. Med.* The temporary withdrawing of blood from circulation, as for exposing it to air or other treatment. Compare TRANSFUSION.
ref·u·ta·tion (ref′yŏŏ·tā′shən) *n.* The act of refuting or proving the falsity or error in a statement, proposition, or argument; evidence applied to overthrow an erroneous statement or position. Also **re·fu·tal** (ri·fyōōt′l). [<L *refutatio, -onis* < *refutare* stop, repel]
re·fute (ri·fyōōt′) *v.t.* **·fut·ed, ·fut·ing** **1** To prove the incorrectness or falsity of (a statement). **2** To prove (a person) to be in error; confute. [<L *refutare*] —**re·fut′a·bil′i·ty** *n.* —**re·fut′a·ble** *adj.* —**re·fut′a·bly** *adv.* —**re·fut′er** *n.*
Synonyms: confound, confute, disprove. To *refute* and to *confute* are to answer so as to admit of no reply. *Refute* applies either to arguments and opinions or to accusations; *confute* is not applied to accusations and charges, but to overwhelming arguments or opinions that confound; a person is *confuted* when his arguments are *refuted.*
re·gain (ri·gān′) *v.t.* **1** To get possession of again, as something lost; gain anew. **2** To reach again; get back to: He *regained* the street. See synonyms under RECOVER. [<MF *regaigner*] —**re·gain′er** *n.*
re·gal (rē′gəl) *adj.* Belonging to or fit for a king; royal; also, stately. See synonyms under IMPERIAL, KINGLY. [<OF <L *regalis* < *rex, regis* king. Doublet of ROYAL.] —**re′gal·ly** *adv.*
re·gale (ri·gāl′) *v.* **·galed, ·gal·ing** *v.t.* **1** To give unusual pleasure to; delight: He *regaled* us with stories. **2** To entertain royally or sumptuously; feast. —*v.i.* **3** To feast. —*n. Obs.* **1** A sumptuous feast. **2** Refreshment. **3** A choice dish. [<F *régaler*; ult. origin uncertain] —**re·gale′ment** *n.*
re·ga·li·a (ri·gā′lē·ə, -gāl′yə) *n. pl.* **1** The insignia and emblems of royalty, as the crown, scepter, verge, vestments, etc. **2** The distinctive symbols, insignia, etc., of any society, order, or rank; hence, fine clothes; fancy trappings. **3** In old English law, royal rights; the six prerogatives of sovereignty: the powers of judicature, life and death, war and peace,

taxation, minting money, and taking masterless goods, as waifs, strays, etc. [<L, neut. pl. of *regalis* kingly <*rex, regis* king]

re·gal·i·ty (ri·gal′ə·tē) *n. pl.* **·ties 1** Sovereign jurisdiction; royalty. **2** A territorial jurisdiction conferred by the crown on a subject. **3** A country subject to royal authority; a kingdom. [<OF *regalité*]

Re·gan (rē′gən) In Shakespeare's *King Lear*, the second daughter of Lear. See LEAR.

re·gard (ri·gärd′) *v.t.* **1** To look at or observe closely or attentively. **2** To look on or think of in a certain or specified manner; consider: I *regard* him as a friend. **3** To take into account; consider. **4** To have relation or pertinence to; concern. **5** *Obs.* To care for. —*v.i.* **6** To pay attention. **7** To gaze or look. See synonyms under ESTEEM, LOOK, PERTAIN. —*n.* **1** Observant attention or notice; heed; consideration. **2** Common estimation or repute, especially good repute: a man of *regard.* **3** Reference; relation. **4** A look or aspect; view. **5** *Usually pl.* Respect; affection: My kindest *regards* to your family. **6** Motive. [<OF *regarder* look at <*re-* again + *garder* guard, heed. Doublet of REWARD.]

Synonyms (noun): esteem, favor, respect. *Regard* is more personal and less distant than *esteem*, and adds a special kindliness; *respect* is a more distant word than *esteem. Respect* may be wholly on one side, while *regard* is more often mutual; *respect* in the fullest sense is given to what is lofty, worthy, and honorable, or to a person of such qualities; we may pay an external *respect* to one of lofty station, regardless of personal qualities, showing *respect* for the office. See ATTACHMENT, ESTEEM, FAVOR, FRIENDSHIP, LOVE. *Antonyms*: abhorrence, antipathy, aversion, contempt, dislike, hatred, loathing, repugnance.

re·gard·ant (ri·gär′dənt) *adj. Her.* Looking backward. Compare GARDANT. [<F, ppr. of *regarder* look at]

re·gard·ful (ri·gärd′fəl) *adj.* **1** Having or showing regard; heedful. **2** Respectful. —**re·gard′ful·ly** *adv.* —**re·gard′ful·ness** *n.*

re·gard·ing (ri·gär′ding) *prep.* In reference to; with regard to.

re·gard·less (ri·gärd′lis) *adj.* Having no regard or consideration; heedless; negligent. See synonyms under INATTENTIVE. —*adv. Colloq.* In spite of everything.

re·gat·ta (ri·gat′ə, -gä′tə) *n.* A boat race, or a series of such races. [<Ital. <*regatar* strive]

re·ge·late (rē′jə·lāt) *v.i.* **·lat·ed, ·lat·ing** To unite by regelation. [<RE- + L *gelatus,* pp. of *gelare* freeze]

re·ge·la·tion (rē′jə·lā′shən) *n.* The refreezing of melting ice by reducing the pressure to which it is subjected, thus raising the freezing point.

re·gen·cy (rē′jən·sē) *n. pl.* **·cies 1** The government or office of a regent or body of regents; vicarious government. **2** The period during which a regent or body of regents governs. **3** A body of regents. **4** The district under the rule of a regent. Also **re′gent·ship.** —**the Regency 1** In English history, the years 1811–20. **2** In French history, the years 1715–1723.

re·gen·er·a·cy (ri·jen′ər·ə·sē) *n.* The state of being regenerate.

re·gen·er·ate (ri·jen′ə·rāt) *v.* **·at·ed, ·at·ing** *v.t.* **1** To cause complete moral and spiritual reformation or regeneration in. **2** To produce or form anew; re–create; reproduce. **3** To make use of (heat or other energy that might otherwise be wasted) by means of various devices. **4** *Biol.* To grow or form by regeneration. **5** *Electronics* To raise the amplification of (a vacuum tube) by transferring to the input circuit some of the power of the output circuit. —*v.i.* **6** To form anew; be reproduced. **7** To become spiritually regenerate. **8** To effect regeneration. —*adj.* (ri·jen′ər·it) **1** Having new life; restored. **2** Spiritually renewed; regenerated. [<L *regeneratus,* pp. of *regenerare* generate again <*re-* again +*generare.* See GENERATE.]

re·gen·er·a·tion (ri·jen′ə·rā′shən) *n.* **1** The act of regenerating, or the state of being regenerated. **2** The impartation of spiritual life by divine grace. **3** *Biol.* **a** The reproduction of a lost part or organ, as in lizards. **b** The renewal or reproduction of cells, tissues, etc., in the ordinary vital processes: the *regeneration* of the ectodermic layers. **4** The process by which, in various devices, heat or other forms of energy are saved and re–utilized. **5** *Electronics* The amplification of radiosignal strength by returning part of the output of a vacuum tube to the grid: an effect of feedback. [<OF] —**re·gen·er·a·tive** (ri·jen′ə·rā′·tiv, -ər·ə·tiv) *adj.* —**re·gen′er·a′tive·ly** *adv.*

re·gen·er·a·tor (ri·jen′ə·rā′tər) *n.* **1** One who or that which regenerates. **2** A device in a furnace, gas burner, or similar apparatus, by which the waste heat of escaping gases is used to heat the gas and air just entering. **3** A furnace containing such a device.

Re·gens·burg (rā′gənz·bŏŏrkh) A city of eastern Bavaria, West Germany, a port on the Danube at its northernmost point: English *Ratisbon.*

re·gent (rē′jənt) *n.* **1** One who rules in the name and place of the sovereign. **2** Any ruler or governor; one who governs. **3** resident master who takes part in the government of a university or college. **4** One of various officers having charge of the higher education, as of a state. —*adj.* **1** Exercising authority in another's place. **2** Governing; ruling. [<OF <L *regens, -entis,* ppr. of *regere* rule]

reg·gae (reg′ā) *n.* A simple, lively, rhythmic kind of rock 'n' roll music, of West Indian origin. [< a native West Indian name]

reg·i·cide (rej′ə·sīd) *n.* **1** The killing of a king or sovereign. **2** The killer of a king or sovereign. [<L *rex, regis* king + -CIDE] —**reg′i·ci′dal** *adj.*

Re·gil·lus (ri·jil′əs) In ancient geography, a small lake near Rome; scene of the victory of the Romans over the Latins in 496 B.C.

re·gime (ri·zhēm′) *n.* **1** System of government or administration. **2** Prevalent mode in social matters; social system. **3** Regimen (def. 1). Also **ré·gime** (rā·zhēm′). [<F *régime* <L *regimen.* Doublet of REGIMEN.]

reg·i·men (rej′ə·mən) *n.* **1** A systematized course of living, as to food, clothing, etc. **2** Government; control. **3** *Gram.* The influence of one word in determining the form of another connected with it; grammatical government. See synonyms under FOOD. [<L *regimen* <*regere* rule. Doublet of REGIME.]

reg·i·ment (rej′ə·mənt) *n.* **1** A body of soldiers constituting the unit of infantry, cavalry, artillery, etc., commanded by a colonel. **2** *Obs.* Government over a people or country. —*v.t.* **1** To form into a regiment or regiments; organize. **2** To assign to a regiment. **3** To form into well–defined or specific units or groups; systematize. **4** To make uniform at the expense of individual differences: Certain types of education *regiment* children. [<OF <LL *regimentum* <L *regere* rule] —**reg′i·men′tal** *adj.*

reg·i·men·tals (rej′ə·men′təlz) *n. pl.* Military uniform; the uniform worn by the men and officers of a regiment.

reg·i·men·ta·tion (rej′ə·men·tā′shən)*n.* **1** The act of regimenting; formation into or as into a regiment. **2** Organization into disciplined, uniform groups.

Re·gin (rā′gin) In Norse mythology, a dwarf, foster father of Sigurd, by whom he was slain. Also **Re′ginn.** See FAFNIR, SIGURD.

re·gi·na (ri·jī′nə) *n. Latin* Queen.

Re·gi·na (ri·jī′nə) The capital of Saskatchewan province, Canada.

re·gi·nal (ri·jī′nəl) *adj.* Pertaining to a queen; queenly; also, supporting or favoring a queen. [<Med. L *reginalis*]

re·gion (rē′jən) *n.* **1** A portion of territory or space; a country or district; also, realm; specifically, one of the strata into which the air or the sea is divided by imaginary boundaries. **2** A zoogeographical division of the earth's surface: the Australian *region.* **3** A portion of the body, arbitrarily circumscribed for anatomical and medical purposes: the abdominal *region.* See synonyms under LAND. [<AF *regiun,* OF *regium* <L *regio, -onis* <*regere* rule]

re·gion·al (rē′jən·əl) *adj.* **1** Of or pertaining to a particular region; sectional; local: *regional* planning. **2** Of or pertaining to an entire region or section, especially a geographic one: *regional* features. —**re′gion·al·ly** *adv.*

re·gion·al·ism (rē′jə·nə·liz′əm) *n.* **1** An emotional loyalty or strong feeling for a particular region. **2** An emphasis on regional flavor in art and literature. **3** A specific habit, custom, or way of speaking of a certain region.

ré·gis·seur (rā·zhē·sœr′) *n. French* Director; manager.

reg·is·ter (rej′is·tər) *n.* **1** An official record, the book containing it, or an entry therein; roll; list; schedule; a registry. **2** A registrar. **3** That which registers; a registering apparatus, as for recording velocity, pressure, etc. **4** A device for regulating the admission of heated air to a room. **5** A machine or apparatus which automatically records cash intake; a cash register. **6** *Music* **a** The range or compass of a voice or musical instrument. **b** A class or series of tones of a particular quality or belonging to a particular portion of the compass of a voice or of some instruments. The normal and natural register of the voice is the chest, or thick, register; a middle and an upper register are also recognized, the latter being also termed a head, or thin, register. **7** *Phot.* Relation of position between the sensitive plate or film and the focusing screen. **8** *Printing* **a** Exact correspondence of the lines and margins on the opposite sides of a printed sheet. **b** Correct relation of the colors in color printing. See synonyms under HISTORY, RECORD. —*v.t.* **1** To enter in or as in a register; enrol; specifically, to record formally, as a document, securities, etc. **2** To indicate on a scale. **3** To express or indicate: His face *registered* his disapproval. **4** To effect the exact correspondence of (parts), as the two sides of a printed sheet, the separate plates or films of a color print, etc. **5** To cause (mail) to be recorded, on payment of a fee, when deposited with the postal system, so as to insure delivery. —*v.i.* **6** To enter one's name in a register, poll, etc. **7** To have effect; make an impression. **8** *Printing* To be in register. See synonyms under ENROL. [<OF *registre* < Med. L *registrum* <L *regesta* records, neut. pl of *regestus,* pp. of *regerere* record <*re-* back + *gerere* carry] —**reg·is·tra·ble** (rej′is·trə·bəl) *adj.*

reg·is·tered (rej′is·tərd) *adj.* **1** Recorded, as a birth, a voter, an animal's pedigree, etc. **2** Having a required or official certificate, as a nurse.

registered mail First–class mail, specially entered and recorded at a higher fee, to insure safe delivery.

registered nurse A graduate nurse licensed to practice by the appropriate State authority and entitled to add R.N. after her name.

reg·is·trant (rej′is·trənt) *n.* One who registers, as a voter; especially, one who registers a trademark or patent. [<F]

reg·is·trar (rej′is·trär, rej′is·trär′) *n.* The authorized keeper of a register or of records; especially, a college or university officer who records the enrolment of students, their grades, etc. [<Med. L *registrarius*]

reg·is·tra·tion (rej′is·trā′shən) *n.* **1** The act of entering in a registry; also, an entry in a registry. **2** The registering of voters; also, the number of voters registered. **3** Enrolment in a school, college, or university. **4** The combination of stops used in playing a composition on the organ. [<Med. L *registratio, -onis*]

reg·is·try (rej′is·trē) *n. pl.* **·tries 1** Registration. **2** A register, or the place where it is kept. **3** The condition of being registered: a certificate of *registry.*

re·gi·us (rē′jē·əs) *adj. Latin* Royal: a designation of certain English university professorships founded by the crown, or of their incumbents, and also of certain Scottish professors appointed by the crown.

reg·let (reg′lit) *n.* **1** A flat, narrow molding. **2** *Printing* A thin wooden strip used for making space between lines of type, as in posters; also, the strips collectively or the material of which they are made. [<OF, dim. of *regle* < L *regula.* See RULE.]

reg·ma (reg′mə) *n.* *pl.* **·ma·ta** (-mə·tə) *Bot.* A capsular fruit made up of two or more carpels, each of which dehisces at maturity. [<NL <Gk. *rhēgma* fracture < *rhēgnynai* break]

reg·nal (reg′nəl) *adj.* Of or pertaining to a reign, a king, or a kingdom. [<LL *regnalis* <L *regnum* reign]

reg·nant (reg′nənt) *adj.* Reigning in one's own right; hence, dominant. [<L *regnans, -antis,* ppr. of *regnare* < *regnum* reign]

reg·nant pop·u·li (reg′nənt pop′yōō·lī) *Latin* The people rule: motto of Arkansas.

Re·gnauld (rə·nyō′) French form of REGINALD. Also **Re·gnault′.**

Ré·gnier (rā·nyā′), **Henri de,** 1864–1936, French author.

re·gorge (ri·gôrj′) *v.* **·gorged, ·gorg·ing** *v.t.* To vomit up; disgorge. —*v.i.* To gush or flow back. [<F *regorger* < *re-* again + *gorger* gorge < *gorge* throat <L *gurges* whirlpool. Related to REGURGITATE.]

re·grade (ri·grād′) *v.t.* **·grad·ed, ·grad·ing** To grade again.

re·grate (ri·grāt′) *v.t.* **·grat·ed, ·grat·ing 1** To buy up, as provisions, for the purpose of selling at a higher price in or near the same market. **2** To retail, as provisions. [<OF *regrater*; ult. origin uncertain]

re·gress (rē′gres) *n.* **1** Passage back; return; also, the power or right of passing back or returning. **2** Retrogression. —*v.i.* (ri·gres′) **1** To go back; move backward; return. **2** *Astron.* To move in a direction opposite to that of the general motion of the heavenly bodies, as the moon's nodes. **3** *Stat.* To return to the mean value of a series of observations. [<L *regressus,* pp. of *regredi* go back < *re-* back + *gradi* walk] —**re·gres′sor** *n.*

re·gres·sion (ri·gresh′ən) *n.* **1** The act of moving back or returning. **2** *Astron.* Motion in a direction opposite to that of the general motion of the heavenly bodies. **3** *Psychoanal.* A retreat of the libido to earlier levels of development or to infantile tendencies belonging to a period preceding the obstacles which prevented their normal fulfilment. **4** *Stat.* The return to a mean or average value. **5** *Med.* The subsidence of a disease or of its symptoms.

re·gres·sive (ri·gres′iv) *adj.* **1** Passing back; returning. **2** Retroactive. **3** Retrogressive. —**re·gres′sive·ly** *adv.*

re·gret (ri·gret′) *v.t.* **·gret·ted, ·gret·ting 1** To look back upon with a feeling of distress or loss. **2** To feel sorrow or grief concerning. See synonyms under MOURN. —*n.* **1** Distress of mind in recalling some past event; a wish that something had or had not happened. **2** Remorseful sorrow; compunction. **3** An expression of sorrow or disappointment. **4** *pl.* A polite declination in response to an invitation. See synonyms under GRIEF, REPENTANCE. [<OF *regreter*; ult. origin uncertain] **re·gret′ter** *n.*

re·gret·ful (ri·gret′fəl) *adj.* Feeling, expressive of, or full of regret. —**re·gret′ful·ly** *adv.* —**re·gret′ful·ness** *n.*

re·gret·ta·ble (ri·gret′ə·bəl) *adj.* Causing or demanding regret; unfortunate; deplorable. —**re·gret′ta·bly** *adv.*

reg·u·la (reg′yə·lə) *n.* *pl.* **·lae** (-lē) *Archit.* A fillet, especially one of a series in a Doric architrave, placed under the taenia and bearing six guttae on the under side. [<L, ruler < *regere* rule, lead straight]

reg·u·lar (reg′yə·lər) *adj.* **1** Made according to rule; symmetrical; normal. **2** Acting according to rule; recurring without fail; methodical; orderly: *regular* habits. **3** Constituted, appointed, or conducted in the proper manner; duly authorized: a *regular* meeting, a *regular* practitioner. **4** *Gram.* Undergoing the inflection that is normal or most common to the class of words to which it belongs; following the rule; not exceptional. **5** *Bot.* Having all the parts or organs of the same kind uniform in structure or shape and size: said mainly of flowers. **6** *Zool.* Conforming to an established type; exhibiting radial or bilateral symmetry. **7** *Music* Following strict and classical rules of composition: a *regular* movement. **8** *Eccl.* Bound by a religious rule; pertaining or belonging to a religious order: the *regular* clergy. **9** *Mil.* Belonging to the standing army; permanent. **10** In politics, adhering loyally to a party organization or platform; also, nominated by the official party organization: said of a candidate. **11** *Geom.* Having equal sides and angles. **12** Controlled or governed by one law or operation throughout: a *regular* equation. **13** *Colloq.* Thorough; unmitigated; absolute. **14** *Slang* Fine; good: a *regular* guy. **15** *U.S.* Designating that component of a branch of the armed services which consists of persons in continuous service on active duty in both peace and war: the **Regular Army, Regular Navy, Regular Air Force.** See synonyms under CONTINUAL, GRADUAL, HABITUAL, NORMAL, SOBER, USUAL. —*n.* **1** A soldier belonging to a standing army as opposed to a volunteer, draftee, or member of a reserve unit. **2** *Colloq.* One regularly employed or engaged; also, a habitual customer. **3** *Eccl.* A member of a religious or monastic order. **4** A person loyal to a certain political party. [<L *regularis* < *regula* rule] —**reg′u·lar·ness** *n.*

reg·u·lar·i·ty (reg′yə·lar′ə·tē) *n.* *pl.* **·ties** The state, quality, or character of being regular: *regularity* of form or in occurrence. See synonyms under SYMMETRY, SYSTEM.

reg·u·lar·ize (reg′yə·lə·rīz′) *v.t.* **·ized, ·iz·ing** To make regular. —**reg′u·lar·i·za′tion** *n.*

reg·u·lar·ly (reg′yə·lər·lē) *adv.* In a regular manner; according to the usual method or order.

reg·u·late (reg′yə·lāt) *v.t.* **·lat·ed, ·lat·ing 1** To direct, manage, or control according to certain rules, principles, etc. **2** To adjust according to a standard, degree, etc.: to *regulate* currency. **3** To adjust to accurate operation: to *regulate* a watch. **4** To put in order; set right. [<LL *regulatus,* pp. of *regulare* rule <L *regula* a rule < *regere* rule, lead straight] —**reg′u·la′tive** *adj.*

Synonyms: adjust, arrange, conduct, direct, dispose, govern, guide, manage, methodize, order, rule, systematize. See SET, SETTLE. *Antonyms*: confuse, derange, disorder, displace, distract, disturb, unsettle.

reg·u·la·tion (reg′yə·lā′shən) *n.* **1** The act of regulating, or the state of being regulated. **2** A rule prescribed for conduct: army *regulations*: also used adjectively. See synonyms under LAW[1], RULE.

reg·u·la·tor (reg′yə·lā′tər) *n.* **1** One who or that which regulates. **2** A clock used as a standard; also, an index arm for regulating the rate of a watch. **3** *Mech.* A contrivance for governing or equalizing motion or flow; the governor of a steam engine; a damper or other device for regulating a draft; a throttle valve. **4** A register (def. 4). **5** A thermostat. **6** *Electr.* A device for keeping at constant strength the current produced by a dynamo. —**reg′u·la′tor·ship** *n.*

Reg·u·la·tor (reg′yə·lā′tər) *n.* **1** A member of any of several bands or committees organized in North Carolina (1768–71) to resist official extortion, and in South Carolina (1767–69) to exterminate horse thieves. **2** One belonging to a volunteer band or committee, which, in the absence of lawful authority, took it upon itself to preserve order and punish crime, but which often deteriorated into lawless bands of violent men.

reg·u·la·to·ry (reg′yə·lə·tôr′ē, -tō′rē) *adj.* Tending or serving to regulate: *regulatory* measures. Also **reg′u·la′tive.**

reg·u·lus (reg′yə·ləs) *n.* *pl.* **·li** (-lī) *Metall.* **1** The metallic mass that sinks to the bottom of the vessel in which slag is being treated. **2** An intermediate product obtained in smelting ores of copper, lead, silver, and nickel. [<L, lit., kinglet, dim of *rex, regis* king] —**reg′u·line** (-lin, -līn) *adj.*

Reg·u·lus (reg′yə·ləs) A white star, Alpha in the constellation Leo; magnitude, 1.34: sometimes called *Cor Leonis.* [<L]

Reg·u·lus (reg′yə·ləs), **Marcus Attilius** Roman general; put to death by the Carthaginians about 250 B.C.

re·gur·gi·tate (ri·gûr′jə·tāt) *v.* **·tat·ed, ·tat·ing** *v.i.* To rush, pour, or surge back; vomit. —*v.t.* To cause to surge back, as partially digested food; vomit. [<LL *regurgitatus,* pp. of *regurgitare* < *re-* back + *gurgitare* flood, engulf < L *gurges, gurgites* whirlpool] —**re·gur′gi·tant** *adj.*

re·gur·gi·ta·tion (ri·gûr′jə·tā′shən) *n.* **1** The act of rushing back or reswallowing. **2** *Physiol.* The backward rush of blood into the heart, due to defective valves.

re·ha·bil·i·tate (rē′hə·bil′ə·tāt) *v.t.* **·tat·ed, ·tat·ing 1** To restore to a former state, capacity, privilege, rank, etc.; reinstate. **2** To make one capable of becoming a useful member of society again: to *rehabilitate* a crippled soldier. [<Med. L *rehabilitatus,* pp. of *rehabilitare* < *re-* back + *habilitare.* See HABILITATE.] —**re′ha·bil′i·ta′tion** *n.*

re·hash (rē·hash′) *v.t.* To work into a new form; go over again. —*n.* (rē′hash′) Something hashed over, or made or served up from something used before, as old matter issued under a new name.

re·hears·al (ri·hûr′səl) *n.* **1** The act of rehearsing, as a play. **2** The act of reciting or telling over again.

re·hearse (ri·hûrs′) *v.* **·hearsed, ·hears·ing** *v.t.* **1** To perform privately in preparation for public performance, as a play or song. **2** To cause to perform or recite by way of preparation; instruct by rehearsal. **3** To say over again; repeat aloud; recite. **4** To give an account of; relate. **5** To enumerate. —*v.i.* **6** To rehearse a play, song, dance, etc. See synonyms under RELATE. [<OF *reherser* harrow over, repeat < *re-* again + *herser* harrow < *herse.* See HEARSE.] —**re·hears′er** *n.*

re·heat (rē·hēt′) *v.t.* To heat again or anew. —**re·heat′er** *n.*

Rehn·quist (ren′kwist), **William H.,** born 1924, U.S. jurist, associate Supreme Court justice 1972–.

Re·ho·bo·am (rē′ō·bō′əm) Son and successor of Solomon; king of Judah after the revolt of the ten tribes. II *Chron.* ix 31.

rei (rā) Erroneous English form for Portuguese *real.* See MILREIS, REAL[2].

Reich (rīkh) Germany or its government. —**First Reich** The Holy Roman Empire from its establishment in the ninth century to its collapse in 1806. —**Second Reich** The German Empire, 1871–1919, or the Weimar Republic, 1919–1933, or both German governments in the period 1871–1933. —**Third Reich** The Nazi state under Adolf Hitler, 1933–45. [<G, realm]

Reich (rīkh), **Wilhelm,** 1897–1957, U.S. psychotherapist and natural scientist, born in Germany.

Reich·en·berg (rīkh′ən·berkh) The German name for LIBEREC.

Reichs·bank (rīkhs′bängk) *n.* The state or national bank of Germany, founded in 1876. [<G]

Reichs·land (rīkhs′länt) **1** From 1806 to 1871, all German crown lands. **2** From 1871 to 1918, Alsace-Lorraine.

reichs·mark (rīkhs′märk) See MARK[2] (def. 1). [<G]

reichs·pfen·nig (rīkhs′pfen′ikh) See PFENNIG. [<G]

Reichs·rat (rīkhs′rät) *n.* **1** The former parliament of the Austrian Empire, excluding Hungary. **2** The Council of the Reich under the Weimar Republic. Also **Reichs′rath.** [<G, lit., council of the empire]

Reichs·tag (rīkhs′täkh) *n.* The former legislative assembly of Germany. [<G, lit., day of the empire. Cf. DIET for analogous development.]

Reid (rēd), **Whitelaw,** 1837–1912, U. S. journalist and diplomat.

reif (rēf) *n. Scot.* Robbery; plunder.

re·i·fy (rē′ə·fī) *v.t.* **·fied, ·fy·ing** To make real or concrete; materialize: to *reify* an idea. [<L *res, rei* thing + -FY] —**re′i·fi·ca′tion** *n.* —**re′i·fi′er** *n.*

reign (rān) *n.* **1** The possession or exercise of supreme political power; sovereignty; dominion. **2** The time or duration of a sovereign's rule. —*v.i.* **1** To hold and exercise sovereign power; be the head of a monarchy. **2** To hold sway; be predominant; prevail: Winter *reigns.* See synonyms under GOVERN. ◆ Homophones: *rain, rein.* [<F *règne* <L *regnum* rule]

Reign of Terror The period of the French Revolution from May, 1793, to August, 1794, during which Louis XVI, Marie Antoinette, and thousands of other persons were guillotined, and confiscation, violence, and terror reigned under the revolutionary leaders.

re·im·burse (rē′im·bûrs′) *v.t.* **·bursed, ·burs·ing 1** To pay back (a person) an equivalent for what has been spent or lost; recompense; indemnify. **2** To pay back; refund. [< RE- + obs. *imburse* <LL *imbursare* <L *in-* in

+ *bursa* purse] — **re'im·burse'ment** *n.* — **re'im·burs'er** *n.*

re·im·plan·ta·tion (rē'im·plan·tā'shən) *n. Surg.* The act of restoring in place a bone, or part of a bone, removed in an operation.

re·im·pres·sion (rē'im·presh'ən) *n.* **1** A new or second impression of anything. **2** A reprint of a book without editorial change.

Reims (rēmz, *Fr.* raṅs) A city in NE France; its cathedral, former coronation place of the French kings, was greatly damaged by German bombardment in 1870 and 1914: also *Rheims.*

rein (rān) *n.* **1** *Usually pl.* A strap attached to the bit to control a horse or other draft animal. **2** Any means of restraint or control; government. — *v.t.* **1** To guide, check, or halt with or as with reins. **2** To furnish with reins. — *v.i.* **3** To check or halt a horse by means of reins: with *in* or *up.* **4** To obey the reins. See synonyms under REPRESS. ◆ Homophones: *rain, reign.* [<AF *redne,* OF *resne* <L *retinere.* See RETAIN.]

Rei·nach (re·nȧk'), **Salomon,** 1858–1932, French archeologist.

re·in·car·nate (rē'in·kär'nāt) *v.t.* **·nat·ed, ·nat·ing** To cause to undergo reincarnation.

re·in·car·na·tion (rē'in·kär·nā'shən) *n.* A rebirth of the soul in successive bodies; specifically, in Vedic religions, the becoming of an avatar again: one of the series in the transmigrations of souls. — **re'in·car·na'tion·ist** *n.*

rein·deer (rān'dir') *n. pl.* **·deer** A deer (genus *Rangifer*) of northern regions, having branched antlers in both sexes: long domesticated for its milk, hide, and flesh, and used as a draft and pack animal. [<ON *hreindȳri* < *hreinn* reindeer + *dȳr* deer]

Reindeer Lake A lake in northern Saskatchewan and Manitoba provinces, Canada; 2,444 square miles.

reindeer moss A gray, branched lichen (*Cladonia rangiferina*) found as far as the extreme limits of arctic vegetation, and furnishing food for reindeer and sometimes man.

re in·fec·ta (rē in·fek'tə) *Latin* The business being unfinished.

re·in·force (rē'in·fôrs', -fōrs') *v.t.* **·forced, ·forc·ing 1** To give new force or strength to. **2** To increase the military or naval strength of by providing with more troops or ships. **3** To add some strengthening part or material to; thicken; strengthen; support. See synonyms under RECRUIT. — *n.* That which strengthens or reinforces, as the part of a cannon near the breech that is cast thicker than the rest. Also spelled *reenforce.* [<RE- + *inforce,* var. of ENFORCE]

reinforced concrete Concrete containing metal bars, rods, or netting disposed through the mass in such a way as to increase its tensile strength and durability; ferroconcrete.

re·in·force·ment (rē'in·fôrs'mənt, -fōrs'-) *n.* **1** The act of reinforcing. **2** Increase of force; a fresh body of troops or additional vessels: often in the plural. See synonyms under INCREASE. Also spelled *reenforcement.*

Rein·hardt (rīn'härt), **Max,** 1873–1943, Austrian theatrical director and producer active in Germany and the United States.

Rein·hold (rīn'hōld; *Dan.* rīn'hōlth, *Ger.* rīn'·hōlt, *Sw.* rīn'hōld) See REGINALD. Also *Ger.* **Rei·nald** (rī'nält), *Du.* **Rei·nold** (rī'nōlt).

reins (rānz) *n. pl. Archaic* **1** The kidneys. **2** The region near the kidneys. **3** The affections and passions, formerly thought to have their seat in the loins. [<OF <L *renes,* pl. of *ren*]

re·in·stall (rē'in·stôl') *v.t.* To install again. — **re·in·stal·la·tion** (rē'in·stə·lā'shən) *n.* — **re'in·stal'ment** or **re'in·stall'ment** *n.*

re·in·state (rē'in·stāt') *v.t.* **·stat·ed, ·stat·ing** To restore to a former state, position, etc. — **re'in·state'ment** *n.*

re·in·sure (rē'in·shŏŏr') *v.t.* **·sured, ·sur·ing 1** To protect (the risk on a policy already issued) by obtaining insurance from a second insurer: said of a first insurer. **2** To insure anew. — **re'in·sur'ance** *n.* — **re'in·sur'er** *n.*

re·in·vest (rē'in·vest') *v.t.* To invest (money) again; especially, to invest earnings from previous investments. — **re'in·vest'ment** *n.*

Rein·wald (rīn'vält) A German form of REGINALD.

reis (rēs) Plural of REAL[2] (def. 2). See MILREIS.

reise (rēs) *n. Scot.* A twig; brush; brushwood.

re·is·sue (rē·ish'ōō) *n.* **1** A second or subsequent issue, as of a publication changed only in form or price. **2** A second printing of postage stamps from the same plates. — *v.t.* **·sued, ·su·ing** To issue again.

reit·bok (rēt'bok) *n.* The reedbuck. [<Du. *rietbok*]

re·it·er·ate (rē·it'ə·rāt) *v.t.* **·at·ed, ·at·ing** To say or do again and again; repeat. [<L *reiteratus,* pp. of *reiterare* < *re-* again + *iterare.* See ITERATE.] — **re·it'er·a'tion** *n.*

re·it·er·a·tive (rē·it'ə·rā'tiv) *adj.* Characterized by reiteration. — *n.* **1** A word or syllable repeated, usually with some slight change, so as to make a reduplicated word; also, the word so formed, as *tittle-tattle.* **2** A word expressing repeated action. — **re·it'er·a'tive·ly** *adv.*

Ré·jane (rā·zhän'), **Gabrielle Charlotte,** 1857–1920, French actress and comedienne: real name *Réju.*

re·ject (ri·jekt') *v.t.* **1** To refuse to accept, recognize, believe, etc. **2** To refuse to grant; deny, as a petition. **3** To refuse (a person) recognition, acceptance, etc. **4** To expel, as from the mouth; vomit. **5** To cast away as worthless; discard. — *n.* (rē'jekt) A person or thing that has been discarded or rejected. [<L *rejectus,* pp. of *reicere* fling back < *re-* back + *jacere* throw] — **re·ject'er** or **re·jec'·tor** *n.*

re·jec·ta·men·ta (ri·jek'tə·men'tə) *n. pl.* Things thrown away; especially, things rejected from a living organism; excrement. [<NL <L *rejectare,* freq. of *reicere* fling back]

re·jec·tion (ri·jek'shən) *n.* **1** The act of rejecting. **2** That which is rejected.

re·joice (ri·jois') *v.* **·joiced, ·joic·ing** *v.i.* To feel joyful; be glad. — *v.t.* To fill with joy; gladden. [<OF *rejoiss-, resjoiss-,* stem of *resjoir* enjoy < *re-* again (<L) + *esjoir* <L *ex-* thoroughly + *gaudere* be joyous < *gaudium* joy] — **re·joic'er** *n.*

Synonyms: cheer, delight, enjoy, enrapture, exhilarate, exult, gladden, gratify, joy, please, ravish, triumph. Compare HAPPINESS, HAPPY. *Antonyms*: afflict, agonize, bewail, grieve, lament, mourn, pain, regret, sadden, sorrow.

re·joic·ing (ri·joi'sing) *adj.* Pertaining to or characterized by joyfulness. See synonyms under HAPPY. — *n.* The feeling or expression of joy. See synonyms under HAPPINESS, LAUGHTER, RAPTURE.

re·join[1] (ri·join') *v.t.* **1** To say in reply; answer. — *v.i.* **2** To answer. **3** *Law* To make answer to the plaintiff's replication. [<F *rejoindre* < *re-* again (<L) + *joindre.* See JOIN.]

re·join[2] (rē·join') *v.t.* **1** To come again into company with. **2** To join together again; reunite. — *v.i.* **3** To come together again. [<RE- + JOIN]

re·join·der (ri·join'dər) *n.* **1** An answer to a reply; also, any reply or retort. **2** *Law* The answer filed by a defendant to a plaintiff's replication. See synonyms under ANSWER. [< F *rejoindre* answer, reply]

re·ju·ve·nate (ri·jōō'və·nāt) *v.t.* **·nat·ed, ·nat·ing 1** To make young; give new vigor or youthfulness to. **2** *Geog.* To restore (a mature or old river) to its youthful condition by the development of lakes, as by obstruction through mountain growth or elevation. Also **re·ju've·nize.** [<RE- again + L *juvenis* young + -ATE[1]] — **re·ju've·na'tion** *n.*

re·ju·ve·nes·cence (ri·jōō'və·nes'əns) *n.* **1** A renewal of youth; the state of being or growing young again. **2** *Biol.* The transformation of the entire protoplasm of a vegetative cell into a primordial cell, which subsequently invests itself with a new cell wall, and forms the starting point of the life of a new individual. [<L *rejuvenescens,* ppr. of *rejuvenescere* renew youth < *re-* again + *juvenescere* grow young < *juvenis* young] — **re·ju've·nes'cent** *adj.*

re·lapse (ri·laps') *v.i.* **·lapsed, ·laps·ing 1** To lapse back, as into disease after partial recovery. **2** To return to bad habits or sin; backslide. — *n.* (*also* rē'laps) A relapsing; lapse into a former evil state. [<L *relapsus,* pp. of *relabi* slide back < *re-* back + *labi* slide] — **re·laps'er** *n.*

relapsing fever *Pathol.* An acute infectious disease occurring in several forms and due to certain spirochetes transmitted by lice and ticks. It is characterized by febrile paroxysms recurring every five or seven days. Also called *recurrent fever.*

re·late (ri·lāt') *v.* **·lat·ed, ·lat·ing** *v.t.* **1** To tell the events or the particulars of; narrate. **2** To bring into connection or relation. — *v.i.* **3** To have relation: with *to.* **4** To have reference: with *to.* [<F *relater* <L *relatus,* pp. to *referre.* See REFER.] — **re·lat'er** *n.*

Synonyms: describe, detail, narrate, recite, recount, rehearse, report, state, tell. See PERTAIN. *Antonyms*: deny, hide, suppress, withhold.

re·lat·ed (ri·lā'tid) *adj.* **1** Standing in relation; connected. **2** Of common ancestry; connected by blood or marriage; akin. **3** Narrated. **4** Belonging to the same harmonic or melodic series. — **re·lat'ed·ness** *n.*

re·la·tion (ri·lā'shən) *n.* **1** The fact or condition of being related or connected, or that by which things are connected, either objectively or in the mind; interdependence; connection. **2** The act of relating or narrating; also, that which is related or told. **3** Connection by blood or marriage; kinship. **4** A person connected by blood or marriage; a kinsman: now mostly supplanted by *relative.* **5** *Law* **a** The statement of the grounds of a complaint or grievance by a relator. **b** The reaching back and taking effect of an act or judicial decree at a date anterior to its actual occurrence: Assignment in bankruptcy operates by *relation* back to the date of filing the petition. **6** Reference; regard; allusion: chiefly in the phrase, **in relation to.** **7** The position of one person with respect to another: the *relation* of ruler to subject. **8** *pl.* Conditions in general which bring an individual in touch with his fellows; also, the various ways in which one country may come into contact with another politically and commercially. See synonyms under ANALOGY, KINDRED, KINSMAN, REPORT, STORY[1]. [<F <L *relatio, -onis* < *relatus,* pp. to *referre.* See REFER.]

re·la·tion·al (ri·lā'shən·əl) *adj.* **1** Pertaining to or expressing relation: said especially of certain parts of speech. **2** Having relation or kinship.

re·la·tion·ship (ri·lā'shən·ship) *n.* The state of being related; connection. See synonyms under AFFINITY, KIN.

rel·a·tive (rel'ə·tiv) *adj.* **1** Having connection; pertinent: an inquiry *relative* to one's health. **2** Resulting from or depending upon relation; comparative: a *relative* truth. **3** Intelligible only in relation to each other: the *relative* terms "father" and "son." **4** Referring to, relating to, or qualifying an antecedent term: a *relative* pronoun. **5** Having the same key signature, as major and minor keys and scales. — *n.* **1** One who is related; a kinsman. **2** A relative word or term; especially, a relative pronoun. See synonyms under KINDRED, KINSMAN. [<F *relatif* <LL *relativus* <L *relatus*] — **rel'a·tive·ly** *adv.* — **rel'a·tive·ness** *n.*

relative pronoun See under PRONOUN.

rel·a·tiv·ism (rel'ə·tiv·iz'əm) *n. Philos.* The theory that truths are relative and may vary according to the individual, the group, the place, or the time. — **rel'a·tiv·ist** *n.* — **rel'a·tiv·is'tic** *adj.*

rel·a·tiv·i·ty (rel'ə·tiv'ə·tē) *n.* **1** The quality or condition of being relative; relativeness. **2** *Philos.* Existence only as an object of, or in relation to, a thinking mind; phenomenality: sometimes called the doctrine of the relativity of existence. **3** A condition of dependence or of close relation, as of the solar system on the sun. **4** *Physics* The principle of the interdependence of matter, energy, space, and time, as mathematically formulated by A. Einstein. The **special theory of relativity** states that the velocity of light is independent of the motion of its source and that motion itself is a meaningless concept except as between two physical systems or material bodies moving relatively to each other. The **general theory of relativity** extends these principles to the law of gravitation and the motions of the heavenly bodies.

relativity of knowledge *Philos.* The theory that knowledge of what things really are is impossible, since knowledge itself is dependent upon the mind's purely subjective forms of relating its objects.

re·la·tor (ri·lā′tər) *n.* **1** One who relates; a relater. **2** *Law* One who institutes a special proceeding by relation or by information: the *relator* in the writ of quo warranto. [<L]

re·lax (ri·laks′) *v.t.* **1** To make lax or loose; make less tight or firm. **2** To make less stringent or severe, as discipline. **3** To abate; slacken, as efforts. **4** To relieve from strain or effort: to *relax* the eyes. —*v.i.* **5** To become lax or loose; loosen. **6** To become less stringent or severe. **7** To rest; engage in relaxation. **8** To unbend; become less formal. [< L *relaxare* <*re-* again + *laxare* loosen < *laxus* loose. Doublet of RELEASE.] —**re·lax′·a·ble** *adj.* —**re·lax′er** *n.*

Synonyms: abate, divert, ease, loose, loosen, mitigate, recreate, reduce, relieve, remit, slacken, unbend. Compare WEAKEN. *Antonyms*: bind, confine, contract, strain, stretch, tighten.

re·lax·a·tion (rē′lak·sā′shən) *n.* **1** The act of relaxing, or the state of being relaxed. **2** Indulgence in diversion, or the diversion indulged in; entertainment. [<L *relaxatio, -onis*] —**re·lax·a·tive** (ri·lak′sə·tiv) *adj. & n.*

re·lay (rē′lā, ri·lā′) *n.* **1** A fresh set, as of men, horses, or dogs, to replace or relieve a tired set. **2** A supply of anything kept in store for anticipated use or need. **3** A relay race, or one of its laps or legs. **4** *Electr.* A device which utilizes variations in the condition or strength of a current in a circuit to effect the operation of similar devices in the same or another circuit: a telegraph *relay.* —*v.t.* **1** To send onward by or as by relays. **2** To provide with relays. **3** *Electr.* To operate or retransmit by means of a relay. [<F *relais* <Ital. *rilascio* <*rilasciare, rilassare* leave behind, release <L *relaxare* loosen again. See RELAX.]

re–lay (rē·lā′) *v.t.* **–laid, –lay·ing** To lay again.

relay race A race between two or more teams of runners, each of whom runs a set part of the course and is relieved by a teammate.

re·lease (ri·lēs′) *v.t.* **·leased, ·leas·ing 1** To set free; liberate; deliver from worry, pain, obligation, etc. **2** To free from something that holds, binds, etc. **3** To permit the circulation, sale, performance, etc., of, as a motion picture, phonograph record, or news item. —*n.* **1** The act of releasing or setting free, or the state of being released; liberation from restraint of any kind. **2** A deliverance or final relief, as from anything grievous or oppressive. **3** A discharge from responsibility or penalty, as from a debt. **4** *Law* An instrument of conveyance by which one of two persons having a mutual interest in lands surrenders and relinquishes all his interest and estate to the other; quitclaim. **5** A motion picture, phonograph record, news item, or the like ready for distribution or circulation. **6** Exhaust of motive fluid in a steam engine; also, the point at which such exhaust begins. **7** *Mech.* Any catch or device to hold and release a mechanism, weights, etc. [<OF *relaisser* let free <L *relaxare.* Doublet of RELAX.] —**re·leas′er** *n.*

Synonyms (verb): deliver, discharge, disengage, emancipate, exempt, extricate, free, liberate, loose, unbind, unfasten, unloose, untie. See ABSOLVE.

released time Time made available by public schools for religious education or other legally authorized instruction outside of school.

rel·e·gate (rel′ə·gāt) *v.t.* **·gat·ed, ·gat·ing 1** To send off or consign, as to an obscure position or place. **2** To assign, as to a particular class or sphere. **3** To refer (a matter) to someone for decision. **4** To banish; exile. See synonyms under COMMIT. [<L *relegatus,* pp. of *relegare* send away <*re-* away, back + *legare* send] —**rel′e·ga′tion** *n.*

re·lent (ri·lent′) *v.i.* To soften in temper; become more gentle or compassionate. —*v.t. Obs.* To cause to relent. [<OF *ralentir* <L *relentescere* grow soft <*re-* again + *lentus* soft]

re·lent·less (ri·lent′lis) *adj.* **1** Indifferent to the pain of others; not relenting; pitiless. **2** Unremitting; continuous. See synonyms under AUSTERE, IMPLACABLE. —**re·lent′less·ly** *adv.* —**re·lent′less·ness** *n.*

rel·e·vant (rel′ə·vənt) *adj.* **1** Fitting or suiting given requirements; pertinent; applicable: commonly with *to.* **2** *Ling.* Designating those features of a phoneme which function to distinguish it from other phonemes in a language, as place of articulation in English consonants. [<Med. L *relevans, -antis,* ppr. of *relevare* bear upon <L, raise up. See RELIEVE.] —**rel′·e·vance, rel′e·van·cy** *n.* —**rel′e·vant·ly** *adv.*

re·li·a·ble (ri·lī′ə·bəl) *adj.* **1** That may be relied upon; worthy of confidence; trustworthy. **2** *Stat.* Exhibiting a reasonable consistency in results obtained, as in a group of repeated tests: distinguished from *valid.* [<RELY + -ABLE] —**re·li′a·bil′i·ty, re·li′a·ble·ness** *n.* —**re·li′a·bly** *adv.*

Synonyms: trustworthy, trusty. *Trusty* and *trustworthy* refer to inherent qualities of a high order, *trustworthy* being especially applied to persons, and denoting moral integrity and truthfulness; we speak of a *trusty* sword, a *trustworthy* man. *Reliable* is inferior in meaning, denoting merely the possession of such qualities as are needed for safe reliance; as, a *reliable* pledge, *reliable* information. A man is said to be *reliable* with reference not only to moral qualities, but to judgment, knowledge, skill, habit, or perhaps pecuniary ability. A *reliable* messenger is one who may be depended on to do his errand correctly and promptly; a *trusty* or *trustworthy* messenger is one who may be admitted to knowledge of the views and purposes of those who employ him.

re·li·ance (ri·lī′əns) *n.* **1** The act of relying or the condition of being reliant; confidence; trust; pendence. **2** That upon which one relies; a ground of confidence. See synonyms under BELIEF, FAITH. [<RELY + -ANCE]

re·li·ant (ri·lī′ənt) *adj.* Confident; manifesting reliance, especially upon oneself. [<RELY + -ANT] —**re·li′ant·ly** *adv.*

rel·ic (rel′ik) *n.* **1** Some remaining portion or fragment of that which has vanished or is destroyed: a *relic* of barbarism. **2** Something cherished in memory of one deceased; an object of sacred reverence or of affection; a keepsake or memento. **3** The body or part of the body of a saint, or an object connected with a saint or his tomb; a sacred memento. **4** *pl. Obs.* A corpse; remains. Also spelled *relique.* [<F *relique* <L *reliquiae* remains, leavings <*relinquere* leave. See RELINQUISH.]

rel·ict (rel′ikt) *n.* **1** A widow; rarely, a widower. **2** *Biol.* A plant or animal species persisting in a given area as a survival from an earlier period or type. —*adj.* (ri·likt′) *Geol.* Left by gradual erosion; residual. [<L *relicta* widow, fem. of *relictus,* pp. of *relinquere* leave behind. See RELINQUISH.]

re·lief (ri·lēf′) *n.* **1** The act of relieving, or the state of being relieved; removal in whole or in part of any evil, hardship, or trial; alleviation; comfort. **2** That which relieves. **3** Charitable aid, given in the form of money or food to the needy. **4** The release, as of a sentinel or guard, from his post or duty, and the substitution of some other person or persons; also, the person or persons so substituted. **5** In architecture and sculpture, the projection of a figure, ornament, etc., from a surface; also, any such figure: opposed to *round.* Sculptural relief is of three principal kinds: *alto–relievo, bas–relief,* and *mezzo–relievo.* Extremely low relief is called *stiacciato.* **6** In painting, the apparent projection of forms and masses from the plane or ground of a picture given by the arrangement of the lines, colors, or gradations of color; hence, sharpness of outline caused by contrast. **7** In feudal law, a tribute of a fee paid to the lord by the vassal–heir of a deceased tenant for the right of assuming the lapsed tenancy. **8** *Geog.* **a** The unevenness of land surface, as caused by mountains, hills, etc. **b** The parts of a map which portray the configuration of the district represented; contour lines. —**on relief** Receiving money, food, clothing, etc., from a local or other government because of need. [< OF <*relever.* See RELIEVE.]

re·li·er (ri·lī′ər) *n.* One who or that which relies. See RELY.

re·lieve (ri·lēv′) *v.t.* **·lieved, ·liev·ing 1** To free wholly or partly from pain, embarrassment, etc. **2** To lessen or alleviate, as pain or anxiety. **3** To give aid or assistance to: to *relieve* a besieged city. **4** To free from obligation, injustice, etc. **5** To release from duty, as a sentinel, by providing or serving as a substitute. **6** To make less monotonous, harsh, or unpleasant; vary. **7** To bring into relief or prominence; display by contrast. See synonyms under ALLAY, ALLEVIATE, RELAX. [< OF *relever* give assistance to, succor <L *relevare* lift up <*re-* again + *levare* lift, raise < *levis* light] —**re·liev′a·ble** *adj.* —**re·liev′er** *n.*

re·lie·vo (ri·lē′vō) *n. pl.* **·vos** Relief (defs. 5 and 6). [<Ital. <*rilevare* emphasize, elevate <L *relevare.* See RELIEVE.]

re·li·gieuse (rə·lē·zhyœz′) *n. pl.* **·gieuses** (-zhyœz′) *French* A nun.

re·li·gieux (rə·lē·zhyœ′) *n. pl.* **·gieux** (-zhyœ′) *French* A man under monastic vows; a monk.

re·lig·ion (ri·lij′ən) *n.* **1** A belief binding the spiritual nature of man to a supernatural being, as involving a feeling of dependence and responsibility, together with the feelings and practices which naturally flow from such a belief. **2** Any system of faith and worship: the Christian *religion.* **3** An essential part or a practical test of the spiritual life. See *James* i 27. **4** An object of conscientious devotion or scrupulous care: His work is a *religion* to him. **5** *Obs.* Religious practice or belief. [< OF <L *religio, -onis*]

Synonyms: devotion, faith, godliness, holiness, pietism, piety, worship. *Piety* is primarily filial duty, and hence, in its purest sense, a loving obedience and service to God as the heavenly Father; *pietism* often denotes a mystical, sometimes an affected *piety; religion* is the reverent acknowledgment of a divine being. *Religion* includes *worship* whether it be external and formal, or the reverence of the human spirit for the divine, seeking outward expression. *Devotion,* which in its fullest sense is self–consecration, is often used to denote an act of *worship,* especially prayer or adoration; as, He is engaged his *devotions. Godliness* is a character and spirit like that of God. *Holiness* is the highest sinless perfection of any spirit, whether divine or human, and often used for purity or for consecration. *Faith,* strictly a firm reliance on the truth of religious doctrines, is often used as a comprehensive word for a whole system of *religion* considered as the object of *faith*; as, the Christian *faith,* the Buddhist *faith. Antonyms*: atheism, blasphemy, godlessness, impiety, infidelity, irreligion, profanity, sacrilege, unbelief, ungodliness.

re·lig·ion·ism (ri·lij′ən·iz′əm) *n.* The practice of or adherence to religion: used derogatorily to imply affectation and insincerity. —**re·lig′ion·ist** *n.*

re·lig·i·os·i·ty (ri·lij′ē·os′ə·tē) *n.* Religiousness; also, pious sentimentality. [<LL *religiositas, -tatis*]

re·lig·ious (ri·lij′əs) *adj.* **1** Feeling and manifesting religion; devout; pious. **2** Of or pertaining to religion; teaching or setting forth religion: a *religious* teacher. **3** Having thorough and genuine fidelity; strict in performance; conscientious: a *religious* loyalty. **4** Belonging to the monastic life; bound by monastic vows; following or devoted to a life of religion and devotion. —*n. pl.* **·ious** A person or people devoted to a life of piety and devotion; a monk or nun. [<OF *religious* <L *religiosus*] —**re·lig′ious·ly** *adv.* —**re·lig′ious·ness** *n.*

re·lin·quish (ri·ling′kwish) *v.t.* **1** To give up; abandon; surrender. **2** To cease to demand; renounce: to *relinquish* a claim. **3** To let go (a hold or something held). See synonyms under ABANDON, SURRENDER. [<OF *relinquiss-,* stem of *relinquir* <L *relinquere* < *re-* back, from + *linquere* leave] —**re·lin′·quish·er** *n.* —**re·lin′quish·ment** *n.*

rel·i·quar·y (rel′ə·kwer′ē) *n. pl.* **·quar·ies** A casket, coffer, shrine, or other repository for relics. [<F *reliquaire* <L *reliquiae* remains. See RELIC.]

rel·ique (rel′ik, ri·lēk′) See RELIC.

re·liq·ui·ae (ri·lik′wi·ē) *n. pl. Latin* Fossil organisms; relics; organic remains.

rel·ish (rel′ish) *n.* **1** Appetite; appreciation; liking: a *relish* for excitement. **2** The flavor, especially when agreeable, in food and drink; figuratively, the quality in anything that lends spice or zest: Danger gives *relish* to adventure. **3** A slight savory dish served to stimulate appetite; also, something taken with food to lend it flavor or zest; a condiment. **4** An admixture or a small but important characteristic; flavoring: no *relish* of nature in his

poetry. — *v.t.* 1 To like the taste or savor of; enjoy: to *relish* a dinner or a joke. 2 To give pleasant flavor to. — *v.i.* 3 To have an agreeable flavor; afford gratification. See synonyms under LIKE. [ME *reles* <OF *reles,* var. of *relais* remainder < *relaisser* leave behind. See RELEASE.] — **rel'ish·a·ble** *adj.*
Synonyms (noun): appetite, appreciation, fondness, gusto, inclination, partiality, predilection, taste, zest. See APPETITE, SAVOR. *Antonyms*: antipathy, aversion, disgust, dislike, distaste, loathing, repugnance.

re·lo·cate (rē·lō'kāt) *v.t.* & *v.i.* **·cat·ed, ·cat·ing** To locate again or anew.

re·lu·cent (ri·lo͞o'sənt) *adj.* Shining back; reflecting light; gleaming. [<L *relucens, -entis,* ppr. of *relucere* < *re-* back + *lucere* shine. See LUCENT.]

re·luct (ri·lukt') *v.i.* 1 To show reluctance; hesitate. 2 To rebel; make opposition. [<L *reluctari.* See RELUCTANT.]

re·luc·tance (ri·luk'təns) *n.* 1 The state of being reluctant; unwillingness. 2 *Electr.* Capacity for opposing magnetic induction: the reciprocal of *permeance.* 3 *Obs.* Resistance; opposition. Also **re·luc'tan·cy.** [<RELUCTANT]

re·luc·tant (ri·luk'tənt) *adj.* 1 Disinclined to yield to some requirement; unwilling. 2 Marked by unwillingness or rendered unwillingly. 3 *Obs.* Struggling; offering opposition. [<L *reluctans, -antis,* ppr. of *reluctari* fight back < *re-* back + *luctari* fight] — **re·luc'tant·ly** *adv.*
Synonyms: averse, backward, disinclined, indisposed, loath, opposed, slow, unwilling. *Reluctant* signifies struggling against what one is urged or impelled to do, or is actually doing; *averse* signifies turned away as with dislike or repugnance; *loath* signifies having a repugnance, disgust, or loathing for, but the adjective *loath* is not so strong as the verb *loathe.* A man may be *slow* or *backward* in entering upon that to which he is by no means *averse.* A man is *loath* to believe evil of his friend, *reluctant* to speak of it, absolutely *unwilling* to use it to his injury. A legislator may be *opposed* to a certain measure, while not *averse* to what it aims to accomplish. Compare ANTIPATHY. *Antonyms*: desirous, disposed, eager, favorable, inclined, willing.

rel·uc·tiv·i·ty (rel'ək·tiv'ə·tē) *n. Electr.* The specific electrical reluctance, or the resistance to magnetization of a given substance per unit of length or cross-section: the reciprocal of *permeability.*

re·lume (ri·lo͞om') *v.t.* **·lumed, ·lum·ing** 1 To light again; rekindle. 2 To illuminate again. Also **re·lu·mine** (ri·lo͞o'min). [<RE- + (IL)LUME]

re·ly (ri·lī') *v.i.* **·lied, ·ly·ing** To place trust or confidence: with *on* or *upon.* See synonyms under LEAN[1]. [<OF *relier* bind (together), adhere to <L *religare* < *re-* again + *ligare* bind]

rem (rem) *n. Physics* That dose of absorbed ionizing radiation which has the same biological effect as one roentgen of high-voltage X-ray radiation. [<R(OENTGEN) + E(QUIVALENT) + M(AN)]

REM (rem) *n.* See REM SLEEP. [Acronym formed from *rapid eye movement*]

Re·ma·gen (rā'mä·gən) A town on the Rhine in northern Rhineland-Palatinate, West Germany.

re·main (ri·mān') *v.i.* 1 To stay or be left behind after the removal, departure, or destruction of other persons or things. 2 To continue in one place, condition, or character: He *remained* in office. 3 To be left as something to be done, dealt with, etc.: It *remains* to be proved. 4 To endure or last; abide. See synonyms under ABIDE, PERSIST, STAND. [<OF *remaindre* <L *remanere* < *re-* back + *manere* stay, remain]

re·main·der (ri·mān'dər) *n.* 1 That which remains; something left after a subtraction, expenditure, or passing over of a part; a residue; remnant. 2 *Math.* **a** That which is left after the subtraction of one quantity from another. **b** In division, the excess of the dividend over the product of the divisor by the integral part of the quotient. 3 *Law* An estate in expectancy, but not in actual possession and enjoyment; that remnant or residue of interest which, on the creation of a particular prior estate, is by the same instrument limited to another to be enjoyed on the termination of that estate. 4 In philately, an obsolete issue of stamps, demonetized by the government and sold at a large discount, generally to dealers. 5 A copy or part of an edition of a book remaining with a publisher after sales have ceased. — *adj.* Left over; remaining. — *v.t.* To sell as a remainder (def. 5). [<AF <OF *remaindre* REMAIN]

re·mains (ri·mānz') *n. pl.* 1 That which is left after a part has been removed or destroyed; remnants. 2 The body of a deceased person; a corpse. 3 Writings of an author published after his death. 4 Survivals of the past, as fossils, monuments, etc.: the *remains* of ancient Troy. See synonyms under BODY.

re·make (rē·māk') *v.t.* **·made, ·mak·ing** To make again or in a different form: to *remake* a silent film. — *n.* (rē'māk) Something that is remade, especially a motion picture.

re·man (rē·man') *v.t.* **·manned, ·man·ning** 1 To furnish with a fresh complement of men. 2 To instil courage or manliness into.

re·mand (ri·mand', -mänd') *v.t.* 1 To order or send back: to *remand* a soldier to his post. 2 *Law* **a** To recommit to custody, as an accused person after a preliminary examination. **b** To send back to a lower court, as a case improperly brought before the court so ordering. — *n.* 1 Recommittal, as of an accused person to custody; also, the recommitted person. 2 A judicial order of recommittal. [< OF *remander* <LL *remandare* <L *re-* back + *mandare* order] — **re·mand'ment** *n.*

rem·a·nence (rem'ə·nəns) *n.* 1 The state or quality of remaining; permanence; also, the remainder. 2 *Electr.* That part of magnetic induction remaining in a material after the removal of an applied magnetomotive force. [<L *remanens, -entis,* ppr. of *remanere* remain] — **rem'a·nent** *adj.*

re·mark (ri·märk') *n.* 1 A comment or saying, oral or written; a casual observation; also, conversational speech in general: I enjoyed his *remarks.* 2 The act of observing or noticing; observation; notice. 3 Remarque. — *v.t.* 1 To say or write by way of comment. 2 To take particular notice of. 3 *Obs.* To mark; distinguish. — *v.i.* 4 To make remarks: with *on* or *upon.* [<F *remarque* observation < *remarquer* notice < *re-* again + *marquer* mark. See MARK.] — **re·mark'er** *n.*
Synonyms (noun): annotation, comment, note, observation, utterance. A *comment* is an explanatory or critical *remark,* as upon some passage in a literary work or some act or speech in common life. A *note* is something to call attention, hence a brief written statement; in correspondence, a *note* is briefer than a letter. *Annotations* are especially brief *notes,* commonly marginal, and closely following the text. *Comments, observations,* or *remarks* may be oral or written, *comments* being oftenest written, and *remarks* oftenest oral. An *observation* is properly the result of fixed attention and reflection; a *remark* may be the suggestion of the instant.

re·mark·a·ble (ri·mär'kə·bəl) *adj.* Worthy of special notice; hence, extraordinary; unusual; conspicuous; distinguished. See synonyms under EMINENT, RARE, EXTRAORDINARY. — **re·mark'a·ble·ness** *n.* — **re·mark'a·bly** *adv.*

re·marque (ri·märk') *n.* 1 A small engraved picture or other distinguishing mark on an engraved plate, appearing on the engraved surface or in the margin, to indicate a stage in its progress before completion. 2 A print bearing such a mark. [<F]

Re·marque (rə·märk'), **Erich Maria,** 1897–1970, U.S. novelist born in Germany: real name *Erich Paul Kramer.*

re·mar·ry (rē·mar'ē) *v.t.* & *v.i.* **·ried, ·ry·ing** To marry again. — **re·mar'riage** (-mar'ij) *n.*

Rem·brandt (rem'brant, *Du.* rem'bränt), 1606–1669, Dutch painter and etcher: full name *Rembrandt Harmenszoon van Rijn* or *van Ryn.*

re·me·di·a·ble (ri·mē'dē·ə·bəl) *adj.* Capable of being cured or remedied. [<F *remédiable*] — **re·me'di·a·bly** *adv.*

re·me·di·al (ri·mē'dē·əl) *adj.* Of the nature of or adapted to be used as a remedy. [<L *remedialis*] — **re·me'di·al·ly** *adv.*

rem·e·di·less (rem'ə·dē·lis) *adj.* Without remedy; incurable; irreparable.

rem·e·dy (rem'ə·dē) *v.t.* **·died, ·dy·ing** 1 To cure or heal, as by medicinal treatment. 2 To make right; repair; correct. 3 To overcome or remove (an evil or defect). — *n. pl.* **·dies** 1 That which cures or affords relief to bodily disease or ailment; a medicine; also, remedial treatment. 2 A means of counteracting or removing evil; relief. 3 *Law* A legal mode for enforcing a right or redressing or preventing a wrong. 4 Tolerance (def. 5). [<AF <L *remedium* < *re-* thoroughly + *mederi* heal, restore]

re·mem·ber (ri·mem'bər) *v.t.* 1 To bring back or present again to the mind or memory; recall; recollect. 2 To keep in mind carefully, as for a purpose. 3 To bear in mind with affection, respect, awe, etc. 4 To bear in mind as worthy of a reward, gift, etc.: She *remembered* me in her will. 5 To reward; tip: *Remember* the steward. 6 *Obs.* To remind. — *v.i.* 7 To have or use one's memory. — **to remember (one) to** To inform a person of the regard of: *Remember* me *to* your wife. [<OF *remembrer* <LL *rememorari* <L *re-* again + *memorare* bring to mind < *memor* mindful] — **re·mem'ber·er** *n.*
Synonyms: recall, recollect, retain. Compare synonyms for MEMORY. *Antonyms*: forget, overlook.

re·mem·brance (ri·mem'brəns) *n.* 1 The act or power of remembering; the state of being remembered; memory. 2 The period within which one can remember. 3 That which is remembered; a reminiscence. 4 A memento; keepsake; also, a token or message of friendship: often in the plural. 5 Mindful regard. See synonyms under MEMORY.

re·mem·branc·er (ri·mem'brən·sər) *n.* 1 One who or that which causes one to remember; a reminder. 2 One of the recording officers of the Exchequer in England, as the **King's** or **Queen's remembrancer,** responsible for collecting debts due to the sovereign: since 1873, an officer of the Supreme Court.

re·mex (rē'meks) *n. pl.* **rem·i·ges** (rem'ə·jēz) *Ornithol.* One of the large quill feathers of a bird's wing: usually in the plural. [<L, oarsman < *remus* oar] — **re·mig·i·al** (ri·mij'ē·əl) *adj.*

re·mind (ri·mīnd') *v.t.* To bring to (someone's) mind; cause to remember. See synonyms under ADMONISH. [<RE- + MIND] — **re·mind'er** *n.*

re·mind·ful (ri·mīnd'fəl) *adj.* 1 Tending to remind; serving as a reminder: said of things. 2 Mindful: said of persons.

Rem·ing·ton (rem'ing·tən), **Frederic,** 1861–1909, U.S. painter and sculptor. — **Philo,** 1816–89, U.S. inventor and gunsmith.

rem·i·nisce (rem'ə·nis') *v.i.* **·nisced, ·nisc·ing** To recall incidents or events of the past; indulge in reminiscences. [Back formation < REMINISCENT]

rem·i·nis·cence (rem'ə·nis'əns) *n.* 1 The recalling to mind of past incidents and events; also, the narration of past experiences. 2 The act or power of reproducing past cognitions in consciousness. 3 An expression, fact, or feature serving as a reminder of something else. See synonyms under MEMORY. [<F]

rem·i·nis·cent (rem'ə·nis'ənt) *adj.* 1 Of the nature of or possessing reminiscence; also, recalling or dwelling upon the past; remembering. 2 Inducing a reminiscence of a person or thing; suggestive. [<L *reminiscens, -entis,* ppr. of *reminisci* recollect < *re-* again + *memini* remember] — **rem'i·nis'cent·ly** *adv.*

re·mise (ri·mīz') *Law v.t.* **·mised, ·mis·ing** To give; surrender; release; relinquish: used in conveyancing. — *n.* The act of remising. [<F, fem. of *remis,* pp. of *remettre* <L *remittere* send back. See REMIT.]

re·miss (ri·mis') *adj.* Slack or careless in matters requiring attention; dilatory; negligent; hence, lacking in earnestness or energy. See synonyms under INATTENTIVE. [<L *remissus,* pp. of *remittere* send back, slacken. See REMIT.] — **re·miss'ness** *n.*

re·mis·si·ble (ri·mis'ə·bəl) *adj.* Capable of being remitted or pardoned, as sins. [<F *rémissible*] — **re·mis'si·bil'i·ty** *n.*

re·mis·sion (ri·mish'ən) *n.* 1 The act of remitting, or the state of being remitted; specifically, discharge from penalty; pardon; deliverance, as from a debt or obligation.

2 Abatement, as of a fine erroneously imposed. 3 Relaxation, as from work or study. 4 Temporary abatement of a disease or of pain. 5 The act of sending a remittance. [<OF <L *remissio, -onis*]

re·mit (ri·mit′) *v.* **·mit·ted, ·mit·ting** *v.t.* **1** To send, as money in payment for goods; transmit. **2** To refrain from exacting or inflicting, as a penalty. **3** To pardon; forgive, as a sin or crime. **4** To abate; relax, as vigilance. **5** To restore; replace. **6** To put off; postpone. **7** To refer or submit for judgment, settlement, etc., as to one in authority. **8** *Law* To refer (a legal proceeding) to a lower court for further consideration. **9** *Rare* To send back, as to prison. **10** *Obs.* To resign; renounce. **11** *Obs.* To free; release. — *v.i.* **12** To send money, as in payment. **13** To diminish; abate. — *n.* The act of remitting; specifically, the sending of a legal cause from one tribunal to another. [<L *remittere* send back < *re-* back + *mittere* send] — **re·mit′ta·ble** *adj.* — **re·mit′ter** or **re·mit′tor** *n.*

re·mit·tal (ri·mit′l) *n.* Remission.

re·mit·tance (ri·mit′ns) *n.* The act of transmitting money or credit; also, that which is remitted, as money.

remittance man A ne'er-do-well living outside his home country on money transmitted at regular intervals by friends or relatives: originally applied to British persons living in the colonies or in the western United States.

re·mit·tent (ri·mit′nt) *adj.* **1** Having remissions. **2** Having partial, irregular, or temporary diminutions of energy or action: a *remittent* fever or geyser. — *n.* A remittent fever. [<L *remittens, -entis,* ppr. of *remittere.* See REMIT.]

remittent fever *Pathol.* A form of malaria in which the fever fluctuates daily but does not entirely disappear.

rem·nant (rem′nənt) *n.* **1** That which remains of anything; specifically, the piece of cloth, silk, etc., left over after the last cutting. **2** A remaining trace or survival of anything, suggestive of former condition, use, or belief. **3** A small piece or quantity. **4** A small remaining number of people. See synonyms under TRACE[1]. — *adj.* Remaining. [<OF *remenant,* ppr. of *remaindre.* See REMAIN.]

re·mod·el (rē·mod′l) *v.t.* **·eled** or **·elled, ·el·ing** or **·el·ling** **1** To model again. **2** To make over or anew.

re·mon·e·tize (ri·mon′ə·tīz) *v.t.* **·tized, ·tiz·ing** To reinstate, especially silver, as lawful money. [<RE- again + L *moneta* money + -IZE] — **re·mon′e·ti·za′tion** *n.*

re·mon·strance (ri·mon′strəns) *n.* **1** The act of remonstrating; protest; expostulation. **2** Expostulatory counsel or reproof. [<OF]

Re·mon·strance (ri·mon′strəns) *n.* The document formulating the five points of Arminian dissent from strict Calvinism, presented to the states of Holland and Friesland in 1610 and condemned by the synod of Dort in 1619. — **the Grand Remonstrance** A document presented by Parliament to King Charles I of England, Nov. 22, 1641, protesting against his misgovernment. — **Re·mon′strant** *n.*

re·mon·strant (ri·mon′strənt) *adj.* Having the character or tendency of a remonstrance; expostulatory. — *n.* One who presents or signs a remonstrance. [<Med. L *remonstrans, -antis,* ppr. of *remonstrare.* See REMONSTRATE.]

re·mon·strate (ri·mon′strāt) *v.* **·strat·ed, ·strat·ing** *v.t.* **1** To say or plead in protest or opposition. **2** *Obs.* To point out; demonstrate. — *v.i.* **3** To urge strong reasons against any course or action; protest; object. [<Med. L *remonstratus,* pp. of *remonstrare* demonstrate <L *re-* again + *monstrare* show] — **re·mon·stra·tion** (rē′mon·strā′shən, rem′ən-) *n.* — **re·mon′·stra·tive** (-strə·tiv) *adj.* — **re·mon′stra·tor** (strā·tər) *n.*

re·mon·ta (rā·mōn′tä) *n. SW U.S.* A group of saddle horses. [<Sp.]

re·mon·tant (ri·mon′tənt) *adj. Bot.* Ascending again: said of roses that bloom more than once in a season. — *n.* A remontant rose. [<F, ppr. of *remonter.* See REMOUNT.]

rem·on·toir (rem′ən·twär′, *Fr.* rə·môn·twär′) *n. Mech.* An apparatus that utilizes force from the train of a clock to give new impulse to the escape wheel at certain intervals, usually once in 30 seconds. [<F]

rem·o·ra (rem′ər·ə) *n.* **1** Any of a genus *(Remora)* of fish (family *Echeneididae*) having on its head an oval suctorial disk by means of which it attaches itself to sharks, other fishes, or floating objects, being thus carried great distances. **2** Any delay or impediment. [<L, hindrance < *re-* back + *mora* delay]

re·morse (ri·môrs′) *n.* **1** The keen or hopeless anguish caused by a sense of guilt; compunction; distressing self-reproach. **2** *Obs.* Compassion; pity. See synonyms under REPENTANCE. [<OF *remors* <LL *remorsus* a biting back <L *remordere* keep biting < *re-* again + *mordere* bite] — **re·morse′ful** *adj.* — **re·morse′ful·ly** *adv.* — **re·morse′ful·ness** *n.*

re·morse·less (ri·môrs′lis) *adj.* Having no compassion; pitiless; cruel. — **re·morse′less·ly** *adv.* — **re·morse′less·ness** *n.*

re·mote (ri·mōt′) *adj.* **1** Located far from a specified place or some place regarded as a point of reference: *remote* regions. **2** Removed far from present time; distant in time: the *remote* future. **3** Having slight relation or connection; separated; foreign; distant in relation: a *remote* cause, *remote* kinship. **4** Not obvious; inconsiderable; slight: a *remote* likeness or analogy. **5** Abstracted; absent-minded; hence, aloof. — *n.* A television or radio broadcast made from a mobile camera or microphone operated at a distance from the station, and sent to the transmitter by cable or through relay towers. See synonyms under ALIEN. [<L *remotus,* pp. of *removere* remove < *re-* again + *movere* move] — **re·mote′ly** *adv.* — **re·mote′ness** *n.*

remote control Control from a distance, as of a machine, apparatus, aircraft, guided missile, etc., by electrical or radio circuits.

re·mo·tion (ri·mō′shən) *n.* **1** The act of removing; removal. **2** *Obs.* Departure. [<OF]

ré·mou·lade (rā′mə·läd′, *Fr.* rā·mōō·làd′) *n.* A sharp sauce made of hard-boiled egg yolks, oil, vinegar, and seasoning. [<F <Ital. *remolata,* lit., vigorously stirred]

re·mount (rē·mount′) *v.t.* & *v.i.* To mount again or anew. — *n.* (rē′mount′) **1** A new setting or framing. **2** A fresh riding horse. [<OF *remonter*]

re·mov·a·ble (ri·mōō′və·bəl) *adj.* Capable of being removed; movable; also, capable of being displaced, dismissed, or obliterated: *removable* walls, officials, or stains. — **re·mov′·a·bil′i·ty** *n.* — **re·mov′a·bly** *adv.*

re·mov·al (ri·mōō′vəl) *n.* **1** The act of removing or the state of being removed. **2** Dismissal, as from office. **3** Changing of place, especially of habitation.

re·move (ri·mōōv′) *v.* **·moved, ·mov·ing** *v.t.* **1** To take or move away or from one place to another. **2** To take off; doff, as a hat. **3** To get rid of; do away with: to *remove* abuses. **4** To kill; assassinate. **5** To displace or dismiss, as from office. **6** To take out; extract: with *from.* — *v.i.* **7** To change one's place of residence or business; move. **8** *Poetic* To go away; depart. See synonyms under ABOLISH, ABSTRACT, ALLEVIATE, CANCEL, CARRY, CONVEY, DISPLACE, EXTERMINATE, SEPARATE. — *n.* **1** A removal; a move; the act of removing, as one's business or belongings. **2** The space moved over in changing an object from one position to another; hence, a degree of difference; step; interval: He is only one *remove* from a fool. **3** *Brit.* A dish or course at dinner removed to give place to another. **4** *Obs.* A period of absence. [<OF *remouvoir* <L *removere* < *re-* again + *movere* move] — **re·mov′er** *n.*

re·moved (ri·mōōvd′) *adj.* **1** Separated, as by intervening space, time, or relationship, or by difference in kind: a cousin twice *removed.* **2** Taken away; transferred.

Rem·scheid (rem′shīt) An industrial city in North Rhine-Westphalia, West Germany.

Rem·sen (rem′sən), **Ira,** 1846–1927, U.S. chemist and educator.

REM sleep A recurrent stage of normal sleep characterized by distinctive patterns of brain waves, rapid movement of the eyes under closed lids, and dreaming: also called *paradoxical sleep.*

re·mu·da (rā·mōō′dä) *n. SW U.S.* The extra mounts or saddle horses of each cowboy herded together, usually a herd of 90 to 100 geldings for an outfit of eight to ten men: called a *saddle band* in the Northwest. [<Sp., lit., exchange < *remudar* replace]

re·mu·ner·ate (ri·myōō′nə·rāt) *v.t.* **·at·ed, ·at·ing** To make just or adequate return to or for; compensate; pay or pay for; reward. See synonyms under PAY, REQUITE. [<L *remuneratus,* pp. of *remunerari* < *re-* again + *munus, muneris* gift] — **re·mu′ner·a·bil′i·ty** *n.* — **re·mu′ner·a·ble** *adj.*

re·mu·ner·a·tion (ri·myōō′nə·rā′shən) *n.* **1** The act or fact of remunerating. **2** That which remunerates; pay; compensation; recompense. See synonyms under RECOMPENSE, RESTITUTION, SALARY.

re·mu·ner·a·tive (ri·myōō′nə·rā′tiv, -nər·ə·tiv) *adj.* **1** Profitable; lucrative. **2** Serving to pay or remunerate: *remunerative* justice. — **re·mu′·ner·a′tive·ly** *adv.* — **re·mu′ner·a′tive·ness** *n.*

Re·mus (rē′məs) In Roman mythology, the twin brother of Romulus, by whom he was killed.

Remus (rē′məs), **Uncle** See UNCLE REMUS.

ren- Var. of RENI-.

ren·ais·sance (ren′ə·säns′, -zäns′, ri·nā′səns; *Fr.* rə·ne·säṅs′) *n.* A new birth; resurrection; renascence. [<F < *renaître* be reborn < *re-* again + L *natus,* pp. of *nasci* be born]

Ren·ais·sance (ren′ə·säns′, -zäns′, ri·nā′səns; *Fr.* rə·ne·säṅs′) *n.* **1** The revival of letters and art in Europe, marking the transition from medieval to modern history: it began in Italy in the 14th century and gradually spread to other countries. **2** The period of this revival, from the 14th to the 16th century; also, the style of art, literature, etc., marked by a classical influence, that was developed in and characteristic of this period. Also *Renascence.* — *adj.* Of or characteristic of the Renaissance.

Renaissance architecture A style of building and decoration that followed the medieval, originating in Italy in the 15th century, and based on the classic Roman style.

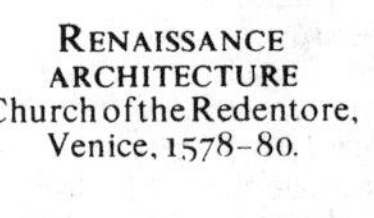

RENAISSANCE ARCHITECTURE
Church of the Redentore, Venice, 1578–80.

re·nal (rē′nəl) *adj. Med.* Of, pertaining to, affecting, or situated near the kidneys. [<F *rénal* <L *renalis* < *renes* kidneys]

renal capsule or **gland** The suprarenal gland.

Re·nan (rə·näṅ′), **Joseph Ernest,** 1823–1892, French historian, philologist, and critic.

Ren·ard (ren′ərd) See REYNARD.

re·nas·cence (ri·nas′·əns) *n.* Rebirth; new birth or life; a renaissance; a revival. [<L *renascens, -entis,* ppr. of *renasci* < *re-* again + *nasci* be born] — **re·nas′cent** *adj.*

Re·nas·cence (ri·nas′əns) *n.* The Renaissance.

Re·naud (rə·nō′) French form of REGINALD.

ren·con·tre (ren·kon′tər, *Fr.* räṅ·kôṅ′tr′) *n. French* A rencounter.

ren·coun·ter (ren·koun′tər) *n.* **1** *Obs.* A sudden hostile collision, as with an enemy. **2** An unexpected encounter, as of travelers. **3** A contest or debate. — *v.t.* & *v.i. Obs.* To meet unexpectedly or by surprise. [<F *rencontrer.* See RE- and ENCOUNTER.]

rend (rend) *v.* **rent** or **rend·ed, rend·ing** *v.t.* **1** To tear apart forcibly; split; break. **2** To pull or remove forcibly: with *away, from, off,* etc. **3** To pass through (the air) violently and noisily. **4** To distress (the heart, etc.), as with grief or despair. — *v.i.* **5** To split; part. [OE *rendan* tear, cut down] — **rend′er** *n.*

Synonyms: break, burst, cleave, lacerate, mangle, rip, rive, rupture, sever, slit, sunder, tear. *Rend* and *tear* are applied usually to the sundering of textile substances, *tear* being the milder, *rend* the stronger word. To *rip,* as applied to articles made by sewing or stitching, is to divide along the line of a seam by cutting or breaking the stitches. *Rive* is a woodworkers' word for parting wood in the way of the grain without a clean cut, as by splitting. To *lacerate* is to *tear* roughly the flesh or animal tissue, as by the teeth of a wild beast. *Mangle* is a stronger word than *lacerate*; *lacerate* is more superficial, *mangle* more complete. To *burst* or *rupture* is to tear or rend by force from within, *burst* denoting the greater violence; as, to *burst* a gun; to *rupture* a blood vessel. Compare BREAK. *Antonyms*: heal, join, mend, reunite, secure, stitch, unite, weld.

ren·der (ren′dər) *v.t.* **1** To give, present, or submit for action, approval, payment, etc. **2** To provide or furnish; give: to *render* aid to the poor. **3** To give as due: to *render* obedience. **4** To perform; do: to *render* great service. **5** To give or state formally: to *render* judgment. **6** To give by way of requital or retribution: to *render* double for one's sins. **7** To represent or depict, as in music or painting. **8** To cause to be or become: to *render* a ship seaworthy. **9** To express in another language; translate. **10** To melt and clarify, as lard. **11** To give back; return: often with *back.* **12** To surrender; give up: to *render* a fortress. See synonyms under INTERPRET. —*n.* **1** A payment, specifically of rent, made to a superior. **2** A coat of plaster applied without intervening lathing. [<F *rendre* <L *reddere* give back < *re-* back + *dare* give] —**ren′der·a·ble** *adj.* —**ren′der·er** *n.*

ren·dez·vous (rän′dā·vōō, -də-; *Fr.* räṅ·de·vōō′) *n. pl.* **·vous** (-vōōz, *Fr.* -vōō′) **1** An appointed place of meeting. **2** A meeting or an appointment to meet. **3** A base for naval ships or for military units. **4** *Obs.* A resort; refuge. —*v.t.* & *v.i.* **·voused** (-vōōd), **·vous·ing** (-vōō′ing) To assemble or cause to assemble at a certain place or time. [<F *rendez-vous,* lit., betake yourself < *se rendre* betake oneself]

ren·di·tion (ren·dish′ən) *n.* **1** A translation; the interpretation of a text. **2** Artistic, dramatic, or musical interpretation; also, the performance or execution of a dramatic or musical composition. **3** A surrendering, especially of a person. **4** The act of rendering, or the amount rendered. [< obs. F < *rendre* render]

Ren·do·va (ren·dō′və) An island in the New Georgia group of the Solomon Islands; of volcanic origin; 75 square miles.

Re·né (rə·nā′, *Fr.* rə·nā′) A masculine personal name. [<F, reborn] —**Re·née** (rə·nā′) *fem.*

ren·e·gade (ren′ə·gād) *n.* **1** An apostate. **2** A traitor; deserter. Also **ren′e·ga′do** (-gā′dō). —*adj.* Traitorous. [<Sp. *renegado,* pp. of *renegar* deny <Med. L *renegare* <L *re-* again and again + *negare* deny]

re·nege (ri·nig′, -neg′, -nēg′) *v.i.* **·neged, ·neg·ing 1** In card games, to fail to follow suit when able to do so. See REVOKE. **2** *Colloq.* To fail to fulfil a promise. **3** *Obs.* To renounce; deny. Also **re·nig′.** [<Med. L *renegare.* See RENEGADE.] —**re·neg′er** *n.*

re·new (ri·nōō′, -nyōō′) *v.t.* **1** To make new or as if new again; restore to a former or sound condition. **2** To begin again; resume: to *renew* an argument. **3** To repeat: to *renew* an oath of loyalty. **4** To acquire again; regain (vigor, strength, etc.). **5** To cause to continue in effect; extend: to *renew* a subscription. **6** To revive; reestablish. **7** To replenish or replace, as provisions. —*v.i.* **8** To become new again. **9** To begin or commence again. See synonyms under RECLAIM. [<RE- again + NEW] —**re·new′a·ble** *adj.*

re·new·al (ri·nōō′əl -nyōō′-) *n.* The act of renewing, or the state of being renewed.

re·newed (ri·nōōd′, -nyōōd′) *adj.* Made new; restored; revived; repeated. See synonyms under FRESH. —**re·new·ed·ly** (ri·nōō′id·lē, -nyōō′-) *adv.*

Renewed Church of the United Brethren See MORAVIAN.

Ren·frew (ren′frōō) A county in SW Scotland; 240 square miles; county town, Renfrew. Also **Ren′frew·shire** (-shir).

Re·ni (rā′nē), **Guido,** 1575–1642, Italian painter.

reni- *combining form* Kidney; of or related to the kidneys: *reniform*: also, before vowels, *ren-*. Also **reno-**. [<L *ren, renis* a kidney]

ren·i·form (ren′ə·fôrm, rē′nə-) *adj.* Kidney-shaped. [<RENI- + -FORM]

ren·in (ren′in) *n. Biochem.* A protein substance secreted by an ischemic kidney or blood vessel and supposed to be responsible for a rise in blood pressure. [<L *ren* kidney]

re·ni·tent (ri·nī′tənt, ren′ə·tənt) *adj.* Offering resistance to any influence or force; continuously reluctant; recalcitrant; specifically, presenting elastic resistance to pressure. [<L *renitens, -entis,* ppr. of *reniti* resist < *re-* back + *niti* struggle] —**re·ni′tence, re·ni′ten·cy** *n.*

Rennes (ren) A city in NW central France; the intellectual center of Brittany.

ren·net (ren′it) *n.* **1** The dried stomach of certain young hoofed animals, especially the mucous membrane lining the fourth stomach of a suckling calf or sheep, which is capable of curdling milk. **2** Anything used to curdle milk. **3** An aqueous or vinous infusion of animal rennet. **4** Rennin. [Alter. of ME *rennels* <OE *rinnan* run together, coagulate]

ren·nin (ren′in) *n. Biochem.* An enzyme present in rennet; the milk-curdling ferment: also called *chymosin.* [<RENN(ET) + -IN]

Re·no (rē′nō) A city in western Nevada.

Re·noir (rə·nwär′), **Pierre Auguste,** 1841–1919, French Impressionist painter.

re·nounce (ri·nouns′) *v.* **·nounced, ·nounc·ing** *v.t.* **1** To give up, especially by formal statement. **2** To disown; repudiate. **3** In card games, to indicate inability to follow (a suit led) by playing a card of another suit. —*v.i.* **4** In card games, to renounce the suit led. [<F *renoncer* <L *renuntiare* protest against, announce < *re-* back, against + *nuntiare* report < *nuntius* messenger] —**re·nounce′ment** *n.* —**re·nounc′er** *n.*

Synonyms: abandon, abjure, deny, disavow, discard, disclaim, disown, forswear, recall, recant, refuse, reject, repudiate, retract, revoke. *Abjure, discard, forswear, recall, recant, renounce, retract,* and *revoke,* like *abandon,* imply some previous connection. *Renounce* is to declare against and give up formally and definitively; as, to *renounce* the pomps and vanities of the world. *Retract* is to take back something that one has said as not true or as what one is not ready to maintain; as, to *retract* a charge or accusation; one *recants* his own opinions or beliefs. *Repudiate* is to put away with emphatic and determined repulsion; as, to *repudiate* a debt. To *deny* is to affirm to be not true or not binding; as, to *deny* a statement or relationship; or to refuse to grant, as a request or petition. To *discard* is to cast away as useless or worthless; thus, one *discards* a worn garment. *Revoke,* etymologically the equivalent of the English *recall,* is to take back something given or granted; as, to *revoke* a command, a will, or a grant; *recall* may be used in the exact sense of *revoke,* but is often applied to persons, as *revoke* is not; we *recall* a messenger and *revoke* an order. Compare ABANDON, ABDICATE, ABJURE, RECANT. *Antonyms*: acknowledge, advocate, assert, avow, cherish, claim, defend, hold, maintain, own, proclaim, retain, uphold, vindicate.

ren·o·vate (ren′ə·vāt) *v.t.* **·vat·ed, ·vat·ing 1** To make as good as new; repair. **2** To renew; refresh; reinvigorate. —*adj.* Renovated. [<L *renovatus,* pp. of *renovare* < *re-* again + *novare* make new < *novus* new] —**ren′o·va′tion** *n.* —**ren′o·va′tor** *n.*

re·nown (ri·noun′) *n.* **1** Exalted reputation; celebrity; the state of being widely known for great achievements or merits; fame. **2** *Obs.* Rumor; report. See synonyms under FAME. —*v.t. Obs.* To spread the fame of; render famous. [<OF *renon* < *renomer* name again, make famous <L *re-* again + *nominare* name < *nomen* a name]

re·nowned (ri·nound′) *adj.* Having renown; famous. See synonyms under ILLUSTRIOUS.

rens·se·laer·ite (ren′sə·lə·rīt′, ren′sə·lâr′īt) *n.* A light-colored variety of talc of such waxlike consistency that it may be worked on a lathe. [after Stephen Van *Rensselaer,* 1764–1839, U. S. soldier and politician]

rent[1] (rent) *n.* **1** Compensation made in any form by a tenant to a landlord or owner for the use of land, buildings, etc.; especially, such compensation paid in money at regular or specified intervals. **2** Similar payment for the use of any property, movable or fixed. **3** *Econ.* **a** Income derived by the owner from the use of his land or property. **b** The return afforded by cultivated land in excess of the costs, as of labor or materials. **c** That which is yielded by land in excess of the yield of the poorest land cultivated under equal conditions: also called **economic rent. d** Hence, a return derived from a similar advantage, as in a monopoly of natural resources. **4** *Obs.* **a** Landed or other property affording revenue. **b** Income or revenue. —**for rent** Available for use or occupancy by the paying of rent. —*v.t.* **1** To obtain the temporary possession and use of for a compensation, usually made at fixed intervals. **2** To grant the temporary possession and use of for a rent. —*v.i.* **3** To be let for rent. [<OF *rente* <LL *rendita,* L *reddita* what is given back or paid, fem. of pp. of *reddere.* See RENDER.] —**rent′a·ble** *adj.*

rent[2] (rent) Alternative past tense and past participle of REND. —*n.* **1** A hole or slit made by rending or tearing; tear; rip; fissure. **2** A schism; violent separation; split. See synonyms under BREACH, HOLE. [<REND]

rent·al (ren′təl) *n.* **1** The revenue derived from rented property. **2** A schedule of rents. —*adj.* Of or pertaining to rent. [<AF]

rente (räṅt) *n. French* **1** *pl.* The bonds and other securities representing the government indebtedness of France; also, the sums paid as interest on this indebtedness: also **rentes sur l'É·tat** (räṅt sür lā·tà′). **2** Income or revenue in general; annuity.

rent·er (ren′tər) *n.* One who rents; specifically, one who rents an estate or tenement; a tenant.

ren·tier (räṅ·tyā′) *n. French* One who owns, or derives a fixed income from, invested capital or lands.

re·nun·ci·a·tion (ri·nun′sē·ā′shən, -shē-) *n.* **1** The act of renouncing or disclaiming; repudiation. **2** A declaration, statement, or formula in which something is renounced. [<L *renunciatio, -onis* a proclamation] —**re·nun′ci·a′tive** *adj.* —**re·nun·ci·a·to·ry** (ri·nun′sē·ə·tôr′ē, -tō′·rē-, -shē-) *adj.*

re·o·pen (rē·ō′pən) *v.t.* & *v.i.* **1** To open again. **2** To begin again; resume.

re·or·gan·i·za·tion (rē′ôr·gən·ə·zā′shən, -ī·zā′-) *n.* **1** The act of reorganizing, or the condition of being reorganized. **2** The legal reconstruction of a corporation, usually after or to avert a failure.

re·or·gan·ize (rē·ôr′gən·īz) *v.t.* & *v.i.* **·ized, ·iz·ing** To organize anew. —**re·or′gan·iz′er** *n.*

re·o·ri·ent (rē·ôr′ē·ənt, -ō′rē-) *adj. Rare* Rising again. [See ORIENT]

rep[1] (rep) *n.* A silk, cotton, rayon, or wool fabric having a distinctive crosswise rib: also spelled *repp.* [<F *reps* <E *ribs*]

rep[2] (rep) *n. Slang* Reputation.

rep[3] (rep) *n. Slang* A representative.

rep[4] (rep) *n. Physics* **1** A unit of absorbed nuclear radiation equivalent to the release of from 83 to 97 ergs per gram of absorbing material. **2** The rad. [<R(OENTGEN) + E(QUIVALENT) + P(HYSICAL)]

re·pair[1] (ri·pâr′) *v.t.* **1** To restore to sound or good condition after damage, injury, decay, etc.; mend. **2** To make amends for (an injury); remedy. **3** To make up, as a loss; compensate for. See synonyms under AMEND, RECRUIT. —*n.* **1** Restoration, as after decay, waste, injury, etc.; reparation. **2** Condition after use or after repairing: in good *repair.* [<OF *reparer* <L *reparare* < *re-* again + *parare* prepare, make ready] —**re·pair′er** *n.*

re·pair[2] (ri·pâr′) *v.i.* **1** To betake oneself; go: to *repair* to the garden. **2** To return. —*n.* **1** The act of repairing, or the place to which one repairs; a haunt. **2** *Scot.* A concourse of people to a certain spot. [<OF *repairer* <LL *repatriare* < *re-* again + *patria* native land]

re·pair·man (ri·pâr′man′, -mən) *n. pl.* **·men** (-men′, -mən) A man whose work is to make repairs.

re·pand (ri·pand′) *adj. Bot.* Having a wavy or uneven outline: said of leaves. [<L *repandus* bent back < *re-* back + *pandus,* pp. of *pandare* bend]

rep·a·ra·ble (rep′ər·ə·bəl) *adj.* Capable of repair or reparation. Also **re·pair·a·ble** (ri·pâr′·ə·bəl). [<F *réparable* <L *reparabilis*] —**rep′·a·ra·bil′i·ty** *n.* —**rep′a·ra·bly** *adv.*

rep·a·ra·tion (rep′ə·rā′shən) *n.* **1** The act of making amends; atonement; amends; indemnity; also, that which is done by way of amends or satisfaction. **2** The act of repairing or the state of being repaired. **3** *pl.* Repairs; specifically, indemnities paid by defeated countries for acts of war. See synonyms under RESTITUTION. [<L *reparatio,*

-onis a renewal] —**re·par·a·tive** (ri·par′ə·tiv) *adj.*

rep·ar·tee (rep′är·tē′, -ər-) *n.* **1** Conversation marked by quick and witty replies. **2** Skill or quickness in such conversation. **3** A witty or quick reply; a sharp rejoinder. See synonyms under ANSWER. [<F *repartie,* pp. of *repartir* depart again, reply < *re-* again + *partir* depart]

re·par·ti·tion (rē′pär·tish′ən) *n.* **1** Distribution; allotment. **2** Redistribution.

re·past (ri·past′, -päst′) *n.* **1** Food taken at a meal; hence, a meal. **2** Food in general; also, mealtime. [<OF *repas* <Med. L *repastum,* orig. pp. of LL *repascere* feed again <L *re-* again + *pascere* feed]

re·pa·ten·cy (ri·pāt′n·sē, -pat′n-) *n.* The reopening of a part or vessel that had been closed. [<RE- + L *patentia,* neut. pl. of *patens, patentis,* ppr. of *patere* be open]

re·pa·tri·ate (rē·pā′trē·āt) *v.t.* & *v.i.* **·at·ed, ·at·ing** To send back or return to his own country, as a soldier interned in a neutral territory; restore to citizenship. —*n.* (rē·pā′trē·it) A person who has been repatriated. [<LL *repatriatus,* pp. of *repatriare* <L *re-* again + *patria* native land] —**re·pa′tri·a′tion** *n.*

re·pay (ri·pā′) *v.* **·paid, ·pay·ing** *v.t.* **1** To pay back; refund. **2** To pay back or refund something to. **3** To make compensation or retaliation for; give a reward or inflict a penalty for. —*v.i.* **4** To make repayment or requital. See synonyms under REQUITE. [<OF *repaier*] —**re·pay′a·ble** *adj.* —**re·pay′ment** *n.*

re·peal (ri·pēl′) *v.t.* **1** To rescind, as a law; revoke. **2** *Obs.* To summon back, as from exile. See synonyms under ABOLISH, ANNUL, CANCEL. —*n.* **1** The act of repealing; revocation; rescission. **2** *Obs.* Recall, as from exile. [<OF *rapeler* recall < *re-* again + *appeler.* See APPEAL.] —**re·peal′a·ble** *adj.* —**re·peal′er** *n.*

re·peat (ri·pēt′) *v.t.* **1** To say again; reiterate: to *repeat* a question. **2** To recite from memory. **3** To say (what another has just said). **4** To tell, as a secret, to another. **5** To do, make, or experience again. —*v.i.* **6** *U.S.* To vote more than once at the same election: an offense punishable by law. —*n.* **1** The act of repeating; a repetition. **2** *Music* **a** A sign consisting of dots placed in the spaces at the left hand of a bar, to indicate that the preceding passage is to be repeated. **b** A repeated passage, song, refrain, etc. **3** Anything repeated, as a new supply of goods, or a renewed order for such supply. [<OF *repeter* <L *repetere* do or say again < *re-* again + *petere* seek]

re·peat·ed (ri·pē′tid) *adj.* Occurring or spoken again and again; reiterated. See synonyms under FREQUENT. —**re·peat′ed·ly** *adv.*

re·peat·er (ri·pē′tər) *n.* **1** One who or that which repeats. **2** A timepiece, especially a watch, which will strike again the hour last struck when a spring is pressed. **3** A repeating firearm. **4** An instrument for automatically retransmitting electromagnetic signals: a telegraph *repeater.* **5** *U.S.* One who votes, or attempts to vote, more than once at the same election. **6** One who has been repeatedly imprisoned for criminal offenses.

repeating decimal *Math.* **1** A decimal fraction in which one figure is repeated indefinitely. **2** A circulating decimal.

repeating firearm A gun, rifle, or pistol arranged to deliver several shots without reloading.

re·pêch·age (rə·pesh·äzh′) *n. French* Consolation race; a second heat to afford another chance to those running second best in preliminary heats.

re·pel (ri·pel′) *v.* **·pelled, ·pel·ling** *v.t.* **1** To force or drive back; repulse. **2** To reject; refuse, as a suggestion. **3** To cause to feel distaste or aversion: His manner *repels* me. **4** To refuse to mix with or adhere to: Mercury *repels* iron. **5** To push or keep away, especially with invisible force: Like magnetic poles *repel* each other: opposed to *attract.* —*v.i.* **6** To act so as to drive something back or away. **7** To cause distaste or aversion. [<L *repellere* < *re-* back + *pellere* drive] —**re·pel′ler** *n.*

Synonyms: check, oppose, repulse, resist. *Repulse* is stronger and more conclusive than *repel*; one may be *repelled* by the very aspect of the person whose favor he seeks, but is not *repulsed* except by a direct refusal of his suit. See DRIVE. *Antonyms*: accept, admit, encourage, entertain, favor, grant, welcome.

re·pel·lent (ri·pel′ənt) *adj.* **1** Serving, tending, or having power to repel. **2** Waterproof. **3** Repugnant. —*n.* **1** A waterproof cloth. **2** A remedial application that tends to repel fluids from a swollen part. **3** A chemical compound intended to be distasteful to insects and other vermin and to keep them at a distance. —**re·pel′len·cy, re·pel′lence** *n.*

re·pent[1] (ri·pent′) *v.i.* **1** To feel remorse or regret, as for something done or undone; be contrite. **2** To change one's mind concerning past action because of disappointment, failure, etc.: with *of*: He *repented* of his generosity to the old man. **3** *Theol.* To feel such sorrow for one's sins as to reform. —*v.t.* **4** To feel remorse or regret for (an action, sin, etc.). **5** To change one's mind concerning (a past action): He *repented* his decision. [<OF *repentir* <L *re-* again + *poenitere* cause to repent < *poena* punishment] —**re·pent′er** *n.*

re·pent[2] (rē′pənt) *adj.* **1** *Bot.* Lying flat and rooting, as certain plants; procumbent. **2** *Zool.* Reptant. [<L *repens, repentis,* ppr. of *repere* creep]

re·pen·tance (ri·pen′təns) *n.* A turning with sorrow from a past course or action; loosely, regret or contrition; also, the condition of being penitent.

Synonyms: compunction, contrition, penitence, regret, remorse, sorrow. *Regret* is *sorrow* for any painful or annoying matter. One is moved with *penitence* for wrongdoing. To speak of *regret* for a fault of our own marks it as slighter than one for which we should express *penitence. Repentance* is *sorrow* for sin with self-condemnation, and complete turning from the sin. *Compunction* is a momentary sting of conscience, in view either of a past or of a contemplated act. *Contrition* is a subduing *sorrow* for sin, as against the divine holiness and love. *Remorse* is, as its derivation indicates, a biting or gnawing back of guilt upon the heart. *Antonyms*: approval, comfort, complacency, content, hardness, impenitence, obduracy, obstinacy, recusancy, stubbornness.

re·pen·tant (ri·pen′tənt) *adj.* Showing, experiencing, or characterized by repentance. [<OF] —**re·pen′tant·ly** *adv.*

re·peo·ple (rē·pē′pəl) *v.t.* **·pled, ·pling** **1** To people anew. **2** To provide again with animals; restock.

re·per·cus·sion (rē′pər·kush′ən) *n.* **1** The act of driving or throwing back, or the state of being driven back; repulse; also, echo; reverberation. **2** A stroke or blow given in return; recoil after impact; hence, the indirect result of something; aftereffect: the *repercussions* of the peace treaty. **3** *Med.* The motion produced on a fetus by the process of ballottement. [<L *repercussio, -onis* < *repercussus,* pp. of *repercutere* rebound < *re-* again + *percutere* strike. See PERCUSS.]

re·per·cus·sive (rē′pər·kus′iv) *adj.* Causing, of the nature of, or produced by repercussion; reverberated.

rep·er·toire (rep′ər·twär, -twôr) *n.* A list of songs, plays, operas, or the like, that a person or company is prepared to perform; also, such pieces collectively. [<F <LL *repertorium.* See REPERTORY.]

rep·er·to·ry (rep′ər·tôr′ē, -tō′rē) *n. pl.* **·ries** **1** A place where things are gathered together, or the things so gathered; a repository; collection. **2** Repertoire. [<LL *repertorium* inventory <L < *repertus,* pp. of *reperire* find, discover < *re-* again + *parire* produce]

repertory company A theatrical group having a repertoire of productions, each typically running for a few weeks, and usually having some acting personnel continuing from one production to the next. Also **repertory theater.**

rep·e·tend (rep′ə·tend, rep′ə·tend′) *n.* **1** *Math.* That part of a circulating decimal which is repeated indefinitely. **2** Something repeated or to be repeated. [<L *repentendus* to be repeated, gerundive of *repetere.* See REPEAT.]

rep·e·ti·tion (rep′ə·tish′ən) *n.* **1** The act of repeating; the doing, making, or saying of something again; recital from memory. **2** *Music* The singing or playing of the same note, chord, or passage over again. **3** That which is repeated; a copy. [<F *répétition*]

rep·e·ti·tious (rep′ə·tish′əs) *adj.* Characterized by or containing useless or tedious repetition. —**rep′e·ti′tious·ly** *adv.* —**rep′e·ti′tious·ness** *n.*

re·pet·i·tive (ri·pet′ə·tiv) *adj.* Marked by repetition; recurrent. —**re·pet′i·tive·ly** *adv.*

re·pine (ri·pīn′) *v.i.* **·pined, ·pin·ing** To be discontented or fretful; complain; murmur. See synonyms under COMPLAIN. [<RE- + PINE[2]] —**re·pin′er** *n.* —**re·pin′ing** *n.*

re·place (ri·plās′) *v.t.* **·placed, ·plac·ing** **1** To put back in place. **2** To take or fill the place of; supersede. **3** To refund; repay. —**re·place′a·ble** *adj.* —**re·plac′er** *n.*

re·place·ment (ri·plās′mənt) *n.* **1** The act of replacing; also, that which takes the place of anything discarded or worn out. **2** *Mineral.* The formation of a new crystal face which obliterates an edge or angle. **3** A soldier available for assignment to fill a vacancy or a quota. **4** The act of putting a thing back in place. **5** *Chem.* A substitution. **6** A substitute.

re·play (rē·plā′) *v.t.* **1** To play again. **2** To show a replay of. —*n.* (rē′plā′) **1** The act of playing again. **2** The playing of a television tape, often in slow motion and usually immediately following the live occurrence of the action shown. **3** The action shown in such a replay.

re·plead·er (ri·plē′dər) *n. Law* **1** An order of court directing the parties to file new pleadings in order to present a better issue for trial. **2** The right of pleading again. [<RE- + obs. *pleader* a pleading in court]

re·plen·ish (ri·plen′ish) *v.t.* **1** To fill again, as something that has been wholly or partially emptied. **2** To bring back to fullness or completeness, as diminished supplies. **3** To repeople. [<OF *repleniss-,* stem of *replenir* < *re-* again + L *plenus* full] —**re·plen′ish·er** *n.* —**re·plen′ish·ment** *n.*

re·plete (ri·plēt′) *adj.* **1** Full to the uttermost. **2** Gorged with food or drink; sated. **3** Abundantly supplied or stocked; abounding. [<OF *replet* <L *repletus,* pp. of *replere* fill again < *re-* again + *plere* fill] —**re·ple′tion** *n.*

re·plev·in (ri·plev′in) *Law n.* **1** An action to regain possession of personal property unlawfully retained, on giving security to try the title and respond to the judgment; recovery of property by such action. **2** The judicial writ or process by which such proceedings are instituted. —*v.t.* To replevy. [<AF *replevine* <OF *replevir* warrant, pledge < *re-* back + *plevir* pledge <Gmc.]

re·plev·y (ri·plev′ē) *Law v.t.* **·plev·ied, ·plev·y·ing** **1** To recover possession of (chattels) by proceedings in replevin. **2** To admit to bail or give bail for. —*n.* Replevin. [<OF *replevir.* See REPLEVIN.] —**re·plev′i·a·ble, re·plev′is·a·ble** *adj.*

rep·li·ca (rep′lə·kə) *n.* **1** A duplicate, as of a picture, executed by the original artist. **2** Any close copy or reproduction. See synonyms under DUPLICATE, MODEL. [<Ital. <L *replicare* reply, answer to. See REPLY.]

rep·li·cate (rep′lə·kit) *adj.* Folded backward, as the upper part of a leaf on the lower, or the wing of an insect. Also **rep′li·cat′ed** (-kā′·tid). —*v.t.* (-kāt) **·cat·ed, ·cat·ing** **1** To fold over. **2** To make a replica of. **3** To answer; reply. [<L *replicatus,* pp. of *replicare* answer. See REPLY.]

rep·li·ca·tion (rep′lə·kā′shən) *n.* **1** A reply. **2** *Law* A plaintiff's reply to a defendant's plea or answer. **3** A repetition or copy. **4** A methodical or systematic doubling over of a surface. [<OF] —**rep′li·ca′tive** *adj.*

re·ply (ri·plī′) *v.* **·plied, ·ply·ing** *v.i.* **1** To give an answer, orally or in writing. **2** To respond by some act, gesture, etc.: He *replied* with a blow. **3** To echo. **4** *Law* To file a pleading in answer to the statement of the defense. —*v.t.* **5** To say in answer: often with a clause as object: She *replied* that she would do it. —*n. pl.* **·plies** Something said, written, or done by way of answer; a response; rejoinder. See synonyms under ANSWER. [<OF *replier* bend back <L *replicare* fold back, answer to, make a reply < *re-* back + *plicare* fold] —**re·pli′er** *n.*

ré·pon·dez s'il vous plaît (rā·pôn·dā′ sēl vōō ple′) *French* Reply, if you please: used on formal invitations: abbr. *R.S.V.P.*

re·port (ri·pôrt′, -pōrt′) *v.t.* **1** To make or give an account of, especially formally: to *report* the minutes of a meeting, or an event for a newspaper. **2** To relate, as information obtained by investigation: Please *report* your findings. **3** To bear back or repeat to another, as an answer. **4** To complain about, especially to a superior: I'll *report* you to the manager. **5** To state the result of consideration concerning: The committee *reported* the bill. — *v.i.* **6** To make a report. **7** To act as a reporter. **8** To present oneself, as for duty. See synonyms under ANNOUNCE. — *n.* **1** That which is reported; an announcement, statement, or account; the formal statement of the result of an investigation: a medical *report.* **2** Common talk; rumor; hence, fame, reputation, or character: good *report; reports* grossly untrue. **3** A record with more or less detail of the transactions of a deliberative body. **4** An account of any occurrence prepared for publication through the press. **5** *Law Usually pl.* A published narration (usually official) of a case or series of cases judicially considered: the Supreme Court *reports.* **6** An explosive sound: the *report* of a gun. [<OF *reporter* carry back <L *reportare* < *re-* back + *portare* carry] — **re·port′a·ble** *adj.*

Synonyms (noun): account, description, narration, narrative, recital, record, rehearsal, relation, rumor, statement, story, tale. *Account,* primarily a commercial summary, carries a similar meaning in the derived sense; an *account* of an occurrence is circumstantial, adequate, complete, and unembellished; we speak of a clear, a full, or a partial *account;* a glowing *account* is still supposed to be circumstantially as well as substantially correct. A *statement* is definite, confined to essentials and properly to matters within the personal knowledge of the one who states them. A *narrative* is a somewhat extended and embellished *account* of events in order of time, ordinarily with a view to please or entertain. A *description* gives especial scope to the pictorial element. A *report* is supposed or intended to bring back the past, and may be concise and formal or highly descriptive and dramatic. Compare ALLEGORY, ANECDOTE, HISTORY, NEWS, RECORD.

report card *U.S.* A periodic statement of a pupil's scholastic record, which is presented to the parents or guardian.

re·port·ed·ly (ri·pôr′tid·lē, -pōr′-) *adv.* According to report.

re·port·er (ri·pôr′tər, -pōr′-) *n.* **1** A bearer of news; specifically, one employed by a newspaper to gather and report news for publication. **2** One who edits reports of important cases in court for official publication. [<OF *reporteur*] — **rep·or·to·ri·al** (rep′ər·tôr′ē·əl, -tō′rē-) *adj.*

re·pose[1] (ri·pōz′) *n.* **1** The act of taking rest, or the state of being at rest; especially, rest in a recumbent posture. **2** Freedom from excitement or anxiety; composure; hence, ease of manner; graceful and dignified calmness. **3** That which conduces to rest or calm. See synonyms under REST. — *v.* **·posed, ·pos·ing** *v.t.* **1** To lay or place in a position of rest: to *repose* oneself on a bed. — *v.i.* **2** To lie at rest. **3** To rely; depend: with *on, upon,* or *in.* See synonyms under REST. [<F *reposer* <LL *repausare* < *re-* again + *pausare* pause] — **re·pos′al** *n.* — **re·pos′er** *n.*

re·pose[2] (ri·pōz′) *v.t.* **·posed, ·pos·ing** **1** To place, as confidence or hope: with *in.* **2** *Rare* To deposit. [<L *repositus,* pp. of *reponere* put back, on analogy with *depose, oppose,* etc.] — **re·pos′al** *n.*

re·pose·ful (ri·pōz′fəl) *adj.* Full of repose; restful.

re·pos·it (ri·poz′it) *v.t.* To put in some secure and proper place; deposit. [<L *repositus.* See REPOSE.] — **re·po·si·tion** (rē′pə·zish′ən, rep′ə-) *n.*

re·pos·i·to·ry (ri·poz′ə·tôr′ē, -tō′rē) *n. pl.* **·ries** **1** A place in which goods are or may be stored; a depository. **2** A person to whom a secret is entrusted. **3** A building used as a place of exhibition and sale. **4** A burial vault. **5** A sepulcher (def. 2). [<L *repositorium* < *repositus.* See REPOSE.]

re·pos·sess (rē′pə·zes′) *v.t.* **1** To have possession of again; regain possession of. **2** To give back possession or ownership to. **3** *Scot.* To reinstate: with *in.* See synonyms under RECOVER. — **re′pos·ses′sion** (-zesh′ən) *n.*

re·pous·sé (rə·pōō·sā′) *adj.* Formed in relief, as a design in metal, or adorned with such designs. [<F, lit., thrust back <L *repulsus.* See REPULSE.]

repp (rep) See REP[1].

Rep·plier (rep′lir), **Agnes,** 1855–1950, U. S. essayist.

rep·re·hend (rep′ri·hend′) *v.t.* To criticize sharply; find fault with; blame. See synonyms under BLAME, REPROVE. [<L *reprehendere* < *re-* back + *prehendere* hold]

rep·re·hen·si·ble (rep′ri·hen′sə·bəl) *adj.* Deserving blame or censure. — **rep′re·hen′si·bil′i·ty, rep′re·hen′si·ble·ness** *n.* — **rep′re·hen′si·bly** *adv.*

rep·re·hen·sion (rep′ri·hen′shən) *n.* A finding fault; expression of blame; rebuke. See synonyms under ANIMADVERSION, REPROOF. — **rep′re·hen′sive** *adj.* — **rep′re·hen′sive·ly** *adv.*

rep·re·hen·so·ry (rep′ri·hen′sər·ē) *adj.* Censorious.

rep·re·sent (rep′ri·zent′) *v.t.* **1** To serve as the symbol, expression, or designation of; symbolize: The letters of the alphabet *represent* the sounds of speech. **2** To express or symbolize in this manner: to *represent* royal power with a scepter. **3** To set forth a likeness or image of; depict; portray, as in painting or sculpture. **4 a** To produce on the stage, as an opera. **b** To act the part of; impersonate, as a character in a play. **5** To serve as or be the delegate, agent, etc., of: He *represents* the State of Maine. **6** To describe as being of a specified character or condition: They *represented* him as a genius. **7** To set forth in words; state; explain: He *represented* the circumstances of his case. **8** To bring before the mind; present clearly. **9** To serve as an example, specimen, type, etc., of; typify: His use of words *represents* an outmoded school of writing. See synonyms under IMITATE. [<OF *representer* <L *repraesentare* < *re-* again + *praesentare.* See PRESENT[2].] — **rep′re·sent′a·ble** *adj.* — **rep′re·sent′a·bil′i·ty** *n.*

re-present (rē′pri·zent′) *v.t.* To present again. — **re′-pre′sen·ta′tion** *n.*

rep·re·sen·ta·tion (rep′ri·zen·tā′shən) *n.* **1** The act of representing, or the state of being represented. **2** That which represents; a likeness; model; picture; statue; statement; description; also, a dramatic performance. **3** The right of acting authoritatively for others, especially in a legislative body; also, the system of electing delegates to act for a constituency. **4** Representatives collectively. **5** The stage or process of mental conservation that consists in the presenting to itself by the mind of objects previously known. **6** *Law* The authorized acting for or in the stead of another in regard to that other's affairs. **7** A setting forth by statement or account; specifically, an argument against some object or proposal. See synonyms under IMAGE, MODEL, PICTURE. [<OF]

rep·re·sen·ta·tive (rep′ri·zen′tə·tiv) *adj.* **1** Typifying or typical of a group or class. **2** Acting, having the power or authority to act, or qualified to act, as an agent. **3** Made up of representatives. **4** Based on or pertaining to the political principle of representation. **5** Presenting, portraying, or representing, or capable of so doing. **6** Having to do with cognition of a memory image: distinguished from *presentative.* — *n.* **1** One who or that which is fit to stand as a type; a typical instance. **2** One who is a qualified agent of any kind. **3** A member of a deliberative or legislative body chosen by vote of the people; specifically, in the United States, a member of the lower house of Congress or of a State legislature. See synonyms under DELEGATE. — **rep′re·sen′ta·tive·ly** *adv.* — **rep′re·sen′ta·tive·ness** *n.*

re·press (ri·pres′) *v.t.* **1** To keep under restraint or control; curb. **2** To put down; quell, as a rebellion. **3** *Psychoanal.* To effect the repression of, as fears, impulses, etc. [<L *repressus,* pp. of *reprimere* < *re-* back + *premere* press] — **re·press′er** or **re·pres′sor** *n.* — **re·press′i·ble** *adj.*

Synonyms: bridle, chasten, check, crush, curb, overcome, overpower, quiet, rein, restrain, stay, still, subdue, suppress. See LIMIT, RESTRAIN, SUBDUE. *Antonyms*: agitate, animate, arouse, awaken, encourage, excite, incite, inspirit, instigate, kindle, provoke, rouse, stimulate.

re·pressed (ri·prest′) *adj.* Suppressed.

re·pres·sion (ri·presh′ən) *n.* **1** The act of repressing, or the condition of being repressed. **2** That which holds in check; a restraint. **3** *Psychoanal.* The exclusion from consciousness of painful, unpleasant, or unacceptable psychic material, as memories, desires, and impulses, which are thus compelled to manifest themselves through the unconcious.

re·pres·sive (ri·pres′iv) *adj.* **1** Tending to repress. **2** Capable of repressing. — **re·pres′sive·ly** *adv.* — **re·pres′sive·ness** *n.*

re·prieve (ri·prēv′) *v.t.* **·prieved, ·priev·ing** **1** To suspend temporarily the execution of a sentence upon. **2** To relieve for a time from suffering, danger, or trouble. **3** To postpone or delay, as a danger. — *n.* **1** The temporary suspension of a sentence, or the instrument officially ordering such a suspension. **2** Temporary relief or cessation of pain or ill; respite. See synonyms under RESPITE. [< earlier *repry* <F *repris,* pp. of *reprendre* take back; infl. in form by ME *repreven* <OF *reprover* reprove]

rep·ri·mand (rep′rə·mand, -mänd) *v.t.* To reprove sharply or formally. See synonyms under ADMONISH, REPROVE. — *n.* Severe reproof or formal censure, public or private. See synonyms under REPROOF. [<F *réprimande* reproof <L *reprimenda,* fem. of *reprimendus* to be repressed, gerundive of *reprimere.* See REPRESS.]

re·print (rē′print′) *n.* An edition of a printed work that is a verbatim copy of the original; specifically, a copy of matter already printed, as in another country. — *v.t.* (rē·print′) To print a new edition or copy of; print anew or again. — **re·print′er** *n.*

re·pri·sal (ri·prī′zəl) *n.* **1** Forcible seizure of anything from an enemy by way of retaliation or indemnity. **2** Anything taken from an enemy as indemnification or in retaliation; also, any act or infliction by way of retaliation; specifically, the infliction of suffering or death on a prisoner of war in retaliation for acts of inhumanity inflicted by him. **3** Any act of retaliation. **4** *Obs.* A prize seized or gained. [<OF *reprisaille* < *repris,* pp. of *reprendre* take back <L *reprehendere.* See REPREHEND.]

re·prise (ri·prīz′ *for def. 1;* rə·prēz′, -prīz′ *for def. 2*) *n.* **1** *pl. Brit. Law* Deductions and payments (as for annuities) out of lands: a manor's yearly value over and above *reprises.* **2** *Music* A repeated phrase; specifically, the repetition of or return to the subject after an intermediate movement. [<OF fem. of *repris.* See REPRISAL.]

re·proach (ri·prōch′) *v.t.* **1** To charge with or blame for something wrong; rebuke; censure; upbraid. **2** To bring discredit and disgrace upon; to disgrace. See synonyms under ABUSE, BLAME, REPROVE, REVILE. — *n.* **1** The act of reproaching, or the words of one who reproaches; censure; reproof; rebuke. **2** A cause of blame or disgrace; hence, disgrace or discredit. See synonyms under BLEMISH, REPROOF, SCANDAL. [<F *reprocher.* Origin uncertain.] — **re·proach′a·ble** *adj.* — **re·proach′a·ble·ness** *n.* — **re·proach′a·bly** *adv.* — **re·proach′er** *n.* — **re·proach′less** *adj.*

re·proach·ful (ri·prōch′fəl) *adj.* **1** Containing or full of reproach; expressing reproach. **2** *Obs.* Reproachable. — **re·proach′ful·ly** *adv.* — **re·proach′ful·ness** *n.*

rep·ro·bate (rep′rə·bāt) *adj.* **1** Abandoned in sin; lost to all sense of duty; utterly depraved; profligate. **2** Abandoned to punishment; condemned. **3** *Obs.* Not enduring proof or trial; inferior or base. — *n.* One lost to all sense of duty or decency; one abandoned to depravity or doom. — *v.t.* **·bat·ed, ·bat·ing** **1** To disapprove of heartily; condemn. **2** *Theol.* To abandon, condemn, or foreordain to damnation. See synonyms under BLAME, CONDEMN. [<LL *reprobatus,* pp. of *reprobare.* See REPROVE.]

rep·ro·ba·tion (rep′rə·bā′shən) *n.* **1** The act of reprobating, or the condition of being reprobated; censure. **2** *Theol.* Rejection or condemnation by God's purpose. See synonyms under OATH.

rep·ro·ba·tive (rep′rə·bā′tiv) *adj.* Of, pertaining to, or expressing reprobation. — **rep′ro·ba′tive·ly** *adv.*

re·proc·ess (rē·pros′es) *v.t.* To process again.

reprocessed wool Wool fibers previously woven or knitted but never used by a consumer, unraveled and spun and rewoven into fabric.

re·pro·duce (rē′prə·do͞os′, -dyo͞os′) *v.* **·duced, ·duc·ing** *v.t.* **1** To make a copy, image, or reproduction of. **2** *Biol.* **a** To give rise to (offspring) by sexual or asexual generation. **b** To replace (a lost part or organ) by regeneration. **3** To cause the reproduction of (plant life, etc.). **4** To produce again; bring forward or exhibit anew. **5** To bring into existence again; recreate; revive. **6** To recall to the mind; visualize again; re-create mentally. — *v.i.* **7** To produce offspring. **8** To undergo copying, reproduction, etc. — **re′pro·duc′i·ble** *adj.*

re·pro·duc·er (rē′prə·do͞o′sər, -dyo͞o′-) *n.* **1** One who or that which reproduces. **2** A diaphragm used for the reproduction of sounds in a phonograph, etc.

re·pro·duc·tion (rē′prə·duk′shən) *n.* **1** The act or power of reproducing. **2** *Biol.* The process by which an animal or plant gives rise to another of its kind; generation. **3** *Psychol.* The process of the memory by which objects that have previously been known are brought back into consciousness. **4** That which is reproduced, as a revival in drama or a copy in art. See synonyms under DUPLICATE.

re·pro·duc·tive (rē′prə·duk′tiv) *adj.* Pertaining to, employed in, or tending to reproduction. — **re′pro·duc′tive·ly** *adv.* — **re′pro·duc′tive·ness** *n.*

re·proof (ri·pro͞of′) *n.* **1** The act of reproving; rebuke; blame; censure. **2** *Obs.* Ignominy; reproach. Also **re·prov·al** (ri·pro͞o′vəl). [<OF *reprove* < *reprover.* See REPROVE.]

Synonyms: admonition, animadversion, blame, censure, check, chiding, comment, condemnation, criticism, denunciation, disapproval, objurgation, rebuke, reflection, reprehension, reprimand, reproach, reproval, upbraiding. *Blame, censure,* and *disapproval* may either be felt or uttered; *comment, criticism, rebuke, reflection, reprehension,* and *reproof* are always expressed. The same is true of *admonition* and *animadversion. Comment* and *criticism* may be favorable as well as censorious; they imply no superiority or authority on the part of him who utters them; nor do *reflection* or *reprehension,* which are simply turning the mind back upon what is disapproved. *Reprehension* is supposed to be calm and just, and with good intent; *reflection* is often from mere ill feeling, and is likely to be more personal and less impartial than *reprehension. Rebuke,* literally a stopping of the mouth, is administered to a forward or hasty person; *reproof* is administered to one intentionally or deliberately wrong; both words imply authority in the reprover, and direct expression of *disapproval* to the face of the person *rebuked* or *reproved. Reprimand* is official *censure* formally administered by a superior to one under his command. *Rebuke* may be given at the outset, or in the midst of an action; *reflection, reprehension, reproof,* always follow the act; *admonition* is anticipatory, and meant to be preventive. *Check* is allied to *rebuke,* and given before or during action; *chiding* is nearer to *reproof,* but with more personal bitterness and less authority. Compare CONDEMN, REPROVE. *Antonyms*: applause, approbation, approval, commendation, encomium, eulogy, panegyric, praise.

re·prove (ri·pro͞ov′) *v.t.* **·proved, ·prov·ing** **1** To censure, as for a fault; rebuke. **2** To express disapproval of (an act). **3** *Obs.* To convince; convict. [<OF *reprover* <LL *reprobare* < *re-* again + *probare* test < *probus* upright] — **re·prov′a·ble** *adj.* — **re·prov′er** *n.* — **re·prov′ing·ly** *adv.*

Synonyms: admonish, blame, censure, chasten, check, chide, condemn, rebuke, reprehend, reprimand, reproach, upbraid. To *censure* is to pronounce an adverse judgment that may or may not be expressed to the person *censured*; to *rebuke* is to *reprove* sharply, and often abruptly; to *blame* is a familiar word signifying to pass *censure* upon, make answerable, as for a fault. To *reproach* is to *censure* openly and vehemently, and with intense personal feeling as of grief or anger; as, to *reproach* one for ingratitude; *reproach* knows no distinction of rank or character; a subject may *reproach* a king or a criminal a judge. Compare REPROOF. See ADMONISH, BLAME, CONDEMN. *Antonyms*: see synonyms for PRAISE.

rep·tant (rep′tənt) *adj. Zool.* Creeping; crawling: also *repent.* [<L *reptans, -antis,* ppr. of *reptare,* intens. of *repere* creep]

rep·tile (rep′til, -tīl) *n.* **1** A cold-blooded, air-breathing vertebrate, especially one with scales, as a lizard, snake, or crocodile; a reptilian; any member of the class *Reptilia.* **2** A groveling, abject person; one morally base or odious. — *adj.* **1** Crawling on the belly; creeping; reptant. **2** Groveling morally; sly and base; treacherous; venomous. **3** Of, pertaining to, or resembling a reptile. [<LL, neut. sing. of *reptilis* crawling < *reptus,* pp. of *repere* creep]

rep·til·i·an (rep·til′ē·ən) *adj.* **1** Of or pertaining to a class *(Reptilia)* of cold-blooded, air-breathing vertebrates, the reptiles, having fully ossified skeletons and bodies usually covered with horny plates or scales. In addition to the limbless snakes, the class includes crocodiles, alligators, lizards, and turtles. **2** Malicious; base; mean. — *n.* One of the *Reptilia*; any reptile.

re·pub·lic (ri·pub′lik) *n.* **1** A state in which the sovereignty resides in the people or a certain portion of the people, and the legislative and administrative powers are lodged in officers elected by and representing the people; a representative democracy: applied to almost every form of government except kingdoms, empires, and dictatorships. **2** A community of persons working freely in or devoted to the same cause: the *republic* of letters. — **The Republic** **1** The United States. **2** Plato's dialog on government. [<F *république* <L *respublica* commonwealth < *res* thing + *publica,* fem. of *publicus* public]

re·pub·li·can (ri·pub′li·kən) *adj.* Pertaining to, of the nature of, or suitable for a republic; agreeable to the nature of a republic; also, of or pertaining to any party supporting republican government. — *n.* One who advocates or upholds a republican form of government or belongs to a party upholding republican government; one who believes in equality and liberty.

Re·pub·li·can (ri·pub′li·kən) *adj.* Pertaining to or belonging to the Republican party of the United States, or to any political group which calls itself by this name: the *Republican* parties of Spain or France. — *n.* A member of the Republican party. — **black Republican** Formerly, a member of the Republican party: derisively so called in allusion to their opposition to Negro slavery.

Republican calendar See under CALENDAR.

re·pub·li·can·ism (ri·pub′li·kən·iz′əm) *n.* **1** The theory or principles of republican government. **2** A liking for republican principles.

Re·pub·li·can·ism (ri·pub′li·kən·iz′əm) *n.* The policy and principles of the Republican party of the United States.

re·pub·li·can·ize (ri·pub′li·kən·īz′) *v.t.* **·ized, ·iz·ing** To make republican in spirit or character. — **re·pub′li·can·i·za′tion** *n.*

Republican party **1** One of the two major political parties of the United States, founded in 1854 in opposition to the extension of slavery. **2** The political party founded by Thomas Jefferson in 1792: full name, *Democratic-Republican party.* One of its several factions became, in 1828, the present Democratic party. **3** One of various political parties of foreign countries, devoted to the overthrow of monarchy or the establishment or extension of democratic ideals.

Republican River A river in Colorado, Nebraska, and Kansas, flowing 445 miles east to the Kansas River.

re·pub·li·ca·tion (rē′pub·lə·kā′shən) *n.* The act of republishing, or that which is republished.

re·pub·lish (rē·pub′lish) *v.t.* **1** To publish again. **2** *Law* To revive, as a canceled will, by executing anew. — **re·pub′lish·er** *n.*

re·pu·di·ate (ri·pyo͞o′dē·āt) *v.t.* **·at·ed, ·at·ing** **1** To refuse to accept as valid, true, or authorized; reject; condemn. **2** To refuse to acknowledge or pay. **3** To cast off; disown, as a son. **4** *Obs.* To divorce; put away (a wife). See synonyms under ABANDON, RECANT, RENOUNCE. [<L *repudiatus,* pp. of *repudiare* divorce < *repudium* divorce, separation, ? < *re-* back + *pudere* feel shame] — **re·pu′di·a′tive** *adj.* — **re·pu′di·a′tor** *n.*

re·pu·di·a·tion (ri·pyo͞o′dē·ā′shən) *n.* **1** The act of repudiating. **2** The state of being repudiated. **3** The rejection of the whole or a part of a contract, debt, or obligation, as by a government.

re·pugn (ri·pyo͞on′) *v.t.* & *v.i. Obs.* To oppose; resist. [<OF *repugner* <L *repugnare* < *re-* back + *pugnare* fight]

re·pug·nance (ri·pug′nəns) *n.* **1** A feeling of aversion and resistance. **2** *Logic* The relation of contradictories; inconsistency. **3** *Obs.* Opposition. Also **re·pug′nan·cy.** See synonyms under ANTIPATHY, HATRED.

re·pug·nant (ri·pug′nənt) *adj.* **1** Offensive to taste or feeling; exciting aversion or repulsion. **2** Being inconsistent or opposed; antagonistic. **3** *Law* Contrary to or in conflict with something else in the same or in another document or statute. **4** Hostile; rebellious; resisting. See synonyms under INCONGRUOUS, INIMICAL. [<OF <L *repugnans, -antis,* ppr. of *repugnare.* See REPUGN.]

re·pulse (ri·puls′) *v.t.* **·pulsed, ·puls·ing** **1** To drive back; repel, as an attacking force. **2** To repel by coldness, discourtesy, etc.; reject; rebuff. See synonyms under DRIVE, REPEL. — *n.* **1** The act of repulsing, or the state of being repulsed. **2** Rejection; refusal. [<L *repulsus,* pp. of *repellere.* See REPEL.] — **re·puls′er** *n.*

re·pul·sion (ri·pul′shən) *n.* **1** The act of repelling or repulsing, or the state of being repelled or repulsed. **2** Aversion; repugnance. **3** *Physics* The mutual action of two bodies which tends to drive them apart: opposed to *attraction.*

re·pul·sive (ri·pul′siv) *adj.* **1** Exciting such feelings, as of dislike, disgust, or horror, that one is repelled; grossly offensive; causing aversion. **2** Such as to forbid approach or familiarity; forbidding. **3** Acting by repulsion: *repulsive* forces. — **re·pul′sive·ly** *adv.* — **re·pul′sive·ness** *n.*

rep·u·ta·ble (rep′yə·tə·bəl) *adj.* **1** Having a good reputation; estimable; honorable. **2** Consistent with honorable standing; complying with the usage of the best writers and speakers. — **rep′u·ta·bil′i·ty** *n.* — **rep′u·ta·bly** *adv.*

rep·u·ta·tion (rep′yə·tā′shən) *n.* **1** The general estimation in which a person or thing is held by others, especially by a community; repute, either good or bad. **2** The state of being in high regard or esteem; good repute: to ruin one's *reputation.* **3** A particular credit or character ascribed to a person or thing: usually with *for*: a *reputation* for honesty. See synonyms under CHARACTER, FAME. [<L *reputatio, -onis* < *reputatus,* pp. of *reputare* be reputed. See REPUTE.]

re·pute (ri·pyo͞ot′) *v.t.* **·put·ed, ·put·ing** To regard or consider to be as specified; esteem: usually in the passive: They are *reputed* to be an intelligent people. — *n.* **1** Reputation, good or bad. **2** Public opinion; general report. [<L *reputare* reckon, be reputed < *re-* again + *putare* think, count]

re·put·ed (ri·pyo͞o′tid) *adj.* Generally thought or supposed; having a specified reputation. — **re·put′ed·ly** *adv.*

re·quest (ri·kwest′) *v.t.* **1** To express a desire for, especially politely; ask for; solicit. **2** To address a request to; ask: to *request* a person to do one a favor. See synonyms under ASK, DEMAND, PRAY. — *n.* **1** The act of requesting; entreaty; petition. **2** That which is asked for. **3** The state of being so esteemed as to be in demand; demand: in *request.* See synonyms under PETITION, PRAYER. — *adj.* Having been asked for; in response to a request: a *request* program. [<OF *requeste* <Med. L *requisita,* orig. fem. of L *requisitus,* pp. of *requirere* seek, again. See REQUIRE.]

re·qui·em (rē′kwē·əm, rek′wē-) *n.* **1** Any musical hymn, composition, or service for the dead. **2** *Often cap. Eccl.* In the Roman Catholic Church, a solemn mass sung for the repose of the souls of the dead, the **Requiem mass.** **3** *Often cap.* A musical setting for such a mass; also a similar piece of music using different words. [<L *Requiem (aeternam dona eis, Domine)* rest (eternal give unto them, O Lord), the opening words of the introit of this mass]

req·ui·es·cat (rek′wē·es′kat) *n.* A prayer for the repose of a departed soul: the first word of the Latin petition **requiescat in pa·ce** (in pā′sē), may he rest in peace. Abbr. *R.I.P.* [<L]

re·quire (ri·kwīr′) *v.* **·quired, ·quir·ing** *v.t.* **1** To have need of; find necessary. **2** To demand authoritatively; insist upon: to *require* absolute silence. **3** To command; order: He *requires* us to be punctual. —*v.i.* **4** To make demand or request. See synonyms under ASK, DEMAND, DICTATE, MAKE. [<L *requirere* seek again, be in want of <*re-* again + *quaerere* ask, seek] —**re·quir′a·ble** *adj.* —**re·quir′er** *n.*

re·quire·ment (ri·kwīr′mənt) *n.* **1** That which is required; a requisite. **2** The act of requiring, or that which requires; a demand. See synonyms under NECESSITY, ORDER.

req·ui·site (rek′wə·zit) *adj.* Required by the nature of things or by circumstances; indispensable. See synonyms under NECESSARY. —*n.* That which cannot be dispensed with; a necessity; requirement. See synonyms under NECESSITY. [<L *requisitus,* pp. of *requirere.* See REQUEST.] —**req′ui·site·ly** *adv.* —**req′ui·site·ness** *n.*

req·ui·si·tion (rek′wə·zish′ən) *n.* **1** A formal request, summons, or demand, as by a government. **2** A necessity or requirement. **3** The state of being required. **4** A demand for the surrender of a fugitive from justice made by the governing official of one state or country upon another. —*v.t.* To make a requisition for or upon; demand or take upon requisition. [<L *requisitio, -onis* <*requisitus,* pp. of *requirere.* See REQUIRE.]

re·qui·tal (ri·kwīt′l) *n.* **1** The act of requiting. **2** That which requites; adequate return for good or ill; in the favorable sense, reward or compensation; in the unfavorable sense, retaliation. See synonyms under RECOMPENSE, REVENGE. [<REQUITE]

re·quite (ri·kwīt′) *v.t.* **·quit·ed, ·quit·ing** **1** To make equivalent return for, as kindness, service, or injury; make up for. **2** To make return to; compensate or repay in kind: Does she *requite* me for my love? **3** To give or do in return. [<RE- + *quite,* obs. var. of QUIT] —**re·quit′a·ble** *adj.* —**re·quit′er** *n.*

Synonyms: avenge, compensate, pay, punish, quit, reciprocate, recompense, remunerate, repay, retaliate, return, revenge, reward, satisfy. *Requite* is often used in the more general sense of *recompense* or *repay,* but always with the suggestion, at least, of the original idea of full equivalent. To *repay* or to *retaliate,* to *punish* or to *reward,* may be to make some return very inadequate to the benefit or injury received or the right or wrong done; but to *requite* is to make such return as to *quit* oneself of all obligation of favor or hostility, of punishment or reward. See PAY. *Antonyms*: absolve, acquit, excuse, forget, forgive, neglect, overlook, pardon, slight.

re–ra·di·a·tion (rē′rā′dē·ā′shən) *n.* **1** *Telecom.* The emission of one or more radio frequencies from the antenna of a radio receiver through improper oscillation of the tubes, with resulting confusion of signals. **2** *Physics* Secondary emission.

rere·dos (rir′dos) *n.* **1** An ornamental screen behind an altar. **2** The back of an open fire hearth; a fireback. **3** In old armor, a backplate. [<AF *areredos* <OF *arere* at the back (<L *ad* to + *retro* behind) + *dos* back <L *dorsum*]

rere·mouse (rir′mous) *n. pl.* **·mice** (-mīs) *Brit. Dial.* A bat: also spelled *rearmouse.* [OE *hreremūs*]

re·run (rē′run′) *n.* **1** A running over again or a second time. **2** The presenting of a motion picture after its original presentation. —*v.t.* (rē·run′) **·ran, ·run·ning** To run again.

Re·sa·ca (ri·sä′kə) A town of NW Georgia; scene of a Civil War battle, 1864.

Re·sa·ca de la Pal·ma (rā·sä′kä dā lä päl′mä) A locality in southern Texas north of Brownsville; scene of an American victory over the Mexicans, 1846.

res ad·ju·di·ca·ta (rēz a·jōō′də·kā′tə) See RES JUDICATA.

re·scind (ri·sind′) *v.t.* To make void, as an act; abrogate; repeal: to *rescind* a resolution. See synonyms under ANNUL, CANCEL. [<L *rescindere* <*re-* back + *scindere* cut] —**re·scind′a·ble** *adj.* —**re·scind′er** *n.*

re·scis·si·ble (ri·sis′ə·bəl) *adj.* Capable of being rescinded.

re·scis·sion (ri·sizh′ən) *n.* The act of rescinding or abrogating.

re·scis·so·ry (ri·sis′ər·ē, -siz′-) *adj.* Having power to rescind; rescinding; revoking. [<LL *rescissorius* <L *rescissus,* pp. of *rescindere.* See RESCIND.]

re·script (rē′skript) *n.* **1** In ancient Rome, an imperial decree, consisting of the emperor's answer to questions on matters of state or law. **2** Any decree, edict, order, or formal announcement, especially one made by a monarch or ruler. **3** A formal, written reply by the pope to a petition or question of morality or canon law submitted to him. **4** A facsimile; counterpart; something written over again. [<L *rescriptum* edict, orig. neut. pp. of *rescribere* write back (in reply) <*re-* again + *scribere* write]

res·cue (res′kyōō) *v.t.* **·cued, ·cu·ing** **1** To save or free from danger, captivity, evil, etc.; deliver. **2** *Law* To take or remove forcibly from the custody of the law. See synonyms under DELIVER, RECLAIM. —*n.* The act of rescuing; deliverance. [<OF *rescourre* <Med. L *rescutere* <L *re-* again + *excutere* shake off <*ex-* off, out + *quatere* shake. Related to QUASH.] —**res′cu·a·ble** *adj.* —**res′cu·er** *n.*

rescue grass A high bromegrass (*Bromus catharticus*), cultivated for hay. [Origin uncertain; perhaps confused with FESCUE]

re·search (ri·sûrch′, rē′sûrch) *n.* **1** Diligent, protracted investigation; studious inquiry. **2** A systematic investigation of some phenomenon or series of phenomena by the experimental method. See synonyms under INQUIRY. —*v.i.* To make research; investigate. [<F *recherche*] —**re·search′er** *n.*

re–search (rē·sûrch′) *v.t.* & *v.i.* To search again or anew.

re·seat (rē·sēt′) *v.t.* **1** To seat again. **2** To put a new seat or seats in or on.

ré·seau (rā·zō′) *n. pl.* **·seaux** (-zō′) **1** In textile work, a laceground composed of regular meshes; netground. **2** *Astron.* The small lines forming squares cut upon a glass plate: used in mapping out the heavens by photography. **3** A network. **4** *Meteorol.* A group of weather stations operating in the same territory or under common direction. **5** *Phot.* A sensitive filter screen for use in making color films. [<F, dim. of OF *roix* net <L *rete*]

re·sect (ri·sekt′) *v.t. Surg.* To cut or pare off: distinguished from *excise.* [<L *resectus,* pp. of *resecare* <*re-* back + *secare* cut, amputate]

re·sec·tion (ri·sek′shən) *n.* **1** A cutting or paring off. **2** *Surg.* The operation of cutting out part of a bone, organ, etc. **3** The determination of a position with reference to points of known location, whether on the ground or on a map or chart. [<L *resectio, -onis*]

re·se·da (ri·sē′də) *n.* **1** An herb of the mignonette family (genus *Reseda*). **2** A light or grayish green. [<L, prob. <*resedare* assuage; because once thought to be a sedative]

res·e·da·ceous (res′ə·dā′shəs) *adj. Bot.* Designating a family (*Resedaceae*) of annual or perennial herbs with alternate simple leaves and terminal spikes of small unsymmetrical flowers; the mignonette family. [<RESEDA + -ACEOUS]

re·sell (rē·sel′) *v.t.* **·sold, ·sell·ing** To sell anew or again. —**re·sell′er** *n.*

re·sem·blance (ri·zem′bləns) *n.* **1** The quality of similarity in nature, form, etc.; relative identity; likeness. **2** That which resembles; a semblance or likeness of a person or thing. **3** *Obs.* A characteristic quality or attribute. **4** *Obs.* Probability or likelihood. See synonyms under ANALOGY, APPROXIMATION, PICTURE. [<AF]

re·sem·ble (ri·zem′bəl) *v.t.* **·bled, ·bling** **1** To be similar to in appearance, quality, or character. **2** *Obs.* To compare; liken. See synonyms under IMITATE. [<OF *resembler* <*re-* again and again + *sembler* seem <L *simulare.* See SIMULATE.] —**re·sem′bler** *n.*

re·sent (ri·zent′) *v.t.* To feel or show resentment at; be indignant at, as an injury or insult. [<F *ressentir* feel the effects <*re-* again + *sentir* feel <L *sentire*]

re·sent·ful (ri·zent′fəl) *adj.* Disposed to resent; full of or characterized by resentment. See synonyms under MALICIOUS. —**re·sent′ful·ly** *adv.* —**re·sent′ful·ness** *n.*

re·sent·ment (ri·zent′mənt) *n.* Anger and ill will in view of real or fancied wrong or injury. See synonyms under ANGER, HATRED, OFFENSE, PIQUE.

re·ser·pine (ri·sûr′pēn, -pin, res′ər-) *n.* An ataractic drug prepared from alkaloids found in certain species of *Rauwolfia,* especially *R. serpentina.*

res·er·va·tion (rez′ər·vā′shən) *n.* **1** The act of reserving. **2** That which is reserved, kept back, or withheld. **3** The unexpressed qualification of a statement, promise, etc., that would, if uttered, so affect or alter its meaning for the person addressed as to vitiate its truth: also **mental reservation.** **4** Hence, any limitation. **5** A tract of government land reserved for the use and occupancy of an Indian tribe or for some other special purpose, as the preservation of forests, wild birds, etc. See synonyms under RESERVE. [<OF <LL *reservatio, -onis*]

re·serve (ri·zûrv′) *v.t.* **·served, ·serv·ing** **1** To hold back or set aside for special or future use; store up. **2** To keep as one's own; retain: He *reserves* that privilege for himself. **3** To arrange for ahead of time; have set aside for one's use: I *reserved* two tickets on the train. **4** To set aside (a portion of the consecrated elements of the Eucharist) for communion of the sick. See synonyms under RETAIN. —*n.* **1** That which is reserved; something stored up for future use, as in a reservoir; something set apart for a particular purpose; specifically, a reservation of land. **2** In banking, the amount of funds reserved from investment, in order promptly to meet regular or emergent demands. **3** The act of reserving; reservation. **4** The state of being reserved; silence as to one's feelings, opinions, or affairs; reticence; also, absence of exaggeration. **5** A fighting force held back from action to meet possible emergencies or demands. **6** That component of the armed forces of a nation composed of civilians trained for military service or assignment and subject to call to active duty in emergencies or under particular circumstances; specifically, *U.S.,* the **Army Reserve, Air Force Reserve, Naval Reserve, Marine Corps Reserve,** and **Coast Guard Reserve.** —*adj.* Held in reserve; constituting a reserve: a *reserve* supply of money. [<OF *reserver* <L *reservare* keep back <*re-* back + *servare* keep] —**re·serv′a·ble** *adj.* —**re·serv′er** *n.*

Synonyms (noun): backwardness, coldness, constraint, coyness, haughtiness, limitation, modesty, pride, reservation, reservedness, restraint, reticence, shyness, taciturnity. *Reserve* is the holding oneself aloof from others, or holding back one's feelings from expression, or one's affairs from communication to others; it may spring from *coldness* or *pride,* but is not identical with either and may arise from timidity or policy. See MODESTY.

reserve bank A member of the Federal Reserve System.

reserve clause In professional sports, the stipulation in a contract that commits a player to work for a particular team until released or traded by the employer or until retirement.

re·served (ri·zûrvd′) *adj.* **1** Showing or characterized by reserve of manner; distant; undemonstrative. **2** Retained; kept back. See synonyms under HAUGHTY, TACITURN. —**re·serv·ed·ly** (ri·zûr′vid·lē) *adv.* —**re·serv′ed·ness** *n.*

re·serv·ist (ri·zûr′vist) *n.* A member of the military reserve.

res·er·voir (rez′ər·vwôr, -vwär, -vôr) *n.* **1** A receptacle where some material, especially of a liquid or gas, may be kept in store. **2** A basin, either natural or artificial, for collecting and containing a supply of water, as for use in a city or for water power. **3** An attachment to a stove, machine, or instrument, for containing a fluid to be used in its operation: the *reservoir* of a lamp. **4** An extra supply; a store of anything. [<F *réservoir*]

re·set (rē·set′) *v.t.* **·set, ·set·ting** To set again. — *n.* (rē′set′) The act of resetting, or that which is reset; specifically, a resetting of type. — **re·set′ter** *n.*

res ges·ta (rēz jes′tə) *pl.* **res ges·tae** (jes′tē) *Latin* **1** Anything done; a transaction. **2** *Usually pl.* All the essential circumstances attending a transaction.

resh (resh) *n.* The twentieth Hebrew letter. See ALPHABET. [<Hebrew *rēsh*, lit., the head]

re·ship (rē·ship′) *v.* **·shipped, ·ship·ping** *v.t.* **1** To ship again. **2** To transfer (oneself) to another vessel. — *v.i.* **3** To go on a vessel again. **4** To sign for another voyage as a crew member or a passenger.

re·ship·ment (rē·ship′mənt) *n.* **1** The act of reshipping. **2** The thing reshipped.

Resht (resht) A city in northern Iran, near the Caspian Sea.

re·side (ri·zīd′) *v.i.* **·sid·ed, ·sid·ing** **1** To dwell for a considerable time; make one's home; live. **2** To exist as an attribute or quality: with *in.* **3** To be vested: with *in.* See synonyms under ABIDE. [<F *résider* <L *residere* sit back, abide < *re-* back + *sedere* sit] — **re·sid′er** *n.*

res·i·dence (rez′ə·dəns) *n.* **1** The place or the house where one resides. **2** The act of residing. **3** Inherence in a thing, as of an attribute in a subject. **4** The fact of being officially present; the statutory presence of an incumbent in a benefice, as a bishop in his diocese: especially in the phrase **in residence:** the canon *in residence.* **5** The seat or place of power or government. **6** The length of time one resides in a place. See synonyms under HOME, HOUSE. [<OF <LL *residentia*]

res·i·den·cy (rez′ə·dən·sē) *n. pl.* **·cies** **1** Residence. **2** In the East Indies, the official abode of the representative of the governor general, as at a native court. **3** Formerly, a government division of the Dutch East Indies.

res·i·dent (rez′ə·dənt) *n.* **1** One who resides or dwells in a place. **2** A diplomatic representative residing at a foreign court or seat of government; specifically, a **minister resident,** a diplomatic agent of the third rank, accredited by the sovereign or head of one country to the sovereign or head of another country; also, an agent in a protectorate. — *adj.* **1** Having a residence; residing. **2** Abiding in a place in connection with one's official work: a *resident* physician. **3** Inherent: Pungency is *resident* in pepper. **4** Not migratory: said of certain birds. [<OF]

res·i·den·tial (rez′ə·den′shəl) *adj.* **1** Pertaining to, fitted for, or resulting from residence; having residence. **2** Used by residents.

res·i·den·ti·ar·y (rez′ə·den′shē·er′ē, -shər·ē) *adj.* **1** Having or maintaining a residence, especially an official residence. **2** Pertaining to residence. — *n. pl.* **·ar·ies** A resident.

re·sid·u·al (ri·zij′o͞o·əl) *adj.* **1** Pertaining to or having the nature of a residue or remainder. **2** Left over as a residue. — *n.* **1** That which is left over from a total mass, magnitude, or quantity which has been acted upon in any specified way; a remainder or remnant. **2** *Stat.* **a** The difference between observed results and those obtained by computation according to formula. **b** The difference between the value of a given observation and the mean of a series to which it belongs. **3** *Often pl.* A payment made to a performer for each rerun of taped or filmed television material in which he or she has appeared. — **re·sid′u·al·ly** *adv.*

re·sid·u·ar·y (ri·zij′o͞o·er′ē) *adj.* Of or pertaining to a residuum or remainder; residual.

res·i·due (rez′ə·do͞o, -dyo͞o) *n.* **1** A remainder or surplus after a part has been separated or otherwise treated. **2** *Chem.* **a** Insoluble matter left after filtration or separation from a liquid. **b** An atom or radical separated from a molecule of a substance. **c** A residuum. **3** *Law* That portion of an estate which remains after all charges, debts, and particular bequests have been satisfied. [<OF *residu* <L *residuum,* neut. of *residuus* remaining < *residere.* See RESIDE.]

re·sid·u·um (ri·zij′o͞o·əm) *n. pl.* **·u·a** (-o͞o·ə) **1** That which remains after any process of subtraction; a residue. **2** *Chem.* A residual product: the *residuum* from the distillation of coal tar. **3** Residue (def. 3). [<L]

re·sign (ri·zīn′) *v.t.* **1** To give up, as a position, office, or trust. **2** To relinquish (a privilege, claim, etc.). **3** To give over (oneself, one's mind, etc.), as to fate or domination. — *v.i.* **4** To resign a position, etc. See synonyms under ABANDON. [<OF *resigner* <L *resignare* sign back, transfer, cancel < *re-* back + *signare* sign] — **re·sign′er** *n.*

re–sign (rē·sīn′) *v.t.* To sign again.

res·ig·na·tion (rez′ig·nā′shən) *n.* **1** The act of resigning, as a position, office, or trust, or the formal document declaring such act. **2** The quality of being submissive; unresisting acquiescence. See synonyms under PATIENCE, SUBMISSION. [<F *résignation*]

re·signed (ri·zīnd′) *adj.* Characterized by resignation; submissive. — **re·sign·ed·ly,** (ri·zī′nid·lē) *adv.* — **re·sign′ed·ness** *n.*

re·sile (ri·zīl′) *v.i.* **·siled, ·sil·ing** **1** To spring back; recoil. **2** To resume original shape or position after being stretched or compressed. [<MF *resiler* <L *resilire* rebound < *re-* back + *salire* leap]

re·sil·ience (ri·zil′yəns) *n.* **1** The act or power of springing back to a former position or shape; elasticity. **2** *Physics* The quantity of work given back by a body that is compressed to a certain limit and then allowed freely to recover its former size or shape. Also **re·sil′·ien·cy.**

re·sil·ient (ri·zil′yənt) *adj.* **1** Springing back to a former shape or position. **2** Capable of recoiling from pressure or shock unchanged or undamaged. **3** Elastic; buoyant. [<L *resiliens, -entis,* ppr. of *resilire.* See RESILE.] — **re·sil′ient·ly** *adv.*

res·in (rez′in) *n.* **1** An amorphous organic substance exuded from plants, especially from fir or pine trees, yellowish or dark in color and usually translucent or transparent: it is soluble in alcohol and ether, and is a non-conductor of electricity. **2** Any of various substances made by chemical synthesis, especially those used in the making of plastics. **3** The resinous precipitate obtained from a vegetable tincture by treatment with water: used in pharmacy. **4** Rosin. — *v.t.* To apply resin to. [<OF *resine* <L *resina* <Gk. *rhētinē*] — **res·i·na·ceous** (rez′ə·nā′shəs) *adj.*

res·in·ate (rez′ən·āt) *v.t.* **·at·ed, ·at·ing** To infuse or impregnate with resin.

res·in·if·er·ous (rez′ən·if′ər·əs) *adj.* Producing resin.

res·in·og·ra·phy (rez′ən·og′rə·fē) *n.* The microscopic study of the etched or polished surfaces of synthetic resins in order to identify the pigments, fillers, or other substances composing them. — **res′in·og′ra·pher** *n.*

res·in·oid (rez′ən·oid) *adj.* Resembling resin. — *n.* **1** A substance either wholly or partially of a resinous nature. **2** Any of a class of thermosetting synthetic resins.

res·i·nous (rez′ə·nəs) *adj.* **1** Of the nature of resins, or containing more or less resin as an ingredient. **2** Obtained from resin: *resinous* electricity; electronegative.

res·in·y (rez′ən·ē) *adj.* Resinous.

re·sist (ri·zist′) *v.t.* **1** To strive against; act counter to for the purpose of stopping, preventing, defeating, etc. **2** To be proof against; withstand; defeat. **3** To refrain from: I can't *resist* teasing him. — *v.i.* **4** To offer opposition. See synonyms under DRIVE, HINDER, OPPOSE, REPEL. — *n.* Any substance used to prevent the action of another substance, as a coating applied to a surface to protect it from an acid. [<OF *resister* <L *resistere* cause to stand back < *re-* back + *sistere,* causative of *stare* stand] — **re·sist′er** *n.*

re·sis·tance (ri·zis′təns) *n.* **1** The act of resisting. **2** Any force tending to hinder motion. **3** *Electr.* **a** The opposition offered by a body to the passage through it of an electric current: expressed in ohms: the reciprocal of *conductance.* **b** Impedance. **4** *Psychol.* The force tending to prevent the return to consciousness of unpleasant incidents and experiences. **5** The underground and guerrilla movement opposing an occupying power. See synonyms under DEFENSE. [<F *résistance*]

re·sis·tant (ri·zis′tənt) *adj.* Offering or tending to produce resistance; resisting. — *n.* One who or that which resists. [<F *résistant*]

Re·sis·ten·cia (rā′sēs·ten′syä) The capital of Chaco province, northern Argentina.

re·sist·i·ble (ri·zis′tə·bəl) *adj.* Capable of being resisted. — **re·sist′i·bil′i·ty** *n.* — **re·sist′i·bly** *adv.*

re·sis·tive (ri·zis′tiv) *adj.* Having or exercising the power of resistance. — **re·sis′tive·ly** *adv.*

re·sis·tiv·i·ty (rē′zis·tiv′ə·tē) *n.* **1** The capacity to resist, or the degree of that capacity. **2** *Electr.* Specific resistance to the electric or magnetic force of a substance as tested in a cube measuring one centimeter: the reciprocal of *conductivity.*

re·sist·less (ri·zist′lis) *adj.* **1** Irresistible. **2** Offering no resistance; powerless. — **re·sist′·less·ly** *adv.* — **re·sist′less·ness** *n.*

re·sis·tor (ri·zis′tər) *n. Electr.* A device, as a coil of wire, for introducing resistance into an electrical circuit.

res ju·di·ca·ta (rēz jo͞o′də·kā′tə) *Latin* Literally, a matter decided; an issue or point of law that has been previously decided by a court of authoritative or competent jurisdiction and which when pleaded is conclusive of the matter in controversy. Also *res adjudicata.*

re·sole (rē·sōl′) *v.t.* **·soled, ·sol·ing** To sole again.

res·o·lu·ble (rez′ə·lo͞o·bəl, ri·zol′yə·bəl) *adj.* Capable of being resolved; soluble. [<LL *resolubilis*] —**res′o·lu·bil′i·ty, res′o·lu·ble·ness** *n.*

res·o·lute (rez′ə·lo͞ot) *adj.* Having a fixed purpose; determined; constant; steady; also, bold; unflinching. See synonyms under FIRM, INFLEXIBLE, OBSTINATE. [<L *resolutus,* pp. of *resolvere.* See RESOLVE.] — **res′o·lute·ly** *adv.* — **res′o·lute·ness** *n.*

res·o·lu·tion (rez′ə·lo͞o′shən) *n.* **1** The act of resolving or of reducing to a simpler form. **2** The state of being resolute; active fortitude; resoluteness. **3** The making of a resolve; also, the purpose or course resolved upon; a resolve; determination. **4** Chemical, mechanical, or mental analysis; separation of anything into component parts. **5** A proposition offered to or adopted by an assembly. **6** *Law* A judgment or decision of a court. **7** *Med.* The termination of an abnormal condition. **8** *Music* **a** The replacement of a dissonant tone or chord by a higher or lower one so that a consonance, or, sometimes, another dissonance occurs. **b** The tone or chord replacing the original dissonant tone or chord. See synonyms under COURAGE, DETERMINATION, FORTITUDE, PURPOSE, PERSEVERANCE, WILL. — **concurrent resolution** A resolution adopted by both of the houses of Congress and having the force of law without the signature of the President. — **joint resolution** A resolution which, when passed by both houses of Congress and approved by the President, has the force of law. [<L *resolutio, -onis* < *resolutus.* See RESOLUTE.] — **res′o·lu′tion·er, res′o·lu′·tion·ist** *n.*

re·solv·a·ble (ri·zol′və·bəl) *adj.* Capable of being resolved, analyzed, or solved. — **re·solv′a·bil′i·ty, re·solv′a·ble·ness** *n.*

re·solve (ri·zolv′) *v.* **·solved, ·solv·ing** *v.t.* **1** To decide; determine (to do something). **2** To cause to decide or determine. **3** To separate or break down into constituent parts; analyze. **4** To make clear; explain or solve, as a problem. **5** To explain away; remove (doubts, etc.). **6** To state or decide by vote, as in a legislative assembly. **7** To transform; convert: He *resolves* his anger into pride. **8** *Music* To change, as a chord, from dissonance to consonance; cause to undergo resolution. **9** *Chem.* To separate (a racemic compound) into its optically active components. **10** *Optics* To make distinguishable the structure or parts of. **11** *Med.* To cause to disperse or be absorbed without the formation of pus. **12** *Obs.* To melt; dissolve. **13** *Obs.* To inform. — *v.i.* **14** To make up one's mind; arrive at a decision: with *on* or *upon.* **15** To become separated into constituent parts. **16** *Music* To undergo resolution. — *n.* **1** Fixity of purpose; resolution. **2** A fixed determination; a resolution. **3** The action of a deliberative body expressing formally its intention or purpose. See synonyms under DETERMINATION, PURPOSE. [<L *resolvere* loosen again, relax < *re-* again + *solvere* loosen] — **re·solv′er** *n.*

re·solved (ri·zolvd′) *adj.* Fixed or set in purpose; determined; also, having formed a resolve. See synonyms under OBSTINATE. — **re·solv·ed·ly** (ri·zol′vid·lē) *adv.*

re·solv·ent (ri·zol′vənt) *adj.* Having the power to cause the dissolution or resolution of a thing into its elements; solvent. — *n.* **1** That which has the power of resolving or dissolving; a solvent. 2 *Med.* A preparation which has the property of reducing or dispersing a swelling. [<L *resolvens, -entis,* ppr. of *resolvere.* See RESOLVE.]

res·o·nance (rez'ə·nəns) *n.* 1 The state or quality of being resonant; resonant sound. 2 *Physics* **a** The phenomenon exhibited by any vibratory system responding with large amplitude to a series of imposed vibrations of equal, or nearly equal, frequency. **b** That property of a molecule by virtue of which it assumes an electronic structure intermediate between two other theoretically possible structures. **c** The prolongation and amplification of sound by reverberation within a cavity. 3 *Electr.* The condition of an electric circuit in which maximum flow of current is obtained by impressing an electromotive force of given frequency. [<L *resonantia* echo]

res·o·nant (rez'ə·nənt) *adj.* 1 Sending back or having the quality of sending back or prolonging sound. 2 Resounding; specifically, having resonance. [<L *resonans, -antis,* ppr. of *resonare* resound, echo < *re-* back, again + *sonare* sound] —**res'o·nant·ly** *adv.*

res·o·nate (rez'ə·nāt) *v.i.* **·nat·ed, ·nat·ing** 1 To have or produce resonance. 2 To manifest sympathetic vibration, as a resonator. [<L *resonatus,* pp. of *resonare.* See RESONANT.]

res·o·na·tor (rez'ə·nā'tər) *n.* 1 That which resounds. 2 *Electronics* Any device used to exhibit or utilize the effects of resonance. 3 *Physics* A set or cluster of electrons which absorbs electromagnetic waves of certain frequencies. [<NL]

re·sorb (ri·sôrb') *v.t.* To reabsorb. [<L *resorbere* drink in again, suck back < *re-* back, again + *sorbere* drink in, suck up] —**re·sorption** (ri·sôrp'shən) *n.*

re·sor·cin·ol (ri·zôr'sin·ōl, -ol) *n. Chem.* A colorless crystalline compound, $C_6H_6O_2$, of peculiar odor and sweetish taste, used as an antiseptic and in the treatment of skin eruptions. Also **re·sor'cin.** [<RES(IN) + ORCINOL] —**re·sor'cin·al** *adj.*

re·sort (ri·zôrt') *v.i.* 1 To go frequently or habitually; repair. 2 To have recourse; apply or betake oneself for relief or aid: with *to.* —*n.* 1 The act of frequenting a place. 2 A place resorted to or frequented to regain health, or for amusement or entertainment. 3 The use of something as a means; a recourse; refuge. [<OF *resortir* < *re-* again + *sortir* go out] —**re·sort'er** *n.*

re·sound (ri·zound') *v.i.* 1 To be filled with sound; echo; reverberate. 2 To make a loud, prolonged, or echoing sound. 3 To ring; echo: said of sounds. 4 *Poetic* To be famed or extolled. —*v.t.* 5 To give back (a sound, etc.); re-echo. 6 *Poetic* To celebrate; extol. 7 *Rare* To utter or repeat loudly. See synonyms under ROAR. [<OF *resoner* <L *resonare.* See RESONANT.]

re–sound (rē·sound') *v.t.* & *v.i.* To sound again.

re·source (ri·sôrs', -sōrs', rē'sôrs, -sōrs) *n.* 1 That which is resorted to for aid or support; resort. 2 *pl.* Available means or property; a supply that can be drawn on; any natural advantages or products: natural *resources.* 3 Capacity for finding or adapting means; power of achievement. 4 Fertility in expedients; resourcefulness; skill or ingenuity in meeting any situation. See synonyms under ALTERNATIVE, PROPERTY. [<OF *ressource* < *resourdre* rise again < *re-* (<L *re-*) back + *sourdre* <L *surgere* rise, surge]

re·source·ful (ri·sôrs'fəl, -sōrs'-) *adj.* 1 Fertile in resources or expedients. 2 Full of resources. —**re·source'ful·ly** *adv.* —**re·source'ful·ness** *n.*

re·spect (ri·spekt') *v.t.* 1 To have deferential regard for; esteem. 2 To treat with propriety or consideration. 3 To regard as inviolable; avoid intruding upon. 4 To have relation or reference to; concern. See synonyms under ADMIRE, DEFER, VENERATE. —*n.* 1 A just regard for and appreciation of worth; honor and esteem: I have great *respect* for the man. 2 Demeanor or deportment indicating deference; courteous regard: to have *respect* for one's elders. 3 *pl.* Expressions of consideration or esteem; compliments: to pay one's *respects.* 4 Conformity to duty or obligation; compliance or observance: *respect* for the law. 5 The condition of being honored or respected: He is held in *respect* by his colleagues. 6 A specific aspect or feature; detail: In what *respect* is he wanting? 7 Reference or relation: usually with *to*: with *respect* to profits. 8 Undue inclination or bias of mind: to have *respect* of persons. 9 *Obs.* Consideration. [<L *respectare* < *respectus,* pp. of *respicere* look back, consider < *re-* again + *specere* look]

re·spect·a·bil·i·ty (ri·spek'tə·bil'ə·tē) *n. pl.* **·ties** 1 The characteristic or quality of being respectable; fair social standing; good repute. 2 The respectable people of a community, collectively. 3 *pl.* Certain conventions and other features of conduct presumed to be signs of gentility, social position, morality, etc. Also **re·spect'a·ble·ness.**

re·spect·a·ble (ri·spek'tə·bəl) *adj.* 1 Deserving of respect; being of good name or repute; also, respected. 2 Being of moderate excellence; fairly good; considerable in number, quantity, size, quality, etc.; average. 3 Having a good appearance; presentable. 4 Conventionally correct or socially acceptable in conduct; of decent character. —**re·spect'a·bly** *adv.*

re·spect·er (ri·spek'tər) *n.* One who respects, usually one who respects persons: often in the phrase **respecter of persons,** one who shows favoritism or is influenced in his opinions or actions by others.

re·spect·ful (ri·spekt'fəl) *adj.* Marked by or manifesting respect; deferential. —**re·spect'ful·ly** *adv.* —**re·spect'ful·ness** *n.*

re·spect·ing (ri·spek'ting) *prep.* In relation to; regarding.

re·spec·tive (ri·spek'tiv) *adj.* 1 Pertaining or relating severally to each of those under consideration; several; particular. 2 *Obs.* Characterized by partiality. 3 *Obs.* Attentive.

re·spec·tive·ly (ri·spek'tiv·lē) *adv.* As singly or severally considered; singly in the order designated: The first, second, and third seats belong to John, James, and William *respectively.*

re·spell (rē·spel') *v.t.* To spell again, especially in a system whereby pronunciation is indicated. —**re·spell'ing** *n.*

Re·spi·ghi (rā·spē'gē), **Ottorino,** 1879–1936, Italian composer.

re·spir·a·ble (ri·spīr'ə·bəl, res'pər·ə·bəl) *adj.* 1 Capable of being respired or breathed; fit for respiration. 2 Able to breathe or respire. [<F]

res·pi·ra·tion (res'pə·rā'shən) *n.* 1 The act of inhaling air into the lungs and expelling it; breathing. 2 The process by which a plant or animal takes in oxygen from the air and gives off carbon dioxide and other products of oxidation in the tissues. [<L *respiratio, -onis*]

res·pi·ra·tor (res'pə·rā'tər) *n.* 1 A screen, as of fine gauze, worn over the mouth or nose, as a protection against dust, etc. 2 A device worn over the nose and mouth for the inhalation of medicated vapors, or to warm or sift the air for lung patients. 3 A gas mask. 4 An apparatus for artificial respiration, as a Pulmotor. [<L *respiratus,* pp. of *respirare.* See RESPIRE.]

respirator cabinet An iron lung.

re·spir·a·to·ry (ri·spīr'ə·tôr'ē, -tō'rē, res'pər·ə-) *adj.* Of, pertaining to, employed in, or caused by respiration.

re·spire (ri·spīr') *v.* **·spired, ·spir·ing** *v.i.* 1 To inhale and exhale air; breathe. 2 To breathe again; recover vitality, hope, ambition, courage, etc. —*v.t.* 3 To inhale and exhale; breathe. 4 *Rare* To breathe or give forth; exhale. [<F *respirer* <L *respirare* < *re-* again + *spirare* breathe]

res·pite (res'pit) *n.* 1 Postponement; delay. 2 Temporary intermission of labor or effort; an interval of rest. 3 *Law* Temporary suspension of the execution of a sentence for a capital offense; reprieve. —*v.t.* **·pit·ed, ·pit·ing** 1 To relieve by a pause or rest. 2 To grant delay in the execution of (a penalty, sentence, etc.). 3 To put off or postpone. [<OF *respit* <Med. L *respectus* delay <L, consideration, regard < *respicere.* See RESPECT.]

Synonyms (noun): delay, forbearance, interval, pause, postponement, reprieve, rest, stay. *Antonyms*: accomplishment, completion, consummation, effect, execution, operation, performance.

re·splen·dence (ri·splen'dəns) *n.* The state or quality of being resplendent; brilliant luster; splendor. Also **re·splen'den·cy.**

re·splen·dent (ri·splen'dənt) *adj.* Shining with brilliant luster; vividly bright; splendid; gorgeous. See synonyms under BRIGHT. [<L *resplendens, -entis,* ppr. of *resplendere* glitter < *re-* again and again + *splendere* shine] —**re·splen'dent·ly** *adv.*

re·spond (ri·spond') *v.i.* 1 To give an answer; reply. 2 To act in reply or return. 3 *Law* To be liable or answerable. —*v.t.* 4 To say in answer; reply. —*n. Archit.* A pilaster, semi column, or similar feature placed against a wall, to receive an arch. [<L *respondere* give back in return < *re-* back + *spondere* pledge, promise] —**re·spond'er** *n.*

re·spon·dence (ri·spon'dəns) *n.* 1 The character or condition of being respondent. 2 The act of responding. 3 Agreement. Also **re·spon'den·cy.**

re·spon·dent (ri·spon'dənt) *adj.* 1 Giving response, or given as a response; answering; responsive. 2 *Law* Occupying the position of defendant. 3 *Obs.* Correspondent. —*n.* 1 One who responds or answers. 2 *Law* The party called upon to answer an appeal or petition; a defendant; especially, the defendant in a suit in equity, admiralty, or divorce. [<L *respondens, -entis,* ppr. of *respondere.* See RESPOND.]

re·sponse (ri·spons') *n.* 1 The act of responding, or that which is responded; words or acts evoked by the words or acts of another or others; an answer; reply. 2 *Eccl.* A portion of a liturgy or church service said or sung by the congregation or choir in reply to the officiating priest; also, an anthem sung or said during or after a reading. 3 *Biol.* The action of an organism or a part, or the cessation of action, resulting from a stimulus or influence; a reaction. [<OF <L *responsum,* neut. of pp. of *respondere.* See RESPOND.]

Synonyms: answer, rejoinder, repartee, reply, retort. A *rejoinder* is strictly an *answer* to a *reply,* while often used in the general sense of *answer,* but always with the implication of something more or less controversial or opposed, yet lacking the conclusiveness implied in *answer.* A *response* is accordant or harmonious, designed or adapted to carry on the thought of the words that called it forth, or to meet the wish of him who seeks it; as, The appeal for aid met a prompt and hearty *response. Repartee* is a prompt, witty, and commonly good-natured *answer* to some argument or attack; a *retort* may also be witty, but is severe and may be even savage in its intensity. See ANSWER.

re·spon·ser (ri·spon'sər) *n. Electronics* The receiving element connected with the transponder of an interrogator assembly. Also **re·spon'sor.**

re·spon·si·bil·i·ty (ri·spon'sə·bil'ə·tē) *n. pl.* **·ties** 1 The state of being responsible or accountable. 2 That for which one is answerable; a duty or trust. 3 Ability to meet obligations or to act without superior authority or guidance. See synonyms under DUTY. Also **re·spon'si·ble·ness.**

re·spon·si·ble (ri·spon'sə·bəl) *adj.* 1 Answerable legally or morally for the discharge of a duty, trust, or debt. 2 Having capacity to perceive the distinctions of right and wrong; having ethical discrimination. 3 Able to meet legitimate claims; having sufficient property or means for the payment of debts. 4 Involving accountability or obligation. 5 Denoting the status of a cabinet or ministry with respect to the legislative body to which it is answerable. [< obs. F *responsible* <L *responsus,* pp. of *respondere.* See RESPOND.] —**re·spon'si·bly** *adv.*

re·spon·sion (ri·spon'shən) *n.* 1 *Rare* A response; reply. 2 *pl.* At Oxford University, the first of the three examinations to be passed by a candidate for a B.A. degree. [<L *responsio, -onis*]

re·spon·sive (ri·spon′siv) *adj.* **1** Inclined or ready to respond; being or reacting in accord, sympathy, or harmony; responding. **2** Constituting, or of the nature of, response or reply. **3** Characterized by or containing responses. **4** *Obs.* Correspondent. — **re·spon′sive·ly** *adv.* — **re·spon′sive·ness** *n.*

re·spon·so·ry (ri·spon′sər·ē) *adj. Obs.* Of or pertaining to response; containing answer; responsive. — *n. pl.* **·ries** *Eccl.* **1** A response sung between readings. **2** A response of the people or congregation to the officiating priest or clergyman. [<Med. L *responsorium*]

res pub·li·ca (rēz pub′li·kə) *pl.* **res pub·li·cae** (pub′li·sē) *Latin* **1** The commonwealth. **2** *pl.* Things that belong to the state.

rest[1] (rest) *v.i.* **1** To cease working, exerting oneself, etc., so as to refresh oneself. **2** To cease from effort or activity for a time. **3** To seek or obtain ease or refreshment by lying down, sleeping, etc. **4** To sleep. **5** To be at peace; be tranquil. **6** To lie in death; be dead. **7** To remain unchanged: And there the matter *rests.* **8** To be supported; stand, lean, lie, or sit: with *against, on,* or *upon.* **9** To be founded or based: with *on* or *upon.* **10** To rely; depend: with *on* or *upon*: Our hopes *rest* on you. **11** To be placed as a burden or responsibility: with *on* or *upon.* **12** To be or lie in a specified place: The blame *rests* with me. **13** To be directed; remain on something, as the gaze or eyes. **14** *Law* To cease presenting evidence in a case. **15** *Agric.* To lie fallow. — *v.t.* **16** To give rest to; refresh by rest. **17** To put, lay, lean, etc., as for support or rest. **18** To found; base. **19** To direct (the gaze, eyes, etc.). **20** *Law* To cease presenting evidence in (a case). — *n.* **1** The act or state of resting; cessation from labor, exertion, action, or motion of any kind; repose; quiet. **2** Freedom from disturbance or disquiet; peace; tranquillity. **3** Sleep; also, death. **4** That on which anything rests; a support; base; basis; foundation; specifically, in billiards and pool, a support for a cue; a bridge. **5** A place of repose or quiet; a stopping place; abode. **6** *Music* **a** A pause, or an interval of silence. **b** A character indicating such pause: an eighth *rest.* **7** In prosody, a pause in a verse; a caesura. **8** *Obs.* Restored or renewed strength. **9** *Mil.* A command given troops, allowing them to relax. ◆ Homophone: *wrest.* [OE *restan*] — **rest′er** *n.*

Synonyms: (verb): abide, acquiesce, cease, desist, halt, hold, lean, lie, pause, recline, repose, sleep, slumber, stand, stay, stop, unbend. See ABIDE, LEAN[1]. *Antonyms*: contend, fight, labor, strive, struggle, toil, wake, watch, work.

Synonyms (noun): calm, calmness, cessation, ease, pause, peace, peacefulness, quiescence, quiet, quietness, quietude, recreation, repose, sleep, slumber, stay, stillness, stop, tranquillity. *Ease* denotes freedom from cause of disturbance, whether external or internal. *Quiet* denotes freedom from agitation, or especially from annoying sounds. *Rest* is a *cessation* of activity, especially of wearying or painful activity. *Recreation* is some pleasing activity of certain organs or faculties that affords *rest* to other parts of our nature that have become weary. *Repose* is a laying down, primarily of the body, and figuratively, a relaxing freedom from toil or strain of mind. *Sleep* is the perfection of *repose,* the most complete *rest; slumber* is a light and ordinarily pleasant form of *sleep.* See REMAINDER, RESPITE. *Antonyms*: agitation, commotion, disquiet, disturbance, excitement, motion, movement, restlessness, stir, strain, toil, tumult, unrest, work.

rest[2] (rest) *n.* **1** That which remains or is left over; a remainder. **2** Those remaining or not enumerated; the others: in this sense a collective noun taking a plural verb. **3** A balance, as of resources. — *v.i.* **1** To be and remain; continue; stay: *Rest* content. **2** *Obs.* To be left: Nothing *rests* but hope. — *v.t.* **3** *Obs.* To cause to remain: God *rest* you well. ◆ Homophone: *wrest.* [<OF *reste* < *rester* remain <L *restare* stop, stand < *re-* again + *stare* stand]

rest[3] (rest) *n.* A support for a lance attached to medieval armor: an aphetic form of *arrest.* ◆ Homophone: *wrest.*

re·state (rē·stāt′) *v.t.* **·stat·ed, ·stat·ing** To state again or anew. — **re·state′ment** *n.*

res·tau·rant (res′tər·ənt, -tə·ränt) *n.* A place where refreshments or meals are provided; a public dining-room. [<F, lit., restoring, ppr. of *restaurer* <OF *restorer.* See RESTORE.]

res·tau·ra·teur (res′tər·ə·tûr′, *Fr.* res·tō·rȧ·tœr′) *n.* The proprietor or keeper of a restaurant. [<F]

rest–balk (rest′bôk′) *n. Agric.* An unplowed ridge between furrows.

rest cure A treatment, as of nervous disorders, prescribing seclusion and quiet, generous diet, massage, etc.

rest·ful (rest′fəl) *adj.* **1** Full of or giving rest; affording freedom from disturbance, work, or trouble. **2** Being at rest or in repose; quiet. — **rest′ful·ly** *adv.* — **rest′ful·ness** *n.*

rest·har·row (rest′har′ō) *n.* A low European undershrub (*Ononis hircina*) of the bean family, with pink and white flowers. [Aphetic form of ARREST + HARROW; from the resistance offered by its tough roots]

res·ti·form (res′tə·fôrm) *adj. Anat.* Ropelike; twisted, as the **restiform bodies,** ropelike bundles of nerve fibers of the medulla oblongata that pass upward to the cerebellum. [<L *restis* cord + -FORM]

rest·ing (res′ting) *adj.* **1** At rest; reposing; also, dead. **2** Dormant.

resting spore *Bot.* A spore that germinates only after a lapse of a number of weeks or months, or at the end of the winter season.

res·ti·tu·tion (res′tə·tōō′shən, -tyōō′-) *n.* **1** The act of restoring something that has been taken away or lost. **2** The act of making good or rendering an equivalent for injury or loss; indemnification. **3** Restoration to, return to, or recovery of a former position or condition. **4** *Physics* The property of elastic bodies by which they tend to recover their shape after compression. **5** Establishment of the true nature or position of objects distorted in an aerial photograph. [<OF <L *restitutio, -onis* < *restitutus,* pp. of *restituere* restore, set up again < *re-* again + *statuere* set up]

Synonyms: amends, compensation, indemnification, indemnity, recompense, remuneration, reparation, repayment, restoration, return. *Antonyms*: cheat, cheating, defrauding, embezzlement, extortion, fraud, plunder, robbery, stealing, theft.

res·tive (res′tiv) *adj.* **1** Impatient of control; unruly. **2** Restless; fidgety; also, stubborn; balky. [<F *restif* < *rester* remain, balk <L *restare.* See REST[2].] — **res′tive·ly** *adv.* — **res′tive·ness** *n.*

Synonyms: fidgety, fractious, fretful, frisky, impatient, intractable, mutinous, rebellious, refractory, restless, skittish, unruly, vicious. The disposition to offer active resistance to control by any means whatever is what is commonly indicated by *restive.* A horse may be made *restless* by flies or by martial music, but with no refractoriness; the *restive* animal impatiently resists or struggles to break from control, as by bolting, flinging his rider, or otherwise. With this the metaphorical use of the word agrees, which is always in the sense of such terms as *impatient, intractable, rebellious,* and the like; a people *restive* under despotism are not disposed to "rest" under it, but to resist it and fling it off. *Antonyms*: docile, gentle, manageable, obedient, peaceable, quiet, submissive, tractable, yielding.

rest·less (rest′lis) *adj.* **1** Having no rest; never quiet; unresting: the *restless* waves. **2** Unable or disinclined to rest. **3** Uneasy; constantly seeking change. **4** Discontented. **5** Devoid of or destructive to rest or repose; obtaining no rest or sleep; sleepless. See synonyms under ACTIVE. — **rest′less·ly** *adv.* — **rest′less·ness** *n.*

re·stock (rē·stok′) *v.t.* To stock again or anew.

res·to·ra·tion (res′tə·rā′shən) *n.* **1** The act of restoring a person or thing to a former place or condition. **2** The state of being restored; rehabilitation; renewal. **3** The bringing back of a building or work of art as nearly as may be to its original state; also, the restored building or object. **4** *Paleontol.* The reconstruction of the skeleton of a fossil animal. **5** *Theol.* The doctrine that all men will eventually be restored to a sinless state and divine favor. See UNIVERSALISM. — **the Restoration** **1** The return of Charles II to the English throne in 1660, after the overthrow of the Cromwellian Protectorate; also, the following period until 1685. **2** The return of the Bourbons to power in 1814 under Louis XVIII; also, the period following the return. **3** The return of the Jews to Palestine after the Babylonian captivity. [<OF *restauration* <LL *restauratio, -onis* <L *restauratus,* pp. of *restaurare.* See RESTORE.]

re·sto·ra·tive (ri·stôr′ə·tiv, -stō′rə-) *adj.* **1** Tending or able to restore. **2** Pertaining to restoration. — *n.* That which restores; specifically, something to restore consciousness after a fainting fit.

re·store (ri·stôr′, -stōr′) *v.t.* **·stored, ·stor·ing** **1** To bring into existence or effect again: to *restore* peace. **2** To bring back to a former or original condition, appearance, etc.: to *restore* a great painting. **3** To put back in a former place or position; reinstate, as a deposed monarch. **4** To bring back to health and vigor. **5** To give back (something lost or taken away); return. See synonyms under RECLAIM, RECOVER. [<OF *restorer* <L *restaurare* < *re-* again + *-staurare* make firm, as in *instaurare* repair] — **re·stor′er** *n.*

re–store (rē·stôr′, -stōr′) *v.t.* **–stored, –stor·ing** To store again or anew.

re·strain (ri·strān′) *v.t.* **1** To hold back from acting, proceeding, or advancing; keep in check; repress. **2** To deprive of freedom or liberty, as by placing in a prison or asylum. **3** To restrict or limit. [<OF *restraindre, restreindre* <L *restringere* < *re-* back + *stringere* draw tight] — **re·strain′a·ble** *adj.* — **re·strain′ed·ly** *adv.*

Synonyms: abridge, bridle, check, circumscribe, confine, constrain, curb, hinder, hold, keep, repress, restrict, suppress. *Constrain* is positive; *restrain* is negative; one is *constrained* to an action; he is *restrained* from an action. *Constrain* refers almost exclusively to moral force, *restrain* frequently to physical force, as when we speak of putting one under restraint. To *restrain* an action is to hold it partially or wholly in check, thus controlling it even in performance; to *restrict* an action is to fix a limit or boundary which it may not pass, but within which it is free. To *repress,* literally to press back, is to hold in check, and perhaps only temporarily, that which is still very active; it is a feebler word than *restrain*; to *suppress* is finally and effectually to put down; *suppress* is a much stronger word than *restrain*; as, to *suppress* a rebellion. See ARREST, BIND, GOVERN, KEEP, LIMIT, REFRAIN, REPRESS, TEMPER. *Antonyms*: aid, animate, arouse, emancipate, encourage, excite, free, impel, incite, release.

re·strain·er (ri·strā′nər) *n.* **1** One who or that which restrains. **2** *Phot.* A chemical agent used to retard the action of the developer.

re·straint (ri·strānt′) *n.* **1** The act of restraining. **2** The state of being restrained; abridgment of liberty; confinement. **3** That which restrains; a restriction. **4** Self-repression; constraint. See synonyms under BARRIER, RESERVE. [<OF *restrainte,* noun use of pp. of *restraindre.* See RESTRAIN.]

re·strict (ri·strikt′) *v.t.* To hold or keep within limits or bounds; confine. See synonyms under BIND, CIRCUMSCRIBE, LIMIT, RESTRAIN. [<L *restrictus,* pp. of *restringere.* See RESTRAIN.]

re·strict·ed (ri·strik′tid) *adj.* **1** Limited; confined. **2** Not for general consumption, use, or service: *restricted* traffic or supplies. **3** Denoting specified defense information the unauthorized publication or dissemination of which is prohibited by law. — **re·strict′ed·ly** *adv.*

re·stric·tion (ri·strik′shən) *n.* **1** The act of restricting, or the state of being restricted; limitation. **2** That which restricts; a restraint. **3** Reservation; self-repression. See synonyms under BARRIER.

re·stric·tive (ri·strik′tiv) *adj.* **1** Serving, tending, or operating to restrict. **2** *Gram. & Logic* Limiting in thought, expression, or application. — **re·stric′tive·ly** *adv.*

rest–room (rest′rōōm′, -rŏŏm′) *n.* A room in a public building, as a railroad station, theater, office building, etc., provided with means and conveniences for the rest and comfort of patrons or employees; also, a toilet in a public building.

re·sult (ri·zult′) *n.* **1** The outcome of an action, course, process, or agency; consequence;

effect; conclusion. **2** *Math.* A quantity or value ascertained by calculation. **3** The final determination of a deliberative assembly. See synonyms under CONSEQUENCE, END, EVENT, HARVEST, OPERATION, PRODUCT. — *v.i.* **1** To be a result or outcome; be a physical or logical consequent; follow: with *from.* **2** To have an issue; terminate; end: with *in.* [<Med. L *resultare* <L, spring back, freq. of *resilire* rebound. See RESILE.]

re·sul·tant (ri·zul′tənt) *adj.* Arising or following as a result. — *n.* **1** That which results; a consequence. **2** *Physics* A force, velocity, etc., resulting from the action of two or more quantities of the same kind. [<L *resultans, -antis,* ppr. of *resultare.* See RESULT.]

re·sume (ri·zo͞om′) *v.* **·sumed, ·sum·ing** *v.t.* **1** To begin again; take up again after cessation or interruption. **2** To take or occupy again: *Resume* your places. **3** To take for oneself again: to *resume* a title. — *v.i.* **4** To continue after cessation or interruption. See synonyms under RECOVER. [<F *résumer* <L *resumere* take up again, take back < *re-* again + *sumere* take, seize] — **re·sum′a·ble** *adj.* — **re·sum′er** *n.*

ré·su·mé (rez′o͞o·mā′, rez′o͞o·mā) *n.* A summary, as of one's employment record. [<F]

re·sump·tion (ri·zump′shən) *n.* The act of resuming. [<L *resumptio, -onis* < *resumptus,* pp. of *resumere.* See RESUME.]

re·su·pi·nate (ri·so͞o′pə·nāt) *adj. Bot.* Having the appearance of being upside down; inverted; reversed: said of the flowers of orchids. [<L *resupinatus,* pp. of *resupinare* bend back < *resupinus.* See RESUPINE.] — **re·su′pi·na′·tion** *n.*

re·su·pine (rē′so͞o·pīn′) *adj.* Lying on the back; supine. [<L *resupinus* < *re-* again + *supinus* on the back]

re·sur·face (rē·sûr′fis) *v.t.* **·faced, ·fac·ing** To provide with a new surface.

re·sur·gam (ri·sûr′gam) *Latin* I shall rise again.

re·surge (ri·sûrj′) *v.i.* **·surged, ·surg·ing** **1** To rise again; be resurrected. **2** To surge or sweep back again, as the tide. [<L *resurgere* < *re-* again + *surgere* rise]

re·sur·gence (ri·sûr′jəns) *n.* A rising again.

re·sur·gent (ri·sûr′jənt) *adj.* **1** Rising again, as from the grave. **2** Surging back or again. [<L *resurgens, -entis,* ppr. of *resurgere*]

res·ur·rect (rez′ə·rekt′) *v.t.* **1** To bring back to life; raise from the dead. **2** To bring back into use or to notice. — *v.i.* **3** To rise again from the dead. [Back formation <RESURRECTION]

res·ur·rec·tion (rez′ə·rek′shən) *n.* **1** A rising again from the dead. **2** The state of those who have risen from the dead. **3** Any revival or renewal, as of a practice or custom, after disuse, decay, etc.; restoration; rebirth. **4** In Christian Science, spiritualization of thought; a new and higher idea of immortality, or spiritual existence; material belief yielding to spiritual understanding. — **the Resurrection** *Theol.* **1** The rising of Christ from the dead. **2** The rising again of all the dead at the day of final judgment. [<L *resurrectio, -onis* < *resurrectus,* pp. of *resurgere.* See RESURGE.] — **res′ur·rec′tion·al** *adj.*

res·ur·rec·tion·ar·y (rez′ə·rek′shən·er′ē) *adj.* **1** Of or pertaining to resurrection. **2** Of or pertaining to the exhuming of dead bodies.

res·ur·rec·tion·ist (rez′ə·rek′shən·ist) *n.* **1** One who steals bodies from the grave; a body-snatcher. **2** One who brings to light anything buried in obscurity. **3** A believer in the rising again of the dead. — **res′ur·rec′tion·ism** *n.*

resurrection plant The rose of Jericho.

re·sus·ci·tate (ri·sus′ə·tāt) *v.t.* & *v.i.* **·tat·ed, ·tat·ing** To bring or come back to life; revive from unconsciousness or apparent death. [<L *resuscitatus,* pp. of *resuscitare* < *re-* again + *suscitare* revive < *sub-* under + *citare* call, rouse. See CITE.] — **re·sus′ci·ta′tive** *adj.* — **re·sus′ci·ta′tor** *n.*

re·sus·ci·ta·tion (ri·sus′ə·tā′shən) *n.* The act of resuscitating, or the state of being resuscitated; revivification; reanimation.

Resz·ke (resh′ke), **Édouard de,** 1856–1917, Polish basso. — **Jean de,** 1853–1925, Polish tenor; brother of the preceding.

ret (ret) *v.t.* **ret·ted, ret·ting** To steep or soak, as flax, to facilitate the separation of the fibers: also *rot.* [ME *reten,* ? <MDu. *reten* soak]

re·ta·ble (ri·tā′bəl) *n.* **1** A shelf or ledge raised above the back of an altar to support ornaments, lights, etc. **2** A panel containing a picture or bas-relief of subjects from sacred history. [<F <OF *rere-table* <Med. L *retrotabulum* <L *retro-* behind + *tabula* plank]

re·tail (rē′tāl) *n.* The selling of goods in small quantities: opposed to *wholesale.* — *adj.* Of, pertaining to, or concerned in the sale of goods in small quantities or parcels. — *v.t.* **1** To sell in small quantities; sell directly to the ultimate consumer. **2** (ri·tāl′) To repeat, as gossip. — *v.i.* **3** To be sold at retail. [<OF, cutting < *retailler* cut up < *re-* again + *tailler* cut <LL *taliare* split]

re·tail·er (rē′tā·lər) *n.* One who sells in small quantities to the consumer.

re·tain (ri·tān′) *v.t.* **1** To keep or continue to keep in one's possession; hold. **2** To maintain in use, practice, etc.: to *retain* one's standards. **3** To keep in a fixed condition or place. **4** To keep in mind; remember. **5** To hire, as a servant; also, to engage (an attorney or other representative) by paying a retainer. [<OF *retenir* <L *retinere* < *re-* back + *tenere* hold]

Synonyms: detain, employ, engage, hire, hold, keep, maintain, preserve, reserve, secure, withhold. See KEEP, REMEMBER. *Antonyms*: abandon, cede, discard, discharge, dismiss, eject, relinquish, renounce, resign, surrender.

re·tain·er[1] (ri·tā′nər) *n.* **1** One retained in the service of a person of rank or position. **2** One who retains or keeps. **3** *Mech.* A device for holding the parts of ball or roller bearings in place.

re·tain·er[2] (ri·tā′nər) *n.* **1** The fee paid, or the agreement made, to employ an attorney to serve in a suit; a retaining fee. **2** A similar fee paid to anyone to retain his services. [<OF *retenir* hold back, in a noun use]

retaining wall A wall to prevent the material of an embankment or cut from sliding.

re·take (rē·tāk′) *v.t.* **·took, ·tak·en, ·tak·ing** **1** To take back; receive again. **2** To recapture. **3** To photograph again. — *n.* (rē′·tāk′) A motion-picture scene or sequence photographed again.

re·tal·i·ate (ri·tal′ē·āt) *v.* **·at·ed, ·at·ing** *v.i.* To return like for like; especially, to repay evil with evil. — *v.t.* To repay (an injury, wrong, etc.) in kind; revenge. See synonyms under AVENGE. [<L *retaliatus,* pp. of *retaliare* < *re-* back + *talio* punishment in kind < *talis* such] — **re·tal′i·a′tive** *adj.*

re·tal·i·a·tion (ri·tal′ē·ā′shən) *n.* The act of retaliating; reprisal; requital. See synonyms under REVENGE.

re·tal·i·a·to·ry (ri·tal′ē·ə·tôr′ē, -tō′rē) *adj.* Of, containing, or of the nature of retaliation.

re·tard (ri·tärd′) *v.t.* To cause to move or proceed slowly; hinder the advance or course of; impede; delay. — *v.i.* To be delayed. See synonyms under HINDER, OBSTRUCT. — *n.* Delay; retardation. [<F *retarder* <L *retardare* < *re-* back + *tardare* make slow < *tardus* slow] — **re·tard′a·tive** *adj.* — **re·tard′er** *n.*

re·tard·ant (ri·tär′dənt) *n.* Something that retards. — *adj.* Tending to hinder.

re·tar·date (ri·tär′dāt) *n.* A mentally retarded person.

re·tar·da·tion (rē′tär·dā′shən) *n.* **1** The act of retarding. **2** The state of being retarded. **3** A lessening of velocity, gain, or progress; a delaying. **4** The amount of delay or hindrance effected. **5** That which retards; a hindrance. **6** Slowness. **7** *Music* A gradual slackening of the time. [<L *retardatio, -onis*]

re·tard·ed (ri·tär′did) *adj.* Abnormally slow in development, especially mentally.

retch (rech) *v.i.* To make an effort to vomit; strain; heave. ◆ Homophone: *wretch.* [OE *hrǣcan* bring up (blood or phlegm)]

re·te (rē′tē) *n. pl.* **·ti·a** (-shē·ə, -tē·ə) A plexiform arrangement, as of vessels or nerves; network. [<L, net]

re·tell (rē·tel′) *v.t.* **·told, ·tell·ing** To count or relate again.

re·tem (rē′təm) *n.* A desert shrub (genus *Retama*) of Arabia and Syria, with small white flowers: the Old Testament juniper. [<Arabic *ratam,* pl. of *ratamah*]

ret·ene (ret′ēn, rē′tēn) *n. Chem.* A colorless crystalline compound, $C_{18}H_{18}$, contained in resinous pine wood and fir wood, also in fossil pine stems found in beds of peat and lignite. [<Gk. *rhētinē* resin]

re·tent (ri·tent′) *n.* That which is retained. [<L *rententus,* pp. of *retinere.* See RETAIN.]

re·ten·tion (ri·ten′shən) *n.* **1** The act of retaining. **2** The ability to remember; memory. **3** The keeping up or maintenance, as of a custom, practice, opinion, or intention. **4** *Med.* A holding within the body of materials normally excreted, as urine, etc. [<OF <L *retentio, -onis*]

re·ten·tive (ri·ten′tiv) *adj.* Having the power or tendency to retain; retaining: a *retentive* memory.

re·ten·tive·ness (ri·ten′tiv·nis) *n.* **1** The capacity of holding or retaining. **2** *Psychol.* The preservative function of memory.

re·ten·tiv·i·ty (rē′ten·tiv′ə·tē) *n.* **1** Retentiveness. **2** *Physics* The capacity of a material to retain magnetism after the withdrawal of the magnetizing force.

re·think (rē·thingk′) *v.t.* **·thought** (-thôt), **·think·ing** To think about again, especially in order to reassess; reconsider.

Re·thondes (rə·tônd′) A village 5 miles east of Compiègne, eastern France; armistice to suspend hostilities of World War I signed here, Nov. 11, 1918; during World War II, armistice to suspend hostilities between Germany and France signed here, June 22, 1940.

re·ti·ar·i·us (rē′shē·âr′ē·əs) *n. pl.* **·ar·i·i** (-âr′ē·ī) One of a class of ancient Roman gladiators, armed with a net to enmesh their adversaries, and a trident and dagger to dispatch them. See illustration under GLADIATOR. [<L < *rete* net]

ret·i·cence (ret′ə·səns) *n.* The quality, act, or an instance of being reserved in speech; reserve; taciturnity. Also **ret′i·cen·cy.** See synonyms under RESERVE. [<L *reticentia,* orig. neut. pl. of *reticens.* See RETICENT.]

ret·i·cent (ret′ə·sənt) *adj.* Habitually silent or reserved in utterance. See synonyms under TACITURN. [<L *reticens, -entis,* ppr. of *reticere* remain silent < *re-* again + *tacere* be silent] — **ret′i·cent·ly** *adv.*

ret·i·cle (ret′i·kəl) *n. Optics* The network of fine threads or lines of reference in the focal plane of a telescope or other optical instrument, serving to determine the position of an observed object: also spelled *reticule.* [<L *reticulum.* Doublet of RETICULUM.]

re·tic·u·lar (ri·tik′yə·lər) *adj.* **1** Like a network; reticulate; intricate. **2** *Anat.* Of or pertaining to a reticulum. Also **re·tic′u·lar′y.** [<NL *reticularis* <L *reticulum.* See RETICULUM.]

re·tic·u·late (ri·tik′yə·lāt) *v.* **·lat·ed, ·lat·ing** *v.t.* **1** To make a network of. **2** To cover with or as with lines of network. — *v.i.* **3** To form a network. — *adj.* (-lit, -lāt) Having the form or appearance of a network; having lines or veins crossing, as in leaves: also **re·tic′u·lat′ed.** [<L *reticulatus* < *reticulum.* See RETICULUM.]

re·tic·u·la·tion (ri·tik′yə·lā′shən) *n.* Any formation that is reticulated; a network. [< RETICULATE]

ret·i·cule (ret′ə·kyo͞ol) *n.* **1** A small bag formerly used by women for carrying personal articles, sewing materials, etc. **2** *Optics* A reticle. [<F *réticule*]

re·tic·u·lum (ri·tik′yə·ləm) *n. pl.* **·la** (-lə) **1** *Anat.* A protoplasmic network of cells or cellular tissue. **2** *Zool.* The honeycomb bag or second stomach of a ruminant, with the lining membrane raised into folds forming hexagonal cells. [<L, dim. of *rete* net. Doublet of RETICLE.]

Re·tic·u·lum (ri·tik′yə·ləm) A southern constellation, the Net. See CONSTELLATION. [<NL]

re·ti·form (rē′tə·fôrm, ret′ə-) *adj.* Arranged like a network; reticulate. [<F *rétiforme* <L *rete* net + *forma* shape]

ret·i·na (ret′ə·nə, ret′nə) *n. pl.* **·nas** or **·nae** (-nē) *Anat.* The inner membrane at the back of the eyeball, containing the light-sensitive rods and cones which receive the optical image. See illustration under EYE. [<LL <L *rete* net] — **ret′i·nal** *adj.*

ret·in·ene (ret′ən·ēn) *n. Biochem.* The yellow

pigment found in visual yellow and associated also in the production of vitamin A. [<RETINA]

ret·i·nite (ret′ə·nīt) *n.* A hard, brittle, vitreous resin obtained from lignite. [<Gk. *rhētinē* + -ITE[1]]

ret·i·ni·tis (ret′ə·nī′tis) *n. Pathol.* Inflammation of the retina.

ret·i·nol (ret′ə·nōl, -nol) *n.* A yellowish liquid hydrocarbon obtained by the distillation of various resins, and used as a solvent, especially in pharmacy. Also called *rosin oil.* [< Gk. *rhētinē* resin + -OL[2]]

ret·i·nos·co·py (ret′ə·nos′kə·pē) *n.* Skiascopy. [<L *retino* (<RETINA) + -SCOPY] —**ret′i·no·scop′ic** (-nō·skop′ik) *adj.*

ret·i·nue (ret′ə·nōō, -nyōō) *n.* The body of retainers attending a person of rank; an escort; cortège. [<F *retenue,* fem. of *retenu,* pp. of *retenir.* See RETAIN.]

re·tire (ri·tīr′) *v.* **·tired, ·tir·ing** *v.i.* **1** To go away or withdraw, as for privacy, shelter, or rest. **2** To go to bed. **3** To withdraw oneself from business, public life, or active service. **4** To fall back; retreat, as troops under attack. **5** To move back; recede or appear to recede. —*v.t.* **6** To remove from active service, as an officer of the army or navy. **7** To pay off and withdraw from circulation: to *retire* bonds. **8** To withdraw (troops, etc.) from action. **9** In baseball, etc., to keep (a batter or runner) from reaching base or scoring by putting him out, or to remove (a side) from an opportunity of scoring. [<F *retirer* < *re-* back + *tirer* draw]

re·tired (ri·tīrd′) *adj.* **1** Withdrawn from public view; existing or passed in seclusion; solitary; secluded: a *retired* life. **2** Withdrawn from active service, business, office, or public life: a *retired* sea captain. **3** Due or received by a person withdrawn from active service: *retired* pay. See synonyms under SECRET.

retired list One of the lists of officers or enlisted men voluntarily or involuntarily retired from an active status in one of the armed services of the United States, either on account of disability, age, or years of service, with or without retired pay.

re·tir·ee (ri·tīr′ē′) *n.* A person who is retired.

re·tire·ment (ri·tīr′mənt) *n.* **1** The act of retiring, or the state of being retired; withdrawal; seclusion. **2** A secluded place; a retreat.

Synonyms: loneliness, privacy, seclusion, solitude. In *retirement* one withdraws from association he has had with others; in *seclusion* one shuts himself off from the society of all except intimate friends or attendants; in *solitude* no other person is present. As private denotes what concerns ourselves individually, *privacy* denotes freedom from the presence or observation of those not concerned or whom we do not wish to have concerned in our affairs; *privacy* is more temporary than *seclusion*; we speak of a moment's *privacy.* There may be *loneliness* without *solitude,* as amid an unsympathizing crowd, and *solitude* without *loneliness,* as when one is glad to be alone. See SECLUSION, SOLITUDE. *Antonyms*: association, companionship, company, fellowship, society.

re·tir·ing (ri·tīr′ing) *adj.* **1** Shy; modest; reserved; unobtrusive. **2** Pertaining to retirement: a *retiring* pension. See synonyms under MODEST.

re·tort[1] (ri·tôrt′) *v.t.* **1** To direct (a word or deed) back upon the originator. **2** To reply to, as an accusation or argument, by a similar one. —*v.i.* **3** To make answer, especially sharply. —*n.* A retaliatory speech; a turning back of an accusation or insult upon the one who makes it; a keen rejoinder or caustic riposte; also, the act of making such reply: to be quick at *retort.* See synonyms under ANSWER. [<L *retortus,* pp. of *retorquere* < *re-* back + *torquere* twist] —**re·tort′er** *n.*

RETORTS
a. Retort with receiver.
b. Common retort.

re·tort[2] (ri·tôrt′) *n.* **1** *Chem.* A vessel with a bent tube, for the heating of substances, or for distillation. **2** *Metall.* A vessel in which ore may be heated for the removal of its metal content. [<L *retortus* bent back. See RETORT[1].]

re·tor·tion (ri·tôr′shən) *n.* **1** The act of retorting. **2** A bending, turning, or twisting back. **3** Retaliation; in international law, the infliction by one nation upon the subjects of another of the same ill treatment that its own citizens have received from the latter government. Also **re·tor′sion.** [<Med. L *retortio, -onis*]

re·touch (rē·tuch′) *v.t.* **1** To add new touches to; modify; revise. **2** *Phot.* To change, or improve, as a print, by a hand process in which a hard, sharp pencil or fine brush is used. —*n.* (*also* rē′tuch′) An additional touch, as to a picture, model, or other work of art, previously regarded as finished. [<F *retoucher*] —**re·touch′er** *n.*

re·trace (ri·trās′) *v.t.* **·traced, ·trac·ing** **1** To go back over; follow backward, as a path. **2** To trace the whole story of, from the beginning. **3** To go back over with the eyes or mind. [<F *retracer*] —**re·trace′a·ble** *adj.*

re–trace (rē·trās′) *v.t.* **–traced, –trac·ing** To trace again, as an engraving, drawing, or map.

re·tract (ri·trakt′) *v.t.* & *v.i.* **1** To take back (an assertion, accusation, admission, etc.); make a disavowal (of); recant. **2** To draw back or in, as the claws of a cat. See synonyms under RECANT, RENOUNCE. [<F *rétracter* <L *retractare* draw back <*re-* back + *tractare* draw violently, freq. of *trahere* draw] —**re·tract′a·ble** or **·i·ble** *adj.* —**re·trac·ta·tion** (rē′·trak·tā′shən) *n.*

re·trac·tile (ri·trak′til) *adj. Zool.* Capable of being drawn back or in, as a cat's claws or the head of a tortoise. [<F *rétractile*] —**re·trac·til·i·ty** (rē′trak·til′ə·tē) *n.*

re·trac·tion (ri·trak′shən) *n.* **1** The act of retracting or drawing something back or in. **2** The state of being retracted. **3** The act of withdrawing or recalling something said or avowed; recantation; revocation.

re·trac·tive (ri·trak′tiv) *adj.* Having the power or tendency to retract; retracting.

re·trac·tor (ri·trak′tər) *n.* **1** One who or that which retracts. **2** *Surg.* An instrument used to hold apart the edges of a wound.

re·tral (rē′trəl) *adj.* Situated at the back; posterior. [<L *retro* backward + -AL[1]]

re·tread (rē′tred′) *n.* A new outer covering of a pneumatic tire, to replace a worn or damaged one. —*v.t.* (rē·tred′) **·tread·ed, ·tread·ing** To fit or furnish (an automobile tire) with a new tread. Also *recap.*

re–tread (rē·tred′) *v.t.* **–trod, –trod·den, –tread·ing** To tread again.

re·treat (ri·trēt′) *v.i.* **1** To go back or backward; withdraw; retire. **2** To curve or slope backward. —*v.t.* **3** In chess, to move (a piece) back. —*n.* **1** The act of retreating, as from contest or danger. **2** The retirement of a naval or land force from a position of danger or from an enemy; also, a signal for retreating, made by trumpet or drum. **3** In the army or navy, a signal, as by bugle, for the lowering of the flag at sunset. **4** Retirement; seclusion; solitude. **5** A place of retirement, quiet, or security; a refuge; shelter; haunt. **6** Religious retirement; also, the time spent in religious retirement. **7** An establishment for the mentally ill, for alcoholics, etc. See synonyms under REFUGE, SECLUSION, SHELTER. Compare RETIREMENT. [<F *retraite,* orig. fem. of pp. of *retraire* draw back <L *retrahere* < *re-* again + *trahere* draw]

re·trench (ri·trench′) *v.t.* **1** To cut down or reduce; curtail (expenditures). **2** To cut off or away; remove; omit. —*v.i.* **3** To make retrenchments; economize. [<MF *retrencher* < *re-* back + *trencher* cut. See TRENCH.]

Synonyms: abridge, clip, curtail, cut, decrease, diminish, economize, lessen, reduce. *Antonyms*: elongate, expand, extend, lavish, lengthen, prolong, protract, squander, waste.

re·trench·ment (ri·trench′mənt) *n.* **1** The act of retrenching. **2** Reduction, as of expenses, for the sake of economy. **3** An interior breastwork or rampart from which the enemy can be resisted should the outer line be taken.

ret·ri·bu·tion (ret′rə·byōō′shən) *n.* **1** The act of requiting; impartial infliction of punishment. **2** That which is done or given in requital. **3** A reward or (especially) a punishment. See synonyms under RECOMPENSE, REVENGE. [<OF <L *retributio, -onis* < *retributus,* pp. of *retribuere* pay back < *re-* back + *tribuere* pay]

re·trib·u·tive (ri·trib′yə·tiv) *adj.* Tending to reward or punish. Also **re·trib′u·to′ry** (-tôr′ē, -tō′rē).

re·triev·al (ri·trē′vəl) *n.* **1** The act of retrieving. **2** Restoration from loss, damage, or failure.

re·trieve (ri·trēv′) *v.* **·trieved, ·triev·ing** *v.t.* **1** To get back; regain. **2** To restore; revive, as flagging spirits. **3** To make up for; remedy the consequences of. **4** To call to mind; remember. **5** To find and bring in (wounded or dead game): said of dogs. —*v.i.* **6** To retrieve game. See synonyms under RECOVER. —*n.* The act of retrieving; retrieval; recovery. [ME *retreve* <OF *retroev-,* stressed stem of *retrouver* find again < *re-* again + *trouver* find] —**re·triev′a·bil′i·ty** *n.* —**re·triev′a·ble** *adj.* —**re·triev′a·bly** *adv.*

re·triev·er (ri·trē′vər) *n.* **1** A sporting dog variously bred and specifically trained to retrieve game. **2** A person who retrieves.

retro– *prefix* **1** Back; backward: *retroflex, retrograde.* **2** Chiefly in scientific terms, behind: *retrolental.* [<L *retro-* < *retro* back, backward]

ret·ro·act (ret′rō·akt′, rē′trō-) *v.i.* **1** To act reciprocally or in return; react. **2** *Law* To affect past acts, obligations, or penalties. [Back formation <RETROACTIVE] —**ret′ro·ac′·tion** *n.*

ret·ro·ac·tive (ret′rō·ak′tiv, rē′trō-) *adj.* Having or designed to have a retrospective effect or reversed action; in effect also during a specified prior period. —**ret′ro·ac′tive·ly** *adv.* —**ret′ro·ac·tiv′i·ty** *n.*

retroactive law A law legalizing past proceedings; a retrospective law.

ret·ro·cede (ret′rō·sēd′) *v.* **·ced·ed, ·ced·ing** *v.t.* To cede, grant, or give back. —*v.i.* To go back; recede. [<L *retrocedere* <*retro-* back + *cedere* go]

ret·ro·ces·sion (ret′rō·sesh′ən) *n.* **1** The act of retroceding or giving back. **2** *Law* The conveyance of an estate to a former owner. [<LL *retrocessio, -onis*]

ret·ro·choir (ret′rə·kwīr) *n.* That part of a church interior which is east of or beyond the altar. [<RETRO- + CHOIR, modeled on Med. L *retrochorus*]

ret·ro·flex (ret′rə·fleks) *adj.* **1** Bent or turned backward; reflexed. **2** *Phonet.* Cacuminal. Also **ret′ro·flexed.** [<LL *retroflexus,* pp. of *retroflectere* <L *retro-* back + *flectere* bend]

ret·ro·flex·ion (ret′rə·flek′shən) *n.* **1** A bending or being bent backward. **2** *Anat.* A position or condition of the uterus in which its body is bent back at an angle with the cervix. Also **ret′ro·flec′tion.**

ret·ro·grade (ret′rə·grād) *v.* **·grad·ed, ·grad·ing** *v.i.* **1** To move or appear to move backward; recede. **2** To grow worse; decline; degenerate. **3** *Astron.* To have a retrograde motion. —*v.t.* **4** To cause to move backward; reverse. —*adj.* **1** Going, moving, or tending backward; contrary; reversed. **2** Declining to or toward a worse state or character. **3** *Astron.* Apparently moving from east to west relatively to the fixed stars. **4** Reversed; inverted. **5** *Obs.* Opposed; contrary. —*n.* A retrograde movement; decline. [<L *retrogradus*] —**ret′·ro·gra·da′tion** (-grā·dā′shən) *n.*

ret·ro·gress (ret′rə·gres) *v.i.* To go back to an earlier or worse condition. [<L *retrogressus,* pp. of *retrogradi* < *retro-* backward + *gradi* walk]

ret·ro·gres·sion (ret′rə·gresh′ən) *n.* **1** A retreat; degeneration; motion in a reverse direction. **2** A moving toward a lower plane. **3** *Biol.* Descent to or toward a less complex or less perfect structure.

ret·ro·gres·sive (ret′rə·gres′iv) *adj.* **1** Retrograde. **2** Deteriorating; degenerating. **3** *Biol.* Descending from a higher to a less complex organization.

ret·ro·len·tal (ret′rō·len′təl) *adj.* Behind the lens of the eye. [<RETRO- + L *lens, lentis.* See LENS.]

retrolental fi·bro·pla·sia (fī′brō·plā′zhə, -zhē·ə) *Pathol.* The persistence or growth of embryonic vascular tissue behind the lens of the eye.

ret·ro–rock·et (ret′rō·rok′it) *n.* An auxiliary jet engine whose thrust acts to lessen the velocity of fall of a rocket or spaceship to the surface of the earth or other celestial body.

re·trorse (ri·trôrs′) *adj.* Turned, bent, or directed backward. [<L *retrorsus*, contraction of *retroversus* <*retro-* backward + *versus*, pp. of *vertere* turn] —**re·trorse′ly** *adv.*

ret·ro·spect (ret′rə·spekt) *v.i. Rare* **1** To think about the past. **2** To look or refer back. —*v.t.* **3** *Rare* To consider or think about in retrospect. —*n.* A looking back on things past; view or contemplation of something past. See synonyms under MEMORY. [<L *retrospectus*, pp. of *retrospicere* reexamine, look back < *retro-* back + *specere* look]

ret·ro·spec·tion (ret′rə·spek′shən) *n.* A calling to remembrance; a looking back upon or recollection of the past.

ret·ro·spec·tive (ret′rə·spek′tiv) *adj.* **1** Looking back on the past; of, pertaining to, or referring to the past. **2** Retroactive: said of some legislation. **3** Characterized by retrospection. —**ret′ro·spec′tive·ly** *adv.*

re·trous·sage (rə·trōō·säzh′) *n.* In etching, a process of wiping a soft cloth across the ink-filled incisions of an etched plate before printing to produce an effect of softness or richness. [<F <*retrousser* turn up]

ret·rous·sé (ret′rōō·sā′, *Fr.* rə·trōō·sā′) *adj.* Turned up at the end: said of noses. [<F, pp. of *retrousser* turn up, tuck up <*re-* back + *trousser* fasten together]

ret·ro·ver·sion (ret′rə·vûr′zhən, -shən) *n.* **1** A tipping or bending backward. **2** The state of being turned backward. **3** The act of looking or turning back.

ret·ro·vert (ret′rə·vûrt) *v.t.* To turn back. [<LL *retrovertere* <L *retro-* back + *vertere* turn]

re·turn (ri·tûrn′) *v.i.* **1** To come or go back, as to or toward a former place or condition. **2** To come back or revert in thought or speech. **3** To revert to a former owner. **4** To answer; respond. —*v.t.* **5** To bring, carry, send, or put back; restore; replace. **6** To give in return for something: to *return* ingratitude for kindness. **7** To repay or requite, especially with an equivalent: to *return* a compliment. **8** To yield or produce, as a profit or interest. **9** To send back; reflect, as light or sound. **10** To render (a verdict, etc.). **11** To submit, as a report or writ, to one in authority. **12** To report or announce officially. **13** To replace (a weapon, etc.) in its holder. **14** In card games, to lead (a suit previously led by one's partner). —*n.* **1** The act, process, state, or result of coming back or returning; also, that which is returned; resumption; restoration or replacement; repayment or requital; response; answer; retort; reappearance or recurrence. **2** That which accrues, as from investments, labor, or use; profit. **3** A coming back, reappearance, or recurrence, as of a periodical event or season. **4** A report, list, etc.; especially, a formal or official report, or, in the plural, a set of tabulated statistics: election *returns.* **5** *Archit.* **a** continuation of a dripstone, hood molding, etc., to form a termination having a different direction from the main part. **b** A part or face of a building at an angle with the main part of the façade. **6** The sending back by a sheriff of a writ to the court from which it was issued; also, a sheriff's report on such writ. **7** *Law* A brief statement, usually endorsed on a writ by the officer to whom it was issued, of what has been done under it; also, the filing of the writ thus endorsed in the office of the clerk or the tribunal whence it was issued. **8** In card games, a returned lead. **9** Any volley, stroke, or thrust received from an opponent; specifically, in a game, the sending of an object, as a tennis ball, from one player to another from whom he has received it. See synonyms under HARVEST, INCREASE, PRODUCT, PROFIT, RESTITUTION. —*adj.* Of or pertaining to a return; given, taken, or done in return; returning: a *return* visit; a *return* ticket. [<OF *returner*] —**re·turn′er** *n.*

re–turn (rē·tûrn′) *v.t. & v.i.* To turn again; fold over or back.

re·turn·a·ble (ri·tûr′nə·bəl) *adj.* **1** Capable of being or suitable to be returned. **2** Due and required: said of a judicial writ in reference to the time when and the place where it is to be returned by the officer to whom it is directed.

re·tuse (ri·tōōs′, -tyōōs′) *adj. Bot.* Having a rounded end or apex in which there is a slight depression, indentation, or notch: said of leaves. [<L *retusus*, pp. of *retundere* beat back <*re-* back + *tundere*]

Retz (rets), **Cardinal de,** 1614–79, Jean François Paul de Gondi, French ecclesiastic and author.

Reu·ben (rōō′bin) A masculine personal name. [<Hebrew, behold, a son]

—**Reuben** The eldest son of Jacob. *Gen.* xxix 32.

Reuch·lin (roikh′lēn, roikh·lēn′), **Johann,** 1455–1522, German humanist and Hebraist. —**Reuch·lin′i·an** *adj.* —**Reuch′lin·ism** *n.*

re·un·ion (rē·yōōn′yən) *n.* **1** The act of reuniting; renewed harmony. **2** A social gathering of persons who have been separated: a family *reunion.*

Ré·un·ion (rē·yōōn′yən, *Fr.* rā·ü·nyôṅ′) A French island of the Mascarene group, east of Madagascar; 970 square miles; capital, Saint-Denis: formerly *Bourbon Island.*

re·un·ion·ism (rē·yōōn′yən·iz′əm) *n.* The principle of renewed union as a policy; specifically, advocacy of reunion of the various Christian churches. —**re·un′ion·ist** *n.* —**re·un′·ion·is′tic** *adj.*

re·u·nite (rē′yōō·nīt′) *v.t. & v.i.* **·nit·ed, ·nit·ing** To unite, cohere, or combine again after separation. —**re′u·nit′er** *n.*

Reu·ter·dahl (roi′tər·däl), **Henry,** 1871–1935, U.S. marine and naval painter born in Sweden.

Reu·ters (roi′tərz) *n.* A British organization for collecting news and distributing it to member newspapers. Also **Reuter's News Agency.** [after Baron Paul Julius von *Reuter,* 1816–99, English founder of the agency]

Reu·ther (rōō′thər), **Walter Philip,** 1907–1970, U.S. labor leader.

rev (rev) *n.* A revolution, as of a motor or machine part. —*v.t. & v.i.* **revved, rev·ving** To alter the speed of (a motor): with *up* or *down.*

Re·val (rā′väl) The German name for TALLINN.

rev·a·len·ta (rev′ə·len′tə) *n. Brit.* Meal made from ground lentils, prepared as food for invalids. [<NL, alter. of earlier *ervalenta* <L *ervum* vetch + *lens, lentis* lentil]

re·vamp (rē·vamp′) *v.t.* **1** To vamp (a boot or shoe) anew. **2** To patch up; make over. —*n.* A thing which is revamped. [<RE- + VAMP]

re·veal (ri·vēl′) *v.t.* **1** To make known; disclose; divulge. **2** To make visible; expose to view; exhibit; show. See synonyms under ANNOUNCE, INFORM, PUBLISH. —*n. Archit.* The vertical side of an aperture or opening in a wall; especially, the portion of the side of a door or window between the line where the window frame or door frame stops and the outer edge of the opening. [<OF *reveler* <L *revelare* unveil <*re-* back + *velum* veil] —**re·veal′a·ble** *adj.* —**re·veal′er** *n.*

re·veal·ment (ri·vēl′mənt) *n.* A revelation; act of revealing; disclosure.

rev·eil·le (rev′i·lē) *n.* **1** A morning signal by drum or bugle, notifying soldiers or sailors to rise. **2** The hour at which this signal is sounded. [<F *reveillez-vous,* imperative of *se reveiller* wake up <*re-* (<L *re-*) again + L *vigilare* watch. See VIGIL.]

rev·el (rev′əl) *v.i.* **·eled** or **·elled, ·el·ing** or **·el·ling** **1** To take delight; indulge freely: with *in*: He *revels* in his freedom. **2** To make merry; engage in boisterous festivities. —*n.* **1** Merrymaking; carousing; noisy festivity. **2** An occasion of boisterous festivity; a celebration. [<OF *reveler* make an uproar <L *rebellare.* Doublet of REBEL.] —**rev′el·er** or **rev′el·ler** *n.*

Synonyms (noun): carnival, carousal, carouse, feast, festivity, jollification, merrymaking, revelry, rout.

Re·vel (re′vel′y′) The Russian name for TALLINN.

rev·e·la·tion (rev′ə·lā′shən) *n.* **1** The act or process of revealing, or the state of being revealed. **2** That which is or has been revealed. **3** *Theol.* **a** The act of revealing or communicating divine truth, especially by divine agency or supernatural means. **b** That which has been so revealed, as concerning God in his relations to man. **c** That which is revealed in the Bible itself. [<OF <LL *revelatio, -onis* < L *revelatus,* pp. of *revelare.* See REVEAL.]

Rev·e·la·tion (rev′ə·lā′shən) The Apocalypse, or Book of Revelation: in full, **The Revelation of Saint John the Divine;** the last book of the Bible.

rev·e·la·tion·ist (rev′ə·lā′shən·ist) *n.* One who holds that God has made a supernatural revelation of himself and his will.

rev·e·la·tor (rev′ə·lā′tər) *n.* A revealer. [<LL]

rev·el·ry (rev′əl·rē) *n. pl.* **·ries** Noisy or boisterous merriment.

rev·e·nant (rev′ə·nənt) *n.* **1** One who or that which returns. **2** A ghost; an apparition. [< F, ppr. of *revenir* come back <*re-* back + *venir* come]

re·venge (ri·venj′) *v.* **·venged, ·veng·ing** *v.t.* **1** To inflict punishment, injury, or loss in return for; to take vengeance for; avenge. **2** To take or seek vengeance in behalf of. —*v.i.* **3** *Obs.* To take vengeance. —*n.* **1** The act of returning injury for injury; the infliction of injury or punishment in the spirit of personal vindictiveness; retaliation. **2** A mode or means of avenging oneself or others. **3** The desire for vengeance. [<OF *revenger* <*re-* (<L *re-*) again + *venger* take vengeance <L *vindicare.* See VINDICATE.] —**re·veng′er** *n.*

Synonyms (noun): avenging, requital, retaliation, retribution, vengeance. *Retaliation* and *revenge* are personal and often bitter. *Retaliation* may be partial; *revenge* is meant to be complete and may be excessive. *Vengeance,* which once meant an indignant vindication of justice, now signifies the most furious and unsparing *revenge. Revenge* emphasizes more the personal injury in return for which it is inflicted. A *requital* is an even return, such as to quit one of obligation for what has been received, and may be good or bad. *Avenging* and *retribution* give a solemn sense of exact justice, *avenging* being more personal in its infliction, and *retribution* the impersonal visitation of the doom of righteous law. See HATRED. *Antonyms*: compassion, excuse, forgiveness, grace, mercy, pardon, pity.

re·venge·ful (ri·venj′fəl) *adj.* Vindictive; disposed to, or full of, revenge. —**re·venge′ful·ly** *adv.* —**re·venge′ful·ness** *n.*

rev·e·nons à nos mou·tons (rəv·nôṅ′ zá nō mōō·tôṅ′) *French* Let us return to our sheep; that is, to our subject.

rev·e·nue (rev′ə·nyōō, -nōō) *n.* **1** Total current income of a government, except duties on imports: also **internal revenue. 2** Income from any form of property. **3** The department of government or civil service which collects the national funds: in the United States, the **Internal Revenue Service** of the Department of the Treasury. **4** A source or an item of income. [<F, fem. of *revenu,* pp. of *revenir* return]

revenue cutter An armed vessel in the government revenue service used to enforce customs regulations and prevent smuggling.

revenue sharing *U.S.* The distribution among state and municipal governments, based on their population, of a part of the revenue from Federal taxes.

re·ver·ber·ant (ri·vûr′bər·ənt) *adj.* Resounding. [<L *reverberans, -antis,* ppr. of *reverberare.* See REVERBERATE.]

re·ver·ber·ate (ri·vûr′bə·rāt) *v.* **·at·ed, ·at·ing** *v.i.* **1** To resound or re-echo. **2** To be reflected or repelled. **3** To bend back, as flames in a reverberatory furnace. **4** To rebound or recoil. —*v.t.* **5** To echo back (a sound); re-echo. **6** To reflect. **7** To cause to bend back, as flames in a reverberatory furnace; deflect. **8** To expose to heat in a reverberatory furnace. See synonyms under ROAR. [<L *reverberatus,* pp. of *reverberare* strike back, cause to rebound <*re-* back + *verberare* beat]

re·ver·ber·a·tion (ri·vûr′bə·rā′shən) *n.* **1** The act or process of reverberating. **2** That which constitutes reverberating. **3** The rebound or reflection of light, heat, or sound waves. —**re·ver′ber·a′tive** *adj.*

re·ver·ber·a·tor (ri·vûr′bə·rā′tər) *n.* **1** One who or that which causes reverberation. **2** A reflecting lamp, or a reverberatory furnace.

re·ver·ber·a·to·ry (ri·vûr′bər·ə·tôr′ē, -tō′rē)

adj. Producing or intended to produce reverberation; reverberative. — *n.* *pl.* **·ries** A reverberatory furnace.

reverberatory furnace A furnace having a vaulted ceiling that deflects the flame and heat toward the hearth or the upper surface of the substance to be treated.

REVERBERATORY FURNACE
A. Flames and gases.
B. Bed of molten iron.

re·vere (ri·vir′) *v.t.* **·vered, ·ver·ing** To regard with veneration; reverence; venerate. See synonyms under ADMIRE, DEFER, VENERATE, WORSHIP. [<L *revereri* feel awe of < *re-* again and again + *vereri* fear] — **re·ver′er** *n.*

Re·vere (ri·vir′), **Paul,** 1735–1818, American silversmith, famous for his midnight ride from Charlestown to Lexington, Mass., the night of April 17–18, 1775, to warn the colonists of the approach of British troops.

rev·er·ence (rev′ər·əns) *n.* **1** A feeling of profound respect often mingled with awe and affection; veneration. **2** An act of respect; an obeisance. **3** The quality or character that commands respect. **4** A reverend person: used as a respectful appellation or title, especially applied to a clergyman. — *v.t.* **·enced, ·enc·ing** To regard with reverence. See synonyms under VENERATE. [<OF <L *reverentia*]

Synonyms (noun): adoration, awe, homage, honor, veneration, worship. See VENERATION. *Antonyms*: contumely, derision, dishonor, insult, irreverence, mockery, outrage, ridicule, scoff, scoffing.

rev·er·end (rev′ər·ənd) *adj.* **1** Worthy of reverence. **2** Being a clergyman; of or pertaining to the clergy or the clerical office. — *n. Colloq.* A clergyman; minister. [<L *reverendus,* gerundive of *revereri.* See REVERE.]

rev·er·ent (rev′ər·ənt) *adj.* **1** Impressed with or feeling reverence. **2** Expressing reverence. [<L *reverens, -entis*] — **rev′er·ent·ly** *adv.*

rev·er·en·tial (rev′ə·ren′shəl) *adj.* Proceeding from or expressing reverence. — **rev′er·en′·tial·ly** *adv.*

rev·er·ie (rev′ər·ē) *n.* *pl.* **·er·ies** **1** Abstracted musing; dreaming. **2** A product of such musing in written or musical composition. Also **rev′er·y.** See synonyms under DREAM, THOUGHT. [<F *rêverie* < *rêver* dream, rave, ? <L *rabere* rage]

re·vers (rə·vir′, -vâr′) *n.* *pl.* **·vers** (-virz′, -vârz′) **1** A part of a garment folded over to show the inside, as the lapel of a coat. **2** Material used to cover such a part. [<OF. See REVERSE.]

re·ver·sal (ri·vûr′səl) *n.* **1** The act of reversing. **2** *Physics* The change of a dark to a bright spectral line, or vice versa. **3** *Law* An annulling or setting aside: the *reversal* of a decree.

re·verse (ri·vûrs′) *adj.* **1** Turned backward; contrary or opposite in direction, character, order, etc. **2** On the other side; backward; inverted. **3** Causing backward motion: the *reverse* gear of an automobile. — *n.* **1** That which is directly opposite or contrary: The *reverse* of what you say is true. **2** The back, rear, or secondary side or surface, as distinguished from the front or principal side. **3** A reversing; change to an opposite position, direction, or state; reversal: a *reverse* of a gun or gun carriage. **4** A change or alteration for the worse; a check or partial defeat; misfortune. **5** *Mech.* A reversing gear or movement. See synonyms under MISFORTUNE. — *v.* **·versed, ·vers·ing** *v.t.* **1** To turn upside down or inside out; invert or overturn. **2** To turn in an opposite direction. **3** To transpose; exchange. **4** To change into something different or opposite; alter: to *reverse* policy. **5** To set aside; annul: to *reverse* a decree. **6** *Mech.* To cause to have an opposite motion or effect: *Reverse* engines! — *v.i.* **7** To move or turn in the opposite direction, as in dancing. **8** To reverse its action: said of engines, etc. See synonyms under ABOLISH. [<OF *revers* <L *reversus,* pp. of *revertere.* See REVERT.] — **re·vers′er** *n.*

reverse fault *Geol.* A thrust fault.

re·verse·ly (ri·vûrs′lē) *adv.* In a reverse or contrary manner.

re·vers·i·ble (ri·vûr′sə·bəl) *adj.* **1** Capable of being reversed in direction or position. **2** Capable of going either forward or backward, as a chemical reaction or physiological process. **3** Capable of being used or worn inside out or backward: a *reversible* coat. **4** Having the finish on both sides, as a fabric. — *n.* A reversible coat. — **re·vers′i·bil′i·ty, re·vers′i·ble·ness** *n.* — **re·vers′i·bly** *adv.*

re·ver·sion (ri·vûr′zhən, -shən) *n.* **1** A return to or toward some former state or condition. **2** The act of reversing or the state of being reversed. **3** A return, as to a former practice or belief. **4** *Biol.* **a** The recurrence or reappearance in an individual of characteristics which had not been evident for two or more generations; atavism. **b** An example of such recurrence. **5** *Law* **a** The return of an estate to the grantor or his heirs after the expiration of the grant. **b** The estate so returning. **c** The right of succession to an estate. **6** *Obs.* Remainder. [<OF <L *reversio, -onis.* See REVERT.]

re·ver·sion·al (ri·vûr′zhən·əl, -shən-) *adj.* Reversionary.

re·ver·sion·ar·y (ri·vûr′zhən·er′ē, -shən-) *adj.* Of, pertaining to, characterized by, or involving reversion.

re·ver·sion·er (ri·vûr′zhən·ər, -shən-) *n. Law* One entitled to an estate in reversion.

re·ver·so (ri·vûr′sō) *n.* *pl.* **·sos** A left-hand page: opposed to *recto.* [<Ital. *riverso* reverse]

re·vert (ri·vûrt′) *v.i.* **1** To go or turn back to a former place, condition, attitude, topic, etc. **2** *Biol.* To return to or show characteristics of an earlier, primitive type. **3** *Law* To return to the former owner or to his heirs. — *n.* **1** One who is reconverted to a former faith. **2** That which reverts. [<OF *revertir* <L *revertere* turn back < *re-* back + *vertere* turn] — **re·vert′i·ble** *adj.* — **re·ver′tive** *adj.*

re·vest (rē·vest′) *v.t.* **1** To vest again, as with rank, authority, or ownership; reinvest. **2** To vest again, as office or powers. — *v.i.* **3** To take effect again, as a title reverting to a former owner. [<OF *revestir* <LL *revestire* reclothe <L *re-* again + *vestire* clothe < *vestis* a garment]

re·vet (ri·vet′) *v.t.* **·vet·ted, ·vet·ting** To face, as an embankment, with masonry. [<F *revêtir* clothe <L *revestire.* See REVEST.]

re·vet·ment (ri·vet′mənt) *n.* A facing, sheathing, or retaining wall, as of masonry, for protecting earthworks, river banks, etc. [<F *revêtement*]

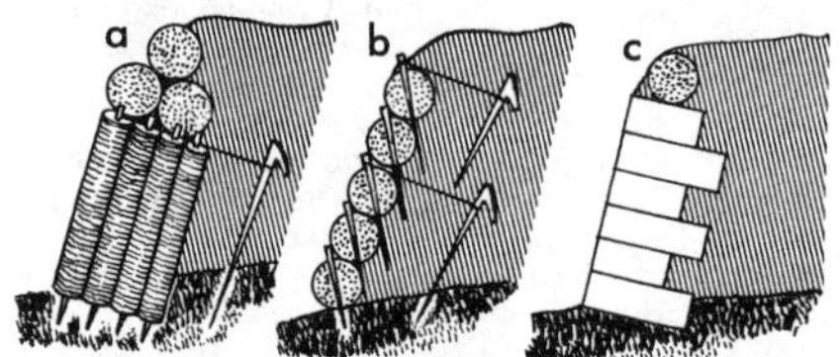

REVETMENTS
a. Built of gabions supporting fascines.
b. Built of fascines only.
c. Built of timbers or concrete.

re·view (ri·vyōō′) *v.t.* **1** To go over or examine again; look at or study again. **2** To look back upon, as in memory; think of retrospectively. **3** To go over, as a manuscript, so as to correct defects. **4** To make an inspection of, especially formally. **5** To write or make a critical review of, as a new book. **6** *Law* To examine (something done or adjudged by a lower court) so as to determine its legality or correctness. — *v.i.* **7** To write a review or reviews, as for a magazine. [<RE- + VIEW; modeled on F *revoir* look at again] — *n.* **1** A second, repeated, or new view, examination, consideration, or study of something; a retrospective survey. **2** A lesson studied or recited again. **3** Critical study or examination. **4** An article or essay containing a critical examination, discussion, or notice of some work; a criticism; critique. **5** A periodical devoted to essays in criticism and on general subjects. **6** A formal or official inspection or view, as of troops. **7** *Law* A judicial revision by a superior court of the order or decree of a subordinate court. **8** A revision, as of a work by its author; examination with a view to correction or improvement. [<MF *reveue* < pp. of *revoir* <L *revidere* < *re-* again + *videre* see]

re·view·al (ri·vyōō′əl) *n.* A review; the act of reviewing.

re·view·er (ri·vyōō′ər) *n.* A critic or examiner; an essayist in critical periodicals; a book reviewer.

re·vile (ri·vīl′) *v.* **·viled, ·vil·ing** *v.t.* To assail with abusive or contemptuous language; vilify; abuse. — *v.i.* To use abusive or contemptuous language. [<OF *reviler* treat as vile < *re-* + *vil* vile] — **re·vile′ment** *n.* — **re·vil′er** *n.* — **re·vil′ing·ly** *adv.*

Synonyms: abuse, asperse, calumniate, defame, malign, reproach, slander, traduce, upbraid, vilify. See ABUSE, ASPERSE. *Antonyms*: see synonyms for PRAISE.

Re·vil·la·gi·ge·do Island (ri·vil′ə·gi·gē′dō) An island in the Alexander Archipelago, SE Alaska; 1,120 square miles.

re·vis·al (ri·vī′zəl) *n.* Revision; the act of revising.

re·vise (ri·vīz′) *v.t.* **·vised, ·vis·ing** **1** To read or read over so as to correct errors, suggest or make changes, etc.: to *revise* a manuscript or the proofs of a book. **2** To change; alter: He has *revised* his opinions. — *n.* **1** The act or result of revising or reviewing; a revision. **2** A corrected proof after revision. [<F *reviser* <L *revisere* look back, see again < *re-* again + *visum,* pp. of *videre* see] — **re·vis′er** or **re·vi′sor** *n.*

Revised Version A translation of the Bible into English, made by two bodies, one of English and one of American scholars, in the years 1870–84.

re·vi·sion (ri·vizh′ən) *n.* The act or result of revising; a revised version or edition. — **re·vi′·sion·al, re·vi′sion·ar′y** *adj.*

re·vi·sion·ism (ri·vizh′ən·iz′əm) *n.* The advocacy of revision.

re·vi·sion·ist (ri·vizh′ən·ist) *n.* **1** One who advocates revision. **2** A reviser.

re·vis·it (rē·viz′it) *v.t.* To visit again. — *n.* A return visit. — **re′vis·i·ta′tion** *n.*

re·vi·so·ry (ri·vī′zər·ē) *adj.* Effecting, or capable of effecting, revision; revising: *revisory* powers.

re·vi·tal·ize (rē·vī′təl·īz) *v.t.* **·ized, ·iz·ing** To restore vitality to; bring back to life; revive. — **re·vi′tal·i·za′tion** *n.*

re·vi·val (ri·vī′vəl) *n.* **1** The act of reviving, or the state of being revived; specifically, a recovery, as from depression. **2** A restoration or resuscitation after neglect, oblivion, or obscurity: the *revival* of letters. **3** A renewal of special interest in and attention to religious services and duties and the subject of personal salvation; a religious awakening. **4** A series of emotional and sensational evangelical meetings.

re·vi·val·ism (ri·vī′vəl·iz′əm) *n.* **1** The spirit and methods of religious revivals or revivalists, or that promote revivals. **2** A tendency to restore former conditions or principles.

re·vi·val·ist (ri·vī′vəl·ist) *n.* A preacher or leader in a religious revival movement.

revival of learning or **literature** See RENAISSANCE.

re·vive (ri·vīv′) *v.* **·vived, ·viv·ing** *v.t.* **1** To bring to life again after real or apparent death; restore to consciousness. **2** To give new vigor, health, etc., to. **3** To bring back into use or currency. **4** To make effective or operative again. **5** To renew in the mind or memory; refresh; reawaken. **6** To produce again, as an old play. — *v.i.* **7** To come back to life again; return to consciousness. **8** To assume new vigor, health, etc. **9** To come back into use or currency. **10** To become effective or operative again. [<F *revivre* <L *revivere* < *re-* again + *vivere* live] — **re·viv′er** *n.*

re·viv·i·fy (ri·viv′ə·fī) *v.t.* **·fied, ·fy·ing** To give new life or spirit to; revive. [<F *revivifier* <L *revivificare* < *re-* again + *vivificare* vivify < *vivus* alive + *facere* make] — **re·viv′i·fi·ca′·tion** *n.*

rev·i·vis·cence (rev′ə·vis′əns) *n.* A renewal of life or of vital activities and vigor; a return to life; restoration; revival. Also **rev′i·vis′·cen·cy.** [<L *reviviscens, -entis,* ppr. of *reviviscere* < *re-* again + *viviscere* come to life, freq. of *vivere* live] — **rev′i·vis′cent** *adj.*

rev·o·ca·ble (rev′ə·kə·bəl) *adj.* Capable of being revoked. [<F *révocable*] — **rev′o·ca·bil′i·ty** *n.* — **rev′o·ca·bly** *adv.*

rev·o·ca·tion (rev′ə·kā′shən) *n.* **1** The act of

revoking, or the state of being revoked; repeal; reversal. **2** *Law* The annulment or cancellation of an instrument, act, or promise by or in behalf of the party who made it. **3** *Obs.* A summoning back or recalling. [<OF *revocacion*] **—rev·o·ca·to·ry** (rev′ə·kə·tôr′ē, -tō′rē) *adj.*

re·voice (rē·vois′) *v.t.* **·voiced, ·voic·ing** **1** To restore or give the proper quality of tone to: to *revoice* an organ pipe. **2** To voice again or in return; echo.

re·voke (ri·vōk′) *v.* **·voked, ·vok·ing** *v.t.* **1** To annul or make void by recalling; cancel; rescind. **2** *Obs.* To call or summon back; recall. **—** *v.i.* **3** In card games, to fail to follow suit when possible and when required by the rules. See synonyms under ABOLISH, ANNUL, CANCEL, RECANT, RENOUNCE. **—** *n.* **1** An annulling or cancellation. **2** In card games, neglect to follow suit; a renege. [<OF *revoquer* <L *revocare* < *re-* back + *vocare* call] **— re·vok′er** *n.*

re·volt (ri·vōlt′) *n.* **1** A throwing off of allegiance and subjection; an uprising against authority; a rebellion or mutiny; insurrection. **2** An act of protest, refusal, revulsion, or disgust. See synonyms under REVOLUTION. **—** *v.i.* **1** To rise in rebellion against constituted authority; renounce allegiance; mutiny; rebel. **2** To turn away in disgust or abhorrence; be shocked or repelled: with *against, at,* or *from.* **—** *v.t.* **3** To cause to feel disgust or revulsion; repel. [<F *révolte* < *révolter* <Ital. *rivoltare* <L *revolutus,* pp. of *revolvere.* See REVOLVE.] **— re·volt′er** *n.*

re·volt·ing (ri·vōl′ting) *adj.* Abhorrent; loathsome; nauseating. **— re·volt′ing·ly** *adv.*

rev·o·lute (rev′ə·lo͞ot) *adj. Bot.* Rolled backward or downward from the margins upon the under surface, as certain leaves. [<L *revolutus.* See REVOLT.]

rev·o·lu·tion (rev′ə·lo͞o′shən) *n.* **1** The act or state of revolving. **2** A motion in a closed curve around a center, or a complete or apparent circuit made by a body in such a course: used generally in this sense in distinction from *rotation.* **3** Rotation about an axis; especially, a complete rotation so that every part of the moving body returns to the position from which it started. **4** *Mech.* Any winding or turning about an axis, as in a spiral or other bend, so as to come to a point corresponding to the starting point. **5** A group, round, or cycle of successive events or changes; a cycle; also, the period of space or time occupied by a cycle or by the accomplishment of a circuit. **6** The overthrow and replacement of a government or political system by those governed. **7** An extensive or drastic change in a condition, method, idea, etc.: a *revolution* in industry. [<OF *revolucion* <LL *revolutio, -onis* <L *revolutus,* pp. of *revolvere.* See REVOLVE.]

Synonyms: anarchy, confusion, disintegration, disorder, insubordination, insurrection, lawlessness, mutiny, rebellion, revolt, riot, sedition, tumult. The essential idea of *revolution,* in definition 6, is a change in the form of government or constitution, or a change of rulers, otherwise than as provided by existing laws of succession, election, etc.; while such change is apt to involve armed hostilities, these make no necessary part of a *revolution,* which may be accomplished without a battle. *Anarchy* refers to the condition of a state when government is superseded or destroyed by factions. A *revolt* is an uprising against existing authority without the comprehensive views of change in the form or administration of government that are involved in *revolution.* See CHANGE. Compare ANARCHY, REBELLION, REVOLT. *Antonyms*: authority, command, control, domination, dominion, empire, government, law, loyalty, obedience, order, rule, sovereignty, submission, supremacy.

— American Revolution The war for independence carried on by the thirteen American colonies against Great Britain, 1775–83. Also *Revolutionary War.* See table under WAR.

— Chinese Revolution The events in China during the years 1911–12, inspired by Sun Yat-sen, which overthrew the authority of the Dowager Empress and the Manchu Empire, and resulted in the establishment of a republic. **— English Revolution** The course of events in England in 1642–89 that brought about the execution of Charles I, the rise of the Commonwealth, the dethronement of James II, and the establishment of a constitutional government under William III and Mary: called in England **The Revolution,** sometimes with reference to the events of 1688. **— French Revolution** The revolution which began in 1789, overthrew the French monarchy, and culminated in the Empire of Napoleon I.

— Russian Revolution The conflict (1917–22), beginning in a Petrograd uprising on March 12, 1917, that resulted in a provisional moderate government and the abdication of Nicholas II. On November 6 (October 24, Old Style), the Bolsheviks under Lenin overthrew this government (the *October Revolution*), and after resisting counter-revolution and libertarian revolution until December, 1922, united the soviet states in the Union of Soviet Socialist Republics under Communist (Bolshevik) control.

rev·o·lu·tion·ar·y (rev′ə·lo͞o′shən·er′ē) *adj.* **1** Pertaining to or of the nature of revolution, especially political; causing or tending to produce revolution. **2** Rotating; revolving. **—** *n. pl.* **·ar·ies** A revolutionist.

Revolutionary calendar See CALENDAR (Republican).

Revolutionary War See AMERICAN REVOLUTION under REVOLUTION.

rev·o·lu·tion·ist (rev′ə·lo͞o′shən·ist) *n.* One who takes part in a revolution.

rev·o·lu·tion·ize (rev′ə·lo͞o′shən·īz) *v.t.* **·ized, ·iz·ing** To effect a radical or entire change in the character, government, or affairs of: to *revolutionize* a country.

re·volve (ri·volv′) *v.* **·volved, ·volv·ing** *v.i.* **1** To move in an orbit about a center; move in a circle. **2** To rotate. **3** To move in cycles; recur periodically. **—** *v.t.* **4** To cause to move in a circle or orbit. **5** To cause to rotate. **6** To turn over mentally; consider; ponder. [<L *revolvere* < *re-* back + *volvere* roll, turn] **— re·volv′a·ble** *adj.* **— re·volv′ing** *adj.*

Synonyms: roll, rotate, turn. Any round body *rolls* which continuously touches with successive portions of its surface successive portions of another surface; a wagon wheel *rolls* along the ground. To *rotate* is said of a body that has a circular motion about its own center or axis; to *revolve* is said of a body that moves about a center outside of itself. A *revolving* body may also either *rotate* or *roll* at the same time; the earth *revolves* around the sun, and *rotates* on its own axis. Any object that is in contact with or connected with a *rolling* body is often said to *roll*; as, The car *rolls* smoothly along the track. Objects whose motion approximates or suggests a rotary motion along a supporting surface are also said to *roll*; as, Ocean waves *roll* in upon the shore. *Antonyms*: bind, chafe, grind, slide, slip, stick.

re·volv·er (ri·vol′vər) *n.* **1** One who or that which revolves. **2** A type of pistol with a revolving cylinder in the breech chambered to hold several cartridges so that it may be fired in succession without reloading.

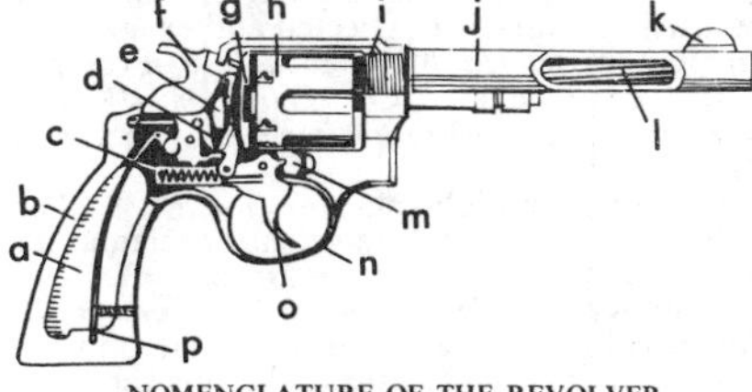

NOMENCLATURE OF THE REVOLVER

a. Stock.	*f.* Hammer.	*l.* Rifling.
b. Frame.	*g.* Extractor.	*m.* Cylinder stop.
c. Trigger spring.	*h.* Cylinder.	*n.* Trigger guard.
	i. Barrel pin.	
d. Sear.	*j.* Barrel.	*o.* Trigger.
e. Bolt.	*k.* Front sight.	*p.* Mainspring.

revolving door A door rotating like a turnstile about a central post and consisting of three or four adjustable leaves so encased in a doorway as to exclude drafts of air.

revolving fund A fund set up to finance loans or operations which yield returns that are placed in the fund for re-use.

revolving stage A circular stage divided in sections, each set for a different scene: by revolving the stage, scenes may be rapidly changed.

re·vue (ri·vyo͞o′) *n.* A kind of musical comedy, without plot or dramatic sequence, characterized by songs and dances, and by a series of skits which lampoon or burlesque contemporary people and events. [<F. See REVIEW.]

re·vul·sion (ri·vul′shən) *n.* **1** A sudden change of feeling, conduct, or conditions; a strong reaction of any kind. **2** The drawing back or away from something; violent withdrawal or recoil. **3** *Med.* A turning or diverting of any disease from one part of the body to another, as by counterirritation. [<OF <L *revulsio, -onis* < *revulsus,* pp. of *revellere* pluck away < *re-* back + *vellere* pluck, pull] **— re·vul′·sive** *adj.*

Re·wa (rē′wə) **1** A trading city in northern Madhya Pradesh State, India; capital of the former state of Vindhya Pradesh, 1948–56; before 1948, capital of the princely state of Rewa. **2** A former princely state of central India; 12,830 square miles.

re·ward (ri·wôrd′) *n.* **1** Something given or done in return; especially, a gift, prize, or recompense for merit, service, or achievement; also, punishment or retribution for evil. **2** Money offered for information, for the return of lost goods, the apprehension of criminals, etc. **3** Merited results; just deserts: He has gone to his *reward.* See synonyms under RECOMPENSE, SUBSIDY. **—** *v.t.* To give a reward to or for; requite; be a reward for; recompense. See synonyms under PAY, REQUITE. [< AF *rewarder,* OF *regarder* look at. Doublet of REGARD.] **— re·ward′er** *n.*

re·ward·ing (ri·wôrd′ing) *adj.* Yielding intangible rewards; worthwhile; satisfying: a *rewarding* career.

re·wind (rē·wīnd′) *v.t.* **·wound, ·wind·ing** To wind or coil anew.

re·wire (rē·wīr′) *v.t.* **·wired, ·wir·ing** To wire again, as a house or a machine.

re·word (rē·wûrd′) *v.t.* **1** To say again in other words; express differently. **2** To utter or say again in the same words; repeat.

re·write (rē·rīt′) *v.t.* **·wrote, ·writ·ten, ·writ·ing** **1** To write over again. **2** In American journalism, to put into publishable form (a story submitted by a reporter). **—** *n.* (rē′rīt′) A news item sent in by a reporter and rewritten for publication.

Rex (reks) A masculine personal name. [<L, king]

Rey·kja·vik (rā′kyä·vēk′) The capital of Iceland, a port on the SW coast.

Rey·mont (rā′mônt), **Wladyslaw Stanislaw,** 1867–1925, Polish novelist.

Rey·nal·do (rā·näl′thō) Spanish form of REGINALD.

Reyn·ard (ren′ərd, rā′nərd) *n.* The fox, especially as the personification of cunning. [< MDu. <OF *Renard* <OHG *Reginhard,* name of the protagonist in *Reynard the Fox,* the medieval beast epic]

Rey·naud (rā·nō′), **Paul,** 1878–1966, French statesman; premier, 1940.

Reyn·old (ren′əld) See REGINALD.

Reyn·olds (ren′əldz), **Sir Joshua,** 1723–92, English painter.

Re·za·i·yeh (ri·zä′ē·yä′) See RIZAIYEH.

rhab·do·man·cy (rab′də·man′sē) *n.* Divination; the discovery of springs, precious metals, etc., by means of a divining rod: also spelled *rabdomancy.* [<LL *rhabdomantia* <Gk. *rhabdomanteia* < *rhabdos* a rod + *manteia* divination] **— rhab′do·man′tist** *n.*

rha·chis (rā′kis) See RACHIS.

Rhad·a·man·thus (rad′ə·man′thəs) In Greek mythology, a son of Zeus and Europa who was noted for justice during his lifetime, and in the afterworld was made a judge, together with Minos and Aeacus. Also **Rhad′a·man′·thys. — Rhad′a·man′thine** (-thin) *adj.*

Rhae·ti·a (rē′shē·ə) An ancient Roman province, including part of modern Tirol and the Grisons, and later extended to the Danube. Also **Rhæ′ti·a. — Rhae·tian** (rē′shən) *adj.* & *n.*

Rhaetian Alps A division of the central Alps

on the Italo-Swiss and Swiss-Austrian borders, within the boundaries of ancient Rhaetia; highest peak, 13,300 feet.

Rhae·tic (rē′tik) *adj.* **1** *Geol.* Of or pertaining to a group of rock strata representing the upper division of the Triassic system in England and western Europe. **2** Of or pertaining to the Rhaetian Alps. Also **Rhe′tic.** [<L *Rhaeticus*]

Rhae·to-Ro·man·ic (rē′tō·rō·man′ik) *adj.* Of or pertaining to the peoples of SE Switzerland, northern Italy, and Tirol, or to their Romance dialects known as Ladin, Romansch, and Friulian. — *n.* These dialects as a group.

-rhage, -rhagia, -rhagy See -RRHAGIA.

rham·na·ceous (ram·nā′shəs) *adj. Bot.* Of, pertaining to, or designating a family *(Rhamnaceae)* of spiny shrubs and small trees, the buckthorn family, having simple leaves and regular flowers in cymes. [<Gk. *rhamnos,* a kind of prickly shrub]

rha·phe (rā′fē) See RAPHE.

-raphy See -RRHAPHY.

rhap·so·dist (rap′sə·dist) *n.* **1** Among the ancient Greeks, a wandering minstrel who recited epic poems, either his own or another's; especially, one who declaimed the Homeric poems. **2** One who expresses himself with exaggeration of sentiment in speech or writing.

rhap·so·dize (rap′sə·dīz) *v.t.* & *v.i.* **·dized, ·diz·ing** To express or recite rhapsodically.

rhap·so·dy (rap′sə·dē) *n. pl.* **·dies 1** A series of disconnected and often extravagant sentences, extracts, or utterances, gathered or composed under excitement; rapt or rapturous utterance. **2** In ancient Greece, an epic poem, or a part of such a poem, especially from the *Odyssey* or *Iliad,* recited by a rhapsodist; also, the recitation itself. **3** *Music* An instrumental composition of irregular form, often suggesting the qualities of improvisation. **4** A miscellaneous collection; a medley. [<F *rapsodie* <L *rhapsodia* <Gk. *rhapsōidia* < *rhapsōidos* rhapsodist < *rhaptein* stitch together + *ōidē* song] — **rhap·sod·ic** (rap·sod′ik) or **·i·cal** *adj.* — **rhap·sod′i·cal·ly** *adv.*

rhat·a·ny (rat′ə·nē) *n.* **1** Either of two perennial, shrubby South American plants of the pea family (genus *Krameria*), the **Peruvian rhatany** *(K. triandra)* or the **Brazilian rhatany** *(K. argentea),* whose dried roots are used in medicine. **2** The roots of these plants, or medicinal substances prepared from them. Also spelled *ratany.* [<NL <Sp. *ratania* <Quechua]

rhe·a (rē′ə) *n.* A ratite bird (genus *Rhea*) of the plains of South America, smaller than true ostriches, and having three toes: also called *ostrich.* [<NL]

Rhe·a (rē′ə) In Greek mythology, the daughter of Uranus and Gaea, wife of her brother Kronos, and mother of Zeus, Poseidon, Hades, Hera, Demeter, and Hestia: identified with the Phrygian *Cybele* and the Roman *Ops*: also called *Mother of the Gods.* See KRONOS.

-rhea See -RRHEA.

Rhea Sylvia In Roman legend, a vestal, the mother by Mars of Romulus and Remus.

Rhee (rē), **Syngman,** 1875–1965, Korean statesman; president 1948–1960.

Rheims (rēmz, *Fr.* rans) See REIMS.

rhe·in (rē′in) *n. Chem.* A yellow crystalline acid, $C_{15}H_8O_6$, obtained from senna leaves and Chinese rhubarb: sometimes used as a purgative. [<Gk. *rhēon* rhubarb + -IN]

Rhein (rīn) The German name for RHINE.

Rhein·fall (rīn′fäl) The German name for SCHAFFHAUSEN FALLS.

Rhein·gold (rīn′gōld, *Ger.* rīn′gōlt) **1** In Wagner's *Der Ring des Nibelungen,* the gold snatched from the Rhine by Alberich, from which he made the magical ring. **2** The title of the first of the tetralogy of music dramas by Wagner forming *Der Ring des Nibelungen.* Also spelled *Rhinegold.* [<G]

Rhein·land (rīn′länt) The German name for RHINELAND.

Rhein·pfalz (rīn′pfälts) The German name for RHINE PALATINATE.

rhe·mat·ic (ri·mat′ik) *adj.* **1** Relating to or derived from a verb. **2** Pertaining to the formation of words. [<Gk. *rhēma* word, verb]

Rhen·ish (ren′ish) *adj.* Pertaining to the river Rhine, or to the adjacent lands. — *n.* Rhine wine. [<L *Rhenus* Rhine]

Rhenish Hesse An administrative division of Rhineland-Palatinate, West Germany; 517 square miles.

Rhenish Prussia See RHINE PROVINCE.

rhe·ni·um (rē′nē·əm) *n.* A heavy, lustrous, metallic chemical element (symbol Re) of the manganese group. See ELEMENT. [<NL <L *Rhenus* Rhine]

Rhe·nus (rē′nəs) Ancient name for the RHINE.

rheo- *combining form* Current or flow, as of water or electricity: *rheostat.* [<Gk. *rheos* a current]

rhe·o·base (rē′ə·bās) *n. Physiol.* The minimum voltage of an electric current required to stimulate a nerve or muscle. Compare CHRONAXY.

rhe·ol·o·gy (rē·ol′ə·jē) *n.* The study of the properties and behavior of flowing substances; the science of flow. [<RHEO- + -LOGY] — **rhe·ol′o·gist** *n.*

rhe·om·e·ter (rē·om′ə·tər) *n.* A device for indicating the force or velocity of blood circulation. [<RHEO- + -METER]

rhe·o·scope (rē′ə·skōp) *n.* A galvanoscope. — **rhe′o·scop′ic** (-skop′ik) *adj.*

rhe·o·stat (rē′ə·stat) *n. Electr.* A device for regulating current-strength of electricity, as by resistance coils. [< RHEO- + Gk. *statos* standing] — **rhe′o·stat′ic** *adj.*

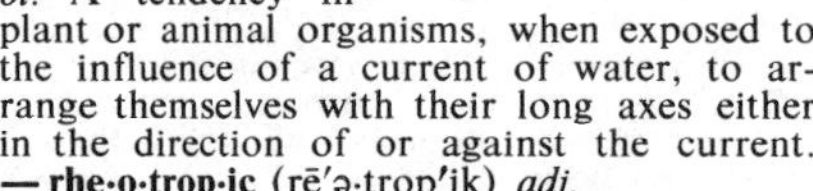

RHEOSTAT
a. Sliding contact.
b. Resistance coil.
c. Lug.

rhe·o·tax·is (rē′ə·tak′sis) *n. Biol.* The response of an organism to the influence of a current, especially of water. — **rhe′o·tac′·tic** (-tak′tik) *adj.*

rhe·ot·ro·pism (rē·ot′rə·piz′əm) *n. Biol.* A tendency in plant or animal organisms, when exposed to the influence of a current of water, to arrange themselves with their long axes either in the direction of or against the current. — **rhe·o·trop·ic** (rē′ə·trop′ik) *adj.*

rhe·sus (rē′səs) *n.* A macaque *(Macaca mulatta)* with a moderate tail, common throughout India. [<NL <Gk. *Rhēsos* Rhesus; arbitrarily assigned]

RHESUS
(From 12 to 18 inches long: tail, 6 to 8 inches)

Rhe·sus (rē′səs) In the *Iliad,* a king of Thrace and ally of the Trojans, killed by Odysseus the night of his arrival before Troy.

Rhe·sus factor (rē′səs) See RH FACTOR.

rhe·tor (rē′tər) *n.* **1** Formerly, one who taught rhetoric. **2** An orator. [<L <Gk. *rhētōr*]

rhet·o·ric (ret′ə·rik) *n.* **1** The art of discourse; skill in the use of language. **2** The power of pleasing or persuading. **3** A textbook treating of discourse; especially, written discourse. **4** Affected and exaggerated display in the use of language. **5** Prose, as opposed to verse. [<F *rhétorique* <L *rhetorica* <Gk. *rhētorikē (technē)* rhetorical (art)]

rhe·tor·i·cal (ri·tôr′i·kəl, -tor′-) *adj.* **1** Pertaining to rhetoric; oratorical; declamatory. **2** Designed for showy oratorical effect. — **rhe·tor′i·cal·ly** *adv.* — **rhe·tor′i·cal·ness** *n.*

rhetorical question A question put only for oratorical or literary effect, the answer being implied in the question.

rhetorical stress The emphasis required by the meaning of a line or the lines in a poem: opposed to *metrical stress.*

rhet·o·ri·cian (ret′ə·rish′ən) *n.* **1** A master or teacher of rhetoric. **2** An orator; one who writes or speaks eloquently. [<F *rhétoricien*]

rheum (ro͞om) *n.* **1** *Pathol.* Catarrhal discharge from the nose and eyes; hence, a cold. **2** *Med.* Any thin watery flux, as tears or saliva. [<OF *reume* <L *rheuma* <Gk. *rheuma* a flow < *rheein* flow] — **rheum′y** *adj.*

rheu·mat·ic (ro͞o·mat′ik) *adj.* Pertaining to, causing, or affected with rheumatism. — *n.* **1** One affected with or liable to rheumatism. **2** *pl. Colloq.* Rheumatic pains. [<OF *reumatique* <L *rheumaticus* <Gk. *rheumatikos* < *rheuma.* See RHEUM.]

rheumatic fever *Pathol.* A severe, probably infectious disease chiefly affecting children and young adults, characterized by painful inflammation around the joints, typically intermittent fever, and inflammation of the pericardium and valves of the heart.

rheu·ma·tism (ro͞o′mə·tiz′əm) *n. Pathol.* **1** A variable, shifting, painful inflammation and stiffness of the muscles, joints, or other structures. **2** Rheumatic fever. **3** Rheumatoid arthritis. [<L *rheumatismus* rheum <Gk. *rheumatismos* < *rheuma* rheum]

rheu·ma·toid (ro͞o′mə·toid) *adj. Pathol.* **1** Resembling rheumatism or rheumatic symptoms: *rheumatoid* arthritis. **2** Afflicted with rheumatism. Also **rheu′ma·toi′dal** (-toid′l). — **rheu′·ma·toi′dal·ly** *adv.*

rheumatoid arthritis *Pathol.* A persisting inflammatory disease of the joints, marked by atrophy, rarefaction of the bones, and deformities.

Rheydt (rīt) A city in western North Rhine-Westphalia, West Germany; the twin city of München-Gladbach.

Rh factor *Biochem.* Any of a group of genetically transmitted agglutinogens present in the blood of most individuals (Rh positive) and which may cause hemolytic reactions under certain conditions, as during pregnancy or following transfusions with blood lacking this factor (Rh negative). Also called *Rhesus factor.*

rhig·o·lene (rig′ə·lēn) *n. Chem.* A colorless, volatile, inflammable liquid distillate of petroleum: used in medicine as a local freezing anesthetic for minor operations. [<Gk. *rhigos* frost + L *oleum* oil]

rhin- Var. of RHINO-.

rhi·nal (rī′nəl) *adj.* Of or pertaining to the nose; nasal. [<RHIN- + -AL]

Rhine (rīn) The principal river of west central Europe, flowing 810 miles north from SE Switzerland, through Germany and Netherlands, to the North Sea, forming part of the SW boundary of Germany, and dividing, in the Netherlands, into the *Waal,* the *Lek,* the *Oude Rijn,* and the *Ijssel*: ancient *Rhenus,* German *Rhein,* Dutch *Rijn.* French **Rhin** (rañ).

Rhine (rīn), **Joseph Banks,** born 1895, U. S. psychologist.

Rhine·gold (rīn′gōld) The hoard of the Nibelungs, secreted in the Rhine. Compare RHEINGOLD.

Rhine·land (rīn′land′) **1** That part of Germany west of the Rhine. **2** The Rhine Province. German *Rheinland.*

Rhine·land-Pa·lat·i·nate (rīn′land′pə·lat′ə·nāt) A state of West Germany; 7,654 square miles; capital, Mainz. *German* **Rhein·land-Pfalz** (rīn′länt·pfälts′).

rhi·nen·ceph·a·lon (rī′nen·sef′ə·lon) *n. pl.* **·la** (-lə) *Anat.* That portion of the brain which forms the olfactory lobe, consisting of the olfactory tubercle, tract, and bulb, which give origin to the sense of smell. [<RHIN- + ENCEPHALON] — **rhi·nen·ce·phal·ic** (rī′nen·sə·fal′ik) *adj.*

Rhine Palatinate See PALATINATE, THE. German *Rheinpfalz.*

Rhine Province A former Prussian province in western Germany, included since 1945 in Rhineland-Palatinate; 9,451 square miles; former capital, Coblenz: also *Rhenish Prussia.*

rhine·stone (rīn′stōn′) *n.* A highly refractive, colorless glass or paste, used as an imitation gemstone. [Trans. of F *caillou du Rhin*; orig. made at Strasbourg]

Rhine wine Wine made from grapes grown in the neighborhood of the Rhine; specifically, the white, still wines of this region, noted for their delicate bouquet; hock.

rhi·ni·tis (rī·nī′tis) *n. Pathol.* Inflammation of the mucous membranes of the nose; nasal catarrh. [<RHIN- + -ITIS]

rhi·no (rī′nō) *n. pl.* **·nos** A rhinoceros.

rhino- *combining form* Nose; nasal: *rhinoplasty.* Also, before vowels, *rhin-.* [<Gk. *rhis, rhinos* nose]

rhi·noc·e·ros (rī·nos′ər·əs) *n. pl.* **·ros·es** or **·ros** A large, herbivorous, odd-toed mammal (family *Rhinocerotidae*) of Africa and Asia, with one or two keratin-fiber horns on the snout, a very thick hide, and the upper lip protruded and prehensile. [<LL <Gk. *rhinokerōs* <*rhis, rhinos* nose + *keras* horn]

RHINOCEROS
a. African: About 5 feet at the shoulder; to 3000 pounds.
b. Indian: About 5 1/2 feet at the shoulder; to 4000 pounds.

rhi·nol·o·gy (rī·nol′ə·jē) *n.* The branch of medicine that relates to the nose and its diseases. [<RHINO- + -LOGY] **—rhi·nol′o·gist** *n.*

rhi·no·plas·ty (rī′nō·plas′tē) *n.* Plastic surgery of the nose. **—rhi′no·plas′tic** *adj.*

rhi·no·scope (rī′nə·skōp) *n.* An instrument for inspecting the nasal cavities.

rhi·nos·co·py (rī·nos′kə·pē) *n.* Inspection of the nasal passages.

rhizo– *combining form* Root; pertaining to a root or to roots: *rhizogenic.* Also, before vowels, **rhiz–.** [<Gk.*rhiza* a root]

rhi·zo·bi·um (rī·zō′bē·əm) *n. pl.* **·bi·a** (-bē·ə) *Bacteriol.* One of a genus *(Rhizobium)* of rod–shaped, nitrogen–fixing bacteria causing nodules on the roots of leguminous plants. [<NL <RHIZO- + Gk. *bios* life]

rhi·zo·car·pous (rī′zō·kär′pəs) *adj. Bot.* Having annual stems and foliage growing from perennial roots: said of perennial plants. Also **rhi′·zo·car′pic.**

rhi·zo·ceph·a·lous (rī′zō·sef′ə·ləs) *adj. Zool.* Naming or pertaining to a suborder *(Rhizocephala)* of parasitic cirripeds, without antennae or feet, which attach themselves to crabs by a short peduncle from which rootlike processes branch out.

rhi·zo·gen·ic (rī′zō·jen′ik) *adj. Bot.* Root–producing: said of the layer of mother cells at the periphery of the central cylinder of a root that gives rise to rootlets. Also **rhi·zog·e·nous** (rī·zoj′ə·nəs).

rhi·zoid (rī′zoid) *adj.* Rootlike; similar to or resembling a root. **—***n. Bot.* A delicate filiform or hairlike organ developed on all kinds of thalli, moss stems, etc.: the analog of the roots of flowering plants, serving for absorption and attachment. **—rhi·zoi·dal** (rī·zoid′l) *adj.*

rhi·zome (rī′zōm) *n. Bot.* A procumbent or subterranean rootlike stem, producing roots from its lower surface and leaves or shoots from its upper surface; a rootstock. Also **rhi·zo·ma** (rī·zō′·mə). [<NL *rhizoma* <Gk. *rhizōma* mass of roots, ult. <*rhiza* root] **—rhi·zom·a·tous** (rī·zom′ə·təs, -zō′mə-) *adj.*

RHIZOME
The bearded iris

rhi·zo·morph (rī′zə·môrf) *n. Bot.* One of the rootlike parts of the mycelium, composed of many united hyphal strands, by which certain fungi attach themselves to and penetrate the higher plants.

rhi·zo·mor·phous (rī′zō·môr′fəs) *adj. Bot.* Branching after the manner of rootlets: said of mycelia.

rhi·zoph·a·gous (rī·zof′ə·gəs) *adj.* Feeding on roots. [<RHIZO- + -PHAGOUS]

rhi·zo·pod (rī′zə·pod) *n.* Any member of a subclass *(Rhizopoda)* of protozoans with pseudopodia for locomotion and the ingestion of food. **—rhi·zop·o·dan** (rī·zop′ə·dən) *adj. & n.* **—rhi·zop′o·dous** *adj.*

rhi·zot·o·my (rī·zot′ə·mē) *n. Surg.* The division of the roots of the spinal nerves, for the relief of pain or spastic paralysis. [<RHIZO- + -TOMY]

rho (rō) *n.* The seventeenth letter and twelfth consonant in the Greek alphabet (Ρ,ρ): equivalent to the English *r* aspirated. As a numeral it denotes 100. [<Gk. *rhō*]

Rho·da (rō′də) A feminine personal name. [< Gk., rose]
—Rhoda A damsel in the house of Mary, the mother of John. *Acts* xii 13.

rho·da·mine (rō′də·mēn, -min) *n. Chem.* Any of various red or pink dyestuffs obtained by condensing an amino derivative of phenol with phthalic anhydride. The solution shows green fluorescence. Also **rho′da·min** (-min). [< Gk. *rhodon* rose + AMINE]

Rhode Island (rōd) A southern New England State of the United States; 1,214 square miles; capital, Providence; entered the Union May 29, 1790, one of the original thirteen States: officially **The State of Rhode Island and Providence Plantations;** the smallest State in the Union; nickname *Little Rhody:* abbr. RI — **Rhode Islander**

Rhode Island Red An American breed of domestic fowls, reddish and black in color, having smooth yellow legs and a small single comb.

Rhodes (rōdz) **1** The largest island of the Dodecanese group; 545 square miles. **2** Its chief city, capital of the Dodecanese Islands. Italian *Rodi. Greek* **Ró·dhos** (rô′thôs). See COLOSSUS OF RHODES.

Rhodes (rōdz), **Cecil (John),** 1853–1902, British South African financier and statesman. — **James Ford,** 1848–1927, U.S. industrialist and historian.

Rho·de·sia (rō·dē′zhə, -zhē·ə) **1** Formerly, a region of south central Africa divided by the Zambezi river into **Northern Rhodesia,** a British Protectorate, and **Southern Rhodesia,** a British Colony. See ZAMBIA. **2** A British Colony in south central Africa consisting of the former Southern Rhodesia; unilaterally declared its independence in 1965; 150,333 sq. mi.; capital, Salisbury. **—Rho·de′sian** *adj. & n.*

Rho·de·sian man (rō·dē′zhən) An African forerunner *(Homo rhodesiensis)* of Neanderthal man, represented by the massive upper jaw and cranium of a skull discovered in 1921 at Broken Hill, Rhodesia.

Rhodes scholarships Any of a number of scholarships, tenable at Oxford University, provided for in the will of Cecil Rhodes, for selected scholars from the United States and the British dominions and colonies.

Rho·di·an (rō′dē·ən) *adj.* Of or pertaining to the island of Rhodes or to the Knights of Rhodes. **—***n.* A Knight of Rhodes; also, a native of that island.

rho·dic (rō′dik) *adj. Chem.* Of, pertaining to, or derived from rhodium: *rhodic* sulfate.

rho·di·um (rō′dē·əm) *n.* A whitish–gray metallic element (symbol Rh) of the platinum group, whose salts are for the most part rose–colored: used for plating silver and in alloys, especially with steel. See ELEMENT. [<NL < Gk. *rhodon* rose; from the color of its salts]

rho·do·chro·site (rō′də·krō′sīt) *n.* A vitreous rose–red or variously colored rhombohedral manganese carbonate, $MnCO_3$. [<G *rhodochrosit* <Gk. *rhodochrōs* rose–colored < *rhodon* rose +*chrōs* color]

rho·do·den·dron (rō′də·den′drən) *n.* Any of a genus *(Rhododendron)* of showy evergreen shrubs or small trees of the heath family, with profuse clusters of beautiful flowers, found growing wild in mountainous regions; especially, the **great rhododendron** *(R. macrophyllum),* the State flower of Washington, and the **rosebay rhododendron** *(R. maximum),* the State flower of West Virginia. [<L <Gk. <*rhodon* rose + *dendron* tree]

rho·do·lite (rō′də·līt) *n.* A pale rose–colored garnet, used as a gem. [<Gk. *rhodon* rose + -LITE]

rho·do·nite (rō′də·nīt) *n.* A vitreous, red or pink manganese silicate, $MnSiO_3$, crystallizing in the triclinic system, and often used as an ornamental stone. [<Gk. *rhodon* rose]

Rhod·o·pe Mountains (rod′ə·pē) A mountain chain of the Balkan Peninsula, dividing Bulgaria from Thrace and Macedonia; highest peak, 9,591 feet.

Rho·do·phy·ce·ae (rō′də·fī′si·ē) *n. pl.* A major division or group of algae characterized by a red, purple, or reddish–brown color and found chiefly in seas of the temperate zone; the red algae. [<NL <Gk. *rhodon* rose + *phykos* seaweed]

rho·dop·sin (rō·dop′sin) *n. Biochem.* The rose–colored component of visual purple, breaking down into retinene on exposure to light. [< Gk. *rhodon* rose + *opsis* appearance]

rho·do·ra (rō·dôr′ə, -dō′rə) *n.* A handsome shrub *(Rhododendron canadense),* from 1 to 3 feet high, with terminal clusters of pale–purple flowers preceding the leaves. It is found in cool bogs, from Pennsylvania to Canada. [<L *rhodora* meadowsweet]

–rhoea See -RRHEA.

rhomb (rom, romb) *n.* A rhombus. [<F *rhombe.* See RHOMBUS.]

rhom·ben·ceph·a·lon (rom′ben·sef′ə·lon) *n. Anat.* The parts of the cerebrospinal axis that develop from the posterior cerebral vesicle; medulla oblongata and cerebellum taken together. [<NL]

rhom·bic (rom′bik) *adj.* **1** Pertaining to or having the shape of a rhombus. **2** Orthorhombic. Also **rhom′bi·cal.**

rhom·bo·he·dral (rom′bə·hē′drəl) *adj. Geom.* Pertaining to a rhombohedron.

rhombohedral system In the classification of some authors, the trigonal division of the hexagonal crystal system.

rhom·bo·he·dron (rom′bə·hē′drən) *n. pl.* **·drons** or **·dra** (drə) *Geom.* A prismatic form included within six equal rhombic faces.

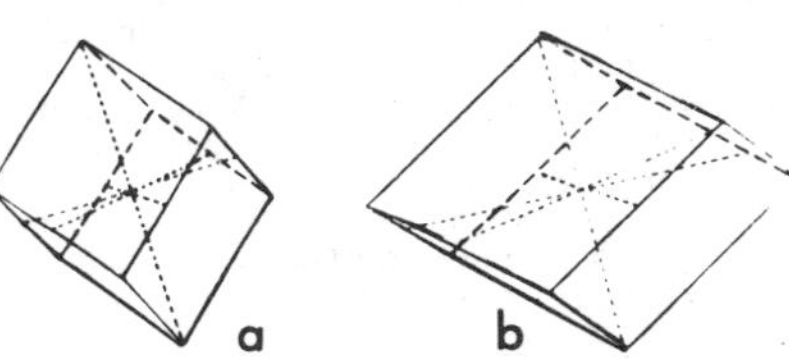

RHOMBOHEDRONS
a. Acute. *b.* Obtuse.

rhom·boid (rom′boid) *n. Geom.* **1** A parallelogram having opposite sides and opposite angles equal but no right angle. **2** A solid bounded by such parallelograms. **—***adj.* **1** Having the character or shape of a rhomboid. **2** Having a shape approaching that of a rhombus, as one of two muscles attached to the shoulder blades. [<F *rhomboïde*] — **rhom·boi·dal** (rom·boid′l) *adj.*

rhom·bus (rom′bəs) *n. pl.* **·bus·es** or **·bi** (-bī) *Geom.* **1** An equilateral parallelogram having the angles usually, but not necessarily, oblique: A square may be considered as a special case of the *rhombus.* **2** A rhombohedron. [<L <Gk. *rhombos* spinning top, rhomb]

rhon·chus (rong′kəs) *n. pl.* **·chi** (-kī) *Pathol.* A rattling or whistling sound in respiration, especially when it resembles snoring; a râle. [< L <Gk. *rhonchos*] **—rhon′chal, rhon′chi·al** *adj.*

Rhond·da (ron′də) An urban district of Glamorganshire, SE Wales: also *Ystradyfodwg.*

Rhond·da (ron′də), **Viscount,** 1856–1918, David Alfred Thomas, British industrialist and administrator.

Rhône (rōn) A river in Switzerland and SE France, flowing 504 miles to the Mediterranean including 45 miles through Lake Geneva above Geneva; enters the Gulf of the Lion below Arles. Also **Rhone.**

rhu·barb (rōō′bärb) *n.* **1** A stout, coarse, perennial herb (genus *Rheum*) of the buckwheat family, having large leaves and small clusters of flowers on tall fleshy stalks; especially, the common rhubarb or pie plant *(R. rhaponticum),* whose acid leaf stalks are used in cooking. **2** The dried roots of the medicinal rhubarb *(R. officinale* and *R. palmatum),* used as a cathartic and bitter tonic. **3** *U.S. Slang* A heated argument; scuffle or quarrel. [<OF *reubarbe* <LL *rhabarbarum* <Gk. *Rha* Volga river, Volga plant, rhubarb + *barbaron* foreign; so called because orig. imported from Russia]

rhumb (rum, rumb) *n. Naut.* **1** One of the 32 points of the mariners' compass, separated by arcs of 11° 15′. **2** One of these arcs or divisions. [<OF *rumb*]

rhum·ba (rum′bə) See RUMBA.

rhumb line A line or course along the surface of a sphere crossing successive meridians at the same angle; a loxodromic curve.

Rhus (rus) *n.* A large genus of trees or shrubs

of the cashew family, including the true sumacs. Poison ivy and poison oak, also often included, are now placed in the genus *Toxicodendron.* [<NL <L <Gk. *rhous* sumac]

rhyme (rīm), **rhym·er** (rī′mər), **rhyme·ster** (rīm′stər), etc. See RIME, etc.

rhyn·cho·ce·pha·li·an (ring′kō·sə·fā′lē·ən) *adj.* Pertaining to or designating a nearly extinct order of lizardlike reptiles *(Rhynchocephalia),* represented by only one genus *(Sphenodon),* the tuatara of New Zealand. —*n.* One of the *Rhynchocephalia.* [<NL *Rhynchocephalia,* name of the order <Gk. *rhynchos* snout + *kephalē* head]

rhy·o·lite (rī′ə·līt) *n.* A highly acidic, variously colored volcanic rock. [<Gk. *rhyax* stream + -LITE]

rhythm (rith′əm) *n.* **1** Movement characterized by regular measured or harmonious recurrence of stress, beat, sound, accent, or motion: the *rhythm* of the pulse, the *rhythm* of moving oars. **2** The musical property dependent on the regular succession of accents or tone–impulses; accent–movement or accent–structure; also, a system or kind of accentuation as determined by the make–up of the accentual divisions. **3** In poetry, the cadenced flow of sound as determined by the succession of long and short syllables **(classical rhythm),** or accented and unaccented syllables **(modern rhythm).** When definitely measured by feet or bars or periods, which make lines or verses, it becomes *meter.* **4** A metrical foot or measure. **5** Verse or rime. See synonyms under METER. [<F *rhythme* < Gk. *rhythmos* <*rheein* flow]

CHARACTERISTIC DANCE RHYTHMS
a. Cracovienne. *b.* Polka. *c.* Mazurka.

rhyth·mic (rith′mik) *adj.* Relating to or characterized by rhythm: contrasted with *harmonic.* Also **rhyth′mi·cal.** —**rhyth′mi·cal·ly** *adv.*

rhyth·mics (rith′miks) *n.* The science of rhythm.

rhyth·mist (rith′mist) *n.* A master of rhythmical composition; also, one versed in rhythmics.

ri·al (rī′al) *n.* The monetary unit of Iran; a silver coin, twenty of which equal one pahlavi. [<OF *rial, real* royal]

ri·al·to (rē·al′tō) *n. pl.* **·tos** A market or place of exchange. [from *Rialto* <*Rivo Alto* ancient name of the island on which Venice was founded about 800 <Ital. *rivo* channel (<L *rivus* brook) + *alto* deep <L *altus*]

Ri·al·to (rē·al′tō, *Ital.* rē·äl′tō) **1** An island comprising the ancient business quarter of Venice. **2** A bridge over the Grand Canal connecting the old Rialto with the island of San Marco at Venice, Italy: short for **Ponte del Rialto. 3** In New York City, the theater district.

ri·ant (rī′ənt) *adj.* Laughing. [<F, laughing, ppr. of *rire* laugh] —**ri′ant·ly** *adv.*

ri·a·ta (rē·ä′tə) *n.* A lasso; lariat. [<Sp. *reata* <*reatar* tie again <L *re-* again +*aptare* fit]

Ri·au Archipelago (rē′ou) See RIOUW ARCHIPELAGO.

rib (rib) *n.* **1** *Anat.* One of the series of bony rods attached to the spine of most vertebrates, and nearly encircling the thoracic cavity. In man there are twelve ribs on each side, forming the walls of the thorax, of which the first seven **(true** or **sternal ribs)** are attached to the sternum, the last five **(false** or **asternal ribs)** being either attached by their edges to the rib above, as in the upper three, or free distally **(floating ribs),** as in the lower two. ◆ Collateral adjective: *costal.* **2** Something likened to the rib of an animal; a ridge, strip, or band. **3** A curved side timber bending away from the keel in a boat or ship, or a curved timber or support in a vault. **4** A raised wale or stripe in cloth or knit goods, as stockings. **5** *Aeron.* An element in the construction of an airplane wing, usually extending fore and and aft and crossing the wing spars, to hold the fabric of the wing in shape. **6** *Bot.* A vein or nerve of a leaf, especially the middle one; any ridge on a plant. **7** A cut of meat including one or more ribs. **8** A wife: in jocular allusion to *Gen.* ii 22. **9** *Slang* A practical joke. —*v.t.* **ribbed, rib·bing 1** To make with ridges; to *rib* a piece of knitting. **2** To strengthen or protect by or enclose within ribs. **3** *Slang* To make fun of; tease. [OE *ribb*]

rib·ald (rib′əld) *adj.* Pertaining to or indulging in coarse or offensive language or vulgar jokes; coarsely jocular. —*n.* One who uses coarse or abusive language. [<OF *ribauld* < Gmc. Cf. MHG *riben* copulate, MDu. *ribe* whore.]

rib·ald·ry (rib′əl·drē) *n.* Coarse or ribald language. [<OF *ribauderie*]

rib·and (rib′ənd) *n. Archaic* A decorative ribbon. [Earlier form of RIBBON]

rib·band (rib′band′, rib′ənd, -ən) *n. Naut.* A lengthwise strip following a vessel's curves and bolted to its ribs, to hold them in place until they receive the planking or plating. Also **rib′–band′.** [<RIB + BAND[1]]

Rib·ben·trop (rib′ən·trôp), **Joachim von,** 1893–1946, German Nazi diplomat; executed.

rib·bing (rib′ing) *n.* An arrangement or collection of ribs,as in ribbed cloth, etc.

rib·bon (rib′ən) *n.* **1** A narrow strip of fine fabric, usually silk or satin, having two selvages, and commonly less than eight inches wide, made in a variety of weaves: used as trimming. **2** Something shaped like or suggesting a ribbon, as a watch spring, or a painted stripe on the side of a vessel. **3** A narrow strip; a shred: torn to *ribbons.* **4** An ink–bearing strip of cloth in a typewriter. **5** A ribband. **6** *pl. Colloq.* Driving reins. **7 a** A colored strip of cloth worn to signify membership in an order, the award of a prize, etc. **b** A similar strip of cloth worn on the left breast of a military or naval uniform to indicate campaigns served in, medals won, etc. **8** A ticker tape. —*v.t.* To ornament with ribbons; also, to form or tear into ribbons. —*adj.* **1** Made of or like ribbon. **2** Having parallel bands or streaks, as certain minerals: *ribbon* jasper. **3** Of a standard to receive a prize in a competitive show: a *ribbon* hog. [<OF *riban;* origin unknown]

rib·bon·fish (rib′ən·fish′) *n. pl.* **·fish** or **·fish·es** A long marine fish with a compressed, ribbonlike body, as an oarfish or dealfish.

ribbon snake The American garter snake.

Ri·be·ra (rē·vä′rä), **José,** 1588–1656, Spanish painter: sometimes called "Lo Spagnoletto."

ri·bo·fla·vin (rī′bō·flā′vin) *n. Biochem.* A member of the vitamin B complex, vitamin B_2, an orange–yellow, crystalline compound, $C_{17}H_{20}N_4O_6$, found in milk, green leafy vegetables, egg yolk, and meats, and also made synthetically: formerly called *lactoflavin, vitamin G.* [<RIBO(SE) FLAVIN]

ri·bon·ic acid (rī·bon′ik) *Chem.* An acid, $C_5H_{10}O_6$, produced by the oxidation of ribose.

ri·bo·nu·cle·ase (rī′bō·nōō′klē·ās, -nyōō′-) *n.* An enzyme that promotes the hydrolysis of ribonucleic acid.

ri·bo·nu·cle·ic acid (rī′bō·nōō·klē′ik, -nyōō-) *Biochem.* A nucleic acid that serves to promote the synthesis of cell proteins. Abbr. *RNA.*

ri·bose (rī′bōs) *n. Chem.* A sugar, $C_5H_{10}O_5$, derived from pentose and occurring in certain nucleic acids. [<RIB(ONIC ACID) + -OSE[2]]

ri·bo·some (rī′bə·sōm) *n. Biol.* One of a class of minute protein particles found in the cytoplasm of plant and animal cells, associated with ribonucleic acid in the transmission of genetic characteristics.

rib·wort (rib′wûrt′) *n.* The English plantain *(Plantago lanceolata),* or a related species. See PLANTAIN.

–ric *combining form* Realm or jurisdiction of: *bishopric.* [OE *rice* kingdom, realm]

Ri·car·do (*Ital.* rē·kär′dō, *Pg.* rē·kär′thōō, *Sp.* -thō) Italian, Portuguese, and Spanish form of RICHARD. Also *Ital.* **Ric·car·do** (rēk·kär′dō), *Lat.* **Ri·car·dus** (rē·kär′dəs).

Ri·car·do (ri·kär′dō), **David,** 1772–1823, English political economist. —**Ri·car′di·an** *adj.* & *n.*

Ric·cio (rēt′chō), **David** See RIZZIO.

rice (rīs) *n.* **1** An annual cereal grass *(Oryza sativa),* widely cultivated on wet land in warm climates. **2** The edible grain or seeds of this plant. [<F *riz* <L *oryza* <Gk. *oryza*]

Rice (rīs), **Elmer,** 1892–1967, U.S. dramatist. —**Grantland,** 1888–1954, U.S. journalist.

rice·bird (rīs′bûrd′) *n.* **1** Any bird frequenting rice fields; especially, in the southern United States, the bobolink: also **rice bunting. 2** The Java sparrow.

rice·braid (rīs′brād′) *n.* Braid made to resemble rice grains strung together lengthwise.

rice paper 1 Paper made from rice straw. **2** A delicate vegetable paper made from the pith of a Chinese shrub, the **rice–paper plant** *(Tetrapanax papyriferus),* pared into thin rolls and flattened into sheets.

ric·er (rī′sər) *n.* A kitchen utensil consisting of a perforated container through which potatoes and other vegetables are pressed, emerging in small particles resembling grains of rice.

rice weevil A small brown weevil *(Sitophilus* or *Calandra oryza)* destructive to growing rice and the stored grain. For illustration see INSECTS (injurious).

rich (rich) *adj.* **1** Having large possessions, as of money, goods, or lands; wealthy; opulent. **2** Composed of rare or precious materials; valuable; costly; *rich* fabrics. **3** Having in a high degree qualities pleasing to the senses; luscious to the taste: often implying an unwholesome excess of butter, fats, flavoring, etc. **4** Full, satisfying, and pleasing, as a tone, voice, color, or perfume. **5** Luxuriant; abundant: *rich* hair; *rich* crops. **6** Yielding abundant returns; fruitful. **7** Abundantly supplied: often with *in* or *with.* **8** Abounding in desirable qualities; of full strength, as blood. **9** *Colloq.* Exceedingly humorous; amusing or ridiculous: a *rich* joke. See synonyms under FERTILE, RACY. [OE *rīce;* infl. in form by OF *riche* < Gmc.] —**rich′ly** *adv.* —**rich′ness** *n.*

Rich·ard (rich′ərd; *Fr.* rē·shär′, *Ger.* rē′khärt) A masculine personal name. Also *Lat.* **Ri·char·dus** (rē·kär′dəs), *Du.* **Ri·chart** (rē′shärt). [<Gmc., strong ruler]

—**Richard I,** 1157–99, king of England 1189–1199; went on Third Crusade: called "Coeur de Lion" or "the Lion–Hearted."

—**Richard II,** 1367–1400, king of England 1377–99, deposed by Henry IV.

—**Richard III,** 1452–85, king of England 1483–85; usurped throne; killed at Bosworth.

Richard Roe See JOHN DOE.

Rich·ards (rich′ərdz), **Ivor Armstrong,** born 1893, English literary critic. —**Theodore William,** 1868–1928, U.S. chemist.

Rich·ard·son (rich′ərd·sən), **Henry Handel** Pseudonym of Henrietta Richardson, 1878?–1946, Australian novelist. —**Henry Hobson,** 1838–1886, U.S. architect. —**Owen Willans,** 1879–1959, English physicist. —**Samuel,** 1689?–1761, English novelist.

Ri·che·lieu (rē·shə·lyœ′), **Duc de,** 1585–1642, Armand Jean Duplessis, French cardinal and statesman; prime minister of Louis XIII.

Ri·che·lieu River (rē·shə·lyœ′, rish′ə·lōō) A river of southern Quebec, flowing 75 miles north from Lake Champlain to the Saint Lawrence.

rich·es (rich′iz) *n. pl.* [In Middle English, this was a singular noun and spelled *richess* or *richesse;* now, from its form, used in the plural] **1** Abundant possessions; wealth. **2** Hence, abundance of whatever is precious. See synonyms under WEALTH. [<F *richesse* < *riche* <Gmc.]

Ri·chet (rē·she′), **Charles Robert,** 1850–1935, French physiologist.

Rich·mond (rich′mənd) **1** The capital of Virginia, a port on the James River: capital of the Confederacy, 1861–65. **2** A borough on the Thames in northern Surrey, England. **3** A borough of New York City coextensive with Staten Island.

Rich·ter (rikh′tər), **Johann Paul Friedrich,** 1763–1825, German author and humorist: pseudonym *Jean Paul.*

Rich·ter scale (rik′tər) A logarithmic measure of the estimated energy released by earthquakes according to which 1 represents an imperceptible tremor and 10 a theoretical maximum about one thousand times greater than any recorded earthquake. [after Charles R. *Richter,* born 1900, U.S. seismologist]

Richt·ho·fen (rikht′hō·fən), **Baron Manfred von,** 1892–1918, German aviator in World War I; killed in action.

rich·weed (rich′wēd′) *n.* **1** An herb *(Pilea pumila)* of the nettle family growing in wet,

cool places: also called *clearweed.* **2** A strong-scented herb *(Collinsonia canadensis)* of the mint family: also called *horse balm.* **3** Ragweed. **4** White snakeroot.
ri·cin (rī′sin, ris′in) *n. Chem.* A very toxic protein isolated from the castor bean in the form of a white powder: it agglutinates red blood corpuscles. [<L *ricinus* castor bean]
ric·in·o·le·ic (ris′in·ō·lē′ik) *adj.* Of, pertaining to, or derived from the castor bean.
ricinoleic acid *Chem.* An unsaturated fatty acid, $C_{18}H_{34}O_3$, present in castor oil and hardening in a thick, yellow, crystalline or viscid mass.
ric·in·o·le·in (ris′in·ō′lē·in) *n. Chem.* The glycerol ester derivative of ricinoleic acid, preponderant in castor oil. [<L *ricinus* castor bean + *oleum* oil + -IN]
rick (rik) *n.* **1** A stack, as of hay, having the top rounded and thatched to protect the interior from rain. **2** A haycock in the field. — *v.t.* To pile in ricks. [OE *hrēac*]
Rick·en·back·er (rik′ən·bak′ər), **Edward Vernon,** 1890–1973, U.S. aviation executive; military aviator in World War I.
rick·ets (rik′its) *n. Pathol.* A disease of early childhood, chiefly due to a deficiency of calcium salts as provided by vitamin D, characterized by softening of the bones and consequent deformity; rachitis. [Origin uncertain]
rick·ett·si·a (rik·et′sē·ə) *n. pl.* **·si·ae** (-si·ē) Any of a genus *(Rickettsia)* of micro-organisms typically parasitic in the bodies of certain ticks and lice, but transmissible to other animals and to man; especially, *R. prowazeki,* the causative agent of typhus. [after Howard T. *Ricketts,* 1871–1910, U. S. pathologist]
rick·ett·si·al (rik·et′sē·əl) *adj.* Pertaining to or designating any of the various infective diseases caused by micro-organisms of *Rickettsia* or related genera, as typhus, Rocky Mountain spotted fever, or trench fever.
rick·et·y (rik′it·ē) *adj.* **1** Ready to fall; tottering. **2** Affected with rickets. — **rick′et·i·ly** *adv.* — **rick′et·i·ness** *n.*
rick·ey (rik′ē) *n.* A cooling drink of which spirits, lime juice, and carbonated water are the chief ingredients. [Origin uncertain]
rick·le (rik′əl) *n. Scot.* **1** A heap or bundle. **2** A small rick of grain or hay; a stook.
rick-rack (rik′rak′) *n.* Flat braid in zigzag form, made of cotton, rayon, silk, or wool; also, the openwork trimming made with this serpentine braid. [Reduplication of RACK[1]]
rick·shaw (rik′shô) *n.* A jinriksha. Also **rick′·sha.** [Short for JINRIKSHA]
ric·o·chet (rik′ə·shā′, -shet′) *v.i.* **·cheted** (-shād′) or **·chet·ted** (-shet′id), **·chet·ing** (-shā′ing) or **·chet·ting** (-shet′ing) To glance from a surface, as a projectile over the water; make a series of skips or bounds. — *n.* **1** A bounding, as of a projectile over a surface. **2** The method of firing by which a projectile is made to rebound. **3** A projectile so rebounding. [<OF]
ri·cot·ta (ri·kot′ə; *Ital.* rē·kôt′tä) *n.* An unripened cheese, Italian in origin and similar to cottage cheese but smoother. [<Ital. <L *recoquere* to cook again]
ric·tus (rik′təs) *n.* **1** The expanse of the open mouth; a gaping. **2** A fissure or cleft. [<L, open, gaping mouth < *ringi* open the mouth wide] — **ric′tal** *adj.*
rid[1] (rid) *v.t.* **rid** or **rid·ded, rid·ding 1** To free, as from a burden or annoyance; clear: usually with *of*: to *rid* a house of vermin. **2** *Obs.* To rescue; deliver. **3** *Obs.* To drive away; expel; banish. — *adj.* Free; clear; quit: with *of*: We are well *rid* of him. [Fusion of OE *geryddan* clear (land) + ON *rythja* clear (land) of trees]
rid[2] (rid) Obsolete past tense and past participle of RIDE.
rid·a·ble (rī′də·bəl) *adj.* That may be ridden on, through, or over, as an animal or a road.
rid·dance (rid′ns) *n.* A ridding of something undesirable, or the state of being rid.
rid·den (rid′n) Past participle of RIDE.
rid·dle[1] (rid′l) *v.t.* **·dled, ·dling 1** To perforate in numerous places, as with shot. **2** To sift through a coarse sieve. **3** To damage, injure, refute, etc., as if by perforating: to *riddle* a theory. [< *n.*] — *n.* **1** A coarse sieve, such as one used in a foundry or in washing for gold. **2** A board set with pins, used for straightening wire. [OE *hriddel* sieve] — **rid′·dler** *n.*
rid·dle[2] (rid′l) *n.* **1** A puzzling question or conundrum; anything ambiguous or puzzling. **2** Any mysterious object or person. — *v.* **·dled, ·dling** *v.t.* To solve; explain. — *v.i.* To utter or solve riddles; speak in riddles. [OE *rǣdels* < stem of *rǣdan* interpret, solve]
Synonyms (noun): conundrum, enigma, paradox, problem, puzzle. *Conundrum* signifies some question or statement in which some hidden and fanciful resemblance is involved, the answer often depending upon a pun; an *enigma* is a dark saying; a *paradox* is a true statement or fact that appears absurd or contradictory. The *riddle* is not so petty as the *conundrum*; it is an ambiguous or paradoxical statement with a hidden meaning to be guessed by the mental acuteness of the one to whom it is proposed; a *problem* may require simply study and scholarship, as a *problem* in mathematics; a *puzzle* may be in something other than a verbal statement, as a dissected map or any perplexing mechanical contrivance. Both *enigma* and *puzzle* may be applied to any matter difficult of answer or solution, *enigma* conveying an idea of greater dignity, *puzzle* applying to something more commonplace and mechanical. *Antonyms*: answer, axiom, explanation, proposition, solution.
ride (rīd) *v.* **rode** (*Obs.* **rid**), **rid·den** (*Obs.* **rid**), **rid·ing** *v.i.* **1** To sit on and be borne along by a horse or other animal, especially while guiding or controlling its motion. **2** To be borne along as if on horseback. **3** To travel or be carried on or in a vehicle or other conveyance. **4** To be supported in moving: The wheel *rides* on the shaft. **5** To move; be borne; float: The ship *rides* on the waves. **6** To support and carry a rider in a specified manner: This car *rides* easily. **7** To seem to float in space, as a star. **8** *Naut.* To lie at anchor, as a ship. **9** To overlap or overlie, as broken bones. **10** To work or move upward out of place: with *up*: His sleeve has *ridden* up. **11** *Slang* To continue unchanged: Let it *ride.* — *v.t.* **12** To sit on and control the motion of (a horse, bicycle, etc.). **13** To move or be borne or supported upon: The glider *rides* air currents. **14** To overlap or overlie. **15** To travel or traverse (an area, etc.) on horseback, in an automobile, etc. **16** To control imperiously or oppressively: usually in the past participle: a king-*ridden* people. **17** To accomplish by riding: to *ride* a race. **18** To cause to ride. **19** To place (someone) astride something and carry him, especially as a punishment: They *rode* him out of town on a rail. **20** *Naut.* To keep at anchor. **21** *Colloq.* To tease or harass by ridicule or petty criticisms; tyrannize. See synonyms under DRIVE. — **to ride out** To survive; endure successfully. — *n.* **1** An excursion by any means of conveyance, as on horseback, by car, etc. **2** A road intended for riding. — **to take for a ride** *Slang* **1** To remove (a person) to a place with the intent to murder. **2** To cheat; swindle. [OE *rīdan*]
rid·er (rī′dər) *n.* **1** One who or that which rides; a horseman; a bicyclist; specifically, one who breaks in horses. **2** Any device that rides upon or weighs down something else, actually or figuratively. **3** A separate piece of writing or print added to a document, record, or the like. **4** An addition or proposed addition to a legislative bill, adding to or modifying its original purport. **5** A metallic weight for use astride the graduated beam of a delicate balance. **6** The top rail of a rail fence.
rid·er·less (rī′dər·lis) *adj.* Without a rider, as a horse.
ridge (rij) *n.* **1** An elevation or protuberance long in proportion to its width and height and generally having sloping sides; a raised strip; especially, a lengthened elevation of land; a long hill, or range of hills. **2** That part of a roof where the rafters meet the ridge pole. **3** A slight elevation of earth in a garden or field thrown up by the plow, hoe, or other implement. **4** The back or backbone of an animal, especially of a whale. **5** *Meteorol.* A relatively narrow band of high pressure between two cyclone areas, as shown on a weather map. — *v.* **ridged, ridg·ing** *v.t.* **1** To mark with ridges. **2** To form into ridges. — *v.i.* **3** To form ridges. [OE *hrycg* spine, ridge]
ridge pole A horizontal timber at the ridge of a roof, to which the upper ends of the rafters are nailed. Also **ridge beam, ridge piece, ridge plate.**
Ridg·way (rij′wā), **Matthew Bunker,** born 1895, U. S. general; chief of staff 1953–55.
ridg·y (rij′ē) *adj.* Having ridges; raised in a ridge; ridged.
rid·i·cule (rid′ə·kyōōl) *n.* **1** Language calculated to make a person or thing the object of contemptuous humorous disparagement; also, looks or acts expressing amused contempt; derision; mockery. **2** An object of mocking merriment; butt. **3** *Obs.* Ridiculousness. — *v.t.* **·culed, ·cul·ing** To make fun of; hold up as a laughingstock; deride. [<OF <L *ridiculum* a jest, joke, orig. neut. of *ridiculus* comical < *ridere* laugh] — **rid′i·cul′er** *n.*
Synonym (noun): derision. *Ridicule* may be merely sportive or thoughtless; *derision* is always hostile or malicious. See BANTER.
Synonyms (verb): banter, chaff, deride, flout, jeer, lampoon, mock, quiz, rally, satirize, scoff, scout, taunt. *Antonyms*: applaud, celebrate, compliment, eulogize, extol, honor, praise.
ri·dic·u·lous (ri·dik′yə·ləs) *adj.* Exciting or calculated to excite ridicule; absurdly comical; unworthy of consideration. [<L *ridiculus*] — **ri·dic′u·lous·ly** *adv.* — **ri·dic′u·lous·ness** *n.*
Synonyms: absurd, comical, droll, farcical, funny, grotesque, laughable, ludicrous, preposterous, risible, silly, trifling, trivial. See ABSURD, QUEER. *Antonyms*: clever, commendable, grave, imposing, judicious, majestic, sensible, venerable, wise.
rid·ing[1] (rī′ding) *n.* The act of one who rides; a ride. — *adj.* **1** To be ridden on or in; suitable for riding: a *riding* horse. **2** To be used while riding: *riding* boots. **3** For use while at anchor: a *riding* light.
rid·ing[2] (rī′ding) *n.* **1** One of the three administrative divisions of Yorkshire, England: North Riding, East Riding, and West Riding. **2** Any similar administrative division, as in Canada, New Zealand, etc. [OE *thrithing* the third part (of a county); the initial *th* having been lost through the influence of the final *t* or *th* of *East, West,* and *North.* Related to THIRD.]
riding habit Apparel worn by horseback riders, especially that designed for women, consisting usually of a jacket and breeches or jodhpurs.
riding horse A horse used for riding.
riding school An establishment where the art of riding on horseback is taught.
Rid·ley (rid′lē), **Nicholas,** 1500?–55, Anglican bishop, reformer, and martyr.
ri·dot·to (ri·dot′ō) *n. pl.* **·tos** A public musical and dancing entertainment much in vogue in England in the 18th century. [<Ital., a festival, redoubt. See REDOUBT.]
Rid·path (rid′path, -päth), **John Clark,** 1840–1900, U. S. historian.
Rie·mann (rē′män), **Georg Friedrich Bernhard,** 1826–66, German mathematician.
Ri·en·zi (rē·en′zē), **Cola di,** 1313–54, Italian popular orator and leader. Also **Ri·en′zo.**
Rie·sen·ge·bir·ge (rē′zən·gə·bir′gə) The highest range of the Sudetes, in Lower Silesia and northern Bohemia; highest point, 5,259 feet. *Czech* **Kr·ko·no·še** (kûr′kô·nô·she′), *Polish* **Kar·ko·no·sze** (kär′kô·nô′she).
Riet (ryet) A river in Orange Free State and Cape of Good Hope Province of the Union of South Africa, flowing 250 miles NW to the Vaal.
Rif (rif) The mountain range of NW Africa, bordering the northern coast of Morocco; highest point, 8,060 feet. Also **Riff.**
ri·fa·ci·men·to (rē·fä′chē·men′tō) *n. pl.* **·ti** (-tē) *Italian* A remaking; recasting: said of literary or musical adaptations.
rife (rīf) *adj.* **1** Great in number or quantity; plentiful; abundant; prevalent; current. **2** Containing in abundance: followed by *with.* [OE *rīfe* abundant]
riff (rif) *n.* In jazz music, a melodic phrase or

motif, played repeatedly as background or used as the main theme. [Prob. back formation of RIFFLE]

Riff (rif) *n.* One of a Berber tribe inhabiting the mountainous region of northern Morocco. — **Rif′fi·an** *adj.* & *n.*

rif·fle[1] (rif′əl) *n.* **1** *U.S.* A shoal or rocky obstruction lying beneath the surface of a river or other stream. **2** A stretch of shallow, choppy water caused by such a shoal; a rapid. **3** A way of shuffling cards. — *v.t.* & *v.i.* **·fled, ·fling 1** To cause or form a rapid. **2** To shuffle (cards) by bending up adjacent corners of two halves of the pack, and permitting the cards to slip together as they are released. **3** To thumb through (the pages of a book). [? Blend of RIPPLE and RUFFLE]

rif·fle[2] (rif′əl) *n. Mining* **1** A groove or indentation set in the bottom of an inclined trough or sluice, for arresting gold contained in sands or gravels. **2** A cross slat or cleat rising above the bottom of such a sluice and adapted for catching gold: also **riffle bar, riffle block.** [Cf. LG *riffel* furrow]

rif·fler (rif′lər) *n.* **1** A file with curved working surfaces at one or both ends and a smooth center serving as a handle: used in sculpture, woodcarving, diemaking, etc. **2** A workman in any of these fields who handles such a tool. [<RIFFLE[2]]

riff-raff (rif′raf′) *n.* **1** The populace; rabble. **2** Miscellaneous rubbish. [<OF *rif et raf* every bit]

ri·fle[1] (rī′fəl) *n.* **1** A firearm, of any size, having grooves, now always spiral, on the surface of the bore for imparting rotation to the projectile and increasing the accuracy of the weapon. **2** One of these grooves. **3** Such a weapon fired from the shoulder, as distinguished from pistols, a carbine, or artillery, and provided with a device for attaching a bayonet. **4** *pl.* A body of soldiers

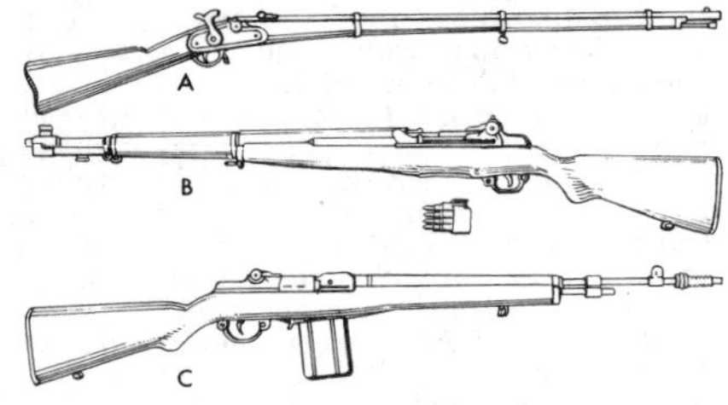

AMERICAN RIFLES
A. Springfield—Civil War.
B. Garand—World War II.
C. M-14, Automatic—1958.

equipped with rifles. **5** An emery-coated stick for whetting scythes. — **magazine rifle** A rifle with a chamber containing extra cartridges which are brought one by one into position for firing; a semi-automatic or repeating rifle. — *v.t.* **·fled, ·fling** To cut a spirally grooved bore in (a firearm, etc.). [Cf. G *reifeln* flute, LG *rifeln* furrow, F *rifler* scratch; *n.*, short for *rifled gun*]

ri·fle[2] (rī′fəl) *v.t.* **·fled, ·fling 1** To search through and rob, as a safe. **2** To search and rob (a person). **3** To seize and take away by force. [<OF *rifler* scratch, plunder <Gmc.]

rifle grenade A grenade designed to be discharged from a rifle by means of a launching device.

ri·fle·man (rī′fəl·mən) *n. pl.* **·men** (-mən) One armed or skilled with the rifle.

rifle pit A trench, the earth from which is thrown up in front, as a protection for riflemen.

ri·fler (rī′flər) *n.* A robber.

rifle salute A salute in the position of right shoulder arms or order arms, with the left hand carried smartly to the rifle, palm down and fingers together.

ri·fling (rī′fling) *n.* **1** The operation of forming the grooves in a rifle. **2** The grooves of a rifle collectively: shallow or deep *rifling.* [<RIFLE[1]]

rift[1] (rift) *n.* An opening made by riving or splitting; a cleft; fissure. — *v.t.* & *v.i.* To rive; burst open; split. [<Scand. Cf. Dan. *rift* cleft, ON *ript* < *ripta* break. Akin to RIVE.]

rift[2] (rift) *n.* **1** A shallow place in a stream; fording place. **2** The wash up the beach after a wave has broken. [? Alter. of *riff,* obs. var. of REEF[1]]

Rift Valley See GREAT RIFT VALLEY.

rig[1] (rig) *v.t.* **rigged, rig·ging 1** To fit out; equip. **2** *Naut.* **a** To fit, as a ship, with rigging. **b** To fit (sails, stays, etc.) to masts, yards, etc. **3** *Colloq.* To dress; clothe, especially in finery. **4** To make or construct hurriedly or by makeshifts: often with *up*: to *rig* up a door from old boards. — *n.* **1** *Naut.* The arrangement of sails, rigging, spars, etc., on a vessel. **2** *Colloq.* A style of dress; costume. **3** *U.S. Colloq.* A turnout for driving; a horse or horses and vehicle. **4** Gear, machinery, or equipment: an oil-well *rig.* **5** Fishing tackle. [<Scand. Cf. ON *rigga* wrap around, Norw. *rigga* bind.]

rig[2] (rig) *v.t.* **rigged, rig·ging** To control fraudulently; manipulate: to *rig* an election. — **to rig the market** To manipulate the exchange market by raising or lowering prices without regard to the value of the security or commodity traded in, in order to derive a profit. — *n.* **1** A practical joke; a trick; jest. **2** A tumult; frolic. [Origin uncertain]

rig[3] (rig) *n. Scot.* & *Brit. Dial.* **1** A ridge or strip of ground. **2** The back of an animal. **3** A path; way. [Var. of RIDGE]

Ri·ga (rē′gə) The capital of Latvia, a port on the **Gulf of Riga,** an arm of the Baltic Sea between Estonia and Latvia.

rig·a·doon (rig′ə·do͞on′) *n.* **1** A gay, quick dance for two, originating probably in Provence. **2** The music for such a dance. [<F *rigodon* a dance]

Ri·gel (rī′jəl, -gəl) A star, Beta in the constellation of Orion; magnitude, 0.34. See STAR. [<Arabic *rijl* foot]

rig·ger (rig′ər) *n.* **1** One who rigs. **2** One who fits the rigging of ships. **3** One who assembles and alines the major parts of an aircraft.

rig·ging (rig′ing) *n.* **1** *Naut.* The entire cordage system of a vessel. **2** Tackle used in logging.

Riggs's disease (rig′ziz) Pyorrhea alveolaris. [after J. M. *Riggs,* 1810–85, U.S. dentist]

Ri·ghi (rē′gē) See RIGI.

right (rīt) *adj.* **1** Done in accordance with or conformable to moral law or to some standard of rightness; equitable; just; righteous. **2** Conformable to truth or fact; correct; true; accurate; not mistaken. **3** Conformable to a standard of propriety or to the conditions of the case; proper; fit; suitable. **4** Most desirable or preferable; also, fortunate. **5** Pertaining to that side of the body which is toward the south when one faces the sunrise: opposed to *left.* **6** Holding one direction, as a line; straight; direct. **7** Properly placed, disposed, or adjusted; well-regulated; orderly; correctly done. **8** Sound in mind or body; healthy; well. **9** *Geom.* Formed with reference to a line or plane perpendicular to another line or plane: a *right* angle. See ANGLE. **10** Designed to be worn outward or placed toward an observer in use: the *right* side of cloth. **11** *Law* Rightful; legal. **12** *Obs.* Real or genuine in character; not spurious. — *adv.* **1** In accordance with justice or moral principle. **2** According to the fact or truth; correctly. **3** In a straight line; directly. **4** Very: used dialectically or in some titles: a *right* good time, *Right* Reverend. **5** Suitably; properly. **6** Precisely; just; also, immediately. **7** Without delay or evasion. **8** Toward the right. **9** Completely or quite: The house burned *right* to the ground. — *n.* **1** That which is right; moral rightness: opposed to *wrong*; also, justice. **2** A just and proper claim or title to anything, or that which may be claimed on just, moral, legal, or customary grounds: often in the plural. **3** *Law* A claim or title to, or interest in, anything whatsoever that is enforceable by law. **4** The right hand, side, or direction. **5** Anything adapted for right-hand use or position. **6** *Often cap.* In politics, a conservative or reactionary position, or a party or group advocating such a position, so designated because of the views of the party occupying seats on the right side of the presiding officer in certain European legislative bodies: used with *the.* Compare LEFT. **7** The outside or front side of a thing: opposed to *reverse.* **8** In boxing, a blow delivered with the right hand. **9** A stockholder's privilege to purchase new stock in a corporation at a special price, usually at par. — **natural rights** Rights with which mankind is supposedly endowed by nature, such as the right to life, liberty, security, and the pursuit of happiness. — *v.t.* **1** To restore to an upright or normal position. **2** To put in order; set right. **3** To make correct or in accord with facts. **4** To make reparation for; redress or avenge: to *right* a wrong. **5** To make reparation to (a person); do justice to. — *v.i.* **6** To regain an upright or normal position. — *interj.* I agree! I understand! — **right on** *Colloq.* An interjectory phrase expressing enthusiastic agreement or encouragement: also used adjectivally. ◆ Homophones: *rite, wright, write.* [OE *riht*] — **right′er** *n.*

Synonyms (adj.): correct, direct, equitable, fair, good, honest, just, lawful, perpendicular, rightful, straight, true, unswerving, upright. See CORRECT, INNOCENT, JUST, MORAL, PRECISE, VIRTUOUS. *Antonyms*: bad, evil, false, improper, incorrect, iniquitous, unjust, wrong.

Synonyms (noun): advantage, claim, exemption, franchise, immunity, liberty, license, prerogative, privilege. In the sense of that which one may rightly claim, a *right* may be either general or special, natural or artificial. "Life, liberty, and the pursuit of happiness" are the natural and inalienable *rights* of all men; *rights* of property, inheritance, etc., are individual and special, and often artificial, as the *right* of inheritance by primogeniture. A *privilege* is always special, exceptional, and artificial. It is something peculiar to one or some, as distinguished from others. A *privilege* may be of doing or avoiding; in the latter case it is an *exemption* or *immunity*; as, a *privilege* of hunting or fishing; *exemption* from military service; *immunity* from arrest. A *franchise* is a specific *right* or *privilege* granted by the government or established as such by governmental authority; as, the elective *franchise,* a railroad *franchise.* A *prerogative* is an official *right* or *privilege,* especially one inherent in the royal or sovereign power; in a wider sense it is an exclusive and peculiar *privilege* which one possesses by reason of being what he is; as reason is the *prerogative* of man; kings and nobles have often claimed *prerogatives* and *privileges* opposed to the inherent *rights* of the people. See DUTY, JUSTICE, PROPERTY.

right-a·bout (rīt′ə·bout′) *n.* **1** The opposite direction. **2** A turning in or to the opposite direction, physically or mentally.

right angle See under ANGLE..

right-an·gled (rīt′ang′gəld) *adj.* Forming or containing a right angle or angles.

right ascension *Astron.* The angular distance of a celestial body from the vernal equinox, measured eastward along the celestial equator in hours, minutes, and seconds from 0 hours to 24 hours.

right away At once; immediately.

right·eous (rī′chəs) *adj.* Conforming in disposition and conduct to a standard of right and justice; upright; virtuous; blameless; morally right; equitable; right-thinking. See synonyms under GOOD, INNOCENT, JUST, MORAL, VIRTUOUS. [OE *rihtwīs* < *riht* right + *wīs* wise] — **right′eous·ly** *adv.*

right·eous·ness (rī′chəs·nis) *n.* **1** The quality or character of being righteous; uprightness; rectitude. **2** A righteous act or quality. **3** Rightfulness; justice. See synonyms under DUTY, JUSTICE, VIRTUE.

right face In military drill, a 90-degree turn to the right, using the ball of the left foot and the heel of the right.

right·ful (rīt′fəl) *adj.* **1** Characterized by or conformed to a right or just claim according to established laws or usage; also, owned or held by just claim: *rightful* heritage. **2** Consonant with moral right or with justice and truth. **3** Proper. **4** Upright; just. See synonyms under JUST, RIGHT. [OE *rihtful*] — **right′·ful·ly** *adv.* — **right′ful·ness** *n.*

right-hand (rīt′hand′) *adj.* **1** Of, pertaining to, or situated on the right side; dextral. **2** Chiefly depended on: my *right-hand* man.

right-hand·ed (rīt′han′did) *adj.* **1** Using the right hand habitually or more easily than the left. **2** Done with the right hand. **3** Turning or moving from left to right, as the hands of a clock. **4** Adapted for use by the right hand, as a tool. **5** In conchology, having the spirals rising from left to right. — **right′-hand′ed·ness** *n.*

right-hand rope Plain-laid rope.

right·ism (rī′tiz·əm) *n.* The advocacy of conservative or reactionary policies. —**right′ist** *n. & adj.*

right·ly (rīt′ē) *adv.* **1** Correctly. **2** Honestly; uprightly. **3** Properly; aptly.

right–mind·ed (rīt′mīn′did) *adj.* Having approved feelings or opinions.

right·ness (rīt′nis) *n.* **1** The quality or condition of being right. **2** Moral rectitude. **3** Correctness. **4** Straightness. See synonyms under VIRTUE.

right·o (rī′tō) *interj. Brit. Colloq.* An exclamation of satisfaction or assent.

right off Right away.

right of search In international law, the right of a belligerent vessel in time of war to verify the nationality of a vessel and to ascertain, if neutral, whether it carries contraband goods. Also **right of visit and search.**

right of way 1 *Law* The right, general or special, of a person to pass over the land of another; also, the path or piece of land over which passage is made. **2** The strip of land, acquired by easement, condemnation, or purchase, over which a railroad lays its tracks, or that land on which a public highway is built; also, the strip of land above which a high-tension power line is built. **3** The legal or customary precedence which allows one vehicle or vessel to cross in front of another.

right on *Informal* An interjectional phrase expressing enthusiastic agreement or encouragement; also used adjectivally: He was *right on* in that speech.

right shoulder arms The position in which the rifle is held at an angle of 45 degrees on the right shoulder, barrel uppermost.

right–to–work law *U.S.* Any law that guarantees a worker's right to a job, whether or not he or she joins a union.

right triangle A plane triangle containing one right angle.

right whale A whale, especially *Balaena mysticetus* of circumpolar seas, having a large head with long, narrow, highly elastic whalebone plates in its mouth, for straining food: it yields more oil than any other species. [Prob. orig. so called because advantageous to pursue]

ATLANTIC, OR SOUTHERN, RIGHT WHALE
(From 50 to 60 feet in length;
the pigmy right whale to 20 feet)

right wing 1 A political party or group advocating moderate or conservative policies. **2** That part of any group advocating conservative policies. Also **Right Wing.** —**right′–wing′** *adj.* —**right′–wing′er** *n.*

rig·id (rij′id) *adj.* **1** Resisting change of form; stiff. **2** Rigorous; inflexible; severe. **3** Strict; exact, as reasoning. **4** *Aeron.* Designating a type of airship whose gas compartments are enclosed within a rigid structure. See synonyms under AUSTERE, HARD, INFLEXIBLE, PRECISE, SEVERE. [<L *rigidus* <*rigere* be stiff] —**rig′id·ly** *adv.* —**rig′id·ness** *n.*

ri·gid·i·ty (ri·jid′ə·tē) *n.* **1** The character of being rigid; inflexibility. **2** The property of bodies by which they resist a change in shape: opposed to *ductility.*

Rig·il Ken·tau·rus (rij′il ken·tôr′əs) A star of .06 magnitude in the constellation Centaurus. See STAR.

rig·ma·role (rig′mə·rōl) *n.* A succession of confused or nonsensical statements; incoherent talk or writing; nonsense. [Alter. of *ragman (roll)* document (with pendant seals), catalog, ME *rageman* document; origin unknown]

rig·ol (rig′əl) *n. Obs.* A ring; circle; hence, a crown. [<F *rigole* groove]

ri·go·let·to (rē′gō·let′tō) *n. Italian* A round dance.

rig·or (rig′ər) *n.* **1** The condition of being stiff or rigid. **2** Stiffness of opinion or temper; harshness. **3** Exactness without allowance or indulgence; inflexibility; strictness; severity. **4** Inclemency, as of the weather; hardship. **5** A severe, harsh, or cruel act. **6** *Med.* **a** A violent chill from cold or nervous shock. **b** The trembling observed in the chill preceding a fever. **7** *Biol.* A rigid state in an organism or in any of its parts, caused by adverse or unfavorable conditions. Also *Brit.* **rig′our.** [<L <*rigere* be stiff]

rig·or·ism (rig′ə·riz′əm) *n.* Stiffness in opinion or conduct; severity in style or living, etc.; strictness; austerity. Also *Brit.* **rig′our·ism.** —**rig′or·ist** *n.* —**rig′or·is′tic** *adj.*

rig·or mor·tis (rig′ər môr′tis, rī′gər) The muscular rigidity that ensues within a few hours after death. [<L, stiffness of death]

rig·or·ous (rig′ər·əs) *adj.* **1** Marked by or acting with rigor; uncompromising; severe. **2** Logically accurate; exact; strict. **3** Inclement; severe; bitter; causing hardship: a *rigorous* climate. See synonyms under AUSTERE, SEVERE. [<OF *rigoureux*] —**rig′or·ous·ly** *adv.* —**rig′·or·ous·ness** *n.*

Rigs·dag (rigz′däg) *n.* The two chambers that form the Danish parliament: the Landsting and Folketing. [<Dan. <*rige* kingdom + *dag* day. See REICHSTAG.]

rigs·da·ler (rigz′dä′lər), **rijks·daal·der** (rēks′·däl′dər) See RIX–DOLLAR.

Rig–Ve·da (rig·vä′də, -vē′-) The oldest collection of hymns and verses in Hindu sacred literature; supposed date, 2000 B.C. See VEDA. [<Skt. *Rigveda* <*ric* praise, hymn + *veda* knowledge]

rig·wid·die (rig·wid′ē) *adj. Scot.* Bony; sapless; scrawny. Also **rig·wood′ie** (-wo͝od′ē).

Riis (rēs), **Jacob August,** 1849–1914, U.S. journalist and sociologist born in Denmark.

Ri·je·ka (rē·ye′kä) A port of NW Croatia, Yugoslavia, on the Adriatic SW of Zagreb: 40 miles, across Istria, from Trieste: Italian *Fiume.*

Rijn (rīn) The Dutch name for the RHINE.

Rijs·wijk (rīs′wīk) The Dutch name for RYSWICK.

Riks·mål (rēks′mōl) *n.* One of the two official forms of Norwegian, based on literary Danish: also called *Dano–Norwegian. Danish* **Rigs·mål** (rēks′mōl). Compare LANDSMÅL. [<Norw., speech of the kingdom]

rile (rīl) *v.t. Colloq.* or *Dial.* **1** To vex; irritate. **2** To roil; make muddy. [Var. of ROIL]

rile·y (rī′lē) *adj.* **1** Roiled; muddy. **2** Ill–tempered; also, irritated.

Ri·ley (rī′lē), **James Whitcomb,** 1849?–1916, U.S. poet.

ri·lie·vo (rē·lye′vō) *n.* Relief (defs. 5 and 6). [Ital.]

Ril·ke (ril′kə), **Rainer Maria,** 1875–1926, German poet born in Prague.

rill (ril) *n.* **1** A small stream; rivulet. **2** A long, narrow, and generally straight valley on the face of the moon: also **rille.** See synonyms under STREAM. [Cf. Du. *dil.* G *rille*]

rill·et (ril′it) *n.* A little rill (def. 1).

rim (rim) *n.* **1** The edge of an object, usually of a circular object; a margin; border. **2** The peripheral part of a wheel, connected to the hub by spokes. **3** On an automobile wheel, the detachable band over which the tire is fitted. **4** The frame of a pair of spectacles surrounding the lenses. See synonyms under BANK. —*v.t.* **rimmed, rim·ming 1** To provide with a rim; border. **2** In sports, to roll around the edge of (the basket, cup, etc.) without falling in: The ball *rimmed* the cup. [OE *rima*]

Rim·baud (raṅ·bō′), **Arthur,** 1854–91, French poet.

rime[1] (rīm) *n.* [The spelling *rhyme,* introduced in the 17th century through association with *rhythm,* is etymologically unjustified.] **1** A correspondence of sounds in two or more words, especially at the ends of lines of poetry. See also NEAR RIME, INTERNAL RIME, TERMINAL RIME. **2** A verse, line, etc., corresponding in terminal sound with another. **3** A word corresponding in sound with another. **4** Poetry; verse; also, a tale in verse. See synonyms under POETRY. —*v.* **rimed, rim·ing** *v.i.* **1** To make rimes or verses; compose poetry. **2** To correspond in sound or in terminal sounds. —*v.t.* **3** To put or write in rime or verse. **4** To use as a rime. **5** To cause to correspond in sound. Also spelled *rhyme.* [Prob. fusion of OF *rime* <Gmc. + OE *rīm* a number] —**rime′less** *adj.*

rime[2] (rīm) *n.* **1** Hoarfrost. **2** *Meteorol.* A rough or feathery coating of ice deposited by fog on terrestrial objects. —*v.t. & v.i.* **rimed, rim·ing** To cover with or congeal into rime. [OE *hrim* frost]

rim·er (rī′mər) *n.* One who makes riming verse, especially inferior verse: also spelled *rhymer.*

rime riche (rēm rēsh′) *French* In prosody, rime involving words identical in sound but of different meaning. Also **rich rime.**

rime royal A stanza of seven lines in iambic pentameter, rimed *ababbcc*: first used in Chaucer's *Complaint unto Pity.*

rime scheme The pattern of rimes in a stanza or poem, usually represented by letters: A standard *rime scheme* is *abab.*

rime·ster (rīm′stər) *n.* One who makes rimes; a mere versifier; a maker of inferior verses: also spelled *rhymester.*

Rim·i·ni (rim′i·nē, *Ital.* rē′mē·nē) A port in north central Italy on the Adriatic: ancient *Ariminum.*

ri·mose (rī′mōs, rī·mōs′) *adj.* Full of fissures or cracks; chinky. Also **ri′mous.** [<L *rimosus* < *rima* chink] —**ri′mose·ly** *adv.* —**ri·mos·i·ty** (rī·mos′ə·tē) *n.*

rim·ple (rim′pəl) *n.* A fold or wrinkle. —*v.t. & v.i.* **·pled, ·pling** To wrinkle; rumple. [OE *hrympel*]

Rim·sky–Kor·sa·kov (rim′skē·kôr′sə·kôf, *Russian* rēm′skē·kor·sä·kôf′), **Nicholas Andreievich,** 1844–1908, Russian composer.

rim·y (rī′mē) *adj.* **1** White with rime. **2** Cold; frosty.

rin (rin) *v.t. & v.i. Scot.* **1** To run. **2** To melt.

Ri·nal·do (rē·näl′dō) Italian form of REGINALD.

rind[1] (rīnd) *n.* The skin or outer coat that may be peeled or taken off, as of flesh, fruit, or trees. [OE *rind* bark, crust]

rind[2] (rind, rīnd) See RYND.

rin·der·pest (rin′dər·pest) *n.* An infectious disease of cattle and sometimes of sheep, characterized by inflammation of the mucous membranes of the intestines; cattle plague: formerly known as *murrain.* [<G <*rinder* cattle + *pest* plague]

Rine·hart (rīn′härt), **Mary Roberts,** 1876–1958, U.S. fiction writer.

rin·for·zan·do (rēn′fôr·tsän′dō) *adj.* Reinforcing or increasing the power and emphasis: a musical direction. [<Ital., ppr. of *rinforzare* reinforce]

ring[1] (ring) *n.* **1** Any circular object having an opening of nearly its own diameter. **2** A circular band of precious metal, worn on a finger. **3** Any metal or wooden band used for holding or carrying something: a napkin *ring;* also, a hoop. **4** A group of persons or things in a circle. **5** A combination of persons, often for corrupt or mercenary cooperation, as in business or politics; a clique. **6** A place where the bark has been cut away around a branch or tree trunk. **7** One of a series of concentric layers of wood in an exogenous stem, formed by annual growth: also **annual ring. 8** An area or arena, as that in which boxers fight; hence prize fighting in general; a circular racecourse or track, as of a circus or horse show. **9** The field of competition or rivalry: He tossed his hat into the *ring.* **10** The area set apart for bookmakers and other betters at a racetrack. **11** *Chem.* An arrangement of atoms in a closed chain: the benzene *ring.* **12** The space between two concentric circles. —*v.* **ringed, ring·ing** *v.t.* **1** To surround with a ring; encircle. **2** To form into a ring or rings. **3** To provide or decorate with a ring or rings. **4** To cut a ring of bark from (a branch or tree); girdle. **5** To put a ring in the nose of (a pig, bull, etc.). **6** To hem in (cattle, etc.) by riding in a circle around them. **7** In certain games, to cast a ring over (a peg or pin). —*v.i.* **8** To form a ring or rings. **9** To move or fly in rings or spirals; circle. ◆ Homophone: *wring.* [OE *hring*]

ring[2] (ring) *v.* **rang, rung, ring·ing** *v.i.* **1** To give forth a resonant, sonorous sound, as a bell when struck. **2** To sound loudly or be filled with sound or resonance; reverberate; resound. **3** To cause a bell or bells to sound, as in summoning a servant. **4** To have or suggest a sound expressive of a specified quality: His story *rings* true. **5** To have a continued sensation of ringing or buzzing: My ears *ring.* — *v.t.* **6** To cause to ring, as a bell. **7** To produce, as a sound, by or as by ringing. **8** To announce or proclaim by ringing: to *ring* the hour. **9** To summon, escort, usher, etc., in this manner: with *in* or *out*: to *ring* out the old year. **10** To strike (coins, etc.) on something so as to test their quality by the sound produced. **11** To call on the telephone: often with *up.* — **to ring the changes** See under CHANGE. — *n.* **1** The sound produced by a bell or other vibrating, sonorous body; the act of sounding a bell; also, a telephone call. **2** Any reverberating sound, as of acclamation. **3** A sound that is characteristic or indicative: His words have the *ring* of truth. **4** A set, chime, or peal of bells. ◆ Homophone: *wring.* [OE *hringan*]

ring-billed (ring′bild′) *adj.* Having a ring of color around the beak: said of certain birds.

ring-billed gull The common gull *(Larus delawarensis)* having a black ring around the bill.

ring bolt A bolt having a ring through an eye in its head.

ring·bone (ring′bōn′) *n.* A bony enlargement or excrescence on the pastern bones of a horse, usually causing lameness.

ring dove **1** The cushat: also called *wood pigeon.* **2** One of several other pigeons related to the turtle dove *(Streptopelia risoria)* of southeastern Europe.

ringed (ringd) *adj.* **1** Having a wedding ring; hence, lawfully married. **2** Encircled by raised or depressed lines or bands, as the stems or roots of some plants. **3** Encircled by a ring or rings of color; composed of rings.

rin·gent (rin′jənt) *adj. Biol.* Gaping, as a two-lipped corolla in which the lips are widely separated, or as the valves of certain bivalves. [<L *ringens, -entis,* ppr. of *ringi* gape]

ring·er[1] (ring′ər) *n.* **1** One who or that which rings (a bell or chime). **2** *Slang* An athlete who illegally enters a contest by concealing facts which would disqualify him. **3** *Slang* A person who bears a marked resemblance to another: You are a *ringer* for Jones.

ring·er[2] (ring′ər) *n.* **1** One who or that which rings or encircles. **2** A quoit or horseshoe that falls around one of the posts.

ring·er[3] (ring′ər) *n. Austral.* **1** The fastest shearer in a crew; hence, a remarkably competent person. **2** A cattleman.

Ring·er's solution (ring′ərz) *Chem.* A physiologically balanced solution of the chlorides of sodium, potassium, and calcium, used to keep organs alive outside the body. [after Sidney *Ringer,* 1835–1910, English physiologist]

ring finger The third finger of the left hand, on which the marriage ring is worn.

ring·hals (ring′hals) *n.* The spitting snake. [<G, lit., ring-neck]

ring·head (ring′hed′) *n.* An instrument for stretching woolen cloth.

ring·lead·er (ring′lē′dər) *n.* A leader or organizer of any undertaking, especially of an unlawful undertaking like a riot.

ring·let (ring′lit) *n.* **1** A long, spiral lock of hair; a curl. **2** A small ring.

ring·mas·ter (ring′mas′tər, -mäs′-) *n.* One who has charge of a circus ring and of the performances in it.

ring·neck (ring′nek′) *n.* **1** The ring snake. **2** The ring plover. **3** The ring-necked duck.

ring-necked (ring′nekt′) *adj.* Having a ring of color around the neck: said of certain birds and animals.

ring-necked duck A North American duck *(Aythya collaris),* blackish with a chestnut collar about the neck: also called *marsh bluebill.* Also spelled *ringneck.*

Ring of the Ni·be·lung (nē′bə·lŏŏng) In German legend, the ring which Alberich made from the Rheingold. In his tetralogy of music dramas, *Das Rheingold, Die Walküre, Siegfried,* and *Die Götterdämmerung,* which collectively bear this title, Richard Wagner traces the story of the ring. Also *German* **Der Ring des Ni·be·lung·en** (der ring des nē′bə·lŏŏng′ən).

ring plover Any of certain small plovers (genus *Charadrius*) marked with a black breast-encircling band; especially *C. semipalmatus* and the smaller piping plover *(C. melodus)* of eastern North America; also, a European plover *(C. niaticula)*; also *ringneck.*

ring·shake (ring′shāk′) *n.* A cupshake.

ring·side (ring′sīd′) *n.* The space or seats immediately surrounding a ring, as at a prize fight.

ring snake **1** A small, harmless, grayish-green snake of North America *(Diadophis punctatus)* having a bright yellow ring around the neck: also *ringneck.* **2** The hoop snake.

ring·ster (ring′stər) *n. U.S. Colloq.* A member of a political ring.

ring-streaked (ring′strēkt′) *adj.* Streaked with encircling rings, as an animal. Also *Archaic* **ring′straked′** (-strākt′).

ring-tailed (ring′tāld′) *adj. Slang* Very extraordinary or superior; stupendous.

ring-tailed roarer In U.S. folklore, a person of extraordinary size, strength, or athletic prowess; a bragging, swaggering fellow.

ring·time (ring′tīm′) *n. Obs.* The time of marriage or betrothal.

ring·worm (ring′wûrm′) *n. Pathol.* One of several contagious skin diseases affecting both man and domestic animals, caused by certain fungi, and marked by the localized appearance of discolored, scaly patches on the skin and by disorders of the scalp.

rink (ringk) *n.* **1** A smooth, artificial surface of ice, usually covered, used for ice-skating. **2** A smooth floor, similarly enclosed, used for roller-skating. **3** A building containing a surface smoothed and prepared for ice-skating or roller-skating. **4** An area on a field of ice marked off for the game of curling. **5** The part of a bowling green occupied by one side. **6** In bowling, quoits, and curling, the players on one side. [<dial. E (Scottish), prob. <OF *renc* row, rank]

rinse (rins) *v.t.* **rinsed, rins·ing** **1** To remove soap from by putting through clear water. **2** To wash lightly, as by dipping in water or by running water over or into. **3** To remove (dirt, etc.) by this process. See synonyms under CLEANSE. — *n.* The act of rinsing. [<OF *rincer, reïncer,* ? ult. <L *recens* recent, fresh] — **rins′er** *n.*

rins·ing (rin′sing) *n.* **1** A rinse. **2** The liquid in which anything is rinsed. **3** That which is removed by rinsing.

Ri·o Bran·co (rē′ŏŏ vrañg′kŏŏ) **1** Capital of Acre territory, western Brazil. **2** A federal territory of northern Brazil; 89,035 square miles; capital, Boa Vista. **3** A river in Río Branco territory, northern Brazil, flowing 350 miles south from the Uraricoera to the Río Negro.

Rí·o Bra·vo (rē′ō brä′vō) The Mexican name for the RIO GRANDE. Also **Río Bravo del Norte** (thel nôr′tā).

Ri·o da Dú·vi·da (rē′ŏŏ thə thŏŏ′vē·thə) A former Portuguese name for the ROOSEVELT RIVER.

Ri·o de Ja·nei·ro (rē′ō də jə·nâr′ō, zhə·nâr′ō; *Pg.* rē′ŏŏ thə zhə·nā′rŏŏ) The capital of Brazil (until the transfer of the federal capital, in April, 1960, to the new city of **Bra·si·li·a** (brə·zē′lē·ə), located in a federal district, on the central plateau of Goiás state, about 120 miles NE of Goiânia, the state capital), a port on Guanabara Bay or **Rio de Janeiro Bay:** also **Rio.** An inhabitant of the city is known as a *Carioca.* **2** A state in SE Brazil; 16,439 square miles; capital, Niterói.

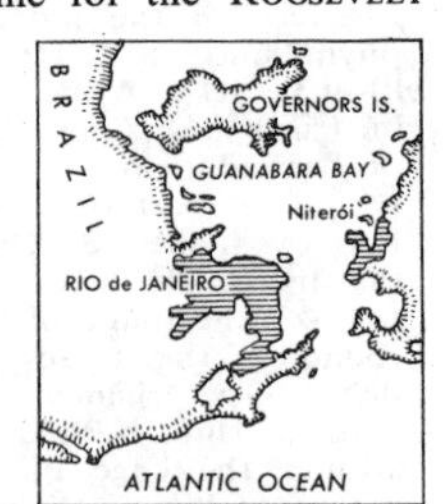

Rí·o de la Pla·ta (rē′ō thā lä plä′tä) See PLATA, RÍO DE LA.

Rí·o de O·ro (rē′ō thā ō′rō) **1** The undefined area of Spanish interest on the NW coast of Africa SW of Morocco. **2** A zone of Spanish Sahara; 73,362 square miles; capital, Villa Cisneros.

Rí·o Gal·le·gos (rē′ō gä·yā′gōs) The capital of Santa Cruz national territory, southern Argentina.

Ri·o Grande (rē′ō grand′) **1** A river flowing 1,800 miles from the Rocky Mountains in SW Colorado to the Gulf of Mexico and forming the boundary between Texas and Mexico: Mexican *Río Bravo.* **2** See RIO GRANDE DO SUL (def. 2).

Ri·o Gran·de do Nor·te (rē′ŏŏ grañn′də thŏŏ nôr′tə) A maritime state in NE Brazil; 20,482 square miles; capital, Natal.

Ri·o Gran·de do Sul (rē′ŏŏ grañn′də thŏŏ sōōl′) **1** The southernmost state of Brazil; 109,037 square miles; capital, Pôrto Alegre. **2** A port in Rio Grande do Sul state: formerly *São Pedro de Rio Grande do Sul*: also *Rio Grande.*

Rio·ja (ryō′hä) See LA RIOJA.

Rí·o Mu·ni (rē′ō mōō′nē) The mainland district of Spanish Guinea, including the islands of Annobon, Corisco, and Great and Little Elobey; mainland area, 10,040 square miles; chief town, Bata: also *Continental Guinea.*

Rí·o Ne·gro (rē′ō nā′grō) **1** A river in the southern Argentine Republic, flowing 400 miles east and SE to the Atlantic. **2** A river in NW Brazil, flowing SE about 1,400 miles to the Amazon. **3** A national territory of south central Argentina; 78,363 square miles; capital, Viedma. **4** A river in central Uruguay, rising in southern Brazil, and flowing 500 miles SW to the Uruguay river.

Ri·on Strait (rē·ôn′) A strait of the Ionian Sea, joining the Gulf of Patras to the Gulf of Corinth: 1 mile wide: formerly *Strait of Lepanto.*

Rí·o Pie·dras (rē′ō pyā′thräs) A city of northern Puerto Rico, the second largest of the commonwealth.

Rí·o Roo·se·velt (rē′ō rō′zə·velt) A Spanish name for the ROOSEVELT RIVER.

ri·ot (rī′ət) *n.* **1** A disturbance consisting of wild and turbulent conduct of a large number of persons, as a mob; uproar; tumult. **2** *Law* Specifically, a tumultuous disturbance of the public peace by three or more assembled persons who, in the execution of some private object, do an act, lawful or unlawful, in a manner calculated to terrorize the people. **3** A state of confusion; a jumble: The garden was a *riot* of color. **4** Boisterous festivity; revelry. **5** *U.S. Slang* An uproariously amusing person, thing, or performance. See synonyms under REVOLUTION, TUMULT. — **to run riot** **1** To act or move wildly and without restraint. **2** To grow rankly, as vines. — *v.i.* **1** To take part in a riot or public disorder. **2** To live a life of unrestrained feasting, drinking, etc.; revel. — *v.t.* **3** To spend (time, money, etc.) in riot or revelry. [<OF *riote* < *rioter,* prob. dim. of *ruir* make an uproar <L *rugire* roar] — **ri′ot·er** *n.*

riot act Any forceful or vigorous warning or reprimand. — **to read the riot act to** To reprimand bluntly and severely.

Riot Act English statute of George I (1715) for preventing tumultuous and riotous assemblages.

Rí·o Té·o·do·ro (rē′ō tā′ō·thō′rō) A Spanish name for the ROOSEVELT RIVER.

riot gun A short-barreled shotgun for use on guard duty or against rioters.

ri·ot·ous (rī′ət·əs) *adj.* **1** Pertaining to riot; engaged in riot or tumultuous disorder; tumultuous. **2** Indulging in revelry; also, profligate: more *riotous* spending. See synonyms under NOISY, TURBULENT. — **ri′ot·ous·ly** *adv.* — **ri′ot·ous·ness** *n.*

Ri·ouw Archipelago (rē′ou) An Indonesian island group south of Singapore; 2,279 square miles; comprising, with other islands, a province of Indonesia; 12,503 square miles; capital, Tandjungpinang. Also *Riau Archipelago.*

rip[1] (rip) *v.* **ripped, rip·ping** *v.t.* **1** To tear or cut apart roughly or violently; slash. **2** To tear or cut from something else in a rough or violent manner: with *off, away, out,* etc. **3** To saw or split (wood) in the direction of the grain. — *v.i.* **4** To be torn or cut apart; split. **5** *Colloq.* To utter with vehemence: with *out.* **6** *Colloq.* To rush headlong. — **to rip into** *Colloq.* To attack violently, as with blows or words. — **to rip off** *Slang* **1** To steal or steal from. **2** To copy, imitate, or reproduce illegally or dishonestly. **3** To swindle; dupe; cheat. — **to rip out** To utter with vehemence. See synonyms under REND. — *n.* **1** A place torn or ripped open, especially along a seam; a tear. **2** A ripsaw. [ME *rippen,* prob. <LG. Cf. Frisian *rippe,* Flemish *rippen.*]

rip[2] (rip) *n.* **1** A ripple; a rapid in a river. **2** A riptide. [? <RIP[1]]

rip[3] (rip) *n. Colloq.* **1** A dissipated or worthless person. **2** A worn-out, worthless animal or object. [? Var. of *rep,* short for REPROBATE]

rip[4] (rip) *n. Scot.* A handful of unthreshed grain or of hay.

ri·par·i·an (ri·pâr′ē·ən, rī-) *adj.* **1** Pertaining to the bank of a river: *riparian* rights. **2** Growing naturally in the sides or banks of watercourses, ponds, etc. [<L *riparius* < *ripa* bank of a river]

ri·par·i·ous (ri·pâr′ē·əs, rī-) *adj.* Growing or living along the banks of streams, as an animal or a plant.

rip·cord (rip′kôrd′) *n. Aeron.* **1** The cord, together with the handle and fastening pins, which, when pulled, releases the canopy of a parachute from its pack. **2** A cord attached to the rip panel of a balloon, which, when pulled, frees the panel from the envelope.

ripe[1] (rīp) *adj.* **1** Grown to maturity and fit for food, as fruit or grain. **2** Brought by keeping and care to a condition for use, as wine. **3** Fully developed; matured. **4** In full readiness to do or try; prepared; ready: The men are *ripe* for mutiny. **5** Fit; opportune: The times are *ripe* for war. **6** Resembling ripe fruit; rosy; luscious. **7** *Surg.* Ready for an operation of removal or opening, as an appendix or an abscess. [OE *rīpe* ready for reaping] — **ripe′ly** *adv.* — **ripe′ness** *n.*

Synonyms: complete, consummate, finished, fit, mature, matured, mellow, perfect, perfected, ready, seasoned. *Antonyms*: budding, callow, crude, green, immature, imperfect, sour, undeveloped.

ripe[2] (rīp) *v.t.* **riped, rip·ing** *Scot. & Brit. Dial.* **1** To cleanse. **2** To examine thoroughly. **3** To search.

rip·en (rī′pən) *v.t. & v.i.* To make or become ripe; mature. — **rip′en·er** *n.*

Rip·ley (rip′lē), **William Zebina,** 1867–1941, U.S. economist.

rip–off (rip′of′, -ôf′) *n. Slang* **1** The act of ripping off; an act of stealing or cheating. **2** Anything dishonest, illegal, or exploitative.

Rip·on (rip′ən) A municipal borough of West Riding, Yorkshire, England.

Rip·on Falls (rip′ən) A waterfall in SE Uganda on the Victoria Nile just below Lake Victoria; about 16 feet high; 900 feet wide.

ri·poste (ri·pōst′) *n.* **1** A return thrust, as in fencing. **2** A quick, clever reply. — *v.i.* **1** To make a riposte. **2** To reply quickly. Also **ri·post′.** [<F *riposte* <Ital. *risposta,* properly fem. of pp. of *rispondere* <L *respondere.* See RESPOND.]

rip panel *Aeron.* A segment of the fabric in a balloon or nonrigid airship that may be ripped open quickly to permit emergency deflation.

rip·per (rip′ər) *n.* **1** One who or that which rips. **2** A tool for ripping, as a ripsaw. **3** A double–ripper. **4** *Brit. Slang* A thoroughgoing or efficient person or thing; something or someone very good.

rip·ping (rip′ing) *Brit. Slang adj.* Splendid; excellent. — *adv.* Very; extraordinarily: a *ripping* good time.

rip·ple[1] (rip′əl) *v.* **·pled, ·pling** *v.i.* **1** To become slightly agitated on the surface, as water running over a rough, pebbly surface or blown on by a light breeze; form small waves or undulations. **2** To flow with small waves or undulations on the surface. **3** To make a sound like water flowing in small waves. — *v.t.* **4** To cause to form ripples. — *n.* **1** One of the wavelets on the surface of water; a ruffle, or slight curling wave. **2** Any sound like that made by rippling. **3** Any appearance like a wavelet. See synonyms under WAVE. [Origin uncertain] — **rip′pler** *n.* — **rip′pling** *adj.* — **rip′·pling·ly** *adv.*

rip·ple[2] (rip′əl) *n.* A toothed tool, especially a comblike instrument for cleaning flax fiber or broomcorn. — *v.t.* **·pled, ·pling** To cleanse, as flax or hemp, by removing the seeds and capsules from the stalk. [<Gmc. Cf. Frisian *ripelje.*]

rip·plet (rip′lit) *n.* A small ripple.

rip·ply (rip′lē) *adj.* Marked by or sounding like ripples.

rip–rap (rip′rap′) *n.* **1** Broken stones loosely thrown together for a foundation, as in deep water or on a soft bottom, or for a sustaining wall, as along a river bank; also, the stones used, or the foundation so made. **2** *pl.* Artificial islands in Chesapeake Bay. — *v.t.* **–rapped, –rap·ping** To make a rip–rap in or upon; strengthen with rip–raps.

rip–roaring (rip′rôr′ing, -rōr′-) *adj. U.S. Slang* **1** Excellent; superior; exciting: a *rip–roaring* time. **2** Lively; full of vigor.

rip–roar·i·ous (rip·rôr′ē·əs, -rōr′-) *adj. U.S. Slang* Uproarious; boisterous; violent. — **rip-roar′i·ous·ly** *adv.*

rip·saw (rip′sô′) *n.* A coarse–toothed saw used for cutting wood in the direction of the grain.

rip·snort·er (rip′snôr′tər) *n.* **1** Any person or thing excessively noisy, violent, or striking. **2** A violent windstorm.

rip·tide (rip′tīd′) *n.* Water agitated and made dangerous for swimmers by conflicting tides or currents. Also called *rip, tiderip.*

Rip·u·ar·i·an (rip′yōō·âr′ē·ən) *adj.* Designating or pertaining to a branch of the Frankish people that dwelt on both sides of the Rhine, near Cologne, in the fourth century. — *n.* A Ripuarian Frank. [<L *ripuarius* < *ripa* bank]

Rip Van Win·kle (rip van wing′kəl) In Washington Irving's tale by that name in *The Sketch Book,* a Dutch villager, who, while out hunting in the Catskills, falls asleep for twenty years, and awakes to find his world changed and himself forgotten.

rise (rīz) *v.* **rose, ris·en, ris·ing** *v.i.* **1** To move upward; go from a lower to a higher position. **2** To slope gradually upward: The ground *rises* here. **3** To have height or elevation; extend upward: The city *rises* above the plain. **4** To gain elevation in rank, status, fortune, or reputation. **5** To swell up: Dough *rises.* **6** To become greater in force, intensity, height, etc. **7** To become greater in amount, value, etc. **8** To become erect after lying down, sitting, etc.; stand up. **9** To get out of bed. **10** To return to life. **11** To revolt; rebel: The people *rose* against the tyrant. **12** To adjourn: The House passed the bill before *rising.* **13** To appear above the horizon: said of heavenly bodies. **14** To come to the surface, as a fish after a lure. **15** To have origin; begin: The river *rises* in the mountains. **16** To become perceptible to the mind or senses: The scene *rose* in his mind. **17** To occur; happen. **18** To be able to cope with an emergency, danger, etc.: Will he *rise* to the occasion? — *v.t.* **19** To cause to rise. **20** *Naut.* To cause, as a ship, to appear above the horizon by drawing nearer to it. — **to rise above** To prove superior to; show oneself indifferent to. — *n.* **1** The act of rising; ascent. **2** Degree of ascent; elevation; also, an ascending course. **3** The act of beginning to be or appear, as from a source: the *rise* of a stream. **4** An elevated place; rising ground; a small hill. **5** The act of appearing above the horizon. **6** Increase or advance, as in price. **7** Advance, as in rank, prosperity, or importance; also, elevation morally, mentally, or spiritually. **8** The spring or height of an arch above the impost level. **9** The height of a stair step. **10** Ascent in the diatonic scale; also, increase in volume of tone; a swell. **11** The ascent of a fish to food or bait; also, the flying up of a game bird. **12** *Colloq.* An emotional reaction; a response or retort. **13** *Brit.* An increase in salary. See synonyms under BEGINNING. [OE *rīsan*]

Synonyms (verb): arise, ascend, flow, spring.

ris·en (riz′ən) Past participle of RISE.

ris·er (rī′zər) *n.* **1** One who rises or gets up, as from bed: He is an early *riser.* **2** The vertical part of a step or stair.

ris·i·bil·i·ty (riz′ə·bil′ə·tē) *n. pl.* **·ties** **1** A tendency to laughter. **2** *pl.* Impulses to laughter; appreciation of what seems ridiculous: also **ris′i·bles.**

ris·i·ble (riz′ə·bəl) *adj.* **1** Having the power of laughing. **2** Of a nature to excite laughter. **3** Pertaining to laughter. See synonyms under RIDICULOUS. [<F <LL *risibilis* <L *risus,* pp. of *ridere* laugh] — **ris′i·bly** *adv.*

ris·ing (rī′zing) *adj.* **1** Increasing in wealth, power, or distinction. **2** Ascending: the *rising* moon; also, sloping upward: a *rising* hill. **3** Advancing to adult years or to a state of vigor and activity; growing: the *rising* generation. — *n.* **1** The act of one who or that which rises. **2** That which rises above the surrounding surface; specifically, a tumor; wen. **3** An insurrection or revolt; an uprising. **4** Yeast or leaven used to make dough rise; also, the quantity of dough prepared at once. — *prep. Dial.* **1** Approaching; going on: He's six years old, *rising* seven. **2** More than; upwards of: a crop *rising* 5,000 bushels.

risk (risk) *n.* **1** A chance of encountering harm or loss; hazard; danger. **2** In insurance, hazard of loss, as of a ship or cargo, or of goods or other property; also, degree of exposure to loss or injury. **3** An obligation or contract of insurance on the part of the insurer: to take a *risk* on a cargo. **4** An applicant for an insurance policy considered with regard to the advisability of placing insurance upon him. See synonyms under DANGER, HAZARD. — *v.t.* **1** To expose to a chance of injury or loss; hazard. **2** To incur the risk of. [<F *risque* <Ital. *rischio* < *risicare* dare, ult. <Gk. *rhiza* cliff, root] — **risk′er** *n.*

risk·y (ris′kē) *adj.* **risk·i·er, risk·i·est** Attended with risk; hazardous; dangerous. See synonyms under PRECARIOUS.

Ri·sor·gi·men·to (rē·sôr′jē·men′tō) *n.* The movement for the liberation and unification of Italy in the 19th century. [<Ital., resurgence]

ri·sot·to (rē·sôt′tō) *n.* Rice cooked in broth and served with meat, cheese, and various condiments. [<Ital. < *riso* rice]

ris·qué (ris·kā′, *Fr.* rēs·kā′) *adj.* Bordering on or suggestive of impropriety; bold; daring; off–color: a *risqué* story or play. [<F]

Riss (ris) See GLACIAL EPOCH. [from *Riss,* name of a German stream]

ris·sole (ris′ōl, *Fr.* rē·sôl′) *n.* In cookery, a sausagelike roll consisting of minced meat or fish, enclosed in a thin puff paste and fried. [<F, <OF *ruissolle, rousole* <LL *russeola,* fem. of L *russeolus* reddish < *russus* red]

ris·so·lé (rē·sô·lā′) *adj. French* Browned by frying.

Rist (rēst), **Charles,** 1874–1955, French economist.

ri·sus (rī′səs) *n.* A grin or laugh, especially the **risus sar·do·ni·cus** (sär·don′i·kəs), the twisted, grinning expression caused by spasm of the facial muscles, as in tetanus. [<L, a grimace < *ridere* laugh]

ri·tar·dan·do (rē′tär·dän′dō) *adj. Music* Slackening the speed gradually; retarding. [<Ital., gerund of *ritardare* delay]

rite (rīt) *n.* **1** A solemn or religious ceremony performed in an established or prescribed manner, or the words or acts constituting or accompanying it. **2** Any formal practice or custom. See synonyms under FORM, SACRAMENT. ◆ Homophones: *right, wright, write.* [<L *ritus*]

rite de pas·sage (rēt də pa·säzh′) *pl.* **rites de pas·sage** (rēt) *Sociol.* A ritual event signifying a change in status in the course of life of an individual, as one marking puberty, marriage, the achievement of adult responsibility, or death. Also **rite of passage.** [<F]

Rit·ter (rit′ər) *n. German* A knight; one of the lowest of the noble orders in Austria and Germany.

rit·u·al (rich′ōō·əl) *n.* A prescribed form or method for the performance of a religious or solemn ceremony; any body of rites or ceremonies; also, a book setting forth such a system of rites or observances. See synonyms under FORM. — *adj.* Of, pertaining to, or consisting of a rite or rites. [<OF <L *ritualis* < *ritus* rite] — **rit′u·al·ly** *adv.*

rit·u·al·ism (rich′ōō·əl·iz′əm) *n.* **1** A system of conducting public worship according to prescribed or established forms. **2** Strenuous insistence upon ritual.

rit·u·al·ist (rich′ōō·əl·ist) *n.* One who practices or advocates ritualism. — *adj.* Ritualistic.

rit·u·al·is·tic (rich′ōō·əl·is′tik) *adj.* **1** Of or pertaining to ritual or ritualism. **2** Advocating ritualism. — **rit′u·al·is′ti·cal·ly** *adv.*

rit·u·al·ly (rich′ōō·əl·ē) *adv.* According to ritual or to a certain ritual.

ritz·y (rit′sē) *adj. U.S. Slang* Smart; elegant; classy. [after César *Ritz,* 1850–1918, Swiss hotelier who founded hotels bearing his name in London, Paris, and New York]

riv·age (riv′ij) *n. Archaic* A shore; coast; bank. [<OF < *rive* <L *ripa* shore]

ri·val (rī′vəl) *n.* **1** One who strives to equal

or excel another, or is in pursuit of the same object as another; a competitor. **2** One equaling or nearly equaling another, in any respect. **3** *Obs.* An associate, or companion in office. See synonyms under ENEMY. —*v.* **·valed** or **·valled, ·val·ing** or **·val·ling** *v.t.* **1** To strive to equal or excel; compete with. **2** To be the equal of or a match for. —*v.i.* **3** *Archaic* To be a competitor. —*adj.* Standing in competition or emulation; having opposing claims to the same object; competing. [<F < L *rivalis*]

ri·val·ry (rī′vəl·rē) *n. pl.* **·ries 1** The act of rivaling. **2** The state of being a rival or rivals; competition. See synonyms under AMBITION, COMPETITION, EMULATION.

rive (rīv) *v.* **rived, rived** or **riv·en, riv·ing** *v.t.* **1** To split asunder by force; cleave. **2** To break (the heart, etc.). —*v.i.* **3** To become split. See synonyms under BREAK, REND. [<ON *rifa* tear, rend] —**riv·er** (rī′vər) *n.*

rived (rīvd) Alternative past participle of RIVE. —*adj.* Split instead of sawed.

riv·en (riv′ən) Alternative past participle of RIVE. —*adj.* Rent, burst, or torn asunder; split; cleaved.

riv·er (riv′ər) *n.* **1** A large, natural stream of water, usually fed by converging tributaries along its course and discharging into a larger body of water, as into the ocean, a lake, or another stream. ◆ Collateral adjective: *fluvial.* **2** A large stream of any kind; copious flow. See synonyms under STREAM. —**to sell down the river 1** Formerly, to sell (a Negro slave) into unsparing and rigorous servitude: from the severe conditions on the lower Mississippi cane and cotton plantations. **2** Hence, to betray the trust of; deceive. —**to send up the river** To send to the penitentiary: from the fact that Sing Sing is up the Hudson from New York. [<OF *rivière* <LL *riparia* < L *riparius.* See RIPARIAN.]

Ri·ve·ra (rē·vä′rä), **Diego,** 1886–1957, Mexican painter.

Ri·ve·ra y Or·ba·ne·ja (rē·vä′rä ē ôr′vä·nā′·hä), **Miguel Primo de,** 1870–1930, Spanish general; chief of state 1923–30.

river basin *Geog.* An extensive area of land drained by a river and its branches.

river bottom Low-lying alluvial land along a river.

riv·er·head (riv′ər·hed′) *n.* The source of a river.

river horse A hippopotamus.

riv·er·ine (riv′ə·rīn, -ər·in) *adj.* Pertaining to or like a river; riparian.

River of Doubt A former name for the ROOSEVELT RIVER.

Riv·ers (riv′ərz), **William Halse,** 1864–1922, English physiologist and anthropologist.

riv·er·side (riv′ər·sīd′) *n.* The space alongside of or adjacent to a river.

riv·er·weed (riv′ər·wēd′) *n.* A small aquatic plant *(Podostemon ceratophyllum)* resembling a seaweed, found in the eastern and southern United States.

Rives (rēvz), **Amélie,** 1863–1945, Princess Troubetzkoy, U.S. novelist.

riv·et (riv′it) *n.* A short, soft metal bolt, having a head on one end, used to join objects, as metal plates, by passing the shank through holes and forming a new head by flattening out the headless end. —*v.t.* **1** To fasten with or as with a rivet. **2** To batter the headless end of (a bolt, etc.) so as to make fast. **3** To fasten firmly. **4** To engross or attract (the eyes, attention, etc.). [<OF <*river* clench] —**riv′et·er** *n.*

Riv·i·er·a (riv′ē·âr′ə, *Ital.* rē·vyā′rä) The coastal strip between the southernmost Alpine ranges and the Mediterranean, extending from Hyères, France, about 230 miles to La Spezia, Italy.

ri·vière (rē·vyâr′) *n. French* A necklace of diamonds or other gems, usually in several strings.

riv·u·let (riv′yə·lit) *n.* A small stream or brook; streamlet. See synonyms under STREAM. [<Ital. *rivoletto,* dim. of *rivolo* <L *rivulus,* dim. of *rivus* brook]

rix-dol·lar (riks′dol′ər) *n.* **1** Any one of several small silver coins formerly current in the Scandinavian countries and the Netherlands: also called *rigsdaler, rijksdaalder.* **2** A former British silver coin of Ceylon, Cape Colony, etc. [<Du. *rijksdaler* dollar of the realm]

Ri·yadh (rē·yäd′) The capital of Nejd and (with Mecca) of Saudi Arabia. Also **Ri·yad′.**

Ri·za·i·yeh (rē·zä′ē′yä) **1** A city of NE Iran: also *Rezaiyeh.* **2** See URMIA.

Ri·zal (rē·säl′), **José,** 1861–96, Filipino patriot and author; shot for alleged conspiracy against Spain.

Rizal Day A holiday observed on December 30 in the Philippine Islands in memory of José Rizal.

Ri·za Shah Pah·la·vi (ri·zä′ shä′ pä′lə·vē), 1877–1944, shah of Iran 1925–41; abdicated.

riz·zer (riz′ər) *v.t. Scot.* To parch or dry in the sun. Also **riz′zar.**

Riz·zi·o (rēt′tsyō), **David,** 1533?–66, Italian musician; secretary of Mary Queen of Scots; assassinated: also *Riccio.*

ro (rō) *n. Archit.* In Japanese houses, a firepan set into the floor and used in connection with formal tea ceremonies.

Ro (rō) *n.* An artificial, international language based on the classification of ideas and dispensing with existing words and roots. [Coined by Rev. E. P. Foster of Ohio, who devised it in 1906]

roach[1] (rōch) *n.* **1** A European fresh-water fish *(Rutilus rutilus)* of the carp family, with a greenish back. **2** One of certain other related cyprinoid fishes, as the American fresh-water sunfish. [<OF *roche*]

roach[2] (rōch) *n.* A cockroach. [See COCKROACH]

roach[3] (rōch) *v.t.* To clip or trim, as the mane of an animal. [Origin unknown] —**roached** *adj.*

road (rōd) *n.* **1** An open way for public passage, especially from one city, town, or village to another; a highway: distinguished from a *street.* **2** Any way of advancing or progressing; any course followed in a journey; a path. **3** A roadstead: commonly in the plural: Hampton *Roads.* **4** *U.S.* A railroad. —**on the road 1** On tour: said of circuses, theatrical companies, etc. **2** Traveling, as a canvasser or salesman. **3** Living the life of a tramp or hobo. [OE *rād* a ride, a riding <*rīdan* ride. Related to RIDE.]

Synonyms: course, highway, lane, passage, path, pathway, route, street, thoroughfare, track, turnpike, way. See WAY.

road-a·gent (rōd′ā′jənt) *n.* A highway robber; highwayman, especially on stage routes of the western United States.

road·bed (rōd′bed′) *n.* **1** The graded foundation of gravel, etc., on which the ties, rails, etc., of a railroad are laid. **2** The graded foundation or surface of a road.

road·block (rōd′blok′) *n.* **1** An obstruction in a road. **2** Any arrangement of men and materials for blocking passage, as of enemy troops along a course of advance or retreat.

road hog An automobilist or other driver who keeps his vehicle in or near the middle of a road, making it difficult for other drivers to pass.

road·house (rōd′hous′) *n.* A restaurant, dance hall, or similar establishment located at the side of the road in a rural area.

road metal Broken stone or the like, used for making or repairing roads.

road·run·ner (rōd′·run′ər) *n.* A long-tailed ground cuckoo (genus *Geococcyx*), especially *G. californianus,* inhabiting open regions of southwestern North America, and running with great swiftness: also called *chaparral cock* or *hen.*

ROADRUNNER
(Length about 22 inches over-all)

road·stead (rōd′sted) *n. Naut.* A sheltered place of anchorage offshore, but less sheltered than a harbor. [< ROAD + STEAD (def. 4)]

road·ster (rōd′stər) *n.* **1** A light, open automobile, usually single-seated and having a luggage compartment or a rumble seat in the rear. **2** A horse adapted for use on the road, as in light driving; also, a buggy or light carriage. **3** One who journeys a great deal on roads.

road test 1 A test of a person's ability to operate a motor vehicle, esp. as part of an official driving-licence examination. **2** A test of a motor vehicle in actual driving situations on a road or highway.

road train *Austral.* A train of trailer trucks carrying livestock.

road·way (rōd′wā′) *n.* A road; specifically, that part over which vehicles pass.

Ro·ald (rō′äl) A Norwegian masculine personal name. [<Norw., lit., famous power <Gmc.]

roam (rōm) *v.i.* To move about purposelessly from place to place; wander; rove. —*v.t.* To wander over; range: to *roam* the fields. See synonyms under RAMBLE, WANDER. —*n.* The act of roaming; a ramble. [ME *romen*; origin unknown] —**roam′er** *n.*

roan (rōn) *adj.* **1** Of a color consisting of bay, sorrel, or chestnut, thickly interspersed with gray or white, as a horse. **2** Made of roan leather. —*n.* **1** A roan color. **2** An animal of a roan color. **3** A soft sheepskin leather, tanned to a roan color and used in bookbinding: also **roan leather.** [<OF <Sp. *roano,* ? ult. <L <*ravus* grayish-yellow]

Ro·a·noke (rō′ə·nōk) A city in western Virginia.

Roanoke Island An island off the eastern coast of North Carolina north of Cape Hatteras; settlements attempted by Raleigh in 1585 and 1587 failed; 12 miles long, 3 miles wide. See CROATAN.

Roanoke River A river in Virginia and North Carolina, flowing 410 miles to the head of Albemarle Sound.

roar (rôr, rōr) *v.i.* **1** To utter a deep, prolonged cry, as of rage or distress. **2** To make a loud noise or din, as the sea or a cannon. **3** To laugh loudly. **4** To move, proceed, or act noisily. **5** To make a labored, rasping sound in breathing, as a horse. —*v.t.* **6** To utter or express by roaring: The crowd *roared* its disapproval. —*n.* **1** A full, deep, resonant cry, as of a beast; a similar cry of a human being, as in pain, grief, or anger. **2** Any loud, prolonged sound, as of wind or waves, or a confused mingling of sounds suggesting the cry of wild beasts. See synonyms under NOISE. [OE *rārian*]

Synonyms (verb): bawl, bellow, boom, bray, shout, shriek, yell. See CALL.

roar·er (rôr′ər, rō′rər) *n.* **1** One who or that which roars. **2** An oil gusher.

roar·ing (rôr′ing, rō′ring) *adj.* **1** Emitting or uttering roars; bellowing. **2** *Archaic* Characterized by riotous merriment; boisterous. **3** *Colloq.* Very prosperous or brisk: a *roaring* business. —*n.* **1** A loud, deep, continued sound, as of some animals, or of the waves. **2** A disease among horses, characterized by labored, rasping breathing.

roast (rōst) *v.t.* **1** To cook by subjecting to the action of heat, as in an oven. **2** Originally, to cook before an open fire, or by placing in hot ashes, embers, etc. **3** To heat excessively, or to an extreme degree. **4** To dry and parch under the action of heat: to *roast* coffee. **5** *Metall.* To heat (ores) with access of air, but without fusing, for the purpose of driving off or volatilizing impurities, or for oxidizing them. **6** *Colloq.* To banter or ridicule severely. —*v.i.* **7** To roast food in an oven, etc. **8** To be cooked or prepared by this method. **9** To be uncomfortably hot. —*n.* **1** Something roasted; a piece of meat that is adapted or prepared for roasting, or that is roasted. **2** The act of roasting. —*adj.* Roasted. [<OF *rostir* <OHG *rosten* < *rost* a gridiron, a roast]

roast·er (rōs′tər) *n.* **1** A person who roasts. **2** A pan for roasting. **3** Something suitable for roasting, especially a pig.

rob (rob) *v.* **robbed, rob·bing** *v.t.* **1** To seize and carry off the property of by unlawful violence or threat of violence; commit robbery upon. **2** To deprive (a person) of something belonging or due; defraud. **3** To plunder; rifle, as a house. **4** To steal. —*v.i.* **5** To commit robbery. See synonyms under STEAL. [<OF *rober* <OHG *roubon.* Akin to REAVE, ROBE.]

Rob (rob) Diminutive of ROBERT.

rob·a·lo (rob′ə·lō, rō′bə-) *n. pl.* **·los** or **·lo** Any of a family *(Centropomidae)* of perchlike fishes of tropical American seas, especially *Centropomus undecimalis,* a large and esteemed food fish; a sergeant fish. [<Sp. *róbalo* <Catalan *elobarro,* ult. <L *lupus* a wolf]

rob·and (rob′ənd) *n. Naut.* A piece of spun yarn for fastening the head of a sail to a spar: sometimes called *rope band.* Also **rob′bin.**

[Earlier *raband,* ult. <ON *rābenda* bend asail on a yard <*ra* a yard for a sail + *benda* bend, bind]

rob•ber (rob′ər) *n.* A plunderer, as a burglar or highwayman.

Synonyms: bandit, brigand, buccaneer, burglar, depredator, footpad, freebooter, highwayman, marauder, pillager, pirate, plunderer, thief. A *robber* seeks to obtain the property of others by force or intimidation; a *thief* by stealth and secrecy.

robber fly The assassin fly.

rob•ber•y (rob′ər•ē) *n. pl.* **•ber•ies** The act of robbing; the taking away of the property of another unlawfully, by force or fear. See synonyms under PLUNDER.

Rob•bia (rôb′byä), **del•la** (del′lä) A family of Italian sculptors and workers in glazed terra cotta; especially **Luca,** 1400–82; his nephew, **Andrea,** 1435–1525; and grandnephew, **Giovanni,** 1469–1529.

robe (rōb) *n.* **1** A long, loose, flowing garment, worn over other dress; a gown. **2** *pl.* Such a garment worn as a badge of office or rank. **3** Any kind of costume; dress; figuratively, anything that covers in the manner of a robe. **4** A blanket or covering, as for use in a carriage or automobile: lap *robe.* **5** The dressed skin of an animal, formerly especially of the American bison, used as a garment or blanket. —*v.* **robed, rob•ing** *v.t.* To put a robe upon; clothe; dress. —*v.i.* To put on robes. [<OF, orig. booty <OHG *roub* spoils, robbery. Akin to ROB.]

robe de chambre (rôb′ də shän′br′) *French* A dressing gown. Also **robe′–de–cham′bre.**

robe de nuit (rôb′ də nwē′) *French* A nightgown.

Rob•ert (rob′ərt; *Du., Ger., Sw.* rō′bert, *Fr.* rō·bâr′) A masculine personal name. Also *Ital., Pg., Sp.* **Ro•ber•to** (rō·ber′tō), *Lat.* **Ro•ber•tus** (rə·bûr′təs). [<Gmc., bright fame]

—**Robert I,** died 1035, duke of Normandy 1028–35; father of William the Conqueror: called "Robert the Devil."

—**Robert II,** 1054?–1134, duke of Normandy 1087–1134; son of William the Conqueror; invaded England, defeated by his brother Henry I.

—**Robert the Bruce** See BRUCE.

Ro•ber•ta (rə·bûr′tə) A feminine personal name. [Fem. of ROBERT]

Rob•erts (rob′ərts), **Frederick Sleigh,** 1832–1914, Earl Roberts of Kandahar, Pretoria, and Waterford, British field marshal: known as *Bobs.* —**Kenneth,** 1885–1957, U.S. novelist.

Rob•ert•son (rob′ərt·sən), **William,** 1721–93, Scottish historian. —**Sir William Robert,** 1860–1933, English field marshal; chief of British general staff 1915–18.

Ro•ber•val (rô·ber·vål′), **Gilles Personne de,** 1602–75, French mathematician.

Robe•son (rōb′sən), **Paul,** 1898–1976, U.S.baritone.

Robes•pierre (rōbz′pir, *Fr.* rô·bəs·pyâr′), **Maximilien François Marie Isidore de,** 1758–1794, French revolutionist; guillotined.

rob•in (rob′in) *n.* **1** A large North American thrush *(Turdus migratorius)* with black head and tail, grayish wings and sides, and reddish–brown breast and underparts. **2** A small European bird *(Erithacus rubecula)* of the thrush family, especially common in Great Britain, with the forehead, cheeks, and breast yellowish–red. [<OF *Robin,* dim. of ROBERT]

Rob•in (rob′in) Diminutive of ROBERT. [<OF]

Rob•in Good•fel•low (rob′in good′fel′ō) **1** In English folklore, a merry and mischievous sprite: originally identified with Puck, but later believed to work his mischief around houses. Compare PUCK. **2** Any fairy or elf.

Robin Hood A legendary medieval hero of England, bold, chivalrous, courteous, and generous, an outlaw of great skill in archery, who robbed the rich to relieve the poor, especially in Sherwood Forest in Nottinghamshire, England. Compare ALLAN–A–DALE, FRIAR TUCK.

robin redbreast The European or American robin.

rob•in's–egg blue (rob′inz·eg′) A light greenish blue; the color of the egg shell of the American robin.

Rob•in•son (rob′in·sən), **Edwin Arlington,** 1869–1935, U.S. poet. —**James Harvey,** 1863–1936, U.S. historian. —**Sir Robert,** born 1886, English biochemist.

Rob•in•son Cru•soe (rob′in·sən kroo′sō) In Defoe's *Robinson Crusoe* (1719), the hero, a sailor shipwrecked on a tropical island, where, by ingenious devices, he maintained himself until rescued. See FRIDAY; SELKIRK, ALEXANDER.

ro•ble (rō′blā) *n.* One of various trees of the oak family, especially the Californian white oak *(Quercus lobata).* [<Sp. <L *robur,* a hard variety of oak]

rob•o•rant (rob′ər·ənt) *adj.* Restoring strength; strengthening. —*n.* Any strengthening medicine; a tonic. [<L *roborans, -antis,* ppr. of *roborare* strengthen <*robur, -oris.* See ROBUST.]

ro•bot (rō′bət, rob′ət) *n.* **1** An automaton; a manufactured, mechanical person that performs all hard work. **2** One who works mechanically and heartlessly. [after a creation introduced by Karel Čapek, Bohemian playwright, in his *Rossom's Universal Robots (R. U. R.)* in 1921; ult. <Czech *robota* work, compulsory service <*robotiti* drudge]

robot bomb See under BOMB.

robot pilot An automatic pilot.

Rob Roy (rob roi) Nickname of Robert Macgregor, 1671?–1734, a Highland outlaw; hero and title of one of Scott's novels.

Rob•son (rob′sən), **Mount** The highest peak in the Canadian Rockies, in eastern British Columbia, near Alberta; 12,972 feet.

ro•bust (rō·bust′, rō′bust) *adj.* **1** Possessing or characterized by great strength or endurance; rugged; healthy. **2** Requiring strength. **3** Violent; rude. **4** Rich, as in flavor: a *robust* soup. See synonyms under FIRM, POWERFUL, STRONG. [<L *robustus* <*robur, roboris,* a hard variety of oak, strength] —**ro•bust′ly** *adv.* —**ro•bust′ness** *n.*

ro•bus•tious (rō·bus′chəs) *adj. Archaic* Of a robust character; also, rough: now often used humorously. —**ro•bus′tious•ly** *adv.* —**ro•bus′•tious•ness** *n.*

roc (rok) *n.* In Arabian and Persian legend, an enormous and powerful bird of prey. [<Arabic *rokh, rukhkh* <Persian *rukh*]

Ro•ca (rō′kä), **Cape** A cape near Lisbon in Portugal; westernmost point of continental Europe. *Portuguese* **Ca•bo da Ro•ca** (kä′voo thə rō′kə).

roc•am•bole (rok′əm·bōl) *n.* A European perennial *(Allium scorodoprasum),* allied to the leek, with bulbs or cloves resembling those of garlic. [<F <G *rokenbolle* rye bulb]

Ro•cham•beau (rō·shäṅ·bō′), **Comte de,** 1725–1807, Jean Baptiste Donatien de Vimeure, French marshal; commanded French allies in the American Revolution.

Roch•dale (roch′dāl) A county borough in SE Lancashire, England, where, in 1844, the first cooperative stores were established.

Roche•fort (rôsh·fôr′) A port on the Charente in western France, 10 miles above the Bay of Biscay. Also **Roche•fort′–sur–mer′** (-sür·mâr′).

Ro•chelle (rô·shel′), **La** See LA ROCHELLE.

Ro•chelle powder (rō·shel′) Seidlitz powder.

Rochelle salt Potassium sodium tartrate, $KNaC_4H_4O_6 \cdot 4H_2O$, a white crystalline salt used as a cathartic. [from LA ROCHELLE]

roches mou•ton•nées (rosh′ moo·tô·nā′, rôsh′) Rounded knobs of rock ground down and smoothed by glacial action: so called because smooth and rounded like a sheep's back: also called *sheepbacks.* [<F, sheep–shaped rocks]

Roch•es•ter (roch′es·tər, -is-) **1** A municipal borough of northern Kent, England. **2** A city of western New York, near Lake Ontario.

Roch•es•ter (roch′es·tər, -is-), **Earl of,** 1648?–1680, John Wilmot, English courtier and poet.

roch•et (roch′it) *n.* A ceremonial garment similar to a surplice, but with closer sleeves or without sleeves: worn by bishops and other high churchmen. [<OF, dim. of *roc* a cloak <Gmc. Cf. G *rock* coat.]

Ro•ci•nan•te (rō′thē·nän′tā) The raw–boned steed of Don Quixote; hence, any ill–looking riding horse: also spelled *Rosinante.* [<Sp. *rocín* nag]

rock[1] (rok) *n.* **1** Any large mass of stone or stony matter; a boulder; also, a stone small enough to throw; stony fragments; a cliff. **2** A firm or immovable support; refuge; defense. **3** That on which one may be wrecked, as a reef; some source of ruin or injury. **4** *Geol.* The consolidated material forming the crust of the earth; any mass of mineral matter forming an essential part of the earth's crust. **5** The rockfish, or striped bass. **6** The rock dove. **7** A hard confection, of varied flavors. **8** Any of several very hard objects, as ice, rock candy, rock salt, etc.; also, a kind of cooky. **9** *U.S. Slang* A dollar; in the plural, money. —**on the rocks** *U.S. Slang* **1** Ruined; also, destitute; bankrupt. **2** Served with ice cubes but without soda or water: said of whisky or other spirituous beverage. —*adj.* Made or composed of rock; hard; stony: a *rock* wall. [<OF *roque, roke;* ult. origin uncertain]

rock[2] (rok) *v.i.* **1** To move backward and forward or from side to side; sway. **2** To sway, reel, or stagger, as from a blow; shake. **3** *Mining* To be washed in a cradle, as ores. —*v.t.* **4** To move backward and forward or from side to side, especially so as to soothe or put to sleep. **5** To cause to sway or reel: The earthquake *rocked* the houses. **6** *Mining* To wash (ores) in a cradle. **7** In mezzotint engraving, to prepare (a plate) by roughing its surface with a rocker (def. 8). See synonyms under SHAKE. —*n.* The act of rocking; a rocking motion. [OE *roccian*]

Rock, the Gibraltar.

rock•a•by (rok′ə·bī) *interj.* Go to sleep: from a nursery song intended to lull a child to slumber. —*n.* A lullaby. Also **rock′a•bye, rock′–a–bye.**

rock•a•hom•i•ny (rok′ə·hom′ə·nē) *n.* Indian corn parched and pounded; hominy. [<N. Am. Ind. (Algonquian) <*roc* corn + *oham* grind + termination *-min*]

rock•air (rok′âr′) *n.* A rocket launched from an aircraft, usually equipped with instruments for the investigation and recording of conditions in the upper atmosphere. Compare ROCKOON.

rock–and–roll (rok′ən·rōl′) *adj.* Describing a form of popular music, derived from hillbilly styles, achieving its effect by repetition of simple melodic elements, strongly marked rhythms, and exaggerated vocal mannerisms. —*n.* Rock–and–roll music. Also **rock 'n' roll.**

rock•a•way (rok′ə·wā) *n.* A four–wheeled, two–seated pleasure carriage with standing top. [from *Rockaway,* town in New Jersey]

rock bass A fresh–water food fish *(Ambloplites rupestris)* common in eastern North America.

rock bottom **1** The very bottom; the lowest possible level: Prices have hit *rock bottom.* **2** The basis or foundation of any issue. —**rock′–bot′tom** *adj.*

rock–bound (rok′bound′) *adj.* Encircled by or bordered with rocks.

rock candy Sugar candied in hard, clear crystals.

rock cork A variety of asbestos. Also called *rock leather.*

rock crystal Colorless transparent quartz.

rock dove The European wild pigeon *(Columba livia),* the parent of domestic varieties.

Rock•e•fel•ler (rok′ə·fel′ər) Name of a family of American capitalists and philanthropists, including **John Davison,** 1839–1937; his son, **John Davison, Jr.,** 1874–1960; and the latter's sons, **John Davison, III,** 1906–1978; **Nelson Aldrich,** 1908–1979, vice president of the United States (1974–77); **Laurance S.,** born 1910; **Winthrop,** born 1912, and **David,** born 1915.

rock•er[1] (rok′ər) *n.* **1** One who or that which rocks, in any sense. **2** One of the curved pieces on which a rocking chair or a cradle rocks. **3** A rocking chair. **4** A rock shaft. **5** A rocking–horse. **6** *Mining* A cradle. **7** An ice skate having a curved runner. **8** A small steel plate with a serrated edge for preparing a copper plate for a mezzotint.

rock•er[2] (rok′ər) *n.* The rock dove.

rocker arm *Mech.* An arm on a rock shaft, as in the valve mechanism of a steam engine.

rocker cam A cam on a rock shaft.

rocker shaft A rock shaft.

rock·er·y (rok′ər·ē) *n. pl.* **·er·ies 1** Rockwork. **2** A rock garden.

rock·et[1] (rok′it) *n.* **1** A firework, projectile, missile, or other device, usually cylindrical in form, that is propelled by the reaction of escaping gases produced during flight. **2** A vehicle operated by rocket propulsion and designed for space travel. — *v.i.* **1** To move like a rocket. **2** To fly straight up into the air, as a bird when alarmed. — *v.t.* **3** To propel by means of a rocket. [<Ital. *rocchetta* spool, dim. of *rocca* distaff <OHG *roccho*; from its resemblance to a distaff]

ROCKET
a. Head.
b. Bursting-charge.
c. Composition.
d. Clay choke.
e. Fuse.
f. Gas exhaust.
g. Stick.

rock·et[2] (rok′it) *n.* **1** Any of several ornamental Old World herbs (genus *Hesperis*), especially the common garden **dame rocket** *(H. matronalis)*, or dame-wort. **2** An annual *(Eruca sativa)* used in southern Europe as a salad. [<F *roquette*, ult. <L *eruca* colewort]

rocket bomb See under BOMB.

rock·et·eer (rok′ə·tir′) *n.* One who designs or launches rockets.

rocket gun A gun having the barrel open at both ends and used for the discharge of rocket projectiles. Compare BAZOOKA.

rocket launcher See under LAUNCHER.

rocket projector A device for aiming and discharging rockets.

rock·et·ry (rok′it·rē) *n.* The science, art, and technology of rocket flight, including all aspects from fundamental research to design, engineering, construction, and operation.

rock·et·sonde (rok′it·sond′) *n. Meteorol.* A radiosonde adapted for use on high-altitude rockets.

Rock fever Undulant fever. [from ROCK (OF GIBRALTAR)]

rock·fish (rok′fish′) *n. pl.* **·fish** or **·fish·es 1** A fish living about rocks. **2** Any of several food fishes (*Sebastodes* and related genera) of the west coast of North America. The black, orange, red, and spotted rockfish, as well as other species, are familiar in California markets. **3** One of various other fishes, as the striped bass, or the killifish.

rock flour Finely pulverized rock produced by the grinding action of glacier ice: also called *glacier meal.*

rock garden A garden with flowers and plants growing in rocky ground or among rocks arranged to imitate this.

rocking chair A chair having the legs set on rockers.

Rock·ing·ham (rok′ing·əm), **Marquis de,** 1730–1782, Charles Watson-Wentworth, English statesman.

rock·ing-horse (rok′ing·hôrs′) *n.* A toy horse mounted on rockers, large enough to be ridden by a child.

rocking stone A stone, often very large, so poised as to rock under little pressure.

rock leather Rock cork.

rock lobster The spiny lobster.

rock maple The sugar maple.

rock milk Agaric mineral.

Rock·ne (rok′nē), **Knute Kenneth,** 1888–1931, U. S. football coach born in Norway.

rock oil Petroleum.

rock·oon (rok·o͞on′) *n.* A small rocket equipped with various meteorological recording devices and attached to a balloon from which it is released at altitudes determined chiefly by its weight. Compare ROCKAIR. [<ROCK(ET) + (BALL)OON]

rock rabbit A hyrax.

rock·rose (rok′rōz′) *n.* One of several plants (genera *Cistus, Helianthemum,* and *Crocanthemum*) having flowers resembling the wild rose.

rock salt Halite.

rock shaft A shaft made to rock on its bearings; particularly, such a shaft for operating a slide valve in an engine: also called *rocker, rocker shaft.*

rock·weed (rok′wēd′) *n.* Any one of various coarse seaweeds (genera *Fucus* and *Sargassum*) growing on rocks.

rock wool Mineral wool.

rock·work (rok′wûrk′) *n.* **1** A mound or wall of stones set with mortar and arranged to imitate a rocky surface. **2** An artificial grotto.

rock·y[1] (rok′ē) *adj.* **rock·i·er, rock·i·est 1** Consisting of, abounding in, or resembling rocks. **2** Tough; unfeeling; hard; also, disreputable.

rock·y[2] (rok′ē) *adj.* **rock·i·er, rock·i·est** *Colloq.* Shaky or dizzy, as if rocking; unsteady in the head, as from past intoxication. — **rock′i·ness** *n.*

ROCKY MOUNTAIN GOAT
(About 40 inches high at the shoulder)

Rocky Mountain goat A conspicuous, typically white antelope *(Oreamnos americanus)* found in the mountains of NW North America.

Rocky Mountain National Park A mountainous region in northern Colorado; 395.5 square miles; established, 1915.

Rocky Mountains The major mountain system of western North America, extending from the Arctic to Mexico; highest peak, Mount Elbert, 14,431 feet. Also **Rock′ies.**

Rocky Mountain sheep The bighorn.

Rocky Mountain spotted fever *Pathol.* An acute infectious rickettsial disease caused by a micro-organism *(Rickettsia rickettsii)* transmitted by the bite of certain ticks (genus *Dermacentor*): it is marked by fever, chills, headache, and diffuse pains, and is endemic in Rocky Mountain and Pacific coast States.

ro·co·co (rə·kō′kō) *n.* **1** A style of decoration and architecture, developed from the baroque and distinguished by profuse, elaborate, and often delicately executed ornament in imitation of rockwork, shells, foliage, and scrolls massed together: prevalent during the 17th and 18th centuries. **2** Anything regarded as florid, fantastic, or odd in literature. — *adj.* **1** Having, or built in, the style of rococo. **2** Overelaborate; florid. [<F, fanciful alter. of *rocaille* shellwork < *roc* rock]

rod (rod) *n.* **1** A shoot or twig of any woody plant; a straight, slim piece of wood or other material, used as an instrument of punishment, a badge of office, etc.; hence, with the definite article, discipline; correction. **2** A scepter; hence, dominion; power. **3** A bar, commonly of metal, forming part of a machine; a connecting rod. **4** A light pole used to suspend and manipulate a fishing line. **5** A measure of length, equal to 5.5 yards or 16.5 feet, or 5.02 meters; also, in England, a **cubic rod,** a unit of volume equal to 1,000 cubic feet. **6** A measuring rule. **7** One of the rod-like bodies of the retina sensitive to faint light. **8** A particular line of family descent. **9** *U.S. Slang* A pistol. **10** A lightning rod. **11** The drawbar of a freight train. — **to ride the rods** *U.S. Slang* To steal a ride by getting on the metal framework underneath a freight train. See synonyms under STICK. [OE *rod.* Related to ROOD.]

rode (rōd) Past tense of RIDE.

ro·dent (rōd′nt) *n.* A gnawing mammal (order *Rodentia*) having in each jaw two (rarely four) incisors, growing continually from persistent pulps, and no canine teeth, as a squirrel, beaver, or rat. — *adj.* **1** Gnawing. **2** Pertaining to the rodents. [<L *rodens, -entis,* ppr. of *rodere* gnaw] — **ro·den·tial** (rō·den′·shəl) *adj.*

rodent ulcer *Pathol.* A malignant ulcer that progressively destroys soft tissues and bones, especially of the face. Also called *noli-me-tangere.*

ro·de·o (rō′dē·ō, rō·dā′ō) *n. pl.* **·de·os 1** The driving of cattle together to be branded, counted, inspected, etc.; a roundup. **2** An enclosure in a stock farm, in which cattle are collected to be counted and branded. **3** A public spectacle in which the more exciting features of a roundup are presented, as the riding of broncos, branding, lariat-throwing, etc. [<Sp. < *rodear* go around < *rueda* wheel <L *rota*]

Rod·er·ick (rod′ər·ik) A masculine personal name. Also **Rod′er·ic,** *Lat.* **Ro·der·i·cus** (rō′·də·rī′kəs), *Ger.* **Ro·de·rich** (rō′də·rikh), *Fr.* **Ro·drigue** (rō·drēg′), *Ital., Sp.* **Ro·dri·go** (*Ital.* rō·drē′gō, *Sp.* -thrē′-). [<Gmc., famous king] — **Roderick,** died 711, last king of the Visigoths.

Rod·gers (roj′ərz), **Richard,** born 1902, U. S. composer.

Ro·di (rô′dē) Italian name for RHODES.

Ro·din (rō·daṅ′), **Auguste,** 1840–1917, French sculptor.

rod·man (rod′mən) *n. pl.* **·men** (-mən) One who uses or carries a surveyor's leveling rod. Also **rods′man.**

Rod·ney (rod′nē), **George Brydges,** 1719?–1792, Baron Rodney, English admiral.

Ro·dó (rō·thō′), **José Enrique,** 1872–1917, Uruguayan essayist.

Ro·dol·fo (*Ital.* rō·dôl′fō, *Sp.* rō·thôl′fō) Italian and Spanish form of RUDOLPH. Also *Fr.* **Ro·dolphe** (rô·dôlf′), *Ital.* **Ro·dol·pho** (rō·dôl′fō), **Ro·dol·phus** (*Du.* rō·dol′fo͞os, *Lat.* rō·dol′fəs).

rod·o·mon·tade (rod′ə·mon·tād′, -täd′) *n.* Vainglorious boasting; bluster. — *adj.* Bragging. — *v.i.* **·tad·ed, ·tad·ing** To boast; bluster; brag. [<F <Ital. *rodomontata* <*Rodomonte,* name of a boastful Saracen king in Ariosto's *Orlando Furioso*]

roe[1] (rō) *n.* **1** The spawn or eggs of female fish. **2** The milt of male fish. **3** The eggs of crustaceans. ◆ Homophone: *row.* [Var. of dial. *roan,* appar. <ON *hrogn*]

roe[2] (rō) *n.* **1** A small, graceful deer (genus *Capreolus*) of Europe and western Asia, with slender antlers rising vertically from the head. Also **roe deer. 2** Improperly, the doe of the red deer. ◆ Homophone: *row.* [OE *rā*]

Roeb·ling (rōb′ling), **John Augustus,** 1806–1869, U. S. engineer born in Germany; built the Niagara and Cincinnati suspension bridges. — **Washington Augustus,** 1837–1926, son of preceding; built Brooklyn Bridge, completed in 1883.

roe·buck (rō′buk′) *n.* A roe, especially the male.

Roe·mer (rœ′mər), **Olaus,** 1644–1710, Danish astronomer.

roent·gen (rent′gən, runt′-; *Ger.* rœnt′gən) *n.* The international unit of X-ray intensity; the quantity of radiation which, with full use of secondary electrons and without loss to the walls of the chamber, produces in 1 cubic centimeter of air at normal temperature and pressure 1 electrostatic unit of electricity of either sign: also spelled *röntgen.* [after Wilhelm Konrad *Roentgen*]

Roent·gen (rent′gən, runt′-; *Ger.* rœnt′gən), **Wilhelm Konrad,** 1845–1923, German physicist; discoverer of Roentgen rays, better known as X-rays.

roentgen equivalent man See REM.

roentgen equivalent physical See REP.

roent·gen·ize (rent′gən·īz, runt′-) *v.t.* **·ized, ·iz·ing** To subject or expose to the action of X-rays. — **roent′gen·i·za′tion** *n.*

roentgeno- *combining form* X-rays; using, produced by, or producing X-rays: *roentgenogram.* Also, before vowels, **roentgen-.** [<ROENTGEN]

roent·gen·o·gram (rent′gən·ə·gram′, runt′-) *n.* An X-ray photograph, especially one taken for medical or therapeutic purposes; a skiagraph.

roent·gen·og·ra·phy (rent′gən·og′rə·fē, runt′-) *n. Med.* Photography by means of X-rays; radiography.

roent·gen·ol·o·gy (rent′gən·ol′ə·jē, runt′-) *n.* The science which treats of the properties, action, and effects of X-rays. — **roent′gen·ol′·o·gist** *n.*

roent·gen·o·paque (rent′gən·ō·pāk′, runt′-) *adj.* Impervious to X-rays.

roent·gen·o·ther·a·py (rent′gən·ō·ther′ə·pē, runt′-) *n. Med.* Treatment of disease by means of X-rays.

Roentgen rays X-rays.

Roer·ich (rœr′ikh), **Nicholas Konstantin,** 1874–1947, Russian painter.

ro·ga·tion (rō·gā′shən) *n.* **1** In ancient Rome, the submission of a proposed law by the executive (consul or tribune) to the people, requesting its adoption; also, a law submitted in this manner and accepted. **2** Litany; supplication. [<L *rogatio, -onis* < *rogatus,* pp. of *rogare* ask]

Rogation days *Eccl.* The three days immediately preceding Ascension Day, observed as days of special supplication by litanies, processions, etc.

ro·ga·to·ry (rō′gə·tôr′ē, -tō′rē) *adj.* **1** Commissioned to gather information. **2** Officially requesting another court to ascertain and report certain facts: letters *rogatory.*

Rog·er (roj′ər) *interj.* **1** Message received: a code signal used in radiotelephone communication. **2** *U.S. Colloq.* All right; O.K. [from *Roger,* personal name]

Roger (roj′ər, *Fr.* rô·zhā′) A masculine personal name. Also *Lat.* **Ro·ger·us** (rō·jir′əs), *Ital.* **Ro·ge·ro** (rō·jā′rō), **Ro·ge·rio** (*Pg.* rō·zhā′ryŏŏ, *Sp.* rō·hā′ryō). [<Gmc., spear of fame]

Rog·ers (roj′ərz), **Will,** 1879–1935, U. S. actor and humorist: full name *William Penn Adair Rogers.*

Ro·get (rô·zhā′), **Peter Mark,** 1779–1869, English physician and philologist; compiled *Roget's Thesaurus of English Words and Phrases,* 1852.

rogue (rōg) *n.* **1** A dishonest and unprincipled person; trickster; rascal. **2** One who is innocently mischievous or playful: sometimes said familiarly and endearingly. **3** An idle, sturdy beggar; a roving vagrant. **4** *Biol.* A variation from a standard. **5** A fierce and dangerous elephant separated from the herd: in this sense also used adjectively: a *rogue* elephant. —*v.* **rogued, ro·guing** *v.t.* **1** To practice roguery upon; defraud. **2** To eliminate (inferior individuals) from a plot of plants undergoing selection. —*v.i.* **3** To live or act like a rogue. [Origin uncertain]

Rogue River A river in SW Oregon, flowing 200 miles SW to the Pacific.

ro·guer·y (rō′gər·ē) *n. pl.* **·guer·ies 1** Knavery, cheating, or dishonesty, or an instance of it. **2** Playful mischievousness.

rogues' gallery A collection of photographs of criminals taken to aid the police in their future identification.

rogues' march Music played in derision of a person when he is expelled or driven away in disgrace, as from a military body or community.

ro·guish (rō′gish) *adj.* **1** Playfully mischievous. **2** Knavish; dishonest. —**ro′guish·ly** *adv.* —**ro′guish·ness** *n.*

Ro·han (rô·än′), **de** A feudal family of France; especially, its descendants, **Henri,** 1579–1638, duke and Huguenot leader; and **Louis René Édouard,** 1734–1803, grand almoner and cardinal.

Ro·hil·khand (rō′hil·kund′) A division of north central Uttar Pradesh State, India; 11,759 square miles; capital, Bareilly.

roil (roil) *v.t.* **1** To make muddy, as a liquid, by stirring up sediment. **2** To irritate or anger. Also spelled *rile.* [<F *rouiller* rust, make muddy <OF *rouil* mud, rust]

roil·y (roi′lē) *adj.* **1** Full of sediment; stirred up; turbid. **2** Irritated; vexed.

roist·er (rois′tər) *v.i.* **1** To act in a blustery manner; swagger. **2** To engage in revelry; riot. [<earlier *roister* loud bully <OF *ruistre* <L *rusticus.* See RUSTIC.] —**roist′er·er** *n.* —**roist′er·ing** *adj.*

rok·e·lay (rok′ə·lā) See ROQUELAURE.

Ro·kos·sov·sky (ro·kə·sôf′skē), **Konstantin,** born 1893?, U.S.S.R. marshal.

Ro·land (rō′lənd, *Dan.* rō′län, *Fr.* rô·län′, *Ger.* rō′länt) A masculine personal name. Also *Du.* **Roe·land** (rōō′länt), *Ital., Sp.* **Ro·lan·do** (rō·län′dō), *Pg.* **Ro·lan·do** (rō·läṅ′dŏŏ), **Rol·dão** (rōl·douṅ′), *Lat.* **Ro·lan·dus** (rō·lan′dəs). [<Gmc., fame of the land]

—**Roland** Hero of the Anglo-Norman epic *Chanson de Roland* and of many other stories of the Charlemagne cycle. According to legend he was the nephew of Charlemagne, and a bulwark of Christianity against the Saracens, dying in battle at Roncesvalles in 788. He is known as *Orlando* in Italian romances concerning Charlemagne. —**a Roland for an Oliver** Action taken in retaliation, or by way of matching something said or done by another; a tit for tat: in allusion to an indecisive battle between Roland and Oliver, his companion-in-arms.

role (rōl) *n.* A part or character taken by an actor; any assumed character or function. Also **rôle.** ◆ Homophone: *roll.* [<F]

Rolfe (rolf), **John,** 1585–1622, English colonist in Virginia; husband of Pocahontas.

roll (rōl) *v.i.* **1** To move forward upon a surface by turning round and round, as the wheel of a vehicle. **2** To move or be moved on wheels: The cart *rolled* down the hill. **3** To rotate wholly or partially: Her eyes *rolled* with pleasure. **4** To assume the shape of a ball or cylinder by turning over and over upon itself. **5** To move or appear to move in undulations or swells, as waves or plains. **6** To sway or move from side to side, as a ship: to pitch and *roll.* **7** To walk with a swaying motion; swagger; also, to stagger. **8** To make a sound as of heavy, rolling wheels; rumble: Thunder *rolled* across the sky. **9** To become spread or flat because of pressure applied by a roller, etc.. The metal *rolls* easily. **10** To perform a periodic revolution, as the sun. **11** To move ahead; progress. —*v.t.* **12** To cause to move along a surface by turning round and round, as a ball, log, etc. **13** To move, push forward, etc., on wheels or rollers. **14** To impel or cause to move onward with a steady, surging motion: The ocean *rolls* its waves upon the shore. **15** To rotate, as the eyes. **16** To impart a swaying motion to. **17** To spread or make flat by means of a roller. **18** To wrap round and round upon itself. **19** To cause to assume the shape of a ball or cylinder by means of rotation and pressure: to *roll* a cigarette. **20** To wrap or envelop in or as in a covering. **21** To utter with a trilling sound: to *roll* one's r's. **22** To emit in a full and swelling manner, as musical sounds. **23** To beat a roll upon, as a drum. **24** To cast (dice) in the game of craps. **25** *Printing* To apply ink to (a form) by means of a roller or rollers. See synonyms under REVOLVE. —**to roll back** To cause (prices or wages) to return to a previous, lower level, as by government order. —**to roll in 1** To arrive. **2** To gather. **3** *Colloq.* To luxuriate; wallow. —**to roll out 1** To unroll. **2** *Colloq.* To leave. **3** To flatten by means of rollers. —**to roll up 1** To assume or cause to assume the shape of a ball or cylinder by turning over and over upon itself. **2** To accumulate; amass: to *roll up* large profits. —*n.* **1** Anything rolled up in cylindrical form: a *roll* of parchment. **2** Hence, an official writing, especially a list of names or a register. **3** *U.S. Slang* A wad of paper money; also, money in general. **4** A long strip, as of ribbon or carpet, rolled upon itself or upon a core: sometimes of an agreed length used as a measure of quantity. **5** Any food rolled up in preparation for use, as bread by rolling up pieces of dough, meat for roasting, or a pudding or cake formed in a similar way: a jelly *roll.* **6** A roller; particularly, a cylinder in fixed bearings used as a roller. **7** A reverberation, as of thunder. **8** A trill. **9** The rapid beating of a drum to make its sound continuous. **10** A rolling gait or movement; also, motion from side to side, as of a ship in a seaway. **11** *Aeron.* A single turn of an airplane about its long axis without change in the direction of flight: also called **barrel roll;** when performed quickly, called a **snap roll. 12** A strip of leather or other material fitted with pockets to hold tools or toilet articles, etc., around which it is rolled and fastened. See synonyms under RECORD. ◆ Homophone: *role.* [<OF *roller* <L *rotula* <*rota* wheel]

Rol·land (rô·läṅ′), **Romain,** 1868–1944, French novelist and dramatist.

roll·a·way (rōl′ə·wā′) *adj.* Mounted on rollers for easy movement into storage: a *rollaway* bed.

roll-back (rōl′bak′) *n.* A return, by government order, to a previous, lower price or wage level.

roll call 1 The act of calling over a roll or list of the names of a number of persons, as soldiers or workmen, to ascertain which are present. **2** The time of or signal for calling the roll.

roll·er (rō′lər) *n.* **1** One who or that which rolls anything. **2** Any cylindrical device that rolls. **3** The wheel of a caster or roller skate. **4** A rod for carrying a curtain, towel, map, or the like. **5** A heavy cylinder for rolling, smoothing, or crushing something: a steam *roller.* **6** *Printing* A cylindrical device, often of hard rubber, to spread the ink on a form before impressing on paper. **7** *Surg.* A long rolled bandage to be wrapped around a limb or the like. **8** One of a series of long, swelling waves which break on a coast, especially after a storm. **9** *Ornithol.* **a** An Old World bird of crowlike form with gaudy colors, remarkable for its irregular rolling or tumbling flight, especially the common roller *(Coracias garrula)* found in Europe. **b** A tumbler pigeon.

roller bearing A bearing employing steel rollers to lessen friction between the parts of a mechanism.

ROLLER BEARING

roller coaster A circular switchback railway with many steep inclines, over which small cars are run: common at amusement parks.

roller derby *U.S.* A race between two teams on roller skates: a player scores points for his team by overtaking opposing players after skating completely around the track within a given time limit.

roll·er-skate (rō′lər·skāt′) *v.i.* **–skat·ed, –skat·ing** To go on roller skates.

roller skate A skate having rollers or wheels instead of a runner.

roller towel An endless towel for use on a roller.

rol·lick (rol′ik) *v.i.* To move in a careless, frolicsome manner; act carelessly and jovially. [Blend of ROMP and FROLIC]

rol·lick·ing (rol′ik·ing) *adj.* **1** Moving in a careless or swaggering manner; jovial. **2** Expressive of a careless, frolicsome spirit: *rollicking* behavior. Also **rol′lick·some** (-səm), **rol′lick·y.**

roll·ing (rō′ling) *adj.* **1** Having a succession of sloping elevations and depressions; undulating: *rolling* prairies. **2** Turned back or down as if over a roll: a *rolling* collar. **3** Of or pertaining to rolling; used in rolling. **4** Moving on or as if on wheels; rotating. **5** Surging in puffs or billows, as smoke, clouds, etc. **6** Recurring; elapsing: said of time. **7** Swaying from side to side: a *rolling* gait. —*n.* The act of a person or thing that rolls, or of one who uses a rolling tool.

rolling barrage *Mil.* An artillery barrage in which the range is steadily increased so that the shells fall just ahead of advancing ground troops.

rolling hitch A hitch with one or more intermediate turns between the first and last hitch. See illustration under HITCH.

rolling kitchen *Mil.* A field kitchen equipped to move with troops.

rolling mill An establishment in which metal is rolled into sheets, bars, etc.

rolling pin A roller, usually of wood, with a handle at each end, for rolling out dough, etc.

rolling stock The wheeled transportation equipment of a railroad.

rolling stone 1 A stone worn smooth by friction and wear. **2** A person of restless, unsettled habits and occupation.

Rol·lo (rol′ō) A masculine personal name. [See RUDOLPH]

—**Rollo,** 860?–932?, Norwegian Viking leader; first duke of Normandy: also *Hrolf.*

roll-top (rōl′top′) *adj.* Having a cover which slides back out of the way: a *roll-top* desk.

roll·way (rōl′wā′) *n.* An inclined way, natural or artificial, down which logs may be rolled or shot; chute.

Röl·vaag (rœl′väg), **Ole Edvart,** 1876–1931, U. S. educator and novelist born in Norway.

ro·ly-po·ly (rō′lē-pō′lē) *adj.* Short and fat; pudgy; dumpy. —*n.* **1** *Brit.* A pudding made of a sheet of pastry dough spread with fruit, preserves, etc., rolled up and cooked. **2** A pudgy person. [Reduplication of ROLL]

Ro·ma·gna (rō·mä′nyä) A region and former province of the Papal States in north central Italy on the Adriatic.

Ro·ma·ic (rō·mā′ik) *adj.* Pertaining to or characteristic of the language or people of modern Greece. —*n.* Modern Greek, especially the popular spoken form. [<LL *Romaicus* <Gk. *Rhōmaikos* Roman <*Rhōmē* Rome]

ro·maine (rō·mān′) *n.* A variety of lettuce *(Lactuca sativa longifolia)* characterized by long, crisp leaves. [<F, fem. of *romain* Roman]

Ro·mains (rô·mañ'), **Jules** Pseudonym of Louis Farigoule, 1885–1972, French novelist.

ro·man[1] (rō'mən) *adj. Printing* Designating or pertaining to a common style of type or letter, characterized chiefly by serifs, perpendicularity, and the greater thickness of its upright strokes than of its horizontal strokes: This line is set in roman: distinguished from *italic.* — *n.* Roman type. Also **Ro'man.**

ro·man[2] (rō·mäñ') *n. French* **1** A type of metrical narrative, especially common in Old French literature, developed from the ancient chansons de geste. **2** A romantic novel.

Ro·man (rō'mən) *adj.* **1** Of, pertaining to, or characteristic of Rome or its people. **2** Belonging to or connected with the Church of Rome or its head; Roman Catholic. **3** Somewhat aquiline: a *Roman* nose. — *n.* **1** A native, resident, or citizen of modern Rome or a citizen of ancient Rome. **2** A Roman Catholic. **3** *pl.* The Epistle to the Romans. — **Epistle to the Romans** One of the books of the New Testament; a letter from the apostle Paul to the Christians at Rome. [<OF *romain* <L *Romanus* < *Roma* Rome]

ro·man à clef (rō·mäñ' à kle') *French* A novel in which actual persons and places appear under fictitious names; literally, a novel with a key.

Roman alphabet The Latin alphabet.

Roman architecture A style of architecture

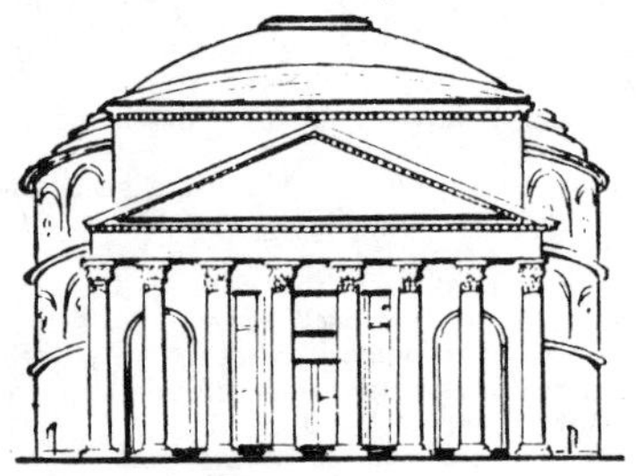

ROMAN ARCHITECTURE
Pantheon, Rome, A.D. 123

which is characterized by the size, massiveness, and boldness of its round arches and vaults, by the somewhat lavish adoption of Greek embellishments, and by excellent stonemasonry and brickmasonry of every kind.

Roman calendar See under CALENDAR.

Roman candle A firework consisting of a tube filled with a composition which discharges colored balls and sparks of fire.

Roman Catholic A member of the Roman Catholic Church.

Roman Catholic Church The church in communion with the pope, whom it recognizes as its supreme head on earth: an official designation. Also called the *Catholic Church.*

ro·mance (rō·mans', rō'mans) *n.* **1** Adventurous, heroic, or picturesque character or nature; strange and fascinating appeal: the *romance* of faraway places. **2** A disposition to delight in the mysterious or adventurous: a child of *romance.* **3** A love affair. **4** A long narrative from medieval legend, presenting chivalrous ideals and aristocratic society and usually involving heroes in strange adventures and affairs of love. **5** Any long fictitious narrative embodying scenes and events remote from common life and filled with extravagant adventures and often long digressions. **6** The class of literature consisting of romances (defs. 4 and 5). **7** An extravagant or fanciful falsehood. **8** *Music* A simple rhythmic melody, often sentimental, suggestive of a love song. See synonyms under DREAM, FICTION. — *v.* (rō·mans') **·manced, ·manc·ing** *v.i.* **1** To tell romances. **2** To think or act in a romantic manner. **3** *Colloq.* To make love. — *v.t.* **4** *Colloq.* To make love to; woo. [<OF *romans* a story written in French <L *Romanice* in Roman style <*Romanicus* Roman]

Ro·mance (rō·mans') *adj.* Pertaining or belonging to one or more, or all, of the languages which have developed from the vulgar Latin speech, and which exist now as French, Italian, Spanish, Portuguese, Catalan, Provençal, Rhaeto-Romanic, and Rumanian. — *n.* One, or all collectively, of the Romance languages.

ro·manc·er (rō·man'sər) *n.* **1** A writer of romances. **2** One who indulges in extravagant fictions or fancies.

Ro·man de la Rose (rō·mäñ' də là rôz') An allegorical Old French verse romance, begun by Guillaume de Lorris about the middle of the 13th century, and completed in satirical tone by Jean de Meung toward the end of the century: source of Chaucer's *Romaunt of the Rose.*

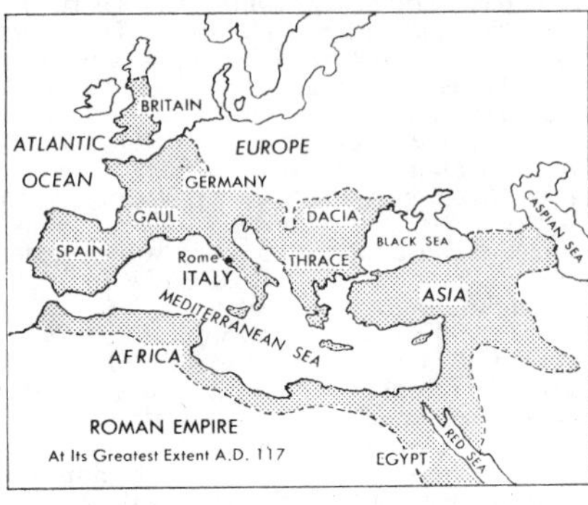

Roman Empire The empire of ancient Rome, established by Augustus in 27 B.C. and continuing until the reign of Theodosius in A.D. 395, when it was divided into the Eastern Roman Empire and the Western Roman Empire.

ro·man·esque (rō'mən·esk') *adj.* Romantic; fabulous; fanciful. [<F <Ital. *romanesco* <Med. L *romaniscus* <L *romanus* Roman]

Ro·man·esque (rō'mən·esk') *adj.* **1** Pertaining to or designating the Romanesque style of architecture. **2** Pertaining to or characterized by the Romance languages, especially Provençal. — *n.* **1** Romanesque architecture. **2** The vernacular of Languedoc and other provinces in southern France.

Romanesque architecture The prevailing style, developed from Roman principles, of Western architecture from the 5th to the 12th centuries, embracing the Saxon, Norman, Lombard, etc., characterized by the round arch and general massiveness. It reached its

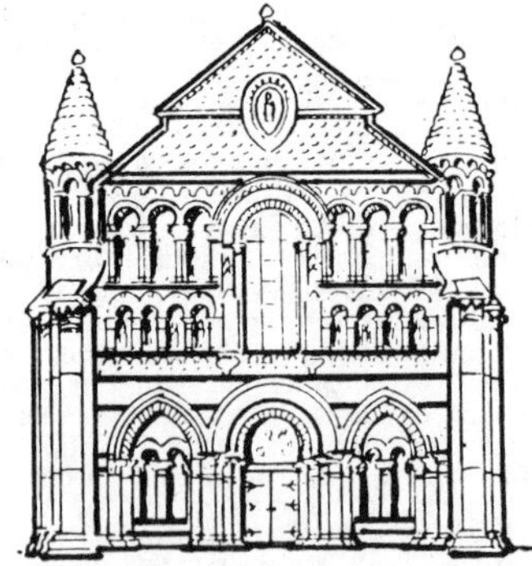

ROMANESQUE ARCHITECTURE
Notre Dame la Grande, Poitiers, France, A.D. 11th Century.

best form in France in the 11th and 12th centuries.

Roman holiday **1** A day of gladiatorial and other contests in ancient Rome. **2** Enjoyment or profit whereby others suffer.

Ro·mâ·nia (rō·mān'ya, *Rumanian* rô·mœ'nyä) The Rumanian name for RUMANIA.

Ro·man·ic (rō·man'ik) *adj.* Roman; also, Romance.

Ro·man·ism (rō'mən·iz'əm) *n.* The dogmas, forms, etc., of the Roman Catholic Church: a term used chiefly in disparagement. — **Ro'·man·ist** *adj.* & *n.*

Ro·man·ize (rō'mən·īz) *v.t* & *v.i.* **·ized, ·iz·ing** **1** To make or become Roman or Roman Catholic. **2** To write or speak in a Latinized style. — **Ro'man·i·za'tion** *n.*

Roman mile See MILE.

Roman nose A nose that is somewhat aquiline.

Roman numerals The letters used by the ancient Romans as symbols in arithmetical notation. See NUMERAL.

Ro·ma·nov (rō'mə·nôf, *Russian* rô·mä'nôf) A Russian dynasty, 1613–1917, founded by *Czar Michael,* 1596–1645. Also **Ro'ma·noff.**

Roman punch An ice consisting of the white of eggs beaten with rum and lemon juice.

Ro·mansch (rō·mansh', -mänsh') *n.* **1** A Rhaeto-Romanic dialect spoken in the Grisons canton, Switzerland. **2** The Rhaeto-Romanic dialects as a group. Also **Ro·mansh'.** [<L *Romanicus* <*Roma* Rome]

ro·man·tic (rō·man'tik) *adj.* **1** Characterized or influenced by romance or the extravagantly ideal; imaginative; marvelous; fanciful: a *romantic* tale. **2** Given to feelings or thoughts of romance; dreamy: a *romantic* girl. **3** Characterized by or conducive to love or amorousness. **4** Visionary; fantastic; impractical: a *romantic* scheme. **5** Strangely wild or picturesque: *romantic* scenery. **6** Of, pertaining to, or characteristic of a style of art and literature tending toward free expression of subjective feeling, impressive picturesqueness, imagination, sensuousness, etc.: opposed to *classic* or *classical.* **7** Of or pertaining to romanticism in art and literature in the 19th century. — *n.* **1** An adherent of romanticism; a romanticist. **2** A romantic person. **3** A romantic trait, idea, etc. [<F *romantique* < *romant, roman* romance, novel] — **ro·man'·ti·cal·ly** *adv.*

Synonyms (adj.): airy, chimerical, dreamy, extravagant, fanciful, fantastic, fictitious, ideal, imaginative, picturesque, poetic, sentimental, visionary, wild. *Antonyms*: exact, historical, literal, precise, truthful, unadorned, unimaginative, unvarnished.

ro·man·ti·cism (rō·man'tə·siz'əm) *n.* **1** The quality or characteristic of being romantic. **2** In art, music, and literature, a romantic style as opposed to the classical. **3** In the late 18th century and the 19th, a social and esthetic movement, beginning as a reaction to neo-classicism, that sought to free the individual from unpleasant realities by appealing to his aspirations for wonder and mystery. It emphasized a love for strange beauty, for the past and the far-away, and for the wild, irregular, or grotesque in nature, and found creative expression in spontaneity, lyricism, reverie, sentimentalism, mysticism, and individualism. — **ro·man'ti·cist** *n.*

ro·man·ti·cize (rō·man'tə·sīz) *v.t.* **·cized, ·ciz·ing** To regard or interpret in a romantic manner.

Romantic Movement See ROMANTICISM (def. 3).

Rom·a·ny (rom'ə·nē) *adj.* Of or pertaining to the Gipsies or their language. — *n.* **1** A Gipsy. **2** The Indic language of the Gipsies, containing elements of the language of each country in which they live: also called *Gipsy.* Also **Rom'ma·ny.** [<Romany *romani* < *rom* man]

ro·maunt (rō·mänt', -mônt') *n.* A romance, usually in verse. [<OF *romant,* var. of *romans.* See ROMANCE.]

Rom·berg (rom'bûrg), **Sigmund,** 1887–1951, U. S. composer born in Hungary.

Rom·blon (rōm·blōn') A Philippine province, comprising a group of Visayan Islands including **Romblon Island** (32 square miles); 512 square miles; capital, Romblon.

Rome (rōm) **1** A city on the Tiber river, capital of Italy and the site of Vatican City, center of the Roman Catholic Church; formerly the capital of the Roman republic, the Roman Empire, and the States of the Church. *Italian* and *Latin* **Ro·ma** (rō'mä). **2** The Roman Catholic Church. **3** Roman Catholicism. **4** A city in central New York.

Ro·me·o (rō'mē·ō) In Shakespeare's tragedy *Romeo and Juliet,* the hero of the play, son of Montague, in love with Juliet, daughter of Capulet who is the enemy of the house of the Montagues.

Rom·ford (rum'fərd, rom'-) A municipal borough in SW Essex, England.

Rom·ish (rō'mish) *adj.* Pertaining to the Roman Catholic Church: an invidious usage.

Rom·mel (rum'əl, *Ger.* rôm'əl), **Erwin,** 1891–1944, German field marshal in World War II.

Rom·ney (rom'nē, rum'-), **George,** 1734–1802, English painter.

romp (romp) *v.i.* **1** To play boisterously. **2** To win easily. — *n.* **1** One, especially a girl, who romps. 2 Noisy, exciting frolic or play. [Var. of RAMP[2]]

romp·er (rom′pər) *n.* 1 One who romps. 2 *pl.* A combination of waist and bloomers, as worn by young children at play.

romp·ing (rom′ping) *n.* Boisterous playing. — **romp′ing·ly** *adv.*

romp·ish (rom′pish) *adj.* Inclined toward boisterousness in play. — **romp′ish·ly** *adv.* — **romp′ish·ness** *n.*

Rom·u·lus (rom′yə·ləs) In Roman mythology, a son of Mars and founder of Rome, later deified as *Quirinus*: abandoned in the Tiber with his twin brother Remus, the infant Romulus was reared by a she-wolf, later killing his brother to become the first ruler of Rome.

Ron·ald (ron′əld, *Norw.* rō·näl′) A masculine personal name. [See REGINALD]

Ron·ces·val·les (ron′sə·valz, *Sp.* rôn′thes·vä′·lyäs) A village in the Pyrenees, northern Spain; nearby **Roncesvalles Pass** was the scene of Roland's death and the defeat of Charlemagne's rear guard, 778. *French* **Ronce·vaux** (rôṅs·vō′).

ron·deau (ron′dō, ron·dō′) *n.* A poem of French origin, consisting of thirteen lines with only two rimes: the opening words of the first line are added, as an unrimed refrain, after the eighth and thirteenth lines. [<F < *rondel* < *rond* round]

ron·del (ron′dəl, -del) *n.* A form of French verse consisting of 13 or 14 lines, in two stanzas of four and one of five or six lines, the first two lines being repeated, as a refrain, in the seventh and eighth lines, and again in the thirteenth and fourteenth. The names *rondeau* and *rondel* are often used interchangeably in English. [<F. See RONDEAU.]

ron·de·let (ron′də·let) *n.* A brief French verse form with a refrain, which generally consists of two or more words of the first line. [<OF, dim. of *rondel.* See RONDEAU.]

ron·do (ron′dō, ron·dō′) *n.* 1 *Music* A composition or movement having a main theme and several contrasting episodes, the former being repeated in its original key after each subordinate theme. 2 The musical setting of a rondeau. [<Ital., round]

Ron·dô·nia (rôn·dô′nyä) A federal territory of western Brazil; 1,381,877 square miles; capital, Porto Velho: formerly *Guaporé.*

ron·dure (ron′jər) *n.* Anything circular or spherical; a curve or swell. [<F *rondeur* roundness]

Rong·e·lap (rông′ə·läp) An atoll in the Ralik chain of the Marshall Islands; 35 miles long; 3 square miles. Also **Rong′e·lab.**

Rong·e·rik (rông′ə·rik) An atoll in the Ralik chain of the Marshall Islands; about 30 miles in circumference.

ron·ion (run′yən) *n. Obs.* A mangy or scabby animal or person. Also **ron′yon.** [<F *rogne* scab]

Rø̸n·ne (rœn′ə) A Danish city, chief port of Bornholm island.

ron·quil (ron′kil) *n.* A deep-water fish (family *Bathymasteridae)* of the North Pacific. [<Sp. *ronquillo,* dim. of *ronco* hoarse <L *raucus* hoarse]

Ron·sard (rôn·sàr′), **Pierre de,** 1524–85, French poet.

Rönt·gen (rent′gən, runt′-; *Ger.* rœnt′gən) See ROENTGEN.

rood (ro͞od) *n.* 1 A cross or crucifix; specifically, a crucifix or a representation of the Crucifixion over the altar screen of a church. 2 A square land measure, **square rood,** equivalent to one fourth of a statute acre, or 40 square rods. 3 A linear measure varying locally between six and eight yards. ◆ Homophone: *rude.* [OE *rōd* rod, measure of land, cross. Related to ROD.]

rood beam A beam over the entrance to a choir for supporting a cross or crucifix.

Roo·de·poort–Ma·rais·burg (rō′də·pôrt·mar′·is·bûrg, -pōrt-, ro͞o′-) A town of southern Transvaal province, Union of South Africa.

rood screen An enriched screen, usually surmounted by a rood, separating the choir presbytery from the nave.

roof (ro͞of, ro͝of) *n.* 1 The exterior upper covering of a building. 2 Any top covering, as of a car or oven. 3 A house; home. 4 The most elevated part of anything; top; summit. — *v.t.* To cover with or as with a roof. [OE *hrōf*]

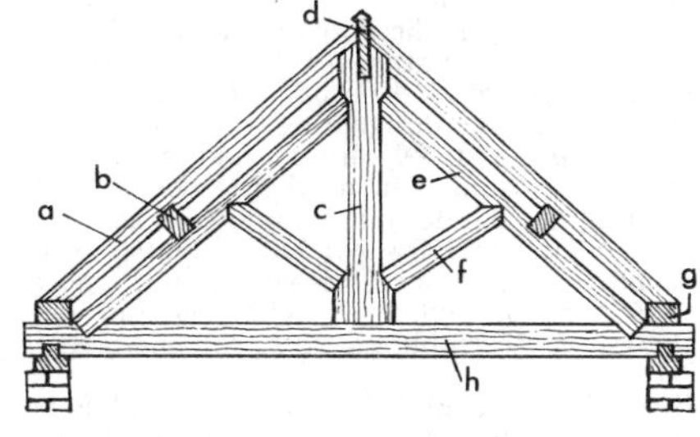

ROOF CONSTRUCTION–KINGPOST TYPE
a. Common rafters. *b.* Purlin. *c.* Kingpost. *d.* Ridge pole. *e.* Principal rafters. *f.* Struts. *g.* Pole plate. *h.* Tie beams.

roof·age (ro͞o′fij, ro͝of′ij) *n.* The material forming a roof; roofing.

roof·er (ro͞o′fər, ro͝of′ər) *n.* One who makes or repairs roofs.

roof garden A garden on the roof of a building; especially, a space on a roof used for public entertainments, restaurants, etc.

roof·ing (ro͞o′fing, ro͝of′ing) *n.* 1 Roofs collectively. 2 Material for roofs. 3 Shelter. 4 The act of covering with a roof.

roof·less (ro͞of′lis, ro͝of′-) *adj.* 1 Having no roof. 2 Destitute of shelter; homeless.

roof of the mouth The hard palate.

roof·tree (ro͞of′trē′, ro͝of′-) *n.* 1 The ridge pole of a roof. 2 The roof. 3 A home or dwelling.

rook[1] (ro͝ok) *n.* 1 An Old World corvine bird with the feathers of the face lost in the adult state; especially, the common *Corvus frugilegus,* noted for its gregariousness. 2 A sharper; cheat; trickster. — *v.t.* & *v.i.* To cheat; defraud. [OE *hrōc*]

rook[2] (ro͝ok) *n.* One of a pair of castle-shaped chessmen which can move any number of unoccupied squares parallel to the sides of the board; a castle. [<OF *roc* <Persian *rukh;* orig. meaning unknown]

rook·er·y (ro͝ok′ər·ē) *n. pl.* **·er·ies** 1 A colony or breeding place of rooks. 2 A breeding place of sea birds, seals, etc. 3 A rambling building; an old tenement densely populated.

rook·ie (ro͝ok′ē) *n. Slang* 1 A raw recruit in the army, police, or any other service. 2 A novice in professional baseball. [Prob. alter. of RECRUIT]

rook·y (ro͝ok′ē) *adj.* 1 Pertaining to rooks and their habits. 2 Gregarious. 3 Abounding in rooks.

room (ro͞om, ro͝om) *n.* 1 Extent of space considered with regard to its sufficiency for some implied or specified purpose; free or open space. 2 A space for occupancy or use enclosed on all sides, as in a building; an apartment; chamber. 3 Suitable or warrantable occasion; opportunity: *room* for doubt. See synonyms under PLACE. — *v.i.* To occupy a room; lodge. [OE *rūm* space]

room·er (ro͞o′mər, ro͝om′ər) *n.* A lodger; especially, one who rents a room and eats elsewhere.

room·ette (ro͞o·met′, ro͝om·et′) *n.* A compartment with a single bed in some railroad sleeping-cars.

room·ful (ro͞om′fo͝ol′, ro͝om′-) *n.* 1 As many or as much as a room will hold. 2 A number of persons present in a room considered collectively.

rooming house A house for roomers; lodging house.

room·mate (ro͞om′māt′, ro͝om′-) *n.* One who occupies a room with another or others.

room·y (ro͞o′mē, ro͝om′ē) *adj.* **room·i·er, room·i·est** Having abundant room; spacious. — **room′i·ly** *adv.* — **room′i·ness** *n.*

roon[1] (ro͞on) *adj. Scot.* Round.

roon[2] (ro͞on) *n. Scot.* A shred; border; strip of cloth.

roop (ro͞op) *n. Brit. Dial.* 1 An outcry; call. 2 Hoarseness. [OE *hrōp* clamor]

roor·back (ro͝or′bak) *n. U.S.* A fictitious report circulated for political purposes. [after *Roorback,* purported author of a (non-existent) book of travel, which was cited as authority for certain defamatory charges made against President Polk in the 1844 campaign]

roose (ro͞oz, rœz) *v.t. Scot.* To praise. — *n.* Praise. — **roos′er** *n.*

Roo·se·velt (rō′zə·velt, rōz′velt, -vəlt), **(Anna) Eleanor,** 1884–1962, *née* Roosevelt, U.S. lecturer, writer, and diplomat; wife of F. D. Roosevelt. — **Franklin Delano,** 1882–1945, president of the United States 1933–45; re-elected to fourth consecutive term 1944. — **Theodore,** 1858–1919, president of the United States 1901–09.

Roosevelt Dam A dam in the Salt River, central Arizona; 280 feet high; 1,125 feet long; completed 1911.

Roosevelt River A river in western Brazil, flowing 400 miles north to the Aripuaña; formerly *River of Doubt* (Portuguese *Río da Dúvida*): Spanish *Río Roosevelt, Río Teodoro.*

roost (ro͞ost) *n.* 1 A perch upon which fowls rest at night; also, any place where birds resort to spend the night. 2 Any temporary resting place. — *v.i.* 1 To sit or perch upon a roost. 2 To come to rest; settle. [OE *hrōst*]

roost·er (ro͞os′tər) *n.* The male of the chicken; cock. [<ROOST + -ER[1]]

roost·it (ro͞os′tit) *adj. Scot.* 1 Rusty. 2 Dry; parched.

root[1] (ro͞ot, ro͝ot) *n.* 1 The underground portion or descending axis of a plant, which absorbs moisture, obtains or stores nourishment, and provides support. It differs from the stem in that it branches irregularly and lacks joints or leaves. 2 Loosely, any underground growth, as a tuber or bulb. 3 One of certain other growths serving for attachment, support, etc., as in the ivy or mistletoe. 4 That from which anything derives origin, growth, or life and vigor: Money is the *root* of evil; Industry is the *root* of prosperity. 5 An antecedent; ancestor. 6 Some rootlike part of an organ or structure: the *root* of a tooth or nerve. 7 *Ling.* A morpheme serving as the common center or basic constituent element of a related group of words, as *know* in *unknown, knowledge, knowable,* and *knowingly.* A root to which affixes or other morphemes may be added directly is equivalent to a stem. 8 *Math.* A quantity that, taken a specified number of times as a factor, will give another quantity called its *power:* 2 is the fourth *root* of 16. The number of times the root is thus taken as a factor is called its *index,* and roots are named from the indices, the words **square root** and **cube root** being often used for *second* and *third root.* 9 A tone on which a chord is built up. — *v.i.* 1 To put forth roots and begin to grow; take root. 2 To be or become firmly fixed or established. — *v.t.* 3 To fix or implant by or as by roots. 4 To pull, dig, or tear up by or as by the roots; extirpate; eradicate: with *up* or *out.* [OE *rōt* <ON *rōt*]

root[2] (ro͞ot, ro͝ot) *v.t.* 1 To turn up or dig with the snout or nose, as swine. — *v.i.* 2 To turn up the earth with the snout. 3 To search for something; rummage. 4 To work hard; toil. [OE *wrōtan* root up < *wrōt* snout]

root[3] (ro͞ot, ro͝ot) *v.i. U.S. Colloq.* To cheer for or encourage a contestant: with *for:* He *rooted* for Harvard. [Prob. var. of ROUT[3]]

Root (ro͞ot, ro͝ot), **Elihu,** 1845–1937, U. S. lawyer and statesman.

root beer A beverage made with yeast and the extracts of several roots.

root climber Any plant that climbs by means of adventitious roots developed from stems.

root·er[1] (ro͞o′tər, ro͝ot′ər) *n.* One who or that which takes root.

root·er[2] (ro͞o′tər, ro͝ot′ər) *n.* One who or that which roots, as a swine, or tears up as by rooting; a destroyer; eradicator.

root·er[3] (ro͞o′tər, ro͝ot′ər) *n. U.S. Colloq.* One who gives encouragement, as by applauding.

root hair *Bot.* Hairlike outgrowths of plant roots, having an absorbent and protective function.

root·less (ro͞ot′lis, ro͝ot′-) *adj.* Without roots.

root·let (ro͞ot′lit, ro͝ot′-) *n.* A small root.

root sheath The tough membrane covering the root portion of a hair. See illustration under HAIR.

root·stalk (ro͞ot′stôk′, ro͝ot′-) *n. Bot.* An underground rootlike stem; a rhizome.

root·stock (ro͞ot′stok′, ro͝ot′-) *n.* **1** A rhizome. **2** Original source; origin.
root·y (ro͞o′tē, ro͝ot′ē) *adj.* **root·i·er, root·i·est** **1** Full of or consisting of roots. **2** Resembling roots. **— root′i·ness** *n.*
rope (rōp) *n.* **1** A construction of twisted fibers, as of hemp, cotton, flax, etc., so intertwined in several strands as to form a thick cord. **2** A collection of things plaited or united in a line. **3** A slimy or glutinous filament or thread. **4** A cord or halter used in hanging; hence, execution or death by strangling or hanging. **5** A lasso. **— to give (one) plenty of rope** To allow (a person) to pursue unchecked a course that will end in disaster. **— to know the ropes** To be familiar with all the conditions in any sphere of activity; hence, to be sophisticated in the ways of the world. **—** *v.* **roped, rop·ing** *v.t.* **1** To tie or fasten with or as with rope. **2** To enclose, border, or divide with a rope: usually with *off*: He *roped* off the arena. **3** To catch with a lasso. **4** *Colloq.* To deceive; take in: with *in.* **—** *v.i.* **5** To become drawn out or extended into a filament or thread. [OE *rāp*]
rope·a·ble (rōp′ə·bəl) *adj. Austral.* Violently angry; irascible.
rope band Roband.
rope–dancer (rōp′dan′sər, -dän′-) *n.* One who performs on the tightrope. **— rope′–danc′ing** *n.*
rope ferry A set of ropes overhanging a stream or defile, over which supplies and equipment may be pulled by a towline.
rope ladder A ladder made of ropes or with rope sides and wooden or other rounds.
rop·er·y (rō′pər·ē) *n.* **1** A ropewalk. **2** *Archaic* Roguery.
rope's end **1** A short piece of rope used for flogging. **2** A hangman's noose.
rope·walk (rōp′wôk′) *n.* A long alley formerly used for the spinning of rope yarn: now in general superseded by some structure using improved machinery.
rope–walk·er (rōp′wô′kər) *n.* One who performs on the tightrope.
rop·y (rō′pē) *adj.* **rop·i·er, rop·i·est** **1** That may be drawn into threads, as a glutinous substance; stringy. **2** Resembling ropes or cordage. **— rop′i·ly** *adv.* **— rop′i·ness** *n.*
roque (rōk) *n.* A form of croquet requiring more skill than the ordinary game. [Aphetic alter. of CROQUET]
Roque·fort (rōk′fərt, *Fr.* rôk·fôr′) A village in south central France. Also **Roquefort–sur–Soul·zon** (-sür·so͞ol·zôn′).
Roquefort cheese A strong cheese with a blue mold (*Penicillium roqueforti*) made from ewe's and goat's milk at Roquefort, France.
roqu·e·laure (rok′ə·lôr, rok′lôr, -lōr) *n.* A form of short cloak worn by men in the 18th century: also spelled *rokelay.* [after Duc de *Roquelaure*, 1656–1738, French nobleman]
ro·quet (rō·kā′) *v.t.* & *v.i.* **·queted** (-kād′), **·quet·ing** (-kā′ing) In croquet, to strike (another player's ball). **—** *n.* The act of roqueting. [See ROQUE]
Ro·rai·ma (rō·rī′mä), **Mount** A peak at the junction of the Brazil–Venezuela–British Guiana boundaries; 9,219 feet.
Ro·rer (rôr′ər, rō′rər), **Sarah Tyson,** 1849–1937, *née* Heston, U. S. home economist and writer.
ror·qual (rôr′kwəl) *n.* Any of a genus (*Balaenoptera*) of whales of the Atlantic and Pacific oceans; especially, *B. physalis* of the North Atlantic: also called *finback, finback whale.* [<F <Norw. *röyrkval*]

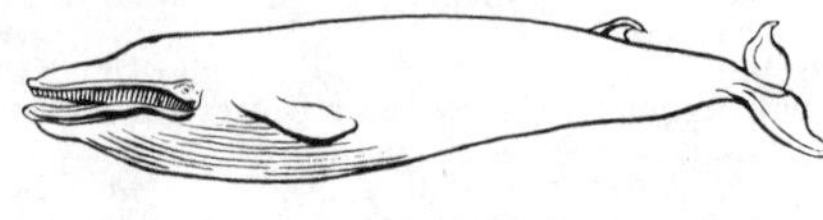

RORQUAL
(About 60 feet in length)

Ror·schach test (rôr′shäk, -shäkh, rōr′-) *Psychol.* A test in which personality characteristics are made accessible to analysis by the subject's interpretation of the nature and meaning of a series of standard inkblot patterns. [after Hermann *Rorschach*, 1884–1922, Swiss psychiatrist]
Ro·sa (rō′zə) A feminine personal name. See ROSE.
Ro·sa (rō′zä), **Monte** The highest mountain group of the Pennine Alps on the Swiss–Italian border; its highest peak, 15,216 feet, is the second highest in the Alps.
Ro·sa (rô′zä), **Salvator,** 1615–73, Italian painter.
ro·sa·ceous (rō·zā′shəs) *adj.* **1** *Bot.* Of, pertaining to, or designating the rose family (*Rosaceae*) of trees, shrubs, and herbs: it is widely distributed in northern temperate regions, and includes many important genera of ornamental and fruit–yielding plants, as the apple, pear, quince, peach, plum, cherry, hawthorn, strawberry, blackberry, and raspberry. **2** Resembling a rose; rosy. [<L *rosaceus*]
Ro·sa·lie (rō′zə·lē) A feminine personal name. Also **Ro·sa·li·a** (rō·zā′lē·ə). [<L, little rose]
Ros·a·lind (roz′ə·lind) A feminine personal name. [<L, pretty rose]
— Rosalind In Shakespeare's *As You Like It,* the heroine, daughter of the banished duke, who assumes male attire.
Ros·a·mond (roz′ə·mənd) A feminine personal name. Also *Fr.* **Rose·monde** (rōz·mônd′), **Ro·sa·mun·da** (*Lat.* rō′zə·mun′də, *Sp.* rō′sä·mo͞on′·dä). [<L, rose of the world]
ro·san·i·line (rō·zan′ə·lin, -lēn) *n. Chem.* **1** A colorless, crystalline organic compound, $C_{20}H_{21}ON_3$, having basic properties, obtained from aniline by treatment with reagents, as arsenic acid, nitric acid, and stannic chloride. It forms reddish salts, used as dyestuffs. **2** Some salt of this base used as a dyestuff, as fuchsin or rosein. [<ROSE[1] + ANILINE]
Ro·sa·rio (rō·sä′ryō) A port on the Paraná in Santa Fé province, Argentina.
ro·sa·ry (rō′zə·rē) *n. pl.* **·ries** **1** *Eccl.* **a** A series of prayers, consisting in its common form **(Dominican rosary)** of fifteen decades, each containing ten Aves preceded by a paternoster and followed by the Gloria Patri, and each related to a mystery or event in the life of Christ or the Virgin Mary which is contemplated during its recitation. **b** A string of beads for keeping count of the prayers thus recited. **2** A garden or bed of roses. **3** A chaplet or garland, as of roses. **4** A collection of literary selections. [<LL *rosarium* a rose garden <L *rosa* a rose]
Ros·cius (rosh′əs), **Gallus Quintus,** died 62? B.C., Roman comic actor. **— Ros′cian** *adj.*
Ros·coe (ros′kō), **Sir Henry Enfield,** 1833–1915, English chemist.
Ros·com·mon (ros·kom′ən) A county of eastern Connacht province, Ireland; 951 square miles; county town, Roscommon.
rose[1] (rōz) *n.* **1** A hardy, erect or climbing shrub (genus *Rosa*) grown in many varieties, with rodlike, prickly stems. In cultivation the stamens are transformed into petals and the flowers become double. It is the national flower of England and the State flower of New York, North Dakota, and Iowa. **2** The flower, having 5, or rarely 4, sepals. **3** Any one of various other plants or flowers having some real or fancied likeness to the true rose. **4** A light pinkish red, like the color of many roses. **5** An ornamental knot, as of ribbon or lace; a rosette. **6** A perforated cap, plate, or nozzle at the end of a pipe, for throwing water in a fine spray. **7** A compass rose. **8** A form in which gems, especially diamonds, are often cut, characterized by a flat base with a hemispherical upper surface covered with small facets; also, a diamond so cut. **9** Erysipelas. **— golden rose** A rose of wrought gold, blessed by the pope and presented, usually to a Roman Catholic sovereign, as a distinguished honor. **— under the rose** In secret. See SUB ROSA. **—** *v.t.* **rosed, ros·ing** To cause to blush; redden; flush. [OE <L *rosa* <Gk. *rhodon*]
rose[2] (rōz) Past tense of RISE.
Rose (rōz) A feminine personal name. Also **Ro·sa** (rō′zə; *Fr.* rō·zä′, *Ger.* rō′zä, *Ital.* rô′zä, *Sp.* rō′sä). [<L, rose]
rose acacia A locust tree (*Robinia hispida*) of the SE United States, bearing racemes of large rose or pale–purple flowers.
ro·se·ate (rō′zē·it, -āt) *adj.* **1** Of a rose color. **2** Rosy; rose–colored; hence, optimistic. [<L *roseus*] **— ro′se·ate·ly** *adv.*
roseate spoonbill A tropical American wading bird (*Ajaia ajaja*) having a bare head and throat and pink plumage.
rose·bay (rōz′bā′) *n.* **1** Any rhododendron, especially *Rhododendron maximum.* **2** The oleander. **3** The willow herb.
rose beetle **1** The goldsmith beetle. **2** The rose chafer.
Rose·ber·y (rōz′bər·ē), **Earl of,** 1847–1929, Archibald Philip Primrose, English statesman and author.
rose–breast·ed grosbeak (rōz′bres′tid) See under GROSBEAK.
rose·bud (rōz′bud′) *n.* **1** The bud of a rose. **2** A young girl; a debutante.
rose bush A rose–bearing shrub or vine.
rose campion **1** Any species of *Lychnis,* especially *L. coronaria.* **2** The corncockle.
rose chafer A hairy, fawn–colored beetle (*Macrodactylus subspinosus*) injurious to roses: also called *rose beetle.* Also **rose bug.** For illustration see INSECTS (injurious).
rose cold *Pathol.* A variety of hay fever, assumed to be caused by rose pollen. Also **rose fever.**
rose–col·ored (rōz′kul′ərd) *adj.* Pink or crimson, as a rose. **— to see through rose–colored glasses** To see things in an unduly favorable light; to look too much or only on the bright side. Compare COULEUR DE ROSE.
Rose·crans (rōz′kranz), **William Starke,** 1819–1898, U. S. general.
rose–cross (rōz′krôs′, -kros′) *n.* The symbol of the Rosicrucians, a rose and cross combined in some form.
rose·fish (rōz′fish′) *n. pl.* **·fish** or **·fish·es** An orange–red scorpaenoid food fish (*Sebastes marinus*) of the North Atlantic.
rose geranium A cultivated geranium (*Pelargonium capitatum*) with rose–scented leaves and dense clusters of rose–purple flowers, grown extensively in South Africa.
Rose Island Easternmost island in the American Samoa group.
rose·mal·low (rōz′mal′ō) *n.* **1** The hibiscus: also called *mallow rose.* **2** The hollyhock.
rose·mar·y (rōz′mâr′ē) *n. pl.* **·mar·ies** An evergreen, fragrant shrub (*Rosmarinus officinalis*) of the mint family of southern Europe and western Asia, with usually blue flowers: cultivated for its stimulating and refreshing perfume, for an oil obtained from it, and for use in cookery. [Alter. of L *rosmarinus* < *ros* dew + *marinus* marine; infl. by *rose, Mary*]
rose moss A garden variety of portulaca (*Portulaca grandiflora*).
Ro·sen·wald (rō′zən·wôld), **Julius,** 1862–1932, U. S. businessman and philanthropist.
rose of Jericho A small annual (*Anastatica hierochuntica*) growing in desert places from Syria to Algeria, which rolls up when dry and expands again when moist: also called *resurrection plant, Jericho rose.*
rose of Sharon **1** In Scripture (*Canticles* ii 1), an unknown flower, perhaps the autumn crocus or the narcissus. **2** The shrub–althea. **3** A species (*Hypericum calycinum*) of St. Johnswort with large, yellow flowers.
ro·se·o·la (rō·zē′ə·lə) *n. Pathol.* A rose–colored rash appearing on the skin. Also **rose rash.** [<NL, dim. of L *roseus* rosy]
rose quartz A translucent to semitransparent variety of quartz, pink or rose in color and often asteriated: used for ornament, as a gemstone, etc.
ros·et (roz′it) *n. Scot.* Resin.
Ro·set·ta (rō·zet′ə) **1** The western branch of the Nile in its delta, Lower Egypt. Ancient **Bol·bi·ti·ne** (bol′bə·tī′nē). **2** A town on the Rosetta.
Ro·set·ta stone (rō·zet′ə) A tablet of basalt containing an inscription in two forms of Egyptian hieroglyphics (demotic and hieratic) and in Greek, found near Rosetta, Egypt, in 1799. It supplied Champollion with the key to the ancient inscriptions of Egypt.
ro·sette (rō·zet′) *n.* **1** An ornament or badge having some resemblance to a rose; specifically, a painted or sculptured architectural ornament with parts circularly arranged. **2** A ribbon badge worn in the lapel buttonhole of civilian clothes to indicate possession of a certain military decoration. **3** A ribbon decoration shaped like a full–blown

ROSETTE

or double rose and made of gathered or pleated silk, lace, etc. 4 A flowerlike cluster or combination of leaves, organs, parts, or markings, arranged in circles, as in certain plants. [<F, little rose]

rose·wa·ter (rōz′wô′tər, -wot′ər) *n.* A fragrant toilet and pharmaceutical water made variously by the distillation of rose petals or rose oil with water. —*adj.* 1 Made with or resembling rosewater. 2 Extremely or affectedly delicate or sentimental: *rosewater* philosophy.

rose window A circular window filled with tracery, called, when this takes the form of spokes, a *wheel window.*

rose·wood (rōz′wŏŏd′) *n.* 1 A hard, close-grained, dark-colored, fragrant wood yielded by different Brazilian trees of the genus *Dalbergia,* etc., especially that produced by *D. nigra,* the most highly prized for cabinet work. Some species are said to be rose-scented when fresh. 2 Any of various other woods in some way resembling the true rosewoods. 3 Any tree yielding such a wood.

Rosh Ha·sha·na (rosh hə·shä′nə, rōsh) The Jewish New Year, celebrated on Tisri 1st and 2nd (September–early October). Also **Rosh Ha·sho′nah** (-shō′-). [<Hebrew *rōsh* head of + *hash-shānāh* the year]

Ro·si·cru·cian (rō′zə·krōō′shən, roz′ə-) *n.* One who is a member of an international fraternity, said to have originated in Egypt, and devoted to the practical application of an occult philosophy to human relationship. See ILLUMINATI. —*adj.* Of or pertaining to this society, its members, or its doctrines. [<L *rosae crucis* roses of the cross; said to be the trans. of the name of Christian *Rosenkranz,* 1387–1484, a German to whom the founding of this order has been attributed] —**Ro′si·cru′cian·ism** *n.*

ros·in (roz′in) *n.* 1 Resin. 2 The hard, amber-colored resin forming the residue after the distillation of oil of turpentine from crude turpentine; colophony. —*v.t.* To apply rosin to. [Var. of RESIN] —**ros′in·y** *adj.*

Ros·i·nan·te (roz′ə·nan′tē) See ROCINANTE.

rosin oil Retinol.

ros·in·weed (roz′in·wēd′) *n.* 1 A coarse perennial herb (genus *Silphium*) of the composite family, with copious resinous juice, growing in the central and western United States. 2 The compass plant.

ro·so·lio (rō·zō′lyō) *n.* A cordial made from raisins and brandy in the Mediterranean countries. [<Ital. <Med. L *ros solis* (<L *ros* dew + *solis* of the sun) sundew, from which it was once extracted]

Ross (rôs), **Betsy,** 1752–1836, American patriot; made first American flag, 1777. —**Sir James Clark,** 1800–62, English Arctic explorer; discovered the north magnetic pole in 1831. —**Sir John,** 1777–1856, Scottish Arctic explorer; uncle of the preceding. —**Sir Ronald,** 1857–1932, English physician; first investigator of malaria-bearing mosquitoes.

Ross and Crom·ar·ty (krom′ər·tē, krum′-) A maritime county of NW Scotland; 3,089 square miles; county town, Dingwall.

Ross Dependency An uninhabited, ice-covered region of the Antarctic Zone under the jurisdiction of New Zealand; 175,000 square miles.

Ros·set·ti (rō·set′ē, -zet′ē), **Christina Georgina,** 1830–94, English poet; sister of Dante Gabriel. —**Dante Gabriel,** 1828–82, English painter and poet.

Ros·si (rôs′sē), **Bruno,** born 1905, Italian physicist.

Ros·si·ni (rôs·sē′nē), **Gioacchino Antonio,** 1792–1868, Italian composer.

Ross Island 1 An island off the NE tip of Palmer Peninsula, Antarctica; 39 nautical miles long, 31 nautical miles wide. 2 A volcanic island in the western Ross Sea off Victoria Land, Antarctica, on which Mount Erebus is located; 43 nautical miles long, 45 nautical miles wide.

Ros·si·ya (ros·sē′yä) The Russian name for RUSSIA.

Ross Sea An inlet of the South Pacific in Antarctica south of New Zealand.

Ross Shelf Ice The extensive area of shelf ice in Antarctica, occupying the southern part of the Ross Sea; about 400 miles wide on its seaward side. Also called **Ross Barrier.**

Ros·tand (rôs·täṅ′), **Edmond,** 1869?–1918, French dramatist and poet.

ros·tel·late (ros′tə·lāt, -lit) *adj.* Having a small beak or rostellum. [<NL *rostellatus*]

ros·tel·lum (ros·tel′əm) *n. pl* **·tel·la** (-tel′ə) 1 *Bot.* A small, beaklike structure developed from the stigma of an orchid. 2 *Zool.* The hooked scolex of a tapeworm. [<L, dim. of *rostrum* beak]

ros·ter (ros′tər) *n.* 1 A list of officers and men enrolled for duty; also, a list of active military organizations. 2 Any list of names. [<Du. *rooster* list]

Ros·tock (ros′tok, *Ger.* rôs′tôk) 1 A port on the Baltic in Rostock district, northern East Germany. 2 A district of East Germany, formerly part of the former state of Mecklenburg; 2,722 square miles.

Ros·tov (ros′tof′) A city in southern Russian S.F.S.R., on the Don near its mouth on the Sea of Azov. Also **Ros·tov′-on-Don′** (-dôn′).

Ro·stov·tzeff (ro·stôf′tsəf), **Michael Ivanovich,** 1870–1952, U. S. historian and archeologist born in Russia.

ros·tral (ros′trəl) *adj.* 1 Of or pertaining to a rostrum. 2 Having a rostrum, or beaklike process; beaked: often used in combination, as in *curvirostral,* having a crossed or curved-down beak. Also **ros′trate** (-trāt). [<LL *rostralis*]

ros·trum (ros′trəm) *n. pl.* **·trums** or **·tra** (-trə) 1 A pulpit or platform. 2 *pl.* **ros·tra** The orators' platform in the Roman forum: embellished with the beaks of the Latin ships captured 338 B.C. 3 A beak or snout; a beaklike process or part. 4 One of various beaklike parts, as the beak or prow of an ancient war galley. [<L *rostrum* beak]

ROSTRUM (*def. 4*)

ros·y (rō′zē) *adj.* **ros·i·er, ros·i·est** 1 Like a rose; rose-red; blooming; blushing. 2 Figuratively, bright, pleasing, or flattering. 3 Made of or ornamented with roses. 4 Auguring success; favorable: *rosy* predictions. 5 Optimistic. —**ros′i·ly** *adv.* —**ros′i·ness** *n.*

rot (rot) *v.* **rot·ted, rot·ting** *v.i.* 1 To undergo decomposition; decompose; decay. 2 To fall or pass by decaying: with *away, off,* etc. 3 To become morally rotten. —*v.t.* 4 To cause to decompose; decay. 5 To ret. See synonyms under DECAY, PUTREFY. —*n.* 1 That which is rotten, or the process of rotting. 2 A wasting disease, as of the lungs. 3 A parasitic disease affecting sheep and other domestic animals. 4 A form of decay in plants, caused by fungi and bacteria. 5 *Colloq.* Trashy and nonsensical opinions or expressions; twaddle; bosh. —*interj.* Nonsense; bosh. [OE *rotian*]

ro·ta (rō′tə) *n.* 1 A roll of names, giving order of duty; a roster. 2 A routine. 3 A wheel. [<L, wheel]

Ro·ta (rō′tə) *n.* In the Roman Catholic Church, an ecclesiastical court composed of ten prelates or auditors, subject only to papal authority, and serving as a court of final appeal: also known as *Sacra Romana Rota.*

Ro·ta (rō′tä) An island in the southern Marianas group; 33 square miles.

Ro·tar·i·an (rō·târ′ē·ən) *n.* A member of a Rotary Club. —*adj.* Of or pertaining to the organization of Rotary Clubs or to their members. —**Ro·tar′i·an·ism** *n.*

ro·ta·ry (rō′tər·ē) *adj.* 1 Turning around its axis, like a wheel, or so constructed as to turn thus. 2 Having some part that so turns: a *rotary* press. [<LL *rotarius* < *rota* wheel]

Rotary Club A club belonging to an international association of clubs, **Rotary International,** whose aim is to improve civic service, and whose motto is "Service."

rotary engine 1 An engine in which rotary motion is directly produced without reciprocating parts, as in a steam turbine: distinguished from *reciprocating engine.* 2 In internal-combustion engines, a radial engine revolving about a fixed crankshaft.

rotary harrow *Agric.* A harrow with many spikes set along the rim of a wheel which turns on a horizontal axis as it is pulled along the ground.

rotary motor See under MOTOR.

rotary plow *Agric.* A set of plowshares arranged on the rim of a rotating, power-driven shaft.

rotary press A printing press using curved type plates which revolve against the paper.

ro·tate (rō′tāt) *v.t.* & *v.i.* **·tat·ed, ·tat·ing** 1 To turn or cause to turn on or as on its axis. 2 To alternate in a definite order or succession. See synonyms under REVOLVE. —*adj.* 1 Wheel-shaped; circular, as the corollas of certain flowers. 2 Forming a circle around a part, as spines or hairs. [<L *rotatus,* pp. of *rotare* turn < *rota*] —**ro′tat·a·ble** *adj.*

ro·tat·ed (rō′tā·tid) *adj.* 1 Turned around. 2 Rotate.

ro·ta·tion (rō·tā′shən) *n.* 1 The act or state of rotating; rotary motion. 2 Change by alternation; order of succession, variation, or sequence: *rotation* of crops or office. 3 The period represented by the age of a forest, or a part of a forest, at the time when it is cut, or intended to be cut. —**ro·ta′tion·al** *adj.*

ro·ta·tive (rō′tə·tiv) *adj.* Pertaining to or causing rotation; turning.

ro·ta·tor (rō′tā·tər) *n.* 1 One who or that which rotates or causes rotation. 2 *pl.* **ro·ta·to·res** (rō′tə·tôr′ēz, -tō′rēz) *Anat.* A muscle that rolls or rotates a part upon its axis. [<L]

Ro·ta·to·ri·a (rō′tə·tôr′ē·ə, -tō′rē·ə) See ROTIFER.

ro·ta·to·ry (rō′tə·tôr′ē, -tō′rē) *adj.* 1 Having, pertaining to, or producing rotation. 2 Following in succession. 3 Alternating or recurring.

rotche (roch) *n.* A bird, the dovekie. Also **rotch.** [Var. of *rotge* <Du. *rotje* petrel]

rote[1] (rōt) *n.* 1 Mechanical routine. 2 Repetition of words as a means of learning them, with slight attention to the sense. —**by rote** Mechanically; without intelligent attention: to learn *by rote.* [Var. of ROUTE]

rote[2] (rōt) *n. Rare* The roar of the surf. [Cf. ON *rōt* breaking of waves]

ro·te·none (rō′tə·nōn) *n. Chem.* A white crystalline substance, $C_{23}H_{22}O_6$, the effective principle in insecticides and fish poisons, obtained from the roots of various plants, especially an Amazonian tree (genus *Lonchocarpus*) and the Indian derris. [Origin unknown]

rot·gut whisky (rot′gut′) *U.S.* An inferior raw whisky. Also **rot′gut′.**

Roth·er·ham (roth′ər·əm) A county borough in the West Riding, southern Yorkshire, England.

Roth·schild (rôth′child, *Ger.* rōt′shilt) A family of European bankers, of whom the first, **Meyer Amschel,** 1743–1812, established a bank in Frankfort on the Main. His sons opened branches: **James,** 1792–1868, at Paris; **Karl,** 1788–1855, at Naples; **Nathan Meyer,** 1777–1836, at London; **Salomon,** 1774–1855, at Vienna.

ro·ti·fer (rō′tə·fər) *n.* One of a division (*Rotifera*) of many-celled, microscopic, aquatic organisms usually found in stagnant fresh water, having rings of cilia which in motion resemble revolving wheels; a wheel animalcule. Some authorities place the *Rotifera* in a separate class or phylum, *Rotatoria.* [<NL <L *rota* wheel + *ferre* bear] —**ro·tif·er·al** (rō·tif′ər·əl), **ro·tif′er·ous** *adj.*

ro·ti·form (rō′tə·fôrm) *adj.* Shaped like a wheel; rotate. [<L *rota* wheel + -FORM]

ro·tis·se·rie (rō·tis′ə·rē′) *n.* 1 A restaurant where patrons select uncooked food and have it roasted and served. 2 A shop where food is roasted and sold. 3 A rotating device for roasting meat, etc. [<F < *rôtir* roast]

rot·l (rot′l) *n. pl.* **ar·tal** (är′täl) A weight used in Moslem countries, varying in different localities between one and five pounds. [< Arabic *ratl*]

ro·to·chute (rō′tə·shōōt′) *n. Aeron.* A long, dartlike, high-altitude parachute equipped with a propeller having rapidly rotating blades for breaking the speed of descent. [<L *rota* wheel + CHUTE]

ro·to·graph (rō′tə·graf, -gräf) *n.* One of a series of photographs printed from a developed roll of sensitized paper that bears the images. [<L *rota* wheel + -GRAPH]

ro·to·gra·vure (rō′tə·grə·vyŏŏr′, -grāv′yər) *n.* **1** A picture engraved on a cylindrical printing surface and run through a rotary press that prints both sides of the paper at the same time. **2** The process of making such pictures. [<L *rota* wheel + GRAVURE]

ro·tor (rō′tər) *n.* **1** *Electr.* The portion of an alternating-current motor which revolves. **2** A revolving part of a machine, as the wheel or wheels of a turbine. Compare STATOR. **3** *Aeron.* The horizontally rotating unit of a helicopter. [Contraction of ROTATOR]

rotor ship A vessel propelled by rotors operated by wind power but fitted with auxiliary power for propulsion when the wind fails.

rot·ten (rot′n) *adj.* **1** Decomposed by natural process; putrid. **2** Unsound; liable to break. **3** Untrustworthy; treacherous; also, venal; corrupt. **4** Afflicted with the rot, as sheep. **5** *Colloq.* Worthless. [<ON *rotinn*] — **rot′·ten·ly** *adv.* — **rot′ten·ness** *n.*

Synonyms: carious, corrupt, decayed, deceitful, decomposed, defective, fetid, offensive, putrefied, putrescent, putrid, tainted, treacherous, unsound. See BAD. *Antonyms*: complete, fresh, healthful, healthy, perfect, pure, sound, sweet, untainted, wholesome.

rotten borough **1** Any English borough prior to 1832 having few voters, yet entitled to send a member to Parliament. **2** Any election district or political unit no longer having sufficient population to justify the representation alloted to it.

rot·ter (rot′ər) *n. Slang* A scoundrel; a worthless scamp; any objectionable person.

rot·ten·stone (rot′n·stōn′) *n.* A soft, friable rock, consisting largely of siliceous particles, used for polishing: also called *tripoli.*

Rot·ter·dam (rot′ər·dam) The largest port of the Netherlands, in the western part.

Ro·tu·ma (rō·tōō′mə) An island dependency of Fiji; 18 square miles.

ro·tund (rō·tund′) *adj.* **1** Rounded out; spherical; plump. **2** Full-toned, as a voice or utterance; in style, using sonorous words. **3** Complete; entire. **4** Circular, or nearly so; orbicular. See synonyms under ROUND. [<L *rotundus* < *rota* wheel. Doublet of ROUND.] — **ro·tund′ly** *adv.* — **ro·tund′ness** *n.*

ro·tun·da (rō·tun′də) *n.* A circular building or an interior hall, surmounted with a dome. [<Ital. *rotonda* <L *rotunda,* fem. of *rotundus.* See ROTUND.]

ro·tun·di·ty (rō·tun′də·tē) *n.* **1** The condition of being rotund; sphericity. **2** A protuberance.

ro·ture (rō·tür′) *n. French* **1** A plebeian condition or rank. **2** In French-Canadian law, a tenure of feudal lands by a constituted rent, without feudal duties and charges.

ro·tu·rier (rō·tü·ryā′) *n. French* **1** A person without rank; plebeian or peasant. **2** In French-Canadian law, one who holds lands by the tenure of roture.

Rou·ault (rōō·ō′), **Georges,** 1871–1958, French painter.

Rou·baix (rōō·be′) A city in northern France, NE of Lille; produces most of France's woolen textiles.

rou·ble (rōō′bəl) See RUBLE.

rouche (rōōsh) See RUCHE.

rou·é (rōō·ā′) *n.* A sensualist; debauchee. [<F, jaded, orig. pp. of *rouer* break on the wheel, beat severely < *roue* wheel <L *rota*; from the appearance of a debauchee]

Rou·en (rōō·än′) A city on the Seine in Normandy, northern France; noted for its cathedral; scene of the burning of Joan of Arc.

rouge (rōōzh) *n.* **1** Any cosmetic used for coloring the cheeks or lips pink or red. **2** A ferric oxide used in polishing metals and glass. — *v.* **rouged, roug·ing** *v.t.* To color, as the face, with rouge. — *v.i.* To apply rouge. [<F, red <L *rubeus* ruby]

rouge et noir (rōōzh′ e nwär′) A gambling game played with cards on a table having four diamond-shaped figures, two red and two black. See TRENTE-ET-QUARANTE. [<F, red and black]

Rou·get de l'Isle (rōō·zhe′ də lēl′), **Claude Joseph,** 1760–1836, French poet; author and composer of the *Marseillaise.*

rough (ruf) *adj.* **1** Having an uneven surface; having small inequalities on the surface; not smooth or polished: *rough* stone. **2** Coarse in texture; shaggy; also, disordered or ragged; shabby: said of dress or appearance: a *rough* suit, a *rough* shock of hair. **3** Having the surface broken; uneven: a *rough* country. **4** Characterized by rude or violent action: *rough* sports. **5** *Naut.* Boisterous or tempestuous; stormy: a *rough* passage. **6** Characterized by harshness of spirit; brutal. **7** Lacking the finish and polish bestowed by art or culture; unpolished; crude. **8** Done or made hastily and without attention to details; approximate. **9** *Phonet.* Uttered with an aspiration; aspirated: a *rough* breathing. **10** Harsh to the ear; grating; inharmonious: *rough* sounds. — *n.* **1** A low, rude, and violent fellow; a ruffian; a rowdy. **2** A crude, incomplete, or unpolished object, material, or condition. **3** Any part of a golf course on which tall grass, bushes, etc., grow. **4** A spike for insertion in a horseshoe, to prevent slipping. — *v.t.* **1** To make rough; roughen. **2** To treat roughly; specifically, in football, to treat (a player) with needless and intentional violence. **3** To make, cut, or sketch roughly: with *in* or *out*: to *rough* in the details of a plan. — *v.i.* **4** To become rough. **5** To behave roughly. — **to rough it** To live under rough, hard, or impoverished conditions; also, to camp out or travel in a rough manner; rusticate. — *adv.* In a rude manner; roughly. ◆ Homophone: *ruff.* [OE *rūh*] — **rough′ly** *adv.* — **rough′ness** *n.*

Synonyms (adj.) coarse, craggy, harsh, jagged, ragged, rude, rugged, shaggy, uneven, unfinished, unhewn, unpolished. See AWKWARD, BLUFF. *Antonyms*: bland, even, glossy, level, plain, polished, sleek, smooth.

rough·age (ruf′ij) *n.* **1** Any coarse or tough substance. **2** Food material containing a high percentage of indigestible constituents, as cellulose.

rough-and-read·y (ruf′ən·red′ē) *adj.* **1** Characterized by or acting with rude but effective promptness. **2** Unpolished but good enough.

rough-and-tum·ble (ruf′ən·tum′bəl) *adj.* **1** Disregarding all rules: said of a certain kind of fighting. **2** Scrambling; disorderly. — *n.* **1** A fight disregarding procedure according to rule, or in which anything goes; also, a scuffle. **2** Rough or adventurous existence.

rough breathing See under BREATHING.

rough-cast (ruf′kast′, -käst′) *v.t.* **-cast, -cast·ing** **1** To shape or prepare in a preliminary or incomplete form. **2** To roughen the surface of (pottery) before firing. **3** To coat, as a wall, with coarse plaster, and cover with thin mortar by dashing it on. — *n.* **1** Very coarse plaster for the outside of buildings. **2** A rude model; the form of a thing in its first rough stage. — **rough′-cast′er** *n.*

rough-draft (ruf′draft′, -dräft′) *v.t.* To make a rough or unfinished draft of; design or sketch hastily, as a plan or discourse.

rough-draw (ruf′drô′) *v.t.* **-drew, -drawn, -draw·ing** To sketch hastily or crudely.

rough-dry (ruf′drī′) *v.t.* **-dried, -dry·ing** To dry without ironing, as washed clothes.

rough·en (ruf′ən) *v.t.* & *v.i.* To make or become rough.

rough·er (ruf′ər) *n.* One who makes things in the rough.

rough-hew (ruf′hyōō′) *v.t.* **-hewed, -hewed** or **-hewn, -hew·ing** **1** To hew or shape roughly or irregularly or without smoothing. **2** To make crudely; rough-cast.

rough-house (ruf′hous′) *Slang n.* A noisy, boisterous or violent game or disturbance; rough play, especially within a room or house. — *v.* **-housed, -hous·ing** *v.i.* To make a disturbance; engage in horseplay or violence. — *v.t.* To handle or treat roughly but without hostile intent.

rough·ie (ruf′ē) *n. Scot.* **1** Brushwood or heath for fuel; a dead and fallen branch. **2** A kind of torch. **3** A clogged wick.

rough-leg·ged hawk (ruf′leg′id, -legd′) A large hawk (*Buteo lagopus sanctijohannis*) of Alaska and Canada, having the legs feathered all the way to the toes.

rough·neck (ruf′nek′) *n. U.S. Slang* A rowdy.

rough-rid·er (ruf′rī′dər) *n. U.S.* **1** One skilled in breaking broncos or performing dangerous feats in horsemanship. **2** A western cowboy.

Rough Riders The 1st U.S. Volunteer Cavalry in the Spanish-American War of 1898, mainly organized and subsequently commanded by Theodore Roosevelt.

rough-shod (ruf′shod′) *adj.* Shod with rough shoes to prevent slipping, as a horse. — **to ride rough-shod (over)** To act overbearingly; domineer without consideration.

rou·lade (rōō·läd′) *n.* **1** In singing, a run of short notes on one syllable; also, a roll or flourish, as on a drum. **2** A slice of meat rolled around a filling and cooked. [<F < *rouler* roll]

rou·leau (rōō·lō′) *n. pl.* **·leaux** (-lōz) or **·leaus** **1** A roll of coins in paper. **2** *Usually pl.* In millinery, a roll or fold of ribbon used for piping. [<F, dim. of *rôle* roll]

Rou·lers (rōō·lâr′) A town in western Belgium south of Bruges; scene of several battles of World War I, 1914, 1917. *Flemish* **Roe·se·la·re** (rōō′sə·lä′rə).

rou·lette (rōō·let′) *n.* **1** A game played at a table divided into spaces numbered and colored red and black, and having in the center a rotating disk on which a ball is rolled until it drops into one of 37 correspondingly numbered and colored spaces, a player winning if he has staked his money on that space or its color or on a combination including it. **2** An engraver's disk of tempered steel, as for tracing points on a copperplate; also, a draftsman's wheel for making dotted lines. **3** In philately, a series of incisions, made in any of several shapes, without removal of paper. Compare PERFORATION. — *v.t.* **·let·ted, ·let·ting** To use or produce a roulette upon. [<F, dim. of *rouelle,* dim. of *roue* wheel <L *rota*]

Roum (rōōm) See RUM.

Rou·ma·ni·a (rōō·mā′nē·ə, -mān′yə), **Rou·ma·ni·an** (rōō·mā′ne·ən, -mān′yən) See RUMANIA, etc.

Rou·me·li·a (rōō·mē′lē·ə) See RUMELIA.

rounce (rouns) *n.* A game of cards with a full pack for two to nine persons, in which each player seeks to efface the score of 15 with which he starts, each trick taken subtracting one from it. [<Du. *rondse*]

round[1] (round) *adj.* **1** Having such a contour that a section in some direction will be circular or approximately so; circular, spherical, or cylindrical. **2** Having a curved contour or surface; not angular or flat; convex or concave. **3** Liberal; ample; large: a good *round* fee. **4** Easy and free, as in motion; brisk: a *round* pace. **5** Of full cadence; well-balanced; full-toned: a *round* sentence or tone. **6** Made without reserve; bold; outspoken: a *round* assertion. **7** Open; just; honorable. **8** Formed or moving in rotation or a circle: a *round* dance. **9** Returning to the point of departure, usually by the same means of transportation: a *round* trip. **10** Passing through the same or a like series of mutations: the *round* year. **11** Free from fractions; also, not exact in the small denominations; especially, evenly divisible by 10: *round* numbers. **12** Semicircular: a *round* arch; also, characterized by the round arch: the *round* style. **13** *Phonet.* Labialized; rounded. — *n.* **1** Something round, as a globe, ring, or cylinder, a rung of a ladder, a crossbar connecting the legs of a chair, a portion of the thigh of a beef, etc. **2** A circular course or range; circuit; beat: often in the plural; also, revolving motion or one revolution. **3** A series of recurrent movements; a routine; a completed succession or order: the daily *round* of life. **4** One of a series of concerted actions performed in succession by a number of persons: a *round* of toasts or applause. **5** One of the divisions of a boxing match; a bout. **6** In archery, the total number of arrows shot; the sum of all arrows in two or three ranges. **7** A short melody taken up at intervals by several voices; a rondo, roundel, or roundelay. **8** A firing by a company or squad in which each soldier fires once; volley. **9** A single charge of ammunition. **10** A round dance. **11** The state of being carved out on all sides: opposed to *relief.* **12** The state or condition of being circular; roundness. **13** A thick slice from a haunch: a *round* of beef. — **to go the rounds** **1** To take the usual walk of inspection. **2** To pass from mouth to mouth or person to person of a certain group. — *v.t.* **1** To make round. 2 To bring to completion; perfect: usually with *off* or *out.* 3 To free of angularity; fill out to fullness of form. 4 *Phonet.* To utter (a vowel) with the lips in a rounded position; labialize. 5 To travel or go around; make a circuit of. 6 *Archaic* To encircle; surround. — *v.i.* 7 To become round. 8 To come to completeness or perfection. 9 To fill out; become plump. 10 To make a circuit; travel a circular course. 11 To turn around. — **to round off** *Math.* To reduce the number of decimal places to which a number is carried in a calculation: usually, a final figure less than 5 is eliminated and a final figure of 5 or greater increases the preceding figure to its next highest value, as, 2.1414, rounded off, becomes 2.141; 3.14159 becomes 3.1416. — **to round up** 1 To collect (cattle, etc.) in a herd, as for driving to market. 2 *Colloq.* To gather together; assemble. — *adv.* 1 On all sides; in such a manner as to encircle: A crowd gathered *round.* 2 With a circular or rotating motion: The wheel turns *round.* 3 Through a circle or circuit; more or less completely from person to person or point to point: provisions enough to go *round.* 4 In circumference: a log 3 feet *round.* 5 From one view or position to another; hither and yon; to and fro. 6 In the vicinity: to hang *round.* See AROUND. — *prep.* 1 Enclosing; encircling: a belt *round* his waist. 2 On every side of, or from every side toward; surrounding. 3 Toward every side from; about: He peered *round* him. [<OF *roonde,* fem. of *roond* <L *rotundus.* Doublet of ROTUND.] — **round′ness** *n.*

Synonyms (adj.): circular, curved, curvilinear, cylindrical, globose, globular, orbed, orbicular, plump, rotund, spherical, spheroidal. See BLUNT. *Antonyms*: angular, conical, cubical, flat, polygonal, quadrangular, quadrilateral, rectangular, square, triangular.

Round may appear as a combining form in hyphemes or solidemes:

round-arched	**round-hoofed**
round-armed	**round-horned**
round-backed	**round-leaved**
round-barreled	**round-limbed**
round-bellied	**round-lobed**
round-billed	**round-mouthed**
round-bodied	**round-nosed**
round-boned	**round-pointed**
round-bottomed	**round-ribbed**
round-bowled	**round-rooted**
round-celled	**round-sided**
round-cornered	**round-skirted**
round-crested	**round-spun**
round-eared	**round-stalked**
round-edged	**round-tailed**
round-faced	**round-toed**
round-fenced	**round-topped**
round-footed	**round-trussed**
round-furrowed	**round-visaged**
round-handed	**round-winged**
round-headed	**round-wombed**

round[2] (round) *v.t.* & *v.i. Obs.* To whisper (to). [OE *rūnian*]

round·a·bout (round′ə·bout′) *adj.* 1 Circuitous; indirect. 2 Covering the whole field; ample. 3 Encircling. — *n.* 1 An outer garment reaching to the waist; a jacket. 2 *Brit.* A merry-go-round.

round-about chair A corner chair.

round clam A quahaug.

round dance 1 A country dance in which the dancers form a circle. 2 A dance with a revolving motion, as a waltz or polka, performed by two persons.

round·ed (roun′did) *adj.* 1 Round or spherical. 2 *Phonet.* Labialized.

roun·del (roun′dəl) *n.* 1 A roundelay. 2 In prosody, a modification of the rondeau, introduced by Swinburne, written in three stanzas of three lines each, with a refrain after the first and third. Compare RONDEL. 3 *Archit.* A semicircular recess, small round window, etc. [<OF *rondel* a roundelay]

roun·de·lay (roun′də·lā) *n.* 1 A simple melody. 2 A musical setting of a poem with a recurrent refrain. 3 A dance performed in a circle. [<OF *rondelet,* dim. of *rondel* < *rond* round]

round·er (roun′dər) *n.* 1 *U.S. Slang* A dissolute person who makes the rounds of public resorts at night, or who is often arrested for misdemeanors. 2 A tool for rounding. 3 *pl.* An old English game of ball somewhat resembling baseball: construed as singular.

round·hand (round′hand′) *n.* A style of handwriting in which the tendency is to make all letters round, full, and distinct.

Round·head (round′hed′) *n.* A member of the Parliamentary party in England in the civil war of 1642–49: so called in contempt by the Royalists, from their close-cropped hair.

round·house (round′hous′) *n.* 1 A cabin on the after part of the quarter-deck of a vessel. 2 A round building with a turntable in the center for housing and switching locomotives. 3 *Obs.* A lockup. 4 A round trip in pinochle.

round·ing (roun′ding) *adj.* 1 Pertaining to or denoting something, as a tool, used in or for rounding. 2 Becoming round; also, somewhat round.

round·ish (roun′dish) *adj.* Somewhat round. — **round′ish·ness** *n.*

round·let (round′lit) *n.* A little circle. [<F *rondelet*]

round·ly (round′lē) *adv.* 1 In a round manner or form; circularly; spherically. 2 Severely; vigorously: to be *roundly* denounced. 3 Frankly; bluntly. 4 Thoroughly; completely.

round-nose (round′nōz′) *adj.* Designating a kind of pliers whose gripping surfaces meet in a round, tapering point. See illustration under PLIERS.

round ringing A method of change-ringing a set of chimes in sequence from the bell of the highest note to that of the lowest, and then repeating this sequence while the earlier overtones are still vibrating, thus producing an effect like a round.

round robin 1 A number of signatures, as to a petition, written in a circle so as to avoid giving prominence to any single name; also, a paper so signed. 2 The cigar fish. 3 A tournament, as in tennis or chess, in which each player meets every other player.

rounds (roundz) *n. pl.* The position of a set of chiming bells when struck in a descending scale from highest to lowest.

round-shoul·dered (round′shōl′dərd) *adj.* Having the back rounded or the shoulders stooping.

rounds·man (roundz′mən) *n. pl.* **·men** (-mən) A police officer having charge of a group of patrolmen.

round table Any meeting place for conference or discussion; also, any discussion group. — **round-ta·ble** (round′tā′bəl) *adj.*

Round Table The table of King Arthur, made exactly circular so as to avoid any question of precedence among his knights; also, collectively, King Arthur and the body of knights having places there.

round-the-clock (round′thə·klok′) *adj.* Through all twenty-four hours of the day.

round tower 1 Any cylindrical tower; especially, a slender, tapering tower of circular plan, with a conical cap. 2 In Ireland, a detached campanile built as a watchtower to guard church treasures, etc., against viking raids.

round trip 1 A trip to a place and back again; a return trip. 2 In pinochle, a meld of four kings and four queens: also called *roundhouse.* — **round′-trip′** *adj.*

round·up (round′up′) *n.* 1 The bringing together of cattle scattered over a range for inspection, branding, or selection for sale. 2 The cowboys, horses, etc., employed in this work. 3 *U.S. Colloq.* A bringing together of several persons: a *roundup* of pickpockets by the police.

round·worm (round′wûrm′) *n.* A nematode worm, especially one parasitic in the human intestines.

roup[1] (ro͞op) *n.* An infectious respiratory and catarrhal disease affecting poultry. [Origin uncertain]

roup[2] (roup, ro͞op) *Scot. n.* An auction. — *v.t.* To auction. [OE *hrōpan*]

roup·et (ro͞o′pit, rou′pit) *adj. Scot.* Roupy.

Rou·phi·a (ro͞o·fē′ə) The former name for the ALPHEUS RIVER.

roup·y (ro͞o′pē) *adj.* 1 Pertaining to, like, or affected with roup. 2 *Scot.* Hoarse.

rouse[1] (rouz) *v.* **roused, rous·ing** *v.t.* 1 To cause to awaken from slumber, repose, unconsciousness, etc. 2 To excite to vigorous thought or action; stir up. 3 To startle or drive (game) from cover. — *v.i.* 4 To awaken from sleep or unconsciousness. 5 To become active. 6 To start from cover: said of game. See synonyms under PIQUE, SPUR, STIR. — *n.* 1 The act of rousing; an awakening to or signal for action. 2 *Brit.* Reveille. [Origin unknown] — **rous′er** *n.*

rouse[2] (rouz) *n.* 1 *Archaic* A full draft of liquor; a bumper. 2 Noisy mirth; a drinking bout; carousal. [Aphetic form of CAROUSE]

rouse[3] (rouz) *v.t.* & *v.i.* **roused, rous·ing** *Naut.* To pull together and with vigor. [? <ROUSE[1]]

rouse·a·bout (rous′ə·bout) *n. Austral.* A handyman, especially one at a sheep or cattle station.

rouse·ment (rouz′mənt) *n.* A stirring up of interest or enthusiasm; especially, a widespread religious awakening or excitement.

rous·ing (rou′zing) *adj.* 1 Able to rouse or excite: a *rousing* speech. 2 Lively; active; vigorous: a *rousing* trade.

Rous·seau (ro͞o·sō′), **Henri,** 1844–1910, French painter: called "Le Douanier." — **Jean Jacques,** 1712–78, French philosopher and author. — **Pierre Étienne Théodore,** 1812–67, French painter.

Rous·sil·lon (ro͞o·sē·yôn′) A region and former province of southern France on the Spanish border; former capital, Perpignan.

roust (roust) *v.t.* & *v.i. Colloq.* To arouse and drive (a person or thing); stir up: usually with *out.* [Blend of ROUSE and ROUT]

roust·a·bout (rous′tə·bout′) *n.* 1 A laborer on river craft or on the waterfront; a deck hand. 2 One employed for casual work, especially, a transient laborer. 3 A man of all work on a cattle ranch or in a cow camp.

rout[1] (rout) *n.* 1 A disorderly and overwhelming defeat or flight. 2 A boisterous and disorderly assemblage; the rabble. 3 An entourage; a retinue. 4 *Law* A disturbance of the peace by three or more persons with riotous intent. 5 *Archaic* A large and festive evening social gathering. 6 *Archaic* Any assembly; a throng. See synonyms under REVEL. — *v.t.* To defeat disastrously; put to flight. See synonyms under CONQUER. [<OF *route* <L *rupta,* fem. of *ruptus,* pp. of *rumpere* break]

rout[2] (rout) *v.i.* 1 To root, as swine. 2 To search; rummage. — *v.t.* 3 To dig or turn up with the snout. 4 To disclose to view; turn up as if with the snout: with *out.* 5 To hollow, gouge, or scrape, as with a scoop. 6 To drive or force out. [Var. of ROOT[2]]

rout[3] (rout, ro͞ot) *v.i. Scot.* or *Obs.* To make a loud noise; snore. — *n. Obs.* 1 Snoring. 2 A roaring noise; uproar. [OE *hrūtan*]

route (ro͞ot, rout) *n.* 1 A course, road, or way taken in passing from one point to another by any person or moving object. 2 The specific course over which mail is sent; also, the territory covered by a newsboy. See synonyms under ROAD, WAY. — *v.t.* **rout·ed, rout·ing** To dispatch or send by a certain way, as passengers, goods, etc. [<OF <L *rupta (via)* broken (road), fem. of *ruptus,* pp. of *rumpere* break] — **rout′er** *n.*

route column Close marching order for troops.

route formation An open formation of military aircraft prior or subsequent to action.

route march A troop march with discipline reduced to permit singing, talking, etc. Also **route step.**

route of march In a military march order, the designation of the way to be taken and the location of headquarters for each evening.

rout·er (rou′tər) *n.* 1 One who scoops or routs. 2 A tool for routing. 3 A plane devised for working a molding around a circular sash. [<ROUT[2]]

routh (ro͞oth, routh) *Scot. adj.* Abundant. — *n.* Plenty; abundance. Also spelled *rowth.*

rou·tine (ro͞o·tēn′) *n.* 1 A detailed method of procedure, regularly followed; prescribed course of action: an official *routine.* 2 Habitual methods of action induced by circumstances. See synonyms under HABIT. — *adj.* Customary; habitual; everyday. [<F < *route* way, road]

rou·tin·ism (ro͞o·tē′niz·əm) *n.* Adherence to routine or routine methods in general. — **rou·tin′ist** *n.*

roux (ro͞o) *n. French* Melted butter mixed with browned flour for thickening soups, gravies, etc.

rove[1] (rōv) *v.* **roved, rov·ing** *v.i.* To wander from place to place; go or move without any definite destination. — *v.t.* To roam over, through, or about. See synonyms under RAMBLE, WANDER. — *n.* The act of roving or roaming; a ramble. [<Du. *rooven* rob]

rove[2] (rōv) *v.t.* **roved, rov·ing** **1** To join and elongate, as a number of slivers from a carding machine, by passing between one or more pairs of rollers. **2** To pass through an eye. **3** To draw into thread; ravel out. **4** To reduce the diameter of with a hooked, flat tool: to *rove* a grindstone. — *n.* **1** A slightly twisted wool, cotton, flax, jute, or silk sliver. **2** A metal ring or washer for use in clinching a nail in boatbuilding. [Origin uncertain]

rove[3] (rōv) Past participle of REEVE[1].

rove beetle Any of a family *(Staphylinidae)* of beetles having elongated bodies with very short elytra: most species are scavengers. For illustration see INSECTS (beneficial).

rov·er[1] (rō′vər) *n.* **1** One who roves; a wanderer. **2** A pirate, or pirate vessel. **3** A croquet ball that has been sent through all the arches and has only to strike the final stake to go out. [<MDu., a robber. Akin to ROBBER.]

rov·er[2] (rō′vər) *n.* In archery, any object, usually distant, chosen as a mark. Also **roving mark.** [Origin unknown]

Ro·vu·ma (rō·vo͞o′mə) The Portuguese name for the RUVUMA.

row[1] (rō) *n.* An arrangement or series of persons or things in a continued line; a rank; file; specifically, a line of houses on a street, or the street: Park *Row*; also, a line of plants, trees, etc., in a field or garden. — **a long row to hoe** A hard task or undertaking. — **at the end of one's row** Exhausted; also, having used up one's resources. — *v.t.* To arrange in a row: with *up.* ◆ Homophone: *roe.* [OE *rāw, rǣw* line]

row[2] (rō) *v.i.* **1** To use oars, sweeps, etc., in propelling a boat. — *v.t.* **2** To propel across the surface of the water with oars, as a boat. **3** To transport by rowing. **4** To be propelled by (a specific number of oars): said of boats. **5** To make use of (oars or rowers), especially in a race. **6** To row against in a race. — *n.* A trip in a rowboat; also, a turn at the oars, or the distance covered. ◆ Homophone: *roe.* [OE *rōwan*]

row[3] (rou) *n.* A noisy disturbance or quarrel; dispute; brawl; hence, any disturbance. — *v.t.* & *v.i.* To engage in a row or brawl. [Prob. back formation <ROUSE[2] (taken as a pl.)]

row[4] (rō) *Scot. n.* A roll, as of wool. — *v.t.* & *v.i.* To roll.

row·an (rō′ən, rou′-) *n.* **1** The European mountain ash *(Sorbus aucuparia).* **2** The related American mountain ash *(S. americana).* **3** The fruit of these trees. [<Scand. Cf. Norw. *raun, roun,* ON *reynir.*]

row·an·ber·ry (rō′ən·ber′ē) *n. pl.* **·ries** The fruit of the rowan.

row·boat (rō′bōt′) *n.* A boat propelled by oars.

row·dy (rou′dē) *n. pl.* **·dies** One inclined to create disturbances or engage in rows; a rough, quarrelsome person. — *adj.* **·di·er, ·di·est** Rough and loud; disorderly. [Origin uncertain] — **row′dy·ish** *adj.* — **row′dy·ism, row′di·ness** *n.*

Rowe (rō), **Nicholas,** 1674–1718, English poet and dramatist; poet laureate 1715.

row·el (rou′əl) *n.* **1** A spiked or toothed wheel, as on a spur. **2** The spur so furnished. **3** A hair or silk thread passed through a horse's skin, to facilitate the discharge of pus. — *v.t.* **·eled** or **·elled, ·el·ing** or **·el·ling** **1** To prick with a rowel; spur. **2** To attach or apply a rowel to. [<OF *roele* <LL *rotella* little wheel <L *rota* wheel]

ROWEL ON SPUR

row·en (rou′ən) *n.* A second growth of grass or hay; aftermath. [<OF *regain*]

Row·lands (rō′ləndz), **John** See STANLEY, HENRY.

Row·land·son (rō′lənd·sən), **Thomas,** 1756–1827, English artist and caricaturist.

row·lock (rō′lok′) *n. Brit.* A device in which an oar plays and which serves as a point for applying its power to a boat: also called *oarlock.* [Alter. of OARLOCK; infl. by *row*[2]]

ROWLOCK

rowth (ro͞oth, routh) See ROUTH.

Rox·an·a (rok·san′ə) A feminine personal name. Also **Rox·y** (rok′sē), *Fr.* **Rox·ane** (rôk·sàn′). [<Persian, dawn of day]
— **Roxane** In Rostand's *Cyrano de Bergerac,* the heroine.

Ro·xas y A·cu·ña (rō′häs ē ä·ko͞o′nyä), **Manuel,** 1892–1948, Philippine statesman; president of the Philippines 1946–48.

Rox·burgh·shire (roks′bûr·ə·shir′) An inland county in southern Scotland; 666 square miles; capital, Jedburgh. Also **Rox′burgh** (-bûr·ə).

roy·al (roi′əl) *adj.* **1** Pertaining to a monarch; kingly. **2** Under the patronage or authority of a king, or connected with a monarchical form of government: the *Royal* Society; a *royal* governor. **3** Like a king; princely; regal. **4** Of superior quality or size: *royal* octavo. **5** Surpassingly pleasant or fine: We had a *royal* time. See synonyms under IMPERIAL, KINGLY. — *n.* **1** A size of paper, 19 × 24 for writing, 20 × 25 for printing. **2** *Naut.* A sail next above the topgallant, used in a light breeze. [<F <L *regalis* kingly < *rex* king. Doublet of REGAL.] — **roy′al·ly** *adv.*

Royal Academy A society established in 1768 by George III of England for the advancement of painting, sculpture, and design: in full, *Royal Academy of Arts.*

Royal Air Force The air force of Great Britain.

Royal Australian Air Force The air force of Australia.

Royal Australian Navy The navy of Australia.

royal blue **1** Originally, the color of smalt, or cobalt blue; also, Prussian blue. **2** A more modern, brilliant blue; a reddish blue.

Royal Canadian Air Force The air force of Canada.

royal fern An attractive, deep-rooted fern *(Osmunda regalis)* of Asia, Africa, and America, having branched stems with oval or elliptical leaflets.

royal flush See under FLUSH.

Royal Gorge A canyon of the Arkansas River in south central Colorado, extending 10 miles; over 1,000 feet deep.

roy·al·ism (roi′əl·iz′əm) *n.* Adherence to the principles or cause of royalty.

roy·al·ist (roi′əl·ist) *n.* A supporter of a royal dynasty. — *adj.* Supporting a royal house; pertaining to royalists: also **roy′al·is′tic.**

Roy·al·ist (roi′əl·ist) *n.* **1** In English history, a Cavalier or adherent of King Charles I, as against the Parliament, in the middle of the 17th century. **2** In French history, a supporter of the Bourbon or Orléans claims to the throne since 1793. **3** In the American Revolution, a supporter of the king; Loyalist; Tory.

roy·al·mast (roi′əl·mast′, -mäst′) *n. Naut.* The section of a mast next above the topgallant mast.

Royal Navy The naval forces of Great Britain.

royal purple **1** A very deep violet color verging toward blue. **2** Originally, a rich crimson.

Royal Society A society founded about 1660 in London and chartered in 1662, concerned with the advancement of science.

royal tine The tine of an antler projecting away from or above the bez tine: also called *trez tine.* For illustration see ANTLER.

royal touch The touch of a reigning monarch once believed to cure scrofula (king's evil).

roy·al·ty (roi′əl·tē) *n. pl.* **·ties** **1** Royal rank, birth, or lineage; kingly nature or quality; kingliness; regal authority; sovereignty. **2** A royal personage; royal persons collectively. **3** A share of proceeds paid to a proprietor, author, or inventor, by those doing business under some right belonging to him. **4** A tax or seigniorage paid to the crown on the produce of royal mines, or on gold and silver coinage. **5** A royal possession or domain; hence, domain or province in general. [<OF *roialté*]

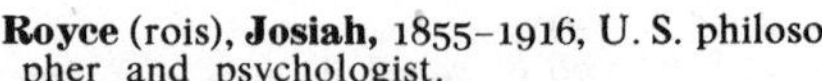

Royce (rois), **Josiah,** 1855–1916, U. S. philosopher and psychologist.

Ro·za·mond (rō′zə·mont) Dutch form of ROSAMOND.

-rrhagia *combining form Pathol.* A morbid or violent discharge or flow; an eruption: *metrorrhagia*: also spelled *-rhagia.* Also **-rrhage, -rrhagy.** Corresponding adjectives are formed in **-rrhagic.** [<Gk. < *rrhag-,* root of *rrhēgnynai* burst]

-rrhaphy *combining form* A sewing together; a suture: *neurorrhaphy,* the suturing of a nerve. Also spelled *-rhaphy.* [<Gk. *rrhaphē* a seam]

-rrhea *combining form Pathol.* An abnormal or excessive flow or discharge: *diarrhea*: also spelled *-rhea, -rhoea.* Also **-rrhoea.** [<Gk. *-rrhoia* < *rheein* flow]

Ru·an·da-U·run·di (ro͞o·än′dä·o͞o·ro͞on′dē) A former United Nations Trust Territory in central Africa, administered by Belgium, and once part of German East Africa. See BURUNDI, RWANDA.

rub (rub) *v.* **rubbed, rub·bing** *v.t.* **1** To move or pass over the surface of with pressure and friction. **2** To cause (something) to move or pass with friction; scrape; grate. **3** To cause to become frayed, worn, or sore from friction: This collar *rubs* my neck. **4** To clean, shine, burnish, etc., by means of pressure and friction, or by means of a substance applied thus. **5** To apply or spread with pressure and friction: to *rub* polish on a table. **6** To force by rubbing: with *in* or *into*: to *rub* oil into wood. **7** To remove or erase by friction: with *off* or *out.* — *v.i.* **8** To move along a surface with friction; scrape. **9** To exert pressure and friction. **10** To become frayed, worn, or sore from friction; chafe. **11** To undergo rubbing or removal by rubbing: with *off, out,* etc. — **to rub it in** *Slang* To harp on someone's errors, faults, etc. — **to rub out** *Slang* To kill. — **to rub the wrong way** *Slang* To irritate; annoy. See synonyms under WEAR. Compare FRICTION. — *n.* **1** A subjection to frictional pressure; rubbing: Give it a *rub.* **2** That which renders progress difficult; a hindrance or a doubt: There's the *rub.* **3** Something that rubs or is rough to the feelings; a sarcasm: a *rub* in debate. **4** A roughness or unevenness of surface, quality, or character. [ME *rubben,* prob. <LG. Cf. G *reiben.*]

rub-a-dub (rub′ə·dub′) *n.* The sound of a drum when beaten; hence, any clatter. [Imit.]

ru·bái·yát (ro͞o′bī·yät, -bē-) *n. pl.* **1** In Persian poetry, four-lined stanzas; quatrains. **2** Hence, **Rubáiyát,** a poem by Omar Khayyám and an English translation of it by Edward FitzGerald. [<Arabic *rubā'īyāt,* pl. of *rubā'īyah* quatrain, fem. of *rubā'ī* fourfold < *rubā* four]

Rub al Kha·li (ro͞ob′ äl khä′lē) The desert region of southern Arabia; 250,000 square miles: English *Empty Quarter*: also *Ar Rimal.*

ru·basse (ro͞o·bas′, -bäs′) *n.* A crystalline variety of quartz stained a ruby red by spangles of hematite. Also **ru·bace′.** [<F *rubace* < *rubi.* See RUBY.]

ru·ba·to (ro͞o·bä′tō) *adj. Music* Literally, robbed; noting the lengthening of one note at the expense of another. — *n. pl.* **·tos** A rubato modification. [<Ital.]

rub·ber[1] (rub′ər) *n.* **1** A tenacious, elastic material obtained by coagulating the milky latex of certain tropical plants, especially the tree *Hevea brasiliensis.* When purified, the crude rubber or caoutchouc is a white polymerized isoprene; it is insoluble in water or alcohol, and for commercial use is mixed with various vulcanizing agents, fillers, and pigments, then heated and molded into the desired form. **2** Anything used for rubbing, erasing, polishing, etc. **3** One who or that which rubs. **4** An article made of rubber, as an elastic band or an overshoe. — *adj.* Made of rubber. [<RUB] — **rub′ber·y** *adj.*

rub·ber[2] (rub′ər) *n.* In bridge, whist, and other card games, a series of two or three games played by the same partners against the same adversaries, terminated when one side has won two games; also, the odd game which breaks a tie between the players. [Origin unknown]

rub·ber·ize (rub′ər·īz) *v.t.* **·ized, ·iz·ing** To coat, impregnate, or cover, as silk, with a preparation of rubber.

rub·ber·neck (rub′ər·nek′) *n. U.S. Slang* One who cranes his neck in order to see something;

a sightseer; tourist. — *v.i.* To stretch or crane one's neck; gape.

rubber plant 1 Any of several plants yielding rubber. 2 An East Indian tree of the mulberry family (*Ficus elastica*) having large, glossy, leathery leaves: much cultivated as an ornamental house plant.

rub·ber–stamp (rub′ər·stamp′) *v.t.* 1 To endorse, initial, or approve with the mark made by a rubber stamping device. 2 *Colloq.* To pass or approve as a matter of course or routine.

rub·bish (rub′ish) *n.* Waste refuse, or broken matter; trash. [Origin unknown]

rub·bish·y (rub′ish·ē) *adj.* Worthless; without value.

rub·ble (rub′əl) *n.* 1 Rough, irregular pieces of broken stone. 2 The debris to which buildings of brick, stone, etc., have been reduced by a violent action, such as earthquake or bombing. 3 (*also* rōō′bəl) **a** In quarrying, the weathered or friable surface layer of rock. **b** Rough pieces of stone for use in construction, especially in residences. 4 Water-worn stones. 5 Rubblework. [Origin uncertain. Prob. related to RUBBISH.]

rub·ble·work (rub′əl·wûrk′) *n.* Masonry composed of irregular or broken stone, or fragments of stone mingled with cement or clay.

rub–down (rub′doun′) *n.* A massage.

rube (rōōb) *n. Slang* A countryman; farmer; rustic. [Abbreviation of REUBEN]

ru·be·fa·cient (rōō′bə·fā′shənt) *adj.* Causing redness, as of the skin. —*n.* A medicament for producing irritation of the skin. [<L *rubefaciens, -entis* < *rubefacere* redden < *rubeus* red + *facere* make] —**ru′be·fa′cience** *n.* —**ru′be·fac′tion** (-fak′shən) *n.*

ru·bel·la (rōō·bel′ə) *n. Pathol.* A contagious eruptive fever intermediate between scarlatina and measles: also called *German measles.* [<NL, neut. pl. of L *rubellus* reddish, dim. of *ruber* red]

ru·bel·lite (rōō′bə·līt) *n.* A red, usually transparent, tourmaline: used as a gem. [<L *rubellus.* See RUBELLA.]

Ru·bens (rōō′bənz, *Flemish* rü′bəns), **Peter Paul,** 1577–1646, Flemish painter.

ru·be·o·la (rōō·bē′ə·lə) *n. Pathol.* 1 Measles. 2 Rubella. [<NL, neut. pl. dim. of L *rubeus* red] —**ru·be′o·lar** *adj.*

Ru·ber·to (rōō·ber′tō) Italian and Spanish form of RUPERT.

ru·bes·cent (rōō·bes′ənt) *adj.* Becoming red; reddening. [<L *rubescens, -entis,* ppr. of *rubescere* grow red, inceptive of *rubere* < *rubeus* red] —**ru·bes′cence** *n.*

ru·bi·a·ceous (rōō′bē·ā′shəs) *adj. Bot.* Belonging or pertaining to a large, chiefly tropical family (*Rubiaceae*) of trees, shrubs, and herbs, the madder family of the order *Rubiales,* with simple opposite or whorled leaves and perfect, often dimorphous, flowers, including plants yielding coffee, quinine, and ipecac. [<L *rubia* madder]

Ru·bi·con (rōō′bi·kon) A river in north central Italy, flowing 15 miles NE to the Adriatic: modern *Fiumicino*; it formed the boundary separating Caesar's province of Gaul from Italy, and by crossing it under arms he committed himself to a civil war with the Roman government then controlled by Pompey; hence, **to cross the Rubicon,** to be committed definitely to some course of action; make an irrevocable move.

ru·bi·cund (rōō′bə·kənd) *adj.* Red, or inclined to redness; rosy. [<L *rubicundus* red] —**ru′bi·cun′di·ty** *n.*

ru·bid·i·um (rōō·bid′ē·əm) *n.* A soft, rare, silvery-white metallic element (symbol Rb) resembling potassium, discovered by Bunsen and Kirchoff with the aid of the spectroscope. See ELEMENT. [<NL <L *rubidus* red]

ru·big·i·nous (rōō·bij′ə·nəs) *adj.* Having a rusty or brownish-red color: *rubiginous* plants. Also **ru·big′i·nose** (-nōs). [<LL *rubiginosus* <L *rubigo, rubiginis* rust]

ru·bi·go (rōō·bī′gō, -bē′-) *n.* Red iron oxide, used as a polishing powder and pigment. [<L, rust]

Ru·bin·stein (rōō′bin·stīn), **Anton Gregor,** 1829–94, Russian pianist and composer. —**Artur,** born 1886, U.S. pianist born in Poland.

ru·bi·ous (rōō′bē·əs) *adj.* Red; ruby-colored. [<RUBY]

ru·ble (rōō′bəl) *n.* The Russian monetary unit containing 100 kopecks, and equivalent to one tenth of a chervonets: also spelled *rouble.* [<Russian *rubl′*]

ru·bric (rōō′brik) *n.* 1 That exceptional part of an early manuscript or a book that appears in red, or in some distinctive type: once used to indicate initial letters, caption words, headings, etc. 2 The heading or title of a statute or of a section in a code of law, formerly written in red. 3 *Eccl.* A direction or rule printed in devotional or liturgical office, as in a prayer book, missal, or breviary; also, such rules collectively. 4 A division, group, or category. 5 The color red. 6 *Obs.* Red ochre or chalk; reddle. 7 Any direction or rule of conduct. 8 A distinguishing flourish or mark after a person's signature. —*adj.* 1 Red or reddish. 2 Written or printed in red. —*v.t.* **·bricked, ·brick·ing** *Rare* To rubricate. [<OF *rubrique* <L *rubrica* red earth < *ruber* red] —**ru′bri·cal** *adj.* —**ru′bri·cal·ly** *adv.*

ru·bri·cate (rōō′brə·kāt) *v.t.* **·cat·ed, ·cat·ing** 1 To mark or tint with red; illuminate with red, as a book. 2 To furnish with a rubric or rubrics; arrange in permanent form. —*adj.* Marked, written, or printed in red. [<L *rubricatus,* pp. of *rubricare* redden < *rubrica.* See RUBRIC.] —**ru′bri·ca′tion** *n.* —**ru′bri·ca′·tor** *n.*

ru·bri·cian (rōō·brish′ən) *n.* One versed in the knowledge of, or punctiliously adhering to, rubric or rubrics.

ru·by (rōō′bē) *n. pl.* **·bies** 1 A translucent gemstone of a deep-red color, usually a variety of corundum, as the **Oriental ruby,** but sometimes a variety of spinel, as the **almandine, balas,** and **spinel rubies.** 2 A rich red color like that of a ruby. 3 Something like a ruby in color, as red wine or a carbuncle. 4 Something made of a ruby; especially, in watchmaking, a bearing or roller made of a ruby or similar material. 5 In England, a size of type (5 1/2 points): equivalent to the American *agate.* —*adj.* Pertaining to or like a ruby; being of a rich crimson: *ruby* lips. —*v.t.* **·bied, ·by·ing** To redden; tint with the color of a ruby. [<OF *rubi* <L *rubeus* red]

ru·by–crowned kinglet (rōō′bē·kround′) See under KINGLET.

ru·by·throat (rōō′bē·thrōt′) *n.* The hummingbird (*Archilochus colubris*) of eastern North America, having in the male a gorget of brilliant metallic red. Also **ruby–throated hummingbird.**

ru·cer·vine (rōō·sûr′vēn, -vin) *adj.* 1 Of or pertaining to a genus (*Rucervus*) of large deer native in southeastern Asia. 2 Denoting the antlers characteristic of this genus. For illustration see ANTLER. [<NL *Rucervus,* name of the genus <Malay *rusa* deer + CERVINE]

ruche (rōōsh) *n.* A quilted or ruffled strip of fine fabric, worn about the neck or wrists of a woman's costume: also spelled *rouche.* [<F, beehive <Med. L *rusca* tree bark, ? <Celtic]

ruch·ing (rōō′shing) *n.* Material for ruches; ruches collectively.

ruck[1] (ruk) *n.* The common herd or run; a crowd; also, trash; rubbish. [<Scand. Cf. Norw. *ruka* heap, crowd.]

ruck[2] (ruk) *v.t. & v.i.* 1 To wrinkle, rumple, crease, etc. 2 To annoy; ruffle: usually with *up.* —*n.* A wrinkle, crease, or ridge, as in cloth or paper; a wrinkled place. [<ON *hrukka* wrinkle]

ruck·sack (ruk′sak′, rŏŏk′-) *n.* A canvas knapsack. [<G, lit., back sack]

ruck·us (ruk′əs) *n. U.S. Slang* An uproar; commotion; rumpus. [Prob. blend of RUMPUS and RUCTION]

ruc·ta·tion (ruk·tā′shən) *n.* Eructation.

ruc·tion (ruk′shən) *n. Colloq.* A riotous outbreak; quarrel; uproar. [Prob. alter. of INSURRECTION]

ruc·tious (ruk′shəs) *adj. Slang* Difficult; quarrelsome. [<RUCTION]

rud·beck·i·a (rud·bek′ē·ə) *n.* Any of a genus (*Rudbeckia*) of North American herbs of the composite family, the coneflowers, with alternate simple or compound leaves and showy yellow heads; especially, the black-eyed Susan. [after Olaus *Rudbeck,* 1630–1702, Swedish botanist]

rudd (rud) *n.* A European fresh-water fish (*Scardinius erythrophthalmus*), olive-brown with red fins: also called *red eye.* [OE *rudu* red color]

rud·der (rud′ər) *n.* 1 *Naut.* A broad, flat device hinged vertically at the stern of a vessel to direct its course. 2 Anything that guides or directs a course. 3 *Aeron.* A hinged or pivoted surface, used to control the position of an aircraft about its vertical axis. [OE *rōthor* oar, scull] —**rud′·der·less** *adj.*

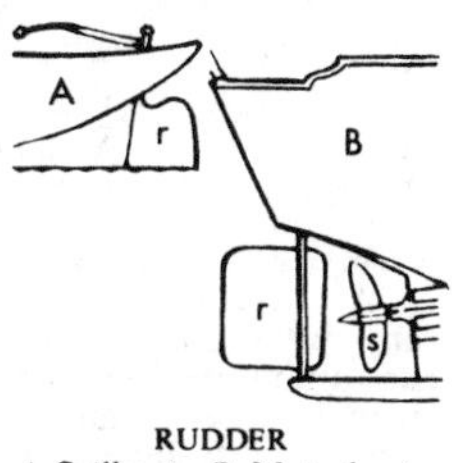

RUDDER
A. Sailboat *B.* Motorboat. *r.* Rudder. *s.* Screw.

rudder bar *Aeron.* A foot-operated rod by which the pilot controls the rudder of an airplane.

rudder fish Any of various fishes that follow vessels, as the pilot fish, etc.

rudder stock The vertical shaft to which the rudder of a ship or boat is attached, having at its upper portion a yoke (the **rudder crosshead**) or tiller by which it may be turned. Also **rudder post.**

rud·dle (rud′l) *n.* A variety of red ocherous iron ore; reddle. —*v.t.* **·dled, ·dling** To color or stain with red ocher. Also spelled *raddle.* [OE *rudu* red color]

rud·dle·man (rud′l·mən) *n. pl.* **·men** (-mən) A reddleman.

rud·dock (rud′ək) *n.* The European robin. [OE *rudduc* robin < *rudu* red color]

rud·dy (rud′ē) *adj.* **·di·er, ·di·est** 1 Tinged with red. 2 Having a healthy glow; rosy: a *ruddy* complexion. See synonyms under FRESH. [OE *rudig*] —**rud′di·ly** *adv.* —**rud′di·ness** *n.*

ruddy duck A small North American duck (*Erismatura jamaicensis rubida*) having the tail feathers stiffened with narrow webs. The adult male is bright chestnut-reddish above. Also called *paddywhack.*

rude (rōōd) *adj.* **rud·er, rud·est** 1 Rough or abrupt; severe or tempestuous; offensively blunt or uncivil; impudent. 2 Characterized by lack of polish or refinement; uncultivated; uncouth. 3 Unskilfully made or done; lacking in skill or training; crude; rough: *rude* workmanship. 4 Characterized by robust vigor; strong: *rude* health. 5 Barbarous; savage. 6 Humble; lowly; rustic. See synonyms under BARBAROUS, BLUFF, IMPUDENT, ROUGH, RUSTIC, VULGAR. ◆ Homophone: *rood.* [<OF <L *rudis* rough] —**rude′ly** *adv.*

rude·ness (rōōd′nis) *n.* 1 The state or quality of being rude. 2 A rude action. See synonyms under IMPUDENCE.

rudes·by (rōōdz′bē) *n. Archaic* An ill-bred boor.

Rü·di·ger (rü′di·ger) German form of ROGER.

ru·di·ment (rōō′də·mənt) *n.* 1 A first principle, step, stage, or condition. 2 That which is as yet undeveloped or only partially developed. 3 *Biol.* **a** Something in a first, embryonic, incomplete, or early stage that may develop by growth; a germ. **b** A part, organ, or other structure that has become aborted or stunted and will always be undeveloped; a vestige; vestigial part. [<F <L *rudiment* first attempt < *rudis* rough]

ru·di·men·ta·ry (rōō′də·men′tər·ē) *adj.* 1 Pertaining to or of the nature of a rudiment: *rudimentary* knowledge. 2 Being or remaining in an imperfectly developed state; germinal; undeveloped; abortive. Also **ru′di·men′tal.** —**ru′di·men′ta·ri·ly** *adv.* —**ru′di·men′ta·ri·ness** *n.*

Ru·dolf (rōō′dolf; *Du.* rü′dolf, *Ger.* rōō′dôlf, *Sw.* rōō′dôlf) A masculine personal name. Also **Ru′dolph.** [<Gmc., wolf of fame]
—**Rudolf I,** 1218–91, Holy Roman Emperor 1273–91; founded the Hapsburg dynasty.
—**Rudolf II,** 1552–1612, Holy Roman Emperor 1576–1612; persecuted Protestants.
—**Rudolf of Hapsburg,** 1858–89, crown prince of Austria; son of Francis Joseph; committed suicide.

Rudolf, Lake A lake in NW Kenya, extending into Ethiopia on the northwest; 3,500 square miles.

rue[1] (rōō) *v.* **rued, ru·ing** *v.t.* To feel sorrow or remorse for; regret extremely. — *v.i.* To feel sorrow or remorse; be regretful. See synonyms under MOURN. — *n.* **1** Sorrowful remembrance; regret. **2** *Scot.* Repentance. [OE *hrēowan* be sorry] — **ru′er** *n.*

rue[2] (rōō) *n.* **1** A small, bushy herb *(Ruta graveolens)* with bitter, acrid leaves, formerly much used in medicine for stimulating effects: formerly also an emblem of bitterness or grief. **2** An infusion made from this plant; hence, any bitter draft. [<F <L *ruta* <Gk. *rhytē*]

rue anemone A delicate little American woodland perennial *(Anemonella thalictroides)*, having white flowers in the spring.

Rue de la Paix (rü də là pe′) A street in Paris, France, famous for its fashionable shops.

rue·ful (rōō′fəl) *adj.* **1** Feeling or causing sorrow, regret, or pity; deplorable; sorrowful. **2** Expressing sorrow or pity. — **rue′ful·ly** *adv.* — **rue′ful·ness** *n.*

ru·fes·cent (rōō·fes′ənt) *adj.* Inclining to reddishness; somewhat reddish or rufous. [<L *rufescens, -entis,* ppr. of *rufescere* redden < *rufus* red] — **ru·fes′cence** *n.*

ruff[1] (ruf) *n.* **1** A pleated, round, heavily starched collar popular in the 16th century. **2** Ruffle[1] (def. 1). **3** A natural collar of projecting feathers or hair around the neck of a bird or mammal. **4** An Old World sandpiper *(Philomachus pugnax)* of which the male in the breeding season has an erectile frill of elongated feathers about the neck. The female is called a *reeve.* — *v.i.* To become ruffled; stand out like a ruff. ◆ Homophone: *rough.* [Short for RUFFLE[1]]

RUFF
17th century.

ruff[2] (ruf) *n.* **1** The playing of a trump upon another suit when one has no cards of that suit. **2** An old game, the predecessor of whist. — *v.t.* & *v.i.* To trump when unable to follow suit. ◆ Homophone: *rough.* [<OF *roffle, rouffle, ronfle,* aphetic alter. of *triomphe* triumph. Cf. Ital. *ronfa* a game at cards < *trionfo* triumph. Related to TRUMP[1].]

ruff[3] (ruf) *n.* A small perchlike fish *(Acerina cernua)* of European fresh waters. Also **ruffe.** ◆ Homophone: *rough.* [<ROUGH]

ruff[4] (ruf) See RUFFLE[3].

ruffed (ruft) *adj.* Having a ruff, ruffle, or frill; ruffled.

ruffed grouse A North American grouse *(Bonasa umbellus)*: called *partridge* in the northern and *pheasant* in the southern United States.

ruf·fi·an (ruf′ē·ən, ruf′yən) *n.* A lawless, brutal, cruel fellow; a rough; one ready for or given to riotous, cruel, or murderous deeds. — *adj.* Lawlessly or recklessly brutal or cruel. [<F *rufian* <Ital. *rufiano* pimp, ? <OHG *ruf* dirty] — **ruf′fi·an·ism** *n.* — **ruf′·fi·an·ly** *adj.*

ruf·fle[1] (ruf′əl) *n.* **1** A pleated strip; frill, as for trim or ornament; also, anything resembling this: also *ruff.* **2** A temporary discomposure. **3** A ripple. — *v.* **·fled, ·fling** *v.t.* **1** To disturb or destroy the smoothness or regularity of: The wind *ruffles* the lake. **2** To draw into folds or ruffles; gather. **3** To furnish with ruffles. **4** To erect (the feathers) in a ruff, as a bird when frightened. **5** To disturb or irritate; upset. **6 a** To riffle (the pages of a book). **b** To shuffle (cards). — *v.i.* **7** To be or become rumpled or disordered. **8** To become disturbed or irritated. [ME *ruffelen.* Cf. LG *ruffelen* rumple, ON *hrufla* scratch.]

ruf·fle[2] (ruf′əl) *n.* A low, continuous beat of a drum, not as loud as a roll: also *ruff.* — *v.t.* **·fled, ·fling** To beat a ruffle upon, as a drum. [<earlier *ruff*; imit.]

ruf·fle[3] (ruf′əl) *v.t.* **·fled, ·fling** To act in a rough or turbulent manner; swagger; bluster. [? Special use of RUFFLE[2]] — **ruf′fler** *n.*

ru·fous (rōō′fəs) *adj.* Dull-red; rust-colored. [<L *rufus* red]

Ru·fus (rōō′fəs) A masculine personal name. [<L, red]

rug[1] (rug) *n.* **1** A heavy textile fabric, made in one piece, to cover a portion of a floor. **2** A covering made from the skins of animals dressed with the hair or wool on. **3** A heavy coverlet or lap robe. [<Scand. Cf. Norw. *rugga* coarse coverlet, *skinrugga* skin rug, ON *rögg* long, rough fleece.]

rug[2] (rug) *v.t.* **rugged, rug·ging** *Scot.* & *Brit. Dial.* To tug or tear roughly.

ru·ga (rōō′gə) *n. pl.* **·gae** (-jē) A fold, wrinkle, or crease. [<L]

ru·gate (rōō′gāt, -git) *adj.* Covered with or having rugae; corrugated; wrinkled. [<L *rugatus,* pp. of *rugare* wrinkle < *ruga* a wrinkle]

Rug·bei·an (rug·bē′ən) *adj.* Of or pertaining to Rugby, England, or to the school there located. — *n.* A native or inhabitant of Rugby; a pupil at Rugby school.

Rug·by (rug′bē) A municipal borough of eastern Warwickshire, England; seat of a boys' school founded in 1567.

Rugby football A form of football played between two teams of fifteen men each, in which the ball is propelled toward the opponents' goal by kicking or carrying, but in which no player of the side in possession of the ball may be ahead of the ball while it is in play.

Rü·gen (rü′gən) The largest German island in the Baltic, NE of Stralsund; 358 square miles.

rug·ged (rug′id) *adj.* **1** Having a surface full of abrupt inequalities; broken into irregular points or crags; steep and rocky; rough; uneven. **2** Shaggy; unkempt; disordered; ragged. **3** Rough in temper, character, or action; harsh; stern. **4** Having strongly marked features; wrinkled; frowning; furrowed. **5** Lacking culture or refinement; rude. **6** Rough to the ear; grating . **7** Robust; sturdy. **8** Tempestuous; stormy. See synonyms under FIRM, ROUGH. [<Scand. Cf. Sw. *rugga* roughen. Prob. related to RUG[1].] — **rug′ged·ly** *adv.* — **rug′ged·ness** *n.*

Rug·gie·ro (rōōd·jā′rō) Italian form of ROGER.

ru·gose (rōō′gōs) *adj.* **1** Covered with or full of rugae or wrinkles; corrugate; rugate. **2** *Bot.* Having a rough or wrinkled surface, as some strongly veined leaves. Also **ru′gous.** [<L *rugosus* < *ruga* wrinkle] — **ru·gos·i·ty** (rōō·gos′ə·tē) *n.*

Ruhr (rōōr) **1** A river of western Germany, flowing 142 miles west to the Rhine. **2** The region south of which the Ruhr river flows, noted as an industrial and coal-mining district; about 2000 square miles; included in North Rhine-Westphalia, West Germany.

ru·in (rōō′in) *n.* **1** Total destruction of value or usefulness; in morals, the loss of character, chastity, or honor; seduction; corruption. **2** That which remains of something demolished, destroyed, or decayed: often in the plural. **3** A condition of desolation or degradation. **4** That which causes destruction, downfall, decay, or injury: Gambling was his *ruin.* **5** The act of falling down; collapse. — *v.t.* **1** To bring to ruin; destroy; demolish. **2** To bring to bankruptcy or poverty. **3** To deprive of chastity; seduce. — *v.i.* **4** To fall into ruin. See synonyms under ABUSE, DEMOLISH. [<OF *ruine* <L *ruina* < *ruere* fall] — **ru′in·a·ble** *adj.* — **ru′in·er** *n.*

Synonyms (noun): collapse, decay, defeat, desolation, destruction, discomfiture, downfall, fall, overthrow, perdition, subversion, undoing, wreck. See ADVERSITY, MISFORTUNE. *Antonyms*: conservation, preservation, prosperity, recovery, regeneration, reparation, success.

ru·in·ate (rōō′in·āt) *v.t.* **·at·ed, ·at·ing** *Rare* To ruin. — *adj.* Ruined. [<Med. L *ruinatus,* pp. of *ruinare* ruin < *ruina*]

ru·in·a·tion (rōō′in·ā′shən) *n.* **1** The act of ruining. **2** The state of being ruined. **3** Something that ruins.

ru·ined (rōō′ind) *adj.* **1** Destroyed; ravaged; in ruins. **2** Bankrupt.

ru·in·ous (rōō′in·əs) *adj.* **1** Causing or tending to ruin. **2** Falling to ruin; decayed; dilapidated; ruined. See synonyms under PERNICIOUS. [<OF *ruineux* <L *ruinosus*] — **ru′in·ous·ly** *adv.* — **ru′in·ous·ness** *n.*

Ruis·dael (rois′däl, *Du.* rœis′däl) See RUYSDAEL.

Ru·iz (rōō·ēth′, -ēs′) A Spanish masculine personal name.

rule (rōōl) *n.* **1** Controlling power, or its possession and exercise; government; dominion; authority. **2** A method or principle of action; common or regular course of procedure, or customary standard or form: I make early rising my *rule.* **3** An authoritative direction or enactment; a concise direction respecting the doing or method of doing something, as one of the regulations of a legislative or deliberative body for the government of its own proceedings, or a regulation to be observed in playing a given game. **4** A regulation for the conduct of religious services or for the government of life; specifically, the body of directions laid down by or for a religious order: the *rule* of St. Francis. **5** A prescribed form, method, or set of instructions for solving a given class of mathematical problems. **6** An established usage or law, fixing the form or use of words or the construction of sentences: a *rule* for forming the plural. **7** What belongs to the ordinary course of events or condition of things: In some communities illiteracy is the *rule.* **8** Regular or proper method; propriety, as of conduct; regularity. **9** *Law* A formal regulation prescribed by authority touching a certain matter: a *rule* of court; also, a judicial decision on some motion or special application: a *rule* to show cause. A **rule of court** is an order made by a court, and is either *general,* as for regulating the practice of the court, or *special,* as an order sending a case before a referee. **10** A straight-edged instrument for use in measuring, or as a guide in drawing lines; a ruler, usually marked in inches, feet, etc. **11** *Printing* A strip of type-high metal for handling type or for printing a rule or line. **12** A ruled line. — **as a rule** Ordinarily; usually. — *v.* **ruled, rul·ing** *v.t.* **1** To have authority or control over; govern. **2** To influence greatly; dominate: Greed has *ruled* his life. **3** To decide or determine judicially or authoritatively. **4** To restrain; keep in check: *Rule* your temper. **5** To mark with straight, parallel lines. **6** To make (such a line) with or as with a ruler. — *v.i.* **7** To have authority or control; be in command. **8** To maintain a standard of rates: Prices *ruled* high. **9** To form and express a decision: The judge *ruled* on that point. — **to rule out** **1** To dismiss from consideration: They *ruled out* a strike. **2** To preclude; prevent. See synonyms under GOVERN, REGULATE. [<OF *reule* <L *regula* ruler, rule < *regere* lead straight, direct. Doublet of RAIL[1].] — **rul′a·ble** *adj.*

Synonyms (noun): canon, formula, guide, maxim, method, order, regulation, standard. See HABIT, LAW, STICK, SYSTEM.

ruled surface *Math.* A surface capable of being generated by a straight line, as a hyperboloid of one sheet.

rule of three *Math.* A rule for finding any term of a proportion, the three others being given.

rule of thumb **1** Measurement by the thumb. **2** Roughly practical rather than scientifically accurate measure.

rul·er (rōō′lər) *n.* **1** One who rules or governs, as a sovereign. **2** A straight-edged strip for guiding a marking implement; a rule; a ruling machine. **3** One who rules lines, as with a ruling machine. See synonyms under CHIEF.

rul·ing (rōō′ling) *adj.* Exercising dominion; controlling; predominant. — *n.* **1** The act of one who rules or governs. **2** A decision, as of a judge or presiding officer. **3** The act of making ruled lines, or the lines so made.

rum[1] (rum) *n.* **1** An alcoholic liquor distilled from fermented molasses or cane juice. **2** Any alcoholic liquor. [Short for obs. *rumbullion* rum, alter. of *Rambouillet,* town in France]

rum[2] (rum) *adj. Brit. Slang* Queer; strange; peculiar. [? <Romany *rom* man]

Rum (rōōm) The Arabic name for the BYZANTINE EMPIRE: also *Roum.*

Ru·ma·ni·a (rōō·mā′nē·ə, -mān′yə), **People's Republic of** A state in SE Europe; 91,671 square miles; capital, Bucharest: also *Romania, Roumania*: Rumanian *România.*

Ru·ma·ni·an (rōō·mā′nē·ən, -mān′yən) *adj.* Of Rumania, its people, or their language. — *n.* **1** A native or inhabitant of Rumania. **2** The Romance language of the Rumanians. Also *Romanian, Roumanian.*

rum·ba (rum′bə, *Sp.* rōōm′bä) *n.* **1** A frenzied dance formerly performed by Cuban Negroes. **2** A modern dance based on this. Also spelled *rhumba.* [<Sp.]

rum·ble (rum′bəl) *v.* **·bled, ·bling** *v.i.* **1** To make a low, heavy, rolling sound, as thunder.

2 To move or proceed with such a sound. — *v.t.* 3 To cause to make a low, heavy, rolling sound. 4 To utter with such a sound. 5 To subject to the action of a tumbling box. — *n.* 1 A continuous low, heavy, rolling sound; a muffled roar. 2 A tumbling box: also **rum′bler.** 3 A seat or baggage compartment in the rear of a carriage. 4 A folding seat in the back of a coupé or roadster: in full, **rumble seat.** 5 *U.S. Slang* A fight involving a group, usually deliberately provoked. [ME *romblen* <MDu. *rommelen*] — **rum′bler** *n.* — **rum′bling·ly** *adv.*

Ru·me·li·a (ro͞o·mē′lē·ə) The possessions of the former Ottoman Empire in the Balkan Peninsula, including Macedonia, Thrace, and Albania: also *Roumelia.*

ru·men (ro͞o′men) *n. pl.* **ru·mi·na** (ro͞o′mə·nə) 1 The first stomach of a ruminant. 2 The cud of a ruminant. [<L, throat]

Rum·ford (rum′fərd), **Count,** 1753–1814, Benjamin Thompson, physicist, born in America, active in Germany, England, and France.

ru·mi·nant (ro͞o′mə·nənt) *n.* One of a division *(Ruminantia)* of even-toed ungulates, as a deer, antelope, sheep, goat, or cow, that has a stomach with four complete cavities: the rumen, the reticulum, the manyplies (omasum, psalterium), and the reed or abomasum, the food entering the first being returned to the mouth, rechewed and swallowed, and digested in the other compartments. — *adj.* 1 Chewing the cud. 2 Of or pertaining to the *Ruminantia.* 3 Meditative or contemplative; thoughtful; drowsily quiet. [<L *ruminans, -antis,* ppr. of *ruminare* ruminate < *rumen* gullet]

ru·mi·nate (ro͞o′mə·nāt) *v.t.* & *v.i.* **·nat·ed, ·nat·ing** 1 To chew (food previously swallowed and regurgitated) over again; chew (the cud). 2 To meditate or reflect (upon); ponder. See synonyms under MUSE. — *adj.* Perforated or mottled, as the albumen of a betelnut or nutmeg: also **ru′mi·nat′ed.** [<L *ruminatus,* pp. of *ruminare.* See RUMINANT.] — **ru′mi·nat′ing·ly** *adv.* — **ru′mi·na′tive** *adj.* — **ru′mi·na′tive·ly** *adv.* — **ru′mi·na′tor** *n.*

ru·mi·na·tion (ro͞o′mə·nā′shən) *n.* 1 The act, process, or characteristic of chewing the cud. 2 The act of ruminating mentally. 3 The regurgitation of imperfectly digested food. See synonyms under REFLECTION.

Ruml (rum′əl, ro͝om′əl), **Beardsley,** 1894–1960, U.S. businessman and financier.

rum·mage (rum′ij) *v.* **·maged, ·mag·ing** *v.t.* 1 To search through (a place, box, etc.) by turning over and disarranging the contents; ransack. 2 To find or bring out by searching: with *out* or *up.* — *v.i.* 3 To make a thorough search. — *n.* 1 Any act of rummaging; especially, disarranging things by searching thoroughly. 2 An upheaval or stirring up; bustle. 3 *Obs.* Room in a ship for stowing cargo; also, the arrangement or stowing of the cargo. 4 A rummage sale. [< obs. F *arrumage* place or act of stowage < *arrumer* stow away, ? < *rum* ship's hold <OE *rūm* room] — **rum′mag·er** *n.*

rummage sale 1 A sale of all sorts of second-hand objects gathered up from benevolent givers, to obtain money for some charitable object. 2 A sale of unclaimed articles, or a clearing-out sale prior to restocking.

rum·mer (rum′ər) *n.* A glass or cup for drinking; specifically, a tall stemless glass; also, its contents. [<Du. *roemer* < *roemen* praise; from its use in drinking toasts]

rum·my[1] (rum′ē) *n.* A card game in which each player in turn draws a card from the talon or the discard pile beside it, and discards another card, the object being to get rid of one's hand in sequences of three cards or more of the same suit. [Origin unknown]

rum·my[2] (rum′ē) *n. pl.* **·mies** *Slang* A drunkard. — *adj.* 1 Of or pertaining to rum: a *rummy* flavor. 2 Affected by rum; befuddled; drunk.

ru·mor (ro͞o′mər) *n.* 1 Popular report; common gossip; also, reputation. 2 A story circulating without known foundation or authority; an unverified report passing from person to person. 3 *Obs.* A confused sound; confusion; murmur. — *v.t.* To tell or spread as a rumor; report abroad. Also *Brit.* **ru′mour.** [<OF <L, noise]

rump (rump) *n.* 1 The hinder parts or buttocks. 2 The fag-end of anything; an inferior remnant. 3 A legislative group having only a remnant of its former membership and therefore lacking authority because unrepresentative. 4 The piece of beef between aitchbone and loin. [<Scand. Cf. Dan. *rumpl,* ON *rumpr.*]

Rum·pel·stilts·kin (rum′pəl·stilt′skin, *Ger.* ro͝om′pəl·shtilts′kin) In German folklore, a dwarf who saves the life of a girl who has married a king, by spinning for her the fabulous quantity of flax her mother has boasted that she can spin. In return for this, the dwarf demands her first child. When it is born the distressed mother begs to be released from her promise. The dwarf consents if she can guess his name within three days. She does so at the crucial moment and Rumpelstiltskin's power is broken. Also **Rum·pel·stiltz·chen** (ro͝om′pəl·shtilts′khən).

rum·ple (rum′pəl) *v.t.* & *v.i.* **·pled, ·pling** To form into creases or folds; wrinkle; ruffle. — *n.* 1 An irregular fold; a rumpled fabric. 2 The condition of being rumpled. [<MDu. *rumpelen*]

Rump Parliament See LONG PARLIAMENT under PARLIAMENT.

rum·pus (rum′pəs) *n. Colloq.* A row; wrangle; to-do. [Origin uncertain]

rumpus room A room for games, informal gatherings, etc.

rum-run·ner (rum′run′ər) *n.* One who illicitly transports or smuggles alcoholic liquors across a border; also, a vessel employed in illegal liquor traffic.

run (run) *v.* **ran, run, run·ning** *v.i.* 1 To move by rapid steps, faster than walking, in such a manner that both feet are off the ground for a portion of each step. 2 To move rapidly; go swiftly. 3 To flee; take flight. 4 To make a brief or rapid journey: We *ran* over to Staten Island last night. 5 To make regular trips; ply: This steamer *runs* between New York and Liverpool. 6 **a** To take part in a race. **b** To be a candidate or contestant: to *run* for dog-catcher. 7 To finish a race in a specified position: I *ran* a poor last. 8 To move or pass easily: The rope *runs* through the block. 9 To pass continuously and rapidly; elapse: The hours *run* by. 10 To proceed in direction or extent: This road *runs* north. 11 To move in or as in a stream; flow. 12 To become liquid and flow, as wax; also, to spread or mingle confusedly, as colors when wet. 13 To move or pass inadvertently: The ship *ran* aground. 14 To pass into a specified condition: to *run* to seed. 15 To come undone; unravel, as a fabric. 16 To give forth a discharge or flow; suppurate. 17 To leak. 18 To continue or proceed without restraint: The conversation *ran* on and on. 19 To be in operation; be operative; work: Will the engine *run*? 20 To continue in existence or effect; extend in time: Genius *runs* in her family. 21 To be reported or expressed: The story *runs* as follows. 22 To migrate, as salmon from the sea to spawn. 23 To occur or return to the mind: An idea *ran* through his head. 24 To occur with specified variation of size, quality, etc.: The corn is *running* small this year. 25 To be performed or repeated in continuous succession: The play *ran* for forty nights. 26 To make a rapid succession of demands for payment, as on a bank. 27 To continue unexpired or unpaid, as a debt; become payable. — *v.t.* 28 To run or proceed along, as a route or path. 29 To make one's way over, through, or past: to *run* rapids. 30 To perform or accomplish by or as by running: to *run* a race or an errand. 31 To compete against in or as in a race. 32 To enter (a horse) for a race. 33 To present and support as a candidate. 34 To hunt or chase, as game. 35 To bring to a specified condition by or as by running: to *run* oneself out of breath. 36 To drive or force: with *out of, off, into, through,* etc. 37 To cause (a vessel) to move rapidly or freely: They *ran* the ship into port. 38 To move (the eye, hand, etc.) quickly or lightly: He *ran* his hand over the table. 39 To cause to move, slide, etc., as into a specified position: to *run* up a flag. 40 To cause to go or ply: to *run* a train between New York and Washington. 41 To transport or convey in a vessel or vehicle. 42 To smuggle. 43 To cause to flow: to *run* water into a pot. 44 To give forth a flow of; emit: Her eyes *ran* tears. 45 To mold, as from melted metal; found. 46 To sew (cloth) in a continuous line, usually by taking a number of stitches with the needle at a time. 47 To maintain or control the motion or operation of. 48 To direct or control; manage; oversee. 49 To allow to continue or mount up, as a bill. 50 In games, to make (a number of points, strokes, etc.) successively. 51 To publish in a magazine or newspaper: to *run* an ad. 52 To mark, set down, or trace, as a boundary line. 53 To suffer from (a fever, etc.). — **to run across** To meet by chance. — **to run down** 1 To pursue and overtake, as a fugitive. 2 To strike down while moving. 3 To exhaust, damage, lessen in worth, vigor, etc., as by abuse or overwork. 4 To speak of disparagingly; decry. — **to run in** 1 To insert; include. 2 *Printing* To print without a paragraph or break. 3 *Slang* To arrest and place in confinement. — **to run into** 1 To meet by chance. 2 To collide with. — **to run off** 1 To produce on a typewriter, printing press, etc. 2 To decide (a tied race, game, etc.) by the outcome of another, subsequent race, game, etc. 3 To flee or escape; elope. — **to run out** To come to an end; be exhausted, as supplies. — **to run out of** To exhaust one's supply of. — **to run over** 1 To ride or drive over; run down. 2 To overflow. 3 To go over or examine hastily or quickly; rehearse. — **to run through** 1 To spend wastefully; squander. 2 To stab or pierce. 3 To run over (def. 3). — **to run up** To produce; make hurriedly, as on a sewing machine. — *n.* 1 The act, or an act, of running or going rapidly. 2 A running pace: to break into a *run.* 3 Flow; movement; sweep: the *run* of the tide. 4 A distance covered by running. 5 A journey or passage, especially between two points, made by a vessel, train, etc.: the *run* from New York to Albany. 6 A rapid journey or excursion, marked by a brief stay at the destination: to take a *run* into town. 7 A swift stream or brook. 8 A migration of fish, especially to up-river spawning grounds. 9 A grazing or feeding ground for animals or fowl; a range: a sheep *run.* 10 The regular trail or path of certain animals: an elephant *run.* 11 The bower of a bowerbird. 12 The privilege of free use or access: to have the *run* of the place. 13 A runway. 14 *Music* A rapid succession of tones; a roulade. 15 A series or succession. 16 A sequence of three or more playing cards in consecutive order. 17 A trend or tendency: the general *run* of the market. 18 The direction or course (of something): the *run* of the grain of wood. 19 A continuous length (of something): a *run* of pipe. 20 A continuous spell (of some condition): a *run* of luck. 21 A surge of demands made upon a bank or treasury to meet its obligations. 22 Any great sustained demand. 23 A period of continuous performance, occurrence, popularity, etc.: a play with a long *run.* 24 Class or type: the general *run* of readers. 25 A period of operation of a machine or device: an experimental *run.* 26 The output during such a period. 27 A period during which a liquid is allowed to run. 28 The amount of liquid allowed to flow at one time. 29 A measure of yarn (about 1,600 yards). 30 A narrow, lengthwise ravel, as in a sheer stocking. 31 An approach to a target made by a bombing plane. 32 In baseball, a complete circuit of the bases from home plate and back before three outs are made, thus scoring a point. 33 In cricket, an act in which both batsmen successfully run to opposite popping creases, thereby scoring a point. 34 A hunt, especially on horseback; a chase. 35 *Naut.* The after part of a ship's bottom where it narrows off from the floor timbers to the sternpost. 36 *Mining* A vein. 37 *Austral.* A sheep or cattle station. — **dry run** Any practice test; specifically, an approach to a target made by a bombing plane, without dropping bombs. — **in the long run** As the ultimate outcome of any train of circumstances. — **on the run** 1 Almost without pausing while doing something else; hastily: to eat *on the run.* 2 In full retreat. 3 While running. — *adj.* 1 Made liquid; melted. 2 Made by a process of melting and casting or molding: *run* metal; *run* butter. 3 Extracted or drained: *run* honey. 4 Smuggled; contraband: *run* liquor. [OE *rinnan* flow]

run-a·bout (run′ə·bout′) *n.* 1 A light, handy, open automobile for ready service. 2 A light, open wagon. 3 A small motorboat.

run·a·gate (run′ə·gāt) *n. Archaic* 1 A deserter; renegade. 2 A vagabond; homeless wanderer. [Alter. of RENEGADE; infl. by *run,* dial. *agate* on the way]

run-a-round (run′ə·round′) *n.* 1 *Slang* Artful deception; evasion. 2 Run-round. 3 *Printing* Type set narrower than the body of the text, as around illustrations.

run·a·way (run′ə·wā′) *adj.* 1 Escaping or escaped from restraint or control; fugitive. 2 Brought about by running away: a *runaway* marriage. 3 Easily won: said of a horse race; hence, decisive; one-sided. — *n.* 1 One who or that which runs away or flees; a fugitive or deserter; also, a horse of which the driver has lost control. 2 An act of running away: said especially of a horse.

run·ci·ble spoon (run′sə·bəl) A fork having three broad tines, of which one has a sharp edge. [<RUNC(INATE) + -IBLE]

run·ci·nate (run′sə·nāt, -nit) *adj. Bot.* Saw-toothed, with the incisions or teeth inclined backward: said of leaves. [<L *runcinatus,* pp. of *runcinare* plane off < *runcina* plane, saw]

run·dle (run′dəl) *n.* 1 A rung, as of a ladder. 2 Something that rotates about an axis, as the drum of a capstan. [Var. of ROUNDEL]

rund·let[1] (rund′lit) *n.* A small barrel, or the wine it contains, about 18 wine gallons. Also *runlet.* [<OF *rondelet.* See ROUNDELAY.]

rund·let[2] (rund′lit) See RUNLET[1].

run-down (run′doun′) *adj.* 1 Debilitated; physically weak; tired out. 2 Dilapidated; shabby. 3 Stopped because not wound: said of a timepiece. — *n.* (run′doun′). 1 A summary; resumé. 2 In baseball, a play in which a base runner is put out when trapped between two bases.

Rund·stedt (ro͝ont′shtet), **Karl Rudolf Gerd von,** 1875–1953, German field marshal in World War II.

rune (ro͞on) *n.* 1 A character of the primitive runic alphabet. 2 A Finnish poem or one of its cantos. 3 *pl.* Old Norse lore expressed, or considered as if expressed, in runes; hence, early rimes or poetry in general. 4 Any obscure or mystic song, poem, verse, or saying; a mystery. [<ON *rūn* mystery, rune] — **ru′nic** *adj.*

RUNES
Tomb inscription, Sweden, eleventh century.

Ru·ne·berg (ro͞o′nə·ber′y′), **Johann,** 1804–77, Finnish poet.

rung[1] (rung) *n.* 1 A round crosspiece of a ladder or chair; a round; also, a spoke of a wheel. 2 *Naut.* **a** One of the handles on the rim of a ship's tiller. **b** A floor timber of a ship. 3 *Scot.* & *Brit. Dial.* A heavy club or staff; cudgel. [OE *hrung* crossbar]

rung[2] (rung) Past participle of RING[2].

ru·nic alphabet (ro͞o′nik) An old Germanic alphabet, probably originating in both the Latin and Greek, consisting originally of 24 characters, or runes, later reduced to 16 in Scandinavian writings. The earliest inscriptions in this alphabet are of the second or third century A.D. In England it was still in occasional use at the end of the Old English period, and was finally completely replaced by the Roman alphabet through the spread of Christian writings. Also called *futhark.*

runic staff A clog almanac.

run-in (run′in′) *n.* 1 A quarrel; bicker. 2 *Printing* Inserted or added matter. — *adj.* (run′in′) *Printing* That is inserted or added.

Run·jeet Singh (run′jēt sin′hə) See RANJIT SINGH.

run·kle (rung′kəl) *n., v.t. Scot.* Wrinkle.

run·let[1] (run′lit) *n.* A little stream; rivulet; a runnel. Also *rundlet.* See synonyms under STREAM.

run·let[2] (run′lit) See RUNDLET[1].

run·nel (run′əl) *n.* A streamlet; brooklet; rivulet. [OE *rynel* < *rinnan* run]

run·ner (run′ər) *n.* 1 One who or that which runs; especially, one who runs a race; also, a fugitive or deserter. 2 One who operates or manages anything; especially, the driver of a locomotive. 3 One who runs errands or goes about on any kind of business; a messenger, as for a bank; specifically, one who drums up or solicits patronage or business, as for a hotel. 4 That part on which an object runs or slides: the *runner* of a skate. 5 *Mech.* A device to assist sliding motion. 6 A slender fish *(Elegatis bipinnulatus)* of warm seas with single dorsal and anal pinnules; also, the jurel of the Atlantic coast of America. 7 A cursorial bird; the water rail. 8 *Bot.* **a** A slender, procumbent stem disposed to root at the end and nodes, as in the strawberry; also, sometimes, the plant itself. **b** Any of various twining plants: the scarlet *runner.* 9 A smuggler. 10 A blacksnake. 11 A long, narrow rug or carpeting, used in hallways, etc. 12 A narrow strip of cloth, usually of fine quality, used on tables, dressers, etc.

run·ner-up (run′ər·up′) *n.* A contestant or team finishing in second place.

run·ning (run′ing) *adj.* 1 Such as runs: said specifically of horses inclined or trained to a running gait rather than to pacing or trotting. 2 Following one another without intermission; successive: used with words expressing periods of time: He talked for three hours *running.* 3 Continuous; repeated: said of a design: a *running* ornament, a *running* molding, etc. 4 Kept up continuously; also, passing; cursory: *running* comments, a *running* glance. 5 Characterized by easy flowing curves; cursive: a *running* hand. 6 Discharging, as pus from a sore. — *n.* 1 The act or movement of one who or that which runs: a horse trained for fast *running.* 2 That which runs or flows; the amount or quantity that runs. 3 A discharge, as from a sore. 4 Ability or power to run. 5 Competition; race; rivalry: He's out of the *running.* 6 Climbing; sending out runners, as certain plants.

running board A footboard on the side of a locomotive, street car, automobile, etc.

running expenses Daily expenses.

running fits Fright disease.

running gear 1 *Mech.* **a** The wheels and axles of any vehicle and their immediate attachments, as distinguished from the body, frame, etc., which they support. **b** Those parts of a mechanism or construction that have partially independent motion: the *running gear* of a watch. 2 *Naut.* The movable ropes and wires on a boat or ship by which sails, etc., are raised, lowered, and trimmed.

running hand Writing done with a continuous easy motion without lifting the pen from the paper and usually having the letters slanted forward.

running knot A knot made so as to slip along a noose and tighten when pulled upon.

running lights The sidelights of a vessel.

running mate 1 A horse that is teammate for another; also, a horse entered to set the pace for another entered to run in a horse race. 2 The candidate for the lesser of two offices closely linked by constitutional provisions, as the vice-presidency with the presidency.

running title *Printing* A title or headline repeated at the head of succeeding pages throughout a book or chapter. Also **running head.**

Run·ny·mede (run′i·mēd) A meadow in Surrey, England, on the Thames west of London, where King John is said to have met his barons to sign the Magna Carta in 1215.

run-off (run′ôf′, -of′) *n.* 1 That part of the rainfall in a particular area which is not absorbed directly by the soil but is drained off in rills or streams. 2 A special contest held to break a tie.

run-of-the-mill (run′əv·thə·mil′) See MILL-RUN.

run-on (run′on′, -ôn′) *n. Printing* Appended or added matter.

run-on line Enjambement.

run-out (run′out′) *n.* That portion of a motion-picture film immediately following the last frame of the picture itself.

run-round (run′round′) *n. Pathol.* A circumscribed inflammation of the skin, as on the fingers or toes; a felon: also called *run-around.*

runt (runt) *n.* 1 An unusually small, weak, or stunted animal; also, the smallest and weakest of a litter. 2 A dwarf. 3 *Scot.* An old ox or cow; a withered old man or hag. 4 *Scot.* & *Brit. Dial.* A stump of a tree or shrub; also, the stem or stalk of a plant. [Origin uncertain] — **runt′i·ness** *n.* — **runt′y** *adj.*

run·way (run′wā′) *n.* 1 A way or path over which something runs. 2 The channel or bed of a stream, or the path over which animals pass to and from their places of feeding or watering. 3 In lumbering, an incline down which logs are slid; a chute. 4 Any track specially laid for wheeled vehicles. Also *run.* 5 *Aeron.* An artificial landing strip for airplanes.

Run·yon (run′yən), **Damon,** 1884–1946, U.S. journalist and writer.

ru·pee (ro͞o·pē′) *n.* The standard monetary unit of British India: it contains 16 annas. [< Hind. *rupīya* <Skt. *rūpya* silver]

Ru·pert (ro͞o′pərt; *Fr.* rü·pâr′, *Ger.* ro͞o′pert) A masculine personal name: variant of ROBERT. Also *Ger.* **Ru·precht** (ro͞o′prekht). [See ROBERT]

— **Rupert, Prince,** 1619–82, Royalist general in English Civil War; born in Bavaria.

ru·pi·ah (ro͞o·pē′ä) *n.* The principal Indonesian currency unit.

rup·ture (rup′chər) *n.* 1 The act of breaking apart or the state of being broken apart. 2 Hernia. 3 Breach of peace and concord between individuals or nations. — *v.t.* & *v.i.* **·tured, ·tur·ing** 1 To break apart; separate into parts. 2 To affect with or suffer a rupture. See synonyms under BREAK, REND. [<F <L *ruptus,* pp. of *rumpere* break] — **rup′tur·a·ble** *adj.*

Synonyms (noun): blast, breach, break, burst, disruption, fracture. See BREACH, QUARREL[1].

ru·ral (ro͝or′əl) *adj.* 1 Pertaining to the country as distinguished from the city or the town; rustic. 2 Pertaining to farming or agriculture. See synonyms under RUSTIC. [<F <L *ruralis* < *rus, ruris* country] — **ru′ral·ism** *n.* — **ru′ral·ist** *n.* — **ru′ral·ly** *adv.* — **ru′ral·ness** *n.*

rural dean Dean (def. 2).

rural free delivery A government service of house-to-house free mail delivery by carrier in rural districts, as distinguished from the general delivery service: in addresses abbreviated *R.F.D.* Often shortened to *R.D.*

ru·ral·i·ty (ro͞o·ral′ə·tē) *n.* 1 Ruralness. 2 A rural peculiarity. 3 A place in the country.

ru·ral·ize (ro͝or′əl·īz) *v.* **·ized, ·iz·ing** *v.t.* To make rural. — *v.i.* To go into or live in the country; rusticate. — **ru′ral·i·za′tion** *n.*

Ru·rik (ro͞o′rik) Russian form of RODERICK. — **Rurik,** died 879, Scandinavian conqueror who founded the Russian monarchy, the **House of Rurik,** which lasted from 862 to 1598.

ruse (ro͞oz) *n.* An action intended to mislead or deceive; a stratagem; trick. See synonyms under ARTIFICE, PRETENSE. [<F < *ruser* dodge, detour, drive back. Related to RUSH[1].]

Ru·se (ro͞o′se) A city on the Danube in NE Bulgaria.

ruse de guerre (rüz də gâr′) *French* A stratagem of war.

rush[1] (rush) *v.i.* 1 To move or go swiftly or with violence. 2 To make an attack; charge: with *on* or *upon.* 3 To proceed recklessly or rashly; plunge: with *in* or *into.* — *v.t.* 4 To drive or push with haste or violence; hurry. 5 To do or perform hastily or hurriedly: to *rush* one's work. 6 **a** To make a sudden assault upon. **b** To capture by such an assault. 7 *Slang* To seek the favor of with assiduous attentions. 8 In football, to move (the ball) toward the goal of the other team. See synonyms under HUSTLE. — *n.* 1 The act of rushing; a sudden turbulent movement, drive, or onset. 2 A sudden pressing demand; a run: a *rush* on foreign bonds. 3 A sudden exigency; urgent pressure: a *rush* of business. 4 A sudden flocking of people to a new region, especially to an area rumored to be rich in a precious mineral: a gold *rush.* 5 *U.S.* A general contest or scrimmage between students from different classes, as between sophomores and freshmen. 6 In football: **a** An attempt to take the ball through the opposing linemen and toward the goal. **b** Formerly, a player in the rush line: a center *rush.* 7 In motion pictures, the first film prints of a scene or series of scenes, before editing or selection. See synonyms under CAREER. —*adj.* 1 Requiring urgency or haste: a *rush* order. 2 Characterized by much traffic, business, etc.: the *rush* hours. 3 Denoting a time or function set aside for fraternity or sorority members to meet new students to consider them for membership: *rush* week; a *rush* smoker. [<AF *russher* push, var. of *russer,* OF *ruser, reuser* push back, dodge <LL *recusare* push back. See RECUSANT.]

rush[2] (rush) *n.* 1 Any one of various grasslike, usually aquatic herbs (family *Juncaceae*). The common or **soft rush** *(Juncus effusus)* grows in marshy ground and has soft and pliant, cylindrical, leafless stems: used for mats, seats of chairs, etc. 2 A thing of little or no value. 3 A rushlight. [OE *rysc*]

Rush (rush), **Benjamin,** 1745–1813, American physician, signer for Pennsylvania of the Declaration of Independence.

rush·er (rush′ər) *n.* 1 One who rushes. 2 In football, a lineman.

rush–hold·er (rush′hōl′dər) *n.* A candlestick with a clip for supporting a rushlight.

rush hour A time when traffic or business is at its height. —**rush–hour** (rush′our′) *adj.*

rush·ing (rush′ing) *n. U.S.* The series of activities in which fraternity and sorority members meet and evaluate new college students wishing to be pledged.

rush·light (rush′līt′) *n.* A candle made by dipping a rush in tallow. Also **rush candle.**

Rush·more (rush′môr), **Mount** A mountain in the Black Hills of western South Dakota, on the side of which are carved gigantic faces of Presidents Washington, Jefferson, Lincoln, Theodore Roosevelt: in **Mount Rushmore National Memorial;** 1,220 acres; established, 1929.

rush·y (rush′ē) *adj.* **rush·i·er, rush·i·est** Abounding in or made of rushes.

ru·sine (rōō′sin, -sīn) *adj.* Of, pertaining to, or designating a genus *(Rusa)* of deer native in the East Indies. Compare SAMBUR. [<Malay *rūsa* deer]

rusine antler An antler having a simple brow tine and a simple fork at the tip of the beam.

rus in ur·be (rus′ in ûr′bē) *Latin* The country in the city.

rusk (rusk) *n.* 1 A light, sweetened bread or biscuit. 2 Bread or cake that has been crisped and browned in an oven, then often pounded fine to be eaten with milk. [<Sp. *rosca,* twisted loaf of bread]

Rus·kin (rus′kin), **John,** 1819–1900, English art critic and author.

Russ (rus) *adj.* & *n.* Russian.

Rus·sell (rus′əl), **Bertrand Arthur William,** 1872–1970, third Earl Russell, English mathematician and philosopher. —**Countess Elizabeth Mary,** 1866–1941, *née* Beauchamp, English novelist: pen name *Elizabeth.* —**George William** See Æ. —**Lord John,** 1792–1878, first Earl Russell, English statesman. —**Lillian,** 1861–1922, U. S. soprano: original name Helen Louise Leonard.

Russell diagram *Astron.* The Hertzsprung–Russell diagram.

rus·set (rus′it) *n.* 1 A color formed by combining orange and purple; popularly, any reddish- or yellowish-brown. 2 Russet cloth, clothing, etc.; hence, any coarse homespun cloth or garment; a country dress. 3 Russet leather. 4 A winter apple of greenish color, mottled with brown. —*adj.* 1 Of a reddish- or yellowish-brown color. 2 Made of russet cloth; hence, coarse; homespun; rustic. 3 Finished, but not blacked: said of leather: *russet* shoes. [<OF *rousset,* dim. of *rous* <L *russus* reddish] —**rus′set·y** *adj.*

Rus·sia (rush′ə) 1 Before 1917, an empire of eastern Europe and northern Asia; capital, Saint Petersburg (Petrograd). 2 The Union of Soviet Socialist Republics. 3 The Russian Soviet Federated Socialist Republic: Russian *Rossiya.*

Rus·sian (rush′ən) *adj.* Pertaining to Russia, its people, or their language. —*n.* 1 An inhabitant of Russia; especially, one of any of the Slavic peoples of the U.S.S.R., including the **Great Russians** of the central and northwestern region, the Ukrainians (or **Little Russians**) of the Ukrainian S.S.R. and eastern Poland, which group includes also the Cossacks and Ruthenians, and the **White Russians** of the west, all speaking Indo–European Balto–Slavic languages, such as Russian, Polish, Lithuanian, and Lettish; also, one of any of the peoples of Russia speaking any of the Uralic languages, especially the Finno–Ugric branch; also, one of any of the native peoples of the Caucasus speaking languages unrelated to these others, as Circassian, Georgian, and the Lesghian group. 2 The language of Russia, belonging to the East Slavic branch of the Balto–Slavic languages, having a separate alphabet including several characters not found in other alphabets. Its subdivisions are **Great Russian,** the principal subdivision and standard literary language in northern and central Russia, Ukrainian or Ruthenian (or **Little Russian**), and **White Russian,** the literary language of western Russia.

Russian Church A division of the Greek Church, independent since 1589, and governed by the Holy Synod. See GREEK CHURCH.

Russian dressing Mayonnaise dressing to which chili sauce, pimientos, and chopped pickles have been added.

Rus·sian·ize (rush′ən·īz) *v.t.* **·ized, ·iz·ing** To make Russian.

Russian leather A smooth, well–tanned, high–grade leather of calfskin or light cattle hide, dressed with birch oil and having a characteristic odor.

Russian Revolution See under REVOLUTION.

Russian Soviet Federated Socialist Republic The largest of the constituent republics of the U. S.S.R., occupying 76 per cent of the U.S.S.R. and extending across northern Asia and eastern Europe; 6,590,564 square miles; capital, Moscow: also *(Soviet) Russia*: abbr. *R.S.F.S.R.*

Russian Turkestan See under TURKESTAN.

Russian wolfhound The borzoi.

Russo– *combining form* Russia; pertaining to the Russians: *Russophobia.* [<RUSSIA]

Rus·so·phile (rus′ə·fīl, -fil) *n.* One who favors Russia, or its principles, policy, or methods.

Rus·so·pho·bi·a (rus′ə·fō′bē·ə) *n.* Fear of the policy or influence of Russia. —**Rus′so·phobe** *n.*

rust (rust) *n.* 1 The reddish or yellow coating caused on iron and steel by oxidation, as by the action of air and moisture, consisting of ferric hydroxide, $Fe(OH)_3$, and ferric oxide, Fe_2O_3. 2 A film of oxide formed on any metal by corrosion. 3 Any of the parasitic fungi of the order *Uredinales,* living on the tissues of higher plants. 4 The diseases caused by such fungi; incorrectly, any one of several diseases not caused by these fungi. 5 Any coating or accretion formed by a corrosive or degenerative process: *rust* on salted meat. 6 A condition, affection, or tendency that destroys or weakens energy or active qualities: the *rust* of idleness. 7 Any of several shades of reddish–brown, somewhat like the color of rust, but containing more orange. —*v.t.* & *v.i.* 1 To become or cause to become rusty; undergo or cause to undergo oxidation. 2 To contract or cause to contract rust. 3 To become or cause to become weakened or impaired because of inactivity or disuse: to allow one's powers to *rust.* 4 To make or become rust-colored. [OE]

rus·tic (rus′tik) *adj.* 1 Rural; hence, plain; homely: *rustic* garments. 2 Uncultured; rude; awkward: *rustic* manners. 3 Unaffected; artless: *rustic* simplicity. 4 Pertaining to any irregular style of work or decoration appropriate to the country or to work in natural, unpolished wood. —*n.* 1 One who lives in the country; a country person of simple manners or character; also, a coarse or clownish person. 2 Rusticwork. 3 Country dialect. [<F *rustique* <L *rusticus* <*rus* country] —**rus′ti·cal·ly** *adv.*

Synonyms (adj.): agricultural, artless, awkward, boorish, bucolic, clownish, coarse, countrified, country, hoydenish, inelegant, outlandish, pastoral, plain, rude, rural, sylvan, uncouth, unpolished, unsophisticated, untaught, verdant. *Rural* refers especially to scenes or objects in the country, considered as the work of nature; *rustic* refers to their effect upon man or to their condition as affected by human agency; as, a *rural* scene; a *rustic* party; a *rustic* lass. We speak, however, of the *rural* population, *rural* simplicity, etc. *Rural* has always a favorable sense; *rustic* often an unfavorable one, as denoting lack of culture and refinement; thus, *rustic* politeness expresses that which is well–meant, but awkward. *Rustic* is, however, often used of a studied simplicity, an artistic rudeness, which is pleasing and perhaps beautiful; as, a *rustic* cottage. *Pastoral* refers to the care of flocks and to the shepherd's life with the pleasing associations suggested by the old poetic ideal of that life; as, *pastoral* poetry. *Bucolic* is kindred to *pastoral,* but is a less elevated term, and sometimes slightly contemptuous. *Antonyms*: accomplished, cultured, elegant, polished, polite, refined, urban, urbane.

rus·ti·cate (rus′tə·kāt) *v.* **·cat·ed, ·cat·ing** *v.i.* 1 To go to the country. 2 To stay or live in the country. —*v.t.* 3 To send or banish to the country. 4 *Brit.* To suspend (a student) and send away temporarily, as from a college. 5 To make rustic. 6 To construct (masonry) with rusticwork. [<L *rusticatus,* pp. of *rusticari* rusticate < *rusticus.* See RUSTIC.] —**rus′ti·ca′tion** *n.* —**rus′ti·ca′tor** *n.*

rus·tic·i·ty (rus·tis′ə·tē) *n. pl.* **·ties** 1 Rustic condition, characters, or manners; simplicity; homeliness; awkwardness. 2 A rustic trait or peculiarity. [<L *rusticitas, -tatis*]

rus·tic·work (rus′tik·wûrk′) *n.* 1 Ashlar masonry, or a method of making it, with rough surfaces, and often with deeply sunk grooves at the joints, to make them conspicuous. 2 Woodwork made of the natural limbs and roots of trees, fancifully arranged.

rus·tle[1] (rus′əl) *v.t.* & *v.i.* **·tled, ·tling** To fall, move, or cause to move with a quick succession of small, light, rubbing sounds, as dry leaves or sheets of paper. —*n.* A rustling sound. [OE *hrūxlian* make a noise. Cf. OE *gehyrstan* murmur.] —**rus′tler** *n.* —**rus′tling** *adj.* —**rus′tling·ly** *adv.*

rus·tle[2] (rus′əl) *v.t.* & *v.i.* **·tled, ·tling** 1 *Colloq.* To act with or obtain by energetic or vigorous action. 2 *U.S. Colloq.* To steal (cattle, etc.). [Blend of RUSH and HUSTLE]

rus·tler (rus′lər) *n. U.S.* 1 *Slang* Any person who is active, pushing, and bustling in any enterprise. Compare HUSTLER. 2 *Colloq.* **a** A cowboy or ranchman. **b** A cook on a ranch. **c** A cattle or horse thief.

rust·y[1] (rus′tē) *adj.* **rust·i·er, rust·i·est** 1 Covered or affected with rust. 2 Consisting of or produced by rust. 3 Having the appearance of rust; having a reddish or yellowish discoloration, as from decomposition: said especially of salted fish or meat that has become rancid. 4 Impaired by inaction or want of exercise; also, lacking nimbleness; stiff. 5 **a** Weakened through neglect of use: My Latin is *rusty.* **b** Having lost skill for want of practice: *rusty* in math. 6 *Biol.* Appearing as if covered with rust; brownish–red. See synonyms under TRITE. [OE *rustig* < *rust* rust] —**rust′i·ly** *adv.* —**rust′i·ness** *n.*

rust·y[2] (rus′tē) *adj. Brit. Dial.* Restive; stubborn; obstinate.

rut[1] (rut) *n.* 1 A sunken track worn by a wheel, as in a road; hence, a groove forming a path for anything. 2 A settled habit or course of procedure; routine. —*v.t.* **rut·ted, rut·ting** To wear or make a rut or ruts in. [? Var. of ROUTE]

rut[2] (rut) *n.* 1 The sexual excitement of various animals, especially deer; estrus; also, the period during which it lasts. 2 A roaring or uproar; especially, the noise made by a rutting stag. —*v.* **rut·ted, rut·ting** *v.i.* To be in rut. —*v.t. Rare* To unite with in copulation; cover. [<F <L *rugitus* a roaring, tumult < *rugire* roar] —**rut′ting** *adj.*

ru·ta·ba·ga (rōō′tə·bā′gə) *n.* 1 A cultivated plant *(Brassica napobrassica)* allied to the common turnip. 2 Its edible, yellowish root. Also *Swedish turnip.* [<dial. Sw. *rotabagge*]

ru·ta·ceous (ro͞o·tā′shəs) *adj. Bot.* Of or pertaining to the rue family *(Rutaceae)* of shrubs, trees, and, rarely, herbs, including the lemon, lime, citron, etc. [<L *ruta* <Gk. *rhytē* rue]

Rut·ger (rut′gər, ro͝ot′gər) Dutch form of ROGER.

ruth (ro͞oth) *n.* Sorrow; compassion; pity; also, grief; misery; repentance; regret. [ME *reuthe, reowthe* <OE *hrēow* sad]

Ruth (ro͞oth, *Fr.* rüt) A feminine personal name. [<Hebrew, companion]
— **Ruth** A woman of Moab, daughter-in-law of the Israelite Naomi; she left her own people and went to Bethlehem, where she married Boaz, thus becoming an ancestress of David. Her story is told in the Old Testament book of this name.

Ru·the·ni·a (ro͞o·thē′nē·ə) A region of western Ukrainian S.S.R.; formerly a province of Czechoslovakia; annexed by Hungary, 1939; ceded to U.S.S.R., 1945; since 1945, the **Transcarpathian Oblast** of the Ukrainian S.S.R.; 5,000 square miles; capital, Uzhgorod: also *Carpatho-Ukraine.*

Ru·then·i·an (ro͞o·thē′nē·ən) *n.* **1** One of a group of Ukrainians living in Ruthenia and eastern Czechoslovakia, formerly in Austria. **2** The East Slavic language of the Ukrainians; Ukrainian. See RUSSIAN. — *adj.* Pertaining to the Ruthenians or their language.

ru·then·ic (ro͞o·then′ik) *adj. Chem.* Of, pertaining to, or derived from ruthenium, especially when combined in its higher valence.

ru·the·ni·ous (ro͞o·thē′nē·əs) *adj. Chem.* Of, pertaining to, or derived from ruthenium, especially when combined in its lower valence.

ru·the·ni·um (ro͞o·thē′nē·əm) *n.* A gray, brittle, rare metallic element (symbol Ru) of the platinum group. See ELEMENT. [<NL, after *Ruthenia*]

ruth·er·ford (ruth′ər·fərd) *n.* A unit of radioactivity larger than the curie: equal to that quantity of a radioisotope which decays at the rate of a million disintegrations per second. [after Sir Ernest *Rutherford*]

Ruth·er·ford (ruth′ər·fərd), **Sir Ernest,** 1871–1937, English physicist. — **Joseph,** 1869–1942, U. S. leader of Jehovah's Witnesses.

ruth·ful (ro͞oth′fəl) *adj. Archaic* **1** Full of sorrow or pity; sorrowful; merciful. **2** Causing sorrow. — **ruth′ful·ly** *adv.* — **ruth′ful·ness** *n.*

ruth·less (ro͞oth′lis) *adj.* Having no compassion; unrestrained by pity; merciless: the *ruthless* cruelty of the barbaric Hun. — **ruth′less·ly** *adv.* — **ruth′less·ness** *n.*

ru·ti·lant (ro͞o′tə·lənt) *adj.* Of a shining red color; glittering. [<L *rutilans, -antis,* ppr. of *rutilare* glow red < *rutilus.* See RUTILE.]

ru·ti·lat·ed (ro͞o′tə·lā′tid) *adj.* Enclosing rutile needles: *rutilated* quartz.

ru·tile (ro͞o′til, -tēl, -tīl) *n.* An adamantine, reddish-brown, transparent to opaque titanium dioxide, TiO_2, usually containing a small quantity of iron. [<F, shining <L *rutilus* red]

Rut·land (rut′lənd) **1** A county of eastern England; 152 square miles: county town Oakham. Also **Rut′land·shire** (-shir). **2** A city in central Vermont, important as a center of the marble-cutting industry.

Rut·ledge (rut′lij), **Ann,** 1816–35, fiancée of Abraham Lincoln. — **Edward,** 1749–1800, American jurist; signer for South Carolina of Declaration of Independence. — **John,** 1739–1800, jurist; a framer of the U. S. Constitution; brother of the preceding.

rut·tish (rut′ish) *adj.* Disposed to rut; lustful; libidinous.

rut·ty (rut′ē) *adj.* Full of ruts. — **rut′ti·ness** *n.*

Ru·vu·ma (ro͞o·vo͞o′mə) A river in eastern Africa, flowing 450 miles north and east to the Indian Ocean, and forming the Tanganyika-Mozambique border: Portuguese *Rovuma.*

Ru·wen·zo·ri (ro͞o′wən·zôr′ē, -zō′rē) A mountain group in east central Africa between Albert and Edward lakes, on the boundary between the Belgian Congo and Uganda: identified with the *Mountains of the Moon* of ancient writers; highest peak, 16,795 feet.

Ru·y (*Sp.* ro͞o·ē′, *Pg.* ro͞o′ē) Spanish and Portuguese form of RODERICK.

Ruys·dael (rois′däl, *Du.* rœis′däl), **Jacob van,** 1625?–82, Dutch painter: also spelled *Ruisdael.*

Ruy·ter (roi′tər), **Michel Adriaanszoon de,** 1607–76, Dutch admiral.

Rwan·da (rwän′də) A republic in central Africa, part of the former UN Trust Territory of Ruanda-Urundi; 10,169 square miles; pop. about 2,500,000; capital Kigali.

-ry Var. of -ERY.

Rya·zan (rē·ə·zän′, *Russian* ryä·zän′) A city near the Oka river in the central European Russian S.F.S.R.

Ry·binsk (ri′binsk) See SHCHERBAKOV.

Ry·binsk Reservoir (ri′binsk) The largest artificial lake of the U.S.S.R. in north central European Russian S.F.S.R. on the upper Volga; 1,800 square miles: also **Rybinsk Sea.**

Ry·der (rī′dər), **Albert Pinkham,** 1847–1917, U. S. painter.

rye[1] (rī) *n.* **1** The grain or seeds of a hardy cereal grass *(Secale cereale)* closely allied to wheat. **2** The plant. **3** Whisky distilled from rye. ◆ Homophone: *wry.* [OE *ryge* rye]

rye[2] (rī) *n.* In Gipsy dialect, a gentleman. ◆ Homophone: *wry.* [<Romany *rei, rae,* prob. <Skt. *rājan* a king]

Rye (rī) A municipal borough of east Sussex, England; an important Channel port before the sea receded in the early 19th century.

rye·grass (rī′gras′, -gräs′) *n.* Common darnel: sometimes called *raygrass.*

ryke (rīk, rēk) *v.i. Scot.* To reach.

rynd (rind, rīnd) *n.* An iron fitting supporting an upper millstone, having a central hollow bearing which rests upon the upper pointed end of the mill spindle: also spelled *rind.* [Prob. <M Du. *rijn*]

Ryo·jun (ryō·jo͞on) The Japanese name for PORT ARTHUR.

ry·ot (rī′ət) *n.* In India, a tenant; tiller of the soil; peasant. [<Hind. *raiyat* <Arabic *ra'īyah*]

Rys·wick (riz′wik) A village in southern Netherlands, near The Hague; site of the signing of a treaty by France, Germany, the Netherlands, England, and Spain, 1697: Dutch *Rijswijk.*

Ryu·kyu Islands (ryo͞o·kyo͞o) An archipelago between Kyushu and Taiwan; 1,803 square miles; chief island, Okinawa; Japanese possessions, administered by the U. S. after 1945; formally returned to Japan, May 15, 1972. Also *Nansei Islands.*

S

s, S (es) *n. pl.* **s's, S's** or **ss, Ss** or **ess·es** (es′iz) **1** The nineteenth letter of the English alphabet, from Phoenician *shin,* through Hebrew *shin,* Greek *sigma,* Roman *S.* **2** The sound of the letter *s,* usually a voiceless sibilant. See ALPHABET. — *symbol* **1** *Chem.* Sulfur (symbol S). **2** Anything shaped like an S.

-s[1] A variant of *-es*[1], inflectional ending of the plurals of nouns, attached to nouns not ending in a sibilant or an affricate: *books, words, cars.* It is pronounced (s) after a voiceless consonant, and (z) after a voiced consonant or a vowel.

-s[2] An inflectional ending used to form the third person singular present indicative of verbs not ending in a sibilant, affricate, or vowel: *reads, walks, sings.* Compare -ES[2].

-s[3] *suffix* On; of a; at: often used in adverbs without appreciable force: *nights, Mondays, always, towards.* [OE *-es,* genitive ending]

-'s[1] An inflectional ending used to form the possessive of singular nouns and of plural nouns not ending in *-s*: a *man's* world, *women's* fashions. In plurals ending in *-s* (or *-es*) a simple apostrophe is used as a sign of the possessive: a *girls'* school, the *churches'* steeples, the *Joneses'* claim to the inheritance.

-'s[2] Contraction of: **1** Is: *He's* here. **2** Has: *She's* left. **3** Us: *Let's* go.

Saa·di (sä′dē), **Muslih-ud-Din,** 1184?–1291?, Persian poet. Also spelled *Sadi.*

Saa·le (zä′lə) **1** A river in central East Germany, flowing 265 miles north to the Elbe. Also **Sax·o·ni·an Saale** (sak·sō′nē·ən). **2** A river in northern Bavaria, West Germany, flowing 84 miles west, south and SW from the East German border to the Main. Also **Fran·co·ni·an Saale** (frang·kō′nē·ən).

Saa·mi (sä′mē) *n.* Lapp.

Saar (zär) A river in NE France and western Germany, flowing 152 miles north from the Vosges Mountains to the Moselle.

Saar (zär), **The** A state and industrial region in the Saar valley, SW West Germany; 989 square miles; capital, Saarbrücken. French *Sarre, German* **Saar·land** (zär′länt). Also **Saar Basin, Saar Territory.**

Saar·brück·en (zär′brük·ən) The capital of The Saar.

Saa·re (sä′re) The largest Estonian island in the Baltic, at the mouth of the Gulf of Riga; 1,046 square miles: Swedish *Ösel*: also *Sarema.* Also **Saa·re·maa** (sä′re·mä). *Russian* **E·zel** (ā′zel).

Saa·ri·nen (sä′ri·nen), **Eero,** born 1910, U. S. architect. — **Eliel,** 1873–1950, U. S. architect born in Finland; father of the preceding.

Saa·ve·dra La·mas (sä·vā′thrä lä′mäs), **Carlos,** 1878–1959, Argentine lawyer and statesman.

sab (sab) *n., v.t.* & *v.i. Scot.* Sob.

sa·ba (sä·bä′) *n.* A fine Philippine fabric made from fibers of a plant resembling the banana. [<Tagalog]

Sa·ba (sä′bä) **1** The Arabic name for SHEBA. **2** An island in the eastern group of the Netherlands West Indies; 5 square miles.

sab·a·dil·la (sab′ə·dil′ə) *n.* **1** The acrid seeds of a Mexican and Central American bulbous plant *(Schoenocaulon officinale),* used as a source of veratrine, and formerly as an anthelmintic. **2** The plant. Also spelled *cebadilla, cevadilla.* [<Sp. *cebadilla,* dim. of *cebada* barley]

Sa·bah (sä′bä) A state of Malaysia in northern Borneo; 29,387 square miles; capital, Jesselton. Formerly *North Borneo.*

Sa·ba·ism (sā′bə·iz′əm) *n.* Star worship. [< Hebrew *tsābhā* (heavenly) host, army + -ISM] — **Sa′ba·ist** *n.*

Sab·a·oth (sab′ē·oth, sə·bā′ōth) *n. pl.* Armies; hosts: chiefly in the phrase *the Lord of Sabaoth. Rom.* ix 29, *James* v 4. [<LL <Gk. *Sabaōth* < Hebrew *tsebāōth,* pl. of *tsābhā* host, army]

Sa·bar·ma·ti (sä′bər·mu′tē) A river in southern Rajasthan and northern Bombay, India, flowing 250 miles south to the Gulf of Cambay.

Sa·ba·tier (sà·bà·tyā′), **Paul,** 1854–1941, French chemist.

sab·bat (sab′ət) *n.* The witches' Sabbath. Also **Sab′bat.** [<OF. See SABBATH.]

sab·ba·tar·i·an (sab′ə·târ′ē·ən) *adj.* Pertaining to the Sabbath or its strict observance. — *n.* **1** A Christian who observes Sunday with strict propriety. **2** A Christian who observes the seventh day as the Sabbath: opposed to *dominical.* [<L *sabbatarius* < *sabbatum* SABBATH] — **Sab′ba·tar′i·an·ism** *n.*

Sab·bath (sab′əth) *n.* **1** The seventh day of the week, appointed in the decalog as a day of rest to be observed by the Jews; now, Saturday. **2** The first day of the week as observed by Christians; Sunday. **3** The institution or observance of a day or time of rest. **4** The sabbatical year of the Jews. *Lev.* xxv 4. [Fusion of OE *sabat* and OF *sabbat, sabat,* both <L *sabbatum* <Gk. *sabbaton* <Hebrew *shabbāth* < *shābath* rest] — **Sab·bat′ic** or **·i·cal** *adj.* — **Sab·bat′i·cal·ly** *adv.*
Synonym: Sunday. *Sabbath* carries a suggestion of rest not in *Sunday,* the first day of the week. See FIRST DAY.

Sabbath school A Sunday school.
sab·bat·i·cal (sə·bat′i·kəl) *adj.* Of the nature of the Sabbath as a day of rest; offering rest at regular intervals. Also **sab·bat′ic.** — *n.* A sabbatical year. [< *sabbatic* <F *sabbatique* <Gk. *sabbatikos* < *sabbaton* SABBATH]
sabbatical year **1** In the ancient Jewish economy, every seventh year, in which the people were required to refrain from tillage. **2** A year's vacation awarded to teachers in some American educational institutions every seven years.
sa·be (sä′bē) *SW U.S. v.i.* To understand; know. — *n.* Understanding; knowledge. [<Sp. *saber* know]
Sa·be·an (sə·bē′ən) *adj.* Of or pertaining to ancient Sheba, its people, or their language. — *n.* **1** One of an ancient people of the kingdom of Sheba in SW Arabia in the first millennium B.C.: noted for their commerce and their wealth. **2** The Southwest Semitic language of these people. Also **Sa·bae′an.** [<L *Sabaeus* <Gk. *Sabaios* <*Saba* Sheba <Arabic *Saba'* <Hebrew *Shebā*]
Sa·bel·li·an (sə·bel′ē·ən) *n.* A branch of the Italic subfamily of Indo-European languages, including the ancient Aequian, Marsian, Sabine, and Volscian. [<L *Sabellus* a Sabine]
sa·ber (sā′bər) *n.* A heavy one-edged cavalry sword, with a thick-backed blade, often curved. — *v.t.* **·bered** or **·bred, ·ber·ing** or **·bring** To strike, wound, kill, or arm with a saber. Also spelled *sabre.* [<F *sabre, sable* <MHG *sabel,* prob. <Slavic]
sa·ber-toothed (sā′bər·tōōtht′) *adj.* Having very long, curved, upper canine teeth, likened to sabers.
saber-toothed tiger *Paleontol.* A large, ferocious, extinct carnivore (subfamily *Machaerodontinae*), characterized by very large, trenchant, upper canine teeth; especially, *Smilodon californicus,* common in the western hemisphere until its extinction in the Pleistocene.

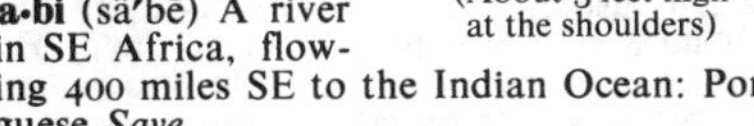
SABER-TOOTHED TIGER (About 3 feet high at the shoulders)

Sa·bi (sä′bē) A river in SE Africa, flowing 400 miles SE to the Indian Ocean: Portuguese *Save.*
Sa·bi·an (sā′bē·ən) *n.* One of an ancient religious sect dwelling in Mesopotamia and described in the Koran as monotheistic: identified by some with the Mandeans. — *adj.* Pertaining to the Sabians or to their religious worship. [<Arabic *sabi'ah* <Aramaic *tsebha'* immerse, baptize] — **Sa′bi·an·ism** *n.*
sab·i·cu (sab′ə·kōō′) Horseflesh (def. 3).
sa·bin (sā′bin) *n. Physics* A unit of sound absorption, equivalent to one square foot of a completely absorbing substance. [after W. C. W. *Sabine,* 1868–1919, U. S. physicist]
sab·ine (sab′in) See SAVIN.
Sa·bine (sā′bīn) *n.* **1** One of an ancient central Italian people, conquered and absorbed by Rome in 290 B.C., whose daughters the early Romans married by force. **2** The language of these people, belonging to the Sabellian branch of the Italic languages. — *adj.* Of or pertaining to the Sabines. [<L *Sabinus*]
Sa·bine River (sə·bēn′) A river in eastern Texas and western Louisiana, flowing 578 miles SE, passing through **Sabine Lake** (17 miles long) and entering the Gulf of Mexico through **Sabine Pass** (7 miles long).
Sa·bir (sa·bēr′) *n.* The lingua franca of the Mediterranean ports, largely a mixture of French, Italian, and Spanish. [<*Se ti sabir,* a jargon phrase in Molière's *Bourgeois Gentilhomme* <Provençal *sabir* knowledge, science]
sa·ble (sā′bəl) *n.* **1** A carnivore (*Martes zibellina*), of northern Asia and Europe, related to the marten. ◆ Collateral adjective: *zibeline.* **2** The dressed fur of a sable, specifically, of the Asian sable. **3** *pl.* Garments made wholly or partly of this fur. **4** The color black; hence, mourning or a mourning garment. **5** *Her.* Black: represented, when uncolored, by a network of lines crossing each other at right angles. — **Alaska sable** A trade name for natural or dyed skunk. — *adj.* **1** Black, especially as the color of mourning. **2** Made of or having the color of sable fur; dark-brown. See synonyms under DARK. [<OF *sable, saible* <Med. L *sabelum* <Slavic]
Sable, Cape **1** The southernmost point of the United States, at the SW tip of Florida. **2** The southernmost extremity of Nova Scotia, on an islet just south of **Cape Sable Island** (7 miles long, 3 miles wide).
sable antelope A large, black, African antelope (*Hippotragus niger*) having annular curved horns.
sa·ble·fish (sā′bəl·fish′) *n. pl.* **·fish** or **·fish·es** The coalfish (def. 2).
Sable Island An island SW of Nova Scotia; 30 miles by 2 miles; opposite Cape Sable, Nova Scotia.
sa·bot (sab′ō, *Fr.* sȧ·bō′) *n.* **1** A wooden shoe, as of a French peasant. **2** A shoe having a wooden sole but flexible shank. See GETA. **3** A disk formerly attached to a projectile to cause it to maintain its position in the bore of a firearm or to take the rifling of the gun. [<F <OF *sabot,* alter. of *savate* an old shoe, ult. <Arabic *sabbāt* a sandal; infl. in form by *bot* a boot]
sab·o·tage (sab′ə·täzh, *Fr.* sȧ·bô·tȧzh′) *n.* An act of malicious damage; deliberately poor workmanship intended to cause damage, obstruction of plans, aims, etc., as in secret resistance to an enemy: sometimes resorted to by workmen to secure compliance with demands. — *v.t.* & *v.i.* **·taged, ·tag·ing** To engage in, damage, or destroy by sabotage. [<F < *saboter* work badly, damage < *sabot* a sabot; with ref. to damage done to machinery with sabots]
sab·o·teur (sab′ə·tûr′, *Fr.* sȧ·bô·tœr′) *n.* One who engages in sabotage. [<F]
sa·bra (sä′brə) *n. Often cap.* An Israeli born in Israel. [<Heb.]
sa·bre (sā′bər) See SABER.
sa·bre·tache (sā′bər·tash, sab′ər-) *n.* A leather pocket hung from the sword belt of a mounted man. [<G *säbeltasche* < *säbel* a saber + *tasche* a pocket]
sab·u·lous (sab′yə·ləs) *adj.* Gritty, like sand. Also **sab′u·lose** (-lōs). [<L *sabulosus* < *sabulum* sand] — **sab′u·los′i·ty** (-los′ə·tē) *n.*
sac (sak) *n. Biol.* A membranous pouch; a cavity or receptacle: the ink *sac* of a squid. [<F <L *saccus.* Doublet of SACK.]
Sac (sak, sôk) See SAUK.
sac·a·ton (sak′ə·tōn′) *n.* A coarse perennial grass (*Sporobolus wrighti*) of the United States and Mexico, yielding hay. [<Sp. *zacatón* < *zacate, sacate* <Nahuatl *çacatl* a kind of grass]
sac·cate (sak′it, -āt) *adj.* **1** Sac-shaped. **2** Having a sac, bag, or pouch. [<Med. L *saccatus* <L *saccus* a sack]
sac·cha·rate (sak′ə·rāt) *n. Chem.* **1** A salt of saccharic acid. **2** A compound of a sugar with a metallic oxide.
sac·char·ic (sə·kar′ik) *adj. Chem.* **1** Of, pertaining to, or derived from sugar or a sweetish substance. **2** Designating a dibasic acid, $C_6H_{10}O_8$, obtained by the oxidation of glucose and other sugars.
sac·cha·ride (sak′ə·rīd, -rid) *n. Chem.* Any of a class of carbohydrates containing sugar, as a *monosaccharide, polysaccharide,* etc.
sac·char·i·fy (sə·kar′ə·fī, sak′ər·ə·fī) *v.t.* **·fied, ·fy·ing** To convert, as starches, into sugar; impregnate with sugar. [<SACCHAR(O)- + (I)FY] — **sac·char′i·fi·ca′tion** *n.*
sac·cha·rim·e·ter (sak′ə·rim′ə·tər) *n.* A polariscope for detecting the strength or concentration of sugar in a solution. [<F *saccharimètre* <Gk. *sakchari* sugar + *metron* measure] — **sac′cha·rim′e·try** *n.*
sac·cha·rin (sak′ər·in) *n. Chem.* A white crystalline compound, $C_7H_5O_3NS$, derived from toluene. It is 300 to 500 times sweeter than cane sugar, and is used as a sweetening agent, especially by diabetics. Also spelled *saccharine.* [<Med. L *saccharum* sugar (<L *saccharon* <Gk. *sakchari, sakcharon,* ult. <Skt. *sharkarā* grit, gravel, sugar) + -IN]
sac·cha·rine (sak′ər·in, -ə·rīn) *adj.* **1** Of, pertaining to, or of the nature of sugar; sweet. **2** Ingratiatingly or cloyingly sweet. — *n.* Saccharin. [<SACCHAR(O)- + -INE[1]] — **sac′cha·rine·ly** *adv.* — **sac′cha·rin′i·ty** *n.*
sac·cha·rize (sak′ə·rīz) *v.t.* **·rized, ·riz·ing** *Chem.* To convert into sugar; ferment. — **sac′·cha·ri·za′tion** *n.*
saccharo- *combining form* Sugar; of or pertaining to sugar: *saccharometer.* Also, before vowels, **sacchar-.** [<Gk. *sakcharon* sugar]
sac·cha·roid (sak′ə·roid) *adj.* **1** Resembling sugar. **2** *Geol.* Having crystalline granular structure: *saccharoid* marble. Also **sac′cha·roi′dal** (-roid′l).
sac·cha·rom·e·ter (sak′ə·rom′ə·tər) *n.* A hydrometer for determining the concentration of sugar in saccharine solutions.
sac·cha·ro·my·ce·tous (sak′ə·rō·mī·sē′təs, -mī′·sə-) *adj.* Of or pertaining to a genus (*Saccharomyces*) of fungi, the yeast family, commonly unicellular, but sometimes developing a septate mycelium. Several produce endogenous spores, while most of them cause alchoholic fermentation with evolution of carbon dioxide. [<NL <Gk. *sakcharon* sugar + *mykēs, -ētos* a mushroom, fungus]
sac·cha·rose (sak′ə·rōs) *adj.* Sucrose.
Sac·co (sak′ō, *Ital.* säk′kō), **Nicola,** 1891–1927, philosophical anarchist in the United States who with *Bartolomeo Vanzetti* was convicted of murder in connection with a payroll robbery, and executed. Their trial aroused international protest because it was thought to have been influenced by political considerations.
sac·cu·late (sak′yə·lāt) *adj.* Formed into a series of saclike expansions; dilated and constricted alternately. Also **sac′cu·lat′ed.**
sac·cule (sak′yōōl) *n.* **1** A little sac. **2** *Anat.* Part of the membranous labyrinth of the ear. [<L *sacculus* a sacculus]
sac·cu·lus (sak′yə·ləs) *n. pl.* **·li** (-lī) A small sac or pouch; a saccule. [<L, dim. of *saccus* a sack]
sac·er·do·tal (sas′ər·dōt′l) *adj.* **1** Pertaining to a priest or priesthood; priestly. **2** Believing in the divine authority of the priesthood. [< OF <L *sacerdotalis* < *sacerdos, -dotis* a priest < *sacer* holy + *do-,* stem of *dare* give] — **sac′·er·do′tal·ly** *adv.*
sac·er·do·tal·ism (sas′ər·dōt′l·iz′əm) *n.* **1** The character and methods of the priesthood; priestcraft. **2** Zeal for priestly things.
sa·chem (sā′chəm) *n.* **1** A North American Indian hereditary chief. **2** Any chief; the head of a political party; specifically, one of the leaders of the Tammany Society in New York. See synonyms under CHIEF. [<Algonquian (Narraganset). Akin to SAGAMORE.]
sa·chet (sa·shā′, *esp. Brit.* sash′ā) *n.* A small ornamental bag for perfumed powder. [<OF, dim. of *sac* <L *saccus* a sack]
Sachs (zäks), **Hans,** 1494–1576, German shoemaker, poet, and playwright; also, the hero of Wagner's *Die Meistersinger.*
Sach·sen (zäkh′sən) The German name for SAXONY.
sack[1] (sak) *n.* **1** A bag for holding bulky articles. **2** A measure or weight of varying amount. **3** A loosely hanging dress without a waistline, often worn without a belt: also spelled *sacque*: also **sack dress.** **4** *Slang* Dismissal: especially in the phrases **to get the sack, to give (someone) the sack.** **5** In baseball slang, a base. **6** *Slang* A bed; mattress. — **to be left holding the sack** *Slang* To be left to take the consequences of a bad situation. — *v.t.* **1** To put into a sack or sacks. **2** To dismiss, as a servant. [OE *sacc* <L *saccus* <Gk. *sakkos* <Hebrew *saq* sackcloth, a grain sack. Doublet of SAC.]

Sack may appear as a combining form in hyphemes or solidemes, or as the first element in two-word phrases, with the meaning of the noun (def. 1):

sack baler	**sack-formed**
sack baling	**sackmaker**
sack carrier	**sackmaking**
sack checker	**sackman**
sack cleaner	**sack mender**
sack cutter	**sack repairer**
sack emptier	**sack-shaped**
sack examiner	**sack sorter**

sack[2] (sak) *v.t.* To plunder or pillage (a town or city) after capturing. — *n.* **1** The pillaging of a captured town or city. 2 Loot; booty obtained by pillage. [<MF *sac* <Ital. *sacco,* orig. plunder <Med. L *saccare* pillage <L *saccus* a sack; from the use of sacks in carrying off plunder] — **sack′er** *n.*

sack[3] (sak) *n.* Light-colored Spanish dry wine; also, any strong white wine from southern Europe. [Earlier *(wyne)seck* <F *(vin) sec* a dry (wine) <L *siccus* dry]

sack·but (sak′but) *n.* 1 A primitive instrument resembling the trombone. 2 In the Bible, a stringed instrument. [<MF *saquebute,* orig. a hooked lance for horseback fighting <OF *saquer* pull + *bouter* push]

sack·cloth (sak′klôth′, -kloth′) *n.* 1 A coarse cloth used for making sacks. 2 Coarse cloth or haircloth worn in penance.

sack coat A man's short, loose-fitting coat with no waist seam, for informal wear.

sack·ful (sak′fo͝ol′) *n. pl.* **·fuls** Enough to fill a sack.

sack·ing (sak′ing) *n.* A coarse cloth made of hemp or flax and used for sacks; bagging.

sack posset A posset formerly brewed with sack.

sack race A race in which each contestant has a sack tied over both feet.

sack suit A man's suit having a sack coat.

Sack·ville (sak′vil), **Thomas,** 1536–1608, first Earl of Dorset and Baron Buckhurst, English poet and diplomat.

Sack·ville–West (sak′vil·west′), **V(ictoria Mary),** 1892–1962, English novelist and poet.

sacque (sak) See SACK[1] (def. 3).

sa·cral[1] (sā′krəl) *adj.* Of, pertaining to, or situated near the sacrum. — *n.* A sacral vertebra or nerve. [<NL *sacralis* < *sacrum* SACRUM]

sa·cral[2] (sā′krəl) *adj.* Pertaining to sacred rites. [<L *sacrum* a rite, orig. neut. sing. of *sacer* holy]

sac·ra·ment (sak′rə·mənt) *n.* 1 *Eccl.* A rite ordained by Christ or by the church as an outward and visible sign of an inward and spiritual grace: in the Greek Church, also called *mystery.* Traditionally they are seven in number (baptism, the Eucharist, confirmation, matrimony, orders, penance, and unction) in the Greek, Roman Catholic, and some other churches; since the Reformation only two of these (baptism and the Eucharist) are recognized by most Protestant churches. 2 *Often cap. Eccl.* **a** The Eucharist; the Lord's Supper. **b** The consecrated bread and wine of the Eucharist: often with *the.* See BLESSED SACRAMENT. 3 Any sign or token of a solemn covenant or pledge. 4 Any thing considered to have a secret or mysterious meaning. [<OF *sacrement* <LL *sacramentum* a mystery <L, an oath, pledge < *sacrare.* See SACRED.]

Synonyms: ceremony, communion, Eucharist, observance, ordinance, rite, service, solemnity. A *ceremony* is a form expressing reverence, or respect; as, religious *ceremonies,* the *ceremonies* of a coronation or of a wedding. An *observance* has more than a formal obligation, approaching a religious sacredness; a religious *observance* viewed as established by authority is called an *ordinance*; viewed as an established custom, it is a *rite.* Any religious act, especially a public act, viewed as a means of serving God is called a *service. Sacrament* and *ordinance* in the religious sense are often used interchangeably; the *ordinance* derives its sacredness from the authority that ordained it, while the *sacrament* possesses a sacredness due to something in itself, even when viewed simply as a memorial. The Lord's Supper is the Scriptural name for the *observance* commemorating the death of Christ; the word *communion* is once applied to it (1 *Cor.* x 16). *Eucharist,* called *The Sacrament,* describes the Lord's Supper as a thanksgiving *service.*

sac·ra·men·tal (sak′rə·men′təl) *n.* 1 One of certain rites, such as the use of holy water, oil, or salt, employed as adjuncts to sacraments, or regarded as analogous to a sacrament. 2 *pl.* The objects, words, or ceremonies used in administering a sacrament. — *adj.* 1 Of or pertaining to a sacrament; constituting or composing a sacrament; having the influence or efficacy of a sacrament. 2 Consecrated, as by sacred vows: the *sacramental* host of God's elect. — **sac′ra·men′tal·ism** *n.* — **sac′ra·men′tal·ist** *n.* — **sac′ra·men′tal·ly** *adv.*

sac·ra·men·tar·i·an (sak′rə·men·târ′ē·ən) *n.* One who regards the sacraments as channels of divine grace. Also **sac′ra·men′ta·rist, sac′·ra·ment·er.** — *adj.* Of or pertaining to a sacrament or sacraments, or to sacramentarians. — **sac′ra·men·tar′i·an·ism** *n.*

Sac·ra·men·tar·i·an (sak′rə·men·târ′ē·ən) *n.* One who regards the sacraments as simply symbols or signs: the name given to Calvinists and followers of Zwingli.

sac·ra·men·ta·ry (sak′rə·men′tər·ē) *n. pl.* **·ries** Any of several books containing the ritual for mass, the sacraments, and various other rites: now used only as a basis for modern rituals.

Sac·ra·men·to (sak′rə·men′tō) The capital of California, on the **Sacramento River,** the largest river in the State, flowing 382 miles south from Central Valley to Suisun Bay.

sa·crar·i·um (sə·krâr′ē·əm) *n. pl.* **·i·a** (-ē·ə) 1 Any sacred or secluded place or shrine of the ancient Romans where venerated things were deposited. 2 The sanctuary of a church. 3 In the Roman Catholic Church, a piscina. [<L < *sacer* holy, sacred]

sa·cred (sā′krid) *adj.* 1 Set apart or dedicated to religious use; hallowed: a *sacred* edifice. 2 Pertaining or related to deity, religion, or hallowed places or things. 3 Consecrated by love or reverence; dedicated to a person or purpose. 4 Entitled to reverence or respect; not to be profaned; inviolable. 5 *Rare* Set apart for evil; accursed. See synonyms under HOLY. [Orig. pp. of obs. *sacre* consecrate <OF *sacrer* <L *sacrare* < *sacer* holy] — **sa′·cred·ly** *adv.* — **sa′cred·ness** *n.*

Sacred College See COLLEGE OF CARDINALS.

sac·ri·fice (sak′rə·fīs) *n.* 1 The act of making an offering to a deity, in worship or atonement. 2 That which is sacrificed; a victim. 3 A giving up of some cherished or desired object. 4 Loss incurred or suffered without return; destruction, as of life. 5 A reduction of price that leaves little or no profit or involves loss. 6 In baseball, a sacrifice hit. — *v.* **·ficed, ·fic·ing** *v.t.* 1 To make an offering or sacrifice of, as to a god or deity in propitiation, supplication, etc. 2 To give up, yield, permit injury to, or relinquish (something valued) for the sake of something else, as a person, thing, or idea. 3 To sell at a reduced price; part with at a loss. 4 In baseball, to advance (one or more runners) by means of a sacrifice hit. — *v.i.* 5 To make a sacrifice. 6 To make a sacrifice hit. See synonyms under SURRENDER. [<OF <L *sacrificium* < *sacra* rites, orig. neut. pl. of *sacer* holy + *facere* make] — **sac′ri·fic′er** *n.* — **sac′·ri·fic′ing·ly** *adv.*

sacrifice hit In baseball, a hit by which the batter is retired but by which a base runner is advanced another base, the batter not being charged with a time at bat: when batted into the air also called **sacrifice fly.**

sac·ri·fi·cial (sak′rə·fish′əl) *adj.* Pertaining to, performing, or of the nature of a sacrifice. — **sac′ri·fi′cial·ly** *adv.*

sac·ri·lege (sak′rə·lij) *n.* The act of violating or profaning anything sacred, including sacramental vows. [<OF <L *sacrilegium* < *sacrilegus* a temple robber < *sacer* holy + *legere* gather] — **sac′ri·le′gist** (-lē′jist) *n.*

sac·ri·le·gious (sak′rə·lij′əs, -lē′jəs) *adj.* 1 Having committed, or being ready to commit, sacrilege; impious. 2 Of the nature of sacrilege. See synonyms under PROFANE. — **sac′ri·le′gious·ly** *adv.* — **sac′ri·le′gious·ness** *n.*

sa·cring bell (sā′kring) A small bell rung at the elevation during mass; the tolling of the church bell at this time; the Sanctus bell. [< *sacring,* ppr. of obs. *sacre* consecrate + BELL]

sa·crist (sā′krist) *n.* 1 A sacristan. 2 A person who takes charge of choir books and copy music; also, a sexton. [<OF *sacrist* <L *sacrista* < *sacra* holy (objects), neut. pl. of *sacer*]

sac·ris·tan (sak′ris·tən) *n.* An officer having charge of the sacristy of a church or religious house and its contents, and of the proper arrangement of all objects needed for divine service. The sacristan of a cathedral is commonly in orders. Compare SEXTON. [<Med. L *sacristanus* <L *sacrista.* Doublet of SEXTON.]

sac·ris·ty (sak′ris·tē) *n. pl.* **·ties** A room in a religious house for the sacred vessels and vestments; a vestry. [<F *sacristie* <Med. L *sacristia* <L *sacrista* a sacrist]

sacro– *combining form Med.* Near, or related to the sacrum: *sacrosciatic.* [<L *(os) sacrum* the sacral (bone)]

sac·ro·il·i·ac (sak′rō·il′ē·ak) *adj. Anat.* Pertaining to the sacrum and the ilium and to the joints or ligaments connecting them. [< SACRO- + ILIAC]

sac·ro·sanct (sak′rō·sangkt) *adj.* Peculiarly and exceedingly sacred; inviolable; preeminent for sanctity: sometimes used ironically. [<L *sacrosanctus* < *sacro,* ablative of *sacrum* a rite (< *sacer* holy) + *sanctus,* pp. of *sancire* make holy, inviolable] — **sac′ro·sanc′ti·ty** *n.*

sa·cro·sci·at·ic (sā′krō·sī·at′ik) *adj. Anat.* Of or pertaining to the sacrum and the ischium: the *sacrosciatic* ligaments, connecting the sacrum and the hip bone.

sa·crum (sā′krəm) *n. pl.* **·cra** (-krə) *Anat.* A composite bone formed by the union of the five vertebrae between the lumbar and caudal regions, constituting the dorsal part of the pelvis. [<NL <L *(os) sacrum* sacred (bone); from its being offered in sacrifices]

Sa·cy (sà·sē′), **Baron de,** 1758–1838, Antoine Isaac Silvestre, French Oriental scholar.

sad (sad) *adj.* **sad·der, sad·dest** 1 Sorrowful or depressed in spirits; expressing, or having the external appearance of grief or sorrow; unhappy; mournful; gloomy. 2 Causing sorrow or pity; distressing; unfortunate. 3 *Dial.* Heavy; soggy: said of food. 4 *Colloq.* Vexatious, mischievous, or bad: often humorously or as a mild intensive: That boy is a *sad* tease. 5 Dark-hued; somber. [OE *sæd,* orig. sated] — **sad′ly** *adv.* — **sad′ness** *n.*

Synonyms: afflicted, dejected, depressed, desolate, despondent, disconsolate, dismal, distressed, doleful, downcast, dreary, dull, gloomy, grave, heavy, lugubrious, melancholy, miserable, mournful, sober, somber, sorrowful, sorry, unhappy, woebegone, woeful. *Sad, melancholy, unhappy,* and many similar words may be used either of the personal experience of grief, sorrow, mental depression, etc., or of that which causes grief or pain; a person is *sad* on account of a *sad* event. See synonyms under BAD. *Antonyms*: see synonyms for HAPPY.

sad·den (sad′n) *v.t.* & *v.i.* To make or become sad or unhappy.

sad·dle (sad′l) *n.* 1 A seat or pad for a rider, as on the back of a horse or on a bicycle. 2 A padded cushion for a horse's back, as part of a harness or to support a pack, etc. For illustration see HARNESS. 3 The two hindquarters of a carcass, as of mutton, veal, or venison; also, the undivided loins of such a carcass. 4 Some part like or likened to a saddle, as the lower part of the back of a fowl. See illustration under FOWL. 5 *Geog.* A depression across the summit of a ridge; a pass. 6 *Meteorol.* A low-pressure area between two anticyclones; a col. 7 Something resembling a saddle in form or position, as a bearing for a car axle. — **in the saddle** In control. — *v.* **·dled, ·dling** *v.t.* 1 To put a saddle on: to *saddle* a horse. 2 To load, as with a burden. 3 To place as a burden or responsibility: with *upon.* — *v.i.* 4 To get into a saddle. [OE *sadol*]

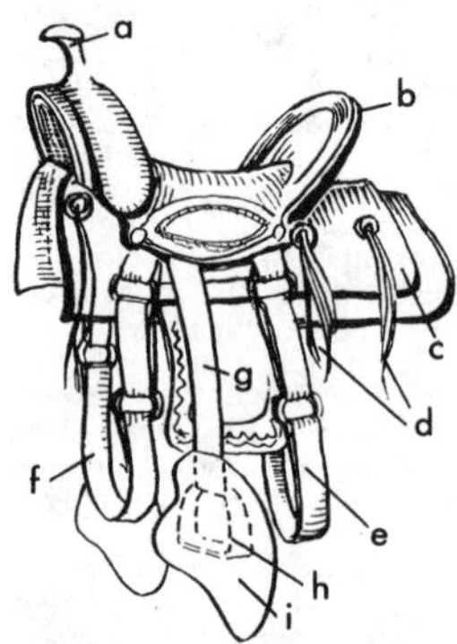

NOMENCLATURE–AMERICAN STOCK SADDLE
a. Pommel or horn.
b. Cantle.
c. Saddle.
d. Saddle strings.
e. Back cinch.
f. Front cinch.
g. Stirrup strap or leather.
h. Stirrup.
i. Tapadera or stirrup hood.

saddle bags A pair of pouches connected by a strap or band and slung over an animal's back or attached to a saddle.

saddle band A remuda.

sad·dle·bow (sad′l·bō′) *n.* The arched front upper part of a saddletree.

sad·dle·cloth (sad′l·klôth′, -kloth′) *n.* A cloth

under and attached to a saddle, or one under the saddle of a harness.
saddle horse A horse used with or trained for the saddle.
sad·dler (sad′lər) *n.* 1 A maker of saddles, harness, etc. 2 A saddle horse.
saddle roof A roof consisting of two gables and one ridge.
sad·dler·y (sad′lər·ē) *n. pl.* **·dler·ies** 1 Saddles, harness, and fittings, collectively. 2 A saddler's shop. 3 The business of a saddler.
saddle shoe A white sport shoe with a dark band of leather across the instep.
saddle soap A softening and preserving soap for leather, containing pure white soap, usually Castile, and neat's-foot oil.
sad·dle·tree (sad′l·trē′) *n.* 1 The frame of a saddle. 2 The tulip tree: so called from its saddle-shaped leaf.
Sad·du·cee (saj′o͝o·sē, sad′yo͝o·sē) *n.* A member of a strict Jewish school that arose in the second century B.C., and later became skeptical and traditionalistic, adhering only to the Mosaic law. [<LL *Sadducaeus* <Gk. *Saddoukaios* <Hebrew *tsaddūqī*, appar. after *Tsaddūq* Zadok (*Ezek.* xl 46)] —**Sad′du·ce′·an, Sad′du·cae′an** *adj.* —**Sad′du·cee′ism** *n.*
sa·de (sä·dā′) *n.* The eighteenth Hebrew letter: also spelled *tsade.* Also **sa·dhe′.** See ALPHABET.
Sade (såd), **Comte Donatien de,** 1740–1814, French writer and libertine: known as *Marquis de Sade.*
Sa·di (sä·dē′) See SAADI.
sad-i·ron (sad′ī′ərn) *n.* A flat iron for smoothing clothes: distinguished from a *box-iron.* [<SAD, in obs. sense "heavy" + IRON]
sad·ism (sā′diz·əm, sad′iz·əm) *n. Psychiatry* 1 Sexual gratification obtained through the infliction of pain upon others. 2 A morbid delight in being cruel. [after Comte Donatien de *Sade*; with reference to the various sexual aberrations described in his writings] —**sad·ist** (sā′dist, sad′ist) *n. & adj.* —**sa·dis·tic** (sə·dis′tik, sā-) *adj.* —**sa·dis′ti·cal·ly** *adv.*
Sa·do·va (sä′dô·vä) A town in southern Bohemia, Czechoslovakia; scene of the culminating defeat of the Austrians by Prussian forces, 1866. *German* **Sa′do·wa.**
sae (sā) *adv. Scot.* So.
sa·fa·ri (sə·fä′rē) *n.* 1 An expedition or journey, often on foot, as for hunting. 2 The caravan and animals employed in this; also, a day's march: also spelled *suffari.* [<Swahili <Arabic *safara* travel]
safe (sāf) *adj.* 1 Free or freed from danger or evil. 2 Having escaped injury or damage; unharmed. 3 Not hazardous; not involving risk or loss; also, conferring safety; of persons, trusty; prudent. 4 Not likely to disappoint; free from doubt or error: It is *safe* to promise. 5 Not likely to cause or do harm or injury. 6 In politics, adhering to party principles; to be depended on to support certain interests: said of a candidate; also, sure to vote for a certain candidate: said of a district. 7 In baseball, having reached base without being retired: He was ruled *safe* at second. See synonyms under SECURE. —*n.* 1 A strong iron-and-steel receptacle, usually fireproof, for protecting valuables, as money or jewels. 2 Any place of safe storage, as a room, tank, refrigerator, or box, for preserving perishable articles, as meator fish. [<OF *sauf* <L *salvus* whole, healthy] —**safe′ly** *adv.* —**safe′·ness** *n.*
safe-blow·ing (sāf′blō′ing) *n.* The act of using explosives to open a safe to be robbed. —**safe′-blow′er** *n.*
safe-break·er (sāf′brā′kər) *n.* A safe-cracker.
safe-con·duct (sāf′kon′dukt) *n. Law* 1 An official document assuring protection on a journey or voyage, as in time of war; a passport. 2 The act of conducting in safety. —*v.t.* (sāf′kən·dukt′) 1 To convoy in safety. 2 To provide with a safe-conduct.
safe-crack·er (sāf′krak′ər) *n.* One who breaks into safes to rob them.
safe-crack·ing (sāf′krak′ing) *n.* The breaking open of safes for robbery.
safe deposit A room, vault, or other fireproof storage place for valuables.
safe-de·pos·it box (sāf′di·poz′it) A box, safe, drawer, or other fireproof receptacle for valuable jewelry, papers, etc., generally in a bank.
safe·guard (sāf′gärd′) *n.* 1 One who or that which guards or keeps in safety, as an escort, guard, or safe-conduct. 2 A mechanical device designed to prevent accident or injury. See synonyms under DEFENSE. —*v.t.* To defend; protect; guard.
safe-hand (sāf′hand′) *n.* 1 A safe method of transmitting official secret papers. 2 A trustworthy courier.
safe hit In baseball, a fair hit by which the batter reaches first base.
safe house A house or apartment used by a spy where he or she may presume to be safe from capture or discovery.
safe·keep·ing (sāf′kē′ping) *n.* The act or state of keeping or being kept in safety; protection.
safe·ty (sāf′tē) *n. pl.* **·ties** 1 The state or condition of freedom from danger or risk. 2 Freedom from injury. 3 A device or catch designed as a safeguard, as in a firearm. 4 In football, the act or play of touching the ball to the ground behind the player's own goal line when the impetus which sent the ball over the goal line was given to it by one of his own side: also **safe′ty-touch′down′** (-tuch′·doun′) 5 In baseball, a safe hit.
safety belt 1 An extensible strap encircling the user and a permanently fixed object so that the user may move freely but be safe from falling or slipping: used by linemen, window cleaners, etc. 2 *Aeron.* A strap fixed to the seat of an aircraft by which the passenger is secured against sudden shocks or turning movements. 3 A life belt.
safety bicycle A bicycle having equal or nearly equal wheels, operated by pedal cranks communicating with the driving wheel.
safety glass See under GLASS.
Safety Islands A group of three islands off the coast of French Guiana, including Devil's Island. *French* **Îles du Sa·lut** (ēl dü så·lü′).
safety lamp 1 A miner's lamp having the flame surrounded by fine wire gauze, which prevents the ignition of explosive gases: called a *davy* from its inventor, Sir Humphry Davy. 2 A specially protected incandescent electric lamp.
safety lever *Mech.* 1 A device for controlling the movement of machine parts. 2 A similar contrivance for preventing the accidental discharge of a grenade, automatic pistol, etc.: also **safety catch.**
safety match A match that will ignite only when struck upon a chemically prepared surface.
safety pin 1 A pin whose point springs into place within a protecting sheath. 2 A pin which prevents the premature detonation of a hand grenade.
safety razor See under RAZOR.
safety valve 1 *Mech.* A valve in a steam boiler, etc., for automatically relieving excessive pressure. 2 Any outlet for pent-up energy or emotion.
saf·flow·er (saf′lou′ər) *n.* 1 A thistlelike herb *(Carthamus tinctorius)* about 2 feet high, with spiny heads of orange-red flowers. 2 The dried flower heads of this plant pressed into small cakes for export: also **safflower cake.** 3 The reddish dyestuff obtained from the dried flowers. [<Du. *saffloer* <OF *saffleur, safour* <Ital. *saffiore*; infl. in form by SAFFRON and FLOWER]
saf·fron (saf′rən) *n.* 1 An autumn-flowering species of crocus *(Crocus sativus).* 2 The dried orange-colored stigmas of this plant used for coloring confectionery, varnishes, etc., and in parts of the Old World as a flavoring and coloring ingredient in cookery. 3 A deep yellow orange: also **saffron yellow.** —*adj.* Of the orange color of saffron. [<OF *safran* <Sp. *azafran* <Arabic *az-za′farān* the saffron]
Sa·fi (sä′fē) A port in Morocco, SW of Casablanca. Formerly **Saf′fi.**
saf·ra·nine (saf′rə·nēn, -nin) *n. Chem.* 1 Any of a class of basic compounds considered as symmetrical diamine derivatives of the azo group bases. Their salts form important dyes. 2 Any of various mixtures of safranine salts used in dyeing. See SAFFRON. Also **saf′·ra·nin** (-nin). [<F *safran* SAFFRON + -INE[2]]
saf·role (saf′rōl) *n. Chem.* A poisonous liquid, $C_{10}H_{10}O_2$, forming a large portion of sassafras oil: contained also in other oils, as oil of camphor: used in medicine and perfumery. Also **saf′rol.** [<F *safran* SAFFRON + -OLE[1]]
saft (saft, säft) *adj. Scot.* 1 Soft. 2 Wet: said of the weather.
sag (sag) *v.* **sagged, sag·ging** *v.i.* 1 To bend or sink downward from weight or pressure, especially in the middle. 2 To hang unevenly. 3 To lose firmness or determination; weaken, as from exhaustion, age, etc. 4 To decline, as in price or value. 5 *Naut.* To drift. —*v.t.* 6 To cause to sag. —*n.* 1 A sagging, or its extent or degree; a sagging place or part, as of a roof. 2 *Naut.* A sidewise drift, as of a vessel. 3 A depressed or sunken place in flat land; a marsh. [ME *saggen,* ? <MDu. *zakken* subside, ? <dial. ON (nautical) *sakka* plummet]
sa·ga (sä′gə) *n.* 1 A medieval Scandinavian (specifically, Icelandic) prose narrative of conventionalized form dealing with legendary or historical exploits, usually of a single hero or a single family. 2 A story, sometimes poetic, having the saga form or manner, often chronicling the history of a family, as Galsworthy's *Forsyte Saga.* [<ON, history, narrative. Akin to SAW[2].]
sa·ga·cious (sə·gā′shəs) *adj.* 1 Ready and apt to apprehend and to decide on a course. 2 Characterized by discernment, shrewdness, and wisdom. 3 Quick of scent, as a hound. [<L *sagax, sagacis* wise, foreseeing] —**sa·ga′·cious·ly** *adv.* —**sa·ga′cious·ness** *n.*
Synonyms: able, acute, apt, clear-sighted, discerning, intelligent, judicious, keen, keen-sighted, keen-witted, perspicacious, quick-witted, rational, sage, sensible, sharp, sharp-witted, shrewd, wise. *Sagacious* refers to a power of tracing the hidden or recondite by slight indications, as by instinct or intuition; with reference to inferior animals it is often applied to special keenness of sense-perception as of a hound in following a trail. In human affairs *sagacious* refers to a power of ready, far-reaching, and accurate inference from observed facts, perhaps in themselves very slight, that seems like a special sense; or to a similar readiness to foresee the results of any action, a kind of prophetic common sense, especially upon human motives or conduct. *Sagacious* is a broader word than *shrewd,* and not capable of the invidious sense which the latter often bears; on the other hand, *sagacious* is less lofty than *wise* in its full sense, and more limited to practical matters. See ACUTE, ASTUTE, KNOWING, POLITIC, WISE[1]. *Antonyms*: absurd, dull, foolish, futile, ignorant, irrational, obtuse, senseless, silly, simple, sottish, stupid, unintelligent.
sa·gac·i·ty (sə·gas′ə·tē) *n.* The quality of being sagacious; discernment and judgment; shrewdness. See synonyms under ACUMEN, WISDOM. [<MF *sagacité* <L *sagax* sagacious]
sa·ga·man (sä′gə·man′, -mən) *n.* The author, singer, or narrator of a saga; a Scandinavian poet or bard. [Trans. of ON *sögumadhr* < *sögu,* genitive of *saga* a saga + *madhr* a man]
Sa·ga·mi Sea (sä·gä·mē) An inlet of the Philippine Sea in central Honshu island, Japan.
sag·a·more (sag′ə·môr, -mōr) *n.* A tribal or lesser chief among the Algonquian Indians of North America, usually inferior to *sachem.* [< Algonquian (Penobscot) *sagamo.* Akin to SACHEM.]
sage[1] (sāj) *n.* A venerable man of recognized experience, prudence, and foresight; a profoundly wise counselor or philosopher. —*adj.* 1 Characterized by or proceeding from calm, far-seeing wisdom and prudence. 2 Befitting a sage; profound; learned; also, grave; serious; shrewd. See synonyms under SAGACIOUS, WISE[1]. [<OF *saige, savie,* ult. <L *sapiens, -entis* wise, ppr. of *sapere* be wise. Doublet of SAPIENT.] —**sage′ly** *adv.* —**sage′ness** *n.*
sage[2] (sāj) *n.* 1 A plant of the mint family (genus *Salvia*), especially the common garden sage *(S. officinalis),* a stiff, shrubby perennial with gray-green leaves and purple, blue, or white flowers: used for flavoring meats, etc. 2 A light, greenish-gray color, like the color of sage leaves. 3 Any other plant of the genus *Salvia,* as the scarlet sage *(S. splendens).* 4 The Jerusalem sage (genus *Phlomis*), also of the mint family. 5 The sagebrush. [<OF

sauge <L *salvia,* ? <*salvus* safe; with ref. to its reputed healing powers]

Sage (sāj), **Russell,** 1816–1906, U.S. financier and philanthropist.

sage·brush (sāj′brush′) *n.* An aromatic, bitter, typically perennial herb or small shrub (genus *Artemisia*) of the composite family, widely distributed on the alkali plains of the western United States; especially, *A. tridentata,* the State flower of Nevada. The Old World species are called *wormwood.*

Sagebrush State Nickname of NEVADA.

sage cock See COCK OF THE PLAINS.

sage hen 1 The female of the sage cock. See GROUSE. **2** *Usually cap.* A native of Nevada: a nickname.

sage sparrow A small, pale–gray, fringilline bird of the western United States *(Amphispiza nevadensis).*

sag·gar (sag′ər) *n.* **1** A vessel of baked fireproof clay in which are fired delicate pieces of pottery that would be injured by direct exposure to the heat. **2** Clay used for making saggars. Also spelled *seggar.* Also **sag′gard** (-ərd). —*v.t.* To place or treat in a saggar, as pottery. Also **sag′ger.** [Contraction of SAFEGUARD]

Sa·ghal·ien (sə·gäl′yən) A former spelling of SAKHALIN.

Sag·i·naw (sag′ə·nô) A city in east central Michigan, a port of entry on the **Saginaw River,** which flows about 22 miles into Saginaw Bay just below Bay City.

Saginaw Bay A SW arm of Lake Huron, extending 60 miles into eastern Michigan.

Sa·git·ta (sə·jit′ə) *Astron.* A northern constellation between Aquila and Cygnus; the Arrow. See CONSTELLATION. [<L, lit., an arrow]

sag·it·tal (saj′ə·təl) *adj.* **1** Pertaining to or resembling an arrow or arrowhead. **2** *Anat.* **a** Straight: the *sagittal* suture between the two parietal bones of the skull. **b** Of or pertaining to the longitudinal plane dividing an animal into right and left halves. [<L *sagitta* an arrow] —**sag′it·tal·ly** *adv.*

Sag·it·ta·ri·us (saj′ə·târ′ē·əs) **1** A zodiacal constellation, pictured as a centaur shooting an arrow; the Archer. See CONSTELLATION. **2** The ninth sign of the zodiac, with the symbol ♐. [<L, lit., an archer <*sagitta* an arrow]

sag·it·tate (saj′ə·tāt) *adj. Bot.* Shaped like an arrowhead, as certain leaves. Also **sag′it·tat′·ed, sa·git·ti·form** (sə·jit′ə·fôrm). [<L *sagitta* an arrow]

sa·go (sā′gō) *n.* **1** Any of several varieties of East Indian palm (genus *Metroxylon*). **2** The dried, powdered pith of this palm used as a thickening agent in puddings, etc. [<Malay *sāgū*]

Sa·guache (sə·wach′) See SAWATCH MOUNTAINS.

sa·gua·ro (sə·gwä′rō, -wä′-) *n. pl.* **·ros** The giant cactus of the SW United States *(Cereus giganteus):* its blossom is the State flower of Arizona. Also **sa·hua′ro** (-wä′-). [<Sp. <Piman]

Sag·ue·nay River (sag′ə·nā′) A river in southern Quebec province, Canada, flowing 110 miles east from Lake St. John to the St. Lawrence River; total length, including sections above and traversing Lake St. John, about 475 miles.

Sa·guia el Ham·ra (sä′gyä el häm′rä) A territory of Spanish West Africa; 32,047 square miles. Also **Se·kia el Hamra** (se′kyä).

sa·gum (sā′gəm) *n. pl.* **·ga** (-gə) The ancient Roman soldiers' military cloak: a symbol of war, as the toga was of peace. [<L, ? ult. < Celtic]

Sa·gun·to (sä·gōōn′tō) An ancient town in eastern Spain near the Gulf of Valencia; destroyed by Hannibal, 219 B.C.: formerly *Murviedro.* Ancient **Sa·gun·tum** (sə·gun′təm).

sag·y (sā′jē) *adj.* Flavored or seasoned with or like sage.

Sa·har·a (sə·har′ə, -hâr′ə, -hä′rə) The world's largest desert area, extending from the Atlantic to the Red Sea in northern Africa; about 3,000,000 square miles. Also **Sahara Desert.**

Sa·ha·ran·pur (sə·hä′rən·pōōr) A city in northern Uttar Pradesh State, India.

Sa·hib (sä′ib) *n.* Master; lord; Mr.; sir: used in India by natives in speaking of or addressing Europeans, also by Hindus and Moslems for people of rank: Raja *Sahib.* Also **Sa′heb.** [< Urdu *sāhib* <Arabic *ṣaḥib,* lit., a friend]

said[1] (sed) Past tense and past participle of SAY[1]. —*adj. Law* Previously mentioned; aforesaid.

sa·id[2] (sä′yid, sī′id) See SAYID.

Sa·i·da (sä′ē·dä) A port in SW Lebanon: ancient *Sidon:* also *Sayida.*

Sai·du (sī′dōō) A market town in northern West Pakistan, NE of Peshawar; the capital of the former princely state of Swat.

sai·ga (sī′gə) *n.* An antelope *(Saiga tatarica)* of the Siberian steppes, resembling a sheep. [< Russian *saiga*]

Sai·gon (sī·gon′, *Fr.* sà·ē·gôṅ′) Former name of Ho Chi Minh City.

sail (sāl) *n.* **1** *Naut.* A piece of canvas, etc., attached to the mast of a vessel, to secure its propulsion by the wind: variously shaped and rigged: fore–and–aft or square *sails.* **2** Sails collectively: full *sail.* **3** A sailing vessel or craft: plural same as singular: 30 *sail* in sight. **4** A trip or passage in a sailing vessel, or in any watercraft. **5** Anything resembling a sail in form or use, as the broad part of the arm of a windmill or a bird's wing. **6** A structure rising from the deck of a submarine that houses detection gear. —**to make sail 1** To unfurl a sail or sails. **2** To set out on a voyage. —**to set sail** To begin a voyage; get under way. —**under sail** Sailing; with sails spread and driven by the wind. —*v.i.* **1** To move across the surface of water by the action of wind or, by extension, steam. **2** To travel over water in a ship or boat. **3** To begin a voyage; set sail. **4** To manage a sailing craft: Can you *sail*? **5** To move, glide, or float in the air; soar. **6** To move along in a stately or dignified manner: She *sailed* by haughtily. **7** *Colloq.* To pass rapidly. **8** *Colloq.* To proceed boldly into action: with *in.* —*v.t.* **9** To move or travel across the surface of (a body of water) in a ship or boat. **10** To navigate (a ship, etc.). —**to sail into 1** To begin with energy. **2** To attack violently. ◆ Homophone: *sale.* [OE *segl*] —**sail′a·ble** *adj.*

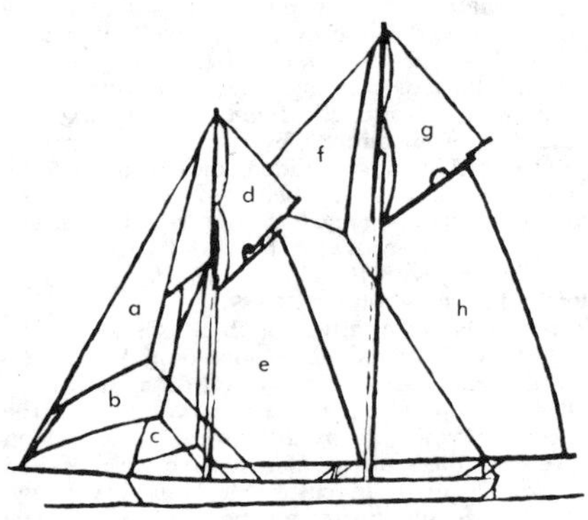

SAILS OF A
CLUB TOPSAIL SCHOONER

a. Jib topsail.
b. Flying jib.
c. Jib.
d. Fore club topsail.
e. Foresail.
f. Maintopmast staysail.
g. Main club topsail.
h. Mainsail.

sail·boat (sāl′bōt′) *n.* A small boat propelled by a sail pr sails.

sail·cloth (sāl′klôth′, -kloth′) *n.* A very strong, firmly woven, cotton canvas suitable for sails: also called *duck.*

sail·fish (sāl′fish′) *n. pl.* **·fish** or **·fish·es 1** Any of a genus *(Istiophorus)* of marine fishes allied to the swordfish, having a large or conspicuous dorsal fin likened to a sail. **2** The basking shark.

SAILFISH
(Up to 6 feet in length)

sail·ing (sā′ling) *n.* **1** The setting forth on or prosecution of a voyage: the *sailing* of a vessel. **2** The art and method of determining the direction and distance sailed by a ship at sea, the point reached, and the course to be taken; navigation; seamanship.

sailing orders Instructions given to a ship's captain, covering alldetails of a voyage.

sail–loft (sāl′lôft′, -loft′) *n.* A room where sails are cut out and sewed.

sail·or (sā′lər) *n.* **1** A seaman; mariner. **2** A sailor hat. —**sail′or·ly** *adj.*

Synonyms: mariner, seafarer, seaman. In nautical language *sailors* and *seamen* are exclusive of officers, but in literary use all whose vocation is navigation are figuratively termed *sailors* or *seamen. Mariner* is one who navigates or assists in navigating a ship; in the United States statutes *mariner* denotes any person, from captain to cook, who serves in any capacity on a ship. *Antonym:* landsman.

sailor hat A low–crowned, flat–topped straw hat with a brim, worn by both sexes. Also *sailor.*

sail·or's–choice (sā′lərz·chois′) *n.* **1** The hogfish. **2** The pinfish. **3** A West Indian grunt *(Haemulon parra)* or related fish.

sail·plane (sāl′plān′) *n. Aeron.* A light, highly maneuverable glider requiring a relatively low speed for flight, used for soaring. —*v.i.* **·planed, ·plan·ing** To fly a sailplane.

Sai·maa (sī′mä) A lake system of SE Finland near the U.S.S.R. border; 1,699 square miles.

sain (sān) *v.t. Scot.* or *Archaic* To sign or bless with the sign of the cross to preserve against malign influence: also spelled *sane.* [OE *segnian* <L *signare* sign, make a sign of the cross <*signum* a sign]

sain·foin (sān′foin) *n.* An Old World perennial, cloverlike herb *(Onobrychis viciaefolia)* of the bean family, with variegated flowers, cultivated for forage: also called *esparcet.* Also **saint′·foin.** [<F <*sain* wholesome (<L *sanus* healthy) + *foin* hay]

saint (sānt) *n.* **1** A holy, godly, or sanctified person; in the New Testament, any Christian believer. *Eph.* i 1. **2** Such a person who has died and been canonized by certain churches, as the Roman Catholic. **3** Any one of the blessed in heaven. **4** An angel. **5** A very patient, unselfish person. —*v.t.* To canonize; venerate as a saint. —*adj.* Holy; canonized: as a title, often abbreviated to *St.* [<OF *seint, saint* <L *sanctus,* orig. holy, consecrated, pp. of *sancire* make sacred]

Saint For entries not found under *Saint,* see under ST.

Saint (sānt) *n.* A member of one of the religious bodies known as **Saints:** Latter–day *Saint.*

Saint–Bar·thé·le·my (saṅ′bàr·tā·lə·mē′) An island dependency of Guadeloupe, 125 miles NW of it, in the Leeward Islands; 9 1/2 square miles.

Saint Bernard A working dog of great size and strength, originally bred in Switzerland, characterized by a massive head, and a thick, white coat combined with red or brindle: used to rescue travelers by the hospice at Great St. Bernard Pass in the Swiss Alps.

SAINT BERNARD
(About 28 inches high at the shoulder)

Saint–Cloud (saṅ·klōō′) A town in northern France, 5 miles west of Paris; former residence of French monarchs.

Saint–Cyr (saṅ·sēr′), **Marquis Laurent de Gouvion,** 1764–1830, French marshal.

Saint–Cyr–l'É·cole (saṅ·sēr·lā·kôl′) A town near Versailles in north central France; site of a national military academy.

Saint–De·nis (saṅ·də·nē′) **1** A northern suburb of Paris; burial place of many French kings. **2** The capital of Réunion island.

Sainte–Beuve (saṅt·bœv′), **Charles Augustin,** 1804–69, French poet, critic, and historian.

saint·ed (sān′tid) *adj.* **1** Canonized. **2** Of holy character; saintly.

Saintes (saṅt), **Les** See LES SAINTES.

Saint–É·tienne (saṅ·tā·tyen′) A city in SE France, SW of Lyon; a key industrial center.

Saint–Ex·u·pé·ry (saṅ·teg·zü·pā·rē′) **Antoine de,** 1900–44, French writer and aviator.

Saint–Gau·dens (sānt·gô′dənz), **Augustus,** 1848–1907, U.S. sculptor born in Ireland.

Saint–Ger·main (saṅ·zher·maṅ′) A NW suburb of Paris; scene of the signing of the peace treaty between France and Austria,

1919. Also **Saint-Germain-en-Laye** (-äṅ·lā′).

saint·hood (sānt′hŏŏd) *n.* 1 The character or condition of a saint. 2 Saints collectively.

Saint-Just (saṅ·zhüst′), **Louis Antoine Léon de,** 1767–94, French revolutionist; one of the triumvirate of the Reign of Terror.

Saint-Lô (saṅ·lō′) A town of NW France; partially destroyed during the Normandy campaign of World War II.

Saint-Lou·is (saṅ·lōō·ē′) 1 A city at the mouth of the Senegal, capital of Senegal and of Mauritania. 2 A town on the SW coast of Réunion island.

saint·ly (sānt′lē) *adj.* Like a saint; godly; pious; holy. See synonyms under HOLY. —**saint′li·ness** *n.*

Saint-Ma·lo (saṅ·mà·lō′) A port in NW France on the **Gulf of Saint-Malo,** an inlet of the English Channel between Normandy and Brittany.

Saint-Mi·hiel (saṅ·mē·yel′) A town on the Meuse in NE France, scene of an American victory of World War I, 1918.

Saint-Na·zaire (saṅ·nà·zâr′) A port in central western France, at the mouth of the Loire.

Saint-O·mer (saṅ·tō·mâr′) A town in northern France, 22 miles SE of Calais.

Saint-Ouen (saṅ·twäṅ′) A northern suburb of Paris, on the Seine.

Saint·paul·i·a (sānt·pô′lē·ə) *n.* The African violet, much cultivated as an ornamental house plant. [<NL, after Baron Walter von *Saint Paul,* German botanist, its discoverer]

Saint-Pierre (saṅ·pyâr′), **Jacques Henri Bernardin de,** 1737–1814, French author.

Saint-Quen·tin (saṅ·kaṅ·taṅ′) A city in NE France, on the Somme.

Saint-Quentin Canal A canal in NE France, connecting the Oise with the Somme and the Scheldt; 58 miles long.

Saint-Saëns (saṅ·säṅs′), **(Charles) Camille,** 1835–1921, French composer.

Saints·bur·y (sānts′ber·ē), **George Edward Bateman,** 1845–1933, English literary critic and historian.

saint·ship (sānt′ship) *n.* Sainthood.

Saint-Si·mon (saṅ·sē·môṅ′), **Comte de,** 1760–1825, Claude Henri, founder of French socialism. —**Duc de,** 1675–1755, Louis de Rouvroy, French historian, memoirist, and diplomat.

Saint-Si·mon·ism (sānt·sī′mən·iz′əm) *n.* The socialistic principles of the Comte de Saint-Simon, advocating the state ownership of all property and the distribution of earnings based on the amount and quality of the work done by each laborer: also called *Simonianism.*

Saint-Vaast-la-Hogue (saṅ·väst′là·ôg′) A port of the NE Cotentin Peninsula, NW France; site of a French naval defeat by English and Dutch forces, 1692: also *La Hogue.*

Sai·pan (sī·pän′, -pan′, sī′pan) The largest island of the Marianas group; 47 square miles; capital, Garapan; captured from Japan by United States forces in World War II, 1944; after 1947, a district of the Trust Territory of the Pacific Islands, administered by the U.S. under the United Nations.

sair[1] (sâr) *v.t.* & *v.i.* *Scot.* To serve.

sair[2] (sâr) *adj.* *Scot.* Sore; sorrowful; heavy, great. —**sair′ly** *adv.*

sair·y (sâr′ē) *adj.* *Scot.* Sorry; sorrowful; wretched; poor. Also **sair′ie.**

Sa·ïs (sā′is) An ancient city of Lower Egypt on the Rosetta branch of the Nile. —**Sa·ite** (sā′īt) *n.* —**Sa·it·ic** (sā·it′ik) *adj.*

saith (seth) *Archaic* Present indicative third person singular of SAY[1].

sai·yid (sī′id, sä′yid) See SAYID.

sa·jou (sə·jōō′) *n.* Sapajou.

Sa·kai (sä·kī) A city on Osaka Bay, southern Honshu, Japan; industrial center; once a port.

Sa·kart·ve·lo (sä·kärt′ve·lô) The Georgian name for GEORGIA, U.S.S.R.

Sa·kar·ya (sä·kär′yä) A river in west central Turkey in Asia, flowing 490 miles to the Black Sea.

sake[1] (sāk) *n.* 1 Purpose of obtaining or accomplishing: preceded by *for* and followed by *of:* to open the window for the *sake* of air. 2 Interest, regard, or affectionate or reverent consideration, felt for any person or thing; account; well-being; advantage: commonly with *for* and a possessive: for your *sake,* for the *sake* of your children. [OE *saccu* a (legal) case]

sa·ke[2] (sä′kē) *n.* A fermented liquor made from rice; by extension, in Japan, any spirituous liquor. Also **sa′ki.** [<Japanese]

Sa·kel (zä′kəl), **Manfred,** 1906–57, Austrian psychiatrist; originator of insulin shock therapy.

sa·ker (sā′kər) *n.* A falcon; specifically, the Old World *Falco cherrug* or *sacer,* and the American prairie falcon (*F. mexicanus*). [< OF *sacre* <Sp. *sacro* <Arabic *ṣaqr* falcon]

Sa·kha·lin (sä′hä·lēn′, sak′ə·lēn) An island of Siberian Russian S.F.S.R. off its eastern coast; 29,700 square miles; the portion south of latitude 50° (13,930 square miles), known as **Japanese Sakhalin** or *Karafuto,* was ceded to Japan by the Treaty of Portsmouth; reoccupied by Russia after World War II. Formerly *Saghalien.*

Sa·ki (sä′kē) Pseudonym of Hector Hugh Munro, 1870–1916, English writer.

Sa·ki·shi·ma Islands (sä·kē·shē·mä) A southern group of the Ryukyu Islands; 343 square miles.

Sak·ka·ra (sə·kä′rə) A village of Upper Egypt; site of excavations of many ancient ruins: also *Saqqara.*

Sak·ti (säk′tē, sak′-; *Sanskrit* shuk′tē) See SHAKTI.

Sa·kun·ta·la (sə·kŏŏn′tə·lä, shə-) The heroine of a famous Sanskrit play of this name by Kalidasa. Also *Shakuntala.*

sal (sal) *n.* Salt. [<L]

sa·laam (sə·läm′) *n.* An oriental salutation or obeisance resembling prostration, the palm of the right hand being held to the forehead; also, a respectful or ceremonious verbal greeting. —*v.t.* & *v.i.* To greet with or make a salaam. [<Arabic *salām,* orig. peace, in *(as)salām ('alaikum)* peace (be upon you), a salutation]

sal·a·ble (sā′lə·bəl) *adj.* Such as can be sold; marketable: also spelled *saleable.* See synonyms under VENAL[1]. —**sal′a·bil′i·ty, sal′a·ble·ness** *n.* —**sal′a·bly** *adv.*

sa·la·cious (sə·lā′shəs) *adj.* Lustful; lecherous. [<L *salax, salacis* <*salire* leap] —**sa·la′cious·ly** *adv.* —**sa·la′cious·ness, sa·lac′i·ty** (-las′ə·te) *n.*

sal·ad (sal′əd) *n.* 1 A dish of green herbs or vegetables, usually uncooked and served with a dressing, sometimes mixed with chopped cold meat, fish, etc. 2 The course consisting of such a dish. [<OF *salade* <Provençal *salada* <L *salata,* pp. of *salare* salt <*sal* salt]

sa·la·dang (sə·lä′däng) *n.* The East Indian ox (*Bos gaurus*): also called *gaur.* Also spelled *seladang.* [Var. of *seladang* <Malay *sĕladaṅ*]

salad days Days of youth, freshness, and inexperience.

salad dressing A savory sauce used on salads, as mayonnaise, or a mixture of salt, oil, and vinegar, etc.

Sal·a·din (sal′ə·din), 1137?–93, sultan of Egypt and Syria, 1174–93; defended Acre against Crusaders.

Sa·la·do (sä·lä′thō), **Río** 1 A river of north central Argentina, flowing 1,250 miles SE from the Andes to the Paraná: also **Salado del Nor·te** (thel nôr′tā). 2 A river of central Argentina, flowing 750 miles south from the Andes to the salt marshes near the Colorado: in its upper courses known as the **Des·a·gua·de·ro** (des′ä·gwä·thā′rō). 3 A river in Buenos Aires province, eastern Argentina, flowing 400 miles SE from the border of Santa Fe province to the Río de la Plata.

Sa·la·jar (sä·lä′yär) An Indonesian island off SW Celebes; 259 square miles. Also **Sa·la′yar.**

Sal·a·man·ca (sal′ə·mang′kə, *Sp.* sä′lä·mäng′·kä) A city in west central Spain; scene of a victory of Wellington against the French, 1812.

sal·a·man·der (sal′ə·man′dər) *n.* 1 Any of an order (*Caudata*) of tailed, lizardlike amphibians having a smooth, moist, scaleless skin and usually two pairs of limbs, as the American **tiger salamander** (*Ambystoma tigrinum*): once popularly believed able to live in fire. 2 One of the genii fabled to live in fire; an elemental fire spirit in Paracelsus' theory of elementals; hence, a creature fabled to live in fire. 3 Any person or thing that can stand great heat. 4 A large poker or other implement used around or in fire, or when red-hot. 5 A mass of hardened metal or slag remaining in the hearth of a furnace after the fires are drawn: also called *shadrach.* [<OF *salamandre* <L *salamandra* <Gk.] —**sal′a·man′drine** (-drin) *adj.*

SPOTTED SALAMANDER
(From 6 to 7 inches long over-all)

Sa·lam·bri·a (sä′läm·brē′ä, *Greek* säläm·brē·ä′) The former name for the PENEUS.

sa·la·mi (sə·lä′mē) *n.* A salted, spiced sausage, originally Italian. [<Ital., pl., preserved meat, salt pork, ult. <L *salare* salt <*sal* salt]

Sal·a·mis (sal′ə·mis) 1 An ancient ruined city of eastern Cyprus. 2 An island in the Saronic Gulf of the Aegean, off the coast of Attica, Greece; 39 square miles; the **Bay of Salamis,** nearly bisecting the island, was the scene of the Greek victory over the Persian fleet, 480 B.C.

sal ammoniac A white, soluble ammonium chloride. [<L *sal Ammoniacum,* lit., salt of Ammon; so called because orig. made from camel's dung near the shrine of Jupiter *Ammon* in Libya]

sal·a·ried (sal′ər·ēd) *adj.* 1 In receipt of a salary. 2 Yielding a salary.

sal·a·ry (sal′ər·ē) *n.* *pl.* **·ries** A periodic allowance as compensation for official or professional services. —*v.t.* **·ried, ·ry·ing** To pay or allot a salary to. [<AF *salarie* <L *salarium* money paid Roman soldiers for their salt, orig. neut. of *salarius* of salt <*sal* salt]

Synonyms (noun): allowance, compensation, earnings, fee, hire, honorarium, pay, payment, recompense, remuneration, requital, stipend, wages. An *allowance* is a stipulated amount furnished at regular intervals, as of food or of money. *Compensation* signifies a return for a service done. *Remuneration* is applied to matters of great amount or importance. *Recompense* has a still wider meaning; there are services for which affection and gratitude are the sole and sufficient *recompense; earnings, fees, hire, pay, salary,* and *wages* are forms of *compensation* and may be included in *compensation, remuneration,* or *recompense. Pay* is commercial, and signifies an exact pecuniary equivalent for a thing or service, except when the contrary is expressly stated, as when we speak of high *pay* or poor *pay.* A *wage* is what a worker receives, and is usually estimated on an hourly or daily rate. *Earnings* is often equivalent to *wages,* but may be used with reference to the real value of work done or service rendered, and even applied to inanimate things; as, the *earnings* of capital. *Hire* is distinctly mercenary or menial. *Salary* is for professional, literary, executive, or clerical work, and is usually estimated on a weekly, monthly, or annual rate. A *fee* is given for a single service or privilege, and is sometimes a gratuity. Compare REQUITE.

Sa·la·zar (sä′lə·zär′), **Antonio de Oliveira,** born 1889, Portuguese statesman; prime minister 1932–.

sale (sāl) *n.* 1 The act of selling; the exchange or transfer of property for money or its equivalent. 2 An auction or selling-off at bargain prices. 3 Opportunity of selling; demand by purchasers; market: Stocks find no *sale.* —**for sale** (or **on sale**) Offered or ready for sale. ◆ Homophone: *sail.* [OE *sala,* prob. <ON]

Synonyms: bargain, barter, change, deal, exchange, trade. A *bargain* is strictly an agreement or contract to buy and sell; (see CONTRACT) but the word is often used to denote the entire transaction and also the thing sold or purchased. *Change* and *exchange* are words of wider signification, applying only incidentally to the transfer of property or value; a *change* secures something different in any way or by any means; an *exchange* secures something as an equivalent or return, but not necessarily as payment for what is given. *Barter* is the *exchange* of one commodity, generally a portable one, for another. *Trade* in the broad sense may apply to vast businesses (as the book *trade*), but as denoting a single transaction is used chiefly in regard to things of moderate value, when it becomes nearly synonymous with *barter. Sale* is commonly limited to the transfer of property for money, or for something estimated at a money value or considered as equivalent to so much money. A *deal* in the political sense is a *bargain,* substitution,' or transfer for the benefit of certain persons or parties against all others; as, The nomination was the result of a *deal*; in business it may have a similar meaning, but it frequently signifies simply a *sale* or *exchange,* a dealing.

Sa·lé (sä·lā′) A port of NW Morocco NE of Rabat. *Arabic* **Sla** (slä).

sale·a·ble (sā′lə·bəl) See SALABLE.

Sa·lem (sā′ləm) **1** A port of entry in NE Massachusetts; the original settlement of the Massachusetts Bay Colony. **2** The capital of Oregon, on the Willamette River in the NW part of the State. **3** An Old Testament name for JERUSALEM. **4** A city in west central Madras State, India.

sal·ep (sal′ep) *n.* A farinaceous meal obtained from the dry tubers of various orchids, used as food and formerly as medicine. [<F <Turkish *sālep* <Arabic *tha'leb, sa'leb,* prob. contraction of *khasyu'th–tha'lab* orchis, lit., fox's testicles]

sal·e·ra·tus (sal′ə·rā′təs) *n.* Sodium (or formerly potassium) bicarbonate, for use in cookery; baking soda. [<NL *sal aëratus* aerated salt <L *sal* salt + *aër* air, gas; so called because it produces carbon dioxide]

Sa·ler·no (sä·ler′nō) A port in SW Italy on the **Gulf of Salerno,** an arm of the Tyrrhenian Sea; scene of fierce fighting in World War II between Germans and Allied landing forces, 1943. Ancient **Sa·ler·num** (sə·lûr′nəm).

sales·clerk (sālz′klûrk′) *n.* A clerk who sells goods in a store.

sales·girl (sālz′gûrl′) *n.* A woman or girl hired to sell merchandise, especially in a store.

Sa·le·sian (sə·lē′shən) *n.* A member of an order of priests and nuns founded in Italy by Don Bosco for the rescue and education of poor and neglected children and named for St. Francis de Sales, patron of the order. —*adj.* Pertaining to the spirit of St. Francis de Sales or to his works.

sales·la·dy (sālz′lā′dē) *n. pl.* **·dies** *Colloq.* A woman or girl hired to sell merchandise, especially in a store.

sales·man (sālz′mən) *n. pl.* **·men** (-mən) A man hired to sell goods, stock, etc., in a store or by canvassing.

sales·man·ship (sālz′mən·ship) *n.* **1** The work or profession of a salesman. **2** Ability or skill in selling.

sales·peo·ple (sālz′pē′pəl) *n. pl.* Salespersons.

sales·per·son (sālz′pûr′sən) *n.* A person hired to sell merchandise, especially in a store.

sales resistance An attitude or state of mind in an individual or in the buying public that resists buying certain goods because of something antipathetic in the salesman, the advertising, or in the product.

sales·room (sālz′ro͞om′, -ro͝om′) *n.* A room where merchandise is displayed for sale.

sales tax A tax on money received from sales of goods.

sales·wom·an (sālz′wo͝om′ən) *n. pl.* **·wom·en** (-wim′in) A woman or girl hired to sell merchandise, especially in a store.

Sal·ford (sôl′fərd) A county borough in SE Lancashire, England.

Sa·li·an (sā′lē·ən) *adj.* Of or pertaining to the **Sal·i·i** (sal′ē·ī), a tribe of Franks who, in the fourth century A.D., settled on both sides of the lower Rhine, near the Zuyder Zee. —*n.* One of the Salii. Also **Salian Frank.** [<LL *Salii*]

sal·ic (sal′ik) *adj. Geol.* Belonging to a group of igneous rocks composed chiefly of silica and alumina, as the feldspars, quartz, etc. [<S(ILICA) + AL(UMINUM) + -IC]

Sal·ic (sal′ik) *adj.* **1** Characterizing a law, the **Salic Law,** derived from Germanic sources in the fifth century, and providing that males only could inherit lands: later applied to the succession to the French and Spanish thrones. **2** Pertaining to the Salian Franks. Also spelled *Salique.* [<MF *salique* <Med. L *salicus* <LL *Salii* the Salii]

sal·i·ca·ceous (sal′ə·kā′shəs) *adj. Bot.* Of or pertaining to a family *(Salicaceae)* of shrubs and trees forming the order *Salicales,* having alternate undivided leaves and dioecious flowers; the willow family. It includes the willows and the poplars. [<NL *salicaceus* <L *salix, -icis* a willow]

sal·i·cin (sal′ə·sin) *n. Chem.* A white, crystalline, bitter glycoside, $C_{13}H_{18}O_7$, contained in the bark of certain willows and poplars, and also made synthetically: used in medicine for rheumatism and as an antiperiodic. Also **sal′i·cine** (-sēn, -sin). [<F *salicine* <L *salix, -icis* a willow + F *-ine* -INE[2]]

sal·i·cyl·ate (sal′ə·sil′āt, sə·lis′ə·lāt) *n. Chem.* A salt or ester of salicylic acid.

sal·i·cyl·ic (sal′ə·sil′ik) *adj.* Of, pertaining to, or derived from certain willows. [<F *salicyle* (<L *salix, -icis* a willow + F *-yle* -YL) + -IC]

salicylic acid *Chem.* A white crystalline compound, $C_7H_6O_3$, occurring naturally in many plants and also made synthetically from phenol. It is an antiseptic and is used sparingly in preserving foods, and, in the form of its salts, for treating rheumatism.

sa·li·ence (sā′lē·əns) *n.* **1** The condition of being salient or, figuratively, noteworthy. **2** A protruding feature or detail. **3** That which arrests attention because of its importance. Also **sa′li·en·cy.**

sa·li·ent (sā′lē·ənt) *adj.* **1** Standing out prominently; striking; conspicuous: a *salient* feature. **2** Extending beyond the general line; projecting. **3** Leaping; springing. —*n.* An angle pointing outwards, as of a fortification (see illustration under BASTION); projecting line or lines of trenches; a sharp curve in a military line protruding toward the enemy. [<L *saliens, -entis,* ppr. of *salire* leap] —**sa′li·ent·ly** *adv.* —**sa′li·ent·ness** *n.*

sa·li·en·ti·an (sā′lē·en′shē·ən) *n.* Any of an order *(Salientia)* of amphibians characterized by broad, stocky bodies and the absence of tails, and having hind legs adapted for leaping, including the frogs and toads. —*adj.* Belonging or pertaining to the *Salientia.* [<NL <L *saliens.* See SALIENT.]

sa·lif·er·ous (sə·lif′ər·əs) *adj.* Containing a considerable proportion of salt in beds or as brine: *saliferous* strata. [<L *sal, salis* salt + -FEROUS]

sal·i·fy (sal′ə·fī) *v.t.* **·fied, ·fy·ing** **1** To combine or impregnate with a salt. **2** To form into a salt, as with an acid. [<F *salifier* <NL *salificare* <L *sal, salis* salt + *facere* make] —**sal′i·fi′a·ble** *adj.* —**sal′i·fi·ca′tion** *n.*

sa·lim·e·ter (sə·lim′ə·tər) *n.* A salinometer. [<L *sal, salis* salt + -METER]

sa·li·na (sə·lī′nə) *n.* **1** A pool, pond, or marsh containing salt water diked in from the sea; also, a salt spring; a saltlick. **2** A saltworks or salt mine. [<Sp. <L *salinae (fodinae)* salt (pits) <*sal, salis* salt]

Sa·li·na Cruz (sä·lē′nä kro͞os′) A port of Oaxaca, southern Mexico, on the Pacific coast.

sa·line (sā′līn) *adj.* Constituting, consisting of, or characteristic of salt; containing salt; salty. —*n.* **1** A metallic salt, especially a salt of one of the alkalis or of magnesium. **2** A salt solution used in the investigation of biological and physiological processes, and also in medicine, as for an injection. **3** A natural deposit of common or other soluble salt; salina. [<F *salin* <LL (assumed) *salinus* <L *sal, salis* salt]

sa·lin·i·ty (sə·lin′ə·tē) *n.* **1** The state or degree of being salt or saline. **2** The quantity of solid material dissolved in one kilogram of water: expressed in parts per thousand. Compare CHLORINITY.

sa·lin·i·za·tion (sā′lin·ə·zā′shən, -ī·zā′-) *n.* **1** The accumulation of salt. **2** The process by which a soil acquires various kinds of salts, as sodium chloride, calcium sulfate, or the like.

sal·i·nom·e·ter (sal′ə·nom′ə·tər) *n.* A hydrometer graduated to show the percentage of salt in a solution and to measure the density of sea water. [<*salino-* (<SALINE) + -METER] —**sal′i·nom′e·try** *n.*

Sa·lique (sə·lēk′, sal′ik, sā′lik) See SALIC.

Salis·bur·y (sôlz′ber·ē, -brē) **1** A municipal borough, county town of Wiltshire, England, on the Avon River; noted for its 13th century cathedral: also *New Sarum.* **2** The capital of Southern Rhodesia.

Salis·bur·y (sôlz′ber·ē, -brē), **Marquis of,** 1830–1903, Robert Gascoigne Cecil, English statesman.

Salisbury Plain An undulating chalk plateau in southern Wiltshire, England; 300 square miles; site of Stonehenge.

Salisbury steak Hamburger (def. 2).

Sa·lish (sā′lish) *n.* **1** A North American Indian of Salishan stock: commonly called *Flathead.* **2** Any of the languages of the Salishan Indians.

Sa·lish·an (sā′lish·ən, sal′ish-) *adj.* Of or pertaining to a linguistic stock of North American Indians, formerly inhabiting Oregon, Washington, British Columbia, and Montana. —*n.* Any of the Salishan languages. Also **Sa′lish.**

sa·li·va (sə·lī′və) *n. Physiol.* The slightly alkaline fluid secreted by the glands of the mouth; spittle. It contains a specific amylase called ptyalin, which converts starch into maltose and is therefore considered a promoter of digestion. [<L] —**sal·i·var·y** (sal′ə·ver′ē) *adj.*

sal·i·vate (sal′ə·vāt) *v.* **·vat·ed, ·vat·ing** *v.i.* To secrete saliva. —*v.t.* To produce salivation in. [<L *salivatus,* pp. of L *salivare* <*saliva* saliva]

sal·i·va·tion (sal′ə·vā′shən) *n.* An abnormally increased flow of saliva, especially when due to the effect of drugs, as mercury.

Salk (sôk, sôlk), **Jonas Edward,** born 1914, U. S. bacteriologist; developed vaccine for poliomyelitis.

sall (sal) *v.i. Dial.* Shall. [Var. of SHALL]

salle à man·ger (sȧl ȧ mäṅ·zhā′) *French* Dining–room.

sal·len·ders (sal′ən·dərz) *n. pl.* An eczematic inflammation about the hock joint of a horse. Compare MALANDERS. [<F *solandre*; ult. origin uncertain]

sal·let (sal′it) *n.* A hemispherical helmet of the 15th century. [<OF *salade* <Ital. *celata* <L *caelata (cassis)* an engraved (helmet), orig. pp. fem. of *caelare* engrave]

SALLET
Of Italian archer, 15th century.

sal·low[1] (sal′ō) *adj.* Of an unhealthy yellowish color: said chiefly of the human skin. [OE *salo*] —**sal′low·ish** *adj.* —**sal′low·ly** *adv.* —**sal′low·ness** *n.*

sal·low[2] (sal′ō) *n.* **1** A European willow with less flexible shoots than the osiers, especially the goat willow *(Salix caprea),* sometimes called the **great sallow,** and the **gray sallow** *(S. caprea cinerea).* **2** An osier; a willow shoot. [OE *sealh*]

sal·low·y (sal′ō·ē) *adj.* Fringed with or abounding in sallows.

Sal·lust (sal′əst), 86–35 B.C., Roman historian: full name *Gaius Sallustius Crispus.*

sal·ly (sal′ē) *v.i.* **·lied, ·ly·ing** **1** To rush out suddenly. **2** To set out energetically. **3** To go out, as from a room or building. —*n. pl.* **·lies** **1** A rushing forth, as of besieged troops against besiegers; sortie. **2** A going forth, as on a walk or excursion. **3** A sudden overflow of spirits; a witticism or bantering remark. [<OF *saillie,* orig. pp. fem. of *saillir* <L *salire* leap]

Sal·ly (sal′ē) A diminutive of SARAH; also, a feminine personal name.

sally lunn (lun) A raised and sweetened teacake resembling a muffin. [after *Sally Lunn,* pastry cook, of Bath, England, in the 18th century]

Sal·ma·cis (sal′mə·sis) In Greek mythology, a nymph of a fountain in ancient Caria, the waters of which were supposed to render effeminate all who drank of them. See HERMAPHRODITUS.

sal·ma·gun·di (sal′mə·gun′dē) *n.* **1** A dish of chopped meat, anchovies, eggs, onions, etc., mixed and seasoned. **2** Hence, any medley or miscellany; a potpourri. [<F *salmigondis,* prob. <Ital. *salami conditi* pickled meats <*salame* preserved meat, sausage + *conditi,* pp. of *condire* flavor <L, preserve, pickle]

Sal·ma·gun·di (sal′mə·gun′dē) A series of humorous and satirical papers published periodically in 1807–08 by Washington Irving and others.

sal·mi (sal′mē) *n.* A spiced dish of birds or game roasted, minced, and stewed in wine; a ragout. Also **sal·mis** (sal′mē, *Fr.* sȧl·mē′). [<F, prob. contraction of *salmigondis* SALMAGUNDI]

salm·on (sam′ən) *n.* **1** A clupeid fish (family *Salmonidae,* genus *Salmo*), especially *S. salar* of the North Atlantic, brownish above, silvery on the sides, with black spots. The salmon ascends to the headwaters of rivers to spawn, and surmounts obstructions, as waterfalls of considerable height. It is a highly prized game and food fish, and has delicate reddish–orange flesh. **2** One of other salmonoid fishes, especially the quinnat, ascending rivers flowing to the North Pacific. **3** A color of a reddish– or pinkish–orange tint: also **salm'on-pink'**. —*adj.* Having the color salmon. [< AF *samoun, saumoun, salmun* <L *salmo, -onis*]

salm·on·ber·ry (sam'ən·ber'ē) *n. pl.* **·ries 1** A hardy raspberry *(Rubus spectabilis)* of the Pacific coast. **2** The cloudberry. **3** A raspberry *(R.parviflorus)* of the United States, having a white blossom.

Sal·mo·nel·la (sal'mō·nel'ə) *n.* A genus of aerobic, rodlike, preponderantly motile bacteria capable of fermenting certain carbohydrates with the formation of acid and gas; especially, *S. paratyphi,* which causes a form of paratyphoid in man. [<NL, after Daniel Elmer *Salmon,* U.S. pathologist, 1850–1914]

sal·mo·nel·lo·sis (sal'mə·ne·lō'səs) *n.* A disease caused by Salmonella bacteria, esp. paratyphoid.

Sal·mo·ne·us (sal·mō'nē·əs) In Greek mythology, a son of Aeolus and king of Elis who was destroyed by thunderbolts for claiming to be the equal of Zeus.

sal·mo·noid (sal'mə·noid) *adj.* Resembling a salmon; belonging to the salmon family. —*n.* A salmonoid.

Salmon River A river in central Idaho, flowing 425 miles NE to the Snake River.

salmon trout 1 The European sea trout *(Salmo trutta).* **2** Certain other salmonoid fish, as the namaycush or the steelhead. See TROUT.

sal·ol (sal'ōl, -ol) *n. Chem.* A colorless crystalline compound, $C_{13}H_{10}O_3$, derived from salicylic acid: used in medicine as a substitute for salicylic acid and as an antineuralgic, antirheumatic, antipyretic, and an internal antiseptic. [<SAL(ICYLIC ACID) + -OL[1]]

Sa·lo·me (sə·lō'mē) The daughter of Herodias, who asked from Herod the head of John the Baptist on a silver charger in return for her dancing. *Matt.* xiv 8.

Sal·o·mon (sal'ə·mən; *Fr.* sȧ·lô·môṅ', *Hungarian* shol'o·mōn, *Polish* sä·lō'môn, *Sp.* sä'lō·mōn') See SOLOMON. Also *Du., Ger.* **Sa·lo·mo** (sä'lō·mō), *Ital.* **Sa·lo·mo·ne** (sä'lō·mō'nā), *Pg.* **Sa·lo·mão** (sä'lō·mouṅ').

Sal·o·mon (sal'ō·mən), **Haym,** 1740?–85, American patriot born in Poland; advanced large loans to American treasury during the Revolutionary War.

sa·lon (sə·lon', *Fr.* sȧ·lôṅ') *n.* **1** A room in which guests are received; a drawing–room. **2** The periodic gathering or reception of noted persons, under the auspices of some distinguished woman, especially in Paris in the 17th and 18th centuries. **3** A hall or gallery used for exhibiting works of art. **4** An exhibition of works of art. **5** An establishment devoted to some specific purpose: a beauty *salon.* [< F <Ital. *salone,* aug. of *sala* a room, hall < OHG *sal*]

Sa·lon (sə·lon', *Fr.* sȧ·lôṅ') *n.* An annual exhibition of works by living artists at the Grand Palais des Champs Elysées in Paris: so called because formerly held in the Salon Carré of the Louvre. Since 1891 there have been two rival Salons in Paris, the Salon of the Champs Élysées, or **Old Salon,** and the Salon of the Champ de Mars, or **New Salon,** which both exhibit in the Grand Palais.

Sa·lo·ni·ka (sä'lō·nē'kä) A port of NE Greece, in Macedonia on the **Gulf of Salonika,** an arm of the Aegean between Thessaly and Macedonia: ancient *Therma*: Greek *Thessalonike.* Also **Sa'lo·ni'ki** (-kē), **Sa'lo·ni'ca.**

sa·loon (sə·lo͞on') *n.* **1** *U.S.* A place where alcoholic drinks are sold; a bar. **2** *Brit.* In a public house, a section of the bar set aside for patrons of a higher social status than those in the public bar. **3** A large apartment or room for assemblies, public entertainment, exhibitions, etc. **4** The main cabin of a passenger ship, used by the passengers in general. **5** A salon (def. 1). **6** *Brit.* A sedan (def. 1). [<F *salon* a salon]

sa·loon–keep·er (sə·lo͞on'kē'pər) *n.* One who keeps a saloon; a liquor dealer.

sa·loop (sə·lo͞op') *n. Brit.* An infusion of sassafras chips, salep, or similiar aromatic herbs, formerly used largely as a beverage, as a cure for rheumatism, etc.; sassafras tea. [Var. of SALEP]

Sal·op (sal'əp) See SHROPSHIRE. —**Sa·lo·pi·an** (sə·lō'pē·ən) *adj. & n.*

sal·pa (sal'pə) *n.* Any of a genus *(Salpa)* of free–swimming, transparent, cylindrical tunicates (class *Thaliacea*) found in warm seas: they exhibit a solitary asexual stage and a colonial sexual one. Also **sal'pi·an, sal'pid.** [< NL <L <Gk. *salpē,* a kind of sea fish] —**sal'pi·form** *adj.*

Sal·pi·glos·sis (sal'pə·glos'is) *n.* A small genus of South American solanaceous, downy herbs having entire leaves and handsome variegated flowers. [<NL <Gk. *salpinx, -ingos* a trumpet + *glōssa* tongue]

sal·pin·gec·to·my (sal'pin·jek'tə·mē) *n. Surg.* The excision of a Fallopian tube; sterilization of women. [<NL *salpinx, salpingos* a Fallopian tube (<Gk., a trumpet) + -ECTOMY]

sal·pinx (sal'pingks) *n. pl.* **sal·pin·ges** (sal·pin'·jēz) *Anat.* A tube in man and other mammals, especially the Eustachian or Fallopian tube. [<NL <Gk., a trumpet]

sal·si·fy (sal'sə·fē) *n.* An Old World plant *(Tragopogon porrifolius)* of the composite family, with a white, edible root: from its flavor called *oyster plant, vegetable oyster.* [<F *salsifis,* prob. <Ital. *sassefrica;* ult. origin unknown]

sal·sil·la (sal·sil'ə) *n.* Any of several tropical American plants of the amaryllis family (genus *Bomarea*), yielding edible tubers resembling those of the Jerusalem artichoke. [<Sp., dim. of *salsa* a sauce]

sal soda Sodium carbonate; washing soda. See SODA.

salt (sôlt) *n.* **1** Sodium chloride, NaCl, a widely distributed compound, used by men from time immemorial as a seasoning preservative: a necessary ingredient of food for most mammals. It is obtained by evaporation or freezing of the water of the ocean, of saline lakes and springs or wells, and by mining in beds of rock salt. ◆ Collateral adjective: *saline.* **2** *Chem.* Any compound produced when all or part of the hydrogen of an acid is replaced by an electropositive radical or a metal. Salts are usually formed by treating a metal with an acid or by the interaction of a base and an acid. Usually the salts derived from acids whose names end in *–ic* take the suffix *–ate,* and those ending in *–ous* take *–ite.* **3** *pl.* A salt used as a laxative or cathartic; also, smelling salts. **4** Piquant humor; dry wit; repartee: from the phrase *Attic salt.* **5** That which preserves, corrects, or purifies: the *salt* of criticism; seasoning. **6** A sailor: an old *salt.* **7** A saltcellar. —**below the salt** In inferior, subordinate, or servile position. —**to take with a grain of salt** To allow for exaggeration; have doubts about. —*adj.* **1** Flavored with salt; salty; briny: opposed to *sweet.* **2** Cured or preserved with salt. **3** Containing, or growing or living in or near, salt water. **4** *Obs.* Salacious; licentious; gross. —*v.t.* **1** To season with salt. **2** To preserve or cure with salt. **3** To furnish with salt: to *salt* cattle. **4** To season as if with salt; add zest or piquancy to. **5** To add something to so as fraudulently to increase the value: to *salt* a mine with gold. —**to salt away 1** To pack in salt for preserving. **2** *Colloq.* To store up; save. —**to salt out** To separate (coal–tar colors) by adding salt to solutions containing them. [OE *sealt.* Akin to SAL.] —**salt'ish** *adj.* —**salt'ness** *n.*

Sal·ta (säl'tä) A province of NW Argentina; 59,743 square miles; capital, Salta.

sal·tant (sal'tənt) *adj.* Leaping; jumping; saltatory. [<L *saltans, -antis,* ppr. of *saltare* dance, freq.of *salire* leap]

sal·ta·rel·lo (sal'tə·rel'ō, *Ital.* säl'tä·rel'lō) *n. pl.* **·rel·li** (-rel'ē, *Ital.* -rel'lē) **1** A quick Italian dance, diversified by skips. **2** Music for such a dance. [<Ital., lit., a firecracker <*saltare* dance, leap <L. See SALTANT.]

sal·ta·tion (sal·tā'shən) *n.* **1** A leaping or leap, as in a dance. **2** A throbbing or palpitation, as of a blood vessel. **3** *Biol.* Mutation. [<L *saltatio, -onis* <*saltatus,* pp. of *saltare.* See SALTANT.]

sal·ta·to·ri·al (sal'tə·tôr'ē·əl, -tō'rē-) *adj.* **1** Built or adapted for leaping. **2** *Zool.* Adapted for or characterized by leaping. [<SALTATORY]

sal·ta·to·ry (sal'tə·tôr'ē, -tō'rē) *adj.* **1** Of or pertaining to leaping or dancing. **2** Moving by leaps; fitted for leaping; specifically, moving the feet synchronously, as certain birds. [<L *saltatorius* <*saltator* a leaper <*saltare.* See SALTANT.]

salt cake Crude sodium sulfate, especially as obtained by the action of sulfuric acid on sodium chloride.

salt·cel·lar (sôlt'sel'ər) *n.* A small receptacle for salt; a saltshaker.

salt chuck *Canadian* In the Pacific Northwest, the sea.

salt·ed (sôl'tid) *adj.* **1** Treated with or as with salt for any purpose; hence, preserved. **2** Immune from infectious disease by reason of previous attack: a term used in South Africa. **3** *Colloq.* Experienced or expert.

salt·er (sôl'tər) *n.* **1** One who applies salt to cure fish, meat, etc. **2** One who manufactures or deals in salt. [OE *sealtere*]

salt·ern (sôl'tərn) *n.* A place or building where salt is manufactured. [OE *sealtærn*]

salt grass Any of certain grasses found growing on salt marshes or on alkaline western plains, as *Distichlis spicata* or some species of *Spartina.*

salt hay Hay made from salt grass.

salt–horse (sôlt'hôrs') *n.* Salted beef; corned beef: a sailor's term. Also **salt'–junk'** (-jungk').

sal·ti·grade (sal'tə·grād) *adj.* Adapted for leaping; said of certain insects, as grasshoppers. [<NL *Saltigradae,* group name of saltigrade spiders <L *saltus* a leap + *gradi* step]

Sal·til·lo (säl·tē'yō) The capital of Coahuila state, NE Mexico.

sal·tine (sôl·tēn') *n.* A crisp, salty cracker.

sal·tire (sal'tir) *n. Her.* An ordinary formed by a bendand a bend sinister crossing as in St. Andrew's cross: also spelled *sautoir.* Also **sal'tier.** [<OF *sauteoir* a stirrup cord <Med. L *saltatorium* <L *saltatorius* SALTATORY]

SALTIRE
Showing cross of St. Andrew.

Salt Lake See GREAT SALT LAKE.

Salt Lake City The capital and largest city of Utah, SE of Great Salt Lake; center of Mormonism.

salt·lick (sôlt'lik') *n.* A place to which animals resort to lick salt from superficial deposits; a salt spring or dried salt pond.

salt marsh Low coastal land frequently overflowed by the tide, usually covered with coarse grass. Also **salt meadow.**

salt of the earth The fundamentally fine people of the world; those who add value to mankind. *Matt.* v 13.

Sal·ton Sink (sôl'tən) A depression in southern California; lowest part, 280 feet below sea level; in 1905 and 1906 became a shallow, saline lake, the **Salton Sea,** by an overflow of the Colorado River; originally about 450 square miles, reduced to about 300 square miles by evaporation.

salt·pan (sôlt'pan') *n.* **1** A vessel in which salt is made by evaporating saline water. **2** A pond or basin from which salt is obtained by natural evaporation.

salt·pe·ter (sôlt'pē'tər) *n.* Niter: so called colloquially and in commerce. —**Chile saltpeter** Mineral sodium nitrate occurring in beds in a desert region near the boundary of Chile and Peru, but chiefly in Chile. Also **salt'pe'tre.** [< OF *saltpetre* <Med. L *sal petrae,* lit., salt of rock <L *sal* salt + *petra* a rock <Gk.]

salt rheum *Pathol.* One of various skin eruptions, as eczema.

salt–ris·ing (sôlt'rī'zing) *n.* Salted batter used as leaven, or bread made from it.

Salt River 1 A river in central Arizona, flowing about 200 miles west to the Gila River. **2** A river in NE Missouri, flowing 125 miles NW to the Ohio. —**to row** (or **be rowed**) **up**

Salt River *Colloq.* To suffer political defeat.
salt·shak·er (sôlt′shā′kər) *n.* A container with small apertures for sprinkling table salt.
salt spring A flow of salt water from the earth.
salt-wa·ter (sôlt′wô′tər, -wot′ər) *adj.* Of, composed of, or living in salt water.
salt well A well from which brine is obtained.
salt·works (sôlt′wûrks′) *n. pl.* **·works** An establishment where salt is made on a commercial scale: in England the form **saltwork** is preferred in describing a single factory.
salt·wort (sôlt′wûrt′) *n.* **1** Any of various maritime plants (genus *Salsola*), especially the common saltwort (*S. kali*), used in making soda ash. **2** Any of various glassworts, as the dwarf glasswort (*Salicornia bigelovi*) of the New England coast. [Prob. trans. of Du. *zoutkruid*]
salt·y (sôl′tē) *adj.* **salt·i·er, salt·i·est** **1** Tasting somewhat like salt; of or containing salt. **2** Reminiscent of the sea; smelling of the sea. **3** Piquant; sharp; pungent, as literature, speech, etc. — **salt′i·ly** *adv.* — **salt′i·ness** *n.*
sa·lu·bri·ous (sə·lo͞o′brē·əs) *adj.* Conducive to health; healthful; wholesome. See synonyms under HEALTHY. [<L *salubris* < *salus* health] — **sa·lu′bri·ous·ly** *adv.* — **sa·lu′bri·ty, sa·lu′bri·ous·ness** *n.*
Sa·lu·da River (sə·lo͞o′də) A river in west central South Carolina, flowing 200 miles SE to the Congaree River.
sa·lu·ki (sə·lo͞o′kē) *n.* A very old breed of hound, having feathered ears, tail, and legs, and a greyhoundlike body; the "dog" of the Bible, known as the Royal Dog of Egypt: introduced into England in 1840. [< Arabic *salūqi* <*Salūq* an ancient Arabian city]

SALUKI
(From 23 to 28 inches high at the shoulder)

Sa·lus (sā′ləs) In Roman mythology, goddess of health and prosperity: later identified with the Greek *Hygeia.* [<L, health]
sal·u·tar·y (sal′yə·ter′ē) *adj.* **1** Calculated to bring about a sound condition by correcting evil or promoting good; corrective; beneficial. **2** Salubrious; wholesome; healthful. See synonyms under HEALTHY, USEFUL. [<F *salutaire* <L *salutaris* < *salus, salutis* health] — **sal′u·tar′i·ly** *adv.* — **sal′u·tar′i·ness** *n.*
sal·u·ta·tion (sal′yə·tā′shən) *n.* **1** The act of saluting. **2** Any form of greeting. **3** The opening words of a letter, as *Dear Sir.* [<OF *salutacion* <L *salutatio, -onis* < *salutatus,* pp. of *salutare* SALUTE]
sa·lu·ta·to·ri·an (sə·lo͞o′tə·tôr′ē·ən, -tō′rē-) *n.* *U.S.* In colleges and schools, the graduating student, usually the second (sometimes the first) honor man, who delivers the salutatory at commencement. [<SALUTATORY]
sa·lu·ta·to·ry (sə·lo͞o′tə·tôr′ē, -tō′rē) *n. pl.* **·ries** An opening oration, as at a college commencement. —*adj.* Pertaining to or consisting in greeting or welcome; specifically, relating to a salutatory address. [<L *salutatorius* pertaining to salutation < *salutare* SALUTE]
sa·lute (sə·lo͞ot′) *n.* **1** A greeting by display of military, naval, or other official honors, as by presenting arms, firing cannon, etc. **2** The act of or attitude assumed in giving a military salute. **3** A gesture of greeting, compliment, respect, or the like, as a bow, kiss, etc. —*v.* **·lut·ed, ·lut·ing** *v.t.* **1** To greet with an expression or sign of welcome, respect, etc.; welcome. **2** To honor in some prescribed way, as by raising the hand to the cap, presenting arms, firing cannon, etc. —*v.i.* **3** To make a salute. See synonyms under ADDRESS. [<L *salutare* < *salus, salutis* health] — **sa·lut′er** *n.*
sal·va·ble (sal′və·bəl) *adj.* Capable of being saved or salvaged. [<LL *salvare* SAVE] — **sal′·va·bil′i·ty** *n.*
Sal·va·dor (sal′və·dôr′, *Sp.* säl′vä·thōr′) **1** El Salvador. **2** The capital of Bahia state, Brazil: formerly *Bahia, São Salvador.*
Sal·va·do·ri·an (sal′və·dôr′ē·ən, -dō′rē-) *adj.* Relating to El Salvador or its people. —*n.* A native or inhabitant of El Salvador. Also **Sal′·va·do′ran.** [<*(El) Salvador* <Sp., the Saviour <LL *salvator* < *salvare* save]
sal·vage (sal′vij) *v.t.* **·vaged, ·vag·ing** To save, as a ship or its cargo, from wreck, capture, etc.; salve. —*n.* **1** The saving of a ship, cargo, etc., from loss; hence, any act of saving property. **2** The compensation allowed to persons by whose voluntary exertions a vessel, her cargo, or the lives of those belonging to her are saved from danger or loss: termed legally **civil salvage,** as distinguished from **military salvage,** which consists in the liberation of property from the enemy in time of war. **3** That which is saved from a wrecked or abandoned vessel or from or after a fire; hence, anything saved from destruction. [< OF < *salver* SAVE] — **sal′vag·er** *n.*
sal·va·gee (sal′və·jē′) *n.* In maritime law, a person in whose favor or behalf salvage has been effected.
Sal·va·ges (səl·vä′zhĕsh) See SELVAGENS.
Sal·var·san (sal′vər·san) *n.* Proprietary name for a brand of arsphenamine. [<G <LL *salvare* save + G *arsen* arsenic]
sal·va·tion (sal·vā′shən) *n.* **1** The process or state of being saved; preservation from impending evil. **2** *Theol.* Deliverance from sin and penalty, realized in a future state; redemption. **3** Any means of deliverance from danger, evil, or ruin. [<OF *sauvacion* <LL *salvatio, -onis* < *salvatus,* pp. of *salvare* SAVE]
Salvation Army A religious and charitable organization on semimilitary lines, founded by William Booth in England in 1865 as the Christian Mission, which took the title of Salvation Army in 1878.
Sal·va·tion·ist (sal·vā′shən·ist) *n.* A member of the Salvation Army.
salve[1] (sav, säv) *n.* **1** A thick, adhesive ointment for local ailments. **2** Anything that heals, soothes, or mollifies; hence, praise or flattery. —*v.t.* **salved, salv·ing** **1** To dress with salve or ointment. **2** To soothe; appease, as conscience, pride, etc. [OE *sealf*]
salve[2] (salv) *v.t.* **salved, salv·ing** To save from loss; salvage. [Back formation <SALVAGE]
sal·ve[3] (sal′vē) *interj.* Hail: literally, be well. [<L, imperative of *salvere* be well]
Sal·ve·mi·ni (säl·vā′mē·nē), **Gaetano,** 1873–1957, Italian historian active in the United States.
sal·ver (sal′vər) *n.* A tray, as of silver. [<OF *salve* <Sp. *salva,* orig. the foretasting of food, as for a king < *salvar* taste, save <LL *salvare* SAVE]
Sal·ve Re·gi·na (sal′vē ri·jī′nə) *Eccl.* **1** A hymn to the Virgin Mary, contained in the Roman Catholic breviary. **2** A translation of this. [<L, Hail, O queen; the opening words]
sal·vi·a (sal′vē·ə) *n.* Any of a genus (*Salvia*) of ornamental plants of the mint family; the sage. [<NL <L, SAGE[2]]
Sal·vi·ni (säl·vē′nē), **Tommaso,** 1829–1916, Italian actor.
sal·vo[1] (sal′vō) *n. pl.* **·vos** or **·voes** **1** A simultaneous discharge of artillery, or of two or more bombs from an aircraft. **2** A salute given by firing all the guns, as at the funeral of an officer; hence, any salute or simultaneous discharge: *salvos* of applause, a *salvo* of rockets. **3** The concentrated fire of many pieces, as in a naval engagement. **4** A successive and specified number of discharges of guns, from right to left, or left to right, at prescribed intervals. [Orig. *salva* <Ital., a salute <L *salve* SALVE[3]]
sal·vo[2] (sal′vō) *n. pl.* **·vos** **1** A saving clause; proviso. **2** An evasion, reservation, or bad excuse. **3** An expedient. [<L *salvo (jure)* (right) being reserved, ablative of *salvus* uninjured, safe]
sal vo·lat·i·le (sal vō·lat′ə·lē) Ammonium carbonate. Compare HARTSHORN. [<NL, volatile salt <L]
sal·vor (sal′vər) *n.* One who or a ship which saves or helps to save vessels or property from loss at sea; a salvager. Also **salv′er.** [<SALVE[2] + -OR]
Sal·ween (sal′wēn′) A river of eastern Tibet, SW China, and eastern Burma, flowing about 1,750 miles east, SE, and south to the Andaman Sea at Moulmein. Also **Sal′win′.**
Salz·burg (zälts′bo͝orkh) A city in west central Austria; the birthplace of Mozart.
Sa·ma·ni (sä·mä′nē) *n. pl.* A Persian dynasty ruling from A.D. 874–1005, celebrated because of its encouragement of literature and the arts.
Sa·mar (sä′mär) One of the Visayan Islands, third largest of the Philippines; 5,050 square miles.
sam·a·ra (sam′ər·ə, sə·mâr′ə) *n. Bot.* A one-seeded indehiscent fruit, as of the elm, ash, or maple, provided with a membrane or wing; a key or key fruit. [<NL <L, elm seed]
Sa·ma·ra (sä·mä′rä) The former name for KUIBYSHEV.
Sa·ma·rang (sə·mä′räng) See SEMARANG.
Sa·mar·i·a (sə·mâr′ē·ə) **1** In the Bible, a city of Palestine, capital of the northern kingdom of Israel, or the hill on which it was built, on the site of modern Sebastye in western Jordan. **2** In the Bible, the territory occupied by the kingdom of Israel, or, later, a restricted portion of central Palestine west of the Jordan occupied by the Samaritans.
Sa·mar·i·tan (sə·mar′ə·tən) *n.* **1** One of the people of Samaria, a mixed population. II *Kings* xvii. **2** The Northwest Semitic language of this people. — **Good Samaritan** A humane, compassionate person who helps one in trouble: from the parable in *Luke* x 30–37. —*adj.* Of or pertaining to Samaria. [<LL *Samaritanus* <Gk. *Samareitēs* < *Samareia* Samaria]
sa·mar·i·um (sə·mâr′ē·əm) *n.* A hard, brittle, yellowish-gray metallic element (symbol Sm) of the lanthanide series. See ELEMENT. [<NL <SAMAR(SKITE); so called because first found in the spectrum of samarskite]
Sam·ar·kand (sam′ər·kand′, *Russian* sä′mär känt′) The second largest city and former capital of the Uzbek S.S.R., in the extreme eastern part; the ancient capital of Tamerlane's empire and the site of his tomb: ancient *Maracanda.* Also **Sam′ar·cand′.**
sa·mar·skite (sə·mär′skīt) *n.* An orthorhombic, vitreous, black mineral, source of several elements, as samarium, etc. [<G *samarskit,* after Col. Samarski, 19th c. Russian mine officer]
sam·ba (sam′bə, säm′bä) *n.* A dance of Brazilian origin in two-four time. —*v.i.* To dance the samba. [<Pg. < a native African name]
sam·bo (sam′bō) *n. pl.* **·bos** A half-breed of mixed Negro and Indian or Negro and mulatto blood. [<Sp. *zambo* a Negro, a mulatto, a monkey, prob. <Bantu *nzambu* a monkey]
Sam·bre (säṅ′br′) A river in northern France and SW Belgium, flowing 100 miles NE to the Meuse.
Sam Browne belt (sam′ broun′) A military belt, with one or two light shoulder straps running diagonally across the chest from right to left: designed by General Sir Samuel J. Browne, 1824–1901, of the British army, to carry the pistol when on horseback, and the sword when dismounted: later used by the armies of the United States and other countries.
sam·bu·ca (sam·byo͞o′kə) *n.* In ancient music, a sharp-toned, triangular, stringed instrument resembling a harp: of Asian origin. Also **sam·buke** (sam′byo͞ok). [<L <Gk. *sambykē,* prob. <Aramaic *sabbĕkhā*]
sam·bur (sam′bər, säm′-) *n.* A rusine deer, especially *Cervus aristotelis,* of hilly districts in India, Burma, and China. Also **sam′bar.** [<Hind. *sābar* <Skt. *shambara*]
same (sām) *adj.* **1** Having individual or specific identity or quality; identical; equal: with *the.* **2** Similar in kind or quality. **3** Aforesaid; identical: said of a person or thing just mentioned or held in mind. **4** Equal in degree of preference; indifferent. **5** Unchanged; monotonous. See synonyms under IDENTICAL, SYNONYMOUS. — **all the same** **1** Nevertheless. **2** Equally significant; equally acceptable or unacceptable. — **just the same** **1** Nevertheless. **2** Exactly identical or corresponding; unchanged. —*pron.* The identical person, thing, event, etc. —*adv.* In like manner; equally: with *the.* [ME <ON *samr, sami.* Akin to OE *same* equally.]
sa·mek (sä′mek) *n.* The fifteenth Hebrew letter. Also **sa′mech, sa′mekh.** See ALPHABET.
same·ness (sām′nis) *n.* **1** Lack of change or variety; dull monotony. **2** Close similarity. **3** Identity.
Sam Hill (sam′ hil′) *U.S. Slang* Hell: a euphemism.
sam·iel (sam′yel) *n.* The simoom. [<Turkish *samyel* < *sam* poison (<Arabic *samm*) + *yel* wind]

sam·i·sen (sam′i·sen) *n.* A Japanese guitarlike instrument with three strings, played with a plectrum. [<Japanese <Chinese *san hsien* three strings]

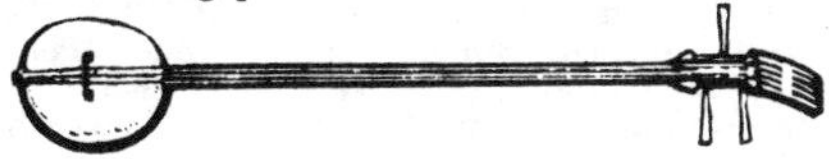

SAMISEN

sa·mite (sā′mīt, sam′īt) *n.* A rich medieval fabric of silk, often interwoven with gold or silver. [<OF *samit* <Med. L *samitum,* var. of *examitum* <Med. Gk. *hexamiton* < *hexamitos,* woven with six threads <Gk. *hex* six + *mitos* a thread]

sam·iz·dat (säm′iz·dät′) *n.* **1** In the Soviet Union, the secret publication and distribution of officially banned literature. **2** The literature that is so published and distributed. [< Russian <*sam* self + *izdat* publishing]

sam·let (sam′lit) *n.* A young salmon; a parr. [Contracted dim. of SALMON; infl. by earlier SALMONET]

Sam·nite (sam′nīt) *adj.* Of or pertaining to ancient Samnium, its people, or their language. —*n.* **1** One of the people of ancient Samnium, descended from the Sabines. **2** The Italic language of these people: also called *Oscan.* [<L *Samnis, Samnitis*]

Sam·ni·um (sam′nē·əm) An ancient country of central Italy, on the Adriatic, conquered by the Romans by 290 B.C.

Sa·mo·a (sə·mō′ə) An island group in the SW Pacific; 1,209 square miles; formerly *Navigators' Islands;* divided by the 171st meridian into: (1) **American** (or **Eastern**) **Samoa,** an unincorporated territory of the United States, comprising Tutuila, Rose, Swains, and Manua; 76 square miles; capital, Pago Pago, on Tutuila. (2) **Western Samoa,** a former trusteeship administered by New Zealand, independent 1962, and comprising Savaii, Upolu, and several smaller islands; 1,133 square miles; capital, Apia, on Upolu.

Sa·mo·an (sə·mō′ən) *adj.* Of or pertaining to Samoa, to its aboriginal Polynesian inhabitants, or to their language. —*n.* **1** A native of the Samoan islands. **2** The Polynesian language of the Samoans.

Sam·o·gi·ti·a (sam′ō·jish′ē·ə) A historical region of western Lithuania.

Sa·mos (sā′mos, *Greek* sä′môs) A Greek island in the Aegean, north of the Dodecanese; 194 square miles. —**Sa·mi·an** (sā′mē·ən) *adj. & n.*

Sam·o·thrace (sam′ə·thrās) A Greek island in the NE Aegean; 71 square miles. *Greek* **Sa·mo·thra·ki** (sä′mô·thrä′kē). —**Sam′o·thra′cian** (-thrā′shən) *adj. & n.*

sam·o·var (sam′ə·vär, sam′ə·vär′) *n.* A metal urn containing a tube for charcoal for heating water, as for making tea. [<Russian, lit., self-boiler <*samo-* self + *varit* boil]

Sam·o·yed (sam′ə·yed′) *n.* **1** One of a Mongoloid people inhabiting the Arctic coasts of Siberia. **2** A large dog characterized by a thick white coat of long hair, originally bred by the Samoyeds as a sled dog and for herding reindeer. —*adj.* Samoyedic. Also **Sam′·o·yede′** (-yed′). [<Russian, lit., self-eater, i.e., a cannibal]

Sam·o·yed·ic (sam′ə·yed′ik) *adj.* Of or pertaining to the Samoyeds or their language. —*adj.* A subfamily of the Uralic languages, including the language of the Samoyeds.

samp (samp) *n.* Coarse, hulled Indian corn; also, a porridge made of it. [<Algonquian (Narraganset) *nasaump* softened with water]

sam·pan (sam′pan) *n.* A small flat-bottomed boat or skiff used along rivers and coasts of China and Japan. [<Chinese *san-pan* <*san* three + *pan* board]

SAMPAN
Shown with typical lateen rig.

sam·phire (sam′fīr) *n.* **1** A European herb *(Crithmum maritimum)* of the parsley family, having fleshy leaves (formerly used in pickles). **2** A species *(Salicornia europaea)* of glasswort. [Earlier *sampere* <F *(l'herbe de) Saint Pierre* (the herb of) Saint Peter; ? infl. in form by CAMPHIRE]

sam·ple (sam′pəl) *n.* A portion, part, or piece taken or shown as a representative of the whole. —*v.t.* **·pled, ·pling** To test or examine by means of a portion or sample. [ME, aphetic var. of *asample* <OF *essample* EXAMPLE]

Synonyms (noun): case, example, exemplification, illustration, instance, specimen. A *sample* is a portion taken at random out of a quantity supposed to be homogeneous, so that the qualities found in the *sample* may reasonably be expected to be found in the whole; as, a *sample* of sugar, a *sample* of cloth. A *specimen* is one unit of a series, or a fragment of a mass, all of which is supposed to possess the same essential qualities; as, a *specimen* of coinage, or of quartz. No other unit or portion may be exactly like the *specimen,* while all the rest is supposed to be exactly like the *sample.* An *instance* is a *sample* or *specimen* of action. See EXAMPLE.

sam·pler[1] (sam′plər) *n.* **1** One who tests by samples; one who exhibits samples. **2** A device for removing a portion of a substance for testing.

sam·pler[2] (sam′plər) *n.* A piece of needlework, as a sample, designed to show a beginner's skill. [Aphetic var. of OF *essamplair* <LL *examplarium* <L *exemplum* EXAMPLE]

sam·pling (sam′pling) *n.* **1** A small part of something or a number of items from a group selected for examination or analysis in order to estimate the quality or nature of the whole. **2** The act or process of making this selection.

Samp·son (samp′sən), **William Thomas,** 1840–1902, U.S. rear admiral.

sam·sa·ra (səṅ·sä′rə) *n.* **1** In Buddhism, the course of mundane existence; the endless cycle of birth, death and rebirth; the wheel of causation. **2** Transmigration; metempsychosis. [<Skt. *samsāra,* lit., a passage through a succession of states]

Sam·son (sam′sən, *Fr.* säṅ·sôṅ′) A masculine personal name. Also **Samp′son.** Also *Pg.* **San·são** (säṅ·souṅ), *Sp.* **San·són** (säṅ·sōn′). [<Hebrew, the sun]

—**Samson** A Hebrew judge of great physical strength, betrayed to the Philistines by Delilah. *Judges* xiii 24.

Sam·u·el (sam′yo͞o·əl; *Ger.* zä′mo͞o·el, *Fr.* sä·mwel′, *Sp.* sä′mo͞o·el′) A masculine personal name. Also *Hungarian* **Sá·mu·el** (shä′mo͞o·el), *Ital.* **Sa·mue·le** (sä·mwā′lā). [<Hebrew, name of God]

—**Samuel** A Hebrew judge and prophet, I *Sam.* i 20; also, either of two historical books of the Old Testament.

Sam·u·rai (sam′o͝o·rī) *n. pl.* **·rai** *Japanese* Under the Japanese feudal system, a member of the soldier class of the lower nobility, acting as a military retainer of the daimios; also, the class itself.

San (sän) A river in SE Poland, flowing 247 miles NW from the Carpathians to the Vistula.

Sa·naa (sä·nä′) The capital of Yemen, Arabia. Also **Sa·na′.**

San An·to·ni·o (san an·tō′nē·ō) A city in south central Texas, the third largest in the State; a port of entry with a free port zone on the **San Antonio River,** which, rising here, flows 195 miles SE to join the Guadalupe River near its mouth on San Antonio Bay.

San Antonio Bay An inlet of the Gulf of Mexico, extending 19 miles into southern Texas.

san·a·tive (san′ə·tiv) *adj.* Healing; sanatory; health-giving. [<OF, fem. of *sanatif* <Med. L *sanativus* <L *sanatus,* pp. of *sanare* heal]

san·a·to·ri·um (san′ə·tôr′ē·əm, -tō′rē-) *n. pl.* **·to·ri·ums** or **·to·ri·a** (-tôr′ē·ə, -tō′rē·ə) **1** A health retreat, especially one in the mountains. **2** An institution for treatment of disease by curative waters or climate, or for the care of invalids. [<NL <LL *sanatorius* SANATORY]

san·a·to·ry (san′ə·tôr′ē, -tō′rē) *adj.* Promotive of health; curative [<LL *sanatorius* <L *sanatus,* pp. of *sanare* heal]

san·be·ni·to (san′bə·nē′tō) *n. pl.* **·tos** A black garment worn by a condemned heretic or a yellow cloak worn by a penitent under the Inquisition. [<Sp. *sambenito* <*San Benito* Saint Benedict; so called from its resemblance to a Benedictine's cloak.]

San Ber·nar·di·no Mountains (san bûr′nər·dē′nō) A range in SE California south of the Mojave Desert; highest peak, 11,485 feet.

San Bernardino Pass A pass in the Lepontine Alps, SE Switzerland; 6,770 feet.

San Blas (sän bläs′), **Gulf of** An inlet of the Caribbean on the north coast of Panama, east of the Panama Canal.

San·cho Pan·za (san′chō pan′zə, *Sp.* sän′chō pän′thä) In Cervantes' *Don Quixote,* a credulous peasant who acts as squire to the Don.

San Cris·to·bal (san kris·tō′bəl) One of the British Solomon Islands; 80 miles long, 25 miles wide. Also **San Cris·to′val** (-tō′vəl).

San Cris·tó·bal Island (san kris·tō′bəl) The chief island of the Galápagos group; 195 square miles; also *Chatham Island.*

sanc·ti·fied (sangk′tə·fīd) *adj.* Made holy; freed from sin; consecrated; also, sanctimonious.

sanc·ti·fy (sangk′tə·fī) *v.t.* **·fied, ·fy·ing 1** To set apart as holy or for holy purposes; consecrate. **2** To free of sin; purify or make holy. **3** To give religious sanction to; render sacred or inviolable, as a vow. **4** To render productive of or conducive to holiness or spiritual blessing. [<OF *saintifier, sanctifier* <LL *sanctificare* <L *sanctus* holy + *facere* make] —**sanc′ti·fi·ca′tion** *n.* —**sanc′ti·fi′er** *n.*

sanc·ti·mo·ni·ous (sangk′tə·mō′nē·əs) *adj.* **1** Making an ostentatious display or a hypocritical pretense of sanctity. **2** *Obs.* Saintly. —**sanc′ti·mo′ni·ous·ly** *adv.* —**sanc′ti·mo′ni·ous·ness** *n.*

sanc·ti·mo·ny (sangk′tə·mō′nē) *n.* Assumed or outward sanctity; a show of holiness or devoutness; exaggerated gravity or solemnity. See synonyms under HYPOCRISY, SANCTITY. [<OF *sanctimonie* <L *sanctimonia* holiness < *sanctus* holy]

sanc·tion (sangk′shən) *v.t.* **1** To approve authoritatively; confirm; ratify. **2** To countenance; allow. See synonyms under ABET, ALLOW, CONFIRM, RATIFY. —*n.* **1** Final and authoritative confirmation; justification or ratification. **2** A formal decree. **3** A provision for securing conformity to law, as by the enactment of rewards or penalties or both; a reward or penalty. **4** *pl.* In international law, a coercive measure adopted, usually by several nations at the same time, to force a nation which is violating international law to desist or yield to adjudication, by withholding loans, limiting trade relations, or by military force and blockade. **5** In ethics, that which makes virtue morally obligatory, or which furnishes a motive for man to seek it. [<MF <L *sanctio, -onis* ordaining something inviolable, a decree <*sanctus,* pp. of *sancire* make, sacred, decree]

sanc·ti·ty (sangk′tə·tē) *n. pl.* **·ties 1** The state of being sanctified; holiness. **2** Sacredness; solemnity. [<OF *sainteté* <L *sanctitas, -tatis* <*sanctus* holy]

Synonyms: holiness, sanctimoniousness, sanctimony. As referring to character, *sanctity* is *holiness,* while *sanctimoniousness,* or *sanctimony* is the pretense or affectation of *holiness.* Compare synonyms for HOLY.

sanc·tu·ar·y (sangk′cho͞o·er′ē) *n. pl.* **·ar·ies 1** A holy or sacred place; especially, a building or space, as a church, mosque, temple, or structure devoted to the worship of any deity. **2** The most sacred part of a place in a sacred structure; especially, the part of a church where the principal altar is situated; in Scripture, the holy of holies of the Jewish tabernacle and temple; also, the adytum of an ancient Greek or Roman temple. **3** A place of refuge; asylum; hence, immunity. See synonyms under REFUGE, SHELTER. [<OF *saintuarie* < LL *sanctuarium* <L *sanctus* holy]

sanc·tum (sangk′təm) *n. pl.* **·tums** or **·ta** (-tə) **1** A sacred place. **2** A private room where one is not to be disturbed. [<L, neut. of *sanctus holy*]

sanc·tum sanc·to·rum (sangk′təm sangk·tôr′·əm, -tō′rəm) **1** The holy of holies. **2** A place

of great privacy: often used humorously. [<L <*sanctum,* neut. nominative sing. + *sanctorum,* neut. genitive pl. of *sanctus* holy]
Sanc·tus (sangk′təs) *n. Eccl.* **1** An ascription of praise to God, occurring at the end of the Preface in many eucharistic liturgies. **2** A musical setting for this. [<L *sanctus* holy, its thrice repeated opening word]
Sanctus bell *Eccl.* In the celebration of the Eucharist, a bell rung at the singing of the Sanctus, the elevation of the Host, etc.: also called *mass bell, sacring bell.*
San·cy (säṅ·sē′), **Puy de** The highest peak of the Massif Central, France; 6,817 feet.
sand (sand) *n.* **1** A hard, granular, comminuted rock material finer than gravel and coarser than dust. **2** *pl.* Sandy wastes; stretches of sandy beach. **3** *pl.* Sandy grains or particles, as those of the hourglass; hence, moments of time or life. **4** *Slang* Strength of character; endurance; grit; courage. **5** A reddish-yellow color. —*v.t.* **1** To sprinkle or cover with sand. **2** To smooth or abrade with sand or sandpaper. **3** To mix sand with: to *sand* sugar. **4** To fill with sand, as a harbor by the action of currents. [OE]
Sand (sand, *Fr.* säṅd), **George** Pseudonym of Amandine Aurore Lucie Dudevant, 1803–76, *née* Dupin, French novelist.
San·da·kan (sän·dä′kän) A port of Sabah, chief town and once capital of the former North Borneo colony.
san·dal[1] (san′dəl) *n.* **1** A foot covering, consisting usually of a sole only, held to the foot by thongs. **2** A light slipper. **3** An overshoe of rubber, cut very low. **4** A strap or latchet for fastening a low shoe on the foot. **5** Sendal. [<L *sandalium* <Gk. *sandalion,* dim. of *sambalon, sandalon*] —**san′daled** *adj.*

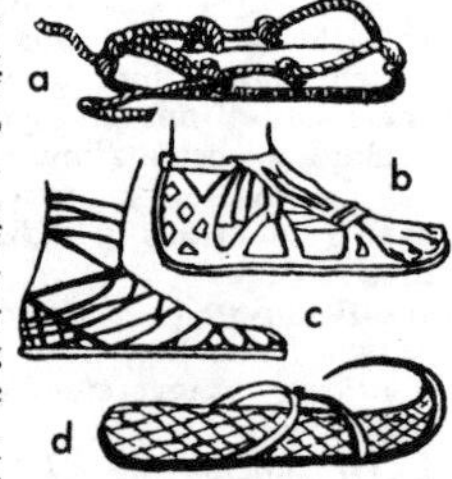

SANDALS
a. Japanese. *c.* Greek.
b. Roman. *d.* Egyptian.

san·dal[2] (san′dəl) *n.* Sandalwood.
sandal tree A Burmese evergreen tree *(Sandoricum koetjape),* extensively cultivated in the tropics. Its fruit is an applelike edible berry.
san·dal·wood (san′dəl·wo͝od′) *n.* **1** The fine-grained, dense, fragrant wood of any of several East Indian trees (genus *Santalum*). **2** The similar wood of other trees, as the East Indian **red sandalwood** *(Pterocarpus santalinus)*: also called *sanderswood.* [<obs. *sandal* sandalwood (<Med. L *sandalum,* ult. <Skt. *śandana*) + WOOD]
Sandalwood Island A former name for SUMBA.
san·da·rac (san′də·rak) *n.* A pale-yellow aromatic gum resin that exudes in drops from the sandarac tree: used as a lacquer and as an incense. See GUM[1]. Also **san′da·rach.** [<L *sandaraca* <Gk. *sandarakē* <an Oriental source]
sandarac tree A medium-sized North African tree *(Tetraclinis articulata),* yielding sandarac gum and a hard, dark-colored, fragrant wood susceptible of a high polish and used in ornamental work. Also **sandarach tree.**
sand·bag (sand′bag′) *n.* **1** A bag filled with or intended for holding sand: used for building fortifications, for ballast, etc. **2** A long, narrow bag filled with sand and used as a club or weapon. —*v.t.* **·bagged, ·bag·ging 1** To fill or surround with sandbags. **2** To strike or attack with or as with a sandbag. **3** To coerce in some forceful way. —**sand′bag′ger** *n.*
sand·bar (sand′bär′) *n.* A ridge of silt or sand in rivers, along beaches, etc., formed by the action of currents or tides.
sand bird Any of various birds frequenting the seashore, as a snipe or sandpiper.
sand·blast (sand′blast′, -bläst′) *n.* **1** An apparatus for propelling a jet of sand, as for engraving patterns on glass. **2** The jet of sand. **3** A sandstorm. —*v.t.* To clean or engrave by means of a sandblast.
sand·blind (sand′blīnd′) *adj.* Partially blind; having the vision affected by appearance of moving specks, etc. —**sand′blind′ness** *n.*
sand·box (sand′boks′) *n.* **1** A box with a perforated top, formerly used for sanding freshly written paper to avoid blotting. **2** A reservoir on a locomotive filled with sand to be poured on the rail treads in front of the forward drivers to prevent slipping. **3** A box of sand for children to play in. **4** The sandbox tree.
sandbox tree A tropical American tree *(Hura crepitans),* often cultivated for its curious woody capsules which burst with a loud report when ripe.
sand·bur (sand′bûr′) *n.* **1** A pernicious weed *(Solanum rostratum)* of the great plains of the western United States, having prickly foliage. **2** An ambrosiaceous weed *(Franseria acanthicarpa)* common in western North America. Also **sand′burr′.**
Sand·burg (sand′bûrg, san′-), **Carl,** 1878–1967, U.S. poet.
sand-cast (sand′kast′, -käst′) *v.t.* **-cast, -cast·ing** To make (a casting) by pouring metal into a mold of sand.
sand·crack (sand′krak′) *n.* A crack running down from the coronet of a horse's hoof and apt to cause lameness if neglected. See QUARTER-CRACK.
sand dab See under DAB[1].
sand dollar Any small, flat sea urchin (genus *Echinarachnius*) having a circular shell, found on sandy bottoms from New Jersey to Labrador and on the Pacific coast.
sand·ed (san′did) *adj.* **1** Filled, covered, or clogged with sand. **2** Of a sandy color; minutely speckled.
sand eel One of a family *(Ammodytidae)* of fishes with elongate bodies. Also **sand lance** or **sand launce.**
sand·er (san′dər) *n.* **1** One who or that which sands, as a locomotive sandbox. **2** A sandpapering machine.
san·der·ling (san′dər·ling) *n.* A small sandpiper *(Crocethia alba)* of arctic breeding habits, the adult gray and white in winter but having a rusty breast in summer. [<SAND + OE *yrthling* a kind of small bird, a ploughman]
san·ders·wood (san′dərz·wo͝od′) *n.* Sandalwood (def. 2). Also **san′ders.**
sand flea 1 The chigoe. **2** A beach flea.
sand fly Any of various minute hairy flies (family *Psychodidae*) found near the seashore and in damp places: some of the genus *Phlebotomus* are carriers of the tropical disease leishmaniasis.
sand grouse An Old World bird (family *Pteroclidae*) of pigeonlike form, with long pointed wings and short feathered legs, inhabiting sandy tracts.
san·dhi (san′dē, sän′-) *n. Ling.* **1** A phonetic environment in which a word undergoes assimilative change from its absolute form under the influence of neighboring words: "Did you" becomes dij′o͞o) in *sandhi.* **2** The assimilative changes occurring in combined sounds in consecutive speech: "Has" becomes (s) by *sandhi* in the sentence "Jack's done that." [<Skt. *saṁdhi* a placing together]
sand-hill·er (sand′hil′ər) *n.* A poor white inhabitant of the sand-hill districts of Georgia and South Carolina; a cracker.
sand·hog (sand′hôg′, -hog′) *n.* One who works under air pressure, as in caisson-sinking, tunnel-building, etc.: also called *ground hog.*
sand hopper A flea (def. 2).
Sand·hurst (sand′hûrst) A village in Berkshire, England; seat of the Royal Military College.
San Di·e·go (san dē·ā′gō) A port and U.S. naval base in SW California, on **San Diego Bay,** a landlocked natural harbor separated from the Pacific Ocean by overlapping peninsulas.
sand lily A low-growing herb *(Leucocrinum montanum)* of the lily family, with fragrant white flowers, native in western and Pacific States: also *star lily.*
sand-lot (sand′lot′) *adj.* Of or in a vacant lot in or near an urban area: applied to games played in such lots: *sand-lot* baseball.
sand·man (sand′man′) *n.* In nursery lore, a mythical person supposed to make children sleepy by casting sand in their eyes.
sand martin The bank swallow.
sand painting An indigenous Amerindian art form practiced especially by the Navaho. Pigments of finely ground sand in five colors are trickled on a ground base of neutral-colored sand to give highly symbolic representations (usually the gods, a rainbow, lightning, etc.). Each painting, whether three or twenty feet in diameter, has to be started at dawn and finished by sunset.
sand·pa·per (sand′pā′pər) *n.* Stout paper coated with sand for smoothing or polishing. —*v.t.* To rub or polish with sandpaper.
sand pine The smooth-barked pine *(Pinus clausa)* of sandy areas of the southern United States, especially common to the Gulf coast of Florida.
sand·pi·per (sand′pī′pər) *n.* Any of certain small wading birds (family *Scolopacidae*), mostly frequenting seashores in flocks. The two best known are the **common sandpiper** *(Actitis hypoleuca)* of Europe, and the **spotted sandpiper** *(A. macularia)* of North America. —**least sandpiper** A tiny, common, American marsh and shore bird *(Enolia minutilla)*: also **sand′peep′** (-pēp′).

SANDPIPER
(From 7 to 9 inches long)

San·dring·ham (san′dring·əm) A royal estate and parish of NW Norfolk, England.
San·dro·cot·tus (san′drō·kot′əs) See CHANDRAGUPTA I.
sand·stone (sand′stōn′) *n.* A rock consisting chiefly of quartz sand cemented with silica.
sand·storm (sand′stôrm′) *n.* A high wind by which sand or dust is carried along.
San·dus·ky (san·dus′kē) A port of entry on Lake Erie in northern Ohio.
sand verbena A trailing annual or perennial plant (genus *Abronia*) with vivid red, yellow, or white flowers, native in deserts of the western United States.
sand viper 1 The hog-nosed snake. **2** The horned viper.
sand·wich (sand′wich, san′-) *n.* Two thin slices of bread, having between them meat, cheese, etc.; hence, any combination of alternating dissimilar things pressed together. —*v.t.* To place between two layers or objects; insert between dissimilar things. [after John Montagu, fourth Earl of *Sandwich,* 1718–92, who is said to have originated it in order to eat without leaving the gaming table]
Sand·wich (sand′wich) A municipal borough in Kent, England, near Dover; the most ancient of the Cinque Ports.
Sandwich Islands A former name for the HAWAIIAN ISLANDS.
sand·wich-man (sand′wich·man′, -mən, san′-) *n. pl.* **-men** (-men′, -mən) A man carrying advertising boards slung in front and behind.
sand·wort (sand′wûrt′) *n.* Any of a genus *(Arenaria)* of low, usually tufted herbs, with opposite sessile leaves and small white flowers.
sand·y (san′dē) *adj.* **sand·i·er, sand·i·est 1** Consisting of or characterized by sand; containing, covered with, or full of sand. **2** Yellowish-red: a *sandy* beard. —**sand′i·ness** *n.*
Sandy Hook A peninsula, 6 miles long, extending north from eastern New Jersey, at the entrance to New York Bay.
sane[1] (sān) *adj.* **1** Mentally sound; not deranged. **2** Proceeding from a sound mind. [<L *sanus* whole, healthy] —**sane′ly** *adv.* —**sane′ness** *n.*
Synonyms: healthy, lucid, rational, sober, sound, underanged, unperverted. See SOBER.
sane[2] (sān) See SAIN.
San·ford (san′fərd), **Mount** The highest peak of the Wrangell Mountains in southern Alaska; 16,208 feet.
San·for·ize (san′fə·rīz) *v.t.* **·ized, ·iz·ing** To treat (cloth) by a special mechanical process so as to prevent more than slight shrinkage: a trade name. [after *Sanford* L. Cluett, U.S. inventor of the process, 1874–1968] —**San′for·ized** *adj.* —**San′for·iz′ing** *adj. & n.*

San Fran·cis·co (san′ frən·sis′kō) The second largest city of California, a port on **San Francisco Bay,** a landlocked inlet of the Pacific Ocean in western California. Colloquially shortened to *Frisco.* —**San′ Fran·cis′can** *n.* & *adj.*

San Francisco Peaks Three peaks of an extinct eroded volcano in northern Arizona; highest peak, also highest in State, 12,655 feet.

sang[1] (sang) Past tense of SING.

sang[2] (sang) *n. Scot.* Song.

San·gal·lo (sän·gäl′lō), **Giuliano da,** 1445–1516, Italian architect and sculptor.

San·ga·mon River (sang′gə·mən) A river in central Illinois, flowing 250 miles west to the Illinois River.

san·ga·ree (sang′gə·rē′) *n.* A tropical drink of wine or brandy and water, spiced and sweetened. [<Sp. *sangría,* lit., bleeding <*sangre* blood <L *sanguis*]

San·gay (säng·gī′) An active volcano in east central Ecuador; 17,454 feet.

sang de bœuf (säṅ də bœf′) *French* Oxblood.

Sang·er (sang′ər), **Margaret,** 1883–1966, U.S. advocate of birth-control education.

sang–froid (säṅ·frwä′) *n.* Calmness amid trying circumstances; coolness; composure. [<F, lit., cold blood]

San·gha (sung′gə) *n.* **1** The assembly; one of the three jewels of the Buddhist triad; the union of the generative power of Buddha with the productive power of the female Dharma. **2** Any order or community of Buddhist monks. **3** The total body of Buddhist monks everywhere. **4** A community of Jain monks. [<Skt. *saṁgha* close contact, an assemblage <*saṁhan* strike together, unite closely]

San·gihe Islands (säng′ir) An Indonesian island group between the Celebes Sea and the Molucca Sea; total, 314 square miles. Also **San·gi Islands** (säng′ē).

San·gre·al (sang′grē·əl) *n.* The Holy Grail. Also **San·graal** (sang·gräl′). [<OF *Saint Graal* <*saint* holy (<L *sanctus*) + *graal* GRAIL]

San·gre de Cris·to Mountains (säng′grā dā krēs′to) A mountain range in southern Colorado, the southernmost range of the Rocky Mountains; highest point, 14,363 feet.

san·gri·a (sang·grē′ə) *n.* An alcoholic drink made from red wine and fruit juice. [<Sp. *sangria* <*sangre* blood]

san·guic·o·lous (sang·gwik′ə·ləs) *adj.* Inhabiting the blood, as a parasite. [<L *sanguis* blood + *colere* inhabit]

san·guif·er·ous (sang·gwif′ər·əs) *adj.* Conducting blood, as the organs of circulation. [<L *sanguis* blood + -FEROUS]

san·gui·nar·i·a (sang′gwə·nâr′ē·ə) *n.* The bloodroot, or its medicinal preparation which is emetic. [<NL <L *(herba) sanguinaria,* fem. of *sanguinarius* SANGUINARY]

san·gui·nar·y (sang′gwə·ner′ē) *adj.* **1** Attended with bloodshed. **2** Prone to shed blood; bloodthirsty. **3** Consisting of blood. [<L *sanguinarius* <*sanguis, -inis* blood] —**san′gui·nar′i·ly** *adv.* —**san′gui·nar′i·ness** *n.*

Synonyms: blood thirsty, bloody, cruel, inhuman, murderous, sanguine, savage. *Sanguinary* applies either to the act of shedding blood or to the spirit that delights in bloodshed; *bloody* applies more directly to the actual staining with blood; we may say either a *sanguinary* or a *bloody* battle, but a *bloody* (not a *sanguinary*) field. *Sanguine* is sometimes used in poetic or elevated style in the sense of *bloody*; as, a *sanguine* stain. See BLOODY.

san·guine (sang′gwin) *adj.* **1** Of buoyant disposition; hopeful; confident; originally, having a temperament supposed to be due to active blood. **2** Having the color of blood; of, like, or full of blood. **3** *Obs.* Bloodthirsty; sanguinary. [<OF *sanguin* <L *sanguineus* <*sanguis, sanguinis* blood] —**san′guine·ly** *adv.* —**san′guine·ness n.**

Synonyms: animated, ardent, buoyant, confident, enthusiastic, hopeful. *Sanguine,* from the same root as *sanguinary,* came to denote full-blooded or plethoric, hence, *ardent, confident, hopeful,* because these qualities were supposed to be associated with fullness of blood. For the rare use of *sanguine* in direct literal sense, see synonyms under SANGUINARY.

san·guin·e·ous (sang·gwin′ē·əs) *adj.* **1** Pertaining to, consisting of, or forming blood. **2** Full-blooded; sanguine; hence, hopeful. **3** Of the color of blood. [<L *sanguineus* SANGUINE]

san·guin·o·lent (sang·gwin′ə·lənt) *adj.* Tinged or mixed with blood; bloody. [<OF <L *sanguinolentus* <*sanguis, sanguinis* blood]

San·he·drin (san′hi·drin, san′i-) *n.* **1** In ancient times, the supreme council and highest court of the Jewish nation: also **Great Sanhedrin. 2** Figuratively, any council or assembly. Also spelled *Synedrion, Synedrium.* Also **San′·he·drim** (-drim). [<Hebrew *sanhedrin* <Gk. *synedrion,* lit., a sitting together <*syn-* together + *hedra* a seat]

san·i·cle (san′i·kəl) *n.* Any of a genus *(Sanicula)* of smooth perennial herbs of the carrot family, reputed to have medicinal roots. [<OF <Med. L *sanicula,* prob. dim. <L *sanus* healthy; with ref. to its reputed healing powers]

sa·ni·es (sā′ni·ēz) *n. Pathol.* A serous, greenish, blood-tinged fluid discharged from ulcers. [<NL <L]

San Il·de·fon·so (sän ēl′thā·fōn′sō) A town in central Spain, 38 miles NW of Madrid; site of royal palace; scene of the signing of a treaty by Spain, France, and England, 1796: also *La Granja.*

sa·ni·ous (sā′nē·əs) *adj.* **1** Of or like sanies; watery and blood-tinged. **2** Producing or discharging sanies.

san·i·tar·i·an (san′ə·târ′ē·ən) *n.* A person skilled in matters relating to sanitation and public health.

san·i·tar·i·um (san′ə·târ′ē·əm) *n. pl.* **·tar·i·ums** or **·tar·i·a** (-târ′ē·ə) A sanatorium. [<NL <L *sanitas* health]

san·i·tar·y (san′ə·ter′ē) *adj.* **1** Relating to the preservation of health. **2** Cleanly; disease-preventing. See synonyms under HEALTHY. —*n. pl.* **·tar·ies** A public watercloset or urinal. [<F *sanitaire* <L *sanitas* health <*sanus* healthy] —**san′i·tar′i·ly** *adv.*

sanitary belt A belt, usually made of elastic, that has tabs to which a sanitary napkin may be attached.

sanitary cordon See CORDON SANITAIRE.

sanitary napkin An absorbent pad used by women during menstruation.

san·i·tate (san′ə·tāt) *v.t.* **·tat·ed, ·tat·ing** To apply sanitary measures to. [Back formation <SANITATION]

san·i·ta·tion (san′ə·tā′shən) *n.* The practical application of sanitary science; the removal or neutralization of elements injurious to health. [<SANIT(ARY) + -ATION]

san·i·ta·tion·man (san′i·tā′shən·man′) *n. pl.* **·men** (-mən) A person, especially a municipal employee, whose work is the collection of refuse and trash.

san·i·tize (san′ə·tīz) *v.t.* **·tized, ·tiz·ing 1** To make sanitary, as by scrubbing, washing, or sterilizing. **2** To make acceptable or unobjectionable, as by deleting offensive parts: a *sanitized* version of the fairy tale.

san·i·ty (san′ə·tē) *n.* **1** The state of being sane or sound; soundness of mind; mental health. **2** Moderation; reasonableness. [<MF *sanité* <L *sanitas* health <*sanus* healthy]

San Ja·cin·to (san′ jə·sin′tō) A locality in eastern Texas, scene of a Texan victory against Mexico, 1836; at the mouth of the **San Jacinto River,** which flows 115 miles south to Galveston Bay.

San Joa·quin River (san′ wô·kēn′, wä·kēn′) A river of south central California, flowing 317 miles through Central Valley to the Sacramento River just above its mouth.

San Jo·sé (sän hō·zā′) **1** The capital of Costa Rica. **2** (san′hō·zā′) A city on San Francisco Bay in western California.

San José scale A scale insect *(Quadraspidiotus perniciosus)* destructive to various fruit trees: so called because it first appeared in the United States at San José, California. For illustration see INSECTS (injurious).

San Juan (san hwän′) **1** A port, capital of Puerto Rico. **2** A province of west central Argentina; 33,249 square miles; capital, San Juan.

San Juan de la Cruz (thä lä krōōth′) See JOHN OF THE CROSS, SAINT.

San Juan de los Mor·ros (thā lōs môr′rōs) The capital of Guàrico state, north central Venezuela.

San Juan Islands An American island group lying between SE Vancouver Island and the mainland of NW Washington at the northern end of Puget Sound.

San Juan Mountains A range of the Rocky Mountains in SW Colorado; highest peak, 14,306 feet.

sank (sangk) Past tense of SINK.

San·key (sang′kē), **Ira David,** 1840–1908, U.S. evangelist and hymn writer.

San·khya (säng′kyə) *n.* The oldest system of Indian philosophy, professing unqualified dualism: founded by Kapila, fabled son of Brahma. [<Skt. *Sāṁkhya* <*saṁkhyā* enumeration; with ref. to its enumeration of twenty-four material principles *(tattva)* and one independent immaterial principle]

Sankt Mo·ritz (zängt mō′rits) The German name for ST. MORITZ.

San Lu·is (sän lōō·ēs′) A province in west central Argentina; 29,625 square miles; capital, San Luis.

San Luis Po·to·sí (pō′tō·sē′) A state in central Mexico; 24,415 square miles; capital, San Luis Potosí.

San Ma·ri·no (mä·rē′nō) An independent republic in eastern Italy near the coast of the Adriatic Sea; 23 square miles; capital, San Marino.

San Mar·tín (mär·tēn′), **José de,** 1778–1850, South American general and statesman.

San Mi·guel Gulf (mē·gel′) The eastern part of the Gulf of Panama, adjacent to eastern Panama.

san·nup (san′up) *n.* A married male American Indian; the husband of a squaw. Also **san′·nop.** [<Algonquian (Narraganset) *sannop*]

San Pa·blo Bay (san′ pä′blō) The northern part of San Francisco Bay, California.

San Re·mo (sän rā′mō) A port and resort on the Gulf of Genoa in NW Italy.

sans (sanz, *Fr.* säṅ) *prep.* Without. [<OF *sens, sanz,* alter. of L *absentia* absence, infl. by *sine* without]

San Sal·va·dor (san′ sal′və·dôr, *Sp.* sän säl′vä·thōr′) The capital of El Salvador.

San Salvador Island An island in the central Bahamas, the first landing place of Columbus in the New World, 1492: also called *Watling Island.*

san·sar (sän′sər) *n.* A sarsar.

sans cé·ré·mo·nie (säṅ sā·rā·mô·nē′) *French* Without ceremony; informal.

sans·cu·lotte (sanz′kyōō·lot′, *Fr.* säṅ·kü·lôt′) *n.* **1** A revolutionary: first applied by the aristocrats as a term of contempt for those who started the revolution of 1789; later it became a popular name for one of a revolutionary mob; a Jacobin. **2** Any revolutionary republican or radical. **3** Any ragged or strangely dressed person. [<F, lit., without knee breeches] —**sans′cu·lot′tic** *adj.* —**sans′·cu·lot′·tism** *n.*

sans·cu·lot·tides (sanz′kyōō·lot′idz, *Fr.* säṅ′·kü·lô·tēd′) See CALENDAR (Republican).

sans doute (säṅ dōōt′) *French* Without doubt; unquestionably.

San Se·bas·tián (san sə·bas′chən, *Sp.* sän sä·väs·tyän′) A port on the Bay of Biscay, in northern Spain.

San·sei (sän·sä) *n. pl.* **·sei** An American citizen of Japanese descent whose grandparents settled in the United States; a third-generation Japanese American. [<Japanese, third generation]

san·se·vi·e·ri·a (san′sə·vi·ir′ē·ə) *n.* Any of a genus *(Sansevieria)* of erect perennial herbs of the lily family, native in Africa but sometimes grown as an ornamental plant. [<NL, after the Prince of *Sanseviero,* 1710–71, a Neapolitan savant]

San·skrit (san′skrit) *n.* The ancient and classical language of the Hindus of India, belonging to the Indic branch of the Indo-Iranian subfamily of Indo-European languages. It includes specifically **Vedic Sanskrit,** the language of the Vedas, and the later **classical Sanskrit** of India's great religious, philosophical, and poetic literature, still used for sacred or learned writings, and distinguished from the vernacular Prakrit. Also **San′scrit.** Abbr. *Skt.* [<Skt. *saṁskṛta* well-formed <*sam-* together + *kṛ* make, do] —**San′skrit·ist** *n.*

San·skrit·ic (san·skrit′ik) *adj.* **1** Of, pertaining to, or written in the ancient and sacred language of India. **2** Designating a group of some 30 to 40 ancient and modern languages and dialects of India, embracing Sanskrit, Prakrit, Pali, Assamese, Bengali, Eastern and Western Hindi, Punjabi, Singhalese, Romany or Gipsy, etc.

San·so·vi·no (sän′sō·vē′nō), 1486?–1570, Italian sculptor and architect: original name *Jacopo Tatti.*

sans pa·reil (säṅ pȧ·rā′y′) *French* Without equal.

sans peur et sans re·proche (säṅ pœr ā säṅ rə·prôsh′) *French* Without fear and without reproach.

sans ser·if (sanz ser′if) *Printing* A style of type without serifs.

sans–sou·ci (säṅ·sōō·sē′) *adj. French* Carefree; free and easy.

San Ste·fa·no (sän stā′fä·nō) A village on the Sea of Marmara west of Istanbul, in Turkey in Europe; scene of the signing of a Russo–Turkish treaty, 1878: Turkish *Yesilköy.*

San·ta An·a (sän′tä ä′nä) A city in NW El Salvador, the second largest; a coffee center and rail junction.

San·ta An·na (sän′tä ä′nä), **Antonio Lopez de,** 1795–1876, Mexican general: president and dictator of Mexico; massacred the surviving defenders of the Alamo, Mar. 6, 1836; defeated by the U. S. Army in 1847. Also **San′ta A′na.**

San·ta Bar·ba·ra Islands (san′tə bär′bər·ə) A chain of small islands, extending 150 miles along the coast of southern California.

San·ta Cat·a·li·na (san′tə kat′ə·lē′nə) One of the Santa Barbara Islands, 24 miles south of Los Angeles, California; 22 miles long: also *Catalina Island.*

San·ta Ca·ta·ri·na (saṅn′tə kä′tə·rē′nə) A maritime state in southern Brazil; 36,592 square miles; capital, Florianópolis.

San·ta Cla·ra (sän′tä klä′rä) A city in central Cuba.

San·ta Claus (san′tə klôz′) In nursery folklore, a friend of children who brings presents at Christmas time: usually represented as a fat, jolly old man. The patron saint of children, figuring in the nursery lore of many countries and identified with *St. Nicholas.* [< dial. Du. *Sante Klaus* Saint Nicholas]

San·ta Cruz (san′tə krōōz′, *Sp.* sän′tä krōōth′) **1** St. Croix. **2** A national territory in southern Patagonia, Argentina; 77,822 square miles; capital, Río Gallegos.

Santa Cruz de Ten·er·ife (də ten′ə·rif′, *Sp.* thā tā′nā·rē′fā) **1** One of the two provinces in the Canary Islands, comprising Tenerife, La Palma, Gomera, and Hierro; 1,238 square miles. **2** A port of NE Tenerife, capital of this province and of Tenerife island.

Santa Cruz Islands An island group north of the New Hebrides, comprising part of the British Solomon Islands protectorate; total, 370 square miles; scene of U. S. naval victory over Japanese, 1942.

San·ta Fe (san′tə fā′) **1** The capital of New Mexico, in the northern part of the State. **2** (sän′tä fā′) A province of NE central Argentina; 51,341 square miles; capital, Santa Fe.

Santa Fe trail The trade route, important from 1821 to 1880, between Independence, Missouri, or a nearby terminus, and Santa Fe, New Mexico.

San·ta Is·a·bel (sän′tä ē′sä·bel) **1** A city on Fernando Pó island, capital of Spanish Guinea. **2** (san′tə iz′ə·bel) One of the British Solomon Islands; 1,800 square miles: also *Ysabel.*

san·ta·la·ceous (san′tə·lā′shəs) *adj. Bot.* Of or pertaining to a family *(Santalaceae)* of apetalous shrubs, herbs, and some trees; the sandalwood family. [<NL <*Santalum,* genus name <Med. L, sandalwood]

san·tal·ic (san·tal′ik) *adj.* Of, pertaining to, or derived from sandalwood, as **santalic acid,** a red crystalline coloring matter, $C_{15}H_{14}O_5$. [<NL *santal(um)* sandalwood (<Med. L) + -IC]

San·ta Ma·ri·a (san′tə mə·rē′ə, *Sp.* sän′tä mä·rē′ä) One of the three ships of Columbus on his maiden voyage to America.

San·ta Ma·ri·a (sän′tä mä·rē′ä) **1** An island in the SE Azores; 37 square miles. **2** An active volcano in SW Guatemala; 12,362 feet.

San·ta Mau·ra (sän′tä mou′rä) The Italian name for LEVKAS.

San·tan·der (sän′tän·der′) A port of northern Spain on the Bay of Biscay.

San·ta·rém (saṅn′tə·rāṅ′) The second largest city of Pará state, Brazil, on the Tapajós at its influx into the Amazon.

San·ta·ya·na (sän′tä·yä′nä), **George,** 1863–1952, U. S. philosopher and author born in Spain.

San·tee River (san·tē′) A river in east central South Carolina, flowing 143 miles SE from the junction of the Congaree and Wateree rivers, over **Santee Dam** (45 feet high, 7.8 miles long; completed 1941), to the Atlantic.

San·ti·a·go (sän′tē·ä′gō) **1** The capital of Chile. Also **Santiago de Chi·le** (thā chē′lā). **2** Santiago de Compostela. **3** Santiago de los Caballeros.

Santiago de Com·po·ste·la (thā kōm′pō·stā′·lä) A city and chief pilgrimage center of NW Spain: also *Santiago.*

Santiago de Cu·ba (thā kōō′bä) **1** The second largest city of Cuba and capital of Oriente province, on the southern coast. **2** The former name for ORIENTE province, Cuba.

Santiago del Es·te·ro (thel es·tā′rō) A province of northern Argentina; 52,208 square miles; capital, Santiago del Estero.

Santiago de los Ca·bal·le·ros (thā lōs kä′vä·yā′rōs) A city in northern Dominican Republic, the second largest city of the Republic: also *Santiago.*

San·to Do·min·go (sän′tō dō·ming′gō) The capital of the Dominican Republic, a port on the south coast; the oldest continuously occupied European settlement in the Western Hemisphere: formerly *Ciudad Trujillo.*

san·ton·i·ca (san·ton′i·kə) *n.* **1** An Old World plant of the composite family, especially the European wormwood *(Artemisia maritima).* **2** The unexpanded flower heads of this plant, used as a vermifuge. [<NL <L *(herba) Santonica* a kind of wormwood, fem. sing. of *Santonicus* of the Santoni <*Santoni* the Santoni, a people of Aquitania]

san·to·nin (san′tə·nin) *n. Chem.* A colorless crystalline poisonous compound, $C_{15}H_{18}O_3$, contained in santonica: used in medicine as a vermifuge. Also **san′to·nine** (-nēn, -nin). [<F *santonine* <NL *santon(ica)* + -INE[2]]

San·to·rin (sän′tō·rēn′) A former name for THERA.

San·tos (saṅn′tōōs) A port and the second largest city in São Paulo state, SE Brazil.

San·tos–Du·mont (saṅn′tōōz·dü·môṅ′), **Alberto,** 1873–1932, Brazilian airship pioneer active in France.

São Fran·cis·co (souṅ frän·sēs′kōō) A river of eastern Brazil, flowing 1,800 miles to the Atlantic; the third largest drainage basin of Brazil; developed for hydroelectric power.

São Jor·ge (souṅ zhôr′zhə) An island in the central Azores; 92 square miles.

São Lu·ís (souṅ lōō·ēs′) A port of NE Brazil, capital of Maranhão state. Formerly **São Luís do Ma·ra·nhão** (thōō mä′rə·nyouṅ′). Also **São Luiz.**

São Ma·nuel (souṅ mə·nwel′) A river of northern Mato Grosso, Brazil, flowing 700 miles NW to the Tapajós.

São Mi·guel (souṅ mē·gel′) An island in the eastern Azores; 288 square miles.

Saône (sōn) A river in eastern France, flowing 268 miles SW to the Rhône at Lyon.

São Pau·lo (souṅm pou′lōō) A maritime state in SE Brazil; 95,428 square miles; capital, São Paulo.

São Paulo de Lo·an·da (thə lō·än′də) A former name for LUANDA.

São Pe·dro de Ri·o Gran·de do Sul (souṅm pā′·thrōō thə rē′ōō graṅn′də thōō sōōl′) A former name for the port of RIO GRANDE DO SUL.

Saor·stat Eir·eann (sâr′stät âr′ən, *Gaelic* ā′rôn) Gaelic name for IRISH FREE STATE.

São Sal·va·dor (souṅ säl′və·thōr′) The former name for Salvador, Brazil.

São Tia·go (souṅ tyä′gōō) Largest of the Cape Verde Islands; 383 square miles; capital, Praia. Also **São Thia′go.**

Saõ To·mé e Prin·ci·pe (souṅ tô·me′ e prēṅ′·sē·pə) A Portuguese province in the Bight of Biafra, comprising the islands of **São Tomé** (also **São Thomé,** English *St. Thomas*); 320 square miles; and **Principe** (English *Prince Island*); 52 square miles.

sap[1] (sap) *n.* **1** The aqueous juices of plants, which contain and transport the materials necessary to vegetable growth. **2** Any vital fluid; vitality. **3** Sapwood. **4** *Slang* A foolish, stupid, or ineffectual person. [OE *sæp*]

sap[2] (sap) *v.* **sapped, sap·ping** *v.t.* **1** To weaken or destroy gradually and insidiously; enervate; exhaust. **2** To approach or undermine (an enemy fortification) by digging a sap or saps. —*v.i.* **3** To dig a sap or saps; undermine an enemy fortification. See synonyms under WEAKEN. —*n.* A deep, narrow trench or tunnel dug so as to approach or undermine a fortification. [<MF *saper, sapper* < *sappe* a spade <Ital. *zappe* < *zappa* a goat; with ref. to resemblance of the handle to a goat's horns]

sap·a·jou (sap′ə·jōō, *Fr.* sȧ·pȧ·zhōō′) *n.* A South American monkey, the capuchin: often seen in captivity. Also called *sajou.* [<F < Tupian]

SAPAJOU
(Head and body about 1 1/2 feet long)

sa·pan·wood (sə·pan′wŏŏd′) *n.* **1** The brownish–red dyewood obtained from a medium–sized East Indian tree *(Caesalpinia sappan)* of the bean family. **2** The tree. Also spelled *sappanwood:* also called *brazil.* [Trans. of Du. *sapanhout* < Malay *sapang* sapanwood + Du. *hout* wood]

Sa·phar (sä·fär′) See under CALENDAR (Mohammedan).

sap·head (sap′hed′) *n. Slang* A soft–headed person; simpleton. [<SAP[1] (def. 4) + HEAD] —**sap′head′ed** *adj.*

sa·phe·na (sə·fē′nə) *n. pl.* **·nae** (-nē) *Anat.* One of the two large superficial veins of the leg. [<Med. L, a vein in the leg <Arabic *ṣāfin*] —**sa·phe′nous** *adj.*

sap·id (sap′id) *adj.* Affecting the sense of taste; savory; agreeable. [<L *sapidus* < *sapere* taste] —**sa·pid′i·ty, sap′id·ness** *n.*

sa·pi·ence (sā′pē·əns) *n.* Wisdom; learning: often ironical. Also **sa′pi·en·cy.** [<OF <L *sapientia* wisdom < *sapiens, -entis* SAPIENT]

sa·pi·ent (sā′pē·ənt) *adj.* Wise; sagacious: often ironical. See synonyms under WISE[1]. [<L *sapiens, -entis,* ppr. of *sapere* know, taste] —**sa′pi·ent·ly** *adv.*

sa·pi·en·tial (sā′pē·en′shəl) *adj.* Of, marked by, or expounding wisdom; especially, the *sapiential* books of the Bible, as Proverbs. —**sa′pi·en′tial·ly** *adv.*

sap·in·da·ceous (sap′in·dā′shəs) *adj. Bot.* Of or pertaining to a family *(Sapindaceae)* of mostly tropical trees, shrubs, and vines, the soapberry family, including some genera with edible fruit, as the litchi tree. [<NL <*Sapindus,* genus name <L *sapo* soap + *Indicus* Indian]

sap·less (sap′lis) *adj.* **1** Destitute of sap; withered. **2** Wanting vitality, spirit, or vivacity; insipid; dull.

sap·ling (sap′ling) *n.* **1** A young tree. **2** A youth. [Dim. of SAP[1]]

sap·o·dil·la (sap′ə·dil′ə) *n.* **1** A large evergreen tree *(Achras zapota)* of the West Indies and Central America. **2** Its luscious apple–shaped fruit, the **sapodilla plum,** for which it is cultivated. Often called *mamey,* *marmalade tree.* Also **sa·po·ta** (sə·pō′tə), **sap′a·dil′lo, sap′o·dil′lo.** [<Sp. *zapotille,* dim of *zapota* <Nahuatl *zapotl, sapotl*]

sap·o·na·ceous (sap′ə·nā′shəs) *adj.* Of the nature of soap; soapy. [<NL *saponaceus* <L *sapo, saponis* soap]

sa·pon·i·fi·ca·tion (sə·pon′ə·fə·kā′shən) *n.* **1** The process or result of making soap. **2** *Chem.* **a** A decomposition in which an ester is changed into an acid and an alcohol. **b** The conversion of certain acid derivatives, as nitrates, acid amides, etc., into the corresponding acids.

sa·pon·i·fy (sə·pon′ə·fī) *v.t.* **·fied, ·fy·ing** To convert (a fat or oil) into soap by the action of an alkali. [<F *saponifier* <NL *saponificare* <L *sapo, saponis* soap + *facere* make] —**sa·pon′i·fi′a·ble** *adj.* —**sa·pon′i·fi′er** *n.*

sap·o·nin (sap′ə·nin) *n. Biochem.* One of several nearly white amorphous glycosides contained in various plants and characterized by their ability to form emulsions and soapy lathers. Also **sap′o·nine** (-nēn, -nin). [<F *saponine* <L *sapo, saponis* soap + F *-ine* -INE[2]]

sap·o·nite (sap′ə·nīt) *n.* A soft, hydrous silicate of magnesium and aluminum, found as an amorphous soaplike mass in nodules, or filling cavities in rock. [<L *sapo, saponis* soap + -ITE[1]]

sa·por (sā′pər, -pôr) *n.* That quality of a substance affecting the sense of taste; flavor; taste. Also *Brit.* **sa′pour.** [<L, taste < *sapere* taste, know] — **sap·o·rif·ic** (sap′ə·rif′ik), **sap′o·rous** *adj.*

sap·o·ta·ceous (sap′ə·tā′shəs) *adj. Bot.* Of or pertaining to a family *(Sapotaceae)* of trees and shrubs yielding a milky juice of considerable economic importance, and also some edible fruits, as the sapodilla family. [<NL < *sapota* <Sp. *zapote* SAPODILLA]

sap·pan·wood (sə·pan′wŏŏd′) See SAPANWOOD.

sap·per (sap′ər) *n.* **1** One who or that which saps. **2** A soldier employed in making trenches, tunnels, and underground fortifications. [<SAP[2] + -ER]

Sap·phic (saf′ik) *adj.* **1** Pertaining to or in the manner of Sappho. **2** Denoting a meter or verse form used by Sappho, especially a stanza of three Sapphics followed by an Adonic. — *n.* A line of trochaic pentameter with a dactyl in the third foot: much used by Sappho. [<F *sapphique, saphique* <L *Sapphicus* <Gk. *Sapphikos* <*Sapphō* Sappho]

Sap·phi·ra (sə·fī′rə) Wife of Ananias. *Acts* v.

sap·phire (saf′īr) *n.* **1** Any one of the hard, transparent, colored varieties of corundum which when cut are used as gems: usually and specifically, the blue variety. **2** Deep pure blue. — **star sapphire** A sapphire cut en cabochon, showing six rays on the dome. [< OF *sapir* <L *sapphirus, sapp(h)ir* <Gk. *sappheiros,* a gemstone <Semitic, ? ult. <Skt. *śanipriya* dear to the planet Saturn]

sap·phi·rine (saf′ər·in, -ə·rēn) *adj.* Consisting of or like sapphire. — *n.* **1** A vitreous pale blue or green silicate of aluminum and magnesium, crystallizing in the monoclinic system. **2** Sapphire quartz. **3** A blue variety of spinel.

Sap·pho (saf′ō) Greek poetess of Lesbos; lived about 600 B.C.

Sap·po·ro (säp·pō·rō) The capital of Hokkaido island, Japan.

sap·py (sap′ē) *adj.* **·pi·er, ·pi·est** **1** Full of sap; juicy. **2** *Slang* Immature; silly. **3** Vital; pithy. — **sap′pi·ly** *adv.* — **sap′pi·ness** *n.*

sa·pre·mi·a (sə·prē′mē·ə) *n. Pathol.* Blood poisoning by the products of putrefaction. Also **sa·prae′mi·a.** [<NL <Gk. *sapros* putrid + *haima* blood] — **sa·pre′mic** *adj.*

sapro– *combining form* **1** Decomposition or putrefaction: *saprogenic.* **2** Saprophytic: *saproplankton.* [<Gk. *sapros* rotten]

sap·ro·gen·ic (sap′rə·jen′ik) *adj.* **1** Productive of putrefaction. **2** Developing in or living upon putrefying matter. Also **sa·prog·e·nous** (sə·proj′ə·nəs).

sap·ro·lite (sap′rə·līt) *n. Geol.* Thoroughly decomposed, earthy rock, lying in its original place. [<SAPRO- + -LITE] — **sap′ro·lit′ic** (-lit′ik) *adj.*

sa·proph·a·gous (sə·prof′ə·gəs) *adj.* Feeding on decaying substances. [<SAPRO- + -PHAGOUS]

sap·ro·phyte (sap′rə·fīt) *n.* An organism that lives on dead or decaying organic matter, as certain fungous or other plants, various bacteria, etc. [<SAPRO- + -PHYTE] — **sap′ro·phyt′ic** (-fit′ik) *adj.*

sap·ro·plank·ton (sap′rə·plangk′tən) *n.* Plankton found on the surface of stagnant water. [<SAPRO- + PLANKTON]

sap·sa·go (sap′sə·gō) *n.* A hard green Swiss cheese flavored with melilot, used chiefly in cooking. [Alter. of G *schabzieger* < *schaben* shave, scrape + *zieger* whey]

sap·suck·er (sap′suk′ər) *n.* Any small black-and-white woodpecker (genus *Sphyrapicus*), especially the **yellow-bellied sapsucker** *(S. varius),* which damages orchard trees by exposing and devouring the sapwood.

YELLOW–BELLIED SAPSUCKER (About 8 1/2 inches long)

sap sugar Maple sugar.

sap·wood (sap′wŏŏd′) *n. Bot.* The new wood next the bark of an exogenous tree; alburnum. See illustration under EXOGEN.

Saq·qa·ra (sə·kä′rə) See SAKKARA.

sar·a·band (sar′ə·band) *n.* A stately Spanish dance in triple time, of the 17th and 18th centuries; also, the music for or in the rhythm of this dance, often used as one of the movements of the classical suite. Also **sar′a·bande.** [<F *sarabande* <Sp. *zarabanda,* ult. <Persian *sarband* a kind of dance and song]

Sa·ra·bat (sä′rä·bät′) Former name of the GEDIZ.

Sar·a·cen (sar′ə·sən) *n.* **1** Originally, a nomad Arab of the Syrian–Arabian desert, who harassed the frontiers of the Roman Empire. **2** A Moslem enemy of the Crusaders. **3** Any Arab. **4** *Obs.* A heathen; pagan. [Fusion of OE *Sarracene* and OF *Sarazin, Saracin,* both <LL *Saracenus* <LGk. *Sarakēnos,* ? <Arabic] — **Sar′a·cen′ic** (-sen′ik) or **·i·cal** *adj.*

Sar·a·gos·sa (sar′ə·gos′ə) A city of NE Spain, on the Ebro; former capital of Aragon: Spanish *Zaragoza.*

Sar·ah (sâr′ə) A feminine personal name. Also **Sar·a** (sâr′ə; *Fr.* sȧ·rȧ′, *Ital., Sp.* sä′rä, *Ger.* zä′rä). [<Hebrew *sārāh* a princess]
— **Sarah** The wife of Abraham. *Gen.* xvii 15.

Sa·ra·je·vo (sä′rä·yā′vō) A city in central Yugoslavia; the former capital of Bosnia where Archduke Francis Ferdinand was assassinated, June 28,1914: also *Serajevo.*

sa·ran (sə·ran′) *n.* Any of a class of synthetic fibers and textile materials obtained by the chemical treatment of petroleum and natural brines. [Coined by Dow Chemical Co.]

Sar·a·nac Lakes (sar′ə·nak) Three lakes in NE New York, in the Adirondack Mountains, **Upper, Middle,** and **Lower Saranac,** linked by the **Saranac River,** which flows 50 miles NE to Lake Champlain at Plattsburg.

Sa·ransk (sä·ränsk′) The capital of Mordvinian Autonomous S.S.R.

Sar·a·to·ga (sar′ə·tō′gə) A former name for SCHUYLERVILLE.

Saratoga Springs A resort city in eastern New York, noted for horse–racing and mineral waters.

Saratoga trunk A very large traveling trunk used formerly by ladies. [after *Saratoga* Springs]

Sa·ra·tov (sä·rä′tôf) A port on the Volga in SE European Russian S.F.S.R.; a major industrial and natural–gas–producing center.

Sa·ra·wak (sə·rä′wäk) A State of Malaysia in NW Borneo; 47,071 square miles; capital, Kuching. — **Sa·ra·wak·ese** (sə·rä′wäk·ēz′, -ēs′) *adj & n.*

sar·casm (sär′kaz·əm) *n.* **1** A keenly ironical or scornful utterance; contemptuous and taunting language. **2** The use of biting gibes or cutting rebukes. See synonyms under BANTER. [<LL *sarcasmus* <Gk. *sarkasmos* < *sarkazein* tear flesh, speak bitterly < *sarx, sarkos* flesh]

sar·cas·tic (sär·kas′tik) *adj.* **1** Characterized by or of the nature of sarcasm. **2** Taunting. Also **sar·cas′ti·cal.** — **sar·cas′ti·cal·ly** *adv.*

sarce·net (särs′nit) See SARSENET.

Sar·ci·na (sär·si′nə) *n.* A genus of parasitic, usually Gram–positive bacteria, which divide to form clusters of individuals: many are saprophytic. See illustration under BACTERIA. [<NL <L, a bundle < *sarcire* patch, mend]

sarco– *combining form* Flesh; of or related to flesh: *sarcogenic.* Also, before vowels, **sarc–.** [<Gk. *sarx, sarkos* flesh]

sar·co·carp (sär′kō·kärp) *n. Bot.* The succulent part of a drupaceous fruit, as the fleshy edible part of a plum or peach. [<F *sarcocarpe* <Gk. *sarx, sarkos* flesh + *karpos* a fruit]

Sar·co·di·na (sär′kō·dī′nə) *n. pl.* A class of marine and fresh–water protozoa which move by means of pseudopodia, including both naked forms, as the *Amoebae,* and those with protective shell covering, as the *Foraminifera.* [<NL <Gk. *sarkōdēs* fleshy < *sarx, sarkos* flesh]

sar·co·gen·ic (sär′kō·jen′ik) *adj.* Flesh–producing. Also **sar·cog·e·nous** (sär·koj′ə·nəs).

sar·co·lem·ma (sär′kō·lem′ə) *n. Anat.* The elastic membrane that invests striated muscular fibers. [<NL <Gk. *sarx, sarkos* flesh + *lemma* a husk]

sar·co·ma (sär·kō′mə) *n. pl.* **·ma·ta** (-mə·tə) *Pathol.* A tumor, or group of tumors, often malignant, composed of embryonal lymphoid or connective tissue in which the cell elements predominate. [<NL <Gk. *sarkōma* < *sarkaein* become fleshy < *sarx, sarkos* flesh] — **sar·co′ma·toid, sar·co′ma·tous** (-kō′mə·təs, -kom′ə-) *adj.*

sar·co·ma·to·sis (sär·kō′mə·tō′sis) *n. Pathol.* The formation of sarcomatous growths in the body. [<NL <Gk. *sarkōma, -ōmatos* SARCOMA + *-ōsis* -OSIS]

sar·coph·a·gus (sär·kof′ə·gəs) *n. pl.* **·gi** (-jī) **1** A stone coffin or tomb; hence, a large ornamental coffin of marble or stone placed in a crypt or exposed to view. **2** A kind of limestone, used by the Greeks for coffins and said to reduce flesh to dust. [<L <Gk. *sarkophagos,* orig. adj., flesh–eating < *sarx, sarkos* flesh + *phagein* eat]

sar·co·plasm (sär′kō·plaz′əm) *n. Anat.* The substance resembling hyaloplasm that lies between the columns of a striated muscle fiber.

sar·cous (sär′kəs) *adj.* Of, pertaining to, or composed of flesh or muscle. [<Gk. *sarx, sarkos* flesh]

sard (särd) *n.* The deep brownish–red variety of chalcedony, translucently blood–red: used as a gem. Also called *sardine, sardius.* [<OF *sarde* <L *sarda* <Gk. *sardios.* See SARDIUS.]

Sar·da·na·pa·lus (sär′də·nə·pā′ləs) Greek form of ASHURBANIPAL.

sar·dine[1] (sär·dēn′) *n.* **1** A small fish preserved in oil as a delicacy, especially the California pilchard *(Sardinia coerulea).* **2** The young of the herring or some like fish similarly prepared. [<OF <Ital. *sardina* <L <Gk. *sardēnē* < *sarda* a kind of fish, prob. <*Sardō* Sardinia]

sar·dine[2] (sär′din) See SARD.

Sar·din·i·a (sär·din′ē·ə) **1** An Italian island in the Mediterranean, west of Italy; 9,196 square miles; forming, with its neighboring islands, an autonomous region of Italy; 9,298 square miles; capital, Cagliari. *Italian* **Sar·de·gna** (sär·dā′nyä). **2** A former kingdom (1720–1860) of northern Italy, including the island of Sardinia with Savoy and Piedmont. — **Sar·din′i·an** *adj. & n.*

Sar·dis (sär′dis) An ancient city of Asia Minor, capital of Lydia; destroyed by Tamerlane. Also **Sar′des.**

sar·di·us(sär′dē·əs)*n.* **1** A sard. **2** A stone in the breastplate of the Hebrew high priest. *Ex.* xxviii 17. [<LL <Gk. *sardios, sardion* <*Sardeis* Sardis]

sar·don·ic (sär·don′ik) *adj.* Scornful or derisive; sneering; mocking; cynical. [<F *sardonique* <L *sardonius* <Gk. *sardonios* < *sardanios* bitter, scornful; infl. in form by *Sardō* Sardinia, because thought to be < *sardanē,* a bitter plant of Sardinia causing fatal, laughterlike convulsions] — **sar·don′i·cal·ly** *adv.* — **sar·don′i·cism** *n.*

sar·do·nyx (sär′də·niks) *n.* A variety of onyx, consisting of alternate layers of light–colored chalcedony and reddish carnelian. [<L <Gk., appar. < *sardios* sardius + *onyx* onyx]

Sar·dou (sȧr·dōō′), **Victorien,** 1831–1908, French dramatist.

Sa·re·ma (sä′re·mä) See SAARE.

Sarg (särg), **Tony,** 1882–1942, U. S. artist born in Germany; maker of marionettes: full name *Anthony Frederick Sarg.*

sar·gas·so (sär·gas′ō) *n.* Any of a large genus *(Sargassum)* of brown algae found growing in tropical seas; the gulfweed. Also **sar·gas′·sum.** [<Pg. *sargaço* < *sarga,* a kind of grape]

Sargasso Sea A part of the North Atlantic, extending from the West Indies to the Azores, known for its relatively still water and its large amounts of floating seaweed.

Sar·gent (sär′jənt), **John Singer,** 1856–1925, U. S. painter.

Sar·gon II (sär′gon), died 705 B.C., king of Assyria 722–705 B.C.

sa·ri (sä′rē) *n.* A long piece of cotton or silk cloth, constituting the principal garment of Hindu women: worn round the waist, one end falling to the feet, and the other crossed over the bosom, shoulder, and sometimes over the head. Also **sa′ree.** [<Hind. *sarī, sarhī* <Skt. *śāṭī*]

sark (särk) *n. Scot.* A shirt or chemise; hence, a shroud. [OE *serc*]

Sark (särk) One of the Channel Islands; 2 square miles. *French* **Sercq** (serk).

sark·it (sär′kit) *adj. Scot.* Provided with shirts.

Sar·ma·ti·a (sär·mā′shē·ə, -shə) An ancient name for a region of NE Europe, in Poland and U.S.S.R. between the Vistulaand the Volga. —**Sar·ma′tian** *adj. & n.* —**Sar·mat′ic** (-mat′ik) *adj.*

sar·men·tose (sär·men′tōs) *adj. Bot.* Having or producing sarmenta; having runners. Also **sar·men·ta·ceous** (sär′mən·tā′shəs), **sar·men′·tous.** [<L *sarmentosus* full of twigs <*sarmentum.* See SARMENTUM.]

sar·men·tum (sär·men′təm) *n. pl.* **·ta**(-tə) *Bot.* The slender runner of a plant, as in a vine. Also **sar′ment.** [<NL <L, a twig lopped off <*sarpere* prune (trees)]

Sar·mien·to (sär·myen′tō), **Domingo,** 1811–88, Argentine educator, journalist, and statesman.

sa·rod (sə·rōd′) *n.* A lutelike Indian stringed instrument. [<Hindi *sarod*]

sa·rong (sə·rong′) *n.* **1** A skirtlike garment of colored silk or cloth worn by both sexes in the Malay Archipelago, etc. **2** The material used for this garment. [<Malay *sārung,* prob. <Skt. *sāranga* variegated]

Sa·ron·ic Gulf (sə·ron′ik) An inlet of the Aegean in central Greece, separating Attica from Peloponnesus; 50 miles long, 30 miles wide: also *Gulf of Aegina.*

Sa·ros (sä′rôs), **Gulf of** An arm of the Aegean in Turkey in Europe north of Gallipoli Peninsula; 37 miles long, 22 miles wide.

Sa·roy·an (sə·roi′ən), **William,** born 1908, U.S. novelist and playwright.

Sar·pe·don (sär·pē′dən) In Greek mythology: **1** A son of Zeus and Europa who was allowed to live for three generations. **2** A Lycian prince and warrior killed by Patroclus in the Trojan War.

sar·ra·ce·ni·a (sar′ə·sē′nē·ə) *n.* Any of a genus plants, having trumpetlike or pitcher–shaped leaves by which insects are entrapped and then digested by the plants; a pitcherplant. [<NL, orig. *Sarracena,* after Dr. D. *Sarrazin,* 17th–18th c. physician of Quebec who sent a specimen to the botanist Tournefort in 1700] —**sar′ra·ce′ni·a′ceous** (-sē′nē·ā′shəs) adj.

Sarre (sår) The French name for THE SAAR.

sar·rus·o·phone (sa·rus′ə·fōn) *n.* A musical instrument resembling a bassoon but with a metal tube. [after *Sarrus,* 19th c. French bandmaster, its inventor + -(O)PHONE]

sar·sa·pa·ril·la (sas′pə·ril′ə, sär′sə·pə·ril′ə) *n.* **1** The dried roots of certain tropical American climbing plants (genus *Smilax*). **2** A medicinal preparation or a beverage made from them. **3** Any one of various plants, so called from some resemblance to true sarsaparilla, as the wild sarsaparilla *(Aralia nudicaulis).* [< Sp. *zarzaparilla* <*zarza* a bramble +*parilla,* dim. of *parra* a vine]

sar·sar (sär′sər) *n.* A cold, whistling wind of Moslem lands: also spelled *sansar.* [<Arabic *ṣarṣar* a cold wind]

sarse·net (särs′nit) *n.* A fine, thin silk, used for linings: also spelled *sarcenet.* [<AF *sarzinet,* dim. of ME *sarzin* a Saracen; prob. infl. by OF *drap sarrasinois,* lit., Saracen cloth <Med. L *pannus saracenicus*]

Sar·to (sär′tō), **Andrea del,** 1487–1531, Florentine painter.

sar·tor (sar′tər) *n.* A tailor: a humorous or literary term. [<L, a patcher, mender <*sartus,* pp. of *sarcire* mend]

sar·to·ri·al (sär·tôr′ē·əl, -tō′rē-) *adj.* **1** Pertaining to a tailor or his work; also, pertaining to men's clothes: *sartorial* perfections. **2** *Anat.* Relating to the sartorius. —**sar·to′·ri·al·ly** *adv.*

sar·to·ri·us (sär·tôr′ē·əs, -tō′rē-) *n. Anat.* A long, narrow muscle of the thigh that aids in flexing the knee; the longest muscle in the human body: so called from its use in crossing the legs, as in the manner in which tailors traditionally sat down to work. [<NL <L <*sartor* a or]

Sar·tre (sår′tr′), **Jean Paul,** born 1905, French philosopher, novelist, and dramatist.

Sar·um (sâr′əm), **New** See SALISBURY.

Sa·se·bo (sä·se·bō) A port on NW Kyushu island, Japan.

Sa·se·no (sä′se·nô) An Albanian island in the Strait of Otranto, at the entrance to the Bay of Valona; 2 square miles. *Albanian* **Sa·zan** (sä′zän).

sash[1] (sash) *n.* An ornamental band or scarf, worn as a girdle, or around the waist or over the shoulder, often as part of a uniform or as a badge of distinction. [Orig. *shash* <Arabic *shāsh* muslin, turban]

sash[2] (sash) *n.* A frame, as of a window, in which glass is set. —*v.t.* To furnish with a sash. [Alter. of CHASSIS, taken as a pl.]

sa·shay (sa·shā′) See CHASSÉ[1].

sa·shi·mi (sä′shē·mē) *n.* In Japan, raw fish slices.

sa·sin (sā′sin) *n.* The common black buck. [< Nepalese]

Sas·katch·e·wan (sas·kach′ə·won) A province of west central Canada; 251,700 square miles; capital, Regina: abbr. *Sask.*

Saskatchewan River A river of west central Canada, flowing 340 miles east to Lake Winnipeg from the confluence of the **North Saskatchewan,** flowing 760 miles east, and the **South Saskatchewan,** flowing 550 miles NE.

sas·ka·toon (sas′kə·tōōn′) *n.* A small tree *(Amelanchier alnifolia)* of the rose family, with thick leaves and a globular purple fruit; a shadbush. [<Algonquian (Cree) *misāskwatomin* <*misāskwat* the shadbush + *min* a fruit, a berry]

Sas·ka·toon (sas′kə·tōōn′) A city in south central Saskatchewan province, Canada, on the South Saskatchewan River.

Sas·quatch (sas′kwach, -kwôch) *n.* A hairy, big-footed creature supposed to live in the forests of the Pacific Northwest.

sass (sas) *Colloq. n.* Impudence; back talk. —*v.t.* To talk to impudently or disrespectfully. [Dial. alter. of SAUCE]

sas·sa·by (sas′ə·bē) *n. pl.* **·bies** A large dark-red South African antelope (genus *Damaliscus*), with almost black back and face. [<Bantu *tsessébe, tsessábi*]

sas·sa·fras (sas′ə·fras) *n.* **1** A tree (genus *Sassafras*) of the laurel family. **2** The bark of the roots, yielding an aromatic stimulant and an essential oil used in cosmetics. [<Sp. *sasafrás,* prob. <N. Am. Ind. name; infl. in form by Sp. *sassifragia* <L *saxifraga* saxifrage]

Sas·sa·nid (sas′ə·nid) *n. pl.* **Sas·sa·nids** or **Sas·san·i·dae** (sa·san′ə·dē) A member of the last national dynasty of ancient Persia (226–651). —*adj.* Of or pertaining to the Sassanids. Also **Sas·sa·ni·an** (sa·sā′nē·ən), **Sas′sa·nide.** [<Med. L *Sassanidae,* pl. <*Sassan* Sasan, grandfather of Ardashir I, the first Sassanid king]

Sas·se·nach (sas′ə·nakh) *n. Scot. & Irish* A person of Saxon blood; an Englishman; a Protestant. [<Irish *sasanach,* Scottish Gaelic *Sasunnach* <Gaelic *Sasunn* a Saxon]

Sas·soon (sa·sōōn′), **Siegfried,** 1886–1967, English poet and author.

sas·sy[1] (sas′ē) *adj.* **·si·er, ·si·est** *U.S. Dial.* Saucy; impertinent.

sas·sy[2] (sas′ē) *n.* A West African tree *(Erythrophleum guineense)* with poisonous bark and juice. Also **sas′sy·wood′** (-wŏŏd′). [<native W. African name, ? <E *saucy*]

sat (sat) Past tense of SIT.

Sa·tan (sā′tən) In the Bible, the great adversary of God and tempter of mankind; the Devil: identified with *Lucifer* who, in Semitic mythology, led a revolt against God, was defeated by the archangel Michael, and cast into hell as punishment for his pride. *Luke* iv 5–8; *Rev.* xii 7–9. [<Hebrew *sātān* an enemy <*sātan* oppose, plot against]

sa·tang (sä·tang′) *n. pl.* **sa·tang** A bronze coin and money of account in Thailand; one one-hundredth of a baht. [<Siamese *satān*]

sa·tan·ic (sā·tan′ik) *adj.* Devilish; infernal; wicked. Also **sa·tan′i·cal.** See synonyms under INFERNAL —**sa·tan′i·cal·ly** *adv.*

Sa·tan·ism (sā′tən·iz′əm) *n.* Satan–worship; specifically, a cult addicted to profane mockeries of the holy rites of Christian worship. —**Sa′tan·ist** *n.*

sat·a·ra (sat′ər·ə, sə·tä′rə) *n.* A lustrous ribbed woolen fabric. [from *Satara,* a town about 100 miles from Bombay, India]

satch·el (sach′əl) *n.* A small handbag. [<OF *sachel* <L *sacellus,* dim. of *saccus* a sack]

sate[1] (sāt) *v.t.* **sat·ed, sat·ing** To satisfy the appetite of; satiate. See synonyms under SATISFY. [Appar. alter. of obs. *sade* sate, OE *sadian;* refashioned after L *sat, satis* enough]

sate[2] (sāt) Archaic past tense of SIT.

sa·teen (sa·tēn′) *n.* A cotton fabric woven so as to give it a satin surface: usually mercerized cotton. [Alter. of SATIN; infl. inform by VELVETEEN]

sat·el·lite (sat′ə·līt) *n.* **1** *Astron.* A smaller body attending upon and revolving round a larger one; a moon. **2** One who attends upon a person in power. **3** Any obsequious attendant. **4** A small nation politically, economically, or militarily dependent on a great power. **5** A town or community whose activities are largely determined by those of a neighboring metropolis. **6** An airfield, base, or installation dependent upon a larger one. **7** A man–made object launched from and revolving around the earth: compare SPUTNIK. [<F <L *satelles, satellitis* an attendant, a guard]

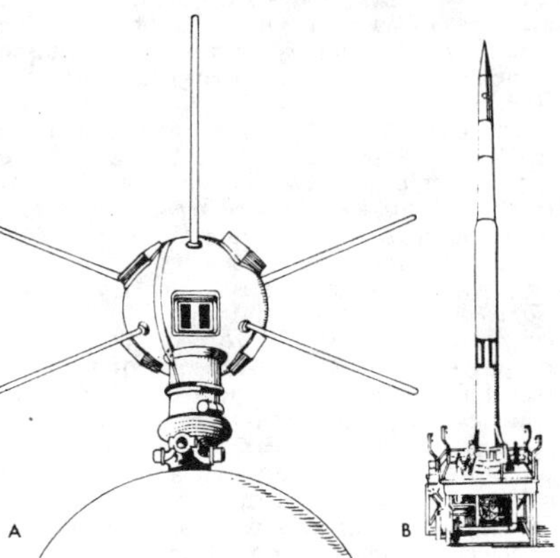

TYPE OF AMERICAN SATELLITE
A. Satellite. *B.* Rocket, which carries satellite into orbit, in position for launching.

sa·tem (sä′təm, sā′-) *n.* The eastern division of the Indo–European family of languages, including the Indo–Iranian, Armenian, Albanian, and Balto–Slavic subfamilies, in which proto–Indo–European palatal (k) is typically sibilated, as in the Avestan word *satem* "hundred." Compare CENTUM.

Sa·than (sā′tən), **Sath·a·nas** (sath′ə·nas) See SATAN.

sa·ti·a·ble (sā′shē·ə·bəl, -shə·bəl) *adj.* Capable of being satiated. —**sa′ti·a·bil′i·ty, sa′ti·a·ble·ness** *n.* —**sa′ti·a·bly** *adv.*

sa·ti·ate (sā′shē·āt) *v.t.* **·at·ed, ·at·ing 1** To satisfy the appetite or desire of; gratify. **2** To fill or gratify beyond natural desire; glut; surfeit. See synonyms under SATISFY. —*adj.* Filled to satiety; satiated. [<L *satiatus,* pp. of *satiare* fill <*satis* enough] —**sa′ti·a′tion** *n.*

Sa·tie (sȧ·tē′), **Erik Alfred Leslie,** 1866–1925, French composer.

sa·ti·e·ty (sə·tī′ə·tē) *n. pl.* **·ties** Repletion; surfeit. [<F *satieté* <L *satietas, -tatis* <*satis* enough]

sat·in (sat′ən) *n.* A silk, cotton, rayon, or acetate fabric of thick texture, with glossy face and dull back. —*adj.* Of or similar to satin; glossy; smooth. [<OF <Med. L *satinus, setinus,* ult. <L *seta* silk]

sat·i·net (sat′ə·net′) *n.* **1** A strong fabric with cotton warp and woolen filling. **2** A thin satin. Also **sat′i·nette′.** [<F, dim. of *satin* satin]

sat·in·flow·er (sat′ən·flou′ər) *n.* The garden flower honesty: so called from the satiny luster of its silvery silicles. Also **sat′in·pod′** (-pod′).

satin spar A silky fibrous mineral, a variety either of calcite, aragonite, orgypsum.

sat·in·wood (sat′ən·wŏŏd′) *n.* **1** The satinlike wood of an East Indian tree *(Chloroxylon swietenia)* of the mahogany family. **2** The tree. **3** A West Indian tree *(Zanthoxylum flavum)* of the rue family, having a fine–textured, golden–yellow wood much used in fine cabinet work.

sat·in·y (sat′ən·ē) *adj.* Resembling or characteristic of satin; glossy.

sat·ire (sat′īr) *n.* **1** The use of sarcasm, irony, or keen wit in denouncing abuses or follies; ridicule. **2** A written composition in which vice, folly, or incapacity is held up to ridicule. See synonyms under BANTER. [< MF <L *satira, satura* a satire, earlier, a discursive verse composition on a number of subjects, orig. a medley <*(lanx) satura* a fruit salad, lit., a full (dish), fem. of *satur* full]

sa·tir·ic (sə·tir′ik) *adj.* Of, pertaining to, or resembling satire, especially literary satire: *satiric* verse.

sa·tir·i·cal (sə·tir′i·kəl) *adj.* **1** Given to or characterized by satire: a *satirical* writer. **2** Severely sarcastic; biting; caustic: a *satirical* laugh. **3** Satiric. —**sa·tir′i·cal·ly** *adv.* —**sa·tir′i·cal·ness** *n.*

sat·i·rist (sat′ə·rist) *n.* A writer of satire; a satirical person.

sat·i·rize (sat′ə·rīz) *v.t.* **·rized, ·riz·ing** To subject to or criticize in satire. See synonyms under RIDICULE. —**sat′i·riz′er** *n.*

sat·is·fac·tion (sat′is·fak′shən) *n.* **1** The act of satisfying, or the state of being satisfied; complete gratification. **2** The making of amends, reparation, or payment; extinguishment of a claim or obligation by payment, performance, restitution, or the rendering of an equivalent. **3** That which satisfies; atonement; compensation. [<OF *satisfactiun* <L *satisfactio, -onis* <*satisfactus,* pp. of *satisfacere* SATISFY]

Synonyms: comfort, complacence, content, contentment, enjoyment, gratification. See COMFORT, HAPPINESS, PROPITIATION, RECOMPENSE. *Antonyms*: annoyance, discontent, dislike, displeasure, dissatisfaction, disturbance, pain, sorrow, trouble, vexation.

sat·is·fac·tion–piece (sat′is·fak′shən·pēs′) *n.* A formal acknowledgment given by one who has received satisfaction of a mortgage or judgment, to authorize the entry of such satisfaction on the record.

sat·is·fac·to·ry (sat′is·fak′tər·ē) *adj.* **1** Giving satisfaction; answering fully all desires, expectations, or requirements; sufficient. **2** Making satisfaction; atoning or expiatory. See synonyms under ADEQUATE, COMFORTABLE. —**sat′is·fac′to·ri·ly** *adv.* —**sat′is·fac′to·ri·ness** *n.*

sat·is·fy (sat′is·fī) *v.* **·fied, ·fy·ing** *v.t.* **1** To supply fully with what is desired, expected, or needed; cause to have enough; gratify; content. **2** To free from doubt or anxiety; assure; convince. **3** To give what is due to. **4** To pay or discharge (a debt, obligation, etc.). **5** To answer sufficiently or convincingly, as a question or objection. **6** To fulfil the conditions or requirements of, as an equation. **7** To make reparation for; expiate. —*v.i.* **8** To give satisfaction. [<OF *satisfier* <L *satisfacere* <*satis* enough + *facere* do] —**sat′is·fi′er** *n.* —**sat′is·fy′ing** *adj.* —**sat′is·fy′ing·ly** *adv.*

Synonyms: cloy, content, fill, glut, sate, satiate, suffice, surfeit. To *satisfy* is to furnish enough to meet physical, mental, or spiritual desire. To *sate* or *satiate* is to gratify desire so fully as to extinguish it for a time. To *cloy* or *surfeit* is to gratify to the point of revulsion or disgust. *Glut* is a strong word applied to the utmost satisfaction of vehement appetites and passions; as, to *glut* a vengeful spirit with slaughter; we speak of *glutting* the market with a supply so excessive as to extinguish the demand. Much less than is needed to *satisfy* may *suffice* a frugal or abstemious person; less than a sufficiency may *content* one of a patient and submissive spirit. See INDULGE, PAY[1], REQUITE. *Antonyms*: check, deny, disappoint, refuse, restrain, restrict, starve, stint, tantalize.

sa·to·ri (sä·tō·rē) *n.* In Japanese Buddhism, enlightenment; especially, the abrupt or "sudden" enlightenment of Zen Buddhism. [<Japanese, lit., comprehension, perception]

Sat·pu·ra Range (sät·pōō′rə) A line of hills in northern India, forming the northern edge of the Deccan Plateau; highest point, 4,429 feet.

sa·trap (sā′trap, sat′rap) *n.* **1** A governor of a province in ancient Persia. **2** Any petty ruler under a despot. **3** A subordinate ruler or governor. [<L *satrapes* <Gk. *satrapēs* <O Persian *shathraparan,* lit., a protector of a province]

sa·trap·y (sā′trə·pē, sat′rə·pē) *n. pl.* **·trap·ies** The territory or the jurisdiction of a satrap. Also **sa·trap·ate** (sā′trə·pit, sat′rə-).

Sa·tsu·ma (sä·tsōō·mä) A former province of southern Kyushu island, Japan.

Satsuma ware A kind of Japanese pottery, originally made at Satsuma.

Sa·tu–Ma·re (sä′tōō·mä′rā) A city in NW Rumania near the Hungarian border.

sat·u·rant (sach′ər·ənt) *adj.* Saturating. —*n.* A substance that fully neutralizes another.

sat·u·rate (sach′ə·rāt) *v.t.* **·rat·ed, ·rat·ing** **1** To soak or imbue thoroughly; fill or impregnate to the utmost capacity for absorbing or retaining. **2** *Chem.* To utilize fully the combining powers of the atoms in (a molecule). —*adj.* **1** Filled to repletion; saturated. **2** Very intense; deep: said of colors. [<L *saturatus,* pp. of *saturare* fill up <*satur* full] —**sat·u·ra·ble** (sach′ər·ə·bəl) *adj.* —**sat′u·ra′·tor** or **sat′u·rat′er** *n.*

sat·u·rat·ed (sach′ə·rā′tid) *adj.* **1** Completely satisfied; replete; incapable of holding more of a substance or material: *saturated* vapor; a *saturated* solution. **2** *Chem.* Designating an organic compound having no free valences and without double or triple bonds, as paraffin, methane, and other *saturated* hydrocarbons. **3** Designating a pure color or hue, as in the spectrum; exhibiting high saturation. **4** *Geol.* Designating rocks or minerals with a maximum content of silica.

sat·u·ra·tion (sach′ə·rā′shən) *n.* **1** The act of saturating, or the state of being saturated; full impregnation. **2** The impregnation of one substance with another till no more can be received. Saturation may be by solution or by chemical combination. **3** *Meteorol.* The filling of the atmosphere with any vapor to the point of condensation. **4** The maximum magnetization of which a body is capable. **5** The degree of vividness or purity of chromatic color, as indicated by its freedom from admixture with white. **6** A massive concentration, in any given area, as of advertising, military force, etc., for a specific purpose: often used attributively: *saturation* bombing.

Sat·ur·day (sat′ər·dē, -dā) *n.* The seventh or last day of the week; the day of the Jewish Sabbath. [OE *Sæterdæg, Sæternesdæg,* trans. of L *Saturni dies* Saturn's day]

Saturday night special *U.S.* A kind of cheap, easily obtainable pistol.

Sat·urn (sat′ərn) **1** The planet next beyond Jupiter and next to Jupiter in size, remarkable for its 9 satellites and its flat, luminous, encircling rings. In astrology it was regarded as a melancholy planet. See PLANET. **2** In Roman mythology, the god of agriculture: identified with the Greek *Kronos* [OE *Sætern, Saturnus* <L *Saturnus*]

sat·ur·na·li·a (sat′ər·nā′lē·ə) *n.* Any season or period of general license or revelry: generally construed as singular: a *saturnalia* of crime. [<L. See SATURNALIA.]

Sat·ur·na·li·a (sat′ər·nā′lē·ə) *n. pl.* The feast of Saturn held at Rome in mid–December, celebrating the winter solstice, and marked by wild reveling and licentious abandon. [<L, orig. neut. pl. of *Saturnalis* of Saturn < *Saturnus* Saturn] —**Sat′ur·na′li·an** *adj.*

Sa·tur·ni·an (sə·tûr′nē·ən) *adj.* Of or pertaining to the god, or to the planet, Saturn, especially to a fabled golden age in the reign of Saturn, marked by simplicity, virtue, and happiness.

sa·tur·ni·id (sə·tûr′nē·id) *n.* Any of a family *(Saturniidae)* of large, hairy, brightly–colored moths widely distributed in most temperate regions. Many of them produce cocoons useful in the production of silk. —*adj.* Of or pertaining to the *Saturniidae.* [<NL <*Saturnia,* genus name <L *Saturnius* of Saturn < *Saturnus* Saturn]

sat·ur·nine (sat′ər·nīn) *adj.* **1** Having a grave, gloomy, or morose disposition or character; heavy; dull. **2** In old chemistry, pertaining to lead. **3** *Pathol.* Pertaining to or produced by lead. [<OF *saturnin* of Saturn, of lead, heavy <Med. L *Saturnus* lead, Saturn <L, Saturn]

Sat·ur·nine (sat′ər·nīn) *adj.* **1** Of or pertaining to the planet Saturn. **2** Born or being under the influence of the planet Saturn; hence, gloomy; heavy.

sat·urn·ism (sat′ərn·iz′əm) *n.* Lead poisoning. [<Med. L *Saturnus.* See SATURNINE.]

Sat·ya·gra·ha (sut′yə·gru′hə) *n.* **1** A movement characterized by non–violent resistance and non–cooperation, adopted in India, 1919, by the followers of M. K. Gandhi in protest against certain civil and religious abuses. **2** The non–violent force characterizing this movement, defined as an active love for one's opponents and a radical insistence on truth. [<Hind., truth–force, lit., a grasping for truth <Skt. *satya* truth + *graha* a grasping]

sat·yr (sat′ər, sā′tər) *n.* **1** In Greek mythology, a woodland deity in human form, having pointed ears, pug nose, short tail and budding horns, and of wanton nature. **2** A very lascivious man. **3** Any butterfly of the family *Agapetidae,* commonly brown and gray with eyelike spots. [<L *satyrus* <Gk. *satyros*] —**sa·tyr·ic** (sə·tir′ik) or **·i·cal** *adj.*

SATYR

sat·y·ri·a·sis (sat′ə·rī′ə·sis) *n. Psychiatry* A morbid lasciviousness in males. [<NL <Gk. *satyriaein* suffer from satyriasis <*satyros* a satyr]

sauce (sôs) *n.* **1** An appetizing dressing or liquid relish for food; loosely, any appetizing garnish of a meal; formerly, any condiment, as salt, pepper. **2** A dish of fruit pulp stewed and sweetened: cranberry *sauce.* **3** *Colloq.* Table vegetables, as roots or greens: also **garden sauce.** **4** *Colloq.* Pert or impudent language. —*v.t.* **sauced, sauc·ing** **1** To flavor with sauce; season. **2** To give zest or piquancy to. **3** *Colloq.* To be saucy to. [<OF < LL *salsa,* orig. fem. of L *salsus* salted, pp. of *salire* salt <*sal* salt]

sauce·box (sôs′boks′) *n. Colloq.* A saucy person: said generally of a child.

sauce·pan (sôs′pan′) *n.* A metal or enamel pan with projecting handle, for cooking food.

sau·cer (sô′sər) *n.* **1** A small dish for holding a cup. **2** Any small, round, shallow vessel of similar shape. [<OF *saussier* <*sauce* sauce]

sau·cy (sô′sē) *adj.* **·ci·er, ·ci·est** **1** Disrespectful to superiors; impudent. **2** Piquant; sprightly; amusing. See synonyms under IMPUDENT. —**sau′ci·ly** *adv.* —**sau′ci·ness** *n.*

Sa·ud (sä·ōōd′), **King,** 1902–1969, king of Saudi Arabia 1953–1964; son of Ibn Saud: full name *Ibn Abdul Aziz al Faisal al Saud.*

Sa·u·di Arabia (sä·ōō′dē) A kingdom (1932) in the northern and central part of Arabia; 927,000 square miles; dual capitals, Mecca and Riyadh.

sauer·bra·ten (sour′brät′n, *Ger.* zou′ər·brä′tən) *n.* Beef marinated in vinegar before being braised. [<G <*sauer* sour + *braten* roast]

sauer·kraut (sour′krout′) *n.* Shredded and salted cabbage fermented in its own juice: also spelled *sourcrout.* [<G <*sauer* sour + *kraut* cabbage, vegetable, a plant]

sau·ger (sô′gər) *n.* A percoid fish, the smaller American pike perch *(Cynoperca canadensis),* resembling the walleye. [<N. Am. Ind.]

saugh (sôkh) *n. Scot.* The sallow; the willow.

Sauk (sôk) *n.* One of a tribe of North American Indians of Algonquian stock, formerly occupying Michigan, later Wisconsin and the Mississippi valley: now on reservations in Oklahoma, Iowa, and Kansas. Also spelled *Sac.*

Saul (sôl) A masculine personal name. [<Hebrew, asked (of God)]

—**Saul** The first king of Israel. I *Sam.* ix 2.

—**Saul** The Hebrew name of the Apostle Paul. *Acts* xiii 9. Also **Saul of Tarsus.**

Sault Sainte Ma·rie (sōō′ sānt′ mə·rē′) **1** A city in northern Michigan, on St. Marys River. **2** A city opposite it in south central Ontario. Also **Sault Ste. Marie.**

Sault Sainte Marie Canals Three ship canals at the rapids in the St. Marys River, connecting Lake Superior with Lake Huron: also, *Colloq., Soo Canals.*

sau·na (sou′nə, sô′-) *n.* **1** A Finnish steam bath in which the steam is produced by running water over heated stones. **2** A bath in which the bather is exposed to very hot, dry air. **3** A room or enclosure for a sauna. [< Finnish]

saun·ter (sôn′tər) *v.i.* To walk in a leisurely or lounging way; stroll. See synonyms under LINGER. —*n.* **1** A slow, aimless manner of walking. **2** An idle stroll. [ME *santren* muse, meditate; ult. origin unknown]

Sau·rash·tra (sou·räsh′trə) A former constituent State of western India, comprising most of Kathiawar peninsula and including 222 former states; merged into Bombay State, 1956; 21,062 square miles; former capital, Rajkot.

sau·rel (sôr′əl) *n.* A horse mackerel (genus *Trachurus*), especially *T. trachurus* and *T. symmetricus* of America and Europe. [<F <Gk. *sauros* a horse mackerel]

sau·ri·an (sôr′ē·ən) *n.* One of a suborder *(Sauria)* of reptiles, the lizards: formerly including also crocodiles, dinosaurians, pterodactyls, and other fossil forms. —*adj.* Pertaining to the *Sauria.* [<NL <Gk. *sauros* a lizard]

sau·ris·chi·an (sô·ris′kē·ən) *adj. Paleontol.* Of, pertaining to, or belonging to an order *(Saurischia)* of reptilelike dinosaurs that flourished through most of the Mesozoic era. —*n.* A member of this order. [<NL <Gk. *sauros* a lizard + *ischion* a hip]

sauro- *combining form* Lizard: *sauropod.* Also, before vowels, **saur-**. [<Gk. *sauros* a lizard]

sau·ro·pod (sôr′ə·pod) *n. Paleontol.* One of a suborder *(Sauropoda)* of amphibious four-footed dinosaurs of the Triassic, Jurassic, and Cretaceous periods. —*adj.* Of or pertaining to the *Sauropoda.* [<NL <Gk. *sauros* a lizard + *pous, podos* a foot] —**sau·rop·o·dous** (sô·rop′ə·dəs) *adj.*

-saurus *combining form Zool.* Lizard: used to form genus names: *Brontosaurus, Plesiosaurus.* Corresponding class names end in **-sauria**, family names in **-sauridae**, and individual names in **-saur** or **-saurid**. [<Gk. *sauros* a lizard]

sau·ry (sôr′ē) *n. pl.* **·ries** An edible fish *(Scomberesox saurus)* of the Atlantic, having the jaws developed into a slim beak. It travels in predatory shoals. Also **saury pike.** [<NL *saurus* <Gk. *sauros* a lizard]

sau·sage (sô′sij) *n.* **1** Finely chopped and highly seasoned meat, commonly stuffed into the cleaned and prepared entrails of some animal or artificial casings. **2** *Aeron.* A type of airship or captive observation balloon, shaped like a sausage. [<AF *saussiche* <LL *salsicia,* ult. <L *salsus.* See SAUCE.]

saus·su·rite (sô·sŏŏr′īt, sôs′yə·rīt) *n.* A tough, compact, impure form of labradorite. [after Prof. H. B. de *Saussure,* 1740–99, Swiss geologist] —**saus·su·rit·ic** (sôs′yə·rit′ik) *adj.*

saut (sät, sôt) *adj. & n. Scot.* Salt.

sau·té (sō·tā′, sô-) *adj.* Fried quickly with little grease. —*v.t.* **·téed, ·té·ing** To fry quickly in a little fat. [<F, pp. of *sauter* leap]

sau·terne (sō·tûrn′, sô-; *Fr.* sō·tern′) *n.* A sweet, white French wine; often, in America, any white wine, dry or sweet. Also **sau·ternes′.** [from *Sauternes,* district in SW France]

sau·toir (sō·twär′) *n. Her.* A saltire. Also **sau·toire′.** —**en sautoir** Worn saltirewise, or diagonally about the body, as a ribbon. [<F. See SALTIRE.]

sauve qui peut (sōv kē pœ′) *French* A stampede; rout; literally, save himself who can.

Sa·va (sä′vä) A river of northern Yugoslavia, flowing about 583 miles east to the Danube near Belgrade; the longest river entirely in Yugoslavia. *French* **Save** (sàv), *German* **Sau** (sou).

sav·age (sav′ij) *adj.* **1** Of a wild and untamed nature; not domesticated; hence, ferocious; fierce. **2** Living in or belonging to the most primitive and rude condition of human life and society; uncivilized; uncultivated: *savage* tribes. **3** Enraged; cruel; furious: said of man or beast. **4** *Obs.* Remote from human abode; belonging to the wilderness: a *savage* trail. See synonyms under BARBAROUS, BITTER, FIERCE, GRIM, SANGUINARY. —*n.* **1** A primitive or uncivilized human being. **2** A brutal, fierce, and cruel person; a barbarian. [<OF *salvage, sauvage* <L *silvaticus, salvaticus* < *silva* a wood] —**sav′age·ly** *adv.*

Sav·age (sav′ij), **Arthur William,** 1857–1938, U.S. inventor; manufacturer of rifles, etc. —**Richard,** 1697?–1743, English poet.

Savage Island See NIUE.

sav·age·ry (sav′ij·rē) *n. pl.* **·ries 1** The state of being savage: also **sav′age·ness. 2** Cruelty in disposition or action; a cruel or savage act. **3** Savages collectively: also **sav′age·dom.** Also **sav′ag·ism.**

Savage's Station A battlefield near Richmond, Virginia; scene of an unsuccessful Confederate attack (1862) during the Civil War.

Sa·vai·i (sä·vī′ē) The largest island in Western Samoa; 700 square miles.

sa·van·na (sə·van′ə) *n.* **1** A tract of level land covered with low vegetation; a treeless plain. **2** Any large area of tropical or subtropical grassland, covered in part with trees and spiny shrubs. Also **sa·van′nah.** [Earlier *zavana* <Sp. <Cariban]

Sa·van·nah (sə·van′ə) A port in eastern Georgia, at the mouth of the **Savannah River,** which flows 314 miles SE to the Atlantic and forms the boundary between Georgia and South Carolina.

sa·vant (sə·vänt′, sav′ənt; *Fr.* sà·väṅ′) *n.* A man of exceptional learning. See synonyms under SCHOLAR. [<F, orig. ppr. of *savoir* know <L *sapere* be wise]

Sa·vart (sà·vàr′), **Felix,** 1791–1841, French physician and physicist.

save[1] (sāv) *v.* **saved, sav·ing** *v.t.* **1** To preserve or rescue from danger, harm, etc. **2** To keep from being spent, expended, or lost; avoid the loss or waste of. **3** To set aside for future use; accumulate: often with *up.* **4** To treat carefully so as to avoid fatigue, harm, etc.: to *save* one's eyes. **5** To avoid the need or trouble of; prevent by timely action: A stitch in time *saves* nine. **6** *Theol.* To deliver from spiritual death or the consequences of sin; redeem. —*v.i.* **7** To avoid waste; be economical. **8** To preserve something from danger, harm, etc. **9** To admit of preservation, as food. See synonyms under DELIVER, PRESERVE, SCRIMP. [<OF *salver, sauver* <LL *salvare* save <L *salvus* safe] —**sav′a·ble** or **save′a·ble** *adj.* —**sav′a·ble·ness** *n.* —**sav′er** *n.*

save[2] (sāv) *prep.* Except; but. —*conj.* **1** Except; but. **2** *Archaic* Unless. See synonyms under BUT[1]. [<OF *sauf* being excepted, orig. safe <L *salvus*]

Sa·ve (sä′və) The Portuguese name for the SABI.

save-all (sāv′ôl′) *n.* **1** A contrivance for preventing waste; anything that saves fragments. **2** A child's savings bank. **3** An overall or pinafore.

saved (sāvd) *adj.* **1** Delivered from punishment after death. **2** Converted to religion. **3** Not spent or lost; amassed.

sav·e·loy (sav′ə·loi) *n.* A kind of highly seasoned, dried sausage made of salted pork. [Alter. of F *cervelas* <Ital. *cervellata* < *cervello* the brain <L *cerebellum.* See CEREBELLUM.]

Sav·ile (sav′il), **Sir Henry,** 1549–1622, English classical and biblical scholar.

Savile Row A street in London famous for fashionable men's tailor shops; hence, sartorially magnificent.

sav·in (sav′in) *n.* **1** A bushy shrub or small tree *(Juniperus sabina)* of the cypress family. **2** The young shoots of this plant, yielding an acrid volatile oil used in medicine. **3** The red cedar *(Juniperus virginiana).* Also called *sabine.* [OE *safine* <OF *savine* <L *(herba) Sabina* the Sabine (herb), fem. of *Sabinus*]

sav·ing (sā′ving) *adj.* **1** That saves; preserving, as from destruction. **2** Redeeming; delivering. **3** Avoiding needless waste or expense; economical; frugal. **4** Incurring no loss, if not gainful: a *saving* investment. **5** Holding in reserve; making an exception; qualifying: a *saving* clause. —*n.* **1** Preservation from loss or danger. **2** Avoidance of waste; economy. **3** The result of this; reduction in cost: a *saving* of 16 percent. **4** That which is saved; especially, in the plural, sums of money not expended. **5** *Law* Reservation; exception. See synonyms under FRUGALITY. —*prep.* **1** With the exception of; save. **2** With due respect for: *saving* your presence. —*conj.* Save. —**sav′ing·ly** *adv.* —**sav′ing·ness** *n.*

savings account An account drawing interest at a savings bank.

savings bank 1 An institution for receiving and investing savings and paying interest on deposits. **2** A container with a slot for coins.

sav·ior (sāv′yər) *n.* One who saves. Also *Brit.* **sav′iour.** [<OF *saveour* <LL *salvator, -oris* <L *salvare* SAVE]

Sav·iour (sāv′yər) *n.* He who saves men from death and sin: a title sometimes applied directly to God, but chiefly to Jesus Christ, as the Redeemer: usually with *the.* Also **Sav′ior.**

sa·voir faire (sà·vwàr fâr′) *French* Ability to see and to do the right thing; readiness in proper and gracious actions and speech; tact; literally, to know how to act.

sa·voir vi·vre (sà·vwàr vē′vr′) *French* Good breeding; good social manners; literally, to know how to live.

Sa·vo·na (sä·vō′nä) A port on the Gulf of Genoa in NW Italy.

Sav·o·na·ro·la (sav′ə·nə·rō′lə, *Ital.* sä′vō·nä·rō′lä), **Girolamo,** 1452–98, Italian monk; reformer; burned at the stake for heresy.

sa·vor (sā′vər) *n.* **1** That quality of a thing that affects the taste and smell, or both; flavor; odor. **2** Specific or characteristic quality or approach to a quality; flavor. **3** Relish; zest: The conversation had *savor.* **4** *Archaic* Character; reputation. —*v.i.* **1** To have savor; taste or smell: with *of.* **2** To have a specified savor or character: with *of.* —*v.t.* **3** To give flavor to; season. **4** To taste or enjoy with pleasure; relish. **5** To have the savor or character of. Also *Brit.* **sa′vour.** [<OF *savour* <L *sapor* taste < *sapere* taste, know] —**sa′vor·er** *n.* —**sa′vor·ous** *adj.*

Synonyms (noun): flavor, fragrance, odor, relish, scent, smell, taste. See SMELL

sa·vor·less (sā′vər·lis) *adj.* Tasteless; insipid.

sa·vor·y[1] (sā′vər·ē) *adj.* **1** Of an agreeable taste and odor; appetizing. **2** Piquant to the taste. **3** In good repute. See synonyms under DELICIOUS. —*n. Brit.* A small, hot serving of food eaten at the end or beginning of a dinner. Also *Brit.* **sa′vour·y.** [<OF *savouré,* pp. of OF *savourer* taste < *savour* SAVOR] —**sa′vor·i·ly** *adv.* —**sa′vor·i·ness** *n.*

sa·vor·y[2] (sā′vər·ē) *n.* A hardy, annual, aromatic culinary herb of the mint family *(Satureia hortensis)* used for seasoning. Also **summer savory.** [<OF *savoreie,* alter. of L *satureia;* infl. in form by OF *savour* savor]

sa·voy (sə·voi′) *n.* A variety of cabbage with wrinkled leaves and a compact head. [<F *(chou de) Savoie* (cabbage of) Savoy]

Sa·voy (sə·voi′) A region and former duchy of the kingdom of Sardinia, between Italy and France; ceded to France in 1860. *French* **Sa·voie** (sà·vwà′).

Sa·voy (sə·voi′), **House of** A family of French nobles, reigning in Italy from 1861–1946. Its members were descended from Humbert I, Count of Savoy (11th century).

Sa·voy·ard (sə·voi′ərd, *Fr.* sà·vwà·yàr′) *n.* **1** A native or inhabitant of Savoy, France. **2** An actor or actress in the Gilbert and Sullivan operas of which most were originally produced at the Savoy Theatre in London. **3** An admirer or producer of these operas. —*adj.* **1** Of or pertaining to Savoy, France. **2** Of the Savoy Theatre, London. [<F < *Savoie* Savoy]

Sa·vu Sea (sä′vōō) That part of the Indian Ocean bounded by the islands of Flores, Sumba, and Timor.

sav·vy (sav′ē) *Slang v.i.* **·vied, ·vy·ing** To understand; comprehend. —*n.* Understanding; good sense. [Alter. of Sp. ¿ *Sabe (usted)*? Do (you) know? < *saber* know <L *sapere* know, taste]

saw[1] (sô) *n.* **1** A cutting instrument with pointed teeth arranged continuously along the edge of the blade: used to cut or divide wood, bone, metal, etc. See illustrations under BUCKSAW, FRET SAW, HACKSAW. **2** A machine for operating a saw or gang of saws. **3** Any tool or instrument without teeth used like a saw, as a steel disk for cutting armor plate, etc. —**circular saw** A disk having saw teeth in or on its periphery, and mounted on an arbor, with which it is rotated, usually at high speed. —*v.* **sawed, sawed** or **sawn, saw·ing** *v.t.* **1** To cut or divide with a saw. **2** To shape or fashion with a saw. **3** To cut or slice (the air, etc.) as if using a saw: The speaker *saws* the air. **4** To cause to move with a to-and-fro motion like that of a saw. —*v.i.* **5** To use a saw. **6** To cut: said of a saw. **7** To be cut with a saw: This wood *saws* easily. [OE *sagu, saga*] —**saw′er** *n.*

saw[2] (sô) *n.* A proverbial or familiar saying; old maxim. See synonyms under ADAGE. [OE *sagu.* Akin to SAGA.]

saw[3] (sô) Past tense of SEE[1].

saw[4] (sô) *v.t. Scot.* To sow.

Sa·watch Range (sə·wach′) A range of the Rocky Mountains in central Colorado; highest peak, 14,431 feet: also *Saguache.*

saw·bill (sô′bil′) *n.* A motmot.

saw·bones (sô′bōnz′) *n. Slang* A surgeon.

saw·buck (sô′buk′) *n.* **1** A rack or frame consisting of two X-shaped ends joined by a connecting bar or bars, for holding sticks of wood while they are being sawed. Compare SAWHORSE. **2** *U.S. Slang* A ten-dollar bill: so called from the resemblance of X, Roman numeral ten, to the ends of a sawbuck. [Trans. of Du. *zaagbok*]

SAWBUCK AND SAWHORSE
a. Sawbuck. *b.* Bucksaw. *c.* Sawhorse.

saw·dust (sô′dust′) *n.* Small particles of wood cut or torn out by sawing.
sawed-off (sôd′ôf′, -of′) **1** *adj.* Having one end sawed off. **2** Short; not of average height or length: a *sawed-off* shotgun.
saw·fish (sô′fish′) *n. pl.* **·fish** or **·fish·es** A sharklike, tropical ray (genus *Pristis*) having an elongated body and the snout prolonged into a flat blade with teeth on each edge.
saw·fly (sô′flī′) *n. pl.* **·flies** A hymenopterous insect (family *Tenthredinidae*) having in the female a sawlike ovipositor for piercing plants, soft wood, etc., in which to lay eggs.
saw·grass (sô′gras′, -gräs′) *n.* A sedge (genus *Mariscus*) with saw-toothed leaves, growing in marshes along the Atlantic coast from North Carolina to Florida and westward.
saw·horse (sô′hôrs′) *n.* **1** A frame consisting of a long wooden bar or plank supported by four extended legs: used by carpenters. Compare SAWBUCK. **2** A packsaddle.
saw log A log of suitable size for sawing.
saw·mill (sô′mil′) *n.* **1** An establishment for sawing logs with power-driven machinery. **2** A large sawing machine.
saw·munt (sô′mənt) See SAUMONT.
sawn (sôn) Alternative past participle of SAW[1].
saw palmetto Either of two palmettos (*Serenoa repens* and *Paurotis wrighti*) of the southern United States and the West Indies.
saw·pit (sô′pit′) *n.* A pit over which a timber is laid to be sawed by two sawyers, one of whom stands in the pit and the other above.
saw set An instrument to give set to, or bend slightly outward, the teeth of a saw.
saw-toothed (sô′tōōtht′) *adj.* Serrate; having teeth or toothlike processes similar to those of a saw.
saw·yer (sô′yər) *n.* **1** One who saws logs; specifically, a lumberman who fells trees by sawing, or one who works in a sawmill: also spelled *sawer.* **2** Any beetle of the genus *Monochamus* having wood-boring larvae. [Alter. of SAWER]
sax[1] (saks) *n.* **1** A chopping tool for trimming edges of roofing slates: also called *slate ax.* **2** A long knife. **3** A short, broad sword. [OE *seax* a knife]
sax[2] (saks) *n. Colloq.* A saxophone. [Short for SAXOPHONE]
sax·a·tile (sak′sə·til) *adj.* **1** Pertaining to rocks. **2** Saxicoline. [<L *saxatilis* < *saxum* a rock]
Saxe (sȧks) The French name for SAXONY.
Saxe (sȧks), **Comte de,** 1696–1750, Hermann Maurice, French marshal.
Saxe-Al·ten·burg (saks′äl′tən·bûrg) A former duchy in central Germany.
Saxe-Co·burg (saks′kō′bûrg) A former duchy in central Germany; united in 1826 with **Saxe-Go·tha** (-gō′thə), another duchy, to form the duchy of **Saxe-Coburg-Gotha,** which was divided between Thuringia and Bavaria in 1918.
Saxe-Mei·ning·en (saks′mī′ning·ən) A former duchy in central Germany.
Saxe-Wei·mar (saks′vī′mär) A former grand duchy in central Germany; became the duchy of **Saxe-Weimar-Ei·se·nach** (ī′zə·näkh) in 1741.
sax·horn (saks′hôrn′) *n.* A brass wind instrument having a long winding tube and cup-shaped mouthpiece, used in military bands. [after Antoine Joseph *Sax,* (called *Adolphe*), 1814–94, Belgian instrument maker + HORN]
sax·ic·o·line (sak·sik′ə·lēn, -lin) *adj. Ecol.* Living or growing among rocks. Also **sax·ic′o·lous.** [<NL *saxicola* <L *saxum* rock + *colere* inhabit]
sax·i·fra·ga·ceous (sak′sə·frə·gā′shəs) *adj. Bot.* Of or pertaining to a widely distributed family (*Saxifragaceae*) of herbs, shrubs, and trees, including gooseberries and witch hazel. [<NL <L *saxifraga.* See SAXIFRAGE.]
sax·i·frage (sak′sə·frij) *n.* **1** Any plant of the genus *Saxifraga,* growing in rocky places. **2** Any of various related plants. Also called *stonebreak.* [<OF <L (*herba*) *saxifraga,* lit., stone-breaking (herb)]
Sax·o Gram·mat·i·cus (sak′sō grə·mat′i·kəs), 1150?–1220?, Danish historian.
Sax·on (sak′sən) *n.* **1** A member of a Germanic tribal group living in the southern part of what is now Schleswig-Holstein in the early centuries of the Christian era. **2** A member of any of the offshoots of this group, as those who, with the Angles and Jutes, invaded England in the fifth and sixth centuries A.D. **3** An Anglo-Saxon. **4** An inhabitant of Saxony. **5** The modern High German dialect of Saxony. **6** A Teuton. **— Old Saxon** The dialect of Low German current in the valley of the lower Elbe in the early Middle Ages. *— adj.* **1** Of or pertaining to the Saxons, or to their language. **2** Germanic; Anglo-Saxon; also, English: said of words, phrases, etc. [<F <L *Saxo, Saxonis* <WGmc.]
Sax·on·ism (sak′sən·iz′əm) *n.* A word, phrase, etc., of English, specifically Anglo-Saxon, origin.
Sax·on·ist (sak′sən·ist) *n.* An authority on pre-Norman England or the Saxon language, especially Old Saxon.
Sax·o·ny (sak′sə·nē) *n. pl.* **·nies 1** A fabric made from wool raised in Saxony, central Germany. **2** A variety of fine yarn. **3** A glossy woolen cloth.
Sax·o·ny (sak′sə·nē) **1** A former duchy, electorate, and kingdom of central Germany. **2** A former Prussian province of central Germany, constituted in 1816, largely from the territories of the kingdom of Saxony; 9,753 square miles; capital, Magdeburg. **3** A former state of east central Germany, 1918–45; 5,789 square miles; capital, Dresden. **4** A former state of SE East Germany, 1949–52; 6,561 square miles; capital, Dresden. French *Saxe,* German *Sachsen.*
Sax·o·ny-An·halt (sak′sə·nē·än′hält) A former state (1949) of east central East Germany; 9,515 square miles; capital, Halle.
sax·o·phone (sak′sə·fōn) *n.* A brass wind instrument with about 20 finger keys, tonally like, but more powerful than, a clarinet. [after Antoine Joseph *Sax* (called Adolphe), 1814–94, Belgian instrument maker, who invented it about 1840 + -PHONE] **— sax′o·phon′ist** *n.*

SAXOPHONE

sax·tu·ba (saks′tōō′bə, -tyōō′-) *n.* A large saxhorn. [<SAX(HORN) + TUBA]
say[1] (sā) *v.* **said, say·ing** *v.t.* **1** To pronounce or utter; speak. **2** To declare or express in words; tell; state. **3** To state positively or as an opinion: *Say* which you prefer. **4** To recite; repeat: to *say* one's prayers. **5** To report; allege. **6** To assume as possibly true or as a hypothesis: He is worth, *say,* a million. *— v.i.* **7** To make a statement; speak. **— that is to say** In other words. *— n.* **1** What one has said or has to say; testimony; word: Let him have his *say.* **2** *Colloq.* Right or turn to speak or choose: Now it is my *say.* **3** Authority: to have the *say.* *— interj. U.S. Colloq.* A hail or an introductory exclamation to command attention: also *Brit.* **I say!** Compare LISTEN. [OE *secgan*] **— say′er** *n.*
Synonyms (verb): allege, assert, speak.
say[2] (sa) *n.* A fine, thin serge used in the 16th century, sometimes partly of silk, later entirely of wool. [<OF *saie* <L *saga,* pl. of *sagum* a military cloak]
Say (sā), **Thomas,** 1787–1834, U.S. zoologist.
Sa·yan Mountains (sä·yän′) A mountain system on the Siberia-Mongolia border.
Say·ers (sā′ərz, sârz), **Dorothy L(eigh),** 1893–1957, English author.
say·id (sī′id, sä′yid) *n.* Lord: a title applied to men who claimed to be descendants of Mohammed through his elder grandson, Husain: also spelled *said, saiyid.* Also **say′yid.** [<Arabic *sayyid*]
Sa·yi·da (sä′yə·dä) See SAIDA.
say·ing (sā′ing) *n.* An utterance; also, a maxim. See synonyms under ADAGE.
says (sez) Third person singular, present indicative of SAY.
say-so (sā′sō′) *n. Colloq.* **1** An unsupported assertion or decision. **2** Right or power to make decisions: He has the *say-so.*
'sblood (zblud) *interj. Archaic* God's blood: an imprecation. [Short for *God's blood*]
S-brack·et (es′brak′it) *n.* In mechanical construction, a bracket or other piece in the shape of the letter S: also called *S-piece.*
scab (skab) *n.* **1** A crust formed on the surface of a wound or sore. **2** A contagious disease among sheep, resembling mange; scabies. **3** Any of certain plant diseases of bacterial or fungous origin, in which there is a roughened or warty exterior. **4** *Slang* A mean, paltry fellow. **5** A workman who does not belong to or will not join or act with a labor union; one who takes the place of a striker; a strikebreaker. *— v.i.* **scabbed, scab·bing 1** To form or become covered with a scab. **2** To take the place of a striker; act as a scab. [Fusion of ON *skabbr* (assumed) and OE *sceabb*; infl. in meaning by L *scabies.* See SCABIES.] **— scabbed** *adj.* **— scab′bi·ly** *adv.* **— scab′bi·ness** *n.* **— scab′by** *adj.*
scab·bard (skab′ərd) *n.* A sheath for a weapon, as for a bayonet or a sword. *— v.t.* To sheathe in or furnish with a scabbard. [<OF *escalberc,* prob. <OHG *scar* a sword + *bergan* hide, protect]
scabbard fish 1 The cutlas fish (*Trichiurus lepturus*) having a long, eel-like body, found in the warm coastal waters of the United States and West Indies. **2** Any long, slender, silvery fish of the genus *Lepidopus* of European coasts.
scab·ble (skab′əl) *v.t.* **·bled, ·bling** In stoneworking, to dress or shape roughly. [Earlier *scapple* <OF *escapeler* dress timber]
scab·bling (skab′ling) *n.* A stone chip or fragment.
sca·bi·es (skā′bi·ēz, -bēz) *n.* The itch; especially, a contagious skin disease of sheep caused by any of certain itch mites, as *Psoroptes communis.* [<L, roughness, an itch < *scabere* scratch, scrape. Akin to SHAVE.] **— sca·bi·et·ic** (skā′bē·et′ik) *adj.*
sca·bi·ous[1] (skā′bē·əs) *adj.* **1** Pertaining to scabies. **2** Having scabs. [<L *scabiosus* < *scabies.* See SCABIES.]
sca·bi·ous[2] (skā′bē·əs) *n.* Any of a genus (*Scabiosa*) of herbs of the teasel family, with involucrate heads of variously colored flowers, as the sweet scabious (*S. atropurpurea*). Also **sca′bi·o′sa** (-ō′sə). [<NL <Med. L (*herba*) *scabiosa* fem. sing. of *scabiosus* SCABIOUS[1]]
sca·brous (skā′brəs) *adj.* **1** Roughened with minute points; rugged; scurfy. **2** Knotty; difficult to handle tactfully. [<LL *scabrosus* < *scabere* scratch] **— sca′brous·ly** *adv.* **— sca′brous·ness** *n.*
scac·cog·ra·phy (ska·kog′rə·fē) *n.* The literature pertaining to the science and art of chess. [<Ital. *scacchi* chess, pl. of *scacco* a square on a chessboard + -(O)GRAPHY] **— scac·chic** (skak′ik) *adj.* **— scac·cog′ra·pher** *n.*
scad (skad) *n.* A saurel. [? Var. of SHAD]
scads (skadz) *n. pl. Colloq.* A large amount or quantity. [? Var. of dial. E *scald* a large amount, great number]
Sca·fell Pike (skô·fel′) A mountain in Cumberland, England, the highest peak in England; 3,210 feet.
scaff (skaf, skäf) *n. Scot. & U.S. Dial.* Food; provisions. *— v.t. & v.i.* **1** To beg for (food). **2** *U.S. Slang* To eat. Also spelled *scauff.* [Prob. <G and Du. *schaffen* provide (food)]
scaf·fold (skaf′əld, -ōld) *n.* **1** A temporary elevated structure for the support of workmen, materials, etc., as in building. **2** A raised wooden framework used for drying hay, tobacco, fish, etc. **3** A platform for the execution of criminals. **4** A stage, as for

exhibition purposes. 5 A raised wooden frame formerly used by certain North American Indians for the disposal of their dead. — *v.t.* 1 To furnish or support with a scaffold: to *scaffold* a building in order to repaint the exterior. 2 To place on a scaffold. [<OF *(e)schaffaut, escadafaut.* Related to CATAFALQUE.]

scaf·fold·ing (skaf′əl·ding) *n.* A scaffold, or system of scaffolds, or the materials for constructing them: wooden *scaffolding.* Also **scaf′fold·age.**

scaff–raff (skaf′raf′, skäf′räf′) *n. Scot.* The rabble.

scag (skag) *n. Slang* Heroin. [Origin unknown]

scagl·ia (skal′yə) *n.* An Italian calcareous rock, corresponding to the chalk of England. [<Ital., a scale, a chip of marble <Med. L *scalia* <Gmc.]

scagl·io·la (skal·yō′lə) *n.* Hard, polished plasterwork imitating marble, granite, or other stone: made of powdered gypsum and glue, colored in various ways. [<Ital. *scagliuola,* dim. of *scaglia* SCAGLIA]

scaith (skāth) *n. Scot.* Scathe; damage; mar. — **scaith′less** *adj.*

sca·lade (skə·lād′) *n.* An escalade. Also **sca·la·do** (skə·lā′dō). [<Ital. *scalada* <*scalare* scale <*scala* a ladder <L. See SCALE[2].]

scal·age (skā′lij) *n.* 1 A percentage by which something is scaled down to allow for shrinkage. 2 The amount of lumber estimated to be in a log or logs being scaled. [<SCALE[2] + -AGE]

sca·lar (skā′lər) *adj.* Completely definable by a single number or by a point on a scale: said of a quantity having magnitude but no direction, as a volume or mass: distinguished from *vector.* — *n. Math.* A pure number, especially one representing only a magnitude. [<L *scalaris* of a ladder <*scala* a ladder. See SCALE[2].]

sca·la·re (skə·lā′rē, -lä′rā) *n.* 1 A deep–bodied cichlid fish of South American rivers (genus *Pterophyllum*), noted for its striking coloration and popular as an aquarium fish: also called *angelfish.* 2 A related fish of the Amazon, the **blue scalare** *(Symphysodon discus),* with a brownish–green, disk–shaped body. [<NL <L *scalaris* of a ladder; so called because marked with dark crossbars]

sca·lar·i·form (skə·lar′ə·fôrm) *adj. Biol.* Ladderlike: said of cells or vessels. [<NL *scalariformis* <L *scalaris* of a ladder + *forma* form]

scal·a·wag (skal′ə·wag) *n.* 1 *Colloq.* A worthless fellow; scamp. 2 *U.S.* A native Southern white who became or remained a Republican during the Reconstruction period: a contemptuous term used by Southern Democrats. Compare CARPETBAGGER. Also spelled *scallawag, scallywag.* [Origin uncertain]

scald[1] (skôld) *v.t.* 1 To burn with or as with hot liquid or steam. 2 To cleanse or treat with boiling water. 3 To heat (a liquid) to a point just short of boiling. 4 To cook in a liquid which is just short of the boiling point. — *v.i.* 5 To be or become scalded. — *n.* 1 A burn or injury to the skin by a hot fluid, as steam or water. 2 An act of scalding. 3 A destructive parasitic disease of cranberries. 4 A discoloration of plant tissue due to improper conditions of growth, bad storage, etc. [<AF *escalder* <LL *excaldare* wash with hot water <*ex-* very + *calidus* hot]

scald[2] (skôld, skäld) *n.* An ancient Scandinavian bard, minstrel, or reciter of eulogies: also spelled *skald.* [<ON *skald*] — **scal·dic** (skôl′dik, skäl′-) *adj.*

scald[3] (skäld, skôld) *v.t.* & *v.i. Scot.* To scold.

scald[4] (skôld) See SCALL.

scald·head (skôld′hed′) *n. Pathol.* Favus. [< *scald,* var. of *scalled* (<SCALL) + HEAD]

scale[1] (skāl) *n.* 1 One of the thin, flat, horny, membranous or bony outgrowths of the skin of various vertebrates, as most fishes, usually overlapping and forming a nearly complete investment. 2 A scab. 3 A scale insect. 4 *Bot.* A rudimentary or metamorphosed leaf, as of a pine cone. 5 *Metall.* The coating of oxide that forms on heated iron, etc.: also, an incrustation, as on the inside of boilers. 6 Any hard, thin, scalelike formation, as a flake, husk, shell, pod, or exfoliation. — *v.* **scaled, scal·ing** *v.t.* 1 To strip or clear of scale or scales. 2 To form scales on; cover with scales. 3 To take off in layers or scales; pare off. 4 To throw (a thin, flat object) so that its edge cuts the air or so that it skips along the surface of water. — *v.i.* 5 To come off in layers or scales; peel. 6 To shed scales. 7 To become incrusted with scales. [<OF *escale* a husk <Gmc.; infl. in meaning by OF *escaille* a fish's scale, an oyster's shell <Med. L *scalia* <Gmc.] — **scal′er** *n.*

scale[2] (skāl) *n.* 1 A piece of metal, wood, or glass bearing accurately spaced lines or graduations for use in measurement, or the series of marks so used. 2 Any system of designating units of measurement or in which a fixed proportion is used in determining quantities: a *scale* of 1 inch to the mile. 3 *Math.* A system of notation in which the successive places determine the value of figures, as the decimal system. 4 Any progressive or graded series; a graduation: the social *scale.* 5 *Music* All the tones or notes of a key in regular ascending or descending order, in an octave or

SCALE
a. Ascending. *b.* Descending.

more. 6 *Phot.* The range of light values which may be reproduced by a photographic paper. 7 An escalade. 8 A succession of steps; ladder; stairs: the original meaning. — **major scale** *Music* A scale having semitones between the 3–4 and 7–8 notes. — **minor scale** *Music* A scale having semitones between 2–3, 5–6, 7–8 notes (the harmonic form); or between 2–3, 7–8 ascending, 6–5, 3–2 descending (the melodic form). — *v.* **scaled, scal·ing** *v.t.* 1 To climb to the top of; go up by or as by means of a ladder. 2 To make according to a scale. 3 To regulate or adjust according to a scale or ratio: with *up, down,* etc. 4 To measure (logs) or estimate the amount of lumber in (standing timber). — *v.i.* 5 To climb; ascend. 6 To rise, as in steps or stages: Mountains *scaling* to the skies. [<Ital. *scala* a ladder <L <*scandere* climb] — **scal′a·ble** *adj.* — **scal′er** *n.*

scale[3] (skāl) *n.* 1 The bowl, scoop, or platform of a weighing instrument or balance. 2 The balance itself; hence, figuratively, the *scale* or *scales* of Justice. 3 *Usually pl.* Any form of weighing machine. — **to turn the scales** To determine; decide. — *v.* **scaled, scal·ing** *v.t.* 1 To weigh in scales. 2 To amount to in weight. — *v.i.* 3 To be weighed in scales. [<ON *skāl* a bowl, in pl. a weighing balance. Akin to SHALE, SHELL.]

scale board 1 A very thin, veneerlike piece of board, as for the back of a picture. 2 *Printing* A narrow strip of wood used in justifying a line of type. [<SCALE[1] + BOARD]

scale insect One of numerous small, hemipterous, plant–feeding insects (family *Coccidae*) which as adults are degenerate, sedentary, and covered with a scalelike, waxy protective shield.

scale moss Any plant belonging to the class *Hepaticae;* any of the liverworts: so called because of their scalelike leaves.

sca·lene (skā′lēn, skā·lēn′) *adj.* 1 *Geom.* **a** Having no two sides equal: said of a triangle. **b** Having the axis inclined to the base: said of a cone or cylinder. 2 *Anat.* Designating one of several deeply placed muscles attached to the cervical vertebrae and first and second ribs and acting to flex or bend the neck. Also **sca·le·nous** (skā·lē′nəs). [<LL *scalenus* <Gk. *skalēnos* uneven]

sca·le·nus (skə·lē′nəs) *n.* A scalene muscle. [<NL *(musculus) scalenus* <L, SCALENE (def. 2)]

Scales (skālz) A sign of the zodiac, called also *Libra* or *The Balance.*

scall (skôl) *n. Pathol.* 1 A cutaneous eruption of small pustular vesicles containing a purulent fluid: often epidemic among children. 2 Any scabby or scaly eruption. Also called *scald.* [<ON *skalle* a bald head]

scal·la·wag (skal′ə·wag), **scal·ly·wag** (skal′ē·wag) See SCALAWAG.

scal·lion (skal′yən) *n.* 1 A young, tender onion with a small, underdeveloped white bulb. 2 A shallot or leek. [<AF *scalun,* OF *eschalogne,* ult. <L *(caepa) Ascalonia* (onion) of Ashkelon, a Palestinian seaport]

scal·lop (skal′əp, skol′-) *n.* 1 A bivalve (genus *Pecten*) having a nearly circular shell with radiating ribs and wavy edge. 2 Its adductor muscle, which as a rule is edible and very succulent. 3 Its shell, formerly worn as a pilgrim's badge. 4 A dish or pan (originally a scallop shell) in which oysters are cooked or served. 5 One of a series of semicircular curves along an edge, as for ornament. — *v.t.* 1 To shape the edge of with scallops; ornament with scallops. 2 To bake (food) in a casserole with a liquid or sauce, often topped with bread crumbs. Also spelled *escallop, scollop.* [ME *scalop* <MF *escalope* shell <Gmc. Akin to SCALE[1].] — **scal′lop·er** *n.*

SCALLOP SHELL

scalp (skalp) *n.* 1 The skin of the top and back of the human skull, usually covered with hair; also, a portion of this, cut or torn away as a war trophy among certain North American Indians, particularly of the St. Lawrence region. 2 A similar piece taken from the head of a wild animal as an evidence that it has been killed for the collection of a bounty. 3 A political victory or defeat. 4 A denuded or bare summit, as of a hill or cliff. 5 On the stock exchange, a small profit taken by a speculator. — *v.t.* 1 To cut or tear the scalp from. 2 *Colloq.* To buy (tickets) and sell again at prices exceeding the established rate. 3 *Colloq.* To buy and sell again quickly in order to make a small profit. — *v.i.* 4 *Colloq.* To scalp bonds, tickets, etc. [ME, prob. <Scand. Cf. ON *skālpr* a sheath.] — **scalp′er** *n.*

scalp dance A ceremonial victory dance of certain North American Indians, in which the women of the tribe display the trophies and perform the dances, accompanied by the singing of the warriors.

scal·pel (skal′pəl) *n.* A small pointed knife with a very sharp, thin blade, used in dissections and in surgery. [<L *scalpellum,* dim. of *scalprum* a knife <*scalpere* cut]

scalp lock A long lock of hair left on the crown of the head by certain North American Indians, often braided and interwoven with feathers or fur: a challenge to an enemy.

scal·y (skā′lē) *adj.* **scal·i·er, scal·i·est** 1 Having a covering of scales; hence, also, exfoliated; scurfy. 2 Of the nature of a scale; squamous. 3 Incrusted, as a boiler. 4 *Slang* Mean; dishonorable. [<SCALE[1] + -Y[1]] — **scal′i·ness** *n.*

scaly ant–eater A pangolin.

scam (skam) *n. U.S. Slang* 1 A fraudulent bankruptcy planned as a swindle. 2 Any fraudulent scheme; swindle. [? Alter. of *scheme*]

Sca·man·der (skə·man′dər) Ancient name for the MENDERES (def. 2).

scam·ble (skam′bəl) *v.* **·bled, ·bling** *Brit. Dial. v.t.* 1 To scatter (something) to a crowd. 2 To gather confusedly. — *v.i.* 3 To scramble. 4 To stumble along. [Cf. SCRAMBLE and SHAMBLE[1]]

scam·mo·ny (skam′ə·nē) *n.* 1 A climbing plant *(Convolvulus scammonia)* of the morning–glory family, native in Asia Minor, with tuberous roots containing a milky juice. 2 The dried resin of scammony roots, used as a strong cathartic. [<L *scammonia* <Gk. *skammōnia*]

scamp[1] (skamp) *n.* A confirmed rogue; good–for–nothing fellow; rascal. [<obs. *scamp, v.,* roam, contraction of SCAMPER] — **scamp′ish, scamp′y** *adj.*

scamp[2] (skamp) *v.t.* To perform (work) carelessly or dishonestly. [Orig. dial. E, ? <ON *skemma* shorten <*skammr* short. Akin to SCANT, SKIMP.] — **scamp′er** *n.*

scam·per (skam′pər) *v.i.* To run quickly or hastily, as from danger; hurry away. — *n.* A hurried flight. [? <obs. Du. *schampen* run away <AF *escamper,* OF *eschamper* decamp, run off hurriedly, escape, ult. <L *ex* out from + *campus* a plain, battlefield] — **scam′per·er** *n.*

scam·pi (skam′pē) *n.pl.* Large shrimp, usually served in a garlic sauce. [<Ital.]

scan (skan) *v.* **scanned, scan·ning** *v.t.* 1 To examine in detail; scrutinize closely. 2 To pass the eyes over quickly; glance at, as a page of manuscript. **3** To separate (verse) into metrical feet; ascertain the rhythm of. **4** To read (verse) aloud so as to ascertain the metrical structure. **5** In television, to pass a beam of light or electrons rapidly over every point of (a surface) so as to reproduce an image being televised. —*v.i.* **6** To scan verse. **7** To conform to metrical rules: said of verse. **8** In television, to scan a surface. See synonyms under LOOK. [<LL *scandere* scan verses <L, climb] —**scan′na·ble** *adj.* —**scan′ner** *n.*

scan·dal (skan′dəl) *n.* **1** The heedless or malicious repetition of evil reports; aspersion of character. **2** Reproach caused by outrageous or improper conduct. **3** A discreditable circumstance, event, or action; cause of reproach. **4** Injury to reputation, or general comment causing it. **5** *Law* Malicious defamation by word of mouth. **6** One whose conduct disgraces. [<AF *escandle* <L *scandalum* a cause of stumbling <Gk. *skandalon* a snare; refashioned after MF *scandale* <L *scandalum*. Doublet of SLANDER.]

Synonyms: aspersion, backbiting, calumny, defamation, detraction, obloquy, odium, reproach, slander. *Scandal* may be odious truth; *slander* is certain falsehood. *Antonyms*: applause, celebrity, credit, eulogy, fame, glory, honor, renown, reputation, repute.

scan·dal·i·za·tion (skan′dəl·ə·zā′shən, -ī·zā′-) *n.* **1** The act of offending moral feelings. **2** That which scandalizes; a scandal.

scan·dal·ize (skan′dəl·īz) *v.t.* **·ized, ·iz·ing** To shock the moral feelings of, as by improper, frivolous, or offensive conduct; outrage. —**scan′dal·iz′er** *n.*

scan·dal·ous (skan′dəl·əs) *adj.* **1** Causing, or tending to cause, scandal; being a scandal; opprobrious; disgraceful; shocking to the sense of truth, decency, or propriety. **2** Consisting of evil or malicious reports; tending to injure reputation. **3** *Law* Libelous; irrelevant. See synonyms under FLAGRANT, INFAMOUS. —**scan′dal·ous·ly** *adv.* —**scan′dal·ous·ness** *n.*

scan·dent (skan′dənt) *adj.* Climbing, or aiding to climb, as a plant. [<L *scandens, -entis,* ppr. of *scandere* climb]

Scan·der·beg (skan′dər·beg), 1403–68, Albanian chief and national hero: real name *George Castriota.*

scan·di·a (skan′dē·ə) *n. Chem.* Scandium oxide, Sc_2O_3, a colorless, amorphous powder soluble in acids. [<NL < *scandium* SCANDIUM]

Scan·di·an (skan′dē·ən) *adj.* **1** Relating to Scandia, the Scandinavian Peninsula. **2** Scandinavian. [<L *Scandia*]

scan·dic (skan′dik) *adj. Chem.* Pertaining to or derived from scandium, especially in its higher valence.

Scan·di·na·vi·a (skan′də·nā′vē·ə) The region of NW Europe occupied by Sweden, Norway, and Denmark; 315,156 square miles; Finland, Iceland, and the Faroe Islands are often included: total area, 485,539 square miles. Ancient **Scan·di·a** (skan′dē·ə).

Scan·di·na·vi·an (skan′də·nā′vē·ən) *adj.* Of or pertaining to Scandinavia, its people, or their languages. —*n.* **1** A native or inhabitant of Scandinavia. **2** The North Germanic group of languages. See under GERMANIC. —**Old Scandinavian** Old Norse. See under NORSE. [<L *Scandinavia,* var. of *Scadinavia* <Gmc.]

Scandinavian Peninsula The peninsula of NW Europe containing Norway and Sweden; 298,550 square miles.

scan·di·um (skan′dē·əm) *n.* A metallic element (symbol Sc) of the lanthanide series, found in certain Swedish yttrium minerals. See ELEMENT. [<NL <L *Scandia* Scandinavia]

scan·ning (skan′ing) *n.* **1** Scansion. **2** The process by which the electron beam of a television transmitting unit passes rapidly over every point of the image on the photosensitive screen.

scan·sion (skan′shən) *n.* The act or art of scanning verse to show its metrical parts. Compare METER[2] (def. 2). [<F <LL *scansio, -onis* <L *scandere.* See SCAN.]

scan·so·ri·al (skan·sôr′ē·əl, -sō′rē-) *adj. Zool.* Pertaining to or adapted for climbing. Also **scan·so′ri·ous.** [<L *scansorius* < *scansus,* pp. of *scandere* climb]

scant (skant) *adj.* **1** Scarcely enough; meager in measure or quantity. **2** Being just short of the measure specified; of limited extent: often with the indefinite article even with a plural noun: a *scant* half-hour, a *scant* five yards. **3** Insufficiently supplied with something: with *of*: We were *scant* of breath. See synonyms under SCANTY. —*v.t.* **1** To restrict or limit in supply; stint. **2** To treat briefly or inadequately. See synonyms under SCRIMP. —*adv. Dial.* Scarcely; barely; not quite. [< ON *skamt,* neut. of *skammr* short] —**scant′ly** *adv.* —**scant′ness** *n.*

scant·ling (skant′ling) *n.* **1** A timber of moderate cross-section, used for studding, etc. **2** Such timbers collectively. **3** The dimensions of a timber in breadth and depth, but not in length; also, the dimensions of a stone in length, breadth, and thickness. **4** A small quantity or part; a sample. [Alter. of obs. *scantillon* <OF *eschantillon* specimen, corner-piece, chip; ? infl. in meaning by SCANT]

scant·y (skan′tē) *adj.* **scant·i·er, scant·i·est** **1** Limited in extent; small; close; cramped. **2** Restricted in quantity or number; scarcely sufficient. **3** Sparing. [<SCANT] —**scant′i·ly** *adv.* —**scant′i·ness** *n.*

Synonyms: deficient, insufficient, limited, narrow, niggardly, parsimonious, poor, scant, scarce, scrimped, scrimping, scrimpy, short, sparing, sparse. *Antonyms*: see synonyms under AMPLE.

Sca·pa Flow (skä′pə flō′, skap′ə) A sea basin and British naval base in the Orkney Islands, northern Scotland; 50 square miles: the Germans scuttled part of their own fleet here, June 21, 1919.

scape[1] (skāp) *n.* **1** *Bot.* A long, naked peduncle rising from a depressed stem, as in the dandelion. **2** *Biol.* A stemlike part, as of an insect antenna, or the shaft of a feather. **3** *Archit.* The shaft of a column, or the apophyge of a shaft. [<L *scapus* < dial. Gk. (Doric) *scapos.* Akin to SCEPTER.]

scape[2] (skāp) *n.* A scene, as of land, sea, clouds, or the like. [Back formation <LANDSCAPE]

scape[3] (skāp) *Archaic v.t.* & *v.i.* To escape: generally written *'scape.* —*n.* **1** An escape or means of escape. **2** A fault; an escapade. [Aphetic var. of ESCAPE]

scape·goat (skāp′gōt′) *n.* **1** The goat upon whose head Aaron symbolically laid the sins of the people on the day of atonement, after which it was led away into the wilderness. *Lev.* xvi. **2** Any animal or person on whom the bad luck or sins of an individual or group are symbolically placed, and which is then turned loose: a world-wide folk custom of great antiquity. **3** Any person bearing blame for others. [<SCAPE[3], *n.* + GOAT]

scape·grace (skāp′grās′) *n.* A mischievous or incorrigible person. [<SCAPE[3] + GRACE (def. 4)]

scape wheel An escape wheel.

scaph·oid (skaf′oid) *adj.* Boat-shaped. —*n. Anat.* A proximal bone of the wrist on the radial side; the navicular; also, a bone of the tarsus. [<NL *scaphoides* <Gk. *skaphoeidēs* < *skaphē* a boat + *eidos* form]

scapi- *combining form* A stalk or stem; a shaft: *scapiform,* resembling a scape. Also, before vowels, **scap-.** [<L *scapus* a stalk]

scap·o·lite (skap′ə·līt) *n.* Any of a definite group of tetragonal silicates, chiefly of aluminum, calcium, and sodium: also called *wernerite.* [<G *skapolith* <Gk. *skapos* a rod + *lithos* stone]

sca·pose (skā′pōs) *adj.* **1** Bearing a scape. **2** Like a scape. [<SCAPE[1] + -OSE]

scap·u·la (skap′yə·lə) *n. pl.* **·lae** (-lē) *Anat.* The shoulder blade; the superior or proximal element of the pectoral girdle in the skeleton of vertebrates. [<LL, shoulder <L *scapulae* shoulder blades]

scap·u·lar (skap′yə·lər) *n.* **1** An outer garment worn by members of certain religious orders and consisting of two strips of cloth hanging down front and back and joined across the shoulders; formerly, a monastic working dress. **2** Two small rectangular pieces of woolen cloth connected by strings: worn as a badge of membership by certain religious orders. **3** *Surg.* A bandage passing over the shoulder blade. **4** *Ornithol.* The shoulder feathers of a bird lying along the sides of the back. —*adj.* Of or pertaining to the scapula or scapulars. Also **scap′u·lar′y** (-ler′ē). [< Med. L *scapulare* <LL *scapula.* See SCAPULA.]

scar[1] (skär) *n.* **1** The mark left on the skin after the healing of a wound or sore; a cicatrix. **2** Any mark resulting from past injury: often applied figuratively to the effects on a character of crimes or sorrows. **3** The mark left on or made by an organ, as by leaves after separation from a stem or branch. **4** An indentation or mark made by use, motion, or contact. —*v.t.* & *v.i.* **scarred, scar·ring** To mark or become marked with a scar. [<OF *escare* <LL *eschara* a scab <Gk.] —**scar′less** *adj.*

scar[2] (skär) *n.* **1** A bare rock standing alone. **2** A cliff or rocky place on the side of a hill or mountain. Also, *Scot.,* *scaur.* [<ON *sker*]

scar·ab (skar′əb) *n.* **1** A scarabaeid beetle, especially the large, black, dung beetle *(Scarabaeus sacer),* held sacred by the ancient Egyptians as the symbol of resurrection and fertility. **2** A gem representing this beetle and inscribed with symbols, used in ancient Egypt as an amulet. Also **scar·a·bee** (skar′ə·bē). [<MF *scarabée* <L *scarabaeus*]

SCARAB

scar·a·bae·id (skar′ə·bē′id) *adj.* Pertaining to a large family *(Scarabaeidae)* of beetles, including cockchafers, etc. —*n.* A member of this family of beetles. Also **scar′a·bae′an, scar′a·bae′oid.** [<NL <L *scarabaeus* scarab]

scar·a·bae·us (skar′ə·bē′əs) *n. pl.* **·bae·i** (-bē′ī) **1** The scarab beetle. **2** A gem or design resembling it. Also **scar′a·be′us.** [<L]

scar·a·boid (skar′ə·boid) *adj.* Resembling or of the nature of a scarab or scarabaeid. —*n.* A scarab or scarabaeid.

scar·a·mouch (skar′ə·mouch, -mōōsh) *n.* A boastful, cowardly character; a swaggering buffoon: so called from a character in old Italian comedy. [<F *Scaramouche* <Ital. *Scaramuccia,* lit., a skirmish <Gmc.]

Scar·bor·ough (skär′bûr·ə) A municipal borough and resort town in North Riding, eastern Yorkshire, England, on the North Sea.

scarce (skârs) *adj.* **1** Rarely met with; infrequent. **2** Not plentiful, scant; insufficient. **3** Characterized or attended by insufficiency or want. See synonyms under RARE[1], SCANTY. —**to make oneself scarce** *Colloq.* To go away, or stay away. [<AF *scars, escars,* OF *eschars* scanty, insufficient, ult. <L *excerptus.* See EXCERPT.] —**scarce′ness** *n.*

scarce·ly (skârs′lē) *adv.* **1** Only just; barely. **2** Not quite; hardly.

scarce·ment (skârs′mənt) *n.* **1** *Archit.* A plain flat ledge or set-off in a wall. **2** *Mining* A ledge or projection left in the side of a shaft, embankment, or wall, as for a ladder. [Appar. < obs. *scarce, v.,* lessen (<SCARCE) + -MENT]

scar·ci·ty (skâr′sə·tē) *n. pl.* **·ties** Scantiness; insufficiency; lack of necessities; dearth. See synonyms under WANT.

scare[1] (skâr) *v.* **scared, scar·ing** *v.t.* **1** To strike with sudden fear; frighten. **2** To drive or force by frightening: with *off* or *away*: to *scare* away an intruder. —*v.i.* **3** To take fright; become scared. See synonyms under FRIGHTEN. —**to scare up** *Colloq.* To get together hurriedly; discover; produce: *to scare up* votes, food, a group of people, etc. —*n.* **1** Sudden fright, especially from slight or imaginary cause; terror. **2** A panic (def. 2). —*adj. Colloq.* Intended or likely to scare, or to provoke alarm or concern: *scare* tactics. [< ON *skirra* frighten < *skiarr* shy] —**scar′er** *n.* —**scar′ing·ly** *adv.*

scare[2] (skâr) *n.* In golf, the smaller end of a club head at the part where, formerly, it was spliced to the handle. [< dial. E (Scottish), a joint <ON *skor*]

scare·crow (skâr′krō′) *n.* **1** Any effigy set up to scare crows and other birds from growing crops. **2** A cause of false alarm. **3** A wretched-looking person.

Synonyms: bogy, bugbear, fright, goblin, hobgoblin.

scare·head (skâr′hed′) *n.* An exceptionally large newspaper headline in very bold type for news of sensational interest.

scare·mon·ger (skâr′mung′gər, -mong′-) *n.* One who spreads an alarming rumor; an alarmist.

scarf[1] (skärf) *n. pl.* **scarfs 1** In carpentry, a lapped joint made as by notching two timbers at the ends, and bolting them together so as to form one continuous piece without increased thickness: also **scarf joint. 2** The notched end of either of the timbers so cut. **3** A cut or incision in the blubber of a whale. —*v.t.* **1** To unite with a scarf joint. **2** To cut a scarf in. [? <ON *skarfr* a notch in a timber]

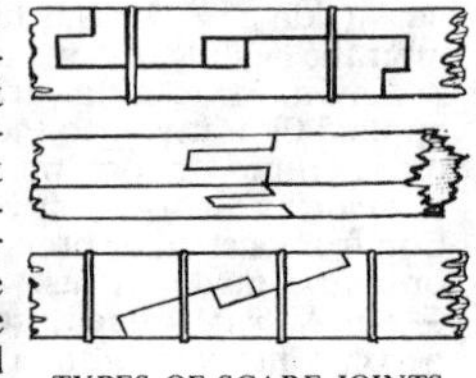

TYPES OF SCARF JOINTS

scarf[2] (skärf) *n. pl.* **scarfs** or **scarves** (skärvz) **1** A long and wide band, especially when worn about the head and neck; also, any sash. **2** A necktie or cravat. **3** A runner for a bureau or dresser. **4** An official sash, denoting rank. **5** A tippet or neckpiece. —*v.t.* **1** To cover or decorate as with a scarf. **2** To use as a scarf; wrap loosely around one. [<AF *escarpe,* OF *escharpe,* ? <*escreppe* a scrip[2]]

scarf[3] (skärf) See SCART[3].

scarf·pin (skärf′pin′) *n.* An ornamental pin worn on a tie or scarf.

scarf·skin (skärf′skin′) *n.* The epidermis; cuticle. [<SCARF[2] + SKIN]

scar·i·fi·ca·tor (skar′ə·fə·kā′tər) *n.* A surgical instrument, consisting of several lancet points, and used for making incisions in the skin to draw blood.

scar·i·fi·er (skar′ə·fī′ər) *n.* One who or that which scarifies.

scar·i·fy (skar′ə·fī) *v.t.* **·fied, ·fy·ing 1** To scratch or make slight incisions in, as the skin in surgery. **2** To criticize severely; make cutting comments on. **3** *Agric.* To stir the surface of, as soil. **4** To prune. [<MF *scarifier* <LL *scarificare* <L *scarifare* <Gk. *skariphasthai* scratch an outline, sketch <*skariphos* a stylus] —**scar′i·fi·ca′tion** *n.*

scar·i·ous (skâr′ē·əs) *adj.* **1** *Bot.* Thin, dry, membranaceous, and not green: said of plants. **2** Scaly. Also **scar′i·ose** (-ōs). [<F *scarieux* <NL *scariosus* <L *scaria* a thorny shrub]

scar·la·ti·na (skär′lə·tē′nə) *n.* Scarlet fever; popularly, a mild form of scarlet fever. [<NL <Ital. *scarlattina,* fem. dim. of *scarlatto* <Med. L *scarlatum* SCARLET]

scar·la·ti·noid (skär′lə·tē′noid, skär·lat′ə·noid) *adj.* Resembling scarlet fever. —*n. Pathol.* One of a group of erythemas closely resembling scarlet fever.

Scar·lat·ti (skär·lät′tē), **Alessandro,** 1659–1725, Italian composer. —**Domenico,** 1683–1757, Italian composer; son of preceding.

scar·let (skär′lit) *n.* **1** A brilliant red, inclining to orange. **2** A bright-red dye formerly obtained from the kermes or cochineal insect. **3** Any one of several coal-tar colors, varying from yellow to brown and used for dyeing. **4** Cloth or clothing of a scarlet color. —*adj.* **1** Brilliant-red, inclining to orange. **2** Clothed in scarlet. [<OF *escarlate* <Med. L *scarlatum,* prob. <Arabic *siqillāt* <Persian *saqalāt* a rich, scarlet cloth]

scarlet fever *Pathol.* An acute infectious fever caused by certain strains of hemolytic streptococci and characterized by a diffused scarlet rash followed by scaling off of the skin. Also *scarlatina.*

scarlet letter A scarlet "A," a badge of shame, which women convicted of adultery were once compelled to wear.

scarlet runner A tall climbing bean (*Phaseolus coccineus*) of tropical America, with vivid red flowers and long seed pods, now widely cultivated as a vegetable; a string bean.

Scarlet Woman The woman of *Rev.* xvii 4-6: an abusive epithet, first applied to pagan Rome, latterly to the Roman Catholic Church.

scarp (skärp) *n.* Any steep slope; an abrupt declivity; an escarpment. Compare illustration under BASTION. —*v.t.* To cut to a steep slope. [<AF *escarpe* <Ital. *scarpa*]

Scar·pan·to (skär′pän·tō) The Italian name for KARPATHOS.

Scarpe (skärp) A river of northern France, flowing 60 miles NE to the Scheldt.

scar·pet·ti (skär·pet′tē) *n. pl.* Rope-soled shoes used by mountain climbers. [<Ital. *scarpetto* a light shoe, dim. of *scarpa* a shoe]

Scar·ron (skà·rôṅ′), **Paul,** 1610–60, French poet and dramatist; first husband of Madame de Maintenon.

scart[1] (skärt) *Scot. n.* **1** A scratch; slight wound. **2** A pen or pencil mark. **3** A scrap or small irregular portion. —*v.t.* & *v.i.* To mark slightly; scratch or scrape. [ME *scratte;* of obscure origin]

scart[2] (skärt) *n. Scot.* A puny- or scrawny-looking person; also, a miserly person.

scart[3] (skärt) *n. Scot.* A cormorant. Also called *scarf.* [<ON *skarfr*]

scarves (skärvz) Alternative plural of SCARF[2].

scar·y (skâr′ē) *adj.* **scar·i·er, scar·i·est** *Colloq.* **1** Easily scared. **2** Somewhat frightened; anxious; timid. **3** Giving cause for alarm.

scat[1] (skat) *v.i.* **scat·ted, scat·ting** *Colloq.* To go away; depart: usually in the imperative. [? <*ss,* imit. of a hiss + CAT]

scat[2] (skat) *n. Slang* A type of jazz singing in which meaningless syllables are improvised on the melodic line. [Prob. <SCAT[1]]

scathe (skāth) *v.t.* **scathed, scath·ing 1** To criticize severely. **2** To injure severely; harm; blast. —*n.* Severe injury; harm; loss. Also **scath** (skath). Also, *Scot., skaith.* [<ON *skatha* <*skathi* harm] —**scathe′ful** *adj.*

scathe·less (skāth′lis) *adj.* Free from harm. Also **scath′less** (skath′-).

scath·ing (skā′thing) *adj.* Damaging by scorching or blasting; withering: now usually figuratively: a *scathing* rebuke. —*n.* Harm; injury. —**scath′ing·ly** *adv.*

scato– *combining form* Dung; excrement: *scatology.* Also, before vowels, **scat–**. [<Gk. *skōr, skatos* dung]

scat·o·log·ic (skat′ə·loj′ik) *adj.* Of or pertaining to scatology; obscene. Also **scat′o·log′i·cal.**

sca·tol·o·gy (skə·tol′ə·jē) *n.* **1** The study of excrement, considered as a branch of paleontology, medicine, and psychiatry. **2** Preoccupation with filth or obscenity, as in literature. Also **scat·o·lo·gi·a** (skat′ə·lō′jē·ə). [<SCATO- + -LOGY] —**sca·tol′o·gist** *n.*

scat·o·man·cy (skat′ō·man′sē) *n.* In folklore, divination, or determination of disease, by means of feces.

scat·ter (skat′ər) *v.t.* **1** To throw about in various places; sprinkle; strew, as seed. **2** To separate and drive away in different directions; disperse; rout. **3** *Physics* To reflect (heat or light) irregularly. —*v.i.* **4** To separate and go in different directions; disperse; dissipate. See synonyms under SPREAD, SQUANDER. [ME *scateren* squander. ? Akin to SHATTER.] —**scat′ter·er** *n.*

scat·ter·brain (skat′ər·brān′) *n.* A person without concentration of mind; a heedless person. —**scat′ter-brained′** *adj.*

scat·ter·good (skat′ər·go͝od′) *n.* **1** One who wastes that which is good; a spendthrift. **2** One who or that which distributes charities.

scat·ter·ing (skat′ər·ing) *n.* **1** Dispersion. **2** *Physics* The deflection of a beam of particles or waves into a variety of directions upon collision with any obstacle preventing continuous propagation in the original direction. **3** The dispersion, over an area, of votes for candidates. —*adj.* Placed at intervals or at a distance. —**scat′ter·ing·ly** *adv.*

scat·ter·ling (skat′ər·ling) *n.* A person without a home; a vagrant. [<SCATTER + -LING[1]]

sca·tu·ri·ent (skə·cho͝or′ē·ənt) *adj. Obs.* Gushing forth, as a fountain. [<L *scaturiens, -entis,* ppr. of *scaturire* <*scatere* flow out]

scaud (skôd) *v.t. Scot.* To scald.

scauff (skôf) See SCAFF.

scaup[1] (skôp) *n.* A sea duck (genus *Aythya*) of northern regions, related to the canvasback, having the head and neck black in the male; especially, the common American bay duck (*A. marila*). Also **scaup duck.** [Short for *scaup duck* <SCAUP[2] + DUCK]

scaup[2] (skôp) *n. Obs.* & *Scot.* **1** The scalp; skull. **2** A mussel bed. [Var. of SCALP]

scaur (skär, skôr) See SCAR[2].

scav·enge (skav′inj) *v.* **·enged, ·eng·ing** *v.t.* **1** To remove filth, rubbish, and refuse from, as streets. **2** To remove exhaust gases from (the cylinder of an internal-combustion engine). **3** *Metall.* To remove impurities from (a metal or alloy). —*v.i.* **4** To act as a scavenger. **5** To search for food. [Back formation <SCAVENGER]

scav·en·ger (skav′in·jər) *n.* **1** A street-cleaner. **2** An animal that feeds on carrion, as the buzzard. [ME *scavager* <AF *scawager* <*scawage* inspection <*escauwer* inspect <Flemish *scauwen* see]

sce·nar·i·o (si·nâr′ē·ō, -när′ē·ō) *n. pl.* **·nar·i·os 1** The plot of a dramatic work, or a skeleton libretto. **2** The written plot and arrangement of incidents of a motion picture. **3** An outline or plan of a projected series of actions or events. [<Ital. <LL *scenarius* of stage scenes <L *scena.* See SCENE.]

sce·nar·ist (si·nâr′ist, -när′ist) *n.* One who writes scenarios.

scend (send) *Naut. v.i.* To heave upward, as a vessel on a wave. —*n.* The upward angular displacement of a vessel: correlative of *pitch.* Also spelled *send.* —**pitch and scend** The longitudinal rocking of a vessel. [Var. of SEND[2]; infl. in form by *ascend*]

scene (sēn) *n.* **1** A locality and all connected with it, as presented to view; a landscape. **2** The place in which the action of a drama is supposed to occur; setting or locality. **3** The place and surroundings of any event, real or imagined, as in literature or art. **4** A division of an act of a play; one comprehensive event in a play. **5** Any incident or episode that may serve as the subject of a description. **6** The painted canvas screen or screens for the background for a play. **7** Any striking exhibition or display; especially, a display of passion or excited feeling. **8** *Slang* A place or realm of a currently popular activity: the pop music *scene.* —**behind the scenes 1** Out of sight of a theater audience; backstage. **2** Privately; in secret. [<OF <L *scena, scaena* <Gk. *skēnē* tent, stage]

Synonyms: action, display, event, exhibition, incident, landscape, place, prospect, situation.

scen·er·y (sē′nər·ē) *n. pl.* **·er·ies** Natural or theatrical scenes collectively. [<Ital. *scenario.* See SCENARIO.]

sce·nic (sē′nik, sen′ik) *adj.* **1** Artistic in grouping and effect. **2** Picturesque. **3** Relating to stage scenery.

sce·nog·ra·phy (sē·nog′rə·fē) *n.* The art of making drawings in perspective. [<F *scénographie* <L *scaenographia* <Gk. *skēnographia* <*skēnē* a scene, tent + *graphein* write] —**scen·o·graph·ic** (sen′ə·graf′ik, sē′nə-) *adj.*

scent (sent) *n.* **1** An odor, pleasant or unpleasant. **2** The effluvium by which an animal can be tracked. **3** A clue aiding investigation. **4** Scraps of paper, in the game of hare and hounds, dropped by the hares in their flight to enable the hounds to follow them. **5** A fluid essence containing extracts from flowers or other fragrant bodies; perfume. **6** The sense of smell. —*v.t.* **1** To perceive by the sense of smell. **2** To form a suspicion of. **3** To cause to be fragrant; perfume. —*v.i.* **4** To hunt by the sense of smell: said of hounds. ◆ Homophone: *cent.* [<OF *sentir* discern by the senses, feel <L *sentire*] —**scent′less** *adj.*

Synonyms (noun): savor, smell.

scep·ter (sep′tər) *n.* **1** A staff or wand carried as the badge of command or sovereignty. **2** Hence, kingly office or power. —*v.t.* **1** To confer the scepter on; invest with royal power. **2** To furnish with or as with a scepter or scepters. Also **scep′tre** (-tər). [<OF *ceptre, sceptre* <L *sceptrum* <Gk. *skēptron* a staff <*skēptesthai* prop oneself, lean on]

SCEPTER

scep·tic (skep′tik), **scep·ti·cal, scep·ti·cism,** etc. See SKEPTIC, etc.

Schac·a·bac (shak′ə·bak) In the *Arabian Nights,* the beggar invited to the Barmecide feast.

Schacht (shäkht), **(Horace Greeley) Hjalmar,** 1877–1970, German financier and economic expert.

Schaff·hau·sen (shäf′hou′zən) A town in northern Switzerland, on the Rhine near **Schaffhausen Falls** (German *Rheinfall*), a group of several cataracts falling a total of 100 feet, now harnessed for hydroelectric power.

schanz (skhäns) *n.* A breastwork of earth and stones. —*v.t.* To protect with a schanz. [< Du. *schans*]

schap·pe (shä′pə) *n.* A fabric woven from spun silk. —*v.t.* **schapped, schap·ping** To ferment (silk) so as to remove its gum coating. [<dial. G (Swiss), a waste, impurity]

Scharn·horst (shärn′hôrst), **Gerhard von,** 1755–1813, Prussian general and military writer.

schat·chen (shät′khən) *n.* One who arranges marriages for a fee; a marriage-broker: chiefly among Russian Jews. Also **schad′chan.** [<Yiddish, a marriage broker <Hebrew *shadhkhān*]

Schaum·burg-Lip·pe (shoum′bŏŏrkh·lip′ə) A former state of NW Germany, comprised in Lower Saxony, northern West Germany, 1945; 131 square miles; former capital, Bückeburg.

sched·ule (skej′ōōl, *Brit.* shed′yōōl) *n.* **1** A written or printed statement, usually in tabular form, specifying the details of some matter, and often annexed to statutes, petitions, and other documents. **2** A list; catalog; an inventory. **3** A timetable; also, a detailed and timed plan for any procedure. **4** A program. —*v.t.* **·uled, ·ul·ing 1** To place in or on a schedule. **2** To make a schedule of. **3** *Colloq.* To appoint or plan for a specified time or date: He *scheduled* his appearance for five o'clock. [Alter. of ME *sedule* <OF *cedule* <LL *scedula,* dim. of L *scida, scheda* a leaf of paper <Gk. *schidē* a wood splinter <*schizein* split; infl. in form by Med. L *schedula*]

Schee·le (shā′lə), **Karl Wilhelm,** 1742–86, Swedish chemist; discovered chlorine in 1774, oxygen in 1777, and other elements.

schee·lite (shē′līt) *n.* A vitreous, variously colored, tetragonal calcium tungstate. [after K. W. *Scheele,* who discovered tungstic acid]

Schef·fel (shef′əl), **Joseph Victor von,** 1826–1886, German poet.

schef·fer·ite (shef′ə·rīt) *n.* A brown manganese pyroxene often containing iron. [after H. T. *Scheffer,* 1710–59, Swedish chemist]

Sche·her·e·za·de (shə·her′ə·zä′də, -zäd′) In the *Arabian Nights,* the bride of a sultan who had sworn to kill each of his wives after her wedding night. Scheherezade tricked the sultan into sparing her life by telling him an exciting story each night, not revealing the ending until the following day. Also **Sche·her′a·za′de.**

scheik (shēk) See SHEIK.

Scheldt (skelt) A river in northern France, Belgium, and the Netherlands, flowing 270 miles NE to North Sea: French *Escaut. Flemish & Dutch* **Schel·de** (skhel′də).

Schel·ling (shel′ing), **Friedrich Wilhelm Joseph von,** 1775–1854, German philospher. —**Schel·lin·gi·an** (she·lin′jē·ən) *adj.*

sche·ma (skē′mə) *n. pl.* **sche·ma·ta** (skē′mə·tə) **1** A scheme, synopsis, or summary. **2** A diagrammatic representation of certain relations in some system of knowledge. **3** Any figure drawn in outline; formerly, a geometric diagram. [<L. See SCHEME.]

sche·ma·tism (skē′mə·tiz′əm) *n.* **1** A particular form or disposition of anything. **2** Orderly arrangement of parts, as in a philosophic system, the classification of knowledge, etc.; design.

sche·ma·tize (skē′mə·tīz) *v.t.* **·tized, ·tiz·ing** To form into or arrange according to a scheme or schema. [<Gk. *schēmatizein* <*schēma, -atos* a form] —**sche′ma·ti·za′·tion** *n.*

scheme (skēm) *n.* **1** A plan of something to be done; a plot or device for the accomplishment of an object. **2** A combination of various things according to a general plan or design; systematic arrangement. **3** A formal plan or arrangement, or a statement of such a plan; also, a table or schedule. **4** An outline drawing or sketch; diagram. **5** In astrology, a plan representing the aspects of the heavenly bodies at any given time. See synonyms under DESIGN, HYPOTHESIS, PLAN, PROJECT. —*v.* **schemed, schem·ing** *v.t.* **1** To make a scheme for; devise; plan. **2** To plan or plot in an underhand manner. —*v.i.* **3** To make schemes; plan or plot; connive. [<L *schema* a shape, figure of speech <Gk. *schēma, -atos* a form, plan] —**sche·mat·ic** (skē·mat′ik) or **·i·cal** *adj.* —**sche·mat′i·cal·ly** *adv.* —**schem′er** *n.* —**schem′ing** *adj.*

Sche·nec·ta·dy (skə·nek′tə·dē) An industrial city on the Mohawk River in eastern New York.

schenk beer (shengk) Beer fermented in 4 to 6 weeks and brewed for immediate use in the winter. [<G *schenkbier* <*schenken* pour out + *bier* beer; so called with ref. to its being put on schenk (draft) as soon as it is made, to keep it from turning sour]

scher·zan·do (sker·tsän′dō) *adv. Music* In a sportive or playful manner. [<Ital., ppr. of *scherzare* play <*scherzo.* See SCHERZO.]

scher·zo (sker′tsō) *n. pl.* **·zos** or **·zi** (-tsē) *Music* A sportive or lightsome movement, usually following a slow movement, especially in a symphony or sonata. [<Ital., a jest <G *scherz*]

Sche·ven·ing·en (skhā′vən·ing′ən) A resort town of western Netherlands just NW of The Hague on the North Sea; scene of a British naval victory over the Dutch, 1653.

Schia·pa·rel·li (skyä′pä·rel′lē), **Giovanni,** 1835–1910, Italian astronomer.

Schick (shik), **Béla,** 1877–1967, Austrian pediatrician, born in Hungary and active in the United States.

Schick test A test to determine the susceptibility of a person to diphtheria by injecting a diluted diphtheria toxin: a positive reaction gives a reddening of the skin. [after Dr. Béla *Schick,* who devised it]

Schie·dam (skhē·däm′) A town of western Netherlands, just west of Rotterdam.

schil·ler (shil′ər) *n. Mineral.* A bronzelike luster or iridescence due to the reflection of particles dispersed in certain minerals. [<G, a play of colors <*schillern* change color]

Schil·ler (shil′ər), **Johann Christoph Friedrich von,** 1759–1805, German poet and dramatist.

schil·ler·ize (shil′ə·rīz) *v.t.* **·ized, ·iz·ing** To impart schiller to. —**schil′ler·i·za′tion** *n.*

schil·ling (shil′ing) *n.* The monetary unit of Austria since 1924; a former North German silver coin. [<G]

Schip·hol (skhip′hôl) A village and international airport in western Netherlands, 6 miles SW of Amsterdam.

schip·per·ke (skip′ər·kē) *n.* A Belgian breed of dog used as a watchdog and sometimes for hunting. It is usually tailless, has a thick-set body, foxlike head, and a rather thick, short, black coat. Formerly called *Spits* or *Spitske.* [<dial. Du., a little boatman, dim. of Du. *schipper*; so called because orig. used as watchdogs on boats]

schism (siz′əm) *n.* **1** A division of a church into factions. **2** The offense of causing division in a church or a religious community. **3** An ecclesiastical body separated from a larger or older body, as from an established church. **4** The act of dividing, or the state of being divided; division. See synonyms under SECT. [<OF *cisme, scisme* <LL *schisma* <Gk., a split <*schizein* split]

schis·mat·ic (siz·mat′ik) *adj.* Relating to, having the character of, implying, or promoting schism: also **schis·mat′i·cal.** —*n.* One who makes or participates in an ecclesiastical schism: a term of opprobrium. [<OF *cismatique, scismatique* <LL *schismaticus* <Gk. *schismatikos* <Gk. *schisma, -atos.* See SCHISM.] —**schis·mat′i·cal·ly** *adv.* —**schis·mat′i·cal·ness** *n.*

schist (shist) *n. Geol.* Any rock that readily splits or cleaves; specifically, a rock that has had a parallel or foliated structure secondarily developed in it: also spelled *shist.* [<F *schiste* <L *schistos* readily split <Gk. <*schizein* split] —**schist′ous, schist·ose** (shis′·tōs) *adj.*

schis·ta·ceous (shis·tā′shəs) *adj.* Bluish-gray; of a light slaty color. [<SCHIST + -ACEOUS]

schisto- *combining form* Split: *schistosome.* Also, before vowels, **schist-.** [<Gk. *schistos* split]

schis·to·some (shis′tə·sōm) *n.* Any of a genus (*Schistosoma*) of trematode worms, including certain species parasitic in the blood of man, as the blood fluke (*S. haematobium*) common in Africa. [<NL <Gk. *schistos* split (<*schizein* split) + *sōma* a body]

schis·to·so·mi·a·sis (shis′tə·sō·mī′ə·sis) *n. Pathol.* A wasting disease caused by infestation with worms of the genus *Schistosoma,* endemic in Egypt and other parts of Africa: also called *bilharziasis.* [<NL <*Schistosoma* a schistosome]

schizo- *combining form* Split; divided: *schizophrenia.* Also, before vowels, **schiz-.** [<Gk. *schizein* split]

schiz·o·carp (skiz′ə·kärp) *n. Bot.* A split fruit; a pericarp splitting at maturity into two or more one-seeded indehiscent portions. Compare illustration under FRUIT. —**schiz′o·car′·pous, schiz′o·car′pic** *adj.*

schiz·o·gen·e·sis (skiz′ō·jen′ə·sis) *n. Biol.* Reproduction by fission.

schi·zog·o·ny (ski·zog′ə·nē) *n. Biol.* Reproduction by multiple fission, as in certain protozoa. [<NL *schizogonia* <Gk. *schizein* split + *genesthai* become]

schiz·oid (skiz′oid) *Psychiatry adj.* Of, pertaining to, or afflicted with schizophrenia. —*n.* One affected with schizophrenia. [< SCHIZ(OPHRENIA) + -OID]

schiz·o·my·cete (skiz′ō·mī·sēt′) *n.* One of the *Schizomycetes*; a bacterium. [<NL <Gk. *schizein* split + *mykēs, -ētos* a mushroom] —**schiz′o·my·ce′tous** *adj.*

Schiz·o·my·ce·tes (skiz′ō·mī·sē′tēz) *n. pl.* A class of widely distributed, minute, unicellular plants reproducing by fission and allied to the fungi: it comprises the bacteria and, in the Bergey classification, includes the following orders:

Eubacteriales	Simple undifferentiated forms
Actinomycetales	Moldlike bacteria
Chlamydobacteriales	Algalike iron bacteria
Caulobacteriales	Aquatic, gum-secreting bacteria
Thiobacteriales	Sulfur bacteria
Myxobacteriales	Slime-mold bacteria
Spirochaetales	Protozoanlike bacteria

schiz·o·my·co·sis (skiz′ō·mī·kō′sis) *n. Pathol.* A morbid condition or disease due to the presence of schizomycetes. [<NL]

schiz·ont (skiz′ont, skī′zont) *n.* The mature trophozoite of a sporozoan, as the malaria parasite, from which new cells, or merozoites, are liberated into the blood by schizogony. [<Gk. *schizōn, -ontos,* ppr. of *schizein* split]

schiz·o·phre·ni·a (skiz′ō·frē′nē·ə) *n. Psychiatry* A mental derangement characterized by the presence of conflicting impulses, emotions, and ideas, and resulting in a disintegration of personality resembling, but more inclusive than, that found in dementia precox. [<NL <Gk. *schizein* split + *phrēn* mind] —**schiz′·o·phren′ic** (-fren′ik) *adj.* & *n.*

schiz·o·phyte (skiz′ə·fīt) *n.* One of a division or phylum (*Schizophyta*) of unicellular or simple multicellular plants which reproduce by fission or by asexual spores: it includes the bacteria and the blue-green algae. —*adj.* Of or pertaining to the *Schizophyta*: also **schiz′o·phyt′ic** (-fit′ik). [<NL <Gk. *schizein* split + *phyton* a plant]

schiz·o·pod (skiz′ə·pod) *n.* Any of a former order (*Schizopoda*) of crustaceans having a soft carapace and resembling the shrimp: now included in the subclass *Malacostraca.* [<NL <Gk. *schizopous, -podos* having parted toes <*schizein* split + *pous, podos* a foot]

schiz·o·thy·mi·a (skiz′ō·thī′mē·ə) *n. Psychiatry* A schizophrenic condition marked by introversion and a withdrawing from the world, but milder than schizophrenia. [<NL <Gk. *schizein* split + *thymos* spirit] —**schiz′o·thyme** *n.* —**schiz′o·thy′mic** *adj.*

Schle·gel (shlā′gəl), **August Wilhelm von,** 1767–1845, German philologist, poet, and literary critic. —**Friedrich von,** 1772–1829, German philosopher and critic: brother of the preceding.

Schlei·er·ma·cher (shlī′ər·mäkh′ər), **Friedrich Ernst Daniel,** 1768–1834, German theologian and philosopher.

schle·miel (shlə·mēl′) *n. Slang* An inept, easily duped person; a bungler; dolt. Also **schle·mihl′.** [<Yiddish, an unlucky person <Hebrew *Shelumiēl,* a personal name]

schlep (shlep) *Slang v.* **schlepped, schlep·ping** *v.t.* 1 To drag awkwardly; lug. —*v.i.* 2 To drag something awkwardly. 3 To proceed wearily or heavily: to *schlep* uptown. —*n.* 1 A difficult journey. 2 A stupid, awkward person. Also **schlepp.** [<Yiddish *shleppen* to drag] —**schlep′per** *n.*

Schle·si·en (shlā′zē·ən) The German name for SILESIA.

Schles·wig (shlās′vikh) 1 A city in NW Germany, former capital of Schleswig–Holstein. 2 The southern part of Jutland Peninsula, divided between Germany and Denmark: Danish *Sleswig.*

Schles·wig-Hol·stein (shlās′vikh·hōl′shtīn) A state of NW Germany (NE West Germany); 6,052 square miles; capital, Kiel.

Schley (slī), **Winfield Scott,** 1839–1911, U. S. rear admiral.

Schlie·mann (shlē′män), **Heinrich,** 1822–90, German archeologist.

schlie·re (shlē′rə) *n. pl.* **·ren** (-rən) *Geol.* In an igneous rock, an irregular, commonly not sharply bounded, portion differing in composition or texture from the general mass of the rock. [<G, lit., a streak] —**schlie′ric** *adj.*

schlie·ren (shlē′rən) *n. Physics* Any disturbance in the light path of an interferometer which alters the density of the air and thus changes the interference pattern of the light waves. [<G, pl. of *schliere,* lit., a streak]

schlock (shlok) *Slang n.* Shoddy, inferior merchandise. —*adj.* Of inferior quality; tawdry. Also spelled *shlock.* [<Yiddish] —**schlock′y** *adj.*

schmaltz (shmälts) *n. Slang* 1 Anything which is overly sentimental, as in music or literature. 2 Extreme sentimentalism. [<Yiddish <G *schmalz,* lit., melted fat] —**schmaltz′y** *adj.*

Schmidt telescope A reflecting telescope that yields undistorted images of a very wide field. [after B. *Schmidt,* died 1935, German optical designer]

Schna·bel (shna′bəl), **Artur,** 1882–1951, U.S. pianist and composer born in Austria.

schnap·per (shnap′ər, snap′-) *n.* A snapper (def. 4). [<G *schnapper* a schnapper]

schnapps (shnäps, shnaps) *n.* Holland gin; Hollands; loosely, any ardent spirits. Also **schnaps.** [<G, a dram, a nip <Du. *snaps,* lit., a gulp, mouthful]

schnau·zer (shnou′·zər) *n.* A small, active terrier originally developed in Germany, having a wiry black or pepper-and-salt coat. —**miniature schnauzer** A toy terrier bred from the standard schnauzer and a pinscher. [<G *Schnauze* snout]

STANDARD SCHNAUZER (From 18 to 20 inches high at the shoulder)

Schnitz·ler (shnits′·lər), **Arthur,** 1862–1931, Austrian playwright and novelist.

schnor·kel (shnôr′kəl) *n.* 1 An apparatus for the ventilation of a submerged submarine, consisting of retractable tubes for the intake of fresh air and the removal of the toxic gases. 2 A snorkel. [<G *schnörkel* spiral]

schnor·rer (shnôr′ər) *n.* A professional or habitual beggar. [<Yiddish <G *schnurrer* < slang *schnurren* go begging, orig. whirr, purr; with ref. to musical instruments of beggars]

schnoz·zle (shnoz′əl) *n. Slang* Nose. [<Yiddish <G *schnauze.* Akin to SNOUT.]

Scho·field (skō′fēld), **John McAllister,** 1831–1906, U. S. general.

schol·ar (skol′ər) *n.* 1 A person eminent for learning. 2 The holder of a scholarship. 3 One who learns under a teacher; a pupil. —**Rhodes scholar** A male student selected from a college or university of the United States or of any British dominion or colony, to receive one of the scholarships established by Cecil Rhodes for attendance at Oxford University, England. [Prob. fusion of OE *scolere* and OF *escoler,* both <LL *scholaris* <L *schola.* See SCHOOL[1].]

Synonyms: disciple, learner, pupil, savant, student. Historically the primary sense of a *scholar* is one who is being schooled; thence the word passes to designate one who is apt in school work, and finally one who is thoroughly schooled, master of what the schools can teach, an erudite or accomplished person: when used without qualification, the word is generally understood in this sense; as, He is manifestly a *scholar. Pupil* signifies one under the close personal supervision or instruction of a teacher or tutor.

schol·arch (skol′ärk) *n.* 1 In Greek antiquity, the head of a school of philosophy in Athens. 2 The head of any school. [<Gk. *scholarchē* <*scholē* a school + *archein* rule]

schol·ar·ly (skol′ər·lē) *adj.* Like a scholar; learned; erudite.

schol·ar·ship (skol′ər·ship) *n.* 1 Learning; erudition. 2 Maintenance or a stipend for a student awarded by an educational institution: also, the position of such a student. See synonyms under KNOWLEDGE, LEARNING.

scho·las·tic (skō·las′tik, skə-) *adj.* 1 Pertaining to or characteristic of scholars, education, or schools. 2 Pertaining to or characteristic of the medieval schoolmen. 3 Precise; pedantic. 4 Pertaining to the theological grade of students of the Jesuit order. Also **scho·las′ti·cal.** —*n.* 1 A student; pupil. 2 *Often cap.* A schoolman; an advocate of scholasticism. 3 A pedant. [<L *scholasticus* <Gk. *scholastikos* <*scholazein* be at leisure, devote leisure to study <*scholē.* See SCHOOL[1].]

scho·las·ti·cate (skō·las′tə·kāt, skə-) *n.* A general house of higher studies for Jesuit scholastics. [<NL *scholasticatus* <L *scholasticus* SCHOLASTIC]

scho·las·ti·cism (skō·las′tə·siz′əm, skə-) *n.* 1 *Often cap.* The systematized Christian logic, philosophy, and theology of medieval scholars from the 10th to the 15th centuries, based on Aristotle's *Logic* and *Metaphysics* and the writings of the early Christian fathers. See HUMANISM. 2 Any system of teaching which insists on traditional doctrines and forms. 3 A similar teaching of the present day given especially in seminaries of the Roman Catholic Church.

scho·li·ast (skō′lē·ast) *n.* A commentator; especially, an ancient grammarian or annotator of classical texts. See SCHOLIUM. [<L *scholiasta* <Gk. *scholiastēs* <*scholion* a commentary <*scholē* a school] —**scho′li·as′tic** *adj.*

scho·li·um (skō′lē·əm) *n. pl.* **·li·ums** or **·li·a** (-lē·ə) 1 An explanatory marginal note, as on a classical text by an ancient grammarian. 2 An interpolated note accompanying a mathematical proof. [<LL *scholium* <Gk. *scholion.* See SCHOLIAST.]

Schön·berg (shœn′berkh), **Arnold,** 1874–1951, Austrian composer and conductor active in the United States.

school[1] (sko͞ol) *n.* 1 An educational institution. 2 The place in which formal instruction is given; also, the instruction itself. 3 A period or session of an educational institution; a course of study at a school: *School* begins tomorrow. 4 The pupils in an educational institution. 5 A subdivision of a university devoted to a special branch of higher education: a *school* of education, medicine, etc. 6 The prescribed drill, duties, instruction, and training of any branch of the army or navy: gunnery *school,* aviation *school*; also, the manual of such instruction. 7 A body of disciples of a teacher or system; a sect, etc.; also, the system, methods, or opinions characteristic of those thus associated: the Scottish *school* of philosophy, a painting of the Flemish *school.* 8 A general style of life, manners, etc. 9 In medieval times, specifically, a seminary of logic, metaphysics, and theology; in the plural, the seats of the scholastic philosophy. 10 Any sphere or means of instruction: the *school* of example. —*v.t.* 1 To instruct in a school; train; educate. 2 To subject to rule or discipline. [OE *scōl* <L *schola* <Gk. *scholē* leisure or that which is done during leisure time, a school]

—**common school** One of the free public elementary schools in the United States.

—**consolidated school** A school, usually rural, consisting of several elementary schools and sometimes a high school, merged into one organization, for pupils from outlying districts.

—**continuation school** Comprehensively, a school for the further education of persons already employed; specifically, a school for employed boys and girls below the legal age for leaving school, attended a few hours a week on the employers' time.

—**dame school** An early form of school kept by a woman who drilled young children in their ABC's and the beginnings of reading.

—**elementary school** A school giving a course of education of from six to nine years, pupils usually entering at about six years of age.

—**finishing school** A school that prepares girls for entrance into society.

—**grammar school** 1 In graded public schools, the grades between primary and high school, grades one to eight inclusive. 2 Popularly, an elementary school. 3 *Brit.* A secondary school, often preparatory for college; originally for the teaching of Latin and Greek, but now offering broader curriculums.

—**high school** The highest division of the common schools, typically comprising grades 9, 10, 11, and 12: often preparatory for college or the vocations. —**junior high school** A school usually consisting of the 7th, 8th, and 9th grades, but sometimes of only 7th and 8th or 8th and 9th grades: also **intermediate school.** —**senior high school** A corresponding division of the public schools, consisting usually of grades 10, 11, and 12.

—**industrial school** 1 An institute for the practical development of manual and industrial skills. 2 A school for the care and training of neglected children.

—**parochial school** A school, usually elementary, supported by the parish of a church, especially by a Roman Catholic church.

—**primary school** A school for the teaching of the youngest pupils; the first grades of common schools beyond kindergarten.

—**private school** A school maintained under private or corporate management, usually for profit: in the United States, contradistinguished from *public school.*

—**public school** 1 A school maintained by public funds for the free education of the children of the community, usually covering elementary and secondary grades. 2 In England, a private or endowed school not run for profit; specifically, the exclusive endowed schools preparing students for the universities, as Eton, Harrow, etc.: so called because it serves the country at large, and not merely one community.

—**secondary school** A high school or preparatory school intermediate between the grammar school and college.

—**trade school** A vocational school designed to give a knowledge of processes and a skill of hand adequate for work in a specific trade.

—**vocational school** In general, a school training in the practical application of knowledge to business, the professions, or the technical arts and crafts.

school[2] (sko͞ol) *n.* A large number of fish, whales, etc., swimming together; shoal. —*v.i.* To swim together in a school. [<Du., a crowd, school of fishes. Akin to SHOAL[2].]

school board A legal board or committee having oversight of public schools.

school·book (sko͞ol′bo͝ok′) *n.* A book for use in school; textbook.

school·boy (sko͞ol′boi′) *n.* A boy attending school.

school bus A bus used to take children to and from school, often making numerous stops along the way and therefore distinctively marked as a warning to other motorists.

school·fel·low (sko͞ol′fel′ō) *n.* A schoolmate.

school·girl (sko͞ol′gûrl′) *n.* A girl attending school.

school·house (sko͞ol′hous′) *n.* A building in which a school is conducted.

school·ing (sko͞o′ling) *n.* 1 Instruction given at school; also, any preparatory training or discipline. 2 Price paid for instructing pupils. 3 The training of horses and riders. See synonyms under EDUCATION, NURTURE.

school·man (sko͞ol′mən) *n. pl.* **·men** (-mən) One of the theologians of the Middle Ages.

school·marm (sko͞ol′märm′) *n. Colloq.* A woman schoolteacher, especially one considered to be prudish, spinsterish, or strict. Also **school′ma′am′** (-mam′).

school·mas·ter (sko͞ol′mas′tər, -mäs′-) *n.* 1 A man who teaches school. 2 One who or that which instructs or disciplines in any way:

Necessity was his *schoolmaster.* **3** A Caribbean fish *(Neomaenis apoda)* of the snapper family. See synonyms under MASTER.

school·mate (sko͞ol′māt′) *n.* A fellow pupil; a schoolfellow.

school·mis·tress (sko͞ol′mis′tris) *n.* A woman who teaches school.

school·room (sko͞ol′ro͝om′, -ro͞om′) *n.* A room in which instruction is given.

school ship A vessel in which boys and young men are trained in seamanship.

school·teach·er (sko͞ol′tē′chər) *n.* One who gives instruction in a school below the college level.

school·yard (sko͞ol′yärd′) *n.* The grounds about a school used for play.

schoon·er (sko͞o′nər) *n.* **1** A fore-and-aft rigged vessel having originally two masts, but now often three or more. **2** A prairie schooner. **3** A large beer glass, holding usually about a pint or more. [Appar. coined in New England < dial. *scoon* skim on water, prob. <Scand.]

SCHOONER

schoon·er-yacht (sko͞o′nər·yot′) *n.* A yacht rigged like a schooner.

Scho·pen·hau·er (shō′pən·hou′ər), **Arthur,** 1788–1860, German philosopher. —**Scho′·pen·hau′er·i·an** *adj.*

Scho·pen·hau·er·ism (shō′pən·hou′ə·riz′əm) *n.* The philosophy (pessimistic determinism) of Arthur Schopenhauer, who taught that egoism, manifested in the "will to live," must be overcome; that the world is evil and should not be perpetuated; and that God, free will, and the immortality of the soul are illusions.

schorl (shôrl) *n.* Tourmaline, especially the black variety: also spelled *shorl.* [<G *schörl*]

schor·la·ceous (shôr·lā′shəs) *adj.* Containing black tourmaline, as granite. [<SCHORL + -ACEOUS]

schot·tische (shot′ish) *n.* A dance in 2/4 time similar to the polka, but somewhat slower; also, the music for such a dance. [<G *(der) schottische (tanz)* (the) Scottish (dance)]

Schou·ten Islands (skhou′tən, -tə) An island group off NW New Guinea, comprising part of Netherlands New Guinea; total, 1,231 square miles.

schrik (skhrik) *n. Afrikaans* Panic or sudden fright.

Schrö·ding·er (shrœ′ding·ər), **Erwin,** 1887–1961, Austrian physicist.

schtick (shtik) *n.* See SHTICK.

Schu·bert (sho͞o′bərt, *Ger.* sho͞o′bert), **Franz Peter,** 1797–1828, Austrian composer.

schuit (skoit) *n.* A Dutch vessel, sloop-rigged, used in rivers and canals. Also **schuyt.** [<Du. *schuit, schuyt* <MDu. *schute*]

schule[1] (skül, skœl) *n. Scot.* A school.

schule[2] (sho͞ol) *n. Scot.* A shovel.

Schu·man (shü·män′), **Robert,** 1886–1963, French political leader born in Luxembourg.

Schu·mann (sho͞o′män), **Robert,** 1810–56, German composer.

Schu·mann-Heink (sho͞o′män·hīngk′), **Ernestine,** 1861–1936, U. S. dramatic contralto singer born in Austria.

Schur·man (shûr′mən), **Jacob Gould,** 1854–1942, U. S. philosopher and diplomat born in Canada; president of Princeton University 1892–1920.

Schurz (sho͝orts), **Carl,** 1829–1906, U. S. statesman, journalist, and general, born in Germany.

Schusch·nigg (sho͝osh′nik), **Kurt von,** born 1897, Austrian statesman.

schuss (sho͝os) *v.i.* To ski down a steep slope at high speed. —*n.* A straight, steep ski course, or the act of skiing this course. [<G, lit., a shot]

Schutz·staf·fel (sho͝ots′shtä′fəl) *n. pl.* **·feln** (-fəln) *German* Hitler's personal bodyguard, known as the Black Shirts; later, the chief section, the Elite Guard, of the Nazi militia, used to maintain order in Germany and occupied countries. Abbr. *SS.*

Schuy·ler (skī′lər), **Philip John,** 1733–1804, American statesman and soldier.

Schuy·ler·ville (skī′lər·vil) A town in eastern New York near Saratoga Springs; scene of Battle of Saratoga and General Burgoyne's surrender, October 17, 1777, in the American Revolution: formerly *Saratoga.*

Schuyl·kill River (sko͞ol′kil, sko͞o′kəl) A river in SE Pennsylvania, flowing 150 miles SE to the Delaware River.

schwa (shwä, shvä) *n.* **1** *Phonet.* A weak or obscure, central vowel sound occurring in most of the unstressed syllables in English speech. The sound, regardless of spelling, is that of the *a* in *alone,* the *o* in *lemon,* or the *u* in *circus*: written ə. **2** In Hebrew, the obscure vowel sound: written : and often transliterated by *e.* [<G <Hebrew *shewa*]

Schwab (shwäb), **Charles M.** 1862–1939, U. S. industrialist.

Schwa·ben (shvä′ben) The German name for SWABIA.

Schwann (shvän), **Theodor,** 1810–82, German physiologist.

schwan·pan (shwän′pän′) See SWANPAN.

Schwarz·wald (shvärts′vält) The German name for the BLACK FOREST.

Schwein·furt (shvīn′fo͝ort) A city in NW Bavaria, West Germany.

Schwei·tzer (shvī′tsər), **Albert,** 1875–1965, Alsatian clergyman, physician, missionary, philosopher, and musicologist.

Schweitzer's reagent *Chem.* An aqueous solution of cupric hydroxide precipitated in ammonium hydroxide: used as a solvent for cellulose, especially in the cuprammonium process. Also called *cuprammonia.* [after Mathias E. *Schweitzer,* 1818–1860, German chemist]

Schweiz (shvīts) The German name for SWITZERLAND.

Schwei·zer·kä·se (shvī′tsər·kā′zə) *n. German* Swiss cheese.

Schwe·rin (shve·rēn′) The capital of the former state of Mecklenburg, northern East Germany.

Schwyz (shvēts) A city of east central Switzerland near Lake Lucerne.

sci·ae·noid (sī·ē′noid) *n.* Any of a family *(Sciaenidae)* of spiny-finned, carnivorous, mostly marine fishes (order *Percomorphi*), as croakers, drums, weakfish, etc. —*adj.* Of or pertaining to the *Sciaenidae.* Also **sci·ae′nid** (-ē′nid). [<NL <L *sciaena* <Gk. *skiaina,* a kind of fish]

sci·at·ic (sī·at′ik) *adj.* Pertaining to or affecting the hip or its nerves; ischial. —*n.* A sciatic nerve or part. [<MF *sciatique* <Med. L *sciaticus,* alter. of L *ischiadicus* <Gk. *ischiadikos* < *ischion* hip, hip joint]

sci·at·i·ca (sī·at′i·kə) *n. Pathol.* **1** Neuralgia, affecting the sciatic nerve traversing the hip and thigh. **2** Any painful affection of these or adjoining parts. [<Med. L *sciatica (passio)* (the) sciatic (disease), fem. of *sciaticus* SCIATIC]

sci·ence (sī′əns) *n.* **1** Knowledge as of facts, phenomena, laws, and proximate causes, gained and verified by exact observation, organized experiment, and correct thinking; also, the sum of universal knowledge. **2** An exact and systematic statement or classification of knowledge concerning some subject or group of subjects. **3** Any department of knowledge in which the results of investigation have been systematized in the form of hypotheses and general laws subject to verification. **4** Expertness, skill, or proficiency resulting from knowledge. **5** Any one of the seven liberal arts (grammar, rhetoric, logic, arithmetic, music, geometry, astronomy): an ancient use. [<OF <L *scientia* < *sciens, -entis,* ppr. of *scire* know]

Synonyms: knowledge, art, learning, scholarship. *Knowledge* may be a medley of facts which gain real value only when coordinated and systematized by the man of *science. Art* relates to something to be done or produced by skill, *science* to something to be known. Creative *art* seeking beauty for its own sake is closely akin to fundamental *science* seeking *knowledge* for its own sake. See ART[1], KNOWLEDGE.

science fiction *n.* Fiction employing scientific ideas or devices as elements of plot or background. —**sci′ence-fic′tion** *adj.*

sci·en·tial (sī·en′shəl) *adj.* Of, characterized by, or producing knowledge or science; also, skilful; scientific; knowing; capable.

sci·en·tif·ic (sī′ən·tif′ik) *adj.* **1** Of, pertaining to, discovered by, derived from, or used in science; of the nature of science. **2** Agreeing with the rules, principles, or methods of science; accurate; systematic; exact. **3** Versed in science or a science; eminently learned or skilful. Also **sci′en·tif′i·cal.** [<F *scientifique* <LL *scientificus* < *scientia* knowledge + *facere* make; orig. trans. of Gk. *epistēmonikos* pertaining to knowledge, science] —**sci′en·tif′i·cal·ly** *adv.*

scientific method A method of inquiry depending upon the reciprocal interplay of observable data and generalizations. It consists typically of the statement of a problem and the accumulation and analysis of relevant data that may lead to the construction of a hypothesis, in turn tested by the reliability and accuracy of deductions from it and by its consistency with other hypotheses and observed data.

sci·en·tism (sī′ən·tiz′əm) *n.* **1** Adherence to or belief in the aims and methods of scientists. **2** Uncritical or unsuitable application of scientific concepts or terms.

sci·en·tist (sī′ən·tist) *n.* One versed in science or devoted to scientific study or investigation.

Sci·en·tist (sī′ən·tist) *n.* A Christian Scientist.

sci·en·tol·o·gy (sī′ən·tol′ə·jē) *n. Often cap.* A religious and psychotherapeutic cult purporting to solve personal problems, cure mental and physical disorders, and increase intelligence. [<L *scientia* science + -LOGY] —**sci′·en·tol′o·gist** *n.*

sci-fi (sī′fī) *Colloq. n.* Science fiction. —*adj.* Science-fiction.

scil·i·cet (sil′ə·set) *adv.* Namely; to wit; that is to say: introducing a word to be supplied, or an explanation: generally abbreviated *scil., sc.,* or *ss.* [<L, contraction of *scire licet* it is permitted to know]

Scil·la (sil′ə) A town at the NE end of the Strait of Messina, southern Italy, on a small promontory supposed to be the site of the cave of the legendary Scylla.

Scil·ly Islands (sil′ē) A group of 140 islands off the SW coast of Cornwall, SW England; 6.3 square miles.

scim·i·tar (sim′ə·tər) *n.* **1** An Oriental sword or saber of extreme curve. **2** A billhook of somewhat similar form. Also **scim′e·tar, scim′i·ter:** formerly variously spelled with *si-, ci-,* etc. [<MF *cimeterre*; infl. in form by Ital. *scimitarra*; both ? <Persian *shamshīr*]

SCIMITAR

scin·coid (sing′koid) *n.* One of a family *(Scincidae)* of lizardlike viviparous reptiles (order *Squamata*) with typically smooth scales; a skink. —*adj.* Of or pertaining to the *Scincidae.* Also **scin·coi·di·an** (sing·koi′dē·ən). [< NL *scincoides* <L *scincus* skink]

scin·til·la (sin·til′ə) *n.* A spark; hence, a trace; iota: usually of something abstract: There was not a *scintilla* of truth in the remark. See synonyms under PARTICLE. [<L]

scin·til·late (sin′tə·lāt) *v.* **·lat·ed, ·lat·ing** *v.i.* **1** To give off sparks. **2** To sparkle; glitter. **3** To twinkle, as a star. —*v.t.* **4** To give off as a spark or sparks. See synonyms under SHINE. [<L *scintillatus,* pp. of *scintillare* scintillate < *scintilla* a spark] —**scin′til·lat′ing** *adj.*

scin·til·la·tion (sin′tə·lā′shən) *n.* **1** The act or state of scintillating; a sparkling, tremulous flashing or twinkling. **2** A spark or sparkle. **3** The twinkling of the stars. See synonyms under LIGHT.

sci·o·lism (sī′ə·liz′əm) *n.* Charlatanism; pretentious superficial knowledge. [<LL *sciolus* a smatterer, dim. of L *scius* knowing < *scire* know]

sci·o·list (sī′ə·list) *n.* One who has a smattering of knowledge, especially a pretender to scientific attainment. —**sci′o·lis′tic, sci′o·lous** *adj.*

sci·on (sī′ən) *n.* **1** *Bot.* A cion. **2** A child or descendant. [<OF *cion,* prob. blend of *scier* saw and L *sectio, -onis* a cutting, both <L *secare* cut]

sci·oph·i·lous (sī·of′ə·ləs) *adj. Ecol.* Shade-loving; able to live in shade; thriving in the shade. [<Gk. *skia* shade + -PHILOUS]

sci·o·phyte (sī′ə·fīt) *n.* A plant growing or adapted to live in the shade. [<Gk. *skia* shade + -PHYTE] — **sci′o·phyt′ic** (-fit′ik) *adj.*

sci·os·o·phy (sī·os′ə·fē) *n.* Any system of thought founded on beliefs which are at variance with contemporary scientific knowledge and resistant to the procedures of scientific method. [<Gk. *skia* a shadow + -SOPHY] — **sci·os′o·phist** *n.*

Sci·o·to River (sī·ō′tə, -tō) A river in central and southern Ohio, flowing 237 miles south to the Ohio River.

Scip·i·o (sip′ē·ō) Name of a great Roman family, especially including **Publius Cornelius Scipio Africanus Major,** 237–183 B.C., general; defeated Hannibal at Zama 202 B.C.: called "The Elder"; and **Publius Cornelius Scipio Aemilianus Africanus Minor,** 185–129 B.C., general; burned Carthage: called "The Younger."

sci·re fa·ci·as (sī′rē fā′shē·əs) *Law Latin* A writ (or the proceeding under it) commanding the party against whom it is issued to show cause why the plaintiff should not have advantage of or execution on a judicial record, or why a nonjudicial record should not be repealed or annulled; literally, that you cause to know: abbr. *sci. fa.*, or *s. f.*

scir·rhus (skir′əs, sir′-) *n. pl.* **scir·rhi** (skir′ī) or **scir·rhus·es** *Pathol.* A hard tumor; specifically, a hard cancerous tumor. [<NL <L *scirros* <Gk. *skirrhos* a tumor < *skiros* hard] — **scir·rhos·i·ty** (ski·ros′ə·tē, si-) *n.* — **scir′·rhous, scir′rhoid** *adj.*

scis·sile (sis′il) *adj.* Capable of being cut or split easily and evenly. [<L *scissilis* < *scissus,* pp. of *scindere* cut]

scis·sion (sizh′ən, sish′-) *n.* The act of cutting or splitting, or the state of being cut; hence, any division. [<OF <LL *scissio, -onis* < *scissus,* pp. of *scindere* cut]

scis·sor (siz′ər) *v.t.* & *v.i.* To cut with scissors.

scis·sor·er (siz′ər·ər) *n.* One using scissors; hence, a compiler.

scis·sors (siz′ərz) *n. pl.* & *sing.* **1** A cutting implement with handles and a pair of blades pivoted face to face: sometimes a **pair of scissors. 2** In wrestling, a hold secured by clasping the legs about the body or head of the opponent. **3** Gymnastic feats in which the movement of the legs suggests the opening and closing of scissors. [<OF *cisoires* <LL *cisoria,* pl. of *cisorium* a cutting instrument < *caedere* cut; infl. in form by L *scissor* one who cuts < *scindere* cut]

scissors kick In swimming, a kick performed usually with the side stroke, in which both legs are thrust apart, the upper leg bent at the knee while the lower is kept straight, then brought sharply together.

scis·sor·tail (siz′ər·tāl′) *n.* A flycatcher (*Muscivora forficata*) of the SW United States and Mexico having a scissorlike tail.

scis·sure (sizh′ər, sish′-) *n.* **1** A lengthwise cut; fissure. **2** Any division, rupture, or schism. [<MF <L *scissura* < *scissus.* See SCISSION.]

sci·u·rine (sī′yōō·rīn, -rin) *adj.* Belonging or pertaining to a family (*Sciuridae*) of rodents, including squirrels, chipmunks, woodchucks, marmots, etc. — *n.* One of the *Sciuridae.* [< L *sciurus* a squirrel <Gk. *skiouros* < *skia* a shadow + *oura* a tail + -INE[1]]

sci·u·roid (sī·yōōr′oid) *adj.* **1** Of or pertaining to the *Sciuridae.* **2** *Bot.* Resembling a squirrel's tail, as the tufted spikes of certain cereal grasses. [<NL <L *sciurus* a squirrel + Gk. *eidos* a form]

sclaff (sklaf) *v.i.* **1** In golf, to strike the ground with the club before hitting the ball. — *v.t.* **2** In golf: **a** To strike (the ball) or make (a stroke) in this manner. **b** To drag (the club) thus. — *n.* **1** A slight slap or blow; the noise so made. **2** A light shoe; a slipper. **3** The golf stroke made by sclaffing. [< dial. E (Scottish) *sclaf* slap, shuffle; imit.]

Sclav (skläv), **Sclav·ic** (sklä′vik), etc. Obsolete forms of SLAV, etc.

scle·ra (sklir′ə) *n. Anat.* The hard, firm, fibrous outer coat of the eye, continuous with the cornea; the white of the eye. Also **scle·rot·i·ca** (sklə·rot′i·kə). See illustration under EYE. [<NL <Gk. *sklēros* hard]

scle·ren·chy·ma (sklə·reng′kə·mə) *n. Bot.* The tough, stony, thick-walled tissue composing the hard parts of plants. [<NL <Gk. *sklēros* hard + *enchyma* an infusion] — **scle·ren·chym·a·tous** (sklir′eng·kim′ə·təs) *adj.*

scle·ri·a·sis (sklə·rī′ə·sis) *n. Pathol.* Any morbid hardening or induration of parts. [<NL <Gk. *sklēriasis* < *sklēria* hardness < *sklēros* hard]

scle·rite (sklir′īt) *n.* **1** *Zool.* **a** One of the definite hard pieces of the integument of an arthropod. **b** A hard element in the integument of a polyp. **2** A spicule. [<Gk. *sklēros* hard + -ITE[1]] — **scle·rit·ic** (sklə·rit′ik) *adj.*

scle·ri·tis (sklə·rī′tis) *n. Pathol.* Rheumatic ophthalmia; inflammation of the sclera of the eye. Also **scle·ro·ti·tis** (sklir′ō·tī′tis, skler′-). [<NL < *sclera* the white of the eye] — **scle′·ro·tit′ic** (-tit′ik) *adj.*

sclero– *combining form* Hardness; hard: *scleroderma.* Also, before vowels, **scler–.** [<Gk. *sklēros* hard]

scle·ro·der·ma (sklir′ō·dûr′mə, skler′-) *n. Pathol.* Hardening of the skin. [<NL <Gk. *sklēros* hard + *derma* skin]

scle·ro·der·ma·tous (sklir′ō·dûr′mə·təs, skler′-) *adj. Zool.* Provided with a horny or bony covering, as an armadillo. [<Gk. *sklēros* hard + *derma, -atos* skin]

scle·roid (sklir′oid) *adj. Biol.* Hard; sclerous; hard in texture, as the shells of nuts, etc. [<Gk. *sklēroeidēs* < *sklēros* hard + *eidos* form]

scle·ro·ma (sklə·rō′mə) *n. Pathol.* Hardening of the cellular tissue; sclerosis; scleroderma. [<NL <Gk. *sklērōma* < *sklēroein* harden < *sklēros* hard]

scle·rom·e·ter (sklə·rom′ə·tər) *n.* An instrument for determining the degree of hardness of a mineral.

scle·rosed (sklə·rōst′) *adj.* Affected with sclerosis; grown abnormally hard. [<SCLEROS(IS) + -ED[3]]

scle·ro·sis (sklə·rō′sis) *n.* **1** *Pathol.* The morbid thickening and hardening of a tissue; especially, the hardening of the coats of the arteries. **2** *Bot.* The hardening of a plant cell wall by the formation of lignin in it. [<Med. L *sclirosis* <Gk. *sklērōsis* < *sklēroein* harden < *sklēros* hard] — **scle·ro′sal** *adj.*

scle·rot·ic (sklə·rot′ik) *adj.* **1** Dense; hard, as the white of the eye. **2** *Pathol.* Pertaining to or affected with sclerosis. [<NL *scleroticus* <Gk. *sklērotēs* hardness < *sklēroein.* See SCLEROMA.]

scle·ro·ti·um (sklə·rō′shē·əm) *n. pl.* **·ti·a** (-shē·ə) *Bot.* A compact horny mass of mycelium, found in certain higher fungi; especially, in the myxomycetes, a plasmodium, or part of a plasmodium, dry and hard, which for some time remains dormant. [<NL <Gk. *sklēros* hard] — **scle·ro′ti·oid** (-shē·oid), **scle·ro′tial** (-shəl) *adj.*

scle·rot·o·my (sklə·rot′ə·mē) *n. Surg.* Incision of the sclera. [<SCLER(A) + -(O)TOMY]

scle·rous (sklir′əs) *adj.* Hard or indurated; bony. [<SCLER(O)- + -OUS]

scob (skob) *n.* A defect in fabric caused by failure of the warp to interlace in the weaving. [? <Irish and Scottish Gaelic *sgolb* a splinter]

scoff (skôf, skof) *v.i.* To speak with contempt or derision; jeer: often with *at.* — *v.t.* To deride; mock. — *n.* An expression or an object of contempt or derision. See synonyms under SNEER. [ME *scof,* prob. <Scand. Cf. Dan. *skof* a jest, mockery.] — **scoff′er** *n.* — **scoff′·ing·ly** *adv.*

Synonyms (verb): deride, flout, gibe, jeer, mock, sneer, taunt. See RIDICULE; SCORN. *Antonyms*: see synonyms for PRAISE.

scoff·law (skôf′lô′, skof′-) *n.* One who scoffs at the law; especially, a habitual or deliberate violator of traffic, safety, or public-health regulations.

scog·ger (skog′ər) *n. Brit. Dial.* A heavy woolen garment worn for protection as a gaiter, or as a sleeve. [Cf. *cocker* a boot, quiver, OE *cocer*]

scold (skōld) *v.t.* To find fault with harshly. — *v.i.* To find fault harshly or continuously. — *n.* One who scolds, especially a virago: also **scold′er.** [Appar. <ON *skāld* a poet, satirist] — **scold′ing** *adj.* & *n.* — **scold′ing·ly** *adv.*

scol·e·cite (skol′ə·sīt, skō′lə-) *n.* A vitreous or silky, colorless, hydrous silicate of calcium and aluminum; a zeolite, isomorphous with natrolite. [<Gk. *skōlēx, -ēkos* a worm; so called because it sometimes curls up when heated]

sco·lex (skō′leks) *n. pl.* **sco·le·ces** (skō·lē′sēz) or **scol·i·ces** (skol′ə·sēz, skō′lə-) *Zool.* The knoblike head of a tapeworm, equipped with a circular disk of hooks and a group of two or four suckers. [<NL <Gk. *skōlēx* a worm]

sco·li·o·sis (skō′lē·ō′sis, skol′ē-) *n. Pathol.* A lateral curvature of the spine. Also **sco′li·o′·ma.** [<NL <Gk. *skoliōsis* < *skolios* curved] — **sco′li·ot′ic** (-ot′ik) *adj.*

scol·lop (skol′əp), etc. See SCALLOP, etc.

scol·o·pen·drid (skol′ə·pen′drid) *n.* One of a family of chilopods (*Scolopendridae*) including the typical centipedes. [<NL <L *scolopendra* <Gk. *skolopendra* a milliped] — **scol′o·pen′·drine** (-drīn, -drin) *adj.*

scom·broid (skom′broid) *adj.* Of or pertaining to a family (*Scombridae*) of acanthopterygian fishes, including mackerels, tunnies, and related genera. — *n.* One of the *Scombridae.* [<NL <L *scomber* a mackerel <Gk. *skombros*]

sconce[1] (skons) *n.* **1** A small earthwork or fort. **2** A protective shelter, covering, or screen. [<Du. *schanz* a fortress, wicker basket; infl. in form by SCONCE[2]]

sconce[2] (skons) *n.* An ornamental wall bracket for holding a candle or other light. [<OF *esconse* a dark lantern, hiding place <Med. L *sconsa,* short for L *absconsa,* pp. fem. of *abscondere* hide]

sconce[3] (skons) *n. Colloq.* **1** The head or skull. **2** Brains; wit. [? Special use of SCONCE[1]]

SCONCE

sconce[4] (skons) *Brit. n.* A light fine or penalty. — *v.t.* **sconced, sconc·ing** To fine; mulct. [? <SCONCE[3]]

scone (skōn, skon) *n. Scot.* Originally, a thin oatmeal cake, baked on a griddle; hence, a teacake or soda biscuit.

Scone (skōōn, skōn) A village in SE Perthshire, Scotland; coronation place of Scottish kings, 1153 to 1488. — **the Stone of Scone** The stone on which early Scottish kings were crowned: brought to England by Edward I and placed under the seat of the Coronation Chair in Westminster Abbey.

scon·ner (skon′ər) *Scot. v.i.* To feel loathing or disgust. — *n.* Loathing; abhorrence. Also spelled *scunner.*

scoop (skōōp) *n.* **1** A shovel-like instrument or large shovel with high sides for scooping. **2** A small shovel-like implement or ladle used by grocers, druggists, etc. **3** An implement for bailing, as water from a boat. **4** A spoon-shaped instrument for using in a cavity: a surgeons' *scoop.* **5** An act of scooping; a movement in a curved line convex downward. **6** The amount scooped at once: a *scoop* of water. **7** *Colloq.* A large gain, especially in speculation: He made a big *scoop* on that deal. **8** A bowl-shaped cavity; hollow excavation. **9** In newspaper slang, a news story obtained and published ahead of rival papers. — *v.t.* **1** To take or dip out with or as with a scoop. **2** To hollow out, as with a scoop; excavate. **3** To empty with a scoop. **4** *Colloq.* To heap up or gather in as if in scoopfuls; amass. **5** In newspaper slang, to obtain and publish a news story before (a rival). [Fusion of MDu. *schope* a vessel for bailing out water, and *schoppe* a shovel] — **scoop′er** *n.* — **scoop′·ful′** *n.*

scoot (skōōt) *v.i. Colloq.* To go quickly; dart off. — *n.* The act of scooting; a darting off hurriedly. [Prob. <Scand.; cf. ON *skiōta* shoot. Akin to SHOOT.]

scoot·er (skōō′tər) *n.* **1** A child's vehicle consisting of a board mounted on two tandem wheels and steered by a long handle attached to the front axle: the rider stands with one foot on the board, using the other foot to push. **2** A similar vehicle powered by an internal-combustion motor and provided with a driver's seat: also *motor scooter.* **3** A sailboat so constructed that it may be sailed in water and on ice. **4** A small plow with a single shovel used for opening the soil: also *scooter plow.*

scop (skop) *n. Obs.* A bard, minstrel, or poet. [OE]

Sco·pas (skō′pəs) Greek sculptor of the fourth century B.C.

scope (skōp) *n.* **1** A range of view or action; outlook. **2** Room for the exercise of faculties or function; extent; capacity for achievement. **3** End in view; aim; purpose. **4** Length or sweep, as of a cable. **5** The range of a missile. [<Ital. *scopo* <L *scopus* <Gk. *skopos* a watcher < *skopeein* look at]

-scope *combining form* An instrument for viewing, observing, or indicating: *microscope.* [<Gk. *skopos* a watcher < *skopeein* watch]

Scopes (skōps), **John T(homas),** 1901–1970, U. S. educator; prosecuted for teaching evolution in Tennessee.

sco·po·drom·ic (skō′pə·drom′ik) *adj.* Pursuing a course in the line of sight; homing: said of guided missiles. [<Gk. *skopos* a watcher + *dromos* a running]

sco·pol·a·mine (skō·pol′ə·mēn, -min, skō′pə·lam′ēn, -in) *n. Chem.* An alkaloid, $C_{17}H_{21}O_4N$, extracted from the dried rhizomes of certain solanaceous plants, as *Scopolia carniolica*: its salts are used in medicine as a mydriatic, hypnotic, and sedative: also called *hyoscine.* [<G *scopolamin* <NL *Scopolia,* genus name of plants from which it is obtained, after G. A. *Scopoli,* 1723–88, Italian naturalist]

sco·po·line (skō′pə·lēn, -lin) *n. Chem.* A crystalline compound, $C_8H_{13}O_2N$, derived from scopolamine: also called *oscine.* [<SCOPOL(AMINE) + -INE[2]]

sco·po·phil·i·a (skō′pə·fil′ē·ə) *n. Psychiatry* Pleasure, especially of a sexual nature, derived from the act of observing, contemplating, or looking at something. Also **scop′to·phil′i·a** (skop′tə-). [<Gk. *skopos* a watcher + -PHILIA]

sco·po·pho·bi·a (skō′pə·fō′bē·ə) *n. Psychiatry* A morbid fear of being looked at. [<Gk. *skopos* a watcher + -PHOBIA]

scop·u·late (skop′yə·lit, -lāt) *adj.* Broom-shaped. [<L *scopulae* a little broom, pl. of *scopula* a broom twig, dim. of *scopa* a twig, a broom]

Sco·pus (skō′pəs), **Mount** A peak in central Palestine, NE of Jerusalem; 2,736 feet.

-scopy *combining form* Observation; viewing: *microscopy.* [<Gk. *-skopia* < *skopeein* watch]

scor·bu·tic (skôr·byōō′tik) *adj.* Relating to, like, or affected with scurvy: also **scor·bu′ti·cal.** — *n.* A person affected with scurvy. [< NL *scorbuticus* <Med. L *scorbutus* SCORBUTUS] — **scor·bu′ti·cal·ly** *adv.*

scor·bu·tus (skôr·byōō′təs) *n. Pathol.* Scurvy. [<NL <Med. L, appar. <MDu. *scheurbot, scheurbuik* < *scheuren* break, lacerate + *bot, buik* belly]

scorch (skôrch) *v.t.* **1** To change the color, taste, etc., of by slight burning; char the surface of. **2** To wither or shrivel by heat. **3** To affect painfully, as if by heat; criticize severely. — *v.i.* **4** To become scorched. **5** *Colloq.* To go at high speed. — *n.* **1** A superficial burn. **2** A mark caused by heat, as a slight burn. [Prob. related to ME *skorken* <ON *skorpna* dry up, shrivel; infl. in form by OF *escorchier* flay <L *excorticare* < *ex-* off + *cortex, -icis* bark] — **scorch′ing** *adj.* — **scorch′·ing·ly** *adv.*

scorched-earth policy (skôrcht′ûrth′) The policy of destroying all crops, industrial equipment, dwellings, etc., before an advancing enemy so as to leave nothing for his use or aid.

scorch·er (skôr′chər) *n.* **1** Something that scorches or is hot enough to scorch: Today was a *scorcher.* **2** Something severe or caustic, as criticism. **3** One who or that which moves or may move at great speed.

scor·da·to (skôr·dä′tō) *adj. Music* Out of tune; altered in tuning; made discordant. [<Ital., pp. of *scordare* be out of tune, short for *discordare* <L. See DISCORD.]

scor·da·tu·ra (skôr′dä·tōō′rä) *n. Music* An intentional changing of the normal tuning of a stringed instrument: resorted to for effect. [<Ital. *scordato* SCORDATO]

score (skôr, skōr) *n.* **1 a** A notch, cut, groove, mark, or line. **b** A notch or line used in keeping a tally or score; hence, an account or reckoning kept by notches or marks. **2** Any record, especially of indebtedness; debt; bill: to run up a *score* at a grocery. **3** Something charged or laid up against one; grudge; difference: to pay off old *scores*; an account; a credit; motive. **4** The record of the winning points, counts, or runs in competitions and games; also, the whole number of such points made by a player or side or in the game. **5** *Music* The collective notes in which a composition is written, when placed on two or more connected staffs one above another. **6** The number twenty, originally indicated by a special notch on a tally; twenty units or things: in the plural often indicating indefinitely large numbers. **7** *Psychol.* A quantitative value assigned to an individual or group response to a test or series of tests, as of intelligence or performance. — *v.* **scored, scor·ing** *v.t.* **1** To mark with notches, cuts, or lines. **2** To mark with cuts or lines for the purpose of keeping a tally or record. **3** To obliterate or cross out by means of a line drawn through: with *out.* **4** To make or gain, as points, runs, etc. **5** To count for a score of, as in games: A touchdown *scores* six points. **6** To rate or grade, as an examination paper; evaluate. **7** *Music* **a** To orchestrate. **b** To arrange or adapt for an instrument. **8** *U.S.* To criticize severely; scourge. **9** In cooking, to make superficial cuts in (meat, etc.). — *v.i.* **10** To make points, runs, etc., as in a game. **11** To keep score. **12** To make notches, cuts, etc. **13** To win an advantage; achieve a success. [OE *scoru* <ON *skor* a notch, tally] — **scor′er** *n.*

score-keep·er (skôr′kē′pər, skōr′-) *n.* One who keeps score.

Scores·by Sound (skôrz′bē, skōrz′-) An inlet and fjord system extending 200 miles into eastern Greenland from the Greenland Sea.

sco·ri·a (skôr′ē·ə, skō′rē·ə) *n. pl.* **·ri·ae** (-i·ē) Fragmentary lava; slag; refuse of ores or metals. [<L <Gk. *skōria* refuse < *skōr* dung] — **sco′ri·a′ceous** (-ā′shəs) *adj.*

sco·ri·form (skôr′ə·fôrm, skō′rə-) *adj.* Resembling scoria; in the form of dross.

sco·ri·fy (skôr′ə·fī, skō′rə-) *v.t.* **·fied, ·fy·ing** *Metall.* **1** To separate, as gold or silver, from an ore by smelting with lead, borax, etc. **2** To reduce to scoria or dross. [< SCORI(A) + -FY] — **sco′ri·fi·ca′tion** *n.*

scorn (skôrn) *n.* **1** Disdain; a feeling entertained toward someone or something as so inferior as to be unworthy of attention. **2** The expression of such a feeling; derision. **3** An object of supreme contempt. — *v.t.* **1** To hold in or treat with contempt; despise. **2** To reject with scorn; disdain; spurn. — *v.i.* **3** *Obs.* To mock; jeer. [<OF *escarn* < *escarnir* <Gmc.] — **scorn′er** *n.* — **scorn′ful** *adj.* — **scorn′ful·ly** *adv.* — **scorn′ful·ness** *n.*

Synonyms (noun): contempt, contumely, derision, despite, disdain, dishonor, mockery, scoff, scoffing, sneer, sneering, taunt. *Antonyms*: admiration, approbation, approval, attention, consideration, courtesy, deference, esteem, honor, regard, respect, reverence.

Synonyms (verb): abhor, contemn, despise, detest, disdain, spurn. *Antonyms*: see synonyms for CHERISH.

scor·pae·noid (skôr·pē′noid) *adj.* Belonging to a family (*Scorpaenidae*) of spiny-finned marine fishes. — *n.* A scorpaenoid fish: also **scor·pae′nid** (-nid). [<NL <L *scorpaena* a kind of fish + Gk. *eidos* form]

Scor·pi·o (skôr′pē·ō) **1** *Astron.* The Scorpion, a zodiacal constellation between Libra and Sagittarius, containing the brilliant red star Antares. See CONSTELLATION. **2** The eighth sign of the zodiac. Also **Scor′pi·on** (-ən), **Scor′·pi·us** (-əs). [<L, a scorpion]

scor·pi·oid (skôr′pē·oid) *adj.* **1** Scorpionlike. **2** Rolled or curled like the tail of a scorpion: specifically said of a terminal unilateral inflorescence, as in the borage family of plants. [<Gk. *skorpioeidēs* < *skorpios* a scorpion + *eidos* form]

scor·pi·on (skôr′pē·ən) *n.* **1** One of an order (*Scorpionida*) of rapacious arachnids with elongated, lobsterlike bodies and segmented tails which bear a poisonous sting: they are chiefly tropical but occur as far north as Canada. **2** The harmless pine lizard (genus *Sceloporus*) of the southern United States. **3** An instrument of chastisement; a whip or scourge. I *Kings* xii 11. **4** An ancient ballistic engine. [<OF <L *scorpio, -onis* <Gk. *skorpios*]

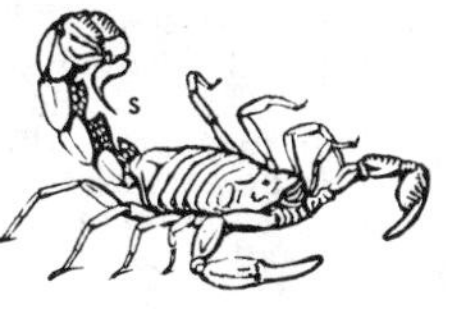

INDIAN SCORPION
s. Stinger.

scorpion fly A mecopterous insect (genus *Panorpa*) living on the banks of shaded streams and in moist woods: in the male, the end of the abdomen is upcurved like a scorpion's sting. See illustration under INSECTS (beneficial).

Scorpion's Heart *Astron.* The star Antares in the constellation Scorpio.

scot (skot) *n.* An assessment; tax; a contribution, reckoning, or fine. [Fusion of ON *skot,* OF *escot*; ? infl. by OE *sceot, scot* payment]

Scot (skot) *n.* **1** A native of Scotland; a Scotsman; formerly, a Gaelic Highlander. **2** One of a Gaelic people who migrated in the fifth century to northwestern Britain from Ireland. [OE *Scottas,* pl., the Irish <LL *Scotus, Scoti* <OIrish *Scuit*]

scot and lot An assessment in Great Britain formerly laid on all of a parish or borough, according to their ability to pay; also, figuratively, obligations of every kind.

scotch[1] (skoch) *v.t.* **1** To cut; scratch. **2** To wound so as to maim or cripple. **3** To put down; crush or suppress. **4** To dress, as stone, with a pick. — *n.* **1** A superficial cut; a scratch; a notch. **2** A line traced on the ground, as for hopscotch. [Origin uncertain]

scotch[2] (skoch) *v.t.* To block, as a wheel or log, with a chock or wedge to prevent moving or slipping. — *n.* A block put behind or under something, as a wheel, to prevent rolling or sliding. [Origin unknown]

Scotch (skoch) *n.* **1** The people of Scotland collectively: with *the.* **2** One or all of the dialects spoken by the people of Scotland. **3** Scotch whisky. — *adj.* Of or pertaining to Scotland, its inhabitants, or their language; Scottish; Scots.

◆ **Scotch, Scots, Scottish** Of these three proper adjectives, the form *Scotch* developed in the dialects of the Midland and southern England, and is accepted even in Scotland as applying to *Scotch* plaid, *Scotch* terriers, *Scotch* whisky, etc.; in Scotland and in northern England, however, the forms *Scots* and *Scottish* (earlier *Scottis*) prevailed, and are preferred as applying to the people, culture, and institutions of Scotland: *Scots* or *Scottish* English, the *Scottish* church. This distinction is now widely accepted.

Scotch broom See under BROOM.

Scotch elm The wych-elm.

Scotch grain Heavy, durable, chrome-tanned leather with pebbled grain, usually of cowhide.

Scotch·man (skoch′mən) *n. pl.* **·men** (-mən) A Scot; Scotsman.

Scotch stone See AYR STONE.

Scotch tape A rolled strip of transparent cellulose tape having an adhesive on one side: a trade name.

Scotch terrier See under TERRIER.

Scotch whisky Whisky having rather a smoky flavor and made (originally in Scotland) from malted barley.

Scotch woodcock Eggs cooked and served on toast or crackers spread with anchovy paste.

sco·ter (skō′tər) *n.* A sea duck (genera *Oidemia* and *Melanitta*) of northern regions, having the bill gibbous or swollen at the base, especially the **American scoter** (*O. americana*) also called *coot,* or **scoter duck.** [< dial. E *scote,* var. of SCOOT]

scot-free (skot′frē′) *adj.* Free from scot; untaxed; unharmed.

sco·ti·a (skō′shē·ə, -shə) *n. Archit.* A concave molding common in the bases of classical columns. [<L <Gk. *skotia* darkness < *skotos*; so called from the darkness in its concavity]

Sco·tia (skō′shə) The Medieval Latin name for SCOTLAND.

Sco·tism (skō′tiz·əm) *n.* The scholastic system and metaphysical doctrines of the Scottish philosopher John Duns Scotus (13th century): a kind of formalism. — **Sco′tist** *n.* — **Sco·tis′·tic** *adj.*

Scot·land (skot′lənd) A political division and the northern part of Great Britain; a separate kingdom until its legislative union with England, 1707; 30,405 square miles; capital, Edinburgh.

Scotland Yard 1 The former headquarters of the London metropolitan police, situated in Great Scotland Yard, a short street in central London; removed to **New Scotland Yard,** on the Thames Embankment, in 1890. 2 The police force at headquarters; specifically, the detective bureau of the London police.

scoto- *combining form* Darkness: *scotophobia.* Also, before vowels, **scot-.** [<Gk. *skotos* darkness]

sco·to·ma (skə·tō′mə) *n. pl.* **·ma·ta** (-mə·tə) *Pathol.* A defect in the field of vision; a blind or dark spot. [<LL <Gk. *skotōma* dizziness < *skotoein* darken < *skotos* darkness]

scot·o·phil·i·a (skot′ə·fil′ē·ə) *n.* A love of darkness. [<SCOTO- + -PHILIA]

scot·o·pho·bi·a (skot′ə·fō′bē·ə) *n.* A morbid fear of darkness: also called *nyctophobia.* [<SCOTO- + -PHOBIA]

sco·to·pi·a (skə·tō′pē·ə) *n. Physiol.* Adaptation of the eye for night vision. [<NL <Gk. *skotos* darkness + *ōps, ōpos* an eye] **—sco·top′ic** (-top′ik) *adj.*

Scots (skots) *adj.* Scottish. **—***n.* The Scottish dialect of English. [Earlier *Scottis.* var. of SCOTTISH]

Scots·man (skots′mən) *n. pl.* **·men** (-mən) A Scot: the preferred term.

Scott (skot), **Dred,** 1795?–1858, U. S. Negro, central figure in Supreme Court decision. **—Sir George Gilbert,** 1811–78, English architect. **—Robert Falcon,** 1868–1912, English Antarctic explorer; reached South Pole, Jan. 17, 1912; perished on return journey. **—Sir Walter,** 1771–1832, Scottish novelist and poet. **—Winfield,** 1786–1866, U. S. general in the War of 1812 and Mexican and Civil Wars.

Scot·ti·cism (skot′ə·siz′əm) *n.* A form of expression or an idiom peculiar to the Scottish people.

Scot·tish (skot′ish) *adj.* Pertaining to or characteristic of Scotland, its inhabitants, or their language. **—***n.* 1 The dialect of English spoken in Scotland, especially in the Lowlands; Scots. 2 The people of Scotland collectively: with *the.* [OE *Scottisc* < *Scotta* a Scot]

Scottish Gaelic The Goidelic language of the Scottish Highlands.

scoun·drel (skoun′drəl) *n.* A mean, thoroughgoing rascal; a rogue; villain. **—***adj.* Scoundrelly. [Prob. dim. <AF *escoundre,* OF *escoundre* abscond <L *ex-* off + *condere* hide]

scoun·drel·dom (skoun′drəl·dəm) *n.* Scoundrels collectively; scoundrelism.

scoun·drel·ism (skoun′drəl·iz′əm) *n.* The conduct or characteristics of scoundrels; rascality.

scoun·drel·ly (skoun′drəl·ē) *adj.* 1 Having the character of a scoundrel. 2 Pertaining to or characteristic of a scoundrel; rascally.

scour[1] (skour) *v.t.* 1 To clean or brighten by thorough washing and rubbing, as with sand or steel wool. 2 To remove dirt, etc., from; clean: to *scour* wool. 3 To remove by or as by rubbing away. 4 To clear by means of a strong current of water; flush. 5 To purge the bowels of. 6 To clean (wheat) before milling. **—***v.i.* 7 To rub something vigorously so as to clean or brighten it. 8 To become bright or clean by rubbing. See synonyms under CLEANSE. **—***n.* 1 The act of scouring. 2 A place scoured, as by running water. 3 A cleanser used in cleaning wool. 4 *Usually pl.* A watery diarrhea in cattle. [Prob. <MDu. *schuren* <OF *escurer,* ult. <L *ex-* out + *curare* take care of < *cura* care]

scour[2] (skour) *v.t.* 1 To range over or through, as in making a search. 2 To move or run swiftly over or along. **—***v.i.* 3 To range about, as in making a search. 4 To move or run swiftly. [ME *scoure.* Cf. ON *skura* rush, run.]

scour·er[1] (skour′ər) *n.* 1 One who or that which cleanses, removes stains, etc. 2 A cathartic. 3 A grain scourer. [<SCOUR[1]]

scour·er[2] (skour′ər) *n.* One who prowls about the streets by night; a vagabond. [<SCOUR[2]]

scourge (skûrj) *n.* 1 A whip for inflicting suffering or punishment. 2 Any instrumentality or means for causing suffering or death; hence, severe punishment; also, a cause of suffering. **—***v.t.* **scourged, scourg·ing** 1 To whip severely; lash; flog. 2 To punish severely; chastise; afflict. See synonyms under BEAT. [<AF *escorge* <LL *excoriare* flay <L *ex-* off + *corium* a hide] **—scourg′er** *n.*

Scourge of God Attila, king of the Huns.

scour·ing rush (skour′ing) Any species of horsetail, formerly much used for polishing wood and metal; scrub grass.

scour·ings (skour′ingz) *n. pl.* The residue after scouring: said especially of grain.

scouse (skous) *n.* A sailor's dish of sea biscuit and vegetables with or without meat; a hasty pudding of corn and rye meal. [Short for LOBSCOUSE]

scout[1] (skout) *n.* 1 One who or that which is engaged in scouting; specifically, a person sent out to observe and get information, as of the position or strength of an enemy in war. 2 The act of scouting. 3 At Oxford University, an undergraduate's manservant. 4 In cricket, a fielder: applied chiefly to one who fields at a distance in practice. 5 A boy scout; a girl scout. See synonyms under SPY. **—***v.t.* To observe or spy upon for the purpose of gaining information; reconnoiter, as an enemy position. **—***v.i.* To go or act as a scout. **—to scout around** To go in search. [<OF *escoute* a listener, listening < *escouter* listen <L *auscultare*] **—scout′er** *n.*

scout[2] (skout) *v.t.* & *v.i.* To reject with disdain; mock; jeer. See synonyms under RIDICULE. [<Scand. Cf. ON *skūta* a taunt.]

scout car A lightly armored motor car for reconnaissance work.

scouth (sko͞oth) *n. Scot.* Room for movement; scope.

scouth·er (skō′thər, sko͞o′-) *v.t. Scot.* To toast over a gridiron; scorch; singe. Also **scowd·er** (sko͞o′dər).

scout·mas·ter (skout′mas′tər, -mäs′-) *n.* The leader of a troop of Boy Scouts.

scow (skou) *n.* A large boat with a flat bottom and square ends: chiefly used as a lighter. [<Du. *schouw* a boat propelled by a pole <MDu. *schoude*]

scowl (skoul) *n.* 1 A lowering of the brows, as in anger, strong disapproval, or sullenness. 2 Gloomy aspect. **—***v.i.* 1 To lower and contract the brows in anger, sullenness, or disapproval. 2 To look threatening; lower. **—***v.t.* 3 To affect or express by scowling. [ME *skoul,* prob. <Scand. Cf. Dan. *skule.*] **—scowl′er** *n.* **—scowl′ing·ly** *adv.*

scrab·ble (skrab′əl) *v.* **·bled, ·bling** *v.i.* 1 To scratch, scrape, or paw, as with the hands. 2 To make irregular or meaningless marks; scribble. 3 To struggle or strive. **—***v.t.* 4 To make meaningless marks on; scribble on. 5 To gather hurriedly; scrape together. **—***n.* 1 The act of scrabbling; a moving on hands and feet or knees. 2 A scrambling effort. 3 A sparse growth: a *scrabble* of underbrush. [<Du. *schrabbelen,* freq. of *schrabben* scratch]

scrag (skrag) *v.t.* **scragged, scrag·ging** *Colloq.* To use roughly; wring the neck of; specifically, to kill by hanging; garrote. [< *n.*] **—***n.* 1 Something thin or lean and rough; a lean or bony piece or end of meat, especially from the neck. 2 *Slang* The neck. 3 A lean, bony person or animal. [Prob. <Scand. Cf. Norw. *skragg* a lean, feeble person.]

scrag·gly (skrag′lē) *adj.* **·gli·er, ·gli·est** Unkempt; shaggy; irregular; jagged. [Prob. <SCRAGG(Y) + -LY]

scrag·gy (skrag′ē) *adj.* **·gi·er, ·gi·est** 1 Rough. 2 Lean; scrawny; bony. [<SCRAG + -Y[1]] **—scrag′gi·ly** *adv.* **—scrag′gi·ness** *n.*

scraich (skrākh) *Scot. v.i.* To scream harshly; screech, as a fowl. **—***n.* A shrill cry; scream; screech. Also **scraigh.**

scram (skram) *v.i.* **scrammed, scram·ming** *U.S. Slang* To go away; leave quickly. [Prob. short for SCRAMBLE]

scram·ble (skram′bəl) *v.* **·bled, ·bling** *v.i.* 1 To move by clambering or crawling on hands and feet. 2 To struggle with others in a disorderly manner; scuffle; also, to strive for something in such a manner. **—***v.t.* 3 To mix together haphazardly or confusedly. 4 To gather or collect hurriedly or confusedly. 5 To cook (eggs) with the yolks and whites stirred together, usually with milk and butter. 6 *Telecom.* To invert or otherwise alter the frequency spectrum of (radio or wireless messages) so as to insure secrecy. **—***n.* The act of scrambling; a disorderly performance or struggle. [Prob. nasalized var. of SCRABBLE]

scrambled eggs Eggs prepared by stirring together the whites and yolks while cooking, usually with milk and butter.

scram·bler (skram′blər) *n.* 1 One who or that which scrambles. 2 *Telecom.* A device for altering the frequencies of radio and wireless signals during transmission.

scran·nel (skran′əl) *Archaic adj.* Thin; lean; reedy; slight; also, harsh. **—***n.* A lean person. [Prob. <Scand. Cf. Norw. *skrann* lean.]

Scran·ton (skran′tən) A city in NE Pennsylvania; an anthracite and manufacturing center.

scrap[1] (skrap) *n.* 1 A small piece cut or broken from something; fragment. 2 A brief extract. 3 *pl.* Pieces of crisp fat tissue after the oil has been expressed by cooking. 4 Old or refuse metal. See synonyms under PARTICLE. **—***v.t.* **scrapped, scrap·ping** 1 To break up into scrap; make scrap of. 2 To discard; throw away. **—***adj.* Having the form of scraps; discarded after use: *scrap* metal. [< ON *skrap* scrapings, scraps < *skrappa* scrape. Akin to SCRAPE.]

scrap[2] (skrap) *v.i.* **scrapped, scrap·ping** To fight; quarrel. **—***n.* A scrimmage; slight disagreement; scuffle; squabble. [<SCRAPE, *n.* (def. 2)]

scrap·book (skrap′bo͝ok′) *n.* 1 A blank book in which to paste pictures, cuttings from periodicals, etc. 2 A personal notebook.

scrape (skrāp) *v.* **scraped, scrap·ing** *v.t.* 1 To rub, as with something rough or sharp, so as to abrade or to remove an outer layer or adherent matter. 2 To remove thus: with *off, away,* etc. 3 To rub (a rough or sharp object) across a surface. 4 To rub roughly across or against (a surface). 5 To dig or form by scratching or scraping. 6 To gather or accumulate with effort or difficulty: usually with *up* or *together.* **—***v.i.* 7 To scrape something. 8 To rub with a grating noise. 9 To emit or produce a grating noise. 10 To draw the foot backward along the ground in bowing: to bow and *scrape.* 11 To manage or get along with difficulty. 12 To be very or overly economical. **—to scrape acquaintance** To make acquaintance without an introduction. **—***n.* 1 The act or effect of scraping; also, the noise made by scraping. 2 A difficult situation; predicament. 3 A scraping or drawing back of the foot in bowing. [Prob. fusion of OE *scrapian* and ON *skrapa* scrape, erase]

scrap·er (skrā′pər) *n.* 1 Any instrument used for scraping. 2 A horse-drawn or motor-driven apparatus having a large metal scoop or scoops, for scraping up, transporting, and dumping dirt: a road *scraper*; a road leveller. 3 One who or that which scrapes. 4 A miser. 5 An unskilful player on the violin.

scrap·ing (skrā′ping) *n.* 1 The act of someone or something that scrapes. 2 The sound so produced. 3 Something scraped off or together.

scrap iron Old pieces of iron suitable for reworking.

scrap·ple (skrap′əl) *n.* A mixture of meal or flour boiled with scraps of pork, seasoned, and allowed to set: usually cooked by frying. [Dim. of SCRAP[1]]

scrap·py[1] (skrap′ē) *adj.* **·pi·er, ·pi·est** Composed of scraps; disconnected; fragmentary. [<SCRAP[1] + -Y[1]] **—scrap′pi·ly** *adv.* **—scrap′·pi·ness** *n.*

scrap·py[2] (skrap′ē) *adj.* **·pi·er, ·pi·est** Pugnacious; given to picking fights. [<SCRAP[2] + -Y[1]] **—scrap′pi·ly** *adv.* **—scrap′pi·ness** *n.*

scratch (skrach) *v.t.* 1 To tear or mark the surface of with something sharp or rough. 2 To scrape or dig with something sharp or rough, as the claws or nails. 3 To scrape lightly with the nails, etc., as to relieve itching. 4 To rub with a grating sound; scrape. 5 To write or draw awkwardly or hurriedly. 6 To erase or cancel by or as by scratches or marks. 7 To erase or cancel the name of (a candidate) from a political ticket, while supporting the rest of the ticket; also, to bolt (a ticket or party) in this way. 8 To withdraw (an entry) from a race, game, etc. **—***v.i.* 9 To use the nails or claws, as in fighting or digging. 10 To scrape the skin, etc., lightly, as to relieve itching. 11 To make a grating noise. 12 To manage or get along with difficulty. 13 To withdraw from a game, race, etc. 14 In billiards and pool, to make a scratch. — *n.* 1 A mark or incision made on a surface by scratching; a shallow mark, groove, furrow, or channel. 2 A slight flesh wound or cut. 3 The line from which contestants start, as in racing: to start from *scratch.* 4 The contestant who competes against an allowance: also **scratch-man.** 5 *Slang* Money. 6 A disease of horses, consisting of dry scabs or chaps on the heel: also **scratch'es.** 7 In billiards, a chance shot; also, a fluke; in billiards and pool, a shot resulting in a penalty; specifically, a shot in which the cue ball goes into a pocket, leaves the table, or fails to hit an object ball. — **from scratch** From the beginning; from nothing. — **up to scratch** *Colloq.* Meeting the standard or requirement in courage, stamina, or performance; in proper or fit condition: He was never *up to scratch* in writing. — *adj.* 1 Done by chance; haphazard. 2 In sports, without handicap or allowance. 3 Made as, or used for, a first try: a *scratch* pad. 4 Chosen at random or by chance: a *scratch* team. [Prob. blend of ME *scratte* scratch (prob. <Scand.; cf. Sw. *kratta* rake) and *cracchen* scratch < MDu. *cratsen*] — **scratch'er** *n.*

scratch test *Med.* A test to determine the substances to which a person is allergic by rubbing allergens in small scratches made in his skin.

scratch·y (skrach'ē) *adj.* **scratch·i·er, scratch·i·est** 1 Characterized by scratches. 2 Making a scratching noise. 3 Straggling; shaggy; rough. — **scratch'i·ly** *adv.* — **scratch'i·ness** *n.*

scrawl (skrôl) *v.t.* & *v.i.* To write hastily or illegibly; scribble. — *n.* Irregular or careless writing. [? < dial. E, var. of CRAWL; ? infl. in meaning by *scribble, scroll,* etc.] — **scrawl'er** *n.*

scrawl·y (skrô'lē) *adj.* **scrawl·i·er, scrawl·i·est** Consisting of or characterized by ill-formed or irregular characters.

scraw·ny (skrô'nē) *adj.* **·ni·er, ·ni·est** Lean and bony; skinny; thin. [< dial. E *scranny,* var. of SCRANNEL] — **scraw'ni·ness** *n.*

screak (skrēk) *v.i.* To creak; screech. — *n.* A screech; also, a creak. [<ON *skrækja*; prob. imit.]

scream (skrēm) *v.i.* 1 To utter a prolonged, piercing cry, as of pain, terror, or surprise. 2 To make a prolonged, piercing sound. 3 To laugh loudly or immoderately. 4 To use heated, hysterical language. 5 To have an effect as of screaming: This color *screams* in contrast to green. — *v.t.* 6 To utter with a scream. — *n.* A loud, shrill, prolonged cry or sound, generally denoting fear or pain. See synonyms under CALL, ROAR. [ME *screamen,* ? <ON *skraema* scare]

scream·er (skrē'mər) *n.* 1 One who or that which screams. 2 A South American bird, related to the ducks (family *Anhimidae* or *Palamedidae*) including the **horned screamer** (*Anhima* or *Palamedea cornuta*) and the **crested screamers** (genus *Chauna*). 3 *U.S. Slang* Something calculated to call forth screams of admiration, astonishment, or the like; hence, a person of great size, strength, or skill. 4 *U.S. Slang* A sensational headline in a newspaper.

scream·ing (skrē'ming) *adj.* 1 Uttering or emitting screams. 2 Provocative of screams or of laughter: a *screaming* farce. 3 Like a scream.

scree (skrē) *n.* Debris of stones and rock fragments at the foot of a cliff or steep, rocky face: usually a sloping mass. See TALUS. [Back formation < *screes,* earlier *screethes* <ON *skridha* a landslide]

screech (skrēch) *n.* A shrill, harsh cry; shriek. — *v.t.* To utter with or as with a screech. — *v.i.* To make a prolonged, harsh, piercing sound; shriek. [Var. of obs. *scritch,* prob. < Scand. Cf. ON *skrækja*; prob. ult. imit.] — **screech'er** *n.* — **screech'y** *adj.*

screech owl 1 Any of various small owls (genus *Otus*) common from Canada to Brazil; especially, the small, gray *O. asio* of the eastern United States. 2 The English barn owl.

screed (skrēd) *n.* 1 A prolonged tirade; harangue. 2 A wooden strip or a strip of mortar laid on a wall at intervals, to gage the thickness of the plastering. 3 A long torn strip or shred; hence, any detached strip or fragment: the original meaning, now chiefly Scottish. 4 *Scot.* A tearing; rent; tear; also, a drinking spree. — *v.t.* 1 To rend or tear into shreds. 2 *Scot.* To repeat glibly. [Var. of SHRED]

screen (skrēn) *n.* 1 That which separates or cuts off, shelters or protects, as a light partition. 2 A sieve or riddle, for sifting. 3 A smooth surface, as a canvas or curtain, on which motion pictures, etc., may be shown. 4 A motion picture or motion pictures collectively. 5 A plate of glass bearing very finely ruled lines, placed between the object and the camera in photographing for reproduction by the half-tone process. 6 a *Mil.* A detachment of troops sent to deceive an enemy as to the movement of the main force. b *Nav.* A formation of ships arranged for the protection of heavier vessels from enemy submarines, etc. 7 *Physics* Any of various devices for confining the action of a physical agency or instrument to a definite area: a magnetic *screen.* 8 *Psychoanal.* A person who stands for someone else or others having some common characteristic, as in a dream: a form of concealment. — *v.t.* 1 To shield from observation or annoyance with or as with a screen. 2 To pass through a screen or sieve; sift. 3 To show or exhibit on a screen, as a motion picture. 4 *Psychol.* To separate from a group (those individuals showing indications of, or tendencies toward, mental or physical incapacity for specified activities): often with *out.* See synonyms under HIDE, PALLIATE, SHELTER. [Prob. <OF *escren, escrin,* prob. < OHG *skirm*] — **screen'a·ble** *adj.* — **screen'er** *n.*

screen·ing (skrē'ning) *n.* 1 A meshlike material, as for a window screen. 2 A showing of a motion picture.

screen·ings (skrē'ningz) *n. pl.* The waste of anything passed through a sieve, as coal or defective grains; siftings.

screw (skro͞o) *n.* 1 A device resembling a nail but having a slotted head and a tapering or cylindrical spiral for driving into wood with a screwdriver, or for insertion into a corresponding grooved part: called **male** or **external screw.** 2 A cylindrical socket with a spiral groove: called **female** or **internal screw.** 3 Anything having the form of a screw. 4 A screw propeller. 5 A turn of or as of a screw. 6 Pressure; force. 7 *Brit. Slang* Salary; pay. 8 *Slang* A prison guard. 9 A haggler over prices; a crafty bargainer. 10 *Brit.* A worthless horse. 11 *Brit.* A small packet of tobacco. 12 *Slang* An act of sexual intercourse: a vulgar term. — **to have a screw loose** *Slang* To be mentally deranged, eccentric, etc. — **to put the screws on** (or **to**) *Slang* To exert pressure or force upon. — *v.t.* 1 To tighten, fasten, attach, etc., by or as by a screw or screws. 2 To turn or twist. 3 To force as if by the pressure of a screw; urge: to *screw* one's courage to the sticking point. 4 To twist out of shape; contort, as one's features. 5 To practice oppression or extortion on; defraud. 6 To obtain by extortion. 7 *Slang* To have sexual intercourse with: a vulgar term. 8 *Slang* To act maliciously toward; harm. — *v.i.* 9 To turn or admit of being turned as a screw. 10 To be attached or become detached by means of a screw or screws: with *on, off,* etc. 11 To have turns like those of a screw. 12 To practice oppression or extortion. 13 *Slang* To have sexual intercourse: a vulgar term. — **to screw up** *Slang* To botch; make a mess of: He *screwed up* his career. [Appar. <OF *escroue* a nut, female screw, ? <L *scrofa* sow; infl. in OF by L *scrobis* vulva] — **screw'er** *n.*

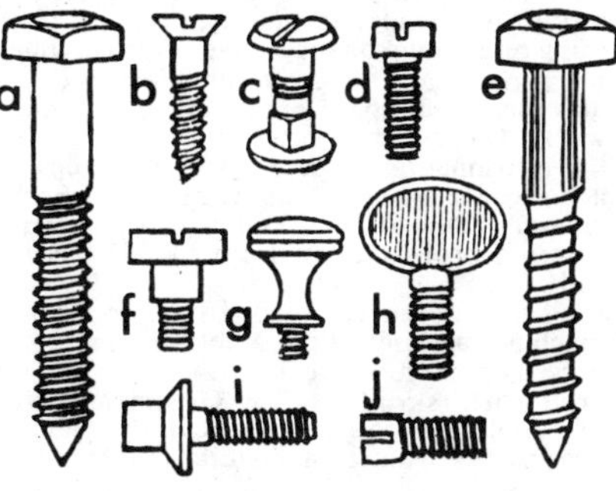

TYPES OF SCREWS

a. Lagscrew. *b.* Wood screw. *c.* Saw screw. *d.* Fillister screw. *e.* Skein screw. *f.* Shoulder screw. *g, h.* Thumbscrews. *i.* Collar screw. *j.* Slotted screw.

screw·ball (skro͞o'bôl') *n.* 1 In baseball, a pitch thrown with a wrist motion opposite to that used for the out-curve, and breaking sharply and often unpredictably. 2 *U.S. Slang* An unconventional or erratic person.

screw·bean (skro͞o'bēn') *n.* 1 The seed of the spirally twisted pod of a species of mesquite (*Strombocarpa odorata*). 2 The tree bearing this seed.

screw·driv·er (skro͞o'drī'vər) *n.* A tool for turning screws.

screwed-up (skro͞od'up') *adj. Slang* 1 Disorganized or disorderly. 2 Mentally ill or emotionally distressed.

screw jack 1 A hoisting or lifting jack operated by a screw; jackscrew. 2 A dental implement for regulating the position of the teeth.

SCREW JACK

screw log A patent log.

screw·pile (skro͞o'pīl') *n.* A pile having a strong metal base with a screw thread to ensure firm penetration of hard ground or bedrock. See illustration under LIGHTHOUSE.

screw·pine (skro͞o'pīn') *n.* Any of a tropical genus (*Pandanus*) of plants having a screwlike arrangement of the clustered leaves and aerial roots.

screw propeller A mechanism consisting of a revolving shaft with radiating blades set at an angle to produce a spiral action: used in propelling ships, etc.

screw thread 1 The projecting spiral ridge of uniform pitch on the outer or inner surface of a cylinder or cone, as of a screw or nut. 2 A complete revolution of any point in this ridge.

screw·worm fly (skro͞o'wûrm') A shiny, blue-green blowfly (genus *Cochliomyia,* family *Calliphoridae*) about twice the size of the common housefly, whose larvae breed in living flesh; especially, *C. americana,* the destructive cattle pest of the southern and western United States.

screw·y (skro͞o'ē) *adj.* **screw·i·er, screw·i·est** *Slang* Extremely irrational; crazy.

Scria·bin (skryä'bēn), **Alexander,** 1872–1915, Russian composer.

scrib·ble (skrib'əl) *v.* **·bled, ·bling** *v.t.* 1 To write hastily and carelessly. 2 To cover with careless or illegible writing or marks. — *v.i.* 3 To write in a careless or hasty manner. 4 To make illegible or meaningless marks. — *n.* 1 Hasty, careless writing. 2 Meaningless lines and marks; any scrawl. [<Med. L *scribillare,* freq. of L *scribere* write]

scrib·bler (skrib'lər) *n.* 1 One who scribbles. 2 A writer of no reputation; a petty or inferior author.

scribe (skrīb) *n.* 1 One who writes or copies manuscripts. 2 A clerk, public writer, or amanuensis. 3 An author, penman, or journalist: used humorously. 4 An ancient Jewish teacher, interpreter, or writer of the Mosaic law. 5 A pointed instrument for marking wood, bricks, etc. — *v.* **scribed, scrib·ing** *v.t.* 1 To mark or scratch with a pointed instrument. 2 To write, inscribe, or engrave. 3 In carpentry, to mark and fit closely. — *v.i.* 4 *Rare* To write; work as a scribe. [<L *scriba* < *scribere* write] — **scrib'al** *adj.*

Scribe (skrēb), **Augustin Eugène,** 1791–1861, French dramatist.

scrib·er (skrī'bər) *n.* 1 One who or that which scribes. 2 Any sharp-pointed tool used in scribing.

scrieve (skrēv) *v.i. Scot.* To glide swiftly along. [Prob. <ON *skrefa* stride]

scrim (skrim) *n.* 1 A lightweight, open-mesh, coarse cotton fabric, usually white or écru, used for draperies, etc. 2 In the theater, a similar fabric, often painted, used as a transparency, to support artificial foliage, etc. [Origin unknown]

scrim·mage (skrim′ij) *n.* **1** A rough-and-tumble contest; fracas; formerly, a skirmish. **2** In American football, a mass play from the line of scrimmage after the ball has been placed on the ground and snapped back, the play ending when the ball is dead. **3** In Rugby football, a scrummage. **—line of scrimmage** In football, the hypothetic line, parallel to the goal lines, on which the ball rests and along which the opposing linemen take position at the start of play. *—v.t. & v.i.* **·maged, ·mag·ing** To engage in a scrimmage. Also spelled *scrummage.* [Alter. of *scrimish,* var. of SKIRMISH]

scrimp (skrimp) *v.i.* **1** To be very or overly economical; be niggardly. *—v.t.* **2** To be overly sparing toward; skimp. **3** To cut too small, narrow, etc. *—adj.* Scanty; short: also **scrimp′y.** See synonyms under SCANTY. *—n.* A miser; niggard. [?. Related to OE *scrimman* shrink, shrivel] **—scrimp′i·ness** *n.*
Synonyms (verb): contract, curtail, economize, limit, pinch, reduce, save, scant, shorten, straiten. *Antonyms*: dissipate, lavish, squander, waste.

scrim·shaw (skrim′shô) *v.t. & v.i.* To ornament (ivory, whale's teeth, etc.) by cutting or carving: a sailor's term. *—n.* A neat example of mechanical work; especially, a scrimshawed article, ornamented with fanciful carving. [?< the surname *Scrimshaw*]

scrip[1] (skrip) *n.* **1** A scrap of paper, especially one containing writing. **2** A writing; a certificate, schedule, or written list. **3** A piece of paper money less than a dollar formerly issued in the United States: also called *shinplaster.* [<SCRIPT, prob. infl. in form by SCRAP]

scrip[2] (skrip) *n.* A provisional document (or documents collectively) certifying that the holder is entitled to receive something else, as shares of stock or land. [Short for obs. *subscription receipt*]

scrip[3] (skrip) *n.* A wallet or small bag. [Prob. fusion of ON *skreppa* a bag and OF *escrepe,* in phrase *escrepe et bordon* wallet and staff]

scrip dividend A distribution of surplus to stockholders in the form of scrip or promises to pay the dividend at a certain time.

Scripps (skrips) Name of a family of U.S. newspaper publishers, including **James Edmund,** 1835–1906, born in England; his half-brother, **Edward Wyllis,** 1854–1926; and **Robert Paine,** 1895–1938, son of Edward Wyllis.

scrip·sit (skrip′sit) *Latin* He (or she) wrote (it): used after an author's name on manuscripts, etc.

script (skript) *n.* **1** Writing of the ordinary cursive form. **2** Type, or printed or engraved matter, in imitation of handwriting. **3** *Law* A writing, especially an original; in English practice, a will; codicil. **4** A piece of writing; a manuscript or typescript; especially, a prepared copy, often containing suggestions, for the use of actors in a theatrical, radio, or television performance. *—v.t. & v.i. U.S. Colloq.* To prepare a script for (a radio, television, or theatrical performance). [<OF *escript* <L *scriptum,* pp. neut. of *scribere* write]

This line is in script.

scrip·to·ri·um (skrip·tôr′ē·əm, -tō′rē-) *n. pl.* **·ri·ums** or **·ri·a** (-ē·ə) The writing-room of a monastery, where records, annals, and manuscripts were written, copied, or illuminated. [<Med. L <L *scriptus,* pp. of *scribere* write]

scrip·tur·al (skrip′chər·əl) *adj.* Relating to writing; written. **—scrip′tur·al·ly** *adv.* **—scrip′tur·al·ness** *n.*

Scrip·tur·al (skrip′chər·əl) *adj.* Pertaining to, contained in, quoted from, or warranted by the Bible; Biblical. **—Scrip′tur·al·ly** *adv.* **—Scrip′tur·al·ness** *n.*

Scrip·tur·al·ism (skrip′chər·əl·iz′əm) *n.* The quality or character of being Scriptural; also, strict or literal adherence to the Scriptures. **—Scrip′tur·al·ist** *n.*

scrip·ture (skrip′chər) *n.* **1** The sacred writings of any people. **2** Originally, anything written, as a document, book, or inscription, or its contents; a writing. [<OF *escripture* <L *scriptura* <*scriptus,* pp. of *scribere* write]

Scrip·ture (skrip′chər) *n.* **1** The books of the Old and New Testaments, including often the Apocrypha; specifically, the Bible: usually plural. **2** A text or passage from the Bible.

script·writ·er (skript′rī′tər) *n.* A writer who prepares copy for the use of a radio or television actor or announcer.

scrive (skrīv) *v.t.* **scrived, scriv·ing** **1** To engrave. **2** *Obs.* To write; scribe. [<OF *escrivre* write <L *scribere*]

scri·vel·lo (skri·vel′ō) *n. pl.* **·loes** or **·los** An elephant's tusk. [<Pg. *escrevelho,* ? var. of *escaravelho* a pin, peg]

scriv·en·er (skriv′ən·ər, skriv′nər) *n.* **1** One who prepares deeds, contracts, and other writings; a clerk or scribe. **2** Formerly, a money-lender. [<obs. *scrivein* <OF *escrivain* <Ital. *scrivano* <L *scribere* write]

scro·bic·u·late (skrō·bik′yə·lit, -lāt) *adj. Biol.* Marked with many small depressions; furrowed or pitted. Also **scro·bic′u·lat′ed** (-lā′·tid). [<L *scrobiculus,* dim. of *scrobis* a trench]

scrod (skrod) *n.* A young codfish, especially when split and prepared for broiling. [? <MDu. *schrode* a piece cut off. Akin to SHRED.]

scrof·u·la (skrof′yə·lə) *n. Pathol.* A tuberculous condition of the lymphatic glands, characterized by enlargement, suppurating abscesses, and cheeselike degeneration; the king's evil. [Orig. pl. <LL *scrofulae,* dim. pl. <*scrofa* a breeding sow; so called because sows were supposed to be subject to the disease]

scrof·u·lous (skrof′yə·ləs) *adj.* **1** Pertaining to, affected with, or of the nature of scrofula. **2** Like scrofula; hence, morally diseased. **—scrof′u·lous·ly** *adv.* **—scrof′u·lous·ness** *n.*

scrog·gy (skrog′ē) *adj. Scot. & Brit. Dial.* Stunted; dwarfed; shriveled; also, abounding with brushwood. [Prob. <Scand. Cf. Dan. *skrog* a lean carcass.]

scroll (skrōl) *n.* **1** A roll of parchment, paper, or the like, especially one containing or intended for writing; also, the writing on such a roll; specifically, an outline; draft. **2** Anything resembling or suggestive of a parchment roll; specifically, a convoluted ornament or an ornamental space or tablet on sculptured work. **3** The curved head of a violin or similar instrument. **4** *Her.* A ribbon bearing a motto. See synonyms under RECORD. [Earlier *scrowle,* alter. of obs. *scrow* <AF *escrowe* a scroll; prob. infl. in form by ME *rowle* a roll]

scroll saw A narrow-bladed saw, or a sawing machine bearing such a blade, for doing curved or irregular work.

scroll·work (skrōl′wûrk′) *n.* Ornamental work of scroll-like pattern; particularly, fanciful designs cut from thin material by means of scroll saws.

Scrooge (skrōōj), **Ebenezer** In Dickens's *Christmas Carol,* a miser whose hard nature is transformed by the revelations of human joy and sorrow given to him by three spirits that visit him on Christmas Eve.

scroop (skrōōp) *v.i.* To give forth a harsh, scraping sound or cry; creak; grate. *—n.* A harsh grating or crunching sound; harsh cry. [Imit.; infl. by SCRAPE]

scroph·u·lar·i·a·ceous (skrof′yə·lâr′ē·ā′shəs) *adj.* Of or pertaining to a family *(Scrophulariaceae)* of herbs, shrubs, and a few trees, the figwort family, including the veronica, snapdragon and digitalis. [<NL *<Scrophularia,* type genus <Med. L *scrophula* SCROFULA; so called from its supposed power to cure scrofula]

scro·tum (skrō′təm) *n. pl.* **·ta** (-tə) *Anat.* The pouch that contains the testes. [<L] **—scro′·tal** *adj.*

scrouge (skrōōj, skrouj) *v.t. Brit. Dial.* To squeeze or grind down; crowd; press. [Earlier *scruze,* blend of SCREW and SQUEEZE]

scrounge (skrounj) *v.t. & v.i.* **scrounged, scroung·ing** *Slang* **1** To hunt about and take (something); pilfer. **2** To mooch; sponge; beg. [? <dial. E *scrunge* steal, var. of SCROUGE] **—scroung′er** *n.*

scroung·y (skroun′jē) *adj.* **scroung·i·er, scroung·i·est** *Slang* **1** Given to scrounging. **2** Unkempt; unclean; grubby.

scrub[1] (skrub) *v.* **scrubbed, scrub·bing** *v.t.* **1** To rub vigorously, as with the hand or a brush, in washing. **2** To remove (dirt, etc.) by such action. **3** To cleanse (a gas). *—v.i.* **4** To rub something vigorously in washing. See synonyms under CLEANSE. *—n.* The act of scrubbing. [? <Scand. Cf. Dan. *skrubbe.*]

scrub[2] (skrub) *n.* **1** A stunted tree. **2** A thicket or tract of stunted trees or shrubs. **3** A domestic animal of inferior or impure breed. **4** A poor, insignificant person. **5** In sports, a player not on the varsity or regular team. **6** A game of baseball contrived hastily by a few players. *—adj.* **1** Undersized or stunted-looking; inferior. **2** Consisting of or participated in by untrained players or scrubs: *scrub* team; *scrub* game. [Dial. var. of SHRUB[1]]

scrub·ber (skrub′ər) *n.* **1** One who or that which scrubs. **2** Any apparatus that removes undesired material through the medium of a liquid by washing.

scrub·by (skrub′ē) *adj.* **·bi·er, ·bi·est** **1** Of stunted growth. **2** Covered with or consisting of scrub or underbrush. [<SCRUB[2]] **—scrub′·bi·ness** *n.*

scrub grass The scouring rush.

scrub·land (skrub′land′) *n.* Land covered with scrub.

scrub oak Any of various dwarf oaks of the United States, as *Quercus ilicifolia* and *Q. prinoides,* common in New England; especially, the turkey oak or *Q. laevis* of the sandy barrens of the South.

scrub pine Any of several American dwarf pines; especially, the common Jersey pine *(Pinus virginiana)* and the shore pine of California, a variety of lodgepole pine *(P. contorta).*

scrub typhus *Pathol.* Tsutsugamushi disease.

scruff (skruf) *n.* The nape or outer back part of the neck. [Earlier *scuff* (<ON *skopt* hair); infl. in form by *scruff,* var. of SCURF]

scrum (skrum) *n. Brit. Colloq.* Scrummage: an abbreviated form.

scrum·mage (skrum′ij) *v.t. & v.i.* **·maged, ·mag·ing** To scrimmage. *—n.* **1** Scrimmage. **2** In Rugby football, a formation, around the ball, of the opposing sets of forwards, each of which endeavors by superior weight or compactness to dislodge the opponent, secure and break away with the ball, or kick it out. [Var. of SCRIMMAGE] **—scrum′mag·er** *n.*

scrump·tious (skrump′shəs) *adj. Slang* **1** Elegant or stylish; fine; delightful; splendid. **2** Fastidious; overly particular; nice. [<dial. E, mean, stingy, ult. <SCRIMP; prob. infl. in meaning by SUMPTUOUS]

scrunch (skrunch) *v.t. & v.i.* To crush; squeeze; crunch. *—n.* A crunch. [Imit. alter. of CRUNCH]

scru·ple (skrōō′pəl) *n.* **1** Doubt or uncertainty regarding a question of moral right or duty; reluctance arising from conscientious disapproval. **2** An apothecaries' weight of twenty grains, or 1.295 grams (symbol: ℈). **3** A minute quantity. **4** An ancient Roman coin. *—v.t. & v.i.* **·pled, ·pling** To have scruples (about); hesitate (doing) from considerations of right or expediency. [<OF *scrupule* <L *scrupulus,* dim. of *scrupus* a sharp stone]

scru·pu·lous (skrōō′pyə·ləs) *adj.* **1** Cautious in action for fear of doing wrong; nicely conscientious. **2** Resulting from the exercise of scruples; exact; careful. See synonyms under PRECISE, SQUEAMISH. [<L *scrupulosus* <*scrupulus* a scruple] **—scru′pu·lous·ly** *adv.* **—scru′pu·lous·ness, scru′pu·los′i·ty** (-los′·ə·tē) *n.*

scru·ti·nize (skrōō′tə·nīz) *v.t.* **·nized, ·niz·ing** To observe carefully; examine in detail. See synonyms under EXAMINE. **—scru′ti·niz′er** *n.*

scru·ti·ny (skrōō′tə·nē) *n. pl.* **·nies** **1** The act of scrutinizing; close investigation. **2** A method of electing the pope by secret ballot. **3** An official examination of votes after an election. See synonyms under INQUIRY. [<LL *scrutinium* <L *scrutari* examine, appar. <*scruta* trash, rags; with ref. to a careful search, including even trash and rags]

scry·ing (skrī′ing) *n. Archaic* Crystal-gazing. [Aphetic var. of DESCRY]

scu·ba (skōō′bə, skyōō′-) *n.* A device worn by a free-swimming diver to provide a supply of air for breathing. [<*s(elf-)c(ontained) u(nderwater) b(reathing) a(pparatus)*]

scud (skud) *v.i.* **scud·ded, scud·ding** **1** To move, run, or fly swiftly. **2** *Naut.* To run rapidly before the wind; especially, to run before a gale with little or no sail set. —*n.* 1 The act of scudding or moving swiftly. 2 Light clouds driven rapidly before the wind; a misty rain. 3 *Brit. Slang* A swift runner. 4 *Scot.* A slap with the open hand. 5 *pl. Scot.* Foaming beer or ale. [Prob. <Scand. (cf. Norw. *skudda* push); ? infl. in meaning by *scut,* in earlier sense of "a hare"]

Scud·der (skud′ər), **Horace,** 1838–1902, U.S. author.

Scu·dé·ry (skü·dā·rē′), **Madeleine de,** 1607–1701, French novelist.

scu·do (skōō′dō) *n. pl.* **scu·di** (skōō′dē) A former Italian and Sicilian silver or gold coin. [<Ital. <L *scutum* a shield]

scuff (skuf) *v.i.* 1 To walk with a dragging movement of the feet; shuffle. —*v.t.* 2 To scrape (the floor, ground, etc.) with the feet. 3 To make the surface of rough by rubbing or scraping. —*n.* The act of scuffing; also, the noise so made. [Prob. <ON *skūfa* shove]

scuf·fle[1] (skuf′əl) *v.i.* **·fled, ·fling** 1 To struggle roughly or confusedly. 2 To drag one's feet; shuffle. —*n.* A disorderly struggle carried on by grappling, pulling, pushing, or the like; confused fracas. [Prob. freq. of SCUFF] —**scuf′fler** *n.*

scuf·fle[2] (skuf′əl) *n.* A form of hoe used by pushing in the manner of a spade. Also **scuffle hoe.** See illustration under HOE. [<Du. *schoffel* a weeding hoe]

scul·dud·der·y (skul·dud′ər·ē) *n. Scot.* Obscenity.

scull[1] (skul) *n.* 1 A long oar worked from side to side over the stern of a boat. 2 A light, short-handled spoon oar, used in pairs by one person. 3 A small boat for sculling. —*v.t.* & *v.i.* To propel (a boat) by a scull or sculls. ◆ Homophone: *skull.* [ME *sculle, skulle*; origin unknown] —**scull′er** *n.*

scull[2] (skul) *n. Scot.* A large, shallow wicker basket. ◆ Homophone: *skull.*

scul·ler·y (skul′ər·ē) *n. pl.* **·ler·ies** A room where kitchen utensils are kept and cleaned; a back kitchen. [<OF *escuelerie* care of dishes < *escuelle* a dish <L *scutella* a tray]

scul·lion (skul′yən) *n.* 1 A servant who washes and scours dishes, pots, and kettles. 2 A low wretch. [<OF *escouillon* a mop < *escouve* a broom <L *scopae* a bundle of twigs, pl. of *scopa* a twig]

sculp (skulp) *v.t.* & *v.i. Colloq.* To sculpture. [Short for SCULPTURE]

scul·pin (skul′pin) *n.* 1 One of several broad-mouthed fishes (family *Cottidae*), of inferior food value, with large, spiny head. The **daddy sculpin** (*Acanthocothus scorpius*) is a common North Atlantic species of which the North American form is a variety. 2 A fish (*Scorpaena guttata*) having a large head and spiny fins, found in southern California. 3 *Brit.* A contemptible fellow; mischief-maker. [Prob. alter. of F *escorpene* <L *scorpaena,* a scorpionlike fish <Gk. *skorpaina* < *skorpios* a scorpion]

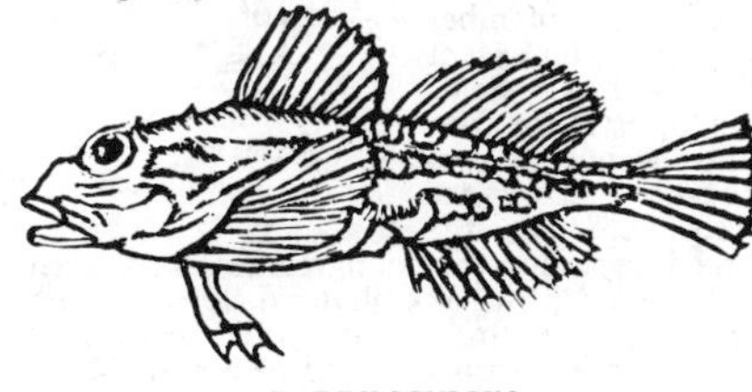

DADDY SCULPIN
(Rarely over 4 inches long)

sculp·sit (skulp′sit) *Latin* He (or she) sculptured it: used on a piece of statuary or sculpture following the name of the person who executed it.

sculp·tor (skulp′tər) *n.* One who designs sculpture by carving wood, modeling plastics, or chiseling stone. [<L < *sculpere* sculpture] —**sculp′tress** (-tris) *n. fem.*

sculp·ture (skulp′chər) *n.* 1 The art of fashioning figures of stone, wood, clay, or bronze. 2 Figures or groups carved, cut, hewn, cast, or modeled in wood, stone, clay, or metal. 3 Raised or incised lines, or markings, as upon a shell. —*v.t.* **·tured, ·tur·ing** 1 To fashion, as statuary, by modeling, carving, or casting. 2 To represent or portray in sculpture. 3 To embellish with sculpture. 4 To change, as the face of a valley or canyon, by erosion and deposition. [<L *sculptura* < *sculptus,* pp. of *sculpere* carve in stone < *scalpere* cut] —**sculp′tur·al** *adj.*

sculp·tur·esque (skulp′chə·resk′) *adj.* Resembling sculpture; coldly, calmly, or grandly beautiful; statuesque; well-proportioned; majestic. —**sculp′tur·esque′ly** *adv.* —**sculp′tur·esque′ness** *n.*

scum (skum) *n.* 1 Impure or extraneous matter that rises to the surface of boiling or fermenting liquids. 2 Minute vegetation on stagnant water. 3 Scoria or dross of molten metals; also, foam; froth. 4 Figuratively, vile element; refuse. See synonyms under WASTE. —*v.* **scummed, scum·ming** *v.t.* To take scum from; skim. —*v.i.* To become covered with or form scum. [<MDu. *schuum*] —**scum′mer** *n.* —**scum′my** *adj.*

scum·ble (skum′bəl) *v.t.* **·bled, ·bling** In drawing and painting, to soften the outlines or blend the colors of by rubbing, as with comparatively dry or opaque color. —*n.* 1 The softening or blending of colors so produced. 2 The material used in scumbling. [Freq. of SCUM]

scun·ner (skun′ər) See SCONNER.

Scun·thorpe (skun′thôrp) A municipal borough of NW Lincolnshire, England.

scup (skup) *n.* 1 A valuable sparoid food fish (*Stenotomus chrysops*) of the eastern coast of the United States; the porgy: also **scup·paug** (skup′ôg, skə·pôg′). 2 A related species (*S. aculeatus*) found southward from Cape Hatteras and on the Gulf Coast to Texas. [<Algonquian (Narraganset) *mishcup* thick-scaled < *mishe* large + *cuppi* a scale]

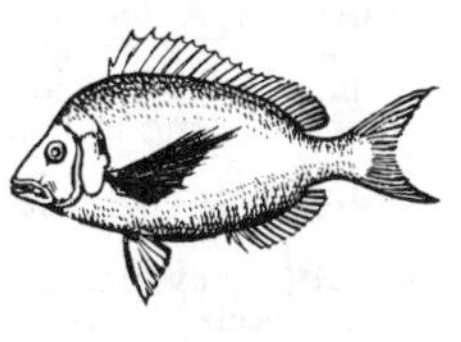

COMMON SCUP
(About 12 inches long)

scup·per[1] (skup′ər) *n. Naut.* A hole or gutter bordering a ship's deck, to let water run off. [Prob. short for *scupper hole* <OF *escope* a bailing scoop <Gmc. Akin to SCOOP.]

scup·per[2] (skup′ər) *v.t. Brit.* To put in great difficulty or danger; surprise or surprise and annihilate. [? <SCUPPER[1]]

scup·per·nong (skup′ər·nông, -nong) *n.* 1 A variety of muscadine grape cultivated in the southern United States. 2 A sweet, straw-colored wine made from this grape. [from the *Scuppernong* River in Tyrrell County, N.C.]

scurf (skûrf) *n.* 1 Loose scarfskin thrown off in minute scales, as in dandruff. 2 Any extraneous scaly matter adhering to a surface. 3 Worthless or impure coating or covering. [OE, alter. of *sceorf*; prob. infl. in form by Scand. Cf. Dan. *skurv.*] —**scurf′i·ness** *n.* —**scurf′y** *adj.*

scur·ril·i·ty (skə·ril′ə·tē) *n. pl.* **·ties** 1 Coarse, vulgar abuse; a scurrilous remark. 2 The quality of being obscenely jocular. [<MF *scurrilité* <L *scurrilitas* < *scurrilis* SCURRILOUS]

scur·ri·lous (skûr′ə·ləs) *adj.* 1 Grossly offensive or vulgar; opprobrious. 2 Expressed with or given to low buffoonery. Also **scur·rile** (skûr′·il), **scur′ril.** [Earlier *scurrile* <L, neut. of *scurrilis* buffoon-like < *scurra* a buffoon] —**scur′ri·lous·ly** *adv.* —**scur′ri·lous·ness** *n.*

scur·ry (skûr′ē) *v.i.* **·ried, ·ry·ing** To move or go hurriedly; scamper. —*n. pl.* **·ries** 1 The act or sound of scurrying; a precipitate movement. 2 A flurry, as of snow; whirl. 3 A short, fast run or race on horseback. [Short for HURRY-SCURRY; ? infl. by SCOUR[2]]

S-curve (es′kûrv′) *n.* A curve shaped like an *S.*

scur·vy (skûr′vē) *adj.* **·vi·er, ·vi·est** 1 Meanly low or contemptible; base. 2 *Obs.* Afflicted with scurvy; also, scabby. See synonyms under BAD[1], BASE[2]. —*n. Pathol.* A disease characterized by livid spots under the skin, swollen and bleeding gums, and great prostration: caused by lack of vitamin C in the diet. [<SCURF] —**scur′vi·ly** *adv.* —**scur′vi·ness** *n.*

scurvy grass A biennial herb (*Cochlearia officinalis*) highly prized by Arctic explorers as a remedy for scurvy.

scut (skut) *n.* 1 A short or docked tail. 2 *Slang* A contemptible person. —*v.t. Obs.* To dock (an animal's tail). —*adj.* Short. [ME, a tail, a hare, prob. <Scand. Cf. Icelandic *skott* a fox's tail.]

scu·tage (skyōō′tij) *n.* A tax exacted from feudal knights instead of personal military service for their lands. [<Med. L *scutagium* <L *scutum* a shield]

Scu·ta·ri (skōō′tä·rē) 1 Üsküdar. 2 The largest city of northern Albania, at the SE end of **Lake Scutari,** a lake in SW Yugoslavia and NW Albania; 205 square miles. *Albanian* **Shko·dër** (shkô′dər), **Shko·dra** (shkô′drə). Ancient **Sco·dra** (skō′drə).

scu·tate (skyōō′tāt) *adj. Biol.* 1 Covered with horny, shieldlike plates or large scales. 2 Shaped like a shield. Also *scutellate.* See PELTATE. [<L *scutatus* provided with a shield < *scutum* a shield]

scutch (skuch) *v.t.* 1 To dress (textile fiber) by beating. 2 To separate the woody parts from the valuable fiber of (flax, etc.) by beating. —*n.* An implement for scutching hemp and flax. [Prob. <OF *escousser* shake, ? <Scand. Cf. Norw. *skoka* a scutch.] —**scutch′er** *n.*

scutch·eon (skuch′ən) *n.* 1 An escutcheon or anything shaped like it. 2 A metal plate or shield; a name plate or the like. [Aphetic var. of ESCUTCHEON]

scute (skyōōt) *n.* 1 *Zool.* A thin plate or scale, as a scale on a reptile. 2 Scutellum. [<L *scutum* a shield]

scu·tel·late (skyōō·tel′it, skyōō′tə·lāt) *adj. Zool.* 1 Platterlike; shield-shaped. 2 Covered with transverse scales; scutate. Also **scu′tel·lat′ed** (-lā′tid). [<NL *scutellatus* <L *scutella* a platter, dim. of *scutra* a tray; infl. in meaning by L *scutum* a shield]

scu·tel·la·tion (skyōō′tə·lā′shən) *n. Ornithol.* The presence or the arrangement of the scales on a bird's tarsus and toes.

scu·tel·lum (skyōō·tel′əm) *n. pl.* **·la** (-ə) 1 *Bot.* A small shieldlike organ or part, as in the cotyledon of a plant. 2 *Ornithol.* A scale on the foot of a bird. [<NL, dim. of L *scutum* a shield] —**scu·tel′lar** *adj.*

scu·ti·form (skyōō′tə·fôrm) *adj.* Shield-shaped. [<NL *scutiformis* <L *scutum* a shield + *forma* form]

scut·ter (skut′ər) *v.i.* To scurry; scuttle. —*n.* A hasty running. [SCUTT(LE)[3] + -ER[4]]

scut·tle[1] (skut′l) *n.* 1 A small opening or hatchway with movable lid or cover, especially in the roof or wall of a house, or in the deck or side of a ship. 2 The lid closing such an opening. 3 A sea cock in the bottom of a ship. —*v.t.* **·tled, ·tling** To sink (a ship) by making holes in the bottom or by opening the sea cocks. [<MF *escoutille* a hatchway <Sp. *escotilla,* prob. <Gmc.]

scut·tle[2] (skut′l) *n.* 1 A metal vessel or hod for coal. 2 Rarely, a vessel or pail for other purposes. [OE *scutel* a dish, platter <L *scutella*]

scut·tle[3] (skut′l) *v.i.* **·tled, ·tling** To run in haste; scurry. —*n.* A hurried run or departure. [? Var. of *scuddle,* freq. of SCUD; prob. infl. in form by dial. E *scut* a hare, a short tail; with ref. to the rapid movement of the hare]

scut·tle·butt (skut′l·but) *n.* 1 A drinking fountain aboard ship; formerly, a cask containing the day's drinking water. 2 *U.S. Slang* Rumor; gossip. [Orig. *scuttled butt* a lidded cask for drinking water]

scut·tler (skut′lər) *n.* The striped lizard of the southern United States.

scu·tum (skyōō′təm) *n. pl.* **·ta** (-tə) 1 The large oval or rectangular shield of the Roman legionaries. 2 *Zool.* Some platelike piece or part in a turtle, fish, etc.; a large scale. [<L]

Scu·tum (skyōō′təm) The Shield, a zodiacal constellation. See CONSTELLATION. [<L]

Scyl·la (sil′ə) In Greek mythology, a six-headed sea monster who dwelt in a cave on the Italian coast opposite the whirlpool Charybdis. See SCILLA. —**between Scylla and Charybdis** Between two dangers, where one cannot be avoided without incurring equally great peril from the other.

scypho- *combining form* Cup; vessel: also,

before vowels, **scyph-**. Also **scyphi-**, as in *scyphiform*, cup-shaped. [<L *scyphus* and Gk. *scyphos* a cup]

scy·pho·zo·an (sī′fə·zō′ən) *n.* Any of a class *(Scyphozoa)* of coelenterates including the sea anemones, corals, and jellyfish. —*adj.* Of or resembling the *Scyphozoa.* [<NL <Gk. *skyphos* a cup + *zōon* an animal]

Scy·ros (sī′rəs) The Latin name for SKYROS.

scythe (sīth) *n.* **1** A long curved blade for mowing, reaping, etc., fixed at an angle to a long bent handle or snath. **2** The implement so formed. **3** A curved blade attached to the axles or wheels of some ancient war chariots. —*v.t.* **scythed, scyth·ing** To cut or mow as with a scythe. [OE *sīthe*]

Scyth·i·a (sith′ē·ə) An ancient region of southern Europe, generally considered as lying north of the Black Sea.

Scyth·i·an (sith′ē·ən) *n.* **1** One of an ancient nomadic and fiercely savage people dwelling along the north shore of the Black Sea and extending as far east as the Aral Sea: last known in history about 100 B.C. **2** The Iranian language of the Scythians. —*adj.* Of or pertaining to the Scythians, their land, or their language. [<L *Scythia* <Gk. *Skythia* <*Skythēs* a Scythian]

'sdeath (zdeth) *interj. Archaic* God's death: an imprecation.

Sdot Yam (sdôt yäm) A settlement in NW Israel, on the site of ancient Caesarea.

sea (sē) *n.* **1** The great body of salt water covering the larger portion of the earth's surface; the ocean. **2** A large or considerable body of oceanic water partly or almost entirely enclosed by land: the Adriatic *Sea.* **3** A large inland body of water, salt or fresh: the Dead *Sea* or the *Sea* of Galilee. **4** The swell of the ocean; the course, flow, or set of the waves. **5** Anything that resembles or suggests the sea, as something vast, boundless, or wide-spread. —**at sea 1** On the ocean. **2** At a loss what to do or think; bewildered. —**to follow the sea** To follow the occupation of a sailor. —**the high seas** The unenclosed expanse of the ocean; also, that part of the ocean beyond a country's territorial waters. —**the seven seas** All the oceans of the world: the North and the South Atlantic, the North and the South Pacific, the Indian, the Arctic, and the Antarctic oceans. ◆ Homophone: *see.* [OE *sǣ*]

sea anchor A drag anchor; a heavy float or canvas bag or sail serving to hold a ship's head to the wind in order to ride out a gale or reduce drifting.

sea anemone A soft-bodied marine coelenterate (class *Anthozoa,* order *Actinaria*), that attaches itself to rocks, etc., suggesting a flower by its coloring and outspread tentacles.

SEA ANEMONE
a. Tentacles contracted.
b. Tentacles extended.

sea bag A cylindrical canvas bag, fastened with a drawstring, in which sailors stow their clothes.

sea bass 1 A dusky-brown or black seranoid food fish *(Centropristes striatus)* common from Cape Cod to Florida: also called *blackfish.* **2** A related fish of California waters *(Stereolepis gigas).* Also **black sea bass. 3** The white sea bass of California *(Cynoscion nobilis).* **4** The related shortfin sea bass *(C. parvipinnis).*

Sea·bee (sē′bē′) *n.* A member of the Construction Battalions of the U. S. Navy, which build base facilities, airfields, etc. [<*C(onstruction) B(attalion)*]

sea bird Any web-footed bird frequenting the oceans or their coasts, as albatrosses, gulls, gannets, petrels, frigate birds, shearwaters, etc.

sea biscuit Hardtack.

sea·board (sē′bôrd′, -bōrd′) *adj.* Bordering on the sea. —*n.* The seashore or seacoast; also, the land or region bordering the sea. [<SEA + *board* a border, OE *bord*]

Sea·borg (sē′bôrg), **Glenn Theodore,** born 1912, U.S. physical chemist.

sea bread An unsalted hard biscuit used at sea; hardtack.

sea bream Any of several Old World sparoid food fishes; specifically, a common migratory species *(Pagellus centrodontus).*

sea breeze A cool breeze blowing from the ocean toward the land.

sea butterfly A pteropod.

sea calf The common harbor seal *(Phoca vitulina)* of the North Atlantic.

sea captain The captain of a seagoing vessel.

sea·coast (sē′kōst′) *n.* The seashore; seaboard.

sea cock A cock or valve controlling connection with the water through a vessel's hull.

sea coconut The very large and heavy bilobate fruit of a palm *(Lodoicea maldivica)* native to islands of the Indian Ocean, weighing 40 or 50 pounds and containing four nuts 18 inches long: also called *double coconut.*

sea cow 1 Any aquatic herbivorous mammal of the order *Sirenia,* sometimes attaining a length of about 25 feet; especially, the manatee or the dugong. **2** The walrus. **3** The hippopotamus.

sea craft 1 Skill in navigation. **2** Seagoing vessels.

sea cucumber A large holothurian (genera *Cucumaria* and *Thyone*) found on both coasts of the Atlantic: named from the form it commonly assumes.

sea devil 1 A devilfish. **2** An angelfish.

sea dog 1 The harbor seal or the California sea lion. **2** The piked or spiny dogfish. **3** A sailor with long experience at sea. **4** A fog dog.

sea drake 1 The male of the eider duck. **2** A cormorant.

sea drift Anything cast up by the sea; flotsam, especially vegetable or animal matter.

sea·drome (sē′drōm′) *n. Aeron.* An airport established at sea for the accommodation and servicing of aircraft making overseas flights. [<SEA + -DROME]

sea duck Any duck that frequents salt water, belonging to the subfamily *Nyrocinae*; especially, the American eider duck *(Somateria mollissima dresseri),* ranging from Labrador to Maine and as far westward as the Great Lakes. See DUCK.

sea eagle 1 An eagle, related to the bald eagle, which lives principally on fish; especially, **Steller's sea eagle** *(Thalassoaëtus pelagicus),* found on the islands off Alaska. **2** The osprey.

sea fan A coral *(Gorgonia flabellum)* of Florida and the West Indies, with fanlike branches.

sea·far·er (sē′fâr′ər) *n.* A seaman; a mariner. See synonyms under SAILOR. [<SEA + FARER]

sea·far·ing (sē′fâr′ing) *adj.* Following the sea as a calling. —*n.* Traveling over the ocean.

sea fight A conflict between vessels on the high seas.

sea fire The phosphorescence of sea water.

sea floor The bottom of the sea.

sea flower A sea anemone or related anthozoan.

sea foam 1 Foam of the ocean. **2** Meerschaum. **3** A fluffy candy made of spun sugar.

sea food Edible fish, shellfish, etc.

sea fowl A sea bird or sea birds collectively.

sea fox The thresher shark.

sea front Land that borders on the sea; buildings, etc., that face the sea.

sea gage 1 The depth to which a vessel sinks in the water; the draft of a vessel. **2** A sounding instrument showing the depth of water by the pressure on a column of fluid Also **sea gauge.**

sea·girt (sē′gûrt′) *adj.* Surrounded by waters of the sea or ocean. [<SEA + GIRT[2]]

sea·go·ing (sē′gō′ing) *adj.* **1** Adapted for use on the ocean. **2** Skilful in navigation; seafaring.

sea grape A tropical American tree *(Coccolobis uvifera)* of the buckwheat family, with glossy, red-veined leaves, white flowers, and clusters of a purple fruit resembling grapes.

sea green A deep bluish green, like the color of sea water.

sea gull Any gull or large tern.

sea hog A porpoise.

sea holly A European coarse herb *(Eryngium maritimum)* of the carrot family.

sea horse 1 A teleost fish, usually 3 inches long, found in warm seas and allied to the pipefish; especially, *Hippocampus guttatus,* having a head resembling that of a horse. **2** A hippopotamus. **3** A walrus. **4** A fabulous animal, half horse and half fish, driven by Neptune. **5** A large white-crested wave.

SEA HORSE
(From 2 to 12 inches in length)

Sea Island cotton A valuable long-staple variety of cotton formerly grown on the Sea Islands, now also cultivated elsewhere.

Sea Islands A chain of small islands off the coasts of South Carolina, Georgia, and northern Florida.

sea kale A hardy perennial herb *(Crambe maritima)* of the mustard family, cultivated for its edible young shoots.

sea king 1 A viking as a maritime leader; Norse pirate king of the Middle Ages. **2** Neptune.

seal[1] (sēl) *n.* **1** An instrument or device used for making an impression upon some tenacious substance, as wax or a wafer; also, the impression made. **2** The wax, wafer, or similar token affixed to a document as a proof of authenticity; also, an impression, scroll, or mark on the paper. **3** A substance employed to secure a letter, door, lid, wrapper, joint, etc., firmly. **4** Anything that confirms or ratifies; a pledge; authentication. **5** Any instrumentality that keeps something close, secret, or unknown. **6** The fluid filling the trap of a drainage pipe and preventing the upward flow of gas. **7** An ornamental stamp for packages, etc. —*v.t.* **1** To affix a seal to, as to prove authenticity or prevent tampering. **2** To stamp or otherwise impress a seal upon in order to attest to weight, fineness, quality, etc. **3** To fasten or close with or as with a seal: to *seal* a letter; to *seal* a glass jar. **4** To grant or assign under seal. **5** To establish or settle finally; determine. **6** In Mormon usage, to solemnize forever, as a marriage or the adoption of a child. **7** To sign with the cross; also, to baptize or confirm. **8** To secure, set, or fill up, as with plaster. **9** To supply with a device or trap for preventing a return flow of gas or air. ◆ Homophone: *ceil.* [<OF *seel* <L *sigillum* a small picture, seal, dim. of *signum* a sign] —**seal′a·ble** *adj.*

GREAT SEAL OF THE UNITED STATES

seal[2] (sēl) *n.* **1** An aquatic carnivorous mammal (order or suborder *Pinnipedia*) mostly of high latitudes, of which some species, as the **fur seal,** yield valuable fur; any member of *Pinnipedia* except the walrus. Seals feed mostly on fish, and frequent seacoast rocks, ice floes, etc. In the breeding season they congregate on seacoasts, wild islands, etc. ◆ Collateral adjective: *phocine.* **2** The fur of a fur seal; sealskin. **3** Leather made from the hide of a seal. **4** Any fur prepared so as to look like sealskin. —*v.i.* To hunt seals. ◆ Homophone: *ceil.* [OE *seolh*]

SEAL
(Species vary from 7 to 12 feet long)

seal·ant (sē′lənt) *n.* Any substance which secures the contents of a container against contamination, evaporation, spoilage, or leakage.

sea lavender Any of a genus *(Limonium)* of mostly Old World maritime herbs bearing lavender-colored flowers.

sea lawyer A sailor given to criticizing and querying at every opportunity; a captious or argumentative person.

sea leather The skins of sharks, porpoises, and dogfishes prepared for use as leather.

sealed orders Orders given in a sealed envelope, with instructions to open at a given time or place under specified conditions; specifically, such orders given to the master of a ship before sailing.

sea legs The ability to walk aboard ship without losing one's balance.

seal·er[1] (sē′lər) *n.* **1** A person or thing that seals. **2** An officer who attests and certifies weights, materials, etc. [<SEAL[1]]

seal·er[2] (sē′lər) *n.* A person or ship employed in hunting seals. [<SEAL[2]]

seal·er·y (sē′lər·ē) *n. pl.* **·er·ies** **1** The business of hunting seals. **2** A place where seals are regularly hunted.

sea lettuce A green seaweed (genus *Ulva*) often used for food.

sea level The level continuous with that of the surface of the ocean at mean tide, between high and low water: used in reckoning altitudes.

sea lily A crinoid; a stalked marine invertebrate resembling a flower.

sealing wax A mixture of shellac and resin with turpentine and pigment that is fluid when heated but becomes solid as it cools: used for sealing papers and bottles.

sea lion One of various large, eared seals (family *Otariidae*), especially the California sea lion *(Zalophus californianus)*.

seal ring A signet ring; a finger ring containing an engraved stone.

seal·skin (sēl′skin′) *n.* **1** The under fur of the fur seal when prepared for use by removing the long hairs and dyeing dark-brown or black. **2** A coat or other article made of this fur.

sea lungwort An attractive American herb *(Mertensia maritima)* of the borage family, with white, long-stalked flowers, common to northern coasts.

Sea·ly·ham terrier (sē′lē·ham, -əm) See under TERRIER.

seam[1] (sēm) *n.* **1** A visible line of junction between parts, especially the edges of two pieces of cloth sewn together. **2** A crack; fissure; rent. **3** A ridge made in joining two pieces or left by a mold upon a casting. **4** A scar or cicatrix; also, a wrinkle. **5** A thin layer or stratum of rock. **6** A suture. — *v.t.* **1** To unite by means of a seam. **2** To mark with a cut, furrow, wrinkle, etc. **3** In knitting, to give the appearance of a seam to; purl. — *v.i.* **4** To crack open; become fissured. **5** In knitting, to form seams. ◆ Homophone: *seem.* [OE *sēam*] — **seam′er** *n.*

seam[2] (sēm) *n. Obs.* Any kind of grease; hence, fatness. ◆ Homophone: *seem.* [<OF *saim,* ult. <L *sagina* a fattening]

sea maiden *Poetic* A sea nymph or a mermaid. Also **sea maid.**

sea·man (sē′mən) *n. pl.* **·men** (-mən) **1** An enlisted man in the Navy or in the Coast Guard, graded according to his rank. **2** One skilled in the work of a ship and the ways of the sea; mariner; sailor. — **sea′man·like′** (-līk′) *adj.* — **sea′man·ly** *adj. & adv.*

sea·man·ship (sē′mən·ship) *n.* The skill and ability of a seaman in the operation and handling of a boat or ship.

sea·mark (sē′märk′) *n.* Any landmark that serves as a guide in navigation; a beacon; lighthouse.

Seam·as (shā′məs) Irish form of JAMES. Also **Seam′us.**

sea mew A gull, especially the European mew *(Larus canus).* [<SEA + MEW[3]]

sea mile See under MILE.

sea milkwort See under MILKWORT.

seam·less (sēm′lis) *adj.* Having no seam.

sea monster **1** Any huge, terrifying, or strange marine creature, as a devilfish or octopus. **2** A fabulous or mythical man-eating monster of the sea.

sea·mount (sē′mount′) *n.* Any of a widely distributed group of orogenic formations which rise to various heights from the ocean floor and serve as indicators of geologic processes; a submarine mountain.

sea mouse One of a family *(Aphroditidae)* of annelids with iridescent hairlike setae.

seam·ster (sēm′stər) *n.* A person employed in sewing. [OE *seamestre*]

seam·stress (sēm′stris) *n. fem.* A woman skilled in needlework, especially one whose occupation is sewing. Also spelled *sempstress.* [<OE *seamestre* a seamster + -ESS]

seam·y (sē′mē) *adj.* **seam·i·er, seam·i·est** **1** Full of seams, as the wrong side of a garment. **2** Showing the worst aspect: the *seamy* side. — **seam′i·ness** *n.*

Seán (shôn, shän) Irish form of JOHN.

Sean·ad Eir·eann (san′ad âr′ən) The Senate, or upper house, of the Irish Free State legislature. [<Irish *seanad* a senate + *Eireann* of Ireland]

sé·ance (sā′äns, *Fr.* sā·äns′) *n.* **1** A session or sitting. **2** A meeting of persons seeking spiritualistic manifestations. [<F <OF *seoir* sit <L *sedere*]

sean·na·chie (shan′ə·kē) *n. Scot.* A bard who preserved and repeated the traditions of the Scottish Highland tribes.

sea onion A bulbous herb *(Urginea maritima)* of the Old World, the source of squill.

sea otter A nearly extinct otter *(Enhydra lutris)* of the rocky shores of the North Pacific, about four feet long, and feeding principally on shellfish. The deep, rich fur, silvery-gray brown superficially, liver-brown beneath, is extremely valuable.

sea palm See under KELP.

sea pen A polyp (genus *Pennatula*) having a rodlike base with the polyps borne on lateral pinnae, giving the appearance of a feather.

sea·plane (sē′plān′) *n.* An airplane designed to rise from and descend upon the water.

sea·port (sē′pôrt′, -pōrt′) *n.* **1** A harbor or port on a coast accessible to seagoing ships. **2** A town located on such a harbor.

sea potato A brown alga (genus *Leathesia*) having a rounded, tuberous appearance.

sea power **1** A nation of great naval importance. **2** The naval strength of a nation.

sea purse *Zool.* The rectangular capsule enclosing the eggs or embryo of certain sharks, skates, and rays.

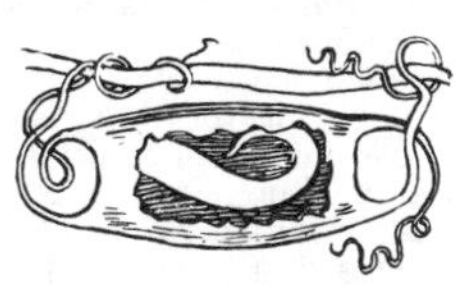

SEA PURSE

sea·quake (sē′kwāk′) *n.* An agitation of the sea from a submarine earthquake; a seismic disturbance under the sea.

sear[1] (sir) *v.t.* **1** To wither; dry up. **2** To burn the surface of; scorch. **3** To burn or cauterize, as with a hot iron; brand. **4** To make callous; harden. — *v.i.* **5** To become withered; dry up. — *adj.* Dried or blasted; withered. — *n.* A scar or brand. Also spelled *sere.* ◆ Homophones: *cere, sere.* [OE *sēarian* wither <*sear* dry]

sear[2] (sir) *n.* The pawl in a gunlock, which holds the hammer at half or full cock. ◆ Homophones: *cere, sere.* [<OF *serre* a grasp <*serrer* close, press <LL *serrare* bolt, bar <L *serare* bolt, bar <*sera* a lock; infl. in LL by L *serrare* saw]

sea raven **1** A deep-water sculpin. **2** The cormorant.

search (sûrch) *n.* **1** The act of seeking or looking diligently. **2** Investigation; inquiry. **3** A critical examination or scrutiny. **4** *Law* Right of search. — *v.t.* **1** To look through or explore thoroughly in order to find something; go over or through in making a search. **2** To subject (a person) to a search, as for concealed weapons, etc. **3** To examine with close attention; probe. **4** To penetrate or pierce: The wind *searches* my clothes. **5** To learn by examination or investigation: with *out.* — *v.i.* **6** To make a search. See synonyms under EXAMINE, HUNT. [<OF *cercher* <L *circare* go round, explore <*circus* a ring] — **search′a·ble** *adj.* — **search′er** *n.*

search·ing (sûr′ching) *adj.* **1** Investigating minutely. **2** Keenly penetrating. — **search′·ing·ly** *adv.* — **search′ing·ness** *n.*

search·light (sûrch′līt′) *n.* An apparatus containing a reflector, and so mounted that a beam of intensely brilliant light may be thrown in various directions for search or signaling; the beam of light from this apparatus.

search warrant A warrant directing an officer to search a house or other specified place for things alleged to be unlawfully concealed there.

sea risk Danger or hazard at sea; specifically, in marine insurance, a peril of the sea.

sea robin One of various gurnards, especially the American brown-finned species *(Prionotus strigatus).*

sea room Sufficient offing or space for a vessel to be maneuvered.

sea·scape (sē′skāp′) *n.* **1** An ocean view, especially when picturesque. **2** A picture presenting a marine view. [<SEA + (LAND)SCAPE]

sea-scout·ing (sē′skou′ting) *n.* Training in seamanship and water activities given to older boy scouts, called **sea scouts.**

sea serpent A snakelike animal, of monstrous size, believed by many to inhabit the ocean in very limited numbers.

sea·shell (sē′shel′) *n.* The shell of a marine mollusk.

sea·shore (sē′shôr′, -shōr′) *n.* Land adjacent to or bordering on the ocean; the ground between high- and low-water marks.

sea·sick (sē′sik′) *adj.* Suffering from seasickness.

sea·sick·ness (sē′sik′nis) *n.* Nausea, dizziness, and prostration caused by the motion of a vessel.

sea·side (sē′sīd′) *n.* The seashore, especially as a place of resort; also, the side abutting or facing the sea.

sea snake **1** A venomous fish-eating snake (subfamily *Hydrophinae*) of tropical seas, especially of the Indian Ocean. **2** A sea serpent.

sea·son (sē′zən) *n.* **1** A division of the year as determined by the earth's position with respect to the sun, and as marked by the temperature, moisture, vegetation, etc. The ancient Greeks had three seasons, spring, summer, and winter (mentioned by Homer and Hesiod); autumn appears first in Alcman: these four seasons are still used. **2** A period of time. **3** Any of the periods into which the Christian year is divided. **4** A period of special activity: usually with the definite article: the opera or hunting *season.* **5** A fit or suitable time. **6** That which imparts relish; seasoning. See synonyms under OPPORTUNITY, TIME. — **in season** **1** In condition and obtainable for use: Clams are *in season* during the summer. **2** In good or sufficient time; opportunely. **3** To be killed or taken by permission of the law. **4** Ready to mate or breed: said of animals. — *v.t.* **1** To increase the flavor or zest of (food), as by adding spices, etc. **2** To add zest or piquancy to. **3** To render more suitable for use, especially by drying or hardening, as timber. **4** To make accustomed or inured; harden: to *season* troops by strict discipline. **5** To mitigate or soften; moderate. — *v.i.* **6** To become seasoned. [<OF *seson* <LL *satio, -onis* sowing time <L, a sowing <*satus,* pp. of *serere* sow] — **sea′son·er** *n.*

sea·son·a·ble (sē′zən·ə·bəl) *adj.* **1** Being in keeping with the season. **2** Done at the proper time. See synonyms under CONVENIENT. — **sea′son·a·ble·ness** *n.* — **sea′son·a·bly** *adv.*

sea·son·al (sē′zən·əl) *adj.* Characteristic of, or occurring at, a certain season. — **sea′son·al·ly** *adv.*

sea·son·er (sē′zən·ər) *n.* **1** One who or that which seasons or gives added relish; a seasoning. **2** *U.S.* One engaged to serve for the season on a fishing vessel.

sea·son·ing (sē′zən·ing) *n.* **1** The act or process by which something, as lumber, is rendered fit for use. **2** Something added to food to give relish; especially, a condiment; hence, figuratively, something added to increase enjoyment or to relieve monotony. **3** The gradual process of acclimation to a new country or climate.

season ticket A ticket or pass entitling the holder to daily trips on a train for a certain period or to admission to a series of entertainments.

sea squirt An ascidian.

seat (sēt) *n.* **1** That on which one sits; a chair, bench, or stool. **2** That part of a thing upon which one rests in sitting, or upon which an object or another part rests. **3** That part of the person which sustains the weight of the body in sitting, or the corresponding portion of a garment. **4** The place where anything is situated, settled, or established: the *seat* of pain, the *seat* of a government; a site. **5** A place of abode; an estate or mansion, especially a country estate. **6** The privilege or right of membership in a legislative body, stock exchange, or the like. **7** The manner of sitting, as on horseback. **8** A surface or part upon which the base of anything rests. **9** A position in a legislature or an office. — *v.t.* **1** To place on a seat or seats; cause to sit down. **2** To have seats for; furnish with seats: The theater *seats* only 299 people. 3 To put a seat on or in; renew or repair the seat of. 4 To locate, settle, or center: usually in the passive: The French government is *seated* in Paris. 5 To fix or set firmly or in place. [<ON *sæti*. Akin to SIT.]

sea tangle A large brown seaweed (genus *Laminaria*) of the temperate zones.

seat·ing (sē′ting) *n.* 1 The act of providing with seats. 2 Fabric for upholstering seats. 3 A fitted support or base; a seat.

SEATO (sē′tō) Southeast Asia Treaty Organization.

seat of government 1 Any city (usually the capital) of a state or nation where the administrative offices of the government are located. 2 A town where a county court sits; a county seat.

sea trout 1 A trout that descends to the sea after spawning. 2 A weakfish.

seat·stone (sēt′stōn′) *n.* Underclay.

Se·at·tle (sē·at′l) A port on Puget Sound in west central Washington.

sea urchin An echinoderm (class *Echinoidea*) having a soft rounded body covered with a variously shaped shell bearing numerous movable spines.

sea wall 1 A wall or an embankment for preventing the encroachments of the sea or for breaking the force of the waves. 2 A ridge of stones, etc., washed up by the sea. — **sea-walled** (sē′wôld′) *adj.*

sea walnut Any of various ctenophores having an ovate body somewhat resembling a walnut, especially of the genus *Pleurobrachia.*

sea·wan (sē′wən) *n.* An oblong bead made from shell; hence, wampum: used by the Algonquian Indians of North America: also spelled *sewan.* Also **sea′want** (-wənt). [<Algonquian (Narraganset) *seawohn* scattered, i.e., unstrung (shell beads)]

sea·ward (sē′wərd) *adj.* 1 Going toward the sea. 2 Blowing, as wind, from the sea. — *adv.* In the direction of the sea: also **sea′wards.**

sea·ware (sē′wâr′) *n.* Seaweed; especially, coarse seaweed thrown up on the beach: used for manure and other purposes. [OE *sǣwār* < *sǣ* sea + *wār* alga]

sea·way (sē′wā′) *n.* 1 A way or lane over the sea. 2 An inland waterway that receives ocean shipping. 3 The headway made by a ship. 4 A rough sea: usually in *in a seaway.*

sea·weed (sē′wēd′) *n.* Any of a widely distributed class *(Algae)* of plants growing in the sea, including the kelps, rockweeds, dulse, sea lettuce, etc.

sea·wor·thy (sē′wûr′thē) *adj.* In fit condition for a voyage: said of a vessel. See synonyms under STAUNCH. — **sea′wor′thi·ness** *n.*

sea wrack Seaweed, especially a kelp or other large species.

se·ba·ceous (si·bā′shəs) *adj. Physiol.* 1 Pertaining to, appearing like, or secreting fat. 2 Designating the compound, saclike glands in the corium of the skin. [<NL *sebaceus* <L, a tallow candle < *sebum* tallow]

se·bac·ic (si·bas′ik, -bā′sik) *adj.* 1 Of or derived from fat. 2 *Chem.* Designating a white crystalline acid, $C_{10}H_{18}O_4$, contained in various oils, from which it is obtained by distillation. [<SEBAC(EOUS) + -IC]

Se·bas·tian (si·bas′chən, *Ger.* zä·bäs′tē·än) A masculine personal name. Also *Du., Sw.* **Se·bas·ti·aan** (sä·bäs′tē·än), *Fr.* **Sé·bas·tien** (sā·bäs·tyaṅ′), *Ital.* **Se·bas·tia·no** (sā′bäs·tyä′nō), *Lat.* **Se·bas·ti·a·nus** (si·bas′tē·ā′nəs); *Pg.* **Se·bas·tião** (sā′bäs·tyouṅ′). [<Gk., venerable]

Se·bas·to·pol (si·bas′tə·pōl) A former spelling of SEVASTOPOL.

Se·bas·tye (sa·bäs′tē·yə) A town in western Jordan, on the site of ancient Samaria.

Se·bat (shi·bät′) See SHEBAT.

Seb·ha (seb′hə) The capital of Fezzan, Libya.

sebi- *combining form* Fat; fatty matter: *sebiferous*: also, before vowels, **seb-**. Also **sebo-**. [<L *sebum* tallow]

se·bif·er·ous (si·bif′ər·əs) *adj.* Secreting or producing fat or fatty matter; sebaceous: *sebiferous* glands; *sebiferous* plants. Also **se·bip·a·rous** (si·bip′ər·əs). [<SEBI- + -FEROUS]

seb·or·rhe·a (seb′ə·rē′ə) *n. Pathol.* A morbid increase of secretion from the sebaceous glands: also called *steatorrhea.* Also **seb′or·rhoe′a.** [<L *sebum* tallow + -RRHEA]

se·bum (sē′bəm) *n. Physiol.* A fatty matter secreted by the sebaceous glands. [<L, tallow]

sec (sek) *adj. French* Dry: said of wines. Also *Italian* **sec·co** (sek′kō).

se·cant (sē′kənt, -kant) *adj.* Cutting, especially into two parts; intersecting. — *n.* 1 *Geom.* A straight line intersecting a given curve. 2 *Trig.* **a** A line drawn from the center of a circle through one extremity of an arc to the tangent drawn from the other extremity of the same arc. **b** The ratio of this line to the radius of the circle: the reciprocal of the cosine. [<L *secans, -antis,* ppr. of *secare* cut]

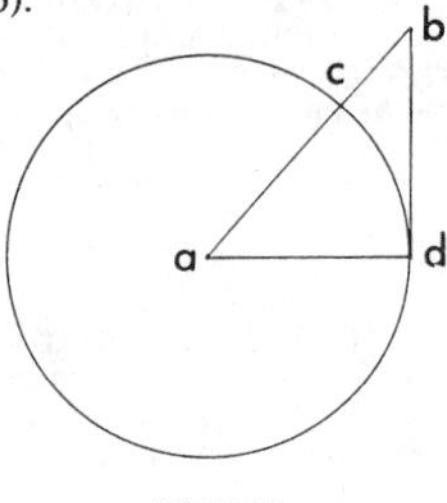

SECANT
Ratio of *ab* to *ad* is the secant of angle *a. ab* is the secant of arc *cd.*

sec·co painting (sek′ō) Painting done on dry plaster, as opposed to fresco painting on wet plaster. [<Ital., dry <L *siccus*]

se·cede (si·sēd′) *v.i.* **·ced·ed, ·ced·ing** To withdraw formally from a union, fellowship, or association, especially from a political or religious organization. [<L *secedere* withdraw < *se-* apart + *cedere* go] — **se·ced′er** *n.*

se·cern (si·sûrn′) *v.t.* 1 To separate; also, to distinguish. 2 *Physiol.* To secrete: said of a gland or follicle. [<L *secernere* < *se-* apart + *cernere* separate] — **se·cern′ent** *adj.* — **se·cern′ment** *n.*

se·cesh (si·sesh′) *n. U.S. Slang* A secessionist during the American Civil War; also, secessionists collectively. — *adj.* Belonging to, supporting, or sympathetic toward the Southern Confederacy. [Short for SECESSIONIST]

se·ces·sion (si·sesh′ən) *n.* 1 The act of seceding; withdrawal from fellowship, especially from political or religious association. 2 *Usually cap. U.S.* The withdrawal of the Southern States from the Union in 1860–61. [<L *secessio, -onis* < *secedere* SECEDE] — **se·ces′sion·al** *adj.*

se·ces·sion·ism (si·sesh′ən·iz′əm) *n. U.S.* The principles and doctrines of those who favored the withdrawal of the Southern States from the Union. — **se·ces′sion·ist** *adj.* & *n.*

seck (sek) *adj.* Barren; profitless; unenforceable by distress: said of rent. [<F *sec* <L *siccus* dry]

Seck·el (sek′əl, sik′əl) *n.* A variety of small, sweet pear. Also called *sickle pear.* [after the Pennsylvania farmer who introduced it]

se·clude (si·klōōd′) *v.t.* **·clud·ed, ·clud·ing** 1 To remove and keep apart from company or society of others; isolate. 2 To screen or shut off, as from view: usually in the past participle. [<L *secludere* < *se-* apart + *claudere* shut]

se·clud·ed (si·klōō′did) *adj.* 1 Separated; withdrawn; living apart from others. 2 Protected or screened. — **se·clud′ed·ly** *adv.* — **se·clud′ed·ness** *n.*

se·clu·sion (si·klōō′zhən) *n.* 1 The act of secluding, or the state or condition of being secluded; solitude; retirement. 2 A secluded place. [<Med. L *seclusio, -onis* <L *seclusus,* pp. of *secludere* SECLUDE]

Synonyms: privacy, retirement, retreat, secrecy, separation, solitude. See RETIREMENT, SOLITUDE. *Antonyms*: crowd, multitude, numbers, publicity, society, throng, world.

se·clu·sive (si·klōō′siv) *adj.* Having a tendency to seclusion. — **se·clu′sive·ly** *adv.* — **se·clu′sive·ness** *n.*

sec·ond[1] (sek′ənd) *n.* 1 A unit of time, 1/60 of a minute. 2 *Geom.* A unit of angular measure, 1/60 of a minute of arc. Symbol: ″ 3 In the duodecimal notation, 1/12 of an inch or prime. [<OF *seconde* <Med. L *seconda (minuta),* lit., second (minute), i.e., the result of the second operation of sexagesimal division, fem. of L *secundus* SECOND[2]]

sec·ond[2] (sek′ənd) *adj.* 1 Next in order, authority, responsibility, etc., after the first: the ordinal of *two.* 2 Ranking next to or below the first or best; of inferior quality or value; secondary; subordinate. 3 Identical in character with another or preceding one; another; other. 4 *Music* Lower in pitch, or rendering a lower part than the principal one. — *n.* 1 The one next after the first in position, rank, importance, or quality. 2 An attendant who supports or aids another, as in a duel. 3 *pl.* Articles of merchandise of imperfect manufacture, of second grade, or of inferior quality. 4 *Music* **a** The interval between any note and the next above or below in the diatonic scale. **b** A note separated by this interval from any other. **c** Two notes at this interval written or sounded together. **d** The resulting dissonance. **e** A second or subordinate part, instrument, or voice. 5 In parliamentary law, an utterance whereby a motion is seconded: Do I hear a *second*? — **major second** *Music* A second between whose tones is a difference of pitch of a step. — *v.t.* 1 To act as a supporter or assistant of; promote; stimulate; encourage. 2 In deliberative bodies, to support formally, as a motion, resolution, etc., as a prerequisite to discussion or adoption. See synonyms under AID, HELP. — *adv.* In the second order, place, or rank: also, in formal discourse, **sec′ond·ly.** [<OF <L *secundus* following < *sequi* follow]

Second Advent The expected second coming of Christ, to judge the world. Also **Second Coming.** — **Second Adventist**

sec·on·dar·y (sek′ən·der′ē) *adj.* 1 Of second rank, grade, or influence; subordinate; auxiliary; subsequent; resultant. 2 Depending on what is primary or original. 3 *Ornithol.* Of or pertaining to the secondaries of a bird's wings. 4 *Electr.* Of, pertaining to, or noting an induced current or its circuit, especially in an induction coil. 5 *Chem.* Formed by replacement of atoms or radicals in the molecules of certain organic compounds: a *secondary* alcohol. 6 *Geol.* Subsequent in origin; involving some chemical or physical change of the original mineral: contrasted with *primary.* 7 Pertaining to instruction in a secondary school. — *n. pl.* **·dar·ies** 1 One who acts in a secondary or subordinate capacity; an assistant; a deputy or delegate. 2 Anything of secondary size, position, or importance. 3 A secondary planet; a satellite. 4 *Ornithol.* One of the feathers that grow on the second joint or forearm of a bird's wing. See illustrations under BIRD, FOWL. 5 One of the hind wings of an insect. — **sec′on·dar′i·ly** *adv.*

Sec·on·dar·y (sek′ən·der′ē) *n. Geol.* 1 The Mesozoic era. 2 The rocks formed in this era. — *adj.* Belonging to or occurring in the Mesozoic era.

secondary education High school or preparatory school education; schooling beyond the elementary or primary, and below the college, level.

secondary electron *Physics* An electron emitted from a surface by the direct impact of electrons or ions, as produced by an X-ray machine.

secondary emission *Physics* The emission of secondary electrons from a substance exposed to direct radiation, as by X-rays, etc. Also **secondary radiation.**

secondary school See under SCHOOL.

second base In baseball, the second base reached by the runner, situated between first and third base. See illustration under BASEBALL.

second childhood A time or condition of foolishness or dotage; senility.

sec·ond-class (sek′ənd·klas′, -kläs′) *adj.* 1 Ranking next below the first or best; inferior; mediocre. 2 Of, pertaining to, or belonging to a class next below the first: *second-class* mail, *second-class* standing, *second-class* ticket, etc. — *adv.* By second-class ticket or by using second-class conveniences: to travel *second-class.*

second class A class of mail including all periodical printed matter.

se·conde (si·kond′, *Fr.* sə·gôṅd′) *n.* The second position in fencing. [<F, fem. of *second* <OF, SECOND]

sec·ond·er (sek′ən·dər) *n.* One who seconds, supports, or approves what is attempted, moved, or proposed by another.

second fiddle 1 The part played by the second violins in an orchestral composition. 2 Any secondary status; a substitute — **to be (or play) second fiddle** To be of secondary importance in an undertaking or in the affections of another.

sec·ond-hand (sek′ənd·hand′) *adj.* 1 Having been previously owned, worn, or used by another; not new. 2 Received from another;

not direct from the original source: *second-hand* information. **3** Employed in handling or dealing in merchandise that is not new. **4** Of inferior grade; being a poor imitation: a *second-hand* statesman. —*n.* That which is second-hand or a poor imitation.

second hand The hand that marks the seconds on a clock or a watch.

sec·on·dine (sek′ən·dīn, -din) See SECUNDINE.

second mortgage A mortgage given next after and subordinate to a first mortgage.

second nature A disposition or character that is acquired and not innate; deep-seated habits that have become fixed.

se·con·do (sā·kôn′dō) *n. pl.* **·di** (-dē) *Italian* The second part in concerted music, especially in a pianoforte duet; also, the performer of this part.

sec·ond-rate (sek′ənd·rāt′) *adj.* Second in quality, size, rank, importance, etc.; second-class. —*n.* That which is mediocre or of inferior value: also **sec′ond-rat′er.**

second sight **1** The faculty or power of seeing the invisible. **2** The power of prophecy; intuition; clairvoyance. —**sec′ond-sight′ed** *adj.*

second sound *Physics* The peculiar vibratory motion, resembling that of sound waves, associated with the rapid transfer of heat by helium atoms cooled to within two degrees of absolute zero.

Second World War See WORLD WAR II in table under WAR.

sec·par (sek′pär) *n. Astron.* Parsec. [< *sec(ond of) par(allax)*]

se·cre·cy (sē′krə·sē) *n. pl.* **·cies** **1** The condition or quality of being secret or hidden; concealment. **2** The character of being secretive; secretiveness. **3** Privacy; retirement; solitude. Also **se′cret·ness.** See synonyms under SECLUSION. [Earlier *secretee* < obs. *secre* <OF *secré* secret; refashioned after *primacy, lunacy,* etc.]

se·cret (sē′krit) *adj.* **1** Kept separate or hidden from view or knowledge, or from all persons except the individuals concerned; not immediately apparent; unseen; occult. **2** Affording privacy; secluded. **3** Good at keeping secrets; close-mouthed. **4** Unrevealed or unavowed as such: a *secret* partner. **5** *U.S.* Designating defense information classified second to top-secret material with regard to required security and protection. Compare TOP-SECRET, CONFIDENTIAL (def. 4). —*n.* **1** Something not to be told. **2** A thing undiscovered or unknown. **3** An underlying reason; that which, when known, explains; key. **4** A secret contrivance. **5** Secrecy. —**in secret** In privacy; in a hidden place. [<OF *secré, secret* <L *secretus,* orig. pp. of *secernere* < *se-* apart + *cernere* separate] —**se′cret·ly** *adv.*

Synonyms (adj.): clandestine, concealed, covered, covert, furtive, hid, hidden, latent, mysterious, obscure, occult, private, recondite, retired, unknown, unrevealed, unseen, veiled. See MYSTERIOUS. *Antonyms*: aboveboard, apparent, clear, evident, manifest, obvious, plain, transparent, unconcealed, undisguised.

se·cret·age (sē′krə·tij) *n.* A process of preparing or dressing furs by means of mercury or some of its salts, in order to facilitate felting and matting; carroting. Also **se′cret·ing.** [<F *sécréter* conceal; because it was at first a secret process]

sec·re·tar·i·at (sek′rə·târ′ē·it, -at) *n.* **1** A secretary's position. **2** The place where a secretary transacts his business and preserves his official records. **3** The entire staff of secretaries in an office; especially, the department headed by a governmental secretary. Also **sec′re·tar′i·ate.** [<F *secrétariat* <Med. L *secretariatus* the office of secretary < *secretarius* SECRETARY]

Sec·re·tar·i·at (sek′rə·târ′ē·it, -at) *n.* The administrative organ of the former League of Nations and of the present United Nations, consisting of the Secretary General, his officials, and secretaries.

sec·re·tar·y (sek′rə·ter′ē) *n. pl.* **·tar·ies** **1** A person employed to deal with correspondence, keep records, and handle clerical business for a person, business, committee, or organization. **2** An executive officer presiding over and managing a department of government. **3** A writing desk with a bookcase or cabinet with pigeonholes on top. —**under-secretary** In a government department, the official who ranks next below the secretary. [<Med. L *secretarius* <L *secretum* a secret, neut. of *secretus* SECRET] —**sec′re·tar′i·al** (-târ′ē·əl) *adj.*

secretary bird A South African bird (genus *Sagittarius*), having long legs and a crested head: so named from the resemblance of its crest to quill pens stuck behind the ear. It preys on serpents.

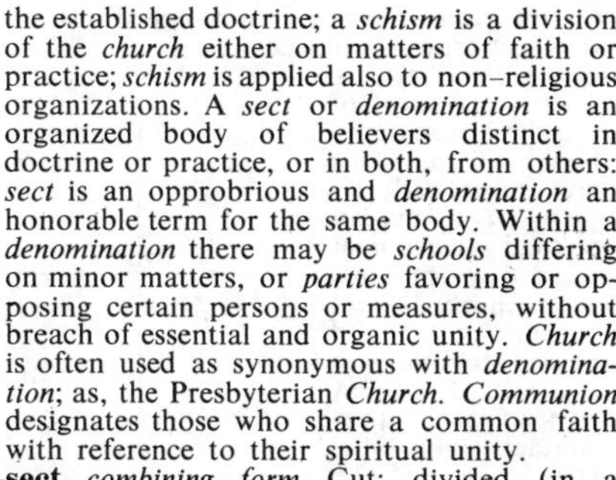

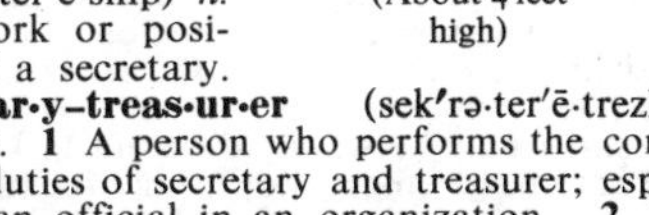

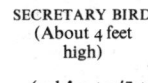

SECRETARY BIRD (About 4 feet high)

secretary general *pl.* **secretaries general** A chief secretary; an assistant to a governor general. —**sec′re·tar′y-gen′er·al·cy** *n.*

sec·re·tar·y·ship (sek′rə·ter′ē·ship) *n.* The work or position of a secretary.

sec·re·tar·y-treas·ur·er (sek′rə·ter′ē·trezh′ər·ər) *n.* **1** A person who performs the combined duties of secretary and treasurer; especially, an official in an organization. **2** In Canada, a town or city clerk.

se·crete (si·krēt′) *v.t* **·cret·ed, ·cret·ing** **1** To remove or keep from observation; conceal; hide. **2** *Biol.* To separate or elaborate from blood or sap. [Alter. of obs. *secret, v.* conceal; refashioned after L *secretus* SECRET] —**se·cre′tor** *n.*

Synonym: conceal. *Secrete* is a stronger word than *conceal,* and is used chiefly of such material objects as may be separated from the person, or from their ordinary surroundings, and put in unlooked-for places; a man *conceals* a scar on his face, but does not *secrete* it; a thief *secretes* stolen goods; an officer may also be said to *secrete* himself to watch the thief. See HIDE.

se·cre·tin (si·krē′tin) *n. Biochem.* A hormone found in the lining of the intestinal wall and stimulating the flow of pancreatic juice. [<SECRET(ION) + -IN]

se·cre·tion (si·krē′shən) *n.* **1** *Biol.* The process by which materials are separated from blood or sap and elaborated into new substances: the *secretion* of milk, gastric juice, or urine. Secretion in animals is generally performed by glandular epithelial cells. Compare EXCRETION. **2** The substance secreted, as saliva or milk. **3** The act of concealing. **4** A deposit of mineral matter in successive coatings, filling cavities, and fissures.

se·cre·tive (si·krē′tiv) *adj.* **1** (*also* sē′krə·tiv) Inclined to secrecy; reticent. **2** Producing or causing secretion. —**se·cre′tive·ly** *adv.* —**se·cre′tive·ness** *n.*

se·cre·to·ry (si·krē′tər·ē) *adj.* Pertaining to secretion. —*n. pl.* **·ries** A secreting vessel or gland.

secret service **1** Investigation conducted secretly for a government. **2** The secret or espionage work of various government agencies in time of war.

Secret Service A section of the Department of the Treasury concerned with the suppression of counterfeiting, the protection of the president of the United States, etc.

secret society A society or association that uses secret signs, oaths, rites, or symbols.

sect (sekt) *n.* **1** A body of persons distinguished by peculiarities of faith and practice from other bodies adhering to the same general system; specifically, the adherents collectively of a particular creed or confession; a denomination, or an organized body of dissenters from an established or older form of faith. **2** Adherents of a particular philosophical system or teacher. **3** Any number of persons united in opinion or interest, as in the state or in society; a party or faction; an order. **4** A cutting in horticulture. [<OF *secte* <L *secta* a following, a faction < *sequi* follow. Doublet of SET.]

Synonyms: church, communion, denomination, heresy, heterodoxy, party, schism, school. *Heresy* or *heterodoxy* is a departure from the established doctrine; a *schism* is a division of the *church* either on matters of faith or practice; *schism* is applied also to non-religious organizations. A *sect* or *denomination* is an organized body of believers distinct in doctrine or practice, or in both, from others: *sect* is an opprobrious and *denomination* an honorable term for the same body. Within a *denomination* there may be *schools* differing on minor matters, or *parties* favoring or opposing certain persons or measures, without breach of essential and organic unity. *Church* is often used as synonymous with *denomination*; as, the Presbyterian *Church. Communion* designates those who share a common faith with reference to their spiritual unity.

-sect *combining form* Cut; divided (in a specified manner or number of parts): *vivisect.* Also **-sected,** as in *bisected.* [<L *sectus,* pp. of *secare* cut]

sec·tar·i·an (sek·târ′ē·ən) *adj.* Pertaining to a sect; bigoted. —*n.* A member of a sect, especially if bigoted.

sec·tar·i·an·ism (sek·târ′ē·ən·iz′əm) *n.* Sectarian character or tendency; excessive devotion to or zeal for a particular sect.

sec·tar·i·an·ize (sek·târ′ē·ən·īz′) *v.t.* **·ized, ·iz·ing** To make sectarian.

sec·ta·ry (sek′tər·ē) *n. pl.* **·ries** **1** A sectarian: mostly used opprobriously. **2** A dissenter from an established church; a nonconformist. **3** *Obs.* A religious sect. Also **sec′ta·rist.** [< MF *sectaire* <Med. L *sectarius* <L *secta* a sect]

sec·tile (sek′til) *adj.* Admitting of being cut or severed smoothly. [<F <L, neut. of *sectilis* < *sectus,* pp. of *secare* cut] —**sec·til·i·ty** (sek·til′ə·tē) *n.*

sec·tion (sek′shən) *n.* **1** A separate part or division; a portion of a book, treatise, or writing; a subdivision of a chapter; also, a division of law. **2** A distinct part of a country, community, etc. **3** *U.S.* An area of public land one mile square, containing 640 acres and constituting 1/36 of a township. **4** A portion of a railway company's tracks under the care of a particular set of men. **5** In a sleeping-car, a space containing two berths. **6** A tactical unit of the U.S. Army, smaller than a platoon and larger than a squad. **7** A division of an animal group, of indeterminate rank. **8** A representation, picture, or drawing of a building, machine, geological formation, etc., as if cut by an intersecting plane; also, the thing so cut or viewed. **9** A very thin slice of anything, especially for microscopic examination. **10** The character §, indicating a subdivision: used also as a reference mark. **11** The act of cutting; division by cutting, as in surgical operations. **12** The figure formed by the intersection of a plane or other surface with a solid. In mechanical drawing the following sections are distinguished: **lengthwise** or **longitudinal section,** usually representing objects as cut lengthwise through the center; **cross-section** or **transverse section,** cut crosswise; **horizontal section,** cut horizontally, and usually through the center; **oblique section,** cut at various angles. See synonyms under PART. —**frozen section** A cutting, slice, or sliced surface of a frozen part: much employed in anatomy. —*v.t.* **1** To cut or divide into sections. **2** To shade (a drawing) so as to designate a section or sections. [<MF <L *sectio, -onis* < *sectus,* pp. of *secare* cut]

-section *combining form* The act or process of cutting or dividing: *vivisection.* [<L *sectio, -onis* a cutting < *secare* cut]

sec·tion·al (sek′shən·əl) *adj.* **1** Pertaining to a section, as of a country; local; characteristic of the people of a certain section or area: a *sectional* dialect. **2** Dividing or alienating one section from another: *sectional* problems. **3** Made up of sections. —**sec′tion·al·ly** *adv.*

sectional feeling Intense consciousness of the differences between the interests of one section of a country and those of another.

sec·tion·al·ism (sek′shən·əl·iz′əm) *n.* Regard for a particular section of the country rather than the whole; sectional feeling. —**sec′tion·al·ist** *n.*

sec·tion·al·ize (sek′shən·əl·īz′) *v.t.* **·ized, ·iz·ing** **1** To make sectional. **2** To divide into sections. —**sec′tion·al·i·za′tion** *n.*

section gang A work crew assigned to a certain section of a railroad.

sec·tor (sek′tər) *n.* 1 *Geom.* A part of a circle bounded by two radii and the arc subtended by them. 2 A mathematical instrument consisting of two arms marked with various scales and hinged together at one end. 3 *Mil.* A part of a front in contact with the enemy. —*v.t.* To divide into sectors. [<LL <L, a cutter <*sectus,* pp. of *secare* cut]

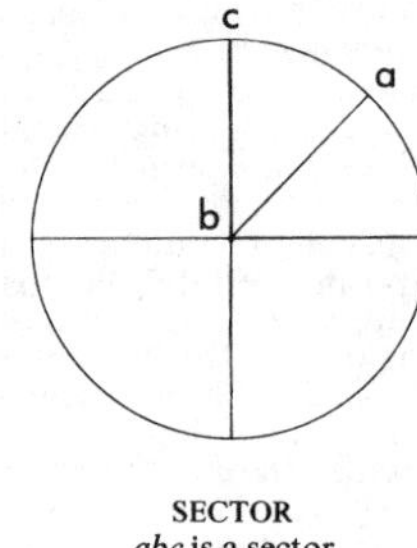

SECTOR
abc is a sector of the circle.

sec·to·ri·al (sek·tôr′ē·əl, -tō′rē-) *adj.* 1 Of or pertaining to a sector. 2 *Zool.* Adapted for cutting; carnassial.

sec·u·lar (sek′yə·lər) *adj.* 1 Of or pertaining to this world or the present life; temporal; worldly: contrasted with *religious* or *spiritual.* 2 Not under the control of the church; civil; not ecclesiastical. 3 Not concerned with religion; not sacred: *secular* art. 4 Not bound by monastic vows: opposed to *regular*: the *secular* clergy. 5 Occurring or observed but once in an age or century. 6 Lasting for ages. See synonyms under PROFANE. —*n.* 1 One in holy orders who is not bound by monastic vows. 2 A layman. [<OF *seculer* <LL *saecularis* <L, belonging to an age <*saeculum* a generation, an age]

sec·u·lar·ism (sek′yə·lə·riz′əm) *n.* Regard for worldly as opposed to spiritual matters; specifically, the belief of secularists.

sec·u·lar·ist (sek′yə·lə·rist) *n.* 1 A person who bases morality on the well-being of mankind in this world without any consideration of religious systems and forms of worship. 2 One who believes that religion should not be introduced into public education or the management of public affairs. —**sec′u·lar·is′tic** *adj.*

sec·u·lar·i·ty (sek′yə·lar′ə·tē) *n.* 1 Secularism; worldliness. 2 Any practice or interest belonging exclusively to the present life.

sec·u·lar·ize (sek′yə·lə·rīz′) *v.t.* **·ized, ·iz·ing** 1 To make secular; convert from sacred to secular uses. 2 To make worldly. 3 To change from a monastic or regular to a secular, as a monk. —**sec′u·lar·i·za′tion** *n.*

se·cund (sē′kund, sek′und) *adj. Bot.* Having the parts or organs arranged on one side only, as certain flowers; unilateral. [<L *secundus* following. See SECOND^2.]

Se·cun·der·a·bad (si·kun′dər·ä·bäd′) A northern suburb of Hyderabad, Andhra Pradesh, India, where conduction of malaria by mosquitoes was discovered by Sir Ronald Ross, 1898.

sec·un·dine (sek′ən·dīn, -din) *n.* 1 *Bot.* The inner, first-developed coat or integument of an ovule. 2 That which remains in the womb to be expelled after childbirth: usually in the plural. Also spelled *secondine.* [<LL *secundinae,* pl., the afterbirth <L *secundus* following. See SECOND^2.]

se·cun·dum na·tu·ram (si·kun′dəm nə·tyo͝or′·əm) *Latin* According to nature.

se·cun·dum u·sum (si·kun′dəm yo͞o′səm) *Latin* According to usage or ritual.

se·cure (si·kyo͝or′) *adj.* 1 Guarded against or not likely to be exposed to danger; safe. 2 Free from fear, apprehension, etc. 3 Confident; careless. 4 Assured; certain; sure: followed by *of,* sometimes by an infinitive. 5 So strong or well made as to render loss, escape, or failure impossible. —*v.* **·cured, ·cur·ing** *v.t.* 1 To make secure; protect. 2 To make firm, tight, or fast; fasten. 3 To make sure or certain; insure; guarantee. 4 To obtain possession of; get. —*v.i.* 5 To be or become secure; take precautions. See synonyms under ARREST, BIND, CATCH, GET, OBTAIN, PRESERVE, PURCHASE, RETAIN. [<L *securus* <*se-* without + *cura* care. Doublet of SURE.] —**se·cur′a·ble** *adj.* —**se·cure′ly** *adv.* —**se·cure′ment** *n.* —**se·cure′ness** *n.* —**se·cur′er** *n.*

Synonyms (adj.): assured, careless, certain, confident, defended, guarded, impregnable, insured, protected, safe, sure, unassailable, undisturbed, unmolested, unsuspecting, untroubled. See FIRM. *Antonyms*: dangerous, dubious, exposed, hazardous, imperiled, insecure, perilous, risky.

Securities and Exchange Commission An agency of the U.S. government which supervises the registration of security issues, prevents fraudulent stock manipulations, and regulates transactions in securities.

se·cur·i·ty (si·kyo͝or′ə·tē) *n. pl.* **·ties** 1 The state of being secure; specifically, freedom from danger, risk, care, poverty, or apprehension. 2 One who or that which secures or guarantees; surety. 3 *pl.* Written promises or something deposited or pledged for payment of money, as stocks, bonds, etc. 4 Methods adopted for insuring freedom or secrecy of action, communications, etc., as in wartime; also, the protection afforded by such methods.

Synonyms: bail, collateral, earnest, gage, pledge, surety. The first four words agree in denoting something given or deposited as an assurance of something to be given, paid, or done. An *earnest* is a portion delivered in advance, as when part of the purchase money is paid, "to bind the bargain." A *pledge* or *security* may be wholly different in kind from that to be given or paid; it may greatly exceed it in value, and may be of real or personal property; a *pledge* (as here considered) is always of personal property or chattels. Every pawnshop contains unredeemed *pledges*; land, merchandise, bonds, etc., are frequently offered and accepted as *security. Collateral* is property, as stocks, bonds, etc., actually deposited as *security,* often termed *collateral security.* A person may become *security* or *surety* for another's payment of a debt, appearance in court, etc.; in the latter case, he is said to become *bail* for that person; the person accused gives *bail* for himself. *Gage* survives only as a literary word, chiefly in certain phrases; as, "the *gage* of battle."

Security Council A permanent organ of the United Nations charged with the maintenance of international peace and security and consisting of five permanent members (China, France, the U.S.S.R., the United Kingdom, and the United States) and six elected members, three of whom are replaced each year.

se·dan (si·dan′) *n.* 1 A closed automobile having one compartment for passengers and driver. 2 A closed chair, for one passenger, carried by two or more men by means of poles at the sides: also **sedan chair.** [? <Ital. *sedere* sit <L]

Se·dan (si·dan′, *Fr.* sə·däṅ′) A city in NE France on the Meuse; scene of the decisive French defeat in the Franco-Prussian War, 1870.

se·date (si·dāt′) *adj.* Characterized by habitual composure; staid. [<L *sedatus,* pp. of *sedare* make calm, settle <*sedere* sit] —**se·date′ly** *adv.* —**se·date′ness** *n.*

Synonyms: calm, contemplative, demure, grave, quiet, serene, serious, sober, solemn, staid, still, thoughtful, tranquil, undisturbed, unruffled. See CALM, SERIOUS, THOUGHTFUL. *Antonyms*: agitated, disturbed, excited, flighty, flurried, frolicsome, gay, lively, mad, merry.

se·da·tion (si·dā′shən) *n. Med.* The act of reducing distress, irritation, excitement, etc., particularly by administering sedatives.

sed·a·tive (sed′ə·tiv) *adj.* 1 Having a soothing tendency. 2 *Med.* Allaying irritation; assuaging pain. —*n.* Any means, as a medicine, of allaying irritation or pain.

sed·en·tar·y (sed′ən·ter′ē) *adj.* 1 Sitting much of the time; accustomed to sit much or to work in a sitting posture; hence, settled in one place, as certain tribes; sluggish; inactive. 2 Characterized by sitting. 3 Resulting from much or long sitting. 4 *Zool.* Remaining in one place; attached or fixed to an object; sessile. [<L *sedentarius* <*sedens, -entis,* ppr. of *sedere* sit] —**sed′en·tar′i·ly** *adv.* —**sed′en·tar′i·ness** *n.*

Se·der (sā′dər) *n. pl.* **Se·da·rim** (sə·där′im) or **Se·ders** In Judaism, a ceremonial dinner commemorating the Exodus, held on the eve of the first day of Passover, and traditionally on the eve of the second day by Jews outside of Israel.

sedge (sej) *n.* 1 A grasslike cyperaceous herb (genus *Carex*) with flowers densely clustered in spikes: widely distributed in marshy places. 2 Any coarse, rushlike or flaglike herb growing in a wet place. [OE *secg*] —**sedged** *adj.* —**sedg′y** *adj.*

Sedge·moor (sej′mo͝or) A tract in Somersetshire, England; scene of the victory of James II over the Duke of Monmouth, 1685.

Sedg·wick (sej′wik), **Anne Douglas,** 1873–1935, U.S. novelist.

se·di·le (si·dī′lē) *n. pl.* **·dil·i·a** (-dil′ē·ə) A seat (usually one of three) near the altar in the chancel of a church, for officiating clergy: usually in the plural. Also **se·dil′i·um.** [<L, a seat <*sedere* sit]

sed·i·ment (sed′ə·mənt) *n.* 1 Matter that settles to the bottom of a liquid; settlings; dregs; lees. 2 *Geol.* Fragmentary material deposited by water or air. See synonyms under WASTE. [<MF *sédiment* <L *sedimentum* a settling <*sedere* sit, settle]

sed·i·men·ta·ry (sed′ə·men′tər·ē) *adj.* 1 Pertaining to or having the character of sediment. 2 *Geol.* Designating rocks, as shale and sandstone, composed of fragments of other rocks deposited after transportation from their sources, and including also rocks formed by precipitation, as gypsum, or by calcareous secretions of animals, as certain limestones. Also **sed′i·men′tal.**

sed·i·men·ta·tion (sed′ə·men·tā′shən) *n.* 1 The accumulation or deposition of sediment. 2 The depositing of an insoluble material.

se·di·tion (si·dish′ən) *n.* 1 Language or conduct directed against public order and the tranquillity of the state. 2 The incitement of such disorder, tending toward treason, but lacking an overt act. 3 Dissension; revolt. See synonyms under REVOLUTION. [<OF <L *seditio, -onis* <*sed-* aside + *itio, -onis* a going <*ire* go]

se·di·tion·ar·y (si·dish′ən·er′ē) *adj.* Seditious. —*n. pl.* **·ar·ies** One who promotes sedition: also **se·di′tion·ist.**

se·di·tious (si·dish′əs) *adj.* 1 Pertaining to, promotive of, or having the character of sedition. 2 Inclined to, taking part in, or guilty of sedition. See synonyms under REBELLIOUS, TURBULENT. [OF *seditieux* <L *seditiosus* <*seditio, -onis* SEDITION] —**se·di′tious·ly** *adv.* —**se·di′tious·ness** *n.*

Se·dl·ča·ny (sed′l·chä′nē) A village in southern Bohemia, Czechoslovakia. *German* **Sed·litz** (zed′lits). Also *Seidlitz.*

se·duce (si·do͞os′, -dyo͞os′) *v.t.* **·duced, ·duc·ing** 1 To lead astray; entice into wrong, disloyalty, etc.; tempt. 2 To induce, as a woman, to surrender chastity; debauch. See synonyms under ALLURE. [<L *seducere* lead apart <*se-* apart + *ducere* lead] —**se·duc′er** *n.* —**se·duc′i·ble** or **se·duce′a·ble** *adj.*

se·duc·tion (si·duk′shən) *n.* 1 The act of seducing. 2 Something which seduces; an enticement. Also **se·duce′ment.** [<MF *séduction* <L *seductio, -onis* <*seductus,* pp. of *seducere.* See SEDUCE.]

se·duc·tive (si·duk′tiv) *adj.* Tending to seduce; enticing. —**se·duc′tive·ly** *adv.* —**se·duc′tive·ness** *n.*

se·duc·tress (si·duk′tris) *n.* A female seducer.

se·du·li·ty (si·do͞o′lə·tē, -dyo͞o′-) *n.* The state or character of being sedulous.

sed·u·lous (sej′o͞o·ləs) *adj.* Constant in application or attention; persevering in effort; assiduous. See synonyms under INDUSTRIOUS. [<L *sedulus* careful, appar. <*sedulo* sincerely <*se dolo* without guile] —**sed′u·lous·ly** *adv.* —**sed′u·lous·ness** *n.*

se·dum (sē′dəm) *n.* Any of a large genus *(Sedum)* of chiefly perennial smooth plants, the stonecrops, having very thick leaves and cymose flowers. [<L, house leek]

SEDUM

see^1 (sē) *v.* **saw, seen, see·ing** *v.t.* 1 To perceive with the eyes; gain knowledge or awareness of by means of one's vision. 2 To perceive with the mind; understand; comprehend. 3 To find out or ascertain; inquire about: *See* who is at the door. 4 To have experience or knowledge of; undergo: We have *seen* more peaceful times. 5 To encounter; chance to meet: I *saw* your husband today. 6 To have a meeting or interview with; visit or receive as a guest, visitor, etc.: The doctor will *see* you now. **7** To attend as a spectator; view. **8** To accompany; escort. **9** To take care; be sure: with a clause as object: *See* that you do it! **10** In poker, to accept (a bet) or equal the bet of (a player) by betting an equal sum. — *v.i.* **11** To have or exercise the power of sight. **12** To find out; inquire: I will go and *see.* **13** To understand; comprehend. **14** To think; consider. **15** To take care; be attentive: *See* to your work. **16** To gain certain knowledge, as by awaiting an outcome: We will *see* if you are right or wrong. — **to see about** **1** To inquire into the facts, causes, etc., of. **2** To take care of; attend to. — **to see through** **1** To penetrate, as a disguise or deception. **2** To aid or protect, as throughout a period of difficulty or danger. See synonyms under LOOK. ◆ Homophone: *sea.* [OE *sēon*]

see[2] (sē) *n.* **1** The local seat from which a bishop, an archbishop, or the pope exercises jurisdiction; espiscopal or papal jurisdiction, authority, or rank; a bishop's or pope's office. **2** *Obs.* A seat, especially of dignity or power. — **Holy See** The pope's jurisdiction, court, or office; erected as an independent state, Feb. 11, 1929: also **See of Rome.** ◆ Homophone: *sea.* [<OF *se, sie, sed* <L *sedes* a seat]

see·catch (sē'kach') *n. pl.* **·catch·ie** An adult male fur seal. [<Russian *sekach*]

seed (sēd) *n.* **1** The ovule from which a plant may be reproduced; the fertilized ovule containing an embryo. **2** That from which anything springs; source. **3** Offspring; children. **4** The male fertilizing element; semen; milt. **5** Any small seedlike fruit; also, any part of a plant from which it may be propagated, as bulbs, tubers, etc. **6** A young oyster fit for transplanting. **7** Race; generation; birth. **8** The seed-bearing stage; hence, overripeness. **9** *U.S. Dial.* An animal or animals used for breeding. — *v.t.* **1** To sow with seed. **2** To sow (seed). **3** To remove the seeds from: to *seed* raisins. **4** To strew (moisture-bearing clouds) with crystals, as of dry ice, silver iodide, etc., in order to initiate precipitation. **5** In sports: **a** To arrange (the drawing for positions in a tournament, etc.) so that the more skilled competitors meet only in the later events. **b** To rank (a skilled competitor) thus. — *v.i.* **6** To sow seed. **7** To grow to maturity and produce or shed seed. — **to go to seed** **1** To develop and shed seed. **2** To become shabby, useless, etc. ◆ Homophone: *cede.* [OE *sǣd*] — **seed'less** *adj.*

seed·bed (sēd'bed') *n.* **1** A bed of earth planted with seeds, especially for later transplanting. **2** A place of early growth or nurture: the *seedbed* of neurosis.

seed bud *Bot.* The germ within a seed; also, the ovule.

seed cake **1** A sweet cake containing aromatic seeds, as caraway. **2** Cottonseed-oil cake.

seed·case (sēd'kās') *n. Bot.* A seed vessel; pericarp.

seed capsule *Bot.* A testa (def. 1).

seed coat *Bot.* The integument of a seed, usually the outer one or testa.

seed corn Corn or grain of high quality, especially maize, used or intended for seed.

seed crystal A crystallon.

seed·er (sē'dər) *n.* **1** One who or that which sows seed, as a machine. **2** A device for removing seeds from fruit.

seed leaf *Bot.* A cotyledon.

seed·ling (sēd'ling) *n.* **1** *Bot.* A plant grown from seed, as distinguished from one propagated by grafting. **2** A very small or young tree or plant.

seed money Funds used to experiment or innovate with a new venture to test its workability.

seed oyster A young oyster, especially one transplanted to another bed: also *oyster seed.*

seed pearl A small pearl, especially one used for ornamenting bags, etc., or in embroidery.

seed plant A plant which bears seeds; spermatophyte.

seeds·man (sēdz'mən) *n. pl.* **·men** (-mən) **1** A dealer in seeds. **2** A sower. Also **seed'man.**

seed·time (sēd'tīm') *n.* The proper time for sowing seed.

seed vessel *Bot.* The part of a plant that contains the seeds; pericarp.

seed·y (sē'dē) *adj.* **seed·i·er, seed·i·est** **1** Abounding with seeds; going to seed. **2** Poor and ragged; shabby. **3** Feeling or looking wretched. — **seed'i·ly** *adv.* — **seed'i·ness** *n.*

See·ger (sē'gər), **Alan,** 1888–1916, U.S. poet.

see·ing (sē'ing) *n.* The act of seeing; vision; sight. — *conj.* Taking into consideration; since; in view of the fact.

Seeing Eye A philanthropic organization located near Morristown, New Jersey, that trains and supplies dogs (**Seeing Eye dogs**) as guides and companions to the blind.

seek (sēk) *v.* **sought, seek·ing** *v.t.* **1** To go in search of; look for. **2** To strive for; try to get or obtain: to *seek* glory. **3** To endeavor or try: with an infinitive as object: He *seeks* to mislead me. **4** To ask or inquire for; request: to *seek* information. **5** To go to; betake oneself to: to *seek* a warmer climate. **6** *Obs.* or *Dial.* To search or explore. — *v.i.* **7** To make a search or inquiry. [OE *sēcan*] — **seek'er** *n.*

See·land (zā'länt) The German name for ZEALAND.

see·ly (sē'lē) *adj. Obs.* Weak; wretched; feeble. [OE *gesǣlig* punctual, happy, innocent < *sǣl* time, due time, happiness]

seem (sēm) *v.i.* **1** To give the impression of being; appear. **2** To appear to oneself: a form of reflexive use: I *seem* to hear strange voices. Compare MESEEMS. **3** To appear to exist: There *seems* no reason for hesitating. **4** To be evident or apparent: It *seems* to be raining. [<ON *sǿma* honor, conform to] — **seem'er** *n.*

seem·ing (sē'ming) *adj.* Having the appearance of reality; apparent: often implying non-reality. See synonyms under APPARENT. — *n.* Appearance; semblance; especially, false show. — **seem'ing·ly** *adv.* — **seem'ing·ness** *n.*

seem·ly (sēm'lē) *adj.* **·li·er, ·li·est** Befitting the proprieties; becoming; proper; decorous; suited to the occasion. See synonyms under BECOMING. — *adv.* Becomingly; decently; appropriately. [<ON *sǿmiligr* honorable, becoming < *sǿmr* fitting] — **seem'li·ness** *n.*

seen (sēn) Past participle of SEE.

seep (sēp) *v.i.* To soak through pores or small interstices; percolate; ooze. — *n.* A small spring; a place out of which water, oil, or other liquid oozes. [OE *sipian* soak]

seep·age (sē'pij) *n.* **1** The oozing or percolation of fluid. **2** The fluid or moisture that oozes.

seer[1] (sē'ər *for def. 1;* sir *for defs. 2 and 3*) *n.* **1** One who sees. **2** One who foretells events; a prophet. **3** One believed to have second sight. [<SEE[1] + -ER] — **seer'ess** *n. fem.*

seer[2] (sir) *n.* **1** A weight used in different parts of India, and having varying local values: also spelled *ser.* **2** A measure of capacity: used chiefly in Bombay and Ceylon. [<Hind. *ser*]

seer·suck·er (sir'suk'ər) *n.* **1** A thin linen or linen and silk fabric, usually striped in colors, with crinkled surface. **2** A similar lightweight cotton or rayon crinkled fabric made by having some of the warp threads slack and others tight. [<Hind. *shirshaker* <Persian *shīr o shakkar,* lit., milk and sugar]

see-saw (sē'sô') *n.* **1** A sport in which persons sit or stand on opposite ends of a balanced plank and make it move up and down. **2** A plank or board balanced for this sport. **3** Any up-and-down or to-and-fro movement. **4** A crossruff. — *v.t.* & *v.i.* To move or cause to move on or as if on a see-saw. — *adj.* Moving to and fro; vacillating. [Reduplication of SAW[1] <*See saw sack a downe,* a sawyer's jingle]

seethe (sēth) *v.* **seethed** (*Obs.* **sod**), **seethed** (*Obs.* **sod·den, sod**), **seeth·ing** *v.i.* **1** To boil. **2** To foam or bubble as if boiling. **3** To be agitated or excited, as by rage. — *v.t.* **4** To soak in liquid; steep. **5** *Archaic* To boil. — *n.* The act of seething; turmoil. [OE *sēothan*]

Se·ges·ta (si·jes'tə) An ancient city of NW Sicily.

seg·gar (seg'ər) See SAGGAR.

seg·ment (seg'mənt) *n.* **1** A part cut off or divided from the other parts of anything; a section. **2** *Geom.* **a** A part of a figure cut off by a line or plane; especially, the part of a circle included within a chord and its arc. **b** A finite part of a divided line. **3** *Zool.* One of the serial divisions of an animal; somite; metamere; also, the portion of a limb between two joints. See synonyms under PART. — *v.t.* & *v.i.* To divide into segments. [<L *segmentum* < *secare* cut] — **seg·men·tal** (seg·men'təl) *adj.* — **seg·men'tal·ly** *adv.* — **seg·men·tar·y** (seg'mən·ter'ē) *adj.*

seg·men·ta·tion (seg'mən·tā'shən) *n.* **1** The act of cutting or dividing into segments. **2** The state of being so divided. **3** The cleavage of a cell into parts.

segmentation cavity *Biol.* The cavity formed by segmentation of a fertilized ovum; blastocele.

se·gno (sā'nyō) *n. pl.* **·gni** (-nyē) *Music* A sign; specifically, the musical sign *:S:* or 𝄋, indicating the beginning or end of a repeat. [<Ital. <L *signum*]

se·go (sē'gō) *n. pl.* **·gos** **1** A perennial herb (*Calochortus nuttalli*) of the lily family, having white flowers lined with purple: it is the State flower of Utah. **2** Its edible bulb. Also **sego lily.** [<Shoshonean (Ute) *sīgo*]

Se·go·via (sā·gō'vyä) A city of Old Castile, central Spain; remarkable for its architecture.

Se·go·via (sā·gō'vyä), **Andrés,** born 1894, Spanish classical guitarist.

seg·re·gate (seg'rə·gāt) *v.* **·gat·ed, ·gat·ing** *v.t.* **1** To place apart from others or the rest; isolate. — *v.i.* **2** To separate from a mass and gather about nuclei or along lines of fracture, as in crystallization or solidification. **3** To undergo segregation. — *adj.* **1** Separated or set apart from others; select. **2** Simple; solitary; not compound. [<L *segregatus,* pp. of *segregare* separate < *se-* apart + *grex, gregis* a flock] — **seg're·ga'tive** *adj.* — **seg're·ga'tor** *n.*

seg·re·ga·tion (seg'rə·gā'shən) *n.* **1** The act or process of segregating. **2** *Biol.* The separation and distribution of inherited characters in the offspring of crossbred parents. **3** The provision for separate facilities, as in housing, schools, and transportation, for whites and non-whites, especially Negroes.

se·gue (sā'gwā, seg'wā) *v.i.* **se·gued, se·gue·ing** *Music* To flow without any break into the next section or theme. [<Ital., (there) follows < *seguire* to follow]

se·gui·dil·la (sā'gē·dē'lyä) *n. Spanish* **1** A lively Spanish dance, in triple time, for two dancers. **2** The music of such a dance, or its movement, based on a stanza of four to seven lines, partly assonant. **3** *pl.* An air to which the dancers sing a group of these stanzas.

sei·cen·to (sā·chen'tō) *n.* The 17th century, in reference to Italian art and literature. [<Ital., short for *mil seicento* one thousand six hundred]

seiche (sāsh) *n.* An occasional oscillation of water above and below the mean level of lakes or landlocked seas, lasting from a few minutes to an hour or more. [< dial. F (Swiss), ? ult. <L *siccus* dry]

Seid·litz (zīd'lits) A German name for SEDLČANY: also *Sedlitz.*

Seid·litz powder (sed'lits) An aperient powder consisting of two separate parts: tartaric acid and sodium bicarbonate mixed with Rochelle salt: a mild cathartic used by dissolving separately, mixing the solutions, and drinking while effervescing: also called *Rochelle* powder. [from *Seidlitz;* so called because of its aperient property, similar to that of the water from the spring there]

seign·ior (sēn'yər) *n.* **1** A lord; in southern Europe, equivalent to English *sir.* **2** A lord or feudal lord. Also **sei·gneur** (sēn·yûr'). [< AF *segnour,* OF *seignor* <L *senior* older] — **sei·gnio·ri·al** (sēn·yôr'ē·əl, -yō'rē-) *adj.*

seign·ior·age (sēn'yər·ij) *n.* **1** Something charged or claimed as a prerogative. **2** A charge made by a government for coining bullion; also, the difference between the cost of bullion and the face value of coin made from it. **3** A royalty. Compare BRASSAGE.

seign·ior·y (sēn'yər·ē) *n.* **1** The territory or jurisdiction of a seignior; a manor. **2** Right or priority belonging to feudal superiority.

Seim (sām) A river in SW European U.S.S.R., rising in SW Russian S.F.S.R. and flowing 435 miles west to the Desna in central northern Ukrainian S.S.R., above Chernigov: also *Seym.*

seine (sān) *n.* Any long fishnet, having floats at the top edge and weights at the bottom, and hauled by its ends to close around a body of fish. — *v.t.* & *v.i.* **seined, sein·ing** To fish or catch with a seine. [OE *segne* <L *sagena* <Gk. *sagēnē* a fishing net]

Seine (sān, *Fr.* sen) A river of NE France, flowing 482 miles NW to the English Channel between Le Havre and Honfleur.

Seine, Bay of the A bay of the Normandy coast, NW France, indented by the estuary of the Seine; 65 miles wide; 25 miles long.

seise (sēz), **sei·sin** (sē′zin) See SEIZE, SEIZIN.

seism (sī′zəm, -səm) *n.* An earthquake. [<Gk. *seismos.* See SEISMIC.]

seis·mic (sīz′mik, sīs′-) *adj.* Pertaining to, characteristic of, or produced by earthquakes. Also **seis′mal, seis′mi·cal.** [<Gk. *seismos* an earthquake < *seiein* shake]

seis·mism (sīz′miz·əm, sīs′-) *n.* The process or phenomena involved in earth movements.

seismo– *combining form* Earthquake: *seismograph.* Also, before vowels, **seism–.** [<Gk. *seismos* an earthquake]

seis·mo·gram (sīz′mə·gram, sīs′-) *n.* The record of an earthquake or earth tremor made by a seismograph.

seis·mo·graph (sīz′mə·graf, -gräf, sīs′-) *n.* An instrument for automatically recording the intensity, direction, and duration of an earthquake shock. — **seis′mo·graph′ic** *adj.* — **seis·mog·ra·pher** (sīz·mog′rə·fər, sīs-) *n.*

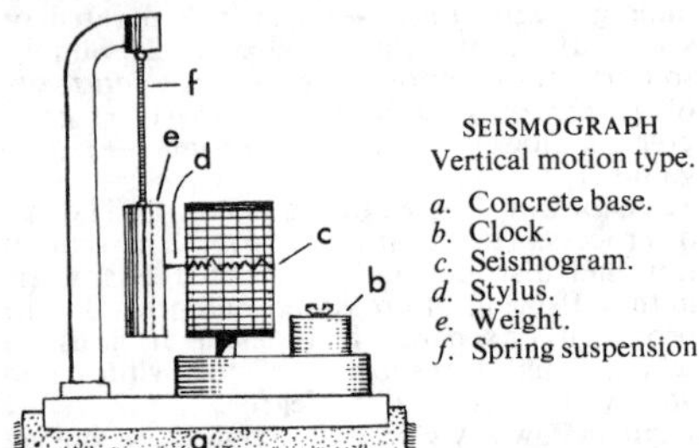

SEISMOGRAPH
Vertical motion type.
a. Concrete base.
b. Clock.
c. Seismogram.
d. Stylus.
e. Weight.
f. Spring suspension.

seis·mog·ra·phy (sīz·mog′rə·fē, sīs-) *n.* The study or description of earthquakes. [<SEISMO- + -GRAPHY]

seis·mol·o·gy (sīz·mol′ə·jē, sīs-) *n.* The science of earthquake phenomena. [<SEISMO- + -LOGY] — **seis·mo·log·ic** (sīz′mə·loj′ik, sīs′-) or **·i·cal** *adj.* — **seis′mo·log′i·cal·ly** *adv.* — **seis·mol′o·gist** *n.*

seis·mom·e·ter (sīz·mom′ə·tər, sīs-) *n.* A seismograph. — **seis·mo·met·ric** (sīz′mō·met′rik, sīs′-) or **·ri·cal** *adj.*

seis·mom·e·try (sīz·mom′ə·trē, sīs-) *n.* The scientific recording of facts regarding earthquake phenomena.

seis·mo·scope (sīz′mə·skōp, sīs′-) *n.* A simple form of seismograph; a device for indicating the time and occurrence of earthquake waves without measuring them. — **seis′mo·scop′ic** (-skop′ik) *adj.*

Seis·tan (sās·tän′) A region and inland lake depression of eastern Iran and SW Afghanistan: also *Sistan.*

seize (sēz) *v.* **seized, seiz·ing** *v.t.* **1** To take hold of suddenly and forcibly; clutch; grasp. **2** To grasp mentally; comprehend; understand. **3** To take possession of by authority or right. **4** To take possession of by or as by force: The usurper *seized* the throne. **5** To take prisoner; capture; arrest. **6** To act upon with sudden and powerful effect; attack; strike: Terror *seized* the attackers and they fled. **7** To take advantage of immediately, as an opportunity. **8** *Law* To put into legal possession: usually spelled *seise.* **9** *Naut.* To fasten or bind by turns of cord, line, or small rope; lash. — *v.i.* **10** To take a sudden or forcible hold. See synonyms under ARREST, CATCH, GRASP. [<OF *saisir, seisir* <Med. L *(ad propriam) sacire* take (into one's own possession), prob. <Gmc.] — **seiz′a·ble** *adj.*

seiz·er (sē′zər) *n.* **1** One who seizes in any sense. **2** *Law* One who takes livery of seizin: also **seiz′or, seis′or.**

sei·zin (sē′zin) *n. Law* **1** The possession of land under a claim of a freehold. **2** That which is possessed; property. **3** The act of taking possession. — **livery of seizin** The delivery of corporeal possession of lands and tenements of freehold. Also spelled *seisin.* [<OF *saisine* < *saisir.* See SEIZE.]

seiz·ing (sē′zing) *n.* **1** The act of grasping or taking forcible possession. **2** The process of fastening or binding together with turns of cord. **3** A small cord used in making such fastenings, and the fastening itself.

sei·zure (sē′zhər) *n.* **1** The act of seizing. **2** A sudden or violent attack, as of epilepsy or neuralgia; fit; spell.

se·jant (sē′jənt) *adj. Her.* Sitting with the fore limbs erect, as a lion. Also **se′jeant.** [<AF *sejant,* OF *seant,* ppr. of AF *seier,* OF *seoir* sit <L *sedere*]

Se·ja·nus (si·jā′nəs), **Lucius Aelius,** died A.D. 31, Roman favorite of Tiberius; executed.

Sejm (sām) *n. Polish* An assembly or diet having legislative power; specifically, the former Constituent Assembly of the Polish Republic.

sel (sel) *n. Scot.* Self. — **a body's sel** Oneself alone.

Se·la·chi·i (si·lā′kē·ī) *n. pl.* An order or subclass of elasmobranch fishes, including the sharks, skates, dogfishes, and rays, with their immediately related fossil allies. [<NL <Gk. *selachos* a shark] — **se·la′chi·an** *adj.* & *n.* — **sel·a·choid** (sel′ə·koid) *adj.* & *n.*

se·la·dang (sə·lä′däng) See SALADANG.

sel·a·gi·nel·la (sel′ə·ji·nel′ə) *n.* One of a widely distributed genus *(Selaginella)* of flowerless branching herbs with scalelike leaves. [<NL, dim. of L *selago, -inis,* a plant like the savin]

se·lah (sē′lə) *n.* A word of unknown meaning in the Psalms and Habakkuk, usually considered as a direction to readers or musicians. [<Hebrew *selāh*]

se·lam·lik (si·läm′lik) *n.* The men's quarters in a Turkish house, where guests are received; formerly, the official visit of the Turkish sultan to a mosque on a Friday. [<Turkish *selāmliq* <Arabic *salām* health, peace]

Se·lan·gor (se·läng′gôr, -gōr) A State of Malaya, on the Strait of Malaya; 3,160 square miles; capital, Kuala Lumpur.

Sel·den (sel′dən), **John,** 1584–1654, English jurist and antiquary.

sel·dom (sel′dəm) *adv.* At widely separated intervals, as of time or space; infrequently. [OE *seldum, seldan,* dative pl. of *seld-* rare, strange]

se·lect (si·lekt′) *v.t.* To take in preference to another or others; pick out; choose. — *v.i.* To make a choice; choose. See synonyms under ALLOT, CHOOSE. — *adj.* **1** Chosen in preference to others; taken as being most fit or desirable; choice. **2** Exclusive. **3** Very particular in selecting. See synonyms under CHOICE, EXCELLENT. [<L *selectus,* pp. of *seligere* < *se-* apart + *legere* choose] — **se·lect′ness** *n.* — **se·lec′tor** *n.*

se·lec·tee (si·lek′tē′) *n.* One selected; specifically, a person called up for military service under selective service.

se·lec·tion (si·lek′shən) *n.* **1** The act of selecting; choice. **2** Anything selected; a collection made with care. **3** *Biol.* The process, natural or artificial, by which certain organisms, or any of their characteristics, are favored in the struggle for perpetuation and survival.

se·lec·tive (si·lek′tiv) *adj.* **1** Pertaining to selection; tending to select. **2** Having or characterized by good selectivity, as a radio receiver. — **se·lec·tive·ly** *adv.*

selective service Compulsory military service according to specified conditions of age, fitness, etc. — **se·lec′tive-ser′vice** *adj.*

selective transmission *Mech.* A transmission for motor vehicles effected by a single lever which directly changes the gear from one speed to another.

se·lec·tiv·i·ty (si·lek′tiv′ə·tē) *n.* **1** The state or condition of being selective. **2** *Telecom.* That characteristic of a radio receiver by which certain frequencies can be received to the exclusion of others.

se·lect·man (si·lekt′mən) *n. pl.* **·men** (-mən) One of a board of town officers, elected annually in New England, except in Rhode Island, to exercise executive authority in local affairs.

selector box A watertight metal box which contains the mechanisms controlling a set of submarine mines and operated electrically from a shore station.

sel·e·nate (sel′ə·nāt) *n. Chem.* A salt of selenic acid. [<SELEN(IC) + -ATE[3]]

Se·le·ne (si·lē′nē) In Greek mythology, goddess of the moon: identified with the Roman *Luna.* Also **Se·le′na** (-nə). [<Gk. *Selēnē,* lit., the moon]

Se·len·ga (se′leng·gä′) A river in the Mongolian People's Republic, flowing 897 miles NE to Lake Baikal.

se·len·ic (si·len′ik, -lē′nik) *adj. Chem.* Of, pertaining to, or derived from selenium, especially in its higher valence. [<SELEN(IUM) + -IC]

selenic acid *Chem.* A transparent, colorless liquid, H_2SeO_4, obtained variously, as by decomposing a selenate with hydrogen sulfide.

se·le·ni·ous (si·lē′nē·əs) *adj. Chem.* Of, pertaining to, or derived from selenium, especially in its lower valence, as the colorless, crystalline **selenious acid,** H_2SeO_3.

sel·e·nite[1] (sel′ə·nīt) *n.* A pearly, usually transparent variety of gypsum. [<L *selenites* <Gk. *selēnitēs (lithos),* lit., moonstone < *selēnē* the moon; so called because it was thought to wax and wane with the moon]

sel·e·nite[2] (sel′ə·nīt) *n.* A salt of selenious acid. [<SELEN(IUM) + -ITE[2]]

sel·e·nite[3] (sel′ə·nīt) *n. Often cap.* An imaginary inhabitant of the moon. [<Gk. *selēnitēs* < *selēnē* the moon]

se·le·ni·um (si·lē′nē·əm) *n.* A gray, crystalline, non-metallic element of the sulfur group (symbol Se) varying greatly in electrical resistance under the influence of light. See ELEMENT. [<NL <Gk. *selēnē* the moon]

selenium cell A photoelectric cell in which plates of selenium respond in accordance with the action of light upon them.

seleno– *combining form* Moon; pertaining to the moon; lunar: *selenography.* Also, before vowels, **selen–.** [<Gk. *selēnē* the moon]

sel·e·nog·ra·phy (sel′ə·nog′rə·fē) *n.* The science or study of the moon's surface. [<SELENO- + -GRAPHY] — **sel′e·nog′ra·pher** or **·phist** *n.* — **sel′e·no·graph′ic** (-nō·graf′ik) or **·i·cal** *adj.*

sel·e·nol·o·gy (sel′ə·nol′ə·jē) *n.* The science that treats of the movements and astronomical relations of the moon. [<SELENO- + -LOGY] — **se·le·no·log·i·cal** (si·lē′nō·loj′i·kəl) *adj.* — **sel′e·nol′o·gist** *n.*

Se·leu·cia (si·lo͞o′shə) **1** An ancient city on the NE Mediterranean, in extreme southern Turkey near Syria; formerly the port of Antioch. Also **Seleucia Pi·e·ri·a** (pī·ir′ē·ə). **2** An ancient city of Mesopotamia, on the Tigris, the site of which is 20 miles SE of Baghdad, Iraq. **3** An ancient city of Cilicia, SW of Tarsus, the site of modern Silifke, Turkey. Also **Seleucia Tra·che·o·tis** (trā′kē·ō′tis).

Se·leu·cid (si·lo͞o′sid) *adj.* Pertaining to the Seleucids: also **Se·leu′ci·dan, Se·leu·cid·i·an** (sē′lo͞o·sid′ē·ən). — *n.* One of the Seleucids. [<L *Seleucides* <Gk. *Seleukidēs,* a descendant of Seleucus <*Seleukos* Seleucus]

Se·leu·cids (si·lo͞o′sids) *n. pl.* The members of the dynasty that ruled Syria from 312 B.C. till the Roman conquest, 64 B.C.: named from Seleucus. Also **Se·leu′ci·dae** (-dē).

Se·leu·cus (si·lo͞o′kəs) Name of six kings of the Seleucid dynasty, especially **Seleucus Ni·ca·tor** (nī·kā′tər), 358?–280 B.C., Macedonian general under Alexander the Great, and founder of the dynasty.

self (self) *adj.* **1** Same; identical: obsolete except in the compound *selfsame.* **2** Pure; unmixed: applied especially to colors. — *n. pl.* **selves 1** An individual known or considered as the subject of his own consciousness; anything considered as having a distinct personality. **2** Personal interest or advantage. **3** Any thing, class, or attribute that, abstractly considered, maintains a distinct and characteristic individuality or identity. [OE]

Self may appear as a combining form with various meanings in solidemes and hyphemes, as shown in the list beginning at the foot of this page.

1 Of the self (the object of the root word); as in:

self–abandonment	**self–abhorrence**	**self–administer**	**self–adornment**	**self–advertise**	**self–aggrandizement**	**self–applause**
self–abasement	**self–accusation**	**self–admiration**	**self–adulation**	**self–advertisement**	**self–analysis**	**self–appreciation**
self–abasing	**self–adaptive**	**self–admission**	**self–advancement**	**self–affliction**	**self–annihilation**	**self–approbation**

self-ab·ne·ga·tion (self′ab′ni·gā′shən) *n.* The complete putting aside of self and claims of self for the sake of some person or object; self-sacrifice.

Synonyms: self-control, self-denial, self-devotion, self-renunciation, self-sacrifice. *Self-control* is holding oneself within due limits in pleasures and duties, as in all things else; *self-denial,* the giving up of pleasures for the sake of duty. *Self-renunciation* surrenders conscious rights; *self-abnegation* forgets that there is anything to surrender. A mother will care for a sick child with complete *self-abnegation,* but without a thought of *self-denial. Self-devotion* is whole-hearted consecration of self to a person or cause with readiness for any needed sacrifice. *Self-sacrifice* is the strongest term of all, and contemplates the gift of self as actually made. *Antonyms*: self-gratification, self-indulgence, self-will.

self-a·buse (self′ə·byōōs′) *n.* **1** The disparagement of one's own person or powers. **2** Masturbation.

self-ad·dressed (self′ə·drest′) *adj.* Addressed to and by oneself.

self-as·sured (self′ə·shŏŏrd′) *adj.* Confident in one's own abilities; self-reliant. **— self′-as·sur′ance** *n.*

self-col·ored (self′kul′ərd) *adj.* **1** Having the natural color. **2** Of but one color or tint. Also *Brit.* **self′-col′oured.**

self-com·mand (self′kə·mand′, -mänd′) *n.* The state of having all the faculties and powers fully and effectively at command: more positive and less repressive than *self-control.*

self-com·posed (self′kəm·pōzd′) *adj.* Calm; controlling one's emotions.

self-con·ceit (self′kən·sēt′) *n.* An unduly high opinion of oneself or of one's own abilities, acquirements, etc.; self-esteem; vanity; egotism. See synonyms under EGOTISM, PRIDE. **— self′-con·ceit′ed** *adj.*

self-con·fi·dence (self′kon′fə·dəns) *n.* Confidence in oneself or in one's own unaided powers, judgment, etc. See synonyms under ASSURANCE, EGOTISM. **— self′-con′fi·dent** *adj.* **— self′-con′fi·dent·ly** *adv.*

self-con·scious (self′kon′shəs) *adj.* **1** Unduly conscious that one is observed by others, or manifesting such consciousness; embarrassed by inability to forget oneself; ill at ease. **2** Conscious of one's existence. **— self′-con′·scious·ly** *adv.* **— self′-con′scious·ness** *n.*

self-con·tained (self′kən·tānd′) *adj.* **1** Keeping one's thoughts and feelings to oneself; uncommunicative; impassive. **2** Exercising self-control. **3** Complete and independent; bearing its own motor, as a machine; mounted on its own boiler, as a steam engine.

self-con·tra·dic·tion (self′kon′trə·dik′shən) *n.* **1** The contradicting of oneself or itself. **2** That which contradicts itself. **— self′-con′·tra·dic′to·ry** *adj.*

self-con·trol (self′kən·trōl′) *n.* The act, power, or habit of having one's faculties or energies under control of the will. Compare SELF-COMMAND.

self-de·fense (self′di·fens′) *n.* Defense of oneself, one's property, or one's reputation. Also **self′-de·fence′. — self′-de·fen′sive** *adj.*

self-de·ni·al (self′di·nī′əl) *n.* The act or power of denying oneself gratification; passive self-sacrifice. See synonyms under ABSTINENCE, SELF-ABNEGATION. **— self′-de·ny′ing** *adj.* **— self′-de·ny′ing·ly** *adv.*

self-de·ter·mi·na·tion (self′di·tûr′mə·nā′shən) *n.* **1** The principle of free will; decision by oneself without extraneous force or influence. **2** Decision by the people of a country or section as to its future political status. **— self′-de·ter′min·ing** *adj.* & *n.*

self-de·vo·tion (self′di·vō′shən) *n.* The devoting of oneself, with one's claims, wishes, or interests, to the service of a person or a cause. See synonyms under SELF-ABNEGATION. **— self′-de·vo′tion·al** *adj.*

self-driv·en (self′driv′ən) *adj.* Driven by itself; automotive.

self-ed·u·cat·ed (self′ej′ŏŏ·kā′tid) *adj.* **1** Educated through one's own efforts without the aid of instructors. **2** Educated at one's own expense. **— self′-ed′u·ca′tion** *n.*

self-es·teem (self′es·tēm′) *n.* A good opinion of oneself; an overestimate of oneself. See synonyms under EGOTISM, PRIDE.

self-ev·i·dent (self′ev′ə·dənt) *adj.* Carrying its evidence or proof in itself; requiring no proof of its truth. **— self′-ev′i·dence** *n.* **— self′-ev′i·dent·ly** *adv.*

self-ex·e·cut·ing (self′ek′sə·kyōō′ting) *adj.* Containing provisions for securing its own execution independent of legislation: said of a law, etc.

self-ex·ist·ence (self′ig·zis′təns) *n.* Inherent, underived, independent existence: an attribute of God. **— self′-ex·ist′ent** *adj.*

self-ex·pres·sion (self′ik·spresh′ən) *n.* Expression of one's own temperament or emotions, as in art.

self-feed·er (self′fē′dər) *n.* A machine, boiler, or other mechanical device that feeds itself automatically. **— self′-feed′ing** *adj.*

self-fer·til·i·za·tion (self′fûr′təl·ə·zā′shən, -ī·zā′shən) *n. Biol.* Fertilization of an ovum by semen from the same animal or of a plant ovule by its own pollen.

self-gov·ern·ment (self′guv′ərn·mənt, -ər·mənt) *n.* **1** Self-control. **2** Government of a country or region by its own people; especially, government of a colony by the inhabitants rather than by the mother country. **— self′-gov′ern·ing, self′-gov′erned** *adj.*

self-hard·en·ing (self′här′də·ning) *adj. Metall.* Pertaining to or designating certain steels which will harden properly without the need for quenching.

self·heal (self′hēl′) *n.* **1** A weedy, perennial herb (genus *Prunella*) with violet or purple flowers, formerly reputed to cure disease, especially the common selfheal of North America *(P. vulgaris).* **2** One of various similar plants, as the sanicle.

self·hood (self′hŏŏd) *n.* **1** The state of being an individual, or that which constitutes such a state; personality. **2** Selfishness.

self-i·den·ti·ty (self′ī·den′tə·tē) *n.* **1** The identity of a thing with itself. **2** *Psychol.* That state of consciousness by or through which the self recognizes itself as one and the same.

self-im·por·tance (self′im·pôr′təns) *n.* Pompous self-conceit. **— self′-im·por′tant** *adj.*

self-in·duced (self′in·dōōst′, -dyōōst′) *adj. Electr.* Characterizing an electromotive force induced in a circuit because of variations of the current in that circuit.

self-in·duc·tion (self′in·duk′shən) *n. Electr.* The production of an induced or extra current in a circuit by the variation of the current in that circuit, especially when it is started or stopped. **— self′-in·duc′tive** *adj.*

self-in·sur·ance (self′in·shŏŏr′əns) *n.* That proportion of the insurance risk which the insured assumes himself by the premium payments he makes.

self-in·ter·est (self′in′tər·ist, -in′trist) *n.* Personal interest or advantage, or the pursuit of it; selfishness. **— self′-in′ter·est·ed** *adj.*

self·ish (sel′fish) *adj.* **1** Caring chiefly for self or for one's own interests or comfort; influenced by personal motives to the disregard of the welfare or wishes of others. **2** Proceeding from or characterized by undue love of self. See synonyms under GREEDY. **— self′ish·ly** *adv.*

self·ish·ness (sel′fish·nis) *n.* The quality of being selfish; undue regard for one's own interest, regardless of others.

Synonym: self-love. *Self-love* is a due care for one's own happiness and well-being, which is perfectly compatible with justice, generosity, or benevolence toward others; *selfishness* is an undue or exclusive care for one's own

self-approval
self-asserting
self-assertion
self-assertive
self-awareness
self-bedizenment
self-betrayal
self-blame
self-castigation
self-chastisement
self-cognizance
self-commendation
self-committal
self-comparison
self-comprehending
self-condemnation
self-condemning
self-conditioning
self-confinement
self-confounding
self-congratulatory
self-conquest
self-conservative
self-conserving
self-consideration
self-consoling
self-consuming
self-contempt
self-contradicting
self-conviction
self-correction
self-corruption
self-creation
self-criticism
self-cure
self-damnation
self-debasement
self-deceit
self-deceiving
self-dedication
self-defeating
self-deflation
self-degradation
self-deifying
self-dejection
self-delation
self-delusion
self-depreciation
self-depreciative
self-destroying
self-destruction
self-destructive
self-direction
self-disapproval
self-discipline
self-disclosure
self-discovery
self-disgrace
self-disparagement
self-display
self-disposal
self-disquieting
self-dissolution
self-distrust
self-doubt
self-easing
self-enriching
self-estimate
self-evacuation
self-exalting
self-examination
self-exculpation
self-excuse
self-expansion
self-expatriation
self-exploiting
self-exposure
self-extermination
self-fearing
self-flatterer
self-flattering
self-flattery
self-folding
self-formation
self-glorification
self-gratification
self-guidance
self-harming
self-help
self-helpful
self-humbling
self-humiliation
self-hypnosis
self-hypnotism
self-hypnotize
self-idolatry
self-idolizing
self-ignorance
self-ignorant
self-imitation
self-immolation
self-immurement
self-impairment
self-improvement
self-indignation
self-indulgence
self-indulgent
self-indulgently
self-indulging
self-inspection
self-instruction
self-insurer
self-integration
self-intensifying
self-interrogation
self-introduction
self-judgment
self-justification
self-justifying
self-knowledge
self-lashing
self-laudatory
self-limitation
self-limited
self-limiting
self-loss
self-loving
self-maceration
self-maintenance
self-martyrdom
self-mastery
self-mistrust
self-mortification
self-murder
self-murderer
self-mutilation
self-neglect
self-neglectful
self-nourishment
self-objectification
self-observation
self-offense
self-opinion
self-painter
self-paying
self-perceiving
self-perceptive
self-perfecting
self-perfection
self-perpetuation
self-persuasion
self-pitiful
self-pity
self-pitying
self-pleasing
self-praise
self-praising
self-preparation
self-presentation
self-preserving
self-projection
self-protecting
self-protection
self-punishment
self-raising
self-realization
self-recollection
self-reconstruction
self-reduction
self-regulation
self-representation
self-repressing
self-repression
self-reproach
self-reproachful
self-restriction
self-revealing
self-revelation
self-ruin
self-satirist
self-scrutinizing
self-scrutiny
self-searching
self-serve
self-slaughter
self-soothing
self-study
self-subjection
self-subordination
self-support
self-supporting
self-suppression
self-surrender
self-suspicious
self-taxation
self-teacher
self-terminating
self-tolerant
self-torment
self-torture
self-treatment
self-trust
self-trusting
self-undoing
self-upbraiding
self-usurp
self-valuing
self-vaunting
self-vindication
self-worship

2 By oneself or itself; by one's own effort (the agent of the root word); as in:

self-abandoned
self-appointed
self-approved
self-authorized
self-balanced
self-beguiled
self-betrayed
self-blinded
self-caused
self-chosen
self-commissioned
self-condemned
self-conducted
self-confuted
self-constituted
self-convicted
self-corrupted
self-declared
self-defended
self-deluded
self-deprived
self-destroyed
self-determined
self-devised
self-divided
self-doomed
self-elaborated
self-elected

comfort or pleasure, regardless of the happiness, and often of the rights, of others. *Self-love* is necessary to high endeavor, and even to self-preservation; *selfishness* limits endeavor to a narrow circle of intensely personal aims. *Antonyms*: See synonyms under BENEVOLENCE.

self·less (self′lis) *adj.* Regardless of self; unselfish.

self-liq·ui·dat·ing (self′lik′wə·dā′ting) *adj.* Designating a business transaction in which goods in great demand are converted into cash over a short period.

self-load·ing (self′lō′ding) *adj.* Automatically reloading: said of a gun using the energy of recoil to eject and reload.

self-love (self′luv′) *n.* Love of oneself; the desire or tendency that leads one to seek to promote his own well-being. See synonym under SELFISHNESS.

self-made (self′mād′) *adj.* **1** Having attained honor, wealth, etc., by one's own efforts. **2** Made by oneself.

self-per·cep·tion (self′pər·sep′shən) *n.* Perception of one's own existence or mental states; introspection.

self-pol·li·na·tion (self′pol′ə·nā′shən) *n. Bot.* The transfer of pollen from stamens to pistils of the same flower.

self-pos·ses·sion (self′pə·zesh′ən) *n.* **1** The full possession or control of one's powers or faculties; freedom from perturbation, perplexity, or excitement. **2** Presence of mind; self-command. **—self′-pos·sessed′** *adj.*

self-pres·er·va·tion (self′prez′ər·vā′shən) *n.* **1** The protection of oneself from destruction. **2** The urge to protect oneself regarded as an instinct.

self-prof·it (self′prof′it) *n.* Self-interest.

self-pro·nounc·ing (self′prə·noun′sing) *adj.* Having marks of pronunciation and stress applied to a word without phonetic alteration of the spelling.

self-re·li·ance (self′ri·lī′əns) *n.* Reliance on one's own abilities, resources, or judgment. See synonyms under ASSURANCE. **—self′-re·li′ant** *adj.*

self-re·nun·ci·a·tion (self′ri·nun′sē·ā′shən) *n.* Renunciation of one's own rights, privileges, or claims. **—self′-re·nun′ci·a·to′ry** (-sē·ə·tôr′ē, -tō′rē) *adj.*

self-re·spect (self′ri·spekt′) *n.* Such regard for one's own character as will restrain one from unworthy action; rational self-esteem. See synonyms under PRIDE **—self′-re·spect′ing** *adj.*

self-re·straint (self′ri·strānt′) *n.* Restraint, as of the passions, by the force of one's own will; self-control.

self-right·eous (self′rī′chəs) *adj.* Righteous in one's own estimation; pharisaic. **—self′-right′eous·ly** *adv.* **—self′-right′eous·ness** *n.*

self-ris·ing (self′rī′zing) *adj.* **1** That rises of itself. **2** Having the leaven already added by the millers, as some flours.

self-sac·ri·fice (self′sak′rə·fīs) *n* The sacrifice or subordination of one's self or one's personal welfare or wishes, for the sake of duty or for others' good. See synonyms under SELF-ABNEGATION. **—self′-sac′ri·fic′ing** *adj.*

self·same (self′sām′) *adj.* Exactly the same; identical. See synonyms under IDENTICAL. **—self′-same′ness** *n.*

self-sat·is·fac·tion (self′sat′is·fak′shən) *n.* Satisfaction with one's own actions and characteristics; conceit; self-complacency. **—self′-sat′is·fied** *adj.* **—self′-sat′is·fy′ing** *adj.*

self-seek·ing (self′sē′king) *adj.* Given to the exclusive pursuit of one's own interests or gain. **—** *n.* Self-aggrandizement; selfishness. **—self′-seek′er** *n.*

self-ser·vice (self′sûr′vis) *adj.* Designating a particular type of café, restaurant, or store where patrons serve themselves.

self-start·er (self′stär′tər) *n.* **1** An internal-combustion engine, with automatic or semi-automatic starting mechanism; also, such mechanism. **2** *Slang* One who requires no outside stimulus to start or accomplish work.

self-styled (self′stīld′) *adj.* Characterized (as such) by oneself: a *self-styled* gentleman.

self-suf·fi·cient (self′sə·fish′ənt) *adj.* **1** Able to support or maintain oneself without aid or cooperation from others. **2** Having overweening confidence in oneself. Also **self′-suf·fic′ing** (-sə·fī′sing). **—self′-suf·fi′cien·cy** *n.*

self-will (self′wil′) *n.* Pertinacious adherence to one's own will or wish, especially with disregard of the wishes of others; obstinacy. **—self′-willed′** *adj.*

self-wind·ing (self′wīn′ding) *adj.* Having a magnetic, electrical, or other attachment which automatically winds a clock or other mechanism at certain times.

self-wrong (self′rông′, -rong′) *n.* Injury done to one's self.

Sel·juk (sel·jo͝ok′) *n.* A member of one of several Turkish dynasties which reigned over a large part of central and western Asia from the 11th to the 13th centuries. **—** *adj.* Pertaining to a Seljuk. Also **Sel·ju·ki·an** (sel·jo͞o′kē·ən). [<Turkish *seljūq*, after *Seljūq*, a Turkish chieftain, reputed ancestor of the Seljuk dynasties]

Sel·kirk (sel′kûrk) A county of SE Scotland; 267 square miles; county burgh, Selkirk. Also **Sel′kirk·shire** (-shir).

Sel·kirk (sel′kûrk), **Alexander**, 1676–1721, Scottish sailor who was marooned on Juan Fernandez Island, Pacific Ocean, for four years. His adventures are said to have suggested Defoe's *Robinson Crusoe.*

Selkirk Mountains A range of the Rocky Mountains in SE British Columbia.

sell[1] (sel) *v.* **sold, sell·ing** *v.t.* **1** To transfer (property) to another for a consideration; dispose of by sale. **2** To deal in; offer for sale. **3** To deliver, surrender, or betray for a price or reward: to *sell* one's honor. **4** *Colloq.* To cause to accept or approve something: They *sold* him on the scheme. **5** *Colloq.* To cause the acceptance or approval of. **6** *Slang* To deceive; cheat. **—** *v.i.* **7** To transfer ownership for a consideration; engage in selling. **8** To be on sale; be sold. See synonyms under CONVEY. **—** *n.* **1** *Slang* A trick; joke; swindle. **2** On the stock exchange, a stock that ought to be sold. ◆ Homophone: *cell.* [OE *sellan* give]

sell[2] (sel) *n.* **1** An elevated seat; an honorable place; also, any seat. **2** A saddle. ◆ Homophone: *cell.* [<OF *selle* <L *sella* a seat, ult. < *sedere* sit]

sell·er (sel′ər) *n.* **1** One who sells. **2** Something with a measure of salability: This book is a good *seller.*

sell·ing-plat·er (sel′ing·plā′tər) *n.* A horse that runs in a selling race.

selling race *Brit.* A horse race in which the entrants may be claimed for a set price, and the winning horse must be offered at auction. Compare CLAIMING RACE. Also **sell′er, sell′·ing·er.**

sell-out (sel′out′) *n.* **1** An act of selling out. **2** *Colloq.* A performance for which all seats have been sold. **3** *Slang* A betrayal through a secret bargain or agreement.

Selt·zer (selt′sər) *n.* An effervescing mineral water. Also **Seltzer water, Sel·ters** (sel′tərz). [Alter. of G *Selterser*, from *Nieder Selters*, a village in SW Prussia, its place of origin]

sel·vage (sel′vij) *n.* **1** The edge of a woven fabric so finished that it will not ravel. **2** An edge. **3** The edge plate of a lock having an opening for a bolt. Also **sel′vedge.** [<SELF + EDGE, trans. of MDu. *selfegghe*]

Sel·va·gens (sel·vä′zhēṅsh) A group of uninhabited islets in Madeira: also *Salvages.*

selves (selvz) Plural of SELF.

se·man·tic (si·man′tik) *adj.* **1** Of or pertaining to meaning. **2** Of or relating to semantics. [<Gk. *sēmantikos* < *sēmainein* signify]

se·man·ti·cist (si·man′tə·sist) *n.* A specialist in semantics.

se·man·tics (si·man′tiks) *n. pl.* (*construed as singular*) **1** *Ling.* The study of the meanings of speech forms, especially of the development and changes in meaning of words and word groups. **2** *Logic* The relation between signs or symbols and what they signify or

self-employed	self-honored	self-instructed	self-maimed	self-pampered	self-proclaimed	self-schooled
self-exhibited	self-idolized	self-invited	self-matured	self-performed	self-professed	self-sown
self-explained	self-illumined	self-irrecoverable	self-misused	self-perpetuated	self-punished	self-subdued
self-exposed	self-improvable	self-judged	self-mortified	self-perplexed	self-renounced	self-supported
self-extolled	self-incurred	self-justified	self-named	self-planted	self-repressed	self-sustained
self-furnished	self-inflicted	self-kindled	self-offered	self-pollinated	self-restrained	self-taught
self-hidden	self-initiated	self-limited	self-paid	self-posed	self-revealed	self-tempted

3 To, toward, in, for, on, or with oneself; as in:

self-absorbed	self-centered	self-contented	self-dissatisfied	self-injurious	self-preference	self-repellent
self-absorption	self-comment	self-delight	self-elation	self-injury	self-preoccupation	self-repose
self-aid	self-communing	self-dependence	self-enamored	self-kindness	self-prescribed	self-reproof
self-aim	self-compassion	self-dependent	self-enclosed	self-liking	self-pride	self-repulsive
self-amusement	self-compensation	self-desire	self-exultation	self-loathing	self-procured	self-resentment
self-angry	self-complacence	self-despair	self-focusing	self-oblivious	self-produced	self-resigned
self-application	self-complacency	self-directed	self-gain	self-occupied	self-profit	self-respectful
self-applied	self-complacent	self-direction	self-helpfulness	self-panegyrical	self-purifying	self-responsibility
self-assumed	self-concentration	self-disdain	self-helpless	self-penetration	self-reflection	self-rigorous
self-assuming	self-conflict	self-disgust	self-hope	self-permission	self-regard	self-sent
self-benefit	self-consistency	self-dislike	self-imposture	self-pictured	self-relation	self-tenderness
self-care	self-consistent	self-dissatisfaction	self-infliction	self-pleased	self-relying	self-vexation

4 From oneself or itself; from one's own nature or power; as in:

self-apparent	self-derived	self-explaining	self-initiative	self-moving	self-refuting	self-rewarding
self-arising	self-desirable	self-explanatory	self-intelligible	self-operative	self-renewing	self-sprung
self-born	self-developing	self-forbidden	self-interpretative	self-originating	self-resourceful	self-stability
self-coherence	self-distinguishing	self-fruition	self-issuing	self-perfect	self-resplendent	self-stimulated
self-complete	self-effort	self-healing	self-luminous	self-poise	self-restoring	self-sustaining
self-defining	self-evolving	self-inclusive	self-manifestation	self-poised	self-reward	self-warranting

5 Independent; as in: self-agency self-authority

self-credit	self-dominance	self-entity	self-existence	self-ownership	self-rule	self-sovereignty

6 *Technol.* Automatic or automatically; as in:

self-acting	self-binder	self-cleaning	self-feed	self-lubricating	self-propelled	self-registering
self-adapting	self-burning	self-closing	self-filling	self-lubrication	self-propelling	self-regulated
self-adjustable	self-changing	self-cocking	self-inking	self-oiling	self-propulsion	self-regulating
self-adjusting	self-charging	self-cooled	self-lighting	self-primer	self-raker	self-righting
self-alining	self-checking	self-emptying	self-locking	self-priming	self-recording	self-setting

denote: also called *semasiology, semiotics.* Compare GENERAL SEMANTICS. **3** Loosely, verbal trickery, especially by adulteration or shift of meaning within a word; amphibology.

sem·a·phore (sem′ə·fôr, -fōr) *n.* An apparatus for making signals, as with movable arms, disks, flags, or lanterns. — *v.t.* To send by semaphore. [<F *sémaphore* <Gk. *sēma* a sign + *pherein* carry] — **sem′·a·phor′ic** (-fôr′ik, -for′ik) or **·i·cal** *adj.*

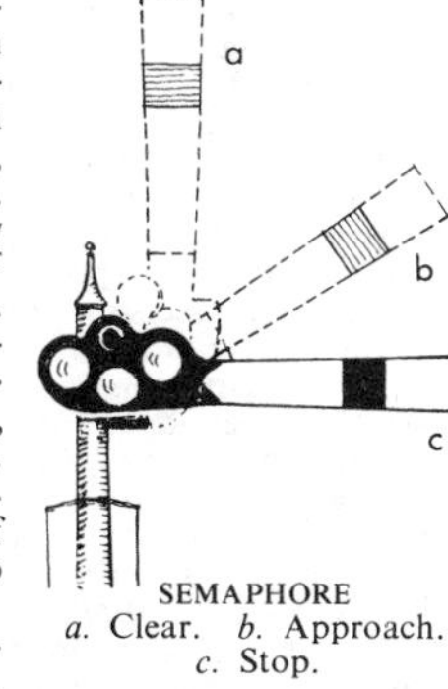

SEMAPHORE
a. Clear. *b.* Approach. *c.* Stop.

Se·ma·rang (sə·mä′·räng) A port of northern Java: also *Samarang.*

se·ma·si·ol·o·gy (si·mā′sē·ol′ə·jē, -zē-) *n.* Semantics (def. 2). [<Gk. *sēmasia* the signification of a word <*sēma* sign + -LOGY] — **se·ma·si·o·log·i·cal** (si·mā′sē·ə·loj′i·kəl, -zē-) *adj.*

se·mat·ic (si·mat′ik) *adj.* Of the nature of a sign; warning; in animal coloration, serving to distinguish as a means of recognition or warning. [<Gk. *sēma, -atos* a sign]

sem·bla·ble (sem′blə·bəl) *adj.* **1** Resembling; similar. **2** Apparent; not real. — *n.* A thing resembling another thing. Also **sem′bla·tive.** [<OF <*sembler.* See SEMBLANCE.]

sem·blance (sem′bləns) *n.* **1** A mere show without reality; pretense. **2** Outward appearance; look; aspect. **3** A pictorial representation; likeness; resemblance. See synonyms under PRETENSE. [<OF <*sembler* seem <L *simulare, similare* simulate <*similis* like]

sem·ble (sem′bəl) *v.i.* **·bled, ·bling** It seems; it would seem: used only in law, and generally in abbreviated form, **sem.** or **semb.** [<F, it seems <*sembler.* See SEMBLANCE.]

se·mé (sə·mā′, *Fr.* se·mā′) *adj. Her.* Strewn or scattered over with small bearings, as fleurs-de-lis; powdered. [<OF, pp. of *semer* sow <L *seminare* <*semen* a seed]

se·mei·ol·o·gy (sē′mī·ol′ə·jē, sē′mē-), **se·mei·ot·ics** (sē′mī·ot′iks, sē′mē-), etc. See SEMIOLOGY, SEMIOTICS, etc.

Sem·e·le (sem′ə·lē) In Greek mythology, the mother of Dionysus by Zeus: she was destroyed by lightning when she asked to see Zeus as he appeared to the gods.

se·meme (sē′mēm) *n. Ling.* The meaning of a morpheme. [<Gk. *sēma* a sign; on analogy with *phoneme*]

se·men (sē′mən) *n.* **1** The impregnating fluid of male animals. **2** Seed. [<L <*serere* sow]

se·mes·ter (si·mes′tər) *n.* A college half-year; hence, a period of instruction, usually lasting 17 or 18 weeks. [<G <L *(cursus) semestris* (a period) of six months <*sex* six + *mensis* a month] — **se·mes′tral** *adj.*

sem·i (sem′ē) *n. pl.* **sem·is** *Colloq.* **1** *U.S.* A semitrailer. **2** *Brit.* A semi-detached house. — **the semis** *Colloq.* The semifinal round of competition in a sports competition.

semi- *prefix* **1** Half; partly; not fully: *semiautomatic, semicivilized.* **2** Exactly half: *semicircle.* **3** Occurring twice (in the period specified): *semiweekly.* [<L]

Semi-, meaning not fully, partially, or partial, is found in solidemes and hyphemes, as in the list beginning at the foot of this page.

sem·i·an·nu·al (sem′ē·an′yo͞o·əl) *adj.* Issued or occurring twice a year; half-yearly. — *n.* A publication issued twice a year. — **sem′i·an′·nu·al·ly** *adv.*

sem·i·a·quat·ic (sem′ē·ə·kwat′ik, -kwot′ik) *adj. Biol.* Adapted for living or growing near water, as certain types of plants and animals.

semi·au·to·mat·ic (sem′ē·ô′tə·mat′ik) *adj.* Only partly automatic: said especially of guns which are self-loading but not self-firing.

sem·i·breve (sem′ē·brēv′) *n. Music* A note equal to half a breve; a whole note.

sem·i·cell (sem′ē·sel′) *n. Biol.* Half of a complete cell, usually joined to the other half by an isthmus, as in certain green algae. Compare DESMID.

sem·i·cen·ten·ni·al (sem′ē·sen·ten′ē·əl) *adj.* Occurring or celebrated at the end of fifty years from some event. — *n.* The fiftieth anniversary of an event, or its celebration.

sem·i·cir·cle (sem′ē·sûr′kəl) *n.* **1** A half-circle; an arc or a segment of 180°. **2** Anything formed or arranged in a half-circle. — **sem′i·cir′·cu·lar** *adj.*

semicircular canal *Anat.* One of the three tubular structures in the inner ear of most vertebrates, which together serve as the organ of balance. See illustration under EAR.

sem·i·cir·cum·fer·ence (sem′ē·sər·kum′fər·əns, -frəns) *n.* One half of a circumference.

sem·i·civ·i·lized (sem′ē·siv′ə·līzd) *adj.* Half or partly civilized.

sem·i·co·lon (sem′ē·kō′lən) *n.* A mark (;) of punctuation, indicating a greater degree of separation than the comma.

sem·i·con·duc·tor (sem′ē·kən·duk′tər) *n. Physics* **1** One of a class of crystalline solids, as germanium, silicon, and lead sulfide, which are electronic conductors at ordinary temperatures: used in the manufacture of transistors. **2** Any substance or material having an electrical conductivity intermediate between metals and dielectrics.

sem·i·con·scious (sem′ē·kon′shəs) *adj.* Partly conscious; half-conscious.

sem·i·de·tached (sem′ē·di·tacht′) *adj.* Joined to another on one side only: said of two houses built side by side with one common wall.

sem·i·di·am·e·ter (sem′ē·dī·am′ə·tər) *n.* A radius; half of a diameter.

sem·i·di·ur·nal (sem′ē·dī·ûr′nəl) *adj.* **1** Pertaining to or continuing during a half-day; occurring or accomplished in a half-day, or once each half-day. **2** Designating either half of the arc described by a heavenly body during its rising or setting. [<SEMI- + DIURNAL]

sem·i·dome (sem′ē·dōm′) *n. Archit.* A roof structure resembling a portion, approximately half, of a dome divided vertically.

SEMIDOME

sem·i·el·lip·ti·cal (sem′ē·i·lip′ti·kəl) *adj.* Having the form of half of an ellipse that has been divided along either diameter.

sem·i·fi·nal (sem′ē·fī′nəl) *n.* **1** A competition which precedes the final in a list of sporting events. **2** One of two competitions in a tournament, the winners of each meeting in the final. — *adj.* Next before the final. — **sem′i·fi′nal·ist** *n.*

sem·i·flu·id (sem′ē·flo͞o′id) *adj.* Fluid, but thick and viscous. — *n.* A thick, viscous fluid. — **sem′i·flu·id′ic** (-flo͞o·id′ik) *adj.*

sem·i·liq·uid (sem′ē·lik′wid) *adj.* Half liquid. — *n.* A partly liquid substance.

sem·i·lu·nar (sem′ē·lo͞o′nər) *adj.* Resembling or shaped like a half-moon; crescentic. Also **sem′i·lu′nate** (-lo͞o′nāt).

semilunar bone *Anat.* The middle bone in the upper row of wrist bones.

semilunar valve *Anat.* One of the crescent-shaped pockets at the entrances to the aorta and to the pulmonary artery respectively: their function is to prevent the backward flow of blood.

sem·i·mo·bile (sem′ē·mō′bēl) *adj.* Partly mobile: said especially of military units not fully equipped with motor vehicles.

sem·i·month·ly (sem′ē·munth′lē) *adj.* Taking place twice a month. — *n. pl.* **·lies** A publication issued twice a month. — *adv.* At half-monthly intervals.

sem·i·mute (sem′ē·myo͞ot′) *adj.* Having imperfectly developed or partially lost speech.

sem·i·nal (sem′ə·nəl) *adj.* **1** Pertaining to or containing seeds, germs, or primal elements. **2** Having productive power; germinal; propagative. **3** Not developed; embryonic; rudimentary. [<OF <L *seminalis* <*semen, seminis* semen, a seed] — **sem′i·nal·ly** *adv.*

sem·i·nar (sem′ə·när) *n.* **1** A group of advanced students at a college or university, meeting regularly and informally with a professor for discussion of research problems. **2** The course thus conducted. [<G <L *seminarium.* See SEMINARY.]

sem·i·nar·y (sem′ə·ner′ē) *n. pl.* **·nar·ies** **1** A special school, as of theology; also, a school of higher education. **2** A seminar. **3** The place where anything is nurtured. **4** A seminary priest. — *adj.* **1** Seminal. **2** Pertaining to a seminary. [<MF *séminaire* <L *seminarium* a seed plot, orig. neut. of *seminarius* seminal <*semen, seminis* a seed, semen]

sem·i·na·tion (sem′ə·nā′shən) *n.* **1** The act of sowing or spreading; dispersion of seeds. **2** Propagation. [<L *seminatio, -onis* <*semen, seminis* a seed, semen]

sem·i·nif·er·ous (sem′ə·nif′ər·əs) *adj.* **1** Carrying or producing semen. **2** Seed-bearing. [<L *semen, seminis* a seed, semen + *ferre* bear]

sem·i·niv·o·rous (sem′ə·niv′ər·əs) *adj.* Feeding on seeds. [<L *semen, seminis* a seed, semen + -VOROUS]

Sem·i·nole (sem′ə·nōl) *n.* One of a Florida tribe of North American Indians of Muskhogean linguistic stock, an offshoot of the Creeks: now chiefly in Oklahoma, a remnant remaining in Florida. [<Muskhogean (Creek) *Simanóle,* lit., a separatist, a runaway]

sem·i-of·fi·cial (sem′ē·ə·fish′əl) *adj.* Having official authority or sanction; official to a certain extent. — **sem′i-of·fi′cial·ly** *adv.*

se·mi·ol·o·gy (sē′mē·ol′ə·jē, sē′mī-) *n.* **1** The science that relates to sign language. **2** *Med.* Symptomatology. **3** The use of signs in signaling. Also spelled *semeiology.* [<Gk. *sēmeion,* dim. of *sēma* a mark + -LOGY]

sem·i·o·paque (sem′ē·ō·pāk′) *adj.* Half-opaque; translucent but not transparent.

se·mi·ot·ic (sē′mē·ot′ik, sē′mī-) *adj.* **1** Of or pertaining to semantics (def. 2). **2** *Med.* Relating to symptomatology. Also spelled *semeiotic.* Also **se′mi·ot′i·cal.** [<Gk. *sēmeiōtikos* <*sēmeion.* See SEMIOLOGY.]

se·mi·ot·ics (sē′mē·ot′iks, sē′mī-) *n. pl. (construed as singular)* **1** Semantics (def. 2). **2** *Med.* Symptomatology. Also spelled *semeiotics.* [<Gk. *sēmeiōtikos.* See SEMIOTIC.]

sem·i·o·vip·a·rous (sem′ē·ō·vip′ər·əs) *adj.* Giving birth to imperfectly developed offspring, as a marsupial.

Se·mi·pa·la·tinsk (sye·mē·pə·lä′tyinsk) A city of eastern Kazakh S.S.R., on the Irtysh.

sem·i·pal·mate (sem′ē·pal′māt, -mit) *adj. Ornithol.* Having the toes connected by webs for less than half their length, as many shore birds. Also **sem′i·pal′mat·ed.**

semipalmated plover A common plover *(Charadrius semipalmatus)* of the Atlantic coast, which breeds only in the Arctic.

sem·i·par·a·sit·ic (sem′ē·par′ə·sit′ik) *adj. Biol.*

semiaccomplishment
semiacquaintance
semiaffectionate
semiagricultural
semialcoholic
semiallegiance
semianarchist
semiangular
semianimal
semianimated
semiarborescent
semiarchitectural
semiarid
semiatheist
semiattached
semi-autonomous
semi-autonomy
semibald
semibarbarian
semibarbarism
semibarbarous
semibarren
semibleached
semiblind
semiblunt
semiboiled
semibourgeois
semichannel
semichaotic
semichivalrous
semi-Christian
semiclerical
semiclosed
semiclosure
semicoagulated
semicollapsible
semicolonial
semicomplete
semiconceal
semiconfident
semiconfinement
semiconformist
semiconnection
semiconservative
semiconversion
semicooperative
semicured
semicylindrical
semidangerous
semidarkness
semideaf
semidelirious
semidenatured
semidependent
semidestructive
semidiaphanous
semidigested
semidirect
semidomesticated
semidry
semi-Empire
semienclosed
semierect
semieremitical
semiexposed
semiextinction
semifailure
semifatalistic
semifeudalism
semifictional
semifinished
semifit
semifitting
semifixed
semiflexed
semifluctuating
semiforeign

Partly parasitic: said especially of certain bacteria and of chlorophyll-bearing plants, as the mistletoe.

Sem·i-Pe·la·gi·an (sem′ē·pə·lā′jē·ən) *n.* One of a theological party in the fifth century which held a middle ground between the predestination doctrine of Augustine and the free-will doctrine of Pelagius. [<SEMI- + PELAGIAN]

sem·i·per·me·a·ble (sem′ē·pûr′mē·ə·bəl) *adj.* Partially permeable: said especially of osmotic membranes that separate a solvent from the dissolved substance.

sem·i·por·ce·lain (sem′ē·pôr′sə·lin, -pōr′-, -pôrs′lin, -pōrs′-) *n.* **1** A grade of porcelain having little or no translucency. **2** Earthenware resembling porcelain.

sem·i·post·al (sem′ē·pōs′təl) *adj.* Designating a postage stamp or series of stamps sold by postal authorities for more than the franking value, the additional proceeds usually going to a philanthropic purpose. —*n.* A semipostal stamp.

sem·i·pre·cious (sem′ē·presh′əs) *adj.* Designating a gem or class of gems that are not as valuable as those classified precious: *semiprecious* stones.

sem·i·qua·ver (sem′ē·kwā′vər) *n. Music* A note one sixteenth the value of a semibreve or whole note.

Se·mir·a·mis (si·mir′ə·mis) In Assyrian legend, the wife of Ninus and founder of Babylon, known for her beauty and wisdom.

sem·i·rig·id (sem′ē·rij′id) *adj. Aeron.* Partly rigid, as an airship in which an exterior stiffener supports the load. —*n.* A semirigid airship.

sem·i·round (sem′ē·round′) *adj.* Having one side round and the other flat. —*n.* A semiround object.

sem·i·skilled (sem′ē·skild′) *adj.* Partly skilled, but not enough to perform highly specialized work.

sem·i·sol·id (sem′ē·sol′id) *adj.* Partly solid; so viscous as to be nearly solid.

Sem·ite (sem′īt, sē′mīt) *n.* **1** A person believed to be or considered as a descendant of Shem. **2** One of a people of Caucasian stock, now represented by the Jews and Arabs, but originally including the ancient Babylonians, Assyrians, Arameans, Phoenicians, etc. Also *Shemite.* [<NL *Semita* <LL *Sem* Shem <Gk. *Sēm* <Hebrew *shēm*]

Se·mit·ic (sə·mit′ik) *adj.* Of or pertaining to the Semites, or to any of their languages. —*n.* A subfamily of the Hamito-Semitic family of languages, divided into three groups — **East Semitic** (Akkadian), **Northwest Semitic** (Phoenician, ancient and modern Hebrew, Aramaic, etc.), and **Southwest Semitic** (Arabic, Ethiopic, Amharic, etc.).

Se·mit·ics (sə·mit′iks) *n.* The scientific study of the history, language, and literature of the Semitic peoples.

Sem·i·tism (sem′ə·tiz′əm) *n.* **1** A Semitic word or idiom. **2** Semitic practices, opinions, or customs collectively. **3** Any political or economic policy favoring the Jews.

sem·i·tone (sem′ē·tōn′) *n. Music* An interval approximately equal to half a major tone on the scale: the smallest interval in most European music. — **sem·i·ton·ic** (sem′ē·ton′ik) *adj.*

sem·i·trail·er (sem′ē·trāl′ər) *n.* **1** A trailer having wheels only at the rear, the front end being attached to the rear of a truck tractor. **2** A tractor and its attached semitrailer considered as a unit: also called *trailer truck.*

sem·i·trans·lu·cent (sem′ē·trans·lōō′sənt, -tranz-) *adj.* Half or partly translucent. — **sem′i·trans·lu′cent·ly** *adv.*

sem·i·trans·par·ent (sem′ē·trans·pâr′ənt, -par′-) *adj.* Half or partly transparent.

sem·i·trop·i·cal (sem′ē·trop′i·kəl) *adj.* Nearly tropical.

sem·i·vit·ri·fied (sem′ē·vit′rə·fīd) *adj.* Half vitrified; partially made into glass.

sem·i·vow·el (sem′i·vou′əl) *n. Phonet.* A vowel-like sound used as a consonant, as (w), (y), and (r): also called *glide.* —**sem′i·vo′cal** (-vō′kəl) *adj.*

sem·i·week·ly (sem′ē·wēk′lē) *adj.* Issued or occurring twice a week. —*n. pl.* **·lies** A publication issued twice a week. —*adv.* At half-weekly intervals.

Sem·lin (zem·lēn′) The German name for ZEMUN.

Sem·mel·weiss (sem′əl·vīs), **Ignaz Philipp,** 1816–65, Austrian obstetrician; pioneer in prevention of puerperal fever.

Semmes (semz), **Raphael,** 1809–77, American Confederate naval officer.

sem·o·li·na (sem′ə·lē′nə) *n.* The gritty or grain-like portions of wheat retained in the bolting machine after the fine flour has been passed through. [Alter. of Ital. *semolino,* dim. of *semola* bran <L *simila* fine flour]

Sem·pach (zem′päkh) A town in central Switzerland; scene of a Swiss victory over the Austrians, 1386.

sem·per fi·de·lis (sem′pər fi·dē′lis, fi·dā′lis) *Latin* Always faithful: motto of the U.S. Marine Corps.

sem·per pa·ra·tus (sem′pər pə·rā′təs) *Latin* Always prepared: motto of the U.S. Coast Guard.

sem·per·vi·rent (sem′pər·vī′rənt) *adj.* Evergreen. [<L *semper* always + *virens, -entis,* ppr. of *virere* be green]

sem·pi·ter·nal (sem′pə·tûr′nəl) *adj.* Enduring or existing to all eternity; everlasting. See synonyms under IMMORTAL, PERPETUAL. [<OF *sempiternel* <LL *sempiternalis* <L *sempiternus* everlasting < *semper* always] — **sem′·pi·ter′ni·ty** *n.*

sem·pli·ce (sem′plē·chā) *adj. Music* Simple; unaffected: a direction to performers. [<Ital. <L *simplex, simplicis*]

sem·pre (sem′prā) *adv. Music* Always; throughout the passage or composition: *sempre* legato, piano, etc. [<Ital. <L *semper*]

semp·stress (semp′stris, sem′-) See SEAMSTRESS.

sen (sen) *n. Japanese* A Japanese copper or bronze coin, equal to 1/100 of a yen.

sen′ (sen) *v.t.* & *v.i., n. Scot.* Send[1].

sen·a·ry (sen′ər·ē) *adj.* Of or pertaining to six; containing six units. [<L *senarius* < *seni* six each < *sex* six]

sen·ate (sen′it) *n.* **1** The governing body of some universities and institutions of learning. **2** An advisory body of members of the faculty and representative students in a school or college. **3** A body of distinguished or venerable men; council; legislative body. [<OF *senat* <L *senatus,* lit., a council of old men < *senex, senis* old]

Sen·ate (sen′it) *n.* **1** The upper branch of national or state legislative bodies of the United States, and of France and other governments; especially, the **United States Senate,** composed of two Senators elected by popular vote from each State. **2** In ancient Rome, the state council, whose originally very extensive powers were curtailed under the empire: limited to 100 patricians under the kings, it consisted, under the republic, of 300 patricians, plebeians, and high officials; under Augustus, there were 600 senators.

sen·a·tor (sen′ə·tər) *n.* A member of a senate. [<OF *senateur* <L *senator* < *senex, senis* an old man, old] — **sen′a·tor·ship′** *n.*

sen·a·to·ri·al (sen′ə·tôr′ē·əl, -tō′rē-) *adj.* **1** Pertaining to or befitting a senator or senate. **2** Entitled to elect a senator, as a district. — **sen′a·to′ri·al·ly** *adv.*

se·na·tus con·sul·tum (sə·nā′təs kən·sul′təm) *Latin* A decree of the ancient Roman Senate, pronounced upon some matter of law or public policy: originally only advisory and finally authoritative as laws. Also **se·na′tus con·sult′.**

send[1] (send) *v.* **sent, send·ing** *v.t.* **1** To cause or direct to go; dispatch, as a messenger. **2** To cause to be conveyed to another place; transmit; forward: to *send* a letter. **3** To cause to issue; emit or discharge, as heat, light, smoke, etc.: with *forth, out,* etc. **4** To throw or drive by force; impel. **5** To cause to come, happen, etc.; grant: God *send* us peace. **6** To bring into a specified state or condition; drive: The decision *sent* him into bankruptcy. **7** To transmit, as a current or electromagnetic impulses. —*v.i.* **8** To dispatch an agent, messenger, or message. —**to send for** To summon by a message or messenger. —**to send in one's papers** To resign. —*n.* A messenger. [OE *sendan*] —**send′er** *n.*

Synonyms (verb): cast, delegate, depute, discharge, dispatch, dismiss, emit, fling, forward, hurl, impel, lance, launch, project, propel, sling, throw, transmit. *Send* in its most common use involves personal efficiency without personal presence; according to the adage, "If you want your business done, go; if not, *send*"; one *sends* a letter or a bullet, a messenger or a message. To *dispatch* is to *send* hastily or very promptly, ordinarily with a destination in view; to *dismiss* is to *send* away from oneself without reference to a destination; as, to *dismiss* a clerk, an application, or an annoying subject. To *discharge* is to *send* away so as to relieve a person or thing of a load; we *discharge* a gun or *discharge* the contents; as applied to persons, *discharge* is a harsher term than *dismiss.* To *emit* is to *send* forth from within, with no reference to a destination; as, The sun *emits* light and heat. *Transmit,* from the Latin, is a dignified term, often less vigorous than the Saxon *send,* but preferable at times in literary or scientific use; as, to *transmit* a charge of electricity. *Transmit* fixes the attention more on the intervening agency, as *send* does upon the points of departure and destination. *Antonyms*: bring, carry, convey, get, give, hand, hold, keep, receive, retain.

send[2] (send) *Naut. n.* **1** The flow or impulse of the waves. **2** Scend. —*v.i.* **1** To move by the force of waves. **2** To scend. [<SEND[1]; prob. infl. in meaning by ASCEND]

Sen·dai (sen·dī) A city on NE Honshu island, Japan.

sen·dal (sen′dəl) *n.* **1** A light, thin, silken fabric much used for dresses, etc., in the Middle Ages. **2** An article made of it. Also spelled *sandal.* [<OF *cendal, sendal,* ult. <Gk. *sidōn* fine linen]

send-off (send′ôf′, -of′) *n.* **1** The act of sending off; a start. **2** A farewell dinner or other celebration or demonstration at parting. **3** Encouragement, as in starting a career.

send-up (send′up′) *n. Brit. Slang* A parody; take-off.

Sen·e·ca (sen′ə·kə) *n.* One of a tribe of North American Indians of Iroquoian stock formerly inhabiting western New York, the largest tribe of the confederation known as the Five Nations: still numerous in New York and Ontario. [<Du. *Sennacaas* the Five Nations <Algonquian (Mohegan) *A'sinnika,* trans. of Iroquoian *Oneñiute,* short for *oneñiute' roñ non* Oneida, lit., people of the standing rock]

Sen·e·ca (sen′ə·kə), **Lucius Annaeus,** 3? B.C.–A.D. 65, Roman Stoic philosopher, statesman, and tragic dramatist.

Sen·e·ca Lake (sen′ə·kə) One of the Finger Lakes in west central New York, extending 35 miles north and south; 67 square miles.

sen·e·ga (sen′ə·gə) *n.* **1** The dried root of an herb (*Polygala senega*) of the milkwort family, used as a stimulating expectorant, as in treating bronchitis. **2** The plant itself. Also **senega**

semifriable
semifrontier
semifunctional
semigala
semigenuflection
semi-Gnostic
semi-Gothic
semigranulate
semihard
semihigh
semihistorical
semihobo
semihostile
semihumanitarian
semihumorous
semi-idle
semi-idleness
semi-incandescent
semi-independence
semi-intoxicated
semi-intoxication
semi-invalid
semileafless
semilegendary
semiliberal
semilined
semilucent
semimilitary
semimonastic
semimonopoly
semimystical
seminationalization
seminecessary
seminervous
semioblivious
semiobscurity
semiopened
semiorganized
semiovoid
semipagan
semipanic
semiparallel
semiparalysis
semipastoral
semipeace
semiperfect
semipermanent
semiperspicuous
semipolitician
semiprivate
semiprofessional
semipublic
semiraw
semirebellion
semireligious
semiresolute
semirespectability
semirespectable
semiretirement
semiriddle
semi-Romanized
semiroyal
semirustic
semisacred
semisatiric
semiscientific
semisecrecy
semiseriousness
semisocial
semisocialism
semisoft
semispontaneity
semistagnation
semistarvation
semistarved
semisuccess
semitailored
semitrained
semitruth
semivirtue
semivital
semivoluntary
semiwarfare
semiwild

root. [<NL, alter. of SENECA; so called because thought, by the Seneca Indians, to be good for snakebites]

Sen·e·gal (sen′ə·gôl′) A river of western Africa, flowing about 1,000 miles NW from SW Guinea to the Atlantic at Saint-Louis, Senegal, forming the border between Senegal and Mauritania.

Sen·e·gal (sen′ə·gôl′), **Republic of** An independent republic of the French Community in west Africa; 76,124 square miles; capital, Dakar: formerly a French overseas territory. — **Sen′e·ga·lese′** (-gə·lēz′, -lēs′) *adj.* & *n.*

Sen·e·gam·bi·a (sen′ə·gam′bē·ə) The former name for the territory between the Senegal and Gambia rivers, in west Africa.

se·nes·cent (si·nes′ənt) *adj.* **1** Growing old. **2** Characteristic of old age. [<L *senescens, -entis,* ppr. of *senescere* grow old <*senex* old] — **se·nes′cence** *n.*

sen·e·schal (sen′ə·shəl) *n.* **1** An official in the household of a medieval prince or noble who had charge of feasts, etc.; a steward or majordomo. **2** A magistrate or governor. **3** *Brit.* A cathedral official. [<OF <Gmc. Cf. OHG *siniskalk* old servant.]

se·nile (sē′nīl, -nil) *adj.* **1** Pertaining to, proceeding from, or characteristic of old age. **2** Infirm; weak; doting. **3** *Geog.* Almost worn away to base level: a *senile* continent. [<L *senilis*< *senex* old] — **se′nile·ly** *adv.*

senile dementia *Psychiatry* The progressive deterioration of cerebral functions and mental faculties associated with old age. Also **senile psychosis.**

se·nil·i·ty (si·nil′ə·tē) *n.* Mental and physical infirmity due to old age.

sen·ior (sēn′yər) *adj.* **1** Older in years; elder; specifically, after personal names (usually in the abbreviated form *Sr.*), to denote the elder of two related persons of the same name, especially a father and his son. **2** Older in office; more advanced in service; superior in rank or dignity. **3** Pertaining to the closing year of a high school or college course. — *n.* **1** One older in years or office, or more advanced in rank or dignity than another. **2** Hence, any elderly person. **3** A member of a senior class. **4** A graduate or one of the older fellows of an English college. [<L, compar. of *senex, senis* old]

senior citizen An elderly person, especially one of or over the age of retirement.

sen·ior·i·ty (sēn·yôr′ə·tē, -yor′-) *n.* *pl.* **·ties** **1** The state of being older in years or in office; priority of age, service, or rank. **2** An assembly of seniors or, in England, senior fellows of a college.

Sen·lac (sen′lak) A hill, near Hastings, in Sussex, England; scene of the battle of Hastings, 1066.

sen·na (sen′ə) *n.* **1** The dried leaflets of any one of several leguminous plants (genus *Cassia*), used medicinally for their purgative properties; especially, the Old World species *C. acutifolia* and *C. angustifolia.* **2** Any one of the plants yielding true senna or a similar product. [<NL *senna, sena* <Arabic *sanā*]

Sen·nach·er·ib (si·nak′ər·ib), died 681 B.C.; king of Assyria 705–681 B.C.

Sen·nar (sen·när′) An ancient city in the Sudan between the White Nile and the Blue Nile, capital of a large native kingdom, 15th to 19th centuries. Also **Sen·naar′.**

sen·net (sen′it) *n.* A signal of exit or entrance sounded on a horn: chiefly as a stage direction in Elizabethan plays. [<OF *senet, sinet, signet.* Double of SIGNET.]

sen·night (sen′īt, -it) *n.* *Archaic* A week. Also **se′n′night, sev′en-night′.** [OE *seofan nihta* <*seofan* seven + *nihta,* pl. of *niht* a night]

sen·nit (sen′it) *n.* **1** Plaited cordage, of from 3 to 9 strands, used for gaskets on ships. **2** Plaited grass or straw for hatmaking. [Earlier *sinnet,* ? <SEVEN + KNIT]

se·no·pi·a (si·nō′pē·ə) *n.* An apparent restoration of normal vision in formerly myopic people who have become hypermetropic in old age. Also called *gerontopia.* [<NL <L *senex* old + Gk. *ōps, ōpos* an eye]

se·ñor (sā·nyôr′) *n.* *pl.* **·ño·res** (-nyō′rās) *Spanish* A Spanish title of courtesy; a gentleman; Mr.; sir: used before a name, like *Mr.,* or alone, like *Sir.*

se·ño·ra (sā·nyō′rä) *n.* *Spanish* A Spanish lady; Mrs.; madam.

se·ño·ri·ta (sā′nyō·rē′tä) *n.* *Spanish* A young, unmarried Spanish lady; miss.

sen·sate (sen′sāt) *adj.* Perceived or appreciated by the senses: *sensate* matters: also **sen′sat·ed.** — *v.t.* **·sat·ed, ·sat·ing** To perceive by the senses. [<LL *sensatus* gifted with sense <L *sensus* sense]

sen·sa·tion (sen·sā′shən) *n.* **1** *Physiol.* **a** That aspect of consciousness resulting from the stimulation of a nerve process beginning at any point in the body and passing through the brain, especially by those stimuli affecting any of the sense organs, as hearing, taste, touch, smell, and sight. **b** The capacity to respond to such stimulation. **2** That which produces interest or excitement; an excited condition: to cause a *sensation.* **3** A condition of mind resulting from inherent feeling; emotion. [<Med. L *sensatio, -onis* <LL *sensatus.* See SENSATE.]

Synonyms: emotion, feeling, perception, sense. *Sensation* is the mind's consciousness due to bodily response to stimuli, as heat or sound; *perception* is the cognition of some external object which causes the *sensation.* While *sensations* are connected with the body, *emotions* add the reactions of the mind. *Feeling* is a term popularly denoting what is felt, whether through the body or by the mind alone, and includes both *sensation* and *emotion.* A *sense* is an organ or faculty of *sensation* or of *perception.* See FEELING.

sen·sa·tion·al (sen·sā′shən·əl) *adj.* **1** Pertaining to emotional excitement. **2** Pertaining to physical sensation. **3** Causing excitement; startling. **4** Causing unnatural emotional excitement; melodramatic; trashy: a *sensational* story. — **sen·sa′tion·al·ly** *adv.*

sen·sa·tion·al·ism (sen·sā′shən·əl·iz′əm) *n.* **1** *Philos.* The theory that all knowledge originates in sensation, or is composed of transformed sense elements, that all consciousness is modified sensation, and all mental phenomena have a sensory basis: a branch of modern empiricism. **2** The use of melodramatic methods in writing or speaking. **3** The theory that feeling is the only criterion of good. — **sen·sa′tion·al·ist** *n.* — **sen·sa′tion·al·is′tic** *adj.*

sense (sens) *n.* **1** The faculty of sensation; sense perception. **2** Any of certain agencies by or through which an individual receives impressions of the external world; popularly, one of the five senses. **3** *Physiol.* Any receptor, or group of receptors, specialized to receive and transmit stimuli, either external, as of sight, taste, smell, etc., or internal, as of hunger, thirst, sex, equilibrium, muscular and visceral movements, etc. **4** Rational perception accompanied by feeling; realization; discriminating cognition: a *sense* of wrong. **5** Normal power of mind or understanding; sound or natural judgment: The fellow has no *sense*; often in the plural: She is coming to her *senses.* **6** Signification; import; meaning. **7** Opinion, view, or judgment of the majority: The *sense* of the meeting was manifest. **8** That which commends itself to the understanding as being in accordance with reason and good judgment: to talk *sense.* **9** Capacity to perceive or appreciate: a *sense* of color. **10** *Geom.* One of two opposite directions in which a magnitude may be described or generated. **11** Direction; trend. See synonyms under FEELING, MIND. — **the five senses** The Aristotelian division of senses into sight, hearing, smell, taste, and touch: now collectively known as the **special senses.** — **sixth sense** **1** Capacity for perception beyond the normal range of the senses; extrasensory perception. **2** Intuitive or premonitory knowledge, especially as affecting or affected by the senses. **3** Cenesthesia. — *v.t.* **sensed, sens·ing** **1** To become aware of through the senses. **2** *Colloq.* To comprehend; understand. [<MF *sens* <L *sensus* perception <*sentire* feel]

sense datum *Psychol.* That which is experienced as a result of the stimulation of a sense organ.

sense·less (sens′lis) *adj.* **1** Deprived of consciousness; unconscious. **2** Incapable of feeling or perception; insensate. **3** Devoid of sense; foolish; stupid. — **sense′less·ly** *adv.* — **sense′less·ness** *n.*

sense organ *Physiol.* A structure specialized to receive sense impressions, as the eye, nose, ear, etc.; a receptor (def. 2).

sense perception Immediate knowledge of things through the senses, as distinguished from mediate or inferred knowledge.

sense stress See SENTENCE STRESS.

sen·si·bil·i·ty (sen′sə·bil′ə·tē) *n.* *pl.* **·ties** **1** The capability of sensation; power to perceive or feel. **2** The capacity of sensation and rational emotion, as distinguished from intellect and will. **3** Susceptibility or sensitiveness to outside influences or mental impressions; sometimes, abnormal sensitiveness: often in the plural. **4** Appreciation accompanying mental apprehension; discerning judgment. **5** Delicacy or sensitiveness of an instrument. **6** Responsiveness to pathos or to artistic or esthetic values. **7** *Archaic* Sentimentality.

Synonyms: sensitiveness, sensibility, susceptibility. In popular use *sensibility* denotes sometimes capacity of feeling of any kind; as, *sensibility* to heat or cold; sometimes, a peculiar readiness to be the subject of feeling, especially of the higher feelings: as the *sensibility* of the artist or the poet. *Sensitiveness* denotes an especial delicacy of *sensibility,* ready to be excited by the slightest cause, as displayed, for instance, in the sensitive plant. *Susceptibility* is rather a capacity to receive, to contain feeling, so that a person of great *susceptibility* is capable of being readily and deeply moved; *sensitiveness* is more superficial, *susceptibility* more pervading. In physics, the *sensitiveness* of a magnetic needle is the ease with which it may be deflected, as by another magnet; its *susceptibility* is the degree to which it can be magnetized by a given magnetic force or the amount of magnetism it will hold. A person of great *sensitiveness* is quickly and keenly affected by any external influence, as by music, pathos, or ridicule, while a person of great *susceptibility* is not only touched, but moved to his utmost soul. See FEELING. *Antonyms*: coldness, deadness, hardness, insensibility, numbness, unconsciousness.

sen·si·ble (sen′sə·bəl) *adj.* **1** Possessed of good mental perception; exhibiting sound sense and judgment; discreet; judicious. **2** Capable of physical sensation; sensitive: *sensible* to pain. **3** Perceptible or appreciable through the senses: *sensible* heat. **4** Emotionally or mentally sensitive. **5** Having a perception or cognition; fully aware; persuaded. **6** Great enough to be perceived; appreciable. **7** *Obs.* Sensitive to minute changes. See synonyms under CONSCIOUS, EXPEDIENT, INTELLIGENT, PHYSICAL, SAGACIOUS. — *n.* **1** A substance capable of being felt or observed. **2** A sentient being. **3** *Music* The leading note; the seventh of a scale: also **sensible note** (or **tone**). [<OF <L *sensibilis* <*sensus,* pp. of *sentire* feel, perceive] — **sen′si·ble·ness** *n.* — **sen′si·bly** *adv.*

sen·si·tive (sen′sə·tiv) *adj.* **1** Easily affected by outside operations or influences; excitable or impressible; touchy; easily offended. **2** *Chem.* & *Phot.* Reacting readily to the proper agents or forces: paper *sensitive* to light. **3** Pertaining to or depending on the senses or sensation: *sensitive* motions. **4** Closing or moving when touched or irritated, as certain plants. **5** Liable to fluctuation. **6** *Obs.* Wise; sensible. **7** Capable of indicating minute changes or differences; delicate. See synonyms under FINE, MOBILE. [<OF *sensitif* <Med. L *sensitivus* <L *sensus.* See SENSIBLE.] — **sen′si·tive·ly** *adv.* — **sen′si·tive·ness** *n.*

sensitive plant A shrubby tropical herb (*Mimosa pudica*), whose leaves close at a touch; often cultivated in hothouses.

sen·si·tiv·i·ty (sen′sə·tiv′ə·tē) *n.* **1** The state or degree of being sensitive; sensitiveness. **2** *Physiol.* The degree of acuteness with which sensations are discriminated; irritability, as of organs: distinguished from *sensibility,* in which the mental side is more prominent. **3** The degree of responsiveness to an electric current or to radio waves. **4** *Phot.* Sensitiveness to light.

sen·si·tize (sen′sə·tīz) *v.t.* **·tized, ·tiz·ing 1** To render sensitive. **2** *Phot.* To make sensitive to light, as a plate or film. **3** *Med.* To make susceptible or hypersensitive to the action of a drug by repeated injections. [<SENSIT(IVE) + -IZE] **—sen′si·ti·za′tion** *n.* **—sen′si·tiz′er** *n.*

sen·si·tom·e·ter (sen′sə·tom′ə·tər) *n.* An apparatus by which the sensitiveness to light of a photographic film or body tissue may be tested or measured. [<SENSIT(IVE) + -(O)-METER]

sen·sor (sen′sər) *adj.* Sensory: applied to nerves and nerve organs. [Short for SENSORY]

sen·so·ri·mo·tor (sen′sə·ri·mō′tər) *adj. Physiol.* Of or pertaining to muscular and nervous responses induced by sensory stimuli. Compare IDEOMOTOR. [<SENSORY + MOTOR]

sen·so·ri·um (sen·sôr′ē·əm, -sō′rē-) *n. pl.* **·ri·a** (-ē·ə) **1** *Anat.* The nervous system, including the cerebrum, as the collective organ of sensation. **2** *Biol.* The entire sensory apparatus of an organism. [<LL <L *sensus.* See SENSIBLE.]

sen·so·ry (sen′sər·ē) *adj.* **1** Pertaining to the sensorium or to sensation. **2** Conveying or producing sense impulses. Also **sen·so·ri·al** (sen·sôr′ē·əl, -sō′rē-). [<LL *sensorium* SENSORIUM]

sen·su·al (sen′shōō·əl) *adj.* **1** Unduly indulgent to the appetites or sexual pleasure; exhibiting a predominance of the animal nature; lewd. **2** Pertaining to the body or the physical senses; also, fleshly; carnal: opposed to *spiritual.* **3** Pertaining to sensualism: usually opprobrious. See synonyms under BRUTISH. [<MF *sensuel* <LL *sensualis* <L *sensus* SENSE] **—sen′su·al·ly** *adv.*

sen·su·al·ism (sen′shōō·əl·iz′əm) *n.* **1** Sensuality. **2** *Philos.* A debased sensationalism. **3** A system of ethics predicating the pleasures of sense to be the highest good. **4** Emphasis on the sensuous elements of beauty, rather than the ideal. **—sen′su·al·ist** *n.* **—sen′su·al·is′tic** *adj.*

sen·su·al·i·ty (sen′shōō·al′ə·tē) *n.* **1** The state of being sensual, or sensual acts collectively. **2** Sensual or animal indulgence. Also **sen′su·al·ness.**

sen·su·al·ize (sen′shōō·əl·īz′) *v.t.* **·ized, ·iz·ing** To make sensual. Also *Brit.* **sen′su·al·ise′. —sen′su·al·i·za′tion** *n.*

sen·su·ous (sen′shōō·əs) *adj.* **1** Pertaining or appealing to or derived from the senses: used in a higher and purer sense than *sensual.* **2** Keenly appreciative of and aroused by beauty, refinement, or luxury. **3** Resembling imagery that appeals to the senses: a *sensuous* portrayal. [<L *sensus* SENSE + -OUS] **—sen′su·ous·ly** *adv.* **—sen′su·ous·ness** *n.*

sent (sent) Past tense and past participle of SEND.

sen·tence (sen′təns) *n.* **1** *Gram.* A word or a related group of words expressing a complete thought, whether a statement of fact (declarative), a question (interrogative), a command (imperative), or an exclamation (exclamatory). Declarative and interrogative sentences usually contain a subject (that which is spoken of) and a predicate (what is said about the subject), but either or both of these elements may be missing in an utterance that, nevertheless, conveys full meaning, as in "Where is John?" "At home." or "Look!" **—simple sentence** A sentence consisting of one independent clause, as *The dog barked.* Its subject and predicate may be simple (having one substantive or one verb) or compound (having two or more substantives or verbs), and there may be modifying words and phrases. **—compound sentence** A sentence consisting of more than one independent clause, as *The sun shone and the birds sang.* **—complex sentence** A sentence consisting of a principal clause and one or more subordinate clauses, as *After I have read it, I shall give the book to you.* **2** *Law* A final judgment; penalty pronounced upon a person convicted. **3** A determination; opinion, especially as expressed formally. **4** An instructive saying; a maxim. **5** *Music* A complete idea or period, usually consisting of several phrases, as the half of a four-line hymn tune or song. **—***v.t.* **·tenced, ·tenc·ing** To pass sentence upon; condemn to punishment. See synonyms under CONDEMN. [<OF <L *sententia* an opinion <*sentire* feel, be of opinion] **—sen·ten·tial** (sen·ten′shəl) *adj.*

sen·tenc·er (sen′tən·sər) *n.* One who pronounces sentence; a judge.

sentence stress The variation in emphasis given to successive words in a sentence to stress the meaning: also called *sense stress.* Also **sentence accent.**

sen·ten·tious (sen·ten′shəs) *adj.* **1** Abounding in or giving terse expression to thought; axiomatic; sometimes, opprobriously, pompously formal, or moralizing. **2** Habitually using terse, laconic, or aphoristic language. See synonyms under TERSE. [<L *sententiosus* <*sententia* a maxim. See SENTENCE.] **—sen·ten′tious·ly** *adv.* **—sen·ten′tious·ness, sen·ten·ti·os·i·ty** (sen·ten′shē·os′ə·tē) *n.*

sen·ti·ence (sen′shē·əns, -shəns) *n.* **1** The state of being sentient. **2** Capacity for sensation or sense perception. **3** Consciousness. **4** Sensation regarded as immediate experience and so distinguished from thought or perception. Also **sen′ti·en·cy.**

sen·ti·ent (sen′shē·ənt, -shənt) *adj.* Possessing powers of sense or sense perception; having or actually experiencing sensation or feeling: opposed to *inanimate* and *vegetal.* **—***n.* One capable of sensation or perception; loosely, the mind, as the seat of consciousness. [<L *sentiens, -entis,* ppr. of *sentire* feel] **—sen′ti·ent·ly** *adv.*

sen·ti·ment (sen′tə·mənt) *n.* **1** Noble, tender, or artistic feeling, or susceptibility to such feeling; sensibility; also, its verbal expression. **2** A mental attitude or response to a person, object, or idea conditioned entirely by feeling instead of reason; loosely, an exaggerated emotional reaction. **3** Idealistic, personal, or esthetic reaction as distinguished from intellectual or practical. **4** An opinion or judgment; thought as distinguished from its expression: often in the plural. **5** An expressive thought or idea dressed in appropriate language, as a toast aptly uttered. See synonyms under FEELING, IDEA. [<OF *sentement* <Med. L *sentimentum* <L *sentire* feel]

sen·ti·men·tal (sen′tə·men′təl) *adj.* **1** Characterized by sentiment or intellectual emotion; involving or exciting tender emotions or aspirations. **2** Experiencing, displaying, or given to sentiment, often in an extravagant or mawkish manner: a *sentimental* person. See synonyms under ROMANTIC. **—sen′ti·men′tal·ly** *adv.*

sen·ti·men·tal·ism (sen′tə·men′təl·iz′əm) *n.* The state of being sentimental, or its manifestation; tendency to be emotional. Also **sen′ti·men·tal′i·ty** (-men·tal′ə·tē). **—sen′ti·men′tal·ist** *n.*

sen·ti·men·tal·ize (sen′tə·men′təl·īz) *v.* **·ized, ·iz·ing** *v.t.* **1** To affect with sentiment. **2** To cherish sentimentally. **—***v.i.* **3** To behave sentimentally. Also *Brit.* **sen′ti·men′tal·ise.**

sen·ti·nel (sen′tə·nəl) *n.* A sentry; hence, any watcher or guard. **—***v.t.* **·neled** or **·nelled, ·nel·ing** or **·nel·ling 1** To watch over as a sentinel. **2** To protect or furnish with sentinels. **3** To station or appoint as a sentinel. [<OF *sentinelle* <Ital. *sentinella* <LL *sentinare* avoid danger <*sentire* perceive]

sen·try (sen′trē) *n. pl.* **·tries 1** A soldier placed on guard to see that only authorized persons pass his post and to give warning of approaching danger; a sentinel. **2** The watch or guard kept by a sentry. [? Short for obs. *centrenel,* var. of SENTINEL]

sentry box A small shelter or cabin to protect a sentry from the weather.

Se·nus·si (se·nōō′sē) *n. pl.* A belligerent Moslem religious sect once influential in northern Africa and Arabia, founded by Sidi Mohammed ben Ali ben Es Senussi about 1842. Also **Se·nu′si, Se·nus′sites. —Se·nus′si·an** *adj.*

Se·oul (sā·ōōl′, sōl; *Korean* syœ·ōōl) The capital of the Republic of Korea (South Korea): also *Kyongsong:* Japanese *Keijo.*

se·pal (sē′pəl) *n. Bot.* One of the individual leaves of a calyx. [<F *sépale* <NL *sepalum* <L *sep(aratus)* separate + *(pet)alum* a petal] **—sep·a·line** (sep′ə·lin, -līn), **sep′a·lous** *adj.*

sep·a·ra·ble (sep′ər·ə·bəl, sep′rə-) *adj.* Capable of being separated or divided. [<L *separabilis* <*separare* separate] **—sep′a·ra·bil′i·ty, sep′a·ra·ble·ness** *n.* **—sep′a·ra·bly** *adv.*

sep·a·rate (sep′ə·rāt) *v.* **·rat·ed, ·rat·ing** *v.t.* **1** To set asunder; disunite or disjoin; sever. **2** To occupy a position between; serve to keep apart: The Hudson River *separates* New York from New Jersey. **3** To divide into components, parts, etc. **4** To isolate or obtain from a compound, mixture, etc.: to *separate* the wheat from the chaff. **5** To consider separately; distinguish between. **6** *Law* To part by separation. **—***v.i.* **7** To become divided or disconnected; draw apart. **8** To part company; withdraw from association or combination. **—***adj.* (sep′ər·it, sep′rit) **1** Existing or considered apart from others; distinct; individual: *separate* rooms. **2** Disembodied; disunited from the body. **3** Separated; disjoined. **—***n.* **1** An offprint. **2** *pl.* Garments to be worn in various combinations, as skirts and blouses. See synonyms under PARTICULAR. [<L *separatus,* pp. of *separare* <*se-* apart + *parare* prepare] **—sep′a·rate·ly** *adv.* **—sep′a·rate·ness** *n.*

Synonyms (verb): alienate, detach, disconnect, disengage, disjoin, dissever, disunite, divide, part, remove, sever, split, sunder, withdraw. *Antonyms:* see synonyms for MIX.

separate school *Canadian* A private school; specifically, a Roman Catholic parochial school.

sep·a·ra·tion (sep′ə·rā′shən) *n.* **1** The act or process of separating; division. **2** The state of being disconnected or apart. **3** A dividing line. **4** *Law* Relinquishment of cohabitation between husband and wife by mutual consent: distinguished from *divorce.* See synonyms under SECLUSION.

separation center A central army or navy point that handles discharges and releases of personnel except medical discharges.

sep·a·ra·tist (sep′ər·ə·tist, sep′rə-) *n.* One who advocates or upholds separation; specifically, a seceder; dissenter. Also **sep′a·ra′tion·ist. —sep′a·ra·tism** *n.*

sep·a·ra·tive (sep′ə·rā′tiv, -rə·tiv) *adj.* Tending to or inducing separation; useful in separating.

sep·a·ra·tor (sep′ə·rā′tər) *n.* **1** Any device, implement, or apparatus for dividing or separating things into their component parts. **2** A machine for separating the chaff from grain. **3** A centrifugal mechanism for separating cream from milk. **4** One who separates.

sep·a·ra·trix (sep′ə·rā′triks) *n.* A separating point or line; decimal point. [<LL *(linea) separatrix* the separating or dividing (line)]

sep·a·ra·tum (sep′ə·rā′təm) *n. pl.* **·ta** (-tə) A paper published separately from a series to which it belongs; a reprint of an article previously published as a part of a report.

Se·phar·dim (si·fär′dim) *n. pl.* The Spanish and Portuguese Jews or their descendants: distinguished from the *Ashkenazim.* Also **Se·phar′a·dim** (-ə·dim). [<Hebrew *sephārādhīm* <*Sephāradh,* a country mentioned in *Ob.* iii 20, identified by the rabbis with Spain, but prob. orig. in Asia Minor] **—Se·phar′dic, Se·phar′a·dic** *adj.*

se·pi·a (sē′pē·ə) *n.* **1** A reddish-brown pigment prepared from the ink of the cuttlefish; the color of this pigment. **2** A picture done in this pigment. **3** The ink of the cuttlefish. **4** Any of a genus *(Sepia)* of decapod mollusks having an internal shell, especially the common Atlantic cuttlefish *(S. officinalis).* **—***adj.* Executed in or colored like sepia; dark-brown with a tinge of red. [<L <Gk. *sēpia* a cuttlefish]

Se·pik (sā′pik) A river in NE New Guinea, in the Australian Territory of New Guinea, rising near the border of Netherlands New Guinea and flowing 700 miles NE to the Bismarck Sea.

se·pi·o·lite (sē′pē·ə·līt′) *n.* Meerschaum. [<G *sepiolith* <NL *sepium* cuttlebone (<Gk. *sēpion,* dim. of *sēpia* a cuttlefish) + Gk. *lithos* a stone]

se·poy (sē′poi) *n.* A native Indian soldier outfitted and trained in European style; especially, one employed in the former British Indian Army. [<Pg. *sipae* <Urdu *sipāhī* a soldier <Persian <*sipāh* an army]

Sepoy Mutiny The Indian Mutiny. Also **Sepoy Rebellion.**

sep·pu·ku (sep·pōō·kōō) *n. Japanese* Hara-kiri.

sep·sis (sep′sis) *n. Pathol.* **1** Poisonous putrefaction. **2** Infection of the blood by putrescent material containing pathogenic microorganisms. [<NL <Gk. *sēpsis* <*sēpein* make putrid]

sept (sept) *n.* A division of a tribe ruled by a hereditary chief, especially in ancient and medieval Ireland; any similar social unit or group descended from a common ancestor. [Prob. <OF *septe,* var. of *secte* SECT] — **sep′tal** *adj.*

sept-[1] Var. of SEPTI-[1].

sept-[2] Var. of SEPTI-[2].

sep·ta (sep′tə) Plural of SEPTUM.

sep·tan·gle (sep′tang′gəl) *n.* A heptagon. [<LL *septangulus* <*septem* seven + *angulus* an angle] — **sep·tan·gu·lar** (sep·tang′gyə·lər) *adj.*

sep·tar·i·um (sep·târ′ē·əm) *n. pl.* **·tar·i·a** (-târ′ē·ə) *Geol.* A rock nodule or concretion, usually several feet in diameter and roughly spherical, having a compact crust and an internal mass broken up by angular radiating or intersecting cracks usually filled with a foreign mineral: also called *turtlestone.* [<NL <L *septum* an enclosure, wall] — **sep·tar′i·an** *adj.*

sep·tate (sep′tāt) *adj.* Divided by or provided with a partition or partitions; having a septum or septa. [<NL *septatus* <LL, surrounded <L *septum* an enclosure, wall]

sep·tec·to·my (sep·tek′tə·mē) *n. Surg.* Excision of a part of the nasal septum. [<SEPT-[2] + -ECTOMY]

Sep·tem·ber (sep·tem′bər) The ninth month of the year, containing 30 days; the seventh month in the old Roman calendar. — **massacre of September** The massacre in Paris in September, 1792, when 10,000 persons were put to death in prison by order of Danton: also **September massacre** or **massacres.** [<L *septem* seven]

Sep·tem·brist (sep·tem′brist) *n.* A member of the Parisian mob that massacred political prisoners in the massacre of September 2 to 6, 1792; hence, a cruel and bloodthirsty person; a butcher; murderer.

sep·te·mi·a (sep·tē′mē·ə) *n.* Septicemia. Also **sep·tae′mi·a.** [<NL <Gk. *sēptos* putrid + *haima* blood]

sep·tem·vir (sep·tem′vər) *n. pl.* **·virs** or **·vi·ri** (-vi·rī) One of seven men in Roman history associated in some office, authority, or work. [<L <*septem* seven + *vir* a man]

sep·te·nar·y (sep′tə·ner′ē) *adj.* **1** Consisting of, pertaining to, or being seven. **2** Septennial. **3** Septuple. — *n. pl.* **·nar·ies 1** The number seven; heptad. **2** A group of seven things of any kind; anything that has some definite relation to the number seven. **3** A verse containing seven feet. Also **sep′te·nar′i·us** (sep′tə·nâr′ē·əs). [<L *septenarius* <*septeni* seven each <*septem* seven]

sep·te·nate (sep′tə·nāt) *adj.* Having seven parts, or the parts in sevens. [<L *septeni* seven each (<*septem* seven) + -ATE[1]]

sep·ten·nate (sep·ten′āt) *n.* A period of seven years; a term of office or the like lasting seven years. [<F *septennat* <L *septennis* (<*septem* seven + *annus* a year)]

sep·ten·ni·al (sep·ten′ē·əl) *adj.* **1** Recurring every seven years. **2** Continuing or capable of lasting seven years. [<L *septennium* a period of seven years <*septem* seven + *annus* a year] — **sep·ten′ni·al·ly** *adv.*

Sep·ten·tri·o (sep·ten′trē·ō) The constellation Ursa Major; the Dipper. See CONSTELLATION. Also **Sep·ten′tri·on.** [<L, sing. of *septentriones,* orig. *septem triones* the seven stars of the Big Dipper <*septem* seven + *triones,* pl. of *trio* a plow ox]

sep·ten·tri·on (sep·ten′trē·on) *adj.* Of, pertaining to, or coming from the north; boreal. — *n.* The north; northern regions. [<L *septentrionalis* <*septentrio* SEPTENTRIO] — **sep·ten′tri·o·nal** (-trē·ə·nəl) *adj.*

sep·tet (sep·tet′) *n.* **1** A group of seven singers, players, or other persons, things, or parts. **2** *Music* A composition for seven voices or instruments. Also **sep·tette′.** [<G <L *septem* seven]

septi-[1] *combining form* Seven: *septilateral.* Also, before vowels, *sept-.* [<L *septem* seven]

septi-[2] *combining form* **1** A partition; fence: *septicidal.* **2** *Med.* The nasal septum: *septectomy.* Also, before vowels, *sept-.* Also **septo-.** [<L *septum* an enclosure, wall]

sep·tic (sep′tik) *adj.* **1** Of, pertaining to, or caused by sepsis. **2** Productive of putrefaction; putrid. Also **sep′ti·cal.** — *n.* Any substance that produces or promotes putrefaction. [<LL *septicus* <Gk. *sēptikos* <*sēpein* putrefy]

sep·ti·ce·mi·a (sep′tə·sē′mē·ə) *n. Pathol.* A morbid condition of the blood due to infection by pathogenic micro-organisms; blood poisoning: also called *septemia.* Also **sep′ti·cae′mi·a.** [<NL <Gk. *sēptikos* putrefactive + *haima* blood] — **sep′ti·ce′mic** (-sē′mik) *adj.*

sep·ti·ci·dal (sep′tə·sīd′l) *adj. Bot.* Dividing at the partitions: said of the dehiscence of a plant capsule that resolves itself at maturity into its component carpels by splitting through the septa. Also **sep′ti·cide.** [<SEPTI-[2] + L *caedere* cut] — **sep′ti·ci′dal·ly** *adv.*

sep·tic·i·ty (sep·tis′ə·tē) *n.* The quality of being septic; sepsis.

septic tank A tank in which sewage is allowed to remain until purified by the action of anaerobic bacteria.

sep·tif·ra·gal (sep·tif′rə·gəl) *adj. Bot.* Breaking away from the partitions: said of a form of dehiscence in plants. [<SEPTI-[2] + L *frangere* break]

sep·ti·lat·er·al (sep′tə·lat′ər·əl) *adj.* Seven-sided. [<SETPI-[1] + LATERAL]

sep·til·lion (sep·til′yən) *n.* A cardinal number: in the French system and in the United States, 1 followed by 24 ciphers; in the English system, 1 followed by 42 ciphers. — *adj.* Numbering a septillion. [<F *septillion* <L *sept(em)* + F *(m)illion* a million] — **sep·til′lionth** *adj.* & *n.*

sep·time (sep′tēm) *n.* The seventh position of a swordsman in fencing. [<L *septimus* seventh <*septem* seven]

sep·tu·a·ge·nar·i·an (sep′cho͞o·ə·jə·nâr′ē·ən, sep′to͞o-) *n.* A person 70 years old, or between 70 and 80. [<L *septuagenarius* <*septuaginta* seventy]

sep·tu·ag·e·nar·y (sep′cho͞o·aj′ə·ner′ē, sep′to͞o-) *adj.* **1** Containing or consisting of 70. **2** Pertaining to a septuagenarian.

sep·tu·a·ges·i·ma (sep′cho͞o·ə·jes′ə·mə, sep′to͞o-) *n.* A period of 70 days. [<L *septuagesima (dies)* the seventieth (day), fem. of *septuagesimus* seventieth <*septuaginta* seventy] — **sep′tu·a·ges′i·mal** *adj.*

Sep·tu·a·ges·i·ma (sep′cho͞o·ə·jes′ə·mə, sep′to͞o-) *n.* The third Sunday before Lent. Also **Septuagesima Sunday.** [<L, seventieth, on analogy with *Quadragesima, Quinquagesima*]

Sep·tu·a·gint (sep′cho͞o·ə·jint′, sep′to͞o-) *n.* An old Greek version of the Old Testament Scriptures, made in Alexandria between 280 and 130 B.C. It is the version used by the Greek Church. [<L *septuaginta* seventy; from a tradition that it was produced for Ptolemy II in 70 days by a group of 72 scholars] — **Sep′tu·a·gin′tal** *adj.*

sep·tum (sep′təm) *n. pl.* **·ta** (-tə) *Biol.* **1** A dividing wall between two cavities: the nasal *septum.* **2** A partition, as in coral or in a spore. [<L <*sepere* enclose <*sepes* a hedge] — **sep′tal** *adj.*

sep·tu·ple (sep′to͞o·pəl, -tyo͞o-, sep·to͞o′-, -tyo͞o′-) *adj.* **1** Consisting of seven; sevenfold. **2** Multiplied by seven; seven times repeated. — *v.t.* & *v.i.* **·pled, ·pling** To multiply by seven; make or become septuple. — *n.* A number or sum seven times as great as another. [<L *septuplus* <*septem* seven]

sep·tu·pli·cate (sep·to͞o′plə·kit, -tyo͞o′-) *adj.* **1** Sevenfold. **2** Raised to the seventh power. — *v.t.* (-kāt) **·cat·ed, ·cat·ing** To multiply by seven; septuple. — *n.* (-kit) One of seven like things. [<L *septuplus,* on analogy with *duplicate, triplicate,* etc.] — **sep·tu′pli·cate·ly** *adv.* — **sep·tu′pli·ca′tion** *n.*

sep·ul·cher (sep′əl·kər) *n.* A burial place, especially one found or made in a rock or solidly built of stone; tomb; vault. **2** A receptacle for relics, especially in an altar slab; a box or urn in a chapel to receive the Holy Sacrament: also called the *repository.* — **the Holy Sepulcher** The rock-hewn tomb in which the body of Jesus was buried. — *v.t.* **·chered** or **·chred, ·cher·ing** or **·chring** To place in a grave; entomb; bury. Also **sep′ul·chre** (-kər). [<OF *sepulcre* <L *sepulcrum* a burial place, tomb <*sepultus,* pp. of *sepelire* bury]

se·pul·chral (si·pul′krəl) *adj.* **1** Pertaining to a sepulcher. **2** Suggestive of burial or the grave; dismal in color or aspect, or unnaturally low or hollow in tone; gloomy: a *sepulchral* color, a *sepulchral* voice. — **se·pul′chral·ly** *adv.*

sep·ul·ture (sep′əl·chər) *n.* **1** The act of entombing; burial. **2** A sepulcher. [<OF <L *sepultura* burial <*sepultus.* See SEPULCHER.]

se·qua·cious (si·kwā′shəs) *adj.* **1** Disposed to follow; following; attendant. **2** Logically consecutive. **3** Ductile; pliable. [<L *sequax, -acis* following, pursuing <*sequi* attend, follow] — **se·qua′cious·ly** *adv.* — **se·quac·i·ty** (si·kwas′ə·tē) *n.*

se·quel (sē′kwəl) *n.* **1** Something which follows and serves as a continuation; a development from what went before. **2** A narrative discourse which, though entire in itself, develops from a preceding one. **3** A consequence; upshot; result. [<OF *sequelle* <L *sequela* <*sequi* follow]

se·que·la (si·kwē′lə) *n. pl.* **·lae** (-lē) **1** One who or that which follows. **2** *Pathol.* A morbid condition resulting from a preceding disease. [<L, a sequel]

se·quence (sē′kwəns) *n.* **1** The process or fact of following in space, time, or thought; succession or order: also **se′quen·cy. 2** Order of succession; arrangement. **3** A number of things following one another, considered collectively; a series. **4** An effect or consequence. **5** *Music* A regular succession of similar melodic phrases at different pitches. **6** *Eccl.* In the Eucharistic liturgy, a prose or hymn sung immediately after the gradual and before the gospel. **7** In card games, a set of three or more cards next each other in value; in poker, a straight. **8** A section of motion-picture film presenting a single episode, without time lapses or interruptions. **9** *Math.* An ordered succession of quantities, as $2x$, $4x^2$, $8x^3$, $16x^4$ . . . 2^nx^n, a finite sequence, and x_1, x_2, x_3, . . . x_n, . . ., or x_n, an infinite sequence. See synonyms under TIME. [<MF *séquence* <L *sequentia* <*sequens, -entis,* ppr. of *sequi* follow]

sequence of tenses See under TENSE[2].

se·quent (sē′kwənt) *n.* That which follows; a consequence; result. — *adj.* **1** Following in the order of time; succeeding. **2** Consequent; resultant. [<OF <L *sequens.* See SEQUENCE.]

se·quen·tial (si·kwen′shəl) *adj.* **1** Characterized by or forming a sequence, as of parts. **2** Sequent. — **se·quen·ti·al·i·ty** (si·kwen′shē·al′ə·tē) *n.* — **se·quen′tial·ly** *adv.*

se·ques·ter (si·kwes′tər) *v.t.* **1** To place apart; separate; segregate. **2** To seclude; withdraw: often used reflexively. **3** *Law* To take (property) into custody until a controversy, claim, etc., is settled or satisfied. **4** In international law, to confiscate and control (enemy property) by preemption. [<OF *sequestrer* <LL *sequestrare* remove, lay aside <*sequester* a trustee] — **se·ques′tra·ble** *adj.*

se·ques·tered (si·kwes′tərd) *adj.* Retired; secluded.

se·ques·trant (si·kwes′trənt) *n.* **1** That which sets apart, divides, or sequesters. **2** *Chem.* A substance which forms a colorless mixture with certain metals precipitated in a solution.

se·ques·trate (si·kwes′trāt) *v.t.* **·trat·ed, ·trat·ing 1** To seize, especially for the use of the government; confiscate. **2** To take possession of for a time, with a view to the just settlement of the claims of creditors. **3** To seclude; sequester. [<LL *sequestratus,* pp. of *sequestrare.* See SEQUESTER.] — **se·ques·tra·tion** (sē′kwes·trā′shən, sek′wəs-) *n.* — **se·ques·tra·tor** (sē′kwes·trā′tər, si·kwes′trā·tər) *n.*

se·ques·trum (si·kwes′trəm) *n. pl.* **·tra** (-trə) *Pathol.* A piece of dead bone remaining in its place, but separated from the living bone. [<NL <L, something separated, orig. neut. of *sequester* standing apart]

se·quin (sē′kwin) *n.* **1** An obsolete gold coin of the Venetian republic later introduced into Turkey: also spelled *zecchino.* **2** A spangle or coinlike ornament sewn on clothing. [<F <Ital. *zecchino* <*zecca* the mint <Arabic *sikka* a coining-die]

se·quoi·a (si·kwoi′ə) *n.* One of a genus *(Sequoia)* of gigantic trees (family *Taxodiaceae*) of the western United States, including only two species, the redwood *(S. sempervirens)* and the mammoth or "big" tree *(S. gigantea* or *Sequoiadendron giganteum),* both natives of California. [<NL, after *Sikwayi,* 1770?-1843,

a half-breed Cherokee Indian who invented the Cherokee alphabet]

Sequoia National Park A government reservation in east central California including Mount Whitney and containing many giant sequoias and redwoods; 602 square miles; established, 1890.

ser (sir) See SEER[2].

ser- Var. of SERO-.

se·ra (sir′ə) Plural of SERUM.

sé·rac (sā·ràk′) *n. Geol.* One of the largest angular blocks or tower-shaped forms into which glacier ice breaks in passing down steep inclines. [< dial. F (Swiss), a cheese put up in cubic form; from its resemblance to the shape of this cheese]

ser·a·file (ser′ə·fīl) See SERREFILE.

se·ra·glio (si·ral′yō, -räl′-) *n.* **1** A harem. **2** Loosely, a place of debauchery. **3** The old palace of the sultans at Constantinople with its mosques, official buildings, and gardens. **4** Hence, any residence of a sultan. Also **se·rail** (se·rāl′). [<Ital. *serraglio* an enclosure, ult. <LL *serrare,* var. of L *serare* lock up < *sera* lock; used to render Turkish *serai* a palace, lodging, because of similarity of sound]

se·ra·i (se·rä′ē) *n.* **1** In the Orient, an inn or caravansary. **2** A Turkish palace. [<Turkish <Persian *sarāī*]

Se·ra·je·vo (se′rä·yā′vō) See SARAJEVO.

se·ra·pe (se·rä′pē) *n.* A shawl or blanketlike outer garment worn in Latin America, especially in Mexico: also spelled *zarape.* [<Sp.]

ser·aph (ser′əf) *n. pl.* **ser·aphs** or **ser·a·phim** (ser′ə·fim) A celestial being; an angel of the highest order. *Is.* vi 2–6. [Back formation from *Seraphim,* pl. <LL <Hebrew *s*ə*rāphīm,* ? ult. < *sāraph* burn] — **se·raph·ic** (si·raf′ik), **se·raph′i·cal** *adj.* — **se·raph′i·cal·ly** *adv.*

Seraphic Doctor Saint Bonaventura: so called because of the religious purity and fervor of his life.

ser·a·phim (ser′ə·fim) *n.* **1** Plural of SERAPH: also **ser′a·phin** (-fin). **2** *pl.* **·phims** A seraph, as in *Isaiah* vi 2, 6: an erroneous usage.

ser·a·phine (ser′ə·fēn) *n.* A coarse-toned musical instrument, a kind of harmonium, played with a keyboard. Also **ser·a·phi·na** (ser′ə·fē′·nə). [<SERAPH + -INE[1]]

Se·ra·pis (si·rā′pis) In Egyptian mythology, a god of the lower world in the form of the dead Apis. — **Se·ra′pic** *adj.*

ser·as·kier (ser′əs·kir′, si·ras′kir) *n.* A Turkish minister of war, or commander in chief. Also **se·ras·ker** (si·ras′kər), **ser·as·quier** (ser′əs·kir′). [<Turkish <Persian *ser asker* head of an army < *ser* head + Arabic *'asker* an army]

Ser·bi·a (sûr′bē·ə) A constituent republic of eastern Yugoslavia; 34,107 square miles; capital, Belgrade; formerly an independent kingdom: formerly *Servia. Serbo-Croatian* **Sr·bi·ja** (sûr′bē·yä). — **Serb, Ser′bi·an** *adj.* & *n.*

Ser·bo-Cro·a·tian (sûr′bō·krō·ā′shən) *n.* **1** The South Slavic language of Yugoslavia, including all the old languages and dialects of Serbia, Montenegro, Bosnia, Herzegovina, Croatia, Slavonia, and Dalmatia. **2** A native of Yugoslavia; any person whose native tongue is Serbo-Croatian. Also spelled *Servo-Croatian.* Also **Ser′bo-Cro′at.** — *adj.* Of or pertaining to the people of Yugoslavia, or to their language.

Ser·bo·ni·an Bog or **Lake** (sûr·bō′nē·ən) A large marshy tract once existing near the Red Sea littoral of Lower Egypt, in which Herodotus said whole armies were engulfed; hence, a strait; difficulty; complication: also spelled *Sirbonian.*

Serbs, Croats, and Slovenes, Kingdom of the See YUGOSLAVIA.

ser·dab (sûr′dab, sûr·däb′) *n.* A secret cell within the masonry of an ancient Egyptian tomb, in which images of the deceased were deposited. [<Arabic *serdāb* a cellar <Persian, an icehouse, a grotto]

sere[1] (sir) See SEAR[1].

sere[2] (sir) *n. Ecol.* The series of changes found in a given plant formation from the initial to the ultimate stage. ◆ Homophones: *cere, sear.* [Back formation <SERIES] — **ser′al** *adj.*

se·rein (sə·ran′) *n. Meteorol.* A fine rain that falls sometimes from an apparently clear sky, especially in the tropics after sunset. [<F]

ser·e·nade (ser′ə·nād′) *n.* **1** An evening song, usually that of a lover beneath his lady's window; also, by extension, music performed in honor of some person in front of his residence in the open air at night. **2** The music for such a song. — *v.t.* & *v.i.* **·nad·ed, ·nad·ing** To entertain with a serenade. [<F *sérénade* <Ital. *serenata* < *sereno* serene, open air <L *serenus* clear, serene; infl. in meaning by L *sera (hora)* the evening (hour), fem. of *serus* late] — **ser′·e·nad′er** *n.*

ser·e·na·ta (ser′ə·nä′tə) *n. Music* **1** A dramatic cantata, often composed as a complimentary offering for a royal personage. **2** A serenade. [<Ital. See SERENADE.]

ser·en·dip·i·ty (ser′ən·dip′ə·tē) *n.* The faculty of happening upon or making fortunate discoveries when not in search of them. [Coined by Horace Walpole (1754), in *The Three Princes of Serendip* (Ceylon), the heroes of which make such discoveries]

se·rene (si·rēn′) *adj.* **1** Clear, or fair and calm; having its brightness undimmed: a *serene* sky. **2** Marked by peaceful repose; tranquil; unruffled; placid: a *serene* spirit. **3** Of exalted rank: chiefly in the titles of certain continental European princes: His *Serene* Highness. See synonyms under SEDATE. — *n. Rare* or *Poetic* **1** Clearness, or a serene or clear region. **2** Calmness; placidity. [<L *serenus*] — **se·rene′ly** *adv.* — **se·ren·i·ty** (si·ren′ə·tē), **se·rene′ness** *n.*

Se·reth (zā′ret) See SIRET.

serf (sûrf) *n.* **1** A person who is attached to the estate on which he lives; loosely, a peasant. **2** Figuratively, one in servile subjection. ◆ Homophone: *surf.* [<OF <L *servus* a slave] — **serf′dom, serf′age, serf′hood** *n.*

serge (sûrj) *n.* **1** A strong twilled fabric made of wool yarns and characterized by a diagonal rib on both sides of the cloth. **2** In the Middle Ages, a coarse woolen cloth. **3** A rayon lining fabric. ◆ Homophone: *surge.* [<OF *sarge, serge* <L *serica (lana)* (wool) of the Seres <*Seres* the Seres, an eastern Asian people]

ser·geant (sär′jənt) *n.* **1** A non-commissioned military officer ranking next above a corporal. See the table under GRADE. **2** In the United States, a police officer of rank next below a captain (sometimes lieutenant); in England, one next below an inspector. **3** *Brit.* Formerly, one who held land of the king by tenure of military service, or a squire or gentleman of less than knightly rank; one of the household officials of a sovereign. **4** A sergeant at arms. **5** A sergeant at law. **6** A constable or bailiff. **7** The sergeant fish. Also *serjeant.* — **color sergeant** A sergeant who standard. — **lance sergeant** A corporal acting carries the regimental or national colors or as sergeant. — **mess sergeant** A non-commissioned officer who plans meals, issues rations, and superintends the company mess under the mess officer. [<OF *sergent, serjant* <L *serviens,* ppr. of *servire* serve] — **ser′gean·cy, ser′geant·cy, ser′geant·ship** *n.*

sergeant at arms **1** An executive officer in a legislative body who enforces order; especially, *Brit.,* the attendant on the lord chancellor or on the speaker of the House of Commons. **2** The title of certain court or city officials who have ceremonial duties.

sergeant at law Formerly, a barrister of high order or rank taking social but not professional precedence of king's counsel.

sergeant fish **1** A large, dusky fish *(Rachycentron canadus)* of warm seas, with a broad black band suggesting a chevron on the sides. **2** The robalo.

sergeant major **1** In the U.S. Army, the principal enlisted assistant to the adjutant of a battalion or higher unit. **2** The highest non-commissioned officer in the U.S. Marine Corps.

Sergeant Major of the Army The highest enlisted rank in the U.S. Army. See the table under GRADE.

ser·geant·y (sär′jən·tē) *n. Brit.* Formerly, a tenure of lands on condition of rendering some personal or menial service directly to the king or to some nobleman; also, the service rendered.

Ser·gi·pe (sər·zhē′pə) A state in eastern Brazil on the Atlantic, 8,502 square miles; capital, Aracajú.

se·ri·al (sir′ē·əl) *adj.* **1** Of the nature of a series. **2** Published in a series at regular intervals. **3** Successive; arranged in rows or ranks: also **se·ri·ate** (sir′ē·it, -āt). — *n.* **1** A novel or other story regularly presented in successive instalments, as in a magazine, on radio or television, or in motion pictures. **2** *Brit.* A periodical. **3** A subdivision of a military unit organized for transport or for marching. ◆ Homophone: *cereal.* [<NL *serialis* <L *series* a row, order] — **se′ri·al·ly, se′ri·ate·ly** *adv.*

serial comma A comma placed before an *and* which joins the last two in a series of three or more substantives, adjectives, phrasal modifiers, or adverbs. ◆ Opinion is evenly divided as to whether the serial comma is needed. The best argument for its use, which is observed in this dictionary, is that it makes the meaning unmistakable and the relation between the various modifiers unmistakably clear: The motion was opposed by Lords Arundel, Salisbury, Somerset, and Say and Sele. If the last comma (the serial comma) were omitted here, there could be confusion as to the name of the last peer, which is *Say and Sele.*

se·ri·al·ize (sir′ē·əl·īz′) *v.t.* **·ized, ·iz·ing** To arrange or publish in serial form. — **se′ri·al·i·za′tion** *n.*

serial number A number assigned to a person, object, item of merchandise, etc., as a means of identification.

serial symmetry **1** The symmetry of serial parts. **2** Metamerism. Also **serial homology.**

se·ri·a·tim (sir′ē·ā′tim, ser′ē-) *adv.* One after another; in connected order; serially. [< Med. L <L *series,* on analogy with *gradatim*]

se·ri·a·tion (sir′ē·ā′shən) *n.* The arrangement of unorganized material or data in an orderly series.

se·ri·ceous (si·rish′əs) *adj.* **1** Lustrous like silk; silky. **2** *Bot.* Having fine, soft, appressed hairs, as the leaves of certain plants. [<L *sericeus* < *sericum* silk, orig. neut. of *sericus* silken, belonging to the Seres. See SERGE.]

ser·i·cin (ser′ə·sin) *n. Biochem.* A viscous substance formed on the surface of raw silk fiber and usually removed by boiling in soapy water. [<L *sericus* silken + -IN]

ser·i·cul·ture (sir′ə·kul′chər) *n.* The raising and care of silkworms for the production of raw silk. [Contraction of F *sériciculture* <L *sericum* silk + *cultura* a raising, culture] — **ser′i·cul′tur·al** *adj.* — **ser′i·cul′tur·ist** *n.*

ser·i·e·ma (ser′i·ē′mə, -ā′mə) *n.* **1** A long-legged crested bird *(Cariama cristata)* of the plains of Brazil and Paraguay. **2** The smaller species, Burmeister's cariama *(Chunga burmeisteri)* of Argentina. [<NL *seriema, cariama* <Tupian *siriema, sariama* crested]

se·ries (sir′ēz) *n. pl.* **se·ries** **1** An arrangement of one thing after another; a connected succession of persons, books, objects, observations, etc., on the basis of like relationships. **2** *Math.* An ordered, finite or infinite arrangement of expressions, each a function of another, the sum of which is indicated, as $x_1 + x_2 + x_3 \ldots + x_n + \ldots$, or $\sum_{i=1}^{\infty} x_i$ for infinite series, and $x_1 + x_2 + x_3 \ldots + x_n$, or $\sum_{i=1}^{n} x_n$ for finite series. **3** *Chem.* A group of compounds or elements resembling one another more or less in their chemical characters and crystalline forms, or differing from each other by a constant difference of certain factors. **4** *Electr.* An arrangement of sources or utilizers of electricity, as batteries or lamps, in which the positive electrode of one is connected with the negative electrode of another. **5** *Gram.* A group of successive coordinate elements of a sentence. [<L <*serere* join, weave together]

series motor A motor whose field and armature windings are in series.

series winding *Electr.* The winding of a dynamo or an electric motor in such a way that the field-magnet coil is a part of the armature and exterior circuit. Compare SHUNT-WOUND. — **se·ries-wound** (sir′ēz·wound′) *adj.*

ser·if (ser′if) *n. Printing* A hairline; a light line or stroke crossing or projecting from the end of a main line or stroke in a letter: also spelled *ceriph.* [<Du. *schreef* a stroke, line < *schrijve* write <L *scribere*]

ser·i·graph (ser′ə·graf, -gräf) *n.* **1** An artist's color print made by serigraphy. **2** A device for testing the tensile strength and elasticity of textile fabrics, paper, leather, rubber, etc., under specified conditions. [<L *sericum* silk + GRAPH]

se·rig·ra·phy (si·rig′rə·fē) *n.* An adaptation of the silk-screen process in which hand-made color prints are made on any desired surface by the use of stencils painted upon or cemented to the screen, one stencil to each color, the finished print being in all details the work of an individual artist in distinction from those commercially reproduced by silk-screen printing. — **se·rig′ra·pher** *n.* — **ser·i·graph·ic** (ser′ə·graf′ik) *adj.*

ser·in (ser′in) *n.* A small greenish finch *(Serinus canarius)*, related to and closely resembling the wild canary, but smaller. [<F; ult. origin unknown]

ser·ine (ser′ēn, -in) *n. Biochem.* A white crystalline amino acid, $C_3H_7NO_3$, obtained as a dissociation product of various proteins. Also **ser′in.** [<L *sericus* silken + -INE[2]; so called because originally obtained from dissociation of sericin]

se·rin·ga (si·ring′gə) *n.* Any of several Brazilian trees (genus *Hevea*) yielding rubber. [<Pg. <L *syringa* SYRINGA]

Se·rin·ga·pa·tam (sə·ring′gə·pə·tam′) A town in southern Mysore, India; former seat of the sultans of Mysore, 7 miles NE of Mysore city.

se·ri·o-com·ic (sir′ē·ō·kom′ik) *adj.* Mingling mirth and seriousness, or the comic with an appearance of gravity. Also **se′ri·o-com′i·cal.** [<*serio-* partly serious (<SERIOUS) + COMIC]

se·ri·ous (sir′ē·əs) *adj.* **1** Grave and earnest in quality, feeling, or disposition; thoughtful; sober. **2** Said, planned, or done with full practical intent; not jesting or making a false pretense; being or done in earnest. **3** Of grave importance; weighty; attended with considerable danger or loss: a *serious* matter, a *serious* accident. **4** Particularly attentive to religion. [<MF *sérieux* <LL *seriosus* <L *serius*] — **se′ri·ous·ly** *adv.* — **se′ri·ous·ness** *n.*

Synonyms: dangerous, demure, earnest, grave, great, important, momentous, sedate, sober, solemn. A *serious* person is *sedate, sober, solemn*; a *serious* purpose is *earnest*; a *serious* illness is *dangerous*; a *serious* business is *important*, and may be *momentous*. See BAD, GOOD, IMPORTANT, SEDATE. *Antonyms*: careless, gay, insignificant, jocose, jolly, light, slight, thoughtless, trifling, trivial, volatile.

ser·jeant (sär′jənt) See SERGEANT.

ser·mon (sûr′mən) *n.* **1** A discourse based on a passage or text of the Bible, delivered as part of a church service; hence, any discourse intended for the pulpit. **2** Any discourse of a serious kind; an exhortation to duty or a formal reproof. See synonyms under SPEECH. [<AF *sermun*, OF *sermon* <L *sermo, -onis* talk]

ser·mon·et (sûr′mən·et′) *n.* A brief sermon. Also **ser′mon·ette′.** [Dim. of SERMON]

ser·mon·ic (sər·mon′ik) *adj.* Pertaining to or of the nature of a sermon or sermonizing; didactic. Also **ser·mon′i·cal.**

ser·mon·ize (sûr′mən·īz) *v.t.* & *v.i.* **·ized, ·iz·ing** To compose or deliver sermons (to); address or discourse at length in a didactic manner. — **ser′mon·iz′er** *n.*

Sermon on the Mount The discourse of Jesus found recorded in *Matt.* v, vi, vii: properly distinguished from the **Sermon on the Plain,** *Luke* vi 20–49.

sero– *combining form* Connected with or related to serum: *serology*. Also, before vowels, *ser–*. [<L *serum* whey]

se·rol·o·gy (si·rol′ə·jē) *n.* The science of serums and their actions: also called *orrhology*. [SERO- + -LOGY] — **se·ro·log·i·cal** (sir′ə·loj′i·kəl) *adj.*

se·roon (si·ro͞on′) *n.* A bale of goods, as Spanish dates, figs, etc., packed in an animal's hide: also spelled *ceroon*. [<Sp. *serón* a hamper, crate <*sera* a large basket]

se·ros·i·ty (si·ros′ə·tē) *n.* **1** The condition of being serous or watery. **2** A watery or serous secretion. Also **se′rous·ness.** [<F *sérosité* <NL *serositas* <*serosus* SEROUS]

se·ro·ther·a·py (sir′ō·ther′ə·pē) *n. Med.* The treatment of disease by injecting into the veins serum from immunized animals.

se·rot·i·nous (si·rot′ə·nəs) *adj.* Produced, blossoming, or developing relatively late in the season: used also figuratively. Also **se·rot′i·nal, ser·o·tine** (ser′ə·tin, -tīn). [<L *serotinus* <*serus* late]

ser·o·to·nin (ser′ə·tō′nin) *n. Biochem.* A crystalline protein found in the serum of clotted blood and in various animals and plants: it is associated with a wide range of physiological processes, especially in the brain and blood vessels. [<SERO- + TON- + -IN]

se·rous (sir′əs) *adj.* Pertaining to, producing, or resembling serum. [<F *séreux* <L *serosus* <*serum* serum, whey]

serous fluid Any of the thin watery fluids secreted by the serous membranes.

serous membrane *Anat.* A tissue of endothelial cells lining the large cavities of the body, as the peritoneum and the pleura.

ser·ow (ser′ō) *n.* Any of a genus *(Capricornis)* of antelopes ranging from the Himalayas to Japan; especially, the large goat antelope *(C. bubalinus)*. [<Tibetan]

Ser·pens (sûr′penz) *Astron.* An equatorial constellation, the Serpent, between Corona Borealis and Libra. See CONSTELLATION. [<L, a serpent]

ser·pent (sûr′pənt) *n.* **1** A scaly, limbless reptile; a snake, especially when of large size. **2** Anything of serpentine form or appearance, as a certain kind of twisting firework. **3** An obsolete musical wind instrument, bent several times in serpentine form. **4** An insinuating and treacherous person. **5** Satan. [<OF <L *serpens, -entis* a serpent, creeping thing, orig. ppr. of *serpere* creep]

serpent fence A worm fence. See under FENCE.

ser·pen·tine (sûr′pən·tēn, -tīn) *adj.* **1** Pertaining to or like a serpent; zigzag or sinuous; crawling sinuously. **2** Subtle; cunning. — *n.* A massive or fibrous, often mottled green or yellow, hydrous magnesium silicate, the fibrous varieties of which are important sources of asbestos, the massive as architecturally decorative stones. [<OF *serpentin* <L *serpentinus* <*serpens* SERPENT]

Ser·pen·to (sûr′pən·tō) *n. pl.* **·to** The Shoshone Indians: a tribe belonging to the Shoshoneans.

ser·pi·go (sər·pī′gō) *n. Pathol.* An eruption on the skin; spreading ringworm. [<Med. L <L *serpere* creep] — **ser·pig·i·nous** (sər·pij′ə·nəs) *adj.*

Ser·ra (ser′rä), **Junípero,** 1713–84, Spanish Franciscan missionary in California.

ser·ra·noid (ser′ə·noid) *adj.* Of or pertaining to the *Serranidae*, a family of fishes including the sea bass, striped bass, and their allies. — *n.* A serranoid fish. [<NL <*Serranus*, genus name (<L *serra* a saw) + Gk. *eidos* form]

ser·rate (ser′āt, -it) *adj.* Toothed or notched like a saw, as the margins of certain leaves. Also **ser′rat·ed.** [<L *serratus* <*serra* a saw]

ser·ra·tion (se·rā′shən) *n.* **1** The state of being edged as with saw teeth. **2** *Biol.* One of the projections of a serrate formation, or a series of such projections. Also **ser·ra·ture** (ser′ə·chər). [<NL *serratio, -onis* <L *serratus*, pp. of *serrare* saw <*serra* a saw]

ser·re·file (ser′ə·fīl) *n.* **1** One of the non-commisioned officers drawn up in line in the rear of a troop or squadron. **2** *pl.* The line of serrefiles. Also spelled *serafile*. [<F <*serrer* tighten (<LL *serrare* lock <L *sera* a lock) + *file* a file[1]]

ser·ried (ser′ēd) *adj.* Compacted in rows or ranks, as soldiers in company formation. [Pp. of obs. *serry* press close together in ranks <MF *serré*, pp. of *serrer*. See SERREFILE.]

ser·ri·form (ser′ə·fôrm) *adj.* Formed like a saw; saw-toothed. [<L *serra* a saw + -FORM]

ser·ru·late (ser′ə·lit, -lāt, ser′yə-) *adj.* Diminutively serrate; serrate with small, fine teeth. Also **ser′ru·lat′ed** (-lā′tid). [<L *serrula*, dim. of *serra* a saw + -ATE[1]]

ser·ru·la·tion (ser′ə·lā′shən, ser′yə-) *n.* **1** The state of being or becoming serrulate; a fine notching. **2** One of the teeth of a serrulate margin.

Ser·to·ri·us (sər·tôr′ē·əs, -tō′rē-), **Quintus,** 121?–72 B.C., Roman general; assassinated.

ser·tu·lar·i·an (sûr′cho͝o·lâr′ē·ən) *n. Zool.* One of a genus *(Sertularia)* of branching colonial hydroids common between tide lines. [<NL <L *sertula*, dim. of *serta* a garland]

se·rum (sir′əm) *n. pl.* **se·rums** or **se·ra** (sir′ə) **1** The more fluid constituent of blood, lymph, milk, and similar animal liquids. **2** The serum of the blood of an animal which has been subjected to the process of immunization; any antitoxic blood serum or lymph. **3** Whey; serum of milk. **4** Any similar secretion. [<L, whey, watery fluid]

serum sickness Illness caused by inoculation of serum.

serum therapy Serotherapy.

ser·val (sûr′vəl) *n.* An African wildcat *(Felis serval)*, yellow with black spots and having a ringed tail and long legs. [<F <Pg. *lobo cerval* <*lobo* a wolf (<L *lupus*) + *cerval* a stag <L *cervus*]

ser·vant (sûr′vənt) *n.* **1** A person employed to work for another; especially, in law, one employed to render service and assistance in some trade or vocation; an employee. **2** A person hired to assist in domestic matters, sometimes living within the employer's house; hired help. **3** A slave or bondman. **4** A government official. [<OF, orig. ppr. of *servir* SERVE]

serve (sûrv) *v.* **served, serv·ing** *v.t.* **1** To work for, especially as a servant; be in the service of. **2** To be of service to; wait on. **3** To promote the interests of; aid; help: to *serve* one's country. **4** To obey and give homage to: to *serve* God. **5** To satisfy the requirements of; suffice for. **6** To perform the duties connected with, as a public office. **7** To go through (a period of enlistment, term of punishment, etc.). **8** To furnish or provide, as with a regular supply. **9** To offer or bring food or drink to (a guest, etc.); wait on at table. **10** To bring and place on the table or distribute among guests, as food or drink. **11** To operate or handle; tend: to *serve* a cannon. **12** To copulate with: said of male animals. **13** In tennis, etc., to put (the ball) in play by hitting it to one's opponent. **14** *Law* **a** To deliver (a summons or writ) to a person. **b** To deliver a summons or writ to. **15** *Naut.* To wrap (a rope, stay, etc.), as with marlin or spun yarn, so as to strengthen or protect. — *v.i.* **16** To work as or perform the functions of a servant; wait at table. **17** To perform the duties of any employment, office, etc. **18** To go through a term of service, as in the army or navy. **19** To be suitable or usable, as for a purpose; perform a function. **20** To be favorable, as weather. **21** In tennis, etc., to put the ball in play. — *n.* **1** In tennis, etc., the delivering of the ball by striking it toward an opponent. **2** The turn of the server. [<OF *servir* <L *servire* <*servus* a slave]

Synonyms: advance, aid, assist, attend, benefit, help, minister, obey, promote, subserve, succor, suffice. See ACCOMMODATE. *Antonyms*: command, control, desert, disobey, hinder, obstruct, oppose, retard, thwart, withstand.

serv·er (sûr′vər) *n.* **1** One who serves; especially, an attendant aiding a priest at low mass. **2** That which is used in serving, as a tray. **3** The male of any domestic animal used for breeding. **4** The player who serves the ball in games.

Ser·ve·tus (sər·vē′təs), **Michael,** 1511–53, Spanish physician and theologian, burned at the stake in Geneva for heresy. Also *Sp.* **Miguel Ser·ve·to** (ser·vā′tō). — **Ser·ve′tian** (-shən) *adj.* & *n.*

Ser·vi·a (sûr′vē·ə) A former name for SERBIA.

ser·vice (sûr′vis) *n.* **1** Assistance or benefit afforded another: to render a *service*; to be of *service*. **2** A useful result or product of labor which is not a tangible commodity: in the plural, often contrasted with *goods*. **3** The manner in which one is waited upon or served: The *service* in this restaurant is only fair. **4** A system of labor and material aids used to accomplish some regular work or accommodation for the public: telephone *service*, train *service*, postal *service*. **5** A division of public employment devoted to a particular function: the diplomatic *service*. **6** Employment as a public servant in government: to enter public *service*. **7** A public duty or function: jury *service*. **8** Any branch of the armed forces: to enter the *service*. **9** Military duty or assignment: to volunteer for foreign *service*.

10 Devotion to God, as demonstrated by obedience and good works. **11** A formal and public exercise of worship: to attend Sunday *services.* **12** A ritual prescribed for a particular ministration or observance: a burial *service;* a marriage *service.* **13** The music for a liturgical office or rite. **14** The state or position of a servant, especially a domestic servant. **15** A set of tableware for a specific purpose: a tea *service.* **16** Installation, maintenance, and repair of an article provided a buyer by a seller. **17** *Law* **a** The legal communication of a writ or process to a designated person. **b** Duty or work rendered by one person for another. **c** A duty rendered by a feudal tenant as recompense to his lord. **18** In tennis and similar games, the act or manner of serving a ball. **19** *Naut.* The protective cordage wrapped around a rope. **20** In animal husbandry, the copulation or covering of a female. — *adj.* **1** Pertaining to or for service. **2** Used by, or for the use of, servants or tradespeople: a *service* entrance. **3** Of, pertaining to, or belonging to a military service: a *service* flag. **4** Worn during active military service: distinguished from *dress*: a *service* cap, hat, or uniform. — *v.t.* **·viced, ·vic·ing 1** To maintain or repair: to *service* a car or radio. **2** To supply service to. [<OF *servise* <L *servitium* < *servus* a slave]

Synonyms (noun): advantage, avail, benefit, good, purpose, serviceableness, use, utility. See PROFIT, SACRAMENT, UTILITY.

Ser·vice (sûr′vis), **Robert William,** 1874–1958, Canadian writer.

ser·vice·a·ble (sûr′vis·ə·bəl) *adj.* **1** That can be made of service; beneficial; such as serves or can serve a useful purpose. **2** Capable of rendering long service; durable. **3** *Obs.* Obliging; attentive. See synonyms under GOOD, USEFUL. — **ser′vice·a·ble·ness, ser′vice·a·bil′i·ty** *n.* — **ser′vice·a·bly** *adv.*

ser·vice·ber·ry (sûr′vis·ber′ē) *n. pl.* **·ries** The Juneberry; the shadberry. [< *service,* the service tree + BERRY]

service book A book containing the offices, or forms of service, of any church that uses liturgical forms.

service cap A military uniform cap of cotton, wool, or felt, with visor.

service club An organization to promote community welfare and further the interests of its members.

service coat A single-breasted jacket worn with the U.S. Army service uniform: also called a *blouse.*

service hat A hat worn in the U. S. Army when full-dress uniform is not worn: its shape and material vary according to requirements of climate. Formerly, a khaki-colored felt hat with broad flat brim, and crown dented in four places.

ser·vice·man (sûr′vis·man′) *n. pl.* **·men** (-men′) A member of one of the armed forces. — **ser′vice·wom′an** *n. fem.*

service man A man who performs services of maintenance, supply, repair, etc.

service ribbon A distinctively colored ribbon worn on the U. S. service uniform to indicate the wearer's right to the corresponding campaign medal or decoration.

service station 1 A place for supplying automobiles with gasoline, oil, water, etc. **2** A place where adjustments and repairs can be made and parts obtained for electrical or mechanical devices.

service stripe A stripe worn on the sleeve of a uniform to denote years of service or employment, as in an army or on a police force: also *hash mark.*

service tree 1 An Old World tree *(Sorbus domestica)* with odd-pinnate leaves, panicled cream-colored flowers, and small edible fruit. **2** The American mountain ash *(S. americana).* **3** The Juneberry. [Orig. *serves,* pl. of obs. *serve,* OE *syrfe* <L *sorbus*]

service uniform The regulation uniform to be worn during routine or active service in the army or navy.

ser·vi·ette (sûr′vē·et′, -vyet′) *n.* A table napkin. [<MF, prob. < *servir* SERVE]

ser·vile (sûr′vil) *adj.* **1** Having the spirit of a slave; slavish; abject: a *servile* flatterer. **2** Pertaining to or appropriate for slaves or servants: a *servile* insurrection, *servile* employment. **3** Being of a subject class; existing in a condition of servitude. **4** Obedient; subject: with *to*: *servile* to applause. **5** *Ling.* Not belonging to the original root; serving only to modify the construction or pronunciation of a word. **6** Designating tenures of land in England subject to conditions distinguished from those of freehold, as labor instead of rent. See synonyms under BASE, OBSEQUIOUS. — *n.* **1** A slave, or one of slavish spirit; menial. **2** *Ling.* A letter, syllable, or sound used only to modify a word, and not part of its radical form. [<L *servilis* < *servus* a slave] — **ser′vile·ly** *adv.* — **ser·vil′i·ty, ser′vile·ness** *n.*

serv·ing (sûr′ving) *n.* **1** A portion of food for one person. **2** The act of one who or that which serves. — *adj.* Used for dealing out food.

ser·vi·tor (sûr′və·tər) *n.* **1** One who waits upon and serves another; an attendant; follower; servant. **2** Formerly, an undergraduate at Oxford University partly supported by a college grant and partly earning his living by service. [<OF <LL <L *servire* SERVE] — **ser′vi·tor·ship′** *n.*

ser·vi·tude (sûr′və·to͞od, -tyo͞od) *n.* **1** The condition of a slave; slavery; bondage; now, especially, enforced service as a punishment for crime: penal *servitude.* **2** A state of subjection to any claim, demand, or control: *servitude* to vice. **3** The condition or duties of a servant; menial service. **4** The subjection of a person to a person or to a thing, or of a thing to a person or thing. **5** *Law* An easement; a right that one man may have to use the land of another for a special purpose. See synonyms under BONDAGE. [<MF <L *servitudo* < *servus* a slave]

servo– *combining form* In technical use, auxiliary: *servomechanism.* [<L *servus* a slave]

Ser·vo-Cro·a·tian (sûr′vō·krō·ā′shən) See SERBO-CROATIAN.

ser·vo·mech·a·nism (sûr′vō·mek′ə·niz′əm) *n.* Any of various relay devices which can be actuated by a comparatively weak force in the automatic control of a complex machine, instrument, operation, or process, as artillery fire, the course of an airplane or ship, etc. [<SERVO- + MECHANISM]

ser·vo·mo·tor (sûr′vō·mō′tər) *n.* An electric motor connected with and supplying power for a servomechanism.

ses·a·me (ses′ə·mē) *n.* An East Indian herb *(Sesamum indicum),* containing seeds which are used as food and as a source of the pale yellow **sesame oil,** used as an emollient. — **open sesame** A charm to secure admission, originally to the robbers' cave in the story of Ali Baba and the Forty Thieves in the *Arabian Nights.* [<F *sésame* <L *sesamum, sesama* <Gk. *sēsamon, sēsamē,* prob. < an Oriental source]

ses·a·moid (ses′ə·moid) *adj. Anat.* **1** Having the shape of a sesame seed; obovate; nodular: said specifically of certain bones, cartilages, and nodules. **2** Pertaining to a sesamoid. — *n.* A sesamoid bone or cartilage, as the kneecap. [<L *sesamoides* <Gk. *sēsamoeidēs* < *sēsamon* sesame + *eidos* form]

sesqui– *prefix* **1** One and a half; one-half more; one and a half times: *sesquicentennial.* **2** *Chem.* Indicating the presence of three atoms of one element and two of another in a compound, as chromium *sesquioxide,* Cr_2O_3. [<L *sesqui-* one-half more < *semis* half + *que* and]

ses·qui·cen·ten·ni·al (ses′kwi·sen·ten′ē·əl) *adj.* Of or pertaining to a century and a half. — *n.* A 150th anniversary, or its celebration.

ses·qui·pe·da·li·an (ses′kwi·pi·dā′lē·ən) *adj.* **1** Measuring a foot and a half. **2** Long and ponderous, as polysyllabic words. Also **ses·quip·e·dal** (ses·kwip′ə·dəl, ses′kwi·pēd′l). — *n.* A very long word. [<L *sesquipedalis* < *sesqui-* more by a half + *pes, pedis* a foot]

ses·qui·plane (ses′kwi·plān′) *n. Aeron.* A type of biplane one wing of which has half or less than half the area of the other.

ses·sile (ses′il) *adj.* **1** *Bot.* Attached by its base, without a stalk, as a leaf. **2** *Zool.* Fixed; sedentary; firmly or permanently attached. [<L *sessilis* sitting down, stunted < *sessus,* pp. of *sedere* sit] — **ses·sil′i·ty** *n.*

ses·sion (sesh′ən) *n.* **1** The sitting together of a legislative assembly, court, etc., for the transaction of business. **2** A single meeting or series of meetings of an assembly, court, or other body, for conducting business. **3** The governing body of a Presbyterian Church congregation. **4** In some educational institutions, a term. **5** *Law* The term for which a court or legislative body sits continuously for the transaction of business. **6** *pl.* The sitting of a certain court: the quarter-*sessions*; and in the United States, the Court of *Sessions,* a court of criminal jurisdiction; any one of certain courts, especially in England: general *sessions,* petty *sessions.* **7** *Obs.* The act of sitting, or the state of one who is seated. ◆ Homophone: *cession.* [<F <L *sessio, -onis* < *sessus,* pp. of *sedere* sit] — **ses′sion·al** *adj.* — **ses′sion·al·ly** *adv.*

sess·pool (ses′po͞ol′) See CESSPOOL.

ses·terce (ses′tûrs) *n. pl.* **·ter·ces** (-tûr′sēz) A coin of ancient Rome equal to 1/4 denarius: originally of silver, later of bronze. Also **ses·ter′ti·us** (-shē·əs). [<L *sestertius (nummus)* (a coin) that is two and a half < *semis* half + *tertius* third; so called because worth two and a half asses]

ses·ter·ti·um (ses·tûr′shē·əm) *n. pl.* **·ti·a** (-shē·ə) An ancient Roman money of account equivalent to 1,000 sesterces. [<L, short for *(mille) sestertium* (a thousand) sesterces, gen. pl. of *sestertius* a sesterce]

ses·tet (ses·tet′) *n.* **1** The last six lines of a sonnet; any six-line stanza. **2** *Music* A sextet. [<Ital. *sestetto* < *sesto* sixth (<L *sextus*) + *-etto,* dim. suffix]

ses·ti·na (ses·tē′nə) *n.* A verse form consisting of six stanzas of six, generally unrimed, lines each and a three-line envoy: the end words of the first stanza are progressively changed in order in the remaining five, and appear medially and terminally in the envoy. Also **ses′tine** (-tin). [<Ital. < *sesto* sixth <L *sextus*]

Ses·tos (ses′tos) A ruined town on the Dardanelles in Turkey in Europe. See ABYDOS.

set[1] (set) *v.* **set, set·ting** *v.t.* **1** To put in a certain place or position; place. **2** To put into a fixed or immovable position, condition, or state: to *set* brick; to *set* one's jaw. **3** To bring to a specified condition or state: *Set* your mind at ease; to *set* a boat adrift. **4** To restore to proper position for healing, as a broken bone. **5** To place in readiness for operation or use: to *set* a trap. **6** To adjust according to a standard: to *set* a clock. **7** To adjust (an instrument, dial, etc.) to a particular calibration or position. **8** To place knives, forks, etc., on (a table) in preparing for a meal. **9** To bend the teeth of (a saw) to either side alternately. **10** To appoint or establish; prescribe: to *set* a time or limit. **11** To fix or establish a time for: We *set* our departure for noon. **12** To assign for performance, completion, etc.; allot: to *set* a task. **13** To assign to some specific duty or function; appoint; station: to *set* a guard. **14** To cause to sit. **15** To present or perform so as to be copied or emulated: to *set* the pace; to *set* a bad example. **16** To give a specified direction to; direct: He *set* his course for the Azores. **17** To put in place so as to catch the wind: to *set* the jib. **18** To place in a mounting or frame, as a gem. **19** To stud or adorn with gems: to *set* a crown with rubies. **20** To place (a hen) on eggs to hatch them. **21** To place (eggs) under a fowl or in an incubator for hatching. **22** To place (a price or value): with *by* or *on*: to *set* a price on an outlaw's head. **23** To point (game): said of hunting dogs. **24** *Printing* **a** To arrange (type) for printing; compose. **b** To put into type, as a sentence, manuscript, etc. **25** *Music* To arrange (music) for words or write (words) to accompany music. **26** To describe (a scene) as taking place: to *set* the scene in Monaco. **27** In the theater, to arrange (a stage) so as to depict a scene. **28** In some games, as bridge, to defeat. — *v.i.* **29** To go or pass below the horizon, as the sun. **30** To wane; decline. **31** To sit on eggs, as fowl. **32** To become hard or firm; solidify; congeal. **33** To begin a journey; start: with *forth, out, off,* etc. **34** To have a specified direction; tend. **35** To hang or fit, as clothes. **36** To point game: said of hunting dogs. **37** *Bot.* To begin development or growth, as a rudimentary fruit. — **to set about** To start doing; begin. — **to set against 1** To balance; compare. **2** To make unfriendly to; prejudice against. — **to set aside 1** To place apart or to one side. **2** To reject; dismiss. **3** To declare null and void. — **to set back** To reverse; hinder. — **to set down 1** To place on a surface. 2 To write or print; record. 3 To judge or consider. 4 To attribute; ascribe. **— to set forth** 1 To state or express. 2 To start, as a journey. **— to set in** 1 To begin. 2 To blow or flow toward shore, as wind or tide. **— to set off** 1 To put apart by itself. 2 To serve as a contrast or foil for; enhance. 3 To cause to explode. **— to set on** To incite or instigate; urge. **— to set out** 1 To present to view; display; exhibit. 2 To lay out or plan. 3 To begin a journey. 4 To begin any enterprise. 5 To plant. **— to set to** 1 To start; begin. 2 To start fighting. **— to set up** 1 To place in an upright position. 2 To raise. 3 To place in power, authority, etc. 4 **a** To construct or build. **b** To put together; assemble. **c** To found; establish. 5 To provide with the means to start a new business. 6 To cause to be heard: to *set up* a cry. 7 To propose or put forward (a theory, etc.). 8 To cause. 9 *Colloq.* **a** To pay for the drinks, etc., of; treat. **b** To pay for (drinks, etc.). 10 *Colloq.* To encourage; exhilarate. — *adj.* 1 Established by authority or agreement; prescribed; appointed: a *set* time; a *set* method. 2 Customary; conventional: a *set* phrase. 3 Deliberately and systematically conceived; formal: a *set* speech. 4 Fixed and motionless; rigid. 5 Fixed in opinion or disposition; obstinate. 6 Formed; built; made: with a qualifying adverb: deep–*set* eyes; a low–*set* man. 7 Ready; prepared: to get *set.* — *n.* 1 The act or condition of setting. 2 Permanent change of form, as by chemical action, cooling, pressure, strain, etc. 3 The arrangement, tilt, or hang of a garment, hat, sail, etc. 4 Carriage or bearing: the *set* of his shoulders. 5 The sinking of a heavenly body below the horizon. 6 The direction of a current or wind. 7 A young plant ready for setting out; a cutting, slip, or seedling. 8 *Mech.* The spread in opposite directions given to the alternate teeth of certain saws. 9 *Psychol.* A temporary condition assumed by an organism preparing for a particular response or activity. 10 In tennis, a group of games completed when one side wins six games, or in the event of a score tied at five games, the group of games terminated when one side wins two more games consecutively. [OE *settan* cause to sit. Akin to SIT.]

Synonyms (verb): adapt, adjust, appoint, arrange, assign, determine, dispose, establish, fix, locate, place, plant, post, prescribe, put, regulate, settle, station. See ALLOT, PLANT, PREPARE, PUT, RAISE. *Antonyms*: detach, disestablish, disturb, eradicate, loosen, overthrow, remove, transfer, unsettle, uproot.

set[2] (set) *n.* 1 A number of persons regarded as associated through status, common interests, etc.: a new *set* of customers. 2 A social group having some exclusive character; coterie; clique: the fast *set.* 3 A number of things belonging together and customarily used together: a *set* of instruments; a *set* of teeth; a *set* of dishes. 4 A number of specific things so grouped as to form a whole: a *set* of lyrics; a *set* of motives; a *set* of features. 5 A group of volumes issued together and related by common authorship or subject. 6 The number of couples needed for a square dance or country dance. 7 The group of movements that compose a square dance. 8 In motion pictures, the complete assembly of properties, structures, etc., required in a scene. 9 Radio or television receiving equipment assembled for use. See synonyms under CLASS, FLOCK. [<OF *sette* <L *secta* a sect; infl. by SET[1]. Doublet of SECT.]

Set (set) In Egyptian mythology, the animal–headed god of darkness, night, and evil; opponent and slayer of Osiris. Also *Seth.*

SET

se·ta (sē′tə) *n. pl.* **·tae** (-tē) *Biol.* 1 A bristle, or slender, bristlelike part or process of an organism. 2 A slender spine or prickle. 3 A coarse, rigid hair. [<L]

set-a·side (set′ə·sīd′) *n.* An amount or quantity of something put in reserve for future use.

se·ta·ceous (si·tā′shəs) *adj.* 1 Bristly; more or less covered with bristles. 2 Of the nature or form of setae. Also **se′tal** (sēt′l). [<NL *setaceus* <L *seta* a bristle]

set·back (set′bak′) *n.* 1 A check; forced return to a point already passed; a reverse in fortune or plan. 2 A countercurrent; eddy. 3 *Archit.* In mammoth buildings, the stepping of sections in such a way that, while the first section is erected on the street line, the remaining sections are erected in step formation, so as to permit of better light and ventilation in the street below.

Sète (set) A port on the Mediterranean in southern France SW of Montpellier: formerly *Cette.*

Set·e·bos (set′ə·bos) A supposed deity of the Patagonians: alluded to in Shakespeare's *The Tempest* as the power worshiped by Sycorax, the witch, mother of Caliban.

Seth (seth) A masculine personal name. [< Hebrew, appointed]

— Seth The third son of Adam. *Gen.* v 3.

— Seth The Egyptian god Set.

set–ham·mer (set′ham′ər) *n.* A hammer the head of which may be easily removed from the handle. See illustration under HAMMER.

seti– *combining form* A bristle: *setiferous.* Also, before vowels, **set–.** [<L *seta* a bristle]

se·tif·er·ous (si·tif′ər·əs) *adj.* Bearing setae; bristly. Also **se·tig·er·ous** (si·tij′ər·əs). [< SETI- + -FEROUS]

se·ti·form (sē′tə·fôrm) *adj.* Having the form of a seta; setaceous.

set–off (set′ôf′, -of′) *n.* 1 An offset or counterpoise. 2 A decorative contrast or setting. 3 A counterclaim or the discharge of a debt by a counterclaim. 4 *Archit.* A ledge; offset.

se·ton (sē′tən) *n. Surg.* A bristle, or a few threads, passed through a fold of the skin and left there to produce an issue for relief of subjacent parts. [<Med. L *seto, -onis,* appar. <*seta* silk <L, a bristle]

Se·ton (sē′tən), **Ernest Thompson,** 1860–1946, U.S. naturalist and writer born in England.

se·tose (sē′tōs) *adj.* Setaceous; bristly. Also **se′tous.** [<L *setosus* <*seta* a bristle]

set·screw (set′skrōō′) *n.* A screw used as a clamp; especially, one having a cup instead of a point: used to screw through one part and slightly into another to bind the parts tightly.

set·tee[1] (se·tē′) *n.* 1 A long wooden seat with a high back. 2 A sofa suitable for two or three people. [<SET[1] + *-ee,* dim. suffix; infl. in meaning by SEAT]

set·tee[2] (se·tē′) *n.* A Mediterranean vessel with long prow, single deck, two or three masts, and lateen sails. [<Ital. *saettia,* prob. <*saetta* an arrow]

set·ter (set′ər) *n.* 1 One who or that which sets. 2 One of a breed of medium–sized, silky–coated, lithe bird dogs of great intelligence, originally trained to indicate the presence of game birds by crouching, now by standing rigid. — **English setter** A setter, white, or white marked with black, tan, yellow, or orange, trained since the 16th century to find and point game. The most famous British strains, the Laveracks and the Llewellins, are popular in field trials and bench shows. **— Gordon setter** A setter having a black coat marked with tan, chestnut, or red, probably crossbred with black–and–tan spaniels: named for the original breeder, the Duke of Gordon, and used especially for cover shooting. — **Irish** (or **red**) **setter** A handsome, useful, and companionable golden–chestnut or red setter, probably a setter–spaniel–pointer combination: extensively bred in America and very popular.

ENGLISH SETTER
(About 25 inches high at the shoulder)

set·ting (set′ing) *n.* 1 The act of anything that sets. 2 An insertion. 3 That in which something is set; a frame; environment. 4 The act of indicating game like a setter. 5 A number of eggs placed together for hatching. 6 The music adapted to a song or poem. 7 The scene or background of a play or narrative. 8 The apparent sinking of the sun, etc., below the horizon. 9 The tableware set out for one person.

set·ting–out (set′ing·out′) *n. Colloq.* The trousseau and household equipment given to a bride or newly married couple by the parents.

set·tle (set′l) *v.* **·tled, ·tling** *v.t.* 1 To put in order; set to rights; to *settle* affairs. 2 To put firmly in place; establish or fix permanently or as if permanently: He *settled* himself on the couch. 3 To free of agitation or disturbance; calm; quiet: to *settle* one's nerves. 4 To cause (sediment or dregs) to sink to the bottom. 5 To cause to subside or come to rest; make firm or compact: to *settle* dust or ashes. 6 To make clear or transparent, as by causing sediment or dregs to sink. 7 *Colloq.* To make quiet or orderly: One blow *settled* him. 8 To decide or determine finally, as an argument or difference. 9 To pay, as a debt; satisfy, as a claim. 10 To establish residents or residence in (a country, town, etc.). 11 To establish as residents. 12 To establish in a permanent occupation, home, etc. 13 To decide (a suit at law) by agreement between the litigants. 14 *Law* To make over or assign (property) by legal act: with *on* or *upon.* — *v.i.* 15 To come to rest, as after moving about or flying. 16 To sink gradually; subside. 17 To sink or come to rest, as dust or sediment. 18 To become more firm or compact. 19 To become clear or transparent, as by the sinking of sediment. 20 To take up residence; establish one's abode or home. 21 To come to a decision; determine; resolve: with *on, upon,* or *with.* 22 To pay a bill, etc. **— to settle down** 1 To start living a regular, orderly life, especially after a period of wandering or irresponsibility. 2 To apply steady effort or attention. — *n.* 1 A long seat or bench, generally of wood, with a high back, originally to direct the draft up the chimney and to provide a warm nook: often with arms and sometimes having a chest from seat to floor. 2 A wide step; platform. 3 *Obs.* A ledge. [OE *setlan* <*setl* a seat]

Synonyms (verb): adjust, allay, arrange, calm, compose, decide, determine, establish, finish, fix, pay, quiet, regulate. Compare CONFIRM, PAY[1], RATIFY, REQUITE, SET. *Antonyms*: agitate, confuse, derange, disarrange, discompose, disorder, disturb, fluster, flutter, mix, muss.

set·tle·ment (set′l·mənt) *n.* 1 The act of settling, or state of being settled; specifically, an adjustment of affairs by public authority. 2 Colonization. 3 Subsidence of a structure, or its effect. 4 An area of country newly occupied by those who intend to live and labor there; a colonized region, village, or town. 5 *Brit.* A regular or settled place of living; one's dwelling place. 6 An accounting; adjustment; liquidation in regard to amounts. 7 The conveyance of property in such form as to provide for some future object, especially the support of members of the settler's family; also, the property so settled. 8 A religious community. 9 *pl.* A collection or series of frontier dwellings and clearings: distinguished from wild, unsettled territory. 10 Formerly, Negro quarters on a southern plantation. 11 A welfare institution established in a congested part of a city, having a resident staff of workers to conduct educational and recreational activities for the community: also **settlement house.**

set·tler (set′lər) *n.* 1 One who settles; especially, one who establishes himself in a colony or new country; a colonist. 2 One who or that which settles or decides something.

set·tling (set′ling) *n.* 1 The act of settling or sinking. 2 *pl.* Dregs; sediment.

set–to (set′tōō′) *n.* A bout at fighting, fencing, arguing, or any other mode of contest. [< *set to*; see under SET]

Se·tú·bal (sə·tōō′bəl) A port of south central Portugal, on **Setúbal Bay,** an inlet of the Atlantic off the west coast of Portugal. Formerly **St. Yves** (sãnt ēvz).

set·u·lose (sech′ōō·lōs) *adj.* Clothed or covered with setae or bristles. [<NL, dim. of L *seta* a bristle]

set–up (set′up′) *n.* 1 Physique; physical build; make-up. 2 Carriage of the body; bearing.

3 *U.S. Slang* A system or scheme of organization or construction; the salient elements of a situation; circumstances. 4 *U.S. Slang* A contest or match arranged to result in an easy victory; a contest in which the strength of the contestants is so unequal that the result is easily foreseen; also, the weaker of two such contestants. 5 *U.S. Colloq.* Ice, soda water, etc., provided to a customer who has brought his own liquor.

Seu·rat (sœ·rä′), **Georges,** 1859–91, French painter.

Se·van (se·vän′), **Lake** The largest lake in Transcaucasia, in central Armenian U.S.S.R.; 546 square miles. *Turkish* **Gök·cha** (gœk′chä).

Se·vas·ti·an (se·väs′tē·än′) Russian form of SEBASTIAN.

Se·vas·to·pol (si·vas′tə·pōl, sev′əs·tō′pəl, *Russian* si′väs·tô′pəl) A port and naval base in the SW Crimea, Russian S.F.S.R.: formerly *Sebastopol.*

sev·en (sev′ən) *adj.* Being one more than six. — *n.* 1 The sum of one and six. 2 The symbols (7, vii, VII) representing that number. 3 A playing card with seven spots. 4 Something composed of seven units. [OE *seofon*]

Seven against Thebes In Greek legend, the seven heroes (Adrastus, Amphiaraus, Capaneus, Hippomedon, Parthenopaeus, Polynices, and Tydeus) who unsuccessfully marched on Thebes to restore Polynices to the throne which had been usurped by his brother Eteocles: all were killed save Adrastus. See ANTIGONE, EPIGONI.

Seven Cities of Ci·bo·la (sē′bō·lä) Seven Zuñi towns sought by the early Spanish explorers as centers of hidden gold and fabulous wealth: found in what is now New Mexico by Coronado about 1540.

Seven Deadly Sins Pride, Lust, Envy, Anger, Covetousness, Gluttony, and Sloth as personified in medieval literature: also known as *cardinal sins.*

sev·en·fold (sev′ən·fōld′) *adj.* 1 Seven times as many or as great. 2 Made up of seven; septuple. 3 Folded seven times. — *adv.* In sevenfold manner or degree.

Seven Hills of Rome The group of seven hills on and around which the city of Rome was built: the Palatine, Caelian, Esquiline, Capitoline, Quirinal, Viminal, and Aventine.

seven lively arts All forms of popular entertainment; originally, motion pictures, vaudeville, popular music, popular dancing, writing in the vernacular, musical shows, comic strips. [from *The Seven Lively Arts* (1924) by Gilbert Seldes]

Seven Pines See FAIR OAKS.

Seven Seas See under SEA.

sev·en·teen (sev′ən·tēn′) *adj.* Being seven more than ten. — *n.* The sum of ten and seven, or the symbols (17, xvii, XVII) representing this number. [OE *seofontȳne*]

sev·en·teenth (sev′ən·tēnth′) *adj.* 1 Seventh in order after the tenth. 2 Being one of seventeen equal parts. — *n.* 1 One of seventeen equal parts of anything. 2 A seventeenth object or unit. [OE *seofontēotha* < *seofontȳne* seventeen]

sev·en·teen–year locust (sev′ən·tēn′yir′) A dark-bodied, wedge-shaped cicada (*Magicicada septemdecim*) native to the eastern United States: the northern variety has an underground nymphal stage of 17 years, and the southern variety of 13 years.

sev·enth (sev′ənth) *adj.* 1 Next in order after the sixth. 2 Being one of seven equal parts. — *n.* 1 One of seven equal parts; the quotient of a unit divided by seven. 2 A seventh object or unit. 3 *Music* **a** The interval between any note and the seventh note above it on the diatonic scale, counting the starting point as one. **b** A note separated by this interval from any other, considered with reference to that other; specifically, the seventh above the keynote. **c** Two notes at this interval written or sounded together. **d** The resulting dissonance. See INTERVAL (def. 5). — *adv.* In the seventh order, place, or rank: also, in formal discourse, **sev′enth·ly.** [ME *seventhe* <SEVEN + -TH, replacing OE *seofande* and *seofotha*]

sev·enth–day (sev′ənth·dā′) *adj.* 1 Pertaining to the seventh day of the week. 2 Advocating the observance of the seventh day as the Sabbath: a *Seventh–Day* Adventist.

seventh day 1 Saturday; the seventh day of the week; the Sabbath of the Jews and of some other religious groups. 2 Saturday, in the speech of the Society of Friends.

Seventh–Day Adventist See under ADVENTIST.

seventh heaven 1 The highest abode or condition of happiness. 2 The highest heaven according to various ancient systems of astronomy or in certain theologies.

sev·en·ti·eth (sev′ən·tē·ith) *adj.* 1 Tenth in order after the sixtieth. 2 Being one of seventy equal parts. — *n.* 1 One of seventy equal parts; the quotient of a unit divided by seventy. 2 A seventieth object or unit. [ME *seventithe* <SEVENTY + -TH]

sev·en·ty (sev′ən·tē) *adj.* Being ten more than sixty, or seven times ten. — *n. pl.* **·ties** The sum of ten and sixty, or the symbols (70, lxx, LXX) representing this number. [OE *(hund-) seofontig*] — **sev′en·ty·fold′** *adj.* & *adv.*

sev·en–up (sev′ən·up′) *n.* A game of cards: also called *all fours, old sledge.*

Seven Wonders of the World The seven works of man considered the most remarkable in the ancient world: generally considered to be the Egyptian pyramids, the hanging gardens of Babylon, the temple of Diana at Ephesus, the statue of Zeus by Phidias at Olympia, the Mausoleum at Halicarnassus, the Colossus of Rhodes, and the Pharos or lighthouse of Alexandria.

sev·er (sev′ər) *v.t.* 1 To put or keep apart; separate. 2 To cut or break into two or more parts. 3 To break off; dissolve, as a relationship or tie. — *v.i.* 4 To come or break apart or into pieces. 5 To go away or apart; separate. See synonyms under BREAK, CUT, REND, SEPARATE. [<AF *severer,* OF *sevrer* <L *separare* SEPARATE]

sev·er·a·ble (sev′ər·ə·bəl) *adj.* 1 Capable of being severed. 2 *Law* That can be severed from something to which it is attached or of which it forms part: said of a contract consisting of several obligations, when non–fulfilment of one obligation does not invalidate the contract.

sev·er·al (sev′ər·əl, sev′rəl) *adj.* 1 Being of an indefinite number, more than two, yet not large; divers. 2 Considered individually; pertaining to an individual; single; separate. 3 *Law* Pertaining individually and separately to each tenant or party to a bond: opposed to *joint*: a joint and *several* note. 4 Individually different; various or diverse. [<AF <Med. L *separalis* <L *separ* separate, distinct]

sev·er·al·ly (sev′ər·əl·ē, sev′rəl·ē) *adv.* 1 Individually; separately. 2 Respectively.

sev·er·al·ty (sev′ər·əl·tē, sev′rəl-) *n. pl.* **·ties** 1 *Law* The holding of land in one's own right without participation; a sole tenancy. 2 The character of being several or distinct.

sev·er·ance (sev′ər·əns, sev′rəns) *n.* The act of severing, or the condition of being severed.

severance pay An amount of money paid to an employee at the termination of employment by the employer, based on regular wages or salary and often related to length of service.

se·vere (si·vir′) *adj.* 1 Trying to one's powers or endurance; hard to bear. 2 Rigorous in the treatment of others; unsparing; harsh; merciless. 3 Conforming to rigid rules; marked by pure and simple excellence; accurate. 4 Serious and austere in disposition or manner; grave; sedate; austerely plain. 5 Causing sharp pain or anguish; extreme: a *severe* pain. [<MF *sévère* <L *severus*] — **se·vere′ly** *adv.*

Synonyms: austere, rigid, rigorous, stern, stiff, unrelenting. That is *severe* which is devoid of all softness, mildness, indulgence, or levity, or (in literature and art) devoid of unnecessary ornament, amplification, or embellishment of any kind; as, a *severe* style; as said of anything painful, *severe* signifies such as heavily taxes endurance or power to resist; as, a *severe* pain, fever, or winter. *Rigid* signifies primarily *stiff,* resisting any effort to change its shape, its will, or course of conduct. *Rigorous* is nearly akin to *rigid,* but is a stronger word, having reference to action or active qualities: a *rigid* rule may be *rigorously* enforced. *Strict* signifies bound or stretched tight, tense, strenuously exact. *Stern* unites harshness and authority with strictness or severity; *stern,* as said even of inanimate objects, suggests something authoritative or forbidding. *Austere* signifies severely simple or temperate, *strict* in self–restraint or discipline, and similarly *unrelenting* toward others. See ARDUOUS, AUSTERE, BAD, DIFFICULT, HARD, IMPLACABLE, MOROSE, VIOLENT.

se·ver·i·ty (si·ver′ə·tē) *n. pl.* **·ties** 1 The quality of being severe. 2 Harshness or cruelty of disposition or treatment; power of paining or distressing. 3 Extreme strictness in character or rigor in operation; exactness. 4 Seriousness; austerity. 5 Strict conformity to truth or law. See synonyms under ACRIMONY, VIOLENCE.

Sev·ern (sev′ərn) A river in northern Wales and western England, flowing 210 miles NE, SE, south, and SW from near Aberystwith to the Bristol Channel.

Severn River A river in NW Ontario, Canada, flowing 610 miles NE to Hudson Bay.

Se·ver·na·ya Zem·lya (sā′vir·nə·yə zim·lyä′) An archipelago in the Arctic Ocean in Krasnoyarsk territory, Russian S.F.S.R.; total, 14,300 square miles.

Se·ver·sky (si·ver′skē), **Alexander de,** 1894–1974, U.S. airplane designer and manufacturer born in Russia.

Se·ve·rus (si·vir′əs), **Lucius Septimius,** 146–211, Roman emperor; rebuilt Hadrian's Wall across northern England.

Sé·vi·gné (sā·vē·nyā′), **Madame de,** 1626–96, Marie de Rabutin–Chantal, French writer.

Se·ville (sə·vil′) A city of SW Spain; the leading city of Andalusia. *Spanish* **Se·vil·la** (sā·vēl′lyä).

Sè·vres (se′vr′) *n.* A fine porcelain originally made at Sèvres, France. Also **Sèvres ware.**

Sè·vres (se′vr′) A city of north central France on the Seine just SW of Paris.

sew (sō) *v.* **sewed, sewed** or **sewn, sew·ing** *v.t.* 1 To make, mend, or fasten with needle and thread. 2 To affect by sewing: often with *up.* — *v.i.* 3 To work with needle and thread. [OE *siwan, siowian*]

sew·age (sōō′ij) *n.* 1 The waste matter from domestic, commercial, and industrial establishments carried off in sewers. 2 Loosely, sewerage. [<SEW(ER) + -AGE]

Sew·all (sōō′əl), **Samuel,** 1652–1730, Massachusetts jurist and diarist.

se·wan (sē′wən) See SEAWAN.

Sew·ard (sōō′ərd), **William Henry,** 1801–72, U. S. statesman; secretary of state 1861–69.

Sew·ard Peninsula (sōō′ərd) The westernmost part of Alaska, extending 210 miles west to Cape Prince of Wales; 90–140 miles wide.

se·wel·lel (si·wel′el) *n.* A brown, burrowing, nocturnal, vegetarian rodent (*Aplodontia rufa*) of the Pacific coast north of California; the mountain beaver. [<Chinook *shewallal* dual, a blanket of two sewellel skins sewn together (mistaken by Lewis and Clark for the animal's name) < *ogwoolal* a sewellel]

sew·er[1] (sōō′ər) *n.* 1 A conduit, usually laid underground, to carry off drainage and excrement. ◆ Collateral adjective: *cloacal.* 2 Any large public drain. [<OF *seuwiere* a channel from a fish pond, ult. <L *ex-* off + *aqua* water]

sew·er[2] (sōō′ər) *n.* Formerly, in England, an attendant who supervised the serving of meals and seating of guests. Also **sew′ar.** [<AF *asseour,* OF *asseoir* cause to sit <L *assidere* < *ad-* to + *sedere* sit]

sew·er[3] (sō′ər) *n.* One who or that which sews.

sew·er·age (sōō′ər·ij) *n.* 1 A system of sewers. 2 Systematic draining by sewers. 3 Sewage.

sew·ing (sō′ing) *n.* 1 The act, business, or occupation of one who sews. 2 That which is sewed; material on which one is at work with needle and thread; needlework.

sewing bee A social gathering of the women and girls of a community to sew for some charitable purpose.

sewing circle 1 A group of women, usually organized within a church or other welfare organization, meeting periodically to sew for some charitable purpose. 2 A meeting of such a group. Also **sewing society.**

sewing machine A machine for stitching or sewing cloth, leather, etc.

sewing silk Finely twisted silk thread used for sewing.

sewn (sōn) Alternative past participle of SEW.

sex (seks) *n.* 1 Either of two divisions, male and female, by which organisms are distinguished with reference to the reproductive functions. 2 Males or females collectively. 3 The character of being male or female. 4 The activity or phenomena of life concerned with sexual desire or reproduction. 5 *Colloq.* Sexual gratification. **—the fair sex** Women. [<OF *sexe* <L *sexus*, prob. orig. division]

sex– *combining form* Six: *sexpartite*. Also spelled *sexi–*. [<L *sex* six]

sex·a·ge·nar·i·an (sek′sə·jə·nâr′ē·ən) *n.* A person between sixty and seventy years of age. *—adj.* **1** Sixty years old, or between sixty and seventy. **2** Of or pertaining to a sexagenarian. [<SEXAGENARY]

sex·ag·e·nar·y (seks·aj′ə·ner′ē) *adj.* **1** Of or pertaining to the number sixty. **2** Sixty years old, or between sixty and seventy. *—n. pl.* **·nar·ies** A sexagenarian. [<L *sexagenarius* < *sexageni* sixty each < *sexaginta* sixty]

Sex·a·ges·i·ma (sek′sə·jes′ə·mə) *n.* The second Sunday before Lent. Also **Sexagesima Sunday.** [<L *sexagesima (dies)* sixtieth (day). See SEXAGESIMAL.]

sex·a·ges·i·mal (sek′sə·jes′ə·məl) *adj.* Pertaining to or founded on the number sixty. [<Med. L *sexagesimalis* <L *sexagesimus* sixtieth < *sexaginta* sixty]

sex·an·gle (seks′ang′gəl) *n.* A six-angled figure; a hexagon. [<L *sexangulus* < *sex* six + *angulus* an angle] **—sex′an′gu·lar** (-ang′gyə·lər), **sex′·an′gled** *adj.* **—sex′an′gu·lar·ly** *adv.*

sex appeal **1** A physical quality or charm which attracts sexual interest. **2** *Slang* The capacity to excite interest or attention: Tax reductions have *sex appeal.*

sex cell A gamete; a sperm or ovum.

sex·cen·te·nar·y (seks·sen′tə·ner′ē, seks′sen·ten′ər·ē) *adj.* Pertaining to or consisting of six hundred, especially six hundred years. *—n. pl.* **·nar·ies** **1** A period of six hundred years or a collection of six hundred units. **2** A six-hundredth anniversary. [<L *sexcenteni* six hundred each < *sexcenti* six hundred < *sex* six + *centum* a hundred]

sex chromosome *Biol.* A chromosome whose presence in the reproductive cells of certain plants and animals is associated with the determination of the sex of offspring. In mammals the ovum carries two X-chromosomes and sperm an X- and a Y-chromosome; females are produced by a paired XX in the fertilized ovum, males by a paired XY.

sex·en·ni·al (seks·en′ē·əl) *adj.* Happening once every six years, or lasting six years. *—n.* A sixth anniversary. [<L *sexennis, sexennium* < *sex* six + *annus* a year] **—sex·en′ni·al·ly** *adv.*

sex·fid (seks′fid) *adj. Bot.* Six-cleft, as a calyx. Also **sex′i·fid.** [<SEX- + -FID]

sex gland A gonad; either of the testes or ovaries.

sex hygiene The division of hygiene having to do with sexual conduct as related to the health of the individual and community.

sexi– Var. of SEX–.

sex·ism (seks′iz·əm) *n.* Sexual prejudice against women. [<SEX + -ISM, on analogy with *racism*] **—sex′ist** *n., adj.*

sex·less (seks′lis) *adj.* Having no sex; neuter. **—sex′less·ly** *adv.* **—sex′less·ness** *n.*

sex linkage *Biol.* That type of inheritance which is associated with the transmission of genes attached to the sex chromosomes. **—sex–linked** (seks′lingkt′) *adj.*

sex·ol·o·gy (seks·ol′ə·jē) *n.* The study of human sexual behavior. [<SEX + -(O)LOGY] **—sex·o·log·ic** (sek′sə·loj′ik) or **·i·cal** *adj.* **—sex·ol′·o·gist** *n.*

sex·par·tite (seks·pär′tīt) *adj.* Divided into or made up of six parts, as a groined arch or other structure. [<NL *sexpartitus* <L *sexus* six + *partitus* PARTITE]

sex·ploi·ta·tion (seks′ploi·tā′shən) *n.* The commercial exploitation of interest in sex, as by means of pornography. [Blend of SEX + EXPLOITATION]

sex·pot (seks′pot′) *n. Slang* A very sexy woman.

sex ratio The ratio of males to females in a given population, usually expressed as the number of males per 100 females.

sext (sekst) *n.* **1** One of the canonical hours; the office for the sixth hour or noon. **2** The sixth book of the decretals. [<LL *sexta* <L *sexta (hora)* the sixth (hour), fem. of *sextus* sixth < *sex* six]

Sex·tans (seks′tənz) An equatorial constellation between Leo and Hydra; the Sextant. See CONSTELLATION. [<L, a sextant]

sex·tant (seks′tənt) *n.* **1** An instrument for measuring angular distance between two objects, as between a heavenly body and the horizon, by a double reflection from two mirrors: used especially in determining latitude at sea. **2** The sixth part of a circle; an arc of 60 degrees. [<L *sextans, -antis* the sixth part < *sextus* sixth]

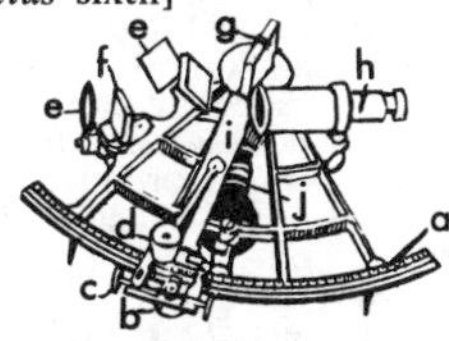

SEXTANT

a. Scale. *b.* Clamp screw. *c.* Tangent screw. *d.* Reading lens. *e.* Glass shades. *f.* Horizon glass. *g.* Index glass. *h.* Telescope. *i.* Movable arm. *j.* Handle.

sex·tar·i·us (seks·târ′ē·əs) *n. pl.* **·tar·i·i** (-târ′ē·ī) An ancient Roman measure of capacity. See CONGIUS. [<L, a sixth part < *sextus* sixth < *sex* six]

sex·tet (seks·tet′) *n.* **1** A band of six singers or players; also, a musical composition for six parts. **2** Any collection of six persons or things. Also **sex·tette′.** [Alter. of SESTET; refashioned after L *sex* six]

sex·tile (seks′til) *adj.* Indicated or measured by a distance of 60 degrees. *—n.* **1** *Astron.* The aspect of two planets at a distance of 60 degrees from each other. **2** *Stat.* One of the divisions of a frequency distribution containing exactly one sixth of the total number of cases or observations included. [<L *sextilis (mensis)* the sixth (month), i.e., August < *sextus* sixth]

sex·til·lion (seks·til′yən) *n.* A cardinal number: in the French system and in the United States, 1 followed by 21 ciphers; in the English system, 1 followed by 36 ciphers. [<F <L *sex* six + F *(m)illion* a million]

sex·to·dec·i·mo (seks′tō·des′ə·mō) *n.* Sixteenmo. [<L *sextusdecimus* sixteenth < *sextus* sixth + *decimus* tenth]

sex·ton (seks′tən) *n.* **1** A janitor of a church having charge also of ringing the bell, overseeing burials, etc.; also, formerly, a grave-digger. **2** Any of certain carrion beetles (genus *Necrophorus*) that bury small dead animals by excavating the ground beneath them: also called *burying beetle.* The larvae feed on the maggots in the rotting flesh. ◆ Homophone: *sextan.* [<AF *segerstaine,* OF *secrestein* <Med. L *sacristanus.* Doublet of SACRISTAN.] **—sex′ton·ship** *n.*

sex·tu·ple (seks′to͞o·pəl, -tyo͞o-, seks·to͞o′-, -tyo͞o′-) *adj.* **1** Sixfold. **2** Multiplied by six; six times repeated. **3** *Music* Having six beats to the measure. *—v.t.* **·pled, ·pling** To make sextuple; multiply by six. *—n.* A number or sum six times as great as another. [<L *sextus* sixth < *sex* six, formed on analogy with *quadruple, quintuple,* etc.]

sex·tu·plet (seks′to͞o·plit, -tyo͞o-, seks·to͞o′-, -tyo͞o′-) *n.* **1** A set of six similar things. **2** One of six offspring produced at a single birth. [<SEXTUPLE on analogy with *triplet*]

sex·tu·pli·cate (seks·to͞o′plə·kit, -tyo͞o′-) *adj.* **1** Sixfold. **2** Raised to the sixth power. *—v.t.* (-kāt) **·cat·ed, ·cat·ing** To multiply by six; sextuple. *—n.* One of six like things. [<Med. L *sextuplicatus,* pp. of *sextuplicare* <*sextuplex* multiplied by six < *sex* six] **—sex·tu′pli·cate·ly** *adv.* **—sex·tu′pli·ca′tion** *n.*

sex·u·al (sek′sho͞o·əl) *adj.* **1** Of, pertaining or peculiar to, characteristic of, or affecting sex, the sexes, or the organs or functions of sex. **2** Characterized by or having sex: opposed to *asexual.* [<LL *sexualis* <L *sexus* sex] **—sex′u·al·ly** *adv.*

sexual intercourse **1** The sexual act, especially between humans, in which the erect penis is introduced into the vagina for the ejaculation of semen and sexual gratification. **2** Any act of sexual connection, especially between humans.

sex·u·al·i·ty (sek′sho͞o·al′ə·tē) *n.* **1** The state of having, or of being distinguished by, sex. **2** Preoccupation with sex. **3** Possession of sexual power.

sexual selection In the theory of evolution, a phase of natural selection whereby characters, as bright colors, or fine song, considered as especially attractive to the opposite sex, have a tendency to become perpetuated or enhanced.

sex·y (sek′sē) *adj.* **sex·i·er, sex·i·est** *Slang* **1** Provocative of sexual desire: a *sexy* dress; a *sexy* woman. **2** Concerned in large or excessive degree with sex: a *sexy* novel.

Sey·chelles (sā·shel′, -shelz′) An island group in the western Indian Ocean, comprising a British colony; 156 square miles; capital, Victoria, on Mahé.

Sey·han (sā·hän′) A river in south central Turkey in Asia, flowing 320 miles SW to the Mediterranean.

Seym (sām) See SEIM.

Sey·mour (sē′môr, -mōr), **Jane,** 1509?–37, third wife of Henry VIII of England; mother of Edward VI.

Sfax (sfäks) A port in central eastern Tunisia, on the north shore of the Gulf of Gabès; the second largest city of Tunisia.

sfer·ics (sfer′iks) *n. Meteorol.* **1** A cathode-ray tube connected with a directional antenna, used for the detection and plotting of electrical discharges in the atmosphere up to distances of several thousand miles. **2** *pl.* Atmospherics. [Short for ATMOSPHERICS]

Sfor·za (sfôr′tsä) A Milanese ducal family which flourished in the 15th century. **—Count Carlo,** 1873–1952, Italian anti-Fascist leader.

sfor·zan·do (sfôr·tsän′dō) *adj. Music* Accented more forcibly than the rhythm requires; especially, sounded, as a note or chord, with sudden explosive force: also spelled *forzando.* Also **sfor·za′to** (-tsä′tō). [<Ital., forcing < *sforzare* force]

′s Gra·ven·ha·ge (skhrä′vən·hä′khə) The Dutch name for THE HAGUE.

Shaa·ban (shä·bän′) See CALENDAR (Mohammedan).

shab·by (shab′ē) *adj.* **·bi·er, ·bi·est** **1** Threadbare; ragged; soiled or defaced, as from hard use. **2** Characterized by worn or defaced garments. **3** Mean; paltry. See synonyms under BAD[1], BASE[2]. [OE *sceabb* a scab + -Y[1]] **—shab′bi·ly** *adv.* **—shab′bi·ness** *n.*

Sha·bu·oth (shä·vo͞o′ōth, shə·vo͞o′əs) *n. pl.* The Jewish festival of Pentecost or Feast of Weeks. [<Hebrew *shebuōth*, lit., weeks]

shach·le (shäkh′əl) *Scot. v.t.* To pull or wrench out of shape, as by excessive use. *—n.* Anything misshapen by or as by excessive use.

shack[1] (shak) *n.* A rude cabin, as of logs. **—shack up** *Slang* **1** To live together and cohabit: said of unmarried persons. **2** To live or stay, usually briefly, at a specific place. [? < dial. Sp. (Mexican) *jacal* a wooden hut <Nahuatl *xacalli*; prob. infl. by RAMSHACKLE]

shack[2] (shak) *n.* **1** Fallen acorns or nuts of any kind; mast. **2** Any bait picked up at sea, as dead sea birds, refuse fish, etc.: distinguished from bait regularly carried or newly caught: also **shack bait.** **3** A catch of miscellaneous, unsorted fish. [< *shack, v.,* dial. var. of SHAKE]

shack[3] (shak) *n.* A slow trot: also **shack gait.** *—v.t.* To go at a slow trot. [Short for *shack-rag,* var. of *shake-rag* a vagabond, a worthless horse <SHAKE + RAG[2]]

shack[4] (shak) *v.t.* To go after; retrieve. [Origin unknown]

shack·le (shak′əl) *n.* **1** A ring, clasp, or braceletlike fastening for encircling and fettering a limb; fetter; gyve. **2** Impediment or restraint. **3** One of various forms of fastenings, as the bow of a padlock, a clevis, or a link for coupling railway cars. See synonyms under FETTER. *—v.t.* **·led, ·ling** **1** To restrain or confine with shackles; fetter. **2** To keep or restrain from free action or speech. **3** To connect or fasten with a shackle. See synonyms under BIND. [OE *sceacul*] **—shack′ler** *n.*

SHACKLES

shackle bolt **1** A bolt having on its end a shackle or clevis, or a bolt that is passed through the eyes of a shackle. **2** The shackle of a padlock, chain, etc. 3 *Her.* Shackle and padlock: used as a bearing.

Shack·le·ton (shak′əl·tən), **Sir Ernest Henry,** 1874–1922, English Antarctic explorer.

shack·o (shak′ō) See SHAKO.

shad (shad) *n. pl.* **shad** A deep-bodied food fish (genus *Alosa*) related to the herring, especially the common or American shad (*Alosa sapidissima*) of the Atlantic coast, which is highly esteemed as food. [OE *sceadd*]

shad–bel·lied (shad′bel′ēd) *adj.* 1 Cutaway: said of a coat. 2 Lean and lank: said of persons.

shad·ber·ry (shad′ber′ē) *n. pl.* **·ries** The shadbush, or its fruit.

shad·bush (shad′bo͝osh′) *n.* 1 The Juneberry. 2 Other smaller and shrublike related forms of the same genus, as *Amelanchier alnifolia* of the northern and western United States. Also **shad′blow′** (-blō′). [<SHAD + BUSH[1]; so called because it flowers when the shad appear in U. S. rivers]

shad·dock (shad′ək) *n.* 1 The large, pale-yellow fruit of a tropical tree (genus *Citrus*), varying in size from the smaller grapefruit or pomelo of the United States to the pompelmous, which may be 8 inches in diameter. 2 The tree. [after Capt. *Shaddock,* commander of an East India ship, who brought the seed to the West Indies from the East Indies in 1696]

shade (shād) *v.* **shad·ed, shad·ing** *v.t.* 1 To screen from light by intercepting its rays; put in shade. 2 To make dim with or as with shade; darken; overcast. 3 To screen or protect with or as with a shade. 4 To cause to change, pass, blend, or soften, by gradations. 5 **a** To represent (degrees of shade, colors, etc.) by gradations of light or dark lines or shading. **b** To represent varying shades, colors, etc., in (a picture or painting) thus. 6 To make slightly lower, as a price. — *v.i.* 7 To change or vary by degrees. [< *n.*] — *n.* 1 Relative obscurity from interception of the rays of light: distinguished from *shadow;* hence, gloom; darkness; obscurity; the state of being outshone. 2 A shady place; secluded retreat. 3 Something that serves to intercept or screen from light; hence, a screen that shuts off light, heat, air, dust, etc. 4 A gradation of color; also, slight degree; minute difference. 5 The unilluminated part of a picture, drawing, or engraving: opposed to *light.* 6 A disembodied spirit; ghost; something unreal. 7 *pl. Slang* Sunglasses. See synonyms under SPECTER. — **the shades** The abode of departed spirits; Hades. [OE *sceadu*] — **shade′less** *adj.*

shade grass Pachysandra.

shad·fly (shad′flī′) *n. pl.* **·flies** Any of several flies that appear when the shad are running; especially, a mayfly.

shad·ing (shā′ding) *n.* 1 Protection against light or heat. 2 The lines, dots, etc., by which degrees of darkness, color, or depth are represented in a picture or painting. 3 A slight difference or variation.

sha·doof (shä·do͞of′) *n.* A water-raising device, operating on the principle of a well sweep: used in the Orient for irrigation, etc., as on the Nile. Also **sha·duf′.** [Arabic *shādūf*]

shad·ow (shad′ō) *n.* 1 A comparative darkness within an illuminated area caused by the interception of light by an opaque body. 2 The dark figure or image thus produced on a surface and representing the approximate shape of the intercepting body: the *shadow* of a man. 3 The shaded or dark portion of a picture. 4 A mirrored image: to see one's *shadow* in a pool. 5 A delusive image or semblance; anything unreal or unsubstantial. 6 A phantom; ghost; shade. 7 A faint representation or indication; a symbol: the *shadow* of things to come. 8 A remnant; vestige: *shadows* of his former glory. 9 An insignificant trace or portion: not a *shadow* of evidence. 10 *Archaic* Shelter; protection. 11 Gloom; a saddening influence. 12 An inseparable companion. 13 One who trails or follows another, as a detective or spy. See synonyms under IMAGE. — *adj.* Of or pertaining to a shadow cabinet. — *v.t.* 1 To cast a shadow upon; overspread with shadow; shade. 2 To darken or cloud; make gloomy. 3 To represent or foreshow dimly or vaguely: with *forth* or *out.* 4 To follow closely or secretly; spy on. 5 To shade in painting, drawing, etc. 6 *Archaic* To screen; shelter. [OE *sceadwe,* genitive and dative of *sceadu* a shade] — **shad′ow·er** *n.*

shad·ow·box (shad′ō·boks′) *v.i.* To spar with an imaginary opponent as a form of exercise. — **shad′ow·box′ing** *n.*

shadow cabinet In the British or other parliamentary government, a group of opposition leaders who would assume specific cabinet positions if the government in power should fall.

shad·ow·graph (shad′ō·graf, -gräf) *n.* 1 A pictorial image formed by casting a shadow, usually of the hands, upon a lighted surface or screen. 2 A drama produced by a series of these images: also **shadow play.** 3 A radiograph.

shadow test Skiascopy.

shad·ow·y (shad′ō·ē) *adj.* 1 Full of or affording shadow; dark; shady: a *shadowy* grove. 2 Like shadows in indistinctness; vague; dim. 3 Unsubstantial or illusory; unreal; ghostly. 4 Symbolic. See synonyms under DARK, IMAGINARY, VAIN. — **shad′ow·i·ness** *n.*

sha·drach (shā′drak, shad′rak) See SALAMANDER (def. 5).

Sha·drach (shā′drak, shad′rak) A Jewish captive in Babylon, who, with Meshach and Abednego, was cast into a fiery furnace by Nebuchadnezzar, but came out unscathed. *Dan.* i 7; iii 1–30.

Shad·well (shad′wel), **Thomas,** 1642?–92, English dramatist and poet.

shad·y (shā′dē) *adj.* **shad·i·er, shad·i·est** 1 Full of shade; casting a shade. 2 Shaded or sheltered. 3 Morally questionable; dubious; suspicious. 4 Quiet; hidden. See synonyms under DARK. — **to keep shady** 1 To stay in hiding; keep out of the way. 2 To hide and protect (another). — **on the shady side of** Older than; past the age of. — **shad′i·ly** *adv.* — **shad′i·ness** *n.*

shaft[1] (shaft, shäft) *n.* 1 The long narrow rod of an arrow, spear, lance, harpoon, etc. 2 An arrow. 3 Anything resembling a missile in appearance or effect: *shafts* of ridicule. 4 A beam or streak of light. 5 A long handle, as of a hammer, ax, etc. 6 *Mech.* A long and usually cylindrical bar, especially if rotating and transmitting motive power. 7 *Archit.* **a** The portion of a column between capital and base. **b** A slender column. 8 An obelisk or memorial column. 9 The vertical part of a cross. 10 The stem of a feather. 11 *Anat.* **a** A long slender portion, as the diaphysis of a bone. **b** The portion of a hair from the root to the end. 12 On a loom, one of the long laths at the ends of the heddles. 13 A thill. 14 *Slang* Malicious or abusive treatment: with *the,* especially in the phrases **to get the shaft, to give (someone) the shaft.** — *v.t. Slang* To act maliciously or abusively toward. [OE *sceaft*]

shaft[2] (shaft, shäft) *n.* 1 A narrow, vertical or inclined, excavation connected with a mine; also, a passage for light or air. 2 The tunnel of a blast furnace. 3 An opening through the floors of a building, as for an elevator. [<LG *schacht* rod, shaft; infl. by SHAFT[1]]

Shaftes·bur·y (shafts′bər·ē, shäfts′-), **Earl of,** 1621–83, Anthony Ashley Cooper, English statesman; lord chancellor 1672–73.

shaft·ing (shaf′ting, shäf′-) *n.* 1 A system of shafts or rods, as in pulleys or gearwheels, for communicating power. 2 Material from which to make shafts.

shag[1] (shag) *n.* 1 A rough coat or mass, as of hair. 2 A wild growth, as of weeds. 3 A long nap on cloth. 4 Cloth having a rough or long nap; formerly, a silk or worsted cloth having a velvet nap. 5 A cormorant. 6 A coarse, strong tobacco: also **shag tobacco.** — *v.* **shagged, shag·ging** *v.t.* 1 To make shaggy or hairy; roughen. 2 In baseball, to catch (flies) in practice. — *v.i.* 3 To become shaggy or rough. — *adj.* Shaggy: also **shag·ged** (shag′id). [OE *sceacga* rough hair, wool]

shag[2] (shag) *n.* A dance of the late 1930's, consisting of hopping quickly on alternate feet. — *v.i.* **shagged, shag·ging** To dance the shag.

shag·a·nap·pi (shag′ə·nap′ē) *Canadian* A rawhide cord or thong.

shag·bark (shag′bärk′) *n.* 1 The white hickory (*Carya ovata*), which yields high-grade nuts. 2 Its wood. Also called *shellbark.*

shag·gy (shag′ē) *adj.* **·gi·er, ·gi·est** 1 Having, consisting of, or resembling rough hair or wool; rugged; rough. 2 Covered with any rough, tangled growth; fuzzy; scrubby. 3 Unkempt; unpolished: said of manners. See synonyms under ROUGH. — **shag′gi·ly** *adv.* — **shag′gi·ness** *n.*

sha·green (shə·grēn′) *n.* 1 The rough skin of various sharks and rays: used for polishing. 2 A rough-grained Russian or Oriental leather or parchment, usually dyed green, or a pressed leather made in imitation of it. 3 Chagrin. [<F *chagrin* <Turkish *sāghrī* horse's hide]

shah (shä) *n.* An eastern king or ruler, especially of Persia. [<Persian *shāh,* short for *pādshāh.* See PADISHAH.]

Sha·hap·ti·an (shä·hap′tē·ən) *n.* A linguistic stock of North American Indians of which the Nez Percés were the chief tribe, formerly occupying the upper Columbia River valley: now on reservations in Oregon.

Shah·ja·han·pur (shä′jə·hän′po͝or) A city in Uttar Pradesh State, northern India.

Shah Je·han (shä jə·hän′), 1592–1666, Mogul emperor, 1627–58, of Delhi, celebrated for his peacock throne and as the builder of the Taj Mahal. Also **Shah Ja·han′.**

shaik (shīk) See SHEIK.

Shairp (shârp, shärp), **John Campbell,** 1819–1885, Scottish educator and critic.

shai·tan (shī·tän′) *n.* 1 In Moslem countries, the devil. 2 Any evil spirit; an evilly disposed person. 3 In India, a duststorm. Also spelled *sheitan.* [<Arabic *shaiṭān* <Hebrew *śāṭān.* See SATAN.]

shake (shāk) *v.* **shook, shak·en, shak·ing** *v.t.* 1 To cause to move to and fro or up and down with short, rapid movements. 2 To affect in a specified manner by or as by vigorous action: with *off, out, from,* etc.: to *shake* out a sail; to *shake* off a tackler. 3 To cause to tremble or quiver; jolt; vibrate: The blows *shook* the door. 4 To cause to stagger or totter. 5 To weaken or disturb; unsettle: I could not *shake* his determination. 6 To agitate or rouse; stir: often with *up.* 7 *Slang* To get rid of or away from. 8 *Music* To trill. 9 In dice games, to mix (the dice) before casting. — *v.i.* 10 To move to and fro or up and down in short, rapid movements. 11 To be affected in a specified way by vigorous action: with *off, out, from,* etc. 12 To tremble or quiver, as from cold or fear. 13 To become unsteady; totter. 14 *Music* To trill a note, etc. — **to shake down** 1 To cause to fall by shaking; bring down. 2 To cause to settle; make compact. 3 *Slang* To extort money from. — **to shake hands** To clasp hands as a form of greeting, agreement, etc. — *n.* 1 A shaking; concussion; agitation; vibration; shock; jolt. 2 The state of being shaken. 3 *pl. Colloq.* The chill or ague of intermittent fever. 4 A rough, unshaved shingle used to cover barns and shanties. 5 A frost or wind crack in timber; also, a tight fissure in rock. 6 An earthquake. 7 *Slang* An instant; a jiffy. 8 *Music* A trill. 9 *Colloq.* A bargain. — **to give (someone) the shake** To get rid of (someone). [OE *scacan*]

Synonyms (verb): agitate, brandish, flap, fluctuate, flutter, jar, joggle, jolt, jounce, oscillate, quake, quaver, quiver, rattle, reel, rock, shiver, shudder, sway, swing, thrill, totter, tremble, vibrate, wave, waver. A thing is *shaken* which is subjected to short and abruptly checked movements as forward and backward, up and down, from side to side, etc. A thing *rocks* that is held up from below; it *swings* if suspended from above, as a pendulum, or pivoted at the side, as a crane or a bridge draw; to *oscillate* is to *swing* with a smooth and regular returning motion; a *vibrating* motion may be tremulous or *jarring.* The pendulum of a clock may be said to *swing* or *oscillate;* a steel bridge *vibrates* under the passage of a heavy train; the term *vibrate* is also applied to molecular movements. *Jolting* is a lifting from and letting down suddenly upon an unyielding surface; a *jarring* motion is abruptly and very rapidly repeated through an exceedingly limited space; the *jolting* of the carriage *jars* the windows. *Rattling* refers directly to the sound produced by *shaking.* To *joggle* is to *shake* slightly; as, A passing touch *joggles* the desk on which one is writing. To *agitate* in its literal use is nearly the same as to *shake,* but we speak of the sea as *agitated* when we could not say it is *shaken;* in the metaphorical use *agitate* is more transitory and superficial, *shake* more fundamental and enduring; a person's feelings are *agitated* by distressing news; his courage, his faith, his credit, or his testimony is *shaken.* Compare FLUCTUATE, QUAKE, SWAY, TREMBLE.

shake-down (shāk′doun′) *n.* **1** A bed of straw shaken down; hence, any makeshift bed. **2** *U.S. Slang* A swindle; a share of graft; extortion money. **3** A noisy, energetic dance common among Negroes of the southern United States. —*adj.* For the purpose of adjusting mechanical parts or habituating people: a *shake-down* cruise.

shak·er (shā′kər) *n.* **1** One who or that which shakes; a container for shaking something: a *saltshaker,* cocktail *shaker,* etc. **2** One who shivers or shakes; a totterer.

Shak·er (shā′kər) *n.* One of a sect practicing celibacy and communal living, introduced in America in 1774 under the leadership of Mother Ann Lee, at Lebanon, New York: so called from their characteristic bodily movements during religious meetings. Their official name is *The United Society of Believers in Christ's Second Appearing.* —**Shak′er·ism** *n.*

Shake·speare (shāk′spir), **William,** 1564–1616, English poet and dramatist. Also **Shake′spere, Shak′speare, Shak′spere.**

Shake·spear·i·an (shāk·spir′ē·ən) *adj.* Of, pertaining to, or characteristic of Shakespeare, his work, or his style. —*n.* A specialist on Shakespeare or his writings. Also **Shake·spear′e·an.**

Shake·spear·i·an·ism (shāk·spir′ē·ən·iz′əm) *n.* **1** An expression peculiar to Shakespeare. **2** Shakespearian style.

Shakespearian sonnet See under SONNET.

shake-up (shāk′up′) *n.* A change of personnel or organization, as in a government administration, a business office, etc.

Shakh·ty (shäkh′tē) A city in southern European Russian S.F.S.R.

shaking palsy *Pathol.* A chronic disorder of the central nervous system, characterized by alternations of muscular rigidity and tremor and peculiar gait: also called *paralysis agitans.*

shak·o (shak′ō) *n. pl.* **·os** A kind of high, stiff military headdress, having a peak and an upright plume: originally of fur: also spelled *shacko.* [<F *schako* <Hungarian *csákó*]

SHAKO

Shak·ti (shuk′tē) *n.* The female energy of the Hindu god, Siva: worshiped under various forms; Devi: also spelled *Sakti.* [<Skt. *śakti* power] —**Shak′tism** *n.*

Sha·kun·ta·la (shə·ko͝on′tə·lə) See SAKUNTALA.

shak·y (shā′kē) *adj.* **shak·i·er, shak·i·est 1** Habitually shaking or tremulous; tottering; weak; unsound. **2** Of doubtful credit or solvency; embarrassed. —**shak′i·ly** *adv.* —**shak′i·ness** *n.*

shale[1] (shāl) *n.* A fissile argillaceous rock resembling slate, with fragile, uneven laminae. [<G *schale* shale] —**shal′y** *adj.*

shale[2] (shāl) *n.* Shell or husk. [OE *scealu*] —**shaled** *adj.*

shale oil Petroleum obtained by the distillation of bituminous shales.

shall (shal) A defective verb having a past tense **should,** an archaic present second person singular, (thou) **shalt,** past (thou) **shouldst** or **shouldest,** and no other inflected forms. It is now used only as an auxiliary followed by the infinitive without *to,* or elliptically with the infinitive unexpressed. Its function is to indicate, now chiefly in formal discourse: **1** In the first person, simple futurity, with a matter-of-fact attitude toward the action or state projected: We *shall* take only the usual precautions. (But see usage note below.) **2** In the second and third persons, futurity combined with a mood or feeling of: **a** Determination: They *shall* not pass. **b** Promise: You *shall* have whatever you need. **c** Threat: You *shall* pay for this. **d** Command: No one *shall* twice be put in jeopardy. **e** Inevitability: When earthly time *shall* end, will life survive? **3** In all persons, indefinite future time in conditional statements: If and when you or we or the divers *shall* locate the treasure, it will (or, in legal use, the mandatory *shall*) be shared out according to the agreement. **4** In all persons, futurity involving ideal certainty, in clauses following expressions of anxiety, demand, or desire: They are anxious, indeed insist, that you or I or both of us *shall* go, rather than any outsider. [OE *sceal* I am obliged, 1st person sing. of *sceolan*]

◆ **shall** vs. **will** The traditional view on the use of *shall* and *will* is that to indicate simple futurity *shall* is used in the first person, *will* in the second and third; their roles are reversed to express determination, promise, threat, command, inevitability, etc.; while in questions, the choice between them depends on which one is expected in the answer. These statements hold fairly well for legal usage, but they are too arbitrary to describe accurately the facts of current American usage in speech and writing, except at the most stilted formal level. *Shall* and *will* have had a tendency gradually to exchange roles once each century since 1500, and during the present century it has been the turn of *will* to make its way into the lead. In the important task of indicating simple future time in the first person, *will* has largely replaced *shall,* aided in doing so by the leveling effect of the contraction *'ll*: *I'll* (= *I will* or *I shall*) be free at ten. *Shall,* thus displaced, takes on one role assigned by traditional formula to *will,* and is used in the first person to express determination plus inevitability, as in General MacArthur's "I *shall* return" and Winston Churchill's " . . . and win we *shall.*" If *will* in the first person is to express determination according to the formula, it must be stressed or qualified in some way: I *will* too go out and play. In questions in the first person, *shall* is still commonly used to express the simple future, but it is also found as the hortatory *shall,* either humorously formal: *Shall* we (= *Let's*) dance? or politely threatening: *Shall* we (= *Let's*) do it my way for once. Again, *will* has won out over *shall* when it comes to giving routine or polite, as distinct from peremptory, commands: You *will* proceed to Hill 90 and occupy it. The peremptory *shall* in the second person is now usually replaced, except in legal usage, by *will* with *have to*: You *will have to* (= *shall*) go whether you want to or not. It is hazardous to try to sum up the present position of these two forms, but with the few exceptions noted, in American usage *will* now usually indicates the simple future in all persons, while *shall* expresses the future complicated by some feeling about it.

shal·loon (sha·lo͞on′) *n.* A light, woven woolen fabric used for linings. [<F *chalon,* from *Châlons*-sur-Marne, France]

shal·lop (shal′əp) *n.* An open boat propelled by oars or sails. [<F *chaloupe* <Du. *sloep.* See SLOOP.]

shal·lot (shə·lot′) *n.* **1** An onionlike culinary vegetable (*Allium ascalonicum*) allied to garlic but having milder bulbs which are used in seasoning and for pickles. **2** A small onion. Also spelled *eschalot.* [<OF *eschalotte,* alter. of *eschaloigne.* See SCALLION.]

shal·low (shal′ō) *adj.* **1** Having the bottom not far below the surface or top; lacking depth; shoal. **2** Lacking intellectual depth; not wise or profound; superficial. —*n.* A shallow place in a body of water; shoal. —*v.t.* & *v.i.* To make or become shallow. [ME *schalowe.* Prob. related to SHOAL[1].] —**shal′low·ly** *adv.* —**shal′low·ness** *n.*

shalt (shalt) Archaic or poetic second person singular, present tense of SHALL: used with *thou.*

shal·war (shul′wâr) *n.* Oriental trousers or pajamas. [<Persian *shalwār*]

sham (sham) *v.* **shammed, sham·ming** *v.t.* **1** To assume or present the appearance of; counterfeit; feign. **2** To represent oneself as; pretend to be. **3** *Obs.* To delude; deceive. —*v.i.* **4** To make false pretenses; feign something. See synonyms under COUNTERFEIT, PRETEND. —*adj.* False; pretended; counterfeit; mock. See synonyms under FACTITIOUS. —*n.* **1** A pretense; imposture; deception. **2** One who affects or simulates a certain character; a pretender: also **sham′mer. 3** A deceptive imitation; simulation; counterfeit. **4** A bordered strip simulating the edge of a sheet on a made-up bed. See synonyms under HYPOCRISY. [Prob. dial. var. of SHAME]

sha·man (shä′mən, shā′-, sham′ən) *n.* **1** A priest of Shamanism; a magician. **2** Among certain northwestern North American Indians, a tribal medicine man or wizard. —*adj.* Of or pertaining to a shaman: also **sha·man·ic** (shə·man′ik). [<Russian <Tungusic *samān* <Skt. *śamaṇa* ascetic]

Sha·man·ism (shä′mən·iz′əm, shā′-, sham′ən-) *n.* A primitive religion of NE Asia and Europe holding that gods, demons, ancestral spirits, etc., work for the good or ill of mankind through the sole medium of its priests, the shamans. Certain Indians of the American Northwest have similar beliefs and practices. —**Sha′man·is′tic** *adj.* & *n.*

Sha·mash (shä′mäsh) In Assyro-Babylonian religion, the sun god, the deity controlling crops and personifying righteousness.

sham·a·teur·ism (sham′ə·to͝or′iz·əm, -ə·tər·iz′-) *n.* The practice in some sports of offering amateur athletes large fees, ostensibly for expenses, but actually as an inducement to participate. [<SHAM + AMATEURISM]

sham·ble (sham′bəl) *v.i.* **·bled, ·bling** To walk with shuffling or unsteady gait. —*n.* A shambling walk. [Origin uncertain]

sham·bles (sham′bəlz) *n. pl.* (*generally construed as singular*) **1** A place where butchers kill animals; slaughterhouse. **2** Any place of carnage or execution: The trench was a *shambles.* **3** A place marked by great destruction or disorder. **4** *Brit. Dial.* A meat market; in the singular, a table or stall in such a market. [OE *scamel* a bench, stool <L *scamellum,* dim. of *scamnum* bench, stool]

shame (shām) *n.* **1** A painful sense of guilt or degradation caused by consciousness of guilt or of anything degrading, unworthy, or immodest. **2** The restraining sense of pride, decency, or modesty. **3** That which brings reproach; a disgrace. **4** A state of ignominy; sensitiveness or susceptibility to humiliation. See synonyms under ABOMINATION, CHAGRIN. —**to put to shame 1** To disgrace; make ashamed. **2** To surpass or eclipse. —*v.t.* **shamed, sham·ing 1** To make ashamed; cause to feel shame. **2** To bring shame upon; disgrace. **3** To impel by a sense of shame: with *into* or *out of.* See synonyms under ABASH. [OE *scamu*]

shame·faced (shām′fāst′) *adj.* Easily abashed; showing shame or bashfulness in one's face; modest; bashful. [Alter. of ME *shamefast,* OE *scamfæst* abashed] —**shame·fac·ed·ly** (shām′fā′·sid·lē, shām′fāst′lē) *adv.* —**shame′fac′ed·ness** *n.*

shame·ful (shām′fəl) *adj.* **1** Deserving or bringing shame or disgrace; disgraceful; scandalous. **2** Exciting shame; indecent. See synonyms under FLAGRANT. —**shame′ful·ly** *adv.* —**shame′ful·ness** *n.*

shame·less (shām′lis) *adj.* **1** Impudent; brazen; immodest. **2** Done without shame, indicating a want of decency. See synonyms under INFAMOUS, IMMODEST, IMPUDENT. —**shame′less·ly** *adv.* —**shame′less·ness** *n.*

sham·my (sham′ē), **sham·ois** (sham′ē) See CHAMOIS (def. 2).

Sha·mo (shä′mō) A Chinese name for the GOBI DESERT.

sham·poo (sham·po͞o′) *v.t.* **1** To lather, rub, and wash (the hair and scalp) thoroughly. **2** To cleanse by rubbing. —*n.* The act or process of shampooing, or a preparation used for it. [<Hind. *chāmpnā* press] —**sham·poo′er** *n.*

sham·rock (sham′·rok) *n.* Any one of several trifoliate plants, accepted as the national emblem of Ireland, especially the wood sorrel (*Oxalis acetosella*), the white clover (*Trifolium repens*), and the black medic (*Medicago lupulina*). [<Irish *seamrōg,* dim. of *seamar* trefoil]

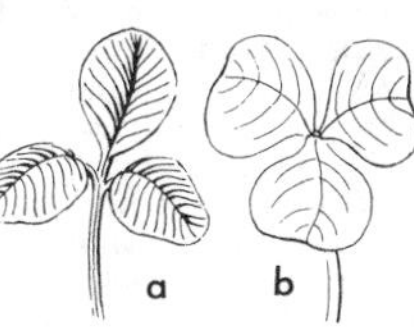

SHAMROCK
a. White clover.
b. Wood sorrel.

Shan (shan, shän) *n.* **1** One of a group of Mongoloid tribes of southern China, Assam, Burma, and Thailand. **2** The Thai language of these tribes, closely related to Siamese. —*adj.* Of or pertaining to the Northern and Southern Shan States, their people, or their language.

shand (shand, shänd) *Scot. adj.* Worthless; mean, paltry. —*n.* Spurious coin.

shan·dry·dan (shan′drə·dan) *n. Irish* **1** A two-wheeled Irish cart, or hooded chaise: also **shan′da·ra·dan′, shan′der·y·dan′.** **2** An old-fashioned or rickety vehicle. [Origin unknown]

shan·dy·gaff (shan′dē·gaf) *n.* An alcoholic drink composed of two liquids mixed, at least one being effervescent: usually ale or beer and ginger beer. [Origin unknown]

shang·hai (shang′hī, shang·hī′) *v.t.* **·haied, ·hai·ing** **1** To drug or render unconscious and kidnap for service aboard a ship. **2** To cause to do something by force or deception. [from *Shanghai*]

Shang·hai (shang′hī′) *n.* One of a former large breed of domestic fowls, with long legs and feathered shanks, said to have originated in Shanghai, China.

Shang·hai (shang′hī′, *Chinese* shäng′hī′) A port of eastern China, the largest city on the Asian continent.

Shan·gri-la (shang′gri·lä′) *n.* **1** Any imaginary hidden utopia or paradise. **2** The reported taking-off place of the United States Army bombers that raided Tokyo April 18, 1942: a term used by Franklin Roosevelt. **3** Any secret base for air force military operations. [From the locale of James Hilton's novel *Lost Horizon*]

Shan·hai·kwan (shän′hī′gwän′) A city in NE Hopeh province, China, on the Gulf of Liaotung on the Manchurian boundary; the easternmost end of the Great Wall. Formerly called **Lin·yü** (lin′yōō′).

shank (shangk) *n.* **1** The leg proper; that part of the lower limb between the knee and the ankle. **2** A cut of meat from the leg of an animal; the shin. **3** The tarsus of a bird. See the illustration under FOWL. **4** Something resembling a leg. **5** The part of a tool connecting the handle with the working part, as the stem of a drill. **6** The projecting piece or loop by which some forms of buttons are attached. **7** The stem of an anchor. **8** The stem of a key between the bow and the bit. **9** The straight part of a hook. **10** The narrow part of a spoon handle. **11** A continuation of the tang of a tool or instrument. **12** *Printing* The body of a type. **13** The narrow part of a shoe sole in front of the heel. See illustration under SHOE. **14** *Bot.* A pedicel. **15** *Colloq.* The remainder or last part of a thing: the *shank* of the evening. —*v.i.* **1** *Bot.* To decay or fall off the stem because of disease. **2** *Scot.* To travel on foot. [OE *sceanca*]

Shan·ka·ra (shung′kə·rə), flourished about 800 A.D., Hindu religious reformer, teacher and writer; foremost exponent of Vedanta philosophy; considered an incarnation of Shiva. Also **Shan·ka·ra·char·ya** (shung′kə·rä·chär′yə).

shanks' mare One's own legs as a means of conveyance.

shan·na (shan′na, shän′nä) *Scot.* Shall not.

Shan·non (shan′ən) An international airport in southern County Clare, Ireland, on the Shannon River west of Limerick.

Shannon River (shan′ən) The chief river of Ireland, in the west central part, flowing 224 miles south and west to the Atlantic.

Shan·si (shän′sē′) A province of NE China; 50,000 square miles; capital, Taiyüan.

Shan State (shän, shan) A constituent unit of Burma in east Upper Burma, consisting of **Northern Shan State** and **Southern Shan State**; 61,090 square miles; capital, Lashio.

sha'nt (shant, shänt) Shall not: a contraction. Also **shan't.**

shan·tung (shan′tung, shan·tung′) *n.* A silk fabric similar to pongee and having the same rough, nubby surface: originally made in China of wild silk, now often made of rayon combined with cotton. [from SHANTUNG]

Shan·tung (shan′tung′, *Chinese* shän′dŏŏng′) A province of NE China, extending as a peninsula in the eastern part into the Yellow Sea; 55,000 square miles; capital, Tsinan.

shan·ty[1] (shan′tē) *n. pl.* **·ties** A hastily built shack or cabin; a ramshackle or rickety dwelling. See synonyms under HOUSE, HUT. [<F (Canadian) *chantier* lumberer's shack]

shan·ty[2] (shan′tē) See CHANTEY.

shan·ty·man (shan′tē·mən) *n. pl.* **·men** (-mən) One who lives in a shanty; specifically, a woodcutter or lumberman.

shan·ty·town (shan′tē·toun′) *n.* **1** That section of a city or town comprised of ramshackle or hastily constructed shacks. **2** The inhabitants collectively of such a section: All *shantytown* turned out for the parade.

Shao·hing (shou′shing′) A city in northern Chekiang province, China. Also **Shao′-hsing′.**

shape (shāp) *n.* **1** Outward form or construction; configuration; contour. **2** A developed expression or definite formulation; realization or application; embodiment; cast: to put an idea into *shape.* **3** A being, image, or appearance considered with reference to its form, generally incorporeal; ghost; phantom. **4** The character or form in which a thing appears; guise; aspect. **5** Something that gives or determines form; a pattern or mold; in millinery, a stiff frame. **6** The lines of a person's body; figure. **7** Manner of execution. **8** Condition as regarding fitness. **9** A blancmange, jelly, etc., cooled and shaped in a mold. —**to take shape** To have or assume a definite form. —*v.* **shaped, shaped** (*Rare* **shap·en**), **shap·ing** *v.t.* **1** To give shape to; mold; form. **2** To adjust or adapt; modify. **3** To devise; prepare. **4** To give direction or character to: to *shape* one's course of action. **5** To put into or express in words. **6** *Obs.* To appoint; ordain. —*v.i.* **7** To take shape; develop; form: often with *up* or *into.* **8** *Rare* To become adapted; conform. **9** *Rare* To happen; come about. See synonyms under MAKE. [OE *gesceap* creation] —**shap′er** *n.*

SHARKS
A. Great white shark (to 40 feet). *B.* Blue shark (to 15 feet). *C.* Hammerhead shark (to 15 feet).

shaped (shāpt) *adj.* **1** Formed. **2** Resembling in shape: used in compounds, as in leaf-*shaped,* club-*shaped,* key-*shaped.*

shaped charge An explosive charge so placed in a shell or projectile as to deliver most of its force directly through the nose of the shell instead of scattering it at random: developed especially for anti-tank guns.

shape·less (shāp′lis) *adj.* Having no definite shape; lacking symmetry; formless. —**shape′·less·ly** *adv.* —**shape′less·ness** *n.*

shape·ly (shāp′lē) *adj.* **·li·er, ·li·est** Having a pleasing shape; well-formed; graceful. —**shape′li·ness** *n.*

shape-up (shāp′up′) *n.* The selection of a work crew by an employer representative, a labor union deputy, or other agent, who chooses from among a number of men assembled for a work shift: a common practice in hiring longshoremen and workers in other industries in which the relationship between an employee and a specific employer is by the day or otherwise casual.

Shap·ley (shap′lē), **Harlow,** 1885–1973, U.S. astronomer.

shard (shärd) *n.* **1** A broken piece of a brittle substance, as of an earthen vessel; a potsherd; a fragment: also spelled *sherd.* **2** *Zool.* A hard, thin shell, or a wing cover, of an insect. [OE *sceard.* Related to SHEAR.]

share (shâr) *n.* **1** A portion; allotted or equitable part. **2** Specifically, one of the equal parts into which the capital stock of a company or corporation is divided. **3** An equitable part of something enjoyed or suffered in common. **4** A plowshare: also spelled *shear.* **5** A blade of a cultivator, seeder, etc. See synonyms under PART. —*v.* **shared, shar·ing** *v.t.* **1** To divide and give out in shares or portions; apportion. **2** To enjoy or endure in common; participate in. —*v.i.* **3** To have a part; participate: with *in.* See synonyms under APPORTION. [OE *scearu* < *sceran* shear. Related to SHEAR.] —**shar′er** *n.*

share·crop·per (shâr′krop′ər) *n.* A tenant farmer who pays a share of his crop as rent for his land.

share·hold·er (shâr′hōl′dər) *n.* An owner of a share or shares of a company's stock; a stockholder.

shares·man (shârz′mən) *n. pl.* **·men** (-mən) A member of a cooperative fishing crew who shares in the risks and profits of the cruise or season. Also **share′man.**

Sha·ri (shä′rē) A river of central French Equatorial Africa, forming the principal tributary of Lake Chad and flowing 500 miles NW: French *Chari.*

shark[1] (shärk) *n.* One of a group of voracious elasmobranch fishes (order *Selachii*), mostly marine, of medium to large size, having a cartilaginous skeleton, lateral gill slits, and dun-colored bodies covered with placoid scales. Most species do not molest man; the great white shark (*Carcharodon carcharias*) is the man-eater frequenting warm seas. —*v.i.* To fish for sharks. [Origin uncertain]

shark[2] (shärk) *n.* **1** A bold and dishonest person; a rapacious swindler. **2** *Slang* A person of exceptional skill or ability in some special line. Also **shark′er.** —*v.t. Archaic* To obtain by unscrupulous or deceitful means. —*v.i.* To live by trickery or deceit. [Prob. <G *schurke* scoundrel]

shark·skin (shärk′skin′) *n.* **1** The skin of a shark. **2** A summer fabric with a smooth, almost shiny surface, made of acetate rayon and used for sports clothes; originally, a weave of woolen yarns of two colors: so called from its resemblance to sharkskin leather.

sharn (shärn) *n. Scot.* Cow dung. —**sharn′y** *adj.*

Shar·on (shar′ən), **Plain of** A part of the coastal plain of western Israel, extending 50 miles between the Hills of Ephraim and the Mediterranean.

sharp (shärp) *adj.* **1** Having a keen edge or an acute point; capable of cutting or piercing. **2** Coming to an acute angle; not obtuse; angular; abrupt: a *sharp* peak. **3** Keen of perception or discernment; also, shrewd in bargaining; artful; overreaching: *sharp* practice. **4** Ardent; quick; eager; keen, as the appetite; impetuous or fiery, as a combat or debate; vigilant or attentive. **5** Affecting the mind or senses, as if by cutting or piercing; afflictive; poignant; painful; harsh; censorious; acrimonious; rigorous; stern; sarcastic; bitter. **6** Shrill. **7** Pinching; cutting, as cold. **8** Having an acid or pungent taste. **9** Distinct, as an outline; not blurred or hazy; well-defined. **10** *Music* Being above the proper or indicated pitch; specifically, being a half-step higher than the indicated note; sharped. **11** Hard and rough; gritty, as sand. **12** *Phonet.* Surd; voiceless: opposed to *flat*: said of consonants. —*adv.* **1** In a sharp manner; sharply. **2** Promptly; exactly; on the instant: at 4 o'clock *sharp.* **3** *Music* Above the proper pitch. —*n.* **1** *Music* A character (♯) used on a natural degree of the staff to make it represent a pitch a half-step higher; the tone so indicated; on the pianoforte, the next higher key; one of the black keys: a loose use in the phrase *sharps and flats.* **2** A sewing needle of long, slender shape. **3** A cheating rogue; sharper: a *cardsharp.* **4** *Obs.* A dueling sword; rapier. —*v.t. Music* To raise in pitch, as by a half-step. —*v.i. Music* To sing, play, or sound above the right pitch. [OE *scearp*] —**sharp′ly** *adv.* —**sharp′ness** *n.*

Synonyms (*adj.*): acute, cutting, keen, penetrating, piercing, pointed. See ACID, ACUTE, ASTUTE, BITTER, CLEVER, FINE, KNOWING, SAGACIOUS, STEEP, VIOLENT. *Antonyms*: blunt, dull, dulled, edgeless, flat, obtuse, pointless, round, rounded.

Sharp (shärp), **William,** 1856?–1905, Scottish poet and novelist: pseudonym, *Fiona McLeod.*

sharp·en (shär′pən) *v.t.* & *v.i.* To make or become sharp. —**sharp′en·er** *n.*

sharp·er (shär′pər) *n.* A swindler; cheat.

sharp–eyed (shärp′īd′) *adj.* 1 Having acute eyesight. 2 Keenly observant; alert.

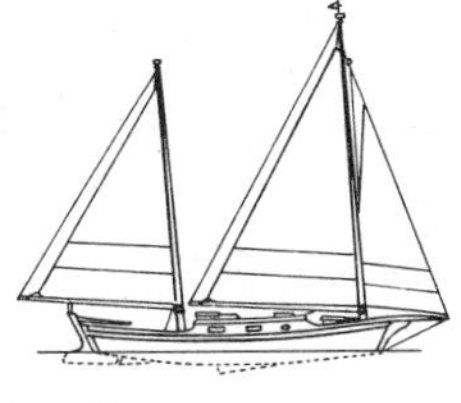
SHARPIE

sharp·ie (shär′pē) *n.* A long, sharp, flat-bottomed sailboat having a center-board and one or two masts, each having a triangular sail: originally used in the oyster and scallop fisheries. [<SHARP; in allusion to its outline]

Sharps·burg (shärps′bûrg) A town in NW Maryland; site of the battle of Antietam, 1862, in the Civil War.

sharp–set (shärp′set′) *adj.* 1 Set at a sharp angle; prepared like a saw for cutting. 2 Keen; eager; fierce. 3 Ravenous; hungry; thin and hungry-looking.

sharp–shinned (shärp′shind′) *adj.* Having slender shanks, somewhat angular in front: specifically said of the North American **sharp–shinned hawk** *(Accipiter velox).*

sharp·shoot·er (shärp′shōō′tər) *n.* 1 A skilled marksman, especially in the use of the rifle. 2 The second grade of skill in small-arms shooting, ranking next above *marksman* and below *expert*; also, a soldier having this grade. — **sharp′shoot′ing** *n.*

sharp–sight·ed (shärp′sī′tid) *adj.* Having keen vision. — **sharp′–sight′ed·ness** *n.*

sharp–tongued (shärp′tungd′) *adj.* Bitter or caustic in speech.

sharp–wit·ted (shärp′wit′id) *adj.* Acute; intelligent; discerning. See synonyms under INTELLIGENT, SAGACIOUS. — **sharp′–wit′ted·ness** *n.*

Sha·si (shä′sē′) A city on the Yangtze in south central Hupeh province, China.

Shas·ta (shas′tə), **Mount** A volcanic cone in the Cascade Range of northern California; 14,161 feet.

Shasta daisy A cultivated variety of a short-lived perennial *(Chrysanthemum maximum)* having large, white-rayed flowers.

Shas·tan (shas′tən) *adj.* & *n.* Comanchean.

Shatt–el–Ar·ab (shat′al·ar′əb) A river in SE Iraq, formed by the Tigris and Euphrates which unite 40 miles NW of Basra and flow 120 miles SE, forming the Iraq-Iran boundary from below Basra to the Persian Gulf.

shat·ter (shat′ər) *v.t.* 1 To break into pieces suddenly, as by a blow. 2 To break the health or tone of, as the body or mind; disorder; damage. 3 *Obs.* To scatter. — *v.i.* 4 To break into pieces; burst. See synonyms under BREAK. — *n. Obs.* 1 A shattered fragment; a splinter: a tree rent into *shatters.* 2 A shattered or disordered condition: His nerves are in a *shatter.* [ME *schateren.* ? Akin to SCATTER.]

shat·ter·proof glass (shat′ər·prōōf′) See under GLASS.

shauch·le (shakh′əl, shä′khəl, shô′-) *Scot. v.t.* To put out of shape; distort, as a shoe. — *v.i.* To shuffle; shamble. Also **shaugh′le.**

shaul (shôl) See SHOAL[1].

shave (shāv) *v.* **shaved, shaved** or **shav·en, shav·ing** *v.i.* 1 To cut hair or beard close to the skin with a razor. — *v.t.* 2 To remove hair or beard from (the face, head, etc.) with a razor. 3 To cut (hair or beard) close to the skin with a razor: often with *off.* 4 To trim closely as if with a razor: to *shave* a lawn. 5 To cut thin slices from, as in preparing the surface; pare; plane. 6 To cut into thin slices: to *shave* ice. 7 To touch or scrape in passing; graze; come close to. 8 *U.S.* To buy (commercial paper) at a greater reduction than the bank discount. — *n.* 1 The act or operation of cutting off the beard with a razor. 2 A knife or blade, mounted between two handles, as for shaving wood: also **draw shave, spoke shave.** 3 A shaving; thin slice. 4 An extra or exorbitant discount paid for cashing a note or draft, as a premium given for an extension of time. 5 *Colloq.* The act of rushing by or barely grazing something; hence, a narrow escape: a close *shave.* 6 One who drives hard bargains. [OE *scafan* shave]

shave·ling (shāv′ling) *n.* 1 One who is shaven; opprobriously, a monk or priest. 2 A youth.

shav·en (shā′vən) Alternative past participle of SHAVE. — *adj.* 1 Shaved; also, tonsured. 2 Trimmed closely.

shav·er (shā′vər) *n.* 1 One who shaves; specifically, a barber. 2 A plunderer; cheat; sharper. 3 *Colloq.* A lad.

shave·tail (shāv′tāl′) *n. U.S. Slang* 1 A second lieutenant, especially one recently commissioned. 2 An untrained or intractable mule. 3 A tenderfoot. [Formerly in allusion to young, unbroken army mules with their tails bobbed]

Sha·vi·an (shā′vē·ən) *n.* An admirer of George Bernard Shaw, his books, or his theories. — *adj.* Of, pertaining to, or like George Bernard Shaw, or his style and methods.

shav·ie (shā′vē) *n. Scot.* A deceptive trick.

shav·ing (shā′ving) *n.* 1 The act of one who shaves; that which shaves. 2 A thin paring shaved from anything, as a board.

shaw[1] (shô) *v.t. Scot.* To show.

shaw[2] (shô) *n. Brit.* 1 A thicket; copse: also **shaugh.** 2 The leaves and tops of vegetables: usually in the plural. [OE *scaga* copse]

Shaw (shô), **George Bernard,** 1856–1950, Irish dramatist, critic, and novelist. — **Henry Wheeler,** 1818–85, U.S. humorist: pseudonym *Josh Billings.* — **Thomas Edward** See LAWRENCE, THOMAS EDWARD.

Shawan·gunk Mountains (shong′gum, -gungk) A range of the Appalachians in SE New York; about 45 miles long; highest point, 2,289 feet.

shawl (shôl) *n.* A wrap, as a square cloth, or large broad scarf, worn over the upper part of the body. [<Persian *shāl*]

shawm (shôm) *n.* An ancient, double-reed instrument; inaccurately, a cornet or horn. [<OF *chalemie* pipe <LL *calamellus,* dim. of L *calamus* reed]

Shaw·nee (shô·nē′) *n.* One of a warlike tribe of North American Indians of Algonquian stock, formerly living in Tennessee and South Carolina: now in Oklahoma. [<Algonquian (Shawnee) *Shawunogi* southerners <*shawun* south]

Shaw·wal (shô·wäl′) See under CALENDAR (Mohammedan).

shay (shā) *n.* A chaise: a back formation due to mistaking *chaise* for a plural.

Shays (shāz), **Daniel,** 1747?–1825, a captain in the American Revolution and leader of **Shays' Rebellion,** 1786–87, a popular insurrection in western Massachusetts, caused by economic distress of that time. — **Shays′ite** *n.*

Shcher·ba·kov (shchir′bə·kôf′) A city on the Volga in north central European Russian S.F.S.R.: formerly *Rybinsk.*

she (shē) *pron.* 1 The female person or being previously mentioned or understood, in the nominative case. 2 That woman or female; any woman: *She* who listens learns. — *n.* A female person or being: This puppy is a *she.* [OE *sēo, sīo,* fem. of *sē* the, replacing *hēo* she]

she– *combining form* Female; feminine: in hyphenated compounds: a *she*-lion.

shea (shē) *n.* A large tree *(Butyrospermum parkis)* growing only in western tropical Africa and yielding **shea butter,** used for food, illumination, and making soap. [<Mundingo *si, se*]

sheaf[1] (shēf) *n. pl.* **sheaves** (shēvz) 1 A quantity of the stalks of cut grain or the like, bound together; a bundle of straw. 2 Any collection of things, as papers, held together by a band or tie. 3 The quiverful of arrows carried by an archer, usually 24. — *v.t.* To bind in a sheaf; sheave. [OE *scēaf*]

sheaf[2] (shēf) See SHEAVE[2].

sheal[1] (shēl) *n. Scot.* & *Brit. Dial.* A shealing.

sheal[2] (shēl) *n. Brit.* A pod or shell. [Var. of SHELL]

sheal·ing (shē′ling) *n.* 1 *Brit. Dial.* A hut or cabin for the use of shepherds or sportsmen in the hills, for fishermen at the shore, etc.: also spelled *shieling.* 2 *Scot.* A shed for sheltering sheep at night in the hills. Also called *sheal.*

shealing hill *Scot.* A hill upon which grain is winnowed by the wind: also spelled *sheeling hill.*

shear (shir) *n.* 1 A two-bladed cutting instrument: obsolete except in the plural. See SHEARS. 2 *Physics* A deformation of a solid body, equivalent to a sliding over each other of adjacent laminar elements, with a progressive relative displacement: also **shearing stress.** 3 The act or result of shearing. 4 A plowshare. 5 *Naut.* Sweep; sheer. — *v.* **sheared** (*Archaic* **shore**), **sheared** or **shorn, shear·ing** *v.t.* 1 To cut the hair, fleece, etc., from. 2 To remove by cutting or clipping: to *shear* wool. 3 To deprive; strip, as of power or wealth. 4 To cut or clip with shears or other sharp instrument: to *shear* a cable. 5 *Dial.* To reap, as grain, with a sickle. — *v.i.* 6 To use shears or other sharp instrument. 7 To slide or break from a shear (def. 2). 8 To proceed by or as by cutting a way: with *through.* 9 *Dial.* To reap with a sickle. See synonyms under CUT. ◆ Homophone: *sheer.* [OE *scēara* scissors <*sceran* shear. Akin to SHARD, SHARE.] — **shear′er** *n.*

shear·ling (shir′ling) *n.* 1 The fleece from the second shearing of a sheep. 2 The sheep from which one fleece has been cut.

shears (shirz) *n. pl.* 1 Any large cutting or clipping instrument worked by the crossing of cutting edges. 2 The ways or guides, as of a lathe. 3 An apparatus for hoisting and moving heavy objects, consisting of two or more spars with lower ends spread out and upper ends jointed to receive the tackle: also **shear legs:** sometimes spelled *sheers.* 4 The side frames of a steam fire engine. [See SHEAR]

shear·wa·ter (shir′wô′tər, -wot′ər) *n.* One of several sea birds (genus *Puffinus*) related to the petrels and albatrosses, found in most seas: so called because they skim close to the water.

sheat·fish (shēt′fish′) *n. pl.* **·fish** or **·fish·es** A catfish *(Siluris glanis)* of the fresh waters of central and eastern Europe. It is the largest fresh-water fish in Europe. [OE *scēota* trout + FISH]

sheath (shēth) *n.* 1 An envelope or case, as for a sword; scabbard. 2 *Bot.* A case enclosing a part or an organ, as the lower part of the leaves in grasses. 3 *Zool.* Any covering in animals that resembles a sheath. 4 *Entomol.* An elytron of a beetle. 5 *Agric.* A bar connecting the beam and sole in a plow [OE *scǣth*] — **sheath′less** *adj.*

sheath–bill (shēth′bil′) *n.* Any of a small number of species of sea birds of the family *Chionididae,* natives of the Antarctic islands. They are pure white in plumage and have a horny sheath at the base of the bill.

sheathe (shēth) *v.t.* **sheathed, sheath·ing** 1 To put into a sheath. 2 To plunge (a sword, etc.) into flesh, as if into a sheath. 3 To incase or protect with a covering, as the hull of a ship with metal. 4 To draw in, as claws. [<SHEATH]

sheath·ing (shē′thing) *n.* 1 A casing, as of a building, or the protective covering of a ship's hull; that which sheathes; also, the material used. 2 The act of one who sheathes. 3 *Archit.* The covering or waterproof material on outside walls or roof

sheath knife A large case knife carried in a sheath attached to a belt, worn by sailors and riggers.

sheave[1] (shēv) *v.t.* **sheaved, sheav·ing** To gather into sheaves; collect. [<SHEAF]

sheave[2] (shēv) *n.* 1 A grooved pulley wheel; also, a pulley wheel and its block. 2 An eccentric, or its disk. 3 *Scot.* A slice or cut. Also spelled *sheaf, sheeve.* [Var. of SHIVE[1]]

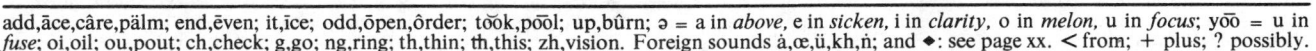

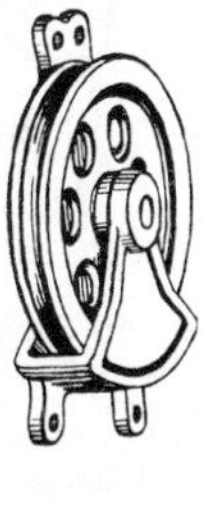

SHEAVE

sheaves (shēvz) Plural of SHEAF.

She·ba (shē′bə) The Old Testament name for a region of the SW Arabian peninsula, corresponding to modern Yemen: Arabic *Saba.*

She·ba (shē′bə), **Queen of** A queen, called Balkis in the Koran, who visited Solomon to test his wisdom. I *Kings* x 1–13.

she·bang (shi·bang′) *n. U.S. Slang* 1 A building, vehicle, saloon, theater, etc. 2 Any matter of present concern; thing; contrivance; outfit: tired of the whole *shebang.* [Var. of SHEBEEN]

She·bat (shi·bät′) See under CALENDAR (Hebrew). Also spelled *Sebat.*

she·been (shi·bēn′) *n. Irish* & *Scot.* A groggery; specifically, a place where liquors are sold without a license; hence, weak ale or beer. [<Irish *sibin* little mug]

She·be·li (shi·bā′lē), **Web·be** (web′ā) See SHIBELI, WEBBE.

She·chem (shē′kem) The ancient name for NABLUS.

shed[1] (shed) *v.* **shed, shed·ding** *v.t.* **1** To pour forth in drops; emit, as tears or blood. **2** To cause to pour forth. **3** To send forth or abroad; diffuse; radiate, as light. **4** To throw off without allowing to penetrate, as rain; repel. **5** To cast off by natural process, as hair, skin, a shell, etc. —*v.i.* **6** To cast off or lose hair, skin, etc., by natural process. **7** To fall or drop, as leaves or seed. —**to shed blood** To kill. —*n.* **1** That which sheds, as a sloping surface or watershed. **2** The act of shedding: *bloodshed.* **3** A separation or division; parting: applied technically to the opening in the warp through which the shuttle is thrown in weaving, and in parts of Great Britain to the parting of the hair. See illustration under LOOM. **4** The slope of a hill. [OE *scēadan* separate, part]

shed[2] (shed) *n.* **1** A small low building, often with front or sides open; also, a lean-to: a wagon *shed.* **2** *Brit.* A storehouse; barn. **3** A temporary covering; cabin. **4** A hangar. See synonyms under HUT. [Var. of SHADE]

she'd (shēd) **1** She had. **2** She would.

shed·der (shed′ər) *n.* **1** One who sheds. **2** An animal that sheds or has lately shed its skin, as a crab.

she–dev·il (shē′dev′əl) *n.* **1** A bad-tempered and spiteful woman. **2** A female demon.

shee (shē) See SID.

sheel·ing hill (shē′ling) See SHEALING HILL.

sheen (shēn) *n.* **1** A glistening brightness, as if from reflection. **2** Bright, shining attire. See synonyms under LIGHT. —*adj.* Shining; radiant; beautiful. —*v.i.* To shine; gleam; glisten. [OE *scēne* beautiful; infl. in meaning by SHINE. Akin to G *schön* beautiful.] —**sheen′y** *adj.*

sheep (shēp) *n. pl.* **sheep** **1** A medium-sized, domesticated ruminant of the genus *Ovis* (family *Bovidae*), highly prized for its flesh, wool, and skin. ◆ Collateral adjective: *ovine.* **2** Leather made from the skin of the sheep, as for bookbinding: also *sheepskin.* **3** Someone with the supposed temperament of a sheep; hence, a meek, bashful, or timid person. [OE *scēap*]

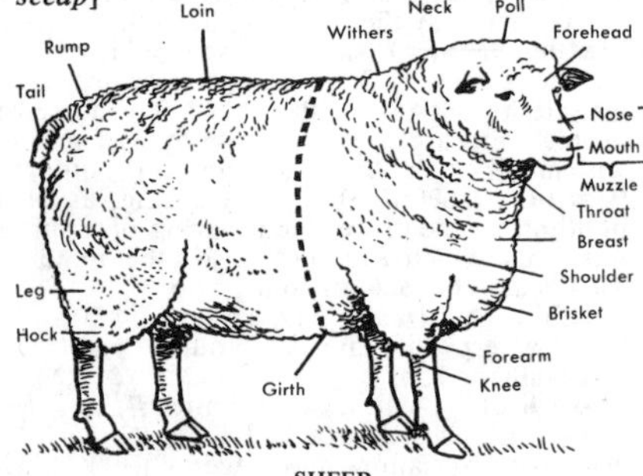

SHEEP
Nomenclature of anatomical parts.

sheep·backs (shēp′baks′) *n. pl.* Roches moutonnées.

sheep·ber·ry (shēp′ber′ē) *n. pl.* **·ries** **1** One of the black, oval, edible drupes of the sweet viburnum *(Viburnum lentago).* **2** The tree itself.

sheep·cote (shēp′kōt′) *n.* A small enclosure for the protection of sheep; a sheepfold. Also **sheep′cot′** (-kot′).

sheep dip Any of several liquid disinfectants which contain creosote, nicotine, cresol, arsenic, etc., used for dipping sheep.

sheep dog **1** A dog trained to guard and control sheep; shepherd's dog: often a collie, but also a rough-coated, heavy, short-tailed dog much used by drovers in England. **2** Figuratively, a chaperon. —**old English sheep dog** A bob-tailed dog of undetermined origin, used as a sporting dog, and, in Great Britain, to herd flocks: characterized by a strong, muscular, thick-set body, covered with a very thick gray, grizzle, or blue-gray shaggy coat.

sheep·fold (shēp′fōld′) *n.* A place where sheep are enclosed at night; a pen for sheep.

sheep·herd·er (shēp′hûr′dər) *n.* A herder of sheep. —**sheep′herd′ing** *n.*

sheep·ish (shē′pish) *adj.* Foolish, as a sheep; awkwardly diffident; abashed. —**sheep′ish·ly** *adv.* —**sheep′ish·ness** *n.*

sheep laurel Lambkill.

sheep ranch A ranch and range where sheep are bred and raised. Also *Brit.* **sheep′walk′**, *Austral.* **sheep run.**

sheep's eyes Bashful, sidelong, or amorous glances.

sheeps·head (shēps′hed′) *n.* **1** A common deep-bodied sparoid food fish *(Archosargus probatocephalus)* of the Atlantic coast of the United States. **2** The Great Lakes drumfish, also found in the Mississippi region. **3** The dollarfish. **4** A foolish or silly person.

sheep·shear·ing (shēp′shir′ing) *n.* **1** The act of shearing sheep. **2** The shearing season; an occasion at which sheep are shorn, and the feast or celebration given at the occasion. —**sheep′shear′er** *n.*

sheep·skin (shēp′skin′) *n.* **1** The skin of a sheep, tanned or untanned, or anything made from it, as parchment. **2** A document written on parchment; hence, a diploma.

sheep sorrel An herb *(Rumex acetosella)* of the buckwheat family, widely distributed in dry places, and having leaves of an acrid taste.

sheer[1] (shir) *v.i.* To swerve from a course; turn aside. —*v.t.* To cause to swerve or deviate. —*n.* **1** *Naut.* **a** The rise, or the amount of rise from a level, of the lengthwise lines of a vessel's hull. **b** A position of a vessel that enables it to swing clear of a single anchor. **2** A swerving or curving course. ◆ Homophone: *shear.* [<SHEAR]

sheer[2] (shir) *adj.* **1** Having no modifying conditions; unmitigated; absolute; downright; utter: *sheer* folly; *sheer* nonsense. **2** Exceedingly thin and fine: said of fabrics. **3** Perpendicular; steep; ascending vertically: a *sheer* precipice. **4** Pure; pellucid. **5** *Obs.* Bright; shining. See synonyms under PURE, STEEP. —*n.* Any very thin fabric used for clothes. —*adv.* Entirely; perpendicularly: also **sheer′ly.** ◆ Homophone: *shear.* [ME *schere.* Cf. ON *skærr* clear, bright and OE *scīr* bright, shining.] —**sheer′ness** *n.*

Sheer·ness (shir′nes′) An urban district and port on the Isle of Sheppey at the mouth of the Medway, in the Thames estuary, northern Kent, England.

sheers (shirz) See SHEARS (def. 3).

sheet (shēt) *n.* **1** A very thin and broad piece of any substance; that which is or can be spread, as upon a surface, or can be laid in broad folds; anything having a considerable expanse with very little thickness. **2** A large rectangular piece of linen or cotton cloth, used in making up a bed. **3** A piece of paper, especially one of a regular size; hence, a newspaper, or a leaf of a book. **4** A piece of metal or other substance hammered, rolled, fused, or cut very thin: a *sheet* of glass. **5** A broad, flat surface; superficial expanse: a *sheet* of water; a *sheet* of flame. **6** *Naut.* **a** A rope or chain from a lower corner of a sail to extend it or move it. **b** *pl.* In an open boat, the space at the bow and stern not occupied by the thwarts. The former is termed the **fore sheets** and the latter the **stern sheets.** **7** A sail: a literary use. **8** *Geol.* **a** An originally horizontal or moderately inclined layer of igneous rock of small thickness as compared with its lateral extent. **b** Any superficial deposit, as of gravel left by a glacier, or of soil or ice. **9** The large, unseparated block of stamps printed by one impression of a plate. —**three sheets in the wind** *Slang* Tipsy; drunk. —*v.t.* **1** To stretch by hauling on a sheet: used only in the expression **to sheet home,** to stretch the clews of a sail to the extremities of the next lower yard. **2** To cover with or wrap in a sheet. **3** To furnish with sheets. —*v.i.* **4** To extend in a particular direction: said of the sheets of a sail. [OE *scēte* linen cloth]

sheet anchor **1** One of two anchors for use only in emergency; formerly, the main anchor. **2** A sure dependence on occasion of danger or emergency.

sheet bend *Naut.* A knot used to join two ropes' ends, made by passing one end through a loop of the other rope, carrying it around the loop, and slipping it under its own running part.

sheet·ing (shē′ting) *n.* **1** The act of sheeting, in any sense. **2** Cotton, muslin, linen, or cotton percale, for making bleached, unbleached, or colored sheets for beds.

sheet lightning Lightning appearing in sheet-like form as a momentary and broadly diffused radiance in the sky, caused by the reflection of a distant lightning flash.

sheet metal Metal rolled and pressed into sheets.

sheet music Music printed on separate sheets of paper.

sheeve (shēv) See SHEAVE[2].

Shef·field (shef′ēld) A city and county borough in West Riding, southern Yorkshire, England.

sheik (shēk, *Brit.* shāk) *n.* **1** A Moslem high priest, a venerable man; the chief or head of an Arab tribe or family: often used as a title of respect. **2** A man who fascinates women; a lady-killer: from *The Sheik,* a novel (1921) by Edith M. Hull. Also **sheikh.** Also spelled *scheik, shaik, sheyk.* [<Arabic *sheikh, shaykh,* lit., an elder, chief < *shakha* grow old]

sheik·dom (shēk′dəm) *n.* The land ruled by a sheik. Also **sheikh′dom.**

Sheik ul Is·lam (shēk′ ŏŏl is·läm′) Formerly, the head of the hierarchy in Turkey; the grand mufti.

shei·tan (shī·tän′) See SHAITAN.

shek·el (shek′əl) *n.* **1** An Assyrian, Babylonian, and, later, Hebrew unit of weight and money; a coin having this weight. **2** *pl. Slang* Money; riches. [<Hebrew *sheqel* < *shāqal* weigh]

She·ki·nah (shi·kī′nə) *n.* A cloud of glory which accompanied the tabernacle of the Jews, especially when over the mercy seat: a symbol and manifestation of the divine presence. [<Hebrew *shekhinah,* lit., dwelling place < *shākhan* dwell]

Shel·don (shel′dən), **Charles Monroe,** 1857–1946, U. S. clergyman and author.

shel·drake (shel′drāk′) *n.* **1** A large Old World duck of either of the genera *Tadorna* or *Casarca,* as the common sheldrake *(T. tadorna),* or the **ruddy sheldrake** *(C. rutila)* of southeastern Europe and North Africa. **2** A merganser, especially the red-breasted merganser or **salt-water sheldrake** *(Mergus serrator).* **3** The canvasback duck. [< dial. E *sheld* piebald, dappled + DRAKE]

shelf (shelf) *n. pl.* **shelves** (shelvz) **1** A board or slab set horizontally into or against a wall to support articles, as books; one of the boards in a bookcase or closet; the contents of a shelf. **2** Any flat projecting ledge, as of rock. **3** A steep-sided bank or shallow place in a body of water; a reef; shoal. **4** The stratum of bedrock met in sinking a shaft. —**on the shelf** No longer in use; discarded. [<LG *schelf* set of shelves]

Shel·i·kof Strait (shel′i·kôf) A channel between Alaska and Kodiak Island, connecting the North Pacific with the Gulf of Alaska, 130 miles long, 30 miles wide.

shell (shel) *n.* **1** A hard structure incasing an animal, as a mollusk, or an egg or fruit. **2** A mollusk; shellfish: much used in composition. **3** A hollow structure or vessel, generally thin and weak; also, a framework with its interior removed or destroyed, or one to be filled out or built upon. **4** A very light, long, and narrow racing rowboat. **5** A hollow metallic projectile filled with an explosive or chemical; especially, an artillery projectile filled with high explosive: used against materiel and fortifications and distinguished from shrapnel used against personnel. **6** The plates, etc., constituting the framework of a steam boiler or the like. **7** A metallic or paper cartridge case for breechloading small arms (see illustration under CARTRIDGE); also, any paper case used to contain the explosives of fireworks, such as torpedos. **8** *Physics* One of the orbits in which the electrons of an atom revolve. **9** A shape or outline that merely simulates a reality; hollow form; external semblance. **10** The external ear; auricle. **11** The lyre: originally a stringed tortoise shell. **12** A reserved or impersonal attitude: to come out of one's *shell.* —*v.t.* **1** To divest of or remove from a shell; strip from the husk, pod, or shell. **2** To separate from the cob, as Indian corn. **3** To bombard with shells, as a fort. **4** To cover with shells. —*v.i.* **5** To shed or become freed from the shell or pod. **6** To fall off, as a shell or scale. —**to shell out** *Colloq.* To hand over, as money. [OE *scell* shell] —**shell′er** *n.* —**shell′-less** *adj.* —**shell′y** *adj.*

she'll (shēl) She will.

shel·lac (shə·lak′) *n.* **1** A purified lac obtained as plates or cakes and extensively used in varnish, sealing wax, insulators, etc. **2** A solution, orange or white, of flake shellac dissolved in methylated spirit: used for coating floors, woodwork, etc. —*v.t.* **·lacked, ·lack·ing 1** To cover or varnish with shellac. **2** *Slang* **a** To belabor; beat. **b.** To defeat utterly. Also **shel·lack′.** [<SHELL +LAC[1], trans. of F *laque en écailles* lac in fine sheets]

shel·lack·ing (shə·lak′ing) *n. Slang* **1** A beating; assault. **2** A thorough defeat.

shellac varnish Any of several varnishes containing dissolved shellac and giving a thin, hard, sometimes glossy, coat.

shell·back (shel′bak′) *n.* A veteran sailor; an old salt; especially, one who has crossed the equator. [Prob. with reference to the shell of the sea turtle]

shell·bark (shel′bärk′) *n.* The shagbark or one of its nuts.

shell bean Any of various beans cultivated for their edible mature seeds.

Shel·ley (shel′ē), **Mary Wollstonecraft,** 1797–1851, *née* Godwin, English novelist; wife of the following. **—Percy Bysshe,** 1792–1822, English poet.

shell·fire (shel′fīr′) *n.* The firing of artillery shells.

shell·fish (shel′fish′) *n. pl.* **·fish** or **·fish·es** Any aquatic animal having a shell, as a mollusk.

shell game 1 A swindling game in which the victim bets on the location of a pea covered by one of three nutshells; thimblerig. **2** Any game in which the victim cannot win.

shell·heap (shel′hēp′) *n.* A kitchen midden. Also **shell′mound′** (-mound′).

shell hole A hole made by an exploding shell; specifically, a craterlike depression in the ground. Also **shell crater.**

shell jacket A snugly fitted jacket, short at the back, worn in place of the tuxedo in tropical countries.

shell pink Any of several shades of light, pure pink, like the color in certain seashells.

shell·proof (shel′prōōf′) *adj.* Built to resist the destructive effect of projectiles and bombs.

shell shock Combat fatigue. **—shell–shocked** (shel′shokt′) *adj.*

shel·ter (shel′tər) *v.t.* To provide protection or shelter for; shield, as from danger or inclement weather. —*v.i.* To take shelter. —*n.* **1** That which covers or shields from exposure or danger; a place of safety. **2** The state of being sheltered or protected. **3** A cover from the weather, as a box for meteorological instruments, etc. **4** One who protects; a guardian. [Appar. alter. of ME *scheltrum* <OE *scēld–truma,* a body of men armed with shields, phalanx, protection] **—shel′ter·er** *n.* **—shel′ter·less** *adj.*

Synonyms (verb): cover, defend, guard, harbor, protect, screen, shield, ward. To *cover* generally means to extend completely over something; a vessel is *covered* with a lid; the head is *covered* with hair. To *shelter* is to *cover* so as to *protect* from injury or annoyance; as, The roof *shelters* from the storm. To *defend* implies the actual, *protect* implies the possible use of force or resisting power; *guard* implies sustained vigilance with readiness for conflict. *Protect* is more complete than *guard* or *defend*; an object may be faithfully *guarded* or bravely *defended* in vain, but that which is *protected* is secure. See CHERISH. Compare synonyms for DEFENSE. *Antonyms*: betray, expel, expose, refuse, reject, surrender.

Synonyms (noun): asylum, cover, covert, defense, harbor, haven, protection, refuge, retreat, sanctuary, shield. See DEFENSE. *Antonyms*: assault, attack, danger, exposure, onslaught, peril.

shelter belt Natural or artificial forest maintained as a protection from wind or snow.

shelter tent A tent large enough to accommodate two men: divided into two sections, each of which, called a **shelter half,** is carried as part of a soldier's field equipment. Also called *pup tent.*

shelt·ie (shel′tē) *n. Scot.* A Shetland pony. Also **shelt′y.**

shelve (shelv) *v.* **shelved, shelv·ing** *v.t.* **1** To place on a shelf. **2** To postpone indefinitely; put aside. **3** To retire. **4** To provide or fit with shelves. —*v.i.* **5** To incline gradually; slope. [<SHELF] **—shelv′y** *adj.*

shelves (shelvz) Plural of SHELF.

shelv·ing (shel′ving) *n.* **1** Shelves collectively. **2** Material for the construction of shelves. **3** The act of putting away on shelves; hence, putting aside; dismissing. **4** A slight inclining.

Shem (shem) The eldest son of Noah. *Gen.* v 32.

Shem·ite (shem′īt) See SEMITE.

Shen·an·do·ah (shen′ən·dō′ə) A river in Virginia and West Virginia, flowing 55 miles to the Potomac at Harper's Ferry. The **Shenandoah Valley,** part of the Great Appalachian Valley, was the scene of many battles during the Civil War.

Shenandoah National Park A region in the Blue Ridge Mountains of NW Virginia; 302 square miles; established 1935.

she·nan·i·gan (shi·nan′ə·gən) *n. Colloq.* Trickery; foolery; nonsense; also, treacherous action or a treacherous act. [Prob. <Irish *sionnach* fox]

Sheng·king (sheng′jing′) A former name for LIAONING.

Shen·si (shen′sē′) A province of NW central China; 75,000 square miles; capital, Sian.

Shen·stone (shen′stən, -stōn), **William,** 1714–1763, English poet.

Shen·yang (shun′yäng′) A city of NE China, capital of Liaoning province; the capital city of the former Manchuria region; a major metal–fabricating center: formerly *Mukden, Fengtien.*

she·ol (shē′ōl) *n.* Hell. [<Hebrew *she'ōl* cave <*shā'al* dig]

She·ol (shē′ōl) In the Old Testament, a place under the earth where the departed spirits were believed to go.

Shep·ard (shep′ərd), **Alan B., Jr.,** born 1923, U.S. naval officer; first American astronaut to make a rocket flight into space and first astronaut to control the space vehicle himself, May 5, 1961.

shep·herd (shep′ərd) *n.* **1** A keeper or herder of sheep. **2** Figuratively, a pastor, leader, or guide. —*v.t.* To watch and tend as a shepherd; guard; protect. [OE *scēaphyrde*] **—shep′·herd·ess** *n. fem.*

shep·herd·clock (shep′ərd·klok′) *n.* Goatbeard. Also **shep′herd's–clock′.**

shepherd dog A sheep dog, as the Scotch collie or the German shepherd dog.

shepherd kings See HYKSOS.

shep·herd's–nee·dle (shep′ərdz·nēd′l) *n.* Venus's–comb.

shep·herd's–purse (shep′ərdz·pûrs′) *n.* A common herbaceous weed *(Capsella bursa–pastoris)* bearing small white flowers and notched triangular pods (whence its name).

Shep·pey (shep′ē), **Isle of** An island in the Thames estuary, northern Kent, England; 36 square miles.

sher·ard·ize (sher′ər·dīz) *v.t.* **·ized, ·iz·ing** *Metall.* To give a coating of zinc to (steel or iron) by packing in zinc dust, placing in a furnace, and subjecting to a heat sufficient to cause the zinc vapor to soak in. [after *Sherard* Cowper–Coles, died 1936, British inventor] **—sher′ard·iz′ing** *n. & adj.*

Sher·a·ton (sher′ə·tən) *adj.* Denoting the graceful, straight–lined style of English furniture developed by Thomas Sheraton.

Sher·a·ton (sher′ə·tən), **Thomas,** 1751–1806, English furniture maker and designer.

sher·bet (shûr′bit) *n.* **1** A flavored water ice. **2** An Oriental drink, made of fruit juice sweetened and diluted with water and sometimes cooled with snow. [<Turkish *sharbat* <Arabic *sharbah* a drink <*shariba* drink. Doublet of SIRUP.]

Sher·brooke (shûr′brŏŏk) A city in southern Quebec province, Canada.

sherd (shûrd) *n.* A fragment of pottery: often in composition: *potsherd*: also spelled *shard.* [Var. of SHARD]

Sher·i·dan (sher′ə·dən), **Philip Henry,** 1831–1888, U.S. general in the Civil War. **—Richard Brinsley,** 1751–1816, English dramatist and politician.

she·rif (she·rēf′) *n.* **1** A member of a princely Moslem family which claims descent from Mohammed through his daughter Fatima. **2** The chief magistrate of Mecca: also **grand sherif. 3** An Arab chief. Also **she·reef′.** [<Arabic *sharīf* noble]

sher·iff (sher′if) *n.* The chief administrative officer of a county, who executes the mandates of courts, etc. In the United States, the sheriff is elected by the legislature or by direct vote of the citizens and must be of age, a citizen of the country, and reside in the county he represents. [OE *scīr–gerēfa* shire reeve] **—sher′·iff·dom** *n.*

Sher·iff·muir (sher′if·myŏŏr) A locality in southern Perthshire, Scotland; scene of a battle between the Scottish Jacobites and the English, 1715.

sher·lock (shûr′lok) *n. Slang* A detective. [after *Sherlock* Holmes]

Sher·lock Holmes (shûr′lok hōmz′) A fictitious English detective, the central character of numerous stories by Arthur Conan Doyle.

Sher·man (shûr′mən), **John,** 1823–1900, U.S. statesman. **—Roger,** 1721–93, American statesman; signer of Declaration of Independence. **—William Tecumseh,** 1820–91, U.S. general in the Civil War; led march from Atlanta to the sea, 1864.

she·root (shə·rōōt′) See CHEROOT.

Sher·ra·moor (sher′ə·mŏŏr) *n. Scot. & Brit. Dial.* The Scottish rebellion of 1715, so called because the Jacobites were stopped in their advance at Sheriffmuir; hence, any turmoil or tumult. Also **Sher′ry·moor.**

Sher·ring·ton (sher′ing·tən), **Sir Charles Scott,** 1861–1952, English physiologist.

sher·ry (sher′ē) *n. pl.* **·ries** The fortified wines of Jerez (formerly Xerez), Spain, or a wine made in imitation of these, as in California. [from *Xerez,* Spain]

sherry cobbler A mixed beverage of sherry, lemon, sugar, water, and ice.

s'Her·to·gen·bosch (ser′tō·khən·bôs′) The capital of North Brabant province in south central Netherlands: French *Bois–le–Duc.*

Sher·wood (shûr′wŏŏd), **Robert Emmet,** 1896–1955, U.S. playwright.

Sherwood Forest An ancient forest, chiefly in Nottinghamshire, central England; celebrated as the home of Robin Hood and his men.

she's (shēz) **1** She is. **2** She has.

Shet·land Islands (shet′lənd) A Scottish island group NE of the Orkney Islands, comprising a county of northern Scotland (**Shetland**: also *Zetland*); 551 square miles; several hundred islands, 24 inhabited; capital, Lerwick, on Mainland, the largest island.

Shetland pony A small, hardy, shaggy breed of pony originally bred on the Shetland Islands.

Shetland sheepdog A long–haired black or brown working dog resembling a small collie, bred in the Shetland Islands.

Shetland wool Thin, very loosely twisted yarn from the wool of Shetland sheep; also, the wool.

sheuch (shükh) *n. Scot.* A ditch or open drain. Also **sheugh.**

sheuk (shœk) *Scot.* Past tense and past participle of SHAKE.

shew (shō) Older spelling of SHOW.

shew·bread (shō′bred′) *n.* Unleavened bread formerly displayed in the Jewish temple: also spelled *showbread.*

she–wolf (shē′wŏŏlf′) *n. pl.* **–wolves** (-wŏŏlvz′) A female wolf.

Shey·enne River (shī·en′) A river in North Dakota, flowing 325 miles east and south to the Red River of the North.

Shi·ah (shē′ə) *n.* **1** One of the two great sects (Sunni and Shiah) of Islam, consisting of followers of Ali, the cousin and son–in–law of Mohammed, who maintain that Ali was the first Imam and true Successor to the Prophet. **2** An adherent of Shiah: also called *Shiite*: also **Shie·ite** (shē′īt). [<Arabic *shi'i* a follower, sect]

shib·bo·leth (shib′ə·leth) *n.* A test word or pet phrase of a party; a watchword: from the Hebrew word *shibboleth,* given by Jephthah (*Judges* xii 4–6) as a test to distinguish his own men from the Ephraimites, who used the pronunciation *sibboleth.* [<Hebrew *shibbōleth* ear of corn]

Shi·be·li (shi·bā′lē), **Web·be** (web′ā) A river in Ethiopia and Somalia, flowing NE, then SE and south 1,200 miles to a swamp 25 miles inland from the Indian Ocean: also *Shebeli.* Also **Webi Shebeli, Webi Shibeli.**

Shi·de·ha·ra (shē·de·hä·rä), **Baron Kijuro,**

1872–1951, Japanese diplomat and statesman.
shied (shīd) Past tense and past participle of SHY.
shield (shēld) *n.* **1** A broad piece of defensive armor, commonly carried on the left arm; a large buckler. **2** Something that protects or defends; a defender; shelter. **3** Any device for covering or protecting something. **4** *Mil.* A screen of steel attached to a gun to protect the men who are serving it. **5** *Mining* A framework or screen of wood or iron protecting the workers: pushed forward as the work advances. **6** *Her.* The escutcheon upon which emblems of heraldry are depicted. **7** *Zool.* A platelike protective part, as the carapace of a crustacean. **8** A policeman's badge. See synonyms under DEFENSE, SHELTER. —*v.t.* **1** To protect from danger as with a shield; defend; guard. **2** *Archaic* To avert; forbid. —*v.i.* **3** To act as a shield or safeguard. See synonyms under SHELTER. [OE *sceld*] —**shield′er** *n.* —**shield′-bear′er** (-bâr′ər) *n.* —**shield′-shaped′** (-shāpt′) *adj.*

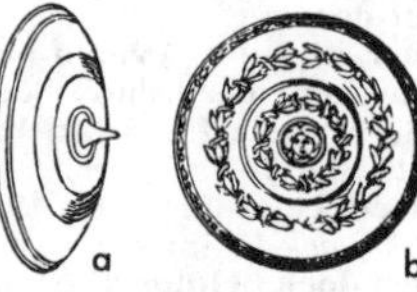

SHIELDS
a. Anglo-Saxon.
b. Greek.

shield bone *Anat.* The scapula or shoulder bone.
shield·fern (shēld′fûrn′) *n.* A fern (genus *Dryopteris*), so called from its shield-shaped sporangia.
Shield of David See MOGEN DAVID.
shiel·ing (shē′ling) *n.* A shepherd's or sportsman's hut: also spelled *shealing*. [Var. of SHEALING]
shi·er[1] (shī′ər) *n.* A horse in the habit of shying: also spelled *shyer*.
shi·er[2] (shī′ər), **shi·est** (shī′ist) Comparative and superlative of SHY.
shift (shift) *v.t.* **1** To change or move from one position, place, etc., to another. **2** To change for another or others of the same class. **3** To change (gears) from one arrangement to another. **4** *Ling.* To alter phonetically as part of a systematic change. —*v.i.* **5** To change position, place, etc. **6** To try varied expedients; do the best one can; manage. **7** To evade; equivocate. **8** To shift gears: The car *shifts* automatically. —*n.* **1** The act of shifting. **2** A recourse or contrivance adopted in the absence of direct means: We'll make *shift* to get along; hence, a dodge; artifice; trick; evasion. **3** *Archaic* or *Dial.* An undergarment; chemise. **4** A change of clothes. **5** A change of place, direction, or form: a *shift* in the wind; transfer, as of a burden. **6** A change of the position of the hand when playing on the fingerboard of an instrument of the viol class. **7** A relay of workers; also, the working time of each group. **8** *Physics* Any of various displacements of spectral lines caused by velocity of the light source, gravitational effect, etc. Compare EINSTEIN SHIFT, DOPPLER EFFECT. **9** *Geol.* The relative displacement of areas on opposite sides of a rock fault and outside of the zone of dislocation. **10** *Ling.* **a** A patterned phonetic or phonemic change, as the consonant *shift* described in Grimm's Law. **b** Functional shift. See synonyms under CHANGE, CONVEY. [OE *sciftan* divide] —**shift′er** *n.*
shift·less (shift′lis) *adj.* **1** Unable or unwilling to shift for oneself; inefficient or lazy. **2** Inefficiently done; showing lack of energy or resource. See synonyms under IMPROVIDENT. —**shift′less·ly** *adv.* —**shift′less·ness** *n.*
shift·y (shif′tē) *adj.* **shift·i·er, shift·i·est** **1** Full of expedients; alert; capable. **2** Artful; tricky; fickle. —**shift′i·ly** *adv.* —**shift′i·ness** *n.*
Shi·ge·mi·tsu (shē·ge·mē·tso͞o), **Mamoru**, 1887–1957, Japanese diplomat.
Shi Huang Ti (shir′ hwäng′ tē′), 259–210 B.C., Chinese emperor.
Shi·ism (shē′iz·əm) *n.* The doctrine held by the Shiah or Persian branch of Moslems, showing traces of the earlier Persian faith. See SHIAH.
Shi·ite (shē′īt) *n.* A Shiah. —**Shi·it′ic** (-it′ik) *adj.*
shi·kar (shi·kär′) *Anglo-Indian v.t.* To hunt. —*n.* Hunting; sport; the chase. [<Urdu <Persian]
shi·ka·ree (shi·kä′rē) *n.* A hunter or sportsman; especially, a native attendant and guide in the chase. Also **shi·kar′ree, shi·ka′ri.** [<Urdu *shikari*]
Shi·kar·pur (shi·kär′po͝or) A city in NE Sind, West Pakistan.
Shi·ko·ku (shē·kō·ko͞o) An island of SW Japan, east of Kyushu; 7,248 square miles.
Shil·ka (shil′kə) A river in SE Siberian Russian S.F.S.R., flowing 345 miles NE to the Amur.
shill[1] (shil) *adj. Scot.* Shrill.
shill[2] (shil) *n. Slang* The assistant of a sidewalk peddler or gambler who makes a purchase or bet to encourage onlookers to buy or bet; a capper. [Origin unknown]
shil·le·lagh (shi·lā′lə, -lē) *n.* In Ireland, a stout cudgel made of oak or blackthorn. See synonyms under STICK. Also **shil·la′lah, shil·lea′lah, shil·le′lah.** [from *Shillelagh,* a town in Ireland famed for its oaks]
shil·ling (shil′ing) *n.* **1** A current silver coin of Great Britain, first issued in 1504; twelvepence. Compare SOLIDUS (def. 2). **2** A former denomination of money in the United States varying in value from 12 1/2 to 16 2/3 cents. —**King's shilling** An English shilling formerly handed to a recruit on his joining the British military service: considered as binding as the signing of a contract: also **Queen's shilling.** [OE *scilling*]

PINE-TREE SHILLING
Issued by Massachusetts in 1652 (actual size).

shilling side Formerly, the west side of lower Broadway, New York, where the shops carried a cheaper grade of merchandise than on the other (the dollar) side.
Shil·long (shi·lông′) The capital of Khasi and Jaintia Hills district, India.
shil·ly-shal·ly (shil′ē·shal′ē) *v.i.* **·lied, ·ly·ing** **1** To act with indecision; be irresolute; vacillate. **2** To trifle. —*adj.* Weak; hesitating. —*n.* Weak or foolish vacillation; irresolution; any trifling. —*adv.* In an irresolute manner. [Dissimilated reduplication of *shall I*?] —**shil′ly-shal′li·er** *n.*
Shi·loh (shī′lō) **1** An ancient Israelite sanctuary in central Palestine, NW of the Dead Sea. **2** A national military park in SW Tennessee; 6 square miles; scene of a Confederate defeat in the Civil War, 1862; established 1894.
shil·pit (shil′pit) *adj. Scot.* **1** Watery and insipid; weak: *shilpit* drink. **2** Sickly; puny: a *shilpit* girl.
shi·ly (shī′lē) See SHYLY.
shim (shim) *n.* In machinery, stoneworking, and railroading, a piece of metal or other material used to fill out space, as where joints are worn loose, or between something and its support. —*v.t.* **shimmed, shim·ming** To wedge up or fill out to a proper position or level by inserting a shim. [Origin uncertain]
Shi·mi·zu (shē·mē·zo͞o) A port on central Honshu island, Japan.
shim·mer (shim′ər) *v.i.* To shine faintly; give off or emit a tremulous light; glimmer. —*n.* A tremulous shining or gleaming; glimmer; gleam. See synonyms under LIGHT. [OE *scimerian,* prob. freq. of *scīnan* shine] —**shim′mer·y** *adj.*
shim·my (shim′ē) *n. pl.* **·mies** *U.S.* **1** *Colloq.* A chemise. **2** A jazz dance accompanied by shaking movements: also **shimmy shake. 3** Unusual vibration, as in automobile wheels. —*v.i.* **·mied, ·my·ing** **1** To vibrate or wobble. **2** To dance the shimmy. [Alter. of CHEMISE]
Shim·o·no·se·ki (shim′ə·nō·sä′kē, *Japanese* shē·mō·nō·sä·kē) A port of SW Honshu island, Japan, on **Shimonoseki Strait,** a narrow channel between Honshu and Kyushu, connecting the Sea of Japan with the Inland Sea.
shin[1] (shin) *n.* **1** The front part of the leg below the knee; also, the shin bone. **2** The lower foreleg: a *shin* of beef. —*v.t.* & *v.i.* **shinned, shin·ning** **1** To climb (a pole) by gripping with the hands or arms and the shins or legs: usually with *up.* **2** To kick (someone) on the shins. [OE *scinu*]
shin[2] (shēn) *n.* The twenty-first Hebrew letter. See ALPHABET.
Shi·nar (shī′när) An ancient country along the lower Tigris and Euphrates. *Gen.* x 10.
shin bone The tibia.
shin·dig (shin′dig) *n. U.S. Slang* A dance or noisy party. [? < *a dig on the shin*]
shin·dy (shin′dē) *n. pl.* **·dies** **1** *Slang* A riotous quarrel; row; also, a dance or shindig. **2** The game of shinny. [Var. of SHINNY]
shine (shīn) *v.i.* **shone** or (*esp. for def.* 5) **shined, shin·ing** **1** To emit light; beam; glow. **2** To gleam, as by reflected light. **3** To excel or be conspicuous in splendor, beauty, or intellectual brilliance; be preeminent. —*v.t.* **4** To cause to shine. **5** To brighten by rubbing or polishing. —**to shine up to** *Slang* To try to please. —*n.* **1** The state or quality of being bright or shining; radiance; luster; sheen. **2** Fair weather; sunshine. **3** *U.S. Colloq.* A liking or fancy. **4** *U.S. Colloq.* A smart trick or prank. **5** A gloss or polish on shoes. See synonyms under LIGHT. —**to take a shine to** *U.S. Colloq.* To become fond of. [OE *scīnan*]

Synonyms (verb): beam, coruscate, glare, gleam, glisten, glitter, glow, scintillate, sparkle.
shin·er (shī′nər) *n.* **1** One who or that which shines or causes to shine. **2** A bright or gold coin. **3** One of various silvery cyprinoid freshwater fishes (genus *Notropis*) common in North America. **4** A bristletail. **5** *Slang* A black eye from a blow.
shin·gle[1] (shing′gəl) *n.* **1** A thin, tapering piece of wood or other material, usually about 18 inches long and 4 or more inches wide, used in courses to cover roofs. **2** A small sign board, as a shingle or a brass plate, bearing the name of a doctor, lawyer, etc., and placed outside his office. **3** A short haircut. —*v.t.* **·gled, ·gling** **1** To cover (a roof, building, etc.) with or as with shingles. **2** To cut (the hair) short all over the head. [Alter. of ME *schindle* <L *scindula,* var. of *scandula* a shingle] —**shin′gler** *n.*
shin·gle[2] (shing′gəl) *n.* **1** Rounded, water-worn detritus, coarser than gravel, found on the seashore. **2** A place strewn with shingle, as a beach. [Cf. Norw. *singl* coarse gravel] —**shin′gly** *adj.*
shin·gle[3] (shing′gəl) *v.t.* **·gled, ·gling** *Metall.* To drive out impurities from (puddled iron) by heavy blows or pressure. [Origin unknown]
shingle oak The jack oak.
shin·gles (shing′gəlz) *n. Pathol.* A skin disease, most commonly due to an infection, but also to nervous trouble, accompanied by neuralgia, with eruptions sometimes extending half round the body like a girdle: also called *herpes zoster.* [Alter. of Med. L *cingulus* <L *cingulum* girdle < *cingere* gird]
shin·ing (shī′ning) *adj.* **1** Emitting or reflecting a continuous light; gleaming; luminous. **2** Of unusual brilliance or excellence; conspicuous. —**shin′ing·ly** *adv.*
shin·leaf (shin′lēf′) *n.* A low perennial herb (*Pyrola elliptica*), with rounded evergreen root leaves, common in the woods of the northern United States. [From the use of its leaves for shinplasters]
shin·ny[1] (shin′ē) *n.* A game resembling hockey, or one of the sticks or clubs used by the players. Also **shin′ney.** [< *shin ye,* a cry used in the game]
shin·ny[2] (shin′ē) *v.i.* **·nied, ·ny·ing** *U.S. Colloq.* To climb using one's shins: usually with *up.*
shin·plas·ter (shin′plas′tər, -pläs′-) *n.* **1** *U.S.* **a** Fractional currency issued by other than the constituted authorities. See FRACTIONAL CURRENCY. **b** Any scrip or paper money issued by private enterprises. **2** A plaster for a sore shin.
shin·ti·yan (shin′tē·yan) *n. pl.* Wide loose trousers worn by Moslem women. [<Arabic < Turkish *chintiyan*]
Shin·to (shin′tō) *n.* The primitive religion of Japan, consisting chiefly in ancestor worship, nature worship, and the worship of many ethnic divinities, from the chief of whom the Emperor is thought to be descended, and thus himself a god: as **State Shinto,** it was the state religion of Japan, 1868–1945, and in that

period incorporated many nationalistic and militaristic elements, later minimized. Also **Shin'to·ism.** [<Japanese, way of the gods < Chinese *shin* god + *tao* way or law] —**Shin'·to·ist** *n.*

shin·y (shī'nē) *adj.* **shin·i·er, shin·i·est 1** Glistening; glossy; polished. **2** Bright; clear.

ship (ship) *n.* **1** Any vessel suitable for deep-water navigation: a *steamship,* sailing *ship.* **2** A large seagoing sailing vessel with at least three masts, carrying square-rigged sails on all three. **3** An airship or airplane. **4** Figuratively, fortune: when my *ship* comes in. — **capital ship** Any vessel of war of the first rank, as a battleship, battle cruiser, or aircraft carrier. —*v.* **shipped, ship·ping** *v.t.* **1** To transport by ship or other mode of conveyance. **2** To send by any established mode of transportation, as by rail. **3** To hire and receive for service on board a vessel, as sailors. **4** *Naut.* To receive over the side, as in rough weather: to *ship* a wave. **5** *Colloq.* To get rid of. **6** To set or fit in a prepared place on a boat or vessel, as a mast, or a rudder; also, to draw (oars) inside a boat from rowlocks. —*v.i.* **7** To go on board ship; embark. **8** To undergo shipment: Raspberries do not *ship* well. **9** To enlist as a seaman. [OE *scip*]

FULL-RIGGED SHIP
With double topsails and staysails.
a. Flying jib. *b.* Jib. *c.* Foretopmast staysail. *d.* Foresail. *e.* Mainsail. *f.* Crossjacksail. *g.* Spanker. *h.* Maintopmast staysail. *i.* Mizzentopmast staysail. *j.* Lower foretopsail. *k.* Lower maintopsail. *l.* Lower mizzentopsail. *m.* Upper foretopsail. *n.* Upper maintopsail. *o.* Upper mizzentopsail. *p.* Foretopgallant sail. *q.* Maintopgallant sail. *r.* Mizzentopgallant sail. *s.* Fore royal. *t.* Main royal. *u.* Mizzen royal. *v.* Main skysail. *w.* Maintopgallant staysail. *x.* Mizzentopgallant staysail. *y.* Main royal staysail.

-ship *suffix of nouns* **1** The state, condition, or quality of: *friendship.* **2** Office, rank, or dignity of: *kingship.* **3** The art or skill of: *marksmanship.* [OE *-scipe*]

ship biscuit Hardtack; sea biscuit.

ship·board (ship'bôrd', -bōrd') *n.* The side or deck of a ship; hence, a vessel: only in phrase **on shipboard.**

ship broker A mercantile agent who buys and sells ships, cargoes, etc. Also **ship·bro·ker** (ship'brō'kər). —**ship'bro'ker·age** *n.*

ship·build·er (ship'bil'dər) *n.* One who designs, superintends, contracts for, or works at the building of vessels. —**ship'build'ing** *n.*

ship canal A waterway or canal deep enough for seagoing vessels.

ship carpenter 1 A carpenter who builds or repairs vessels; a shipwright. **2** A carpenter attached to a vessel.

ship chandler One who deals in cordage, canvas, and other furniture of vessels.

ship fever Prison fever.

Ship·ka Pass (ship'kä) A pass in the central Balkan Mountains, central Bulgaria; elevation, 4,166 feet; scene of a defeat of the Turks by the Bulgarians, 1877.

ship·load (ship'lōd') *n.* The quantity that a ship carries or can carry; a cargo.

ship·man (ship'mən) *n. pl.* **·men** (-mən) A sailor; mariner.

ship·mas·ter (ship'mas'tər, -mäs'-) *n.* The captain or master of a merchant ship.

ship·mate (ship'māt') *n.* A fellow sailor.

ship·ment (ship'mənt) *n.* The act of shipping, or that which is shipped; a consignment.

ship money An impost levied by the sovereign on English maritime towns and counties, for providing and arming a fleet for the protection of the coast: originated about 1007 and declared illegal by Parliament in 1640.

ship of the line Formerly, a man-of-war large enough to take a position in a line of battle.

ship owner A person owning a ship, ships, or shares in them. —**ship owning**

ship·pa·ble (ship'ə·bəl) *adj.* That can be shipped or transported.

ship·pen (ship'ən) *n. Scot.* A cow shed; barn. Also **ship'pon.**

ship·per (ship'ər) *n.* **1** One who or that which ships. **2** Any appliance for shifting some part of a machine, as in a loom. **3** A skipper; mariner.

ship·ping (ship'ing) *n.* **1** Ships collectively; the body of vessels belonging to a country or port; also, tonnage. **2** The act of shipping, in any sense. **3** *Obs.* A voyage.

shipping ton A freight ton. See under TON (def. 3).

ship-rigged (ship'rigd') *adj. Naut.* Rigged as a ship; square-rigged. See illustration under SHIP.

ship·shape (ship'shāp') *adj.* Well arranged; trim; orderly; neat. —*adv.* In a seamanlike manner; neatly.

ship's papers The documents required by international law to be carried by a ship, as bills of lading, bill of health, invoices, logbook, proofs of ownership; also, certificate of registry, crew-list, clearance, license, and shipping articles. Compare MANIFEST.

ship's time *Naut.* The time as shown by the deck clock: usually local mean time at whatever meridian a vessel happens to be.

ship·way (ship'wā') *n.* **1** The ways on which a ship is built or examined. **2** A ship canal.

ship·worm (ship'wûrm') *n.* One of a family *(Teredinidae)* of marine bivalves, resembling worms, especially *Teredo navalis,* which burrows into the timbers of ships, piers, wharfs, etc.: also called *borer.*

ship·wreck (ship'rek') *n.* **1** The partial or total destruction of a ship at sea. **2** Utter or practical destruction; ruin. **3** Scattered remnants, as of a wrecked ship; wreckage. —*v.t.* **1** To wreck, as a vessel. **2** To bring to disaster; ruin; destroy.

ship·wright (ship'rīt') *n.* A ship carpenter or builder; one who works on the wooden parts of ships.

ship·yard (ship'yärd') *n.* An enclosure where ships are built or repaired.

shipyard eye *Pathol.* Kerato-conjunctivitis.

Shi·raz (shē·räz') A city in SW Iran.

shire (shīr) *n.* **1** A territorial division of Great Britain; a county. **2** A county in America: used only in compounds and proper names borrowed from England. [OE *scīr*]

Shi·ré (shē'rā) A river of southern Nyasaland and central Mozambique, SE Africa, flowing 250 miles south from Lake Nyasa to the Zambezi. *Portuguese* **Chi·re** (shē'rə).

shire horse One of a breed of large draft horses originating in the shires or midland counties of England. Also **Shire.**

shire town The capital of a county; county seat; county town.

shirk (shûrk) *v.t.* **1** To avoid the doing of; evade doing (something that should be done). **2** *Obs.* To obtain by trickery. —*v.i.* **3** To avoid work or evade obligation. [<*n.*] —*n.* One who shirks; also **shirk'er.** [Prob. <G *Schurke* rascal. Akin to SHARK[2].]

Shir·ley (shûr'lē), **James,** 1596–1666, English dramatist.

Shir·pu·la (shir·pŏŏ'lə) See LAGASH.

shirr (shûr) *v.t.* **1** To gather on parallel gathering threads. **2** To bake with crumbs in a buttered dish, as eggs. —*n.* **1** A fulling or gathering by threads. **2** A rubber thread woven into a fabric to make it elastic. [Origin unknown]

shirt (shûrt) *n.* **1** A loose garment for the upper part of the body, usually having collar and cuffs and a front closing. **2** A closely fitting undergarment for the upper part of the body. **3** The inner lining of a blast furnace. —**to keep one's shirt on** *Slang* To remain calm; keep one's temper. —**to lose one's shirt** *Slang* To lose everything. [OE *scyrte* shirt, short garment. Akin to SKIRT.] —**shirt'less** *adj.*

shirt·ing (shûr'ting) *n.* Closely woven material of cotton, linen, silk, etc., used for making shirts, blouses, dresses, etc.

shirt-waist (shûrt'wāst') *n.* A tailored, sleeved blouse or shirt: usually worn tucked in under skirt or trousers.

Shir·wa (shir'wä) See CHILWA.

shish ke·bab (shish' kə·bäb') Beef or lamb, cut into cubes and cooked on skewers with onions, green peppers, and tomatoes. [<Arm. *shish kabab*]

shist (shist) See SCHIST, etc.

shit·tim·wood (shit'im·wŏŏd') *n.* In the Bible, the wood of a species of acacia (the **shit'tah** or **shittah tree**) used in making the furniture of the Jewish tabernacle. Also **shit'tim.** [<Hebrew *shiṭṭīm,* pl. of *shiṭṭāh*]

shiv (shiv) *n. Slang* In the criminal underworld, a knife or razor: often spelled *chevy, chiv.* Also **shive, shiv'y.** [<Romany *chiv* goad]

Shi·va (shē'və) See SIVA.

shiv·a·ree (shiv'ə·rē') *n. U.S.* A charivari, especially in the sense of the burlesque serenade of newly-weds. [Alter. of CHARIVARI]

shive[1] (shīv) *n. Brit. Dial.* **1** A short flat cork; a thin wooden bung. **2** *Brit.* A slice cut off, as of bread. [Cf. ON *skifa* slice]

shive[2] (shīv) *n.* A thin fragment; sliver; a woody fragment separated from flax by breaking. [Back formation <SHIVER[2]]

shiv·er[1] (shiv'ər) *v.i.* To tremble, as with cold or fear; shake; vibrate; quiver. —*v.t. Naut.* To cause to flutter in the wind, as a sail. See synonyms under QUAKE. —*n.* The act of shivering; a shaking or quivering from any cause. [? Blend of SHAKE and QUIVER]

shiv·er[2] (shiv'ər) *v.t. & v.i.* To break suddenly into fragments; shatter. See synonyms under BREAK, SHAKE. —*n.* A splinter; sliver. [ME *schivere;* origin uncertain]

shiv·er·y[1] (shiv'ər·ē) *adj.* Chilly; tremulous.

shiv·er·y[2] (shiv'ər·ē) *adj.* Easily shivered; brittle.

Shi·zu·o·ka (shē·zōō·ō·kä) A city on central Honshu island, Japan.

shlock (shlok) See SCHLOCK.

shoal[1] (shōl) *n.* **1** A shallow place in any body of water. **2** A sandbank or bar, especially one seen at low water. Compare BANK and REEF. —*v.i.* **1** To become shallow. —*v.t.* **2** To make shallow. **3** To sail into a lesser depth of (water), as shown by soundings: The ship *shoaled* her water off Cape Hatteras. —*adj.* Of little depth; shallow. Also, *Scot., shaul.* [OE *sceald* shallow]

shoal[2] (shōl) *n.* An assemblage or multitude; throng, as of fish. —*v.i.* **1** To throng in shoals or multitudes. **2** To school: said of fish. [OE *scolu* shoal of fish. Akin to SCHOOL[2].]

shoal duck The American eider duck: so called from Isles of Shoals, off Portsmouth, New Hampshire.

shoal·y (shō'lē) *adj.* Abounding in shoals.

shoat (shōt) *n.* **1** A young hog. **2** A worthless fellow. Also spelled *shote.* [Cf. West Flemish *schote* young pig]

shock[1] (shok) *n.* **1** A violent collision or concussion; impact; blow. **2** A sudden and violent sensation, as if causing one to shake or tremble; a stroke: a *shock* of paralysis. **3** A sudden agitation of the mind; startling emotion. **4** *Pathol.* Prostration of bodily functions, as from sudden injury. **5** The passage of a strong electric current through the body, or the phenomena it produces: characterized by involuntary muscular contractions. See synonyms under BLOW, COLLISION. —*v.t.* **1** To shake by sudden collision; jar; give a shock to. **2** To disturb the emotions or mind of; horrify; disgust. **3** To encounter with hostile intent; meet with sudden encounter. —*v.i.* **4** *Archaic* To come into violent contact; collide. [<F *choc* <*choquer* <Gmc. Cf. MDu. *schokken* collide.]

shock[2] (shok) *n.* A number of sheaves of grain, stalks of maize, or the like, stacked for drying upright in a field. —*v.t. & v.i.* To gather (grain) into a shock or shocks. [ME *schokke* <Gmc. Cf. MLG *schok.*] —**shock'er** *n.*

shock[3] (shok) *adj.* Shaggy; bushy. —*n.* **1** A coarse, tangled mass, as of hair. **2** A dog with a woolly coat. [? Var. of SHAG]

shock absorber *Mech.* **1** A device designed to absorb the energy of sudden impacts or of abrupt changes in velocity, as the springs of an automobile, or an airplane landing gear. **2** A type of damper which absorbs motion, as of a part or mechanism, by hydraulic action, friction, etc.

shock action *Mil.* A sudden, violent attack by mobile and massed military units, as tanks, artillery, infantry with bayonets fixed, etc.

shock·er (shok′ər) *n.* **1** One who or that which shocks or startles. **2** *Brit. Colloq.* A sensational novel.

shock excitation *Electr.* The excitation of an oscillatory circuit by an impulse of different frequency, as in radio: also called *impulse excitation.*

shock·head (shok′hed′) *adj.* Having thick, bushy hair. Also **shock′-head′ed.**

shock·ing (shok′ing) *adj.* Causing a mental shock; striking as with horror or disgust; repugnant; distressing. See synonyms under AWFUL, FLAGRANT, FRIGHTFUL. — **shock′ing·ly** *adv.* — **shock′ing·ness** *n.*

shock tactics *Mil.* The use of a preponderating mass of picked troops in an attack in which hand-to-hand encounter is relied upon more than gunfire.

shock therapy *Med.* The treatment of certain nervous and mental disorders by the subcutaneous injection of drugs, as Metrazol, insulin, camphor, etc., or by electrical shocks.

shock troops *Mil.* Seasoned or picked men selected to lead an attack.

shock wave *Physics* A wave (of air, sound, etc.) having a pattern of flow which changes abruptly, with corresponding changes in temperature, pressure, and density: characteristic of bodies moving at or above the speed of sound.

shod (shod) Past tense and alternative past participle of SHOE.

shod·dy (shod′ē) *n. pl.* **·dies** **1** Reclaimed wool obtained by shredding discarded woolens or worsteds: longer fiber than mungo and better quality. **2** Fiber or cloth manufactured of inferior material or of shredded woolen rags. **3** Vulgar assumption or display; pretension; sham. **4** Refuse; waste. — *adj.* **·di·er, ·di·est** **1** Made of or containing shoddy. **2** Sham; inferior. [Origin uncertain] — **shod′di·ly** *adv.* — **shod′di·ness** *n.*

shoe (shōō) *n. pl.* **shoes** (*Obs.* **shoon**) **1** An outer covering, usually of leather, for the human foot, usually distinguished from a *boot* by not reaching above the ankle. **2** Something resembling a shoe in position or use. **3** A rim or plate of iron to protect the hoof of an animal from wear or injury. **4** A strip of iron, steel, or other hard material fitted under a sleigh or sledge runner to receive friction. **5** A drag of iron or wood placed under the wheel of a vehicle to retard its motion in going downhill; also, the part of a brake that presses upon the wheel. **6** An iron socket or ferrule for protecting the point of a wooden pile, or the end of a handspike, pole, or staff. **7** The tread or outer covering of a pneumatic tire, as for an automobile. **8** The part of a bridge on which the superstructure rests. **9** The sliding contact plate on an electric car. — *v.t.* **shod, shod** or **shod·den, shoe·ing** **1** To furnish with shoes or the like. **2** To furnish with a guard of metal, wood, etc., for protection, as against wear. [OE *scōh*]

PARTS OF A SHOE

a.	Tongue.	*h.*	Slipsole.
b.	Top.	*i.*	Insole.
c.	Lacing.	*j.*	Shank.
d.	Eyelets.	*k.*	Heel.
e.	Vamp.	*l.*	Counter.
f.	Toe cap.	*m.*	Backstay.
g.	Outsole.	*n.*	Backstrap.

shoe·bill (shōō′bil′) *n.* A heron (*Balaeniceps rex*) of central Africa, with a huge vaulted and hooked bill.

shoe·black (shōō′blak′) *n.* A bootblack.

shoe findings Shoemakers' tools and supplies, with the exception of leather.

shoe·horn (shōō′hôrn′) *n.* A smooth curved implement of horn or other material shaped to aid in putting on a shoe.

shoe·mak·er (shōō′mā′kər) *n.* **1** One who makes shoes, boots, etc. **2** A cobbler. — **shoe′mak′ing** *n.*

sho·er (shōō′ər) *n.* One who supplies or fits on shoes; specifically, a blacksmith.

shoe·shine (shōō′shīn′) *n.* **1** The waxing and polishing of a pair of shoes. **2** The polished appearance thus given to the shoes.

shoe string A lace, cord, or ribbon for tying a shoe. Also **shoe lace.**

shoe·tree (shōō′trē′) *n.* A wooden or metal form for inserting in boots and shoes to preserve their shape or to stretch them: also called *boot-tree.*

sho·far (shō′fär) *n.* A ram's horn used in Jewish ritual, sounded on solemn occasions and in war. It is still blown on the Jewish New Year and on the Day of Atonement: also spelled *shophar.* [<Hebrew *shōphār*]

sho·gun (shō′gun, -gōōn) *n.* The hereditary commander in chief of the Japanese army until 1868: known to foreigners as the *tycoon.* [<Japanese <Chinese *chiang-chün* leader of an army] — **sho′gun·ate** (-it, -āt) *n.*

Sho·la·pur (shō′lə·pŏŏr) A town in central southern Bombay State, India.

shone (shōn, shon) Past tense and past participle of SHINE.

shoo (shōō) *interj.* Begone! be off! away!: used in driving away fowls. — *v.t.* To drive away by crying "shoo." — *v.i.* To cry "shoo." [Imit.]

shoo·fly (shōō′flī) *n. U.S.* **1** A shuffling dance; also, the music for it. **2** An enclosed child's rocker with sides representing horses, swans, etc. **3** A kind of pie with a sirupy filling made with molasses and brown sugar: also **shoofly pie.**

shoo-in (shōō′in′) *n. Colloq.* One who is virtually certain to win, as an election.

shook[1] (shŏŏk) Past tense of SHAKE.

shook[2] (shŏŏk) *n.* **1** A collection of barrel staves, shaped, chamfered, and arranged for assembling, conveniently bundled for transportation. **2** A set of boards in order for nailing together into a packing box, and conveniently bundled for transportation. **3** A shock of sheaves. [? Var. of SHOCK[2]]

shoon (shōōn) Obsolete plural of SHOE.

shoot (shōōt) *v.* **shot, shoot·ing** *v.t.* **1** To hit, wound, or kill with a missile discharged from a weapon. **2** To discharge (a missile) from a bow, rifle, etc. **3** To discharge (a weapon): often with *off*: to *shoot* a cannon. **4** To take the altitude of with a sextant, etc.: to *shoot* the sun. **5** To send forth as if from a weapon, as questions, glances, etc. **6** To pass over or through swiftly: to *shoot* rapids. **7** To go over (an area) in hunting game. **8** To emit, as rays of light. **9** To photograph; film. **10** To cause to stick out or protrude; extend. **11** To put forth in growth; send forth (buds, leaves, etc.). **12** To push into or out of the fastening, as the bolt of a door. **13** To propel, discharge, or dump, as down a chute or from a container. **14** To variegate, as with streaks of color: usually in the past participle: The morning clouds were *shot* with silver. **15** In games: **a** To score (a goal, point, etc.) by kicking or otherwise forcing the ball, etc., to the objective. **b** To play (golf, craps, pool, etc.). **c** To propel (a marble) from between the thumb and forefinger; play (marbles). **d** To cast (the dice). **16** *Slang* To inject (a drug, especially a narcotic). — *v.i.* **17** To discharge a missile from a bow, firearm, etc.: Don't *shoot*! **18** To go off; discharge. **19** To move swiftly; dart. **20** To hunt game. **21** To jut out; extend or project. **22** To put forth buds, leaves, etc.; germinate; sprout. **23** To take a photograph. **24** To start the cameras, as in motion pictures. **25** In games, to make a play by propelling the ball, puck, etc., in a certain manner. — **to shoot at** (or **for**) *Colloq.* To strive for; attempt to attain or obtain. — **to shoot down** To bring to earth by shooting. — **to shoot off one's mouth** *Slang* To talk too freely or too much. — **to shoot up** **1** To move or grow upward quickly. **2** To strike with several or many shots. **3** *SW U.S.* To ride through (a town, etc.) shooting recklessly in all directions. — *n.* **1** A young branch or sucker of a plant; offshoot. **2** A narrow passage in a stream; a rapid. **3** An inclined passage down which anything may be shot; a chute. **4** The act of shooting. **5** A shooting match, hunting party, etc. **6** The thrust of an arch. **7** An antler or horn just pushing up. **8** Shooting distance; range. **9** A rapid thrusting movement. [OE *scēotan*]

shoot·ing (shōō′ting) *n.* The act of one who or that which shoots.

shooting box A small house in a game district, furnishing accommodation for sportsmen. Also **shooting lodge.**

shooting gallery A place where one can go for target practice.

shooting iron *U.S. Slang* A firearm.

shooting star **1** A meteor. **2** Any of certain small perennial herbs (genus *Dodecatheon*); especially, the American cowslip (*D. meadia*) with oblong leaves and clusters of cyclamenlike flowers.

shoot-out (shōōt′out′) *n.* A battle involving an exchange of gunfire.

shop (shop) *n.* **1** A place for the sale of goods at retail: in the United States commonly called a *store.* **2** A place for making or repairing any article, or the carrying on of a craft. **3** One's own craft or business as a subject of conversation: to talk *shop.* — *v.i.* **shopped, shop·ping** To visit shops or stores to purchase or look at goods. [OE *sceoppa* booth]

shop·boy (shop′boi′), **shop·girl** (-gûrl′) *n.* A boy or a girl who works in a shop.

sho·phar (shō′fär) See SHOFAR.

shop·keep·er (shop′kē′pər) *n.* One who keeps a shop or store; a tradesman.

shop·lift·er (shop′lif′tər) *n.* One who steals goods exposed for sale in a shop. — **shop′·lift′ing** *n.*

shop·per (shop′ər) *n.* One who purchases or inspects goods in shops. — **shop′ping** *n.*

shopping center A group of retail stores, restaurants, etc., including an ample parking area, usually built as a unit and accessible chiefly by automobile.

shop talk Conversation limited to one's job or profession.

shop·walk·er (shop′wô′kər) *n. Brit.* A floorwalker; a person who walks about a shop to supervise employees and help customers.

shop·worn (shop′wôrn′, -wōrn′) *adj.* Soiled or otherwise deteriorated from having been handled or on display in a shop.

sho·ran (shôr′an, shō′ran) *n.* A high-precision electronic navigation system which transmits pulses, usually from an aircraft or ship, to ground stations at distances determined by the elapsed time between emission and return of the pulses. [<SHO(RT) RA(NGE) N(AVIGATION)]

shore[1] (shôr, shōr) *n.* **1** The coast or land adjacent to an ocean, sea, lake, or large river. ◆ Collateral adjective: *littoral.* **2** *Law* The ground between the ordinary high-water mark and low-water mark. See synonyms under BANK[1], LAND, MARGIN. — **in shore** Near or toward the shore. — *v.t.* **shored, shor·ing** **1** To set on shore. **2** To surround as with a shore. [ME *schore*; origin uncertain]

shore[2] (shôr, shōr) *v.t.* **shored, shor·ing** To prop, as a wall, by a vertical or sloping timber: usually with *up.* — *n.* A beam set endwise as a prop, as against the side of a building, a ship on the stocks, etc., especially as a temporary support. See illustration under DRYDOCK. [Cf. Du. *schoor* prop, ON *skordha* stay]

shore[3] (shôr, shōr) Archaic past tense of SHEAR.

shore bird Any of various birds (suborder *Charadrii*) which frequent beaches and also the shores of inland waters.

shore·less (shôr′lis, shōr′-) *adj.* Having no shore; boundless.

shore·line (shôr′līn′, shōr′-) *n.* The line or contour of a shore.

shore patrol A detail of the U. S. Navy, Coast Guard, or Marine Corps assigned to police duties ashore.

shore·ward (shôr′wərd, shōr′-) *adj.* & *adv.* Toward the shore. Also **shore′wards.**

shor·ing (shôr′ing, shō′ring) *n.* **1** The operation of propping, as with shores. **2** Shores, collectively.

shorl (shôrl) See SCHORL.

shorn (shôrn, shōrn) Alternative past participle of SHEAR.

short (shôrt) *adj.* **1** Having little linear extension; not long; of little extent; of no great distance. **2** Being below the average stature; not tall. **3** Having little extension in time; of limited duration; brief. **4** Abrupt in manner or spirit; curt; petulant; cross. **5** Not reaching or attaining a requirement, result, or mark; deficient; inadequate; scant: often with *of* **6** In finance or commerce, not having in possession when selling, but having to procure in time to deliver as contracted; not being in possession of the seller, as stocks or shares; of or pertaining to short stocks or commodities: *short* sales. **7** Not comprehensive or retentive; at fault; in error; narrow: said of persons or their faculties: *short* memory. **8** Breaking easily; friable; crisp. **9** *Phonet.* **a** Relatively brief in pronunciation: said of vowels. **b** Designating a set of vowel sounds which contrast with the "long" vowels. See LONG[1] (def. 9). **10** In classical prosody, requiring a relatively short time to pronounce: said of syllables containing a short vowel (epsilon, omicron, etc.) not followed by two consonants or a double consonant. **11** In English prosody, unaccented. **12** Less than: with *of.* **13** Concise; compressed. See synonyms under LITTLE, SCANTY, TERSE, TRANSIENT. — *n.* **1** The compressed substance or pith of a matter. **2** Anything that is short; a short syllable or vowel. **3** A deficiency, as in a payment. **4** A short contract or sale; one who has sold short; a bear. **5** *pl.* Bran mixed with coarse meal or flour. **6** *pl.* Trousers with legs extending part way to the knees: worn by both men and women. **7** *pl.* A man's undergarment covering the loins and often a portion of the legs. **8** In baseball slang, a shortstop. **9** *pl.* Clippings, scraps, etc., left over in the manufacture of different products and used to make an inferior quality of the product. **10** *Electr.* A short circuit. **11** A motion picture of relatively short duration as compared with the feature attraction on a program. — **for short** For brevity: Edward was called Ed *for short.* — **in short** In a word; briefly. — **the short and the long** The whole; the entire sum and substance. — *adv.* In a short manner or method, in any sense of the adjective: to stop *short,* to turn *short,* to sell *short.* — *v.t.* & *v.i.* To short-circuit. [OE *sceort* short] — **short′·ish** *adj.* — **short′ness** *n.*

Short (shôrt), **Walter Campbell,** 1880–1949, U. S. general.

short account **1** The account of a person who sells short on the stock market. **2** The open short sales as a whole.

short·age (shôr′tij) *n.* The amount by which anything is short; deficiency.

short·bread (shôrt′bred′) *n.* A rich, dry cake or cooky made with shortening.

short·cake (shôrt′kāk′) *n.* **1** A cake made short and crisp with butter or other shortening. **2** Cake or biscuit served with fruit usually between layers: strawberry *shortcake.*

short·change (shôrt′chānj′) *v.t.* **·changed, ·chang·ing** To give less change than is due to; hence, to cheat or swindle. — **short′chang′er** *n.*

short–cir·cuit (shôrt′sûr′kit) *v.t.* & *v.i.* To make a short circuit (in).

short circuit *Electr.* **1** A path of low resistance established between any two points in an electric circuit, thus shortening the distance traveled by the current. **2** Any defect in an electric circuit or apparatus which may result in a dangerous or wasteful leakage of current.

short·com·ing (shôrt′kum′ing) *n.* **1** Failure; remissness; delinquency. **2** A falling off; shortage, as of a crop.

short commons A scanty supply of food; a meager ration.

short covering The buying of stocks or securities to close out a short sale.

short–cut (shôrt′kut′) *v.t.* & *v.i.* To take a short cut (in).

short cut **1** A byway or path between two places shorter than the regular road. **2** A means or method that saves distance or time.

short–eared owl (shôrt′ird′) See under OWL.

short·en (shôr′tən) *v.t.* **1** To make short or shorter; curtail. **2** To reduce; diminish; lessen. **3** To furl or reef (a sail) so that less canvas is exposed to the wind. **4** To make brittle or crisp, as pastry, by adding shortening. — *v.i.* **5** To become short or shorter. See synonyms under ABBREVIATE, SCRIMP. — **short′en·er** *n.*

short·en·ing (shôr′tən·ing) *n.* **1** A fat, such as lard or butter, used to make pastry crisp. **2** An abbreviation. **3** The act of one who shortens.

short·hand (shôrt′hand′) *n.* Any system of rapid writing, as stenography or phonography. — *adj.* **1** Written in shorthand. **2** Using shorthand.

short–hand·ed (shôrt′han′did) *adj.* Not having a sufficient or the usual number of assistants, workmen, or hands.

short·head (shôrt′hed′) *n.* A brachycephalic individual. — **short′–head′ed** *adj.*

short·horn (shôrt′hôrn′) *n.* One of a breed of cattle with short horns, originally from northern England.

shor·ti·a (shôr′tē·ə) *n.* Any of a genus *(Shortia)* of perennial evergreen herbs with bell–shaped, nodding, white flowers. [after C. W. *Short,* 1794–1863, U. S. botanist]

Short·land Islands (shôrt′lənd) A group in the British Solomon Islands SE of Bougainville; total, 200 square miles.

short–lived (shôrt′līvd′, -livd′) *adj.* Living or lasting but a short time.

short·ly (shôrt′lē) *adv.* **1** At the expiration of a short time; quickly; soon. **2** In few words; briefly. **3** Curtly; abruptly.

short sale A sale for future delivery of goods or stocks not in possession at time of sale.

short shrift **1** A short time in which to confess before dying. **2** Little or no mercy or delay in dealing with a person or disposing of a matter.

short–sight·ed (shôrt′sī′tid) *adj.* **1** Unable to see clearly at a distance; myopic; nearsighted. **2** Lacking foresight. **3** Resulting from or characterized by lack of foresight. See synonyms under IMPRUDENT. — **short′–sight′ed·ly** *adv.* — **short′–sight′ed·ness** *n.*

short–spo·ken (shôrt′spō′kən) *adj.* Characterized by shortness or curtness of speech or manner; abrupt in address; gruff.

short–sta·ple (shôrt′stā′pəl) *adj.* Having a short fiber: in the United States, said of cotton fibers less than 1 1/8 inches long.

short·stop (shôrt′stop′) *n.* In baseball, an infielder stationed between second and third bases.

short story A narrative prose story presenting a central theme or impression, usually subordinated to a single mood or characterization: shorter than a novel or novelette, usually under 10,000 words.

short–tem·pered (shôrt′tem′pərd) *adj.* Easily aroused to anger.

short–term (shôrt′tûrm′) *adj.* Payable a short time after issue: said of securities.

short ton See under TON.

short wave A radio wave having a length of about 100 meters or less, corresponding to a frequency ranging upwards from about 3000 kilocycles. — **short′–wave′** *adj.*

short–wind·ed (shôrt′win′did) *adj.* Affected with difficulty of breathing; becoming easily out of breath.

Sho·sho·ne (shō·shō′nē) *n.* **1** One of a large and important tribe of North American Indians of northern Shoshonean stock of the Uto–Aztecan family, formerly occupying western Wyoming, central and southern Idaho, northeastern Nevada, and western Utah. **2** The Shoshonean language of this tribe. Also **Sho·sho′ni.**

Sho·sho·ne·an (shō·shō′nē·ən, shō′shə·nē′ən) *n.* The largest branch of the Uto–Aztecan linguistic family of North American Indians, including the Comanche, Paiute, Ute, and Shoshone plateau tribes, and the Hopi Indians. — *adj.* Of or pertaining to this linguistic branch. Also **Sho·sho′ni·an.**

Shoshone Cavern A national monument on the Shoshone River SW of Cody, Wyoming; 212.4 acres; established 1909.

Shoshone Falls A cascade in the Snake River, southern Idaho; over 200 feet high.

Shoshone River A river in NW Wyoming, flowing 100 miles NE to the Bighorn River.

Shos·ta·ko·vich (shos′tə·kô′vich), **Dmitri,** 1906–75, Russian composer.

shot[1] (shot) *n.* **1** *pl.* **shot** A solid missile, as a ball of iron, or a bullet or pellet of lead, to be discharged from a firearm; also, such spherules or pellets collectively. See illustration under CARTRIDGE. **2** The act of shooting; any stroke, hit, or blow. **3** One who shoots; a marksman. **4** The distance traversed or that can be traversed by a projectile; reach; range. **5** A blast, as in mining. **6** A stroke, especially in certain games, as in billiards. **7** A conjecture; guess. **8** An attempted performance. **9** A metal sphere which a competitor puts, pushes, or slings, in a distance contest. **10** A hypodermic injection. **11** A drink of liquor. **12** An action or scene recorded on motion–picture film. **13** A picture taken with a camera. **14** *Naut.* A unit of chain length: in the United States, 15 fathoms; in Great Britain, 12 1/2 fathoms. **15** *Obs.* Any projectile. — *v.t.* **shot·ted, shot·ting** To load or weight with shot. — *adj.* **1** Of changeable color, as when warp and weft are of different colors. **2** *Slang* More or less intoxicated. **3** *Colloq.* Completely done for; ruined. [OE *scot*]

shot[2] (shot) Past tense and past participle of SHOOT.

shot[3] (shot) *n.* A reckoning or charge, or a share of such a reckoning; scot. [Var. of SCOT]

shote (shōt) See SHOAT.

shot effect *Electronics* The background noise resembling the patter of small shot, developed in a vacuum tube by the fluctuating emission of electrons from the heated filament. Also **shot noise.**

shot glass A small glass for holding or measuring out one shot of liquor.

shot·gun (shot′gun′) *n.* A light, smoothbore gun, either single– or double–barreled, adapted for the discharge of shot at short range. — *adj.* **1** Having a clear passageway straight through: a *shotgun* house. **2** Coerced with, or as with, a shotgun: a *shotgun* wedding.

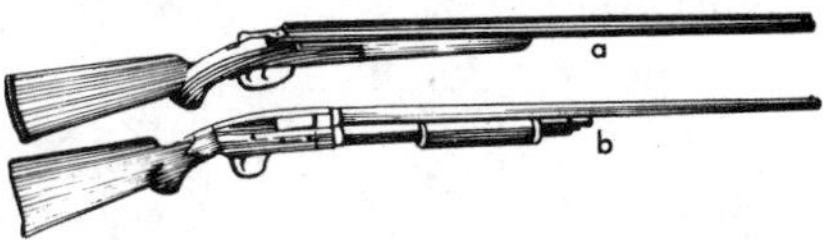

SHOTGUNS
a. Double–barrel hammerless shotgun.
b. Repeating shotgun.

shot peening A method for improving the mechanical properties of steel parts by bombarding the surfaces with metallic shot delivered under pressure or by centrifugal action.

shot–put (shot′po͝ot′) *n.* **1** An athletic contest in which a shot is thrown, or put, for distance. **2** A single put of the shot. — **shot′–put′ter** *n.*

shot·ten (shot′n) *adj.* Having spawned: said of a fish, especially a herring. [Obs. pp. of SHOOT]

should (sho͝od) Past tense of SHALL, but rarely a true past, rather chiefly used as a modal auxiliary which, while conveying varying shades of present and future time, expresses a wide range of subtly discriminated feelings and attitudes: **1** Obligation or propriety in varying degrees, but milder than *ought*: You *should* write that letter; *Should* we tell him the truth about his condition? His father thought that he *should* go; You *should* really taste that cake! **2** Condition: **a** Simple contingency, but involving less probability than *shall* or the present with future sense: If I *should* die before I wake . . . If I *should* go, he would go too. **b** Assumption: *Should* (=*Assuming that*) the space platform prove practicable, as seems almost certain, a trip to the moon will be easy. **3** Surprise at an unexpected event in the past: When I reached the station, whom *should* I run into but the detective! **4** Expectation: I *should* be at home by noon. ("I said that I *should* be home by noon" implies expectation, whereas "I said that I *would* be home by noon" implies intention.) **5** *U.S. Colloq.* Irony, in positive statement with negative force: He'll be fined heavily, but with all his money he *should* (=*need not*) worry! **6** Hesitation or deprecatory modesty, in the first person: I *should* hardly think so; We *should* like to have you come to dinner, if you are free and have nothing better to do. (Ordinarily, in American usage, but not in British, *would* is used in the first person, as well as in the second and third, before *like, prefer,* etc.: We *would,* or We'*d,* like to have you come to visit us.) See usage note under WOULD. [OE *scolde,* pt. of *sculan* owe]

shoul·der (shōl′dər) *n.* **1** The part of the trunk between the neck and the free portion of the arm or forelimb; also, the joint connecting the arm or forelimb with the body. **2** Anything which supports, bears up, or projects like a shoulder. 3 The forequarter of various animals. 4 An enlargement, projection, or offset, as for keeping something in place, or preventing movement past the projection. 5 *Printing* The top of the shank of a type when extending above or below the face of the letter. 6 Either edge of a road or highway. 7 The angle of a bastion included between a face and the adjacent flank: also **shoulder angle.** — **shoulder to shoulder** 1 Side by side and close together. 2 With united effort; in cooperation. — **straight from the shoulder** *Colloq.* Candidly; straightforwardly. — *v.t.* 1 To assume as something to be borne; sustain; bear. 2 To push with or as with the shoulder or shoulders. 3 To fashion with a shoulder or abutment; make a shoulder on. — *v.i.* 4 To push with the shoulder or shoulders. — **to shoulder arms** To rest a rifle against the shoulder, holding the butt with the hand on the same side, the arm being held bent and close to the side. [OE *sculder* shoulder]

shoulder blade The scapula.

shoulder loop 1 A strap worn on or over the shoulder to support an article of dress. 2 A strap of cloth marked with insignia of rank, worn by army and navy officers. Also **shoulder strap.**

shoulder patch A cloth insignia worn on the upper part of the sleeve of a uniform to indicate the branch or unit to which the wearer belongs.

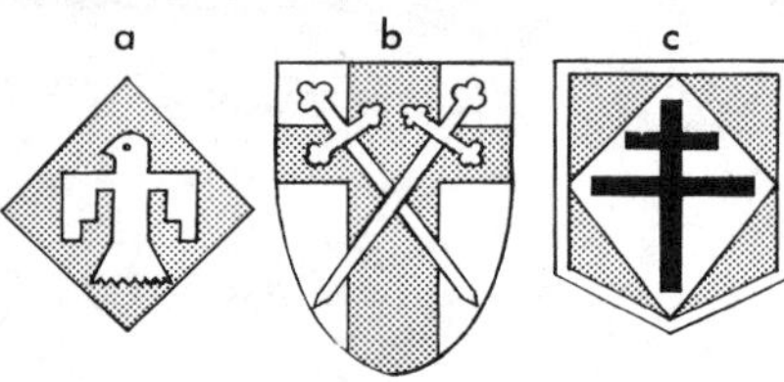

SHOULDER PATCHES
a. United States — 45th Division.
b. Great Britain — Army of Liberation.
c. France — Fighting French Commandos.

shoulder screw A screw having a shoulder, as for limiting the depth to which it may be sunk. See illustration under SCREW.

shoulder weapon Any small-arm weapon designed to be held against the shoulder in firing, as a rifle, carbine, etc.

should·na (shōōd′nə) *Scot.* Should not.

should·n't (shōōd′nt) Should not.

shout (shout) *n.* 1 A sudden and loud outcry, such as a call or command, but also expressing emotion, as of joy, exultation, courage, or derision; a loud burst of voice or voices. 2 *Austral. Slang* **a** A free drink or round of drinks. **b** One's turn to buy drinks. **c** One's turn to pay. — *v.t.* To utter with a shout; say or express loudly. — *v.i.* 1 To utter a shout; cry out loudly. 2 *Austral. Slang* To buy drinks for another or others. See synonyms under CALL, ROAR. [Origin unknown]

shout·er (shou′tər) *n.* One who shouts.

shouth·er (shōō′thər) *n. Scot.* The shoulder.

shove (shuv) *v.t.* & *v.i.* **shoved, shov·ing** 1 To push, as along a surface: to *shove* a boat with a pole. 2 To press forcibly (against); jostle. See synonyms under PUSH. — **to shove off** 1 To push along or away, as a boat. 2 *Colloq.* To depart. — *n.* 1 The act of pushing or shoving; strong push. 2 The woody center of flax. 3 *Can.* A forward movement of ice in a river. [OE *scūfan*] — **shov′er** *n.*

shov·el (shuv′əl) *n.* 1 A flattened scoop with a handle, as for digging, lifting earth, rock, etc. 2 *Colloq.* A shovel hat. — *v.* **·eled** or **·elled, ·el·ing** or **·el·ling** *v.t.* 1 To take up and move or gather with a shovel. 2 To toss hastily or in large quantities as if with a shovel. 3 To clear or clean with a shovel, as a path. — *v.i.* 4 To work with a shovel. [OE *scofl*]

shov·el·board (shuv′əl·bôrd′, -bōrd′) *n.* Shuffleboard.

shov·el·er (shuv′əl·ər, shuv′lər) *n.* 1 One who or that which shovels. 2 A large river duck (genus *Spatula*) with spatulate bill broadening roundly toward the end; especially, the **common shoveler** (*S. clypeata*) of the northern hemisphere: also *shovelbill.* Also **shov′el·ler.**

shovel hat A hat with broad brim turned up at the sides and projecting in front.

shov·el·head (shuv′əl·hed′) *n.* 1 A shark (*Sphyrna tiburo*) resembling the hammerhead, about 5 feet long. 2 The paddlefish. 3 The shovelnose (def. 1).

shov·el·nose (shuv′əl·nōz′) *n.* 1 A sturgeon (*Scaphirhynchus platyrhynchus*), common in the Mississippi valley, having a broad, depressed, shovel-shaped snout. 2 Any of several varieties of shark with a shovel-like nose; especially, the cow shark (*Hexanchus corinus*), found on the Pacific coast of the United States.

shov·el–nosed (shuv′əl·nōzd′) *adj.* Having a broad, flattened snout or beak.

show (shō) *v.* **showed, shown** or **showed, show·ing** *v.t.* 1 To cause or permit to be seen; present to view; exhibit; manifest; display. 2 To give in a marked or open manner; confer; bestow: to *show* favor. 3 To cause or allow (something) to be understood or known; explain; reveal; tell. 4 To cause (someone) to understand or see; explain something to; convince; teach. 5 *Law* To advance an allegation; plead: to *show* cause. 6 To make evident by logical process; prove; demonstrate. 7 To guide; lead; introduce, as into a room or building: with *in* or *up*: to *show* a caller in. 8 To indicate: The thermometer *shows* the temperature. 9 To enter in a show or exhibition. — *v.i.* 10 To become visible or known; be manifested or displayed. 11 To appear; seem. 12 To make one's or its appearance; be present. 13 *Colloq.* To give a theatrical performance; appear: to *show* in Newark. 14 *Colloq.* In racing, to be the third (horse, dog, etc.) to finish in a race. — **to show off** 1 To exhibit proudly or ostentatiously. 2 To make an ostentatious display of oneself, or of one's accomplishments. — **to show up** 1 To expose or be exposed, as faults. 2 To be evident or prominent. 3 To attend; arrive; make an appearance. 4 *Colloq.* To be better than. — *n.* 1 That which is shown; a public spectacle; a theatrical performance, circus, or motion picture; exhibition. 2 The act of showing; specifically, display; parade. 3 Pretense; semblance. 4 That which shows; an indication; promise; specifically, a sign of precious metal in a mine: a *show* of ore. 5 *Colloq.* An opportunity or chance. 6 *U.S. Colloq.* The third place in a race. — **the whole show** The center of interest or notice. [OE *scēawian*]

show·bill (shō′bil′) *n.* A poster announcing a play or show.

show biz *U.S. Slang* Show business.

show·boat (shō′bōt′) *n.* A boat, such as the old stern-wheelers on the Mississippi, on which a traveling troupe gives a theatrical performance.

show·bread (shō′bred′) See SHEWBREAD.

show business The entertainment arts, especially the theater, motion pictures, television, etc., collectively considered as an industry.

show·case (shō′kās′) *n.* A glass case for exhibiting and protecting articles for sale.

show·down (shō′doun′) *n.* 1 In poker, the play in which the hands are laid on the table face up. 2 Any action or any disclosure of facts, plans, etc., that brings an issue to a head.

show·er[1] (shou′ər) *n.* 1 A fall of rain, hail, or sleet, especially heavy rain of short duration within a local area. 2 A copious fall, as of tears, sparks, or other small objects. 3 A shower bath. 4 A variety of fireworks for simulating a shower of stars. 5 A party for the bestowal of gifts, as to a bride; also, the gifts. — *v.t.* 1 To sprinkle or wet with or as with showers. 2 To discharge in a shower; pour out. 3 To bestow with liberality. — *v.i.* 4 To fall as in a shower. 5 To take a shower bath. [OE *scūr*] — **show′er·y** *adj.*

show·er[2] (shō′ər) *n.* One who shows.

shower bath A bath in which water is sprayed on the body from an overhead, perforated nozzle.

show·folk (shō′fōk′) *n. pl.* Persons engaged in the entertainment business.

show–how (shō′hou′) *n. U.S. Colloq.* The teaching which imparts know-how: used especially in connection with the export of U.S. technological and agricultural aid and skills to backward areas of the world. [First in print in State Department publication on Point 4, Nov. 1949.]

show·ing (shō′ing) *n.* 1 Show; display, as of a quality. 2 Presentation; statement, as of a subject.

show·man (shō′mən) *n. pl.* **·men** (-mən) 1 One who exhibits or owns a show. 2 One who is skilled in presenting shows, etc. — **show′·man·ship** *n.*

Show Me State Nickname of MISSOURI.

shown (shōn) Past participle of SHOW.

show–off (shō′ôf′, -of′) *n. Colloq.* One who makes a pretentious display of himself; a swaggerer.

show·piece (shō′pēs′) *n.* 1 A prized object considered worthy of special exhibit. 2 An object on display.

show place A place exhibited for its beauty, historic interest, etc.

show ring A circular enclosure at a fair, cattle show, or other exhibition, where animals are shown to compete for prizes, or for sale.

show·y (shō′ē) *adj.* **show·i·er, show·i·est** 1 Making a great display; gaudy; gay; splendid. 2 Given to display; ostentatious. — **show′i·ly** *adv.* — **show′i·ness** *n.*

shrank (shrangk) Past tense of SHRINK.

shrap·nel (shrap′nəl) *n. pl.* **·nel** *Mil.* 1 A field artillery projectile for use against personnel, containing a quantity of metal balls and a time fuze and base charge which expel the balls in mid-air. 2 Shell fragments. [after Henry *Shrapnel,* 1761–1842, British artillery officer]

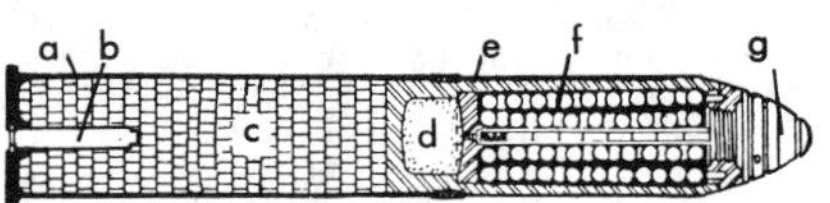

SHRAPNEL SHELL
a. Brass casing. *b.* Percussion primer. *c.* Smokeless powder. *d.* Black powder. *e.* Steel shell body. *f.* Shrapnel balls. *g.* Time fuze.

shred (shred) *n.* 1 A small irregular strip torn or cut off. 2 A bit; fragment; particle. See synonyms under PARTICLE. — *v.t.* **shred·ded** or **shred, shred·ding** 1 To tear or cut into shreds, as fibrous material. 2 *Brit. Dial.* To lop off; trim. [OE *scrēade* cutting]

shred·der (shred′ər) *n.* 1 One who or that which shreds. 2 A machine for cutting up corn or cane stalks, or for shredding wheat.

Shreve·port (shrēv′pôrt, -pōrt) A city on the Red River in NW Louisiana.

shrew (shrōō) *n.* 1 Any of numerous diminutive, mouse-like, insectivorous mammals (family *Soricidae*) having a long pointed snout and soft fur, as the **long-tailed shrew** (*Sorex longicauda*): also **shrew′mouse′.** ◆ Collateral adjective: *soricine.* 2 A woman of vexatious, scolding, or nagging disposition. — *v.t. Obs.* To berate; curse. [OE *scrēawa*]

SHREW
(Species vary from 1 1/2 to 6 inches in body length)

shrewd (shrōōd) *adj.* 1 Having keen insight; sharp; sagacious. 2 Artful; sly. 3 *Obs.* Keen or sharp; biting. 4 *Obs.* Shrewish; also, vexatious, vicious; dangerous. See synonyms under ACUTE, ASTUTE, INTELLIGENT, KNOWING, POLITIC, SAGACIOUS. [ME *shrewed,* pp. of *schrewen* curse < *shrew* malicious person] — **shrewd′ly** *adv.* — **shrewd′ness** *n.*

shrew·ish (shrōō′ish) *adj.* Like a shrew; ill-tempered. — **shrew′ish·ly** *adv.* — **shrew′ish·ness** *n.*

Shrews·bur·y (shrōōz′ber·ē, -bər·ē) A municipal borough and county town of Shropshire, England.

shriek (shrēk) *n.* A sharp shrill outcry or scream. — *v.i.* To utter a shriek. — *v.t.* To utter with or in a shriek. See synonyms under CALL, ROAR. [<ON *skrækja*] — **shriek′er** *n.*

shriev·al·ty (shrē′vəl·tē) *n. pl.* **·ties** The office, term, or jurisdiction of a sheriff. — **shriev′al** *adj.*

shrieve (shrēv) *n. Obs.* A sheriff. [Contraction of SHERIFF]

shrift (shrift) *n.* The act of shriving; confession; absolution. [OE *scrift*]

shrike (shrīk) *n.* Any of numerous birds (family *Laniidae*) with hooked bill, short wings, and long tail; especially, the **loggerhead shrike** (*Lanius ludovicianus*) of the southern Atlantic coast. [OE *scrīc* thrush]

shrill (shril) *adj.* **1** Having a high and piercing quality; sharp and piercing, as a sound. **2** Emitting a sharp, piercing sound. **3** *Poetic* Sharp to other senses than that of hearing; keen. —*v.t.* To cause to utter a shrill sound. —*v.i.* To make a shrill sound. —*adv.* Shrilly. [<Gmc. Cf. LG *schrell* having a sharp tone.] —**shrill'ness** *n.*

shrill·y (shril'ē) *adj. Poetic* Shrill, or somewhat shrill. —*adv.* (shril'lē) In a shrill manner.

shrimp (shrimp) *n. pl.* **shrimp** or **shrimps 1** Any of numerous diminutive, long-tailed, principally marine crustaceans (genus *Crago*), especially the edible shrimp *(C. vulgaris)* of the northern hemisphere. **2** *Slang* A small or insignificant person. [Akin to OE *scrimman* shrink]

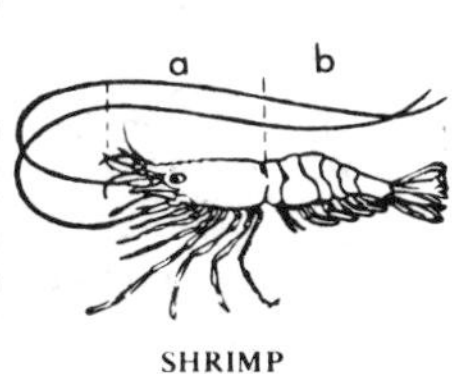

SHRIMP
a. Cephalothorax.
b. Abdomen.

shrine (shrīn) *n.* **1** A receptacle for sacred relics. **2** A place, as a tomb or a chapel, sacred to some holy personage, or considered as sanctified by the remains or presence of such. **3** A thing or spot made sacred by historic or other association. —*v.t.* **shrined, shrin·ing** To enshrine. [OE *scrīn* <L *scrinium* case, chest]

Shrine (shrīn) *n.* A secret fraternal order said to have been founded in Mecca, A.D. 646, and established in the United States in 1872: officially called *Ancient Arabic Order of Nobles of the Mystic Shrine.*

Shrin·er (shrī'nər) *n.* A member of the Shrine.

shrink (shringk) *v.* **shrank** or **shrunk, shrunk** or *less commonly* **shrunk·en, shrink·ing** *v.i.* **1** To draw together; contract, as from heat, cold, etc. **2** To diminish; become less or smaller. **3** To draw back, as from disgust, horror, or timidity; withdraw; recoil: with *from.* **4** To flinch; wince. —*v.t.* **5** To cause to shrink, contract, or draw together. See synonyms under WITHER. —*n.* **1** The act of shrinking; contraction. **2** *Slang* A psychiatrist or psychoanalyst. [OE *scrincan*] —**shrink'a·ble** *adj.* —**shrink'er** *n.*

shrink·age (shringk'ij) *n.* **1** Contraction, as of metal by cooling, or wood by drying. **2** The amount lost by contraction, depreciation, etc. **3** Decrease in value; depreciation.

shrive (shrīv) *v.* **shrove** or **shrived, shriv·en** or **shrived, shriv·ing** *v.t.* **1** To receive the confession of and give absolution to. **2** To obtain absolution for (oneself) by confessing one's sins and doing penance. —*v.i.* **3** To make confession. **4** To hear confession. [OE *scrifan*, ult. <L *scribere* write, prescribe] —**shriv'er** *n.*

shriv·el (shriv'əl) *v.t. & v.i.* **·eled** or **·elled, ·el·ing** or **·el·ling 1** To contract into wrinkles; shrink and wrinkle: often with *up.* **2** To make or become impotent; wither. [Origin uncertain. Cf. Sw. *skryvla.*]

shriv·en (shriv'ən) Alternative past participle of SHRIVE.

shroff (shrof) *n.* **1** In China and Japan, an expert detector of counterfeit money or base coin. **2** In India, a money-changer. [< Hind. *sarrāf* <Arabic]

Shrop·shire (shrop'shir, -shər) *n.* A breed of black-faced hornless sheep, noted for heavy fleece and superior mutton, originating in Shropshire.

Shrop·shire (shrop'shir, -shər) A county in western England on the border of Wales; 1,347 square miles; county town, Shrewsbury: also *Salop.*

shroud[1] (shroud) *n.* **1** A dress or garment for the dead; winding sheet. **2** Something that envelops or conceals like a garment. —*v.t.* **1** To dress for the grave; clothe in a shroud. **2** To envelop, as with a garment. **3** *Archaic* To shelter. —*v.i.* **4** *Obs.* To take shelter; go under cover; also, to gather together, as beasts, for warmth. See synonyms under MASK[1]. [OE *scrūd* a garment] —**shroud'less** *adj.*

shroud[2] (shroud) *n.* **1** *Naut.* **a** One of a set of ropes fitted in pairs and constituting part of the standing rigging of a vessel; specifically, one of the ropes, often of wire, stretched from a masthead to the sides or rims of a top, serving as means of ascent and as a lateral strengthening stays to the masts. **b** One of a pair or set of stay ropes or chains to give lateral support to a topmast, bowsprit, etc. **2** A guy, as a support for a smokestack: usually in the plural. **3** One of the supporting ropes attached to the edges of a parachute canopy. [< SHROUD[1]]

SHROUDS
a. Chain plates.
b. Shrouds.
c. Swifter.
d. Deadeyes.
e. Lanyards.
f. Ratlines.
g. Topmast backstays.

shroud-laid (shroud'lād') *adj.* Made of four strands twisted around a core: said of rope.

shrove (shrōv) Alternative past tense of SHRIVE.

Shrove·tide (shrōv'tīd') *n.* The three days immediately preceding Ash Wednesday **(Shrove Sunday, Shrove Monday, Shrove Tuesday),** on which confession is made in preparation for Lent. Compare QUINQUAGESIMA. [ME *schroftide* <stem of SHRIVE + TIDE[1], *n.* (def. 4)]

shrub[1] (shrub) *n.* A woody perennial plant of low stature, characterized by persistent stems and branches springing from the base. ◆ In popular language a shrub is a *bush.* [OE *scrybb* brushwood] —**shrub'by** *adj.*

shrub[2] (shrub) *n.* A beverage of sweetened fruit juice, sometimes with spirits. [<Arabic *sharāb.* See SHERBET.]

shrub-al·the·a (shrub'al·thē'ə) *n.* A hardy shrub *(Hibiscus syriacus)* of the mallow family: also called *rose of Sharon.*

shrub·ber·y (shrub'ər·ē) *n. pl.* **·ber·ies 1** Shrubs collectively. **2** A shrubby place; a collection of shrubs, as in a garden.

shrug (shrug) *v.t. & v.i.* **shrugged, shrug·ging** To draw up (the shoulders), as in displeasure, doubt, surprise, etc. —*n.* The act of shrugging the shoulders. [Origin uncertain]

shrunk (shrungk) Alternative past tense and past participle of SHRINK.

shrunk·en (shrungk'ən) Alternative past participle of SHRINK. —*adj.* Contracted and atrophied.

shtick (shtik) *n. U.S. Slang* An artificial or contrived device, mannerism, special area of knowledge, etc., intended to make one appear distinctive or unique; gimmick. Also spelled *schtick.* [<Yiddish <G *stück* piece, bit]

shuck (shuk) *n.* **1** A husk, shell, or pod, as of maize or peas; the outer covering of nuts. **2** A shell of an oyster or a clam. **3** *U.S. Colloq.* Something of little or no value: usually plural: not worth *shucks.* —*v.t.* **1** To remove the shucks of or from; remove the husk or shell from (corn, oysters, etc.). **2** *Colloq.* To take off or cast off, as clothes, or any outer covering. [? Metathetic alter. of HUSK] —**shuck'er** *n.*

shuck·ing (shuk'ing) *n. U.S. Colloq.* **1** A husking bee. **2** The removing of shucks, especially from corn.

shucks (shuks) *interj. U.S. Colloq.* A mild ejaculation expressing annoyance, disgust, etc.

shud·der (shud'ər) *v.i.* To tremble or shake, as from fright or cold; shiver; quake. —*n.* The act of shuddering; convulsive shiver, as from horror or fear; tremor. See synonyms under QUAKE, SHAKE. [Prob. freq. of OE *scūdan* move, shake] —**shud'der·ing** *adj.* —**shud'der·ing·ly** *adv.*

shuf·fle (shuf'əl) *n.* **1** A mixing or changing of the order of things, as of cards in a pack before each deal. **2** A hesitating, evasive, or tricky course; prevarication; artifice. **3** A scraping of the feet, as in walking; a slow, dragging gait. **4** A dance, or the step used in it, where the dancer pushes his foot along the floor at each step. —*v.* **·fled, ·fling** *v.t.* **1** To shift this way and that; mix; confuse; disorder; especially, to change the order of by mixing, as cards in a pack. **2** To move (the feet) along the ground or floor with a dragging gait. **3** To change from one place to another. **4** To make up or remove fraudulently or hastily; also, to put aside carelessly: with *up, off,* or *out.* —*v.i.* **5** To change position; shift ground. **6** To resort to indirect methods; prevaricate. **7** To dance the shuffle. **8** To scrape the feet along. **9** To scrape or struggle along awkwardly. [Prob. <LG *schuffeln* move with dragging feet, mix cards, etc.]

shuf·fle·board (shuf'əl·bôrd', -bōrd') *n.* **1** A game in which wooden or composition disks are slid by means of a pronged cue along a smooth surface toward numbered spaces. **2** The board or surface on which the game is played. Also spelled *shovelboard.*

shuf·fler (shuf'lər) *n.* **1** One who shuffles. **2** The scaup duck. **3** The coot.

shuf·fling (shuf'ling) *adj.* **1** Marked by awkward or clumsy movements. **2** Evading the truth; prevaricating.

shul (sho͞ol) *n.* A synagogue. [<Yiddish]

Shu·lam·ite (sho͞o'ləm·īt) The chief female character in the Song of Solomon, vi 13.

shun (shun) *v.t.* **shunned, shun·ning 1** To keep clear of; avoid; refrain from. **2** *Obs.* To escape; evade. **3** *Obs.* To abhor. See synonyms under ABHOR, ESCAPE. [OE *scunian*] —**shun'ner** *n.*

shun·pike (shun'pīk') *n.* A road taken by a motorist to avoid a turnpike or other express highway. —**shun'pik'ing,** *n.*

shunt (shunt) *n.* **1** A turning aside; the act of using a switch or shunt. **2** A railroad switch. **3** *Electr.* A conductor joining two points in a circuit and serving to divert part of the current. The proportion of the current diverted is regulated by the resistance of the shunt employed. —*v.t.* **1** To turn aside. **2** In railroading, to switch, as a train or car, from one track to another. **3** *Electr.* To distribute by means of shunts. **4** To evade by turning away from; put off on someone else, as a task. —*v.i.* **5** To move to one side. **6** *Electr.* To be diverted by a shunt: said of current. **7** To shift or transfer one's views or course. [Origin uncertain] —**shunt'er** *n.*

shunt-wound (shunt'wound') *adj. Electr.* Designating a type of direct-current motor in which the armature circuit and field circuit are connected in parallel: distinguished from *series-wound.*

shush (shush) *v.t.* To try to quiet; hush up, especially by making a noise like the sound (sh). [Imit.; infl. in form by HUSH]

Shu·shan (sho͞o'shän) Old Testament name for SUSA.

shut (shut) *v.* **shut, shut·ting** *v.t.* **1** To bring into such position as to close an opening or aperture; close, as a door, lid, or valve. **2** To close (an opening, aperture, etc.) so as to prevent ingress or egress. **3** To close and fasten securely, as with a latch or lock. **4** To forbid entrance into or exit from. **5** To keep from entering or leaving; confine or exclude; bar: with *in, out, from,* etc. **6** To close, fold, or bring together, as extended, expanded, or unfolded parts: to *shut* an umbrella. **7** To hide from view; obscure. —*v.i.* **8** To be or become closed or in a closed position. —**to shut down 1** To cease from operating, as a factory or mine; close up; stop work. **2** To lower; come down close: The fog *shut down.* **3** *Colloq.* To suppress: with *on.* —**to shut one's eyes to** To ignore. —**to shut out** In sports, to keep (an opponent) from scoring during the course of a game. —**to shut up 1** *Colloq.* To stop talking or cause to stop talking. **2** *Colloq.* To become exhausted and stop running, as a horse in a race. **3** To close all the entrances to, as a house. **4** To imprison; confine. —*adj.* **1** Made fast or closed. **2** Not sonorous; dull: said of sound. **3** *Phonet.* **a** Formed by closing the oral and nasal passages completely, preparatory to uttering certain sounds: said of certain consonants, as *t, p, k, b,* and *d.* **b** Cut off sharply by succeeding consonants: said of vowels, as *i* in *pit* and *o* in *top.* **4** *Dial.* Freed, as from something disagreeable; rid: with *of.* —*n.* **1** The act of shutting; also, the time of shutting, closing, or ending: the *shut* of day. **2** The place of shutting or closing together; specifically, the junction between welded pieces of metal. [OE *scyttan*]

Synonyms (verb): bar, beleaguer, block, blockade, close, confine, enclose, exclude, imprison, intercept, preclude, prohibit, seal, stop. *Antonyms:* expand, liberate, open, unbar, unclose, undo, unfasten.

shut·down (shut′doun′) *n.* The closing of or ceasing of work in a mine, mill, factory, or other industrial plant.

Shute (sho͞ot), **Nevil,** 1899–1960, English aeronautical engineer and writer: full name Nevil Shute Norway.

shut–eye (shut′ī′) *n. Slang* Sleep.

shut–in (shut′in′) *n.* An invalid who has to stay at home. —*adj.* **1** Obliged to stay at home. **2** Inclined to avoid people.

shut·off (shut′ôf′, -of′) *n. Mech.* A device for shutting something off.

shut·out (shut′out′) *n.* **1** A shutting out; especially, a lock–out. **2** In sports, a game in which one side is prevented from scoring; also, the action or the play that prevents scoring.

shut·ter (shut′ər) *n.* **1** One who or that which shuts. **2** That which shuts out or excludes; specifically, a cover, usually hinged, for closing an opening. **3** A hinged screen or cover for a window. **4** *Phot.* Any of various mechanisms for momentarily admitting light through a camera lens to the film or plate. —*v.t.* To furnish, close, or divide off with shutters.

shut·ter·bug (shut′ər·bug′) *n. Slang* A photography enthusiast. [<SHUTTER + BUG[1]]

shut·tle (shut′l) *n.* **1** A device used in weaving to carry the weft to and fro between the warp threads. **2** A similar rotating or other device in a sewing machine or the like. **3** A transport system operating between two near-by points. —*v.t.* & *v.i.* **·tled, ·tling** To move to and fro, like a shuttle. —*adj.* Pertaining to or designating any contrivance, action, etc., intended to operate back and forth between two points: *shuttle* bombing. [OE *scytel* missile; so called because shot to and fro in weaving]

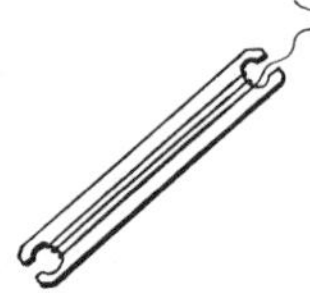
SHUTTLE (*def. 1*)

shuttle armature An H–armature.

shut·tle·cock (shut′l·kok′) *n.* A rounded piece of cork, with a crown of feathers, used in the game of badminton and of battledore and shuttlecock; the game itself. —*v.t.* To send or knock back and forth like a shuttlecock. [<SHUTTLE + COCK[1]]

shwan·pan (shwän′pän′) See SWANPAN.

shy[1] (shī) *v.i.* **shied, shy·ing 1** To start suddenly aside, as in fear: said of a horse. **2** To draw back, as from doubt or caution: with *off* or *away.* [< *adj.*] —*adj.* **shy·er, shy·est,** or **shi·er, shi·est 1** Easily frightened or startled, timorous. **2** Bashful; reserved; coy. **3** Circumspect, as from motives of caution; watchful; wary: with *of.* **4** Not easy to perceive, seize, or secure; elusive: a *shy* expression. **5** Not prolific: said of plants, trees, or, rarely, birds. **6** *Colloq.* Having a less amount of money than is called for or required. **7** Short; lacking: often with *on.* —*n.* A starting aside, as in fear. [OE *scēoh* timid. Akin to ESCHEW.] —**shy′ly** *adv.* —**shy′ness** *n.*

shy[2] (shī) *v.t.* & *v.i.* **shied, shy·ing** To throw with a swift, sidelong motion. —*n. pl.* **shies 1** A careless throw; fling, hence, a verbal fling; a sneer. **2** A trial; experiment. [Origin unknown]

shy·er (shī′ər) *n.* **1** One who shies. **2** A shying horse. Also spelled *shier.*

Shy·lock (shī′lok) In Shakespeare's *Merchant of Venice,* a revengeful usurer who endeavors to exact a pound of flesh from Antonio's body as a forfeit for non-payment of a debt; hence, any relentless creditor.

shy·ster (shīs′tər) *n.* **1** Anyone who conducts his business in an unscrupulous or tricky manner. **2** A lawyer who practices in an unprofessional manner, preys on petty criminals, etc. [? <SHY[1], in slang sense of "disreputable" + -STER]

si[1] (sē) See TI[1].

si[2] (sē) *adv.* Italian, Portuguese, and sometimes French, for "yes". [<L *sic* thus]

si·al (sī′al) *n. Geol.* A rock formation rich in silica and alumina which underlies sedimentary rock in continental land masses. —**si·al′·ic** *adj.* [<SI(LICA) + AL(UMINA)]

si·a·lid (sī′ə·lid) *n.* Any member of a family of insects (*Sialidae,* order *Megaloptera*), with enlarged or elongated thorax, including the hellgrammite and related genera. —*adj.* Of or pertaining to the *Sialidae.* Also **si·al·i·dan** (sī·al′ə·dən). [<Gk. *sialis,* kind of bird]

Si·al·kot (sē·äl′kōt) A city in the NE part of the former province of Punjab, NE West Pakistan.

sialo– *combining form* Saliva; pertaining to saliva: *sialogog.* Also, before vowels, **sial–.** [<Gk. *sialon* saliva]

si·al·o·gog (sī·al′ə·gog) *n.* Any agent exciting a flow of saliva. Also **si·al′a·gogue, si·al′o·gogue.** [<SIAL(O)- + -AGOG] —**si·a·lo·gog·ic** (sī′ə·lō·goj′ik) *adj.* & *n.*

si·a·loid (sī′ə·loid) *adj.* Like or resembling saliva.

Si·am (sī·am′) See THAILAND.

Siam, Gulf of An arm of the South China Sea, separating the Malay Peninsula from Indochina; 300 to 350 miles wide, 450 miles long.

si·a·mang (sē′ə·mang) *n.* A large black gibbon (genus *Symphalangus*) found in Sumatra. [<Malay *siaman* < *iaman* black]

Si·a·mese (sī′ə·mēz′, -mēs′) *adj.* **1** Pertaining to Thailand (Siam), its people, or their language. **2** Closely connected; twin. —*n.* **1** A native or the natives of Siam, belonging to the Thai stock. **2** The Thai language of these people.

Siamese cat A breed of short–haired cat native in Siam, now extensively bred in the United States, typically fawn–colored or pale cream, with dark–tipped ears, tail, feet, and dark mask, a wedge–shaped head, and bright– or deep–blue, gently slanting eyes.

SIAMESE CAT (About 11 inches at the shoulder)

Siamese twins 1 Originally, the two Chinese males, Eng and Chang, 1811–74, born in Siam, whose bodies were joined by a fleshy band from the navel to the xiphoid cartilage. **2** Any twins joined together at birth.

Si·an (sē′än′, shē′-) **1** The capital of Shensi province, NW China: formerly *Singan.* **2** A city in northern Lianoing province, south central Manchuria, China.

Siang (syäng, shyäng) **1** A river in Hunan province, China, flowing 715 miles NE to Tungting Lake. **2** See YÜ RIVER.

Siang·tan (syäng′tän′, shyäng′-) A city in eastern Hunan province, China.

sib (sib) *n.* **1** A blood–relation; kinsman. **2** Kinsmen collectively; relatives. —*adj.* **1** Related by blood; akin. **2** Related; similar. Also **sibb.** [OE *sibb*]

Sib·bo·leth (sib′ə·leth) See SHIBBOLETH.

Si·be·li·us (si·bā′lē·əs, -bāl′yəs; *Finnish* si·bā′·lyo͞os), **Jean,** 1865–1957, Finnish composer.

Si·be·ri·a (sī·bir′ē·ə) A region of the U.S.S.R. in Asia extending from the Ural Mountains and the Caspian Sea to the Pacific Ocean in northern Asia and roughly corresponding to the Asiatic part of Russian S.F.S.R.; 5,000,000 square miles. *Russian* **Si·bir** (si·bēr′). —**Si·be′ri·an** *adj.* & *n.*

Siberian husky A breed of working dog of medium size with a strong, closely knit body, head resembling that of a fox, brush tail, and thick, soft outer coat.

Siberian Sea, East A section of the Arctic Ocean north of NE Siberia, east of the New Siberian Islands and west of Wrangell Island (def. 2): Russian *Vostochno–Sibirskoye More.*

sib·i·lant (sib′ə·lənt) *adj.* **1** Hissing. **2** *Phonet.* Describing those consonants which are uttered with a hissing sound, as (s), (z), (sh), and (zh). —*n. Phonet.* A sibilant consonant. [<L *sibilans, -antis,* ppr. of *sibilare* hiss] —**sib′i·lance, sib′i·lan·cy** *n.* —**sib′i·lant·ly** *adv.*

sib·i·late (sib′ə·lāt) *v.t.* **·lat·ed, ·lat·ing** To give a hissing sound to, as in pronouncing the letter *s.* [<L *sibilatus,* pp. of *sibilare* hiss] —**sib′i·la′tion** *n.*

Si·biu (si·byo͞o′) A city in central Rumania: German *Hermannstadt.*

sib·ling (sib′ling) *n.* A blood–relation; a relative: used in eugenics, psychology, and anthropology to denote brothers and sisters. [OE, a relative]

Si·bu·yan Sea (si·bo͞o′yän) A part of the Pacific in the central Philippines, bounded by Mindoro, Luzon, Masbate, and Panay.

sib·yl (sib′əl) *n.* **1** In ancient Greece and Rome, any of several women who prophesied under the supposed inspiration of some deity, chiefly of Apollo, and delivered their oracles in a frenzied state. **2** A fortune–teller; sorceress. [<L *sibylla* <Gk.]

Sib·yl (sib′əl) A feminine personal name. Also *Du.* **Si·byl·la** (sē·bil′ə), *Fr.* **Si·bylle** (sē·bēl′), *Ger.* **Si·byl·le** (sē·bē′lə), *Lat.* **Si·byl·la** (si·bil′ə). [<L, soothsayer]

sib·yl·line (sib′əl·īn, -ēn, -in) *adj.* **1** Pertaining to or characteristic of the sibyls; uttered or composed by sibyls; hence, prophetic; oracular; occult. **2** Exorbitant; excessive. Also **si·byl·ic** (si·bil′ik), **si·byl′lic.**

Sibylline Books A collection of nine books which were reputed to set forth the destiny of Rome. The last three were bought from the Cumaean sibyl by Tarquin the Proud and placed in the temple of Jupiter Capitolinus, and were consulted by the senate on momentous occasions.

sic[1] (sik) *adv.* So; thus: sometimes inserted in brackets after something quoted, to indicate that the quotation is literal, and that, in the opinion of the one making the insertion, what immediately precedes is questionable or incorrect. [<L]

sic[2] (sik) *adj. Scot.* Such. Also **sic′can.**

sic[3] (sik) See SICK[2].

Si·ca·ni·an (si·kā′nē·ən) *adj.* Sicilian.

sic·ca·tive (sik′ə·tiv) *adj.* Causing to dry; drying. —*n.* That which has a drying effect; a drying agent or medicine. [<LL *siccativus* <L *siccatus,* pp. of *siccare* dry < *siccus* dry]

sice (sīs) See SYCE.

Sic·el (sis′əl) *n.* **1** A member of an ancient people of Sicily. **2** The Indo–European language of the Sicels, possibly related to Ligurian or Latin. —*adj.* Of or pertaining to the Sicels or their language.

sicht (sikht) *n.* & *v. Scot.* Sight.

Si·cil·i·an Vespers (si·sil′ē·ən, -sil′yən) A general massacre of the French in Sicily (1282) by Sicilians rising against the French rule of Charles of Anjou: so called because the toll that called to Vespers on Easter Monday was the signal for attack.

Sic·i·lies (sis′ə·lēz), **The Two** See TWO SICILIES, THE.

Sic·i·ly (sis′ə·lē) The largest island in the Mediterranean, just SW of Italy (9,831 square miles); comprising with some small neighboring islands an autonomous region of Italy; 9,926 square miles; capital, Palermo: ancient *Trinacria. Italian* **Si·ci·lia** (sē·chē′lyä). —**Si·cil′i·an** *adj.* & *n.*

sick[1] (sik) *adj.* **1** Affected with disease; ill; ailing. **2** Of or used by ill persons: often used in combination: *sickroom.* **3** Affected by nausea; nauseated; desiring to vomit. **4** Expressive or suggestive of nausea; sickly: a *sick* laugh. **5** Impaired or unsound from any cause; weakened; out of condition. **6** Pallid; wan: said of colors. **7** Depressed and longing because of some unattained desire; languishing: *sick* for the sea. **8** Disinclined by reason of satiety or disgust; surfeited: with *of*: *sick* of music. **9** Exhausted, as soil; unable to produce a profitable yield; also, diseased. —*n.* Sick people collectively: with *the.* [OE *sēoc*]

sick[2] (sik) *v.t.* **1** To seek or attack: used in the imperative to order a dog to attack. **2** To urge to attack: I'll *sick* the dog on you. Also spelled *sic.* [Var. of SEEK]

sick·bay (sik′bā′) *n.* That part of a ship or of a naval base set aside for the care of the sick, including operating room, dispensary, and hospital.

sick·bed (sik′bed′) *n.* The bed upon which a sick person lies.

sick call *Mil.* **1** The daily period for reporting to the medical officer all non–hospitalized sick or injured military personnel. **2** The call or signal which announces it.

sick·en (sik′ən) *v.t.* & *v.i.* To make or become sick or disgusted. —**sick′en·er** *n.*

sick·en·ing (sik′ən·ing) *adj.* Disgusting; nauseating. —**sick′en·ing·ly** *adv.*

sick·er[1] (sik′ər) *adj.* More sick.

sick·er[2] (sik′ər) *adj. Scot.* & *Brit. Dial.* Safe; sure; also, cautious. —*adv.* Surely; securely. Also spelled *siker.* [OE *sicor* <L *securus* safe]

sick headache Headache accompanied by nausea and stomach disorders; migraine.

sick·ish (sik′ish) *adj.* **1** Somewhat sick. **2** Slightly nauseating: a sweet, *sickish* odor. See synonyms under SQUEAMISH. —**sick′ish·ly** *adv.* —**sick′ish·ness** *n.*

sick·le (sik′əl) *n.* A reaping implement with a

long, curved blade mounted on a short handle. —*v.t.* **·led, ·ling** To cut with a sickle, as grass, hay, etc. [OE *sicel* <L *secula* <*secare* cut]

Sickle A sickle-shaped group of stars in the constellation Leo.

sick·le·bill (sik′əl·bil′) *n.* Any of several birds having a strongly curved bill, as a hummingbird or the long-billed curlew *(Numenius americanus).*

sick·le-cell anemia (sik′əl·sel′) A severe, hereditary anemia occurring among the offspring of parents who both have sickle-cell trait.

sickle-cell trait A tendency in erythrocytes to become deformed into a sickle shape and to clog small blood vessels, occurring chiefly among Negroes and due to the presence of a genetic hemoglobin abnormality inherited from one parent. Also **sickl·e·mi·a** (sik′əl·ē′mē·ə).

sickle feather One of the long curved feathers in the tail of the domestic cock. See illustration under FOWL.

sickle pear A seckel.

sick·list (sik′list′) *n.* A list of those incapacitated by illness, especially in an army or navy.

sick·ly (sik′lē) *adj.* **·li·er, ·li·est 1** Habitually indisposed; ailing; unhealthy: a *sickly* child. **2** Marked by the prevalence of sickness: a *sickly* summer. **3** Nauseating; disgusting; also, mawkish; sickening. **4** Pertaining to or characteristic of the sick or sickness: a *sickly* appearance. **5** Weak- or sick-looking; faint: a *sickly* moon. —*adv.* In a sick manner; poorly. —*v.t.* **·lied, ·ly·ing** To make sickly or sickish, as in color or complexion. —**sick′li·ly** *adv.* —**sick′li·ness** *n.*

sick·ness (sik′nis) *n.* **1** Illness; the state of being sick. **2** A particular form of disease. **3** Specifically, nausea. **4** Any disordered and weakened state: the soul's *sickness.* See synonyms under DISEASE, ILLNESS.

sick-out (sik′out′) *n.* An absence from work by workers who say they are sick so they may not be penalized for an illegal strike action.

sick·room (sik′ro͞om′, -ro͝om′) *n.* A room for the sick.

sic·like (sik′līk′) *adj. Scot.* Similar; such.

sic pas·sim (sik pas′im) *Latin* Thus everywhere (as throughout a book).

sic sem·per ty·ran·nis (sik sem′pər ti·ran′is) *Latin* Thus ever to tyrants: motto of Virginia.

sic tran·sit glo·ri·a mun·di (sik tran′sit glō′·rē·ə mun′dī) *Latin* Thus passes away the glory of the world.

Sic·y·on (sish′ē·on) An ancient city NW of Corinth in Peloponnesus, southern Greece: Greek *Sikyon.*

Sid·dons (sid′nz), **Sarah,** 1755–1831, *née* Kemble, English tragic actress.

sid·dur (sid′o͝or) *n.* The Jewish prayer book, containing the year's prayers for weekdays, Sabbaths, fast days, and holy days. [<Hebrew *siddūr* arrangement]

side[1] (sīd) *n.* **1** Any one of the bounding lines of a surface or of the bounding surfaces of a solid object: often limited to a particular bounding line or surface, as distinguished from top, or bottom: the *side* of a box, house, or mountain. **2** A lateral part of a surface or object. **3** One of two or more contrasted surfaces, parts, or places: *inside* and *outside.* **4** Any distinct party or body of competitors or partisans; a faction. **5** An opinion, aspect, or point of view considered with respect to its opposite: my *side* of the question. **6** Family connection, especially by descent through one parent: my grandfather on my father's *side.* **7** The lateral half of a slaughtered animal or of a tanned skin or hide. **8** Either half of the human body as divided by the median plane. **9** The space beside someone. **10** A page of written or printed paper. **11** *Naut.* The part of a ship's hull from stem to stern above the waterline. **12** In billiards, a lateral spin given to the cue ball; english. **13** Abounding line of a geometrical figure. **14** *Brit. Slang* Superciliousness of manner; pretentiousness. —**off side** See OFFSIDE. —*adj.* **1** Situated at or on one side; lateral: a *side* window. **2** Being or viewed as if from one side; oblique: a *side* glance; incidental: a *side* issue. —*v.t.* **sid·ed, sid·ing 1** To provide with sides, as a building. **2** To cut into sides, as a carcass. **3** To thrust aside. —**to side with** To range oneself on the side of; take the part of. [OE]

side[2] (sīd) *adj.* **1** *Scot. & Brit. Dial.* Relatively long or wide; large: said of garments. **2** *Scot.* Far; distant.

side arms Weapons worn at the side, as swords, pistols, bayonets, etc.

side·bands (sīd′bandz′) *n. pl. Telecom.* The bands of frequencies on either side of the carrier wave within which fall the frequencies produced by modulation.

side·board (sīd′bôrd′, -bōrd′) *n.* **1** A piece of dining-room furniture for holding tableware. **2** *pl. Brit.* Sideburns.

side·burns (sīd′bûrnz′) *n. pl.* **1** Whiskers grown on the cheeks; burnsides. **2** The hair growing on the sides of a man's face below the hairline: usually worn with the rest of the beard shaved off. [Alter. of BURNSIDES]

side-by-side (sīd′bī′sīd′) *adj.* Beside or next to each other; together.

side·car (sīd′kär′) *n.* **1** A small, one-wheeled passenger car attached to the side of a motorcycle. **2** A cocktail containing equal parts of lemon juice, brandy, and curaçao or Cointreau. **3** A jaunting car.

side chain *Chem.* A group of atoms, specifically an alkyl group, attached to a carbon atom of a ring compound.

side dish A portion of food subordinate to the main dish or dishes of a course; also, the small dish in which it is served.

side-dress (sīd′dres′) *v.t. Agric.* To apply fertilizer along only one side of (a row of growing plants). —**side′-dress′ing** *n.*

side effect *Med.* A secondary, often injurious effect resulting from a drug or other form of therapy whose action is not restricted to the condition for which it was administered.

side·kick (sī′kik′) *n. U.S. Slang* A close friend; buddy.

side·light (sīd′līt′) *n.* **1** A side window. **2** A light coming from the side; hence, incidental illustration or information. **3** *Naut.* One of the colored lights (red on the port side, green on the starboard) displayed on the sides of ships at night; a running-light; also, a nightlight in the gangway of a war vessel.

side·line (sīd′līn′) *n.* **1** An auxiliary line of goods sold by a store or a commercial traveler. **2** Any additional or secondary work differing from one's main job. **3** A track or road, especially of a railroad, branching off from the main line. **4** A line used to hobble a horse by connecting the fore and hind feet of the same side: also **side′-hob′ble** (-hob′əl). **5** One of the lines bounding the two sides of a football field, tennis court, or the like; also, the area just outside these lines: often in the plural. **6** The point of view of an outsider or non-participant.

side·ling (sīd′ling) *adj.* Having a slanting or oblique position or motion; indirect. —*adv.* Sidewise; obliquely; indirectly.

side·long (sīd′lông′, -long′) *adj.* Inclining or tending to one side; lateral. —*adv.* **1** In a lateral or oblique direction. **2** Steeply inclined.

side·man (sīd′man′) *n. pl.* **·men** (-men′) One of the supporting musicians, as distinguished from the featured performers, of a band, especially a jazz band.

side meat A side of salt pork or bacon.

side·piece (sīd′pēs′) *n.* **1** A piece at or forming the side of anything. **2** The jamb or check in any finished aperture in a wall, as of a doorway.

si·de·re·al (sī·dir′ē·əl) *adj.* **1** Pertaining or relative to stars; constituted of or containing stars. **2** Measured by means of the stars: said of periods of time. [<L *sidereus* <*sidus sideris* star] —**si·de′re·al·ly** *adv.*

sidereal time See under TIME.

sid·er·ite (sid′ə·rīt) *n.* **1** A vitreous, native ferrous carbonate, $FeCO_3$; spathic iron ore: also called *chalybite.* **2** An indigo-blue variety of quartz. **3** An iron meteorite. [<L *siderites* <Gk. *sidēritēs* of iron <*sidēros* iron] —**sid′er·it′ic** (-rit′ik) *adj.*

sidero-[1] *combining form* Iron; of or pertaining to iron: *siderolite.* Also, before vowels, **sider-.** [<Gk. *sidēros* iron]

sidero-[2] *combining form* Star; stellar: *siderostat.* Also, before vowels, **sider-.** [<L *sidus, sideris* a star]

sid·er·o·lite (sid′ər·ə·līt′) *n.* **1** A spongy meteoric iron containing embedded grains of certain minerals, as chrysolite. **2** A meteorite. [<SIDERO-[1] + -LITE]

sid·er·o·scope (sid′ər·ə·skōp′) *n.* A magnetic device for detecting the presence of iron or steel particles in the eyes.

sid·er·o·sis (sid′ə·rō′sis) *n. Pathol.* **1** Abnormal deposit of iron in the tissues of the body, and especially of the lungs. **2** Any lung disease caused by the inhalation of metallic dust; pneumonoconiosis.

sid·er·o·stat (sid′ər·ə·stat′) *n. Astron.* A mirror turning by clock motion so as to reflect the light of a star in an invariable direction into a fixed telescope or other astronomical instrument. [<SIDERO-[2] + Gk. *statos* standing] —**sid′er·o·stat′ic** *adj.*

side-sad·dle (sīd′sad′l) *n.* A woman's saddle having but one stirrup and a cushioned horn on the same side, about which the right knee fits.

side show 1 A small show incidental to a larger or more important one; especially, one connected with a circus but charging an extra entrance fee; also, a minor exhibit at a fair. **2** Any subordinate issue or attraction.

side-slip (sīd′slip′) *v.i.* **-slipped, -slip·ping** To slip or skid sideways. —*n.* **1** A lateral skid, as of an automobile. **2** A downward, sidewise slipping of an airplane along the lateral axis: executed to lose altitude without a gain in forward speed.

side-split·ting (sīd′split′ing) *adj.* Having a tendency as if to split the sides with laughter; mirth-provoking.

side-step (sīd′step′) *v.* **-stepped, -step·ping** *v.i.* To step to one side; avoid responsibility. —*v.t.* To avoid, as an issue, or postpone, as a decision; evade. —*n.* **1** A step or a movement to one side, as of a pugilist. **2** A step on the side of a thing for ascending and descending. —**side′-step′per** *n.*

side stroke In swimming, a stroke made while lying on the side, the arms being thrust forward alternately, the upper arm above the water, the lower arm below the water: performed with a scissors kick.

side·swipe (sīd′swīp′) *n.* A sweeping blow along the side. —*v.t. & v.i.* **·swiped, ·swip·ing** To strike or collide with such a blow.

side·track (sīd′trak′) *v.t. & v.i.* **1** To move to a siding, as a railroad train. **2** To divert or depart from the main issue or subject; distract or be distracted. —*n.* A railroad siding; also, a branch line.

side·walk (sīd′wôk′) *n.* A path or pavement at the side of the street for the use of pedestrians.

side·wall (sīd′wôl′) *n.* The side surface of a rubber tire, between the tread and the rim.

side·ward (sīd′wərd) *adj.* Directed or moving toward or from the side; lateral. —*adv.* Toward or from the side; laterally: also **side′·wards.**

side·ways (sīd′wāz′) *adv.* **1** From one side. **2** So as to incline toward the side, or with the side forward: Hold it *sideways.* **3** Toward one side; askance; obliquely; indirectly. —*adj.* Moving to or from one side: a *sideways* glance. Also **side′way′, side′wise′.**

side wheel A wheel at the side; specifically, one of two paddle wheels on either side of a steamboat. —**side′-wheel′** *adj.* —**side′-wheel′er** *n.*

MARY POWELL

SIDE WHEEL

side-wind·er (sīd′·wīn′dər) *n.* **1** One of several small rattlesnakes found in the American Southwest, and particularly the horned rattler *(Crotalus cerastes):* so called because of its characteristic lateral motion. **2** A heavy, swinging, sideways blow with the fist.

Si·di If·ni (sē′dē ēf′nē) The capital of Ifni.

sid·ing (sī′ding) *n.* **1** A railway track by the side of the main track. **2** The boarding that covers the side of a wooden house or is prepared for that purpose: often in the plural. **3** The act of dressing timbers to correct breadths, as in shipbuilding, or the timbers themselves. **4** The act of taking sides, as in a controversy.

si·dle (sīd′l) *v.i.* **·dled, ·dling** To move sideways, especially in a cautious or stealthy manner. — *n.* A sideways step or movement. [< obs. *sidling* sidelong] — **si′dler** *n.*

Sid·ney (sid′nē) A masculine personal name. Also *Sydney.* [<F, St. Denis]

Sid·ney (sid′nē), **Sir Philip,** 1554–86, English soldier, courtier, poet, and writer: also spelled *Sydney.*

Si·don (sīd′n) The capital of ancient Phoenicia, on the site of modern *Saida.* — **Si·do·ni·an** (sī·dō′nē·ən) *adj.* & *n.*

Sid·ra (sid′rə), **Gulf of** An inlet of the Mediterranean in the coast of Libya; 275 miles wide: ancient *Syrtis Major.*

Sie·ben·ge·bir·ge (zē′bən·gə·bir′gə) A range of hills along the Rhine south of Bonn in West Germany; highest point, 1,509 feet.

siè·cle (sye′kl′) *n. French* Century; age; period.

Sie·dl·ce (she′dəl·tse) A city in eastern Poland; formerly, capital of a political subdivision of Russian Poland.

Sieg·bahn (sēg′bän), **Karl Manne Georg,** born 1886, Swedish physicist.

siege (sēj) *n.* **1** The besieging of a town or fortified place; beleaguerment. ◆ Collateral adjective: *obsidional.* **2** A steady attempt to win something; also, the protracted period spent in the effort: He laid *siege* to her heart. **3** The time during which one undergoes a protracted illness or difficulty. **4** *Obs.* A seat; chair; throne. **5** *Obs.* Rank, station. — *v.t.* **sieged, sieg·ing** To besiege. [<OF <L *sedes* seat < *sedere* sit; infl. in meaning by L *obsidium* siege]

Siege Perilous A seat at King Arthur's Round Table, fatal to all occupants save Sir Galahad, the knight destined to find the Holy Grail.

Sieg·fried (sēg′frēd, *Ger.* zēkh′frēt) The hero of the *Nibelungenlied* and several other Germanic legends. [<G, peace of victory]

Siegfried Line See LIMES.

Sieg Heil (zēkh′ hīl′) *German* Hail to victory: a Nazi salute.

Sie·mens (sē′mənz, *Ger.* zē′məns), **Ernst Werner von,** 1816–92, German electrical engineer, inventor, and manufacturer. — **Sir William,** 1823–83, Karl Wilhelm Siemens, German engineer who settled in England; invented the electrodynamometer; brother of the preceding.

Si·en·a (sē·en′ə, *Ital.* syā′nä) A city in Tuscany, central Italy. — **Si·en·ese** (sē′ən·ēz′, -ēs′) *adj.* & *n.*

si·en·ite (sī′ən·īt) See SYENITE.

Sien·kie·wicz (shen·kyā′vich), **Henryk,** 1846–1916, Polish novelist.

si·en·na (sē·en′ə) *n.* **1** A brownish orange-yellow natural clay colored with oxides of iron and manganese: used as a pigment. **2** Orange-yellow, the color of this pigment. [<Ital. *(terra di) Siena* (earth of) Siena]

sier·o·zem (sir′ə·zem) *n.* A grayish-brown soil that merges gradually into a calcareous or hardpan layer: formed usually in a temperate to cool climate. [<Russian, gray earth]

si·er·ra (sē·er′ə) *n.* **1** A mountain range or chain, especially one having a jagged or serrated outline: a term occurring in the names of ranges in Spain and former Spanish colonies. **2** Any of several large mackerel-like fishes, as the cero. [<Sp. <L *serra* saw]

Si·er·ra de Cór·do·ba (sē·er′rä thā kôr′thō·vä) A mountain range of central Argentina; highest point, 9,450 feet.

Si·er·ra de Gre·dos (sē·er′rä thā grā′thōs) A mountain range in central Spain, 25 miles west of Madrid; highest point, 8,504 feet.

Si·er·ra de Gua·dar·ra·ma (sē·er′rä thā gwä′·thär·rä′mä) A mountain range in central Spain, NW of Madrid; highest point, 7,972 feet.

Si·er·ra Le·o·ne (sē·er′rä lā·ō′nā) **1** An independent state on the west coast of Africa; 27,925 square miles, mostly on the **Sierra Leone Peninsula,** extending 25 miles into the Atlantic; capital, Freetown: formerly a British dependency. **2** An estuary in western Sierra Leone, flowing 25 miles past Freetown to the Atlantic.

Si·er·ra Ma·dre (sē·er′rä mä′thrā) A Mexican mountain chain bordering the central plateau on the east and west and divided into the **Sierra Madre del Sur** in the south, the **Sierra Madre Occidental** in the west, and the **Sierra Madre Oriental** in the east; highest point, 18,700 feet.

Si·er·ra Mo·re·na (sē·er′rä mō·rā′nä) A mountain range in southern Spain; highest point, 4,340 feet.

Si·er·ra Ne·vad·a (sē·er′ə nə·vad′ə, -vä′də; *Sp.* sē·er′rä nā·vä′thä) **1** A mountain range of eastern California, extending 400 miles north and south; highest point, 14,495 feet. **2** A mountain range in southern Spain; highest peak, 11,411 feet.

si·es·ta (sē·es′tə) *n.* A midday or afternoon nap. [<Sp. <L *sexta (hora)* sixth (hour), noon < *sex* six]

sieur (syœr) *n.* Sir; master: a former French title of respect. [<F <L *senior* older]

sieve (siv) *n.* **1** A utensil or apparatus for sifting, consisting of a frame provided with a bottom of mesh wire. **2** A garrulous person. — *v.t.* & *v.i.* **sieved, siev·ing** To sift. [OE *sife* sieve]

sieve cell *Bot.* A thin-walled, elongated cell having perforations, **sieve pores,** and sieve plates that permit communication between contiguous cells, forming sieve tubes.

sieve plate *Bot.* One of the thickened terminal sections of a sieve cell.

sieve tissue *Bot.* Phloem tissue containing or made up of vascular bundles of sieve cells.

sieve tube *Bot.* An arrangement of sieve cells in plants by means of which conduction is accomplished.

Sie·yès (syā·yes′), **Emmanuel,** 1748–1836, French revolutionist: called "Abbé Sieyès."

si·fak·a (si·fak′ə) *n.* Any of a genus *(Propithecus)* of lemuroid primates characterized by long tails, black skin, short arms, and powerful hind limbs: native in Madagascar: also called *propitheque.* [<Malagasy]

sif·fle (sif′əl) *v.t.* & *v.i.* **·fled, ·fling** To whistle; hiss. — *n.* A sibilant râle. [<F *siffler* <L *sibilare* hiss]

sift (sift) *v.t.* **1** To pass through a sieve in order to separate the fine parts from the coarse. **2** To scatter by or as by a sieve. **3** To examine carefully. **4** To separate as if with a sieve; distinguish: to *sift* fact from fiction. — *v.i.* **5** To use a sieve; sift something. **6** To fall or pass through or as through a sieve: The light *sifts* through the trees. [OE *siftan* sift] — **sift′er** *n.*

sift·ings (sif′tingz) *n. pl.* Something removed or separated by a sieve.

sigh (sī) *v.i.* **1** To draw in and exhale a deep, audible breath, as in expressing sorrow, weariness, pain, etc. **2** To make a sound suggestive of a sigh, as the wind. **3** To yearn; long. — *v.t.* **4** To express with a sigh. **5** To lament with sighs. — *n.* The act or sound of or as of sighing. [Back formation <ME *sighte,* pt. of *siken* <OE *sīcan* sigh]

sight (sīt) *n.* **1** The faculty, act, or fact of seeing; vision. **2** That which is seen; a view; spectacle; show; as used absolutely, something remarkable and strange. **3** *pl.* Things worth seeing: the *sights* of the town. **4** The range or scope of vision; limit of eyesight. **5** A point of view; estimation. **6** Insight; opportunity for investigation or study. **7** A device to assist aim, as on a gun, leveling instrument, etc. **8** An aim or observation taken with a telescope or other sighting instrument. **9** A view; glimpse. **10** The part of a drawing or painting within the marginal lines or the frame. **11** *Colloq.* A great quantity or number: a *sight* of people. — **at** (or **on**) **sight** **1** As soon as seen: to read or shoot *at sight.* **2** On presentation for payment: said of drafts, bills, and notes. — **battle sight** The position of the rear sight on a rifle in which the leaf is laid down. — **bore sight** An auxiliary sighting device with parts attached to the muzzle and breech of a gun, used to secure alinement of the axis of the bore with the axis of the gun sight. — **leaf sight** A rear sight for small arms, containing a movable peep sight and hinged to permit raising and lowering. — **peep sight** A sight attached to the breech end of a firearm, and provided with a small hole in the center for close aiming. — *v.t.* **1** To perceive with the eyes; see: to *sight* a whale. **2** To take a sight of; observe; look at through a telescope or similar instrument. **3** To furnish with sights, or adjust the sights of, as a gun. **4** To give the proper aim or elevation to, as a gun; take aim with. **5** *Colloq.* To bring to notice; present, as a bill to its drawee. — *v.i.* **6** To take aim. **7** To make an observation or sight. — *adj.* **1** Understood or performed on sight without previous familiarity or preparation. **2** Payable when presented: a *sight* draft. ◆ Homophones: *cite, site.* [OE *gesiht*]

sight-hole (sīt′hōl′) *n.* A peephole.

sight·less (sīt′lis) *adj.* **1** Without the power of sight; blind. **2** Invisible. — **sight′less·ly** *adv.* — **sight′less·ness** *n.*

sight·ly (sīt′lē) *adj.* **·li·er, ·li·est** **1** Pleasant to the view; comely. **2** Affording a grand view. — **sight′li·ness** *n.*

sight-read (sīt′rēd′) *v.t.* & *v.i.* **-read** (red), **-read·ing** (rē′ding) To understand or perform (something requiring interpretation or translation) on sight without previous familiarity or preparation: to *sight-read* music or a foreign language. — **sight reader** — **sight reading**

sight·see·ing (sīt′sē′ing) *n.* The visiting of objects of interest. — **sight′se′er** *n.*

sight unseen Without examing: to exchange stamps *sight unseen.*

sig·il (sij′il) *n.* A seal or signature; also, a mark or sign supposed to exercise occult power. [<L *sigillum* seal] — **sig′il·lary** (-ə·ler′ē) *adj.*

Sig·is·mund (sij′əs·mənd, sig′-; *Ger.* zē′gis·mo͝ont) A masculine personal name. Also *Fr.* **Si·gis·mond** (sē·zhēs·môn′), *Ital.* **Si·gis·mon·do** (sē′jēs·mōn′dō) [<Gmc., protecting conqueror]

— **Sigismund,** 1368–1437, king of Hungary 1387–1437, Holy Roman Emperor 1411–37.

sig·ma (sig′mə) *n.* **1** The 18th letter in the Greek alphabet, written Σ (capital), σ (small initial), or ς (small final): corresponding to English *s* in *so.* As a numeral it denotes 200. **2** *Math.* The symbol signifying that the sum is to be taken of a series or sequence following. **3** Something shaped like a sigma. [<Gk. *sigma* the letter *s*]

sig·mate (sig′māt) *adj.* Having the shape or form of S or of sigma.

sig·moid (sig′moid) *adj.* **1** Shaped like the Greek capital letter sigma (Σ), or like the letter S. **2** Pertaining to the sigmoid flexure. Also **sig·moi·dal** (sig·moid′l). [<Gk. *sigmoeidēs*]

sigmoid flexure *Anat.* A fold in the colon just above the rectum.

sign (sīn) *n.* **1** A motion or action indicating thought, desire, or command; a pantomimic gesture. **2** A board, plate, or representation of any sort, generally bearing an inscription and used to indicate a place of business or resort. **3** An arbitrary mark used to express meaning, rank, condition, value, etc. **4** Any evidence of a recent presence, as tracks, droppings, etc.; a vestige; trace. **5** A mark used in place of a signature by persons unable to write. **6** *Music* Any mark used in musical notation, as a flat or sharp. **7** *Math.* A conventional mark to indicate an operation or relation, as one of the symbols +, −, ×, ÷, indicating the four fundamental operations of addition, subtraction, multiplication, and division. **8** Any indicative or significant object or event; a symbol; token. **9** In the Bible, a miraculous deed as a proof of divine commission or supernatural power; a miracle. **10** *Astron.* One of the twelve equal divisions of the zodiac, named from the constellations that formerly occupied them. See ZODIAC. **11** In hunting, a trace left by an animal; spoor. **12** *Med.* A symptom of disease that is apparent to someone other than the patient. **13** *Eccl.* The sign of the Cross: used in service books and before signatures of bishops. — *v.t.* **1** To write one's signature or initials on. **2** *Law* To acknowledge an instrument by affixing a mark or seal to. **3** To indicate or represent by a sign; stand for. **4** To mark or consecrate with a sign, especially with a cross. **5** To engage by obtaining the signature of to a contract: to *sign* a baseball player; also, to hire (oneself) out for work: often with *on.* **6** To dispose of by signature: with *off* or *away.* **7** To express or indicate with a sign. — *v.i.* **8** To make signs or signals. **9** To write one's signature or initials. — **to sign off** *Telecom.* To announce the close of a program from a broadcasting station and stop transmission. — **to sign up** To enlist, as in a branch of military service.

◆ Homophone: *sine.* [<OF *signe* <L *signum*] — **sign'er** *n.*

Synonyms (noun): emblem, indication, manifestation, mark, note, omen, pattern, presage, prognostic, signal, symbol, symptom, token, type. A *sign* is any distinctive *mark* by which a thing may be recognized or its presence known, and may be intentional or accidental, natural or artificial, suggestive, descriptive or wholly arbitrary. While a *sign* may be involuntary, and even unconscious, a *signal* is always voluntary; a ship may show *signs* of distress to the casual observer, but *signals* of distress are a distinct appeal for aid. A *symptom* is a vital phenomenon resulting from a diseased condition; in medical language a *sign* is an *indication* of any physical condition, whether morbid or healthy; thus, a hot skin and rapid pulse are *symptoms* of pneumonia; dulness of some portion of the lungs under percussion is one of the physical *signs.* See CHARACTERISTIC, EMBLEM, LETTER, MARK[1], TRACE[1].

sig·nal (sig'nəl) *n.* **1** A sign or means of communication agreed upon or understood, and used to convey information or command, as at a distance. **2** *Telecom.* A radio wave or electric current which transmits intelligence, whether direct or in code. **3** An event that incites to action or movement. **4** In some card games, a lead or play that conveys certain information to one's partner. See synonyms under SIGN. — *adj.* **1** Distinguished by some special sign or characteristic; notable; conspicuous. **2** Used to signal: a *signal* fire. See synonyms under EMINENT, EXTRAORDINARY. — *v.* **·naled** or **·nalled, ·nal·ing** or **·nal·ling** *v.t.* **1** To make signals to; inform or notify by signals. **2** To communicate by signals. — *v.i.* **3** To make a signal or signals. [<F <L *signalis* < *signum* sign] — **sig'nal·er** or **sig'·nal·ler** *n.*

Signal Corps A branch of the U. S. Army; a body of officers and enlisted men in charge of signaling apparatus and the transmitting of intelligence by telegraph, telephone, radio, visual signs, etc.

signal fire A fire used as a signal; a beacon fire.

signal generator An electromagnetic oscillator used to supply currents of known frequencies through a specified range in testing the performance of a radio receiver.

sig·nal·ize (sig'nəl·īz) *v.t.* **·ized, ·iz·ing** **1** To render noteworthy. **2** To point out with care.

sig·nal·ly (sig'nəl·ē) *adv.* In a signal manner; eminently.

sig·nal·man (sig'nəl·mən) *n. pl.* **·men** (-mən) **1** One who makes or interprets signals; a signaler. **2** One who operates a railroad signal.

sig·nal·ment (sig'nəl·mənt) *n.* **1** The act of signaling. **2** Description of a person for identification by peculiar or characteristic marks, as in the case of a criminal. [<F *signalement*]

signal smoke A smoke from a fire used to signal to a distance, by a system either of puffs, spirals, or clouds.

signal tower **1** Any tower from which signals are displayed. **2** A small railroad tower from which semaphore or block-system signals are controlled.

sig·na·to·ry (sig'nə·tôr'ē, -tō'rē) *adj.* Bound by the terms of a signed document; having signed: *signatory* powers. — *n.* One who has signed or is bound by a document; specifically, a nation so bound. [<L *signatorius* < *signatus,* pp. of *signare* sign < *signum* a sign]

sig·na·ture (sig'nə·chər) *n.* **1** The name of a person, or something representing his name, written, stamped, or inscribed by himself or by deputy, as a sign of agreement or acknowledgment. **2** *Printing* **a** A distinguishing mark, letter, or number on the first page of each form or sheet of a book, as a guide to the binder. **b** The form or sheet on which this mark is placed. **c** One of the fractional parts of a book; a folded printed sheet, usually comprising 16 pages. **3** *Music* A symbol or group of symbols at the beginning of a staff, indicating time or key. See KEY SIGNATURE, TIME SIGNATURE. **4** In radio, the musical number or sound effect that introduces or closes a given program. **5** *Zool.* A color mark resembling a letter. **6** *Med.* The part of a physician's or pharmacist's prescription that indicates how the medicine is to be taken: usually preceded by *S.* or *Sig.* [<F <Med. L *signatura* <L *signatus.* See SIGNATORY.]

sign·board (sīn'bôrd', -bōrd') *n.* A board on which a sign, direction, or advertisement is displayed.

sig·net (sig'nit) *n.* **1** A seal; especially, in England, one of the seals of the sovereign, used in sealing his private letters and bills of grants, etc. **2** An impression made by or as if by a seal. — *v.t.* To mark or make official with a signet or seal. ◆ Homophone: *cygnet.* [<F, dim. of *signe* sign <L *signum*]

sig·nif·i·cance (sig·nif'ə·kəns) *n.* **1** The character or state of being significant; expressiveness. **2** That which is signified or intended to be expressed; meaning. **3** Importance; consequence: opposed to *insignificance.* Also **sig·nif'i·can·cy.**

sig·nif·i·cant (sig·nif'ə·kənt) *adj.* **1** Having or expressing a meaning; bearing or embodying a meaning. **2** Betokening or standing as a sign for something; having some covert meaning; significative: His manner was *significant.* **3** Important, as pointing out something weighty; momentous: opposed to *insignificant.* **4** *Math.* Having value or the determining or influential value: the *significant* figures in a number. See synonyms under IMPORTANT. — *n.* Something bearing a meaning; specifically, a token or letter. [<L *significans, -antis,* ppr. of *significare* make a sign, mean < *signum* sign + *facere* do, make] — **sig·nif'i·cant·ly** *adv.*

sig·ni·fi·ca·tion (sig'nə·fə·kā'shən) *n.* **1** That which is signified; meaning; sense; import. **2** The act of signifying; communication. [<OF *significaciun* <L *significatio, -onis.* See SIGNIFICANT.]

sig·nif·i·ca·tive (sig·nif'ə·kā'tiv) *adj.* **1** Representing, as a sign; symbolical. **2** Conveying, or tending to convey, a meaning; significant.

sig·ni·fy (sig'nə·fī) *v.* **·fied, ·fy·ing** *v.t.* **1** To make known by signs or words; express; communicate; announce; declare. **2** Hence, to betoken in any way; mean; import. **3** To amount to; mean: What does his opinion *signify*? **4** To denote (medical use) by signature or markings. — *v.i.* **5** To have some meaning or importance; matter. See synonyms under ALLUDE, IMPORT. — **sig'ni·fi'er** *n.*

sign language **1** Dactylology. **2** A system of communication by means of signs, largely manual; specifically, the system used by the Plains Indians to communicate with tribes speaking other languages.

sign manual *pl.* **signs manual** **1** The personal signature of the British sovereign written at the top of state papers. **2** A sign made with the hand; also, any code consisting of manual signs.

si·gnor (sēn'yôr) *n.* **1** An Anglicized form of the Italian title **signore,** used in respectful address to a gentleman: in society equivalent to the English *sir* when no name follows, to *Mr.* with a name, and to the French *monsieur.* **2** A lord or gentleman; especially, an Italian of rank, official position, or social distinction. Also **si'gnior.** [<Ital. *signore* <L *senior* senior]

si·gno·ra (sē·nyō'rä) *n. Italian* Madam; Mrs.: a title of respectful address.

Si·gno·rel·li (sē'nyō·rel'lē), **Luca,** 1442?–1524?, Italian painter.

si·gno·ri·na (sē'nyō·rē'nä) *n. Italian* The equivalent to *miss*: diminutive of Italian *signora.*

si·gno·ri·no (sē'nyō·rē'nō) *n. Italian* A title of respectful address to a young man: diminutive of Italian *signore,* sir.

si·gno·ry (sēn'yə·rē) See SEIGNIORY.

sign·post (sīn'pōst') *n.* A post bearing a sign; sometimes, a guideboard.

Sigs·bee (sigz'bē), **Charles Dwight,** 1845–1923, U. S. admiral.

Sig·urd (sig'ərd, *Ger.* zē'gŏŏrt) In the *Volsunga Saga,* the hero who slays Fafnir. He corresponds to Siegfried, the hero of the *Nibelungenlied.*

Si·kang (sē'kang', *Chinese* shē'käng') A former province of SW China bordering on Tibet, incorporated, 1955, in Szechwan province; 204,194 square miles; former capital, Yaan.

sike (sīk, sik) *n. Scot. & Brit. Dial.* **1** A gutter; rill. **2** A marshy bottom with a stream flowing through it: also spelled *syke.* [OE *sīc* streamlet]

sik·er (sik'ər) See SICKER[2].

Sikh (sēk) *n.* One of a religious and military sect founded by Guru Nának (1469–1538) in India early in the 16th century. — *adj.* Of or pertaining to the Sikhs. [<Hind., lit., disciple]

Sikh·ism (sēk'iz·əm) *n.* The creed and practices of the Sikhs: it is a monotheistic system, combining the teachings of the Persian Sufis with those of Hinduism, rejecting caste, and enjoining purity of life and toleration.

Si·kho·te–A·lin Range (sē'khō·tā·ä·lēn') A mountain range along the Sea of Japan in Russian S.F.S.R.; highest point, 5,200 feet.

Si Kiang (sē' kyäng', shē' jyäng') The Chinese name for the WEST RIVER.

Sik·kim (sik'im) A protectorate of India in the eastern Himalayas, south central Asia; 2,818 square miles; capital, Gangtok.

Si·kor·sky (si·kôr'skē), **Igor,** born 1889, U. S. aeronautical engineer born in Russia: inventor of the helicopter.

Sik·y·on (sik'ē·on) The Greek name for SICYON.

si·lage (sī'lij) *n.* Ensilage. [<ENSILAGE]

sil·ane (sil'ān) *n. Chem.* **1** A compound of silicon and hydrogen, SiH_4; silicon hydride or monosilane. **2** Any of a series of similar compounds, named according to the number of silicon atoms present in the molecule. [< SIL(ICON) + -ANE[1]]

Si·las (sī'ləs) A masculine personal name. [See SILVANUS]

sil·a·zane (sil'ə·zān) *n. Chem.* Any of a class of nitrogen-containing silicon compounds having the general formula $H_3Si(NHSiH_2)_n$-$NHSiH_3$. [<SIL(ICON) + AZ(OTE) + -ANE[1]]

sile (sīl) *Brit. Dial. v.t.* **1** To strain; skim. **2** To glide or pass through. — *v.i.* **3** To sink; subside. **4** To boil gently; simmer. — *n.* **1** A strainer. **2** Filth; sediment. [Cf. Sw. & Norw. *sila* strain]

si·le·na·ceous (sī'lə·nā'shəs) *adj.* Caryophyllaceous. [<NL *Silene,* a genus of plants <L *Silenus* Silenus + -ACEOUS]

si·lence (sī'ləns) *n.* **1** The state or quality of being silent; abstinence from speech or noise; taciturnity. **2** Absence of sound or noise; stillness. **3** Absence of note; failure to mention; oblivion; secrecy. **4** *Music* A rest. — *v.t.* **·lenced, ·lenc·ing** **1** To render silent; take away the authority to speak or the power of reply from. **2** To stop the motion or activity of; put to rest; quiet. **3** To force (guns, etc.) to cease firing, as by return fire, bombing, or the like. — *interj.* Be silent. [<F <L *silentium* < *silere* be silent]

si·lenc·er (sī'lən·sər) *n.* **1** A tubular device attached to the muzzle of a firearm rendering the discharge noiseless. **2** A muffler (def. 2). **3** A device to prevent the buzzing of telegraph or telephone wires.

MAXIM SILENCER
a. Socket for attaching to gun.
b. Vortex chamber for gases.
c. Passage groove for bullet.

si·lent (sī'lənt) *adj.* **1** Not making any sound or noise; noiseless; still; also, unspoken; unuttered: *silent* grief. **2** Not speaking, or not given to speech; mute; taciturn. **3** Making no mention or allusion; passing by without notice or record. **4** Free from activity, motion, or disturbance; calm; quiet: a *silent* retreat. **5** Interested financially in a business, but having no authority to act: a *silent* partner. **6** Written, but not pronounced: said of a letter, as the *b* in *debt.* [<F <L *silens, -entis,* ppr. of *silere* be silent] — **si'lent·ly** *adv.* — **si'lent·ness** *n.*

silent butler A small receptacle with a handle and hinged lid, used for collecting refuse from ashtrays, etc.

si·len·ti·ar·y (sī·len'shē·er'ē) *n. pl.* **·ar·ies** **1** One appointed to keep silence and order in court. **2** A Byzantine official sworn not to divulge secrets of state; a privy councilor.

3 An observer of silence because of religious beliefs. [<LL *silentiarius*]
silent partner See under PARTNER.
silent system A system of prison discipline imposing silence on all prisoners.
si·le·nus (sī·lē′nəs) *n. pl.* **·ni** (-nī) In Greek mythology, any woodland deity resembling a satyr.
Si·le·nus (sī·lē′nəs) In Greek mythology, the foster father and teacher of Bacchus and leader of the satyrs: traditionally represented as a fat, drunken old man with pointed ears and goat's legs, riding on an ass. [<L <Gk. *Seilēnos* Silenus]
si·le·sia (si·lē′shə, sī-) *n.* **1** A glazed linen cloth first made in Prussian Silesia. **2** A thin, twilled cotton fabric for linings.
Si·le·sia (si·lē′shə, sī-) A region of east central Europe divided between north central Czechoslovakia and SW Poland; formerly a province of Prussia and a crownland of Austria; total area, about 20,000 square miles: German *Schlesien,* Polish *Śląsk,* Czech *Slezsko.* — **Si·le′sian** *adj.* & *n.*
si·lex (sī′leks) *n.* Silica. [<L, flint]
sil·hou·ette (sil′o͞o·et′) *n.* **1** A profile drawing or portrait having its outline filled in with uniform color, commonly black: often cut out, as from cardboard. **2** The figure or likeness cast by a shadow; the outline of a solid figure. — *v.t.* **·et·ted, ·et·ting** To cause to appear in silhouette; outline; make a silhouette profile of. [after Étienne de *Silhouette,* 1709–1767, French minister of finance; in mockery of the petty economies for which he was notorious]

SILHOUETTE Abraham Lincoln

silic– Var. of SILICO–.
sil·i·ca (sil′i·kə) *n.* A white or colorless, extremely hard, crystalline silicon dioxide, SiO_2, the principal constituent of quartz and sand. [<NL <L *silex, silicis* flint]
silica gel A highly adsorbent colloidal silica, used for deodorizing and cleaning air, purifying blast–furnace gases, etc.
sil·i·cane (sil′i·kān) *n. Chem.* Silane.
sil·i·cate (sil′i·kit) *n. Chem.* A salt of silicic acid. The silicates are mineralogically of great importance, and make up a large part of the earth's crust.
si·li·ceous (si·lish′əs) *adj.* **1** Pertaining to, resembling, or containing silica. **2** Growing or living on siliciferous soil. Also **si·li′cious.** [<L *siliceus*]
si·lic·ic (si·lis′ik) *adj.* Pertaining to, derived from, or consisting of silica or silicon. [< SILIC- + -IC]
silicic acid *Chem.* Any of several gelatinous and easily decomposed compounds of silica and water; especially, orthosilicic acid, H_4SiO_4, associated in the formation of many metallic silicates.
sil·i·cide (sil′ə·sīd) *n. Chem.* A binary compound of silicon with a metal, such as iron, cobalt, nickel, chromium, copper, or magnesium.
sil·i·cif·er·ous (sil′ə·sif′ər·əs) *adj.* Containing or producing silica; united partially with silica. [<SILIC- + -(I)FEROUS]
si·lic·i·fied wood (si·lis′ə·fīd) Wood that has been replaced by silica crystallizing out from solution so as to become a mass of quartz of the original form and structure of the wood; petrified wood. See PETRIFIED FOREST.
si·lic·i·fy (si·lis′ə·fī) *v.* **·fied, ·fy·ing** *v.t.* To convert into silica, as wood. — *v.i.* To become silica, or become impregnated with it. [< SILIC- + -(I)FY] — **si·lic′i·fi·ca′tion** *n.*
sil·i·cle (sil′i·kəl) *n.* A very short, flat silique. [<L *silicula,* dim. of *siliqua* pod]
silico– *combining form* Silicon; of, related to, or containing silicon. Also, before vowels, *silic–,* as in *silicosis.* [<L *silex, silicis* flint]
sil·i·con (sil′ə·kən) *n.* A widely–distributed nonmetallic element (symbol Si) prepared as a dull–brown amorphous powder, as shining metallic scales resembling graphite, or as a steel–gray crystalline mass, by heating silica with carbon in an electric furnace. See ELEMENT. Also **si·li·ci·um** (si·lish′ē·əm, -lis′-). [<L *silex, silicis* flint]
sil·i·cone (sil′ə·kōn) *n. Chem.* Any of various organosilicon compounds containing a silicon–carbon bond: their great physical, chemical, and electrical stability adapts them for many industrial uses as lubricants, greases, polishes, insulating resins, waterproofing materials, and for the making of a special type of synthetic rubber. [<SILICON]
sil·i·co·sis (sil′ə·kō′sis) *n. Pathol.* A pulmonary disease caused by the inhalation of finely powdered silica or quartz.
si·lic·u·lose (si·lik′yə·lōs), **si·lic·u·lous** (-ləs) *adj.* Siliquose. [<SILIQUOSE]
Si·lif·ke (si·lif·ke′) A town in central southern Turkey near the Mediterranean: ancient *Seleucia Trachea.*
si·lique (si·lēk′, sil′ik) *n. Bot.* A narrow, dry, two–valved pod or fruit characteristic of plants of the mustard family. Also **sil·i·qua** (sil′ə·kwə). [<F <L *siliqua* pod]
sil·i·quose (sil′ə·kwōs) *adj.* Silique–bearing; pertaining to or resembling a silique. Also **sil′i·quous** (-kwəs). [<NL *siliquosus* <L *siliqua* pod]
Si·lis·tri·a (si·lis′trē·ə) A city on the Danube, in NE Bulgaria. Also **Si·li·stra** (sē·lē′strä). Ancient **Du·ros·to·rum** (do͝o·ros′tə·rəm, dyo͝o-).
silk (silk) *n.* **1** The creamy–white or yellowish, very fine natural fiber produced by various insects, especially by the larvae of silkworms, to form their cocoons. **2** A similar thread spun by other insects or arachnids. **3** Cloth, thread, or garments made of silk. **4** Anything resembling or suggestive of silk, as the fine soft styles of an ear of corn. — **to hit the silk** *Slang* To descend from an aircraft by parachute. — *adj.* Consisting of silk; silken; silky. — *v.t.* To clothe or cover with silk: grand ladies plumed and *silked.* — *v.i.* To produce the portion of the flower called silk: said of corn. [OE *seoloc,* ult. <L *sericus* silken, lit., pertaining to the Seres (Chinese), from whom silk was bought. Related to SERGE.]
silk·a·line (sil′kə·lēn′) *n.* A soft and thin mercerized cotton fabric resembling silk. Also **silk′a·lene′.**
silk cotton The silky seed covering of various species of a genus *(Bombax)* of tropical American trees, and of the West Indian god tree *(Ceiba pentandra)* or corkwood *(Ochroma pyramidale).* Its principal use is for stuffing cushions, packing, etc.
silk–cot·ton tree (silk′kot′n) Any tree producing silk cotton.
silk·en (sil′kən) *adj.* **1** Made of silk. **2** Like silk; glossy; delicate; smooth. **3** Dressed in silk; hence, luxurious.
silk hat A high cylindrical hat covered with fine silk plush: worn by men and used as a dress hat.
silk·man (silk′mən) *n. pl.* **·men** (-mən) A dealer in or a manufacturer of silk; also, an operative in a silk factory.
silk paper A granite paper made with occasional silk fibers in the pulp.
silk–screen print (silk′skrēn′) A reproduction made by the silk–screen process.
silk–screen process A printing process which forces ink through the meshes of a silk screen on which the desired pattern or design has been imposed.
silk–stock·ing (silk′stok′ing) *adj.* Wearing silk stockings; hence, wealthy; luxurious. — *n.* **1** One who wears silk stockings; a member of the wealthy class. **2** A supporter of a branch of the Whig party in the United States in the early 19th century.
silk vine A deciduous shrub of the milkweed family *(Periploca graeca)* growing in the neighborhood of the Black Sea: its bark yields periplocin. Also called *wolf's–bane.*
silk·weed (silk′wēd′) *n.* Milkweed.
silk·worm (silk′wûrm′) *n.* The larva of a moth that produces a dense silken cocoon, especially the common silkworm *(Bombyx mori),* from whose cocoon commercial silk is made.
silk·y (sil′kē) *adj.* **silk·i·er, silk·i·est 1** Like silk in any way; soft; lustrous. **2** Made of or consisting of silk; silken. **3** Long, fine, and appressed, as hairs, or covered with such hairs, as leaves. **4** Gentle or insinuating in manner; smooth and persuasive: usually in a bad sense, implying insincerity. — **silk′i·ly** *adv.* — **silk′i·ness** *n.*
silky oak See under LACEWOOD.
sill (sil) *n.* **1** A horizontal member forming the foundation, or part of the foundation, of a structure of any kind, as at the bottom of a casing in a building; especially, a door sill or a window sill. **2** A timber in the frame of the floor of a railroad car: end *sill;* side *sill.* **3** *Geol.* A relatively thin stratum of igneous rock intruded between level or gently inclined beds of other rock. [OE *syll*]
sil·la·bub (sil′ə·bub) *n.* **1** A dish made by combining milk or cream with wine or cider, and thus forming a soft curd, which is then flavored. It may be whipped into a froth, or made solid by boiling after adding water and gelatin. **2** Figuratively, something frothy, as flowery language. Also spelled *syllabub.* [Alter. of obs. *sillibouk* <SILLY + OE *būc* belly]
Sil·lan·pää (sil′län·pa), **Frans Eemil,** 1888–1964, Finnish writer.
sil·ler (sil′ər) *adj.* & *n. Scot.* Silver; money.
Sil·li·man (sil′i·mən), **Benjamin,** 1779–1864, U. S. chemist and geologist.
sil·ly (sil′ē) *adj.* **·li·er, ·li·est 1** Destitute of ordinary good sense; simple; foolish; imbecile; fatuous; sometimes, senile. **2** Characterized by or resulting from foolishness or imbecility; stupid: *silly* talk. **3** *Rare* Simple; plain; rustic. **4** *Colloq.* Stunned; dazed, as by a blow. **5** *Obs.* or *Brit. Dial.* Frail; feeble; weak; helpless. **6** *Scot.* Mentally or physically incapable; idiotic; imbecilic. **7** *Obs.* Scanty; meager. See synonyms under CHILDISH, RIDICULOUS. — *n. pl.* **·lies** *Colloq.* A silly person. [OE *gesælig* happy] — **sil′li·ly** *adv.* — **sil′li·ness** *n.*
si·lo (sī′lō) *n. pl.* **·los 1** A structure, usually of wood or concrete, as a cylindrical pit or a tower, in which fodder, grain, or other food is stored green to be fermented and used as feed for cattle, etc. See ENSILAGE. **2** A deep cylindrical structure built underground for the housing and launching of guided missiles. — *v.t.* **·loed, ·lo·ing** To put or preserve in a silo; turn into ensilage. [<Sp. <L *sirus* <Gk. *siros* pit for corn]

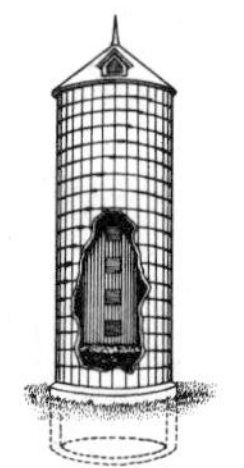
SILO Stave type, showing interior construction and pit.

Si·lo·am (si·lō′əm, sī-) A spring and pool outside Jerusalem. *John* ix 7.
sil·ox·ane (sil′ok′sān) *n. Chem.* Any of a class of oxygen–containing silicon compounds.
silt (silt) *n.* **1** An earthy sediment consisting of extremely fine particles of rock and soil suspended in and carried by water. **2** A deposit of such sediment, as at the mouth of a river. — *v.i.* **1** To become filled or choked with silt: usually with *up.* **2** To ooze; drift. — *v.t.* **3** To fill or choke with silt or mud: usually with *up.* [ME *sylte.* Cf. Dan. *sylt* salt marsh, Norw. *sylta* coast–land washed by the sea.] — **silt′y** *adj.*
sil·ta·tion (sil·tā′shən) *n.* The process of depositing silt.
sil·thi·ane (sil′thē·ān) *n. Chem.* Any of a class of sulfur–containing silicon compounds having the general formula $H_3Si(SSiH_2)_nSSiH_3$. [<SIL(ICON) + THI- + -ANE[1]]
Sil·u·res (sil′yə·rēz) *n. pl.* The pre–Celtic inhabitants of ancient Britain, occupying what is now SE Wales, described by Tacitus as of Iberian origin. [<L]
Si·lu·ri·an (si·lo͝or′ē·ən, sī-) *adj.* **1** *Geol.* Of or pertaining to the period or rock system of the Paleozoic era following the Ordovician and preceding the Devonian, sometimes called the era of invertebrates: so called because first identified in southern Wales, the home of the ancient Silures. **2** Of or pertaining to the Silures. — *n.* **1** The Silurian period or system. **2** Originally, the period between the Cambrian and the Devonian.
si·lu·rid (si·lo͝or′id, sī-) *n.* Any one of a large family of fishes *(Siluridae),* the catfishes, including many fresh–water food fishes of the United States. — *adj.* Of or pertaining to the *Siluridae.* Also **si·lu′roid.** [<NL *Siluridae,* name of the family <L *silurus* a river fish <Gk. *silouros*]
sil·va (sil′və), **sil·van** (sil′vən), etc. See SYLVA, etc.
Sil·va·nus (sil·vā′nəs) In Roman mythology, a god of woods and farming: also *Sylvanus.* [<L < *silva* forest]
Sil·va·nus (sil·vā′nəs, *Du., Ger.* sēl·vä′no͞os) A masculine personal name. Also *Fr.* **Sil·vain** (sēl·vaṅ′) or **Sil·vie** (sēl·vē′), *Ital., Sp.* **Sil·va·no** (sēl·vä′nō) or **Sil·vio** (sēl′vyō). [<L, of the forest]
sil·ver (sil′vər) *n.* **1** A white, ductile, and very

malleable metallic element (symbol Ag), crystallizing in the isometric system and possessing a high electric conductivity: one of the precious metals. It is found native, as well as in combination. See ELEMENT. **2** Silver regarded as a commodity or as a standard of currency. **3** Silver coin considered as money; hence, ready cash or change; money in general. **4** Articles for domestic use, as tableware, made of silver; silver plate; silverware. **5** A luster or color resembling that of silver; also, the color of silver. **6** *Phot.* Silver nitrate or one of the other salts of silver, used for sensitizing paper. — *adj.* **1** Made of or coated with silver. **2** Resembling silver; having a silvery lustre. **3** Having the soft, clear tones of a silver bell; hence, enticing; persuasive; eloquent. **4** Relating to, connected with, or producing silver. **5** Designating a 25th wedding anniversary. **6** White; hoary: said of the hair or beard. **7** Favoring the use of silver as a monetary standard. — *v.t.* **1** To coat or plate with silver. **2** To coat with some substance having a resemblance to silver; specifically, to coat with amalgam of tin and mercury, as a mirror. **3** To make silverlike; cause to glitter like silver. **4** To coat, as photographic paper, with a film of a silver salt. — *v.i.* **5** To become silver or white, as with age; to become silverlike. [OE *siolfor*] — **sil′ver·er** *n.*

silver age **1** In Latin literature, the age, following the Augustan age, of which Martial and Tacitus are representatives. **2** In classical mythology, the age of Jupiter's rule, succeeding that of Kronos or Saturn and preceding the brazen age.

sil·ver·bell (sil′vər·bel′) *n.* A small tree *(Halesia carolina)* of the southern United States, with showy white flowers: sometimes called *snowdrop tree.* Also **silverbell tree.**

sil·ver·ber·ry (sil′vər·ber′ē) *n.* *pl.* **·ber·ries** A shrub *(Elaeagnus commutata)* of the northwestern United States, with silvery foliage, flowers, and edible fruit.

silver bromide *Chem.* A photosensitive compound, AgBr, of silver salts and a bromide: used in photography.

silver certificate Paper currency issued by the United States treasury and validated by silver currency or bullion.

silver chloride *Chem.* A white, curdy precipitate, AgCl, made by treating silver salts with chloride solutions: used in photography for developing and printing.

sil·ver·fish (sil′vər·fish′) *n.* *pl.* **·fish** or **·fish·es** **1** A silvery-white variety of the goldfish. **2** The tarpon. **3** The silversides. **4** Any of numerous primitive, flat-bodied, wingless insects (genus *Lepisma,* order *Thysanura*) having three bristlelike tails and feeding on starchy matter: often called *bristletail.* **5** Any of several similar insects, as the firebrat.

silver fox **1** The red fox *(Vulpes fulva)* of the United States and Canada, in that color phase when the pelage is black with interspersed silver-tipped hairs. **2** The fur.

silver glance Silver sulfide, Ag_2S; argentite.

silver gray A slightly bluish gray, the color of silver.

sil·ver·ing (sil′vər·ing) *n.* **1** A plating or covering of silver, or an imitation of it, as applied to any surface. **2** The art or process of coating surfaces with or as with silver. **3** Sensitization of photographic paper with a silver salt.

sil·ver·ling (sil′vər·ling) *n.* **1** An old Hebrew or Persian silver coin. **2** A tarpon.

sil·ver·ly (sil′vər·lē) *adv.* In the manner of silver; brightly; with sweet tone.

silver maple White maple.

sil·vern (sil′vərn) *adj. Archaic* or *Poetic* Made of or like silver.

silver nitrate *Chem.* A white, crystalline, poisonous compound, $AgNO_3$, obtained by treating silver with nitric acid. It is widely used in industry and photography, and in medicine as an astringent, antiseptic, etc.

silver plate **1** Table utensils made of silver. **2** *U.S.* Plated silverware: a trade term.

silver point **1** A drawing implement consisting of a slender silver rod pointed at one end, or of silver wire held in an etching-needle holder. **2** The process of drawing with such an implement. **3** A drawing made with a silver point on paper coated with a white pigment, as Chinese white, characterized by delicacy of line, and often by a tarnish which is highly esteemed. **4** *Physics* The melting point of silver at normal atmospheric pressure, 960.5° C.: one of the basic points in the international temperature scale.

silver poplar The white poplar.

sil·ver·sides (sil′vər·sīdz′) *n.* **1** Any of certain small fishes (family *Atherinidae*) related to the mullets and blennies, having a silver band along each side of the body; especially, the **common silversides** *(Menidia notata)* of the coast of the eastern United States. **2** Any small cyprinoid; a fresh-water minnow. Also **sil′ver·side′.**

sil·ver·smith (sil′vər·smith′) *n.* A worker in silver; a maker of silverware.

silver standard A monetary standard or system based on silver.

Silver Star A U. S. military decoration in the form of a bronze star inset with a small raised silver star, awarded for gallantry in action: first issued in 1932, and ranking next in honor to the Distinguished Service Cross.

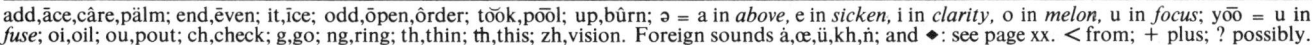

Silver State Nickname of Nevada: so called from its native silver ores.

sil·ver–tongued (sil′vər·tungd′) *adj.* Persuasive; eloquent.

sil·ver·ware (sil′vər·wâr′) *n.* Articles made of silver; silver plate; especially, tableware.

SILVER STAR

sil·ver·weed (sil′vər·wēd′) *n.* A perennial herb *(Potentilla anserina)* of the rose family, growing on shores and meadows, with pinnate silvery leaves and large yellow flowers.

sil·ver·y (sil′vər·ē) *adj.* **1** Containing or adorned with silver. **2** Resembling silver, as in luster, hue, or sound: a *silvery* laugh. — **sil′ver·i·ness** *n.*

Sil·ves·ter (sil·ves′tər) A masculine personal name. Also *Fr.* **Sil·ves·tre** (sēl·ves′tr′). *Ital.* **Sil·ves·tro** (sēl·ves′trō). [<L, forest dweller]

sil·vi·cul·ture (sil′vi·kul′chər) *n.* The art of producing and tending a forest and forest trees. See FORESTRY. [<L *silva* forest + CULTURE] — **sil′vi·cul′tur·al** *adj.* — **sil′vi·cul′·tur·al·ly** *adv.* — **sil′vi·cul′tur·ist** *n.*

s'il vous plaît (sēl vo͞o ple′) *French* If you please; please.

si·ma (sī′mə) *n. Geol.* An igneous rock rich in silica and magnesium underlying sial formations in continental land masses. [<SI(LICA) + MA(GNESIUM)]

si·mar (si·mär′) *n.* A light, flowing robe for women. [<F *simarre* <Ital. *cimarra* <Arabic *sammūr* sable]

sim·a·ru·ba (sim′ə·ro͞o′bə) *n.* Any of a genus *(Simaruba)* of tropical American trees of the quassia family, having diclinous flowers and drupaceous fruits. *S. amara* yields a bark used in pharmacy. Also **sim′a·rou′ba.** [<NL < native Carib name] — **sim′a·ru·ba′ceous** or **·rou·ba′ceous** *adj.*

Sim·bor (sim·bôr′) A continental territory of Diu district, Portuguese India, on the southern coast of the Kathiawar peninsula at the mouth of the Gulf of Cambay.

Sim·chath To·rah (sim′khäs tō′rə) Literally, the rejoicing over the law; a Jewish holiday which falls on the 23rd of Tishri and closes the feast of Sukkoth. See CALENDAR (Hebrew), JEWISH HOLIDAYS. Also **Sim′hath To′rah.**

Sim·coe (sim′kō), **Lake** A lake in southern Ontario, Canada; 280 square miles.

Sim·e·on (sim′ē·ən, *Ger.* zē′mā·ōn) A masculine personal name. Also *Fr.* **Si·mé·on** (sē·mā·ôṅ′), *Pg.* **Si·ma·ão** (sē′mä·ouṅ′) or **Si·mão** (sē·mouṅ′), *Sp.* **Si·ma·on** (sē′mä·ōn′). See also SIMON. [<Hebrew, obedient]
— **Simeon** The second son of Jacob, or the tribe descended from him. *Gen.* xxix 33.
— **Simeon** A Biblical personage. See NUNC DIMITTIS.
— **Simeon Sty·li·tes** (stī·lī′tēz), 390?–459, Syrian ascetic and stylite.

Sim·fer·o·pol (sim′fər·ō′pəl, *Russian* sēm′fi·rô′pəl) The capital of the Crimea, SW Russian S.F.S.R., in the south central part of the peninsula.

sim·i·an (sim′ē·ən) *adj.* Like or pertaining to the apes and monkeys. — *n.* An ape or monkey. [<L *simia* ape]

sim·i·lar (sim′ə·lər) *adj.* **1** Bearing resemblance to one another or to something else; like, but not completely identical. **2** Of like characteristics, nature, or degree; of the same scope, order, or purpose. **3** *Music* Having motion in the same direction; ascending or descending together, as two parts. **4** *Geom.* Shaped alike: said of two figures, each of which may become congruous with the other by altering all its linear dimensions in one and the same ratio, its angles remaining unchanged. See synonyms under ALIKE, SYNONYMOUS. [<F *similaire* <L *similis* like]

similar fraction See under FRACTION.

sim·i·lar·i·ty (sim′ə·lar′ə·tē) *n. pl.* **·ties** **1** The quality or state of being similar. **2** The point in which the objects compared are similar. **3** *pl.* Things that coincide with or resemble each other. See synonyms under ANALOGY, APPROXIMATION.

sim·i·lar·ly (sim′ə·lər·lē) *adv.* Likewise.

sim·i·le (sim′ə·lē) *n.* A rhetorical figure expressing comparison or likeness, by the use of such terms as *like, as, so,* etc.: distinguished from *metaphor* and *comparison* proper. [<L, neut. of *similis* similar]

Synonyms: comparison, figure, illustration, image, imagery, likeness, metaphor, similitude, symbol. The *simile* carries its note of *comparison* on the surface, in the words *as, like, such as,* or similar expressions; the *metaphor* is given directly without any note of *comparison.* "God is *like* a rock" is a *simile*; "God *is* a rock" is a *metaphor.* In order that a *comparison* may become a *simile,* objects of different classes must be compared, bringing in some imaginative element. To say, "The Hudson is like the Rhine" is not *simile,* but direct and literal *comparison*; but to say, "The Hudson flows like the march of time" is to lift the river out of its class and associate it with a great elemental conception, and thus to transform the *comparison* into a *simile. Similitude* is broader in meaning than *simile* or *metaphor,* and may include direct and literal *comparison.* Compare ALLEGORY, ANALOGY, EMBLEM.

si·mil·i·a si·mil·i·bus cu·ran·tur (si·mil′ē·ə si·mil′ə·bəs ko͞o·ran′tər) *Latin* Like (ailments) are cured by like, i.e., by remedies that produce the effects of the disease itself: the principle of homeopathy.

si·mil·i·tude (si·mil′ə·to͞od, -tyo͞od) *n.* **1** Similarity. **2** One who or that which is similar. **3** A rhetorical figure involving comparison or likeness; loosely, a metaphor or a simile. **4** *Geom.* The relation of identity between two figures irrespective of magnitude. See synonyms under ANALOGY, IMAGE, PICTURE, SIMILE. [<L *similitudo* < *similis* like]

sim·i·ous (sim′ē·əs) *adj.* Simian. Also **sim′i·oid.** [See SIMIAN]

sim·i·tar (sim′ə·tər), **sim·i·ter** See SCIMITAR.

Sim·la (sim′lə) A city of far northern central India; capital of Himachal Pradesh. Formerly the summer capital of India under British rule.

sim·lin (sim′lin) *n.* A cymlin. [Var. of SIMNEL]

sim·mer[1] (sim′ər) *v.i.* **1** To boil gently or with a singing sound; be or stay at or just below the boiling point. **2** To be on the point of breaking forth, as with rage. — *v.t.* **3** To keep at or just below the boiling point. — *n.* The state or process of simmering; figuratively, a busy pondering over something, or a state of repressed emotion. [< obs. *simper* boil; origin unknown; prob. imit.]

sim·mer[2] (sim′ər) *n. Scot.* Summer.

Simms (simz), **William Gilmore,** 1806–70, U. S. novelist and poet.

sim·nel (sim′nəl) *n. Brit.* **1** A brittle cake or bread made of fine flour. **2** A rich cake for mid-Lent Sunday, Easter, or Christmas. [<OF *simenel* <LL *siminellus* <L *simila* fine wheat flour, prob. <Gk. *semidalis,* ult. <Babylonian *samidu* fine flour]

si·mo·le·on (si·mō′lē·ən) *n. Slang* A dollar. [Origin unknown]

Si·mon (sī′mən; *Fr.* sē·môn′; *Ger.* zē′mōn; *Sp.,*

Sw. sē·mōn′; *Hungarian* shē′mōn) A masculine personal name. Also *Ital.* **Si·mo·ne** (sē·mō′nā). See also SIMEON. [<Hebrew, obedient]
— **Simon Ma·gus** (mā′gəs) A Samarian magician of the first century, founder of the Simonians, a sect competing with Gentile Christianity.
— **Simon Peter** See PETER.
— **Simon Ze·lo·tes** (zē·lō′tēz) One of the twelve apostles: also called "Simon the Canaanite."
Si·mon (sī′mən) *n.* A credulous unsophisticated person: from the Mother Goose nursery rime *Simple Simon.*
Si·mon (sī′mən), **Sir John Allsebrook,** 1873–1954, first viscount Simon, English lawyer and statesman.
si·mo·ni·ac (si·mō′nē·ak) *n.* One who carries on or is guilty of simony. [<Med. L *simoniacus.* See SIMONY.] — **sim·o·ni·a·cal** (sim′ə·nī′ə·kəl) *adj.* — **sim′o·ni′a·cal·ly** *adv.*
Si·mo·ni·an (si·mō′nē·ən, sī-) *adj.* Of or pertaining to Simon Magus or his sect. — *n.* One of an early sect that held Simon Magus to be the Messiah.
Si·mo·ni·an·ism (si·mō′nē·ən·iz′əm, sī-) *n.* Saint-Simonism.
Si·mon·i·des of Ceos (sī·mon′ə·dēz) A Greek lyric poet of the sixth and early fifth centuries B.C.
Simon Le·gree (li·grē′) In Harriet Beecher Stowe's *Uncle Tom's Cabin,* the cruel overseer; hence, any brutal master.
si·mon-pure (sī′mən·pyŏŏr′) *adj.* Real; genuine; authentic. [after a character in a 17th c. comedy, who is impersonated by a rival; the rival is discomfited when the real Simon Pure appears]
si·mo·ny (sī′mə·nē, sim′ə-) *n.* Traffic in sacred things; the purchase or sale of ecclesiastical preferment. [<Med. L *simonia* <*Simon (Magus),* who offered Peter money for the gift of the Holy Spirit]
si·moom (si·mōōm′, sī-) *n.* A hot, dry, dust-laden, exhausting wind of the desert, as in Africa and Arabia: also spelled *samoun.* Also **si·moon′** (-mōōn′). [<Arabic *samūm* < *samma* poison]
simp (simp) *n. U.S. Slang* A simpleton.
sim·per (sim′pər) *v.i.* To smile in a silly, self-conscious manner; smirk. — *v.t.* To say with a simper. — *n.* A silly, self-conscious smile; smirk. [Prob. <Scand. Cf. Sw. and Norw. *semper* affected, coy.] — **sim′per·er** *n.* — **sim′per·ing·ly** *adv.*
sim·ple (sim′pəl) *adj.* **·pler, ·plest 1** Consisting of one thing; single; uncombined; unmingled. **2** Not complex or complicated; easy. **3** Without embellishment; plain; unadorned. **4** Free from affectation; sincere; artless; unsophisticated; also, of humble rank or condition; lowly. **5** Of weak intellect; silly; feeble-minded. **6** Not worth much consideration; insignificant; trifling; ordinary. **7** Without luxury; frugal. **8** Having nothing added; mere: the *simple* truth. **9** *Chem.* That cannot be or has not been decomposed; elementary; also, unmixed. **10** *Bot.* Not subdivided: a *simple* leaf; entire; not divided. **11** *Music* **a** Single. **b** Without overtones. **c** Not developed or elaborated: *simple* harmony. — *n.* **1** That which is simple; an unartificial, uncomplex, or natural thing; an element. **2** A medicinal plant, or the medicine extracted from it: from the former supposition that each single herb was or provided a specific for some disease. **3** A simpleton; a stupid or ignorant person; also, a person of humble position or birth. **4** *Eccl.* A feast of lowest rank which is merely commemorated at the canonical hours. **5** *pl. Colloq.* Foolishness; insanity: He suffers from the *simples.* [<OF <L *simplex, simplus*]
Synonyms (adj.): chaste, modest, natural, neat, plain, quiet, unadorned, unaffected, unembellished, unpretentious, unstudied, unvarnished. See CANDID, PURE. *Antonyms*: affected, artful, artificial, complex, complicated, elaborate, intricate, involved, ostentatious, pretentious, showy.
simple fraction See under FRACTION.
simple fruit *Bot.* A fruit consisting of a single enlarged and matured ovary, as the date, cherry, peach, apple, and quince.
sim·ple-heart·ed (sim′pəl·här′tid) *adj.* **1** Tender-hearted. **2** Ingenuous in disposition; open; sincere.
simple honors In bridge, three honors of the trump suit held by a player and his partner.
simple interest Interest computed on the original principal alone.
simple machine 1 Any one of certain elementary mechanical contrivances, as the lever, the wedge, the inclined plane, the screw, the wheel and axle, and the pulley. **2** A hand tool having no parts, as a hammer or chisel, or two parts working in simple combination, as shears.
sim·ple-mind·ed (sim′pəl·mīn′did) *adj.* **1** Artless or unsophisticated in character. **2** Defective in intellect; mentally imbecile. — **sim′ple-mind′ed·ly** *adv.* — **sim′ple-mind′ed·ness** *n.*
sim·pler (sim′plər) *n.* A collector or dispenser of herbs or medicinal remedies extracted from them; herbalist.
simple sentence See under SENTENCE.
Simple Simon A simpleton: from a character in an old English nursery rime of this name.
simple sugar A monosaccharide.
sim·ple·ton (sim′pəl·tən) *n.* A weak-minded or silly person.
sim·plex (sim′pleks) *adj.* **1** Simple. **2** Noting a form of telegraphy in which only one message is sent over a wire at a time. [<L, simple]
simplici- *combining form* Simple. Also, before vowels, **simplic-.** [<L *simplex, simplicis* simple]
sim·pli·ci·den·tate (sim′plə·si·den′tāt) *adj.* Pertaining or belonging to a suborder of rodents *(Simplicidentata)* with a single pair of upper incisors, which includes mice, squirrels, porcupines, and all others with the exception of hares and pikas.
sim·plic·i·dent (sim·plis′ə·dənt) *adj.* Simplicidentate. — *n.* A simplicidentate rodent.
sim·plic·i·ty (sim·plis′ə·tē) *n. pl.* **·ties 1** The state of being simple; freedom from admixture, ornament, formality, ostentation, subtlety, or difficulty; sincerity; unaffectedness. **2** Deficiency of intelligence or good sense, or an instance of it. See synonyms under INNOCENCE. Also **sim′ple·ness.** [<L *simplicitas, -tatis*]
sim·pli·fy (sim′plə·fī) *v.t.* **·fied, ·fy·ing** To make more simple or less complex. [<F *simplifier* <Med. L *simplificare* <L *simplex* simple + *facere* make] — **sim′pli·fi·ca′tion** *n.* — **sim′pli·fi′er** *n.*
sim·plis·tic (sim·plis′tik) *adj.* Tending to ignore or overlook underlying questions, complications, or details; overly simple: *simplistic* attitudes. — **sim·plis′ti·cal·ly** *adv.*
Sim·plon Pass (sim′plon, *Fr.* saṅ·plôṅ′) A pass over the Alps in SW Switzerland; elevation, 6,592 feet; traversed by a road built (1800–06) by Napoleon near the **Simplon Tunnel** (1906), 12 1/4 miles, the longest in the world.
sim·ply (sim′plē) *adv.* **1** In a simple manner; intelligibly; without ostentation or extravagance; without subtlety or affectation; unassumingly. **2** Merely. **3** Without sense or discretion; foolishly. **4** Really; absolutely: *simply* charming: often used ironically.
Sims (simz), **William Sowden,** 1858–1936, U. S. admiral born in Canada.
Sim·son (sim′sôn) Swedish form of SAMSON.
sim·u·la·cre (sim′yə·lā′kər) *n. Obs.* An image.
sim·u·la·crum (sim′yə·lā′krəm) *n. pl.* **·cra** (-krə) **1** That which is made in the likeness of a being or thing; an image. **2** An imaginary, visionary, or shadowy semblance. **3** A sham. [<L, image < *simulare.* See SIMULATE.]
sim·u·lant (sim′yə·lənt) *adj.* Simulating. — *n.* One who or that which simulates. [<L *simulans, -antis,* ppr. of *simulare.* See SIMULATE.]
sim·u·lar (sim′yə·lər) *n.* One who simulates; a pretender. — *adj.* **1** Given to simulation; pretending. **2** Counterfeit.
sim·u·late (sim′yə·lāt) *v.t.* **·lat·ed, ·lat·ing 1** To assume or have the appearance or form of, without the reality; counterfeit; imitate. **2** To make a pretense of. See synonyms under IMITATE, PRETEND. — *adj.* (-lāt, -lit) Simulated; pretended. [<L *simulatus,* pp. of *simulare* imitate < *similis* like] — **sim′u·la′tor** *n.*
sim·u·la·tion (sim′yə·lā′shən) *n.* The act of simulating; counterfeit; sham. See synonyms under PRETENSE. — **sim′u·la′tive, sim′u·la·to′ry** (-lə·tôr′ē, -tō′rē) *adj.* — **sim′u·la′tive·ly** *adv.*
si·mul·cast (sī′məl·kast′, -käst′) *v.t.* **·cast, ·cast·ing** To broadcast by radio and television simultaneously. — *n.* A broadcast transmitted by radio and television simultaneously. [< SIMUL(TANEOUS) + (BROAD)CAST]
si·mul·ta·ne·ous (sī′məl·tā′nē·əs, sim′əl-) *adj.* Occurring, done, or existing at the same time. [<LL *simultaneus* <L *simul* at the same time] — **si′mul·ta′ne·ous·ly** *adv.* — **si′mul·ta′ne·ous·ness, si′mul·ta·ne′i·ty** (-tə·nē′ə·tē) *n.*
simultaneous equations *Math.* A series of algebraic equations such that each will satisfy the conditions of two or more variables, as, $x + y = 7$ and $2x + 3y = 19$, where $x = 2$, $y = 5$.
si·murg (si·mŏŏrg′) *n.* In Persian mythology, an immense bird possessing great knowledge, who has witnessed the destruction of the world three times; perhaps, the roc. Also **si·murgh′.** [<Persian *simurgh*]
sin[1] (sin) *n.* **1** A lack of conformity to, or a transgression, especially when deliberate, of a law, precept, or principle regarded as having divine authority. **2** The state or condition of having thus transgressed; wickedness. **3** A particular instance of such transgression. **4** Any fault or error; an offense against a standard: a literary *sin.* — *v.* **sinned, sin·ning** *v.i.* **1** To commit sin, transgress, neglect, or disregard the divine law or any requirement of right, duty, or propriety; do wrong. — *v.t.* **2** To commit or do wrongfully: to *sin* a great sin. **3** To effect, consume, drive, etc., by sin. [OE *synn*]
Synonyms (noun): crime, criminality, delinquency, depravity, evil, guilt, ill-doing, immorality, iniquity, misdeed, offense, transgression, ungodliness, unrighteousness, vice, viciousness, wickedness, wrong, wrong-doing. *Sin,* in religious teaching, is any lack of holiness, any defect of moral purity and truth, whether in heart or life, whether of commission or of omission. *Transgression,* as its etymology indicates, is the stepping over a specific enactment, whether of God or man, ordinarily by overt act, but in the broadest sense in volition or desire. *Sin* may be either act or state; *transgression* is always an act, mental or physical. *Crime* is often used for a flagrant violation of right, but in the technical sense denotes specific violation of human law. *Depravity* denotes no act, but a perverted moral condition from which any act of *sin* may proceed. *Immorality* denotes outward violation of the moral law. Compare OFFENSE. *Antonyms*: decorum, godliness, goodness, holiness, integrity, morality, purity, right, righteousness, sinlessness, uprightness, virtue. Compare synonyms for VIRTUE.
sin[2] (sin) *adv., prep., & conj. Scot. & Brit. Dial.* Since.
Si·nai (sī′nī, -nē·ī′) A peninsula between the Mediterranean and the Red Sea, constituting the easternmost part of Egypt NW of Arabia. Also **Sinaitic Peninsula.** — **Si·na·ic** (sī·nā′ik), **Si·na·it·ic** (sī′nā·it′ik) *adj.*
Si·nai (sī′nī, -nē·ī′), **Mount** The mountain where Moses received the law from God: generally identified with a mountain in the southern part of Sinai. *Ex.* xix.
sin·al·bin (sin·al′bin) *n. Chem.* A white, bitter, crystalline alkaloid, $C_{30}H_{42}O_{15}N_2S_2$, found in the seeds of the white mustard. [<L *sinapi* mustard + *albus* white]
Si·na·lo·a (sē′nä·lō′ä) A state in western Mexico, on the Gulf of California; 22,580 square miles; capital, Culiacán.
Sin·an·thro·pus (sin·an′thrə·pəs, sī′nan·thrō′·pəs) *n. Paleontol.* A large-brained, well-developed hominid primate identified from extensive fossil remains discovered between 1927 and 1939 in the Pleistocene deposits of a cave near Peking, China. Also called *Peking man.* [<NL <Gk. *Sinai* Chinese + *anthropos* man]
sin·a·pine (sin′ə·pēn, -pin) *n. Chem.* A bitter, unstable alkaloid, $C_{16}H_{25}O_6N$, contained in the seed of the black mustard. Also **sin′a·pin** (-pin). [<L *sinapi* mustard + -INE[2]]
sin·a·pism (sin′ə·piz′əm) *n.* A mustard plaster. [<L *sinapismus* <Gk. *sinapismos* < *sinapi* mustard]
Sin·ar·quist (sin′är·kwist) *n.* A member of an armed fascist group *(Unión Nacional Sinarquista),* formed about 1937, pledged to destroy liberalism and democracy in Mexico and to establish an authoritarian clerical state. [< Sp. *sinarquista* < *sinarquismo* < *sin-* (<L *sine*) without + *anarquismo* anarchism] — **Sin′ar·quism** *n.* — **Sin′ar·quis′tic** *adj.*
Sin·bad (sin′bad) See SINDBAD THE SAILOR.
since (sins) *adv.* **1** From a past time, mentioned or referred to, up to the present. **2** At some time between a certain past time or

event and the present: He was willing at first, but has *since* refused. **3** In time before the present; ago; before now. — *prep.* **1** During or within the time after or later than: Things have changed *since* you left. **2** Continuously throughout the time after: He has been working *since* noon. — *conj.* **1** During or within the time after which. **2** Continuously from the time when: She has been ill *since* she arrived. **3** Because of or following upon the fact that; inasmuch as. See synonyms under BECAUSE. [ME *sithens* <OE *siththan* afterwards + *-s* (adverbial termination)]

sin·cere (sin·sir′) *adj.* **1** Being in reality as it is in appearance; real; genuine: *sincere* regret. **2** Intending precisely what one says or what one appears to intend; free from hypocrisy; honest in one's action or profession: a *sincere* friend. **3** *Obs.* Being without admixture; free; pure. **4** *Obs.* Blameless. **5** *Obs.* Sound; whole. See synonyms under CANDID, HONEST. [<L *sincerus* uncorrupted <*sin-* without + stem of *caries* decay] — **sin·cere′ly** *adv.*

sin·cer·i·ty (sin·ser′ə·tē) *n.* The state or quality of being sincere; honesty of purpose or character; freedom from hypocrisy, deceit, or simulation. See synonyms under INNOCENCE. Also **sin·cere′ness.**

sin·ci·put (sin′si·put) *n. Anat.* The top of the head, especially the anterior portion. Compare OCCIPUT. [<L <*semi-* half + *caput* head] — **sin·cip·i·tal** (sin·sip′ə·təl) *adj.*

Sin·clair (sin·klâr′), **Upton,** 1878–1968, U. S. author and socialist.

sind (sind) *Scot. v.t.* To rinse; wash down (food) with drink; quench. — *n.* A slight washing; a drink with or after food.

Sind (sind) A former province of West Pakistan, on the Arabian Sea; incorporated into West Pakistan province, 1955; 47,569 square miles; former capital, Hyderabad; total area of Sind and Khairpur, 56,447 square miles, divided into the Commissioners' Divisions of Hyderabad and Khairpur, 1955.

Sind·bad the Sailor (sind′bad) In the *Arabian Nights,* a traveling merchant of Baghdad, who relates the marvelous adventures that befell him on his seven voyages. Also spelled *Sinbad.*

sin·dry (sin′drē) *Scot. adj.* Sundry; several. — *adv.* Asunder.

sine[1] (sīn) *n. Trig.* **1** A function of an angle in a right triangle expressible as the ratio of the side opposite the angle to the hypotenuse. **2** A function of any acute angle expressible, when plotted in Cartesian coordinates, as the ratio of the ordinate to the distance from the point where the ordinate crosses one leg of the angle to the origin. Abbreviated *sin,* as, *sin A.* See TRIGONOMETRIC FUNCTION. — **versed sine** One of the trigonometric functions, equal to one minus the cosine: also *versine.* ◆ Homophone: *sign.* [<L *sinus* bend (trans. of Arabic *jayb* bosom of a garment, sine). Doublet of SINUS.]

B A C O

SINE

AB. Arc.
AO. Radius.
BC. Perpendicular.
$\frac{BC}{AO}$ is sine of the arc *AB.*

si·ne[2] (sī′nē) *prep. Latin* Without.

sin eater One who takes upon himself the sins of a dead person by eating food placed upon the breast of the dead: an ancient Celtic custom closely related to the scapegoat theory.

si·ne·cure (sī′nə·kyŏŏr, sin′ə-) *n.* **1** An office having emoluments but few or no duties. **2** A benefice without cure of souls. [<L *sine* without + *cura* care] — **si′ne·cur·ism** *n.* — **si′ne·cur·ist** *n.*

sine curve *Math.* The plane curve of the equation $y = \sin x$. The curve has a period of $x = 2\pi$ (radians) along the abscissa and a limit along the ordinate of $y = \pm 1$.

si·ne di·e (sī′nē dī′ē) *Latin* Without a day; indefinitely: an adjournment *sine die* (that is, without setting a day for reassembling).

si·ne mo·ra (sī′nē mō′rə) *Latin* Without delay.

si·ne pro·le (sī′nē prō′lē) *Latin* Without offspring: used in genealogical tables: abbr. *s.p.*

si·ne qua non (sī′nē kwā non′) *Latin* That which is indispensable; an essential: literally, without which not.

sin·ew (sin′yōō) *n.* **1** A tendon or other fibrous cord. **2** Strength, or that which supplies strength. **3** *Obs.* A nerve. — *v.t.* To strengthen or knit together, as with sinews; supply with sinews. [OE *sinu, seonu*]

sin·ew·less (sin′yōō·lis) *adj.* **1** Without sinews. **2** Without strength or vigor.

sinews of war Money as a means of carrying on war.

sin·ew·y (sin′yōō·ē) *adj.* **1** Characteristic or consisting of a sinew or nerve. **2** Well braced with sinews; strong; brawny. See synonyms under STRONG.

sin·fo·ni·a (sin·fō′nē·ə, *Ital.* sēn′fō·nē′ä) *n. Italian* **1** A symphony. **2** The overture, in operas of early date.

sin·ful (sin′fəl) *adj.* Consisting in, suggestive of, or tainted with sin. [OE *synfull*] — **sin′·ful·ly** *adv.* — **sin′ful·ness** *n.*

Synonyms (adj.): bad, criminal, depraved, evil, faulty, flagitious, immoral, iniquitous, nefarious, unholy, unrighteous, unworthy, vicious, vile, villainous, wicked, wrong. See BAD[1], CRIMINAL, IMMORAL. Compare synonyms for SIN[1]. *Antonyms*: godly, good, holy, immaculate, incorrupt, incorruptible, innocent, just, right, righteous, sinless, spotless, stainless, undefiled, unfallen, unperverted, unstained, unsullied, untainted, upright, virtuous, worthy.

sing (sing) *v.* **sang** or *(now less commonly)* **sung, sung, sing·ing** *v.i.* **1** To utter words or sounds with musical inflections of the voice. **2** To perform vocal compositions professionally or in a specified manner: She *sings* well. **3** To utter melodious sounds, as a bird. **4** To make a continuous, melodious sound suggestive of singing, as a teakettle, the wind, etc. **5** To buzz or hum; ring: My ears are *singing*. **6** To be suitable for singing. **7** To relate something in verse; hence, to compose poetry. **8** *Slang* To confess the details of a crime, and so implicate others. — *v.t.* **9** To perform (a song, etc.) vocally. **10** To chant; intone. **11** To bring to a specified condition by singing: *Sing* me to sleep. **12** To accompany or escort with songs. **13** To acclaim or relate in or as in song: Generations *sing* his deeds. — *n.* **1** The humming sound made by a bullet in flight. **2** *Colloq.* A social gathering at which songs are sung: a community *sing*. [OE *singan*] — **sing′a·ble** *adj.*

Synonyms (verb): carol, chant, chirp, chirrup, hum, warble. To *sing* is primarily and ordinarily to utter a succession of articulate musical sounds with the human voice. The word has come to include any succession of musical sounds; we say the bird or the rivulet *sings*, or the teakettle or the cricket *sings*. To *chant* is to *sing* in solemn and somewhat uniform cadence; *chant* is ordinarily applied to non-metrical religious compositions. To *carol* is to *sing* joyously, and to *warble* is to *sing* with trills or quavers, usually also with the idea of joy. *Carol* and *warble* are especially applied to the *singing* of birds. To *chirp* is to utter a brief musical sound, perhaps often repeated in the same way, as by certain small birds, insects, etc. To *chirrup* is to utter a somewhat similar sound; the word is often used of a brief sharp sound uttered as a signal to animate or rouse a horse or other animal. To *hum* is to utter murmuring sounds with somewhat monotonous musical cadence, usually with closed lips; we speak also of the *hum* of machinery, etc.

Si·ngan (sē′ngän′) A former name for SIAN (def. 1).

Sin·ga·pore (sing′gə·pôr, -pōr, sing′ə-) **1** An island (224 square miles) off the southern end of the Malay Peninsula, comprising with adjacent islands and Christmas Island the State of Malaysia; a former part of the Straits Settlements, 1826–1946; 286 square miles. **2** Its capital, a port on **Singapore Strait,** a channel between Singapore island and the Malay Peninsula, connecting the South China Sea and the Strait of Malacca; 10 miles wide.

Sin·ga·ra·dja (sing′gə·rä′jə) The capital of Bali, and of Nusa Tenggara province, Indonesia, near the north coast of Bali; site of many Hindu temples. Also **Sin′ga·ra′ja.**

singe (sinj) *v.t.* **singed, singe·ing** **1** To burn slightly or superficially; discolor by burning; scorch: to *singe* the nap of cloth. **2** To remove bristles or feathers from by passing through flame. **3** To burn the ends of (hair, etc.). See synonyms under BURN[1]. — *n.* **1** The act of singeing, especially as performed by a barber. **2** A heat that singes. **3** An injury or risk, as if from or of singeing. [OE *sengan* scorch, hiss, causative of *singan* sing; from the singing sound produced]

sing·er[1] (sing′ər) *n.* **1** One who sings, especially as a profession; also, a poet. See synonyms under POET. **2** That which produces a songlike utterance, as a songbird.

sing·er[2] (sin′jər) *n.* One who or that which singes.

Sing·er (sing′ər), **Isaac Merrit,** 1811–75, U. S. inventor; first manufacturer of the sewing machine.

Sin·gha·lese (sing′gə·lēz′, -lēs′) *adj.* Of or pertaining to Ceylon, to the people constituting the majority of the inhabitants of Ceylon, or to their language. — *n.* **1** One of the Singhalese people. **2** The language of the Singhalese, belonging to the Indic branch of the Indo-Iranian languages, but containing many Dravidian words: the official language of Ceylon since 1956. Also spelled *Sinhalese.* [<Skt. *Sinhala* Ceylon]

sin·gle (sing′gəl) *adj.* **1** Consisting of one only; separate; individual. **2** Having no companion or assistant; alone. **3** Unmarried; also, pertaining to the unmarried state. **4** Of or pertaining to one alone; hence, uncommon; singular; unique. **5** Consisting of only one part; simple; uncompounded. **6** In good condition; sound; also, upright; sincere. **7** Designed for use by only one person: a *single* bed. **8** Designed for use with one thing of which there might be more: a *single* harness (for one horse). **9** *Bot.* Solitary, as a flower when it is the only one on a stem: opposed to *clustered*; in popular usage, having only one row of petals: opposed to *double*. **10** *Obs.* Of medium strength; mild; not double or strong: said of malt liquors. **11** Simplex. See synonyms under PARTICULAR, SOLITARY. — *n.* **1** That which or one who is single; a unit; individual. **2** In baseball, a hit by which the batter reaches first base. **3** A hotel room for one person. **4** A golf match between two players only: opposed to *foursome*. **5** In cricket, a hit which scores one run. **6** In falconry, a talon. — *v.* **·gled, ·gling** *v.t.* **1** To choose or select (one) from others: usually with *out*. — *v.i.* **2** To go with the single-foot gait, as a horse. **3** In baseball, to make a single. [<OF <L *singulus*] — **sin′gle·ness** *n.* — **sin′gly** *adv.*

sin·gle-act·ing (sing′gəl·ak′ting) *adj.* Doing effective work in only one direction, as a motor having a reciprocating motion.

sin·gle-ac·tion (sing′gəl·ak′shən) *adj.* Designating a type of firearm of which the trigger must be cocked by one action and released by another.

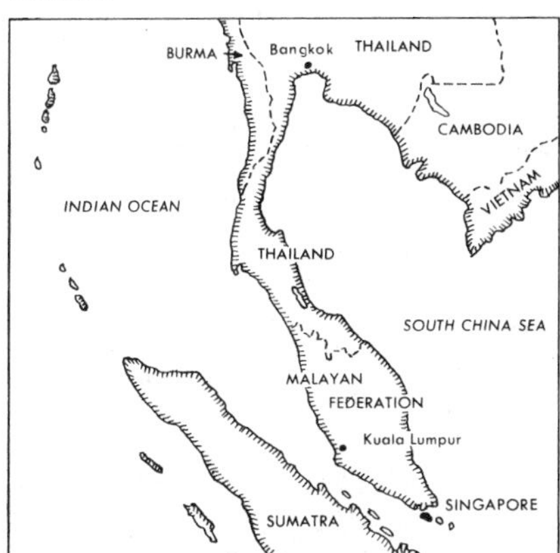

sin·gle-breast·ed (sing′gəl·bres′tid) *adj.* Having only one thickness of cloth over the breast; fastening in front with a single row of buttons, loops, or like means of engagement: said of a coat, waistcoat, etc.

sin·gle-cross (sing′gəl·krôs′, -kros′) *n. Genetics*

The first generation of a cross between two inbred lines.

single entry A method of bookkeeping in which the daybook and ledger are the essential books, transactions being carried to a single account only. — **sin′gle–en′try** *adj.*

single file A line of people, animals, etc., disposed one behind the other, with no two abreast.

sin·gle–foot (sing′gəl·fo͝ot′) *n.* The gait of a horse in which the footfall sequence is right hind, right fore, left hind, left fore, the support of the body being alternately upon one foot and two feet: sometimes called *amble* or *rack.* — *v.i.* To go at this gait.

sin·gle–hand·ed (sing′gəl·han′did) *adj.* 1 Without assistance; unaided. 2 Having but one hand. 3 Capable of being used with a single hand. 4 Having only one workman. Also **sin′gle–hand′.** — **sin′gle–hand′ed·ly** *adv.*

sin·gle–heart·ed (sing′gəl·här′tid) *adj.* Of sincere and frank disposition. — **sin′gle–heart′·ed·ly** *adv.*

sin·gle–mind·ed (sing′gəl·mīn′did) *adj.* 1 Having but one purpose or end in view. 2 Free from duplicity; ingenuous; sincere. — **sin′gle–mind′ed·ly** *adv.* — **sin′gle–mind′ed·ness** *n.*

sin·gle–phase (sing′gəl·fāz′) *adj. Electr.* Applied to the current generated by a two–pole alternating dynamoelectric machine.

sin·gles (sing′gəlz) *n. pl.* In lawn tennis, table tennis, etc., a match with only one person on each side: opposed to *doubles.* — *adj.* Having but one player on a side: a *singles* match.

sin·gle·stick (sing′gəl·stik′) *n.* 1 A cudgel; specifically, a basket–hilted stick used in fencing. 2 The art of fencing with singlesticks; also, a bout with cudgels.

sin·gle–stick·er (sing′gəl·stik′ər) *n. Colloq.* A one–masted sailboat; a sloop.

sin·gle–sur·faced (sing′gəl·sûr′fist) *adj.* Surfaced, covered, or finished on one side only.

sin·glet (sing′glit) *n.* 1 A woolen or cotton undershirt or jersey. 2 An unlined waistcoat.

sin·gle·ton (sing′gəl·tən) *n.* 1 A single card of a suit in the hand of a player at the deal. 2 Any single thing, distinct from a pair.

sin·gle·tree (sing′gəl·trē′) *n.* A swingletree.

sin·gly (sing′glē) *adv.* 1 Without companions or associates; alone; unaided, as an individual. 2 One by one; one at a time. 3 *Obs.* Uprightly; honestly.

Sing Sing (sing′ sing′) 1 A State prison near Ossining, New York. 2 The former name of OSSINING.

sing·song (sing′sông′, -song′) *n.* 1 Monotonous cadence in speaking or reading. 2 Inferior verse; doggerel. — *adj.* 1 Monotonous; droning. 2 Rising and falling in pitch.

sing·spiel (sing′spēl, *Ger.* zing′shpēl) *n.* 1 A dramatic representation in which dialog and song alternate. 2 Opera in which music is subordinated to words, especially in dramatic movement. [<G, lit., sing–play]

sin·gu·lar (sing′gyə·lər) *adj.* 1 Extraordinary; remarkable; uncommon: her *singular* beauty. 2 Odd; unconventional; peculiar; not customary or usual: to be *singular* in one's dress. 3 Representing the only one of its type; unique: a *singular* instance. 4 *Gram.* Of or designating a word form which denotes one person or thing, or a class considered as a unit, as *man, dog, he*; not dual or plural. 5 *Logic* Embodying something specific or individual; not general: a *singular* idea. See synonyms under EXTRAORDINARY, QUEER, RARE[1]. — *n. Gram.* The singular number, or a word form having this number. [<OF *singuler* <L *singularis* < *singuli* single] — **sin′gu·lar·ly** *adv.* — **sin′gu·lar·ness** *n.*

sin·gu·lar·i·ty (sing′gyə·lar′ə·tē) *n. pl.* **·ties** 1 The state or quality of being singular; uncommonness; oddity; eccentricity. 2 A character or quality by which a person or thing is distinguished from all or many others; a peculiarity. 3 Something or someone of uncommon or remarkable character.

sin·gu·lar·ize (sing′gyə·lə·rīz′) *v.t.* **·ized, ·iz·ing** To make singular; convert into the singular number.

Sin·ha·lese (sin′hə·lēz′, -lēs′) See SINGHALESE.

Sin·i·cism (sin′ə·siz′əm) *n.* Something peculiar to the Chinese, as their manners or customs. [<LL *Sinae* the Chinese]

sin·i·grin (sin′ə·grin) *n. Chem.* A white crystalline glycoside, $C_{10}H_{16}KNO_9S_2$, found principally in the seeds of the black mustard. [<NL *sinapis negra* black mustard]

Si·ning (shē′ning′) The capital of Tsinghai province, NW China.

sin·is·ter (sin′is·tər) *adj.* 1 Morally wrong; malevolent; evil; bad; perverse: *sinister* purposes; a *sinister* expression on the face. 2 Boding, tending toward, or attended with disaster; unlucky; inauspicious: from a superstition that omens seen on the left boded ill. 3 Situated on the left side or hand: opposed to *right* or *right–hand.* 4 *Her.* Of a shield, left as regards the wearer; hence, right as regards the observer: opposed to *dexter.* Compare illustration under ESCUTCHEON. [<F *sinistre* <L *sinister* left] — **sin′is·ter·ly** *adv.* — **sin′is·ter·ness** *n.*

sin·is·trad (sin′is·trad) *adv.* Toward the left aspect of the body: opposed to *dextrad.* [<L *sinister* left]

sin·is·tral (sin′is·trəl) *adj.* Of, pertaining to, or turned toward the left side or left hand. [<OF] — **sin′is·tral·ly** *adv.*

sin·is·trorse (sin′is·trôrs, sin′is·trôrs′) *adj.* 1 Sinistral. 2 Twined or twining from right to left, as the hop. Compare DEXTRORSE. [<L *sinistrorsus,* contraction of *sinistroversus* turned toward the left side < *sinister* left + *versum* turned, pp. of *vertere*] — **sin′is·tror′sal** *adj.* — **sin′is·tror′sal·ly** *adv.*

sin·is·trous (sin′is·trəs) *adj.* 1 Of, pertaining to, or directed toward the left; sinistral. 2 Sinister; unpropitious; ill–omened. [<L *sinister* left] — **sin′is·trous·ly** *adv.*

sink (singk) *v.* **sank** or **sunk, sunk** (*Obs.* **sunk·en**), **sink·ing** *v.i.* 1 To go beneath the surface or to the bottom, as of water or snow. 2 To descend to a lower level; go down, especially slowly or by degrees: The flames are *sinking.* 3 To descend toward or below the horizon, as the sun. 4 To incline downward; slope, as land. 5 To pass into a specified state: to *sink* into sleep or a coma. 6 To fail, as from ill–health or lack of strength; approach death: He's *sinking* fast. 7 To become less in force, volume, or degree: His voice *sank* to a whisper. 8 To become less in value, price, etc. 9 To decline in moral level, prestige, wealth, etc.: to *sink* into vice. 10 To penetrate a softer body: The oil *sank* into the wood. 11 To be impressed or fixed, as in the heart or mind: with *in*: I think that lesson will *sink* in. — *v.t.* 12 To cause to go beneath the surface or to the bottom. 13 To cause to fall or drop; lower: He *sank* his head upon his breast. 14 To force or drive into place: to *sink* a fence post. 15 To make (a mine shaft, well, etc.) by digging or excavating. 16 To reduce in force, volume, or degree. 17 To debase or degrade, as one's character or honor. 18 To suppress or hide; also, to omit. 19 To defeat; ruin. 20 To invest. 21 To invest and subsequently lose: I *sank* a million in that deal. — *n.* 1 A box–shaped, basinlike, porcelain or metal receptacle with a drainpipe and usually with a water supply; a cesspool or the like. 2 A place where corruption and vice gather or are rampant. 3 A natural pool, marsh, or basin in which a river terminates by evaporation or percolation. [OE *sincan*] — **sink′a·ble** *adj.*

sink boat A boat sunk to the rim in water: used in duck shooting: also called *surface boat.*

sink·er (singk′ər) *n.* 1 One who or that which sinks, or causes to sink: a die–*sinker.* 2 A weight for sinking a fishing or sounding line. 3 In baseball, a pitch that curves sharply downward as it approaches home plate.

sink·hole (singk′hōl′) *n.* A natural cavity, especially a drainage cavity, as a hole worn by water through a rock along a joint or fracture.

Sin·kiang–Ui·gur Autonomous Region (shin′·jyäng′wē′go͝or′) The westernmost division of China, formerly **Sinkiang,** comprising all of northwestern China between Mongolia and Tibet; 700,000 square miles; capital, Urumchi (Tihwa): also *Chinese Turkestan.*

sinking fund A fund so instituted and invested that its gradual accumulations will wipe out a debt at maturity.

sin·less (sin′lis) *adj.* Having no sin; guiltless; innocent. See synonyms under INNOCENT, PERFECT. — **sin′less·ly** *adv.* — **sin′less·ness** *n.*

sin·ner (sin′ər) *n.* 1 One who has sinned. 2 An irreligious person.

Sinn Fein (shin fān) Literally, we ourselves; an Irish society aiming at both independence and the cultural development of the Irish people. It originated about 1905 and in 1916 became active politically, advocating republicanism and causing a revolt in the spring of that year. — **Sinn Fein′er** — **Sinn Fein′ism**

Sino– *combining form* Chinese; of or pertaining to the Chinese people, language, etc. See CHINO–. [<LL *Sinae* the Chinese]

sin offering An offering made in atonement for sin.

Sin·o·log (sin′ə·lôg, -log, sī′nə-) *n.* One who studies or is versed in Sinology. Also **Sin′o·logue.** [<SINO- + Gk. *logos* discourse]

Si·nol·o·gy (sī·nol′ə·jē, si-) *n.* The systematic study or investigation of the Chinese people, language, literature, history, and characteristics. — **Sin·o·log·i·cal** (sin′ə·loj′i·kəl, sī′nə-) *adj.* — **Si·nol′o·gist** *n.*

Si·non (sī′nən) In the *Aeneid,* the Greek who induced the Trojans to drag the wooden horse into Troy.

Si·no·phile (sī′nə·fīl, sin′ə-) *n.* An admirer of the Chinese. — *adj.* Having admiration for the Chinese or things Chinese.

Si·no·phobe (sī′nə·fōb, sin′ə-) One antipathetic toward the Chinese. — *adj.* Having hostility toward the Chinese or Chinese customs.

Si·no–Ti·bet·an (sī′nō·ti·bet′n) *n.* A family of tone languages spoken over a wide area in central and SE Asia, including the languages of China, Burma, Tibet, and Indochina: characterized by monosyllabic, uninflected word–forms which indicate their syntactic roles by position only. Also called *Indochinese.*

Sin·siang (shin′shyäng′) A city on the Wei in northern Honan province, east central China; from 1949 to 1952, capital of the former province of Pingyuan, NE central China.

sin·syne (sin′sīn) *adv. Scot.* Since; ago.

sin·ter (sin′tər) *n.* 1 Calcareous or siliceous material deposited by springs. 2 That which is produced by sintering. — *v.t.* & *v.i. Metall.* To bring about the cohesion of (metal particles) by the combined action of heat and pressure. [<G, dross of iron]

Sint Eu·sta·ti·us (sint o͞o·stä′tē·o͞os) See under ST. EUSTATIUS.

Sint Maar·ten (sint mär′tən) See under ST. MARTIN.

Sin·tra (sēn′trə) The Portuguese spelling of CINTRA.

sin·u·ate (sin′yo͞o·it, -āt) *adj.* 1 Winding in and out, as a margin; tortuous; sinuous; wavy. 2 *Bot.* Having a sinus, or sinuses: a *sinuate* leaf. Also **sin′u·at′ed.** — *v.i.* (sin′yo͞o·āt) **·at·ed, ·at·ing** To curve in and out; turn; wind. [<L *sinuatus,* pp. of *sinuare* turn, wind < *sinus* curve] — **sin′u·ate·ly** *adv.* — **sin′u·a′tion** *n.*

Sin·ui·ju (shin·ē·jo͞o) A city of NW North Korea, on the Yalu; heavily bombed in the Korean war, 1950.

sin·u·os·i·ty (sin′yo͞o·os′ə·tē) *n.* 1 Sinuous quality. 2 A winding; deflection.

sin·u·ous (sin′yo͞o·əs) *adj.* 1 Characterized by bends or folds; winding; undulating. 2 *Bot.* Sinuate. 3 Devious; erring. [<L *sinuosus* < *sinus* bend] — **sin′u·ous·ly** *adv.* — **sin′u·ous·ness** *n.*

si·nus (sī′nəs) *n.* 1 A recess formed by a bending or folding; an opening or cavity. 2 *Anat.* **a** An air cavity in one of the cranial bones communicating with the nostrils: the frontal *sinus.* **b** A channel or receptacle for venous blood; also, a dilated part of a blood vessel. 3 *Pathol.* Any narrow opening leading to an abscess. 4 *Bot.* A recess or rounded curve between two projecting lobes or teeth of a leaf. [<L. Doublet of SINE.]

si·nu·si·tis (sī′nə·sī′tis) *n. Pathol.* Inflammation of a sinus. Also **sin·u·i·tis** (sin′yo͞o·ī′tis). [< SINUS + -ITIS]

si·nu·sot·o·my (sī′nə·sot′ə·mē) *n. Surg.* Incision of a sinus.

-sion Var of –TION.

Si·on (sī′ən) See ZION.

Sion (syôn) The capital of Valais canton, SW Switzerland: German *Sitten.*

Siou·an (so͞o′ən) *n.* A large linguistic stock of North American Indians, formerly ranging from the west banks of the Mississippi to the Rocky Mountains, and comprising the languages of the Dakota or Sioux tribes proper, those of a group including the Omaha, Osage, etc., those of the Iowa, Missouri, and Oto, also Winnebago, Mandan, Crow, Catawba, and several others now extinct. — *adj.* Of or pertaining to this linguistic stock.

Sioux (sōō) *n. pl.* **Sioux** One of a group of North American Indian tribes of Siouan linguistic stock formerly occupying the Dakotas and parts of Minnesota and Nebraska. They were Plains Indians and called themselves Dakota.

Sioux City A city on the Missouri River in western Iowa.

Sioux Falls A city in SE South Dakota.

sip (sip) *v.* **sipped, sip·ping** *v.t.* **1** To imbibe in small quantities. **2** To drink from by sips. **3** To take in; absorb. — *v.i.* **4** To drink in sips. — *n.* **1** A very small draft; a mere taste. **2** The act of sipping. [OE *sypian* drink in]

sipe (sīp) *v.i. Scot.* To seep.

si·phon (sī′fən) *n.* **1** A tube having a bend used for transferring liquids from a higher to a lower level over an intervening elevation by making use of atmospheric pressure. **2** A siphon bottle. **3** *Zool.* A tubular structure in certain aquatic animals, as the squid, for drawing in or expelling liquids. — *v.t.* To draw off by or cause to pass through or as through a siphon. — *v.i.* To pass through a siphon. Also spelled *syphon.* [<F <L *sipho, -onis* <Gk. *siphōn*] — **si′phon·al** *adj.*

SIPHON

si·phon·age (sī′fən·ij) *n.* The use or action of a siphon.

si·pho·nap·ter·ous (sī′fə·nap′tər·əs) *adj.* Of or pertaining to the order of insects *(Siphonaptera)* including the fleas: small, flattened, wingless, bloodsucking insects with great jumping ability. [<NL *Siphonaptera,* name of the order <SIPHON + A-⁴ + -PTEROUS]

siphon bottle A bottle containing aerated or carbonated water, which is expelled through a bent tube in the neck of the bottle by the pressure of the gas.

si·pho·no·phore (sī′fə·nə·fôr′, -fōr′, sī·fon′ə-) *n.* A marine organism (order *Siphonophora*) with free-swimming pelagic colonies arising by budding, as the Portuguese man-of-war. [<NL *Siphonophora,* name of the order <Gk. *siphōnophŏros* tube-carrying < *siphōn* tube + *pherein* bear]

si·pho·no·stele (sī′fə·nə·stēl′, -stē′lē) *n. Bot.* The hollow tubular stem of certain plants, as ferns. [<Gk. *siphōn* tube + STELE]

sip·pet (sip′it) *n.* **1** A triangular or finger-shaped piece of toasted or fried bread used to garnish a dish of hash or minced meat; a crouton. **2** Any eatable, especially bread, cut into small pieces and soaked in some liquid: frequently used in the plural. **3** Hence, any very small quantity. [Blend of SIP and SOP in a dim. form]

Si·quei·ros (sē·kā′rōs), **David Alfaro,** born 1898, Mexican painter and muralist.

sir (sûr) *n.* **1** The conventional term of respectful address to men: used absolutely, and not followed by a proper name. **2** A title given to persons of rank or to officials: *sir* herald, *sir* clerk. **3** An influential or important person. **4** *Archaic* A title of respect for a priest. [<SIRE]

Sir (sûr) *n.* A title of baronets and knights, used before the Christian name or the full name.

Sir·bo·ni·an (sər·bō′nē·ən) See SERBONIAN.

sir·dar (sər·där′) *n.* **1** In India and Oriental countries, a chief or lord. **2** In Egypt, the commander in chief of the army. **3** In India, a head servant; a leader of palanquin-bearers; also, a body-servant or valet: also **sir·dar′-bear′er.** [<Hind. *sardār* leader < *sar* head + *dār* holding] — **sir·dar′ship** *n.*

sire (sīr) *n.* **1** A father; begetter: used also in composition: *grandsire.* The feminine correlative is *dame.* **2** The male parent of a mammal, the female parent (of lower animals) being usually termed the *dam.* **3** A form of address to a superior: now used only in addressing a king or other sovereign. **4** *Obs.* A master; lord; also, a gentleman. — *v.t.* **sired, sir·ing** To beget; procreate: now used chiefly of domestic animals. [<OF <L *senior* older. See SENIOR.]

si·ren (sī′rən) *n.* **1** One of two, or, in later Greek legend, three nymphs, living on an island, who lured sailors to destruction by their sweet singing. They are represented as birds with women's heads, later as women with birds' feet and wings. Odysseus escaped them by sealing his companions' ears with wax and having himself bound to his ship's mast. **2** Hence, a fascinating, dangerous woman; also, a sweet singer. **3** An eel-like amphibian (genus *Siren*) having well developed gills and lacking hind legs; a mud eel. **4** An apparatus having a device with a perforated rotating disk or disks through which sharp puffs of steam or compressed air are permitted to escape in such rapid succession as to produce a continued musical note or a loud whistle: used in acoustical investigations and as a warning signal. — *adj.* Of or pertaining to a siren; hence, alluring; bewitching; dangerously fascinating. Also spelled *syren.* [<L <Gk. *seirēn*]

si·re·ni·an (sī·rē′nē·ən) *n.* One of an order *(Sirenia)* of aquatic mammals, including the manatee, dugong, etc., of somewhat fishlike form with the lower jaw as in ordinary mammals, and having mostly molariform teeth for a herbivorous diet. — *adj.* Of or pertaining to the *Sirenia.* [<NL *Sirenia,* name of the order <L *siren.* See SIREN.]

Si·ret (sē·ret′) A river in eastern Rumania, flowing 270 miles SE to the Danube: also *Sereth.*

si·ri·a·sis (si·rī′ə·sis) *n. Pathol.* Sunstroke or thermic fever. [<Gk. *seiriasis* < *seirios* hot, scorching]

Sir·i·us (sir′ē·əs) The Dog Star, Alpha in the constellation of Canis Major; magnitude, −1.6. [<Gk. *seirios* hot, scorching]

sir·loin (sûr′loin) *n.* A loin of beef, especially the upper portion: also spelled *surloin.* [Alter. (after *Sir,* from a legend that the cut was knighted for its excellence) of obs. *surloyn* <OF *surlonge* < *sur-* over, above + *longe* loin <L *lumbus*]

si·roc·co (si·rok′ō) *n. pl.* **·cos** **1** A hot, dry, and dusty southerly wind blowing from the African coast to Italy, Sicily, and Spain. **2** A warm, sultry wind blowing from a warm region toward a center of low barometric pressure. **3** A southeast wind: the popular Italian name. [<Ital. *scirocco* <Arabic *sharq* the east, the rising sun < *sharaqa* rise]

Si·ros (sī′ros, *Greek* sē′rôs) See SYROS.

sir·rah (sir′ə) *n. Archaic* Fellow; sir: used in contempt or annoyance. [Var. of *sir,* after Provençal *sira*]

Sir·rah (sir′ə) See ALPHERATZ.

sir-rev·er·ence (sûr·rev′ər·əns) *interj. Obs.* Save your reverence; begging your pardon: used as an apology before any unbecoming expression. [Misspelling of *sa' reverence,* contraction of *save (your) reverence,* erroneous trans. of L *salva reverentia* with due regard for decency]

sir·up (sir′əp) *n.* A thick, sweet liquid, as the boiled juice of fruits, sugarcane, etc.: also spelled *syrup.* [<OF *sirop* <Turkish *sharbat.* Doublet of SHERBET.] — **sir′up·y** *adj.*

sir·vente (sēr·väṅt′) *n.* A lyric in Provençal troubadour literature, characterized by great formal elaboration and a satirical treatment of themes of a political and courtly nature. [<F <Provençal <L *servens, -entis* ppr. of *servire* serve]

sis (sis) *n. Colloq.* Sister.

si·sal (sī′səl, sis′əl, sē′səl) *n.* **1** The strong, tough fiber obtained from the leaves of a West Indian agave *(Agave sisalina).* **2** Henequen. Also **sisal grass, sisal hemp.** [from *Sisal,* town in Yucatán, Mexico]

sis·co·wet (sis′kə·wet) *n.* **1** The namaycush. **2** The cisco. Also **sis′ka·wet, sis′ki·wit.** [<F (Canadian) *ciscoette* <Algonquian (Ojibwa) *pemitewiskawet* oily-fleshed creature]

Sis·er·a (sis′ər·ə) A Canaanite chieftain defeated by the Israelites; murdered by Jael. *Judges* iv 2; v 20, 26.

sis·er·ar·y (sis′ə·rer′ē) *n. Brit. Dial.* **1** An effective proceeding. **2** A writ of certiorari. — **with a siserary** With a vengeance; like a thunderclap. [Alter. of CERTIORARI]

sis·kin (sis′kin) *n.* A finch (genus *Spinus*) related to the goldfinch, as the **European siskin** *(S. spinus)* olive-green and yellow barred with black, or the North American **pine siskin** *(S. pinus).* [<MDu. *cijsken* <LG *zieske* <Polish *czyżik,* dim. of *czyż* finch]

Sis·ley (sēs·lē′), **Alfred,** 1839–99, French painter of English descent.

Sis·mon·di (sēs·môṅ·dē′), **Jean Charles Léonard Simonde de,** 1773–1842, Swiss historian and economist.

siss (sis) *v.i.* To hiss; sizzle. — *n.* A hissing or sizzling sound. [Imit.]

sis·si·fied (sis′i·fīd) *adj. U.S. Colloq.* Like a sissy; effeminate.

sis·sy (sis′ē) *U.S. Colloq. n. pl.* **·sies** An effeminate man or boy; a milksop; a weakling, male or female. — *adj.* Being a sissy; effeminate; sissified. [<SIS] — **sis′sy·ish** *adj.*

Si·stan (se·stän′) See SEISTAN.

sis·ter (sis′tər) *n.* **1** A female person or animal having the same parent or parents as another person or animal. Daughters of the same parents are **full** or **whole sisters,** called in law **sisters german.** Those having only one parent in common are **half-sisters.** **2** A woman or girl allied to another or others by some association: *sisters* in spirit: also used figuratively: Astronomy and astrology are *sisters.* **3** *Eccl.* A member of a sisterhood; a nun. **4** A head nurse in the ward of a hospital; also, popularly, any nurse. — **the three** (or **Fatal) Sisters** The Fates. — *adj.* Bearing the relationship of a sister or one suggestive of sisterhood. [<ON *systir*] — **sis′ter·ly** *adj.*

sis·ter·hood (sis′tər·ho͝od) *n.* **1** A body of sisters united by some bond of fellowship or sympathy. **2** *Eccl.* **a** A community of women bound by monastic vows. **b** An association of women set apart for works of mercy and faith, sometimes bound by a revocable vow. **3** The sisterly relationship.

sis·ter-in-law (sis′tər·in·lô′) *n. pl.* **sis·ters-in-law** A sister by marriage: a sister of one's husband, a sister of one's wife, a brother's wife, or, loosely, a brother-in-law's wife.

Sis·tine (sis′tēn, -tin) *adj.* Belonging or relating to one of the five popes named Sixtus (Italian *Sisto*), particularly to Sixtus IV and Sixtus V. [<Ital. *Sistino* <*Sisto* <L *sextus* sixth]

Sistine Chapel The principal chapel in the Vatican Palace at Rome, constructed by Sixtus IV, and afterward decorated with frescos by Michelangelo and others.

Sistine choir Formerly, a select choir of thirty-two cultivated voices attached to the court of the pope.

Sistine Madonna The Madonna painted by Raphael for the Church of St. Sixtus (Italian *di San Sisto*) in 1515.

sis·troid (sis′troid) *adj. Geom.* Included by the convex sides of two intersecting curves: said of an angle and opposed to *cissoid.* [<SISTR(UM) + -OID]

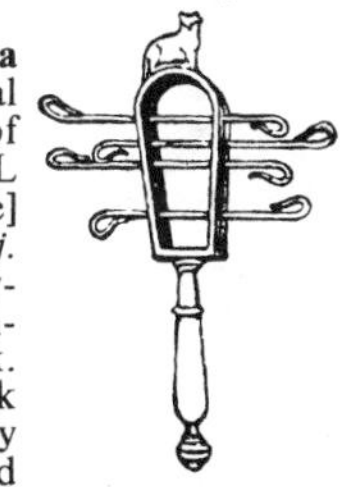

SISTRUM

sis·trum (sis′trəm) *n. pl.* **·tra** (-trə) or **·trums** A musical rattle used in the worship of Isis in ancient Egypt. [<L <Gk. *seistron* < *seiein* shake]

Sis·y·phe·an (sis′ə·fē′ən) *adj.* **1** Of or pertaining to Sisyphus. **2** Difficult and interminable: a *Sisyphean* task.

Sis·y·phus (sis′ə·fəs) In Greek mythology, a crafty, greedy king of Corinth, condemned in Hades forever to roll uphill a huge stone that always rolled down again.

sit (sit) *v.* **sat** (*Archaic* **sate), sat, sit·ting** *v.i.* **1** To rest, as upon a chair, with the body bent at the hips, and the spine nearly vertical; rest upon the haunches; take or occupy a seat. **2** To perch or roost, as a bird; brood; also, to cover eggs so as to give warmth for hatching. **3** To be or remain in a seated or settled position. **4** To remain passive or inactive, or in a position of idleness or rest. **5** To assume an attitude of readiness; take a position for a special purpose; pose, as for a portrait. **6** To meet in assembly for deliberation or business; hold a session. **7** To occupy or be entitled to a seat in a deliberative body. **8** To have or exercise judicial authority. **9** To fit or be adjusted; suit: That dress *sits* well. **10** To be suffered or borne, as a burden. **11** To be situated or located; be in some position or direction: The wind *sits* in the east. — *v.t.*

12 To have or keep a seat or a good seat upon: to *sit* a horse. **13** To seat (oneself): *Sit* yourself down. **— to sit in (on)** To join: to *sit in on* a game of cards, or a business deal. **— to sit on** (or **upon**) **1** To belong to (a jury, commission, etc.) as a member. **2** To hold discussions about and look into carefully, as a case. **3** *Colloq.* To suppress or squelch. **— to sit out** **1** To sit quietly till the end of: to *sit out* an entertainment. **2** To sit aside during: They *sat out* a dance. **3** To stay longer than. **— to sit tight** *Colloq.* To wait quietly for the next move on the part of somebody else: Just *sit tight* until I get back. [OE *sittan*]

si·tar (si·tär′) *n.* A stringed instrument used in Hindu music, somewhat resembling the guitar, having a variable number of strings, some of which are plucked, others vibrating sympathetically. [<Hind. *sitār*]

sit·com (sit′kom′) *n. Slang* A situation comedy. [Blend of SIT(UATION) + COM(EDY)]

sit–down (sit′doun′) *n.* **1** A strike during which strikers refuse to leave the factory or other place of employment until agreement is reached. Also **sit–down strike.** **2** A sit–in (def. 2).

site (sīt) *n.* **1** Situation; local position. **2** A plot of ground set apart for some specific use. **3** The degree of inclination from the horizontal of a line joining the target and the muzzle of a gun: also **angle of site.** See synonyms under PLACE. ◆ Homophones: *cite, sight.* [<F <L *situs* position]

sith (sith) *adv., prep., & conj. Archaic* Since. Also **sith·ence** (sith′əns). [OE *siththan* after]

sit–in (sit′in′) *n.* **1** An organized demonstration in which a protesting group occupies an area prohibited to them, as by taking seats in a restricted restaurant, etc. **2** A form of civil disobedience in which demonstrators obstruct some activity by sitting down and refusing to move: also called *sit–down.* **— sit′–in·ner** *n.*

Sit·ka (sit′kə) A town and naval base on Baranof Island in SE Alaska.

sito– *combining form* Food; related to food: *sitotropism.* [<Gk. *sitos* food]

si·tol·o·gy (sī·tol′ə·jē) *n.* The science of foods, diet, and nutrition. **— si·to·log·ic** (sī′tə·loj′ik) or **·i·cal** *adj.*

si·tos·ter·ol (sī·tos′tə·rōl, -rol) *n. Biochem.* Any of a group of sterols found in higher plants and related to cholesterol, especially *a–sitosterol,* $C_{30}H_{50}O$, from wheat embryos. [< SITO- + STEROL]

si·to·tox·in (sī′tō·tok′sin) *n.* Any poison evolved in vegetable foods, especially in cereals, by the action of micro–organisms. [<SITO- + TOXIN]

si·to·tro·pism (sī′tō·trō′piz·əm) *n.* The automatic response of an organism to the positive or negative influence of food. [<SITO- + TROPISM]

Si·tsang (sē′tsäng′) The Chinese name for TIBET.

Sit·tang (sit′täng) A river in south central Burma, flowing 350 miles south to the Andaman Sea.

Sit·ten (zit′n) The German name for SION.

sit·ter (sit′ər) *n.* **1** One who sits. **2** A baby sitter (which see). **3** A person sitting as a model. **4** A setting hen.

Sit·ter (sit′ər), **Willem de,** 1872–1934, Dutch astronomer.

sit·ting (sit′ing) *adj.* Being in the position of a sitter; also, used for sitting: a *sitting*–room. **—** *n.* **1** The act or position of one who sits; hence, a seat; also, the place of or the right to a seat, as in a church. **2** A single period of uninterrupted application, as for the painting of a portrait. **3** A session or term. **4** An incubation; period of hatching; also, the number of eggs on which a bird sits at one incubation.

Sitting Bull, 1834?–90, Sioux Indian chief; defeated Custer at the battle of Little Big Horn, 1876.

sitting duck **1** A duck resting on water, and therefore an easy target for a hunter. **2** *Colloq.* Any easy target.

sit·ting–room (sit′ing·ro͝om′, -ro͞om′) *n.* A parlor; living–room.

sit·u·ate (sich′o͞o·āt) *v.t.* **·at·ed, ·at·ing** **1** To fix a site for. **2** To place in a certain position or under certain conditions or circumstances; locate. [<Med. L *situatus,* pp. of *situare* place < *situs* a place]

sit·u·at·ed (sich′o͞o·ā′tid) *adj.* **1** Having a fixed place or location; placed. **2** Placed in (usually specified) circumstances or conditions: He is *well* situated.

sit·u·a·tion (sich′o͞o·ā′shən) *n.* **1** The place in which something is situated; relative local position; locality. **2** Condition as modified or determined by surroundings; status. **3** A salaried post of employment, usually subordinate. **4** A combination of circumstances; complication; specifically, in the drama, a conjuncture, climax, or crisis. See synonyms under CIRCUMSTANCE, PLACE, SCENE. **— sit′u·a′tion·al** *adj.*

situation comedy A television or radio show typically centered about a few characters involved in comical situations and presented in separate episodes.

si·tus (sī′təs) *n.* **1** Site; situation; place. **2** A fitting or natural position, as of a part of a plant. [<L]

Sit·well (sit′wel) Name of an English literary family, including **Edith,** 1887–1964, and her brothers, **Osbert,** 1892–1969, and **Sacheverell,** born 1897, all three poets, essayists, biographers, and critics.

sitz bath (zits) **1** A small bathtub in which one bathes in a sitting posture. **2** A bath taken in such a tub. [<G *sitzbad*]

Si·va (sē′və, shē′-) The Hindu god of destruction and reproduction: forming with Brahma and Vishnu the Hindu trinity: also called *Shiva.* [<Hind. *Shiva* <Skt. *śivá* propitious]

Si·va·ism (sē′və·iz′əm, shē′-) *n.* The worship of Siva. **— Si′va·ist** *n.* **— Si′va·is′tic** *adj.*

Si·va·ji (sē·vä′jē), 1627–80, founder of the Mahratta power in India.

Si·van (sē·vän′) A Jewish month. See under CALENDAR (Hebrew). Also **Si·wan′.**

Siv·a·pi·the·cus (siv′ə·pi·thē′kəs) *n. Paleontol.* An extinct ape related to Dryopithecus. [<NL <SIVA + Gk. *pithēkos* ape]

Si·vas (sē·väs′) A city in central Turkey in Asia.

si·ver (sī′vər) *n. Scot.* An open drain; sewer.

Si·wa·lik Range (si·wä′lik) The southernmost range of the Himalayas in south central Asia; highest peak about 5,000 feet.

Si·wash (sī′wosh) *n.* **1** An Indian of the northern Pacific coast. **2** The lingua franca used between the Siwashes and white traders. [< Chinook jargon <F *sauvage* savage]

six (siks) *n.* The cardinal number following five and preceding seven, or any of the symbols (6, vi, VI) used to represent it; also, anything made up of six units or members, as a playing card with six pips. **— *adj.*** Being one more than five; twice three. [OE] **— six′fold′** *adj. & adv.*

six bits Seventy–five cents.

Six Nations The Iroquois confederation known as the Five Nations, plus the Tuscarora, who joined them in the 18th century. Also **Six Allied Nations.**

six·pence (siks′pəns) *n.* A British coin of the value of six English pennies.

six·pen·ny (siks′pen′ē, -pən·ē) *adj.* **1** Worth, valued at, or sold for sixpence; hence, paltry; trashy. **2** Denoting a size of nails. See -PENNY.

six·score (siks′skôr′, -skōr′) *adj.* One hundred and twenty.

six–shoot·er (siks′sho͞o′tər) *n. Colloq.* A revolver that will fire six shots without reloading. **— six′–shoot′ing** *adj.*

sixte (sikst) *n.* In fencing, a parry in which the hand is opposite the right breast and the foil is carried to the right. [<F <L *sextus* sixth]

six·teen (siks′tēn′) *n.* The cardinal number following fifteen and preceding seventeen, or any of the symbols (16, xvi, XVI) representing it. **— *adj.*** Being one more than fifteen; four times four. [OE *sixtēne*]

six·teen·mo (siks·tēn′mō) *n. pl.* **·mos** **1** The page size of a book or pamphlet made up of printer's sheets folded 16 leaves to the sheet, the pages being usually 4 1/2 × 6 7/8 inches. **2** A book having pages of this size. Often written *16mo.* Also called *sextodecimo.* **— *adj.*** Consisting of pages of this size.

six·teenth (siks′tēnth′) *adj.* **1** Sixth in order after the tenth: the ordinal of *sixteen.* **2** Being one of sixteen equal parts. **— *n.*** **1** One of sixteen equal parts of anything; the quotient of a unit divided by sixteen. **2** *Music* A sixteenth note.

sixteenth note *Music* A note of one sixteenth of the value of a whole note; semiquaver.

sixth (siksth) *adj.* **1** Next in order after the fifth. **2** Being one of six equal parts. **— *n.*** **1** One of six equal parts. **2** *Music* **a** The interval between any note and the sixth note above or below it on the diatonic scale. **b** A note separated by this interval from any other, considered with reference to that other. **c** The sixth above the keynote. **d** Two notes at this interval written or sounded together, or the resulting consonance. **— chord of the sixth** *Music* A chord consisting of a tone with its minor third and its sixth: also **sixth chord.** **— *adv.*** In the sixth order, place, or rank: also, in formal discourse, **sixth′ly.** [OE *sixta*; refashioned to conform to *fourth*]

sixth sense Intuitive perception supposedly not employing the five senses.

six·ti·eth (siks′tē·ith) *adj.* **1** Tenth in order after fiftieth: the ordinal of *sixty.* **2** Being one of sixty equal parts. **— *n.*** One of sixty equal parts of anything; the quotient of a unit divided by sixty.

Six·tine (siks′tēn, -tin) See SISTINE.

Six·tus (siks′təs) Appellation of five popes including:

— Sixtus IV, 1414–84, pope 1471–84, real name Francesco della Rovere; built the Sistine Chapel.

— Sixtus V, 1521–90, pope 1585–90, real name Felice Peretti; built the Lateran Palace.

six·ty (siks′tē) *n. pl.* **·ties** The cardinal number following fifty–nine and preceding sixty–one, or any of the symbols (60, lx, LX) representing it. **— *adj.*** Being one more than fifty–nine; ten times six. [OE *sixtig*]

siz·a·ble (sī′zə·bəl) *adj.* Of comparatively large or convenient size. Also **size′a·ble.** **— siz′a·ble·ness** *n.* **— siz′a·bly** *adv.*

siz·ar (sī′zər) *n.* At Cambridge University, England, and Trinity College, Dublin, a student allowed free commons, etc.: formerly required to perform menial services. [<SIZE[1] (def. 4)] **— siz′ar·ship** *n.*

size[1] (sīz) *n.* **1** Measurement or extent of a thing as compared with some standard; comparative magnitude or bulk: when unqualified, implying relative largeness. **2** One of a series of graded measures, or the magnitude between two such limits, as of hats, shoes, etc. **3** A standard of measurement; specified quantity. **4** At Cambridge University, an allotted quantity of provisions; ration. **5** Mental caliber; importance; character. **6** *Colloq.* State of affairs; true situation: That's the *size* of it. **7** Measure or amount. See synonyms under MAGNITUDE. **— *v.t.* sized, siz·ing** **1** To estimate the size of. **2** To distribute or classify according to size. **3** To cut or otherwise shape (an article) to the required size. **— to size up** *Colloq.* **1** To form an estimate, judgment, or opinion of. **2** To meet specifications. [<F *assise.* See ASSIZE.]

size[2] (sīz) *n.* **1** A solution of gelatinous material, usually glue, casein, wax, or clay, used to finish fabrics. **2** A gelatinous substance used to glaze paper, or applied to walls before papering, etc. **3** A viscous preparation used as in fixing gilding. Also *sizing.* **— *v.t.* sized, siz·ing** **1** To treat with size or any size-like substance. **2** To make plastic, as clay. [<OItal. *sisa* painter's glue, aphetic var. of *assisa,* orig., pp. of *assidere* make sit down <L *assidere.* See ASSIZE.]

sized (sīzd) *adj.* **1** Having graded dimensions or a definite size: chiefly in composition: large-*sized.* **2** Arranged according to size.

siz·ing (sī′zing) *n.* **1** Size[2], *n.* **2** The process of adding size to a fabric, yarn, etc., to give it additional strength, stiffness, smoothness, weight, etc.

siz·y (sī′zē) *adj.* Glutinous. [<SIZE[2]]

sizz (siz) *v.i.* To make a hissing sound; sizzle. [Imit.]

siz·zle (siz′əl) *v.i.* **·zled, ·zling** To burn or scorch with or as with a hissing sound; emit a hissing sound under the action of heat. **— *n.*** A hissing sound as from frying or effervescence. [Freq. of SIZZ]

siz·zler (siz′lər) *n. Colloq.* Anything extremely hot, especially a summer day. [<SIZZLE]

siz·zling (siz′ling) *adj.* **1** Extremely hot. **2** That sizzles: a *sizzling* steak.

Sjael·land (shel′län) The Danish name for ZEELAND.

sjam·bok (sham′bok) *n.* A short, heavy whip of rhinoceros hide. [<Afrikaans <Du. <Malay *chamboq* <Persian *chābuq* whip]

Ska·gen (skä′gən), **Cape** The northernmost point of Jutland, Denmark, at the junction of the Skagerrak and the Kattegat: also *The Skaw.*

Skag·er·rak (skag′ə·rak, *Norw.* skäg′ûr·räk) An arm of the North Sea between Jutland and Norway; 150 miles long, 80 to 90 miles wide.

Skag·way (skag′wā) A city of SE Alaska near Chilkoot Pass: gateway to the Yukon and Klondike gold fields in the 1890's.

skail (skāl) *v.t. Brit. Dial.* **1** To scatter; spill. **2** To separate; disperse, as the members of an assembly. [Cf. ON *skilja* divide, part]

skaith (skāth) *v.t.* & *n. Scot.* Scathe; damage.

skald (skôld, skäld) See SCALD[2].

skat (skät) *n.* **1** A three-handed game played with 32 cards. Any of several varieties of the game can be chosen by the highest bidder who, alone, must oppose the other players. **2** In the game of skat, two cards dealt face down and taken into his hand by the successful bidder or otherwise treated according to rule. [<G, orig. *skart* <Ital. *scartare* discard]

skate[1] (skāt) *n.* **1** A keel-shaped metal runner attached to a plate or frame, with suitable clamps or straps for fastening it to the sole of a boot or shoe, enabling the wearer to glide rapidly over ice; also, such a runner affixed to a shoe or boot. **2** A similar contrivance with wheels instead of a runner, for use on a floor or other smooth surface; a roller skate. **3** An ice-boat runner. —*v.i.* **skat·ed, skat·ing** To glide or move over ice or some other smooth surface, on or as on skates. [< earlier *skates* <Du. *schaats* <OF *escache* stilt <Gmc.]

skate[2] (skāt) *n.* Any of several flat-bodied rays (genus *Raia*) with enlarged pectoral fins, ventral gill slits, and a pointed snout; especially, the **barn-door skate** *(R. laevis)* of eastern North America, or the common European **gray skate** *(R. batis).* [<ON *skata*]

skate[3] (skāt) *n. Slang* **1** A miserable, contemptible person. **2** An old, worn-out horse. [Origin uncertain]

skat·er (skā′tər) *n.* **1** One who skates. **2** One of various insects with long legs that run over the surface of the water, as if skating: also called *water strider.*

skat·ole (skat′ōl) *n. Biochem.* A white crystalline compound, C_9H_9N, contained in the feces and urine, and formed in the alimentary canal by the decomposition of proteins. Also **skat′·ol.** [<Gk. *skōr, skatos* dung + -OLE]

Skaw (skô), **The** See SKAGEN, CAPE.

skean (shkēn, skēn) *n.* An early Irish double-edged dagger or short sword. Also **skeen.** [<Irish *sgian* knife]

Skeat (skēt), **Walter William,** 1835–1912, English lexicographer and philologist.

ske·dad·dle (ski·dad′l) *Colloq. v.i.* **·dled, ·dling** To flee in haste; run away; scamper. —*n.* The act of running away; hasty flight. [< dial. E, spill, scatter. Cf. Gk. *skedannynai* scatter.]

skee (skē) See SKI.

Skee·na River (skē′nə) A river in western British Columbia, Canada, flowing 360 miles south and SW to the Pacific.

skeet[1] (skēt) *n.* A variety of trapshooting in which a succession of saucer-shaped targets hurled in such a way as to resemble the flight of quail are fired at from various angles by the shooter. [Origin unknown]

skeet[2] (skēt) *n.* A long-handled scoop or dipper, used for wetting sails and decks. [Origin unknown]

skeet gun A short-barreled shotgun.

skeg (skeg) *n. Naut.* The after part of a vessel's keel, or a projection on or continuation of it, as for supporting the lower end of the rudder of a screw steamer. [<Du. *schegge,* prob. <Scand. Cf. ON *skegg* beard.]

skeigh (skekh, skēkh) *Scot. adj.* **1** Shy; skittish; mettlesome: said of a horse. **2** Coy; disdainful; proud: said especially of women. —*adv.* Proudly.

skein (skān) *n.* **1** A fixed quantity of yarn, thread, silk, wool, etc., wound to a certain length and then doubled and knotted. **2** A measure of length, 360 feet, or 109.73 meters. [<OF *escaigne,* prob. <Celtic. Cf. Irish *sgainne.*]

skein screw A screw with a broad shallow thread. See illustration under SCREW.

skel·dock (skel′dok) *n. Scot.* Wild mustard *(Brassica kaber).* Also **skel′lock.**

skel·e·tal (skel′ə·təl) *adj.* Of, pertaining to, forming, or like a skeleton.

skel·e·ton (skel′ə·tən) *n.* **1** The framework of an animal body, composed of bone and cartilage. The skeletal structure either surrounds and shields the vital organs, as the *exoskeleton* of a turtle, or is embedded within the body, as the *endoskeleton* of man and the vertebrates. **2** Any open framework constituting the main supporting parts of a structure: the *skeleton* of a house. **3** A mere sketch or outline of anything, especially of some literary production: the *skeleton* of an address. **4** A person or animal very thin by nature or loss of flesh; also, a band or troop whose numbers have been greatly thinned out. See synonyms under SKETCH. —**skeleton in the closet** A secret source of shame or discredit. See FAMILY SKELETON. —*adj.* Consisting merely of a framework or outline; resembling a skeleton in use or appearance; meager; emaciated. [<NL <Gk. *skeleton (sōma)* dried (body), mummy < *skeletos* dried up]

skeleton construction A construction in which the main support is an internal framework of steel, to which the outer walls are affixed, their weight being carried, story by story, by the framework.

skel·e·ton·ize (skel′ə·tən·īz′) *v.t.* **·ized, ·iz·ing** **1** To reduce to a skeleton or framework by removing soft tissues or parts; make a skeleton of. **2** To reduce greatly in size or numbers. **3** To draft in outline.

skeleton key A slender false key designed to avoid the wards of a lock, for use as a master key.

skel·lum (skel′əm) *n. Scot.* A scamp.

skelp[1] (skelp) *Brit. Dial.* & *Scot. v.t.* **1** To kick severely. **2** To slap with the hand; spank. **3** To cause to move rapidly. —*n.* A glancing blow with the open hand; slap.

skelp[2] (skelp) *n.* A strip of iron or steel; especially, one from which tubes are made. —*v.t.* To beat out into a skelp, as iron. [Origin unknown]

Skel·ton (skel′tən), **John,** 1460?–1529, English poet, scholar, and clergyman.

skep (skep) *n.* **1** A beehive, especially one made of straw. **2** A receptacle of wickerwork or wood, especially for grain; a basket. [<ON *skeppa* basket]

skep·tic (skep′tik) *n.* **1** One who questions the fundamental doctrines of religion, especially of the Christian religion. **2** One who refuses concurrence in generally accepted conclusions in science, philosophy, etc. **3** An adherent of any philosophical school of skepticism; especially, an adherent of the **Skeptic school** in ancient Greece, of which the Pyrrhonists, with their doctrine of the relativity of knowledge, were the first systematic exponents. **4** One who doubts any particular statement. —*adj.* Skeptical. Also, *Brit., sceptic.* [<F *sceptique* <L *scepticus* <Gk. *skeptikos* reflective < *skeptesthai* consider]

Synonyms (noun): agnostic, atheist, deist, disbeliever, freethinker, infidel, unbeliever. The *skeptic* doubts divine revelation; the *disbeliever* and the *unbeliever* reject it, the *disbeliever* with more of intellectual dissent, the *unbeliever* (in the common acceptation) with indifference or with opposition of heart as well as of intellect. *Infidel* is an opprobrious term that is commonly applied to any decided opponent of an accepted religion. The *atheist* denies that there is a God; the *deist* admits the existence of God, but denies that the Christian Scriptures are a revelation from him; the *agnostic* denies either that we do know or that we can know whether there is a God. *Antonyms*: believer, Christian.

skep·ti·cal (skep′ti·kəl) *adj.* Doubting; questioning; of or pertaining to a skeptic or skepticism. Also, *Brit., sceptical.* —**skep′ti·cal·ly** *adv.* —**skep′ti·cal·ness** *n.*

skep·ti·cism (skep′tə·siz′əm) *n.* **1** A doubting or incredulous state of mind. **2** *Philos.* The doctrine that absolute knowledge is unattainable and that judgments must be continually questioned and doubted in order to attain approximate or relative certainty: opposed to *dogmatism.* Also, *Brit., scepticism.*

sker·ry (sker′ē) *n. pl.* **·ries** *Scot.* An insulated rock or reef.

sketch (skech) *n.* **1** An incomplete but suggestive delineation or presentation of anything, whether graphic or literary; an outline. **2** An artist's preliminary study, graphic or plastic, of a work of art intended for elaboration. **3** A literary or dramatic composition, short, discursive, and of slight construction. **4** A short scene, play, or musical act, especially in vaudeville. —*v.t.* To make a sketch or sketches of; outline. —*v.i.* To make a sketch or sketches. [<Du. *schets* <Ital. *schizzo* <L *schedium* improvisation <Gk. *schedios*] —**sketch′a·ble** *adj.* —**sketch′er** *n.*

Synonyms (noun): brief, delineation, draft, drawing, outline, picture, plan, skeleton. An *outline* gives only the bounding or determining lines of a figure or a scene; a *sketch* may give lines, shading and color, but is hasty and incomplete. The lines of a *sketch* are seldom so full and continuous as those of an *outline. Draft* and *plan* apply especially to mechanical drawing, of which *outline, sketch,* and *drawing* are also used; a *plan* is strictly a view from above, as of a building or machine, giving the lines of a horizontal section, originally at the level of the ground, now in a wider sense at any height; as, a *plan* of the cellar; a *plan* of the attic. A *design* is such a preliminary *sketch* as indicates the object to be accomplished or the result to be attained, and is understood to be original. One may make a *drawing* of any well-known mechanism, or a *drawing* from another man's *design*; but if he says "The *design* is mine," he claims it as his own invention or composition. In written composition an *outline* gives simply the main divisions, and is often called a *skeleton*; a somewhat fuller suggestion of illustration, treatment, and style is given in a *sketch.* A lawyer's *brief* is a succinct statement of the main facts in a case, and of the main heads of his argument on points of law, with reference to authorities. See PICTURE.

sketch·book (skech′bo͝ok′) *n.* **1** A blank book used for sketching. **2** A printed volume of literary sketches. Also **sketch book.**

sketch·y (skech′ē) *adj.* **sketch·i·er, sketch·i·est** Like or in the form of a sketch; roughly suggested without detail; hence, incomplete; superficial; slight. —**sketch′i·ly** *adv.* —**sketch′·i·ness** *n.*

skew (skyo͞o) *v.i.* **1** To take an oblique direction; move or turn aside; swerve. **2** To look obliquely or askance; squint. —*v.t.* **3** To put askew; give an oblique position or direction to. **4** To shape or form in an oblique manner; distort. —*adj.* **1** Placed or turned obliquely; twisted to one side; askew; hence, perverted in use or meaning. **2** *Stat.* Having some elements on opposite sides of a median line reversed or unbalanced; distorted: a *skew* curve. —*n.* **1** A deviation from symmetry or straightness; distortion. **2** A sidelong glance; squint. **3** A slanting coping, as at the corner of a gable. [<AF *eskiuer,* OF *eschiuver* shun <Gmc. Related to ESCHEW.] —**skew′ly** *adv.*

skew arch *Archit.* An arch whose axis is in a vertical plane making other than right angles with its abutments.

skew·back (skyo͞o′·bak′) *n. Archit.* **1** An abutment with inclined face receiving the thrust of a segmented arch. See also illustration under ARCH. **2** A cap or other casting, on the end of a truss, to receive the pull of a tie rod.

SKEWBACK
a. Skewback *(def. 1).*

skew·bald (skyo͞o′·bôld′) *adj.* Piebald, especially when the spots are white and some other color than black. [ME *skewed* piebald]

skew·er (skyo͞o′ər) *n.* **1** A long pin of wood or metal, used chiefly for fastening meat to keep it in shape while roasting. **2** Any of various articles of similar shape or use. —*v.t.* To run through or fasten with or as with a skewer. [Var. of SKIVER]

skew–gee (skyōō′jē) *adj. U.S. Colloq.* Crooked; off center; hence, mentally confused; uncertain.

skew•ness (skyōō′nis) *n.* **1** The state of being unsymmetrical or distorted. **2** *Stat.* The deviation of a frequency distribution curve from a symmetrical form.

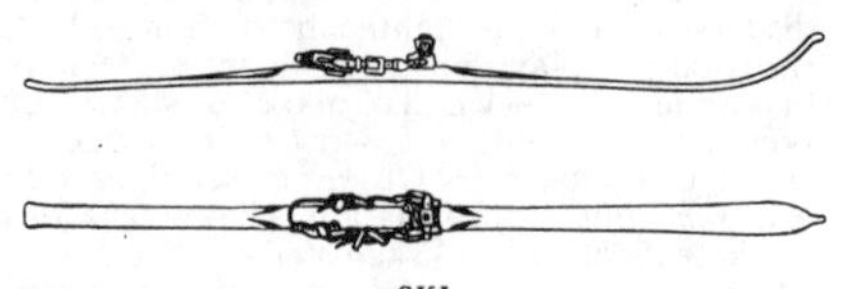

SKI
Side and top view.

ski (skē, *Norw.* shē) *n. pl.* **skis** or **ski** One of a pair of wooden runners, about 7 feet long and 3½ inches wide, attached to the feet and used in gliding over snow or ice. —*v.i.* **skied, ski•ing 1** To glide or travel on skis. **2** To engage in the sport of gliding over snow–covered inclines on skis. Also spelled *skee.* [< Norw. <ON *skidh* snowshoe] —**ski′er** *n.*

ski•a•graph (skī′ə•graf, -gräf) *n.* Roentgenogram. [<Gk. *skia* shadow + -GRAPH]

Ski•ap•o•des (skī•ap′ə•dēz) *n. pl.* In Greek mythology, an ancient people of Libya who had feet so enormous that they used them for sunshades. [<Gk. *skia* shadow + *podes,* pl. of *pous* foot]

ski•a•scope (skī′ə•skōp) *n.* An instrument for examining the refractive power of the eye by the response of the retina to lights and shadows. [<Gk. *skia* shadow + -SCOPE]

ski•as•co•py (skī•as′kə•pē) *n.* Examination of the eye by the skiascope: also called *retinoscopy, shadow test.*

skid (skid) *n.* **1** One of a pair of timbers used to support a heavy tilting or rolling object, as a cask, boat, or cannon; also, a log used as a track in sliding heavy articles about, or forming an inclined plane to ease their descent. **2** In lumbering, one of several logs used to make a track on which other logs are slid or piled; also, one of the cross–logs of a skid road. **3** A shoe or drag on a wagon wheel. **4** *Naut.* A fender hung over a vessel's side to protect it from rubbing and scraping: usually in the plural. **5** *Aeron.* A runner in an airplane's landing gear. **6** The act of skidding; a side–slip. **7** A small frame or platform upon which merchandise is stacked to be moved about or temporarily stored. —**on the skids** *Slang* Rapidly declining in prestige or power. —*v.* **skid•ded, skid•ding** *v.i.* **1** To slide instead of revolving, as a wheel which does not rotate though the vehicle is in motion. **2** To slip sideways through inability to grip the road: said of wheels, and, by extension, of vehicles. **3** *Aeron.* To slide sideways away from the center of curvature when turning, by reason of insufficient banking. —*v.t.* **4** To furnish with skids; put, drag, or haul on skids. **5** To brake or hold back with a skid. [? <ON *skidh* piece of wood]

Skid•daw (skid′ô, ski•dô′) A mountain in central Cumberland, England; 3,054 feet.

skid•doo (ski•dōō′) *interj. Slang* Go away; get out. [<SKEDADDLE]

skid fin *Aeron.* A lengthwise vertical surface formerly placed above the upper wing of an airplane to improve lateral stability.

skid road 1 A road or track along which logs are hauled to the skidway. **2** A road made of logs laid transversely and spaced about five feet apart. **3** Skid row.

skid row *Slang* An urban section inhabited by vagrants and derelicts and consisting mainly of cheap bars, flophouses, etc.

skid•way (skid′wā′) *n.* A structure made of two logs or skids, about 10 feet apart and laid alongside a log road, on which logs are piled before loading.

skied[1] (skīd) Past tense and past participle of SKY.

skied[2] (skēd) Past tense and past participle of SKI.

skiff (skif) *n.* A light rowboat; formerly, a small sailing vessel. —**St. Lawrence skiff** A small boat, carrying centerboard and spritsail, light enough to be rowed with ease. [<F *esquif* <Ital. *schifo* <OHG *scif* ship, boat]

ski•ing (skē′ing) *n.* The act or sport of gliding on skis.

ski•jor•ing (skē•jôr′ing, -jō′ring) *n.* The sport of traveling over ice or snow on skis, towed by a horse or motor vehicle. [<Norw. *skikjöring* <*ski* ski + *kjöring* driving]

ski jump 1 A jump or leap made by a person wearing skis. **2** A course prepared for making such jumps.

skil•ful (skil′fəl) *adj.* **1** Having skill; clever; dexterous; able. **2** Showing or requiring skill. Also **skill′ful.** —**skil′ful•ly** *adv.* —**skil′ful•ness** *n.*

Synonyms: adept, adroit, apt, deft, dexterous, expert, handy, happy, proficient, skilled, trained. One is *adept* in that for which he has a natural gift, improved by practice; he is *expert* in that of which training, experience, and study have given him a thorough mastery; he is *dexterous* in that which he can do effectively with or without training, especially in work of the hand or bodily activities. A *skilled* workman is one who has thoroughly learned his trade, but he may be naturally quite dull: a *skilful* workman has some natural brightness, ability, and power of adaptation, in addition to his acquired knowledge and dexterity. See CLEVER, GOOD. *Antonyms*: awkward, bulky, clumsy, helpless, inexpert, maladroit, unskilled, untaught, untrained.

ski lift An arrangement of seats usually attached to an overhead rope or cable for carrying skiers to the top of a slope.

skill[1] (skil) *n.* **1** The familiar knowledge of any science, art, or handicraft, as shown by dexterity in execution or performance, or in its application to practical purposes; technical ability. **2** A specific art or trade; also, a gift; accomplishment. **3** *Obs.* Intellect; understanding. See synonyms under ABILITY, DEXTERITY, INGENUITY, WISDOM. [<ON *skil* knowledge] —**skill′–less** *adj.*

skill[2] (skil) *v.i. Obs.* To matter; make a difference: usually used impersonally and with a negative: It *skills* not what I do. [<ON *skilja* separate]

skilled (skild) *adj.* Possessing or requiring skill; expert; proficient. See synonyms under SKILFUL.

skil•let (skil′it) *n.* **1** A frying pan. **2** A small kettle or stew pan, often with a bail and short legs. [? <OF *escuellete,* dim. of *escuelle* porringer <L *scutella,* dim. of *scutra* dish]

skill•y (skil′ē) *adj. Scot. & Brit. Dial.* Skilful.

skim (skim) *v.* **skimmed, skim•ming** *v.t.* **1** To remove floating matter from the surface of, as with a ladle: to *skim* milk. **2** To remove thus: to *skim* cream. **3** To cover with a thin film, as of ice. **4** To move lightly and quickly across or over. **5** To cause to pass swiftly and lightly, as a coin across a pond. **6** To read or glance over hastily or superficially. —*v.i.* **7** To move quickly and lightly across or near a surface; glide. **8** To make a hasty and superficial perusal; glance: with *over* or *through.* **9** To become covered with a thin film. —*n.* **1** The act of skimming. **2** That which is skimmed off; scum. **3** Something from which floating matter has been removed, as skim milk. **4** A thin scum of ice. —*adj.* Skimmed: *skim* milk. [Var. of SCUM]

skim•ble–scam•ble (skim′bəl•skam′bəl) *adj.* Incoherent; rambling. —*n.* Meaningless talk; nonsense. Also **skim′ble–skam′ble.** [Prob. reduplication of dial. *scamble* ramble, struggle on the ground (said of horses)]

skim•mer (skim′ər) *n.* **1** A flat ladle or other utensil for skimming. **2** One who or that which skims. **3** A ternlike bird (genus *Rhynchops*) having the lower mandible compressed, that skims up the small fishes from near the surface of the water. *R. nigra* is the **black skimmer.**

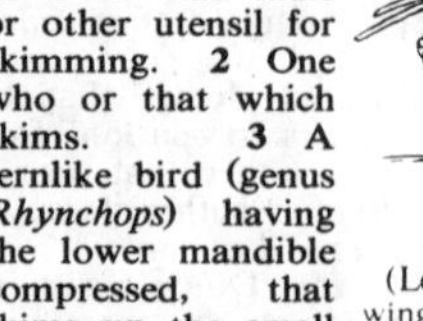

SKIMMER
(Length 16 to 20 inches; wingspread 42 to 50 inches)

skim–milk (skim′milk′) *adj.* Weak; inferior.

skim milk Milk from which the cream has been removed: often used to designate a type of inferiority.

skim•ming (skim′ing) *n.* **1** The act of one who or that which skims. **2** That which is skimmed off: usually in the plural.

skimp (skimp) *v.t. & v.i.* To scrimp or scamp. —*adj.* Scant; meager. [Prob. <ON *skemma* shorten; infl. in meaning by SCRIMP]

skimp•y (skim′pē) *adj.* **skimp•i•er, skimp•i•est 1** Carelessly done. **2** Scanty. **3** Niggardly. —**skimp′i•ly** *adv.* —**skimp′i•ness** *n.*

skin (skin) *n.* **1** The membranous external investment of an animal; the integument. ◆ Collateral adjective: *dermal.* **2** The pelt of a small animal, removed from its body, whether raw or dressed, as distinguished from the *hide* of a large animal. **3** A vessel for holding liquids, made of the skin of an animal: a wine-*skin.* **4** An outside layer, coat, or covering resembling skin, as the epidermis of a plant, fruit, etc.; rind; of pearls, the outermost layer of nacreous matter. **5** Planking or plating of a vessel. **6** A membrane resembling the integument. **7** *Slang* A mean person; skinflint; also, a sharper; blackleg. **8** One's life or physical existence: to save one's *skin.* —**by the skin of one's teeth** Very closely or narrowly; barely. —**under one's skin** Provoking; beneath the surface of control (of irritation, excitation, emotion, etc.). —*v.* **skinned, skin•ning** *v.t.* **1** To remove the skin of; flay; peel. **2** To cover with or as with skin. **3** To remove as if taking off skin: to *skin* a dollar from a roll of bills. **4** *Slang* To cheat or swindle. —*v.i.* **5** To become covered with skin; cicatrize. **6** *Slang* To make off hastily; run away: usually with *off.* [<ON *skinn*]

skin–bound (skin′bound′) *adj.* Affected with a rigid contraction of the skin and hardening of the connective tissue.

skin–deep (skin′dēp′) *adj.* Superficial. —*adv.* Superficially.

skin diving Underwater exploration in which the swimmer is equipped with a self–contained breathing apparatus, goggles, foot fins, rubber garments, etc. —**skin diver**

skin effect *Electr.* An increase of current density on the surface of an alternating–conductor, giving an increase in resistance: especially marked at high frequencies, as in radio.

skin•flint (skin′flint) *n.* A miser; one who drives a hard bargain.

skin friction 1 *Physics* The component of a fluid force tangential to a given point on a surface. **2** *Aeron.* Resistance of air particles due to friction while in contact with the moving surfaces of an airplane: also **skin drag.**

skin•game (skin′gām′) *n.* **1** A gambling game at cards in which the players have no chance of winning against the house or the bank. **2** Any swindle.

skink[1] (skingk) *n.* One of a group of lizards (family *Scincidae*) with short limbs and a conical tail; especially, the **blue–tailed skink** *(Eumeces skiltonianus)* of the United States. [<L *scincos* <Gk. *skinkos,* kind of lizard]

SKINK
(Up to 8 inches long)

skink[2] (skingk) *v.t. Brit. Dial.* **1** To draw or pour out. **2** To fill with liquor. [<MDu. *schenken*]

skink•er (skingk′ər) *n. Brit. Dial.* A bartender; also, an inn keeper. [<SKINK[2]]

skink•ing (skingk′ing) *adj. Scot.* Thin; sloppy.

skin•less (skin′lis) *adj.* Without skin.

skin•ner (skin′ər) *n.* **1** One who skins; a flayer of animals. **2** *U.S. Slang* A cheat; swindler. **3** A dealer in skins. **4** *U.S. Slang* A mule driver.

Skin•ner (skin′ər), **Cornelia Otis,** 1901–1979, U.S. actress and author; daughter of the following. —**Otis,** 1858–1942, U.S. actor.

skin•ny (skin′ē) *adj.* **•ni•er, •ni•est 1** Wanting flesh; lean. **2** Consisting of or like skin. See synonyms under MEAGER. —**skin′ni•ly** *adv.* —**skin′ni•ness** *n.*

skin–tight (skin′tīt′) *adj.* Fitting tightly to the skin, as a garment.

skip (skip) *v.* **skipped, skip•ping** *v.i.* **1** To move with light springing steps; caper; leap lightly. **2** To be deflected from a surface; ricochet; skim. **3** To pass from one point to another without noticing what lies between. **4** *Colloq.* To leave or depart hurriedly; flee. **5** To be advanced in school beyond the next grade in order —*v.t.* **6** To leap lightly over. **7** To cause to ricochet. **8** To pass over or by without notice. **9** *Colloq.* To leave (a place) hurriedly. —*n.* **1** A light bound or spring; especially, a hop alternating between steps in walking. **2** A passing over without notice;

omission. [Prob. <Scand. Cf. Sw. *skuppa* skip.]
skip distance That area within which signals from a radio transmitter are not received: it is between the farthest point reached by the ground wave and the nearest point at which the reflected sky wave strikes the earth.
skip·jack (skip′jak) *n.* **1** Any of various fishes that skip along the surface of the water, as the bonito. **2** Any snapping or click beetle (family *Elateridae*). **3** A Chesapeake Bay sailing vessel with a centerboard and one mast: used in dredging oysters.
skip·per[1] (skip′ər) *n.* **1** One who or that which skips. **2** The saury. **3** A butterfly of the family *Hesperiidae*: so named from its flight. **4** A cheese maggot.
skip·per[2] (skip′ər) *n.* The master or captain of a small vessel; hence, one in charge of any craft. [<Du. *schipper* < *schip* ship]
skip·pet (skip′it) *n.* A round flat box for containing and protecting the large heavy seal formerly tied to a document. [Dim. of SKEP]
skirl (skûrl, skirl) *Scot. v.i.* To shriek shrilly, as a bagpipe. — *v.t.* To play the bagpipe. — *adj.* Shrill. — *n.* A shrill cry; a squall of wind with rain or snow. [Metathetic var. of ME *scrille* <Scand. Cf. Norw. *skrylla.*]
skir·mish (skûr′mish) *v.i.* To fight in a preliminary or desultory way. — *n.* **1** A light engagement, as between small parties; desultory fighting between two armies on a skirmish line. **2** Figuratively, any light movement or operation evasive of the main contention or business. See synonyms under BATTLE. [<OF *eskermiss-*, stem of *eskermir* fence, fight <Gmc. Cf. OHG *skirman* defend < *skirm* shield. Related to SCRIMMAGE.] — **skir′·mish·er** *n.*
skirmish line A line of infantry spread out in extended order for attack.
skirr (skûr) *v.t.* **1** To scour. **2** To skim over. — *v.i.* **3** To move rapidly. — *n.* A whirring sound. [Imit.]
skir·ret (skir′it) *n.* An Old World herb (*Sium sisarum*) formerly much cultivated in Europe for its white tubers, which are cooked and served like salsify. [ME *skirwhit,* prob. OF *eschervis* <Arabic *karawya.* Cf. CARAWAY.]
skirt (skûrt) *n.* **1** That part of a dress, gown, or robe that hangs from the waist downward. **2** A separate garment hanging from the waist and covering the lower portion of the body. **3** A cloth or other material that hangs or covers like a skirt: the *skirt* of a dressing table. **4** *Slang* A girl; woman. **5** The margin, border, or outer edge of anything. **6** *pl.* The border, fringe, or edge of a particular area, path, geographical feature, etc.: on the *skirts* of the town, forest, highway, etc. **7** One of the flaps or loose, hanging parts of a saddle: also **saddle skirt.** **8** *Naut.* The leech of a sail. **9** The diaphragm or midriff of a butchered animal. See synonyms under MARGIN. — *v.t.* **1** To lie along or form the edge of; to border. **2** To surround or border: with *with.* **3** To pass around or about, usually to avoid crossing: to *skirt* the town. — *v.i.* **4** To be or pass along the edge or border: to *skirt* along the coast. [ON *skyrt* shirt. Akin to SHIRT.]
ski–run·ner (skē′run′ər) *n.* One who travels on skis.
skit (skit) *n.* **1** A short literary article, theatrical sketch, etc., usually humorous or satirical. **2** A bantering jest. [<Scand.; cf. ON *skjota* shoot. Prob. akin to SHOOT.]
skite (skīt) *Scot. n.* **1** A quick, sharp slap. **2** A quick, heavy, splashing shower; dash, as of rain. **3** A trick. **4** A squire. — *v.i.* **1** To squirt. **2** To glide away quickly; scoot.
ski troops Soldiers equipped and trained for action on skis.
skit·ter (skit′ər) *v.i.* **1** To glide or skim along, touching ground or water at intervals. **2** To fish by the method known as skittering. [Freq. of SKIT]
skit·ter·ing (skit′ər·ing) *n.* A style of fishing with a hook twitched along the water.
skit·tish (skit′ish) *adj.* **1** Easily frightened, as a horse; hence, shy; timid. **2** Capricious; uncertain; unreliable. **3** Tricky; deceitful. See synonyms under RESTIVE. [< dial. E *skit* caper (said of horses)] — **skit′tish·ly** *adv.* — **skit′tish·ness** *n.*
skit·tle (skit′l) *n.* **1** *pl.* A game of ninepins, in which a flattened ball or thick rounded disk is thrown to knock down the pins. **2** One of the pins used in this game: also **skittle–pin.** — **beer and skittles** Carefree existence, consisting of drink and play; unruffled enjoyment: usually with a negative: Life is not all *beer and skittles.* [Prob. <Dan. *skyttel* a child's earthen ball]
skive[1] (skīv) *v.t.* **skived, skiv·ing** To shave or pare the surface of, as leather. [<ON *skīfa* slice]
skive[2] (skīv) *n.* A gem–cutter's diamond wheel. — *v.t.* **skived, skiv·ing** To grind off, as the surface of a gem. [<Du. *schijf*]
skiv·er (skī′vər) *n.* **1** Leather split with a knife: used for bookbinding. **2** One who skives. **3** A knife or machine used in skiving.
skiv·vies (skiv′ēz) *n. pl. Slang* Men's underwear. [Origin uncertain]
sklent (sklent) *Scot. v.i.* **1** To move in a slanting manner. **2** To glance hostilely; squint. **3** To tell a lie. — *n.* **1** A slant. **2** A lie. — *adj.* Slanting.
skoal (skōl) *interj.* Hail: a toast or salutation in Scandinavian use. — *n.* The act of saluting or toasting with the word "skoal!" [<Scand. Cf. Dan. *skaal* bowl, toast, ON *skāl* bowl.]
Ško·da (shkō′dä), **Emil von,** 1839–1900, Czech engineer and industrialist.
skook·um (sko͝ok′əm) *adj. U.S. Slang* Strong; powerful. [<N. Am. Ind. *skukum* powerful, evil spirit]
Skop·lje (skôp′lye) A city in SE Yugoslavia: the economic, cultural, and Islamic religious center of modern Macedonia: Turkish *Usküb.*
skreigh (skrēkh, skrākh) *v.* & *n. Scot.* Shriek; screech. Also **skreegh.**
Skry·mer (skrī′mər) See UTGARD–LOKI.
sku·a (skyo͞o′ə) *n.* A gull–like bird; a jaeger. Also **skua gull.** [<Faroese *skügver* <ON *skūfr*]
Skuld (sko͝old) In Norse mythology, one of the Norns.
skul·dug·ger·y (skul·dug′ər·ē) *n. U.S.* Trickery; underhandedness. [Var. of dial. *sculduddery*; origin uncertain]
skulk (skulk) *v.i.* **1** To move about furtively or slily; lie close or keep hidden; lurk. **2** To shirk; evade work or responsibility. — *n.* **1** One who skulks. **2** A troop of foxes. [<Scand. Cf. Dan. *skulke.*] — **skulk′er** *n.*

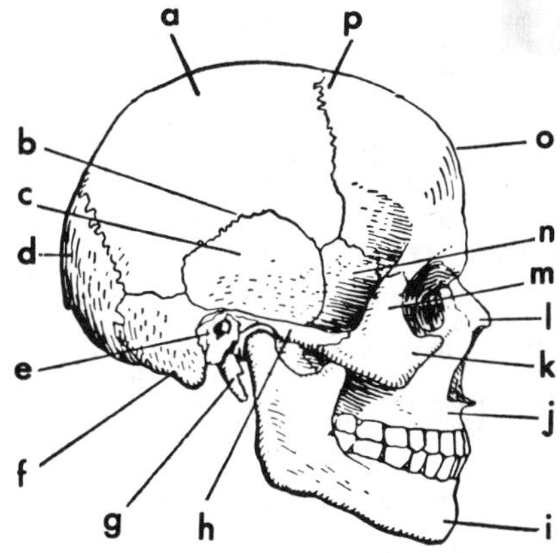

HUMAN SKULL

a.	Parietal bone.	*i.*	Inferior maxillary.
b.	Squamosal suture.	*j.*	Superior maxillary.
c.	Temporal bone.	*k.*	Malar bone.
d.	Occipital bone.	*l.*	Nasal bone.
e.	Opening of ear.	*m.*	Zygomatic bone.
f.	Mastoid process.	*n.*	Sphenoid bone.
g.	Styloid process.	*o.*	Frontal bone.
h.	Zygomatic arch.	*p.*	Coronal suture.

skull (skul) *n.* **1** The bony framework of the head of a vertebrate animal; the cranium. **2** The head considered as the seat of the brain; the mind. ◆ Homophone: *scull.* [<Scand. Cf. dial. Norw. *skul* shell.]
skull and crossbones A representation of the human skull over two crossed thigh bones: used as a symbol of death, as a warning label on poisons, etc., and as an emblem of piracy.
skull·cap (skul′kap′) *n.* **1** The sinciput. **2** Any plant of the genus *Scutellaria,* especially *S. galericulata,* of wet shady places, with large blue flowers.
skull cap **1** A cap closely fitting the skull. **2** A light cap without brim or peak.
skunk (skungk) *n.* **1** A nocturnal, burrowing carnivore of North America (family *Mustelidae*), usually black with a white stripe running from the nape of the neck to a large, bushy tail: under the tail are perineal glands that secrete a liquid of very offensive odor ejected at will. The common striped skunk (*Mephitis mephitis*) of the United States is about the size of a cat, and there are spotted varieties (genus *Spilogale*). **2** *Colloq.* A low, contemptible person. — *v.t. Slang* To defeat, as in a contest, so thoroughly as to keep from scoring. [<Algonquian *seganku*]

SKUNK
(Up to 16 inches in length; tail: 7 inches)

skunk cabbage **1** A stemless perennial herb (*Symplocarpus foetidus*) of the United States, producing in the early spring a horn–shaped, brownish–purple spathe which encloses the oval spadix and emits a strong odor, especially when crushed or bruised: also called *swamp cabbage.* **2** A somewhat similar plant (*Lysichitum americanum*) of western North America. Also **skunk′weed′** (-wēd′).
sky (skī) *n. pl.* **skies** **1** The blue vault, or a part of it, that seems to bend over the earth; the firmament. **2** The upper atmosphere; especially, the region of the clouds. **3** The celestial regions or powers; heaven. **4** Climate; weather. **5** *Obs.* A cloud. — *v.t.* **skied, sky·ing** *Colloq.* In games, to bat or throw (a ball) high into the air. [<ON *skȳ* cloud]
sky–blue (skī′blo͞o′) *adj.* Of the color of the sky; azure.
sky blue A blue like the color of the sky.
sky·cap (skī′kap′) *n.* A porter employed at an airport.
sky·dive (skī′dīv′) *v.i.* **·dived, ·div·ing** To engage in skydiving. — **sky′div′er** *n.*
sky·div·ing (skī′dī′ving) *n.* The sport of jumping from an airplane and performing various maneuvers and assuming various positions before opening the parachute.
Skye (skī), **Isle of** Largest of the Inner Hebrides Islands; 670 square miles.
Skye terrier See under TERRIER.
sky·ey (skī′ē) *adj.* Pertaining to or resembling the sky; heavenly.
sky–high (skī′hī′) *adj.* & *adv.* Extremely high.
sky·jack (skī′jak′) *v.t. Colloq.* To hijack (def. 3). [<SKY + (HI)JACK] — **sky′jack′er** *n.* — **sky′·jack′ing** *n.*
sky·lark (skī′lärk′) *n.* A lark (*Alauda arvensis*) that utters a sweet song as it flies. — *v.i.* To indulge in hilarious or boisterous frolic. — **sky′lark′er** *n.* — **sky′lark′ing** *n.*
sky·light (skī′līt′) *n.* A window facing skyward.
sky line **1** The line where earth and sky appear to meet; horizon. **2** The outline of buildings, trees, etc., against the sky.
sky pilot *Slang* A clergyman; also, a chaplain.
sky·rock·et (skī′rok′it) *n.* A rocket that is shot high into the air, where it explodes, often with brilliant pyrotechnic effect. — *v.i.* To rise or cause to rise or ascend steeply, like a skyrocket: used figuratively of wages, prices, etc.
Sky·ros (skē′ros) The largest island of the Northern Sporades group, in the Aegean east of Euboea; 80 square miles: Latin *Scyros.*
sky·sail (skī′səl, -sāl′) *n. Naut.* A light sail above the royal in a square–rigged vessel.
sky·scrap·er (skī′skrā′pər) *n.* A very high building.
sky·ward (skī′wərd) *adv.* Toward the sky: also **sky′wards.** — *adj.* Moving or directed toward the sky.
sky wave A radio wave projected into the upper atmosphere by a transmitter and reflected back to earth from the Kennelly–Heaviside layer.
sky·writ·ing (skī′rī′ting) *n.* The forming of

words in the air by an aviator, by releasing a jet of vapor from the tail of an airplane. — **sky′writ′er** *n.*

slab[1] (slab) *n.* **1** The outside cut made from a log in sawing it into boards, planks, etc., often bearing the bark on one side. **2** A flat plate, piece, mass, or slice, as of metal, stone, chocolate, or the like. **3** *U.S. Slang* In baseball, the pitcher's plate. — *v.t.* **slabbed, slab·bing** **1** To saw slabs from, as a log; to square by removing the slabs. **2** To cover with, or form of or into slabs. [ME; origin uncertain]

slab[2] (slab) *n.* Slime; viscous mud; mire. — *adj. Archaic* Slimy; viscous. [<ON *slabb* mud]

slab·ber (slab′ər) *v.* & *n.* Slobber. [Prob. <LG. Cf. Du. *slabberen.*]

slab·by (slab′ē) *adj.* **·bi·er, ·bi·est** *Archaic* **1** Thick; viscous. **2** Sloppy; wet. [<SLAB[2]]

slab·sid·ed (slab′sī′did) *adj. U.S. Colloq.* **1** Having flat sides. **2** Lanky; gawky; ungainly.

slack[1] (slak) *adj.* **1** Hanging or extended loosely. **2** Loose or careless in performance; remiss; tardy; slovenly; slow; also, weak; loose: a *slack* mouth. **3** Lacking activity; not brisk or pressing: a *slack* season. **4** Listless; limp: a *slack* grip. **5** Flowing sluggishly, as water between the ebb and flow of the tide; also, blowing slowly, as a wind. **6** Incomplete; underdone; unfinished. See synonyms under SLOW. — *v.t.* **1** To slacken. **2** To slake, as lime. — *v.i.* **3** To be or become slack. — *n.* **1** The part of anything, as a rope, that is slack or loose; also, a slack condition; looseness. **2** A period of inactivity; a slack season. **3** An extent of water where there is no current. **4** *pl.* Loose-fitting trousers worn by both men and women as part of a casual sports costume; also, cotton or wool trousers in a military uniform. — *adv.* In a slack manner; slackly. [OE *slæc*] — **slack′ly** *adv.* — **slack′·ness** *n.*

slack[2] (slak) *n.* Small coal; screenings. [Cf. LG *slacke*]

slack[3] (slak) *n. Scot. & Brit. Dial.* **1** A dry hollow or gully. **2** A bog. **3** A common. **4** A natural slope of ground. [<ON *slakki* dip, depression]

slack-baked (slak′bākt′) *adj.* Not thoroughly cooked; underdone.

slack·en (slak′ən) *v.i.* **1** To become slack, as business; diminish; retard. **2** To become less tense or tight; loosen. **3** To become slow or less intense. — *v.t.* **4** To be or become negligent of or remiss in; to avoid, as duty, especially a military duty; shirk. **5** To make slack.

slack·er (slak′ər) *n.* One who shirks his duties or avoids military service in wartime; shirker.

slae (slē) *n. Scot.* The sloe or blackthorn.

slag (slag) *n.* **1** *Metall.* **a** The fused residue separated in the reduction of ores; metallic dross. **b** A basic iron silicate that floats on the surface of molten iron. **2** Volcanic scoria. — *v.t.* & *v.i.* **slagged, slag·ging** To form into slag. [<MLG *slagge*] — **slag′gy** *adj.*

slag wool Mineral wool.

slain (slān) Past participle of SLAY.

slake (slāk) *v.* **slaked, slak·ing** *v.t.* **1** To render inoperative or harmless, especially by satisfying, as an appetite. **2** To lessen the force of in any way; quench; appease; assuage: to *slake* thirst or flames. **3** To mix with water or moist air, so that a chemical combination shall ensue. **4** To disintegrate and hydrate, as lime. **5** To make loose, slow, or less tense. — *v.i.* **6** To become disintegrated and hydrated: said of lime. **7** To slacken; become loose, slow, or less tense. **8** To ease up on one's efforts; slow down. — *n.* The act or period of slackening; an abatement. [OE *slacian* retard < *slæc* SLACK[1]]

sla·lom (slä′ləm, slā′-) *n.* In skiing, a race over a downhill, serpentine course laid out between posts and marked with flags, victory going to the skier who makes the best speed with the best grace and form. — *v.i.* To ski in or as in a slalom. [<Norw.]

slam (slam) *v.* **slammed, slam·ming** *v.t.* **1** To shut with violence and a loud noise; pull or push to loudly: to *slam* a door. **2** To put, dash, throw, or bring with violence and a loud noise; bang: to *slam* a book down. **3** *Slang* To strike with the fist. **4** *Colloq.* To take to task; criticize severely. — *v.i.* **5** To be shut, enter a place, etc., with force and noise. — *n.* **1** A closing or striking with a bang; the act or noise of slamming. **2** *Colloq.* Severe criticism. **3** A card game of the 16th century, resembling ruff. **4** In bridge, the winning of more than eleven tricks: **grand slam** is the winning of all 13 tricks; **little slam** is the winning of 12 tricks. [<Scand. Cf. dial. Norw. *slamra* slam.]

slam-bang (slam′bang′) *adv.* Violently; noisily; also, recklessly. — *v.i.* To move with noise and violence.

slan·der (slan′dər) *n.* A false tale or report, or such tales or reports collectively, uttered with malice and designed or tending to injure the reputation of another; calumny; also, the utterance of such tales or reports; defamation. See synonyms under SCANDAL. — *v.t.* To injure by maliciously uttering a false report; defame; calumniate. — *v.i.* To utter slander. See synonyms under ABUSE, ASPERSE, REVILE. [<AF *esclaundre,* OF *esclandre,* ult. <L *scandalum.* Doublet of SCANDAL.] — **slan′der·er** *n.*

slan·der·ous (slan′dər·əs) *adj.* **1** Uttering slander; guilty of slander. **2** Containing slander; calumnious. — **slan′der·ous·ly** *adv.* — **slan′der·ous·ness** *n.*

slang (slang) *n.* **1** A type of popular language comprised of words and phrases of a vigorous, colorful, or facetious nature, which are invented as needed or derive from the unconventional use of the standard vocabulary. The vocabulary of slang, although usually ephemeral, may achieve wide colloquial currency, and, in the evolution of language, many words originally slang have been adopted by good writers and speakers, and ultimately taken their place as accepted English. **2** The special vocabulary of a certain class, group, or profession: college *slang.* **3** Originally, the argot or jargon of thieves and vagrants. — *v.t.* To abuse or address with slang; also, to scold. — *v.i.* To use slang. [Origin uncertain]

Synonyms: argot, cant, jargon, lingo. The language of the underworld is *argot,* stressing its secrecy; *cant* often signifies the vocabulary of a special occupational group; *jargon* emphasizes unintelligibility and cacophonous sound. *Cant,* originally the beggar's whine, then the preacher's drone, acquired, in later usage, the more common meaning of sanctimonious moralizing. *Jargon* has as its commonest sense barbarous-sounding gabble. *Lingo* commonly designates foreign-sounding speech, or a language with which we are unfamiliar.

slang·y (slang′ē) *adj.* **slang·i·er, slang·i·est** **1** Of the nature of or containing slang. **2** Using or given to using slang. — **slang′i·ly** *adv.* — **slang′i·ness** *n.*

slank (slangk) Obsolete past tense of SLINK.

slant (slant) *v.t.* **1** To give an oblique or sloping direction to; turn from a direct line or level; incline; lean. **2** To write or edit (news or other literary matter) so as to express a special attitude, bias, or opinion. — *v.i.* **3** To have or take an oblique or sloping direction. **4** To have a certain bias or attitude. — *adj.* Lying at an angle; oblique; sloping — *n.* **1** A slanting direction, course, or plane; inclination from a direct line or level; slope; also, a mental or moral bent, opinion, attitude, etc. **2** An oblique reflection; a sarcastic remark. See synonyms under TIP[1]. [< earlier *slent* <Scand. Cf. Norw. *slenta* slope.] — **slant′·ing** *adj.* — **slant′ing·ly** *adv.* — **slant′ing·ness** *n.*

slant·wise (slant′wīz′) *adj.* Slanting; oblique. — *adv.* At a slant or slope; obliquely; slantingly: also **slant′ways′** (-wāz′).

slap (slap) *n.* A blow delivered with the open hand or with something flat; also, an insult; slur. — *v.* **slapped, slap·ping** *v.t.* **1** To hit or strike with the open hand or with something flat; also, to rebuff; insult. **2** To put or place violently or carelessly. — *v.i.* **3** To strike or beat as if with slaps: The waves *slapped* against the dock. — *adv.* **1** Suddenly and forcibly; abruptly. **2** *Colloq.* Directly; straight: *slap* into his face. [<LG *slapp*] — **slap′per** *n.*

slap·bang (slap′bang′) *adj.* & *adv. Slang* Slap-dash.

slap-dash (slap′dash′) *adj.* Done or acting in a dashing or reckless way; impetuous; careless. — *n.* **1** Offhand or careless work, or thoughtless conduct. **2** Rough casting, or rough plastering. — *adv.* In a dashing or heedless manner.

slap-hap·py (slap′hap′ē) *adj. Slang* Giddy and weak-minded because of concussion of the brain; punch-drunk.

slap·jack (slap′jak) *n.* **1** A griddlecake; flapjack. **2** A children's game of cards.

slap·stick (slap′stik′) *n.* **1** A flexible, double paddle formerly used in farces and pantomimes to make a loud report when an actor was struck with it. **2** The use of this apparatus, or the type of rough comedy in which it is used. — *adj.* Using or suggestive of the slapstick: *slapstick* comedy.

slash (slash) *v.t.* **1** To cut by striking violently and without attempt at accuracy; cut with long sweeping strokes; strike violently with or as with an edged instrument; slit; gash. **2** To strike with long sweeping blows of a whip; lash; scourge. **3** To make long gashes, cuts, or slits in; specifically, to slit, as a garment, so as to expose ornamental material or lining in or under the slits. **4** To criticize severely; censure harshly. **5** To cut down wastefully, as timber in a forest. **6** To reduce sharply, as salaries. — *v.i.* **7** To make a long sweeping stroke or several such strokes with or as with something sharp; cut. — *n.* **1** The act or result of slashing; a sweeping, random cut with a cutting weapon or whip; a slit or gash; specifically, an ornamental slit or cut in a garment showing some other material in or through the slit. **2** An opening or gap made in a forest. **3** The loose tops and branches of trees left in a forest after logging or a high wind. **4** A swampy thicket; low-lying boggy land: usually in the plural. **5** *Printing* A virgula. [? <OF *esclachier* break] — **slash′er** *n.*

slash·ing (slash′ing) *adj.* **1** Striking or cutting at random: a *slashing* warrior or critic. **2** *Colloq.* Of uncommonly high degree; very large; very fine, swift, etc.; exceptionally brilliant. — *n.* **1** A slash; the act of slashing; especially, the wasteful destruction of timber. **2** A region where timber trees have been cut down. **3** A mass of felled trees heaped for burning. — **slash′ing·ly** *adv.* — **slash′ing·ness** *n.*

slash pine **1** A pine *(Pinus caribae)* growing in the slashes along the southeastern coast of the United States; also, its wood. **2** The loblolly pine.

Slask (shlôṅsk) The Polish name for SILESIA.

slat[1] (slat) *n.* **1** One of a number of thin, flat, narrow strips of wood used to support the springs or mattress of a bed. **2** Any thin, narrow strip of wood or metal; a lath. **3** *Aeron.* A movable auxiliary airfoil attached to the leading edge of an airplane wing. — *v.t.* **slat·ted, slat·ting** To provide or make with slats. [<OF *esclat* splinter, chip]

slat[2] (slat) *v.* **slat·ted, slat·ting** *v.t. Dial.* **1** To throw or dash violently; fling carelessly. **2** To beat; slap. — *v.i.* **3** To flap, as sails against yards. — *n. Dial.* A sudden, sharp blow. [? <ON *sletta* slap]

slate[1] (slāt) *n.* **1** Any rock that splits readily into thin and even laminae; specifically, an argillaceous, fine-grained rock that so splits; also, an artificial material made in imitation of it. **2** A piece, slab, or plate of slate used for roofing, writing upon, etc. **3** A record of one's past performance or behavior: a clean *slate.* **4** A list of political candidates made up before their nomination or election; any prearranged list. **5** A dull bluish-gray color resembling that of slate: also **slate gray.** — *adj.* **1** Made of slate: a *slate* roof. **2** Slate-colored. — *v.t.* **slat·ed, slat·ing** **1** To roof with slate. **2** To put on a political slate or a list of any sort; hence, to register or designate as if by writing on a slate: He is *slated* for promotion. **3** To remove hair from (hides) with a slater. [<OF *esclate,* fem. of *esclat* a chip, splinter] — **slat′y** *adj.*

slate[2] (slāt) *v.t.* **slat·ed, slat·ing** **1** To censure, criticize, or review severely; berate. **2** To punish severely. [OE *slætan* bait]

slate ax See SAX[1] (def. 1).

slate pencil A pencil made of soft slate: used for writing on a slate.

slat·er[1] (slā′tər) *n.* **1** A person whose trade is to lay slates. **2** A slate-edged implement for removing hair from hides. **3** A terrestrial isopod crustacean, as the common pill bug or wood louse.

slat·er[2] (slā′tər) *n.* One who censures severely; a caustic critic.

slath·er (slath′ər) *Colloq.* or *Dial. v.t.* To daub thickly; spend or use profusely; lavish. — *n.* **1** A thick layer or spread. **2** *pl.* A lot; very

much: *slathers* of fun. [Var. of dial. E *slither* slip]
slat·ing (slā′ting) *n.* 1 The act or occupation of laying slates. 2 Slates or slate collectively. 3 A liquid for giving a slatelike surface to blackboards, etc.
slat·tern (slat′ərn) *n.* An untidy or slovenly woman. — *adj.* Untidy; slovenly. [<dial. E *slatter* slop, spill] — **slat′tern·li·ness** *n.* — **slat′tern·ly** *adj.* & *adv.*
slaugh·ter (slô′tər) *n.* 1 The act of killing; specifically, the butchering of cattle and other animals for market. 2 Wanton or savage killing, especially of human beings; massacre; carnage. 3 *Slang* A sweeping or ruinous reduction in prices. See synonyms under MASSACRE. — *v.t.* 1 To kill for the market; butcher. 2 To kill wantonly or savagely, especially in large numbers. 3 *Slang* To reduce greatly the price of; sell at a low figure. See synonyms under KILL[1]. [<ON *slātr* butcher's meat. Akin to SLAY.] — **slaugh′ter·er** *n.* — **slaugh′ter·ous** *adj.* — **slaugh′ter·ous·ly** *adv.*
slaugh·ter·house (slô′tər·hous′) *n.* A place where animals are butchered; a scene of carnage.
Slav (släv, slav) *n.* A member of any of the Slavic-speaking peoples of northern or eastern Europe, the northern group comprising the Russians, Poles, Czechs, Moravians, Sorbs or Wends, Slovaks, etc.; the southeastern group comprising the Bulgarians, Serbians, Croats, and Slovenes. Also, *Obs.*, *Sclav.* [<G *Sklave* <Med. L *Sclavus* <LGk. *Sklabos* <Slavic]
slave (slāv) *n.* 1 One whose person is held as property; a person in slavery; a bondsman; serf. 2 *Law* A person over whose life, liberty, and property someone has absolute control. 3 A person in mental or moral subjection to a habit, vice, or influence: a *slave* of tobacco. 4 One who labors like a slave; a drudge. 5 A person of slavish disposition; an abject creature. — *v.* **slaved, slav·ing** *v.i.* To work like a slave; toil; drudge. — *v.t. Rare* To enslave. [<F *esclave* <Med. L *slavus, sclavus,* orig. a Slav; because many Slavs were conquered and enslaved]
slave ant An ant enslaved by members of another species.
slave auction An auction at which slaves are sold.
Slave Coast The coastal region of western Africa extending westward from the mouths of the Niger along the Bight of Benin to Ghana: named for its former trade in slaves.
slave-driv·er (slāv′drī′vər) *n.* 1 A person hired for or charged with the overseeing of slaves at work. 2 Any severe or exacting employer.
slave·hold·er (slāv′hōl′dər) *n.* An owner of slaves. — **slave′hold′ing** *adj.* & *n.*
slav·er[1] (slav′ər) *v.t.* To dribble saliva over. — *v.i.* To dribble saliva; drool. — *n.* Saliva issuing or dribbling from the mouth. [Prob. <ON *slafra*] — **slav′er·er** *n.*
slav·er[2] (slā′vər) *n.* 1 A person or a vessel engaged in the slave trade. 2 One who procures white slaves.
Slave River A river in NE Alberta and the southern region of Mackenzie district, Northwest Territories, Canada, flowing 258 miles NW to Great Slave Lake: also *Great Slave River.*
slav·er·y (slā′vər·ē, slāv′rē) *n.* 1 Involuntary servitude; specifically, the legalized social institution in which humans are held as property or chattels; complete subjection of one person to another. 2 Mental, moral, or spiritual bondage. 3 Slavish toil; drudgery. See synonyms under BONDAGE.
Slave State Any of the United States in which slavery was not prohibited by statute before the Civil War: Alabama, Arkansas, Delaware, Florida, Georgia, Kentucky, Louisiana, Maryland, Mississippi, Missouri, North Carolina, South Carolina, Tennessee, Texas, Virginia.
slave trade The business of dealing in slaves; specifically, the bringing of Negro slaves to America for sale. — **slave′trad′er** *n.*
slav·ey (slā′vē, slav′ē) *n. Brit.* A household servant; drudge; usually, a maidservant.
Slav·ic (slä′vik, slav′ik) *adj.* Of or pertaining to the Slavs or their language. — *n.* A branch of the Balto-Slavic subfamily of the Indo-European language family, consisting of three groups — **East Slavic** (Russian or Great Russian, Ukrainian or Ruthenian or Little Russian, White Russian), **West Slavic** (Czechoslovakian, Sorbian or Wendish, Polish), **South Slavic** (Church Slavonic, Bulgarian, Serbo-Croatian, Slovenian). Also *Slavonic.*
slav·ish (slā′vish) *adj.* 1 Pertaining to or befitting a slave; servile; base. 2 Extremely hard or laborious. 3 Enslaved. See synonyms under BASE[2], OBSEQUIOUS. — **slav′ish·ly** *adv.* — **slav′ish·ness** *n.*
Slav·ism (slä′viz·əm, slav′iz·əm) *n.* The characteristics or aims of the Slavs, collectively.
Slavo- *combining form* Slavic; of or pertaining to the Slavs: *Slavophobe.* [<SLAV]
slav·oc·ra·cy (slāv·ok′rə·sē) *n. pl.* **·cies** Slaveholders or slaveholding interests as a political power, especially for the maintenance of slavery. [<SLAV(E) + -(O)CRACY] — **slav·o·crat** (slā′və·krat) *n.* — **slav′o·crat′ic** *adj.*
Sla·vo·ni·a (slə·vō′nē·ə) A region of Croatia, northern Yugoslavia, between the Sava and Drava rivers. — **Sla·vo′ni·an** *adj.* & *n.*
Sla·von·ic (slə·von′ik) *adj.* & *n.* Slavic. — **Church Slavonic** A member of the South Slavic group of the Balto-Slavic languages: now in use only as the language of the Slavic Greek Orthodox Church and certain Roman Catholic dioceses. See GLAGOL.
Slav·o·phile (släv′ə·fīl, -fil, slav′-) *n.* An admirer of the Slavs or their ideas, art, etc.
slaw[1] (slô) *n.* Cabbage sliced, shredded, or chopped, and served, usually raw, as a salad. [<Du. *sla,* short for *salade* salad]
slaw[2] (slô) *adj. Scot.* Slow.
slay (slā) *v.t.* **slew, slain, slay·ing** 1 To kill, especially by violence; put to death; destroy by, or as by, killing. 2 *Obs.* To smite; strike. See synonyms under KILL[1]. ◆ Homophones: *sleigh, sley.* [OE *slēan*] — **slay′er** *n.*
sleave (slēv) *v.t.* **sleaved, sleav·ing** To separate, as a mass of threads; disentangle. —*n.* Something tangled, matted, knotted, or unspun, as silk or thread. ◆ Homophone: *sleeve.* [OE *slǣfan* divide]
sleave silk Raw untwisted silk; floss.
slea·zy (slē′zē, slā′-) *adj.* **·zi·er, ·zi·est** 1 Lacking firmness of texture or substance. 2 Cheap; shoddy; run-down: a *sleazy* bar. [Origin uncertain] — **slea′zi·ly** *adv.* — **slea′zi·ness** *n.*
sled (sled) *n.* 1 A vehicle on runners, designed for carrying people or loads over snow and ice; a sledge. 2 A small, light frame mounted on runners, used especially by children for sliding on snow and ice. — *v.* **sled·ded, sled·ding** *v.t.* To convey on a sled. — *v.i.* To ride on or use a sled. [<MLG *sledde*]
sled·der (sled′ər) *n.* 1 One who rides on or hauls with a sled. 2 An animal that draws a sled.
sled·ding (sled′ing) *n.* 1 Condition of roads admitting of the use of sleds: usually with a qualifying word: fine *sledding.* 2 The act of using a sled; use of sleds in hauling, traveling, etc. 3 State or circumstances of progress, work, etc.: We have had hard *sledding.*

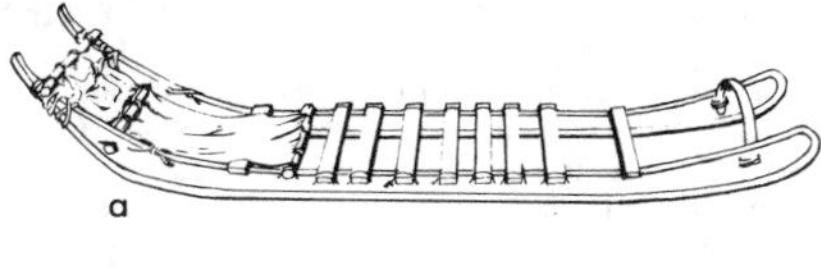

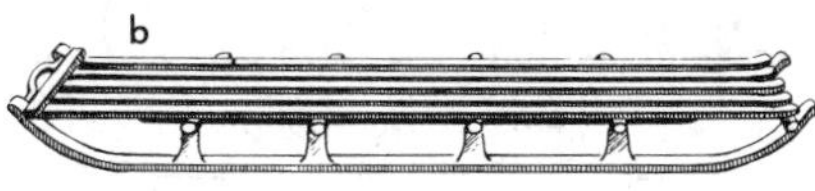

SLEDGES
a. Peary North Pole Expedition.
b. Byrd Antarctic Expedition.

sledge[1] (slej) *n.* A vehicle mounted on low runners for moving loads; especially, one designed to be drawn over snow and ice by dogs, horses, or reindeer, or one designed to be drawn on the ground by draft animals; also, a sled. — *v.t.* & *v.i.* **sledged, sledg·ing** To travel or convey on a sledge. [<MDu. *sleedse*]
sledge[2] (slej) *n.* A heavy hammer wielded with one or both hands, for blacksmiths' use, or for breaking stone, coal, etc.: also **sledge′-ham′mer** (-ham′ər). — *v.t.* **sledged, sledg·ing** To hammer, break, or strike with a sledge. [OE *slecg*]
slee (slē) *adj. Scot.* Sly; dexterous.
sleek (slēk) *adj.* 1 Smooth and glossy; polished. 2 Smooth-spoken; flattering; unctuous; insinuating. See synonyms under SMOOTH. — *v.t.* 1 To make smooth, even, or glossy; polish. 2 To soothe; mollify; also, to make less disagreeable or offensive. Also, *U.S., slick.* [Var. of SLICK] — **sleek′ly** *adv.* — **sleek′ness** *n.* — **sleek′y** *adj.*
sleek·it (slēk′it) *adj. Scot.* 1 Sleek. 2 Deceitful.
sleep (slēp) *n.* 1 A state or period of complete or partial unconsciousness, normal and periodic in man and the higher animals. In animals it is sometimes much prolonged, as in hibernation. 2 A period of slumber. 3 Any condition of inactivity, torpor, or rest; specifically, the rest of the grave; death. 4 Nyctitropism. See synonyms under REST[1]. — **to go to sleep** 1 To fall asleep. 2 To become numb, often with a tingling sensation, from retarded circulation. — *v.* **slept, sleep·ing** *v.i.* 1 To be or fall asleep; slumber. 2 To be in a state resembling sleep; to be dormant, inactive or quiet, or to rest in death. 3 To be in a benumbed state from retarded circulation of the blood: My foot *sleeps.* 4 To spin with such velocity as to be without apparent motion, as a top. 5 To undergo nyctitropism. 6 *Bot.* To assume a different position at night, as petals. — *v.t.* 7 To rest or repose in: with a cognate object: to *sleep* the sleep of the dead. 8 To provide with sleeping quarters; lodge: The hotel can *sleep* a hundred guests. See synonyms under REST[1]. — **to sleep away** (or **off** or **out**) To pass or get rid of by or as by sleep: to *sleep off* a hang-over. — **to sleep on** To postpone a decision upon. [OE *slēp*]

Sleep may appear as a combining form in hyphemes; as in:

sleep-bringing	**sleep-inducing**
sleep-compelling	**sleep-inviting**
sleep-dispelling	**sleep-loving**
sleep-disturber	**sleep-producing**
sleep-disturbing	**sleep-provoking**
sleep-filled	**sleep-resisting**

sleep·er (slē′pər) *n.* 1 One who sleeps; figuratively, a dead person. 2 A railroad sleeping-car. 3 A hibernating animal. 4 In football, a member of the backfield or an end stationed far out at either side before the ball is put in motion. 5 A heavy beam resting on or in the ground, as a support for a roadway, rails, etc.; a like support of iron or stone; also, a timber on or near the ground for the lower joists of a building. 6 A deadman. 7 *U.S. Colloq.* A play, motion picture, or book which achieves unexpected and striking success.
sleep·ing-car (slē′ping·kär′) *n.* A passenger railroad car with accommodations for sleeping.
sleeping partner See under PARTNER.
sleeping pill *Med.* A sedative; especially, one of the barbiturates taken to relieve acute or persistent insomnia.
sleeping sickness *Pathol.* 1 The terminal stage of a form of trypanosomiasis prevalent in tropical Africa: it is caused by the presence in the cerebrospinal fluid of certain trypanosomes usually transmitted by the bite of the tsetse fly, and is marked by progressive lethargy, recurrent fever and headaches, terminating in somnolence and death. 2 Epidemic encephalitis lethargica.
sleep·less (slēp′lis) *adj.* Unable to sleep; wakeful; restless; unquiet. See synonyms under VIGILANT. — **sleep′less·ly** *adv.* — **sleep′less·ness** *n.*
sleep·walk·er (slēp′wô′kər) *n.* A somnambulist. — **sleep′walk′ing** *n.*
sleep·y (slē′pē) *adj.* **sleep·i·er, sleep·i·est** 1 Inclined to sleep. 2 Drowsy; sluggish; dull; heavy. 3 Conducive to sleep. — **sleep′i·ly** *adv.* — **sleep′i·ness** *n.*
sleep·y-head (slē′pē·hed′) *n.* A sleepy person. — **sleep′y-head′ed** *adj.*
sleet (slēt) *n.* 1 A mixture of snow or hail and rain. 2 A drizzle or shower of partly frozen

rain, or rain that freezes as it falls. **3** A thin coating of ice, as on rails, wires, roads, etc. —*v.i.* To pour or shed sleet. [Akin to MLG *slote* hail] —**sleet'y** *adj.*

sleeve (slēv) *n.* **1** The part of a garment that serves especially as a covering for the arm. **2** *Mech.* **a** A tube surrounding something, as a shaft, for protection or to permit motion of itself or of the shaft. **b** A short pipe receiving the ends of two other pipes or rods; a sleeve coupling or sleeve valve. **3** *Electr.* The cylindrical contacting part of a telephone-circuit plug. —**up one's sleeve** Hidden but at hand. —*v.t.* **sleeved, sleev·ing** To furnish with a sleeve or sleeves. ◆ Homophone: *sleave.* [OE *slēfe*]

sleeve coupling *Mech.* A short tube for connecting shafts or pipes.

sleeve·less (slēv'lis) *adj.* **1** Having no sleeves. **2** *Archaic* Unprofitable; fruitless; futile: a *sleeveless* errand.

sleeve valve *Mech.* A valve consisting of a hollow slotted sleeve in the cylinder of an internal-combustion engine, operating with the piston to allow for intake or exhaust of gases.

sleigh (slā) *n.* A light vehicle with runners for use on snow and ice, adapted especially for pleasure use or travel, as distinguished from hauling. Compare SLED, SLEDGE[1]. —*v.i.* To ride or travel in a sleigh. ◆ Homophones: *slay, sley.* [<Du. *slee,* contraction of *slede* sledge] —**sleigh'er** *n.*

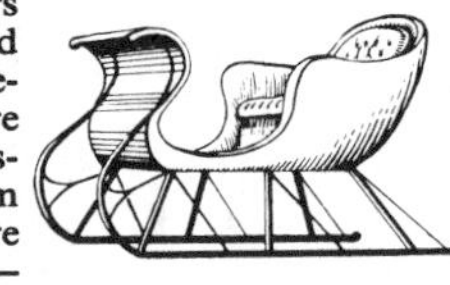
SLEIGH

sleigh·ing (slā'ing) *n.* **1** The act of riding in a sleigh. **2** The condition of the snow or ice that admits of using a sleigh.

sleight (slīt) *n.* **1** The quality of being skilful in manipulation; mechanical expertness; skill; dexterity. **2** A juggler's trick so deftly done that the manner of performance escapes observation; feat of legerdemain. **3** Craft; cunning. ◆ Homophone: *slight.* [<ON *slœgdh* slyness]

sleight of hand **1** Skill in performing tricks in juggling. **2** The art or practice, or an instance, of legerdemain.

slen·dang (slen'däng) *n.* A scarf or shawl worn over the shoulders by women in the Philippines. [<Malay *sĕlendañ*]

slen·der (slen'dər) *adj.* **1** Having a small diameter or circumference, in proportion to the length or height; slim; thin. **2** Having little strength or vigor; feeble; frail; delicate. **3** Having slight basis or foundation; of little validity. **4** Small or inadequate; moderate; insignificant: a *slender* income or diet. **5** Meagerly or insufficiently supplied: a *slender* table. **6** Thin in sound or quality; lacking volume. **7** *Phonet.* Denoting vowels which are pronounced with a narrow opening above the tongue, as (ē); close; narrow; opposed to *broad.* See synonyms under FINE[1], LITTLE, MINUTE[2]. [ME *slendre,* prob. <OF *esclendre*] —**slen'der·ly** *adv.* —**slen'der·ness** *n.*

slen·der·ize (slen'də·rīz) *v.t.* & *v.i.* **·ized, ·iz·ing** To make or become slender.

slept (slept) Past tense and past participle of SLEEP.

Sle·svig (sles'vikh) The Danish name for SCHLESWIG.

sleuth (slōōth) *n.* **1** *U.S. Colloq.* A detective. **2** A sleuthhound. **3** *Obs.* The track of a man or beast, as followed by the scent. —*v.t.* To follow, as a detective. —*v.i.* To play the detective. [<ON *slōdh* track, trail. Doublet of SLOT[2].]

sleuth·hound (slōōth'hound') *n.* A bloodhound.

slew[1] (slōō) Past tense of SLAY[1].

slew[2] (slōō) See SLOUGH[2].

slew[3] (slōō) *n. U.S. Colloq.* A large number, crowd, or amount; a lot: also spelled *slue.* [Cf. Irish *sluagh* a large crowd]

slew[4] (slōō) See SLUE[1].

sley (slā) *n.* **1** The reed guiding the warp threads of a loom. **2** In knitting machines, a groove, slot, or bar for directing the action of a part. —*v.t.* To separate and arrange the threads of (yarn) in a reed for weaving. ◆ Homophones: *slay, sleigh.* [OE *slege*]

Slez·sko (sles'kô) The Czech name for SILESIA.

slice (slīs) *n.* **1** A piece; especially, a thin, broad piece cut off from a larger body. **2** One of various tools or devices, used for slicing or resembling a slice in broadness and thinness; specifically, a broad knife used for serving fish, or a broad flat knife used by printers to remove ink; also, a druggist's spatula. **3** In golf, a blow delivered crosswise from right to left, causing the ball to curve to the right. —*v.* **sliced, slic·ing** *v.t.* **1** To cut or remove from a larger piece: often with *off.* **2** To cut into broad, thin pieces; divide; apportion. **3** To sunder, as with a sharp knife; split. **4** To clear out with a slice bar. **5** In golf, to hit (the ball) with a slice. —*v.i.* **6** In golf, to slice a ball. See synonyms under CUT. [<OF *esclice* < *esclicer* <OHG *slizan* slit] —**slic'er** *n.*

slice bar A thin, wide iron tool for cleaning clinkers from the grate bars of a furnace.

slick (slik) *adj.* **1** Smooth; slippery; sleek. **2** Flattering obsequious; smooth-tongued; plausible. **3** *Colloq.* Dexterously done; cleverly said; specious; tricky. **4** Smart; clever: said of people. **5** Healthy; plump: said of animals. **6** Smooth; oily, as the surface of water. **7** Glazed, as paper; also, printed on glazed paper: *slick* magazines. **8** *Slang* Agreeable; excellent: a *slick* time. —*n.* **1** A smooth place on a surface of water, as from oil or the presence of fish; also, a sleek place in the fur or hair of an animal. **2** A broad chisel for paring or slicking: also **slick chisel.** **3** *pl. U.S.* Magazines printed on glazed paper: distinguished from *pulps.* —*adv. Slang* In a slick or smooth manner; deftly; quickly. —*v.t.* **1** To make smooth, trim, glossy, or oily. **2** *Colloq.* To trim up; make presentable: often with *up.* [ME *slike* <OE *slician* make smooth]

slick·en·sides (slik'ən·sīdz) *n. pl. Geol.* Polished and scratched or striated rock surfaces, exhibited on the opposed faces of veins or faults where they have moved one upon another. [<dial. E *slicken* slick + SIDE] —**slick'en·sid'ed** *adj.* —**slick'en·sid'ing** *n.*

slick·er (slik'ər) *n.* **1** An implement for dressing leather, having a wooden handle. **2** *U.S.* A waterproof overcoat of oilskin. **3** *Colloq.* A cheat; clever person.

slid (slid) Past tense and past participle of SLIDE.

slid·den (slid'n) Alternative past participle of SLIDE.

slide (slīd) *v.* **slid, slid** or **slid·den, slid·ing** *v.i.* **1** To pass along over a surface with a smooth, slipping movement: to *slide* on ice. **2** To slip off, as scales in shedding. **3** To move or pass imperceptibly, smoothly, deftly, or easily; pass gradually or imperceptibly: The years *slide* away swiftly. **4** To move, pass, or proceed by sufferance merely; also, to take care of oneself or itself; go by default or without heed: with *let*: to let the matter *slide.* **5** *Music* To glide from tone to tone without breaking the sound. **6** To make a moral slip; err; sin. **7** To slip; lose one's equilibrium or foothold. **8** In baseball, to throw oneself along the ground toward a base, in order to avoid being tagged by the baseman. —*v.t.* **9** To cause to slide, as over a surface. **10** To move, put, enter, etc., with quietness or dexterity: with *in* or *into.* —*n.* **1** An act of sliding. **2** The slipping of a mass of earth, snow, etc., from a higher to a lower level; an avalanche. **3** An inclined plane or channel on which persons, goods, logs, etc., slide downward to a lower level. **4** A small plate of glass on which a specimen is mounted and examined through a microscope. **5** A small plate of transparent material bearing a single image for projection on a screen. **6** *Phot.* In a camera, that part of a plate holder which covers and uncovers the negative. **7** *Music* **a** A series of short musical notes leading smoothly to a principal note: a type of ornamentation. **b** A portamento. **c** In a trumpet or trombone, a U-shaped portion of the tubing which is pushed in and out to vary the pitch. **8** *Mech.* **a** A sliding part. **b** A groove, rail, etc., on which something slides. [OE *slīdan*]

slide fastener A fastening device for use on fabrics, dress goods, etc., having two rows of interlocking teeth or scoops which may be closed or separated by a sliding element: often called *zipper.*

slide·knot (slīd'not') *n.* A slipknot, particularly one made of two half-hitches on a fishing line.

Sli·dell (slī·del'), **John,** 1793–1871, American lawyer; Confederate agent to France in 1861.

Slide Mountain The highest peak of the Catskill Mountains, in SE New York, 18 miles west of Kingston; 4,204 feet.

slid·er (slī'dər) *n.* **1** One who or that which slides. **2** In baseball, a fast pitch that curves slightly at or near the strike zone.

slide rule A device consisting of a rigid ruler with a central sliding piece, both ruler and slide being graduated in a similar logarithmic scale to permit of rapid calculations.

slide valve *Mech.* **1** A sliding piece in the cylinder of a steam engine, regulated to move back and forth over the ports and connect them alternately with the boiler and the exhaust passage, thus imparting reciprocating motion to the piston. **2** A valve that slides on its seat.

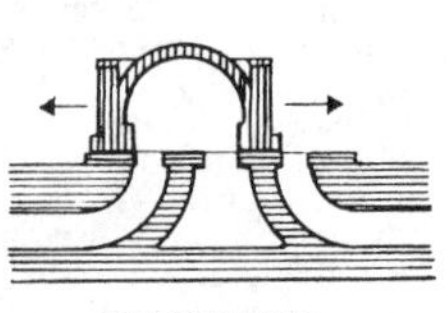
SLIDE VALVE
Arrows show reciprocal action.

sliding board A child's slide, used in play.

sliding scale **1** A schedule affecting imports, prices, or wages, varying under conditions of consumption, demand, or market price of some article. **2** Any graduated scale, as in a clinometer or slide rule, designed to move against a fixed scale in order to facilitate rapid and accurate measurements and computations.

slight (slīt) *adj.* **1** Of small importance; small in quantity, intensity, or degree; inconsiderable. **2** Slender; frail; delicate; flimsy. **3** Of weak intellect or character. **4** *Scot.* Smooth; slippery; unscrupulous. See synonyms under FINE[1], FRAGILE, INSIGNIFICANT, LITTLE, SMALL. —*v.t.* **1** To manifest intentional neglect of or disregard for; snub; omit due courtesy toward or respect for: to *slight* a friend. **2** To omit due care in the doing or performance of; do imperfectly or thoughtlessly; shirk. **3** To treat as trivial or insignificant. —*n.* An act or omission involving failure in courtesy or respect toward another; any contemptuous or neglectful action. ◆ Homophone: *sleight.* [ME. Akin to ON *slettr* smooth.] —**slight'ness** *n.*

Synonyms (noun): disregard, neglect, scorn. *Disregard* is chiefly a matter of intellectual estimate; *slight* is a matter of outward action; *neglect* may be of thought or act. *Disregard* of a thing is setting it aside as not worthy of regard. *Neglect* of a person or thing may be the result of ignorance, thoughtlessness, or preoccupation with other things; a *slight* is an intentional omission of kindness, courtesy, or attention. *Scorn* expresses mingled contempt and bitterness. See NEGLECT. *Antonyms*: esteem, honor, regard, respect, reverence.

slight·ing (slī'ting) *adj.* Conveying, containing, or characterized by a slight: a *slighting* remark. —**slight'ing·ly** *adv.*

slight·ly (slīt'lē) *adv.* In a slight manner; inconsiderably; partially; carelessly.

Sli·go (slī'gō) **1** A county of NW Ireland in Connacht province; 694 square miles. **2** Its county town, a port on **Sligo Bay,** an inlet of the Atlantic extending 7 miles into County Sligo; 10 miles wide.

sli·ly (slī'lē) *adv.* In a sly manner: also spelled *slyly.*

slim (slim) *adj.* **slim·mer, slim·mest** **1** Small in thickness in proportion to height or length, as a human figure or a tree. **2** Having little logical strength; weak. **3** Constructed unsubstantially; flimsy. **4** Lacking robustness; frail. **5** Insufficient; narrow; meager: a *slim* attendance; a *slim* chance. **6** *Brit. Dial.* Sly; crafty; worthless; bad. —*v.t.* & *v.i.* **slimmed, slim·ming** To make or become thin or thinner. [<Du. *slim* bad] —**slim'ly** *adv.* —**slim'·ness** *n.*

slime (slīm) *n.* **1** Any soft, sticky or dirty thing; hence, any offensive quality or thing. **2** Soft, moist, adhesive mud or earth; muck. **3** A mucous exudation from the bodies of certain animals, as fishes and snails, and certain plants. **4** Bitumen; asphalt. **5** *Usually pl.* A mudlike substance formed of ore in an almost impalpable powder, mixed with water. —*v.* **slimed, slim·ing** *v.t.* **1** To smear or cover with or as with slime. **2** To remove slime. **2** To remove slime from, as fishes. —*v.i.* **3** To become covered with or as with slime. [OE *slim*]

slime flux A watery or viscous flow from the injured bark of various deciduous trees, sometimes providing a medium for parasitic growths.
slime mold A fungus belonging to the class *Myxomycetes*. Also **slime fungus.**
slim·sy (slim′zē) *adj. Colloq.* **1** Utterly limp, as from fatigue or illness. **2** Lacking in stiffness or texture, as limp fabric; flimsy. Also **slimp·sy** (slimp′sē). [Blend of SLIM and FLIMSY]
slim·y (slī′mē) *adj.* **slim·i·er, slim·i·est 1** Covered or bedaubed with slime. **2** Containing slime. **3** Slimelike; foul. **— slim′i·ly** *adv.* **— slim′i·ness** *n.*
sling[1] (sling) *n.* **1** A strap or pocket with a string attached to each end, for hurling a stone or other missile by centrifugal force. **2** One of various ropes, straps, chains, or the like, for suspending or hoisting something, for holding up an injured limb, lifting and supporting an animal, in case of lameness or other need, carrying a rifle, etc. **3** *Naut.* A rope or chain by which a lower yard or a gaff is suspended; also, in the plural, the middle portion of a yard. **4** The act of slinging; a sudden throw; cast; fling. [< *v.*] **—** *v.* **slung, sling·ing** *v.t.* **1** To fling from or as from a sling; hurl. **2** To place or hang up in or as in a sling; move or hoist, as by a rope or tackle. **—** *v.i.* **3** To move at an easy gait. See synonyms under SEND[1]. [<ON *slyngva* hurl] **— sling′er** *n.*
sling[2] (sling) *n. U. S.* A drink of brandy, whisky, or gin, with sugar and nutmeg, lemon juice, and hot or cold water. **—** *v.i. U. S. Colloq.* To drink slings; take an alcoholic drink. [Cf. G *schlingen* swallow]
sling·shot (sling′shot′) *n.* A weapon or toy consisting of a forked stick with an elastic strap attached to the prongs for catapulting small missiles.
slink (slingk) *v.* **slunk** (*Obs.* **slank**), **slunk, slink·ing** *v.i.* To creep or steal along furtively or stealthily, as in fear. **—** *v.t.* To give birth to prematurely; miscarry: said of animals, especially cows. **—** *adj.* Produced prematurely, as a calf; too immature to be eaten. **—** *n.* An animal, especially a calf, prematurely born; also, its flesh, too immature for proper food. [OE *slincan* creep] **— slink′ing·ly** *adv.*
slink·y (slingk′ē) *adj.* **slink·i·er, slink·i·est 1** Sneaking; stealthy. **2** *Slang* Sinuous or feline in movement or form.
slip[1] (slip) *v.* **slipped** or **slipt, slip·ping** *v.t.* **1** To cause to move smoothly and easily; cause to glide or slide. **2** To put on or off easily, as a ring or a loose garment. **3** To convey slily or secretly. **4** To free oneself or itself from, as a fetter or bridle. **5** To let loose; unleash, as hounds. **6** To release from its fastening and let run out, as a cable. **7** To give birth to prematurely; slink; cast: said of animals. **8** To dislocate, as a bone. **9** To escape or pass unobserved: It *slipped* my mind. **10** To overlook; omit negligently: to *slip* an opportunity. **—** *v.i.* **11** To slide so as to cause harm or inconvenience; lose one's footing; become misplaced by failing to hold. **12** To fall into an error or fault; err. **13** To escape, as a ship. **14** To move smoothly and easily; slide; glide. **15** To get free of restraint; be unleashed. **16** To go or come stealthily or unnoticed: often with *off, away,* or *from.* **— to let slip** To say without intending to. **—** *n.* **1** An act of slipping; a sudden slide. **2** A lapse or error in speech, writing, or conduct; a slight mistake. **3** *U.S.* A narrow space between two wharves. **4** An artificial pier sloping down to the water, serving as a landing place. **5** An inclined plane leading down to the water, on which vessels are repaired or constructed. **6** A woman's undergarment. **7** A pillowcase. **8** A leash containing a device which permits quick release of the dog. **9** In cricket, a position on the off side a few yards behind the wicket; also, the player who stands at this position. **10** *Naut.* **a** The difference between the speed of a screw propeller and that of the ship. **b** The velocity of the back current generated by a propeller. **11** *Physics* The difference between the advance made by a propeller moving in a fluid and the advance it would make if moving in a solid substance. **12** *Mech.* **a** The relative motion of two surfaces which are meant to be immovable with respect to each other, as a belt on a pulley. **b** Allowance made for slipping or play, as between connected members of a mechanism; slippage. **13** *Geol.* A small dislocation of rock strata. **— to give (someone) the slip** To elude (someone). [<MLG *slippen*]
slip[2] (slip) *n.* **1** A cutting from a plant for planting or grafting; a cion. **2** A small, slender person, especially a youthful one. **3** A small piece of something, as of paper or cloth, rather long relative to its width; a strip. **4** A small piece of paper for jotting down memoranda, a record, etc. **5** *U.S.* A narrow pew in a church. **—** *v.t.* **slipped, slip·ping** To cut off for planting; make a slip or slips of. [<MDu. *slippe* < *slippen* cut]
slip[3] (slip) *n.* Liquid potter's clay, used for decorating and coating rough surfaces. [OE *slype, slypa*]
slip·cov·er (slip′kuv′ər) *n.* **1** A fitted cloth cover for a chair, couch, sofa, or other piece of furniture, that can be readily removed. **2** A paper or cloth jacket for a book.
slip·knot (slip′not′) *n.* **1** A knot so formed, by having part of the material drawn through in a bow, as to be readily untied: also called *bowknot.* **2** A running knot.
slip-on (slip′on′, -ôn′) *n.* A garment which can be easily donned or taken off. **—** *adj.* Denoting such a garment: a *slip-on* blouse.
slip-o·ver (slip′ō′vər) *adj.* Designating a garment easily donned by drawing over the head: a *slip-over* shirt. **—** *n.* A garment of this type.
slip·page (slip′ij) *n.* **1** The amount by which or distance through which anything slips, as a screw propeller. **2** The difference between actual and calculated speed, due to slipping. **3** The act of slipping; slip.
slip·per[1] (slip′ər) *n.* **1** A low, light shoe, chiefly for indoor wear, into or out of which the foot is easily slipped. **2** One who or that which slips. [<SLIP[1] + -ER[2]]
slip·per[2] (slip′ər) *adj. Archaic* Slippery; deceitful; unreliable; forgetful; voluble. [OE *slipor*]
slip·pered (slip′ərd) *adj.* Wearing slippers.
slip·per·wort (slip′ər·wûrt′) *n.* Calceolaria.
slip·per·y (slip′ər·ē) *adj.* **·per·i·er, ·per·i·est 1** Having a surface so smooth that bodies slip or slide easily on it. **2** That evades one's grasp; tricky; elusive. **3** Unreliable; undependable; tricky. **4** *Obs.* Wanton. [<SLIPPER[2] + -Y[3]] **— slip′per·i·ly** *adv.* **— slip′per·i·ness** *n.*
slippery elm 1 A tree *(Ulmus fulva)* of eastern North America. **2** Its hard wood. **3** Its mucilaginous inner bark, used in medicine as a nutritious demulcent.
slip-ring (slip′ring′) *n. Electr.* One of two or more metal rings of an electric machine serving, through contact with stationary brushes, to deliver or transmit a current.
slip-sheet (slip′shēt′) *Printing n.* A blank piece of paper interleaved between newly printed press sheets to prevent offset. **—** *v.t.* To insert slip-sheets in.
slip·shod (slip′shod′) *adj.* Wearing shoes or slippers down at the heels; hence, slovenly. [<SLIP[1] + SHOE]
slip·slop (slip′slop′) *n. Colloq.* **1** Sloppy victuals; any weak drink; slop. **2** A blunder, as in speaking.
slip·stream (slip′strēm′) *n. Aeron.* The stream of air driven backwards by the propeller of an aircraft: also called *race.*
slip-up (slip′up′) *n. Colloq.* A mistake; error.
slip·way (slip′wā′) *n.* A slip (def. 5).
slit (slit) *n.* A cut that is relatively straight and long; also, a long, narrow opening. [< *v.*] **—** *v.t.* **slit, slit·ting 1** To make a long incision in; slash. **2** To cut lengthwise into strips. See synonyms under REND. [ME *slitten* cut] **— slit′ter** *n.*
slith·er (slith′ər) *v.i.* **1** To slide; slip, as on a loose surface. **2** To glide, as a snake. **—** *v.t.* **3** To cause to slither. [Var. of dial. E *slidder* <OE *slidrian*, freq. of *slīdan* slide] **— slith′er·y** *adj.*
slit trench A narrow, shallow trench, similar to a foxhole.
sliv·er (sliv′ər) *n.* **1** A slender piece, as of wood, cut or torn off lengthwise; a splinter. **2** Corded textile fibers drawn into a fleecy strand. **3** A piece cut longitudinally from the side of a fish: used as bait; also, a filet. **—** *v.t.* & *v.i.* To cut or split into long thin pieces; splinter. [< dial. E *slive* cleave] **— sliv′·er·er** *n.*
Sliv·no (slēv′nō) A city in east central Bulgaria. Also **Sliv·en** (slē′vən).
sli·vo·vitz (slē′vô·vēts) *n.* A white, dry plum brandy drunk especially in central European countries. [<Serbo-Croatian < *sliva* a plum]
Sloan (slōn), **John,** 1871–1951, U. S. painter.
slob (slob) *n.* **1** Mud; mire. **2** Slush; mushy snow. **3** *Slang* A stupid, careless, or unclean person. [<Irish *slab,* prob. <SLAB[2]]
slob·ber (slob′ər) *v.t.* **1** To wet and foul with liquids oozing from the mouth. **2** To shed or spill, as liquid food, in eating. **—** *v.i.* **3** To drivel; slaver. **4** To talk or act gushingly. **—** *n.* **1** Liquid spilled as from the mouth; slaver. **2** Gushing, sentimental talk. [Var. of SLABBER] **— slob′ber·er** *n.* **— slob′ber·y** *adj.*
slock (slok) *v.t. Brit. Dial.* To slake; drench; extinguish (a fire). Also **slock′en.**
sloe (slō) *n.* **1** A small, plumlike, astringent fruit. **2** The shrub *(Prunus spinosa)* that bears it; the blackthorn. **3** The blackhaw. **4** The wild yellow plum *(Prunus americana)*; also, the Allegheny plum *(P. alleghaniensis).* ◆ Homophone: *slow.* [OE *slā*]
sloe-eyed (slō′īd′) *adj.* Having eyes dark as sloes.
sloe gin A cordial with a gin base, flavored with sloes.
slog (slog) *v.t.* & *v.i.* **slogged, slog·ging 1** To slug, as a pugilist. **2** To plod (one's way), as through deep mud. **—** *n.* A heavy blow. [Var. of SLUG[3]] **— slog′ger** *n.*
slo·gan (slō′gən) *n.* **1** A battle or rallying cry: originally of the Highland clans. **2** A catchword or motto adopted by a manufacturer, political party, or the like. [<Scottish Gaelic *sluagh* army + *gairm* yell]
sloid (sloid), **slojd** See SLOYD.
sloop (slo͞op) *n. Naut.* A single-masted, fore-and-aft rigged sailing vessel with or without a bowsprit and carrying at least one jib: now used principally as a racing vessel. [<Du. *sloep*]

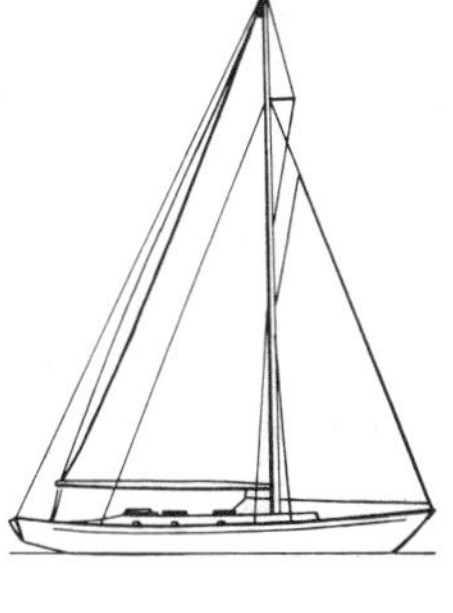
SLOOP

sloop of war In old navies, a vessel rigged either as ship, brig, or schooner, and mounting between 18 and 32 guns; later, any war vessel larger than a gunboat and carrying guns on one deck only.
slop[1] (slop) *v.* **slopped, slop·ping** *v.i.* **1** To splash or spill. **2** To walk or move through slush. **—** *v.t.* **3** To cause (a liquid) to spill or splash. **4** *U.S.* To feed (a domestic animal) with slops. **— to slop over 1** To overflow and splash. **2** To do or say more than is necessary, because of excess zeal, sentimentality, etc. **—** *n.* **1** Slush; watery mud. **2** A dash or puddle of liquid that has been slopped. **3** An unappetizing liquid or watery food. **4** Refuse liquid. **5** *pl.* Waste food or swill, as from a kitchen, used to feed cattle, pigs, etc. **6** *pl.* Distiller's mash which has been deprived of its alcohol. [ME *sloppe*]
slop[2] (slop) **1** *Obs.* A loose outer garment; a smock; in the plural, wide baggy breeches. **2** *pl.* Articles of clothing and other merchandise sold to sailors on shipboard. [ME *sloppe*]
slope (slōp) *v.* **sloped, slop·ing** *v.i.* **1** To be inclined from the level or the vertical; slant. **2** To move on an inclined path; go obliquely. **3** *Colloq.* To leave suddenly; run off. **—** *v.t.* **4** To cause to slope. See synonyms under TIP[1]. [< *adj.*] **—** *n.* **1** Any slanting surface or line; a declivity or acclivity; an inclined plane: the Atlantic *slope* of North America. **2** The degree of inclination of a line or surface from the plane of the horizon. **3** *Math.* **a** The tangent of the positive angle of less than 180° made between the *x*-axis and a tangent to a curve traced in the Cartesian coordinate system; also, the derivative of such a curve at a given point. **b** The tangent of the positive

angle of less than 180° made between the *x*-axis and a straight line traced in the Cartesian coordinate system. — *adj.* Slanting; oblique. [Aphetic var. of *aslope,* OE *aslopen,* ppr. of *aslupan* slip away] — **slop′er** *n.* — **slop′ing** *adj.* — **slop′ing·ly** *adv.* — **slop′ing·ness** *n.*

slop·o·ver (slop′ō′vər) *n.* A breakover.

slop·py (slop′ē) *adj.* **·pi·er, ·pi·est** **1** Slushy; splashy; wet. **2** Watery or pulpy: *sloppy* pudding. **3** Splashed with liquid or slops. **4** *Colloq.* Messy; slovenly; extremely untidy. **5** *Colloq.* Slipshod; careless. **6** *Colloq.* Maudlin; overly sentimental. — **slop′pi·ly** *adv.* — **slop′pi·ness** *n.*

slop·work (slop′wûrk′) *n.* **1** The manufacture of cheap ready-made clothing; also, the clothing itself. **2** Any inferior, slovenly work.

slosh (slosh) *v.t.* To throw about, as a liquid. — *v.i.* To splash; flounder: to *slosh* through a pool. — *n.* Slush. [Var. of SLUSH] — **slosh′y** *adj.*

slot[1] (slot) *n.* **1** A long narrow groove or opening; slit. **2** A comparatively long and narrow depression or cavity, particularly one that is rectangular, cut to receive some corresponding part in a mechanism. **3** The opening to receive the coin in a slot machine. **4** *Colloq.* An opening or position, as a job category or place in a sequence. **5** *Aeron.* An opening in an airplane wing to improve the conditions of airflow at high angles of flight. — *v.t.* **slot·ted, slot·ting** **1** To adjust in a slot. **2** To cut a slot in; groove. [<OF *esclot* the hollow between the breasts]

slot[2] (slot) *n.* The trail of an animal, especially a deer. [<AF *esclot* <ON *slōdh.* Doublet of SLEUTH.]

sloth (slôth, slōth, sloth) *n.* **1** Disinclination to exertion; habitual indolence; laziness. **2** A slow-moving, tree-dwelling edentate mammal (family *Bradypodidae*) of tropical America. The **three-toed sloth** (genus *Bradypus*) has three toes on each foot; the **two-toed sloth** (genus *Choloepus*) has two on the front and three on the hind feet. **3** A related fossil edentate (family *Megatheriidae*). [<SLOW + -TH[1]]

THREE-TOED SLOTH
(Head and body about 21 inches long)

sloth bear A black bear of India and Ceylon (genus *Melursus*), feeding mainly on honey and fruit.

sloth·ful (slôth′fəl, slōth′-, sloth′-) *adj.* Sluggish; lazy; indolent. See synonyms under IDLE. — **sloth′ful·ly** *adv.* — **sloth′ful·ness** *n.*

slot machine A vending machine or gambling machine having a slot in which a coin is dropped to cause operation.

slouch (slouch) *v.i.* **1** To have a downcast or drooping gait, look, or posture. **2** To hang or droop in a careless manner, as a hat. — *n.* **1** A hanging down awkwardly or carelessly; movement or appearance caused by depression or drooping. **2** An awkward or incompetent person. [Origin uncertain] — **slouch′y** *adj.* — **slouch′i·ly** *adv.* — **slouch′i·ness** *n.*

slough[1] (slou *for defs. 1 and 4*; sloo *for defs. 2 and 3*) *n.* **1** A place of deep mud or mire; bog. **2** A depression in a prairie, often dry but sometimes deeply miry, forming part of the natural drainage system. **3** A stagnant swamp, backwater, bayou, inlet, or pond in which water backs up: also spelled *slew, slue.* **4** A state of moral depravity or of despair. [OE *slōh*] — **slough′y** *adj.*

slough[2] (sluf) *n.* **1** Dead tissue separated and thrown off from the living parts, as in gangrene; also, a scab. **2** The skin of a serpent that has been or is about to be shed; cast. — *v.t.* **1** To cast off, as dead from living tissue; shed. **2** To discard; shed, as a habit or a growth; get rid of as useless or needless. — *v.i.* **3** To be cast off. **4** To cast off a slough or tissue; form a scab. [ME *slouh*] — **slough′y** *adj.*

Slough (slou) A municipal borough of SE Buckingham, England.

Slo·vak (slō′vak, slō·vak′) *n.* **1** One of a Slavic people of NW Hungary and parts of Moravia, who united with the Czechs to form the Czechoslovak republic in 1918: now in central Czechoslovakia. **2** The dialect of Czechoslovakian spoken by the Slovaks. — *adj.* Of or pertaining to the Slovaks or to their language. Also **Slo·vak·i·an** (slō·vak′ē·ən, -vä′kē·ən). [<Czech *slovák* a Slav]

Slo·vak·i·a (slō·vak′ē·ə, -vä′kē·ə) The eastern geographical region and a former province (1920–39 and 1945–49) of Czechoslovakia; an independent state, under German protection, 1939–45; divided into six administrative regions, 1949; 18,897 square miles; capital, Bratislava. *Czech* **Slo·ven·sko** (slô′ven·skô).

slov·en (sluv′ən) *n.* One who is careless of dress or of cleanliness; one habitually untidy. [Cf. Flemish *sloef* dirty] — **slov′en·li·ness** *n.* — **slov′en·ly** *adj.* & *adv.*

Slo·vene (slō′vēn, slō·vēn′) *n.* One of a group of southern Slavs now living in NW Yugoslavia. — *adj.* Of or pertaining to the Slovenes or to their language. [<G *Slowene*]

Slo·ve·ni·a (slō·vē′nē·ə) A constituent republic of NW Yugoslavia; 7,717 square miles; capital, Ljubljana: formerly part of Austria.

Slo·ve·ni·an (slō·vē′nē·ən) *adj.* Of or pertaining to Slovenia, its people, or their language. — *n.* The South Slavic language of the Slovenes.

slow (slō) *adj.* **1** Having relatively small velocity; not quick in motion, performance, or occurrence; not advancing or growing rapidly. **2** Behind the standard time: said of a timepiece. **3** Taking sufficient time; not precipitate or hasty: *slow* to anger. **4** Dull or tardy in comprehending; mentally sluggish: a *slow* student. **5** Lacking promptness, spirit, or liveliness; also, colloquially, dull or tedious in character. **6** Denoting a condition of a racetrack that retards the horses' speed, but in less degree than a muddy or heavy track: a *slow* track. — *v.t.* **1** To make slow or slower; cause to go at a slower pace; slacken in speed: often with *up* or *down.* **2** To retard; delay. — *v.i.* **3** To go or become slow or slower: often with *up* or *down.* — *adv.* In a slow or cautious manner or speed. ◆ Homophone: *sloe.* [OE *slāw*] — **slow′ly** *adv.* — **slow′ness** *n.*

Synonyms (adj.): deliberate, dilatory, drowsy, dull, gradual, inactive, inert, lingering, moderate, slack, sluggish, tardy. *Tardy* is applied to that which is behind the proper or desired time, especially in doing work or arriving at a place; *slow* applies to that which is a relatively long time in passing from one point to another, or in beginning or executing something. A person is *deliberate* who takes a noticeably long time to consider and decide before acting, or who acts or speaks as if he were deliberating at every point; a person is *dilatory* who lays aside, or puts off as long as possible, necessary or required action. *Gradual* signifies advancing by steps, and refers to *slow* but regular and sure progression. *Slack* refers to action that seems to indicate a lack of tension, as of muscle or of will, *sluggish* to action that seems as if reluctant to advance. See GRADUAL, HEAVY, RELUCTANT, TEDIOUS. *Antonyms*: see synonyms for IMPETUOUS, NIMBLE.

slow-down (slō′doun′) *n.* A slackening of pace.

slow match A slowly burning fuse used in firing explosives.

slow-mo·tion (slō′mō′shən) *adj.* Pertaining to or designating a motion picture filmed at greater than standard speed so that the action appears slow in normal projection.

slow·poke (slō′pōk′) *n. Slang* A person who works or moves at an exceedingly slow pace; a laggard.

slow·worm (slō′wûrm′) *n.* A blindworm.

sloyd (sloid) *n.* A system of elementary manual training originating in Sweden, having exercises graduated from the simplest use of tools to the most complete joinery: also spelled *sloid, slojd.* [<Sw. *slöjd* skill]

slub (slub) *v.t.* **slubbed, slub·bing** To twist (slivers of wool) slightly in preparation for spinning. — *n.* **1** A slightly twisted roll of cotton, wool, or silk. **2** A thick, uneven lump in yarn. [Origin unknown]

sludge (sluj) *n.* **1** Soft, water-soaked mud; mire. **2** A slush of snow or broken or half-formed ice. **3** Muddy or pasty refuse of various kinds, as that produced by the action of a rock drill and in the purification of sewage. **4** The sediment in a water tank or boiler. [<earlier *slutch.* ? Related to SLUSH.] — **sludg′y** *adj.*

slue[1] (sloo) *v.* **slued, slu·ing** *v.t.* **1** To cause to move sidewise, as if some portion were pivoted; swing, slide, or skid to the side. **2** To cause to twist or turn in its seat or fastenings: said of a boom or mast. — *v.i.* **3** To move sidewise. — *n.* The act of sluing around sidewise; a skidding or pivoting about; also, the position of a body that has slued. Also spelled *slew.* [Origin unknown]

slue[2] (sloo) See SLEW[3].

slue[3] (sloo) See SLOUGH[1] (def. 3).

slug[1] (slug) *n.* **1** A bullet or shot of irregular or oblong shape, especially as used in old muskets. **2** *Printing* **a** A strip of type metal, thicker than a lead and less than type-high, for spacing matter, etc. **b** A metal strip bearing a type-high number, abbreviated title, or the like, used as a compositor's mark. **3** A slungshot, or its metal weight. **4** Any small chunk of metal; especially, one used as a coin in automatic machines, as dial telephones. **5** *Physics* A unit of mass; the mass of a body which, when acted upon by a force of one pound, acquires an acceleration of one foot per second per second: it has the value of about 32.174 pounds or 14.59 kilograms, and is also called *geepound.* — *v.* **slugged, slug·ging** *v.i.* To take shape to fit the grooves of a rifle, as a bullet. — *v.t.* To load with slugs. [Origin uncertain. ? Akin to SLAG.]

slug[2] (slug) *n.* **1** A gastropod (order *Pulmonata*) related to the snail, having an elongated body and a rudimentary shell concealed in the mantle, especially of the genus *Limax.* **2** The larva of a sawfly or other insect resembling a gastropod. **3** A sluggard. [ME *slugge* a sluggard, ? < Scand. Cf. dial. Norw. *slugg* a large, heavy object.]

SLUG

slug[3] (slug) *Colloq. n.* **1** A heavy blow, as with the fist or a baseball bat. **2** A drink of undiluted liquor. — *v.t.* **slugged, slug·ging** To strike heavily or brutally, or without science, as with the fist or a baseball bat. [Origin uncertain] — **slug′ger** *n.*

slug·a·bed (slug′ə·bed′) *n.* One who lounges late in bed, because of laziness.

slug·gard (slug′ərd) *n.* A person habitually lazy or idle; a drone. — *adj.* Lazy; sluggish. [< SLUG[2] + -ARD]

slug·gish (slug′ish) *adj.* **1** Having little motion or power of motion; slow; inactive; torpid. **2** Habitually idle and lazy. **3** Not active; slow; stagnant: a *sluggish* season. See synonyms under HEAVY, IDLE, SLOW, TEDIOUS. — **slug′gish·ly** *adv.* — **slug′gish·ness** *n.*

sluice (sloos) *n.* **1** Any artificial channel for conducting water, or the stream so conducted; specifically, a body of water controlled by a floodgate. **2** A floodgate. **3** A flume. **4** *Mining* A board trough having at the bottom baffles holding quicksilver to separate gold from placer dirt carried through the trough by a current of water. **5** That through which anything issues or flows. — *v.* **sluiced, sluic·ing** *v.t.* **1** To wet or drench, water or irrigate by or as by means of a sluice. **2** To wash in or by a sluice. **3** To draw out or conduct by or through a sluice. **4** To send (logs) down a sluiceway. — *v.i.* **5** To flow out or issue from a sluice. [<OF *escluse* <L *exclusa,* pp. fem. of *excludere* shut out]

sluice·gate (sloos′gāt′) *n.* The gate of a sluice; a watergate or floodgate.

sluice·way (sloos′wā′) *n.* An artificial channel for the passage of water; a sluice, as in mining; flume.

sluit (sloot) *n. Afrikaans* A narrow, natural or artificial channel, through which water flows; a gully.

slum[1] (slum) *n.* A squalid, dirty, overcrowded street or section of a city, marked by the poverty and poor living conditions of its inhabitants. — *v.i.* **slummed, slum·ming** To visit slums, as for reasons of curiosity or philanthropy. [< slang E, a room; ult. origin unknown] — **slum′mer** *n.* — **slum′ming** *n.*

slum[2] (slum) *n. Slang* Slumgullion.

slum·ber (slum′bər) *v.i.* **1** To sleep, especially lightly or quietly. **2** To be inactive; stagnate. — *v.t.* **3** To spend or pass in sleeping. See synonyms under REST. — *n.* Sleep; formerly, light sleep; more recently, complete, quiet sleep. [OE *slumerian* <*slūma*] **—slum′ber·er** *n.* **—slum′ber·ing·ly** *adv.* **—slum′ber·less** *adj.*

slum·ber·ous (slum′bər·əs) *adj.* Inviting to, being in, suggesting, or resembling slumber; soporific; drowsy; sleepy. Also **slum·brous** (slum′brəs). **—slum′ber·ous·ly** *adv.* **—slum′·ber·ous·ness** *n.*

slum·ber·y (slum′bər·ē) *adj.* Slumberous; somnolent.

slum·gul·lion (slum·gul′yən) *n.* **1** *Slang* **a** A stew made principally of meat and vegetables. **b** A weak beverage. **2** A servant, especially one who performs menial chores. **3** Refuse drainage from blubber; also, fish offal. **4** A reddish, muddy deposit in mine sluiceways. [<slang E; origin uncertain]

slum·gum (slum′gum′) *n.* The residue of propolis, cocoons, etc., after beeswax is extracted from honeycombs.

slum·lord (slum′lôrd′) *n.* A landlord of a slum dwelling. [<SLUM + (LAND)LORD]

slump (slump) *v.i.* **1** To break through a crust, as of snow or ice, and sink; sink, as a foot, into any soft material. **2** To slide with perceptible motion down a declivity: said of loose earth or rock. **3** To fall or fail suddenly, as in value or quality. **4** To stand, walk, or proceed with a stooping posture; slouch: He *slumps* badly. **—*n.*** **1** The act of slumping; a collapsing fall. **2** A collapse or failure; also, a sudden fall of prices: a *slump* in stocks. **3** A decline, as of interest, excitement, etc. [Prob. imit.]

slung (slung) Past tense and past participle of SLING.

slung·shot (slung′shot′) *n.* A weight attached to a thong or cord, used as a weapon.

slunk (slungk) Past tense and past participle of SLINK. **—*n.*** The body of a stillborn animal, especially of a calf when cut away from the mother's womb. See SLINK.

slur (slûr) *v.t.* **slurred, slur·ring** **1** To slight; disparage; depreciate. **2** To pass over lightly or hurriedly; suppress; conceal: to *slur* a fact. **3** To pronounce, as a syllable, hurriedly and indistinctly. **4** *Music* **a** To sing or play as indicated by the slur. **b** To mark with a slur. **5** To smear; soil; contaminate. **—*n.*** **1** A disparaging remark or insinuation; also, the occasion for it, or the resulting state; a stigma. **2** *Music* **a** A curved line (‿ or ⁀) indicating that tones so tied are to be sung to the same syllable or performed without a break between them. **b** The legato effect indicated or produced by this mark. **3** A blur. **4** A slurred pronunciation. [<dial. E, orig. fluid mud]

slurp (slûrp) *v.t.* & *v.i.* *Slang* To sip noisily. [Imit.]

slur·ry (slûr′ē) *n.* *pl.* **·ries** **1** Any one of several watery mixtures used to make repairs in furnace linings, to neutralize poisonous chemicals, etc. **2** A mixture used in making Portland cement. [See SLUR.]

slush (slush) *n.* **1** Soft, sloppy material, as melting snow or soft mud. **2** Greasy material used for lubrication, etc. **3** The greasy refuse of cooking, especially from a ship's galley: used on shipboard for lubricating the masts. **4** A mixture of lime with white lead or tallow, for coating bright iron or steel parts of machinery to keep them from rusting. **5** Emotional talk or writing; gush; drivel. **—*v.t.*** **1** To cover or daub with slush, as for lubrication. **2** To fill (spaces in masonry) with mortar: usually with *up.* **3** To wash by throwing water upon, as a deck. [Origin unknown] **—slush′y** *adj.*

slush fund *U.S.* **1** Formerly, on naval vessels, money obtained from the sale of garbage and used to buy small luxuries. **2** Money collected or spent for corrupt purposes, as bribery, lobbying, propaganda, etc.

slut (slut) *n.* **1** A female dog; bitch. **2** A slatternly woman. **3** A drudge. **4** A woman of loose character; hussy. [Origin uncertain]

slut·tish (slut′ish) *adj.* Slatternly; dirty. **—slut′·tish·ly** *adv.* **—slut′tish·ness** *n.*

sly (slī) *adj.* **sli·er** or **sly·er, sli·est** or **sly·est** **1** Artfully dexterous in doing things secretly; cunning in evading notice or detection. **2** Playfully clever; roguish; mischievous. **3** Meanly or stealthily clever; crafty. **4** Done with or marked by artful secrecy: a *sly* trick. **5** Skilful; possessed of practical ability; wise. See synonyms under INSIDIOUS. **—on the sly** In a stealthy way; with concealment. [<ON *slœgr*] **—sly′ness** *n.*

sly·boots (slī′bo͞ots′) *n.* *Colloq.* A roguish, cunning, and sly person or animal.

sly·ly (slī′lē) See SLILY.

smack[1] (smak) *n.* **1** A quick, sharp sound, as of the lips when separated rapidly; a noisy kiss. **2** A sounding blow or slap. **3** The sound of a snapping whip. **—*v.t.* & *v.i.*** To give or make a smack, as in tasting, kissing, striking, etc.; slap. [Cf. MDu. *smack* a blow]

smack[2] (smak) *v.i.* **1** To have a taste or flavor, especially as tested by smacking: usually with *of.* **2** To have, keep, or disclose a slight suggestion: with *of.* **—*n.*** **1** A suggestive tincture, taste, or flavor. **2** A mere taste; smattering. [OE *smæc* taste]

smack[3] (smak) *n.* A small, decked or half-decked vessel of various rig used chiefly for fishing; especially, one having a well for fish in its hold. [<Du. *smak, smacke*]

smack·ing (smak′ing) *adj.* Making a sharp sound; hence, brisk; lively: a *smacking* breeze. **—*n.*** A quick, sharp sound; smack.

smaik (smāk) *n.* *Scot.* A rascal; petty rogue; mean, contemptible, or silly fellow.

Smal·kal·dic League (smôl·kôl′dik) See SCHMALKALDIC LEAGUE.

small (smôl) *adj.* **1** Comparatively less than another or than a standard; diminutive; little. **2** Being of slight moment, weight, or importance. **3** Lacking in moral or mental breadth; narrow; ignoble; mean; paltry. **4** Lacking in the qualities of greatness; not largely gifted. **5** Acting or transacting business in a limited way. **6** Weak in characteristic properties; mildly alcoholic: said of liquors: *small* beer. **7** Having little body or volume; slender; fine; soft, as a voice. **8** Of low degree; obscure. **9** Lacking in power or strength. **—to feel small** To feel humiliated. **—*adv.*** **1** In a low or faint tone: to sing *small.* **2** Into small pieces. **3** In a small way; trivially; also, timidly; to talk *small.* **—*n.*** **1** A small or slender part: the *small* of the back. **2** A small thing or quantity. [OE *smæl*] **—small′ness** *n.*

Synonyms (adj.): diminutive, fine, little, mean, microscopic, minute, narrow, petty, puny, tiny. See FINE[1], INSIGNIFICANT, LITTLE.

small·age (smô′lij) *n.* Celery, especially in the wild state. [<SMALL + F *ache* wild celery <L *apium* parsley]

small arms Arms that may be carried on the person, as a rifle, automatic pistol, or revolver.

small beer **1** Insipid or weak beer. **2** *Brit.* An insignificant person or thing.

small calorie See under CALORIE.

small capital A capital letter cut slightly larger than the lower-case letters of a specified type size. Abbr. *s.c., s. cap., small cap., sm. cap.*

THIS LINE IS IN CAPITAL LETTERS
THIS LINE IS IN SMALL CAPITAL LETTERS
this line is in lower-case letters

small circle The circumference formed by a plane cutting a sphere but not passing through its center.

small-clothes (smôl′klōthz′, -klōz′) *n.* *pl.* Close-fitting knee breeches worn by men in the 18th century. Also *smalls.*

small craft **1** Small vessels collectively. **2** Small things or persons generally.

small-fry (smôl′frī′) *n.* *pl.* **1** Small, young fish. **2** Young children. **3** Small or insignificant people or things.

small hours The early hours of the morning.

small·ish (smô′lish) *adj.* Somewhat small.

small-minded (smôl′mīn′did) *adj.* **1** Having a petty mind; interested in trivialities. **2** Narrow; intolerant; ungenerous.

small·mouth (smôl′mouth′) *n.* An American black bass (*Micropterus dolomieu*).

small potatoes *U.S. Colloq.* Unimportant, insignificant persons or things.

small·pox (smôl′poks′) *n.* *Pathol.* An acute, infectious, highly contagious disease caused by a filtrable virus and characterized by high inflammatory fever, followed by an eruption of deep-seated pustules; variola.

smalls (smôlz) *n.* *pl.* **1** Small-clothes. **2** *Brit. Colloq.* The first examination after matriculation; responsions: used at Oxford to denote the first university examination counting toward a degree. [<SMALL]

small stores Small, miscellaneous items, as tobacco, soap, thread, etc., stocked by a ship's store to be sold to the crew.

small sword **1** A light sword used on dress occasions. **2** The straight sword of modern fencing, introduced about 1700.

small talk Unimportant or trivial conversation.

small-time (smôl′tīm′) *adj.* *U.S. Slang* Petty; unimportant.

smalt (smôlt) *n.* A deep-blue glass colored with cobalt oxide: used when pulverized for painting, etc. [<F <Ital. *smalto* <Gmc.]

smalt·ite (smôl′tīt) *n.* A tin-white to steel-gray cobalt arsenide, crystallizing in the isometric system. Also **smalt·ine** (smôl′tin, -tēn). [<SMALT]

smal·to (smäl′tō) *n.* *pl.* **·ti** (-tē) *Italian* Colored glass, or a piece of it, employed in mosaics.

smar·agd (smar′agd) *n.* *Obs.* A green precious stone, as the beryl or the emerald. Also **smar′·agde.** [<L *smaragdus* <Gk. *smaragdos.* Doublet of EMERALD.] **—sma·rag·dine** (smə·rag′dēn, -din) *adj.*

sma·rag·dite (smə·rag′dīt) *n.* A thin, foliated, light grass-green variety of amphibole.

smarm (smärm) *Brit. Colloq.* *v.t.* To smear or plaster (the hair) with oil. **—*v.i.*** To behave in a servilely flattering manner; toady. [Var. of dial. E *smalm* smear, plaster]

smarm·y (smär′mē) *adj.* *Brit. Colloq.* Unctuously flattering; oily; toadying.

smart (smärt) *v.i.* **1** To experience a stinging sensation, generally superficial, either bodily or mental. **2** To cause a stinging sensation. **3** To experience remorse. **4** To have one's feelings hurt. **5** To pay a severe penalty. **—*v.t.*** **6** To cause to smart. **—*adj.*** **1** Quick in thought or action; bright; acute; clever. **2** Impertinently witty: often used contemptuously. **3** Vigorous; emphatic; severe; brisk. **4** Causing a smarting sensation; stinging; pungent. **5** Keen or sharp, as at trade; shrewd. **6** In active health; well. **7** *Colloq.* Superior, as in speed, strength, or skill. **8** *Colloq.* Large; considerable: a *smart* crop of wheat. **9** Sprucely dressed; showy. **10** Belonging to the stylish classes; fashionable: a *smart* set. **11** Making a creditable showing: a *smart* regiment. See synonyms under CLEVER. **—*n.*** **1** An acute stinging sensation, as from a scratch or an irritant. **2** Any distress; poignant mental suffering. **3** *Dial.* A degree, number, or amount: with ***right***: a **right** *smart* of people. [OE *smeortan*] **—smart′ly** *adv.* **—smart′ness** *n.*

smart al·eck (al′ik) *Colloq.* A cocky, offensively conceited person. **—smart-al·eck·y** (smärt′al′ik·ē) *adj.*

smart·en (smär′tən) *v.t.* To improve in appearance; make smart, as oneself or one's habitation: with *up.*

smart money **1** *Law* Damages awarded against a defendant because of great aggravation attending the wrong committed. **2** Money paid for a release from an engagement or from a painful situation. **3** Money paid by an employer to a workman injured in his service. **4** *Brit.* Money allowed to soldiers or sailors for injuries received in the service. **5** *Colloq.* Money bet by gamblers who supposedly know the result of a contest beforehand.

smart set Fashionable society.

smart·weed (smärt′wēd′) *n.* Any of several species of widely distributed herbs (genus *Polygonum*) having jointed stems, long, grasslike leaves, and inconspicuous, greenish flowers, especially the **common smartweed** or water pepper. Also called *knotweed.*

smart·y (smär′tē) *n.* *pl.* **smart·ies** *Slang* A person affecting to be smart or witty; a smart aleck.

smash (smash) *v.t.* **1** To break in many pieces suddenly, as by a blow, pressure, or collision. **2** To flatten; crush: to *smash* a hat. **3** To dash or fling violently so as to crush or break in pieces. **4** To strike with a sudden blow. **5** To make bankrupt. **6** To destroy, as a theory. **7** In tennis, to strike (the ball) with a hard, swift, overhand stroke. **—*v.i.*** **8** To go bankrupt; fail, as a business, etc. **9** To move or be moved with force; come into violent contact so as to crush or be crushed; collide; dash: The boats *smashed* together. See synonyms under BREAK. **— to go to smash** *Colloq.* To be ruined; fail. **—** *n.* **1** An act or instance of smashing, or the state of being smashed: often compounded with *up*: a *smash-up* on a railroad. **2** Any disaster or sudden break-up of any kind: a *smash* in business. **3** A beverage of spirituous liquors, usually brandy, with mint, water, sugar, and ice. **4** In tennis, a strong overhand shot. **5** *Colloq.* Something acclaimed by the public: The film is a box-office *smash.* [Prob. imit.] **— smash′er** *n.*

smash·ing (smash′ing) *adj. Colloq.* Extremely impressive; overwhelmingly good: a *smashing* success.

smash-up (smash′up′) *n.* A smash; a disastrous collision.

smat·ter (smat′ər) *v.t.* To talk of, dabble in, study, or use superficially. **—** *n.* A slight knowledge. [ME *smateren,* ? <Scand. Cf. Sw. *smattra* patter.] **— smat′ter·er** *n.*

smat·ter·ing (smat′ər·ing) *n.* **1** A superficial degree or kind of anything, especially of knowledge. **2** A little bit or a few.

smear (smir) *v.t.* **1** To spread, rub, or cover with grease, paint, dirt, etc.; bedaub. **2** To spread or apply in a thick layer or coating: to *smear* grease on an axle. **3** To sully the reputation of; defame; slander. **4** *U.S. Slang* To defeat utterly; overwhelm or stop. **5** To cover with smear (def. 3). **6** *Obs.* To anoint. **—** *v.i.* **7** To be or become smeared. **—** *n.* **1** A soiled spot; stain. **2** A small quantity of material, as blood, sputum, etc., placed on a microscope slide or bacterial culture for analysis. **3** A volatile flux for glazing ware. **4** *Obs.* Ointment; grease. **5** A slanderous attack; defamation. **6** *Slang* Anything to spread on bread, as butter, jam, etc. [OE *smerian* < *smeoru* grease]

smear·case (smir′kās′) *n. U.S.* Cottage cheese. [<G *schmierkäse*]

smear·y (smir′ē) *adj.* **smear·i·er, smear·i·est** Greasy, viscous, or staining; also, smeared. **— smear′i·ness** *n.*

smeath (smēth) *n.* A smew. Also **smee** (smē).

smed·dum (smed′əm) *n. Scot. & Brit. Dial.* **1** Fine ore particles that have passed through a wire sieve; fine coal slack. **2** Powder; especially, ground malt. **3** Vigor of mind; sense.

smeek (smēk) *v. & n. Scot.* Smoke. **— smeek′y** *adj.*

smell (smel) *v.* **smelled** or **smelt, smell·ing** *v.t.* **1** To perceive by means of the nose and its olfactory nerves. **2** To perceive the odor or perfume of; scent. **3** To test by odor or smell. **4** To discover, detect, or seek to know, as if by smelling: often with *out.* **—** *v.i.* **5** To emit an odor or perfume; give off a particular odor: frequently with *of*; also, to give indications of, as if by odor: to *smell* of treason. **6** To be malodorous. **7** To use the sense of smell. **8** To pry; investigate: with *about.* **—** *n.* **1** That special sense by means of which odors are perceived. **2** The sensation excited through the olfactory nerves. **3** That which is directly perceived by this sense; an odor; perfume. **4** A faint suggestion; hint; trace. **5** An act of smelling. [ME *smellen*]

Synonyms (noun): aroma, bouquet, fragrance, odor, perfume, savor, scent, stench, stink. *Smell* is the generic word including all the rest. *Aroma, fragrance,* and *perfume* are ordinarily pleasing; *odor, savor,* and *scent* may be so. *Odor* is nearly synonymous with *smell,* but is susceptible of more delicate use; as, the *odor* of incense. An *aroma* is a delicate and spicy *odor,* as of fine coffee; *bouquet* is said chiefly of the delicate *odor* of certain wines. We speak of the *fragrance* or *perfume* of flowers, but *fragrance* is more delicate; a *perfume* may be so strong and rich as to be repulsive by excess. There is a tendency to restrict the application of *perfume* to the artificial preparations called collectively "perfumery." *Scent* is chiefly used for the characteristic *odor* of an animal by which it is tracked or avoided by other animals; the word is also applied to any *odor,* natural or artificial, especially when faintly diffused through the air; as, the *scent* of mignonette or of new-mown hay. *Savor* is chiefly said of the appetizing *odor* evolved from articles of food by the processes of cooking. Any *smell* that is at once foul, strong, and pervasive may be called a *stench.* See SAVOR.

smell·er (smel′ər) *n.* **1** One who smells (anything). **2** *Slang* The nose. **3** A feeler, as of an animal.

smell·feast (smel′fēst′) *n. Archaic* **1** A person who frequents good tables. **2** A greedy sponger; parasite.

smelling salts Pungent or aromatic salts, or mixtures of such, often scented, used as stimulants by smelling; specifically, a preparation of ammonium carbonate.

smell·y (smel′ē) *adj.* **smell·i·er, smell·i·est** Having an unpleasant smell; malodorous.

smelt[1] (smelt) *v.t. Metall.* **1** To reduce (ores) by fusion in a furnace. **2** To obtain (a metal) from the ore by a process including fusion. **—** *v.i.* **3** To melt or fuse, as a metal. [<MDu. *smelten* melt]

smelt[2] (smelt) *n. pl.* **smelts** or **smelt** Any of certain small silvery food fishes (genus *Osmerus* or a related genus), of the northern Atlantic and Pacific. [OE]

smelt[3] (smelt) Alternative past tense and past participle of SMELL.

smelt·er (smel′tər) *n.* **1** One engaged in smelting ore. **2** An establishment for smelting: also **smelt′er·y.**

Sme·ta·na (sme′tä·nä), **Bedřich,** 1824–84, Czech composer.

Smeth·wick (smeth′wik) A county borough of southern Staffordshire, England.

smew (smyōō) *n.* A small merganser *(Mergus albellus)* of northern parts of the Old World. The male is black and white, with a white crest. Also called *smeath, smee.* [Origin unknown]

smid·die (smid′ē) *n. Scot.* A smithy. Also **smid′dy.**

smidg·en (smij′ən) *n. U.S. Colloq.* A tiny bit or part; mite; trifle.

Smig·ly-Rydz (shmēg′wē·rēts), **Edward,** 1886–1943?, Polish marshal; ruled Poland 1935–39.

smi·la·ca·ceous (smī′lə·kā′shəs) *adj. Bot.* Of or pertaining to a family *(Smilacaceae)* of herbs or woody-stemmed vines, having dioecious flowers and globular fruits. [<NL <L *smilax.* See SMILAX.]

smi·la·cin (smī′lə·sin) *n.* Parillin.

smi·lax (smī′laks) *n.* **1** Any of a large, widely scattered genus *(Smilax)* of shrubby or herbaceous plants having net-veined leaves, dioecious flowers in umbels, and globular fruit, especially *S. aristolochiifolia,* a source of sarsaparilla: also called *catbrier, greenbrier.* **2** A delicate twining plant *(Asparagus asparagoides)* of the lily family, from South Africa, with greenish flowers: cultivated in greenhouses and extensively used for bouquets, etc. [<L <Gk. *smilax* yew]

SMILAX
Greenbrier.

smile (smīl) *n.* **1** A pleased or amused expression of the face, characterized by lateral upward extension of the lips. **2** A pleasant aspect: the *smile* of spring. **3** Propitious or favorable disposition; favor; blessing: the *smile* of fortune. **—** *v.* **smiled, smil·ing** *v.i.* **1** To give a smile; wear a cheerful aspect. **2** To show approval or favor: often with *upon.* **—** *v.t.* **3** To express by means of a smile; effect as by a smile. [ME *smilen,* prob. <LG] **— smil′er** *n.* **— smil′ing** *adj.* **— smil′ing·ly** *adv.* **— smil′ing·ness** *n.*

Smiles (smīlz), **Samuel,** 1812–1904, Scottish writer and physician.

smirch (smûrch) *v.t.* **1** To soil, as by contact with grime; smear. **2** Figuratively, to defame; degrade: to *smirch* a reputation. **—** *n.* The act of smirching, or the state of being smirched; a smutch; smear; a moral stain or defect. See synonyms under BLEMISH. [ME *smorchen,* appar. <OF *esmorcher* hurt, torment]

smirk (smûrk) *v.i.* To smile in a silly, self-complacent, or affected manner. **—** *n.* An affected or artificial smile. Also *Obs.* **smerk.** [OE *smercian*] **— smirk′ing·ly** *adv.*

smit (smit) *Brit. Dial. v.t.* **1** To destroy. **2** To infect. **—** *n.* **1** A smutch; spot. **2** Infection.

smite (smīt) *v.* **smote** (*Obs.* **smit**), **smit·ten** or **smit** or **smote, smit·ing** *v.t.* **1** To strike (something). **2** To strike a blow with (something); cause to strike. **3** To cut, sever, or break by a blow: usually with *off* or *out.* **4** To strike with disaster; afflict; destroy by a catastrophe. **5** To affect powerfully with sudden feeling; in the passive, to affect with love. **6** To cause to feel regret or remorse: His conscience *smote* him. **7** To affect as if by a blow; come upon suddenly: The thought *smote* him. **8** To kill by a sudden blow. **—** *v.i.* **9** To come with sudden force; also, to knock against something: His knees *smote* together. See synonyms under BEAT. [OE *smītan*] **— smit′er** *n.*

smith (smith) *n.* **1** One who shapes metals by hammering: often used in combination: *goldsmith, tinsmith.* **2** A blacksmith. [OE]

Smith (smith), **Adam,** 1723–90, Scottish economist. **— Alfred Emanuel,** 1873–1944, U.S. politician. **— Edmund Kirby,** 1824–93, American Confederate general and educator. **— Francis Hopkinson,** 1838–1915, U.S. civil engineer, artist, and author. **— Goldwin,** 1823–1910, English historian. **— Captain John,** 1579–1631, English adventurer; president of Virginia Colony 1608. **— Joseph,** 1805–44, founder and first prophet of the Mormon Church; assassinated. **— Sydney,** 1771–1845, English clergyman and author. **— Theobald,** 1859–1934, U.S. pathologist. **— Walter Bedell,** 1895–1961, U.S. Army officer and diplomat. **— William,** 1769–1839, English geologist. **— Sir William,** 1813–93, English classical scholar. **— William Robertson,** 1846–94, Scottish theologian and author.

smith·er·eens (smith′ə·rēnz′) *n. pl. Colloq.* Fragments produced as by a blow. Also **smith′·ers.** [Cf. dial. E (Irish) *smidirin* a fragment]

smith·er·y (smith′ər·ē) *n. pl.* **·er·ies** **1** The art or trade of a smith. **2** A smith's shop; a smithy.

Smith·son (smith′sən), **James,** 1765–1829, English chemist: known in his youth as James Lewis Macie.

Smith·so·ni·an Institution (smith·sō′nē·ən) An institution founded in 1846 at Washington, D.C., from funds left by James Smithson "for the increase and diffusion of knowledge among men."

smith·son·ite (smith′sən·īt) *n.* **1** A vitreous zinc carbonate, $ZnCO_3$. **2** *Brit.* Hemimorphite. [after James *Smithson*]

Smith Sound (smith) A sea passage between Ellesmere Island and NW Greenland; 45 miles wide.

smith·y (smith′ē, smith′ē) *n. pl.* **smith·ies** A blacksmith's shop; a forge.

smit·ten (smit′n) Alternative past participle of SMITE. **—** *adj.* **1** Struck with sudden force; gravely afflicted. **2** Having the affections suddenly attracted.

smock (smok) *n.* **1** A loose outer garment of light material worn like a coat to protect one's clothes. **2** In colonial times, a woman's undergarment; chemise. **—** *v.t.* **1** To furnish with or clothe in a smock. **2** To shirr (def. 1). See SMOCKING. [OE *smoc*]

smock-frock (smok′frok′) *n.* A loose-fitting outer garment or jacket worn by laborers.

smock·ing (smok′ing) *n.* Shirred work; decorative stitching holding fullness in regular patterns.

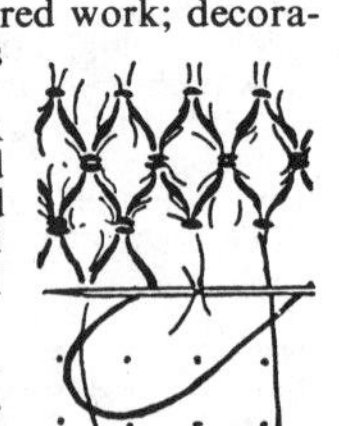
SMOCKING

smog (smog) *n. Colloq.* A combination of smoke and fog, especially as seen in and about heavy industry and manufacturing areas. [Blend of SM(OKE) + (F)OG]

smok·a·ble (smō′kə·bəl) *adj.* Capable of being smoked. **—** *n.* Something to be smoked, as a cigarette, cigar, etc.: usually in the plural.

smoke (smōk) *n.* **1** The volatilized products of the combustion of an organic compound, as coal, wood, etc., charged with fine particles of carbon or soot; less properly, fumes, steam, etc. **2** *Chem.* A colloid system of solid particles in a gas. See COLLOID SYSTEM. **3** Anything transient and unsubstantial; a useless or ephemeral result. **4** The act of smoking a pipe, cigar, etc. **5** A period of time during which one smokes tobacco. **6** *Colloq.* A cigarette, cigar, or pipeful of tobacco. **7** A chemical-warfare agent producing a smoke-like cloud; also, a smudge. **8** A column of smoke, used as a signal by the North American Indians. **9** *U.S. Slang* In baseball, speed in a pitch. **10** A cheap drink, usually of wood alcohol. — *v.* **smoked, smok·ing** *v.i.* **1** To emit or give out smoke: The embers *smoke*; also, to emit smoke excessively or in an undesired direction, as a stove or lamp. **2** To raise dust in rapid riding or driving; hence, to travel rapidly; speed. — *v.t.* **3** To inhale and exhale the smoke of (tobacco, opium, etc.); also, to use, as a pipe, for this purpose. **4** To treat or affect with smoke; treat by the application of smoke; cure; medicate; fumigate; tinge; flavor with smoke. **5** To apply smoke to in order to drive away or expel: to *smoke* bees; hence, to force out of hiding: usually with *out*: to *smoke* out a criminal. **6** To get the scent of; hence, to suspect. **7** To change the color of (glass, etc.) by darkening with smoke. [OE *smoca*]

smoke candle A small, portable, short-burning smokepot.

smoke helmet A protective headdress, such as worn by soldiers, firemen, etc., for protection against poisonous gas fumes and smoke.

smoke·house (smōk′hous′) *n.* **1** A building or close room in which meat, fish, hides, etc., are cured by the action of smoke. **2** A building in which anything is disinfected by the use of smoke.

smoke·jack (smōk′jak′) *n.* A mechanism by which to turn a roasting spit, operated by the ascending combustion gases in a chimney.

smoke·jump·er (smōk′jum′pər) *n.* A fireman trained and equipped to fight forest fires when parachuted to the affected area by aircraft.

smoke·less (smōk′lis) *adj.* Having or emitting little or no smoke: *smokeless* powder.

smoke·pot (smōk′pot′) *n.* A small container for generating a dense cloud of smoke.

smok·er (smō′kər) *n.* **1** One who or that which smokes; one who smokes tobacco habitually. **2** A firebox for blowing smoke upon bees to quiet them. **3** A smoking car. **4** A social gathering of men. **5** A smoking jacket.

smoke screen A dense cloud of smoke emitted to screen an attack or bombardment by land or sea, or to cover a retreat. Also **smoke blanket.**

smoke·stack (smōk′stak′) *n.* **1** An upright pipe, usually of sheet or plate iron, through which combustion gases from a boiler furnace are discharged into the air. **2** The funnel of a steamboat or locomotive, or the tall chimney of a factory, etc.

smoke·tree (smōk′trē′) *n.* **1** An ornamental Old World shrub or tree (*Cotinus coggygria*) with long feathery stalks resembling smoke or mist. **2** A related American species (*C. americanus*).

smoking jacket A short coat worn instead of a regular suit coat as a lounging jacket.

smok·y (smō′kē) *adj.* **smok·i·er, smok·i·est** **1** Giving forth smoke. **2** Mixed with or containing smoke: *smoky* air. **3** Liable to be filled with smoke, as a house. **4** Emitting smoke improperly and unpleasantly, as from bad draft. **5** Discolored with smoke. **6** Smoke-colored; dark-gray. **7** Covered with mist: said of certain mountains. — **smok′i·ly** *adv.* — **smok′i·ness** *n.*

Smoky Hill River A river in Colorado and Kansas, flowing 560 miles east, SE, north, and NE, joining the Republican River to form the Kansas River.

Smoky Mountains See GREAT SMOKY MOUNTAINS.

smol·der (smōl′dər) *v.i.* **1** To burn and smoke in a smothered way, showing little smoke and no flame. **2** Figuratively, to exist in a latent state; to manifest suppressed feeling: His wrath was *smoldering.* — *n.* Smother; smoke. Also spelled *smoulder.* [Dissimilated var. of ME *smorther.* See SMOTHER.]

Smo·lensk (smô·lyensk′) A city on the Dnieper in western Russian S.F.S.R.

Smol·lett (smol′it), **Tobias George,** 1721–71. English novelist and physician.

smolt (smōlt) *n.* A young salmon on its first descent from the river to the sea. [? Related to SMELT[2]]

smooch (smōōch) *n.* A smear; a smutch. — *v.t.* To smear; smudge. — *v.i. Slang* To neck. [Cf. SMUTCH]

smoor (smōōr) *Scot. v.t.* To smother. — *n.* Stifling smoke or atmosphere.

smooth (smōōth) *adj.* **1** Having a surface without irregularities; not rough; continuously even. **2** Having no impediments or obstructions; easy; free from shocks or jolts. **3** Calm and unruffled; bland; pleasant; mild. **4** Flowing melodiously: opposed to *rugged*: a *smooth* style. **5** Suave, as in speech; flattering: often implying deceit. **6** *Phonet.* Sounded without the aspirate: opposed to *rough*: a *smooth* breathing. **7** Free from hair; beardless. **8** Having no acidulous or astringent taste or quality: said of liquors. **9** Without lumps; having the elements perfectly blended: a *smooth* mayonnaise. **10** Offering no resistance to a body sliding along its surface; without friction. **11** Having the high points removed by wear, as the surface of a tire. — *adv.* Calmly; evenly. — *v.t.* **1** To make smooth or even on the surface. **2** To make easy or less difficult: to *smooth* one's path. **3** To free from obstructions. **4** To remove (an obstruction): often with *away*: to *smooth* away a mound. **5** To render less harsh or softer and more flowing: to *smooth* one's verses. **6** To soften the worst features of; palliate; extenuate: usually with *over.* **7** To make calm; mollify: to *smooth* one's feelings. — *v.i.* **8** To become smooth. Also **smooth′en.** — **to smooth (someone's) ruffled feathers** To mollify. — *n.* **1** The smooth portion or surface of anything: the *smooth* of the neck. **2** The act of smoothing. [OE *smōth*] — **smooth′er** *n.* — **smooth′ly** *adv.* — **smooth′ness** *n.*

Smooth may appear as a combining form in hyphemes; as in:

smooth-ankled	**smooth-headed**
smooth-barked	**smooth-limbed**
smooth-billed	**smooth-necked**
smooth-bodied	**smooth-paced**
smooth-browed	**smooth-polished**
smooth-cheeked	**smooth-riding**
smooth-combed	**smooth-rimed**
smooth-cut	**smooth-sculptured**
smooth-edged	**smooth-sided**
smooth-filed	**smooth-skinned**
smooth-fibered	**smooth-sliding**
smooth-flowing	**smooth-speaking**
smooth-fronted	**smooth-stalked**
smooth-gliding	**smooth-stemmed**
smooth-going	**smooth-surfaced**
smooth-grained	**smooth-tempered**
smooth-haired	**smooth-voiced**
smooth-handed	**smooth-woven**

Synonyms (adj.): even, flat, glossy, level, plain, plane, polished, sleek, undisturbed, unruffled. An *even* surface is free from any considerable irregularities, as knobs, or splinters, or abrupt changes of direction or curvature; a *smooth* surface is one that the hand may be passed over without friction or in which the eye discerns no noticeable break or flaw. That which is *polished* is brought to a very high degree of smoothness, so as to be not only frictionless to touch but lustrous to the eye. A board is sawed to an *even* surface, planed till it is *smooth,* and sandpapered till it is *polished.* A thing may be *smooth* or *polished* and yet very uneven, as a warped piece of veneering. See BLAND, BLUNT, CALM, FINE[1], LEVEL, PACIFIC. *Antonyms*: see synonyms for ROUGH.

smooth·bore (smōōth′bôr′, -bōr′) *n.* A firearm, as a shotgun, with an unrifled bore. Also **smooth bore.**

smooth breathing See under BREATHING.

smooth-faced (smōōth′fāst′) *adj.* **1** Beardless. **2** Of smooth surface, as a wall, etc. **3** Bland or mild in expression, especially with deceitful intent.

smooth-shod (smōōth′shod′) *adj.* Shod without sharp projections on the shoes, as a horse.

smör·gås·bord (smôr′gəs·bôrd, *Sw.* smœr′·gōs·bōrd) *n.* Scandinavian hors d'oeuvres. Also spelled **smor′gas·bord.** [<Sw.]

smor·zan·do (zmôr·tsän′dō) *adj. Music* Fading away; growing softer. [<Ital.]

smote (smōt) Past tense of SMITE.

smoth·er (smuth′ər) *v.t.* **1** To prevent the respiration of, as by filling or covering the mouth and nostrils; also, to kill by such means; suffocate; stifle. **2** To cover, or cause to smolder, as a fire. **3** Figuratively, to hide or suppress: to *smother* a scandal. **4** In cooking, to enclose and cook in a covered dish or under a close mass of some other substance. **5** To daub; smear. — *v.i.* **6** To be covered without vent or air, as a fire. **7** To be hidden or suppressed, as wrath. — *n.* **1** That which smothers, as stifling vapor or dust. **2** The state of being smothered; suppression; also, a smoldering fire. **3** A surging of foam or water; a welter. [Earlier *smorther.* Related to OE *smorian* suffocate] — **smoth′er·y** *adj.*

smouch (smōōch, smouch) *v.t. Dial.* To lift; pilfer.

smoul·der (smōl′dər) See SMOLDER.

smout·y (smōō′tē) *adj. Scot.* Smutty; obscene. Also **smout′ie, smoot′ie.**

smudge (smuj) *v.* **smudged, smudg·ing** *v.t.* **1** To smear; soil. **2** To protect (from frost, insects, etc.) by a heavy, smoky pall. — *v.i.* **3** To cause a smudge. **4** To be smudged. — *n.* **1** A soiling, as of dry dirt or soot; smear; stain. **2** A smoky fire or its smoke for driving away insects, preventing frost, etc. **3** Paint-pot scrapings and cleanings. [Var. of SMUTCH] — **smudg′i·ly** *adv.* — **smudg′i·ness** *n.* — **smudg′y** *adj.*

smug (smug) *adj.* **smug·ger, smug·gest** **1** Characterized by a smoothly self-satisfied or extremely complacent air. **2** Trim; neat; spruce, especially with suggestions of respectability or self-satisfaction. [Cf. LG *smuk* neat] — **smug′ly** *adv.* — **smug′ness** *n.*

smug-faced (smug′fāst′) *adj.* Having a prim, self-satisfied face or expression.

smug·gle (smug′əl) *v.* **·gled, ·gling** *v.t.* **1** To take (merchandise) into or out of a country without payment of lawful duties. **2** To bring in or introduce illicitly or clandestinely. — *v.i.* **3** To engage in or practice smuggling. [<LG *smuggeln*]

smug·gler (smug′lər) *n.* **1** One who smuggles. **2** A vessel used in smuggling.

smug·gling (smug′ling) *n.* The offense or practice of fraudulently and illegally importing or exporting merchandise without payment of lawful duties.

smut (smut) *n.* **1** The blackening made by soot, smoke, etc. **2** Obscenity; obscene language. **3** Any of various fungus diseases of plants, in which the affected parts change into a dusty black powder. **4** The parasitic fungus (order *Ustiliginales*) causing such a disease. — *v.* **smut·ted, smut·ting** *v.t.* **1** To blacken or stain, as with soot or smoke. **2** To affect with smut, as growing grain. **3** To remove the smut from (grain). **4** Figuratively, to pollute; defame. — *v.i.* **5** To give off smut. **6** To be or become stained. **7** To be affected with smut, as growing grain. [<LG *schmutt* dirt]

smutch (smuch) *v.* & *n.* Soil; smear; smudge. [Cf. MHG *smutzen* smear] — **smutch′y** *adj.*

Smuts (smuts), **Jan Christiaan,** 1870–1950, South African statesman and general.

smut·ty (smut′ē) *adj.* **·ti·er, ·ti·est** **1** Soiled with smut; black; stained. **2** Affected by smut: *smutty* corn. **3** Obscene; coarse; indecent. — **smut′ti·ly** *adv.* — **smut′ti·ness** *n.*

Smyr·na (smûr′nə) A port of western Turkey in Asia, on the **Gulf of Smyrna,** an inlet of the Aegean 35 miles long: Turkish *Izmir.* — **Smyr′ni·ot** (-nē·ot), **Smyr′ni·ote** (-nē·ōt) *adj.* & *n.*

smyte·rie (smī′trē, smit′rē) *n. Scot.* A numerous collection of small things. Also **smy′trie.**

Smyth (smith), **Henry De Wolf,** born 1898, U. S. physicist.

snack (snak) *n.* **1** A sip or bite. **2** A slight, hurried meal. **3** A share of something. [Orig. a verb <MDu. *snacken* bite, snap]

snaf·fle (snaf′əl) *n.* A horse's bit without a curb, jointed in the middle. Also **snaf′fle·bit′** (-bit′). — *v.t.* **·fled, ·fling** To control with a snaffle. [<Du. *snavel* muzzle]

sna·fu (sna·fōō′) *Slang adj.* In a state of utter confusion; chaotic. — *v.t.* **·fued, ·fu·ing** To put into a confused or chaotic condition. — *n.* Anything which is confused or chaotic. [From the initial letters of the words "Situation normal, all fouled up"]

snag (snag) *n.* **1** A jagged or stumpy knot or protuberance, especially the stumpy base of a branch left in pruning. **2** The root or remnant of a tooth remaining in the jaw; also, a projecting tooth. **3** A branch or point of a deer's antler. **4** The trunk of a tree fixed in the bottom of a river, bayou, etc., by which boats are sometimes pierced. 5 Hence, any unsuspected or hidden obstacle or difficulty. — *v.* **snagged, snag·ging** *v.t.* 1 To injure, destroy, or impede by or as by a snag. 2 To clear of snags. 3 *Colloq.* To block; impede. — *v.i.* 4 To run upon a snag: said especially of river craft. [Prob. <Scand. Cf. dial. Norw. *snag* sharp point, projection.] —**snagged** *adj.*

snag boat A vessel equipped with machinery for removing snags from river beds.

snag chamber A watertight room or compartment in the bow of a river steamboat to keep the boat from sinking if snagged.

snag·gle–tooth (snag′əl·tōōth′) *n.* A tooth that is broken, projecting, or conspicuously out of alinement with the others. —**snag′gle-toothed′** (-tōōtht′, -tōōthd′) *adj.*

snag·gy (snag′ē) *adj.* **·gi·er, ·gi·est** 1 Full of snags, as a river. 2 Full of knots or stubs, as a tree or swamp. 3 Like a snag.

snail (snāl) *n.* 1 Any of numerous slow-moving gastropod mollusks of largely terrestrial habits, with a spiral shell; especially, the common garden snail (*Helix aspersa*) and the edible snail (*H. pomatia*). 2 A slow or lazy person. [OE *snægl*]

SNAIL

snail hawk The small, bluish-gray everglade kite (*Rostrhamus sociabilis plumbeus*) ranging from Florida to Mexico, that feeds on snails.

snail pace A very slow gait or advance movement. Also **snail's pace.** —**snail′-paced′** *adj.*

snake (snāk) *n.* 1 An ophidian reptile (suborder *Serpentes*), having a greatly elongated, scaly body, no limbs, and a specialized swallowing apparatus. The bite of most snakes is non-venomous, but some have much enlarged fangs, connected with venom glands from which a deadly poison flows into the punctures they make. ◆ Collateral adjective: *anguine.* 2 A treacherous or insinuating person. 3 A flexible, resilient wire used to clean clogged drains, etc. — *v.* **snaked, snak·ing** *v.t. Colloq.* To drag by seizing an end or limb and pulling forcibly or quickly; haul along the ground, as a log. — *v.i.* To wind or move like a snake. [OE *snaca*]

Snake (snāk) *n.* A member of any of various Shoshonean tribes of North American Indians, but especially the Walpapi and Yahuskin of eastern Oregon.

snake·bird (snāk′bûrd′) *n.* One of several birds (genus *Anhinga*), with very long slender neck, frequenting southern swamps and feeding upon fish; the water turkey; the darter.

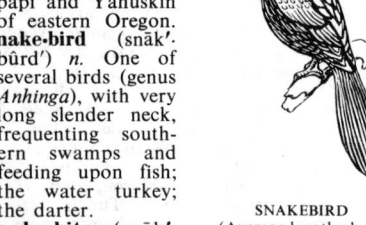

SNAKEBIRD
(Average length about 33 inches)

snake·bite (snāk′bīt′) *n.* 1 The bite of a snake. 2 Poisoning caused by the venom of a snake.

snake charmer 1 An entertainer who charms venomous snakes by rhythmic motions of his body, and, supposedly, by music. 2 Any entertainer who handles snakes.

snake dance A ceremonial dance of the Hopi Indians of Arizona in which live rattlesnakes are carried in the mouths of the dancers. The Hopis believe the snakes to be influential with the rain gods.

snake fence A worm fence; a stake-and-rider. See under FENCE.

snake hawk The swallow-tailed kite (*Elanoides forficatus*) of North and South America.

snake·head (snāk′hed′) *n.* The turtlehead.

Snake Mountains A range in eastern Nevada; highest point, 12,049 feet.

snake·mouth (snāk′mouth′) *n.* A terrestrial orchid (*Pogonia ophioglossoides*) native in eastern North America, with fragrant rose-pink flowers.

Snake River The principal tributary of the Columbia River, flowing 1,038 miles from NW Wyoming through southern Idaho, then northwards to form part of the boundary between Oregon and Idaho, to SE Washington.

snake·root (snāk′ro͞ot′, -ro͝ot′) *n.* 1 One of various plants having roots reputed to be effective against snakebite; especially, the bugbane; the **Seneca snakeroot** (*Polygala senega*), growing east of the Mississippi; the **Virginia snakeroot** (*Aristolochia serpentaria*), with purplish-brown flowers and fibrous roots; and the **white snakeroot** (*Eupatorium rugosum*) of Europe and the United States. 2 The root of any of these plants.

snake·skin (snāk′skin′) *n.* The skin of a snake.

snake·stone (snāk′stōn′) *n.* 1 An ammonite: so called because it resembles a fossil coiled snake. 2 Any absorbent stone-like material popularly believed to cure snakebite.

snake·weed (snāk′wēd′) *n.* The bistort.

snak·y (snā′kē) *adj.* **snak·i·er, snak·i·est** 1 Of or like a snake; serpentine; winding. 2 Insinuating; cunning; treacherous. 3 Full of snakes. —**snak′i·ly** *adv.* —**snak′i·ness** *n.*

snap (snap) *v.* **snapped, snap·ping** *v.i.* 1 To make a sharp, quick sound, as of percussion. 2 To break suddenly with a cracking noise; part with a snap. 3 To fly off or give way quickly, as when tension is suddenly relaxed. 4 To make the jaws come suddenly together in an effort to bite: often with *up* or *at.* 5 To seize or snatch suddenly: often with *up* or *at.* 6 To speak sharply, harshly, or irritably: often with *at.* 7 To emit, or seem to emit, a spark or flash of light: said of the eyes. 8 To close, fasten, etc., with a click or snapping sound, as a lock. 9 To move or act with sudden, neat gestures: He *snapped* to attention. — *v.t.* 10 To seize suddenly or eagerly, with or as with the teeth; snatch: often with *up.* 11 To sever with a snapping sound. 12 To utter, address, or interrupt harshly, abruptly, or irritably: often with *out.* 13 To cause to make a sharp, quick sound. 14 To close, fasten, etc., with a snapping sound. 15 To strike, press, etc., with a snap: to *snap* a whip. 16 To cause to move suddenly, neatly, etc. 17 To photograph instantaneously with a camera. 18 In football, to put in play: said of the ball when sent to a back by the center. —**to snap out of it** *Colloq.* 1 To recover. 2 To change one's attitude. — *n.* 1 The act of snapping, or a sharp, quick sound produced by it: the *snap* of a whip. 2 A sudden breaking of anything, or the sound so produced. 3 Any catch, fastener, or other device that closes or springs into place with a snapping sound. 4 A sudden seizing or effort to seize with or as with the teeth; a sharp shutting, as of the jaws or of a trap. 5 A quick blow of the thumb sprung from the finger or of the finger from the thumb. 6 The sudden release of the tension of a spring or elastic cord. 7 A small, thin, crisp cake, usually containing ginger; a gingersnap. 8 Brisk energy; vigor; vim; zip. 9 A brief spell; a sudden turn: said chiefly of cold weather. 10 A hasty meal; snack. 11 Any task or duty easy to perform: often in the phrase **a soft snap.** 12 A bit: It is not worth a *snap.* 13 The instantaneous taking of a photograph; also, the photograph so taken; a snapshot. 14 A stringbean. — *adj.* 1 Made or done suddenly and without consideration; offhand. 2 Contrived to take unawares and at an advantage: a *snap* policy. 3 Fastening with a snap. — *adv.* With a snap; quickly. [<MDu. *snappen* bite at]

snap·back (snap′bak′) *n.* 1 Formerly, the center in football. 2 The act of snapping back.

snap bean A wax bean.

snap·drag·on (snap′drag′ən) *n.* 1 A plant (genus *Antirrhinum*) of the figwort family, especially the **large-flowered snapdragon** (*A. majus*) having solitary axillary flowers, likened to dragons' heads. 2 Flapdragon.

snap·per (snap′ər) *n.* 1 One who or that which snaps, as a cracker. 2 A large food fish (genus *Lutianus*) of the Gulf coast, as the **red snapper** (*L. blackfordii*). 3 One of various other fishes, as the bluefish, rosefish, etc. 4 A sparoid fish (*Pagrosomus auratus*), reddish with blue bars or spots; one of the most important food fishes of Australasia: also called *schnapper.* 5 A snapping turtle.

snapping beetle An elaterid beetle which by a quick, snapping movement of its body is able to right itself when on its back; especially, the eyed elater (*Alaus oculatus*) of eastern North America: also called *click beetle, skipjack.* For illustration see under INSECTS (injurious).

snapping turtle 1 A large voracious turtle of North America, especially *Chelydra serpentina,* much used as food. 2 The alligator turtle (*Macrochelys temminckii*), a related species.

SNAPPING TURTLE
(Up to 2 feet in length; weight to 100 pounds or more)

snap·pish (snap′ish) *adj.* 1 Apt to speak crossly or tartly. 2 Disposed to snap, as a dog. See synonyms under FRETFUL. —**snap′pish·ly** *adv.* —**snap′pish·ness** *n.*

snap·py (snap′ē) *adj.* **·pi·er, ·pi·est** 1 *Colloq.* Brisk, vivid, and energetic; vivacious. 2 Smart or stylish in appearance. 3 Snappish. —**snap′pi·ly** *adv.* —**snap′pi·ness** *n.*

snap·shot (snap′shot′) *n.* A photograph taken with a small camera without timing.

snap shot A shot made without aim.

snap·weed (snap′wēd′) *n.* Any plant of the genus *Impatiens*; a touch-me-not.

snare[1] (snâr) *n.* 1 A device, as a noose, for catching birds or other animals; a gin; trap. 2 Anything by which one is brought into trouble or caused to sin; an allurement; wile. 3 *Surg.* A loop of wire used to remove tumors and other growths from the body. — *v.t.* **snared, snar·ing** 1 To catch with a snare; ensnare; entrap. 2 To capture by trickery; entice; inveigle. [<ON *snara.* Akin to SNARE[2].] —**snar′er** *n.*

snare[2] (snâr) *n.* 1 A cord to produce a rattling on a drumhead. 2 A snare drum. [<MDu., a string. Akin to SNARE[1].]

snare drum A small drum to be beaten on one head and having snares or strings of catgut stretched across the other.

snarl[1] (snärl) *n.* A sharp, harsh, angry growl; harsh or quarrelsome utterance. — *v.i.* 1 To growl harshly, as a dog. 2 To speak angrily and resentfully. — *v.t.* 3 To utter or express with a snarl. [Freq. of obs. *snar* growl] —**snarl′er** *n.* —**snarl′ing·ly** *adv.* —**snarl′y** *adj.*

snarl[2] (snärl) *n.* 1 A tangle, as of hair or yarn. 2 Any complication, perplexity, or entanglement. 3 *Colloq.* A wrangle; quarrel. 4 A knot or gnarl in wood. — *v.i.* 1 To get into a snarl or tangle; become entangled. — *v.t.* 2 To put into a snarl or tangle. 3 To confuse; entangle mentally; embarrass; make entanglements in. 4 To emboss or flute (thin metalware). [<SNARE[1]] —**snarl′er** *n.* —**snarl′y** *adj.*

snarling iron A curved tool for snarling hollow metalware, etc. Also **snarling tool.**

snash (snash, snäsh) *n. Scot.* Impertinent, abusive, or sneering language.

snatch (snach) *v.t.* 1 To seize or lay hold of suddenly, hastily, or eagerly. 2 To take or remove suddenly. 3 To take or obtain as the opportunity arises: to *snatch* a few hours of sleep. 4 *Slang* To kidnap. — *v.i.* 5 To attempt to seize swiftly and suddenly: with *at.* 6 To accept with great eagerness: with *at.* — *n.* 1 An act of snatching; a hasty grab or grasp: usually with *at.* 2 A brief period: a *snatch* of rest. 3 A small amount; fragment: *snatches* of a conversation; *snatches* of melody. 4 *Slang* A kidnaping. [ME *snacchen.* ? Related to SNACK.] —**snatch′er** *n.*

snatch block *Naut.* A single block having an opening in one cheek to receive a rope, and usually having a swivel hook.

snatch·y (snach′ē) *adj.* Interrupted; spasmodic.

snath (snath) *n.* The long curved handle of a scythe. Also **snathe** (snāth). [Var. of dial. E *snead,* OE *snǣd*]

snaw (snô, snä) *v.* & *n. Scot.* Snow.

sneak (snēk) *v.i.* 1 To move or go in a stealthy manner. 2 To act with covert cowardice or servility. — *v.t.* 3 To put, give, transfer, move, etc., secretly or stealthily. 4 *Colloq.* To pilfer. — *n.* 1 One who sneaks; a mean, cowardly fellow. 2 *pl. Colloq.* Sneakers. 3 A stealthy movement. — *adj.* Stealthy; covert: a *sneak* attack. [Akin to OE *snīcan* creep]

sneak boat A small, shallow boat used for duck hunting. Also **sneak-box** (snēk′boks′).

sneak·er (snē′kər) *n.* 1 One who sneaks; a sneak. 2 *pl. U.S. Colloq.* Rubber-soled canvas shoes.

sneak·ing (snē′king) *adj.* 1 Cringing; meanly secret and underhand. 2 Secretly entertained or cherished; unavowed: a *sneaking* suspicion. See synonyms under BASE[2]. — **sneak′ing·ly** *adv.*

sneak thief One who steals small miscellaneous articles, without violence, by sneaking in through unfastened doors or windows.

sneak·y (snē′kē) *adj.* **sneak·i·er, sneak·i·est** Like a sneak; sneaking. — **sneak′i·ly** *adv.* — **sneak′i·ness** *n.*

snecked (snekt) *adj.* **1** Twisted to one side of the vertical plane of the shank, as the point of a fish hook. **2** Built of rubblework. [? Related to SNATCH]

sned (sned) *v.t. Scot.* To cut; trim; lop off.

sneer (snir) *n.* **1** A grimace of contempt or derision made by slightly raising the upper lip and nostrils. **2** A mean or contemptuous insinuation; a fling. — *v.i.* **1** To make or show a sneer. **2** To express derision or contempt in speech, writing, etc. — *v.t.* **3** To utter with a sneer or in a sneering manner. See synonyms under SCOFF. [ME *sneren*; ult. origin uncertain] — **sneer′er** *n.* — **sneer′ing** *adj.* — **sneer′·ing·ly** *adv.*

Synonyms (noun): fling, gibe, jeer, scoff, taunt. A *sneer* may be simply a contemptuous facial contortion or some brief satirical utterance that throws a contemptuous sidelight on what it attacks without attempting to prove or disprove. The *jeer* and *gibe* are uttered; the *gibe* is bitter, and often sly or covert; the *jeer* is rude and open. A *scoff* may be in act or word, and is commonly directed against that which claims honor, reverence, or worship. A *fling* is careless and commonly pettish; a *taunt* is intentionally insulting and provoking; the *sneer* is supercilious; the *taunt* is defiant. See SCORN.

sneesh (snēsh) *n. Scot.* Snuff. Also **sneesh′ing.**

sneeze (snēz) *v.i.* **sneezed, sneez·ing** *v.i.* To drive air forcibly and audibly out of the mouth and nose by a spasmodic involuntary action. — *v.t.* To utter with or as with a sneeze: often with *out.* — **not to be sneezed at** *Colloq.* Of a character entitling to consideration. — *n.* An act of sneezing: also **sneez′ing.** [Misreading of ME *fnese,* OE *fnēosan* sneeze] — **sneez′er** *n.* — **sneez′y** *adj.*

sneeze gas A sternutator.

sneeze·weed (snēz′wēd′) *n.* Any plant of a genus *(Helenium)* of the composite family, especially *H. autumnale*: from the effect of the powdered leaves and flowers when snuffed up: also called *bitterweed.*

sneeze·wort (snēz′wûrt′) *n.* **1** A perennial Eurasian plant *(Achillea ptarmica)* resembling the yarrow. Its powdered dry leaves produce sneezing. **2** Sneezeweed.

snell[1] (snel) *n.* A short line of gut, horsehair, etc., bearing a fish hook, to be attached to a longer line. [Origin unknown]

snell[2] (snel) *adj.* **1** *Scot.* Sharp; keen; piercing. **2** Austere; severe. **3** Nimble; quick.

Snel·len test (snel′ən) *Med.* A test for determining visual acuity performed by reading a standard set of graded letters at a specified distance. [after Herman *Snellen,* 1834–1908, Dutch opthalmologist, who devised it]

snick (snik) *n.* **1** A small cut; nick; snip. **2** A knot in thread or the like. **3** In cricket, a glancing hit. — *v.t.* **1** To cut a nick in. **2** To hit (a ball) a glancing blow. — **to snick and snee** To thrust and cut. [Back formation < *snick or snee.* See SNICKERSNEE.]

snick·er (snik′ər) *n.* A half-suppressed or smothered laugh. — *v.i.* To utter a snicker; laugh slyly and foolishly with audible catches of the voice; giggle. — *v.t.* To utter or express with a snicker. Also *snigger.* [Imit.]

snick·er·snee (snik′ər·snē′) *n.* **1** A fight with knives. **2** A knife suitable for thrusting and cutting. Also **snick and snee, snick′-a-snee, snick or snee.** [Alter. of earlier *snick or snee* thrust or cut, ult. <Du. *steken* thrust + *snijen* cut]

snide (snīd) *adj.* Malicious or derogatory; nasty. — *n.* A snide person. [Origin unknown]

sniff (snif) *v.i.* **1** To breathe through the nose in short, quick, audible inhalations. **2** To express contempt, etc., by sniffing: often with *at.* **3** To inhale a scent in sniffs. — *v.t.* **4** To breathe in through the nose; inhale. **5** To smell or attempt to smell with sniffs: to *sniff* smoke. **6** To perceive as if by sniffs: to *sniff* peril. **7** To express (contempt) by sniffs. — *n.* **1** An act or the sound of sniffing. **2** Perception by or as by sniffing; that which is inhaled by sniffing. [Appar. back formation <SNIVEL]

snif·fle (snif′əl) *v.i.* **·fled, ·fling** **1** To snuffle. **2** To snivel or whimper; whine; sniff. — *n.* A snuffle. [Freq. of SNIFF]

snif·fy (snif′ē) *adj.* **·fi·er, ·fi·est** *Colloq.* Disposed to sniff or be disdainful or scornful.

snif·ter (snif′tər) *n.* **1** A liquor glass, pear-shaped, with a small opening to concentrate the aroma. **2** *U.S. Slang* A small drink of liquor, usually a dram. [< *snift,* var. of SNIFF]

snig·ger (snig′ər) *n.* A snicker, especially a derisive snicker. — *v.i.* To snicker, especially in derision. [Var. of SNICKER] — **snig′ger·er** *n.*

snig·gle (snig′əl) *v.t.* **·gled, ·gling** *Brit.* **1** To fish for or catch, as eels, by thrusting the bait into their hiding places. **2** To entrap, as in a net; ensnare. [< dial. E *snig* eel]

snip (snip) *v.* **snipped, snip·ping** *v.t.* To clip, remove, or cut with a short, light stroke or strokes of scissors or shears: often with *off.* — *v.i.* To cut with small, quick strokes. — *n.* **1** An act of snipping. **2** A small piece snipped off. **3** *U.S. Colloq.* A small or insignificant person or thing. **4** *pl.* Small shears for cutting metal. [<Du. *snippen*]

snipe (snīp) *n. pl.* **snipe** or **snipes** **1** A shore bird (genus *Capella*), allied to the woodcock and much esteemed as a game bird; especially, the common **European** or **whole snipe** *(C. gallinago),* and the common **American** or **Wilson's snipe** *(C. delicata).* **2** One of other snipelike birds, as the **lesser snipe** or **jack snipe** of Europe *(Limnocryptes minimus).* **3** *U.S. Slang* A cigarette or cigar butt. — *v.i.* **sniped, snip·ing** **1** To hunt or shoot snipe. **2** To shoot at or pick off individual enemies from cover or ambush. **3** *U.S. Slang* To hunt for cigarette or cigar butts. [<ON *snipa*]

snip·er (snī′pər) *n.* One who shoots an enemy from cover; a sharpshooter.

snip·er·scope (snī′pər·skōp′) *n.* An electronic optical device which may be mounted on a carbine or rifle in order to permit accurate night-firing by means of infrared rays focused on a fluorescent screen.

snip·pet (snip′it) *n.* **1** A small piece snipped off. **2** A small portion or share.

snip·pet·y (snip′it·ē) *adj.* **1** Arrogant; brusk; snippy. **2** Trivial, as if composed of little pieces snipped off; small; trifling.

snip·py (snip′ē) *adj.* **·pi·er, ·pi·est** *Colloq.* **1** Supercilious; pert; impertinent. **2** Fragmentary.

snit (snit) *n. Colloq.* An irritable or angry mood: usually preceded by *in* or *into*: The affront put him in a *snit.* [Origin unknown]

snitch (snich) *Slang v.t.* To grab quickly; steal. — *v.i.* To inform; peach: usually with *on.* [? Var. of SNATCH]

snits (snits) *n. pl.* Slices of dried fruit, especially of dried apples. [<Pennsylvania Dutch *schnitz* sections of apple]

sniv·el (sniv′əl) *v.i.* **·eled** or **·elled, ·el·ing** or **·el·ling** To cry in a snuffling manner; run at the nose; snuffle; make affectedly tearful professions. — *n.* **1** Discharge from the nose. **2** The act of sniveling. [OE (assumed) *snyflan* < *snyflung* mucus from the nose] — **sniv′el·er** *n.* — **sniv′el·ing** *adj.* & *n.*

snob (snob) *n.* **1** One who makes birth, wealth, or education the sole criterion of worth. **2** One who is cringing to superiors and overbearing with inferiors in position. **3** *Obs. Brit.* A scab; rat: said of a workingman. [Origin uncertain] — **snob′ber·y** *n.*

snob·bish (snob′ish) *adj.* Pertaining to, characteristic of, or befitting a snob or snobs. — **snob′bish·ly** *adv.* — **snob′bish·ness** *n.*

snod (snod) *Scot. v.t.* To make trim or neat; prune; tidy. — *adj.* Neat; also, sly; demure.

snood (sno͝od) *n.* **1** A small meshlike cap or bag attached to the back of a hat, worn by women to keep the hair in place. **2** *Scot.* A fillet formerly worn about the hair by an unmarried woman in Scotland as an emblem of virginity. — *v.t.* To bind with a snood, as hair. [OE *snōd*]

snook (sno͝ok, sno͞ok) *v.i.* **1** *Scot.* To sniff. **2** To lurk. — *n.* **1** A smell; sniff; a bite. **2** *Slang* An informer.

snook·er (sno͝ok′ər) *n.* A pool game played with fifteen red object balls (one point each) and six variously colored object balls (2 to 7 points). The player pocketing a red ball may try for any varicolored ball. When all red balls have been pocketed, the varicolored balls must be played in order. Also **snooker pool.** [Origin uncertain]

snool (sno͞ol) *Scot. v.i.* **1** To snivel. **2** To yield submissively. — *n.* One who is meanly subservient.

snoop (sno͞op) *Colloq. v.i.* To look or pry into things with which one has no business; thrust one's nose into things. — *n.* One who snoops: also **snoop′er.** [<Du. *snoepen* eat goodies on the sly] — **snoop′y** *adj.*

snoop·er·scope (sno͞o′pər·skōp) *n.* An optical device operating on the same principle as the sniperscope but designed for carrying in the hand or on the head.

snoot (sno͞ot) *n. Colloq.* A person's nose or face; also, a grimace. [Var. of SNOUT]

snoot·y (sno͞o′tē) *adj.* **snoot·i·er, snoot·i·est** *U.S. Colloq.* Conceited or supercilious.

snooze (sno͞oz) *Colloq. v.i.* **snoozed, snooz·ing** To sleep lightly; doze. — *n.* A short and light sleep. [Origin uncertain]

Sno·qual·mie Falls (snō·kwol′mē) A waterfall of 270 feet in the **Snoqualmie River,** a river flowing 45 miles west and NW in central Washington from the Cascade Range east of Seattle.

snore (snôr, snōr) *v.i.* **snored, snor·ing** To breathe in sleep through the nose and open mouth, with a hoarse rough noise and rattling vibrations of the soft palate. — *n.* An act or the noise of snoring. [Imit.] — **snor′er** *n.*

snor·kel (snôr′kəl) *n.* **1** A long ventilating tube capable of extending from a submerged submarine to the surface of the water. **2** A similar device used for underwater breathing. — *v.i.* To swim with a snorkel. [<G *Schnorkel*] — **snor′kel·er** *n.*

snort (snôrt) *v.i.* **1** To force the air violently and noisily through the nostrils, as spirited horses. **2** To express indignation, ridicule, etc., by a snort. **3** *Colloq.* To laugh with a boisterous outburst. — *v.t.* **4** To utter or express by snorting. **5** To expel by or as by a snort. — *n.* **1** The act or sound of snorting. **2** *Slang* A small drink. [ME *snorten.* ? Related to SNORE.] — **snort′er** *n.*

snot (snot) *n.* **1** Mucus from or in the nose: a vulgar usage. **2** *Slang* A low or mean fellow. [OE *gesnot*]

snot·ty (snot′ē) *adj.* **·ti·er, ·ti·est** **1** Dirtied with snot: a vulgar usage. **2** *Slang* Contemptible; mean; paltry. **3** *Slang* Impudent; proudly conceited; saucy.

snout (snout) *n.* **1** The forward projecting part of a beast's head, especially of a swine's; proboscis; muzzle. **2** Some similar anterior prolongation of the head of an animal, as the rostrum of a gastropod or that of a weevil. **3** Something resembling a hog's snout, such as the nozzle of a hose, a pipe, or the like; a blunt projection, as of rock; or, contemptuously, a person's nose. — *v.t.* To provide with a snout or nozzle. [ME *snūte.* Related to OE *snȳtan* blow the nose.]

snout beetle The curculio.

snow[1] (snō) *n.* **1** Precipitation taking the form of minute ice crystals formed from an aqueous vapor in the air when the temperature is below 32° F., and usually falling in irregular masses or flakes. ◆ Collateral adjective: *nival.* **2** A similar aggregation that resembles snow in being white or composed of flakes: a *snow* of blossoms. **3** A fall of snow; snowstorm. **4** A winter. **5** *Slang* Cocaine. **6** The pattern of snowlike drops appearing on a television screen as a result of weakened signals in a receiver. — *v.i.* **1** To fall as snow: usually used impersonally: It is *snowing.* — *v.t.* **2** To scatter or cause to fall as or like snow. **3** To cover, enclose, or

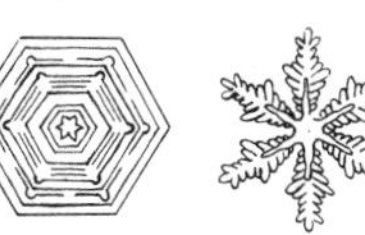

SNOW CRYSTALS

obstruct with snow: with *in, over, under,* or *up.* [OE *snāw*]

Snow may appear as a combining form in hyphemes or solidemes, or as the first element in two-word phrases; as in:

snowbank	**snow-driven**
snow-beaten	**snow-field**
snow-blast	**snow-haired**
snow-blown	**snowland**
snow-bright	**snowless**
snow-clad	**snowlike**
snow cloud	**snow-lined**
snow-cold	**snow peak**
snow-colored	**snowscape**
snow-covered	**snow-tipped**
snow-crested	**snow-topped**

snow[2] (snō) *n. Naut.* A two-masted square-rigged vessel characterized by having a trysail mast close behind the main mast. [<MDu. *snauw* snout]

Snow (snō), **C(harles) P(ercy),** born 1905, English physicist and novelist.

snow apple The Fameuse.

snow·ball (snō′bôl′) *n.* **1** A small round mass of snow compressed to be thrown, as in sport. **2** The guelder-rose *(Viburnum opulus)*: so called from its ball-shaped clusters of white flowers: also **snowball bush** or **tree.** —*v.i.* **1** To throw snowballs. **2** To gain in size, importance, etc., as a snowball that rolls over snow. —*v.t.* **3** To throw snowballs at.

snow·bell (snō′bel′) *n.* Any of a genus *(Styrax)* of trees and shrubs of warm regions, bearing showy white flowers in racemes; especially, *S. americana* of the SE United States.

snow·ber·ry (snō′ber′ē) *n. pl.* **·ries 1** A bushy American shrub *(Symphoricarpos albus)* having a loose, leafy cluster of snow-white berries. **2** A West Indian shrub *(Chiococca alba)* of the madder family: it produces the cainca root and is often cultivated in greenhouses for its white berries: also called *milkberry.*

snow·bird (snō′bûrd′) *n.* **1** A small finch (genus *Junco*) of northern North America, commonly seen in flocks during the winter. **2** The snow bunting. **3** *Slang* A cocaine or heroin addict.

snow blindness An impairment of vision, caused by exposure of the eye to the glare of snow. —**snow′-blind′** *adj.*

snow·blink (snō′blingk′) *n.* The dazzling scintillation of light reflected from a field of ice or snow.

snow-bound (snō′bound′) *adj.* Hemmed in or forced to remain in a place by heavy snow; snowed in.

snow bridge A natural arch formation of snow bridging a crevasse.

snow·broth (snō′brôth′, -broth′) *n.* **1** Melted snow or snow and water mixed. **2** Any very cold liquid.

snow bunting A bird (genus *Plectrophenax*), especially *P. nivalis* of northern regions, the male of which in the breeding season is snow-white with black markings. Also called *snowbird, snowflake.*

snow·bush (snō′boosh′) *n.* A California shrub ofthe genus *Ceanothus,* as *C. cordulatus,* that bears numerous small white flowers.

snow·cap (snō′kap′) *n.* A crest of snow, as on a mountain peak. —**snow′-capped′** *adj.*

snow cover The blanket of snow, variable in thickness and duration, which covers the ground over a given area, affecting ground temperatures and vegetation.

Snow·don (snōd′n) A mountain in Caernarvonshire, the highest point in Wales; 3,560 feet. *Welsh* **Er·y·ri** (er′i·rē).

snow·drift (snō′drift′) *n.* A pile of snow heaped up by the wind.

snow·drop (snō′drop′) *n.* **1** A low, European, early-blooming bulbous plant *(Galanthus nivalis)* bearing a single, white, drooping flower. **2** The common anemone.

snowdrop tree The silverbell.

snow-eat·er (snō′ē′tər) *n.* The chinook.

snow·fall (snō′fôl′) *n.* **1** A fall of snow. **2** The amount of snow that falls in a given period.

snow fence Portable fencing consisting of thin, closely placed pickets, used to prevent the drifting of snow over roads, fields, etc.

snow·flake (snō′flāk′) *n.* **1** One of the small feathery masses in which snow falls. **2** The snow bunting. **3** Any of certain plants (genus *Leucojum*) allied to and resembling the snowdrop; especially, the **spring snowflake** *(L. vernum),* the **summer snowflake** *(L. aestivum),* and the **autumn snowflake** *(L. autumnale).*

snow goose Any of certain North American geese (genus *Chen*) which breed in the Arctic, snow-white with black primary feathers.

snow leopard The ounce.

snow lily An attractive spring-blooming herb *(Erythronium grandiflorum)* of the lily family native in the Rocky Mountains.

snow line 1 The limit of perpetual snow on the sides of mountains, varying in position with the latitude, the season, and the climate. **2** The extreme distance north and south of the equator within which snow never falls. Also **snow limit.**

snow·man (snō′man′, -mən) *n. pl.* **·men** (-men′, -mən) A statue of a man, made of snow, and often having a hat, broom, scarf, etc.

snow·mo·bile (snō′mō·bēl) *n.* Any of various motor vehicles, often with caterpillar treads and steerable front runners, used for traveling over snow, ice, etc. [<SNOW + (AUTO)MOBILE]

snow pellets Snowlike particles sometimes precipitated from a cloud during showers.

snow plant A handsome, blood-red saprophytic herb *(Sarcodes sanguinea)* found in the rich humus of mountain forests in southern California, frequently covered with snow in its blooming season.

snow·plow (snō′plou′) *n.* Any large, plowlike device for turning fallen snow aside from a road or railroad, or for the removal of snow from such surfaces. Also **snow′plough′.**

snow pudding A pudding containing gelatin, sugar, and white of egg whipped into a snowlike foam.

snow·shed (snō′shed′) *n.* A timber structure, as one built over portions of a railway, as a protection from snow slides.

snow·shoe (snō′shōō′) *n.* A device, usually a network of sinew in a wooden frame, to be fastened on the foot by a strap across the toes, as a support in walking over snow. —*v.i.* **·shoed, ·shoe·ing** To walk on snowshoes.

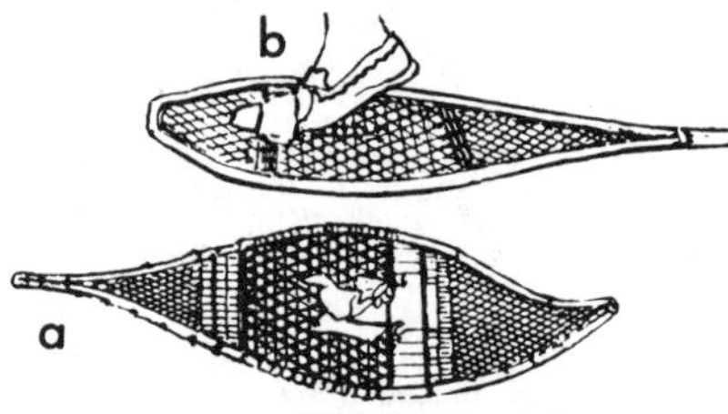

SNOWSHOES
a. Sioux Indian. *b.* Iroquois Indian.

snow·slide (snō′slīd′) *n.* An avalanche of snow.

snow·storm (snō′stôrm′) *n.* A storm with a heavy fall of snow.

snow·suit (snō′sōōt′) *n.* A heavy outer garment worn by young children in cold weather, consisting either of one piece or of ankle-length, tight-fitting pants and a snug jacket with a hood.

snow tire An automobile tire with a heavy tread designed to provide more traction on snow or ice.

snow·y (snō′ē) *adj.* **snow·i·er, snow·i·est 1** Abounding in or full of snow. **2** Snow-white; hence, pure; unblemished; spotless: *snowy* linen. —**snow′i·ly** *adv.* —**snow′i·ness** *n.*

snowy heron The common small white egret *(Egretta thula)* of the southern United States and northern South America.

snowy owl See under OWL.

snub (snub) *v.t.* **snubbed, snub·bing 1** To treat with contempt or disdain; slight. **2** To rebuke or check with a sharp or cutting remark. **3** To stop or check, as a rope in running out, by taking a turnabout a post, etc.; also, to make fast (a boat, etc.) thus. **4** *Obs.* To clip; stunt; nip. —*adj.* Short; pug: said of the nose. —*n.* **1** An act of snubbing; a deliberate and intentional slight. **2** A sudden checking, as of a running rope or cable. **3** A snub nose. [<ON *snubba* snub] —**snub′ber** *n.*

snub-nosed (snub′nōzd′) *adj.* Having a pug or snub nose.

snuff[1] (snuf) *v.t.* **1** To draw in (air, etc.) through the nose. **2** To catch the scent of; smell; sniff; also, to examine by smelling. —*v.i.* **3** To snort; sniff. **4** To inhale air in disdain or anger. —*n.* **1** An act of snuffing; sniff; also, perception by smelling. **2** Resentment expressed by sniffing. [<MDu. *snuffen*]

snuff[2] (snuf) *n.* The charred portion of a wick. —*v.t.* **1** To crop the snuff from (a wick). **2** To put out or extinguish: with *out.* [Cf. G *schnuppe* snuff of a candle]

snuff[3] (snuf) *n.* **1** Pulverized tobacco to be inhaled into the nostrils. **2** The quantity of it taken at one time. **3** Any medicinal powder to be drawn into the nostrils. —**up to snuff** *Colloq.* **1** Meeting the usual standard, as in quality, health, etc. **2** Not easily deceived; sharp-witted. —*v.i.* To take or use snuff. [< Du. *snuf,* appar. short for *snuiftabak,* lit., tobacco to be inhaled]

snuff·box (snuf′boks′) *n.* A small box for carrying snuff about the person.

snuff color The color of snuff; yellowish brown. —**snuff′-col′ored** *adj.*

snuf·fer[1] (snuf′ər) *n.* **1** One who or that which snuffs. **2** A porpoise.

snuf·fer[2] (snuf′ər) *n.* **1** One who or that which snuffs (a candle). **2** *pl.* A scissorlike instrument for removing the snuff from a candle: also called **pair of snuffers.**

snuf·fle (snuf′əl) *v.* **·fled, ·fling** *v.i.* **1** To breathe through the nose noisily and with difficulty, as when it is obstructed by mucus. **2** To breathe noisily, as a dog following a scent. **3** To talk through the nose; snivel. —*v.t.* **4** To utter in a nasal tone. —*n.* **1** An act of snuffling, or the sound made by it. **2** *pl.* Nasal catarrh. **3** An affected nasal or emotional voice or twang; hence, cant. [Freq. of SNUFF[1]] —**snuf′fler** *n.* —**snuf′fly** *adj.*

snuff·y (snuf′ē) *adj.* **snuf·fi·er, snuf·fi·est 1** Pertaining to or like snuff. **2** Soiled with or smelling of snuff; hence, offensive; unattractive. —**snuf′fi·ly** *adv.* —**snuf′fi·ness** *adj.*

snug (snug) *adj.* **snug·ger, snug·gest 1** Closely and comfortably sheltered, covered, or situated. **2** Close or compact; having room enough, but not too much; comfortable; cozy; also, having everything closely secured; trim: said of a ship. **3** Fitting closely but comfortably, as a garment. See synonyms under COMFORTABLE. —*v.* **snugged, snug·ging** *v.t.* To make snug. —*v.i.* To snuggle; move close. —**to snug down** To make a vessel ready for a storm by reducing sail, etc. [Prob. <LG. Cf. Du. *snugger* clean, smooth.] —**snug′ly** *adv.* —**snug′ness** *n.*

snug·ger·y (snug′ər·ē) *n. pl.* **·ger·ies** A cozy and comfortable place or room.

snug·gle (snug′əl) *v.t. & v.i.* **·gled, ·gling** To lie or draw close; nestle; cuddle: often with *up* or *together.* [Freq. of SNUG, *v.*]

so[1] (sō) *adv.* **1** To this or that or such a degree; to this or that extent; in the same degree, quantity, or proportion: either used alone, the degree being implied or understood: Why *so* long; or followed by or preceded by a dependent expression introduced by *as, that,* or *but.* **2** In this, that, or such a manner; in the same or a like or corresponding manner; in the manner mentioned: often following a clause beginning with *as,* or preceding one beginning with *that.* **3** Just as said, directed, suggested, or implied; also, according to fact: referring to a preceding (sometimes following) statement or suggestion. **4** To an extreme degree; extremely; very. **5** The fact being thus: used as an expletive. **6** About as many or as much as stated; thereabouts: I shall stay a day or *so.* **7** At all events; in any case; at all: now only in the compounds *whosoever, whichsoever,* etc. **8** According to the truth of what is sworn to or averred: said in oaths or asseverations: *So* help me God. **9** Indeed! elliptical for *Is it so?* **10** To such an extent: used elliptically for *so much*: I love him *so*! **11** Too: used in emphatic denial: You can *so*! **12** Indicative of surprise or disapproval: *So* there you are. **13** So as to follow immediately; then; therefore. **14** Let it be that way; very well. —*conj.* **1** With the purpose that: often with *that*: They left the hotel early *so* (that) they would not encounter him. **2** In such a way that; as a consequence of which: He consented, *so* they went away. **3** *Obs.* As. —*interj.* **1** Stay still! **2** Is that so! **3** In nautical parlance, steady! [OE *swā*]

so[2] (sō) *n. Music* The fifth of the syllables used in singing the scale: also *sol.* [See GAMUT]

soak (sōk) *v.t.* **1** To place in liquid till thoroughly saturated; steep. **2** To wet thoroughly;

drench: The rain *soaks* the earth. 3 To take in through or as through pores or interstices; suck up; absorb: with *in* or *up*. 4 *Colloq.* To drink, especially to excess. 5 *U.S. Slang* a To charge exorbitantly. b To pawn. c To strike hard; beat. — *v.i.* 6 To remain or be placed in liquid till saturated. 7 To penetrate; pass: with *in* or *into*. 8 *U.S. Slang* To drink to excess. — *n.* 1 The process or act of soaking, or state of being soaked. 2 Liquid in which something is soaked. 3 *Slang* A hard drinker; a drinking spree. ◆ Homophone: *soke*. [OE *socian*. Akin to SUCK.]

soak·age (sō′kij) *n.* 1 The process of soaking, or the state of being soaked. 2 The quantity of liquid that soaks in or through, or seeps out.

soak·er (sō′kər) *n.* 1 One who or that which soaks. 2 *Slang* A habitual drunkard.

soak·ers (sō′kerz) *n. pl.* Short pants of absorbent material, usually wool, worn by babies over diapers.

soak·y (sō′kē) *adj.* **soak·i·er, soak·i·est** Covered or filled with moisture; steeped; soggy.

so-and-so (sō′ən·sō′) *n.* 1 An unnamed or undetermined person or thing. 2 *Colloq.* A euphemism for many offensive epithets.

soap (sōp) *n.* 1 A cleansing agent consisting of sodium or potassium salts of fatty acids, made by decomposing the glyceryl esters of fats and oils with alkalies; a detergent. *Hard* soaps are made by the use of soda, while the potash soaps are *soft*. 2 A metallic salt of one of the fatty acids. 3 *U.S. Slang* Money used for sinister purposes; hence, any means of obtaining an end. — *v.t.* To rub with soap; treat with soap. [OE *sāpe*]

soap·bark (sōp′bärk′) *n.* 1 The bark of the quillai. 2 The bark of a tropical American shrub (genus *Pithecellobium*), used as a substitute for soap. Also **soapbark tree.**

soap·ber·ry (sōp′ber′ē) *n. pl.* **·ries** 1 The fruit of any one of several trees or shrubs (genus *Sapindus*) of the family *Sapindaceae*. 2 Any one of the trees producing it, especially *S. saponaria*, of tropical America and southern Florida, the pulp of whose fruit is used in washing textile fabrics.

soap·box (sōp′boks′) *n.* 1 A box or crate for soap. 2 Any box or crate used as a platform by street orators. — **soapbox oratory** Impromptu or crude oratory, marked by vigor rather than logic. Also **soap box.**

soap·box·er (sōp′bok′sər) *n. Colloq.* A loud and ranting speaker; a street-corner orator; a tubthumper.

soap bubble 1 An inflated bubble of soapsuds, forming a hollow globule. 2 Anything attractive but unsubstantial.

soap opera A daytime television or radio drama presented serially and usually dealing with domestic themes of a highly emotional character: so called in reference to the soap commercials often presented on such programs.

soap plant Any of several plants whose bulbs are used for soap, especially a lilywort (*Chlorogalum pomeridianum*) of California.

soap·stone (sōp′stōn′) *n.* Steatite: so called from its soapy feel.

soap·suds (sōp′sudz′) *n. pl.* Soapy water, especially when worked into a foam.

soap·wort (sōp′wûrt′) *n.* A perennial herb (*Saponaria officinalis*) of the pink family having clusters of pink or whitish, often double, flowers: so called because its juice forms a lather with water. Also called *bouncing Bet.*

soap·y (sō′pē) *adj.* **soap·i·er, soap·i·est** 1 Resembling, containing, or consisting of soap. 2 Smeared with soap. 3 *Slang* Flattering.

soar (sôr, sōr) *v.i.* 1 To float aloft through the air on wings, as a bird. 2 To sail through the air without perceptibly moving the wings, as a hawk or vulture. 3 To glide without losing altitude, as an airplane. 4 To rise above any usual level: Prices will *soar* if the ceilings are removed. See synonyms under FLY[1]. — *n.* An act of soaring; a range of upward flight. [<F *essorer* <L *ex* out + *aura* breeze, air] — **soar′er** *n.*

sob (sob) *n.* A convulsive, audible inhalation of air under the impulse of painful or hysterical emotion, and usually accompanied with tears; the act or the sound of sobbing; also, any similar sound, as of the wind. Also **sob′·bing.** — *v.* **sobbed, sob·bing** *v.i.* 1 To weep with audible, convulsive catches of the breath. 2 To make a sound like a sob, as the wind. — *v.t.* 3 To utter with sobs. 4 To bring to a specified condition by sobbing: to *sob* oneself to sleep. [Imit.]

So·bat (sō′bat) A river in SE Sudan, flowing 205 miles NW from the Ethiopian border to the White Nile.

so·be·it (sō·bē′it) *n.* An amen. — *conj.* If so; if only; provided: originally **so be it.**

so·ber (sō′bər) *adj.* 1 Possessing properly controlled faculties; even-tempered; well-balanced; temperate in action or thought. 2 Grave; sedate; realizing the importance and seriousness of life. 3 Not under the influence of an intoxicant; not drunk. 4 Moderate in or abstinent from the use of intoxicating drink. 5 Of subdued or modest color. — *v.t.* & *v.i.* To make or become sober. [<OF *sobre* <L *sobrius*] — **so′ber·ly** *adv.* — **so′ber·ness** *n.*

Synonyms (adj.): abstemious, abstinent, calm, collected, cool, dispassionate, moderate, quiet, regular, sane, staid, steady, temperate, unimpassioned, unintoxicated. See SAD, SANE[1], SEDATE, SERIOUS. *Antonyms*: agitated, crazy, drunk, drunken, ecstatic, excited, extravagant, extreme, frantic, furious, immoderate, impassioned, intemperate, intoxicated, passionate, unreasonable.

So·bies·ki (sô·byes′kē), **John** See JOHN III OF POLAND.

So·bran·je (sô·brän′yə) *n.* The national assembly or legislature of Bulgaria. Also **So·bran·i·ye** (sô·brän′ē·yə), **So·bran′ye.**

so·bri·e·ty (sō·brī′ə·tē) *n. pl.* **·ties** 1 The state of being sober. 2 Moderateness in temper or conduct; sedateness; seriousness; temperance. See synonyms under ABSTINENCE. [<L *sobrietas, -tatis* <*sobrius* sober]

so·bri·quet (sō′bri·kā) *n.* A fanciful or humorous appellation; a nickname: also spelled *soubriquet*. [<F; ult. origin unknown]

sob sister *U.S. Slang* A journalist who writes mawkishly sentimental news stories.

sob story *Slang* A sad personal narrative told to elicit pity or sympathy.

soc·age (sok′ij) *n.* The feudal tenure of land by certain determinate services other than knight-service; hence, later, tenure by any fixed service other than military. [<*soc*, var. of SOKE] — **soc′ag·er** *n.*

so-called (sō′kôld′) *adj.* Called as stated; generally styled thus: usually implying a doubtful or improper form.

soc·cer (sok′ər) *n.* A form of football in which the ball is propelled toward the opponents' goal by kicking or by striking with the head or body, other than the shoulders or arms, the goalkeepers being the only players allowed to use their hands and arms in deflecting or carrying the ball: officially called *association football*. [Alter. of ASSOCIATION]

So·che (sō′che′) The Chinese name for YARKAND.

So·chi (sô′chē) A port on the Black Sea in southern Krasnodar territory, European Russian S.F.S.R.

so·cia·bil·i·ty (sō′shə·bil′ə·tē) *n.* The quality or character of being sociable. Also **so′cia·ble·ness.**

so·cia·ble (sō′shə·bəl) *adj.* 1 Inclined to seek company; social. 2 Agreeable in company; companionable; genial. 3 Characterized by or affording occasion for agreeable conversation and friendliness. See synonyms under AMICABLE, FRIENDLY. — *n.* 1 An informal social gathering: also *social*. 2 A four-wheeled open carriage with facing seats. [<F <L *sociabilis* <*socius* friend] — **so′cia·bly** *adv.*

so·cial (sō′shəl) *adj.* 1 Of or pertaining to society or its organization; relating to persons as living in society or to the public as an aggregate body: *social* life, *social* questions. 2 Disposed to hold friendly intercourse with others; sociable. 3 Constituted to live in society; having developed or fulfilled tendencies to organize in society as a race or people: *social* beings. 4 Of or pertaining to public welfare: *social* insurance. 5 Pertaining to or characteristic of persons of fashion: *social* register. 6 Living in communities: *social* ants or bees; aggregate; compound; colonial. 7 Grouping compactly, as individual plants; partly or wholly covering a large area of land: said of plant species. 8 Venereal: *social* disease: a euphemism. 9 Pertaining to or between allies or confederates, as the wars waged by Rome in 90–89 B.C., and by Athens in 357–355 B.C. against their allies. See synonyms under FRIENDLY, GOOD. — *n.* A sociable. [<L *socialis* <*socius* ally]

social climber A person who attempts to become friendly with prominent or wealthy people.

social contract *Philos.* The supposed original agreement by which individuals were united in political associations for their mutual protection, the surrender of their individual sovereignty having been made not through force but by mutual consent: a theory of Hobbes, Locke, Rousseau, etc.

Social Democrat 1 A member of the Social Democratic party of Germany, founded by Bebel and Liebknecht in 1869 and based on Marxian principles. In 1875 it was merged with Lassalle's General German Workmen's Association. Under the Republic (1918–33) it advocated the principles embedded in the Weimar Constitution. 2 A member of a similar party in other countries. — **so′cial-dem′o·crat′ic** *adj.*

social evil Prostitution.

social insurance Government insurance designed to protect wage earners against unemployment, illness, accident, or the like, and not always requiring the payment of a premium on the part of the insured.

so·cial·ism (sō′shəl·iz′əm) *n.* Public collective ownership or control of the basic means of production, distribution, and exchange, with the avowed aim of operating for use rather than for profit, and of assuring to each member of society an equitable share of goods, services, and welfare benefits: as a system of social and economic organization planned, attempted, or achieved through various methods—in **Utopian** or **Christian Socialism,** through cooperative communal groups holding all things in common (approximating the philosophic anarchism of Thoreau, Tolstoy, and Kropotkin, and the communalism and commensalism of the early and undivided church); in **Guild Socialism,** through organization of producer groups and the professions in syndicalist guilds to be represented in a federal legislative body; in **Fabian** or **British Labour Party Socialism,** through parliamentary democracy using gradualist evolutionary processes; in **Marxist-Leninist State Socialism,** through revolution, expropriation, and dictatorship of the so-called proletariat, in short, Communism. Compare MIXED ECONOMY. — **creeping socialism** Anything considered as a gradual or piecemeal encroachment upon the system of private property and free enterprise through state action: used as an epithet.

so·cial·ist (sō′shəl·ist) *n.* An advocate of socialism. — *adj.* Socialistic.

so·cial·is·tic (sō′shəl·is′tik) *adj.* Of, pertaining to, advocating, like, or practicing socialism.

Socialist Labor party A U. S. political party, originally formed in 1877 as the **Socialistic Labor party** and renamed in 1891.

Socialist party A U. S. political party formed in 1901 by the combination of a dissident group from the Socialist Labor party with the **Social Democratic party** (established in 1898 by E. V. Debs and others). After the **Social Democratic Federation,** a dissident group formed in 1936, rejoined in 1957, the name **Socialist party-Social Democratic Federation** was officially adopted.

so·cial·ite (sō′shəl·īt) *n.* A person prominent in fashionable society.

so·ci·al·i·ty (sō′shē·al′ə·tē) *n. pl.* **·ties** 1 The state or character of being social; sociability. 2 A social custom or action. 3 The instinct or tendency which is the basis of social organization.

so·cial·ize (sō′shəl·īz) *v.* **·ized, ·iz·ing** *v.t.* 1 To convert from an anti-social to a social attitude; make friendly, cooperative, or sociable. 2 To arouse to an interest in humanity. 3 To convert or adapt to social uses or needs. 4 To put under group control; especially, to regulate according to socialistic principles. — *v.i.* 5 To take part in social activities. Also *Brit.* **so'cial·ise.** —**so'cial·i·za'tion** *n.*

socialized medicine A system proposing to supply the public with medical care at nominal cost, by regulating services and fees, by government subsidies to physicians and medical projects, or by cooperative projects.

social register A directory of persons prominent in fashionable society.

social science 1 The body of knowledge that relates to man as a member of society, or of any component part of society, as the state, family, or any systematized human institution. **2** Any field of knowledge dealing with human society, as economics, history, sociology, education, politics, ethics, etc.

social security 1 Any public system which provides welfare services for members of the community in need. **2** *U.S.* A Federal program of old–age and unemployment insurance, public assistance to the blind, disabled, and dependent, and maternal and child welfare services, administered by the **Social Security Administration.**

social service Activity intended to advance human welfare. —**so'cial–ser'vice** *adj.*

social settlement An institution or settlement, usually in the poor quarters of a large city, devoted to the aid and instruction of the poor.

social work Any clinical, social, or recreational service for improving community welfare, as through health clinics, recreational facilities, aid to the poor and the aged, etc. —**social worker**

so·ci·e·ty (sə·sī'ə·tē) *n. pl.* **·ties 1** The system of community life, in which individuals, ordinarily in a territorial establishment, form a continuous and regulatory association for their mutual benefit and protection. **2** The body of persons composing such a community. **3** A number of persons in a community regarded as forming a class having certain common interests, status, etc.: high *society.* **4** The fashionable or cultured portion of a community, considered as constituting a class. **5** A body of persons associated for a common purpose or object; an association: a medical *society.* **6** *U.S.* In some States, an incorporated religious congregation. **7** A club or fraternity. **8** Association based on friendship or intimacy; companionship; company: to enjoy the *society* of working men. **9** *Ecol.* A group of plants or animals living together under the same physiographic conditions and influences and characterized by a principal species. See synonyms under ASSOCIATION. [<OF *societe* <L *societas, -tatis* <*socius* a friend]

Society Islands A part of French Oceania, comprising an island group south of the Tuamotu Islands; 690 square miles; capital, Papeete, on Tahiti; divided into two clusters: the *Windward Islands,* including Tahiti, Moorea, and other adjacent islands; and the *Leeward Islands,* including the major island of Raiatea.

Society of Friends A Christian religious group, founded in England by George Fox in the middle of the seventeenth century, characterized by their doctrine of "waiting upon the Spirit" for direct guidance and their repudiation of ritual, formal sacraments, oaths, and violence: commonly known as *Quakers.*

Society of Jesus See JESUIT.

So·cin·i·an (sō·sin'·ē·ən) *adj.* Pertaining to either or both of the Italian theologians named Socinus or to their religious teachings, as the denial of the Trinity, of the natural depravity of man, of vicarious atonement, and of the efficacy of sacraments. —*n.* A believer in the Socinian theory. —**So·cin'·i·an·ism** *n.*

socio– *combining form* **1** Society; social: *sociology.* **2** Sociology; sociological: *sociobiology.* [<F <L *socius* a companion]

so·ci·o·bi·ol·o·gy (sō'sē·ō·bī·ol'ə·jē, sō'shē-) *n.* A theory of sociology that utilizes biological principles. —**so'ci·o·bi·ol'ogist,** *n.*

so·ci·o·ec·o·nom·ic (sō'sē·ō·ek'ə·nom'ik, sō'·shē-, -ē'kə-) *adj.* Social and economic: considered as a unit based upon the interrelationship of social and economic factors. —**so'ci·o·ec'o·nom'·i·cal·ly** *adv.*

so·ci·o·ge·net·ic (sō'sē·ō·jə·net' -shē·ō-) *adj.* Of or pertaining to the origin, development, and preservation of human society in any of its aspects.

so·ci·o·lin·guis·tics (sō'sē·ō·ling·gwis'tiks, sō'·shē-) *n.* The study of language as a social instrument and in its social context, in which the principles and investigative techniques of both sociology and linguistics are employed. [<SOCIO- + LINGUISTICS] —**so'ci·o·lin·guis'·tic** *adj.* —**so'ci·o·lin·guis'ti·cal·ly** *adv.*

so·ci·o·log·i·cal (sō'sē·ə·loj'i·kəl, -shē·ə-) *adj.* **1** Of or concerned with human social relations or conditions. **2** Of or pertaining to sociology. Also **so'ci·o·log'ic.** —**so'ci·o·log'i·cal·ly** *adv.*

so·ci·ol·o·gy (sō'sē·ol'ə·jē, sō'shē-) *n.* The science that treats of the origin and evolution of human society and social phenomena, the progress of civilization, and the laws controlling human institutions and functions. —**so'ci·ol'o·gist** *n.*

so·ci·om·e·try (sō'sē·om'ə·trē, sō'shē-) *n.* The study of the interrelationships of individuals within a community or social group, especially as expressed by attitudes of acceptance or rejection. —**so'ci·o·met'ric** (-ə·met'rik) *adj.*

so·ci·o·path (sō'sē·ə·path, sō'shē-) *n.* One who suffers from a mental disorder that causes a lack of moral restraint or responsibility toward fellow members of society.

sock[1] (sok) *n.* **1** A short stocking. **2** The light shoe worn by comic actors in the Greek and Roman drama; hence, comedy. Compare BUSKIN. [OE *socc* <L *soccus* slipper]

sock[2] (sok) *Slang v.t.* To strike or hit, especially with the fist; to punch. —*n.* A hard blow. [Origin unknown]

sock·dol·a·ger (sok·dol'ə·jər) *n. Slang* **1** That which gives the finishing stroke, or is decisive, especially in a dispute; a decisive blow, a conclusive reply or argument, or the like. **2** Something of great size; a rouser. Also **sock·dol'o·ger.** [Alter. of DOXOLOGY]

sock·et (sok'it) *n.* **1** *Mech.* A cavity or an opening specially adapted to receive and hold some corresponding piece or fixture: the *socket* for an electric–light bulb. **2** *Anat.* A cavity or hollowed depression for the reception of an organ or part. —*v.t.* To furnish with, hold by, or put into a socket. [<AF *soket,* dim. of OF *soc* a plowshare <Celtic]

sock·eye (sok'ī) *n.* The red salmon of the Pacific coast *(Oncorhynchus nerka),* highly valued as a food fish. [Alter. of Salishan *sukkegh*]

so·cle (sō'kəl) *n. Archit.* **1** A plain, square block, higher than a plinth, supporting a statue or other work of art. **2** A base supporting a wall or a range of ornaments. [<F <Ital. *zoccolo* a pedestal, shoe <L *socculus,* dim. of *soccus* a sock]

soc·man (sok'mən) *n. pl.* **·men** (-mən) In old English law, one who holds land in socage: often spelled *sokeman.* Also **sock'man.**

Soc·ra·tes (sok'rə·tēz), 469?–399 B.C., Athenian philosopher; the chief character in the dialogs of Plato: accused of impiety and innovation, he was imprisoned, condemned to death, and forced to drink an infusion of hemlock.

So·crat·ic (sō·krat'ik) *adj.* Pertaining to or characteristic of Socrates: also **So·crat'i·cal.** —*n.* A disciple of Socrates. —**So·crat'i·cal·ly** *adv.* —**Soc·ra·tism** (sok'rə·tiz'əm) *n.* —**Soc'·ra·tist** *n.*

Socratic irony A pretense of ignorance, though one may be wise, in order to expose the errors in an opponent's reasoning.

Socratic method The dialectic method of instruction by questions and answers, as adopted by Socrates in his disputations, leading either to a foreseen conclusion or to admissions damaging to an opponent.

sod[1] (sod) *n.* **1** Grassy surface soil held together by the matted roots of grass and weeds; sward; also, a piece of such soil. **2** Grassy ground; lawn; the earth or soil. — **the old Sod** Ireland. —*v.t.* **sod·ded, sod·ding** To cover with sod. [<MDu. *sode* piece of turf]

sod[2] (sod) Obsolete past tense of SEETHE.

so·da (sō'də) *n.* **1** Any of several white alkaline compounds widely used in medicine, industry, and the arts, especially sodium bicarbonate (baking soda), sodium carbonate, sodium hydroxide, and sodium oxide. **2** Soda alum. **3** Soda salts. **4** Soda water; also, a soft drink containing carbonated water, flavoring, and, sometimes, ice–cream. **5** In faro, the first card to appear face up in the dealing box before the start of play. [<Med. L <Ital. *soda (cenere)* solid (ash) <L *solidus*]

soda alum *Chem.* A double salt of sodium sulfate and aluminum.

soda ash Crude sodium carbonate.

soda biscuit 1 A biscuit leavened with sodium bicarbonate. **2** A soda cracker.

soda cracker A thin, crisp cracker made with yeast–leavened dough containing soda.

soda fountain 1 An apparatus from which soda water is drawn, usually containing receptacles for sirups, ice, and ice–cream. **2** A counter at which soft drinks and ice–cream are dispensed.

soda jerk *U.S. Slang* A clerk who serves at a soda fountain.

soda lime A mixture made from sodium hydroxide and calcium oxide.

so·da·lite (sō'də·līt) *n.* A vitreous, translucent silicate of sodium and aluminum, with some lorine. [<SODA + -LITE]

so·dal·i·ty (sō·dal'ə·tē) *n. pl.* **·ties** A brotherhood or fraternity; especially, a brotherhood for devotional or charitable purposes. [<L *sodalitas, -tatis* <*sodalis* companion]

so·dar (sō'där) *n.* A device for obtaining information on local weather conditions by projecting sound waves directly overhead and alyzing the echoes as recorded on an oscilloscope. [<SO(UND) D(ETECTING) A(ND) R(ANGING)]

soda water 1 An effervescent drink consisting of water strongly charged under pressure with purified carbon dioxide gas, formerly generated from sodium bicarbonate: often flavored with a fruit sirup. **2** Alkaline water as found in natural reservoirs or springs.

sod·den (sod'n) *adj.* **1** Soaked with moisture: *sodden* ground. **2** Doughy; soggy, as bread, biscuits, etc. **3** Flabby and pale; flaccid, especially from dissipation: said of persons or their features. **4** Dull; dreary: a *sodden* life. —*v.t.* & *v.i.* To make or become sodden. [ME *sothen,* orig. pp. of SEETHE] —**sod'den·ly** *adv.* —**sod'den·ness** *n.*

Sod·dy (sod'ē), **Frederick,** 1877–1956, English chemist and physicist.

Sö·der·blom (sœ'dər·blo͝om), **Nathan,** 1866–1931, Swedish theologist.

sod house A dwelling built of sod or turf walls, often having a wooden roof: used by early settlers on the prairies.

so·di·um (sō'dē·əm) *n.* A silver–white, highly reactive, alkaline, metallic element (symbol Na), very similar to potassium. It is soft, malleable, and lighter than water, which it decomposes with the liberation of hydrogen. See ELEMENT. [<NL <Med. L *soda* SODA]

Sodium Am·y·tal (am'i·tôl, -tal) Proprietary name of a white, hygroscopic powder, $C_{11}H_{17}O_3N_2Na$, used in medicine as a sedative and hypnotic.

sodium benzoate *Chem.* A white, odorless, amorphous, granular or crystalline powder, $NaC_7H_5O_2$, used as an antipyretic, antirheumatic, antiseptic, as a food preservative, and to disguise taste, as of poor–quality food.

sodium bicarbonate *Chem.* A white crystalline compound, $NaHCO_3$, of alkaline taste, used in medicine and cookery; baking soda.

sodium borate *Chem.* Any sodium salt of boric acid; specifically, borax.

sodium carbonate *Chem.* A strongly alkaline compound, Na_2CO_3: in crystalline hydrated form known as washing soda, $Na_2CO_3 \cdot 10H_2O$, used in the manufacture of glass, soap, paper, etc., and in medicine and photography.

sodium chlorate *Chem.* A white crystalline compound, $NaClO_3$, used as a mordant, insecticide, weed–killer, and as an oxidizing agent.

sodium chloride Common salt, NaCl.

sodium cyanide *Chem.* A white, extremely poisonous salt of hydrocyanic acid, NaCN: used in electroplating and case hardening of metals, as a fumigant and chemical reagent.

sodium dichromate *Chem.* A red crystalline compound, $Na_2Cr_2O_7 \cdot 2H_2O$, used as a dye and in making inks.

sodium hydroxide *Chem.* A white, caustic, fusible compound, NaOH: used in various solutions in chemistry, metallurgy, as a bleaching agent, etc.; caustic soda.

sodium hypochlorite *Chem.* An oxidizing and

bleaching compound, NaOCl, used also as a decontaminating agent for war gases.

sodium hyposulfite 1 Sodium thiosulfate. 2 A colorless crystalline salt, $Na_2S_2O_4$.

sodium nitrate A white compound, $NaNO_3$, used in the manufacture of nitric acid and as a manure. It occurs abundantly in nature.

sodium oxide A gray, highly reactive compound, Na_2O; sodium monoxide.

sodium perborate *Chem.* A colorless crystalline compound, $NaBO_3 \cdot 4H_2O$, used as a bleaching agent and disinfectant.

sodium peroxide *Chem.* A yellowish solid, Na_2O_2, used in combination with other chemicals as a bleaching agent.

sodium phosphate *Chem.* A sodium salt of phosphoric acid, Na_2HPO_4, crystallizing in the presence of water: the tribasic form is used as a laxative and also as a fixing agent in textile coloring.

sodium propionate *Chem.* A colorless, crystalline, water-soluble compound, $NaC_3H_5O_2$, used in medicine as a fungicide and to retard bacterial and mold growth in foods.

sodium silicate A material used in making artificial stone and in various industrial processes: known also as *soluble glass* or *waterglass.*

sodium sulfate *Chem.* A compound, Na_2SO_4, made by the action of sulfuric acid on common salt or on Chile saltpeter. It is used in glassmaking, and in one form (Glauber's salt) is important in medicine.

sodium sulfide *Chem.* A bleaching and decontaminating agent, Na_2S, especially effective against mustard gas.

sodium sulfite *Chem.* A decontaminating agent, Na_2SO_3, effective against chlorpicrin.

sodium thiosulfate *Chem.* A crystalline salt, $Na_2S_2O_3$, used industrially and in photography as a fixing agent: also called *hypo.*

Sod·om (sod′əm) In the Bible, a city on the Dead Sea, destroyed with Gomorrah because of the wickedness of its people. *Gen.* xiii 10.

sod·om·ite (sod′əm·īt) *n.* One guilty of sodomy.

Sod·om·ite (sod′əm·īt) *n.* One of the people of Sodom.

sod·om·y (sod′əm·ē) *n.* Carnal copulation between male persons or with beasts. [<OF *sodomie* <LL *Sodoma* Sodom, to whose people this practice was imputed]

Soem·ba (sōōm′bä) The Dutch name for SUMBA.

Soem·ba·wa (sōōm·bä′wä) The Dutch name for SUMBAWA.

Soe·ra·ba·ja (sōō′rä·bä′yä) The Dutch name for SURABAYA.

so·ev·er (sō·ev′ər) *adv.* To or in some conceivable degree: used in generalizing and emphasizing what follows: a word often added to *who, which, what, where, when, how,* etc., to form the compounds *whosoever,* etc., giving them specific force. Often used separately: *how* great *soever* he might be.

so·fa (sō′fə) *n.* A wide seat, upholstered and having a back and raised ends. [<F <Arabic *soffah* a part of a floor raised to form a seat]

sofa bed A sofa which may be opened up to form a large bed.

so·far (sō′fär) *n.* A system for locating stranded ships or aircraft by means of underwater sound waves, set up by depth charges released by the survivors and detected by hydrophones operated from ground stations. [<SO(UND) F(IXING) A(ND) R(ANGING)]

sof·fit (sof′it) *n. Archit.* The under side of a staircase, entablature, lintel, archway, or cornice. [<F *soffite* <Ital. *soffita* <L *suffixus.* Doublet of SUFFIX.]

So·fi·a (sō·fē′ä) German, Italian, Russian, Spanish, and Swedish form of SOPHIA.

So·fi·a (sō′fē·ə, sō·fē′ə) The capital of Bulgaria, in the western part. *Bulgarian* **So·fi·ya** (sô′fē·yä).

soft (sôft, soft) *adj.* 1 Being or composed of a substance whose shape is changed easily by pressure, without fracture; impressible; pliable, ductile, or malleable; easily worked: *soft* wood: opposed to *hard.* 2 Smooth and delicate to the touch: *soft* skin. 3 Gentle in its effect upon the ear; not loud or harsh. 4 Mild in any mode of physical action; gentle; bland: a *soft* breeze; a *soft* ripple. 5 Of subdued coloring or delicate shading; not glaring or abrupt: *soft* tints; *soft* outline. 6 Gentle; conciliatory; expressing mildness or sympathy; courteous: *soft* words. 7 Giving or enjoying rest; placid: *soft* sleep. 8 Easily or too easily touched in feeling; tender; sympathetic: a *soft* heart. 9 Incapable of bearing hardship; susceptible; tender; delicate: *soft* muscles. 10 Of yielding character; weak; effeminate. 11 *Colloq.* Of weak intellect; also, yielding to emotion; maudlin. 12 Free from mineral salts which prevent the detergent action of water and soap: said of water. 13 Bituminous, as opposed to anthracite: said of coal. 14 Describing *c* and *g* when articulated fricatively as in *cent* and *gibe*: opposed to *hard*; also, voiced and weakly articulated; also, palatalized, as certain consonants in the Slavic languages. 15 *Colloq.* Easy: a *soft* job. 16 *Scot. & Brit. Dial.* Characterized by moisture or thawing: said of the weather. See synonyms under BLAND, SUPPLE. —*n.* 1 That which is soft; softness; a soft part or material. 2 *Colloq.* One who is soft or foolish; a softy. —*adv.* 1 Softly. 2 Quietly; gently. —*interj. Archaic* Proceed softly; be quiet or slow. [OE *sōfte*] —**soft′ly** *adv. & interj.* —**soft′·ness** *n.*

sof·ta (sof′tə) *n. Turkish* A student at a Moslem mosque.

soft·back (sôft′bak′, soft′-) *adj.* Soft-cover. —*n.* A soft-cover book.

soft·ball (sôft′bôl′, soft′-) *n.* A variation of baseball, requiring a smaller diamond, a larger, softer ball, ten players on a team, and seven innings for play.

soft-boiled (sôft′boild′) *adj.* 1 Boiled, as an egg, for only a short while, so that the yolk and albumen are soft or semiliquid. 2 *Colloq.* Mild in disposition: lenient.

soft·bound (sôft′bound′, soft′-) *adj.* Soft-cover.

soft clam The common long clam *(Mya arenaria)* of the north Atlantic coast.

soft coal Bituminous coal.

soft-cov·er (sôft′kuv′ər, soft′-) *adj.* Designating a book having flexible sides, as of paper: contrasted to *hard-cover.*

soft drink A nonalcoholic beverage, as sweetened soda water, ginger ale, etc.

sof·ten (sôf′ən, sof′-) *v.t. & v.i.* To make or become soft or softer. See synonyms under ALLAY, ALLEVIATE, CHASTEN, TEMPER. —**sof′·ten·er** *n.*

softening of the brain 1 *Pathol.* Degeneration of the brain tissue, especially as resulting from paresis; encephalomalacia. 2 *Colloq.* Dementia.

soft-finned (sôft′find′, soft′-) *adj. Zool.* Having fins whose membrane is supported on flexible or jointed rays: opposed to *spiny-finned.*

soft focus *Phot.* A slightly blurred effect obtained by an imperfect focusing of the lens upon a scene or object.

soft·head (sôft′hed′, soft′-) *n.* A foolish or simple person. —**soft′-head′ed** *adj.*

soft·heart·ed (sôft′här′tid, soft′-) *adj.* Tenderhearted; merciful. —**soft′heart′ed·ly** *adv.* —**soft′heart′ed·ness** *n.*

soft-ped·al (sôft′ped′l, soft′-) *v.t.* **·aled** or **·alled, ·al·ing** or **·al·ling** 1 To mute the tone of by depressing the soft pedal. 2 *Colloq.* To render less emphatic; moderate; tone down.

soft pedal A pedal which mutes the tone, as in a piano.

soft sell *U.S. Colloq.* The use of subtle, noninsistent methods of salesmanship.

soft-shell (sôft′shel′, soft′-) *adj.* 1 Having a soft shell, as certain clams, or a crab or lobster after shedding its shell: also **soft′-shelled′.** 2 *U.S. Colloq.* Somewhat moderate in opinion or doctrine; somewhat liberal; not hidebound: a *soft-shell* Baptist. —*n.* A crab which has lately shed its shell: also **soft-shelled crab.**

soft-shelled turtle Any member of a family *(Trionychidae)* of turtles having a long snout and a soft, leathery shell, especially *Trionyx* (or *Amyda*) *spinifera,* common from the Gulf States to the St. Lawrence River.

soft-soap (sôft′sōp′, soft′-) *v.t.* To flatter. —**soft′-soap′er** *n.*

soft soap 1 Fluid or semifluid soap. 2 *Colloq.* Flattery; blarney.

soft·ware (sôft′wâr′, soft′-) *n.* In a digital computer, any of the programs designed to control various aspects of the operation of the machine, such as input and output operations: distinguished from *hardware* (def. 4).

soft·wood (sôft′wŏŏd′, soft′-) *n.* 1 A coniferous tree or its wood. 2 Any soft wood, or any tree with soft wood.

soft·y (sôf′tē, sof′-) *n. pl.* **soft·ies** *Colloq.* 1 An extremely sentimental person. 2 A weak or effeminate man or boy; one not inured to hardship; a sissy.

Sog·di·an (sog′dē·ən) *n.* 1 One of an ancient Iranian people inhabiting Sogdiana. 2 Their extinct Iranian language.

Sog·di·a·na (sog′dē·ā′nə) An ancient region of central Asia comprising part of the Persian Empire; capital, Samarkand: also *Transoxiana.*

sog·gy (sog′ē) *adj.* **·gi·er, ·gi·est** 1 Saturated with water or moisture; wet and heavy; soaked. 2 Heavy: said of pastry. 3 Soft; boggy: said of land. 4 Dull; logy: said of a person or an animal. Also **sog·ged** (sog′id). [<dial. E *sog* a swamp, bog <Scand. Cf. dial. Norw. *soggjast* get wet.] —**sog′gi·ly** *adv.* —**sog′gi·ness** *n.*

Sog·ne Fjord (sông′nə) The longest and deepest fjord in Norway, in the western part; 112 miles long; an inlet of the North Sea.

So·ho (sō·hō′, sō′hō) The foreign quarter of London, noted for its restaurants.

soi-di·sant (swä·dē·zäṅ′) *adj. French* Self-styled; pretended: usually implying false pretense.

soi·gné (swä·nyā′) *adj. French* Cared for; well-groomed.

soil[1] (soil) *n.* 1 Finely divided rock mixed with decayed vegetable or animal matter, constituting that portion of the surface of the earth in which plants grow. 2 The ground in general; native land; country. 3 A mixture of lampblack, glue, and water used in plumbing. See synonyms under LAND. [<OF *soile, sueil* <L *solium* a seat, mistaken for *solum* the ground]

soil[2] (soil) *v.t.* 1 To make dirty; smudge. 2 To disgrace; defile. 3 *Obs.* To manure. —*v.i.* 4 To become dirty. See synonyms under BLEMISH, DEFILE[1], POLLUTE, STAIN. —*n.* 1 That which soils; foul matter; a foul spot; hence, a taint. 2 Manure: confused in use with *soil*[1]. 3 A slough or marshy place in which a hunted boar takes refuge; hence, water or a wet place resorted to by other game. [<OF *soillier,* ult. <L *suculus,* dim. of *sus* a pig]

soil[3] (soil) *v.t.* 1 To feed and fatten, as stalled cattle, with freshly cut, green food. 2 To purge with green food. [? <OF *saoler, saouler* fill <L *satullare* <*satullus,* dim. of *satur* sated]

soil·age (soi′lij) *n.* Green crops for feeding animals.

soil·ure (soil′yər) *n.* Soiling, or the condition of being soiled.

soi·rée (swä·rā′, *Fr.* swà·rā′) *n.* A party or reception given in the evening. Also **soi·ree′.** [<F <*soir* evening]

Sois·sons (swà·sôṅ′) A city in NE France on the Aisne.

so·ja (sō′jə, sō′yə) *n.* The soybean. [<NL <Du. *soya* the soybean]

so·journ (sō′jûrn, sō·jûrn′) *v.i.* To stay or dwell temporarily; abide for a time. See synonyms under ABIDE. —*n.* (sō′jûrn) A temporary residence or stay, as of one in a foreign land. [<OF *sojorner, sojourner,* ult. <L *sub-* under + *diurnus* daily] —**so′journ·er** *n.*

soke (sōk) *n.* 1 In feudal law, a franchise, privilege, or liberty; jurisdiction; a privilege to administer justice within a certain territory, as a manor. 2 The district within which such privilege was exercised. ◆ Homophone: *soak.* [<Med. L *soca* <OE *sōcn* jurisdiction]

soke·man (sōk′mən) See SOCMAN.

Soke of Peterborough An administrative county in NE Northamptonshire, England; 83 square miles.

So·kol (sō′kôl) *n.* 1 A Czech patriotic organization of gymnasts started (1862) as a democratic fraternal body to develop strength, litheness, alertness, and fearlessness. 2 A member of this organization. [<Czechoslovakian *sokol* falcon]

So·ko·to (sō′kō·tō) A province of northern

Nigeria; 39,965 square miles; capital, Sokoto.
So·ko·tra (sō·kō′trə) See SOCOTRA.
sol[1] (sōl) *n. Music* The fifth note of the diatonic scale. [See GAMUT]
sol[2] (sol) *n.* A former French silver or copper coin, equivalent to 12 deniers. [<OF <LL *solidus,* a gold coin <L, solid]
sol[3] (sōl) *n. pl.* **so·les** (sō′lās) A Peruvian monetary unit, equivalent to 1/10 libra. [<Sp., sun]
sol[4] (sol, sōl) *n.* A colloidal suspension in a liquid. [<(HYDRO)SOL]
sol[5] (sol) *n.* In alchemy, gold. [<L, sun]
Sol (sol) **1** The sun. **2** In Roman mythology, the god of the sun. [<L]
so·la (sō′lə) See SOLUS.
sol·ace (sol′is) *v.t.* **·aced, ·ac·ing 1** To comfort or cheer in trouble, grief, or calamity; console. **2** To alleviate, as grief; soothe; assuage; mitigate. —*n.* Comfort in grief, trouble, or calamity; also, that which supplies such comfort or alleviation: also **sol′ace·ment.** [<OF *solacier, solasier* < *solas* comfort <L *solacium*] —**sol′ac·er** *n.*
so·lan (sō′lən) *n.* The gannet, a bird related to the pelicans. Also **so·land** (sō′lənd, -lən), **solan goose.** [<ON *sūla* the gannet]
sol·a·na·ceous (sol′ə·nā′shəs) *adj. Bot.* Pertaining or belonging to a widely distributed family (*Solanaceae*) of frequently narcotic poisonous plants, the nightshade family, having colorless juice and alternate simple leaves. The family includes belladonna, tobacco, eggplant, and potato. [<NL <L *solanum* nightshade]
so·lan·der (sə·lan′dər) *n.* A hinged case or box, usually in the form of a book, adapted to hold a variety of objects, as jewelry, cigarettes, writing materials, pamphlets, maps, rare books and the like. [after Daniel C. *Solander,* 1736–82, English inventor born in Sweden]
so·la·no (sō·lä′nō) *n.* A hot, violent, southeasterly wind of the Mediterranean. [<Sp. <L *sol* sun]
so·la·num (sə·lā′nəm) *n.* Any of a genus (*Solanum*) of herbs and shrubs, the nightshades, typifying the family *Solanaceae,* especially *S. tuberosum,* the common potato. [<NL <L, nightshade]
so·lar (sō′lər) *adj.* **1** Pertaining to, proceeding from, or connected with the sun. **2** Affected, determined, or measured by the sun. **3** Operated by the action of the sun's rays: a *solar* engine. [<L *solaris* < *sol* sun]
solar constant The amount of solar energy falling on one square centimeter of the earth's surface at normal incidence, having a mean value of 1.92 small calories per minute.
solar energy Energy radiated by the sun, the primary source of chemical and other forms of energy, but utilized directly in only minor applications.
so·lar·im·e·ter (sō′lə·rim′ə·tər) *n.* An instrument for measuring solar radiation.
so·lar·i·um (sō·lâr′ē·əm) *n. pl.* **·i·a** (-ē·ə) A room or enclosed porch exposed to the sun's rays, as in a sanatorium. [<L]
so·lar·i·za·tion (sō′lər·ə·zā′shən, -ī·zā′-) *n.* **1** Exposure to the sun's rays. **2** *Phot.* Injury to a sensitized film resulting from overexposure to strong light, or from overprinting.
so·lar·ize (sō′lə·rīz) *v.* **·ized, ·iz·ing** *v.t.* **1** To affect or injure by the action of the sun's rays. **2** *Phot.* To overexpose. —*v.i.* **3** *Phot.* To be overexposed.
solar month A twelfth of a solar year; the time during which the sun is passing through one of the signs of the zodiac.
solar myth A primitive etiological story explaining symbolically some natural phenomenon of the sun; also, a folk tale arising among an agricultural people explaining or symbolizing the power or influence of the sun.
solar plexus 1 *Anat.* The large network of the sympathetic nervous system, found behind the stomach, and containing important ganglia serving the abdominal viscera. **2** *Colloq.* The pit of the stomach.
solar system The sun and the heavenly bodies that revolve about it.
solar time See under TIME.
solar wind The streams of charged particles emanating outward in all directions from the surface of the sun.
solar year See under YEAR.
sol·ate (sol′āt) *v.i.* **·at·ed, ·at·ing** *Chem.* To change from a gel to a sol. [<SOL[4] + -ATE[1]] —**so·la·tion** (sə·lā′shən) *n.*
so·la·ti·um (sə·lā′shē·əm) *n. pl.* **·ti·a** (-shē·ə) **1** Compensation; solace. **2** *Law* Compensation for injury to the feelings as distinguished from pecuniary loss or physical suffering. [<L, var. of *solacium* solace]
sold (sōld) Past tense and past participle of SELL.
sol·dan (sol′dən) *n. Archaic* A ruler or sovereign of a Moslem country, especially Egypt: also spelled *suldan, soudan.* [<OF *soudan* <Arabic *sulṭān* king, sovereign]
sol·der (sod′ər) *n.* **1** A fusible metal or alloy used for joining metallic surfaces or margins: applied in a melted state, either as a **hard solder,** melting only at a red heat, or as a **soft solder,** melting below a red heat. **2** Anything that unites or cements. —*v.t.* **1** To unite or repair with solder. **2** To join together; bind. —*v.i.* **3** To work with solder. **4** To be united by or as by solder. [<OF *soldure* < *souder* make hard <L *solidare* < *solidus* firm, hard] —**sol′der·er** *n.*
sol·dier (sōl′jər) *n.* **1** A person serving in an army. **2** A private in an army, as distinguished from a commissioned officer. **3** A brave, skilful, or experienced warrior. **4** One who serves loyally in any cause. **5** *Colloq.* One who makes a show of working but does little; a shirker; malingerer. **6** *Entomol.* **a** An asexual form (neuter or worker) of a termite or white ant, in which the head and jaws are largely developed, and whose office is to defend the community. **b** A similar neuter of certain true ants. See synonyms under ARMY. —*v.i.* **1** To be a soldier; perform military service. **2** To make a show of working; shirk; malinger. [<OF < *soude* pay, wages <LL *solidus.* See SOL[2].]
sol·dier·ly (sōl′jər·lē) *adj.* Like a true soldier; brave; martial. See synonyms under WARLIKE.
soldier of fortune A military adventurer; a soldier who serves where fortune summons him.
Soldier's Medal A decoration in the form of a bronze octagon on which is displayed an eagle standing on fasces between two groups of stars: awarded to any member of the U.S. Army, or of a military organization connected with it, for heroism not involving actual conflict with the enemy.
sol·dier·y (sōl′jər·ē) *n. pl.* **·dier·ies 1** Soldiers collectively. **2** Military service.
sol·do (sol′dō, *Ital.* sôl′dō) *n. pl.* **·di** (-dē) A small Italian copper coin worth, generally, one twentieth of a lira. [<Ital. <LL *solidus,* a gold coin <L, solid]
sole[1] (sōl) *n.* **1** The bottom surface of the foot. ◆ Collateral adjectives: *plantar, volar*[2]. **2** The bottom surface of a shoe, boot, etc. **3** The lower part of a thing, or the part on which it rests when standing; especially, the bottom part of a plowshare. **4** The bottom part of the head of a golf club. —*v.t.* **soled, sol·ing 1** To furnish with a sole; resole, as a shoe. **2** In golf, to allow (the clubhead) to rest flat on the ground, just behind the ball. ◆ Homophone: *soul.* [<OF <Med. L *sola,* var. of L *solea* a sandal]
sole[2] (sōl) *n.* **1** Any of several flatfishes allied to the flounders, having a small mouth and small eyes set close together on one side of the head; especially, the common **European sole** (*Solea solea*), highly esteemed as food, and the **American sole** (genus *Achirus*), common on the Atlantic coast of the United States. **2** One of various flounders, as *Psettichthys melanostictus,* a food fish of the Pacific coast of the United States. ◆ Homophone: *soul.* [<OF <L *solea*]
sole[3] (sōl) *adj.* **1** Being alone or the only one; existing or acting without another; only; individual. **2** *Law* **a** Unmarried; single: feme *sole* (an unmarried woman). **b** Having exclusive rights; absolute: opposed to *joint*: a *sole* tenant. **3** *Archaic* Solitary. See synonyms under SOLITARY. ◆ Homophone: *soul.* [<OF *sol* <L *solus* alone]
sol·e·cism (sol′ə·siz′əm) *n.* **1** A violation of grammatical rules or of the approved idiomatic usage of language. **2** Any impropriety or incongruity. [<L *soloecismus* <Gk. *soloikismos* < *soloikos* speaking incorrectly < *Soloi,* a Cilician town whose people spoke a substandard Attic dialect] —**sol′e·cist** *n.* —**sol′e·cis′tic** or **·ti·cal** *adj.*
sol·e·cize (sol′ə·sīz) *v.i.* **·cized, ·ciz·ing** *Rare* To use solecisms. Also *Brit.* **sol′e·cise.**
sole·ly (sōl′lē) *adv.* **1** By oneself or itself alone; singly. **2** Completely; entirely. **3** Without exception; exclusively.
sol·emn (sol′əm) *adj.* **1** Characterized by majesty, mystery, or power; exciting grave or serious thought; impressive; awe-inspiring. **2** Characterized by ceremonial observances; religious; sacred. **3** Marked by gravity; serious; earnest; also, affectedly serious. **4** *Law* Done in due form of law; executed formally: a *solemn* protest. **5** *Obs.* Of great reputation, dignity, or importance. **6** *Obs.* Somber; sober: said of color. See synonyms under AWFUL, SEDATE, SERIOUS. [<OF *solemne* <L *solemnis*] —**sol′em·ness, sol′emn·ness** *n.* —**sol′emn·ly** *adv.*
so·lem·ni·ty (sə·lem′nə·tē) *n. pl.* **·ties 1** The state or quality of being solemn; solemn feeling; gravity; reverence. **2** A rite expressive of religious reverence; also, any ceremonious observance. **3** A thing of a solemn or serious nature. **4** Mock seriousness; affected gravity. **5** *Law* A formality to be seriously observed and requisite to the validity or legality of an act. See synonyms under SACRAMENT.
sol·em·nize (sol′əm·nīz) *v.t.* **·nized, ·niz·ing 1** To perform as a ceremony or solemn rite, or according to legal or ritual forms: to *solemnize* a marriage. **2** To dignify as with a ceremony; celebrate. **3** To make solemn, grave, or serious. Also *Brit.* **sol′em·nise.** See synonyms under CELEBRATE. —**sol′em·ni·za′tion** *n.* —**sol′em·niz′er** *n.*
Solemn League and Covenant See under COVENANT.
so·le·noid (sō′lə·noid) *n. Electr.* A conducting wire in the form of a cylindrical coil or helix, capable of setting up a magnetic field by the passage through it of an electric current. [<Gk. *sōlēn* a channel + -OID] —**so′le·noi′dal** *adj.* —**so′le·noi′dal·ly** *adv.*

SOLENOID

So·lent (sō′lənt), **The** A strait between the Isle of Wight and Southampton, England; 3/4 to 5 miles wide, 15 miles long.
sol·er·et (sol′ə·ret′) See SOLLERET.
sole trader See FEME-SOLE TRADER.
So·leure (sô·lœr′) The French name for SOLOTHURN.
sol-fa (sōl′fä′) *Music v.t.* & *v.i.* **-faed, -fa·ing** To sing syllables instead of words to (notes); sing solfeggi. —*n.* **1** Syllables collectively used in solmization; the act of singing them. **2** Rarely, a scale. —**tonic sol-fa** See TONIC. [<Ital. *solfa* the gamut. See GAMUT.] —**sol′-fa′ist** *n.*
sol·fa·ta·ra (sōl′fä·tä′rä) *n. Geol.* An area or phase of volcanic action characterized by the escape of steam, various gases, and sublimates. [<Ital., a dormant crater near Naples, Italy < *solfo* sulfur] —**sol′fa·ta′ric** *adj.*
sol·feg·gio (sōl·fej′ō) *n. pl.* **·feg·gi** (-fej′ē) or **·feg·gios** *Music* **1** A singing exercise of runs, broken chords, etc., sung either to different syllables or all to the same syllable or vowel. **2** Solmization. [<Ital. < *solfa.* See SOL-FA.]
sol·fe·ri·no (sol′fe·rē′nō) *n.* **1** A bright purplish red. **2** Fuchsin. [from *Solferino*; named in honor of a battle fought there in 1859]
Sol·fe·ri·no (sōl′fā·rē′nō) A village in northern Italy; scene of a French and Sardinian victory over Austria, 1859.
so·lic·it (sə·lis′it) *v.t.* **1** To ask for earnestly; seek to obtain by persuasion or entreaty. **2** To beg or entreat (a person) persistently. **3** To influence to action; tempt; especially, to entice (one) to an unlawful or immoral act. —*v.i.* **4** To make petition or solicitation. See synonyms under ASK, PLEAD. [<OF *solliciter* <L *sollicitare* agitate]
so·lic·i·ta·tion (sə·lis′ə·tā′shən) *n.* **1** Importunity; the act of soliciting. **2** An attempt to entice.
so·lic·i·tor (sə·lis′ə·tər) *n.* **1** A person who does any kind of soliciting; especially, one who solicits gifts of money or subscriptions to magazines. **2** The legal advisor to certain branches of the public service. **3** In England, a lawyer who may advise clients or who prepares cases for presentation in court, but who may appear as an advocate in the lower courts only. See BARRISTER. Also **so·lic′i·ter.** —**so·lic′i·tor·ship′** *n.*

Solicitor General *pl.* **Solicitors General** 1 In the United States, an officer who ranks after the Attorney General, and, in the absence of the latter, acts in his place. 2 The principal law officer in some of the States, corresponding to the Attorney General in others. 3 In England, a law officer of the Crown, ranking next after the Attorney General.

so·lic·i·tous (sə·lis′ə·təs) *adj.* 1 Full of anxiety or concern, as for the attainment of something. 2 Full of eager desire; willing. See synonyms under URGENT. —**so·lic′i·tous·ly** *adv.* —**so·lic′i·tous·ness** *n.*

so·lic·i·tude (sə·lis′ə·to͞od, -tyo͞od) *n.* 1 The state of being solicitous; uneasiness of mind. 2 That which makes one solicitous. See synonyms under ANXIETY, CARE.

sol·id (sol′id) *adj.* 1 Having its constituent particles so firmly coherent as to resist stress; compact, firm, and unyielding: opposed to *fluid.* 2 Substantial; firm and stable. 3 Filling the whole of the space occupied by its apparent form; completely filled; not hollow. 4 Having no aperture or crevice; compact. 5 Manifesting strength and firmness; not weak or sickly; sound. 6 Characterized by reality; substantial or satisfactory. 7 Exhibiting united and unbroken characteristics, opinions, etc.; being or acting in unison; unanimous: the *solid* vote; This county is *solid* for the Democratic party; also, blindly or unreasonably partisan. 8 Financially sound or safe. 9 *U.S. Colloq.* Certain and safe in approval and support: They were *solid* with the boss. 10 Having or relating to the three dimensions of length, breadth, and thickness. 11 Written without a hyphen: said of a compound word. See SOLIDEME. 12 Cubic in shape: a *solid* yard. 13 Unadulterated; unalloyed: *solid* gold. 14 Carrying weight or conviction: a *solid* argument. 15 Serious; reliable; exhibiting sound judgment: a *solid* citizen. 16 Continuous; unbroken: a *solid* hour. 17 *Printing* Having no leads or slugs between the lines; not open. See synonyms under FIRM[1], HARD, IMPENETRABLE. —*n.* 1 A mass of matter of which the shape cannot be changed permanently and greatly without fracture. 2 A magnitude that has length, breadth, and thickness, as a cone, cube, pyramid, prism, or sphere. [<F *solide* <L *solidus*] —**sol′id·ly** *adv.* —**sol′id·ness** *n.*

sol·i·da·go (sol′ə·dā′gō) *n. pl.* **·gos** Any of a large North American genus *(Solidago)* of perennial plants of the composite family; a goldenrod: the State flower of Alabama, Kentucky, and Nebraska. [<NL <L *solidare* strengthen; with ref. to its alleged curative powers]

solid angle See under ANGLE.

sol·i·dar·i·ty (sol′ə·dar′ə·tē) *n. pl.* **·ties** Coherence and oneness in nature, relations, or interests, as of a race, class, etc.

sol·i·dar·y (sol′ə·der′ē) *adj.* United in nature or interests.

sol·i·deme (sol′ə·dēm) *n.* A solid compound word. Compare HYPHEME. [<SOLID + *-eme,* as in *phoneme*]

solid geometry That part of geometry which includes all three dimensions of space in its reasoning.

so·lid·i·fy (sə·lid′ə·fī) *v.t. & v.i.* **·fied, ·fy·ing** 1 To make or become solid, hard, firm, or compact, as water crystallizing into ice. 2 To bring or come together in unity. —**so·lid′i·fi·ca′tion** *n.*

so·lid·i·ty (sə·lid′ə·tē) *n. pl.* **·ties** 1 The quality or state of being solid; the property of occupying space; extension in the three dimensions of space; incompressibility. 2 Mental, moral, or financial soundness; substantial or reliable character or quality; firm standing; stability. 3 *Aeron.* The ratio of the total blade area of a rotor or propeller to the area of the disk swept by the blades. 4 *Geom.* Cubic contents; volume.

Solid South The Southern States of the United States, regarded as a political unit because of their support of the Democratic party.

solid state physics That branch of physics which deals with the physical properties of solids, especially as exhibited by atoms and molecules when in the solid state. It includes the study of crystal structure, elasticity, and friction, semiconductors and plastics, defects in materials, thermal properties, and a wide range of electrical and magnetic phenomena.

sol·i·dus (sol′ə·dəs) *n. pl.* **·di** (-dī) 1 A gold coin of the Byzantine Empire: first issued under Constantine, it remained the standard unit of currency during the Middle Ages, when it was called a *bezant.* 2 A medieval coin, equal to 12 denarii: often called *shilling.* 3 The sign (/) used to divide shillings from pence: 10/6 (10*s.* 6*d.*), being originally the long *ſ* written for shilling: sometimes also used instead of a horizontal line to express fractions: 3/4. See VIRGULE. [<LL]

sol·i·fid·i·an (sol′ə·fid′ē·ən) *n.* One who maintains that faith alone, without works, is the one requisite to salvation. —*adj.* Maintaining that faith alone is necessary to insure salvation; also, pertaining to such belief. [<L *solus* alone + *fides* faith]

so·lil·o·quize (sə·lil′ə·kwīz) *v.i.* **·quized, ·quiz·ing** To discourse to oneself; utter a soliloquy. Also *Brit.* **so·lil′o·quise.**

so·lil·o·quy (sə·lil′ə·kwē) *n. pl.* **·quies** A talking to oneself, regardless of the presence or absence of others; a monolog. [<LL *soliloquium* <L *solus* alone + *loqui* talk]

So·li·mões (sô′lē·moinzh′) The upper reaches of the Amazon river, extending from the Peruvian border to the Río Negro.

So·ling·en (zō′ling·ən) A city in North Rhine–Westphalia, West Germany.

sol·i·on (sol′ī′ən) *n. Physics* A small electrochemical cell so constructed that the movement of ions in solution serves to indicate minute changes in temperature, pressure, sound or light waves, acceleration, and other external conditions: used as an electronic control device. [<*ion(s in) sol(ution)*]

sol·ip·sism (sol′ip·siz′əm) *n.* The theory or belief that only knowledge of the self is possible, and that, for each individual, the self itself is the only thing really existent, and therefore that reality is subjective. [<L *solus* alone + *ipse* self] —**sol′ip·sist** *n.*

sol·i·taire (sol′ə·târ′) *n.* 1 A diamond or other gem set alone. 2 One of many games, especially of cards, played by one person. 3 A bird *(Pezophaps solitarius)* somewhat resembling the dodo but more slender and graceful: formerly a native of Réunion but now extinct. [<F <L *solitarius* solitary]

sol·i·tar·y (sol′ə·ter′ē) *adj.* 1 Living, being, or going alone. 2 Made, done, or passed alone: a *solitary* life. 3 Unfrequented by human beings; secluded; lonely; desolate. 4 Lonesome; lonely. 5 Single; one; sole: Not a *solitary* soul was there. —*n. pl.* **·tar·ies** A hermit; recluse; one who lives alone. [<L *solitarius* <*solus* alone] —**sol′i·tar′i·ly** *adv.* —**sol′i·tar′i·ness** *n.*

Synonyms (adj.): alone, companionless, deserted, lone, lonely, lonesome, only, single, sole, unaccompanied, unattended. *Antonyms*: manifold, many, multiplied, multitudinous, myriad, numerous.

sol·i·ter·ra·ne·ous (sol′ə·tə·rā′nē·əs) *adj.* Pertaining to the joint influence of solar and terrestrial forces, especially in relation to meteorological phenomena. [<L *sol, solis* the sun + *terra* the earth]

sol·i·tude (sol′ə·to͞od, -tyo͞od) *n.* 1 Loneliness; seclusion. 2 A deserted or lonely place; hence, a desert. [<OF <L *solitudo* <*solus* alone]

Synonyms: isolation, loneliness, privacy, retirement. See RETIREMENT, SECLUSION.

sol·ler·et (sol′ə·ret′) *n.* In medieval armor, a mounted warrior's steel shoe or one of its overlapping splints: also spelled *soleret.* [<OF, dim. of *soller, soler* a shoe <L *solea* sole of the foot]

sol·mi·zate (sol′mə·zāt) *v.i.* **·zat·ed, ·zat·ing** To sing by syllables; sol-fa.

sol·mi·za·tion (sol′mə·zā′shən) *n. Music* The use of syllables as names for the notes or tones of the scale. The syllables now commonly used are *do, re, mi, fa, sol, la, ti.* [<SOL + MI]

so·lo (sō′lō) *n. pl.* **·los** or **·li** (-lē) 1 A musical composition or passage for a single voice or instrument, with or without accompaniment. 2 Any of several card games, especially one in which the player who bids to take the highest number of tricks plays alone against the others. 3 Any performance accomplished alone or without assistance. —*adj.* 1 Composed or written for, or executed by, a single voice or instrument; performed as a solo. 2 Done by a single person alone: a *solo* flight. —*v.i.* **·loed, ·lo·ing** To fly an airplane alone, especially for the first time. [<Ital. <L *solus* alone]

So·lo (sō′lō) 1 A city in central Java: formerly *Surakarta.* 2 The longest river of Java, flowing 335 miles north, east, and NE from south central Java to the Java Sea, opposite Madura.

so·lo·ist (sō′lō·ist) *n.* One who performs a solo.

So·lo man (sō′lō) *Paleontol.* A species of early man *(Homo soloensis)* identified from a group of skulls found near the Solo river at Ngandong, Java, in 1931: it is thought to be an evolutionary advance over Pithecanthropus. Also called *Ngandong man.*

Sol·o·mon (sol′ə·mən) A masculine personal name. Also (diminutive) **Sol.** See also SALOMON. [<Hebrew, peaceful]

—**Solomon** King of Israel during the tenth century B.C.; noted for his wisdom and magnificence; a son of David.

Solomon Islands An archipelago in the SW Pacific east of New Guinea; about 16,500 square miles; the SE islands, including Guadalcanal, Santa Isabel, San Cristobal, Choiseul, New Georgia, and Malaita, comprise a British protectorate; total, 11,500 square miles; capital, Honiara, on Guadalcanal; the NW islands, including Bougainville, Buka and adjacent islands (total 4,320 square miles) are part of the Territory of Papua and New Guinea, administered by Australia.

Sol·o·mon's-seal (sol′ə·mənz·sēl′) *n.* Any one of several rather large perennial herbs of the lily family (genus *Polygonatum*), having tubular, six-toothed flowers and rootstocks marked at intervals by circular scars.

Solomon's seal A six-pointed star. See MOGEN DAVID.

So·lon (sō′lən), 638?–558? B.C., Athenian lawgiver; hence, **solon,** any wise lawmaker. —**So·lo·ni·an** (sə·lō′nē·ən) *adj.*

so long *Colloq.* Good-by.

So·lor Islands (sô·lôr′) An island group east of Flores, part of the Lesser Sunda Islands, Nusa Tenggara, Indonesia; total, 785 square miles.

So·lo·thurn (zō′lō·to͝orn) 1 A canton of NW Switzerland; 305 square miles. 2 The capital of Solothurn canton, NW Switzerland, on the Aar river: French *Soleure.*

sol·pu·gid (sol·pyo͞o′jid) *n.* A predatory, spider-like arachnid (order *Solpugida*) of warm climates that hides by day. [<L *solpuga, solipuga,* a kind of venomous ant or spider]

sol·stice (sol′stis) *n.* 1 *Astron.* The time of year when the sun is at its greatest distance from the celestial equator, either north or south, and seems to pause before returning on its course; either the **summer solstice,** about June 22 in the northern hemisphere, or the **winter solstice,** about December 22. 2 A culminating or high point; epoch; limit. [<F <L *solstitium* <*sol* sun + *sistere* cause to stand] —**sol·sti·tial** (sol·stish′əl) *adj.*

sol·u·bil·i·ty (sol′yə·bil′ə·tē) *n. pl.* **·ties** The state of being soluble, or the capability of being dissolved. Also **sol′u·ble·ness.**

sol·u·bil·ize (sol′yə·bəl·īz′) *v.t.* **·ized, ·iz·ing** *Chem.* To make soluble; specifically, to disperse (normally insoluble oils and fats) by the action of detergents and certain protein molecules. —**sol′u·bil·i·za′tion** *n.*

sol·u·ble (sol′yə·bəl) *adj.* 1 Capable of being uniformly dissolved in a liquid: Sugar is *soluble* in water. 2 Susceptible of being solved or explained. [<OF <L *solubilis* <*solvere* solve, dissolve] —**sol′u·bly** *adv.*

soluble cotton Nitrocellulose which is soluble in acetone, amyl acetate, ethanol, and certain other solvents: used in making nail polish and similar lacquers.

soluble glass Sodium silicate.

so·lum (sō′ləm) *n.* That part of a soil profile above the parent material in which the processes of soil formation take place; the soil proper. [<L *solum* ground]

so·lus (sō′ləs) *adj. Latin* Alone: used in stage directions. —**so·la** (sō′lə) *adj. fem.*

sol·ute (sol′yōōt, sō′lōōt) *n.* The substance dissolved in a solution as distinguished from the solvent.

so·lu·tion (sə·lōō′shən) *n.* **1** A homogeneous mixture formed by dissolving one or more substances, whether solid, liquid, or gaseous, in another substance, usually a liquid but sometimes a solid or a gas. **2** Any homogeneous mixture of which the solute is uniformly dispersed through the solvent, and whose composition may undergo continuous variation within certain limits. **3** The act or process by which such a mixture is made. **4** The act or process of explaining, settling, or disposing, as of a difficulty, problem, or doubt. **5** *Law* Payment or satisfaction of a claim or debt. **6** *Med.* The crisis of a disease; termination of a disease with critical signs. **7** *Math.* The answer to a problem; also, the method of finding the answer. **8** Separation; disruption: the *solution* of continuity. [<OF <L *solutio, -onis* < *solutus,* pp. of *solvere* dissolve]

solution pressure *Chem.* The pressure caused by the tendency of atoms or molecules to dissolve. In the case of metals it produces the current in a primary battery.

sol·u·tive (sol′yə·tiv) *adj.* **1** Loosening; laxative. **2** Soluble.

So·lu·tre·an (sə·lōō′trē·ən) *adj. Anthropol.* Pertaining to or characteristic of an Upper Paleolithic culture preceding the Magdalenian in western Europe: it is typified by a skilled technique in the making of bladed flint implements and by marked improvements in polychrome cave painting. Also **So·lu′tri·an.** [after *Solutré,* a village in central France, where remains were discovered]

solv·a·ble (sol′və·bəl) *adj.* **1** That may be solved. **2** That may be dissolved. —**solv′a·bil′i·ty, solv′a·ble·ness** *n.*

sol·va·tion (sol·vā′shən) *n. Chem.* A loose combination sometimes formed by the solute and solvent of a solution, as copper sulfate crystallizing from water.

Sol·vay process (sol′vā) A process of making soda by treating a concentrated solution of common salt with ammonia and carbon dioxide, yielding sodium bicarbonate, which is converted into soda by heat, carbon dioxide and water being expelled. [after Ernst *Solvay,* 1838–1922, Belgian chemist]

solve (solv) *v.t.* **solved, solv·ing** To arrive at or work out the correct explanation or solution of; find the answer to; resolve. [<L *solvere* solve, loosen] —**solv′er** *n.*

Synonyms: clear, decipher, do, elucidate, explain, guess, interpret, resolve, understand, unfold. *Antonyms*: confound, confuse, perplex.

sol·ven·cy (sol′vən·sē) *n.* The condition of being solvent.

sol·vent (sol′vənt) *adj.* **1** Having means sufficient to pay all debts; having more assets than liabilities. **2** Having the power of dissolving. —*n.* **1** That which solves. **2** A substance, generally a liquid, capable of dissolving other substances; that in which another substance is dissolved. **3** A medicine used for dissolving morbid concretions or obstructions in or upon some organ. [<L *solvens, -entis,* ppr. of *solvere* solve, loosen]

sol·vol·y·sis (sol·vol′ə·sis) *n. Chem.* Any of various double-decomposition reactions similar to hydrolysis, as the reaction of mercuric chloride with liquid ammonia to form a basic salt. [<L *solvere* loosen + Gk. *lysis* a loosening] —**sol·vo·lyt·ic** (sol′və·lit′ik) *adj.*

Sol·way Firth (sol′wā) An inlet of the Irish Sea on the boundary between England and Scotland; extends 40 miles inland; 20 miles wide at its mouth.

Sol·y·man (sol′i·mən) See SULEIMAN.

Sol·zhe·ni·tsyn (sôl′zhə·nē′tsin), **Alexander Isaevich,** born 1918, U.S.S.R. author.

so·ma (sō′mə) *n. pl.* **·ma·ta** (-mə·tə) *Biol.* The body of any organism, excluding the germ, or germ plasm. [<Gk. *sōma* body]

-soma See -SOME².

So·ma·li (sō·mä′lē) *n.* **1** A member of one of certain Hamitic tribes of Somaliland. **2** The Hamitic language of the Somalis. Also **So·mal** (sō·mäl′).

So·ma·lia (sō·mä′lyə) An independent republic in eastern Africa comprising the former United Nations Trust Territory of Somalia, administered by Italy, and British Somaliland; about 270,000 square miles; capital, Mogadishu. —**So·ma′li** *adj.* & *n.*

So·ma·li·land (sō·mä′lē·land), **French** A French overseas territory in eastern Africa; 8,494 square miles; capital, Djibouti.

so·ma·scope (sō′mə·skōp) *n.* A photographic device combining the principles of sonar, radar, and television to facilitate the detection of cancer and other diseases. —*v.t.* **·scope, ·scop·ing** To apply the somascope to (a patient). [<Gk. *sōma* body + -SCOPE] —**so·mas·co·py** (sō·mas′kə·pē) *n.*

so·mas·the·ni·a (sō′məs·thē′nē·ə) *n. Pathol.* General debility, accompanied by poor appetite, insomnia, and chronic exhaustion. [<Gk. *sōma* body + ASTHENIA] —**so′mas·then′ic** (-then′ik) *adj.*

so·ma·tal·gi·a (sō′mə·tal′jē·ə) *n. Pathol.* Pain due to physical causes: distinguished from *psychalgia.* [<SOMAT(O)- + Gk. *algos* a pain]

so·mat·ic (sō·mat′ik) *adj. Biol.* **1** Of or relating to the body, as opposed to the spirit; physical; corporeal. **2** Of or pertaining to the framework or walls of a body, as distinguished from the viscera; parietal. **3** Pertaining to those elements or processes of an organism which are concerned with the maintenance of the individual as distinguished from the reproduction of the species: *somatic* cells. [<Gk. *sōmatikos* < *sōma* body]

somatic cell *Biol.* A cell that assists with maintenance of the body rather than reproduction of the species: distinguished from *germ cell.*

so·mat·ics (sō·mat′iks) *n. pl. (construed as singular)* Somatology.

so·ma·tism (sō′mə·tiz′əm) *n.* Materialism. —**so′ma·tist** *n.*

somato- *combining form* Body; of, pertaining to, or denoting the body: *somatology.* Also, before vowels, **somat-.** [<Gk. *sōma, sōmatos* the body]

so·ma·to·gen·ic (sō′mə·tō·jen′ik) *adj. Biol.* Originating in the soma or body cells of an organism: said of variations due to the direct influence of environment: *somatogenic* or acquired characters. Also **so′ma·to·ge·net′ic** (-jə·net′ik). —**so′ma·to·gen′e·sis** *n.*

so·ma·tol·o·gy (sō′mə·tol′ə·jē) *n.* **1** The science of organic bodies, especially of the human body: embracing anatomy and physiology. **2** The branch of anthropology that treats of the physical nature of man. [< SOMATO- + -LOGY] —**so′ma·to·log′ic** (-tō·loj′ik), **so′ma·to·log′i·cal** *adj.* —**so′ma·to·log′i·cal·ly** *adv.* —**so′ma·tol′o·gist** *n.*

so·ma·to·pleure (sō′mə·tō·plōōr′) *n. Biol.* In the embryonic development of vertebrates, the outer of the two layers into which the mesoblast divides, together with its investing epiblast. [<SOMATO- + Gk. *pleura* side]

som·ber (som′bər) *adj.* **1** Partially deprived of light or brightness; dusky; murky; gloomy. **2** Somewhat melancholy; producing or denoting gloomy feelings; depressing. Also **som′·bre,** *Obs.* **som′brous.** See synonyms under DARK, SAD. [<F *sombre*; ult. origin uncertain] —**som′ber·ly** *adv.* —**som′ber·ness** *n.*

som·bre·ro (som·brâr′ō) *n. pl.* **·ros** A broad-brimmed hat, usually of felt, much worn in Spain, Latin America, and the southwestern United States: humorously called a *ten-gallon hat.* [<Sp. < *sombra* shade]

Som·bre·ro (sôm·brâr′ō) See ST. CHRISTOPHER, NEVIS, AND ANGUILLA.

some (sum) *adj.* **1** Of indeterminate quantity, number, or amount. **2** Limited in degree or amount; moderate. **3** Conceived or thought of, but not definitely known: *some* person. **4** *Logic* Part (more than one) but not all of a class. **5** *U.S. Slang* Of considerable account; worthy of notice; extraordinary: That was *some* birthday party. —*pron.* **1** A certain undetermined quantity or part; a portion. **2** Certain particular ones not definitely known or not specifically designated. —*adv.* **1** *U.S. Colloq.* In an approximate degree; as nearly as may be estimated; about: *Some* eighty people were present. **2** *Slang* Somewhat. ◆ Homophone: *sum.* [OE *sum* some]

-some¹ *suffix of adjectives* Characterized by, or tending to be (what is indicated by the main element): *blithesome, frolicsome, darksome.* [OE *-sum* like, resembling]

-some² *suffix of nouns* A body: *chromosome, merosome.* Also spelled *-soma.* [<Gk. *sōma* a body]

-some³ *suffix of nouns* A group consisting of (a specified number): *twosome, foursome.* [<SOME]

some·bod·y (sum′bod′ē, -bəd·ē) *pron.* A person unknown or unnamed: *Somebody* loves me. —*n. pl.* **·bod·ies** A person of consequence or importance: She thinks herself a *somebody.*

some·day (sum′dā′) *adv.* At some future time.

some·deal (sum′dēl′) *adv. Archaic* Somewhat.

some·how (sum′hou′) *adv.* In some way or in some manner not explained.

some·one (sum′wun′, -wən) *pron.* Some person; somebody. —*n.* A somebody.

som·er·sault (sum′ər·sôlt) *n.* A leap in which a person turns heels over head and lights on his feet. —*v.i.* To perform a somersault. Also spelled *summersault, summerset.* Also **som′·er·set.** [<OF *sombresault,* alter. of *sobresault,* ult. <L *supra* above + *saltus* a leap]

Som·er·set (sum′ər·set) A maritime county in SW England; 1,613 square miles; county town, Taunton. Also **Som′er·set·shire′** (-shir′).

Som·er·vell (sum′ər·vel), **Brehon,** 1892–1955, U. S. general.

So·meș (sô·mesh′) A river in northern Rumania and NE Hungary, flowing 145 miles NW to the Tisza river; including either headstream, 250 miles.

so·mes·the·sis (sō′məs·thē′sis) *n.* A diffuse, generalized awareness of the body and of bodily sensation. Also **so′mes·the′si·a** (-thē′·zhē·ə, -zhə). [<Gk. *sōma* body + *esthesis*] —**so′mes·thet′ic** (-thet′ik) *adj.*

some·thing (sum′thing) *n.* **1** A particular thing indefinitely conceived or stated. **2** Some portion or quantity. **3** A person or thing of importance. —*adv.* Somewhat: archaic except in special phrases, as **something like.**

some·time (sum′tīm′) *adv.* **1** At some future time not precisely stated; eventually. **2** At some indeterminate time or occasion. —*adj.* Former; quondam: a *sometime* student at Oxford.

some·times (sum′tīmz′) *adv.* **1** At times; occasionally. **2** *Obs.* Formerly; once.

some·way (sum′wā′) *adv.* In some way or other; somehow. Also **some way, some′ways′.**

some·what (sum′hwot′, -hwət) *n.* **1** An uncertain quantity or degree; something. **2** An individual or thing of consequence. —*adv.* In some degree.

some·when (sum′hwen′) *adv.* At some time.

some·where (sum′hwâr′) *adv.* **1** In, at, or to some place unspecified or unknown. **2** In one place or another. **3** In or to some existent place: opposed to *nowhere.* **4** Approximately. —*n.* An unspecified or unknown place.

some·wheres (sum′hwârz′) *adv. Chiefly Dial.* Somewhere: not considered an acceptable form in standard English.

some·whith·er (sum′hwith′ər) *adv. Archaic* To some indefinite or unknown place; somewhere.

some·why (sum′hwī′) *adv.* For some reason.

some·wise (sum′wīz′) *adv.* In some way or other: obsolete except in the phrase, **in somewise.**

so·mite (sō′mīt) *n. Zool.* A serial segment of the body of an animal, especially of an annelid or arthropod. [<Gk. *sōma* body + -ITE¹] —**so·mi·tal** (sō′mə·təl), **so·mit·ic** (sō·mit′ik) *adj.*

Somme (sôm) A river in northern France, flowing 150 miles west to the English Channel; scene of battles in World War I (1916, 1918), and in World War II (1940, 1944).

som·me·lier (sô·me·lyā′) *n. French* A wine steward.

som·nam·bu·late (som·nam′byə·lāt) *v.* **·lat·ed, ·lat·ing** *v.i.* To walk or wander about while asleep. —*v.t.* To walk over or through while asleep. [<L *somnus* sleep + AMBULATE]

som·nam·bu·lism (som·nam′byə·liz′əm) *n.* The act or state of walking during sleep. Also **som·nam′bu·la′tion.** —**som·nam′bu·lant** (-lənt) *adj.* —**som·nam′bu·list** *n.* —**som·nam′bu·lis′tic** *adj.*

somni- *combining form* Sleep; of or pertaining to sleep: *somnifacient.* [<L *somnus* sleep]

som·ni·fa·cient (som′nə·fā′shənt) *adj.* Promoting sleep; hypnotic. —*n.* A drug which induces sleep. [<SOMNI- + -FACIENT]

som·nif·er·ous (som·nif′ər·əs) *adj.* Tending to produce sleep; soporiferous; narcotic. Also **som·nif′ic.** [<SOMNI- + -FEROUS]

som·nil·o·quy (som·nil′ə·kwē) *n.* **1** The act of talking when asleep, especially in mesmeric sleep. 2 The words so spoken. [<SOMNI- + L *loqui* speak] — **som·nil'o·quist** *n.*

som·no·lence (som'nə·ləns) *n.* Oppressive drowsiness or inclination to sleep. Also **som'·no·len·cy.**

som·no·lent (som'nə·lənt) *adj.* **1** Inclined to sleep; drowsy. **2** Tending to induce drowsiness. [<F <L *somnolentus* < *somnus* sleep] — **som'no·lent·ly** *adv.*

Som·nus (som'nəs) In Roman mythology, the god of sleep: identified with the Greek *Hypnos.*

son (sun) *n.* **1** A male child considered with reference to either parent or to both parents. **2** Any male descendant. **3** One who occupies the place of a son, as by adoption, marriage, or regard. **4** A person regarded as a native of a particular country or place. **5** A male person who is characterized or influenced by some quality or thing or by a being representing some quality or character: a *son* of liberty; *sons* of Belial. Homophone: *sun.* [OE *sunu*]

Son (sun) Jesus Christ; the second person of the Trinity.

so·nance (sō'nəns) *n.* **1** A sound, as of music; also, a tune or air. **2** The state or quality of being sonant.

so·nant (sō'nənt) *adj.* **1** Sounding; resonant. **2** *Phonet.* Voiced: opposed to *surd, voiceless.* — *n. Phonet.* **1** A voiced speech sound. **2** A syllabic sound; in the Indo-European languages, a sonorant. [<L *sonans, -antis,* ppr. of *sonare* resound]

so·nar (sō'när) *n.* **1** A method of using underwater sound waves, at either audible or ultrasonic frequencies, for sounding, navigating, range finding, detection of submerged objects, communication, etc. **2** The equipment for accomplishing the transmission or reception of underwater sound waves. — *adj.* Of, or pertaining to, the equipment, personnel, or methods employed in underwater acoustic signaling. [<SO(UND) NA(VIGATION AND) R(ANGING)]

so·na·ta (sə·nä'tä) *n. Music* A composition for one or two instruments, written in three or four movements, each of which is distinct from the others in tempo and mood but akin to them in style and key. [<Ital. < *sonare* sound]

sonata form *Music* The outline upon which the construction of a movement, specifically the first, of a sonata, quartet, symphony, etc., is based. A movement written in sonata form falls into three sections, called *exposition,* or statement of themes, *development,* and *recapitulation.*

so·na·ti·na (son'ə·tē'nə) *n.* *pl.* **·ti·ne** (-tē'nā) *Music* A short or easy sonata. [<Ital., dim. of *sonata* SONATA]

son·der (zon'dər) *n. Naut.* A class of small yachts, of which the sum of the water-line length, extreme beam, and extreme draft must not be greater than thirty-two feet. Also **son'·der·class'** (-klas', -kläs'). [Short for G *sonderklasse* < *sonder* particular + *klasse* class]

sone (sōn) *n. Physics* A unit of loudness, equivalent to a simple tone having a frequency of 1,000 cycles per second at 40 decibels above the threshold of hearing. [<L *sonus* sound]

song (sông, song) *n.* **1** The rendering of vocal music; more widely, any melodious utterance, as of a bird. **2** A musical composition for the voice or for several voices. **3** A short poem whether intended to be sung or not; a lyric or ballad. **4** Poetry; verse. **5** A mere trifle: to sell something for a *song.* [OE] — **song'less** *adj.*
Synonyms: air, anthem, ballad, canticle, carol, chant, descant, ditty, hymn, lay, lyric, melody, poem, poesy, poetry, psalm, sonnet, strain. Compare synonyms for SING.

song and dance **1** A short theatrical act consisting of a song and dance, often having no connection with the rest of the program; especially, a vaudeville act. **2** *Colloq.* Any highly interesting or entertaining statement of no pertinence to the subject under consideration; a rigmarole.

song·bird (sông'bûrd', song'-) *n.* A bird that utters a musical call; an oscine bird.

Song Bo (sông' bō') The Annamese name for the BLACK RIVER, North Vietnam.

Song Coi (sông' koi') The Annamese name for the RED RIVER, North Vietnam.

song·ful (sông'fəl, song'-) *adj.* Full of song or melody.

Song of Solomon A Hebrew dramatic love poem in the Old Testament, attributed to Solomon; Canticles. Also **Song of Songs.**

song sparrow A common sparrow (*Melospiza melodia*) of the eastern United States, noted for its song.

song·ster (sông'stər, song'-) *n.* **1** A person or bird given to singing; one skilled in song; a poet. **2** A book of favorite songs.

song·stress (sông'stris, song'-) *n.* A female songster.

son·ic (son'ik) *adj.* **1** Of, pertaining to, determined or affected by sound: *sonic* vibrations. **2** Having a speed approaching that of sound. [<L *sonicus* < *sonus* sound]

sonic barrier *Aeron.* The transonic barrier.

so·nif·er·ous (sō·nif'ər·əs) *adj.* Producing or conducting sound. [<L *sonus* sound + -FEROUS]

son-in-law (sun'in·lô') *n.* *pl.* **sons-in-law** The husband of one's daughter.

son·net (son'it) *n.* **1** A poem of fourteen decasyllabic or (rarely) octosyllabic lines, originally composed of an octave and a sestet, properly expressing two successive phases of a single thought or sentiment. In the **Petrarchan,** or **Italian, sonnet** the rime scheme for the octave is *abbaabba,* followed by two or three other rimes in the sestet, with a slight change in thought after the octave. In the **Elizabethan,** or **Shakespearean, sonnet** the rime scheme is *ababcdcdefefgg.* **2** A short poem; an amatory lyric. See synonyms under SONG. — *v.t.* To celebrate in sonnets. — *v.i.* To compose sonnets. [<F <Ital. *sonnetto* <Provençal *sonet,* dim. of *son* a sound <L *sonus*]

son·net·eer (son'ə·tir') *n.* A composer of sonnets. — *v.i.* To compose sonnets.

son·ny (sun'ē) *n.* *pl.* **·nies** *Colloq.* Youngster: a familiar form of address.

son of liberty Originally, one who fought against the British in the American Revolution, or a member of any of various organizations formed to oppose the Stamp Act.

So·no·ra (sō·nô'rä, -nō'rä) **1** A state in NW Mexico; 70,465 square miles; capital, Hermosillo. **2** A river in Sonora state, flowing 250 miles south and SW to the Gulf of California.

so·no·rant (sə·nôr'ənt, -nō'rənt) *n. Phonet.* A voiced consonant of relatively high resonance, as (l), (r), (m), and (n), capable of constituting a syllable.

so·nor·i·ty (sə·nôr'ə·tē, -nor'-) *n.* Sonorous quality or state; resonance. Also **so·no'rous·ness.**

so·no·rous (sə·nôr'əs, -nō'rəs) *adj.* **1** Productive or capable of sound vibrations; sounding. **2** Loud and full-sounding; resonant. **3** *Phonet.* Sonant. [<L *sonorus* < *sonare* resound] — **so·no'rous·ly** *adv.*

son·ship (sun'ship) *n.* The state or relation of being a son.

Sons of Liberty The various patriotic societies, or members thereof, organized to oppose British rule in the American colonies.

son·sy (son'sē) *adj. Scot. & Brit. Dial.* Having sweet, engaging looks; happy; jolly; well-conditioned. Also **son'sie.**

Soo Canals (sōō) A colloquial name for the SAULT SAINTE MARIE CANALS.

soo·chong (sōō'chong', -jong') See SOUCHONG.

Soo·chow (sōō'chou', *Chinese* sōō'jō') See SÜCHOW.

soom (sōōm) *v. & n. Scot.* Swim.

soon (sōōn) *adv.* **1** At a future or subsequent time not long distant; shortly. **2** Without delay; in a speedy manner; also, with ease; readily. **3** With willingness or readiness: usually with *would as, had as,* etc. **4** In good season; early. **5** *Obs.* At once; immediately. [OE *sōna* immediately]

soon·er (sōō'nər) *n. U.S. Slang* **1** A person who goes before the appointed time to take up free public land, and thus obtains one of the most desirable sites. **2** One who makes an unfair and premature start.

Soon·er (sōō'nər) *n. U.S.* A nickname for a native of Oklahoma.

Sooner State Nickname for OKLAHOMA.

Soong (sōōng) Name of a distinguished Chinese family influential in politics, whose members include **Tse-ven,** born 1891, banker; **Ai-ling,** born 1888, the wife of H. H. Kung; **Ching-ling,** born 1890, the widow of Sun Yat-sen, and **Mei-ling,** born 1898, the wife of Chiang Kai-shek.

soop (sōōp) *v.t. & v.i. Scot.* To sweep.

soor (sōōr) *adj. Scot.* Sour.

soot (sŏŏt, sōōt) *n.* A black substance, essentially carbon from the combustion of wood or coal, as deposited on the inside of chimneys and other surfaces in contact with smoke. — *v.t.* To soil or cover with soot. [OE *sōt*]

sooth (sōōth) *Archaic adj.* **1** True; real. **2** Soothing; smooth. — *n.* Truth. Also spelled *soth.* [OE *sōth*] — **sooth'ly** *adv.*

soothe (sōōth) *v.* **soothed, sooth·ing** *v.t.* **1** To restore to a quiet or normal state; calm. **2** To mitigate, soften, or relieve, as pain or grief. **3** *Obs.* To yield assent to; agree with. — *v.i.* **4** To afford relief; have a calming or relieving effect. See synonyms under ALLAY, TEMPER, TRANQUILIZE. [OE *sōthian* verify < *sōth* truth] — **sooth'er** *n.*

sooth·fast (sōōth'fast', -fäst') *adj. Archaic* **1** Truthful; also, steadfast; loyal. **2** Real; true. — **sooth'fast'ly** *adv.* — **sooth'fast'ness** *n.*

sooth·ing (sōō'thing) *adj.* Calming; quieting, as a sedative; pacifying. — **sooth'ing·ly** *adv.*

sooth·say (sōōth'sā') *v.i.* **·said, ·say·ing** To announce the future, as a soothsayer. — **sooth'·say'ing** *n.*

sooth·say·er (sōōth'sā'ər) *n.* **1** One who claims to have supernatural insight and to be able to foretell events. **2** *Obs.* A truthful person: the original meaning.

soot·y (sŏŏt'ē, sōō'tē) *adj.* **soot·i·er, soot·i·est** **1** Blackened or stained by soot. **2** Producing or consisting of soot. **3** Black like soot. — **soot'i·ly** *adv.* — **soot'i·ness** *n.*

sooty grouse A blue grouse (*Dendrogapus fuliginosus*).

sop (sop) *v.* **sopped, sop·ping** *v.t.* **1** To dip or soak in a liquid. **2** To drench. **3** To take up by absorption: often with *up.* — *v.i.* **4** To be absorbed; soak in. **5** To be or become saturated or drenched. — *n.* **1** Anything softened in liquid, as bread. **2** Anything given to pacify, as a bribe. **3** Any soggy mass. [OE *sopp*] — **sop'py** *adj.*

So·phi·a (sō·fī'ə, -fē'ə) A feminine personal name. Also **So·phie** (sō'fē; *Dan., Du.* sō·fē'ə, *Fr.* sō·fē'). [<Gk., wise]

soph·ism (sof'iz·əm) *n.* **1** A false argument intentionally used to deceive. **2** The doctrine or method of the sophists. See synonyms under SOPHISTRY. [<L *sophisma* <Gk., ult. < *sophos* wise]

soph·ist (sof'ist) *n.* **1** A philosopher; a learned man; a thinker. **2** One who argues cleverly but fallaciously or unnecessarily minutely. — *adj.* Pertaining to the art or method of sophists, or to sophistry. [<L *sophista* <Gk. *sophistēs,* ult. < *sophos* wise]

Soph·ist (sof'ist) *n.* **1** A member of a certain school of early Greek philosophy, preceding the Socratic school. **2** One of the later Greek teachers of philosophy and rhetoric, who acquired great skill in subtle disputation under logical forms.

soph·is·ter (sof'is·tər) *n.* **1** A student in one of the later years of a course in some English universities. At Cambridge, students of the second year are called **junior sophisters** or **junior sophs,** and the third-year men **senior sophisters.** **2** A sophist or a Sophist.

so·phis·tic (sə·fis'tik) *adj.* Pertaining to a Sophist, sophists, or sophistry. — *n.* The art or method of the Sophists. Also **so·phis'ti·cal.** — **so·phis'ti·cal·ly** *adv.* — **so·phis'ti·cal·ness** *n.*

so·phis·ti·cate (sə·fis'tə·kāt) *v.* **·cat·ed, ·cat·ing** *v.t.* **1** To make less simple or ingenuous in mind or manner; render worldly-wise or artificial. **2** To mislead or corrupt (a person). **3** To adulterate. **4** To falsify (a text, statement, etc.) by unauthorized or deceptive alterations. — *v.i.* **5** To indulge in sophistry; be sophistic. — *n.* (-kit, -kāt) A sophisticated person. [<Med. L *sophisticatus,* pp. of *sophisticare* < *sophisticus* sophistic] — **so·phis'ti·ca'·tor** *n.*

so·phis·ti·cat·ed (sə·fis'tə·kā'tid) *adj.* **1** Worldly-wise; deprived of natural simplicity; disillusioned. **2** Pretentiously wise; possessing

superficial information. 3 Of a kind that appeals to the worldly-wise. 4 Very complicated in design, capabilities, etc.: said of mechanical and electronic devices.
so·phis·ti·ca·tion (sə·fis′tə·kā′shən) *n.* 1 The act of sophisticating; a quibble; a misrepresentation in reasoning or argument. 2 The state of being sophisticated. 3 Adulteration or falsification.
soph·is·try (sof′is·trē) *n. pl.* **·tries** 1 Subtly fallacious reasoning or disputation. 2 The art or methods of the Greek Sophists.
Synonyms: casuistry, chicanery, evasion, fallacy, hair-splitting, paralogism, prevarication, quibbling, sophism, subterfuge, trickery.
Soph·o·cles (sof′ə·klēz), 495?–406 B.C., Athenian tragic poet. — **Soph′o·cle′an** *adj.*
soph·o·more (sof′ə·môr, -mōr) *n.* In American high schools, colleges, and universities having a four-year course, a second-year student. [Earlier *sophomer* a dialectician < *sophom*, var. of SOPHISM (def. 1), because they studied dialectics; later infl. in meaning by Gk. *sophos* wise + *mōros* a fool]
soph·o·mor·ic (sof′ə·môr′ik, -mōr′-) *adj.* Of, pertaining to, or like a sophomore; hence, marked by a shallow assumption of learning or by empty grandiloquence; immature; callow. Also **soph′o·mor′i·cal.** — **soph′o·mor′i·cal·ly** *adv.*
So·phy (sō′fē) *n. Obs.* A title formerly given to kings of Persia: also **So′phi.** [<Persian *Safawi*, a Persian royal family]
So·phy (sō′fē) A diminutive of SOPHIA.
-sophy *combining form* Knowledge pertaining to a (specified) field: *theosophy.* [<Gk. *sophia* wisdom]
so·por (sō′pər) *n.* Deep lethargic sleep. [<L]
so·po·rif·er·ous (sō′pə·rif′ər·əs, sop′ə-) *adj.* Bringing sleep. — **so′po·rif′er·ous·ly** *adv.* — **so′·po·rif′er·ous·ness** *n.*
so·po·rif·ic (sō′pə·rif′ik, sop′ə-) *adj.* 1 Causing or tending to cause sleep. 2 Drowsy; sleepy; characterized by lethargy. — *n.* A medicine that produces sleep.
sop·ping (sop′ing) *adj.* Wet through; drenched; soaking.
sop·py (sop′ē) *adj.* **·pi·er, ·pi·est** Saturated and softened with moisture; soft and sloppy; very wet.
so·pran·o (sə·pran′ō, -prä′nō) *n. pl.* **so·pran·os** or **so·pra·ni** (sə·prä′nē) 1 A woman's or boy's voice of the highest range, usually extending from middle C upward about two octaves. 2 The music intended for such a voice; the treble. 3 A person having a treble or high-range voice, or singing such a part. — *adj.* Of or pertaining to a soprano voice or part. [<Ital. < *sopra* above <L *supra.* Related to SOVEREIGN.]
Sop·ron (shōp′rōn) A city in western Hungary near the Austrian border: German *Ödenburg.*
So·qo·tra (sō·kō′trə) See SOCOTRA.
so·ra (sôr′ə, sō′rə) *n.* A small grayish-brown North American rail (*Porzana carolina*), esteemed as food. Also **sora rail.** [? <N. Am. Ind.]
So·ra·ta (sô·rä′tä) See ILLAMPU.
sorb (sôrb) *n.* 1 The service tree, or the rowan. 2 The fruit of either of these. [<F *sorbe* <L *sorbus* service tree]
Sorb (sôrb) *n.* A Wend.
sorb apple The fruit of the service tree.
sor·be·fa·cient (sôr′bə·fā′shənt) *adj.* Conducive to absorption; absorptive. — *n.* A medicine that promotes absorption. [<L *sorbere* absorb + -FACIENT]
Sorb·i·an (sôr′bē·ən) *adj.* Of or pertaining to the Sorbs or Wends or to their language. — *n.* 1 A Sorb or Wend. 2 The West Slavic language of the Sorbs; Wendish.
sor·bite (sôr′bīt) *n. Metall.* A mixture of ferrite and cementite forming an important constituent of tempered steels. [after H. C. *Sorby*, 1826–1908, British metallurgist]
sor·bi·tol (sôr′bə·tōl, -tol) *n. Chem.* A white, sweetish, crystalline alcohol, $C_6H_{14}O_6$, found in mountain-ash berries, cherries, apples, pears, and some other fruits: it is used as a plasticizer and moistening agent and in the manufacture of ascorbic acid. [<SORB + -IT(E)[1] + -OL[1]]
Sor·bon·ist (sôr′bən·ist) *n.* A doctor of the Sorbonne; a student at the Sorbonne.
Sor·bonne (sôr·bôn′) 1 A former theological college founded in Paris by Robert de Sorbon in 1255–59. 2 The seat of the faculties of literature and science of the University of Paris.
sor·bose (sôr′bōs) *n.* A non-fermentable monosaccharide, $C_6H_{12}O_6$, obtained from sorbitol by bacterial action and important in the synthesis of vitamin C. [<SORB + -OSE[2]]
sor·cer·er (sôr′sər·ər) *n.* A wizard; conjurer; magician. — **sor′cer·ess** *n. fem.*
sor·cer·y (sôr′sər·ē) *n. pl.* **·cer·ies** 1 Pretended employment of supernatural agencies; magic; witchcraft. 2 Any remarkable or inexplicable means of accomplishment; witchery. [<OF *sorcerie* < *sorcier* <L *sors* fate] — **sor′cer·ous** *adj.* — **sor′cer·ous·ly** *adv.*
Synonyms: divination, enchantment, incantation, magic, necromancy, spell, voodoo, witchcraft.
sor·del·li·na (sôr′del·lē′nä) *n. Italian* A kind of small bagpipe.
Sor·del·lo (sôr·del′ō, *Ital.* sôr·del′lō), 1180?–1255?, Provençal troubadour.
sor·did (sôr′did) *adj.* 1 Of, pertaining to, or actuated by a low desire for gain; mercenary. 2 Of degraded character; vile; base; squalid. 3 Of a dull, dirty, or muddy hue. 4 Foul: the old sense. See synonyms under AVARICIOUS, BASE[2]. [<L *sordidus* squalid] — **sor′did·ly** *adv.* — **sor′did·ness** *n.*
sor·di·no (sôr·dē′nō) *n. pl.* **·ni** (-nē) *Music* A mute. [<Ital.]
sore (sôr, sōr) *n.* 1 A place on an animal body where the skin or flesh is bruised, broken, or inflamed; an ulcer or diseased spot. 2 A painful memory; distressing evil; trouble; grief; controversy. — *adj.* **sor·er, sor·est** 1 Morbidly tender; having a sore or sores. 2 Pained or distressed in mind; aggrieved; touchy. 3 Arousing painful feelings; irritating; distressing. 4 Causing extreme distress; severe; also, very great; extreme: He was in *sore* need of money. 5 *Colloq.* Offended; aggrieved; angry. — *adv. Archaic* Sorely. [OE *sār*] — **sore′ness** *n.*
so·re·di·um (sə·rē′dē·əm) *n. pl.* **·di·a** (-dē·ə) *Bot.* A scalelike structure of algal cells in a lichen, enveloped in a network of hyphae and capable of independent vegetative growth. Also **so·rede** (sō′rēd). [<NL <Gk. *sōros* a heap]
sore·head (sôr′hed′, sōr′-) *U.S. Slang n.* A disgruntled or offended person. — *adj.* Dissatisfied; discontented.
sor·el (sôr′əl, sor-) See SORREL[2].
sore·ly (sôr′lē, sōr′-) *adv.* 1 Grievously; distressingly. 2 Greatly; in high degree: His aid was *sorely* needed.
sor·ghum (sôr′gəm) *n.* 1 A stout canelike tropical grass (genus *Sorghum*) cultivated for its saccharine juice and as fodder, especially any of the varieties of *Sorghum vulgare.* 2 Molasses prepared from the sweet juices of the plant. [<NL <Ital. *sorgo*, ult. <L *Syricus* of Syria, where originally grown]
sor·go (sôr′gō) *n. pl.* **·gos** *Spanish* Any variety of sorghum cultivated for its sweet juices and for forage. Also **sor′gho.**
so·ri (sôr′ī, sō′rī) Plural of SORUS.
sor·i·cine (sôr′ə·sin, -sin, sor′-) *adj.* Pertaining or belonging to a subfamily (*Soricinae*) typical of a family (*Soricidae*) of small, mouselike mammals, the shrews, widely distributed in the northern hemisphere; shrewlike. [<NL <L *sorex, soricis* a shrew]
so·ri·tes (sō·rī′tēs, sō-) *n. Logic* A form of compound syllogism made up of successive coordinate members: Bucephalus is a horse; a horse is a quadruped; a quadruped is an animal; therefore Bucephalus is an animal. [<L <Gk. *sōreitēs* < *sōros* a heap] — **so·rit′·i·cal** (-rit′i·kəl) *adj.*
sorn (sôrn) *v.i. Scot.* To force oneself on others for food and lodging. — **sorn′er** *n.*
So·ro·ca·ba (sō′rōō·kä′və) A city in SE São Paulo state, Brazil.
so·ro·che (sō·rō′chā) *n. Spanish* Mountain sickness; puna.
So·rol·la y Bas·ti·da (sō·rō′lyä ē väs·tē′thä), **Joaquín,** 1863–1923, Spanish painter.
so·ror·ate (sôr′ə·rāt, sō′rə·rāt) *n. Anthropol.* The marriage of a man with the sister or sisters of his wife, or with other close female relatives. Compare LEVIRATE. [<L *soror* a sister]
so·ror·i·cide (sə·rôr′ə·sīd) *n.* 1 The killing of a sister. 2 One who kills a sister. [<LL *sororicidium* < *soror* a sister + *caedere* kill; def. 2 <L *sororicida*]
so·ror·i·ty (sə·rôr′ə·tē, -ror′-) *n. pl.* **·ties** A sisterhood; specifically, a women's national or local association having chapters in a secondary school, college, or university. [< Med. L *sororitas, -tatis*, <L *soror* a sister]
so·ro·sis (sə·rō′sis) *n. Bot.* A type of multiple fruit consisting of a fleshy mass formed by the merging of many flowers, as in the mulberry. [<NL <Gk. *sōros* a heap]
So·ro·sis (sə·rō′sis) *n.* A women's club, the first to be organized (1868) in America; hence, **sorosis,** any women's club or society.
sorp·tion (sôrp′shən) *n.* Any process by which one substance takes up and holds the molecules of another substance, as by absorption or adsorption. [<NL *sorptio, -onis* <L *sorbere*]
sor·rel[1] (sôr′əl, sor′-) *n.* 1 Any of several low perennial herbs (genus *Rumex*) with acid leaves, especially the common sorrel (*R. acetosa*). 2 The wood sorrel (genera *Oxalis* or *Xanthoxalis*). [<F *surele* < *sur* <OHG, sour]
sor·rel[2] (sôr′əl, sor′-) *n.* 1 A reddish- or yellowish-brown color. 2 An animal of this color. 3 A buck of the third year. Also spelled *sorel.* [<OF *sorel* < *sor*, a hawk with red plumage]
sorrel tree An American tree (*Oxydendrum arboreum*) of the heath family, with drooping clusters of white flowers and sour evergreen leaves.
Sor·ren·to (sôr·ren′tō) A port on the Bay of Naples, SW Italy.
sor·row (sor′ō, sôr′ō) *n.* 1 Pain or distress of mind because of loss, injury, or misfortune, the commission of sin, or sympathy with suffering; grief. 2 An event that causes pain or distress of mind; affliction; a trial; misfortune; woe. 3 The expression of grief; lamentation; mourning. See synonyms under GRIEF, MISFORTUNE, REPENTANCE. — *v.i.* To feel sorrow; grieve; lament; be sad. See synonyms under MOURN. [OE *sorg* care] — **sor′row·er** *n.*
sor·row·ful (sor′ə·fəl, sôr′-) *adj.* Sad; unhappy; mournful. See synonyms under BAD[1], PITIFUL, SAD. — **sor′row·ful·ly** *adv.* — **sor′row·ful·ness** *n.*
sor·ry (sor′ē, sôr′ē) *adj.* **·ri·er, ·ri·est** 1 Grieved or pained; affected by sorrow from any cause. 2 Causing sorrow; melancholy; dismal. 3 Pitiable or worthless; poor; paltry. 4 Painful; grievous. See synonyms under BAD, SAD. [OE *sārig* < *sār* sore] — **sor′ri·ly** *adv.* — **sor′ri·ness** *n.*
sort (sôrt) *n.* 1 Any number or collection of persons or things characterized by the same or similar qualities; a kind; species; class; set. 2 Form of being or acting; character; nature; quality; also, manner; way; style. 3 *Printing* A character or type considered as a portion of a font: usually in the plural. 4 *Obs.* Social rank, especially high rank. 5 *Obs.* A lot; destiny. — **of sorts** Originally, of various or different kinds; now, of a poor or unsatisfactory kind: used disparagingly: an actor *of sorts.* — **sort of** Somewhat. — *v.t.* 1 To arrange or separate into grades, kinds, or sizes; classify; assort. — *v.i.* 2 To agree; be suitable; correspond. 3 To associate; consort. [<OF *sorte* <L *sors, sortis* lot, condition] — **sort′a·ble** *adj.* — **sort′a·bly** *adv.* — **sort′er** *n.*
Synonyms (noun): character, condition, degree, denomination, description, kind, nature, order, race, rank, style.
sor·tie (sôr′tē) *n. Mil.* 1 A sally of troops from a besieged place to attack the besiegers. 2 A single trip of an aircraft on an assigned military or naval mission. [<F < *sortir* go forth]
sor·ti·lege (sôr′tə·lij) *n.* The act or practice of drawing lots; divination by lot; also, sorcery. [<OF *sortilege* <LL *sortilegus* a diviner <L *sors, sortis* a lot + *legere* pick, choose]
so·rus (sôr′əs, sō′rəs) *n. pl.* **so·ri** (sôr′ī, sō′rī) *Bot.* In ferns and fernlike plants, a cluster of spore cases (sporangia); a fruit dot. [<NL <Gk. *sōros* a heap]
S O S The code signal of distress adopted by the Radiotelegraphic Convention in 1912, and used by airplanes, ships, etc.; hence, any call for assistance.
So·sno·wiec (sô·snô′vyets) A city in SW Poland, important as an industrial center.
so-so (sō′sō′) *adj.* Passable; neither very good nor very bad; mediocre. — *adv.* Indifferently; tolerably.
sos·te·nu·to (sôs′te·nōō′tō) *Music adj.* Sustained or continuous in tone; prolonged or held. — *n.* A sostenuto passage or movement.

Also **sos'ti·nen'to** (-tē·nen'tō), **sos'te·nen'do** (-te·nen'dō). [<Ital.]

sot (sot) *n.* A habitual drunkard. [OE <OF <LL *sottus* a drunkard]

so·te·ri·ol·o·gy (sə·tir'ē·ol'ə·jē) *n.* The branch of theology that treats of salvation by Jesus Christ. [<Gk. *sōtērios* <*sōtēr* savior + -LOGY] — **so·te'ri·o·log'i·cal** (-ə·loj'ə·kəl) *adj.*

soth (sōth) See SOOTH.

Soth·ern (suth'ərn), **Edward Hugh,** 1859–1933, U. S. actor.

So·thic cycle (sō'thik, soth'ik) A period of about 1,460 years, based on an ordinary year of 365 days; or 1,461 years, based on a Sothic year of the Egyptians. See under YEAR. Also **Sothic period.**

So·this (sō'this) Sirius, the Dog Star. [<Gk. <Egyptian] — **So'thic** *adj.*

So·tho (sō'thō) *n.* A Bantu language of southern Africa.

so·tol (sō'tōl) *n.* Any one of a genus (*Dasylirion*) of yuccalike plants found in the SW United States. [<Mexican Sp. <Nahuatl *tzotolli*]

sot·ted (sot'id) *adj.* Drunk; besotted.

sot·tish (sot'ish) *adj.* Having the manner or character of a sot; stupefied with drink; hence, stupid; doltish. — **sot'tish·ly** *adv.*

sot·to vo·ce (sot'ō vō'chē, *Ital.* sôt'tō vō'chā) Softly; in an undertone; privately; under the breath. [<Ital., under the (normal) voice]

sou (sōō) *n.* A former French coin of varying value; now, colloquially, something trivial or negligible. [<F <LL *solidus,* a gold coin]

sou·a·ri (sōō·ä'rē) *n.* Any of several tropical American trees (genus *Caryocar*), yielding a durable timber known as **souari wood,** and edible nuts called **souari nuts** or butternuts; especially, *C. nuciferum.* [<F *saouari* < native name]

sou·bise (sōō·bēz') *n. French* A sauce of onions, butter, and white sauce: also **soubise sauce.**

sou·brette (sōō·bret') *n.* **1** An actress in light comedy; originally, a pert, intriguing lady's maid. **2** A frivolous or coquettish maid-servant. [<F <Provençal *soubreto* <*soubret* shy, coy] — **sou·bret'tish** *adj.*

sou·bri·quet (sōō'bri·kā) See SOBRIQUET.

sou·car (sou·kär') *n. Anglo-Indian* A native banker: also spelled *sowcar.*

sou·chong (sōō'chong', -shong') *n.* A variety of black tea, made from the youngest leaves of the earliest pickings, or the infusion made from it: also spelled *soochong.* [<F <Chinese *siao* small + *chung* plant]

sou·dan (sou'dən) See SOLDAN.

Sou·dan (sōō·dän') The French name for SUDAN.

souf·fle (sōō'fəl) *n.* A low whispering or blowing sound or murmur heard on auscultation: the respiratory *souffle.* [<F <*souffler* blow]

souf·flé (sōō·flā') *adj.* Made light and frothy, and fixed in that condition by heat: also **souf·fléed'** (-flād'). — *n.* A light, baked dish made fluffy with beaten egg whites combined with the yolks, and often with cheese, mushrooms, or other ingredients. [<F, orig. pp. of *souffler* blow <L *sufflare* <*sub-* under + *flare* blow]

Sou·fri·ère (sōō·frē·âr') **1** La Soufriere. **2** Either of two dormant volcanoes, one on Guadaloupe, French West Indies, the other on St. Lucia, The West Indies.

sough (suf, sou) *v.i.* To make a sighing sound, as the wind. — *n.* A deep, murmuring sound, as of wind through trees. — **to keep a calm sough** *Scot.* To be silent. [OE *swōgan* sound, roar, rustle]

sought (sôt) Past tense and past participle of SEEK.

soul (sōl) *n.* **1** The rational, emotional, and volitional faculties in man, conceived of as forming an entity distinct from, and often existing independently of, his body. **2** *Theol.* **a** The divine principle of life in man. **b** The moral or spiritual part of man as related to God, considered as surviving death and liable to joy or misery in a future state. **3** The emotional faculty of man as distinguished from his intellect: He puts his *soul* into his acting. **4** Fervor; emotional force; heartiness; vitality; nobleness: His music lacks *soul.* **5** The animating principle of a thing; an essential or vital element: Justice is the *soul* of law. **6** The leading figure or inspirer of a cause, movement, party, etc.: Lee was the *soul* of the Confederacy. **7** A person considered as the embodiment of a quality or attribute: He is the *soul* of generosity. **8** A living person; a human being: Every *soul* trembled at the sight. **9** The disembodied spirit of one who has died; a ghost. **10** In Christian Science, Spirit; Deity. **11** Among U.S. Negroes: **a** The awareness of a black African heritage. **b** A strongly emotional pride and solidarity based on this awareness. **c** The qualities that arouse such feelings, especially in black culture and art. **12** Soul music. **13** Soul food. — *adj.* Of or pertaining to soul (def. 11). ◆ Homophone: *sole.* [OE *sawol*] — **souled** *adj.*

Synonyms: mind, spirit. The *soul* includes the intellect, sensibilities, and will; beyond what is expressed by the word *mind,* the *soul* denotes especially the moral, the immortal nature. *Spirit* is used especially in contradistinction from matter; it may in many cases be substituted for *soul,* but *soul* has commonly a fuller and more determinate meaning. In the figurative sense, *spirit* denotes animation, excitability, perhaps impatience; as, a lad of *spirit. Soul* denotes energy and depth of feeling, as when we speak of *soulful* eyes; or it may denote the very life of anything; as, the *soul* of harmony. Compare MIND.

soul brother A Negro male: used by other Negroes.

soul food Any of various Southern foods or dishes popular with American Negroes, as fried chicken, ham hocks, chitterlings, yams, etc.

soul·ful (sōl'fəl) *adj.* Full of that which appeals to or satisfies the higher feelings; emotional; spiritual. — **soul'ful·ly** *adv.* — **soul'ful·ness** *n.*

soul·less (sōl'lis) *adj.* **1** Having no soul. **2** Heartless; unemotional. **3** Devoid of activity or expression. — **soul'less·ly** *adv.* — **soul'less·ness** *n.*

soul music A type of popular music strongly emotional in character and influenced chiefly by the blues and gospel hymns.

soul-search·ing (sōl'sûrch'ing) *n.* A deep examination of one's motives, desires, etc.

soul sister A Negro female: used by other Negroes.

sou mar·qué (sōō mär·kā') *French* **1** An 18th century copper coin of France. **2** Hence, a trifle; something of little value. Also **sou mar·kee'** (-kē'), **sou mar·quee'** (-kē').

sound[1] (sound) *n.* **1** The sensation of hearing, produced by stimulation of the auditory centers of the brain by vibratory waves propagated through the atmosphere or other elastic medium. **2** The vibrations that produce sound waves, having for the normal human ear frequencies from about 20 to 20,000 cycles per second. **3** Noise of any specified quality: the *sound* of bugles; any tone, voice, or note. **4** Significance; implication: The story has a sinister *sound.* **5** Sounding or hearing distance; earshot: We were within the *sound* of battle. **6** Mere noise without significance: full of *sound* and fury. **7** *Obs.* Rumor. — *v.i.* **1** To give forth a sound or sounds. **2** To give a specified impression; seem: The story *sounds* true. — *v.t.* **3** To cause to give forth sound. **4** To give a signal or order for or announcement of: to *sound* retreat; to *sound* the hour. **5** To utter audibly; pronounce. **6** To make known or celebrated: to *sound* a hero's fame. **7** To test or examine by sound; auscultate. — **to sound in tort** To act as or have the nature of a tort. [<OF *son* <L *sonus*]

Synonyms (noun): noise, note, tone. *Sound* is the most comprehensive word, applying to anything that is audible. *Tone* is sound considered from the point of view of quality or pitch, or as expressive of some feeling; *noise* is *sound* considered without reference to musical quality or as distinctly unmusical or discordant. In music, *tone* may denote a musical *sound* or the interval between two such *sounds,* but in the most careful usage the latter is now distinguished as the "interval." *Note* in music strictly denotes the character representing a *sound,* but in loose popular usage it denotes the *sound* also, and becomes practically equivalent to *tone.*

sound[2] (sound) *adj.* **1** Having all the organs or faculties complete and in normal action and relation; healthy. **2** Free from injury, flaw, mutilation, defect, or decay: *sound* timber. **3** Founded in truth; right; substantial; valid; legal. **4** Correct in views or processes of thought. **5** Solvent. **6** Profound, as rest; deep; unbroken; also, resting profoundly. **7** Complete and effectual; thorough. **8** Solid; stable; firm; safe; hence, trustworthy. **9** Based on good judgment. See synonyms under HEALTHY, SANE[1], STAUNCH, WISE[1]. [OE *gesund*] — **sound'ly** *adv.* — **sound'·ness** *n.*

sound[3] (sound) *n.* **1** A long and narrow body of water, more extensive than a strait, connecting larger bodies. **2** The air bladder of a fish. [Fusion of OE *sund* sea, a swimming and ON *sund* a strait, swimming]

sound[4] (sound) *v.t.* **1** To test the depth of (water, etc.), especially by means of a lead weight at the end of a line. **2** To measure (depth) thus. **3** To explore or examine (the bottom of the sea, etc.) by means of a sounding lead adapted for bringing up adhering particles. **4** To discover or try to discover the views and attitudes of (a person) by means of conversation and round-about questions: usually with *out.* **5** To try to ascertain or determine (beliefs, attitudes, etc.) in such a manner. **6** *Surg.* To search or examine, as with a sound. — *v.i.* **7** To measure depth, as with a sounding lead. **8** To dive down suddenly and deeply, as a whale when harpooned. **9** To make investigation; inquire. — *n. Surg.* An instrument for exploring a cavity; a probe. [<OF *sonder,* ? <L *sub-* under + *unda* a wave] — **sound'a·ble** *adj.*

Sound (sound), **The** See ÖRESUND.

sound barrier *Aeron.* The transonic barrier.

sound·board (sound'bôrd', -bōrd') *n.* A thin board, as in a piano or violin, forming the upper plate of a resonant box: also called *belly.*

sound·box (sound'boks') *n.* That part of a phonograph which by means of a sensitive diaphragm relays to the surrounding air the acoustic vibrations transmitted to it by the stylus in the record groove.

sound effects In motion pictures, radio, etc., the incidental and often mechanically produced sounds, as of rain, hoofbeats, fire, etc., required to heighten the illusion of reality.

sound·er (soun'dər) *n.* **1** One who or that which sounds or gives a sound. **2** An apparatus for taking soundings, as at sea. **3** A probe. **4** A telegraphic device for converting electromagnetic code impulses into sound, thus enabling messages to be interpreted.

sound·ing[1] (soun'ding) *adj.* **1** Giving forth a full sound; sonorous. **2** Having much sound with little significance; noisy and empty. — **sound'ing·ly** *adv.*

sound·ing[2] (soun'ding) *n.* **1** The act of one who or that which sounds, in any sense. **2** Measurement of the depth of water. **3** *pl.* The depth of water as sounded; also, water of such depth that the bottom may be reached by sounding.

sounding board **1** A structure or suspended dome over a pulpit or speaker's platform to amplify and clarify the speaker's voice. **2** Any device that gives force to an opinion or speech.

sounding lead The lead or other weight used on a sounding line; a plummet.

sounding line A weighted line marked at fathom intervals with pieces of leather, cloth, etc., used for determining the depth of water.

sound·less (sound'lis) *adj.* Having or making no sound; silent. — **sound'less·ly** *adv.* — **sound'·less·ness** *n.*

sound locator An apparatus for locating the position of aircraft by means of the sound waves which they emit.

sound picture A motion picture with a sound track.

sound·proof (sound'prōōf') *adj.* Resistant to the penetration or spread of sound. — *v.t.* To make soundproof.

sound ranging A method of locating the point of origin of a sound by checking time intervals as recorded from microphones of known position.

sound spectrograph See under SPECTROGRAPH.

sound track That portion along the edge of a motion-picture film which carries the sound record.
sound truck A truck with a mounted loud-speaker.
soup (so͞op) *n.* **1** Liquid food made by boiling meat, vegetables, etc., in water: distinguished from *broth,* which is usually strained. **2** *Phot.* A developer. **3** *U.S. Slang* Nitroglycerin. —**in the soup** *U.S. Slang* In difficulties; in a quandary. —**to soup up** *U.S. Slang* To supercharge or otherwise modify (an automobile) for high speed. [<F *soupe* <Gmc.]
soup·çon (so͞op·sôṅ′) *n. French* Literally, a suspicion; hence, a minute quantity; a taste.
soup kitchen A place where soup is served to the needy either free or at very low cost.
sou·ple (so͞o′pəl) *adj. Scot.* **1** Supple. **2** Swift.
soup·spoon (so͞op′spo͞on′) *n.* A spoon used in eating soup.
soup·y (so͞o′pē) *adj.* **soup·i·er, soup·i·est** Like soup in appearance or consistency.
sour (sour) *adj.* **1** Sharp to the taste; acid; tart, like vinegar: designating one of the four fundamental taste sensations. **2** Having an acid or rancid taste as the result of fermentation; also, pertaining to fermentation. **3** Having a rancid, acid smell or vapor; dank. **4** Misanthropic and crabbed; cross; morose: a *sour* person, a *sour* smile. **5** Cold and wet; unpleasant: *sour* weather. **6** Acid; harsh to crops: said of land. **7** Containing sulfur compounds: said of gasoline. —*v.t. & v.i.* To become or make sour. —*n.* **1** Something sour or distasteful. **2** An acid solution used in bleaching or in curing skins. **3** A treatment with such a solution. **4** A sour or acid beverage: a whisky *sour.* [OE *sūr*] —**sour′ly** *adv.* —**sour′ness** *n.*
source (sôrs, sōrs) *n.* **1** That from which any act, movement, or effect proceeds; an originator; creator; origin. **2** A place where something is found or whence it is taken or derived. **3** The spring or fountain from which a stream of water proceeds; a fountainhead; fountain. **4** A person, writing, or agency from which information is obtained. **5** The initiator of a payment, dividend, etc. [<OF, orig. pp. of *sourdre* rise <L *surgere*]
Synonyms: beginning, fountain, fountainhead, origin, spring. See BEGINNING, CAUSE. *Antonyms:* close, completion, conclusion, end, expiration, result, termination.
sour·crout (sour′krout′) See SAUERKRAUT.
sour·dine (so͞or·dēn′) *n.* **1** A mute, especially a trumpet mute. **2** A stop on the harmonium producing a soft effect. **3** An obsolete, soft-toned musical instrument. **4** In telegraphy, a silencer. [<F <Ital. *sordino* <*sordo* <L *surdus* deaf]
sour·dough (sour′dō′) *n.* **1** *Dial.* Fermented dough for use as leaven in making bread. **2** *U.S. & Can. Slang* A pioneer or prospector; especially, an Alaskan or Canadian prospector who carries fermented dough for use in making bread.
sour gourd **1** One of a genus *(Adansonia)* of trees with huge trunk, having a woody gourdlike capsule; especially, the Australian tree *(A. gregorii).* **2** The acid fruit of this tree. **3** The Madagascar baobab.
sour grapes That which a person affects to despise, because it is beyond his attainment: in allusion to the fable of the fox and the grapes.
sour·gum (sour′gum′) *n.* Any of several species of trees of the genus *Nyssa,* especially the blackgum tree and the tupelo.
Sou·ris (so͞or′is) A river in North Dakota and Canada, flowing 435 miles SE and north from SE Saskatchewan, through northern North Dakota, to the Assiniboine river in southern Manitoba.
sour·puss (sour′po͝os′) *n. Slang* A person with a sullen, peevish expression or character.
sour·sop (sour′sop′) *n.* **1** A tree *(Annona muricata)* of tropical America. **2** The pulpy, somewhat acid fruit of this tree.
Sou·sa (so͞o′zə), **John Philip,** 1854–1932, U.S. bandmaster and composer.
sou·sa·phone (so͞o′zə·fōn, -sə-) *n.* A large brass wind instrument, resembling a tuba, but circular and with flaring bell frontward: used in military bands. [after John P. *Sousa*]
souse[1] (sous) *v.t. & v.i.* **soused, sous·ing** **1** To dip or steep in a liquid. **2** To pickle. **3** *Slang* To make or get drunk. —*n.* **1** Pickled meats; especially, the feet and ears of swine, pickled or soused in brine; formerly, any salt pickle. **2** A plunge in water. **3** Brine. **4** *Slang* A drunkard; sot. [<OF *sous* <OHG *sulza* brine]
souse[2] (sous) *Archaic v.* **soused, sous·ing** *v.t.* To pounce upon. —*v.i.* To swoop suddenly, as a hawk: with *on* or *upon.* [<*n.*] —*n.* A swoop, as of a hawk on its prey; a downright blow or stroke. —*adv.* Suddenly; with a plunge or swoop headlong; all over. [Var. of SOURCE, in earlier sense of "arising"]
Sousse (so͞os) A port of eastern Tunisia: ancient *Hadrumetum*: formerly *Susa.*
sou·tache (so͞o·tàsh′) *n. French* **1** A very narrow, flat, decorative braid in a herringbone effect. **2** Mohair or silk rounded braid.
sou·tane (so͞o·tän′) *n.* A Roman Catholic priest's cassock. [<F <Ital. *sottana* <*sotto* under <L *subtus*]
sou·ter (so͞o′tər) *n. Scot.* A shoemaker; cobbler: also spelled *sowter.* Also **sou′tar.**
south (south) *n.* **1** That one of the four cardinal points of the compass which is directly opposite to north, and at the right hand of an observer who faces the sunrise. **2** The direction in which the point lies. **3** A region lying in this direction. **4** A south wind. —*adj.* **1** Situated in a southern direction relatively to the observer or to any given place or point. **2** Facing toward the south. **3** Belonging to or proceeding from the south. —*v.i.* **1** To turn southward. **2** *Astron.* To cross the meridian. —*adv.* **1** Toward or at the south. **2** From the south. [OE *sūth*]
South, the **1** The portion of the United States lying south of the Mason–Dixon line, and east and south of the western and northern borders of Missouri. **2** The Confederacy.
South Africa, Republic of An independent republic at the southern end of Africa, consisting of four provinces; 472,359 square miles; seat of government, Pretoria; seat of legislature, Cape Town. Formerly *Union of South Africa.*

South African **1** Pertaining to South Africa, especially to the Republic of South Africa. **2** A native of the Republic of South Africa; an Afrikander.
South African Dutch Afrikaans.
South African Republic A former state of South Africa, coextensive with the Transvaal.
South African War See BOER WAR in table under WAR.
South America The southern continent of the western hemisphere; about 6,900,000 square miles. —**South American.**
South·amp·ton (south·hamp′tən, sou·thamp′-) **1** An administrative county and the mainland part of Hampshire, southern England; 1,503 square miles; county town, Winchester. **2** A port and county borough of southern Hampshire, England, the major European terminal of most transatlantic shipping lines, at the head of **Southampton Water,** an inlet of The Solent in Southampton county, 6 miles long.
South Australia A state of southern Australia; 380,070 square miles; capital, Adelaide.
South Bass Island An island in Lake Erie, 15 miles NW of Sandusky, Ohio; site of Put–in–Bay; 3½ miles long, 1½ miles wide.
South Bend A city in northern Indiana.
south–bound (south′bound′) *adj.* Going southward. Also **south′bound′.**
south by east One point east of south on the mariner's compass. See COMPASS CARD.
south by west One point west of south on the mariner's compass. See COMPASS CARD.
South Carolina A SE State of the United States, on the Atlantic; 31,055 square miles; capital, Columbia; entered the Union May 23, 1788; one of the thirteen original States; nickname *Palmetto State*: abbr. SC —**South Carolinian**
South China Sea The arm of the Pacific between the SE Asian mainland and the Malay Archipelago.
South Dakota A State in the north central United States; 77,047 square miles; capital, Pierre; entered the Union Nov. 2, 1889; nickname *Coyote State*: abbr. SD —**South Dakotan**
South·down (south′doun′) *n.* One of a breed of hornless sheep with brown legs and faces: originally bred in the South Downs.
South Downs A range of hills in southern England, chiefly in Sussex, terminating at Beachy Head.
south·east (south′ēst′, *in nautical usage* sou′·ēst′,) *n.* That point on the mariner's compass midway between south and east; any region lying toward that point on the horizon. —*adj.* Of, pertaining to, toward, or from the southeast. —*adv.* Toward or from the southeast. —**south′east′ern** *adj.* —**south′east′ern·most** *adj.* —**south′east′ward** *adj. & adv.* —**south′·east′·ward·ly, south′east′wards** *adv.*
southeast by east One point east of southeast on the mariner's compass. See COMPASS CARD.
southeast by south One point south of southeast on the mariner's compass. See COMPASS CARD.
south·east·er (south′ēs′tər, *in nautical usage* sou′ēs′tər) *n.* A gale from the southeast.
south·east·er·ly (south′ēs′tər·lē, *in nautical usage* sou′ēs′tər·lē) *adj. & adv.* **1** Toward the southeast. **2** From the southeast: said of wind.
South·end–on–Sea (south′end′on·sē′) A resort and county borough in SE Essex, England.
south·er[1] (sou′thər) *n.* A gale from the south.
sou·ther[2] (sô′thər) *n. Brit. Dial.* Solder: also spelled *sowther.*
south·er·ly (suth′ər·lē) *adj.* **1** Situated in or tending toward the south. **2** Proceeding from the south. —*adv.* Toward or from the south. —**south′er·li·ness** *n.*
southerly buster See under BUSTER.
south·ern (suth′ərn) *adj.* **1** Pertaining to the south or a place relatively in the south. **2** Proceeding from the south, as a wind. [OE *sutherne*] —**south′ern·er** *n.* —**south′ern·ly** *adv.* —**south′ern·most** *adj.*
South·ern (suth′ərn) *adj.* Of or pertaining to the South.
Southern Alps A mountain range in west central South Island, New Zealand; highest peak, 12,349 feet.
Southern Cross A southern constellation having four bright stars in the form of a cross. See CONSTELLATION.
Southern Crown A southern constellation near Sagittarius; Corona Australis.
South·ern·er (suth′ərn·ər) *n.* A native of the South.
Southern Kar·roo (ka·ro͞o′) A plateau region in SW Cape of Good Hope Province, Republic of South Africa: also *Little Karroo.*
southern lights The aurora australis.
Southern Pines A resort town in central North Carolina.
Southern Protectorate of Morocco A former Spanish protectorate on the NW coast of Africa, part of Spanish West Africa; 10,039 square miles.
Southern Rhodesia See under RHODESIA.
Southern Territories **1** A division of southern Algeria; 769,827 square miles. **2** A former French military territory of southern Tunisia; about 17,800 square miles. *French* **Ter·ri·toires du Sud** (ter·ē·twår′ dü süd′).
south·ern·wood (suth′ərn·wo͝od′) *n.* A European plant *(Artemisia abrotanum)* allied to wormwood.
South·ey (suth′ē), **Robert,** 1774–1843, English poet; poet laureate 1813–43.
South Georgia A barren island between the Falkland Islands and Cape Horn, considered part of the Falkland Island Dependencies in the South Atlantic; 1,600 square miles. See FALKLAND ISLAND DEPENDENCIES.

South Holland A province of western Netherlands; 1,085 square miles; capital, The Hague. *Dutch* **Zuid·hol·land** (zoit′hô′länt).

south·ing (sou′thing) *n.* **1** The difference of latitude measured toward the south between any position and the last one determined. **2** *Astron.* **a** The passage across the meridian, in its diurnal motion, of a celestial object that culminates south of the zenith. **b** The attainment of this position, or the time at which it is reached. **3** Deviation or progression toward the south.

South Island The largest island of the New Zealand group; 58,093 square miles.

South Jutland The southern part of the Jutland peninsula, northern Germany and southern Denmark, coextensive with the former duchy of Schleswig.

South Korea See under KOREA.

south·land (south′land′) *n.* A land or region situated to the south. **—south′land′er** *n.*

South Mountain The northernmost part of the Blue Ridge, in western Pennsylvania, Maryland, and northern Virginia; highest peak, 2,145 feet; scene of a Union victory in the Civil War, Sept. 14, 1862.

South Orkney Islands An island group in the South Atlantic NE of the Palmer Peninsula; 240 square miles: claimed by Great Britain and by Argentina; administered by Great Britain as a dependency of the Falkland Islands.

South Os·se·tian Autonomous Region (o·sē′shən) An administrative division of northern Georgian S.S.R.; 1,428 square miles; capital, Staliniri.

south·paw (south′pô′) *Slang n.* **1** In baseball, a left-handed pitcher. **2** Any left-handed person or player. **—***adj.* Left-handed.

South Platte River A river in Colorado and Nebraska, flowing 450 miles east and NE to join the North Platte, forming the Platte River.

South Pole The southern extremity of the earth's axis; the 90th degree of south latitude, from which all terrestrial directions are north.

South·port (south′pôrt, -pōrt) A county borough on the Irish Sea in SW Lancashire, England, north of Liverpool.

south·ron (suth′rən, south′-) *adj.* Southern. **—***n.* A person who lives in the south. [Alter. of dial. E *southren,* var. of SOUTHERN; infl. in form by *Saxon, Briton,* etc.]

South·ron (suth′rən, south′-) *n. Scot.* An Englishman or native of southern Britain: formerly used by the Scots as a term of derision: also *Suthron.*

South Sandwich Islands An island group in the South Atlantic, included in the Falkland Island Dependencies; 130 square miles.

South Sea Islands The islands of the South Pacific Ocean.

South Seas **1** The South Pacific Ocean. **2** The seas of the world south of the Equator.

South Shetland Islands An archipelago in the South Atlantic, between South America and Antarctica: claimed by Great Britain, Argentina, and Chile; administered by Great Britain as a dependency of the Falkland Islands; 1,800 square miles.

South Shields A port and county borough of NE Durham, England, at the mouth of the Tyne on the North Sea.

south-south·east (south′south′ēst′, *in nautical usage* sou′sou′ēst′) *n.* That point on the mariner's compass midway between south and southeast. **—***adj. & adv.* Midway between south and southeast. See COMPASS CARD.

south-south·west (south′south′west′, *in nautical usage* sou′sou′west′) *n.* That point on the mariner's compass midway between south and southwest. **—***adj. & adv.* Midway between south and southwest. See COMPASS CARD.

South Vietnam **1** The Republic of Vietnam, comprising the former French colony of Cochin China and the southern part of the former Empire of Annam; 65,709 square miles; capital, Saigon. **2** Cochin China alone, now the southern part of the Republic of Vietnam; 24,750 square miles; capital, Saigon.

south·ward (south′wərd, *in nautical usage* suth′ərd) *adj.* Situated in or toward the south. **—***adv.* In a southerly direction: also **south′ward·ly, south′wards.** **—***n.* The direction of south; also, a region to the south.

South·wark (suth′ərk) A borough of London, England, on the south bank of the Thames.

South·well (south′wel, suth′əl) A town in central Nottinghamshire, England; known for its Norman cathedral.

south·west (south′west′, *in nautical usage* sou′west′) *n.* That point on the mariner's compass midway between south and west; any region lying toward that point on the horizon. **—***adj.* Of, pertaining to, facing, or toward the southwest; blowing from the southwest. **—***adv.* Toward or from the southwest. **—south′west′ern, south′west′ern·most** *adj.* **—south′west′ward** *adj. & adv.* **—south′·west′ward·ly, south′west′wards** *adv.*

Southwest, the The SW part of the United States: generally including Oklahoma, Texas, New Mexico, Arizona, and southern California.

South-West Africa A self-governing mandated territory on the Atlantic north of and administered by the Union of South Africa; 317,887 square miles; capital, Windhoek: formerly *German Southwest Africa.*

southwest by south One point south of southwest on the mariner's compass. See COMPASS CARD.

southwest by west One point west of southwest on the mariner's compass. See COMPASS CARD.

south·west·er (south′wes′tər, *in nautical usage* sou′wes′tər) *n.* **1** A wind, gale, or storm from the southwest. **2** A waterproof hat of oilskin, canvas, etc., with a broad brim behind to protect the neck: worn in stormy weather. Also **sou′west′er.**

south·west·er·ly (south′wes′tər·lē, *in nautical usage* sou′wes′tər·lē) *adj. & adv.* **1** Toward the southwest. **2** From the southwest: said of wind.

Southwest Semitic See under SEMITIC.

South Yemen, People's Republic of A republic on the southern coast of the Arabian peninsula, containing most of the territory of the former Aden and Aden Protectorate; about 110,000 square miles; capital Medina al-Eshaab.

sou·ve·nir (so͞o′və·nir′, so͞o′və·nir) *n.* A token of remembrance; memento. [<F, remember <L *subvenire* come to mind]

sov·er·eign (sov′rin, suv′-) *n.* **1** One who possesses supreme authority, especially a person or a determinate body of persons in whom the supreme power of the state is vested; a monarch. **2** An English gold coin equivalent to one pound sterling or twenty shillings, first issued by Henry VII. **3** A former gold coin of Austria. See synonyms under MASTER. **—***adj.* **1** Exercising or possessing supreme jurisdiction or power; royal. **2** Free, independent, and in no way limited by external authority or influence: a *sovereign* state. **3** Possessing supreme excellence or greatness; preeminent; paramount. **4** Superior in efficacy; potent: a *sovereign* remedy. See synonyms under IMPERIAL, PREDOMINANT. Also, *Poetic, sovran.* [<OF *soverain,* ult. <L *super* above. Related to SOPRANO.] **—sov′er·eign·ly** *adv.*

sov·er·eign·ty (sov′rin·tē, suv′-) *n. pl.* **·ties** **1** The state of being sovereign; supreme authority. **2** The ultimate, supreme power in a state. **3** A sovereign state. **4** The status or dominion of a sovereign. Also, *Poetic, sovranty.* **—popular sovereignty** The theory that the right to legislate and choose a government belongs to the body of the people.

So·vetsk (so·vyetsk′) A city on the Neman River in western European Russian S.F.S.R.: formerly *Tilsit.*

So·vet·ska·ya Ga·van (so·vyet′skə·yə gä′vən·y′) A port and naval base on the Sea of Japan, Russian S.F.S.R.

so·vi·et (sō′vē·et, sō′vē·et′) *n.* **1** In the Soviet Union, any of the legislative bodies existing at various governmental levels. See SUPREME SOVIET. **2** Any of various similar legislative bodies. [<Russian *sovyet* a council]

So·vi·et (sō′vē·et, sō′vē·et′) *adj.* Of or pertaining to the Soviet Union.

Soviet Central Asia The constituent Soviet republics of Russian Turkestan: the Kazakh, Kirghiz, Tadzhik, Turkmen, and Uzbek Soviet Socialist Republics; 1,541,530 square miles: also *Central Asia.*

soviet congress The administrative body of each constituent republic of the Union of Soviet Socialist Republics, empowered to adopt its own constitution based on the Union constitution: autonomous republics are governed by executive committees elected by the local Congress of Soviets.

Soviet Far East The easternmost part of Siberia, together with Sakhalin and the Kurile Islands, in Russian S.F.S.R.; 1,204,700 square miles.

so·vi·et·ism (sō′vē·ə·tiz′əm) *n.* The policies and principles of, or goverment by peoples' councils or congresses, especially as practiced in Soviet Russia. **—so′vi·et·ist** *n.*

so·vi·et·ize (sō′vē·ə·tīz′) *v.t.* **·ized, ·iz·ing** To bring under a soviet form of government. **—so′vi·et·i·za′tion** *n.*

so·vi·et·ol·o·gist (sō′vē·ə·tol′ə·jist) *n.* A student of the policies and history of the Soviet Union. **—so′vi·et·ol′o·gy** *n.*

Soviet Russia **1** The Union of Soviet Socialist Republics. **2** The Russian Soviet Federated Socialist Republic.

Soviet Union The Union of Soviet Socialist Republics.

sov·ran (sov′rən, suv′-), **sov·ran·ty** (sov′rən·tē, suv′-), etc. See SOVEREIGN, etc.

sow[1] (sō) *v.* **sowed, sown** or **sowed, sow·ing** *v.t.* **1** To scatter (seed) over land for growth. **2** To scatter seed over (land). **3** To spread abroad; disseminate; implant: to *sow* the seeds of distrust. **4** To cover or sprinkle. **—***v.i.* **5** To scatter seed. See synonyms under PLANT. [OE *sāwan*] **—sow′er** *n.* **—sow′ing** *n.*

sow[2] (sou) *n.* **1** A female hog. **2** *Metall.* **a** The connection between pieces of pig iron before breaking up. **b** The conduit to the pig bed for molten metal. [OE *sū, sugu*]

so·war (sō·wär′, -wôr′) *n. Anglo-Indian* Formerly, in the British-Indian army, an Indian trooper of the cavalry; a mounted orderly.

sow-bel·ly (sou′bel′ē) *n. U.S. Colloq.* Salt pork.

sow·bread (sou′bred) *n.* The cyclamen.

sow bug A small crustacean (family *Oniscidae*) found under logs and stones; a wood louse.

sow·car (sou·kär′) See SOUCAR.

sow·ens (sō′ənz) *n. Scot.* **1** Sour porridge made from the husks of oatmeal.

sowth (so͞oth) *v.t. & v.i. Scot.* To hum or whistle (an air) softly.

sow·ther (sou′thər) See SOUTHER[2].

sow thistle Any of a genus *(Sonchus)* of spiny plants, especially the common sow thistle.

soy (soi) *n.* **1** A small, erect herb *(Glycine soja)* of the bean family, growing in India and China and cultivated for forage. **2** Its edible bean, a source of oil, flour, and other products: also **soy·a** (soi′ə), **soy′bean′.** **3** A sauce prepared in China and Japan from soybeans that have been fermented and steeped in brine: also **soy sauce.** [<Japanese *soy, shoy,* short for *shōyū* soy]

so·zin (sō′zin) *n. Biochem.* Any protein normally contained in the body of an animal and forming a natural protection against germs. Also **so′zine.** [<Gk. *sōzein* save + -IN]

spa (spä) *n.* Any locality frequented for its mineral springs; a mineral spring. [from SPA]

Spa (spä) A resort town in eastern Belgium.

Spaak (spåk), **Paul Henri,** 1899–1972, Belgian and international statesman.

Spaatz (späts), **Carl,** 1891–1974, U. S. general.

space (spās) *n.* **1** An interval between points or objects; a limited portion of extension; distance; area. **2** The abstract possibility of extension; that which is characterized by illimitable dimension; continuous boundless extension in all directions. **3** An interval of time; period; hence, a little while. **4** An occasion or opportunity. **5** *Printing* A piece of type metal, less than type-high, used for spacing between lines; specifically, one less than one en in width. **6** One of the degrees of a musical staff. **7** One of the intervals during the transmission of a telegraph message when the key is open or not in contact. **8** Reserved accommodations, as on a train or airplane. **9** *Math.* A system of continuous, unlimited, corresponding points in a series; an ordered set of infinite numbers. **10** Outer space. See synonyms under PLACE. **—***v.t.*

spaced, spac·ing 1 To separate by spaces. 2 To divide into spaces. [<OF *espace* <L *spatium*] —**space'less** *adj.* —**spac'er** *n.*

Space, meaning for, pertaining to, or concerned with travel in outer space, may appear as a combining form in solidemes or as the first element in two-word phrases; as in:

space age **spaceman** **space sociology**
space crew **space patrol** **space suit**
spaceflight **space rocket** **space vehicle**

space band *Printing* In Linotype operation, an adjustable wedge-shaped metal strip used for spacing.
space-cab·in simulator (spās'kab'in) A chamber built to resemble the cabin of a spaceship, for testing human or animal reactions under physiological conditions simulating those in actual space travel.
space charge *Physics* 1 An electric charge uniformly distributed through a given space. 2 A grouping of electrons around the filament of a vacuum tube, imparting a negative charge which inhibits the free emission of other electrons.
space·craft (spās'kraft', -kräft') *n.* 1 Any vehicle, manned or unmanned, designed for flight in outer space. 2 Spacemanship.
spaced-out (spāst'out') *adj. U.S. Slang* Dazed or drugged, as by the use of narcotics.
space·flight (spās'flīt') *n.* Flight in outer space by a man-made object or vehicle.
space lattice *Physics* The characteristic arrangement of the atoms or structural units in a crystal, such that corresponding units are separated by constant intervals along any straight line drawn through their centers.

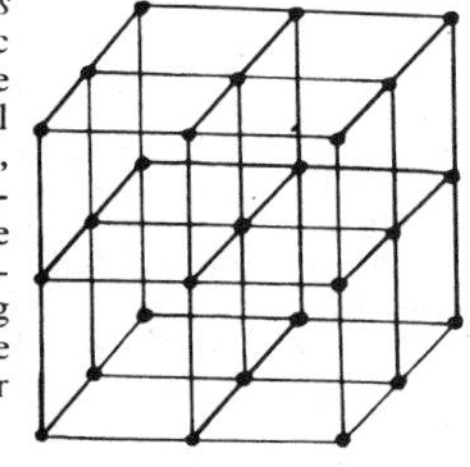
SPACE LATTICE

space·man·ship (spās'mən·ship) *n.* The science and art of space travel, especially as regards the design, construction, fueling, launching, and operation of vehicles and missiles equipped for flight beyond the earth's atmosphere.
space medicine The branch of aviation medicine which deals with the biological, physiological, and psychological aspects of travel in outer space.
space·port (spās'pôrt', -pōrt') *n.* A base for rockets and other spacecraft, including the equipment necessary for their testing, storage, maintenance, launching, etc.
space probe A spacecraft designed and equipped to obtain information of phenomena and conditions in outer space.
space·ship (spās'ship') *n.* Any of various vehicles designed for the transport of men and materials through outer space, especially between and among the planets.
space shuttle A vehicle used for transferring passengers and freight from earth to an orbiting space station.
space station A large, usually manned satellite orbiting the earth, used for observation, experiments, as a relay station, etc.
space time A four-dimensional continuum within which may be precisely located any magnitude having both extension and duration: it consists of three spatial coordinates and one coordinate of time. Also **space-time continuum.**
space travel Travel in regions above the earth's atmosphere or beyond its gravitational field, whether within or outside of the solar system.
spa·cial (spā'shəl) See SPATIAL.
spac·ing (spā'sing) *n.* 1 The arrangement of spaces. 2 A space or spaces, as in a line of print.
spa·cious (spā'shəs) *adj.* 1 Of indefinite or vast extent. 2 Affording ample room; capacious. See synonyms under LARGE. —**spa'·cious·ly** *adv.* —**spa'cious·ness** *n.*
Spack·le (spak'əl) *n.* A dry powder which, in the form of a paste, is used for filling cracks, holes, and other surface defects before painting and decorating: a trade name. —*v.t.* **·led, ·ling** To apply Spackle to (a crack, etc.).
spade[1] (spād) *n.* 1 An implement used for digging in the ground, ditching, cutting turf, etc., heavier than a shovel and having a flatter blade. 2 A tool or implement resembling a spade; specifically, a large chisel-like implement for flensing whales. 3 A heavy piece of metal at the end of a gun-carriage trail which helps to keep the carriage in position when the gun recoils. —**to call a spade a spade** To call a thing by its right name; speak the plain, uncompromising truth. —*v.t.* **spad·ed, spad·ing** To dig or cut with a spade. [OE *spadu*] —**spade'ful** *n.* —**spad'er** *n.*
spade[2] (spād) *n.* 1 A figure, resembling a heart with a triangular handle, on a playing card. 2 A card so marked. 3 The suit of cards so marked: usually in the plural. [< Sp. *espada* a sword <L *spatha* <Gk. *spathē*]
spade·fish (spād'fish') *n. pl.* **·fish** or **·fish·es** 1 A spiny-finned food fish *(Chaetodipterus faber)* of the Atlantic coast from Massachusetts to the West Indies. 2 The paddlefish.
spade·work (spād'wûrk') *n.* 1 Work done with a spade. 2 Any preliminary work necessary to get a project under way.
spa·di·ceous (spā·dish'əs) *adj.* 1 Of or like a spadix. 2 Of a clear brown or bay color.
spa·dix (spā'diks) *n. pl.* **spa·di·ces** (spā·dī'sēz) *Bot.* A spike or head of flowers with a fleshy axis, usually enclosed within a spathe. [<Gk. *spadix* <*spaein* break]
spae (spā) *v.t. Scot.* To foretell; divine. —**spae'·man** (-mən), **spae'wife'** (-wīf') *n.*
spa·ghet·ti (spə·get'ē) *n.* 1 A cordlike food paste, in size between macaroni and vermicelli. 2 Insulated cloth tubing through which wire is passed, as in a radio circuit. [<Ital., pl. dim. of *spago* a small cord]
spa·gyr·ic (spə·jir'ik) *adj.* Alchemical. Also **spa·gir'ic, spa·gyr'i·cal.** [<NL *spagyricus*; prob. coined by Paracelsus]
spa·hi (spä'hē) *n.* 1 Formerly, a Turkish corps of irregular cavalry; a member of such a corps. 2 One of a native Algerian cavalry corps in the French service. Also **spa'hee.** [< Turkish *sipāhi* <Persian *sipāh* an army. Cf. SEPOY.]
Spain (spān) A nominal monarchy in SW Europe; continental Spain alone, 189,626 square miles; including the Balearic and Canary Islands, 194,368 square miles; capital, Madrid: Spanish *España.*
spake (spāk) Archaic past tense of SPEAK.
Spa·la·to (spä'lä·tō) The Italian name for SPLIT.
spall (spôl) *v.t.* To break up; chip; prepare for sorting, as ore. —*v.i.* To chip at the edges, as a stone under pressure. —*n.* A chip, splinter, or flake, as from a stone. [ME *spalle.* ? Related to MLG *spalden* split.]
Spal·lan·za·ni (späl'län·dzä'nē), **Lazzaro,** 1729–99, Italian naturalist; disproved theory of spontaneous generation.
spal·la·tion (spa·lā'shən) *n.* 1 The act or process of reducing to fragments. 2 *Physics* The splitting of an atomic nucleus into numerous parts instead of the two or three characteristic of ordinary fission. [<SPALL + -ATION]
spal·peen (spal·pēn', spal'pēn) *n.* A wandering harvester; hence, a good-for-nothing. [<Irish *spailpín* laborer]
span[1] (span) *v.t.* **spanned, span·ning** 1 To measure, especially with the hand with the thumb and little finger extended. 2 To encircle or grasp with the hand, as in measuring. 3 To stretch across; extend over or from side to side of: This road *spans* the continent. 4 To provide with something that stretches across or extends over. [<*n.*] —*n.* 1 The extreme space over which the hand can be expanded: 9 inches, or 22.86 centimeters. 2 Any small interval or distance, in space or in time. 3 *Archit.* The space or distance between the supports of an arch, abutments of a bridge, etc. 4 That which spans. 5 *Aeron.* The maximum lateral distance from tip to tip of airplane wings. [OE *spann*]
span[2] (span) *v.* **spanned, span·ning** *v.t.* To bind; make fast; fetter. —*v.i.* To match in color and size: said of horses. —*n.* 1 A rope or chain used as a fastening on a ship. 2 A pair of matched horses or oxen. 3 In South Africa, a team of oxen or bullocks, of two or more yokes. [<MDu. *spannen* fasten, join, draw together]
span[3] (span) Archaic past tense of SPIN.
Span·dau (shpän'dou) A district of western Berlin, Germany: formerly an independent city.
span·drel (span'drəl) *n. Archit.* 1 The triangular space between the outer curve of an arch and the rectangular figure formed by the moldings or framework surrounding it. 2 The space between the shoulders of two adjoining arches. See illustration under ARCH. Also **span'dril.** [Dim. of AF *spaundre,* prob. <OF *espandre* expand]
spa·ne·mi·a (spə·nē'mē·ə) *n. Pathol.* Poverty of blood; anemia. Also **spa·nae'mi·a.** [<NL < Gk. *spanos* lacking + *haima* blood] —**spa·ne'mic** (-nē'mik, -nem'ik) *adj.*
spang (spang) *v.t. Brit. Dial.* To throw or bang down. —*v.i. Brit. Dial.* To spring. —*adv. U.S. Colloq.* Abruptly; straight: He ran *spang* into the wall.
span·gle (spang'gəl) *n.* 1 A small bit of brilliant tin or other metal foil, or other substances, used for decoration in dress, as in theatrical costume. 2 Any small sparkling object. —*v.* **·gled, ·gling** *v.t.* To adorn with or as with spangles; cause to glitter. —*v.i.* To sparkle as spangles; glitter. [Dim. of MDu. *spang* a clasp, brooch] —**span'gly** *adj.*
Span·iard (span'yərd) *n.* 1 A native or citizen of Spain. 2 A prickly bush of New Zealand *(Aciphylla colensoi).*
span·iel (span'yəl) *n.* 1 A small or medium-sized dog having large pendulous ears and long silky hair: used especially for hunting small game in the fields, retrieving water birds, etc. 2 One who follows like a dog; an obsequious follower. [<OF *espaignol* Spanish (dog)]
—**Blenheim spaniel** A variety of English toy spaniel having a white coat with rich chestnut or ruby-red markings: originally bred at Blenheim, England, from cocker spaniels sent to the Duke of Marlborough from China: formerly used for woodcock shooting, now usually a pet.
—**Clumber spaniel** A small, stout-bodied, short-legged spaniel having a straight silky coat usually white with lemon markings: named from Clumber, the estate of the second Duke of Newcastle, where they were bred.
—**cocker spaniel** The smallest of the sporting spaniels, of solid or various coloring, characterized by sturdy body and rather short legs: an excellent retriever, especially in thick covers and swamps, and named for its special skill in woodcock hunting.
—**English springer spaniel** A spaniel of moderate size, strongly built, with a long and broad skull, deep chest, and wavy or flat coat; usually liver and white or tan, black and white or tan, etc.: named for its characteristic method of flushing game.
—**field spaniel** A black or varicolored spaniel used for hunting small game, having a long, low body, short legs, and a larger, stronger appearance than the cocker.
—**Irish water spaniel** A sporting dog of a breed developed in Ireland, having a curly, waterproof, liver-colored coat: used especially as a duck retriever.
—**Japanese spaniel** A breed of toy dog, thought to have originated in China, squarely built with small-boned feathered legs, a proportionately large head, and a long, straight coat which may be black and white or red and white.
—**King Charles spaniel** An English toy spaniel, originating in the Far East at an unknown date, having a long, silky, black-and-tan coat, feathery ears and feet, rounded head, and a short, turned-up nose.
—**Sussex spaniel** A field spaniel bred in Sussex county, England, somewhat slow in speed, having a very keen nose, massive muscular body, heavy head, rather large ears, long back, short large-boned legs, and a thick coat of a rich, golden-liver color.
—**Welsh springer spaniel** A dark, rich red-and-white sporting spaniel of uncertain origin, found chiefly in Wales and the west of England: larger than the cocker, and an excellent watchdog.
Span·ish (span'ish) *adj.* Pertaining to Spain, the Spaniards, or their language. —*n.* 1 The Romance language of Spain, Spanish America, and the Philippine Islands. 2 The inhabitants of Spain collectively: with *the.*
Spanish America The parts of the western hemisphere in which Spanish is the common language: Mexico, the countries of Central America, except British Honduras, the countries of South America except Brazil and

the Guianas, and most of the Caribbean islands: also *Hispanic America.*

Span·ish-A·mer·i·can (span′ish·ə·mer′ə·kən) *adj.* **1** Pertaining to the parts of America where Spanish is the vernacular tongue or is in common use. **2** Designating or pertaining to the war between the United States and Spain, 1898. — *n.* One of Spanish blood living in America, especially Central or South America; a citizen of a Spanish-American country.

Spanish-American War See table under WAR.

Spanish Armada See under ARMADA.

Spanish cedar Cedar (def. 4).

Spanish dagger Any of various species of yucca, with sword-shaped leaves. Also **Spanish bayonet.**

SPANISH DAGGER

Spanish fly A bright-green blister beetle *(Lytta vesicatoria)* of the Mediterranean region, used in the preparation of the drug cantharidin. See illustration under INSECTS (beneficial).

Spanish Guinea A Spanish colony in western Africa, divided into the two districts of Fernando Pó and Río Muni (continental Guinea, together with Annobon, Corisco, Great Elobey, and Little Elobey); total area, 10,853 square miles; capital, Santa Isabel, on Fernando Pó.

Spanish mackerel **1** The chub. **2** The cero.

Spanish Main **1** The mainland of Spanish America, especially the coastal region of northern South America between Panama and the mouth of the Orinoco. **2** That part of the Caribbean comprising the course of Spanish merchantmen formerly sailing between the eastern and western hemispheres.

Spanish Morocco Formerly, a Spanish protectorate on the coastal strip of Morocco north of French Morocco; incorporated in Morocco, 1956; 10,808 square miles; former capital, Tetuán.

Spanish moss A long, pendent, epiphytic plant *(Tillandsia* or *Dendropogon usneoides)* that grows upon trees of the southern United States near the seacoast: not a true parasite: sometimes called *long moss, Florida moss.* Also **Spanish beard.**

Spanish needles **1** A smooth annual plant *(Bidens bipinnata)* of the composite family, with bipinnate leaves and spiny achenia. **2** The barbed, prickly fruit of this plant.

Spanish onion A large, fleshy variety of onion, usually mild flavored.

Spanish paprika A cultivated variety of paprika, widely used as a condiment.

Spanish Peaks Two peaks in the Sangre de Cristo Mountains of southern Colorado; 13,623 feet and 12,683 feet.

Spanish Sahara A subdivision of Spanish West Africa, comprising Río de Oro and Saguia el Hamra; 105,409 square miles.

Spanish West Africa The Spanish possessions in NW Africa: Spanish Sahara (Río de Oro and Saguia el Hamra), Ifni, and the Southern Protectorate of Morocco; 116,189 square miles.

spank (spangk) *v.t.* To slap or strike, especially on the buttocks with the open hand as a punishment. — *v.i.* To move briskly. — *n.* A smack on the buttocks; a spanking. [Imit.]

spank·er (spangk′ər) *n.* **1** One who or that which spanks. **2** *Naut.* A fore-and-aft sail extended by a boom and a gaff from the mizzenmast of a ship or bark. **3** Any person or thing uncommonly large or fine. **4** One who or that which proceeds rapidly.

spank·ing (spangk′ing) *adj.* **1** Moving or blowing rapidly; swift; dashing; lively; strong. **2** *Brit. Colloq.* Uncommonly large or fine. — *n.* A series of slaps on the buttocks; the act of administering such punishment.

span·less (span′lis) *adj.* That cannot be spanned.

span·ner (span′ər) *n.* **1** One who or that which spans. **2** *Brit.* A hand-tool used to turn nuts, bolts, etc.: a form of wrench. **3** A measuring worm. [def. 2 <G]

span-new (span′nōō′, -nyōō′) *adj. Dial.* Really or freshly new. [<ON *spān-nȳr* < *spānn* chip + *nȳr* new]

span worm A measuring worm.

spar[1] (spär) *n.* **1** *Naut.* A round timber for extending a sail, as a mast, yard, or boom. **2** A similar heavy, round timber forming part of a derrick, crane, etc., or used for various other purposes. **3** *Aeron.* That part of an airplane wing which carries the ribs. **4** *Naut.* A spar buoy: see under BUOY. — *v.t.* **sparred, spar·ring** **1** To furnish with spars. **2** *Archaic* To fasten, as with a bolt. [<ON *sparri* a beam]

spar[2] (spär) *v.i.* **sparred, spar·ring** **1** To box, especially with care and adroitness. **2** To bandy words; wrangle. **3** To fight, as cocks, by striking with spurs. — *n.* The act or practice of boxing, as by pugilists; a boxing match: also **spar′ring.** [<OF *esparer* <Ital. *sparare* kick <L *parare* prepare]

spar[3] (spär) *n.* A vitreous, crystalline, easily cleavable, lustrous mineral. [<MDu. Akin to OE *spær* gypsum.]

Spar (spär) *n.* A member of the women's reserve of the United States Coast Guard. Also **SPAR.** [<L *s(emper) par(atus)* always ready, the motto of the U. S. Coast Guard]

spar·a·ble (spar′ə·bəl) *n.* A species of small headless nail used by shoemakers in soling boots. [Alter. of *sparrow bill*; so called from resemblance in shape]

spar buoy *Naut.* See under BUOY.

spar deck *Naut.* The light upper deck of a vessel extending from bow to stern: including the quarter-deck and the forecastle; the deck on which extra spars are stowed.

spare (spâr) *v.* **spared, spar·ing** *v.t.* **1** To refrain from injuring, molesting, or killing; treat with mercy or lenience. **2** To free or relieve (someone) from (pain, expense, etc.): *Spare* us the sight. **3** To use frugally; refrain from using or exercising: *Spare* the rod and spoil the child. **4** To dispense or dispense with; do without: Can you *spare* a dime? — *v.i.* **5** To be frugal; live or act economically. **6** To be lenient or forgiving; show mercy. — *adj.* **spar·er, spar·est** **1** That can be spared or used at will; disposable; available. **2** Held in reserve; additional; extra; surplus. **3** Having little flesh; thin; lean. **4** Not lavish or abundant; scanty. **5** Economical; chary; stingy; parsimonious. See synonyms under MEAGER. — *n.* **1** That which has been saved or stored away; something unused. **2** A duplicate; an item kept as a substitute in case the original breaks down, as an automobile tire or a mechanical part. **3** In bowling, the act of overturning all the pins with the first two balls; also, the score thus made. [OE *sparian*] — **spare′ly** *adv.* — **spare′ness** *n.* — **spar′er** *n.*

spare·rib (spâr′rib′) *n.* A piece of meat, especially pork, consisting of ribs somewhat closely trimmed.

sparge (spärj) *v.t.* & *v.i.* **sparged, sparg·ing** To scatter; sprinkle; shower. — *n.* A sprinkling. [<OF *espargier* <L *spargere* sprinkle]

sparg·er (spär′jər) *n.* **1** A sprinkler or sprinkling apparatus. **2** In brewing, a hot-water sprinkler for use in a mashing tub.

spar·ing (spâr′ing) *adj.* **1** Scanty; slight. **2** Frugal; stingy. **3** Merciful; forbearing. See synonyms under SCANTY. — *n.* The act of one who spares; frugality; parsimony. See synonyms under FRUGALITY. — **spar′ing·ly** *adv.* — **spar′ing·ness** *n.*

spark[1] (spärk) *n.* **1** An incandescent particle thrown off from a red-hot or burning body or struck from a flint. **2** Any glistening or brilliant point or transient luminous particle. **3** Anything that kindles or animates. **4** *Electr.* **a** The luminous effect of a disruptive electric discharge, or the discharge itself. **b** A small transient arc or an incandescent particle thrown off from such an arc. **5** A small diamond, or bit of diamond used as in cutting glass. **6** A small trace or indication. — *v.i.* **1** To give off sparks; sparkle; scintillate. **2** In an internal-combustion engine, to have the electric ignition operating. — *v.t.* **3** To bring into action or being; activate or cause: The shooting *sparked* a revolution. [OE *spearca*]

spark[2] (spärk) *n.* **1** A man fond of gallantry. **2** A lover; suitor; gallant. — *v.t.* & *v.i.* To play the spark (to); woo; court. [Special use of SPARK[1]]

spark arrester **1** A sievelike device for catching sparks, as on a locomotive. **2** *Electr.* An apparatus to prevent injurious sparking at the opening of a circuit made and broken frequently.

spark coil *Electr.* An induction coil used with an internal-combustion engine, wireless telegraph equipment, etc., to secure sparking.

spark·er (spär′kər) *n.* **1** One who or that which sparks. **2** An electrical spark arrester.

spark gap *Electr.* **1** An arrangement of two electrodes between which a disruptive electric charge may pass. **2** The space so covered.

spark generator *Electr.* Any device capable of generating a sufficiently high voltage to discharge across a spark gap.

spark·ish (spär′kish) *adj.* **1** Jaunty; sprightly; airy; gay. **2** Showy; fine; well-dressed.

spark killer *Electr.* A device, usually a condenser, or condenser and resistance in series, for reducing harmful sparking at frequently interrupted points in a circuit. Also **spark suppressor.**

spar·kle (spär′kəl) *v.i.* **·kled, ·kling** **1** To give off flashes of light; scintillate; glitter. **2** To emit sparks. **3** To effervesce. **4** To be brilliant or vivacious: His words *sparkle* with wit. See synonyms under SHINE. — *n.* A spark; gleam. See synonyms under LIGHT[1]. [Freq. of SPARK[1]]

spar·kler (spär′klər) *n.* **1** Something that sparkles. **2** A sparkling gem. **3** A thin, rodlike firework that emits sparks. **4** A person who shines with spirit or vivacity.

spar·kling (spär′kling) *adj.* Giving out sparks or flashes; glittering; figuratively, brilliant; vivacious. — **spar′kling·ly** *adv.* — **spar′kling·ness** *n.*

spark plug A device for igniting the charge in an internal-combustion engine by means of an electric current.

Sparks (spärks), **Jared,** 1789–1866, U. S. editor and historian.

spark transmitter *Telecom.* A radio transmitter which obtains its alternating current from the discharge of a condenser across a spark gap.

spar·ling (spär′ling) *n.* **1** A smelt, parr, or other young fish. **2** A young herring. [<OF *esperlinge* <Gmc.]

spar·oid (spâr′oid, spar′-) *adj.* Of or pertaining to a family *(Sparidae)* of spiny-finned marine fishes allied to the grunts and including the porgy, sheepshead, etc. — *n.* A sparoid fish; the sea bream. [<L *sparus* <Gk. *sparos* gilthead + -OID]

spar·row (spar′ō) *n.* **1** Any of various small, plainly colored, passerine birds (family *Fringillidae)* related to the finches, grosbeaks, and buntings; especially, the European **house sparrow** *(Passer domesticus),* known in the United States as the **English sparrow.** **2** Some other singing bird like or likened to the house sparrow, as the song sparrow. [OE *spearwa*]

sparrow bill A sparable.

spar·row·grass (spar′ō·gras′, -gräs′) *n. Dial.* Asparagus: a corruption. Also **spar′ry·grass′** (spar′ē-).

sparrow hawk **1** A small falconine bird that preys on sparrows, as the kestrel, or the **eastern sparrow hawk** *(Falco sparverius).* **2** A small European hawk *(Accipiter nisus)* that preys on other birds.

spar·ry (spär′ē) *adj.* **·ri·er, ·ri·est** Of, abounding in, or like spar.

sparse (spärs) *adj.* Scattered at considerable distances apart; thinly diffused; not dense. [<L *sparsus,* pp. of *spargere* sprinkle, scatter] — **sparse′ly** *adv.* — **sparse′ness, spar·si·ty** (spär′sə·tē) *n.*

Spar·ta (spär′tə) An ancient city in the Peloponnesus, southern Greece; capital of ancient Laconia: also *Lacedaemon.*

Spar·ta·cist (spär′tə·sist) *n.* A member of a party of extreme socialists in Germany (1918–19): name derived from the pseudonym *Spartacus* used by their leader, Karl Liebknecht. Also **Spar′ta·cide** (-sīd).

Spar·ta·cus (spär′tə·kəs) Thracian leader of slaves in the gladiatorial war against Rome 73–71 B.C.

Spar·tan (spär′tən) *adj.* Pertaining to Sparta or the Spartans; heroically brave and enduring. — *n.* A native or citizen of Sparta; hence, one of exceptional valor and fortitude. — **Spar′tan·ism** *n.*

spar·te·ine (spär′ti·ēn, -tē·in) *n. Chem.* A colorless, oily, poisonous alkaloid, $C_{15}H_{26}N_2$, contained in the common broom: it resembles digitalis in action. [<Gk. *spartos* broom + -INE[2]]

spasm (spaz′əm) *n.* **1** Any sudden or convulsive action or effort, as of the body, mind, or nature, especially such a one as is abnormal or temporary. **2** *Pathol.* Any involuntary convulsive contraction of muscles: when manifested by alternate contractions and relaxations it is a **clonic spasm;** when persistent and steady, it is a **tonic spasm.** [<L *spasma, spasmus* <Gk. *spasmos* < *spaein* draw, pull]

spas·mod·ic (spaz·mod′ik) *adj.* **1** Of the nature of a spasm; convulsive. **2** Violent, or impulsive and transitory. Also **spas·mod′i·cal.** — **spas·mod′i·cal·ly** *adv.*

spas·mol·y·sis (spaz·mol′ə·sis) *n. Med.* The checking or relief of spasms. — **spas·mo·lyt·ic** (spaz′mə·lit′ik) *adj.*

spas·mo·phil·i·a (spaz′mə·fil′ē·ə) *n. Pathol.* A constitutional tendency to spasms and convulsions. — **spas′mo·phil′ic** *adj.*

spas·tic (spas′tik) *adj.* Of, pertaining to, or characterized by spasms; spasmodic; tetanic: *spastic* hemiplegia. — *n.* A person afflicted with spastic seizures. [<L *spasticus* <Gk. *spastikos* < *spaein* draw, pull] — **spas′ti·cal·ly** *adv.*

spat[1] (spat) Past tense and past participle of SPIT[1].

spat[2] (spat) *n.* **1** Spawn of shellfish; specifically, spawn of the oyster. **2** A young oyster, or young oysters collectively. — *v.i.* **spat·ted, spat·ting** To spawn, as oysters. [? Related to SPIT[1]]

spat[3] (spat) *n.* **1** A slight blow; slap. **2** A splash, as of rain; spatter. **3** A petty dispute. — *v.* **spat·ted, spat·ting** *v.i.* **1** To strike with a slight sound; slap. **2** To engage in a petty quarrel. — *v.t.* **3** To slap. [Prob. imit.]

spat[4] (spat) *n.* A short gaiter worn over a shoe and fastened underneath with a strap: usually in the plural. [Short for SPATTERDASH]

spate (spāt) *n.* **1** A freshet; overflow. **2** A sudden, violent rainstorm; also, a waterspout. **3** A sudden or vigorous outpouring, as of words, feeling, etc. Also **spait.** [Origin uncertain]

spa·tha·ceous (spə·thā′shəs) *adj. Bot.* Bearing or of the nature of a spathe. Also **spa·thal** (spā′thəl).

spathe (spāth) *n. Bot.* A large bract or pair of bracts sheathing a flower cluster, as a spadix. [<L *spatha* <Gk. *spathē* broadsword] — **spa·those** (spā′thōs, spath′ōs) *adj.*

spath·ic (spath′ik) *adj. Mineral.* Of, pertaining to, or resembling spar. Also **spath·ose** (spath′ōs). [<G *spath* spar]

spa·tial (spā′shəl) *adj.* Pertaining to space; involving or having the nature of space. Also *spacial.* [<L *spatium* space] — **spa·ti·al·i·ty** (spā′shē·al′ə·tē) *n.* — **spa′tial·ly** *adv.*

spa·ti·o–tem·po·ral (spā′shē·ō·tem′pər·əl) *adj.* Of or pertaining to both space and time.

spat·ter (spat′ər) *v.t.* **1** To scatter in drops or splashes, as mud or paint. **2** To splash with such drops; bespatter. **3** To defame. — *v.i.* **4** To throw off drops or splashes; sputter. **5** To fall in a shower, as raindrops. — *n.* **1** The act of spattering, or the matter spattered; a splash. **2** A pattering noise, as of falling rain. [OE *spat-*, stem of *spatlian* spit out + -ER[4]]

spat·ter·dash (spat′ər·dash′) *n.* A legging reaching to the knee, worn as a protection from mud, especially when riding: used chiefly in the plural. — **spat′ter·dashed′** *adj.*

spat·ter·dock (spat′ər·dok′) *n.* The yellow pondlily (*Nuphar advena*).

spat·u·la (spach′ŏŏ·lə) *n.* **1** A knifelike instrument with a flat, flexible blade, used to spread plaster, cake icing, etc. **2** *Med.* An instrument used to press the tongue down or aside, as in examinations. [<L, dim. of *spatha.* See SPATHE.] — **spat′u·lar** *adj.*

spat·u·late (spach′ŏŏ·lit, -lāt) *adj.* **1** Shaped like a spatula. **2** *Bot.* Oblong, with an attenuated base, as many leaves.

spav·in (spav′in) *n.* A disease of the hock joint of horses, occurring either as an infusion of lymph within the joint (**blood spavin** or **bog spavin**) or as a bony deposit stiffening the joint (**bone spavin**). Also *Scot.* **spa·vie** (spā′vē, spav′ē). [<OF *espavain, esparvain;* ult. origin uncertain] — **spav′ined** *adj.*

spawn (spôn) *n.* **1** *Zool.* The eggs of fishes, amphibians, mollusks, etc., especially in masses. **2** Derisively, the offspring of any animal; also, outcome or results; product; yield. **3** The spat of the oyster. **4** Very small fish; fry. **5** *Bot.* The mycelium of mushrooms or other fungi. [< *v.*] — *v.i.* **1** To produce spawn; deposit eggs or roe. **2** To come forth as or like spawn. — *v.t.* **3** To produce (spawn). **4** To give rise to; originate. **5** To bring forth abundantly or in great quantity. **6** To plant with spawn or mycelium. [<AF *espaundere,* OF *espendre* <L *expandere.* Doublet of EXPAND.]

spay (spā) *v.t.* To remove the ovaries from (a female animal). [<AF *espeier,* OF *espeer* cut with a sword < *espee* a sword <L *spatha*]

speak (spēk) *v.* **spoke** (*Archaic* **spake**), **spo·ken** (*Archaic* **spoke**), **speak·ing** *v.i.* **1** To employ the vocal organs in ordinary speech; utter words. **2** To express or convey ideas, opinions, etc., in or as in speech: to *speak* about a matter; Actions *speak* louder than words. **3** To make a speech; deliver an address. **4** To converse. **5** To make a sound; also, to bark, as a dog. — *v.t.* **6** To express or make known in or as in speech. **7** To utter in speech: to *speak* words of love. **8** To use or be capable of using (a language) in conversation. **9** To speak to. **10** *Naut.* To hail and exchange communications with (a vessel) at sea. — **to speak daggers** To express hatred. — **to speak for 1** To speak in behalf of; represent officially. **2** To lay claim to; bespeak; engage. [OE *specan, spreccan*]

Synonyms: announce, articulate, converse, declaim, declare, deliver, dictate, enunciate, express, pronounce, say, talk, tell, utter. See TALK.

speak–eas·y (spēk′ē′zē) *n. pl.* **–eas·ies** A saloon where liquor is sold contrary to law.

speak·er (spē′kər) *n.* **1** One who speaks; an orator. **2** The presiding officer in any one of various legislative bodies. **3** A volume of oratorical selections, for declamation. **4** A loudspeaker. — **speak′er·ship** *n.*

speak·ing (spē′king) *adj.* **1** Having the power of effective speech; uttering speech. **2** Expressive; vivid; telling; lifelike. — *n.* **1** The act of utterance; vocal expression. **2** Oratory; public declamation. — **speak′ing·ly** *adv.*

spean (spēn) *v.t. Brit. Dial.* To wean. [<MDu. *spene* a teat]

spear (spir) *n.* **1** A weapon consisting of a pointed head on a long shaft. **2** A similar instrument, barbed and usually forked, as for spearing fish. **3** A spearman. **4** A leaf or slender stalk, as of grass: sometimes called a *spire.* — *v.t.* **1** To pierce or capture with a spear. — *v.i.* **2** To pierce as a spear does. **3** To send forth spears or spires, as a plant. [OE *spere* spear] — **spear′er** *n.*

spear·fish (spir′fish′) *n. pl.* **·fish** or **·fish·es** A powerful marine fish (genus *Tetrapturus*) with a long snout, related to the swordfish.

spear·head (spir′hed′) *n.* **1** The point of a spear or lance. **2** The military units which lead in a massed attack on enemy positions. — *v.t.* To be in the lead of (an attack, etc.).

spear·man (spir′mən) *n. pl.* **·men** (-mən) A man armed with a spear. Also **spears′man.**

spear·mint (spir′mint′) *n.* An aromatic herb (*Mentha spicata*) similar to peppermint.

spear side *Archaic* The male branch of a family: opposed to the female or *distaff* or *spindle side.* Also **spear half.**

spear·wort (spir′wûrt′) *n.* Any of several species of crowfoot having lance-shaped or linear leaves, especially, the **lesser spearwort** (*Ranunculus flammula*).

spe·cial (spesh′əl) *adj.* **1** Having some peculiar or distinguishing characteristic or characteristics; out of the ordinary; uncommon; particular. **2** Designed for or assigned to a specific purpose; limited or specific in range, aim, or purpose. **3** Of or pertaining to, constituting, or designating a species; specific; distinguishing; differential. **4** Unique; singular; exceptional. **5** Extra or additional, as a dividend. **6** Intimate; esteemed; beloved: a *special* favorite. See synonyms under PARTICULAR. — *n.* **1** A person or thing made, detailed for, or appropriated to a specific service or occasion, as a train, a newspaper edition, etc. **2** A featured dish or course in a restaurant or cafeteria. **3** A temporary sale. **4** A television show that is not regularly scheduled but is produced for a single presentation. [<OF *especial* <L *specialis* < *species* kind, species] — **spe′cial·ly** *adv.*

special delivery *U.S.* Mail delivery by special courier in advance of regular delivery: a postal service obtained for an additional fee.

Special Drawing Rights International monetary credit that can be drawn by member nations from the International Monetary Fund to be used in lieu of gold: also called *paper gold.* Abbr. *SDR, S.D.R., SDRs, S.D.R.s.*

spe·cial·ism (spesh′əl·iz′əm) *n.* The confining of oneself to a particular line of work.

spe·cial·ist (spesh′əl·ist) *n.* A person devoted to some one line of study, occupation, or professional work. — **spe′cial·is′tic** *adj.*

spe·ci·al·i·ty (spesh′ē·al′ə·tē) *n. pl.* **·ties 1** A specific or individual characteristic; peculiarity. **2** Specialty (defs. 3, 4, 5). ◆ In British usage, this form is preferred instead of *specialty.*

spe·cial·i·za·tion (spesh′əl·ə·zā′shən, -ī·zā′-) *n.* **1** The act or process of specializing; also, the state of being or becoming specialized. **2** *Biol.* The development of an organ or part for a special function; differentiation.

spe·cial·ize (spesh′əl·īz) *v.* **·ized, ·iz·ing** *v.i.* **1** To concentrate on one particular activity or subject; engage in a specialty. **2** *Biol.* To take on a special form or forms by specialization or adaptation. — *v.t.* **3** To adapt for some special use or purpose; endow with a particular character. **4** *Biol.* To develop by specialization or adaptation, as an organ or part. **5** To endorse, as a check, to a payee. **6** To mention specifically. Also *Brit.* **spe′cial·ise.**

special pleading 1 *Law* **a** A pleading made with reference to some new or particular matter instead of the general issue. **b** The allegation of new or special matter in reply to the opposing party's averments, rather than an offer of a direct denial. **2** A presentation of the favorable aspects of an argument while avoiding or suppressing the unfavorable.

spe·cial·ty (spesh′əl·tē) *n. pl.* **·ties 1** The state of being special or of having peculiar characteristics. **2** An individual characteristic; peculiarity; distinguishing mark. **3** An occupation or study limited to one particular line. **4** An article dealt in exclusively or chiefly, or a manufactured product of peculiar character. **5** *Law* A sealed contract; deed. — **specialty of the house** A featured dish or course in a restaurant.

spe·ci·a·tion (spē′shē·ā′shən) *n. Biol.* The formation of a species by the action of evolutionary processes upon plant and animal organisms.

spe·cie (spē′shē) *n.* Coined money; coin. See synonyms under MONEY. — **in specie 1** In coin. **2** *Law* In kind; in the shape mentioned; in sort. [<L *(in) specie* (in) kind]

spe·cies (spē′shēz, -shiz; *Lat.* spē′shi·ēz) *n. pl.* **·cies 1** *Biol.* A category of animals or plants subordinate to a genus but above a breed, race, strain, or variety. The species name follows immediately after the name of the genus to which it belongs, and with it forms the scientific name of the individual plant or animal, as *Oreamnos americanus,* the Rocky Mountain goat. **2** A group of individuals or objects agreeing in some common attribute or attributes and designated by a common name. **3** A mental image considered as having the likeness of some object in nature. **4** A kind; sort; variety; form. **5** *Eccl.* **a** The visible form of bread or of wine retained by the eucharistic elements after consecration. **b** The consecrated elements of the Eucharist. **6** *Obs.* Specie; coin. [<L, form, kind. Doublet of SPICE.]

spec·i·fi·a·ble (spes′ə·fī′ə·bəl) *adj.* Such as can be specified.

spe·cif·ic (spi·sif′ik) *adj.* **1** Distinctly and plainly set forth; definite or determinate; particular; explicit. **2** Of, pertaining to, or distinguishing a species: a *specific* name of an animal. **3** Peculiar; special. **4** Having some distinct medicinal or pathological property;

distinguishable or determinate: a *specific* medicine, a *specific* germ. 5 Having or designating a particular property, composition, ratio, or quantity serving to identify a given substance or phenomenon in relation to some arbitrary but constant standard of comparison: *specific* heat, *specific* volume, etc. 6 Denoting a customs duty chargeable upon imported merchandise by quantity, weight, or number, without regard to value: contrasted with ad valorem duty. Also *Rare* **spe·cif'i·cal.** — *n.* Anything specific or adapted to effect a specific result, as a medicine specially indicated to cure or prevent some particular disease. [<L *specificus* < *species* kind, class + *facere* make] — **spec·i·fic·i·ty** (spes'ə·fis'ə·tē) *n.*

spe·cif·i·cal·ly (spi·sif'ik·lē) *adv.* 1 In a specific manner; explicitly; particularly; definitely. 2 As to or in respect to species: *specifically* distinct. 3 In a particular sense or case.

spec·i·fi·ca·tion (spes'ə·fə·kā'shən) *n.* 1 The act of specifying. 2 A definite and complete statement, as in a contract; also, one detail in such a statement. 3 In patent law, the detailed statement of an inventor's scheme, setting forth the nature of the invention and the precise method of constructing and applying it. 4 A specific description of certain dimensions, types of material, etc., to be used in a construction or engineering project; also, any item in this description.

specific gravity *Physics* The ratio of the mass of a body to that of an equal volume of some standard substance, water in the case of solids and liquids, and air or hydrogen in the case of gases.

specific heat *Physics* The amount of heat required to raise the temperature of a given quantity of a substance one degree.

specific impulse The thrust in pounds produced in one second by the burning with its oxidizer of one pound of a specified fuel, as in a rocket motor or jet engine.

spec·i·fy (spes'ə·fī) *v.t.* **·fied, ·fy·ing** 1 To mention specifically; state in full and explicit terms. 2 To embody in a specification. [<OF *specifier* <L *species* kind, species + *facere* make]

spec·i·men (spes'ə·mən) *n.* 1 One of a class of persons or things regarded as representative of the class; an example; sample. 2 *Biol.* A plant or an animal, entire or in part, prepared and kept as an example to illustrate a species or variety. 3 A sample for urinalysis. 4 *Colloq.* A person of pronounced or curious type; a character; a case: What a *specimen*! See synonyms under EXAMPLE, SAMPLE. [<L < *specere* look at]

spe·ci·os·i·ty (spē'shē·os'ə·tē) *n. pl.* **·ties** 1 One who or that which is specious; a thing that appears just and plausible at first view but actually is not. 2 *Obs.* The state of being beautiful.

spe·cious (spē'shəs) *adj.* 1 Apparently good or right, but without merit; plausible: *specious* reasoning. 2 Pleasing or attractive in appearance, but deceptive; fair-seeming: a *specious* promise. 3 Beguiling, but lacking in sincerity: a *specious* hypocrite. 4 *Archaic* Showy; pleasing to the view. See synonyms under OSTENSIBLE. [<L *speciosus* fair] — **spe'cious·ly** *adv.* — **spe'cious·ness** *n.*

speck (spek) *n.* 1 A small spot; a little stain or discoloration. 2 Any very small thing; a particle. See synonyms under BLEMISH. — *v.t.* To mark with spots or specks; speckle. [OE *specca*]

speck·le (spek'əl) *v.t.* **·led, ·ling** To mark with specks or speckles. — *n.* A diminutive spot; speck.

speck·led (spek'əld) *adj.* 1 Dotted with specks or spots. 2 Of motley appearance or mixed character.

specs (speks) *n. pl. Colloq.* Spectacles. Also **specks.**

spec·ta·cle (spek'tə·kəl) *n.* 1 That which is exhibited to public view; a grand display; pageant; parade; show. 2 An unwelcome or deplorable exhibition; a painful sight. 3 *pl.* A pair of eyeglasses, with hinged bows to secure them before the eyes: used to correct defects in vision, or to protect the eyes, as from glare. 4 *pl.* A marking on animals resembling a pair of spectacles. — **compound spectacles** *Optics* 1 Spectacles having supplementary colored glasses hinged to them for use when desired. 2 Supplementary lenses of greater power, similarly hinged. 3 Bifocals; trifocals. [<F <L *spectaculum* < *spectare*, freq. of *specere* see]

Synonyms: display, exhibition, pageant, parade, scene, show, sight. See SIGHT.

spec·ta·cled (spek'tə·kəld) *adj.* 1 Wearing spectacles. 2 Having markings resembling a pair of spectacles: the *spectacled* cobra.

spec·tac·u·lar (spek·tak'yə·lər) *adj.* Characterized by grand scenic display; exciting wonder by dramatic or unusual display. — *n.* 1 An imposing exhibition. 2 In television, a lavish dramatic or musical production of 90 minutes duration, especially designed for reproduction in color. 3 An elaborate, illuminated sign. — **spec·tac'u·lar·ly** *adv.* — **spec·tac'u·lar'i·ty** (-lar'ə·tē) *n.*

spec·ta·tor (spek'tā·tər, spek·tā'-) *n.* 1 One who beholds; an eyewitness; an onlooker. 2 One who is present at and views a show, game, spectacle, etc. [<L < *spectare* look at]

Synonyms: beholder, bystander, onlooker, observer, witness.

Spec·ta·tor (spek'tā·tər, spek·tā'-), **The** An English periodical, conducted by Joseph Addison and Richard Steele from March, 1711, to Dec., 1712; revived by Addison, June–Dec., 1714.

spec·ter (spek'tər) *n.* A phantom of the dead or of a disembodied spirit; especially, one of a grisly or horrible nature; ghost; apparition. Also **spec'tre.** [<F *spectre* <L *spectrum* vision]

Synonyms: apparition, phantom, ghost, shade, spirit.

specter of the Brocken See BROCKEN.

spec·tra (spek'trə) Plural of SPECTRUM.

spec·tral (spek'trəl) *adj.* 1 Pertaining to a specter; ghostly. 2 Pertaining to the spectrum or to spectra. See synonyms under GHASTLY. — **spec'tral·ly** *adv.* — **spec·tral·i·ty** (spek·tral'ə·tē) *n.*

spectro– *combining form* 1 Radiant energy, as exhibited in the spectrum: *spectroscope.* 2 Spectroscope; spectroscopic: *spectrobolometer.* [<SPECTRUM]

spec·tro·bo·lom·e·ter (spek'trō·bō·lom'ə·tər) *n.* A bolometer combined with a spectroscope for measuring the heat of different parts of the spectrum.

spec·tro·chem·is·try (spek'trō·kem'is·trē) *n.* The study of chemical phenomena and properties by means of spectrum analysis. — **spec'·tro·chem'i·cal** *adj.*

spec·tro·gram (spek'trə·gram) *n.* The record of a spectrograph.

spec·tro·graph (spek'trə·graf, -gräf) *n. Physics* 1 An apparatus for photographing a spectrum or for forming a representation of the spectrum in any way. 2 A photograph of a spectrum. — **sound spectrograph** An electronic instrument designed to record the frequencies of speech sounds as measured in cycles per second, and the amplitude at any given frequency: used in acoustic phonetics.

spec·tro·he·li·o·gram (spek'trō·hē'lē·ə·gram') *n.* A photograph made by the spectroheliograph.

spec·tro·he·li·o·graph (spek'trō·hē'lē·ə·graf', -gräf') *n.* An instrument for photographing the sun with its prominences by means of monochromatic light.

spec·trom·e·ter (spek·trom'ə·tər) *n.* 1 An instrument by means of which the angular deviation of a ray of light produced by a prism or by a refraction grating can be determined, or a wavelength of a ray of light can be accurately measured. 2 A spectroscope provided with such an instrument. — **spec·tro·met·ric** (spek'trō·met'rik) *adj.*

spec·tro·pho·tom·e·ter (spek'trō·fō·tom'ə·tər) *n.* An instrument for determining the relative intensity of two spectra or of the corresponding bands of color in two spectra.

spec·tro·ra·di·om·e·ter (spek'trō·rā'dē·om'ə·tər) *n.* A form of spectrometer for determining the distribution of the intensity of any type of radiation, especially in the infrared region of the spectrum. — **spec'tro·ra'di·om'e·try** *n.*

spec·tro·scope (spek'trə·skōp) *n.* An optical instrument for forming and analyzing spectra emitted by bodies or substances. — **spec'tro·scop'ic** (-skop'ik) or **·i·cal** *adj.* — **spec'tro·scop'i·cal·ly** *adv.*

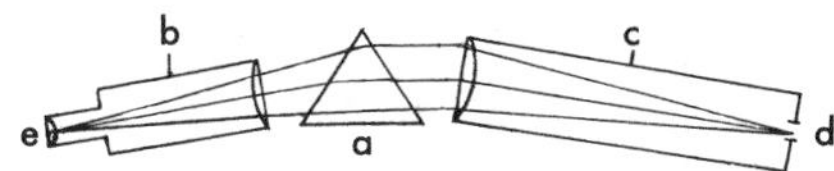

PRINCIPLE OF SIMPLE SPECTROSCOPE
a. Prism. *b.* Telescope for viewing prism through eyepiece *(e)*. *c.* Collimator with slit *(d)*.

spec·tros·co·py (spek·tros'kə·pē) *n.* 1 The branch of physical science treating of the phenomena observed with the spectroscope. 2 The art of using the spectroscope. — **spec·tros'co·pist** *n.*

spec·trum (spek'trəm) *n. pl.* **·tra** (-trə) 1 The continuously varying band of color observed when a beam of white light is passed through a prism which separates each component of the light according to frequencies ranging from low for red to high for violet: also **visible spectrum, chromatic spectrum.** 2 An image formed by radiant energy directed through a spectroscope and brought to a focus in which each wavelength corresponds to a specific band or line in a progressive series characteristic of the emitting source. 3 An after-image. [<L, a vision]

spectrum analysis The investigation or qualitative analysis of bodies or substances by means of their spectra; spectroscopy.

spec·u·la (spek'yə·lə) Plural of SPECULUM.

spec·u·lar (spek'yə·lər) *adj.* 1 Pertaining to or assisted by a speculum or a mirror; reflecting. 2 *Obs.* Affording a view; aiding vision. [<L *specularis* < *speculum* mirror]

specular iron A lustrous, crystalline variety of hematite.

specular pig iron Spiegeleisen.

spec·u·late (spek'yə·lāt) *v.i.* **·lat·ed, ·lat·ing** 1 To form conjectures regarding anything without experiment; theorize; conjecture. 2 To make an investment involving a risk, but with hope of gain. [<L *speculatus*, pp. of *speculari* look at, examine < *specere* see]

spec·u·la·tion (spek'yə·lā'shən) *n.* 1 The act of theorizing or conjecturing; speculating. 2 A theory or conjecture. 3 A conclusion reached by or based upon conjecture. 4 An investment involving risk with hope of large profit. 5 The act of engaging in risky business transactions that offer a possibility of large profit. 6 *Archaic* Vision; observation; intuition. See synonyms under HYPOTHESIS, THOUGHT[1].

spec·u·la·tive (spek'yə·lā'tiv, -lə·tiv) *adj.* 1 Of, pertaining to, engaged in, or given to speculation: opposed to *experimental.* 2 Strictly theoretical or purely scientific: opposed to *practical.* 3 Engaging in or involving financial speculation. 4 *Archaic* Pertaining to vision or observation; affording a good view. 5 *Archaic* Prying; observing. — **spec'u·la'tive·ly** *adv.* — **spec'u·la'tive·ness** *n.*

spec·u·la·tor (spek'yə·lā'tər) *n.* One who speculates, in any sense. — **spec'u·la·to'ry** (-lə·tôr'ē, -tō'rē) *adj.*

spec·u·lum (spek'yə·ləm) *n. pl.* **·la** (-lə) or **·lums** 1 A mirror of polished metal or of glass coated with a metal film used for telescope reflectors and other optical instruments. 2 *Med.* An instrument that dilates a passage of the body for examination. 3 *Ornithol.* A specially colored, typically iridescent area on the wings of certain birds, as ducks. [<L, a mirror < *specere* see]

sped (sped) Alternative past tense and past participle of SPEED.

Spee (shpā), **Count Maximilian von,** 1861–1914, German rear admiral in World War I.

speech (spēch) *n.* 1 The faculty of expressing thought and emotion by spoken words; the power of speaking. 2 The act of speaking, involving the production of meaningful combinations of distinctive speech sounds. 3 That which is spoken; conversation; talk; a saying or remark. 4 A public address; a discourse. 5 A characteristic manner of speaking: His *speech* is loud and unpleasant. **6** A particular language, idiom, or dialect: American *speech.* **7** Any audible or visible method of communication, including cries, gestures, and sign language. **8** The study of oral communication, including the physiology of articulation, the nature of speech sounds, and the techniques of effective expression. [OE *spec, sprec* < *specan, sprecan* speak]

Synonyms: address, discourse, discussion, disquisition, dissertation, eloquence, harangue, oration, oratory, sermon. *Speech* is the general word for utterance of thought in language. A *speech* is the simplest mode of delivering one's sentiments; an *oration* is an elaborate and prepared *speech*; a *harangue* is a vehement appeal to passion, or a *speech* that has something disputatious and combative in it. A *discourse* is a set *speech* on a definite subject intended to convey instruction. See LANGUAGE. *Antonyms*: hush, silence, stillness.

speech clinic A place where speech disorders are corrected by training and re-education.

speech community All the speakers of a given language or dialect in both contiguous and geographically distributed areas.

speech defect The manifestation or end product of a speech disorder.

speech disorder Disorganization or impairment of speech caused either by physical defect or by mental disorder, such as aphasia, stuttering, etc.

speech·i·fy (spē′chə·fī) *v.i.* **·fied, ·fy·ing** To make speeches: often used derisively. — **speech′i·fi′er** *n.*

speech·less (spēch′lis) *adj.* **1** Unable to speak or temporarily deprived of speech because of physical weakness or strong emotion, etc.: *speechless* with rage. **2** Mute; dumb. **3** Silent; reticent. **4** *Archaic* Unspoken in words: the *speechless* message in her eyes. **5** Unaccompanied by speech: *speechless* joy. **6** *Archaic* Inexpressible. — **speech′less·ly** *adv.* — **speech′less·ness** *n.*

speech·mak·er (spēch′mā′kər) *n.* One who delivers a speech or speeches. — **speech′mak′·ing** *n.*

speech sound An articulation which functions in oral communication.

speed (spēd) *n.* **1** The act or state of moving or progressing swiftly; rapidity of motion; celerity; swiftness. **2** *Physics* **a** Rate of motion, especially as considered without reference to direction: a scalar quantity distinguished from *velocity.* **b** Rate of performance, as shown by the ratio of work done to time spent. **3** *Mech.* A transmission gear in a motor vehicle. **4** *Phot.* In a camera lens, the minimum time required for an effective exposure under given conditions, expressed as the ratio of focal length to effective aperture. **5** *Slang* One of the amphetamines taken illicitly, especially by injection. **6** *Archaic* Good luck; success; prosperity. — *v.* **sped** or **speed·ed, speed·ing** *v.i.* **1** To move or go with speed. **2** *Obs.* To prosper. **3** *Obs.* To fare in a specified manner. — *v.t.* **4** To promote the forward progress of; cause to move or go with speed. **5** To promote the success of. **6** To wish Godspeed to: *Speed* the parting guest. — **to speed up** To accelerate in speed or action. See synonyms under FLY[1]. — *adj.* Having, pertaining to, characterized by, regulating, or indicating speed: used chiefly in compounds:

speed-cone **speed-gage** **speed-gear** **speed-lathe** **speed-pulley** **speed-recorder** **speed-test** **speed-trap**

[OE *spēd* power]

speed·boat (spēd′bōt′) *n.* A motorboat capable of high speed.

speed·er (spē′dər) *n.* Someone or something that speeds; specifically, a motorist who drives at a speed exceeding a safe or legal limit.

speed indicator **1** An instrument showing the rotation speed of a machine or part of a machine. **2** A speedometer.

speed·ing (spē′ding) *adj.* Moving with speed. — *n.* Travel at high speed; especially, by motor vehicles, travel at an unsafe or reckless speed or above a specified speed limit.

speed limit A legally set maximum speed at which vehicles may travel on certain stretches of roads or through specified districts.

speed·om·e·ter (spi·dom′ə·tər) *n.* A device for indicating the speed of a vehicle or the distance traveled.

speed·ster (spēd′stər) *n.* **1** A speeder. **2** An automobile, usually having two seats, designed for speed.

speed-up (spēd′up′) *n.* An acceleration in work, output, movement, etc.

speed·way (spēd′wā′) *n.* A specially reserved or prepared road for vehicles traveling at high speed.

speed·well (spēd′wel) *n.* One of various low herbs (genus *Veronica*) of the figwort family, bearing blue or white flowers, especially the common speedwell (*V. arvensis*) and the **germander speedwell** (*V. chamaedrys*), with bright-blue flowers: also called *birdseye.*

speed·y (spē′dē) *adj.* **speed·i·er, speed·i·est** **1** Characterized by speed. **2** Without delay. See synonyms under NIMBLE, SWIFT[1]. — **speed′·i·ly** *adv.* — **speed′i·ness** *n.*

speed·y-cut (spē′dē·kut′) *n.* An injury on the side of the knee or carpus of a horse caused by a blow from the shoe of the foot of the opposite leg when trotting or moving at any other rapid gait.

speel (spēl) *v.t.* & *v.i. Scot.* To climb.

speer (spir) *v.t.* & *v.i. Scot.* To inquire; ask: also spelled *spier.* — **to speer at** To question.

speer·ing (spir′ing) *n. Scot.* Inquiry; news; information.

speiss (spīs) *n.* An impure mixture consisting of the arsenides of certain metals, as copper, iron, and nickel, that concentrate in smelting certain ores. Also *Ger.* **spei·se** (shpī′zə). [<G *speise* amalgam]

spe·le·an (spi·lē′ən) *adj.* **1** Dwelling in a cave or caves. **2** Of or pertaining to a cave or caverns. Also **spe·lae′an.** [<L *spelaeum* <Gk. *spēlaion* a cave]

spe·le·ol·o·gy (spē′lē·ol′ə·jē) *n.* **1** The scientific study of caves in their physical, geological, and biological aspects. **2** The exploration of caves as a sport or profession. [<L *spelaeum* a cave + -LOGY] — **spe′le·o·log′i·cal** (-ə·loj′i·kəl) *adj.* — **spe′le·ol′o·gist** *n.*

spell[1] (spel) *v.* **spelled** or **spelt, spell·ing** *v.t.* **1** To pronounce or write the letters of (a word); especially, to do so correctly. **2** To form or be the letters of: C-a-t *spells* cat; hence, to compose; make up. **3** To read with difficulty; hence, to puzzle out and learn: sometimes with *over* or *out.* **4** To signify; mean: Extravagance *spells* disaster. — *v.i.* **5** To form words out of letters, especially correctly. [<OF *espeler* <Gmc. Akin to SPELL[2].]

spell[2] (spel) *n.* A formula used as a charm; incantation; charm; hence, fascination. — *v.t.* **spelled, spell·ing** To cast a spell upon; fascinate; bewitch. [OE, story, statement. Akin to SPELL[1].]

spell[3] (spel) *n.* **1** A period of time, usually of short length. **2** *Colloq.* A continuous period characterized by a certain type of weather. **3** *Colloq.* A short distance. **4** *Colloq.* A fit of illness, debility, etc. **5** A turn of duty in relief of another. **6** A period of work or employment. **7** *Austral.* A period of relaxation; rest. — *v.t.* **1** To relieve temporarily from some work or duty. **2** *Austral.* To give a rest to, as a horse. — *v.i.* **3** To take a rest. [OE *gespelia* a substitute, one who spells another]

spell·bind (spel′bīnd′) *v.t.* **·bound, ·bind·ing** To bind or enthral, as if by a spell.

spell·bind·er (spel′bīn′dər) *n.* One who casts a spell over others; specifically, a political orator.

spell·bound (spel′bound′) *adj.* Bound as by a spell; fascinated.

spell·er (spel′ər) *n.* **1** One who spells. **2** A spelling book.

spell·ing (spel′ing) *n.* **1** The act of one who spells. **2** The art of correct spelling; orthography. **3** The way in which a word is spelled.

spelling bee A gathering at which contestants engage in spelling words, those who spell wrongly usually being retired until only one remains.

spelling book A book of exercises for training students to spell.

Spell·man (spel′mən), **Francis Joseph,** 1889–1967, U.S. cardinal; archbishop of New York.

spelt[1] (spelt) Alternative past tense and past participle of SPELL[1].

spelt[2] (spelt) *n.* A species of wheat (*Triticum spelta*) or any of its winter or spring varieties. [OE]

spel·ter (spel′tər) *n.* Zinc: a commercial term. — **brazing spelter** See BRAZING SOLDER. [Var. of PEWTER]

spe·lun·ker (spē·lung′kər) *n.* An enthusiast in the exploration and study of caves; a speleologist. [<L *spelunca* a cave]

Spe·mann (shpā′män), **Hans,** 1869–1941, German zoologist.

spence (spens) *n. Brit. Dial.* **1** A pantry or larder. **2** The parlor of a cottage. [<OF *despense* <L *dispendere* DISPENSE]

spen·cer[1] (spen′sər) *n.* A trysail.

spen·cer[2] (spen′sər) *n.* **1** A man's short jacket of the early 19th century. **2** A similar outer garment for women, usually tight-fitting and often knitted or fur-trimmed. [after 2nd Earl *Spencer,* 1758–1834, English nobleman]

Spen·cer (spen′sər), **Herbert,** 1820–1903, English philosopher.

Spen·cer Gulf (spen′sər) An inlet of the Indian Ocean in South Australia; 200 miles long; 80 miles wide.

Spen·ce·ri·an (spen·sir′ē·ən) *adj.* **1** Pertaining to Herbert Spencer, or to his doctrine. **2** Pertaining to a system of freehand penmanship devised by P. R. Spencer about 1855. — *n.* A follower of Herbert Spencer and his system.

Spen·cer·ism (spen′sə·riz′əm) *n.* The doctrine of Herbert Spencer that the universe has evolved through mechanical forces from relative simplicity to relative complexity; synthetic philosophy. Also **Spen·ce·ri·an·ism** (spen·sir′ē·ən·iz′əm).

spend (spend) *v.* **spent, spend·ing** *v.t.* **1** To pay out or disburse (money). **2** To expend by degrees; use up. **3** To apply or devote, as thought or effort, to some activity, purpose, etc. **4** To pass: to *spend* one's life in jail. **5** To lose: now chiefly in the nautical phrase **to spend a mast.** **6** To emit, as a milt or spawn. — *v.i.* **7** To pay out or disburse money, etc. **8** *Obs.* To be wasted or exhausted. See synonyms under SQUANDER. [OE *aspendan* <L *expendere* EXPEND] — **spend′er** *n.*

Spen·der (spen′dər), **Stephen,** born 1909, English poet and critic.

spend·thrift (spend′thrift′) *n.* One who is wastefully lavish of money: also **spend′er.** — *adj.* Excessively lavish; wasteful; prodigal.

Speng·ler (speng′glər, *Ger.* shpeng′lər), **Oswald,** 1880–1936, German philosopher of history.

Spen·ser (spen′sər), **Edmund,** 1552–99, English poet.

Spen·se·ri·an (spen·sir′ē·ən) *adj.* Of or pertaining to Edmund Spenser or to his style.

Spenserian sonnet See under SONNET.

Spenserian stanza A nine-line stanza consisting of eight lines of ten syllables and one of twelve syllables and riming *ababbcbcc*: used by Edmund Spenser in *The Faerie Queene.*

spent (spent) Past tense and past participle of SPEND. — *adj.* **1** Worn out or exhausted. **2** Deprived of force: a *spent* bullet or cannon ball.

Sper·lon·ga (sper·lông′gä) A village and port of south central Italy; site of a cave containing numerous ancient statues.

sperm[1] (spûrm) *n.* **1** The male fertilizing fluid; semen. **2** A male reproductive cell; spermatozoon. [<Gk. *sperma* a seed < *speirein* sow]

sperm[2] (spûrm) *n.* **1** A sperm whale. **2** Spermaceti. **3** Sperm oil. [Short for SPERMACETI]

-sperm *combining form Bot.* A seed (of a specified kind): *gymnosperm.* [<Gk. *sperma, spermatos* a seed]

sper·ma·ce·ti (spûr′mə·sē′tē, -set′ē) *n.* A white, waxy substance separated from the oil contained in the head of the sperm whale: used for making candles, ointments, etc. [<F <L *sperma ceti* seed of a whale]

sper·ma·ry (spûr′mər·ē) *n. pl* **·ries** The sperm-generating gland of the male; testis.

sper·ma·the·ca (spûr′mə·thē′kə) *n. pl.* **·cae** (-sē) *Zool.* A receptacle for receiving and retaining spermatozoa in the females of many invertebrates, as insects, worms, and mollusks. [<L *sperma* a seed + THECA] — **sper′·ma·the′cal** (-thē′kəl) *adj.*

sper·mat·ic (spûr·mat′ik) *adj.* Of or pertaining to sperm or a spermary.

spermatic cord *Anat.* The cord, made up of the spermatic duct and its accompanying vessels and nerves, that passes from the testis through the inguinal canal into the abdominal cavity.

spermatic fluid *Physiol.* Semen.

spermatic sac *Anat.* The scrotum.
sper·ma·tid (spûr′mə·tid) *n. Biol.* A cell resulting from the division of the secondary spermatocytes, and developing into a spermatozoon.
sper·ma·ti·um (spûr·mā′shē·əm) *n. pl.* **·ti·a** (-shē·ə) *Bot.* **1** A minute spore in certain lichens and fungi: formerly regarded as a non-motile male gamete. **2** A non-motile gamete which, in the red algae, unites with the carpogonium. [<NL <Gk. *spermation,* dim. of *sperma* a seed]
spermato– *combining form* **1** Seed; pertaining to seeds: *spermatophyte.* **2** Spermatozoa; of or related to spermatozoa: *spermatophore.* Also spelled *spermo–*. Also, before vowels, **spermat–.** [<Gk. *sperma, spermatos* a seed]
sper·ma·to·cyte (spûr′mə·tə·sīt′) *n. Biol.* A primary cell from which spermatozoa are developed through primary and secondary divisions, resulting in the spermatids.
sper·ma·to·gen·e·sis (spûr′mə·tə·jen′ə·sis) *n. Biol.* The development of spermatozoa. — **sper·ma·to·ge·net·ic** (spûr′mə·tō·jə·net′ik) *adj.*
sper·ma·to·go·ni·um (spûr′mə·tə·gō′nē·əm) *n. pl.* **·ni·a** (-nē·ə) *Biol.* One of the cells of the seminal tubules that produce the spermatocytes. — **sper′ma·to·go′ni·al** *adj.*
sper·ma·toid (spûr′mə·toid) *adj.* Resembling sperm.
sper·ma·to·phore (spûr′mə·tə·fôr′, -fōr′) *n. Zool.* A capsule or case containing spermatozoa, as in many mollusks, worms, and other invertebrates. — **sper′ma·toph′o·ral** (-tof′ər·əl) *adj.*
sper·ma·to·phyte (spûr′mə·tə·fīt′) *n.* Any plant of a phylum or division *(Spermatophyta)* of the most highly developed plants; a flowering and seed-bearing plant. — **sper′ma·to·phyt′ic** (-fit′ik) *adj.*
sper·ma·tor·rhe·a (spûr′mə·tə·rē′ə) *n. Pathol.* Excessive or frequent seminal discharge without sexual excitement. Also **sper′ma·tor·rhoe′a.**
sper·ma·to·zo·id (spûr′mə·tə·zō′id) *adj.* Resembling a spermatozoon. — *n.* **1** A spermatozoon. **2** *Bot.* A motile male germ cell in plants. Also **sper′ma·to·zo′oid** (-zō′oid).
sper·ma·to·zo·on (spûr′mə·tə·zō′on) *n. pl.* **·zo·a** (-zō′ə) *Biol.* The male fertilizing element of an animal, usually in the form of a nucleated cell with a long flagellate process or tail by which it swims actively about. [< SPERMATO- + Gk. *zōion* an animal] — **sper′ma·to·zo′al, sper′ma·to·zo′ic** *adj.*
sper·mic (spûr′mik) *adj.* Of or pertaining to sperm or semen; spermatic.
sper·mine (spûr′mēn, -min) *n. Biochem.* A colorless, crystalline, strongly basic compound, $C_{10}H_{26}N_4$, salts of which are contained in semen and other animal tissues. [<SPERM + -INE[2]]
sperm·ism (spûr′miz·əm) *n.* The old theory that the spermatozoon alone is responsible for the development of the future animal.
sperm·ist (spûr′mist) *n.* A believer in spermism.
spermo– See SPERMATO–.
sper·mo·go·ni·um (spûr′mə·gō′nē·əm) *n. pl.* **·ni·a** (-nē·ə) *Bot.* In fungi, a cup- or flask-shaped receptacle bearing a great number of spermatia.
sperm oil Oil obtained from the head and blubber cavities of the sperm whale.
sperm·o·phile (spûr′mə·fīl, -fil) *n.* A squirrel-like burrowing rodent (*Citellus* and related genera), as the striped gopher or the suslik.
–spermous *combining form* Having (a specified number or kind of) seeds; -seeded: *polyspermous.* Also **–spermal, –spermic.** [<-SPERM + -OUS]

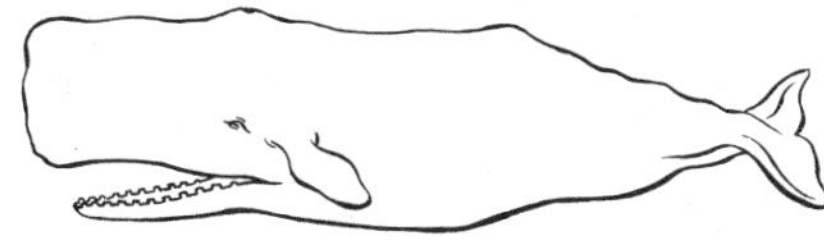

SPERM WHALE
(Up to 80 feet in length)

sperm whale A large, toothed whale *(Physeter catodon)* of warm seas, having a huge truncate head containing a reservoir of sperm oil; the cachalot.
Sper·ry (sper′ē), **Elmer Ambrose,** 1860–1930. U.S. engineer and inventor.
sper·ry·lite (sper′i·līt) *n.* A metallic tin-white platinum arsenide, $PtAs_2$, crystallizing in the isometric system. [after F. L. *Sperry,* Canadian mineralogist + -LITE]
spet (spet) *Obs. v.t. & v.i.* To spit. — *n.* Spittle. [OE *spǣtan*]
spetch·es (spech′iz) *n. pl.* The offal of skins, hides, etc., used for making glue. [Origin uncertain]
spew (spyōō) *v.t. & v.i.* To vomit; throw up. — *n.* That which is spewed; vomit. [OE *spīwan*]
Spey·er (shpī′ər) A city in SE Rhineland-Palatinate, West Germany; former capital of Rhine Palatinate: English *Spires.*
Spe·zia (spe′tsyä) La Spezia, a port on the **Gulf of Spezia,** an inlet of the Gulf of Genoa in NW Italy.
sphac·e·late (sfas′ə·lāt) *v.i.* **·lat·ed, ·lat·ing** *Pathol.* To become gangrenous; decay; die. [<Gk. *sphakelos* gangrene] — **sphac′e·la′·tion** *n.*
sphag·num (sfag′nəm) *n.* Any of a genus *(Sphagnum)* of whitish-gray mosses constituting the family *Sphagnaceae,* the bog or peat mosses: used as packing and in surgical dressings. [<Gk. *sphagnos,* kind of moss] — **sphag′nous** *adj.*
sphal·er·ite (sfal′ər·īt) *n.* A resinous to adamantine native zinc sulfide, ZnS, crystallizing in the isometric system; zinc blende. [<Gk. *sphaleros* deceptive + -ITE[1]]
sphene (sfēn) *n.* An adamantine, variously colored silicate of calcium and titanium, crystallizing in the monoclinic system: also called *titanite.* [<F *sphène* <Gk. *sphēn* wedge]
sphe·nic (sfē′nik) *adj.* Wedge-shaped.
sphenic number See under NUMBER.
spheno– *combining form* **1** Wedge-shaped: *sphenogram.* **2** *Med.* Pertaining to the sphenoid bone. Also, before vowels, **sphen–.** [<Gk. *sphēn, sphēnos* a wedge]
sphe·no·don (sfē′nə·don) *n.* A lizardlike reptile *(Sphenodon punctatum),* the sole surviving representative of the order *Rhynchocephalia;* the hatteria or tuatara of New Zealand. [<NL <Gk. *sphēn, sphēnos* a wedge + *odous, odontos* a tooth]
sphe·no·gram (sfē′nə·gram) *n.* A cuneiform character or symbol.
sphe·noid (sfē′noid) *n.* **1** *Mineral.* In the tetragonal and orthorhombic crystal systems, a hemihedral form enclosed by four faces, each of which cuts all three axes. **2** The sphenoid bone. — *adj.* Wedge-shaped: the *sphenoid* bone. [<SPHEN(O)- + -OID] — **sphe·noi·dal** (sfi·noid′l) *adj.*
sphenoid bone *Anat.* An irregular, compound bone situated at the base of the skull.
sphe·ra·di·an (sfi·rā′dē·ən) *n.* A steradian.
spher·al (sfir′əl) *adj.* **1** Shaped like a sphere; spherical; rounded; symmetrical. **2** Of or pertaining to a sphere. **3** Belonging to or relating to the celestial sphere; harmonious.
sphere (sfir) *n.* **1** The surface described by a semicircle making one complete rotation on its diameter as a fixed axis; a globular figure enclosed by a surface, every point of which is equidistant from a point within called the center. **2** An approximately globular body; a globe; ball; orb. **3** One of the heavenly bodies; a planet, sun, or star. **4** The apparent outer dome of the heavens on which the heavenly bodies appear to lie. **5** In old astronomy, one of the concentric and transparent globes believed to revolve about the earth and carry the various heavenly bodies, their movement supposedly producing mysteriously beautiful music. **6** Compass or field of activity, endeavor, influence, etc.; range; scope; province. **7** Social rank or position. — *v.t.* **sphered, spher·ing 1** To place in or as in a sphere; encircle; encompass. **2** To set among the celestial spheres. **3** To make spherical. [<OF *espere* <L *sphaera* < Gk. *sphaira* a ball]
–sphere *combining form* **1** Denoting an enveloping spherical mass: *hydrosphere, atmosphere.* **2** A sphere-shaped body: *oosphere.* **3** Denoting a spherical form: *planisphere.* [<Gk. *sphaira* a ball, sphere]
sphere of influence A country or region, usually backward politically or economically undeveloped, in which a state or states claim and are allowed exclusive rights to colonize, exploit natural and economic resources, or eventually annex.
spher·ic (sfer′ik) *adj.* Pertaining to a sphere or spheres; spherical.
spher·i·cal (sfer′i·kəl) *adj.* **1** Shaped like a sphere; globular. **2** Pertaining to a sphere or spheres. **3** Pertaining to the heavenly bodies; celestial. See synonyms under ORBICULATE, ROUND[1] — **spher′i·cal·ly** *adv.* — **spher′i·cal·ness** *n.*
spherical aberration See under ABERRATION.
spherical angle See under ANGLE.
spherical coordinate system *Math.* A three-dimensional system for indicating the shape of a solid by means of a sphere with the pole at the center. A point is located in terms of its distance along its radius vector from the pole, and in terms of two angles—the colatitude, or angle the radius vector forms with the vertical or polar axis of the sphere; and the longitude, or angle the radius vector makes with a fixed, vertical plane or initial meridian axis.
spherical sailing Navigation in which calculations are based upon a consideration of the spherical or spheroidal shape of the earth: distinguished from *plane sailing.*
spherical triangle *Math.* A spherical polygon the three sides of which are arcs of great circles of a sphere.
spherical trigonometry *Math.* The study of spherical triangles.
sphe·ric·i·ty (sfi·ris′ə·tē) *n. pl.* **·ties** The state of being a sphere; spherical form; roundness.
spher·ics (sfer′iks) *n.* **1** The geometry and trigonometry of figures on the surface of a sphere. **2** Atmospherics.
sphe·roid (sfir′oid) *n. Geom.* A body having nearly the form of a sphere; an ellipsoid. — **sphe·roi′dal** (sfi·roid′l), **sphe·roi′dic** or **·di·cal** *adj.* — **sphe·roi′dal·ly** *adv.*
sphe·roi·dic·i·ty (sfir′oi·dis′ə·tē) *n.* The state or character of being a spheroid. Also **sphe·roi·di·ty** (sfi·roi′də·tē).
sphe·rom·e·ter (sfi·rom′ə·tər) *n.* An instrument for measuring curvature or radii of spherical and other curved surfaces. [<SPHERE + -(O)METER]
spher·ule (sfer′ōōl) *n.* A small or minute sphere; globule. — **spher·u·lar** (sfer′ōō·lər) *adj.*
spher·u·lite (sfer′ōō·līt) *n.* A radiating spherical group of minute acicular crystals common in acidic glassy rocks. [<SPHERULE + -ITE[1]] — **spher′u·lit′ic** (-lit′ik) *adj.*
spher·y (sfir′ē) *adj. Poetic* **1** Like a sphere or star. **2** Of or relating to the celestial spheres.
sphinc·ter (sfingk′tər) *n. Anat.* A muscle that surrounds an opening or tube and serves to close it. [<LL <Gk. *sphinktēr* < *sphingein* close] — **sphinc′ter·al** *adj.*
sphinx (sfingks) *n. pl.* **sphinx·es** or **sphin·ges** (sfin′jēz) **1** In Egyptian mythology, a wingless monster with a lion's body and the head of a man *(androsphinx,* or simply *sphinx),* or of a ram *(criosphinx),* or of a hawk *(hieracosphinx);* also, any monumental representation of such a creature. **2** In Greek mythology, a winged monster with a woman's head and breasts and a lion's body, that destroyed those unable to guess her riddle. See OEDIPUS. **3** A mysterious or enigmatical person. **4** A large, stout-bodied, swift-flying moth. — **the Sphinx** The colossal androsphinx at Gizeh, having the body of a couchant lion, representing Harmachis, the Egyptian god of the morning, and dating to the IV dynasty. [<L <Gk. *sphinx* < *sphingein* close, strangle]

SPHINX *(def. 2)*

sphinx moth A hawk moth.
sphra·gis·tics (sfrə·jis′tiks) *n.* The study of signet rings or engraved seals, including their

authenticity, age, history, etc. [<Gk. *sphragistikos* of sealing < *sphragis* seal] —**sphra·gis'tic** *adj.*

sphyg·mic (sfig'mik) *adj. Physiol.* Pertaining to the pulse; pulsatory. [<Gk. *sphygmikos* < *sphygmos* pulse]

sphygmo– *combining form* Pulse; of or related to the pulse: *sphygmogram.* Also, before vowels, **sphygm–.** [<Gk. *sphygmos* pulse]

sphyg·mo·gram (sfig'mə·gram) *n.* A series of connected curves traced by a sphygmograph.

sphyg·mo·graph (sfig'mə·graf, -gräf) *n.* An instrument that, when applied over the heart or an artery, notes and records the character of the pulse and its rate, force, and variations: also called *pulsimeter.* —**sphyg'mo·graph'ic** *adj.* —**sphyg·mog'ra·phy** (sfig·mog'rə·fē) *n.*

sphyg·moid (sfig'moid) *adj. Physiol.* Pulselike.

sphyg·mo·ma·nom·e·ter (sfig'mō·mə·nom'ə·tər) *n.* An instrument for measuring the pressure of the blood in the arteries. Also **sphyg·mom'e·ter** (-mom'ə·tər).

sphyg·mo·scope (sfig'mə·skōp) *n.* An apparatus designed to make the pulse beat visible and to exhibit the varying pressures of the blood in the arteries during circulation.

sphyg·mus (sfig'məs) *n.* The pulse. [<NL <L <Gk. *sphygmos* pulse]

spi·ca (spī'kə) *n. pl.* **·cae** (-sē) **1** An ear of grain; a spike. **2** *Surg.* A bandage having a reversed spiral form, somewhat resembling an ear of wheat. [<L, spike, ear of grain]

Spi·ca (spī'kə) *Astron.* A spectroscopic binary star, Alpha in the constellation Virgo; magnitude, 1.21.

spi·cate (spī'kāt) *adj.* **1** *Bot.* Arranged in spikes: said of flowers. **2** *Ornithol.* Having a spur, as the legs of some birds. Also **spi'cat·ed.** [<L *spicatus* < *spica* spike]

spic·ca·to (spēk·kä'tō) *adj. & adv. Music* Detached; not legato. [<Ital., pp. of *spiccare* detach]

spice (spīs) *n.* **1** An aromatic, pungent vegetable substance, as cinnamon, cloves, etc., used to flavor food and beverages. **2** Such substances collectively. **3** That which gives zest or adds interest. **4** An aromatic odor; an agreeable perfume. **5** *Obs.* Sort; kind; species: the original meaning; also, a specimen. —*v.t.* **spiced, spic·ing** To season with spice; hence, to add zest or piquancy to. [< OF *espice* <L *species.* Doublet of SPECIES.] —**spic'er** *n.*

spice·ber·ry (spīs'ber'ē) *n. pl.* **·ries 1** A small tree (*Eugenia rhombea*) found in the West Indies and Florida. **2** The black or orange fruit of this tree. **3** The wintergreen or checkerberry.

spice·bush (spīs'bŏŏsh') *n.* An aromatic American shrub (*Lindera benzoin*) of the laurel family, the leaves of which have been used for tea, and the drupes, when powdered, for allspice. Also **spice'wood'** (-wŏŏd').

Spice Islands A former name for the MOLUCCA ISLANDS.

spic·er·y (spī'sər·ē) *n. pl.* **·er·ies 1** Spices collectively. **2** *Obs.* A place where spices are kept. **3** Spicy property or character; also, that which has spiciness.

spick (spik) *n. U.S. Slang* A Spanish-speaking person: an offensive term. Also **spic, spig** (spig).

spick-and-span (spik'ən·span') *adj.* **1** Neat and clean. **2** Perfectly new, or looking as if new. [Prob. < *spick,* var. of SPIKE[1] + SPAN-NEW]

spic·ule (spik'yŏŏl) *n.* **1** A small, slender, sharp-pointed body; a spikelet. **2** *Zool.* One of the small, needlelike, calcareous growths supporting the soft tissues of certain invertebrates, as sponges, radiolarians, etc. Also **spic·u·la** (spik'yə·lə). [<L *spiculum,* dim. of *spicum* point, spike] —**spic'u·lar, spic'u·late** (-lāt, -lit) *adj.*

spic·u·lum (spik'yə·ləm) *n. pl.* **·la** (-lə) **1** A spicule. **2** *Zool.* Any small, dartlike organ, as the spines of a sea urchin. [<L]

spic·y (spī'sē) *adj.* **spic·i·er, spic·i·est 1** Containing, flavored, or fragrant with spices. **2** Producing spices. **3** Highly flavored; pungent; having zest; hence, somewhat improper; risqué. See synonyms under RACY. —**spic'i·ly** *adv.* —**spic'i·ness** *n.*

spi·der (spī'dər) *n.* **1** Any one of a large number of wingless arachnids (order *Araneae*) having an unsegmented abdomen and capable of spinning silk in the construction of webs for the capture of prey such as flies or other insects. **2** A long-handled iron frying pan, often having legs. **3** A portable electric switching apparatus for use in motion-picture studios. **4** A three-legged iron stool for the support of pots and pans over a fire; a trivet. **5** An apparatus for pulverizing the ground during cultivation. **6** *Electr.* The central part of an armature core. **7** *Naut.* **a** An iron hoop around the mast of a ship for the attachment of shrouds. **b** A magnifying glass for a ship's compass. **8** Any of several vehicles of different types having unusually light frames. [OE *spithra* < *spinnan* spin]

spider crab Any of a genus (*Libinia*) of decapod crustaceans with long legs, retractable eyes, and spiny growths on the carapace, especially *L. emarginata,* common on the Atlantic coast of North America.

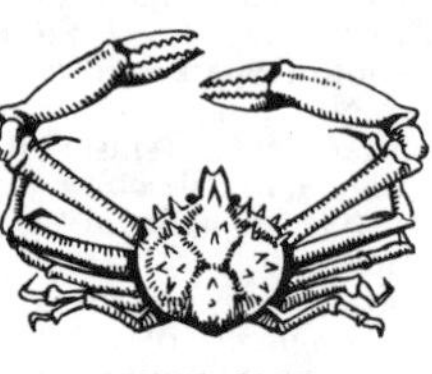

SPIDER CRAB
(Up to 10 inches in breadth)

spi·der·flow·er (spī'·dər·flou'ər) *n.* A cleome.

spider monkey An arboreal American monkey (genus *Ateles*) of slender form, with very long limbs, thumbs absent or vestigial, and a long prehensile tail: range from Mexico to Paraguay.

spider phaeton A type of carriage of light construction, having a covered seat in front, and a rear seat for a footman or attendant.

spi·der·wort (spī'dər·wûrt') *n.* **1** Any species of a genus (*Tradescantia*) of plants, especially *T. virginiana,* an American perennial with deep-blue, three-petaled flowers in umbels. **2** Any plant of the same family (*Commelinaceae*).

spi·der·y (spī'dər·ē) *adj.* Spiderlike.

S-piece (es'pēs') *n.* An S-bracket.

spied (spīd) Past tense and past participle of SPY.

spie·gel·ei·sen (spē'gəl·ī'zən) *n.* A white, very hard and brittle cast iron containing manganese, largely used in the manufacture of steel: when more than about 20 percent of manganese is in the alloy it is called *ferromanganese.* Also **spie'gel, spiegel iron.** [<G < *spiegel* a mirror + *eisen* iron]

spiel (spēl) *U.S. Slang v.i.* To talk; orate. —*n.* A speech, especially a long speech. [<G, a game, play < *spielen* play]

spi·er[1] (spī'ər) *n. Brit. Dial.* A spy; scout.

spier[2] (spir) See SPEER.

spif·fy (spif'ē) *adj. Slang* Smartly dressed; spruce. [< dial. E *spiff* a dandy]

spi·ge·li·a (spī·jē'lē·ə) *n.* Pinkroot: used as a vermifuge. [<NL, after Adrian van den *Spiegel,* 1578–1625, Flemish anatomist]

spig·ot (spig'ət) *n.* **1** A plug or faucet for the bunghole of a cask. **2** A turning plug fitting into a faucet, or the faucet itself. [ME *spigote.* Prob. akin to SPIKE[1].]

spike[1] (spīk) *n.* **1** A stout piece of metal, like a large nail, but thicker in proportion. **2** A projecting, pointed piece of metal, or any similar object, as in the soles of shoes to keep the wearer from slipping. **3** A very high heel on a woman's shoe, narrow at the bottom. **4** A steel pin for plugging cannon vents. **5** A straight, unbranched antler, as of a young deer. **6** A young mackerel. —*v.t.* **spiked, spik·ing 1** To fasten with spikes. **2** To set or provide with spikes. **3** To block the vent of (a cannon) with a spike, rendering it useless. **4** To block; put a stop to. **5** To pierce with or impale on a spike. **6** In baseball, to injure (another player) with the spikes on one's shoes. **7** *Colloq.* To add spirituous liquor to. [ME <Scand. Cf. ON *spikr* a nail.]

spike[2] (spīk) *n.* **1** An ear of corn, barley, wheat, or other grain. **2** *Bot.* A flower cluster in which there are numerous flowers arranged closely on an elongated common axis. [<L *spica* ear of grain]

spike lavender See under LAVENDER.

spike·let (spīk'lit) *n. Bot.* A small spike bearing few flowers and forming the compound inflorescence of cereal grasses and sedges.

spike·nard (spīk'nərd, -närd) *n.* **1** An ancient fragrant and costly ointment prepared mainly from a plant of the same name. **2** A perennial East Indian herb (*Nardostachys jatamansi*) of the valerian family. **3** An American herb (*Aralia racemosa*) of the ginseng family. [<L *spica* spike + *nardus* nard]

spik·er (spī'kər) *n.* One who or that which spikes; specifically, a workman who drives spikes in railroad ties.

spik·y (spī'kē) *adj.* **spik·i·er, spik·i·est 1** Resembling a spike; pointed. **2** Having spikes.

spile[1] (spīl) *n.* **1** A large timber driven into the ground to serve as a foundation; a pile. **2** A wooden pin or plug used as a vent in a cask; a spigot. **3** A spout driven into a sugar-maple tree to lead the sap to a bucket. —*v.t.* **spiled, spil·ing 1** To pierce for and provide with a spigot. **2** To drive spiles into. [<MDu., skewer, splinter]

spile[2] (spīl) *v.t. & v.i. Dial.* To spoil.

spil·i·kin (spil'i·kin) *n.* **1** A jackstraw; one of the thin straws used in playing jackstraws. **2** *pl.* The game of jackstraws. Also **spil'li·kin.** [Dim. of SPILL[2]]

spil·ing (spī'ling) *n.* Spiles collectively; piling.

spill[1] (spil) *v.* **spilled** or **spilt, spill·ing** *v.t.* **1** To allow or cause to fall or run out or over, as a liquid or a powder. **2** To shed, as blood. **3** *Naut.* To empty (a sail) of wind. **4** *Colloq.* To cause to fall, as from a horse. **5** *Colloq.* To divulge; make known, as a secret. —*v.i.* **6** To fall or run out or over: said of liquids, etc. —**to spill the beans** *Colloq.* To divulge, especially a secret. —*n.* **1** *Colloq.* A fall to the ground, as from a horse or vehicle; tumble. **2** *Colloq.* A downpour, as of rain. **3** A crack, seam, or other defect in iron or steel castings, forgings, etc. [OE *spillan* destroy] —**spill'·age** *n.* —**spill'er** *n.*

spill[2] (spil) *n.* **1** A slip of wood, or rolled strip of paper, used for lighting lamps, etc.; a lamplighter. **2** A slender peg, pin, or bar of wood or metal; especially, a slender plug for stopping a hole in a cask; a spile. [Var. of SPILE[1]]

spill·way (spil'wā') *n.* **1** A passageway in or about a dam to release the water in a reservoir. **2** The paved upper surface of a dam over which surplus water escapes.

SPILLWAY

spil·o·site (spil'ə·sīt) *n.* A greenish schistous rock spotted with chlorite, produced by the shearing of a basic amygdaloid. [<Gk. *spilos* spot + -ITE[1]]

spilt (spilt) Alternative past tense and past participle of SPILL[1].

spilth (spilth) *n.* That which is spilled or poured out profusely; effusion; excess of supply.

spin (spin) *v.* **spun** (*Archaic* **span**), **spun, spin·ning** *v.t.* **1** To draw out and twist into threads; also, to draw out and twist fiber into (threads, yarn, etc.). **2** To make or produce as if by spinning. **3** To form (a net, etc.) from filaments of a viscous substance extruded from the body: said of spiders, silkworms, etc. **4** To tell, as a story or yarn. **5** To protract; prolong, as a period of time by delays or a story by additional details: with *out.* **6** To cause to whirl rapidly: to *spin* a top. —*v.i.* **7** To make thread or yarn. **8** To extrude filaments of a viscous substance from the body: said of spiders, etc. **9** To whirl rapidly; rotate. **10** To seem to be whirling, as from dizziness: My head is *spinning.* **11** To move rapidly. **12** To fish with a spoon bait or swivel. —*n.* **1** An act or instance of spinning; a rapid whirling. **2** Any rapid movement or action. **3** *Aeron.* The downward spiral motion of an airplane about a vertical axis, with its longitudinal axis steeply inclined. **4** *Physics* The angular momentum of an atomic particle or nuclide, commonly given in units of Planck's constant divided by 2π. [OE *spinnan* spin]

spi·na·ceous (spi·nā'shəs) *adj.* Of, relating to, or resembling spinach or plants allied to it.

spin·ach (spin'ich, -ij) *n.* **1** An edible garden pot herb (*Spinacia oleracea*) of the goosefoot family. **2** Its fleshy, edible leaves. Also **spin'·age.** [<OF *espinage* <LL *spinacia* <Arabic *isbānah*; infl. in form by L *spina* a thorn]

spi·nal (spī'nəl) *adj.* **1** Pertaining to the backbone; vertebral. **2** Pertaining to a spine, spines, or spinous processes. **3** Dependent upon or functioning with a spinal cord, as the vertebrates.

spinal canal *Anat.* The tubular cavity on the dorsal side of the spinal column, in which the spinal cord and its membranes are lodged.
spinal column *Anat.* The series of articulated vertebrae which, with their associated structures, enclose the spinal cord and provide dorsal support for the ribs; the backbone or spine.
spinal cord *Anat.* That portion of the central nervous system enclosed by the spinal column. It is composed of an inner region of gray matter and an outer, larger region of white matter, the whole divided into the cervical, thoracic, lumbar, sacral, and coccygeal areas.
spi·nate (spī′nāt) *adj.* Spinelike, or bearing spines or thorns. Also **spi′nat·ed.**
spin·dle (spin′dəl) *n.* **1** A rod having a slit or catch in the top and a whorl of wood or metal at its lower end, formerly used in hand spinning, and on which was wound the thread from the distaff. **2** The slender rod in a spinning wheel by the rotation of which the thread is twisted and wound on a spool or bobbin on the same rod; also, a small rod or pin bearing the bobbin of a spinning machine or a shuttle. **3** *Mech.* A rotating rod, pin, axis, arbor, or shaft, especially when small and bearing something that rotates: the *spindle* of a lathe. **4** The pin on which rotates a fusee in a watch, or the fusee itself. **5** The tapering end of a vehicle axle that enters the hub. **6** A small shaft passing through the lock of a door and bearing the knobs or handles. **7** *Biol.* A spindle-shaped structure of elongated achromatic fibers formed during the mitosis of a cell. **8** A measure of length for cotton or linen yarn, varying according to the number of hanks or cuts: generally 18 hanks, or 15,120 yards. **9** *Naut.* An iron pile or pipe, surmounted by a lantern or other conspicuous object, placed on a rock or shoal for the guidance of seamen. **10** A hydrometer. **11** A needlelike rod mounted on a weighted base, for impaling bills, checks, etc. — *v.* **·dled, ·dling** *v.i.* **1** To grow into a long, slender stalk or body; become extremely long and slender. — *v.t.* **2** To form into or as into a spindle. **3** To provide with a spindle. [OE *spinel* < *spinnan* spin]
spin·dle-leg·ged (spin′dəl·leg′id, -legd′) *adj.* Having long, slender legs. Also **spin′dle-shanked′** (-shangkt′).
spin·dle-legs (spin′dəl·legz′) *n.* **1** Long, slender legs. **2** *Colloq.* A person having long, slender legs. Also **spin′dle-shanks′** (-shangks′).
spindle side The female or distaff side of a family.
spindle tree A European shrub or low-spreading tree *(Euonymus europaeus)*, so called from the use of its compact wood in making spindles, slender pins, skewers, etc.
spin·dling (spind′ling) *adj.* Long and thin; disproportionately slender. — *n.* A spindling person or plant shoot.
spin·dly (spind′lē) *adj.* Of a slender, lanky growth or form, suggesting weakness.
spin·drift (spin′drift) *n.* Blown spray or scud: also called *spoondrift.* [Alter. of *spoondrift* < *spoon,* var. of SPUME + DRIFT]
spine (spīn) *n.* **1** The spinal column of a vertebrate; backbone. **2** *Zool.* Any of various hard, pointed outgrowths on the bodies of certain animals, as the porcupine and starfish; a spicule; the fin ray of a fish. **3** *Bot.* A stiff, short-pointed woody process on the stems of certain plants, as the honey locust; thorn. **4** The back of a bound book. **5** A projecting eminence or ridge. **6** Any slender, thornlike process, as of a vertebra or nerve. **7** The central ridge on the underside of a horse's hoof. [<OF *espine* <L *spina* spine, thorn]
spi·nel (spi·nel′, spin′əl) *n.* A hard isometric mineral of various colors and composition, the red variety of which is used as a gem under the name of **ruby spinel.** Compare BALAS. [<F *spinelle* <Ital. *spinella,* dim. of L *spina* spine]
spine·less (spīn′lis) *adj.* **1** Having no spine or backbone; invertebrate. **2** Lacking spines. **3** Having a very flexible backbone; limp. **4** Figuratively, lacking decision of character or steadfastness. — **spine′less·ness** *n.*
spi·nes·cent (spī·nes′ənt) *adj.* **1** *Bot.* Bearing spines; spinous; terminating in a spine. **2** *Zool.* Tending to become spinous, as certain animals during the period of racial decline. — **spi·nes′cence** *n.*
spin·et (spin′it) *n.* **1** A small keyboard musical instrument of the harpsichord class. **2** A small upright piano. [Perhaps after G. *Spinetti,* 16th-century Venetian inventor]
Spin·garn (spin′gärn), **Joel Elias,** 1875–1939, U. S. poet and critic.
spini- *combining form* A spine; thorn: *spiniferous.* [<L *spina* a thorn]
spi·nif·er·ous (spī·nif′ər·əs) *adj.* Bearing or producing spines. Also **spi·nig′er·ous** (-nij′·ər·əs).
spin·i·fex (spin′i·feks, spī′ni-) *n.* An Australian grass (genus *Spinifex*) with pointed leaves.
spin·na·ker (spin′ə·kər) *n. Naut.* A large jib-shaped sail sometimes carried on the mainmast of a racing vessel, opposite the mainsail, and used when sailing before the wind. The foot slides on a spar called the **spinnaker boom.** [? < *spinx,* a mispronunciation of *Sphinx,* the name of the first vessel to carry this kind of sail]
spin·ner (spin′ər) *n.* **1** One who or that which spins, as a spider or a machine. **2** In angling, a whirling spoon bait. **3** *Aeron.* A streamlined fairing fitted over the boss of an airplane propeller and revolving with it. See illustration under AIRPLANE. **4** A play in football wherein the ball carrier spins around to conceal the direction of the play from his opponents.
spin·ner·et (spin′ə·ret) *n.* **1** An organ, as of spiders and silkworms, for spinning silk. **2** A metal plate pierced with holes through which filaments of plastic material are forced, as in the making of rayon fibers.
spin·ner·y (spin′ər·ē) *n. pl.* **·ner·ies** A spinning mill.
spin·ney (spin′ē) *n.* A small wood or thicket. Also **spin′ny.** [<OF *espinei* <LL *spinetum* <L *spina* a thorn]
spin·ning (spin′ing) *n.* **1** The action of, or activities involved in, converting fibers into thread or yarn. **2** The product of spinning. — *adj.* **1** That spins, in any sense. **2** Of or used in the process of spinning.
spinning gland A gland that secretes silk or a silky substance, as in silkworms.
spinning house A house of correction for prostitutes: so called because the inmates were formerly forced to spin yarn, etc.
spinning jenny A framed mechanism for spinning more than one strand of yarn at a time: also called *jenny.*
spinning mill A mill or factory devoted to spinning.
spinning mule A kind of spinning jenny.
spinning wheel A household implement formerly used for spinning yarn or thread, consisting of a rotating spindle operated by a treadle and flywheel.

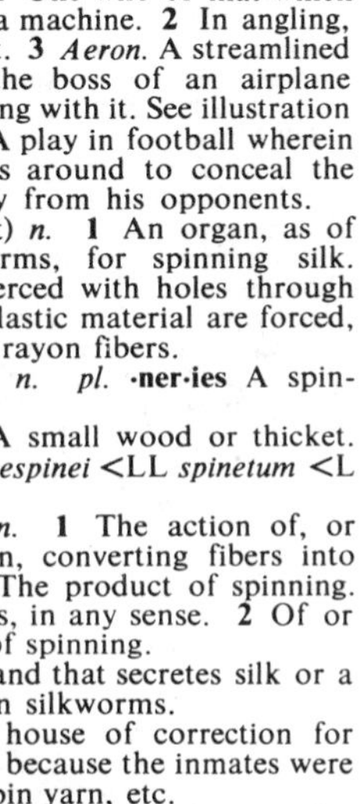

SPINNING WHEEL

spin-off (spin′ôf′, -of′) *n.* **1** Action of a corporation in divesting itself, tax free, of a segment or division of its operations by transfer to a new, independently owned and managed company, the stockholders of the original corporation receiving the new shares pro rata. **2** A new application or incidental result, especially if beneficial; offshoot or by-product; also, such applications or results considered collectively: commercial *spin-off* from the government's aerospace program: also **spin′off′.**
spi·nose (spī′nōs) *adj.* Bearing, armed with, or having many spines. [<L *spinosus* < *spina* a thorn] — **spi′nose·ly** *adv.*
spi·nos·i·ty (spī·nos′ə·tē) *n. pl.* **·ties** **1** The state of being spinous or spinose. **2** A spinous part or thing.
spi·nous (spī′nəs) *adj.* **1** Spinelike; prickly. **2** Spinose.
Spi·no·za (spi·nō′zə), **Baruch,** 1632–77, Dutch philosopher and pantheist: also known as *Benedict Spinoza.*
Spi·no·zism (spi·nō′ziz·əm) *n. Philos.* A system of absolute monism developed from Cartesianism by Spinoza. This system regards the entire universe as one infinite and universal substance, namely, God. — **Spi·no′zist** *n.* — **Spin·o·zis·tic** (spin′ō·zis′tik) *adj.*
spin·ster (spin′stər) *n.* **1** An unmarried woman, especially when no longer young; an old maid. **2** *Law* In England, a woman who has never married: a legal title. **3** A woman who spins; a spinner. [ME <SPIN + -STER] — **spin′·ster·hood** *n.* — **spin′ster·ish** *adj.*
spin·thar·i·scope (spin·thar′ə·skōp) *n.* A device for showing the radioactivity of a substance by the scintillations of the alpha rays emitted from a minute particle of the substance and thrown against a fluorescent screen. [<Gk. *spintharis* spark + -SCOPE] — **spin·thar′i·scop′ic** (-skop′ik) *adj.*
spi·nule (spī′nyōōl, spin′yōōl) *n.* A small spine; spicule. Also **spin·u·la** (spin′yə·lə). [<L *spinula,* dim. of *spina* spine]
spin·u·les·cent (spin′yə·les′ənt, spī′nyə-) *adj.* Furnished with or producing spinules; spiny.
spin·u·lose (spin′yə·lōs, spī′nyə·lōs) *adj.* Having spinules. Also **spin′u·lous** (-ləs).
spin·y (spī′nē) *adj.* **spin·i·er, spin·i·est** **1** Having spines; thorny. **2** Difficult; perplexing. — **spin′i·ness** *n.*
spiny ant-eater The echidna.
spin·y-finned (spī′nē·find′) *adj.* Characterized by fins bearing one or more sharp, unsegmented rays, as the perch, mackerel, and bass. Also **spine′-finned′.**
spiny lobster One of various large-bodied marine crustaceans (genus *Palinurus*) with spiny shells but lacking claws; especially, the California spiny lobster *(P. interruptus),* valued as a sea food. Also called *crayfish.*
Spi·on Kop (spē′ən kop) A hill in NW Natal province, Union of South Africa; scene of a battle in the Boer War, 1900.
spir- Var. of SPIRO-.
spir·a·cle (spir′ə·kəl, spī′rə-) *n.* **1** *Zool.* **a** An aperture or orifice for the passage of air or water in the respiration of terrestrial arthropods, as the grasshopper and locust. **b** A breathing hole, as the blowhole or nostril of a cetacean. **2** A minute cone formed on a stream of lava by escaping gases. **3** Any opening to admit or expel air; an airhole. [< OF <L *spiraculum* airhole < *spirare* breathe]
spi·rae·a (spī·rē′ə) *n.* Any of a genus *(Spiraea)* of ornamental shrubs of the rose family, having alternate simple or pinnate leaves and small, white or pink flowers; especially, an American variety, the meadowsweet. Also **spi·re′a.** [<L, meadowsweet <Gk. *speiraia* < *speira* coil]
spi·ral (spī′rəl) *adj.* **1** Winding about and constantly receding from a center. **2** Winding and advancing; helical. **3** Winding and rising in a spire, as some springs. — *n.* **1** *Geom.* Any plane curve formed by a point that moves around a fixed center and continually increases its distance from it. **2** A curve winding like a screw thread. **3** Something wound as a spiral or having a spiral shape, as a spring or a whorled shell. **4** A sharp or disproportionate rise, as in prices. **5** *Aeron.* A flight of an airplane in a spiral path. **6** In football, the motion of a ball rotating on its long axis. — *v.* **·raled** or **·ralled, ·ral·ing** or **·ral·ling** *v.t.* **1** To cause to take a spiral form or course. — *v.i.* **2** To take a spiral form or course. **3** To rise sharply or disproportionately, as prices, costs, etc. [< Med. L *spiralis* <L *spira* SPIRE[2]] — **spi′ral·ly** *adv.*
spiral binding A binding consisting of a wire in spiral form looped through holes in the covers on either side.
spiral nebula *Astron.* An extragalactic system of celestial bodies exhibiting a spiral configuration, known to be composed of aggregates of stars resembling the Milky Way, as the *spiral nebula* in Andromeda.
spiral of Archimedes *Math.* The polar curve traced by a point starting at the pole and moving along its radius vector at a constant velocity while the radius vector moves at a constant angular velocity.

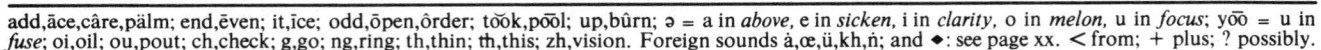

spi·rant (spī′rənt) *n.* & *adj.* *Phonet.* Fricative.

spire[1] (spīr) *n.* **1** The tapering or pyramidal roof of a tower; a pinnacle; also, loosely, a steeple. **2** A slender stalk or blade. **3** The summit or tapering end of anything; a sharp point. — *v.* **spired, spir·ing** *v.t.* **1** To furnish with a spire or spires. — *v.i.* **2** To shoot or point up in or as in a spire. **3** To put forth a spire or spires; sprout. [OE *spīr* a stalk, stem] — **spired** *adj.*

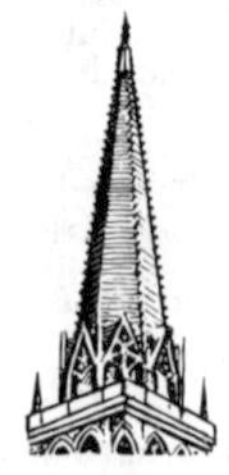

SPIRE

spire[2] (spīr) *n.* **1** A spiral or a single turn of one; whorl; twist. **2** The portion of a spiral formed by a single revolution about the central point. **3** *Zool.* The convoluted portion of a spiral shell. [<F <L *spira* <Gk. *speira* coil] — **spired** *adj.*

spi·reme (spī′rēm) *n.* *Biol.* **1** The stage in the division of a cell during which the chromatin appears like a skein of filaments. **2** One of these filaments. Also **spi′rem** (-rem). [<Gk. *speirēma* a coil]

Spires (spīrz) The English name for SPEYER.

spi·rif·er·ous (spī·rif′ər·əs) *adj.* **1** Bearing spiral appendages. **2** Having a spire, as a univalve. Also **spi·rig′er·ous** (-rij′ər·əs). [<L *spira* coil + -(I)FEROUS]

spir·il·lo·sis (spir′ə·lō′sis) *n.* **1** *Pathol.* Any disease caused by the presence of spirilla in the body. **2** A disease of domestic fowls caused by a spirochete transmitted by a tick. [<SPIRILLUM + -OSIS]

spi·ril·lum (spī·ril′əm) *n.* *pl.* **·ril·la** (-ril′ə) Any of a genus *(Spirillum)* of flagellate bacteria with cells in spirally twisted and rigid filaments. See illustration under BACTERIUM. [< NL, dim. of L *spira* a coil]

spir·it (spir′it) *n.* **1** The principle of life and energy in man and animals, at one time regarded as being composed of an especially refined substance, such as breath or warm air, separable from the body, mysterious in nature, and ascribable to a divine origin. **2** An entity conceived of as that part of a human being that is incorporeal and invisible and is characterized by intelligence, personality, self-consciousness, and will; the mind: opposed to *body.* **3** The substance or universal aspect of reality, regarded as independent of and opposed to matter. **4** In the Bible, the creative, animating power or divine influence of God. *Joel* ii 28. **5** A rational, supernatural being without a material body, as an angel, demon, elf, fairy, etc.; specifically, such a being with a certain character or a particular abode or area of activity: an evil *spirit.* **6** A disembodied soul regarded as manifested to the senses, often as visible or having some kind of immaterial body: a ghost; specter: Hamlet saw his father's *spirit.* **7** A person regarded with reference to any peculiar activity, characteristic, or temper: a leading *spirit* in the community. **8** *Usually pl.* A state of mind; mood; temper: Success raised his *spirits.* **9** Vivacity or energy; ardor; dash; fire: an attack made with *spirit.* **10** Ardent loyalty or devotion: school *spirit.* **11** True intent or meaning as opposed to outward, formal signification: to keep the *spirit* of the law. Compare LETTER (def. 5). **12** The emotional or affective faculty of man; the heart: Great poetry stirs the *spirit.* **13** The characteristic temper or disposition of a period or of a movement: the *spirit* of the Reformation. **14** *pl.* A strong alcoholic liquor or liquid obtained by distillation. **15** *Usually pl.* *Chem.* **a** The essence or distilled extract of a substance: *spirits* of turpentine. **b** Ethanol. **16** *Often pl.* In pharmacy, a solution of a volatile principle in alcohol; a tincture; essence: *spirits* of ammonia. **17** In dyeing, a solution of a tin salt in acid. **18** In alchemy, one of four substances, mercury, sal ammoniac, sulfur, and arsenic (or orpiment). **19** In medieval physiology, one of the three degrees of spirit inherent in the human body: **natural spirit,** located in the liver and underlying the processes of nutrition, growth, and reproduction; **vital spirit,** located in the heart, which circulated heat and life through the body; **animal spirit,** located in the brain, which guided reason and conveyed the powers of motion and sensation to and through the nerves. **20** *Obs.* Breathed air; breeze; wind. **21** *Obs.* The breath; life. See synonyms under CHARACTER, COURAGE, MIND, SPECTER. — *v.t.* **1** To carry off secretly or mysteriously, as if by the agency of a spirit: with *away, off,* etc. **2** To infuse with spirit or animation; inspirit; encourage: often with *up.* — *adj.* **1** Of or pertaining to ghosts or the belief in the existence of departed souls; spiritualistic. **2** Operated by the burning of alcohol: a *spirit* lamp. [<OF *espirit* <L *spiritus* breathing < *spirare* breathe. Doublet of SPRITE.]

Spir·it (spir′it) *n.* In Christian theology, the Holy Spirit.

spir·it·ed (spir′it·id) *adj.* Full of spirit; animated: used in various compound adjectives: high-*spirited,* mean-*spirited.* See synonyms under RACY. — **spir′it·ed·ly** *adv.* — **spir′it·ed·ness** *n.*

spir·it·ing (spir′it·ing) *n.* Movement as of a spirit; hence, something dexterously done; the work or ministering of a spirit; inspiration; encouragement.

spir·it·ism (spir′i·tiz′əm) *n.* **1** Loosely, spiritualism. **2** *Rare* Animism; the theory that inanimate objects possess spirits. — **spir′it·ist** *n.* — **spir′it·is′tic** *adj.*

spirit lamp A lamp that burns alcohol: used in laboratory work, etc.

spir·it·less (spir′it·lis) *adj.* Lacking in enthusiasm, energy, or courage; lacking in the sense of well-being. — **spir′it·less·ly** *adv.* — **spir′it·less·ness** *n.*

spirit level An instrument for adjusting any deviation from the horizontal or perpendicular by reference to the position of a bubble of air in a tube of alcohol or other liquid.

spi·ri·to·so (spir′i·tō′sō, *Ital.* spē′rē·tō′sō) *Music adj.* Spirited; animated. — *adv.* With spirit. [<Ital. < *spirito* spirit]

spir·it·ous (spir′i·təs) *adj.* **1** Like spirits; refined. **2** Spirituous. **3** Spirited; ardent.

spirit rapping The professed communication with the spirits of departed persons by raps, as on a table; also, the rapping believed to be made by spirits.

spirits of hartshorn See under AMMONIA.

spirits of turpentine Oil of turpentine.

spirits of wine Rectified alcohol.

spir·i·tu·al (spir′i·cho͞o·əl) *adj.* **1** Of or pertaining to spirit, as distingushed from matter; having the nature of spirit; consisting of spirit; incorporeal. **2** Pertaining to or affecting the immaterial nature or soul of man. **3** Of or pertaining to God, his Spirit, or his law, or to the soul as acted upon by the Holy Spirit; holy; pure; not carnal. **4** Sacred or religious; not lay or temporal; ecclesiastical: *spiritual* authorities: contrasted with *secular.* **5** Marked or characterized by the highest qualities of the human mind; intellectualized. — *n.* **1** Anything pertaining to spirit or to sacred matters. **2** A religious folk song originating among the Negroes of the southern United States, typified by colorful rhythm and emotion: sometimes in narrative or ballad form; also, any song composed in imitation of a Negro spiritual. — **the Spirituals** See under FRATICELLI. [<L *spiritualis* < *spiritus* spirit] — **spir′i·tu·al·ly** *adv.* — **spir′i·tu·al·ness** *n.*

spiritual incest *Eccl.* Sexual intercourse between persons spiritually related, as between godparent and godchild.

spir·i·tu·al·ism (spir′i·cho͞o·əl·iz′əm) *n.* **1** The belief that the spirits of the dead in various ways communicate with and manifest their presence to the living, usually through the agency of a person called a medium; also, the doctrines and practices of those so believing. **2** The doctrine that there are beings not cognizable by the senses or characterized by the properties of matter, and that are therefore spiritual, as distinguished from material: opposed to *materialism.* **3** The doctrine that man is an immortal spirit and as such may know, love, or worship God. **4** A non-materialistic philosophy, a form of idealism which identifies ultimate reality as one universal conscious mind. **5** The state or character of being spiritual. — **spir′i·tu·al·ist** *n.* — **spir′i·tu·al·is′tic** *adj.*

spir·i·tu·al·i·ty (spir′i·cho͞o·al′ə·tē) *n.* *pl.* **·ties** **1** The state of being spiritual. **2** That which belongs to the church or to an ecclesiastic: opposed to *temporality.*

spir·i·tu·al·ize (spir′i·cho͞o·əl·īz′) *v.t.* **·ized, ·iz·ing** **1** To make spiritual; free of grossness or materialism: to *spiritualize* the thoughts. **2** To imbue with spirit; animate. **3** To treat as having a spiritual meaning or sense. Also *Brit.* **spir′i·tu·al·ise′.** — **spir′i·tu·al·i·za′tion** *n.* — **spir′i·tu·al·iz′er** *n.*

spir·i·tu·al·ty (spir′i·cho͞o·əl·te) *n.* *pl.* **·ties** Ecclesiastical bodies collectively; the clergy.

spiritual wife Among the Mormons, a woman who has been married for eternity in accordance with the doctrine of the Mormon gospel; hence, **spiritual wifeism, spiritual wifehood.**

spir·i·tu·el (spir′i·cho͞o·el′, *Fr.* spē·rē·tü·el′) *adj.* Characterized by esprit, or wit, and by the higher and finer qualities of the mind generally. [<F] — **spir′i·tu·elle′** *adj. fem.*

spir·i·tu·ous (spir′i·cho͞o·əs) *adj.* **1** Containing alcohol. **2** Intoxicating; distilled. **3** *Obs.* Spiritlike; ethereal. **4** *Rare* Lively. — **spir′i·tu·ous·ness** *n.*

spir·i·tus (spir′i·təs) *n.* *pl.* **·tus** **1** A breathing or an aspirate. In Greek grammar the rough breathing is called **spiritus asper,** the smooth **spiritus lenis.** See BREATHING. **2** Any liquid product of distillation; especially, alcoholic liquor. See SPIRIT. [<L, a breathing]

spirit writing Visible but automatic writing done without the conscious will of the writer, and believed to be a manifestation of spirit guidance; pneumatography.

spiro-[1] *combining form* Breath; respiration: *spirograph.* Also, before vowels, *spir-.* [<L *spirare* breathe]

spiro-[2] *combining form* Spiral; coiled: *spirochete.* Also, before vowels, *spir-.* [<Gk. *speira* a coil]

spi·ro·chete (spī′rə·kēt) *n.* **1** Any of a genus *(Spirochaeta)* of typically saprophytic bacteria commonly found in water and sewage, and characterized by spiral flexible filaments with apparently rotary movements. See illustration under BACTERIUM. **2** Any of various other similar micro-organisms of the order *Spirochaetales,* including those which cause syphilis and relapsing fever. Also **spi′ro·chaete.** [<Gk. *speira* coil + *chaitē* bristle] — **spi′ro·che′tal** *adj.*

spi·ro·che·to·sis (spī′rə·kē·tō′sis) *n.* **1** *Pathol.* Infection by spirochetes. **2** An infectious septicemia in chickens caused by a spirochete *(Borrelia anserina).*

spi·ro·graph (spī′rə·graf, -gräf) *n.* An instrument for recording the breathing movement. [<SPIRO-[1] + -GRAPH] — **spi′ro·graph′ic** *adj.* — **spi·rog·raph·y** (spī·rog′rə·fē) *n.*

spi·ro·gy·ra (spī′rə·jī′rə) *n.* Any of a genus *(Spirogyra)* of bright-green, fresh-water algae forming dense masses or beds of growth in slow-running or stagnant water, and characterized by having the chlorophyll bands winding spirally to the right. [<SPIRO-[2] + Gk. *gyros* ring, coil]

spi·roid (spī′roid) *adj.* Resembling a spiral.

spi·rom·e·ter (spī·rom′ə·tər) *n.* An instrument for measuring the capacity of the lungs. [<SPIRO-[1] + -METER] — **spi·ro·met·ric** (spī′rə·met′rik) *adj.* — **spi·rom′e·try** *n.*

spirt (spûrt) See SPURT.

spir·u·la (spir′yə·lə, spir′o͞o-) *n.* *pl.* **·lae** (-lē) Any of a genus *(Spirula)* of cephalopods with an internal spiral chambered shell having whorls detached and in the same plane. [<NL <Gk. *speira* coil]

spir·y[1] (spīr′ē) *adj.* **1** Pertaining to or having the form of a spire. **2** Abounding in spires, as a city.

spir·y[2] (spīr′ē) *adj.* Having the form of a spiral; coiled; whorled.

spis·sat·ed (spis′ā·tid) *adj.* Thickened. [<L *spissatus,* pp. of *spissare* thicken]

spit[1] (spit) *v.* **spat** or **spit, spit·ting** *v.t.* **1** To eject (saliva, blood, etc.) from the mouth. **2** To throw off, eject, or utter with violence. **3** To light, as a fuse. — *v.i.* **4** To eject saliva from the mouth. **5** To make a noise like that made in ejecting saliva. **6** To fall in scattered drops or flakes, as rain or snow. — *n.* **1** Spittle; saliva. **2** An act of spitting or expectorating. **3** A frothy, spit-like secretion of the spittle insect; also, a spittle insect. **4** A light, scattered fall or short, driving flurry of snow or rain. **5** *Colloq.* Exact image; likeness; counterpart: He's the *spit* of John. [OE *spittan*] — **spit′ter** *n.*

spit[2] (spit) *n.* **1** A pointed rod on which meat is turned and roasted before a fire. **2** A point of low land, or a long, narrow shoal, extending from a shore into the water. — *v.t.* **spit·ted, spit·ting** To transfix or impale with or as with a spit. [OE *spitu* spit]

spit·al (spit′l) *n. Obs.* A hospital. Also **spital house, spit′tle, spittle house.**

spit·ball (spit′bôl′) *n.* **1** Paper chewed in the mouth and shaped into a ball for use as a missile. **2** In baseball, a pitched ball wet with saliva, and rotating deceptively in its course: no longer permitted by the rules. — **spit′ball′er** *n.*

spitch·cock (spich′kok) *v.t.* To split and broil, as a bird or fish. — *n.* An eel split and broiled. [Origin unknown]

spite (spīt) *n.* **1** Malicious bitterness prompting to vexatious acts; mean hatred; grudge. **2** That which is done in spite. **3** *Archaic* Trouble; bad luck: a Shakespearean usage. See synonyms under ENMITY, HATRED. — **in spite of** (or **spite of**) Formerly, in contempt of; now, notwithstanding. — *v.t.* **spit·ed, spit·ing** **1** To show one's spite toward; vex maliciously; thwart. **2** *Obs.* To fill with spite; offend; vex. [Short for DESPITE]

spite fence *U.S.* A fence or wall put up to spite a neighbor, usually of such a nature as to detract from the desirability or value of the adjoining property: now illegal.

spite·ful (spīt′fəl) *adj.* **1** Filled with spite. **2** Prompted by spite. See synonyms under MALICIOUS. — **spite′ful·ly** *adv.* — **spite′ful·ness** *n.*

spit·fire (spit′fīr′) *n.* A quick-tempered person who is given to saying spiteful things.

Spit·head (spit′hed) A roadstead between the Isle of Wight and southern England, at Portsmouth.

Spits·ber·gen (spits′bûr·gən) A group of Norwegian islands in the Arctic Ocean, east of Greenland and north of Norway, and comprising most of Svalbard; 23,658 square miles. Also **Spitz′ber·gen.**

Spits (spits), **Spits·ke** (spits′kē) See SCHIPPERKE.

Spit·te·ler (shpit′ə·lər), **Carl,** 1845–1924, Swiss writer; pseudonym *Felix Tandem.*

spit·ter (spit′ər) *n.* **1** A young deer whose antlers have emerged, but have not branched. **2** One who cooks meat on a spit.

spit·ting image (spit′ing) *Colloq.* An exact likeness or counterpart. Also **spit and image.**

spitting snake A venomous snake of South Africa *(Sepedon haemachates)* related to the cobras, that is able to eject its poison for some distance; the ringhals.

spit·tle (spit′l) *n.* **1** The fluid secreted by the mouth; saliva; spit. **2** The salivalike matter in which the larvae of spittle insects live. [OE *spātl*; infl. in form by *spit*[1]]

spittle insect A froghopper.

spit·toon (spi·to͞on′) *n.* A receptacle for spit; a cuspidor.

spitz (spits) *n.* One of a breed of small dogs with a tapering muzzle; a Pomeranian. Also **spitz dog.** [<G, short for *spitzhund*]

Spitz·en·burg (spit′sən·bûrg) *n.* A variety of apple, yellow and red in color, prized for its delicate flavor. [Prob. <Du. *spits* a point + *berg* a hill; so called because it is pointed and was found on an upstate New York hillside]

spiv (spiv) *n.* **1** *Brit. Colloq.* A flashy chiseler, sharper, or one who lives by his wits. **2** A low and common thief.

spiv·er·y (spiv′ər·ē) *n. Brit. Colloq.* The obtaining of a livelihood by the least possible personal effort, relying on government subsidy, sinecures, or private income.

splake (splāk) *n. Canadian* A hybrid fish, a cross between the speckled trout and the lake trout: also called *mendigo.*

splanch·nic (splangk′nik) *adj. Anat.* Pertaining to or supplying the viscera: a *splanchnic* nerve. [<Gk. *splanchnikos* <*splanchnon* entrail]

splanchno- *combining form Anat. & Med.* The viscera; of or related to the viscera. Also, before vowels, **splanchn-.** [<Gk. *splanchnon* entrail]

splanch·nol·o·gy (splangk·nol′ə·jē) *n.* The anatomy and physiology of the viscera. [< SPLANCHNO- + -LOGY]

splash (splash) *v.t.* **1** To dash or spatter (a liquid, etc.) about. **2** To spatter, wet, or soil with a liquid dashed about. **3** To make with splashes: to *splash* one's way. **4** To decorate with splashed ornament. — *v.i.* **5** To make a splash or splashes. **6** To move, fall, or strike with a splash or splashes. — *n.* **1** The act or noise of splashing. **2** The result of splashing; a spot made by a liquid or color splashed on. **3** In logging, a head of water released suddenly from a splash dam to drive a body of logs. [Var. of PLASH[1]]

splash·board (splash′bôrd′, -bōrd′) *n.* **1** Any of various devices to protect against splashes, especially a dashboard for a vehicle. **2** A board for closing the spillway or sluice of a dam. Also **splash′wing′** (-wing′).

splash·down (splash′doun′) *n.* The setting down of a spacecraft or a part of it in the seas following its flight.

splash·er (splash′ər) *n.* **1** One who or that which splashes. **2** A piece of oilcloth, toweling, rug, or other device to protect a surface against splashing, as at the back of a washstand or over a wheel.

splash·y (splash′ē) *adj.* **1** Slushy; wet. **2** Marked by or as by splashes; blotchy. **3** *Colloq.* Sensational; showy: They made a *splashy* appearance.

splat (splat) *n.* A thin, broad piece of wood, as that forming the middle of a chair back. [Origin uncertain]

splat·ter (splat′ər) *v.t. & v.i.* To spatter or splash. — *n.* A spatter; splash. [Blend of SPLASH and SPATTER]

splay (splā) *adj.* Spread out; displayed; broad; clumsy; clumsily formed: a *splay* mouth. — *n. Archit.* A slanted surface or beveled edge, as of the sides of a doorway or window, or of a joist. — *v.t.* **1** To make with a splay; bevel or chamfer away a corner or angle of, as a window opening. **2** To open to sight; spread; cut open; display. **3** In farriery, to dislocate. — *v.i.* **4** To spread out; open. **5** To slant; slope. [Aphetic var. of DISPLAY]

splay·foot (splā′fo͝ot′) *n.* **1** Abnormal flatness and turning outward of the feet. **2** A foot so deformed. — **splay′-foot′ed** *adj.*

spleen (splēn) *n. Anat.* **1** A highly vascular, flattened, ductless organ found near the stomach of most vertebrates, which effects certain modifications in the blood. ◆ Collateral adjective: *lienal.* **2** This organ regarded as the seat of various emotions. **3** Ill temper; spitefulness: to vent one's *spleen.* **4** *Archaic* Lowness of spirits; melancholy; hypochondria. **5** *Obs.* Mode or state of mind; also, caprice; a fit of pique. **6** *Obs.* Violent mirth. [<L *splen* <Gk. *splēn*] — **spleen′ish** *adj.* — **spleen′y** *adj.*

spleen·ful (splēn′fəl) *adj.* Affected with spleen; peevish; ill-tempered. — **spleen′ful·ly** *adv.*

spleen·wort (splēn′wûrt′) *n.* Any of a genus *(Asplenium)* of hardy and cultivated ferns with simple or compound fronds: so called from the use formerly made of some species in disorders of the spleen.

splen·dent (splen′dənt) *adj.* **1** Shining; lustrous. **2** Illustrious. [<L *splendens, -entis,* ppr. of *splendere* shine]

splen·did (splen′did) *adj.* **1** Magnificent; imposing. **2** Inspiring to the imagination; glorious; illustrious. **3** Giving out or reflecting brilliant light; shining. **4** *Colloq.* Very good; excellent: a *splendid* offer. See synonyms under FINE[1], BRIGHT. [<L *splendidus* <*splendere* shine] — **splen′did·ly** *adv.* — **splen′did·ness** *n.*

splen·di·de men·dax (splen′di·dē men′daks) *Latin* Splendidly false; nobly untruthful.

splen·dif·er·ous (splen·dif′ər·əs) *adj. Colloq.* Exhibiting great splendor; very magnificent: a facetious usage. [<SPLEND(OR) + -(I)FEROUS]

splen·dor (splen′dər) *n.* **1** Exceeding brilliance from emitted or reflected light. **2** Magnificence. **3** Conspicuous greatness of achievement; preeminence. Also *Brit.* **splen′dour.** [<L, brightness <*splendere* shine] — **splen′dor·ous, splen′drous** *adj.*

sple·net·ic (spli·net′ik) *adj.* **1** Pertaining to the spleen. **2** Fretfully spiteful; peevish. See synonyms under MOROSE. Also **sple·net′i·cal, splen·i·tive** (splen′ə·tiv). — *n.* **1** One suffering from disease of the spleen. **2** A peevish person. — **sple·net′i·cal·ly** *adv.*

splen·ic (splen′ik, splē′nik) *adj.* Of, in, or pertaining to the spleen.

sple·ni·tis (spli·nī′tis) *n. Pathol.* Inflammation of the spleen.

sple·ni·um (splē′nē·əm) *n. pl.* **·ni·a** (-nē·ə) **1** *Surg.* A compress or bandage. **2** *Anat.* The rounded posterior end of the corpus callosum. [<NL <Gk. *splēnion* a bandage] — **sple′ni·al** *adj.*

sple·ni·us (splē′nē·əs) *n. pl.* **·ni·i** (-nē·ī) *Anat.* A large, thick muscle of the back of the neck, extending in two parts from the skull to the vertebral spines in the cervical and upper thoracic region. [<NL <Gk. *splēnion* a bandage] — **sple′ni·al** *adj.*

spleno- *combining form Anat. & Med.* The spleen; of or related to the spleen. Also, before vowels, **splen-,** as in *splenitis.* [<Gk. *splēn, splēnos* the spleen]

spleu·chan (splo͞o′khən) *n. Scot. & Irish* A small bag or wallet to hold tobacco, etc.: sometimes used as a purse. [<Irish *spliūcán* a leather pouch]

splice (splīs) *v.t.* **spliced, splic·ing** **1** To unite, as two ropes or parts of a rope, so as to form one continuous piece, by intertwining the strands. **2** To connect, as timbers, by beveling, scarfing, or overlapping at the ends. **3** *Slang* To join in marriage: usually in the passive. — **to splice the main brace** To serve or take a glass of grog: chiefly jocular. — *n.* **1** A union at the ends of joined parts, especially of ropes, made by intertwining the strands. **2** The place at which two parts are spliced. [<MDu. *splissen*]

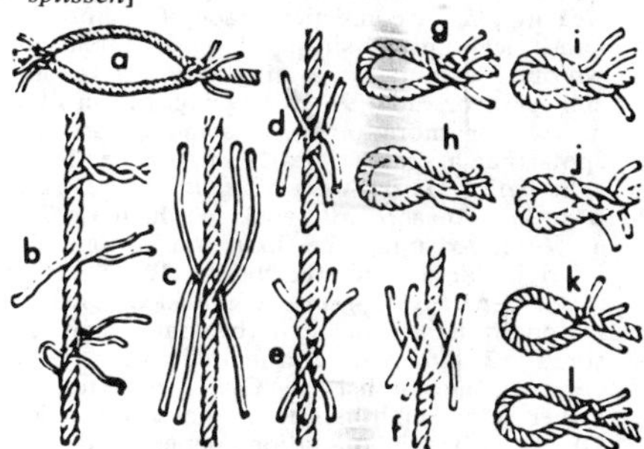

SPLICES

a. Cut splice. *b–c.* Long splices. *d–f.* Short splices. *g–l.* Eye splices.

splic·er (splī′sər) *n.* **1** One who makes splices. **2** An implement by which a splice is made in a rope; a fid for splicing.

spline (splīn) *n.* **1** *Mech.* A metal key permanently set into a slot in one of two connected rotating mechanical parts, as a shaft and a pulley, and engaging with a similar slot cut in the other, thus permitting both parts to have relative lengthwise motion, but not to rotate upon each other: also called *feather, feather key.* **2** A long, flexible strip of wood or hard rubber, used by mechanical draftsmen to lay down ship lines, railway curves, or similar work. **3** A thin strip or tongue of wood or metal used in matching grooved planks, making partitions, filling air spaces, etc. — *v.t.* **splined, splin·ing** **1** To make a slot or groove in for a spline. **2** To fit with a spline. [? Related to SPLINT] — **splined** *adj.*

splint (splint) *n.* **1** A thin, flat piece split off; a splinter. **2** A thin, flexible strip of split wood used for basket-making, chair bottoms, etc. **3** In plate armor, one of the flexibly adjusted overlapping laminae. **4** *Surg.* An appliance, as of wood or metal, used for keeping a fractured limb or other injured part in a fixed position. **5** A splint bone. **6** An osseous tumor on the splint bone of a horse, due to inflammation of the periosteum; also, a bony callosity resulting from disease of the splint bones. — *v.t.* To confine, support, or brace, as a fractured limb, with or as with splints. [<MDu. *splinte*]

splint armor Armor made of overlapping metal plates.

splint bone **1** One of the small rudimentary bones of the metacarpus or metatarsus of the horse and related animals. Compare illustration under HORSE. **2** The fibula.

splin·ter (splin′tər) *n.* A thin, sharp piece of wood, glass, metal, etc., split or torn off lengthwise; a sliver. —*v.t. & v.i.* To split into thin sharp pieces or fragments; shatter; shiver. [<MDu.] —**splin'ter·y** *adj.*

splin·ter·proof (splin'tər·prōōf') *adj.* Resistant to the penetration of splinters: said especially of shelters affording protection from machine-gun fire and shell fragments.

split (split) *v.* **split, split·ting** *v.t.* **1** To separate into parts by force, especially into two approximately equal parts. **2** To break or divide lengthwise or along the grain; rive; separate into layers. **3** To divide into groups or factions; disrupt, as a political party. **4** To divide and distribute by portions or shares. —*v.i.* **5** To break apart; divide lengthwise or along the grain. **6** To become divided or disunited through disagreement, etc. **7** To share something with others. **8** *Slang* To leave quickly or abruptly. —**to split hairs** To make fine distinctions; be unnecessarily precise or subtle. —**to split off 1** To break off by splitting. **2** To separate by or as by splitting. —**to split the difference** To divide equally a sum in dispute. —**to split up 1** To separate into parts and distribute. **2** To cease association; separate. —*n.* **1** The act or result of splitting; a longitudinal fissure; cleft; rent. **2** Separation of an aggregate body into factions; rupture; schism: a *split* in the church. **3** A sliver; splinter. **4** A share or portion, as of loot or booty. **5** A six-ounce bottle of an alcoholic beverage or of mineral water. **6** A split osier, used in certain phases of basket weaving. **7** A confection made of a sliced banana, ice-cream, sirup, chopped nuts, and whipped cream. **8** A single thickness of a split skin or hide. **9** In bowling, the position of two or more pins left standing on such spots that a spare is nearly impossible. **10** A split ballot: There were 47 *splits* in the ballot box. **11** An acrobatic trick in which the legs are extended upon the floor in a straight line at right angles to the body. **12** *Slang* A quick departure. —*adj.* **1** Divided, especially longitudinally or with the grain; cleft; fissured. **2** Dressed and cured after being cleaned: said of fish. **3** Given in sixteenths, rather than eighths, as a stock quotation: 10 1/16 is a *split* quotation: opposed to *regular.* **4** Divided: a *split* ballot. [<MDu. *splitten*] —**split'ter** *n.*

Split (splēt) The chief Dalmatian city of southern Croatia, Yugoslavia; a major port on the Adriatic: Italian *Spalato.*

split decision In boxing, a decision in which only two of three officials agree on the winner.

split infinitive See under INFINITIVE.

split-lev·el (split'lev'əl) *adj.* Designating a type of dwelling in which the floors of adjoining parts are at different levels, connected by short flights of stairs, permitting a compact arrangement of living and service rooms.

split product *Chem.* Any product of a decomposition, as of a protein into amino acids.

split saw A ripsaw.

split ticket 1 A ballot on which the voter has distributed his vote among candidates of different parties. **2** A ballot containing names of candidates of more than one party or party faction. Compare STRAIGHT TICKET.

split·ting (split'ing) *adj.* Acute or extreme in kind or degree: a *splitting* pain.

splotch (sploch) *n.* A discolored spot, as of ink, etc.; a daub; splash; spot. —*v.t.* To soil or mark with a splotch or splotches. [Cf. OE *splot* spot] —**splotch'y** *adj.*

splurge (splûrj) *Colloq. n.* **1** An ostentatious display. **2** An extravagant expenditure. —*v.i.* **splurged, splurg·ing 1** To show off; be ostentatious. **2** To spend money lavishly or wastefully. [Imit.] —**splurg'y** *adj.*

splut·ter (splut'ər) *v.i.* **1** To make a series of slight, explosive sounds, or throw off small particles, as meat frying in fat. **2** To speak hastily, confusedly, or incoherently, as from surprise or indignation. —*v.t.* **3** To utter excitedly or confusedly; sputter. **4** To spatter or bespatter. —*n.* A noise as of spluttering; bustle; confused stir. [Blend of SPLASH and SPUTTER] —**splut'ter·er** *n.*

spode or **Spode** (spōd) *n.* Fine porcelain or china made at the works founded by Josiah Spode (1754–1827) in Staffordshire, England.

spod·u·mene (spoj'oo·mēn) *n.* A vitreous, transparent to translucent lithium-aluminum silicate, belonging to the pyroxene group and crystallizing in the monoclinic system. [<Gk. *spodoumenos,* ppr. of *spodoesthai* be burned to ashes <*spodos* ashes]

spoil (spoil) *v.* **spoiled** or **spoilt, spoil·ing** *v.t.* **1** To impair or destroy the value, usefulness, or beauty of; injure: to *spoil* a book. **2** To weaken or impair the character or personality of, especially by overindulgence: Spare the rod and *spoil* the child. **3** *Obs.* To take property from by force; despoil. **4** *Obs.* To seize by force. —*v.i.* **5** To lose normal or useful qualities; specifically, to become tainted or decayed, as food. **6** *Obs.* To plunder; rob. See synonyms under CORRUPT, DECAY, DEFILE[1], INDULGE, PAMPER. —**to be spoiling for** To long for; crave: He is *spoiling for* a fight. —*n.* **1** Plunder seized by violence; booty; loot. **2** *pl.* The emoluments of public office as the objects of political contests and rewards of political service. **3** The act of pillaging; spoliation. **4** An object to be forcibly seized and taken away. **5** *Obs.* Ruin; destruction. **6** Material removed in digging trenches or excavations. **7** *Obs.* Damage; waste. See synonyms under PLUNDER. [<OF *espoillier* <L *spoliare* <*spolium* booty]

spoil·age (spoi'lij) *n.* **1** Spoiled material collectively. **2** Something that is or has been spoiled. **3** The process of spoiling. **4** The state of being spoiled.

spoil·er (spoi'lər) *n.* **1** One who takes spoil; a robber; despoiler. **2** One who or that which causes to spoil; a corrupter.

spoil-five (spoil'fīv') *n.* A card game played by 2 to 10 persons, in which each player tries to take the pool or to spoil it, taking being accomplished by winning, spoiling by preventing the other players from winning, three out of five possible tricks in a deal.

spoils·man (spoilz'mən) *n. pl.* **·men** (-mən) One who advocates the spoils system or works for a political party for spoils.

spoil-sport (spoil'spôrt', -spōrt') *n.* A person whose actions or attitudes spoil the pleasures of others.

spoils system The theory, or the practice of a political party after a victorious campaign, of making public offices the rewards of partisan services.

Spo·kane (spō·kan') The second largest city in Washington, located on a falls in the **Spokane River,** a river which flows 100 miles west from western Idaho to the Columbia River in eastern Washington.

spoke[1] (spōk) *n.* **1** One of the members of a wheel which serve to support the rim (or felly) by connecting it to the hub. **2** One of the radial handles of a ship's steering wheel. **3** A stick or bar for insertion in a wheel to prevent it from turning, as in descending a hill. **4** A rung of a ladder. —**to put a spoke in (someone's) wheel** To hinder or prevent (someone's) action. —*v.t.* **spoked, spok·ing 1** To provide with spokes. **2** To fasten (a wheel) with a stick or spoke to prevent its turning. [OE *spāca*]

spoke[2] (spōk) Past tense and archaic past participle of SPEAK.

spo·ken (spō'kən) Past participle of SPEAK. —*adj.* **1** Uttered orally, as opposed to written. **2** Speaking or having a specified kind of speech: smooth-*spoken.*

spoke·shave (spōk'shāv') *n.* A wheelwright's tool having a blade set between two handles, used with a drawing motion in rounding and smoothing wooden surfaces.

spokes·man (spōks'mən) *n. pl.* **·men** (-mən) One who speaks in the name and behalf of another or others. —**spokes'wom'an** (-wŏŏm'·ən) *n. fem.*

Spo·le·to (spō·lā'tō) A town of central Italy, site of extensive Roman ruins and several medieval churches, including an 11th century cathedral. Ancient **Spo·le·ti·um** (spō·lē'shē·əm).

spo·li·a·tion (spō'lē·ā'shən) *n.* **1** The act of despoiling; specifically, the plundering of neutral commerce by a belligerent. **2** *Law* Destruction; mutilation; alteration; specifically, the erasure, alteration, mutilation, or destruction of a paper to prevent its being used as evidence. **3** In English canon law, the taking of the fruits of a benefice under a pretended but illegal title, or a writ or suit brought on such grounds. **4** *Law* The destruction of a ship's papers so as to conceal its nationality, the character of its trade, cargo, etc. [<L *spoliatio,* *-onis* <*spoliare* despoil] —**spo'li·a'tor** *n.*

spo·li·a·tive (spō'lē·ā'tiv) *adj.* Tending to abstract from or lessen; in medicine, resulting in a considerable loss of blood.

spon·da·ic (spon·dā'ik) *adj.* **1** Pertaining to or of the nature of a spondee; composed of spondees. **2** Having a spondee in a position where another kind of metrical foot is usual. Also **spon·da'i·cal.** [<L *spondaicus* <Gk. *spondeiakos* <*spondē.* See SPONDEE.]

spon·dee (spon'dē) *n.* A metrical foot consisting of two long syllables or, in English verse, of two accented syllables. [<F *spondée* <Gk. *spondeios (pous)* libation (meter) <*spondē* a libation; because used in the solemn chants accompanying a libation]

spon·du·lics (spon·dōō'liks) *n. U.S. Slang* Cash money. Also **spon·du'licks, spon·du'lix.**

spon·dy·li·tis (spon'də·lī'tis) *n. Pathol.* Pott's disease.

spondylo- *combining form Anat. & Med.* A vertebra; of or pertaining to vertebrae. Also, before vowels, **spondyl-.** [<Gk. *spondylos* a vertebra]

sponge (spunj) *n.* **1** Any of a phylum *(Porifera)* of fixed, usually marine organisms characterized by a highly porous body without specialized internal organs. **2** The skeleton or network of elastic fibers that remains after the removal of the living matter from certain sponges and that readily absorbs liquids: used as an absorbent, for bathing, etc. **3** Some spongelike implement or substance that serves as an absorbent, as a swabbing implement for cleaning a cannon bore after discharge. **4** Leavened dough, or dough in the process of leavening and before kneading. **5** A porous, spongelike form assumed by finely divided metals, as iron and platinum. **6** *Surg.* An absorbent pad, as of sterilized gauze, used in operations, etc., to absorb blood or other fluid matter. **7** One who consumes or absorbs a great deal, as of food or drink. **8** *Colloq.* A person who lives at the expense of another or others; a parasite. —**to throw** (or **toss) up** (or **in) the sponge** *Colloq.* To yield; give up; abandon the struggle. —*v.* **sponged, spong·ing** *v.t.* **1** To wipe, wet, or clean with a sponge. **2** To wipe out; expunge; erase. **3** To absorb; suck in, as a sponge does. **4** *Colloq.* To get by mean device or at another's expense. —*v.i.* **5** To be absorbent. **6** To gather or fish for sponges. **7** *Colloq.* To live at the expense of others. See synonyms under CLEANSE. [OE <L *spongia,* ult. <Gk. *spongos.* Akin to FUNGUS.]

sponge cake A cake of sugar, eggs, and flour, containing no shortening and beaten very light.

spong·er (spun'jər) *n.* **1** One who or that which sponges in any sense. **2** A person or vessel that gathers sponges. **3** A human parasite.

spon·gi·form (spun'jə·fôrm, spon'-) *adj.* Resembling a sponge in form or structure.

spon·gin (spun'jin) *n. Biochem.* A protein from the skeletal tissue of sponges and corals.

spon·gi·o·blast (spon'jē·ə·blast') *n. Biol.* **1** An epithelial cell of the embryonic neural tube which becomes transformed into a cell of the tissue lining the central cavities of the brain and spinal cord. **2** A spongoblast. [<Gk. *spongia,* var. of *spongos* a sponge + -BLAST]

spon·go·blast (spon'gō·blast) *n. Biol.* An ameboid cell in the mesenchyme of sponges by which spongin is secreted. Also **spon·gin·blast** (spun'jin·blast, spon'-). [<Gk. *spongos* a sponge + -BLAST]

spong·y (spun'jē) *adj.* **1** Having the nature or character of a sponge; elastic, compressible, and porous. **2** Having the quality of imbibing fluids; absorptive. **3** Existing in a condition of fine division and loose coherence. **4** *Obs.* Wet; soaked. Also **spon·gi·ose** (spun'jē·ōs). —**spong'i·ness** *n.*

spon·sal (spon'səl) *adj.* Relating to marriage or to a spouse. [<L *sponsus,* pp. of *spondere* promise]

spon·sion (spon'shən) *n.* **1** The act of becoming surety or sponsor for another. **2** In international law, an undertaking on behalf of his state by a public officer not specifically empowered to enter into it.

spon·son (spon'sən) *n.* **1** A curved projection from the hull of a vessel or seaplane, to give greater stability or increase the surface area. **2** A similar protuberance on a ship or tank, for storage purposes or for the training of a gun. **3** An air tank built into the side of a canoe, to improve stability and prevent sinking. [Appar. alter. of EXPANSION]

spon·sor (spon′sər) *n.* **1** One who makes himself responsible for a statement by, or the debt or duty of, another; a surety. **2** One who makes the required professions and promises for an infant at baptism and becomes responsible for its religious training; a godfather or godmother. **3** A business firm or enterprise that assumes all the costs of a radio or television program which advertises its product or service. — *v.t.* To act as sponsor for; answer or vouch for. — **spon·so·ri·al** (spon·sôr′ē·əl, -sō′rē-) *adj.* — **spon′sor·ship** *n.*

spon·ta·ne·i·ty (spon′tə·nē′ə·tē) *n. pl.* **·ties** **1** Spontaneous quality. **2** The tendency to action or behavior independent of external forces, conditions, or influences.

spon·ta·ne·ous (spon·tā′nē·əs) *adj.* **1** Arising from inherent qualities or tendencies without external efficient cause; done or acting from one's own impulse, prompting, or desire. **2** Not having material causation outside itself. **3** Generated or produced without human labor; wild or sporadic; indigenous. **4** *Biol.* Apparently arising independently of external stimulus, influence, or conditions. [<LL *spontaneus* <L *sponte* of free will] — **spon·ta′ne·ous·ly** *adv.* — **spon·ta′ne·ous·ness** *n.*

Synonyms: automatic, instinctive, involuntary, unbidden, voluntary, willing. That is *spontaneous* which is freely done, with no external compulsion and, in human actions, without special premeditation or distinct determination of the will; that is *voluntary* which is freely done with distinct act of will; that is *involuntary* which is independent of the will, and perhaps in opposition to it; a *willing* act is not only in accordance with will, but with desire. Thus *voluntary* and *involuntary*, which are antonyms of each other, are both partial synonyms of *spontaneous*. An infant's smile in answer to that of its mother is *spontaneous*; the smile of a pouting child wheedled into good humor is *involuntary*. In physiology the action of the heart and lungs is *involuntary* action; the growth of the hair and nails is *spontaneous*; the action of swallowing is *voluntary* up to a certain point, beyond which it becomes *involuntary* or *automatic*.

spontaneous combustion The oxidation of a substance with such rapidity as to engender heat sufficient to ignite it, as masses of oiled rags, finely powdered ores, coal, and certain metals.

spontaneous generation *Biol.* Abiogenesis.

spon·toon (spon·to͞on′) *n.* A half-pike usually armed with a hook, carried by infantry officers in the 18th century: also spelled *espontoon*. [<F *sponton* <Ital. *spontone* pike < *puntone* a point]

spoof (spo͞of) *Colloq. v.t. & v.i.* To deceive or hoax; joke. — *n.* Deception; humbug; hoax. [after a nonsensical game invented by Arthur Roberts, 1852–1933, English comedian]

spook (spo͝ok) *Colloq. n.* A ghost; an apparition; specter. — *v.t.* **1** To haunt (a person or place). **2** To frighten, disturb, or annoy. **3** To startle or frighten (an animal) into flight, stampeding, etc. [<Du.] — **spook′ish** *adj.*

spook·y (spo͞o′kē) *adj.* **spook·i·er, spook·i·est** *Colloq.* **1** Of or like a spook; ghostly; eerie. **2** Frightened; nervous; skittish. — **spook′i·ly** *adv.* — **spook′i·ness** *n.*

spool (spo͞ol) *n.* **1** A small cylinder, commonly of wood and with a flange at each end and an axial bore, upon which thread or yarn is or may be wound. **2** The quantity of thread held by a spool; also, the spool and the thread upon it. **3** Anything resembling a spool in shape or purpose. — *v.t.* To wind on a spool. [<MLG *spole*]

spoon (spo͞on) *n.* **1** A utensil having a shallow, generally ovoid bowl and a handle, used in preparing, serving, or eating food. **2** Something resembling a spoon or its bowl. **3** A metallic lure attached to a fishing line: also **spoon bait, trolling spoon.** **4** A concave overhanging extension on a torpedo tube to keep the launched torpedo in a straight course. **5** A wooden golf club with lofted face and comparatively short, stiff shaft, used by some players for approaching. — *v.t.* **1** To lift up or out with a spoon. **2** To hollow out like the bowl of a spoon. **3** In certain games, to play or hit (the ball) with little force up into the air; in croquet, to shove or scoop (the ball) with the mallet. — *v.i.* **4** To fish with a spoon. **5** In certain games, to spoon the ball. **6** *Colloq.* To make love, especially openly and demonstratively. [OE *spōn* sliver, chip]

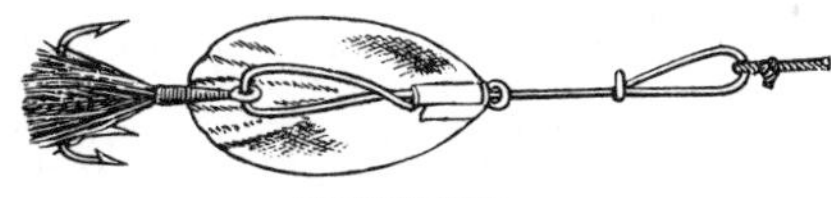

SPOON BAIT

spoon·bill (spo͞on′bil′) *n.* **1** A wading bird (genera *Platalea* or *Ajaia*) related to the ibises, having the bill broad and flattened. **2** The shoveler (def. 2). **3** The paddlefish. — **spoon′-billed′** *adj.*

spoon·bread (spo͞on′bred′) *n.* A quick bread made of cornmeal, eggs, milk, and shortening, baked soft enough to be served with a spoon: also called *batter bread*.

spoon·drift (spo͞on′drift) *n.* Spindrift.

spoon·er·ism (spo͞o′nə·riz′əm) *n.* The unintentional transposition of sounds or of parts of words in speaking, as in "half-*w*armed *f*ish" for "half-*f*ormed *w*ish". [after William A. *Spooner*, 1844–1930, of New College, Oxford, who was renowned for such slips of the tongue]

spoon-feed (spo͞on′fēd′) *v.t.* **-fed** (fed), **-feed·ing** (fē·ding) **1** To feed with a spoon. **2** To pamper; spoil. **3** To present (information) in such a manner that little or no thought, initiative, etc., is required of the recipient. **4** To instruct or inform (a person) in this manner.

spoon·ful (spo͞on′fo͝ol′) *n. pl.* **·fuls** As much as a spoon will hold; especially, a teaspoonful.

spoon hook A fish hook with a bright, revolving, spoon-shaped piece of metal attached.

spoon·y (spo͞o′nē) *Colloq. adj.* **spoon·i·er, spoon·i·est** Sentimental or silly, as in lovemaking; soft. — *n. pl.* **spoon·ies** A foolish, demonstrative lover; sentimental simpleton. Also **spoon′ey.**

spoor (spo͝or) *n.* **1** A track; trail. **2** Footprint or other trace of a wild animal. — *v.t. & v.i.* To track by or follow a spoor. [<Du.]

Spor·a·des (spôr′ə·dēz, *Greek* spô·rä′thes) **1** Loosely, all the Greek islands in the Aegean, exclusive of the Cyclades. **2** Anciently, the islands of the SE Aegean, off western Asia Minor, including the Dodecanese, Icaria, Samos, and, in some usages, Chios and Lesbos. **3** Strictly, the **Northern Sporades,** a group of Greek islands in the western Aegean, off the coasts of Euboea and Thessaly, the chief of which is Skyros: Greek *Voriai Sporades*.

spo·rad·ic (spô·rad′ik, spō-) *adj.* **1** Occurring here and there; occasional. **2** Separate; isolated. **3** Not widely diffused; neither epidemic nor endemic: said of disease. Also **spo·rad′i·cal.** [<Med. L *sporadicus* <Gk. *sporadikos* < *sporas* scattered] — **spo·rad′i·cal·ly** *adv.* — **spo·rad′i·cal·ness** *n.*

spor·a·do·sid·er·ite (spôr′ə·dō·sid′ər·īt, spō′rə-) *n.* A meteorite consisting of a typically crystalline mass with disseminated particles of nickel-iron alloy. [<SPORADIC + SIDERITE]

spo·ran·gi·o·spore (spô·ran′jē·ə·spôr′, spō·ran′jē·ə·spōr′) *n. Bot.* A spore produced within a sporangium.

spo·ran·gi·um (spô·ran′jē·əm, spō-) *n. pl.* **·gi·a** (-jē·ə) *Bot.* A sac in which asexual spores are produced endogenously, as in certain algae and fungi. Also called *spore case*. [<SPOR(O)- + Gk. *angeion* a vessel] — **spo·ran′gi·al** *adj.*

spore (spôr, spōr) *n.* **1** *Bot.* The reproductive body in flowerless plants, but containing no embryo. They are free, usually single-celled and highly resistant bodies, produced externally or in some closed sac or cavity, and are capable of developing at once or after a time into an independent organism or individual. **2** A minute body that develops into a new individual; any minute organism; a germ. — *v.i.* **spored, spor·ing** To develop spores: said of plants. [<Gk. *spora* seed, sowing] — **spo·ra·ceous** (spô·rā′shəs, spō-) *adj.*

spore case A sporangium.

spore fruit *Bot.* An ascocarp; any plant structure producing spores.

spo·rif·er·ous (spô·rif′ər·əs, spō-) *adj.* Bearing spores.

sporo- *combining form* Seed; spore: *sporophyte*. Also, before vowels, **spor-.** [<Gk. *spora* a seed]

spo·ro·carp (spôr′ə·kärp, spō′rə-) *n. Bot.* **1** A many-celled form of fruit produced from a fertilized archicarp in certain of the lower cryptogams, especially red algae and ascomycetous fungi: also called *cystocarp*. **2** The sporogonium in mosses.

spo·ro·cyst (spôr′ə·sist, spō′rə-) *n. Zool.* **1** An asexual form of a trematode worm that develops directly from the embryo and in which mouth and intestinal tract are wanting. **2** An encysted organism, especially a protozoan, that gives rise to spores.

spo·ro·cyte (spôr′ə·sīt, spō′rə-) *n. Biol.* The mother cell from which spores are produced.

spo·ro·gen·e·sis (spôr′ə·jen′ə·sis, spō′rə-) *n. Biol.* **1** Reproduction by spores. **2** Sporogony. — **spo·rog·e·nous** (spô·roj′ə·nəs, spō-) *adj.*

spo·ro·go·ni·um (spôr′ə·gō′nē·əm, spō′rə-) *n. pl.* **·ni·a** (-nē·ə) *Bot.* An elongated stalk having upon its summit a capsule in which the asexual spores of liverworts and mosses are produced.

spo·rog·o·ny (spô·rog′ə·nē, spō-) *n. Biol.* Spore formation; specifically, in sporozoans, the development of spores from a mature zygote. [<SPORO- + -GONY]

spo·ro·phore (spôr′ə·fôr, spō′rə·fōr) *n.* **1** A spore-bearer or seed-bearer. **2** *Bot.* In fungi, a branch from the thallus which bears the spores.

spo·ro·phyll (spôr′ə·fil, spō′rə-) *n. Bot.* The leaf, or modified leaf, which bears the sporangia. Also **spo′ro·phyl.**

spo·ro·phyte (spôr′ə·fīt, spō′rə-) *n. Bot.* The spore-bearing individual or generation in certain plants which reproduce by alternation of generations.

spo·ro·tri·cho·sis (spôr′ə·tri·kō′sis, spō′rə-) *n. Pathol.* A chronic disease caused by a fungus (genus *Sporotrichum*) and marked by the formation of ulcerated lesions in the lymph nodes or subcutaneous tissue. [<NL *Sporotrichum*, genus of fungi + -OSIS]

-sporous *combining form* Having (a specified number or kind of) spores: *homosporous*. [<SPOR(O)- + -OUS]

spo·ro·zo·an (spôr′ə·zō′ən, spō′rə-) *adj.* Designating or belonging to a class (*Sporozoa*) of parasitic protozoans developing by asexual and sexual stages and reproducing by sporulation, as the malaria parasite. — *n.* One of the class *Sporozoa*. [<SPORO- + Gk. *zōion* animal]

spo·ro·zo·ite (spôr′ə·zō′īt, spō′rə-) *n. Zool.* An aggregation of protoplasm of a sporozoan zygote, segmented off as a minute sickle-shaped germ: the initial phase of the malaria parasite in its host.

spor·ran (spor′ən) *n.* A skin pouch, generally with the fur on, worn in front of the kilt by Highlanders. [<Scottish Gaelic *sporan* <LL *bursa* purse]

sport (spôrt, spōrt) *n.* **1** That which amuses in general; diversion; pastime. **2** A particular game or play pursued for diversion, especially an outdoor or athletic game, as baseball, football, track, tennis, swimming, etc. **3** A spirit of jesting or raillery. **4** That with which one sports; a toy; plaything. **5** Mockery; an object of derision: to make *sport* of someone; also, a laughingstock; butt. **6** *Biol.* An animal or plant, or one of its parts, that exhibits sudden and spontaneous variation from the normal type; a mutation. **7** *Bot.* A bud variation. **8** *Colloq.* One whose interest in sport lies chiefly in gambling; a gamester or gambler. **9** *Colloq.* One who lives a fast, gay, or flashy life. **10** A person characterized by his observance of the rules of fair play, or by his ability to get along with others: a good *sport*. **11** *Archaic* Amorous fondling; wanton dalliance. — *v.i.* **1** To amuse oneself; play; frolic.

2 To participate in games. 3 To make sport or jest; trifle. 4 *Bot.* **a** To vary suddenly or spontaneously from the normal type; mutate. **b** To display bud variation. 5 *Archaic & Dial.* To make love in a sportive or trifling manner. — *v.t.* 6 *Colloq.* To display or wear ostentatiously; show off. 7 *Obs.* To amuse; divert. See synonyms under FRISK. — *adj.* Of, pertaining to, or fitted for sports; also, appropriate for informal outdoor wear: a *sport* coat: also **sports.** [Aphetic var. of DISPORT] — **sport′er** *n.* — **sport′ful** *adj.* — **sport′ful·ly** *adv.* — **sport′ful·ness** *n.*

Synonyms (noun): amusement, diversion, entertainment, frolic, fun, gaiety, gambol, game, jollity, joviality, merriment, merrymaking, mirth, pastime, play, playfulness, pleasantry, pleasure, prank, recreation. See ENTERTAINMENT, FROLIC. Compare RIDICULE.

sport·ing (spôr′ting, spōr′-) *adj.* 1 Pertaining to, engaged in, or used in connection with athletic games or field sports. 2 Characterized by the spirit of sportsmanship; conforming to the codes or standards of sportsmanship. 3 Interested in or associated with sports for gambling or betting: a *sporting* man. — **sport′ing·ly** *adv.*

sporting chance *Colloq.* A chance involving the risk of loss.

spor·tive (spôr′tiv, spōr′-) *adj.* 1 Relating to or fond of sport or play; frolicsome. 2 Interested in, active in, or related to sports. 3 *Obs.* Wanton or amorous. See synonyms under HUMOROUS, JOCOSE, MERRY, VIVACIOUS, WANTON. — **spor′tive·ly** *adv.* — **spor′tive·ness** *n.*

sports car A low, rakish automobile, usually seating two persons, and built for high speed and maneuverability.

sports·cast·er (spôrts′kas′tər, -käs′-, spōrts′-) *n. U.S.* One who broadcasts sports events, news, and comment.

sport shirt A shirt for informal wear, often cut square at the bottom so as to be worn inside or outside slacks. Also **sports shirt.**

sports·man (spôrts′mən, spōrts′-) *n. pl.* **·men** (-mən) 1 One who pursues field sports, especially hunting and fishing. 2 A professional gambler; also, one who bets on horse races. 3 One who abides by a code of fair play in games or in daily practice.

sports·man·like (spôrts′mən·līk′, spōrts′-) *adj.* Pertaining to sportsmen; honorable; generous; conforming to the rules of sportsmanship. Also **sports′man·ly.**

sports·man·ship (spôrts′mən·ship, spōrts′-) *n.* 1 The art or practice of field sports. 2 Honorable or sportsmanlike conduct.

sports·wear (spôrts′wâr′, spōrts′-) *n.* Clothes made for informal or outdoor activities.

sports·wom·an (spôrts′wo͝om′ən, spōrts′-) *n. pl.* **·wom·en** (-wim′in) A woman who participates in sports.

sport·y (spôr′tē, spōr′-) *adj.* **sport·i·er, sport·i·est** *Colloq.* Relating to or characteristic of a sport; hence, gay, loud, or dissipated. — **sport′i·ly** *adv.* — **sport′i·ness** *n.*

spor·u·late (spôr′yə·lāt, spor′-) *v.i.* **·lat·ed, ·lat·ing** To form spores.

spor·u·la·tion (spôr′yə·lā′shən, spor′-) *n. Biol.* The act or condition of spore formation, especially by multiple cell division after encystment.

spor·ule (spôr′yo͞ol, spor′-) *n.* A spore; sometimes, a little spore. [Dim. of SPORE]

spot (spot) *n.* 1 A particular place of small extent; a definite locality. 2 Any small portion of a surface differing as in color from the rest; blot. 3 A stain or blemish on character; a fault; a reproach. 4 A congenital birthmark. 5 A food fish *(Leiostomus xanthurus)* of the Atlantic coast of the United States, marked with a spot above each pectoral fin; the oldwife. 6 One of the figures or pips with which a playing card is marked; also, a card having (a certain number of) such marks: the five *spot* of clubs. 7 *Slang* A currency note having a specified value: a ten *spot.* 8 *Chiefly Brit.* A portion or bit: a *spot* of tea. 9 *Slang* Position or situation: He was in a good *spot.* 10 *U.S. Slang* A spotlight. See synonyms under BLEMISH, PLACE. — **in a spot** *Slang* In a difficult or embarrassing situation; in trouble. — **in spots** Now and then, in some respects: He is bright *in spots.* — **to go to the spot** To satisfy a definite need or craving. — **to hit the spot** *Slang* To gratify an appetite or need. — **on the spot** 1 At once; immediately. 2 At the very place. 3 *Slang* **a** In danger of death. **b** Accountable or in danger of being held accountable for some action. — *v.* **spot·ted, spot·ting** *v.t.* 1 To mark or soil with spots. 2 To decorate with spots; dot. 3 To place on a designated spot; locate; station. 4 *Colloq.* To recognize or detect; see. 5 *Colloq.* To yield (an advantage or handicap) to someone: We *spotted* them five points. — *v.i.* 6 To become marked or soiled with spots. 7 To make a stain or discoloration. 8 *Mil.* To observe the effect of gunfire to obtain data for improving its accuracy. See synonyms under STAIN. — *adj.* 1 Being on the place or spot. 2 Paid or prepared for payment on delivery; also, ready for instant delivery following sale. 3 *Telecom.* Designed for presentation between regular programs and usually very brief: a *spot* TV commercial. [ME <LG. Cf. MDu. *spotte* a spot.] — **spot′ta·ble** *adj.*

spot brake Disk brake.

spot cash Immediate payment on actual delivery.

spot·less (spot′lis) *adj.* Free from spot, stain, or impurity. See synonyms under INNOCENT, PERFECT, PURE. — **spot′less·ly** *adv.* — **spot′less·ness** *n.*

spot·light (spot′līt′) *n.* 1 A circle of powerful light thrown on the stage to bring an actor or actors into clearer view. 2 The apparatus that produces such a light. 3 A pivoted automobile lamp. 4 Notoriety; publicity.

Spot·syl·va·ni·a (spot′sil·vā′nē·ə) A village in NE Virginia; scene of a 13-day battle in the Civil War, May, 1864. Formerly called **Spotsylvania Courthouse.**

spot·ted (spot′id) *adj.* 1 Discolored in spots; stained; soiled. 2 Characterized or marked by spots. 3 Blazed: said of trees, trails, etc.

spotted adder The house snake.

spotted crake A small European rail *(Porzana porzana),* allied to the American sora.

spotted cranebill See under CRANEBILL.

spotted fever *Pathol.* 1 Meningitis. 2 Typhus. 3 Rocky Mountain spotted fever.

spotted sandpiper See under SANDPIPER.

spot·ter (spot′ər) *n.* 1 One who or that which spots. 2 *Colloq.* A private detective. 3 An observation balloon. 4 A device on a railroad car that marks irregularities along the track. 5 In drycleaning, one who removes spots.

spot·ty (spot′ē) *adj.* **·ti·er, ·ti·est** 1 Having many spots. 2 Occurring in spots; unevenly distributed. — **spot′ti·ly** *adv.* — **spot′ti·ness** *n.*

spous·al (spou′zəl) *adj.* Pertaining to marriage. See synonyms under MATRIMONIAL. — *n.* Marriage; espousal.

spouse (spouz, spous) *n.* A partner in marriage; one's husband or wife. — *v.t.* **spoused, spous·ing** *Obs.* To wed; marry; espouse. [<OF *espous, espouse* <L *sponsus,* pp. of *spondere* promise, betroth]

spout (spout) *v.i.* 1 To pour out copiously and forcibly, as a liquid under pressure. 2 To discharge a fluid either continuously or in jets. 3 *Colloq.* To speak or orate pompously; declaim. — *v.t.* 4 To cause to pour or shoot forth. 5 To utter grandiloquently or pompously. 6 *Brit. Slang* To pawn or pledge. — *n.* 1 A tube, trough, etc., for the discharge of a liquid. 2 A continuous stream of fluid. 3 Formerly, the shoot or lift in a pawnbroker's shop. 4 *Brit. Slang* A pawnbroker's shop. [ME *spoute*; origin uncertain] — **spout′er** *n.*

sprag (sprag) *n.* A billet of wood used to prevent a vehicle from slipping backward, or in mining as a prop to support coal when undermined. [Origin uncertain]

Sprague's pipit (sprāgz) The Missouri skylark.

sprain (sprān) *n.* 1 A violent straining or twisting of the ligaments surrounding a joint. 2 The condition due to such strain. [< *v.*] — *v.t.* To cause a sprain in; wrench the muscles of (a joint). [<OF *espreindre* squeeze <L *exprimere.* See EXPRESS.]

sprang (sprang) Alternative past tense of SPRING.

sprat (sprat) *n.* 1 A herringlike fish *(Clupea sprattus)* found in shoals on the Atlantic coast of Europe. 2 The young of the herring. [OE *sprott*]

sprat·tle (sprat′l) *Scot. v.i.* To struggle or scramble. — *n.* A struggle; scramble.

sprawl (sprôl) *v.i.* 1 To sit or lie with the limbs stretched out ungracefully. 2 To be stretched out ungracefully, as the limbs. 3 To move with awkward motions of the limbs. 4 To spread out in a straggling manner, as handwriting, vines, etc. — *v.t.* 5 To cause to spread or extend awkwardly or irregularly. — *n.* 1 The act or position of sprawling; an awkward recumbent posture or movement. 2 An unplanned or disorderly group, as of houses, spread out over a broad area: urban *sprawl*; a vast *sprawl* of lights. [OE *spreawlian* move convulsively] — **sprawl′er** *n.*

spray[1] (sprā) *n.* 1 Water or other liquid dispersed in fine particles. 2 An instrument for discharging small particles of liquid; an atomizer. [< *v.*] — *v.t.* 1 To disperse (a liquid) in fine particles. 2 To apply spray to, as with an atomizer. — *v.i.* 3 To send forth or scatter spray. 4 To go forth as spray. [Akin to MDu. *sprayen* sprinkle] — **spray′er** *n.*

spray[2] (sprā) *n.* 1 A small branch bearing dependent branchlets or flowers. 2 Any ornament, pattern, etc., resembling a collection of twigs or flowers. [ME; origin uncertain]

spread (spred) *v.* **spread, spread·ing** *v.t.* 1 To open or unfold to full width, extent, etc., as wings, sail, a map, etc. 2 To distribute over a surface, especially in a thin layer; scatter or smear. 3 To cover with a layer of something: to *spread* toast with marmalade. 4 To force apart or farther apart: The heavy train has *spread* the rails. 5 To extend over a period of time; prolong: He *spread* the payments over a six-month period. 6 To make more widely known, active, etc.; promulgate or diffuse: to *spread* a rumor; to *spread* contagion. 7 To set (a table, etc.), as for a meal. 8 To arrange or place on a table, etc., as a meal or feast. 9 To set forth or record in full. — *v.i.* 10 To be extended or expanded; increase in size, width, etc. 11 To be distributed or dispersed, as over a surface or area; scatter. 12 To become more widely known, active, etc. 13 To be forced farther apart; separate. — *n.* 1 The act of spreading: the *spread* of the gospel. 2 An open extent or expanse. 3 The limit or extent of expansion of some designated object, as of sail or a bird's wings. 4 *Aeron.* The maximum distance from tip to tip of an airplane wing. 5 A cloth or covering for a bed, table, or the like. 6 *Colloq.* An informal feast or banquet; also, a table with a meal set out on it. 7 Anything used to spread on bread: a cheese *spread.* 8 Two pages of a magazine or newspaper facing each other and covered by related material; also, print spread across two or more columns or on facing pages for advertising or display. 9 In finance and commerce, a straddle. 10 Diffusion; dispersion. — *adj.* Having a broad surface; expanded; outstretched. [OE *sprǣdan*]

Synonyms (verb): circulate, diffuse, disperse, disseminate, distribute, divulge, expand, extend, promulgate, propagate, scatter. See PUBLISH, STRETCH. *Antonyms*: check, confine, condense, contract, restrain.

spread-ea·gle (spred′ē′gəl) *adj.* 1 Having the arms and legs spread wide apart. 2 Extravagant; bombastic: applied especially to patriotic American oratory. — *v.* **-ea·gled, -ea·gling** *v.t.* To lash to the mast or shrouds in spread-eagle position as a punishment: a former practice. — *v.i.* To deliver an oration in bombastic, patriotic style. — **spread′-ea′gle·ism** *n.*

spread eagle 1 The figure of an eagle with extended wings: used as an emblem of the United States. 2 Any position or movement resembling this, as a figure in skating. 3 Extravagant speech; especially, American bombastic, patriotic oratory.

spread·er (spred′ər) *n.* 1 One who or that which spreads, as a small knife for spreading butter. 2 A bar of wood, metal, etc., to keep stays or wires apart, etc. 3 *Agric.* An implement for spreading hay, manure, etc.

spreagh (sprākh) *n. Scot.* Property, particularly cattle, taken as plunder; booty; prey; a foray. Also **spreagh′er·y.**

spreck·le (sprek′əl) *n. & v. Scot. & Brit. Dial.* Speckle.

spree (sprē) *n.* 1 A drinking spell; drunken carousal. 2 A gay frolic. See synonyms under FROLIC. Compare SPORT. [Origin uncertain]

Spree (sprā, shprā) A river of eastern East Germany, flowing 250 miles north to the Havel River.

sprig (sprig) *n.* 1 A shoot or sprout of a tree or plant; an ornament in this form. 2 An offshoot from an ancestral stock; a young man. 3 One of various small, pointed implements.

4 A brad without a head. 5 A small, wedge-shaped piece of metal used to hold glass in a window sash. — *v.t.* **sprigged, sprig·ging** 1 To ornament with a design of sprigs. 2 To form (twigs or plants) into sprays. 3 To fasten with sprigs or brads. 4 To pluck sprigs from. [ME *sprigge*; origin uncertain] — **sprig'ger** *n.*

sprig·gy (sprig'ē) *adj.* **·gi·er, ·gi·est** Abounding in sprigs or small branches.

spright (sprīt) See SPRITE.

spright·ly (sprīt'lē) *adj.* **·li·er, ·li·est** Full of animation and spirits; vivacious; lively. — *adv.* Spiritedly; briskly; gaily. — **spright'li·ness** *n.*

Synonyms: airy, animated, brisk, bustling, cheerful, lively, nimble, spry, vivacious. The *sprightly* display a cheerful, pleasing lightness and quickness, spiritlike; *lively* has a similar meaning, as abounding in cheerful life. The *brisk* and *bustling* are full of stir, the former generally to some purpose. See ACTIVE, AIRY, CHEERFUL, HAPPY, NIMBLE, VIVACIOUS, VIVID.

spring (spring) *v.* **sprang** or **sprung, sprung, spring·ing** *v.i.* 1 To move or rise suddenly and rapidly; leap; dart: He *sprang* across the creek; The cat *sprang* into the air. 2 To move suddenly as by elastic reaction; snap: The jaws of the heavy trap *sprang* shut. 3 To move as if with a leap: An angry retort *sprang* to his lips. 4 To rise up suddenly, as birds from cover. 5 To work or snap out of place, as a mechanical part. 6 To become warped or bent, as boards. 7 To explode: said of a mine. 8 To rise above surrounding objects. 9 To come into being: New towns have *sprung* up. 10 To originate; proceed, as from a source. 11 To develop; grow, as a plant. 12 To be descended: He *springs* from good stock. 13 *Poetic* To begin to appear, as light or dawn. — *v.t.* 14 To cause to spring or leap. 15 To cause to act, close, open, etc., unexpectedly or suddenly, as by elastic reaction: to *spring* a trap. 16 To cause to happen, become known, or appear suddenly: to *spring* a surprise. 17 To leap over; vault. 18 To start (game) from cover; flush. 19 To explode (a mine). 20 To warp or bend; split. 21 To cause to snap or work out of place. 22 To force into place, as a beam or bar. 23 To suffer (a leak). 24 *Slang* To obtain the release of (a person) from prison or custody. See synonyms under LEAP, RISE. — *n.* 1 *Mech.* An elastic body or contrivance that yields under stress, and returns to its normal form when the stress is removed. 2 Elastic quality or energy. 3 The act of flying back from a position of tension; recoil. 4 An energy or power; a cause of action; impelling motive. 5 The act of leaping up or forward suddenly; a jump; bound. 6 The season in which vegetation starts anew; in the north temperate zone, the three months of March, April, and May; in the astronomical year, the period from the vernal equinox to the summer solstice. 7 A flow or fountain, as of water; hence, any source or origin of continued supply; a flow of curative water. 8 A crack or break, as of a plank, beam, or spar, or a thing sprung or warped. 9 *Archit.* The commencement of curvature in an arch. 10 A hinge. See illustration under HINGE. 11 *Scot.* A quick, lively tune. See synonyms under BEGINNING, CAUSE, SOURCE. — *adj.* 1 Pertaining to the season of spring. 2 Resilient; acting like or having a spring. 3 Hung on springs. [OE *springan*]

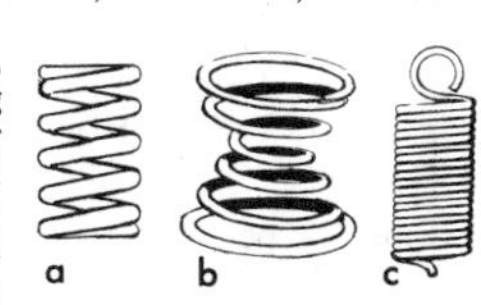

SPRING
a. Compression coil.
b. Double spiral.
c. Extension coil.

spring·al¹ (spring'əl) *n.* An engine like the ballista, used in medieval warfare: also *espringal.* Also **spring'ald** (-əld). [<AF *springalde,* OF *espringale* < *espringuer* spring < Gmc.]

spring·al² (spring'əl) *n. Scot.* A youth.

spring balance A weighing device, often used in classroom experiments, consisting essentially of a spring with a hook at one end to which objects to be weighed may be hung.

spring·beau·ty (spring'byōō'tē) *n. pl.* **·ties** One of a genus *(Claytonia)* of perennial wild flowers of the purslane family; especially, *C. virginica* of the eastern United States, with pink-tinged white flowers. See CLAYTONIA.

spring·board (spring'bôrd', -bōrd') *n.* 1 An elastic board used to aid in leaping; a springy board secured at one end, used to give impetus to a dive into the water below. Also *diving board.* 2 A short board inserted by one end in a notch in a tree, on which a workman stands when felling large trees.

spring·bok (spring'bok) *n.* A small South African gazelle *(Antidorcas marsupialis)* noted for its ability to leap high in the air. Also **spring'·buck'** (-buk'). [< Afrikaans]

SPRINGBOK
(About 2 feet high at the shoulder)

spring chicken 1 A young chicken, 10 weeks to 10 months old, especially tender for cooking: so called because usually hatched in the spring. 2 *Colloq.* A young, immature, or unsophisticated person.

springe (sprinj) *n.* A snare or noose, arranged with a spring to catch small game. [ME *sprenge.* Related to SPRING.]

spring·er (spring'ər) *n.* 1 One who or that which springs. 2 *Archit.* The bottom stone of an arch, lying upon the impost (see illustration under ARCH); the lowest stone in the coping of a gable; a rib in a groined roof or vault. 3 A spaniel valuable for flushing birds. See under SPANIEL. 4 The springbok. 5 The grampus. 6 A spring chicken.

spring fever The listlessness and restlessness that overtakes a person with the first warm days of spring.

Spring·field (spring'fēld) 1 The capital of Illinois. 2 A city in southern Massachusetts; site of a U. S. arsenal. 3 A city in SW Missouri. 4 A city in SW Ohio.

Springfield rifle A magazine-fed, bolt-action, .30-caliber U. S. Army rifle. Also **Springfield.** [from the U. S. arsenal at *Springfield,* Mass.]

spring·halt (spring'hôlt') *n.* A stringhalt.

spring·head (spring'hed') *n.* A fountainhead; source.

spring hinge A hinge the leaves of which are connected with a spring to insure automatic closing.

spring·house (spring'hous') *n.* A small building constructed over a spring, and used for keeping milk, meats, etc., cool.

spring·ing (spring'ing) *n.* 1 The act of one who or that which springs. 2 *Archit.* A springer: also **springing line.**

spring·let (spring'lit) *n.* A small spring; streamlet or rill.

Springs (springz) A city of southern Transvaal province, Republic of South Africa.

spring·tail (spring'tāl') *n.* Any of certain very small wingless insects (order *Collembola*) having a tail comprised of two united parts, which bends beneath it and enables it to jump.

spring tide 1 A high tide occurring under the combined attraction of sun and new or full moon. 2 Any great wave of feeling, etc.

spring·time (spring'tīm') *n.* The season of spring. Also **spring'tide'** (-tīd').

spring water Water found in or obtained from a spring.

spring·y (spring'ē) *adj.* **spring·i·er, spring·i·est** 1 Elastic. 2 Spongy; wet. — **spring'i·ly** *adv.* — **spring'i·ness** *n.*

sprin·kle (spring'kəl) *v.* **·kled, ·kling** *v.t.* 1 To scatter in drops or small particles. 2 To besprinkle; specifically, to apply drops of water to, as a form of baptism: opposed to *immerse.* — *v.i.* 3 To fall or rain in scattered drops. — *n.* A falling in drops or particles, or that which so falls; a sprinkling; hence, a small quantity. [ME *sprenkelen.* Akin to LG *sprinkeln* scatter.]

sprin·kler (spring'klər) *n.* 1 A nozzle or other device for spraying water on lawns, built either as a portable apparatus or as a unit in a stationary network fed by underground pipes. 2 An outlet in a sprinkler system.

sprinkler system An arrangement of pipes distributed through a building, with outlets suitably placed for sprinkling water or other extinguishing fluid to put out fire: often with automatic temperature control.

sprin·kling (spring'kling) *n.* 1 That which is sprinkled. 2 A small number or quantity. 3 A mottling. 4 The act of scattering drops of liquid.

sprint (sprint) *n.* A short race run at top speed. [< *v.*] — *v.i.* To run fast, as in a sprint. [ME *sprenten* <Scand. Cf. ON *spretta* run.] — **sprint'er** *n.*

sprit¹ (sprit) *n. Naut.* 1 A small spar reaching diagonally from a mast to the peak of a fore-and-aft sail. 2 *Brit.* A pole used for propelling a boat. 3 A bowsprit. [OE *sprēot* pole]

sprit² (sprit) *n. Scot.* A rush or rushlike plant. — **sprit'tie** *adj.*

sprite (sprīt) *n.* 1 A fairy, elf, or goblin. 2 A disembodied spirit; a ghost. Also spelled *spright.* [<OF *esprit* <L *spiritus.* Doublet of SPIRIT.]

sprit·sail (sprit'səl, sprit'sāl') *n. Naut.* A sail extended by a sprit.

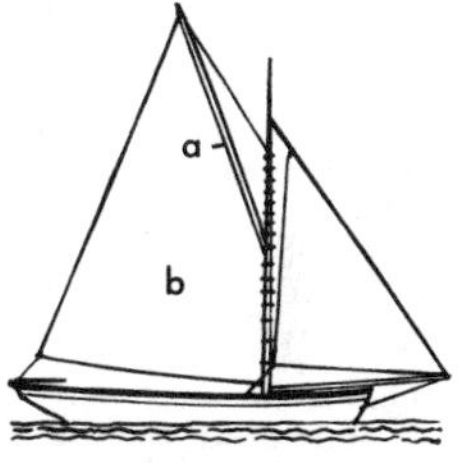

SPRITSAIL
a. Sprit. *b.* Spritsail.

sprock·et (sprok'it) *n. Mech.* 1 A projection, as on the periphery of a wheel, for engaging with the links of a chain. 2 A wheel bearing such projections: also **sprocket wheel.** [Origin uncertain]

sprout (sprout) *v.i.* 1 To put forth shoots; begin to grow; germinate. 2 To develop or grow rapidly. — *v.t.* 3 To cause to sprout. 4 To remove shoots from. — *n.* 1 A new shoot or bud on a plant; hence, something like or suggestive of a sprout; a scion. 2 *pl.* Brussels sprouts. — **a course of sprouts** A period of training. [OE *sprūtan*]

sprout·ling (sprout'ling) *n.* A little sprout.

spruce¹ (sprōōs) *n.* 1 Any of a genus *(Picea)* of evergreen trees of the pine family, having a sharp-pointed pyramidal crown, needle-shaped leaves, and pendulous cones; especially, the ornamental **Norway spruce** *(P. abies),* and the **Engelmann spruce** *(P. engelmanni)* of the Pacific coast. 2 The wood of any of these trees. 3 Any of certain other coniferous trees, as the Douglas fir. [Earlier *pruce* Prussian <*Pruce* Prussia <Med. L *Prussia*; so called because first known as a product of Prussia]

spruce² (sprōōs) *adj.* 1 Having a smart, trim appearance. 2 Fastidious. See synonyms under NEAT¹. — *v.* **spruced, spruc·ing** *v.t.* To make spruce; dress or arrange neatly: often with *up.* — *v.i.* To make oneself spruce: usually with *up.* [Special use of SPRUCE³] — **spruce'ly** *adv.* — **spruce'ness** *n.*

spruce³ (sprōōs) *n.* A kind of superior Prussian leather. Also **spruce leather.** [See SPRUCE¹]

spruce beer A slightly fermented beverage made by boiling leaves and twigs of spruce with sugar or molasses.

sprue¹ (sprōō) *n.* 1 In founding, a channel connecting with the gate through which the melted metal is poured into the mold; also, dross. 2 A pouring hole in a mold; gate. [Origin uncertain]

sprue² (sprōō) *n. Pathol.* 1 A disease of tropical regions marked by anemia, emaciation, and gastrointestinal disturbances; psilosis. 2 Thrush. [<Du *spruw*]

sprug (sprug) *n. Scot. & Brit. Dial.* The common sparrow.

sprung (sprung) Past participle and alternative past tense of SPRING.

sprung rhythm In prosody, a rhythm involving feet of varying number of syllables but of equal time length, the stress usually falling on the first syllable: a term coined by Gerard Manley Hopkins.

sprung weight In automobiles, the weight supported by the suspension system: opposed to *unsprung weight.*

spry (sprī) *adj.* **spri·er** or **spry·er, spri·est** or **spry·est** Quick and active; agile. See synonyms under ACTIVE, SPRIGHTLY. [<dial. E *sprey* <Scand. Cf. Sw. *sprygg* active.] —**spry′ly** *adv.* —**spry′ness** *n.*

spud (spud) *n.* **1** A spadelike tool with narrow blade or prongs for removing the roots of weeds by digging or cutting. **2** *Colloq.* A potato. —*v.t.* **spud·ded, spud·ding** To remove, as weeds, with a spud. [ME *spudde* <Scand. Cf. Dan. *spyd* a spear.]

spud·der (spud′ər) *n.* A tool for removing bark from trees; also, one who uses such an implement.

spul·yie (spül′yē) *Scot. n.* The act of despoiling; spoil; booty. Also **spul′yie·ment.** —*v.t.* & *v.i.* To plunder. Also **spuil′zie, spul′zie** (-yē).

spume (spyōōm) *n.* Froth, as on an agitated or effervescing liquid; foam; scum. —*v.i.* **spumed, spum·ing** To foam; froth. [<F <L *spuma* foam] —**spu′mous** *adj.* —**spum′y** *adj.*

spu·mes·cent (spyōō·mes′ənt) *adj.* Resembling or producing froth or foam; spumy. —**spu·mes′cence** *n.*

spu·mo·ne (spə·mō′nē, *Ital.* spōō·mō′nā) *n. pl.* **·ni** (-nē) A dessert or mousse of ice-cream or water ice containing fruit, nuts, or other candied products, in a base of whipped cream. [<Ital., aug. of *spuma* froth <L *spuma*]

spun (spun) Past tense and past participle of SPIN.

spunk (spungk) *n.* **1** Dry wood that burns easily; touchwood; also, a kind of tinder made from a species of fungus; punk. **2** A small fire, spark, or flame; also, a match. **3** *Colloq.* Quick, fiery temper; mettle; pluck; courage. —**to get one's spunk up** To become defiant or angry; also, to take heart; show courage. —*v.i.* To take fire; flare up; kindle. [<Irish *sponnc* tinder <L *spongia* sponge]

spunk·ie (spungk′ē) *Scot. n.* **1** The ignis fatuus. **2** A small flame. **3** Liquor; whisky. —*adj.* Spunky.

spunk·y (spungk′ē) *adj.* **spunk·i·er, spunk·i·est** *Colloq.* Spirited; courageous; also, touchy. —**spunk′i·ly** *adv.* —**spunk′i·ness** *n.*

spun rayon Yarns or fabrics made from short rayon fibers instead of from one long filament.

spun silk **1** Short fibers of silk from cocoons which the worms have pierced, and which cannot be reeled. **2** Yarn or cloth made from these fibers.

spun yarn *Naut.* A two- to four-stranded, left-handed line made from loosely twisted rope yarn: used for seizings, etc.

spur (spûr) *n.* **1** A pricking or goading instrument worn on a horseman's heel, and bearing a sharp point or a series of points on a rotating wheel. **2** Anything that incites or urges; instigation; incentive. **3** A part or attachment projecting like or suggestive of a spur, as a crag or mountain peak, a steel gaff fastened to a gamecock's leg, the ergot of rye, etc. **4** A stiff, sharp spine, as on the legs of some insects and the wings of some birds; especially, the spine on the tarsus of the domestic cock. See illustration under FOWL. **5** *Archit.* A buttress or other offset from a wall; also, a claw or the like projecting upon the plinth at the four angles of the base of a column. **6** In carpentry, a brace reinforcing a rafter or post; a strut. **7** *Bot.* A tubular expansion of a foliaceous part, usually some part of the flower, as in the columbine and larkspur. **8** A branch of a lode, railroad, etc. —**on the spur of the moment** Hastily; prompted by an impulse. —*v.* **spurred, spur·ring** *v.t.* **1** To prick or urge with or as with spurs. **2** To furnish with spurs. **3** To injure or gash with the spur, as a gamecock. —*v.i.* **4** To spur one's horse. **5** To hasten; hurry. [OE *spura*] —**spur′rer** *n.*

Synonyms (verb): goad, impel, incite, instigate, provoke, rouse, stimulate, sting, stir, urge. *Antonyms*: check, deter, discourage, dissuade, hold, moderate, rein, restrain.

spur·gall (spûr′gôl′) *n.* A galled place on a horse's side, caused by the spur. —*v.t.* To injure or gall with a spur.

spurge (spûrj) *n.* **1** Any of several shrubs (genus *Euphorbia*) having fertile flowers with 3-lobed ovaries on long pedicels and yielding a milky juice of bitter taste. **2** One of various related plants of the spurge family (*Euphorbiaceae*). [<OF *espurge* < *espurgier* purge <L *expurgare* < *ex-* out + *purgare* cleanse]

spur gear *Mech.* **1** A spur wheel. **2** Spur gearing.

spur gearing *Mech.* Gearing composed of spur wheels.

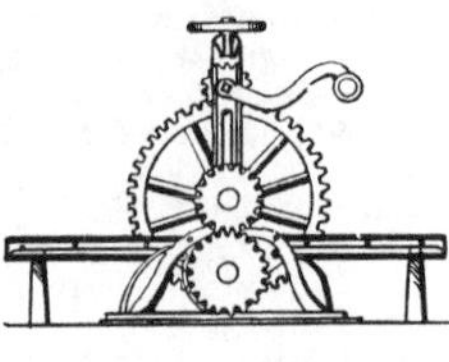

SPUR GEARING

spurge laurel An evergreen shrub of Europe and Asia (*Daphne laureola*), with oblanceolate leaves and yellowish-green flowers.

Spur·geon (spûr′jən), **Charles Haddon,** 1834–92, English Baptist preacher and writer.

spu·ri·ous (spyŏŏr′ē·əs) *adj.* **1** Not proceeding from the source pretended; not genuine; false. **2** Illegitimate. **3** Apparent, but not real; resembling in appearance but not in structure: a *spurious* fruit. See synonyms under COUNTERFEIT, FACTITIOUS. [<L *spurius*] —**spu′ri·ous·ly** *adv.* —**spu′ri·ous·ness** *n.*

spurn (spûrn) *v.t.* **1** To reject with disdain; refuse contemptuously; scorn. **2** To strike with the foot; kick. —*v.i.* **3** To reject something with disdain. See synonyms under SCORN. —*n.* The act of spurning; also, a kick. [OE *spurnan* kick, reject] —**spurn′er** *n.*

spurred (spûrd) *adj.* Wearing or having spurs; having sharp spikes, claws, or shoots.

spur·ri·er (spûr′ē·ər) *n.* A maker of spurs.

spur·ry (spûr′ē) *n. pl.* **·ries** Any of several low annual herbs (genus *Spergula*); especially, the **corn spurry** (*S. arvensis*), which is a common weed. Also **spur′rey.** [<Du. *spurrie*]

spurt (spûrt) *n.* **1** A sudden gush of liquid. **2** Any sudden outbreak, as of anger. **3** An extraordinary effort of brief duration; a sudden rise in activity or price. **4** A brief period. —*v.i.* **1** To come out in a jet; gush forth. **2** To make a sudden and extreme effort. —*v.t.* **3** To force out in a jet; squirt. Also spelled *spirt.* [Var. of earlier *spirt,* metathetic var. of *sprit* <OE *spryttan* come forth]

spur·tle (spûr′təl) *n. Scot.* A stirring stick for porridge.

spur track A short side track connecting with the main track of a railroad. Also **spur.**

spur wheel A toothed wheel having external radial teeth on the periphery; a spur gear.

sput·nik (spŏŏt′nik, sput′-) *n.* A Russian artificial earth satellite: the first to be recorded in world history, called Sputnik I, containing various scientific instruments, was launched October 4, 1957, to an initial height of 560 miles, orbiting at a mean velocity of 18,000 miles per hour. [<Russian, a satellite; lit., that which travels with something else]

sput·ter (sput′ər) *v.i.* **1** To throw off solid or fluid particles in a series of slight explosions. **2** To emit particles of saliva from the mouth, as when speaking excitedly. **3** To speak rapidly or confusedly. —*v.t.* **4** To throw off or emit in small particles. **5** To utter in a confused or excited manner. —*n.* **1** The act or sound of sputtering; especially, excited talk; jabbering. **2** That which is thrown out in sputtering. **3** Trouble; fuss. [Freq. of SPOUT, *v.*] —**sput′ter·er** *n.*

spu·tum (spyōō′təm) *n. pl.* **·ta** (-tə) Saliva; spittle; expectorated matter. [<L < *spuere* spit]

Spuy·ten Duy·vil Creek (spīt′n dī′vəl) A narrow stream in New York City, connecting the Hudson and Harlem rivers and separating Manhattan Island from the mainland on the north; used as a ship canal.

spy (spī) *n. pl.* **spies** **1** One who enters an enemy's military lines covertly to get information; a secret agent. **2** One who watches others secretly: often used contemptuously. **3** A peep; glance; hence, an eye. **4** The act of watching secretly. —*v.* **spied, spy·ing** *v.i.* **1** To keep watch closely or secretly; act as a spy. **2** To make careful examination; pry: with *into.* —*v.t.* **3** To observe stealthily and with hostile intent: usually with *out.* **4** To catch sight of; see; espy. **5** To discover by careful or secret investigation: with *out.* **6** To examine or scrutinize carefully. [<OF *espie* < *espier* espy <Gmc.]

Synonyms (noun): emissary, scout. The *scout* and the *spy* are both employed to obtain information of the numbers, movements, etc., of an enemy. The *scout* lurks on the outskirts of the hostile army with such concealment as the case admits of, but without disguise; a *spy* enters in disguise within the enemy's lines. A *scout,* if captured, has the rights of a prisoner of war; a *spy* is held to have forfeited all rights, and is liable, in case of capture, to capital punishment. Soldiers not in disguise or military aviators are not considered *spies,* even while passing through or over hostile territory. An *emissary* is rather political than military, sent to influence opponents secretly rather than to bring information concerning them.

spy·glass (spī′glas′, -gläs′) *n.* A small field glass or telescope.

Spy·ri (shpē′rē), **Johanna,** 1827–1901, *née* Heusser, Swiss author of *Heidi.*

squab (skwob) *n.* **1** A young pigeon, especially when an unfledged nestling. **2** A fat, short person. **3** A soft, stuffed cushion; sofa; ottoman. —*adj.* **1** Fat and short; low and bulky; squat. **2** Unfledged or but half-fledged; half-grown, as a pigeon, or figuratively, any fowl. [<dial. E <Scand. Cf. dial. Norw. *skvabb* a soft, wet mass.]

squab·ble (skwob′əl) *v.* **·bled, ·bling** *v.i.* To engage in a petty wrangle or scuffle; quarrel. —*v.t. Printing* To twist (composed type) so as to mix the lines. —*n.* The act of squabbling; a petty wrangle. See synonyms under QUARREL[1]. [Cf. dial. Sw. *skvabbel* dispute, argue] —**squab′bler** *n.*

squab·by (skwob′ē) *adj.* **·bi·er, ·bi·est** Short and fat. Also **squab′bish.**

squad (skwod) *n.* **1** A small group of persons organized for the performance of a specific function; a small detachment of troops or police; specifically, the smallest tactical unit in the infantry of the U. S. Army. **2** Hence, a team: a football *squad.* —*v.t.* **squad·ded, squad·ding** **1** To form into a squad or squads. **2** To assign to a squad. [<F *escouade* <OF *esquadre* a square <Ital. *squadra* <L *quattuor* four]

squad car An automobile used by police for patrolling, and equipped with radiotelephone for communicating with headquarters.

squad·ron (skwod′rən) *n.* **1** An assemblage of war vessels smaller than a fleet; one of the divisions of a fleet. **2** A division of a cavalry regiment. **3** The basic unit of the United States Air Force, usually consisting of two or more flights operating as a unit. **4** Any regularly arranged or organized body, as of men. —*v.t.* To arrange in a squadron or squadrons. [<Ital. *squadrone,* aug. of *squadra* SQUAD]

squail (skwāl) *n.* A disk used in the game of squails.

squails (skwālz) *n. pl.* A game played with small wooden disks on a table, the object being to approach as nearly as possible to a mark at the center of the board, by snapping the disks from the edge. [Origin uncertain]

squal·id (skwol′id) *adj.* Having a foul, mean, or poverty-stricken appearance; dirty, neglected, and wretched. See synonyms under BASE[2]. [<L *squalidus* < *squalere* be foul] —**squal′id·ly** *adv.* —**squal′id·ness, squa·lid·i·ty** (skwo·lid′ə·tē) *n.*

squall[1] (skwôl) *n.* A loud, screaming outcry. —*v.i.* To cry loudly; scream; bawl. [Cf. ON *skvala* shout, bawl] —**squall′er** *n.*

squall[2] (skwôl) *n.* A sudden, violent burst of wind, often accompanied by rain or snow. —*v.i.* To blow a squall; be squally. [Cf. Sw. *skval-regn* a sudden rainstorm]

squall cloud A grayish cloud rolling beneath an approaching thunderstorm.

squall line *Meteorol.* A cold front characterized along its edge by a sharp change of wind and the occasional formation of line squalls.

squall·y (skwô′lē) *adj.* **squall·i·er, squall·i·est** **1** Stormy; blustering. **2** *Colloq.* Threatening a squall or trouble of any kind.

squal·or (skwol′ər) *n.* The state of being squalid, or the filth of thriftless poverty. [<L < *squalere* be foul]

squa·lus (skwā′ləs) *n.* Any of a genus (*Squalus*) of cartilaginous fishes (class *Chondrichthyes*), including the spiny dogfish or shark (*S. acanthias*) common in shore waters of the Atlantic. [<L, large marine fish]

squa·ma (skwā′mə) *n. pl.* **·mae** (-mē) A thin, scalelike structure; a scale. [<L] —**squa′·mate** (-māt) *adj.*

Squa·ma·ta (skwə·mā′tə) *n. pl.* An order of reptiles, including lizards, chameleons, and serpents. [<NL <L *squama* a scale]

squa·ma·tion (skwə·mā′shən) *n.* 1 The state of being scaly. 2 The arrangement of epidermal scales.

squa·mo·sal (skwə·mō′səl) *adj.* 1 Like a scale; squamous. 2 *Anat.* Relating to the squamous portion of the temporal bone or the analogous bone in lower animals. — *n.* The squamosal bone.

squa·mous (skwā′məs) *adj.* 1 Covered with scales; scaly; scalelike. 2 *Anat.* Designating the vertical plate of the temporal bone. Also **squa′mose** (-mōs). [<L *squamosus* < *squama* a scale] — **squa′mous·ly** *adv.* — **squa′mous·ness** *n.*

squam·u·lose (skwam′yə·lōs, skwā′myə-) *adj.* *Bot.* Provided with small bracts or scales, as a plant; minutely squamate.

squan·der (skwon′dər) *v.t.* 1 To spend (money, time, etc.) wastefully; lavish profusely; dissipate. 2 *Obs.* To scatter. — *n.* Prodigality; the act of squandering. [Cf. dial. E *squander* scatter] — **squan′der·er** *n.* — **squan′der·ing·ly** *adv.*

Synonyms (verb): dissipate, expend, lavish, scatter, spend, waste. *Antonyms*: economize, hoard, hold, husband, preserve, reserve, save.

squan·tum[1] (skwon′təm) *n.* Among North American Indians, especially the Narragansets, a spirit or god; an evil spirit.

squan·tum[2] (skwon′təm) *n.* In New England, a picnic or shore dinner; a chowder party; hence, any merrymaking or frolic. [from *Squantum*, Mass., after *Tisquantum*, a Massachuset chief]

square (skwâr) *n.* 1 A parallelogram having four equal sides and four right angles. 2 Any object, part, or surface that is square or nearly so, as a pane of glass, or one of the spots on a checkerboard. 3 An instrument by which to measure or lay out right angles, consisting usually of two legs or branches at right angles to each other, in L-shape or T-shape (in the latter case called a *T-square*). 4 An open area in a city or village, left between streets at their intersection or formed by their expansion. 5 A town or city block; also, the distance between one street and the next. 6 *Math.* The product of a number or quantity multiplied by itself. 7 Formerly, a body of troops formed in a four-sided array. 8 *Obs.* A standard or pattern; rule. 9 *Slang* A person not conversant with developments in the popular arts, especially the latest fashions in jazz, slang, etc. — **on the square** 1 At right angles. 2 On equal terms. 3 *Colloq.* In a fair and honest manner. 4 In Freemasonry, in good standing: said of members. — **out of square** 1 Not at right angles; obliquely. 2 Incorrectly; askew; out of order. — *adj.* 1 Having four equal sides and four right angles; loosely, approaching a square in form. 2 Formed with or characterized by a right angle; rectangular. 3 Adapted to forming squares or computing in squares: a *square* measure. 4 Direct; fair; just; equitable; honest. 5 Having debit and credit balanced; even; settled. 6 Absolute; complete; unequivocal. 7 Having a broad, stocky frame; hence, strong, sturdy. 8 *Colloq.* Solid; full; satisfying: a *square* meal. 9 *Naut.* At right angles to the mast and keel: said of the yards of a square-rigged ship. 10 *Math.* Raised to the second power; squared: 10 *square* equals 100. 11 Steady: said of a horse's gait. 12 *Mech.* Having the cylinder bore equal, or nearly equal to the piston stroke: said of engines. See synonyms under JUST[1]. — *v.* **squared, squar·ing** *v.t.* 1 To make square; form with four equal sides and four right angles. 2 To shape or adjust so as to form a right angle, or a right angle with something else. 3 To mark with or divide into squares. 4 To test for the purpose of adjusting to a straight line, right angle, or plane surface. 5 To bring to a position suggestive of a right angle: *Square* your shoulders. 6 To make satisfactory settlement or adjustment of: to *square* accounts. 7 To make (the score of a game or contest) equal. 8 To cause to conform; adapt; reconcile: to *square* one's opinions to the times. 9 *Math.* **a** To multiply (a number or quantity) by itself. **b** To determine the contents of in square measure. **c** To find the square equivalent of: to *square* a circle. 10 *Slang* To bribe: to *square* a jockey. — *v.i.* 11 To be at right angles. 12 To conform; agree; harmonize. 13 In golf, to make the ·scores equal. 14 *Obs.* To squabble; quarrel. — **to square away** 1 *Naut.* To set (the yards) at right angles to the keel. 2 To square up. — **to square off** To assume a position for attack or defense; prepare to fight. — **to square up** To adjust satisfactorily. — *adv.* 1 So as to be square, or at right angles. 2 Honestly; fairly. 3 Directly; firmly. [<OF *esquire, esquarre,* ult. <L *quattuor* four] — **square·ness** *n.*

SQUARES
a. T-square.
b. Steel square.
c. Try square.

square bracket Bracket (def. 4).

square dance Any dance, as a quadrille, in which the couples form sets in squares.

squared circle *Colloq.* A boxing ring; the prize ring. Also **squared ring.**

square deal *Colloq.* 1 In card games, an honest deal. 2 Hence, fair or just treatment.

square·head (skwâr′hed′) *n.* *U.S. Slang* 1 A Scandinavian. 2 A German.

square knot A common knot, formed of two overhand knots: also called *reef knot.* See illustration under KNOT.

square league An old Spanish land measure equal to 4,438 acres.

square·ly (skwâr′lē) *adv.* 1 In a direct or straight manner: He looked her *squarely* in the eyes. 2 Honestly; fairly. 3 *U.S.* Plainly; unequivocally. 4 In a square form: *squarely* built. 5 At right angles (to a line or plane).

square meal *Colloq.* A full and substantial meal.

square measure A unit or system of units for measuring areas, as in the following table of principal customary standards. See also METRIC SYSTEM.

144 square inches (sq. in.; in²)	=	1 square foot (sq. ft.; ft²)
9 square feet	=	1 square yard (sq. yd.; yd²)
30.25 square yards	=	1 square rod (sq. rd.; rd²)
160 square rods	=	1 acre (A.)
640 acres	=	1 square mile (sq. mi.)

square number See under NUMBER.

square piano See under PIANO[1].

squar·er (skwâr′ər) *n.* 1 One who squares. 2 *Archaic* A brawler.

square–rigged (skwâr′rigd′) *adj.* *Naut.* Having the principal sails extended by horizontal yards; ship-rigged: distinguished from *fore-and-aft-rigged.* Compare illustrations under BARK, BRIG, SHIP.

square–rig·ger (skwâr′rig′ər) *n.* A square-rigged ship.

square root *Math.* A number or quantity that, multiplied by itself, produces the given number or quantity: 4 is the *square root* of 16; a second root. See under CUBE[1], ROOT[1].

square sail *Naut.* A quadrilateral sail usually rigged on a yard set at right angles to the mast.

square shooter *Colloq.* An upright person; one who acts honestly and justly.

square–toed (skwâr′tōd′) *adj.* Having the toes square, as the shoes worn by the Puritans; hence, exact; punctilious.

square–toes (skwâr′tōz′) *n.* An old-fashioned, exact person.

squaring a log Sawing a log so as to give it four equal sides.

squaring the circle Quadrature of the circle.

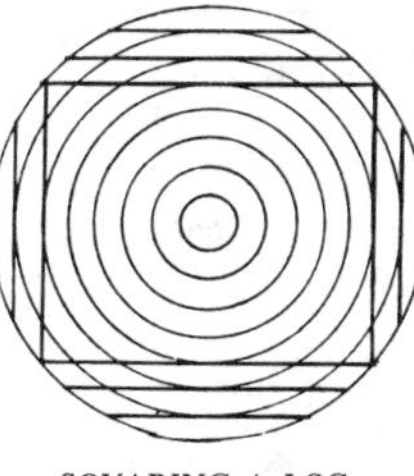

SQUARING A LOG

squar·rose (skwar′·ōs, skwo·rōs′) *adj.* 1 *Biol.* Rough with projecting scalelike processes. 2 *Bot.* Crowded and rigid: *squarrose* leaves. Also **squar·rous** (skwar′əs). [<L *squarrosus* scurfy]

squash[1] (skwosh) *v.t.* 1 To beat or press into a pulp or soft mass; crush. 2 To quell or suppress. — *v.i.* 3 To be smashed or squashed. 4 To make a splashing or sucking sound. — *n.* 1 A soft or overripe object; also, a crushed mass. 2 The sudden fall of a heavy, soft, or bursting body; also, the sound made by such a fall. 3 The sucking, squelching sound made by walking through ooze or mud. 4 Either of two games played on an indoor court with rackets and a ball. In one (**squash rackets**) a slow rubber ball is used; in the other (**squash tennis**), a livelier, smaller ball. 5 A beverage of which one ingredient is a fruit juice: lemon *squash.* — *adv.* With a squelching, oozy sound. [<OF *esquasser,* ult. <L *ex-* thoroughly + *quassare* crush] — **squash′er** *n.*

squash[2] (skwosh) *n.* 1 The edible fruit of various trailing annuals (genus *Cucurbita*) of the gourd family. 2 The plant that bears it. [<Algonquian. Cf. Massachuset *askootasquash,* lit., eaten raw.]

squash bug A large, brownish-black, evil-smelling North American hemipterous insect (*Anasa tristis*) which is destructive to squash vines.

squash·y (skwosh′ē) *adj.* **squash·i·er, squash·i·est** Soft and moist; easily squashed. — **squash′·i·ly** *adv.* — **squash′i·ness** *n.*

squat (skwot) *v.* **squat·ted** or **squat, squat·ting** *v.i.* 1 To sit on the heels or hams, or with the legs near the body. 2 To crouch or cower down, as to avoid being seen. 3 To settle on a piece of land without title or payment. 4 To settle on government land in accordance with certain government regulations that will eventually give title. — *v.t.* 5 To cause (oneself) to squat. — *adj.* 1 Short and thick; squatty. 2 Being in a squatting position. — *n.* A squatting attitude or position. [<OF *esquatir* < *es-* thoroughly (<L *ex-*) + *quatir* press down <L *coactus,* pp. of *cogere* force < *co-* together + *agere* drive]

squat tag A game of tag in which the players cannot be tagged while squatting.

squat·ter (skwot′ər) *n.* 1 One who or that which squats; specifically, one who settles on land without permission or right, as on public or unimproved land. 2 In the United States and Australia, one who settles on government land subject to regulations with a view to obtaining title.

squatter sovereignty 1 The political theory that the people or settlers of a Territory had the right to make their own laws, specifically whether or not slavery should be permitted; popular sovereignty. 2 The right of settlers to the lands they have settled.

squat·ty (skwot′ē) *adj.* Disproportionately short and thick.

squaw (skwô) *n.* 1 An American Indian woman or wife. 2 *Colloq.* Any woman or girl. [<Algonquian, woman]

squaw·bush (skwô′bŏŏsh′) *n.* 1 Any shrub of the genus *Cornus*; especially, the red-osier dogwood. 2 The cranberry tree.

squaw·fish (skwô′fish′) *n.* *pl.* **·fish** or **·fish·es** 1 A cyprinoid fish (genus *Ptychocheilus*) found in the rivers of the northern Pacific coast. 2 A surf fish.

squawk (skwôk) *v.i.* 1 To utter a shrill, harsh cry, as a parrot. 2 *Slang* To utter loud complaints or protests. — *n.* 1 The harsh cry of certain birds; also, the act of squawking. 2 *Slang* A loud protest or complaint. 3 The black-crowned night heron (*Nycticorax nycticorax*). [Prob. imit.] — **squawk′er** *n.*

squaw man 1 Among the American Indians, a man who lives and works among the women. 2 A white man married to an Indian woman and in possession of tribal rights on that account.

squaw·root (skwô′rōōt′, -rŏŏt′) *n.* 1 A yellowish-brown leafless North American herb (*Conopholis americana*) parasitic on roots. 2 One of certain other plants, as the blue cohosh.

squaw vine The partridgeberry.

squeak (skwēk) *n.* 1 A thin, sharp, penetrating sound. 2 *Colloq.* A narrow margin; the least amount; a hairbreadth: in the phrase **a narrow** (or **close**) **squeak.** — *v.i.* 1 To make a squeak. 2 *Colloq.* To let out information; squeal. 3 To succeed or otherwise progress after narrowly averting failure or reversal: He just managed to *squeak* through. — *v.t.* **4** To utter or effect with a squeak. **5** To cause to squeak. [ME *squeke,* prob. <Scand. Cf. Sw. *sqväka* croak.] — **squeak′er** *n.*

squeak·y (skwē′kē) *adj.* **squeak·i·er, squeak·i·est** Making a squeaking noise. — **squeak′i·ly** *adv.* — **squeak′i·ness** *n.*

squeal (skwēl) *v.i.* **1** To utter a sharp, shrill, somewhat prolonged cry. **2** *Slang* To turn informer; betray an accomplice or a plot. — *v.t.* **3** To utter with a squeal. — *n.* A shrill, prolonged cry, as of a pig. [Imit.] — **squeal′er** *n.*

squeam·ish (skwē′mish) *adj.* **1** Easily disgusted or shocked; unduly scrupulous. **2** Easily nauseated. [< earlier *squeamous* <AF *escoymous;* ult. origin unknown] — **squeam′·ish·ly** *adv.* — **squeam′ish·ness** *n.*

Synonyms: affected, dainty, difficult, fastidious, finical, foolish, hypercritical, overnice, oversensitive, particular, prudish, qualmish, scrupulous, sickish.

squee·gee (skwē′jē) *n.* **1** A wooden implement having a stout straight-edged strip of rubber or leather inserted in its blade, used for removing water from wet decks or floors, window panes, etc. **2** *Phot.* A smaller similar implement, made in the same way or in the form of a roller, used for pressing a film closer to its mount, or for squeezing the moisture from a print. — *v.t.* **1** To smooth down, as a photographic film, with a squeegee. **2** To cleanse with a squeegee. Also spelled *squilgee, squillagee.* [< *squeege,* var. of SQUEEZE]

squeeze (skwēz) *v.* **squeezed, squeez·ing** *v.t.* **1** To press hard upon; compress. **2** To extract something from by pressure: to *squeeze* oranges. **3** To draw forth by pressure; express: to *squeeze* juice from apples. **4** To force or push; cram. **5** To oppress, as with burdensome taxes. **6** To exert pressure upon (someone) to act as one desires, as by blackmailing. **7** To take a squeeze (def. 4) of. — *v.i.* **8** To apply pressure. **9** To force one's way; push: with *in, through,* etc. **10** To be pressed; yield to pressure: These lemons *squeeze* well. See synonyms under JAM[1]. — **to squeeze out** To force out of business, or ruin financially, by unscrupulous methods. — *n.* **1** The act or process of squeezing; pressure. **2** A firm grasp of someone's hand; a hearty handclasp; also, an embrace; hug. **3** Something, as juice, extracted or expressed. **4** A facsimile, as of a coin or inscription, produced by pressing some soft substance upon it. **5** *Colloq.* A crowded social gathering. **6** *Colloq.* Pressure exerted for the extortion of money or favors; also, financial pressure. [? <OF *es-* thoroughly (<L *ex-*) + ME *queisen,* OE *cwēsan* crush] — **squeez′a·ble** *adj.*

squeeze play In baseball, a play in which the batter bunts the ball so that a man on third base may score by starting while the pitcher is about to deliver the ball.

squeez·er (skwē′zər) *n.* One who or that which squeezes; especially, a mechanical device for applying pressure on fruit.

squeez·ing (skwē′zing) *n.* **1** The act or process of squeezing. **2** *Often pl.* That which is squeezed out. **3** A crowding together.

squelch (skwelch) *v.t.* **1** To crush; squash. **2** *Colloq.* To subdue utterly; silence, as with a crushing reply. — *v.i.* **3** To make a splashing or sucking noise, as when walking in deep mud. **4** To walk with such a sound. — *n.* **1** A noise made when walking in wet boots. **2** A heavy fall or blow. **3** *Colloq.* A squelcher. [Prob. imit.]

squelch·er (skwel′chər) *n.* **1** One who or that which squelches. **2** *Colloq.* A silencing retort; crushing reply.

sque·teague (skwi·tēg′) *n.* A weakfish. [<Algonquian (Narraganset) *pesukwiteaug* they make glue]

squib (skwib) *n.* **1** A roll or case filled with gunpowder, to be thrown or rolled swiftly, finally exploding like a rocket. **2** A tubular case filled with gunpowder and connected with an electric circuit, used for firing a charge in a blasthole, igniting a smokepot, or the like. **3** A broken firecracker that burns with a spitting sound. **4** A short speech or writing in a witty or satirical vein; a mild lampoon. **5** An undistinguished or petty person. — *v.* **squibbed, squib·bing** *v.i.* **1** To write or use squibs. **2** To fire a squib. **3** To explode or sound like a squib. **4** To move quickly or restlessly. — *v.t.* **5** To attack with squibs; lampoon. **6** To fire or use as a squib. [Origin unknown]

squid (skwid) *n.* **1** One of various ten-armed cephalopods (genera *Loligo* and *Ommastrephes*) with a slender conical body, ink sac, and broad caudal fins; especially, the common squid (*L. pealei*) of the Atlantic coast. **2** Fish bait prepared from squid; also, an artificial fish bait, often made in imitation of a squid. — *v.i. Aeron.* To assume a narrow, squidlike shape, as a parachute under excess wind or air pressure. [Origin uncertain]

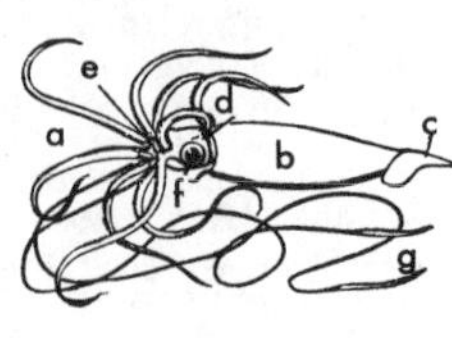

SQUID
a. Arm. *b.* Body. *c.* Fluke. *d.* Eye. *e.* Mouth. *f.* Siphon. *g.* Tentacles.

squig·gle (skwig′əl) *Colloq. n.* A meaningless scrawl. — *v.i.* To wriggle. [Blend of SQUIRM and WRIGGLE]

squil·gee (skwil′jē, skwil·jē′) See SQUEEGEE.

squill[1] (skwil) *n.* **1** A bulbous plant (*Urginea maritima*) of the lily family, growing in the Mediterranean region; the sea onion. **2** Its bulb, dried and sliced, the white variety having diuretic and expectorant properties, and the red variety yielding a rat poison. **3** Any plant of the genus *Scilla,* the more common ones usually called by some other name, as the common English bluebell or wild hyacinth. [<L *squilla* <Gk. *skilla* sea onion]

squill[2] (skwil) *n.* Any of a genus (*Squilla*) of burrowing crustaceans having the form and appearance of a mantis: sometimes called *mantis shrimp.* Also **squil·la** (skwil′ə). [<L *squilla* shrimp]

squil·la·gee (skwil′ə·jē) See SQUEEGEE.

squinch (skwinch) *n. Archit.* A small stone arch or series of arches, or of projecting courses, across an interior angle of a square tower, to support an oblique side of an octagonal spire or lantern. [Alter. of obs. *scunch,* abbreviation of *scuncheon* <OF *escoinson*]

SQUINCH
Salisbury Cathedral, England.

squin·ny (skwin′ē) *v.i.* & *n. Obs.* Squint. Also **squin′y.** [Var. of SQUINT]

squint (skwint) *v.i.* **1** To look with half-closed eyes, as into bright light. **2** To look with a side glance; look askance. **3** To be cross-eyed. **4** To incline or tend: with *toward,* etc. — *v.t.* **5** To hold (the eyes) half shut, as in glaring light. **6** To cause to squint. — *adj.* **1** Having the optic axes not coincident; affected with strabismus: said of the eyes. **2** Looking obliquely or askance; indirect. — *n.* **1** *Pathol.* An affection of the eyes in which their axes are differently directed; strabismus. **2** The act or habit of squinting. **3** Hence, an indirect leaning, tendency, or drift. **4** A hagioscope. [Origin uncertain] — **squint′er** *n.*

squint-eye (skwint′ī′) *n.* Strabismus, or one afflicted with it.

squint-eyed (skwint′īd′) *adj.* **1** Affected with strabismus; cross-eyed. **2** Looking sidewise; aiming in two directions. **3** Apt to see awry; malignant; evil.

squire (skwīr) *n.* **1** A knight's attendant; an armorbearer. **2** A title of dignity, office, or courtesy ranking in England below that of *knight,* and applied in the United States especially to rural or village lawyers and justices of the peace; also, in England, a landed proprietor. **3** A gentleman who acts as the escort of a lady in public; a gallant. — *v.t.* & *v.i.* **squired, squir·ing** To attend or serve (someone) as a squire or escort. [Aphetic var. of ESQUIRE]

squire·ar·chy (skwīr′är·kē) *n. pl.* **·chies** **1** English country gentlemen collectively; also, any body of squires. **2** Government by squires. Also **squir′ar·chy.**

squire·ling (skwīr′ling) *n.* A petty squire. Also **squire′let** (-lit).

squirm (skwûrm) *v.i.* **1** To bend and twist the body; wriggle; writhe. **2** To show signs of pain or distress. — *n.* A squirming motion; a wriggle. [Origin uncertain] — **squirm′er** *n.* — **squirm′y** *adj.*

squir·rel (skwûr′əl, *Brit.* skwir′əl) *n.* **1** Any of various slender rodents (family *Sciuridae*) with a very long bushy tail, living mainly in trees and feeding chiefly on nuts, but occasionally on eggs and small birds. The **red squirrel** (*Sciurus hudsonicus*), the **gray squirrel** (*S. carolinensis*), and the **fox squirrel** (*S. niger*) are North American types. ◆ Collateral adjective: *sciurine.* **2** One of various sciuroid rodents, as the **rock squirrel** (*Otospermophilus grammurus*) of the western United States. **3** The fur of a squirrel. [<OF *esquireul* <LL *scurellus,* dim. of L *sciurus* <Gk. *skiouros* < *skia* shadow + *oura* tail]

GRAY SQUIRREL
(Body to 10 inches; tail to 8 inches)

squirrel corn A smooth and delicate plant (*Dicentra canadensis*) of the northern United States, having white or cream-colored flowers with the spurs rounded and yellow tubers resembling grains of corn.

squirrel glider A flying phalanger (*Petaurus norfolcensis*) of Australia.

squirrel monkey A marmoset.

squirt (skwûrt) *v.i.* **1** To come forth in a thin stream or jet; spurt out. **2** To eject water, etc., thus. — *v.t.* **3** To eject (water or other liquid) forcibly and in a jet. **4** To wet or bespatter with a squirt or squirts. — *n.* **1** The act of squirting or spurting; also, a jet of liquid squirted forth. **2** A syringe or squirt gun. **3** *Colloq.* A conceited, brainless fellow. [Cf. LG *swirtjen*] — **squirt′er** *n.*

squirt gun An instrument or toy shaped like a gun and used for squirting.

squirting cucumber The fruit of a procumbent branching herb (*Ecballium elaterium*) of the gourd family, which, when ripe, ejects its seeds and juice.

squish (skwish) *v.t.* & *v.i. Colloq.* To squash. — *n.* A squashing sound. [Var. of SQUASH[1]] — **squish′y** *adj.*

Sri·nag·ar (srē·nug′ər) The capital of Jammu and Kashmir State, NW India; site of extensive eighth century Buddhist ruins.

St. For entries not found under *St.,* see under SAINT.

-st See -EST[2].

stab (stab) *v.* **stabbed, stab·bing** *v.t.* **1** To pierce with a pointed weapon; wound, as with a dagger. **2** To thrust (a dagger, etc.), as into a body. **3** To penetrate; pierce. — *v.i.* **4** To thrust or lunge with a knife, sword, etc. **5** To inflict a wound thus. See synonyms under PIERCE. — *n.* A thrust made with any pointed weapon. [? <Irish *stob* push, thrust, fix a stake < *stob* a stake] — **stab′ber** *n.*

Sta·bat Ma·ter (stä′bät mä′tər, stā′bat mā′tər) *Latin* A 13th century hymn commemorating the agony of Mary at the crucifixion of Christ and so called from its opening words: literally, the mother was standing.

sta·bile (stā′bil, stab′il) *adj.* **1** Not kept in motion. **2** *Med.* **a** Not affected by moderate heat. **b** Denoting a form of electrotherapy in which one of the electrodes is kept stationary on a part. Compare LABILE. — *n.* An amorphous piece of stationary sculpture. Compare MOBILE. [<L *stabilis.* See STABLE[1].]

sta·bil·i·ty (stə·bil′ə·tē) *n. pl.* **·ties** **1** The condition of being stable; steadiness. **2** The quality or character of being steady or constant; steadfastness of purpose or resolution. **3** *Physics* The state of being in stable equilibrium, or the degree of such equilibrium as measured by the force with which a body tends to maintain its condition of rest or steady motion. **4** *Aeron.* The ability of an aircraft to resume equilibrium when disturbed. **5** A vow to continue in the same profession and order, taken by some Benedictine monks. **6** *Obs.* Rigidity: opposed to *fluidity.* [<L *stabilitas, -tatis* < *stabilis.* See STABLE[1].]

sta·bi·lize (stā′bə·līz) *v.t.* **·lized, ·liz·ing** **1** To make firm or stable. **2** To keep steady; keep from fluctuating, as money or currency: to *stabilize* prices. **3** *Aeron.* To secure or maintain the equilibrium of (an aircraft) by means of fixed surfaces, gyroscopes, etc. [<L

stabilis steady + -IZE] **—sta′bi·li·za′tion** *n.*
sta·bi·liz·er (stā′bə·lī′zər) *n.* **1** *Aeron.* An automatic balancing device; especially, one which steadies the flight of an airplane. See illustration under AIRPLANE. **2** *Chem.* A substance which increases the stability of another substance or compound, especially one which reduces the spontaneous combustion of an explosive.
sta·ble[1] (stā′bəl) *adj.* **1** Standing firmly in place; not easily moved, shaken, or overthrown; fixed. **2** Marked by fixity of purpose; steadfast; inflexible. **3** Having durability or permanence; abiding. **4** *Chem.* Not easily decomposed: said of compounds. **5** *Physics* Resisting forces which tend to cause or distort motion. See synonyms under FIRM, PERMANENT. [<F <L *stabilis* < *stare* stand] **—sta′bly** *adv.* **—sta′ble·ness** *n.*
sta·ble[2] (stā′bəl) *n.* **1** A building set apart for lodging and feeding horses or cattle. **2** Specifically, race horses belonging to a particular stable; also, the owner and personnel of a particular stable collectively. **—***v.t.* & *v.i.* **·bled, ·bling** To put or lodge in a stable. [<OF *estable* <L *stabulum* < *stare* stand]
sta·ble·boy (stā′bəl·boi′) *n.* A boy employed in a stable.
sta·ble·man (stā′bəl·man′, -mən) *n.* *pl.* **·men** (-men′, -mən) One who works in a stable; a hostler; groom.
sta·bling (stā′bling) *n.* **1** The act of one who stables. **2** Room or accommodation in a stable.
stab·lish (stab′lish) *v.t.* *Archaic* To establish. [Aphetic var. of ESTABLISH]
stac·ca·to (stə·kä′tō) *adj.* **1** *Music* Played, or to be played, in an abrupt, disconnected manner: opposed to *legato.* **2** Marked by abrupt, sharp emphasis: a *staccato* style of speaking. [<Ital., pp. of *staccare* detach]
stack (stak) *n.* **1** A large, orderly pile of unthreshed grain, hay, or straw, usually conical. **2** Any systematic pile or heap, as a pile of poker chips purchased or won by a player. **3** A group of rifles (usually three) set upright and supporting one another. **4** A case composed of several rows of bookshelves one above the other. **5** *pl.* That part of a library where most of the books are shelved. **6** A vertical main smoke flue, especially of a furnace or boiler; a chimney; smokestack; also, a collection of such chimneys or flues. **7** *Brit.* A measure of fuel (coal or wood), equal to 108 cubic feet or 4 cubic yards. **8** *Colloq.* A great amount; plenty. **—***v.t.* To gather or place in a pile; pile up in a stack: to *stack* arms; to *stack* firewood. **—to stack the cards 1** To arrange cards in the pack in a manner favorable to the dealer. **2** To have an unfair advantage secured beforehand. [<ON *stakkr*]
stack·er[1] (stak′ər) *n.* *Agric.* An attachment or apparatus for depositing straw from a threshing machine on a wagon or on a stack.
stack·er[2] (stak′ər) *v.* & *n.* *Scot.* Stagger.
stac·te (stak′tē) *n.* One of the spices, of uncertain composition, anciently used by the Jews in preparing incense. *Ex.* xxx 34. [<L, oil of myrrh <Gk. *staktē* < *stazein* drip]
stac·tom·e·ter (stak·tom′ə·tər) *n.* A tube having a minute orifice in one end, for measuring a liquid in drops: also called *stalagmometer.* [<Gk. *staktos* trickling + -METER]
stad·dle (stad′l) *n.* *Brit. Dial.* **1** Anything that serves as a foundation or support; a prop; staff; crutch. **2** *Agric.* A raised platform or frame, or an arrangement of short posts, for a stack of hay or straw, to keep it dry and free from vermin. [OE *stathol* base]
stad·hold·er (stad′hōl·dər) *n.* Formerly, a viceroy or governor of a province or town of the Netherlands as the representative of the sovereign; specifically, the chief magistrate of the Netherlands, a hereditary office in the family of the princes of Orange. Also **stadt′·hold·er** (stat′-). [<Du. *stadhouder* lieutenant < *stad* place + *houder* holder]
sta·di·a (stā′dē·ə) *n.* **1** A temporary surveying station. **2** A form of sighting instrument for measuring distances used in connection with a vertical graduated rod (**stadia rod**). **3** The rod alone or the method of using it. [Prob. <F *stade* a stage, a measure of length <L *stadium.* See STADIUM.]
sta·di·um (stā′dē·əm) *n.* *pl.* **·di·a** (-dē·ə), *for def.* **2 ·di·ums 1** In ancient Greece, a course for footraces, with banked seats for spectators, as at Olympia and Athens, where games were held. **2** A similar modern structure in which athletic games are played: the *stadium* at Harvard. **3** An ancient Greek measure of length, equaling 606.75 feet. **4** A degree of progress or development. **5** *Med.* A given stage or period in the course of a disease. [<L <Gk. *stadion,* a measure of length]
Staël (stäl), **Madame de,** 1766–1817, Baronne de Staël–Holstein, *née* Anne Louise Germaine Necker, French writer; famous for her salon.
staff[1] (staf, stäf) *n.* *pl.* **staves** (stāvz) or **staffs** *for defs. 1–3,* **staffs** *for defs. 4–6.* **1** A stick or piece of wood carried for some special purpose, as an aid in walking or climbing, or as a cudgel or weapon, or as an emblem of authority. **2** A shaft or pole that forms a support or handle: the *staff* of a spear; a *flagstaff.* **3** A stick used in measuring or testing, as a surveyors' leveling rod. **4** *Mil.* **a** A body of officers not having command but attached in an executive or advisory capacity to an army or navy unit as assistants to the officer in command. The central body is known as the **general staff. b** The personnel of a military establishment, as the officers in charge of construction, ordnance, repairs, equipment, provisions, medicine and surgery, the paymasters, and engineers. **5** A body of persons associated in carrying out some special enterprise under the supervision of a manager or chief: the editorial *staff* of a newspaper. **6** *Music* The combined lines and spaces used to represent the pitches of tones. The staff has always five long horizontal lines and the accompanying long spaces, but is enlarged as the occasion may require, by short lines above or below and the short spaces they bring. See synonyms under STICK. **—***v.t.* To provide (an office, etc.) with a staff: to *staff* a management group. [OE *stæf* stick]
staff[2] (staf, stäf) *n.* A composition of plaster, fiber, etc., for temporary buildings, statues, etc. [Prob. <G *staffieren* fill, decorate]
Staf·fa (staf′ə) An islet of the Inner Hebrides group, NW Argyll, Scotland, on which is Fingal's Cave.
staff officer An officer serving on a staff.
Staf·ford (staf′ərd) A county in west central England; 1,153 square miles; county town, Stafford. Also **Staf′ford·shire** (-shir). Shortened form **Staffs.**
stag (stag) *n.* **1** The male of the red deer *(Cervus elaphus),* especially the matured male. **2** The male of other large deer, as the caribou, and of certain other animals. **3** A castrated bull or boar. **4** *Scot.* A colt: also spelled *staig.* **5** *U.S. Slang* A man, especially when not in the company of women. **6** *U.S. Slang* A social gathering for men only. **—***adj.* *U.S. Slang* Of or for men only: a *stag* party. **—***v.i.* **stagged, stag·ging** *Slang* **1** *Brit.* To turn informer; squeal. **2** *U.S.* To attend a social affair unaccompanied by a woman. [OE *stagga*]

STAG HEAD
Showing antlers.

stag beetle A large, lamellicorn beetle (family *Lucanidae*), the male of which has the jaws enormously developed and branched like the antlers of a stag; specifically, the European *Lucanus cervus* and the American *L. dama*: also called *pinchbug.* They are injurious to trees.
stage (stāj) *n.* **1** The raised platform, with its scenery and mechanical appliances, on which the performance in a theater or hall takes place. **2** The theater. **3** The drama. **4** The dramatic profession. **5** The field or plan of action of some notable event: to set the *stage* for a counter–offensive. **6** A definite portion of a journey. **7** The distance traveled between two stopping points. **8** One of the regular stopping places on the route of a stagecoach or postrider. **9** A stagecoach. **10** A step in some development, progress, or process. **11** *Med.* A definite period in the course of a disease, characterized by a certain group of symptoms. **12** *Biol.* Any of the periods of growth in animals or plants: the larval *stage* of insects. **13** *Electronics* One of the radio elements in cascade amplification. **14** A water level: The river rose to flood *stage.* **15** A horizontal section or story of a building. **16** An elevated platform or scaffold for the use of workmen. **17** The horizontal shelf on a microscope which supports the slide or object to be examined. **18** Any raised platform or floor. **19** *Geol.* The stratigraphic subdivision next below a series, corresponding to an *age* in the time scale. **20** *Aerospace* One of the separate propulsion units of a rocket vehicle. Each becomes operational after the preceding one reaches burnout and is jettisoned. **—***v.t.* **staged, stag·ing 1** To put or exhibit on the stage. **2** To plan, conduct, or carry out: to *stage* a rally. **3** To organize, perform, or carry out so as to appear authentic, legitimate, or spontaneous when actually not so: The entire incident was *staged* for the benefit of press photographers. [<OF *estage,* ult. <L *status,* pp. of *stare* stand]
stage·coach (stāj′kōch′) *n.* A large four–wheeled vehicle having a regular route from town to town.
stage·craft (stāj′kraft′, -kräft′) *n.* Skill in writing or staging plays.
stage door A door to a theater used by actors and stagehands which leads to the stage or behind the scenes.
stage–door Johnny (stāj′dôor′) *U.S. Slang* A man who frequents stage doors seeking the companionship of actresses.
stage·hand (stāj′hand′) *n.* A worker in a theater who handles scenery and props, etc.
stage–man·age (stāj′man′ij) *v.t.* **·aged, ·ag·ing 1** To be a stage manager for. **2** To plan, organize, or direct, especially so as to create a desired impression.
stage manager One who superintends the stage during the production of a play.
stag·er (stā′jər) *n.* **1** One who has had long experience at anything; an old hand: often **old stager. 2** *Archaic* An actor.
stage–set·ting (stāj′set′ing) *n.* **1** The scene or background of a stage presentation. **2** The act of arranging scenery.
stage–struck (stāj′struk′) *adj.* Possessed of the idea of becoming an actor or an actress; enamored of theatrical life.
stage whisper A loud whisper, as one uttered on the stage for the audience to hear.
stag·fla·tion (stag′flā′shən) *n.* *Econ.* Inflation combined with abnormally slow economic growth, resulting in high unemployment. [<STAG(NATION) + (IN)FLATION)]
stag·y (stā′jē) See STAGY.
stag·gard (stag′ərd) *n.* The male of the red deer in its fourth year. Also **stag′gart** (-ərt). [<STAG + -ARD]
stag·ger (stag′ər) *v.i.* **1** To move unsteadily; totter; reel. **2** To begin to give way; become less confident or resolute; waver; hesitate. **—***v.t.* **3** To cause to stagger. **4** To affect strongly; overwhelm, as with surprise or grief. **5** To place in alternating rows or groups. **6** To arrange so as to prevent congestion or confusion, as by distributing: to *stagger* lunch hours. **7** *Aeron.* To adjust (two surfaces, as the wings of a biplane) so that the edge of one extends beyond the other. **—***n.* **1** The act of staggering; a reeling motion. See STAGGERS. **2** *Aeron.* The amount of advance of the leading edge of one wing of a biplane over that of the other. [< obs. *stacker* <ON *stakra*] **—stag′ger·er** *n.* **—stag′ger·ing·ly** *adv.*
stag·ger·bush (stag′ər·bŏŏsh′) *n.* A shrub *(Lyonia mariana),* 2 to 4 feet high, with white or pale–red flowers, common to Tennessee and the North Atlantic seaboard: poisonous to stock.
stag·gers (stag′ərz) *n. pl.* *(construed as singular)* **1** Any of various diseases of domestic animals, as horses, characterized by vertigo, staggering, and sudden falling, due to disorder of the brain and spinal cord: also called *blind staggers.* **2** A giddy sensation.

stag·hound (stag′hound′) *n.* One of a breed of nearly extinct, large hounds, somewhat resembling the foxhound, formerly used for hunting deer, wolves, etc.: also called *buckhound, deerhound.*

stag·ing (stā′jing) *n.* **1** A scaffolding or temporary platform. **2** The act of putting a play upon the stage. **3** The business of driving or running stagecoaches; also, traveling by stagecoach.

Sta·gi·ra (stə·jī′rə) A city of ancient Macedonia, on the Chalcidice peninsula, NE Greece, near the Strymonic Gulf; birthplace of Aristotle. Also **Sta·gi·rus** (stə·jī′rəs).

Stag·i·rite (staj′ə·rīt) *n.* A native of Stagira; specifically, Aristotle. —*adj.* Of or pertaining to Stagira; also, Aristotelian.

stag·nant (stag′nənt) *adj.* **1** Standing still; not flowing: said of water, as in a pool; hence, foul from long standing. **2** Lacking briskness or activity, as life or business; dull; inert; sluggish. [<F <L *stagnans, -antis,* pp. of *stagnare* stagnate <*stagnum* a pool] —**stag′nan·cy** *n.* —**stag′nant·ly** *adv.*

stag·nate (stag′nāt) *v.i.* **·nat·ed, ·nat·ing 1** To be or become stagnant. **2** To become dull or inert. [<L *stagnatus,* pp. of *stagnare.* See STAGNANT.]

stag·na·tion (stag·nā′shən) *n.* **1** The condition of being stagnant: the *stagnation* of water; *stagnation* in trade. **2** *Physiol.* Accumulation and retardation of a circulating fluid in the body.

St. Agnes' Eve The evening of January 20th, when, by old superstition, a girl might have prevision of her future husband. Also **St. Agnes's Eve.**

stag·y (stā′jē) *adj.* **stag·i·er, stag·i·est** Having a theatrical manner; of or suited to the stage. Also spelled *stagey.* —**stag′i·ly** *adv.* —**stag′i·ness** *n.*

staid (stād) *adj.* Fixed; steady and sober; sedate. See synonyms under SOBER, SEDATE. [Orig. pt. and pp. of STAY[1]] —**staid′ly** *adv.* —**staid′ness** *n.*

staig (stag) See STAG (def. 4).

stain (stān) *n.* **1** A discoloration from foreign matter; a spot; smirch; blot. **2** The act of discoloring, or the state of being discolored. **3** A dye or thin pigment used in staining. **4** A chemical reagent for coloring microscopic specimens. **5** A moral taint; tarnish. [<*v.*] —*v.t.* **1** To make a stain upon; discolor; soil. **2** To color by the use of a dye or stain. **3** To bring a moral stain upon; blemish. **4** To impregnate, as a microscopic specimen, with a substance whose reaction colors some part without affecting others, thus rendering form or structure visible. —*v.i.* **5** To take or impart a stain. [Aphetic var. of DISTAIN] —**stain′a·ble** *adj.* —**stain′er** *n.* —**stain′less** *adj.* —**stain′less·ly** *adv.*

Synonyms (verb): blot, color, discolor, disgrace, dishonor, dye, soil, spot, sully, tarnish, tinge, tint. To *color* is to impart a color desired or undesired, temporary or permanent, or, in the intransitive use, to assume a color in any way. To *dye* is to impart a color intentionally and with a view to permanence, and especially so as to pervade the substance or fiber of that to which it is applied. To *stain* is primarily to *discolor,* to impart a color undesired and perhaps unintended, and which may or may not be permanent. *Stain* is, however, used of giving an intended and perhaps pleasing color to wood, glass, etc., by an application of coloring matter which enters the substance a little below the surface, in distinction from painting, in which coloring matter is spread upon the surface; *dyeing* is generally said of wool, yarn, cloth, or similar materials which are dipped into the *coloring* liquid. To *tinge* is to *color* slightly. It may be used of giving a slight flavor, or a slight admixture of one ingredient or quality with another that is more pronounced. See BLEMISH, DEFILE[1], POLLUTE. Compare FOUL.

stained glass See under GLASS.

stainless steel A steel alloy made resistant to corrosion and atmospheric influences by the addition of from 10 to 30 percent chromium, and other ingredients.

stair (stâr) *n.* **1** A step, or one of a series of steps, for mounting or descending from one level to another. **2** A series of steps: usually in the plural. ◆ Homophone: *stare.* [OE *stǣger*]

stair·case (stâr′kās′) *n.* A flight or set of stairs, usually from one floor to another, complete with the supports, balusters, etc.

stair·head (stâr′hed′) *n.* The top of a staircase.

stair·way (stâr′wā′) *n.* A flight of stairs.

stair·well (stâr′wel′) *n.* A vertical shaft enclosing a staircase.

stake (stāk) *n.* **1** A stick or post, as of wood sharpened for driving into the ground: used as a boundary mark, sign of ownership, to support the rails of a fence, etc. **2** A post to which a person is bound to be burned alive; hence, death by burning at the stake. **3** An upright, set in a socket at the edge of the floor of a car or wagon, to confine loose material. **4** Something wagered or risked, as the money bet on a race. **5** A prize in a contest: sometimes in the plural. **6** An interest in an enterprise; contingent gain or loss. **7** An organizational unit of the Mormon Church, consisting of several wards. **8** A grubstake. —**at stake** In hazard or jeopardy; in question: My whole future was *at stake.* —**to pull up stakes** To wind up one's business in a place and move on; move out. —*v.t.* **staked, staking 1** To fasten or support by means of a stake; tether to a stake. **2** To mark the boundaries of with stakes: often with *off* or *out.* **3** *Colloq.* To put at hazard; wager; risk. **4** *Colloq.* To grubstake; also, to supply with working capital; finance. ◆ Homophone: *steak.* [OE *staca*]

stake-and-rid·er (stāk′ən·rī′dər) *n.* A split rail fence having the ends of the rails or riders laid at an angle across each other and supported by pairs of stakes: also called *snake fence.* —**staked′-and-rid′ered** *adj.*

Staked Plain See LLANO ESTACADO.

Sta·kha·no·vism (stä·khä′no·viz′əm) *n.* The efficiency system of Stakhanovite competition and awards. [after Aleksei G. *Stakhanov,* a Russian miner who originated it in 1935]

Sta·kha·no·vite (stä·khä′no·vīt) *n.* In the U.S.S.R., a worker awarded special privileges and bonuses for having displayed marked efficiency and initiative.

sta·lac·ti·form (stə·lak′tə·fôrm) *adj.* Resembling or having the form of a stalactite.

sta·lac·tite (stə·lak′tīt) *n.* **1** An elongated, downward-hanging form in which certain minerals, especially calcium carbonate, are sometimes deposited by slow dripping, as in a cave. **2** Any similar formation. **3** A downward-projecting ornament of a vaulted surface. [<NL *stalactites* < Gk. *stalaktitos* dripping <*stalassein* trickle, drip] —**stal·ac·tit·ic** (stal′ək·tit′ik) or **·i·cal** *adj.*

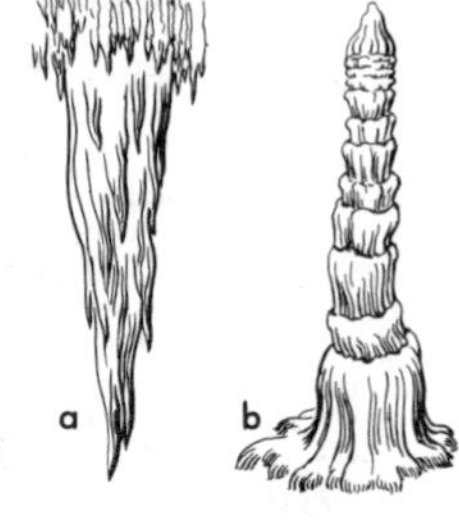

STALACTITE *(a)*
STALAGMITE *(b)*

sta·lag (stal′ag, *Ger.* shtä′läkh) *n.* A German prison camp for captured enlisted men. [<G, contraction of *stammlager* <*stamm* base + *lager* camp]

sta·lag·mite (stə·lag′mīt) *n.* **1** An incrustation, usually cylindrical, or conical, on the floor of a cavern: the counterpart of a stalactite, often fusing with it into the stalactite column. **2** Any similar formation. [<NL *stalagmites* <Gk. *stalagmos* a dripping <*stalassein* drip] —**stal·ag·mit·ic** (stal′əg·mit′ik) or **·i·cal** *adj.*

stal·ag·mom·e·ter (stal′əg·mom′ə·tər) *n.* A stactometer.

St. Al·bans (sānt′ ôl′bənz) A city in southern Hertfordshire, England: scene of a Yorkist victory in the Wars of the Roses, 1455; site of one of the oldest inhabited houses in England: Roman *Verulamium.*

stale[1] (stāl) *adj.* **1** Having lost freshness; slightly changed or deteriorated by standing, as air, vapid wine or beer, old bread, etc. **2** Lacking in interest from age or familiarity; worn out; trite: a *stale* joke. **3** In poor condition from prolonged activity, as from overstudy or, in athletics, from overtraining: especially in the phrase **gone stale. 4** Inactive; dull: said of a stock market after a period of overactivity. **5** *Law* In courts of equity, impaired in legal force, due to long neglect in pressing or asserting a claim or to a change in the condition or situation of the parties. See synonyms under TRITE. —*v.i.* **staled, stal·ing** To become stale or trite. [Origin uncertain] —**stale′ly** *adv.* —**stale′ness** *n.*

stale[2] (stāl) *n.* The urine of cattle or horses. —*v.i.* **staled, stal·ing** To urinate: said of horses and cattle. [Prob. <MLG *stal* horse urine]

stale[3] (stāl) *n. Obs.* **1** A prostitute; drab. **2** A snare; trap. **3** Concealment; stealth; also, theft. [? <AF *estale, estal* a decoy]

stale·mate (stāl′māt′) *n.* **1** In chess, a position in which a player, not in check, can make no move without putting his king in check. The result is a drawn game. **2** Hence, any tie or deadlock. —*v.t.* **·mat·ed, ·mat·ing 1** To put into a condition of stalemate. **2** To bring to a standstill. [<AF *estale* a fixed position + MATE[2]]

Sta·lin (stä′lin, -lēn) **1** See VARNA. **2** A city in Transylvania, central Rumania: Rumanian *Braşov,* German *Kronstadt.* **3** See STALINO.

Sta·lin (stä′lin, -lēn), **Joseph,** 1879–1953, U.S.S.R. statesman: real name *Iosif Dzhugashvili.*

Sta·li·na·bad (stä′lyi·nä·bät′) The capital of Tadzhik S.S.R., in the eastern part: formerly *Dyushambe.*

Sta·lin·grad (stä′lin·grad, *Russian* stä′lyin·grät′) A city on the lower Volga in SE European Russian S.F.S.R.; scene of a battle and ultimate Russian victory over German forces in World War II, Sept., 1942, to Jan., 1943: formerly *Tsaritsyn.*

Sta·li·ni·ri (stä′lyi·nyē′rē) The capital of the South Ossetian Autonomous Region, north central Georgian S.S.R. Formerly **Tskhin·va·li** (tskhin′vä·lē).

Sta·lin·ism (stä′lin·iz′əm) *n.* The doctrines or practices of Stalin; especially, communism involving a rigid implementation of government policy, through coercion, intimidation, and ruthless suppression of opposition, and characterized by ardent patriotism focused upon the Soviet Union and its leader. —**Sta′lin·ist** *n.*

Sta·li·no (stä′lyi·no) A city in the Donbas in SE Ukrainian S.S.R.: formerly *Yuzovka*: also *Stalin.*

Stalin Peak 1 The highest peak of the Carpathians and of Czechoslovakia; 8,737 feet: formerly *Gerlachovka.* **2** The highest point in the U.S.S.R., in SE Tadzhik S.S.R.; 24,590 feet: formerly *Garmo Peak.* **3** The highest peak of the Rhodope Mountains and of Bulgaria, in SW Bulgaria: formerly *Mus Allah.*

Sta·linsk (stä′lyinsk) A city on the Tom river in SW Asiatic Russian S.F.S.R.: formerly *Novo Kuznetsk.*

stalk[1] (stôk) *n.* The stem or axis of a plant, especially when herbaceous. **2** Any support on which an organ is borne, as a pedicel. **3** A supporting part or stem: the jointed *stalk* of a sea lily, the *stalk* of a quill. **4** Any stem or main axis, as of a goblet. [ME *stalke,* dim. of OE *stæla* stem of a plant] —**stalked** *adj.* —**stalk′less** *adj.*

stalk[2] (stôk) *v.i.* **1** To approach game, etc., stealthily. **2** To walk in a stiff, dignified manner: also used figuratively: Murder *stalked* through the streets. **3** *Obs.* To go stealthily; creep. —*v.t.* **4** To approach (game, etc.) stealthily. **5** To pace through: Famine *stalked* the countryside. —*n.* **1** The act of stalking game. **2** A stately step or walk. [OE *bestealcian* move stealthily] —**stalk′er** *n.*

stalk·ing-horse (stô′king·hôrs′) *n.* **1** A horse behind which a hunter conceals himself in stalking game. **2** Anything serving to conceal one's intention.

stalk·y (stô′kē) *adj.* **stalk·i·er, stalk·i·est 1** Long and slender, like a stalk. **2** Consisting of stalks.

stall (stôl) *n.* **1** A compartment in which a horse or bovine animal is confined and fed. **2** A small booth or compartment in a street, market, etc., for the sale or display of small articles. **3** A partially enclosed seat, as in the orchestra of a theater or the choir of a cathedral. **4** A working compartment in a coal mine. **5** A space set aside for the parking of an automobile. **6** A sheath or covering for a finger or thumb; a cot. **7** *Aeron.* The condition of an airplane which has lost the relative speed necessary for control; the act of stalling. **8** *Colloq.* An evasion or argument made to postpone action or decision. —*v.t.* **1** To place or keep in a stall. **2** To keep in a stall for fattening, as cattle. **3** To bring to a standstill; stop the progress or motion of, especially unintentionally. **4** To cause to stick fast in mud, snow, etc. —*v.i.* **5** To come to a standstill; stop, especially unintentionally. **6** To stick fast in mud, snow, etc. **7** *Colloq.* To make delays; be evasive: to *stall* for time. **8** To live or be kept in a stall. **9** *Aeron.* To go into a stall. [OE *steall*]

stall-feed (stôl′fēd′) *v.t.* **-fed, -feed·ing** To feed (cattle) in a stall or stable; fatten. —**stall′-fed′** *adj.*

stal·lion (stal′yən) *n.* An uncastrated male horse. [<OF *estalon* <OHG *stal* stable]

stal·wart (stôl′wərt) *adj.* **1** Strong and brawny; robust. **2** Resolute; determined; unwavering. **3** Brave; courageous. —*n.* **1** An uncompromising partisan, as in politics. **2** *U.S.* A member of a conservative faction of the Republican party (1874–85) which opposed civil service reform and liberal policies toward the South. [Var. of STALWORTH] —**stal′wart·ly** *adv.* —**stal′wart·ness** *n.*

stal·worth (stôl′wərth) *adj. Obs.* Stalwart. [OE *stǣlwierthe* serviceable < *stǣl* place + *wierthe* worth]

stam·bou·line (stam′bə·lēn′) *n.* A coat for formal occasions, worn by officials in Turkey. [from *Stamboul,* var. of *Stambul*]

Stam·bul (stäm·bo͞ol′) **1** Istanbul. **2** The old part of the city of Istanbul. Also **Stam·boul′.**

sta·men (stā′mən) *n. pl.* **sta·mens,** *Rare* **stam·i·na** (stam′ə·nə) *Bot.* The pollen-bearing floral organ of a flower, standing inside the floral envelopes and consisting of two parts: the *filament,* or support, and the *anther,* or pollen sac. [<L, warp, thread < *stare* stand]

STAMEN (*a, b, c*) *a.* Filament. *b.* Anther. *c.* Pollen. *d.* Pistil.

Stam·ford (stam′fərd) **1** A municipal borough in SW Lincolnshire, England; a 14th century center of learning, at that time comparable to Oxford. **2** A city on Long Island Sound in SW Connecticut.

stam·i·na (stam′ə·nə) *n.* **1** Supporting vitality; strength; vigor; physical or moral capacity to endure or withstand hardship or difficulty. **2** The supporting part of a body. [<L, pl. of *stamen* warp, thread. See STAMEN.]

stam·i·nal (stam′ə·nəl) *adj.* **1** Of or pertaining to a stamen. **2** Relating to or furnishing stamina or lasting strength and vigor; essential.

stam·i·nate (stam′ə·nit, -nāt) *adj. Bot.* **1** Having stamens but no pistils, as certain flowers. **2** Having stamens.

stamini- *combining form Bot.* Stamen; of or pertaining to stamens: *staminiferous,* bearing stamens. Also, before vowels, **stamin-.** [<L *stamen, -inis* a fiber, thread]

stam·i·no·di·um (stam′ə·nō′dē·əm) *n. pl.* **·di·a** (-dē·ə) *Bot.* An abortive or sterile stamen, or an organ resembling one. Also **stam′i·node** (-nōd). [<NL <L *stamen, -inis* a stamen + Gk. *eidos* form]

stam·i·no·dy (stam′ə·nō′dē) *n. Bot.* The conversion of other parts of a flower, such as bracts, sepals, petals, or pistils, into stamens.

stam·mel (stam′əl) *n.* A linsey-woolsey of a dull-scarlet color; also, a dull scarlet. —*adj.* Of or pertaining to stammel or its color; dull-red. [<OF *estamel* < *estamine* <L *stamen* thread]

stam·mer (stam′ər) *v.t.* & *v.i.* To speak or utter with a halting articulation, commonly with nervous repetitions or prolongations of a sound or syllable, and involuntary pauses: to *stammer* an apology. —*n.* A halting, defective utterance. [OE *stamerian*] —**stam′·mer·er** *n.*

Synonym: stutter. *Stammer* and *stutter* are virtually interchangeable in general use. Frequently, however, *stammer* is associated with nervousness, excitement, or embarrassment, while *stutter* is reserved by the speech therapists for a particular speech disorder of obscure origin.

stamp (stamp) *v.t.* **1** To strike heavily with the sole of the foot. **2** To bring down (the foot) heavily and noisily. **3** To affect in a specified manner by or as by stamping with the foot: to *stamp* a fire out; to *stamp* out opposition. **4** To make marks or figures upon by means of a die, stamp, etc. **5** To imprint or impress with a die, stamp, etc. **6** To fix or imprint permanently: The deed was *stamped* on his memory. **7** To assign a specified quality to; characterize; brand: to *stamp* a story false. **8** To affix an official seal, stamp, etc., to. **9** To crush, break, or pulverize, as ore. —*v.i.* **10** To strike the foot heavily on the ground. **11** To walk with heavy, resounding steps. See synonyms under IMPRESS[1], INSCRIBE. —*n.* **1** A characteristic mark made by stamping; a device or design impressed upon any object, as by a die. **2** An implement or machine for stamping; specifically, a die having a pattern as for coinworking; any instrument for impressing a mark, design, or copy upon any object or surface: a hand *stamp.* **3** The weight or block as in an ore mill, which by its impact crushes the ore; by extension, the stamping mill itself. **4** A cutting tool for making articles of outline corresponding to the cutting edges: operated by pressure or by blows. **5** Any characteristic mark, as a label or imprint; a brand. **6** Hence, figuratively, characteristic quality or form; kind; sort: I dislike men of his *stamp.* **7** The act of stamping. **8** A printed device prepared and sold by a government, for attachment, as to a letter (**postage stamp**), commodity (**revenue stamp**), etc., as proof that the tax or fee has been paid; also, a trading stamp. See synonyms under MARK[1]. —**trading stamp** A stamp of fixed value given by a tradesman to a purchaser and exchangeable, in quantities, for goods selected from a premium list. [ME *stampen.* Akin to OE *stempan* pound.]

Stamp Act An act of the British Parliament, passed in March, 1765, and repealed in March, 1766, which required the American colonists to affix to various legal and commercial papers, as well as to pamphlets, newspapers, vellum, parchment, or paper, a government stamp varying in price from a halfpenny up to £10.

stam·pede (stam·pēd′) *n.* **1** A sudden starting and rushing off through panic: said primarily of a herd of cattle, horses, etc. **2** Any sudden, impulsive, tumultuous running movement of a crowd, as of a mob. **3** A movement or rush of people toward a certain region or object, as a gold rush or for homestead sites. **4** The sudden unplanned movement to support a certain candidate at a political convention, as from common impulse. —*v.* **·ped·ed, ·ped·ing** *v.t.* To cause a stampede or panic in. —*v.i.* To rush or flee in a stampede. [<Am. Sp. *estampida* crash < *estampar* stamp] —**stam·ped′er** *n.*

stamp·er (stam′pər) *n.* **1** One who stamps, in any sense. **2** One who cancels stamps, as in a post office. **3** Any tool or machine for stamping.

stamping ground **1** A place where horses or other animals gather in numbers. **2** A favorite resort; a habitual gathering place.

stamp mill A machine for pulverizing rock for the purpose of extracting the ore it contains.

stance (stans) *n.* **1** Mode of standing; posture. **2** In golf, the position of a player's feet, with reference to the ball and to each other, when making a stroke. **3** *Scot.* A position; a station; hence, a site; foundation. [<OF *estance* <L *stans, stantis,* ppr. of *stare* stand]

stanch (stanch, stänch) *v.t.* **1** To stop or check the flow of (blood, etc.). **2** To stop the flow of blood from (a wound). **3** *Obs.* To quench; quell; put an end to. Also spelled *staunch.* —*adj.* & *n.* Staunch. [<OF *estanchier* halt, bring to a stop, make stand, ult. <L *stare* stand] —**stanch′er** *n.*

◆ The spelling *stanch* is preferred for the verb in both England and the United States, and *staunch* for the adjective. Many writers use one or the other spelling for both.

stan·chion (stan′shən) *n.* **1** An upright bar forming a principal support. **2** A vertical bar or pair of bars used to confine cattle in a stall. —*v.t.* **1** To provide with stanchions. **2** To support or confine with stanchions. [<OF *estanchon* < *estance* situation, position. See STANCE.]

stand (stand) *v.* **stood, stand·ing** *v.i.* **1** To assume or maintain an erect position on the feet: distinguished from *sit, lie, kneel,* etc. **2** To be in a vertical position; be erect. **3** To measure a specified height when standing: He *stands* six feet. **4** To assume a specified position: to *stand* aside. **5** To be situated; have position or location; lie. **6** To have or be in a specified state, condition, or relation: We *stand* ready to fight; He *stood* in fear of his life. **7** To assume an attitude for defense or offense: *Stand* and fight! **8** To be or remain firm or resolute, as in determination. **9** To be consistent; accord; agree. **10** To remain unimpaired, unchanged, or valid: My decision still *stands.* **11** To collect and remain; also, to be stagnant, as water. **12** To be of a specified rank or class: He *stands* third. **13** To stop or pause; halt. **14** To scruple; hesitate. **15** *Naut.* To take a direction; steer: The brig *stood* into the wind. **16** To point, as a hunting dog. **17** *Brit.* To be a candidate, as for election. —*v.t.* **18** To place upright; set in an erect position. **19** To put up with; endure; tolerate. **20** To be subjected to; undergo: He must *stand* trial. **21** To withstand; resist. **22** *Colloq.* To pay for; bear the expense of: to *stand* a treat. —**to stand a chance** (or **show**) To have a chance or likelihood, as of success. —**to stand by** **1** To stay near and be ready to help or operate. **2** To help; support. **3** To abide by; make good; adhere to. **4** To remain passive and watch, as when help is needed. **5** *Telecom.* To wait, as for the continuance of an interrupted transmission. —**to stand clear** To remain at a safe distance. —**to stand down** *Law* To leave the witness stand. —**to stand for** **1** To represent; symbolize. **2** To put up with; tolerate. —**to stand from under** To move from beneath, as something about to fall. —**to stand in** *Colloq.* To cost. —**to stand in for** To act as a substitute for. —**to stand off** *Colloq.* **1** To keep at a distance. **2** To fail to agree or comply. —**to stand on** **1** To be based on or grounded in; rest. **2** To insist on or demand observance of: to *stand on* ceremony. **3** *Naut.* To keep on the same tack or course. —**to stand on one's own (two) feet** (or **legs**) To be independent; manage one's own affairs. —**to stand out** **1** To stick out; project or protrude. **2** To be prominent; appear in relief or contrast. **3** To refuse to consent or agree; remain in opposition. —**to stand over** **1** To remain near and watch, as a subordinate. **2** To be postponed. —**to stand pat** **1** In poker, to play one's hand as dealt, without drawing new cards. **2** To resist change. See STAND-PATTER. —**to stand to reason** To conform to reason. —**to stand up** **1** To stand erect. **2** To withstand wear, criticism, analysis, etc. **3** *Slang* To fail, usually intentionally, to keep an appointment with. —**to stand up for** To side with; take the part of. —**to stand up to** To confront courageously; face. —**to stand up with** To be best man or bridesmaid for. —*n.* **1** A structure upon which persons or things may stand, or on which articles may be kept or displayed. **2** A small table on which things may be placed conveniently. **3** A rack or other piece of furniture on which hats may be hung, or canes, umbrellas, etc., supported: a hall *stand.* **4** A stall, counter, or the like, where merchandise is displayed: a *bookstand.* **5** A structure upon which persons may sit or stand, as a platform, or a series of raised seats: a *bandstand,* a judges' *stand*; also, a small platform in court from which a witness testifies. **6** Any place where or in which something stands; position; place; specifically, the place of one's customary occupation; an assigned or chosen location. **7** The act of standing, especially of standing firmly: to make a *stand* against the enemy. **8** Cessation from motion or progress; a standstill. **9** A complete set; outfit: chiefly in the phrase **stand of arms.** **10** A growth on the field, as of corn or grass. **11** A tree grown from seed; also, a young tree left when others are cut down.

12 The growing trees in a forest or in part of a forest. **13** In the theater, a stop made while on tour to give a performance; also, the place: a one-night *stand.* **14** *Obs.* A troop; force. **15** A curved metal bar attached to the base of a force pump and serving as a fulcrum for the brake which moves the piston up and down. **16** In prosody, an epode: so called because it was originally sung while the chorus stood still. [OE *standan*] **— stand′er** *n.*
Synonyms (verb): abide, continue, endure, halt, pause, remain, stay, stop. See REST[1]. *Antonyms*: decline, droop, drop, fail, faint, falter, flee, fly, sink, succumb, yield.

stan·dard (stan′dərd) *n.* **1** A flag, ensign, or banner, used as a distinctive emblem of a government, body of men, or special cause: the *standard* of freedom or revolt. **2** A figure or an image adopted as the emblem of a nation. **3** A long, narrow flag carried by mounted and motorized units of the U. S. Army. **4** Any established measure of extent, quantity, quality, or value. **5** Any type, model, or example for comparison; a criterion of excellence; test: a *standard* of conduct or taste. **6** In coinage, the established proportion by weight of fine metal and alloy. **7** An upright timber, post, pole, or beam, especially as a support. **8** *Bot.* **a** Any tree, shrub, bush, or herb not dwarfed by grafting, and growing on a vigorous upright stem without support of a wall or trellis. **b** The vexillum (def. 2). **9** A heavy or stationary article of furniture. See synonyms under EXAMPLE, IDEAL, RULE. **— National Bureau of Standards** A branch of the U. S. Department of Commerce that maintains scientific, technical, and industrial standards, and acts as a research and testing agency for the government. **—** *adj.* **1** Having the accuracy or authority of a standard; serving as a gage, test, or model; hence, of recognized excellence or authority: a *standard* book or author. **2** Designating or belonging to the form of a language which, through its use in a region of economic and cultural importance, has gained acceptance and social prestige among all the speakers of the language. ◆ In this dictionary, words and meanings not considered to be at the level of the standard language are appropriately labeled colloquial, slang, dialectal, or illiterate. [<OF *estandard* banner <Gmc.]

stan·dard-bear·er (stan′dərd·bâr′ər) *n.* **1** An officer or soldier of a regiment or other military body who carries the flag or ensign. **2** Hence, one who leads, as a candidate; specifically, a presidential nominee.

stan·dard·bred (stan′dərd·bred′) *n.* A breed of horse notable for its trotters and pacers: descendent from the thoroughbred stallion *Messenger,* imported from England in 1788.

stan·dard-bred (stan′dərd·bred′) *adj.* Bred so as to be of a required strain, quality, or pedigree, as poultry, horses, etc.

standard candle *Physics* A candela.

standard cell *Electr.* A voltaic cell which serves as a standard of electromotive force.

standard deviation *Stat.* The square root of the arithmetic average of the squares of all the deviations from the mean value of a series of observations.

standard dollar See under DOLLAR.

standard gage **1** A gage for determining whether tools, etc., are of a recognized standard size. **2** A railroad track width of 56 1/2 inches, considered as standard. **3** A railroad having such a gage, or a locomotive or car made to run on this gage. **— stan′dard-gage′** (-gāj′) *adj.*

stan·dard·ize (stan′dər·dīz) *v.t.* **·ized, ·iz·ing** To make to or regulate by a standard: to *standardize* equipment. **— stan′dard·i·za′tion** *n.* **— stan′dard·iz′er** *n.*

standard lamp **1** Any of several standard lighting units used in photometric determinations. **2** In the United States, the pentane-burning lamp, equal to 10 international candles, or the Hefner lamp, burning amyl acetate, equal to 0.9 international candle.

standard time Civil time as reckoned from a certain meridian officially established as standard over a large area. Reckoning from the meridian of Greenwich, each time zone, comprising a sector of 15 degrees of longitude, is considered to represent a time interval of one hour, although in practice these zones are adjusted to meet various geographic and other regional conditions, as along the International

STANDARD TIME IN PRINCIPAL CITIES

Referred to noon in Washington, D.C. (*Time Zone +5*) and in Greenwich, England (*Time Zone 0*). Times have been calculated to the even hour, disregarding a few deviations (up to 30 minutes) resulting from local time-zone adjustments. All hours are for the same day except as indicated by (*) when the time is for the *following* day. Compare the table under TIME ZONE for explanation of the plus and minus factor in column 4.

(1) *City*	(2) *When* NOON *Washington Time*	(3) *When* NOON *Greenwich Time*	(4) *Time Zone Number*
Alexandria	7 P.M.	2 P.M.	–2
Amsterdam	5 P.M.	NOON	0
Athens	7 P.M.	2 P.M.	–2
Auckland	*4 A.M.	11 P.M.	–11
Baghdad	8 P.M.	3 P.M.	–3
Bangkok	MIDNIGHT	7 P.M.	–7
Belfast	5 P.M.	NOON	0
Berlin	6 P.M.	1 P.M.	–1
Bogotá	NOON	7 A.M.	+5
Bombay	10 P.M.	5 P.M.	–5
Boston	NOON	7 A.M.	+5
Brussels	5 P.M.	NOON	0
Bucharest	7 P.M.	2 P.M.	–2
Budapest	6 P.M.	1 P.M.	–1
Buenos Aires	1 P.M.	8 A.M.	+4
Cairo	7 P.M.	2 P.M.	–2
Calcutta	11 P.M.	6 P.M.	–6
Cape Town	6 P.M.	1 P.M.	–1
Caracas	1 P.M.	8 A.M.	+4
Chicago	11 A.M.	6 A.M.	+6
Copenhagen	6 P.M.	1 P.M.	–1
Delhi	10 P.M.	5 P.M.	–5
Denver	10 A.M.	5 A.M.	+7
Detroit	11 A.M.	6 A.M.	+6
Dublin	5 P.M.	NOON	0
Geneva	6 P.M.	1 P.M.	–1
Greenwich	5 P.M.	NOON	0
Halifax	1 P.M.	8 A.M.	+4
Havana	1 P.M.	8 A.M.	+4
Hong Kong	*1 A.M.	8 P.M.	–8
Istanbul	7 P.M.	2 P.M.	–2
Jakarta	MIDNIGHT	7 P.M.	–7
Johannesburg	7 P.M.	2 P.M.	–2
LeHavre	5 P.M.	NOON	0
Leningrad	7 P.M.	2 P.M.	–2
Lima	NOON	7 A.M.	+5
Lisbon	5 P.M.	NOON	0
Liverpool	5 P.M.	NOON	0
London	5 P.M.	NOON	0
Madrid	6 P.M.	1 P.M.	–1
Manila	*1 A.M.	8 P.M.	–8
Melbourne	*3 A.M.	10 P.M.	–10
Mexico City	11 A.M.	6 A.M.	+6
Montreal	NOON	7 A.M.	+5
Moscow	7 P.M.	2 P.M.	–2
New York	NOON	7 A.M.	+5
Oslo	6 P.M.	1 P.M.	–1
Ottawa	NOON	7 A.M.	+5
Paris	5 P.M.	NOON	0
Peking	*1 A.M.	8 P.M.	–8
Philadelphia	NOON	7 A.M.	+5
Quebec	NOON	7 A.M.	+5
Río de Janeiro	2 P.M.	9 A.M.	+3
Rome	6 P.M.	1 P.M.	–1
St. Louis	11 A.M.	6 A.M.	+6
San Francisco	9 A.M.	4 A.M.	+8
Shanghai	*1 A.M.	8 P.M.	–8
Singapore	MIDNIGHT	7 P.M.	–7
Stockholm	6 P.M.	1 P.M.	–1
Sydney	*3 A.M.	10 P.M.	–10
Teheran	8 P.M.	3 P.M.	–3
Tokyo	*2 A.M.	9 P.M.	–9
Toronto	NOON	7 A.M.	+5
Vancouver	9 A.M.	4 A.M.	+8
Vienna	6 P.M.	1 P.M.	–1
Vladivostok	*2 A.M.	9 P.M.	–9
Warsaw	6 P.M.	1 P.M.	–1
Washington	NOON	7 A.M.	+5
Winnipeg	11 A.M.	6 A.M.	+6
Yokohama	*2 A.M.	9 P.M.	–9
Zurich	6 P.M.	1 P.M.	–1

Date Line. See table above. In the conterminous United States the four standard time zones are the Eastern, Central, Mountain, and Pacific, using respectively the mean local time of the 75th, 90th, 105th, and 120th meridians west of Greenwich, and being 5, 6, 7, and 8 hours slower or earlier than Greenwich time. Canada has in addition a fifth zone, the Atlantic (or Provincial), based on the local time of the 60th meridian, which is 4 hours earlier than Greenwich time. See also TIME ZONE.

standard wavelength *Physics* The wavelength of the red cadmium line observed in dry air at 15 degrees Celsius and 760 millimeters of mercury: equal to 6438.4696 angstrom units.

stand-by (stand′bī′) *n.* *pl.* **-bys** Any person or thing that can be relied on in time of stress or emergency.

stand·ee (stan·dē′) *n.* *Colloq.* A person who must stand for lack of chairs or seats, as at a theater or on a train.

stand-fast (stand′fast′, -fäst′) *n.* That which stands firm and strong; a solid or settled position. **—** *adj.* Firm; settled.

stand-in (stand′in′) *n.* **1** A position of influence or favor; a pull. **2** A person who relieves a motion-picture player from tedious waiting intervals and substitutes for him in hazardous actions.

stand·ing (stan′ding) *adj.* **1** Remaining erect; not prostrated or cut down, as grain. **2** Continuing for regular or permanent use; remaining the same indefinitely; not special or temporary: a *standing* rule, a *standing* army. **3** Stagnant; not flowing: *standing* water. **4** Begun while standing: distinguished from *running*: a *standing* high jump. **5** Established; permanent: the *standing* church. **—** *n.* **1** Place; relative position, as in social, commercial, or moral relations; repute; grade; especially, high grade or rank; good reputation: a man of *standing.* **2** A place to stand in; station. **3** Time in which something stands or goes on; continuance; duration: a feud of long *standing.* **4** The act of one who stands; erectness; stance. **—** *adv.* At or to a sudden stop or standstill, especially in the phrase **to bring up standing.**

standing order **1** A military order always in force and not subject to change or modification. **2** In parliamentary procedure, a general regulation governing the manner in which the business of a body shall be conducted: in force from session to session until rescinded or voided.

standing rigging *Naut.* The heavy ropes or cables which support the masts and fixed spars of a ship.

standing room Place in which to stand, as in a building, theater, etc., where the seats are all occupied.

stand·ish (stan′dish) *n.* A receptacle for pens and ink. [<STAND + DISH]

Stan·dish (stan′dish), **Miles,** 1584?–1656, English soldier and emigrant in the "Mayflower"; military leader of the Pilgrims; subject of Longfellow's *The Courtship of Miles Standish.*

stand-off (stand′ôf′, -of′) *n.* **1** A draw or tie, as in a game. **2** A counterbalancing or neutralization. **3** A feeling or state of indifference or coldness; aloofness. **4** A postponement. **— stand′-off′ish** *adj.*

stand oil Linseed or other oil heated for several hours at a temperature of about 300° C. to thicken it and remove coagulated impurities: used in varnishes and paints.

stand-out (stand′out′) *n.* **1** Someone or something that is outstanding, excellent, etc. **2** *Colloq.* One who stubbornly refuses to agree, consent, or cooperate.

stand-pat (stand′pat′) *adj.* Characterized by or pertaining to the policy of opposition to change; conservative.

stand-pat·ter (stand′pat′ər) *n.* In U. S. politics, one who adheres obstinately to a policy or party; specifically, a politician who advocates maintaining the existing tariff schedules; a conservative. **— stand′-pat′tism** *n.*

stand·pipe (stand′pīp′) *n.* A vertical pipe, as at a reservoir, into which the water is pumped to give it a head; a water tower.

stand·point (stand′point′) *n.* A position from which things are viewed or judged; point of view; basal principle.

St. An·drews (sānt an′drōōz) A port and burgh in eastern Fifeshire, Scotland; the rules of golf are established at a famous course nearby, founded 1754.

St. Andrew's cross The oblique cross; also, a saltire. See under CROSS.

stand·still (stand′stil′) *n.* A pause; cessation of motion or action; halt; rest. **—** *adj.* In a state of rest or inactivity; standing still.

stand-up (stand′up′) *adj.* **1** Having an erect

position: a *stand-up* collar. 2 Done, consumed, etc., while standing.

Stan·ford revision (stan′fərd) *Psychol.* A modification of the Binet-Simon scale designed to cover a wider range of mental age and to provide a constant number of tests, usually six, for each year group. [from *Stanford* University, Calif., where it was originated]

stang[1] (stang) *Scot. & Brit. Dial. v.t.* To sting. — *v.i.* To throb with pain. — *n.* A sting; throbbing pain.

stang[2] (stang) Obsolete past tense of STING.

stan·hope (stan′hōp) *n.* A light, open, one-seated carriage. [after Fitzroy *Stanhope*, 1787–1864, English clergyman, for whom it was first made]

stan·iel (stan′yəl) *n.* The kestrel. Also **stan·nel** (stan′əl). [OE *stāngella* < *stān* stone + *gellan* scream]

sta·nine (stā′nīn) *n. Psychol.* A composite weighted score of aptitudes and performance based on a scale of nine: it is a form of frequency distribution about a median of 5, 1 being lowest and 9 highest: originally developed to test air crews in the U. S. Army Air Forces. [< STA(NDARD SCALE OF) NINE]

Sta·ni·slav (stä′ni·släf) A city in western Ukrainian S.S.R., formerly, 1919–45, in Poland. *German* **Stan·is·lau** (stän′is·lou), *Polish* **Sta·ni·sla·wow** (stä′nē·swä′vo͞of).

Stan·is·lav·sky (stä′ni·släf′skē), **Constantin,** 1863–1938, Russian actor, director, and producer: real name *Konstantin Sergeyevich Alekseyev.*

stank[1] (stangk) Past tense of STINK.

stank[2] (stangk) *n. Brit. Dial.* A pool; reservoir; pond; ditch; dam. [< OF *estanc* < L *stagnum* < *stagnare* stagnate. See STAGNANT.]

Stan·ley (stan′lē) A masculine personal name. [OE, stone lea]

Stan·ley (stan′lē), **Arthur Penrhyn,** 1815–81, English author and divine. — **Sir Henry Morton,** 1841–1904, British journalist and explorer active in the United States; sent out to find David Livingstone in Africa; original name *John Rowlands.* — **Wendell Meredith,** born 1904, U. S. biochemist.

Stanley, Mount See RUWENZORI.

Stanley Falls The seven cataracts of the upper Congo river, near the equator; total fall, 200 feet.

Stanley Pool A lakelike expansion of the Congo river on the border between SW Belgian Congo and SE French Equatorial Africa; 320 square miles.

stan·na·ry (stan′ər·ē) *n. pl.* **·ries** A tin mine or region of tin mines. [< Med. L *stannaria* < L *stannum* tin]

stan·nic (stan′ik) *adj. Chem.* Of, pertaining to, or containing tin, especially in its higher valence. [< L *stannum* tin]

stannic acid *Chem.* Any of three compounds derived from stannic chloride by the action of alkalis.

stannic chloride *Chem.* A thin, colorless liquid, $SnCl_4$, made by exposing metallic tin to the action of chlorine: used as a mordant in dyeing.

stannic oxide *Chem.* A white, amorphous, pulverulent compound, SnO_2, found native or formed by heating the lower (stannous) oxide in air: extensively used as a polishing agent called *putty powder.*

stannic sulfide *Chem.* A yellow compound, SnS_2, precipitated from a solution of a stannic salt by hydrogen sulfide: used in bronzing.

stan·nif·er·ous (stə·nif′ər·əs) *adj.* Yielding or containing tin. [< L *stannum* tin + -FEROUS]

stan·nite (stan′īt) *n.* A granular, metallic, steel-gray to iron-black mineral containing tin, copper, iron, sulfur, and sometimes zinc; tin pyrites. [< L *stannum* tin + -ITE[1]]

stan·nous (stan′əs) *adj. Chem.* Of, pertaining to, or containing tin, especially in its lower valence. [< L *stannum* tin + -OUS]

stan·num (stan′əm) *n.* Tin. [< L]

Sta·no·voi Range (stä′nô·voi′) A mountain chain in SE Siberian Russian S.F.S.R.; highest point, 8,143 feet; forms the watershed between the Lena and Amur river basins. Also **Sta·no·vy Range** (stä·nō′vē).

St. Anthony's fire *Pathol.* Erysipelas.

St. Anthony's nut An earthnut (*Conopodium denudatum*), fed to pigs: so called because St. Anthony was once a swineherd: also called *pignut, groundnut.*

Stan·ton (stan′tən), **Edwin McMasters,** 1814–1869, U. S. statesman; secretary of war 1862–1868. — **Elizabeth Cady,** 1815–1902, U. S. woman-suffrage leader.

stan·za (stan′zə) *n.* A certain number of lines of verse grouped in a definite scheme of meter and sequence; a metrical division of a poem: often incorrectly called a *verse.* [< Ital., room, stanza < L *stans, stantis* standing. See STANCE.] — **stan·za·ic** (stan·zā′ik) *adj.*

sta·pe·li·a (stə·pē′lē·ə) *n.* Any of a genus (*Stapelia*) of fleshy African plants of the milkweed family, having leafless toothed stems and showy, starlike, ill-smelling, purple or yellowish flowers sometimes a foot in diameter; a carrion flower. [< NL, after J. B. van *Stapel*, died 1636, Dutch botanist]

sta·pes (stā′pēz) *n. Anat.* The innermost ossicle of the middle ear of mammals. See illustration under EAR. [< LL *stapes* a stirrup] — **sta·pe·di·al** (stə·pē′dē·əl) *adj.*

staphylo- *combining form* 1 *Anat.* The uvula: *staphyloplasty.* 2 *Med.* Staphylococcic. Also, before vowels, **staphyl-.** [< Gk. *staphylē* bunch of grapes]

staph·y·lo·coc·cus (staf′ə·lō·kok′əs) *n. pl.* **·coc·ci** (-kok′sī) Any of a genus (*Staphylococcus*) of typically parasitic bacteria occurring singly, in pairs, or in irregular clusters; especially, *S. aureus,* an infective agent in boils, furuncles, and suppurating wounds. See illustration under BACTERIUM. [< NL < Gk. *staphylos* bunch of grapes + *kokkos* a berry] — **staph′y·lo·coc′cic** (-kok′sik) *adj.*

staph·y·lo·plas·ty (staf′ə·lō·plas′tē) *n.* Reparative surgery of the soft palate and uvula. — **staph′y·lo·plas′tic** *adj.*

staph·y·lor·rha·phy (staf′ə·lôr′ə·fē, -lor′-) *n. Surg.* The operation of uniting a cleft palate. Also **staph′y·lor′a·phy.** [< STAPHYLO- + -RHAPHY]

sta·ple[1] (stā′pəl) *n.* 1 A principal commodity or production of a country or region; a well-established article of commerce. 2 A chief element or main constituent of something. 3 The carded or combed fiber of cotton, wool, or flax. 4 Raw material. 5 A commercial emporium; mart. 6 Hence, a source of supply; storehouse. — *adj.* 1 Regularly and constantly produced or sold; hence, main; chief. 2 Commercially established; having regular commercial channels. 3 Marketable. — *v.t.* **·pled, ·pling** To sort or classify according to length, as wool fiber. [< OF *estaple* market, support < Gmc.]

sta·ple[2] (stā′pəl) *n.* A U-shaped piece of metal with pointed ends, or a loop of thin wire, driven into wood, fabrics, paper, etc., to serve as a fastening. — *v.t.* **·pled, ·pling** To fix or fasten by a staple or staples. [OE *stapol* post, prop]

sta·pler[1] (stā′plər) *n.* 1 A sorter of wool according to its staple. 2 A merchant who participated in one of the monopolies formerly granted by royal authority.

sta·pler[2] (stā′plər) *n.* A wire-stitching machine that binds pamphlets, books, etc.

star (stär) *n.* 1 *Astron.* One of a class of self-luminous celestial bodies, exclusive of comets, meteors, and nebulae, but including the sun. The stars are classified according to their relative brightness in what are known as magnitudes, the first being the brightest and the sixth the faintest visible to the naked eye. The table below gives the names of the principal navigational stars and their apparent magnitudes, with the constellation in which each may be found. ◆ Collateral adjectives: *astral, sidereal, stellar.* 2 Loosely, any heavenly body; a planet. 3 A conventional figure having five or more radiating points: used as an emblem or device, as on the shoulder strap of a general. 4 An asterisk (*). 5 A white spot on the forehead of a horse or bovine animal. 6 An actor or actress who plays the leading part; hence, anyone who shines prominently in a calling or profession: a literary *star.* 7 A heavenly body considered as influencing one's fate; hence, fortune; destiny. — **binary star** A pair of stars revolving about a common center. Three types have been noted: *eclipsing,* in which the members successively eclipse each other; *spectroscopic,* in which the members are distinguishable only by shifts in their spectral lines; and *visual,* in which the members may be distinguished through the telescope. — **dark star** An invisible star, non-shining or dimly shining: known only through relation to visible stars, as during eclipsing action. — **double star** Two stars so near to each other as to be almost indistinguishable except through a telescope. — **dwarf star** Any of a class of stars which have reached their greatest temperature and are in the phase of contraction, with luminosity passing from bluish to orange. — **giant star** Any of a class of stars of great mass and high luminosity which are passing through the early stages of their evolution. — **variable star** Any of several groups of stars whose apparent magnitude varies at different times. The cause may be external, as with binary stars, one of which regularly eclipses the other; or internal, as with true variable stars whose periodic fluctuations in light are caused by internal changes. See CEPHEID VARIABLE, NOVA. — *v.* **starred, star·ring** *v.t.* 1 To set or adorn with spangles or stars. 2 To mark with an asterisk. 3 To transform into a star. 4 To present as a star in a play or motion picture. — *v.i.* 5 To shine brightly as a star; be prominent or brilliant. 6 To play the leading part; be the star. — *adj.* 1 Of or pertaining to a star or stars. 2 Prominent; brilliant: a *star* football player. [OE *steorra*]

TABLE OF PRINCIPAL STARS

Star	*Constellation*	*Magnitude*
Achernar	Eridanus	0.60
Acrux	Crucis	1.05
Aldebaran	Taurus	1.06
Alpheratz	Andromeda	2.15
Altair	Aquila	0.89
Antares	Scorpio	1.22
Arcturus	Boötes	0.24
Betelgeuse	Orion	1.20
Canopus	Argo	−0.86
Capella	Auriga	0.21
Deneb	Cygnus	1.33
Fomalhaut	Piscis Austrinus	1.29
Peacock	Pavo	2.12
Polaris	Ursa Minor	2.12
Pollux	Gemini	1.21
Procyon	Canis Minor	0.48
Regulus	Leo	1.34
Rigel	Orion	0.34
Rigil Kentaurus	Centaurus	0.06
Sirius	Canis Major	−1.58
Spica	Virgo	1.21
Vega	Lyra	0.14

star apple 1 The edible fruit of a West Indian tree (*Chrysophyllum cainito*), resembling an apple in size and appearance, and having ten cells and as many seeds disposed stellately around its center. 2 The tree itself.

star·board (stär′bərd) *Naut. n.* The right-hand side of a vessel as one looks from stern to bow: opposed to *larboard, port.* — *adj.* Of or pertaining to the right of the observer on a vessel when facing the bow. — *adv.* Toward the starboard side. — *v.t.* To put, move, or turn (the helm) to the starboard side. [OE *steorbord* steering side]

star boarder The senior boarder in a boarding house, or one who pays more than the others, considered as entitled to special privileges.

starch (stärch) *n.* 1 *Biochem.* A white, odorless, tasteless, amorphous, powdery carbohydrate $(C_6H_{10}O_5)_n$, insoluble in cold water, alcohol, and other liquids, found in the seeds, pith, or tubers of most plants. Starch is an exceedingly important component of vegetable foods, reacting with certain digestive enzymes to produce maltose and dextrin; it is also used in the commercial production of glucose, for stiffening linen, and for many industrial purposes. 2 Stiffness or formality; a stiff or formal manner. 3 *U.S. Slang* Energy; vigor. — *v.t.* To apply starch to; stiffen with or as with starch. [ME *sterche* < OE *stercan* stiffen < *stearc* stiff. Related to STARK.]

Star Chamber A former English court which met in secret and dispensed justice without jury, and which was noted for its arbitrary

and inquisitorial proceedings: abolished by Parliament in 1641; hence, any arbitrary or secret tribunal. [Prob. because it met in Westminster Palace in a chamber whose ceiling was decorated with stars]
starch gum Dextrin.
starch sugar Dextrose.
starch·y (stär′chē) *adj.* **starch·i·er, starch·i·est** **1** Stiffened with starch; stiff; figuratively, prim; formal; precise: also **starched.** **2** Formed of or combined with starch; farinaceous. **— starch′i·ly** *adv.* **— starch′i·ness** *n.*
star cluster *Astron.* Any of numerous groupings of stars associated in the same region of space, as the Pleiades and Coma Berenices: they are classified as open or galactic, and globular.
star-crossed (stär′krôst′, -krost′) *adj.* Astrologically ill-fated; unfortunate; ill-starred: a *star-crossed* love affair.
star·dom (stär′dəm) *n.* The status of a movie or theatrical star.
star drift *Astron.* A common proper motion of stars in the same region of the heavens: noticed in close groups of stars and in pairs of widely separated stars.
stare (stâr) *v.* **stared, star·ing** *v.i.* **1** To gaze fixedly, usually with the eyes open wide, as from admiration, fear, or insolence. **2** To be conspicuously or unduly apparent; glare. **3** To stand on end, as hair. **—** *v.t.* **4** To stare at. **5** To affect in a specified manner by a stare: to *stare* a person into silence. See synonyms under LOOK. **—** *n.* A steady, fixed gaze with wide-open eyes. ◆ Homophone: *stair.* [OE *starian*] **— star′er** *n.*
sta·re de·ci·sis (stā′rē di·sī′sis) *Law Latin* The doctrine that precedents are law and should be followed; literally, to stand by decisions.
star facet One of eight triangular facets adjoining the table in the crown of a brilliant-cut gem. For illustration see DIAMOND.
star·fish (stär′fish′) *n. pl.* **·fish** or **·fish·es** Any of various radially symmetrical echinoderms (class *Asteroidea*), commonly with a star-shaped body having five or more arms. Starfish feed mainly on mollusks, including oysters.

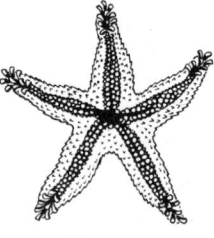

STARFISH
Ventral side showing tube feet.

star·flow·er (stär′flou′ər) *n.* **1** Any of various plants with conventionally star-shaped flowers; especially, a low perennial *(Trientalis borealis)* with one or more white star-shaped flowers. **2** A starwort. **3** A star of Bethlehem.
star-gaze (stär′gāz′) *v.i.* **-gazed, -gaz·ing** **1** To gaze at or study the stars. **2** To daydream.
star-gaz·er (stär′gā′zər) *n.* **1** One who gazes at or studies the stars; especially, an astrologer or astronomer. **2** A marine carnivorous fish with eyes small and near the front of the top of the head, as *Uranoscopus scaber* of the Mediterranean, and *Astroscopus anoplus* of the Atlantic coast of the United States.
star-gaz·ing (stär′gā′zing) *adj.* Given to watching the stars. **—** *n.* **1** The act or practice of watching or studying the stars. **2** An absent-minded state; abstraction.
star·grass (stär′gras′, -gräs′) *n.* Any of various grasslike plants (genus *Hypoxis*) of the amaryllis family, with starlike flowers.
stark (stärk) *adj.* **1** Stiff or rigid, as in death. **2** *Obs.* Stubborn; inflexible. **3** Severe; tempestuous, as weather; strict or grim, as a person; also, deserted or barren, as a landscape. **4** *Obs.* Strong and powerful. **5** Without ornamentation; blunt; complete; utter; downright: *stark* misery. **6** Naked: short for *stark naked.* **—** *adv.* **1** In a stark manner. **2** Completely; utterly: *stark* mad. [OE *stearc* stiff. Related to STARCH.] **— stark′ly** *adv.*
Stark (shtärk), **Johannes,** 1874–1957, German physicist.
Stark (stärk), **John,** 1728–1822, American Revolutionary general.
stark naked Entirely without clothing. [Alter. of ME *stert-naked* <OE *steort* tail + *nacod* naked; infl. in form by STARK]
star·less (stär′lis) *adj.* Being without stars or starlight.
star·let (stär′lit) *n.* **1** A small star. **2** *Colloq.* A young movie actress aspiring to stardom.
star·light (stär′līt) *n.* The light given by a star or stars. **—** *adj.* Lighted by or only by the stars: also **star′lit′** (-lit′).
star·like (stär′līk′) *adj.* Like a star; bright; luminous; shining.
star lily The sand lily.
star·ling[1] (stär′ling) *n.* Any of several Old World passerine birds (genus *Sturnus*). The common starling *(S. vulgaris)* is brown glossed with black, with metallic purple and green reflections and a buff tip to each feather. It is often caged. [OE *stærling* < *stær* starling]
star·ling[2] (stär′ling) *n.* **1** An enclosure of close piling, as around a pier of a bridge for protection. **2** One of the piles of such an enclosure. [OE *statholung* foundation]
Starn·ber·ger·see (shtärn′ber′gər·zā′) A lake SW of Munich, in southern Bavaria, West Germany; 22 square miles: also *Würmsee.*
star·nose (stär′nōz′) *n.* A North American mole *(Condylura cristata)* having a radiate arrangement of fleshy processes around the end of the nose. Also **star-nosed mole.**
star of Bethlehem **1** The large star by which the three Magi were guided to the manger in Bethlehem where the child Jesus lay. **2** An Old World plant *(Ornithogalum umbellatum)* of the lily family, having white stellate flowers striped with green on the outside: naturalized in the eastern United States.
star of David The six-pointed star used as a symbol by the Hebrews; the mogen David.

STAR OF DAVID

star of Jerusalem Goatbeard.
starred (stärd) *adj.* **1** Spangled with stars; marked with stars or a star; specifically, marked with an asterisk. **2** Affected by astral influence: chiefly in composition: ill-*starred.* **3** Presented or advertised as the star of a play or motion picture; featured.
star·ry (stär′ē) *adj.* **·ri·er, ·ri·est** **1** Set with stars or starlike spots or points; abounding in stars. **2** Lighted by the stars. **3** Shining as or like the stars. **4** Star-shaped. **5** Of, pertaining to, proceeding from, or connected with stars. **6** Consisting of stars; stellar. **— star′ri·ness** *n.*
star·ry-eyed (stär′ē·īd′) *adj.* Given to fanciful wishes or yearnings.
Stars and Bars The first flag authorized by the Congress of the Southern Confederacy, consisting of a field of three bars, red, white, and red, and a blue canton with a circle of white stars, one for each State of the Confederacy.
Stars and Stripes The flag of the United States of America, a field of thirteen horizontal stripes, alternate red and white, and blue union with as many white stars as States: with the definite article.
star sapphire See under SAPPHIRE.
star·shell (stär′shel′) *n.* An artillery shell that explodes in mid-air with a shower of bright light: used for illuminating objectives, signaling, etc.
star shower A meteoric shower.
star-span·gled (stär′spang′gəld) *adj.* Spangled with stars or starlike spots or points: said especially of the United States flag.
Star-Spangled Banner, The **1** The flag of the United States. **2** A poem written by Francis Scott Key in 1814 during the bombardment by the British of Fort McHenry, Md., and adopted by Congress in 1931 as the national anthem of the United States. The music to which it is sung is that of an old English drinking song, *To Anacreon in Heaven.*
start[1] (stärt) *v.i.* **1** To make an involuntary, startled movement, as from fear or surprise. **2** To move suddenly, as with a spring, leap, or bound; jump. **3** To make a beginning or start; set out. **4** To begin; commence: The play *starts* at eight o'clock. **5** To protrude; seem to bulge: His eyes *started* from his head. **6** To be displaced or dislocated; become loose, warped, etc.: The rivets have *started.* **—** *v.t.* **7** To set in motion: to *start* an engine; to *start* a rumor. **8** To begin; commence: to *start* a lecture. **9** To set up; establish. **10** To introduce (a subject) or propound (a question). **11** To displace or dislocate; loosen, warp, etc.: The collision *started* the ship's seams. **12** To rouse from cover; cause to take flight; flush, as game. **13** To draw the contents from; tap, as a cask. **14** *Archaic* To startle. See synonyms under INSTITUTE. **— to start in** To begin. **— to start off** To begin a journey; set out. **— to start out** **1** To start off. **2** To make a beginning or start. **— to start up** **1** To rise or appear suddenly. **2** To begin or cause to begin operation, as an engine. **— to start with** In the first place; to begin with. **—** *n.* **1** A quick, startled movement or feeling; a sudden quickening of sense, pulse, or nerve at something unexpected. **2** A setting out or going forth; beginning. **3** A temporary or spasmodic action or attempt; a brief, intermittent effort: by fits and *starts.* **4** *Archaic* A sudden impulse or effusion; burst; sally: *starts* of wit. **5** Advantage or distance in advance at the outset; lead: I had a *start* of five miles in the race. **6** Impetus at the beginning of motion or, figuratively, of a course of action: to get a *start* in business. **7** A loosened place or condition; crack: a *start* in a ship's planking. See synonyms under BEGINNING. [ME *sterten* start, leap, fusion of ON *sterta* overturn and OE *styrtan* start, jump]
start[2] (stärt) *n.* **1** The sharp point of an antler. **2** A tail-like piece. **3** The tail of a bird or animal: the original sense, now obsolete except in compounds: a *redstart.* [OE *steort* tail]
start·er (stär′tər) *n.* **1** One who or that which starts; specifically, one who sees to it that buses, trolleys, etc., leave on schedule. **2** A self-starter. **3** A competitor at the start of a race. **4** A person who gives the signal for the start of a race.
star thistle An Old World weed *(Centaurea calcitrapa)* with spiny heads of tubular flowers, naturalized in the United States; also, another species *(C. solstitialis)* with yellow flowers.
star·tle (stär′təl) *v.* **·tled, ·tling** *v.t.* To arouse or excite suddenly; cause to start involuntarily; alarm. **—** *v.i.* To be aroused or excited suddenly; take alarm. **—** *n.* A sudden fright or shock; a scare. [OE *steartlian* kick, struggle] **— star′tler** *n.*
star·tling (stärt′ling) *adj.* Rousing sudden surprise, alarm, or the like. **— star′tling·ly** *adv.*
star·va·tion (stär·vā′shən) *n.* **1** The act of starving. **2** The state of being starved.
starve (stärv) *v.* **starved, starv·ing** *v.i.* **1** To die or perish from lack of food. **2** To suffer from extreme hunger. **3** To suffer from lack or need: to *starve* for friendship. **4** *Dial.* To die of cold. **5** *Obs.* To die. **—** *v.t.* **6** To cause to die of hunger; deprive of food. **7** To bring to a specified condition by starving: to *starve* an enemy into surrender. [OE *steorfan* die] **— starv′er** *n.*
starve·ling (stärv′ling) *n.* A person or animal that is starving, starved, or emaciated. **—** *adj.* **1** Starving; emaciated; hungry. **2** Failing to meet needs; inadequate: a *starveling* religion. See synonyms under MEAGER.
star·wort (stär′wûrt′) *n.* A stitchwort.
stase (stās) *n. Ecol.* A deposit of fossil plants which has not moved from its original position, often occurring as a series of layers of related species. [<Gk. *stasis.* See STASIS.]
stash (stash) *v.t. Slang* To hide or conceal (money or valuables), for storage and safekeeping: often with *away.* [? Blend of STORE + CACHE]
sta·sis (stā′sis, stas′is) *n. Pathol.* **1** Stoppage of the blood in its circulation, especially in the small vessels and capillaries: caused by abnormal resistance of the capillary walls, rather than by any lessening of the heart's action. **2** Retarded movement of the intestinal contents due to obstruction or muscular malfunction. [<NL <Gk., a standing < *histanai* stand]
Stass·furt (shtäs′fo͝ort) A town in the former state of Saxony-Anhalt, eastern East Germany.
stat- Var. of STATO-.
-stat *combining form* A device which stops or makes constant: *thermostat, rheostat.* [<Gk. *-statēs* causing to stand < *histanai* stand]
state (stāt) *n.* **1** Mode of existence as determined by circumstances, external or internal; nature; condition; situation. **2** Frame of mind; mood: a *state* of anxiety. **3** Mode or style of living; station; especially, grand and ceremonious style; pomp; formality. **4** A sovereign political community organized under a distinct government recognized and

conformed to by the people as supreme, and having jurisdiction over a given territory; a nation. **5** One of a number of political communities or bodies politic united to form one sovereign state; specifically, one of the United States: in this sense usually written **State.** **6** *pl.* The legislative bodies of a nation; estates. **7** Authority of government; the territorial, political, and governmental entity comprising a state or nation. **8** *Obs.* A person of rank; a noble. **9** *Obs.* An estate; order; class of persons. See synonyms under PEOPLE. — **Department of State** An executive department of the U.S. government (established in 1789), headed by the Secretary of State, which supervises the conduct of foreign affairs, directs the activities of all diplomatic and consular representatives, protects national interests abroad, and assists in the formulation of policies in relation to international problems. Also **State Department.** — **to lie in state** To be placed on public view, with ceremony and honors, before burial. — *adj.* **1** Of or pertaining to the state, nation, or government: *state* papers. **2** Intended for use on occasions of ceremony. — *v.t.* **stat·ed, stat·ing 1** To set forth explicitly in speech or writing; assert; declare. **2** To fix; determine; settle. **3** *Law* To make known specifically; declare as a matter of fact. See synonyms under AFFIRM, ALLEGE, ASSERT, RELATE. [Aphetic var. of OF *estat* <L *status* condition, state < *stare* stand; defs. 4, 5, and 7 directly <L, as in *status rei publicae* the state of the republic. Doublet of STATUS.] — **sta·tal** (stā′·tal) *adj.*

state·craft (stāt′kraft′, -kräft′) *n.* The art of conducting affairs of state.

stat·ed (stā′tid) *adj.* Established; regular; fixed. See synonyms under HABITUAL. — **stat′ed·ly** *adv.*

State flower A flower or plant adopted by popular consent or official designation as the floral emblem of one of the United States.

State·hood (stāt′hŏŏd) *n.* The condition or status of one of the United States as opposed to that of a Territory.

State House A building used for sessions of a State legislature and for other public purposes; a State capitol.

state·less (stāt′lis) *adj.* **1** Without nationality: a *stateless* person. **2** Without a state or community of states: a *stateless* society.

state·ly (stāt′lē) *adj.* **·li·er, ·li·est** Dignified; lofty. See synonyms under AWFUL, GRAND, HAUGHTY, SUBLIME. — *adv.* Loftily: also **state′·li·ly.** — **state′li·ness** *n.*

state·ment (stāt′mənt) *n.* **1** A summary of facts; narration; the act of stating. **2** That which is stated. **3** *Law* A formal narration of facts filed as the foundation for judicial proceeding; a pleading. **4** A summary of the assets and liabilities of a bank or firm, showing the balance due. **5** A report sent, usually at monthly intervals, to a debtor of a business firm or to a depositor in a bank. See synonyms under REPORT.

Stat·en Island (stat′n) An island SW of the mouth of the Hudson River, at the entrance to New York Harbor, coextensive with the borough of Richmond, New York City; 57 square miles.

State prison A prison built and controlled by a State, usually for felons.

stat·er[1] (stā′tər) *n.* One who makes a statement.

sta·ter[2] (stā′tər) *n.* Any of several standard coins of the ancient Greek city-states, made variously of gold, silver, and electrum, and differing widely in value. [<Gk. *statēr*]

State rights 1 The rights and powers not delegated to the United States by the Constitution, nor prohibited by it to the States: reserved by the Constitution to the respective States, or to the people of the States, under the Tenth Amendment. **2** That construction of the Constitution which makes these rights and powers as large as possible. **3** The doctrine that the States, being sovereign, have the right to judge and nullify an act of the Federal government. See NULLIFICATION. Also **States' rights.**

state·room (stāt′rŏŏm′, -rŏŏm′) *n.* **1** A small private room having sleeping accommodations on a passenger boat. **2** A private sleeping compartment on a railroad car.

State's attorney *U.S.* A lawyer appointed by a State to represent it in court.

state's evidence 1 One who confesses himself guilty of a crime and testifies as a witness against his accomplices. **2** Evidence produced by the State in criminal prosecutions. Also, in Great Britain, Canada, Australia, etc., *king's* or *queen's evidence.*

States General A general as opposed to a provincial legislature: the name of the legislative body of the Netherlands and that of France before the Revolution.

state·side (stāt′sīd′) *adj.* Of or in the continental United States. — *adv.* In or to the continental United States.

states·man (stāts′mən) *n. pl.* **·men** (-mən) One skilled in the science of government; a political leader of distinguished ability; also, one engaged in government matters, or influential in state affairs or policy. — **states′man·like′, states′man·ly** *adj.* — **states′man·ship** *n.*

state socialism A political theory advocating government ownership of utilities and industries for the purpose of equalizing income.

States of the Church A part of central Italy which, before the unification of Italy in 1870, was under the sovereignty of the pope: also *Papal States.*

States' Rights party A political party founded during May, 1948, in Jackson, Miss., by southern Democrats who were opposed to the civil rights program of the regular Democratic party. It nominated Gov. James Strom Thurmond of South Carolina as its candidate for president. Popularly called *Dixiecrats.*

states·wom·an (stāts′wŏŏm′ən) *n. pl.* **·wom·en** (-wim′in) A woman engaged or skilled in the conduct of government affairs.

state-wide (stāt′wīd′) *adj.* Throughout a state.

stat·ic (stat′ik) *adj.* **1** Pertaining to bodies at rest or forces in equilibrium: opposed to *dynamic.* **2** *Physics* Acting as weight, but not moving: *static* pressure. **3** *Electr.* Pertaining to electricity at rest, or to stationary electric charges. **4** At rest; quiescent; dormant; not active. **5** Of or pertaining to non-active elements. **6** In art, simply posed; monumental. **7** Treating of fixed or stable conditions rather than of fluctuations of sales: said of capital or goods. Also **stat′i·cal.** — *n. Electr.* A condition in which electromagnetic waves produced by atmospheric disturbances affect a radio receiving set, interfering with normal reception. [<Gk. *statikos* causing to stand < *histanai* stand] — **stat′i·cal·ly** *adv.*

stat·ics (stat′iks) *n. pl.* (*construed as singular*) The science of bodies at rest and of the relations required to produce equilibrium. Compare DYNAMICS.

static tube *Aeron.* A small closed tube with openings around the side, facing into the wind on an airplane and designed to measure the static pressure of the air.

sta·tion (stā′shən) *n.* **1** A place where a person or thing usually stands or is; an assigned location. **2** The headquarters of some official person or body of men: a police *station.* **3** An established building or place serving as a starting point, stage, stopping place, or post; specifically, a building for the accommodation of passengers or freight, as on a railroad or bus line; terminal; depot. **4** Social condition; rank; standing. **5** *Mil.* A military post; the place to which an individual, unit, or ship is assigned for duty. **6** The administrative offices, studios, and technical installations of a radio broadcasting unit operating on its assigned frequency. **7** *Mining* A recess in a shaft or passage of a mine. **8** *Austral.* A cattle or sheep run with its appertaining buildings and grounds. **9** In surveying, a point around or from which measurements of angles or distances are made; also, the distance adopted for the standard length. **10** *Eccl.* **a** A stopping place, as a church, shrine, etc., for a solemn religious procession, at which certain prayers are said. **b** A Station of the Cross. — *v.t.* To assign to a station; set in position. [<F <L *statio, -onis* < *status,* pp. of *stare* stand]

Synonym (noun): depot. Properly, a train stops at a *station* to take on and discharge passengers or freight. Freight is kept in a *depot,* which is a storage room or a storehouse. However, the *station* and the *depot* were so often located in one building in the early days of railroads that the word *depot,* which formerly was thought to be more elegant but now has less dignity than *station,* came to be used for both. See PLACE.

sta·tion·ar·y (stā′shən·er′ē) *adj.* **1** Remaining in one place. **2** Fixed: opposed to *portable.* **3** Exhibiting no change of character or condition. — *n. pl.* **·ar·ies** One who or that which is stationary; especially, a member of a stationary military force. ◆ Homophone: *stationery.*

sta·tion·er (stā′shən·ər) *n.* **1** A dealer in stationery and kindred wares. **2** *Obs.* A bookseller; publisher. [<Med. L *stationarius* stationary, having a fixed location (for business)]

Stationers' Company A guild incorporated in London in 1577 comprising printers, bookbinders, booksellers, etc., which until 1911 in England exercised a copyright monopoly requiring all publications to be registered at its office, **Stationers' Hall.**

sta·tion·er·y (stā′shən·er′ē) *n.* Writing materials in general; paper, pens, pencils, ink, notebooks, etc. — *adj.* Dealing in or pertaining to stationery. ◆ Homophone: *stationary.*

station house A police station.

sta·tion·mas·ter (stā′shən·mas′tər, -mäs′-) *n.* The person having charge of a bus or railroad station.

Stations of the Cross The fourteen images or pictures ranged in a church or on church property, which form in series the representation of the successive scenes of the Passion of Christ, and before which devotions are performed.

station wagon An automotive vehicle with one or more rows of removable or folding seats located behind the front seat and with a hinged tailgate for admitting luggage, or the like.

stat·ism (stā′tiz·əm) *n.* **1** A theory of government which holds that the returns from group or individual enterprise are vested in the state, as in communism. **2** Loosely, adherence to state sovereignty, as in a republic. **3** *Obs.* Statecraft.

stat·ist (stā′tist) *n.* **1** An adherent of statism. **2** A statistician. **3** *Obs.* A statesman; politician.

sta·tis·tic (stə·tis′tik) *adj.* Statistical. — *n.* **1** Any element entering into a statistical statement or array, as the mean, the standard deviation, number of cases, etc. **2** Statistics. [<G *statistik* <Med. L *statisticus* statesmanlike, ult. <L *status.* See STATE.]

stat·is·ti·cian (stat′is·tish′ən) *n.* One skilled in collecting and tabulating statistical data.

sta·tis·tics (stə·tis′tiks) *n.* **1** Quantitative data, collectively, pertaining to any subject or group, especially when systematically gathered and collated; specifically, such data relating to a large body of people: *statistics* of population: construed as plural. **2** The science that deals with the collection, tabulation, and systematic classification of quantitative data, especially with reference to frequency distribution and as a basis for inference and induction respecting probable future trends: construed as singular. — **sta·tis′ti·cal** *adj.* — **sta·tis′ti·cal·ly** *adv.*

Sta·tius (stā′shəs), **Publius Papinius,** A.D. 45?–96?, Roman poet.

stato- *combining form* Position: *statoscope.* Also, before vowels, *stat-.* [<Gk. *statos* standing, fixed < *histanai* stand]

stat·o·blast (stat′ə·blast) *n. Zool.* One of the chitinous internal buds developed in fresh-water sponges and on the funiculus of fresh-water polyzoans.

stat·o·cyst (stat′ə·sist) *n. Anat.* One of the sacs in the labyrinth of the internal ear, provided with sensitive hairs and otoliths which are believed to aid in maintaining body equilibrium.

stat·o·lith (stat′ə·lith) *n.* **1** *Bot.* A starch grain or other minute particle in a plant cell, believed to influence the response of a plant organ to the action of gravity. **2** *Anat.* An otolith.

sta·tor (stā′tər) *n.* The stationary portion of a dynamo, turbine, or other power generator.

Compare ROTOR. [<NL <L, a supporter < *status*. See STATE.]

stat·o·scope (stat′ə·skōp) *n.* 1 *Meteorol.* A very sensitive form of aneroid barometer having a large reservoir of air, for indicating minute fluctuations in pressure. 2 *Aeron.* A device which indicates small variations in air pressure: used to show changes in altitude of an aircraft.

stat·u·ar·y (stach′o͞o·er′ē) *n. pl.* **·ar·ies** 1 Statues collectively. 2 One who makes statues; a sculptor. 3 The art of making statues. —*adj.* Of or suitable for statues. [<L *statuaria* < *statua* statue. See STATUE.]

stat·ue (stach′o͞o) *n.* A representation of a human or animal figure in marble, bronze, etc., especially when nearly life-size or larger, and preserving the proportions in all directions: distinguished from *painting* or *relief.* See synonyms under IMAGE. —*v.t.* **·ued, ·u·ing** To make a statue of. [<F <L *statua* < *status,* pp. of *stare* stand]

Statue of Liberty National Monument The site of Bartholdi's giant bronze statue *Liberty Enlightening the World* (presented to the U. S. by France, unveiled 1886) on Liberty Island in Upper New York Bay; 10 acres; established 1924. The statue is over 150 feet high and depicts a crowned woman holding aloft a burning torch.

stat·u·esque (stach′o͞o·esk′) *adj.* Resembling a statue, as in grace, pose, or dignity. [<STATUE + -ESQUE] —**stat′u·esque′ly** *adv.* —**stat′u·esque′ness** *n.*

stat·u·ette (stach′o͞o·et′) *n.* A statue not more than half life-size. [<F, dim. of *statue*]

stat·ure (stach′ər) *n.* 1 The natural height of an animal body, especially of a human body. 2 The height of anything, especially of a tree. 3 Development; growth: used figuratively: moral *stature.* [<OF <L *statura* < *status.* See STATE.]

sta·tus (stā′təs, stat′əs) *n.* 1 State, condition, or relation. 2 Relative position or rank. [<L. Doublet of STATE.]

sta·tus quo (stā′təs kwō, stat′əs) The condition or state in which (a person or thing is or has been): often used with the definite article: to maintain the *status quo.* Also **status in quo.** [<L]

sta·tus quo an·te bel·lum (stā′təs kwō an′tē bel′əm) *Latin* The state of affairs existing before the war.

stat·u·ta·ble (stach′o͞o·tə·bəl) *adj.* Statutory; agreeing or conforming with statute. —**stat′u·ta·bly** *adv.*

stat·ute (stach′o͞ot) *n.* 1 *Law* A legislative enactment duly sanctioned and authenticated by constitutional rule; act of Parliament, Congress, etc.; also, any authoritatively declared rule, ordinance, decree, or law. 2 The act of a corporation or its founder, intended as a permanent rule or law: the *statutes* of a university. See synonyms under LAW[1]. —*adj.* Consisting of or regulated by statute. [<F *statut* <LL *statutum,* neut. of L *statutus,* pp. of *statuere* set, found, constitute]

statute law The law as set forth in statutes.

statute mile See under MILE.

statute of limitations A statute which imposes time limits upon the right of action in certain cases, as by obliging a creditor to demand payment of a debt within a specified time.

stat·u·to·ry (stach′ə·tôr′ē, -tō′rē) *adj.* Pertaining to a statute; created by or dependent upon legislative enactment.

St. Augustine (sānt ô′gəs·tēn) A city on the Atlantic in NE Florida; oldest permanent town in the United States; founded by Spain in 1565.

staum·rel (stôm′rəl) *Scot. adj.* Half-witted. —*n.* A half-wit.

staunch (stônch, stänch) *adj.* 1 Firm in principle; constant; faithful; loyal; trustworthy: a *staunch* friend. 2 Stout; sound; tight; seaworthy: a *staunch* ship; having firm constitution or construction; strong and vigorous; hearty. —*v.t.* To stanch. —*n. Brit. Dial.* A floodgate; weir; dam. Also spelled *stanch.* [<OF *estanche* watertight, reliable < *estanchier* make stand. See STANCH.] —**staunch′ly** *adv.* —**staunch′ness** *n.*

Synonyms (adj.): firm, seaworthy, sound, stout, strong, taut, tight, trim, trustworthy, trusty. See FAITHFUL. *Antonyms*: crazy, leaky, rotten, unseaworthy, untrustworthy.

stau·ro·lite (stôr′ə·līt) *n.* A brown to brownish-black native silicate of iron and aluminum, found in prismatic crystals and sometimes used as a gem. [<Gk. *stauros* cross + -LITE; from the crosslike twin crystals] —**stau′ro·lit′ic** (-lit′ik) *adj.*

stau·ro·scope (stôr′ə·skōp) *n. Optics* An instrument used to determine the directions of the planes of vibration of polarized light in crystals. [<Gk. *stauros* cross + -SCOPE] —**stau′ro·scop′ic** (-skop′ik) *adj.*

Sta·vang·er (stä·väng′ər) A port in SW Norway; a fishing and industrial center; site of an 11th century cathedral.

stave (stāv) *n.* 1 A curved strip of wood, forming a part of the sides of a barrel, tub, or the like; hence, any narrow strip of material used for a like purpose: iron *staves.* 2 A straight board forming part of a curb, as about a well. 3 *Music* A staff. 4 A stanza; verse. 5 A rod, cudgel, or staff. 6 A rung of a rack or ladder. —*v.* **staved** or **stove, stav·ing** *v.t.* 1 To break in the staves or strakes of (a cask or a boat); crush the shell or surface of; smash. 2 To make (a hole) by crushing or collision. 3 To furnish with staves. 4 To ward off, as with a staff; keep at a distance: usually with *off*: to *stave* off hunger. —*v.i.* 5 To be broken in, as a vessel's hull. [Back formation < *staves,* pl. of STAFF]

staves (stāvz) 1 Alternative plural of STAFF. 2 Plural of STAVE.

staves·a·cre (stāvz′ā′kər) *n.* 1 A tall larkspur (*Delphinium staphisagria*) of southern Europe. 2 Its seeds, yielding a poisonous alkaloid formerly used as a purgative and antispasmodic. [<OF *stafisagre* <Med. L *staphis agria* <Gk. *staphis* raisin + *agrios* wild]

Stav·ro·pol (stav·rô′pəl) A city on the Volga in southern European Russian S.F.S.R.: formerly (1935–43) *Voroshilovsk.*

staw (stô) *Scot.* Past tense of STEAL.

stay[1] (stā) *v.i.* 1 To cease motion; stop; halt. 2 To continue in a specified place, condition, or state: to *stay* indoors; to *stay* healthy. 3 To remain temporarily as a guest, resident, etc.: Where are you *staying*? 4 To pause; wait; tarry. 5 *Colloq.* To have endurance; stand up; last. 6 *Colloq.* To keep pace with a competitor, as in a race. 7 In poker, to remain in a hand by meeting an ante, bet, or raise. 8 *Archaic* To cease. 9 *Archaic* To stand firm. —*v.t.* 10 To bring to a stop; halt; check. 11 To hinder; delay. 12 To put off; postpone. 13 To satisfy the demands of temporarily; quiet; appease: to *stay* the pangs of hunger. 14 To remain for the duration of: I will *stay* the night. 15 To remain till or beyond the end of: with *out*: to *stay* out one's welcome. 16 *Archaic* To quell, as strife. 17 *Obs.* To wait for. See synonyms under ABIDE, HINDER[1], OBSTRUCT, PERSIST, REPRESS, REST[1], STAND. —*n.* 1 The act or time of staying; continuance in a place; sojourn; visit. 2 That which checks or stops; specifically, a suspension of judicial proceedings. 3 Staying power; endurance; persistence. 4 A state of rest; standstill. See synonyms under RESPITE, REST. [<AF *estaier,* OF *ester* <L *stare* stand] —**stay′er** *n.*

stay[2] (stā) *v.t.* 1 To be a support to; prop or hold up. 2 To support mentally; comfort; sustain. 3 To cause to depend or rely, as for support: with *on* or *upon.* —*n.* 1 Anything which props or supports; a prop, buttress, or the like. 2 *pl.* A corset. [<OF *estayer*]

stay[3] (stā) *Naut. n.* 1 A large, strong rope, often of wire, used to support, steady, or fasten a mast or spar. 2 Any rope supporting a mast or funnel; a guy rope. —**in stays** In the act of turning about on another tack. —*v.t.* 1 To support with a stay or stays, as a mast. 2 To put (a vessel) on the opposite tack. —*v.i.* 3 To tack: said of vessels. [OE *stæg*]

stay-at-home (stā′at·hōm′) *adj.* Given to remaining at home; not in the habit of traveling. —*n.* A person accustomed to staying home.

staying power The ability to endure.

stay·sail (stā′səl, -sāl′) *n. Naut.* A sail, usually triangular, extended on a stay.

St. Ber·nard (sānt bər·närd′, *Fr.* saṅ ber·när′) Either of two passes in the Alps: (1) **Great St. Bernard,** between Switzerland and Italy, east of Mont Blanc; elevation 8,120 feet; **St. Bernard hospice,** founded in the 11th century for the rescue of snowbound travelers, is at its summit. (2) **Little St. Bernard,** between France and Italy, south of Mont Blanc; elevation, 7,180 feet; site of a 10th century hospice for travelers.

St. Chris·to·pher (kris′tə·fər), **Ne·vis** (nē′vis, nev′is) **and An·guil·la** (ang·gwil′ə) A British colony, and a federating unit of The West Indies (federation), formerly a presidency of the British Leeward Islands, comprising the islands of **St. Christopher** (commonly *St. Kitts*); 68 square miles; *Nevis*; 50 square miles; and *Anguilla*; 34 square miles; capital, Basseterre, on St. Kitts.

St. Clair (klâr), **Lake** A lake between southern Ontario, Canada, and SE Michigan; 460 square miles; connected with Lake Huron by the **St. Clair River,** a river which flows 40 miles south, forming part of the boundary between Ontario, Canada, and Michigan.

St. Croix (sānt kroi′) The largest of the Virgin Islands of the United States; 82 square miles; capital, Christiansted: also *Santa Cruz.*

St. Croix River 1 A river forming the boundary between NW Wisconsin and eastern Minnesota and flowing 164 miles SW and south, through **Lake St. Croix** (a natural widening of the river extending 24 miles south) to the Mississippi River. 2 A river forming the boundary between Maine and New Brunswick and flowing 75 miles south and east to Passamaquoddy Bay.

stead (sted) *n.* 1 Place of another person or thing: preceded by *in*: Serfdom came *in* the *stead* of slavery. Compare INSTEAD. 2 Place or attitude of support; use; avail; service: in the phrase **to stand one in stead** or **in good stead.** 3 A steading or farm: used chiefly in compounds: *homestead, Hempstead.* 4 *Archaic* Position; condition; place, in general. —*v.t. Archaic* To be of advantage to; help; benefit; support. [OE *stede* place]

stead·fast (sted′fast′, -fäst′, -fəst) *adj.* 1 Firmly fixed in faith or devotion to duty; constant; unchanging. 2 Directed fixedly at one point or to one end, as the gaze or purpose; steady. Also spelled *stedfast.* See synonyms under FIRM, INFLEXIBLE, PERMANENT. [OE *stedefæst*] —**stead′fast′ly** *adv.* —**stead′fast′ness** *n.*

stead·ing (sted′ing) *n. Brit. Dial.* A farmhouse, sheds, and offices; a farmstead.

stead·y (sted′ē) *adj.* **stead·i·er, stead·i·est** 1 Stable in position; firmly supported; fixed. 2 Moving or acting with uniform regularity; constant; unfaltering: a *steady* light; hence, not readily disturbed or upset: *steady* nerves. 3 Free from intemperance and dissipation; industrious, sober, and reliable: *steady* habits. 4 Constant in mind or conduct: not wavering; steadfast; also, regular: a *steady* customer. 5 Uninterrupted; continuous: a *steady* flow of conversation. 6 *Naut.* Having the direction of the ship's head unchanged. See synonyms under FIRM, SOBER. —*v.t.* & *v.i.* **stead·ied, stead·y·ing** To make or become steady. —*interj.* 1 *Naut.* Keep her steady: an order to a helmsman to keep the ship's head pointed in the same direction. 2 Not so fast; keep calm: an order enjoining self-control or composure. —*n. Slang* A sweetheart or steady companion. [<STEAD + -Y[3]] —**stead′i·er** *n.* —**stead′i·ly** *adv.* —**stead′i·ness** *n.*

steak (stāk) *n.* 1 A slice of meat, as of beef, usually broiled or fried; specifically, beefsteak. 2 Meat, chopped for cooking like a steak: hamburger *steak.* ◆ Homophone: *stake.* [<ON *steik*]

steal (stēl) *v.* **stole, sto·len, steal·ing** *v.t.* 1 To take from another without right, authority, or permission, and usually in a secret manner. 2 To take or obtain in a surreptitious, artful, or subtle manner: He has *stolen* the hearts of the people. 3 To move, place, or convey stealthily: with *away, from, in, into,* etc. 4 In baseball, to reach (a base) without the aid of a hit or error. —*v.i.* 5 To commit theft; be a thief. 6 To move secretly or furtively. —*n.* 1 The act of stealing or that which is stolen; a theft. 2 In baseball, the act of stealing a base. 3 Any financial transaction or other deal that benefits no one but the originators. ◆ Homophones: *steel, stele.* [OE *stelan*] —**steal′er** *n.* —**steal′ing** *n.*

Synonyms (verb): abstract, embezzle, extort, filch, pilfer, pillage, plunder, purloin, rob, swindle. To *steal* is, in law, to commit simple *larceny*; but the word may be applied to any furtive, covert, or surreptitious taking of anything, whether material or immaterial. To *pilfer* is to *steal* petty articles. *Filch* especially emphasizes the secrecy and slyness of the act, and is ordinarily applied to things of little value, but may apply to the most precious, as in Shakespeare, "he that *filches* from me my good name." To *purloin* is etymologically to carry far away, and is commonly applied to the dishonest removal of articles of value or importance. To *rob* is, in law, to take feloniously from the person by force or fear, as in highway robbery; it is also applied to the felonious taking of articles of value from places as well as persons generally with suggestion of force and violence. To *abstract* is to take secretly and feloniously from among other things belonging to another. To *embezzle* is to appropriate fraudulently to oneself funds received and held in trust. To *swindle* is to cheat grossly, commonly by false pretenses, but is not a recognized legal offense under that name; one form of *swindling*, "obtaining money by false pretenses," is an indictable offense, but much *swindling* may be carried on under the forms of law. To *plunder* is to take property from an enemy in time of war, and is not a crime at law. See ABSTRACT. *Antonyms*: refund, repay, restore, return, surrender.

steal·age (stē′lij) *n.* Losses suffered from stealing.

stealth (stelth) *n.* **1** The quality or habit of acting secretly; a concealed manner of acting; a secret or clandestine act, movement, or proceeding. **2** *Obs.* Theft or the thing stolen. [ME *stelthe, stalthe* <OE *stelan* steal]

stealth·y (stel′thē) *adj.* **stealth·i·er, stealth·i·est** Moving or acting secretly or slily; done or characterized by stealth; furtive. — **stealth′·i·ly** *adv.* — **stealth′i·ness** *n.*

steam (stēm) *n.* **1** Water in the form of vapor. **2** The gas or vapor into which water is changed by boiling. **3** The visible mist into which aqueous vapor is condensed by cooling. **4** Any kind of vaporous exhalation. **5** Energy, force, or power derived from water vapor under pressure, as in cooking, heating, etc. **6** *Colloq.* Vigor; force; speed. — **to let off steam** *Colloq.* To give expression to pent-up emotions or opinions. — *v.i.* **1** To give off or emit steam or vapor. **2** To rise or pass off as steam. **3** To become covered with condensed water vapor: often with *up.* **4** To generate steam. **5** To move or travel by the agency of steam. — *v.t.* **6** To treat with steam, as in softening, cooking, cleaning, etc. — *adj.* **1** Of, driven, or operated by steam: a *steam* gage, *steam* shovel. **2** Containing or conveying steam: a *steam* boiler. **3** Treated by steam. [OE *stēam*]

steam·boat (stēm′bōt′) *n.* A boat or vessel propelled by steam.

steam boiler A closed vessel used in generating steam.

steam chest The box or chest through which steam is delivered from a boiler to an engine cylinder. Also **steam box.**

steam engine An engine that derives its motive force from the action of steam, usually by pressure against a piston sliding within a closed cylinder.

steam·er (stē′mər) *n.* **1** Something propelled or worked by steam, as a steamship. **2** A vessel in which something is steamed, as for cooking, washing, etc.

steamer trunk A trunk small enough to fit under a berth in a ship's cabin.

steam·fit·ter (stēm′fit′ər) *n.* A man who sets up or repairs steampipes and their fittings. — **steam′fit′ting** *n.*

steam point *Physics* The boiling point of water at standard atmospheric pressure; 100° C.: one of the fixed points of the international temperature scale.

steam roller **1** A road-rolling machine driven by steam. **2** Any force that ruthlessly overcomes opposition. — **steam′roll′er** *adj.*

steam·ship (stēm′ship′) *n.* A large vessel used for ocean traffic and propelled, usually, by one or more screws operated by steam; a steamer.

steam shovel A steam-operated shovel for digging and excavation.

steam table A long table with openings in which containers of food are placed to be kept warm by hot water or steam circulating beneath them.

steam·tight (stēm′tīt′) *adj.* Preventing the escape of steam.

steam turbine A turbine operated by steam power.

steam·y (stē′mē) *adj.* **steam·i·er, steam·i·est** Consisting of, like, or full of steam; misty. — **steam′i·ly** *adv.* — **steam′i·ness** *n.*

Ste. Anne de Beau·pré (sānt an′ də bō·prā′) A village and shrine on the north bank of the St. Lawrence River, 21 miles NE of Quebec, Canada.

ste·ap·sin (stē·ap′sin) *n. Biochem.* A lipase contained in pancreatic juice. [<STEA(RIN) + (pe)PSIN]

ste·a·rate (stē′ə·rāt) *n. Chem.* A salt or ester of stearic acid.

ste·ar·ic (stē·ar′ik, stir′ik) *adj. Chem.* **1** Of, pertaining to, or derived from stearin. **2** Designating a white fatty acid, $C_{17}H_{35}COOH$, contained in the more solid animal fats and in many vegetable oils. [<F *stéarique* <Gk. *stear* suet]

ste·a·rin (stē′ə·rin, stir′in) *n. Chem.* **1** A white, crystalline ester of glycerol and stearic acid, $C_3H_5(C_{18}H_{35}O_2)_3$, obtained from various animal and vegetable fats: more correctly called *glyceryl stearate* or *tristearin.* **2** Stearic acid, especially as combined with palmitic acid for making candles, etc. **3** Fat in solid form. Also **ste′a·rine** (-rin, -rēn). [<Gk. *stear* suet]

ste·a·rop·tene (stē′ə·rop′tēn) *n. Chem.* A solid crystalline compound that separates from a volatile oil on standing or exposure to cold. Compare ELAEOPTENE. [<STEAR(IC) + (ELAE)-OPTENE]

ste·ar·rhe·a (stē′ə·rē′ə) *n. Pathol.* Steatorrhea. [<Gk. *stear* suet + -RRHEA]

ste·a·tite (stē′ə·tīt) *n.* Massive talc; soapstone: found in extensive beds and quarried for hearths, sink linings, coarse utensils, etc. See TALC. [<L *steatitis* <Gk. *stear, steatos* suet, tallow] — **ste′a·tit′ic** (-tit′ik) *adj.*

ste·a·to·py·gi·a (stē′ə·tō·pī′jē·ə, -pij′ē·ə) *n.* Abnormal growth of fat on the buttocks: noted especially in women among the Bushmen and Hottentots of Africa. Also **ste′a·to·py′ga** (-pī′gə). [<NL <Gk. *stear, steatos* suet, fat + *pygē* buttock] — **ste′a·to·py′gous** (-pī′gəs) *adj.*

ste·a·tor·rhe·a (stē′ə·tə·rē′ə) *n. Pathol.* **1** Seborrhea. **2** Excess fat in the stools. Also **ste·a·tor·rhoe′a.** [<Gk. *stear, steatos* suet + -RRHEA]

stech (stekh) *v.t.* & *v.i. Scot.* To cram; stuff.

sted·fast (sted′fast′, -fäst′, -fəst) See STEADFAST.

steed (stēd) *n.* A horse; especially, a spirited war horse: now chiefly a literary use. [OE *stēda* studhorse]

Steed (stēd), **Henry Wickham,** 1871–1956, English journalist.

steek (stēk) *Scot. v.t.* & *v.i.* To shut; close. — *n.* A stitch.

steel (stēl) *n.* **1** A tough alloy of iron containing carbon in variable amounts up to about 2.0 percent, malleable under proper conditions, and greatly hardened by sudden cooling. Commercial grades are classified, on the basis of carbon content, as: **mild** or **soft steel,** with up to about 0.30 percent of carbon; **medium steel,** 0.30 to 0.60 percent of carbon, and **high** or **hard steel,** containing more than 0.60 percent of carbon. The addition of other components gives a large range of alloys having special properties, as **chrome steel, nickel steel,** etc. **2** Something made of steel, as an implement or weapon; a sword; a knife sharpener. **3** Hardness of character; steel-like nature or quality. **4** A strip or band of steel, as for stiffening a corset. **5** The quotation for shares in a steel company. — *adj.* Made or composed of steel; also, resembling steel; hence, hard; obdurate; adamant; unyielding. — *v.t.* **1** To cover with steel; plate, edge, point, or face with steel. **2** To make hard or strong like steel; make unfeeling or unyielding; harden: to *steel* one's heart against misery. ◆ Homophones: *steal, stele.* [OE *stēl*]

steel-blue (stēl′blōō′) *adj.* Having a color similar to the bluish tinge of certain steels.

steel blue A steel-blue color.

steel-die printing (stēl′dī′) Intaglio printing.

Steele (stēl), **Sir Richard,** 1672–1729, English dramatist and essayist.

steel engraving **1** The art and process of engraving on a steel plate. **2** The impression made from such a plate.

steel gray Any of several shades of dark, dull gray, like the color of finished steel.

steel·head (stēl′hed′) *n.* **1** A species of migratory trout (*Salmo gairdneri*), found from California to Alaska. **2** The black spotted trout (*S. purpuratus*) of the western United States, especially in its adult marine stage.

steel·ing (stē′ling) *n.* **1** The coating of an engraved copper plate with a protective film of iron by electrolysis to increase its durability. **2** Casehardening.

steel·mak·er (stēl′mā′kər) *n.* A maker of steel; especially, the operator or owner of a steel mill.

steel wool Steel fibers matted together for use as an abrasive or in cleaning, polishing, and finishing utensils and the like.

steel·work (stēl′wûrk′) *n.* **1** Any article or construction of steel. **2** *pl.* A shop or factory where steel is made or fabricated. — **steel′·work′ing** *n.*

steel·work·er (stēl′wûr′kər) *n.* One who works in a steel mill.

steel·y (stē′lē) *adj.* **steel·i·er, steel·i·est** Made of, resembling, or containing steel; suggesting steel; figuratively, having a steel-like hardness: a *steely* obduracy; a *steely* gaze. — **steel′i·ness** *n.*

steel·yard (stēl′yärd′, -yərd) *n.* A simple device for weighing, consisting of a scaled beam, counterpoise, and hooks, the article to be weighed being hung at the short end, and the counterpoise weight on the long arm. Also **steel′yards.** [from *Steelyard,* formerly, the London headquarters for Hanseatic traders; a mistranslation of MLG *stalhof* a court where samples of goods are displayed]

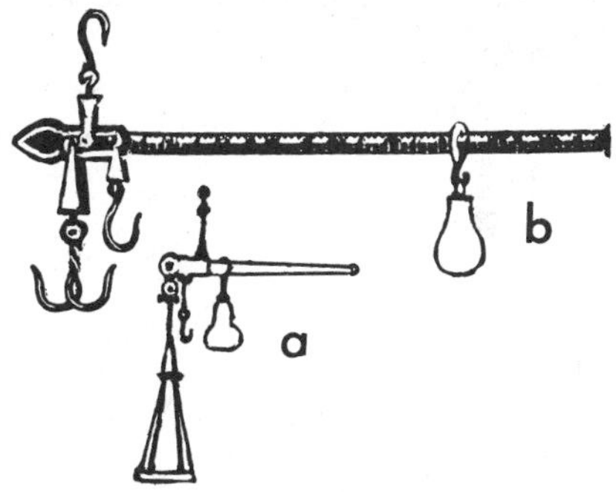

STEELYARDS
a. Pompeian. *b.* Modern.

Steen (stān), **Jan,** 1626–79, Dutch painter.

steen·bok (stān′bok, stēn′-) See STEINBOK.

steep[1] (stēp) *adj.* **1** Making a large angle with the plane of the horizon; precipitous. **2** *Colloq.* Exorbitant; excessive; high, as a price. — *n.* A cliff; hill; precipice; a precipitous place. [OE *stēap*] — **steep′ly** *adv.* — **steep′·ness** *n.*

Synonyms (adj.): abrupt, high, precipitous, sharp, sheer. *High* is used of simple elevation; *steep* is said only of an incline where the vertical measurement is sufficiently great in proportion to the horizontal to make it difficult of ascent. *Steep* is relative; an ascent of 100 feet to the mile on a railway is a *steep* grade; a rise of 500 feet to the mile makes a *steep* wagon road; a roof is *steep* when it makes with the horizontal line an angle of more than 45°. A *sharp* ascent or descent is one that makes a sudden, decided angle with the plane from which it starts; a *sheer* ascent or descent is perpendicular, or nearly so; *precipitous* applies to that which is of the nature of a precipice, and is used especially of a descent; *abrupt* is as if broken sharply off, and applies to either acclivity or declivity. See HIGH. *Antonyms*: easy, gentle, gradual, level, low, slight.

steep[2] (stēp) *v.t.* **1** To soak in a liquid, as for softening, cleansing, etc. **2** To saturate; imbue thoroughly: *steeped* in crime. — *v.i.* **3** To undergo soaking in a liquid. — *n.* **1** The process of steeping, or the state of being steeped. **2** A liquid or bath in which anything is or is to be steeped; especially, a fertilizing liquid for seeds. [ME *stepen*, ? <Scand. Cf. ON *steypa* pour.] — **steep′er** *n.*

steep·en (stē′pən) *v.t.* & *v.i.* To make or become steep or steeper.

stee·ple (stē′pəl) *n.* A lofty structure rising above the tower of a church; a spire. [OE *stēpel, stȳpel*]

stee·ple·bush (stē′pəl·bo͝osh′) *n.* An erect shrub (*Spirae tomentosa*) of the rose family, with dense terminal clusters of rose–colored flowers; the hardhack.

stee·ple·chase (stē′pəl·chās′) *n.* **1** A race on horseback across country, in which obstacles are to be leaped: originating from a race to see which of several riders could first reach a distant church steeple. **2** A race over a course artificially prepared, as with hedges, rails, and water jumps. **3** Any cross–country run. — **stee′ple·chas′ing** *n.*

stee·ple·chas·er (stē′pəl·chā′sər) *n.* A person who takes part in a steeplechase; also, a horse used in or trained for steeplechasing.

stee·ple·jack (stē′pəl·jak′) *n.* A man whose occupation is to climb steeples and other tall structures to inspect or make repairs. [<STEEPLE + obs. *jack* workman]

steer[1] (stir) *v.t.* **1** To direct the course of (a vessel or vehicle) by means of a rudder, steering wheel, or other device. **2** To follow (a course). **3** To direct; guide; control. — *v.i.* **4** To direct the course of a vessel, vehicle, etc. **5** To undergo guiding or steering: The car *steers* easily. **6** To follow a course: to *steer* for land. — **to steer clear of** To avoid; keep away from. — *n. U.S. Slang* A tip; piece of advice. [OE *stēoran*] — **steer′a·ble** *adj.* — **steer′er** *n.*

steer[2] (stir) *n.* **1** A young male of the ox kind, especially when castrated and from two to four years old. **2** An ox of any age raised for beef. [OE *stēor*]

steer[3] (stir) *Scot. v.t.* To disturb; molest. — *n.* A disturbance; a nudge.

steer·age (stir′ij) *n.* **1** That part of an ocean passenger vessel, formerly near the stern, but now usually situated in the forward lower decks, allotted to passengers paying the lowest fares. **2** In a war vessel, the portion of the berth deck just forward of the wardroom, appropriated as the quarters of junior officers, clerks, etc. See GUNROOM. **3** The act of steering. **4** The state of being steered; direction; the effect of the helm on a vessel.

steer·age·way (stir′ij·wā′) *n. Naut.* **1** Sufficient movement of a vessel to enable it to answer the helm. **2** The lowest speed at which a vessel can be accurately steered.

steering committee A committee in a legislature or other assemblage that arranges or directs the course of the business that is to be considered.

steering gear *Mech.* Any arrangement of parts for converting action on the steering wheel into corresponding motion of the rudder of a ship, or, on an automotive vehicle, of the steering axle and its connected members.

steering wheel *Mech.* **1** A vertical wheel with handles along the rim, by which motion is communicated to the rudder of a ship by the wheel ropes or other connections. **2** A hand wheel for guiding an automobile or other heavy vehicle.

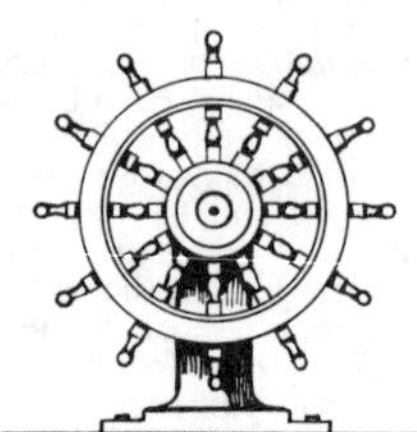

SHIP'S STEERING WHEEL

steers·man (stirz′·mən) *n. pl.* **·men** (-mən) One who steers a boat; a helmsman.

steer·y (stir′ē) *Scot. n.* A stir; bustle. — *adj.* Busy; bustling.

steeve[1] (stēv) *n.* A derrick or a spar with a block at one end used in stowing cargo. [<*v.*] — *v.t.* **steeved, steev·ing** **1** To stow, as cargo in the hold of a vessel, by using a steeve or a jackscrew. **2** *Scot.* To pack; cram. [<F *estiver* <L *stipare* compress]

steeve[2] (stēv) *Naut. n.* The angular elevation of a bowsprit from the horizontal: also **steev′ing.** — *v.t.* & *v.i.* **steeved, steev·ing** To set or be set upward at an angle with the horizon. [? <OF *estive* tail of a plough <L *stiva*]

Stef·ans·son (stef′ən·sən), **Vilhjalmur,** 1879–1962, U.S. Arctic explorer, born in Canada of Icelandic parentage.

Stef·fens (stef′ənz), **(Joseph) Lincoln,** 1866–1936, U.S. journalist.

steg·o·my·ia (steg′ə·mī′ə) *n.* Any of a former genus (*Stegomyia*) of mosquitos; especially, the yellow–fever mosquito (*S. fasciata* or *S. calopus*), which is now called *Aëdes aegypti.* [<NL <Gk. *stegos* a roof + *myia* fly]

steg·o·sau·rus (steg′ə·sôr′əs) *n. pl.* **·sau·ri** (-sôr′ī) *Paleontol.* Any of a genus (*Stegosaurus*) of herbivorous armored dinosaurs of great size which flourished in the western United States during the Upper Jurassic and Lower Cretaceous periods. [<NL <Gk. *stegos* roof + -SAURUS]

Stei·er·mark (shtī′ər·märk) The German name for STYRIA.

stein (stīn) *n.* A beer mug, holding usually a pint; also, the quantity of beer it contains. [<G]

Stein (shtīn), **Baron vom und zum,** 1757–1831, Heinrich Friedrich Karl, Prussian statesman.

Stein (stīn), **Gertrude,** 1874–1946, U.S. writer, resident in France.

Stein·am·ang·er (shtīn′äm·äng′ər) See SZOMBATHELY.

Stein·beck (stīn′bek), **John Ernst,** 1902–1968, U.S. novelist.

stein·bok (stīn′bok) *n.* A small fawn–colored African antelope (*Raphicerus campestris*): also spelled *steenbok.* Also **stein′buck′** (-buk′). [<Du. *steenbok* <*steen* stone + *bok* buck]

STEINBOK (About 20 inches shoulder height)

Stein·metz (stīn′mets), **Charles Proteus,** 1865–1923, U.S. electrical engineer born in Germany.

St. E·li·as (sānt i·lī′əs), **Mount** A peak (18,008 feet) in the **St. Elias Mountains** in SW Yukon and SE Alaska; filled by the world's most extensive glacier system apart from the polar ice caps; highest point, 19,850 feet.

ste·le[1] (stē′lē) *n. pl.* **·lae** (-lē) or **·les** (-lēz) An upright sculptured slab or tablet of stone, either sepulchral or intended for public use, as for laws, decrees, treaties, milestones, etc. Also **ste·la** (stē′lə). [<L *stela* <Gk. *stēlē*] — **ste′lar, ste′lene** (-lēn) *adj.*

stele[2] (stēl) *n. Bot.* An axial cylinder of vascular tissue in plants, sometimes more than one. ◆ Homophones: *steal, steel.* [<STELE[1]] — **ste′lic** *adj.*

Stel·la (stel′ə) A feminine personal name. [<L, star]

stel·lar (stel′ər) *adj.* **1** Of or pertaining to the stars; astral. **2** Of or pertaining to an actor or actress who plays a principal role, or to other persons prominent in the arts. [<LL *stellaris* <L *stella* star]

stel·lar·a·tor (stel′ə·rā′tər) *n. Physics* A device for the study of controlled thermonuclear reactions, consisting essentially of a series of magnetizing coils surrounding a hollow glass tube in which ionized gases may be briefly heated to temperatures of several million degrees. [<STELLAR + -ATOR; from the great temperatures developed]

stel·late (stel′it, -āt) *adj.* Star–shaped or starlike; radiating. See illustration under FROST. Also **stel·lat·ed** (stel′ā·tid). [<L *stellatus,* pp. of *stellare* cover with stars <*stella* star] — **stel′late·ly** *adv.*

stel·lif·er·ous (ste·lif′ər·əs) *adj.* Abounding with stars. [<L *stella* star + -(I)FEROUS]

stel·li·form (stel′ə·fôrm) *adj.* Star–shaped. [<NL *stelliformis* <L *stella* star + *forma* form]

Stell·ite (stel′īt) *n.* A class of hard cobalt alloys containing varying amounts of tungsten and chromium: used chiefly in the manufacture of cutting tools: a trade name.

stel·lu·lar (stel′yə·lər) *adj.* Bespangled with fine stars; shaped like or resembling little stars. [<LL *stellula* little star]

St. El·mo's fire or **light** (sānt el′mōz) A luminous charge of atmospheric electricity sometimes appearing on the masts and yardarms of ships, on church steeples, etc.: also called *corposant.*

stem[1] (stem) *n.* **1** The ascending axis or stalk of a plant, as distinguished from the descending axis or *root*; the main body or stalk of a tree, shrub, or other plant, rising above the ground or other rooting place. **2** The relatively slender growth supporting the fruit, flower, or leaf of a plant; a stalk, peduncle, pedicel, or petiole. ◆ Collateral adjective: *cauline.* **3** A bunch of bananas. **4** The main line of descendants from a particular ancestor. **5** An ethnic line; race. **6** The long, slender, usually cylindrical portion of an instrument: a pipe *stem.* **7** The slender upright support of a goblet, wineglass, vase, etc. **8** A shaft, as of a hair or feather. **9** In a watch, the small projecting rod used for winding the mainspring. **10** In some locks, the central circular part about which the key turns. **11** *Printing* The upright stroke of a type face or letter. **12** *Music* The line attached to the head of a written musical note. **13** *Ling.* The element common to all the members of a given inflection or related groups of words. A stem often consists of more than one morpheme, as the Latin stem *luci–* "light" in *lucifer* "light-bearer" is composed of the root *luc–* plus the thematic vowel *–i–.* **14** *Electr.* The air–sealed, tubular glass section at the base of an incandescent lamp, serving to lead the filaments into the evacuated bulb. See illustration under INCANDESCENT. — *v.* **stemmed, stem·ming** *v.t.* **1** To remove the stems of or from. **2** To supply with stems. — *v.i.* **3** To be descended or derived: to *stem* from John Alden. [OE *stemm, stemn, stæfn* stem of a tree, prow of a ship] — **stem′less** *adj.*

stem[2] (stem) *n. Naut.* **1** A nearly upright timber or metal piece uniting the two sides of a vessel at the fore–end. **2** The bow or prow of a vessel. — **from stem to stern** From end to end; hence, thoroughly. — *v.* **stemmed, stem·ming** *v.t.* **1** To resist or make progress against, as a current: said of a vessel. **2** To stand firm or make progress against (any opposing force): to *stem* the tide of public opinion. **3** To strike with the stem (of a vessel). [<STEM[1], in obs. sense "a tree trunk"]

stem[3] (stem) *v.t.* **stemmed, stem·ming** **1** To stop, hold back, or dam up, as a current; stanch. **2** To make tight, as a joint; to plug. [<ON *stemma* stop]

stem·mer (stem′ər) *n.* **1** One who stems. **2** In tobacco manufacture, one who takes out the main stem from the tobacco plant in making strips. **3** A device for stemming fruits, as grapes.

stem·son (stem′sən) *n. Naut.* A curved supporting timber bolted to the stem and keelson of a vessel near the bow. [<STEM[2] + (KEEL)SON]

stem turn In skiing, a turn made by placing the points of the skis nearly together and the ends wide apart, then placing the weight on the outside ski.

stem·ware (stem′wâr′) *n.* Drinking vessels with stems, as goblets, taken collectively.

stem–wind·er (stem′wīn′dər) *n.* **1** A watch wound by turning the crown of the stem. **2** *U.S. Slang* A very superior person or thing.

stem–wind·ing (stem′wīn′ding) *adj.* Wound by turning a knob on an outside stem connected with inside mechanism.

stench (stench) *n.* A foul or offensive odor; stink. See synonyms under SMELL. [OE *stenc*]

sten·cil (sten′səl) *n.* **1** A thin sheet or plate in which a pattern is cut by means of spaces or dots, through which applied paint or ink penetrates to a surface beneath. **2** A decoration or the like produced by stenciling. — *v.t.* **·ciled** or **·cilled, ·cil·ing** or **·cil·ling** To mark with a stencil. [Prob. ME *stansel* decorate with many colors <OF *estenceler,* ult. <L *scintilla* a spark] — **sten′cil·er** or **sten′cil·ler** *n.*

Sten·dhal (stän·dàl′) Pen name of *Marie Henri Beyle,* 1783–1842, French novelist.

steno– *combining form* Tight; narrow; contracted: *stenography.* Also, before vowels, **sten–.** [<Gk. *stenos* narrow]

sten·o·graph (sten′ə·graf, -gräf) *n.* **1** A character or writing in shorthand. **2** A keyboard machine for printing in shorthand.

ste·nog·ra·pher (stə·nog′rə·fər) *n.* One who writes stenography or is skilled in shorthand; especially, a writer of phonography. Also **ste·nog′ra·phist.**

ste·nog·ra·phy (stə·nog′rə·fē) *n.* **1** The art of writing by the use of contractions or arbitrary symbols; shorthand. **2** Loosely, phonography. **— sten·o·graph·ic** (sten′ə·graf′·ik) or **·i·cal** *adj.* **— sten′o·graph′i·cal·ly** *adv.*

sten·o·morph (sten′ə·môrf) *n. Ecol.* A plant form that is abnormally undersized because of a cramped habitat. **— sten′o·mor′phic** *adj.*

sten·o·phyl·lous (sten′ō·fil′əs) *adj. Bot.* Characterized by narrow leaves, as certain plants.

ste·no·sis (sti·nō′sis) *n. Pathol.* Narrowing of a duct or canal in the body. [<NL <Gk. *stenōsis* < *stenos* narrow]

sten·o·ther·mal (sten′ō·thûr′məl) *adj. Ecol.* Adapted to a limited range of temperature variations: said especially of certain plants. **— sten′o·ther′my** *n.*

sten·o·trop·ic (sten′ə·trop′ik) *adj. Ecol.* Having a narrow range of adaptability to environmental changes: said of plant and animal species.

sten·o·type (sten′ə·tīp) *n.* A letter or combination of letters representing a word or phrase, especially in shorthand.

Sten·o·type (sten′ə·tīp) *n.* A keyboard-operated machine used in stenotypy: a trade name.

sten·o·typ·y (sten′ə·tī′pē) *n.* A system of shorthand representing, by ordinary letters or type, shortened forms of words or phrases.

stent[1] (stent) *Scot. v.t.* To assess for taxation; rate; tax. **—** *n.* A tax, levy, or due.

stent[2] (stent) *n., v.t.* & *v.i. Brit. Dial.* Stint.

stent[3] (stent) *adj. Scot.* Drawn tight; taut.

sten·tor (sten′tôr) *n.* **1** One who possesses an uncommonly strong, loud voice. **2** Any of a genus *(Stentor)* of fresh-water protozoans (class *Ciliata*) having contractile trumpet-shaped bodies capable of attachment by their lower ends. [after *Stentor*]

Sten·tor (sten′tôr) In the *Iliad,* a herald famous for his loud voice.

sten·to·ri·an (sten·tôr′ē·ən, -tō′rē-) *adj.* Extremely loud.

step (step) *n.* **1** An act of progressive motion that requires one of the supporting limbs of the body to be thrust in the direction of the movement, and to reassume its function of support; a pace. **2** The distance passed over in making such a motion; in military quick-time marching, 30 inches. **3** Any short distance; a space easily traversed. **4** That upon which the foot rests in ascending or descending, as a stair or ladder rung. **5** A single action or proceeding regarded as leading to something: a *step* toward emancipation. **6** An advance or promotion that forms one of a series, especially in military usage; grade; degree. **7** The manner of stepping; walk; gait; also, the sound of a footfall. **8** A footprint; track. **9** *pl.* Progression by walking; walk. **10** A combination of foot movements in dancing, forming a pattern that may be repeated, varied, or elaborated: the tango *step.* **11** An interval measuring a difference of musical pitch, corresponding to a degree of the scale or staff. **12** A socket, supporting framework, pocket, or the like: the *step* of a mast. **13** A steplike projection or part, as of the bit of a key. **14** *Mech.* The radial distance between the face of one pulley and that of another stepped on the same shaft. **15** A break in the contour of a float or hull, as of a seaplane, designed to lessen resistance and improve control. **16** A stage in cascade amplification. **— in step** In agreement or synchronism when marching, dancing, etc.; walking evenly with another by taking corresponding steps. **— out of step** Not in step. **— to take steps** To adopt measures, as to attain an end. **—** *v.* **stepped, step·ping** *v.i.* **1** To move forward or backward by taking a step or steps. **2** To go by foot; walk a short distance: to *step* across the street. **3** To move with measured, dignified, or graceful steps. **4** To move or act quickly or briskly: The old man was *stepping* down the road. **5** To pass into a situation, circumstance, etc., as if in a single step: He *stepped* into a fortune. **—** *v.t.* **6** To take (a pace, stride, etc.). **7** To perform the steps of: to *step* a quadrille. **8** To place or move (the foot) in taking a step. **9** To measure by taking steps: often with *off:* to *step* off five yards. **10** To cut or arrange in steps. **11** *Naut.* To place the lower end of (a mast) in its step. **— to step down** **1** To decrease gradually, or by steps or degrees. **2** To resign from an office or position; abdicate. **— to step in** To begin to take part; intervene. **— to step on** (or **upon**) **1** To put the foot down on; tread upon. **2** To put the foot on so as to activate, as a brake or treadle. **3** *Colloq.* To reprove or subdue. **— to step on it** To hurry; hasten. **— to step out** **1** To go outside, especially for a short while. **2** *Colloq.* To go out for fun or entertainment. **3** To step down (def. 2). **4** To walk vigorously and with long strides. **— to step up** To increase; raise. ◆ Homophone: *steppe.* [OE *stæpe*]

step– *combining form* Related through the previous marriage of a parent or spouse, but not by blood: *stepchild.* [OE *steop-* < stem of *astypan, astepan* bereave, orphan]

step·broth·er (step′bruth′ər) *n.* The son of one's step-parent by a former marriage.

step·child (step′chīld′) *n.* The child of one's husband or wife by a former marriage.

step·dame (step′dām′) *n. Archaic* A stepmother.

step·daugh·ter (step′dô′tər) *n.* A female stepchild.

step–down (step′doun′) *adj.* **1** That decreases gradually. **2** *Electr.* Converting a small current of high voltage into a large one of low voltage: said of the usual form of transformer: opposed to *step-up.* **3** Designating a ratio-reducing gear.

step·fa·ther (step′fä′thər) *n.* The husband of one's mother other than one's own father.

Steph·a·nie (stef′ə·nē) A feminine personal name: feminine of STEPHEN. Also **Steph′a·na,** *Fr.* **Sté·pha·nie** (stā·fà·nē′).

Ste·phen (stē′vən) A masculine personal name: often spelled *Steven.* Also *Sw.* **Ste·fan** (stā′·fän), *Ital.* **Ste·fa·no** (stā·fä′nō), *Russian* **Ste·pan** (stā·pän′), *Dan., Ger.* **Ste·phan** (shtā′·fän). [<Gk., crown]

— Stephen The first Christian martyr. *Acts* vii 60.

— Stephen I, 975?–1038, first king of Hungary: known as *St. Stephen.*

— Stephen of Blois, 1097?–1154, king of England 1135–54.

Ste·phen (stē′vən), **Sir Leslie,** 1832–1904, English biographer and critic.

Ste·phens (stē′vənz), **Alexander Hamilton,** 1812–83, U. S. statesman; vice president of the Confederate States. **— James,** 1882–1950, Irish poet and novelist.

Ste·phen·son (stē′vən·sən), **George,** 1781–1848, English engineer; invented the locomotive. **— Robert,** 1803–59, English engineer; son of the preceding.

step–in (step′in′) *n.* **1** An undergarment like short drawers, without actual legs: also **step′–ins′.** **2** A pumplike shoe. **—** *adj.* Put on, as undergarments or shoes, by being stepped into.

step·lad·der (step′lad′ər) *n.* A set of portable steps with, usually, a hinged frame at the back, which may be extended to support the steps in an upright position.

step·moth·er (step′muth′ər) *n.* The wife of one's father, other than one's own mother.

Step·ney (step′nē) A metropolitan borough of eastern London, including the districts of Whitechapel and Limehouse.

step–par·ent (step′pâr′ənt) *n.* A stepfather or stepmother.

steppe (step) *n.* A vast plain devoid of forest; specifically, one of the extensive plains in Russia and Siberia. ◆ Homophone: *step.* [<Russian *step′*]

step·per (step′ər) *n.* **1** One who or that which steps: The horse is a high *stepper.* **2** *Slang* A dancer.

Steppes (steps), **The** See KIRGHIZ STEPPE.

step·ping·stone (step′ing·stōn′) *n.* **1** A stone affording a footrest, as for crossing a stream, etc. **2** That by which one advances or rises: *steppingstones* to fortune.

step·re·la·tion (step′ri·lā′shən) *n.* A person related through the remarriage of a parent or spouse and not by blood. **— step′re·la′tion·ship** *n.*

step·sis·ter (step′sis′tər) *n.* The daughter of one's step-parent by a former marriage.

step·son (step′sun′) *n.* A male stepchild.

step–up (step′up′) *adj.* **1** Increasing by stages: a *step-up* transformer: opposed to *step-down.* **2** Designating a ratio-increasing gear.

step·wise (step′wīz′) *adv.* In the manner of steps; step by step.

-ster *suffix of nouns* **1** One who makes or is occupied with: often with pejorative force: *songster, prankster.* **2** One who belongs or is related to: *gangster.* **3** One who is: *youngster.* [OE *-estre,* feminine suffix]

ste·ra·di·an (sti·rā′dē·ən) *n.* The unit of measurement for solid angles; that solid angle which, on a sphere, encloses a surface equivalent to the square of the radius: also called *spheradian.* [<Gk. *stereos* solid + RADIAN]

ster·co·ra·ceous (stûr′kə·rā′shəs) *adj.* Consisting of or pertaining to excrement or dung: *stercoraceous* vomiting.

stercori– *combining form* Dung; excrement: *stercoricolous:* also, before vowels, **stercor–.** Also **sterco–.** [<L *stercus, stercoris* dung]

ster·co·ric·o·lous (stûr′kə·rik′ə·ləs) *n.* Living in manure, as some insects.

ster·cu·li·a·ceous (stûr·kyōō′lē·ā′shəs) *adj. Bot.* Designating or belonging to a family *(Sterculiaceae)* of chiefly tropical herbs, shrubs, and trees, including the cacao and the colanut tree. [<NL <L *Sterculius,* the deity of manuring < *stercus* dung]

stere (stir) *n.* A measure of capacity in the metric system, equal to one cubic meter. See METRIC SYSTEM. [<F *stère* <Gk. *stereos* solid]

ster·e·o (ster′ē·ō, stir′-) *n. pl.* **·e·os** **1** A stereophonic record player, record, tape, etc. **2** Stereophonic sound. **3** A stereotype (defs. 1 & 3). **4** A stereoscopic method; also, a stereoscopic photograph. **—** *adj.* **1** Stereophonic. **2** Stereotyped. **3** Of or pertaining to the stereoscope.

stereo– *combining form* Solid; firm; hard: *stereoscope.* Also, before vowels, **stere–.** [<Gk. *stereos* hard]

ster·e·o·bate (ster′ē·ə·bāt′, stir′-) *n. Archit.* A substructure, continuous base, or solid platform without columns, as distinguished from a *stylobate,* which has them. [<STEREO- + Gk. *batēs* that which steps] **— ster′e·o·bat′ic** (-bat′ik) *adj.*

ster·e·o·chem·is·try (ster′ē·ō·kem′is·trē, stir′-) *n.* The branch of chemistry that treats of the spatial arrangement of atoms and molecules.

ster·e·o·chro·my (ster′ē·ō·krō′mē, stir′-) *n.* The art or process of painting with pigments mixed with waterglass. [<STEREO- + Gk. *chrōma* color] **— ster′e·o·chro′mic** *adj.*

ster·e·o·com·pa·ra·graph (ster′ē·ō·kom′pər·ə·graf′, -gräf′, stir′-) *n.* A mapmaking device utilizing data provided by stereoscopic photographs. [<STEREO- + COMPARE + -GRAPH]

ster·e·og·no·sis (ster′ē·og·nō′sis, stir′-) *n.* Perception of shape, solidity, and weight, especially by the sense of touch. [<STEREO- + Gk. *gnōsis* knowing] **— ster′e·og·nos′tic** (-nos′tik) *adj.*

ster·e·o·gram (ster′ē·ə·gram′, stir′-) *n.* **1** A picture or diagram giving the impression of a solid in relief, or two pictures of an object combined so as to produce the effect of a solid, as in a stereoscopic picture. **2** A stereograph.

ster·e·o·graph (ster′ē·ə·graf′, -gräf′, stir′-) *n.* **1** A photograph or pair of photographs representing objects so that they appear solid; a stereoscopic photograph. **2** An instrument for making projections of solid objects.

ster·e·og·ra·phy (ster′ē·og′rə·fē, stir′-) *n.* **1** The art of representing solids on a plane by means of lines; perspective. **2** The branch of geometry that treats of solids and of the construction of regularly bounded solids. **— ster′·e·o·graph′ic** (-ə·graf′ik) or **·i·cal** *adj.* **— ster′e·o·graph′i·cal·ly** *adv.*

ster·e·o·i·som·er·ism (ster′ē·ō·ī·som′ə·riz′əm, stir′-) *n. Chem.* An isomerism which depends on the spatial arrangement of the atoms or groups in an organic compound. **— ster′e·o·i′so·mer′ic** (-ī′sō·mer′ik), **ster′e·o·mer′ic** *adj.*

ster·e·ome (ster′ē·ōm, stir′-) *n. Bot.* The solid supporting elements of the fibrovascular tissues of plants. [<Gk. *stereōme* solid body < *stereos* solid]

ster·e·om·e·try (ster′ē·om′ə·trē, stir′-) *n.* The art of measuring the volume and other spatial elements of solids. [<STEREO- + -METRY] —**ster′e·o·met′ric** (-ō·met′rik) or **·ri·cal** *adj.* —**ster′e·o·met′ri·cal·ly** *adv.*

ster·e·o·phone (ster′ē·ə·fōn′, stir′-) *n.* Any sound–transmitting system equipped with stereophonic devices.

ster·e·o·phon·ic (ster′ē·ə·fon′ik, stir′-) *adj.* **1** Pertaining to, designed for, or characterized by the perception of sound by both ears; binaural. **2** Denoting a system of sound transmission in which two or more microphones or loudspeakers are so placed as to give the effect of hearing with both ears simultaneously, as in wide–screen motion pictures and certain types of radio receivers. —**ster′e·o·phon′i·cal·ly** *adv.*

ster·e·o·phon·ics (ster′ē·ə·fon′iks, stir′-) *n. pl.* (*construed as singular*) The branch of acoustics which investigates the stereophonic reproduction of sound and develops its practical applications.

ster·e·o·phon·ism (ster′ē·ə·fō′niz·əm, stir′-) *n.* The condition of being stereophonic; binaural hearing.

ster·e·oph·o·ny (ster′ē·of′ə·nē, stir′-) *n.* The art and techniques of designing, producing, and applying stereophonic devices for the recording and transmission of sound.

ster·e·op·sis (ster′ē·op′sis, stir′-) *n.* Vision characterized by stereoscopy; stereoscopic vision. [<STERE(O)- + -OPSIS]

ster·e·op·ti·con (ster′ē·op′ti·kon, stir′-) *n.* A double magic lantern arranged to combine two images of the same object or scene, or used to bring one image after another on the screen by the alternate use of the lanterns; a projection lantern. [<STEREO- + Gk. *optikos* of sight]

ster·e·o·scope (ster′ē·ə·skōp, stir′-) *n.* An instrument for blending into one image two pictures of an object from slightly different points of view, so as to produce upon the eye the impression of relief and solidity. [<STEREO- + -SCOPE] —**ster′e·o·scop′ic** (-skop′ik) or **·i·cal** *adj.* —**ster′e·o·scop′i·cal·ly** *adv.*

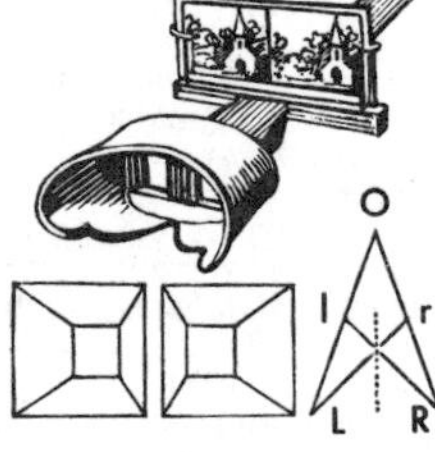

STEREOSCOPE
Line of sight, *Ll* and *Rr*, of the eyes, combines the images of points *l* and *r* at *O*. A card (at dotted line) shuts off two side images otherwise seen along *Rl* at *l* and *Lr* at *r*.

ster·e·os·co·py (ster′ē·os′kə·pē, stir′-) *n.* **1** The art of making or using stereoscopes and stereoscopic slides. **2** The viewing of objects as in three dimensions. —**ster′e·os′co·pism** *n.* —**ster′e·os′co·pist** *n.*

ster·e·o·ski·ag·ra·phy (ster′ē·ō·skī·ag′rə·fē, stir′-) *n.* Stereoscopic photography by means of X–rays. [<STEREO- + SKIAGRAPHY]

ster·e·ot·ro·pism (ster′ē·ot′rə·piz′əm, stir′-) *n.* Involuntary response of an organism to contact with a foreign body. Also **ster′e·o·tax′is** (-ō·tak′sis) —**ster′e·o·trop′ic** (-trop′ik) *adj.*

ster·e·o·type (ster′ē·ə·tīp′, stir′-) *n.* **1** A plate taken in type metal from a matrix, as of paper, reproducing the surface from which the matrix was made. **2** Stereotypy. **3** Anything made or processed in this way. **4** A conventional or hackneyed expression, custom, or mode of thought. —*v.t.* **·typed, ·typ·ing 1** To make a stereotype of. **2** To fix firmly or unalterably.

ster·e·o·typed (ster′ē·ə·tīpt′, stir′-) *adj.* Formalized as if produced from a stereotype; hackneyed; without originality.

ster·e·o·typ·er (ster′ē·ə·tī′pər, stir′-) *n.* **1** One who makes stereotype plates. **2** A stereotype–making machine for making embossed plates from which printing for the blind is done. Also **ster′e·o·typ′ist.** —**ster′e·o·typ′ic** (-tip′ik), **ster′e·o·typ′i·cal** *adj.*

ster·e·o·typ·y (ster′ē·ə·tī′pē, stir′-) *n.* The art or act of making stereotypes. Also **ster′e·o·typ′er·y** (-tī′pər·ē).

ster·e·o·vi·sion (ster′ē·ō·vizh′ən, stir′-) *n.* Three–dimensional vision.

ster·ic (ster′ik, stir′-) *adj. Chem.* Denoting relative position in space: said of the component atoms in a molecule. Also **ster′i·cal.** [<Gk. *stereos* solid]

ster·il·ant (ster′əl·ənt) *n.* **1** That which makes sterile or induces sterility. **2** *Agric.* Any of various chemical compounds whose use as weed–killers renders the soil infertile for one or more growing seasons.

ster·ile (ster′əl) *adj.* **1** Having no reproductive power; barren. **2** *Bot.* Producing no pistil or no spores; incapable of germinating, as certain plants. **3** Lacking productiveness or fertility; hence, useless; being without result: *sterile* soil. **4** Containing no pathogenic bacteria or other micro–organisms; aseptic: a *sterile* fluid. **5** Destitute of attractiveness or suggestiveness: said especially of literary work: *sterile* verse. [<L *sterilis* barren] —**ster′ile·ly** *adv.* —**ste·ril·i·ty** (stə·ril′ə·tē), **ster′ile·ness** *n.*

ster·il·i·za·tion (ster′əl·ə·zā′shən, -ī·zā′-) *n.* **1** The act or process of making sterile. **2** The condition of being sterile. **3** The deliberate procedure of destroying reproductive power by surgical means.

ster·il·ize (ster′əl·īz) *v.t.* **·ized, ·iz·ing 1** To deprive of productive or reproductive power, especially by surgical operation on the Fallopian tubes or on the vas deferens. **2** To destroy bacteria in; free from germs. **3** To make barren; exhaust the productiveness of. **4** To make powerless. —**ster′il·iz′er** *n.*

ster·let (stûr′lit) *n.* A small sturgeon (*Acipenser ruthenus*) found in the Black, Caspian, and Azov seas, and in rivers of Russia, yielding superior caviar and isinglass. [<Russian *sterlyad′*]

ster·ling (stûr′ling) *n.* **1** The official standard of fineness for British coins: for silver (**sterling silver**), 0.925 until 1920, 0.500 since then; for gold, 0.91666 or 11/12. **2** Sterling silver, 0.925 fine, as used in manufacturing articles, as tableware, etc.; also, an article or articles made of it. **3** A former silver penny of England and Scotland, in circulation as early as the 12th century. —*adj.* **1** Made of or payable in sterling: pounds *sterling.* **2** Made of sterling silver. **3** Having accepted worth; genuine; hence, valuable; esteemed: *sterling* qualities. See synonyms under GOOD. [Prob. OE *steorra* star + -LING; because a star was stamped on some of the coins]

stern[1] (stûrn) *adj.* **1** Proceeding from or marked by severity or harshness; unyielding: a *stern* command. **2** Having an austere disposition; strict; severe: a *stern* judge. **3** Inspiring fear; repelling. **4** Resolute; stout: a *stern* resolve. See synonyms under AUSTERE, GRIM, HARD, SEVERE. [OE *styrne*] —**stern′ly** *adv.* —**stern′ness** *n.*

stern[2] (stûrn) *n.* **1** *Naut.* The aft part of a ship, boat, etc. **2** The buttocks or tail part of an animal: now chiefly humorous. **3** The hindmost part of any object. —*adj.* Situated at or belonging to the stern. [<ON *stjoren* steering, rudder < *styra* steer]

Stern (stûrn), **Otto,** born 1888, U. S. physicist born in Germany.

ster·nal (stûr′nəl) *adj.* Pertaining to the breastbone or sternum.

stern chase *Naut.* A chase in which the pursuing vessel follows in the other's course.

stern chaser A cannon mounted in the stern to fire at a pursuing ship.

Sterne (stûrn), **Laurence,** 1713–68, English clergyman and novelist.

stern·fore·most (stûrn′fôr′mōst′, -məst, -fōr′-) *adv.* Hind side foremost; moving with the stern in advance; backward; hence, awkwardly.

stern·most (stûrn′mōst′, -məst) *adj.* Farthest to the rear or stern.

sterno– *combining form Anat. & Med.* The sternum: *sternotomy,* cutting through the sternum. Also, before vowels, **stern–.** [<L *sternum* breast]

stern·post (stûrn′pōst′) *n. Naut.* The main vertical post of the stern frame of a vessel, to which the rudder is attached.

stern·sheets (stûrn′shēts′) *n. Naut.* The inside stern portion of a boat; the space in a boat abaft the thwarts.

stern·son (stûrn′sən) *n. Naut.* An inner sternpost attached to the center keelson, to strengthen the stern frame. Also **stern′knee′** (-nē′), **stern′son–knee′.** [<STERN + (KEEL)SON]

ster·num (stûr′nəm) *n. pl.* **·na** (-nə) or **·nums 1** *Anat.* The breastbone which forms the ventral support of the ribs in most vertebrates. **2** *Zool.* The ventral portion of a somite in an arthropod, as an insect or crustacean. [<L <Gk. *sternon* breast]

ster·nu·ta·tion (stûr′nyə·tā′shən) *n.* **1** The act of sneezing. **2** A sneeze or the noise produced by it. [<L *sternutatio, -onis* < *sternutare,* freq. of *sternuere* sneeze]

ster·nu·ta·tor (stûr′nyə·tā′tər) *n.* One of a class of chemical–warfare agents having a strongly irritant effect upon the nasal and respiratory passages, with resulting physical exhaustion; a sneeze gas.

ster·nu·ta·to·ry (stər·nyōō′tə·tôr′ē, -tō′rē, -nōō′-) *adj.* Causing or tending to cause sneezing: also **ster·nu′ta·tive** (-tə·tiv). —*n. pl.* **·ries** Any substance tending to cause sneezing, as snuff.

stern·ward (stûrn′wərd) *adj. & adv.* Toward the stern; astern. Also **stern′wards.**

stern·way (stûrn′wā′) *n. Naut.* Backward or sternforemost movement of a vessel: opposed to *headway.*

stern–wheel·er (stûrn′hwē′lər) *n.* A steamboat of small draft propelled by one large paddle wheel at the stern.

STERN–WHEELER

ster·oid (ster′oid) *n. Biochem.* Any of a sizable group of organic compounds widely distributed in nature, including the sterols, the bile acids, and the sex hormones. [<STER(OL) + -OID]

ster·ol (ster′ōl, -ol) *n. Biochem.* Any of a class of complex, chiefly unsaturated, solid alcohols widely distributed in plant and animal tissue, as cholesterol. [Contraction of CHOLESTEROL]

Ster·o·pe (ster′ə·pē) One of the Pleiades: also called *Asterope.*

ster·tor (stûr′tər) *n.* A deep snore or snoring. [<NL <L *stertere* snore]

ster·tor·ous (stûr′tər·əs) *adj.* Characterized by snoring; accompanied by a snoring sound: *stertorous* breathing. —**ster′tor·ous·ly** *adv.* —**ster′tor·ous·ness** *n.*

ster·ule (ster′ōōl, -yōōl) *n.* A small glass container holding a sterile solution. Compare AMPOULE. [<STER(ILE) + -ULE]

stet (stet) Let it stand: a direction used in proofreading to indicate that a word, letter, etc., marked for omission or correction is to remain. —*v.t.* **stet·ted, stet·ting** To cancel a former correction or omission of by marking with the word *stet.* Compare DELE. [<L, 3rd person sing. subjunctive of *stare* stand, stay]

stetho– *combining form* The breast or chest; pectoral: *stethoscope.* Also, before vowels, **steth–.** [<Gk. *stēthos* breast]

ste·thom·e·ter (ste·thom′ə·tər) *n.* An instrument to measure the expansion of the chest in breathing. [<STETHO- + -METER]

steth·o·scope (steth′ə·skōp) *n. Med.* An apparatus for auscultation, of various forms, sizes, and materials, adapted for conveying the sounds of the body to the examiner's ear or ears. —**steth′o·scop′ic** (-skop′ik), **steth′o·scop′i·cal** *adj.* —**steth′o·scop′i·cal·ly** *adv.* —**ste·thos·co·py** (ste·thos′kə·pē) *n.*

Stet·son (stet′sən) *n.* A hat; especially, one of felt with high crown and wide brim: a trade name. [after John Batterson *Stetson,* 1830–1906, U. S. hatmaker]

Stet·tin (stet′in, *Ger.* shte·tēn′) A port on the Oder in NW Poland, formerly the capital of Pomerania. *Polish* **Szcze·cin** (shche·tsēn′).

Stet·tin·i·us (stə·tin′ē·əs, -tin′yəs), **Edward Riley,** 1900–49, U. S. industrialist and statesman; secretary of state December 1944–June 1945.

Steu·ben (stōō′bən, *Ger.* shtoi′bən), **Baron Friedrich Wilhelm von,** 1730–94, Prussian general; served in American Revolutionary War.

St. Eu·sta·tius (sānt yōō·stā′shəs, -shē·əs) An island in the eastern group of the Netherlands West Indies; 8 square miles. *Dutch* **Sint Eu·sta·ti·us** (sint ōō·stä′tē·ōōs).

Steve (stēv) Familiar shortening of STEPHEN. Also **Ste′vie.**

ste·ve·dore (stē′və·dôr, -dōr) *n.* One whose business is stowing or unloading the holds of vessels. —*v.t. & v.i.* **·dored, ·dor·ing** To load or unload (a vessel or vessels). [<Sp. *estivador* <*estivar* stow <L *stipare* compress, stuff]

stevedore knot A knot used by stevedores to prevent unreeving.

STEVEDORE KNOT

Ste·ven (stē′vən) See STEPHEN.

Ste·vens (stē′vənz), **Thaddeus,** 1792–1868, U.S. statesman; abolitionist. —**Wallace,** 1879–1955, U.S. poet and businessman.

Ste·ven·son (stē′vən·sən), **Adlai Ewing,** 1900–1965, U.S. lawyer and political leader. —**Robert Louis,** 1850–94, Scottish novelist and essayist.

ste·vi·o·side (stē′vē·ə·sīd) *n. Chem.* A glycoside extracted from the dried leaves of a small South American shrub *(Stevia rebaudiana)* and having a sweetness 300 times that of cane sugar. [<STEVI(A) the genus of the shrub + (GLYC)OSIDE]

stew (sto͞o, styo͞o) *v.t. & v.i.* **1** To boil slowly and gently; seethe; keep or be at the simmering point. **2** *Colloq.* To worry. —*n.* **1** Stewed food, especially a preparation of meat or fish cooked by stewing. **2** *Colloq.* Mental agitation; worry. **3** *pl. Archaic* A brothel. **4** *Obs.* A room heated for bathing or drying purposes. [<OF *estuver,* prob. ult. <L *ex-* out + Gk. *typhos* steam, vapor]

stew·ard (sto͞o′ərd, styo͞o′-) *n.* **1** A person entrusted with the management of estates or affairs not his own; an administrator. **2** A person put in charge of the domestic affairs of an establishment. **3** On shipboard, a petty officer in charge of the service of provisions, or a man who waits on table and takes care of passengers' rooms. **4** *Brit.* A fiscal officer in certain ancient guilds. [OE *stīweard* <*stī* hall, sty + *weard* ward, keeper] —**stew′ard·ess** *n. fem.* —**stew′ard·ship** *n.*

Stew·art (sto͞o′ərt, styo͞o′-), **Dugald,** 1753–1828, Scottish philosopher.

Stewart Island An island of New Zealand south of South Island; 670 square miles.

stewed (sto͞od, styo͞od) *adj.* **1** Cooked by stewing. **2** *Slang* Drunk.

stew pan A cooking vessel used for stewing.

stey (stā) *adj. Scot.* **1** Steep. **2** Haughty; lofty.

St. Fran·cis River (sānt fran′sis) **1** A river in southern Quebec, Canada, flowing 150 miles SW to the St. Lawrence. **2** A river in SW Missouri and NE Arkansas, flowing 470 miles south to the Mississippi.

St. Gall (sānt gôl′) **1** A canton in NE Switzerland; 778 square miles. **2** Its capital, site of a seventh century Benedictine abbey. *German* **Sankt Gal·len** (zängt gäl′ən). Also **Saint Gal·len** (sānt gal′in).

St. George's (sānt jôr′jiz) The capital of Grenada, The West Indies (federation); former administrative capital of the Windward Islands. Also **St. George.**

St. George's Channel A strait between SE Ireland and Wales, connecting the Irish Sea with the Atlantic Ocean; 100 miles long, 50 to 95 miles wide.

St. George's cross The Greek cross, used on the British flag. See under CROSS.

St. Gott·hard (sānt got′ərd, *Fr.* saṅ gô·tår′) A mountain group in the Lepontine Alps, south central Switzerland; highest peak 10,483 feet; site of the **St. Gotthard Pass,** at 6,929 feet, and of the **St. Gotthard tunnel,** extending 9 1/4 miles at an elevation of 3,786 feet.

St. He·le·na (sānt hə·lē′nə) An island in the South Atlantic, 1,200 miles west of Africa, to which Napoleon was exiled from 1815–21; 47 square miles; comprising a British crown colony with the dependencies of Ascension Island and the Tristan da Cunha group; 133 square miles; capital, Jamestown, on St. Helena.

St. Hel·ens (sānt hel′ənz) A county borough in SW Lancashire, England.

St. Hel·ier (sānt hel′yər) Capital of Jersey, Channel Islands.

sthe·ni·a (sthē′nē·ə, sthi·nī′ə) *n.* Unusual energy or vigor; excited force: opposed to *asthenia.* [<NL <Gk. *sthenos* strength]

sthen·ic (sthen′ik) *adj.* **1** Exhibiting activity or energy, especially in morbid states. **2** Having power to inspire or animate; indicating vigor. [<Gk. *sthenos* strength]

Sthe·no (sthē′nō, sthen′ō) One of the Gorgons.

stiac·cia·to (styät·chä′tō) *n.* Sculpture or a piece of sculpture in lower relief than bas-relief, as the very low relief used on coins. —*adj.* Of or pertaining to this kind of sculpture; in very low relief. [<Ital., crushed, flattened, pp. of *stiacciare*]

stib·ble (stib′əl) *n. Scot.* Stubble. Also **stib′bul.**

stib·bler (stib′lər) *n. Scot.* **1** A gleaner. **2** A minister without a ministerial charge.

stib·ine (stib′ēn, -in) *n. Chem.* A colorless poisonous gas, SbH_3, resembling arsine, formed by decomposing antimony or any of its compounds in the presence of hydrogen. [<STIB(IUM) + -INE[2]]

stib·i·um (stib′ē·əm) *n.* Antimony. [<L <Gk. *stibi*] —**stib′i·al** *adj.*

stib·nite (stib′nīt) *n.* A metallic steel-gray antimony sulfide, Sb_2S_3, crystallizing in the orthorhombic system: the most important ore of antimony. [<STIB(I)N(E)+ -ITE[2]]

stich (stik) *n.* **1** A line of the Bible. **2** A line of poetry; a verse: used often in composition: *hemistich.* [<Gk. *stichos* row]

stich·ic (stik′ik) *adj.* **1** Relating to or consisting of stichs. **2** Metrically the same throughout: said of verses.

sti·chom·e·try (sti·kom′ə·trē) *n.* **1** The measurement of the text of a manuscript by lines of measured length into which it is divided; also, the appendix stating the number of lines. **2** The practice of writing prose in line lengths corresponding to the sense of the phrasal cadence. [<Gk. *stichos* line + -METRY] —**stich·o·met·ric** (stik′ə·met′rik) or **·ri·cal** *adj.*

sti·chom·y·thy (sti·kom′ə·thē) *n.* The arrangement of a dialog in alternate lines of verse: characteristic of ancient Greek drama, poetry, and disputation: also spelled *stychomythia.* [< Gk. *stichos* line + *mythos* speech] —**stich·o·myth·ic** (stik′ə·mith′ik) *adj.*

-stichous *combining form* Having (a specified number of) rows: *tristichous.* [<Gk. *stichos* a row, line]

stich·wort (stich′wûrt′) See STITCHWORT.

stick (stik) *n.* **1** A piece of wood that is long, compared with its cross-section; a stiff shoot or branch cut from a tree or bush and used as a rod, wand, staff, club, etc.; also, sometimes one much bigger: a *stick* of timber. **2** *Brit.* A cane. **3** Anything resembling a stick in form: a *stick* of candy or dynamite. **4** *Printing* **a** A composing stick. **b** As much type as a composing stick will hold: about two inches in depth. **c** Copy which will fill this space in a newspaper column: also **stick′ful′.** **5** A piece of wood of any size, cut for fuel, lumber, or timber. **6** *Aeron.* The control lever of an airplane which operates the elevators and ailerons. **7** A poke, stab, or thrust with a stick or pointed instrument. **8** *Archaic* A difficulty or obstacle; hesitation; stop. **9** The state of being stuck together; adhesion. **10** In sports, a baseball bat, hockey stick, racing hurdle, etc. **11** A timber tree. **12** *Colloq.* A stiff, inert, or dull person. **13** *Slang* Any alcoholic ingredient in an otherwise non-alcoholic drink. **14** A revolver or rifle. **15** *Colloq.* The mast of a ship. **16** *Mil.* A group of bombs released consecutively in a straight line crossing the target area. **17** A stalk, as of asparagus. **18** *Colloq.* A conductor's baton. —**the sticks 1** A timber forest. **2** *Colloq.* The backwoods; an obscure rural district. —*v.* **stuck** or (*for defs.* **15, 16**) **sticked, stick·ing** *v.t.* **1** To pierce, stab, or penetrate with a pin, knife, or other pointed object. **2** To kill or wound by piercing; stab. **3** To thrust or force, as a sword or pin, into or through something else. **4** To force the end of (a nail, etc.) into something so as to be fixed in place: to *stick* a nail in a wall. **5** To fasten in place with or as with pins, nails, etc.: to *stick* a ribbon on a dress. **6** To cover with objects piercing the surface: a paper *stuck* with pins. **7** To fix on a pointed object; impale; transfix. **8** To put or thrust: He *stuck* his hand into his pocket. **9** To fasten to a surface by or as by an adhesive substance. **10** To bring to a standstill; obstruct; halt: usually in the passive: We were *stuck* in Rome. **11** *Colloq.* To smear with something sticky. **12** *Colloq.* To baffle; puzzle. **13** *Slang* To impose upon; cheat. **14** *Slang* To force great expense, an unpleasant task, responsibility, etc., upon. **15** To provide with sticks or brush on which to grow, as a vine. **16** *Printing* To set or compose (type). —*v.i.* **17** To be or become fixed in place by being thrust in: The pins are *sticking* in the cushion. **18** To become or remain attached by or as by adhesion; adhere; cling. **19** To come to a standstill; become blocked or obstructed; stop; halt. **20** To be baffled or disconcerted. **21** To hesitate; scruple: with *at* or *to.* **22** To persist; persevere, as in a task or undertaking: with *at* or *to.* **23** To remain firm or resolute; be faithful, as to an ideal or bargain. **24** To be extended; protrude: with *from, out, through, up,* etc. —**to be stuck on** *Colloq.* To be enamored of. —**to stick around** *Slang* To remain near or near at hand. —**to stick by** To remain faithful to; be loyal to. —**to stick it out** To persevere to the end. —**to stick up** *Slang* To stop and rob. —**to stick up for** *Colloq.* To take the part of; support; defend. [OE *sticca*]

stick·ball (stik′bôl′) *n.* A kind of baseball played on streets or in vacant lots, with a rubber ball and a narrow stick or a broom handle for a bat.

stick·er (stik′ər) *n.* **1** One who holds tenaciously to anything. **2** One who or that which fastens with or as with paste. **3** A paster. **4** *Colloq.* Anything that confuses or silences a person; a puzzle. **5** A prickly stem, thorn, or bur.

sticking plaster An adhesive material for covering slight cuts, etc.; a court plaster.

stick insect An orthopterous insect (family *Phasmidae*), typically wingless and characterized by a long, sticklike body, as the green or pinkish *Timema* of the Pacific coast.

stick-in-the-mud (stik′in·thə·mud′) *n. Colloq.* A person too sluggish or lacking in initiative to take any progressive action.

stick·it (stik′it) *adj. Scot.* Stuck; unsuccessful; having failed in or given up something.

stickit minister *Scot.* A probationer who fails to qualify for a license, or a licentiate without pastoral charge.

stick·le[1] (stik′əl) *v.i.* **·led, ·ling 1** To contend about trifling matters. **2** To insist or hesitate for petty reasons. [ME *stightlen* set in order, freq. of OE *stihtan* arrange, dispose]

stick·le[2] (stik′əl) *n.* A prickle; spine: obsolete except in compounds. [OE *sticel* sting]

stick·le·back (stik′əl·bak′) *n.* A small fresh- or salt-water fish (genera *Gasterosteus* and *Eucalia*) of northern regions, having sharp dorsal spines. The male builds nests for the reception of the eggs laid by the female.

stick·ler (stik′lər) *n.* **1** One who contends over trifles. **2** *Obs.* A referee.

stick·pin (stik′pin′) *n.* An ornamental pin for a necktie.

stick·seed (stik′sēd′) *n.* Any of a genus *(Lappula)* of coarse weeds, whose prickly seeds stick in clothing, the wool of sheep, etc.

stick shift A gearshift operated by hand rather than automatically, located either on the floor or on the steering column.

stick·tight (stik′tīt′) *n.* A coarse herb (genus *Bidens*) of the composite family with prickly achenes; a bur marigold.

stick-to-it-ive (stik·to͞o′it·iv) *adj. Colloq.* Persevering; dogged; pertinacious. —**stick-to′-it·ive·ly** *adv.* —**stick-to′-it·ive·ness** *n.*

stick-up (stik′up′) *n. Slang* **1** A robbery or hold-up. **2** A robber who intimidates his victims with a weapon, compelling them to hold their hands in the air.

stick·weed (stik′wēd′) *n.* Ragweed.

stick·y (stik′ē) *adj.* **stick·i·er, stick·i·est 1** Adhering to a surface; adhesive. **2** Warm and humid. See synonyms under ADHESIVE. —**stick′i·ly** *adv.* —**stick′i·ness** *n.*

Stieg·litz (stēg′lits), **Alfred,** 1864–1946, U.S. photographer and art patron.

stiff (stif) *adj.* **1** Resisting the action of a bending force; not flaccid, limp, pliant, or flexible; rigid. **2** Not easily moved; acting with difficulty or friction. **3** Not natural, graceful, or easy; constrained and awkward; formal. **4** Not liquid or fluid; thick; viscous. **5** Taut; tightly drawn. **6** Having a strong, steady movement: a *stiff* breeze. **7** Firm in resistance; obstinate; stubborn. **8** Difficult to achieve, understand, or accept; harsh; severe: a *stiff* penalty. **9** High; dear: a *stiff* price. **10** Firm in prices; strong and steady: a *stiff* market. **11** *Naut.* Heeling over but little, while carrying much sail; not crank: a *stiff* ship. **12** *Scot.* & *Brit. Dial.* Lusty; strong; sturdy. **13** Dense; not porous, as soil. **14** Strong; potent: a *stiff* drink. **15** Difficult; arduous: a *stiff* climb. **16** *Obs.* Formidable; serious: said of news. See synonyms under INFLEXIBLE, SEVERE. — *n. Slang* **1** A corpse. **2** An awkward or unresponsive person; especially, a bore. **3** A man; fellow: *working* stiff; also, a roughneck. **4** A hobo. **5** An accomplice in dishonest dealings; also, a prospective victim. [OE *stīf*] — **stiff′ly** *adv.* — **stiff′ness** *n.*

stiff·en (stif′ən) *v.t.* & *v.i.* To make or become stiff or stiffer.

stiff·en·er (stif′ən·ər) *n.* One who or that which stiffens. — **bow stiffener** *Aeron.* A rigid structural member to reinforce the bow of a dirigible or other airship: also **nose stiffener.**

stiff-necked (stif′nekt′) *adj.* Not yielding; stubborn; incorrigible; obstinate.

sti·fle[1] (stī′fəl) *v.* **·fled, ·fling** *v.t.* **1** To kill by stopping respiration; suffocate; choke. **2** To keep back; suppress or repress, as sobs. — *v.i.* **3** To die of suffocation. **4** To experience difficulty in breathing, as in a stuffy room. [<ON *stīfla* stop up, choke] — **sti′fler** *n.* — **sti′fling** *adj.* — **sti′fling·ly** *adv.*

sti·fle[2] (stī′fəl) *n.* **1** The stifle joint. **2** Any abnormal condition of the stifle joint or stifle bone. [Origin unknown]

stifle bone The patella or kneepan of a horse, situated at the stifle joint, formerly thought of as stopping or damming up the joint.

sti·fled (stī′fəld) *adj.* Having some disease of the stifle joint; affected with stifle.

stifle joint The joint in the upper leg of a horse or a dog. See illustration under DOG, HORSE.

stig·ma (stig′mə) *n. pl.* **stig·ma·ta** (stig′mə·tə, stig·mä′tə) or *(for defs.* 1–3, *usually)* **stig·mas** **1** A mark of infamy, or token of disgrace; blemish; a blot on one's good name. **2** Formerly, a brand made with a branding iron on slaves and criminals. **3** *Bot.* That part of a pistil which receives the pollen. **4** *Biol.* **a** A mark or spot, as on the wings of certain insects. **b** An aperture, as the gill slit of a tunicate. **5** A small mark or scar; a birthmark. **6** *Pathol.* A small red or bleeding spot on the skin caused by nervous tension or by capillary congestion. **7** *pl.* The wounds that Christ received during the Passion and Crucifixion; also, marks on the body corresponding to these wounds: said to be miraculously impressed on certain persons as a token of divine favor. **8** One of the characteristic signs or marks of a disease. See synonyms under BLEMISH. [<L, mark, brand <Gk., pointed end, mark <*stizein* prick, brand]

stig·mas·ter·ol (stig·mas′tər·ōl, -ol) *n. Biochem.* A sterol, $C_{29}H_{47}OH$, obtained chiefly from the calabar bean, and in lesser amounts from soybean oil. [<STIGMA + STEROL]

stig·mat·ic (stig·mat′ik) *adj.* **1** Of, pertaining to, or marked with a stigma or stigmata. **2** Infamous; ignominious or vicious; hence, deformed. **3** Anastigmatic. Also **stig·mat′i·cal** — *n.* One marked with or bearing a stigma or stigmata.

stig·ma·tism (stig′mə·tiz′əm) *n.* **1** The state of being affected with stigmas. **2** *Optics* The quality or condition of a lens or of the cornea of the eye through which rays of light are accurately focused.

stig·ma·tist (stig′mə·tist) *n.* One bearing miraculous stigmata.

stig·ma·tize (stig′mə·tīz) *v.t.* **·tized, ·tiz·ing** **1** To characterize or brand as ignominious. **2** To mark with a stigma. **3** To cause stigmata to appear on. Also *Brit.* **stig′ma·tise.** [<Med. L *stigmatizare* <Gk. *stigmatizein* mark < *stigma* pointed end, mark] — **stig′ma·ti·za′tion** *n.* — **stig′ma·tiz′er** *n.*

Sti·kine River (sti·kēn′) A river in NW British Columbia and SE Alaska flowing 335 miles SW to the Pacific from the **Stikine Mountains,** a range in northern British Columbia; highest point 8,200 feet.

stilb (stilb) *n.* A unit of illumination, equal to one candle per square centimeter. [<Gk. *stilbein* glitter]

stil·bene (stil′bēn) *n. Chem.* A crystalline unsaturated hydrocarbon, $C_{14}H_{12}$, used in making dyestuffs. [<Gk. *stilbein* glitter + -ENE]

stil·bes·trol (stil′bəs·trōl, -trol) *n. Chem.* A synthetic sex hormone, $C_{18}H_{20}O_2$, similar in action to but more potent than the naturally occurring estrogens. [<STILB(ENE) + ESTR(ONE) + -OL[1]]

stil·bite (stil′bīt) *n.* A vitreous native hydrous silicate of aluminum, calcium, and sodium crystallizing in the monoclinic system. [<Gk. *stilbein* glitter + -ITE[1]]

stile[1] (stīl) *n.* A step, or series of steps, on each side of a fence or wall to aid in surmounting it; loosely, a turnstile. ◆ Homophone: *style.* [OE *stigel* < *stīgan* climb]

STILE
Over wire fence.

stile[2] (stīl) *n.* One of the vertical sidepieces in a door or a window sash. ◆ Homophone: *style.* [< Du. *stijl* doorpost]

sti·let·to (sti·let′ō) *n. pl.* **·tos** or **·toes** **1** A small dagger with a slender blade. **2** A small, sharp-pointed instrument, as of bone, for puncturing eyelets. — *v.t.* To pierce with a stiletto; stab. Also **sti·let′, sti·lette′.** [<Ital., dim. of *stilo* dagger <L *stilus.* See STYLE[1].]

Stil·i·cho (stil′ə·kō), **Flavius,** 359?–408, Roman general and statesman.

still[1] (stil) *adj.* **1** Being without movement; motionless. **2** Free from disturbance or agitation; peaceful; tranquil. **3** Making no sound; silent. **4** Low in sound; hushed. **5** Subdued; soft. **6** Dead; inanimate. **7** Having no effervescence: opposed to *sparkling*: said of wines. **8** *Phot.* Showing no movement. See synonyms under CALM, PACIFIC, SEDATE. — *n.* **1** Absence of sound or noise; stillness; calm. **2** A still-life picture. **3** *Phot.* A still photograph; especially, one taken with a still camera on a motion-picture set, for advertising, promotion, etc. **4** A still alarm. — *adv.* **1** Now as previously; up to this or that time; yet: He is *still* here. **2** After or in spite of something; all the same; nevertheless. **3** In increasing degree; even more; even yet: *still* more. **4** *Poetic* & *Dial.* Always; constantly. See synonyms under BUT[1], NOTWITHSTANDING, YET. — *conj.* Nevertheless. — *v.t.* **1** To cause to be still or calm. **2** To silence or hush. **3** To quiet or allay, as fears. — *v.i.* **4** To become still. See synonyms under ALLAY, REPRESS, TRANQUILIZE. [OE *stille*] — **still′ness** *n.*

still[2] (stil) *n.* **1** An apparatus in which a substance is vaporized by heat, and the vapor then liquefied in a condenser and collected: used especially for distilling liquors. **2** A distillery: also **still house.** — *v.t.* & *v.i.* To distil. [<L *stillare* drip < *stilla* a drop]

STILL

Still (stil), **Andrew Taylor,** 1828–1917, U. S. physician; founder of osteopathy.

still alarm A fire alarm given by telephone or other call without sounding the regular signal apparatus.

still·birth (stil′bûrth′) *n.* The bringing forth or birth of a dead child.

still·born (stil′bôrn′) *adj.* Dead at birth.

still-hunt (stil′hunt′) *v.t.* & *v.i.* To hunt (game) stealthily; stalk. — *n.* **1** The hunting of game by stealth. **2** The cautious, guarded pursuit of anything; specifically, secret or underhand methods in politics.

stil·li·form (stil′ə·fôrm) *adj.* Drop-shaped. [<NL *stilliformis* <L *stilla* drop + *forma* shape]

still-life (stil′līf′) *n.* **1** In painting, the representation of fruit, flowers, lifeless animals, and inanimate objects. **2** A picture of such a subject.

Still·son wrench (stil′sən) A wrench closely resembling a monkey wrench, but with one serrated jaw capable of slight angular movement about the other, so that the grip is increased by pressure on the handle: a trade name.

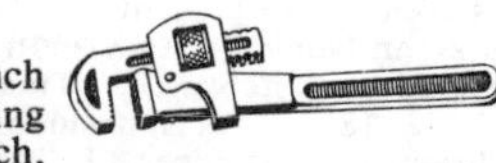

STILLSON WRENCH

Still·wa·ter (stil′wô′tər, -wot′ər) A village near Saratoga Springs, eastern New York; scene of several battles of the Revolutionary War, 1777.

still·y (stil′ē) *adj.* Still; silent, calm. — *adv.* (stil′lē) Calmly; quietly; without noise.

stilt (stilt) *n.* **1** One of a pair of slender poles made with a projection to support the foot above the ground in walking. **2** A tall post or pillar used as a support for a dock or building. **3** Any of several long-legged, three-toed birds (genera *Himantopus* and *Cladorhynchus*) related to the avocet, inhabiting ponds and fresh- and salt-water marshes. The American stilt *(H. mexicanus)* is mostly white with back, wings, crown, and nape a greenish black. The Old World stilt *(H. candidus)* is white except for wings and back. **4** *Scot.* A crutch. — *v.t.* To raise on stilts. — *v.i. Scot.* To hobble on crutches. [ME *stilte,* ? <LG. Cf. MLG *stelte.*]

stilt·ed (stil′tid) *adj.* Artificially elevated in manner; bombastic; inflated. — **stilt′ed·ly** *adv.* — **stilt′ed·ness** *n.*

stilted arch *Archit.* An arch whose curve springs from a level some distance above that of the impost.

Stil·ton cheese (stil′tən) A rich cheese permeated when ripe with a blue-green mold: originally made at Stilton, England. Also **Stil′ton.**

stilt-walk·er (stilt′wô′kər) *n.* One who walks or runs on stilts.

Stil·well (stil′wel), **Joseph Warren,** 1883–1946, U. S. general.

stime (stīm) *n. Scot.* A particle of light; a glimpse.

stim·part (stim′pərt) *n. Scot.* The fourth of a peck.

Stim·son (stim′sən), **Henry Lewis,** 1867–1950, U. S. statesman; secretary of war 1911–13, 1940–45; secretary of state 1929–33.

stim·u·lant (stim′yə·lənt) *n.* **1** Anything that quickens or promotes the activity of some physiological process, as a drug. **2** Popularly, an alcoholic beverage. — *adj.* Acting as a stimulant; serving to stimulate. [<L *stimulans, -antis,* ppr. of *stimulare.* See STIMULATE.]

stim·u·late (stim′yə·lāt) *v.* **·lat·ed, ·lat·ing** *v.t.* **1** To rouse to activity or to quickened action by some agency or motive; spur. **2** To arouse, or to increase action in, by applying some form of stimulus: to *stimulate* the skin. **3** To affect by intoxicants. — *v.i.* **4** To act as a stimulant. See synonyms under ENCOURAGE, PIQUE[1], SPUR, STIR[1]. [<L *stimulatus,* pp. of *stimulare* prick, goad < *stimulus* a goad] — **stim′u·lat′er, stim′u·la′tor** *n.* — **stim′u·la′tion** *n.*

stim·u·la·tive (stim′yə·lā′tiv) *adj.* Having the power or tendency to stimulate. — *n.* A stimulus.

stim·u·lus (stim′yə·ləs) *n. pl.* **·li** (-lī) **1** Anything that rouses the mind or spirits; an incentive; a stimulant; a sting; a spur, or goad. **2** *Physiol.* **a** Any agent or form of excitation which influences the activity of an organism as a whole or in any of its parts. **b** That which initiates an impulse, as in a nerve or muscle, or produces an altered state of consciousness, as by arousing new or stronger sensations. [<L]

sti·my (stī′mē) See STYMIE.

sting (sting) *v.* **stung** (*Obs.* **stang**), **stung, sting·ing** *v.t.* **1** To pierce or prick painfully, as with a sharp, poisonous organ: The bee *stung* me. **2** To cause to suffer sharp, smarting pain from or as from a sting: The blow *stung* his cheek. **3** To cause to suffer mentally; pain: His heart was *stung* with remorse. **4** To stimulate or rouse as if with a sting; goad; spur. **5** *Slang* To impose upon; get the better of; also, to overcharge. — *v.i.* **6** To have or use a sting, as a bee. **7** To suffer or cause a sharp, smarting pain. **8** To suffer or cause mental distress; pain. See synonyms under INCENSE[1], PIQUE[1], SPUR. — *n.* **1** *Zool.* A sharp offensive or defensive organ, as of a bee or wasp, capable of inflicting a painful and especially a poisonous wound. **2** The act of stinging; the wound made by a sting, or the pain caused by it. **3** Any sharp, smarting sensation; stinging quality: the *sting* of remorse. **4** A keen stimulus; spur; goad. **5** *Bot.* One of the sharp-pointed hairs of a nettle; a stinging hair. **6** The point of an epigram. [OE *stingan*] — **sting′ing·ly** *adv.*

sting-and-ling (sting′ən·ling′) *adv. Scot.* As a whole: forcibly.

sting·a·ree (sting′ə·rē, sting′ə·rē′) *n.* A sting ray. [Alter. of STING RAY]

stinge (stinj) *v.i.* **stinged, stinge·ing** To act in a miserly, stingy way. [Back formation <STINGY]

sting·er (sting′ər) *n.* **1** One who or that which stings. **2** A plant or animal that stings. **3** An insect's sting. **4** A cocktail made of brandy and white crème de menthe.

stinging hair *Bot.* One of the hairs of a nettle, charged at the base with an irritating fluid which is injected beneath the skin when touched.

stin·go (sting′gō) *n. Brit. Slang* **1** A strong ale or beer. **2** Zest; vim. [<STING; from the sharpness of the taste]

sting ray One of the various flat-bodied selachian fishes (*Dasyatis* and related genera) with broad pectoral fins and a whiplike tail having one or more stinging spines which are capable of inflicting severe, often poisoned, wounds. Also called *stingaree.*

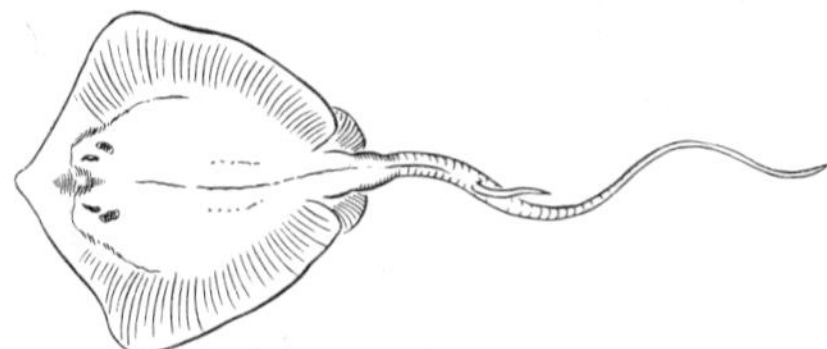

STING RAY
(Body about 20 inches in length; the stinger, 8 to 15 inches)

stin·gy[1] (stin′jē) *adj.* **·gi·er, ·gi·est** **1** Extremely penurious or selfish; miserly. **2** Scanty, as from penurious giving. See synonyms under AVARICIOUS. [<dial. E *stinge* a sting] — **stin′gi·ly** *adv.* — **stin′gi·ness** *n.*

sting·y[2] (sting′ē) *adj. Colloq.* Stinging; piercing. — **sting′i·ly** *adv.*

stink (stingk) *n.* A strong, foul odor; stench. See synonyms under SMELL. — *v.* **stank** or **stunk, stunk, stink·ing** *v.i.* **1** To give forth a foul odor. **2** To be extremely offensive or hateful. — *v.t.* **3** To cause to stink. — **to stink out** To drive from a den, hideaway, etc., by a foul or suffocating odor. [OE *stincan* smell] — **stink′ing** *adj.* — **stink′ing·ly** *adv.*

stink·ard (stingk′ərd) *n.* **1** A mean, detestable fellow. **2** The dogfish.

stink·ball (stingk′bôl′) *n.* A jar containing a mixture of various compounds, as gunpowder, asafetida, etc., formerly used for throwing from one warship to another when at close quarters: also called *stinkpot.* Also **stink′bomb′** (-bom′).

stink·bug (stingk′bug′) *n.* Any of a family (*Pentatomidae*) of hemipterous insects, including mostly rather large, broad, flattened bugs which emit a sickening, sweetish odor when disturbed.

stink·er (stingk′ər) *n.* **1** One who or that which stinks, as a stinkball. **2** The fulmar or other petrel that feeds on carrion. **3** *Slang* An unpleasant, disgusting, or irritating person.

stink·horn (stingk′hôrn′) *n.* Any of an order (*Phallales*) of basidiomycetous, ill-smelling fungi, especially the carrion fungus (*Ithyphallus impudicus*).

stinking hellebore Helleboraster.

stinking smut The bunt disease of wheat.

stink·pot (stingk′pot′) *n.* **1** A stinkball. **2** The musk turtle.

stink·stone (stingk′stōn′) *n.* Any kind of rock that gives off a fetid odor under percussion, as certain limestones.

stink·weed (stingk′wēd′) *n.* The jimsonweed or stramonium.

stink·wood (stingk′wŏŏd′) *n.* **1** Any of various trees having wood of a disagreeable odor. **2** The wood.

Stin·nes (shtin′əs), **Hugo,** 1870–1924, German industrialist.

stint (stint) *v.t.* **1** To limit, as in amount or share; be stingy with: Don't *stint* yourself. **2** *Archaic* To stop. — *v.i.* **3** To be frugal or sparing. **4** *Archaic* To stop. — *n.* **1** A fixed amount, as of work; a task to be performed within a specified time; allowance. **2** A bound; restriction. **3** A small sandpiper. **4** *Obs.* A cessation. See synonyms under TASK, TOIL[1]. [ME *stynten* cause to stop <OE *styntan* stupefy < *stunt* stupid] — **stint′er** *n.* — **stint′ing** *adj.* — **stint′ing·ly** *adv.*

stipe (stīp) *n.* **1** *Zool.* A stalk or support. **2** *Bot.* **a** A stalklike support of a gynoecium or carpel. **b** The petiole or support of a fern's frond. **c** The stem supporting the cap of a mushroom or similar fungus. See illustration under MUSHROOM. [<F <L *stipes* branch]

sti·pel (stī′pəl) *n. Bot.* A secondary or small stipule standing at the base of a leaflet. [<NL *stipella,* dim. of *stipes* a branch] — **sti·pel·late** (stī·pel′it, stī′pəl·it, -āt) *adj.*

sti·pend (stī′pend) *n.* **1** An allowance or salary; a fixed payment for services, especially a salary that affords a bare livelihood. **2** *Scot.* A clergyman's salary. **3** *Eccl.* In the Roman Catholic Church, an offering given to a priest for saying a mass with a special intention. See synonyms under SALARY. [<L *stipendium* tax, tribute < *stips* coin, payment in coin + *pendere* weigh, pay out]

sti·pen·di·ar·y (stī·pen′dē·er′ē) *adj.* **1** Receiving a stipend. **2** Paying tribute; owing feudal service; performing services for a fixed payment. — *n. pl.* **·ar·ies** **1** One who receives a stipend, as a clergyman. **2** A person owing feudal service. **3** A province paying a special tribute to a Roman emperor, instead of a tax. [<L *stipendiarius* < *stipendium* STIPEND]

sti·pes (stī′pēz) *n.* **1** A stipe. **2** *Entomol.* The subbasal, central, and usually the largest part of an insect's maxilla. [<L] — **sti′pi·form** (-pə·fôrm), **stip·i·ti·form** (stip′ə·tə·fôrm′) *adj.*

stip·i·tate (stip′ə·tāt) *adj.* Having or borne on a stipe; stalked. [<NL *stipitatus* <L *stipes* stock]

stip·ple (stip′əl) *v.t.* **·pled, ·pling** To draw, paint, or engrave with dots or short touches instead of lines, so as to produce a shaded effect. — *n.* In painting, etching, etc., a method of representing light and shade by employing dots instead of lines, or the effect thus produced: also **stip′pling.** [<Du. *stippelen* < *stippen* speckle < *stip* dot] — **stip′pler** *n.*

stip·u·lar (stip′yə·lər) *adj. Bot.* **1** Growing on stipules. **2** Of, resembling, or pertaining to stalks or stems.

stip·u·late[1] (stip′yə·lāt) *v.* **·lat·ed, ·lat·ing** *v.t.* **1** To specify as the terms of an agreement, contract, etc. **2** To specify as a requirement or condition for agreement. **3** To promise; guarantee. — *v.i.* **4** To demand something as a requirement or condition: with *for.* **5** To make an agreement. [<L *stipulatus,* pp. of *stipulari* bargain] — **stip′u·la′tor** *n.*

stip·u·late[2] (stip′yə·lit, -lāt) *adj.* Furnished with stipules. Also **stip′u·lat′ed** (-lā′tid).

stip·u·la·tion (stip′yə·lā′shən) *n.* **1** The act of stipulating, or the condition of being stipulated. **2** An agreement or contract. See synonyms under CONTRACT. — **stip′u·la·to′ry** (-lə·tôr′ē, -tō′rē) *adj.*

stip·ule (stip′yōōl) *n. Bot.* One of a pair of leaflike appendages at the base of the petiole of certain leaves. [<L *stipula* stalk]

stir[1] (stûr) *v.* **stirred, stir·ring** *v.t.* **1** To agitate so as to alter the relative position of the particles or components of, as soup with a spoon. **2** To cause to move, especially slightly or irregularly; disturb: The tide *stirred* the boat. **3** To move vigorously; bestir: *Stir* yourself! **4** To rouse, as from sleep, indifference, or inactivity; stimulate. **5** To incite; provoke: often with *up.* **6** To affect strongly; move with emotion. — *v.i.* **7** To move, especially slightly: The log wouldn't *stir.* **8** To be active; move about: They heard him *stirring* in his room. **9** To take place; happen. **10** To undergo stirring: This molasses *stirs* easily. — *n.* **1** The act of stirring, or state of being stirred; activity. **2** Public interest; excitement; to-do; commotion. **3** A poke; nudge. [OE *styrian*] — **stir′rer** *n.*

Synonyms (verb): agitate, animate, arouse, awake, awaken, excite, incite, instigate, move, prompt, provoke, rouse, stimulate, wake. See ACTUATE, INFLUENCE, SPUR. *Antonyms:* see synonyms for ALLAY, ALLEVIATE.

stir[2] (stûr) *n. Slang* A jail; prison. [Origin uncertain]

stir·a·bout (stûr′ə·bout′) *n. Brit.* A porridge made of oatmeal or cornmeal stirred in boiling milk or water; a hasty pudding.

stirk (stûrk) *n.* **1** A yearling ox or cow. **2** *Scot.* A stupid fellow. [OE *stirc* calf < *stēor* steer]

Stir·ling (stûr′ling) A county in central Scotland; 451 square miles; county town, Stirling. Also **Stir′ling·shire** (-shir).

stir·pi·cul·ture (stûr′pə·kul′chər) *n.* The breeding of special races or strains of animals and plants. [<L *stirps, stirpis* stem, stock + CULTURE] — **stir′pi·cul′tur·al** *adj.* — **stir′pi·cul′tur·ist** *n.*

stirps (stûrps) *n. pl.* **stir·pes** (stûr′pēz) **1** Race; family. **2** A stock as regards lineage: a source of property-descent: Descent per *stirpes* (as a family) is distinguished from descent per capita (as an individual). **3** *Biol.* The number of organic units existing in and determining the development of a fertilized ovum. [<L]

stir·ring (stûr′ing) *adj.* **1** Stimulating; inspiring. **2** Full of activity or stir; lively. See synonyms under VIVID. — **stir′ring·ly** *adv.*

stir·rup (stûr′əp, stir′-) *n.* **1** A loop, as an inverted U-shaped piece of metal or wood with flat footpiece, suspended from a saddle to support the rider's foot in and after mounting. **2** A loop or metal strap, as for supporting a beam. **3** *Naut.* A rope on a ship depending from a yard and having at its end an eye or thimble to carry a footrope. [OE *stigrāp* mounting rope]

stirrup bone *Anat.* The stapes.

stir·rup-cup (stûr′əp·kup′, stir′-) *n.* A cup of liquor, as that taken by a mounted horseman on departing; hence, a farewell drink.

stirrup leather The strap by which the stirrup iron is hung from the saddle. Also **stirrup strap.**

stitch[1] (stich) *n.* **1** A single passage of a threaded needle or other implement through fabric and back again, as in sewing or embroidery, or, in surgery, through skin or flesh. **2** A single turn of thread or yarn around a needle or other implement, as in knitting or crocheting; also, the link or loop resulting from such a turn. **3** Any peculiar or individual arrangement of a thread or threads used in sewing, embroidery, or crocheting: a chain *stitch.* **4** A sharp sudden pain, especially in the back or side. **5** A ridge between two furrows. **6** *Colloq.* A garment: I haven't a *stitch* to wear. — **to be in stitches** *Colloq.* To laugh uproariously; be overcome with laughter. — *v.t.* **1** To join together with stitches. **2** To ornament with stitches. — *v.i.* **3** To make stitches; sew. [OE *stice* prick, stab]

stitch[2] (stich) *n. Brit. Dial.* **1** A space passed over; a span of time; distance. **2** A fragment. [OE *stycce* piece]

stitch·er (stich′ər) *n.* One who or that which stitches; especially, a machine for that purpose, as in bookbinding.

stitch·wort (stich′wûrt′) *n.* Any of various plants (genus *Stellaria*), especially the common chickweed: also called *starwort, stichwort.* [OE *sticwyrt* < *stice* prick + *wyrt* plant]

stith·y (stith′ē, stith′ē) *n. pl.* **stith·ies** **1** A smithy or forge. **2** An anvil. — *v.t.* **stith·ied, stith·y·ing** *Archaic* To forge on an anvil. [<ON *stedhi*]

stive (stīv) *v.t. Obs.* To stow closely; cram; stifle. [<OF *estiver* <L *stipare* crowd]

sti·ver (stī′vər) *n.* **1** A small Dutch coin, 1/20 of a guilder. **2** Anything of little value. [<Du. *stuiver*]

St. James's Palace (sānt jām′ziz) The Tudor palace in Pall Mall, London, residence of the British sovereigns from Henry VIII to the accession of Victoria: the British royal court is still called the **Court of Saint James's.**

St. John (sānt jon′) **1** One of the Virgin Islands of the United States; 19 square miles. **2** A port on the Bay of Fundy, in southern New Brunswick, Canada. **3** St. John's, Leeward Islands.

St. John (sānt jon′, sin′jən), **Henry** See BOLINGBROKE.

St. John, Lake A lake in south central Quebec, Canada; 375 square miles.

St. John River A river flowing 400 miles NE and east through northern Maine and western New Brunswick to the Bay of Fundy, forming part of the boundary between Maine and New Brunswick.

St. John's (jonz) **1** The capital and largest city of Newfoundland, a port on the SE coast. **2** The capital of Antigua, The West Indies (federation), and former administrative capital of the Leeward Islands.

St. John's bread See CAROB.

St. Johns River A river in NE Florida, flowing 285 miles north and east to the Atlantic.

St. Johns·wort (sānt jonz′wûrt′) Any of a genus *(Hypericum)* of hardy perennial shrubs and herbs, with deep-yellow flowers: found in dry fields. Also **St.-John's-wort.**

St. Jo·seph (sānt jō′zif) A city in NW Missouri on the Missouri River.

St. Kitts (sānt kits′) See ST. CHRISTOPHER, NEVIS, AND ANGUILLA.

St. Lau·rent (san lô·rän′), **Louis,** born 1882, Canadian prime minister 1948–57.

St. Law·rence Island (sānt lôr′əns, lor′-) An island of western Alaska in the Bering Sea; 90 miles long, 8 to 22 miles wide.

St. Lawrence River A river of SE Canada, the outlet of the Great Lakes system, flowing 744 miles NE from the NE end of Lake Ontario to the **Gulf of St. Lawrence,** an inlet of the North Atlantic between Newfoundland and eastern Canada; together with the Great Lakes and the St. Marys River it forms a waterway about 2,350 miles long, from the western end of Lake Superior to the Atlantic.

St. Lou·is (sānt lo͞o′is, lo͞o′ē) A city in eastern Missouri, on the Mississippi River below the influx of the Missouri; a major center of transportation, industry, and commerce.

St. Lu·ci·a (sānt lo͞o′shē·ə, lo͞o·sē′ə, lo͞o′shə) A British colony in the Windward Islands, a federating unit of The West Indies (federation); 233 square miles; capital, Castries.

St. Mar·tin (sānt mär′tin) An island in the NW Leeward Islands; the southern part, *Dutch* **Sint Maar·ten** (sint mär′tən), 13 square miles, in the Netherlands Antilles; the northern part, *French* **Saint-Mar·tin** (san·mär·tan′), 20 square miles, a dependency of Guadeloupe; total 33 square miles.

St. Mar·y·le·bone (sānt mâr′ē·lə·bōn′) See MARYLEBONE.

St. Mar·ys River (sānt mâr′ēz) **1** A river flowing 63 miles SE from Lake Superior to Lake Huron and forming the boundary between northern Michigan and Ontario. **2** A river in SE Georgia and NE Florida, flowing 175 miles south, east, and north from the Okefinokee Swamp to the Atlantic, and forming part of the Georgia-Florida border.

St. Mau·rice River (sānt môr′is, mor′is; *Fr.* san mô·rēs′) A river in Quebec province, Canada, flowing 325 miles SE and south to the St. Lawrence.

St. Mo·ritz (sānt môr′its, mō′rits) A resort town in SE Switzerland; elevation, 6,080 feet: German *Sankt Moritz. French* **Saint-Mo·ritz** (san·mô·rēts′).

sto·a (stō′ə) *n. pl.* **sto·ae** (stō′ē) or **sto·as** In Greek architecture, a covered colonnade, portico, cloister, or promenade. [<Gk., porch]

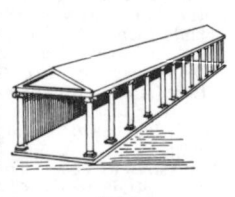

STOA

stoat¹ (stōt) *n.* The ermine, especially in its summer coat, red-brown above, yellow below. [ME *stote*; origin uncertain]

stoat² (stōt) *v.t.* To sew with an invisible stitch that passes only half-way through the cloth. [Origin unknown] — **stoat′ing** *n.*

stob (stob) *Dial. n.* A stake or post, usually short; also, the stump of a tree. — *v.t.* To stab. [Var. of STUB]

stoc·ca·do (stə·kä′dō, -kä′-) *n. Archaic* A stabbing or thrusting movement with a rapier. Also **stoc·ca′ta** (-tə). [<Ital. *stoccata* < *stocco* rapier]

sto·chas·tic (stō·kas′tik) *adj.* **1** Of, pertaining to, characterized by, or skilled in conjecture; conjectural. **2** *Physics* Subject to the laws of probability; not predictable within a given time limit or spatial framework, as the disintegration of a single radioactive element: the *stochastic* phenomena of microphysics. **3** Denoting the process of selecting, from among a group of theoretically possible alternatives, those elements or factors whose combination will most closely approximate a desired result: a *stochastic* model. [<Gk. *stochastikos* < *stochazesthai* guess at < *stochos* mark, aim]

stock (stok) *n.* **1** The trunk or main stem of a tree or other plant, as distinguished from a branch or root. **2** A line of familial descent. **3** The original progenitor of a family line. **4** An ethnic group; race. **5** *Ling.* A family of languages. **6** A related group or family of plants or animals. **7** *Bot.* **a** A rhizome. **b** A stem upon which a graft is made. **8** *Zool.* A zooid which reproduces by generation. **9** Livestock: in Australia, cattle, not livestock in general. **10** A quantity of something acquired or kept for future use: to lay in a *stock* of provisions. **11** The merchandise or goods which a trader or merchant has on hand. **12** In card games and dominoes, the part of the pack or group of dominoes that is left on the table and drawn from. **13** The broth from boiled meat or fish used in preparing soups, etc. **14** Raw material: paper *stock.* **15** *pl.* A timber frame with holes for confining the ankles and often the wrists, formerly used in punishing petty offenders. **16** *pl.* The timber frame on which a vessel rests during construction. **17** *pl.* A frame for confining an animal for shoeing or veterinary treatment. **18** *Naut.* An anchor crossbar. **19** The wooden block suspending a bell. **20** In firearms: **a** The rear wooden portion of a rifle, musket, or shotgun, to which the barrel and mechanisms are secured. **b** The arm on rapid-fire guns connecting the shoulder piece to the slide. **c** The handle of a pistol or similar firearm. **d** That member of a gun carriage which usually bears the prolonge and trails along the ground. **21** The handle of certain instruments, as of a whip or fishing rod. **22** A theatrical stock company. **23** The collection of dramas produced by a theatrical stock company. **24** A broad stiffened band, formerly worn as a cravat. **25** *Geol.* The rounded mass of plutonic rock rising above ground level: also called *boss.* **26** *Mech.* An adjustable wrench used for grasping and turning thread-cutting dies. **27** An ornamental garden plant, as the gilliflower, or common stock *(Mathiola incana).* **28** In finance: **a** The capital or fund raised by a corporation through the sale of shares, which entitle the holder to interest or dividends and to part ownership of the corporation. The stockholder may not claim repayment of the principal, though he may sell his shares to other investors at the current market value. **b** The proportional part of this capital credited to an individual stockholder and represented by the number of shares he owns. **c** A certificate showing ownership of a specific number of shares. — **common stock** The stock of a corporation which entitles the holder to dividends, or a share in the profits, only after all other obligations have been met and dividends have been rendered to the owners of preferred stock. Direction of a corporation is usually vested in the owners of common stock. — **debenture stock** *Brit.* A debenture of a corporation or public body issued in the form of stock, the certificates of which are usually transferable but not redeemable and entitle the holder to a perpetual annuity. — **no-par stock** Stock issued without a face value on the certificate and sold at whatever price it will command on the market. — **preferred stock** The stock of a corporation which gives the holder prior claim to dividends up to a certain amount. — **to take stock 1** To take an inventory. **2** To make a careful estimate or appraisal. — **to take stock in** To have trust or belief in; give credence to. — *v.t.* **1** To furnish with stock; supply with cattle, as a farm, or with merchandise, as a store. **2** To keep for sale: to *stock* black ink. **3** To put aside for future use. **4** To provide with a handle or stock. **5** *Obs.* To put (a person) in the stocks for punishment. — *v.i.* **6** To lay in supplies or stock: often with *up.* **7** To send out new shoots; sprout. — *adj.* **1** Kept continually ready or constantly brought forth, like old goods: a *stock* joke. **2** Kept on hand: a *stock* size. **3** Banal; commonplace: a *stock* phrase. **4** Used for breeding purposes: a *stock* mare. **5** Employed in handling or caring for the stock: a *stock* clerk. — *adv.* Motionlessly; like a stump or block of wood: used in combination: *stockstill.* [OE *stocc*]
Synonyms (noun): accumulation, capital, fund, hoard, material, provision, store, supply. See STICK.

stock·ade (sto·kād′) *n.* **1** A line of stout posts, stakes, etc., set upright in the earth to form a fence or barrier; also, the area thus enclosed. **2** Specifically, a strong, high barrier of upright posts, stakes, etc., formerly used by American settlers as a defense against Indians. **3** A breakwater of piling, as for protecting a pier. — *v.t.* **·ad·ed, ·ad·ing** To surround or fortify with a stockade. [<OF *estocade, estacade* < *estaque* a stake <Gmc.]

stock·breed·er (stok′brē′dər) *n.* One who breeds and raises livestock.

stock·breed·ing (stok′brē′ding) *n.* The breeding and raising of livestock.

stock·bro·ker (stok′brō′kər) *n.* One who buys and sells stocks or securities for others. — **stock′bro′ker·age, stock′bro′king** *n.*

stock car 1 An automobile, as one selected at random, typifying the regular factory stock. **2** Such an automobile, usually a sedan, modified for racing.

stock company 1 An incorporated company that issues stock. **2** A more or less permanent dramatic company under one management, which presents a series of theater pieces.

stock dove (duv) The common wild pigeon of Europe *(Columba oenas).*

stock exchange 1 A place where securities are bought and sold. **2** An association of stockbrokers who transact business in stocks, bonds, and other shares.

stock farm A farm which specializes in the breeding of livestock.

stock fish Cod, haddock, or the like, cured by splitting and drying in the air, unsalted.

stock·hold·er (stok′hōl′dər) *n.* One who holds certificates of ownership in a company or corporation.

Stock·holm (stok′hōm, *Sw.* stôk′hôlm) The capital of Sweden, a port on the east coast, on the Baltic Sea; called "the Venice of the North" because of its waterways.

stock·i·net (stok′i·net′) *n.* **1** An elastic knitted fabric used chiefly for undergarments. **2** A style of knitting in which the rows are alternately knitted and purled: also **stockinet stitch.** Also **stock′i·nette′.** [Alter. of *stockinget* <STOCKING + -ET]

stock·ing (stok′ing) *n.* **1** A close-fitting woven or knitted covering for the foot and lower leg. **2** Something resembling such a covering. [<STOCK, in obs. sense of "a stocking" + -ING³] — **stock′ing·less** *adj.*

stock in trade 1 The goods which a storekeeper has for sale. **2** Resources, either material or spiritual.

stock·ish (stok′ish) *adj.* Like a stock or block of wood; stupid.

stock·job·ber (stok′job′ər) *n.* A dealer or speculator in stocks in his own interest; also, a stockbroker. — **stock′job′ber·y, stock′job′·bing** *n.*

stock·man (stok′mən) *n. pl.* **·men** (-mən) **1** A man having charge of stock. **2** One who raises or owns livestock; a cattleman.

stock market 1 A stock exchange. **2** The business transacted in such a place: The *stock market* was active. **3** The rise and fall of prices of securities.

stock·pile (stok′pīl′) *n.* A storage pile of materials or supplies. Also **stock pile.** — *v.t.* & *v.i.* **·piled, ·pil·ing** To accumulate a supply or stockpile (of).

Stock·port (stok′pôrt, -pōrt) A county borough of NE Cheshire, England.

stock·pot (stok′pot′) *n.* A pot for preparing and keeping soup stock.

stock-rais·ing (stok′rā′zing) *n.* Breeding and raising of livestock. — **stock′-rais′er** *n.*

stock·room (stok′ro͞om′, -ro͝om′) *n.* A room where reserve stocks of goods are stored.

stock route *Austral.* A road or track used only for livestock drives.

stock·still (stok′stil′) *adj.* Still as a stock or post; motionless.

Stock·ton (stok′tən), **Frank,** 1834–1902, U.S. author; full name Francis Richard Stockton. —**Richard,** 1730–81, American statesman; signer of the Declaration of Independence.

Stock·ton–on–Tees (stok′tən·on·tēz′) A port and borough in SE Durham, England.

stock·whip (stock′wip′) *Austral.* A whip used by stockmen, usually of kangaroo hide with a seven- to eight-foot lash and a cord or horsehair cracker.

stock·work (stok′wûrk′) *n. Geol.* An irregular mass of rock interlaced by a network of small ore-bearing veins.

stock·y (stok′ē) *adj.* **stock·i·er, stock·i·est** Short and stout; thick-set. —**stock′i·ly** *adv.* —**stock′·i·ness** *n.*

stock·yard (stok′yärd′) *n.* A large yard with pens, stables, etc., where cattle are kept ready for shipping, slaughter, etc.

stodge (stoj) *v.* **stodged, stodg·ing** *v.t.* To render dull and heavy by stuffing with food. —*v.i.* To become muddy or marshy. [<dial. E *stodge* fill to distention]

stodg·y (stoj′ē) *adj.* **stodg·i·er, stodg·i·est 1** Distended; crammed full; bulky; lumpy. **2** Stupid; dull; heavy. **3** Indigestible; satiating. **4** Sticky; muddy. **5** Thick-set; clumsy and stiff. —**stodg′i·ly** *adv.* —**stodg′i·ness** *n.*

sto·gy (stō′gē) *n. pl.* **·gies 1** A stout, coarse boot or shoe. **2** A long, slender, inexpensive cigar: also **sto′gie.** [Earlier *stoga* <(CONE)-STOGA (WAGON), because their drivers wore heavy boots and smoked coarse cigars]

sto·ic (stō′ik) *n.* A person apparently unaffected by pleasure or pain. —*adj.* Indifferent to pleasure or pain; impassive; uncomplaining. Also **sto′i·cal.** —**sto′i·cal·ly** *adv.* —**sto′i·cal·ness** *n.*

Sto·ic (stō′ik) *n.* A member of a school of Greek philosophy founded by Zeno about 308 B.C., holding the pantheistic beliefs that the world is a manifestation of a divine mind, that there is no reality but matter, even the human soul being doomed to dissolution, that wisdom lies in being superior to passion, joy, grief, etc., and in submission to the divine will. —*adj.* Of or pertaining to the Stoics or Stoicism. [<L *Stoicus* <Gk. *Stoikos* <*Stoa (Poikilē)* (Painted) Porch, the colonnade at Athens where Zeno taught]

stoi·chi·ol·o·gy (stoi′kē·ol′ə·jē) *n.* T Also **stoe′·chi·ol′o·gy, stoi′·chei·ol′o·gy.** [<Gk. *stoicheion* element + -LOGY] —**stoi′chi·o·log′·i·cal** (-ə·loj′i·kəl) *adj.*

stoi·chi·om·e·try (stoi′kē·om′ə·trē) *n.* The branch of chemistry that treats of the proportions of elements or compounds involved in reactions, and the methods of calculating them. Also **stoe′chi·om′e·try, stoi′chei·om′e·try.** [<Gk. *stoicheion* element + -METRY] —**stoi′chi·o·met′ric** (-ə·met′rik) or **·ri·cal** *adj.*

sto·i·cism (stō′ə·siz′əm) *n.* Indifference to pleasure or pain; stoicalness. See synonyms under APATHY.

Sto·i·cism (stō′ə·siz′əm) *n.* The doctrines of the Stoics.

stoit (stōt, stoit) *v.i. Scot. & Irish* **1** To walk in a reeling, stumbling manner: also **stoit′er, stoit′ur. 2** To rebound; bounce. **3** To leap from the water: said of certain fish.

stoke[1] (stōk) *v.t. & v.i.* **stoked, stok·ing** To supply (a furnace) with fuel; stir up or tend (a fire or furnace). [Back formation <STOKER]

stoke[2] (stōk) *n. Physics* A unit of kinematic viscosity, equivalent to 1 poise in a fluid having a density of 1 gram per cubic centimeter referred to a specified temperature. [after Sir George G. *Stokes,* 1819–1903, English mathematician and physicist]

stoke·hold (stōk′hōld′) *n. Naut.* **1** The furnace room of a steamer. **2** The space in front of the furnaces from which they are stoked.

stoke·hole (stōk′hōl′) *n.* **1** The space about the mouth of a furnace; the fireroom. **2** The mouth of a furnace. **3** A stokehold.

Stoke–on–Trent (stōk′on·trent′) A county borough in NW Stafford, England. Also **Stoke′–up·on′–Trent′.**

Stoke Po·ges (pō′jis) A village in SE Buckingham, England; generally regarded as the scene of Gray's *Elegy.*

stok·er (stō′kər) *n.* **1** One who or that which supplies fuel to a furnace, especially of a steam boiler, as in a ship or locomotive; a fireman on a locomotive, ship, etc. **2** A device for feeding coal to a furnace. [<Du. < *stoken* stir a fire <*stok* stick]

Stokes mortar A light, muzzleloading mortar for high-angle, short-range fire. [after Sir Frederick W. S. *Stokes,* 1860–1927, English inventor]

Sto·kow·ski (stə·kôf′skē, -kou′skē), **Leopold,** 1882–1977, U.S. orchestra conductor born in England.

stole[1] (stōl) *n.* **1** *Eccl.* A long, narrow band, usually of decorated silk or linen, worn about the shoulders by priests and bishops, and over the left shoulder only by deacons, when officiating; loosely, any ecclesiastical vestment. **2** A fur, scarf, or garment resembling a stole, worn by women. **3** In ancient Rome, a long outer garment worn by matrons. [OE <L *stola* a robe <Gk. *stolē* a garment] —**stoled** *adj.*

stole[2] (stōl) Past tense of STEAL.

sto·len (stō′lən) Past participle of STEAL.

stol·id (stol′id) *adj.* Having or expressing no power of feeling or perceiving; impassible; dull. See synonyms under BRUTISH, HEAVY. [<L *stolidus* dull]—**sto·lid·i·ty** (stə·lid′ə·tē), **stol′id·ness** *n.* —**stol′id·ly** *adv.*

sto·lon (stō′lon) *n.* **1** *Bot.* **a** A trailing branch that is capable of taking root. **b** A runner or rootstock by which grasses may propagate. **2** *Zool.* A prolongation of the body of various animals, as corals. [<NL <L *stolo, stolonis*]

sto·ma (stō′mə) *n. pl.* **sto·ma·ta** (stō′mə·tə, stom′ə·tə) **1** A minute orifice; pore. **2** *Biol.* An aperture in the walls of blood vessels or in serous membranes, or in the epidermis of leaves, young stems, etc. [<Gk. *stoma* mouth]

–stoma See -STOME.

stom·ach (stum′ək) *n.* **1** The pouchlike, highly vascular dilation of the alimentary canal, situated in most vertebrates between the esophagus and the small intestine, and serving as one of the principal organs of digestion. ◆ Collateral adjective: *gastric.* **2** Any digestive cavity, as of an invertebrate. **3** The abdomen; belly: an anatomically incorrect use. **4** Desire for food; appetite; hence, any desire or inclination. **5** Temper; spirit. **6** *Obs.* Pride; haughtiness. —*v.t.* **1** To accept without apparent opposition; to put up with; endure. **2** To take into and retain in the stomach; digest. **3** *Obs.* To resent. [<OF *estomac* <L *stomachus* <Gk. *stomachos* gullet, stomach < *stoma* a mouth]

stomach ache Pain in the stomach, as from indigestion or inflammation.

stom·ach·er (stum′ək·ər) *n.* A former ornamental article of dress for the breast and stomach.

sto·mach·ic (stō·mak′ik) *adj.* **1** Pertaining to the stomach. **2** Strengthening the activity of the stomach. Also **stom·ach·al** (stum′ək·əl), **sto·mach′i·cal.** —*n.* Any medicine strengthening or stimulating the stomach.

stomach tooth *Dent.* A lower canine tooth of the first dentition: so called because its emergence is frequently accompanied by digestive disturbances.

stomach worm Any of various nematode worms which are parasitic in the stomachs of man and animals, especially the sheep stomach worm *(Haemonchus contortus).*

stom·ach·y (stum′ək·ē) *adj.* **1** Having a paunch. **2** *Brit. Dial.* Spirited; haughty; proud; also, choleric; resentful.

sto·ma·ta (stō′mə·tə, stom′ə·tə) Plural of STOMA.

sto·ma·tal (stō′mə·təl, stom′ə-) *adj.* Of or pertaining to stomata.

sto·mat·ic (stō·mat′ik) *adj.* **1** Of or pertaining to the mouth. **2** Of, pertaining to, or like a stoma.

sto·ma·tif·er·ous (stō′mə·tif′ər·əs, stom′ə-) *adj.* Bearing stomata. [<STOMAT(O)- + -(I)FEROUS]

sto·ma·ti·tis (stō′mə·tī′tis, stom′ə-) *n. Pathol.* Inflammation of the mouth.

stomato– *combining form* The mouth; of or pertaining to the mouth: *stomatoplasty.* Also, before vowels, **stomat–.** [<Gk. *stoma, stomatos* the mouth]

sto·ma·tol·o·gy (stō′mə·tol′ə·jē, stom′ə-) *n.* The science treating of the mouth and of its diseases.

sto·ma·to·plas·ty (stō′mə·tə·plas′tē, stom′ə-) *n.* Plastic surgery of the mouth.

sto·ma·to·pod (stō′mə·tə·pod′, stom′ə-) *n.* Any of an order *(Stomatopoda)* of crustaceans having abdominal gills and legs near the mouth, including the squills. —**sto′ma·top′o·dous** (-top′ə·dəs) *adj.*

sto·ma·tous (stō′mə·təs, stom′ə-) *adj.* Having a stoma or stomata.

–stome *combining form* Mouth; mouthlike opening: *peristome.* Also spelled *-stoma.* [< Gk. *stoma* the mouth]

sto·mo·de·um (stō′mə·dē′əm, stom′ə-) *n. pl.* **·de·a** (-dē′ə) *Biol.* The invagination of the ectoderm, or outer layer of the embryo, that forms the mouth. Also **sto′mo·dae′um.** [<NL <Gk. *stoma* mouth + *hodaios* on the way < *hodos* way] —**sto′mo·de′al** or **·dae′al** *adj.*

–stomous *combining form* Having a (specified kind of) mouth: *microstomous.* Also **–stomatous.** [<Gk. *stoma, stomatos* the mouth]

stomp (stomp) *Dial. v.t. & v.i.* To stamp; tread heavily (upon). —*n.* A dance involving a heavy and lively step. [Var. of STAMP]

–stomy *combining form Surg.* An operation to form an artificial opening for or into (a specified organ or part): *colostomy, ileostomy.* [< Gk. *stoma* the mouth]

stone (stōn) *n.* **1** A small piece of rock, as a cobble or pebble. **2** Rock, or a piece of rock hewn or shaped; a milestone; a gravestone; hard, concreted mineral or earthy matter. **3** A precious stone; gem. **4** Anything resembling a stone in shape or hardness: a *hailstone.* **5** *Pathol.* A stony concretion in the bladder, or a disease characterized by such concretions. **6** *Bot.* The hard covering of the kernel in a fruit. **7** *(pl.* **stone)** *Brit.* A measure of weight, avoirdupois, usually 14 pounds. **8** A testicle: usually in the plural. **9** *Printing* An imposing table for type, whether made of stone or metal. —*adj.* **1** Made of stone: a *stone* ax. **2** Made of coarse hard earthenware: a *stone* bottle. **3** Characterized by the use of stone implements: the *Stone* Age. —*v.t.* **stoned, ston·ing 1** To hurl stones at; pelt or kill with stones. **2** To remove the stones or pits from. **3** To furnish or line, as a well, with stone. **4** To castrate; geld, as a hog. **5** *Obs.* To make hard or unyielding, as the heart. [OE *stān*] —**ston′er** *n.*

Stone (stōn), **Harlan Fiske,** 1872–1946, U.S. educator; Supreme Court justice 1941–46. —**Lucy,** 1818–93, U.S. suffragist: wife of *Henry Broun Blackwell.*

Stone Age The earliest known period of the cultural evolution of mankind, marked by the creation and use of stone implements and weapons, preceding the Bronze Age, and subdivided into the Eolithic, Paleolithic, and Neolithic periods.

stone–blind (stōn′blīnd′) *adj.* Blind as a stone; totally blind.

stone·boat (stōn′bōt′) *n. U.S.* A runnerless plank sled used for transporting rocks or similar heavy objects or, when weighted, dragged across a field to break clods of earth, etc.; also, a platform swung under the axles of a wagon.

stone·break (stōn′brāk′) *n.* Saxifrage.

stone–broke (stōn′brōk′) *adj. Colloq.* Without any money; having no funds. Also **ston′y–broke′.**

stone·chat (stōn′chat′) *n.* A small thrushlike European bird (genus *Saxicola*) with upper parts black and breast dark-reddish. [< STONE + CHAT[1] (def. 2); from its cry suggesting the knocking together of pebbles]

stone coal Hard or anthracite coal.

stone color Bluish gray. —**stone′–col′ored** *adj.*

stone·crop (stōn′krop′) *n.* A low spreading mosslike herb *(Sedum acre)* with small fleshy leaves and yellow flowers.

stone·cut·ter (stōn′kut′ər) *n.* One who or that which cuts stone; specifically, a machine for facing stone. —**stone′cut′ting** *n.*

stoned (stōnd) *adj.* **1** Having the stones removed: *stoned* peaches. **2** *U.S. Slang* Intoxicated, as by liquor, marihuana, or a narcotic.

stone–deaf (stōn′def′) *adj.* Completely deaf.

stone fly A plecopteran.

stone fruit A fruit having a stone; a drupe.

Stone·henge (stōn′henj) A prehistoric megalithic structure on Salisbury Plain, SE Wiltshire, England. It consists primarily of circles of dressed stones, some with lintels, the main structure dating probably from 1500 B.C.

STONEHENGE

stone lily A fossil sea lily or other crinoid.
stone·ma·son (stōn′mā′sən) *n.* One whose occupation or trade is to prepare and lay stones in building. —**stone′ma′son·ry** *n.*
stone·mint (stōn′mint′) *n.* Dittany (def. 1).
Stone Mountain A granite dome (1,686 feet) of NW central Georgia; a Confederate monument is carved on one side.
stone parsley An Old World herb of the parsley family, especially a British perennial *(Sison amomum)* with cream–colored flowers and aromatic seeds.
stone roller 1 A cyprinoid fish *(Campostoma anomalum)* of North America. **2** A North American sucker *(Catastomus nigricans).*
Stones River A river of central Tennessee, flowing 39 miles NW to the Cumberland River; scene of a Union victory in the Civil War, 1862–63.
stone's throw (stōnz) **1** The distance a stone may be cast by hand. **2** A short distance.
stone·still (stōn′stil′) *adj.* Perfectly motionless.
stone·wall (stōn′wôl′) *v.i.* **1** In cricket, to play on the defensive so as to secure a draw. **2** *Austral.* To oppose by a policy of obstruction; filibuster: a political term. **3** *U.S. Slang* To act in a calculatedly obstructive way, as by lying or failing to respond to inquiry. —*v.t.* **4** *U.S. Slang* To respond to by stonewalling.
stone wall A wall built of stone; especially, a fence built of stones.
Stone·wall Jack·son (stōn′wôl′ jak′sən) See JACKSON, THOMAS JONATHAN.
stone·ware (stōn′wâr′) *n.* A variety of very hard, glazed pottery, made from siliceous clay or clay mixed with flint or sand.
stone·work (stōn′wûrk′) *n.* **1** Work concerned with cutting or setting stone; work made of stone. **2** *pl.* A place where stone is shaped or stoneware is made. —**stone′work′er** *n.*
stone·wort (stōn′wûrt′) *n.* Any of a genus *(Chara)* of green algae growing submerged in fresh or brackish waters and often incrusted with deposits of calcium carbonate.
ston·ish (ston′ish) *v.t. Obs.* To astonish. [Aphetic var. of ASTONISH] —**ston′ish·ment** *n.*
ston·y (stō′nē) *adj.* **ston·i·er, ston·i·est 1** Abounding in stone. **2** Made or consisting of stone. **3** Hard as stone; hence, unfeeling or inflexible. **4** Converting into stone; petrifying; cold and stiff. **5** *Slang* Stone–broke; having no money. —**ston′i·ly** *adv.* —**ston′i·ness** *n.*
stony coral A coral having a calcareous skeleton.
ston·y–heart·ed (stō′nē·här′tid) *adj.* Hard–hearted; unfeeling; pitiless.
Stony Point A village in SE New York; scene of an American victory in the Revolutionary War, July, 1779.
stood[1] (sto͝od) Past tense and past participle of STAND.
stood[2] (sto͝od) *Illit. & Dial.* Stayed: He should have *stood* in bed.
stooge (sto͞oj) *Colloq. n.* **1** An actor placed in the audience to heckle a comedian on the stage. **2** An actor who feeds lines to the principal comedian, acts as a foil for his jokes, etc. **3** Anyone who acts as or is the tool or dupe of another. —*v.i.* **stooged, stoog·ing** To act as a stooge: usually with *for.* [Origin unknown]
stook (sto͞ok, sto͝ok) *n.* A collection of sheaves set together in the field; a shock of corn. —*v.t.* To set up in stooks.[Cf. MLG *stuke* a bundle] —**stook′er** *n.*
stool (sto͞ol) *n.* **1** A backless and armless seat intended for one person. **2** A low bench or portable support for the feet or for the knees in kneeling. **3** A seat used in defecating; a privy. **4** The matter evacuated from the bowels. **5** *Bot.* **a** A plant from which young plants are produced, as from runners. **b** A stump or root of any kind from which suckers or sprouts shoot up. **c** The shoots from such a root or stump. **6** A decoy, as a bird or likeness of one. —*v.i.* **1** To send up shoots or suckers. **2** To decoy wild fowl with a stool or stools. **3** To void feces. **4** *U.S. Slang* To be a stool pigeon; inform. [OE *stōl*]
stool pigeon 1 A living or artificial pigeon attached to a stool or perch to decoy others. **2** Any decoy, as a person employed to decoy others into a gambling house, etc. **3** *U.S. Slang* An informer or spy, especially for the police.
stoop[1] (sto͞op) *v.i.* **1** To bend or lean the body forward and down; bow; crouch. **2** To stand or walk with the upper part of the body habitually bent forward; slouch. **3** To bend; lean; sink: said of trees, cliffs, etc. **4** To lower or degrade oneself; condescend; deign. **5** To pounce or swoop, as a hawk on prey. **6** *Obs.* To submit; yield. —*v.t.* **7** To bend (one's head, shoulders, etc.) forward. **8** *Obs.* To humble or subdue. See synonyms under BEND[1]. —*n.* **1** An act of stooping; a downward and forward bending of the body; also, a habitual forward inclination of the head and shoulders. **2** A decline from dignity or superiority. **3** A swoop, as of a bird of prey. [OE *stūpian*]
stoop[2] (sto͞op) *n. U.S.* **1** Originally, a platform at the door of a house approached by steps and having seats. **2** A small porch or platform at the entrance to a house. [<Du. *stoep*]
stoop[3] (sto͞op) *n. Brit. Dial.* A post set in the ground; a pillar. [<ON *stolpi*]
stoop[4] (sto͞op) See STOUP.
stop (stop) *v.* **stopped** or *(chiefly Poetic)* **stopt, stop·ping** *v.t.* **1** To bring (something in motion) to a halt; arrest the progress of: to *stop* an automobile. **2** To prevent the doing or completion of: to *stop* a revolution. **3** To prevent (a person) from doing something; restrain. **4** To keep back, withhold, or cut off, as wages or supplies. **5** To cease doing; desist from; discontinue: *Stop* that! **6** To intercept in transit, as a letter. **7** To block up, obstruct, or clog (a passage, road, etc.): often with *up.* **8** To fill in, cover over, or otherwise close, as a hole, cavity, etc. **9** To close (a bottle, barrel, etc.) with a cork, plug, or other stopper. **10** To stanch (a wound, etc.). **11** To order a bank not to pay or honor: to *stop* a check. **12** To defeat; also, to kill. **13** *Music* To press down (a string) on the fingerboard, or to close (a finger hole) in order to vary pitch. **14** To punctuate. **15** In boxing, etc., to parry. —*v.i.* **16** To come to a halt; cease progress or motion. **17** To cease doing something; pause or desist. **18** To come to an end. See synonyms under ABIDE, ARREST, CEASE, END, HINDER[1], OBSTRUCT, REST[1], SHUT, STAND, SUSPEND. —**to stop off** To stop for a brief stay before continuing on a trip or journey. —**to stop over** *Colloq.* **1** To stay at a place temporarily. **2** To interrupt a journey; make a stopover. —*n.* **1** The act of stopping, or the state of being stopped; a halt; pause; cessation; end. **2** That which stops or limits the range or time of a movement: a camera *stop*; an obstruction or obstacle; a hindrance. **3** *Music* The pressing down of a string or the closing of an aperture on a musical instrument, to change the pitch of the tone emitted; a key, lever, or handle for stopping a string or an aperture; a fret for a guitar. **4** *Music* In an organ, a set of pipes or reeds producing tones of the same quality, and arranged in regular musical progression. **5 a** *Brit.* A punctuation mark; a period. **b** In cables, etc., a period. **6** In joinery, a block, pin, or the like to check sliding motion, as of a drawer. **7** *Naut.* A small line for lashing or fastening anything temporarily on a ship. **8** *Phonet.* **a** Complete blockage of the breath stream (implosion), as with the lips or tongue, followed by a sudden release (explosion). **b** A consonant so produced; a plosive: opposed to *continuant.* The stops in English are the bilabials (p) and (b), the alveolars (t) and (d), and the velars (k) and (g); the nasals (m) and (n) may also be included in this category. **9** In dogs, the short incline between the forepart of the skull and the face. See illustration under DOG. **10** *pl.* A card game in which certain cards, called **stop cards,** terminate play when they appear: a variety of *newmarket.* [OE *-stoppian,* as in *forstoppian* stop up]
stop·cock (stop′kok′) *n.* A faucet or short pipe having a valve for stopping or regulating the passage of liquid, gas, etc.
stope (stōp) *Mining n.* An excavation from which the ore is removed, either above or below a level, in a series of steps. —*v.t. & v.i.* **stoped, stop·ing** To excavate in stopes. [Appar. related to STEP]
stop·gap (stop′gap′) *n.* That which stops a gap; also, an expedient.
stop key A key so made that when inserted in one side of a lock no key may be used on the other.
stop knob The knob by which a set of organ pipes is opened.
stop light 1 A red light on a traffic sign, directing a motorist or pedestrian to stop. **2** A red light on the rear of a motor vehicle which shines upon application of the brakes.
stop–loss (stop′lôs′, -los′) *adj.* Intended to prevent further loss, in a brokerage account, from falling prices on financial markets.
stop net A small net joined to a seine, to increase its length or prevent the escape of fish.
stop order An order to an agent or stockbroker to buy or sell a stock at the market only when it reaches a specified price.
stop·out (stop′out′) *n. U.S.* A student who interrupts his college education for a year in order to pursue some other activity.
stop·o·ver (stop′ō′vər) *adj.* Giving permission to stop over, as a railway ticket. —*n.* A stopover check, the act of stopping over, or permission to stop over, as from one train to a later train. Also **stop′– off′**.
stop·page (stop′ij) *n.* **1** The act of stopping or the state of being stopped. **2** A deduction from pay to repay something.
stop payment An order to a bank to refuse payment on a certain check.
stop·per (stop′ər) *n.* **1** One who or that which stops up or closes. **2** A plug or cork, as in a bottle. **3** In card games, as bridge, a card that can be used to stop an opponent's successful play of cards of one suit. —*v.t.* To secure or close with a stopper.
stop·ple (stop′əl) *n.* A stopper, plug, cork, or bung. —*v.t.* **·pled, ·pling** To close with or as with a stopple. [ME *stoppel,* prob. <*stoppen* stop]
stop sign A sign in a traffic system, instructing a pedestrian or vehicle to stop.
stop thrust In fencing, a slight thrust designed to frustrate the attack of an opponent.
stop·watch (stop′woch′) *n.* A watch which has a hand indicating fractions of a second and which may be stopped or started by the pressure of a spring: used for timing races, etc.
stop·way (stop′wā′) *n. Aeron.* An extension of an airfield runway to permit safe landing in the event of engine failure during take–off.
stor·age (stôr′ij, stō′rij) *n.* **1** The depositing of articles in a warehouse for safekeeping. **2** Space for storing goods. **3** A charge for storing. **4** A section of a computer in which data is held for later use; memory.

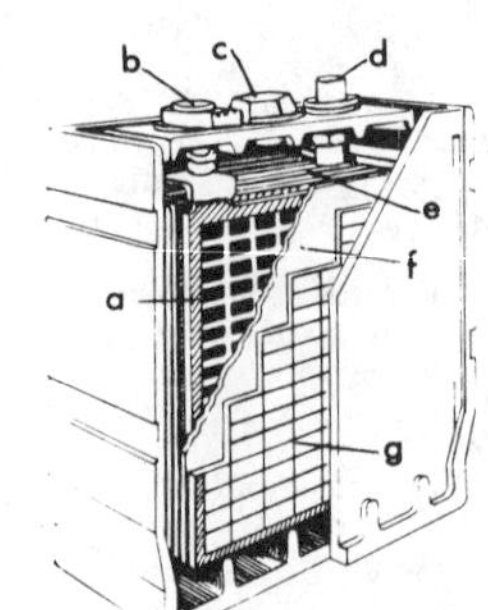

STORAGE BATTERY
a. Positive plate.
b. Positive terminal
c. Vent cap or plug
d. Negative terminal
e. Electrolyte space
f. Separator.
g. Negative plate.

storage battery A connected group of two or more electrolytic cells for the generation of electric energy by the passage of a current which, on being reversed in direction, serves to recharge the cells for another period of use.
sto·rax (stôr′aks, stō′raks) *n.* **1** A fragrant

balsam obtained from the wood and inner bark of either of two trees *(Liquidambar orientalis,* or *L. styraciflua)* of Asia Minor: used in medicine and as a perfume. **2** A gum resin obtained from certain trees of a family *(Styracaceae)*, especially *Styrax officinalis.* [<L <Gk. *styrax*]

store (stôr, stōr) *v.t.* **stored, stor·ing 1** To put away for future use; to accumulate. **2** To furnish or supply; provide. **3** To place in a warehouse or other place of deposit for safekeeping. — *n.* **1** That which is stored or laid up against future need; hence, a large amount at hand. **2** *pl.* Supplies, as of ammunition, arms, or clothing; necessary articles, especially of food. **3** A place where commodities are stored; warehouse. **4** *U.S.* A place where merchandise of any kind is kept for sale; a shop. See synonyms under HEAP, STOCK. — **department store** A large retail establishment selling various types of merchandise and service, and organized by departments. — **in store** Set apart for the future; forthcoming; impending. — **to set store by** To value or esteem; regard. [Aphetic var. of earlier *astore* <OF *estorer* erect, equip, store <L *instaurare* restore, erect]

store·house (stôr′hous′, stōr′-) *n.* A building in which goods are stored; a warehouse; depository.

store·keep·er (stôr′kē′pər, stōr′-) *n.* **1** A person who keeps a retail store or shop; a shopkeeper. **2** One who has charge of receiving and distributing stores; especially, one in charge of naval or military stores.

store·room (stôr′rōōm′, -rŏŏm′, stōr′-) *n.* A room in which things are stored, as supplies.

sto·rey (stôr′ē, stō′rē) See STORY².

sto·ried[1] (stôr′ēd, stō′rēd) *adj.* Having or consisting of stories, as a building: usually in compounds: a six-*storied* house. Also **sto′·reyed.**

sto·ried[2] (stôr′ēd, stō′rēd) *adj.* **1** Having a notable history. **2** Related in a story. **3** Ornamented with designs representing scenes from history or story.

sto·ri·ette (stôr′ē·et′, stō′rē-) *n.* A short story or tale.

stork (stôrk) *n.* A wading bird with a long neck and long legs (family *Ciconiidae*), related to the herons and ibises, especially the Old World **migratory** or **white stork** *(Ciconia ciconia)*, which often nests on buildings. [OE *storc*]

WHITE STORK
(About 20 inches tall)

stork's-bill (stôrks′bil′) *n.* **1** Heronbill. **2** Any species of pelargonium.

storm (stôrm) *n.* **1** A disturbance of the atmosphere, generally a great whirling motion of the air, accompanied by rain, snow, etc. **2** In the Beaufort scale, a wind force of the 11th degree. **3** Figuratively, a furious flight or shower of objects, especially of missiles. **4** A violent outburst, as of passion or excitement: a *storm* of applause or rage. **5** *Mil.* A violent and rapid assault on a fortified place. **6** A violent commotion, as in politics, society, or domestic life. — *v.i.* **1** To blow with violence; rain, snow, hail, etc., heavily: used impersonally: It *stormed* all day. **2** To be very angry; rage. **3** To move or rush with violence or rage: He *stormed* about the room. — *v.t.* **4** *Mil.* To take or try to take by storm. [OE]

Synonyms (noun): agitation, disturbance, tempest. A *storm* is properly a *disturbance* of the atmosphere, with or without rain, snow, hail, or thunder and lightning. Thus we have *rainstorm, snowstorm,* etc., and by extension, magnetic *storm,* etc. A *tempest* is a *storm* of extreme violence, always attended with some precipitation, as of rain, from the atmosphere. In the moral and figurative use *tempest* commonly implies greater intensity. We speak of *agitation* of feeling, *disturbance* of mind, a *storm* of passion, a *tempest* of rage. See WIND. *Antonyms*: calm, hush, peace, serenity, stillness, tranquillity.

Storm may appear as a combining form in hyphemes or solidemes, or as the first element in two-word phrases:

storm area	**storm god**	**storm-rocked**
storm-beaten	**storm goddess**	**storm shutter**
storm blast	**storm gust**	**storm-swept**
storm-boding	**storm jacket**	**stormtight**
stormbound	**storm lane**	**storm-tossed**
storm-bringer	**stormlike**	**storm-washed**
storm cloud	**storm path**	**stormwind**
storm coat	**storm-rent**	**storm-worn**

Storm (shtôrm), **Theodor Woldsen,** 1817–88, German poet and novelist.

storm·belt (stôrm′belt′) *n.* A strip of territory along which storms most frequently move.

storm cellar A cyclone cellar.

storm center 1 *Meteorol.* The center or place of lowest pressure and comparative calm in a cyclonic storm. **2** The central point of a heated argument; the focus of any trouble or turmoil.

storm door A strong outer door for added protection during storms and inclement weather.

Stor·month (stôr′mənth), **James,** 1825–82, Scottish lexicographer.

storm petrel Any of certain petrels of the North Atlantic; especially, *Hydrobates pelagicus,* thought to portend storm. Also **stormy petrel.**

storm·proof (stôrm′prōōf′) *adj.* Capable of keeping out storms.

storm trooper A member of the Nazi party militia unit, the *Sturmabteilung.*

storm warning A signal, as a flag or light, used to warn mariners of coming storm. Also **storm signal.**

storm window An extra window outside the ordinary one as a protection against storms or for greater insulation against cold.

storm·y (stôr′mē) *adj.* **storm·i·er, storm·i·est 1** Characterized by storms; boisterous; also, turbulent; violent: a *stormy* life. **2** Accompanying storms; also, passionate. See synonyms under BLEAK¹. [OE *stormig*] — **storm′·i·ly** *adv.* — **storm′i·ness** *n.*

Stor·thing (stôr′ting′, stōr′-) *n.* The Norwegian parliament. Also **Stor′ting′.** [<Norw. <*stor* great + *thing* meeting]

sto·ry[1] (stôr′ē, stō′rē) *n. pl.* **·ries 1** A narrative or recital of an event, or a series of events, whether real or fictitious. **2** A narrative, usually of fictitious events, intended to entertain a reader or hearer; a short tale. **3** An account or allegation of the facts relating to a particular person, thing, or incident: He tells a more plausible *story* of the conflict. **4** A news article in a newspaper or magazine. **5** The material for a news article. **6** An anecdote. **7** *Colloq.* A lie; falsehood. **8** The series of events in a novel, play, etc. **9** Celebrated or romantic legend or history: to live on in *story.* — *v.t.* **·ried, ·ry·ing 1** To relate as a story. **2** To adorn with designs representing scenes from history, legend, etc. [<OF *estoire* <L *historia.* Doublet of HISTORY.]

Synonyms (noun): allegory, anecdote, incident, narrative, recital, record, relation, tale. *Tale* is nearly synonymous with *story,* but is somewhat archaic; it is used for an imaginative, legendary, or fictitious *recital,* especially if of ancient date; as, a fairy *tale*; also, for an idle or malicious report; as, Do not tell *tales.* See FICTION, HISTORY, REPORT.

sto·ry[2] (stôr′ē, stō′rē) *n. pl.* **·ries** A division in a building comprising the space between two successive floors; a floor; habitable rooms on the same level; also, a horizontal architectural division of a building: also spelled *storey.* [Special use of STORY¹; ? from earlier sense of "a tier of painted windows or sculptures that narrated an event"]

Sto·ry (stôr′ē, stō′rē), **Joseph,** 1779–1845, U. S. jurist. — **William Wetmore,** 1819–95, U. S. sculptor; son of preceding.

story board 1 A bulletin board in a newspaper office on which are posted reportorial assignments to specific stories. **2** The set of original drawings illustrating each stage in the sequence of a motion picture, television program, animated cartoon, etc.

sto·ry·tell·er (stôr′ē·tel′ər, stō′rē-) *n.* **1** One who relates stories or anecdotes. **2** *Colloq.* A prevaricator; liar; fibber. — **sto′ry·tell′ing** *n.* & *adj.*

stoss (stos, *Ger.* shtōs) *adj. Geol.* Facing the direction whence a glacier moves. [<G *stoss* a thrust, push]

sto·tin·ka (stô·ting′kä) *n. pl.* **·ki** (-kē) A small copper coin of Bulgaria; one one-hundredth of a lev. [<Bulgarian]

stound (stound) *n. Obs.* **1** A short time. **2** A sharp pain; pang; heavy blow. — *v.i. Scot.* To ache; hurt. [OE *stund*]

stoup (stōōp) *n.* **1** *Eccl.* A basin for holy water at the entrance of a church. **2** *Scot.* A pail; bucket; flagon; cup; also, its contents. **3** A measure for liquids: a pint *stoup.* Also spelled *stoop, stowp.* [<ON *staup* bucket]

stour[1] (stŏŏr) *n. Obs.* **1** A battle; conflict. **2** Dust in motion; chaff. Also **stoure.** [<OF *estour* tumult] — **stour′ie, stour′y** *adj.*

stour[2] (stŏŏr) *Scot. adj.* **1** Sturdy; also, harsh; rough; surly. **2** Grievous; painful. — *n.* Pressure of circumstances.

stout (stout) *adj.* **1** Strong or firm of structure or material; sound; tough. **2** Determined; resolute. **3** Fat; bulky; thick-set. **4** Strong in effects or active qualities; substantial; solid. **5** Having muscular strength; robust. **6** Proud; stubborn. See synonyms under CORPULENT, STAUNCH, STRONG. — *n.* **1** A stout person. **2** A dress or suit made for a stout person.

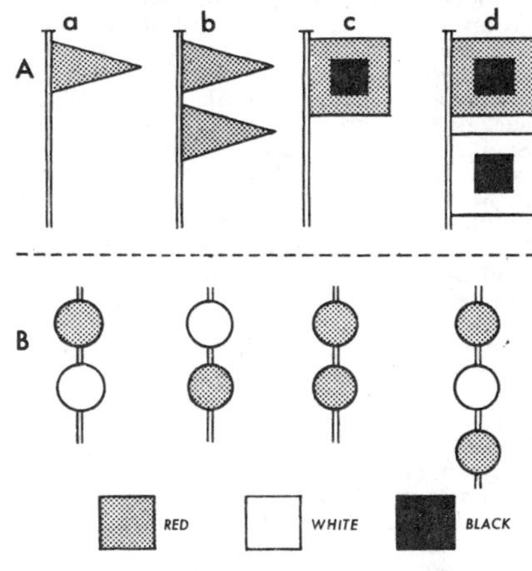

STORM WARNINGS
A. Daylight signals. *B.* Night signals.
a. Small-craft warning. *b.* Gale. *c.* Whole gale.
d. Hurricane.

3 A strong, very dark porter or ale: also **brown stout.** [<OF *estout* bold, strong <Gmc. Cf. MDu. *stolt* bold.] — **stout′ly** *adv.* — **stout′·ness** *n.*

stout·heart·ed (stout′här′tid) *adj.* Brave; courageous. — **stout′heart′ed·ly** *adv.* — **stout′·heart′ed·ness** *n.*

Sto·va·ine (stō′və·ēn, stō·vā′in) *n.* Proprietary name for a local anesthetic, $C_{14}H_{21}NO_2 \cdot HCl$, used especially intraspinally: invented by E. F. A. Fourneau, born 1872, French chemist.

stove[1] (stōv) *n.* **1** An apparatus, usually of metal, in which fuel is consumed for heating or cooking. **2** A drying room or box used in some factories. **3** An artificially heated greenhouse. **4** A pottery kiln. [OE *stofa* a heated room]

stove[2] (stōv) Alternative past tense and past participle of STAVE.

stove·pipe (stōv′pīp′) *n.* **1** A pipe, usually of thin sheet iron, for conducting the smoke and gases of combustion from a stove to a chimney flue. **2** *U.S. Colloq.* A tall silk hat: also **stovepipe hat.**

sto·ver (stō′vər) *n.* Fodder or feed for cattle; cornstalks. [<OF *estover.* See ESTOVERS.]

stow[1] (stō) *v.t.* **1** To place or arrange compactly; pack. **2** To fill by packing. **3** To have room for; hold: said of a room, receptacle, etc. **4** *Slang* To stop; cease. **5** *Obs.* To furnish lodging for. — **to stow away 1** To put in a place of safekeeping, hiding, etc. **2** To be a stowaway. [OE *stōwian* < *stōw* a place]

stow[2] (stō) *v.t. Scot.* & *Brit. Dial.* To lop or cut off; crop.

stow[3] (stō) *n. Scot. & Brit. Dial.* A stump or shoot of a tree; also, a slice; cut.

Stow (stō), **John,** 1525?–1605, English historian and antiquary.

stow·age (stō′ij) *n.* **1** The act or manner of stowing, or the state of being packed away. **2** Space for stowing goods. **3** Charge for stowing goods. **4** The goods stowed.

stow·a·way (stō′ə·wā′) *n.* One who conceals himself, as on a vessel, to obtain free passage.

Stowe (stō), **Harriet Beecher,** 1811–96, U.S. author; wrote *Uncle Tom's Cabin.*

stowp (stōōp) See STOUP.

STP (es′tē′pē′) *n.* A hallucinogenic drug chemically related to mescaline and amphetamine. [< *STP*, a trade name for a gasoline additive supposed to increase engine power]

St. Pat·rick's Day (sānt pat′riks) March 17. See under PATRICK.

St. Paul (sānt pôl′) The capital of Minnesota, in the SE part of the State, on the Mississippi River: one of the Twin Cities.

St. Pe·ter (sānt pē′tər), **Lake** An expansion of the St. Lawrence River in southern Quebec, Canada; 130 square miles.

St. Pe·ters·burg (sānt pē′tərz·bûrg) **1** The capital of the former Russian Empire; renamed *Petrograd* in 1914 and *Leningrad* in 1924. **2** A city on Tampa Bay, western Florida.

St. Pierre (sānt pyâr′, *Fr.* saṅ pyâr′) An island group off Newfoundland; 10 square miles; with the adjacent island group of **Mi·que·lon** (mē·kə·lôṅ′), 83 square miles, it constitutes the French territory of **St. Pierre and Miquelon;** total area, 93 square miles; capital, St. Pierre. *French* **Saint–Pierre–et–Mi·que·lon** (saṅ·pyâr′ā·mē·kə·lôṅ′). **2** A former town in Martinique, completely destroyed by the eruption of Mont Pelée on May 8, 1902. See PELÉE. **3** A town of southern Réunion Island.

stra·bis·mus (strə·biz′məs) *n. Pathol.* A condition in which the eyes cannot be simultaneously focused on the same spot: when one or both eyes turn inward, the patient is *cross–eyed*: when outward, *walleyed.* [<NL <Gk. *strabismos* < *strabizein* squint < *strabos* twisted] — **stra·bis′mal, stra·bis′mic** *adj.*

Stra·bo (strā′bō), 63? B.C.–A.D. 24?, Greek geographer and historian.

stra·bot·o·my (strə·bot′ə·mē) *n. Surg.* The cutting of the eyeball muscles to correct strabismus. [<Gk. *strabos* oblique + -TOMY]

Stra·chey (strā′chē), **(Evelyn) John,** 1901–1963, English politician and writer. — **(Giles) Lytton,** 1880–1932, English author.

strad·dle (strad′l) *v.* **·dled, ·dling** *v.i.* **1** To stand, walk, or sit with the legs spread apart. **2** To stand wide apart: said of the legs. **3** *Colloq.* To appear to favor both sides of an issue; refuse to commit oneself. — *v.t.* **4** To stand, walk, or sit with the legs on either side of. **5** To spread (the legs) wide apart. **6** *Colloq.* To appear to favor both sides of (an issue). **7** *Mil.* To fire shots both beyond and in front of (a target) so as to determine the range. — *n.* **1** A going, standing, or sitting with legs wide apart; the space between the feet or legs of one who straddles. **2** A noncommittal or vacillating position in any issue. **3** A stock transaction in which the holder obtains the privilege of either delivering or calling for a stock at a fixed price. **4** A long position in some stocks while being short in others. **5** *Mil.* Successive range settings that have bracketed the target. [Freq. of STRIDE] — **strad′dler** *n.* — **strad′dling·ly** *adv.*

Stra·di·va·ri (strä′dē·vä′rē), **Antonio,** 1644–1737, violin-maker of Cremona, Italy. Also **Strad·i·var·i·us** (strad′i·vâr′ē·əs).

Strad·i·var·i·us (strad′i·vâr′ē·əs) *n.* One of the famous violins produced by the fine workmanship of Antonio Stradivari.

strafe (strāf, sträf) *v.t.* **strafed, straf·ing** **1** To attack (troops, emplacements, etc.) with machine–gun fire from low–flying airplanes. **2** To bombard or shell heavily. **3** *Slang* To punish. — *n.* A heavy bombardment. [<G *strafen* punish] — **straf′er** *n.*

Straf·ford (straf′ərd), **Earl of,** 1593–1641, Thomas Wentworth, English statesman; beheaded.

strag·gle (strag′əl) *v.i.* **·gled, ·gling** **1** To wander from the road, main body, etc.; stray. **2** To wander aimlessly about; ramble. **3** To occur at irregular intervals. [? Freq. of obs. *strake* move, go about] — **strag′gler** *n.*

strag·gly (strag′lē) *adj.* **·li·er, ·li·est** Scattered or spread out irregularly.

straight (strāt) *adj.* **1** Extending uniformly in the same direction without curve or bend. **2** Free from kinks; not curly, as hair. **3** Not stooped or inclined; erect, as in posture. **4** Not deviating from truth, fairness, or honesty; accurate; honest; upright; reliable; also, candid. **5** Free from obstruction; uninterrupted; unbroken. **6** Correctly kept, ordered, or arranged. **7** Sold without discount for number or quantity taken. **8** *Colloq.* Adhering without reservation or exception to a particular party or policy; representing the regular or older organization; accepting the whole, as of a plan, party, or policy: a *straight* ticket. **9** In poker, consisting of five cards forming a sequence: a *straight* flush. **10** Having nothing added; unmixed; undiluted: *straight* whisky. **11** *Slang* Conforming to what is accepted as usual, normal, or conventional, especially according to middle–class standards. **12** *Slang* Heterosexual. — *n.* **1** A straight part or piece. **2** The part of a racecourse between the winning post and the last turn. **3** In poker, a numerical sequence of five cards not of the same suit, or a hand containing this. **4** A straight line. **5** *Slang* A conventional person. **6** *Slang* A heterosexual. — *adv.* **1** In a straight line or a direct course. **2** Closely in line; correspondingly. **3** At once; straightway. ◆ Homophone: *strait.* [ME *stregt* <OE *streht,* pp. of *streccan* stretch] — **straight′ly** *adv.* — **straight′·ness** *n.*

straight angle See under ANGLE.

straight–arm (strāt′ärm′) *v.t.* In football, to ward off (an opposing tackler) with the outstretched arm.

straight·a·way (strāt′ə·wā′) *adj.* Having no curve or turn; straightforward. — *n.* A straight course or track. — *adv.* At once; straightway.

straight·edge (strāt′ej′) *n.* A bar of wood or metal having one edge true to a straight line: used for ruling, etc. — **straight′–edged′** *adj.*

straight·en (strāt′n) *v.t.* **1** To make straight. **2** To lay out (a corpse). — *v.i.* **3** To become straight. — **to straighten out** To restore order to; set right; rectify. — **to straighten up** **1** To free from disorder; make neat; tidy. **2** To stand in erect posture. **3** To reform; become honorable or honest. — **straight′ener** *n.*

straight face A sober, expressionless, or unsmiling face. — **straight–faced** (strāt′fāst′) *adj.*

straight flush See under FLUSH.

straight·for·ward (strāt′fôr′wərd) *adj.* Proceeding in a straight course or direct manner; frank. See synonyms under CANDID, CLEAR, HONEST, JUST[1], PLAIN[1]. — **straight′for′ward·ly** *adv.* — **straight′for′ward·ness** *n.*

straight·for·wards (strāt′fôr′wərdz) *adv.* In a straight course or direct manner.

straight–line (strāt′līn′) *adj. Mech.* Designating a linkage or similar apparatus intended to copy or generate motion in a straight or nearly straight line.

straight man *U.S. Colloq.* An entertainer who acts as a foil for a comedian.

straight–out (strāt′out′) *adj.* **1** Showing the true sentiments or feelings; unreserved; also, shown without reserve. **2** Real; genuine.

straight ticket **1** A political party ballot or ticket that presents the regular party candidates without addition or change. **2** A ballot cast for all the candidates of one party. Compare SPLIT TICKET.

straight·way (strāt′wā′) *adv.* Immediately; straightaway.

straik[1] (strāk) *v.t. Scot.* To stroke.

straik[2] (strāk) *Scot.* Past participle of STRIKE.

strain[1] (strān) *v.t.* **1** To pull or draw tight; stretch. **2** To exert to the utmost. **3** To injure by overexertion; sprain; also, to wrench or twist. **4** To deform in structure or shape as a result of pressure or stress. **5** To stretch beyond the true intent, proper limit, etc.: to *strain* a point. **6** To embrace tightly; hug. **7** To pass through a strainer (def. 2). **8** To remove by filtration. **9** *Mech.* To alter in size or shape by applying external force. **10** *Obs.* To force; constrain. — *v.i.* **11** To make violent efforts; strive. **12** To be or become wrenched or twisted. **13** To filter, trickle, or percolate. See synonyms under STRETCH. — **to strain at** **1** To push or pull with violent efforts. **2** To strive for. **3** To scruple or balk at accepting. — *n.* **1** An act of straining or the state of being strained; a violent effort or exertion. **2** The injury due to excessive tension or effort. **3** *Physics* Change of shape or size of a body, especially of a solid, produced by the action of a stress; deformation, temporary or permanent; thrust; force. [<OF *estrein-*, stem of *estreindre* <L *stringere* bind tight]

strain[2] (strān) *n.* **1** Line of descent, or the individuals, collectively, in that line; race; stock. **2** Inborn or hereditary disposition; natural tendency; trace; an element or admixture: to have a heroic *strain* in one's character. **3** *Biol.* A special line of individuals belonging to a certain race or species and maintained at a high standard of perfection by selection: said of animals or plants. **4** *Rare* Distinguishing nature or quality; kind; sort. **5** A section, in hymn tunes, divided off by a double bar; a melody; tune; air. **6** A distinctive portion of a poem; also, a composition in verse. **7** Prevailing tone, style, or manner; mood. [? Var. of ME *strene,* OE *strēon* offspring]

strain·er (strā′nər) *n.* **1** One who or that which strains. **2** A utensil or device, containing meshes or porous parts, through which liquids are passed to separate them from coarse particles. **3** A device used for tightening, strengthening, or stretching.

straining arch Any arch erected to exert a corrective strain or to resist a destructive strain in a building.

straining beam A tie beam receiving a lengthwise pulling stress, and connecting the rafters of a roof with the tops of the queenposts. Also **straining piece.**

strait (strāt) *adj.* **1** Of small transverse dimensions; narrow. **2** *Archaic* Restricted as to space or room; close; tight. **3** Destitute, as of money; needy. **4** *Archaic* Strict; rigorous. **5** *Obs.* Difficult; hard–pressed. — *n.* **1** A narrow passage of water connecting two larger bodies of water. **2** Any narrow pass or passage. **3** A position of perplexity or distress; necessity: frequently plural. **4** *Obs.* An isthmus. ◆ Homophone: *straight.* [<OF *estreit* <L *strictus,* pp. of *stringere* bind tight. Doublet of STRICT.] — **strait′ly** *adv.* — **strait′·ness** *n.*

strait·en (strāt′n) *v.t.* **1** To make strait or narrow; contract; restrict. **2** To embarrass, as in finances; also, to distress; hamper. Also **strait.** See synonyms under SCRIMP.

strait·ened (strāt′nd) *adj.* **1** Contracted; narrowed. **2** Suffering privation or hardship, especially from pecuniary difficulties.

strait·jack·et (strāt′jak′it) *n.* **1** A tight jacket of strong canvas, for confining the arms of violent mental patients or prisoners. **2** Anything that unduly confines or restricts. — *v.t.* To confine in or as if in a straightjacket.

strait–laced (strāt′lāst′) *adj.* **1** Tightly laced, as stays; encased in tight corsets. **2** Strict, especially in morals or manners.

Straits (strāts), **The** The Bosporus and the Dardanelles considered as a single passage from the Mediterranean to the Black Sea.

Straits Settlements A former British crown colony comprising Singapore, Penang, Malacca, and Labuan: dissolved, 1946.

strake (strāk) *n. Naut.* A breadth of planking or a line of plating on a vessel's hull from stem to stern: also spelled *streak.* [Appar. akin to STRETCH; infl. in meaning by STREAK]

Stral·sund (shträl′zōōnt) A port on the Baltic Sea in northern East Germany, in the former state of Mecklenburg.

stra·min·e·ous (strə·min′ē·əs) *adj.* **1** Straw–colored. **2** Strawlike; chaffy. [<L *stramineus* < *stramen* straw]

stra·mo·ni·um (strə·mō′nē·əm) *n.* **1** The jimsonweed. **2** A drug prepared from the dried leaves and flowering tops of this plant, used as a sedative, especially in asthma. Also **stram·o·ny** (stram′ə·nē). [<NL <Med. L *stramonia,* ? ult. <Tatar *turman,* a medicine for horses]

strand[1] (strand) *n.* A shore or beach; especially, that portion of an ocean shore between high and low tides. See synonyms under BANK[1]. — *v.t. & v.i.* **1** To drive or run aground. **2** To leave or be left in straits or difficulties: usually in the passive. [OE *strand*]

strand[2] (strand) *n.* **1** One of the principal twists or members of a rope. **2** A fiber, hair, or the like. **3** Wires twisted into a cable.

4 Anything plaited or twisted. —*v.t.* 1 To break a strand of (a rope). 2 To make by twisting strands. [? <OF *estran* <Gmc.]

strand line A line marking the boundary between the shore and the ocean, especially a line higher than the present one.

strang (strang) *adj. Scot.* Strong.

strange (strānj) *adj.* 1 Previously unknown, unseen, or unheard of; unfamiliar. 2 Not according to the ordinary way; unaccountable; remarkable. 3 Pertaining to another or others; of a different class, character, or kind. 4 Foreign; alien. 5 Distant in manner; reserved; shy. 6 Inexperienced; unskilled; unaccustomed. See synonyms under ALIEN, EXTRAORDINARY, ODD, QUEER, RARE[1]. —*adv.* Strangely. [<OF *estrange* <L *extraneus* foreign <*extra* on the outside. Doublet of EXTRANEOUS.] —**strange′ly** *adv.* —**strange′·ness** *n.*

stran·ger (strān′jər) *n.* 1 One who is not an acquaintance. 2 An unfamiliar visitor; guest. 3 A foreigner. 4 One unversed in or unacquainted or unfamiliar with something specified: with *to.* 5 *Law* Any person who is neither a party to a transaction nor privy to it. See synonyms under ALIEN. [<OF *estrangier* <*estrange.* See STRANGE.]

stran·gle (strang′gəl) *v.* **·gled, ·gling** *v.t.* 1 To choke to death; throttle; suffocate; stifle. 2 To repress; suppress. —*v.i.* 3 To suffer or die from strangulation. [<F *estrangler* <L *strangulare* <Gk. *strangalaein* <*strangalē* a halter <*strangos* twisted] —**stran′gler** *n.*

strangle hold 1 In wrestling, a hold which chokes one's opponent: usually forbidden. 2 Any influence or power that chokes freedom or progress.

stran·gles (strang′gəlz) *n. pl.* An infectious bacterial disease of the horse characterized by fever and inflammation of the respiratory mucous membrane.

stran·gu·late (strang′gyə·lāt) *v.t.* **·lat·ed, ·lat·ing** 1 To strangle. 2 *Pathol.* To compress, contract, or obstruct, especially so as to cut off circulation of the blood or flow of fluid. —*adj.* Strangulated. [<L *strangulatus,* pp. of *strangulare.* See STRANGLE.]

stran·gu·lat·ed (strang′gyə·lā′tid) *adj. Pathol.* Characterized by strangulation.

strangulated hernia *Pathol.* A form of hernia in which the protruded organ or part is so tightly constricted as to cut off normal circulation of the blood, with possible necrosis and mortification.

stran·gu·la·tion (strang′gyə·lā′shən) *n.* 1 The act of strangling or the state of being strangled. 2 *Pathol.* The state of being strangulated; constriction of a part, as of the intestine in strangulated hernia, to cut off circulation.

stran·gu·ry (strang′gyə·rē) *n. Pathol.* Difficult and painful urination. [<L *stranguria* <Gk. *strangouria* <*stranx, strangos* a drop + *ouron* urine]

strap (strap) *n.* 1 A long, narrow, and flexible strip of leather or the like, usually having a buckle or other fastener, for binding about objects. 2 A razor strop. 3 A shoulder strap. 4 Something made of, resembling, or used as a strap. 5 A thin metal band or plate. —*v.t.* **strapped, strap·ping** 1 To fasten or bind with a strap. 2 To beat with a strap. 3 To sharpen or strop. 4 *Scot.* To hang. 5 To embarrass financially. [Var. of STROP] —**strap′less** *adj.*

strap hinge A hinge having long leaves, designed for attaching to the flat surfaces of a door and jamb. See illustration under HINGE.

strap·pa·do (strə·pā′dō, -pä′dō) *n. pl.* **·does** 1 A former punishment in which one was drawn up by a rope attached usually to the wrists, and let fall to the length of the rope; also, the machine used. 2 Erroneously, a beating with a strap. [<Ital. *strappata* a pulling, orig. fem. pp. of *strappare* pull]

strap·pan (strap′ən) *adj. Scot.* Tall and handsome; strapping.

strap·per (strap′ər) *n.* 1 One who uses a strap or straps. 2 One who bolts the straps to rails. 3 *Colloq.* A strong, tall person. 4 One who grooms horses.

strap·ping (strap′ing) *adj. Colloq.* Large and muscular; robust.

Stras·bourg (stras′bûrg, sträz′-; *Fr.* strȧz·bo͞or′) A city in NE France, the chief city of Alsace. *German* **Strass·burg** (shträs′bo͝orkh).

strass (stras) *n.* A lead glass of great brilliance used in the manufacture of gems; paste. [after Josef *Strasser,* 18th century German jeweler]

strasse (stras) *n.* Refuse of silk left in making skeins. [<F *strasse* <Ital. *straccio* rag, something torn <*stracciare* tear, lacerate]

stra·ta (strā′tə, strat′ə) Plural of STRATUM.

strat·a·gem (strat′ə·jəm) *n.* 1 A maneuver designed to deceive or outwit an enemy in war. 2 A deception; any device for obtaining advantage. See synonyms under ARTIFICE. [<F *stratagème* <L *strategema* <Gk. *stratēgēma* piece of generalship <*stratēgos* a general <*stratos* army + *agein* lead]

stra·tal (strāt′l) *adj.* Pertaining to, derived from, characteristic of, or caused by a stratum or strata.

stra·te·gic (strə·tē′jik) *adj.* Of or pertaining to strategy; characterized by, used in, or having relation to strategy. Also **stra·te′gi·cal, strat·e·get·ic** (strat′ə·jet′ik) or **·i·cal.** —**stra·te′gi·cal·ly, strat′e·get′i·cal·ly** *adv.*

strategic material Any of several, chiefly raw, materials essential to national defense and industry, especially those that are wholly lacking or in insufficient supply within a nation's boundaries and have to be obtained from sources outside the country: the stockpiling of *strategic materials.*

stra·te·gics (strə·tē′jiks) *n. pl. (construed as singular)* The art or science of strategy; generalship.

strat·e·gist (strat′ə·jist) *n.* One versed in strategy, or skilled in managing affairs.

strat·e·gy (strat′ə·jē) *n. pl.* **·gies** 1 The science and art of conducting a military campaign by the combination and employment of means on a broad scale for gaining advantage in war; generalship: distinguished from *tactics.* 2 The use of stratagem or artifice, as in business, politics, etc. 3 Skill in management. [<F *stratégie* <Gk. *stratēgia* <*stratēgos* general. See STRATAGEM.]

Strat·ford-on-A·von (strat′fərd·on·ā′von) A town on the Avon river in SW Warwickshire, England; birthplace and place of burial of Shakespeare.

strath (strath) *n. Scot.* A wide, open valley; a river course.

Strath·clyde and Cum·bri·a (strath′klīd; kum′·brē·ə) An early medieval British kingdom comprising territory now in southern Scotland and northern England.

Strath·co·na and Mount Royal (strath·kō′·nə), **Lord,** 1820–1914, Donald Alexander Smith, Canadian railroad builder and administrator born in Scotland.

Strath·more (strath′môr) A plain extending 100 miles across Scotland, south of the Grampians, between Dumbarton and the North Sea coast of Kincardine.

strati– *combining form* A stratum; of or pertaining to a stratum or to strata: *stratiform.* Also, before vowels, **strat–.** [<L *stratum* a covering]

stra·tic·u·late (strə·tik′yə·lit, -lāt) *adj. Geol.* Arranged in thin layers or strata: said of sedimentary rocks and certain minerals, as the agate. [<NL *straticulum,* dim. of L *stratum* a layer + -ATE[1]] —**stra·tic′u·la′tion** *n.*

strat·i·form (strat′ə·fôrm) *adj.* 1 *Geol.* Having the form of or constituting a stratum. 2 *Anat.* Denoting a fibrous cartilage enclosed in a channel in a bone as a support for tendons. 3 *Meteorol.* Resembling a stratus. [<STRATI- + -FORM]

strat·i·fy (strat′ə·fī) *v.* **·fied, ·fy·ing** *v.t.* 1 To form or arrange in strata. 2 To preserve (seeds) by spreading in alternating layers of earth and sand. —*v.i.* 3 To form in strata. 4 To be formed in strata. [<F *stratifier* <Med. L *stratificare* <L *stratum* layer + *facere* make] —**strat′i·fi·ca′tion** *n.*

stra·tig·ra·phy (strə·tig′rə·fē) *n.* 1 The order and relative position of the strata of the earth's crust. 2 The study or description of such strata; stratigraphic geology. [< STRATI- + -GRAPHY] —**strat·i·graph·ic** (strat′·ə·graf′ik) or **·i·cal** *adj.* —**strat′i·graph′i·cal·ly** *adv.*

stra·toc·ra·cy (strə·tok′rə·sē) *n. pl.* **·cies** Government by the military. [<Gk. *stratos* army + -CRACY] —**strat·o·crat·ic** (strat′ə·krat′ik) *adj.*

stra·to·cu·mu·lus (strā′tō·kyo͞o′myə·ləs) *n. pl.* **·li** (-lī) *Meteorol.* Large rolls or globular masses of cloud, gray to dark in color, disposed in waves, groups, or bands, and often covering the whole sky: also called *cumulo-stratus.* See table under CLOUD. [<*strato-* (<STRATUS) + CUMULUS]

strat·o·pause (strat′ə·pôz) *n. Meteorol.* The zone of transition between the stratosphere and the mesosphere.

strat·o·sphere (strat′ə·sfir, strā′tə-) *n. Meteorol.* The portion of the atmosphere lying above the troposphere and beginning at a height of about six miles. In it the systematic fall of temperature with increasing altitude, characteristic of the region below it, ceases, often giving place to a more or less uniform temperature. —**strat′o·spher′ic** (-sfer′ik) *adj.*

stra·tum (strā′təm, strat′əm) *n. pl.* **·ta** (-tə) or **·tums** 1 A natural or artificial layer, bed, or thickness. 2 *Geol.* A more or less homogeneous layer of rock, often in two or more beds, and serving to identify a geological group, system, or series. 3 *Biol.* A sheet or layer of tissue. 4 Something corresponding to a stratum of the earth: a low *stratum* of society. [<L, orig. neut. of *stratus,* pp. of *sternere* spread]

stra·tus (strā′təs, strat′əs) *n. pl.* **·ti** (-tī) *Meteorol.* A cloud of foglike appearance, low-lying and arranged in a uniform layer. See table under CLOUD. [<L, orig. pp. of *sternere* spread]

Straus (strous, *Ger.* shtrous), **Oscar,** 1870–1954, Austrian composer.

Strauss (strous, *Ger.* shtrous), **David Friedrich,** 1808–74, German rationalistic theologian. —**Johann,** 1804–49, Austrian composer of dance music. —**Johann,** 1825–99, Austrian composer; son of the preceding. —**Richard,** 1864–1949, German composer.

Stra·vin·sky (strə·vin′skē, *Russian* strä·vēn′·skē), **Igor Fëdorovich,** 1882–1971, U. S. composer born in Russia.

straw (strô) *n.* 1 A dry or ripened stalk. 2 Stems or stalks of grain, collectively, after the grain has been thrashed out. 3 A mere trifle or slight indication. 4 A slender tube, originally a wheat straw, now made of paper, glass, etc., used to suck up a beverage. —**the last straw** The final test of patience or endurance; the culminating element in any state of circumstances. —**straw in the wind** A sign or indication of the course of future events. —*adj.* 1 Like or of straw; of straw color. 2 Of no value; worthless; sham. 3 Made of straw. [OE *strēaw* straw] —**straw′y** *adj.*

straw·ber·ry (strô′ber′ē, -bər·ē) *n. pl.* **·ries** 1 The edible fruit of any plant of the genus *Fragaria,* technically neither a fruit nor a berry, but an enlarged fleshy achene receptacle. 2 The plant that bears this fruit, a stemless perennial of the rose family, with radical trifoliolate leaves, usually white flowers on scapes, and slender runners by which it propagates: also **strawberry vine.** [OE *strēaw* straw + BERRY]

strawberry bass The calico bass.

strawberry blond A person having reddish-blond hair; a red-headed person.

strawberry bush 1 An upright or straggling shrub *(Euonymus americanus)* of the United States and Canada, with rough, warty, depressed crimson pods and scarlet aril. 2 The wahoo or burningbush.

strawberry festival A sociable gathering, church bazaar, etc., at which strawberries are served.

strawberry shrub A shrub (genus *Calycanthus),* named for the strawberrylike fragrance of its purple or dark-red flowers.

strawberry tomato The ground cherry.

strawberry tree A small evergreen tree *(Arbutus unedo)* of southern Europe, having racemose white flowers and edible fruit resembling strawberries.

straw·board (strô′bôrd′, -bōrd′) *n.* Coarse board, made of straw, used for paper boxes and book covers.

straw boss *U.S. Colloq.* In construction work, logging, etc., an under-foreman.

straw color A pale-yellow color, as of clean ripe straw. — **straw'-col'ored** (-kul'ərd) *adj.*
straw man 1 A figure of a man made of straw. 2 A position, as in debate, set forth as one's opponent's view but typically misrepresenting it so that it may be convincingly refuted. 3 A person used to misrepresent or otherwise conceal the real nature of an activity or undertaking.
straw vote A vote taken at a chance gathering to test the strength of opposing candidates; an unofficial test vote.
straw wine A sweet wine made from grapes dried or partly dried in the sun on straw.
straw worm The larva of a caddis fly.
stray (strā) *v.i.* 1 To wander from the proper course, an area, group, etc.; straggle; roam. 2 To wander about; rove. 3 To deviate from right or goodness; go astray. See synonyms under RAMBLE, WANDER. — *adj.* 1 Having strayed; straying. 2 Irregular; occasional; casual; unrelated. — *n.* 1 A domestic animal that has strayed; an estray. 2 A person who is lost or wanders aimlessly. 3 The act of straying or wandering. 4 *pl. Electronics* Electromagnetic waves, affecting a radio receiver, produced by atmospheric electric discharges and electrical storms. [<OF *estraier* wander about, ult. <L *extra vagare* wander outside] — **stray'er** *n.*
streak (strēk) *n.* 1 A long, narrow, somewhat irregularly shaped mark, line, or stripe: a *streak* of lightning. 2 A not very marked characteristic; a vein; trace; dash: a *streak* of meanness; also, a transient mood; whim. 3 *Mineral.* The color of the line of powder left when a mineral is rubbed on an unglazed porcelain plate known as a **streak plate.** 4 A strake. 5 A layer or strip: meat with a *streak* of fat and a *streak* of lean. 6 *Bacteriol.* The application of an inoculum in a thin stripe, as across the surface of a culture. 7 *Slang* The act or an instance of streaking (*v.* def. 3). — *v.i.* 1 To form a streak or streaks. 2 To move, run, or travel at great speed. 3 *Slang* To appear naked in a public place, usually briefly and especially while running, as for a thrill. — *v.t.* 4 To mark with a streak; form streaks in or on. 5 *Slang* To appear naked in (a public place), usually briefly and especially while running, as for a thrill. [OE *strica.* Akin to STRIKE.] — **streaked** *adj.* — **streak'er** *n.*
streak·y (strē'kē) *adj.* **streak·i·er, streak·i·est** 1 Marked with or occurring in streaks; streaked. 2 Variable in character; not uniform. — **streak'i·ly** *adv.* — **streak'i·ness** *n.*
stream (strēm) *n.* 1 A current or flow of water or other fluid. 2 Anything continuously flowing, moving, or passing, as people. 3 A continuous course or advance; drift; current. 4 Anything issuing out or flowing from a source; a ray. — **on stream** In full commercial production, as an oil refinery, chemical plant, etc. — *v.i.* 1 To pour forth or issue in a stream. 2 To pour forth a stream: eyes *streaming* with tears. 3 To move in continuous succession; proceed uninterruptedly, as a crowd. 4 To float with a waving movement, as a flag. 5 To move with a trail of light, as a meteor. 6 In mining or dyeing, to wash in running water. [OE *strēam*] — **stream'y** *adj.*
Synonyms (noun): brook, channel, course, creek, current, drift, eddy, flow, flume, flux, race, rill, river, rivulet, run, runlet, runnel, streamlet, tide, watercourse.
stream·er (strē'mər) *n.* 1 An object that streams forth, or hangs extended. 2 A flag, pennant, or ensign; a long, narrow flag or standard. 3 A stream or shaft of light, such as shoots up from the horizon into or across the sky in the aurora borealis. 4 A newspaper headline that runs across the whole page.
stream·let (strēm'lit) *n.* A rivulet.
stream·line (strēm'līn') *n.* 1 The course of a fluid relative to a solid body past which it is moving, especially a course free of turbulence or eddies. 2 Any shape or contour designed to lessen air resistance. — *adj.* 1 Designating an uninterrupted flow or drift. 2 Denoting a form, body, or the like so constructed as to permit an uninterrupted flow of fluid around it: a *streamline* flow, a *streamline* shape, a *streamline* body for a motor car. — *v.t.* **·lined, ·lin·ing** 1 To design with a streamline shape. 2 To make more simple, efficient, or up to date, especially by reorganization.
stream·lin·er (strēm'lī'nər) *n.* A fast, streamlined train.
stream of consciousness *Psychol.* The uninterrupted series of individual conscious states moving continuously as though in a stream. Also **stream of thought.**
stream-of-con·scious·ness technique (strēm'·əv·kon'shəs·nis) A method of writing fiction in which an author objectifies the inward thoughts, feelings, and sometimes sensations of the characters to supplement or replace dialog and narrated action.
streek (strēk) *Scot. v.t.* 1 To stretch or extend; hence, to lay out, as a corpse. 2 To stretch forth; stretch. — *n.* Extent; progress.
street (strēt) *n.* 1 A public way, with buildings on one or both sides, in a city, town, or village. 2 The highway on which buildings front; also, the roadway for vehicles, between sidewalks. 3 *Colloq.* The people living, habitually gathering, or doing business in a street. — *adj.* 1 Working in the streets: a *street* musician; a *street* beggar. 2 Opening onto the street: a *street* door. 3 Performed or taking place on the street: *street* crime; *street* fair. 4 Habituated to the ways of life in the streets, especially in cities: *street* people. See synonyms under ROAD, WAY. [OE *strǣt* <LL *strata (via)* paved (road)]
Street may appear as a combining form in hyphemes or as the first element in two-word phrases, with the following meanings:
1 Of or pertaining to a street or streets:

street-cleaner	**street-sprinkler**
street-cleaning	**street-sprinkling**
street directory	**street-sweeper**
street layer	**street-sweeping**
street name	**street-widening**

2 In the streets:

street beggar	**street music**	**street-pacing**
street-bred	**street musician**	**street peddler**
street fight	**street noise**	**street singer**

3 On or abutting a street:

street corner	**street entrance**	**street gate**
street door	**street floor**	**street lamp**

street Arab A homeless or outcast child who lives in the streets; a gamin.
street car A passenger car that runs on rails laid on the surface of the streets.
street people People, especially young people of the early 1970s, typically without a permanent home and having a life style like that of hippies, marked by the rejection of family life and other middle-class values and by the use of drugs for pleasure.
street-walk·er (strēt'wô'kər) *n.* A prostitute who solicits in the streets. — **street'-walk'ing** *n. & adj.*
strength (strength) *n.* 1 The quality or property of being strong; power; muscular force; physical vitality. 2 The capacity of material bodies to sustain the application of force without yielding or breaking; solidity; tenacity; toughness. 3 Power in general; operative energy; ability to do or bear. 4 Binding force or validity, as of a law. 5 Vigor or force of style. 6 Available numerical force in a military unit or other organization. 7 Degree of intensity; vehemence: *strength* of passion. 8 The degree in which a thing possesses its distinctive properties or essential elements; concentration. 9 Potency, as of a drug, chemical, or liquor. 10 Rising prices; firmness of prices. 11 One regarded as an embodiment of sustaining or protecting power; in archaic or poetic use, a fortress. See synonyms under POWER, PROWESS. [OE *strengthu* <*strang* strong]
strength·en (streng'thən) *v.t.* 1 To make strong. 2 To encourage; hearten. — *v.i.* 3 To become or grow strong or stronger. See synonyms under CONFIRM. — **strength'en·er** *n.*
stren·u·ous (stren'yoo͞·əs) *adj.* 1 Eagerly pressing or urgent; earnest. 2 Necessitating or marked by strong effort or exertion. [<L *strenuus.* Akin to Gk. *strēnēs* strong.] — **stren'u·ous·ly** *adv.* — **stren'u·os'i·ty** (-os'ə·tē), **stren'u·ous·ness** *n.*
streph·o·sym·bo·li·a (stref'ō·sim·bō'lē·ə) *n.* 1 *Pathol.* A defect of vision in which objects are seen in reverse, as in a mirror. 2 *Psychol.* A condition marked by an inability to differentiate between certain oppositely oriented letters, as *b, d; p, q,* resulting in difficulty in learning to read. [<NL <Gk. *strephein* twist + *symbolon* sign, symbol]
strep·to·coc·cus (strep'tə·kok'əs) *n. pl.* **·coc·ci** (-kok'sī) Any of a genus *(Streptococcus)* of Gram-positive, typically non-motile ovoid or spherical bacteria, grouped in long chains, and dividing in one plane, including highly pathogenic species causing many diseases, as pneumonia, erysipelas, etc. See illustration under BACTERIUM. [<NL <Gk. *streptos* twisted + COCCUS] — **strep'to·coc'cal** (-kok'əl), **strep'to·coc'cic** (-kok'sik) *adj.*
strep·to·my·cin (strep'tō·mī'sin) *n.* A potent antibiotic isolated from a moldlike organism *(Streptomyces griseus)*, effective against certain pathogenic bacteria. [<Gk. *streptos* twisted + *mykēs* fungus]
strep·to·thri·cin (strep'tō·thrī'sin, -thris'in) *n.* A bactericidal substance isolated from a soil fungus *(Actinomyces lavendulae)*: used therapeutically in certain intestinal infections. [<NL *Streptothrix,* former genus name <Gk. *streptos* twisted + *thrix* hair + -IN]
Stre·se·mann (shtrā'zə·män), **Gustav,** 1878–1929, German statesman.
stress (stres) *n.* 1 Special weight, importance, or significance. 2 *Physics* Force exerted between contiguous portions of a body or bodies and generally expressed in pounds per square inch; strain; tension. 3 *Mech.* A force or system of forces which tends to produce deformation in a body on which it acts. 4 Influence exerted forcibly; pressure; compulsion. 5 In pronunciation and oral reading, the relative force with which a sound, syllable, or word is uttered. See also METRICAL STRESS, RHETORICAL STRESS. — *v.t.* 1 To subject to mechanical stress, as a timber. 2 To put stress or emphasis on; accent, as a syllable. 3 To put into straits or difficulties; distress. [<OF *estrece* <*estrecier* constrain <L *strictus,* pp. of *stringere* draw tight] — **stress'ful** *adj.* — **stress'less** *adj.*
-stress *suffix of nouns* Feminine form of -STER: *songstress.* [<-STER + -ESS]
stretch (strech) *v.t.* 1 To extend or draw out, as to full length or width. 2 To extend or draw out forcibly, especially beyond normal or proper limits: The weight has *stretched* the cable; to *stretch* the truth. 3 To cause to reach, as from one place to another or over an area; extend: They *stretched* telegraph wires across the continent. 4 To put forth, hold out, or extend (the hand, an object, etc.): often with *out*: to *stretch* out the hands in appeal. 5 To draw tight; tighten. 6 To strain or exert to the utmost: to *stretch* every nerve. 7 *Slang* To fell with a blow. — *v.i.* 8 To reach or extend over an area or from one place to another: The road *stretches* on and on. 9 To become extended, especially beyond normal or proper limits. 10 To extend one's body or limbs, as in relaxing or reaching for something. 11 To lie down and extend one's limbs to full length: usually with *out.* — *n.* 1 An act of stretching, or the state of being stretched; tension. 2 Extent or reach of that which stretches; scope; especially, an overstrain. 3 A continuous extent of space or time. 4 In racing, the straight part of the track; the straight-away. 5 Direction. 6 *Slang* A term of imprisonment. — *adj.* Capable of being stretched; elastic: said especially of clothing and fabrics: *stretch* socks. [OE *streccan* stretch] — **stretch'a·ble** *adj.* — **stretch'i·ness** *n.* — **stretch'y** *adj.*
Synonyms (verb): elongate, exaggerate, expand, extend, lengthen, reach, spread, strain, tighten.
stretch·er (strech'ər) *n.* 1 One who or that which stretches; any device for stretching, as a device for loosening the fit of gloves, shoes, etc., a frame for drying curtains, sweaters, etc., in shape. 2 A frame, as of stretched canvas, for carrying the wounded or dead; a litter. 3 In masonry, a brick or stone lying lengthwise of a course. 4 A tie beam in the frame of a building.
stretch·er-bear·er (strech'ər·bâr'ər) *n.* One who carries one end of a stretcher or litter. Also **stretch'er·man'** (-man').
stretch-out (strech'out') *n.* 1 A system of industrial operation in which employees are required to perform more work per unit of time worked, as by tending additional machines, usually without proportionate increase in pay. 2 A slow-down practiced by employees so as to make the work last longer: see CA' CANNY.
stret·to (stret'tō) *n. pl.* **·ti** (-tē) or **·tos** *Music*

1 A portion of a fugue, near the close, in which the answer crowds closely on the subject. 2 In an oratorio or operatic piece, the portion at the close accelerated in time to produce a climax: also **stret'ta** (-tä). [<Ital., lit., drawn tight <L *strictus.* See STRESS.]

strew (strōō) *v.t.* **strewed, strewed** or **strewn, strew·ing** 1 To spread about loosely or at random; scatter; sprinkle. 2 To cover with something scattered or sprinkled. 3 To be scattered over (a surface). [OE *strēawian*]

stri·a (strī'ə) *n. pl.* **stri·ae** (strī'ē) 1 A narrow streak, stripe, or band of distinctive color, structure, or texture, often parallel with others. 2 *Geol.* A small groove, channel, or ridge on a rock surface, due to the action of glacier ice. [<L, a groove]

stri·ate (strī'āt) *adj.* 1 Having fine linear markings; grooved. 2 Constituting a stria or striae. Also **stri'at·ed.** — *v.t.* **·at·ed, ·at·ing** To mark with striae. [<L *striatus,* pp. of *striare* groove < *stria* a groove]

stri·a·tion (strī·ā'shən) *n.* 1 The act of striating, or the state of being striated. 2 A striate form or appearance. 3 One of a series of parallel striae, as in a muscle or mineral.

stri·a·ture (strī'ə·chər) *n.* 1 The manner in which striae are disposed or arranged; striation. 2 A stria.

strick (strik) *n. Brit. Dial.* 1 A bunch of fibers, as flax, hackled or ready for hackling. 2 A bundle of silk fibers prepared for the second combing. [Prob. <STRICKEN (def. 4)]

strick·en (strik'ən) *adj.* 1 Wounded, especially by a missile: a *stricken* hare. 2 Struck down; afflicted, as by calamity or disease: *stricken* with polio. Compare STRIKE *v.* 3 Advanced or far gone, as in age: *stricken* in years. 4 Having the contents leveled off even with the top of a container. [OE *stricen,* pp. of *strican* strike]

strick·le (strik'əl) *n.* 1 A straightedge used for striking off an even measure of grain. 2 A template or curved piece of wood used in smoothing a sand or loam mold to form a core. 3 A straightedge, to which emery is applied, for sharpening rotary knives. — *v.t.* **·led, ·ling** To shape or smooth with a strickle. [OE *stricel*]

strict (strikt) *adj.* 1 Observing or enforcing rules exactly; also, containing exact or severe rules or provisions; exacting. 2 Strenuously enjoined and maintained; rigidly observed. 3 Exactly defined, distinguished, or applied; not indefinite or loose. 4 Stretched tight; not lax; tense. 5 Close, narrow, and upright; straight: said of the panicles of certain plants. See synonyms under AUSTERE, PRECISE. [<L *strictus,* pp. of *stringere* draw tight. Doublet of STRAIT.] — **strict'ly** *adv.* — **strict'ness** *n.*

stric·tion (strik'shən) *n.* Constriction. [<L *strictio, -onis* < *strictus.* See STRICT.]

stric·ture (strik'chər) *n.* 1 Severe criticism. 2 *Pathol.* A morbid contraction of some duct or channel of the body. 3 *Obs.* Strictness. [<L *strictura* < *strictus* strict]

strid·den (strid'n) Past participle of STRIDE.

strid·dle (strid'l) *v.t.* & *v.i. Brit. Dial.* To straddle. Also **strid'dul.** [Freq. of STRIDE; infl. in meaning by STRADDLE]

stride (strīd) *n.* 1 A long and sweeping or measured step; also, the space passed over by such a step. 2 In animal locomotion, an act of progressive motion, completed when all the feet are returned to the same relative positions they occupied at the beginning of the movement. 3 A stage of progress. — **to hit one's stride** To attain one's normal speed. — **to make rapid strides** To make quick progress. — **to take (something) in one's stride** To do (something) without undue effort as part of one's normal activity. — *v.* **strode, strid·den, strid·ing** *v.i.* 1 To walk with long steps, as from haste or pride. 2 *Archaic* To straddle. — *v.t.* 3 To walk through, along, etc., with long steps. 4 To pass over with a single stride. 5 To straddle; bestride. [OE *strīdan* stride] — **strid'er** *n.*

stri·dent (strīd'nt) *adj.* Giving a loud and harsh sound; shrill; grating. [<L *stridens, -entis,* ppr. of *stridere* creak] — **stri'dence, stri'den·cy** *n.* — **stri'dent·ly** *adv.*

stri·dor (strī'dər) *n.* 1 A harsh, shrill, creaking, screechy, or grating noise. 2 *Pathol.* A harsh grating noise, particularly one heard in laryngeal obstruction. [<L]

strid·u·late (strij'ōō·lāt) *v.i.* **·lat·ed, ·lat·ing** To make a shrill, creaking noise, as a locust, cicada, or the like. [<NL *stridulatus,* pp. of *stridulare* < *stridulus* rattling < *stridere* rattle, rasp] — **strid'u·la'tion** *n.* — **strid'u·la·to'ry** (-lə·tôr'ē, -tō'rē), **strid'u·lous** *adj.* — **strid'u·lous·ly** *adv.* — **strid'u·lous·ness** *n.*

strife (strīf) *n.* 1 Angry contention; fighting. 2 Any contest for advantage or superiority; rivalry. 3 The act of striving; strenuous endeavor. See synonyms under BATTLE, FEUD[1], QUARREL[1]. [<OF *estrif* < *estriver.* See STRIVE.]

strig·il (strij'əl) *n.* 1 In ancient Greece and Rome, a scraper, as of metal, bone, or ivory, used for scraping the skin, as at the bath. 2 *Archit.* One of a group of wavy flutings carved on flat or curved surfaces, as in Roman architecture. [<L *strigilis* scraper]

strig·i·la·tion (strij'ə·lā'shən) *n.* 1 The application of a strigil to the skin. 2 The friction thus caused.

strig·il·lose (strij'ə·lōs) *adj.* Diminutively or minutely strigose. [<NL *strigilla,* dim. of *striga* a furrow]

stri·gose (strī'gōs, stri·gōs') *adj.* 1 *Bot.* Rough with short, sharp, appressed stiff hairs or bristles, as a leaf; hispid. 2 *Zool.* Marked with stripes or striae. [<NL *strigosus* <L *striga* a furrow]

strike (strīk) *v.* **struck, struck** (*chiefly Archaic* **strick·en**), **strik·ing** *v.t.* 1 To come into violent contact with; hit; crash into: The car *struck* the wall. 2 To hit with a blow; deal a blow to; smite: It *struck* him in the face. 3 To deal (a blow, etc.). 4 To cause to hit forcibly: He *struck* his hand on the table. 5 To attack; assault: We *struck* the enemy on his left flank. 6 To remove, separate, or take off by or as by a blow: with *off, from,* etc.: *Strike* it from the record. 7 **a** To ignite (a match, etc.). **b** To produce (a light, etc.) thus. 8 To form by stamping, printing, etc.; impress; coin. 9 To announce; sound: The clock *struck* two. 10 To fall upon; reach; catch: A sound of crying *struck* his ear. 11 To arrive at; come upon: to *strike* a trail. 12 To discover; find: to *strike* oil. 13 To affect suddenly or in a specified manner: He was *struck* speechless. 14 To come to the mind of; occur to: An idea *strikes* me. 15 To impress in a specified manner; seem to: He *strikes* me as an honest man. 16 To attract the attention of; impress: The dress *struck* her fancy. 17 To assume; take up: to *strike* an attitude. 18 To cause to enter or penetrate deeply or suddenly: to *strike* dismay into one's heart. 19 To lower or haul down; take or let down, as a sail, or a flag in token of surrender. 20 To cease working at in order to compel compliance to a demand, etc. 21 In the theater, to dismantle (a set or scene). 22 To make level (a measure of grain, etc.); strickle. 23 To make and confirm, as a bargain. 24 To harpoon (a whale). 25 To hook (a fish that has taken the lure) by a sharp pull on the line. 26 To arrive at by reckoning: to *strike* a balance. — *v.i.* 27 To come into violent contact; crash; hit. 28 To deal or aim a blow or blows. 29 To make an assault or attack. 30 To sound from a blow or blows. 31 To be indicated by the sound of blows or strokes: Noon has just *struck.* 32 To ignite. 33 To run aground, as on a reef or shoal: The ship *struck* and heeled over. 34 To lower a flag in token of surrender or in salute. 35 To come suddenly or unexpectedly; chance: with *on* or *upon*: to *strike* upon an unknown path. 36 To take a course; start and proceed: to *strike* for home. 37 To move quickly; dart. 38 To cease work in order to enforce demands, etc. 39 To snatch at or swallow the lure: said of fish. — **to strike camp** To take down the tents of a camp. — **to strike down** 1 To fell with a blow. 2 To affect disastrously; incapacitate completely. — **to strike dumb** To astonish; amaze. — **to strike hands** To clasp hands, especially in confirming a bargain. — **to strike home** 1 To deal an effective blow. 2 To have telling effect. — **to strike it rich** 1 To find a valuable vein or pocket of ore. 2 To come into wealth or good fortune. — **to strike off** 1 To remove or take off by or as by a blow or stroke. 2 To cross out or erase by or as by a stroke of the pen. 3 To deduct. — **to strike out** 1 To strike off (def. 2). 2 To aim a blow or blows. 3 To originate; devise; contrive. 4 To begin; start. 5 In baseball: **a** To put out (the batter) by pitching three strikes. **b** To be put out because of taking three strikes. — **to strike up** 1 To begin to play, sing, or sound, as a band or musical instrument. 2 To start up; begin, as a friendship. — *n.* 1 An act of striking or hitting; a blow. 2 In baseball, an unsuccessful attempt by the batter to hit the ball; a pitched ball that passes over home plate above the level of the batter's knees and below that of his shoulders; a foul bunt; any foul tip held by the catcher; any ball hit foul except when there have been two strikes. 3 In bowling, the knocking down by a player of all the pins with the first bowl in any frame. 4 The quitting of work by a body of workers to enforce some demand. 5 A new or unexpected discovery, as of oil or ore. 6 Any unexpected or complete success. 7 A straight-edged implement for leveling something, as grain in a measure; strickle. 8 *Geol.* The direction, referred to the meridian, of a horizontal line in a given structural plane, or of the intersection of the structural plane with a horizontal surface. 9 In coining, the quantity of coin or the number of medals made or struck at one time. 10 Full measure; hence, excellence. 11 The act of attempting to obtain money or some valuable thing, as by simple request, or by the introduction of a bill in a legislative body for the purpose of being bought off. 12 The sudden rise and taking of the bait by a fish; a bite. — **general strike** Concerted cessation of work on the part of the employees of all or nearly all industries, including public utilities, in a certain town, region, or nation. — **sit-down strike** See SIT-DOWN. [OE *strīcan* stroke, move. Akin to STREAK.]

strike·break·er (strīk'brā'kər) *n.* 1 One who takes the place of a workman on strike. 2 A person who supplies workmen to take the place of strikers. — **strike'break'ing** *n.*

strike fault *Geol.* A fault lying parallel with the strike of the rocks through which it cuts.

strike figure A percussion figure.

strike-out (strīk'out') *n.* An instance of striking out, especially in baseball.

strik·er (strī'kər) *n.* 1 One who or that which strikes. 2 In certain torpedoes, a plunger which strikes the priming cap and ignites the charge. 3 An employee who is on strike. 4 One whose business is to strike something in a mechanical occupation, as in forging. 5 *U.S. Colloq.* One who makes a blackmailing strike in politics. 6 In the U. S. Navy, an apprentice in training for a specific technical rating: a radioman *striker.* 7 Formerly, the engineer's apprentice on a river steamboat. 8 In the U. S. Army, a soldier assigned to run errands and do odd jobs for an officer.

strik·ing (strī'king) *adj.* Notable; impressive. See synonyms under EXTRAORDINARY. — **strik'ing·ly** *adv.* — **strik'ing·ness** *n.*

Strind·berg (strind'bûrg, *Sw.* strēn'ber·y'), **John August,** 1849–1912, Swedish dramatist and novelist.

string (string) *n.* 1 A slender line, thinner than a cord and thicker than a thread, used for tying or lacing; twine; also, a slender strip, as of cloth or leather; the cord of a bow; prepared wire or catgut for musical instruments. 2 A stringlike organ or formation; a fibrous vegetable formation; an animal nerve or tendon. 3 A thin cord upon which anything is strung; a row or series of things connected by a small cord: a *string* of pearls. 4 A connected series or succession as of things, acts, or events: sometimes implying unusual length: a *string* of carriages; a *string* of lies. 5 *U.S. Colloq.* A drove or small collection of stock, especially of saddle horses. 6 *pl.* Stringed instruments, especially those of an orchestra; those who play on these. 7 In billiards, the score; the buttons, strung on a wire, by which the score is kept; the string line; the act of stringing. 8 *Archit.* **a** A string-course, as of bricks. **b** A stout inclined plank, notched and set edgewise as a support for the steps of a wooden stairway; a ramp or sidepiece of solid-built stairs. **9** In sports, a group of contestants ranked as to skill. **10** The conditions, limitations, or restrictions attached to any proposition, gift, or donation, whereby the terms may not be binding, or whereby the donor retains some control. **—to pull strings** To manipulate or influence others, secretly or underhandedly, to gain some advantage. **—***v.* **strung, string·ing** *v.t.* **1** To thread, as beads, on or as on a string. **2** To fit with a string or strings, as a guitar. **3** To bind, fasten, or adorn with a string or strings. **4** To tighten the strings of (a musical instrument). **5** To brace; strengthen. **6** To make tense or nervous. **7** To arrange or extend like a string. **8** To remove the strings from (vegetables). **9** *Colloq.* To hang: usually with *up.* **—***v.i.* **10** To extend, stretch, or proceed in a line or series. **11** To form into strings. **12** In billiards, to drive the cue ball from within the string against the farther cushion and back. **—to string along** *Slang* **1** To follow with trust or confidence. **2** To fool; deceive; cheat. **3** To keep (someone) waiting or on tenterhooks. [OE *streng* string]

string bass The double bass.

string bean **1** Any of several varieties of beans (genus *Phaseolus*) cultivated for their edible pods, especially *P. vulgaris.* **2** The pod itself. **3** *Colloq.* A tall, skinny person.

string·board (string′bôrd′, -bōrd′) *n. Archit.* A board serving as a stringpiece in which the ends of steps of a staircase are set.

string-course (string′kôrs′, -kōrs′) *n. Archit.* A horizontal molding or ornamental course, often projecting along the face of a building.

stringed (stringd) *adj.* **1** Furnished with strings. **2** Produced from stringed instruments. **3** Tied with string.

strin·gen·do (strin·jen′dō) *adj. Music* Hastening the tempo as toward a climax; accelerando. [<Ital., ppr. of *stringere* draw tight <L]

strin·gent (strin′jənt) *adj.* **1** Keeping one closely to strict requirements; rigid; severe, as regulations. **2** Hampered by obstructing conditions or scarcity of money; close or tight: The money market is very *stringent.* **3** Convincing; forcible. [<L *stringens, -entis,* ppr. of *stringere* draw tight] **—strin′gen·cy, strin′gent·ness** *n.* **—strin′gent·ly** *adv.*

string·er (string′ər) *n.* **1** A heavy timber, generally horizontal, supporting other members of a structure, and usually running in the direction of the greatest length of the collection of supported members. **2** Any horizontal framing timber, as a tie beam; a stringpiece. **3** A lengthwise timber on which rails are laid, as distinguished from a *cross-tie* or *sleeper.* **4** A news reporter employed on a free-lance basis, often in out-of-town or foreign locations. **5** A person having a specific rating as to excellence, skill, etc.: used in combination: a *second-stringer.*

string·halt (string′hôlt′) *n.* A convulsive movement of the hind legs of a horse: also called *springhalt.* **—string′halt′ed, string′halt′y** *adj.*

string line In billiards, a line passing across the table through the cue spot.

string·piece (string′pēs′) *n.* A heavy supporting timber, horizontal or inclined, forming the margin or edge of a framework, as of a floor or staircase; a stringer, or stringboard.

string·y (string′ē) *adj.* **string·i·er, string·i·est** **1** Containing fibrous strings. **2** Forming in strings, as thick glue; ropy. **3** Having tough sinews. **4** Tall and wiry in build. **—string′·i·ly** *adv.* **—string′i·ness** *n.*

strip[1] (strip) *n.* **1** A narrow piece, comparatively long, as of cloth, wood, etc. **2** A number of stamps attached in a row. **3** A narrow piece of land; a minor civil division in Maine. **4** An act of destruction or spoliation. **5** A comic strip. **—Cherokee strip** A strip of land formerly leased to the Cherokee Indians but now part of Oklahoma. **—***v.t.* **stripped, strip·ping** To cut or tear into strips. [? <MLG *strippe* a strap]

strip[2] (strip) *v.* **stripped** (*Rare* **stript**), **strip·ping** *v.t.* **1** To pull the covering, clothing, etc., from; denude; lay bare. **2** To pull off (the covering or clothing). **3** To rob or plunder; spoil. **4** To make bare or empty. **5** To remove; take away. **6** To deprive of something; divest: He was *stripped* of his rank. **7** To separate the leaves of (tobacco) from the stalks. **8** To milk (a cow) dry by a downward stroke and compression of the thumb and forefinger. **9** *Mech.* To damage or break the teeth, thread, etc., of (a gear, bolt, or the like). **—***v.i.* **10** To remove one's clothing; undress. **11** *Mech.* To suffer breaking or jamming of the teeth or thread. [ME <OE *-strȳpan,* as in *bestrȳpan* despoil, plunder]

stripe[1] (strīp) *n.* **1** A line, band, or long strip of material of different color or finish from the adjacent surface. **2** Distinctive quality or character; kind; sort; also, a certain kind of religious or political belief or opinion: a man of Democratic *stripe.* **3** Striped cloth. **4** *pl.* Prison uniform. **5** A piece of material or braid on the sleeve of a uniform to indicate rank, etc.; a chevron; a service or wound stripe. **—***v.t.* **striped, strip·ing** To mark with a stripe or stripes. [<MDu.]

stripe[2] (strīp) *n.* **1** A blow struck with a whip or rod, as in flogging. **2** A weal or welt on the skin caused by such a blow. See synonyms under BLOW[2]. [Prob. <LG. Cf. Du. *strippen* whip.]

striped (strīpt, strī′pid) *adj.* Having stripes; marked with stripes.

striped bass See under BASS[1] (def. 1).

striped snake A garter snake.

striped squirrel A chipmunk.

strip·er (strī′pər) *n. U.S. Colloq.* A person who wears stripes on his or her sleeves: a one-*striper* or ensign in the Navy.

strip·ling (strip′ling) *n.* A mere youth; a lad. [<STRIP[1] + -LING]

strip-mine (strip′mīn′) *v.t.* **-mined, -min·ing** **1** To extract (material, as coal) from a strip mine. **—***v.i.* **2** To work a strip mine. **—strip miner —strip mining**

strip mine A mine, especially a coal mine, the seams of which are close to the surface of the earth, and which is worked by stripping away the topsoil and the material beneath it.

strip·per (strip′ər) *n.* **1** One who or that which strips. **2** *Slang* A female performer of a strip-tease. **3** A partially depleted oil well producing few barrels a day: also **stripper well.** **4** An owner or operator of a strip mine; also, a worker on a strip mine.

strip·ping (strip′ing) *n.* **1** The act or process of one who or that which strips. **2** *pl.* The milk drawn from a cow by stripping. **3** The operation of strip mines; strip mining.

strip-tease (strip′tēz′) *n.* In burlesque, a gradual disrobing by a female performer. **—strip′-teas′er** *n.*

strip·y (strī′pē) *adj.* **strip·i·er, strip·i·est** Being in or suggesting stripes or streaks; having or marked with stripes.

strive (strīv) *v.i.* **strove, striv·en** (striv′ən) or **strived, striv·ing** **1** To make earnest effort. **2** To engage in strife; contend; fight. **3** To vie; emulate. See synonyms under CONTEND, ENDEAVOR, STRUGGLE. [<OF *estriver,* prob. <Gmc.] **—striv′er** *n.*

strobe (strōb) *n.* **1** A stroboscope. **2** An electronically controlled device that emits light in very brief, brilliant flashes, used in photography, in the theater, etc.: also **strobe light.**

strob·ic (strō′bik) *adj.* **1** Resembling a top. **2** Seeming to spin: said of concentric circles that appear to spin when moved. [<Gk. *strobos* whirling]

stro·bi·la (strō·bī′lə) *n. pl.* **·lae** (-lē) *Zool.* **1** A stage in the life cycle of a jellyfish characterized by a series of annular plates each of which separates as a new organism. **2** The segmented body of a tapeworm. [<NL <Gk. *strobilē* plug of lint shaped like a fir cone <*strobilos* fir cone, anything twisted <*strobos* twisted, ult. <*strephein* twist]

strob·i·la·ceous (strob′ə·lā′shəs) *adj.* **1** Resembling or relating to a strobile or cone. **2** Producing strobiles.

strob·i·late (strob′ə·lāt) *v.i.* **·lat·ed, ·lat·ing** To divide metamerically; undergo strobilation.

strob·i·la·tion (strob′ə·lā′shən) *n. Zool.* Asexual reproduction by division, as in jellyfish and tapeworms; metameric division.

strob·ile (strob′il) *n. Bot.* **1** A multiple fruit consisting of an oblong, oval, or conical mass of dry imbricated scales, as in the pines, spruces, firs, etc.; a cone. **2** A cone-shaped mass of sporophylls producing spore cases, as in the horsetails, clubmosses, etc. Also **strob′il.** [See STROBILA]

strob·o·scope (strob′ə·skōp) *n.* An instrument for observing or studying periodic motion by rendering the moving body visible only at certain points of its path. [<Gk. *strobos* twisting + -SCOPE] **—strob′o·scop′ic** (-skop′·ik) or **·i·cal** *adj.* **—strob·os·co·py** (strob·os′·kə·pē) *n.*

strob·o·tron (strob′ə·tron) *n.* A low-pressure electron tube filled with a rare gas or a mixture of rare gases and used in stroboscopic photography, or to transmit supersonic impulses by means of its periodic discharges.

strode (strōd) Past tense of STRIDE.

stroke (strōk) *n.* **1** The act or movement of striking; a knock; an impact. **2** One of a series of recurring movements, as of oars, a piston, etc.; also, the rate, extent, or manner of such movement. **3** Stroke oar. **4** A single movement, as of the hand, arm, or some instrument, by which something is made or done. **5** A single movement of some instrument, as of a pen or pencil. **6** A blow or any ill effect caused as if by a blow: a *stroke* of misfortune, a *sunstroke.* **7** *Pathol.* An attack of paralysis or apoplexy. **8** A blow or the sound of a blow of a striking mechanism, as of a clock. **9** A sudden or brilliant mental act; feat; coup: a great *stroke* of diplomacy, a *stroke* of wit. **10** A pulsation, as of the heart. **11** A mark or dash of a pen or tool. **12** A light caressing movement; a stroking. See synonyms under BLOW[2], MISFORTUNE. **—***v.t.* **stroked, strok·ing** **1** To pass the hand over gently or caressingly, or with light pressure. **2** To set the pace for (a rowboat or its crew); act as stroke for. **3** To sound (time), as a gong or clock. [ME *strok, strak* <OE *strācian* strike]

stroke oar **1** The aftmost oar of a boat, whose movement sets the rate of rowing. **2** The person who rows with this oar: also **stroke-oars·man** (strōk′ôrz′mən, -ōrz′-), **strokes·man** (strōks′mən). **3** The position occupied by such an oarsman.

stroll (strōl) *v.i.* **1** To walk in a leisurely or idle manner; saunter. **2** To go from place to place. **—***n.* An idle or leisurely walk; a wandering. See synonyms under RAMBLE. [Origin uncertain]

stroll·er (strō′lər) *n.* **1** One who strolls; especially, a strolling showman or player. **2** A tramp. **3** A small, light baby carriage, often collapsible.

stro·ma (strō′mə) *n. pl.* **·ma·ta** (-mə·tə) **1** *Physiol.* The ground substance or connective tissue that forms the framework of an organ or cell. **2** *Bot.* In fungi, the union of mycelial threads into a dense crust on or in which the sporophores are borne. [<Gk. *strōma* bed] **—stro·mat·ic** (strō·mat′ik) *adj.*

Strom·bo·li (strôm′bō·lē) The northernmost of the Lipari Islands in the Tyrrhenian Sea; 5 square miles; site of an active volcano, 3,040 feet.

stro·mey·er·ite (strō′mī·ər·īt) *n.* A metallic, lustrous, steel-gray native sulfide of copper and silver, crystallizing in the orthorhombic system. [after F. *Stromeyer,* 1786–1835, German chemist]

strong (strông, strong) *adj.* **1** Physically or bodily powerful; muscular; vigorous. **2** Healthy; robust: a *strong* constitution. **3** Morally powerful; firm; resolute; courageous. **4** Mentally powerful or vigorous. **5** Especially competent or able (in a certain subject or field): *strong* in mathematics. **6** Abundantly or richly supplied (with something): *strong* in trumps; *strong* in literary interest. **7** Solidly made or constituted; not easily destroyed, injured, or strained: *strong* walls, paper, etc. **8** Powerful as a rival or combatant: a *strong* team, army, etc. **9** Easy to defend; difficult to capture: a *strong* hill position. **10** In numerical force: an army 20,000 *strong.* **11** Well able to exert influence, authority, etc.: a *strong* government. **12** Financially sound: a *strong* bank. **13** Powerful in effect: *strong* poison, medicine, etc. **14** Concentrated; not diluted or weak: *strong* coffee. **15** Containing much alcohol: a *strong* drink. **16** Powerful in flavor or odor; also, rank; unpleasant: a *strong* breath. **17** Intense in degree or quality; not mild: a *strong* pulse; *strong* light, heat, etc. **18** Loud and firm: a *strong* voice. **19** Firm; tenacious: a *strong* grip; a *strong* opinion. **20** Deeply earnest; fervid: a *strong* desire. **21** Cogent; convincing: *strong* evidence. **22** Distinct; marked; definite: a *strong* resemblance. **23** Extreme; high-handed: *strong* measures. **24** Emphatic; not moderate: *strong* language. **25** Moving with great force: said of a wind, stream, or tide; specifically, *Meteorol.*, designating a breeze (No. 6) or a gale (No. 9) on the Beaufort scale. **26** Characterized by steady or rising prices: a *strong* market. **27** *Phonet.* Stressed; accented, as a syllable. **28** *Gram.* In Germanic languages: **a** Of verbs, indicating changes in tense by means of ablaut vowel alteration in the stem, rather than by the addition of inflectional endings; as, English *drink, drank, drunk*; *write, wrote, written*; German *singen, sang, gesungen*: also called *irregular*. **b** Of nouns and adjectives (in German and Old English), showing distinctive declensional endings for case, number, and gender. For example, in German, a descriptive adjective is used in the strong form when not preceded by a limiting word *(guter Mann)* or when preceded by one having no distinctive case and gender inflection *(mein guter Mann)*. Compare WEAK (def. 12). —*adv.* Strongly: usually employed in combination: *strong*-talking. Many self-explaining compound adjectives have *strong* as the first element: *strong*-armed, *strong*-smelling, etc. [OE] —**strong'ly** *adv.*

Synonyms (adj.): cohesive, compact, hardy, robust, sinewy, stalwart, stout, stubborn, sturdy, tenacious, vigorous, See FIRM, HEALTHY.

strong-arm (strông'ärm', strong'-) *Colloq. adj.* Using physical or coercive power: *strong-arm* tactics. —*v.t.* **1** To use physical force upon; assault. **2** To coerce; compel.

strong·bark (strông'bärk', strong'-) *n.* A small tree *(Bourreria ovata)*, native to the West Indies and Florida. The wood is brown, hard, and strong; the berries are edible.

strong·box (strông'boks', strong'-) *n.* A strongly built chest or safe for keeping valuables.

strong drink Alcoholic liquors.

strong·hold (strông'hōld', strong'-) *n.* A place that nature or man has made strongly defensible; hence, a refuge. See synonyms under FORTIFICATION, REFUGE.

strong·man (strông'man', strong'-) *n.* A political leader having considerable or preeminent power, as from a military coup or other extralegal means.

strong-mind·ed (strông'mīn'did, strong'-) *adj.* Having a determined, vigorous mind. —**strong'-mind'ed·ly** *adv.* —**strong'-mind'ed·ness** *n.*

strong·room (strông'ro͞om', -ro͝om', strong'-) *n.* A room especially equipped for the safekeeping of valuables.

strong-willed (strông'wild', strong'-) *adj.* Having a strong will; decided; often, obstinate.

stron·gyle (stron'jil) *n.* Any of an order *(Strongyloidea)* of parasitic nematode worms, many of them very injurious to man and certain animals; especially, the hookworm and the gapeworm. [<Gk. *strongylos* round]

stron·ti·a (stron'shē·ə) *n. Chem.* **1** A grayish-white, infusible strontium monoxide, SrO. **2** Strontium hydroxide, $Sr(OH)_2$. [<NL <STRONTIUM]

stron·ti·an·ite (stron'shē·ən·īt') *n.* A vitreous, native strontium carbonate, $SrCO_3$, occurring in various forms and colors.

stron·ti·um (stron'shē·əm, -shəm, -tē·əm) *n.* A hard yellowish metallic element (symbol Sr) of the alkaline earth group, known chiefly through its salts, which burn with a red flame and are used in pyrotechnics. See ELEMENT. [< NL, from *Strontian*, Argyll, Scotland, where first discovered] —**stron'tic** (-tik) *adj.*

strontium 90 *Physics* A radioactive isotope of strontium chemically resembling calcium and with a half-life of about 28 years: as a component in the fall-out of a thermonuclear bomb it contaminates the soil and is a radiation hazard through progressive concentration in the bones of men and animals. Also called *radiostrontium*.

strop (strop) *n.* **1** A strip of leather or canvas on which to sharpen a razor; also, a rectangular implement with strops on it. **2** A strap. —*v.t.* **stropped, strop·ping** To sharpen on a strop. [OE *stropp* <L *struppus* <Gk. *strophos* a band, cord]

stro·phan·thin (strō·fan'thin) *n.* A bitter, poisonous, crystalline glycoside contained in certain varieties of a tropical plant (genus *Strophanthus*) and resembling digitalis in its action on the heart. [<NL *Strophanthus*, a genus name (<Gk. *strophos* cord + *anthos* flower) + -IN]

stro·phe (strō'fē) *n.* **1** In ancient Greek poetry, the verses sung by the chorus in a play while moving from right to left. **2** In classical prosody, the lines of an ode comprising a stanza and alternating with the antistrophe. **3** The first of two alternating metrical systems in a poem. [<Gk. *strophē* a turning, twist < *strephein* turn] —**stroph·ic** (strof'ik, strō'fik) or **·i·cal** *adj.*

stroph·i·ole (strof'ē·ōl, strō'fē-) *n. Bot.* An aril-like appendage attached to the base of certain seeds. [<L *strophiolum*, dim. of *strophium* a band <Gk. *strophos* cord < *strephein* twist] —**stroph'i·o·late'** (-lāt'), **stroph'i·o·lat'ed** *adj.*

stroph·u·lus (strof'yə·ləs) *n. Pathol.* Any of various types of miliaria common in children: also called *tooth rash, red gum*. [<NL, dim. of Gk. *strophos* a cord. See STROPHE.]

stross·ers (stros'ərz) *n. pl. Obs.* Trousers.

stroud (stroud) *n.* A coarse, heavy, woolen material used for blankets; also, a blanket made of this material, formerly used for trading with North American Indians. [from *Stroud*, England]

strove (strōv) Past tense of STRIVE.

strow (strō) *v.t. Obs.* To strew.

struck (struk) Past tense and past participle of STRIKE.

struck jury A jury specially selected by a process in which each party strikes twelve names from a list of forty-eight eligible persons, and the remaining twenty-four are summoned as the panel from which the jury of twelve men is drawn.

struck measure A measure, as of meal, smoothed down: opposed to *heaped measure*.

struck mine, plant, etc. A mine, manufacturing plant, etc., in which work has been stopped by a strike.

struc·tur·al (struk'chər·əl) *adj.* **1** Of, pertaining to, possessing, characterized, or caused by structure. **2** *Geol.* Having a form, position, or character determined by the preexistent structure of the earth's crust; tectonic. **3** *Biol.* Morphological. **4** *Chem.* Pertaining to or denoting the spatial arrangements of atoms in a molecule: a *structural* formula. **5** Used in or essential to construction. —**struc'tur·al·ly** *adv.*

structural iron **1** Shapes of iron used in constructing buildings, bridges, etc. **2** Iron cast in shapes for this purpose.

structural steel **1** Steel prepared after the manner of structural iron for use in building. **2** Rolled steel adapted for use in construction: of considerable toughness and strength.

struc·ture (struk'chər) *n.* **1** That which is constructed; a combination of related parts, as a building or machine. **2** *Biol.* The arrangement and functional union of parts, tissues, and organs of a plant or animal. **3** *Geol.* **a** The spatial arrangement of rock strata in a larger formation. **b** The gross physical characteristics of a rock. **4** *Chem.* The disposition of atoms within a molecule or of molecules in a compound. **5** The manner of construction or organization: the social *structure* of a primitive society. **6** *Archaic* The act of constructing. —*v.t.* **·tured, ·tur·ing** **1** To form into an organized structure; build. **2** To conceive as a structural whole; ideate: He *structured* the plan before proposing it. See synonyms under FRAME. [<F <L *structura* < *structus*, pp. of *struere* build]

stru·del (stro͞od'l, *Ger.* shtro͞o'dəl) *n.* A kind of pastry made of a thin sheet of dough, spread with fruit or cheese, nuts, etc., rolled, and baked. [<G, lit., eddy]

strug·gle (strug'əl) *n.* A violent effort or series of efforts; a labored contest; sometimes, a war; battle. See synonyms under ENDEAVOR. [< *v.*] —*v.* **·gled, ·gling** *v.i.* **1** To contend with an adversary in physical combat; fight. **2** To put forth violent efforts; strive: to *struggle* against odds. **3** To make one's way by violent efforts: to *struggle* through mud. —*v.t.* **4** To accomplish with a struggle. [ME *strogelen*; origin unknown] —**strug'gler** *n.* —**strug'gling·ly** *adv.*

Synonyms (verb): battle, contend, contest, endeavor, fight, labor, strain, strive, toil, try, vie, wrestle, writhe.

Struld·brug (struld'brug) *n.* One of a class of immortal human beings, described in Swift's *Gulliver's Travels* (Voyage to Laputa), who became senile after the age of eighty, gradually losing all power of communication and becoming wards of the state.

strum (strum) *v.t.* & *v.i.* **strummed, strum·ming** To play (on a stringed instrument) without expression; thrum. —*n.* The act of strumming. [Prob. imit.] —**strum'mer** *n.*

stru·ma (stro͞o'mə) *n. pl.* **·mae** (-mē) **1** *Pathol.* **a** Scrofula. **b** Goiter. **2** *Bot.* A wenlike cushion or swelling of or on an organ, as at the base of the capsule in certain mosses. [<L < *struere* build] —**stru·mat·ic** (stro͞o·mat'ik), **stru'mose** (-mōs), **stru'mous** (-məs) *adj.*

Stru·ma (stro͞o'mä) A river in SW Bulgaria and NE Greece, flowing 215 miles SE to the Aegean: Greek *Strymon*.

strum·pet (strum'pit) *n.* A whore; harlot. [? Ult. <OF *strupe* concubinage <L *stuprum* dishonor]

strung (strung) Past tense and past participle of STRING.

strunt (strunt, stro͝ont) *Scot. v.i.* **1** To strut. **2** To be sullen. —*n.* **1** A sullen mood; umbrage. **2** Spirituous liquor; whisky and water; toddy. —**to take the strunt** To be or become sulky.

strut (strut) *n.* **1** A proud or pompous step or walk. **2** A compression member in a framework, keeping two others from approaching nearer together, as the vertical members of the wing truss of a biplane. **3** An instrument used in adjusting the plaits of a ruff. —*v.* **strut·ted, strut·ting** *v.i.* To walk pompously, conceitedly, and affectedly. —*v.t.* To brace or support, as a framing or structure, by compression pieces, as struts or posts. [OE *strūtian* be rigid, stand stiffly] —**strut'ter** *n.* —**strut'ting** *adj.* —**strut'ting·ly** *adv.*

Stru·thi·on·i·dae (stro͞o'thē·on'i·dē) *n. pl.* A family of large, terrestrial, swift-running ratite birds; the ostriches, especially *Struthio camelus* of Africa and Arabia. [<NL <L *struthio* <Gk. *strouthiōn* ostrich]

stru·thi·ous (stro͞o'thē·əs) *adj.* **1** Like an ostrich. **2** Pertaining to the *Struthionidae*. [<L *struthio* an ostrich]

strych·nine (strik'nin, -nēn, -nīn) *n.* A white, crystalline, bitter, extremely poisonous alkaloid, $C_{21}H_{22}N_2O_2$, contained in various plants (genus *Strychnos*) of the logania family, especially *S. nuxvomica*. Its salts are used in medicine, chiefly as a neural stimulant; a large dose produces tetanic spasms. Also **strych'ni·a** (-nē·ə), **strych'nin** (-nin). [<F <L *strychnos* <Gk., nightshade]

strych·nin·ism (strik'nin·iz'əm) *n. Pathol.* The morbid condition resulting from the excessive or improper use of strychnine.

Stry·mon (strī'mən) The Greek name for the STRUMA.

Stry·mon·ic Gulf (strī·mon'ik) **1** An inlet of the northern Aegean in Greek Macedonia; 14 miles wide, 17 miles long. **2** The entire section of the Aegean between Thasos and Akti: also *Gulf of Orfani*.

St. Si·mons Island (sānt sī'mənz) One of the Sea Islands off the coast of SE Georgia; about 13 miles long, 3 to 7 miles wide; site of a national monument and of a decisive battle between England and Spain, 1742.

St. Swith·in's Day (sānt swith'ənz) July 15th, the day that commemorates St. Swithin, a former patron saint of Winchester Cathedral, England: rain occurring on this day is said to foretell wet weather for the following 40 days. Also **St. Swith'un's Day.**

St. Thom·as (sānt tom'əs) **1** An island of the Virgin Islands of the United States; 28 square miles; capital, Charlotte Amalie. **2** The English name for SÃO TOMÉ.

Stu·art (sto͞o'ərt, styo͞o'-) Name of the royal family of Scotland, 1371–1603, and of Great Britain, 1603–1714: also spelled *Stewart*. —**Charles Edward,** 1720–88, English prince, grandson of James II: called "Bonnie Prince Charlie" and the "Young Pretender." —**James Edward,** 1688–1766, English prince, son of James II: called the "Old Pretender."

Stuart (sto͞o′ərt, styo͞o′-), **Gilbert Charles,** 1755–1828, U. S. portrait painter. — **James Ewell Brown,** 1833–64, American Confederate cavalry general: nickname *Jeb.*

stub (stub) *n.* **1** The part of a tree trunk, bush, etc., that remains when the main part is cut down. **2** Any short projecting part or piece; a remnant, as of a pencil, candle, cigarette, cigar, or broken tooth. **3** In a checkbook or the like, one of the inner ends upon which a memorandum is entered, and which remains when the check is detached; also, the detachable coupon of a theater or other ticket. **4** Anything blunt, short, or stumpy, as a worn horseshoe nail or a stub pen. **5** *Obs.* A log; block; blockhead. **6** The title of a row in a statistical table; also, the first or reading column in such a table. — *v.t.* **stubbed, stub·bing 1** To strike, as the toe, against a low obstruction or projection. **2** To grub up, as roots; root out. **3** To clear or remove the stubs or roots from. — *adj.* Thick-set; stocky. [OE *stubb*]

stub·bed (stub′id, stubd) *adj.* **1** Made into or resembling a stub. **2** Full of stubs. **3** Sturdy; blunt in manner; stout and rough; rugged. — **stub′bed·ness** *n.*

stub·ble (stub′əl) *n.* **1** The stubs of grain stalks, sugarcane, etc., covering a field after the crop has been cut. **2** The field itself. **3** Any surface or growth resembling stubble, as short bristly hair or beard. [<OF *stuble,* ult. <L *stipula* stalk] — **stub′bled** *adj.* — **stub′·bly** *adj.*

stub·born (stub′ərn) *adj.* **1** Inflexible in opinion or intention; unreasonably obstinate. **2** Not easily handled, bent, or overcome; intractable: *stubborn* facts. **3** Characterized by perseverance or persistence: *stubborn* fighting. See synonyms under HARD, INFLEXIBLE, OBSTINATE, PERVERSE, STRONG. [Prob. OE *stubb* a stump] — **stub′born·ly** *adv.* — **stub′·born·ness** *n.*

Stubbs (stubz), **William,** 1825–1901, English bishop and historian.

stub·by (stub′ē) *adj.* **·bi·er, ·bi·est 1** Short, stiff, and bristling: a *stubby* beard. **2** Short and thick; like a stub: a *stubby* pencil. **3** Having many stubs. — **stub′bi·ly** *adv.* — **stub′bi·ness** *n.*

stub nail 1 A short thick nail. **2** An old horseshoe nail.

stub pen A very blunt-pointed pen for writing.

stuc·co (stuk′ō) *n. pl.* **·coes** or **·cos 1** A fine plaster for walls or their relief ornaments, usually of Portland cement, sand, and a small amount of lime. **2** Any plaster or cement used for the external coating of buildings. — *adj.* Stucco-coated. — *v.t.* **·coed, ·co·ing** To apply stucco to; decorate with stucco. [<Ital. <Gmc. Akin to OHG *stucchi* crust.] — **stuc′·co·er** *n.*

stuck (stuk) Past tense and past participle of STICK.

stuck–up (stuk′up′) *adj. Colloq.* Conceited; very vain; supercilious and arrogant; snobbish. — **stuck′–up′ness** *n.*

stud[1] (stud) *n.* **1** A short intermediate post, as in a building frame; a post to which laths are nailed; a scantling. **2** A knob, round-headed nail, or small protuberant ornament, as an ornamental button in a shirt front. **3** A crosspiece in a link, as in a chain cable. **4** A small pin such as is used in a watch. **5** Stud poker. — *v.t.* **stud·ded, stud·ding 1** To set thickly with small points, projections, or knobs. **2** To be scattered or strewn over: Daisies *stud* the meadows. **3** To support or stiffen by means of studs or upright props. [OE *studu* post]

stud[2] (stud) *n.* **1** A collection of horses and mares for breeding. **2** The place where they are kept. **3** A collection of horses for riding, hunting, or racing. **4** A stallion: also *studhorse.* — *adj.* **1** Of or pertaining to a stud. **2** Kept for breeding: a *stud* mare. [OE *stōd*]

stud book A record of the pedigree of a stud, or of thoroughbred racing stock collectively.

stud·die (stud′ē) *n. Brit. Dial.* An anvil; a stithy. [Prob. var. of STITHY]

stud·ding (stud′ing) *n.* **1** Studs or joists collectively, or material from which to make them. **2** The height of a room from floor to ceiling.

stud·ding·sail (stun′səl, stud′ing·sāl′) *n. Naut.* A light auxiliary sail set out beyond one of the principal sails by extensible booms during a following wind.

student (sto͞od′nt, styo͞od′nt) *n.* **1** A person engaged in a course of study; especially, one in a secondary school, college or university. **2** One who closely examines or investigates; one devoted to study. See synonyms under SCHOLAR. [<OF *estudiant* <L *studens, -entis,* ppr. of *studere* be eager, apply oneself, study]

student lamp A reading lamp easily adjustable for direction or distance of light rays.

student nurse One who is in training in a hospital school of nursing.

stu·dent·ship (sto͞od′nt·ship, styo͞od′nt-) *n.* **1** A scholarship. **2** The condition of being a student.

stud·fish (stud′fish′) *n. pl.* **·fish** or **·fish·es** Any of several minnows (genus *Fundulus*) having the sides studded with orange or brown spots, as *Fundulus stellifer* of the Alabama River.

stud·horse (stud′hôrs′) *n.* A stallion kept for breeding. Also **stud horse.**

stud·ied (stud′ēd) *adj.* **1** Deliberately and intentionally designed or undertaken; planned; premeditated: a *studied* insult. **2** Acquired or prepared by study. **3** *Rare* Learned; versed. — **stud′ied·ly** *adv.* — **stud′ied·ness** *n.*

stu·di·o (sto͞o′dē·ō, styo͞o′-) *n. pl.* **·di·os 1** The workroom of an artist, photographer, etc. **2** A place where motion pictures are filmed. **3** A room or rooms where radio or television programs are broadcast or recorded. [<Ital. <L *studium* zeal <*studere* apply oneself, be diligent]

studio couch A backless couch with a bed frame underneath which may be drawn out and made level with the couch to form a double bed or twin beds.

stu·di·ous (sto͞o′dē·əs, styo͞o′-) *adj.* **1** Given to study; devoting oneself to the acquisition of knowledge. **2** Earnest in the use of means; assiduous: *studious* to please. **3** Done with deliberation; studied: *studious* politeness. **4** Favorable to study; for study: *studious* halls. [<L *studiosus* <*studium* zeal. See STUDIO.] — **stu′di·ous·ly** *adv.* — **stu′di·ous·ness** *n.*

stud poker A game of poker in which the cards of the first round are dealt face down and the rest face up, betting opening on the second round.

stud·work (stud′wûrk′) *n.* **1** Walls of brickwork between studs. **2** Studded leather armor. **3** Anything set or supported with studs.

stud·y (stud′ē) *v.* **stud·ied, stud·y·ing** *v.t.* **1** To apply the mind in acquiring a knowledge of: to *study* physics. **2** To examine; search into: to *study* a problem. **3** To look at attentively; scrutinize: to *study* one's reflection in a mirror. **4** To endeavor to memorize, as a part in a play. **5** To give thought and attention to, as something to be done or devised: often with *out.* — *v.i.* **6** To apply the mind in acquiring knowledge. **7** To follow a regular course of instruction; be a student. **8** To muse; meditate. See synonyms under CONSIDER, EXAMINE, MUSE. — **to study up on** To acquire more complete information concerning, as by investigation. — *n. pl.* **stud·ies 1** The act of studying; the process of acquiring information; application of the mind to books, to art or science, etc. **2** A particular instance or form of mental work. **3** Something to be studied; a branch or department of knowledge. **4** A specific product of studious application. **5** In art, a first sketch; a student's art exercise. **6** A carefully elaborated literary treatment of a subject. **7** A room devoted to study, reading, etc. **8** A studious state of mind; profound thought; absent-mindedness: in a brown *study.* See BROWN STUDY. **9** Earnest endeavor; thoughtful care or its object: Our *study* is to please you. **10** *Music* A composition designed to aid development in technical facility; an étude. See synonyms under EDUCATION, INQUIRY, LEARNING, REFLECTION, TASK, THOUGHT[1]. [<OF *estudier* <*estudie* a study <L *studium* zeal. See STUDIO.] — **stud′·i·a·ble** *adj.*

study hall In a school, a large room equipped and reserved for study.

stuff (stuf) *v.t.* **1** To fill completely; pack; cram full. **2** To fill (an opening, etc.) with something forced in; plug. **3** To obstruct or stop up; choke. **4** To fill or expand with padding, as a cushion. **5** To fill (a fowl, roast, etc.) with stuffing. **6** In taxidermy, to fill the skin of (a bird, animal, etc.) with a material preparatory to mounting. **7** To fill too full; overload; distend. **8** To fill or cram with food: He *stuffed* himself with oysters. **9** To fill with knowledge, ideas, or attitudes, especially unsystematically: His head is *stuffed* with prejudices. **10** To force or cram, as into a small space. **11** To fill the pores of (a skin or pelt) with a preservative of oil and tallow. — *v.i.* **12** To eat to excess; gluttonize. — **to stuff a ballot box** To put fraudulent votes into a ballot box. [<*n.*] — *n.* **1** The material out of which something may be shaped or made; hence, raw or unwrought material. **2** Figuratively, the fundamental element of anything, material or spiritual. **3** Possessions generally, especially household goods. **4** A worthless collection of things; rubbish; hence, worthless ideas: often used as an interjection: *Stuff* and nonsense! **5** Woven material, especially of wool. **6** Any textile fabric. **7** Any one of various substances, mixtures, or compounds prepared for use, as paper pulp; in leathermaking, dubbing or stuffing. **8** A medicinal mixture or potion. **9** *Scot.* Luggage; belongings; corn; grain. **10** *Slang* Money; means. **11** In journalism, copy ready for the printer or engraver. [<OF *estoffe,* prob. <L *stuppa* tow] — **stuff′er** *n.*

stuffed shirt *Colloq.* A pretentious person; especially, a pompous boob.

stuff·ing (stuf′ing) *n.* **1** The material with which anything is stuffed. **2** A mixture, as of bread or cracker crumbs with meat and seasoning, used in stuffing fowls, etc., for cooking. **3** The process of stuffing anything.

stuff·ing box *Mech.* A device consisting of a chamber affording passage and lengthwise or rotary motion of a piece, as of a piston rod or shaft, while preventing leakage about the moving part by using packing material to fill the free space.

stuffing nut The nut which encloses a stuffing box.

stuff·y (stuf′ē) *adj.* **stuff·i·er, stuff·i·est 1** Badly ventilated. **2** Impeding respiration. **3** *U.S. Colloq.* Angry; sulky. **4** Old-fashioned; stodgy; stiffly precise; strait-laced. — **stuff′·i·ly** *adv.* — **stuff′i·ness** *n.*

Stu·ka (sto͞o′kə, *Ger.* shto͞o′kä) *n.* A German dive bomber: contraction of *Sturzkampfflugzeug.*

stull (stul) *n. Mining* A cross-timbering or platform in an excavation, especially in a stope to support workmen or to protect workers from falling stones. [Prob. <G *stollen* post, prop]

Stülp·na·gel (shtülp′nä·gəl), **Otto von,** 1880–1948, German general.

stul·ti·fy (stul′tə·fī) *v.t.* **·fied, ·fy·ing 1** To cause to appear absurd; give an appearance of foolishness to. **2** To bring to naught; nullify. **3** *Law* To allege to be of unsound mind. [<LL *stultificare* make foolish <L *stultus* foolish + *facere* make] — **stul′ti·fi·ca′tion** *n.* — **stul′ti·fi′er** *n.*

stum (stum) *n.* **1** Unfermented or partly fermented grape juice. **2** Wine revived, as by adding must, to produce increased fermentation; must. — *v.t.* **stummed, stum·ming 1** To stop fermentation in by some admixture. **2** To revive (wine), as by adding must, so as to increase fermentation. [<Du. *stom* must, lit., silent]

stum·ble (stum′bəl) *v.* **·bled, ·bling** *v.i.* **1** To miss one's step in walking or running; trip. **2** To walk or proceed unsteadily or in a blundering manner. **3** To happen upon something by chance: with *across, on, upon,* etc. **4** To fall into sin or error. — *v.t.* **5** To cause to stumble. — *n.* The act of stumbling; hence, a blunder; false step. [Cf. Norw. *stumla* stumble in the dark] — **stum′bler** *n.* — **stum′bling** *adj.* — **stum′bling·ly** *adv.*

stum·bling·block (stum′bling·blok′) *n.* Any obstacle or hindrance; something that may cause one to err: now only figurative.

stump (stump) *n.* **1** That portion of the trunk of a tree left standing when the tree is felled. **2** The part of anything, as of a limb, that remains when the main part has been removed; a stumplike part; a stub. **3** *pl. Colloq.* The legs: chiefly in the phrase **to stir one's stumps. 4** A place or platform where a stump speech is made; hence, any place or platform from which speeches are made; also, political haranguing. 5 *Colloq.* A challenge; a dare. 6 In cricket, any one of the three posts (the **off stump**, the **middle stump**, and the **leg stump**) forming the wicket. 7 A pencil-like soft leather or rubber bar, with conical ends, used to soften drawings of crayon or charcoal or to apply powdered pigments. 8 A short, thick-set person or animal. 9 A heavy step; a clump. — **to be up a stump** To be in trouble or in a dilemma. — **to take the stump** To electioneer in a political campaign. — *adj.* 1 Being or resembling a stump; stumpy. 2 Of or pertaining to political oratory or campaigning: a *stump* speaker, *stump* speech. — *v.t.* 1 To reduce to a stump; truncate; lop. 2 To remove stumps from (land). 3 To canvass (a district) by making political speeches: The candidate *stumped* the State. 4 *Colloq.* To challenge, as to a contest; dare; defy. 5 *Colloq.* To bring to a halt by real or fancied obstacles; nonplus; baffle. 6 To strike against an obstacle; stub, as one's toe. 7 To shade (a drawing) by rubbing with a stump (def. 7). — *v.i.* 8 To go about on or as on stumps; hence, to walk heavily, noisily, and stiffly; hobble. [<MLG]

stump·age (stum′pij) *n.* 1 Standing timber considered with reference to its value for cutting; also, its price. 2 A tax on lumber cut, rated by the amount cut and the price.

stump·er (stum′pər) *n.* 1 One who or that which stumps. 2 A political speaker. 3 Any problem, situation, etc., beyond one's powers of decision.

stump·y (stum′pē) *adj.* **stump·i·er, stump·i·est** 1 Full of stumps. 2 Like a stump; short and thick. — **stump′i·ness** *n.*

stun (stun) *v.t.* **stunned, stun·ning** 1 To render unconscious or incapable of action by a blow, fall, etc. 2 To astonish; astound. 3 To daze or overwhelm by loud or explosive noise. — *n.* A stupefying blow, shock, or concussion; also, the condition of being stunned. [<OF *estoner* resound, stun <L *ex-* thoroughly + *tonare* thunder, crash]

Stun·dist (shtŏŏn′dist) *n.* A member of a Russian body of Christians originating among peasants about 1860. As fundamentalists, the Stundists rejected forms and ceremonies, took only the Bible as their guide, and emphasized brotherly love and the need to labor: they were subjected to persecution. [<Russian *shtundist′* <G *stunde* hour, lesson] — **Stun′dism** *n.*

stung (stung) Past tense and past participle of STING.

stunk (stungk) Past participle and alternative past tense of STINK.

stun·ner (stun′ər) *n.* 1 One who or that which stuns. 2 *Slang* A person or thing of extraordinary or surprising qualities, such as beauty.

stun·ning (stun′ing) *adj.* 1 Rendering unconscious. 2 *Colloq.* Surprising; impressive; wonderful; beautiful. — **stun′ning·ly** *adv.*

stun·sail (stun′səl) *n. Naut.* A studdingsail. Also **stun′s′le.** [Contraction of STUDDINGSAIL]

stunt[1] (stunt) *v.t.* To check the natural development of; dwarf; cramp. — *n.* 1 A check in growth, progress, or development. 2 A stunted animal or thing. [OE *stunt* dull, foolish; prob. infl. in meaning by ON *stuttr* short] — **stunt′ed** *adj.* — **stunt′ed·ness** *n.*

stunt[2] (stunt) *U.S. Colloq. n.* 1 A sensational feat, as of bodily skill. 2 Any remarkable feat, enterprise, or undertaking. — *v.i.* To perform a stunt or stunts. — *v.t.* To perform stunts with (an airplane, etc.). [Prob. <G *stunde* lesson; orig. college slang]

stunt man In motion pictures, a man employed to perform dangerous actions, such as falling, jumping, etc., often as a temporary substitute for an actor.

stu·pa (stōō′pə) *n.* Tope[4]. [<Skt., heap]

stupe (stōōp, styōōp) *n. Med.* A compress or medicated cloth to be applied to a wound. [<L *stupa, stuppa* tow]

stu·pe·fa·cient (stōō′pə·fā′shənt, styōō′-) *adj.* Having power to stupefy; stupefying: also **stu′pe·fac′tive.** (-fak′tiv). — *n.* Anything that stupefies, as a narcotic. [<L *stupefaciens, -entis,* ppr. of *stupefacere* stun. See STUPEFY.]

stu·pe·fac·tion (stōō′pə·fak′shən, styōō′-) *n.* The act of stupefying or state of being stupefied; stupor. See synonyms under STUPIDITY.

stu·pe·fy (stōō′pə·fī, styōō′-) *v.t.* **·fied, ·fy·ing** 1 To dull the senses or faculties of; stun. 2 To amaze; astound. [<F *stupéfier* <L *stupefacere* stun <*stupere* be stunned + *facere* make] — **stu′pe·fied** *adj.* — **stu′pe·fi′er** *n.*

stu·pen·dous (stōō·pen′dəs, styōō-) *adj.* Of prodigious size, bulk, or degree; characterized by any highly impressive feature: a *stupendous* structure, a *stupendous* error. See synonyms under IMMENSE. [<L *stupendus* amazed, orig. gerundive of *stupere* be benumbed, stunned] — **stu·pen′dous·ly** *adv.* — **stu·pen′dous·ness** *n.*

stu·pid (stōō′pid, styōō′-) *adj.* 1 Very slow of apprehension or understanding; dull-witted; sluggish. 2 Affected with stupor; stupefied: *stupid* from drink. 3 Marked by, or resulting from, lack of understanding, reason, or wit; senseless; doltish: *stupid* acts. See synonyms under ABSURD, BRUTISH, FLAT[1], HEAVY. [<L *stupidus* struck dumb <*stupere* be stunned] — **stu′pid·ly** *adv.* — **stu′pid·ness** *n.*

stu·pid·i·ty (stōō·pid′ə·tē, styōō-) *n.* The state, quality, or character of being stupid; great mental dulness. [<L *stupiditas, -tatis* <*stupidus.* See STUPID.]

Synonyms: apathy, dulness, insensibility, obtuseness, slowness, sluggishness, stupefaction, stupor. *Stupidity* is sometimes loosely used for temporary *dulness* or partial *stupor,* but chiefly for innate and chronic *dulness* and *sluggishness* of mental action, *obtuseness* of apprehension, etc. *Apathy* may be temporary, and be dispelled by appeal to the feelings or by the presentation of an adequate motive, but *stupidity* is inveterate and often incurable. Compare APATHY, IDIOCY, STUPOR. *Antonyms*: acuteness, alertness, animation, brilliancy, cleverness, intelligence, keenness, quickness, readiness, sagacity, sense, sensibility.

stu·por (stōō′pər, styōō′-) *n.* 1 A condition of the body in which the senses and faculties are suspended or greatly dulled, as by drugs or intoxicants. 2 Extreme intellectual or moral dulness; gross stupidity. [<L <*stupere* be stunned] — **stu′por·ous** *adj.*

Synonyms: apathy, asphyxia, coma, fainting, insensibility, lethargy, swoon, swooning, syncope, unconsciousness. The *apathy* of disease is a mental state of morbid indifference; *lethargy* is a morbid tendency to heavy and continued sleep, from which the patient may perhaps be momentarily aroused. *Coma* is a deep, abnormal sleep, from which the patient cannot be aroused, or is aroused only with difficulty, a state of profound *insensibility* perhaps with full pulse and deep, stertorous breathing, and is due to brain-oppression. *Syncope* or *swooning* is a sudden loss of sensation and of power of motion, with suspension of pulse and of respiration, and is due to failure of heart action, as from sudden nervous shock or intense mental emotion. *Insensibility* is a general term denoting loss of feeling from any cause, as from cold, intoxication, or injury. *Stupor* is especially profound and confirmed *insensibility,* properly comatose. *Asphyxia* is a special form of *syncope* resulting from partial or total suspension of respiration, as in strangulation or drowning. See STUPIDITY.

stupp (stup, *Ger.* shtŏŏp) *n.* A deposit of finely divided metallic mercury, as in the condensers of mercury smelters. Also **stup.** [<G]

stur·dy[1] (stûr′dē) *adj.* **·di·er, ·di·est** 1 Possessing rugged health and strength; hardy; enduring; vigorous; lusty: *sturdy* health, *sturdy* blows. 2 Firm and unyielding; resolute: a *sturdy* defense. See synonyms under POWERFUL, STRONG. [<OF *estourdi* dazed, reckless <*estourdir* stun, amaze <LL *exturdire* deafen; ult. origin uncertain] — **stur′di·ly** *adv.* — **stur′di·ness** *n.*

stur·dy[2] (stûr′dē) *n.* A disease of sheep; gid. [Special use of STURDY[1]] — **stur′died** *adj.*

stur·geon (stûr′jən) *n.* A large ganoid fish of northern regions (family *Acipenseridae*), with coarse, edible flesh, especially *Acipenser sturio,* the common sturgeon of both coasts of the Atlantic, which ascends rivers. Sturgeons are the principal source of isinglass and caviar. [<AF *sturgeon,* OF *sturgiun* <Med. L *sturio, -onis* <OHG *sturjo*]

Stur·gis (stûr′jis), **Russell,** 1836–1909, U. S. architect and writer.

stur·ine (stûr′ēn, -in) *n.* A bactericidal protamine from the sperm of sturgeons. [< STUR(GEON) + (PROTAM)INE]

Stur·lu·son (stûr′lə·sən, stŏŏr′-), **Snorri** See SNORRI STURLUSON.

Sturm·ab·teil·ung (shtŏŏrm′äp·tī′lŏŏng) *n. pl.* **·teil·ung·en** *German* Literally, storm detachment; a political militia of the Nazi party, organized to keep order at Nazi mass meetings. After 1934, as *Brown Shirts,* the organization became a national army of political soldiers in charge of pre- and post-military indoctrination.

Sturm und Drang (shtŏŏrm′ ŏŏnt dräng′) *German* Storm and stress: used to designate the late 18th century period of German literary romanticism.

sturt (stûrt) *Brit. Dial. v.t.* 1 To annoy; vex; trouble. 2 To startle. — *v.i.* 3 To start with fear; be frightened. — *n.* 1 Vexation. 2 Strife; wrath. 3 Unrest. [Prob. var. of START[1]]

sturt·in (stûr′tin) *adj. Scot.* Frightened; overwhelmed.

stut·ter (stut′ər) *v.t.* & *v.i.* To utter or speak with spasmodic repetition, blocking, and prolongation of sounds and syllables, especially those in initial position in a word. — *n.* The act or habit of stuttering. See synonyms under STAMMER. [Freq. of ME *stutten* stutter] — **stut′ter·er** *n.* — **stut′ter·ing** *adj.* & *n.* — **stut′ter·ing·ly** *adv.*

Stutt·gart (stut′gärt, *Ger.* shtŏŏt′gärt) A city in SW West Germany, capital of Baden-Württemberg.

Stuy·ve·sant (stī′və·sənt), **Peter,** 1592–1672, last Dutch governor of New Amsterdam 1647–64.

St. Val·en·tine's Day (sānt val′in·tīnz) See under VALENTINE.

St. Vin·cent (sānt vin′sənt) A British colony of the Windward Islands; 150 square miles including dependencies in the Grenadines; capital, Kingstown; a component unit of The West Indies (federation).

St. Vincent, Cape The SW extremity of Portugal and of continental Europe. *Portuguese* **Ca·bo de São Vi·cen·te** (kä′bōō thə souṅ vē·sāṅn′tə).

St. Vi·tus's dance (sānt vī′təs·iz) *Pathol.* Chorea. Also **St. Vitus dance.**

sty[1] (stī) *n. pl.* **sties** 1 A pen for swine. 2 Any filthy habitation or place of bestiality or debauchery. — *v.t.* & *v.i.* **stied, sty·ing** To keep or live in a sty or hovel. [OE *stī, stig*]

sty[2] (stī) *n. pl.* **sties** *Pathol.* A small, inflamed swelling of a sebaceous gland on the edge of the eyelid. Also **stye.** [<obs. *styanye* <OE *stīgend,* ppr. of *stīgan* rise + *ye* eye]

stych·o·myth·i·a (stik′ə·mith′ē·ə) See STICHOMYTHY.

Styg·i·an (stij′ē·ən) *adj.* 1 Pertaining to the river Styx; hence, infernal; dark and gloomy. 2 Inviolable, like the oath, "By the Styx." [<L *Stygius* <Gk. *Stygios* <*Styx* the Styx, prob. <*stygein* hate]

style (stīl) *n.* 1 Manner of expressing thought, in writing or speaking; distinctive or characteristic form of expression: a florid *style*; the *style* of Mark Twain. 2 A good or suitable mode of expression: His writing lacks *style.* 3 A particular form of composition, construction, or appearance, as in art, music, etc.: the Gothic *style*; the American *style* of automobile. 4 The manner in which some action or work is performed: The horse ran in fine *style.* 5 A good or exemplary manner of performing: a team with *style.* 6 A mode of conduct or behavior; a way of living: to live in makeshift *style.* 7 A fashionable manner or appearance: to live in *style.* 8 A particular fashion in clothing. 9 A particular type or fashion suitable for or agreeable to a person: That coat is not my *style.* 10 *Printing* The

STURGEON
(Length up to 10 feet)

conventions of typography, design, etc., observed in a given printing office. **11** The legal or official title or appellation of a person, organization, etc. **12** A stylus (in any sense). **13** The gnomon of a sundial. **14** *Surg.* A slender probe with a blunt point: also called *stylet.* **15** *Bot.* The prolongation of a carpel or ovary, bearing the stigma. **16** *Zool.* A stylet. **17** A system of arranging the length of the calendar years so as to average that of the true solar year: called **New Style,** when following the arrangement made by Pope Gregory XIII (Gregorian calendar) and used in nearly all Christian countries; and **Old Style** when following the Julian calendar. England adopted the New Style by act of Parliament in 1752. Since 1900 New Style has been 13 days later than Old Style. See synonyms under AIR[1], CUSTOM, DICTION, MANNER, NAME. — *v.* **styled, styl·ing** *v.t.* **1** To name; give a title to. **2** To make consistent in typography, spelling, punctuation, etc., as copy to be printed; stylize. — *v.i.* **3** In ornamentation, to use a style or stylus. ◆ Homophone: *stile.* [<OF <L *stilus, stylus* writing instrument] — **sty′lar, sty′li·form** *adj.* — **styl′er** *n.*

sty·let (stī′lit) *n.* **1** Any slender pointed instrument, as a poniard or stiletto. **2** *Surg.* A style. **3** *Zool.* Any pointed, bristlelike process or appendage. [<F <Ital. *stiletto.* See STILETTO.]

sty·li·form (stī′lə·fôrm) *adj.* Resembling or shaped like a stylus. [<NL *styliformis* <L *stylus* a stylus + *forma* a form]

styl·ish (stī′lish) *adj.* Having style; especially, very fashionable. — **styl′ish·ly** *adv.* — **styl′·ish·ness** *n.*

styl·ist (stī′list) *n.* **1** One who is a master of literary or rhetorical style. **2** An adviser concerning style in clothes, interior decoration, etc.

sty·lis·tic (stī·lis′tik) *adj.* Pertaining to style, especially literary style. — *n.* Stylistics. — **sty·lis′ti·cal·ly** *adv.*

sty·lis·tics (stī·lis′tiks) *n. pl.* (*construed as singular*) The art or study of literary expression.

sty·lite (stī′līt) *n.* One of a class of early religious ascetics who lived most of the time on the tops of pillars, without shelter. The practice was originated by Simeon Stylites in A.D. 420. [<Gk. *stylitēs* < *stylos* column]

styl·ize (stī′līz) *v.t.* **·ized, ·iz·ing** To conform to a distinctive mode or style; conventionalize. Also *Brit.* **styl′ise.** — **styl′i·za′tion** *n.* — **styl′·iz·er** *n.*

stylo– *combining form* **1** A pillar: *stylobate.* **2** *Bot.* & *Zool.* A style; of or related to a style: *stylopodium.* **3** *Anat.* Denoting relationship to a styloid process. Also, before vowels, **styl–.** [<Gk. *stylos* a column, pillar]

sty·lo·bate (stī′lə·bāt) *n. Archit.* A continuous base for two or more columns, in contradistinction to a pedestal, which is a base for only one column or object. Compare STEREOBATE. [<L *stylobates* <Gk. *stylobatēs* < *stylos* pillar + *-batēs* a treader < *bainein* walk, step]

STYLOBATE (*a*)

sty·lo·graph (stī′lə·graf, -gräf) *n.* A fountain pen from which ink is fed to a conical writing point. Also **stylographic pen.** — **sty′lo·graph′ic** or **·i·cal** *adj.*

sty·log·ra·phy (stī·log′rə·fē) *n.* The art or process of writing, engraving, etc., with a stylus or other pointed instrument.

sty·loid (stī′loid) *adj.* Resembling a style or peg; styliform.

styloid process *Anat.* One of various bony processes, as the spine that projects from the base of the temporal bone; a projection on the head of the fibula; the pointed lower extremity of either the radius or the ulna; the proximal end of the third metacarpal bone.

sty·lo·lite (stī′lə·līt) *n. Geol.* A small columnar body of the same composition as the surrounding rock. — **sty′lo·lit′ic** (-lit′ik) *adj.*

sty·lo·po·di·um (stī′lə·pō′dē·əm) *n. pl.* **·di·a** (-dē·ə) *Bot.* The fleshy disk that bears the style in umbelliferous flowers. [<NL]

sty·lus (stī′ləs) *n.* **1** An ancient writing instrument, having one end pointed for writing on wax tablets and the other end blunt for erasure. **2** A pointed instrument for marking or engraving, as on carbons, stencils, etc. **3** The needle of a phonograph or of a sound-recording instrument. [<L]

sty·mie (stī′mē) *n.* A condition obtaining in golf when an opponent's ball lies in the line of the player's putt on the green, the balls being more than six inches apart. — *v.t.* **·mied, ·my·ing 1** To block (an opponent) by or as by a stymie. **2** To baffle or perplex. Also spelled *stimy.* [Origin uncertain]

Stym·pha·lus (stim·fā′ləs) A district of NE Arcadia, central Peloponnesus, Greece.

styp·sis (stip′sis) *n.* The application or the action of a styptic. [<LL <Gk., a contraction < *styphein* contract]

styp·tic (stip′tik) *adj.* **1** Causing contraction of living tissues, as blood vessels. **2** Preventing hemorrhage; astringent: a *styptic* pencil. Also **styp′ti·cal.** — *n.* A substance or agent that arrests bleeding. [<L *stypticus* <Gk. *styptikos* < *stypsis* a contraction. See STYPSIS.]

Styr (stir) A river in western Ukrainian S.S.R., flowing 280 miles north to the Pripet River.

Sty·ra·ca·ce·ae (stī′rə·kā′si·ē) *n. pl.* An order of gamopetalous trees or shrubs yielding resins and gums, the storax family, having alternate simple leaves and usually white racemed flowers with a corolla of 4 to 8 united petals. They are found in all parts of the world. [<NL <L *styrax* storax] — **sty′·ra·ca′ceous** (-shəs) *adj.*

sty·rene (stī′rēn, stir′ēn) *n. Chem.* A colorless aromatic hydrocarbon, C_8H_8, contained in liquid storax, from which it may be derived by distillation. [<L *styrax* storax + -ENE]

Styr·i·a (stir′ē·ə) A province and former duchy in central and SE Austria; 6,324 square miles; capital, Graz: German *Steiermark.*

Sty·ro·foam (stī′rə·fōm) *n.* A lightweight, rigid, cellular material formed from a synthetic hydrocarbon polymer: a trade name.

stythe (stīth) *n.* Chokedamp. [OE *stith* harsh]

Styx (stiks) In Greek mythology, the river of hate, one of the five rivers surrounding Hades.

su·a·ble (sōō′ə·bəl) *adj.* Legally subject to civil process; able to be sued. — **su′a·bil′i·ty** *n.*

Sua·kin (swä′kēn) A port on the Red Sea in NE Sudan.

sua·sion (swā′zhən) *n.* The act of persuading; persuasion: archaic except in the phrase **moral suasion.** [<OF <L *suasio, -onis* < *suadere* persuade] — **sua·sive** (swā′siv), **sua·so·ry** (swā′sər·ē) *adj.*

suave (swäv, swāv) *adj.* Smooth and pleasant in manner; bland; gracious. [<F <L *suavis* sweet] — **suave′ly** *adv.* — **suave′ness** *n.*

suav·i·ty (swä′və·tē, swav′ə-) *n. pl.* **·ties 1** The state of being suave; urbanity. **2** Something that is suave, bland, or agreeable. [<F *suavité* <L *suavitas, -tatis* < *suavis* sweet]

sub (sub) *n. Colloq.* Short for: **1** A substitute. **2** A subordinate or subaltern. **3** A subway. **4** A submarine.

sub– *prefix* **1** Under; beneath; below; as in:

subaquatic **subastral** **subcoastal** **subcurrent** **subfloor** **subfluvial** **subsurface** **subtext**

2 *Anat.* Situated under or beneath, or on the ventral side of; as in:

subabdominal **subalar** **subapical** **subauricular** **subaxial** **subcerebellar** **subclavicular** **subcortical** **subcostal** **subcranial** **subcuticular** **subdental** **subdermal** **subdiaphragmatic** **subdorsal** **subepiglottic** **subgenital** **subgingival** **subglottic** **subintegumental** **subintestinal** **submammary** **submuscular** **subnasal** **subneural** **subnodal** **subocular** **suboptic** **suboral** **suborbital** **subpelvic** **subphrenic** **subpleural** **subpubic** **subpulmonary** **subrectal** **subretinal** **subspinal** **subspinous** **substernal** **subungual** **suburethral** **subvaginal** **subvertebral**

3 Almost; nearly; slightly; imperfectly: chiefly in scientific terms; as in:

subacid **subacidity** **subacidulous** **subacrid** **subacuminate** **subalkaline** **subangular** **subastringent** **subaudible** **subcalcareous** **subcarbureted** **subcentral** **subconcave** **subconchoidal** **subconical** **subcolumnar** **subconvex** **subcubical** **subdelirium** **subfebrile** **subfluid** **subhorizontal** **subinflammation** **sublateral** **sublinear** **subluminous** **submedial** **submetallic** **subnarcotic** **suboval** **subparallel** **subparalytic** **subpolar** **subsaline** **subserrate** **subsibilant** **subtetanic** **subtypical** **subvertical** **subvirile**

4 Lower in rank or grade; secondary; subordinate; as in:

subadministration **subadministrator** **subagency** **subagent** **subassociation** **subcantor** **subcause** **subchanter** **subclerk** **subcommission** **subconstellation** **sub–echo** **sub–editor** **sub–element** **subflavor** **subforeman** **subfunction** **subholding** **sub–idea** **sublessee** **sublessor** **sublieutenancy** **sublieutenant** **submeaning** **submediator** **submortgage** **subofficer** **subpart** **subrector** **subrent** **subsecretary** **subtone** **subvicar** **subworker**

5 Forming a subdivision; as in:

sub–branch **sub–bureau** **subcavity** **subclass** **subclassification** **subcorporation** **subcouncil** **subdepartment** **subdialect** **subdistrict** **submember** **suboffice** **subprovince** **subscience** **subsegment** **subseries** **subshaft** **subtype** **subunit** **subzone**

6 *Math.* Denoting a ratio, the inverse of a given ratio: The *subtriplicate* ratio is the inverse of the ratio of the cube. **7** *Chem.* **a** Present (in a compound) in less than normal amount: *subchloride, suboxide.* **b** Designating a basic salt compound: *subacetate, subcarbonate.*

Also: *suc–* before *c,* as in *succumb*; *suf–* before *f,* as in *suffer*; *sug–* before *g,* as in *suggest*; *sum–* before *m,* as in *summon*; *sup–* before *p,* as in *support*; *sur–* before *r,* as in *surrogate*; *sus–* before *c, p, t,* as in *susceptible, suspect, sustain.* [<L *sub–* < *sub* under]

sub·a·cute (sub′ə·kyōōt′) *adj.* **1** Somewhat acute. **2** Intermediate between acute and chronic: said of a disease. — **sub′a·cute′ly** *adv.*

sub·aer·i·al (sub′âr′ē·əl, -ā·ir′-) *adj.* Of, pertaining to, or formed at the earth's surface, in open air: contrasted with *aerial, submarine,* and *subterranean.*

su·bah (sōō′bä) *n.* **1** A province or governmental district of India. **2** A subahdar. Also **su′ba.**

su·bah·dar (sōō′bä·där′) *n.* The chief native officer of a company of sepoys in the former British East-Indian Army: also spelled *subah.* Also **su′ba·dar′.** [<Urdu *sūbahdār* <Persian <Arabic *sūbah* a province + Persian *dār* a possessor, master]

sub·al·pine (sub·al′pīn, -pin) *adj.* **1** Lower than alpine. **2** Of or pertaining to mountainous regions near but below the timber line.

sub·al·tern (sub·ôl′tərn) *adj.* **1** *Brit. Mil.* Ranking below a captain. **2** Of inferior rank or position; subordinate, as a species to a genus, or as a particular proposition under a universal. — *n.* **1** A person of subordinate rank or position. **2** *Brit. Mil.* An officer ranking below a captain. **3** (sub′əl·tûrn) *Logic* A specific class as included under a general one, or a particular statement as deducible from a universal one. [<MF *subalterne* <LL *subalternus* <L *sub-* under + *alternus* alternate]

sub·al·ter·nant (sub′ôl·tûr′nənt) *adj.* Universal, as opposed to *particular.* —*n.* A universal proposition in its relation to the particular proposition containing the same terms. [<NL *subalternans, -antis,* ppr. of Med. L *subalternare* subordinate <LL *subalternus.* See SUBALTERN.]

sub·al·ter·nate (sub·ôl′tər·nit, -al′-) *adj.* 1 Subordinate; subaltern. 2 Successive, or succeeding by turns. 3 *Bot.* Alternate, with a tendency to become opposite. —*n.* A particular as opposed to a universal proposition. [< Med. L *subalternatus,* pp. of *subalternare.* See SUBALTERNANT.]

sub·al·ter·na·tion (sub·ôl′tər·nā′shən, -al′-) *n.* A succession; a subordination.

sub·ant·arc·tic (sub′ant·ärk′tik, -är′tik) *adj.* Denoting or pertaining to a region contiguous to that within the Antarctic Circle.

sub·a·qual (sub·ā′kwəl) *adj.* Situated below the level of the water table, as soils formed on lake or river beds. [<SUB- + L *aqua* water]

sub·a·que·ous (sub·ā′kwē·əs) *adj.* 1 Being, formed, or operating under water; submarine. 2 Occurring under or in water; adapted for use under water. 3 Having an appearance like that produced under water.

sub·arc·tic (sub·ärk′tik, -är′tik) *adj.* Denoting or pertaining to a region contiguous to that within the Arctic Circle.

sub·ar·cu·ate (sub·är′kyōō·it) *adj.* Moderately arched or bent. Also **sub·ar′cu·at′ed** (-ā′tid).

sub·ar·e·a (sub·âr′ē·ə) *n.* A small part of a given area, as in a field of gunfire.

sub·ar·id (sub·ar′id) *adj.* Partly arid; moderately dry.

sub·a·tom·ic (sub′ə·tom′ik) *adj.* Within the atom.

sub·au·di·tion (sub′ô·dish′ən) *n.* 1 The understanding or supplying of something not expressed. 2 A thought thus understood or supplied.

sub·ax·il·lar·y (sub·ak′sə·ler′ē) *adj.* 1 *Bot.* Lying under or beneath the axil. 2 *Anat.* Beneath the armpit.

sub–base (sub′bās′) *n.* 1 *Archit.* The lowest member of a base or pedestal. 2 A subdivision of a main base, as in a field of military operations. 3 The section of a base line between two fixed points, as the line connecting two microphones in a sound-ranging system.

sub–base·ment (sub′bās′mənt) *n.* An underground story, or any one of several below the first or true basement.

sub–bass (sub′bās′) *n.* In an organ, a 16-foot or 32-foot pedal stop. Also **sub′-base′.**

sub·cal·i·ber (sub·kal′ə·bər) *adj.* *Mil.* Of smaller caliber than the firearm from which it is to be fired: said of a projectile. A tube or disk is used to make up the deficit. Also **sub·cal′i·bre.**

sub·car·bide (sub·kär′bīd) *n.* *Chem.* A carbide containing less than the usual amount of carbon.

sub·car·ti·lag·i·nous (sub·kär′tə·laj′ə·nəs) *adj.* *Anat.* 1 Beneath cartilage or under tissue. 2 Partly cartilaginous.

sub·ce·les·tial (sub′si·les′chəl) *adj.* 1 Lower than celestial; beneath the heavens; mundane. 2 Directly beneath the zenith. —*n.* A subcelestial being.

sub·cel·lar (sub′sel′ər) *n.* A cellar under another cellar.

sub·chlo·ride (sub·klôr′īd, -klō′rīd, -rid) *n.* A basic chloride: copper *subchloride,* Cu_2Cl_2.

sub·cla·vi·an (sub·klā′vē·ən) *Anat. adj.* 1 Situated beneath the clavicle. 2 Of or pertaining to the subclavian vessels. —*n.* A subclavian nerve, muscle, vein, etc. [<NL *subclavius* <L *sub-* under + *clavis* a key]

subclavian artery *Anat.* The large main artery that passes under the clavicle to convey blood to the arm.

subclavian groove *Anat.* A groove made by the subclavian artery or vein on the first rib.

subclavian vein *Anat.* That portion of the main venous trunk of the arm that lies under the clavicle.

sub·cli·max (sub·klī′maks) *n.* 1 A stage prior to or below the climax. 2 *Ecol.* **a** Any stage in the development of a plant or animal community determined by agencies other than climate which prevent attainment of the normal climax. **b** Any community so acted upon. —**sub·cli·mac·tic** (sub′klī·mak′tik) *adj.*

sub·com·mit·tee (sub′kə·mit′ē) *n.* An under-committee; part of a committee appointed for special work.

sub·con·scious (sub·kon′shəs) *adj.* 1 Only dimly conscious; not clearly discerned by the conscious subject; lacking intellectual clearness. 2 *Psychol.* Denoting such phenomena of mental life as are not attended by full consciousness, as the many automatic processes involved in the performance of familiar actions. —*n.* 1 That portion of mental activity not directly in the focus of consciousness but sometimes susceptible to recall by the proper stimulus. 2 *Psychoanal.* The preconscious. —**sub·con′scious·ly** *adv.* —**sub·con′scious·ness** *n.*

sub·con·ti·nent (sub·kon′tə·nənt) *n.* A great land mass forming part of a continent but having considerable geographical independence, as India.

sub·con·tract (sub·kon′trakt) *n.* A contract subordinate to another contract and assigning part of the work to a third party. —*v.t.* & *v.i.* (sub′kən·trakt′) To make a subcontract (for); arrange for part or all of (work) to be performed by a third party. —**sub′con·tract′ed** *adj.*

sub·con·trac·tor (sub′kən·trak′tər, -kon′trak-) *n.* One who enters into a contract with a contractor to do work embraced in the latter's contract.

sub·cor·tex (sub·kôr′teks) *n.* *pl.* **·ti·ces** (-tə·sēz) *Anat.* That part of the brain which underlies the cortex. [<NL <L *sub-* under + *cortex* bark]

sub·cul·ture (sub·kul′chər) *n.* 1 *Bacteriol.* A culture of bacteria or other material derived from a preexisting culture. 2 *Sociol.* A group having specific patterns of behavior that set it off from other groups within a culture or society.

sub·cu·ta·ne·ous (sub′kyōō·tā′nē·əs) *adj.* 1 Situated, found, or applied beneath the skin. 2 Hypodermic. [<LL *subcutaneus* <L *sub-* under + *cutis* skin] —**sub′cu·ta′ne·ous·ly** *adv.*

sub·dea·con (sub·dē′kən) *n.* A member of the order of the ministry next below that of deacon, who assists at the Eucharist. [<AF *soudiakene, subdiacne* <Med. L *subdiaconus* (<*sub-* under + *diaconus* deacon), trans. of LGk. *hypodiakonos*] —**sub·dea′con·ate** (-it) *n.*

sub·dean (sub′dēn′) *n.* An assistant or substitute dean. [<OF *soudeien* <*sou-* SUB- + *deien* a dean]

sub·dean·er·y (sub·dē′nər·ē) *n.* *pl.* **·er·ies** The office of a subdean.

sub·deb·u·tante (sub′deb·yōō·tänt′, -deb′yōō·tant) *n.* A young girl the year before she becomes a debutante.

sub·del·e·gate (sub·del′ə·gāt, -git) *n.* One who represents a delegate. —*v.t.* (-gāt) **·gat·ed, ·gat·ing** 1 To appoint as a subdelegate. 2 *Obs.* To delegate (authority, etc.) to another.

sub·de·pot (sub·dē′pō, -dep′ō) *n.* An auxiliary depot located near a base of operations.

sub·di·ac·o·nate (sub′dī·ak′ə·nit, -nāt) *adj.* Of or pertaining to the office, rank, or order of subdeacon: also **sub′di·ac′o·nal.** —*n.* The office, rank, or order of subdeacon. [<Med. L *subdiaconatus* <*subdiaconus.* See SUBDEACON.]

sub·di·vide (sub′di·vīd′) *v.t.* & *v.i.* **·vid·ed, ·vid·ing** 1 To divide (a part) resulting from a previous division; divide again. 2 To divide (land) into lots for sale or improvement. [< LL *subdividere* <L *sub-* under + *dividere* DIVIDE]

sub·di·vi·sion (sub′di·vizh′ən) *n.* 1 Division following upon division. 2 A part, as of land, resulting from subdividing. See synonyms under PART.

sub·dom·i·nant (sub·dom′ə·nənt) *n.* *Music* The tone next below the dominant; fourth tone or degree of a major or minor scale. —*adj.* Less important than the dominant.

sub·duce (sub·dōōs′, -dyōōs′) *v.t.* **·duced, ·duc·ing** *Obs.* 1 To withdraw; take away. 2 To take as a part from a whole; subtract. Also **sub·duct′** (-dukt′). [<L *subducere* <*sub-* from + *ducere* lead] —**sub·duc′tion** (-duk′shən) *n.*

sub·due (sub·dōō′, -dyōō′) *v.t.* **·dued, ·du·ing** 1 To gain dominion over, as by war or force; subjugate; vanquish. 2 To overcome by training, influence, or persuasion; tame. 3 To repress (emotions, impulses, etc.). 4 To reduce the intensity of; soften, as a color or sound. 5 To bring (land) under cultivation. [<OF *soduire* seduce <L *subducere* SUBDUCE; infl. in meaning by L *subdere* overcome] —**sub·du′a·ble** *adj.* —**sub·du′al** *n.* —**sub·du′er** *n.*

Synonyms: beat, break, bridle, conquer, control, crush, master, overbear, overcome, overpower, overwhelm, reduce, repress, subject, suppress, train, vanquish. See CHASTEN, CONQUER, REPRESS.

sub·el·a·phine (sub·el′ə·fīn, -fin) *adj.* *Zool.* Designating a modified form of elaphine antlers. For illustration see ANTLER.

sub·e·qua·to·ri·al (sub·ē′kwə·tôr′ē·əl, -tō′rē-) *adj.* 1 Nearly equatorial. 2 Denoting or belonging to a region adjoining the equatorial region.

su·ber (sōō′bər) *n.* Cork. [<L] —**su·be·re·ous** (sōō·bir′ē·əs) *adj.*

su·ber·ic (sōō·ber′ik) *adj.* Of, pertaining to, or derived from cork.

suberic acid *Chem.* A white crystalline diacid, $C_8H_{14}O_4$, obtained by the action of nitric acid on cork and on various fatty oils.

su·ber·in (sōō′bər·in) *n.* A waxlike, fatty substance formed in cork cells.

su·ber·i·za·tion (sōō′bər·ə·zā′shən, -ī·zā′-) *n.* *Bot.* The transformation of plant cell walls into suberin or cork tissue.

su·ber·ize (sōō′bə·rīz) *v.t.* **·ized, ·iz·ing** To make corky, as cell walls.

su·ber·ose (sōō′bər·ōs) *adj.* 1 Corky. 2 Of or pertaining to suberin. Also **su′ber·ous** (-əs).

sub·fam·i·ly (sub·fam′ə·lē, -fam′lē) *n.* *pl.* **·lies** 1 A division of plants or animals next below a family but above the genus. 2 *Ling.* A division of languages below a family and above a branch.

sub·ge·nus (sub·jē′nəs) *n.* *pl.* **·gen·e·ra** (-jen′·ər·ə) A primary subdivision of a genus including one or more species with common characters. —**sub′ge·ner′ic** (-ji·ner′ik) *adj.*

sub·gla·cial (sub·glā′shəl) *adj.* Deposited or formed at the bottom of or beneath a glacier.

sub·group (sub′grōōp′) *n.* 1 An inferior order, or one of the biological divisions of an order. 2 *Chem.* A group that is included within a superior group, as in the periodic table of the elements.

sub·head (sub′hed′) *n.* 1 A heading or title of a subdivision: also **sub·head′ing.** 2 An official next below the head in a college or school.

sub·hu·man (sub·hyōō′mən) *adj.* 1 Less than or imperfectly human. 2 *Anthropol.* Below the level of the primate type represented by *Homo sapiens.*

sub·hu·mid (sub·hyōō′mid) *adj.* Intermediate between semiarid and humid: said especially of a climate with sufficient precipitation to support a moderate to dense growth of tall and short grasses.

Su·bic (sōō′bik) A municipality of central Luzon, Philippines, at the head of **Subic Bay,** an inlet of the South China Sea near Bataan Peninsula; site of U. S. landing in World War II, January, 1945.

sub·in·ci·sion (sub′in·sizh′ən) *n.* 1 A cutting beneath or under. 2 Among certain primitive peoples, a slitting open of the urethra of the penis.

sub·in·dex (sub·in′deks) *n.* *pl.* **·in·dices** (-in′·də·sēz) An indicative figure, letter, or sign following and slightly underneath a figure, letter, or sign: in M_n, X_2, Y_4, the subindices are *n,* 2, and 4.

sub·in·fec·tion (sub′in·fek′shən) *n.* *Pathol.* 1 Infection of cells weakened by prolonged resistance to toxin. 2 Infection by the toxic wastes of destroyed bacteria.

sub·in·feu·date (sub′in·fyōō′dāt) *v.t.* & *v.i.* **·dat·ed, ·dat·ing** To sublet by subinfeudation. Also **sub′in·feud′.**

sub·in·feu·da·tion (sub·in′fyōō·dā′shən) *n.* 1 The granting of lands by a feudal vassal to a tenant who thus becomes his vassal. 2 The feud or fief resulting from subinfeudation. —**sub·in·feu·da·to·ry** (sub′in·fyōō′də·tôr′ē, -tō′·rē) *adj.*

sub·in·trant (sub·in′trənt) *adj.* 1 Occurring

or entering secretly. 2 *Pathol.* Anticipating a recurrence of, as a paroxysm, a malarial fever, etc. [<L *subintrans, -antis,* ppr. of *subintrare* <*sub-* secretly + *intrare* enter] — **sub·in′·trance** (-trəns) *n.*

sub·ir·ri·gate (sub·ir′ə·gāt) *v.t.* **·gat·ed, ·gat·ing** To irrigate through underground pipes, etc. — **sub′ir·ri·ga′tion** *n.*

su·bi·to (sōō′bē·tō) *adv. Music* Quickly; suddenly. [<Ital. <L *subitus,* pp. of *subire* come or go stealthily <*sub-* secretly + *ire* go]

sub·ja·cent (sub·jā′sənt) *adj.* 1 Situated underneath. 2 Being at a lower elevation. [<L *subjacens, -entis,* ppr. of *subjacere* <*sub-* under + *jacere* lie] — **sub·ja′cen·cy** *n.*

sub·ject (sub′jikt) *adj.* 1 Being under the power of another; owing or yielding obedience to sovereign authority. 2 Exposed to some agency or tendency: *subject* to headache; a climate *subject* to storms. 3 Being under discretionary authority: a treaty *subject* to ratification. — *n.* 1 One who is under the governing power of another, as of a ruler or government, especially of a monarch. 2 One who or that which is employed or treated in a specified way, as a body for dissection, a person used in hypnotic experiments, one attacked by or liable to any disease. 3 Something upon which thought or the artistic constructive faculty is employed, as a theme of consideration or the general idea or plan of an artistic work. 4 *Gram.* The word, phrase, or clause of a sentence about which something is stated or asked in the predicate. 5 *Music* The melodic phrase on which a composition or a part of it is based. 6 A branch of learning. 7 The originating clause or motive. 8 The ego or self; that of which qualities or attributes are affirmed; substance; essential being; the thinking, feeling agent. 9 *Logic* In a proposition, that term about which something is affirmed or denied. See PROPOSITION. See synonyms under TOPIC. — *v.t.* (səb·jekt′) 1 To bring under dominion or control; subjugate. 2 To cause to undergo some experience or action. 3 To offer for consideration or approval; submit. 4 To make liable; expose: His inheritance was *subjected* to heavy taxation. 5 *Obs.* To place beneath. See synonyms under CONQUER, SUBDUE. [<OF *suget, sujet* <L *subjectus,* pp. of *subjicere* <*sub-* under + *jacere* throw; refashioned after L]

Synonyms (adj.): dependent, disposed, exposed, inferior, liable, obnoxious, prone, subordinate. *Antonyms*: clear, exempt, free, supreme, uncontrolled, unrestrained.

sub·jec·tion (səb·jek′shən) *n.* The act of making subject or bringing into a state of subjection.

sub·jec·tive (səb·jek′tiv) *adj.* 1 Relating to, or conditioned by, mental states or the ego; proceeding from or taking place within the thinking subject: opposed to *objective.* 2 Pertaining to the real nature or essence or substance of a person or thing; inherent; essential. 3 Peculiar to an individual; fanciful; illusory. 4 Inclined to be submissive; obedient. 5 *Gram.* Designating that case of the substantive used to denote its function as subject of a finite verb. 6 In literature and art, giving prominence to the subject or author as treating of his inner experience and emotion. 7 Introspective. — **sub·jec′tive·ly** *adv.* — **sub·jec′·tive·ness, sub·jec·tiv·i·ty** (sub′jek·tiv′ə·tē) *n.*

◆ *Subjective* and *objective,* paired words, are strictly speaking neither synonyms nor antonyms. In scholasticism and philosophies of idealism they are both concerned with the object perceived, but represent different approaches to it. *Objective* signifies the relating of mental states to an object, that is, to something outside the perceiving mind which is recognized as having an existence outside that mind. *Subjective* relates to a feeling, attitude, or cognition that is recognized as being a construct within the mind of the perceiver, even though it takes the external object as its point of departure. Different individuals may receive different *subjective* impressions from the same *objective* fact. See INHERENT, OBJECTIVE.

sub·jec·tiv·ism (səb·jek′tiv·iz′əm) *n.* 1 The doctrine that knowledge is merely subjective and relative and is derived from one's own consciousness. 2 The doctrine that we know directly no external object. 3 The doctrine that there is no objective standard, test, or measure of truth; relativism. 4 The doctrine that individual feeling is the standard by which to judge right and wrong. — **sub·jec′tiv·ist** *n.* — **sub·jec′tiv·is′tic** *adj.*

subject matter The object of consideration or study; the subject of thought.

sub·join (sub·join′) *v.t.* To add at the end; attach; affix. See synonyms under ADD. [<MF *subjoindre* <L *subjungere* <*sub-* in addition + *jungere* join]

sub·join·der (sub·join′dər) *n.* Something subjoined. [<SUBJOIN, on analogy with *rejoinder*]

sub ju·di·ce (sub jōō′di·sē) *Latin* Under judicial consideration.

sub·ju·gate (sub′jōō·gāt) *v.t.* **·gat·ed, ·gat·ing** 1 To bring under dominion; conquer; subdue. 2 To make subservient in any way; enslave. See synonyms under CONQUER. [<L *subjugatus,* pp. of *subjugare* <*sub-* under + *jugum* a yoke] — **sub′ju·ga′tion** *n.* — **sub′ju·ga′·tor** *n.*

sub·junc·tion (səb·jungk′shən) *n.* 1 The act of subjoining, or the state of being subjoined. 2 That which is subjoined. [<LL *subjunctio, -onis* <L *subjungere* SUBJOIN]

sub·junc·tive (səb·jungk′tiv) *Gram. adj.* Of or pertaining to that mood of the finite verb that is used to express a future contingency, a supposition implying the contrary, a mere supposition with indefinite time, or a wish or desire. In English the forms of the subjunctive mood are introduced by conjunctions of condition, doubt, contingency, possibility, etc., as *if, though, lest, unless, that, till,* or *whether,* but verbs in conditional clauses are not always in the subjunctive mood, for the use of these conjunctions with the indicative is very common. — *n.* 1 The subjunctive mood. 2 A verb form or construction in this mood. [<L *subjunctivus* <*subjunctus,* pp. of *subjungere* SUBJOIN]

sub·king·dom (sub·king′dəm) *n.* A phylum.

sub·lap·sar·i·an (sub′lap·sâr′ē·ən) *n.* A believer in the predestinarian view held by moderate Calvinists that God foresaw the fall of man and decreed to save some by election. — *adj.* Relating to the sublapsarians or to their tenets. [<NL *sublapsarius* <L *sub-* consequent upon, under + *lapsus* a fall] — **sub′·lap·sar′i·an·ism** *n.*

sub·la·tion (sub·lā′shən) *n. Med.* The detachment, displacement, or removal of a part. [<L *sublatio, -onis* <*sublatus,* pp. to *tollere* lift up, take away]

sub·lease (sub·lēs′) *v.t.* **·leased, ·leas·ing** To obtain or let (property) on a sublease. — *n.* (sub′lēs′) A lease of property from a tenant or lessee.

sub·let (sub·let′, sub′let′) *v.t.* **·let, ·let·ting** 1 To let to another (property held on a lease); underlet. 2 To let (work that one has contracted to do) to a subordinate contractor.

sub·le·thal (sub·lē′thəl) *adj.* Having an effect short of death: a *sublethal* dose of poison.

sub·li·mate (sub′lə·māt) *v.* **·mat·ed, ·mat·ing** *v.t.* 1 *Chem.* To convert from a solid to a vapor by heat, and then solidify again by cooling, with no apparent intermediate liquefaction. 2 To refine; purify. 3 *Psychol.* To convert the energy of (primitive impulses) into acceptable social and cultural manifestations. — *v.i.* 4 To undergo or engage in sublimation. — *adj.* Sublimated; refined. — *n. Chem.* The product of sublimation, especially when regarded as purified by the process. [<L *sublimatus,* pp. of *sublimare* <*sublimis* SUBLIME]

sub·li·ma·tion (sub′lə·mā′shən) *n.* 1 The act or process of sublimating. 2 That which has been sublimated; the pure essence of a thing. 3 *Psychol.* The transfer of psychic energy into socially acceptable channels of endeavor.

sub·lime (sə·blīm′) *adj.* 1 Characterized by elevation, nobility, or awe; grand; solemn. 2 Preeminent for nobility of character or attainment; majestic; noble: said of persons. 3 Being of the highest degree; supreme; utmost. 4 *Poetic* Of lofty bearing; haughty; proud; elated. — *n.* That which is sublime, in any sense: usually with the definite article. — *v.* **·limed, ·lim·ing** *v.t.* 1 To make sublime; ennoble. 2 To purify by sublimating. — *v.i.* To become sublimated. [<L *sublimis* lofty, prob. <*sub-* up to, under + *limen* a lintel] — **sub·lime′ly** *adv.* — **sub·lim′er** *n.* — **sub·lim·i·ty** (sə·blim′ə·tē), **sub·lime′ness** *n.*

Synonyms (adj.): beautiful, exalted, grand, lofty, magnificent, majestic, stately. *Sublime* represents the ultimate, the quintessence, and is seldom applied to persons. What is *beautiful* attracts, but what is *sublime* transcends the beautiful and inspires awe rather than simple delight. *Majestic* refers exclusively to superficial effect which makes an impression but has no connection with moral greatness. *Magnificent* denotes the possession at once of greatness, splendor, and richness; as, *magnificent* array. See GRAND. *Antonyms*: base, contemptible, insignificant, little, mean, petty, ridiculous.

Sublime Porte See PORTE.

sub·lim·i·nal (sub·lim′ə·nəl) *adj. Psychol.* 1 Below the threshold of consciousness: opposed to *supraliminal*: said of psychophysical changes of too small intensity to produce definite sensations or a clear awareness: a *subliminal* stimulus. 2 Belonging to the subconscious. [<SUB- + L *limen, liminis* a threshold, trans. of G *unter der Schwelle (des Bewusstseins)* under the threshold (of consciousness)]

sub·lin·gual (sub·ling′gwəl) *adj.* 1 Situated beneath the tongue. 2 Of or pertaining to the salivary gland situated beneath the tongue.

sub·lit·to·ral (sub·lit′ər·əl) *adj.* 1 Close to the seashore. 2 Pertaining to or designating the area between low-tide mark and a depth of 20 fathoms or of 40 meters.

sub·lu·nar·y (sub′lōō·ner′ē, sub·lōō′nər·ē) *adj.* 1 Situated beneath the moon: also **sub·lu·nar** (sub·lōō′nər). 2 Terrestrial; earthly. [<NL *sublunaris* <L *sub-* under + *luna* the moon]

sub·ma·chine gun (sub′mə·shēn′) A lightweight, gas-operated gun, automatic or semi-automatic in action, designed for firing from the shoulder or hip. — **Thompson submachine gun** An air-cooled, .45-caliber submachine gun with automatic firing action: also called *Tommy gun*: named for its inventor, John T. *Thompson,* 1860–1940, U.S. Army officer.

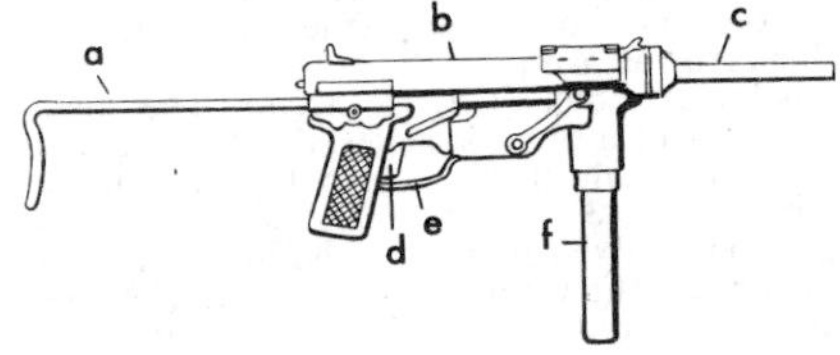

SUBMACHINE GUN
a. Stock. *b.* Housing. *c.* Barrel.
d. Trigger. *e.* Trigger guard. *f.* Clip.

sub·mar·gin·al (sub·mär′jən·əl) *adj.* 1 Below the margin. 2 Below economic sufficiency: *submarginal* land. 3 *Biol.* Situated close to the margin of an organ or structure.

submarginal land *Agric.* Land of such low degree of fertility or productivity as to be incapable of furnishing an economic return.

sub·ma·rine (sub′mə·rēn′) *adj.* Existing, done, or operating beneath the surface of the sea: a *submarine* mine: contrasted with *subaerial.* — *n.* (sub′mə·rēn) A boat designed to operate both on, and at various depths below, the surface of the sea, and now often powered by a reactor using nuclear fuel.

submarine chaser A small patrol vessel designed for action against submarines.

sub·mar·i·ner (sub·mar′ə·nər) *n.* A trained and qualified member of a submarine crew.

sub·max·il·lar·y (sub·mak′sə·ler′ē) *Anat. adj.* 1 Of, pertaining to, or situated beneath the lower jaw. 2 Of or pertaining to one of the salivary glands situated near the angle of the lower jaw. — *n. pl.* **·lar·ies** The lower jaw bone: also **sub·max·il·la** (sub′mak·sil′ə).

sub·me·di·ant (sub·mē′dē·ənt) *n. Music* The sixth tone of a major or minor scale.

sub·men·tal (sub·men′təl) *adj.* 1 *Anat.* Situated beneath the chin: the *submental* artery. 2 Of or pertaining to the submentum.

sub·men·tum (sub·men′təm) *n. Entomol.* The basal sclerite of the labium of an insect, between the gula and the mentum. [<NL <L *sub-* under + *mentum* the chin]

sub·merge (səb·mûrj′) *v.* **·merged, ·merg·ing** *v.t.* 1 To place under or plunge into water. 2 To cover; hide. — *v.i.* 3 To sink or dive beneath the surface of water. Also **sub·merse′**

(-mûrs′). See synonyms under IMMERSE. [<L *submergere*, var. of *summergere* < *sub-* under + *mergere* plunge] — **sub·mer′gence, sub·mer′·sion** (-mûr′shən, -zhən) *n.*

sub·mer·gi·ble (səb·mûr′jə·bəl) *adj.* Capable of being submerged. — **sub·mer′gi·bil′i·ty** *n.*

sub·mersed (səb·mûrst′) *adj.* 1 *Bot.* Growing under water. 2 Submerged. [<L *submersus*, pp. of *submergere* SUBMERGE]

sub·mers·i·ble (səb·mûr′sə·bəl) *adj.* That may be submerged. — *n.* A submarine.

sub·mi·cron (sub·mī′kron) *n.* A particle of from 50 to 1,000 angstroms in diameter.

sub·mi·cro·scop·ic (sub·mī′krə·skop′ik) *adj.* Below the limit of vision in a microscope.

sub·mine (sub′mīn′) *n.* A small, electrically actuated mine located near a submarine mine and used in the training of navy personnel.

sub·min·i·a·ture camera (sub′min′ē·ə·cho͝or) A miniature camera using 16–mm. film for taking still photographs.

sub·min·i·a·tur·ize (sub·min′ē·ə·chə·rīz′) *v.t.* **·ized, ·iz·ing** To reduce, as certain delicate instruments, to the smallest size compatible with efficient use and service, as in the design and production of hearing aids. — **sub·min′i·a·tur·i·za′tion** *n.*

sub·miss (səb·mis′) *adj. Archaic* Submissive; soft; subdued. [<L *submissus*, pp. of *submittere* SUBMIT]

sub·mis·sion (səb·mish′ən) *n.* 1 The act of submitting; a yielding to the power or authority of another; obedience. 2 The state or quality of being submissive; the spirit of subjection or obedience; an acquiescent temper; humility; resignation; meekness. 3 The act of referring, or the agreement to refer, a matter of controversy to arbitration. 4 *Archaic* Acknowledgment of error.

Synonyms: obedience, patience, resignation, subjection, submissiveness. See PATIENCE.

sub·mis·sive (səb·mis′iv) *adj.* Willing or inclined to submit; yielding; obedient; docile. See synonyms under DOCILE, HUMBLE, OBSEQUIOUS, PASSIVE, SUPPLE. — **sub·mis′sive·ly** *adv.* — **sub·mis′sive·ness** *n.*

sub·mit (səb·mit′) *v.* **·mit·ted, ·mit·ting** *v.t.* 1 To place under or yield to the authority, will, or power of another; surrender. 2 To present for the consideration, decision, or approval of others; refer. 3 To present as one's opinion; suggest. — *v.i.* 4 To give up; surrender. 5 To be obedient or submissive; be acquiescent. See synonyms under BEND[1], DEFER, OBEY. [<L *submittere*, var. of *summittere* < *sub-* underneath + *mittere* send] — **sub·mit′tal** *n.* — **sub·mit′ter** *n.*

sub·mon·tane (sub·mon′tān) *adj.* 1 Situated at the foot of a mountain or mountain range. 2 Beneath a mountain. — **sub·mon′tane·ly** *adv.*

sub·mul·ti·ple (sub·mul′tə·pəl) *n. Math.* A number or quantity that is contained in another without remainder; an aliquot part. — *adj.* Contained in something an exact number of times. [<LL *submultiplus* < *sub-* opposite of, lesser + *multiplus* MULTIPLE]

sub·nor·mal (sub·nôr′məl) *adj.* 1 Below the normal. 2 *Psychol.* Of less than normal intelligence. — *n.* 1 *Math.* That portion of the axis of a curve included between the ordinate of one of its points and the normal to that point. 2 A subnormal individual. — **sub·nor·mal·i·ty** (sub′nôr·mal′ə·tē) *n.*

sub·o·ce·an·ic (sub′ō·shē·an′ik) *adj.* Occurring, formed, or happening beneath the ocean floor.

sub·or·der (sub′ôr′dər) *n.* 1 *Biol.* A category of animals or plants next below an order. 2 A subordinate architectural order modifying the principal order, generally for decoration. — **sub·or·di·nal** (sub·ôr′də·nəl) *adj.*

sub·or·di·nar·y (sub·ôr′də·ner′ē) *n. pl.* **·nar·ies** *Her.* One of a class of armorial charges usually considered less honorable than the ordinaries. Among them are the *bordure, flanch, orle, tressure,* etc.

sub·or·di·nate (sə·bôr′də·nit) *adj.* 1 Belonging to an inferior order in a classification; secondary; minor. 2 Subject or subservient to another; inferior in any way. 3 Dependent; joining dependent words to others. See synonyms under AUXILIARY, SUBJECT. — *n.* One who is subordinate; an inferior in rank or official position. — *v.t.* (-nāt) **·nat·ed, ·nat·ing** 1 To make subordinate; assign to a lower order or rank; hence, to hold as of less importance. 2 To make subject or subservient. [<L *subordinatus*, pp. of *subordinare* < *sub-* under + *ordinare* order] — **sub·or′di·nate·ly** *adv.* — **sub·or′di·nate·ness** *n.* — **sub·or′di·na′tion** *n.*

subordinate conjunction See under CONJUNCTION.

sub·or·di·na·tion·ism (sə·bôr′də·nā′shən·iz′əm) *n. Theol.* The doctrine that the second and third persons of the Trinity are inferior to the first person. — **sub·or′di·na′tion·ist** *n.*

sub·or·di·na·tive (sə·bôr′də·nā′tiv) *adj.* Having a tendency to or expressive of subordination.

sub·orn (sə·bôrn′) *v.t.* 1 To bribe or procure (someone) to commit perjury. 2 To incite or instigate to an evil act, especially a criminal act. 3 *Obs.* To decorate or adorn. [<L *subornare* < *sub-* secretly + *ornare* equip] — **sub·orn′er** *n.* — **sub·or·na·tion** (sub′ôr·nā′shən) *n.*

Su·bo·ti·ca (so͞o′bô′ti·tsä) A city in northern Serbia, Yugoslavia: German *Maria Theresiopel*, Hungarian *Szabadka*. Also **Su′bo′ti·tsa.**

sub·ox·ide (sub·ok′sīd) *n. Chem.* An oxide having the minimum amount of oxygen.

sub·phy·lum (sub·fī′ləm) *n. Biol.* A primary division of a phylum, superior to the class.

sub·plinth (sub′plinth′) *n. Archit.* A block or base supporting a plinth; a second or lower plinth.

sub–plot (sub′plot′) *n.* A plot subordinate to the principal one in a novel, play, etc.

sub·poe·na (sə·pē′nə, səb-) *n.* A judicial writ requiring a person to appear at a specified time and place under penalty for default. — *v.t.* To notify or summon by writ or subpoena. Also **sub·pe′na.** [<Med. L <L *sub poena* < *sub* under + *poena* penalty]

sub–port (sub′pôrt′, -pōrt′) *n.* An auxiliary port, equipped to handle traffic diverted from the main port.

sub–post (sub′pōst′) *n.* An administrative subdivision of a military post.

sub·pre·fect (sub·prē′fekt) *n.* A subordinate prefect; in France, the administrative officer of an arrondissement. — **sub·pre′fec·ture** (-fek·chər) *n.*

sub·prin·ci·pal (sub·prin′sə·pəl) *n.* 1 A vice principal. 2 A rafter or brace next to or auxiliary to one of the main timbers of the frame. 3 *Music* An open diapason sub–bass in an organ.

sub·ra·mose (sub·rā′mōs) *adj. Bot.* 1 Branching moderately, as a plant. 2 Having few branches. [<NL *subramosus* <L *sub-* somewhat, under + *ramosus* RAMOSE]

sub·re·gion (sub′rē′jən) *n.* A subdivision of a region, especially with reference to the distribution of animals. — **sub·re′gion·al** *adj.*

sub·rep·tion (səb·rep′shən) *n.* 1 A procuring of some favor or reward by means of a fraudulent concealment or suppression of the truth. 2 Inference resulting from concealment, or misrepresentation of essential elements or facts. [<L *subreptio, -onis* < *subreptus*, pp. of *subripere* < *sub-* secretly + *rapere* snatch, seize]

sub·ro·gate (sub′rō·gāt) *v.t.* **·gat·ed, ·gat·ing** 1 To substitute (one thing) for another. 2 To substitute (one person) for another when attributing or assigning rights or appointing to an office. [<L *subrogatus*, pp. of *subrogare* substitute < *sub-* in place of + *rogare* ask]

sub·ro·ga·tion (sub′rō·gā′shən) *n.* 1 The succession or substitution of one person or thing by or for another. 2 *Law* The putting of a person who (as a surety) has paid the debt of another in the place of the creditor to whom he has paid it.

sub ro·sa (sub rō′zə) *Latin* Confidentially; in secret: literally, under the rose: because, in Egypt, the rose was the emblem of Horus, (Roman Harpocrates), mistakenly regarded by the Greeks and Romans as the god of silence, for he was often depicted as a child with finger on mouth.

sub·scap·u·lar (sub·skap′yə·lər) *adj. Anat.* Situated underneath the scapula. Also **sub·scap′u·lar′y** (-ler′ē). [<NL *subscapularis* <L *sub-* under + *scapula* a shoulder blade]

sub·scribe (səb·skrīb′) *v.* **·scribed, ·scrib·ing** *v.t.* 1 To write, as one's name, at the end of a document; sign. 2 To sign one's name to as an expression of assent, acceptance, etc.; attest to by signing. 3 To promise, especially in writing, to pay or contribute (a sum of money). — *v.i.* 4 To write one's name at the end of a document. 5 To give sanction, support, or approval; agree. 6 To promise to pay or contribute money. 7 To agree to receive and pay for an article, as a periodical, usually by written agreement: with *to.* [<L *subscribere* < *sub-* underneath + *scribere* write] — **sub·scrib′er** *n.*

sub·script (sub′skript) *adj.* 1 Written following and slightly beneath, as a small letter: iota *subscript.* 2 *Math.* Of a subindex. — *n.* A subscript sign, symbol, or letter. Compare SUPERSCRIPT. [<L *subscriptus*, pp. of *subscribere.* See SUBSCRIBE.]

sub·scrip·tion (səb·skrip′shən) *n.* 1 The act of subscribing; signature; hence, consent, confirmation, or agreement. 2 That which is subscribed; a signed paper or statement. 3 A signature written at the end of a document. 4 A signed acceptance of religious articles. 5 The individual or total sum or number subscribed for any purpose. 6 A formal agreement or undertaking evinced by signature, as payment of a certain price for the receipt of a magazine, book, ticket, etc. 7 *Archaic* Submission; obedience. 8 The part of a doctor's prescription which gives directions for compounding the ingredients. 9 The sale of books, magazines, tickets, etc., by mail or by personal canvass. — **to take up a subscription** To collect money (for some special purpose or cause) from a large number of people. — **sub·scrip′tive** *adj.* — **sub·scrip′tive·ly** *adv.*

subscription list A list of the names of people and the amounts they have subscribed, as for a periodical, a charity, or other cause.

sub·sec·tion (sub·sek′shən, sub′sek′shən) *n.* A subdivision of a section.

sub·sec·tor (sub·sek′tər, sub′sek′tər) *n.* A portion of a military sector or coastal frontier marked out for convenience in operations.

sub·se·quence (sub′sə·kwəns) *n.* 1 The condition of being subsequent. 2 The act of following. Also **sub′se·quen·cy.**

sub·se·quent (sub′sə·kwənt) *adj.* 1 Following in time, place, or order, or as a result. 2 Succeeding; consequent. [<L *subsequens, -entis*, ppr. of *subsequi* < *sub-* next below + *sequi* follow] — **sub′se·quent·ly** *adv.* — **sub′se·quent·ness** *n.*

sub·serve (səb·sûrv′) *v.t.* **·served, ·serv·ing** 1 To be of use or help in furthering (a process, cause, etc.); serve; promote. 2 To serve as a subordinate to (a person). See synonyms under SERVE. [<L *subservire* < *sub-* under + *servire* SERVE]

sub·ser·vi·ent (səb·sûr′vē·ənt) *adj.* 1 Adapted to promote some end or purpose; being of service; useful as a subordinate. 2 Hence, acting in the interests of another; servile; obsequious; truckling. — *n.* One who or that which subserves. See synonyms under BASE[2]. [<L *subserviens, -entis*, ppr. of *subservire* SUBSERVE] — **sub·ser′vi·ent·ly** *adv.* — **sub·ser′vi·ent·ness, sub·ser′vi·ence, sub·ser′vi·en·cy** *n.*

sub–shrub (sub′shrub′) *n.* An undershrub or very small shrub. — **sub′–shrub′by** *adj.*

sub·side (səb·sīd′) *v.i.* **·sid·ed, ·sid·ing** 1 To sink to a lower level. 2 To become less violent or agitated; become calm or quiet; abate. 3 To sink to the bottom, as sediment; settle. See synonyms under ABATE, FALL. [<L *subsidere* < *sub-* under + *sidere* settle < *sedere* sit]

sub·sid·ence (səb·sīd′ns, sub′sə·dəns) *n.* 1 The settling of heavy parts to the bottom; precipitation. 2 The sinking of water or other liquids to a lower or usual level: *subsidence* of a flood. 3 A gradual settling into a quiet or inactive state. 4 A gradual settling of the earth to a lower level, because of ground movements or underground workings. [<L *subsidentia* sediment < *subsidere* SUBSIDE]

sub·sid·i·ar·y (səb·sid′ē·er′ē) *adj.* 1 Assisting in an inferior capacity; supplementary; auxiliary; secondary. 2 Of, pertaining to, or in the nature of a subsidy; helping by a subsidy. — *n. pl.* **·ar·ies** 1 One who or that which furnishes supplemental aid or supplies; an auxiliary; assistant. 2 *Music* A theme subordinate to or dependent on the main theme or subject. [<L *subsidiarius* <*subsidium* <*subsidere* SUBSIDE] — **sub·sid′i·ar′i·ly** *adv.*

subsidiary coin Coin of small denomination, legal tender only to a limited amount; in the United States, any coin worth less than a dollar.

subsidiary company A company controlled by another company which owns the greater part of its shares.

sub·si·dize (sub′sə·dīz) *v.t.* **·dized, ·diz·ing 1** To furnish with a subsidy; grant a regular allowance or pecuniary aid to. **2** To obtain the assistance of by a subsidy: now often implying bribery. Also *Brit.* **sub′si·dise.** — **sub′si·di·za′tion** *n.* — **sub′si·diz′er** *n.*

sub·si·dy (sub′sə·dē) *n. pl.* **·dies 1** Pecuniary aid directly granted by government to an individual or private commercial enterprise deemed beneficial to the public. **2** Formerly, an aid or tax granted by the House of Commons to the king for urgent needs of the kingdom. **3** Any financial assistance afforded by one individual or government to another. [<AF *subsidie,* OF *subside* <L *subsidium* auxiliary forces, aid <*subsidere* SUBSIDE]

Synonyms: aid, allowance, bonus, bounty, gift, grant, indemnity, pension, premium, reward, support, subvention, tribute. A nation grants a *subsidy* to an ally, pays a *tribute* to a conqueror. An *indemnity* is a single reparation demanded for a specific injury, while a *tribute* may be exacted indefinitely. A nation may also grant a *subsidy* to its own citizens as a means of promoting the public welfare; as, a *subsidy* to a steamship company. The somewhat rare term *subvention* is especially applied to a *grant* of governmental aid to a literary or artistic enterprise. The word *bounty* may be applied to almost any regular or stipulated *allowance* by a government to a citizen or citizens; as, a *bounty* for enlisting in the army, a *bounty* for killing wolves, a land *bounty* to encourage settlement of sparsely populated areas. A *bounty* is reward for a single act; a *pension* is earned by long service.

sub·sist (səb·sist′) *v.i.* **1** To have existence or reality; continue to exist. **2** To remain alive; manage to live. **3** To continue unchanged; abide. **4** To have existence in or by something; inhere. — *v.t. Obs.* **5** To provide with food and clothing; support. See synonyms under LIVE. [<MF *subsister* <L *subsistere* <*sub-* under + *sistere* cause to stand <*stare* stand] — **sub·sist′er** *n.*

sub·sis·tence (səb·sis′təns) *n.* **1** The act of subsisting. **2** That on which one subsists; sustenance; means of support; livelihood. **3** The state of being subsistent; inherent quality. **4** That which subsists; real being. **5** A basis; a logical substance; hypostasis. Also **sub·sis′ten·cy.** [<LL *subsistentia* <*subsistere* SUBSIST]

subsistence department A former department of the army that provided and had charge of subsistence stores: these are now purchased and issued by the Quartermaster Corps: also called *commissary department.*

sub·sis·tent (səb·sis′tənt) *adj.* **1** That subsists or is inherent. **2** Existing; having real being or action. **3** Having subsistence.

sub·soil (sub′soil′) *n.* The stratum of earth next beneath the surface soil. — *v.t.* To turn up the subsoil of; plow with a subsoil plow. — **sub′·soil′er** *n.*

subsoil plow *Agric.* A plow specially designed for loosening or turning up the subsoil.

sub·so·lar (sub·sō′lər) *adj.* **1** Situated directly beneath the sun, as at high noon at the equinoxes; also, between the tropics. **2** Mundane; earthly.

sub·son·ic (sub·son′ik) *adj.* **1** Designating those sound waves beyond the lower limits of human audibility, or with frequencies of less than about 25 cycles per second; infrasonic. **2** Of, pertaining to, characterized, or operated by such waves. Compare SUPERSONIC.

sub·spe·cies (sub·spē′shēz, -shiz) *n. Biol.* A subdivision of a species, variously ranked but usually distinguished by minor differences in characteristics and by having a particular geographic range within a larger area. [<NL <L *sub-* under + *species* an appearance, sort]

sub·stance (sub′stəns) *n.* **1** The material of which anything is made or constituted. **2** The essential part of anything said or written, put into a brief, condensed statement; the gist or purport. **3** The vital part of that which is spiritual or emotional. **4** Material possessions; wealth; property. **5** That which gives stability or solidity; confidence; ground. **6** *Philos.* The essential nature that underlies phenomena; the permanent cause underlying outward manifestations; that in which qualities or attributes inhere. **7** In Christian Science, Spirit. **8** Any particular kind of material. **9** Essential components or characteristic elements of ideas: The tenets are the same in *substance.* See synonyms under MASS[1]. [<OF <L *substantia* <*substare* be present <*sub-* under + *stare* stand]

sub·stan·dard (sub·stan′dərd) *adj.* **1** Below the standard. **2** Lower than the established rate or authorized requirements.

sub·stan·tial (səb·stan′shəl) *adj.* **1** Solid; strong; firm. **2** Of real worth and importance; of considerable value; valuable. **3** Considerable and sure. **4** Possessed of wealth or sufficient means; responsible. **5** Of or pertaining to substance; having real existence; not illusory; actual; permanent; lasting. **6** Containing or conforming to the essence of a thing; giving the correct idea; essential; material; fundamental. **7** Ample and nourishing. — *n.* **1** That which has substance; a reality. **2** The more important part. — **sub·stan′ti·al′i·ty** · (-shē·al′ə·tē), **sub·stan′tial·ness** *n.* — **sub·stan′tial·ly** *adv.*

sub·stan·tial·ism (səb·stan′shəl·iz′əm) *n. Philos.* The doctrine that substantial realities are the sources or underlying ground of all phenomena, material and mental; the doctrine that matter is a real substance. — **sub·stan′tial·ist** *n.*

sub·stan·ti·ate (səb·stan′shē·āt) *v.t.* **·at·ed, ·at·ing 1** To establish, as a position or a truth, by substantial evidence; verify. **2** To give form to; embody. **3** To make substantial, existent, or real; give substance to. See synonyms under CONFIRM, RATIFY. [<NL *substantiatus,* pp. of *substantiare* establish <L *substantia* SUBSTANCE] — **sub·stan′ti·a′tion** *n.* — **sub·stan′ti·a′tive** *adj.*

sub·stan·ti·val (sub′stən·tī′vəl) *adj.* **1** Of or pertaining to a substantive. **2** Self-existent. — **sub′stan·ti′val·ly** *adv.*

sub·stan·tive (sub′stən·tiv) *n.* **1** A noun. **2** Anything used in place of a noun, as a verbal form, phrase, or clause. **3** One who or that which is independent; a self-subsisting person or thing. — *adj.* **1** Capable of being used as a noun. **2** Expressive of or denoting existence: The verb "to be" is called the *substantive* verb. **3** Having substance or reality; hence, lasting. **4** Being an essential part or constituent. **5** Relating to what is essential. **6** Having distinct individuality. **7** Independent in resources; self-supporting, as a country. **8** Of considerable amount; substantial. **9** In dyeing, not needing a mordant. [<OF *substantif* <LL *substantivus* <L *substantia* SUBSTANCE] — **sub′stan·tive·ness** *n.*

substantive dye See under DYE.

sub·stan·tiv·ize (sub′stən·tiv·īz′) *v.t.* **·ized, ·iz·ing** To treat or use as a substantive: The adjective "meek" is *substantivized* in "Blessed are the meek."

sub·sta·tion (sub′stā′shən) *n.* A subsidiary station, as an electric power station for switching, transforming, or converting purposes, a branch post office, etc.

sub·stit·u·ent (səb·stich′o͞o·ənt) *n. Chem.* A radical, atom, or group, substituting or replacing another in a chemical reaction. — *adj.* Of a substituting atom or molecule. [<L *substituens, -entis,* ppr. of *substituere* SUBSTITUTE]

sub·sti·tute (sub′stə·to͞ot, -tyo͞ot) *v.* **·tut·ed, ·tut·ing** *v.t.* **1** To put in the place of another person or thing. **2** To take the place of. — *v.i.* **3** To act as a substitute. **4** *Chem.* To exchange one constituent of a compound for, or replace it with, another. See synonyms under CHANGE. — *n.* **1** One who or that which takes the place or serves in lieu of another. **2** In the American Civil War, one hired to serve in the place of a man drafted into military service. **3** Any substance or material adapted to replace another in a given product or process, or for a specified purpose: Gelatin is a *substitute* for agar, synthetic rubber for cork, etc.: also called *alternative, replacement.* See synonyms under DELEGATE. [<L *substitutus,* pp. of *substituere* <*sub-* in place of + *statuere* set up]

sub·sti·tu·tion (sub′stə·to͞o′shən, -tyo͞o′-) *n.* **1** The act of substituting, or the state of being substituted. **2** *Chem.* Any reaction which involves the replacement of certain elements or radicals by others: said especially of organic compounds. — **sub′sti·tu′tion·al** *adj.* — **sub′·sti·tu′tion·al·ly** *adv.*

sub·sti·tu·tive (sub′stə·to͞o′tiv, -tyo͞o′-) *adj.* Acting or tending to act as a substitute; admitting of substitution.

sub·strate (sub′strāt) *n.* **1** *Biochem.* The material or substance acted upon by an enzyme or ferment. **2** A substratum. [<SUBSTRATUM]

sub·stra·tum (sub·strā′təm, -strat′əm) *n. pl.* **·stra·ta** (-strā′tə, -strat′ə) **1** An underlying stratum or layer, as of earth or rock; subsoil. **2** That which forms the foundation or groundwork. **3** Matter or mind considered as the ground of qualities and phenomena; the substance possessing attributes. **4** The substance in which something takes root, as vegetable or animal tissue. [<NL <L, pp. neut. of *substernere* spread underneath <*sub-* underneath + *sternere* strew] — **sub·stra′tive** *adj.*

sub·struc·tion (sub·struk′shən) *n.* A foundation. [<F <L *substructio, -onis* <*substruere* <*sub-* underneath + *struere* build] — **sub·struc′tion·al** *adj.*

sub·struc·ture (sub·struk′chər, sub′struk′-) *n.* **1** A structure serving as a foundation of a building, etc. **2** Groundwork. **3** The earthen roadway supporting railroad tracks. — **sub·struc′tur·al** *adj.*

sub·sume (səb·so͞om′) *v.t.* **·sumed, ·sum·ing 1** To place in some particular class; classify. **2** To include, as the specific or individual in the general. [<NL *subsumere* <L *sub-* underneath + *sumere* take] — **sub·sum′a·ble** *adj.*

sub·sump·tion (səb·sump′shən) *n.* **1** The act of subsuming. **2** That which is subsumed; an assumption; especially, the minor premise of a syllogism as stated after the major premise. **3** Formerly, a narrative of an alleged crime giving minute particulars. [<NL *subsumptio, -onis* <*subsumere* SUBSUME] — **sub·sump′·tive** *adj.*

sub·tan·gent (sub·tan′jənt) *n. Geom.* The portion of the axis of a curve cut off between the tangent to a given point and the ordinate of that point. [<NL *subtangens, -entis* <L *sub-* under + *tangens,* ppr. of *tangere* touch]

sub·tem·per·ate (sub·tem′pər·it) *adj.* **1** Pertaining to the colder parts of the temperate zone. **2** Slightly temperate.

sub·ten·ant (sub·ten′ənt) *n.* A person who rents or leases from a tenant; a sublessee. — **sub·ten′an·cy** *n.*

sub·tend (sub·tend′) *v.t.* **1** *Geom.* To extend under or opposite to, as the chord of an arc or the side of a triangle opposite to an angle. **2** *Bot.* To enclose in its axil: A leaf *subtends* a bud. [<L *subtendere* <*sub-* underneath + *tendere* stretch]

sub·tense (sub·tens′) *Geom. n.* **1** A line that subtends an arc or angle. **2** The chord of an arc. — *adj.* Pertaining to or used in estimating distance by measuring the subtended angle. [<NL *subtensa (linea)* (a) subtended (line), pp. fem. of L *subtendere* SUBTEND]

subter- *prefix* Under; less than: opposed to *super-*: *subteraqueous.* [<L *subter* below, beneath]

sub·ter·a·que·ous (sub′tə·rā′kwē·əs, -rak′wē-) *adj.* Situated beneath the surface of the water. Also **sub′ter·ra′que·ous.** [<L (assumed) *subteraqueus* <*subter-* beneath + *aqua* water]

sub·ter·fuge (sub′tər·fyo͞oj) *n.* That to which one resorts for escape or concealment; an evasion of an issue; a plan to avoid censure; a false excuse. See synonyms under ARTIFICE, SOPHISTRY. [<L *subterfugium* <*subterfugere* <*subter-* below, in secret + *fugere* flee, take flight]

sub·ter·nat·u·ral (sub′tər·nach′ər·əl) *adj.* Below the norms of nature.

sub·ter·rane (sub′tə·rān) *n.* **1** A basal or underlying terrane. **2** An underground room; a cave. [<L *subterraneus* <*sub-* under + *terra* the earth]

sub·ter·ra·ne·an (sub′tə·rā′nē·ən) *adj.* **1** Situated or occurring below the surface of the earth: contrasted with *subaerial* and *surficial*; underground. **2** Hidden. Also **sub′ter·ra′ne·al, sub′ter·ra′ne·ous, sub′ter·rene′** (-tə·rēn′).

sub·ter·res·tri·al (sub′tə·res′trē·əl) *adj.* Subterranean; lower than the terrestrial. —*n.* A creature that lives underground.

sub·tile (sut′l, sub′til) *adj.* 1 Having fine structure; delicately formed; ethereal. 2 Characterized by material rarity; rarefied; refined; hence, penetrating; pervasive. 3 Subtle. [< OF *subtil,* alter of *soutil* SUBTLE; refashioned after L] —**sub′tile·ly** *adv.* —**sub′tile·ness** *n.*
Synonym: subtle. *Subtile* and *subtle* have been constantly used as interchangeable by good writers; but there is a present tendency to distinguish them by making *subtile* an attribute of things and *subtle* a characteristic of mind. *Subtle,* the later form of the word, is used preferably when the derogatory sense of crafty is to be expressed. See ACUTE, ASTUTE, FINE[1].

sub·til·i·ty (sub·til′ə·tē) *n.* The quality or state of being subtile; thinness; fineness.

sub·til·ize (sut′l·īz, sub′tə·līz) *v.* **·ized, ·iz·ing** *v.t.* 1 To make subtle or subtile; refine. 2 To make acute; sharpen, as the senses. 3 To discuss or argue subtly. —*v.i.* 4 To make subtle distinctions; use subtlety. [<Med. L *subtilizare* <L *subtilis* SUBTLE] —**sub′til·i·za′tion** *n.*

sub·til·ty (sut′l·tē, sub′təl·tē) *n. pl.* **·ties** 1 Refinement or niceness, or an instance of it; a nicety. 2 Subtlety.

sub·ti·tle (sub′tīt′l) *n.* A subordinate or explanatory title, as in a book, play, or document; a book title repeated, as on top of the first page of the text.

sub·tle (sut′l) *adj.* 1 Characterized by cunning, craft, or artifice; wily; crafty. 2 Keen; penetrative; discriminating: *subtle* humor; overrefined. 3 Apt; skilful. 4 Executed with nice art; ingenious; clever. 5 Insidious; secretly active. 6 Hard to understand; abstruse. 7 Of delicate texture. 8 Subtile. See synonyms under ACUTE, ASTUTE, FINE[1], INSIDIOUS, SUBTILE. [<OF *soutil* <L *subtilis* fine, orig. closely woven <*sub-* under + *tela* a web] —**sub′tle·ness** *n.* —**sub′tly** *adv.*

sub·tle·ty (sut′l·tē) *n. pl.* **·ties** 1 The state or quality of being subtle. 2 The ability to make fine distinctions; keenness of perception. 3 Something subtle, as a nice distinction.

sub·ton·ic (sub·ton′ik) *adj. Phonet.* Sonant or voiced, as certain consonants. —*n.* 1 *Phonet.* A subtonic sound. 2 *Music* The seventh of the scale; a semitone below the tonic.

sub·tor·rid (sub·tôr′id, -tor′-) *adj.* Subtropical.

sub·tract (səb·trakt′) *v.t.* & *v.i.* To take away or deduct, as a portion from the whole, or one quantity from another. [<L *subtractus,* pp. of *subtrahere* <*sub-* away + *trahere* draw] —**sub·tract′er** *n.*

sub·trac·tion (səb·trak′shən) *n.* 1 The act or process of subtracting; a deducting; something deducted. 2 *Math.* The operation of finding the difference between two quantities (symbol −).

sub·trac·tive (səb·trak′tiv) *adj.* 1 Serving or tending to diminish. 2 *Math.* Having the minus sign; to be subtracted.

subtractive process *Phot.* A method of making two or more negatives through filters which exclude all but a desired color: used in color printing and engraving.

sub·tra·hend (sub′trə·hend) *n. Math.* That which is to be subtracted from a number or quantity (the minuend) to give the difference. [<L *subtrahendus (numerus)* (the number) to be subtracted, gerundive of *subtrahere* SUBTRACT]

sub·trans·lu·cent (sub′trans·lōō′sənt, -tranz-) *adj.* Not fully translucent, as certain gemstones and other minerals.

sub·treas·ur·y (sub·trezh′ər·ē) *n. pl.* **·ur·ies** 1 A branch of the U. S. Treasury Department maintained for receipt and safekeeping of government revenues: established in 1840 and abolished in 1920. 2 The building that housed such a branch. —**sub·treas′ur·er** *n.*

sub·trop·i·cal (sub·trop′i·kəl) *adj.* 1 Of, pertaining to, or designating regions adjacent to the tropical zone. 2 Designating either of two irregular belts of high atmospheric pressure roughly between 30° and 40° latitude, north and south. Also **sub·trop′ic.**

sub·trop·ics (sub·trop′iks) *n. pl.* Subtropical regions.

su·bu·late (sōō′byə·lāt, -lit) *adj. Biol.* Shaped like an awl; slender and tapering to a point. [<NL *subulatus* <L *subula* an awl]

sub·um·brel·la (sub′um·brel′ə) *n. Zool.* The under surface of the swimming bell of a jellyfish, or that surface situated in the region of the mouth. —**sub·um·bral** (sub·um′brəl), **sub′·um·brel′lar** *adj.*

sub·urb (sub′ûrb) *n.* A place adjacent to a city; in the plural, collectively, environs; outskirts; outlying residential districts; purlieus. [<OF *suburbe* <L *surburbium* <*sub-* near to + *urbs, urbis* a city]

sub·ur·ban (sə·bûr′bən) *adj.* Of or pertaining to a suburb; dwelling or located in a place which is a combination of the rural and urban. —*n.* A suburbanite.

sub·ur·ban·ite (sə·bûr′bən·īt) *n.* A resident of a suburb.

sub·ur·bi·a (sə·bûr′bē·ə) *n.* 1 The social and cultural world of suburbanites. 2 Suburbs or suburbanites collectively.

sub·ur·bi·car·i·an (sə·bûr′bə·kâr′ē·ən) *adj.* Being in the suburbs (of Rome): applied to the six sees that compose the province of the pope as metropolitan. [<LL *suburbicarius* <L *suburbium* SUBURB]

sub·vene (səb·vēn′) *v.i.* **·vened, ·ven·ing** To come or happen so as to be of aid or support, especially by preventing something; intervene. [<L *subvenire* come to one's assistance <*sub-* up from under + *venire* come]

sub·ven·tion (səb·ven′shən) *n.* 1 The act of subvening; giving of succor; aid. 2 That which aids, especially a grant, as of money; subsidy. See synonyms under SUBSIDY. [<OF *subvencion* <LL *subventio, -onis* <L *subvenire.* See SUBVENE.] —**sub·ven′tion·ar′y** (-er′ē) *adj.*

sub·ver·sion (səb·vûr′shən, -zhən) *n.* 1 The act of subverting, or the state of being subverted; a demolition; overthrow. 2 A cause of ruin. Also **sub·ver′sal** (-səl). See synonyms under RUIN. [<OF <LL *subversio, -onis* <L *subvertere* SUBVERT]

sub·ver·sive (səb·vûr′siv) *adj.* Tending to subvert or overthrow. —*n.* A person who engages in subversion.

sub·vert (səb·vûrt′) *v.t.* 1 To overthrow from the very foundation; destroy utterly. 2 To corrupt; undermine the morals or character of. [<OF *subvertir* <L *subvertere* overturn <*sub-* up from under + *vertere* turn] —**sub·vert′er** *n.* —**sub·vert′i·ble** *adj.*
Synonyms: destroy, extinguish, overthrow, overturn, supersede, supplant. To *supersede* implies the putting of something that is preferred in the place of that which is removed; to *subvert* does not imply substitution. To *supplant* is more often personal, signifying to take the place of another, usually by underhand means; one is *superseded* by authority, *supplanted* by a rival. See ABOLISH. *Antonyms*: conserve, perpetuate, preserve, sustain, uphold.

sub·vit·re·ous (sub·vit′rē·əs) *adj.* Having a luster resembling that of glass, but less brilliant.

sub·way (sub′wā) *n.* 1 An artificial passage below the surface of the ground; specifically, one for traffic, water and gas mains, electric cables, etc. 2 An underground railroad, usually electrically operated; also, a tunnel for such a railroad.

suc– Assimilated var. of SUB–.

suc·ce·da·ne·um (suk′si·dā′nē·əm) *n. pl.* **·ne·ums** or **·ne·a** (-nē·ə) One who or that which is a substitute. [<NL, neut. sing. of L *succedaneus* <*succedere* succeed, replace] —**suc′ce·da′ne·ous** *adj.*

suc·ceed (sək·sēd′) *v.i.* 1 To come next in order or sequence; follow; ensue. 2 To come after another into office, ownership, etc.; be the successor: often with *to.* 3 To be successful; accomplish what is attempted or intended; also, formerly, to achieve an end in a specified manner: They *succeeded* badly. 4 *Law* To devolve: said of an estate. —*v.t.* 5 To be the successor or heir of. 6 To come after in time or sequence; follow. [<OF *succeder* <L *succedere* go under, follow after <*sub-* under + *cedere* go] —**suc·ceed′er** *n.*
Synonyms: achieve, attain, flourish, prevail, prosper, thrive, win. To *win* implies that someone loses, but one may *succeed* where no one fails. A solitary swimmer *succeeds* in reaching the shore; if we say he *wins* the shore we place him in competition with the water. Many students may *succeed* in study; a few *win* the special prizes for which all compete. See FOLLOW.

suc·cen·tor (sək·sen′tər) *n.* 1 A deputy precentor; subcantor; subchanter. 2 The leading bass or bass soloist in a church or cathedral choir. [<LL <L *succinere* sing to <*sub-* subordinately + *canere* sing]

suc·cès d'es·time (sük·se′ des·tēm′) *French* Success marked by the praise of critics but not by widespread popular approval: said of a play, book, etc.

suc·cess (sək·ses′) *n.* 1 A favorable or prosperous course or termination of anything attempted; prosperous or advantageous issue. 2 A successful person or affair. 3 *Obs.* The outcome or result, favorable or unfavorable. 4 *Obs.* Succession. See synonyms under VICTORY. [<L *successus* <*succedere* SUCCEED]

suc·cess·ful (sək·ses′fəl) *adj.* 1 Of persons, obtaining what one desires or intends; especially, having reached a high degree of worldly prosperity. 2 Of things, terminating in or meeting with success; resulting favorably: said of a course of action, etc. See synonyms under AUSPICIOUS, FORTUNATE, HAPPY. —**suc·cess′ful·ly** *adv.* —**suc·cess′ful·ness** *n.*

suc·ces·sion (sək·sesh′ən) *n.* 1 The act of following in order, or the state of being successive; a following consecutively. 2 A group of things that succeed in order; a series, either in time or in place; sequence. 3 The act or right of legally or officially coming into a predecessor's office, possessions, etc.; also, the order of so succeeding, or that which is or is to be so taken. 4 The right or act of succeeding to a throne. 5 Descendants collectively; issue. See synonyms under TIME. —**suc·ces′sion·al** *adj.* —**suc·ces′sion·al·ly** *adv.*

suc·ces·sive (sək·ses′iv) *adj.* Following in succession; consecutive. —**suc·ces′sive·ly** *adv.* —**suc·ces′sive·ness** *n.*

suc·ces·sor (sək·ses′ər) *n.* One who or that which follows in succession; especially, a person who succeeds to a throne, property, or office.

suc·ci·nate (suk′si·nāt) *n. Chem.* A salt of succinic acid. [<SUCCIN(IC) + -ATE[3]]

suc·cinct (sək·singkt′) *adj.* 1 Reduced or comprised within a narrow compass; terse; concise. 2 Supported by an encircling silken thread, as a butterfly chrysalis. 3 *Archaic* Encircled or held in position by or as by a girdle. See synonyms under TERSE. [<L *succinctus,* pp. of *succingere* <*sub-* underneath + *cingere* gird] —**suc·cinct′ly** *adv.* —**suc·cinct′ness** *n.*

suc·cinc·to·ri·um (suk′singk·tôr′ē·əm, -tō′rē-) *n. pl.* **·to·ri·a** (-tôr′ē·ə, -tō′rē·ə) A band or scarf embroidered with an Agnus Dei, worn pendent from the girdle: used by the pope on solemn occasions. [<LL <L *sub-* under + *cinctorium* a girdle <*cinctus,* pp. of *cingere* gird]

suc·cin·ic (sək·sin′ik) *adj.* Derived from or found in amber. [<F *succinique* <L *succinum* amber]

succinic acid *Chem.* Either of two white crystalline isomeric compounds, $C_4H_6O_4$, contained in amber and in certain plants, and also made synthetically.

suc·cor (suk′ər) *n.* 1 Help or relief rendered in danger, difficulty, or distress. 2 One who or that which affords relief. —*v.t.* To go to the aid of; help; rescue. See synonyms under AID, HELP, SERVE. Also *Brit.* **suc′cour.** [<OF *sucurs* <Med. L *succursus* <L *succurrere* <*sub-* up from under + *currere* run] —**suc′cor·a·ble** *adj.* —**suc′cor·er** *n.*

suc·co·ry (suk′ər·ē) *n.* Chicory. [Alter. of *cicoree, sichorie,* earlier vars. of CHICORY; infl. in form by MDu. *sukerie* chicory]

suc·co·tash (suk′ə·tash) *n.* A dish of Indian corn kernels and beans boiled together. [<Algonquian (Narraganset) *misickquatash* an ear of corn]

Suc·coth (sōōk′ōth, sōōk′ōs) See SUKKOTH.

suc·cu·bus (suk′yə·bəs) *n. pl.* **·bi** (-bī) One of a class of demons in female form fabled to have intercourse with men in their sleep. [<Med. L <LL *succuba* a strumpet <L *succubare* <*sub-* underneath + *cubare* lie]

suc·cu·lent (suk′yə·lənt) *adj.* 1 *Bot.* Juicy;

fleshy, as the tissues of certain plants. **2** Rich or vigorous: a *succulent* theme. [<L *succulentus* <*succus* juice] —**suc′cu·lence, suc′cu·len·cy** *n.* —**suc′cu·lent·ly** *adv.*

suc·cumb (sə·kum′) *v.i.* **1** To give way; yield, as to force or persuasion. **2** To die. [<OF *succomber* <L *succumbere* <*sub-* underneath + *cumbere* lie] —**suc·cum′bent** (-bənt) *adj.*

suc·cuss (sə·kus′) *v.t.* To shake suddenly or forcibly. [<L *succussus,* pp. of *succutere* < *sub-* up from under + *quatere* shake] —**suc·cus′sive** *adj.*

suc·cus·sion (sə·kush′ən) *n.* **1** The act of shaking. **2** *Med.* A vigorous shaking of the patient to detect liquids in the thorax or other cavities of the body. Also **suc·cus·sa·tion** (suk′ə·sā′shən). —**suc·cus·sa·to·ry** (sə·kus′ə·tôr′ē, -tō′rē) *adj.*

such (such) *adj.* **1** Of that kind; of the same or like kind: often with *as* or *that* completing the comparison: *Such* wit *as* this is rare. **2** Specifically, being the same as what has been mentioned or indicated: *Such* was the king's command. **3** Being the same in quality: Let the truthful continue *such.* **4** Being the same as something understood by the speaker or the hearer, or purposely left indefinite: a concise and elliptical use by which specification is avoided: the chief of *such* a clan. **5** So extreme, unpleasant, or the like: an emphatic or expletive use: We have come to *such* a pass. —*pron.* **1** Such a person or thing, or (more commonly) such persons or things: by ellipsis of the noun: The friend of *such* as are in trouble. **2** The same; the aforesaid: I bring good tidings, for *such* the general sent. —*adv.* So: *such* destructive criticism. [OE *swelc, swilc, swylc*]

such–and–such (such′ən·such′) *adj.* Being a particular person, thing, or time, not specifically named: He visited *such–and–such* a place. Also **such and such.**

such·like (such′līk′) *adj.* Of a like or similar kind. —*pron.* Persons or things of that kind: mosses, ferns, and *suchlike.*

Sü·chow (shü′jō′) **1** A city in SW Shantung province, China: formerly (1912–45) *Tungshan.* **2** A former name for IPIN.

suck (suk) *v.t.* **1** To draw into the mouth by means of a partial vacuum created by action of the lips and tongue. **2** To draw in or take up in a manner resembling this; inhale; absorb: The sponge *sucked* the water up. **3** To draw liquid or nourishment from with the mouth: to *suck* a lemon; also, to take into and hold in the mouth as if to do this: to *suck* one's thumb. **4** To consume by licking, or by holding in the mouth: to *suck* candy. **5** To bring to a specified state or condition by sucking: He *sucked* the lemon dry. —*v.i.* **6** To draw in liquid, air, etc., by suction. **7** To suckle. **8** To draw in air instead of water, as a defective pump does. **9** To make a sucking sound. —*n.* **1** The act of sucking; suction. **2** That which is sucked or comes by sucking. **3** A slight draft or drink. **4** A mother's milk. **5** A whirlpool or powerful eddy. [OE *sūcan*] —**suck′ing** *adj.* —**suck′ing·ly** *adv.*

suck·er (suk′ər) *n.* **1** One who or that which sucks; a suckler, as a suckling pig or a newly born whale. **2** A North American fresh–water fish (family *Catostomidae*), related to the cyprinoids, having the mouth usually protractile with thick and fleshy lips adapted for sucking in food. **3** *Zool.* An organ by which an animal adheres to other bodies; a suctorial organ. **4** *Slang* A toady; sponger; parasite; hanger–on. **5** *U.S. Slang* A foolish fellow; dolt; one easily deceived; a gull. **6** A piston, as of a syringe or a suction pump; a tube or pipe used for suction. **7** *Bot.* **a** A shoot or branch originating on a subterranean portion of a stem. **b** A shoot or sprout arising from the root near or remote from the trunk of certain trees. **8** A haustorium. **9** A sweetmeat; also, sugar. —*v.t.* To strip of suckers or shoots. —*v.i.* To form or send out suckers or shoots. [<SUCK]

Sucker State Nickname for ILLINOIS.

suck·fish (suk′fish′) *n. pl.* **·fish** or **·fish·es 1** A remora. **2** A fish *(Caularchus maeandricus)* of the Pacific coast, with a ventrally placed sucker by which it attaches itself to stones, shells, etc.

suck·le (suk′əl) *v.* **·led, ·ling** *v.t.* **1** To give suck to, as at the breast. **2** To bring up; nourish. —*v.i.* **3** To take nourishment at the breast; suck. [ME *sucklen,* freq. of *suken* SUCK] —**suck′ler** *n.*

suck·ling (suk′ling) *n.* **1** An unweaned mammal. **2** A young, inexperienced person.

Suck·ling (suk′ling), **Sir John,** 1609–42, English poet and dramatist.

su·crate (so͞o′krāt) *n. Chem.* A compound in which sucrose or some analogous carbohydrate combines with a base to form a salt: calcium *sucrate.* [<F <*sucre* sugar + *-ate* -ATE[3]]

su·cre (so͞o′krā) *n.* The monetary unit of Ecuador. [<Sp., after Antonio José de *Sucre*]

Su·cre (so͞o′krā) The nominal capital of Bolivia. La Paz is the seat of government.

Su·cre (so͞o′krā), **Antonio José de,** 1795?–1830, South American soldier; first president of Bolivia.

su·crose (so͞o′krōs) *n. Chem.* **1** Any one of the group of carbohydrates, including cane sugar, milk sugar, maltose, etc., having the common composition $C_{12}H_{22}O_{11}$, and deviating the plane of polarized light to the right. **2** Cane sugar as obtained from the sugarcane, maple, beet, etc. Also called *saccharose.* [<F *sucre* sugar + *-ose* -OSE[2]]

suc·tion (suk′shən) *n.* **1** The act or process of sucking. **2** The production of a partial vacuum in a space connected with a fluid or gas under pressure. **3** The tendency of a fluid to fill a vacuum contiguous with it. [<OF <L *suctio, -onis* <*sugere* suck]

suction pump A pump operating by suction, consisting of a piston working up and down in a cylinder, both equipped with valves: the most common form of house pump. Compare illustration under FORCE PUMP.

suction stop *Phonet.* A click, as in the Bushman and Hottentot languages. See CLICK (def. 3).

Suc·to·ri·a (suk·tôr′ē·ə, -tō′rē·ə) *n. pl.* A class or subclass of aquatic protozoans having in the adult stage long hollow tentacles for piercing and sucking. [<NL <L *suctus,* pp. of *sugere* suck]

suc·to·ri·al (suk·tôr′ē·əl, -tō′rē·əl) *adj.* **1** Adapted for sucking or for adhesion. **2** *Zool.* Living by sucking; having organs for sucking.

sud (so͝od) *v. Scot.* Should.

su·dan (so͞o·dan′) *adj. Chem.* Designating any of a class of diazo compounds widely used as red and yellow dyes. [from *Sudan*]

Su·dan (so͞o·dan′) A region extending across Africa from the Atlantic Ocean to the Red Sea, south of the Sahara: formerly *Nigritia.*

Sudan, Republic of the An independent country in NE Africa; 967,500 square miles; capital, Khartoum.

Su·da·nese (so͞o′də·nēz′, -nēs′) *adj.* Of or pertaining to the Sudan or its people. —*n. pl.* **·nese** One living in the Sudan; the people of the Sudan collectively, including Negro and Negroid peoples, Hamites and certain Arab tribes.

Su·dan·ic (so͞o·dan′ik) *n.* A family of languages spoken in central Africa from the Atlantic to the Indian oceans, including Dinka, Ewe, Nubian, and Yoruba. —*adj.* Of or pertaining to this family.

su·dar·i·um (so͞o·dâr′ē·əm) *n. pl.* **·dar·i·a** (-dâr′·ē·ə) **1** A handkerchief or cloth for drying or removing perspiration; specifically, the sweat cloth or handkerchief of St. Veronica, said to have been miraculously impressed with the features of Jesus when she wiped his face on his way to crucifixion. **2** The napkin about the head of Christ in the tomb. *John* xx 7. **3** Any miraculous picture of Christ; a veronica. **4** A sudatory (def. 2). Also **su·da·ry** (so͞o′·dər·ē). [<L <*sudor, -oris* sweat]

su·da·tion (so͞o·dā′shən) *n.* Morbid or excessive sweating. [<L *sudatio, -onis* <*sudatus,* pp. of *sudare* sweat]

su·da·to·ry (so͞o′də·tôr′ē, -tō′rē) *adj.* **1** Producing perspiration; sudorific. **2** Perspiring. —*n. pl.* **·ries 1** An agent that causes sweating; a sudorific. **2** A sweating bath; specifically, a hot–air room in a Roman bath: also **su′da·to′ri·um.** [<L *sudatorius*]

sudd (sud) *n.* A floating mass of vegetation that frequently obstructs navigation on the White Nile. [<Arabic <*sudd* obstruct]

sud·den (sud′n) *adj.* **1** Happening quickly and without warning: *sudden* death. **2** Hurriedly or quickly contrived, used, or done; hasty. **3** Come upon unexpectedly; causing surprise. **4** Quick–tempered; precipitate; rash. See synonyms under IMPETUOUS, SWIFT[1]. —*n.* The state of being sudden, or that which is sudden: obsolete except in a few phrases. —**all of a sudden, all on a sudden, on a sudden** Without warning; on the spur of the moment. [< AF *sodein,* OF *soudain* <L *subitaneus* < *subitus,* pp. of *subire* come or go stealthily < *sub-* secretly + *ire* go] —**sud′den·ly** *adv.* —**sud′den·ness** *n.*

sudden death 1 Death that occurs suddenly or instantaneously, esp. violently. **2** *Sports* An extra period played in order to break a tie score, in which the first score ends the game.

Su·der·mann (zo͞o′dər·män), **Hermann,** 1857–1928, German dramatist and novelist.

Su·de·ten·land (so͞o·dāt′n·land, *Ger.* zo͞o·dā′·tən·länt) The border district of Bohemia and Moravia, Czechoslovakia; 8,976 square miles.

Su·de·tes (so͞o·dē′tēz) A mountainous system along the German–Czechoslovak and Polish–Czechoslovak border; highest point, 5,259 feet. Also **Su·det·ic Mountains** (so͞o·det′ik).

su·dor (so͞o′dôr) *n.* Visible perspiration; sweat. [<L] —**su·dor·al** (so͞o′dər·əl) *adj.*

su·dor·if·er·ous (so͞o′də·rif′ər·əs) *adj.* Secreting or producing sweat. [<NL *sudoriferus* <L *sudor, -oris* sweat + *ferre* carry] —**su′dor·if′·er·ous·ness** *n.*

su·dor·if·ic (so͞o′də·rif′ik) *adj.* Causing perspiration. —*n.* A medicine that produces or promotes sweating. [<NL *sudorificus* <L *sudor, -oris* sweat + *facere* make]

suds (sudz) *n. pl.* **1** Soapy water worked up into bubbles and froth; foam; lather. **2** *Slang* Beer: so called from its foamy properties. [Prob. <MDu. *sudde, sudse* a marsh, marsh water] —**suds′y** *adj.*

sue (so͞o) *v.* **sued, su·ing** *v.t.* **1** *Law* **a** To institute proceedings against for the recovery of some right or the redress of some wrong. **b** To prosecute (an action). **c** To seek a grant from (a court). **2** To endeavor to persuade by entreaty; beg; urge; petition. **3** To seek to win in marriage; woo. —*v.i.* **4** To institute legal proceedings. **5** To make entreaty. **6** *Archaic* To pay court; woo. [<AF *suer,* OF *suivre,* ult. <L *sequi* follow] —**su′er** *n.*

Sue (so͞o) Diminutive of SUSANNA.

Sue (so͞o, *Fr.* sü), **(Marie Joseph) Eugène,** 1804–57, French novelist.

suède (swād) *n.* Undressed kid: often attributively: *suède* gloves. [<F *Suède* Sweden, in phrase *gants de Suède* Swedish gloves]

suède fabric A woven or knitted fabric of cotton, rayon, or wool, finished to resemble suède leather: used for sports coats and jackets, linings, gloves, etc.

su·et (so͞o′it) *n.* The fatty tissues about the loins and kidneys of sheep, oxen, etc.: used in cookery and for making tallow. [Dim. of AF *sue,* OF *seu* <L *sebum* tallow, fat] —**su′et·y** *adj.*

Sue·to·ni·us (swi·tō′nē·əs), **Gaius Tranquillus,** A.D. 70?–140?, Roman historian.

Su·ez (so͞o·ez′, so͞o′ez) A port in NE Egypt at the northern end of the **Gulf of Suez,** the NW arm of the Red Sea (about 180 miles long, 20 miles wide).

Suez, Isthmus of The neck of land joining Asia and Africa; between the Gulf of Suez and the Mediterranean; 72 miles wide at its narrowest point; traversed by the **Suez Canal,** a ship canal 107 miles long, 197 feet wide, constructed (1859–69) by Ferdinand de Lesseps.

suf– Assimilated var. of SUB–.

suf·fa·ri (sə·fä′rē) See SAFARI.

suf·fer (suf′ər) *v.i.* **1** To feel pain or distress. **2** To be affected injuriously; suffer loss or injury. **3** To undergo punishment; especially, to be put to death. **4** *Archaic* To tolerate or endure pain, injury, etc. — *v.t.* **5** To have inflicted on one; sustain, as an injury or loss. **6** To undergo; pass through, as change. **7** To bear; endure: He cannot *suffer* more pain. **8** To allow; permit: Will he *suffer* us to leave? See synonyms under ALLOW, ENDURE, PERMIT. [<AF *suffrir,* OF *sofrir,* ult. <L *sufferre* < *sub-* up from under + *ferre* bear] — **suf′·fer·er** *n.*

suf·fer·a·ble (suf′ər·ə·bəl, suf′rə-) *adj.* Such as can be suffered or endured; endurable. — **suf′·fer·a·ble·ness** *n.* — **suf′fer·a·bly** *adv.*

suf·fer·ance (suf′ər·əns, suf′rəns) *n.* **1** Permission given or implied by failure to prohibit; negative consent. **2** In customs, a permit for the shipment of certain kinds of goods to specified ports. **3** The act or state of suffering; wretchedness; experience of pain or evil; power to endure. **4** Patience or endurance under suffering; submission; submissiveness. **5** *Rare* Loss; injury; damage. See synonyms under PATIENCE. [<AF, OF *suf-rance* <LL *sufferentia* < *sufferre* SUFFER]

suf·fer·ing (suf′ər·ing, suf′ring) *n.* **1** The state of anguish or pain of one who suffers; the bearing of pain, injury, or loss. **2** The pain so borne; distress; loss; injury. See synonyms under AGONY, PAIN. — *adj.* Inured to pain and loss; submissive. — **suf′fer·ing·ly** *adv.*

suf·fice (sə·fīs′) *v.* **·ficed, ·fic·ing** *v.i.* To be sufficient or adequate; meet the requirements or answer the purpose. — *v.t.* To be satisfactory or adequate for; satisfy. See synonyms under SATISFY, SERVE. [<OF *suffis-,* stem of *suffire* <L *sufficere* < *sub-* under + *facere* make] — **suf·fic′er** *n.*

suf·fi·cien·cy (sə·fish′ən·sē) *n. pl.* **·cies** **1** The state of being sufficient. **2** That which is sufficient; especially, adequate pecuniary means or income; a competency. **3** Full capability or qualification; efficiency. **4** Conceit; self-sufficiency. See synonyms under COMFORT.

suf·fi·cient (sə·fish′ənt) *adj.* **1** Being all that is needful; adequate; enough. **2** *Archaic* Capable; competent. **3** *Obs.* Financially competent; responsible. See synonyms under ADEQUATE, AMPLE, ENOUGH. [<OF <L *sufficiens, -entis,* ppr. of *sufficere* SUFFICE] — **suf·fi′cient·ly** *adv.*

suf·fix (suf′iks) *n.* **1** *Ling.* A letter or letters added to the end of a word or root, and functioning as a formative, derivative, or inflectional element, as *-er* in shorter, *-ful* in faithful, *-s* and *-es* in dogs, boxes, *-ed* in loved, *-ness* in kindness, etc. Compare COMBINING FORM, PREFIX. **2** Any added title or the like. **3** *Math.* A subindex. — *v.t.* To add as a suffix; append. [<NL *suffixum* <L *suffixus,* pp. of *suffigere* < *sub-* underneath + *figere* fix. Doublet of SOFFIT.] — **suf′fix·al** *adj.* — **suf·fix·ion** (sə·fik′shən) *n.*

suf·flate (sə·flāt′) *v.t.* **·flat·ed, ·flat·ing** *Obs.* To blow up or inflate. [<L *sufflatus,* pp. of *sufflare* < *sub-* up from under + *flare* blow] — **suf·fla′tion** *n.*

suf·fo·cant (suf′ə·kənt) *n.* Any substance or agent that produces suffocation.

suf·fo·cate (suf′ə·kāt) *v.* **·cat·ed, ·cat·ing** *v.t.* **1** To kill by obstructing respiration in any manner. **2** To obstruct or oppress, as by an inadequate supply of air. **3** To stifle; extinguish; smother, as a fire. — *v.i.* **4** To become choked or stifled; die from suffocation. [<L *suffocatus,* pp. of *suffocare* < *sub-* under + *fauces* throat] — **suf′fo·cat′ing·ly** *adv.* — **suf′fo·ca′tion** *n.* — **suf′fo·ca′tive** *adj.*

Suf·folk (suf′ək) *n.* **1** A breed of hardy, chestnut-colored English working horse, smaller and freer from feather than the Shire and Clydesdale breeds. It is heavy in body and has rather short legs. Also **Suffolk punch.** **2** A breed of hornless, short-wool Southdown sheep, with black face and legs: preeminent for the quality of its mutton. [from *Suffolk,* England]

Suf·folk (suf′ək) A county in eastern England; 1,507 square miles; administratively divided into **East Suffolk** (879 square miles; county town, Ipswich) and **West Suffolk** (628 square miles; county town, Bury St. Edmunds).

suf·fra·gan (suf′rə·gən) *Eccl. n.* An auxiliary or assistant bishop, who assists a bishop in the administration of the diocese, or is consecrated for service in a limited portion of the diocese: also **suffragan bishop.** — *adj.* Of or pertaining to a suffragan; assisting; auxiliary; subordinate to an archiepiscopal see. [<AF, OF <Med. L *suffraganeus* <L *suffragari* vote for, support] — **suf′fra·gan·ship′** *n.*

suf·frage (suf′rij) *n.* **1** A vote in support of some measure or candidate; hence, approbation; assent. **2** Voting; also, the right or privilege of voting; franchise: also **political suffrage.** **3** *Eccl.* Any short intercessory prayer or petition. — **woman suffrage** Political suffrage as belonging to or exercised by women. In the United States suffrage was granted to women in 1920 by the 19th amendment to the Constitution: also **female suffrage.** [<OF <L *suffragium* a voting tablet, vote]

suf·fra·gette (suf′rə·jet′) *n. Colloq.* A woman who advocated female suffrage; specifically, a member of a militant organization demanding it. [<SUFFRAGE + -ETTE] — **suf′fra·get′·tism** *n.*

suf·fra·gist (suf′rə·jist) *n.* **1** A voter. **2** An advocate of some particular form of suffrage, especially of woman suffrage.

suf·fru·tex (suf′rə·teks) *n. Bot.* **1** An undershrub; a small plant having a decidedly woody stem. **2** An herb with a permanent woody base. [<NL <L *sub-* under, less than + *frutex, -icis* a shrub] — **suf′fru·tes′cent** (-tes′ənt) *adj.*

suf·fru·ti·cose (sə·frōō′tə·kōs) *adj. Bot.* Somewhat shrubby; woody; shrubby or woody at base and herbaceous above. [<NL *suffruticosus* < *suffrutex, -icis.* See SUFFRUTEX.]

suf·fu·mi·gate (sə·fyōō′mə·gāt) *v.t.* **·gat·ed, ·gat·ing** To fumigate from or as from underneath. [<L *suffumigatus,* pp. of *suffumigare* < *sub-* up from under + *fumigare* FUMIGATE]

suf·fu·mi·ga·tion (sə·fyōō′mə·gā′shən) *n.* **1** The act of suffumigating. **2** The act of burning perfumes. **3** A fume or vapor.

suf·fuse (sə·fyōōz′) *v.t.* **·fused, ·fus·ing** To overspread, as with a vapor, fluid, or color. [<L *suffusus,* pp. of *suffundere* < *sub-* underneath, up from under + *fundere* pour] — **suf·fu·sive** (sə·fyōō′siv) *adj.*

suf·fu·sion (sə·fyōō′zhən) *n.* **1** The act of welling up or spreading over. **2** The state of being suffused; a blush. **3** That which suffuses: a *suffusion* of blood.

Su·fi (sōō′fē) *n.* A follower of a system of Moslem philosophical and devotional mysticism, especially in Persia. [<Arabic *sūfī,* lit., a man of wool < *sūf* wool] — **Su′fic, Su·fis·tic** (sōō·fis′tik) *adj.*

Su·fism (sōō′fiz·əm) *n.* The doctrine of the Sufis, which has inspired a mass of symbolical religious poetry.

sug– Assimilated var. of SUB–.

sug·ar (shŏŏg′ər) *n.* **1** A sweet crystalline disaccharide having the formula $C_{12}H_{22}O_{11}$, obtained chiefly from the juice of the sugarcane or sugar beet; called, according to its source, **beet sugar, cane sugar, date sugar, grape sugar, maple sugar,** etc. ◆ Collateral adjective: *saccharine.* **2** Any of a large class of sweet, soluble, optically active carbohydrates which are ketone or aldehyde derivatives of the higher alcohols. They are widely distributed in plants and animals, play an important role in nutrition, and are generally classified on the basis of chemical structure as monosaccharides, disaccharides, trisaccharides. **3** Flattering or honeyed words, especially if used to disguise or soften an unpleasant or severe reality. **4** *Slang* Sweet one: a pet name. — *v.t.* **1** To sweeten, cover, or coat with sugar. **2** To make agreeable or less distasteful, as by flattery. — *v.i.* **3** *U.S. & Can.* To make maple sugar. **4** To form or produce sugar; granulate. [<OF *sucre* < Med. L *succarum,* ult. <Arabic *sukkar.* Prob. related to SACCHARIN.]

sugar apple The sweetsop.

sugar beet Any sugar-producing variety of the common garden beet.

sug·ar·ber·ry (shŏŏg′ər·ber′ē) *n. pl.* **·ries** The hackberry.

sug·ar·bird (shŏŏg′ər·bûrd′) *n.* **1** Any bird that sucks the nectar of flowers, as the honey creepers, honey-eaters, sunbirds, etc. **2** The evening grosbeak (*Hesperiphona vespertina*): so named by North American Indians from its fondness for maple sugar.

sugar bush A grove of sugar-maple trees: sometimes designating a grove of 200 or more trees.

sugar camp The collection of cabins and other buildings in a sugar bush where the maple sap is boiled.

sug·ar·cane (shŏŏg′ər·kān′) *n.* A tall, stout, perennial grass (*Saccharum officinarum*) of tropical regions with a solid jointed stalk rich in sugar.

sug·ar–coat (shŏŏg′ər·kōt′) *v.t.* **1** To cover with sugar. **2** To cause to appear attractive or less distasteful. — **sug′ar–coat′ed** *adj.* — **sug′ar–coat′ing** *n.*

sugar corn Sweet corn (def. 1).

sug·ar–cured (shŏŏg′ər·kyŏŏrd′) *adj.* Cured by using sugar in the curing process: said of ham and pork.

sugar daddy *U.S. Slang* A wealthy old man who gives a young woman presents in return for her favors.

sug·ared (shŏŏg′ərd) *adj.* Sugar-coated; honeyed; pleasant; sweetened.

sug·ar·house (shŏŏg′ər·hous′) *n.* **1** A building in which the juices are extracted from sugarcane, sugar beets, etc., and made into raw sugar; a sugar refinery. **2** A building in which sugar is stored. **3** A building in a sugar camp in which maple sap is boiled.

sugaring off **1** The boiling of maple sap until it crystallizes into sugar. **2** The time of year at which this is done. **3** A community social gathering to take part in making maple sugar.

sugaring over Making palatable the unpalatable, especially facts.

sugar loaf **1** A conical mass of hard refined sugar. **2** A conical hat or hill. — **sug′ar–loaf′** *adj.*

Sugar Loaf Mountain A peak in Río de Janeiro, Brazil, at the entrance to Guanabara Bay; 1,296 feet: Portuguese *Pão de Açúcar.*

sugar maple The maple (*Acer saccharum*) of eastern North America from the sap of which maple sugar is made: also called *hard maple, rock maple.*

sugar of lead Lead acetate.

sugar of milk Lactose.

sugar orchard An orchard of sugar maples.

sugar pine A tall pine (*Pinus lambertiana*) of the Pacific coast, bearing very large cones and having wood much used in construction work.

sug·ar·plum (shŏŏg′ər·plum′) *n.* **1** A small sweetmeat; a small ball or disk of candy; a bon-bon. **2** The shadbush.

sugar tree The sugar maple.

sug·ar·y (shŏŏg′ər·ē) *adj.* **1** Composed of or as of sugar; sweet. **2** Fond of sugar. **3** Figuratively, honeyed; alluring. **4** Granular. — **sug′ar·i·ness** *n.*

sug·gan (sug′ən) *n.* **1** A type of rope made of twisted straw. **2** A saddle, collar, or bolster so made. **3** A heavy bed coverlet. [<Irish *sūgān*]

sug·gest (səg·jest′, sə·jest′) *v.t.* **1** To bring or put forward for consideration, action, or approval; propose. **2** To arouse in the mind by association or connection; connote: Hallowe'en *suggests* witches and black cats. **3** To give a hint or indirect suggestion of; intimate: This poem *suggests* a great deal of care and thought. **4** To act as or provide a motive for; prompt: The success of his novel *suggested* a sequel. See synonyms under ALLUDE, IMPORT. [<L *suggestus,* pp. of *suggerere* < *sub-* underneath + *gerere* carry] — **sug·gest′er** *n.*

sug·gest·i·bil·i·ty (səg·jes′tə·bil′ə·tē, sə-) *n.* **1** *Psychol.* Responsiveness to suggestion, normal in children and diminishing in adults, but heightened or abnormal in hypnosis, light sleep, and certain nervous conditions. **2** Readiness to believe and agree without reflection; compliancy of mind and will.

sug·gest·i·ble (səg·jes′tə·bəl, sə-) *adj.* **1** That can be suggested. **2** Easily led; yielding, especially to hypnosis: a *suggestible* patient.

sug·ges·tion (səg·jes′chən, sə·jes′-) *n.* **1** The act of suggesting. **2** A hint; insinuation. **3** The spontaneous calling up of an idea in the mind by a connected idea. **4** *Psychol.* **a** The inducing in a person of some idea, impulse, action, or mode of behavior through a stimulus, verbal or other, coming from another person but independent of critical argument or rational persuasion, as in hypnosis. **b** The idea, impulse, etc., so induced.

Synonyms: hint, innuendo, insinuation, intimation. A *suggestion* brings something before the mind less directly than by formal or explicit statement, as by a partial statement, an incidental allusion, an illustration, a question, or the like. *Suggestion* is often used of an unobtrusive statement of one's views or wishes to another, leaving consideration and any consequent action entirely to that person's judgment, and is hence, in many cases, the most respectful way in which to convey one's views to a superior or a stranger. An *intimation* is a *suggestion* in brief utterance, or sometimes by significant act, gesture, or token, of one's meaning or wishes; in the latter case it is often the act of a superior. A *hint* is still more limited in expression and more remote, and is always covert, but frequently with good intent; as, to give one a *hint* of danger or of opportunity. *Insinuation* and *innuendo* usually imply discredit; an *insinuation* is a covert or partly veiled injurious utterance; an *innuendo* is commonly secret as well as sly, as if pointing to something derogatory. See COUNSEL.

sug·ges·tive (səg·jes′tiv, sə-) *adj.* **1** Fitted or tending to suggest; stimulating to thought or reflection. **2** Hinting at indecent thoughts; suggesting the improper. **— sug·ges′tive·ly** *adv.* **— sug·ges′tive·ness** *n.*

sugh (sŏŏkh) *n. Scot.* A rushing sound; sough.

su·i·ci·dal (sōō′ə·sīd′l) *adj.* Self-destructive; ruinous; pertaining to, or leading to, suicide; fatal to one's prospects or interests. **— su′i·ci′dal·ly** *adv.*

su·i·cide (sōō′ə·sīd) *n.* **1** The intentional taking of one's own life. **2** Self-inflicted political, social, or commercial ruin. **3** One who commits self-murder. — *v.i.* **·cid·ed, ·cid·ing** *Colloq.* To commit suicide. [<NL *suicidium* <L *sui* of oneself + *caedere* kill]

su·i gen·e·ris (sōō′ī jen′ər·is) *Latin* Literally, of his (her, its) particular kind; forming a kind by itself; unique.

su·i· ju·ris (sōō′ī jŏŏr′is) *Latin* In one's own right; having legal capacity to act for oneself.

su·int (sōō′int, swint) *n.* Natural wool grease from wool-washings: it consists of fatty substances combined with potash salts. [<F < *suer* sweat <L *sudare*]

Suisse (swēs) The French name for SWITZERLAND.

Sui·sun Bay (sə·sōōn′) The easternmost arm of San Francisco Bay.

suit (sōōt) *n.* **1** A set of outer garments or armor to be worn together. **2** A set of garments consisting of a coat and trousers or skirt, made of the same fabric. **3** An outfit or garment for a particular purpose: a bathing *suit*; a space *suit*. **4** A group of things of like kind or pattern composing a series or set: now usually *suite*. **5** In card-playing, any one of the four sets of thirteen cards each that make up a pack, as spades, hearts, diamonds, or clubs. **6** *Law* A proceeding in a court of law or chancery in which a plaintiff demands the recovery of a right or the redress of a wrong: a term rarely applied to criminal prosecution. **7** *Archaic* Entreaty; petition; supplication. **8** The courting or courtship of a woman. See synonyms under PRAYER. **— to follow suit** **1** To play a card identical in suit to the card led. **2** To do as somebody or something else has done; follow an example. — *v.t.* **1** To meet the requirements of, or be appropriate to; be in accord with; befit. **2** To please; satisfy. **3** To render appropriate or accordant; accommodate; adapt. **4** *Archaic* To furnish with clothes. — *v.i.* **5** To be befitting; agree; correspond. **6** To be or prove satisfactory. **7** *Obs.* To clothe oneself. See synonyms under ACCOMMODATE, ADAPT. [< AF *siwte*, OF *sieute*, ult. <L *sequi* follow. Doublet of SUITE.]

suit·a·ble (sōō′tə·bəl) *adj.* Capable of suiting; appropriate; applicable; proper. See synonyms under APPROPRIATE, BECOMING, CONVENIENT, EXPEDIENT, GOOD. **— suit′a·bil′i·ty, suit′a·ble·ness** *n.* **— suit′a·bly** *adv.*

suit·case (sōōt′kās′) *n.* A flat, rectangular valise used for carrying clothing, etc.

suite (swēt; *for def.* 3, *also* sōōt) *n.* **1** A succession of things forming a series; a set of things having a certain dependence upon each other and intended to go or be used together. **2** A number of connected apartments. **3** A set of furniture. **4** A collection of pictures illustrating consecutive events. **5** *Music* A form of instrumental composition formerly consisting of a series of dances, but now often written for an orchestra and varying freely in its construction and movements. **6** A retinue; a company of attendants or followers. ◆ Homophone: *sweet*. [<F <OF *sieute*. Doublet of SUIT.]

suit·ing (sōō′ting) *n.* Cloth from which to make entire suits of clothes.

suit·or (sōō′tər) *n.* **1** One who institutes a suit in court. **2** A wooer. **3** A petitioner. [<AF *seutor* <LL *secutor*, *-oris* <L *secutus*, pp. of *sequi* follow]

Sui·yü·an (swā′yû·än′) A former province of northern China, incorporated in the Inner Mongolian Autonomous Region, June, 1954; 135,000 square miles; capital, Kweisui.

Su·khu·mi (sōō′khōō·mē) A port on the Black Sea, capital of Abkhaz Autonomous S.S.R.

su·ki·ya·ki (sōō′kē·yä′kē, -yak′ē) *n.* A Japanese dish, usually cooked rapidly at the table, made of meat in thin slices, vegetables, and condiments. [<Japanese]

Suk·koth (sŏŏk′ōth, sŏŏk′ōs) *n. pl.* The feast of Tabernacles, a Jewish holiday beginning on the 15th of Tishri (late September–October): originally a harvest festival: also spelled *Succoth*. Also **Suk′kos, Suk′kot.** [<Hebrew *sŭkōth* tabernacles, booths]

Suk·kur (sŏŏk′kŏŏr) A city in SE central West Pakistan, on the Indus.

Su·ky (sōō′kē) Diminutive of SUSANNA.

Su·la Islands (sōō′lə) An Indonesian island group between the Banggai and the Obi island groups; total, 1,873 square miles. *Dutch* **Soe·la** (sōō′lä).

sul·cate (sul′kāt, -kit) *adj. Biol.* Having long narrow furrows or channels; grooved; fluted. Also **sul′cat·ed.** [<L *sulcatus*, pp. of *sulcare* plow < *sulcus* a furrow] **— sul·ca′tion** *n.*

sul·cus (sul′kəs) *n. pl.* **·ci** (-sī) **1** A narrow channel or furrow. **2** *Anat.* One of a large number of shallow grooves on the surface of the mammalian brain. [<L]

sul·dan (sul′dən) See SOLDAN.

Su·lei·man (sü′lā·män′) Name of three Turkish rulers: also spelled *Solyman*. **— Suleiman the Magnificent,** 1496?–1566, Ottoman sultan 1520–66; added extensive territories to the Turkish Empire in Europe and encouraged arts and science.

sulfa– *combining form Chem.* Sulfur; related to or containing sulfur: also spelled *sulpha–*. Also, before vowels, **sulf–**, as in *sulfarsenide*. See also SULFO–. [<SULFUR]

sul·fa·di·a·zine (sul′fə·dī′ə·zēn) *n. Chem.* A white, crystalline, relatively non-toxic derivative of sulfanilamide, $C_{10}H_{10}N_4SO_2$, used in the treatment of infections due to streptococci, pneumococci, and staphylococci.

sul·fa drug (sul′fə) *Chem.* Any of a group of organic compounds consisting mainly of substituted sulfanilamide derivatives and having a wide range of therapeutic effects in the treatment of bacterial infections.

sul·fa·gua·ni·dine (sul′fə·gwä′nə·din, -dēn, -gwan′ə-) *n. Chem.* A white, crystalline, relatively non-toxic sulfonamide, $C_7H_{10}N_4O_2S$, used in the treatment of certain infections.

sul·fal·de·hyde (sul·fal′də·hīd) *n. Chem.* An oily liquid compound, C_3H_6S, sometimes used as a hypnotic.

sul·fa·nil·a·mide (sul′fə·nil′ə·mīd, -mid) *n. Chem.* A colorless, crystalline sulfonamide, $C_6H_8N_2O_2S$, originally widely developed and used as a chemotherapeutic agent in the treatment of various bacterial infections. [< SULF(A)- + ANIL(INE) + AMIDE]

sul·fa·pyr·i·dine (sul′fə·pir′ə·dēn, -din) *n. Chem.* A white, crystalline derivative of sulfanilamide, $C_{11}H_{11}N_3O_2S$, once widely used in the treatment of various infections.

sulf·ar·se·nide (sulf·är′sə·nīd, -nid) *n. Chem.* A compound of the arsenide and sulfide of a metal or metals.

sulf·ars·phen·a·mine (sulf′ärs·fen′ə·mēn, -fen·am′in) *n. Chem.* A yellow, almost odorless, water-soluble powder containing from 18 to 20 percent arsenic: used in the treatment of syphilis.

sul·fate (sul′fāt) *n. Chem.* A salt of sulfuric acid. Sulfates are widely distributed in nature and are important in the arts and in medicine. — *v.* **·fat·ed, ·fat·ing** *v.t.* **1** To form a sulfate of; treat with a sulfate or sulfuric acid. **2** *Electr.* To form a coating of lead sulfate on (the plate of a secondary battery). **3** To make (red lead) into lead sulfate by the action of sulfuric acid. — *v.i.* **4** To become sulfated. Also **sul′phate.** [<F <NL *sulfas*, *-atis* a sulfate <L *sulfur* sulfur]

sulfate process A method for manufacturing tough kraft paper by introducing sulfate of soda in the digesters containing the wood pulp.

sul·fa·thi·a·zole (sul′fə·thī′ə·zōl) *n. Chem.* A sulfanilamide derivative, $C_9H_9N_3O_3S_2$, considered particularly effective in treating certain pneumococcal and staphylococcal infections.

sul·fa·tize (sul′fə·tīz) *v.t.* **·tized, ·tiz·ing** To turn (ores, etc.) into sulfate, by roasting. Also **sul′pha·tize.**

sulf·hy·dryl (sulf·hī′dril) *n. Chem.* The univalent thiol radical SH: also called *mercapto.* [<SULF(A)- + HYDR- + -YL]

sul·fide (sul′fīd) *n. Chem.* A compound of sulfur with an element or radical. Also **sul′fid** (-fid), **sul′phide, sul′phid.** [<SULF(A)- + -IDE]

sul·fi·nyl (sul′fə·nil) *n. Chem.* Thionyl. [< *sulfine*, var. of SULFONIUM + -YL]

sul·fite (sul′fīt) *n. Chem.* A salt or ester of sulfurous acid. Also **sul′phite.** [<SULF(A)- + -ITE[2]] **— sul·fit′ic** (-fit′ik) *adj.*

sulfite process The production of chemical wood pulp by the use of calcium sulfite.

sulfo– *combining form Chem.* **1** Sulfur; containing sulfur. **2** Denoting the replacement of oxygen by sulfur in a compound. **3** Indicating the presence of the sulfonic or sulfonyl group. Also spelled *sulpho–*. Compare THIO–. [<SULFUR]

Sul·fo·nal (sul′fə·nal, sul′fə·nal′) *n.* Proprietary name for a brand of sulfonmethane.

sul·fon·a·mide (sul·fon′ə·mīd, sul′fən·am′īd, -id) *n. Chem.* Any group of organic compounds containing the univalent radical SO_2NH_2, especially those derived from para-amino-benzene-sulfonamide, $p\text{-}H_2N{\cdot}C_6H_4{\cdot}SO_2NH_2$, used in the treatment of certain bacterial infections. [<SULFON(E) + AMIDE]

sul·fo·nate (sul′fə·nāt) *v.t.* **·nat·ed, ·nat·ing** *Chem.* **1** To form into a sulfonic acid. **2** To subject to the treatment of sulfonic acid. — *n.* A salt or ester of sulfonic acid. [<SULFON(E) + -ATE[3]] **— sul′fo·na′tion** *n.*

sul·fone (sul′fōn) *n. Chem.* Any of several compounds consisting of two organic radicals in combination with the sulfonyl group and corresponding to the formula R_2SO_2. [<G *sulfon*] **— sul·fon·ic** (sul·fon′ik) *adj.*

sul·fon·eth·yl·meth·ane (sul′fōn·eth′il·meth′ān) *n. Chem.* A colorless crystalline compound, $C_8H_{18}O_4S_2$, used as a hypnotic and sedative: a form of sulfonmethane. [<SULFON(E) + ETHYL + METHANE]

sulfonic acid *Chem.* Any of several compounds consisting of an organic radical in combination with the sulfonic radical and corresponding to the formula $R{\cdot}SO_2OH$: used in organic synthesis.

sul·fo·ni·um (sul·fō′nē·əm) *n. Chem.* The ion, H_3S, resulting from the addition of a proton to hydrogen sulfide. [<SULF(A) + (AMM)ONIUM]

sul·fon·meth·ane (sul′fōn·meth′ān) *n. Chem.* A white, crystalline, organic compound, $C_7H_{16}O_4S_2$, used in medicine as a sedative and hypnotic. [<SULFON(E) + METHANE]

sul·fo·nyl (sul′fə·nil) *n. Chem.* The bivalent radical SO_2: also called *sulfuryl.* [<SULFON(E) + -YL]

sul·fur (sul′fər) *n.* **1** A pale-yellow, nonmetallic element (symbol S) in the oxygen group, found both free and combined in the native state. It exists in several allotropic forms, of which the more important are the two crystalline modifications, one orthorhombic (native) and the other monoclinic. Sulfur burns to form sulfur dioxide, which has a penetrating odor; it is used for making matches, gunpowder, vulcanized rubber, sulfuric acid, etc. See ELEMENT. **2** Any one of various yellowish pieridine butterflies, as the common North American **clouded sulfur** *(Colias philodice)* or the **cloudless sulfur** *(Callidryas eubule).* **—flowers of sulfur** A fine yellow powder obtained by the distillation of sulfur. **—***v.t.* To treat or fume, as a wine cask or a hive, with sulfur or with sulfurous acid. Also **sul′phur.** [<AF *sulfre,* OF *soufre* <L *sulfur, -uris*]

sul·fu·rate (sul′fyə·rāt, -fə-) *v.t.* **·rat·ed, ·rat·ing** To sulfurize. [<SULFUR + -ATE[1]]

sul·fur–bot·tom (sul′fər·bot′əm) *n.* A very large baleen whale *(Sibbaldius musculus)* found in Atlantic and Pacific waters, having a yellowish belly and attaining an average length of 60–80 feet, with a maximum of about 100 feet.

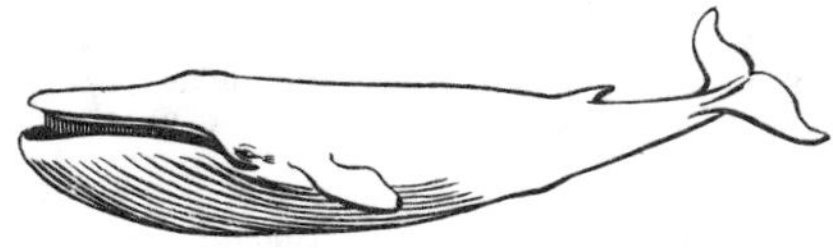

SULFUR–BOTTOM

sulfur dioxide *Chem.* A colorless, gaseous compound, SO_2, with a sharp odor and readily soluble in water: used in the manufacture of sulfuric acid, in bleaching, as a preservative, etc.

sul·fu·re·ous (sul·fyŏŏr′ē·əs) *adj.* Of or like sulfur. [<L *sulfureus* <*sulfur* sulfur]

sul·fu·ret (sul′fyə·ret) *v.t.* **·ret·ed** or **·ret·ted, ·ret·ing** or **·ret·ting** To sulfurize. **—***n.* (-rit) A sulfide. [<F *sulfuret* a sulfide <NL *sulfuretum* <L *sulfur*] **—sul′fu·ret′ed** or **sul′fu·ret′ted** *adj.*

sul·fu·ric (sul·fyŏŏr′ik) *adj. Chem.* Pertaining to or derived from sulfur, especially in its higher valence.

sulfuric acid *Chem.* A colorless, exceedingly corrosive, oily liquid, H_2SO_4, essentially a combination of sulfur trioxide and water, extensively employed in the manufacture of soda, batteries, guncotton, and in almost all chemical operations. Formerly called *vitriol.*

sul·fur·ize (sul′fyə·rīz, -fə-) *v.t.* **·ized, ·iz·ing 1** To impregnate, treat with, or subject to the action of sulfur. **2** To bleach or fumigate with sulfur. **—sul′fur·i·za′tion** *n.*

sul·fur·ous (sul′fər·əs, sul·fyŏŏr′əs) *adj.* **1** *Chem.* Of, pertaining to, or derived from sulfur: specifically applied to compounds that contain sulfur in its lower valence. **2** Fiery; hellish; blasphemous, as language.

sulfurous acid *Chem.* A compound corresponding to the formula H_2SO_3, and known only in solution and by its salts.

sulfur point *Physics* The boiling point of pure liquid sulfur at standard atmospheric pressure, 444.60° C.: one of the fixed points of the international temperature scale.

sulfur trioxide *Chem.* A compound, SO_3, formed by the union of sulfur dioxide and oxygen in the presence of a catalytic agent. With water, sulfur trioxide forms sulfuric acid; hence, it is often called **sulfuric anhydride.**

sul·fur·y (sul′fər·ē) *adj.* Resembling or suggesting sulfur; sulfureous.

sulfur yellow A light greenish–yellow color of very high brilliance, like the color of refined sulfur.

sul·fur·yl (sul′fər·il, -fyə·ril) *n.* Sulfonyl. [<SULFUR + -YL]

sulfuryl chloride *Chem.* A colorless, very pungent liquid compound, SO_2Cl_2, used in the manufacture of dyes, drugs, and poison gas.

sulk (sulk) *v.i.* To be sulky or morose. **—***n.* A sulky mood or humor: often plural. [Back formation <SULKY]

sulk·y[1] (sul′kē) *adj.* **sulk·i·er, sulk·i·est 1** Sullenly cross; doggedly or resentfully ill–humored. **2** Stunted; sluggish; dismal. See synonyms under MOROSE. [? OE *(ā)solcen* slothful, orig. pp. of *(ā)seolcan* be weak, slothful] **—sulk′i·ly** *adv.* **—sulk′i·ness** *n.*

sulk·y[2] (sul′kē) *n. pl.* **sulk·ies** A light, two–wheeled, one–horse vehicle for one person. **—***adj.* Resembling this vehicle: a *sulky* plow. [<SULKY[1]; so called because one rides alone]

sull (sul) *v.i. Dial.* To sulk. [<SULLEN]

Sul·la (sul′ə), **Lucius Cornelius,** 138–78 B.C., Roman general and dictator.

sul·lage (sul′ij) *n.* **1** Mud or silt deposited by flowing water. **2** Refuse; sewage. [<AF *souiller, soillier* SOIL[2]; infl. in form by *sully*]

sul·len (sul′ən) *adj.* **1** Obstinately and gloomily ill–humored; morose; glum. **2** Depressing; somber: *sullen* clouds. **3** Slow; sluggish: a *sullen* tread. **4** Melancholy. **5** Ill–omened; threatening. See synonyms under GRIM. [Earlier *solein,* appar. <AF <*sol* SOLE[3]] **—sul′len·ly** *adv.* **—sul′len·ness** *n.*

Sul·li·van (sul′ə·vən), **Sir Arthur Seymour,** 1842–1900, English composer (often in collaboration with W. S. Gilbert). **—Harry Stack,** 1892–1949, U. S. psychiatrist, editor, and writer. **—John L(awrence),** 1858–1918, U. S. pugilist. **—Louis Henri,** 1856–1924, U. S. architect.

Sul·li·vant (sul′ə·vənt), **William Starling,** 1803–73, U. S. botanist.

sul·ly (sul′ē) *v.* **·lied, ·lying** *v.t.* To mar the brightness or purity of; soil; defile; tarnish. **—***v.i.* To become soiled or tarnished: also figuratively. See synonyms under DEFILE, STAIN. **—***n. pl.* **·lies** Anything that tarnishes; a stain; spot; blemish. [<MF *souiller* SOIL[2]]

Sul·ly (sul′ē, *Fr.* sü·lē′), **Duc de,** 1560–1641, Maximilien de Béthune, French statesman. **—Thomas,** 1783–1872, U. S. portrait painter born in England.

Sul·ly–Prud·homme (sü·lē′·prü·dôm′), **René François Armand,** 1839–1907, French poet and critic.

sulph– For all words so spelled, see the forms beginning SULF–.

sulpha– Var. of SULFA–.

sulpho– Var. of SULFO–.

sul·tan (sul′tən) *n.* **1** The ruler of a Moslem country. **2** A gallinule with deep–blue or purple plumage and white lower tail coverts. *Ionornis martinica* is the purple gallinule or sultan of the warmer parts of America. **3** A small white–crested variety of the domestic fowl, originating in Turkey, having heavily feathered legs and feet. **4** Formerly, any ruler. **—the Sultan** The title of the sovereign of Turkey: office abolished, 1922. [<F <Med. L *sultanus* <Arabic *sulṭān* a sovereign, dominion]

sul·tan·a (sul·tan′ə, -tä′nə) *n.* **1** A sultan's wife, daughter, sister, or mother: also **sul·tan·ess** (sul′tən·is). **2** The mistress of a king or prince. **3** A variety of raisin from the district of Smyrna, Asia Minor. **4** Sultan (def. 3): also **sul·tan′a–bird′.** [<Ital., fem. of *sultano* a sultan <Arabic *sulṭān*]

sul·tan·ate (sul′tən·āt, -it) *n.* The authority or territorial jurisdiction of a sultan. Also **sul′tan·ship.**

sul·try (sul′trē) *adj.* **·tri·er, ·tri·est 1** Hot, moist, and still; close: said of weather. **2** Emitting an oppressive heat; burning; hot with anger. **3** Showing or suggesting passion; sensual. [<obs. *sulter,* var. of SWELTER] **—sul′tri·ly** *adv.* **—sul′tri·ness** *n.*

Su·lu (sōō′lōō) *n.* **1** A member of the chief Moro tribe occupying the Sulu Archipelago. **2** The Indonesian language of this tribe, closely related to Tagalog. **—Su·lu′an** *adj.* & *n.*

Sulu Archipelago An island group between Basilan and the NE coast of Borneo, comprising a province of the Philippines; 1,086 square miles; capital, Jolo.

Sulu Sea An arm of the Pacific Ocean between the SW Philippines and Borneo; over 400 miles long, east to west.

sum (sum) *n.* **1** The result obtained by addition. **2** The entire quantity, number, or substance; the whole; all: the *sum* total of my means; the *sum* and substance of the case. **3** Any indefinite amount: said chiefly of money. **4** A problem in arithmetic propounded for solution. **5** The summit; topmost or highest point; also, the maximum; the complement. **6** A summary; the pith or essence. See synonyms under AGGREGATE. **—***v.* **summed, sum·ming** *v.t.* **1** To present in brief; recapitulate succinctly: usually with *up*: to *sum up* evidence. **2** To add into one total; ascertain the sum of: often with *up.* **3** To ascertain the sum of (the terms of a series). **—***v.i.* **4** To make a summation or recapitulation: generally with *up.* ◆ Homophone: *some.* [<AF, OF *summe, somme* <L *summa (res)* highest (thing), fem. of *summus* highest]

sum– Assimilated var. of SUB–.

su·mac (sōō′mak, shōō′-) *n.* **1** Any of a genus *(Rhus)* of woody, erect, or root–climbing plants (family *Anacardiaceae*), with panicles of small flowers, small drupaceous fruits, and yielding a resinous or milky juice; especially, the **smooth sumac** *(R. glabra)* used in medicine. **2** The poison sumac. **3** The dried and powdered leaves of certain species of sumac, used for tanning and dyeing, especially of **tanner's sumac** *(Rhus coriaria).* Also **su′mach.** [<OF <Med. L *sumach* <Arabic *summāq*]

Su·ma·tra (sōō·mä′trə) An Indonesian island south of the Malay Peninsula, comprising, with adjacent islands, six provinces of Indonesia; 163,557 square miles; chief city, Palembang. **—Su·ma′tran** *adj.* & *n.*

Sum·ba (sōōm′bä) One of the Lesser Sunda Islands, SE of Sumbawa, in south central Nusa Tenggara province, Indonesia; 4,300 square miles: formerly *Sandalwood Island*: Dutch *Soemba.*

Sum·bar (sōōm′bär) A river in SW Turkmen S.S.R. and Iran, flowing 150 miles west to its confluence with the Atrek river, on the U.S.S.R.–Iran border.

Sum·ba·wa (sōōm·bä′wä) One of the Lesser Sunda Islands, east of Lombok, in NW central Nusa Tenggara province, Indonesia; 5,965 square miles: Dutch *Soembawa.*

sum·bul (sum′bəl) *n.* Muskroot. Also **sum′bal, sum′bul–root′** (-rōōt′, -rŏŏt′). [<F <Arabic *sunbul*] **—sum·bu·lic** (sum·bōō′lik) *adj.*

sumbul tree See under AMMONIAC[2].

Su·mer (sōō′mər) A region and ancient country of Mesopotamia, later the southern division of Babylonia; the sites of its once great cities are in south central Iraq.

Su·me·ri·an (sōō·mir′ē·ən) *adj.* Of or pertaining to ancient Sumer, its people, or their language. **—***n.* **1** One of an ancient non–Semitic people formerly occupying a part of lower Babylonia: culturally important in the Near East from about 3300–1800 B.C. **2** The agglutinative, unclassified language of these people, written in cuneiform characters and preserved on rocks and clay tablets the earliest of which date from about 4000 B.C. Also **Su·mir′i·an.**

sum·less (sum′lis) *adj.* Too great for computation; incalculable; without number.

sum·ma cum lau·de (sum′ə kum lô′dē, sōōm′ə kŏŏm lou′de) See under CUM LAUDE.

sum·mand (sum′and) *n.* That which is added; any of the numbers forming part of a sum. [<Med. L *summandus (numerus)* (the number) to be added <*summare* add <L *summa.* See SUM.]

sum·ma·rize (sum′ə·rīz) *v.t.* **·rized, ·riz·ing** To make a summary of; sum up; epitomize. Also *Brit.* **sum′ma·rise. —sum′ma·ri·za′tion** *n.* **—sum′ma·riz′er** *n.*

sum·ma·ry (sum′ər·ē) *adj.* **1** Giving the substance or sum; greatly condensed; concise. **2** Performed without ceremony or delay; instant; offhand: used specifically in law. **—***n. pl.* **·ries** An abridgment or epitome; abstract; compendium. See synonyms under ABRIDGMENT. [<Med. L *summarius* <L *summarium* a summary <*summa.* See SUM.] **—sum·ma·ri·ly** (sum′ər·ə·lē, *emphatic* sə·mer′ə·lē) *adv.* **—sum′ma·ri·ness** *n.* **—sum′ma·rist** *n.*

sum·mate (sum·āt′) *v.t.* & *v.i.* **·mat·ed, ·mat·ing 1** To arrive at the sum of (a series). **2** To sum up. [Back formation <SUMMATION]

sum·ma·tion (sum·ā′shən) *n.* **1** The act or operation of obtaining a sum; the computation or statement of an aggregate sum or result; addition. **2** A speech or a portion of a speech summing up the principal points. [<NL *summatio, -onis* <Med. L *summare* add <*summa.* See SUM.]

sum·mer[1] (sum′ər) *n.* **1** The hottest or warmest season of the year: including June, July, and August, in the northern hemisphere. In the southern hemisphere the summer occurs during the months of the northern winter. ◆ Collateral adjective: *estival.* **2** Figuratively, a year of life, especially of early or happy life; a bright and prosperous period. **—Indian summer** A period of mild weather occurring in the autumn, with hazy atmosphere usually along the horizon, and a clear sky. It corresponds to the English St. Luke's or St. Martin's summer. — **St. Luke's summer** or **little summer of St. Luke** A short period of warm weather in England expected for a few days beginning with St. Luke's day, the 18th of October. — **St. Martin's summer** A season of mild weather about St. Martin's day, the 11th of November, corresponding to the American Indian summer. — *v.t.* To keep or care for through the summer. — *v.i.* To pass the summer. — *adj.* Of, pertaining to, or occurring in summer. [OE *sumor, sumer*] — **sum′mer·ly** *adj.* & *adv.*

sum·mer[2] (sum′ər) *n. Archit.* **1** A heavy horizontal timber or girder serving as a support for some superstructure in a building, etc.; a lintel. **2** A large stone, as on a column or pilaster, for supporting one or more arches, or any similar structure. **3** A horizontal beam resting upon the walls or external frame of a building, and supporting the ends of joists: also **sum′mer-beam′**. [<OF *somier* a pack horse, beam <LL *saumarius* <L *sagmarius* < *sagma* a pack saddle <Gk.]

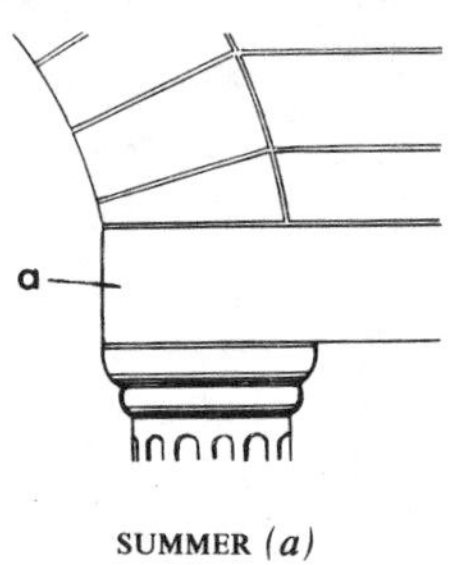

SUMMER *(a)*

summer flounder A flounder (*Paralichthys dentatus*) of the Atlantic coast of North America.

sum·mer·house (sum′ər·hous′) *n.* A rustic structure, as in a garden, for rest or shade.

summer house A house or cottage in the country or at the seashore, used during the summer.

summer kitchen A kitchen in a separate building or in a separate room attached to a house, for use in hot weather.

sum·mer·sault (sum′ər·sôlt), **sum·mer·set** (sum′ər·set) See SOMERSAULT.

summer squash Any of various squashes derived from the variety *Cucurbita pepo melopepo* and picked as vegetables before mature, while their rinds and seeds are tender.

sum·mer·time (sum′ər·tīm′) *n.* Summer; the summer season. Also **sum′mer·tide′**.

sum·mer·y (sum′ər·ē) *adj.* Pertaining to or resembling summer.

sum·mit (sum′it) *n.* **1** The highest part; the top; vertex. **2** The highest degree; maximum. **3** The highest level or office, as of a government or business organization. **4** A meeting of executives of the highest level, as heads of government. — *adj.* Of or involving those at the highest level: a *summit* conference. [<OF *sommette,* dim. of *som* a summit, top <L *summum,* neut. of *summus* highest] — **sum′mit·al** *adj.* — **sum′mit·less** *adj.*

Synonyms: acme, apex, cap, climax, crown, height, peak, pinnacle, top, vertex. *Antonyms*: abyss, base, bottom, chasm, deep, depth, gorge, gulf, pit, vale, valley.

sum·mit·ry (sum′it·rē) *n.* **1** Meetings of officials of the highest rank, as heads of government. **2** The use or dependency upon such meetings to solve international problems.

sum·mon (sum′ən) *v.t.* **1** To order to come; send for. **2** To call together; cause to convene, as a legislative assembly. **3** To order (a person) to appear in court by a summons. **4** To call forth or into action; arouse: usually with *up*: to *summon* up courage. **5** To bid or call on for a specific act: The garrison was *summoned* to surrender. See synonyms under ARRAIGN, CONVOKE. [<AF, OF *somondre* <L *summonere* suggest, hint < *sub-* secretly + *monere* warn] — **sum′mon·er** *n.*

sum·mons (sum′ənz) *n.* **1** A call to attend or act at a particular place or time. **2** *Law* A notice to a defendant summoning him to appear in court: either a judicial writ or process, or a notice signed by the plaintiff or his attorney; any citation issued to a party to an action to appear before a court or judge at chambers. See WRIT OF SUMMONS. **3** A notice to a person requiring him to appear in court as a witness or as a juror. **4** A military demand to surrender. **5** Any signal or sound that is a peremptory call. [<AF *somonse,* OF *sumunse* < *somondre* SUMMON]

sum·mum bo·num (sum′əm bō′nəm) *Latin* The chief, supreme, or highest good.

Sum·ner (sum′nər), **Charles,** 1811–74, U.S. statesman and abolitionist. — **James Batcheller,** 1887–1955, U.S. biochemist. — **William Graham,** 1840–1910, U.S. sociologist.

su·mo (sōō′mō) *n.* A highly stylized form of wrestling popular in Japan. [<Japanese *sumō*]

sump (sump) *n.* **1** *Mining* **a** A depression sunk below the lowest level in a mine shaft, to receive water and form a pool from which it may be pumped. **b** A sump winze. **2** *Mech.* The lowest part of the crankcase of an internal-combustion engine, acting as a reservoir for lubricating oil. **3** A cesspool or other reservoir for drainage. [<MDu. *somp, sump* a marsh. Akin to SWAMP.]

sump·ter (sump′tər) *n.* A pack animal; beast of burden. [<OF *sometier* a driver of a pack horse, ult. <L *sagma.* See SUMMER[2].]

sump·tu·ar·y (sump′chōō·er′ē) *adj.* Pertaining to expense; limiting or regulating expenditure, as some laws. [<L *sumptuarius* < *sumptus* expenditure < *sumere* take]

sumptuary law **1** A law limiting or regulating expenditure in order to prevent extravagance and inflation. **2** A law regulating private life on moral or religious grounds.

sump·tu·ous (sump′chōō·əs) *adj.* Involving or showing lavish expenditure; hence, luxurious; magnificent. [<OF *sumptueux, somptueux* <L *sumptuosus* < *sumptus.* See SUMPTUARY.] — **sump′tu·ous·ly** *adv.* — **sump′tu·ous·ness** *n.*

sump·weed (sump′wēd′) *n.* Marsh elder.

sun (sun) *n.* **1** The heavenly body that is the center of attraction and the main source of light and heat in the solar system, with a mean distance from the earth of about 93,000,000 miles and a diameter of 864,000 miles. Its mass is 332,000 times that of the earth, but its density only about one-fourth. **2** Any star, especially one that is the center of a system revolving around it. **3** The light and heat radiated from the sun; sunshine. **4** Anything brilliant and magnificent, or that is a source of splendor. **5** The time of the earth's revolution round the sun; a year. **6** The daily appearance of the sun; a day; also, the time of its appearance or shining; sunrise. — **a place in the sun** A dominant position in international affairs; hence, a position in the spotlight; publicity. — *v.* **sunned, sun·ning** *v.t.* **1** To expose to the light or heat of the sun. **2** To warm or dry (something) in the sun. — *v.i.* **3** To bask in the sun; expose oneself to the light or heat of the sun. ◆ Homophone: *son.* [OE *sunne*]

Sun may appear as a combining form in hyphemes or solidemes, or as the first element in two-word phrases, with the following meanings:

1 Of the sun; of sunshine:

sun blaze	**sun-loving**
sun-eclipsing	**sun-worship**
sun glare	**sun-worshiper**
sunland	**sun-worshiping**

2 By or with the sun:

sun-bake	**sun-filled**
sun-baked	**sun-flooded**
sun-blind	**sun-gilt**
sun-blinded	**sun-heated**
sun-blistered	**sun-kissed**
sun-brown	**sunlit**
sun-browned	**sun-scorched**
sun-cracked	**sun-scorching**
sun-dappled	**sun-streaked**
sun-dried	**sun-warmed**
sun-dry	**sun-withered**

sun bath Exposure to direct sunlight.

sun-bathe (sun′bāth′) *v.i.* **-bathed, -bath·ing** To bask in the sun, especially as a method of tanning the skin. — **sun′-bath′er** *n.* — **sun′-bath′ing** *n.*

sun·beam (sun′bēm′) *n.* **1** A ray or beam of the sun; light from the sun in a visible path. **2** *pl.* Sunlight.

sun·bird (sun′bûrd′) *n.* **1** A brilliantly colored oriental singing bird (family *Nectariniidae*) resembling the hummingbird. **2** A sun bittern.

sun bittern Either of two birds of Central and South America (genus *Eurypyga*) related to the rails and herons, having a slender neck and bill, long wings and tail, and moderately long legs.

sun·bon·net (sun′bon′it) *n.* A bonnet of light material with projecting brim and sometimes a cape covering the neck.

sun·bow (sun′bō′) *n.* A rainbow formed by the sun, as opposed to a lunar bow.

sun·burn (sun′bûrn′) *n.* Discoloration or inflammation of the skin, produced by exposure to the sun. — *v.t.* & *v.i.* To affect or be affected with sunburn. — **sun′burnt′, sun′burned′** *adj.*

sun·burst (sun′bûrst′) *n.* **1** A strong burst of sunlight, as through rifted clouds. **2** A brooch or pin with jewels so set around a larger central gem as to suggest sun rays.

sun compass A compass serving to establish Greenwich time in relation to the position of the sun: used chiefly in polar regions, where the magnetic compass is unreliable.

sun·dae (sun′dē) *n.* A refreshment consisting of ice-cream and crushed fruit, flavoring, sirup, nuts, etc. [Prob. <*Sunday*; prob. so called because orig. sold only on that day]

Sun·da Islands (sun′də, *Du.* sōōn′dä) An Indonesian island group of the Malay Archipelago, between the Indian Ocean and the Java Sea; divided into *Greater Sunda Islands,* including Sumatra, Java, Borneo, and Celebes, and *Lesser Sunda Islands,* the smaller islands east of Java. *Dutch* **Soen′da.**

sun dance The greatest ceremonial dance of the Plains Indians, usually a summer solstice ceremony, comprising fast days, dance days, secret rites, and a public performance.

Sun·da Strait (sun′də, *Du.* sōōn′dä) The channel between Java and Sumatra, connecting the Java Sea with the Indian Ocean 16 to 70 miles wide.

Sun·day (sun′dē, -dā) *n.* The first day of the week; the Lord's day; the Christian Sabbath: sometimes used attributively. See synonyms under SABBATH. [OE *sunnan dæg* < *sunnan* of the sun + *dæg* a day; trans. of LL *dies solis* day of the sun]

Sun·day (sun′dē, -dā), **Billy,** 1862–1935, U.S. preacher and evangelist: full name *William Ashley Sunday.*

Sun·day-go-to-meet·ing (sun′dē·gō′tə·mē′·ting) *adj. Colloq.* Best: *Sunday-go-to-meeting* clothes or manners.

Sunday school A school, generally attached to some church, in which religious instruction is given on Sunday, especially to the young; also, the pupils, or teachers and pupils, collectively: also called *Sabbath school.*

sun·der (sun′dər) *v.t.* To break apart; disunite; sever. — *v.i.* To be parted or severed. See synonyms under BREAK, CUT, REND, SEPARATE. — *n.* Division into parts; separation. — **in sunder** Apart; separate from other parts. Compare ASUNDER. [OE *syndrian, sundrian*] — **sun′der·ance** *n.*

Sun·der·land (sun′dər·lənd) A port and county borough in NE Durham, England.

sun·dew (sun′dōō′, -dyōō′) *n.* Any of a genus (*Drosera*) of marsh plants that exude a viscid liquid from the tips of the hairs on the leaves. Insects are caught by the secretions and are utilized by the plant for its own nutrition.

sun·di·al (sun′dī′əl) *n.* A device that measures time and shows the time of day by means of the shadow of a style or gnomon thrown on a dial.

SUNDIAL

sun disk The winged disk. See under DISK.

sun·dog (sun′dôg′, -dog′) *n.* **1** A parhelion, appearing near the sun, sometimes with a luminous train, due to the presence of ice crystals in the air; a mock sun. **2** A small rainbow lying near the horizon.

sun·down (sun′doun′) *n.* **1** Sunset: originally colloquial, like *sunup,* but now in good literary usage. **2** A broad-brimmed hat worn by women. [? Contraction of *sun-go-down*]

sun·down·er (sun′dou′nər) *n.* **1** *Colloq.* A tramp. **2** *Austral.* A vagrant who seeks food and lodging at back-country ranches, often about the time of sundown. **3** *Slang* A strict, rigidly uncompromising ship's officer; originally, a ship's captain who granted liberty only until sundown.

sun·dries (sun′drēz) *n. pl.* Items or things too small or too numerous to be separately specified. [<SUNDRY]

sun·drops (sun′drops′) *n.* Any of several American species of evening primrose (genus *Oenothera*), having large yellow flowers, and blooming in the daytime.

sun·dry (sun′drē) *adj.* Of an indefinite small number; various; several; miscellaneous. See synonyms under MANY. [OE *syndrig* separate, private]

sune (so͞on) *adv. Scot.* Soon.

sun·fish (sun′fish′) *n. pl.* **·fish** or **·fish·es** 1 A large pelagic plectognath fish (genus *Mola*), having a deep compressed body truncate behind, as *Mola mola* of warm and tropical seas. It has tough and leathery flesh. 2 Any of several North American freshwater perchlike fishes (family *Centrarchidae*) of the genus *Lepomis*, as the pumpkinseed.

SUNFISH (*def. 1*)
(Up to 8 feet in length)

sun·flow·er (sun′flou′ər) *n.* Any of a genus (*Helianthus*) of tall, stout, rough herbs of the composite family, with large leaves and circular heads of flowers, those in the center tubular and usually purple, and those on the margin strap-shaped and bright-yellow; especially, the common sunflower (*H. annuus*), the source of an edible oil, and the State flower of Kansas.

Sunflower State Nickname of KANSAS.

sung (sung) Past participle and occasional past tense of SING.

Sung (so͝ong) *n.* A dynasty in Chinese history, 960 to 1280, noted for its achievements in art and philosophy.

Sun·ga·ri (so͝ong′gä·rē′) The largest river of Manchuria, flowing 1,150 miles NW to the Amur river. *Chinese* **Sung·hwa** (so͝ong′hwä′).

Sung·kiang (so͝ong′jyäng′) A former province of NE Manchuria region, NE China, incorporated in Heilungkiang province; 75,000 square miles; capital, Harbin.

sun·glass (sun′glas′, -gläs′) *n.* 1 A burning glass; a glass used for concentrating the rays of the sun. 2 *pl.* Spectacles that protect the eyes from the glare of the sun by their colored lenses.

sun·glow (sun′glō′) *n.* 1 The rose tint or faint yellow of the sky that precedes sunrise or follows sunset. 2 The warm glow of the sun.

sun-god (sun′god′) *n.* In the religions of some primitive agricultural peoples, a deity conceived of as life-giving and beneficent, and symbolized by the sun, as the ancient Egyptian Ra, ancient Irish Lug, Inti of the Incas, etc.: not to be confused with personifications of the sun in many cosmogonic myths (Greek Helios, for instance) which are mere explanatory etiological tales and do not posit a sun cult.

sunk (sungk) Past participle and alternative past tense of SINK.

sunk·en (sung′kən) Obsolete past participle of SINK. — *adj.* 1 Lying at the bottom of a body of water: a *sunken* ship. 2 Located beneath a surface. 3 Lower than the surrounding or usual level: *sunken* gardens. 4 Deeply depressed or fallen in: *sunken* cheeks.

sun·ket (sung′kit, so͝ong′-) *n. Scot.* A dainty; tidbit.

sunk fence A ditch having a retaining wall on one side to divide lands; a ha-ha.

sunk·ie (sungk′ē) *n. Scot.* A low stool or small seat.

sunk panel A panel so depressed as to form a recess below the surface of its frame.

sun lamp 1 A lamp giving illumination of high intensity, usually reflected by parabolic mirrors: used in motion-picture studios. 2 A lamp radiating ultraviolet rays: used for therapeutic treatments and as a protection against airborne bacteria in operating rooms, etc.

sun·less (sun′lis) *adj.* Dark; cheerless. — **sun′less·ness** *n.*

sun·light (sun′līt′) *n.* The light of the sun.

sun·lit (sun′lit′) *adj.* Lighted by the sun.

sunn (sun) *n.* An East Indian shrub (*Crotalaria juncea*) of the bean family, with bright-yellow flowers and tough, durable fiber: used for making cordage, bagging, and other coarse textiles: also called *Bombay* or *Madras hemp*. Also **sunn hemp.** [<Hind. *san*]

Sun·na (so͝on′ə) *n.* A path or manner of life; that part of the orthodox Moslem creed or law based on traditions of the Prophet's words and deeds: regarded by a numerous sect as of equal importance with the Koran, which it supplements; hence, the theory and practice of orthodox Islam. Also **Sun′nah.** [<Arabic *sunnah*, lit., a form, way]

Sun·nite (so͝on′īt) *n.* An orthodox Moslem of the sect accepting Sunna (tradition) and the Koran as of equal authority, and acknowledging the first four caliphs as rightful successors of the Prophet: opposed to *Shiah*. Also **Sun·ni** (so͝on′ē).

sun·ny (sun′ē) *adj.* **·ni·er, ·ni·est** 1 Filled with the light and warmth of the sun; exposed to the sun. 2 Bright like the sun; of the sun or sunshine; hence, genial; cheery: a *sunny* smile. See synonyms under BRIGHT, CHEERFUL, HAPPY. — **sun′ni·ly** *adv.* — **sun′ni·ness** *n.*

sunny side 1 The side, as of a hill, facing the sun. 2 The cheerful view of any situation, question, etc.

sun parlor A room enclosed in glass and having a sunny exposure.

sun pillar A column of variously tinted light sometimes seen projecting vertically above or below the sun at sunrise or sunset. It is caused by the reflection of sunlight from small snow crystals.

sun·rise (sun′rīz′) *n.* 1 The daily first appearance of the sun above the horizon, with the atmospheric phenomena just preceding and following. 2 The time at which the sun rises. 3 The east; Orient.

sun·room (sun′ro͞om′, -ro͝om′) *n.* A room built to admit a profusion of sunlight.

sun-scald (sun′skôld′) *n.* A diseased condition of plants induced by exposure to intense sunlight.

sun-scorch (sun′skôrch′) *n.* A scorched or burnt condition of plants.

sun·set (sun′set′) *n.* 1 The apparent daily descent of the sun below the horizon. 2 The time when the sun sets; the early evening. 3 The colors in the sky when the sun sets. 4 The west; Occident. 5 Figuratively, the ending or decline, as of life.

sun·shade (sun′shād′) *n.* Something used as a shade or protection from the rays of the sun, as a parasol, an awning, etc.

sun·shine (sun′shīn′) *n.* 1 The shining light of the sun; the direct rays of the sun. 2 The warmth of the sun's rays. 3 The place where the rays fall. 4 Figuratively, brightness; any cheering influence. — **sun′shin′y** *adj.*

Sunshine State Nickname of NEW MEXICO.

sun·spot (sun′spot′) *n.* 1 *Astron.* One of many dark irregular spots appearing periodically on the surface of the sun: believed to have connection with terrestrial magnetic storms. 2 An incandescent sun lamp used in color photography.

sun·stone (sun′stōn′) *n.* A variety of feldspar; aventurine.

sun·stroke (sun′strōk′) *n. Pathol.* A sudden onset of high fever induced by exposure to the sun and often marked by convulsions and coma; insolation. — **sun′struck′** (-struk′) *adj.*

sun tan A bronze-colored condition of the skin, produced by exposure to the sun. — **sun′-tanned′** (-tand′) *adj.*

sun·tans (sun′tanz′) *n. pl.* The lightweight summer uniform made of khaki worn by U. S. Army personnel: officially known as *cotton khakis*, and often called *khakis*. They are worn in the Navy by officers.

sun·up (sun′up′) *n.* Sunrise. [<SUN + UP; on analogy with *sundown*]

Sun Valley A resort village in south central Idaho; altitude, 6,000 feet.

sun·ward (sun′wərd) *adj.* Facing toward the sun. — *adv.* Toward the sun: also **sun′wards.**

sun·wise (sun′wīz′) *adv.* With the sun; in the direction of the sun; clockwise.

Sun Yat-sen (so͝on′ yät′sen′), 1865?–1925, Chinese statesman; president of China 1911–1912.

su·o ju·re (so͞o′ō jo͝or′ē) *Latin* In one's own right.

su·o lo·co (so͞o′ō lō′kō) *Latin* In its own or proper place.

Su·o·mi (so͞o·ō′mē) *n. pl.* 1 The people of Finland; the Finns. 2 The language of the Finns; Finnish. — **Su·o′mic** *adj.* & *n.*

Su·o·mi (so͞o·ō′mē) The Finnish name for FINLAND.

sup[1] (sup) *v.t.* & *v.i.* **supped, sup·ping** To take (fluid food) in successive mouthfuls, a little at a time; sip. — *n.* A mouthful or taste of liquid or semiliquid food. [OE *sūpan* drink]

sup[2] (sup) *v.* **supped, sup·ping** *v.i.* To eat supper. — *v.t. Obs.* To furnish with or invite to supper. [<OF *soper, super*; ult. origin unknown]

sup- Assimilated var. of SUB-.

supe (so͞op) *n. Slang* A supernumerary actor. [Short for SUPERNUMERARY]

su·per[1] (so͞o′pər) *n. Colloq.* Shortened form of SUPERINTENDENT.

su·per[2] (so͞o′pər) *n. Slang* Shortened form of SUPERNUMERARY (def. 2).

su·per[3] (so͞o′pər) *n.* 1 An article of superior size or quality; also, such size or quality. 2 In bookbinding, a thin, starched cotton fabric used in reinforcement. — *adj.* 1 *Slang* First-rate; superfine. 2 Showing excessive loyalty: a *super* American. — *v.t.* To reinforce (a book) with super. [Short for SUPERIOR, SUPERFINE, etc.]

super- *prefix* 1 Above in position; over: *superstructure, superimpose.* 2 *Anat.* & *Zool.* Situated above, or on the dorsal side of: *superorbital.* 3 Above or beyond; more than: *supersonic, supersensible.* 4 Excessively: *supersaturate.* 5 *Med.* Exceeding the normal: *superacidity.* 6 *Chem.* Denoting a high proportion of the ingredient indicated (now superseded by PER-, BI-): *superphosphate.* 7 Surpassing in power or size all others of its class: *superhighway, supermarket.* In this sense the prefix is sometimes doubled to intensify the degree of superiority: a *super-supernavy* a navy far superior to any other. 8 Extra; additional: *supertax.* [<L *super-* < *super* above, beyond]

In the following list of words *super-* denotes excess or superiority, as *supercritical* excessively critical, *superexcellence* superior excellence.

superabhor
superabominable
superabsurd
superaccession
superaccommodating
superaccomplished
superaccumulate
superachievement
superacquisition
superacute
superadaptable
superadequate
superadmiration
superadorn
superaffluence
superagency
superaggravation
superagitation
superambitious
superangelic
superappreciation
superarbitrary
superarduous
superarrogant
superaspiration
superastonish
superattachment
superattraction
superattractive
superbelief
superbeloved
superbenefit
superbenevolent
superbenign
superbias
superblessed
superblunder
superbold
superbrave
superbusy
supercandid
supercapable
supercatastrophe
supercatholic
supercaution
superceremonious
superchivalrous
supercivil
supercivilized
superclassified
supercolossal
supercombination
supercommendation
supercommercial
supercompetition
supercomplex
supercomprehension
supercompression
superconfident
superconformist
superconformity
superconfusion
supercongestion
superconservative
supercontrol
supercordial
supercritic
supercritical
supercultivated
supercurious
supercynical
superdainty
superdanger
superdeclamatory

superdeficit
superdejection
superdelicate
superdemand
superdemonic
superdesirous
superdevelopment
superdevilish
superdevotion
superdiabolical
superdifficult
superdiplomacy
superdistribution
superdividend
superdonation
supereconomy
supereffective
supereffluence
superelastic
superelated
superelegance
supereligible
supereloquent
superemphasis
superendorsement
superendow
superenforcement
superenrolment
superestablishment
superesthetic
superethical
superevident
superexacting
superexalt
superexaltation
superexcellence
superexcellent
superexcitation
superexcited
superexcitement
superexiguity
superexpansion
superexpectation
superexpenditure
superexpressive
superexquisiteness
superextension
superfecundity
superfeminine
superfervent
superfoliation
superfolly
superformal
superformation
superformidable
superfriendly
superfructified
superfulfilment
supergaiety
supergallant
supergenerosity
superglorious
supergoodness
supergovernment
supergratification
supergravitation
superhandsome
superhearty
superhero
superheroic
superhistorical
superhypocrite
superideal
superignorant
superillustrate
superimpending
superimpersonal
superimportant
superimprobable
superimproved
superincentive
superinclination
superinclusive
superincomprehensible
superindependent
superindifference
superindignant
superindividualism
superindividualist
superindulgence
superindustrious
superinference
superinfinite
superinfirmity
superinfluence
superingenious
superinitiative
superinjustice
superinquisitive
superinsistent
superintellectual
superintolerable
superjurisdiction
superjustification
superknowledge
superlaborious
superlenient
superlie
superlogical
superloyal
superlucky
superluxurious
supermagnificently
supermanhood
supermarvelous
supermasculine
supermechanical
supermediocre
supermental
supermentality
supermetropolitan
supermishap
supermodest
supermoisten
supermorose
supermundane
supermystery
supernecessity
supernegligent
supernotable
supernumerous
superobedience
superobese
superobjectionable
superobligation
superobstinate
superoffensive
superofficious
superofficiousness
superopposition
superoratorical
superordinary
superorganize
superornamental
superoutput
superpatient
superpatriotic
superpatriotism
superperfection
superpious
superplease
superpolite
superpositive
superpraise
superprecise
superpreparation
superproduce
superprosperous
superpublicity
superpure
superpurgation
superradical
superrational
superrefined
superreform
superreliance
superremuneration
superrespectable
superresponsible
superrestriction
superreward
superrighteous
superromantic
supersacrifice
supersafe
supersagacious
supersanguine
supersarcastic
supersatisfaction
superscholarly
superscientific
supersensitive
supersensitiveness
supersensuousness
supersentimental
superserious
supersevere
supersignificant
supersimplify
supersmart
supersolemn
supersolemnly
supersolicitation
superspecialize
superspiritual
superspirituality
superstimulation
superstoical
superstrain
superstrenuous
superstrict
superstrong
superstylish
supersufficient
supersurprise
supersweet
supertension
superthankful
superthorough
supertoleration
supertragic
supertrivial
superugly
superunity
superurgent
supervexation
supervigilant
supervigorous
supervirulent
supervital
superwise
superworldly
superwrought
superzealous

su·per·a·ble (sōō′pər·ə·bəl) *adj.* That can be surmounted, overcome, or conquered. [<L *superabilis* < *superare* overcome < *super* over]

su·per·a·bound (sōō′pər·ə·bound′) *v.i.* To abound to excess or to an unusual extent. [<LL *superabundare* <L *super-* exceedingly + *abundare* overflow]

su·per·a·bun·dant (sōō′pər·ə·bun′dənt) *adj.* Excessive; more than sufficient. See synonyms under REDUNDANT. [<LL *superabundans, -antis,* ppr. of *superabundare.* See SUPERABOUND.] — **su′per·a·bun′dance** *n.* — **su′per·a·bun′dant·ly** *adv.*

su·per·a·cid·i·ty (sōō′pər·ə·sid′ə·tē) *n. Med.* An excess of acid, especially in the gastric juices; hyperacidity.

su·per·add (sōō′pər·ad′) *v.t.* To add in addition to something already added. [<LL *superaddere* < *super-* over and above + *addere* ADD] — **su′per·ad·di′tion** (-ə·dish′ən) *n.*

su·per·al·tar (sōō′pər·ôl′tər) *n. Eccl.* **1** A consecrated slab laid on an unconsecrated altar when mass is said in oratories or temporary chapels. **2** Sometimes, incorrectly, a retable. [<Med. L *superaltare* <L *super-* over + *altare* an altar]

su·per·an·nu·ate (sōō′pər·an′yōō·āt) *v.t.* **·at·ed, ·at·ing** **1** To retire or retire and pension on account of age: chiefly in past participle. **2** To set aside or discard as obsolete or too old. [<Med. L *superannuatus* more than a year old (said of cattle) <L *super annum* < *super* beyond + *annus* a year] — **su′per·an′nu·at′ed** *adj.* — **su′per·an′nu·a′tion** *n.*

su·per·aq·ual (sōō′pər·ak′wəl, -ā′kwəl) *adj.* Of, pertaining to, or denoting those soils lying just above the water table, from which they derive the greater part of their moisture. [<L *super* above + *aqua* water]

su·perb (sōō·pûrb′, sə-) *adj.* **1** Having grand, impressive beauty; majestic; imposing: a *superb* edifice. **2** Luxurious; rich and costly; elegant. **3** Very good; supremely fine. [<L *superbus* proud < *super-* over] — **su·perb′ly** *adv.* — **su·perb′ness** *n.*

su·per·bomb (sōō′pər·bom′) *n.* A hydrogen bomb.

su·per·cal·en·der (sōō′pər·kal′ən·dər) *n.* A calender having a number of polished rollers for giving a high finish to paper. See CALENDER[1]. — *v.t.* To give a high finish to (paper). — **su′per·cal′en·dered** *adj.*

su·per·car·go (sōō′pər·kär′gō) *n. pl.* **·goes** or **·gos** An agent on board ship in charge of the cargo and its sale and purchase. [Alter. of obs. *supracargo* <Sp. *sobrecargo* < *sobre-* over (<L *super-*) + *cargo* CARGO]

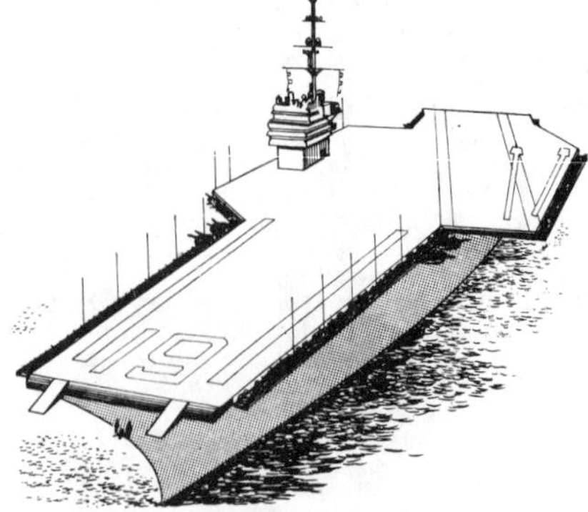

SUPERCARRIER OF THE FORRESTAL CLASS

su·per·car·ri·er (sōō′pər·kar′ē·ər) *n.* An aircraft–carrier of exceptional size.

su·per·charge (sōō′pər·chärj′) *v.t.* **·charged, ·charg·ing** **1** To adapt (an engine) to develop more power, as by fitting with a supercharger. **2** To charge to excess; overload. — *n.* (sōō′·pər·chärj′) **1** An excess charge, in any sense. **2** *Her.* One charge or device borne on another.

su·per·charg·er (sōō′pər·chär′jər) *n.* A compressor for supplying air or combustible mixture to an internal–combustion engine at a pressure greater than that developed by the suction of the pistons alone.

su·per·cil·i·ar·y (sōō′pər·sil′ē·er′ē) *adj.* **1** Of or pertaining to the eyebrow. **2** Situated over the eyebrow; supraorbital: the *superciliary* arches. [<NL *superciliaris* <L *supercilium* an eyebrow < *super-* above + *cilium* an eyelid]

su·per·cil·i·ous (sōō′pər·sil′ē·əs) *adj.* Exhibiting haughty contempt or indifference; arrogant. See synonyms under HAUGHTY. [<L *superciliosus* < *supercilium.* See SUPERCILIARY.] — **su′per·cil′i·ous·ly** *adv.* — **su′per·cil′i·ous·ness** *n.*

su·per·class (sōō′pər·klas′, -kläs′) *n. Biol.* A division of plants or animals below a phylum but above a class.

su·per·co·lum·nar (sōō′pər·kə·lum′nər) *adj. Archit.* **1** Erected above a colonnade or another column. **2** Having one order placed above another.

su·per·con·duc·tiv·i·ty (sōō′pər·kon′duk·tiv′ə·tē) *n. Electr.* The property, exhibited by certain metals and alloys, of becoming almost perfect conductors of electricity when their temperatures fall below transition points in the neighborhood of absolute zero. — **su′per·con·duc′tive** (-kən·duk′tiv) *adj.* — **su′per·con·duc′tor** *n.*

su·per·cool (sōō′pər·kōōl′) *v.t.* To cool, as a liquid, below the freezing point without solidification.

su·per·dom·i·nant (sōō′pər·dom′ə·nənt) *n. Music* The tone just above the dominant; the sixth or submediant.

su·per–du·per (sōō′pər·dōō′pər) *Slang adj.* Superlative: an intensive formation. — *n.* Anything especially fine. [Reduplication of SUPER[3]]

su·per·e·go (sōō′pər·ē′gō, -eg′ō) *n. Psychoanal.* A largely unconscious element of the personality, regarded as dominating the conscious ego, for which it acts principally in the role of conscience and critic.

su·per·em·i·nent (sōō′pər·em′ə·nənt) *adj.* Excelling or surpassing others; of a superior or remarkable quality; supremely exalted. [<L *supereminens, -entis,* ppr. of *supereminere* rise above < *super-* above + *eminere* rise. See EMINENT.] — **su′per·em′i·nence** *n.* — **su′per·em′i·nent·ly** *adv.*

su·per·er·o·gate (sōō′pər·er′ə·gāt) *v.i.* **·gat·ed, ·gat·ing** To do more than is required or ordered. [<L *supererogatus,* pp. of *supererogare* < *super-* over and above + *erogare* pay out <*ex-* out + *rogare* ask]

su·per·er·o·ga·tion (sōō′pər·er′ə·gā′shən) *n.* The performance of an act in excess of the demands or requirements of duty. — **works of supererogation** Good deeds done by saints of the Roman Catholic Church in excess of the requirements of divine law; also, voluntary good deeds performed by men over and above God's commandments.

su·per·e·rog·a·to·ry (sōō′pər·ə·rog′ə·tôr′ē, -tō′·rē) *adj.* Of, pertaining to, or of the nature of supererogation; superfluous. Also **su′per·e·rog′a·tive.**

su·per·fam·i·ly (sōō′pər·fam′ə·lē, -fam′lē) *n. pl.* **·lies** *Biol.* A division of plants or animals ranking next above the family but below an order or superorder.

su·per·fe·cun·da·tion (sōō′pər·fē′kən·dā′shən, -fek′ən-) *n. Physiol.* The successive impregnation of two or more ova.

su·per·fe·male (sōō′pər·fē′māl) *n. Biol.* A supersexual organism, characterized in the fruit fly by a ratio of 3 X–chromosomes to 2 sets of autosomes.

su·per·fe·tate (sōō′pər·fē′tāt) *v.i.* **·tat·ed, ·tat·ing** *Physiol.* To conceive again prior to the birth of an embryo or fetus already conceived. [<L *superfetatus,* pp. of *superfetare* < *super-* over and above + *fetus* a foetus]

su·per·fe·ta·tion (sōō′pər·fi·tā′shən) *n.* **1** *Physiol.* **a** The second impregnation of a female already pregnant. **b** The progeny resulting from such second impregnation; hence, any unusual additional growth. 2 *Bot.* Fertilization of the same ovule by two or more kinds of pollen. Also **su′per·foe·ta′tion.**

su·per·fi·cial (sōō′pər·fish′əl) *adj.* 1 Of, pertaining to, lying near, or forming the surface; affecting only the surface. 2 Of or pertaining to only the ordinary and the obvious; not profound; shallow: a *superficial* writer. 3 Marked by partial knowledge; cursory; hasty; slight: *superficial* treatment of a subject. 4 Not real or genuine. 5 Square: said of measure. [<LL *superficialis* <L *superficies* SUPERFICIES] — **su′per·fi′ci·al′i·ty** (-fish′ē·al′ə·tē), **su′per·fi′cial·ness** *n.* — **su′per·fi′cial·ly** *adv.*

su·per·fi·ci·ar·y (sōō′pər·fish′ē·er′ē) *adj.* 1 Belonging or pertaining to the superficies; superficial. 2 *Law* Situated on another's land, or resulting from such situation.

su·per·fi·ci·es (sōō′pər·fish′i·ēz, -fish′ēz) *n. pl.* **·ci·es** 1 A surface or its area; superficial area. 2 External appearance; exterior part. [<L *super-* over + *facies* a face]

su·per·fine (sōō′pər·fīn′) *adj.* 1 Of surpassing fineness and delicacy; of the best quality. 2 Overrefined; unduly elaborate; overnice. [<MF *superfin* <*super-* over (<L) + *fin* FINE[1]] — **su′per·fine′ness** *n.*

su·per·flu·id (sōō′pər·flōō′id) *n. Physics* A peculiar state of matter noted in helium cooled to within a degree of absolute zero: it is characterized by an exceptional heat conductivity, a ready permeation of very dense substances, and the ability to flow upward against gravity: also called *quantum liquid.* —*adj.* (sōō′pər·flōō′id) Of or pertaining to such a state.

su·per·flu·i·ty (sōō′pər·flōō′ə·tē) *n. pl.* **·ties** 1 The state of being superfluous; superabundance. 2 That, or that part, which is superfluous. See synonyms under EXCESS. [<OF *superfluité* <Med. L *superfluitas, -tatis* <L *superfluus* excessive <*super-* over + *fluere* flow]

su·per·flu·ous (sōō·pûr′flōō·əs) *adj.* 1 Exceeding what is needed; excessively abundant; surplus. 2 *Music* Augmented: sometimes said of an interval. 3 *Archaic* Supererogatory; officious. 4 *Obs.* Overfed, overequipped, or oversupplied. See synonyms under REDUNDANT, WASTE. [<L *superfluus.* See SUPERFLUITY.] — **su·per′flu·ous·ly** *adv.* — **su·per′flu·ous·ness** *n.*

Su·per·for·tress (sōō′pər·fôr′tris) *n.* A heavy, four-engine bombing plane; the B-29: a trade name. Also **Su′per·fort′.**

su·per·fuse (sōō′pər·fyōōz′) *v.* **·fused, ·fus·ing** *v.t.* To pour so as to cover something else, as cod-liver oil on wine. —*v.i.* To be poured over or on something. [<L *superfusus,* pp. of *superfundere* <*super-* over + *fundere* pour] — **su′per·fu′sion** (-fyōō′zhən) *n.*

su·per·gla·cial (sōō′pər·glā′shəl) *adj. Geol.* Resting upon or deposited from the surface of a glacier.

su·per·heat (sōō′pər·hēt′) *v.t.* 1 To heat to excess; overheat. 2 To raise the temperature of (a vapor not in contact with its liquid) above the saturation point for a given pressure. 3 To heat (a liquid) above the boiling point for a given pressure, but without conversion into vapor. —*n.* (sōō′pər·hēt′) The degree to which steam has been superheated, or the heat so imparted.

su·per·heat·er (sōō′pər·hē′tər) *n.* A mechanical contrivance for superheating steam, as by causing it to traverse small tubes in the lower part of a chimney.

su·per·het·er·o·dyne (sōō′pər·het′ər·ə·dīn′) *adj. Electronics* Pertaining to or designating a type of radio reception in which the modulated incoming signals have the frequency of their carrier waves changed to an intermediate (inaudible) frequency, and are then rectified to reproduce the original sounds. —*n.* A radio receiving set for this method of reception. [<SUPER(SONIC) + HETERODYNE]

su·per·high·way (sōō′pər·hī′wā′) *n.* A highway for high-speed traffic, generally with four or more traffic lanes divided by a safety strip.

su·per·hu·man (sōō′pər·hyōō′mən) *adj.* 1 Above the range of human power or skill; above and beyond what is human; miraculous; divine. 2 Beyond normal human ability or power. See synonyms under SUPERNATURAL. — **su′per·hu·man′i·ty** (-hyōō·man′ə·tē) *n.* — **su′per·hu′man·ly** *adv.*

su·per·im·pose (sōō′pər·im·pōz′) *v.t.* **·posed, ·pos·ing** 1 To lay or impose upon something else. 2 To add to something else. — **su′per·im′po·si′tion** (-im′pə·zish′ən) *n.*

su·per·in·cum·bent (sōō′pər·in·kum′bənt) *adj.* Resting or lying upon something else. [<L *superincumbens, -entis,* ppr. of *superincumbere* <*super-* over + *incumbere* rest on. See INCUMBENT.] — **su′per·in·cum′bence** or **·ben·cy** *n.*

su·per·in·duce (sōō′pər·in·dōōs′, -dyōōs′) *v.t.* **·duced, ·duc·ing** To introduce additionally; bring in or cause as an addition. [<LL *superinducere* cover over, add <L *super-* over + *inducere* INDUCE] — **su′per·in·duc′tion** (-duk′·shən) *n.*

su·per·in·tend (sōō′pər·in·tend′) *v.t.* To have the charge and direction of; manage; supervise. [<LL *superintendere* <*super-* over + *intendere* aim at. See INTEND.]

su·per·in·ten·dence (sōō′pər·in·ten′dəns) *n.* Direction and management; guiding and controlling supervision. See synonyms under OVERSIGHT.

su·per·in·ten·den·cy (sōō′pər·in·ten′dən·sē) *n. pl.* **·cies** 1 The office or rank of a superintendent. 2 Superintendence.

su·per·in·ten·dent (sōō′pər·in·ten′dənt) *n.* 1 One whose function is to superintend some particular work, office, or undertaking: a school *superintendent,* road *superintendent.* 2 The person charged with supervising maintenance and repair in an office or apartment building. —*adj.* Of or pertaining to superintendence or a superintendent; superintending. [<LL *superintendens, -entis,* ppr. of *superintendere* superintend]

Synonyms (noun): conductor, curator, custodian, director, guardian, inspector, intendant, manager, master, overseer, superior, supervisor, warden.

su·pe·ri·or (sə·pir′ē·ər, sōō-) *adj.* 1 Surpassing in quantity, quality, or degree; more excellent; preferable; in an absolute sense, of great excellence: a *superior* man. 2 Of higher grade, rank, or dignity. 3 Too great or dignified to be under the influence of something specified; serenely unaffected or indifferent: with *to*: *superior* to envy. 4 Locally higher; more elevated; upper. 5 Situated relatively nearer the top of the head when the body is standing erect: opposed to *inferior.* 6 *Bot.* Situated above or over another organ or part, as an ovary when free from the calyx, or, in an axillary flower, a petal or lip which is the one next to the main axis of the plant. 7 *Printing* Set above the level of the line: said of type; thus, in C^4D^n, 4 and n are *superior.* 8 *Logic* Of wider application; generic: said of terms, conceptions, and propositions. 9 Supercilious; affecting superiority: a *superior* smile. See synonyms under EXCELLENT, PARAMOUNT, PREDOMINANT. —*n.* 1 One who surpasses another in rank or excellence. 2 The ruler of an ecclesiastical order or house, as an abbey, convent, or monastery. 3 *Printing* A superior letter or character. See synonyms under SUPERINTENDENT. [<OF <L, compar. of *superus* on high, above <*super* above] — **su·pe·ri·or·i·ty** (sə·pir′ē·ôr′ə·tē, -or′-, sōō-) *n.* — **su·pe′ri·or·ly** *adv.*

Su·pe·ri·or (sə·pir′ē·ər, sōō-) A port and industrial city in Wisconsin at the western end of Lake Superior.

Superior, Lake The northernmost, westernmost, and largest of the Great Lakes, in the United States and Canada; 31,820 square miles; length, 350 miles; width, 160 miles.

superior court See under COURT.

su·per·ja·cent (sōō′pər·jā′sənt) *adj.* Lying or resting immediately upon or above something else; overlying. [<LL *superjacens, -entis,* ppr. of *superjacere* <*super-* above + *jacere* lie]

su·per·la·tive (sə·pûr′lə·tiv, sōō-) *adj.* 1 Elevated to the highest degree; consummate; of supreme excellence or eminence. 2 *Gram.* Expressing or involving the extreme degree: said of a form of comparison of adjectives or adverbs: The *superlative* degree of "wise" is "wisest." See COMPARISON (def. 2). 3 Excessive. —*n.* 1 That which is of the highest possible excellence or superior to all others. 2 *Gram.* The highest degree of comparison of the adjective or adverb; any word or phrase in the superlative degree. [<OF *superlatif* <LL *superlativus* <L *superlatus* excessive <*super-* above + *latus,* pp. to *ferre* carry] — **su·per′la·tive·ly** *adv.* — **su·per′la·tive·ness** *n.*

su·per·lu·nar (sōō′pər·lōō′nər) *adj.* Being above or beyond the moon; celestial. Also **su′per·lu′na·ry.**

su·per·male (sōō′pər·māl′) *n. Biol.* A supersexual individual having, in the fruit fly, a ratio of 1 X-chromosome to 3 sets of autosomes.

su·per·man (sōō′pər·man′) *n. pl.* **·men** (-men′) 1 A hypothetical superior being, characterized by perfection of physique, capacity for power, and a moral nature beyond good and evil, regarded as the product of evolutionary survival of the fittest; the *Ubermensch* of Nietzsche. 2 An intellectually and morally improved man; a superior man; one possessing superhuman powers. [Trans. of G *übermensch*]

su·per·mar·ket (sōō′pər·mär′kit) *n.* A large store or market selling food and household supplies and operating generally on a self-service, cash-and-carry basis. Also **super market.**

su·per·mo·ron (sōō′pər·môr′on, -mō′ron) *n. Psychiatry* A mentally deficient person ranking above the moron; one only slightly deficient mentally.

su·per·nal (sōō·pûr′nəl) *adj.* 1 Heavenly; celestial. 2 Placed or located above; lofty; overhead; towering. 3 Coming from above or from the sky. [<OF <L *supernus* <*super* over] — **su·per′nal·ly** *adv.*

su·per·na·tant (sōō′pər·nā′tənt) *adj.* 1 Floating uppermost, above something, or on the surface. 2 *Chem.* Denoting a liquid from which a precipitate has been thrown down. [<L *supernatans, -antis* <*super-* above + *natare* swim] — **su′per·na·ta′tion** (-nā·tā′·shən) *n.*

su·per·na·tion·al (sōō′pər·nash′ən·əl) *adj.* Pertaining to all mankind, rather than to one nation only. — **su′per·na′tion·al·ism** *n.* — **su′·per·na′tion·al·ist** *n.*

su·per·nat·u·ral (sōō′pər·nach′ər·əl) *adj.* 1 Existing or occurring through some agency beyond the known forces of nature. 2 Lying outside the sphere of natural law, whether psychic or physical. 3 Believed to be miraculous or caused by the immediate exercise of divine power. 4 Pertaining to the miraculous. —*n.* That which is outside the accepted and known order of nature; that which transcends nature. [<Med. L *supernaturalis* <L *super-* above + *natura* NATURE] — **su′per·nat′u·ral·ly** *adv.* — **su′per·nat′u·ral·ness** *n.*

Synonyms (adj.): miraculous, preternatural, superhuman. The *supernatural* is above or superior to the known powers of nature; the *preternatural* is aside from or beyond what we have been accustomed to regard as the result of natural law, often in the sense of inauspicious; as, a *preternatural* gloom. *Miraculous* is more emphatic and specific than *supernatural,* as referring to the direct personal intervention of divine power. *Miraculous* might be termed "extranatural," rather than *supernatural.* All that is beyond human power is *superhuman*; as, Prophecy gives evidence of *superhuman* knowledge; the word is sometimes applied to remarkable manifestations of human power, surpassing all that is ordinary. *Antonyms*: common, natural, ordinary, usual.

su·per·nat·u·ral·ism (sōō′pər·nach′ər·əl·iz′əm) *n.* 1 The quality of being supernatural. 2 Belief in the supernatural; especially, the doctrine that there is a power not to be identified with nature, but which is the ground of its existences and is manifested in its forces, laws, and events: opposed to *naturalism.* 3 The doctrine of spiritual revelation together with the belief in Providence, the efficacy of prayer, and related doctrines: opposed to *rationalism.* Also spelled *supranaturalism.* — **su′per·nat′u·ral·ist** *adj.* & *n.* — **su′per·nat′u·ral·is′tic** *adj.*

su·per·nor·mal (sōō′pər·nôr′məl) *adj.* 1 *Psychol.* Above the normal in characteristics, properties, or intelligence: a *supernormal* child. 2 Pertaining to or designating phenomena incapable of rigorous scientific explanation but conceivably in accord with still undiscovered natural laws.

su·per·nu·mer·ar·y (sōō′pər·nōō′mə·rer′ē, -nyōō′-) *adj.* 1 Being beyond a fixed or standard number. 2 Beyond a customary or necessary number; superfluous. —*n. pl.* **·ar·ies** 1 A person or thing in excess of the regular, necessary, or customary number. 2 A stage performer, as in mob scenes or processions, without any speaking part: often contracted to *supe* or *super.* [<LL *supernumerarius* a soldier added to a legion after it is complete <L *super numerum* < *super* over + *numerus* a number]

su·per·or·der (sōō′pər·ôr′dər) *n. Biol.* A plant or animal division intermediate between a class and an order.

su·per·pa·tri·ot (sōō′pər·pā′trē·ət, -ot) *n.* A person who is or claims to be a great patriot, often one whose patriotic fervor is marked by a readiness to regard dissent as unpatriotic or subversive. —**su′per·pa′tri·ot′ic** *adj.* —**su′per·pa′tri·ot·ism** *n.*

su·per·phos·phate (sōō′pər·fos′fāt) *n. Chem.* 1 An acid phosphate. 2 Any fertilizing material mostly consisting of soluble phosphates: *superphosphate* of lime.

su·per·phys·i·cal (sōō′pər·fiz′i·kəl) *adj.* Beyond or above the physical.

su·per·pose (sōō′pər·pōz′) *v.t.* **·posed, ·pos·ing** 1 To lay over or upon something else, as one layer upon another. 2 *Geom.* To suppose (one figure) to be placed upon another so that all like parts coincide. Compare SUPERIMPOSE. 3 *Physics* To combine additively, as forces or wave amplitudes. [<F *superposer* < *super-* over + *poser* POSE¹] —**su′per·pos′a·ble** *adj.* —**su′per·po·si′tion** (-pə·zish′ən) *n.*

su·per·pow·er (sōō′pər·pou′ər) *n.* One of a few great, dominant nations characterized by superior economic or military strength and by large population.

su·per·pres·sure (sōō′pər·presh′ər) *n.* 1 Excessive pressure under given conditions. 2 *Aeron.* The amount by which the pressure within the gas cell of a dirigible exceeds atmospheric pressure.

su·per–roy·al (sōō′pər·roi′əl) *n.* A size of ledger paper, 20 by 28 inches.

su·per·sat·u·rate (sōō′pər·sach′ŏŏ·rāt) *v.t.* **·rat·ed, ·rat·ing** 1 To saturate to excess or beyond the normal point. 2 To cause (a solution) to contain more of a dissolved substance than can be held under normal conditions of temperature. —**su′per·sat′u·ra′tion** *n.*

su·per·scribe (sōō′pər·skrīb′) *v.t.* **·scribed, ·scrib·ing** To write or engrave on the outside or on the upper part of; inscribe with a name or address; specifically, to address, as a letter. [<LL *superscribere* <L *super-* over + *scribere* write]

su·per·script (sōō′pər·skript′) *adj.* Written above or overhead: opposed to *subscript.* —*n.* 1 Superscription. 2 *Math.* An index or other mark following and above a letter or figure, as a^3, c'. [<LL *superscriptus,* pp. of *superscribere* SUPERSCRIBE]

su·per·scrip·tion (sōō′pər·skrip′shən) *n.* 1 The act of superscribing an address on a letter. 2 An upper or outer inscription, as a title or a direction; especially, an address on a letter. 3 That portion of a medical prescription that begins with the word *recipe* (generally abbreviated ℞, and meaning "take"). [<OF <LL *superscriptio, -onis* < *superscribere.* See SUPERSCRIBE.]

su·per·sede (sōō′pər·sēd′) *v.t.* **·sed·ed, ·sed·ing** 1 To take the place of, as by reason of superior worth, right, or appropriateness; replace; supplant. 2 To put something in the place of; set aside; suspend; annul. See synonyms under SUBVERT. [<OF *superceder* <L *supersedere* sit over, forbear < *super-* above + *sedere* sit] —**su′per·sed′er** *n.* —**su′per·se′dure** (-sē′jər), **su′per·ses′sion** (-sesh′ən) *n.*

su·per·se·de·as (sōō′pər·sē′dē·əs) *n. Law* A proceeding, as a writ, that operates to supersede or check proceedings. [<L, you shall desist]

su·per·sen·si·ble (sōō′pər·sen′sə·bəl) *adj.* Being above or beyond the range of the senses; supersensual; psychical. —**su′per·sen′si·bly** *adv.*

su·per·sen·su·al (sōō′pər·sen′shōō·əl) *adj.* 1 Being above the senses; supersensible. 2 Spiritual; ideal. Also **su′per·sen′so·ry** (-sen′sər·ē).

su·per·ser·vice·a·ble (sōō′pər·sûr′vis·ə·bəl) *adj.* Trying needlessly or disagreeably to be of service; officious. —**su′per·ser′vice·a·bly** *adv.*

su·per·sex (sōō′pər·seks′) *n. Biol.* A sterile organism having a mixture of male and female characteristics due to a disturbed ratio of autosomes to X–chromosomes, as in the fruit fly. —**su′per·sex′u·al** (-sek′shōō·əl) *adj.*

su·per·son·ic (sōō′pər·son′ik) *adj. Aeron.* Of, pertaining to, or characterized by a speed greater than that of sound: distinguished from *ultrasonic.*

su·per·son·ics (sōō′pər·son′iks) *n. pl. (construed as singular)* The science which treats of the phenomena of supersonic speed, with especial reference to their practical applications to aircraft, guided missiles, rockets, etc.: distinguished from *ultrasonics.*

su·per·star (sōō′pər·stär′) *n.* A public performer, as an actor, singer, or professional athlete, regarded as one of the best or most popular. —**su′per·star′dom** *n.*

su·per·state (sōō′pər·stāt′) *n.* A state established as the governing power of a union or federation of subordinate states.

su·per·sti·tion (sōō′pər·stish′ən) *n.* 1 A belief founded on irrational feelings, especially of fear, and marked by credulity; also, any rite or practice inspired by such belief. 2 Specifically, a belief in a religious system regarded (by others than the believer) as without reasonable support; also, any of its rites. 3 Credulity regarding or reverence for the occult or supernatural, as belief in omens, charms, and signs; loosely, any unreasoning or unreasonable belief or impression. 4 *Obs.* Undue scrupulousness. See synonyms under FANATICISM. [<OF <L *superstitio, -onis* excessive fear of the gods, amazement, dread < *superstare* < *super-* over + *stare* stand still]

su·per·sti·tious (sōō′pər·stish′əs) *adj.* 1 Disposed to believe in or be influenced by superstitions. 2 Of, pertaining to, or manifesting superstition. —**su′per·sti′tious·ly** *adv.* —**su′per·sti′tious·ness** *n.*

su·per·stra·tum (sōō′pər·strā′təm, -strat′əm) *n. pl.* **·stra·ta** (-strā′tə, -strat′ə) A layer superimposed upon another; a superficial stratum.

su·per·struct (sōō′pər·strukt′) *v.t.* To build or erect upon a foundation.

su·per·struc·ture (sōō′pər·struk′chər) *n.* 1 Any structure or any part of a structure above the basement or considered in relation to its foundation. 2 The sleepers, rails, etc., of a railway, as distinguished from the roadbed. 3 *Naut.* The parts of a ship's structure, especially of a warship, above the main deck. Compare SUBSTRUCTURE.

su·per·sub·tle (sōō′pər·sut′l) *adj.* Extremely subtle; oversubtle.

su·per·tank·er (sōō′pər·tangk′ər) *n.* A very large tanker capable of carrying a vast cargo, as of oil.

su·per·tax (sōō′pər·taks′) *n.* An extra tax in addition to the normal tax; especially, a graded additional tax on incomes above certain amounts; a surtax.

su·per·ton·ic (sōō′pər·ton′ik) *n. Music* The tone above the tonic or keynote; the second.

su·per·vene (sōō′pər·vēn′) *v.i.* **·vened, ·ven·ing** 1 To follow closely upon something; come as something extraneous or additional. 2 To take place; happen. See synonyms under HAPPEN. [<L *supervenire* < *super-* over and above + *venire* come] —**su′per·ven′ient** (-vēn′yənt) *adj.* —**su′per·ven′tion** (-ven′shən) *n.*

su·per·vise (sōō′pər·vīz) *v.t.* **·vised, ·vis·ing** To have a general oversight of; superintend; oversee. [<Med. L *supervisus,* pp. of *supervidere* <L *super-* over + *videre* see]

su·per·vi·sion (sōō′pər·vizh′ən) *n.* 1 The act of supervising; superintendence. 2 The authority to direct or supervise.

su·per·vi·sor (sōō′pər·vī′zər) *n.* 1 One who supervises or oversees; a superintendent; an inspector. 2 *U.S.* A township officer in administrative charge of its business; one of a board of such officers constituting a body having charge of the business of a county; a borough officer who has charge of road repairs, etc. 3 A person supervising teachers of special subjects in a school. 4 *Obs.* A beholder. —**su′per·vi′sor·ship** *n.* —**su′per·vi′so·ry** (-zər·ē) *adj.*

su·pi·nate (sōō′pə·nāt) *v.t.* & *v.i.* **·nat·ed, ·nat·ing** 1 To make or become supine. 2 To turn, as the hand or forelimb, so that the palm is upward or forward. [<L *supinatus,* pp. of *supinare* throw (someone) on the back < *supinus* SUPINE]

su·pi·na·tion (sōō′pə·nā′shən) *n. Physiol.* 1 The act of turning the palm of the hand, or the corresponding surface of the forelimb, upward. 2 The position of a limb so turned: opposed to *pronation.* 3 The act or state of lying supine.

su·pi·na·tor (sōō′pə·nā′tər) *n. Anat.* A muscle of the forearm by which supination is effected.

su·pine¹ (sōō·pīn′) *adj.* 1 Lying on the back, or with the face turned upward. 2 Having no interest or care; inactive; indolent; negligent; indifferent; listless. 3 Having an inclined position; sloping, as a hill. [<L *supinus* < *sup-,* root of *super* above] —**su·pine′ly** *adv.* —**su·pine′ness** *n.*

su·pine² (sōō′pīn) *n.* In Latin grammar, one of two parts of the verb, generally regarded as verbal nouns. The **first** or **former supine,** an accusative form in *-um,* is used after verbs of motion to express purpose, as in *Processit libatum* He went forth to sacrifice; the **second** or **latter supine,** an ablative form in *-u,* is used for specification, as in *Mirabile dictu!* Wonderful to relate! [<L *supinum (verbum)* (a) supine (word), neut. of *supinus* SUPINE¹]

sup·per (sup′ər) *n.* The last meal of the day: frequently used of an evening banquet. [<OF *soper, super* sup, dine] —**sup′per·less** *adj.*

sup·plant (sə·plant′, -plänt′) *v.t.* 1 To take the place of; displace. 2 To take the place of (someone) by scheming, treachery, etc. 3 To replace (one thing) with another; remove; uproot. See synonyms under ABOLISH, SUBVERT. [<OF *supplanter* <L *supplantare* trip up < *sub-* up from below + *planta* the sole of the foot] —**sup·plan·ta·tion** (sup′lan·tā′shən) *n.* —**sup·plant′er** *n.*

sup·ple (sup′əl) *adj.* 1 Easily bent; flexible; pliant: a *supple* bow. 2 Yielding to the humor or wishes of others; especially, servilely compliant; obsequious. 3 Of the mind, showing adaptability; elastic; easily changing. —*v.t.* & *v.i.* **·pled, ·pling** To make or become supple. [<OF *supple, sople* <L *supplex, -icis* submissive, lit., bending under < *sub-* under + stem of *plicare* fold] —**sup′ple·ly** *adv.* —**sup′ple·ness** *n.*

Synonyms (adj.): compliant, elastic, fawning, flexible, limber, lissom, lithe, lithesome, obsequious, pliable, pliant, soft, submissive, willowy, yielding. See ACTIVE, OBSEQUIOUS. *Antonyms*: firm, fixed, inflexible, obstinate, pertinacious, rigid, stiff, stubborn, unbending, unyielding.

sup·ple·jack (sup′əl·jak) *n.* 1 Any of various woody climbers with tough and lithe stems; specifically, a high–climbing vine (genus *Berchemia*) of the southern United States. 2 A walking stick made from the wood of such a plant.

sup·ple·ment (sup′lə·ment) *v.t.* To make additions to; provide for what is lacking in. —*n.* (-mənt) 1 Something added that supplies a deficiency; especially, an addition to a publication. 2 A supplementary angle. See synonyms under APPENDAGE. [<L *supplementum* < *supplere* SUPPLY¹]

sup·ple·men·tal (sup′lə·men′təl) *adj.* Like a supplement; supplementing; additional. Also **sup·ple·to·ry** (sup′lə·tôr′ē, -tō′rē).

sup·ple·men·ta·ry (sup′lə·men′tər·ē) *adj.* Supplemental.

supplementary angle See under ANGLE.

sup·pli·ance (sup′lē·əns) *n.* The act of supplicating; an urgent petition or prayer.

sup·pli·ant (sup′lē·ənt) *adj.* 1 Entreating earnestly and humbly; beseeching. 2 Manifesting entreaty or submissive supplication. —*n.* One who supplicates. [<MF, ppr. of *supplier* <L *supplicare* SUPPLICATE] —**sup′pli·ant·ly** *adv.* —**sup′pli·ant·ness** *n.*

sup·pli·cant (sup′lə·kənt) *n.* One who supplicates; a suppliant. —*adj.* Asking or entreating humbly; beseeching. [<L *supplicans, -antis,* ppr. of *supplicare* SUPPLICATE]

sup·pli·cate (sup′lə·kāt) *v.* **·cat·ed, ·cat·ing** *v.t.* 1 To ask for humbly or by earnest prayer. 2 To beg something of; entreat. —*v.i.* 3 To beg or pray humbly; make an earnest request. See synonyms under ASK, PRAY. [<L *supplicatus,* pp. of *supplicare* supplicate < *sub-* under + *plicare* bend, fold] —**sup′pli·ca′tion** *n.* —**sup′pli·ca·to′ry** (-kə·tôr′ē, -tō′rē) *adj.*

sup·ply¹ (sə·plī′) *v.* **·plied, ·ply·ing** *v.t.* 1 To give or furnish (something needful or desirable):

to *supply* milk for a city. **2** To furnish with what is needed: to *supply* an army with ammunition. **3** To provide for adequately; satisfy: to *supply* a demand. **4** To make up for; make good or compensate for, as a loss or deficiency. **5** To fill (the place of another); also, to fill (an office, etc.) or occupy (a pulpit) as a substitute. — *v.i.* **6** To take the place of another temporarily. See synonyms under ACCOMMODATE, GIVE, PROVIDE. — *n. pl.* **·plies** **1** That which is or can be supplied; the available aggregate of things needed or demanded. **2** The amount of a commodity offered at a given price or available for meeting a demand. **3** Accumulated stores reserved for distribution, as for an army or a fleet: usually in the plural: He was cut off from his base of *supplies.* **4** A grant of money to the crown or for the public service; appropriation: usually in the plural. **5** An amount sufficient for a given use; store or quantity on hand. **6** A substitute or temporary incumbent. **7** *Obs.* Reinforcements. **8** The act of supplying. See synonyms under STOCK. [<OF *sopleer, soupleier* <L *supplere* <*sub-* up from under + *ple-,* root of *plenus* full] — **sup·pli′er** *n.*

sup·ply[2] (sup′lē) *adv.* In a supple manner; supplely. [<SUPPLE]

sup·port (sə·pôrt′, -pōrt′) *v.t.* **1** To bear the weight of, especially from underneath; hold in position; keep from falling, sinking, etc. **2** To bear or sustain (weight, etc.). **3** To keep (a person, the mind, etc.) from failing or declining; strengthen. **4** To serve to uphold or corroborate (a statement, theory, etc.); substantiate; verify. **5** To provide (a person, institution, etc.) with maintenance; provide for. **6** To give approval or assistance to; uphold; advocate; aid. **7** To endure or tolerate: I cannot *support* his insolence. **8** To carry on; keep up; maintain: to *support* a war. **9** In the theater: **a** To act (a role or part). **b** To act in a subordinate role to. — *n.* **1** The act of supporting. **2** One who or that which supports. **3** Subsistence. See synonyms under SUBSIDY. [<OF *supporter* <L *supportare* convey <*sub-* up from under + *portare* carry] — **sup·por′tive** *adj.*

Synonyms (verb): bear, carry, maintain, prop, sustain, uphold. *Support* and *sustain* alike signify to hold up or keep up, to prevent from falling or sinking; but *sustain* has a special sense of continuous exertion or strength, as when we speak of *sustained* endeavor or a *sustained* note; a flower is *supported* by the stem or a temple roof by arches; the foundations of a great building *sustain* an enormous pressure; to *sustain* life implies a greater exigency and need than to *support* life; to say one is *sustained* under affliction emphasizes the severity of the trial and the completeness of the *upholding* more than if we say he is *supported.* To *bear* is the most general word, denoting all holding up or keeping up of any object, whether in rest or motion; it refers to something that is a tax upon strength or endurance; as, to *bear* a strain; to *bear* pain or grief. To *maintain* is to keep in a state or condition, especially in an excellent and desirable condition; as, to *maintain* health, reputation, position, etc. *Maintain* is a word of more dignity than *support;* a man *supports* his family; a state *maintains* an army or navy. To *prop* is always partial, signifying to add support to something that is insecure. See ABET, AID, ENDURE, KEEP, LEAN, PROP. *Antonyms*: abandon, betray, demolish, desert, destroy, drop, overthrow, wreck.

sup·port·a·ble (sə·pôr′tə·bəl, -pōr′-) *adj.* That may be supported or borne; bearable; endurable. — **sup·port′a·ble·ness, sup·port′a·bil′i·ty** *n.* — **sup·port′a·bly** *adv.*

sup·port·er (sə·pôr′tər, -pōr′-) *n.* **1** One who or that which supports, in any sense. **2** One who countenances or supports; an adherent. **3** *Her.* One of a pair representing living objects, standing on the dexter and sinister sides of a shield, as if supporting it. **4** An elastic or other support for some part of the body.

SUPPORTER (*def. 3*)

sup·pos·a·ble (sə·pō′zə·bəl) *adj.* That may be supposed. — **sup·pos′a·ble·ness** *n.* — **sup·pos′a·bly** *adv.*

sup·pos·al (sə·pō′zəl) *n.* The act or an instance of supposing; supposition.

sup·pose (sə·pōz′) *v.* **·posed, ·pos·ing** *v.t.* **1** To think or imagine to oneself as true; believe or believe probable; think; presume. **2** To assume as true for the sake of argument or illustration. **3** To require to exist as true; imply as cause or consequence; involve as an inference: Design in creation *supposes* the existence of a God. **4** To expect: I am *supposed* to follow. **5** To presuppose; assume. — *v.i.* **6** To make a supposition. [<OF *suposer* <*sup-* under (<L *sub-*) + *poser* POSE[1]] — **sup·pos′er** *n.*

Synonyms: conjecture, deem, guess, imagine, surmise, think. To *suppose* is temporarily to assume a thing as true, either with the expectation of finding it so or for the purpose of ascertaining what would follow if it were so. To *conjecture* is to put together the nearest available materials for a provisional opinion, always with some expectation of finding the facts to be as *conjectured.* To *imagine* is to form a mental image of something as existing, while its actual existence may be unknown, or even impossible. To *think,* in this application, is to hold as the result of thought what is admitted not to be matter of exact or certain knowledge; as, I do not know, but I *think* this to be the fact: a more conclusive statement than would be made by the use of *conjecture* or *suppose.* See GUESS. *Antonyms*: ascertain, conclude, discover, know, prove.

sup·posed (sə·pōzd′) *adj.* Accepted as genuine; believed; often, falsely imagined. — **sup·pos·ed·ly** (sə·pō′zid·lē) *adv.*

sup·po·si·tion (sup′ə·zish′ən) *n.* **1** The act of supposing, or that which is supposed; conjecture. **2** A hypothetical proposition made for the purpose of explaining certain facts, relating them, or of deducing consequences from them; hypothesis. See synonyms under FANCY, GUESS, HYPOTHESIS, IDEA, THOUGHT. [<Med. L *suppositio, -onis* <L, a substitute <*suppositus,* pp. of *supponere* suppose, substitute <*sub-* under + *ponere* place] — **sup′po·si′tion·al** *adj.* — **sup′po·si′tion·al·ly** *adv.*

sup·po·si·tious (sup′ə·zish′əs) *adj.* Supposed or assumed; hypothetical; also, imaginary.

sup·pos·i·ti·tious (sə·poz′ə·tish′əs) *adj.* Put in the place of or made to represent, in order to deceive or defraud; spurious. See synonyms under COUNTERFEIT. [<L *suppositus.* See SUPPOSITION.] — **sup·pos′i·ti′tious·ly** *adv.* — **sup·pos′i·ti′tious·ness** *n.*

sup·pos·i·tive (sə·poz′ə·tiv) *adj.* Including or implying supposition; supposed. — *n.* A conjunction introducing a supposition, as *if,* or *provided.* — **sup·pos′i·tive·ly** *adv.*

sup·pos·i·to·ry (sə·poz′ə·tôr′ē, -tō′rē) *n. pl.* **·ries** *Med.* A solid, readily fusible, medicated preparation for introduction into some canal, cavity, or internal organ. [<LL *suppositorium,* orig. neut. sing. of *suppositorius* placed underneath or up <L *suppositus.* See SUPPOSITION.]

sup·press (sə·pres′) *v.t.* **1** To put an end or stop to; quell; crush, as a rebellion. **2** To stop or prohibit the activities of, as a rival political group; abolish. **3** To withhold from knowledge or publication, as a book, news, etc. **4** To repress, as a groan or sigh. **5** To stop (a hemorrhage, etc.). See synonyms under ABOLISH, HIDE, REPRESS, RESTRAIN, SUBDUE. [<L *suppressus,* pp. of *supprimere* <*sub-* under + *premere* press] — **sup·press′er, sup·pres′sor** *n.* — **sup·press′i·ble** *adj.*

sup·pres·sion (sə·presh′ən) *n.* **1** The act of suppressing, or the state of being suppressed. **2** *Psychoanal.* The deliberate exclusion from consciousness and action of ideas, memories, or emotions, especially those regarded as unpleasant or as socially unacceptable.

sup·pres·sive (sə·pres′iv) *adj.* Tending to suppress.

sup·pu·rate (sup′yə·rāt) *v.i.* **·rat·ed, ·rat·ing** To form or generate pus; maturate. [<L *suppuratus,* pp. of *suppurare* <*sub-* under + *pus, puris* pus]

sup·pu·ra·tion (sup′yə·rā′shən) *n.* **1** The act or process of suppurating. **2** Pus.

sup·pu·ra·tive (sup′yə·rā′tiv) *adj.* Tending to or producing suppuration. — *n.* A remedy promoting suppuration.

supra– *prefix* Above; beyond: *supraliminal.* Used to form adjectives and often the equivalent of *super–* which is preferred in general words. [<L *supra-* <*supra* above, beyond]
In anatomical and zoological terms *supra–* means above in position, on the dorsal side of; as in:

supra–abdominal **suprahepatic** **supranasal**
supra–auditory **supralabial** **supra–ocular**
supracaudal **supramaxillary** **supraspinal**

su·pra·lap·sar·i·an (so͞o′prə·lap·sâr′ē·ən) *n.* A high Calvinist or holder of the doctrine that predestination preceded creation and the fall of man in the divine order of decrees. See INFRALAPSARIAN. [<NL *supralapsarius* <L *supra-* before + *lapsus* a fall] — **su′pra·lap·sar′i·an·ism** *n.*

su·pra·lim·i·nal (so͞o′prə·lim′ə·nəl) *adj. Psychol.* Above the threshold of normal consciousness or sensation: opposed to *subliminal.*

su·pra·mo·lec·u·lar (so͞o′prə·mə·lek′yə·lər) *adj.* **1** Containing more than one molecule. **2** Of greater complexity than a molecule.

su·pra·mun·dane (so͞o′prə·mun′dān, -mun·dān′) *adj.* Being or placed beyond, or superior to, the world; supernatural; celestial.

su·pra·na·tion·al (so͞o′prə·nash′ə·nəl) *adj.* Of or concerning several or a number of nations; involving more than one nation. — **su′pra·na′tion·al·ism** *n.*

su·pra·nat·u·ral·ism (so͞o′prə·nach′ər·əl·iz′əm) See SUPERNATURALISM.

su·pra·or·bi·tal (so͞o′prə·ôr′bi·təl) *adj. Anat.* Situated above the orbit of the eye. [<NL *supraorbitalis* <L *supra-* above + *orbita* ORBIT]

su·pra·pro·test (so͞o′prə·prō′test) *n. Law* Acceptance or payment of a bill of exchange by one not a party to it after protest for non-acceptance or non-payment. [<Ital. *sopra protesta* upon protest <*sopra* (<L *supra* above) + *protesta* <L *protestari* PROTEST]

su·pra·re·nal (so͞o′prə·rē′nəl) *Anat. adj.* Situated above the kidneys, or pertaining to the ductless glands above the kidneys. — *n.* A suprarenal gland.

suprarenal gland *Anat.* A ductless gland lying outside the upper or anterior part of either kidney in most vertebrates: also called *adrenal gland.*

su·pra·ren·a·lin (so͞o′prə·ren′ə·lin) *n.* Epinephrine. [<SUPRARENAL + -IN]

su·pra·ster·ol (so͞o′prə·ster′ōl, -ol) *n. Biochem.* One of two inactive sterols produced as end products by the ultraviolet irradiation of ergosterol. [<SUPRA- + STEROL]

su·pra·tem·po·ral (so͞o′prə·tem′pər·əl) *Anat. adj.* Situated in the upper part of the temporal bone or region. — *n.* A supratemporal bone.

su·prem·a·cy (sə·prem′ə·sē, so͞o-) *n. pl.* **·cies** The state of being supreme; supreme power or authority. See synonyms under PRECEDENCE, VICTORY. — **royal supremacy** The judicial and executive supremacy of a sovereign as the head of the Christian church within his realm: used especially of English sovereigns.

su·preme (sə·prēm′, so͞o-) *adj.* **1** Highest in power or authority; dominant. **2** Highest in degree, importance, or estimation; most extreme or momentous; utmost: *supreme* devotion. **3** Ultimate; last and greatest. See synonyms under ABSOLUTE, FIRST, IMPERIAL, PARAMOUNT, PREDOMINANT. — **the Supreme Being** God; the Deity. — *n.* **1** The supreme or highest point; acme. **2** One who is above the rest; a superior; chief. [<L *supremus* highest, superl. of *superus* that is above <*super* above] — **su·preme′ly** *adv.* — **su·preme′ness** *n.*

su·prême (sü·prem′) *n. French* **1** An especially choice portion of breast of fowl, fish, etc.: a culinary term. **2** A rich cream sauce.

Supreme Bench The United States Supreme Court.

Supreme Court See under COURT.

supreme sacrifice The sacrifice of one's life.

Supreme Soviet The Russian Congress consisting of two legislative chambers, the Soviet (Council) of the Union and the Soviet (Council) of Nationalities, which have equal rights and whose members are elected for a period of four years.

Supreme War Council An international body with headquarters at Versailles, composed of representatives of the Entente nations, of their allies, and of the United States, established at the end of World War I, to determine the terms of peace. This was accomplished by the signing of the Treaty of Versailles, June 28, 1919.

Sur (sŏŏr, sür) A port of SW Lebanon, on the Mediterranean; site of ancient Tyre: also *Tyre. Arabic* **El Sur.**

sur-[1] *prefix* A form of the Latin *super-* found in words which came into English through Old French. [<OF *sur-* <L *super-* SUPER-]

sur-[2] Assimilated var. of SUB-.

su·ra (sŏŏr′ə) *n.* A chapter or section of the Koran. [<Arabic *sūrah,* lit., a step, degree]

Su·ra·ba·ya (sŏŏ′rä·bä′yä) A port and industrial city of NE Java: Dutch *Soerabaja.* Also **Su′ra·ba′ja.**

su·rah (sŏŏr′ə) *n.* A soft, usually twilled, silk fabric, used for women's wear, ties, etc.: now sometimes mixed with rayon. Also **surah silk.** [from *Surat,* India]

Su·ra·jah Dow·lah (sə·rä′jə dou′lə), 1728?–1757, nawab of Bengal; executed by the British. Also *Siraj-ud-daula.*

Su·ra·kar·ta (sŏŏr′ə·kär′tə) Former name for SOLO.

su·ral (sŏŏr′əl) *adj. Anat.* Of or pertaining to the calf of the leg. [<NL *suralis* <L *sura* the calf of the leg]

sur·ance (sŏŏr′əns, shŏŏr′-) *n. Obs.* Assurance. [<OF < *sur* SURE; infl. in meaning by ASSURANCE]

Su·rat (sŏŏ·rat′, sŏŏ′rət) A port on the Gulf of Cambay, northern Bombay State, India; the first British settlement in India, 1612.

sur·base (sûr′bās′) *n. Archit.* A molding or border above the dado and base of a pedestal or above the baseboard of a room. [<SUR-[1] + BASE[1]]

sur·based (sûr′bāst′) *adj. Archit.* **1** Having a surbase, as a pedestal. **2** Flattened; depressed. **3** Having the rise of the curve less than half the span: a *surbased* arch.

sur·cease (sûr·sēs′, sûr′sēs) *n.* Absolute cessation; end. —*v.t.* & *v.i.* **·ceased, ·ceas·ing** To cease entirely or finally; end. [<AF *sursise* omission, orig. pp. of *surseoir* refrain <L *supersedere* SUPERSEDE]

sur·charge (sûr′chärj′) *n.* **1** An excessive burden, load, or charge. **2** In chancery law, the showing of an omission of items in an account for which credit ought to be allowed: opposed to *falsification.* **3** An additional or excessive amount charged, especially an unlawful charge; an overcharge. **4** A new valuation or something additional printed on a postage or revenue stamp; also, a stamp so imprinted. —*v.t.* (sûr·chärj′) **·charged, ·charg·ing 1** To charge (a person) too much; overcharge. **2** To show an omission of credits in (an account), or of something for which credit should have been allowed. **3** To overload. **4** To fill to excess. **5** To imprint a surcharge on (postage stamps). [<F < *surcharger* < *sur-* over + *charger* <OF *chargier* CHARGE] —**sur·charg′er** *n.*

sur·cin·gle (sûr′sing·gəl) *n.* **1** A girth or strap encircling the body of a beast of burden, for holding a saddle, etc. **2** A girdle, as of a cassock. —*v.t.* **·gled, ·gling** To gird or fasten with a surcingle. [<OF *surcengle* < *sur-* over + L *cingulum* a belt]

sur·coat (sûr′kōt′) *n.* An outer coat or garment; in the Middle Ages, a loose robe or cloaklike garment worn over armor. [<OF *surcot* < *sur-* over + *cot, cote* a coat]

sur·cu·lose (sûr′kyə·lōs) *adj. Bot.* Producing or having suckers: said of plants. [<L *surculosus* < *surculus* a twig, sucker, dim. of *surus* a twig]

surd (sûrd) *n.* **1** *Math.* An irrational number or quantity, especially an indicated root that can only be approximated, as $\sqrt{2}$. **2** *Phonet.* A speech sound made without vibration of the vocal cords. —*adj.* **1** *Math.* Incapable of being expressed in rational numbers; irrational. **2** *Phonet.* Voiceless: opposed to *sonant, voiced.* [<L *surdus* deaf, silent]

sure (shŏŏr) *adj.* **1** Not liable to change or failure; firm; unyielding; stable; infallible. **2** Fit, proper, or deserving to be depended on; reliable; trustworthy. **3** Free from doubt; certain; positive. **4** Certain of obtaining, attaining, or retaining something: with *of.* **5** Safe; secure from danger or harm. **6** Bound to happen. —*adv. Colloq.* Surely; certainly. —**to be sure** Indeed; certainly. —**to make sure** To make certain; secure. [<OF *sur* <L *securus.* Doublet of SECURE.] —**sure′ness** *n.*

Synonyms (adj.): actual, assured, aware, certain, clear, confident, indisputable, positive, real. See AUTHENTIC, FAITHFUL, SECURE.

sure-e·nough (shŏŏr′i·nuf′) *U.S. Colloq. adj.* Real; genuine. —*adv.* Really; surely.

sure-fire (shŏŏr′fīr′) *adj. Colloq.* Reliable; sure or certain to succeed, win, or come out as expected.

sure-foot·ed (shŏŏr′fŏŏt′id) *adj.* Not liable to fall or stumble; figuratively, not liable to err.

sure·ly (shŏŏr′lē) *adv.* **1** Without doubt; certainly. **2** Securely; safely.

sure thing A certainty; any project or undertaking bound to succeed.

sure·ty (shŏŏr′tē, shŏŏr′ə·tē) *n. pl.* **·ties 1** A person who engages to be responsible for the debt, default, or miscarriage of another; bail. **2** An individual or corporation that, in consideration of the payment of a premium, acts as security for a principal (as a State, city, bank, etc.), against possible loss through the act of an associate or employee who is required to furnish such security. **3** A pledge of money deposited, or of credit given, to secure against loss or damage; security for payment or performance. **4** That which gives security or confidence; ground or basis of certainty or security. **5** The state of being sure; sureness; security; safety; certainty. **6** A sponsor. See synonyms under CERTAINTY, SECURITY. [<OF *surte* <L *securitas, -atis* < *securus* SECURE] —**sure′ty·ship** *n.*

surf (sûrf) *n.* **1** The swell of the sea that breaks upon a shore. **2** The foam caused by the billows. —*v.i.* To ride the surf on a surfboard; engage in surfing. ◆ Homophone: *serf.* [Earlier *suff,* ? var. of SOUGH] —**surf′y** *adj.*

sur·face (sûr′fis) *n.* **1** The exterior part or face of anything that has length, breadth, and thickness. **2** That which has length and breadth, but not thickness; a superficies. **3** A superficial aspect; external view or appearance. **4** That portion of the side of a fortification which is bounded by the angle of the nearest bastion and the prolongation of the flank. —*v.* **·faced, ·fac·ing** *v.t.* **1** To put a surface on; especially, to make smooth, even, or plain. —*v.i.* **2** To mine at or near the surface. **3** To rise to the surface, as a submarine. [<F < *sur-* above + *face* FACE] —**sur′fac·er** *n.*

sur·face-ac·tive (sûr′fis·ak′tiv) *adj. Chem.* Pertaining to or denoting any of a class of substances which have the property of reducing the surface tension of a liquid in which they are dissolved: said especially of detergents.

surface boat A sink boat.

surface mail Mail sent by land or sea rather than by air.

surface noise The mechanical noise produced by friction of the needle against the granular surface of a phonograph record.

surface plate *Mech.* A plate having a very accurate surface: used for testing other surfaces.

surface tension *Physics* That property of a liquid by virtue of which the surface molecules exhibit a strong inward attraction, thus forming an elastic skin which tends to contract to the minimum area.

sur·fac·tant (sûr·fak′tənt) *n. Chem.* A surface-active agent or a solute which tends to reduce the surface tension of the solvent, as a soap or detergent. [<SURF(ACE)–ACT(IVE) + -ANT]

surf·bird (sûrf′bûrd′) *n.* A ploverlike bird *(Aphriza virgata)* of the Pacific coast of America from Alaska to Chile.

surf·board (sûrf′bôrd′, -bōrd′) *n.* A long, narrow board used in surfing. Compare AQUAPLANE.

surf·boat (sûrf′bōt′) *n.* A boat of extra strength and buoyancy, for launching and landing through surf. —**surf′boat′man** (-mən) *n.*

surf duck One of various scoters or sea ducks, especially the surf scoter. Also **surf coot.**

sur·feit (sûr′fit) *v.t.* **1** To feed to fullness or satiety; overfeed. **2** To supply to satiety. —*v.i.* **3** To partake of food or drink to excess; overeat. **4** To overindulge. See synonyms under SATISFY. —*n.* **1** The act of surfeiting oneself; excess in eating or drinking; also, the excessive quantity partaken of. **2** The result of such excess; satiety; superfluity. **3** The state of being surfeited; oppressive fullness of the system caused by excess in eating or drinking. [<OF *sorfait* < *surfaire* overdo < *sur-* above + *faire* make <L *facere*]

surf·er (sûrf′ər) *n.* One who engages or is adept in the sport of surfing. Also **surf·rid·er** (sûrf′rī′dər).

surf fish Any of a family *(Embiotocidae)* of viviparous sea fishes, perchlike in form, numerous near shore all along the northern Pacific coast of North America.

sur·fi·cial (sûr·fish′əl) *adj. Geol.* Originally belonging to or being on the surface, as of the earth: contrasted with *subterranean.* [< SURFACE]

surf·ing (sûrf′ing) *n.* A water sport in which a person standing on a surfboard is borne by the surf toward the shore. Also **surf·rid·ing** (sûrf′rī′ding).

surf scoter A North American scoter *(Melanitta perspicillata).* The adult male is black with a white spot on the forehead and the nape. Also **surf′er.**

surge (sûrj) *v.* **surged, surg·ing** *v.i.* **1** To rise high and roll onward, as waves; swell or heave. **2** To move or go in a manner suggestive of this: The mob *surged* through the square. **3** To increase or vary suddenly, as an electric current. **4** To slip, as a rope on a windlass. —*v.t.* **5** To cause to move in surges. **6** To let go suddenly, as a rope or cable. —*n.* **1** A large swelling wave; billow; also, such billows collectively. **2** The act of surging; a heaving and rolling motion, as of great waves. **3** *Naut.* The tapered drum of a capstan or windlass around which the rope surges. **4** *Electr.* A sudden fluctuation of voltage due to lightning, switching, etc. See synonyms under WAVE. ◆ Homophone: *serge.* [<OF *sourge-,* stem of *sourdre* rise <L *surgere*] —**surg′er** *n.* —**surg′y** *adj.*

sur·geon (sûr′jən) *n.* **1** One who practices surgery. **2** A medical officer in the military or naval service; a ship's doctor. **3** A surgeon fish. [<AF *surgien,* var. of OF *cirugien.* See CHIRURGEON.]

sur·geon·cy (sûr′jən·sē) *n. pl.* **·cies** The office, duties, or rank of a surgeon.

surgeon fish A West Indian fish *(Teuthis hepatus)* having erectile lancetlike spines at the sides of the tail.

Surgeon General **1** Chief officer of the Medical Department in the United States Army or Navy. **2** Chief medical officer of the United States Public Health Service.

surgeon's knot A knot used in tying ligatures, stitching up wounds, etc. See illustration under KNOT.

sur·ger·y (sûr′jər·ē) *n. pl.* **·ger·ies 1** The branch of medical science that relates to body injuries, deformities, and morbid conditions that require being remedied by operations or instruments. **2** A place where surgical treatment or advice is regularly given; a surgeon's office; an operating room. **3** The work of a surgeon. **4** The treatment of diseases or injuries to nonhuman organisms by like methods: tree *surgery.* [<OF *surgerie,* contraction of *serurgerie,* ult. <LL *chirurgia* <Gk. *cheirourgia* a handicraft < *cheir, cheiros* the hand + *ergein* work]

sur·gi·cal (sûr′ji·kəl) *adj.* **1** Of or pertaining to surgery. **2** Designating a degree of anesthesia deep enough to permit major surgical operations. —**sur′gi·cal·ly** *adv.*

Su·ri·ba·chi (sŏŏr′ə·bä′chē), **Mount** An extinct volcano (546 feet) in southern Iwo Jima; scene of an American victory over the Japanese in World War II, February, 1945.

su·ri·cate (sŏŏr′ə·kāt) *n.* A small burrowing viverrine carnivore *(Suricata tetradactyla)* of South Africa, having only four toes: often domesticated. [<F *surikate* <Afrikaans, ? < a native South African name]

Su·ri·nam (sŏŏr′ə·näm′) Part of the Kingdom of the Netherlands, on the NE coast of South America; 55,129 square miles; capital, Paramaribo: also called *Dutch Guiana, Netherlands Guiana. Dutch* **Su·ri·na·me** (sü′rē·nä′mə).

Surinam River A river in central Surinam, flowing 300 miles north to the Atlantic near Paramaribo.

sur·loin (sûr′loin) *n.* Sirloin: the older spelling.

sur·ly (sûr′lē) *adj.* **·li·er, ·li·est 1** Persistently rude and ill-humored; crabbed; cross; gruff. **2** Characterized by rudeness or gruffness, as a reply. **3** *Obs.* Haughty. See synonyms under HAUGHTY, MOROSE. [Earlier *sirly* like a lord

< *sir* a lord + *-ly* like] — **sur'li·ly** *adv.* — **sur'li·ness** *n.*

Sur·ma (sŏŏr'mä) A river in Manipur and SE Assam, NE India, and East Pakistan, flowing 320 miles north and west to the Meghna River, and forming numerous arms, especially in Assam.

sur·mise (sər·mīz') *v.* **·mised, ·mis·ing** *v.t.* To infer on slight evidence; guess. — *v.i.* To make a conjecture thus. See synonyms under GUESS, SUPPOSE, SUSPECT. — *n.* (sər·mīz', sûr'mīz) A conjecture made on slight evidence; supposition. See synonyms under GUESS, HYPOTHESIS. [<OF, an accusation, pp. fem. of *surmettre* accuse < *sur-* upon + *mettre* put <L *mittere* send]

sur·mount (sər·mount') *v.t.* **1** To overcome; prevail over (a difficulty, etc.). **2** To mount to the top or cross to the other side of; get over, as an obstacle or mountain. **3** To be or lie over or above. **4** To place something above or on top of; cap. **5** *Obs.* To surpass; exceed. See synonyms under CONQUER. [<OF *surmunter* <Med. L *supermontare* <L *super-* over + *mons, montis* a hill, mountain] — **sur·mount'a·ble** *adj.* — **sur·mount'a·ble·ness** *n.* — **sur·mount'er** *n.*

sur·mul·let (sər·mul'it) See MULLET[1] (def. 2).

sur·name (sûr'nām') *n.* A name subjoined to a given or Christian name; hence, a family name. — *v.t.* (sûr'nām', sûr·nām') **·named, ·nam·ing** To give a surname to; call by a surname. [Alter. of obs. *surnoun* <OF *surnom* < *sur-* above, beyond + *nom* a name <L *nomen, -inis;* infl. in form by NAME] — **sur'·nam'er** *n.*

sur·pass (sər·pas', -päs') *v.t.* **1** To go beyond or past in degree or amount; exceed; excel. **2** To transcend; be beyond the reach or powers of. [<MF *surpasser* < *sur-* above + *passer* PASS] — **sur·pass'a·ble** *adj.*

Synonyms: eclipse, outdo, outstrip, transcend. See BEAT, LEAD. *Antonyms*: fail, yield.

sur·pass·ing (sər·pas'ing, -päs'-) *adj.* Preeminently excellent. — *adv. Poetic* Surpassingly. — **sur·pass'ing·ly** *adv.* — **sur·pass'ing·ness** *n.*

sur·plice (sûr'plis) *n. Eccl.* A loose white vestment with full sleeves, worn over the cassock by the clergy of the Anglican, Moravian, and Roman Catholic churches, and also by choristers in a vested choir. [<AF *surpliz,* OF *sourpeliz* < Med. L *superpellicium (vestimentum)* an overgarment < *super-* over + *pellicia* a fur garment < *pellis* skin]

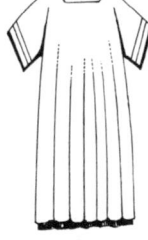

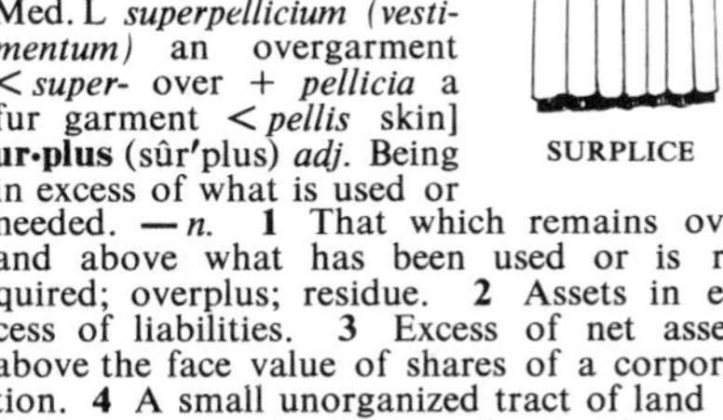
SURPLICE

sur·plus (sûr'plus) *adj.* Being in excess of what is used or needed. — *n.* **1** That which remains over and above what has been used or is required; overplus; residue. **2** Assets in excess of liabilities. **3** Excess of net assets above the face value of shares of a corporation. **4** A small unorganized tract of land in Maine set apart by State authority. See synonyms under EXCESS. [<OF <Med. L *superplus* < *super-* over and above + *plus* more]

sur·plus·age (sûr'plus·ij) *n.* **1** That which is over and above; surplus; overplus. **2** *Law* Matter in an instrument not necessary to the meaning; irrelevant matter.

sur·print (sûr'print') *v.t.* To print again on or over (matter once printed). — *n.* That which is surprinted.

sur·pris·al (sər·prī'zəl) *n.* The act of surprising; surprise. Also *Rare* **sur·priz'al.**

sur·prise (sər·prīz') *v.t.* **·prised, ·pris·ing 1** To cause to feel wonder or astonishment because unusual or unexpected. **2** To come upon suddenly or unexpectedly; take unawares. **3** To attack suddenly and without warning; capture by surprise. **4** To lead unawares, as into doing something not intended: with *into.* **5** To elicit in this manner: They *surprised* the truth from him. — *n.* **1** The act of surprising; a coming upon unawares. **2** A surprised state; astonishment. **3** Something that causes surprise, as a sudden and unexpected event, fact, or gift. Also *Rare* **sur·prize'.** [<OF *surpris,* pp. of *surprendre* < Med. L *superprendere* <L *super-* over + *prehendere* take] — **sur·pris'er** *n.*

surprise party A prearranged social gathering of persons, usually at a friend's home, but without previous notice to him.

sur·pris·ing (sər·prī'zing) *adj.* Causing wonder or astonishment; amazing. — **sur·pris'ing·ly** *adv.* — **sur·pris'ing·ness** *n.*

sur·re·al·ism (sə·rē'əl·iz'əm) *n.* A movement in 20th century literature and art which attempts to express and exhibit the workings of the subconscious mind, especially as manifested in dreams and uncontrolled by the reason or any conscious process: characterized by the incongruous and startling arrangement and presentation of subject matter. [<F *surréalisme* < *sur-* beyond, above + *réalisme* realism < *réal* REAL] — **sur·re'al·ist** *adj.* & *n.* — **sur·re'al·is'tic** *adj.* — **sur·re'al·is'ti·cal·ly** *adv.*

sur·re·but·tal (sûr'ri·but'l) *n. Law* A plaintiff's evidence or presentation of evidence, to support or maintain a surrebutter.

sur·re·but·ter (sûr'ri·but'ər) *n.* In common-law pleading, the plaintiff's reply to a defendant's rebutter. [<SUR-[1] + REBUTTER; on analogy with *surrejoinder*]

sur·reined (sə·rānd') *adj. Obs.* Overridden; worn out. [? <SUR-[1] + *reined,* pp. of REIN]

sur·re·join·der (sûr'ri·join'dər) *n. Law* The plaintiff's answer to the defendant's rejoinder. [<SUR-[1] + REJOINDER]

sur·ren·der (sə·ren'dər) *v.t.* **1** To yield possession of or power over to another; give up because of demand or compulsion. **2** To give up; abandon, as hope. **3** To give up or relinquish, especially in favor of another; resign. **4** To give (oneself) over to a passion, influence, etc. — *v.i.* **5** To give oneself up, as to an enemy in warfare; yield. — *n.* The act of surrendering one's person to another, or the possession of something to another. [< AF *surrender,* OF *surrendre* < *sur-* over + *rendre* RENDER] — **sur·ren'der·er,** *Law* **sur·ren'der·or** *n.*

Synonyms (verb): abandon, alienate, capitulate, cede, give, relinquish, sacrifice, yield. A state *cedes* territory for a consideration, *surrenders* it to a conqueror; a military commander *abandons* an untenable position or unavailable stores. We *relinquish* a claim, *sacrifice* something precious through error, friendship, or duty, *yield* to convincing reasons, a stronger will, winsome persuasion, or superior force. To *yield* is to give place or give way under pressure, and hence under compulsion; it implies more softness or concession than *surrender.* See ABANDON.

surrender value The reserve value of an insurance policy payable to the insured or to the beneficiary when the policy is discontinued.

sur·rep·ti·tious (sûr'əp·tish'əs) *adj.* **1** Accomplished by secret or improper means; clandestine. **2** Acting secretly or by stealth. [<L *surreptitius, subrepticius* < *subreptus,* pp. of *subripere* steal < *sub-* secretly + *rapere* snatch] — **sur'rep·ti'tious·ly** *adv.* — **sur'rep·ti'tious·ness** *n.*

sur·rey (sûr'ē) *n.* A light pleasure vehicle, having two seats, both facing forward, four wheels, and sometimes a top. [Prob. from *Surrey,* England]

Sur·rey (sûr'ē) A county in SE England; 722 square miles; county town, Guildford.

Sur·rey (sûr'ē), **Earl of,** 1516?–47, Henry Howard, English courtier, soldier, and poet: executed for treason.

sur·ro·gate (sûr'ə·gāt) *n.* **1** One who or that which is substituted for another; a substitute. **2** *Brit.* A deputy appointed by an ecclesiastical judge to act in his place. **3** A probate judge. — *v.t.* **·gat·ed, ·gat·ing 1** To put in the place of another; substitute; subrogate. **2** To appoint (another) to succeed oneself. [<L *surrogatus* < *subrogatus,* pp. of *subrogare* < *sub-* in place of another + *rogare* ask]

sur·round (sə·round') *v.t.* **1** To extend completely around; be on all sides of; encircle: Chairs *surrounded* the table. **2** To place something completely around; enclose. **3** To shut in or enclose, as enemy troops, on all sides so as to cut off communication or retreat; beset; invest. — *n.* That which surrounds; the surrounding area. [<AF *surunder,* OF *soronder* overflow <LL *superundare* < *super-* over + *undare* rise in waves < *unda* a wave]

Synonyms: compass, encompass, environ, invest. See EMBRACE.

sur·round·ing (sə·roun'ding) *n.* **1** That which surrounds, or any part of it; environment; conditions of life: usually in the plural. **2** The act of one who surrounds. — *adj.* Encompassing; enveloping.

sur·sum cor·da (sûr'səm kôr'də) *Latin* **1** *Eccl.* **a** Lift up your hearts: the opening words of the Preface in the mass. **b** A translation of this, used in other eucharistic liturgies. **2** A cry of encouragement, exhortation, etc.

sur·tax (sûr'taks') *n.* An extra or additional tax; specifically, a graduated income tax over and above the usual or fixed income tax, levied on the amount by which net income exceeds a certain sum. — *v.t.* To assess with an extra or additional tax. [<F *surtaxe* < *sur-* above + *taxe* < *taxer* TAX]

Sur·tees (sûr'tēz), **Robert Smith,** 1803–1864, English novelist and editor.

sur·tout[1] (sər·tōōt', -tōō'; *Fr.* sür·tōō') *n.* A long, close-fitting overcoat. [<F < *sur-* above + *tout* all <L *totus*]

sur·tout[2] (sür·tōō') *adv. French* Above all; chiefly; especially.

Su·ru·ga Bay (sōō·rōō·gä) An inlet of the Philippine Sea in central Honshu, Japan; 35 miles long, 15 to 35 miles wide.

sur·veil·lance (sər·vā'ləns, -vāl'yəns) *n.* The act of watching, or the state of being watched; a very close watch; a spying supervision. See synonyms under OVERSIGHT. [<F < *surveiller* superintend < *sur-* over + *veiller* watch <L *vigilare*]

sur·veil·lant (sər·vā'lənt, -vāl'yənt) *adj.* Exercising surveillance; watching; watchful. — *n.* One who keeps watch so as to control; an overseer or a spy.

sur·vey (sər·vā') *v.t.* **1** To look at in its entirety; view as from a height. **2** To look at carefully and minutely; scrutinize; inspect. **3** To determine accurately the area, contour, or boundaries of by measuring lines and angles according to the principles of geometry and trigonometry. — *v.i.* **4** To survey land. See synonyms under LOOK. — *n.* (sûr'vā, sər·vā') **1** The operation, act, process, or results of finding the contour, area, boundaries, etc., of a surface. **2** A department or corps for carrying on such operations; also, an area that has been surveyed. **3** A general or comprehensive view; an overlooking. **4** A scrutinizing view; inspection. [<AF *survey-,* stem of *surveier,* OF *sorveir* <Med. L *supervidere* < *super-* over + *videre* look]

sur·vey·ing (sər·vā'ing) *n.* **1** The science and art of determining the area and configuration of portions of the surface of the earth and representing them on maps. **2** The work of one who makes surveys.

sur·vey·or (sər·vā'ər) *n.* **1** One who surveys lands, roads, mines, oil fields, etc.; especially, one engaged in the business of land surveying. **2** One who examines a thing for the purpose of ascertaining its condition, quality, or character; an inspector, as of customs. **3** A customs officer who examines merchandise brought into a port.

sur·vey·or·ship (sər·vā'ər·ship) *n.* The office of a surveyor.

surveyor's level A form of spirit level with telescope and tripod attachment, for use in surveying.

surveyor's measure A system of measurement used in surveying and based on the chain as a unit.

sur·viv·al (sər·vī'vəl) *n.* **1** The act of surviving; an outliving. **2** Something surviving. **3** *Sociol.* The persistence in a society of customs and beliefs originating under circumstances not fully understood or no longer valid. **4** One who or that which lives longer than others. Also *Archaic* **sur·viv'ance.**

survival of the fittest Natural selection.

sur·vive (sər·vīv') *v.* **·vived, ·viv·ing** *v.i.* To live or continue beyond the death of another, the occurrence of an event, etc.; remain alive or in existence. — *v.t.* To live or exist beyond the death, occurrence, or end of; outlive; outlast. See synonyms under LIVE.

[<AF *survivre,* OF *sorvivre* <LL *supervivere* < *super-* above, beyond + *vivere* live] **—sur·viv′ing** *adj.* **—sur·vi′vor, sur·viv′er** *n.*

sur·vi·vor·ship (sər·vī′vər·ship) *n.* **1** The state of surviving. **2** *Law* The right of a surviving party, having a joint interest with others in property, to take the whole estate.

sus– Assimilated var. of SUB–.

Su·sa (sōō′sə) **1** An ancient city of Persia, capital of Elam, the site of which is in SW Iran: Old Testament *Shushan. Persian* **Shush** (shōōsh). **2** A former name for SOUSSE, Tunisia.

Su·san·na (sōō·zan′ə; *Dan., Du., Sw.* sōō·zä′nä, *Ital.* sōō·zän′nä, *Sp.* sōō·sä′nä) A feminine personal name. Also **Su·san** (sōō′zən), **Su·san·nah** (-zä′nə). [Hebrew, a lily]
—Susanna A Jewish captive in Babylon, falsely accused of adultery, whose life Daniel saved; also, the book of the Old Testament Apocrypha containing the story of Susanna.

sus·cep·ti·bil·i·ty (sə·sep′tə·bil′ə·tē) *n. pl.* **·ties** **1** The state or quality of being susceptible to influences or of easily receiving impressions. **2** The ability to receive or be impressed by deep emotions or strong feelings; sensibility. **3** *Physics* The ratio of the magnetization of a material to the magnetic force producing it.

sus·cep·ti·ble (sə·sep′tə·bəl) *adj.* **1** Yielding readily; capable of being influenced, acted on, or determined; unresistant; open; liable: usually with *of* or *to.* **2** Having delicate sensibility; sensitive; impressionable; easily affected. [<Med. L *susceptibilis* <L *suscipere* receive, undertake < *sub-* under + *capere* take] **—sus·cep′ti·ble·ness** *n.* **—sus·cep′ti·bly** *adv.*

sus·cep·tive (sə·sep′tiv) *adj.* Receptive; sensitive to; susceptible. **—sus·cep′tive·ness, sus·cep·tiv·i·ty** (sus′ep·tiv′ə·tē) *n.*

Su·si·an (sōō′zē·ən) *n.* The Elamite language.

Su·si·a·na (sōō′zē·ā′nə, -an′ə) See ELAM.

Su·sie, Su·sy (sōō′zē) Diminutives of SUSANNA.

sus·lik (sōōs′lik) *n.* A sciuroid rodent (*Citellus citellus*) of NE Europe and NW Asia, with a very short tail; a pouched marmot; spermophile. [<Russian]

sus·pect (sə·spekt′) *v.t.* **1** To think (a person) guilty as specified on little or no evidence. **2** To have distrust of; doubt: They *suspected* my motives. **3** To have an inkling or suspicion of; think possible: The police *suspect* arson. **—*v.i.*** **4** To have suspicions. **—*adj.*** (sus′pekt) Suspected; exciting suspicion. **—*n.*** (sus′pekt) A person suspected of a crime or other action. [<F *suspecter* <L *suspectus,* pp. of *suspicere* look under, mistrust < *sub-* from under + *specere* look] **—sus·pect′er** *n.*
Synonyms (verb): conjecture, distrust, doubt, mistrust, surmise. See DOUBT, GUESS.

sus·pend (sə·spend′) *v.t.* **1** To bar for a time from a privilege, office, or function as a punishment; debar. **2** To cause to cease for a time; interrupt; withhold temporarily: to *suspend* payments on a debt. **3** To hold in a state of indecision or abeyance; withhold or defer action on: to *suspend* a sentence. **4** To hang from a support so as to allow free movement. **5** To sustain in a body of nearly the same specific gravity; keep in suspension, as dust motes in the air. **—*v.i.*** **6** To stop for a time. **7** To fail to meet obligations; stop payment. [<OF *suspendre* <L *sub-* under + *pendere* hang]
Synonyms: debar, defer, delay, discontinue, fail, hang, hinder, intermit, interrupt, stay, stop, withhold. See ADJOURN. *Antonyms*: begin, continue, expedite, prolong, protract.

suspended animation Temporary loss of a vital force, simulating death.

sus·pend·er (sə·spen′dər) *n.* **1** One who or that which suspends. **2** One of a pair of straps for supporting the trousers: usually in the plural, **pair of suspenders.** **3** *Brit.* A garter.

sus·pense (sə·spens′) *n.* **1** The state of being uncertain, undecided, or insecure; anxiety. **2** The state of being suspended or stopped temporarily. **3** *Obs.* Cessation. See synonyms under DOUBT. [<OF *suspens, suspense* delay, abeyance <Med. L *suspensum,* orig. pp. neut. of L *suspendere* SUSPEND]

suspense account An account in which charges or credits are entered temporarily pending determination of their proper place.

sus·pen·sion (sə·spen′shən) *n.* **1** The act of suspending or hanging. **2** The state of deferment. **3** *Physics* A uniform dispersion of the fine particles of a solid in a liquid which does not dissolve them. Compare BROWNIAN MOVEMENT, COLLOID. **4** Cessation of payments in business; a going into liquidation: the *suspension* of a bank. **5** Any device used for the purpose of suspension, as in a compass. **6** *Mech.* A system of flexible or absorbent members, as springs in a vehicle, intended to insulate the chassis and body against road shocks transmitted by the wheels. **7** *Music* The prolongation of any note of a chord into the succeeding chord, causing at first dissonance which disappears by resolution; the note so prolonged. **8** The act of debarring from an office or its privileges.

suspension bridge See under BRIDGE.

suspension point One of a series of dots used to indicate the omission of words or sentences.

sus·pen·sive (sə·spen′siv) *adj.* **1** Tending to suspend or to keep in suspense. **2** Having the power of suspending operation: a *suspensive* veto. **—sus·pen′sive·ly** *adv.*

sus·pen·sor (sə·spen′sər) *n.* **1** A suspensory bandage. **2** *Bot.* The thread or chain of cells, in flowering plants and certain cryptogams, which produces at its extremity the developing embryo.

sus·pen·so·ry (sə·spen′sər·ē) *adj.* Suspending; sustaining; delaying. **—*n.*** *pl.* **·ries** A truss, bandage, or supporter.

suspensory ligament *Anat.* A fibrous membrane sustaining the lens of the eye.

sus·pi·cion (sə·spish′ən) *n.* **1** Conjecture; doubt; mistrust; imagining something wrong without proof or clear evidence. **2** *Colloq.* The least particle, as of a flavor. See synonyms under DOUBT. **—*v.t. Dial.*** To suspect. [<AF *suspecioun,* OF *sospeçon* <Med. L *suspectio, -onis* <L *suspicere.* See SUSPECT.] **—sus·pi′cion·al** *adj.*

sus·pi·cious (sə·spish′əs) *adj.* **1** Inclined to suspect. **2** Questionable. **3** Indicating suspicion. See synonyms under ENVIOUS, EQUIVOCAL. **—sus·pi′cious·ly** *adv.* **—sus·pi′cious·ness** *n.*

sus·pire (sə·spīr′) *v.i.* **·pired, ·pir·ing** **1** To sigh. **2** To breathe. [<L *suspirare* < *sub-* up from below + *spirare* breathe] **—sus·pi·ra·tion** (sus′pə·rā′shən) *n.*

Sus·que·han·na (sus′kwə·han′ə) A river in New York, Pennsylvania, and Maryland, flowing 444 miles south to Chesapeake Bay.

Sus·sex (sus′iks) **1** A county in SE England; administratively divided into **East Sussex** (829 square miles; county town, Lewes) and **West Sussex** (628 square miles; county town, Chichester). **2** A former Anglo-Saxon kingdom in southern England.

Sussex spaniel See under SPANIEL.

sus·tain (sə·stān′) *v.t.* **1** To keep from sinking or falling, especially by bearing up from below; uphold; support. **2** To endure without yielding; withstand. **3** To have inflicted on one; undergo; suffer, as loss or injury. **4** To keep up the courage, resolution, or spirits of; comfort. **5** To keep up or maintain; keep in effect or being: to *sustain* friendly relations. **6** To maintain by providing with food, drink, or other necessities; support. **7** To uphold or support as being true or just. **8** To prove the truth or correctness of; corroborate; confirm. See synonyms under AID, ASSENT, CARRY, CONFIRM, ENDURE, HELP, KEEP, PRESERVE, PROP, SUPPORT. [<OF *sustein-,* stem of *sustenir, sostenir* <L *sustinere* < *sub-* up from under + *tenere* hold] **—sus·tain′a·ble** *adj.* **—sus·tain′er** *n.* **—sus·tain′ment** *n.*

sustaining program A radio or television program that has no commercial sponsor but is paid for by the network or station.

sus·te·nance (sus′tə·nəns) *n.* **1** The act or process of sustaining; especially, maintenance of life or health; subsistence. **2** That which sustains; especially, that which supports life; food. **3** Livelihood; means of support. See synonyms under FOOD, NUTRIMENT. [<AF *sustenaunce,* OF *sostenance* < *sostenir* SUSTAIN]

sus·ten·tac·u·lar (sus′ten·tak′yə·lər) *adj. Anat.* Supporting; sustaining. [<L *sustentaculum* a support < *sustentare* hold up, intens. of *sustinere* SUSTAIN]

sus·ten·ta·tion (sus′ten·tā′shən) *n.* **1** The act or process of sustaining; specifically, support of life; maintenance. **2** That which provides the means of support. **3** Upkeep or maintenance of an estate, building, etc. **4** Physical support. **5** Preservation on a certain level. [<OF *sustentacion* <L *sustentatio, -onis* < *sustentatus,* pp. of *sustentare* hold up < *sustinere* SUSTAIN] **—sus′ten·ta′tive** *adj.*

sus·ten·tion (sə·sten′shən) *n.* **1** Support. **2** The act of being sustained. [<SUSTAIN; on analogy with *retention, detention,* etc.]

su·sur·rant (sōō·sûr′ənt) *adj.* Softly murmuring; rustling; whispering. [<L *susurrans, -antis,* ppr. of *susurrare* whisper < *susurrus* a humming, whispering]

su·sur·rate (sōō·sûr′āt) *v.i.* **·rat·ed, ·rat·ing** To speak softly; whisper. [<L *susurratus,* pp. of *susurrare.* See SUSURRANT.] **—su·sur·ra·tion** (sōō′sə·rā′shən) *n.*

su·sur·rus (sōō·sûr′əs) *n.* A gentle sibilant murmur; whisper; rustling. [<L, a humming, whispering]

Suth·er·land (suth′ər·lənd) A county in northern Scotland; 2,028 square miles; county seat, Dornoch. Also **Suth′er·land·shire** (-shir).

Sutherland Falls Falls in SW South Island, New Zealand; 1,904 feet.

Suth·ron (suth′rən) See SOUTHRON.

Sut·lej (sut′lej) A river in SW Tibet, central Himachal Pradesh, and northern Punjab State, northern India and West Pakistan, flowing 850 miles SW to the Indus river on the former SW border of Bahawalpur.

sut·ler (sut′lər) *n.* A peddler who follows an army to sell goods and food to the soldiers. [<Du. *soeteler* a petty tradesman < *soetelen* perform mean duties] **—sut′ler·ship** *n.*

su·tra (sōō′trə) *n.* **1** A formulated doctrine, often so short as to be unintelligible without a key; literally, a rule or precept. **2** In Sanskrit literature, a short grammatical rule. **3** *pl.* A collection of writings or aphorisms, as the dialogs of the Buddha, the Laws of Manu. **4** In Buddhism, an extended writing, usually in verse, and often in dialog form, embodying important religious and philosophical propositions, sometimes directly, sometimes in highly allegorical or metaphorical language. Also **sut·ta** (sōōt′ə). [<Skt. *sūtra* a thread, rule < *siv* sew]

sut·tee (su·tē′, sut′ē) *n.* Formerly, the sacrifice of a Hindu widow on the funeral pyre of her husband: now forbidden; also, the widow so immolated. [<Hind. *satī* <Skt., a faithful wife, fem. of *sat* good, wise, orig. ppr. of *as* be] **—sut·tee′ism** *n.*

Sut·ter (sut′ər), **John Augustus,** 1803–80, U. S. pioneer in California, born in Germany.

Sut·ter's Mill (sut′ərz) A mill in eastern California: gold was discovered on its site in 1848.

sut·tle (sut′l) *adj.* Formerly, taken after the tare has been deducted and before the tret has been allowed; designating that allowance has been made for the container: said of weight. **—*n.*** Suttle weight. [Earlier var. of SUBTLE]

su·ture (sōō′chər) *n.* **1** The junction of two contiguous surfaces or edges along a line by or as by sewing. **2** *Anat.* The interlocking of two bones at their edges, as in the skull. **3** *Zool.* The line of junction between contiguous parts. **4** *Bot.* The line of dehiscence in plants. **5** *Surg.* **a** The act or operation of uniting parts by or as by stitching. **b** The sewing together of the cut or cleft edges of divided parts. **c** The thread, silver wire, or other material used in this operation. **—*v.t.*** **·tured, ·tur·ing** To unite by means of sutures; sew together. [MF <L *sutura* < *sutus,* pp. of *suere* sew] **—su′tur·al** *adj.* **—su′tur·al·ly** *adv.*

su·um cui·que (sōō′əm kī′kwē, kwī′-) *Latin* To each his own.

Su·va (sōō′vä) A port on the south coast of Viti Levu, capital of the Fiji Islands.

Su·vo·rov (sōō·vô′rôf), **Count Alexander Vasilievich,** 1729–1800, Russian field marshal.

Su·wal·ki (sōō·vä′ōō·kē) A town of NE Poland; formerly in Russia.

Su·wan·nee River (sōō·wô′nē, -won′ē) A river in Georgia and Florida, flowing 250 miles south, west, and SW to the Gulf of Mexico: also *Swanee.*

su·ze·rain (sōō′zə·rān, -rin) *n.* **1** One invested with superior or paramount authority; formerly, a feudal lord. **2** A nation having paramount control over a locally autonomous region. **—*adj.*** Sovereign; supreme. [<F *sus* above <L *susum, sursum* upwards; on analogy with *souverain* a sovereign] **—su′ze·rain·ty** *n.*

Su·zu·ki (sōō·zōō·kē), **Daisetz Teitaro,** 1870–1966, Japanese scholar, author, and teacher, active in the U. S.; leading authority on Zen Buddhism, especially as its expositor to the West.

Su·zy (sōō′zē) Diminutive of SUSANNA.

Sval·bard (sväl′bär) An archipelago in the Arctic Ocean, including Spitsbergen and other smaller islands and comprising a possession of Norway; 23,951 square miles; administrative capital, Longyear City on West Spitsbergen.

sva·raj (svä·räj′) See SWARAJ.

Sved·berg (svā′berkh), **The (Theodor),** born 1884, Swedish chemist.

svelte (svelt) *adj.* Slender; slim; willowy. [<F *svelte* <Ital. *svelto* <L *ex-* out + *vellere* pluck]

Sverd·lovsk (sverd·lôfsk′) A city in the central Ural Mountains in western Asiatic Russian S.F.S.R.: formerly *Ekaterinburg.*

Sver·drup (svar′drōōp), **Otto,** 1855–1930, Norwegian Arctic explorer.

Sver·drup Islands (svar′drōōp) An archipelago of northern Franklin District, Northwest Territories, in the Arctic Ocean.

Sve·rige (svā′ryə) The Swedish name for SWEDEN.

Sviz·ze·ra (svēt·tsā′rä) The Italian name for SWITZERLAND.

swab (swob) *n.* **1** One of various utensils consisting essentially of a soft absorbent substance on the end of a handle: used for cleaning, etc. **2** A mop for cleaning decks, floors, etc. **3** A sailor who uses such a mop; a menial; a worthless person. **4** A cylindrical brush for cleaning firearms. **5** *Med.* **a** A bit of sponge or cloth for cleansing the mouth of, or used as a means of applying nourishment or medicine to, a sick person. **b** A specimen of mucus, etc., taken for examination; also, the cotton-wound wire used in obtaining it. — *v.t.* **swabbed, swab·bing** To clean or apply with a swab. Also spelled *swob.* [Back formation <SWABBER]

swab·ber (swob′ər) *n.* **1** One who uses a swab. **2** One fit only for swabbing. **3** A swab. [<MDu. *zwabber* < *zwabben* do dirty work, swab]

Swa·bi·a (swā′bē·ə) A region and former duchy of SW West Germany, which contains the Black Forest; the eastern section comprises an administrative province of SW Bavaria; 3,818 square miles; capital, Augsburg: German *Schwaben.* — **Swa′bi·an** *adj.* & *n.*

swad·dle (swod′l) *v.t.* **·dled, ·dling** To wrap with a bandage; especially, to wrap (an infant) with a long strip of linen or flannel; swathe. — *n.* A swaddling band. [OE *swæthel* swaddling clothes, a bandage < *swathian* swathe]

swaddling clothes **1** Bands or strips of linen or cloth wound around a newborn infant. **2** A time of immaturity, or the limitations that restrict the immature. Also **swaddling bands, swaddling clouts.**

Swa·de·shi (swə·dā′shē) *n.* A former political movement originating in Bengal, India, advocating the boycott of British goods as one means of obtaining swaraj or home rule. [<Skt. *svadeśin* native, national < *svadeśa* native country]

swag (swag) *n.* **1** *Slang* Property obtained by robbery or theft; plunder; booty. **2** *Austral.* A swagman's bundle or pack. **3** Baggage; luggage. **4** A swaying; a lurch. — *v.i.* **swagged, swag·ging** **1** *Brit. Dial.* To swing heavily. **2** *Austral.* To tramp, bearing a swag. **3** To sag; sway; lurch. [Prob. <Scand. Cf. dial. Norw. *svagga* sway.]

swag·bel·ly (swag′bel′ē) *n.* A person having a protuberant abdomen. [<SWAG, *v.* (def. 3) + BELLY] — **swag′bel′lied** *adj.*

swage (swāj) *n.* **1** A tool or form, often one of a pair, for shaping metal by hammering or pressure. **2** An ornamental border or molding. **3** A groove on an anvil for use in shaping metal. **4** A swage block. — *v.t.* **swaged, swag·ing** To shape (metal) with or as with a swage or swage block. [<OF *souage;* ult. origin uncertain]

swage block A heavy iron block or anvil having grooves or holes for shaping metal, heading bolts, etc.: also called *swage.*

swag·ger (swag′ər) *v.i.* **1** To walk with a proud or insolent air; strut. **2** To boast; bluster. — *n.* Braggadocio; expression of superiority in words or deeds. — *adj.* Showy or ostentatious in style, manner, or appearance. [Appar. freq. of SWAG] — **swag′ger·er** *n.* — **swag′ger·ing·ly** *adv.*

swagger coat A sports coat without a belt.

swagger stick A short canelike stick; specifically, one carried by a British soldier when off duty: also called *swanking stick.*

swagger suit A short flared coat and a skirt that matches.

swag·man (swag′man′) *n.* *pl.* **·men** (-men′) *Austral.* One who seeks work, carrying his bundle or swag.

Swa·hi·li (swä·hē′lē) *n.* *pl.* **·hi·li** **1** One of a Bantu people of Zanzibar and the adjacent coast, having an admixture of Arab blood. **2** These people collectively: with *the.* **3** The agglutinative language of the Swahili, belonging to the Bantu family of languages. [<Arabic, coastal < *sawāḥil,* pl. of *sāḥil* a coast] — **Swa·hi′li·an** *adj.*

swain (swān) *n.* **1** A youthful rustic; a lover. **2** *Obs.* A squire; a male servant. [<ON *sveinn* a boy, servant] — **swain′ish** *adj.* — **swain′ish·ness** *n.*

swaird (swârd) *n.* *Scot.* Sward.

swale[1] (swāl) *n.* **1** Low, marshy ground. **2** *Dial.* Shade; a shady place. Also **swail.** [Prob. <Scand. Cf. ON *svalr* cool.]

swale[2] (swāl) See SWEAL.

swall (swäl) *v.* & *n.* *Scot.* Swell.

swal·low[1] (swol′ō) *v.t.* **1** To cause (food, etc.) to pass from the mouth into the stomach by means of muscular action of the gullet or esophagus. **2** To take in or engulf in a manner suggestive of this; absorb; envelop: often with *up.* **3** To put up with or endure; submit to, as insults. **4** *Colloq.* To believe credulously. **5** To refrain from expressing or giving vent to; suppress. **6** To take back; recant: to *swallow* one's words. — *v.i.* **7** To perform the act or the motions of swallowing. See synonyms under ABSORB. — *n.* **1** That which is swallowed at once; a small amount; a mouthful. **2** The gullet; throat; gorge. **3** The act of swallowing; appetite; inclination. **4** The channel in a hoisting block for the passage of the rope. **5** An abyss; whirlpool; also, a pit. [OE *swelgan* swallow] — **swal′·low·er** *n.*

swal·low[2] (swol′ō) *n.* **1** Any of various small, widely distributed passerine birds (family *Hirundinidae*) with short, broad, depressed bill, long, pointed wings, and forked tail: noted for swiftness of flight and migratory habits, as the common **bank swallow** (*Riparia riparia*), the American **tree swallow** (*Iridoprocne bicolor*), and the **barn swallow** (*Hirundo erythrogaster*). ◆ Collateral adjective: *hirundine.* **2** A similar bird, as the swift. [OE *swealwe*]

swallow dive A swan dive.

swal·low·tail (swol′ō·tāl′) *n.* **1** *Colloq.* A man's dress coat with two long, tapering skirts or tails. **2** A butterfly (family *Papilionidae*) having a posterior, tail-like prolongation on each hind wing. —**swal′low-tailed′** *adj.*

swal·low·wort (swol′ō·wûrt′) *n.* **1** A twining perennial herb (*Cynanchum vincetoxicum*) with greenish-white flowers and roots, the latter formerly used in medicine. **2** The common celandine: said to blossom with the arrival of the swallows and to wither when they depart. **3** One of several plants of the milkweed family.

swam (swam) Past tense of SWIM.

swa·mi (swä′mē) *n.* **1** Master; lord: used by Hindus as a title of respect. **2** A Hindu teacher, especially a religious teacher; a pundit. **3** Loosely, a yogi or fakir. Also **swa′my.** [<Hind. *svāmi* lord, master <Skt. *swāmin*]

swamp (swomp, swômp) *n.* A tract or region of low land saturated with water; a wet bog. Also **swamp′land′** (-land′). ◆ Collateral adjective: *paludal.* — *v.t.* **1** To drench or submerge with water or other liquid. **2** To overwhelm with difficulties; crush; ruin. **3** *Naut.* To sink or fill (a vessel) with water. — *v.i.* **4** To sink in water, a swamp, etc. [Cf. LG *swampen* quake (said of a bog). Akin to SUMP.] — **swamp′y, swamp′ish** *adj.*

swamp angel **1** A person who lives in a swamp; a swamper. **2** The hermit thrush.

Swamp Angel A 200-pound Parrott gun used in the siege of Charleston, S.C., in 1863: so called because it was mounted in a swamp.

swamp blackbird The redwing (def. 1).

swamp boat A small, flat-bottomed, blunt-prowed boat powered by an engine with an airplane propeller mounted high in the stern: used in swampy or boggy areas.

swamp cabbage Skunk cabbage.

swamp·er (swom′pər, swôm′-) *n.* **1** One who lives in a swamp or in a swampy district. **2** One who clears a way in a swamp or forest for skidding logs; also, one who clears away underbrush, fallen trees, and other debris for logging operations.

swamp fever **1** Malaria. **2** An infectious anemia of equine animals, caused by a filtrable virus.

Swamp Fox Sobriquet of FRANCIS MARION.

swamp hare A rabbit (*Sylvilagus aquaticus*) frequenting the swamps of the southern United States.

swamp honeysuckle The swamp azalea (*Azalea viscosa*) of the SE United States.

swamp land **1** Land covered with swamps. **2** Fertile, arable land in a swamp.

swamp law Lynch law.

swamp locust The water locust.

swamp maple The red maple of North America (*Acer rubrum*).

swamp oak **1** An oak (*Quercus bicolor*) common in swamps of the eastern United States: also **swamp white oak.** **2** The pin oak.

swamp owl **1** The short-eared owl. **2** The barred owl. See under OWL.

swamp pine Any of certain pines common in swamps or swampy regions; especially, the loblolly pine and the slash pine.

swamp privet See under PRIVET.

swamp sparrow An American sparrow (*Melospiza georgiana*) resembling the song sparrow, inhabiting the swamps of the southern and eastern United States.

swamp willow The pussy willow.

swan[1] (swon, swôn) *n.* **1** A large, web-footed, long-necked bird (subfamily *Cygninae*), allied to but heavier than the goose, and noted for its grace on the water, as the whooper, the trumpeter swan, and the common North American whistling swan (*Cygnus columbiana*). The male is a *cob,* and the female is a *pen.* **2** Figuratively, a poet or singer. [OE]

TRUMPETER SWAN (Body length from 4 to 4 1/2 feet)

swan[2] (swon, swôn) *v.i.* *U.S. Dial.* Swear: chiefly in the phrase *I swan,* an exclamation of amazement. [Prob. < dial. E (Northern) *Is' wan,* lit., I shall warrant, used as euphemism for *swear*]

Swan (swon, swôn) The constellation Cygnus. See under CONSTELLATION.

swan dive A fancy dive performed with head tilted back and arms held like the wings of a swallow until near the water: also called *swallow dive.*

Swa·nee River (swô′nē, swon′ē) See SUWANNEE RIVER.

swang (swang) Dialectal past tense of SWING.

swan·herd (swon′hûrd′, swôn′-) *n.* One who tends swans; especially, a royal officer of England having charge of marking the swans on the Thames which belong to the crown. Also **swan′mas′ter.** Compare SWAN-UPPING.

swank (swangk) *v.* & *n.* *Slang* Swagger; bluster. — *adj.* *Slang* **1** Ostentatiously fashionable; pretentious. **2** *Scot.* Slim; pliant; agile; jolly; lively. Also **swank′y.** [< dial. E. Appar. akin to MLG *swank* flexible, MHG *swanken* sway.] — **swank′i·ly** *adv.* — **swank′i·ness** *n.*

swank·ie (swangk′ē) *n.* *Scot.* An active, clever lad: sometimes said of a lass. Also **swank′y.**

swanking stick A swagger stick.

swan maiden In many ancient folk myths, a beautiful fairy maiden able to transform herself into a swan by means of a magic robe, ring, or chain, and living under an enchantment or tabu affecting her life with a human lover.

swan-neck (swon′nek′, swôn′-) *n.* Any of several mechanical contrivances resembling in outline the neck of a swan.

swan·ner·y (swon′ər·ē, swôn′-) *n. pl.* **·ner·ies** A place where swans are bred or kept.

swan·pan (swän′pän′) *n.* A Chinese abacus or frame of beads to aid reckoning: also spelled *schwanpan, shwanpan.* [<Chinese *suan p'an* a reckoning board]

Swan River (swon, swôn) A river in SW Western Australia, flowing 240 miles NW and SW to the Indian Ocean at Fremantle.

swan's-down (swonz′doun′, swônz′-) *n.* **1** The down of a swan: used for trimming, powder puffs, etc. **2** Canton or cotton flannel. **3** A soft, thick, fine woolen cloth resembling down. Also **swans′down′.**

Swan·sea (swon′sē) A port and industrial county borough in SW Glamorganshire, southern Wales.

swan·skin (swon′skin′, swôn′-) *n.* **1** The unplucked skin of a swan. **2** A soft, fine-twilled flannel or cotton fabric having a soft nap. —*adj.* Made of swanskin.

swan-song (swon′sông′, -song′, swôn′-) *n.* A last or dying work, as of a poet or composer: in allusion to the ancient fable that the swan sings a last song before dying.

swan-up·ping (swon′up′ing, swôn′-) *n. Brit.* The annual inspection and marking on the beak of the royal and other privileged young swans or cygnets on the Thames; also, the annual expedition for this purpose.

swap (swop) *v.t.* & *v.i.* **swapped, swap·ping** *Colloq.* To exchange (one thing for another); trade. —**to swap lies** To exchange tales; tell stories. —*n.* The act of swapping. Also spelled *swop.* [ME *swappen* strike (a bargain), slap; prob. ult. imit. of the sound of clapping the hands, as in bargaining]

swa·raj (swə·räj′) *n.* **1** Formerly in British India, self-government; by extension, cultural and political development under native influence as distinguished from such development under British influence. **2** Home rule: the watchword of the Indian Nationalists; the party itself. Also spelled *svaraj.* [Skt. *svarāj* self-ruling <*sva-* own + *rāj* rule] —**swa·raj′ist** *n.* —**swa·raj′ism** *n.*

sward (swôrd) *n.* **1** Land thickly covered with grass; turf. **2** *Obs.* A skin; rind. Also **swarth** (swôrth). —*v.t.* & *v.i.* To cover or become covered with sward. [OE *sweard* a skin]

sware (swâr) Obsolete past tense of SWEAR.

swarm[1] (swôrm) *n.* **1** A large number or body of insects or small living things of any kind. **2** A hive of bees; also, a large number of bees leaving the parent stock at one time, to take up new lodgings, accompanied by a queen. **3** A crowd or throng of persons, animals, or things, especially when in motion or advancing under pressure. **4** *Biol.* A collection of free-swimming unicellular organisms, especially zoospores. See synonyms under FLOCK. —*v.i.* **1** To leave the hive in a swarm: said of bees. **2** To come together, move, or occur in great numbers. **3** To be crowded or overrun; teem: with *with.* **4** *Biol.* To come forth in a swarm. —*v.t.* **5** To fill with a swarm or crowd; throng. [OE *swearm*]

swarm[2] (swôrm) *v.t.* & *v.i.* To climb (a tree, etc.) by clasping it with the hands and limbs. [Orig. nautical cant. Prob. akin to SWARM[1].]

swarm·er (swôr′mər) *n.* **1** A swarm spore. **2** An insect that swarms, as a bee or gnat; one who or that which swarms.

swarm spore *Biol.* **1** A zoospore. **2** A flagellate spore. **3** A ciliated sponge embryo.

swart (swôrt) *adj.* **1** Swarthy; also, poetically, absolutely black. **2** Malignant; gloomy. Also **swarth** (swôrth). [OE *sweart*] —**swart′ness** *n.*

swart·back (swôrt′bak′) *n. Scot.* The great black-backed gull *(Larus marinus).*

swarth[1] (swôrth) *n.* **1** *Obs.* Sward (*n.* def. 1). **2** *Dial.* An unripe crop of hay. [OE *sweardh*]

swarth[2] (swôrth) *n. Dial.* The apparition of a person about to die; a wraith. [? Var. of SWART]

swarth·y (swôr′thē) *adj.* **swarth·i·er, swarth·i·est** Having a dark hue; of dark or sunburned complexion; tawny; swart. Also **swart′y.** See synonyms under DARK. [Var. of obs. *swarty* <SWART] —**swarth′i·ly** *adv.* —**swarth′i·ness, swarth′ness** *n.*

swarve[1] (swôrv) *v.t.* & *v.i. Obs.* To swerve. [<dial. var. of SWERVE]

swarve[2] (swôrv) *v.t.* & *v.i.* To climb. [Origin uncertain. Prob. akin to SWARM[2].]

swarve[3] (swôrv) *v.i.* To swoon. [? <ON *svarfa* upset]

swash (swosh, swôsh) *v.i.* **1** To move or wash noisily, as waves. **2** To swagger. —*v.t.* **3** To splash (water, etc.). **4** To splash or dash water, etc., upon or against. —*n.* **1** The splash of a liquid. **2** A narrow channel through which tides flow. **3** A bar over which the waves pass freely. **4** Swill or wet refuse for pigs. **5** A swaggerer or his behavior. **6** *Slang* Worthless sentimental literature; trash. [Imit.]

swash·buck·ler (swosh′buk′lər, swôsh′-) *n.* A swaggering soldier; a bravo[2]. [<SWASH + BUCKLER; with ref. to striking one's own or one's opponent's shield with a sword] —**swash′buck′ler·ing** *n.* —**swash′buck′ling** *adj.* & *n.*

swash·er (swosh′ər, swôsh′-) *n.* A blusterer; braggart; bully.

swash·ing (swosh′ing, swôsh′-) *adj.* **1** Splashing. **2** Swaggering; blustering. **3** Crushing; violent.

swash letters Italic special letters having a top or bottom flourish on the side where there is most blank space.

SWASH LETTERS

swas·ti·ka (swos′ti·kə) *n.* **1** A primitive religious ornament or symbol, originally in the form of a gammadion, but variously modified, the most typical being a Greek cross with the ends of the arms bent at right angles, and prolonged to the length of the upright arms, clockwise, or counterclockwise. See *b* in illustration. It dates back to the Bronze Age in Europe, and still exists as a religious symbol in India, Persia, China, Japan, and among North, Central, and South American Indians: believed to be a token of good luck or blessing. **2** The emblem of the Nazis: as *b* in illustration. See HAKENKREUZ. Compare FYLFOT. Also **swas′ti·ca.** [<Skt. *svastika* <*svastí* well-being, fortune <*sú* good + *astí* being <*as* be]

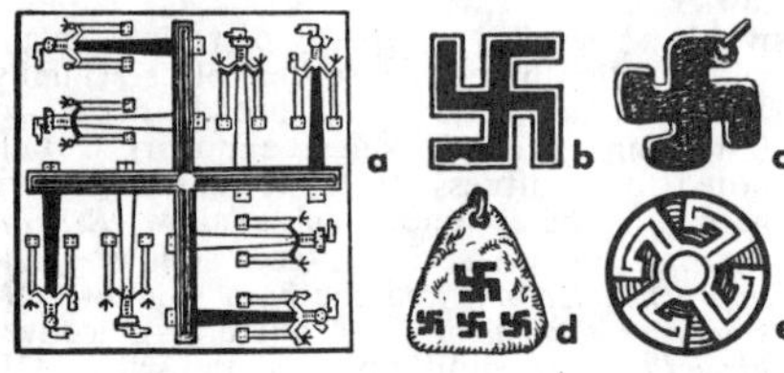

SWASTIKA
a. Navaho Indian. *b.* Indian. *c.* Caucasian. *d.* Siberian. *e.* Pima Indian.

swat (swot) *v.t.* **swat·ted, swat·ting** To hit with a sharp blow. —*n.* A smart blow. Also spelled *swot.* [Var. of SQUAT, in dial. sense of "squash"]

Swat (swot) *n. pl.* **Swa·ti** (swä′tē) One of an East Indian Moslem people of Indo-European linguistic stock, dwelling in northern West Pakistan. Also **Swa′ti.**

Swat (swot) **1** A former princely state, in the former North-West Frontier Province, northern West Pakistan; 4,000 square miles; capital, Saidu. **2** A river in northern West Pakistan, flowing about 200 miles south, SW, and SE to the Kabul.

swatch (swoch) *n.* A strip, as of cloth, especially one cut off for a sample. [<dial. E (Northern), a cloth tally]

swath (swoth, swôth) *n.* **1** A row or line of cut grass. **2** The space cut by a machine or implement in a single course. **3** The width of grass cut by the sweep of a scythe. Also spelled *swathe.* —**to cut a wide swath** To accomplish much; hence, to make a fine impression. [OE *swæth* a track]

swathe[1] (swāth, swäth) *v.t.* **swathed, swath·ing** **1** To bind or wrap, as in bandages; swaddle. **2** To envelop; enwrap; surround. —*n.* A bandage for swathing. [OE *swathian*] —**swath′er** *n.*

swathe[2] (swāth) See SWATH.

Swa·tow (swä′tou′) An industrial city and former treaty port on the South China Sea in eastern Kwangtung province, China.

swat·ter[1] (swot′ər) *n.* **1** One who or that which crushes with a blow. **2** A perforated rubber or meshed wire device for killing flies. **3** A hard-hitting baseball player.

swat·ter[2] (swot′ər) *v.i. Dial.* To splash water about, as geese and ducks in drinking. [Imit.]

sway (swā) *v.i.* **1** To swing from side to side or to and fro; oscillate. **2** To bend or incline to one side; lean; veer. **3** To tend in opinion, sympathy, etc. **4** To have influence or control; rule. —*v.t.* **5** To cause to swing from side to side. **6** To cause to bend or incline to one side. **7** *Naut.* To swing into place; hoist, as a yard or mast. **8** To cause (a person, opinion, etc.) to tend in a given way; influence. **9** To cause to swerve; deflect or divert, as from a course of action. **10** *Archaic* **a** To wield, as a weapon or, especially, a scepter. **b** To rule over; govern. See synonyms under GOVERN, INFLUENCE, SHAKE. —*n.* **1** Power exercised in governing; dominion; control. **2** The act of swaying, literal or figurative; a sweeping, swinging, or turning from side to side. **3** Momentum; inclination; bias. **4** Overpowering force or influence. [Prob. fusion of ON *sveigja* bend and LG *swajen* be moved to and fro by the wind]

sway·back (swā′bak′) *n.* **1** A hollow or unnaturally sagging condition of the back, as in a horse. **2** An animal with a swayback.

sway-backed (swā′bakt′) *adj.* **1** Having a sagged or hollow back. **2** Hence, strained or weakened, as by overwork.

Swa·zi (swä′zē) *n.* One of a tribe belonging to the Bantu peoples, and dwelling in Swaziland, Africa.

Swa·zi·land (swä′zē·land) An independent member of the Commonwealth of Nations, between Mozambique and South Africa; 6,704 sq. mi.; capital, Mbabane. See map of SOUTH AFRICA.

sweal (swēl) *v.i. Brit. Dial.* **1** To melt and run down, as the tallow of a candle. **2** To burn away slowly; waste away. Also spelled *swale.* [OE *swelan, swǣlan* burn]

swear (swâr) *v.* **swore** (*Obs.* **sware**), **sworn, swear·ing** *v.i.* **1** To make a solemn affirmation with an appeal to God or to some deity, or with invocation of something held sacred, as in attestation of truth or proof of good intentions: He *swore* by all the gods. **2** To make a vow; utter a solemn promise. **3** To use profanity; invoke or mention sacred beings or things irreverently or blasphemously; curse. **4** *Law* To give testimony under oath. —*v.t.* **5** To affirm or assert solemnly by invoking sacred beings or things. **6** To promise with an oath or solemn affirmation; vow. **7** To declare or affirm upon oath: to *swear* treason against a man. **8** To take or utter (an oath). **9** To administer a legal oath to. —**to swear by** **1** To appeal to by oath. **2** To have complete confidence in. —**to swear in** To administer a legal oath to. —**to swear off** *Colloq.* To promise to renounce or give up: to *swear off* drink. —**to swear out** To obtain (a warrant for arrest) by making a statement or charge under oath. [OE *swerian*] —**swear′er** *n.*

swear·word (swâr′wûrd′) *n.* A word used in profanity or cursing.

sweat (swet) *v.* **sweat** or **sweat·ed, sweat·ing** *v.i.* **1** To exude or excrete sensible moisture from the pores of the skin; perspire. **2** To exude moisture in drops; ooze. **3** To gather and condense moisture in drops on its surface. **4** To pass through pores or interstices in drops. **5** To ferment, as tobacco leaves. **6** *Colloq.* To work hard; toil; drudge. **7** *Colloq.* To suffer: You will *sweat* for that! —*v.t.* **8** To exude (moisture) from the pores. **9** To gather or condense drops of (moisture). **10** To soak or stain with sweat. **11** To cause to sweat. **12** To cause to work hard. **13** *Colloq.* To force (employees) to work for low wages and under unfavorable conditions. **14** *Slang* To extort money from. **15** To heat (solder, etc.) until it melts. **16** To join, as metal objects, by applying heat after binding together with solder. **17** *Metall.* To heat so as to extract an element that is easily fusible; also, to extract thus. **18** To force moisture from, as wood in a charcoal kiln. **19** To subject to fermentation, as hides or tobacco. **20** To remove particles of (coins) illegally, as by shaking them in a bag. **21** *Slang* To subject to torture or rigorous interrogation for the purpose of extracting information; put through the third degree. **— to sweat (something) out** *Slang* To wait through anxiously and helplessly: to *sweat out* a long delay. — *n.* **1** Sensible perspiration of animals, or any gathering of moisture in minute drops like those of perspiration on the skin. **2** The act or state of sweating; specifically, sweating induced by drugs or artificial means. **3** Figuratively, hard labor; drudgery. **4** *Colloq.* Fuming impatience; worry; hurry. **5** The act or process of causing to sweat, as a short rapid exercise given to a horse or the process of sweating hides or bricks. **6** *Obs.* The sweating sickness. [OE *swǣtan* < *swāt* sweat] **— sweat′i·ly** *adv.* **— sweat′i·ness** *n.* **— sweat′y** *adj.*

sweat·band (swet′band′) *n.* A band, usually of leather, inside the crown of a hat to protect it from sweat.

sweat·box (swet′boks′) *n.* **1** A device for sweating such products as hides and dried fruits. **2** Any very hot, close room. **3** *Colloq.* Formerly, a narrow cell where an unruly prisoner was confined; now, any place of confinement; specifically, a place where a prisoner is questioned or put through the third degree.

sweat·ed (swet′id) *adj.* **1** Saturated or covered with sweat; that has been made to perspire. **2** Employed in hard work for low pay; overworked and underpaid: a *sweated* industry.

sweat·er (swet′ər) *n.* **1** One who or that which sweats; specifically, an employer who underpays and overworks his employees. **2** A jerseylike knitted garment with or without sleeves. **3** A medicine that induces sweating; a sudorific.

sweat gland *Anat.* One of the convoluted tubules that secrete sweat, found in subcutaneous tissue and terminating externally in a small orifice or pore.

sweating sickness *Pathol.* A febrile infective disease epidemic in England in the 15th and 16th centuries, characterized by profuse sweating; miliaria. Also **sweating fever.**

sweat shirt A collarless pull-over sweater, sometimes lined with fleece: used by athletes.

sweat·shop (swet′shop′) *n.* A place where work is done under poor conditions, for insufficient wages, and for long hours.

Swede (swēd) *n.* **1** A native or naturalized inhabitant of Sweden. **2** A Swedish turnip; the rutabaga.

Swe·den (swēd′n) A kingdom in NE Europe, in the eastern part of the Scandinavian peninsula; 173,577 square miles; capital, Stockholm: Swedish *Sverige.*

Swe·den·borg (swēd′n·bôrg, *Sw.* svā′dən·bôr′y′), **Emanuel,** 1688–1772, Swedish mystic, philosopher, and scientist. **— Swe′den·bor′gi·an** (-bôr′jē·ən) *adj.* & *n.*

Swe·den·bor·gi·an·ism (swē′dən·bôr′jē·ən·iz′·əm) *n.* The system of philosophy or the theology developed by Emanuel Swedenborg, or from his writings, which teaches that Jesus Christ is the only God, and emphasizes a symbolic interpretation of the Bible. The Swedenborgian church, first organized in London in 1783, is called the *New Church,* or the *New Jerusalem Church.* Also **Swe′den·borg′ism** (-bôrg′iz·əm).

Swed·ish (swē′dish) *adj.* Pertaining to Sweden, the Swedes, or their language. — *n.* **1** The North Germanic language of Sweden, including Old Swedish (the pre-Reformation language), Modern Swedish, and several dialects. **2** The inhabitants of Sweden collectively: with *the.*

Swedish clover Alsike.

Swedish massage Massage given in combination with Swedish movements.

Swedish movements A system of muscular movements employed in treating certain diseases or developing the body.

Swedish turnip The rutabaga.

swee·ny (swē′nē) *n.* Atrophy of the shoulder muscles of a horse. [Perhaps < dial. G *schweine* atrophy < *schweinen* become emaciated]

sweep (swēp) *v.* **swept, sweep·ing** *v.t.* **1** To collect, remove, or clear away with a broom, brush, etc. **2** To clear or clean with or as with a broom or brush: to *sweep* a floor; to *sweep* the plains of buffalo. **3** To touch or brush with a motion as of sweeping: Her dress *swept* the ground; to *sweep* the strings of a harp. **4** To pass over or through swiftly, as in searching: His eyes *swept* the sky. **5** To cause to move with an even, continuous action: He *swept* the cape over her shoulders. **6** To move, carry, bring, etc., with strong or continuous force: The flood *swept* the bridge away. **7** To move over or through with strong or steady force: The gale *swept* the bay. **8** To drag the bottom of (a body of water, etc.). — *v.i.* **9** To clean or brush a floor or other surface with a broom, etc. **10** To move or go strongly and evenly, especially with speed: The train *swept* by. **11** To walk with or as with trailing garments: She *swept* into the room. **12** To trail, as a skirt. **13** To extend with a long reach or curve: The road *sweeps* along the lake shore on the north. See synonyms under CLEANSE. — *n.* **1** The act or result of sweeping. **2** The motion of a long stroke or movement: a *sweep* of the hand. **3** The act of clearing out or getting rid of; hence, removal from office or place: a clean *sweep* of the office-holders; also, a clearance. **4** A turning of the eye or of optical instruments over the field of vision. **5** The winning of a great success, as in an election. **6** The range, area, or compass reached by sweeping, as extent of stroke, range of vision, etc.; direction or extent of motion; hence, a curve or bend, as of a scythe blade, etc. **7** One who or that which sweeps. **8** A piece, as of a machine, along which something sweeps. **9** *Brit.* A chimneysweeper. **10** A long, heavy oar. **11** A well sweep. **12** A curved roadway or approach before a building. **13** *pl.* Sweepings, as of a place where precious metals are worked. **14** *Physics* An irreversible process in which a substance settles to thermal equilibrium or tends to do so. **15** In card games, a winning of all the points in a hand, as by taking of all the tricks in whist; in casino, the taking or capture of all the cards on the table. **16** *Colloq.* Sweepstakes. [ME *swepen,* alter. of *swopen* brush away <OE *swāpen*] **— sweep′er** *n.*

sweep·back (swēp′bak′) *n. Aeron.* **1** The backward inclination of the leading edge of an airplane wing. **2** The acute angle between the line of this inclination and the lateral axis of the airplane.

sweep·ing (swē′ping) *adj.* **1** Carrying off or clearing away with a driving movement. **2** Carrying all before it; covering a wide area; comprehensive. **3** General and thorough-going. — *n.* **1** The action of one who or that which sweeps. **2** *pl.* Things swept up; refuse. **— sweep′ing·ly** *adv.* **— sweep′ing·ness** *n.*

sweep·stakes (swēp′stāks′) *n. pl.* **·stakes** **1** A gambling arrangement by which all the sums staked may be won by one or by a few of the betters, as in a horse race. **2** A race for all the stakes. **3** A prize in a sporting contest comprising several stakes. **4** A lottery which offers sweepstakes as prizes. Also **sweep′stake′.**

sweep ticket A ticket which gives the holder a chance to win in a sweepstakes.

sweep·y (swē′pē) *adj.* **sweep·i·er, sweep·i·est** **1** Having a sweeping, swaying, or trailing motion. **2** Sweeping in curves, as a river.

sweer (swir) *adj. Dial.* **1** Heavy; lazy; indolent. **2** Reluctant; unwilling. [OE *swǣr*]

sweet (swēt) *adj.* **1** Agreeable to the sense of taste; having a flavor like that of sugar; especially, containing or due to sugar in some form. **2** Fresh, as opposed to *salt, sour,* or *rancid*; not fermented or decaying. **3** Gently pleasing to the senses; agreeable to the smell; pleasing in sound; melodious; fair; restful. **4** Agreeable or delightful to the mind; arousing gentle, pleasant emotions. **5** Having gentle, pleasing, and winning qualities; marked by kindness and amiability; dear; beloved. **6** Easy; smooth; noiseless: said of machines or contrivances. **7** Sound; rich; productive: said of soil. **8** Not dry: said of wines. **9** *Chem.* Free from acid, etc. — *n.* **1** The quality of being sweet; sweetness. **2** Something sweet: chiefly in the plural, as confections, preserves, candy. **3** A beloved person; darling. **4** Something agreeable or pleasing; pleasure. **5** A sweet smell; perfume. **6** *Brit.* A dessert. ◆ Homophone: *suite.* [OE *swēte*] **— sweet′ly** *adv.* **— sweet′ness** *n.*

Synonyms (adj.): honeyed, luscious, nectared, saccharine, sugared, sugary. See AMIABLE, LOVELY.

Sweet (swēt), **Henry,** 1845–1912, English philologist.

sweet alyssum A perennial Mediterranean herb *(Lobularia maritima)* of the mustard family, having very fragrant white blossoms.

sweet basil Basil (def. 1).

sweet bay **1** Laurel (def. 1). **2** A highly ornamental tree or shrub *(Magnolia virginiana),* with evergreen or deciduous leaves and large handsome flowers.

sweet·bread (swēt′bred′) *n.* The pancreas (**stomach sweetbread**) or the thymus gland (**neck sweetbread** or **throat sweetbread**) of a calf or other animal, when used as food. [<SWEET + BREAD, in obs. sense of "a morsel"]

sweet·bri·er (swēt′brī′ər) *n.* A stout prickly rose *(Rosa eglanteria)* with aromatic leaves. Also **sweet′bri′ar.**

sweet cicely **1** A small European perennial *(Myrrhis odorata)* having white fragrant flowers. **2** A related American herb (genus *Osmorhiza*) with white or purplish flowers and fleshy aromatic root.

sweet clover Melilot.

sweet corn **1** Any of several varieties of Indian corn rich in sugar, and shriveling when ripe. **2** Indian corn in the milky stage.

sweet·en (swēt′n) *v.t.* **1** To make sweet or sweeter. **2** To make more endurable; lighten. **3** To make pleasant or gratifying. **4** In poker, to increase the chips in (the pot). **5** To add gilt-edge securities to others so as to increase the value of (collateral for a loan). — *v.i.* **6** To become sweet or sweeter. — **sweet′en·er** *n.*

sweet·en·ing (swēt′n·ing) *n.* **1** The act of making sweet. **2** That which sweetens. **— long sweetening** Molasses; treacle. **— short sweetening** Sugar.

sweet fennel Finochio.

sweet fern **1** A shrub of the northern United States and Canada (genus *Comptonia*) with long, fernlike, fragrant leaves. **2** Any of several ferns (genus *Dryopteris*).

sweet·flag (swēt′flag′) *n.* A marsh-dwelling plant *(Acorus calamus),* with sword-shaped leaves and a thick creeping rootstock with an aromatic flavor; the calamus.

sweet·gale (swēt′gāl′) *n.* A branching shrub *(Myrica gale),* with both fertile and sterile flowers in short scaly catkins, and resinous, dotted, fragrant leaves. [<SWEET + GALE[2]]

sweet·gum (swēt′gum′) *n.* **1** A balsamiferous tree *(Liquidambar styraciflua)* of Atlantic North America, the wood of which is sometimes used to imitate mahogany. **2** The balsam or gum yielded by it.

sweet·heart (swēt′härt′) *n.* One who is particularly loved by or as a lover; a lover.

sweet·ing (swē′ting) *n.* **1** A sweet apple. **2** A sweetheart; dear one; darling.

sweet·ish (swē′tish) *adj.* Somewhat sweet; slightly sweet; also, nauseatingly sweet. — **sweet′ish·ly** *adv.* **— sweet′ish·ness** *n.*

sweet·leaf (swēt′lēf′) *n.* The horse sugar.

sweet marjoram Marjoram.

sweet·meat (swēt′mēt′) *n.* **1** A confection, preserve, or the like. **2** A candy or crystallized fruit. **3** *pl.* Very sweet candy, cakes, etc.

sweetness and light The essence of esthetic and moral culture, consisting of sympathy, appreciation, open-mindedness, and capacity to enlighten or be enlightened: phrase taken from Swift and popularized by Matthew Arnold.

sweet pea An ornamental annual climber *(Lathyrus odoratus)* of the bean family cultivated for its fragrant, varicolored flowers.

sweet pepper A mild variety of capsicum used for pickling and as a vegetable.

sweet potato **1** A perennial tropical vine *(Ipomoea batatas)* of the morning-glory family, with rose-violet or pink flowers and a fleshy tuberous root. **2** The root itself, eaten as a vegetable. 3 *Colloq.* An ocarina.

sweets (swēts) *n. pl.* 1 Sweet things to eat, as puddings, cakes, tarts, jellies, etc. 2 The pleasures and gratifying things in life: the *sweets* of success.

sweet·sop (swēt′sop′) *n.* 1 A tropical American tree *(Annona squamosa)* allied to the custard apple. 2 Its egg-shaped, scaly fruit; the sugar apple.

sweet-talk (swēt′tôk′) *Colloq. v.t.* 1 To persuade by coaxing or flattering. —*v.i.* 2 To flatter or coax someone. —**sweet talk**

sweet tooth *Colloq.* A fondness or appetite for candy or sweets.

sweet william A perennial species of pink *(Dianthus barbatus)* with large lanceolate leaves and closely clustered, showy flowers.

swell (swel) *v.* **swelled, swelled** or **swol·len, swell·ing** *v.i.* 1 To increase in bulk or dimension, as by inflation with air or by absorption of moisture; dilate; expand. 2 To increase in size, amount, degree, etc. 3 To grow in volume or intensity, as a sound. 4 To rise in waves or swells, as the sea. 5 To bulge; protrude or belly, as a sail. 6 To become puffed up with pride. 7 To grow within one: My anger *swells* at the sight. —*v.t.* 8 To cause to increase in size or bulk. 9 To cause to increase in amount, extent, or degree. 10 To cause to bulge; belly. 11 To puff with pride. 12 *Music* To sing or play with combined crescendo and diminuendo. —*n.* 1 The act, process, or effect of swelling; expansion. 2 The long continuous body of a wave; a billow; hence, a rise of, or undulation in, the land. 3 A bulge or protuberance. 4 *Music* The union of crescendo and diminuendo; also, the signs (< >) indicating it. 5 A device by which the loudness of a musical instrument, as an organ, may be increased or diminished. 6 *Slang* A person of the ultrafashionable set. See synonyms under WAVE. —*adj. Slang* 1 Of or pertaining to swells or ultrafashionable people; hence, in the height of fashion; smart. 2 First-rate; distinctive. [OE *swellan*]

Synonyms (verb): bulge, dilate, distend, enlarge, expand, increase, inflate. See PUFF. *Antonyms*: contract, decrease, dwindle, shrink.

swell·box (swel′boks′) *n.* A chamber containing the pipes of the organ and having a front of movable slats which muffle the sound or allow it to be heard clearly.

swell·fish (swel′fish′) *n. pl.* **·fish** or **·fish·es** A puffer or globefish.

swell·head (swel′hed′) *n. Slang* A conceited person.

swell·ing (swel′ing) *n.* 1 The act of expanding, inflating, or augmenting. 2 *Pathol.* Morbid enlargement of a part of the body. 3 A protuberance. —*adj.* Increasing; bulging.

swell mob *Brit. Slang* Well-dressed pickpockets collectively.

swel·ter (swel′tər) *v.i.* 1 To suffer from oppressive heat; perspire from heat. —*v.t.* 2 To cause to swelter. 3 *Obs.* To exude. —*n. Rare* A hot, sweltering condition; oppressive humid heat. [Freq. of obs. and dial. *swelt* be faint, die <OE *sweltan* die]

swel·ter·ing (swel′tər·ing) *adj.* 1 Oppressive; overpoweringly hot. 2 Overcome by heat. Also **swel′try** (-trē). —**swel′ter·ing·ly adv.**

swept (swept) Past tense and past participle of SWEEP.

swept·back (swept′bak′) *adj. Aeron.* Having the front edge (of a wing) tilted backward at an angle with the lateral axis of an airplane. Also called *backswept.*

swept·wing (swept′wing′) *n.* A sweptback wing. —*adj.* Having a sweptback wing.

swerve (swûrv) *v.t. & v.i.* **swerved, swerv·ing** To turn or cause to turn aside from a course or purpose; deflect. See synonyms under FLUCTUATE, WANDER. —*n.* The act of swerving; a sudden turning aside. [OE *sweorfan* file or grind away]

swev·en (swev′ən) *n. Obs.* A dream. [OE *swefn* sleep, a dream]

swift[1] (swift) *adj.* 1 Traversing space or performing movements in a brief time; rapid; quick. 2 Capable of quick motion; fleet; speedy. 3 Passing rapidly, as time or events; also, coming without warning; unexpected. 4 Acting with readiness; prompt. —*adv.* Quickly: a poetic use. [OE] —**swift′ly** *adv.* —**swift′ness** *n.*

Synonyms (adj.): expeditious, fast, fleet, flying, hasty, quick, rapid, speedy, sudden. See IMPETUOUS, NIMBLE. *Antonyms*: deliberate, dilatory, dull, lingering, slow, sluggish, tardy.

swift[2] (swift) *n.* 1 A bird of swallowlike form (family *Micropodidae*), possessing extraordinary powers of flight, including the builders of edible birds' nests (genus *Collocalia*) and the common American swift *(Chaetura pelagica).* 2 One of various small lizards (genera *Sceloporus* and *Uta*) common in the western United States. 3 A reel having an adjustable diameter for winding yarn, etc. 4 The main cylinder of a carding machine; also, a similar part in other machines. [< SWIFT[1]]

CHIMNEY SWIFT
(About 9 1/2 inches long)

Swift (swift), **Jonathan,** 1667–1745, English satirist born in Dublin: called "Dean Swift."

swift·er (swif′tər) *v.t.* To make taut, as shrouds of a ship, by means of a block and tackle. —*n. Naut.* 1 A rope around the extremities of the capstan bars to connect and steady them, and to give a hold for extra men. 2 One of the forward lower shrouds. 3 A rope for encircling a boat, to strengthen her or prevent chafing of her sides. [<obs. *swift* tie with ropes drawn taut, prob. <Scand. Cf. ON *svifta* reef (a sail).]

swift lizard The fence lizard.

swig[1] (swig) *n. Colloq.* A deep draft. —*v.t. & v.i.* **swigged, swig·ging** *Colloq.* To drink swigs (of). [Origin unknown]

swig[2] (swig) *Naut. v.t.* **swigged, swig·ging** To tighten (a rope that is fast at both ends) by hauling at right angles to its lead. —*n.* 1 A hauling on the bight of a rope fast at both ends. 2 A tackle having diverging ropes. [Akin to SWAG]

swill (swil) *v.t.* 1 To drink greedily and to excess. 2 *Brit.* To drench, as with water; rinse; wash. —*v.i.* 3 To drink to excess; tope. —*n.* 1 Liquid food for domestic animals; especially, the mixture of liquid and solid food given to swine; garbage. 2 Liquor drunk greedily or grossly; loosely, liquor in general. [OE *swillan, swillian* wash]

swim[1] (swim) *v.* **swam** (*Dial.* **swum**), **swum, swim·ming** *v.i.* 1 To move through water by working the legs, arms, fins, etc. 2 To be supported on water or other liquid; float. 3 To move with a smooth or flowing motion, as if swimming in water. 4 To be immersed in or covered with liquid; be flooded; overflow. —*v.t.* 5 To cross or traverse by swimming. 6 To cause to swim. See synonyms under FLOAT. —*n.* 1 The action or pastime of swimming. 2 A gliding, swaying motion or movement. 3 The air bladder of a fish; the sound: also **swim bladder, swimming bladder.** 4 *Colloq.* The current of affairs, especially of fashionable life: in the *swim.* [OE *swimman*] —**swim′mer** *n.*

swim[2] (swim) *v.i.* To be dizzy; reel; have a giddy sensation; seem to go round. —*n.* A sudden dizziness; temporary unconsciousness; swoon. [OE *swima* dizziness]

swim·mer·et (swim′ə·ret) *n. Zool.* One of a series of fringed, typically biramous abdominal appendages of a crustacean, adapted for swimming, for aid in respiration, and for carrying the eggs on females. [Dim. of *swimmer*]

swim·ming[1] (swim′ing) *n.* The act of one who swims. —*adj.* 1 Used for swimming; having the capacity of swimming. 2 Watery; flooded with tears, as the eyes. [<SWIM[1]]

swim·ming[2] (swim′ing) *adj.* Affected by dizziness. [<SWIM[2]]

swimming hole A deep hole in a shallow running stream, used for swimming.

swim·ming·ly (swim′ing·lē) *adv.* In a swimming manner; easily, rapidly, and successfully.

swim·suit (swim′so͞ot′) *n.* A garment designed to be worn while swimming.

Swin·burne (swin′bûrn), **Algernon Charles,** 1837–1909, English poet and critic.

swin·dle (swin′dəl) *v.* **·dled, ·dling** *v.t.* 1 To cheat of money or property by deliberate fraud; defraud. 2 To obtain by such means. —*v.i.* 3 To practice fraud; be a swindler. See synonyms under STEAL. —*n.* The act or pro-

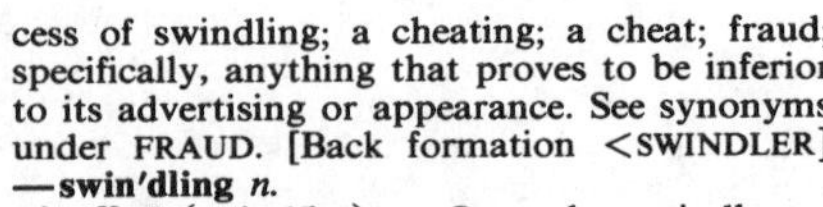

cess of swindling; a cheating; a cheat; fraud; specifically, anything that proves to be inferior to its advertising or appearance. See synonyms under FRAUD. [Back formation <SWINDLER] —**swin′dling** *n.*

swin·dler (swind′lər) *n.* One who swindles; a rogue. [<G *schwindler* giddy-minded person, cheat <*schwindeln* act thoughtlessly]

swindle sheet *U.S. Slang* An expense account.

swine (swīn) *n. pl.* **swine** 1 An omnivorous mammal (family *Suidae*) having a long mobile snout and cloven hoofs. 2 A domesticated hog. 3 A low, greedy, stupid, or vicious person. [OE *swīn*]

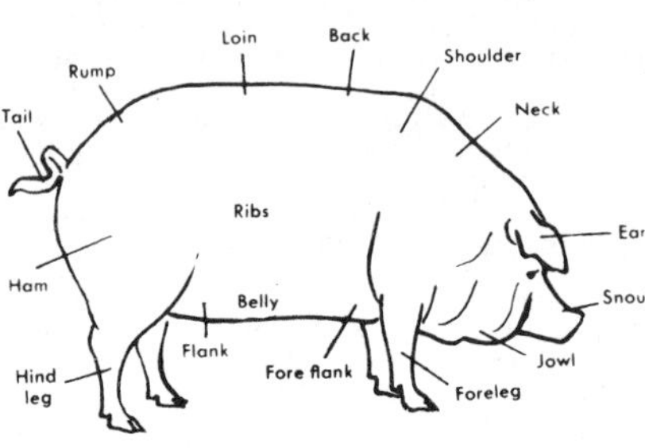

SWINE
Nomenclature of anatomical parts.

swine fever Hog cholera.

swine·herd (swīn′hûrd′) *n.* A tender of swine.

Swi·ne·mün·de (svē′nə·mün′də) The German name for ŚWINOUJŚCIE.

swine·pox (swīn′poks′) *n.* A form of chicken pox affecting swine.

swing (swing) *v.* **swung** (*Dial.* **swang**), **swung, swing·ing** *v.i.* 1 To move to and fro or backward and forward rhythmically, as something suspended; oscillate. 2 To move in a swing (def. 3). 3 To move with an even, swaying motion; walk with vigorous strides. 4 To turn; pivot: We *swung* around and went home. 5 To be suspended; hang. 6 *Colloq.* To be executed by hanging. 7 *Slang* To be very up-to-date and sophisticated, especially in one's amusements and pleasures. 8 *Colloq.* To sing or play with or to have a compelling, usually jazzlike rhythm. 9 *Slang* To be sexually promiscuous. —*v.t.* 10 To cause to move to and fro or backward and forward. 11 To cause to move with a sweeping or circular motion, as a sword, ax, etc.; brandish; flourish. 12 To cause to turn on or as on a pivot or central point. 13 To lift or hoist: They *swung* the mast into place. 14 *Colloq.* To bring to a successful conclusion; manage successfully. 15 *Colloq.* To arrange, sing, or play in the style of swing music. —*n.* 1 The action of swinging. 2 A free swaying motion. 3 A contrivance of hanging ropes with a seat on which a person may move to and fro through the air as a pastime. 4 Free course or scope; full liberty or license. 5 Compass; sweep. 6 The movement or rhythm characterizing certain styles of prose and poetry. 7 That which swings or is swung; a swinging blow or stroke. 8 The course of a career or period of activity. 9 Swing music. 10 *Colloq.* A trip or tour. [OE *swingan* scourge, beat up]

swing back *Phot.* 1 A camera back provided with a hinge to allow free movement in any direction so as to minimize distortion of perspective or focus. 2 A camera so equipped.

swing bridge A bridge constructed to rotate in a horizontal plane to permit the passage of large vessels, etc.

swinge[1] (swinj) *v.t.* **swinged, swinge·ing** *Archaic* To flog; chastise. [OE *swengan* shake, beat]

swinge[2] (swinj) *v.t.* **swinged, swinge·ing** *Dial.* To singe. [? Alter. of SINGE]

swinge·ing (swin′jing) *adj. Colloq.* Very large; heavy; extravagant. [<SWINGE[1]]

swing·er (swing′ər) *n.* 1 *Slang* A lively and up-to-date person. 2 *Slang* A person who indulges freely in sex.

swing·ing (swing′ing) *adj. Slang* 1 Lively and compelling in effect: a *swinging* jazz quartet. 2 Lively and modern.

swinging door A door that will open in either direction and swing shut when not held.

swin·gle (swing′gəl) *n.* 1 A large, knifelike

wooden implement for beating flax: also **swing′·knife.** 2 The short wooden bar of a flail; a swiple. —*v.t.* **·gled, ·gling** To cleanse, as flax, by beating with a swingle; scutch. [< MDu. *swinghel.* Akin to SWING.]

swin·gle·tree (swing′·gəl·trē′) *n.* A horizontal crossbar, to the ends of which the traces of a harness are attached; a whiffletree or singletree. See illustration under HARNESS. Also **swing·tree** (swing′trē′), **swin′gle·bar′** (-bär′).

SWINGLETREE
a, a. Swingletrees.
b. Traces.
c. Double-tree.
d. Plow beam.

swing music 1 A development of jazz after about 1935 which achieved its effects by large bands of musicians, contrapuntal styles, and arranged ensemble playing rather than improvised solo performances. 2 The particular rhythmic quality in such music. Also called *swing.*

swing shift An evening work shift, usually lasting from about 4 p.m. to midnight.

swin·ish (swī′nish) *adj.* Of or like swine; degraded; sensual; beastly. See synonyms under BRUTISH. —**swin′ish·ly** *adv.* —**swin′ish·ness** *n.*

swink (swingk) *v.i. Archaic & Brit. Dial.* To toil hard; drudge. [OE *swincan*]

Swin·ner·ton (swin′ər·tən), **Frank (Arthur),** ,born 1884, English novelist and critic.

Swi·no·ujś·cie (shvē′nô·ōō′əsh·che) A port of NW Poland: German *Swinemünde.*

swipe (swīp) *v.t.* **swiped, swip·ing 1** *Colloq.* To give a strong blow; strike with a full swing of the arm. 2 *Slang* To steal; snatch. —*n. Colloq.* 1 A hard blow, especially in field games. 2 A well sweep, lever, pump handle, or the like. [Var. of SWEEP]

swipes (swīps) *n. pl. Brit. Slang* Poor, spoiled, or weak beer; small beer; beer in general. [< SWIPE, in obs. sense of "drink hastily"]

swip·le (swip′əl) *n.* That part of a threshing flail that strikes the grain; a swingle. Also **swip′ple.** [ME *swepelles* a broom. Akin to SWEEP.]

swirl (swûrl) *v.t. & v.i.* To move or cause to move along in irregular eddies; whirl. —*n.* 1 A whirling along, as in an eddy; whirl. 2 A curl or twist; spiral. [<dial. E (Scottish) *swyrle.* Prob. akin to dial. Norw. *svirla* whirl.]

swirl·y (swûr′lē) *adj.* 1 Full of swirls. 2 *Scot.* Tangled; knotty; gnarled: also **swirl′ie.**

swish (swish) *v.i.* 1 To move with a sweeping motion and whistling sound, as a whip. —*v.t.* 2 To cause to swish. 3 To thrash; flog. —*n.* 1 A hissing, swishing sound, as of a lash through the air, or the swing of a silk skirt. 2 A movement producing such a sound. 3 An implement, as a broom, used with such a movement. [Imit.]

swiss (swis) *n. Often cap.* A sheer, crisp cotton fabric, similar to muslin, and often dotted or figured, when it is called *dotted swiss.*

Swiss (swis) *adj.* Pertaining to Switzerland; characteristic of Switzerland. —*n. pl.* **Swiss** A native or naturalized inhabitant of Switzerland.

Swiss chard Chard (def. 2).

Swiss cheese A pale-yellow cheese with many large holes, made in, or similar to that made in, Switzerland.

Swiss guards Mercenary soldiers from Switzerland formerly used as bodyguards by European monarchs, now as guards at the Vatican.

Swiss steak A thick cut of steak floured and cooked, often with a sauce of tomatoes and onions.

switch (swich) *n.* 1 A small flexible rod; light whip. 2 A tress of human or false hair, fastened together at one end and used by women in building a coiffure. 3 A mechanism for shifting a railway train or other rail vehicles from one track to another. 4 The act or operation of switching, shifting, or changing. 5 The end of the tail in certain animals, as a cow. 6 *Electr.* A device to make or break a circuit, or transfer a current from one conductor to another. 7 A connecting trench between two lines of defensive trenches. 8 A blow with a switch. See synonyms under STICK. —*v.t.* 1 To whip or lash with or as with a switch. 2 To move, jerk, or whisk suddenly or sharply: The woman *switched* her skirts aside. 3 To turn aside or divert; shift. 4 To exchange: They *switched* plates. 5 To shift, as a railroad car, to another track. 6 *Electr.* To connect or disconnect with a switch. —*v.i.* 7 To turn aside; change; shift. 8 To be shifted or turned. 9 *Dial.* To walk with a jerky or uneven gait. [Earlier *swits.* Akin to LG *zwuske* a thin rod.]

switch·back (swich′bak′) *n.* 1 A railway ascending or descending a steep incline in a series of zigzag tracks. 2 A zigzag mountain road. 3 A railroad at amusement resorts in which the cars are hoisted to a starting point and descend along a circuitous route by gravity.

switch·board (swich′bôrd′, -bōrd′) *n.* A panel or arrangement of panels bearing switches for connecting and disconnecting electric circuits, as a telephone exchange.

switch·er (swich′ər) *n.* 1 A switch-tender. 2 One who or that which switches.

switch hitter In baseball, a batter who bats either right- or left-handed.

switch·man (swich′mən) *n. pl.* **·men** (-mən) One who handles railway switches.

switch plant A plant in which green shoots take the place of absent or reduced leaves.

switch·yard (swich′yärd′) *n.* A railroad yard for the assembling and breaking up of trains.

swith (swith) *adv. Scot.* or *Obs.* Strongly; very much; quickly. —*interj.* Begone! quick! Also **swithe** (swīth).

swith·er (swith′ər) *Dial. & Scot. v.i.* To doubt; hesitate; fear. —*n.* 1 A state of doubt or hesitation. 2 A fright; perspiration; faint.

Swith·in (swith′in), **Saint,** died A.D. 862, bishop of Winchester. See under ST. SWITHIN'S DAY.

Swit·zer (swit′sər) *n.* 1 A Swiss. 2 Specifically, Swiss mercenary soldier. Also **Swiss·er** (swis′ər).

Swit·zer·land (swit′sər·lənd) A republic in central Europe; 15,940 square miles; capital, Bern: French *Suisse,* German *Schweiz,* Italian *Svizzera,* Latin *Helvetia.* Also **Swiss Confederation.**

swiv·el (swiv′əl) *n.* 1 A coupling device, link, ring, or pivot that permits either half of a mechanism, as a chain, to rotate independently. 2 A rest on a boat's gunwale, on which a gun may be swept or swung in a horizontal plane. 3 Anything that turns on a pin or headed bolt. 4 A cannon that swings on a pivot: also **swivel gun.** 5 The shuttle of a ribbon loom. —*v.* **·eled** or **·elled, ·el·ing** or **·el·ling** *v.t.* 1 To turn on or as on a swivel. 2 To provide with or secure by a swivel. —*v.i.* 3 To turn or swing on or as on a swivel. [ME *swyuel* <OE *swif-,* stem of *swīfan* move]

SWIVEL (*a*

swiv·et (swiv′it) *n. Colloq.* Hurry; anxiety; eager, nervous haste or excitement: Don't be in such a *swivet.* Also **swiv′vet.** [Cf. obs. *swive* copulation <OE *swīfan* move] —**swiv′et·ty** *adj.*

swiz·zle (swiz′əl) *n.* One of various compounded intoxicating drinks; specifically, a drink made with rum or other spirit, sugar, bitters, and ice. —*v.t. & v.i.* **·zled, ·zling** *Slang* To guzzle. [Origin unknown] —**swiz′·zler** *n.*

swizzle stick 1 A stick, usually with prongs set at right angles to one end, used to mix swizzle by whirling between the palms of the hands. 2 A slender rod of glass, plastic, etc., used to mix drinks.

swob (swob), **swob·ber** (swob′ər) See SWAB, etc.

swol·len (swō′lən) Alternative past participle of SWELL.

swoon (swōōn) *v.i.* To fall in a faint; faint. —*n.* The act of swooning; a fainting fit. See synonyms under STUPOR. Also, *Obs., swoun, swound.* [ME *swounen,* back formation < *swoweninge* SWOONING]

swoon·ing (swōō′ning) *n.* A fainting fit; swoon. —*adj.* Fainting. [ME *swoweninge* <OE *geswōgen* unconscious]

swoop (swōōp) *v.i.* To drop or descend suddenly, as a bird pouncing on its prey. —*v.t.* To take or seize suddenly, as with a swoop. —*n.* A sweeping down or pouncing down, as by a bird of prey: often figuratively. [Var. of obs. *swope* <OE *swāpan* sweep; prob. infl. in form by dial. E *soop* sweep <ON *sōpa*]

swop (swop) See SWAP.

sword (sôrd, sōrd) *n.* 1 A weapon consisting of a long blade fixed in a hilt: used for cutting or thrusting, as a rapier, scimitar, or claymore. 2 The power of the sword; sovereignty; the power of life and death; especially, military as opposed to civil power. 3 War; also, the cause of death or ruin. 4 An end bar from which the lay of a hand loom hangs; also, the upright support of the lay of a power loom. **—at swords' points** Very unfriendly; hostile; ready for a fight. **—to put to the sword** To kill with a sword; slaughter in battle. [OE *sweord*]

sword bayonet A bayonet having the shape of a sword and used like one. See illustration under BAYONET.

sword·bill (sôrd′bil′, sōrd′-) *n.* A tropical American hummingbird (genus *Ensifera*) with a very long, slender bill.

sword cane A cane made to carry a sword or dagger.

sword·craft (sôrd′kraft′, -kräft′, sōrd′-) *n.* 1 Dexterity or skill in the use of the sword. 2 Exercise of authority by the sword, or by military power.

sword dance 1 A dance among or over naked swords laid on the ground. 2 A dance in which the female dancers pass under a double line of swords crossed over their heads by the men.

sword·er (sôr′dər, sōr′-) *n. Obs.* One skilled in the use of, or who fights with, a sword; hence, a cut-throat.

sword·fish (sôrd′fish′, sōrd′-) *n. pl.* **·fish** or **·fish·es** A large fish of the open sea (genus *Xiphias*) having the bones of the upper jaw consolidated to form an elongated swordlike process.

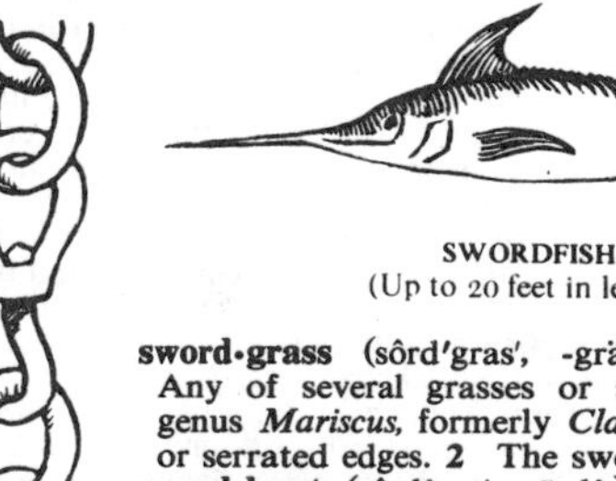

SWORDFISH
(Up to 20 feet in length)

sword·grass (sôrd′gras′, -gräs′, sōrd′-) *n.* 1 Any of several grasses or sedges (especially genus *Mariscus,* formerly *Cladium*) with sharp or serrated edges. 2 The sword lily.

sword·knot (sôrd′not′, sōrd′-) *n.* Formerly, a loop of leather used to fasten the hilt of a sword to the wrist; now, a tassel of cord of ribbon tied to a sword hilt.

sword lily A gladiolus.

sword play 1 Attack and defense with the sword. 2 Skill in fighting with the sword or in fencing; fencing. **—sword′-play′er** *n.*

swords·man (sôrdz′mən, sōrdz′-) *n. pl.* **·men** (-mən) 1 One skilled in the use of or armed with a sword. 2 A soldier. Also **sword′·man.** **—swords′man·ship, sword′man·ship** *n.*

swore (swôr, swōr) Past tense of SWEAR.

sworn (swôrn, swōrn) Past participle of SWEAR.

swot[1] (swot) *Brit. Slang v.i.* **swot·ted, swot·ting** To sweat or work hard over a task; grind. —*n.* Hard work; also, one who works hard, especially in studying. [Dial. var. of SWEAT]

swot[2] (swot) See SWAT[1].

swoun (swoun), **swound** (swound) See SWOON.

swounds (zwoundz, zoundz), **swouns** (zwounz, zounz) See ZOUNDS.

swum (swum) Past participle and dialectal past tense of SWIM.

swung (swung) Past tense and past participle of SWING.

swy (swī) *n. Austral. Slang* The game of two-up. Also **swy′-up** (swī′up). [G *zwei* two]

sy- Var. of SYN-.

Syb·a·ris (sib′ər·is) An ancient Greek city on the Gulf of Tarentum in southern Italy, famous as a center of luxurious living; founded in 720 B.C.; destroyed, 510 B.C.

syb·a·rite (sib′ə·rīt) *n.* A luxurious person; epicure; voluptuary. [<L *Sybarita* <Gk. *Sybaritēs* <*Sybaris* Sybaris]

Syb·a·rite (sib′ə·rīt) *n.* A native or citizen of Sybaris.

Syb·a·rit·ic (sib′ə·rit′ik) *adj.* **1** Of or pertaining to Sybaris or the Sybarites. **2** Hence, given to luxury; voluptuous. Also **Syb′a·rit′i·cal.** — **Syb′a·rit′i·cal·ly** *adv.* — **Syb·a·rit·ism** (sib′ə·rīt·iz′əm) *n.*

sy·bo (sī′bō) *n. pl.* **·boes** The cibol or Welsh onion. [< dial. E (Scottish), var. of CIBOL]

syc·a·mine (sik′ə·min) *n.* The mulberry tree (*Morus nigra*) of the New Testament. [<LL *sycaminus* <Gk. *sykaminos* a mulberry tree <Aramaic *shiqmīn,* pl. <Hebrew *shiqmah*]

syc·a·more (sik′ə·môr, -mōr) *n.* **1** A medium-sized bushy tree of Syria and Egypt (*Ficus sycomorus*) allied to the common fig. **2** Any of various plane trees widely distributed in the United States, especially the American sycamore (*Platanus occidentalis*) and the buttonwood of California. **3** An ornamental shade tree of Europe and Asia (*Acer pseudo-platanus*); the sycamore maple. Also *Obs.* **syc′o·more.** [<OF *sicamor* <LL *sycomorus* <Gk. *sykomoros* < *sykon* a fig + *moron* a mulberry]

syce (sīs) *n.* A groom; a man servant: also spelled *sice, saice.* [<Hind. *sā′is* <Arabic < *sūs* tend a horse]

sy·cee (sī·sē′) *n.* Pure uncoined silver ingots of various weight and size: used by the Chinese as a medium of exchange. Also **sycee silver.** — *adj.* Pure; unalloyed. [< dial. Chinese (Cantonese) *sai sze,* var. of Chinese *si szĕ* fine silk; so called because if pure it may be drawn out into fine threads]

sy·con (sī′kon) *adj. Zool.* Designating a type of sponge having an infolded body wall provided with radial canals for the reception of water, as in the typical genus *Sycon.* [<NL <Gk. *sykon* a fig]

sy·co·ni·um (sī·kō′nē·əm) *n. pl.* **·ni·a** (-nē·ə) *Bot.* An aggregate or multiple fruit in which many flowers have been developed on a fleshy receptacle, which is a flattened disk or forms a nearly closed cavity, as in the fig. [<NL <Gk. *sykon* a fig]

syc·o·phan·cy (sik′ə·fən·sē) *n. pl.* **·cies** The practices of a sycophant; base flattery; fawning.

syc·o·phant (sik′ə·fənt) *n.* **1** A servile flatterer; parasite. **2** *Obs.* An informer; accuser: the original meaning. **3** *Obs.* An impostor; deceiver. [<L *sycophanta* <Gk. *sykophantēs* an informer < *sykon* a fico + *phan-,* stem of *phainein* show] — **syc′o·phan′tic** (-fan′tik) or **·ti·cal** *adj.* — **syc′o·phan′ti·cal·ly** *adv.*

Syc·o·rax (sik′ō·raks) In Shakespeare's *Tempest,* Caliban's mother, a witch.

sy·co·sis (sī·kō′sis) *n. Pathol.* An inflamed staphylococcic infection of the skin involving the hair follicles, generally of the face and scalp. ◆ Homophone: *psychosis.* [<NL <Gk. *sykōsis* a fig-shaped ulcer < *sykon* a fig]

Syd·ney (sid′nē) A masculine personal name. Also *Sidney.* [from a surname, orig. <AF *St. Denis.* See DENIS]

Syd·ney (sid′nē) **1** The chief port and capital of New South Wales, Australia. **2** A port on Cape Breton Island, NE Nova Scotia, Canada.

Syd·ney (sid′nē), **Sir Philip** See SIDNEY.

Sy·e·ne (sī·ē′nē) The ancient name for ASWAN. — **Sy·e·nit·ic** (sī′ə·nit′ik) *adj.*

sy·e·nite (sī′ə·nīt) *n.* An igneous granular rock composed principally of feldspar and containing little or no quartz: also spelled *sienite.* [<F *syénite* <L *syenites* (*lapis*) (stone) of Syene <*Syene* Syene <Gk. *Syēnē*] — **sy′e·nit′ic** (-nit′ik) *adj.*

syke (sīk) *n. Scot.* A small stream from a bog: also spelled *sike.*

Syk·tyv·kar (sik′tif·kär′) The capital of Komi Autonomous S.S.R., in NE central European Russian S.F.S.R.

syl- Assimilated var. of SYN-.

syl·la·bar·y (sil′ə·ber′ē) *n. pl.* **·bar·ies** A list of characters representing syllables; the syllabic characters, collectively, of a language, as Chinese or Japanese, answering the function of an alphabet in writing. [<NL *syllabarium,* neut. of Med. L *syllabarius* < *syllaba* SYLLABLE]

syl·lab·ic (si·lab′ik) *adj.* **1** Of, pertaining to, or consisting of a syllable or syllables. **2** *Phonet.* Designating a consonant capable of forming a complete syllable without a vowel, as *l* in *middle* (mid′l) and *n* in *sudden* (sud′n). See SONORANT. **3** Having every syllable distinctly pronounced. **4** Designating a type of poetry based on a definite number of syllables per line rather than on stress or rhythm. Also **syl·lab′i·cal.** — *n. Phonet.* A syllabic consonant; a sonorant. — **syl·lab′i·cal·ly** *adv.*

syl·lab·i·cate (si·lab′ə·kāt) *v.t.* **·cat·ed, ·cat·ing** To form or divide into syllables. Also **syl·lab′i·fy.** — **syl·lab′i·ca′tion, syl·lab′i·fi·ca′tion** *n.*

syl·la·bism (sil′ə·biz′əm) *n.* **1** The use of characters representing syllables instead of letters in a written language. **2** The theory of syllables; division into syllables.

syl·la·bist (sil′ə·bist) *n.* One skilled in syllabicating.

syl·la·bize (sil′ə·bīz) *v.t.* **·bized, ·biz·ing** To divide (words) or form (letters) into syllables.

syl·la·ble (sil′ə·bəl) *n.* **1** *Phonet.* A word or part of a word uttered in a single vocal impulse, and consisting of a vowel (or diphthong) alone or with one or more consonants, or of a syllabic consonant. An **open syllable** is one ending in a vowel, as the first syllable of *si·lent* (sī′lənt); a **closed syllable** is one ending in a consonant, as the first and third syllables of *cat·a·pult* (kat′ə·pult). **2** A part of a written or printed word corresponding, more or less, to the spoken division. In this dictionary, syllable breaks are indicated by centered dots. **3** The smallest particle of expression; the least detail, mention, or trace: Please don't repeat a *syllable* of what you've heard here. — *v.* **·bled, ·bling** *v.t.* **1** To pronounce the syllables of; utter; speak. **2** *Obs.* To syllabicate. — *v.i.* **3** To pronounce syllables. [<AF *sillable,* OF *sillabe* <L *syllaba* <Gk. *syllabē* < *syllambanein* < *syn-* together + *lambanein* take]

syl·la·bub (sil′ə·bub) See SILLABUB.

syl·la·bus (sil′ə·bəs) *n. pl.* **·bus·es** or **·bi** (-bī) A concise statement of the main points of a subject; outline, as of a course of study; schedule; epitome; abstract; specifically, a short statement at the beginning of a brief of the legal points involved. [<NL <Med. L *syllabos,* a misprint for L *sittybas,* accusative pl. of *sittyba* label on a book <Gk.]

syl·lep·sis (si·lep′sis) *n. pl.* **·ses** (-sēz) A figure of speech, common in classical Greek and Roman literature, by which an adjective or a verb is made to modify or govern two nouns, but must be understood in a different sense for each noun. This figure conveys a double meaning, often with humorous effect, as in Pope's comment on Queen Anne: Dost sometimes *counsel take* —and sometimes *tea.* Compare ZEUGMA. [<LL *syllepsis* <Gk. *syllēpsis* < *syn-* together + *lēpsis* a taking < *lēb-, lab-,* stem of *lambanein* take] — **syl·lep′tic** *adj.*

syl·lo·gism (sil′ə·jiz′əm) *n.* **1** *Logic* **a** A formula of argument consisting of three propositions. The first two propositions, called *premises,* have one term in common furnishing a logical connection between the two other terms, which are then linked in the third proposition, called the *conclusion.* Example: All men are mortal (*major premise*); kings are men (*minor premise*); therefore, kings are mortal (*conclusion*). In this example, the *major term* is "mortal," the *minor term* is "kings," and the *middle term* is "men." **b** Deductive reasoning. **2** A subtle or crafty argument. [<OF *silogime* <L *syllogismus* <Gk. *syllogismos* < *syllogizesthai* SYLLOGIZE]

syl·lo·gis·tic (sil′ə·jis′tik) *adj.* Pertaining to, or having the nature or form of, a syllogism: also **syl′lo·gis′ti·cal.** — *n.* The art of reasoning by syllogism; the department of logic dealing with syllogisms: also **syl′lo·gis′tics.** — **syl′lo·gis′ti·cal·ly** *adv.*

syl·lo·gize (sil′ə·jīz) *v.t.* & *v.i.* **·gized, ·giz·ing** To reason or argue by syllogisms. [<OF *silogiser* <Med. L *syllogizare* <Gk. *syllogizesthai* < *syn-* together + *logizesthai* calculate, infer < *logos* discourse] — **syl′lo·gi·za′tion** (-jə·zā′shən) *n.*

sylph (silf) *n.* **1** Originally, in the system of Paracelsus, a being, male or female, mortal but without a soul, living in and on the air, and intermediate between material and immaterial beings. **2** A slender, graceful young woman or girl. **3** A South American hummingbird (*Cyanolesbia gorgo*), with a long, forked, brilliantly colored tail. [<NL *sylphes,* pl., ? coined by Paracelsus]

sylph·id (sil′fid) *n.* A young or diminutive sylph. — *adj.* Having qualities suggesting a sylph: also **sylph·i·dine** (sil′fə·din, -dīn). [<F *sylphide,* dim. of *sylphe* <NL *sylphes* SYLPH]

sylph·like (silf′līk′) *adj.* Like a sylph; slender; graceful. Also **sylph′ish, sylph′y.**

syl·va (sil′və) *n. pl.* **·vas** or **·vae** (-vē) **1** The forest trees, collectively, of a territory or region. **2** A treatise on forest trees, or a description or list of the forest trees of a certain region. Also spelled *silva.* [<L *silva* a forest]

syl·van (sil′vən) *adj.* **1** Of, pertaining to, or located in a forest or woods. **2** Composed of or abounding in trees or woods. **3** Characteristic of a forest or wood; rustic. — *n.* **1** In mythology, a spirit or deity of the forest. **2** *Archaic* or *Poetic* A person or animal dwelling in the woods. [<MF *sylvain* a sylvan <L *sylvanus, silvanus* < *silva* a wood]

syl·van·ite (sil′vən·īt) *n.* A metallic, steel-gray to silver-white telluride of gold or silver, crystallizing in the monoclinic system: when the crystals are arranged in patterns suggesting runic symbols, it is called *graphic gold, graphic tellurium.* [from (TRAN)SYLVAN(IA) + -ITE[1]]

Syl·va·nus (sil·vā′nəs) See SILVANUS.

Syl·ves·ter (sil·ves′tər) Silvester; a masculine personal name. Also *Sp.* **Syl·ves·tre** (sēl·ves′·trā). [<L, living in the wood]

syl·ves·tral (sil·ves′trəl) *adj.* Adapted to growing in woody and shady places, as certain plants; also, relating to the woods; wild. [<L *silvester, silvestris* < *silva* a forest]

Syl·vi·a (sil′vē·ə) A feminine personal name. [<L, of the forest]

Syl·vi·an fissure (sil′vē·ən) *Anat.* A deep fissure that separates the temporal lobe of the cerebrum from the parietal and frontal lobes. [<F *sylvien,* after François de la Boë *Sylvius,* 1614–72, Flemish anatomist]

syl·vite (sil′vīt) *n.* A vitreous, native potassium chloride, crystallizing in the isometric system. Also **syl′vin** (-vin), **syl′vine** (-vin, -vīn), **syl′·vin·ite.** [<NL (*sal digestivus*) *sylvii* (digestive salt) of Sylvius + -ITE[1]]

sym- Assimilated var of SYN-.

sym·bi·ont (sim′bī·ont, -bē-) *n. Biol.* An organism living in a state of symbiosis. Also **sym′·bi·on.** [<Gk. *symbioōn, -ontos,* ppr. of *bioein.* See SYMBIOSIS.] — **sym′bi·on′tic** *adj.*

sym·bi·o·sis (sim′bī·ō′sis, -bē-) *n. Biol.* The consorting together or partnership of dissimilar organisms, as of the algae and fungi in lichens. The term ordinarily connotes an association which is mutually advantageous. Compare CONSORTISM. [<NL <Gk. *symbiōsis* a living together, companionship < *symbioein* live together < *symbios* a companion, living together < *syn-* together + *bios* life] — **sym′bi·ot′ic** (-ot′ik) or **·i·cal** *adj.* — **sym′bi·ot′i·cal·ly** *adv.*

sym·bol (sim′bəl) *n.* **1** Something chosen to stand for or represent something else, usually because of a resemblance in qualities or characteristics; an object used to typify a quality, abstract idea, etc.: The oak is a *symbol* of strength. **2** A character, mark, abbreviation, conventional sign, or letter indicating something, as a quantity in mathematics, a substance in chemistry, a planet or celestial body, a quality, operation, relationship, etc. **3** A confession of faith; creed. **4** The disguised representation of an unconscious trend involving a person, object, act, etc. See synonyms under EMBLEM, LETTER, MARK, SIGN, SIMILE. ◆ Homophone: *cymbal.* [<LL *symbolum* <Gk. *symbolon* a mark, token < *symballein* put together < *syn-* together + *ballein* throw]

sym·bol·ae·og·ra·phy (sim′bəl·ē·og′rə·fē) *n.* The drawing up or framing of legal instruments. Also **sym′bol·e·og′ra·phy.** [<Gk. *symbolaiographia* < *symbolaiographos* a notary < *symbolaion* a mark, contract + *graphein* write]

sym·bol·ic (sim·bol′ik) *adj.* **1** Of or pertaining to a symbol or symbols; expressed by a symbol. **2** Serving as signs of relation or connection; relational; connective: distinguished from *presentive*: said of certain classes of words, as prepositions and conjunctions. **3** Characterized by or involving the use of symbols: *symbolic* poetry. Also **sym·bol′i·cal.** — **sym·bol′i·cal·ly** *adv.* — **sym·bol′i·cal·ness** *n.*

symbolical books Books containing the symbols or confessions of faith of a church, religious body, or inspired writer.

symbolic logic A development of formal logic in which the ambiguity of verbal propositions and of operations upon them is reduced to a minimum by the rigorous use of symbols each of which has only one referent within the given context. Also called *mathematical logic.*

sym·bol·ics (sim·bol′iks) *n. pl. (construed as singular)* The science or study of symbols or of ancient symbolic rites or creeds.

sym·bol·ism (sim′bəl·iz′əm) *n.* **1** Representation by symbols; treatment or interpretation of things as symbolic; also, the quality of being symbolic. **2** A system of symbols or symbolical representation. **3** The theories and practice of a group of symbolists. **4** Artistic imitation as a means of suggesting or expressing ideal or intangible states or ideas; also, the expression or representation of the invisible by conventional signs or figures.

sym·bol·ist (sim′bəl·ist) *n.* **1** One who uses symbols; one versed or ardent in the interpretation or use of symbols; especially, one who regards the elements in the Eucharist as mere symbols. **2** One of a class of French and Belgian writers and artists of the late 19th century, including Verlaine, Mallarmé and Maeterlinck, who sought to exalt the metaphysical by suggesting ideas and emotions by patterns of color and form and by symbolic meanings of objects, words, and sound.

sym·bol·is·tic (sim′bəl·is′tik) *adj.* **1** Expressed by symbols; characterized by the use of symbols. **2** Of or pertaining to symbolism; symbolic. Also **sym′bol·is′ti·cal.**

sym·bol·ize (sim′bəl·īz) *v.* **·ized, ·iz·ing** *v.t.* **1** To be a symbol of; represent symbolically; typify. **2** To represent by a symbol or symbols. **3** To treat as symbolic or figurative. —*v.i.* **4** To use symbols. **5** *Psychol.* To transfer emotional values from one person, object, or act to another. Also *Brit.* **sym′bol·ise.** —**sym′bol·i·za′tion** *n.*

sym·bol·o·gy (sim·bol′ə·jē) *n.* The art of representing by, or of interpreting, symbols. [< SYMBO(L) + -LOGY]

sym·met·al·ism (sim·met′l·iz′əm) *n.* A money system in which the unit of coinage is composed of two or more metals combined. [< SYM- + METAL + -ISM]

sym·met·ri·cal (si·met′ri·kəl) *adj.* **1** Exhibiting symmetry; having harmonious proportions or a correspondence in shape and size of parts; well-balanced; regular: a *symmetrical* structure. **2** *Biol.* Having parts or organs on one side corresponding to those on the other. **3** *Bot.* Regular as to number or shape of parts: said especially of a flower when the parts or divisions in each cycle (that is, the sepals, petals, stamens, and pistils) are of the same number or multiples of the same. **4** *Chem.* Denoting an arrangement of atoms of a molecule at equal relative intervals when graphically represented. **5** *Med.* Affecting corresponding organs or parts similarly. Also **sym·met′ric.** [<SYMMETRY] —**sym·met′ri·cal·ly** *adv.* —**sym·met′ri·cal·ness** *n.*

sym·me·trist (sim′ə·trist) *n.* A student or advocate of symmetry.

sym·me·trize (sim′ə·trīz) *v.t.* **·trized, ·triz·ing** To make symmetrical or proportional. —**sym′me·tri·za′tion** *n.*

sym·me·try (sim′ə·trē) *n. pl.* **·tries 1** Corresponding arrangement or balancing of the parts or elements of a whole in respect to size, shape, and position on opposite sides of an axis or center; hence, loosely, congruity; harmony; also, an instance of such arrangement. **2** The element of beauty in nature or art that results from such arrangement and balancing. **3** *Biol.* Regular arrangement of parts or organs in an animal body so that a division will give halves corresponding in shape, size, function, relative position, etc.; similarity of structure. **4** *Bot.* Equality of number in the whorls of a flower, as of sepals, petals, etc. **5** *Math.* An arrangement of pairs of points in a general system such that the set of lines joining them together is divided into equal parts by a line, a plane, or a point. **6** *Mineral.* The symmetrical distribution of non-parallel but equivalent directions (faces, edges, etc.) in a crystal with reference to certain planes or lines called **planes** or **axes of symmetry.** [<MF *symmetrie* <LL *symmetria* <Gk. < *symmetros* measured together < *syn-* together + *metron* a measure]

Synonyms: agreement, conformity, harmony, order, parity, proportion, regularity, shapeliness. See HARMONY. *Antonyms*: deformity, discordance, disproportion, shapelessness.

Sym·onds (sim′əndz), **John Addington,** 1840–1893, English author.

Sy·mons (sī′mənz), **Arthur,** 1865–1945, English poet and critic born in Wales.

sym·pa·thec·to·my (sim′pə·thek′tə·mē) *n. Surg.* The operation of interrupting some portion of the sympathetic nervous system, as by transection or resection of a nerve pathway. [<SYMPATH(ETIC) + -ECTOMY]

sym·pa·thet·ic (sim′pə·thet′ik) *adj.* **1** Pertaining to, expressing, or proceeding from sympathy. **2** Having a fellow feeling for others; sympathizing; compassionate. **3** Being in accord or harmony; congenial. **4** Referring to sounds produced by responsive vibrations. **5** *Anat.* Designating the entire autonomic nervous system. Also **sym′pa·thet′i·cal.** See synonyms under HUMANE. [<NL *sympatheticus* <Gk. *sympathētikos* < *sympatheia.* See SYMPATHY.] —**sym′pa·thet′i·cal·ly** *adv.*

sympathetic ink An ink that is colorless and invisible until brought out by heat, light, or chemical action: also called *invisible ink.*

sympathetic nervous system *Anat.* That part of the autonomic nervous system which serves the viscera, glands, heart, blood vessels, and smooth muscles. It consists of a chain of ganglia on each side of the spinal column between the cervical and sacral regions, connected with nerve plexuses, and in general produces effects opposite to those coming from the parasympathetic system.

sym·path·i·co·to·ni·a (sim·path′i·kō·tō′nē·ə) *n. Physiol.* Increased dominance of the sympathetic nervous system over other body functions, marked by vascular spasm and high blood pressure. [<NL <E *sympathic,* var. of SYMPATHETIC + Gk. *tonos* tension] —**sym·path′i·co·ton′ic** (-ton′ik) *adj.*

sym·pa·thin (sim′pə·thin) *n. Biochem.* A substance liberated by the stimulation of certain fibers of the sympathetic nervous system and acting as a chemical mediator in associated nerve impulses. [<SYMPATH(ETIC) + -IN]

sym·pa·thism (sim′pə·thiz′əm) *n.* Suggestibility; the state of being susceptible to hypnotic or other influences.

sym·pa·thize (sim′pə·thīz) *v.i.* **·thized, ·thiz·ing 1** To share the sentiments or ideas of another; have the same feelings as another: with *with.* **2** To feel or express compassion, as for another's sorrow or affliction: with *with.* **3** To be in harmony or agreement. Also *Brit.* **sym′pa·thise.** See synonyms under CONSOLE. —**sym′pa·thiz′er** *n.* —**sym′pa·thiz′ing·ly** *adv.*

sym·pa·thy (sim′pə·thē) *n. pl.* **·thies 1** The quality of being affected by the state of another with feelings correspondent in kind; a fellow feeling; a mutual affinity or susceptibility; reaction to such relationship. **2** A feeling of compassion for another's sufferings; pity; commiseration. **3** An agreement of affections or inclinations, or a conformity of natural temperaments, which makes persons agreeable to one another; congeniality; accord. **4** That quality of inanimate things by virtue of which they attract or influence one another, or are supposed to do so; affinity: a sense once much used in alchemy and astrology: the *sympathy* of the lodestone for iron. See synonyms under BENEVOLENCE, PITY. [<L *sympathia* <Gk. *sympatheia* < *sympathēs* feeling compassion with another < *syn-* together + *pathos* a feeling, passion]

sympathy strike A strike in which the strikers support the demands of another group of workers but demand nothing for themselves.

sym·pa·try (sim′pə·trē) *n. Ecol.* The distribution of plant and animal species in coextensive areas. [<SYM- + L *patria* fatherland]

sym·pet·al·ous (sim·pet′l·əs) *adj. Bot.* Gamopetalous. [<NL *Sympetalae,* a division of dicotyledons <Gk. *syn-* together + *petalon* a leaf, petal]

sym·phon·ic (sim·fon′ik) *adj.* **1** Relating to or having the form of a symphony: also **sym·pho·net·ic** (sim′fə·net′ik). **2** Agreeing in sound; harmonious.

symphonic poem *Music* A composition in free form for symphony orchestra, composed either as a unit (as Liszt's *Les Préludes* or Strauss's *Death and Transfiguration*) or as a short series of pieces (as Debussy's *La Mer*), and following a descriptive, literary, or "program" outline; a tone poem: a form developed by Liszt in the 19th century.

sym·pho·ni·ous (sim·fō′nē·əs) *adj.* According in sound; harmonious; concordant; agreeing; sounding together or in harmony. —**sym·pho′ni·ous·ly** *adv.*

sym·pho·nize (sim′fə·nīz) *v.t.* & *v.i.* **·nized, ·niz·ing** To harmonize.

sym·pho·ny (sim′fə·nē) *n. pl.* **·nies 1** A harmonious or agreeable mingling of sounds, whether vocal, instrumental, or both; figuratively, any concord or agreeable blending: *symphonies* in gray. **2** *Music* A composition for orchestra, consisting usually of four movements, of which one or more generally follow sonata form, and which are of diverse individuality united by homogeneous elements. **3** A symphony orchestra. [<OF *simphonie* <L *symphonia* <Gk. *symphōnia* < *syn-* together + *phōnē* a sound]

symphony orchestra A large orchestra composed usually of the string, brass, woodwind, and percussion sections needed to present symphonic works.

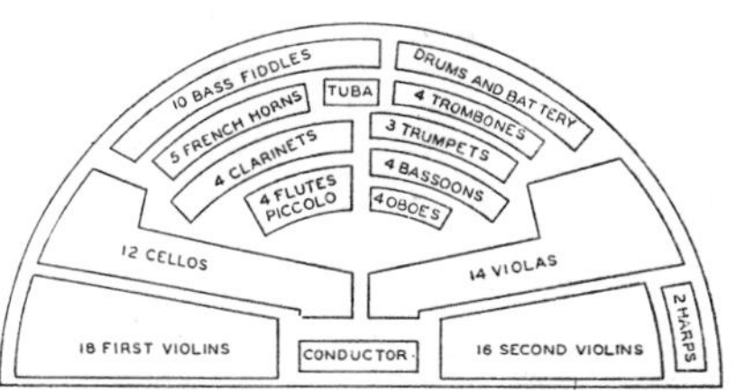

TRADITIONAL SEATING PLAN OF MODERN SYMPHONY ORCHESTRA

sym·phy·sis (sim′fə·sis) *n. pl.* **·ses** (-sēz) **1** *Anat.* A junction of two parts of the skeleton, formed either by a growing together *(synostosis)* or by the intervention of cartilage *(synchondrosis).* **2** *Bot.* The union of similar parts, or of parts normally separate. [<NL <Gk., a growing together, esp. of the bones < *syn-* together + *phyein* grow]

sym·plec·tic (sim·plek′tik) *adj. Geol.* Denoting a rock texture formed by the intermingling of two different minerals. [<Gk. *symplektikos* plaiting together < *symplekein* < *syn-* together + *plekein* plait]

Sym·pleg·a·des (sim·pleg′ə·dēz) In Greek mythology, twin rocks forming a gateway to the Black Sea and supposed to swing together and crush whatever tried to pass between them. [<L <Gk. *(petrai) Symplēgades* the clashing (rocks) < *symplēgas, -ados* striking together < *syn-* together + *plēssein* strike]

sym·po·di·um (sim·pō′dē·əm) *n. pl.* **·di·a** (-dē·ə) *Bot.* A false axis or stem of a plant, morphologically made up of a series of superposed branches imitating a simple stem; a pseudaxis. [<NL <Gk. *syn-* together + *podion,* dim. of *pous, podos* a foot] —**sym·po′di·al** *adj.* —**sym·po′di·al·ly** *adv.*

sym·po·si·ac (sim·pō′zē·ak) *adj.* Pertaining to, of the nature of, or occurring at a symposium; specifically, denoting convivial songs, glees, etc.: also **sym·po′si·al.** —*n.* A symposium. [<LL *symposiacus* <Gk. *symposiakos* < *symposion.* See SYMPOSIUM.]

sym·po·si·arch (sim·pō′zē·ärk) *n.* **1** The master or director of an ancient Greek symposium; hence, the master of a feast; a toastmaster. **2** Familiarly, a ruling spirit of a social or convivial company. [<Gk. *symposiarchos* < *symposion* a symposium (def. 3) + *archos* a ruler]

sym·po·si·um (sim·pō′zē·əm) *n.* **1** A meeting for discussion of a particular subject. **2** A collection of comments or opinions brought together; especially, a series of several brief essays or articles on the same subject by different writers, as in a magazine. 3 In ancient Greece, an after-dinner drinking party, characterized by conversation, music, dancing, and other amusements. 4 Any similar social gathering. Also called *symposiac.* Also **sym·po'si·on** (-zē·on). [<L <Gk. *symposion* < *syn-* together + *posis* a drinking < *po-*, stem of *pinein* drink]

symp·tom (simp'təm) *n.* 1 *Pathol.* An organic or functional condition indicating the presence of disease, especially when regarded as an aid in diagnosis. 2 That which serves to point out the existence of something else; any sign, token, or indication. See synonyms under SIGN. [<L *symptoma* <Gk. *symptōma* a chance, a disease < *sympiptein* happen to < *syn-* together + *piptein* fall]

symp·to·mat·ic (simp'tə·mat'ik) *adj.* 1 Pertaining to, of the nature of, or constituting a symptom or symptoms; indicative: Fever is *symptomatic* of inflammation. 2 According to symptoms: a *symptomatic* classification of diseases. Also **symp'to·mat'i·cal.** [<F *symptomatique* <LL *symptomaticus* <Gk. *symptōmatikos* < *symptōma, -atos* a symptom] — **symp'to·mat'i·cal·ly** *adv.*

symp·tom·a·tol·o·gy (simp'təm·ə·tol'ə·jē) *n.* 1 The branch of medicine that has for its object the observation and classification of symptoms. 2 The combined symptoms of a disease: also *semeiology, semeiotics.* Compare DIAGNOSIS. [<NL *symptomatologia* <Gk. *symptōma, -atos* a symptom + *logos* study]

syn– *prefix* With; together; associated with or accompanying: *syntax, syndrome.* Also: *sy–* before *sc, sp, st,* and *z,* as in *system*; *syl–* before *l,* as in *syllable*; *sym–* before *b, p,* and *m,* as in *sympathy*; *sys–* before *s,* as in *syssarcosis.* [<Gk. < *syn* together]

syn·aer·e·sis (si·ner'ə·sis) See SYNERESIS.

syn·aes·the·sia (sin'is·thē'zhə, -zhē·ə) See SYNESTHESIA.

syn·a·gog (sin'ə·gôg, -gog) *n.* 1 A place of meeting for Jewish worship and religious instruction. 2 A Jewish congregation or assemblage for religious instruction and observances. 3 The Jewish religion or communion. Also **syn'a·gogue.** [<OF *sinagoge* <LL *synagoga* <Gk. *synagōgē* an assembly, synagog < *synagein* bring together < *syn-* together + *agein* lead, bring] — **syn'a·gog'i·cal** (-goj'i·kəl), **syn'a·gog'al** (-gôg'əl, -gog'əl) *adj.*

syn·a·le·pha (sin'ə·lē'fə) *n.* The blending into a single syllable of two successive vowels of different syllables; especially, the suppression of a final vowel or diphthong before one that begins the next word: *th' Omnipotent* for *the Omnipotent.* Compare APOCOPE. Also **syn'a·le'·phe** (-lē'fē), **syn'a·loe'pha, syn'a·loe'phe.** [<LL <Gk. *synaloiphē* < *synaleiphein* smear together < *syn-* together + *aleiphein* anoint]

syn·al·gi·a (si·nal'jē·ə) *n. Pathol.* Sympathetic pain transmitted to a remote organ through associated nerves. [<NL <Gk. *synalgeein* share in suffering < *syn-* together + *algeein* feel bodily pain < *algos, -eos* bodily pain] — **syn·al'gic** *adj.*

syn·an·ther·ous (si·nan'thər·əs) *adj. Bot.* Having the stamens cohering by their anthers, as in composite flowers. [<NL *Synanthereae,* former family name <Gk. *syn-* together + NL *anthera* an anther]

syn·apse (si·naps') *n. Physiol.* The junction point of two neurons, across which a nerve impulse passes. [<NL *synapsis* <Gk., a junction < *syn-* together + *hapsis* a joining < *haptein* join]

syn·ap·sis (si·nap'sis) *n.* 1 *Biol.* The conjugation of maternal and paternal chromosomes preceding maturation, or the reduction division in the nucleus; syndesis. 2 A synapse. [<NL. See SYNAPSE.] — **syn·ap'tic** *adj.* — **syn·ap'ti·cal·ly** *adv.*

syn·ar·thro·sis (sin'är·thrō'sis) *n. pl.* **·ses** (-sēz) *Anat.* A joint that permits no motion between the parts articulated. Also **syn'ar·thro'di·a** (-dē·ə). [<NL <Gk. *synarthrōsis* < *syn-* together + *arthrōsis* a jointing < *arthron* a joint] — **syn'ar·thro'di·al** *adj.* — **syn'ar·thro'·di·al·ly** *adv.*

syn·ax·is (si·nak'sis) *n.* A congregation assembled for public worship, especially for celebrating the Lord's Supper. [<LL <Gk. < *synagein.* See SYNAGOG.]

sync (singk) See SYNCH.

syn·carp (sin'kärp) *n. Bot.* An aggregate fruit composed of several more or less coherent carpels, as in the blackberry, or a multiple fruit, as in the fig. Also **syn·car·pi·um** (sin·kär'pē·əm). [<NL *syncarpium* <Gk. *syn-* together + *karpos* a fruit]

syn·car·pous (sin·kär'pəs) *adj. Bot.* Characterized by or characteristic of a syncarp; consisting of united carpels: contrasted with *apocarpous.*

syn·cat·e·gor·e·mat·ic (sin·kat'ə·gôr'ə·mat'ik, -gor'-) *adj.* Pertaining to words that can only form parts of terms, as adverbs, prepositions, and conjunctions: opposed to *categorematic.* Also **syn·cat'e·gor'e·mat'i·cal.** [<Gk. *synkatēgorēmatikos* < *synkatēgorēma* < *synkatēgorein* predicate jointly < *syn-* together + *katēgoreein.* See CATEGORY.]

synch (singk) *Slang v.i.* & *v.t.* To synchronize or cause to be synchronized. — *n.* The state of being synchronous; synchronization: usually in the phrases **in synch** and **out of synch.** [<SYNCHRONIZATION]

syn·chon·dro·sis (sing'kən·drō'sis) See under SYMPHYSIS. [<NL <Gk. *synchondrōsis* < *syn-* together + *chondros* cartilage]

syn·chro·mesh (sing'kro·mesh') *n. Mech.* 1 A gear system by which driving and driven members are brought to the same speed before engaging. 2 The mechanism by which this uniform speed of gears is obtained. [<SYNCHRO(NIZED) + MESH]

syn·chron·ic (sin·kron'ik) *adj.* 1 Synchronous. 2 *Ling.* Pertaining to the study of some aspect of a language at a given stage in its development: *synchronic* grammar. Also **syn·chron'i·cal.** See DIACHRONIC. [<LL *synchronus* SYNCHRONOUS] — **syn·chron'i·cal·ly** *adv.*

syn·chro·nic·i·ty (sing'krə·nis'ə·tē) *n.* The temporal coincidence of two or more events linked together by meaning, but without any causal connection; meaningful cross-connection between separate causal chains. [Trans. of G *synchronizität*; used by C. G. Jung]

syn·chro·nism (sing'krə·niz'əm) *n.* 1 The state of being synchronous. 2 Coincidence in time of different events or phenomena; simultaneousness. 3 A tabular grouping of historic personages or events according to their dates. 4 In art, representation in the same picture of events having differing dates. [<LL *synchronismus* <Gk. *synchronismos* < *synchronos* SYNCHRONOUS] — **syn'chro·nis'·tic** or **·ti·cal** *adj.* — **syn'chro·nis'ti·cal·ly** *adv.*

syn·chro·nize (sing'krə·nīz) *v.* **·nized, ·niz·ing** *v.i.* 1 To occur at the same time; coincide. 2 To move or operate in unison. — *v.t.* 3 To cause (timepieces) to agree in keeping or indicating time. 4 To cause to operate in unison: to *synchronize* video and audio portions. 5 To assign the same date or period to; make contemporaneous. [<SYNCHRONISM] — **syn'·chro·ni·za'tion** *n.* — **syn'chro·niz'er** *n.*

synchronized shifting A change in the speed of an automotive vehicle by means of synchromesh gearing.

syn·chron·o·scope (sin·kron'ə·skōp) *n.* A synchroscope. [<SYNCHRON(ISM) + -(O)SCOPE]

syn·chro·nous (sing'krə·nəs) *adj.* 1 Occurring at the same time; coincident. 2 Happening at the same rate. 3 *Physics* Having the same period or rate of vibration: *synchronous* currents. Also **syn'chro·nal.** [<LL *synchronus* <Gk. *synchronos* < *syn-* together + *chronos* time] — **syn'chro·nous·ly** *adv.* — **syn'chro·nous·ness** *n.*

synchronous converter *Electr.* A machine adapted for the conversion of direct into alternating current or vice versa.

synchronous machine *Electr.* A machine whose normal speed of operation is exactly proportional to the frequency of the current to which it is connected, as a motor or generator.

synchronous speed *Electr.* The speed of an alternating-current machine as determined by the frequency of the circuit.

syn·chro·scope (sing'krə·skōp) *n. Electr.* An apparatus for visually indicating the degree of synchronization in the working, speed, etc., of two or more engines, as in an airplane. Also *synchronoscope.* [<SYNCHRO(NISM) + -SCOPE]

syn·chro·tron (sing'krə·tron) *n. Physics* An accelerator in which the particles being accelerated travel in nearly constant orbits, the change in orbital period being compensated by a synchronous change in the frequency of the alternating voltage providing the acceleration. [<SYNCHRO(NIZE) + (ELEC)TRON]

syn·clas·tic (sin·klas'tik) *adj.* Having the same kind of curvature in all directions; concave or convex in every direction: said of a surface: opposed to *anticlastic.* [<SYN- + Gk. *klastos* broken < *klaein* break]

syn·cli·nal (sin·klī'nəl) *adj.* 1 Sloping downward on each side toward a common line or point. 2 *Geol.* Dipping downward on each side toward the axis of the fold, as rock strata: opposed to *anticlinal.* Also **syn·clin·i·cal** (sin·klin'i·kəl). — *n.* A syncline. [<Gk. *synklinein* < *syn-* together + *klinein* incline]

syn·cline (sing'klīn) *n. Geol.* 1 A trough or structural basin toward which rocks dip. 2 A synclinal fold. [<Gk. *synklinein.* See SYNCLINAL.]

syn·clit·ism (sing'klə·tiz'əm) *n. Med.* The lateral turning of the fetal head in a natural presentation at childbirth, thus bringing the cranial planes into parallelism with the planes of the maternal pelvis. [<Gk. *syn-* together + *klitikos* < *klinein* incline, turn aside] — **syn·clit'ic** *adj.*

syn·co·pate (sing'kə·pāt) *v.t.* **·pat·ed, ·pat·ing** 1 To contract, as a word, by syncope. 2 *Music* To treat or modify, as a tone, by syncopation. [<LL *syncopatus,* pp. of *syncopare* affect with syncope < *syncope* SYNCOPE]

syn·co·pa·tion (sing'kə·pā'shən) *n.* 1 The act of syncopating or state of being syncopated; also, that which is syncopated; a dance or rhythm in syncopated time. 2 *Music* The beginning of a tone on an unaccented beat and its continuation through the following accented beat, or the beginning of a tone on the last half of a beat and continuing it through the first half of the next beat; also, the tone so treated, generally receiving an accent. 3 Any music featuring syncopation, as ragtime, jazz, etc. 4 Syncope of a word, or an example of it.

syn·co·pe (sing'kə·pē) *n.* 1 The elision of a sound or syllable in the middle part of a word, as *e'er* for *ever.* 2 *Music* Syncopation. 3 *Pathol.* Sudden faintness; swooning, with loss of sensation, motion, and consciousness. See synonyms under STUPOR. [Earlier *sincopis* <OF *sincopin,* ult. <LL *syncope* <Gk. *synkopē* < *syn-* together + *kop-*, stem of *koptein* strike, cut; refashioned after LL] — **syn'co·pal, syn·cop·ic** (sin·kop'ik) *adj.*

syn·cra·sy (sing'krə·sē) *n.* The blending, harmonizing, or massing of different or antagonistic elements. [<Gk. *synkrasis* a commixture < *syn-* together + *krasis* a mixing < *kerannynai* mix]

syn·cre·tism (sing'krə·tiz'əm) *n.* 1 A tendency or effort to reconcile and unite various systems of philosophy or religious opinion on the basis of tenets common to all and against a common opponent. 2 *Ling.* The fusion of two or more inflectional forms which were originally different, as of two cases. [<F *syncrétisme* <NL *syncretismus* <Gk. *synkrētismos* a union of two parties against a third < *synkrētizein* combine] — **syn'cre·tist** *n.* — **syn'cre·tis'tic** or **·ti·cal, syn·cret·ic** (sin·kret'ik) *adj.*

syn·cre·tize (sing'krə·tīz) *v.t.* **·tized, ·tiz·ing** To attempt to blend and reconcile, as various religions or philosophies. [<NL *syncretizare* <Gk. *synkrētizein* combine]

syn·cri·sis (sing'krə·sis) *n.* A figure of speech formed by comparison of opposite persons or things. [<LL <Gk. *synkrisis* < *synkrinein* compare < *syn-* together + *krinein* separate]

sync signal (singk) *Telecom.* The electromagnetic signal pulses by which the scanning process in television is synchronized for proper transmission and reception.

syn·cyt·i·um (sin·sit'ē·əm, -sish'əm) *n. pl.* **·cyt·i·a** (-sit'ē·ə, -sish'ə) *Biol.* 1 A multinucleate cell, or a mass of non-cellular, undifferentiated protoplasm. 2 Plasmodium. [<NL <Gk. *syn-* together + *kytos* a hollow] — **syn·cyt'i·al** *adj.*

syn·dac·tyl (sin·dak'til) *adj. Anat.* Having two or more digits either of the hand or of the foot wholly or partly united; web-footed: also **syn·dac'tyle, syn·dac'ty·lous.** — *n.* A mammal or bird which is syndactyl. [<F *syndactyle* <Gk. *syn-* together + *daktylos* a finger]

syn·dac·tyl·ism (sin·dak′til·iz′əm) *n.* 1 The condition of being syndactyl. 2 The union of two or more digits or toes.

syn·de·sis (sin′də·sis) *n. pl.* **·ses** (-sēz) Synapsis.

syndesmo– *combining form Anat.* A ligament; of or pertaining to a ligament or ligaments: *syndesmology.* Also, before vowels, **syndesm–.** [<Gk. *syndesmos* a ligament]

syn·des·mol·o·gy (sin′des·mol′ə·jē) *n.* The study of the anatomy and physiology of the ligaments.

syn·des·mo·sis (sin′des·mō′sis) *n. Anat.* The joining of two portions of the skeleton by means of ligamentous tissue. [<NL <Gk. *syndesmos* a ligament] **—syn′des·mot′ic** (-mot′ik) *adj.*

syn·det·ic (sin·det′ik) *adj.* Serving to unite or connect; connective, as a word. Also **syn·det′i·cal.** [<Gk. *syndetikos* <*syndeein* bind together <*syn-* together + *deein* bind] **— syn·det′i·cal·ly** *adv.*

syn·dic (sin′dik) *n.* A civil magistrate or officer representing a government or a community; also, one chosen to transact business for others: used also collectively for a body of officers or a council. [<F *syndic, syndique* a delegated representative <LL *syndicus* an advocate, delegate <Gk. *syndikos* a defendant's advocate <*syn-* together + *dikē* judgment] **—syn′di·cal** *adj.*

syn·di·cal·ism (sin′di·kəl·iz′əm) *n.* A social and political theory proposing the taking over of the means of production by syndicates of workers, preferably by means of the general strike, with consequent political control and the disappearance of the bourgeois state. [<F *syndicalisme* <*syndical* of a labor union <*(chambre) syndicale* a labor union <*syndic* a syndic] **—syn′di·cal·ist** *n.* **—syn′di·cal·is′tic** *adj.*

syn·di·cate (sin′də·kit) *n.* 1 An association of individuals united to negotiate some business or to prosecute some enterprise requiring large capital. 2 A combination of persons associated for purchasing manuscripts and selling them again to a number of periodicals, as newspapers, for simultaneous publication. 3 The office or jurisdiction of a syndic; syndics collectively: the original meaning. —*v.t.* (-kāt) **·cat·ed, ·cat·ing** 1 To combine into or manage by a syndicate. 2 To sell for publication in many newspapers or magazines. [<F *syndicat* office of a syndic <*syndic.* See SYNDIC.]

syn·drome (sin′drōm) *n.* 1 *Med.* An aggregate or set of concurrent symptoms together indicating the presence and nature of a disease. 2 A group of traits regarded as being characteristic of a certain type, condition, etc. [<NL <Gk. *syndromē* <*syn-* together + *dramein* run] **—syn·drom·ic** (sin·drom′ik) *adj.*

syne (sīn) *adv. Scot.* 1 Since; ago: auld lang *syne.* 2 Afterward. 3 Then; moreover. Also **syn.**

sy·nec·do·che (si·nek′də·kē) *n.* A figure of speech in which a part is put for a whole or a whole for a part, an individual for a class, or a material for the thing, as a *roof* for a *house, marble* for a *statue.* [<LL <Gk. *synekdochē* <*synekdechesthai* take something with something else <*syn-* together + *ekdechesthai* take from <*ek-* from + *dechesthai* take] **—syn·ec·doch·ic** (sin′ek·dok′ik), **syn′·ec·doch′i·cal** *adj.*

sy·ne·cious (si·nē′shəs) See SYNOECIOUS.

syn·e·col·o·gy (sin′ə·kol′ə·jē) *n.* The study of plant and animal communities in relation to their environment; the ecology of organisms taken collectively. [<SYN- + ECOLOGY]

Syn·e·dri·on (sin·ē′drē·ən), **Syn·e·dri·um** (-drē·əm) See SANHEDRIN.

syn·er·e·sis (si·ner′ə·sis) *n.* 1 The coalescence of two vowels or syllables generally pronounced separately, as *seest* for *see-est*: opposed to *dieresis*; crasis. Compare SYNIZESIS. 2 *Chem.* The contraction of a gel, with the expulsion of water or other liquids, as in the clotting of blood. Also spelled *synaeresis.* [<LL *synaeresis* <Gk. *synairesis* a drawing together <*syn-* together + *haireein* take]

syn·er·get·ic (sin′ər·jet′ik) *adj.* Working together; cooperative, as the flexor muscles of the leg. [<Gk. *synergētikos* <*synergeein* cooperate <*syn-* together + *ergeein* work]

syn·er·gism (sin′ər·jiz′əm) *n.* 1 The doctrine that human effort cooperates with divine grace in the salvation of the soul. 2 *Med.* The mutually cooperating action of separate substances which together produce an effect greater than that of any component taken alone, as certain drug mixtures. [<NL *synergismus* <Gk. *synergos* working together <*synergeein.* See SYNERGETIC.]

syn·er·gist (sin′ər·jist) *n.* 1 One holding to synergism. 2 A cooperating organ, part, or medicine. **—syn′er·gis′tic** or **·ti·cal** *adj.*

syn·er·gy (sin′ər·jē) *n.* 1 Combined and correlated force; united action. 2 *Med.* Correlation or concurrence of action between different organs in health or disease, or between different drugs. Also **syn·er·gi·a** (si·nûr′jē·ə). [<NL *synergia* <Gk. *synergos.* See SYNERGISM.] **—syn·er′gic** *adj.*

syn·e·sis (sin′ə·sis) *n. Gram.* Construction in accordance with the sense rather than the syntax, as the use of a plural form of a verb with a collective noun to emphasize the individuals in the group. [<Gk., a joining together, understanding <*synienai* perceive <*syn-* together + *hienai* send]

syn·es·the·sia (sin′is·thē′zhə, -zhē·ə) *n. Physiol.* 1 Transferred sensation; sensation produced at a point different from the point of stimulation. 2 The producing of a subjective response normally associated with one sense by stimulation of another sense, as of a color from hearing a certain sound. Also spelled *synaesthesia.* [<NL *synaesthesia* <Gk. *synaisthēsis* joint perception <*synaisthanesthai* perceive simultaneously <*syn-* together + *aisthanesthai* perceive, feel] **—syn′es·thet′ic** (-thet′ik) *adj.*

syn·ga·my (sing′gə·mē) *n. Biol.* The union of male and female gametes in fertilization. [<SYN- + -GAMY] **—syn·gam·ic** (sin·gam′ik), **syn′ga·mous** *adj.*

Synge (sing), **John Millington,** 1871–1909, Irish dramatist and poet.

syn·gen·e·sis (sin·jen′ə·sis) *n. Biol.* 1 Sexual reproduction. 2 The theory that the sexually fertilized germ contains within itself the germs of all future generations: opposed to *epigenesis.* [<NL <Gk. *syn-* together + *genesis* GENESIS] **—syn·ge·net·ic** (sin′jə·net′ik) *adj.*

syn·i·ze·sis (sin′ə·zē′sis) *n.* 1 In Greek prosody, the union in pronunciation of two vowels that cannot form a diphthong, so as to pass for one syllable: differing from *contraction* in not being made in the written word, but only in pronunciation. Compare SYNERESIS. 2 *Biol.* The contractile massing of the chromatin during meiotic cell division: associated with *synapsis.* 3 *Med.* Contraction of the pupil of the eye. Also **syn′e·zi′sis** (-zī′sis). [<LL <Gk. *synizēsis* <*synizanein* sink down <*syn-* together + *izanein* settle down, sit <*izein* seat, sit]

syn·od (sin′əd) *n.* 1 An ecclesiastical council, stated or special, local or general; hence, any deliberative assembly. 2 *Astron.* A conjunction (def. 2). [OE *synoth* <LL *synodus* <Gk. *synodos,* lit., a coming together <*syn-* together + *hodos* a way; refashioned after MF *synode* <LL]

Syn·od (sin′əd) *n.* 1 One of certain ecclesiastical councils distinguished by their extent or locality. 2 In the Presbyterian churches, a council intermediate between presbyteries and General Assembly. 3 In the Dutch Reformed, German Reformed, and Lutheran churches in the United States, a supreme council, known as **General Synod,** and also a more limited one, known as **Particular** or **District Synod.**

sy·nod·i·cal (si·nod′i·kəl) *adj.* 1 Of, pertaining to, or of the nature of a synod; transacted in a synod. 2 *Astron.* Pertaining to the conjunction of two heavenly bodies one of which revolves round the other, or to the interval between two successive conjunctions: a *synodical* month. Also **syn·od·al** (sin′ə·dəl), **sy·nod′ic.** **—sy·nod′i·cal·ly** *adv.*

sy·noe·cious (si·nē′shəs) *adj. Bot.* Having male and female organs, either stamens and pistils or antheridia and archegonia, in the same inflorescence or receptacle, as in most composite plants and many mosses: also spelled *synecious.* [<Gk. *synoikia* living together <*syn-* together + *oikos* a house; formed on analogy with *dioecious, monoecious,* etc.]

syn·o·nym (sin′ə·nim) *n.* 1 A word having the same or almost the same meaning as some other; hence, one of a number of words that have one or more meanings in common: opposite of *antonym.* 2 The equivalent of a word in another language. 3 *Biol.* A scientific name, as of a genus or species, superseded or discarded, as by the law of priority or because of incorrect application. Also **syn′o·nyme.** [<LL *synonymum* <Gk. *synōnymon,* neut. of *synōnymos* having like meaning or name <*syn-* together + *onyma, onoma* a name] **—syn′o·nym′ic** or **·i·cal** *adj.* **—syn′·o·nym′i·ty** *n.*

sy·non·y·mize (si·non′ə·mīz) *v.t.* **·mized, ·miz·ing** To give the synonyms of; express by words of similar or equivalent meaning.

sy·non·y·mous (si·non′ə·məs) *adj.* Being a synonym or synonyms; equivalent or similar in meaning; closely related or nearly alike in significance. Also **syn·o·ny·mat·ic** (sin′·ə·ni·mat′ik), **syn′o·nym′ic** (-nim′ik) or **·i·cal.** **—sy·non′y·mous·ly** *adv.*

Synonyms: alike, correspondent, corresponding, equivalent, identical, interchangeable, like, same, similar, synonymic. In the strictest sense, *synonymous* words scarcely exist; rarely, if ever, are any two words in any language *equivalent* or *identical* in meaning; where a difference in meaning cannot be easily shown, a difference in usage, often involving connotation, usually exists, so that the words are not *interchangeable.* By *synonymous* words we usually understand words that coincide or nearly coincide in some part of their meaning, and may hence within certain limits be used interchangeably, while outside of these limits they may differ very greatly in meaning and use. To consider *synonymous* words *identical* is fatal to accuracy; to forget that they are *similar,* to some extent *equivalent,* and sometimes *interchangeable,* is destructive of freedom and variety.

sy·non·y·my (si·non′ə·mē) *n. pl.* **·mies** 1 The quality of being synonymous; the expressing or extending of an idea by the use of synonyms. 2 The science or systematic collection and study of synonyms; the use and nice discrimination of synonyms: also **syn·o·nym·ics** (sin′ə·nim′iks). 3 A book treating of or discriminating the meaning of synonyms or of allied terms. 4 An index, list, or collection of synonyms, as in scientific nomenclature. [<LL *synonymia* <Gk. *synōnymia* <*synōnymos.* See SYNONYM.]

sy·nop·sis (si·nop′sis) *n. pl.* **·ses** (-sēz) A general view, as of a subject or its treatment; an abstract; syllabus; a summary. See synonyms under ABRIDGMENT. [<LL <Gk., a general view <*syn-* together + *opsis* a view]

sy·nop·tic (si·nop′tik) *adj.* 1 Giving a general view. 2 Presenting the same or a similar point of view; containing parts that, when compared, are virtually identical: said of the first three Gospels (**Synoptic Gospels**) as distinguished from the fourth. Also **sy·nop′·ti·cal.** [<NL *synopticus* <Gk. *synoptikos* <*synopsis* a synopsis] **—sy·nop′ti·cal·ly** *adv.*

syn·os·to·sis (sin′os·tō′sis) See under SYMPHYSIS. Also **syn·os·te·o·sis** (si·nos′tē·ō′sis). [Contraction of *synosteosis* <NL <Gk. *syn-* together + *osteon* a bone]

sy·nou·si·acs (si·nōō′shē·aks, -nou′-) *n.* That branch of knowledge pertaining to societies: a term used in cataloging, as in libraries. [<Gk. *synousia* society <*synousa,* ppr. fem. of *syneinai* be with <*syn-* together + *einai* be]

sy·no·vi·a (si·nō′vē·ə) *n. Physiol.* The viscid, transparent, albuminous fluid secreted in the interior of joints and at other points where lubrication is necessary. [<NL *sinovia, synovia, synophia*; coined by Paracelsus, appar. <Gk. *syn-* together + L *ovum* an egg <Gk. *ōon*] **—sy·no′vi·al** *adj.*

syn·o·vi·tis (sin′ō·vī′tis) *n. Pathol.* Inflammation of a synovial membrane.

syn·sep·a·lous (sin·sep′ə·ləs) *adj. Bot.* Gamosepalous. [<SYN- + SEPAL + -OUS]

syn·tax (sin′taks) *n.* 1 The arrangement and interrelationship of words in grammatical constructions. 2 The branch of linguistics dealing with this. [<F *syntaxe* <LL *syntaxis* <Gk. <*syntassein* join together <*syn-* together + *tassein* arrange] —**syn·tac·tic** (sin·tak′tik) or **·ti·cal** *adj.* —**syn·tac′ti·cal·ly** *adv.*

syn·tech·nic (sin·tek′nik) *adj. Ecol.* Denoting resemblance among dissimilar animal forms due to influences of common environment. See CONVERGENCE (def. 7). [<Gk. *syntechnos* practicing the same art <*syn-* together + *technē* an art]

syn·the·sis (sin′thə·sis) *n. pl.* **·ses** (-sēz) **1** The assembling of separate or subordinate parts into a new form; also, the complex whole resulting from this. **2** *Ling.* The combination of radical and formative or inflectional elements in one word, as in *un-think-ing, home-wards.* **3** *Logic* **a** Combination of separate elements into a whole, as of species into genera: contrasted with *analysis.* **b** A process of reasoning from the whole to a part, from the general to the particular; deductive reasoning. **4** *Surg.* The operation of reuniting broken or divided parts, as of bones. **5** *Chem.* **a** The building up of compounds from a series of reactions involving elements, radicals, or simpler compounds. **b** The preparation by such means of organic compounds which have specific properties or are identical in certain respects with naturally occurring substances. Compare ANALYSIS. [<L <Gk. <*syntithenai* <*syn-* together + *tithenai* place] —**syn′the·sist** *n.*

syn·the·size (sin′thə·sīz) *v.t.* **·sized, ·siz·ing** **1** To unite or produce by synthesis. **2** To apply synthesis to. Also *Brit.* **syn′the·sise.**

syn·thet·ic (sin·thet′ik) *adj.* **1** Pertaining to or of the nature of synthesis; characterized by or consisting in synthesis; specifically, tending to reduce particulars to inclusive wholes: a *synthetic* mind. **2** *Chem.* Produced by the synthesis of simpler materials or substances: *synthetic* rubber. **3** Artificial; spurious. **4** *Ling.* Describing a language that utilizes inflectional affixes for the expression of relationships between words, as in Latin; inflectional: opposed to *analytic.* Also **syn·thet′i·cal.** —*n.* **1** Anything produced by synthesis. **2** *Chem.* A synthesized compound adapted for use as a substitute for some other material or substance. [<F *synthétique* <NL *syntheticus* <Gk. *synthetikos* <*synthetos* compounded <*syntithenai* <*syn-* together + *tithenai* place] —**syn·thet′i·cal·ly** *adv.*

synthetic philosophy Spencerism: so called by Spencer as being an attempt to combine all the sciences into a connected whole.

syn·to·nize (sin′tə·nīz) *v.t.* **·nized, ·niz·ing** *Electr.* **1** To place in resonance with each other, as radio frequencies. **2** To tune or tone together, as electrical instruments. [<SYNTON(Y) + -IZE] —**syn·ton·ic** (sin·ton′ik) or **·i·cal** *adj.* —**syn·ton′i·cal·ly** *adv.* —**syn′·to·ni·za′tion** *n.*

syn·to·ny (sin′tə·nē) *n. Electr.* **1** The harmonizing or tuning of particular transmitters and receivers each to the other. **2** Resonance. [<Gk. *syntonia* agreement <*syn-* together + *tonos* a tone]

syn·u·ra (sin·yŏŏr′ə) *n. pl.* **·u·rae** (-yŏŏr′ē) Any of a genus (*Synura*) of flagellate protozoans, uniting in subspherical clusters and discharging oil globules. They are common in swamp waters and render drinking water unpalatable by giving it a cucumberlike flavor. [<NL <Gk. *synouros, synoros* bordering on <*syn-* together + *oros* a boundary]

sy·pher (sī′fər) *v.t.* To make a lap joint with (two chamfered or beveled plank edges) so as to leave a flush surface. [Var. of CIPHER] —**sy′pher·ing** *n.*

syph·i·lis (sif′ə·lis) *n. Pathol.* An infectious, chronic, venereal disease caused by a spirochete (*Treponema pallidum*) transmissible by direct contact or congenitally. It usually progresses by three stages of increasing severity: primary, secondary, and tertiary. [after *Syphilis, sive Morbus Gallicus,* a Latin poem by Fracastoro, published in 1530, the hero of which, *Syphilus,* a shepherd, was the first sufferer from the disease] —**syph′i·loid, syph′·i·lous** *adj.*

syph·i·lit·ic (sif′ə·lit′ik) *adj.* Relating to or affected with syphilis. —*n.* A person suffering from syphilis. [<NL *syphiliticus* <*syphilis* SYPHILIS]

syph·i·lol·o·gy (sif′ə·lol′ə·jē) *n.* The science of syphilis, its cognate diseases, and their treatment. [<SYPHIL(IS) + -(O)LOGY] —**syph′i·lol′o·gist** *n.*

syph·i·lo·pho·bi·a (sif′ə·lə·fō′bē·ə) *n. Psychiatry* A morbid fear of syphilis. [<SYPHIL(IS) + -(O)PHOBIA] —**syph′i·lo·pho′bic** *adj.*

syphon (sī′fən) See SIPHON.

Syr·a·cuse (sir′ə·kyōōs) **1** A port of SE Sicily: Italian *Siracusa.* Ancient **Syr·a·cu·sae** (sir′ə·kyōō′sē, -zē). **2** A city in central New York. —**Syr′a·cu′san** *adj.* & *n.*

Syr Dar·ya (sir där′yä) A river in SW Asiatic U.S.S.R. flowing about 1,327 miles NW to the Aral Sea: ancient *Jaxartes.*

sy·ren (sī′rən) See SIREN.

Syr·ette (si·ret′) *n.* A miniature syringe; especially, a small disposable tube for the emergency administration of morphine, for use on the battlefield, by paratroopers, etc.: a trade name.

Syr·i·a (sir′ē·ə) *n.* **1** A former republic, 1941–1958, south of Asia Minor on the NE coast of the Mediterranean, a part of the United Arab Republic from 1958–61; 72,234 square miles; capital, Damascus. *Arabic* **Esh Shan.** **2** A former French mandated territory, 1920–1941, roughly comprising Syria (def. 1) and Lebanon. **3** An ancient country including Syria (def. 1), Lebanon, Palestine (def. 2), and adjacent districts of western Asia.

Syr·i·ac (sir′ē·ak) *n.* The language of the Syrians, belonging to the eastern Aramaic subgroup of the Northwest Semitic languages. [<L *Syriacus* <Gk. *Syriakos* <*Syria* Syria]

Syr·i·an (sir′ē·ən) *adj.* Of or pertaining to Syria, ancient or modern. —*n.* **1** A native of Syria, especially one of the native Semitic people of Arabic, Phoenician, and Aramean descent. **2** One who is a member of the Christian church in Syria. [<OF *sirien* <L *Syrius* a Syrian <Gk. *Syrios* <*Syria* Syria]

Syrian Desert An arid wasteland of SW Asia between the lands along the eastern Mediterranean and the Euphrates valley.

sy·rin·ga (si·ring′gə) *n.* **1** Any of a genus (*Philadelphus*) of ornamental shrubs of the saxifrage family having cream-colored flowers resembling those of the orange in form and fragrance, especially the Lewis mock orange (*P. lewisii*), the State flower of Idaho. **2** Any of a genus (*Syringa*) of ornamental shrubs of the olive family having panicles of showy white or purple flowers; the lilacs. [<NL <Gk. *syrinx, -ingos* a pipe]

SYRINGA (Plant to 10 feet)

syr·inge (sir′inj, si·rinj′) *n. Med.* An instrument used to withdraw a fluid from a reservoir and eject it in one or more jets or streams. The simplest forms are valveless single-acting devices; other forms consist of an elastic bag supplied with flexible inlet and outlet pipes each having a suitable check valve. —*v.t.* **·inged, ·ing·ing** To spray or inject by a syringe; cleanse or treat with injected fluid. [<Med. L *siringa* <Gk. *syrinx, -ingos* a tube, a pipe]

sy·rin·go·my·e·li·a (si·ring′gō·mī·ē′lē·ə) *n. Pathol.* A morbid condition of the spinal cord, due to the presence of liquid in abnormally formed cavities. [<NL <Gk. *syrinx, -ingos* a tube + *myelos* marrow]

syr·inx (sir′ingks) *n.* **1** *Ornithol.* A special modification of the windpipe serving as the song organ in birds. **2** A tube, pipe, or fistula. **3** Panpipes. [<Gk., a pipe] —**sy·rin·ge·al** (si·rin′jē·əl) *adj.*

Syr·inx (sir′ingks) In Greek mythology, a nymph pursued by Pan and changed into a reed, from which Pan made his pipes.

Sy·ros (sī′rəs) One of the Cyclades group, SW of Tenos; 33 square miles. Also *Siros.* Latin **Sy′rus.**

syr·phus fly (sûr′fəs) A fly of *Syrphus* or a related genus (family *Syrphidae*). The group is large and widely distributed, and contains many species which deceptively resemble bees and wasps. The larvae of many feed upon harmful plant lice. For illustration see INSECTS (beneficial). Also **syr·phid** (sûr′fid), **syr′phi·an.** [<NL <Gk. *syrphos* a gnat]

Syr·tis Ma·jor (sir′tis mā′jər) The ancient name for the GULF OF SIDRA.

Syrtis Minor An ancient name for the GULF OF GABÈS.

syr·up (sir′əp), **syr·up·y** See SIRUP, etc.

sys- Assimilated var. of SYN-.

sys·sar·co·sis (sis′är·kō′sis) *n. Anat.* The union of bones by means of muscles. [<NL <Gk. *syssarkōsis* <*syssarkoein* unite by or cover over with flesh] —**sys′sar·co′sic, sys′sar·cot·ic** (-kot′ik) *adj.*

sys·tal·tic (sis·tal′tik) *adj. Physiol.* Alternately contracting and dilating: the *systaltic* motion of the heart; pulsatory. Compare PERISTALSIS. [<LL *systalticus* <Gk. *systaltikos* depressing <*systellein* draw together <*syn-* together + *stellein* send]

sys·tem (sis′təm) *n.* **1** Orderly combination or arrangement, as of parts or elements, into a whole; specifically, such combination according to some rational principle; any methodical arrangement of parts. **2** In science and philosophy, an orderly collection of logically related principles, facts, or objects. **3** Any group of facts and phenomena regarded as constituting a natural whole and furnishing the basis and material of scientific investigation and construction: the solar *system.* **4** The connection or manner of connection of parts as related to a whole, or the parts collectively so related; a whole as made up of constitutive parts: a railroad *system.* **5** The state or quality of being in order or orderly; orderliness; method: He works with *system.* **6** *Physiol.* An assemblage of organic structures composed of similar elements and combined for the same general functions: the nervous *system*; also, the entire body, taken as a functional whole. **7** *Physics* An aggregation of matter in, or tending to approach, equilibrium. **8** *Mineral.* One of the six divisions into which all crystal forms may be grouped, depending upon the relative lengths and mutual inclinations of the assumed crystal axes. **9** *Geol.* A category of rock strata next below a group and above a series and corresponding with a period in the time scale. [<LL *systema* a musical interval <Gk. *systēma, -atos* an organized whole <*syn-* together + *histanai* stand, set up]

Synonyms: manner, method, mode, order, regularity, rule. *Order* in this connection denotes a fact or a result; as, These papers are in *order. Method* denotes a process; *rule* an authoritative requirement or an established course of things; *system,* not merely a law of action or procedure, but a comprehensive plan; *manner* refers to the external qualities of actions, and to those often as settled and characteristic; we speak of a *system* of taxation, a *method* of collecting taxes, the *rules* by which assessments are made; or we say, As a *rule* the payments are heaviest at a certain time of year; a just tax may be made odious by the *manner* of its collection. *Regularity* applies to even disposition of objects or uniform recurrence of acts in a series. There may be *regularity* without *order,* as in the recurrence of paroxysms of disease or insanity; there may be *order* without *regularity,* as in the arrangement of furniture in a room, where the objects are placed at varying distances. *Order* commonly implies the design of an intelligent agent or the appearance or suggestion of such design; *regularity* applies to an actual uniform disposition or recurrence with no suggestion of purpose, and as applied to human affairs is less intelligent and more mechanical than *order.* See BODY, FRAME, HABIT, HYPOTHESIS. *Antonyms*: chaos, confusion, derangement, disarrangement, disorder, irregularity.

sys·tem·at·ic (sis′tə·mat′ik) *adj.* **1** Of, pertaining to, of the nature of, or characterized by system. **2** Acting by system or method; methodical: *systematic* thieving. **3** Forming a system; systematized. **4** Carried out with organized regularity. **5** Taxonomic: *systematic* botany. Also **sys′tem·at′i·cal.** [<LL *systematicus* <LGk. *systēmatikos* <*systēma, -atos* a system] —**sys′tem·at′i·cal·ly** *adv.*

sys·tem·at·ics (sis′tə·mat′iks) *n. pl.* (*construed as singular*) **1** The art or principles of classification and nomenclature. **2** *Biol.* The science of the classification of organisms; taxonomy.

sys·tem·a·tism (sis′tə·mə·tiz′əm) *n.* **1** Systematic arrangement or classification. **2** Adherence to or reduction of principles, etc., to a system.

sys·tem·a·tist (sis′tə·mə·tist) *n.* **1** One who reduces things to systems, as a taxonomist. **2** One who forms or adheres to a system or to a systematic view of things.

sys·tem·a·tize (sis′tə·mə·tīz′) *v.t.* **·tized, ·tiz·ing** To reduce to a system; dispose methodically. See synonyms under REGULATE. Also **sys′tem·ize,** *Brit.* **sys′tem·a·tise′.** —**sys′tem·a·ti·za′tion, sys′tem·i·za′tion** *n.* —**sys′tem·a·tiz′er, sys′tem·iz′er** *n.*

sys·tem·ic (sis·tem′ik) *adj.* **1** Of or pertaining to system or a system; systematic. **2** *Physiol.* Pertaining to or affecting the body as a whole: a *systemic* poison. —**sys·tem′i·cal·ly** *adv.*

systems analysis The technique of reducing complex processes, as of industry, government, research, etc., to basic operations that can be treated quantitatively and reordered into sequences amenable to control. —**systems analyst**

sys·to·le (sis′tə·lē) *n.* **1** *Physiol.* The regular contraction of the heart, especially of the ventricles, that impels the blood outward. Compare DIASTOLE. **2** The shortening of a syllable that is naturally or by position long. [<NL <Gk. *systolē* a contraction < *systellein.* See SYSTALTIC.] —**sys·tol·ic** (sis·tol′ik) *adj.*

syz·y·gy (siz′ə·jē) *n. pl.* **·gies** **1** *Astron.* One of two opposite points in the orbit of a celestial body when it is in conjunction with or opposition to the sun; especially, the points on the moon's orbit when the moon is most nearly in line with the earth and the sun. **2** The union of parts or organisms. **3** A dipody or group of two feet in one verse. [<LL *syzygia* <Gk., a yoke, conjunction < *syzygos* yoked, paired < *syn-* together + *zeugnynai* yoke < *zygon* a yoke] —**sy·zyg·i·al** (si·zij′ē·əl) *adj.*

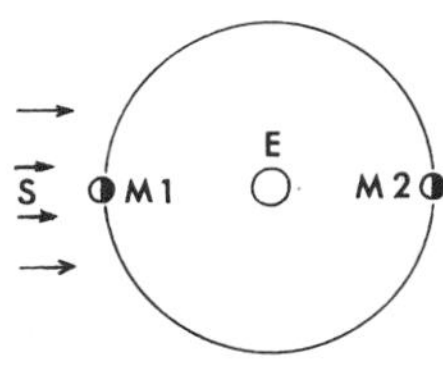

SYZYGY
S. Sun's rays. *E.* Earth. *M1, M2.* Syzygy of the moon.

Sza·bad·ka (sô′bôd·kô) The Hungarian name for SUBOTICA.

Sze·chwan (se′chwän′, su′-) A province of SW and central western China; 338,136 square miles; capital, Chengtu.

Sze·ged (se′ged) A city of southern Hungary. Formerly **Sze·ge·din** (se′ge·din).

Sze·ming (su′ming′) A former name for AMOY.

Szent-Gyor·gyi von Nagy·ra·polt (sent′·dyûr′dyē fon nod′y′ro′pōlt), **Albert,** born 1893, Hungarian biochemist.

Szi·lard (si·lärd′), **Leo,** 1898–1964, U. S. physicist born in Hungary.

Szom·bat·hely (som′bôt·hāy′) A city of western Hungary: German *Steinamanger.*

T

t, T (tē) *n. pl.* **t's, T's** or **ts, Ts, tees** (tēz) **1** The twentieth letter of the English alphabet, from Greek *tau* (a modification of Phoenician *tau*) and Latin *T.* **2** The sound of the letter *t,* the voiceless alveolar stop. See ALPHABET. — *symbol* Anything shaped like a T. —**to a T** Precisely; with exactness: probably in allusion to a T-square.

T (tē) *adj.* Shaped or having a cross-section like a T, as *T*-beam, *T*-pipe, etc. —*n.* Anything having the shape of a T.

't Contraction for IT: used initially, as in *'tis,* and finally, as in *on't.*

-t Inflectional ending used to indicate past participles and past tenses, as in *bereft, lost, spent*: equivalent to *-ed.*

Taal (täl) *n.* A form of Dutch spoken in South Africa; Afrikaans. [<Du., speech, language]

Ta·al (tä·äl′), **Mount** An active volcano (984 feet) on an island in **Lake Taal** (94 square miles) in southern Luzon, Philippines.

tab (tab) *n.* **1** A flap, strip, tongue, or appendage of something, as a garment. **2** *Colloq.* Tally: to keep *tab.* **3** *Aeron.* An auxiliary airfoil attached to the control surface of an airplane. [Origin uncertain]

tab·a·cin (tab′ə·sin) *n. Chem.* A waxy, lemon-yellow, poisonous glycoside extracted from the leaves of Kentucky tobacco. [<F *tabac* tobacco + -IN]

tab·a·nid (tab′ə·nid) *n.* Any of a family (*Tabanidae*) of large, bloodsucking insects; a horsefly or deerfly. —*adj.* Of the *Tabanidae.* [< NL, family name <L *tabanus* a horsefly]

tab·ard (tab′ərd) *n.* **1** Formerly, a short, sleeveless or short-sleeved, outer garment. **2** A knight's cape or cloak, worn over his armor and emblazoned with his own arms; also, a similar garment worn by a herald and embroidered with his lord's arms. **3** A banner attached to a trumpet or bugle. [<OF *tabard,* ult. <L *tapete* tapestry]

tab·a·ret (tab′ə·rit) *n.* A strong, silk upholstery fabric with varicolored stripes of satin or moiré. [Prob. <TABBY]

Ta·bas·co (tə·bas′kō) *n.* A pungent sauce made from the red-pepper plant (genus *Capsicum*): a trade name.

Ta·bas·co (tə·bas′kō, *Sp.* tä·väs′kō) A state in SE Mexico; 9,782 square miles; capital, Villahermosa.

tab·by (tab′ē) *n. pl.* **·bies** **1** Any of several plain-woven fabrics, as a striped or watered taffeta, or a moreen. **2** A garment made of a watered fabric. **3** A brindled or striped cat; popularly, any domestic cat, especially a female. **4** A gossiping old maid. **5** A building material of equal parts of lime and shells, and gravel, mixed with water. —*adj.* **1** Watered; mottled, as a fabric; also, brindled, as a cat. **2** Made of tabby. **3** Woven in the same way as fabric that is to be watered. —*v.t.* **·bied, ·by·ing** To give a wavy or watered appearance to (silk, etc.) by pressure between hot rollers; water; calender. [<F *tabis, atabis* <Arabic *'attābi* <*'Attabi,* name of a quarter of Baghdad where it was manufactured]

ta·ber (tā′bər) See TABOR.

tab·er·nac·le (tab′ər·nak′əl) *n.* **1** A tent or similar structure; slight shelter, fixed or portable. **2** Specifically, the portable sanctuary used by the Jews in the wilderness; later, the Jewish temple; hence, any house of worship, especially one of large size and not of specially ecclesiastical architecture: in England, the place of worship of some nonconformists. **3** The human body as the dwelling place of the soul. **4** The ornamental receptacle for the consecrated eucharistic elements, or for the pyx. **5** An ornamental recess or a structure sheltering something. **6** A socket or hinged post to unstep or lower a mast. —*v.i.* **·led, ·ling** To dwell in a tent; hence, to dwell transiently: The soul *tabernacles* in the body. [<OF <L *tabernaculum,* dim. of *taberna* shed] —**tab·er·nac·u·lar** (tab′ər·nak′·yə·lər) *adj.*

ta·bes (tā′bēz) *n. Pathol.* **1** Emaciation with general languor, progressive atrophy, and hectic fever; a decline. **2** Locomotor ataxia: also **tabes dor·sa·lis** (dôr·sā′lis). [<L, a wasting away < *tabere* waste away] —**ta·bes·cence** (tə·bes′əns) *n.* —**ta·bes′cent** *adj.* —**ta·bet′ic** (-bet′ik) *n.* & *adj.* —**tab·id** (tab′id) *adj.*

Tab·i·tha (tab′i·thə) A feminine personal name. [<Aramaic, gazelle]
—**Tabitha** A woman of Joppa noted for her good works. *Acts* ix 36.

Tab·las (täb′läs) The largest island in the Romblon group, central Philippines; 265 square miles.

tab·la·ture (tab′lə·chər) *n.* **1** *Anat.* One of the plates of bony tissue that form the walls of the cranium. **2** A tablelike painting or design. [<F <L *tabula* board]

ta·ble (tā′bəl) *n.* **1** An article of furniture with a flat horizontal top upheld by one or more supports. **2** Such a table around which persons sit for a meal: to set the *table.* **3** The food served or entertainment provided at a meal or dinner. **4** The company of persons at a table. **5** A gaming table, as for roulette, dice, etc. **6** A collection of related numbers, values, signs, or items of any kind, arranged for ease of reference or comparison, often in parallel columns: a *table* of logarithms; a *table* of statistics. **7** A synoptical statement; list: *table* of contents. **8** A tableland; plateau. **9** *Geol.* A horizontal stratum of rock. **10** The flat facet cut across the top of a precious stone. **11** *Archit.* **a** A raised horizontal surface or band of molding on a wall; a stringcourse. **b** A raised or sunken panel on a wall. **12** In palmistry, the quadrangle formed by four lines of the hand. **13** In backgammon: **a** Either of the two leaves of a backgammon board. **b** *pl. Obs.* Backgammon. **14** *Anat.* One of the flat bony plates forming the inner or outer part of the cranium. **15** A tablet or slab bearing an inscription; especially, one of those which bore the Ten Commandments or certain Roman laws. —**to turn the tables** To thwart an opponent's action and turn the situation to his disadvantage. —*v.t.* **·bled, ·bling** **1** To place on a table, as a playing card. **2** To postpone discussion of (a resolution, bill, etc.) until a future time, or for an indefinite period. **3** *Rare* To make into or enter in a list or table; tabulate. [Fusion of OF *table* and OE *tabule,* both <L *tabula* board]

tab·leau (tab′lō, ta·blō′) *n. pl.* **·leaux** (-lōz) or **·leaus** (-lōz) **1** Any picture or picturesque representation; especially, an unexpected situation produced suddenly and dramatically. **2** A tableau vivant. [<F, dim. of *table.* See TABLE.]

ta·bleau vi·vant (tȧ·blō′ vē·väṅ′) *pl.* **ta·bleaux vi·vants** (tȧ·blō′ vē·väṅ′) *French* A picture-like scene represented by silent and motionless persons standing in appropriate attitudes: also called *living picture.*

Table Bay An inlet of the Atlantic in SW Cape of Good Hope Province, Republic of South Africa: the harbor of Cape Town.

table book An ornamental book to be kept on a table.

ta·ble-chair (tā′bəl·châr′) *n.* An armchair or small bench having a hinged back which when tilted up forms a table-top: also called *chair-table.*

ta·ble·cloth (tā′bəl·klôth′, -kloth′) *n.* A cloth, often white, covering a table at meals.

ta·ble d'hôte (tab′əl dōt′, tä′bəl) *pl.* **ta·bles d'hôte** (tab′əlz dōt′, tä′bəlz) **1** A common table for guests, as at a hotel. **2** A complete meal of several specified courses, served in a restaurant at a fixed price. [<F, lit., table of the host]

ta·ble·land (tā′bəl·land′) *n.* A broad, level, elevated region, usually treeless; a plateau; specifically, a precipitous mesa.

table linen Tablecloths, napkins, doilies, etc., made of linen, cotton, etc.

ta·ble·mount (tā′bəl·mount′) *n.* A guyot.

Table Mountain A flat-topped mountain in SW Cape of Good Hope Province, near Cape Town, Republic of South Africa; 3,550 feet.

ta·ble·spoon (tā′bəl·spōōn′, -spŏŏn′) *n.* A large spoon, larger than a dessertspoon, with a capacity of 15 cc. or three times the capacity of a teaspoon: used for serving food.

ta·ble·spoon·ful (tā′bəl·spōōn·fŏŏl′, -spŏŏn-) *n. pl.* **·fuls** As much as a tablespoon will hold:

usually reckoned as equivalent to half a fluid ounce, 15 cc., or three teaspoonfuls.

tab·let (tab′lit) *n.* **1** A thin leaf or sheet of solid material, as ivory or wood, for writing, painting, or drawing. **2** One of a set of leaves pivoted or joined together at one end and used for writing; also, a set of such leaves; hence, a pad, as of writing paper or note paper. **3** A small table or flat surface, especially one designed for or containing an inscription or design. **4** A small, flat or nearly flat piece of some prepared substance, as chocolate or soap. **5** A definite portion or weight of drug brought by pressure and the addition of a gum into a solid form; a troche or lozenge; also, an electuary. **6** A flat or tablelike surface. [<OF *tablete*, dim. of *table*. See TABLE.]

table tennis A game resembling tennis in miniature, played indoors with a small celluloid ball and wooden paddles on a large table; Ping-pong.

ta·ble·ware (tā′bəl·wâr′) *n.* Ware for table use; dishes, knives, forks, spoons, etc., collectively: called **table furniture** when napery is included.

tab·loid (tab′loid) *n.* A newspaper, one half the size of an ordinary newspaper, in which the news is presented by means of pictures and concise reporting. —*adj.* **1** Compact; concise; condensed. **2** Sensational: *tabloid* journalism. [<TABL(ET) + -OID]

Tab·loid (tab′loid) *n.* Proprietary name for any of various medical preparations and drugs in concentrated or condensed tablet form.

ta·boo (tə·bōō′, ta-) See TABU.

ta·bor (tā′bər) *n.* A small drum or tambourine on which a fife-player beats his own accompaniment; a timbrel. —*v.i.* To beat or play on a timbrel or small drum; beat lightly and repeatedly. Also spelled *taber*. Also **ta′bour.** [<OF *tabour*, prob. <Persian *tabīrah* drum] —**ta′bor·er** *n.*

Ta·bor (tā′bər), **Mount** A mountain near Nazareth in Galilee, northern Israel; 1,929 feet.

tab·o·ret (tab′ər·it, tab′ə·ret′) *n.* **1** A small tabor. **2** A stool or small seat, usually without arms or back. **3** An embroidery frame. **4** A needle case. Also **tab′ou·ret.** [<F *tabouret*, dim. of *tabour* TABOR]

tab·o·rine (tab′ə·rēn, tab·ə·rēn′) *n.* A small tabor, tambourine, or side drum. Also **tab′o·rin, tab′ou·rine.** [<OF *tabourin*, dim. of *tabour* TABOR]

Ta·briz (tä·brēz′) A city in NW Iran: ancient *Tauris*: also *Tebriz*.

ta·bu (tə·bōō′, ta-) *n.* **1** Among primitive peoples, especially the Polynesians, a religious and social interdict against the touching or mentioning of a certain person, thing, or place, the uttering of a certain name, or the performing of a certain action, because it is considered sacred, protective, dangerous, unclean, or possessed of mysterious powers. **2** The system or practice of such interdicts or prohibitions. **3** Any restriction or ban founded on custom or social convention. —*adj.* **1** Consecrated or prohibited by tabu. **2** Banned or forbidden by social authority or convention. —*v.t.* **1** To place under tabu. **2** To exclude; ostracize. Also spelled *taboo*. [<Tonga]

tab·u·lar (tab′yə·lər) *adj.* **1** Pertaining to or consisting of a table or list. **2** Computed from or with a mathematical table. **3** Having a flat surface; tablelike. [<L *tabularis* < *tabula* table] —**tab′u·lar·ly** *adv.*

tab·u·la ra·sa (tab′yōō·lə rä′sə) *Latin* **1** An empty or clean tablet; a clean slate. **2** The concept of the mind of a newborn child as a blank, to be written on by experience.

tab·u·lar·ize (tab′yə·lə·rīz′) *v.t.* **·ized, ·iz·ing** To arrange in tabular form, or in a table or tables; tabulate. —**tab′u·lar·i·za′tion** *n.*

tab·u·late (tab′yə·lāt) *v.t.* **·lat·ed, ·lat·ing 1** To arrange in a table or list: to *tabulate* results. **2** To form with a tabular surface. —*adj.* **1** Having a flat surface or surfaces; broad and flat. **2** *Zool.* Having tabulated horizontal plates extending across the visceral cavity: said of certain corals. [<L *tabula* table + -ATE[1]] —**tab′u·la′tion** *n.*

tab·u·la·tor (tab′yə·lā′tər) *n.* **1** One who or that which tabulates. **2** A device built into a typewriter with which statistical matter may be speedily written in tabulated form. **3** An automatic high-speed accounting machine for tabulating reports.

tac·a·ma·hac (tak′ə·mə·hak′) *n.* **1** A yellowish resinous substance with a strong odor, derived from various trees and used as incense. **2** Any of the trees producing this substance, especially the balsam poplar (*Populus tacamahaca*) of the United States. Also spelled *tacmahack*. Also **tac′a·ma·hac′a** (-hak′ə), **tac′a·ma·hack′.** [<Sp. *tacamaca, tacamahaca* <Nahuatl *tecomahca*, lit., fetid copal]

ta·can (ta·kan′) *n. Aeron.* A system for indicating the distance and bearing of an aircraft from a known fixed point by means of ultrahigh-frequency signals transmitted from the aircraft to a ground station. [<TAC(TICAL) A(IR) N(AVIGATION)]

tace (tās) *n.* Tasset.

ta·cet (tā′set) *Latin* Literally, it is silent: a musical direction for silence.

tache (tach) *n. Archaic* A hook or fastening; a clasp; buckle. Also **tach.** [<OF *tache* nail, fastening. Doublet of TACK.]

tach·e·om·e·ter (tak′ē·om′ə·tər) *n.* **1** A tachymeter. **2** A tachometer. [<Gk. *tachos, tacheos* speed + -METER] —**tach′e·om′e·try** *n.*

tach·i·na fly (tak′ə·nə) A fly (family *Tachinidae*) often resembling the house fly, whose larvae develop as parasites in the caterpillar or other insect. For illustration see under INSECTS (beneficial). [<NL *tachina* <Gk. *tachinos* swift]

Ta Ch'ing (dä′ jing′) The Manchu dynasty of China. See MANCHU.

tach·i·nid (tak′ə·nid) *n.* A tachina fly. —*adj.* Of or pertaining to the *Tachinidae*.

ta·chis·to·scope (tə·kis′tə·skōp) *n.* An apparatus for giving a brief but accurately measurable exposure to visual objects, for the purpose of determining the speed and conditions of their apperception. [<Gk. *tachistos* swiftest + -SCOPE]

tach·o·graph (tak′ə·graf, -gräf) *n.* **1** A registering tachometer. **2** The record it makes. [<Gk. *tachos* swiftness + -GRAPH]

ta·chom·e·ter (tə·kom′ə·tər) *n.* **1** An instrument for measuring linear and angular velocity, as of a machine, the flow of a current, blood, etc. **2** A device for indicating the speed of rotation of an engine, etc. [See TACHEOMETER]

ta·chom·e·try (tə·kom′ə·trē) *n.* The art or science of using a tachometer. —**tach·o·met·ric** (tak′ə·met′rik) *adj.*

tachy- *combining form* Speed; swiftness: *tachycardia*. [<Gk. *tachys* swift]

tach·y·car·di·a (tak′i·kär′dē·ə) *n. Pathol.* Abnormal rapidity of the heartbeat, usually indicating a pulse rate above 100 per minute. —**tach′y·car′di·ac** *adj.* & *n.*

tach·y·graph (tak′ə·graf, -gräf) *n.* **1** A tachygraphic manuscript or symbol. **2** A tachygrapher.

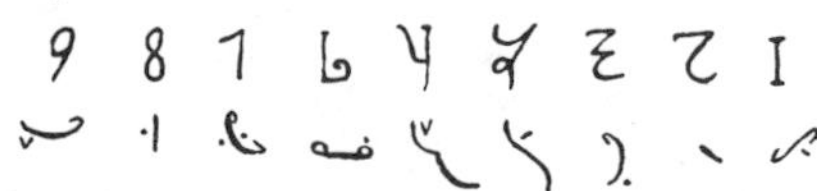

TACHYGRAPHS
Numerals: *Upper* Arabic, A.D. 976; *Lower* Modern Shorthand.

ta·chyg·ra·pher (tə·kig′rə·fər) *n.* **1** One who writes in shorthand; a stenographer. **2** One of the shorthand writers of the ancient Greeks and Romans. Also **ta·chyg′ra·phist.**

ta·chyg·ra·phy (tə·kig′rə·fē) *n. Archaic* Stenography; shorthand. —**tach·y·graph·ic** (tak′ə·graf′ik) or **·i·cal** *adj.* —**tach′y·graph′i·cal·ly** *adv.*

tach·y·lyte (tak′ə·līt) *n.* A pitch-black basaltic glass which is rapidly decomposed by acids. [<TACHY- + -LYTE[1]; so called because easily decomposed] —**tach′y·lyt′ic** (-lit′ik) *adj.*

ta·chym·e·ter (tə·kim′ə·tər) *n.* **1** A surveying instrument for stadia surveying, having a level, telescope, vertical arc or circle, horizontal compass, and stadia wires. **2** A tachometer.

ta·chym·e·try (tə·kim′ə·trē) *n.* The art or science of using, or measuring with, the tachymeter. —**tach·y·met·ric** (tak′ə·met′rik) *adj.*

ta·chys·ter·ol (tə·kis′tə·rōl, -rol) *n. Biochem.* One of the substances formed by the ultraviolet irradiation of ergosterol, and the immediate predecessor of calciferol. [<TACHY- + STEROL]

tac·it (tas′it) *adj.* **1** Existing, inferred, or implied without being directly stated; implied by silence or silent acquiescence. **2** *Law* Not expressed but understood by provision or operation of the law. **3** Silent; emitting no sound; noiseless. ◆ Homophone: *tasset*. [<F *tacite* <L *tacitus*, pp. of *tacere* be silent] —**tac′it·ly** *adv.* —**tac′it·ness** *n.*

Synonyms: implicit, implied, understood, unexpressed, unspoken.

tacit mortgage A lien in the nature of a mortgage created by operation of law.

tac·i·turn (tas′ə·tûrn) *adj.* Habitually silent or reserved; disinclined to conversation. [<L *taciturnus* <L *tacere* be silent] —**tac′i·tur′·ni·ty** *n.* —**tac′i·turn·ly** *adv.*

Synonyms: close, dumb, mute, reserved, reticent, silent, uncommunicative. *Dumb, mute*, and *silent* refer to fact or state; *taciturn* refers to habit and disposition. The talkative person may be stricken *dumb* with terror; the obstinate may remain *mute*; one may be *silent* through preoccupation or set purpose; but the *taciturn* person is averse to the utterance of thought or feeling and to communication with others. One who is *silent* does not speak at all; one who is *taciturn* speaks when compelled, but in a grudging way. *Reserved* suggests more of method and intention than *taciturn*, applying often to some special time or topic. *Reserved* is thus closely equivalent to *uncommunicative*, but is a somewhat stronger word, often suggesting pride or haughtiness, as when we say one is *reserved* toward strangers. *Antonyms*: communicative, free, garrulous, loquacious, talkative, unreserved.

Tac·i·tus (tas′ə·təs), **Gaius Cornelius**, A.D. 55?– after 117, Roman historian.

tack[1] (tak) *n.* **1** A small sharp-pointed nail, commonly with tapering sides and a flat head. **2** *Naut.* **a** A rope which holds down the weather clew of a course. **b** The weather clew of a square sail. **c** The lower forward corner of a fore-and-aft sail. **d** A rope by which the lower outer corner of a studdingsail is pulled to the end of the boom. **e** The direction in which a vessel sails when sailing close-hauled, considered in relation to the position of her sails: the starboard *tack* when the wind is coming from the right-hand side. **f** The distance or the course run at one time in such direction. **g** The act of tacking. **h** Any veering of a vessel to one side, as to take advantage of a side wind. **3** A change of policy; a new course of action. **4** A fastening; in needlework, a temporary stitch. **5** In Scots law, a contract; a lease; also, leased land. **6** The saddle, bridle, martingale, etc., used in riding horseback. —*v.t.* **1** To fasten or attach with tacks. **2** To secure temporarily, as with tacks or long stitches. **3** To attach as supplementary; append. **4** *Naut.* **a** To bring (a vessel) momentarily into the wind so as to go on the opposite tack. **b** To navigate (a vessel) to windward by making a series of tacks. —*v.i.* **5** *Naut.* **a** To tack a vessel. **b** To go on the opposite tack, or sail to windward by a series of tacks: said of vessels. **6** To change one's course of action; veer. [<AF *taque*, OF *tache* a nail <Gmc. Doublet of TACHE.] —**tack′er** *n.*

tack[2] (tak) *n.* Food in general: usually used contemptuously, and often in compounds: *hardtack*. [Origin uncertain]

tack·et (tak′it) *n. Scot.* A hobnail or clout.

tack hammer A small hammer for driving tacks.

tack·le (tak′əl, *in nautical usage* tā′kəl) *n.* **1** A rope, pulley, or combination of ropes and pulleys, used for hoisting or moving objects. **2** *Naut.* A mechanism for raising and lowering heavy weights, or managing sails and spars, as on shipboard. **3** A windlass or winch, together with ropes and hooks. **4** The instruments collectively used in any work or sport; gear; equipment: fishing *tackle*. **5** Formerly, the implements of war; weapons. **6** The act of tackling, or seizing and stopping, especially in

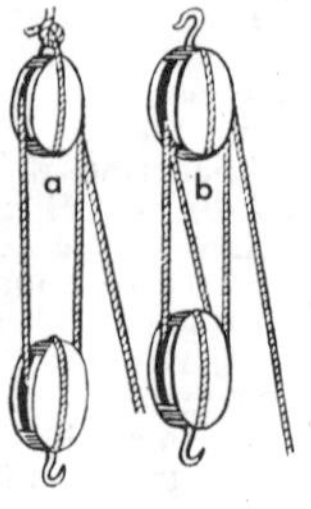

TACKLE
a. Gun.
b. Luff.

football. 7 In football, either of two linemen stationed between the guard and end: called **right** and **left tackle.** 8 A ship's rigging collectively. — *v.t.* **·led, ·ling** 1 To harness (a horse). 2 To deal with; undertake to master, accomplish, or solve: to *tackle* a task or a problem. 3 To seize suddenly and forcefully, usually in order to stop or throw to the ground: to *tackle* a fleeing burglar. 4 In football, to seize and stop (an opponent carrying the ball). [<MLG *takel* < *taken* seize] — **tack'ler** *n.*

tack·ling (tak'ling) *n. Naut.* Tackle, collectively.

tack·y[1] (tak'ē) *adj.* **tack·i·er, tack·i·est** Having adhesive properties; sticky: said especially of surfaces covered with partly dried varnish. Also **tack'ey.** [Prob. <TACK[1], *v.* (def. 2)]

tack·y[2] (tak'ē) *adj. U.S. Colloq.* Unfashionable; plain; in bad taste; common. [Cf. dial. G *taklig* untidy]

tac·ma·hack (tak'mə·hak) See TACAMAHAC.

Tac·na (täk'nä) A department of southern Peru on the Pacific; 4,920 square miles.

tac·node (tak'nōd) *n. Math.* A point of osculation. [<L *tactus,* pp. of *tangere* touch + NODE]

ta·co (tä'kō) *n. pl.* **·cos** A fried tortilla folded around any of several fillings, as chopped meat or cheese. [<Sp., wad]

Ta·co·ma (tə·kō'mə) A port on Puget Sound in western Washington.

Ta·con·ic Mountains (tə·kon'ik) A range of the Appalachian system in New England and New York; highest point, 3,816 feet.

tac·o·nite (tak'ə·nīt) *n. Geol.* A variously tinted ferruginous chert enclosing the iron ores of the Mesabi district in Minnesota. [from *Tacon(ic Mountains)* + -ITE[1]]

tact (takt) *n.* 1 A quick or intuitive appreciation of what is fit, proper, or right; fine or ready mental discernment shown in saying or doing the proper thing, or especially in avoiding what would offend or disturb; skill or facility in dealing with men or emergencies; adroitness; cleverness; address. 2 The sense of touch; feeling; also, a touch or touching. 3 A perception or feeling, other than tactile, of the qualities of things. See synonyms under ADDRESS. [<L *tactus* a touching < *tangere* touch]

tact·ful (takt'fəl) *adj.* Possessing or manifesting tact; considerate. — **tact'ful·ly** *adv.* — **tact'ful·ness** *n.*

tac·tic (tak'tik) *n.* 1 A detail of tactics. 2 *Colloq.* A device or strategem: a clever *tactic.*

tac·ti·cal (tak'ti·kəl) *adj.* 1 Pertaining to or of the nature of tactics. 2 Exhibiting adroit maneuvering. — **tac'ti·cal·ly** *adv.*

tactical unit A military combat unit, running in size from the squad through the army group.

tac·ti·cian (tak·tish'ən) *n.* An expert in tactics; an adroit maneuverer.

tac·tics (tak'tiks) *n. pl.* 1 The science and art of military and naval evolutions; specifically, the art of handling troops in the presence of the enemy or for immediate objectives, as distinguished from *strategy*: construed as singular. 2 Any maneuvering or adroit management to effect an object. [<Gk. *taktika,* pl. of *taktikos* suitable for arranging or organizing < *tassein, tattein* arrange, order]

tac·tile (tak'til, -təl) *adj.* 1 Pertaining to the organs or sense of touch; caused by or consisting of contact; tactual. 2 That may be touched; tangible. [<F <L *tactilis* < *tactus* touch. See TACT.]

tac·til·i·ty (tak·til'ə·tē) *n.* Tangibility.

tac·tion (tak'shən) *n.* 1 The act of touching. 2 The state of being in contact. [<L *tactio, -onis* < *tactus,* pp. of *tangere* touch]

tact·less (takt'lis) *adj.* Without tact. — **tact'less·ly** *adv.* — **tact'less·ness** *n.*

tac·tom·e·ter (tak·tom'ə·tər) *n.* An esthesiometer. [<L *tactus* touch + -METER]

tac·tu·al (tak'cho͞o·əl) *adj.* 1 Pertaining to the sense or the organs of touch. 2 Derived from or caused by touch. [<L *tactus* touch. See TACT.] — **tac'tu·al·ly** *adv.*

Ta·cu·ba·ya (tä'ko͞o·bä'yä) A western section of Mexico City; site of the national astronomical observatory.

tad (tad) *n.* A little boy or girl; young child. [Prob. short for TADPOLE]

Tad·de·o (täd·dā'ō) Italian form of THADDEUS.

Ta·de·o (tä·thā'ō) Spanish form of THADDEUS.

tad·pole (tad'pōl) *n.* The aquatic larva of an amphibian, as a frog or toad, breathing by external gills and having a tail with extended membrane giving it a fishlike form. See FROG. [ME *taddepol* < *tadde* toad + *poll* head]

Ta·dzhik (tä·jēk', -jik') *n. pl.* **·dzhik** One of a people of Iranian descent inhabiting the Tadzhik S.S.R. and adjacent regions: also spelled *Tajik.*

Ta·dzhik Soviet Socialist Republic (tä·jēk', -jik') A constituent republic of the U.S.S.R. in central Asia; 55,043 square miles; capital, Stalinabad: also *Tajik S.S.R.* Also **Tad·zhik·i·stan** (tä·jē'kə·stän, -jik'ə-).

tae (tā) *n. Scot.* 1 A toe. 2 The prong of a fork.

tae·di·um vi·tae (tē'dē·əm vī'tē) *Latin* Weariness of life.

Tae·dong (tī·do͝ong) A river of central and SW North Korea, flowing 245 miles SW to the Yellow Sea at Korea Bay near Chinnampo.

Tae·gu (tī·go͞o) A city in SE South Korea. *Japanese* **Tai·kyu** (tī·kyo͞o).

Tae·jon (tī·jôn) A city of SW central South Korea. *Japanese* **Tai·den** (tī·den).

tael (tāl) *n.* 1 An Oriental weight varying from 1 to 2 1/2 ounces, commonly about 1 1/3 ounces. 2 A Chinese monetary unit of varying value. [<Pg. <Malay *tahil*]

ta'en (tān) *Scot.* Taken: a contraction.

tae·ni·a (tē'nē·ə) *n.* 1 In classical antiquity, a band, ribbon, or fillet for containing the hair. 2 *Archit.* A band or fillet between the Doric frieze and the architrave. 3 *Anat.* A band or strip of tissue, especially one of several ribbonlike arrangements of white substance in the brain, or one of the three longitudinal muscular bands of the colon. 4 *Zool.* A tapeworm (genus *Taenia*). Also spelled *tenia.* [<L <Gk. *tainia* fillet, tape]

tae·ni·a·cide (tē'nē·ə·sīd'), **tae·ni·a·fuge** (tē'nē·ə·fyo͞oj'), etc. See TENIACIDE, etc.

taf·fer·el (taf'ər·əl, -ə·rel) *n. Naut.* 1 A taffrail. 2 Originally, the upper part of a vessel's stern. [<MDu. *tafereel* panel, picture, dim. of *tafel* table, panel <L *tabula* board]

taf·fe·ta (taf'ə·tə) *n.* A fine, glossy, uncorded, somewhat stiff silk fabric: a term variously applied at different times, as to certain silk-and-linen or silk-and-wool mixtures, now also to rayon. — *adj.* Made of or resembling taffeta; also, lacy; filmy; delicate. [<OF *taffetas* <Med. L *taffeta* <Persian *tāftah* < *tāftan* twist]

taff·rail (taf'rāl') *n. Naut.* 1 The rail around a vessel's stern. 2 The upper part of a vessel's stern. [Alter. of TAFFEREL, after RAIL[1]]

taffrail log A screw log.

taf·fy (taf'ē) *n.* 1 A confection made of brown sugar or molasses, mixed with butter, boiled down, and pulled into long ropes until it cools sufficiently to hold its shape: also spelled *toffee, toffy.* 2 *Colloq.* Flattery; blarney. [Origin unknown]

taf·i·a (taf'ē·ə) *n.* A spirituous liquor resembling rum, distilled in the West Indies from impure molasses or from refuse sugar. Also **taf'fi·a.** [<native name, prob. ult. <Malay *tāfīa* spirit distilled from molasses]

Ta·fi·lelt (tä·fē'lelt) The largest Saharan oasis in SE Morocco; 200 square miles. Also **Ta·fi'lalt, Ta·fi'let** (-let).

Taft (taft), **Lorado,** 1860–1936, U. S. sculptor. — **Robert A.,** 1899–1953, U. S. lawyer and politician; son of W. H. Taft. — **William Howard,** 1857–1930, U. S. statesman; president of the United States 1909–13.

tag[1] (tag) *n.* 1 Something tacked on or attached to something else; appendage. 2 A label tied or tacked on, as to a trunk; loosely, any label. 3 A loose, ragged edge of anything; tatter. 4 The tail or tip of the tail of any animal. 5 A matted and ragged lock of wool on a sheep; a loose lock of hair. 6 A worthless leaving; remnant; ort. 7 A flap or loop, as for drawing on a boot. 8 An aglet. 9 A decorative flourish, as on a signature. 10 In angling, a piece of bright material surrounding the shank of the hook in an artificial fly. 11 A lamb or yearling sheep. 12 A well-known quotation or saying, as in a song, poem, or book. 13 The refrain of a song or poem; also, the final lines of a speech in a play; catchword; cue. 14 The crowd; rabble: often in the phrases **rag and tag** and **rag, tag, and bobtail.** — *v.* **tagged, tag·ging** *v.t.* 1 To supply, adorn, fit, mark, or label with a tag. 2 To shear away tags from (sheep). 3 To follow closely or persistently. — *v.i.* 4 To follow closely at one's heels: The little boy *tagged* along. [Prob. <Scand. Cf. Sw. *tagg* spike, tooth, Norw. *tagge* tooth.]

tag[2] (tag) *n.* A juvenile game in which the object of the players is to keep from being caught or touched by one, the tagger (usually called "it"), who chases them for that purpose. — *v.t.* **tagged, tag·ging** To overtake and touch, as in the game of tag. [<TAG[1]]

Ta·ga·log (tä·gä'log, tag'ə·log, -lôg) *n.* 1 A member of a Malay people native to the Philippines, especially Luzon. 2 One of the principal native languages and, since 1940, the official language of the Philippines, belonging to the Indonesian subfamily of the Austronesian family of languages.

Ta·gan·rog (tä'gän·rôk') A port in SW European Russian S.F.S.R., on the **Gulf of Taganrog,** a NE arm of the Sea of Azov.

tag day A day on which contributions are solicited for eleemosynary and other institutions: so called from the custom of giving a tag to each donor.

tagged atom *Physics* A radioisotope which betrays its presence in any part of a system into which it has been introduced.

tag·ger (tag'ər) *n.* 1 One who or that which tags or is tagged. 2 *pl.* Very thin tin plate.

tag·lock (tag'lok') *n.* Daglock. [Var. of DAGLOCK]

tag·meme (tag'mēm) *n. Ling.* The smallest unit of grammatical form having meaning. [<Gk. *tagma* arrangement + *-eme,* on analogy with *phoneme* and *morpheme*] — **tag·me'mics** *n.*

Ta·gore (tə·gôr', -gōr', tä'gôr), **Sir Rabindranath,** 1861–1941, Hindu philosopher and poet.

ta·gua nut (tä'gwä) The ivory nut. [<native Colombian name]

Ta·gus (tā'gəs) A river in west central Spain and central Portugal, flowing 566 miles SW to the Atlantic at Lisbon: Spanish *Tajo,* Portuguese *Tejo.*

Ta·hi·ti (tä·hē'tē, tī'tē) The largest island of the Society group; 600 square miles; capital, Papeete; formerly *Otaheite.*

Ta·hi·ti·an (tä·hē'tē·ən, -shən) *adj.* Of or relating to Tahiti, its people, or their language. — *n.* 1 One of the native Polynesian people of Tahiti. 2 The Polynesian language of the Tahitians.

Ta·hoe (tä'hō, tā'-), **Lake** A lake on the boundary between California and Nevada; 195 square miles; elevation, 6,225 feet.

tah·sil·dar (tä'sēl·där') *n.* An Indian officer of customs; a tax-collector. Also **tah'seel·dar'.** [<Hind. *tahṣīldār* <Arabic *taḥṣīl* a collection + Persian *dār* holder]

Tai (tī) See THAI.

Tai·an (tī'än') A city of western Shantung province, China.

Tai·chung (tī'cho͝ong') A city in west central Taiwan; an agricultural and industrial center.

tai·ga (tī'gə) *n.* The far northern coniferous forest of Siberia and by extension of Eurasia and America, extending to the northern limit of trees. [<Russian]

Tai·ho·ku (tī·hō·ko͞o) The Japanese name for TAIPEH.

tail[1] (tāl) *n.* 1 The hindmost part or rear end of an animal's body, especially when prolonged beyond the rest of the body. ◆ Collateral adjective: *caudal.* 2 Any slender, flexible, terminal prolongation of the body of a structure: the *tail* of a shirt or kite. 3 *Astron.* The luminous sheaf extending from the nucleus of a comet. 4 The hind, back, or inferior portion of anything. 5 *pl. Colloq.* The reverse side of a coin. 6 The lower end of a stream or pool. 7 Anything of tail-like appearance; a body of persons in single file; a queue; also, a retinue or suite. 8 A pigtail. 9 *Aeron.* One of several fixed horizontal or vertical surfaces of an airplane structure placed at some distance to the rear of the main bearing surfaces. 10 The rear portion of a bomb, projectile, rocket, or guided missile, usually equipped with vanes. 11

The bottom of a printed page. **12** *pl. Colloq.* A man's full-dress suit; also, a swallow-tailed coat. **13** The back end of a wagon. **14** *Colloq.* The trail or course taken by a fugitive: The police were on his *tail.* — *v.t.* **1** To furnish with a tail. **2** To cut off the tail of. **3** To be the tail or end of: to *tail* a procession. **4** To join (one thing) to the end of another. **5** To insert and fasten by one end, as a beam into a wall: with *in* or *on.* **6** *Colloq.* To follow secretly and stealthily; shadow. — *v.i.* **7** To extend or proceed in a line. **8** *Colloq.* To follow close behind. **9** To diminish gradually: His voice *tailed* off. **10** To be inserted and fastened at one end, as a beam. **11** *Naut.* To swing or go aground stern foremost: The ship *tailed* into the wind. — *adj.* **1** Rearmost; hindmost: the *tail* end. **2** Following; coming from behind: a *tail* wind. ◆ Homophone: *tale.* [OE *tægl*] — **tail′less** *adj.*

tail² (tāl) *Law adj.* Restricted; limited; abridged; restricted in succession to particular heirs: an estate *tail.* — *n.* A cutting off, abridgment, or limitation of ownership; an entail: an estate in *tail.* ◆ Homophone: *tale.* [<OF *taillié,* pp. of *taillier* cut]

Tai Lake (tī) One of China's largest lakes, on the Kiangsu–Chekiang border, between Shanghai and Nanking; 40 miles long, 30 miles wide. *Chinese* **T'ai Hu** (tī′hōō′).

tail beam Tailpiece (def. 4).

tail coverts *Ornithol.* The feathers that lie at the base of the tail feathers above and below.

tail·first (tāl′fûrst′) *adv.* Backward; with the hind side foremost. Also **tail′fore′most** (-fôr′·mōst, -fōr′-).

tail·gate (tāl′gāt′) *n.* **1** A hinged or vertically sliding board or gate closing the back end of a truck, wagon, etc. Also **tail·board** (tāl′bôrd′, -bōrd′). **2** One of the gates at the lower level of a canal lock. — *v.t.* & *v.i.* **·gat·ed, ·gat·ing** *U.S. Slang* To drive too close behind for safety: impatient drivers *tailgating* in a no-passing zone.

tail gun A gun mounted in the tail section of an airplane.

tail-heav·y (tāl′hev′ē) *adj.* Having too much weight at the rear: a *tail-heavy* airplane: opposed to *nose-heavy.*

tail·ing (tā′ling) *n.* **1** Refuse or residue from grain after milling, or from ground ore after washing: usually plural. **2** The inner, covered portion of a projecting brick or stone.

taille (tāl, *Fr.* tā′y′) *n.* In feudal France, a tax levied by a king or lord from which nobles and clergy were exempt. [<OF < *taillier* cut]

tail light A light attached to the rear of a vehicle. Also **tail lamp.**

tai·lor (tā′lər) *n.* One who makes to order or repairs men's or women's outer garments. — *v.i.* **1** To do a tailor's work. — *v.t.* **2** To fit with garments: He is well *tailored.* **3** To work at or make by tailoring: to *tailor* a coat. ◆ Collateral adjective: *sartorial.* [<OF *tailleor* < *taillier* cut <LL *taliare* split, cut, prob. <L *talea* rod]

tailor bee Any of certain leaf-cutting bees (family *Megachilidae*) that line their nests with pieces of leaves.

tai·lor·bird (tā′lər·bûrd′) *n.* A bird (genus *Sutoria*) of Asia and Africa, related to the warblers, that stitches leaves together to form a receptacle for its nest. See illustration under NEST.

tai·lor·ing (tā′lər·ing) *n.* **1** A tailor's trade or occupation. **2** The making or altering of a garment by a tailor. **3** The style and fit resulting from the work of a tailor.

tai·lor-made (tā′lər·mād′) *adj.* Made by a tailor: said especially of women's clothes of a plain, close-fitting, usually heavier type, as for walking, etc.: opposed to *ready-made.* — *n. Colloq.* A commercially prepared cigarette, as opposed to one which is rolled by hand.

tail·piece (tāl′pēs′) *n.* **1** Any endpiece or appendage. **2** In a violin or similar instrument, a piece of wood, as ebony, at the sounding-board end, having the strings fastened to it. **3** *Printing* An ornamental design on the lower blank portion of a short page. **4** A piece inserted by tailing, as a floor timber.

tail·race (tāl′rās′) *n.* **1** That part of a millrace below the water wheel, bearing away the spent water. **2** *Mining* The channel for water to remove tailings.

tail·skid (tāl′skid′) *n. Aeron.* A runner fixed beneath the tail of an airplane.

tail·spin (tāl′spin′) *n.* **1** *Aeron.* The descent of an airplane along a helical path at a steep angle, either by accident or with power of recovery by manipulation of the controls. **2** *Colloq.* A sudden, sharp, emotional upheaval, often resulting in loss of control: He went into a *tailspin* over her.

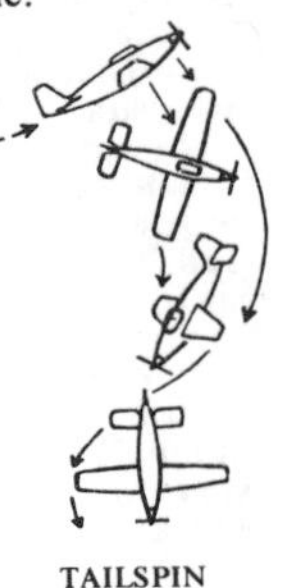

TAILSPIN

tail·stock (tāl′stok′) *n.* That standard or stock of a lathe through which passes the non-rotating spindle or dead center.

tail wind A wind blowing in the same general direction as the flight of an aircraft or course of a ship.

Tai·mir Peninsula (tī·mir′, tī′mir) A large peninsula of northern Asiatic Russian S.F.S.R., extending 700 miles NE to SW, between the Kara and Laptev seas. Also **Tai·myr′.**

tain¹ (tān) *n.* **1** Very thin plate. **2** Tinfoil suitable for backing mirrors. [Prob. aphetic var. of F *étain* tin]

tain² (tôn) *n.* Literally, a cattle raid; by extension, any of numerous Old Irish epics about a cattle raid. [<Irish *táin*]

Tai·nan (tī′nän′) A city of west central Taiwan.

Tai·na·ron (te′nä·rôn), **Cape** See MATAPAN, CAPE.

Tain Bo Cuail·gne (tôn bō kōōl′nyē) The Cattle Raid of Cooley: title of the most famous epic in the Ulster cycle of Old Irish literature, and the oldest epic of all western Europe, embodying the life and exploits of Cuchulain and his single-handed defense of Ulster against the hosts of Connacht. [<Irish *táin* cattle raid + *bo* cow (<L *bos* ox) + *Cuailgne* Cooley, a hill district in County Louth]

Taine (tān, *Fr.* ten), **Hippolyte Adolphe,** 1828–93, French literary critic and historian.

Tai·no (tī′nō) *n. pl.* **·nos** **1** A member of an extinct tribe of Indian aborigines of the West Indies, especially Haiti, probably the first encountered by Columbus. **2** The Arawakan language of this tribe.

taint (tānt) *v.t.* **1** To imbue with an offensive, noxious, or deteriorating quality or principle; infect with decay; render corrupt or poisonous. **2** To render morally corrupt or vitiated; contaminate; pollute. **3** *Obs.* To tincture; tinge. — *v.i.* **4** To be or become tainted. See synonyms under POLLUTE. — *n.* **1** A trace or germ of decay; a cause or result of corruption. **2** A moral stain or blemish; spot. [Fusion of aphetic form of ATTAINT and F *teint,* pp. of *teindre* tinge, color <L *tingere*]

Tai·pei (tī′pā′) The capital of Taiwan, in the northern part: Japanese *Taihoku.* Also **Tai′·peh′, T'ai′-pei′.**

Tai·ping (tī′ping′) *n.* An insurgent in the **Taiping Rebellion** in China (1850–64) led by one Hung-siu-tsuen, who sought to replace the Manchu dynasty with a native dynasty called the T'ai-p'ing Chao (Great Peace Dynasty): suppressed with the aid of a corps of Chinese led by Charles George Gordon. [<Chinese, great peace]

Tai·ping (tī′ping′) A tin-mining center and city in Perak state, NW Malaya.

Tai·sho (tī·shō) The title of the reign (1912–26) of Yoshihito, emperor of Japan. [<Japanese, great righteousness]

Tai·wan (tī′wän′) An island off the coast of SE China, comprising a province, and, together with the Pescadores, the National Republic of China; 13,890 square miles; capital, Taipei; ceded to Japan, 1895–1945: formerly *Formosa.* — **Tai′wan′ese′** (-ēz, -ēs) *n.* & *adj.*

Tai·yü·an (tī′yü·än′) The capital of Shansi province, China.

Ta'iz (ta·iz′) **1** A province of SW Yemen. **2** The capital of Ta'iz province, residence of the Imam of Yemen and the second capital of the country.

taj (täj) *n. Persian* A diadem or crown; a head-dress of distinction; specifically, a tall cap worn by Moslem dervishes.

Ta·jik (tä·jēk′, -jik′) See TADZHIK.

Ta·jik S.S.R. (tä·jēk′, -jik′) See TADZHIK S.S.R.

Taj Ma·hal (täj′ mə·häl′, täzh′) A mausoleum of white marble built (1631–45) by the emperor Shah Jehan at Agra, India, containing the tombs of his favorite wife and of himself.

TAJ MAHAL, AGRA, INDIA.

Ta·jo (tä′hō) The Spanish name for the TAGUS.

Ta·ju·mul·co (tä′hōō·mōōl′kō) An extinct volcano in SW Guatemala; highest point in central America; 13,816 feet.

Ta·ka·mat·su (tä·kä·mät·sōō) A port in northern Shikoku, Japan.

Ta·ka·o·ka (tä·kä·ō·kä) A port of north central Honshu, Japan, a rice-trading and manufacturing center.

take (tāk) *v.* **took, tak·en, tak·ing** *v.t.* **1** To lay hold of; grasp. **2** To get possession of; seize. **3** To seize forcibly; capture; catch. **4** To catch in a trap or snare. **5** To gain in competition; win. **6** To choose; select. **7** To obtain by purchase; buy. **8** To rent or hire; lease: to *take* lodgings. **9** To receive regularly by payment; subscribe to, as a periodical. **10** To assume occupancy of: to *take* a chair. **11** To assume the responsibilities or duties of: to *take* office. **12** To bring or accept into some relation to oneself: He *took* a wife. **13** To assume as a symbol or badge: to *take* the veil. **14** To impose upon oneself; subject oneself to: to *take* a vow. **15** To remove or carry off: with *away.* **16** To remove from the proper place; misappropriate; steal. **17** To remove by death. **18** To subtract or deduct. **19** To be subjected to; undergo: to *take* a beating. **20** To submit to; accept passively: to *take* an insult. **21** To become affected with; contract: He *took* cold. **22** To affect: The fever *took* him at dawn. **23** To captivate; charm or delight: The dress *took* her fancy. **24** To conduct oneself in response to; react to: How did she *take* the news? **25** To undertake to deal with; contend with; handle: to *take* an examination. **26** To consider; deem: I *take* him for an honest man. **27** To understand; comprehend. **28** To strike in a specified place; hit: The blow *took* him on the forehead. **29** *Colloq.* To aim or direct: He *took* a shot at the target. **30** To carry with one; transport; convey: *Take* your umbrella! **31** To lead: This road *takes* you to town. **32** To escort; conduct: Who *took* her to the dance? **33** To receive into the body, as by eating, inhaling, etc.: *Take* a deep breath. **34** To accept, as something offered, due, or given; have conferred on one: to *take* a bribe; to *take* a degree. **35** To let in; admit: The ship is *taking* water; The car will *take* only six people. **36** To indulge oneself in; enjoy: to *take* a nap. **37** To perform, as an action: to *take* a stride. **38** To avail oneself of (an opportunity, etc.). **39** To put into effect; adopt: to *take* measures; to *take* advice. **40** To use up or consume; require as necessary; demand: The piano *takes* too much space; That *takes* a lot of nerve. **41** To make use of; apply: They *took* clubs to him; to *take* pains. **42** To travel by means of: to *take* a train to Boston. **43** To go to; seek: to *take* cover. **44** To ascertain or obtain by measuring, computing, etc.: to *take* a census. **45** To obtain or derive from some source; adopt or copy. **46** To obtain by writing; write down or copy: to *take* notes. **47** To obtain a likeness or representation of, as by drawing or photographing; also, to obtain (a likeness, picture, etc.) in such a manner. **48** To experience; feel: to *take* pride in an achievement. **49** To conceive or feel: She *took* a dislike to him. **50** To become impregnated with; absorb: The cloth will not *take* the pattern. **51** *Slang* To cheat; deceive. **52** *Gram.* To require by construction or usage: The verb *takes* a direct object. — *v.i.* **53** To get possession. **54** To engage; catch, as mechanical parts. **55** To begin to grow; germinate. **56** To have the intended effect: The vaccination *took.* **57** To become popular; gain favor or currency, as a play. **58** To admit of being photographed: His face *takes* well. **59** To detract: with *from.* **60** To become (ill or sick). **61** To make one's way; go. See synonyms under ABSTRACT, ASSUME, CARRY, CATCH. — **to take after** **1** To resemble. **2** To follow as an example. — **to take amiss** To be offended by. — **to take at one's word** To believe. — **to take back** **1** To regain. **2** To retract. — **to take breath** To pause, as from working. — **to take down** **1** To pull down, as a building. **2** To dismantle; disassemble. **3** To humble. **4** To write down; make a record of. — **to take heart** To gain courage or confidence. — **to take in** **1** To admit; receive. **2** To lessen in size or scope. **3** To furl or brail (sail). **4** To include; embrace. **5** To understand. **6** To cheat or deceive. **7** To visit as part of a tour: Did you *take in* the Louvre? **8** To receive into one's home for pay, as lodgers or work. — **to take in vain** To use profanely or blasphemously, as the name of a deity. — **to take it** **1** To assume; understand. **2** To endure hardship, abuse, etc. — **to take off** **1** To remove, as a coat. **2** To carry away. **3** To kill. **4** To deduct. **5** To mimic; burlesque. **6** To rise from the ground or water in starting a flight, as an airplane. **7** To leave; depart. — **to take on** **1** To hire; employ. **2** To undertake to deal with; handle. **3** *Colloq.* To exhibit violent emotion. — **to take out** **1** To extract; remove. **2** To obtain from the proper authority, as a license or patent. **3** To lead or escort. — **to take over** **1** To assume control of. **2** To convey. — **to take place** To happen. — **to take stock** **1** To make an inventory. **2** To estimate probability, position, etc.; consider. — **to take the field** To begin a campaign or game. — **to take to** **1** To betake oneself to: to *take to* one's bed. **2** To develop the practice of, or an addiction to: He *took to* drink. **3** To become fond of; be attracted by. — **to take to heart** To be deeply affected by. — **to take up** **1** To raise or lift. **2** To make smaller or less; shorten or tighten. **3** To pay, as a note or mortgage. **4** To accept as stipulated: to *take up* an option. **5** To begin or begin again; resume. **6** To reprove or criticize. **7** To occupy, engage, or consume, as space or time. **8** To acquire an interest in or devotion to: to *take up* a cause. — **to take up with** *Colloq.* To become friendly with; associate with. — *n.* **1** The act of taking, or that which is taken. **2** An uninterrupted run of the camera and sound apparatus in recording any portion of a motion picture. **3** *Slang* The money collected; receipts. **4** The quantity collected at one time: the *take* of fish. [OE *tacan* <ON *taka*]

take-down (tāk′doun′) *adj.* Fitted for being taken apart or down easily: a *take-down* shack; a *take-down* rifle. — *n.* **1** Any article so constructed as to be taken apart easily. **2** The part of a take-down mechanism by means of which it is taken apart or down. **3** *Colloq.* The act of humiliating any one; humiliation.

take-home pay (tāk′hōm′) The remainder of one's wages or salary after tax and other payroll deductions.

take-in (tāk′in′) *n. Colloq.* An act of cheating or hoaxing.

take-off (tāk′ôf′, -of′) *n.* **1** *Colloq.* A satirical representation; caricature. **2** In horsemanship and athletics, the spot at which the feet leave the ground in leaping. **3** *Aeron.* The act of rising from and leaving the ground or water in an aircraft flight.

tak·er (tā′kər) *n.* One who takes; specifically, one who accepts a wager; also, a collector: a ticket *taker.*

take-up (tāk′up′) *n.* **1** *Mech.* A device for taking up lost motion or drawing in the slack of a thing, as in a loom. **2** The act of tightening or taking up.

tak·ing (tā′king) *adj.* **1** Fascinating; captivating. **2** *Colloq.* Contagious; infectious. — *n.* **1** The act of one who takes. **2** The thing or things taken; in fishing, a catch; haul; in the plural, receipts, as of money. **3** *Obs.* Agitation; perplexity; distress. — **tak′ing·ly** *adv.* — **tak′ing·ness** *n.*

Ta·kla·ma·kan (tä′klä·mä′kän′) A desert in the SW third of the Sinkiang-Uigur Autonomous Region, NW China. Also **Ta′kla′ Ma′kan′.**

Ta·ku (tä′ko͞o′) A port on the Gulf of Chihli, eastern Hopeh province, NE China.

tal·a·poin (tal′ə·poin) *n.* **1** A Buddhist priest or monk. **2** A West African monkey (*Cercopithecus talapoin*) of the guenon group, smallest of the Old World monkeys. [<Pg. *talapões,* pl. of *talapão* <Burmese *tala poi* our master]

ta·lar (tā′lər) *n. Archaic* A cloak or robe reaching to the ankles. [<L *talaris* of the ankles < *talus* ankle]

ta·lar·i·a (tə·lâr′ē·ə) *n. pl. Latin* Winged boots or sandals, or wings springing directly from the ankles: used in antique art as attributes of Mercury, Perseus, etc.

TALARIA

Ta·laud Islands (tä′lout) An Indonesian island group NE of Celebes; 495 square miles. Also **Ta·laur Islands** (tä′·lour).

Ta·la·ve·ra de la Rei·na (tä′lä·vā′rä thā lä rā′nä) A city of central Spain on the Tagus river; scene of a battle between Wellington and Joseph Bonaparte, 1809.

tal·bot (tôl′bət, tal′-) *n.* A sleuthhound, supposed to be related to the bloodhound. [after *Talbot,* English family name]

talc (talk) *n.* A soft, hydrous magnesium silicate, $H_2Mg_3(SiO_3)_4$, used in making paper, soap, toilet powder, lubricants, etc. Soapstone and French chalk are varieties of talc. — *v.t.* **talcked** or **talced, talck·ing** or **talc·ing** To treat with talc: to *talc* a photographic plate. [<F <Med. L *talcum* <Arabian *talq* <Persian *talk*]

Tal·ca (täl′kä) A city of central Chile; birthplace of Chile's independence, 1818; destroyed by earthquake, 1928.

talc·ose (tal′kōs) *adj.* Composed of or containing talc. Also **talc′ous** (tal′kəs).

tal·cum (tal′kəm) *n.* Talc. [<Med. L. See TALC.]

talcum powder Finely powdered and purified talc, used as a dusting agent, filter, and for the relief of chafed skin and prickly heat.

tale (tāl) *n.* **1** That which is told or related; a story; recital. **2** Hence, a connected narrative or account, whether oral or written, of an actual, legendary, or fictitious event or series of events. **3** An idle or malicious report; a piece of gossip. **4** A deliberately untrue story; a lie; falsehood. **5** *Archaic* A counting or enumeration; reckoning; numbering. **6** *Archaic* That which is counted; an amount; total; sum. **7** *Obs.* Speech; talk; also, the language of a country. ◆ Homophone: *tail.* [OE *talu* speech, narrative. Akin to TELL, TALK.]

tale·bear·er (tāl′bâr′ər) *n.* One who tells mischievous tales about other persons. — **tale′·bear′ing** *adj.* & *n.*

tal·ent (tal′ənt) *n.* **1** Mental endowments or capacities of a superior character; marked mental ability; also, mental ability in general. **2** A particular and uncommon aptitude for some special work or activity; a faculty or gift: a usage founded on a Scriptural parable (*Matt.* xxv 14–30), mental power being considered as a divine trust. **3** People of skill or ability, collectively: the *talent* of stage, screen, and radio. **4** *U.S. Slang* In horse-racing circles, those who make bets or take odds on their individual judgment and responsibility: distinguished from the bookmakers. **5** An ancient weight and denomination of money, varying in weight and value among different nations and in different periods. **6** *Obs.* Inclination; disposition. See synonyms under ABILITY, GENIUS. [OE *talente* appetite, will, inclination <L *talentum,* a sum of money <Gk. *talanton* weight, thing weighed]

tal·ent·ed (tal′ən·tid) *adj.* Having mental ability; gifted. See synonyms under CLEVER.

talent scout One whose business it is to discover talented or exceptionally gifted people, especially those suitable for dramatic or motion-picture careers.

ta·ler (tä′lər) *n.* A former German silver coin, the prototype of all dollars, issued in Bohemia and first dated 1518; a dollar: also spelled *thaler.* [<G. See DOLLAR.]

ta·les (tā′lēz) *n. pl.* **·les** (-lēz) *Law* **1** Persons to be summoned for jury duty to make up a deficiency when the regular panel is exhausted by challenges. **2** The writ for summoning such persons. [<L *tales (de circumstantibus)* such (of the bystanders), pl. of *talis* such a one; the phrase is from the writ summoning them]

tales·man (tālz′mən) *n. pl.* **·men** (-mən) One summoned to make up a jury when the regular panel is exhausted. [<TALES + MAN]

tale·tel·ler (tāl′tel′ər) *n.* **1** One who tells stories, etc.; a raconteur. **2** A talebearer. — **tale′tell′ing** *adj.* & *n.*

Ta·lien (dä′lyen′) The Chinese name for DAIREN.

tal·i·grade (tal′ə·grād) *adj. Zool.* Walking on the outer surface of the foot. [<L *talus* ankle + -GRADE]

tal·i·on (tal′ē·ən) *n.* Retaliation, as a form of justice. [<F <L *talio, -onis* < *talis* such]

tal·i·ped (tal′ə·ped) *adj.* Suffering from or afflicted with talipes; clubfooted. — *n.* A clubfooted person. [See TALIPES]

tal·i·pes (tal′ə·pēz) *n. Pathol.* **1** Malformation of the foot. **2** A clubfoot. [<NL <L *talus* ankle + *pes, pedis* foot]

tal·i·pom·a·nus (tal′ə·pom′ə·nəs) *n. Pathol.* Clubhand. [< *talipo-* (<TALIPES) + L *manus* a hand]

tal·i·pot (tal′ə·pot) *n.* A stately and valuable East Indian palm (*Corypha umbraculifera*) crowned by large leaves often used as fans, umbrellas, and as a house covering. Also **talipot palm.** [<Bengali *tālipāt* palm leaf <Skt. *tālī* fan palm + *pattra* leaf]

tal·is·man (tal′is·mən, -iz-) *n. pl.* **·mans** **1** Something supposed to produce or capable of producing extraordinary effects; a charm. **2** An astrological charm or symbol supposed to benefit or protect the possessor, especially by exerting magical or occult influence; in a wider sense, any amulet. [<F <Sp. <Arabic *ṭilsam, ṭilasm* magic figure <LGk. *telesma* a sacred rite <Gk. *teleein* initiate < *telos* end, completion]

Synonyms: amulet, charm. An *amulet* or *talisman* is strictly a material object; a *charm* may be a movement or a form of words. An *amulet* is ordinarily worn upon the person as a protection against disease, injury, or death. A *talisman* is any object supposed to work wonders, like Aladdin's lamp, whether kept in one's possession or not.

tal·is·man·ic (tal′is·man′ik) *adj.* Exerting magical or occult power. Also **tal′is·man′i·cal.**

talk (tôk) *v.i.* **1** To express or exchange thoughts in audible words; communicate by speech; speak or converse. **2** To communicate by means other than speech: to *talk* with one's fingers. **3** To speak irrelevantly; prate; chatter. **4** To confer; consult. **5** To gossip. **6** To make sounds suggestive of speech. **7** *Colloq.* To give information; inform. — *v.t.* **8** To express in words; utter. **9** To use in speaking; converse in: to *talk* Spanish. **10** To converse about; discuss: to *talk* business. **11** To bring to a specified condition or state by talking: to *talk* one into doing something. **12** To pass or spend, as time, in talking. — **to talk back** To answer impudently. — **to talk big** *Slang* To brag; boast. — **to talk down** To silence by talking; outtalk. — **to talk down to** To speak to (an audience of lower or supposedly lower intelligence than one's own) in simple, obvious words; speak to patronizingly. — **to talk shop** To talk about one's work. — **to talk up** **1** To discuss, especially so as to promote; praise; extol. **2** *Colloq.* To speak loudly or boldly. — *n.* **1** The act of talking; conversation; speech, especially when informal. **2** Report, rumor: We heard *talk* of war. **3** That which is talked about; a topic; theme; subject of conversation. **4** A conference for discussion or deliberation; a council. **5** Mere words; verbiage. **6** A language, dialect, or lingo; an argot:

baseball *talk*. See synonyms under CONVERSATION. [ME *talken*, prob. freq. of *talen*, OE *talian* reckon, speak. Related to TELL, TALE.]

Synonyms (verb): chat, chatter, converse, discourse, speak. To *talk* is to utter a succession of connected words, ordinarily with the expectation of being listened to. To *speak* is to give articulate utterance even to a single word; the officer *speaks* the word of command, but does not *talk* it. To *chat* is ordinarily to utter in a familiar, conversational way; to *chatter* is to *talk* in an empty, ceaseless way like a magpie. See SPEAK.

talk·a·thon (tô′kə·thon′) *n. Colloq.* A prolonged session of talking, debating, etc. [< TALK + (MAR)ATHON]

talk·a·tive (tô′kə·tiv) *adj.* Given to much talking. See synonyms under GARRULOUS. — **talk′a·tive·ly** *adv.* — **talk′a·tive·ness** *n.*

talk·er (tô′kər) *n.* One who talks; also, a loquacious person.

talk·ie (tô′kē) *n. Colloq.* A motion picture with spoken words and sound effects. Also **talking picture.**

talking machine A phonograph.

talk·ing–to (tô′king·tōō′) *n. pl.* **·tos** *Colloq.* A scolding; berating.

talk show A television or radio show in which a well–known personality interviews invited guests, often celebrities, in TV usually before a live audience.

talk·y (tô′kē) *adj.* **talk·i·er, talk·i·est** Talkative.

tall (tôl) *adj.* **1** Having more than average height; high or lofty: a *tall* building. **2** Having specified height: He is five feet *tall.* **3** *Colloq.* Inordinate; extravagant; boastful: *tall* talk; also, unbelievable; remarkable: a *tall* story. **4** *Colloq.* Large; excellent; grand: a *tall* dinner. **5** *Obs.* Handsome; fine; proud. **6** *Obs.* Brave; sturdy; spirited. — *adv. Colloq.* Proudly; handsomely: He walks *tall.* [OE *getæl* swift, prompt] — **tall′ness** *n.*

tal·lage (tal′ij) *n.* In old English law, any form of assessment or taxation for raising revenue, including subsidies and customs. — *v.t.* **·laged, ·lag·ing** To tax. [<OF *taillage* < *taille* a tax, a cutting < *taillier* cut. See TAILOR.]

Tal·la·has·see (tal′ə·has′ē) The capital of Florida, in the northern part.

tall·boy (tôl′boi′) *n.* **1** *Brit.* A highboy. **2** A variety of chimney pot.

Tal·ley·rand–Pé·ri·gord (tal′ē·rand·pā′ri·gôr, *Fr.* tà·le·rän′pā·rē·gôr′), **Charles Maurice de,** 1754–1838, French statesman.

Tal·linn (täl′lin) The capital of Estonia, a port in the NW part, on the Gulf of Finland: German *Reval*, Russian *Revel*. Also **Tal′lin.**

tall·ish (tô′lish) *adj.* Rather tall.

tal·lith (tal′ith, tä′lis) *n.* A fringed mantle of fine linen, originally covering the head and falling over the shoulders, now worn around the shoulders by Jews engaged in prayer. [< Hebrew *tallīth* cover, sheet, robe]

tall oil A fatty resinous liquid obtained as a by–product from wood pulp: it is used as an emulsifying agent in various manufacturing processes. [<Sw. *tallöl* pine oil]

tal·low (tal′ō) *n.* **1** A mixture of the harder animal fats, as of beef or mutton, refined for use in candles, soaps, oleomargarine, etc. **2** A vegetable fat obtained from the bayberry. — *v.t.* **1** To smear with tallow. **2** To fatten. [ME *talgh*, prob. <MLG *talg, talch*] — **tal′low·y** *adj.*

tal·ly (tal′ē) *n. pl.* **·lies** **1** A piece of wood on which notches or scores are cut as marks of number. **2** A score or mark; hence, a reckoning; account. **3** A counterpart; duplicate. **4** A mark indicative of tale or number: used to denote one in a series. **5** A label; tag. — *v.* **·lied, ·ly·ing** *v.t.* **1** To score on a tally; mark; record. **2** To reckon; count; estimate: often with *up.* **3** To mark or cut corresponding notches in; cause to correspond. — *v.i.* **4** To correspond; agree precisely; fit: His story *tallies* with yours. **5** To keep score. [<AF *tallie* <L *talea* rod, cutting] — **tal′li·er** *n.*

tal·ly·ho (tal′ē·hō′) *interj.* A huntsman's cry to hounds when the quarry is sighted. — *n.* **1** The cry of "tallyho." **2** A four–in–hand coach. — *v.t.* To urge on, as hounds, with the cry of "tallyho." — *v.i.* To cry "tallyho." [Alter. of F *taïaut*, a hunting cry]

tal·ly·man (tal′ē·mən) *n. pl.* **·men** (-mən) **1** One who keeps a count or a tally, especially of votes. **2** One who keeps a record of number, volume, and measurement, as of timber.

Tal·mi gold (tal′mē) Gold shell. [<G, orig. a trade name]

Tal·mud (tal′mud, täl′mŏŏd) *n.* The body of Jewish civil and religious law (and related commentaries and discussion) not comprised in the Pentateuch, commonly including the Mishna and the Gemara, but sometimes limited to the latter. [<Hebrew *talmūdh* instruction < *lāmadh* learn] — **Tal·mud′ic** or **·i·cal** *adj.* — **Tal′mud·ist** *n.*

tal·on (tal′ən) *n.* **1** The claw of a bird or other animal, especially of a bird of prey: often applied figuratively, as to a grasping human hand. **2** A projection on the bolt of a lock on which the key presses in shooting the bolt. **3** In card games, the part of a pack left on the table after the deal; the stock. **4** The heel of a sword blade. [<OF, spur <L *talus* heel] — **tal′oned** *adj.*

Ta·los (tā′los) In Greek mythology: **1** A giant man of brass presented by Zeus to Minos, king of Crete, who used him as a watchman. **2** A Greek inventor killed by his uncle, Daedalus, because of jealousy. Also **Ta′lus** (-ləs).

ta·luk (tä·lŏŏk′) *n.* In parts of India, a government district from which a revenue is derived; also, a tract of proprietary land; an estate. [< Arabic *ta'alluq* estate]

ta·lus (tā′ləs) *n. pl.* **·li** (-lī) **1** *Anat.* The astragalus. **2** A slope, as of a tapering wall. **3** *Geol.* The sloping mass of rock fragments below a cliff. Compare SCREE. **4** The slope given to the face of an earthwork or other fortification. [<L, ankle, heel]

tam (tam) *n.* A tam–o'–shanter.

tam·a·ble (tā′mə·bəl) *adj.* Capable of being tamed. Also **tame′a·ble.**

ta·ma·le (tə·mä′lē) *n.* A Mexican dish made of crushed Indian corn and meat, seasoned with red pepper, wrapped in corn husks, dipped in oil, and cooked by steam. Also **ta·mal** (tə·mäl′). [<Am. Sp. *tamales*, pl. of *tamal* < Nahuatl *tamalli*]

Tam·al·pais (tam′əl·pī′əs), **Mount** A peak in western California, across the Golden Gate from San Francisco; 2,604 feet.

ta·man·dua (tə·man′dwə, tä′män·dwä′) *n.* A small arboreal ant–eater (*Tamandua tetradactyla*) of Central and South America. Also **tam·an·du** (tam′ən·dōō). [<Pg. <Tupian < *taixi* ant + *mondê* catch]

tam·a·rack (tam′ə·rak) *n.* **1** The American larch (*Larix laricina*) common all over northern North America. **2** Its wood: also called *hackmatack*. **3** The lodgepole pine of the Pacific coast. [<Algonquian]

ta·ma·rau (tä′mə·rou′) *n.* A small, dark–brown, short–horned buffalo (genus *Anoa*) of the island of Mindoro, standing about 40 inches high. Also spelled *timarau*. [< native name]

tam·a·rin (tam′ə·rin) *n.* One of various squirrel–like marmosets of Guiana and the Amazon valley; especially, the **silky tamarin** (*Leontocebus rosalia*). [<F < native Cariban name]

tam·a·rind (tam′ə·rind) *n.* **1** A tropical tree (*Tamarindus indica*) of the bean family, with hard yellow wood, pinnate leaves, and showy yellow flowers striped with red. **2** The fruit of this tree, a flat pod with soft acid pulp used in preserves and as a laxative drink. [<Sp. *tamarindo* <Arabic *tamr hindi* Indian date]

tam·a·risk (tam′ə·risk) *n.* An evergreen shrub (genus *Tamarix*) of the Mediterranean region, western Asia, and India, with slender branches bearing small, pinkish–white flowers in racemes. [<LL *tamariscus*, var. of L *tamarix* a tamarisk]

ta·ma·sha (tə·mä′shə) *n.* In India, any form of public procession, display, or entertainment; a show. [<Arabic *tamāsha* sightseeing, walking around]

Ta·ma·tave (tä′mä·täv′) A port of Madagascar, on the Indian Ocean, chief port of Malagasy Republic.

Ta·ma·u·li·pas (tä′mä·ōō·lē′päs) A state of NE Mexico, bordering on the United States and the Gulf of Mexico; 30,731 square miles; capital, Ciudad Victoria.

Ta·ma·yo (tä·mä′yō), **Rufino,** born 1899, Mexican painter.

tam·bac (tam′bak) See TOMBAC.

Tam·bo·ra (täm′bō·rä) A volcano on northern Sumbawa; 9,255 feet.

tam·bour (tam′bŏŏr) *n.* **1** A drum. **2** A light wooden frame, usually circular, on which material for embroidering may be stretched; also, a fabric embroidered on such a frame. **3** A palisade for defending an entrance to a fortified work. — *v.t.* & *v.i.* To embroider on a tambour. [<F <Arabic *ṭambūr* a stringed instrument; prob. infl. in meaning by OF *tabour* a tabor]

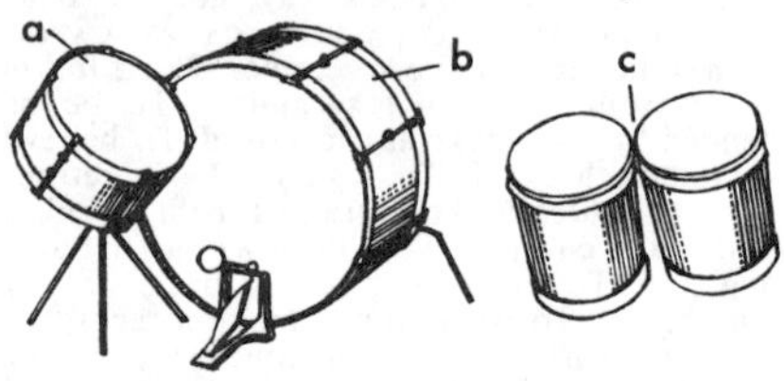

TAMBOURS
a. Snare drum. *b.* Bass drum. *c.* Bongo drums.

tam·bou·rin (tam′bə·rin) *n.* **1** A long, narrow, oblong drum, originating in Provence. **2** A gay, 18th century Provençal dance, or the music accompanying it. [<F, dim. of *tambour*]

tam·bou·rine (tam′bə·rēn′) *n.* A musical instrument like the head of a drum, with jingles in the rim, played by striking it with the hand; a timbrel. [<F]

Tam·bov (täm·bôf′) A city in south central European Russian S.F.S.R.

tame (tām) *adj.* **tam·er, tam·est** **1** Having lost its native wildness or shyness; domesticated. **2** In agriculture, brought under or produced by cultivation: *tame* hay or land. **3** Docile; tractable; hence, subdued or subjugated; spiritless; also, gentle; harmless. **4** Lacking in effectiveness; uninteresting; dull; flat; insipid. See synonyms under DOCILE, FLAT, MEAGER. — *v.t.* **tamed, tam·ing** **1** To make tame; domesticate. **2** To bring into subjection or obedience; conquer or take the spirit or heart from; render spiritless. **3** To tone down; soften, as glaring colors. See synonyms under RECLAIM. [OE *tam*] — **tame′ly** *adv.* — **tame′·ness** *n.* — **tam′er** *n.*

ta·mein (tä·mīn′) *n.* A draped garment, similar to an Indian sari, worn by Burmese women. [<Burmese *thameiṅ*]

tame·less (tām′lis) *adj.* Untamable. — **tame′·less·ness** *n.*

Tam·er·lane (tam′ər·lān), 1336?–1405, Tatar conqueror of Asia: also called *Timour, Timur.* Also **Tam·bur·laine** (tam′bər·lān).

Tam·il (tam′əl, tum′əl) *n.* **1** One of an ancient Dravidian people, and still the most numerous of the inhabitants of southern India and northern Ceylon. **2** Their language, the oldest and most widely used of the Dravidian languages.

tam·is (tam′is) *n.* **1** A strainer of cloth or gauze. **2** A fabric used for straining. Also **tam′my.** [<F, sieve]

Tam·ma·ny (tam′ə·nē) *n.* A fraternal society in New York City (founded 1789) serving as the central organization of the city's Democratic party: more commonly **Tammany Hall,** from its meeting place. The name has often been associated with political bossism. Also called **Tammany Society.** [Alter. of *Tamanend*, lit., the affable, name of a 17th c. Delaware Indian chief noted for his friendliness toward white men]

Tam·mer·fors (täm′mər·fôrs′) The Swedish name for TAMPERE.

Tam·mer·kos·ki (täm′mer·kōs′kē) The Finnish name for TAMPERE.

Tam·muz (täm′mōōz, *in Biblical usage* tam′uz) **1** In Babylonian mythology, the husband of Ishtar and god of agriculture, whose annual death and resurrection symbolize the cycle of months. **2** A Hebrew month. See CALENDAR (Hebrew). Also spelled *Thammuz*. Also **Tam·uz** (tam′uz). [<Hebrew]

tam–o'–shan·ter (tam′ə·shan′tər) *n.* A Scottish cap with a tight headband and a full, flat top, sometimes with a pompon or tassel. [after TAM O' SHANTER]

Tam o' Shan·ter (tam′ ə shan′tər) In Robert Burns's poem *Tam o' Shanter*, the hero, a drunken farmer, who fancies himself pursued by witches.

tamp (tamp) *v.t.* **1** To force down or pack closer by firm, repeated blows. **2** To ram down, as a packing on a charge in a blasthole, in order to increase the explosive effect. —*n.* A tamper. [Back formation <TAMPION]

Tam·pa (tam′pə) A port of entry on **Tampa Bay,** an arm of the Gulf of Mexico in central western Florida.

tam·pa·la (tam′pə·lə) *n.* A horticultural variety of an Asian plant *(Amaranthus tricolor),* cultivated in the United States and esteemed for its edible, spinachlike leaves. [<Hind.]

tam·pan (tam′pan) *n.* A soft-bodied tick (genus *Argas*) of cosmopolitan distribution, a dangerous bloodsucking parasite of poultry whose bite is often injurious to men. Also called *miana bug.* [< native S. African name]

tam·per[1] (tam′pər) *v.i.* **1** To meddle; interfere: usually with *with.* **2** To make changes, especially so as to damage, corrupt, etc.: with *with*: to *tamper* with a manuscript. **3** To use corrupt measures, as bribery; scheme or plot. [Var. of TEMPER] —**tam′per·er** *n.*

tamp·er[2] (tam′pər) *n.* **1** One who tamps. **2** An instrument for tamping. **3** *Physics* A reflector (def. 4).

Tam·pe·re (täm′pe·re) A city in SW Finland: Swedish *Tammerfors,* Finnish *Tammerkoski.*

Tam·pi·co (tam·pē′kō, *Sp.* täm·pē′kō) A port on the Gulf of Mexico in SE Tamaulipas state, NE Mexico.

Tampico fiber Istle.

tam·pi·on (tam′pē·ən) *n.* A tompion. [<F *tampon,* nasal var. of *tapon, tape* a bung < Gmc.]

tam·pon (tam′pon) *n. Med.* A plug of cotton or lint for insertion in a wound or body cavity. —*v.t.* To plug up, as a wound, with a tampon. [See TAMPION]

tam-tam (tum′tum′) *n.* **1** A type of drum, used in the East Indies and western Africa. See TOM-TOM. **2** A Chinese gong. —*v.i.* To play on a tam-tam. [<Hind.; imit. in origin]

tan (tan) *v.* **tanned, tan·ning** *v.t.* **1** To convert into leather, as hides or skins, by treatment with an infusion of tannin obtained from the bark of the oak, hemlock, etc. **2** To make durable or hard, as fishnets or sails. **3** To bronze, as the skin, by exposure to sunlight. **4** *Colloq.* To thrash; flog. —*v.i.* **5** To become tanned, as hides or the skin. —*n.* **1** *Chem.* **a** Tanbark. **b** Tannin. **2** A yellowish-brown color tinged with red. **3** A dark or brown coloring of the skin, resulting from exposure to the sun: a coat of *tan.* —*adj.* **1** Of a yellowish- or reddish-brown; tan-colored. **2** Used in or pertaining to tanning. [OE *tannian* <Med. L *tannare* < *tanum* tanbark, prob. <Celtic. Cf. Breton *tann* oak.]

Ta·na (tä′nä) A river in SE Kenya, Africa, flowing about 500 miles east and south to the Indian Ocean.

Ta·na (tä′nä), **Lake** A lake in northern Ethiopia, source of the Blue Nile; the largest lake in Ethiopia; about 1,400 square miles: also *Tsana.*

tan·a·ger (tan′ə·jər) *n.* Any of a family *(Thraupidae)* of arboreal oscine American birds related to the finches and noted for the brilliant plumage of the male. Most of the species are tropical, but a few migrate to the United States, especially the **scarlet tanager** *(Piranga erythromelas)* and the **western tanager** *(P. ludoviciana).* [<NL *tanagra* <Pg. *tangara* <Tupian] —**tan′a·grine** (-grēn) *adj.*

Tan·a·gra (tan′ə·grə, tə·nag′rə) A village in eastern Boeotia, east central Greece; known for the terra-cotta figurines excavated there.

Tan·a·is (tan′ə·is) An ancient name for the DON (def. 1).

Ta·na·na·rive (tä·nä′nä·rēv′) The capital of Malagasy Republic, in the central part: English *Antananarivo.* Also **Ta·na′na·ri′vo** (-rē′vō).

Ta·na·na River (tä′nä·nä′) A river of western Yukon and central and eastern Alaska, flowing 600 miles from near the Alaskan border to the Yukon River in central Alaska.

tan·bark (tan′bärk′) *n.* **1** The bark of certain trees, especially oak or hemlock, containing tannin in quantity, and used in tanning leather. **2** Spent bark from the tan vats, used on circus arenas, racetracks, etc.

Tan·cred (tang′krid), 1078?–1112, Norman hero of the first crusade.

tan·dem (tan′dəm) *adv.* One in front of or before another: said of two or more persons or things so arranged, and of horses harnessed in single file instead of abreast. —*n.* **1** Two or more horses harnessed and driven in single file; also, such a turnout, including both horses and vehicle. **2** A bicycle with seats for two persons, one behind the other: also **tandem bicycle.** **3** Any arrangement of two or more persons or things placed one before another. —*adj.* Consisting of or being two arranged one before another. [<L, at length (of time); used in puns in sense of "lengthwise"]

Tan·djung·pi·nang (tän·jŏŏng′pē·näng′) A seaport SE of Singapore, capital of the Riouw Archipelago province of Indonesia.

Tan·djung·pri·ok (tän′jŏŏng·prē′ōk) See TANJUNGPRIOK.

Ta·ney (tā′nē), **Roger Brooke,** 1777–1864, U. S. jurist; chief justice of Supreme Court 1836–64.

tang[1] (tang) *n.* **1** A slender shank or tongue projecting from some metal part, as the end of a sword blade or of a chisel, for inserting into or fixing upon a handle, hilt, etc.; also, a tonguelike part, as of a belt buckle. **2** A penetrating taste, flavor, or odor, sometimes a disagreeable one; also, a trace; hint: a *tang* of pepper. **3** Any distinct quality, other than one that is sweet. —*v.t.* To provide with a tang. [<ON *tongi* a point, dagger]

tang[2] (tang) See TWANG.

Tang (täng) A Chinese dynasty, 618–907, under which China enjoyed its greatest period of literature and art.

Tan·gan·yi·ka (tan′gən·yē′kə, tang′-) A region of Tanzania in eastern Africa; 361,800 square miles; capital, Dar es Salaam.

Tan·gan·yi·ka (tan′gən·yē′kə, tang′-), **Lake** A lake in the Great Rift Valley of east central Africa, SW of Victoria Nyanza; 12,700 square miles; 400 miles long; the longest and deepest (4,700 feet) lake in Africa, second deepest fresh-water body in the world.

tan·ge·lo (tan′jə·lō) *n. pl.* **·los** **1** A loose-skinned orangelike fruit, a hybrid of the tangerine and the pomelo. **2** The tree (genus *Citrus*) on which it grows. [<TANG(ERINE) + (POM)ELO]

tan·gen·cy (tan′jən·sē) *n. pl.* **·cies** The state of being tangent. Also **tan′gence.**

tan·gent (tan′jənt) *adj.* **1** *Geom.* Meeting at a point or along a line without further coincidence or intersection: said of either or both of two lines or surfaces so touching. **2** Touching; in contact. —*n.* **1** *Geom.* **a** A line tangent to a curve at any point. **b** The straight line through two coincident points of a curve. **c** The length of a tangent line from the point of contact to the axis of abscissas. **2** *Trig.* One of the functions of an angle; the quotient of the ordinate divided by the abscissa. **3** A sharp change in course or direction. —**to fly** (or **go**) **off on a tangent** *Colloq.* To make a sharp or sudden change in direction or course of action. [<L *tangens, -entis,* ppr. of *tangere* touch]

tan·gen·tial (tan·jen′shəl) *adj.* **1** Of, pertaining to, or moving in the direction of a tangent. **2** Touching slightly. **3** Divergent. Also **tan·gen′tal** (-jen′təl). —**tan·gen′ti·al′i·ty** (-shē·al′ə·tē) *n.* —**tan·gen′tial·ly** *adv.*

tan·ger·ine (tan′jə·rēn′) *n.* **1** A small, juicy orange with a loose, easily removed skin; a variety of mandarin (def. 2). **2** A slightly burnt-orange color, like the color of the tangerine. [from *Tangier*]

Tan·ger·ine (tan′jə·rēn) *adj.* Of or pertaining to Tangier, Morocco. —*n.* A native or inhabitant of Tangier.

tan·gi·ble (tan′jə·bəl) *adj.* **1** Perceptible by touch; also, within reach by touch. **2** Figuratively, capable of being apprehended by the mind; of definite shape; not elusive or unreal: *tangible* evidence. **3** *Law* Perceptible to the senses; corporeal; material: *tangible* property. See synonyms under EVIDENT, PHYSICAL. —*n.* **1** That which is tangible. **2** *pl.* Material assets. [<F <L *tangibilis* < *tangere* touch] —**tan′gi·bil′i·ty, tan′gi·ble·ness** *n.* —**tan′gi·bly** *adv.*

Tan·gier (tan·jir′) A port on the northernmost coast of Morocco; formerly an international zone (**Tangier International Zone;** 225 square miles). *French* **Tan·ger** (täṅ·zhā′).

tan·gle[1] (tang′gəl) *v.* **·gled, ·gling** *v.t.* **1** To twist or involve in a confused and not readily separable mass. **2** To complicate; ensnare as in a tangle; trap; enmesh. —*v.i.* **3** To be or become entangled. —**to tangle with** *Colloq.* To embroil oneself with. —*n.* **1** A confused intertwining, as of threads or hairs; a snarl. **2** Hence, a state of confusion or complication; a jumbled mess. **3** A state of perplexity or bewilderment. [Nasalized var. of obs. *tagle* <Scand. Cf. dial. Sw. *taggla* disorder.] —**tan′gler** *n.*

tan·gle[2] (tang′gəl) *n.* **1** An edible seaweed (genus *Laminaria*). **2** *Scot.* A tall, lean person. [<ON *thöngull*]

tan·gle·ber·ry (tang′gəl·ber′ē) *n. pl.* **·ries** The blue huckleberry *(Gaylussacia frondosa)* of the eastern United States: also called *dangleberry.*

tan·gly (tang′glē) *adj.* Consisting of or being in a tangle.

tan·go (tang′gō) *n. pl.* **·gos** **1** Any of several Latin-American dances, originally from Argentina, in 2/4 time and characterized by deliberate gliding steps and low dips. **2** Any syncopated tune or melody to which the tango may be danced. —*v.i.* To dance the tango. [<Am. Sp., fiesta <Sp., gipsy dance]

tan·gram (tang′grəm) *n.* A Chinese puzzle consisting of a square card or board cut by straight incisions into different-sized pieces (5 triangles, a square, and a rhomboid) to be combined into a variety of figures. [Arbitrary coinage, after ANAGRAM]

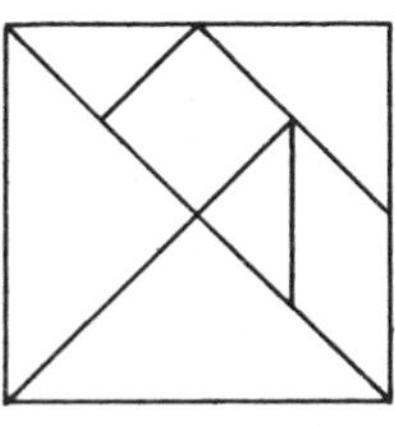

TANGRAM

tang·y (tang′ē) *adj.* **tang·i·er, tang·i·est** Having a tang in taste or odor; pungent.

Ta·nim·bar Islands (tə·nim′bär, tan′im·bär) An Indonesian island group in the Banda Sea; total, 2,172 square miles: also *Timorlaut.*

Ta·nis (tā′nis) An ancient city of Lower Egypt in the Nile delta: Old Testament *Zoan.*

tan·ist (tan′ist, thôn′-) *n.* Among the ancient Celts, the heir apparent to a chieftainship, elected in the lifetime of a chief from among the chief's kinsmen. [<Irish *tānaiste* second, heir presumptive]

tan·ist·ry (tan′ist·rē, thôn′-) *n.* The succession and life tenure relating to a tanist.

tan·jib (tun·jēb′) *n.* A kind of fine muslin fabric made in India. [<Bengali <Persian *tan-zib,* lit., ornament of the body]

Tan·jore (tan·jôr′, -jōr′) A city in SE Madras State, India.

Tan·jung·pri·ok (tän′jŏŏng·prē′ôk) A port of NW Java, the principal port of Indonesia and port for Jakarta: also *Tandjungpriok.*

U. S. ARMY TANK M48A2

tank (tangk) *n.* **1** A large vessel, basin, or receptacle for holding a fluid. **2** Any natural pool or pond. **3** *Mil.* A heavily armored combat vehicle of the Caterpillar tractor type, propelled by internal-combustion engines and mounting guns of various calibers.

—*v.t.* To place or store in a tank. [<Pg. *tanque,* aphetic var. of *estanque* <L *stagnum* pool] —**tank′less** *adj.* —**tank′like′** *adj.*

tan·ka[1] (tang′kə) *n.* **1** A Japanese verse form consisting of five lines, of which the first and third have five syllables, and the rest seven. **2** A poem imitating the Japanese tanka in verse form. [<Japanese]

tan·ka[2] (tang′kə) *n. pl.* **·ka** A descendant of an aboriginal race living on watercraft at Canton, China. [<Chinese *tankia* < *tan* egg + *chia* family, people]

tank·age (tangk′ij) *n.* **1** The act, process, or operation of putting in tanks. **2** The price for storage in tanks. **3** The capacity or contents of a tank. **4** Slaughterhouse waste, as bones and entrails, from which the fat has been rendered: used, when dried, as a fertilizer or coarse feed.

tank·ard (tangk′ərd) *n.* A large, one–handled drinking cup, usually made of pewter or silver, often with a cover. [<MDu. *tanckaert* <Med. L *tancardus,* prob. metathetic var. of L *cantharus* tankard, large goblet]

tank destroyer A motor vehicle equipped with an anti–tank gun.

tank·er (tangk′ər) *n.* A cargo vessel especially constructed for the transport of oil and gasoline.

tank farming Hydroponics. —**tank farmer**

tank·ful (tangk′fŏŏl′) *n.* The quantity that fills a tank.

tank town *U.S. Colloq.* A small town where trains stopped to refill from a water tank.

tank trap A camouflaged ditch excavated along the probable route of enemy tanks for the purpose of trapping them.

tan·nage (tan′ij) *n.* The act, process, or operation of tanning.

tan·nate (tan′āt) *n. Chem.* A salt or ester of tannic acid.

tanned (tand) Past tense and past participle of TAN.

Tan·nen·berg (tän′ən·berkh) A village in NE Poland; scene of major Russian defeat by German forces, 1914.

tan·ner[1] (tan′ər) *n.* One who tans hides.

tan·ner[2] (tan′ər) *n. Brit. Colloq.* A sixpence. [Origin unknown]

tan·ner·y (tan′ər·ē) *n. pl.* **·ner·ies** A place where leather is tanned.

Tann·häu·ser (tän′hoi·zər) A German minnesinger and crusader of the 13th century, identified with a legendary knight who gives himself up to revelry with Venus and her court, then makes a trip to Rome to seek absolution; hero of an opera by Wagner.

tan·nic (tan′ik) *adj.* Pertaining to or derived from tannin or tanbark.

tan·nif·er·ous (ta·nif′ər·əs) *adj.* Having or yielding tannin. [<TANNI(N) + -FEROUS]

tan·nin (tan′in) *n. Chem.* Any of a group of amorphous, brownish–white, astringent compounds that form shiny scales when extracted, as with water, from gallnuts, sumac, etc. Their principal applications in the arts are in the preparation of ink and the manufacture of leather. Also **tannic acid.** [<F *tanin* < *tan* tan]

tan·ning (tan′ing) *n.* **1** The art or process of converting hides into leather. **2** A bronzing, as of the skin, by exposure to the sun, etc.

Tan·nu–tu·va People's Republic (tan′ōō·tōō′·və) A former name for TUVA AUTONOMOUS REGION.

tan·rec (tan′rek) See TENREC.

tan·sy (tan′zē) *n. pl.* **·sies** Any of a genus (*Tanacetum*) of coarse perennial herbs; especially, a species (*T. vulgare*) with yellow flowers and a strongly aromatic and bitter taste, used in medicine for its tonic properties. [<OF *tanesie,* aphetic var. of *athanasie* <LL *athanasia* <Gk., immortality]

Tan·ta (tän′tä) A city in Lower Egypt in the Nile delta.

tan·ta·late (tan′tə·lāt) *n. Chem.* A salt of tantalic acid.

tan·tal·ic (tan·tal′ik) *adj.* **1** Pertaining to tantalum; containing tantalum in its higher valence. **2** Designating a colorless crystalline acid, $HTaO_3$, derived from tantalum oxide, Ta_2O_5.

tan·ta·lite (tan′tə·līt) *n.* An iron–black ferrous tantalate, $FeTa_2O_6$, having a submetallic luster.

tan·ta·lize (tan′tə·līz) *v.t.* **·lized, ·liz·ing** To tease or torment by repeated frustration of hopes or desires. Also *Brit.* **tan′ta·lise.** [from *Tantalus*] —**tan′ta·li·za′tion** *n.* —**tan′·ta·liz′er** *n.* —**tan′ta·liz′ing·ly** *adv.*

tan·ta·lum (tan′tə·ləm) *n.* A silver–white, ductile, metallic element (symbol Ta) occurring in tantalite and other rare minerals. It becomes hard when hammered, and forms alloys with tungsten, molybdenum, and iron. See ELEMENT. [<TANTALUS; from its inability to absorb water]

Tan·ta·lus (tan′tə·ləs) In Greek mythology, a rich king, son of Zeus and father of Pelops and Niobe, who was punished in Hades for revealing the secrets of Zeus by being made to stand in water that receded when he tried to drink, and under fruit–laden branches he could not reach.

tan·ta·mount (tan′tə·mount) *adj.* Having equivalent value, effect, or import; equivalent: with *to.* [<AF *tant amunter* amount to as much <L *tantus* as much + OF *amonter* amount. See AMOUNT.]

tan·ta·ra (tan′tə·rä′, tan·tar′ə, -tä′rə) *n.* A quick succession of notes from a horn; also, a hunting cry. [Imit.]

tan·tiv·y (tan·tiv′ē) *adj.* Swift; rapid. —*n. pl.* **·tiv·ies 1** A hunting cry indicating that the chase is at full speed. **2** *Obs.* A rapid, rushing movement. —*adv.* Swiftly; with all speed. [Prob. imit. of the horse's gallop]

tant mieux (täṅ myœ′) *French* So much the better.

tan·to (tän′tō) *adv. Italian* So much; too much: especially in the musical direction **non tanto,** not too much.

tant pis (täṅ pē′) *French* So much the worse.

tan·trum (tan′trəm) *n.* A petulant fit of passion. [Origin unknown]

Tan·zan·i·a (tan′zə·nē′ə) An independent member of the Commonwealth of Nations consisting of a federation of Tanganyika and Zanzibar in eastern Africa; 362,800 square miles; capital, Dar es Salaam.

Tao·ism (dou′iz·əm, tou′-) *n.* One of the principal religions or philosophies of China, founded about 500 B.C. by Lâo–tse, who taught that happiness could be acquired through obedience to the requirements of man's nature and the simplification of social and political relations, in accordance with the Tao, or Way, the basic principle of the cosmos from which all of nature proceeds. [<Chinese *tao* way, road] —**Tao′ist** *adj.* & *n.* —**Tao·is′tic** *adj.*

Ta·os (tä′ōs) A resort town in northern New Mexico.

tap[1] (tap) *n.* **1** An arrangement for drawing out liquid, as beer from a cask. **2** A faucet or cock; spigot; also, a plug or stopper to close an opening in a cask or other vessel. **3** Liquor drawn from a tap; also, a particular liquor or quality of liquor contained in casks. **4** *Brit.* A place where liquor is served; a bar; taproom. **5** A tool for cutting internal screw threads. **6** A point of connection for an electrical circuit. **7** The act or an instance of wiretapping. —**on tap 1** Contained in a cask; ready for tapping: beer *on tap.* **2** Provided with a tap. **3** Available; ready. —*v.t.* **tapped, tap·ping 1** To provide with a tap or spigot. **2** To pierce or open so as to draw liquid from: to *tap* a sugar–maple tree. **3** To draw (liquid) from a container. **4** To make connection with: to *tap* a gas main. **5** To make connection with secretly: to *tap* a telephone wire. **6** To make an internal screw thread in with a tap: to *tap* a nut. [OE *tæppa*]

tap[2] (tap) *v.* **tapped, tap·ping** *v.t.* **1** To touch or strike gently. **2** To make or produce by tapping. **3** To apply leather to (the sole or heel of a shoe) in repair. —*v.i.* **4** To strike a light blow or blows, as with the finger tip. —*n.* **1** A gentle or playful blow. **2** Leather, etc., affixed to a shoe sole or heel; also, a metal plate on the toe or heel of a tap–dancer's shoe. **3** *pl.* A military signal by trumpet or beat of drum, sounded after tattoo, for the extinguishing of all lights in soldiers' quarters: often played after a military burial. [<OF *taper*]

ta·pa (tä′pä) *n.* The bark of the Asian paper–mulberry tree (*Broussonetia papyrifera*), used in making a kind of cloth, **tapa cloth.** [< native Polynesian name]

tap·a·der·a (tap′ə·dâr′ə) *n.* The leather hood of the stirrup of a Mexican saddle. Also **tap′a·der′o.** [<Sp., cover < *tapar* stop up]

Ta·pa·jós (tä′pə·zhôs′) A river of central and NE Brazil, flowing 500 miles NE from SW Pará state to the Amazon at Santerém.

tap·a·lo (tap′ə·lō) *n. pl.* **·los** A scarf or shawl of coarse cloth worn in Latin–American countries. [<Am. Sp., lit., cover it, imperative of *tapar* cover + *lo* it]

tap–dance (tap′dans′, -däns′) *v.i.* To dance or perform a tap dance. —**tap′–danc′er** *n.*

tap dance A dance, usually solo, in which the dancer emphasizes his steps by tapping the floor with the heels or toes of shoes or clogs designed to make audible the rhythm.

tape (tāp) *n.* **1** A narrow, stout strip of woven fabric. **2** Any long, narrow, flat strip of paper, metal, or the like, as the magnetic strip used in a tape recorder. **3** A tapeline. **4** Red tape. **5** A string or thread stretched breast–high across the finishing point of a racetrack and broken by the winner of the race. —*v.t.* **taped, tap·ing 1** To wrap or secure with tape; also, to bandage: to *tape* a boxer's hands. **2** To measure with or as with a tapeline. **3** To record on magnetic tape. [OE *tæppe* strip of cloth] —**tap′er** *n.*

tape deck An assembly of magnetic head, tape reels, and drive for tape recording and playback.

tape·line (tāp′līn′) *n.* A tape for measuring distances. Also **tape measure.**

ta·per (tā′pər) *n.* **1** A small candle; a burning wick or other light substance giving but feeble illumination. **2** A gradual diminution of size in an elongated object: the *taper* of a mast; also, any tapering object, as a cone. —*v.t.* & *v.i.* **1** To make or become smaller or thinner toward one end. **2** To lessen gradually; diminish: with *off.* —*adj.* Growing small by degrees in one direction. ◆ Homophone: *tapir.* [OE, dissimilated var. of Med.L *papyrus* taper, wick <L, papyrus; from the use of the pith of the papyrus as a wick]

tape–re·cord (tāp′ri·kôrd′) *v.t.* To tape (*v.* def. 3).

tape recorder An electromagnetic apparatus which records by the effect of sound waves upon the particles adhering to a magnetic tape: in the playback the magnetic patterns are reconverted into the original electrical impulses and sound waves.

tap·es·try (tap′is·trē) *n. pl.* **·tries 1** A loosely woven, ornamental fabric used for hangings, in which the woof is supplied by a spindle, the design being formed by stitches across the warp. **2** Loosely, a fabric imitating this process. —*v.t.* **·tried, ·try·ing** To adorn with tapestry. [<OF *tapisserie* < *tapis* carpet <L *tapete* <Gk. *tapētion,* dim. of *tapēs* rug]

tapestry carpet A carpet in which the fabric is woven after the designs are first printed.

ta·pe·tum (tə·pē′təm) *n. pl.* **·ta** (-tə) **1** *Bot.* A cell or layer of cells just outside the spore case of a plant, lining the cavity of an anther or sporangium. **2** *Zool.* A portion of the choroid coat of the eye in cats and certain other animals. **3** *Anat.* The fibers of the corpus callosum. [<LL <L *tapete* carpet. See TAPESTRY.]

tape·worm (tāp′wûrm′) *n.* Any of various cestode worms (class *Cestoda*) with segmented, ribbonlike bodies, parasitic on the intestines of vertebrates; especially, the common pork tapeworm (*Taenia solium*) of man.

taph·e·pho·bi·a (taf′ə·fō′bē·ə) *n. Psychiatry* A morbid fear of being buried alive. [<Gk. *taphē* a grave + -PHOBIA] —**taph′e·pho′bic** *adj.*

tap house An inn; tavern; also, a barroom.

tap·i·o·ca (tap′ē·ō′kə) *n.* A nutritious starchy substance having irregular grains, obtained from cassava. [<Sp. <Tupi *tipioca* juice of the cassava < *ty* juice + *pya* heart + *ocô* be removed]

ta·pir (tā′pər) *n.* A large, ungulate, herbivorous, typically nocturnal mammal (family *Tapiridae*), having short stout limbs and flexible proboscis, with the nostrils near the end. The tapir of South and Central America is brownish–black, that of the Malay Peninsula black and white. ◆ Homophone: *taper.* [<Sp. <Tupi *tapy′ra* tapir]

BRAZILIAN TAPIR
(From 3 to 3 1/2 feet high)

tap·is (tap′ē, tap′is; *Fr.* tȧ·pē′) *n.* Tapestry, formerly used as a cover of a council table: now only in the phrase **on the tapis** (up for consideration). [<F. See TAPESTRY.]

ta·pis·sier (tȧ·pē·syā′) *n. French* **1** A tapestry-maker. **2** An upholsterer. —**ta·pis·sière** (tȧ·pē·syâr′) *n. fem.*

Tap·pan Zee (tap′ən zā′) An expansion of the Hudson River in SE New York above New York City; 10 miles long and 3 miles wide.

tap·per (tap′ər) *n.* One who or that which taps, in any sense.

tap·pet (tap′it) *n. Mech.* A projecting arm of a mechanism, to operate an unattached part automatically, as to impart the motion of a cam to a valve. [<TAP[2]]

tappet rod *Mech.* A reciprocating rod bearing one or more tappets.

tap·ping (tap′ing) *n.* **1** The act of one who or that which taps in any sense. **2** Something taken by tapping, or running from a tap.

tap·pit (tap′it) *adj. Scot.* Having a tuft; crested.

tap·pit-hen (tap′it·hen′) *n.* **1** A hen having a topknot. **2** An Engish pewter measure for liquors, holding three quarts: named for the knob on the lid resembling a hen's topknot. [<dial. E (Scottish) *tappit* topped + HEN]

tap·poon (tə·po͞on′) *n.* A semicircular gate of heavy sheet iron, serving as a temporary dam for a small irrigating ditch. [<Sp. *tapón* plug <*tapar* stop up]

tap·room (tap′ro͞om′, -ro͝om′) *n.* A bar; bar-room.

tap·root (tap′ro͞ot′, -ro͝ot′) *n. Bot.* The principal descending root of a plant. —**tap′root′ed** *adj.*

taps (taps) See TAP[2] (*n.* def. 3).

tap·sal·tee·rie (tap′səl·tir′ē) *adv. Scot.* Upside down and in confusion; topsy-turvy.

tap·ster (tap′stər) *n.* One who draws and serves liquor; a bartender. [OE *tæppestre* barmaid]

Tap·ti (täp′tē) A river of west central India, flowing 450 miles west from west central Madhya Pradesh to the Gulf of Cambay just below Surat.

Ta·pu·ya (tä·po͞o′yä) *n.* A Tapuyan Indian.

Ta·pu·yan (tä·po͞o′yən) *n.* A large linguistic stock of South American Indians; Ge. —*adj.* Of or pertaining to this stock.

Ta·qua·rí (tä·kwə·rē′) **1** A river in south central Mato Grosso, Brazil, flowing 350 miles SW from the Goiás border to the Paraguay river near the Bolivian border. **2** A river in NE Río Grande do Sul, Brazil, flowing 200 miles west and south to the Jacuí river.

tar[1] (tär) *n.* **1** A dark, oily, viscid mixture of hydrocarbons, especially phenols, obtained by the dry distillation of resinous woods, coal, etc. **2** Coal tar. Compare ASPHALT, PITCH[1]. —*v.t.* **tarred, tar·ring** To cover with or as with tar. —**to tar and feather** To smear with tar and then cover with feathers: an old form of punishment. —*adj.* Made of, derived from, or resembling tar. [OE *teru*]

tar[2] (tär) *n. Colloq.* A sailor. [Short for TARPAULIN]

Tar·a (tar′ə) A village of central County Meath, Ireland; seat of the ancient Irish kings until the sixth century.

tar·a·did·dle (tar′ə·did′l) See TARRADIDDLE.

Ta·ra·na·ki (tä′rä·nä′kē) The Maori name for EGMONT.

tar·an·tass (tar′ən·tas′) *n.* A large four-wheeled vehicle on longitudinal bars in place of springs and mounted on a sledge in winter. Also **tar′an·tas′**. [<Russian *tarantas*]

tar·an·tel·la (tar′ən·tel′ə) *n.* A lively Neapolitan dance in 6/8 time: once thought to be a remedy for tarantism; also, the music written for it. [<Ital., dim. of *Taranto* Taranto; infl. by *tarantola* a tarantula]

tar·ant·ism (tar′ən·tiz′əm) *n.* A nervous and hysterical disorder characterized by stupor and hypochondria which, it was supposed, could be cured only by inordinate dancing and music; dancing disease. Formerly prevalent in southern Italy, it was believed to follow the bite of a tarantula. [<Ital. *tarantismo* <*Taranto* Taranto]

Ta·ran·to (tä′rän·tō) A port in SE Italy on the **Gulf of Taranto,** an arm of the Ionian Sea forming the instep of the Italian boot: ancient *Tarentum.*

ta·ran·tu·la (tə·ran′cho͞o·lə) *n. pl.* **·las** or **·lae** (-lē) **1** A large, hairy, venomous spider (*Lycosa tarentula*) of southern Europe, still popularly but erroneously supposed to cause tarantism by its bite. **2** Any of various large, hairy American spiders (family *Theraphosidae*), especially of the genus *Eurypelma* of the SW United States, dreaded for their painful but not dangerous bite. [<Med. L <Ital. *tarantola* <*Taranto* Taranto]

TARANTULA (Body from 2 to 3 1/2 inches)

tarantula hawk A large wasp (genus *Pepsis*) which paralyzes tarantulas with its sting and places them in its nest as food for its young. Also **tarantula killer.**

Ta·ra·pon (tä′rä·pōn) *n.* Micronesian.

Ta·ra·wa (tä·rä′wä, tä′rä·wä) The island headquarters of the Gilbert Islands and capital of the Gilbert and Ellice Islands colony; 8 square miles; scene of a United States victory over Japanese forces in World War II, November, 1943.

ta·rax·a·cum (tə·rak′sə·kəm) *n.* **1** Any of a genus (*Taraxacum*) of composite plants that includes the dandelion. **2** A medicinal preparation from the dried root of the common dandelion, used as a diuretic and laxative. [<NL <Arabic *tarakhshaqūq* bitter herb]

Tar·bell (tär′bel), **Ida Minerva,** 1857–1944, U. S. author.

tar·boosh (tär·bo͞osh′) *n.* A brimless, usually red, felt cap with colored silk tassel, worn by Moslems. Also **tar·bush′.** [<Arabic *ṭarbūsh*]

TARBOOSH

tar camphor Naphthalene.

Tar·de·noi·si·an (tär′də·noi′zē·ən) *adj.* Of, pertaining to, or designating a subdivision of the Mesolithic culture epoch of the late Paleolithic period, related to the Azilian and characterized by small flint implements. [from Fère-en-*Tardenois,* town in NE France where remains were discovered]

Tar·dieu (tȧr·dyœ′), **André Pierre Gabriel Amédée,** 1876–1945, French statesman: pseudonym *George Villiers.*

tar·di·grade (tär′də·grād) *adj.* **1** Slow in motion or action; stepping or walking slowly. **2** Of or pertaining to a group (*Tardigrada*) of slow-moving microscopical arthropods, the water bears, found especially in water and damp moss. —*n.* One of the *Tardigrada.* [<F <L *tardigradus* <*tardus* slow + *gradi* walk]

tar·do (tär′dō) *adj. Music* Slow: a direction to performers. [<Ital.]

tar·dy (tär′dē) *adj.* **·di·er, ·di·est** **1** Not coming at the appointed time; dilatory; late. **2** Slow; reluctant. See synonyms under SLOW, TEDIOUS. [<F *tardif* <L *tardus* slow] —**tar′·di·ly** *adv.* —**tar′di·ness** *n.*

tare[1] (târ) *n.* **1** An unidentified weed that grows among wheat, supposed to be the darnel; hence, a seed of wickedness. *Matt.* xiii 25. **2** Any one of various species of vetch; especially, the common vetch (*Vicia sativa*). ◆ Homophone: *tear*[1]. [? <F *tare* defect, rejectable thing. See TARE[2].]

tare[2] (târ) *n.* **1** An allowance made to a buyer of goods by deducting from the gross weight of his purchase the weight of the container. **2** *Chem.* An empty flask or vessel used as a counterweight. —*v.t.* **tared, tar·ing** To weigh, as a vessel or package, in order to determine the amount of tare. ◆ Homophone: *tear*[1]. [<F <Arabic *ṭarḥah* <*ṭaraḥa* reject, throw away]

Ta·ren·tum (tə·ren′təm) Ancient name for TARANTO.

targ (tärg) *n.* A device for indicating on a plotting board the changing positions of a target. [Back formation <TARGET]

targe[1] (tärj) *n.* A shield; rarely, a target. [<OF <OE *targa* <ON]

targe[2] (tärj) *v.t. Scot.* **1** To censure severely; thrash. **2** To cross-question rigidly. **3** To subject to strict discipline.

tar·get (tär′git) *n.* **1** An object presenting a surface that may be used as a mark or butt, as in rifle or archery practice; anything that is shot at. **2** One who or that which is made an object of attack or a center of attention or observation; a butt: He was the *target* of the crowd's sneers. **3** A small, variously shaped and colored signal, usually placed near a railroad track, to indicate the position of the switches. **4** The vane or sliding sight on a surveyor's rod. **5** *Electronics* That electrode of a vacuum tube on which cathode rays are focused and from which X-rays are emitted. **6** A small round shield or buckler; a targe. [OE *targette, targuete,* dim. of *targe* shield. See TARGE[1].]

tar·get·eer (tär′gə·tir′) *n.* A soldier armed with a shield.

Tar·gum (tär′gum, *Hebrew* tär·go͞om′) *n. pl.* **Tar·gums** or *Hebrew* **Tar·gu·mim** (tär′go͞o·mēm′) One of various ancient paraphrases of portions of the Hebrew scriptures in Aramaic or Chaldee. [<Aramaic *targūm* interpretation] —**Tar′gum·ic** or **·i·cal** *adj.* —**Tar′gum·ist** *n.*

Tar·heel (tär′hēl′) *n. Colloq.* A native of the pine barrens of North Carolina; hence, any North Carolinian. Also **Tar Heel.**

Tarheel State Nickname of NORTH CAROLINA.

Ta·ri·fa (tä·rē′fä) A port on the Strait of Gibraltar in southern Spain.

tar·iff (tar′if) *n.* **1** A schedule of articles of merchandise with the rates of duty to be paid for their importation or exportation. **2** A duty, or duties collectively. **3** The law by which duties are imposed; also, the principles governing their imposition. **4** Any schedule of charges. —*v.t.* **1** To make a list or table of duties or customs on. **2** To fix a price or tariff on. [<Ital. *tariffa* <Arabic *ta'rif* information <*'arafa* know, inform]

Ta·rim (tä′rēm′) The principal river of the Sinkiang-Uigur Autonomous Region, NW China, flowing 1,300 miles east from the west central part, forming the northern boundary of the Taklamakan desert.

Tark·ing·ton (tär′king·tən), **Booth,** 1869–1946, U. S. novelist.

tar·la·tan (tär′lə·tən) *n.* A thin, open-mesh transparent muslin, slightly stiffened and often rather coarse. [<F *tarlatane*; ult. origin unknown]

Tar·mac (tär′mak) *n.* A paving material made from coal tar: a trade name.

tarn (tärn) *n.* A small mountain lake. [ME *terne* <ON *tjörn*]

Tarn (tȧrn) A river in south central France, flowing 235 miles west from the Cévennes to the Garonne below Montauban.

tar·nal (tär′nəl) *U.S. Slang adj.* Eternal; infernal; hence, damned. —*adv.* Very; damn. [Alter. of ETERNAL] —**tar′nal·ly** *adv.*

tar·na·tion (tär·nā′shən) *interj.* & *n. Dial.* Damnation: a euphemism. [Blend of TAR(NAL) + (DAM)NATION]

tar·nish (tär′nish) *v.t.* **1** To dim the luster of. **2** To dim the purity of; stain; disgrace. —*v.i.* **3** To lose luster, as by oxidation; become blemished. See synonyms under DEFILE[1], STAIN. —*n.* **1** Loss of luster; hence, a blemish. **2** The thin film of color on the exposed surface of a metal or mineral. [<OF *terniss-,* stem of *ternir* <*terne* dull, wan] —**tar′nish·a·ble** *adj.*

tarnished plant bug A common, brown-marked hemipterous insect (*Lygus pratensis*) of North America, which attacks many fruits and vegetables. For illustration see INSECTS (injurious).

Tar·no·pol (tär·nô′pôl) The Polish name for TERNOPOL.

Tar·nów (tär′no͞of) A city in southern Poland, 45 miles east of Cracow.

ta·ro (tä′rō) *n. pl.* **·ros** **1** Any one of several tropical plants (genus *Colocasia*) of the arum family, grown for their edible, cormlike root-stocks. **2** The rootstock of this plant. [<native Polynesian name]

tar·ot (tar′ō, -ət) *n.* One of a set of playing

cards with grilled or checkered backs used in Italy as early as the 14th century; also, a game played with such cards in which 22 are trumps and the other 56 are the usual Italian playing cards: used by fortune-tellers and gipsies in foretelling future events. [<F <Ital. *tarocco* < *taroccare* wrangle, play at cards; ult. origin obscure]

tar·pau·lin (tär·pô′lin, tär′pə-) *n.* **1** A waterproof canvas, impregnated with tar, for covering merchandise. **2** A sailor's wide-brimmed storm hat. **3** *Rare* A sailor. [<TAR[1] + PALL[1] + -ING[1]]

Tar·pe·ia (tär·pē′ə) The daughter of the governor of the citadel of Rome, who treacherously opened its gates to the Sabines on condition of receiving what they wore on their arms, meaning their golden bracelets. As they entered they crushed her with their shields instead. —**Tar·pe′ian** *adj.*

Tarpeian Rock A cliff upon the Capitoline Hill at Rome, from which state criminals were hurled to their death.

tar·pon (tär′pon, -pən) *n.* *pl.* **·pon** or **·pons** A large marine game fish with conspicuous silvery scales (*Tarpon atlanticus*) of the West Indies and the coast of Florida. [Origin unknown]

Tar·quin (tär′kwin) Anglicized name of two legendary kings of Rome, **Lucius Tarquinius Priscus** and **Lucius Tarquinius Superbus,** respectively fifth and seventh kings, of the sixth century B.C.

tar·ra·did·dle (tar′ə·did′l) *n.* *Colloq.* A prevarication; lie: also spelled *taradiddle.* [Origin uncertain]

tar·ra·gon (tar′ə·gon) *n.* **1** A European perennial plant (*Artemisia dracunculus*) allied to wormwood, and cultivated for its aromatic leaves which are used as seasoning. **2** The leaves of this plant. [<Sp. *taragona* <Arabic *ṭarkhun* <Gk. *drakōn* dragon]

Tar·ra·go·na (tar′ə·gō′nə) **1** A province in Catalonia, NE Spain; 2,425 square miles. **2** A manufacturing city, capital of Tarragona province, and formerly of a Roman province.

tar·ri·ance (tar′ē·əns) *n.* *Archaic* A tarrying; delay. [<TARRY + -ANCE]

tar·ri·er (tar′ē·ər) *n.* One who or that which tarries.

tar·row (tar′ō) *v.i.* *Scot.* **1** To show reluctance or hesitation; delay; tarry. **2** To feel loathing.

tar·ry[1] (tar′ē) *v.* **·ried, ·ry·ing** *v.i.* **1** To put off going or coming; linger. **2** To remain in the same place; abide; stay. **3** To wait. —*v.t.* **4** *Archaic* To wait for; await: to *tarry* his coming. See synonyms under ABIDE. —*n.* Sojourn; stay. [ME *tarien* vex, hinder, delay, fusion of OE *tergan* vex + OF *targer* delay <LL *tardicare* <L *tardare* delay < *tardus* slow]

tar·ry[2] (tär′ē) *adj.* Covered with tar; like tar.

tar·sal (tär′səl) *adj.* **1** Of, pertaining to, or situated near the tarsus or ankle. **2** Of or pertaining to the tarsi of the eye. See TARSUS.

Tar·shish (tär′shish) In the Bible, an ancient maritime country, often identified with Tartessus, in southern Spain. I *Kings* x 22.

tar·si·er (tär′sē·ər) *n.* A small, arboreal, insectivorous East Indian primate (*Tarsius spectrum*) of nocturnal habits, with large eyes and ears, long tail, and adhesive pads on elongated digits: it is the sole member of the suborder *Tarsioidea.* [<F < *tarse* tarsus; so called from its unusually long tarsal bones]

TARSIER (Size of a small rat)

tarso- *combining form* **1** The tarsus; pertaining to the tarsus. **2** The tarsus of the eye; pertaining to the tarsal plate: *tarsoplasty,* plastic surgery of the eyelid. Also, before vowels, **tars-.** [<Gk. *tarsos* flat of the foot, edge of the eyelid]

tar·so·met·a·tar·sus (tär′sō·met′ə·tär′səs) *n.* *pl.* **·si** (-sī) *Ornithol.* The so-called tarsus of birds; the bone reaching from the tibia to the toes, consisting of the confluent proximal tarsal and metatarsal bones. [<NL]

tar·sus (tär′səs) *n.* *pl.* **·si** (-sī) **1** *Anat.* **a** The ankle, or, in man, the group of seven bones of which it is composed. **b** A plate of connective tissue in the eyelid. **2** *Zool.* **a** The shank of a bird's leg. **b** The distal part of the leg of certain arthropods. [<NL <Gk. *tarsos* flat of the foot, any flat surface]

Tar·sus (tär′səs) **1** A port near the NE Mediterranean in southern Turkey in Asia; anciently, the capital of Cilicia, and the birthplace of St. Paul. **2** A river in southern Turkey, flowing 95 miles south from the Taurus mountains to the Mediterranean below Tarsus: ancient *Cydnus.*

tart[1] (tärt) *adj.* **1** Having a sharp, sour taste. **2** Figuratively, severe; cutting; caustic: a *tart* remark. See synonyms under BITTER. [OE *teart*] —**tart′ly** *adv.* —**tart′ness** *n.*

tart[2] (tärt) *n.* **1** A small pastry shell with fruit or custard filling, and without a top crust, as distinguished from a pie. **2** In England, an uncovered fruit pie. **3** *Slang* A girl or woman of loose morality. [<OF *tarte*]

tar·tan[1] (tär′tən) *n.* **1** A woolen fabric having varicolored lines or stripes at right angles, forming a distinctive pattern; a woolen plaid; the characteristic dress of the Scottish Highlanders, each clan having its particular pattern or patterns; hence, any similar pattern; a plaid. **2** A garment made of tartan. —*adj.* Made of tartan; also, striped or checkered in a manner similar to the Scottish tartans. [? <OF *tiretaine* linsey-woolsey]

tar·tan[2] (tär′tən) *n.* **1** A Mediterranean vessel having one mast with a large lateen sail. **2** A variety of long, covered carriage. [<F *tartane* <Arabic *ṭarīdah,* kind of ship]

tar·tar (tär′tər) *n.* **1** An acid substance deposited from grape juice during fermentation as a pinkish sediment; crude potassium bitartrate. See ARGOL, CREAM OF TARTAR. **2** *Dent.* A yellowish incrustation on the teeth, chiefly calcium phosphate. [<F *tartre* <LL *tartarum* <Med. Gk. *tartaron,* ? <Arabic]

Tar·tar (tär′tər) *n.* **1** Tatar. **2** A person of intractable or savage temper; also, especially in the phrase **to catch a Tartar,** an opponent who turns out to be unexpectedly formidable: also **tar′tar.** —*adj.* Of or pertaining to the Tatars of Tartary. [<F *Tartare* <LL *Tartarus* <Persian *Tātar* Tatar; prob. infl. by L *Tartarus* Hell]

Tar·tar (tär′tər) *Obs.* Tartarus.

Tar·tar·e·an (tär·târ′ē·ən) *adj.* Of or pertaining to Tartarus.

tartar emetic *Chem.* A white, crystalline, poisonous tartrate of antimony and potassium, $K(SbO)C_4H_4O_6 \cdot 1/2H_2O$, with a sweet, afterward disagreeable, metallic taste: used in medicine, chiefly as an emetic, and in dyeing as a mordant.

tar·tar·e·ous (tär·târ′ē·əs) *adj.* Resembling tartar.

tar·tare sauce (tär′tər) A fish sauce consisting of mayonnaise, capers, chopped olives, and pickles. Also **tar′tar sauce.**

Tar·tar·i·an (tär·târ′ē·ən) *adj.* Of or pertaining to the Tatars or Tartary.

tar·tar·ic (tär·tar′ik, -tär′ik) *adj.* Pertaining to or derived from tartar or tartaric acid.

tartaric acid *Chem.* Any one of four isomeric organic compounds, $HOOC(CHOH)_2COOH$, differing from each other in their optical properties, especially the dextrorotatory form, occurring in the free state or as a potassium or calcium salt, as in grape juice, various unripe fruits, etc.

tar·tar·ize (tär′tə·rīz) *v.t.* **·ized, ·iz·ing** To impregnate or treat with tartar, cream of tartar, or tartar emetic. —**tar′tar·i·za′tion** *n.*

tar·tar·ous (tär′tər·əs) *adj.* Pertaining to or derived from tartar.

Tartar sable The kolinsky.

Tar·ta·rus (tär′tər·əs) **1** In Greek mythology, the abyss below Hades where Zeus confined the Titans. **2** Hades.

Tar·ta·ry (tär′tər·ē) A region of Asia and eastern Europe, mostly in central and western Asiatic Russian S.F.S.R., Soviet Central Asia, southern European Russian S.F.S.R., and Ukrainian S.S.R., ruled by the Tatars, under Mongol leadership, in the 13th and 14th centuries A.D. At its greatest extent, under Genghis Khan, it reached the Pacific; after his death, the Asian portion became known as **Great Tartary,** or **Asiatic Tartary,** while the European portion, ruled by the Golden Horde, became **Little Tartary,** or **European Tartary:** also *Tatary.*

Tar·tes·sus (tär·tes′əs) An ancient city and region in the SW part of the Iberian Peninsula near the Pillars of Hercules, often identified with Biblical Tarshish.

tart·let (tärt′lit) *n.* A small tart.

tar·trate (tär′trāt) *n.* *Chem.* A salt or ester of tartaric acid.

tar·trat·ed (tär′trā·tid) *adj.* *Chem.* Containing or combined with tartaric acid.

Tar·tu (tär′tōō) A city in SE central Estonia: German *Dorpat,* Russian *Yurev.*

tar·tufe (tär·tōōf′, *Fr.* tȧr·tüf′) *n.* Any hypocrite or toady. Also **tar·tuffe′.** [after TARTUFE]

Tar·tufe (tär·tōōf′, *Fr.* tȧr·tüf′) In Molière's comedy of the same name, the chief character, a person of pretended devoutness. Also **Tar·tuffe′.**

Tar·ve·si·um (tär·vē′sē·əm) The ancient name for TREVISO.

Tar·zan (tär′zan, tär·zan′) The hero of a series of novels by Edgar Rice Burroughs (1875–1950): an English child of noble birth abandoned in the African jungle, raised by apes, and possessing incredible strength, agility, and a knowledge of the speech of animals. Also **Tarzan of the Apes.**

Tash·kent (täsh·kent′) The largest city of Soviet Central Asia, capital of Uzbek S.S.R. Also **Tash·kend′** (-kend′).

ta·sim·e·ter (tə·sim′ə·tər) *n.* An electrical apparatus for detecting changes in pressure by the resulting variations in the conductivity of a solid, and so measuring changes, as in length, temperature, or moisture, that produce alteration of pressure. [<Gk. *tasis* extension (< *teinein* stretch) + -METER] —**tas·i·met·ric** (tas′ə·met′rik) *adj.* —**ta·sim′e·try** *n.*

task (task, täsk) *n.* **1** A specific amount of labor or study imposed by authority or required by duty or necessity. **2** Any work voluntarily undertaken and imposed on oneself. **3** An exhausting or vexatious employment; burden. **4** A specific military mission. **5** *Obs.* A tax; duty. —**to take to task** To reprove; lecture. —*v.t.* **1** To assign a task to. **2** To overtax with labor; burden. **3** To censure; reprimand. **4** *Obs.* To tax. [<AF *tasque* <LL *tasca, taxa* <L *taxare* appraise. Related to TAX.]

Synonyms (noun): business, drudgery, job, labor, lesson, stint, toil, work. See TOIL[1].

task·er (tas′kər, täs′-) *n.* **1** A reaper. **2** A thresher of grain. **3** A laborer who performs allotted work.

task force **1** *Mil.* A tactical unit drawn from different branches of the armed services assigned to execute a specific mission. **2** Any group assigned to handle a specific task.

task·mas·ter (task′mas′tər, täsk′mäs′tər) *n.* One who assigns tasks; figuratively, one who or that which loads with heavy burdens.

Tas·lan (taz′lan) *n.* A mechanical process for imparting bulk and texture to any standard textile yarn without altering basic chemical properties: a trade name.

Tas·man (täs′män), **Abel Janszoon,** 1603?–1659?, Dutch navigator who discovered Tasmania and New Zealand.

Tas·ma·nia (taz·mā′nē·ə) An island state in the Commonwealth of Australia, south of Victoria; 26,215 square miles; capital, Hobart: formerly *Van Diemen's Land.* —**Tas·ma′ni·an** *adj.* & *n.*

Tasmanian devil A ferocious burrowing carnivorous marsupial (*Sarcophilus harrisii*) of the dasyure family, with white markings on the black fur.

Tasmanian wolf The thylacine. Also **Tasmanian tiger.**

Tas·man Sea (taz′mən) The arm of the South Pacific Ocean between SE Australia and Tasmania on the west and New Zealand on the east.

tass (tas) *n.* *Scot.* A drinking cup, or its contents.

Tass (täs, tas) *n.* Russian news agency: from the initials of *Telegrafnoe Agentstvo Sovetskovo Soyuza* (Telegraph Agency Soviet Union).

tas·sel[1] (tas′əl) *n.* **1** A pendent ornament, for curtains, cushions, and the like, consisting of a tuft of loosely hanging threads or cords; formerly, a clasp for holding a cloak. **2** Something resembling a tassel, as the pendent head of some plants or flowers, or the pyramidal inflorescence on a stalk of Indian corn. — *v.* **·seled** or **·selled, ·sel·ing** or **·sel·ling** *v.t.* **1** To provide or adorn with tassels. **2** To form in a tassel or tassels. **3** To remove the tassels from (Indian corn). — *v.i.* **4** To put forth tassels, as Indian corn. [<OF, clasp]

tas·sel[2] (tas′əl) *n.* The tercel.

tas·set (tas′it) *n.* One of a series of overlapping metal plates pendent from the cuirass to protect the waist and thighs: often called *tace.* Also **tasse.** ◆ Homophone: *tacit.* [<F *tassette,* dim. of OF *tasse* a pouch]

tas·sie (tas′ē) *n. Scot.* A drinking cup.

Tas·so (täs′sō), **Torquato,** 1544–95, Italian epic poet.

taste (tāst) *v.* **tast·ed, tast·ing** *v.t.* **1** To perceive the flavor of (something) by taking into the mouth or touching with the tongue. **2** To take a little of (food or drink); eat or drink a little of. **3** To test the quality of (a product) thus: His business is *tasting* tea. **4** *Archaic* To have a relish for; like. **5** *Obs.* To prove or try by or as by touch. — *v.i.* **6** To take a small quantity into the mouth; take a taste: usually with *of.* **7** To have experience or enjoyment; be or become acquainted through experience: with *of:* to *taste* of great sorrow. **8** To have specified flavor when in the mouth: Sugar *tastes* sweet. — *n.* **1** The sensation excited when a soluble substance comes into contact with any of the taste buds; also, the quality thus perceived; flavor. **2** *Physiol.* Any of the four fundamental sensations, salt, sweet, bitter, or sour, excited alone or in any combination by the sole action of the gustatory nerves. **3** A small quantity tasted, eaten or sipped; a sample: often used figuratively. **4** Special fondness and aptitude for a pursuit; bent; inclination: a *taste* for music. **5** The power or faculty of apprehending and appreciating the beautiful in nature, art, and literature; critical perception or discernment. **6** Style or form with respect to the rules of propriety or etiquette: She behaves in very poor *taste.* **7** Individual preference or liking: That tie suits my *taste.* **8** The act of tasting. **9** *Obs.* The act of examining or testing. See synonyms under RELISH, SAVOR. [<OF *taster* taste, try, feel, prob. ult. <L *taxare* touch, handle, appraise] — **tast′a·ble** *adj.*

taste bud *Physiol.* One of the clusters of cells situated in the mucous membrane chiefly of the tongue and containing sensitive receptors for the discriminatory perception of taste.

taste·ful (tāst′fəl) *adj.* **1** Conforming to taste. **2** Possessing good taste. **3** Savory: a rare use. — **taste′ful·ly** *adv.* — **taste′ful·ness** *n.*

Synonyms: artistic, dainty, delicate, delicious, elegant, esthetic, esthetical, exquisite, fastidious, fine, nice. That which is *elegant* is made so not merely by nature, but by art and culture. *Nice* and *delicate* both refer to exact adaptation to some standard; as regards matters of taste, *delicate* is a higher and more discriminating word than *nice,* and is always used in a favorable sense; a *delicate* distinction is one worth observing; a *nice* distinction may be so, or may be overstrained and unduly subtle. *Esthetic* or *esthetical* refers to beauty or the appreciation of the beautiful, especially from the philosophic point of view. *Exquisite* denotes the utmost perfection of the *elegant* in minute details; we speak of an *elegant* garment, an *exquisite* lace. *Exquisite* is also applied to intense keenness of any feeling; as, *exquisite* pain. *Antonyms:* clumsy, coarse, deformed, disgusting, displeasing, distasteful, fulsome, gaudy, grotesque, harsh, hideous, horrid, inartistic, inharmonious, meretricious, offensive, rude, tawdry.

taste·less (tāst′lis) *adj.* **1** Having no flavor; insipid; dull. **2** Having lost the sense of taste. **3** Devoid of esthetic taste. **4** Lacking, or showing a lack of, good taste. — **taste′less·ly** *adv.* — **taste′less·ness** *n.*

tast·er (tās′tər) *n.* **1** One who tastes; specifically, one who tests the quality of for trade: a tea-*taster.* **2** A device to assist in testing or sampling. **3** A pipette, or a small, flat, circular metal vessel used in testing wines.

tast·y (tās′tē) *adj.* **tast·i·er, tast·i·est** *Colloq.* **1** Having a fine flavor; savory. **2** Tasteful. — **tast′i·ly** *adv.* — **tast′i·ness** *n.*

tat[1] (tat) *v.* **tat·ted, tat·ting** *v.t.* To make, as an edging, by tatting. — *v.i.* To make tatting. [Back formation <TATTING] — **tat′ter** *n.*

tat[2] (tat) *n.* A tap or blow: in the phrase **tit for tat.** [? Var. of TAP[2], *n.*]

Ta·tar (tä′tər) *n.* **1** One belonging to any of the Turkic peoples of eastern, western, and Ural Asiatic Russian S.F.S.R. and Soviet Central Asia; also, one of the Turkic Tatars of the Tatar Republic, the Crimea, the Kalmuck area, and the northern Caucasus. **2** Any of the Turkic languages of the Tatars, as Uzbek. **3** Originally, any of the Tungus of Manchuria and Mongolia. — *adj.* Of or pertaining to the Tatars. Also *Tartar.* [< Persian]

Ta·tar Autonomous Soviet Socialist Republic (tä′tər) An administrative division of east central European Russian S.F.S.R.; 26,100 square miles; capital, Kazan.

Ta·tar·i·an (tä·târ′ē·ən) *adj.* Of or pertaining to the Tatars: also **Ta·tar·ic** (tä·tar′ik). — *n.* A Tatar.

Ta·ta·ry (tä′tər·ē) See TARTARY.

tate (tāt) *n. Scot.* A wisp or tuft, as of hay or hair.

Tate (tāt), **Nahum,** 1652–1715, English dramatist; poet laureate 1692–1715.

ta·tie (tā′tē) *n. Brit. Dial.* A potato. Also **ta′ter, ta′ty.**

Tat·ler (tat′lər), **The** An English periodical, published thrice weekly by Sir Richard Steele from 1709 to 1711, chiefly written by Steele, occasionally by Addison: predecessor of *The Spectator.*

tat·ou·ay (tat′o͞o·ā, tä·to͞o′ī) *n.* A large South American armadillo (genus *Cabassous*). [<Sp. *tatuay* <Guarani *tatu-aí* < *tatu* armadillo + *aí* worthless; so called because it is inedible]

Ta·tra (tä′trä), **High** The highest group of the central Carpathian Mountains, in northern Czechoslovakia; highest peak, 8,737 ft. Also **Tatra Mountains.**

tat·ter (tat′ər) *n.* **1** A torn and hanging shred; rag. **2** *pl.* Ragged clothing. — *v.t.* To make ragged; tear into tatters. — *v.i.* To become ragged. [<Scand. Cf. ON *tötturr* rags.]

tat·ter·de·mal·ion (tat′ər·di·māl′yən, -mal′-) *n.* A person wearing ragged clothes; a ragga-muffin. — *adj.* Ragged. [Origin unknown]

tat·tered (tat′ərd) *adj.* **1** Torn into tatters. **2** Clothed in rags; ragged.

Tat·ter·sall check (tat′ər·sôl) A check or plaid design of dark lines on a light ground: used especially in men's vests. Also **Tattersall plaid.** [From a pattern on blankets used in the London market of Richard *Tattersall,* 18th century horse merchant]

tat·ting (tat′ing) *n.* A lacelike threadwork, made by hand; also, the act or process of making it. [Origin unknown]

tat·tle (tat′l) *v.* **·tled, ·tling** *v.i.* **1** To talk idly; prate; chatter. **2** To tell tales about others; gossip. — *v.t.* **3** To reveal by gossiping. See synonyms under BABBLE. — *n.* **1** Idle talk or gossip. **2** Prattling speech, as of children. [Prob. <MDu. *tatelen*] — **tat′tling·ly** *adv.*

tat·tler (tat′lər) *n.* **1** One who tattles; a talebearer; tattletale. **2** Any long-billed bird of the genus *Totanus,* as the redshank and the yellowlegs. **3** The willet. **4** The wandering tattler (*Heteroscelus incanus*), a shore bird of the Pacific coast of the United States.

tat·tle·tale (tat′l·tāl′) *n.* A talebearer; tattler. — *adj.* Revealing; betraying.

tat·too[1] (ta·to͞o′) *v.t.* **1** To prick and mark (the skin) in patterns with indelible pigments. **2** To mark the skin with (designs, etc.) in this way. — *n. pl.* **·toos** A pattern or picture so made. [<Polynesian. Cf. Tahitian, Tongan *tatau,* Marquesan *tatu* < *ta* mark.] — **tat·too′er** *n.* — **tat·too′·ing** *n.*

TATTOOING ON MAORI CHIEFTAIN

tat·too[2] (ta·to͞o′) *n.* **1** A continuous beating or drumming. **2** In military or naval usage, a signal by drum or bugle to repair to quarters, usually occurring about 9 p.m. [Var. of earlier *taptoo* <Du. *taptoe* < *tap* tap, faucet + *toe* shut]

tat·ty (tat′ē) *n. pl.* **·ties** *Anglo-Indian* An East Indian matting usually hung in doorways and window openings, and kept wet to cool the air. Also **tat′tie.** [<Hind. *ṭaṭṭi*] — **tat′tied** *adj.*

tau (tou) *n.* The nineteenth letter in the Greek alphabet: (Τ,τ) equivalent to the English *t.* As a numeral it denotes 300. [<Gk.]

Tauch·nitz (toukh′nits), **Baron Christian,** 1816–95, German publisher.

tau cross See under CROSS.

taught (tôt) Past tense and past participle of TEACH.

Taungs skull (toungz) A fossil skull assumed to represent Australopithecus. [from *Taungs,* South Africa, where remains were discovered]

taunt[1] (tônt) *n.* **1** A sarcastic, biting speech or remark; insulting reproach. **2** *Obs.* A butt of contemptuous reproach. See synonyms under SCORN, SNEER. — *v.t.* **1** To reproach with sarcastic or contemptuous words; mock; upbraid. **2** To tease in any way; provoke with taunts. See synonyms under MOCK, RIDICULE, SCOFF. [? <OF *tanter,* var. of *tenter* provoke, tempt. See TEMPT.] — **taunt′er** *n.* — **taunt′·ing·ly** *adv.*

taunt[2] (tônt) *adj. Naut.* Unusually tall: said of masts. [Aphetic var. of ATAUNT]

Taun·ton (tän′tən, tôn′-) The county town of Somerset, England; in the west central part.

tau particle *Physics* A rare, unstable atomic particle of the meson group, positively charged and with a mass about 1,000 times that of the electron.

taupe (tōp) *n.* **1** A mole. **2** The color of moleskin; dark gray, often tinged with brown, purple, or yellow. ◆ Homophone: *tope.* [<F <L *talpa* mole]

Tau·ric Cher·so·nese (tô′rik kûr′sō·nēz, -nēs) An ancient name for the CRIMEA.

tau·ri·form (tôr′ə·fôrm) *adj.* Shaped like a bull. [<L *tauriformis* < *taurus* bull + *forma* shape]

tau·rine[1] (tôr′ēn) *adj.* **1** Of or like a bull. **2** Related to or connected with the constellation or sign Taurus. [<L *taurinus* < *taurus* a bull]

tau·rine[2] (tôr′ēn, -in) *n. Chem.* A colorless crystalline compound, $C_2H_7NSO_3$, contained in the bile and muscles of oxen and other animals: also derived synthetically. [<L *taurus* bull + -INE[2]]

Tau·ris (tôr′is) **1** The Tauric Chersonese. **2** The ancient name for TABRIZ.

tauro– *combining form* Bull; ox; bovine. Also, before vowels, **taur–.** [<Gk. *tauros* a bull]

tau·ro·cho·lic acid (tôr′ə·kō′lik, -kol′ik) *Chem.* A bitter crystalline compound, $C_{26}H_{45}NSO_7$, contained in the bile of man and some animals, as the ox. [<TAURO- + Gk. *cholē* bile]

tau·rom·a·chy (tô·rom′ə·kē) *n.* The art of bull-fighting. Also **tau·ro·ma·chi·a** (tôr′ə·mā′kē·ə). [<Gk. *tauromachia* < *tauros* a bull + *machesthai* fight]

Tau·rus (tôr′əs) **1** A zodiacal constellation, the Bull, containing the Hyades, the Pleiades, and Aldebaran. **2** The second sign of the zodiac, which the sun enters April 20. See CONSTELLATION, ZODIAC. [<L, bull]

Tau·rus (tôr′əs) A mountain range in southern Turkey; highest point, 12,251 feet: Turkish *Toros Dağlari.*

Taus·sig (tou′sig), **Frank William,** 1859–1940, U. S. political economist.

taut (tôt) *adj.* **1** Hard-drawn; stretched tight. **2** In proper shape; ready; tidy. **3** Tense; tight: *taut* muscles. **4** *Obs.* Filled to distention; firm. [ME *toyt, toht;* origin uncertain] — **taut′ly** *adv.* — **taut′ness** *n.*

taut·ed (tô′tid) *adj. Scot.* Tangled; tousled; matted: said of wool or hair.

taut·en (tôt′n) *v.t.* & *v.i.* To make or become taut; tighten.

tauto– *combining form* Same; identical: *tautomerism.* Also, before vowels, **taut–.** [<Gk. *tauto* the same]

tau·tog (tô·tôg′, -tog′) *n.* A blackish, edible, labroid fish (*Tautoga onitis*) of the North American Atlantic coast. Also **tau·taug′.** [<Algonquian *tautauog,* pl. of *tautau,* a kind of blackfish]

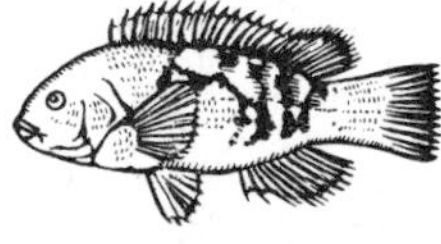

TAUTOG
(About 16 inches long)

tau·tol·o·gism (tô·tol′ə·jiz′əm) *n.* Use of needlessly repetitious speech, or an instance of it; pleonasm. — **tau·tol′o·gist** *n.*

tau·tol·o·gize (tô·tol′ə·jīz) *v.i.* **·gized, ·giz·ing** To repeat needlessly the same idea in different words.

tau·tol·o·gy (tô·tol′ə·jē) *n. pl.* **·gies** Unnecessary repetition of the same idea in different words; pleonasm; also, an instance of such repetition; as, He is writing his own autobiography. See REDUNDANCE. [<LL *tautologia* <Gk. < *tauto* the same + *logos* discourse] — **tau·to·log·ic** (tô′tə·loj′ik) or **·i·cal** *adj.* — **tau′to·log′i·cal·ly** *adv.*

tau·to·mer·ic (tô′tə·mer′ik) *adj.* Having the property of tautomerism.

tau·tom·er·ism (tô·tom′ə·riz′əm) *n. Chem.* The property, exhibited by certain substances and compounds when subjected to appropriate chemical reaction, of assuming either of two interconvertible atomic structures, **tau·to·mers** (tô′tə·mərz), which are in equilibrium with each other. [<TAUTO- + Gk. *meros* part]

tau·tom·er·i·za·tion (tô·tom′ər·ə·zā′shən, -ī·zā′-) *n. Chem.* Conversion into a tautomeric structure.

tau·to·nym (tô′tə·nim) *n.* An instance of tautonymy.

tau·ton·y·my (tô·ton′ə·mē) *n. pl.* **·mies** *Biol.* **1** The possession by two or more distinct plants or animals of the same generic and specific names: prohibited by the rules of scientific nomenclature. **2** Identity of the generic, specific, and subspecific names of a given plant or animal, as *Bison bison bison*: a permitted practice. [<TAUTO- + Gk. *onyma* name] — **tau·to·nym·ic** (tô′tə·nim′ik) *adj.*

tav (täv) *n.* The twenty-second Hebrew letter. Also **taw.** See ALPHABET.

tav·ern (tav′ərn) *n.* **1** A public house where travelers and other guests are accommodated with lodging, food, and drink. **2** A house licensed to retail liquors to be drunk on the premises. [<OF *taverne* <L *taberna* hut, booth]

tav·ern·er (tav′ər·nər) *n. Archaic* A tavern-keeper; also, one who frequents taverns.

taw[1] (tô) *v.t.* **1** To convert into leather by some process other than soaking in tanning liquor, as by using alum and salt. **2** *Brit. Dial.* To beat; torture; vex; also, to harden or prepare. [OE *tawian* prepare, harass] — **taw′er** *n.*

taw[2] (tô) *n.* **1** A game of marbles. **2** The line from which marble-players shoot. **3** A marble used for shooting. — *v.i.* To shoot a marble or come to the mark before shooting. [<Scand. Cf. ON *taug* string.]

taw·dry (tô′drē) *adj.* **·dri·er, ·dri·est** Showy without elegance; excessively ornamental; gaudy. — *n.* Cheap, pretentious finery. [Short for *tawdry lace,* alter. of *St. Audrey's lace,* a type of silk neckpiece sold at St. Audrey's Fair at Ely, England] — **taw′dri·ly** *adv.* — **taw′dri·ness** *n.*

taw·ie (tô′ē) *adj. Scot.* Docile; tame: said of a horse, etc.

Taw·ney (tô′nē), **R(ichard) H(enry),** 1880–1962, English economist and historian.

taw·ny (tô′nē) *adj.* **·ni·er, ·ni·est** Tan-colored; brownish-yellow. Also **taw′ney.** [<AF *taune* <OF *tanné,* pp. of *tanner* tan] — **taw′ni·ness** *n.*

taw·pie (tô′pē) *n. Scot.* A foolish young woman.

taws (tôz) *Scot. n.* A whip made of a leather strap cut into thongs or of several thongs on a handle. — *v.t.* To flog; scourge. Also **tawse.**

tax (taks) *n.* **1** A compulsory contribution levied upon persons, property, or business for the support of government; by extension, any proportionate assessment, as on the members of a society. **2** A heavy demand on one's powers or resources; an onerous duty or requirement; a burden. — **direct tax** A tax, as on property or income, which the taxpayer cannot shift to another person. — **excise tax** An internal-revenue tax on domestic manufactures, levied before they are sold to the consumer. The term has been extended to include license duties. — **income tax** A tax levied on the income or profits of individuals and of corporations. See CAPITAL LEVY. — **indirect tax** A tax, such as a customs duty, paid by one person but ultimately shifted to the consumer. — **nuisance tax** A tax which yields little benefit in proportion to the amount of discontent it causes. — **single tax** A tax to be obtained from a single source, especially from a levy on land and natural resources, as a substitute for all other forms of taxation. The theory was first proposed by John Locke, and was elaborated and popularized in the 19th century by Henry George. [< *v.*] — *v.t.* **1** To impose a tax on; subject to taxation. **2** *Law* To settle or fix (amounts) as duly chargeable in any judicial matter: to *tax* costs. **3** To subject to a severe demand; impose a burden or load upon; task: He *taxes* my patience. **4** To make an accusation against; charge; also, to blame; censure: usually with *with.* [<OF *taxer* <L *taxare* estimate, appraise. Related to TASK.] — **tax′·a·bil′i·ty, tax′a·ble·ness** *n.* — **tax′a·ble** *adj.* — **tax′a·bly** *adv.* — **tax′er** *n.*

Synonyms (noun): assessment, custom, demand, duty, exaction, excise, impost, rate, rating, toll, tribute.

Tax may appear as a combining form in hyphemes or solidemes, or as the first element in two-word phrases, with the meaning of definition 1:

tax-assessor	**tax-evader**	**tax payment**
tax burden	**tax-evading**	**tax proposal**
tax-burdened	**tax-exempt**	**tax receipt**
tax claim	**tax-free**	**tax-repeal**
tax-collecting	**tax-laden**	**tax revenue**
tax-collector	**tax law**	**tax-ridden**
tax-cut	**tax levy**	**tax-supported**
tax-dodger	**taxman**	**tax system**
tax-dodging	**tax-paid**	**taxwise**

tax·a·ceous (tak·sā′shəs) *adj. Bot.* Designating or belonging to a widely distributed family *(Taxaceae)* of typically evergreen shrubs and trees, the yew family, having one or two integuments and drupelike or, rarely, cone fruits. [<NL <L *taxus* yew]

tax·a·tion (tak·sā′shən) *n.* The act of taxing; the amount assessed as a tax.

Tax·co (tas′kō, *Sp.* täs′kō) A resort city in Guerrero, SW Mexico. Officially **Tax·co de Al·ar·cón** (täs′kō thā äl′är·kōn′).

tax·gath·er·er (taks′gath′ər·ər) *n.* A collector of taxes. — **tax′gath′er·ing** *n.* & *adj.*

tax·i (tak′sē) *n.* A taxicab. — *v.* **tax·ied, tax·i·ing** or **tax·y·ing** *v.i.* **1** To ride in a taxicab. **2** To move along the ground or on the surface of the water under its own power, as an airplane before taking off or after landing. — *v.t.* **3** To cause (an airplane) to taxi. [< TAXI(CAB)]

tax·i·arch (tak′sē·ärk) *n.* The commander of a division of an ancient Greek army. [<Gk. *taxiarchēs* < *taxis* division of an army + *archos* leader < *archein* rule]

tax·i·cab (tak′sē·kab′) *n.* A passenger vehicle, usually an automobile fitted with a taximeter, available for hire. [Short for *taximeter cab*]

taxi dancer *U.S.* A girl employed by a dance hall or cabaret to dance with patrons for a certain fee. [< *taxi-* hired, as in *taxicab* + DANCER]

tax·i·der·mist (tak′sə·dûr′mist) *n.* One who practices taxidermy.

tax·i·der·my (tak′sə·dûr′mē) *n.* The art or process of stuffing and mounting the skins of dead animals for preservation or exhibition. [<Gk. *taxis* arrangement + *derma* skin] — **tax′i·der′mal, tax′i·der′mic** *adj.*

tax·i·me·ter (tak′si·mē′tər) *n.* **1** An instrument for measuring distances and recording fares. **2** A taxicab equipped with a taximeter. [<F *taximètre* < *taxe* tariff + *mètre* a meter]

tax·ine (tak′sēn, -sin) *n. Chem.* A yellow-white, poisonous alkaloid, $C_{37}H_{51}O_{10}N$, from the needles and seed of the English yew *(Taxus baccata).* It produces convulsion and paralyzes the heart. Also **tax·in** (tak′sin). [<L *taxus* yew + -INE[2]]

tax·i·plane (tak′sē·plān′) *n.* An airplane available for hire as a public vehicle.

tax·is (tak′sis) *n.* **1** *Surg.* A methodical application of manual pressure, as on a hernial tumor, for restoring the parts to their normal place. **2** *Zool.* The involuntary movement of an organism or cell, as a zoospore, in response to an external stimulus; specifically, a movement involving locomotion or change of place. Compare TROPISM. **3** In ancient Greece, a body of troops of varying size. **4** *Obs.* Order; arrangement, as of words in a sentence. [< Gk., arrangement < *tassein* arrange]

-taxis *combining form* Order; disposition; arrangement: *thermotaxis.* Also spelled **-taxy.** [<Gk. *taxis* arrangement]

tax·ite (tak′sīt) *n.* A volcanic rock which has crystallized in such manner as to have a clastic appearance. [<Gk. *taxis* arrangement + -ITE[1]] — **tax·it·ic** (tak·sit′ik) *adj.*

tax·on·o·mist (tak·son′ə·mist) *n.* One versed in taxonomy. Also **tax·on′o·mer.**

tax·on·o·my (tak·son′ə·mē) *n.* **1** The department of knowledge that embodies the laws and principles of classification. **2** *Biol.* The systematic arrangement of plant and animal organisms according to accepted diagnostic criteria which determine their assignment to each of the following major groups, beginning with the most inclusive: kingdom, phylum or division, class, order, family, genus, and species. [<F *taxonomie* <Gk. *taxis* arrangement + *nomos* law] — **tax·o·nom·ic** (tak′sə·nom′ik) or **·i·cal** *adj.* — **tax′o·nom′i·cal·ly** *adv.*

tax·pay·er (taks′pā′ər) *n.* **1** One who pays any tax. **2** A building, the rental from which is intended to cover merely the taxes on the land.

tax title The title conveyed to a purchaser of property sold for non-payment of taxes.

Ta·yg·e·ta (tā·ij′ə·tə) One of the Pleiades.

Tay·lor (tā′lər), **Bayard,** 1825–78, U. S. writer. — **Frederick Winslow,** 1856–1915, U. S. engineer; developed scientific shop management. — **Jeremy,** 1613–67, English bishop and author. — **(Joseph) Deems,** 1885–1966, U. S. composer. — **Laurette,** 1887–1946, *née* Cooney, U.S. actress. — **Myron,** 1874–1959, U.S. lawyer, businessman, and diplomat. — **Tom,** 1817–80, English dramatist. — **Zachary,** 1784–1850, U. S. general; president of the United States 1849–50.

Tay River (tā) The largest river in Scotland, flowing 118 miles SW and SE, from eastern Perthshire, near the Argyll border, to the **Firth of Tay,** an estuary of the North Sea extending 25 miles into central Scotland.

taz·za (tät′tsä) *n. Italian* A flat ornamental cup, especially one supported on a high foot.

T-base (tē′bās′) *n.* Two strips of wood nailed together in the form of a T and serving as a base for the tripod of a machine-gun.

Tbi·li·si (tpi′li·sē) The Georgian name for TIFLIS.

Tchad (chȧd) The French name for CHAD.

Tchai·kov·sky (chī·kôf′skē), **Peter (Pëtr) Ilich,** 1840–93, Russian composer.

tchick (chik) *n.* A sound made by pressing the tongue against the roof of the mouth and sucking it back, as in urging a horse. — *v.i.* To make a *tchick.* [Imit.]

tea (tē) *n.* **1** An evergreen Asian shrub or small tree *(Thea sinensis),* having a compact head of leathery, toothed leaves and white or pink flowers. **2** The prepared leaves of this plant, or an infusion of them used as a beverage. The difference between **black tea** and **green tea** is the result of manipulation, the latter being withered by steaming, thus retaining the green color, while leaves simply dried turn black. **3** Any infusion, decoction, solution, or extract to be used as a beverage or medicinally: beef *tea.* **4** The leaves of a particular variety of plant, prepared for making a beverage, or for medicinal purposes: senna *tea.* **5** A light evening or afternoon meal; also, a social gathering at which tea is served. [<Chinese *ch'a,* dial. Chinese *t'e*]

Tea may appear as a combining form in hyphemes or solidemes, or as the first element in two-word phrases; as in:

tea-blending	**tea-making**
tea bowl	**tea merchant**
teabox	**tea-packer**
teacart	**tea-packing**
tea china	**tea plant**
tea-colored	**tea-planter**
tea crop	**tea-planting**
tea dealer	**tea-producer**
tea-drinker	**tea-producing**
tea-drinking	**tea table**
tea-farming	**tea-taster**
tea-grower	**tea-tasting**
tea-growing	**teatime**
tea jar	**tea trade**
tea leaf	**tea tray**
tea-loving	**tea tree**
tea-maker	**teaware**

tea bag A small porous sack of cloth or paper

containing tea leaves, which is immersed in water to make tea.

tea ball 1 A perforated metal ball, filled with tea leaves, to be dropped or suspended in boiling water to make tea. 2 A tea bag.

tea·ber·ry (tē′ber′ē) *n. pl.* **·ries** 1 The wintergreen, whose leaves are sometimes mixed with or used as tea. 2 The berry of this plant.

tea biscuit A biscuit or cracker, usually short and sweetened, served with tea.

tea caddy See CADDY[1] (def. 1).

teach (tēch) *v.* **taught, teach·ing** *v.t.* 1 To impart knowledge to by lessons; give instruction to; guide by precept or example; instruct: to *teach* a class. 2 To give instruction in; make known; communicate the knowledge of: to *teach* French. 3 To train by practice or exercise. — *v.i.* 4 To follow the profession of teaching. 5 To impart knowledge or skill. [OE *tǣcan, tǣcean*]

Synonyms: discipline, drill, educate, enlighten, indoctrinate, inform, initiate, instruct, nurture, school, train, tutor. To *teach* is to communicate knowledge; to *instruct* is to impart knowledge with special method and completeness; *instruct* has also an authoritative sense nearly equivalent to command. To *educate* is to draw out or develop the mental powers. To *train* is to direct to a certain result powers already existing. *Train* is used in preference to *educate* when the reference is to the inferior animals or to the physical powers of man; as, to *train* a horse; to *train* the hand or eye. To *discipline* is to bring into habitual and complete subjection to authority. To *nurture* is to furnish the care and sustenance necessary for physical, mental, and moral growth; *nurture* is a more tender word than *educate*. See INFORM[1], LEARN.

teach·a·ble (tē′chə·bəl) *adj.* 1 Capable of being taught; willing to learn; docile. 2 Capable of being imparted by teaching. See synonyms under DOCILE. — **teach′a·bil′i·ty, teach′a·ble·ness** *n.* — **teach′a·bly** *adv.*

teach·er (tē′chər) *n.* One who teaches; specifically, one whose occupation is to teach others. See synonyms under MASTER.

teacher bird 1 The ovenbird. 2 The North American red-eyed vireo. [Imit. of its cry]

teachers' institute See under INSTITUTE.

teach-in (tēch′in′) *n.* An extended meeting, as at a college or university, during which faculty and students participate in lectures, discussions, etc., on a controversial issue, often as a form of social protest.

teach·ing (tē′ching) *n.* 1 The profession of a teacher. 2 That which is taught. See synonyms under DOCTRINE, EDUCATION, NURTURE.

teaching machine Any of various manually-operated devices that present educational material in a series of steps designed to enable each student to learn at a rate commensurate with his ability.

tea cozy See COZY, *n.*

tea·cup (tē′kup′) *n.* 1 A small cup suitable for serving tea. 2 As much as a teacup will hold: also **tea′cup·ful′** (-fo͝ol′).

tea·house (tē′hous′) *n.* In the Orient, a public place serving tea and other light refreshments.

teak (tēk) *n.* 1 A large East Indian tree (*Tectona grandis*) of the vervain family, yielding a very hard, durable timber highly prized for shipbuilding. 2 The wood of this tree. [<Malayalam *tēkka*]

tea·ket·tle (tē′ket′l) *n.* A kettle with a spout, used for boiling water for culinary purposes.

teal (tēl) *n.* 1 Any of several small, short-necked river ducks (genera *Nettion* and *Querquedula*); especially, the common teal (*N. crecca*) of the Old World and the similar North American **green-winged teal** (*N. carolinense*) having grayish wing coverts and the head slightly crested. 2 A darkish, dull-blue color with a greenish cast. [ME *tele*]

team (tēm) *n.* 1 Two or more beasts of burden harnessed together: often including harness and vehicle; also, a single horse and vehicle. 2 A set of workers, or players competing in a game: a baseball *team.* 3 *Dial.* A flock; brood. 4 *Obs.* Race; lineage. — *v.t.* 1 To convey with a team. 2 To harness together in a team. — *v.i.* 3 To drive a team as a business. 4 To form a team; work as a team: to *team* up. — *adj.* Of or pertaining to a team. ◆ Homophone: *teem.* [OE *tēam* offspring, succession, row. Related to TEEM[1].] — **team′ing** *n.*

team boat A paddle-wheel ferryboat propelled by horse power.

team·mate (tēm′māt′) *n.* A fellow player on a team.

team play Cooperation.

team·ster (tēm′stər) *n.* 1 One who drives or owns a team. 2 One who drives a truck or other commercial vehicle.

team teaching *U. S.* A method of organizing instruction in schools so that students in a given course are taught by several teachers, each of whom sometimes teaches the whole group and sometimes a part of it.

team·work (tēm′wûrk′) *n.* 1 Work done by or requiring to be done by or with a team of horses: distinguished from manual labor. 2 Unity of action by the players on an athletic team to further the success of the team. 3 Cooperation.

tea party A social gathering at which tea and light sandwiches or cakes are the principal refreshments.

tea·pot (tē′pot′) *n.* A vessel with a spout and handle in which tea is made and from which it is served.

tea·poy (tē′poi) *n.* A small three- or four-legged table for holding a tea service. [<Hind. *tipāī* < *tīn* three + Persian *pāē* foot]

tear[1] (târ) *v.* **tore, torn, tear·ing** *v.t.* 1 To pull apart, as cloth; part or separate by pulling; rip; rend. 2 To make by rending or tearing: to *tear* a hole in a dress. 3 To injure or lacerate, as skin. 4 To divide; disrupt: a party *torn* by dissension. 5 To distress or torment; anguish: The sight *tore* his heart. — *v.i.* 6 To become torn or rent. 7 To move with haste and energy. See synonyms under REND. — *n.* 1 A fissure made by tearing; a rent; an act of tearing. 2 *Slang* A carouse; a spree; frolic. 3 A rushing motion: to start off with a *tear*; also, any violent outburst, as of anger, enthusiasm, etc. ◆ Homophone: *tare.* [OE *teran*]

tear[2] (tir) *n.* 1 A drop of the saline liquid secreted by the lacrimal gland, for moistening the eye. 2 Something resembling or suggesting a drop of the lacrimal fluid. 3 A drop of any liquid. 4 A droplike portion, as of glass, amber, etc. 5 *pl.* Sorrow; lamentation. ◆ Homophone: *tier.* [OE *tēar*] — **tear′less** *adj.* — **tear′y** *adj.*

Tear may appear as a combining form in hyphemes or solidemes, with the meaning of definition 1:

tear-baptized	**tear-marked**
tear-blinded	**tear-moistened**
tear-compelling	**tear-mourned**
tear-dimmed	**tear-provoking**
tear-filled	**tear-salt**
tear-freshened	**tear-shedding**
tear-glistening	**tear-stained**
tear-kissed	**tear-swollen**

tear·drop (tir′drop′) *n.* A tear.

tear·ful (tir′fəl) *adj.* 1 Weeping abundantly. 2 Causing tears. — **tear′ful·ly** *adv.* — **tear′·ful·ness** *n.*

tear gas (tir) A lacrimator.

tear·ing (târ′ing) *adj. Colloq.* 1 Rushing along as in a hurry or rage. 2 Tremendous; mighty.

tear-jerk·er (tir′jûr′kər) *n. U.S. Slang* A story, play, or motion picture charged with sentimental sadness.

tea·room (tē′ro͞om′, -ro͝om′) *n.* A restaurant serving tea and other refreshments.

tea rose 1 Any of numerous garden roses thought to be tea-scented, primarily hybrids bred from the Chinese *Rosa odorata.* 2 A yellowish-pink color of many hues.

tear-sheet (târ′shēt′) *n.* A page torn or cut from a magazine, book, or newspaper, containing matter of particular interest.

Teas·dale (tēz′dāl), **Sara**, 1884–1933, U. S. poet.

tease (tēz) *v.* **teased, teas·ing** *v.t.* 1 To annoy or harass with continual importunities, raillery, etc.; pester. 2 To scratch or dress in order to raise the nap, as cloth with teasels. 3 To tear or pull apart with instruments, as tissues in examination. 4 To comb or card, as wool or flax; also, to pick or shred, as hard-packed tobacco. 5 To comb (hair) in such a way as to form fluffy layers and give an effect of fullness. — *v.i.* 6 To annoy a person in a facetious or petty way. See synonyms under AFFRONT. — *n.* 1 One who or that which teases. 2 The act of teasing or the state of being teased. [OE *tǣsan* tease, pluck, pull about] — **teas′ing** *n.* & *adj.* — **teas′ing·ly** *adv.*

tea·sel (tē′zəl) *n.* 1 A coarse, prickly Old World herb (genus *Dipsacus*) of which the flower head is covered with hooked bracts, especially the **fuller's teasel** (*D. fullonum*). 2 The rough bur of this plant, or a mechanical substitute: used in dressing cloth. — *v.t.* **·seled** or **·selled, ·sel·ing** or **·sel·ling** To use a teasel on; raise the nap of with a teasel. Also **tea′zel, tea′zle.** [OE *tǣsel*] — **tea′sel·er** or **tea′sel·ler** *n.*

TEASEL (Plant to 5 feet or more)

teas·er (tē′zər) *n.* 1 One who or that which teases, as a machine used for teasing wool. 2 Anything tempting or whetting the appetites. 3 The border at the front of the stage. Compare BORDER.

tea service The articles used in serving tea: a silver *tea service.* Also **tea set.**

tea·shop (tē′shop′) *n.* 1 A tearoom. 2 *Brit.* A lunchroom.

tea·spoon (tē′spo͞on′, -spo͝on′) *n.* 1 A small spoon used for stirring tea, etc. 2 As much as a teaspoon will hold, 1/3 of a tablespoon, usually 1 1/3 fluid drams: also **tea′spoon·ful′** (-fo͝ol′).

teat (tēt) *n.* The protuberance on the breast or udder of most female mammals, through which the milk is drawn; a nipple; pap; dug. [<OF *tete* <Gmc.]

tea wagon A table on wheels for use in serving tea or refreshments.

Te·bet (tā·vāth′, tā′ves) A Hebrew month. Also **Te·beth′.** See CALENDAR (Hebrew).

Te·briz (tə·brēz′) See TABRIZ.

tech·ne·ti·um (tek·nē′shē·əm) *n.* The chemical element of atomic number 43 (symbol Tc), artificially produced by the bombardment of molybdenum with neutrons or deuterons: it displaces the hypothetical element *masurium.* [<NL <Gk. *technētos* artificial]

tech·nic (tek′nik) *n.* 1 Technique. 2 *pl.* The theory of an art or of the arts; specifically, the study of the techniques of an art. 3 *pl.* Technical rules, methods, etc. 4 *pl.* Technology. — *adj.* Technical.

tech·ni·cal (tek′ni·kəl) *adj.* 1 Pertaining to some particular art, science, or trade. 2 Peculiar to a specialized field of knowledge. 3 Of or pertaining to the mechanical arts. 4 Employing a specialized vocabulary, as in a treatise or textbook. 5 Considered in terms of an accepted body of rules and regulations: a *technical* defeat. 6 Designating a money market in which prices are for the most part determined by speculation or manipulation. [<Gk. *technikos* < *technē* art] — **tech′ni·cal·ly** *adv.* — **tech′ni·cal·ness** *n.*

tech·ni·cal·i·ty (tek′ni·kal′ə·tē) *n. pl.* **·ties** 1 The state of being technical. 2 The use of technical terms. 3 A technical point peculiar to some profession, art, trade, etc. 4 A petty distinction; quibble. Also **tech′nism.**

technical knockout In boxing, a victory awarded when one fighter has been beaten so severely that the referee discontinues the fight. Abbr. *t.k.o., T.K.O.,* or *TKO*

tech·ni·cian (tek·nish′ən) *n.* 1 One skilled in the handling of instruments or in the performance of tasks requiring specialized training. 2 A rating in the armed services including those qualified for technical work; also, one having such a rating.

Tech·ni·col·or (tek′ni·kul′ər) *n.* A process used in making color motion pictures: a trade name. Also **tech′ni·col·or.**

tech·nique (tek·nēk′) *n.* Working methods or manner of performance, as in art, science, etc. [<F <Gk. *technikos.* See TECHNICAL.]

techno- *combining form* 1 Art; skill; craft: *technology.* 2 Technical; technological. Also, before vowels, **techn-.** [<Gk. *technē* an art, skill]

tech·noc·ra·cy (tek·nok′rə·sē) *n. pl.* **·cies** 1 A

community governed by experts in applied and theoretical science; national government by organized technologists and engineers. 2 A non-political fact-finding body of experts in the various departments of applied and theoretical sciences, whose aim is to re-evaluate industrial output in terms of energy factors. —**tech′no·crat** (tek′nə·krat) *n.* —**tech′·no·crat′ic** *adj.*

tech·nog·ra·phy (tek·nog′rə·fē) *n.* 1 Description of the arts and crafts. 2 The scientific study of the development and geographic distribution of technical processes.

tech·nol·a·tor (tek·nol′ə·tər) *n.* One who has an excessive admiration for or belief in technology, especially in relation to social problems; immoderate worship of techniques, gadgets, machinery, and the like. [<TECHNO- + Gk. *latris* servant < *latron* pay, hire] —**tech·nol′a·try** *n.*

tech·no·lith·ic (tek′nə·lith′ik) *adj. Anthropol.* Pertaining to or designating those stone implements which were deliberately fashioned for some intended purpose.

tech·no·log·i·cal (tek′nə·loj′i·kəl) *adj.* Of, pertaining to, associated with, produced or affected by technology, especially in relation to improvements resulting from the application of technical advances in industry, manufacturing, commerce, and the arts. Also **tech′no·log′ic.** —**tech′no·log′i·cal·ly** *adv.*

tech·nol·o·gy (tek·nol′ə·jē) *n.* 1 Theoretical knowledge of industry and the industrial arts. 2 The application of science to the arts. 3 That branch of ethnology which treats of the development of the arts. —**tech·nol′o·gist** *n.*

tech·y (tech′ē) *adj.* **tech·i·er, tech·i·est** Peevishly sensitive; irritable; touchy. Also spelled *tetchy.* [<OF *teche* mark, quality] —**tech′i·ly** *adv.* —**tech′i·ness** *n.*

tec·tol·o·gy (tek·tol′ə·jē) *n.* The branch of morphology that treats of the manner in which organic forms are built up. [<Gk. *tektōn* carpenter, builder + -LOGY] —**tec·to·log·i·cal** (tek′tə·loj′i·kəl) *adj.*

tec·ton·ic (tek·ton′ik) *adj.* 1 Of or pertaining to building or construction. 2 *Geol.* **a** Characteristic of or relating to the structure of the earth's crust, especially as due to deformation. **b** Denoting the forces producing such structures. [<L *tectonicus* <Gk. *tektonikos* < *tektōn* carpenter]

tec·ton·ics (tek·ton′iks) *n. pl.* (*construed as singular*) 1 The science or art of constructing functionally beautiful buildings or things. 2 The geology of earth structure.

tec·tri·ces (tek·trī′sēz, tek′tri-) *n. pl. of* **tec·trix** (tek′triks) *Ornithol.* The wing coverts of a bird. [<NL <L *tectus,* pp. of *tegere* cover] —**tec·tri′cial** (-trish′əl) *adj.*

Te·cum·seh (ti·kum′sə), 1768?–1813, Shawnee chief, an ally of Britain in the War of 1812, during which he was killed.

ted (ted) *v.t.* **ted·ded, ted·ding** To turn over and strew about, or spread loosely for drying, as newly mown grass. [Prob. <Scand. Cf. ON *tethja* spread manure.]

Ted (ted), **Ted·dy** (ted′ē) Diminutives of EDWARD, THEODORE.

ted·der (ted′ər) *n.* 1 One who or that which teds. 2 *Agric.* A machine for spreading hay to dry.

ted·dy (ted′ē) *n. pl.* **·dies** A short undergarment combining chemise and drawers in one. [Origin unknown]

ted·dy bear (ted′ē) A toy bear, usually covered with plush. Also **Teddy bear.** [after *Teddy,* a nickname of Theodore Roosevelt]

Te De·um (tē dē′əm) 1 An ancient Christian hymn beginning with these words. 2 The music to which this hymn is set. 3 Any thanksgiving service in which it is sung. [<L *Te Deum (laudamus)* (we praise) Thee, O God]

te·di·ous (tē′dē·əs) *adj.* 1 Causing weariness; wearisome; boring. 2 *Obs.* Moving slowly. [<LL *taediosus* <L *taedium* tedium, weariness] —**te′di·ous·ly** *adv.* —**te′di·ous·ness** *n.*
Synonyms: dilatory, dreary, dull, fatiguing, irksome, monotonous, slow, sluggish, tardy, tiresome, wearisome. See WEARISOME. *Antonyms*: active, alert, animated, brilliant, energetic, exciting, lively, prompt, quick, stirring, vigorous, vivid.

te·di·um (tē′dē·əm) *n.* Tediousness; wearisomeness. [<L *taedium* < *taedere* vex, weary]

tee[1] (tē) *n.* 1 The letter T. 2 Something resembling the form of the letter T. 3 *Mining* The point of the meeting of two veins lying nearly at right angles to each other without intersecting. —*adj.* T-shaped. [OE *te* <L *te,* name of the letter T]

tee[2] (tē) *n.* 1 A little cone, as of damp sand or of wood, on which a golf ball is placed in making the first play to a hole. 2 The teeing ground in golf. —*v.t.* & *v.i.* **teed, tee·ing** To place (the ball) on a tee before striking it. —**to tee off** To strike (the ball) in starting play. [Prob. <TEE[3]]

tee[3] (tē) *n.* In certain games, a mark toward which the balls, quoits, etc., are directed, as in curling. —**to a tee** Exactly; as precisely as possible. [? <TEE[1]]

tee[4] (tē) *n.* A finial in the form of a conventionalized umbrella, used on pagodas, etc. [<Burmese *h'ti* umbrella]

teem[1] (tēm) *v.i.* 1 To be full, as if at the point of producing; be full to overflowing; abound. 2 *Obs.* To bear young. —*v.t.* 3 To produce or bring forth, as offspring: often figuratively. ◆ Homophone: *team.* [OE *tīeman,* prob. < *tēam* progeny. Related to TEAM.] —**teem′er** *n.*

teem[2] (tēm) *v.i.* To pour; come down heavily: said of rain. —*v.t. Obs.* To pour out; empty. ◆ Homophone: *team.* [<ON *tœma* empty]

teem·ing[1] (tē′ming) *adj.* 1 Prolific. 2 Full; overflowing. 3 Produced in great quantity. See synonyms under FERTILE.

teem·ing[2] (tē′ming) *adj.* Raining heavily.

teen[1] (tēn) *n. Scot.* & *Brit. Dial.* Grief; trouble; also, provocation; vexation; anger. [OE *tēona* injury, vexation] —**teen′ful** *adj.*

teen[2] (tēn) *adj.* Teen-age.

-teen *suffix* Plus ten: used in cardinal numbers from 13 to 19 inclusive: *fifteen.* [OE *-tēne* < *tēn* ten]

teen age The age from 13 to 19 inclusive; hence, adolescence. —**teen′-age** *adj.*

teen-ag·er (tēn′ā′jər) *n.* A person of teen age.

teens (tēnz) *n. pl.* The numbers that end in *-teen*; the years of one's age from 13 to 19 inclusive.

tee·ny (tē′nē) *adj.* **·ni·er, ·ni·est** *Colloq.* Tiny. [Var. of TINY]

teen·y·bop·per (tē′nē·bop′ər) *n. Slang* A modern, hip teen-ager, especially a girl. [<Negro slang *teenybop, teenybopper* a troublesome or tough teen-ager <TEEN(-AGE) + -Y[3] + *bop* fight (Cf. BOP[1]) + -ER[1]]

tee·pee (tē′pē) See TEPEE.

tee shirt (tē) See T-SHIRT.

Tees River (tēz) A river in northern England, flowing 70 miles east from eastern Cumberland, between Durham and York, to the North Sea.

tee·ter (tē′tər) *v.i.* 1 To see-saw. 2 To walk or move with a swaying or tottering motion. 3 To vacillate; waver. —*v.t.* 4 To cause to teeter. —*n.* 1 An oscillating motion. 2 A see-saw. 3 The spotted sandpiper: so called from its jerky motions. [<dial. E *titter,* prob. <ON *titra* tremble, shiver]

teeter board A see-saw.

tee·ter-tot·ter (tē′tər·tot′ər) *n.* A see-saw. [<TEETER + TOTTER]

teeth (tēth) Plural of TOOTH.

teethe (tēth) *v.i.* **teethed, teeth·ing** To cut or develop teeth.

teeth·ing (tē′thing) *n.* The process of developing and cutting teeth; dentition.

teething ring A ring of hard rubber, bone, or ivory for a teething baby to bite on.

tee·to·tal (tē·tōt′l) *adj.* 1 Pertaining to total abstinence from intoxicants. 2 Total; entire. [<TOTAL, with emphatic repetition of initial letter] —**tee·to′tal·ism** *n.* —**tee·to′tal·ly** *adv.*

tee·to·tal·er (tē·tōt′l·ər) *n.* One who abstains totally from intoxicants as beverages. Also **tee·to′tal·ist, tee·to′tal·ler.**

tee·to·tum (tē·tō′təm) *n.* 1 A kind of top having lettered and numbered sides: used in the game of put and take. 2 A child's toy, often four-sided, pierced by a peg and spun by the fingers. Also spelled *tetotum*: sometimes called *toddle-top.* [<*T-totum* <*T* + L *totus* all; from the fact that the side marked with a T wins the entire stake]

Tef·lon (tef′lon) *n.* A chemically resistant, heat-stable plastic polymer of fluorine and ethylene having wide application in industry and electronics: a trade name.

teg·men (teg′mən) *n. pl.* **·mi·na** (-mə·nə) 1 A covering or coat. 2 *Bot.* The soft inner covering of a seed. Also **teg′u·men** (-yə·min). [<L < *tegere* cover] —**teg′mi·nal** *adj.*

Teg·nér (teng·nâr′), **Esaias,** 1782–1846, Swedish poet: also **Teng′ner.**

Te·gu·ci·gal·pa (tā·gōō′sē·gäl′pä) The capital of Honduras, in the SW part of the country.

teg·u·la (teg′yə·lə) *n. pl.* **·lae** (-lē) A tile. [<L *tegula* roof tile < *tegere* cover]

teg·u·lar (teg′yə·lər) *adj.* 1 Pertaining to or resembling tiles. 2 Arranged like tiles. 3 Formed of overlapping plates or scales. Also **teg′u·lat′ed.** —**teg′u·lar·ly** *adv.*

teg·u·ment (teg′yə·mənt) *n.* A covering or envelope; an integument. [<L *tegumentum* < *tegere* cover] —**teg·u·men·ta·ry** (teg′yə·men′tər·ē), **teg′u·men′tal** *adj.*

te-hee (tē·hē′) *v.i.* **-heed, -hee·ing** To laugh frivolously or with derision; titter; giggle. —*interj.* An imitative exclamation. —*n.* A restrained laugh; titter. [Imit.]

Te·he·ran (te′ə·rän′, -ran′; *Persian* te·hrän′) The capital of Iran, in the north central part; Roosevelt, Churchill, and Stalin conferred here in November, 1943. Also **Te·hran′.**

Teh·ri (tā′rē) A district of northern Uttar Pradesh State, India; 4,516 square miles; before 1949 a princely state; capital, Tehri. Also **Teh′ri-Garh·wal′** (-gûr·wäl′).

Te·huan·te·pec (te·wän′te·pek′), **Isthmus of** The narrowest part of southern Mexico (125 miles wide) between the **Gulf of Tehuantepec,** an arm of the Pacific Ocean, about 300 miles long, NW to SE, on the coast of southern Mexico, and the Gulf of Campeche.

Te·huan·te·pec Winds (te·wän′te·pek′) *n. pl.* Violent NE winds striking the Gulf of Tehuantepec in winter and early spring.

Te·huel·che (te·wel′che) *n.* One of a group of tribes of South American Indians inhabiting Patagonia, noted for their great height. —**Te·huel′che·an** (-chē·ən) *adj.*

te ig·i·tur (tē ij′ə·tər) The prayer or paragraph beginning the canon of the mass in Latin liturgies. [<L, thee therefore]

teil (tēl) *n.* 1 The linden. 2 The terebinth pistache (*Pistacia terebinthus*) of the Bible. Also called *teyl tree.* [<OF <L *tilia* lime tree]

teind (tēnd) *n. Scot.* A tithe or tithes.

Te·jo (tā′zhōō) The Portuguese name for the TAGUS.

Te·ju·co (tə·zhōō′kōō) A former name for Diamantina, Brazil.

tek·non·y·my (tek·non′ə·mē) *n. Anthropol.* The custom of renaming a parent after his or her child. [<Gk. *teknon* child + *onyma, onoma* name]

tek·tite (tek′tīt) *n. Geol.* One of several kinds of rounded, glasslike objects, variously named and of unknown origin, found in widely scattered parts of the world and believed by some to be fragments of a shattered planet. [<Gk. *tēktos* molten + -ITE[1]]

tel- Var. of TELO-[1].

te·la (tē′lə) *n. pl.* **·lae** (-lē) 1 A tissue or weblike membrane. 2 *Anat.* One of the thin membranes (**tela choroidea**), prolongations of the pia mater, that cover the third and fourth ventricles of the brain. [<L, web]

tel·aes·the·sia (tel′əs·thē′zhə, -zhē·ə) See TELESTHESIA.

tel·a·mon (tel′ə·mon) *n. pl.* **tel·a·mo·nes** (tel′ə·mō′nēz) *Archit.* A male figure used as a pillar to support an entablature, etc. Compare ATLANTES, CARYATID. [<L <Gk. *telamōn* < *tlēnai* bear]

TELAMON

Tel·a·mon (tel′ə·mon) In Greek legend, the father of Ajax.

tel·an·gi·ec·ta·sia (tel·an′ jē·ek·tā′zhə, -zhē·ə) *n. Pathol.* Permanent dilatation of the small arteries or capillaries, producing a vascular tumor: often seen in the form of maternal birthmarks; wine spots. Also **tel·an·gi·ec·ta·sis** (tel′ən·jē·ek′tə·sis). [<NL <Gk. *telos* end + *angeion* vessel + *ekstasis* dilatation] —**tel·an′gi·ec·tat′ic** (-tat′ik) *adj.*

tel·au·to·gram (tel·ô′tə·gram) *n.* A record made by a telautograph.
tel·au·to·graph (tel·ô′tə·graf, -gräf) *n.* An electromagnetically operated device for reproducing writing or drawings at a distance.
Tel A·viv (tel′ ə·vēv′) The largest city of Israel, on the Mediterranean: since 1950 includes Jaffa.
tel·e (tel′ē) *n. Psychoanal.* The development between two or more persons of a relationship based on the gradual recognition of mutual attractions or repulsions either within or between social groups. [<Gk. *tēle* far off]
tele- *combining form* **1** Far off; operating at a distance: *telegraph.* **2** Television; related to or transmitted by television: *telecast.* Also spelled *telo-*. Also, before vowels, **tel-**. [<Gk. *tēle* far]
tel·e·car·di·o·gram (tel′ə·kär′dē·ə·gram′) *n.* A cardiogram electrically produced at a distance from the subject.
tel·e·cast (tel′ə·kast, -käst) *v.t.* & *v.i.* **·cast** or **·cast·ed, ·cast·ing** To broadcast by television. — *n.* A program broadcast by television.
tel·e·com·mu·ni·ca·tion (tel′ə·kə·myōō′nə·kā′·shən) *n.* **1** The art and science of communicating at a distance, especially by means of electromagnetic impulses, with or without wires, as in radio, radar, television, telegraphy, telephony, etc. Also **tel′e·com·mu′ni·ca′·tions.** **2** Any message so transmitted.
tel·e·du (tel′ə·dōō) *n.* A small, short-tailed East Indian mammal (genus *Mydaus*) which resembles the skunk in color and in its ability to emit a fetid odor when disturbed. [<Malay]
tel·e·fi·nal·ist (tel′ə·fī′nəl·ist) *n.* One who believes in final causes or the working out of a final purpose in life or the universe; a teleologist, especially one who seeks scientific proof of the existence of God.
te·le·ga (te·le′gä) *n. Russian* A rude four-wheeled wagon without springs, used in Russia.
tel·e·gen·ic (tel′ə·jen′ik) *adj.* Videogenic.
tel·eg·no·sis (tel′əg·nō′sis) *n.* Knowledge of remote happenings by other than normal sensory means, as by clairvoyance. [<TELE- + Gk. *gnōsis* knowing]
Te·leg·o·nus (tə·leg′ə·nəs) In Greek legend, the son of Odysseus and Circe, who unknowingly killed his father in Ithaca and married Penelope, his father's wife.
te·leg·o·ny (tə·leg′ə·nē) *n. Biol.* The alleged influence of a previous sire on the progeny of the same mother from subsequent matings with other males. [<TELE- + -GONY] — **tel·e·gon·ic** (tel′ə·gon′ik), **te·leg′o·nous** *adj.*
tel·e·gram (tel′ə·gram) *n.* A message sent by telegraph. [<TELE- + -GRAM]
tel·e·graph (tel′ə·graf, -gräf) *n.* Any of various devices, systems, or processes for transmitting messages or signals to a distance, especially any form of such apparatus utilizing electromagnetic impulses transmitted by conducting wires between sending and receiving points. — *v.t.* **1** To send (a message) by telegraph. **2** To communicate with by telegraph. — *v.i.* **3** To transmit a message by telegraph. [<TELE- + -GRAPH]
te·leg·ra·pher (tə·leg′rə·fər) *n.* One who is employed in sending telegrams or is skilled in telegraphy. Also **te·leg′ra·phist.**
tel·e·graph·ic (tel′ə·graf′ik) *adj.* Of or pertaining to the telegraph; transmitted by means of telegraphy. Also **tel′e·graph′i·cal.** — **tel′e·graph′i·cal·ly** *adv.*
te·leg·ra·phone (tə·leg′rə·fōn) *n.* An instrument for recording and reproducing sound, similar in principle to the tape recorder but adapted for connection with a transmitter or microphone. [<TELE- + -GRA(PH) + - PHONE]
tel·e·graph·o·scope (tel′ə·graf′ə·skōp) *n.* An instrument for transmitting and reproducing a picture telegraphically. [<TELE- + GRAPHO- + -SCOPE]
te·leg·ra·phy (tə·leg′rə·fē) *n.* **1** The process of conveying messages by telegraph. **2** The art or science of the construction and operation of telegraphs.
Tel·e·gu (tel′ə·gōō) See TELUGU.
tel·e·ki·ne·sis (tel′ə·ki·nē′sis) *n.* **1** Movement of an object or inanimate body without apparent external cause. **2** The alleged power of a spiritualist medium to bring about such movements without direct or observable contact. — **tel′e·ki·net′ic** (-net′ik) *adj.*
tel·e·lec·tric (tel′i·lek′trik) *adj.* Denoting the transmission, as of music, to a distance by electricity. [<TEL(E)- + ELECTRIC]
Te·lem·a·chus (tə·lem′ə·kəs) In Greek legend, son of Odysseus and Penelope, who helped his father kill his mother's suitors.
tel·e·mark (tel′ə·märk) *n.* In skiing, a turn effected by shifting the weight to one advanced ski and turning its tip inward: used to change direction or stop quickly. [from *Telemark,* Norway]
tel·e·me·chan·ics (tel′ə·mə·kan′iks) *n.* **1** The theory and practice of operating mechanisms from a distance. **2** Remote control operation, as by electromagnetic and radio impulses.
te·lem·e·ter (tə·lem′ə·tər, tel′ə·mē′tər) *n.* **1** An apparatus for determining distances by the measurement of angles. **2** An electrical apparatus for indicating or measuring various quantities and for transmitting the data to a distant point. — **te·lem′e·try** *n.* — **tel·e·met·ric** (tel′e·met′rik) *adj.*
tel·e·mo·tor (tel′ə·mō′tər) *n.* A hydraulic or electrical device by which power is applied at a distance, especially in operating the steering gear of a vessel by turning the wheel on the bridge.
tel·en·ceph·a·lon (tel′en·sef′ə·lon) *n. Anat.* The terminal division of the neural tube of the embryo from which are developed the cerebral hemispheres and olfactory lobes; the endbrain. [<TEL(E)- + ENCEPHALON] — **tel·en·ce·phal·ic** (tel′en·si·fal′ik) *adj.*
teleo- Var. of TELO-¹.
tel·e·ol·o·gy (tel′ē·ol′ə·jē, tē′lē-) *n.* **1** The branch of cosmology that treats of final causes. See FINAL CAUSE. **2** The philosophical and biological doctrine of design which holds that the phenomena of organic life and development can be explained by conscious or purposive causes directed to definite ends and not by mechanical causes; vitalism as opposed to *mechanism.* **3** The explanation of nature in terms of utility or purpose, especially divine purpose; the study of a creative design in the processes of nature. [<NL *teleologia* <Gk. *telos, teleos* end + *logos* discourse] — **tel′e·o·log′i·cal** (-ə·loj′i·kəl) or **tel′e·o·log′ic** *adj.* — **tel′e·o·log′i·cal·ly** *adv.* — **tel′e·ol′o·gist** *n.*
tel·e·ost (tel′ē·ost, tē′lē-) *n.* Any of a large and widely distributed group or order (*Teleostei*) of fishes having true bones: distinguished from cyclostomes and elasmobranchs. — *adj.* Of, pertaining to, or having the characteristics of the teleosts. Also **tel′e·os′te·an.** [<Gk. *telos* end + *osteon* bone]
te·lep·a·thy (tə·lep′ə·thē) *n.* The supposed communication of one mind with another at a distance by other than normal sensory means; thought-transference. [<TELE- + -PATHY] — **tel·e·path·ic** (tel′ə·path′ik) *adj.* — **tel′e·path′i·cal·ly** *adv.* — **te·lep′a·thist** *n.*
tel·e·phone (tel′ə·fōn) *n.* An instrument for reproducing sound or speech at a distant point, by the electromagnetic transmission of variable audio frequencies over a conducting wire or other communication channel. — **wireless telephone** A radiotelephone. — *v.* **·phoned, ·phon·ing** — *v.t.* **1** To send by telephone, as a message. **2** To communicate with by telephone. — *v.i.* **3** To communicate by telephone. [<TELE- + -PHONE] — **tel′e·phon′er** *n.*
telephone receiver That part of a telephone in which a diaphragm is caused to vibrate by electric impulses, converting the varying current into sound.
tel·e·phon·ic (tel′ə·fon′ik) *adj.* **1** Of or pertaining to the telephone. **2** Conveying sound to a great distance. Also **tel′e·phon′i·cal.** — **tel′e·phon′i·cal·ly** *adv.*
tel·e·pho·no·graph (tel′ə·fō′nə·graf, -gräf) *n.* A combination of a phonograph and a telephone receiver by which telephone messages can be recorded and then reproduced. — **tel′·e·pho′no·graph′ic** *adj.*
te·leph·o·ny (tə·lef′ə·nē) *n.* The art or process of communicating by telephone, with or without wires directly connecting the terminal points.
tel·e·pho·to (tel′ə·fō′tō) *adj.* **1** Denoting a combination of lenses which produces a large image of a distant object in a camera; telephotographic. **2** Pertaining to telephotography.
tel·e·pho·to·graph (tel′ə·fō′tə·graf, -gräf) *n.* **1** A picture transmitted by wire or radio. **2** A picture made with a telephoto lens. — **tel′e·pho′to·graph′ic** *adj.*
tel·e·pho·tog·ra·phy (tel′ə·fə·tog′rə·fē) *n.* **1** The art of producing photographic images of distant objects on a larger scale than is possible with an ordinary camera. **2** The reproduction of photographs or other picture material by radio or wire communication.
tel·e·plasm (tel′ə·plaz′əm) *n.* Ectoplasm (def. 2). [<TELE- + -PLASM]
tel·e·print·er (tel′ə·prin′tər) *n.* A teletypewriter.
Tel·e·prompt·er (tel′ə·promp′tər) *n.* A prompting device for television whereby a prepared script, unseen by the audience, is shown to a speaker or performer, enlarged line by line: a trade name.
tel·e·ra·di·o (tel′ə·rā′dē·ō) *n. pl.* **·di·os** Television and radio taken collectively, especially with reference to their use as advertising media. — *adj.* Pertaining to or by means of teleradio. [<TELE- (def. 2) + RADIO]
tel·e·ran (tel′ə·ran) *n. Telecom.* A system of air navigation which combines the principles of television and radar, the information being gathered by ground stations and transmitted to all aircraft within range. [<TELE- (def. 2) + R(ADAR) A(IR) N(AVIGATION)]

REFRACTING TELESCOPE
Yerkes Observatory
40 inch.

tel·e·scope (tel′ə·skōp) *n.* **1** An optical instrument for enlarging the image of a distant object, consisting of an object glass for collecting light beams from the object and an eyepiece for viewing the image. The **refracting telescope** transmits the rays to a focus through a combination of lenses called the object glass; the **reflecting telescope** brings them to a focus by reflection from a concave mirror. **2** A valise or traveling bag that shuts with one section inside the other, and thus can be extended, like a telescope. — *v.* **·scoped, ·scop·ing** *v.t.* **1** To drive or slide together so that one part fits into another in the manner of the sections of a small telescope. **2** To crush by driving something into or upon. **3** To represent in a compressed or shortened form, as a period of time. — *v.i.* **4** To crash or be forced into one another, as railroad cars in a collision. [<TELE- + -SCOPE]
telescope word A blend (def. 2).
tel·e·scop·ic (tel′ə·skop′ik) *adj.* **1** Pertaining to the telescope. **2** Visible only through a telescope. **3** Far-seeing. **4** Having sections that slide within or over one another. Also **tel′e·scop′i·cal.** — **tel′e·scop′i·cal·ly** *adv.*
tel·e·scop·tics (tel′ə·skop′tiks) *n. pl.* (*construed as singular*) The art of designing, constructing, and using telescopes.
te·les·co·py (tə·les′kə·pē) *n.* The art of using or making telescopes. — **te·les′co·pist** *n.*
tel·e·script (tel′ə·skript) *n.* A script written or adapted for a television program. [<TELE- (def. 2) + SCRIPT]
tel·e·set (tel′ə·set) *n.* A television receiving set.
tel·e·sis (tel′ə·sis) *n. Sociol.* Satisfactory progress toward an intended purpose, especially as the result of skilled direction of forces and intelligent planning. [<NL <Gk. *telein* fulfil < *telos, teleos* end]
tel·e·spec·tro·scope (tel′ə·spek′trə·skōp) *n.* **1** A combined telescope and spectroscope. **2** A spectroscope for attachment to a telescope.
tel·e·ster·e·o·scope (tel′ə·ster′ē·ə·skōp′, -stir′-) *n.* An optical instrument that presents images of objects at a distance from the observer in enhanced relief.

tel·es·the·sia (tel′is·thē′zhə, -zhē·ə) *n.* Susceptibility to stimuli coming from a distance and beyond the normal range of the senses: also spelled *telaesthesia.* [<NL <Gk. *tēle* far + *aisthēsis* feeling] **—tel′es·thet′ic** (-thet′ik) *adj.*

tel·e·stich (tel′ə·stik, tə·les′tik) *n.* An acrostic in which the significant letters are at the ends of the lines. [<Gk. *telos* end + *stichos* line]

tel·e·ther·a·py (tel′ə·ther′ə·pē) *n. Med.* **1** Treatment by radiation administered in massive doses at a distance from the body. **2** The prescribing of medical treatment by telephone, letter, etc.: also called **absent treatment.**

tel·e·ther·mom·e·ter (tel′ə·thûr·mom′ə·tər) *n.* Any apparatus used to indicate the temperature of a distant point, as a thermocouple. **—tel′e·ther·mom′e·try** *n.*

tel·e·thon (tel′ə·thon) *n.* A long telecast, usually to raise funds for a charity. [<TELE- + (MARA)THON]

tel·e·tran·scrip·tion (tel′ə·tran·skrip′shən) *n.* A method for transcribing television programs on films for subsequent presentation; also, the transcription itself.

tel·e·type (tel′ə·tīp) *v.t. & v.i.* **·typed, ·typ·ing** To communicate (with) by teletypewriter or Teletype. **—***n.* A teletypewriter. **—tel′e·typ′er** *n.*

Tel·e·type (tel′ə·tīp) *n.* A teletypewriter: a trade name.

tel·e·type·writ·er (tel′ə·tīp′rī′tər) *n.* A telegraphic instrument resembling a typewriter, by which the work done on one machine is simultaneously typed on electrically connected typewriters a distance away.

te·leu·to·spore (tə·lo͞o′tə·spôr, -spōr) *n. Bot.* The one- or two-celled, usually stalked, thick-walled spore produced as the final stage in the growth of rust fungi. [<Gk. *teleutē* fulfilment + SPORE] **—te·leu′to·spor′ic** (-spôr′ik, -spor′ik) *adj.*

tel·e·view (tel′ə·vyo͞o) *v.t. & v.i.* To observe by means of television. **—tel′e·view′er** *n.*

tel·e·vise (tel′ə·vīz) *v.t. & v.i.* **·vised, ·vis·ing** To transmit or receive by television.

tel·e·vi·sion (tel′ə·vizh′ən) *n.* The exact and continuous transmission of visual images, still or in motion but without permanent recording, for instantaneous viewing at a distance: effected by a combined optical and electrical system for converting light waves into corresponding electrical impulses which are reconverted into their visual form in a receiving set. **—tel′e·vi′sion·al, tel′e·vi′sion·ar′y** (-vizh′ən·er′ē) *adj.*

tel·ex (tel′iks) *n.* **1** A communication system using teletypewriters connected by wire through exchanges which operate automatically. **2** A message sent by such a system. **—***v.t.* To send by telex. [<TEL(ETYPEWRITER) + EX(CHANGE)]

tel·fer (tel′fər) See TELPHER.

tel·ford (tel′fərd) *adj.* Designating a road made of large broken stone packed with smaller pieces, covered with a layer of finely broken stone or gravel, and rolled hard and smooth. **—***n.* A road having such a surface. [after Thomas *Telford,* 1757–1834, Scottish engineer]

tel·ford·ize (tel′fər·dīz) *v.t.* **·ized, ·iz·ing** To make or cover (a road) with a telford surface.

tel·har·mo·ni·um (tel′här·mō′nē·əm) *n.* An instrument by which an operator at a central station playing on a keyboard controlling alternating electric currents is able to produce music at a distance. [<TEL(E)- + HARMONIUM] **—tel′har·mon′ic** (-mon′ik) *adj.* **—tel·har′mo·ny** (-här′mə·nē) *n.*

tel·ic (tel′ik, tē′lik) *adj.* Connected with, tending toward, or denoting a purpose; teleological. [<Gk. *telikos* < *telos* end] **—tel′i·cal·ly** *adv.*

te·li·o·stage (tē′lē·ə·stāj′, tel′ē-) *n. Bot.* The last stage in the life cycle of rust fungi. [<TELIUM + STAGE]

te·li·um (tē′lē·əm, tel′ē-) *n. Bot.* The sorus of the teliostage of the rust fungi. [<NL <Gk. *telos, teleos* end] **—te′li·al** *adj.*

tell (tel) *v.* **told, tell·ing** *v.t.* **1** To relate in detail; narrate, as a story. **2** To make known by speech or writing; communicate. **3** To make known; reveal; disclose: to *tell* secrets. **4** To decide; ascertain: I cannot *tell* who is to blame. **5** To utter; express in words: to *tell* a lie. **6** To give a command to; bid; order: I *told* him to go home. **7** To let know; inform. **8** *Colloq.* To inform or assure emphatically: It's cold out, I *tell* you! **9** To count; enumerate: to *tell* one's beads. **—***v.i.* **10** To give an account or description: usually with *of.* **11** To disclose something; inform: with *on.* **12** To serve as indication or evidence: with *of:* Their rags *told* of their poverty. **13** To produce a marked effect: Every blow *told.* See synonyms under AFFIRM, ASSERT, INFORM[1], PUBLISH, RELATE, SPEAK. **—all told** Everyone or everything being counted; in all. **—to tell off 1** To count and set apart. **2** *Colloq.* To reprimand severely. **—***n. Dial.* **1** Something told; story; say. **2** Account; story; explanation: according to his *tell.* [OE *tellan.* Akin to TALE, TALK.] **—tell′a·ble** *adj.*

Tell (tel), **William** A legendary Swiss hero in the struggle for independence from Austria. He refused to salute the governor's cap, which had been set up as a symbol of Austrian authority, and was forced to shoot an apple off his son's head with bow and arrow.

Tell el A·mar·na (tel el ə·mär′nə) Site of the ruins of an ancient city on the east bank of the Nile, Upper Egypt; Ikhnaton's capital, built about 1360 B.C.

tell·er (tel′ər) *n.* **1** One who relates or informs. **2** A person who receives or pays out money, as in a bank. **3** A person appointed to collect and count ballots in a legislative body or other assembly.

Tel·ler (tel′ər), **Edward,** born 1908, U.S. atomic physicist born in Hungary.

tell·ing (tel′ing) *adj.* Producing a great effect; impressive; effective; striking. See synonyms under VIVID. **—tell′ing·ly** *adv.*

tell·tale (tel′tāl′) *adj.* **1** Tattling; talebearing. **2** Betraying. **—***n.* **1** One who improperly gives information concerning the private affairs of others; a tattler. **2** That which conveys information, especially in an involuntary way; a token. **3** An instrument or device, usually automatic, for giving information as to number, position, condition, etc. **4** A row of dangling straps or ropes suspended above a railway track to warn anyone standing on a car roof of the approach of a low overhead structure. **5** A clock to record the times of coming and going, as of workmen, or as a watchman's clock. **6** An index showing the position of a vessel's helm. **7** A yellowlegs or tattler.

telltale sandpiper The yellowlegs.

tel·lu·rate (tel′yə·rāt) *n. Chem.* A salt of telluric acid.

tel·lu·ri·an (te·lo͝or′ē·ən, tel·yo͝or′-) *adj.* Of or pertaining to the earth or its inhabitants. **—***n.* An inhabitant of the earth. [<L *tellus, -uris* the earth]

tel·lu·ric (te·lo͝or′ik, tel·yo͝or′-) *adj.* **1** Of or pertaining to the earth; terrestrial; earthly. **2** *Chem.* Derived from or containing tellurium, especially in its higher valence.

telluric acid *Chem.* A weak acid, H_6TeO_4, obtained by oxidizing tellurium. It is analogous to sulfuric acid.

tel·lu·ride (tel′yə·rīd, -rid) *n. Chem.* A compound of tellurium with an element or an organic radical: *telluride* of lead.

tel·lu·rite (tel′yə·rīt) *n.* **1** A white or yellow native tellurium dioxide, TeO_2. **2** *Chem.* A salt of tellurous acid.

tel·lu·ri·um (te·lo͝or′ē·əm, tel·yo͝or′-) *n.* A rare non-metallic element (symbol Te) resembling sulfur and selenium, occasionally found native as tin-white, rhombohedral crystals, but usually combined with metals, as telluride of gold. See ELEMENT. [<NL <L *tellus, -uris* the earth]

tel·lu·rize (tel′yə·rīz) *v.t.* **·rized, ·riz·ing** To cause to combine with tellurium.

tel·lur·nick·el (tel′ər·nik′əl) *n.* Melonite. [< TELLUR(IUM) + NICKEL]

tel·lu·rous (tel′yər·əs, te·lo͝or′əs, tel·yo͝or′-) *adj. Chem.* Of, pertaining to, or derived from tellurium, especially in its lower valence: *tellurous* acid, H_2TeO_3.

Tel·lus (tel′əs) In Roman mythology, the goddess of the earth: identified with the Greek *Gaea.* Also **Tellus Mater.**

tel·ly (tel′ē) *n. pl.* **tel·lies** *Chiefly Brit. Colloq.* Television.

telo-[1] *combining form* Final; complete; perfect: *telophase:* also, before vowels, *tel-.* Also *teleo-.* [<Gk. *telos* end]

telo-[2] Var. of TELE-.

tel·o·blast (tel′ə·blast) *n. Zool.* A large cell at the growing end of the embryo, in annelids, etc., which produces rows of smaller cells. [<TELO-[1] + -BLAST]

tel·o·dy·nam·ic (tel′ə·dī·nam′ik, -di-) *adj.* Of, related to, or employed in the transmission of power to a distance, specifically by cables and pulleys. [<TELO-[2] + DYNAMIC]

tel·o·lec·i·thal (tel′ə·les′ə·thəl) *adj. Biol.* Having the nutritive part of the yolk at one pole: said of ova, as of birds, with unequal or partial segmentation. [<TELO-[1] + LECITHAL]

tel·o·phase (tel′ə·fāz) *n. Biol.* The closing phase of mitosis, when the cell divides and the daughter nuclei are formed. [<TELO-[1] + PHASE]

tel·pher (tel′fər) *n.* A light car suspended from cables and usually propelled by electricity: used for aerial transportation. **—***v.t.* To transport by telpher. Also spelled *telfer.* [<TEL(E)- + Gk. *pherein* bear] **—tel′pher·ic** *adj.* **—tel′pher·age** (-ij) *n.*

tel·son (tel′sən) *n. Zool.* The last abdominal segment of the body of an arthropod, as of a lobster, shrimp, or scorpion. [<Gk. *telson* boundary]

Tel·star (tel′stär′) One of several U.S. communication satellites, the first of which was launched July 10, 1962.

Tel·u·gu (tel′o͞o·go͞o) *n. pl.* **·gu** **1** A Dravidian language, spoken by more than 30 million people, most important in literary culture. **2** One of a Dravidian people of Telugu speech, inhabiting NW Andhra Pradesh, India. **—***adj.* Of or pertaining to the Telugu or to Telugu. Also spelled *Telegu.*

tem·blor (tem·blôr′) *n. pl.* **·blors** or **·blo·res** (-blô′rās) An earthquake. [<Sp.]

Tem·bu·land (tem′bo͞o·land) A district of eastern Cape of Good Hope Province, Republic of South Africa; 3,448 square miles; capital, Umtata.

tem·e·rar·i·ous (tem′ə·râr′ē·əs) *adj.* Unreasonably adventurous; rash; reckless. [<L *temerarius* < *temere* rashly] **—tem′e·rar′i·ous·ly** *adv.* **—tem′e·rar′i·ous·ness** *n.*

te·mer·i·ty (tə·mer′ə·tē) *n.* Venturesome or foolish boldness; rashness; disregard of personal danger or consequences. [<L *temeritas, -tatis* < *temere* rashly]

Synonyms: audacity, foolhardiness, hardihood, hastiness, heedlessness, precipitancy, precipitation, presumption, rashness, recklessness, venturesomeness. *Rashness* applies to the actual impulsive rushing into danger without counting the cost; *temerity* denotes the needless exposure of oneself to peril because of lack of foresight. *Rashness* is used chiefly of bodily acts, *temerity* often of mental or social matters. We say it is amazing that one should have had the *temerity* to make a statement which could be readily proved a falsehood; in such use *temerity* is often closely allied to *hardihood, audacity,* or *presumption. Venturesomeness* dallies on the edge of danger and experiments with it; *foolhardiness* rushes in for want of sense, *heedlessness* for want of attention, *rashness* for want of reflection, *recklessness* from disregard of consequences. *Antonyms:* care, caution, circumspection, cowardice, hesitation, timidity, wariness.

Tem·es·vár (te′mesh·vär) The Hungarian name for TIMISOARA.

Tem·pe (tem′pē), **Vale of** A valley, about 5 miles long, between Mount Olympus and Mount Ossa in Thessaly, Greece: famous for its beauty and in ancient times regarded as sacred to Apollo. *Greek* **Tem·be** (tem′bē).

Tem·pel·hof (tem′pəl·hof, *Ger.* tem′pəl·hōf) A southern district of West Berlin, Germany; site of the city's chief airport.

tem·per (tem′pər) *n.* **1** Heat of mind or passion; disposition to become angry; also, a fit of anger. **2** Quality of mind with reference to the passions, emotions, or affections; disposition. **3** Composure of mind; equanimity; self-command; calmness: used only in the phrases **to keep, or to lose, one's temper. 4** *Metall.* The condition of a metal as regards hardness and brittleness, especially when due to heating and sudden cooling. **5** Consistency due to mixture, as of mortar, etc. **6** Lime or an equivalent used in clarifying sugar. **7** An alloy, as that added to tin to make pewter. **8** *Obs.* Constitutional condition, resulting, according to the ancients, from the proportion in which the four humors were mixed. **9** *Archaic* A mean; medium. [<*v.*] — *v.t.* **1** To bring to a state of moderation or suitability, as by addition of another quality; free from excess; moderate; mitigate: to *temper* justice with mercy. **2** To bring to the proper consistency, texture, etc., by moistening and working: to *temper* clay. **3** To bring (metal) to a required hardness and elasticity by heating and suddenly cooling. **4** *Music* To adjust the tones of (an instrument) by temperament; tune. **5** *Obs.* To adjust. — *v.i.* **6** To be or become tempered. [Fusion of OE *temprian* mingle, regulate and OF *temprer, tremper* soak, temper (steel), both <L *temperare* combine in due proportion. For sense development of noun defs. 1, 2, and 3, see def. 8.] — **tem′per·a·bil′i·ty** *n.* — **tem′per·a·ble** *adj.* — **tem′per·er** *n.*

Synonyms (noun): constitution, disposition, frame, grain, humor, mood, nature, organization, temperament. See ANGER, CHARACTER. *Synonyms (verb)*: accommodate, adapt, adjust, appease, assuage, attemper, calm, fit, moderate, modify, mollify, pacify, qualify, restrain, soften, soothe.

tem·per·a (tem′pər·ə, *Ital.* tem′pä·rä) *n.* **1** A painting medium which is essentially an emulsion prepared by any of numerous recipes, and composed characteristically of oil usually thickened, with or without a resin such as dammar varnish, and egg and water. **2** The method of painting by this medium, which falls into three principal divisions: *unvarnished tempera, varnished tempera,* and *tempera,* as underpainting for oil glazes: widely used in the Renaissance and revived in modern times, sometimes in combination with oil techniques. [<Ital. <*temperare* temper <L]

tem·per·a·ment (tem′pər·ə·mənt, -prə-) *n.* **1** The characteristic physical and mental peculiarities of an individual as manifested in his reactions. **2** *Music* The tuning of an instrument so that the intervals of the scale shall follow a suitable law of succession. **3** Mental constitution; make-up; disposition. **4** Adjustment or compromise. **5** *Obs.* Temperature. See synonyms under CHARACTER, TEMPER. [<L *temperamentum* proper mixture <*temperare* mix in due proportions]

tem·per·a·men·tal (tem′pər·ə·men′təl, -prə-) *adj.* **1** Of or pertaining to temperament. **2** Having a strongly marked temperament. **3** Sensitive; easily excited; changeable. — **tem′per·a·men′tal·ly** *adv.*

tem·per·ance (tem′pər·əns) *n.* **1** The state or quality of being temperate; habitual moderation, especially in the indulgence of any appetite. **2** Specifically, the principle and practice of total abstinence from intoxicants. **3** *Obs.* Calmness; self-control. See synonyms under ABSTINENCE. — *adj.* **1** Of or pertaining to public places where alcoholic beverages are not sold. **2** Of, relating to, practicing, or promoting total abstinence from intoxicants. [<OF <L *temperantia,* orig. neut. pl. of *temperans, -antis,* ppr. of *temperare* mix in due proportions]

temperance pledge A pledge not to indulge in alcoholic drinks.

tem·per·ate (tem′pər·it) *adj.* **1** Observing moderation or self-control; specifically, by extension, not indulging in intoxicating liquors. **2** Moderate as regards temperature; free from extremes of heat or cold; mild. **3** Characterized by moderation or the absence of extremes; not excessive. **4** Calm; restrained; self-controlled. **5** *Music* Tempered: said of an interval or scale. See synonyms under SOBER. [<L *temperatus,* pp. of *temperare* mix in due proportions] — **tem′per·ate·ly** *adv.* — **tem′per·ate·ness** *n.*

temperate zone See ZONE (def. 1).

tem·per·a·ture (tem′pər·ə·chər, -prə-) *n.* **1** Condition as regards heat or cold. **2** The degree of heat in a body or substance, as measured on the graduated scale of a thermometer. See table below. **3** Sensible heat of the human body; also, excess of this above the normal. **4** *Obs.* Constitution; temperament; mixture; temperateness; temperance. [<L *temperatura* due measure <*temperatus.* See TEMPERATE.]

To convert from Fahrenheit to Celsius (Centigrade): Subtract 32 from the Fahrenheit reading, multiply by 5, and divide the product by 9. *Example*: 65° F. −32 = 33; 33 × 5 = 165; 165 ÷ 9 = 18.3° C. To convert from Celsius to Fahrenheit: Multiply the Celsius reading by 9, divide the product by 5, add 32. *Example*: 30° C. × 9 = 270; 270 ÷ 5 = 54; 54 + 32 = 86° F.

CONVERSION TABLE

Fahrenheit	*Celsius*	*Fahrenheit*	*Celsius*
500	260.0	−10	−23.3
400	204.4	−20	−28.9
300	149.0	−30	−34.4
212	100.0	−40	−40.0
200	93.3	−50	−45.6
100	37.8	−60	−51.1
90	32.2	−70	−56.7
80	26.7	−80	−62.2
70	21.1	−90	−67.8
60	15.6	−100	−73.3
50	10.0	−200	−129.0
40	4.4	−300	−184.0
32	0.0	−400	−240.0
30	−1.1	*−459.4	−273.0
20	−6.6		
10	−12.2		
0	−17.8		

*Absolute zero

temperature coefficient *Physics* The amount of change in some specified physical quantity per unit change in temperature: it may be positive or negative and is usually expressed as the quotient of the change observed after a rise of 1° C. divided by the constant value of the quantity at 0° C.

temperature gradient The rate of change in temperature with change in altitude or other variable factors.

tem·pered (tem′pərd) *adj.* **1** Having temper or a temper, in any sense; mostly in compounds: quick-*tempered,* ill-*tempered.* **2** *Music* Adjusted in pitch to some mean temperament. **3** Moderated by admixture. **4** Having the right degree of hardness and elasticity: well-*tempered* steel.

tem·per-pin (tem′pər·pin′) *n.* **1** A wooden screw used to regulate the motion of a spinning wheel. **2** A tuning peg of a violin.

tem·pest (tem′pist) *n.* **1** An extensive and violent wind, usually attended with rain, snow, or hail. **2** A violent commotion or agitation; a fierce tumult. See synonyms under STORM. — *v.t.* To agitate violently; affect as a tempest does. [<OF *tempeste* <L *tempestas* space of time, weather <*tempus* time]

tem·pes·tu·ous (tem·pes′cho͞o·əs) *adj.* Stormy; turbulent; violent. [<OF *tempestueux* <LL *tempestuosus* <L *tempestas* weather. See TEMPEST.] — **tem·pes′tu·ous·ly** *adv.* — **tem·pes′tu·ous·ness** *n.*

tem·plar (tem′plər) *n.* A law student or a barrister who has apartments in the buildings known as the Inner and the Middle Temple in London. [<OF *templier* <Med. L *templarius* <L *templum.* See TEMPLE.]

Tem·plar (tem′plər) *n.* A Knight Templar.

tem·plate (tem′plit) *n.* **1** A pattern or gage, as of wood or metal, used as a guide in shaping something or in checking the accuracy of work. **2** In building, a stout stone or timber for distributing weight or thrust. **3** A wedge for a building block under a ship's keel. Also spelled *templet.* [<F *templette* stretcher, dim. of *temple* small timber <L *templum*]

tem·ple[1] (tem′pəl) *n.* **1** A stately edifice consecrated to one or more deities and forming a seat of their worship. **2** An edifice dedicated to public worship; especially, in the United States, a Reform synagog. **3** In France, a Protestant church. **4** Figuratively, any place considered as occupied by God; specifically, a sanctified human body. **5** A building erected and dedicated for the administration of Mormon ordinances; a Mormon church. — **the Temple 1** Either of two medieval establishments in London and Paris, once occupied by the Knights Templar. In London, since 1185, the district lying between Fleet Street and the Thames river, the site of the **Inner** and **Middle Temple.** See INNS OF COURT. **2** Any of three successive sacred edifices built in Jerusalem for the worship of Jehovah. [OE *tempel* <L *templum* temple]

tem·ple[2] (tem′pəl) *n.* The region on each side of the head above the cheek bone. [<OF <L *tempora,* pl. of *tempus* temple]

tem·ple[3] (tem′pəl) *n.* An attachment to a loom that serves to keep the last woven part of the fabric stretched and to prevent chafing of the warp. [<F <L *templum* a small timber]

Tem·ple (tem′pəl), **Sir William,** 1628–99, English statesman, diplomat, and writer. — **William,** 1881–1944, English prelate; archbishop of Canterbury 1942–44.

Temple Bar A historic three-arched gateway in London marking the western boundary of the city proper and on which the heads of traitors and other malefactors were exposed. It was dismantled in 1878 but re-erected at Waltham Cross, in Essex, in 1888.

tem·pled (tem′pəld) *adj.* Honored with or enshrined in a temple: a *templed* god.

tem·plet (tem′plit) See TEMPLATE.

tem·po (tem′pō) *n. pl.* **·pos** or **·pi** (-pē) **1** *Music* Relative speed at which a composition is rendered; time; rhythm of a tune. **2** Characteristic manner or style; rate of speed or activity in general. [<Ital. <L *tempus* time]

tem·po·la·bile (tem′pō·lā′bil) *adj. Biol.* Subject to decay or destruction within a certain period of time, as a serum. [<L *tempus* time + *labilis* perishable]

tem·po·ral[1] (tem′pər·əl) *adj.* **1** Pertaining to affairs of the present life, as contrasted with those of a future life; earthly, as opposed to heavenly. **2** Pertaining to or limited by time; transitory, as opposed to eternal. **3** Related to or concerned with worldly affairs; worldly; material, as opposed to spiritual. **4** Pertaining to civil law or authority; lay; secular: contrasted with *clerical.* **5** *Gram.* Of, pertaining to, or denoting time: *temporal* conjunctions. See synonyms under PROFANE. — **lords temporal** English, Scottish, and Irish lay peers with seats in the House of Lords. [<OF *temporel* <L *temporalis* <*tempus, temporis* time] — **tem′po·ral·ly** *adv.* — **tem′po·ral·ness** *n.*

tem·po·ral[2] (tem′pər·əl) *adj. Anat.* Of, pertaining to, or situated at the temple or temples: the *temporal* bone. [<L *temporalis* <*tempora.* See TEMPLE².]

tem·por·al[3] (tem′pər·äl′) *n. SW U.S.* A field or portion of land; a farm, especially one not requiring irrigation. [<Sp. *temporal* storm, tempest; ? <*terreno de temporal* land where heavy rains fall]

temporal bone *Anat.* A compound bone situated at the side of the head in man and other mammals, and containing the organ of hearing.

tem·po·ral·i·ty (tem′pə·ral′ə·tē) *n. pl.* **·ties** **1** *Usually pl.* A temporal or material matter, interest, revenue, etc.; specifically, an ecclesiastical possession or revenue. **2** The state of being temporal or temporary: opposed to *perpetuity.*

tem·po·ra mu·tan·tur (tem′pər·ə myo͞o·tan′tər) *Latin* The times are changed.

tem·po·rar·y (tem′pə·rer′ē) *adj.* **1** Lasting or intended to be used for a short time only; transitory; of passing interest: opposed to *permanent.* **2** *Obs.* Contemporary. See synonyms under TRANSIENT. [<L *temporarius* <*tempus, temporis* time] — **tem′po·rar′i·ly** *adv.* — **tem′po·rar′i·ness** *n.*

TEMPLE OF HORUS, EDFU, BEGUN 237 B.C.
Greco-Egyptian style.

tem·po·rize (tem′pə·rīz) *v.i.* **·rized, ·riz·ing** **1** To act evasively so as to gain time or put off decision or commitment. **2** To give real or apparent compliance to the circumstances;

comply. **3** To parley so as to gain time: with *with.* **4** To effect a compromise; negotiate: with *with* or *between.* Also *Brit.* **tem'po·rise.** [<F *temporiser* <L *temporis* time] —**tem'po·ri·za'tion** *n.* —**tem'po·riz'er** *n.* —**tem'po·riz'·ing·ly** *adv.*

tempt (tempt) *v.t.* **1** To attempt to persuade (a person) to do wrong, as by promising pleasure or gain. **2** To be attractive to; invite: Your offers do not *tempt* me. **3** To provoke or risk provoking: to *tempt* fate. **4** *Obs.* To test; prove. See synonyms under ALLURE. [< OF *tempter, tenter* <L *temptare, tentare* test, try, prob. intens. of *tendere* stretch] —**tempt'·a·ble** *adj.* —**tempt'er** *n.* —**tempt'ress** *n. fem.*

temp·ta·tion (temp·tā'shən) *n.* **1** That which tempts, especially to evil. **2** The state of being tempted, or enticed to evil; the act of tempting or testing. **3** A state of mental conflict between heavenly and infernal influences.

tempt·ing (temp'ting) *adj.* Alluring; attractive; seductive. —**tempt'ing·ly** *adv.* —**tempt'·ing·ness** *n.*

tem·pu·ra (tem·pŏŏr'ə, tem'pŏŏr'ə, -pōō·ra') *n.* A Japanese dish of seafood or vegetables, dipped in batter and deep-fried. [<Jap., fried food]

tem·pus fu·git (tem'pəs fyōō'jit) *Latin* Time flies.

ten (ten) *n.* **1** The cardinal number following nine and preceding eleven, or any of the symbols or combinations of symbols (10, x, X) used to represent it. **2** Anything containing or representing ten units or members; a playing card marked with ten pips; also, a ten-dollar bill. —*adj.* Being or consisting of one more than nine; decennary. [OE]

ten– Var. of TENO–.

ten·a·ble (ten'ə·bəl) *adj.* Capable of being held, maintained, or defended. [<F <*tenir* hold < L *tenere*] —**ten'a·bil'i·ty, ten'a·ble·ness** *n.* —**ten'a·bly** *adv.*

ten·ace (ten'ās) *n.* The combination in the same hand of the best and third best cards **(major tenace)** or of the second and fourth best cards **(minor tenace)** of any suit. [<Sp. *tenaza* pincers, tongs <*tenaz* tenacious <L *tenax, tenacis.* See TENACIOUS.]

te·na·cious (ti·nā'shəs) *adj.* **1** Having great cohesiveness of parts; tough. **2** Adhesive; sticky. **3** Holding or tending to hold strongly, as opinions, rights, etc.: followed by *of;* hence, stubborn; obstinate; unyielding; persistent. **4** Apt to retain; strongly retentive, as memory. See synonyms under STRONG. [<L *tenax, tenacis* holding fast <*tenere* hold, grasp, embrace] —**te·na'cious·ly** *adv.* —**te·na'·cious·ness** *n.*

te·nac·i·ty (ti·nas'ə·tē) *n.* **1** The state or quality of being tenacious. **2** That quality of a body in consequence of which it resists being pulled or forced apart.

te·nac·u·lum (ti·nak'yə·ləm) *n. pl.* **·la** (-lə) *Surg.* A hooked instrument for seizing and holding parts of the body, as arteries, during surgical operations. [<LL, holder <L *tenax, tenacis.* See TENACIOUS.]

te·naille (te·nāl') *n.* A low outwork, usually with one or two reentering angles, in the main ditch between two bastions. —*v.t.* To equip with tenailles. Also **te·nail'.** [<F <LL *tenacula,* pl. of *tenaculum.* See TENACULUM.]

ten·an·cy (ten'ən·sē) *n. pl.* **·cies 1** The holding of lands or tenements by any form of title; occupancy. **2** The period of holding or occupying lands, tenements, or office; temporary possession. **3** A habitation or dwelling place held of another.

ten·ant (ten'ənt) *n.* **1** One who holds or possesses lands or property by any kind of title; especially, one who holds under another; a lessee. **2** A defendant in an action concerning real property. **3** A dweller in any place; an occupant. —*v.t.* To hold as tenant; occupy. —*v.i.* To be a tenant. [<F, orig. ppr. of *tenir* hold <L *tenere*] —**ten'ant·a·ble** *adj.* —**ten'ant·less** *adj.*

tenant farmer One who farms land owned by another and pays rent usually in a share of the crops.

ten·ant–right (ten'ənt·rīt') *n.* A customary right belonging to a tenant, even if not specifically stipulated, as a right to continuous occupancy without increase of rent, or a right to compensation for improvements.

ten·ant·ry (ten'ən·trē) *n. pl.* **·ries 1** Tenants collectively. **2** Tenantship; tenancy.

Te·nas·se·rim (tə·nas'ər·im) A former administrative division of SE Burma extending in a narrow strip of coast 400 miles down the Malay Peninsula to the Isthmus of Kra; 31,588 square miles; capital, Moulmein.

ten–cent store (ten'sent') See FIVE– AND TEN–CENT STORE.

tench (tench) *n.* A European fresh–water cyprinoid fish *(Tinca tinca),* very tenacious of life, and having small, deeply embedded scales. [<F *tenche* <LL *tinca* tench]

Ten Commandments See under COMMANDMENT.

tend[1] (tend) *v.i.* **1** To have an aptitude, tendency, or disposition; incline: He *tends* to talk too much. **2** To have influence toward a specified result; lead or conduce: Education *tends* to refinement. **3** To go in a certain direction. [<OF *tendre* <L *tendere* extend, tend]

tend[2] (tend) *v.t.* **1** To attend to the needs or requirements of; take care of; minister to: to *tend* a fire. **2** To watch over; look after: to *tend* children. **3** To watch (a vessel at anchor) with the intention of so managing her when the tide changes as to prevent fouling the anchor and chain. —*v.i.* **4** To be in attendance; serve or wait: with *on* or *upon.* **5** *Colloq.* To give attention or care: with *to.* [Aphetic var. of ATTEND]

ten·dance (ten'dəns) *n.* **1** The act of tending; attendance; service. **2** *Archaic* Attendants collectively. Also **ten'dence.**

Ten Degree Channel A passage from the Bay of Bengal to the Andaman Sea between the Andaman and Nicobar Islands, along 10° N; about 90 miles wide.

ten·den·cy (ten'dən·sē) *n. pl.* **·cies 1** The state of being directed toward some purpose, end, or result; inclination; bent; aptitude. **2** That which tends to produce some specified effect. **3** Bias; propensity. **4** Trend of a speech; purpose of a story. See synonyms under AIM, DIRECTION, INCLINATION. [<Med. L *tendentia,* orig. neut. pl. of *tendens, -entis,* ppr. of *tendere* extend, tend]

ten·den·tious (ten·den'shəs) *adj.* Having a purposed aim or intentional tendency. [<G *tendenziös* <*tendenz* tendency <Med. L *tendentia.* See TENDENCY.] —**ten·den'tious·ly** *adv.* —**ten·den'tious·ness** *n.*

Ten·denz (ten·dens') *n. German* Tendency or drift; partisan or biased attitude, as in a work of literature or art; angle; slant.

ten·der[1] (ten'dər) *adj.* **1** Yielding easily to force that tends to crush, bruise, break, or injure; soft or delicate. **2** Easily chewed or cut: said of food, especially meat. **3** Delicate or weak; not strong or hardy. **4** Youthful and delicate; not strengthened by maturity: a *tender* age. **5** Characterized by or expressive of a delicate sensibility; kind; affectionate; gentle: *tender* mercy; a *tender* father. **6** Capable of arousing sensitive feelings; touching: *tender* memories; a *tender* sight. **7** Susceptible to spiritual or moral feelings: a *tender* conscience. **8** Painful if touched; easily pained: a *tender* sore. **9** Of delicate effect or quality; soft: a *tender* light. **10** Requiring deft or delicate treatment; ticklish; touchy: a *tender* subject. **11** *Naut.* Careening too easily under sail: said of a ship. See synonyms under BLAND, FRAGILE, FRIENDLY, HUMANE, MERCIFUL. —*v.t.* To make tender; soften. [<OF *tendre* <L *tener, teneris*] —**ten'der·ly** *adv.* —**ten'·der·ness** *n.*

ten·der[2] (ten'dər) *v.t.* **1** To present for acceptance, as a resignation; offer. **2** *Law* To proffer, as money, in payment, in discharge of a debt, or to fulfil a contract. —*n.* **1** The act of tendering; an offer; specifically, in law, a formal offer of satisfaction. **2** That which is offered as payment, especially money: legal *tender.* [<F *tendre* <L *tendere* extend, tend] —**ten'der·er** *n.*

tend·er[3] (ten'dər) *n.* **1** A vessel used to bring supplies, passengers, and crew back and forth between a larger vessel and a nearby shore; also, a vessel which services another at sea. **2** A boat used to carry provisions, etc., to whalers and lighthouses. **3** A vehicle attached to the rear of a steam locomotive to carry fuel and water for it. **4** One who tends or ministers to. [<TEND[2]]

ten·der·foot (ten'dər·fŏŏt') *n. pl.* **·foots** or **·feet** (-fēt') *U.S.* **1** A newcomer in the West; one not yet inured to the hardships of or not yet experienced in the life of the plains, the mining camp, etc.; a greenhorn: opposed to *longhorn.* **2** Any inexperienced person. **3** A boy scout in the beginning class or group. —*adj.* Inexperienced; also, made up of inexperienced people: a *tenderfoot* gang.

ten·der–heart·ed (ten'dər·här'tid) *adj.* Having deep or quick sensibility, as to love, pity, etc.; compassionate; sympathetic; easily impressed by sorrow or pain. —**ten'der–heart'·ed·ly** *adv.* —**ten'der–heart'ed·ness** *n.*

ten·der·ize (ten'də·rīz) *v.t.* **·ized, ·iz·ing** To make tender, as meat.

ten·der·iz·er (ten'də·rī'zər) A substance, as papain, for softening the tough fibers and connective tissues of meat in order to make it more palatable.

ten·der·loin (ten'dər·loin') *n.* The tender part of the loin of beef, pork, etc., lying close to the ventral side of the lumbar vertebrae. —**the tenderloin district 1** A former district of New York City, coinciding with a certain police precinct from 23rd to 42nd streets, west of Broadway, where vice flourished and police corruption was common. **2** Hence, any district in any city which is noted for its night life, a high incidence of crime, and police leniency.

ten·di·nous (ten'də·nəs) *adj.* **1** Of, pertaining to, resembling, or formed by a tendon. **2** Having or full of tendons; sinewy. [<F *tendineux* <Med. L *tendo, -inis.* See TENDON.]

ten·don (ten'dən) *n. Anat.* One of the bands of tough, fibrous connective tissue forming the termination of a muscle and serving to transmit its force to some other part; a sinew. [<F <Med. L *tendo, -inis* <Gk. *tenōn* a sinew < *teinein* stretch]

tendon of Achilles *Anat.* Achilles' tendon.

ten·dril (ten'dril) *n. Bot.* One of the slender, leafless, coiling organs which serve a climbing plant as a means of attachment to a wall, tree trunk, or other supporting surface. [<F *tendrillon,* dim. of *tendron* sprout <*tendre* tender; infl. in meaning by F *tendre* stretch] —**ten'dril·lar, ten'dril·ous** *adj.*

ten·e·brae (ten'ə·brē) *n. pl.* The matins and lauds of Thursday, Friday, and Saturday of Holy Week, sung on the afternoon or evening of the preceding days. [<L, shadows]

ten·e·brif·ic (ten'ə·brif'ik) *adj.* Making dark or gloomy. [<L *tenebrae* darkness + -FIC]

ten·e·brous (ten'ə·brəs) *adj.* Gloomy; dark; obscure. [<L *tenebrosus* <*tenebrae* darkness] —**ten'e·bros'i·ty** (-bros'ə·tē) *n.*

Ten·e·dos (ten'ə·dos, *Gk.* ten'ə·dôs) A Turkish island in the Aegean near the western entrance to the Dardanelles; 15 square miles: Turkish *Bozcaada.*

ten·e·ment (ten'ə·mənt) *n.* **1** A room, or set of rooms, designed for one family. See TENEMENT HOUSE. **2** *Law* Anything of a permanent nature that may be held by one person of another as property, as land, houses, offices, rents, franchises, etc. **3** A house or building; especially, a dwelling house rented or intended for rent; a tenement house. **4** Figuratively, an abode. [<OF <LL *tenementum* tenure <L *tenere* hold] —**ten'e·men'ta·ry** (-men'tər·ē), **ten'e·men'tal** (-men'təl) *adj.*

tenement house A building or house, usually of inferior type and situated in the poorer sections of a city, rented, leased, or let, to be occupied as the home of three or more families living independently of one another, or by more than two families on a floor, all having a common right in stairways, yards, etc.

te·nen·dum (ti·nen'dəm) *n. Law* The clause in a deed in which, before the abolition of feudal tenures, the tenure was defined: now part of the habendum clause. See HABENDUM. [<L, that which must be held, gerundive of *tenere* hold]

Ten·er·ife (ten'ə·rif', -rēf'; *Sp.* tā'nā·rē'fā) The largest of the Canary Islands; 794 1/2 square miles; capital, Santa Cruz de Tenerife; contains the **Peak of Tenerife** (also *Teyde*), a dormant volcano and the highest peak on Spanish soil; 12,200 feet. Also **Ten'er·iffe'.**

te·nes·mus (ti·nes'məs, -nez'-) *n. Pathol.* A painful straining and ineffectual effort to evacuate the bladder or the bowels. [<NL <L *tenesmos* a straining <Gk. *teneismos* <*teinein* stretch] —**te·nes'mic** *adj.*

ten·et (ten'it, tē'nit) *n.* An opinion, principle,

dogma, or doctrine that a person or organization believes or maintains as true. See synonyms under DOCTRINE. [<L, he holds < *tenere* hold]

ten·fold (ten′fōld′) *adj.* Made up of ten; ten times as many or as much; ten times repeated; decuplicate. —*adv.* In a tenfold manner or degree.

Ten·gri Khan (teng′grē khän′) The second highest peak of the Tien Shan, in NE Kirghiz S.S.R.; 22,949 feet. Also **Khan Tengri.**

Ten·gri Nor (teng′grē nôr′, nōr′) The Mongolian name for NAM TSO.

te·ni·a (tē′nē·ə) See TAENIA.

te·ni·a·cide (tē′nē·ə·sīd′) *n.* A substance which destroys tapeworms, as the oleoresin of certain ferns, carbon tetrachloride, etc.: also spelled *taeniacide.* Also **te′ni·a·fuge′** (-fyōōj′) [<L *taenia* <Gk. *tainia* tapeworm + -CIDE] —**te′ni·a·ci′dal** *adj.*

te·ni·a·sis (ti·nī′ə·sis) *n. Pathol.* Any morbid or toxemic condition due to the presence of tapeworms in the body: also spelled *taeniasis.* [<Gk. *tainia* tapeworm + -IASIS]

Ten·iers (ten′yərz, *Flemish* te·nirs′), **David,** 1582–1649, Flemish painter: called "the Elder." —**David,** 1610–90, Flemish painter: called "the Younger"; son of preceding.

Ten·nes·se·an (ten′ə·sē′ən) *n.* A native or inhabitant of Tennessee. —*adj.* Of or pertaining to Tennessee.

Ten·nes·see (ten′ə·sē′) A State in the SE United States; 42,246 square miles; capital, Nashville; entered the Union June 1, 1796; nicknamed *Volunteer State*: abbr. TN

Tennessee River A river of the east central United States, rising in eastern Tennessee and flowing 652 miles SW, NW, and north through Alabama, Tennessee, and Kentucky to the Ohio River at Paducah, Kentucky.

Tennessee Valley Authority A Federal corporation established in 1933 by the U.S. government to take custody of the Wilson Dam and associated plants at Muscle Shoals in Tennessee, developing and operating them in the national interest, with special reference to electric power, irrigation, fertilizers, and flood control. Abbr. *TVA, T.V.A.*

Ten·niel (ten′yəl), **Sir John,** 1820–1914, English illustrator and cartoonist.

ten·nis (ten′is) *n.* A game played by striking a ball to and fro with rackets over a net stretched perpendicularly across a space called a court. It has two forms, **court tennis,** played indoors in a specially prepared building, and **lawn tennis,** played out-of-doors on a court of grass, clay, concrete, etc. [<AF *tenetz* take, receive, imperative of *tenir* hold; from the call of the server]

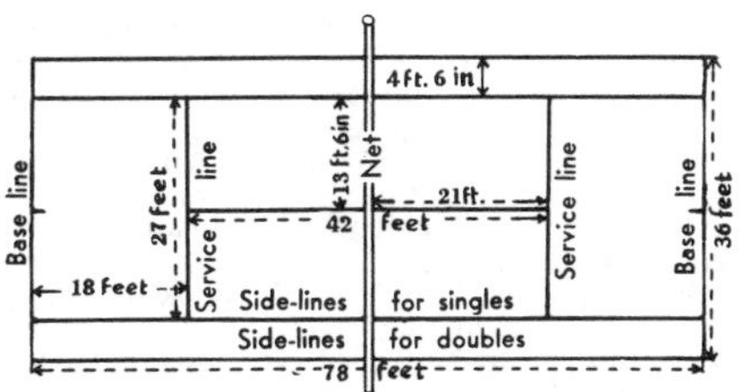

TENNIS COURT — PLAN AND DIMENSIONS

Ten·ny·son (ten′ə·sən), **Alfred,** 1809–92, Lord Tennyson, English poet laureate 1850–92.

Ten·ny·so·ni·an (ten′ə·sō′nē·ən) *adj.* Relating to or characteristic of Alfred Tennyson, or his verse or style.

teno– *combining form Med.* Tendon; related to a tendon, or to tendons: *tenotomy*: also, before vowels, *ten–.* Also **tenonto–.** [<Gk. *tenōn* a tendon]

Te·noch·ti·tlán (tā·nōkh′tē·tlän′) The capital of the ancient Aztec Empire, on the site of Mexico City.

ten·on (ten′ən) *n.* A projection on the end of a timber, etc., for inserting in a socket to form a joint. —*v.t.* **1** To form a tenon on. **2** To join by a mortise and tenon. [<F <*tenir* hold]

ten·o·ni·tis (ten′ə·nī′tis) *n. Pathol.* Inflammation of a tendon. [<NL <Gk. *tenōn* a tendon]

ten·or (ten′ər) *n.* **1** A settled course or manner of progress. **2** Course of thought; general purport. **3** *Law* The purport or substance and effect of a document; an exact transcript, as of a record. **4** General character and tendency; nature. **5** The highest adult male voice (except the falsetto); a singer having such a voice, or a part to be sung by it. **6** An instrument playing the part intermediate between the bass and the alto; especially, the viola. **7** In bell ringing, the lowest bell, irrespective of peal. —*adj.* **1** Of or pertaining to a tenor. **2** Having a relation to other instruments that the tenor bears to other musical parts: a *tenor* violin. [<OF *tenour* <L *tenor* a course <*tenere* hold; in def. 5, so called because this voice originally sang or "held" the melody]

ten·or·ite (ten′ə·rīt) *n.* Native oxide of copper, occurring in minute black scales; black copper. [after Prof. G. *Tenore,* president (1841) of Naples Academy]

te·nor·rha·phy (ti·nôr′ə·fē, -nor′-) *n. Surg.* Suture of the ends of a divided tendon. [<TENO- + -RRHAPHY]

te·not·o·my (ti·not′ə·mē) *n. Surg.* The operation of cutting a tendon. [<TENO- + -TOMY]

ten·pen·ny (ten′pen′ē, -pə·nē) *adj.* **1** Valued at tenpence. **2** Designating the size of nails three inches long. See -PENNY.

ten·pin (ten′pin′) *n.* One of the pins used in the game of tenpins.

ten·pins (ten′pinz′) *n.* A game, played in a bowling alley, in which the players attempt to bowl down ten pins set up at the far end of the alley.

ten·rec (ten′rek) *n.* One of several insectivorous mammals of Madagascar; especially, the spiny-coated, tailless *Tenrec ecaudatus,* from 12 to 16 inches long: also spelled *tanrec.* [<F <Malagasy *trändraka*]

Ten·sas River (ten′sô) A river in eastern Louisiana, flowing 175 miles south and SW to the Ouachita River in east central Louisiana.

tense[1] (tens) *adj.* **1** Stretched tight; taut. **2** Under mental or nervous strain; strained. **3** *Phonet.* Pronounced with the tongue and its muscles taut, as (ē) and (ōō); narrow: opposed to *lax.* —*v.t.* & *v.i.* **tensed, tens·ing** To make or become strained or drawn tight. [<L *tensus,* pp. of *tendere* stretch] —**tense′ly** *adv.* —**tense′ness** *n.*

tense[2] (tens) *n.* A form of a verb that relates it to time viewed either as finite past, present, or future, or as non-finite. —**sequence of tenses** In inflected languages, the customary choice of tense for a verb that follows another in a sentence, particularly in reported or indirect discourse. ◆ The general principle of sequence of tenses in English is that present follows present and past follows past. Thus, the tense of the subordinate clause tends to shift back to agree with the tense of the main verb. "He *wants* to go," becomes, in indirect discourse, "They said that he *wanted* to go." However, if continued, habitual, future, or universal action is expressed, the present tense may be retained in the subordinate clause: They told me that he *is* still in town; Columbus proved that the world *is* round. The present tense is also retained in the subordinate clause for emphasis: They just learned he *is* going after all. In subordinate clauses of purpose the general rule of tense sequence holds true: We *are working* so that we *can* go to Europe; We *worked* so that we *could go* to Europe. In conditional sentences expressing a simple fact or open question, the main and subordinate verbs remain independent: If he *said* that, I *can't* prove it. However, sequence of tenses is strictly observed in a highly improbable or contrary-to-fact statement. Time present is then expressed by the use of the past tense: If he *had* any sense, he *wouldn't drive* that car. Time past is expressed by the past perfect tense: If I *had had* my wits about me, I *would have* telephoned immediately. [< OF *tens* <L *tempus* time, tense]

ten·si·ble (ten′sə·bəl) *adj.* **1** Extensible. **2** Capable of being made tense; tensile.

ten·sile (ten′sil, *Brit.* ten′sīl) *adj.* **1** Of or pertaining to tension. **2** Capable of extension. **3** Producing tones from stretched strings: said instruments. [<NL *tensilis* <L *tensus.* See TENSE[1].] —**ten·sil·i·ty** (ten·sil′ə·tē) *n.*

tensile strength *Physics* The resistance of a material to forces of rupture and longitudinal stress: usually expressed in pounds or tons per square inch.

ten·sim·e·ter (ten·sim′ə·tər) *n.* An instrument for measuring the tension of gases; a manometer. [<*tensi-* (<TENSION) + -METER]

ten·si·om·e·ter (ten′sē·om′ə·tər) *n.* A device for determining tensile strength. [See TENSIMETER]

ten·sion (ten′shən) *n.* **1** The act of stretching; the condition of being stretched tight. **2** Mental strain; intense nervous anxiety. **3** Any strained relation, as between governments. **4** *Physics* **a** Stress on a material caused by pulling: opposed to *compression,* and distinguished from *torsion.* **b** The condition of a body when acted on by such stress. **5** The expansive force of a gas. **6** A regulating device, as that on a sewing machine to regulate the tightness of the thread. **7** *Electr.* Electromotive force; also, electric potential. [< L *tensio, -onis* <*tensus.* See TENSE[1].] —**ten′·sion·al** *adj.*

ten·si·ty (ten′sə·tē) *n.* The state of being tense; tension.

ten·sive (ten′siv) *adj.* **1** Caused by or causing tension. **2** Causing a sensation of stiffness or contraction.

ten·sor (ten′sər, -sôr) *n.* **1** *Anat.* A muscle that stretches a part. **2** *Math.* A vector quantity which may be fully described only with reference to more than three components. [<NL <L *tensus.* See TENSE[1].]

ten-strike (ten′strīk′) *n.* **1** In bowling, the knocking down by a player of all the pins at one bowl: also called *strike.* **2** *U.S. Colloq.* Hence, a stroke of unexampled success; a very profitable bargain.

tent[1] (tent) *n.* A shelter of canvas or the like, supported by poles and fastened by cords to pegs (called **tent pegs**) driven into the ground. —*v.t.* To cover with or as with a tent. —*v.i.* To pitch a tent; camp out. [<F *tente* <LL *tenta,* orig. neut. pl. of *tentus,* pp. of *tendere* stretch. Cf. L *tentorium* awning.]

TENTS
a. Pup tent. *b.* Pyramid tent. *c.* Wall tent.

tent[2] (tent) *Surg. n.* A small roll, as of lint, placed in a wound or orifice to prevent its closing. —*v.t.* To keep open with a tent; also, to probe. [<F *tente* <*tenter* test, probe <L *tentare*]

tent[3] (tent) *Scot. v.t.* **1** To pay attention to; observe. **2** To hinder; prevent. **3** To attend upon; look after. —*n.* **1** Attention; note; heed. **2** An open-air wooden pulpit. —**tent′·less** *adj.*

tent[4] (tent) *n.* A deep-red wine obtained chiefly from Spain. [<Sp. *tinto* deep-colored <L *tinctus* dyed. See TINT.]

ten·ta·cle (ten′tə·kəl) *n.* **1** *Zool.* A protruding flexible process or appendage (usually of the head) of invertebrate animals, functioning as an organ of touch, prehension, or motion. Some examples are the hollow fleshy processes about the mouth of a polyp communicating with the body cavity, the eyestalks of a gastropod, and the arms of a cuttlefish, especially one of the two longer arms of a decapod. **2** *Bot.* A sensitive glandular hair, as on the leaves of the sundew. **3** Something resembling a tentacle; a tendril. Also **ten·tac·u·lum** (ten·tak′yə·ləm). [<L *tentaculum* < *tentare* touch, try] —**ten·tac′u·lar adj.**

tent·age (ten′tij) *n.* **1** The supply of tents available for any purpose. **2** Tents collectively.

ten·ta·tion (ten·tā′shən) *n.* The act or process of adjusting by experimentation until a desired effect is secured. [<F <L *tentatio, -onis* < *tentare* try. See TEMPT.]

ten·ta·tive (ten′tə·tiv) *adj.* **1** Used in making a trial; provisional or conjectural; experimental and subject to change. **2** *Med.* Based on subjective and objective symptoms: said of a diagnosis subject to change. — *n.* An experiment; conjecture. [<Med. L *tentativus* <L *tentatus*, pp. of *tentare* try, probe] — **ten′ta·tive·ly** *adv.* — **ten′ta·tive·ness** *n.*

tent caterpillar The gregarious larva of several North American moths (family *Lasiocampidae)* that spins a large silken web which shelters the colony, especially the **orchard caterpillar** (genus *Malacosoma).*

tent·ed (ten′tid) *adj.* **1** Overspread or covered with or sheltered by tents: the *tented* field. **2** Resembling a tent.

tented arch A fingerprint pattern in which the skin ridges have an upward thrust in the shape of a tent, arranging themselves on both sides of a spine or axis.

ten·ter[1] (ten′tər) *n.* **1** A frame or machine for stretching cloth to prevent shrinkage while drying. **2** *Obs.* A tenterhook. — *v.t.* To stretch on or as on a tenter. — *v.i.* To be or admit of being stretched thus. [<L *tentus* extended. See TENT[1].]

tent·er[2] (ten′tər) *n. Brit.* One who especially attends to anything; particularly, one who attends to machinery in a factory. [<TENT[3]]

ten·ter·hook (ten′tər·ho͝ok′) *n.* A sharp hook for holding cloth while being stretched on a tenter. — **to be on tenterhooks** To be in a state of anxiety or suspense.

tenth (tenth) *adj.* **1** Next in order after the ninth. **2** Designating one of ten equal parts. — *n.* **1** One of ten equal parts. **2** *Music* An interval compounded of an octave and a third; a note separated from another by this interval. **3** An organ stop tuned a tenth above the diapasons. **4** A tax of one tenth of one's income; a tithe. [ME *tenthe*] — **tenth′ly** *adv.*

ten·tie (ten′tē) *adj. Scot.* Attentive; cautious. Also **ten′ty.**

tent pegging A cavalry exercise in British military tournaments in which the horseman, riding at full speed, endeavors to uproot a tent peg with his lance.

tent stitch Petit point.

te·nue (tə·nü′) *n. French* **1** Appearance or style of dress. **2** Bearing; manner.

ten·u·is (ten′yo͞o·is) *n. pl.* **·u·es** (-yo͞o·ēz) In Greek, one of the three voiceless stops, κ, π, τ, considered in relation to their voiced counterparts, γ, β, δ, or voiceless fricatives, χ, φ, θ; also, corresponding voiceless sounds in other languages, as *k, t, p.* [<L, thin, trans. of Gk. *psilos* bare, unaspirated]

ten·u·ous (ten′yo͞o·əs) *adj.* **1** Thin; slim; delicate; also, weak; flimsy. **2** Having slight density; rare: opposed to *dense.* See synonyms under FINE. [<L *tenuis* thin] — **ten′u·ous·ly** *adv.* — **ten′u·ous·ness, ten·u·i·ty** (ten·yo͞o′ə·tē, ti·no͞o′-) *n.*

ten·ure (ten′yər) *n.* **1** A holding, as of land. **2** The act of holding in general, or the state of being held. **3** The term during which a thing is held, as an office. **4** The conditions or manner of holding. See synonyms under OCCUPATION. [<F < *tenir* hold <L *tenere]* — **ten·u·ri·al** (ten·yo͝or′ē·əl) *adj.* — **ten·u′ri·al·ly** *adv.*

te·nu·to (te·no͞o′tō) *adj. Music* Sustained; held for the full time. [<Ital.]

te·nu·to-mark (te·no͞o′tō·märk′) *n. Music* A horizontal stroke over a note or chord that is to be held for its full value.

Te·o·bal·do (tā′ō·bäl′dō) Italian form of THEOBALD.

te·o·cal·li (tē′ə·kal′ē, *Sp.* tā′ō·kä′yē) *n.* **1** A temple peculiar to the ancient Mexicans and Central Americans, usually erected on a truncated pyramid. **2** A mound of similar form. Also **te·o·pan** (tā′ō·pän′). [<Sp. < Nahuatl, house of the god < *teotl* a god + *calli* house]

Te·o·do·ri·co (*Ital.* tā′ō·dō·rē′kō, *Sp.* -thō-) Italian and Spanish form of THEODORIC.

Te·o·do·ro (*Ital.* tā′ō·dō′rō, *Sp.* -thō′rō) Italian and Spanish form of THEODORE. — **Te′o·do′ra** (-rä) *fem.*

Te·o·fi·lo (tā·ō′fē·lō) Italian and Spanish form of THEOPHILUS.

te·o·sin·te (tē′ə·sin′tē) *n.* A stout, hardy perennial grass *(Euchlaena mexicana),* closely allied to Indian corn, and used for fodder. [<Sp. <Nahuatl *teocentli,* lit., divine maize < *teotl* a god + *centli* corn]

te·pee (tē′pē) *n.* A conical tent of the North American Plains Indians, usually covered with skins or other material: also spelled *teepee, tipi.* [<Dakota *tīpi* < *ti* dwell + *pi* used for]

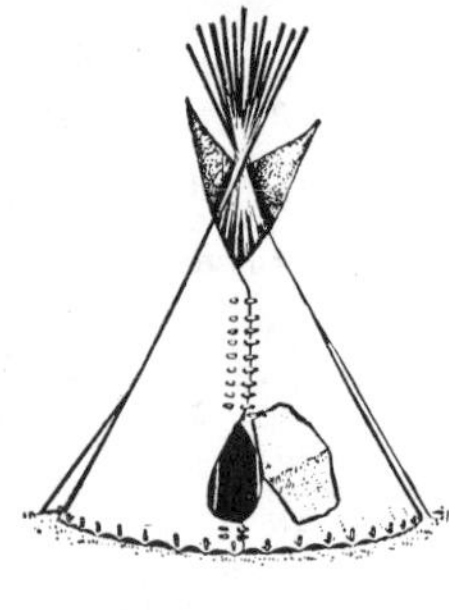
TEPEE
Western Plains Indian.

tep·e·fy (tep′ə·fī) *v.t.* & *v.i.* **·fied, ·fy·ing** To make or become tepid. [<L *tepefacere* make tepid < *tepere* be lukewarm + *facere* make] — **tep′e·fac′tion** (-fak′·shən) *n.*

teph·rite (tef′rīt) *n.* An ash-gray to black volcanic rock, essentially an alkaline andesite, with either nepheline or leucite. [<L *tephritis* <Gk. *tephra* ashes] — **te·phrit·ic** (tə·frit′ik) *adj.*

te·phro·sin (tə·frō′sin) *n. Chem.* A white crystalline compound, $C_{23}H_{22}O_7$, extracted from the leaves of a leguminous plant *(Tephrosia vogeli),* from derris, and cube: used as a fish poison. [<NL <Gk. *tephros* ash-colored < *tephra* ashes]

te·phro·sis (tə·frō′sis) *n.* Cremation; incineration. [<NL <Gk. *tephrōsis* < *tephra* ashes]

tep·id (tep′id) *adj.* Moderately warm; lukewarm, as a liquid. [<L *tepidus* < *tepere* be lukewarm] — **te·pid·i·ty** (tə·pid′ə·tē), **tep′id·ness** *n.* — **tep′id·ly** *adv.*

tep·i·dar·i·um (tep′ə·dâr′ē·əm) *n. pl.* **·dar·i·a** (-dâr′ē·ə) In the Roman baths, the intermediate apartment between the cold- and the hot-bath rooms. [<L < *tepidus.* See TEPID.]

Te·quen·da·ma Falls (tā′ken·dä′mä) A falls in the Bogotá river, west of Bogotá, central Colombia; 482 feet high.

te·qui·la (tə·kē′lə) *n.* A Mexican alcoholic liquor made from the maguey. [from *Tequila,* Jalisco, Mexico]

ter- *combining form* Three; third; threefold; three times: *tercentenary.* [<L *ter* thrice]

ter·a·phim (ter′ə·fim) *n. pl. sing.* **ter·aph** (ter′·əf) or **ter·a·phim** Images, small idols, or household gods consulted as oracles by some of the ancient Hebrews: used as a plural or collective singular in the Bible. [<Hebrew *terāphīm*]

ter·a·tism (ter′ə·tiz′əm) *n. Biol.* A monstrosity; especially, a malformed human or animal fetus. [<Gk. *teras* monster]

terato- *combining form* A wonder; monster: *teratogeny.* Also, before vowels, **terat-.** [< Gk. *teras, teratos* a wonder]

ter·a·tog·e·ny (ter′ə·toj′ə·nē) *n. Biol.* The production of monsters or abnormal organisms. Also **ter′a·to·gen′e·sis** (-tō·jen′ə·sis). [<TERATO- + -GENY] — **ter′a·to·gen′ic** (-tō·jen′ik) *adj.*

ter·a·toid (ter′ə·toid) *adj.* Like a monstrosity; abnormal. [<TERAT(O)- + -OID]

ter·a·tol·o·gy (ter′ə·tol′ə·jē) *n.* The branch of biology and medicine treating of abnormal growths or monstrosities. [<TERATO- + -LOGY] — **ter′a·to·log′ic** (-tō·loj′ik) or **·i·cal** *adj.* — **ter′a·tol′o·gist** *n.*

Te·ra·u·chi (te·rä·o͞o·chē), **Count Juichi,** 1879–1946, Japanese general.

ter·bi·a (tûr′bē·ə) *n. Chem.* Oxide of terbium, Tb_2O_3.

ter·bi·um (tûr′bē·əm) *n.* A metallic element (symbol Tb) belonging to the lanthanide series, found in gadolinite and other rare-earth minerals. See ELEMENT. [<NL < *Ytterby,* a town in Sweden] — **ter′bic** *adj.*

terbium metal One of a group in the lanthanide series of elements, including gadolinium, europium, and terbium.

Ter Borch (tûr bôrkh), **Gerard,** 1617?–81, Dutch painter.

Ter·cei·ra (tûr·sâr′ə) The easternmost island of the central Azores; 153 square miles.

ter·cel (tûr′səl) *n.* A male falcon, especially the peregrine falcon: also spelled *tassel.* Also **tierce·let** (tûrs′lit). [<OF <L *tertius* third; said to be so called because every third egg in a falcon's nest was thought to produce a male]

ter·cen·te·nar·y (tûr·sen′tə·ner′ē, tûr′sen·ten′·ər·ē) *adj.* Of or pertaining to a period of 300 years or to a 300th anniversary. — *n. pl.* **·nar·ies** The 300th anniversary. Also *tricentennial.* Also **ter·cen·ten·ni·al** (tûr′sen·ten′ē·əl).

ter·cet (tûr′sit, tûr·set′) *n.* **1** *Music* A triplet. **2** A group of three lines riming together or connected with adjacent triplets by double or triple rime. [<F <Ital. *terzetto,* dim. of *terzo* <L *tertius* a third]

ter·e·bene (ter′ə·bēn) *n. Chem.* A colorless, aromatic liquid hydrocarbon mixture of terpenes from oil of turpentine: used as an antiseptic and expectorant. [<TEREB(INTH) + (TERP)ENE]

te·reb·ic (te·reb′ik, -rē′bik) *adj. Chem.* Of, pertaining to, or derived from a white crystalline acid, $C_7H_{10}O_4$, derived from oil of turpentine. [<TEREBINTH]

ter·e·binth (ter′ə·binth) *n.* A small tree *(Pistacia terebinthus)* with winged pinnate leaves resembling those of the common ash but smaller: the original source of turpentine. [<L *terebinthus* <Gk. *terebinthos*]

ter·e·bin·thine (ter′ə·bin′thin) *adj.* Of or pertaining to the terebinth or turpentine. Also **ter′e·bin′thic.**

te·re·do (tə·rē′dō) *n.* One of a genus *(Teredo)* of marine mollusks (family *Teredinidae*); a shipworm. [<L, borer <Gk. *terēdōn* < *terein* rub hard, bore]

Te·rek (te′rek, *Russian* tye′rik) A river in northern Caucasus, Russian S.F.S.R., flowing 367 miles north and NE from north central Georgian S.S.R. to the NW Caspian Sea.

Ter·ence (ter′əns), 190?–159 B.C., Roman playwright: full name *Publius Terentius Afer.*

Te·re·sa (tə·rē′sə; *Ital., Sp.* tā·rā′sä) Italian and Spanish form of THERESA.

Te·re·sian (ti·rē′shən) *n.* A Carmelite friar or nun of the order founded by St. Teresa of Avila in 1562.

Te·re·si·na (tā′rə·zē′nə) The capital of Piauí state, Brazil.

te·rete (tə·rēt′, ter′ēt) *adj.* Cylindrical and slightly tapering; round in cross-section. [<L *teres, teretis* round, rounded off < *terere* rub]

Te·reus (tir′yo͞os, tir′ē·əs) In Greek mythology, a Thracian king who was transformed into a hoopoe by the gods after he had raped his sister-in-law. See PHILOMELA.

ter·fa (tûr′fə) *n.* An edible fungus (genera *Terfezia* and *Tirmania)* of the deserts of North Africa, having a subterranean fruit body resembling truffles and eaten by the Arabs. [<Arabic *tirfāsh* truffle]

ter·gal (tûr′gəl) *adj.* Of or pertaining to the tergum; dorsal.

ter·gem·i·nate (tər·jem′ə·nit) *adj. Bot.* Having three pairs of forked leaflets. [<TER- + GEMINATE]

ter·gi·ver·sate (tûr′ji·vər·sāt′) *v.i.* **·sat·ed, ·sat·ing** **1** To be evasive; equivocate or prevaricate. **2** To change sides, attitudes, etc.; become a renegade; apostatize. [<L *tergiversatus,* pp. of *tergiversari* < *tergum* back + *versare* turn] — **ter′gi·ver·sa′tor** *n.*

ter·gi·ver·sa·tion (tûr′ji·vər·sā′shən) *n.* **1** Evasion of a point, as by prevarication or subterfuge. **2** Fickleness or insincerity of conduct; shiftiness.

ter·gum (tûr′gəm) *n. Zool.* The back or dorsal part of an arthropod. [<L]

Ter·hune (tər·hyo͞on′), **Albert Payson,** 1872–1942, U. S. author.

term (tûrm) *n.* **1** A word or expression used to designate some definite thing; a technical expression: a scientific *term.* **2** Any word or expression conveying some conception or thought: a *term* of reproach; to speak in general *terms.* **3** *pl.* The conditions or stipulations according to which something is to be done or acceded to: the *terms* of sale; peace *terms.* **4** *pl.* Mutual relations; footing: usually preceded by *on* or *upon*: England was on friendly *terms* with France. **5** *Math.* **a** The antecedent or consequent of a ratio. **b** The numerator or denominator of a fraction. **c** One of the quantities of an algebraic expression that are connected by the plus and minus signs. **d** One of the quantities which compose a series or progression. **6** *Logic* **a** In a proposition, either of the two parts, the subject and predicate, which are joined by a copula. **b** Any of the three elements of a syllogism, each of which appears twice. In a syllogism, the **major term** is the predicate of both the major premise and the conclusion. The **minor term** is the subject of both the minor premise and the conclusion. See SYLLOGISM. 7 A fixed period or definite length of time: a *term* of office. 8 One of the periods of the year appointed for holding instruction in colleges and schools. 9 *Law* **a** One of the prescribed periods of the year during which a court may hold a session. **b** A specific extent of time during which a termor may hold an estate. **c** A space of time allowed a debtor to meet his obligation. **10** *Med.* The time for childbirth. **11** *Archaic* An utmost limit; boundary. **12** *Archit.* A pillar of tapering form, ending in a sculptured head or bust. — *v.t.* To designate by means of a term; name or call. [<OF *terme* <L *terminus* a limit]

Synonyms (noun): article, condition, expression, member, name, phrase, word. *Term* in its figurative use always retains something of its literal sense of a boundary or limit. The *articles* of a contract or other instrument are simply the portions into which it is divided for convenience; the *terms* are the essential statements on which its validity depends—as it were, the landmarks of its meaning or power; a *condition* is a contingent *term*, which may become fixed upon the happening of some contemplated event. In logic a *term* is one of the essential members of a proposition, the boundary of statement in some one direction. Thus in general use *term* is more restricted than *word, expression,* or *phrase*; a *term* is a *word* that limits meaning to a fixed point of statement or to a special class of subjects; as, when we speak of the definition of *terms,* that is of the key *words* in any discussion; or we say "that is a legal or scientific *term.*" See BOUNDARY, DICTION.

ter·ma·gant (tûr′mə·gənt) *n.* A scolding or abusive woman; shrew. —*adj.* Violently abusive and quarrelsome; vixenish. [<TERMAGANT] —**ter′ma·gan′cy** *n.*

Ter·ma·gant (tûr′mə·gənt) An idol or imaginary deity of very turbulent, overbearing character that the medieval romances represented Moslems as worshiping. Also **Ter′·ma·gaunt, Ter′ma·gund** (-gənd).

Ter·man–Mer·rill test (tûr′mən·mer′il) *Psychol.* An extension of the Stanford revision intelligence test which includes ages down to two years and adds many more items at upper levels, with a choice of two alternative scales.

term day 1 A designated day; specifically, quarter–day. 2 At hiring fairs, the day from which the contract of service dates.

term·er (tûr′mər) *n.* 1 *Law* A termor. 2 *Colloq.* A prisoner serving a certain term: usually with an ordinal: a first–*termer.*

ter·mes (tûr′mēz) *n.* A termite.

ter·mi·na·ble (tûr′mə·nə·bəl) *adj.* That may be terminated; limitable; not perpetual. —**ter′·mi·na·bil′i·ty, ter′mi·na·ble·ness** *n.* —**ter′mi·na·bly** *adv.*

ter·mi·nal (tûr′mə·nəl) *adj.* 1 Pertaining to or creative of a boundary, limit, or terminus: a *terminal* railroad station. 2 Pertaining to the delivery or storage of freight or baggage: *terminal* charges. 3 Pertaining to a term or name. 4 Situated at or forming the end of a series or part. 5 *Bot.* Borne at the end of a stem or branch. 6 Of, pertaining to, or occurring in or at the end of a period of time; of a fixed period. —*n.* 1 That which terminates; a terminating point or part; termination; end. 2 *Electr.* One of the two free ends of a conductor, particularly if proceeding from an electric source, as a battery or dynamo. 3 *Archit.* A terminal figure or pedestal; terminus. 4 The edges or planes that form the end of a crystal. 5 A railroad terminus. 6 *pl.* Charges for the use of terminal facilities, or for the handling of freight at railroad terminuses. 7 *Physiol.* The end structure or end of a neuron or nerve fiber. [<F <LL *terminalis* <L *terminus* boundary] —**ter′mi·nal·ly** *adv.*

Ter·mi·na·li·a (tûr′mə·nā′lē·ə) *n. pl. Latin* The ancient Roman festival of Terminus, celebrated on Feb. 23 by the decoration of the boundary markers between private properties, and the offering of sacrifices.

terminal rime The riming of a word or group of syllables at the end of a verse with that at the end of another verse in the same stanza or poem.

terminal velocity *Physics* The velocity acquired by a freely falling body when the resistance of the medium equals the weight of the body.

ter·mi·nate (tûr′mə·nāt) *v.* **·nat·ed, ·nat·ing** *v.t.* 1 To put an end or stop to. 2 To form the conclusion of; finish. 3 To bound or limit. —*v.i.* 4 To have an end; come to an end. See synonyms under ABOLISH, CEASE, END. [<L *terminatus,* pp. of *terminare* end, limit < *terminus* a limit]

ter·mi·na·tion (tûr′mə·nā′shən) *n.* 1 The act of setting bounds or limits. 2 The act of ending or concluding. 3 That which bounds or limits; close; end; limit in time or space. 4 Outcome; result; conclusion. 5 The final letters or syllable of a word; a suffix. See synonyms under BOUNDARY, END.

ter·mi·na·tion·al (tûr′mə·nā′shən·əl) *adj.* Of, pertaining to, or formative of a syllable or other termination; formed by suffixes.

ter·mi·na·tive (tûr′mə·nā′tiv) *adj.* Designed or tending to terminate; determining; definitive; bounding; conclusive. —**ter′mi·na′tive·ly** *adv.*

ter·mi·na·tor (tûr′mə·nā′tər) *n.* 1 One who or that which terminates. 2 *Astron.* The boundary between the illuminated and dark portions of the moon or of a planet.

ter·mi·ner (tûr′mə·nər) *n. Law* The act or function of determining. See OYER AND TERMINER. [<AF *terminour* <F *terminer* end <L *terminare. See* TERM.]

ter·mi·nism (tûr′mə·niz′əm) *n.* 1 *Theol.* The doctrine that God has ordained a limit in the life of each man and of mankind beyond which the opportunity for salvation is lost. 2 A form of nominalism; specifically, the doctrine of William of Ockham, who stated that universals are abstract terms or predicables, rather than either real existents or mere vocal sounds. [<L *terminus* term]

ter·mi·nol·o·gy (tûr′mə·nol′ə·jē) *n.* 1 The study or the use of terms. 2 The technical terms used in a science, art, trade, etc. 3 Nomenclature. [<L *terminus* + -LOGY] —**ter′mi·no·log′i·cal** (-nə·loj′i·kəl) *adj.* —**ter′·mi·no·log′i·cal·ly** *adv.* —**ter′mi·nol′o·gist** *n.*

ter·mi·nus (tûr′mə·nəs) *n. pl.* **·nus·es** or **·ni** (-nī) 1 The final point or goal; end; terminal. 2 The farthermost station on a railway; also, the town in which such station is situated. 3 A boundary or border; also, a boundary mark. See synonyms under END. [<L]

Ter·mi·nus (tûr′mə·nəs) In Roman mythology, the god of boundaries and landmarks.

ter·min·us ad quem (tûr′mə·nəs ad kwem) *Latin* The end or limit to which; the goal; the terminating point of an argument, period, etc.

ter·mi·nus a quo (tûr′mə·nəs ā kwō) *Latin* The starting point.

ter·mite (tûr′mīt) *n.* A white ant. Also *termes.* For illustration see INSECTS (injurious). [<L *termes, termitis*]

term·less (tûrm′lis) *adj.* 1 Of boundless extent or duration. 2 Independent of conditions; unconditional. 3 *Archaic* Incapable of being expressed by terms; indescribable.

term·ly (tûrm′lē) *adj.* Happening or done every term. —*adv.* Periodically.

term·or (tûr′mər) *n. Law* A person who holds lands or tenements for a definite number of years or for life.

tern[1] (tûrn) *n.* Any of several gull–like birds (subfamily *Sterninae*), having the bill pointed and the mandibles co–terminal, smaller than most gulls, with wings more pointed, and the tail usually deeply forked; especially, the common tern *(Sterna hirundo)* of the Atlantic coasts, white with a black cap, and the **least** or **minute tern** *(S. antillarum).* ◆ Homophones: *terne, turn.* [< Scand. Cf. Dan. *terne* tern.]

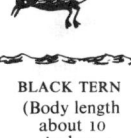

BLACK TERN
(Body length about 10 inches; wingspread, 25 inches)

tern[2] (tûrn) *n.* 1 That which is composed of three; specifically, three numbers in a lottery that, when drawn together, secure a large prize. 2 In New England, a three–masted schooner. ◆ Homophones: *terne, turn.* [<L *terni* by threes < *ter* thrice]

ter·na·ry (tûr′nər·ē) *adj.* 1 Formed or consisting of three; grouped in threes. 2 *Math.* Containing three variables; also, pertaining to systems of notation, having three as a base, or radix. 3 *Chem.* Having three separate parts, as atoms, elements, etc. 4 *Metall.* Made of an alloy which contains three metals. —*n. pl.* **·ries** A group of three; a triad. [<L *ternarius* < *terni* by threes]

ter·nate (tûr′nāt) *adj.* 1 Classified or arranged in threes. 2 *Bot.* Trifoliolate; consisting of threes. [<NL *ternatus* <L *terni* by threes] —**ter′nate·ly** *adv.*

Ter·na·te (ter·nä′tā) An Indonesian island of the northern Moluccas; 41 square miles.

terne (tûrn) *v.t.* **terned, tern·ing** To cover with a thin layer of lead and tin. —*n.* Terne plate. ◆ Homophones: *tern, turn.* [<F *terne* dull; from the resulting finish]

terne plate Steel plate with a coating of lead and tin, having a dull finish and inferior in quality to standard tin plate.

Ter·ni (ter′nē) A city in Umbria, central Italy.

ter·ni·on (tûr′nē·ən) *n.* 1 A set of three. 2 A section of a book composed of three sheets in double folds, or 12 pages. [<L *terni* by threes]

Ter·no·pol (tûr·nō′pəl, *Russian* tyir·nô′pəl) A city in western Ukrainian S.S.R.: *Polish* **Tar·no·pol** (tär·nô′pəl).

Ter·pan·der (tər·pan′dər) Greek poet and musician of the seventh century B.C.

ter·pene (tûr′pēn) *n. Chem.* Any of a class of isomeric hydrocarbons, $C_{10}H_{16}$, contained chiefly in the essential oils of coniferous plants. [<*terp(entin),* earlier form of TURPENTINE + -ENE]

ter·pin·e·ol (tər·pin′ē·ōl, -ol) *n. Chem.* A colorless, unsaturated, tertiary alcohol, $C_{10}H_{17}OH$, derived from the essential oils of various plants and also made synthetically: it has an odor of lilacs and is used in perfumery. [< *terpin,* earlier form of TERPENE + -OL[1]]

ter·pi·nol (tûr′pə·nōl, -nol) *n.* An oily, colorless, liquid mixture of various terpenes, having an odor of hyacinth. [See TERPINEOL]

Terp·sich·o·re (tûrp·sik′ə·rē) The Muse of dancing. [<Gk. *Terpsichorē* < *terpsichoros* delighting in the dance < *terpsis* enjoyment + *choros* dance] —**Terp·si·cho·re·an** (tûrp′·si·kə·rē′ən) *adj.*

terp·si·cho·re·an (tûrp′si·kə·rē′ən) *adj.* Of or relating to dancing: also **terp′si·cho·re′al.** —*n. Colloq.* A dancer.

ter·ra (ter′ə) *n. Latin* The earth; earth.

ter·ra al·ba (ter′ə al′bə) 1 Pipe clay. 2 The pigment made from ground gypsum. 3 Magnesia. 4 A grade of kaolin used as an adulterant of paints. [<L, white earth]

ter·race (ter′is) *n.* 1 An artificial raised level space, as of lawn, having one or more vertical or sloping sides; also, such levels collectively. 2 A raised level supporting a row of houses, or the houses occupying such a position. 3 The flat roof of an Oriental or Spanish house. 4 A relatively narrow step in the face of a steep natural slope. 5 An open gallery; balcony. —*v.t.* **·raced, ·rac·ing** To form into or provide with a terrace or terraces. [<OF <Ital. *terraccia* <L *terra* earth]

ter·ra cot·ta (ter′ə kot′ə) 1 A hard, durable, kiln–burnt clay, reddish–brown in color and usually unglazed: widely used as a structural material and also, in glazed and colored forms, for tiles, building façades, etc. 2 A statue or figure made of this clay. 3 A brownish–orange color resembling that of terra cotta. [<Ital., cooked earth]

ter·ra fir·ma (ter′ə fûr′mə) Solid ground, as distinguished from the sea or the air. [<L]

ter·rain (te·rān′, ter′ān) *n.* 1 Battleground, or a region suited for defense, fortifications, etc. 2 A piece or plot of ground; a region or territory viewed with regard to its suitability for some particular purpose. 3 A terrane. [<F <L *terrenum* < *terrenus* earthen < *terra* earth]

ter·ra in·cog·ni·ta (ter′ə in·kog′nə·tə) 1 An unknown land or region. 2 An unexplored field of study or knowledge. [<L]

Ter·ra·my·cin (ter′ə·mī′sin) *n.* Proprietary name for an antibiotic isolated from a soil mold *(Streptomyces rimosus),* of value in the treatment of a wide variety of pathogenic infections.

ter·rane (te·rān′, ter′ān) *n.* **1** *Geol.* A continuous formation or continuous series of related formations; an area of particular rocks. **2** A tract or region considered with reference to some special purpose. [<F *terrain.* See TERRAIN.]

ter·ra·pin (ter′ə·pin) *n.* One of the several North American edible tortoises (family *Testudinidae*); especially, the diamond-back terrapin. [<Algonquian]

DIAMOND-BACK TERRAPIN (Shell from 4 to 7 inches)

ter·ra·que·ous (te·rā′kwē·əs) *adj.* Composed of, living in, or consisting of, both land and water. [<L *terra* earth, land + AQUEOUS]

ter·rar·i·um (te·râr′ē·əm) *n. pl.* **·rar·i·ums** or **·rar·i·a** (-râr′ē·ə) **1** A small enclosure or box with glass sides for live lizards, growing plants, etc. **2** A vivarium for land animals. [<L *terra* earth + -ARIUM, on analogy with *aquarium*]

ter·raz·zo (ter·rät′sō) *n.* Flooring made of small pieces of marble or colored stone set in concrete. Also **ter·raz′zo Ve·ne·zia·no** (vā′nā·tsyä′nō). [<Ital. <L *terra* earth]

terre (târ) *n. French* Earth. See TERRA.

Terre·bonne (ter′bon′, -bôn′), **Bayou** A lagoon in SE Louisiana, flowing 55 miles south to **Terrebonne Bay,** a shallow inlet of the Gulf of Mexico SW of New Orleans.

ter·reen (te·rēn′) See TERRINE.

Ter·re Haute (ter′ə hōt′) A city in western Indiana, on the Wabash River.

ter·rene[1] (te·rēn′) *adj.* **1** Pertaining to earth; earthy. **2** Earthly; worldly; mundane. —*n.* **1** The surface of the earth. **2** The earth; a land or terrain. [<L *terrenus* < *terra* earth]

ter·rene[2] (te·rēn′) See TERRINE.

terre·plein (ter′plān) *n.* **1** The upper surface of a rampart behind the parapet, on which the guns are mounted. **2** An embankment with a level top. [<F *terre* earth + *plein* level]

ter·res·tri·al (tə·res′trē·əl) *adj.* **1** Belonging to the earth: opposed to *celestial* or *cosmic.* **2** Pertaining to land or earth: *terrestrial* magnetism. **3** *Biol.* Living on or growing in the earth or land: opposed to *aquatic, aerial,* etc. **4** Belonging to or consisting of land, as distinct from water, trees, etc. **5** Worldly; mundane. —*n.* An inhabitant of the earth. [<L *terrestris* <L *terra* land] —**ter·res′tri·al·ly** *adv.* —**ter·res′tri·al·ness** *n.*

ter·ret (ter′it) *n.* **1** One of two metal rings projecting from the saddle of a harness, through which the reins are passed. **2** A ring for attaching a leash to a dog's collar, etc. Also **ter′rit.** [ME *toret* <F *touret* small wheel, dim. of *tour* a turn]

terre-ten·ant (ter′ten′ənt) *n. Law* **1** The person who is in actual possession of lands. **2** The owner or holder of the legal estate in lands. Also spelled *ter-tenant.* [<AF *terre tenaunt* holding land <F *terre* (<L *terra* land) + *tenaunt* holding, ppr. of *tenir* hold <L *tenere*]

terre-verte (ter′vert′) *n.* **1** An earthy silicate resembling glauconite and used as a green pigment by artists. **2** Glauconite. [<F *terre verte* green earth]

ter·ri·ble (ter′ə·bəl) *adj.* **1** Of a nature to excite terror; appalling. **2** *Colloq.* Characterized by excess; severe; extreme. **3** Inspiring awe. See synonyms under AWFUL, FORMIDABLE, FRIGHTFUL, GRIM. [<F <L *terribilis* < *terrere* terrify] —**ter′ri·ble·ness** *n.* —**ter′ri·bly** *adv.*

ter·ric·o·lous (te·rik′ə·ləs) *adj. Biol.* Living on or in the ground. Also **ter·ric′o·line** (-lēn, -lin). [<L *terricola* earth dweller < *terra* earth + *colere* dwell]

ter·ri·er[1] (ter′ē·ər) *n.* A small, active, wiry dog of several breeds, formerly used to hunt burrowing animals and noted for the courage and eagerness with which it "goes to earth" in pursuit of its quarry. See AIREDALE, DANDIE DINMONT, SCHNAUZER. [<OF <L *terrarius* pertaining to earth. See TERRIER².]

— Bedlington terrier A liver-colored or blue terrier with muscular body, long neck, narrow skull, and thick coat. It is very game in attacking badgers, foxes, or vermin. [<*Bedlington,* shire in Northumberland County, England]

— Boston terrier A small, non-sporting terrier of dark brindle color marked with white, crossbred from the English bulldog and the white English terrier, and having a square skull, short tail, and short, smooth coat.

— bull terrier A white terrier first crossbred from the bulldog and the white English terrier, then crossed with the Spanish pointer. It has a muscular, well-balanced body, long head, flat skull, and short, stiff coat.

— Cairn terrier A small, stocky, alert terrier of Scotland, having a broad head, a rough outer coat of any color except white, pointed ears, and a black nose: used as a retriever and to exterminate vermin.

— Clydesdale terrier A straight-eared, silky-haired dog, with tiny, erect ears and short legs, bred from but smaller than the Skye terrier.

— fox terrier A small white terrier, either smooth or wire-haired: formerly bred for bringing the fox out of his burrow, now usually a pet.

— Irish terrier A small, red or golden-red, rough-haired terrier having a rather long body built on racing lines: used for hunting small or big game and vermin and also for retrieving in water.

— Kerry blue terrier A breed of terrier originating in County Kerry, Ireland, having a long straight back, straight legs, long head, and soft, wavy, bluish-black coat: used to hunt and retrieve small game and as a herd dog, watchdog, and companion.

— Lakeland terrier A courageous breed of terrier having a dense, harsh coat of black, blue, or grizzle and tan: originally from Cumberland County, England, and used in hunting the otter or the fox.

— Lhasa terrier A breed of terrier native to Tibet, with a heavy yellow, black, white, or brown coat, straight forelegs, and tail curled over its back.

— Manchester terrier A small, speedy, short-haired, black-and-tan terrier, originally bred in Manchester, England, and known at one time as **Black-and-Tan terrier.**

— Norwich terrier A breed of small, wire-haired terrier, native in England, and usually red, black-and-tan, or grizzled: used in hunting.

Welsh Terrier

Airedale

Lakeland Terrier

Irish Terrier

West Highland White Terrier

Cairn Terrier

Yorkshire Terrier

Skye Terrier

Norwich Terrier

Dandie Dinmont

Boston Terrier

Bull Terrier

Scottish Terrier

Schnauzer

Wire-haired Fox Terrier

Smooth-haired Fox Terrier

Bedlington Terrier

Manchester Terrier

Sealyham Terrier

Kerry Blue Terrier

— **Scottish terrier** A Scotch breed of small, wire-haired, alert, and intelligent terrier, having a compact body, short legs, small eyes and skull, and gray, brindled, grizzled, black, sandy, or wheaten coat. Also **Scotch terrier, Scottie.**

— **Sealyham terrier** A terrier of mixed ancestry, native of Sealyham, Wales, with short legs, a wide skull, square jaws, and wiry coat, usually solid white, but sometimes marked with lemon or brown on ears and head: used in hunting badger, fox, and otter.

— **Skye terrier** The smallest, lowest-set, and longest-bodied of all useful terriers, unrivaled for acute scent, hearing, sight, and alacrity. Its coat is long and straight, usually blue, gray, or fawn with black points.

— **Welsh terrier** An old breed of rough-haired, black-and-tan terrier, a native of Wales, having a broader head than a fox terrier and a flat skull: used for hunting otter, fox, and badger.

— **West Highland white terrier** A breed of small terrier, with long, low, compact body, short legs, and a pure white, coarse, wiry outer coat: said to have existed in Scotland prior to 1600 A.D.

— **Yorkshire terrier** A toy breed, among the smallest of all varieties of terriers. It has semi-erect ears and a coat of long, silky, dark steel-blue hair, with golden tan on chest and head. At first a pet of the working classes, especially of weavers, it later became a fashionable pet.

ter·ri·er[2] (ter′ē·ər) *n. Law* **1** A land survey setting forth in detail the number of acres, names of tenants, etc., in a given district: the *terrier* of glebe lands. **2** A book containing the lists of the lands either of a private person or a corporation; a rent roll. [<OF, list of tenants <LL *terrarius* a roll describing landed property <L, pertaining to land < *terra* land]

ter·rif·ic (tə·rif′ik) *adj.* **1** Arousing or calculated to arouse great terror or fear. **2** *Colloq.* Excessive; extreme; tremendous. See synonyms under AWFUL, FRIGHTFUL. — **ter·rif′i·cal·ly** *adv.*

ter·ri·fy (ter′ə·fī) *v.t.* **·fied, ·fy·ing** To fill with extreme terror. See synonyms under FRIGHTEN. [<L *terrificare* < *terrificus* causing fear < *terrere* frighten + *facere* make]

ter·rig·e·nous (te·rij′ə·nəs) *adj.* **1** Produced from or of the earth. **2** *Geol.* Derived from the land: said of marine deposits formed of material washed from the land, as contrasted with those of organic, chemical, or other origin, formed in the sea. **3** Earthborn. Also **ter·ri·gene** (ter′ə·jēn). [<L *terrigenus* < *terra* earth + *gignere* be born]

ter·rine (te·rēn′) *n.* **1** An earthenware jar containing some delicacy for the table and sold with its contents: a *terrine* of preserved ginger. **2** A kind of ragout or stew. Also spelled *terreen, terrene.* [<F <LL *terrineus* made of earth <L *terra* earth. Doublet of TUREEN.]

ter·ri·to·ri·al (ter′ə·tôr′ē·əl, -tō′rē-) *adj.* **1** Pertaining to a territory or territories; limited to a particular territory. **2** Designating military forces intended for territorial defense. **3** Belonging to a particular locality. **4** Organized or intended primarily for national defense: a *territorial* reserve. — **ter′ri·to′ri·al·ly** *adv.*

Ter·ri·to·ri·al (ter′ə·tôr′ē·əl, -tō′rē-) *adj.* Of or pertaining to any or all of the Territories of the United States: the *Territorial* system. — *n.* A member of the Territorial Army in Great Britain who enlisted for home defense but volunteered for overseas service in World War I.

ter·ri·to·ri·al·ism (ter′ə·tôr′ē·əl·iz′əm, -tō′rē-) *n.* The organizations, theories, or doctrines of the territorial systems. — **ter′ri·to′ri·al·ist** *n.*

ter·ri·to·ri·al·i·ty (ter′ə·tôr′ē·al′ə·tē, -tō′rē-) *n.* Territorial condition, status, or position.

ter·ri·to·ri·al·ize (ter′ə·tôr′ē·əl·īz′, -tō′rē-) *v.t.* **·ized, ·iz·ing** **1** To enlarge by annexation of territory. **2** To reduce to the political status of a territory. **3** To distribute among certain territories. — **ter′ri·to′ri·al·i·za′tion** *n.*

territorial jurisdiction *Law* The sovereign jurisdiction exercised by a state over all lands, waters, persons, and properties within its boundaries.

territorial system **1** A system of church government in which all inhabitants of a territory are required to belong to the same religion as the civil ruler. **2** Local organization for militia service. **3** Landlordism; a system giving predominance to landowners.

territorial waters The belt of sea under a state's territorial jurisdiction: formerly, the range of a cannon shot, or three miles: now often controversial. Also **territorial sea.**

ter·ri·to·ry (ter′ə·tôr′ē, -tō′rē) *n. pl.* **·ries** **1** The domain over which a sovereign state exercises jurisdiction. **2** Any considerable tract of land; a region; district; figuratively, sphere; province. **3** An area assigned for a special purpose: the *territory* of a commercial traveler. [<L *territorium* < *terra* earth]

Ter·ri·to·ry (ter′ə·tôr′ē, -tō′rē) *n. U.S.* A region having a certain degree of self-government, but not having the status of a State. Alaska and Hawaii were formerly Territories.

ter·ror (ter′ər) *n.* **1** An overwhelming impulse of fear; extreme fright or dread. **2** That which or one who causes extreme fear. **3** *Colloq.* An intolerable nuisance: That child is a holy *terror.* See synonyms under ALARM, FEAR, FRIGHT. [<F *terreur* <L *terror* fright < *terrere* frighten]

ter·ror·ism (ter′ər·iz′əm) *n.* **1** The act of terrorizing. **2** A system of government that seeks to rule by intimidation. **3** Unlawful acts of violence committed in an organized attempt to overthrow a government.

ter·ror·ist (ter′ər·ist) *n.* **1** One who adopts or supports a policy of terrorism. **2** A Jacobin or Republican of the French Revolution of 1789, especially during the Reign of Terror. **3** A member of political extremist groups in czarist Russia. **4** An alarmist; a scaremonger. — **ter′ror·is′tic** *adj.*

ter·ror·ize (ter′ə·rīz) *v.t.* **·ized, ·iz·ing** **1** To reduce to a state of terror; terrify. **2** To coerce through intimidation. Also *Brit.* **ter′·ror·ise.** — **ter′ror·i·za′tion** *n.* — **ter′ror·iz′er** *n.*

ter·ry (ter′ē) *n. pl.* **·ries** **1** The loop raised for the nap in weaving pile fabrics. **2** A pile dressmaking fabric in which the loops are uncut: also **terry cloth.** **3** A looped cotton fabric, very water-absorbent, used chiefly for towels and beach robes. [Prob. <F *tiré,* pp. of *tirer* draw <L *trahere*]

Ter·ry (ter′ē), **Dame Ellen,** 1848–1928, English actress.

terse (tûrs) *adj.* **1** Elegantly concise; short and to the point. **2** Rubbed to a polish; clean; polished; refined. [<L *tersus,* pp. of *tergere* rub off, rub down] — **terse′ly** *adv.* — **terse′ness** *n.*

Synonyms: brief, compact, compendious, concise, condensed, laconic, pithy, sententious, short, succinct. Anything *short* or *brief* is of relatively small extent. That which is *concise* is trimmed down, and that which is *condensed* is, as it were, pressed together, so as to include as much as possible within a small space. That which is *compendious* gathers the substance of a matter into a few weighty and effective words. *Succinct* writing is taut and lean without extraneous detail. *Summary* implies compression to the utmost, often to the point of abruptness; as, a *summary* statement or a *summary* dismissal. That which is *terse* has an elegant and finished completeness within the smallest possible compass. A *sententious* style is one abounding in maxims or short, pithy phrases. A *pithy* utterance gives the gist of a matter effectively, whether in rude or elegant style. *Antonyms*: diffuse, lengthy, long, prolix, tedious, verbose, wordy.

ter–ten·ant (ter′ten′ənt) See TERRE-TENANT.

ter·tial (tûr′shəl) *Ornithol. adj.* Of or pertaining to the third row of flight feathers in a bird's wing. — *n.* A tertiary feather. [<L *tertius* third < *ter* thrice]

ter·tian (tûr′shən) *adj.* Recurring every third day, reckoned inclusively, hence every alternate day. — *n. Pathol.* A disease, the paroxysms of which return every other day; a tertian fever. [<L *(febris) tertiana* tertian (fever) < *tertius* third]

ter·ti·ar·y (tûr′shē·er′ē, -shə·rē) *adj.* **1** Third in point of time, number, degree, or standing. **2** Tertial. **3** *Eccl.* Pertaining to the third order of a religious body. **4** *Chem.* **a** Having three substituted atoms or radicals: a *tertiary* amine. **b** Denoting a radical in which three bonds of the combining carbon atoms are directly connected with three other carbon atoms: *tertiary* butyl. — *n. pl.* **·ar·ies** **1** *Ornithol.* One of the feathers attached to the humerus joint of the wing of a bird. **2** Any member of the third order of a monastic body. [<L *tertiarius* < *tertius* third]

Ter·ti·ar·y (tûr′shē·er′ē, -shə·rē) *Geol. adj.* Of or pertaining to the earlier of the two geological periods or systems comprising the Cenozoic era, following the Cretaceous and succeeded by the Quaternary. — *n.* The Tertiary period or system, characterized by the rise of mammals.

ter·ti·um quid (tûr′shē·əm kwid) *Latin* **1** A third something; an indefinite or undefined thing related in some way to two definite or known things. **2** A mediating factor between essentially opposite things.

Ter·tul·li·an (tər·tul′ē·ən) Anglicized name of Quintus Septimius Florens Tertullianus, A.D. 160?–230?, Latin church father.

Te·ru·el (tā′rōō·el′) **1** A province in NE Spain; 6,710 square miles. **2** The capital city of Teruel province; scene of fierce fighting in the Spanish Civil War, 1937.

ter·va·lent (tûr′və·lənt, tər·vā′lənt) *adj. Chem.* Trivalent.

ter·za–ri·ma (ter′tsä·rē′mä) *n. pl.* **ter·ze–ri·me** (ter′tsā·rē′mā) A form of Italian triplet, in iambic decasyllables or hendecasyllables, in which the middle line of the first triplet rimes with the first and third lines of the following triplet: used by Dante in the *Divine Comedy.* [<Ital., third or triple line]

ter·zet·to (ter·tset′tō) *n. pl.* **·ti** (-tē) *Music* A short composition for three performers or singers; a trio. [See TERCET]

Tesch·en (tesh′ən) A territory and former principality in southern Poland and eastern Silesia, Czechoslovakia; 850 square miles; incorporated in Germany, 1939–45. *Czech* **Tě·šín** (tye′shēn), *Polish* **Cie·szyn** (che′shin).

Te·sho La·ma (te′shō lä′mə) See under DALAI LAMA.

Tes·la (tes′lə), **Nikola,** 1857–1943, U. S. electrical inventor born in Yugoslavia.

Tes·lin Lake (tez′lin, tes′-) A lake between NW British Columbia and southern Yukon, Canada; about 200 square miles; 80 miles long, 1 to 3 miles wide.

tes·sel·late (tes′ə·lāt) *v.t.* **·lat·ed, ·lat·ing** To construct in the style of checkered mosaic; lay or adorn with squares or tiles, as pavement. [<L *tessellatus* checkered < *tessella,* dim. of *tessera* cube. See TESSERA.] — **tes′sel·lat′ed** *adj.*

tes·sel·la·tion (tes′ə·lā′shən) *n.* **1** Tessellated work. **2** The art or act of doing such work.

tes·ser·a (tes′ər·ə) *n. pl.* **·ser·ae** (-ər·ē) **1** A small square, as of stone, glass, etc., used in mosaic work. **2** A small object, often a square or cube, as of bone or wood, used as a die in gambling or as a token, voucher, or the like. [<L <dial. Gk. (Ionic) *tesseres* four]

tes·ser·act (tes′ər·akt) *n. Math.* **1** A construct intended to illustrate graphically or in the form of a model the general appearance of a four-dimensional figure. **2** A hypercube bounded by 8 cubes or cells, with 16 vertices, 24 faces, and 32 edges. [<dial. Gk. (Ionic) *tesseres* four + *aktis* ray]

Tes·sin (te·sēn′) See TICINO.

test[1] (test) *v.t.* **1** To subject to a test or trial; try. **2** *Chem.* **a** To refine, as gold or silver, by means of lead, as in the process of cupellation. **b** To examine by means of some reagent, as in testing for sulfuric acid. — *v.i.* **3** *Chem.* To undergo testing; also, to show specified qualities or properties under testing: The alcohol *tested* 75 percent. See synonyms under EXAMINE. [<*n.*] — *n.* **1** Subjection to conditions that disclose the true character of a person or thing in relation to some particular quality. **2** An examination made for the purpose of proving or disproving some matter in doubt, as mental condition. 3 A criterion or standard of judgment. 4 An oath or other confirmatory evidence of principles or belief. 5 *Chem.* **a** A reaction by means of which the identity of a compound or one of its constituents may be determined. **b** Its agent or the result. 6 An earthen vessel similar to a cupel, formerly used in testing metals. 7 A series of questions, problems, etc., intended to measure the extent of knowledge, aptitudes, intelligence, and other mental traits: an intelligence *test.* See synonyms under PROOF. [<OF, a cupel, pot <L *testum* an earthen vessel < *testa* potsherd, shell] —**test'a·ble** *adj.*

test[2] (test) *n.* 1 *Zool.* A rigid external case or covering of many invertebrates, as a sea urchin or mollusk; a shell. 2 *Bot.* A testa. [<L *testa* shell]

test[3] (test) *v.t.* To attest. [<OF *tester* bequeath <L *testari* be a witness. See TESTAMENT.]

tes·ta (tes'tə) *n. pl.* **·tae** (-tē) 1 *Bot.* The outer, usually hard and brittle coat or integument of a seed. 2 *Zool.* A test. [See TEST[2]]

tes·ta·ce·an (tes·tā'shē·ən, -shən) *adj.* Pertaining or belonging to an order *(Testacea)* of rhizopods enclosed in a single-chambered cell. [<NL <L *testaceum* shellfish < *testaceus.* See TESTACEOUS.]

tes·ta·ceous (tes·tā'shəs) *adj.* 1 Of or derived from shells or shellfish. 2 Having a hard shell. 3 Dull brick-red or brownish-yellow. [<L *testaceus* of shell, brick < *testa* a shell]

tes·ta·cy (tes'tə·sē) *n. Law* The state of being testate or of having left a will at death: opposed to *intestacy.*

tes·ta·ment (tes'tə·mənt) *n.* 1 The written declaration of one's last will: usually **last will and testament.** In strictness, a testament differs from a will in that it bequeaths personal property only, but the words are commonly used interchangeably. 2 In Biblical use, a covenant; dispensation. [<F <L *testamentum* < *testari* testify < *testis* a witness] —**tes'ta·men'tal** *adj.*

Tes·ta·ment (tes'tə·mənt) *n.* 1 One of the two volumes of the Bible, distinguished as the **Old** and the **New Testament.** 2 Specifically, a volume containing the New Testament.

tes·ta·men·ta·ry (tes'tə·men'tər·ē) *adj.* 1 Derived from, bequeathed by, or set forth in a will. 2 Appointed or provided by, or done in accordance with, a will. 3 Pertaining to a will, or to the administration or settlement of a will; testamental. 4 *Often cap.* Pertaining to a Testament.

tes·tate (tes'tāt) *adj.* Having made a will before decease. [<L *testatus,* pp. of *testari* be a witness. See TESTAMENT.]

tes·ta·tor (tes·tā'tər, tes'tā·tər) *n.* 1 The maker of a will. 2 One who has died leaving a will. [<L] —**tes·ta'trix** (-triks) *n. fem.*

test·er[1] (tes'tər) *n.* One who tests; a device for testing.

tes·ter[2] (tes'tər) *n.* A flat canopy over a tomb, pulpit, or bed. [<OF *testiere* < *teste* head <L *testa* shell, skull]

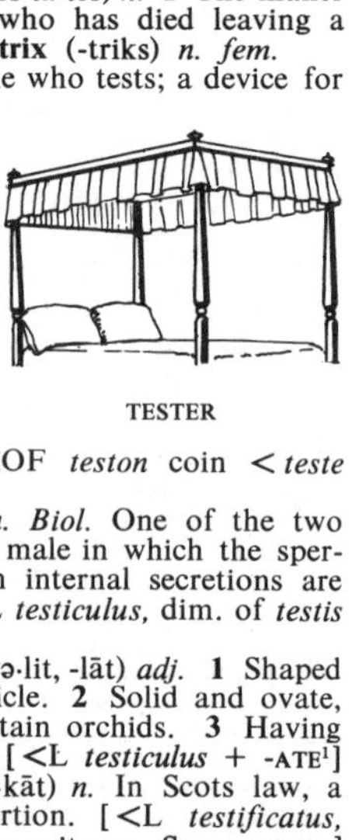

TESTER

tes·ter[3] (tes'tər) *n. Obs.* A silver coin of the Tudor period, originally equal to twelve pence, later worth sixpence. [<OF *teston* coin < *teste* head. See TESTER[2].]

tes·ti·cle (tes'ti·kəl) *n. Biol.* One of the two genital glands of the male in which the spermatozoa and certain internal secretions are formed; a testis. [<L *testiculus,* dim. of *testis* testicle]

tes·tic·u·late (tes·tik'yə·lit, -lāt) *adj.* 1 Shaped or formed like a testicle. 2 Solid and ovate, like the roots of certain orchids. 3 Having organs like testicles. [<L *testiculus* + -ATE[1]]

tes·tif·i·cate (tes·tif'ə·kāt) *n.* In Scots law, a solemn written assertion. [<L *testificatus,* pp. of *testificari* bear witness. See TESTIFY.]

tes·ti·fi·ca·tion (tes'tə·fə·kā'shən) *n.* 1 The act of testifying or the giving of testimony. 2 The testimony given. —**tes'ti·fi·ca'tor** *n.*

tes·ti·fy (tes'tə·fī) *v.* **·fied, ·fy·ing** *v.i.* 1 To make solemn declaration of truth or fact. 2 *Law* To give testimony; bear witness. 3 To serve as evidence or indication: Her rags *testified* to her poverty. —*v.t.* 4 To bear witness to; affirm positively. 5 *Law* To state or declare on oath or affirmation. 6 To be evidence or indication of. 7 To make known publicly; declare. See synonyms under AFFIRM, AVOW. [<L *testificari* < *testis* witness + *facere* make] —**tes'ti·fi'er** *n.*

tes·ti·mo·ni·al (tes'tə·mō'nē·əl) *n.* 1 A formal token of regard. 2 A written certificate; an acknowledgment of services or worth; a letter of recommendation. —*adj.* Pertaining to or constituting testimony or a testimonial. [<L *testimonialis* < *testimonium.* See TESTIMONY.]

tes·ti·mo·ny (tes'tə·mō'nē) *n. pl.* **·nies** 1 A statement or affirmation of a fact, as before a court; evidence; proof. 2 The aggregate of proof offered in a case. 3 The act of testifying; attestation. 4 Public declaration regarding some experience. 5 The Decalog; the Old Testament Scriptures. [<L *testimonium* < *testis* a witness] —**tes'ti·mo'nied** *Obs. adj.*

Synonyms: affidavit, affirmation, attestation, deposition, proof, witness. *Testimony,* in legal as well as in common use, denotes the statements of witnesses. *Deposition* and *affidavit* denote *testimony* reduced to writing. The *deposition* differs from the *affidavit* in that the latter is voluntary and without cross-examination, while the former is made under interrogatories and subject to cross-examination. *Evidence* is a broader term, including the *testimony* of witnesses and all facts of every kind that tend to prove a thing true; we have the *testimony* of a traveler that a fugitive passed this way; his footprints in the sand are additional *evidence* of the fact. Compare PROOF.

tes·tis (tes'tis) *n. pl.* **·tes** (-tēz) A testicle. [<L]

test meal A meal of prescribed materials and quantity taken as a preliminary to a subsequent examination of the contents of the stomach.

tes·ton (tes'tən, tes·to͞on') *n. Obs.* 1 A European silver coin: so called from the head on the obverse side. 2 A French coin of the 16th century. 3 An English silver coin; a tester. Also **tes·toon** (tes·to͞on'). [<F <Ital. *testone,* aug. of *testa* head <L, skull]

tes·tos·ter·one (tes·tos'tə·rōn) *n. Biochem.* A male sex hormone, $C_{19}H_{28}O_2$, isolated as a white crystalline substance from the testes, and also made synthetically. [<TESTIS + STER(OL) + -ONE]

test paper 1 *Chem.* A paper saturated with some reagent that readily changes color when exposed to certain others, as litmus paper. 2 A list of questions, problems, etc., for the testing of students.

test pilot An aviator who flies airplanes of new design to test their performance under various conditions.

test tube A glass tube, open at one end, and usually with a rounded bottom, used in making chemical or biological tests.

tes·tu·di·nal (tes·to͞o'də·nəl, -tyo͞o'-) *adj.* Pertaining to or like a turtle or tortoise shell: also **tes·tu'di·nate.** [<L *testudo, -inis* tortoise]

Tes·tu·din·i·dae (tes'to͞o·din'i·dē, -tyo͞o-) *n. pl.* A family of reptiles having a dorsal shell or carapace constituted chiefly by the vertebrae and ribs and a ventral shell or plastron; tortoises and turtles. [<NL <L *testudo, -inis* tortoise]

tes·tu·do (tes·to͞o'dō, -tyo͞o'-) *n. pl.* **·di·nes** (-də·nēz) 1 A shed or screen used by the Romans for the protection of soldiers in siege operations. 2 A protecting cover formed by soldiers in ranks by overlapping their shields above their heads. [<L < *testa* shell]

Tes·tu·do (tes·to͞o'dō, -tyo͞o'-) *n.* A genus typical of land tortoises. [<L]

tes·ty (tes'tē) *adj.* **·ti·er, ·ti·est** Having an irritable disposition; touchy. See synonyms under FRETFUL. [<AF *testif* heady <OF *teste* head <L *testa* skull] —**tes'ti·ly** *adv.* —**tes'ti·ness** *n.*

te·tan·ic (ti·tan'ik) *adj.* Relating to or productive of tetanus: also **te·tan'i·cal.** —*n.* A drug capable of causing convulsions, as strychnine or nux vomica.

tet·a·nize (tet'ə·nīz) *v.t.* **·nized, ·niz·ing** To affect with tetanic spasms. —**tet'a·ni·za'tion** *n.*

tet·a·nus (tet'ə·nəs) *n.* 1 *Pathol.* An acute infectious disease caused by a bacillus *(Clostridium tetani)* and characterized by rigid spasmodic contraction of various voluntary muscles, especially that form affecting the muscles of the jaw, called *lockjaw.* 2 *Physiol.* A state of contraction in a muscle excited by a rapid series of shocks. [<L <Gk. *tetanos* spasm < *teinein* stretch]

tet·a·ny (tet'ə·nē) *n. Pathol.* 1 Intermittent tetanic spasms, usually due to defective metabolism. 2 Tetanus.

tetarto- *combining form* Four; fourth. Also, before vowels, **tetart-.** [<Gk. *tetartos* fourth < *tettares* four]

te·tar·to·he·dral (ti·tär'tō·hē'drəl) *adj.* Possessing one fourth of the planes necessary for true symmetry: said of crystals.

tetch·y (tech'ē) See TECHY.

tête-à-tête (tāt'ə·tāt', *Fr.* tet·à·tet') *adj.* Being face to face; literally, head to head; hence, confidential, as between two persons. —*n.* 1 A private interview; a confidential chat between two persons. 2 An S-shaped sofa on which two persons may face each other. —*adv.* In private or personal talk. [<F]

tête-bêche (tet·besh') *adj. French* Literally, head to foot: said of a pair of stamps so printed that one is reversed in relation to the other.

tête-de-pont (tet·də·pôn') *n. pl.* **têtes-de-pont** (tet·də·pôn') *French* A bridgehead.

teth (teth) *n.* The ninth Hebrew letter. See ALPHABET.

teth·er (teth'ər) *n.* 1 Something used to check or confine, as a rope for fastening an animal. 2 The range, scope, or limit of one's powers or field of action. —**at the end of one's tether** At the extreme end or limit of one's resources. —*v.t.* To fasten or confine by a tether. [ME *tethir* <Scand. Cf. ON *tiodhr* a tether.]

Te·thys (tē'this) In Greek mythology, a Titaness, sister and wife of Oceanus and mother of the Oceanids.

Te·ton Range (tē'ton, tēt'n) A range of the Rocky Mountains, chiefly in NW Wyoming; highest peak, 13,776 feet.

te·to·tum (tē·tō'təm) See TEETOTUM.

tetra- *combining form* Four; fourfold: *tetrachord.* Also, before vowels, **tetr-.**

tet·ra·ba·sic (tet'rə·bā'sik) *adj. Chem.* 1 Containing four atoms of hydrogen replaceable by a base or basic radicals: said of certain acids. 2 Denoting a compound with four atoms of a univalent metal or the equivalent.

tet·ra·brach (tet'rə·brak) *n.* A Greek or Latin word or foot made up of four short syllables. [<Gk. *tetrabrachys* < *tessares, tettares* four + *brachys* short]

tet·ra·cene (tet'rə·sēn) *n. Chem.* A yellow, solid, nitrogen compound, $C_2H_8N_{10}$, used as a sensitizer or combustion initiator in priming compositions. Also *tetrazine.*

tet·ra·chlo·ride (tet'rə·klôr'īd, -id, -klō'rīd, -rid) *n. Chem.* A compound containing four atoms of chlorine. Also **tet'ra·chlo'rid** (-klôr'id, -klō'rid).

tet·ra·chord (tet'rə·kôrd) *n. Music* 1 A scale series of half an octave. 2 The interval of a perfect fourth. [<Gk. *tetrachordon* a musical instrument < *tetras* group of four + *chordē* string] —**tet'ra·chor'dal** *adj.*

te·trac·id (te·tras'id) *Chem. adj.* Denoting a base which is capable of combination with four molecules of a monobasic acid to form a salt or ester. —*n.* A base having four replaceable hydroxyl radicals. [<TETR(A)- + ACID]

tet·ra·cy·cline (tet'rə·sī'klin) *n. Chem.* A nitrogenous compound, $C_{22}H_{24}N_2O_8$, isolated as a yellow, odorless, crystalline powder from certain species of a soil bacillus (genus *Streptomyces*). It forms the base of several antibiotics, as Aureomycin and Terramycin. [< *tetracyclic,* containing four atomic rings + -INE[2]]

tet·rad (tet'rad) *n.* 1 A collection of four, or the number four. 2 An atom, radical, or element that is quadrivalent. 3 *Biol.* The group of four chromatids into which two bivalent chromosomes divide in the last stages of meiosis. 4 A crystal having an axis showing fourfold symmetry. [<Gk. *tetras, -ados* group of four]

te·trad·y·mite (te·trad'ə·mīt) *n.* A soft, metallic, pale steel-gray, bismuth telluride, Bi_2Te_3, crystallizing in the rhombohedral system. [<G *tetradymit* <Gk. *tetradymos* fourfold; from its occurring in compound twin crystals]

tet·ra·dyn·a·mous (tet'rə·din'ə·məs, -dī'nə-) *adj. Bot.* Having six stamens, of which four, arranged in opposite pairs, are longer than the other two and inserted above them, as in flowers of the mustard family. [<TETRA- + Gk. *dynamis* power]

tet·ra·eth·yl lead (tet'rə·eth'il led) Lead tetraethyl.

tet·ra·gon (tet'rə·gon) *n. Geom.* A plane figure having four angles; a quadrangle. [<Gk. *tetragōnon* a quadrangle <*tetra-* four + *gōnia* angle]

tet·rag·o·nal (tet·rag'ə·nəl) *adj.* **1** Being or pertaining to a tetragon; having four angles; quadrangular. **2** Belonging to or designating a crystal system characterized by four alternately dissimilar planes of symmetry intersecting at angles of 45 degrees and a fifth symmetrical plane at right angles to the others.

tet·ra·gram (tet'rə·gram) *n.* A word of four letters.

Tet·ra·gram·ma·ton (tet'rə·gram'ə·ton) *n.* In Hebrew texts, the group of four letters (JHVH, JHWH, YHVH, or YHWH) representing the holy and ineffable name of God. The common transliteration Jehovah is the result of a combination of the Tetragrammaton with the vowel points of *Adonai* "my Lord," which is substituted in reading the name. [<Gk. *tetragrammaton* <*tetra-* four + *gramma* a letter <*graphein* write]

tet·ra·he·dral (tet'rə·hē'drəl) *adj.* **1** Of or pertaining to a tetrahedron. **2** Made up of or having four sides. [<Gk. *tetraedros.* See TETRAHEDRON.]

tet·ra·he·drite (tet'rə·hē'drīt) *n.* A steel-gray, fine-grained mineral, usually a sulfide of copper and antimony but having other elements, found in tetrahedral crystals. [<TETRAHEDRON]

tet·ra·he·dron (tet'rə·hē'·drən) *n. pl.* **·dra** (-drə) **1** *Geom.* A solid bounded by four plane triangular faces. **2** An anti-tank obstacle shaped like a pyramid. [<Gk. *tetraedron,* neut. of *tetraedros* <*tetra-* four + *hedra* base]

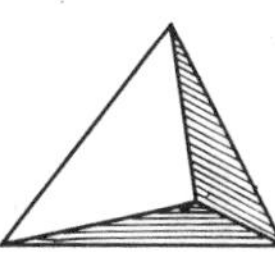
TETRAHEDRON

te·tral·o·gy (te·tral'ə·jē) *n. pl.* **·gies 1** A group of four dramas, three tragic and one satyric, presented together at the festivals of Dionysus at Athens. **2** Hence, any series of four related dramatic or operatic works. [<Gk. *tetralogia* <*tetra-* four + *logos* word, speech]

te·tram·er·ous (te·tram'ər·əs) *adj.* **1** Having four parts. **2** *Bot.* Having the parts or organs in four; arranged in fours or multiples of four: often written *4-merous.* **3** *Zool.* Having four joints; having four-jointed tarsi. Also **te·tram'·er·al.** [<Gk. *tetramerēs* four-parted <*tetra-* four + *meros* part]

te·tram·e·ter (te·tram'ə·tər) *adj.* Having four measures. In classical trochaic, iambic, and anapestic verse a measure consists of two feet (a dipody); hence, a trochaic tetrameter contains eight feet to the line. In English, a tetrameter has four feet or measures. —*n.* A verse (line) thus composed. [<LL *tetrametrus* <Gk. *tetrametros* <*tetra-* four + *metron* measure]

tet·ra·morph (tet'rə·môrf) *n.* The union of the four attributes of the four Evangelists in one composite figure, winged, and standing on winged wheels of fire, the wings being full of eyes. [<Gk. *tetramorphon* four-shaped <*tetra-* four + *morphē* form]

tet·ra·pet·al·ous (tet'rə·pet'l·əs) *adj. Bot.* Having four petals.

tet·ra·pod (tet'rə·pod) *adj.* Four-footed. [<NL *tetrapodus* <Gk. *tetrapous, tetrapodos* four-footed <*tetra-* four + *pous* foot]

te·trap·o·dy (te·trap'ə·dē) *n. pl.* **·dies** A group of four feet, as a colon, meter, or verse containing that number. [<Gk. *tetrapodia* <*tetrapous.* See TETRAPOD.] —**tet·ra·pod·ic** (tet'rə·pod'ik) *adj.*

te·trap·ter·ous (te·trap'tər·əs) *adj. Biol.* Having four wings, as certain fruits and insects. [<NL *tetrapterus* <Gk. *tetrapteros* four-winged <*tetra-* four + *pteron* wing]

tet·ra·py·lon (tet'rə·pī'lon). *n. Archit.* A structure having four gateways or penetrated by two intersecting passages, as some arches. [<Gk. *tetrapylos* with four gates <*tetra-* four + *pylē* a gate]

tet·rarch (tet'rärk, tē'trärk) *n.* **1** The governor of one of four divisions of a country or province. **2** A tributary prince under the Romans; a subordinate ruler. **3** Anciently, in the Greek army, the commander of a subdivision of a phalanx. [<LL *tetrarcha* <L *tetrarches* <Gk. *tetrarchēs* <*tetra-* four + *archos* ruler] —**tet·rar·chy** (tet'rär·kē, tē'·trär-), **tet·rarch·ate** (tet'rär·kāt, -kit, tē'trär-) *n.*

tet·ra·seme (tet'rə·sēm) *n.* A long syllable or a foot equal to four short syllables. [<TETRA- + Gk. *sēma* sign] —**tet'ra·se'mic** *adj.*

tet·ra·spore (tet'rə·spôr, -spōr) *n. Bot.* An asexual spore produced by certain algae: named from the fact that often four are produced together from a mother cell.

tet·ra·stich (tet'rə·stik) *n.* A poem or stanza of four lines; a quatrain. [<TETRA- + Gk. *stichos* row, line] —**tet'ra·stich'ic** *adj.*

te·tras·ti·chous (te·tras'tə·kəs) *adj. Bot.* Four-ranked; having organs, as leaves on a stem, arranged in four vertical rows or ranks.

tet·ra·style (tet'rə·stīl) *adj.* Having four pillars. —*n. Archit.* **1** A temple having four columns in the front or end row. **2** Any building or structure having four pillars in a row or rows. [<L *tetrastylos* <Gk. <*tetra-* four + *stylos* column]

tet·ra·syl·la·ble (tet'rə·sil'ə·bəl) *n.* A word of four syllables. —**tet'ra·syl·lab'ic** or **·i·cal** *adj.*

tet·ra·tom·ic (tet'rə·tom'ik) *adj. Chem.* **1** Containing four atoms. **2** Containing four replaceable univalent atoms or molecules. **3** Quadrivalent.

tet·ra·va·lent (tet'rə·vā'lənt) *adj. Chem.* Quadrivalent.

tet·ra·zine (tet'rə·zēn, -zin) *n. Chem.* Tetracene.

Te·traz·zi·ni (tä'trät·tsē'nē), **Luisa,** 1874?–1940, Italian coloratura soprano active in the United States.

tet·rode (tet'rōd) *n. Electronics* A vacuum tube containing four elements, the fourth usually being an additional grid interposed between the first grid and the plate. [<TETR(A)- + -ODE[1]]

te·trox·ide (te·trok'sīd, -sid) *n. Chem.* An oxide containing four atoms of oxygen to the molecule. Also **te·trox'id** (-sid). [<TETR (A)- + OXIDE]

tet·ryl (tet'ril) *n. Chem.* A yellowish, crystalline nitrogen compound, $C_7H_5N_5O_8$, used as an explosive in boosters and detonators. [<TETR(A)- + -YL]

tet·ter (tet'ər) *n. Pathol.* A vesicular skin disease, as eczema. [OE *teter*]

Te·tuán (tā·twän') A port on the Mediterranean Sea in NE Morocco; former capital of Spanish Morocco.

Tet·zel (tet'səl), **Johann,** 1465–1519, German Dominican monk, opponent of Luther. Also spelled *Tezel.*

Teu·cer (to͞o'sər, tyo͞o'-) In Greek legend: **1** The half-brother of Ajax, who founded Salamis in Cyprus: noted as an archer. **2** The first king of Troy.

Teu·cri·a (to͞o'krē·ə, tyo͞o'-) See TROAS.

Teu·cri·an (to͞o'krē·ən, tyo͞o'-) *adj.* **1** Trojan. **2** Of or pertaining to Teucer.

teugh (to͝okh, tyo͝okh) *adj. Scot.* Tough. Also **teuch.** —**teugh'ly** *adv.* —**teugh'ness** *n.*

Teu·to·bur·ger Wald (toi'tō·bo͝or'gər vält) A range of hills in western Germany; highest point, 1,465 feet; scene of a German victory by Arminius over the Roman army commanded by Varus, 9 A.D.

Teu·ton (to͞ot'n, tyo͞ot'n) *n.* **1** One of an ancient German tribe that dwelt in Jutland north of the Elbe, appearing in history as **Teu·to·nes** (to͞o'tə·nēz, tyo͞o'-), together with the **Cim·bri** (sim'brī), a possibly related tribe, in 113 B.C. **2** One belonging to any of the Teutonic peoples; especially, a German.

Teu·ton·ic (to͞o·ton'ik, tyo͞o-) *adj.* **1** Of or pertaining to the Teutons; especially, designating the blond peoples of northern Europe, formerly including the Angles, Saxons, Danes, Normans, Norwegians, the Goths, Franks, Lombards, Vandals, etc.; now embracing also the English, Germans, Dutch, etc. **2** Of or pertaining to that subfamily of Indo-European languages now called *Germanic,* including Gothic, the Scandinavian languages, and all the High and Low German languages and dialects, among which are German, Dutch, Flemish, and English. —*n.* The Germanic subfamily of languages.

Teutonic Knights The Knights of St. Mary's Hospital at Jerusalem, an order of military monks deriving their name and office from a German hospital founded at Jerusalem in 1128. One of the three great military orders founded during the Crusades to convert the heathen, help pilgrims, and nurse the sick, the knights later moved to eastern Europe and during the Middle Ages became the spearhead of German expansion toward Slavic and Baltic territories. Their costume was a white mantle with a black cross. See HOSPITALER, KNIGHT TEMPLAR.

Teu·ton·ism (to͞ot'n·iz'əm, tyo͞ot'n-) *n.* **1** A custom or mode of expression peculiar to Germans or Teutons; Germanism: also **Teu·ton·i·cism** (to͞o·ton'ə·siz'əm, tyo͞o-). **2** A belief in the superiority of the Teutonic race. **3** Teutonic character and civilization. —**Teu'·ton·ist** *n.*

Teu·ton·ize (to͞ot'n·īz, tyo͞ot'n-) *v.t. & v.i.* **·ized, ·iz·ing** To make or become Teutonic or German. —**Teu'ton·i·za'tion** *n.*

Te·ve·re (tā'vā·rā) The Italian name for the river TIBER.

tew (to͞o, tyo͞o) *Brit. Dial. v.i.* To work hard; fuss or bustle. —*n.* A state of excitement, worry, or bustling.

Tewkes·bur·y (to͞oks'ber·ē, -bər·ē, tyo͞oks'-) A municipal borough in NW Gloucestershire, England; scene of the final defeat of the Lancastrian forces in the Wars of the Roses, 1471.

Tex·ar·kan·a (teks'är·kan'ə) A dual city in NE Texas and SW Arkansas, with two municipal governments.

tex·as (tek'səs) *n. U.S.* The uppermost structure on a river steamboat, containing the pilot house, officers' cabins, etc.; often, a row of staterooms behind the pilot house, or having the pilot house set on top of it. [from *Texas;* so called from the former custom of naming staterooms after the States, those of the officers being the largest]

Tex·as (tek'səs) *n.* A Caddo Indian.

Tex·as (tek'səs) A State in the SW United States, bordering on Mexico and the Gulf of Mexico; 267,339 square miles; capital, Austin; entered the Union Dec. 29, 1845; nicknamed *Lone Star State*: abbr. TX —**Tex'an** *n. & adj.*

Texas cattle Cattle bred from the old longhorn stock of early Texas.

Texas fever A destructive cattle disease caused by a blood parasite transmitted by the cattle tick, *Margaropus annulatus.* Also **Texan fever.**

Texas leaguer *U.S. Colloq.* In baseball, a looping fly ball that falls safe between an infielder and an outfielder.

Texas Ranger 1 A member of the mounted State police force of Texas. **2** Originally, one of a band of armed and mounted men organized in Texas to fight Indians and keep order on the frontiers.

Texas sparrow A plain, olive-backed fringilline bird *(Arremonops rufivirgatus)* found in Mexico and southern Texas.

Texas tower A radar station having several tall towers erected on a platform which may be moored permanently in the sea as part of a radar-warning network.

Texas trail The old Chisholm cattle trail from Red River, Texas, to Abilene, Kansas.

Tex·o·ma (tek·sō'mə), **Lake** A reservoir in northern Texas and southern Oklahoma created by damming the Red River; one of the largest in the U.S.; 227 square miles.

text (tekst) *n.* **1** The actual or original words of an author; the body of matter on a written or printed page, as distinguished from notes, commentary, illustrations, etc. **2** A written or printed version of the matter of an author's works: the folio *text* of Shakespeare. **3** Any one of various recensions that are taken to represent the authentic words, or portion of the words, of the original Scriptures. **4** A verse of Scripture, particularly when cited as the basis of a discourse or sermon. **5** Any subject of discourse; a topic; theme. **6** One of several styles of letters or types. **7** A textbook. [<OF *texte* <L *textus* fabric, structure <*texere* weave]

text·book (tekst′bo͝ok′) *n.* A book used as a standard work or basis of instruction in any branch of knowledge; schoolbook; manual.

tex·tile (teks′til, -tīl) *adj.* **1** Pertaining to weaving or woven fabrics. **2** Such as may be woven; manufactured by weaving. — *n.* **1** A woven fabric; textile material. **2** Material capable of being woven. [<L *textilis* < *textus* fabric. See TEXT.]

tex·tu·al (teks′cho͞o·əl) *adj.* **1** Pertaining to, contained in, or based on the text of a book, especially of the Scriptures; literal; word for word. **2** Versed in texts. [<OF *textuel* < *texte.* See TEXT.] — **tex′tu·al·ly** *adv.*

tex·tu·al·ism (teks′cho͞o·əl·iz′əm) *n.* **1** Rigid adherence to the letter of a text. **2** The method or principles of textual criticism.

tex·tu·al·ist (teks′cho͞o·əl·ist′) *n.* **1** A close adherent to the letter of a text. **2** One who is versed in or cites texts readily.

tex·tu·ar·y (teks′cho͞o·er′ē) *adj.* **1** Contained in a text. **2** Of, belonging to, or adhering to a text. — *n. pl.* **·ar·ies** A textualist.

tex·ture (teks′chər) *n.* **1** The arrangement or character of the threads, etc., of a woven fabric. **2** The mode of union or disposition of elementary constituent parts, as in a photograph, or surface of paper, etc.; minute structure or make; structural order. **3** The structure, especially as regards detail, of a work of art. **4** Any woven fabric; a web. [<L *textura* < *textus* fabric. See TEXT.] — **tex′tur·al** *adj.* — **tex′tur·al·ly** *adv.*

Tey·de (tā′thā) See PEAK OF TENERIFE under TENERIFE.

teyl tree (tēl) See TEIL.

Tez·el (tet′səl) See TETZEL.

T-group (tē′gro͞op) *n.* A group of people, often business or industrial personnel, who meet with a trained leader whose function is to guide them to a more insightful awareness of themselves and others through the free and uninhibited expression of their thoughts, feelings, etc. [< *t(raining) group*]

-th[1] *suffix of nouns* **1** The act or result of the action expressed in the root word: *growth.* **2** The state or quality of being what is indicated in the root word: *health.*

-th[2] *suffix* Used in ordinal numbers: *tenth.* Also, after vowels, *-eth,* as in *fortieth.* [OE *-tha, -the*]

-th[3] See -ETH[1].

Thack·er·ay (thak′ər·ē), **William Makepeace,** 1811–63, English novelist.

Thad·de·us (thad′ē·əs) A masculine personal name. Also **Thad′dae·us,** *Ger.* **Thad·dä·us** (tä·dā′o͝os), *Polish* **Ta·de·usz** (tä·dā′o͝osh), *Pg.* **Thad·de·o** (täd·dā′o͞o). [<Aramaic, praise]

Thai (tī) *n.* **1** The people collectively of Thailand, Laos, and parts of Burma, including the Laos, Shan, and Siamese. **2** A family of languages spoken by these people: considered by some a branch of the Sino-Tibetan family. — *adj.* Of or pertaining to the Thai, their culture, or their languages. Also spelled *Tai.*

Thai·land (tī′land) A constitutional monarchy in SE Asia; 198,404 square miles; capital, Bangkok: formerly *Siam. Thai* **Mu·ang Thai** (mo͞o′äng tī′).

thal·a·men·ceph·a·lon (thal′ə·men·sef′ə·lon) *n. Anat.* Diencephalon. [<THALAM(US) + ENCEPHALON]

tha·lam·ic (thə·lam′ik) *adj.* Of or pertaining to a thalamus, especially to the optic thalamus.

thal·a·mus (thal′ə·məs) *n. pl.* **·mi** (-mī) **1** *Anat.* The optic thalamus. **2** *Bot.* The receptacle of a flower. [<L <Gk. *thalamos* chamber]

thal·as·se·mi·a (thal′ə·sē′mē·ə) *n.* Any of a group of often fatal familial diseases associated with abnormal red blood cells and characterized by anemia, changes in the bones, enlargement of the spleen and liver, and other symptoms, first described in children of Mediterranean regions; Cooley's anemia. [<Gk. *thalassa* sea + -EMIA] — **thal′as·se′mic** *adj.*

tha·las·sic (thə·las′ik) *adj.* **1** Of or pertaining to the seas. **2** Pelagic; oceanic. [<Gk. *thalassa* sea]

thalasso- *combining form* The sea; of or pertaining to the sea: *thalassophobia.* Also, before vowels, **thalass-.** Also **thalassi-.** [<Gk. *thalassa* the sea]

thal·as·sog·ra·phy (thal′ə·sog′rə·fē) *n.* Oceanography. [<THALASSO- + -GRAPHY]

tha·las·so·pho·bi·a (thə·las′ə·fō′bē·ə) *n.* Morbid fear of the sea. [<THALASSO- + -PHOBIA]

tha·ler (tä′lər) See TALER.

Tha·les of Miletus (thā′lēz), 640?–546? B.C., Greek philosopher and scientist.

Tha·li·a (thə·lī′ə) **1** The Muse of comedy and pastoral poetry. **2** One of the three Graces. [<L <Gk. *Thaleia* < *thallein* bloom]

Tha·lic·trum (thə·lik′trəm) *n.* A genus of perennial herbs of the crowfoot family, the meadow rues. [<L <Gk. *thaliktron* < *thallein* bloom]

thal·i·do·mide (thə·lid′ə·mīd) *n. Med.* A mild sedative, illegalized when its use by pregnant women resulted in phocomelia and other birth anomalies.

thal·lic (thal′ik) *adj. Chem.* Of, pertaining to, or derived from thallium, especially in its higher valence.

thal·line (thal′ēn, -in) *n. Chem.* A white, crystalline, synthetic alkaloid, $C_{10}H_{13}NO$: its salts are used as antipyretics and antiseptics.

thal·li·um (thal′ē·əm) *n.* A soft, white, crystalline metallic element (symbol Tl) closely resembling lead: its salts are used in rat poison, insecticides, and in making optical glass. See ELEMENT. [<NL <Gk. *thallos* a green shoot; from the bright green line in its spectrum, which led to its discovery]

thal·loid (thal′oid) *adj.* Resembling a thallus. Also **thal·loi·dal** (thə·loid′l).

thal·lo·phyte (thal′ə·fīt) *n.* Any plant belonging to a major division or phylum of plants *(Thallophyta),* comprising the bacteria, fungi, algae, and lichens. Many of the forms are unicellular and those more highly developed are without true roots, stems, or leaves. [< *thallo-* (<THALLUS) + -PHYTE] — **thal′·lo·phyt′ic** (-fit′ik) *adj.*

thal·lous (thal′əs) *adj. Chem.* Derived from thallium, especially in its lower valence. Also **thal·li·ous** (thal′ē·əs).

thal·lus (thal′əs) *n. pl.* **·lus·es** or **·li** (-ī) *Bot.* A plant body without true root, stem, or leaf, as in thallophytes. [<L, a shoot <Gk. *thallos* < *thallein* bloom]

Thames (temz) A river of southern England, rising in the Cotswold Hills, south central Gloucestershire, and flowing 209 miles east through London to the North Sea between northern Kent and southern Essex; the principal river of England.

Thames River **1** (temz) A river in SE Ontario, Canada, flowing SW 160 miles to Lake St. Clair. **2** (thāmz, tāmz) A river and estuary in SE Connecticut, flowing about 15 miles south to Long Island Sound.

Tham·muz (täm′mo͞oz, tam′uz) See TAMMUZ.

than (than, *unstressed* thən) *conj.* **1** When, as, or if compared with: after an adjective or adverb to express comparison between what precedes and what follows: I am stronger *than* he (is); I know her better *than* (I know) him. **2** Except; but: used after *other, else,* etc: no other *than* you. *Than* is sometimes considered a preposition in the one phrase, *than whom*: an eminent judge *than whom* no other is more just. [OE *thanne* then]

than·age (thā′nij) *n.* **1** In early English law, the state, jurisdiction, or office of a thane. **2** The land held by a thane or the tenure by which he held it. Also spelled *thenage.* [<AF *thaynage* <OE *thegn* a thane]

thanato- *combining form* Death; of or pertaining to death: *thanatophobia.* Also, before vowels, **thanat-.** [<Gk. *thanatos* death]

than·a·toid (than′ə·toid) *adj.* Resembling death; deadly.

than·a·to·pho·bi·a (than′ə·tə·fō′bē·ə) *n.* Morbid fear of death. [<THANATO- + PHOBIA] — **than′a·to·pho′bic** *adj.*

than·a·top·sis (than′ə·top′sis) *n.* A musing or meditation upon death; a view of death. [<THANAT(O)- + -OPSIS]

Than·a·tos (than′ə·tos) **1** In Greek mythology, the god of death: identified with the Roman *Mors.* **2** *Psychoanal.* The death instinct: opposed to *Eros,* the life instinct.

thane (thān) *n.* **1** Originally, a warrior companion of an English king before the Conquest. **2** Later, a man who ranked above an ordinary freeman or ceorl (churl) but below an earl or nobleman. **3** *Scot.* The chief of a clan; a baron; one of the old nobility in the service of the king. Also spelled *thegn.* [OE *thegn*]

Than·et (than′it), **Isle of** An island comprising the NE corner of Kent county, England; 10 miles long, 5 miles wide.

thank (thangk) *v.t.* **1** To express gratitude to; give thanks to. **2** To hold responsible; blame: often used ironically. [OE *thancian* < *thanc* thanks, thought]

thank·ful (thangk′fəl) *adj.* **1** Deeply sensible of favors received; grateful. **2** Done or made to express thanks; manifesting thanks. — **thank′ful·ly** *adv.* — **thank′ful·ness** *n.*

thank·it (thangk′it) *Scot.* Past participle of THANK.

thank·less (thangk′lis) *adj.* **1** Not feeling or expressing gratitude; ungrateful; unresponsive. **2** Not gaining or likely to gain thanks; unthanked; unappreciated. — **thank′less·ly** *adv.* — **thank′less·ness** *n.*

thanks (thangks) *n. pl.* Expressions of gratitude; grateful acknowledgment. — *interj.* My thanks to you; I thank you. — **thanks to** **1** Thanks be given to. **2** Because of.

thanks·giv·ing (thangks′giv′ing) *n* **1** The act of giving thanks, as to God; the expression of gratitude. **2** A form of words or worship in recognition of divine mercies. **3** A public celebration in recognition of divine favor. **4** A day set apart for such celebration.

Thanksgiving Day *U.S.* The fourth Thursday in November, set apart as an annual festival of thanksgiving to God for the year's blessings. Also **Thanksgiving.**

Thant (thänt, tänt), **U,** 1909–, Burmese statesman; secretary general of the United Nations 1961–71.

Thap·sus (thap′səs) An ancient ruined town on the coast of eastern Tunisia; scene of Julius Caesar's defeat of Cato the Younger, 46 B.C.

Thar Desert (tär) A sandy waste in NW India (much of western Rajasthan and southern Punjab) and West Pakistan; over 15,000 square miles: also *Indian Desert.*

Tha·sos (thā′sos) A Greek island in the north Aegean Sea; 170 square miles.

that (that, *unstressed* thət) *adj. pl.* **those** **1** Pertaining to some person or thing previously mentioned, understood, or specifically designated: *that* man. **2** Denoting something more remote in place, time, or thought: correlative to *this.* — *pron.* **1** As a demonstrative, the person or thing implied, mentioned, or understood; or the person or thing there or in the second place: *That* is the dress I like. **2** As a relative, who or which: used as a correlative to *such* or *so.* ◆ In earlier English, *that* was the relative pronoun, *who, what,* and *which* being only interrogatives until they gradually assumed the force of relatives, and in some uses superseded *that.* When the relative clause qualifies or makes an addition to the main clause, *who* or *which* is generally preferred, whereas *that* usually introduces a restrictive clause. Thus we say: Washington, *who* was the first president, is often called Father of his Country. But: *The* Washington *that* emigrated to this country was his ancestor. — *adv.* **1** *Colloq.* In such a manner or degree; so. **2** To that extent: I can't see *that* far. — *conj.* *That* is used primarily to connect a subordinate clause with its principal clause, with the following meanings: **1** As a fact that: introducing a fact: I tell you *that* it is so. **2** So that; in order that: I tell you *that* you may know. **3** For the reason that; seeing that; because: She wept *that* she was growing old. **4** As a result: introducing a result, consequence, or effect: He bled so profusely *that* he died. **5** At which time; when: It was only yesterday *that* I saw him. **6** Introducing an exclamation: O *that* he would come! See synonyms under BUT. — **so that** **1** To the end that. **2** With the result that. **3** Provided. See THOSE. [OE *thæt,* neut. of *se* the]

thatch (thach) *n.* **1** A covering of reeds, straw, etc., arranged on a roof so as to shed water. **2** Any of various palms whose leaves are used for thatching, especially those of the genera *Thrinax* and *Sabal.* **3** Any of certain tall, coarse American grasses (genus *Spartina*) of the northern Atlantic coasts. — *v.t.* To cover with a thatch. [OE *thæc* cover] — **thatch′er** *n.* — **thatch′y** *adj.*

thatch·ing (thach′ing) *n.* **1** The act or process of covering a roof with a thatch. **2** Material used for a thatch.

thaumato- *combining form* A wonder; a miracle: *thaumatology.* Also, before vowels, **thaumat-.** [<Gk. *thauma, -atos* a wonder]

thau·ma·tol·o·gy (thô′mə·tol′ə·jē) *n.* The scientific study of miracles. [<THAUMATO- + -LOGY]

thau·ma·trope (thô′mə·trōp) *n.* An optical toy or instrument in which pictures on opposite sides of a card appear to blend together when the card is rapidly twirled. [<Gk. *thauma* wonder + -TROPE]

thau·ma·turge (thô′mə·tûrj) *n.* One who performs wonders or miracles; a wonder-worker; magician. Also **thau′ma·tur′gist.** [<Gk. *thaumatourgos* < *thauma* wonder + *ergon* work]

thau·ma·tur·gy (thô′mə·tûr′jē) *n.* Magic; the performance or working of wonders or miracles. — **thau′ma·tur′gic** or **·gi·cal** *adj.*

thaw (thô) *v.i.* **1** To melt or dissolve; become liquid or semi-liquid, as snow or ice. **2** To rise in temperature so as to melt ice and snow: said of weather and used impersonally. **3** To become less cold and unsociable. — *v.t.* **4** To cause to thaw. See synonyms under MELT. — *n.* **1** The act of thawing, or the state of being thawed. **2** Warmth of weather such as melts things frozen; also, figuratively, state of warmer feeling or expression. [OE *thawian*] — **thaw′er** *n.*

Thax·ter (thaks′tər), **Celia,** 1835–94, *née* Laighton, U. S. poet.

Thay·er (thā′ər), **Sylvanus,** 1785–1872, U. S. Army officer: called "Father of West Point." — **William Roscoe,** 1859–1923, U. S. historian and biographer.

the[1] (*stressed* thē; *unstressed before a consonant* thə; *unstressed before a vowel* thi) *definite article* or *adj.* *The* is opposed to the indefinite article *a* or *an*, and is used, especially before nouns, to render the modified word more particular or individual. It is used specifically: **1** When reference is made to a particular person, thing, or group: *The* natives are getting restless; He left *the* room. **2** To give an adjective substantive force, or render a notion abstract: *the* quick and *the* dead; *the* doing of the deed. **3** Before a noun to make it generic: *The* dog is a friend of man. **4** With the force of a possessive pronoun: He kicked me in *the* (my) leg. **5** To give distributive force: equivalent to *a, per, each,* etc.: a dollar *the* volume. **6** *Scot.* & *Irish* To designate the head of a clan or group: *the* MacIntosh. **7** To designate a particular one as emphatically outstanding: usually stressed in speech and italicized in writing: He is *the* officer for the command. **8** As part of a title: *The* Duke of York. [OE *the,* later form of *sē*]

the[2] (thə) *adv.* By that much; by so much; to this extent: *the* more, *the* merrier: used to modify words in the comparative degree. [OE *thȳ,* oblique case of *sē* the]

the– Var. of THEO–.

the·a·ceous (thē·ā′shəs) *adj. Bot.* Designating a family (*Theaceae*) of shrubs and trees having alternate, simple leaves, large flowers, and a typically capsular fruit; the tea family. [<NL <*Thea,* genus name <dial. Chinese *t'e* tea; incorrectly taken by Linnaeus as "divine herb" <Gk. *thea* a goddess]

the·an·throp·ic (thē′ən·throp′ik) *adj.* **1** Being both divine and human. **2** Having or pertaining to a nature both divine and human. Also **the′an·throp′i·cal.** [<Gk. *theanthrōpos* < *theos* god + *anthrōpos, -ōpou* man]

the·an·thro·pism (thē·an′thrə·piz′əm) *n.* **1** The doctrine of the manifestation of God in man, or of the union of the divine and human in Christ. **2** The ascription of human characteristics to a deity; anthropomorphism. **3** Belief in the possibility of the combination in one being of a nature both human and divine. — **the·an′thro·pist** *n.*

the·ar·chy (thē′är·kē) *n. pl.* **·chies** **1** Government by God or by a god. **2** A theocracy. **3** A body or class of deities. [<Gk. *thearchia* < *theos* god + *archein* rule]

the·a·ter (thē′ə·tər) *n.* **1** A building especially adapted to dramatic, operatic, or spectacular representations; playhouse. **2** The theatrical world and everything relating to it. **3** A room or hall arranged with seats that rise as they recede from a platform, especially adapted to lectures, surgical demonstrations, etc. **4** Any place of semicircular form with seats rising by easy gradations. **5** Any place or region that is the scene of events: a *theater* of operations in war. Also **the′a·tre.** [<OF *theatre* <Gk. *theatron* < *theasthai* behold]

the·a·ter-go·er (thē′ə·tər·gō′ər) *n.* One who frequents theaters. Also **the′a·tre-go′er.** — **the′a·ter-go′ing, the′a·tre-go′ing** *n.*

the·a·ter-in-the-round (thē′ə·tər·in·thə·round′) *n.* An arena theater.

The·a·tin (thē′ə·tin) *n.* **1** A member of a congregation founded in 1524 by Bishop Carafa and St. Cajetan. **2** A member of an order of nuns founded by Ursula Benincasa, who died in 1618. Also **The′a·tine** (-tēn, -tin). [<NL *theatinus,* from *Teate,* ancient name of Chieti, Italy]

the·at·ri·cal (thē·at′ri·kəl) *adj.* **1** Pertaining to the theater or to dramatic performances. **2** Designed for show, display, or effect; showy; artificial. **3** Suited to dramatic presentation. **4** Like the manner of actors; histrionic. Also **the·at′ric.** — *n. pl.* Dramatic performances: especially when given by amateur performers. [<LL *theatricus* <Gk. *theatrikos* < *theatron.* See THEATER.] — **the·at′ri·cal·ly** *adv.* — **the·at′ri·cal·ness** *n.*

the·at·ri·cal·ism (thē·at′ri·kəl·iz′əm) *n.* Theatrical or melodramatic manner or style.

the·at·rics (thē·at′riks) *n. pl.* (*construed as singular*) The art of bringing about effects appropriate for dramatic performances.

The·ba·id (thē′bā·id, thi·bā′-) *n.* A Latin epic by Statius, narrating the story of the siege of Boeotian Thebes.

The·ba·id (thē′bā·id, thi·bā′-) The territory about Thebes in either Egypt or Greece.

the·ba·ine (thē′bə·ēn, thi·bā′ēn, -in) *n. Chem.* A silvery-white, poisonous, crystalline alkaloid, $C_{19}H_{21}O_3N$, found in opium and resembling strychnine in action: also called *paramorphine.* Also **the′ba·in** (-in). [from Egyptian *Thebes,* where a kind of opium was produced + -INE[2]]

Thebes (thēbz) **1** The ancient capital of Upper Egypt; Luxor and Karnak occupy part of its site on the Nile: Greek *Diospolis.* **2** The chief city of ancient Boeotia, Greece; destroyed in 336 B.C. by Alexander the Great: also **The·bae** (thē′bē). **3** A commercial city in east central Greece on the site of ancient Thebes; important in the Middle Ages: *Greek* **The·vai** or **Thi·vai** (thē′vā). — **The·ban** (thē′bən) *adj.* & *n.*

the·ca (thē′kə) *n. pl.* **·cae** (-sē) **1** A sheath or case. **2** *Anat.* The investment of the spinal cord formed by the dura mater, sometimes called **theca vertebralis.** **3** *Bot.* A spore case, sac, or capsule. [<L <Gk. *thēkē* case] — **the′cal** *adj.*

the·cate (thē′kit, -kāt) *adj.* Having a sheath; sheathed.

thé dan·sant (tā′ däṅ·säṅ′) *pl.* **thés dan·sants** (tā′ däṅ·säṅ′) *French* Literally, a dancing tea; an afternoon tea at which there is dancing.

thee (thē) *pron.* **1** The objective case of *thou.* **2** Thou: used generally by Quakers with a verb in the third person singular: *Thee* knows my mind. [OE *thē,* accusative case of *thū* thou]

theek (thēk) *v.t. Brit. Dial.* To thatch. [Scottish var. of THATCH] — **theek′ing** *n.*

Thee·lin (thē′lin) *n.* Proprietary name for a brand of estrone.

Thee·lol (thē′lōl, -lol) *n.* Proprietary name for a brand of estriol.

theft (theft) *n.* **1** The act of thieving; larceny. **2** *Rare* That which is stolen. [OE *thēoft, thīefth*]

the·gith·er (thi·gith′ər) *adv. Scot.* Together.

thegn (thān) See THANE.

the·ine (thē′ēn, -in) *n. Chem.* The alkaloid found in the tea plant: chemically identical with caffeine. Also **the′in** (-in). [<F *théine* <NL *thea* tea <dial. Chinese *t'e*]

their (thâr) *pronominal adj.* The possessive case of the pronoun *they* employed attributively; belonging or pertaining to them: *their* homes. [ME <ON *theirra* of them]

theirs (thârz) *pron.* **1** The possessive case of *they,* used predicatively; belonging or pertaining to them: That house is *theirs.* **2** The things or persons belonging or relating to them: our country and *theirs.* — **of theirs** Belonging or pertaining to them; their: the double possessive. [<THEIR + *-s,* on analogy with *his*]

the·ism[1] (thē′iz·əm) *n.* **1** Belief in, or in the existence of, God, a god, or gods: opposed to *atheism.* **2** Belief in a personal God as creator and supreme ruler of the universe, who transcends his creation but works in and through it in revealing himself to men. Compare DEISM, PANTHEISM. **3** Belief in one god; monotheism: opposed to *polytheism.* **4** Formerly, deism. **5** *Philos.* The doctrine that one supreme reality, intrinsically complete and perfect, is the final ground and source of everything other than itself: a doctrine resembling monotheism and some types of monism, but opposed to atheism, agnosticism, deism, materialism, pantheism, and polytheism. [<Gk. *theos* god] — **the′ist** *n.* — **the·is′tic** or **·ti·cal** *adj.* — **the·is′ti·cal·ly** *adv.*

the·ism[2] (thē′iz·əm) *n. Pathol.* The toxic effects of excessive tea-drinking. [<NL *thea* tea. See THEINE.]

Theiss (tīs) The German name for TISZA.

Thé·lème (tā·lem′), **Abbey of** An abbey described by Rabelais in *Gargantua,* and having only one rule, "Do what you like."

the·li·tis (thi·lī′tis) *n. Pathol.* Inflammation of the nipple. [<NL <Gk. *thēlē* teat + -ITIS]

Thel·ma (thel′mə) A feminine personal name. [<Gk., nursling]

The·lon River (thi·lon′) A river in Northwest Territories, Canada, rising in eastern Mackenzie district and flowing about 550 miles north, NE, and east to NW Hudson Bay on the central eastern coast of Keewatin district.

them (them, *unstressed* thəm) *pron.* The objective case of *they.* [ME *theim* <ON, to them]

the·mat·ic (thē·mat′ik) *adj.* **1** Of, constituting, or pertaining to a theme or themes. **2** *Ling.* Constituting a stem. Also **the·mat′i·cal.** — **the·mat′i·cal·ly** *adv.*

theme (thēm) *n.* **1** A subject of discourse; a topic to be discussed or developed in speech or writing; hence, any topic. **2** An essay or dissertation; loosely, a brief composition in any form, written as an exercise. **3** *Ling.* The stem of a word, to which are attached the inflectional endings, consisting of the root unmodified or with some internal change and, often, a thematic vowel common to the particular stem class. **4** A melodic subject usually developed with variations in a musical composition. **5** One of the administrative divisions of the Byzantine Empire. See synonyms under TOPIC. [<OF *teme* <L *thema* <Gk. *the-,* stem of *tithenai* place]

theme song **1** A melody used throughout a dramatic presentation to furnish the key to the mood. **2** A strain of music which, from repetition, identifies a daily or periodical radio or television presentation, a dance band, etc.

The·mis (thē′mis) In Greek mythology, a goddess of law and justice, daughter of Uranus and Gaea. [<Gk., law]

The·mis·to·cles (thi·mis′tə·klēz), 527?–460? B.C., Athenian statesman and soldier.

them·selves (them′selvz′, *unstressed* thəm-) *pron.* Emphatic or reflexive form of THEY, THEM: the plural of HIMSELF, HERSELF, ITSELF.

then (then) *adv.* **1** At that time. **2** Soon or immediately afterward; next in space or time. **3** At another time: often introducing a sequential statement following *now, at first,* etc. — *conj.* **1** For that reason; as a consequence; accordingly. **2** In that case: I will *then,* since you won't. — *adj.* Being or acting in, or belonging to, that time: the *then* secretary of state. — *n.* A specific time already mentioned or understood; that time. [OE *thanne*]

then·age (then′ij) See THANAGE

the·nar (thē′när) *n. Anat.* **1** The palm of the hand. **2** The prominence on the palm at the base of the thumb. — *adj.* Of or pertaining to the palm of a hand or the sole of a foot: also **the′nal.** [<Gk. *thenar* palm of the hand]

thence (thens) *adv.* **1** From that place. **2** From the circumstance, fact, or cause; therefore. **3** From that time; after that time. **4** *Archaic* Away from there; elsewhere; absent. [ME *thannes* <OE *thanon* from there + *-s*[3]]

thence·forth (thens′fôrth′, -fōrth′, thens′fôrth′, -fōrth′) *adv.* From that time on; thereafter.

thence·for·ward (thens′fôr′wərd) *adv.* 1 Thenceforth. 2 From that place or time forward. Also **thence′for′wards.**

theo– *combining form* God; of or pertaining to God, a god, or gods: *theophany, theodicy.* Also, before vowels, *the–.* [<Gk. *theos* a god]

The·o·bald (thē′ə·bôld, tib′əld; *Dan.* tä′ō·bäl, *Ger.* tä′ō·bält, *Sw.* tä′ō·bäld) A masculine personal name. Also *Lat.* **The·o·bal·dus** (tä′ō·bôl′dəs), *Pg.* **The·o·bal·do** (tä′o͞o·bäl′tho͞o), *Sp.* **The·u·de·bal·do** (tä′o͞o·thā·väl′thō). [<Gmc., bold patriot]

The·o·bro·ma (thē′ə·brō′mə) *n.* A genus of small trees indigenous in tropical America, especially *Theobroma cacao,* source of the cocoa and chocolate of commerce, now cultivated also in the Old World tropics. [<NL <Gk. *theos* god + *brōma* food]

the·o·bro·mine (thē′ə·brō′mēn, -min) *n. Chem.* A bitter, colorless, crystalline alkaloid, $C_7H_8N_4O_2$, resembling caffeine, contained in cacao beans: used in medicine as a diuretic and myocardial stimulant. [<THEOBROM(A) + -INE[2]]

the·o·cen·tric (thē′ə·sen′trik) *adj.* Having God for its center; proceeding from and returning to God.

the·oc·ra·cy (thē·ok′rə·sē) *n. pl.* **·cies** 1 A state, polity, or group of people that claims a deity as its ruler, as ancient Israel after the Exodus. 2 Government of a state by a god, or by a priestly class claiming to have divine authority, as in the Papacy. [<Gk. *theokratia* < *theos* god + *krateein* rule] — **the·o·crat·ic** (thē′ə·krat′ik) or **·i·cal** *adj.*

the·oc·ra·sy (thē·ok′rə·sē) *n.* 1 The mingling of several deities or divine attributes in one personality. 2 The mystical intimacy or union of the soul with God. [<LGk. *theokrasia* <Gk. *theos* god + *krasis* mingling]

the·o·crat (thē′ə·krat) *n.* 1 A theocratic or divine ruler. 2 An advocate of theocracy.

The·oc·ri·tus (thē·ok′rə·təs) Greek pastoral poet of the third century B.C.

the·od·i·cy (thē·od′ə·sē) *n. pl.* **·cies** 1 Justification of the divine providence by the attempt to reconcile the existence of evil with the goodness and sovereignty of God: a term established by Leibnitz in 1710. 2 The branch of philosophy that treats of the being, perfections, and government of God and the immortality of the soul. [<F *théodicée* <Gk. *theos* god + *dikē* justice]

the·od·o·lite (thē·od′ə·līt) *n.* One of several surveying and astronomical instruments for measuring horizontal and vertical angles by means of a small telescope turning on both a horizontal and a vertical axis. [An arbitrary formation] — **the·od′o·lit′ic** (-lit′ik) *adj.*

The·o·dore (thē′ə·dôr, -dōr) A masculine personal name. Also *Dan., Ger., Sw.* **The·o·dor** (tā′ō·dôr), *Fr.* **Thé·o·dore** (tā·ō·dôr′), *Gk.* **The·o·do·ros** (thē·o′dō·ros), *Du.* **The·o·do·rus** (tā′ō·dôr′əs). [<Gk., gift of God] — **The·o·do·ra** (thē′ə·dôr′ə) *fem.*

The·od·o·ric (thē·od′ər·ik) A masculine personal name. Also **The·od′e·rick, The·od′o·rick,** *Fr.* **Thé·o·do·ric** (tā·ō·dō·rēk′), *Ger.* **The·o·do·rich** (tā·ō′dō·rikh), *Lat.* **The·o·do·ri·cus** (tā′ō·də·rī′kəs). [<Gmc., ruler of the people]
— **Theodoric,** 454?–526, king of the Ostrogoths; invaded and conquered Italy.

The·o·do·si·us (thē′ə·dō′shē·əs), 346?–395, Roman emperor 379–395.

the·og·o·ny (thē·og′ə·nē) *n.* The generation or genealogy of the gods, especially as recited in ancient poetry. [<Gk. *theogonia* < *theos* god + *gonos* generation < *gignesthai* be born] — **the·o·gon·ic** (thē′ə·gon′ik) *adj.* — **the·og′o·nist** *n.*

the·o·log (thē′ə·lôg, -log) *n.* A theological student. Also **the′o·logue.** [<L *theologus* <Gk. *theologos* one who treats of the gods < *theos* god + *logos* discourse < *legein* speak]

the·o·lo·gi·an (thē′ə·lō′jē·ən, -jən) *n.* One versed in theology, especially that of the Christian church; a professor of divinity; a divine.

the·o·log·i·cal (thē′ə·loj′i·kəl) *adj.* 1 Pertaining or relating to theology. 2 Linked to, based on, or referring to divine revelation. 3 Pertaining to the exposition or expounders of theology. Also **the′o·log′ic.** — **the′o·log′i·cal·ly** *adv.*

theological virtues See under VIRTUE.

the·ol·o·gize (thē·ol′ə·jīz) *v.* **·gized, ·giz·ing** *v.t.* To devise or fit (something) into a system of theology. — *v.i.* To reason theologically. Also *Brit.* **the·ol′o·gise.**

the·ol·o·gy (thē·ol′ə·jē) *n. pl.* **·gies** 1 The study of religion, culminating in a synthesis or philosophy of religion; also, a critical survey of religion, especially of the Christian religion. 2 A body of doctrines concerning God, including his attributes and relations with man; especially, such a body of doctrines as set forth by a particular church or religious group: Catholic *theology.* [<OF *theologie* <LL *theologia* <Gk. < *theos* god + *logos* discourse]

the·om·a·chy (thē·om′ə·kē) *n.* 1 A combat with the gods, as that waged by the Titans. 2 A battle among the gods. [<Gk. *theomachia* < *theos* god + *machē* combat]

the·o·mor·phic (thē′ə·môr′fik) *adj.* Having the form or likeness of God. [<Gk. *theomorphos* < *theos* god + *morphē* form]

the·o·mor·phism (thē′ə·môr′fiz·əm) *n.* The doctrine that man has the likeness or form of God.

the·o·pa·thet·ic (thē′ō·pə·thet′ik) *adj.* Pertaining to or of the nature of theopathy: *theopathetic* mysticism. Also **the·o·path·ic** (thē′ə·path′ik).

the·op·a·thy (thē·op′ə·thē) *n.* Religious emotion aroused by meditation on God; mystical ecstasy. [<Gk. *theopathia* the suffering of God < *theos* a god + *path-,* stem of *paschein* suffer]

the·oph·a·ny (thē·of′ə·nē) *n. pl.* **·nies** A manifestation or appearance of a deity or of the gods to man. [<L *theophania* <Gk. < *theos* god + *phainein* show]

The·oph·i·lus (thē·of′ə·ləs; *Du., Ger.* tā·ō′fē·lo͝os) A masculine personal name. Also *Fr.* **Thé·o·phile** (tā·ō·fēl′), *Pg.* **The·o·phi·lo** (tā·ō′fē·lo͞o). [<Gk., lover of God]

The·o·phras·tus (thē′ə·fras′təs), 372?–287? B.C., Greek philosopher.

the·o·phyl·line (thē′ə·fil′ēn, -in) *n. Chem.* A white, bitter, crystalline alkaloid, $C_7H_8O_2N_4$, obtained from tea leaves and also made synthetically: it is an isomer of theobromine. [<NL *thea* tea + Gk. *phyllon* leaf + -INE[2]]

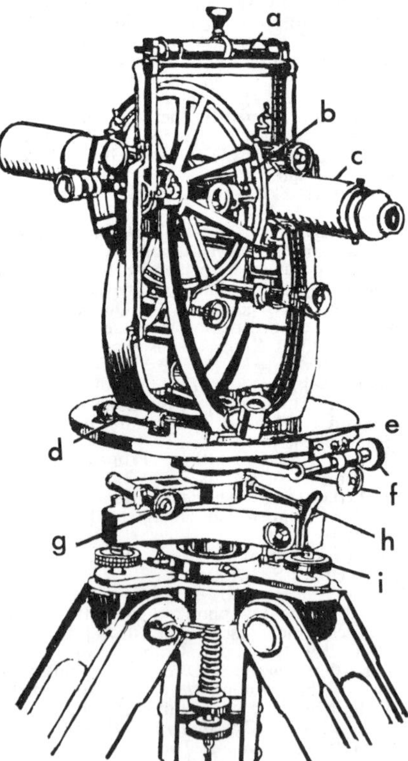

THEODOLITE
a. Striding level. *b.* Vertical limb and vernier. *c.* Telescope. *d.* Plate bubble. *e.* Horizontal limb and vernier. *f.* Clamp and tangent screw. *g.* Lower clamp screw. *h.* Tangent screw. *i.* Leveling screw.

the·or·bo (thē·ôr′bō) *n.* A 17th century lute having two necks. [<F *théorbe* <Ital. *tiorba,* prob. after the name of the inventor]

the·o·rem (thē′ər·əm, thir′əm) *n.* 1 A proposition demonstrably true or acknowledged as such. 2 *Math.* **a** A proposition setting forth something to be proved. **b** A proposition that has been proved or assumed to be true. **c** A rule or statement of relations formulated in symbols. [<F *théorème* <Gk. *theōrēma* sight, theory < *theōreein* look at] — **the·o·re·mat·ic** (thē′ər·ə·mat′ik), **the′o·rem′ic** (-ə·rem′ik) *adj.*

the·o·ret·ic (thē′ə·ret′ik) *n.* 1 Theory, as distinct from practice. 2 *pl.* Theoretical matters; specifically, the theoretical aspect of a science. — *adj.* Theoretical.

the·o·ret·i·cal (thē′ə·ret′i·kəl) *adj.* 1 Of, relating to, or consisting of theory. 2 Relating to knowledge or pure science without reference to its application: compare EXPERIMENT (def. 3). 3 Existing only in theory; hypothetical. 4 Addicted to theorizing; unaffected by practical considerations; hence, impractical; visionary. Also *theoretic.* — **the′o·ret′i·cal·ly** *adv.*

the·o·re·ti·cian (thē′ər·ə·tish′ən) *n.* One who deals with the speculative, hypothetical, or ideal rather than with the practical and executive aspects of a subject.

the·o·rist (thē′ər·ist) *n.* One who theorizes.

the·o·rize (thē′ə·rīz) *v.i.* **·rized, ·riz·ing** To form or express theories; speculate. Also *Brit.* **the′·o·rise.** — **the′o·ri·za′tion** *n.* — **the′o·riz′er** *n.*

the·o·ry (thē′ər·ē, thir′ē) *n. pl.* **·ries** 1 A plan or scheme existing in the mind only, but based on principles verifiable by experiment or observation. 2 A body of the fundamental principles underlying a science or the application of a science: the *theory* of relativity. 3 Abstract knowledge of any art, as opposed to the practice of it. 4 A proposed explanation or hypothesis designed to account for any phenomenon. 5 Loosely, mere speculation or hypothesis; an individual idea or guess. 6 *Math.* An arrangement of results, or a body of theorems, presenting a systematic view of some subject: the *theory* of functions. 7 The science of musical composition, as distinguished from the art of execution. See synonyms under HYPOTHESIS, IDEA. [<F *théorie* <Gk. *theōria* view, speculation < *theōreein* look at]

the·os·o·phy (thē·os′ə·fē) *n.* Mystical speculation applied to deduce a philosophy of the universe. In its modern phase, a system that claims to embrace the essential truth underlying all systems of religion, science, and philosophy. Its doctrines resemble closely those of Buddhism and Brahmanism, teaching the existence of an omnipotent, infinite, eternal, and immutable principle transcending the power of human conception, and the identity of all souls, through the cycle of incarnation with a universal spirit. [<Med. L *theosophia* <Gk. < *theosophos* wise in divine matters < *theos* god + *sophos* wise] — **the·o·soph·ic** (thē′ə·sof′ik) or **·i·cal** *adj.* — **the′o·soph′i·cal·ly** *adv.* — **the·os′o·phist** *n.*

The·o·to·co·pu·li (tā′ō·tō·kō′po͞o·lē), **Domenico** See GRECO, EL.

The·ra (thir′ə, thē′rə) The southernmost island of the Cyclades in the Aegean; 31 square miles: formerly *Santorin.*

ther·a·peu·tic (ther′ə·pyo͞o′tik) *adj.* 1 Having healing qualities; curative. 2 Pertaining to therapeutics. Also **ther′a·peu′ti·cal.** [<NL *therapeuticus* <Gk. *therapeutikos* < *therapeutēs* an attendant < *therapeuein* serve, take care of < *therapōn* an attendant] — **ther′a·peu′ti·cal·ly** *adv.*

therapeutic dose That quantity of a drug which will produce the greatest beneficial effect in the given instance; the optimal dose.

ther·a·peu·tics (ther′ə·pyo͞o′tiks) *n. pl.* (*construed as singular*) 1 The department of medical science that treats of remedies for disease and their application. 2 The art and science of healing. — **ther′a·peu′tist** *n.*

ther·a·py (ther′ə·pē) *n. pl.* **·pies** 1 The treatment of disease by drugs or other curative processes: chiefly used in compounds: *hydrotherapy.* 2 Healing or curative quality. [<NL *therapia* <Gk. *therapeia* < *therapeuein* take care of. See THERAPEUTIC.] — **ther′a·pist** *n.*

there (thâr) *adv.* 1 In or at that place; in a place other than that of the speaker: opposed to *here.* 2 To, toward, or into that place; thither. 3 At that stage or point of action or proceeding. 4 In that respect, relation, or connection. [OE *thǣr*]

◆ *There* is also used: as a pronominal expletive introducing a clause or sentence, the subject usually following the verb: *There* once lived three bears; with independent phrases or clauses, as an equivalent of *that*, expressing encouragement, approval, etc.: *There's* a little dear; as an exclamation expressing triumph, etc.: *There*! I told you so.

there·a·bout (thâr′ə·bout′) *adv.* Near that number, quantity, degree, place, or time; approximately. Also **there′a·bouts′**.

there·af·ter (thâr′af′tər, -äf′-) *adv.* 1 Afterward; from that time on. 2 Accordingly.

there·a·gainst (thâr′ə·genst′) *adv.* Against or in opposition to that thing; on the other hand.

there·at (thâr′at′) *adv.* At that event, place, or time; at that incentive; upon that.

there·by (thâr′bī′) *adv.* 1 Through the agency of that. 2 Connected with that. 3 Conformably to that. 4 Nearby; thereabout. 5 By it or that; into possession of it or that: How did you come *thereby*?

there·for (thâr′fôr′) *adv.* For this, that, or it; in return or requital for this or that: We return thanks *therefor*.

there·fore (thâr′fôr′, -fōr′) *adv.* & *conj.* For that or this reason; on that ground or account; hence; consequently: He did not run fast enough; *therefore* he lost the race.

Synonyms (conj.): accordingly, because, consequently, hence, since, then, thence, whence, wherefore. *Therefore* is the most precise and formal word for expressing the direct conclusion of a chain of reasoning; *then* carries a similar but slighter sense of inference, which it gives incidentally rather than formally; as, If this is true, *then* we can go. *Consequently* denotes a direct result, but more frequently of a practical than a theoretical kind; as, Important matters demand my attention; *consequently* I shall not sail today. *Accordingly* denotes correspondence, which may or may not be consequence; it is often used in narration; as, The soldiers were eager and confident; *accordingly* they sprang forward at the word of command. *Thence* is a word of more sweeping inference than *therefore*, applying not merely to a single set of premises but often to all that has gone before, including the reasonable inferences that have not been formally stated. *Wherefore* is the correlative of *therefore*, and *whence* of *hence* or *thence*, appending the inference or conclusion to the previous statement without a break. Compare synonyms for BECAUSE.

there·from (thâr′frum′, -from′) *adv.* From this, that, or it; from this or that time, place, state, event, or thing.

there·in (thâr′in′) *adv.* 1 In that place. 2 In that time, matter, or respect.

there·in·af·ter (thâr′in·af′tər, -äf′-) *adv.* In a subsequent part of that (book, document, speech, etc.).

there·in·to (thâr′in·tōō′) *adv.* Into this, that, or it.

Ther·e·min (ther′ə·min) *n.* A musical instrument played by manual interference with two sets of radio-frequency waves issuing from a pair of oscillators adapted for tone variation and volume control: a trade name. [after Léon *Thérémin*, born 1896, Russian-French inventor]

there·of (thâr′uv′, -ov′) *adv.* 1 Of or relating to this, that, or it. 2 From or because of this or that cause or particular; therefrom.

there·on (thâr′on′, -ôn′) *adv.* 1 On this, that, or it. 2 Thereupon; thereat.

there's (thârz) There is: a contraction.

The·re·sa (tə·rē′sə, -res′ə) A feminine personal name. Also *Fr.* **Thé·rèse** (tā·rez′). [<Gk., harvester]

— **Saint Theresa of Ávila**, 1515–82, Spanish Carmelite nun and mystic: also *Teresa*.

there·to (thâr′tōō′) *adv.* 1 To this, that, or it. 2 In addition; furthermore. Also **there′·un·to′** (-un·tōō′).

there·to·fore (thâr′tə·fôr′, -fōr′) *adv.* Before this or that; previously to that.

there·un·der (thâr′un′dər) *adv.* 1 Under this or that. 2 Less, as in number. 3 In a lower or lesser status or rank.

there·up·on (thâr′ə·pon′, -ə·pôn′) *adv.* 1 Upon that; upon it. 2 Following upon or in consequence of that. 3 Immediately following; at once.

there·with (thâr′with′, -with′) *adv.* 1 With this, that, or it. 2 Thereupon; thereafter; immediately afterward.

there·with·al (thâr′with·ôl′) *adv.* 1 With all this or that; besides. 2 *Obs.* Therewith; with this, that, or it.

the·ri·a·ca (thi·rī′ə·kə) *n.* 1 An ancient antidote for the bite of venomous creatures, containing numerous drugs mixed with honey. 2 Molasses; treacle. Also **the·ri·ac** (thir′ē·ak). [<LL *theriaca*, an antidote for poison <Gk. *thēriakos* pertaining to wild beasts < *thērion*, dim. of *thēr* wild beast] — **the·ri′a·cal** *adj.*

the·ri·an·thro·pism (thir′ē·an′thrə·piz′əm) *n.* Representation of preternatural beings in combined forms of man and beast, especially in primitive polytheistic worship: the religions of *therianthropism*. [<Gk. *thērion* wild beast + *anthrōpos*, *-ōpou* man] — **the′ri·an·throp′ic** (-an·throp′ik) *adj.*

the·ri·o·mor·phic (thir′ē·ə·môr′fik) *adj.* Beastlike in form: *theriomorphic* gods. Also **the′ri·o·mor′phous.** [<Gk. *thērion* wild beast + *morphē* form]

therm (thûrm) *n.* 1 A unit of heat used as a basis for the sale of illuminating gas in England, equal to 100,000 British thermal units. 2 One thousand great calories. 3 The great calorie. 4 The lesser calorie. Also **therme.** [<Gk. *thermē* heat]

therm- Var. of THERMO-.

Ther·ma (thûr′mə) Ancient name for THESSALONIKE.

ther·mae (thûr′mē) *n. pl.* 1 Hot springs or baths. 2 Specifically, the public baths of the ancient Romans; also, the bathhouses. [<L <Gk. *thermai*, pl. of *thermē* heat]

ther·mal (thûr′məl) *adj.* 1 Pertaining to, determined by, or measured by heat. 2 Hot or warm. Also **ther′mic.** — **ther′mal·ly** *adv.*

thermal barrier *Aeron.* The limit imposed upon the operating speed of jet engines, rockets, motors, and the like by temperatures above the melting point of their materials.

thermal death Heat death.

thermal diffusion 1 The diffusion of heat. 2 *Physics* A method for the separation of isotopes by passing a gas through a vertical tube containing an electrically heated wire which produces a concentration of the heavier components at the bottom and of the lighter components at the top.

therm·an·es·the·sia (thûr′mən·is·thē′zhə, -zhē·ə) *n. Pathol.* Loss of ability to recognize sensations of heat or cold; absence of temperature sense. Also **therm′an·aes·the′sia.** [< THERM(O)- + ANESTHESIA]

therm·el (thûr′mel) *n.* A thermocouple or group of thermocouples when used to determine temperatures. [<Gk. *thermē* heat]

therm·es·the·sia (thûr′mis·thē′zhə, -zhē·ə) *n. Physiol.* The ability to recognize changes of temperature; temperature sensitivity. Also **therm′aes·the′sia.** [<THERM(O)- + ESTHESIA]

Ther·mi·dor (thûr′mə·dôr′, *Fr.* ter·mē·dôr′) See under CALENDAR (Republican). [<F <Gk. *thermē* heat + *dōron* gift]

therm·i·on (thûrm′ī′ən, thûr′mē·ən) *n. Physics* An electrically charged particle emitted by a heated body: it may be either positive or negative. [<THERM(O)- + ION] — **therm·i·on·ic** (thûr′mē·on′ik) *adj.*

therm·i·on·ics (thûr′mē·on′iks) *n. pl. (construed as singular)* The science and practical application of thermionic phenomena.

thermionic tube A vacuum tube emitting thermions from a heated electrode. Also *Brit.* **thermionic valve.**

therm·is·tor (thər·mis′tər) *n. Electr.* A small, compact thermometric device consisting of a semiconducting material having a large temperature coefficient of resistance: widely used in the measurement of microwave power, of temperatures, and as a protective device in circuits. [<THERM(O)- + (RES)ISTOR]

ther·mit (thûr′mit) *n.* A mixture composed of finely divided aluminum and oxide of iron, chromium, or manganese. When such a mixture is brought to a sufficient temperature, the oxygen of the oxide unites with the aluminum, producing an intense heat. Also **ther′mite** (-mīt). [<Gk. *thermē* heat]

thermo- *combining form* Heat; of, related to, or caused by heat: *thermolysis, thermostat.* Also, before vowels, *therm-*. [<Gk. *thermos* heat, warmth]

ther·mo·bar·o·graph (thûr′mō·bar′ə·graf, -gräf) *n.* An apparatus for measuring the pressure and temperature of a gas simultaneously.

ther·mo·ba·rom·e·ter (thûr′mō·bə·rom′ə·tər) *n.* 1 An apparatus for measuring atmospheric pressure by the boiling point of water: used in determining altitudes. 2 A form of barometer that can be inverted and made to serve as a thermometer.

ther·mo·cau·ter·y (thûr′mō·kô′tər·ē) *n.* Cautery by means of heated wires or points.

ther·mo·chem·is·try (thûr′mō·kem′is·trē) *n.* The branch of chemistry that treats of the relations between chemical reactions and the evolution and absorption of heat observed to accompany them. — **ther′mo·chem′i·cal** (-kem′·i·kəl) *adj.* — **ther′mo·chem′ist** *n.*

ther·mo·cline (thûr′mō·klīn) *n.* A gradient indicating marked changes in temperature with depth, especially between discontinuous layers of ocean waters.

ther·mo·coup·le (thûr′mō·kup′əl) *n.* A pair of dissimilar metals so joined as to produce a thermoelectric effect when the contact surfaces are at different temperatures. Also **ther′mo·e·lec′tric couple.**

ther·mo·dy·nam·ics (thûr′mō·dī·nam′iks, -di-) *n. pl. (construed as singular)* That branch of physical science which treats of the relations between heat and energy, especially the convertibility of one into the other and the mechanical work involved. — **ther′mo·dy·nam′ic** or **·i·cal** *adj.* — **ther′mo·dy·nam′i·cist** (-nam′ə·sist) *n.*

ther·mo·e·lec·tric (thûr′mō·i·lek′trik) *adj.* Of or pertaining to thermoelectricity. Also **ther′mo·e·lec′tri·cal.** — **ther′mo·e·lec′tri·cal·ly** *adv.*

ther·mo·e·lec·tric·i·ty (thûr′mō·i·lek′tris′ə·tē) *n.* Electricity generated by differences of temperature, especially between two different metals in contact when one of the junctions is heated.

ther·mo·e·lec·tro·mo·tive (thûr′mō·i·lek′trə·mō′tiv) *adj.* Of, pertaining to, or designating electromotive force caused by difference of temperature.

ther·mo·gal·va·nom·e·ter (thûr′mō·gal′və·nom′·ə·tər) *n.* A combination of a galvanometer and a thermocouple used to measure minute variations of temperature.

ther·mo·gen·e·sis (thûr′mō·jen′ə·sis) *n.* The production of heat, especially of animal heat by organic action. — **ther′mo·gen′ic, ther·mog·e·nous** (thər·moj′ə·nəs), **ther′mo·ge·net′ic** (-jə·net′ik) *adj.*

ther·mo·gram (thûr′mə·gram) *n.* The record made by a thermograph.

ther·mo·graph (thûr′mə·graf, -gräf) *n.* An instrument for recording temperature variations; a self-registering thermometer.

ther·mog·ra·phy (thər·mog′rə·fē) *n.* 1 Photography by means of heat waves emitted by an object which has been coated with luminescent paint and exposed to ultraviolet light. 2 *Printing* Any process of reproducing written or printed characters that employs heat. — **ther·mo·graph·ic** (thûr′mə·graf′ik) *adj.*

ther·mo·hal·ine (thûr′mō·hal′ēn, -īn, -in) *adj.* Pertaining to or characterized by variations in the temperature and salinity of sea water. [<THERMO- + Gk. *hals* salt + -INE[1]]

ther·mo·junc·tion (thûr′mō·jungk′shən) *n.* The point of contact between the pair of conductors forming a thermocouple.

ther·mo·kin·e·mat·ics (thûr′mō·kin′ə·mat′iks) *n. pl. (construed as singular)* The study of heat in motion or of the motive power of heat.

ther·mo·la·bile (thûr′mō·lā′bil) *adj. Biochem.* Decomposed, destroyed, affected, or liable to be adversely affected by heat, as some enzymes and toxins: opposed to *thermostable*. [<THERMO- + LABILE]

ther·mo·lu·mi·nes·cence (thûr′mō·lōō′mə·nes′·əns) *n.* 1 The emission of light from a substance or material under the action of heat. 2 A luminous effect in rock crystals from which electrons displaced by radioactivity have been released at definite temperatures, with or without pressure: sometimes indicative of the age of sedimentary rocks. — **ther′mo·lu′mi·nes′cent** *adj.*

ther·mol·y·sis (thər·mol′ə·sis) *n.* 1 *Chem.* The resolution of a compound substance into its component elements by the application of heat. 2 *Physiol.* The dissipation of heat from the animal body by physical processes. [< THERMO- + -LYSIS] — **ther·mo·lyt·ic** (thûr′mə·lit′ik) *adj.*

ther·mo·mag·net·ic (thûr′mō·mag·net′ik) *adj.* Of or pertaining to the relations between heat and magnetism.

ther·mom·e·ter (thər·mom′ə·tər) *n.* An instrument for measuring the temperature of a substance, body, or space. The ordinary thermometer consists of a graduated glass capillary tube or stem with a bulb containing mercury which expands or contracts as the temperature rises or falls. The **differential thermometer** has two air bulbs connected by a U–tube, containing colored liquid, so that when the bulbs are exposed to different temperatures a shifting of the liquid in the tube will be caused by the difference of expansion of air in the bulbs. A **resistance thermometer** indicates, by means of the change in electrical conductivity of wires with temperature, the temperature of any given wire or its environment. — **clinical thermometer** A thermometer accurately calibrated for determining body temperature, especially of a person. [<THERMO- + METER]

ther·mom·e·try (thər·mom′ə·trē) *n.* The measurement of temperature, or the art thereof, by means of the thermometer; specifically, the use of the thermometer in medical diagnosis. — **ther·mo·met·ric** (thûr′mō·met′rik) or **·ri·cal** *adj.* — **ther′mo·met′ri·cal·ly** *adv.*

ther·mo·mo·tor (thûr′mō·mō′tər) *n.* A heat engine; especially, a hot–air engine. Compare MOTOR.

ther·mo·nu·cle·ar (thûr′mō·nōō′klē·ər, -nyōō′-) *adj. Physics* Pertaining to or characterized by the mass–energy reactions involving the fusion of light atomic nuclei subjected to very high temperatures, especially with reference to stellar energy and the hydrogen bomb.

ther·mo·pen·e·tra·tion (thûr′mō·pen′ə·trā′·shən) *n.* Diathermy.

ther·mo·phil·ic (thûr′mō·fil′ik) *adj.* Fond of heat: used mainly of certain bacteria. Also **ther′mo·phile** (-fil, -fīl). [<THERMO- + Gk. *philos* loving]

ther·mo·pile (thûr′mō·pīl) *n.* A group of thermocouples acting jointly to produce electric energy, especially when used with a galvanometer to measure heat.

ther·mo·plas·tic (thûr′mō·plas′tik) *adj.* Plastic in the presence of or under the application of heat: said especially of certain synthetic molding materials. — *n.* A thermoplastic substance or material.

Ther·mop·y·lae (thər·mop′ə·lē) A narrow mountain pass in Greece; scene of a battle, 480 B.C., in which the Spartans under the command of Leonidas held off the Persians under Xerxes and finally died to the last man rather than yield.

ther·mos bottle (thûr′məs) A container shaped like a bottle or flask, having two walls separated by a vacuum which serves to insulate the contents so that they retain their temperature.

ther·mo·scope (thûr′mə·skōp) *n.* An instrument for detecting changes or differences of temperature without accurately measuring them. [<THERMO- + -SCOPE] — **ther′mo·scop′ic** (-skop′ik) or **·i·cal** *adj.*

ther·mo·set·ting (thûr′mō·set′ing) *adj.* Having the property of assuming a fixed shape after being molded under heat, as certain phenol and other synthetic resins.

ther·mo·si·phon (thûr′mō·sī′fən) *n.* A device consisting of siphon tubes to increase or induce circulation by making use of temperature differential in a water–cooling system, as in that of an internal–combustion engine.

ther·mo·sta·ble (thûr′mō·stā′bəl) *adj.* 1 Resistant to heat, as certain plastics and chemicals. 2 *Biochem.* Unaffected by moderate heats; denoting immune substances, as certain toxins or ferments, which may be heated to 55° C. without loss of special properties: opposed to *thermolabile.* Also **ther′mo·sta′bile.** — **ther′·mo·sta·bil′i·ty** (-stə·bil′ə·tē) *n.*

ther·mo·stat (thûr′mə·stat) *n.* A device for the automatic regulation of temperature by means of a relay utilizing the expansion and contraction caused by temperature changes in certain metals: used for actuating fire alarms, opening or closing dampers, regulating steam pressures, etc. [<THERMO- + Gk. *statos* standing] — **ther′mo·stat′ic** *adj.* — **ther′mo·stat′i·cal·ly** *adv.*

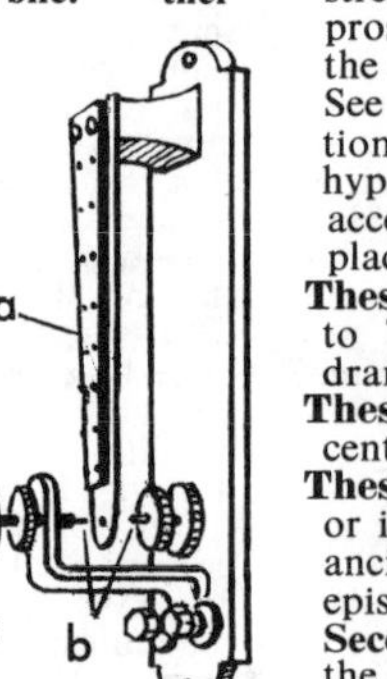

THERMOSTAT
a. Bimetal bar.
b. Contact points.
c. Control knob.

ther·mo·stat·ics (thûr′mō·stat′iks) *n. pl. (construed as singular)* The science that deals with the equilibrium of heat.

ther·mo·tank (thûr′mō·tangk′) *n.* A tank or box in which steam, water, air, or the like circulates through pipes and thus heats or cools the air passing through the tank.

ther·mo·tax·is (thûr′mō·tak′sis) *n. Biol.* 1 The regulation or normal adjustment of the animal heat in an organism. 2 The determination of movement by heat. — **ther′mo·tax′ic, ther′mo·tac′tic** (-tak′tik) *adj.*

ther·mo·ten·sile (thûr′mō·ten′sil) *adj.* Relating to variation of tensile strength caused by temperature.

therm·o·ther·a·py (thûr′mō·ther′ə·pē) *n. Med.* The treatment of disease by the application of heat.

ther·mot·ics (thər·mot′iks) *n. pl. (construed as singular)* The science of heat. [<Gk. *thermotēs* heat]

ther·mot·ro·pism (thər·mot′rə·piz′əm) *n. Biol.* 1 The property or phenomenon of movement in growing plants or other organisms brought about by the influence of heat or cold. 2 The attraction or repulsion from a source of heat evinced by some bacteria. — **ther·mo·trop·ic** (thûr′mō·trop′ik) *adj.*

the·roid (thir′oid) *adj.* Resembling or like a beast. [<Gk. *thēroeidēs* < *thēr, thēros* a wild beast + *eidos* form]

the·ro·phyte (thir′ə·fīt) *n. Bot.* An annual plant which completes its life cycle in one vegetative season. [<Gk. *theros* summer + -PHYTE]

the·ro·pod (thir′ə·pod) *n.* Any of a suborder *(Theropoda)* of saurischian dinosaurs of the Triassic and Cretaceous periods, including the true carnivorous types, as *Allosaurus* and *Tyrannosaurus.* — *adj.* Of or pertaining to the *Theropoda.* [<NL *Theropoda* <Gk. *thēr, thēros* a wild beast + *pous, podos* foot] — **the·rop·o·dan** (thi·rop′ə·dən) *adj.* & *n.*

Ther·si·tes (thər·sī′tēz) In the *Iliad,* an ugly and scurrilous Greek soldier in the Trojan War, killed by Achilles for troublemaking.

ther·sit·i·cal (thər·sit′i·kəl) *adj.* Characteristic of Thersites; hence, loud and scurrilous; abusive.

the·sau·ric (thi·sôr′ik) *adj.* Encyclopedic; having or containing large stores of miscellaneous information.

the·sau·ro·sis (thē′sô·rō′sis) *n. Pathol.* A condition marked by the storage in the body of excessive amounts of normal or foreign substances. [<Gk. *thēsauros* treasure + -OSIS]

the·sau·rus (thi·sôr′əs) *n. pl.* **·sau·ri** (-sôr′ī) 1 A place where treasure is laid up; a storehouse. 2 A repository of words or knowledge; hence, a lexicon or cyclopedia. [<L <Gk. *thēsauros* treasure house. Doublet of TREASURE.]

these (t͟hēz) Plural of THIS.

The·seus (thē′sōōs, -sē·əs) In Greek mythology, the chief hero of Attica, son of Aegeus and king of Athens, celebrated for many adventures, chiefly the killing of the Minotaur, and for unifying Attica with Athens as its capital. See ARIADNE, HIPPOLYTUS, PHAEDRA, PIRITHOUS. — **The′se·an** (-sē·ən) *adj.*

the·sis (thē′sis) *n. pl.* **·ses** (-sēz) 1 A proposition. 2 Specifically, a formal proposition, advanced and defended by argumentation. 3 A formal treatise on a particular subject, especially, a dissertation presented by a candidate for an academic degree. 4 In early prosody, that part of a foot which had the ictus or stress. 5 In later Roman usage and in modern prosody, the unaccented part of a foot; also, the depression of the voice in pronouncing it. See ARSIS. 6 *Logic* An affirmative proposition; a premise or postulate, as opposed to a hypothesis. 7 *Music* The down beat; the accented part of a measure. [<L <Gk., a placing, proposition < *tithenai* put, place]

Thes·pi·an (thes′pē·ən) *adj.* 1 Of or relating to Thespis. 2 Of or relating to drama; dramatic; tragic. — *n.* An actor or actress.

Thes·pis (thes′pis) Greek poet of the sixth century B.C.; reputed father of Greek tragedy.

Thes·sa·lo·ni·an (thes′ə·lō′nē·ən) *n.* 1 A native or inhabitant of modern Thessalonike or of ancient Thessalonica. 2 *pl.* Either of two epistles in the New Testament (**First** and **Second Thessalonians**) written by St. Paul to the Christians of Thessalonica. — *adj.* Of or pertaining to Thessalonike.

Thes·sa·lo·ni·ke (thes′ä·lô·nē′kē) The Greek name for SALONIKA. Ancient **Thes·sa·lo·ni·ca** (thes′ə·lō·nī′kə, -lon′i·kə).

Thes·sa·ly (thes′ə·lē) A division of north central Greece; 5,399 square miles; chief town, Larissa. — **Thes·sa·li·an** (the·sā′lē·ən) *adj.* & *n.*

the·ta (thā′tə, thē′tə) *n.* The eighth letter in the Greek alphabet (Θ, ϑ, θ): equivalent in classical Greek to *t* + *h,* as in *right–hand,* but in modern Greek to spirant *th,* as in *thin.* [<Gk. *thēta*]

thet·ic (thet′ik) *adj.* 1 In ancient prosody, beginning with, bearing, relating to, or of the nature of a thesis. 2 Characterized by positive statement; arbitrary; dogmatic. Also **thet′i·cal.** [<Gk. *thetikos* fit for placing < *thetos* placed < *the-,* stem of *tithenai* place] — **thet′i·cal·ly** *adv.*

The·tis (thē′tis) In Greek mythology, a Nereid, wife of Peleus and mother of Achilles: by dipping Achilles into the Styx, she made him invulnerable, except in the right heel, by which she had held him.

the·ur·gy (thē′ûr·jē) *n. pl.* **·gies** 1 Divine or supernatural intervention in human affairs. 2 The working of miracles through divine or supernatural aid. 3 Magic, as practiced by the Neo–Platonists, by means of which miraculous effects were supposedly produced through the intervention of beneficent spirits; white magic. [<Gk. *theourgia* < *theourgos* divine worker < *theos* god + *ergon* work] — **the·ur·gic** (thē·ûr′jik), **the·ur′gi·cal** *adj.* — **the·ur′gi·cal·ly** *adv.* — **the′ur·gist** *n.*

thew (thyōō) *n.* 1 A sinew or muscle, especially when strong or well–developed. 2 *pl.* Bodily strength or vigor. [ME *theawes* good qualities, strength <OE *thēau* habit, characteristic quality] — **thew′y** *adj.*

thew·less (thyōō′lis) *adj. Scot.* 1 Having no thews; inactive; weak. 2 Spiritless; inert.

they (t͟hā) *pron.* 1 The persons, beings, or things previously mentioned or understood: the nominative plural of *he, she, it.* 2 People in general; men: *They* say rain is expected. [<ON *their,* pl. of *sā* this, that]

they'd (t͟hād) Contraction of: 1 They had. 2 They would.

they'll (t͟hāl) They will: a contraction.

they're (t͟hâr) They are: a contraction.

they've (t͟hāv) They have: a contraction.

thi- Var. of THIO-.

thi·a·mine (thī′ə·mēn, -min) *n. Biochem.* A white crystalline compound, $C_{12}H_{18}ON_4SCl_4$; vitamin B_1, found in various natural sources, as cereal grains, green peas, liver, egg yolk, etc., and also made synthetically. Thiamine is the anti–beriberi vitamin. Also **thi′a·min** (-min). [<THI- + -AMINE]

thi·a·zine (thī′ə·zēn, -zin) *n. Chem.* One of a class of organic ring compounds of one atom of nitrogen, one of sulfur, and four of carbon. Also **thi′a·zin** (-zin). [<THI- + -AZINE]

thi·a·zole (thī′ə·zōl) *n. Chem.* A colorless, stable, liquid compound, C_3H_3NS, whose derivatives yield dyestuffs and certain sulfa drugs. Also **thi′a·zol** (-zōl, -zol). [<THI- + AZOLE]

Thi·bault (tē·bō′), **Jacques Anatole** See FRANCE, ANATOLE.

Thi·baut (tē·bō′) French form of THEOBALD.

Thi·bet (ti·bet′) See TIBET.

thick (thik) *adj.* 1 Having relatively large depth or extent from one surface to its opposite; having the dimension that is commonly least, comparatively great; not thin: distinguished from *long* and *broad.* 2 Having a specified dimension of this kind, whether great or small: an inch *thick.* 3 Arranged compactly; close: a *thick* forest; also, following at brief intervals; frequent, as blows, raindrops, etc. 4 Set or furnished closely or abundantly with objects; abounding. 5 Having considerable density or consistency; dense; hence, turbid; impure; heavy. 6 Overcharged with vapor; foggy; misty. 7 Lacking quickness of apprehension; dull; stupid. 8 Indistinct; muffled: a *thick* sound; also, guttural; husky; throaty. 9 *Colloq.* Very friendly; intimate. 10 *Colloq.* Excessive; going too far; being beyond the bounds of what is tolerable. — *adv.* In a thick manner; placed or following closely. — **to lay it on thick** *Colloq.* 1 To overstate; exaggerate. 2 To praise fulsomely. — *n.* 1 The dimension of thickness; the thickest part. 2 The thickest or most intense time or place of anything: the *thick* of the fight. — **through thick and thin** Through good times and bad; loyally; through good fortune and adversity. [OE *thicce*] — **thick′ly** *adv.*

Synonyms (adj.): close, cloudy, compact, condensed, dense, dull, foggy, gross, hazy, inspissate, misty, muddy, turbid. See BLUNT.

thick·en (thik′ən) *v.t.* & *v.i.* 1 To make or become thick or thicker. 2 To make or become more intricate or intense: The plot *thickens.* — **thick′en·er** *n.*

thick·en·ing (thik′ən·ing) *n.* 1 The act of making or becoming thick. 2 Something added to a liquid to increase its consistency. 3 That or that part which is or has been thickened.

thick·et (thik′it) *n.* A thick growth, as of underbrush, through which a passage is not easily effected; a coppice; jungle. [OE *thiccet* < *thicce* thick]

thick·head (thik′hed′) *n.* A stupid person; numskull. Also **thick′skull′** (-skul′).

thick·ish (thik′ish) *adj.* Somewhat thick.

thick·ness (thik′nis) *n.* 1 The state or quality of being thick. 2 The dimension or measure of a solid other than its length or width. 3 A sheet, layer, etc., as of paper.

thick–set (thik′set′) *adj.* 1 Having a short, thick body; stout. 2 Set like a thicket; closely planted. — *n.* 1 A thicket; also, a thick hedge. 2 A fustianlike fabric with a velveteen nap.

thick–skinned (thik′skind′) *adj.* 1 Having a thick skin; pachydermatous. 2 Insensitive; callous to hints or insults.

thick–wit·ted (thik′wit′id) *adj.* Stupid; obtuse; dense.

thief (thēf) *n. pl.* **thieves** (thēvz) 1 One who takes something belonging to another; one who steals. 2 *Law* One guilty of simple or compound larceny, embezzlement, or swindling. 3 That which causes loss: Procrastination is the *thief* of time. See synonyms under ROBBER. [OE *thēof*]

Thiers (tyâr), **Louis Adolphe,** 1797–1877, French statesman and historian.

thieve (thēv) *v.* **thieved, thiev·ing** *v.t.* To take by theft; purloin; steal. — *v.i.* To be a thief; commit theft. [OE *thēofian*]

thieve·less (thēv′lis) *adj. Scot.* 1 Ungracious; hard. 2 Listless.

thiev·er·y (thē′vər·ē) *n. pl.* **·er·ies** The practice or act of thieving; theft; also, an instance of thieving.

thiev·ish (thē′vish) *adj.* 1 Addicted to thieving. 2 Acting by stealth; furtive. 3 Relating to or like a thief. 4 Partaking of the nature of theft. — **thiev′ish·ly** *adv.* — **thiev′ish·ness** *n.*

thigh (thī) *n.* 1 The leg between the hip and the knee of man or the corresponding portion in other animals. ◆ Collateral adjective: *femoral.* 2 The femur of an insect. [OE *thēoh*]

thigh bone The femur.

thig·mo·tax·is (thig′mə·tak′sis) *n. Biol.* Stereotropism. [<Gk. *thigma* touch + -TAXIS] — **thig′mo·tac′tic** (-tak′tik) *adj.* — **thig′mo·tac′·ti·cal·ly** *adv.*

thig·mot·ro·pism (thig·mot′rə·piz′əm) *n. Biol.* Involuntary response to mechanical stimulation of any kind, as displayed by many insects and by the tendrils, leaves, etc., of certain plants. [<Gk. *thigma* touch + TROPISM] — **thig·mo·trop·ic** (thig′mə·trop′ik) *adj.*

thill (thil) *n.* One of the shafts of a vehicle, between which a horse is harnessed. [OE *thille* board]

thim·ble (thim′bəl) *n.* 1 A caplike cover with a pitted surface, worn in sewing to protect the end of the finger that pushes the needle. 2 *Mech.* A sleeve through which a bolt passes, or which unites two rods, tubes, or the like. 3 *Naut.* **a** A metal anti–chafing ring forming a guard over a loop or eye in a sail. **b** The metal piece about which a rope is bent and spliced to the main body of the rope to form an eye. [OE *thȳmel* < *thūma* thumb]

thim·ble·ber·ry (thim′bəl·ber′ē) *n. pl.* **·ries** Any of certain American raspberries or blackberries having a thimble–shaped fruit; especially, the blackcap raspberry, the **fragrant thimbleberry** *(Rubus odoratus),* and the **western thimbleberry** *(R. parviflorus).*

thim·ble·rig (thim′bəl·rig′) *n.* 1 A swindling trick in which a pea or ball is shifted by sleight of hand from one to another of three inverted thimble–shaped cups. 2 A gambler who operates a thimblerig. — *v.t.* **·rigged, ·rig·ging** To cheat by or as by thimblerig. — **thim′ble·rig′ger** *n.*

thim·ble·weed (thim′bəl·wēd′) *n.* Any of various plants (genus *Rudbeckia*) with thimble–shaped receptacles, as the rudbeckia and the American wood anemone.

thin (thin) *adj.* **thin·ner, thin·nest** 1 Having opposite surfaces relatively close to each other; being of little depth or width; not thick. 2 Lacking roundness or plumpness of figure; lean; slender. 3 Having the component parts or particles scattered or diffused; not dense or abundant; sparse; rare: *thin* ranks, *thin* gas. 4 Having little body or substance; of a loose texture; hence, insufficient to conceal or cover: *thin* clothing; flimsy: a *thin* excuse. 5 Having little or no consistency, as a liquid: *thin* molasses. 6 Lacking in essential ingredients or qualities: *thin* blood. 7 Having little volume or richness; shrill or metallic, as a voice. 8 Not abundantly supplied or furnished; bare; scant: a *thin* table. 9 Not having sufficient contrasts of shade to print well: said of a photographic negative. 10 Lacking vigor or force; feeble; superficial: *thin* wit. See synonyms under FINE[1], GAUNT, MEAGER. — *v.t.* & *v.i.* **thinned, thin·ning** To make or become thin or thinner. [OE *thynne*] — **thin′ly** *adv.* — **thin′ness** *n.*

thine (t͟hīn) *pron.* 1 The possessive case of thou, used predicatively; belonging or pertaining to thee: *Thine* is the kingdom. 2 The things or persons belonging or pertaining to thee. — **of thine** Belonging or relating to thee; thy: the double possessive. — *pronominal adj. Archaic* Thy: *thine* eyes. [OE *thīn,* genitive of *thū* thou]

thing[1] (thing) *n.* 1 That which exists or is conceived to exist as a separate entity; an entity; being. 2 That which is designated, as contrasted with the word or symbol used to denote it. 3 A matter or circumstance; an affair; concern: *Things* have changed. 4 An act or deed; transaction: That was a shameless *thing* to do. 5 A statement or expression; utterance: to say the right *thing.* 6 An idea; opinion; notion: Stop putting *things* in her head. 7 A quality; attribute; characteristic: Kindness is a precious *thing.* 8 An inanimate object, as distinguished from a living organism. 9 An organic being: usually with a qualifying word: Every living *thing* dies. 10 An object that is not or cannot be described or particularized: The *thing* disappeared in the shadows. 11 A person, regarded in terms of pity, affection, or contempt: that poor *thing;* You stupid *thing!* 12 *pl.* Possessions; belongings: to pack one's *things.* 13 *pl.* Clothes; especially, outer garments: Take off your *things* and stay awhile. 14 A piece of literature, art, music, etc.: He read a few *things* by Byron. 15 The proper or befitting act or result: with *the*: That was not the *thing* to do. 16 The important or remarkable point: with *the*: The *thing* we learned from the war was this. 17 *Law* A subject or property or dominion, as distinguished from a person. — **to do one's (own) thing** *Slang* To express oneself by doing what one wants to do or can do well or is in the habit of doing. — **to see things** To have hallucinations. [OE, thing, cause, assembly. Akin to THING[2].]

thing[2] (ting) *n.* A Scandinavian legislative or judicial body: the *Storthing,* the Norwegian parliament: also spelled *ting.* [<ON, assembly. Akin to THING[1].]

thing·a·ma·bob (thing′ə·mə·bob′) *n. Colloq.* A thing the specific name of which is unknown or forgotten; a dingus. Also **thing′um·a·bob′, thing′um·bob.**

thing·a·ma·jig (thing′ə·mə·jig′) *n. Colloq.* A thingamabob. Also **thing′um·a·jig′.**

T–hinge (tē′hinj′) *n.* A hinge the two sections of which have the form of the letter T. See illustration under HINGE.

thing in itself *Philos.* A noumenon; the ultimate, metaphysical reality behind the physical phenomena perceived by the senses, which, according to Kant, can never be known: the English rendering of the German *Ding an sich.*

think[1] (thingk) *v.* **thought** (thôt), **think·ing** *v.t.* 1 To produce or form in the mind; conceive mentally: to *think* evil thoughts. 2 To examine in the mind; meditate upon, or determine by reasoning: He was *thinking* what to do next; to *think* a plan through. 3 To believe; consider: I *think* him guilty. 4 To expect; anticipate: They did not *think* to meet us. 5 To bring to mind; remember; recollect: I cannot *think* what he said. 6 To have the mind preoccupied by: to *think* business morning, noon, and night. 7 To intend; purpose: Do they *think* to rob me? — *v.i.* 8 To use the mind or intellect in exercising judgment, forming ideas, etc.; engage in rational thought; reason. 9 To have a particular opinion, sentiment, or feeling: I don't *think* so. — **to think better of** 1 To abandon a course of action; alter one's intentions: I was going to call but I *thought better of* it. 2 To form a better opinion of. — **to think fit, proper, right,** etc. To regard as worth doing. — **to think nothing of** 1 To have a low opinion of; ignore. 2 To consider easy to do. — **to think of** 1 To bring to mind; remember; recollect. 2 To conceive in the mind; invent; imagine. 3 To have a specified opinion or attitude toward; regard. 4 To be considerate of; have regard for. — **to think over** To reflect upon; ponder. — **to think up** To devise, arrive at, or invent by thinking. — *n.* An act of thinking; a thought. [OE *thencean*; influenced in form by THINK[2]]

think[2] (thingk) *v.i.* To seem; appear: now obsolete except with the pronoun as indirect object in the combinations *methinks, methought.* [OE *thyncan* seem]

think·a·ble (thingk′ə·bəl) *adj.* Susceptible of being thought; conceivable; hence, possible to be believed.

think·er (thingk′ər) *n.* 1 One who thinks. 2 A person of powerful mind who devotes himself to abstract thought.

think·ing (thingk′ing) *adj.* 1 Exercising the mental capacities. 2 Capable of such exercise; rational. — *n.* 1 Mental action; thought. 2 The product of such action, as an idea. See synonyms under REFLECTION, THOUGHT. — **think′ing·ly** *adv.*

think tank *Colloq.* 1 A group of people **(think tankers),** usually academics, business executives, or government employees, organized for the investigation and study of social, scientific, and technological problems. 2 The place in which such a group works.

thin·ner (thin′ər) *n.* 1 One who or that which thins. 2 A liquid, as turpentine or petroleum spirits, mixed with paint in order to give it a proper consistency for working.

thin·nish (thin′ish) *adj.* Somewhat thin.

thin–skinned (thin′skind′) *adj.* 1 Having a thin skin. 2 Hence, easily hurt or offended; sensitive.

thio– *combining form Chem.* Containing sulfur; denoting a compound of sulfur, especially one in which sulfur has displaced oxygen: *thiocyanic.* Also, before vowels, sometimes *thi–.* Compare SULFURO–. [<Gk. *theion* sulfur]

thi·o·a·ce·tic (thī′ō·ə·sē′tik, -ə·set′ik) *adj. Chem.* Designating a yellow, fuming, pungent acid, C_2H_4OS, used in ammonia solutions as a precipitant of metals. [<THIO- + ACETIC]

thi·o·al·co·hol (thī′ō·al′kə·hôl) *n. Chem.* Thiol.

thi·o·al·de·hyde (thī′ō·al′də·hīd) *n. Chem.* An aldehyde containing sulfur as a substitute for oxygen.

thi·o·bac·te·ri·um (thī′ō·bak·tir′ē·əm) *n.* Any

of an order *(Thiobacteriales)* of bacteria which utilize the sulfur of decaying organic matter.

thi·o·car·bam·ide (thī′ō·kär·bam′īd, -id, -kär′·bə·mīd) *n.* Thiourea. [<THIO- + CARBAMIDE]

thi·o·cy·a·nate (thī′ō·sī′ə·nāt) *n. Chem.* A salt or ester of thiocyanic acid.

thi·o·cy·an·ic (thī′ō·sī·an′ik) *adj. Chem.* Designating or pertaining to a colorless liquid acid, HSCN, soluble in water and having a pungent odor. [<THIO- + CYANIC]

thi·o·gen (thī′ə·jen) *n.* A bacterial organism producing sulfur. [<THIO- + -GEN]

Thi·o·kol (thī′ə·kōl, -kol) *n.* A synthetic material consisting of organic polysulfides and resembling natural rubber in its physical properties: a trade name.

thi·ol (thī′ōl, -ol) *n. Chem.* Any of a class of sulfur compounds which are analogs of the alcohols and have the general formula RSH, in which R is a hydrocarbon radical: used largely in compounding, as *ethanethiol,* C_2H_5SH. Formerly called *mercaptan.* [<THI- + -OL[1]]

thi·on·ic (thī·on′ik) *adj. Chem.* **1** Of, pertaining to, containing, or derived from sulfur. **2** Denoting any of a group of unstable acids having the general formula $H_2S_nO_6$. [<Gk. *theion* sulfur]

thi·o·nine (thī′ə·nēn, -nin) *n. Chem.* A dark-green thiazine derivative, $C_{12}H_9N_3S$, made by synthesis, with a glistening metallic luster that yields purplish colors to silk and wool. Also **thi′o·nin** (-nin). [<Gk. *theion* sulfur + -INE[2]]

thi·o·nyl (thī′ə·nil) *n. Chem.* The bivalent sulfur radical SO: also called *sulfinyl.* [<Gk. *theion* sulfur + -YL]

thi·o·phene (thī′ə·fēn) *n. Chem.* A colorless liquid hydrocarbon, C_4H_4S, with an odor resembling that of benzene, found in coal tar and also made by synthesis. Also **thi′o·phen** (-fen). [<THIO- + PH(ENYL) + -ENE]

thi·o·sin·am·ine (thī′ō·sin·am′in, -sin′ə·mēn) *n. Chem.* A crystalline compound, $C_4H_8N_2S$, formed by the union of allyl mustard oil and alcohol with ammonia: used in photography. Also **thi′o·sin·am′in** (-am′in). [<THIO- + Gk. *sin(api)* mustard + AMINE]

Thi·o·spi·ril·lum (thī′ō·spī·ril′əm) *n.* A genus of motile, sulfur-containing bacteria found in fresh or salt water. [<THIO- + SPIRILLUM]

thi·o·sul·fate (thī′ō·sul′fāt) *n. Chem.* A salt of thiosulfuric acid.

thi·o·sul·fu·ric (thī′ō·sul·fyŏŏr′ik) *adj. Chem.* Designating or pertaining to an unstable acid, $H_2S_2O_3$, known chiefly by its salts, which have extensive applications in bleaching and photography.

thi·o·u·re·a (thī′ō·yŏŏ·rē′ə) *n. Chem.* A white, solid compound, NH_2CSNH_2, prepared from urea by replacement of oxygen by sulfur: used in organic synthesis, in photography, and as an insecticide: also called *thiocarbamide.* [<THIO- + UREA]

thir (thûr, thir) *pron. Scot.* These.

third (thûrd) *adj.* **1** Next in order after second: the ordinal of *three.* **2** Being one of three equal parts. —*n.* **1** One of three equal parts of anything. **2** The person or thing coming after the second, as in a series. **3** *pl. Law* The third part of a husband's personal estate, allotted to the widow in case of his dying intestate and leaving an heir; also, loosely, a dower. **4** A unit of time or of an arc, equal to one sixtieth of a second. **5** *Music* **a** The interval between any note and the next note but one above it on a diatonic scale, known as a **major third** when such interval is two whole steps or degrees of the staff, and as a **minor third** when it is a step and a half. **b** A note separated by this interval from any other, considered in relation to that other; specifically, the third above the keynote. **c** Two notes at this interval written or sounded together, or the consonance so produced. **6** In baseball, the third base. —*adv.* In the third order, rank, or place: also, in formal discourse, **third′ly.** [OE *thridda* < *thrī* three]

third base In baseball, the third base reached by the runner, at the left-hand angle of the infield. Compare illustration under BASEBALL.

third class **1** In the U. S. postal system, a classification of mail that includes all miscellaneous printed matter but not newspapers and periodicals legally entered as second class. **2** A classification of accommodations on some ships and trains, usually the cheapest and least luxurious available; formerly, on a ship, steerage; also, the passengers traveling in this classification.

third degree **1** *Colloq.* Severe or brutal examination of a prisoner by the police for the purpose of securing information or a confession; hence, any brutal treatment. **2** In Freemasonry, the degree of Master Mason.

third estate The commons or common people; the third political class of a kingdom, following the nobility and the clergy. See under ESTATE.

third eyelid The nictitating membrane.

Third Order *Eccl.* A confraternity, generally for laymen, associated with a religious order and following a modified rule. [after the *Third Order* of St. Francis, founded 1221]

third person The person or thing spoken of, or the grammatical form indicating such person or thing.

third rail An insulated rail placed as a conductor on the track of an electric railway, from which the current is taken by means of a contact device, the running rails acting as return conductors. —**third′-rail′** *adj.*

Third Reich See under REICH.

third world **1** Any or all of the underdeveloped countries in the world, especially such countries in Asia or Africa that are not aligned with either the Communist or non-Communist nations. **2** Those not resident in the countries of the third world but collectively identified with their peoples, as because of ideology, ethnic background, or disadvantaged status. Also **Third World.**

thirl (thûrl) *v.t. Scot. & Brit. Dial.* **1** To thrill. **2** To drill or bore. [OE *thyrlian* < *thӯrel* hole < *thurh* through]

thirl·age (thûr′lij) *n.* A feudal obligation upon certain tenants or the inhabitants of certain districts to bring their grain to a certain mill for grinding; also, the fee for such grinding. Also **thirl.** [Metathetic var. of obs. *thrillage* < obs. *thrill* enthrall <OE *thræl* thrall]

thirst (thûrst) *n.* **1** A distressful feeling of dryness in the throat and mouth, accompanied by an increasingly urgent desire for liquids. **2** The physiological condition which produces this feeling. **3** Any eager desire; a longing or craving: a *thirst* for glory. See synonyms under APPETITE. —*v.i.* **1** To feel thirst; be thirsty. **2** To have an eager desire or craving; long; yearn. [OE *thurst*] —**thirst′er** *n.*

thirst·y (thûrs′tē) *adj.* **thirst·i·er, thirst·i·est** **1** Affected with thirst. **2** Lacking moisture; arid; parched. **3** Eagerly desirous. **4** *Colloq.* Causing thirst, [OE *thurstig*] —**thirst′i·ly** *adv.* —**thirst′i·ness** *n.*

thir·teen (thûr′tēn′) *n.* The cardinal number preceding fourteen and following twelve, or any of the symbols (13, xiii, XIII) which represent it. —*adj.* Consisting of or being one more than twelve. [OE *thrēotēne*]

thir·teenth (thûr′tēnth′) *adj.* **1** Third in order after the tenth: the ordinal of *thirteen.* **2** Being one of thirteen equal parts. —*n.* **1** One of thirteen equal parts. **2** The next one after the twelfth.

thir·ti·eth (thûr′tē·ith) *adj.* **1** Tenth in order after the twentieth: the ordinal of *thirty.* **2** Being one of thirty equal parts. —*n.* **1** One of thirty equal parts of anything. **2** The tenth in order after the twentieth.

thir·ty (thûr′tē) *n.* The cardinal number preceding thirty-one and following twenty-nine; thrice ten; also, any of the symbols (30, xxx, XXX) used to represent it. —*adj.* Consisting of or being ten more than twenty, or thrice ten; tricennial. [OE *thrītig*]

thir·ty-sec·ond note (thûr′tē·sek′ənd) *Music* A note having one thirty-second of the time of a whole note; a demisemiquaver.

thir·ty-two·mo (thûr′tē·tōō′mō) *n. pl.* **·mos** A sheet of paper folded so as to make 32 leaves about 3 1/8 by 4 3/4 inches; hence a book or pamphlet having 32 leaves to the sheet. —*adj.* Having 32 leaves to a sheet. Commonly written *32mo.*

Thirty Years' War See table under WAR.

this (*th*is) *adj. pl.* **these** **1** That is near or present, either actually or in thought: *This* house is for sale; I shall be there *this* evening. **2** That is understood or has just been mentioned: *This* offense justified my revenge. **3** That is nearer than or contrasted with something else: opposed to *that*: *This* tree is still alive, but that one is dead; He ran *this* way and that. **4** These: used of a number or collection considered as a whole: He has been dead *this* fourteen nights. —*pron.* **1** The person or thing near or present, being understood or just mentioned: *This* is where I live; *This* is the guilty man. **2** The person or thing nearer than or contrasted with something else: opposed to *that*: *This* is a better painting than that. **3** The idea, statement, etc., about to be made clear: I will say *this*: he is a hard worker. —*adv.* To this degree; thus or so: I was not expecting you *this* soon. [OE]

This·be (thiz′bē) See PYRAMUS AND THISBE.

this·tle (this′əl) *n.* **1** One of various vigorous prickly plants (genera *Carduus, Cirsium, Cnicus,* and *Onopordum*) with cylindrical or globular heads of tubular purple flowers; especially, the **bull thistle** *(Cirsium lanceolatum)* of Scotland, and the **Canada thistle** *(Cirsium canadense).* **2** Any of several prickly plants of other genera. [OE *thistel*] —**this′·tly** *adj.*

thistle butterfly A butterfly *(Vanessa cardui)* resembling the painted beauty but having usually four eyespots on the under side of each wing: also called *painted lady.*

this·tle·down (this′əl·doun′) *n.* The pappus of a thistle; the ripe silky fibers from the dry flower of a thistle.

thith·er (thith′ər, *th*ith′-) *adv.* **1** To that place; in that direction: opposed to *hither.* **2** *Archaic* To that end, point, or result. —*adj.* Situated or being on the other side; farther; more distant: the *thither* bank of the river. [OE *thider*]

thith·er·to (thith′ər·tōō′, *th*ith′-) *adv.* Up to that time.

thith·er·ward (thith′ər·wərd, *th*ith′-) *adv.* In that direction; toward that place. Also **thith′·er·wards.**

thix·ot·ro·py (thik·sot′rə·pē) *n. Chem.* The property possessed by certain gels of liquefying under the action of vibrating forces. [<Gk. *thixis* touch + *tropē* turning] —**thix·o·trop·ic** (thik′sə·trop′ik) *adj.*

tho (*th*ō) See THOUGH.

thole[1] (thōl) *n.* A pin or pair of pins serving as a fulcrum for an oar in rowing. Also **thole pin.** [OE *thol* pin]

thole[2] (thōl) *v.t. & v.i. Archaic* To endure: suffer; tolerate. [OE *tholian* suffer]

Thom·as (tom′əs; *Dan., Du., Ger., Sw.* tō′mäs; *Fr.* tō·mä′) A masculine personal name. [< Hebrew, twin]

—**Thomas** One of the Twelve Apostles, known for his doubting disposition. *John* xx 25.

—**Thomas à Becket** See BECKET.

—**Thomas à Kempis** See KEMPIS.

—**Thomas of Er·cel·doune** (ûr′səl·dōōn), 1220?–97, Scottish seer and poet: best known as *Thomas the Rhymer.*

Tho·mas (tō·mä′), **Ambroise,** 1811–96, French composer.

Tho·mas (tom′əs), **Dylan,** 1914–53, Welsh poet and author. —**George Henry,** 1816–70, U. S. general. —**Norman,** 1884–1968, U. S. socialist leader and writer. —**Seth,** 1785–1859, U. S. clock manufacturer. —**Theodore,** 1831?–1905, U. S. orchestra conductor born in Germany.

Tho·mism (tō′miz·əm, thō′-) *n.* The doctrine of St. Thomas Aquinas, who attempted to combine Aristotelian metaphysics, ontology, logic, and method with Christian theology into one comprehensive system, including theology, natural philosophy, esthetics, ethics, psychology, and politics. He held that human reason was the faculty by which men apprehended many truths, but that the divinely revealed truths necessary for salvation could be known only through faith; that reason was distinct from faith, though not opposed to it when rightly used; and that reason served faith by preparing men's minds to receive revealed truth, by expounding and systematizing that truth, and by defending it against attack. The system of dogmatic theology constructed by St. Thomas remains the standard within the Roman Catholic Church, and has had a wide influence in many other communions. —**Tho′·mist** *adj. & n.* —**Tho·mis′·tic** or **·ti·cal** *adj.*

Thomp·son (tomp′sən), **Benjamin** See RUMFORD, COUNT. —**Francis,** 1859–1907, English poet.

Thomp·son River (tomp′sən) A river in southern British Columbia, Canada, flowing 304 miles west and south to the Fraser River.

Thompson submachine gun See under SUBMACHINE GUN.

Thom·son (tom′sən), **Sir George Paget,** 1892–1975, English physicist; son of Sir Joseph John. —**James,** 1700–48, Scottish poet. —**Sir John Arthur,** 1861–1933, Scottish biologist. —**Sir Joseph John,** 1856–1940, English physicist.

thong (thông, thong) *n.* **1** A narrow strip, properly of leather, as for tying or fastening. **2** A whiplash. [OE *thwang* thong]

Thor (thôr, tôr) In Norse mythology, the god of war, thunder, and strength, and son of Odin: he destroyed the enemies of the gods with his magic hammer.

tho·rac·ic (thô·ras′ik, thō-) *adj.* Of, relating to, or situated in or near the thorax. [<NL *thoracicus* <Gk. *thōrax* the chest]

thoracic duct *Anat.* The canal emptying into the left subclavian vein which collects the lymph from parts of the body below the diaphragm.

thoraco– *combining form Med. & Surg.* The thorax or the chest; of or related to the thorax: *thoracotomy.* Also, before vowels, **thorac–.** [<Gk. *thōrax* the chest]

tho·ra·co·plas·ty (thôr′ə·kō·plas′tē, thō′rə-) *n. Surg.* An operation for the removal and replacement of several ribs in order to provide a thoracic cavity within which the underlying lung is kept permanently collapsed: used in the treatment of tuberculosis. [<THORACO- + -PLASTY]

tho·ra·cot·o·my (thôr′ə·kot′ə·mē, thō′rə-) *n. Surg.* Incision of the wall of the chest. [< THORACO- + -TOMY]

tho·rax (thôr′aks, thō′raks) *n. pl.* **tho·rax·es** or **tho·ra·ces** (thôr′ə·sēz, thō′·rə-) **1** *Anat.* The part of the body between the neck and the abdomen, enclosed by the ribs. **2** *Entomol.* The middle region of the body of an insect, between the head and the abdomen. **3** *Zool.* The corresponding region of the body in other arthropods. [<L <Gk. *thōrax*]

THORAX
a. Manubrium.
b. Gladiolus.
c. Ensiform cartilage.
d. Clavicle.
e. Scapula.
f. Sternal ribs.
g. False ribs.
h. Floating ribs.
i. Costal arch.
j. Costal cartilage.

Tho·reau (thôr′ō, thō′rō, thə·rō′), **Henry David,** 1817–1862, U.S. author.

Tho·rez (tô·rez′), **Maurice,** born 1900–1964, French Communist.

tho·ri·a (thôr′ē·ə, thō′rē·ə) *n.* A white, very heavy oxide of thorium, ThO_2, used with zirconia and other earths in the mantle of Welsbach's incandescent lamp. [<NL <*thorium* THORIUM]

tho·ri·a·nite (thôr′ē·ə·nīt, thō′rē-) *n.* A black radioactive mineral composed chiefly of thorium, cerium, and uranium oxides.

tho·rite (thôr′īt, thō′rīt) *n.* A vitreous, yellow to black, thorium silicate, $ThSiO_4$. [<THOR(IUM) + -ITE[1]]

tho·ri·um (thôr′ē·əm, thō′rē-) *n.* A gray, radioactive, metallic element (symbol Th) of the actinide series, found only in small quantities in certain rare minerals. Its oxide, ThO_2, is used in the manufacture of gas mantles, and its isotope of mass 232 has been used in the generation of atomic energy. See ELEMENT. [after *Thor*] —**tho′ric** *adj.*

thorium series *Physics* The group of radioactive elements beginning with thorium of mass 232 and a half–life of 1.39×10^{10} years, with successive disintegrations terminating in the stable isotope of lead of mass 208.

thorn (thôrn) *n.* **1** An indurated, leafless spine or sharp–pointed process from a branch. **2** One of various other sharp processes, as the spine of a porcupine. **3** Any of various thorn–bearing shrubs or trees; especially, any of a genus *(Crataegus)* of rosaceous plants, as the hawthorn. **4** Anything or anyone that occasions discomfort, pain, or annoyance; a vexation. **5** The name of the Old English rune Þ; also, the corresponding Icelandic character: equivalent originally to *th,* both voiced and unvoiced, but finally only to the unvoiced sound, as in *thorn,* from which it derives its name. *Y* or *y* is sometimes used as a makeshift for it in early English, as in the contraction y[e]. Compare EDH. —*v.t.* To pierce or prick with a thorn. [OE] —**thorn′less** *adj.*

Thorn (tôrn) The German name for TORUN.

thorn apple 1 Jimsonweed: so called from its spiny capsule. **2** Any plant of the same genus. **3** The fruit of the hawthorn; a haw.

thorn·back (thôrn′bak′) *n.* **1** A European ray *(Raia clavata)* whose back is studded with short stout spines. **2** The common European spider crab *(Maia squinado).* **3** Any of certain American skates or sticklebacks.

thorn·bill (thôrn′bil′) *n.* Any of certain bright–colored hummingbirds of South America (genera *Rhamphomicron* and *Chalcostigma*) characterized by a long, sharp bill.

thorn broom The furze.

thorn tree 1 The hawthorn. **2** The honey locust.

thorn·y (thôr′nē) *adj.* **thorn·i·er, thorn·i·est 1** Full of thorns; spiny. **2** Sharp like a thorn, literally orfiguratively; painful; vexatious; presenting difficulties or trials. —**thorn′i·ness** *n.*

Thorn·dike (thôrn′dīk), **Ashley,** 1871–1933, U.S. educator. —**Edward Lee,** 1874–1949, U.S. psychologist; brother of the preceding. —**Lynn,** 1882–1965, U.S. historian; brother of the preceding. —**Dame Sybil,** 1882–1976, English actress.

tho·ron (thôr′on, thō′ron) *n.* A gaseous radioactive emanation produced during the atomic disintegration of thorium: it has a half–life of 54.5 seconds. [<NL <THOR(IUM) + *-on,* as in *neon*]

thor·ough (thûr′ō, thûr′ə) *adj.* **1** Carried to completion; thoroughgoing: a *thorough* search; also, carrying (a task) to completion; persevering: a very *thorough* worker. **2** Marked by careful attention throughout; not superficial; hence, complete; perfect. **3** Completely (such and such); through and through: a *thorough* nincompoop. **4** Painstakingly conforming to a standard. **5** *Obs.* Going or passing through. See synonyms under RADICAL. —*adv. & prep. Obs.* Through. Also *Obs.* **thor′o.** [Emphatic var. of THROUGH] —**thor′ough·ly** *adv.* —**thor′·ough·ness** *n.*

Thor·ough (thûr′ō) *n.* The administrative policy of Charles I's minister, the Earl of Strafford: so called by himself as being a method of carrying through his ideas in spite of all opposition.

THOROUGH–BASS
The numbers under the bass indicate the notes of the chords in the treble.

thor·ough–bass (thûr′ō·bās′) *n. Music* **1** A bass part accompanied by shorthand marks, as numerals, below the staff, to indicate the general harmony: now disused. **2** Loosely, the science of harmony or the art of harmonic composition.

thorough brace A strong leather strap extending under each side of the body of a carriage and serving as a support and a spring. —**thor′ough–braced′** *adj.*

thor·ough·bred (thûr′ō·bred′, thûr′ə-) *n.* **1** Pure stock. **2** *Colloq.* A person of culture and good breeding. —*adj.* **1** Belonging to the strain of horses known as Thoroughbred. **2** Bred from pure stock. **3** Possessing the traits of a thoroughbred.

Thor·ough·bred (thûr′ō·bred′, thûr′ə-) *n.* A horse whose ancestry is recorded in the English Stud Book, and which is therefore descended from one of three Eastern sires: the Byerly Turk, the Darley Arabian, or the Godolphin.

thor·ough·fare (thûr′ō·fâr′, thûr′ə-) *n.* **1** A frequented way or course; especially, a road or street through which the public have unobstructed passage; highway. **2** A traveling or passing through, or the right or possibility of doing so; a passage: now chiefly in the phrase *no thoroughfare.* **3** An outlet to an enclosed place, as to a court. **4** Any place through which much traffic passes, as a strait, river, or other waterway. See synonyms under ROAD, WAY. [ME *thurghfare* <OE *thurh* through + *faru* going]

thor·ough·go·ing (thûr′ō·gō′ing, thûr′ə-) *adj.* **1** Characterized by extreme thoroughness or efficiency. **2** Unmitigated: a *thoroughgoing* scoundrel.

thor·ough–paced (thûr′ō·pāst′, thûr′ə-) *adj.* **1** Perfectly trained, as a horse. **2** Hence, thoroughgoing; accomplished: a *thorough–paced* villain.

thor·ough·pin (thûr′ə·pin′) *n.* Dropsical swelling of the sheath of the tendon of a flexor muscle connected with the hock of a horse: it appears on both sides of the leg, as if the latter had been pierced by a pin. Also **thor′·ough·shot′** (-shot′).

thor·ough·wort (thûr′ō·wûrt′, thûr′ə-) *n.* **1** A stout, hairy herb, the boneset, 2 to 5 feet high, with white flowers, common in the United States and Canada. **2** Any other eupatorium.

THOROUGHWORT
(Plant to 5 feet high)

thorp (thôrp) *n.* A hamlet; small cluster of houses in the country: now chiefly in names of places. Also **thorpe.** [OE. Akin to DORP.]

Thors·havn (tôrs·houn′) Capital of the Faeroe Islands, in the central part of the group.

Thor·vald·sen (tôr′väl·sən), **Albert Bertel,** 1770–1844, Danish sculptor. Also **Thor′wald·sen.**

those (thōz) *adj. & pron.* Plural of THAT. [OE *thās*]

Thoth (thōth, tōt) In Egyptian mythology, the god of wisdom, inventor of art, science, and letters: identified with the Greek *Hermes Trismegistus*: represented with the head of an ibis or a dog.

THOTH

Thoth·mes (thōth′mēz, tōt′·mes) Any of several Egyptian kings, between 1587–1328 B.C.: also *Thuthmose.*

thou (thou) *pron.* The person spoken to, as denoted in the nominative case: archaic except in Biblical, homiletic, elevated, or poetic language, in prayers to a deity, or in certain dialects. [OE *thū*]

though (thō) *conj.* **1** Notwithstanding the fact that: introducing a clause expressing an actual fact. **2** Conceding or granting that; even if: introducing a clause assumed or admitted as supposedly true. **3** And yet; still; however: introducing a modifying clause or statement added as an afterthought: I am well, *though* I do not feel very strong. **4** Notwithstanding what has been done or said; nevertheless: But they have, *though.* As used in this sense, *though* is sometimes regarded as a conjunctive adverb. Also spelled *tho.* Compare HOWEVER. See synonyms under BUT[1]. [Prob. fusion of OE *thēah* and ON *tho*]

thought[1] (thôt) *n.* **1** The act or process of using the mind actively and deliberately; meditation; cogitation. **2** The product of thinking; an idea, concept, judgment, opinion, or the like. **3** Intellectual activity of a specific kind: Greek *thought.* **4** Consideration; attention; heed: to take *thought* on how to do something. **5** Intention or idea of doing something; plan; design: All *thought* of returning was abandoned. **6** Expectation; anticipation: He had no *thought* of finding her there. 7 A trifle; a small amount: Be a *thought* more cautious. [<THOUGHT[2]]

Synonyms: cogitation, conception, conclusion, consideration, contemplation, deliberation, fancy, idea, imagination, judgment, meditation, musing, notion, opinion, reflection, reverie, speculation, study, supposition, thinking, view. See IDEA, MIND, REFLECTION.

thought[2] (thôt) Past tense and past participle of THINK. [OE *thōht*]

thought·ful (thôt′fəl) *adj.* **1** Full of thought; meditative: a *thoughtful* face. **2** Showing, characterized by, or employed in thought; promotive of thought. **3** Attentive; careful; especially, manifesting regard for others; considerate: often with *of* or an infinitive: *thoughtful* of one's reputation; *thoughtful* to lay up a store for winter. — **thought′ful·ly** *adv.* — **thought′ful·ness** *n.*

Synonyms: attentive, careful, circumspect, considerate, heedful, mindful, provident. An *attentive* person waits upon another to supply what is needed or desired. A *thoughtful* person provides in advance for needs and wishes not yet manifested. A *considerate* person carefully spares another all that would harm, grieve, or annoy; one who is *circumspect* carefully avoids all that might compromise himself. See SEDATE. *Antonyms*: careless, gay, giddy, heedless, inadvertent, inattentive, inconsiderate, neglectful, negligent, reckless, remiss.

thought·less (thôt′lis) *adj.* **1** Manifesting lack of thought or care; heedless; also, giddy. **2** Stupid. See synonyms under IMPROVIDENT, IMPRUDENT. — **thought′less·ly** *adv.* — **thought′·less·ness** *n.*

thought-trans·fer·ence (thôt′trans·fûr′əns) *n.* Telepathy.

thou·sand (thou′zənd) *n.* The cardinal number following 999; one hundred times ten, or any of the symbols (1,000, m, M) used to represent it; also, loosely, an indefinitely large number. — *adj.* Consisting of a hundred times ten; millenary. [OE *thusend*] — **thou′sand·fold′** (-fōld′) *adj.* & *adv.*

Thousand Islands A group of 1,500 islets in an expansion of the upper St. Lawrence River, near Lake Ontario.

thou·sandth (thou′zəndth) *adj.* **1** Last in a series of a thousand: an ordinal numeral. **2** Being one of a thousand equal parts. — *n.* **1** One of a thousand equal parts. **2** The next in order after the 999th.

thowe (thō) *n. Scot.* Thaw. Also **thow.**

thow·less (thou′lis) *adj. Scot.* Inactive; lazy; without ambition or energy. See THEWLESS.

Thrace (thrās) An ancient region, later a Roman province, NE of Macedonia in the eastern part of the Balkan Peninsula: modern Thrace is divided into a Greek division (3,315 square miles); and a Turkish division corresponding to Turkey in Europe. Ancient **Thra·cia** (thrā′shə).

Thra·cian (thrā′shən) *adj.* Pertaining to Thrace or its people. — *n.* **1** One of the people of Thrace. **2** The Indo-European language of the ancient Thracians, related to Phrygian. **3** A gladiator who fought in the native dress of the Thracians. See illustration under GLADIATOR.

Thracian Chersonese An ancient name for GALLIPOLI PENINSULA.

thral·dom (thrôl′dəm) *n.* **1** The state of being a thrall. **2** Figuratively, any sort of bondage or servitude. See synonyms under BONDAGE. Also **thrall′dom.**

Thrale (thrāl), **Mrs.** See PIOZZI, HESTER LYNCH.

thrall (thrôl) *n.* **1** A person in bondage; a slave; serf; hence, figuratively, one controlled by a passion or vice. **2** The condition of bondage; thraldom. — *v.t. Archaic* To reduce to thraldom; enslave. — *adj.* Held in subjection; enslaved. [OE *thrǣl* <ON]

thrang (thrăng) *Scot. adj.* Occupied fully; busy. — *n.* A throng; crowd.

thrash (thrash) *v.t.* **1** To thresh, as grain. **2** To beat as if with a flail; flog; whip. **3** To defeat utterly. — *v.i.* **4** To move or swing about with flailing, violent motions. **5** *Naut.* To work to windward, against the tide, etc. See synonyms under BEAT. — **to thrash out** To discuss fully and to a conclusion. — *n.* **1** The act of thrashing. **2** In swimming, a kick used with the crawl and back strokes. [Dial. var. of THRESH]

thrash·er[1] (thrash′ər) *n.* **1** One who or that which thrashes. **2** *Agric.* A threshing machine. **3** The thresher shark.

thrash·er[2] (thrash′ər) *n.* Any of several long-tailed American songbirds (genus *Toxostoma*) resembling the thrushes and related to the mockingbirds, especially the common eastern **brown thrasher** (*T. rufum*), colored foxy-red with black spots. [<dial. E *thresher* <THRUSH[1]]

thrash·ing (thrash′ing) *n.* A sound beating or whipping.

thra·son·i·cal (thrā·son′i·kəl) *adj.* Characterized by boasting or ostentation; bragging; boastful. [<L *Thraso,* a braggart soldier in Terence's *Eunuch* <Gk. *Thrasōn* < *thrasus* rash] — **thra·son′i·cal·ly** *adv.*

Thras·y·bu·lus (thras′ə·byōō′ləs) Greek patriot and naval commander, died 389 B.C.

thrave (thrāv) *n. Scot. & Brit. Dial.* **1** Twenty-four sheaves of grain. **2** An indefinite number; a company; throng; also, a bundle.

thraw[1] (thrô) *Scot. n.* **1** A wrench or twist. **2** A throe. — *v.t.* **1** To twist or wrench. **2** To thwart; frustrate. — *adj.* Awry.

thraw[2] (thrô) *v. & n. Scot. & Brit. Dial.* Throw.

thrawn (thrôn) *adj. Scot.* **1** Wrenched; awry; twisted; crooked. **2** Obstinate; contrary.

thread (thred) *n.* **1** A very slender cord or line composed of two or more yarns or filaments, as of flax, cotton, silk, or other fibrous substance, twisted together. **2** A filament of any substance, as of metal, glass, or tissue; a hair. **3** A fine stream or beam: a *thread* of light. **4** A fine line of color. **5** Anything suggestive of a thread; something that runs a continuous course through a series, serving to give sequence to the whole: the *thread* of his discourse. **6** *Mining* A very thin seam or vein of ore. **7** *Mech.* The spiral ridge of a screw. **8** Thread of life. — *v.t.* **1** To pass a thread through the eye of: to *thread* a needle. **2** To arrange or string on a thread, as beads. **3** To cut a thread on or in, as a screw. **4** To make one's way through or over: to *thread* a maze. **5** To make (one's way) carefully. **6** To be present throughout; pervade. — *v.i.* **7** To make one's way carefully; step. **8** To drop from a fork or spoon in a fine thread: said of boiling sirup when it has reached a certain consistency. — *adj.* Pertaining to, resembling, or made of thread; filar. [OE *thrǣd*] — **thread′er** *n.* — **thread′like′** *adj.*

thread·bare (thred′bâr′) *adj.* **1** Worn so that the threads show, as a rug or garment. **2** Clad in worn garments. **3** Commonplace; hackneyed. See synonyms under COMMON, TRITE. — **thread′bare′ness** *n.*

thread feather *Ornithol.* An extremely slender feather, having the vane rudimentary or absent; filoplume.

thread·fin (thred′fin′) *n.* A fish of tropical seas (family *Polynemidae*), having three or more threadlike rays below the pectoral fins. Also **thread′fish′.**

thread mark A marking made in paper currency by running colored silk fibers in with the pulp, as a safeguard against counterfeiting. Compare GRANITE PAPER, SILK PAPER.

Thread·nee·dle Street (thred′nēd′l) A short street in London faced by the Bank of England. — **The Old Lady of Threadneedle Street** The Bank of England.

thread of life The course of existence, represented by the ancient Greeks and Romans as a thread being spun and cut off by the three Fates, Atropos being the one who cut it.

thread·worm (thred′wûrm′) *n.* A threadlike nematode worm; a pinworm or filaria.

thread·y (thred′ē) *adj.* **1** Resembling a thread; filamentous; tenuous. **2** Consisting of, containing, or covered with thread.

threap (thrēp) *v.t. & v.i. Scot. & Brit. Dial.* To contradict; dispute; also, to rebuke; insist. Also **threep.**

threat (thret) *n.* **1** A declaration of an intention to inflict injury or pain; a menace. **2** An announcement or omen of impending danger or evil. **3** A menace or danger of any sort. — *v.t. Archaic* To threaten. [OE *thrēat* crowd, oppression]

threat·en (thret′n) *v.t.* **1** To utter menaces or threats against. **2** To be menacing or dangerous to. **3** To be ominous or portentous of. **4** To utter threats of (injury, vengeance, etc.). — *v.i.* **5** To utter threats. **6** To have a menacing aspect; lower: The rising waters seemed to *threaten.* [OE *thrēatnian* urge, compel] — **threat′en·er** *n.* — **threat′en·ing·ly** *adv.*

Synonym: menace. *Threaten* is applied alike to vast and trivial matters; *menace* only to those of moment. Either persons or things may *threaten*; *menace* is chiefly used of persons or of things personified. One may *threaten* by word or act; *menace* is for the most part limited to actions or concrete things; one *threatens* another with death; he *menaces* him with a revolver.

three (thrē) *n.* **1** The cardinal number following two and preceding four, or any of the symbols (3, iii, III) used to represent it. **2** Any group of three persons or things; a playing card with three pips. — *adj.* Being one more than two; ternary. [OE *thrī*]

three-base hit (thrē′bās′) A fair hit in baseball that enables the batter to reach third base without the help of an error. Also **three′-bag′ger** (-bag′ər).

three-cent piece (thrē′sent′) A copper and nickel coin of the United States from 1865–1890.

three-col·or (thrē′kul′ər) *adj.* Pertaining to or denoting a process of color printing based on three primary colors, each of which is transferred to the printing surface from a separate, accurately registered plate.

three-deck·er (thrē′dek′ər) *n.* **1** A vessel having three decks or gun decks. **2** Any structure having three levels. **3** A sandwich made with three slices of bread.

three·fold (thrē′fōld′) *adj.* Made up of three; three times as many or as great; triplicate. — *adv.* Triply; in a threefold manner or degree.

three-mile limit (thrē′mīl′) See under LIMIT.

three·pence (thrip′əns, threp′-, thrup′-) *n. Brit.* **1** The sum of three pennies. **2** A small coin of Great Britain, made of alloy, formerly of silver, worth three pennies: also **threepenny bit.**

three-pen·ny (thrip′ə·ni, threp′-, thrup′-, thrē′pen′ē) *adj. Brit.* **1** Worth or costing threepence. **2** Hence, of little value.

three-phase (thrē′fāz′) *adj. Electr.* Designating a combination of alternating currents or circuits each of which differs in phase by one third of a cycle or 120 degrees.

three-piled (thrē′pīld′) *adj.* **1** Having a triple pile or nap: said of velvet; also, figuratively, costly or extravagant. **2** Clad in or wearing such velvet; hence, wealthy. **3** Piled in a set or sets of three.

three-ply (thrē′plī′) *adj.* Consisting of three thicknesses, strands, layers, etc.

three-point landing (thrē′point′) **1** *Aeron.* A perfect airplane landing, with the front wheels and tail skid or wheel touching the ground simultaneously. **2** Any successful outcome.

three-quar·ter binding (thrē′kwôr′tər) A style of bookbinding having the strip of leather over the back and corners projecting to a greater width than in half-binding.

Three Rivers The English name for TROIS RIVIÈRES, Canada.

three R's See under R.

three·score (thrē′skôr′, -skōr′) *adj. & n.* Sixty.

three·some (thrē′səm) *adj.* Performed by three; triple: a *threesome* reel. — *n.* A golf match in which one plays against two, the latter playing one ball between them alternately.

three-square (thrē′skwâr′) *adj.* Having three plane faces of equal width: said especially of certain files of triangular cross-section.

threm·ma·tol·o·gy (threm′ə·tol′ə·jē) *n.* The science of breeding animals and plants. [< Gk. *thremma, -atos* a nursling + -LOGY]

thren·o·dy (thren′ə·dē) *n. pl.* **·dies** An ode or song of lamentation; a dirge. Also **thren′ode** (-ōd). [<Gk. *thrēnōidia* < *thrēnos* lament + *ōidē* song] — **thre·no·di·al** (thri·nō′dē·əl), **thre·nod·ic** (thri·nod′ik) *adj.* — **thren′o·dist** *n.*

thre·o·nine (thrē′ə·nēn, -nin) *n. Biochem.* A crystalline amino acid, $C_4H_9NO_3$, isolated as a product of the hydrolysis of certain proteins and regarded as an essential to proper nutrition.

thresh (thresh) *v.t.* **1** To beat stalks of (ripened grain) with a flail or machine so as to separate the grain from the straw or husks. **2** To beat; flog. — *v.i.* **3** To thresh grain. **4** To move or thrash about. — **to thresh out** (or **over**) To discuss fully and to a conclusion. — *n.* The act of threshing; a threshing. [OE *therscan*] — **thresh′ing** *n.*

thresh·er (thresh′ər) *n.* **1** One who or that which threshes; specifically, a machine for threshing. **2** A large shark *(Alopias vulpes)* of warm seas, having the dorsal lobe of the tail extremely long, supposedly for splashing the water to round up its prey: also **thresher shark.**

thresh·old (thresh′ōld, -hōld) *n.* **1** The plank, timber, or stone lying under the door of a building; doorsill. **2** The entrance, entering point, or beginning of anything: the *threshold* of the 20th century. **3** *Physiol.* The point at which a stimulus, as of a nerve or muscle, just produces a response; especially, the minimum degree of stimulation necessary for conscious perception: the *threshold* of consciousness: also called *limen.* ◆ Collateral adjective: *liminal.* [OE *therscold*]

threw (thro͞o) Past tense of THROW.

thrice (thrīs) *adv.* **1** Three times. **2** In a threefold manner; hence, fully; repeatedly. [ME *thries* <OE *thriwa* thrice + -s[3]]

thrift (thrift) *n.* **1** Care and wisdom in the management of one's resources; frugality. **2** A flourishing condition; vigorous growth, as of a plant. **3** Any of a genus *(Armeria,* formerly *Statice)* of tufted herbs of the north temperate zone growing on mountains and the seashore; especially, the common thrift *(A. maritima),* having white or pink flower heads. **4** *Obs.* The state of one who thrives; prosperity. **5** *Scot.* & *Brit. Dial.* Effort; occupation; work. [<ON. Akin to THRIVE.] — **thrift′less** *adj.* — **thrift′less·ly** *adv.* — **thrift′·less·ness** *n.*

Synonyms: gain, profit, prosperity. See FRUGALITY.

thrift·y (thrif′tē) *adj.* **thrift·i·er, thrift·i·est** **1** Displaying thrift or good management; economical; frugal. **2** Prosperous; thriving. **3** Growing vigorously. See synonyms under PRUDENT. — **thrift′i·ly** *adv.* — **thrift′i·ness** *n.*

thrill[1] (thril) *v.t.* **1** To cause to feel a sudden wave of emotion; move to great or tingling excitement. **2** To cause to vibrate or tremble. — *v.i.* **3** To feel a sudden wave of emotion or excitement. **4** To vibrate or tremble; quiver. See synonyms under SHAKE. — *n.* **1** A tremor of feeling or excitement. **2** A pulsation. **3** *Med.* An abnormal vibratory or tremulous resonance perceived in auscultation; fremitus. [Metathetic var. of THIRL[1]] — **thrill′ing** *adj.* — **thrill′ing·ly** *adv.*

thrill[2] (thril) See TRILL[1].

thrill·er (thril′ər) *n.* **1** One who or that which thrills. **2** *Colloq.* An exciting book, play, or motion picture.

thrip (thrip) *n. Brit. Slang* A threepenny piece.

thrips (thrips) *n.* A small insect (order *Thysanoptera*), many species of which are injurious to grain and plants. [<L <Gk., woodworm]

thrive (thrīv) *v.i.* **throve** (thrōv) or **thrived, thrived** or **thriv·en** (thriv′ən), **thriv·ing** **1** To prosper; be successful, especially by being thrifty. **2** To grow with vigor; flourish. See synonyms under FLOURISH, SUCCEED. [<ON *thrīfast,* orig. reflexive of *thrīfa* grasp. Akin to THRIFT.] — **thriv′er** *n.* — **thriv′ing·ly** *adv.*

throat (thrōt) *n.* **1** The anterior part of the neck, extending from the back of the mouth and containing the epiglottis, larynx, trachea, and pharynx. **2** Anything resembling a throat; an entrance, inlet, or orifice: the *throat* of a bottle. **3** *Naut.* The end of a gaff nearest the mast. — *v.t.* **1** *Rare* To utter in a guttural tone. **2** To provide with a throat; channel; groove. [OE *throte*]

HUMAN THROAT
a. Soft palate.
b. Tonsils.
c. Pharynx.
d. Epiglottis.
e. Vocal cords.
f. Larynx.
g. Esophagus.

throat·latch (thrōt′lach′) *n.* A strap passing under the neck of a draft animal and aiding in holding a bridle or halter in place.

throat·y (thrō′tē) *adj.* **throat·i·er, throat·i·est** Uttered in the throat; guttural. — **throat′i·ly** *adv.* — **throat′i·ness** *n.*

throb (throb) *v.i.* **throbbed, throb·bing** **1** To beat or pulsate rhythmically, as the heart; especially, to beat rapidly or violently; palpitate. **2** To feel or show emotion. — *n.* **1** The act or state of throbbing. **2** A pulsation or beat, especially one caused by excitement or emotion. [? Imit.] — **throb′ber** *n.*

throe (thrō) *n.* **1** A violent pang or pain; agony: said especially of the pains of death and childbirth. **2** Any agonized or agonizing activity. See synonyms under AGONY, PAIN. — *v.t.* & *v.i.* **throed, throe·ing** *Rare* To put in, suffer, or undergo agony. ◆ Homophone: *throw.* [ME *throwe,* prob. fusion of OE *throwian* suffer and *thrāwan* twist, throw]

throm·bin (throm′bin) *n. Biochem.* The enzyme present in blood serum that reacts with fibrinogen to form fibrin in the process of clotting. [<THROMBUS]

throm·bo·cyte (throm′bə·sīt) *n.* A blood platelet. [<Gk. *thrombos* clot + -CYTE]

throm·bo·gen (throm′bə·jen) *n. Biochem.* Prothrombin. [<Gk. *thrombos* clot + -GEN]

throm·bo·plas·tin (throm′bō·plas′tin) *n. Biochem.* A complex substance present in the blood and other animal tissues, which reacts with calcium ions to give prothrombin. Also **throm′bo·kin′ase** (-kin′ās, -kī′nās). [<Gk. *thrombos* clot + -PLAST + -IN] — **throm′bo·plas′tic** *adj.*

throm·bo·sis (throm·bō′sis) *n. Pathol.* Local coagulation of blood in the heart, arteries, veins, or capillaries, forming by its clot an obstruction to circulation. [<NL <Gk. *thrombōsis* < *thrombos* clot] — **throm·bot′ic** (-bot′ik) *adj.*

throm·bus (throm′bəs) *n. pl.* **·bi** (-bī) *Pathol.* The blood clot formed in thrombosis. [<Gk. *thrombos* clot, lump]

throne (thrōn) *n.* **1** The royal chair occupied by a sovereign on state occasions. **2** The chair of state of a pope or of some other dignitary, as a cardinal, archbishop, or bishop. **3** Royal estate or dignity; sovereign power. **4** One invested with sovereign power; sometimes, the rank or authority of any high dignitary. **5** *pl.* The third of the nine orders of angels in the celestial hierarchy. — *v.t.* & *v.i.* **throned, thron·ing** To place or sit on a throne; enthrone; exalt. [<OF *trone* <L *thronus* <Gk. *thronos* seat]

throng (thrông, throng) *n.* **1** A multitude of people crowded closely together. **2** Any numerous collection. — *v.t.* **1** To crowd into and occupy fully; jam. **2** To press or crowd upon. — *v.i.* **3** To collect or move in a throng. See synonyms under JAM[1]. [OE *gethrang*]

Synonyms (noun): concourse, crowd, host, jam, mass, multitude, press. A *crowd* is a company of persons filling to excess the space they occupy and pressing inconveniently upon one another; the total number in a *crowd* may be great or small. *Throng* implies that the persons are numerous as well as pressed or pressing closely together; there may be a dense *crowd* in a small room, but there cannot be a *throng. Host* and *multitude* both imply vast numbers, but a *multitude* may be diffused over a great space so as to be nowhere a *crowd*; *host* is a military term, and properly denotes an assembly too orderly for crowding. *Concourse* signifies a spontaneous gathering of many persons moved by a common impulse, and suggests less massing and pressure than is indicated by the word *throng.* Compare ASSEMBLY, COMPANY.

throp·ple (throp′əl) *n. Scot.* & *Brit. Dial.* The windpipe or throttle.

thros·tle (thros′əl) *n.* **1** *Scot.* A thrush, as the song thrush. **2** A machine for twisting and winding fibers from roves. [OE. Related to THRUSH[1].]

throt·tle (throt′l) *n.* **1** The throat or windpipe. **2** *Mech.* A valve controlling the supply of steam to a steam engine, or of vaporized fuel to the cylinders of an internal-combustion engine: also **throttle valve.** **3** The lever which operates the throttle valve: also **throttle lever.** — *v.t.* **·tled, ·tling** **1** To press or constrict the windpipe or throat of; strangle; choke or suffocate. **2** To silence, stop, or suppress by or as by choking. **3** To reduce or shut off the flow of (steam, or fuel in an internal-combustion engine). **4** To reduce the speed of by means of a throttle; slow down. — *v.i.* **5** To suffocate; choke. [Dim. of ME *throte* throat] — **throt′tler** *n.*

through (thro͞o) *prep.* **1** From end to end, side to side, or limit to limit of; into at one side, end, or point, and out of at another. **2** Covering, entering, or penetrating all parts of; throughout; also, over the surface of. **3** From the first to the last of; during the time or period of. **4** In the midst of; here and there upon or in. **5** By way of: He departed *through* the door. **6** By means of; by the instrumentality or aid of. **7** Having reached the end of, especially with success: He got *through* his examinations easily. **8** On account of; because or as a result of. See synonyms under BY. — *adv.* **1** From one end, side, surface, etc., to or beyond another. **2** From beginning to end. **3** To a termination or conclusion, especially a successful one: to pull *through.* **4** Completely; entirely: He is wet *through.* — **through and through** Thoroughly; completely. — *adj.* **1** Going from beginning to end without stops or with very few stops, and without reshipment or change: a *through* train; also, pertaining to or serving an entire distance or route: a *through* ticket. **2** Extending from one side or surface to another. **3** Unobstructed; open; clear: a *through* road. **4** Arrived at an end; finished: Are you *through* with my pen? **5** At the end of all relations or dealings: He is *through* with his old friends. Also spelled *thru.* [OE *thurh*]

through·ith·er (thro͞o′ith′ər) *Scot. adj.* Disorderly; harum-scarum. — *adv.* Pell-mell. Also **through′-oth′er** (-uth′ər), **throu·ther** (thro͞o′thər).

through·ly (thro͞o′lē) *adv. Archaic* Thoroughly.

through·out (thro͞o·out′) *adv.* Through or in every part: The house was searched *throughout.* — *prep.* All through; everywhere in: *throughout* the nation.

through·put (thro͞o′po͝ot′) *n.* The quantity of raw materials which may be processed for intended final use in a given time, as in an oil refinery or a chemical plant.

throve (thrōv) Past tense of THRIVE.

throw (thrō) *v.* **threw** (thro͞o), **thrown, throw·ing** *v.t.* **1** To propel through the air by means of a sudden straightening or whirling of the arm. **2** To propel or hurl: The mortar *threw* shells into the town. **3** To put hastily or carelessly: He *threw* a coat over his shoulders. **4** To direct or project (light, shadow, a glance, etc.). **5** To bring to a specified condition or state by or as by throwing: to *throw* the enemy into a panic. **6** To cause to fall; overthrow: The horse *threw* its rider. **7** In wrestling, to force the shoulders of (an opponent) to the ground. **8** To cast (dice). **9** To make (a specified cast) with dice. **10** To cast off or shed; lose: The horse *threw* a shoe. **11** *Colloq.* To lose purposely, as a race. **12** To give birth to (young): said of domestic animals. **13** To move, as a lever or switch, in connecting or disconnecting a circuit, mechanism, etc.; also, to connect or disconnect in this manner. **14** *Slang* To give (a party, etc.). **15** In card games, to play or discard. **16** In ceramics, to shape on a potter's wheel. **17** To spin (filaments, as of silk) into thread. — *v.i.* **18** To cast or fling something. — **to throw away** **1** To cast off; discard. **2** To waste; squander. — **to throw back** To revert to ancestral characteristics. — **to throw cold water on** To discourage. — **to throw in** **1** To cause (gears or a clutch) to mesh or engage. **2** To contribute; add. **3** To join with others. — **to throw off** **1** To cast aside; reject; spurn. **2** To rid oneself of. **3** To do or utter in an offhand manner. **4** To disconnect, as a machine; release. — **to throw oneself at** To strive to gain the affections or love of. — **to throw oneself into** To engage or take part in vigorously. — **to throw oneself on** (or **upon**) To entrust oneself to; rely on. — **to throw open** **1** To open suddenly or completely, as a door. **2** To free from restrictions or obstacles. **— to throw out** 1 To put forth; emit. 2 To cast out or aside; discard; reject. 3 To utter as if accidentally: to *throw out* hints. 4 In baseball, to retire (a runner) by throwing the ball to the base toward which he is advancing. **— to throw over** 1 To overturn. 2 To discard. **— to throw together** To put together hastily or roughly. **— to throw up** 1 To erect hastily. 2 To give up; relinquish. 3 To vomit. 4 *Colloq.* To mention or repeat, as a fault or taunt. — *n.* 1 An act of throwing or hurling; a cast; fling. 2 The distance over which a missile may be thrown: a stone's *throw.* 3 A cast of dice, or the resulting number; hence, a hazard; venture. 4 *Mech.* **a** The radius of the circle described by a crank, cam, or the like. **b** The travel or extent of reciprocating motion obtainable, as from a crank, piston, slide valve, etc. 5 A scarf used for draping an easel or picture frame; also, a woman's scarf or boa. 6 *Geol.* **a** A faulting, or dislocation of rock strata. **b** The amount of vertical displacement produced by dislocation of strata. 7 The sudden fluctuation of a magnetic needle when the force is suddenly changed. 8 The distance from a motion-picture projector to the screen. 9 In wrestling, a flooring of one's opponent so that both his shoulders touch the mat simultaneously for ten seconds. ◆ Homophone: *throe.* [OE *thrāwan* turn, twist, curl] **— throw′er** *n.*

throw·back (thrō′bak′) *n.* 1 *Biol.* **a** Reversion to an earlier ancestral or primitive type, phase, or condition of physical being or development. **b** An example of such reversion. 2 Anything returned for revision, correction, redirection, etc.

throw·ster (thrō′stər) *n.* 1 A thrower of dice; gamester. 2 One who throws silk.

thru (thro͞o) See THROUGH.

thrum[1] (thrum) *v.* **thrummed, thrum·ming** *v.t.* 1 To play on or finger (a stringed instrument) idly and without expression. 2 To drum or tap monotonously or listlessly. 3 To recite or repeat in a droning, monotonous way. — *v.i.* 4 To thrum a stringed instrument. 5 To sound when played thus, as a guitar. 6 *Scot.* To purr. — *n.* Any monotonous drumming. [Prob. imit.]

thrum[2] (thrum) *n.* 1 The fringe of warp threads remaining on a loom beam after the web has been cut off; also, one of such threads. 2 Any loose thread or fringe, or a tuft of filaments or fibers; a tassel. 3 *pl.* Coarse or waste yarn. 4 *pl. Naut.* Bits of rope yarn for sewing on canvas to make chafing gear or collision mats. 5 *Bot.* A threadlike organ or part of a flower; stamen. 6 *Scot.* A bit; particle: I don't care a *thrum.* 7 *Scot.* A tangle. — *v.t.* **thrummed, thrum·ming** 1 To cover or trim with thrums or similar appendages. 2 *Naut.* To insert bits of rope yarn in (canvas) to produce a rough surface or mat to be used to prevent chafing. [OE *-thrum* ligament, as in *tungethrum* the ligament of the tongue]

thrum·my (thrum′ē) *adj.* **·mi·er, ·mi·est** Made of or with thrums or resembling a thrum; shaggy; rough.

thrush[1] (thrush) *n.* Any one of many migratory, passerine birds of the family *Turdidae,* having typically a long and slightly graduated tail, long wings, and spotted under parts. The robin, **hermit thrush** *(Hylocichla guttata),* **wood thrush** *(H. mustelina),* and the European **song thrush** *(Turdus philomelus)* are examples. ◆ Collateral adjective: *turdine.* [OE *thrysce*]

WOOD THRUSH
(To 8 1/2 inches in length)

thrush[2] (thrush) *n.* 1 *Pathol.* A vesicular disease of the mouth, lips, and throat caused by a fungus *(Monilia albicans)*: generally confined to infants. 2 A disease of a horse's foot characterized by suppuration. Also called *sprue.* [Cf. Dan. *tröske,* Sw. *trosk* a mouth disease]

thrust (thrust) *v.* **thrust, thrust·ing** *v.t.* 1 To push or shove with force or sudden impulse. 2 To pierce with a sudden forward motion; stab, as with a sword or dagger. 3 To interpose; put in. — *v.i.* 4 To make a sudden push or thrust. 5 To force oneself on or ahead; push one's way; crowd: with *through, into, on,* etc. See synonyms under DRIVE, PUSH. — *n.* 1 A sudden and forcible push, especially with a long, pointed weapon: distinguished from *cut.* 2 A vigorous attack; sharp onset. 3 *Engin.* A stress or strain tending to push a member of a structure outward or sidewise: the *thrust* of an arch. 4 The driving force exerted by certain propulsive devices, as a jet or rocket engine, an airplane's or ship's propellor, etc. 5 Salient force or meaning: the *thrust* of his remarks. 6 *Geol.* A rock fault due to horizontal compression; also, the plane of such a fault. [<ON *thrȳsta*] **— thrust′er** *n.*

thrust fault *Geol.* A fault resulting from horizontal compression in which the hanging wall appears to have moved upward, with a corresponding shortening of the entire rock mass: opposed to *gravity fault.* Also called *reverse fault.*

thru·way (thro͞o′wā′) *n.* A long-distance express highway.

Thu·cyd·i·des (tho͞o·sid′ə·dēz, thyo͞o-), 471?–399? B.C., Athenian statesman and historian. **— Thu·cyd′i·de′an** (-dē′ən) *adj.*

thud (thud) *n.* A dull, heavy sound, as of a hard body striking upon a comparatively soft one; also, the blow causing such a sound; a thump. — *v.i.* **thud·ded, thud·ding** To make a thud. [OE *thyddan* strike, thrust, press]

thug (thug) *n.* 1 Formerly, one of an organization of religious, professional assassins in northern India. 2 Any cutthroat or ruffian. [<Hind. *thag* <Skt. *sthaga* swindler] **— thug′ger·y** *n.* **— thug′gish** *adj.*

thug·gee (thug′ē) *n.* The system of secret assassination formerly practiced by thugs in India. [<Hind. *thagī*]

thu·ja (tho͞o′jə) *n.* Any of a genus *(Thuja)* of evergreen trees and shrubs of the pine family, including the arborvitae, source of the medicinal **oil of thuja.** Also spelled *thuya.* [<NL <Gk. *thyia,* an African tree]

Thu·le (tho͞o′lē, to͞o′-) 1 In ancient geography, the northernmost limit of the habitable world: identified with Iceland or Mainland in the Shetland Islands. See ULTIMA THULE. 2 A settlement in NW Greenland; site of a major United States military installation.

thu·li·a (tho͞o′lē·ə) *n. Chem.* Oxide of thulium, Tm_2O_3, found in samarskite. [<THULIUM]

thu·li·um (tho͞o′lē·əm) *n.* A metallic element (symbol Tm) of the erbium family in the lanthanide series. See ELEMENT. [from THULE]

thumb (thum) *n.* 1 The inner digit of a limb when set apart from and apposable to the other fingers; especially, the short, thick digit on the radial side of the human hand; the pollex. 2 *Ornithol.* The first radial digit of the wing of certain birds. 3 The division in a glove or mitten that covers the thumb. 4 *Archit.* An ovolo. **— all thumbs** *Colloq.* Clumsy with the hands; not deft. **— thumbs down** A sign of negation or disapproval. **— under one's thumb** Under one's influence or power. — *v.t.* 1 To press, rub, soil, or wear with the thumb in handling, as the pages of a book. 2 To perform with or as with the thumbs; hence, to do or handle clumsily. 3 To run through the pages of (a book, manuscript, etc.,) rapidly and perfunctorily. 4 To solicit or obtain (a ride) in an automobile by standing by the road and indicating with the thumb the direction one wishes to go; also, to make (one's way) thus: He *thumbed* his way from Boston to New York. [OE *thūma*]

thumb-in·dex (thum′in′deks) *v.t.* To provide with a thumb index.

thumb index A series of scalloped indentations cut along the right-hand edge of a book and labeled to indicate its various sections.

thumb·kin (thum′kin) *n.* A thumbscrew or pair of thumbscrews.

thumb·ling (thum′ling) *n.* A diminutive being; dwarf. Compare FINGERLING.

thumb·nail (thum′nāl′) *n.* 1 The nail of the thumb. 2 Anything as small and essentially complete as a thumbnail. — *adj.* Small and essentially complete: a *thumbnail* sketch.

thumb·nut (thum′nut′) *n.* A threaded nut having one or more wings or projections for screwing by the thumb and fingers; wing-nut. See illustration under NUT.

thumb·print (thum′print′) *n.* An impression or print made by the thumb.

thumb·screw (thum′skro͞o′) *n.* 1 A screw to be turned by thumb and fingers. See illustration under SCREW. 2 An instrument of torture for compressing the thumb or thumbs.

thumb·stall (thum′stôl′) *n.* A covering or sheath, as of leather, for the thumb.

thumb·tack (thum′tak′) *n.* A broad-headed tack that may be pushed in with the thumb.

Thum·mim (thum′im) See under URIM.

thump (thump) *n.* A blow with a blunt or heavy object; also, the sound made by such a blow; a dull thud. See synonyms under BLOW. — *v.t.* 1 To beat or strike so as to make a heavy thud or thuds. 2 *Colloq.* To beat or defeat severely. — *v.i.* 3 To strike with a thump. 4 To make a thump or thumps; pound or throb. [Imit.] **— thump′er** *n.*

thump·ing (thum′ping) *adj.* 1 That thumps. 2 *Colloq.* Huge; whopping.

thumps (thumps) *n. pl.* 1 Hiccups in a horse. 2 A lung disease in swine, caused by infestation with the larvae of a roundworm (genus *Ascaris*). [<THUMP; from the sound of the contractions of the diaphragm]

Thun (to͞on) A town on the Aar river in central Switzerland. *French* **Thoune** (to͞on).

Thun (to͞on), **Lake of** An expansion of the Aar river in central Switzerland; 10 miles long; 18 square miles. *German* **Thu·ner·see** (to͞o′nər·zā).

thun·der (thun′dər) *n.* 1 The sound that accompanies lightning, caused by the sudden heating and expansion of the air along the path of the lightning flash. 2 Any loud, rumbling or booming noise, suggestive of thunder. 3 An awful denunciation or threat; a vehement or powerful utterance, oratorical or other. 4 *Rare* A lightning stroke; thunderbolt. **— to steal one's thunder** To take for one's own use anything especially popular or effective originated by another: said especially of an argument. — *v.i.* 1 To give forth a peal or peals of thunder: used impersonally: It *thunders.* 2 To make a noise like thunder. 3 To utter vehement denunciations or threats. — *v.t.* 4 To utter or express with a noise like or suggestive of thunder: The cannon *thundered* defiance. [OE *thunor*] **— thun′der·er** *n.*

thun·der·a·tion (thun′də·rā′shən) *interj.* & *n. Slang* Damnation: a euphemism. [<THUNDER + (DAMN)ATION]

thun·der·bird (thun′dər·bûrd′) *n.* An enormous bird believed to produce thunder by flapping its wings, lightning by opening and closing its eyes, and rain by allowing a huge lake to run off its back: common to the folklore of the North American Indians of the Plains and the Canadian forests.

thun·der·bolt (thun′dər·bōlt′) *n.* 1 One electric discharge accompanied by a clap of thunder: formerly conceived of as a molten ball or bolt hurled by the lightning flash. 2 Any person or thing acting with or as with the force and speed or destructiveness of lightning.

thun·der·clap (thun′dər·klap′) *n.* 1 A sharp, violent detonation of thunder. 2 Anything having the violence or suddenness of a clap of thunder.

thun·der·cloud (thun′dər·kloud′) *n.* A dark, heavy mass of cloud highly charged with electricity.

thun·der·head (thun′dər·hed′) *n.* A rounded mass of cumulus cloud, either silvery-white or dark with silvery edges, often developing into a thundercloud.

thun·der·ing (thun′dər·ing) *adj.* 1 Giving forth, or accompanied by, thunder. 2 Unusually great or extreme; superlative.

thun·der·ous (thun′dər·əs) *adj.* Producing or emitting thunder or a sound like thunder. Also **thun′drous** (-drəs). **— thun′der·ous·ly** *adv.*

thun·der·peal (thun′dər·pēl′) *n.* A clap of thunder.

thun·der·show·er (thun′dər·shou′ər) *n.* A shower of rain with thunder and lightning.

thunder snake The house snake: so called because forced out of its hole by heavy rain.

thun·der·squall (thun′dər·skwôl′) *n.* A squall accompanied by thunder.

thun·der·stone (thun′dər·stōn′) *n.* 1 *Archaic* A thunderbolt. 2 A stone or rock supposed to have accompanied a thunderbolt. 3 A belemnite.

thun·der·storm (thun′dər·stôrm′) *n.* A local storm accompanied by lightning and thunder.

thun·der·stroke (thun′dər·strōk′) *n.* A stroke of lightning.

thun·der·struck (thun′dər·struk′) *adj.* 1 Struck by lightning. 2 Amazed, astonished, or confounded, as with fear, surprise, or the like. Also **thun′der·strick′en** (-strik′ən).

thun·der·y (thun′dər·ē) *adj. Colloq.* Thunderous; indicative of, or accompanied by thunder.

Thur·ber (thûr′bər), **James Grover,** 1894–1961, U. S. humorous artist and writer.

thu·ri·ble (thŏŏr′ə·bəl) *n.* A censer. [<L *thuribulum* < *thus, thuris* frankincense]

thu·ri·fer (thŏŏr′ə·fər) *n.* A censer-bearer; an acolyte or altar boy who carries a thurible. [<L < *thus, thuris* frankincense + *ferre* bear, carry]

thu·rif·er·ous (thŏŏ·rif′ər·əs) *adj.* Yielding or bearing incense.

Thu·rin·gi·a (thŏŏ·rin′jē·ə, -jə) A former state of central Germany in southwestern East Germany; 6,022 square miles; capital, Weimar; formerly a region of central Germany including several duchies and principalities. *German* **Thü·ring·en** (tü′ring·ən).

Thu·rin·gi·an (thŏŏ·rin′jē·ən) *adj.* 1 Of or relating to Thuringia or its inhabitants. 2 *Geol.* Denoting the upper division of the Permian in Europe. — *n.* 1 One of an ancient Teutonic tribe which occupied a kingdom in central Germany until the sixth century, when they were conquered by the Franks. 2 A citizen or inhabitant of modern Thuringia.

Thuringian Forest A wooded mountain range of central Germany; highest point, 3,222 feet. *German* **Thü·ring·er Wald** (tü′ring·ər vält).

Thurs·day (thûrz′dē, -dā) *n.* The fifth day of the week. [Fusion of OE *Thunres dæg* day of Thunor and ON *Thōrsdagr* day of Thor; trans. of LL *dies Jovis* day of Jove]

Thursday Island An island of NE Australia in Torres Strait, comprising a municipality of Queensland; 1 1/2 miles long, 1 mile wide.

thus (thus) *adv.* 1 In this or that or the following way or manner. 2 To such degree or extent; so: *thus* far. 3 In these circumstances or conditions; in this case; therefore. [OE]

thu·ya (thŏŏ′yə) See THUJA.

thwack (thwak) *v.t.* To strike with something flat; whack. — *n.* A blow with some flat or blunt instrument. [Prob. OE *thaccian* smack; infl. in form by *whack*] — **thwack′er** *n.*

thwart (thwôrt) *v.t.* 1 To prevent the accomplishment of, as by interposing an obstacle; also, to prevent (one) from accomplishing something; foil; frustrate; balk. 2 *Obs.* To move or place over or across. See synonyms under BAFFLE, HINDER[1]. — *n.* An oarsman's seat extending athwart a boat. — *adj.* 1 Lying, moving, or extending across something; transverse. 2 *Obs.* Perverse or cross-grained; ill-natured. — *adv.* & *prep.* Athwart. [<ON *thvert*, neut. of *thverr* transverse] — **thwart′er** *n.*

Thwing (twing), **Charles Franklin,** 1853–1937, U. S. educator.

thy (thī) *pronominal adj.* The possessive case of the pronoun *thou* used attributively; belonging or pertaining to thee: *Thy* kingdom come. [Apocopated var. of THINE]

Thy·es·te·an banquet (thī·es′tē·ən) A cannibal feast: so called from the feast at which Thyestes was served his own sons. See ATREUS.

Thy·es·tes (thī·es′tēz) In Greek legend, a son of Pelops and brother of Atreus. — **Thy·es′·te·an, Thy·es′ti·an** *adj.*

thy·la·cine (thī′lə·sīn, -sin) *n.* A nearly extinct, carnivorous, doglike marsupial (*Thylacinus cynocephalus*) of Tasmania, grayish-brown with dark transverse bands on the hinder part of the back: also called *Tasmanian wolf, Zebra wolf.* [<NL <Gk. *thylax, thylakos* pouch]

THYLACINE
(About 18 inches high at the shoulder)

thyme (tīm) *n.* Any of a genus (*Thymus*) of small shrubby plants of the mint family, having aromatic leaves and cultivated for seasoning in cookery; especially, the **wild thyme** (*T. serpyllum*). [<F *thym* <L *thymum* <Gk. *thymon*] — **thym′y** *adj.*

thym·e·lae·a·ceous (thim′ə·lē·ā′shəs) *adj. Bot.* Designating a family (*Thymelaeaceae*) of apetalous trees or shrubs having very tough bark; the mezereon family. [<NL, family name <L *thymelaea* <Gk. *thymelaia* < *thymon* thyme + *elaia* olive tree]

thym·ic[1] (tī′mik) *adj.* Pertaining to or derived from thyme.

thy·mic[2] (thī′mik) *adj.* Of, pertaining to, or derived from the thymus.

thy·mol (tī′mōl, -mol, thī′-) *n. Chem.* A crystalline compound, $C_{10}H_{13}OH$, contained in certain volatile oils, as those of thyme and horsemint, and also made synthetically: used as an antiseptic. [<THYME + -OL[2]]

thymol iodide *Chem.* A reddish-brown mixture of iodine derivatives and thymol, used as a deodorant and antiseptic.

thy·mus (thī′məs) *n. Anat.* A lymphoid organ of glandular character and unknown function, developed in the region of the neck in many vertebrates. In man and other mammals it lies at the root of the neck, just above the heart, and is most prominent in the young. It is the neck sweetbread of calves and lambs. [<NL <Gk. *thymos*]

thy·re·oid (thī′rē·oid) *adj.* Thyroid.

thyro– *combining form Med. & Surg.* The thyroid; of or related to the thyroid: *thyrotropin.* Also, before vowels, **thyr–.** Also **thyreo–.** [<Gk. *thyreoeidēs* thyroid]

thy·ro·hy·oid (thī′rō·hī′oid) *adj. Anat.* Having a relationship to the thyroid gland and the hyoid bone: the *thyrohyoid* ligament. See illustration under LARYNX. [<THYRO- + HYOID]

thy·roid (thī′roid) *adj.* 1 Relating or pertaining to the thyroid cartilage or the thyroid gland. 2 Shaped like a shield; also, having a shield-shaped marking. — *n.* 1 The thyroid cartilage or gland. 2 The dried and powdered thyroid gland of certain domesticated food animals, used in the treatment of myxedema, goiter, obesity, and other disorders. [<Gk. *thyreoeidēs* shield-shaped < *thyreos* large shield + *eidos* form]

thyroid cartilage *Anat.* The largest cartilage of the larynx, composed of two blades whose juncture in front forms the Adam's apple.

thy·roid·ec·to·my (thī′roid·ek′tə·mē) *n. Surg.* Excision of the thyroid gland. [<THYROID + -ECTOMY]

thyroid gland *Anat.* A bilobate endocrine gland situated in front of and on each side of the trachea, close to the larynx. It secretes thyroxin, vitally important in growth and in the prevention of such disorders as goiter, cretinism, etc.

thy·roid·i·tis (thī′roid·ī′tis) *n. Pathol.* Inflammation of the thyroid gland.

thy·ro·tox·i·co·sis (thī′rō·tok′sə·kō′sis) *n. Pathol.* A morbid or diseased condition resulting from excessive activity of the thyroid gland, as in exophthalmic goiter. [<THYRO- + TOXICOSIS] — **thy′ro·tox′ic** (-tok′sik) *adj.*

thy·rot·ro·pin (thī·rot′rə·pin) *n. Biochem.* A hormone from the anterior lobe of the pituitary gland, regarded as having an affinity for the thyroid gland. [<THYRO- + -TROP(E) + -IN]

thy·rox·in (thī·rok′sin) *n. Biochem.* A white, odorless, crystalline compound, $C_{15}H_{11}O_4NI_4$, obtained as the hormone of the thyroid gland and also made synthetically: used in the treatment of thyroid disorders. Also **thy·rox′ine** (-sēn, -sin). [<THYR(O)- + OXY- + -IN] — **thy·rox·in·ic** (thī′rok·sin′ik) *adj.*

thyrse (thûrs) *n.* A thyrsus.

thyr·soid (thûr′soid) *adj. Bot.* Resembling or shaped like a thyrsus. Also **thyr·soi·dal** (thûr·soid′l).

thyr·sus (thûr′səs) *n. pl.* **·si** (-sī) 1 A staff wreathed in ivy and crowned with a pine cone or a bunch of ivy leaves with grapes or berries: an attribute of Dionysus and the satyrs. 2 *Bot.* A branched panicle in which the middle branches are longer than those above or below them, as in the lilac and grape. [<L <Gk. *thyrsos*]

thy·sa·nu·ran (thī′sə·nŏŏr′ən, -nyŏŏr′-, this′ə-) *adj.* Designating or belonging to an order (*Thysanura*) of primitive wingless insects, including the silverfish and the firebrat. — *n.* One of the *Thysanura.* [<NL, name of the order <Gk. *thysanos* fringe + *oura* tail] — **thy′sa·nu′rous** *adj.*

thy·self (thī·self′) *pron.* Emphatic or reflexive form of the second person singular pronouns *thee* and *thou*: I love thee for *thyself.*

Thys·sen (tis′ən), **Fritz,** 1873–1951, German industrialist.

ti[1] (tē) *n. Music* In solmization, a syllable representing the seventh note of the diatonic scale: formerly called *si.* [See GAMUT]

ti[2] (tē) *n.* One of several Asian trees (genus *Cordyline*) of the lily family, especially the **ti palm** (*C. terminalis*) of eastern Asia, having many foliage forms. [<Polynesian]

Ti·a Jua·na (tē′ə wä′nə) See TIJUANA.

ti·ar·a (tī·âr′ə, tē·är′ə, -ar′ə) *n.* 1 The pope's triple crown, emblematic of his claim to spiritual and temporal authority; hence, the papal dignity. Compare MITER. 2 The upright headdress worn by the ancient Persian kings. 3 A coronet or form of headdress denoting princely rank; also, anything in imitation of it worn for personal adornment. 4 A Phrygian cap for men and women, long, conical, and falling over the brow: found in Greco-Roman art as the attribute of Paris, Mithras, and others. [<L <Gk. *tiara* Persian headdress]

PAPAL TIARA

Tib·bett (tib′it), **Lawrence,** 1896–1960, U. S. baritone.

Ti·ber (tī′bər) A river of central Italy, flowing 251 miles south from the Apennines through Rome to the Tyrrhenian Sea, SE of Rome: Italian *Tevere.*

Ti·be·ri·as (tī·bir′ē·əs), **Lake** See GALILEE, SEA OF.

Ti·be·ri·us (tī·bir′ē·əs), 42 B.C.–A.D. 37, second emperor of Rome, A.D. 14–37: full name Tiberius Claudius Nero Caesar.

Ti·bes·ti Massif (ti·bes′tē) The highest mountain group of the Sahara and of western equatorial Africa, lying mostly in NW Chad, partly in Libya and in Niger; highest point, 11,204 feet.

Ti·bet (ti·bet′) A former independent theocracy of central Asia, south of the Sinkiang-Uigur Autonomous Region, China, and north of India, Nepal, Sikkim, and Bhutan; incorporated, 1950–57, in China, as the **Tibetan Autonomous Region;** about 470,000 square miles; capital, Lhasa: Chinese *Sitsang*: also *Thibet. Tibetan* **Pö** (pœ).

Ti·bet·an (ti·bet′n) *adj.* Of or pertaining to Tibet, the Tibetans, or to their language, religion, or customs. — *n.* 1 One of the native Mongoloid people of Tibet, now intermixed with Chinese and various peoples of India. 2 The Sino-Tibetan language of Tibet. Also spelled *Thibetan.*

Tibetan lion dog The Lhasa apso.

tib·i·a (tib′ē·ə) *n. pl.* **tib·i·ae** (tib′i·ē) or **tib·i·as** 1 *Anat.* The inner and larger of the two bones of the leg below the knee; the shin bone. See illustration under FOOT. 2 *Entomol.* The fourth or penultimate joint of the leg of an insect, between the femur and the tarsus. 3 An ancient flute or pipe provided with holes for the fingers, originally made of an animal's leg bone. [<L] **— tib′i·al** *adj.*

Ti·bul·lus (ti·bul′əs), **Albius,** 54?–18 B.C., Roman elegiac poet.

Ti·bur (tī′bər) Ancient name of TIVOLI.

tic (tik) *n.* **1** An involuntary spasm or twitching of muscles, usually of the face and sometimes of neurotic origin. **2** Tic douloureux. [<F]

ti·cal (ti·käl′, -kôl′, tē′kəl) *n.* **1** The former name for the baht, a Thai unit of currency. **2** A Thai unit of weight, equivalent to about half an ounce: also called *baht.* [<Malay *tikal*]

tic dou·lou·reux (tik do͞o′lo͞o·ro͞o′, *Fr.* tēk′ do͞o·lo͞o·rœ′) *Pathol.* An acutely painful neuralgia of the face with paroxysmal muscular twitchings. [<F, painful tic]

Ti·ci·no (tē·chē′nō) A river of Switzerland and Italy, flowing 150 miles south through Lake Maggiore to the Po below Pavia. Ancient **Ti·ci·nus** (ti·sī′nəs).

tick[1] (tik) *n.* **1** A light recurring sound made by a watch, clock, or similar mechanism. **2** *Brit. Colloq.* The length of time occupied by one tick of a watch or clock: I'll be through in five *ticks.* **3** A mark, as a dot or dash, used in checking off something. **—** *v.i.* To make or sound a tick or ticks; make a recurrent clicking sound, as a running watch or clock. **—** *v.t. Brit.* To mark or check with ticks. **— to tick off** *Brit. Colloq.* To tell off. [Prob. imit.]

tick[2] (tik) *n.* **1** One of numerous flat, leathery, bloodsucking arachnids (order *Acarida*) that attack the skin of man and other animals; especially, the **cattle tick** (*Margaropus annulatus*), causative agent of Texas fever. **2** Any of certain two-winged or wingless parasitic insects (family *Hippoboscidae*), as the **sheep ticks** and **bat ticks.** [Cf. LG *tieke,* G *zecke* a tick]

tick[3] (tik) *n.* **1** The stout outer covering of a mattress; also, the material for such covering. **2** *Colloq.* Ticking. [Earlier *teke, tyke,* ult. <L *teca, theca* <Gk. *thēke* a case]

tick[4] (tik) *n. Brit. Colloq.* Credit; trust: to buy something on *tick.* [Short for TICKET]

tick·er (tik′ər) *n.* **1** One who or that which ticks. **2** A telegraphic receiving instrument which records stock quotations on a paper ribbon (**ticker tape**). **3** *Slang* A watch. **4** *Slang* The heart.

tick·et (tik′it) *n.* **1** A note or notice; a memorandum; also, a slip of paper containing a notice or memorandum. **2** A card with words or characters on it showing that the holder is entitled to something, as transportation in a public vehicle, admission to a theater, or the like. **3** A certificate or license, as of an airplane pilot or the captain of a ship. **4** A label or tag for attachment or identification. **5 a** A list of candidates of a single party on a ballot: the Democratic *ticket.* **b** The group of candidates running for the offices of a party. **—** *v.t.* **1** To fix a ticket to; label. **2** To present or furnish with a ticket or tickets. [<MF *etiquet* a little note <OF *estiquette* < *estiquer* stick, fix <OLG *stekan.* Doublet of ETIQUETTE.]

ticket agent **1** One who sells tickets, especially railroad or theater tickets. **2** An agency, or one who runs an agency, for the sale of railroad or theater tickets.

ticket of leave Formerly, in Great Britain and Australia, a written permit granted to a penal convict to be at large before the expiration of his sentence on certain specified conditions.

tick fever Any of several fevers caused by ticks, especially the Texas fever of cattle, and Rocky Mountain spotted fever, transmitted to man by the bite of a wood tick.

tick·ing (tik′ing) *n.* A strong, closely woven cotton or linen fabric: used for mattress covering, awnings, etc. [<TICK[3] + -ING[1]]

tick·le (tik′əl) *v.* **·led, ·ling** *v.t.* **1** To excite the nerves of by touching or scratching on some sensitive spot, producing a thrilling sensation resulting in spasmodic laughter or twitching; titillate. **2** To arouse or excite agreeably; please: Compliments *tickle* our vanity. **3** To amuse or entertain; delight. **4** To move, stir, or get by or as by tickling. **—** *v.i.* **5** To have or experience a thrilling or tingling sensation: My foot *tickles.* **—** *n.* The sensation produced by tickling; titillation; also, the touch or action producing such sensation. [ME *tikelen,* ? metathetic var. of ON *kitla* tickle]

tick·le-grass (tik′əl·gras′, -gräs′) *n.* Rough bent grass (*Agrostis hiemalis*).

tick·ler (tik′lər) *n.* **1** One who or that which tickles. **2** A memorandum book or file, as of bills receivable, notes due, etc.

tickler coil In radio, a coil of the regenerative type coupled in series with the plate circuit and employed to intensify sound on a receiving circuit by means of a feedback action.

tick·lish (tik′lish) *adj.* **1** Sensitive to tickling. **2** Liable to be upset; unstable; also, easily offended; sensitive. **3** Attended with risk; difficult; delicate. **— tick′lish·ly** *adv.* **— tick′·lish·ness** *n.*

Tick·nor (tik′nər), **George,** 1791–1871, U.S. historian and educator.

tick·seed (tik′sēd′) *n.* **1** The coreopsis. **2** The tick trefoil. [<TICK[2] + SEED]

tickseed sunflower A square-stemmed species of bur marigold (genus *Bidens*), with a panicle of large-rayed yellow flowers.

tick-tack (tik′tak′) *n.* **1** A recurrent sound like that of the ticking of a clock. **2** Anything that makes a tapping or rattling noise; specifically, a device for making a rattling noise against a window or door, worked from a distance: used in playing pranks. [Imit. reduplication of TICK[1]]

tick-tack-toe (tik′tak·tō′) *n.* A game for two players, who alternately put circles or crosses in the spaces of a figure formed by two sets of parallel lines crossing at right angles. Each player tries to get a row of three circles or crosses before his opponent does.

tick-tock (tik′tok′) *n.* The oscillating sound of a clock. **—** *v.i.* To make this sound. [Imit.]

tick trefoil Any of several leguminous plants (genus *Desmodium*) whose leaves and pods cling to the coats of animals and to clothing. [<TICK[2] + TREFOIL]

tick·y tack·y (tik′ē tak′ē) *Slang* **1** Shoddy, inferior materials: rows of little houses built of *ticky tacky.* **2** Dull, tedious uniformity. **— tick′y-tack′y** *adj.*

Ti·con·der·o·ga (tī′kon·də·rō′gə) A town on Lake George in New York; site of **Fort Ticonderoga,** captured from the French in 1759 and from the British by the American revolutionists in 1775.

tid·al (tīd′l) *adj.* **1** Of, pertaining to, or influenced by the tides; periodically flowing and ebbing: a *tidal* river. **2** Dependent on the rise of the tide as to time of starting or leaving: a *tidal* steamship.

tidal wave **1** Any great incoming rise of waters along a shore, caused by windstorms at sea or by excessively high tides. **2** A tsunami. **3** A great movement in popular feeling or in the affairs of men.

tid·bit (tid′bit′) *n.* A choice bit, as of food. Also, *Brit.,* *titbit.* [< dial. E *tid* a small object + BIT[1]]

tid·dle·dy·winks (tid′l·dē·wingks′) *n.* A game in which the players attempt to snap little disks of bone, ivory, or the like, from a plane surface into a cup. Also **tid′dly·winks′** (tid′·lē-). [Prob. < *tiddly,* a child's word for *little*]

tide[1] (tīd) *n.* **1** The periodic rise and fall of the surface of the ocean, and of the waters connected with the ocean, caused by the attraction of moon and sun. In each lunar day of 24 hours and 51 minutes there are two high tides and two low tides, alternating at equal intervals of flood and ebb. **Spring tides** are high tides above the average, occurring when the moon is new or full; **neap tides** are high tides below the average, occurring when the moon is in the first or third quarter. See FLOOD, EBB. **2** Anything that comes like the tide at flood; the time at which something is most flourishing. **3** The natural drift or tendency of events; also, a current; stream. **4** Season; time; especially, a season of the ecclesiastical year: used chiefly in composition and in the phrase *time and tide*: *Christmastide.* **5** *Archaic* A suitable or favorable occasion; opportunity. See synonyms under STREAM. **—** *v.* **tid·ed, tid·ing** *v.i.* **1** To ebb and flow like the tide. **2** To float with the tide. **—** *v.t.* **3** To carry or help like a boat buoyed up by the tide: Charity *tided* us over the depression. **4** To surmount; survive; endure, as a difficulty: with *over*: to *tide* over hard times. [OE *tīd* a period, season] **— tide′less** *adj.*

tide[2] (tīd) *v.i. Archaic* To betide; happen. [OE *tīdan*]

tide·land (tīd′land′) *n.* Land alternately covered and uncovered by the tide.

tide·rip (tīd′rip′) *n.* Riptide. [<TIDE[1] + RIP[2]]

tide·waiter (tīd′wā′tər) *n.* A customs officer who boards vessels entering port, to enforce customs regulations.

tide·wa·ter (tīd′wô′tər, -wot′ər) *n.* Water which inundates land at high tide; also, water affected by the tide on the seacoast or in a river; hence, loosely, the seacoast. **—** *adj.* Pertaining to the tidewater; also, situated on the seacoast: the *tidewater* country.

tide·way (tīd′wā′) *n.* A channel where the tide runs.

ti·dings (tī′dingz) *n. pl.* (*sometimes construed as singular*) A report or information; news. [OE *tīdung*; infl. in meaning by ON *tithindi* news, a message]

Synonyms: advice, information, intelligence, news. *News* is the most general of these words, signifying something that has either just happened or just become known. *Advices* are communications of fact by a trusted informant with the design of guiding or influencing the action of the recipient; the word signifies *news* with a practical purpose and value. *Intelligence* is *news* or *information,* often secret *information,* specifically communicated, usually in certain form. See NEWS.

ti·dy (tī′dē) *adj.* **·di·er, ·di·est** **1** Marked by neatness and order; trim. **2** Of an orderly disposition. **3** *Colloq.* Moderately large; considerable: a *tidy* sum. **4** *Colloq.* Tolerable; fairly good. See synonyms under NEAT[1]. **—** *v.t.* & *v.i.* **ti·died, ti·dy·ing** To make (things) tidy; put (things) in order. **—** *n. pl.* **·dies** A light, detachable covering, to protect the back or arms of a chair or sofa. [ME *tidi* <OE *tīd* time] **— ti′di·ly** *adv.* **— ti′di·ness** *n.*

ti·dy·tips (tī′dē·tips′) *n. pl* **·tips** Any of a genus (*Layia*) of ornamental annual plants of California, having yellow flower heads tipped with white; especially, *L. elegans.*

tie (tī) *v.* **tied, ty·ing** *v.t.* **1** To fasten with cord, rope, etc., the ends of which are then drawn into a knot. **2** To draw the parts of together or into place by a cord or band fastened with a knot: to *tie* one's shoes. **3** To form (a knot). **4** To form a knot in, as string. **5** To fasten, attach, or join in any way. **6** To restrain or confine; restrict; bind. **7 a** To equal (a competitor) in score or achievement. **b** To equal (a competitor's score). **8** *Colloq.* To unite in marriage. **9** *Music* To unite by a tie. **—** *v.i.* **10** To make a tie or connection. **11** To make the same score; be equal. See synonyms under BIND. **— to tie down** To hinder; restrict. **— to tie up** **1** To fasten with rope, string, etc. **2** To wrap, as with paper, and then fasten with string, cord, etc. **3** To moor (a vessel). **4** To block; hinder. **5** To have or be already committed, in use, etc., so as to be unavailable. **—** *n.* **1** A flexible bond or fastening secured by drawing the ends into a knot or loop. **2** Any bond or obligation, mental, moral, or legal: *ties* of affection. **3** An exact equality in number, as of a score, votes, etc.; hence, a contest which neither side wins; a draw. **4** Something that is tied or intended for tying, as a shoelace, necktie, or the like. **5** *Engin.* A structural member fastening parts together and receiving tensile stress: distinguished from a *strut.* **6** *Music* A curved line placed over or under two musical notes of the same pitch on the staff to make them represent one tone length. **7** *pl.* Low shoes fastened with lacings: Oxford *ties.* **8** One of a set of timbers laid crosswise on the ground as supports for railroad tracks. [OE *tīgan* bind < *tēah, tēag* a rope]

tie beam A timber that serves as a tie in a roof, etc.

Tie·bout (tē′bout) Dutch form of THEOBALD.

tie-dye (tī′dī′) *v.t.* **-dyed, -dye·ing** To create designs on fabric by tying parts of it in clumps that will not absorb the dye. **—** *n.* **1** The process of decorating fabrics by tie-dying. **2** Fabric so decorated; also, a design so made.

tie-in (tī′in′) *n.* Connection; association.

tie-in sale A sale in which the buyer, in order to get the article he wants, is required to buy a second article.

tie·man·nite (tē′mə·nīt) *n.* A metallic, steel-to lead-gray, opaque mercuric selenide, HgSe.

[<G *tiemannit,* after W. *Tiemann,* 19th c. German mineralogist, its discoverer]

Tien Shan (tyen′ shän′) A mountain chain of central Asia, chiefly in the Tadzhik S.S.R., Kirghiz S.S.R., and Sinkiang-Uigur Autonomous Region, China; highest point, 24,406 feet.

Tien·tsin (tin′tsin′, *Chinese* tyen′jin′) A port near the Gulf of Chihli, NE China; formerly included in Hopeh Province; since 1935, an independent municipality under direct control of the central government; the leading transportation and industrial center of northern China.

Tie·po·lo (tye′pō·lō), **Giovanni Battista,** 1696?–1770?, Venetian painter.

tier[1] (tir) *n.* A rank or row in a series of things placed one above another. —*v.t.* & *v.i.* To place or rise in tiers. ◆ Homophone: *tear.* [Earlier *tire* <OF, a sequence < *tirer* draw, elongate]

ti·er[2] (tī′ər) *n.* **1** One who or that which ties; also, that used for or in tying. **2** A child's apron.

tierce (tirs) *n.* **1** A former liquid measure equivalent in the United States to 42 wine gallons; a third of a pipe or butt. **2** A cask holding this amount, intermediate between a hogshead and a barrel. **3** In card games, a sequence of three cards of the same suit. **4** In fencing, the third standard position from which a guard, parry, or thrust can be made. **5** *Eccl.* The third canonical hour, nine a.m., or the office or service of that hour: often called *undernsong.* **6** *Music* An interval of a third. **7** A set of three. [<OF *tierce, terce* a third <L *tertia,* fem. of *tertius*]

Tier·ra del Fue·go (tyer′ä del fwā′gō) **1** An archipelago at the southern tip of South America, belonging to Chile and to Argentina; separated from the mainland by the Strait of Magellan; total, 27,476 square miles: 7,996 square miles in Argentina, the rest in Chile. **2** The largest island of the group; 18,000 square miles: 7,750 square miles in Argentina, the rest in Chile.

tiers é·tat (tyâr zā·tȧ′) *French* The third estate, especially in prerevolutionary France.

tie-up (tī′up′) *n.* **1** A situation, resulting from a strike, the breakdown of machinery, etc., in which further progress or operation is impossible: a *tie-up* in traffic. **2** *Dial.* The part of a barn where cows and oxen are kept.

tiff[1] (tif) *n.* **1** A peevish display of irritation; a pet; huff. **2** A light quarrel; a spat. —*v.i.* To be in or have a tiff. [Prob. imit.]

tiff[2] (tif) *Obs. n.* A small draft of liquor; a sip; drink. —*v.t.* To sip; taste. [Cf. ON *thefr* a smell, taste]

tiff[3] (tif) *v.i. Anglo-Indian* To take tiffin or lunch. [Back formation < *tiffing* TIFFIN]

tif·fa·ny (tif′ə·nē) *n. pl.* **·nies** **1** A very thin transparent cotton gauze. **2** Formerly, a very thin silk. [<OF *tifinie, tiphanie* Epiphany <LL *theophania* THEOPHANY; ? so called because its transparency manifests the wearer]

Tif·fa·ny (tif′ə·nē), **Charles Lewis,** 1812–1902, U. S. jeweler.

tif·fin (tif′ən) *Anglo-Indian n.* Midday luncheon. —*v.i.* To lunch; tiff. [Appar. < *tiffing,* ppr. of TIFF[2]]

Tif·lis (tif′lis, *Russian* tif·lēs′) The capital of Georgian S.S.R., on the Kura River: Georgian *Tbilisi.*

ti·ger (tī′gər) *n.* **1** A large carnivorous feline mammal (*Felis tigris*) of Asia, with vertical black wavy stripes on a tawny body and black bars or rings on the limbs and tail. **2** One of several other large ferocious animals, as the South American jaguar or the African leopard; also, the thylacine of Tasmania. **3** A fierce, cruel person. **4** *U.S.* An additional cheer or yell (often the word "tiger") given at the conclusion of a round of cheering. [<OF *tigre* <L *tigris* <Gk., ?< Avestan *tīghri* an arrow, a dart]

BENGAL TIGER
(About 6 1/2 feet long; tail, 3 feet)

tiger beetle Any of certain very active, predacious beetles (genus *Cicindela*) having spotted or striped wings, which dart upon their prey from a concealment. For illustration see INSECTS (beneficial).

tiger cat **1** A wildcat, resembling, but smaller than, the tiger, as the Asian **marbled tiger cat** (*Felis marmorata*), the African serval, the American ocelot, and the margay. **2** A domestic cat having striped markings.

ti·ger-eye (tī′gər·ī′) *n.* **1** A gemstone, usually the mineral crocidolite altered by oxidation, showing a beautiful chatoyant luster. One variety is called *hawk's-eye.* Also **ti′ger's-eye′.** **2** A tiger cat.

ti·ger·ish (tī′gər·ish) *adj.* Of, pertaining to, or resembling the tiger or its habits; predacious; bloodthirsty: also spelled *tigrish.*

tiger lily **1** A tall cultivated lily (*Lilium tigrinum*) from China, with nodding orange flowers spotted with black. **2** Any of various lilies with similar flowers, especially the leopard lily (*L. pardalinum*).

tiger moth A stout-bodied moth (family *Arctiidae*) with striped or spotted wings.

tight (tīt) *adj.* **1** So closely held together or constructed as to be impervious to fluids; not leaky: a *tight* roof; a *tight* vessel. **2** Firmly fixed or fastened in place; secure. **3** Fully stretched, so as not be slack; taut; tense: *tight* as a drum. **4** Strict; stringent: a *tight* schedule. **5** Fitting closely; especially, fitting too closely: said of a garment, shoe, cork, etc. **6** *Colloq.* Difficult to cope with; troublesome: a *tight* spot; a *tight* squeeze. **7** *Colloq.* Parsimonious; tight-fisted; close. **8** Characterized by a feeling of constriction: a *tight* cough. **9** *Slang* Drunk; intoxicated. **10** Evenly matched: said of a race or contest. **11** Difficult to obtain because of scarcity or financial restrictions: said of money or of commodities. **12** Straitened from lack of money or commodities: a *tight* market. **13** Yielding very little or no profit: said of a bargain. —*adv.* **1** Firmly; securely: Hold me *tight.* **2** Closely; with much constriction: The dress fits too *tight.* —**to sit tight** To remain firm in one's position; refrain from budging. [ME *thight,* appar. <Scand. Cf. ON *thēttr* dense.] —**tight′·ly** *adv.* —**tight′ness** *n.*

-tight *combining form* Impervious to: *watertight.*

tight·en (tīt′n) *v.t.* & *v.i.* To make or become tight or tighter. —**tight′en·er** *n.*

tight-fist·ed (tīt′fis′tid) *adj.* Stingy; parsimonious.

tight-lipped (tīt′lipt′) *adj.* Having the lips held tightly together; hence, unwilling to talk; reticent or secretive.

tight·rope (tīt′rōp′) *n.* A tightly stretched rope on which acrobats perform. —*adj.* Pertaining to or performing on a tightrope: a *tightrope* walker.

tights (tīts) *n. pl.* Skin-fitting garments, commonly for the legs and lower torso.

tight·wad (tīt′wod′) *n. U. S. Slang* A skinflint; miser. [<TIGHT + WAD[1]]

Tig·lath-pi·le·ser (tig′lath·pi·lē′zər, -pī-) Any of several Assyrian kings and conquerors; especially, Tiglath-pileser III, reigned 745–727 B.C.

tig·lic (tig′lik) *adj. Chem.* **1** Derived from croton oil. **2** Designating a white, crystalline, poisonous acid, $C_5H_8O_2$, contained as an ester in croton oil. Also **tig·lin·ic** (tig·lin′·ik). [<NL (*Croton*) *tiglium* the croton oil plant, prob. ult. <Gk. *tilos* thin feces; so called because of its purgative properties]

Ti·gré (tē·grā′) *n.* A modern Semitic language of Ethiopia, descended from the ancient Ethiopian.

Ti·gré (tē·grā′) A province of northern Ethiopia, bordering on Eritrea; formerly an independent kingdom; about 26,000 square miles; capital, Makale. Also **Ti·gre** (tēg′r′).

ti·gress (tī′gris) *n.* A female tiger.

Ti·gri·ña (tē·grē′nyä) *n.* A Southwest Semitic language spoken in Ethiopia.

Ti·gris (tī′gris) A river of SW Asia, flowing about 1,150 miles SE from east central Turkey in Asia through Iraq to the Euphrates NW of Basra.

ti·grish (tī′grish) See TIGERISH.

Ti·hwa (dē′hwä′) See URUMCHI.

Ti·jua·na (tē·hwä′nä) A border town in NW Lower California, Mexico: also *Tia Juana.*

tike (tīk) *n.* **1** A low-bred dog; a cur. **2** *Scot.* An uncouth fellow; a boor. **3** *Colloq.* A small child. Also spelled *tyke.* [<ON *tīk* a bitch]

Ti·ki (tē′kē) In Maori mythology, the creator of the first man.

til (til, tēl) *n.* Sesame. [<Hind. <Skt. *tilá*]

Til·burg (til′bûrg, *Du.* til′bûrkh) A city in North Brabant province, south Netherlands.

til·bur·y (til′ber·ē) *n. pl.* **·bur·ies** A form of gig seating two persons. [after *Tilbury,* an early 19th c. London coachmaker who invented it]

Til·da (til′də) Diminutive of MATILDA.

til·de (til′də, -dē) *n.* **1** A sign (~) used in Spanish over *n* to indicate nasal palatalization or the sound of *ny,* as in *cañon,* canyon. **2** The same sign (usually called **til**) used in Portuguese over a vowel or the first vowel of a dipthong to indicate nasalization, as in *lã, Camões.* [<Sp. <L *titulus* superscription, title]

Til·den (til′dən), **Samuel Jones,** 1814–86, U. S. statesman.

Til·dy (til′dē), **Zoltán,** 1889–1961, Hungarian politician; president of Hungary 1946–48.

tile (tīl) *n.* **1** A thin piece or plate of baked clay, sometimes decorated, used for covering roofs, floors, etc., and as an ornament. **2** A short earthenware pipe, used in forming sewers. **3** Tiles collectively; tiling. **4** *Colloq.* A high silk hat. —*v.t.* **tiled, til·ing** **1** To cover with tiles. **2** To secure against intrusion; specifically, in Freemasonry, to place the doorkeeper or tiler at the door of (a lodge) to keep out unauthorized persons. [OE *tigule, tigele,* ult. <L *tegula* < *tegere* cover]

tile·fish (tīl′fish′) *n. pl.* **·fish** or **·fishes** A large marine fish (*Lopholatilus chamaeleonticeps*) of the western Atlantic, marked with large yellow spots, and esteemed as food. [<NL (*Lophola*)*til*(*us*), genus name; infl. by *tile,* because its markings resemble ornamental tiles]

til·er (tī′lər) *n.* **1** A maker or layer of tiles. **2** The doorkeeper of a Masonic lodge.

til·i·a·ceous (til′ē·ā′shəs) *adj. Bot.* Designating or belonging to a widely distributed family (*Tiliaceae*) of trees, shrubs, and herbs, the linden family, having clusters of often fragrant flowers. [<NL <L *tiliaceus* <*tilia* the linden tree]

til·ing (tī′ling) *n.* **1** The act, operation, or system of using tiles for roofing or drainage. **2** Tiles collectively. **3** Something made of or faced with tiles.

till[1] (til) *v.t.* & *v.i.* To put and keep (soil) in order for the production of crops, as by plowing, harrowing, hoeing, sowing, etc.; cultivate. [OE *tilian* strive, acquire] —**till′a·ble** *adj.*

till[2] (til) *prep.* **1** To the time of; up to; until: He slept *till* noon. **2** Before: with the negative: He couldn't leave *till* today. **3** *Scot.* & *Brit. Dial.* To; unto; as far as. —*conj.* **1** Up to such time as; until: *till* death do us part. **2** Before: with the negative: They couldn't go *till* the carriage came for them. [OE *til* <ON, to]

till[3] (til) *n.* A drawer, compartment, or tray; a money drawer. [Earlier *tille,* prob. <ME *tillen, tyllen* draw]

till[4] (til) *n. Geol.* An unassorted, commingled, and chiefly unstratified mass of clay, sand, pebbles, and boulders, deposited by masses of ice. [Var. of ME *thill,* ? <OE *thille* a board, flooring]

till·age (til′ij) *n.* The cultivation of land. See synonyms under AGRICULTURE. [<TILL[1] + -AGE]

til·land·si·a (ti·land′zē·ə) *n.* Any of a genus (*Tillandsia*) of mainly epiphytic bromeliaceous plants of tropical America and the southern United States, having narrow, entire, often scurfy leaves, and flowers in a terminal spike. [<NL, after Elias *Tillands,* 18th c. Swedish botanist]

till·er[1] (til′ər) *n.* One who or that which tills; a plowman; a farmer. [<TILL[1]]

till·er[2] (til′ər) *n.* **1** A lever to turn a rudder. **2** A means of guidance. [<OF *telier* stock

of a crossbow <Med. L *telarium* a weaver's beam <L *tela* a web; prob infl. in meaning by ME *tillen* draw]

till·er[3] (til'ər) *n.* **1** A shoot from the base of a stem; sucker. **2** A sapling. —*v.i.* To put forth stems from the root; send forth new shoots. [Prob. OE *telgor* a twig <*telga* a branch]

til·lot (til'ət) *n. Brit.* A type of cloth used for wrapping fabric. Also **til'let.** [Earlier *tillet,* appar. <OF *tellette,* var. of *teilete, toilete* a wrapper of cloth. See TOILET.]

Til·lot·son (til'ət·sən), **John,** 1630–94, English theologian.

Til·ly (til'ē), **Count von,** 1559–1632, Johann Tserklaes, Flemish general of the imperial league in the Thirty Years' War.

til·ly-val·ly (til'ē·val'ē) *interj. Brit.* Nonsense; bosh. Also **til'ly-fal'ly** (-fal'ē). [Origin unknown]

Til·sit (til'zit) A former name for SOVETSK.

tilt[1] (tilt) *v.t.* **1** To cause to rise at one end or side; incline at an angle; slant; lean; tip. **2** To aim or thrust, as a lance. **3** To charge or overthrow in a tilt or joust. **4** To hammer or forge with a tilt hammer. —*v.i.* **5** To incline at an angle; lean. **6** To contend with the lance; engage in a joust. See synonyms under TIP[1]. —*n.* **1** An inclination from the vertical or horizontal position; slant; slope; also, the act of inclining, or the state of being inclined. **2** A medieval sport in which mounted knights, charging with lances, endeavored to unseat each other. **3** Any encounter resembling or suggestive of that between two tilting knights; hence, a quarrel; dispute; altercation; also, a thrust or blow, as with a lance. **4** A tilt hammer. **5** A seesaw. **6** The American black-necked stilt. —**at full tilt** At full speed; at full charge. [ME *tylten* be overthrown, totter <OE *tealt* unsteady] —**tilt'er** *n.*

tilt[2] (tilt) *n.* A canvas canopy or awning on a boat, wagon, booth, or the like. —*v.t.* To furnish or cover with an awning or tilt. [Var. of ME *tild, teld,* OE *teld* a tent]

tilth (tilth) *n.* **1** The act of tilling; cultivation of soil; tillage. **2** That part of the surface soil affected by tillage; cultivated land. [OE < *tilian* till]

tilt hammer A trip hammer.

tilt roof A round-topped roof: so called from its resemblance to the canopy or tilt of a covered wagon.

tilt-up (tilt'up') *n.* The spotted sandpiper: so called from its teetering habits.

tilt·yard (tilt'yärd') *n.* A courtyard or other place for tilting.

Tim (tim) Diminutive of TIMOTHY.

Ti·ma·ga·mi (ti·mä'gə·mē), **Lake** A lake in east central Ontario, Canada; 90 square miles.

ti·ma·rau (tē'mə·rou') See TAMARAU.

Tim·a·ru (tim'ə·rōō) A port on eastern South Island, New Zealand.

tim·bal (tim'bəl) *n.* **1** A kettledrum. **2** *Entomol.* The drumlike, sound-producing, folding membrane of the shrilling organ of a male cicada or harvest fly. Also spelled *tymbal.* [<F• *timbale,* appar. alter. of *attabale* <Sp. *atabal* ATABAL]

tim·bale (tim'bəl, *Fr.* taṅ·bȧl') *n.* **1** A dish made of chicken, fish, cheese, or vegetables, pounded fine and mixed with the white of eggs, sweet cream, etc., cooked in a drum-shaped mold, then turned out and served with sauce. **2** A small cup made of fried pastry, in which food may be served. [<F. See TIMBAL.]

tim·ber (tim'bər) *n.* **1** Wood suitable for building purposes, prepared for use. **2** Growing or standing trees; also, woodland. **3** A single piece of squared wood prepared for use or already in use. **4** Any principal beam in a vessel's framing. **5** The wooden part or handle of any implement. **6** Loosely, the materials for any structure; hence, also, human material: That boy has good *timber* in him. See synonyms under STICK. —*v.t.* To provide or shore with timber. [OE] —**tim'ber·er** *n.*

tim·bered (tim'bərd) *adj.* **1** Covered with growing trees; wooded. **2** Constructed of timber.

tim·ber·head (tim'bər·hed') *n. Naut.* **1** An end of a timber projecting above the deck, and used for attaching lines, etc. **2** An upright post fastened to the deck at the point where a timber's end would come.

timber hitch *Naut.* A knot by which a rope is fastened around a spar.

tim·ber·ing (tim'bər·ing) *n.* **1** Timberwork; timbers collectively. **2** The act or process of furnishing with timber.

tim·ber·land (tim'bər·land') *n.* Land covered with forests.

timber line **1** The upper limit of tree growth on mountains and in arctic regions; the line above which no trees grow. **2** The boundary line of a tract of timber. —**tim'ber-line'** (-līn') *adj.*

timber wolf The large gray or brindled wolf (*Canis occidentalis*) of the forests of the northern United States and Canada: distinguished from the *coyote* or *prairie wolf.*

TIMBER WOLF
(About 4 feet long; 26 inches high)

tim·ber·work (tim'·bər·wûrk') *n.* Work constructed of wood, especially the framing of a structure.

tim·bre (tim'bər, tam'-; *Fr.* taṅ'br') *n.* **1** The inherent quality of tone which serves to distinguish one musical instrument or voice from another and renders it unique: sometimes called *tone color.* **2** In acoustics, the character or quality of a sound that is produced by the relative number and strength of its harmonics: distinguished from *intensity* (amplitude of vibrations) and *pitch* (frequency of vibrations). **3** *Phonet.* The degree of resonance of a voiced sound, especially a vowel. [<F <OF, a small bell, sound of a bell, orig. a timbrel <L *tympanum* a kettledrum <Gk. *tympanon*]

tim·brel (tim'brəl) *n.* An ancient Hebrew instrument resembling a tambourine. [Dim. of earlier *timbre* a timbrel <OF. See TIMBRE.]

tim·breled (tim'brəld) *adj.* Chanted to the accompaniment of a timbrel. Also **tim'brelled.**

Tim·buk·tu (tim·buk'tōō, tim'buk·tōō') A town of central French Sudan, French West Africa, near the Niger; formerly a major center of the slave trade: French *Tombouctou.*

time (tīm) *n.* **1** The general idea, relation, or fact of continuous or successive existence; infinite duration or its measure. **2** A definite portion of duration; a moment; period; season. **3** A considerable period marked off by some special characteristics; era. **4** The portion of duration allotted to some specific purpose, as that allotted to human life or to any particular life, military service, a prison sentence, etc. **5** The length of an apprenticeship. **6** Period of gestation. **7** A portion of duration available or sufficient for, or allotted to, some special purpose or event; also, leisure: I have no *time* to read. **8** Indefinite duration viewed in the concrete as measurable and terminable, but not precisely limited: You build for *time,* we for eternity. **9** A general term indicating a subdivision of one of the grander divisions of geological history. **10** A point in duration; date; occasion; especially, the hour of death or of travail: Your *time* has come! **11** A portion of duration considered as having some quality or experience of its own, personal or general: in the latter sense usually in the plural: *Times* are hard. **12** A system of reckoning or measuring duration, especially with reference to the rotation and revolution of the earth, or to the movements of the celestial bodies. See also DAYLIGHT-SAVING TIME, STANDARD TIME, and lists given below. **13** A case of recurrence or repetition: many a *time,* three *times* a day. **14** The temporal relation of a verb. **15** *Music* **a** The characteristic tempo suited to a particular style of composition. **b** The division of musical composition into measures of equal length; rhythm: common *time,* triple *time.* Rhythms which are divisible by two are called **duple** or **common time,** as 2/2, 2/4, 2/8, 4/2, 4/4, 4/8, etc. Rhythms which are divisible by three are called **triple time,** as 3/2, 3/4, 3/8. **Compound triple times** are 9/4, 9/8, 9/16, 5/4, and 5/8. **16** A measured interval in verse; a unit of duration in rhythmical utterance; a mora. **17** One of the Aristotelian unities of the drama. See under UNITY. **18** Period during which work has been, or remains to be done; also, the amount of pay due one, especially on an hourly rate: *time* and a half for overtime. **19** Rate of movement, as in dancing, marching, etc.; tempo. **20** *pl.* In arithmetic, the fact or process of being multiplied or added to or by: Five *times* four is twenty; also, the multiplication sign ×. **21** Fit or proper occasion: This is no *time* to quibble. —**at the same time** **1** At the same moment. **2** Despite that; however; nevertheless. —**at times** Now and then. —**to bring to time** To call to account; discipline; force to conform. —**to have a time** To experience unusual pleasure, difficulty, etc. —**high time** The expiration of, or a time past the expiration of, a period of which something should have been accomplished. —**in time** **1** While time permits or lasts; before it is too late. **2** In the progress of time; ultimately. —**to keep time** **1** To indicate time correctly, as a clock; run in time, as a train. **2** To make regular or rhythmic movements in unison with another or others. **3** To render a musical composition in proper time or rhythm. **4** To make a record of the number of hours worked by an employee or employees. —**to make a time** To make a fuss or to-do. —**to make time** **1** To gain time; especially, to make up for lost time by extra speed, as a train. **2** To perform, achieve, or arrive in a certain time: to *make* good *time.* **3** *Slang* To impress or influence favorably: with *with.* —**on time** **1** Promptly; according to schedule: The train left *on time.* **2** Paid for, or to be paid for, later or in instalments. —*adj.* **1** Of or pertaining to time. **2** Devised so as to operate, explode, etc., at a specified time: a *time* bomb, *time* lock. **3** Payable at, or to be paid for at, a future date. —*v.t.* **timed, tim·ing** **1** To regulate as to time. **2** To cause to correspond in time: They *timed* their steps to the music. **3** To choose or arrange the time or occasion for: He *timed* his arrival for five o'clock. **4** To mark the rhythm or measure of. **5** To assign metrical or rhythmic qualities to (a syllable or note). **6** To ascertain or record the speed or duration of: to *time* a horse or a race. [OE *tīma*]

—**astronomical time** Prior to Jan. 1, 1925, the 24-hour period reckoned from noon to noon: since that date reckoned from midnight to midnight in order to bring civil and navigational practice into conformity with each other.

—**civil time** (or **civil day**) The 24-hour period extending from midnight to midnight: generally divided into two sections of 12 hours each, but in navigation, aeronautics, and other technical uses reckoned from 0 (midnight) to 24 hours. The same reckoning now applies to *astronomical time.*

—**Greenwich mean time** See CIVIL TIME.

—**Greenwich time** Time as reckoned from the zero meridian of Greenwich, England. To each hour in advance of, or behind, Greenwich time there corresponds a difference of 15 degrees longitude east or west of the Greenwich meridian.

—**local time** Time, whether sidereal or solar, as reckoned from a local meridian other than the standard meridian.

—**mean time** Time reckoned from the hour angle of the mean sun; the *mean solar day* is the 24-hour interval between two successive lower transits of the mean sun across the meridian of a place and corresponds exactly with civil time.

—**sidereal time** Time computed from the hour angle of a fixed point on the celestial sphere known as the first point in Aries, coincident with the vernal equinox; the *sidereal day* is the interval between two successive upper transits of the vernal equinox across the meridian.

—**solar time** Time reckoned from the hour angle of the central point of the sun's disk; the *apparent solar day* is the slightly variable interval between two successive lower transits of the sun across the meridian of a place, noon being the moment of upper transit or the hour angle plus 12 hours.

—**zone time** Time corresponding to that within a zone of 7 1/2 degrees on either side of a meridian; used in the determination of a ship's longitude.

Synonyms (noun): age, date, duration, epoch, era, period, season, sequence, succession. *Sequence* and *succession* apply to events viewed as following one another; *time* and *duration* denote something conceived of as enduring while events take place and acts are done. According to the necessary conditions of human thought, events are contained in *time* as objects are in space, *time* existing before the event, measuring it as it passes, and still existing when the event is past. *Duration* and *succession* are more general words than *time*; we can speak of infinite or eternal *duration* or *succession*, but *time* is commonly contrasted with eternity. *Time* is measured or measurable *duration*.

time and again Frequently. Also **time after time.**

time belt A time zone.

time·card (tīm′kärd′) *n.* A card for recording the time of arrival and departure of an employee.

time clock A clock equipped for automatically recording times of arrival and departure, or for actuating release mechanisms, as on vault doors, etc.

time exposure *Phot.* A film exposure made at spaced intervals by two separate manual operations of the shutter instead of automatically.

time-hon·ored (tīm′on′ərd) *adj.* Observed or honored from former times; claiming veneration as of long existence. See synonyms under ANCIENT[1]. Also *Brit.* **time′-hon′oured.**

time immemorial A considerable and indefinite length of time; specifically, in law, time beyond legal memory, now reckoned at twenty years: the period of the statute of limitations relating to realty; formerly, "a time whereof the memory of man runneth not to the contrary," fixed, in England, as the commencement of the reign of Richard I.

time·keep·er (tīm′kē′pər) *n.* **1** One who or that which keeps time. **2** One who declares the time in a race, game, athletic match, etc., or records the hours worked by employees. **3** A railroad train starter. **4** A timepiece.

time·less (tīm′lis) *adj.* **1** Independent of, or unaffected by, time; unending. **2** *Archaic* Untimely. **3** Not assigned or limited to any special time, era, or epoch; without a date. See synonyms under ETERNAL. **—time′less·ly** *adv.* **—time′less·ness** *n.*

time lock A lock, having a clock mechanism attached, so devised as to prevent its being unlocked before a specified time.

time·ly (tīm′lē) *adj.* **·li·er, ·li·est** **1** Being or occurring in good or proper time; opportune; seasonable; also, well-timed. **2** *Archaic* Early. **—*adv.*** Opportunely; seasonably; early. **—time′li·ness** *n.*

ti·me·ma (ti·mē′mə) *n.* A stick insect. [<NL]

tim·e·o Dan·a·os et do·na fe·ren·tes (tim′ē·ō dan′ā·ōs et dō′nə fə·ren′tēz) *Latin* I fear the Greeks, even when they bring gifts; hence, the motives of a foe offering a gift are suspect.

time·ous (tī′məs) *adj. Scot.* Seasonable; timely.

time-out (tīm′out′) *n.* **1** A short recess requested by a team during play. **2** Any interval of rest taken during the course of a regular period of work. Also **time out.**

time out of mind Longer than is known or can be remembered; time immemorial.

time·piece (tīm′pēs′) *n.* A chronometer; a clock, or watch.

tim·er (tī′mər) *n.* **1** A timekeeper, or one who gives or officially records time. **2** A stopwatch, as for timing a race. **3** A device attached in an adjustable form to an internal-combustion engine so as to time the spark automatically.

time-sav·ing (tīm′sā′ving) *adj.* Calculated or devised to save time by facilitating work: Vacuum cleaners are *time-saving* devices.

time-serv·er (tīm′sûr′vər) *n.* One who yields to the apparent demands of the time, without reference to principle; a temporizer. Also **time′-pleas′er** (-plē′zər). **—time′-serv′ing** *adj.* & *n.*

time signature *Music* A sign placed at the beginning of a composition, immediately after the key signature, to indicate the rhythm or time.

Times Square A square in New York City formed by the intersection of Broadway and Seventh Avenue, extending from 42nd to 45th street; by extension, the area around it, the city's entertainment district.

time·ta·ble (tīm′tā′bəl) *n.* A tabular statement of the times at which certain things, as arrivals and departures of trains, boats, high and low tides, etc., are to take place.

time·work (tīm′wûrk′) *n.* Work paid for on the basis of a set wage per hour, day, week, etc. **—time′work′er** *n.*

time-worn (tīm′wôrn′, -wōrn′) *adj.* Showing the ravages of time; affected by time.

time zone One of the 24 established divisions or sectors into which the globe is divided for convenience in reckoning standard time from the meridian of Greenwich: each sector represents 15 degrees of longitude, or a time interval of 1 hour. See table below. See also STANDARD TIME.

WORLD TIME ZONES

Each zone comprises (with certain geographic adjustments) an area 7 1/2 degrees on each side of the reference longitude from Greenwich, and the zone number is equivalent to the number of hours later (−) or earlier (+) than Greenwich time. The places given in parentheses are for convenience of reference.

Zone No. East of Greenwich	*Longitude from Greenwich*	*Zone No. West of Greenwich*
0 (Greenwich)	0°	0 (Greenwich)
− 1 (Berlin)	15°	+ 1 (Iceland)
− 2 (Leningrad)	30°	+ 2 (Azores)
− 3 (Baghdad)	45°	+ 3 (Rio de Janeiro)
− 4 (Bokhara)	60°	+ 4 (Halifax)
− 5 (Bombay)	75°	+ 5 (Washington)
− 6 (Lhasa)	90°	+ 6 (Chicago)
− 7 (Singapore)	105°	+ 7 (Denver)
− 8 (Manila)	120°	+ 8 (Vancouver)
− 9 (Kyoto)	135°	+ 9 (Dawson)
−10 (Melbourne)	150°	+10 (Tahiti)
−11 (Kamchatka)	165°	+11 (Nome)
−12 (Fiji Is.)	180°	+12 (Samoa)

(International Date Line)

Tim·gad (tim·gad′) An ancient ruined city in NE Algeria.

tim·id (tim′id) *adj.* Shrinking from danger or publicity; easily frightened; shy; lacking self-confidence. See synonyms under FAINT, PUSILLANIMOUS. [<L *timidus* < *timere* fear] **—ti·mid·i·ty** (ti·mid′ə·tē), **tim′id·ness** *n.* **—tim′id·ly** *adv.*

tim·ing (tī′ming) *n.* **1** In music, oratory, acting, etc., the act or art of regulating the speed of performance, utterance, etc., so as to accentuate the impressiveness of certain parts; also, the effect produced by such regulation. **2** In certain sports, as swimming, boxing, etc., the regulation of the speed of a blow or stroke so that it reaches its highest effectiveness at just the right moment.

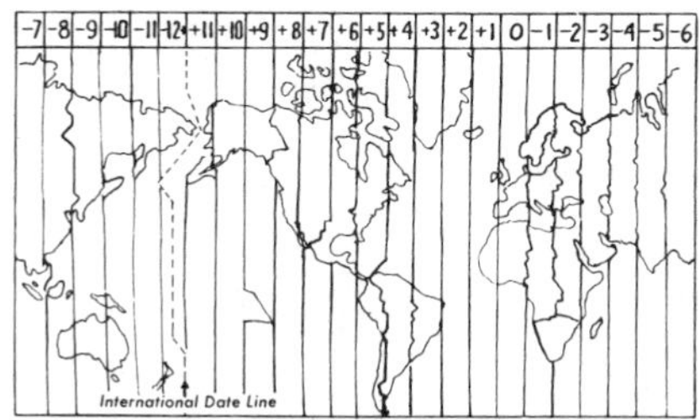

WORLD TIME ZONES
The system of keeping standard time at sea has been adopted by most of the world's navies.

Ti·mi·soa·ra (tē′mē·shwä′rä) A city in western Rumania: Hungarian *Temesvár.*

ti·moc·ra·cy (tī·mok′rə·sē) *n. pl.* **·cies** **1** A state in which the honor attaching to the position of ruler becomes an object of contention, and is sought by the ambitious with intrigue, rather than accepted as a trust. **2** A state in which honors are bestowed according to property owned. [<OF *tymocracie* <Med. L *timocratia* <Gk. *timokratia* < *timē* honor + *krateein* rule] **—ti·mo·crat·ic** (tī′mə·krat′ik) or **·i·cal** *adj.*

ti·mol·o·gy (tī·mol′ə·jē) *n. Philos.* A study or theory of value or excellence, especially of inherent rather than relative value. [<Gk. *timē* honor, valuation + -LOGY] **—ti·mo·log·ic** (tī′mə·loj′ik) or **·i·cal** *adj.* **—ti·mol′o·gist** *n.*

Ti·mon (tī′mən) An Athenian of the fifth century B.C.; called "the Misanthrope"; hero of Shakespeare's *Timon of Athens.*

Ti·mor (tē′môr, ti·môr′) The largest and easternmost of the Lesser Sunda Islands; divided into *Indonesian Timor,* included in Nusa Tenggara province, in the western portion; 5,765 square miles; capital, Kupang: formerly *Netherlands Timor*; and into *Portuguese Timor,* a Portuguese province, in the eastern portion; 5,761 square miles, including the exclave of Ambeno and the islands of Atauro and Jaco; capital, Dili.

Timor Archipelago See LESSER SUNDA ISLANDS.

Ti·mor·laut (tē′môr·lout) See TANIMBAR ISLANDS. Also **Ti·mor·laoet** (tē′môr·lout).

tim·or·ous (tim′ər·əs) *adj.* **1** Fearful of danger; timid. **2** Indicating or produced by fear. See synonyms under PUSILLANIMOUS. [<OF *timoureus, temeros* <Med. L *timorosus,* ult. <L *timor, -oris* fear] **—tim′or·ous·ly** *adv.* **—tim′or·ous·ness** *n.*

Timor Sea An arm of the Indian Ocean between northern Australia and Timor.

Ti·mo·shen·ko (tē′mō·sheng′kō), **Semion Konstantinovich,** born 1895, Russian marshal in World War II.

tim·o·thy (tim′ə·thē) *n.* A perennial fodder grass *(Phleum pratense)* having its flowers in a long, dense, cylindrical, spikelike panicle. Also **timothy grass.** [after *Timothy* Hanson, who took the seed from New York to the Carolinas about 1720]

TIMOTHY (Plant to 6 feet high)

Tim·o·thy (tim′ə·thē) A masculine personal name. Also *Dan., Du., Ger., Sw.* **Ti·mo·the·us** (tē·mō′·tē·o͞os), *Fr.* **Ti·mo·thée** (tē·mō·tā′), *Ital., Sp.* **Ti·mo·te·o** (tē′mō·tā′ō), *Pg.* **Ti·mo·the·o** (tē′mō·tā′o͞o). [< Gk., honoring a god]
—Timothy A convert and companion of the apostle Paul; also, either of two pastoral epistles in the New Testament, addressed to Timothy and attributed to Paul.

Ti·mour, Ti·mur (ti·mo͝or′, tē-) See TAMERLANE.

tim·pa·ni (tim′pə·nē) *n. pl. sing.* **·pa·no** (-pə·nō) Kettledrums; a set of kettledrums in an orchestra: also spelled *tympani.* [<Ital., pl. of *timpano* <L *tympanum* a drum <Gk. *tympanon*] **—tim′pa·nist** *n.*

tim·pa·num (tim′pə·nəm) See TYMPANUM.

tin (tin) *n.* **1** A white, malleable, metallic element (symbol Sn) of low tensile strength and crystalline structure, found chiefly in combination and extensively used in making alloys. See ELEMENT. **2** Tin plate. **3** An article of tinware; a container or box made of tin. **4** *Brit.* A tin container for preserved foods; a can. **5** *Slang* Money. **—*v.t.*** **tinned, tin·ning** **1** To coat or cover with tin or tin plate. **2** To pack or put up in tins. **—*adj.*** Made of tin. [OE]

Ti·na (tē′nə) Diminutive of CHRISTINA.

tin·a·mou (tin′ə·mo͞o) *n.* Any of certain South American birds (family *Tinamidae*), resembling quails, and hunted as game birds. [<F <Cariban *tinamu*]

tin·cal (ting′kəl, -käl, -kôl) *n.* Native borax. [<Malay *tiṅkal* <Persian *tiṅkāl, tiṅkar* <Skt. *ṭankaṇa* borax]

tinct (tingkt) *v.t.* To tinge; tint. **—*adj.*** *Poetic* Slightly tinged. **—*n.*** **1** *Poetic* A tint. **2** *Obs.* A tincture; specifically, the elixir vitae. [<L *tinctus,* pp. of *tingere* dye, color]

tinc·to·ri·al (tingk·tôr′ē·əl, -tō′rē-) *adj.* **1** Of or pertaining to color or hue. **2** Affording or imbuing with tint or color. [<L *tinctorius* < *tinctus.* See TINCT.]

tinc·ture (tingk′chər) *n.* **1** A solution, usually in alcohol, of some principle used in medicine. **2** A tinge of color; tint. **3** A slight flavor superadded; modicum; spice. **4** That part of a substance which is extracted by a solvent. **5** One of the metals, colors, or furs used in heraldic description. **—*v.t.*** **·tured, ·tur·ing** **1** To impart a slight hue or tinge to. **2** To imbue with flavor, odor, etc. **3** To imbue with a specified moral or mental quality. [<L *tinctura* a dyeing < *tinctus.* See TINCT.]

tin·der (tin′dər) *n.* Any readily combustible substance, as charred linen or touchwood, that will ignite (without explosion) on contact with a spark. [OE *tynder*] —**tin'der·y** *adj.*

tin·der·box (tin'dər·boks') *n.* **1** A portable metallic box containing tinder, and usually flint and steel to ignite it. **2** A highly inflammable mass of material. **3** A person with an easily excitable temper.

tine (tīn) *n.* A spike or prong, as of a fork or of an antler. [OE *tind*] —**tined** *adj.*

tin·e·a (tin'ē·ə) *n.* **1** Any of a genus (*Tinea*) of small, narrow-winged moths, including the case-making clothes moth (*T. pellionella*). **2** *Pathol.* Ringworm; any fungous skin disease. [<NL <L, a moth, gnawing worm]

tin·e·id (tin'ē·id) *adj.* Of or pertaining to a family (*Tineidae*) of moths. —*n.* One of the *Tineidae*. [<NL <*Tinea* TINEA]

tin·foil (tin'foil') *n.* Tin or an alloy of tin made into thin sheets for use as wrapping material and in decoration.

ting[1] (ting) *n.* A single high metallic sound, as of a small bell. —*v.t.* & *v.i.* To give forth or cause to give forth a ting. [Imit.]

ting[2] (ting) See THING[2].

ting-a-ling (ting'ə·ling') *n.* The sound of a little bell.

tinge (tinj) *v.t.* **tinged, tinge·ing** or **ting·ing** **1** To imbue with a faint trace of color; impart a tint to. **2** To impart a slight characteristic quality of some other element to. See synonyms under STAIN. —*n.* **1** A faint trace of added color. **2** A quality or peculiar characteristic imparted to something by the slight admixture of some foreign element. [<L *tingere* dye]

tin·gle (ting'gəl) *v.* **·gled, ·gling** *v.i.* **1** To experience a prickly, stinging sensation, as the skin from exposure to cold, or the ears from a sharp blow. **2** To cause such a sensation. —*v.t.* **3** To cause to tingle. —*n.* **1** A prickly, stinging sensation; a tingling. **2** A jingle or tinkling. [Appar. var. of TINKLE] —**tin'gler** *n.* —**tin'gly** *adj.*

Ting·ley (ting'lē), **Katherine,** 1847–1929, *née* Wescott, U.S. theosophist.

tin·horn (tin'hôrn') *Slang n.* **1** A pretentious person without any real ability, power, influence, etc. **2** A gambler who bets with low stakes. —*adj.* **1** Resembling or characteristic of a cheap gambler. **2** Pretentious. [With ref. to the fine appearance, but poor quality, of a tin horn]

Tin·i·an (tin'ē·ən, tē'nē·än') One of the southern Marianas Islands; 39 square miles.

tink (tingk) *v.i.* To make a single or separate tinkling sound; chink. —*n.* A tinkle or tinkling. [Imit.]

tink·er (tingk'ər) *n.* **1** An itinerant mender of domestic tin utensils, as pots and pans. **2** Loosely, one who does repairing work of any kind; a jack-of-all-trades. **3** A clumsy workman; a botcher. **4** The act of roughly repairing; hasty workmanship. **5** A young mackerel about two years old. **6** The chub mackerel. **7** The razor-billed auk. —*v.i.* **1** To work as a tinker. **2** To work in a clumsy, makeshift fashion on anything. **3** To potter; fuss. —*v.t.* **4** To mend as a tinker. **5** To repair clumsily or inexpertly. [Var. of earlier *tinekere* a worker in tin]

tinker's damn *Slang* Any useless or worthless article: commonly in the phrase *not worth a tinker's damn.* Also **tinker's dam.** [<TINKER + DAMN; with ref. to the reputed profanity of tinkers]

tin·kle (ting'kəl) *v.* **·kled, ·kling** *v.i.* **1** To produce slight, sharp, metallic sounds, as a small bell. —*v.t.* **2** To cause to tinkle. **3** To summon or signal by a tinkling. —*n.* A sharp, clear, tinkling sound. [Freq. of TINK] —**tin'kling** *adj.* & *n.* —**tin'kly** *adj.*

tin lizzie *U.S. Slang* The Model T automobile.

tin·ner (tin'ər) *n.* **1** A miner employed in tin mines. **2** A maker of or dealer in tinware; a tinsmith.

tin·ni·tus (ti·nī'təs) *n. Pathol.* A subjective ringing, rushing, or buzzing sound in the ears, not caused by any external stimulus. [<NL <L *tinnire* ring]

tin·ny (tin'ē) *adj.* **·ni·er, ·ni·est** **1** Pertaining to, composed of, or abounding in tin. **2** Sounding as if a tin pan were being struck: a *tinny* sound. **3** Tasting of tin, as food from a can. —**tin'ni·ly** *adv.* —**tin'ni·ness** *n.*

tin-pan (tin'pan') *adj.* Noisy; clanging; inharmonious; tinny. Also **tin'-pan'ny.**

tin-pan alley (tin'pan') **1** A street or section of a city frequented by musicians and song writers and occupied by publishers of popular music: originally used to designate a section of New York where cheap, tinny-sounding pianos were supposedly heard in publishers' offices. **2** The composers and publishers of popular music, collectively.

tin-plate (tin'plāt') *v.t.* **-plat·ed, -plat·ing** To plate with tin. —**tin'-plat'er** *n.*

tin plate Sheet iron or steel plated with tin.

tin·sel (tin'səl) *n.* **1** Very thin glittering bits of brass, copper, and other cheap metals, used for display and to ornament articles of dress; also, the thin metal from which they are cut. **2** A fabric in which such spangles or bits of metal are woven, or to which they are attached; also, a fabric or yarn containing gold or silver thread. **3** Anything sparkling and showy, with little real worth; superficial adornment and brilliancy. —*adj.* **1** Made or covered with tinsel. **2** Of tinsel-like qualities; superficially brilliant; tawdry. —*v.t.* **·seled** or **·selled, ·sel·ing** or **·sel·ling** **1** To adorn or decorate with or as with tinsel. **2** To give a metallic appearance to (ceramic ware) by washing with a metallic substance. [<MF *étincelle* <OF *estincelle* <L *scintilla* a spark]

tin·smith (tin'smith') *n.* One who works with tin or tin plate.

tin spirits *Chem.* A solution of a tin salt in acid, used in dyeing.

tin·stone (tin'stōn') *n.* Cassiterite.

tint[1] (tint) *n.* **1** A variety of color; tincture; specifically, a tendency toward or slight admixture of a different color; tinge: red with a blue *tint.* **2** A gradation or shading of a color made by dilution with white to lessen its chroma and saturation. **3** Any color having a brilliance higher than that of median gray. **4** In engraving, an effect of light, shade, texture, etc., produced by the spacing of lines or by hatching. **5** An impression from a block bearing a design to be printed in a faint color as a background: used on checks as a safeguard against erasure. —*v.t.* **1** To give a tint to; tinge. **2** In engraving, to form a tint upon. See synonyms under STAIN. [Alter. of TINCT; ? infl. in form by Ital. *tinta* color] —**tint'er** *n.*

tint[2] (tint) *Scot.* Past tense and past participle of TINE[2].

Tin·tag·el Head (tin·taj'əl) A promontory with castle ruins in western Cornwall, England; traditionally, the birthplace of King Arthur.

Tin·tern Abbey (tin'tərn) The ruins of a Cistercian abbey founded in the 12th century in Monmouth, England, on the Wye.

tin·tin·nab·u·lar (tin'ti·nab'yə·lər) *adj.* Characterized by tinkling, as of bells. Also **tin'tin·nab'u·lar'y, tin'tin·nab'u·lous.**

tin·tin·nab·u·la·tion (tin'ti·nab'yə·lā'shən) *n.* The pealing, tinkling, or ringing of bells.

tin·tin·nab·u·lum (tin'ti·nab'yə·ləm) *n. pl.* **·la** (-lə) A bell; especially, a small tinkling or signaling bell. [<L, a small bell <*tintinnare* ring]

Tin·to·ret·to (tin'tə·ret'ō, *Ital.* tēn'tō·ret'tō), 1518–94, Venetian painter: real name *Jacopo Robusti.*

tin·type (tin'tīp') *n.* A photograph taken on a sensitized film supported on a thin sheet of enameled tin or iron; a ferrotype.

tin·ware (tin'wâr') *n.* Household articles, collectively, made of tin plate.

tin·work (tin'wûrk') *n.* **1** Articles made of tin; work with tin. **2** *pl.* A place or establishment where tin is manufactured or mined.

ti·ny (tī'nē) *adj.* **·ni·er, ·ni·est** Very small; minute; wee. See synonyms under LITTLE, MINUTE[2], SMALL. [<obs. *tine* a small amount, bit + -Y[3]; ult. origin unknown]

-tion *suffix of nouns* **1** Action or process of: *rejection.* **2** Condition or state of being: *completion.* **3** Result of: *connection.* Also *-ation, -cion, -ion, -sion, -xion.* [<F *-tion* <OF *-cion* <L *-tio, -tionis*]

tip[1] (tip) *n.* A slanting or inclined position; a tilt. —*v.* **tipped, tip·ping** *v.t.* **1** To cause to lean by lowering or raising one end or side; cant; tilt. **2** To overturn or upset: often with *over.* —*v.i.* **3** To become tilted; slant. **4** To overturn; topple: with *over.* [ME *tipen* overturn; origin uncertain] —**tip'per** *n.*

Synonyms (verb): cant, careen, heel, incline, lean, list, slant, slope, tilt. To *tilt* or *tip* is to throw out of a horizontal position by raising one side or end or lowering the other. *Slant* and *slope* are said of things somewhat fixed or permanent in a position out of the horizontal or perpendicular: the roof *slants,* the hill *slopes. Incline* is a more formal word for *tip,* and also for *slant* or *slope.* To *cant* is to set slantingly; in many cases *tip* and *cant* might be interchanged, but *tip* is more temporary, often momentary; one *tips* a pail so that the water flows over the edge; a mechanic *cants* a table by making or setting one side higher than the other. *Careen, heel,* and *list* are used of vessels which from any cause, as leakage, shifting of cargo, etc., are off an even keel.

tip[2] (tip) *v.t.* **tipped, tip·ping** **1** To strike lightly, or with something light; tap. **2** In baseball, to strike (the ball) a light, glancing blow. —*n.* A tap; light blow. [Earlier *tippe,* prob. <LG. Cf. Du. *tippen* tap.]

tip[3] (tip) *n.* **1** A small gift of money for services rendered, given to a servant, waiter, porter, or the like. **2** A friendly, helpful hint; specifically, secret information presumed to increase a better's or speculator's chance of winning. [<*v.*] —*v.* **tipped, tip·ping** *v.t.* **1** To give a small gratuity to. **2** *Colloq.* To give secret information to, as in betting and speculation: often with *off.* —*v.i.* **3** To give tips. [Orig. <thieves' cant, ? <TIP[2]] —**tip'·per** *n.*

tip[4] (tip) *n.* **1** The point or extremity of anything tapering; end: the *tip* of the tongue. **2** A piece or part made to form the end of anything, as a nozzle, ferrule, etc. **3** The upper part of a hat crown; also, the lining in the upper part of the crown. —*v.t.* **tipped, tip·ping** **1** To furnish with a tip. **2** To form the tip of. **3** To cover or adorn the tip of. [Prob. <MDu., a point]

ti palm See TI[2].

tip·cart (tip'kärt') *n.* A cart having a body that can be tipped for unloading.

tip·cat (tip'kat') *n.* A game played with a stick or bat and a small piece of wood pointed at the ends and called a *cat,* which the batter hits lightly into the air and then hits again, trying to drive it as far as possible; also, the cat. [<TIP[1] + CAT]

ti·pi (tē'pē) See TEPEE.

tip-off (tip'ôf', -of') *n. Colloq.* A hint or warning.

Tip·pe·ca·noe (tip'ē·kə·no͞o') The nickname of William Henry Harrison: from his victory over Tecumseh's Indians at Tippecanoe River in 1811. The name provided the presidential campaign slogan, **Tippecanoe and Tyler too,** for Harrison and his vice-presidential running mate, John Tyler, in 1840.

Tip·pe·ca·noe River (tip'ē·kə·no͞o') A river in north central Indiana, flowing 166 miles NW, west, and SW to the Wabash River near Lafayette; scene of General W. H. Harrison's victory over Indians, 1811.

Tip·per·ar·y (tip'ə·râr'ē) A county of NE Munster province, Ireland; 1,643 square miles; county town, Clonmel.

tip·pet (tip'it) *n.* **1** An outdoor covering for the neck, or neck and shoulders, hanging well down in front. **2** *Eccl.* A long scarf worn by clergymen in the Anglican Church. **3** A ruff of feathers on birds, etc. [Prob. dim. of TIP[4]]

tip·ple[1] (tip'əl) *v.t.* & *v.i.* **·pled, ·pling** To drink (alcoholic beverages) frequently and habitually. —*n.* Liquor consumed in tippling. [Cf. Norw. *tipla* drip, tipple] —**tip'pler** *n.*

tip·ple[2] (tip'əl) *n.* **1** An apparatus for tipping loaded cars. **2** The place where such tipping is done. [<dial. E *tipple* topple, freq. of TIP[1]]

tip·py (tip'ē) *adj.* **·pi·er, ·pi·est** *Colloq.* Shaky; unsteady; apt to tip over. [<TIP[1] + -Y[3]]

tip·staff (tip'staf', -stäf') *n.* **1** *pl.* **·staffs** In England, a sheriff's subordinate; bailiff; constable; also, a court crier. **2** *pl.* **·staves** (-stāvz') A staff having a metal tip: a badge of office. [<TIP(PED) STAFF]

tip·ster (tip'stər) *n. Colloq.* One who sells tips for betting, as on a race. [<TIP[3]]

tip·sy (tip'sē) *adj.* **·si·er, ·si·est** **1** Befuddled with drink, but not really drunk; partially intoxicated; high. **2** Tippy; shaky; also, crooked; askew. [<TIP[1]] —**tip'si·ly** *adv.* —**tip'si·ness** *n.*

tip·toe (tip'tō') *n.* **1** The tip of a toe, or the tips of all the toes collectively. **2** Topmost height; also, alertness of expectation: usually in the phrase **to be on tiptoe** or **a-tiptoe,** to be eagerly expectant. — *v.i.* **·toed, ·toe·ing** To walk on tiptoe; go stealthily. — *adj.* **1** Standing on tiptoe. **2** Quiet; gentle; stealthy. — *adv.* On tiptoe, in any sense.

tip-top (tip′top′) *Colloq. adj.* Best of its kind; first-rate. — *n.* The highest point, quality, or degree; the very top; the best. — *adv.* In a tip-top manner. [<TIP[4] + TOP[1]] — **tip′-top′per** *n.*

Ti·pu Sa·hib (tï′pōō sä′hib), 1753?–99, sultan of Mysore; fought against the British 1775–79. Also **Tip′poo Sa′hib.**

Ti·rach Mir (tē′rəch mēr′) See TIRICH MIR.

ti·rade (tī′rād, tə·rād′) *n.* **1** A prolonged declamatory outpouring, as of censure. **2** *Music* A diatonic run, filling the interval between two musical notes. [<F <Ital. *tirata* a volley, pp. of *tirare* fire, pull]

ti·rail·leur (tir′ə·lûr′, *Fr.* tē·rà·yœr′) *n.* A sharpshooter; skirmisher. [<F]

Ti·ra·na (tē·rä′nə) The capital of Albania, in the central part. Also **Ti·ra′në.**

tire[1] (tīr) *v.* **tired, tir·ing** *v.t.* **1** To reduce the strength of, as by toil; weary; fatigue. **2** To reduce the interest or patience of, as with tediousness. — *v.i.* **3** To become weary or exhausted. **4** To lose patience, interest, etc. — **to tire of** To become weary of or impatient with. — **to tire out** To weary completely. — *n. Dial.* The sensation of fatigue; weariness. [OE *tīorian, tēorian*]

Synonyms (verb): exhaust, fag, fatigue, harass, jade, weary. To *tire* is to reduce one's strength in any degree by exertion; one may be *tired* just enough to make rest pleasant, or even unconsciously *tired,* becoming aware of the fact only when he ceases the exertion. One who is *fatigued* suffers from painful lack of strength as the result of overtaxing; an invalid may be *fatigued* with very slight exertion; when one is *wearied,* the painful lack of strength is the result of long-continued demand or strain; one is *exhausted* when the strain has been so severe and continuous as utterly to consume the strength, so that further exertion is for the time impossible. One is *fagged* by drudgery; he is *jaded* by incessant repetition of the same act until it becomes increasingly difficult or well-nigh impossible; as, a horse is *jaded* by a long and unbroken journey. See WEAR[1].

tire[2] (tīr) *n.* **1** A band or hoop surrounding the rim of a wheel. **2** A flexible tube, usually of inflated rubber, set in a rim and protected by an outer covering: used on automobiles, bicycles, etc., to reduce vibration. — *v.t.* **tired, tir·ing** To furnish with a tire; put a tire on. Also, *Brit., tyre.* [Special use of TIRE[4]]

tire[3] (tīr) *Archaic v.t.* **1** In falconry, to rend and devour; draw; pull. — *v.i.* **2** To prey. **3** To be preoccupied; dote; gloat. [<OF *tirer;* ult. origin uncertain]

tire[4] (tīr) *Obs. v.t.* To attire; dress; adorn. — *n.* **1** A tiara; headdress. **2** Attire. [Aphetic var. of ATTIRE]

tire[5] (tīr) *n.* A volley of cannon; a broadside. [<OF *tir* < *tirer* draw, shoot; ult. origin uncertain]

tired (tīrd) *adj.* Weary; exhausted; jaded; fatigued. [Orig. pp. of TIRE[1]] — **tired′ly** *adv.* — **tired′ness** *n.*

tire·less (tīr′lis) *adj.* Proof against fatigue; untiring. See synonyms under INDEFATIGABLE. [<TIRE[1] + -LESS] — **tire′less·ly** *adv.* — **tire′·less·ness** *n.*

Ti·re·si·as (tī·rē′sē·əs) In Greek mythology, a Theban soothsayer, blinded by Athena whom he saw bathing: in recompense she gave him power to foretell the future. — **Ti·re′si·an** *adj.*

tire·some (tīr′səm) *adj.* Tending to tire, or causing one to tire; tedious. See synonyms under TEDIOUS, TROUBLESOME, WEARISOME. — **tire′some·ly** *adv.* — **tire′some·ness** *n.*

tire·wom·an (tīr′wōōm′ən) *n.* *pl.* **·wom·en** (-wim′in) *Obs.* A lady's maid; an abigail. Also **tir′ing-wom′an.** [<TIRE[4] + WOMAN]

Ti·rich Mir (tē′rich mēr′) The highest mountain in the Hindu Kush, in extreme NW West Pakistan near the border of Afghanistan; 25,263 feet: also *Tirach Mir.*

tiring room *Archaic* A dressing-room, especially in a theater. [<*tiring,* ppr. of TIRE[4] + ROOM]

tirl (tûrl) *Scot. v.t.* To cause to produce a vibrating or thrilling noise, as by plucking a string. — *n.* A vibrating or thrilling noise.

tirl·ing pin (tûr′ling) *Scot.* A vertical twisted iron bar passed through a loose ring and fastened to a door: formerly used as a knocker.

Tir·no·vo (tir′nô·vô) A city in northern Bulgaria; scene of the declaration of the country's independence, 1908: also *Trnovo.*

ti·ro (tī′rō) See TYRO.

Ti·rol (ti·rōl′, tir′ōl, tī′rōl) An autonomous province of western Austria in the eastern Alps north of Italy; 4,883 square miles; capital, Innsbruck: also *Tyrol.* — **Ti·ro′le·an** *adj.* & *n.*

Tir·o·lese (tir′ō·lēz′, -lēs′) *adj.* Of or pertaining to Tirol or its inhabitants. — *n.* *pl.* **·lese** A native of Tirol. Also *Tyrolese.*

Tir·pitz (tir′pits), **Alfred von,** 1849–1930, German admiral.

tir·ri·vee (tir′ə·vē) *n. Scot.* A burst of ill-humor; fit of passion; tantrum.

Tir·so de Mo·li·na (tir′sō thä mō·lē′nä), 1571?–1648, Spanish dramatist: real name Gabriel Téllez.

Ti·ruch·i·rap·pal·li (ti·rōōch′ē·räp′ə·lē) A city in east central Madras State, India: also *Trichinopoly.*

'tis (tiz) It is: a contraction.

Ti·sa (tē′sä) The Czech and Rumanian name for the Tisza.

ti·sane (ti·zan′, *Fr.* tē·zàn′) *n.* A slightly medicated decoction, usually of herbs, prepared for the sick; a ptisan. [<F <L *ptisana* a ptisan]

Tish·ri (tish′rē) The first month of the Hebrew calendar. See CALENDAR (Hebrew). Also **Tis·ri** (tiz′rē). [<Hebrew <Aramic *tishrī* < *sherā* begin; infl. by Babylonian *tashrītu* the seventh month, first month of the second half of the year]

Ti·siph·o·ne (ti·sif′ə·nē) In Greek mythology, one of the three Furies.

tis·sue (tish′ōō) *n.* **1** Any light or gauzy textile fabric, usually of silk; originally, cloth interwoven with gold or silver thread. **2** *Biol.* One of the elementary aggregates of cells and their products, developed by plants and animals for the performance of a particular function: connective *tissue.* **3** A connected or interwoven series; chain; fabrication: a *tissue* of lies. **4** Tissue paper. — *v.t.* **·sued, ·su·ing** *Rare* **1** To make into tissue. **2** To adorn with tissue; weave. [<OF *tissu* a rich stuff, orig. pp. of *tistre* weave <L *texere*]

tissue culture The science and art of growing body tissues in a culture medium.

tis·sued (tish′ōōd) *adj.* **1** Clad in tissue. **2** Variegated.

tissue paper Very thin, unsized, almost transparent paper for wrapping delicate articles, protecting engravings, etc.

Ti·sza (ti′so) A river flowing 800 miles from the Carpathian Mountains, in SW Ukrainian S.S.R., south through Hungary and Yugoslavia to the Danube north of Belgrade: German *Theiss,* Czech and Rumanian *Tisa.*

tit[1] (tit) *n.* **1** A titmouse. **2** One of various other small birds, as a titlark, etc. [Short for TITMOUSE, TITLARK, etc]

tit[2] (tit) *n.* A light blow; tap: chiefly in the phrase *tit for tat.* [Var. of TIP[2]]

tit[3] (tit) *n.* Teat; breast; nipple. [OE *titt*]

tit[4] (tit) *n.* **1** A small or worn-out horse; a nag. **2** *Slang* A young woman or girl: a disrespectful term. [ME, a little thing, ? <Scand. Cf. dial. Norw. *titta* little girl.]

ti·tan (tī′tn) *n.* Any person having gigantic strength or size; a giant. — *adj.* Titanic. [after *Titan*] — **ti′tan·ess** *n. fem.*

Ti·tan (tīt′n) **1** In Greek mythology, one of a race of giant gods, children of Uranus and Gaea, who were vanquished and succeeded by the Olympian gods, who imprisoned them in Tartarus. **2** Helios: so called by some Latin poets.

ti·tan·ate (tī′tə·nāt) *n. Chem.* A salt or ester of titanic acid. [<TITAN(IC)[2] + -ATE[3]]

Ti·tan·esque (tīt′n·esk′) *adj.* Of or befitting the Titans; gigantic.

Ti·tan·ess (tīt′n·is) A female Titan.

Ti·ta·ni·a (ti·tā′nē·ə, tī-) Queen of fairyland and wife of Oberon in Shakespeare's *A Midsummer Night's Dream.*

ti·tan·ic[1] (tī·tan′ik) *adj.* Gigantic; huge; tremendous. [<Gk. *titanikos* <*Titanes* the Titans]

ti·tan·ic[2] (tī·tan′ik, ti-) *adj. Chem.* Of or pertaining to titanium, especially in its higher valence. [<TITAN(IUM) + -IC]

Ti·tan·ic (tī·tan′ik) *adj.* Pertaining to, characteristic of, or resembling the Titans.

titanic acid *Chem.* **1** A white pulverulent titanium dioxide, TiO_2, found native as rutile, etc.: a common constituent of iron ores: also **titanic oxide.** **2** One of various weak acids derived from titanium dioxide.

ti·tan·if·er·ous (tī′tən·if′ər·əs) *adj.* Containing or yielding titanium. [<TITAN(IUM) + -(I)FEROUS]

Ti·tan·ism (tīt′n·iz′əm) *n.* Defiance of, or rebellion against, constituted authority or social conventions: a characteristic attributed to the Titans in Greek mythology.

ti·tan·ite (tī′tən·īt) *n.* Sphene. [<G *titanit* < *titanium* titanium]

ti·ta·ni·um (tī·tā′nē·əm, ti-) *n.* A widely distributed dark-gray metallic element (symbol Ti) resembling tin and silicon, found in small quantities in many minerals and used to toughen steel alloys. See ELEMENT. [<NL <L *Titani* the Titans <Gk. *Titanes;* named on analogy with *uranium*]

titanium tetrachloride *Chem.* A colorless liquid compound, $TiCl_4$, used as a smoke-producing agent in warfare.

Ti·tan·om·a·chy (tī′tən·om′ə·kē) *n.* In Greek mythology, the war of the Titans against the Olympian gods. [<Gk. *Titanomachia* <*Titan* a Titan + *machē* a battle]

ti·tan·o·there (tī′tən·ə·thir′, tī·tā′nə-, ti-) *n.* *Paleontol.* Any of an extinct family (*Titanotheriidae*) of large, odd-toed ungulates resembling the rhinoceros and common in the Lower Eocene of the Tertiary period. [<NL <Gk. *Titan* a Titan + *thērion,* dim. of *thēr* a wild beast]

ti·tan·ous (tī′tən·əs, tī·tan′əs, ti-) *adj. Chem.* Of or pertaining to titanium, especially in its lower valence. [<TITAN(IUM) + -OUS[2]]

tit·bit (tit′bit′) See TIDBIT.

Tite (tēt) French form of TITUS.

ti·ter (tī′tər, tē′-) *n. Chem.* **1** The strength or concentration of a solution as determined by titration. **2** The temperature at which a molten fatty acid or wax solidifies. Also spelled *titre.* [<F *titre* the fineness of gold or silver alloy]

tit for tat Retaliation in kind; blow for blow. [? Alter. of *tip for tap;* ? infl. in form by MF *tant pour tant* tit for tat]

tith·a·ble (tī′thə·bəl) *adj.* Liable to be tithed, as property.

tithe (tīth) *n.* **1** A tax or assessment of one tenth, especially when payable in kind; loosely, any ratable tax. **2** Specifically, in England, a tenth part of the yearly proceeds arising from lands and from the personal industry of the inhabitants, for the support of the clergy and the church. **3** The tenth part of anything; hence, a small part. — *v.t.* **tithed, tith·ing** **1** To give or pay a tithe, or tenth part of. **2** To tax with tithes. [ME *tithe, tethe,* OE *tēotha, tēogotha* a tenth] — **tith′er** *n.*

tith·ing (tī′thing) *n.* **1** The act of levying tithes. **2** A tenth part. **3** In old English law, a civil division composed of ten freeholders and their families.

tith·ing·man (tī′thing·mən) *n.* *pl.* **·men** (-mən) **1** Anciently, in England, the chief of a tithing; more recently, a constable. **2** In the New England colonies, an officer for enforcing Sunday observance and order.

Ti·tho·nus (ti·thō′nəs) In Greek mythology, a son of Laomedon who was loved by Eos. She persuaded Zeus to grant him immortality but neglected to request for him eternal youth, so that Tithonus shriveled as he grew older and older, and was finally changed into a grasshopper. [<L <Gk. *Tithōnos*]

ti·ti[1] (tē′tē) *n.* **1** An evergreen shrub or small tree (*Cliftonia monophylla*) with fragrant white flowers, native in swamps of the southern United States. **2** Any of a genus (*Cyrilla*) of related trees of tropical America; especially, the **white titi** (*C. racemiflora*). [<Sp. <Aymaran]

ti·ti[2] (tē·tē′) *n.* One of several small South American monkeys (genus *Callicebus*). [<Sp. *tití* <Guarani *titi*]

ti·tian (tish′ən) *n.* A reddish-yellow color

much used by Titian, especially in painting women's hair. — *adj.* Having or pertaining to the color titian. [after *Titian*]

Ti·tian (tish'ən), 1477–1576, Venetian painter: real name *Tiziano Vecellio.*

Ti·ti·ca·ca (tē'tē·kä'kä), **Lake** The largest lake in South America, in the Andes between SE Peru and west central Bolivia; 3,200 square miles; elevation, 12,500 feet; the highest large lake in the world.

tit·il·lant (tit'ə·lənt) *n.* An excitant. [<L *titillans, -antis,* ppr. of *titillare* tickle]

tit·il·late (tit'ə·lāt) *v.t.* **·lat·ed, ·lat·ing 1** To cause a tickling sensation in. **2** To excite pleasurably in any way. [<L *titillatus,* pp. of *titillare* tickle]

tit·il·la·tion (tit'ə·lā'shən) *n.* **1** The act of titillating, or the state of being titillated. **2** Any momentary exciting or gratifying sensation. — **tit'il·la'tive** *adj.*

tit·i·vate (tit'ə·vāt) *v.t.* & *v.i.* **·vat·ed, ·vat·ing** *Colloq.* To put on decorative touches; smarten; dress up: also spelled *tittivate.* [Earlier *tidivate, tiddivate,* ? <TIDY, on analogy with *cultivate*] — **tit'i·va'tion** *n.*

tit·lark (tit'lärk') *n.* A pipit. [ME *tit* a little thing + LARK]

ti·tle (tīt'l) *n.* **1** *Law* **a** The means whereby the owner of lands has the just possession of his property; the union of possession, the right of possession, and the right of property in lands and tenements; also, the legal evidence of one's right of property, or the means by or source from which one's right to property has accrued: *title* by purchase. **b** The distinguishing form of words that heads or opens a legal document or statute; also, the opening clause containing the name of the court in which any action is pending, together with the names of the parties, etc. **2** A claim based on an acknowledged or alleged right: What is his *title* to credence? **3** A section or division of a statute, legal document, treatise, or the like. **4** An inscription that serves as a name for designating something, as a book or legal document. **5** A name; descriptive designation. **6** An appellation significant of office, rank, etc.; especially, a designation of nobility. **7** In or near Rome, a church or parish headed by a cardinal: so called because dedicated to or named after the title of some martyr or saint. **8** A source of maintenance, as a patrimony, or a place of duty, especially with income attached, a right or nomination to which is a canonical prerequisite to ordination. **9** In some sports, supremacy; championship: to play for the *title.* See synonyms under NAME. — *v.t.* **·tled, ·tling 1** To give a name to; entitle; call. **2** To confer an honorary title upon; ennoble. [<OF <L *titulus* a label, an inscription. Doublet of TITTLE.] — **ti'tle·less** *adj.*

ti·tled (tīt'ld) *adj.* Having a title, especially of nobility.

ti·tle·hold·er (tīt'l·hōl'dər) *n.* One who possesses a title, especially a championship title. Also **ti'tlist.** — **ti'tle·hold'ing** *adj.*

title page A page containing the title of a work and the names of its author and its publisher.

title rolè The character in a play, opera, or motion picture for whom it is named.

tit·man (tit'mən) *n. pl.* **·men** (-mən) *U.S. Colloq.* **1** The smallest pig in a litter; the runt of a litter of pigs. **2** A man small or stunted either physically or mentally. [ME *tit* a little thing + MAN]

tit·mouse (tit'mous') *n. pl.* **·mice** (-mīs') Any of several small oscine birds (family *Paridae*), related to the nuthatches; especially, the **tufted titmouse** (*Baeolophus bicolor*) of the United States, having a conspicuous crest. [Alter. of ME *titmose* < *tit-* little + *mose,* alter. of OE *mase* a titmouse; infl. in form by MOUSE]

TITMOUSE
(About 5 1/2 inches long)

Ti·to (tē'tō) Italian, Spanish, and Portuguese form of TITUS.

Ti·to (tē'tō), **Marshal,** born 1891?, Yugoslav guerrilla leader in World War II; premier 1945–53; president 1953–: real name *Josip Broz.*

Ti·to·grad (tē'tô·gräd) The capital of Montenegro in southern Yugoslavia: formerly **Pod·go·ri·ca** (pod'gô·rē'tsä).

Ti·to·ism (tē'tō·iz'əm) *n.* The assertion by a Communist state of its national interests in opposition to Soviet domination, such as occurred under Marshal Tito in Yugoslavia.

ti·trate (tī'trāt, tit'rāt) *v.t.* & *v.i.* **·trat·ed, ·trat·ing** *Chem.* To determine the strength of (a solution) by means of standard solutions or by titration. [<F *titrer* < *titre.* See TITER.]

ti·tra·tion (tī·trā'shən, ti-) *n. Chem.* The process of determining the strength or concentration of a given solution by adding to it measured amounts of a standard solution until the desired chemical reaction has been effected.

ti·tre (tī'tər, tē'-) See TITER.

tit·ter (tit'ər) *v.i.* To laugh in a suppressed way, as from nervousness or in ridicule; snicker; giggle. — *n.* The act of tittering; a giggling. [Imit.] — **tit'ter·er** *n.* — **tit'ter·ing·ly** *adv.*

tit·tie (tit'ē) *n. Scot.* A sister. Also **tit'ty.**

tit·tle (tit'l) *n.* **1** The minutest quantity; iota. **2** Originally, a very small mark in writing, as the dot over an *i,* etc.; any diacritical mark. [<L *titulus.* Doublet of TITLE.]

tit·tle-tat·tle (tit'l·tat'l) *n.* **1** Foolish or trivial talk; gossip. **2** An idle, trifling or tattling talker. — *v.i.* **·tled, ·tling** To talk foolishly or idly; gossip; chatter. [Reduplication of TATTLE]

tit·tup (tit'əp) *v.i.* **·tuped** or **·tupped, ·tup·ing** or **·tup·ping** To act in a restless or lively manner; dance along; prance. — *n.* A prancing or curveting action, indicating gaiety or frolicsomeness; a caper. [Appar. imit. of hoof beats]

tit·u·ba·tion (tich'ōō·bā'shən, tit'yə-) *n. Pathol.* A stumbling; tottering; a disturbance of equilibrium resulting in the stumbling gait characteristic of spinal disease. [<L *titubatio, -onis* < *titubatus,* pp. of *titubare* stagger]

tit·u·lar (tich'ōō·lər, tit'yə-) *adj.* **1** Existing in name or title only; nominal. **2** Pertaining to a title. **3** Bestowing or taking title. See TITLE (def. 8). — *n.* One having a title in virtue of which he holds an office or benefice, whether he performs its duties or not; in ecclesiastical law, one holding a sinecure title. Also **tit'u·lar'y** (-ler'ē). [<L *titulus* a title] — **tit'u·lar·ly** *adv.*

Ti·tus (tī'təs) A masculine personal name. [<L, safe]

— **Titus** A disciple of the apostle Paul; also, the epistle in the New Testament addressed to Titus and attributed to Paul.

— **Titus,** A.D. 40?–81, emperor of Rome A.D. 79–81: full name *Titus Flavius Sabinus Vespasianus.*

Ti·u (tē'ōō) In Teutonic mythology, god of war and sky: identified with the Norse *Tyr.*

Tiv·o·li (tiv'ə·lē, *Ital.* tē'vō·lē) A town in central Italy NE of Rome: ancient *Tibur.*

tiv·y (tiv'ē) *adv.* With great speed: a hunting cry. [Appar. short for TANTIVY]

tiz·zy[1] (tiz'ē) *n. pl.* **·zies** *Slang* A bewildered or excited state of mind; a dither. [Origin unknown]

tiz·zy[2] (tiz'ē) *n. pl.* **·zies** *Brit. Slang* A sixpence. [Prob. alter. of TESTER[3]; infl. in form by slang *tilbury* a sixpence]

Tji·la·tjap (chē·lä'chäp) A port of southern Java, Indonesia. Also **Chi·la'chap.**

Tji·re·bon (chē're·bôn') A port of NW central Java, Indonesia, SE of Jakarta: also *Cheribon.*

Tlax·ca·la (tläs·kä'lä) A state of central Mexico; 1,555 square miles; capital, Tlaxcala.

Tlem·cen (tlem·sen') A city of NW Algeria. Also **Tlem·sen'.**

Tlin·git (tling'git) *n. pl.* North American Indians belonging to any of eighteen tribes comprising the Koluschan linguistic stock, and inhabiting the Alexander Archipelago of SE Alaska. They are a seafaring people of fairly advanced culture. Also **Tlin·kit** (tling'kit).

tme·sis (tmē'sis, mē'sis) *n.* The separation of the elements of a compound word by an intervening word, as in the phrase *to us ward,* meaning "toward us." [<L <Gk. *tmēsis* a cutting < *temnein* cut]

TNT (tē'en'tē') *n.* **1** Trinitrotoluene. **2** *Colloq.* Any explosive and dangerous circumstance, force, or person. Also **T.N.T.** [<T(RI)N(ITRO)-T(OLUENE)]

to (tōō, *unstressed* tə) *prep.* **1** In a direction toward or terminating in: going *to* town. **2** Opposite, in contact with, or near: face *to* face; Hold me *to* your breast. **3** Intending or aiming at; having as an object or purpose: Come *to* my rescue. **4** Resulting in; having as a condition or effect: frozen *to* death; flattered *to* his ruin. **5** Belonging in connection or accompaniment with; denoting the relation of things made to go together or between which there is correspondence: the key *to* the barn; March *to* the music. **6** In honor of: Drink *to* me only with thine eyes. **7** In comparison, correspondence, or agreement with: often denoting ratio: 9 is *to* 3 as 21 *to* 7; four quarts *to* the gallon. **8** Until; approaching as a limit; denoting the end of a period of time, or a time not reached: *to* my dying day; five minutes *to* one. **9** For the utmost duration of; as far as: a miser *to* the end of his days. **10** In respect of; concerning: blind *to* her charms; a speech *to* the point. **11** In close application toward: Buckle down *to* work; Fall *to* dinner. **12** For; with regard for: The contest is open *to* everyone. **13** Noting an indirect or limiting object after verbs, adjectives, or nouns, and designating the recipient of the action: taking the place of the dative case in other languages: Give the ring *to* me; That fact is not apparent *to* me. **14** By: known *to* the world. **15** From the point of view of: It seems *to* me. **16** *Dial.* At or in (a place): He is not *to* home now. **17** *Colloq.* With: The land was planted *to* potatoes. **18** About; involved in: That's all there is *to* it. ◆ *To* also serves to indicate the infinitive, and is often used elliptically for it: You may come if you care *to.* See synonyms under AT, INTO. — *adv.* **1** To or toward something. **2** In a direction, position, or state understood or implied; especially, shut or closed: Pull the door *to.* **3** Into a normal condition; into consciousness: She soon came *to.* **4** *Naut.* With head to the wind: said of a sailing vessel: to lie *to.* **5** Upon the matter at hand; into action or operation: They fell *to* with good will. **6** Nearby; at hand. — **to and fro** In opposite or different directions; back and forth. [OE *tō*]

toad (tōd) *n.* **1** A tailless, jumping, insectivorous amphibian (family *Bufonidae*), resembling the frog but without teeth in the upper jaw, and resorting to water only to breed. **2** Some similar amphibian; especially, the **Surinam toad** (*Pipa pipa*) or the European **midwife toad** (*Alytes obstetricans*). **3** Any person regarded scornfully or contemptuously. [OE *tādige*]

TOAD
(Species vary from 2 to 6 inches)

toad-eat·er (tōd'ē'tər) *n.* A fawning parasite; a sycophant. [Orig. an assistant to a charlatan, who ate, or pretended to eat, toads (held to be poisonous) to show the efficacy of a patent medicine]

toad·fish (tōd'fish') *n. pl.* **·fish** or **·fish·es** Any of a family (*Batrachoididae*) of fishes with scaleless skin and mouth and head resembling those of a toad.

toad·flax (tōd'flaks') *n.* **1** A common, showy perennial weed (*Linaria vulgaris*) of the figwort family, having terminal spikes of spurred yellow flowers marked with an orange spot: also called *butter-and-eggs.* **2** Any other plant of the genus *Linaria.* [So called because spotted like toads and having a flaxlike foliage]

toad spit Cuckoo spit. Also **toad spittle.**

toad·stone[1] (tōd'stōn') *n. Dial.* A volcanic rock, generally decomposed, occurring in limestone in Derbyshire, England. [? So called from a resemblance of its markings to those of a toad]

toad·stone[2] (tōd'stōn') *n.* A natural or artificial stone resembling a toad in color and form, and long believed to be formed in a toad: worn as a talisman. [<TOAD + STONE; trans. of L *batrachites* <Gk.]

toad·stool (tōd'stōōl') *n.* **1** Any one of many umbrella-shaped fungi, growing on decaying vegetable matter, common in woods and damp places; a mushroom. **2** *Colloq.* A poisonous mushroom.

toad·y (tō′dē) *n. pl.* **toad·ies** An obsequious flatterer; a fawning, servile person; a toad-eater. — *v.t* & *v.i.* **toad·ied, toad·y·ing** To act the toady (to). ◆ Homophone: *tody.* [Short for TOAD-EATER] — **toad′y·ish** *adj.* — **toad′y·ism** *n.*

to-and-fro (to͞o′ən·frō′) *adj.* Moving back and forth; undulating; alternating. — *n.* Motion back and forth.

toast[1] (tōst) *v.t.* **1** To brown before or over a fire; especially, to brown (bread or cheese) before a fire or in a toaster. **2** To warm thoroughly before a fire. — *v.i.* **3** To become warm or toasted. — *n.* Sliced bread browned in a toaster or at a fire; toasted bread. [<OF *toster* roast, grill <L *tostus* < *torrere* parch, roast]

toast[2] (tōst) *n.* **1** The act of drinking to someone's health or to some sentiment. **2** The person or sentiment named in thus drinking: She was the *toast* of the town. — *v.t.* To drink to the health of or in honor of. — *v.i.* To drink a toast or toasts. [<TOAST[1] in obs. sense of "a spiced piece of toast put in a drink to flavor it"]

toast·er[1] (tōs′tər) *n.* A device for making toast.

toast·er[2] (tōs′tər) *n.* One who proposes a toast.

toast·mas·ter (tōst′mas′tər, -mäs′tər) *n.* A person who, at public dinners, announces the toasts, calls upon the various speakers, etc. — **toast′mis′tress** (-mis′tris) *n. fem.*

to·bac·co (tə·bak′ō) *n. pl.* **·cos** or **·coes 1** An annual plant of the nightshade family (genus *Nicotiana*), especially *N. tabacum,* the chief source of the tobacco of commerce, originally of tropical America, but now cultivated in various parts of the world. **2** Its leaves prepared in various ways, as for smoking, chewing, snuffing, etc. **3** The use of tobacco for smoking. **4** The various products prepared from tobacco leaves, as cigarettes, cigars, etc. [<Sp. *tabaco* <Cariban, a tube or pipe in which the natives smoked tobacco]

TOBACCO (Plant to 8 feet or more)

tobacco heart *Pathol.* A cardiac disorder brought about by excessive smoking and characterized by a rapid or uneven pulse; nicotinism.

to·bac·co·nist (tə·bak′ə·nist) *n. Brit.* One who deals in tobacco.

tobacco worm Either of two large green worms (*Protoparce sexta* and *P. quinquemaculata*) with white stripes and a slender horn at the rear end of the body, destructive to tobacco plants.

To·ba·go (tō·bā′gō) See TRINIDAD AND TOBAGO.

To·bi·as (tə·bī′əs, tō-; *Dan., Du., Ger., Sp.* tō·bē′äs) A masculine personal name. Also **To·bi′ah** (-bī′ə), *Fr.* **To·bie** (tō·bē′), *Ital.* **To·bi·a** (tō·bē′ä). [<Hebrew, the Lord is (my) good]

To·bit (tō′bit) A pious Hebrew captive in Nineveh, hero of the Apocryphal book of the Old Testament bearing his name.

to·bog·gan (tə·bog′ən) *n.* **1** A light sledlike vehicle, consisting of a long thin board or boards curved upward at the forward end: used for transporting goods or coasting, especially on prepared slides. **2** A luge. — *v.i.* **1** To coast on a toboggan. **2** To move downward swiftly: Wheat prices *tobogganed.* [< dial. F (Canadian) *tabagan* a sleigh <Algonquian. Cf. Micmac *tobākun.*] — **to·bog′gan·er, to·bog′gan·ist** *n.*

toboggan slide A slope prepared for coasting with toboggans: often a winding track with banked curves.

To·bol (tô·bôl′y′) A river in northern Kazakh S.S.R. and SW Asiatic Russian S.F.S.R., flowing 1,042 miles NE from the Ural Mountains of NW central Kazakh S.S.R., near the Russian border, to the Irtish River at Tobolsk.

To·bolsk (tô·bôlsk′) A city in SW Asiatic Russian S.F.S.R., at the junction of the Tobol and Irtish rivers.

To·bruk (tō·bro͝ok′, tō′bro͝ok) A port of eastern Cyrenaica, Libya; scene of several battles of World War II, 1941–42. *Italian* **To·bruch** (tō′·bro͝ok).

to·by (tō′bē) *n. pl.* **·bies 1** A mug or jug for ale or beer, often made in the form of an old man wearing a three-cornered hat. **2** *Colloq.* A form of stogie cigar. [<TOBY]

TOBY JUG

To·by (tō′bē) Diminutive of TOBIAS.

To·can·tins (tō′kän·tēns′) A river in north central and north Brazil, flowing 1,640 miles north to the Pará River.

toc·ca·ta (tə·kä′tə, *Ital.* tôk·kä′tä) *n. Music* A rapid free composition for piano, organ, or other keyboard instrument, often preceding a fugue. [<Ital., lit., a touching, orig. pp. fem. of *toccare* touch]

To·char·i·an (tō·kâr′ē·ən, -kär′-) *n.* **1** One of an ancient cultured people known to the Greeks and Chinese as having inhabited central Asia in the first Christian millennium: conquered by the Uigurs. **2** The language of the Tocharians, belonging to the centum division of the Indo-European language family: unknown before 1904, when it was brought to light through manuscripts of the seventh century found in ruined temples in Chinese Turkestan. Two dialects have been distinguished, usually referred to as *Tocharian A* and *Tocharian B.* Also spelled *Tokharian.*

toch·er (tokh′ər) *Scot.* & *Brit. Dial. n.* The dowry of a bride. — *v.t.* To give a dowry to; dower. [<Irish *tochar* an assigned portion < *tochuirim* I put to, assign < *chuirim* I put]

toco- *combining form* Child; pertaining to children or to childbirth: *tocology.* Also, before vowels, **toc-.** [<Gk. *tokos* child, childbirth]

to·col·o·gy (tō·kol′ə·jē) *n.* The science and art of midwifery; obstetrics: also spelled *tokology.* [<TOCO- + -LOGY]

to·coph·er·ol (tō·kof′ə·rōl, -rol) *n. Biochem.* Any of three closely related alcohols, widely distributed in nature and also made synthetically; especially, alpha-tocopherol, $C_{29}H_{50}O_2$, an active principle of vitamin E. [<TOCO- + Gk. *pherein* bear + -OL[1]; so called because thought to be effective against sterility]

Tocque·ville (tōk·vēl′), **Alexis Charles Henri Maurice Clérel de,** 1805–59, French statesman and political writer.

toc·sin (tok′sin) *n.* **1** A signal sounded on a bell; alarm. **2** An alarm bell. [<MF <OF *toquassen* <Provençal *tocasenh* < *tocar* strike, touch + *senh* a bell <LL *signum* a signal bell <L, a sign]

tod[1] (tod) *n.* **1** A bushy clump. **2** A former weight for wool, about 28 pounds. [ME *todde,* prob. <LG. Cf. East Frisian *todde* small load, bundle.]

tod[2] (tod) *n. Scot.* & *Brit. Dial.* A fox.

to·day (tə·dā′) *adv.* **1** On or during this present day. **2** At the present time; nowadays. — *n.* The present day, time, or age. Also **to-day′.** ◆ Collateral adjective: *hodiernal.* [OE *tō dæg* <*tō* to + *dæg* a day]

Todd (tod), **Sir Alexander R.,** born 1907, English chemist.

tod·dle (tod′l) *v.i.* **·dled, ·dling** To walk unsteadily and with short steps, as a little child. — *n.* The act of toddling; a child's walk; also, a stroll. [? Freq. of TOTTER] — **tod′dler** *n.*

tod·dle-top (tod′l·top′) *n.* Teetotum.

tod·dy (tod′ē) *n. pl.* **·dies 1** A drink made with spirits, hot water, sugar, and a slice of lemon. **2** The sap or juice that flows from the incised spathes of certain East Indian palms; also, a spirituous liquor distilled from it. The principal palms yielding toddy are called **toddy palms,** as the wild date of India (*Phoenix sylvestris*). [<Hind. *tāṛī* toddy (def. 2) < *tāṛ* palm tree <Skt. *tāla* a palmyra]

Tod·le·ben (tōt′lā·bən) See TOTLEBEN.

to-do (tə·do͞o′) *n. Colloq.* Confusion or bustle, as on account of something disturbing; a demonstration; a fuss. [OE *to-dōn* < *to-* asunder + *dōn* do, put]

Todt (tōt), **Fritz,** 1891–1942, German military engineer.

to·dy (tō′dē) *n. pl.* **·dies** Any of numerous very small insectivorous West Indian birds (genus *Todus*) related to the kingfishers; especially, the **green tody** (*Todus godus*) of Jamaica, bright green with a scarlet throat. ◆ Homophone: *toady.* [<F *todier* <L *todus,* a kind of small bird]

toe (tō) *n.* **1** One of the digits of the foot; also, the forward part of the foot, as distinguished from the *heel.* **2** That portion of a shoe, boot, sock, stocking, skate, or the like that covers, or corresponds in position with, the toes. **3** The lower end or projection of something, resembling or suggestive of a toe. **4** *Mech.* **a** A pivot or journal in a bearing. **b** A horizontally projecting arm on a stem, as for operating a valve, raised by a cam or lifted. **5** The end of the head of a golf club. **6** In a railroad switch, the space between the rails at the unchanneled end of a frog. — **on one's toes** Alert; wide-awake. — **to tread on (someone's) toes** To offend (a person); trespass on (someone's) feelings, opinions, prejudices, etc. — *v.* **toed, toe·ing** *v.t.* **1** To touch with the toes: to *toe* the line. **2** To kick with the toe. **3** To furnish with a toe. **4** To drive (a nail or spike) obliquely; also, to attach (beams, etc.) end to end, by nails driven thus. **5** To strike (a golf ball) with the toe of the club. — *v.i.* **6** To stand or walk with the toes pointing in a specified direction: to *toe* out. — **to toe the mark** To touch a certain line or mark with the toes preparatory to starting a race; hence, to abide by the rules; conform to discipline or a standard. [OE *tā*] — **toe′less** *adj.*

toe cap A cap covering for the tip or toe of a boot or shoe. See illustration under SHOE.

toe crack A sandcrack.

toed (tōd) *adj.* **1** Having toes: chiefly in composition: pigeon-*toed.* **2** Fastened or fastening by obliquely driven nails; also, driven obliquely, as a nail.

toe-dance (tō′dans′, -däns′) *v.i.* **-danced, -danc·ing** To dance on tiptoe; perform a toe dance. — **toe′-danc′er** *n.*

toe dance A dance performed on tiptoe.

toe·hold (tō′hōld′) *n.* **1** In climbing, a small space which supports the toes. **2** Any means of entrance, support, or the like; a footing: The Marines gained a *toehold* on the island. **3** A hold in which a wrestler bends back the foot of his opponent.

toe·nail (tō′nāl′) *n.* **1** A nail growing on the toe. **2** A nail driven obliquely to hold the foot of a stud or brace. — *v.t.* To fasten with obliquely driven nails.

toff (tof, tôf) *n. Brit. Slang* A dandy; also, a gentleman. [Earlier *toft* <TUFT (def. 3)]

tof·fee, tof·fy (tôf′ē, tof′ē) See TAFFY.

toft (tôft, toft) *n. Brit.* **1** Land once occupied as a messuage, on which the buildings have decayed or been burned; a homestead. **2** A hillock or knoll. [OE, a homestead <ON *topt, tupt*]

tog (tog) *Colloq. n.* **1** A coat. **2** *pl.* Clothes; outfit: football *togs.* — *v.t.* **togged, tog·ging** To dress; clothe: often with *up* or *out.* [Short for vagabond's cant *togemans, togman* coat, cloak <F *toge* a toga <L *toga*]

to·ga (tō′gə) *n. pl.* **·gas** or **·gae** (-jē) **1** The distinctive outer garment worn in public by a citizen of ancient Rome. **2** Any gown or cloak characteristic of a calling or profession: the lawyer's *toga.* [<L < *tegere* cover]

ROMAN TOGA

to·gaed (tō′gəd) *adj.* Robed in the toga; hence, classical and stately. Also **to·gat·ed** (tō′gā·tid).

to·ga vi·ri·lis (tō′gə vi·rī′lis) *Latin* The toga assumed by a male citizen of ancient Rome at the age of 14 as a token of manhood.

to·geth·er (to͝o·geth′ər, tə-) *adv.* **1** Into union or contact with each other; conjointly. **2** In the same place or at the same spot; with each other; in company. **3** At the same moment of time; simultaneously. **4** Without cessation or intermission. **5** With one another; mutually. [OE *tōgædere, tōgadore* < *tō* to + *gædre* together. Akin to GATHER.]

to·geth·er·ness (to͝o·geth′ər·nis, tə-) *n.* The state of being associated or united.

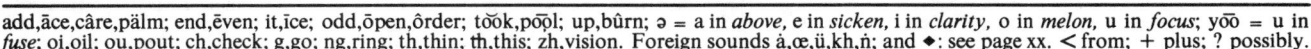

tog·ger·y (tog′ər·ē) *n.* *pl.* **·ger·ies** *Colloq.* Togs collectively; clothes.

tog·gle (tog′əl) *n.* **1** A pin, or short rod, properly attached in the middle, as to a rope, and designed to be passed through a hole or eye and turned. **2** A toggle iron. **3** A toggle joint. — *v.t.* **·gled, ·gling** To fix, fasten, or furnish with a toggle or toggles. [Prob. nautical var. of dial. *tuggle,* appar. freq. of TUG]

toggle iron A harpoon, as for killing whales, so arranged as to turn crosswise when it enters the animal's body. Also **toggle harpoon.**

toggle joint *Mech.* A joint having a central hinge like an elbow, and operable by applying the power at the junction, thus changing the direction of motion and giving indefinite mechanical pressure.

TOGGLE JOINT Level Type

toggle switch *Electr.* A switch in the form of a projecting lever whose movement through a small arc opens or closes an electric circuit.

To·gliat·ti (tō·lyät′tē), **Palmiro,** 1893–1964, leader of the Italian Communist party.

To·go (tō′gō) An independent republic in western Africa; 22,008 square miles; capital, Lomé: formerly French Togoland, a United Nations Trust Territory. — **To′go·lese′** (-lēs, -lēz) *adj.* & *n.*

To·go (tō·gō), **Count Heihachiro,** 1847–1934, Japanese admiral; defeated the Russian fleet at the battle of Tsushima, 1905.

To·go·land (tō′gō·land), **British** See GHANA.

Togoland, French See TOGO.

toil[1] (toil) *n.* **1** Fatiguing work; labor; hence, any oppressive task. **2** Any notable work accomplished by labor. **3** *Obs.* Strife; struggle. — *v.i.* **1** To work arduously; labor painfully and tiringly. **2** To progress or make one's way with slow and labored steps. — *v.t.* **3** To accomplish or obtain by toil. See synonyms under STRUGGLE. [<AF *toil* a dispute, OF *tooil* trouble <AF *toiler* strive, OF *tooillier* soil, agitate <L *tudiculare* stir about < *tudicula* a machine for bruising olives, dim. of *tudes* a mallet] — **toil′er** *n.*

Synonyms (noun): drudgery, labor, stent, stint, task, travail, work. *Work* is exertion of body or mind that taxes the powers for the accomplishment of some end. The term is a broad one; *work* may be light and pleasant, or severe and exhausting. *Labor* is always strenuous; it is hard *work. Toil* is still more severe. One may enjoy *work* and be cheerful in *labor,* but *toil* oppresses. *Drudgery* is often applied to menial service, but also to any *work* that is not only hard, but dull and mechanical. A *task* is a definite amount of *work* appointed and required by another; yet we sometimes speak of a *task* which one imposes upon himself; this in popular language is called a *stint* or *stent.* See TASK, WORK. *Antonyms*: amusement, ease, idleness, leisure, play, recreation, relaxation, repose, rest.

toil[2] (toil) *n.* A net, snare, or other trap: now generally used figuratively and commonly in the plural. [<MF *toiles* nets < *toile* cloth <OF *teile* <L *tela* a web]

toile (twäl) *n.* A sheer linen fabric; also, a fine cretonne with scenic designs printed in one color. [<F. See TOIL[2].]

toi·let (toi′lit) *n.* **1** A fixture in the shape of a bowl, used for urination and defecation. **2** A lavatory or watercloset; also, a bathroom. **3** The act or process of dressing oneself; formerly, especially of dressing the hair. **4** Attire; toilette; also, a toilette or costume. — *adj.* Used in dressing or grooming: *toilet* articles. [<F *toilette* orig. a cloth dressing gown, dim. of *toile* cloth. See TOIL[2].]

toi·let·ry (toi′lit·rē) *n.* *pl.* **·ries** Any of the several articles used in making one's toilet, as soap, comb, brush, etc.

toi·lette (toi·let′, *Fr.* twà·let′) *n.* **1** The act or process of grooming oneself, usually including bathing, hair–dressing, application of cosmetics and perfume, and costuming. **2** A person's actual dress or style of dress; also, any specific costume or gown: an elaborate *toilette.* [<F. See TOILET.]

toilet water A scented liquid containing a small amount of alcohol, used in or after the bath, after shaving, etc.

toil·ful (toil′fəl) *adj.* Replete with toil; laborious. — **toil′ful·ly** *adv.*

toil·some (toil′səm) *adj.* Accomplished with fatigue; involving toil. See synonyms under ARDUOUS, DIFFICULT. — **toil′some·ly** *adv.*

toil·worn (toil′wôrn′, -wōrn′) *adj.* Exhausted by toil; showing the effects of toil.

toit (toit) *v.i.* *Brit. Dial.* **1** To dawdle; saunter. **2** To totter. Also spelled *toyte.* [Origin uncertain]

To·jo (tō·jō), **Hideki,** 1885–1948, Japanese general and statesman in World War II.

To·kay (tō·kā′) *n.* **1** A white or reddish–blue grape from Tokay, Hungary. **2** A wine made from it. [from *Tokay,* a town in northern Hungary]

To·ke·lau (tō′kə·lou′) A New Zealand island group north of Samoa; 4 square miles: also *Union Islands.*

to·ken (tō′kən) *n.* **1** Anything indicative of some other thing; a visible sign; indication; evidence: in *token* of respect. **2** A symbol: This gift is a *token* of my affection. **3** *Obs.* A signal. **4** Some tangible proof or evidence of a statement or of one's identity, authority, etc. **5** A memento; keepsake; souvenir. **6** A characteristic mark or feature. **7** A piece of metal issued as currency and having a face value greater than its actual value. **8** A piece of metal issued by a transportation company and good for one fare. See synonyms under EMBLEM, MARK[1], SIGN, TRACE[1]. — *v.t.* To evidence by a token; betoken. — *adj.* Done or given as a token, especially in partial fulfilment of an obligation or engagement: a *token* payment. [OE *tācen, tācn*]

to·kened (tō′kənd) *adj.* *Obs.* Marked by spots: the *tokened* pestilence. [<TOKEN, in obs. sense "a spot on the body indicating disease"]

to·ken·ism (tō′kən·iz·əm) *n.* The policy of attempting to meet certain obligations or conditions by symbolic or token efforts.

To·khar·i·an (tō·kâr′ē·ən, -kär′-) See TOCHARIAN.

to·kol·o·gy (tō·kol′ə·jē) See TOCOLOGY.

To·ku·shi·ma (tō·ko͞o·shē·mä) A port of eastern Shikoku, Japan.

To·ky·o (tō′kē·ō, *Japanese* tō·kyō) The capital of Japan, a port on **Tokyo Bay,** an inlet of the Philippine Sea in central Honshu, Japan: formerly *Edo* or *Yedo.* Also **To′ki·o.**

to·la (tō′lä) *n.* *Anglo–Indian* A weight, about 180 grains, for gold and silver; the weight of one rupee. [<Hind. <Skt. *tulā* a balance, weight < *tul-* weigh]

to·lan (tō′lan) *n.* A white crystalline unsaturated hydrocarbon, $C_{14}H_{10}$, prepared by synthesis. Also **to·lane** (tō′lān). [<TOL(UENE) + -ANE[2]]

tol·booth (tōl′bo͞oth′, -bo͞oth′) See TOLLBOOTH.

told (tōld) Past tense and past participle of TELL.

tole[1] (tōl) *v.t.* **toled, tol·ing** **1** *Dial.* To draw as with a lure; entice; decoy. **2** *Obs.* To pull; drag; draw. Also spelled *toll.* [Var. of TOLL[2]]

tole[2] (tōl) *n.* A metalware, enameled or lacquered in various colors and frequently gilded: esteemed as an ornamental material. Also **tôle.** ◆ Homophone: *toll.* [<F *tôle* sheet iron, dial. var. of *table* a table]

To·le·do (tə·lē′dō) *n.* *pl.* **·dos** A sword or sword blade from Toledo, Spain. Also **to·le′do.**

To·le·do (tə·lē′dō) **1** A city in NW Ohio near Lake Erie. **2** (*Sp.* tō·lā′thō) An ancient city of central Spain on the Tagus.

tol·er·a·ble (tol′ər·ə·bəl) *adj.* **1** Passably good; commonplace. **2** Endurable; capable of being borne. **3** Allowable. **4** *Colloq.* In passably good health. [<OF <L *tolerabilis* able to endure < *tolerare* endure] — **tol′er·a·ble·ness** *n.* — **tol′er·a·bly** *adv.*

tol·er·ance (tol′ər·əns) *n.* **1** The character, state, or quality of being tolerant. **2** Indulgence or forbearance in judging the opinions, customs, or acts of others; freedom from bigotry or from racial or religious prejudice. **3** The act of enduring, or the capacity for endurance. **4** *Mech.* A fractional allowance for variations from the specified standard weight, dimensions, etc., of mechanical constructions. **5** A legally permissible variation from the standard of weight, fineness, etc., of coins: also called *remedy.* **6** *Med.* Natural or acquired ability to endure without ill effects large or increasing amounts of specified substances, particularly drugs.

tol·er·ant (tol′ər·ənt) *adj.* **1** Of a long–suffering disposition. **2** Indulgent; liberal. **3** *Med.* Capable of taking with impunity unusual or excessive doses of dangerous drugs. [<F <L *tolerans, -antis,* ppr. of *tolerare* endure] — **tol′er·ant·ly** *adv.*

tol·er·ate (tol′ə·rāt) *v.t.* **·at·ed, ·at·ing** **1** To allow to be or be done without active opposition. **2** To concede, as the right to opinions or participation. **3** To bear, sustain, or be capable of enduring or sustaining. **4** *Med.* To endure, as a poisonous amount of dose, with impunity. See synonyms under ABIDE, ALLOW, ENDURE, PERMIT. [<L *toleratus,* pp. of *tolerare* endure] — **tol′er·a′tive** *adj.* — **tol′er·a′tor** *n.*

tol·er·a·tion (tol′ə·rā′shən) *n.* **1** The act or practice of tolerance. **2** The recognition of the rights of the individual to his own opinions and customs, as in matters pertaining to religious worship, when they do not interfere with the rights of others or with decency and order. **3** The spirit and desire to be tolerant in matters of opinion; forbearance; freedom from bigotry or race prejudice.

tol·i·dine (tol′ə·dēn, -din) *n.* *Chem.* One of several isomeric bases, $(CH_3 \cdot C_6H_3 \cdot NH_2)_2$, derived from dimethyl benzidine: one form is used in making dyes. Also **tol′i·din** (-din). [<TOL(UOL) + (BENZ)IDINE]

To·li·ma (tō·lē′mä), **Ne·va·da del** (nā·vä′thä thel) A volcano in the Andes Mountains of west central Colombia; 18,438 feet; last eruption, 1829.

toll[1] (tōl) *n.* **1** A fixed compensation for some privilege granted or service rendered, especially for one granted in a general or public way, as passage on a bridge or turnpike, or that taken by a miller for grinding grain (commonly a portion of the grain). **2** The right to levy such charge. **3** Something taken or elicited like a toll; price: The train wreck took a heavy *toll* of lives. **4** A due charged for the privilege of shipping or landing goods. **5** A charge for transportation of goods, especially by rail or canal. **6** A charge for a long–distance telephone call. See synonyms under TAX. — *v.t.* To take as a toll. — *v.i.* To take or exact a toll. ◆ Homophone: *tole.* [OE, ? <LL *toloneum* <L *telonium* <Gk. *telōnion* a customhouse < *telōnes* a tax collector < *telos* a tax]

toll[2] (tōl) *v.t.* **1** To cause (a bell) to sound slowly and at regular intervals. **2** To announce thus; especially, to announce (a death, funeral, etc.) by tolling. **3** To call or summon by tolling. **4** To decoy (game, especially ducks). **5** *Rare* To entice. — *v.i.* **6** To sound slowly and at regular intervals. — *n.* The sound of a bell rung slowly and with single, regularly repeated strokes. ◆ Homophone: *tole.* [Prob. <TOLL[1], in obs. sense of "pull, draw"]

toll·age (tō′lij) *n.* **1** A charge in the nature of a toll. **2** The toll itself.

toll·bar (tōl′bär′) *n.* A tollgate, properly one with a single bar.

toll·booth (tōl′bo͞oth′, -bo͞oth′) *n.* **1** *Scot.* A jail; prison: also spelled *tolbooth.* **2** A tollhouse.

toll bridge A bridge at which toll for passage is paid.

toll call A long–distance telephone call, charged for at more than local rates.

toll collector A collector of tolls.

toll·er (tō′lər) *n.* **1** One who tolls a bell. **2** A bell used for tolling. **3** A small dog trained to toll or decoy ducks.

Tol·ler (tôl′ər), **Ernst,** 1893–1939, German dramatist and politician.

toll·gate (tōl′gāt′) *n.* A gate at the entrance to a bridge, or on a road, at which toll is paid.

toll·house (tōl′hous′) *n.* A toll collector's lodge adjoining a tollgate.

toll·keep·er (tōl′kē′pər) *n.* One who keeps a tollgate.

toll line A telephone line or channel, as between two central offices in different exchanges, for the use of which a toll is charged; a long–distance circuit.

Tol·stoy (tol′stoi, tōl′-; *Russian* tol·stoi′), **Count Leo Nikolaevich,** 1828–1910, Russian novelist and social reformer. Also **Tol′stoi.**

Tol·tec (tol′tek, tōl′-) *n.* One of certain ancient Nahuatlan tribes that dominated central and southern Mexico about A.D. 900–1100 and through contact with Mayan culture founded the highly civilized Nahua culture of the Aztecs: referred to in Aztec and Mayan legend. See NAHUA. — *adj.* Of or pertaining to the Toltecs. [<Nahuatl *Tolteca*] — **Tol′tec·an** *adj.*

to·lu (tə·lo͞o′) *n.* Balsam of Tolu. [<Sp. *tolú,*

from Santiago de *Tolu*, a seaport in Colombia]

tol·u·ate (tol′yo͞o·āt) *n. Chem.* A salt or ester of a toluic acid. [<TOLU(IC) + -ATE[3]]

To·lu·ca (tō·lo͞o′kä) The capital of Mexico state, central Mexico. Also **Toluca de Ler·do** (thā ler′thō).

tol·u·ene (tol′yo͞o·ēn) *n. Chem.* A limpid hydrocarbon, $C_6H_5CH_3$, of the aromatic series, homologous with benzene, and obtained from coal tar by distillation: it is used in making dyestuffs and explosives. [<TOLU + -ENE; so called because orig. obtained from tolu]

to·lu·ic (tə·lo͞o′ik, tol′yo͞o·ik) *adj. Chem.* Designating or pertaining to any one of four isomeric acid derivatives of toluene, $C_8H_8O_2$, occurring as white crystalline compounds. [<TOLU(ENE) + -IC]

tol·u·ide (tol′yo͞o·īd, -id) *n. Chem.* One of a series of compounds obtained from toluene by substituting a tolyl radical for hydrogen in the amino group. Also **tol′u·id** (-id). [<TOLU(ENE) + -IDE]

to·lu·i·dine (tə·lo͞o′ə·dēn, -din) *n. Chem.* One of three isomeric compounds, C_7H_9N, homologous with aniline and derived from the nitro-compounds of toluene. Also **to·lu′i·din** (-din). [<TOLUID(E) + -INE[2]]

tol·u·ol (tol′yo͞o·ōl, -ol) *n. Chem.* Crude commercial toluene. Also **tol′u·ole** (-ōl). [<TOLU + (BENZ)OL]

tol·u·yl (tol′yo͞o·il) *n. Chem.* The univalent acid radical C_8H_7O. [<TOLU(IC) + -YL]

tol·yl (tol′il) *n. Chem.* The univalent radical $C_6H_4CH_3$, derived from toluene; cresyl. [<TOL(UIC) + -YL]

tom (tom) *n.* **1** The male of various animals, especially the cat. **2** *U.S. Slang* An Uncle Tom; a servile Negro. —*adj.* Male: a *tom* pheasant. [from the personal name *Tom*]

Tom (tom) Diminutive of THOMAS.

Tom (tom) A river in SW central Asiatic Russian S.F.S.R., flowing 440 miles west and NW, from east Stalinsk to the Ob river NW of Tomsk.

tom·a·hawk (tom′ə·hôk) *n.* A war weapon used by the Algonquian Indians of North America, originally a carved club about three feet long, having a knob of solid wood on the end in which a piece of bone or metal was inserted; later, the light ax or hatchet-shaped weapon with an iron blade obtained in trade with Europeans. Tomahawks were either thrown or wielded in the hand. —*v.t.* To strike or kill with a tomahawk. [<Algonquian *tamahak*, short for *tamahaken* a cutting utensil < *tamahaken* he uses for cutting < *tamaham* he cuts]

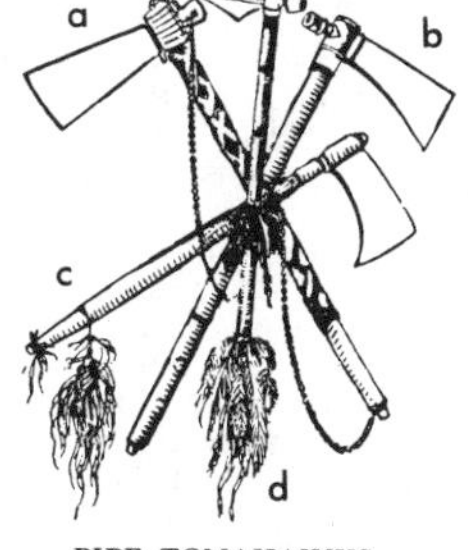

PIPE TOMAHAWKS
a. Cree. *b.* Iroquois. *c.* Omaha. *d.* Osage.

tom·al·ley (tom′al·ē) *n.* The liver of the lobster, turning green when cooked: considered a great delicacy. Also **to·mal·ly** (tə·mal′ē). [Prob. <Cariban]

to·man (tō·män′) *n.* A Persian gold coin of varying value: formerly a money of account. [<Persian *tūmān, tumān, tuman* <Turki, lit., ten thousand]

Tom-and-Jer·ry (tom′ən·jer′ē) *n.* A drink made with brandy, rum, beaten egg, hot milk or water, sugar, and nutmeg. [after Corinthian *Tom* and *Jerry* Hawthorn, two main characters in *Life in London*, 1821, by Pierce Egan, 1772–1849, English writer on sports and sports jargon]

To·más (tō·mäs′) Spanish form of THOMAS.

to·ma·tin (tə·mā′tin, -mä′-) *n.* An antibiotic extracted from the leaves and plants of the tomato plant and also from the leaf juices of potatoes and green peppers. [<TOMAT(O) + -IN]

to·ma·to (tə·mā′tō, -mä′-) *n. pl.* **·toes** **1** The pulpy edible berry, yellow or red when ripe, of a tropical American perennial plant (*Lycopersicon esculentum*) of the nightshade family, highly esteemed as a vegetable. **2** The plant itself. **3** *U.S. Slang* A girl or woman. [<Sp. *tomate* <Nahuatl *tomatl*]

tomato fruitworm The bollworm.

tomb (to͞om) *n.* **1** A place for the burial of the dead; a vault; grave. **2** A place where the dead lie. **3** Death itself. **4** A tombstone. —*v.t.* To entomb; bury; inter. [<AF *tumbe*, OF *tombe* <LL *tumba* <Gk. *tymbos* a mound]

tom·bac (tom′bak) *n.* Any of several copper-and-zinc alloys used to make gongs and bells in the East, and cheap jewelry in Europe: often spelled *tambac*. Also **tom′back, tom′·bak.** [<F <Pg. <Malayan *tambāga* copper <Skt. *tāmraka*]

Tom·big·bee River (tom·big′bē) A river in NE Mississippi and SW Alabama, flowing 384 miles SE and south to a junction with the Alabama River, forming the Mobile River, 30 miles north of Mobile Bay.

Tom·bouc·tou (tôṅ·bo͝ok·to͞o′) The French name for TIMBUKTU.

tom·boy (tom′boi′) *n.* A girl of romping and boisterous conduct; hoyden. [<TOM + BOY] —**tom′boy′ish** *adj.* —**tom′boy′ish·ness** *n.*

Tombs (to͞omz), **the** Formerly, the New York City police prison: so called from the funereal appearance of the building in which it was housed until 1948; also, loosely, the prison which replaced the original Tombs.

tomb·stone (to͞om′stōn′) *n.* A stone, usually inscribed, marking a place of burial.

Tomb·stone (to͞om′stōn) A city in SE Arizona; formerly the site of the richest gold mines in Arizona.

tom·cat (tom′kat′) *n.* A male cat. [after *Tom*, a male cat, hero of *The Life and Adventures of a Cat*, 1760, a very popular anonymous work]

tom·cod (tom′kod) *n.* Any of several small edible fishes (genus *Microgadus*) common on the Atlantic coast of North America. [<TOM + COD]

Tom Collins A drink consisting of gin, lemon or lime juice, sugar, and carbonated water.

Tom, Dick, and Harry Any persons taken at random from the crowd: used disparagingly, and often preceded by *every*.

tome (tōm) *n.* A volume, particularly if large; originally, one of a series of volumes. [<MF <L *tomus* <Gk. *tomos* a fragment, volume < *temnein* cut]

-tome *combining form* A cutting instrument (of a specified kind): *microtome*. [<Gk. *tomos* a cutting < *temnein* cut]

to·men·tose (tə·men′tōs, tō′men·tōs) *adj. Biol.* Covered with matted woolly hairs; flocculent. Also **to·men′tous** (-təs). [<L *tomentosus* < *tomentum* a stuffing for cushions]

to·men·tum (tə·men′təm) *n. pl.* **·ta** (-tə) **1** *Anat.* A network of small blood vessels of the pia mater where applied to the brain or spinal cord. **2** *Bot.* A form of pubescence composed of matted woolly hairs. [<L. See TOMENTOSE.]

tom·fool (tom′fo͞ol′) *n.* **1** An idiotic or silly person. **2** An amusing trifler. —*adj.* Ridiculous; very stupid. [after *Tom Fool*, a name formerly applied to mental defectives]

tom·fool·er·y (tom′fo͞ol′ər·ē) *n. pl.* **·er·ies** **1** Nonsensical behavior. **2** Kickshaws. Also **tom′fool′ish·ness.**

tom-ful·ler (tom′fo͝ol′ər) *n.* Sour or fermented hominy prepared as food: originally a Choctaw Indian dish. Also **tom′ful′la** (-fo͝ol′ə), **tom fuller.** [<Choctaw *tahfula* hominy]

Tom·ma·si·ni (tôm′mä·zē′nē), **Vicenzo,** 1880–1950, Italian composer.

tom·my[1] (tom′ē) *n. pl.* **·mies** *Slang* A roll; a loaf or piece of bread. [< *brown Tommy* < *Tommy Brown*, appar. a personification of brown bread]

tom·my[2] (tom′ē) *n. pl.* **·mies** Provisions or goods given instead of money in payment of wages; also, the system of paying workmen partly or entirely in kind. [Short for *tommy-shop*, a store run on the truck system]

tom·my[3] (tom′ē) *n. pl.* **·mies** A Tommy Atkins; a British soldier: also **Tom′my.** [Short for TOMMY ATKINS]

Tom·my (tom′ē) Diminutive of THOMAS.

Tommy At·kins (at′kinz) A British private of the regular army. [after *Thomas Atkins*, a name used on specimen forms in the official regulations of the British Army after 1815]

Tommy gun A Thompson submachine gun. [<*Tommy*, dim. of *Thompson* + GUN]

to·mo·dro·mic (tō′mə·drō′mik, -drom′ik) *adj.* Having a flight path which cuts athwart a moving target; heading to cut or intercept: said of guided missiles. [<Gk. *tomos* cutting (< *temnein* cut) + *dromos* a running < *dramein* run]

to·mog·ra·phy (tō·mog′rə·fē) *n. Med.* X-ray photography of a predetermined plane of the body, with a blurring or elimination of details in other planes. [<Gk. *tomos* a slice (< *temnein* cut) + (PHOTO)GRAPHY]

to·mor·row (tə·môr′ō, -mor′ō) *adv.* On or for the next day after today. —*n.* The next day after today; the morrow. Also **to-mor′row.** [OE *tō morgen* < *tō* to + *morgen* morning, morrow]

tom·pi·on (tom′pē·ən) *n. Mil.* A stopper, as the plug put into the mouth of a cannon, to exclude moisture, etc.: also called *tampion*. [Var. of TAMPION]

Tomsk (tomsk, *Russian* tômsk) A city in west central Siberia, Russian S.F.S.R.

Tom Thumb In English folklore, the son of a plowman, as big as his father's thumb, who undergoes many adventures, including being swallowed by a cow and a giant. —**General Tom Thumb** The stage name of Charles Sherwood Stratton, 1838–83, a dwarf exhibited by P. T. Barnum.

tom·tit (tom′tit′) *n.* **1** A tit; titmouse. **2** Any of various small birds, as a chickadee or a wren. [<TOM + TIT[1]]

tom-tom (tom′tom′) *n.* **1** The native drum of India, Africa, etc., variously shaped, and usually beaten with the hands. **2** A percussion instrument of monotonous tone, used in some modern orchestras for special effects. **3** A copper or copper-alloy disk-shaped instrument sounded with a felt-covered hammer or stick; a Chinese gong. Also spelled *tam-tam*. [<Hind. *tamtam*, imit. of the instrument's sound]

-tomy *combining form* **1** *Surg.* A cutting of a (specified) part or tissue: *osteotomy*. **2** A (specified) kind of cutting or division: *dichotomy*. [<Gk. *tomē* a cutting < *temnein* cut]

ton[1] (tun) *n.* **1** Any of several large measures of weight; particularly, the **short ton** of 2000 pounds avoirdupois, commonly used in the United States and Canada; the **long ton** of 2240 pounds of Great Britain; or the **metric ton** of 1000 kilograms. **2** A unit for reckoning the displacement or weight of vessels, 35 cubic feet of sea water weighing about one long ton: called **displacement ton. 3** A unit for reckoning the freight-carrying capacity of a ship, usually equivalent to 40 cubic feet of space but varying with the cargo: called **freight ton, measurement ton. 4** A unit for reckoning the internal capacity of merchant vessels for purposes of registration, equivalent to 100 cubic feet or 2.832 cubic meters: called **register ton.** [Var. of TUN; infl. in form by OF *tonne* a cask]

ton[2] (tôṅ) *n. French* Tone; style; the prevailing fashion; vogue.

ton- Var. of TONO-.

-ton *suffix* Town: used in place names: *Charleston, Brockton*. [OE *-tun* < *tun* a town]

to·nal (tō′nəl) *adj.* Of or pertaining to tone or tonality. —**to′nal·ly** *adv.*

to·nal·ite (tō′nəl·īt) *n.* A quartz-mica diorite. Also **to′nal·yte.** [from *Tonale*, in the Tirol, where it was first described]

to·nal·i·ty (tō·nal′ə·tē) *n. pl.* **·ties** **1** *Music* The quality and peculiarity of a tonal system; the melodic and harmonic relations between the tones of a scale or system of tones; a key or mode. **2** The general color scheme or collective tones of a painting. **3** Tonicity.

to-name (to͞o′nām′) *n. Scot.* **1** Some special distinguishing name; nickname. **2** A surname. [OE *tō-nama*]

to·na·pha·si·a (tō′nə·fā′zhē·ə, -zhə) *n. Psychiatry* Inability to recall a familiar tune; musical aphasia. [<NL <L *tonus* TONE + Gk. *aphasia* inability to speak]

tone (tōn) *n.* **1** Sound in relation to quality, volume, duration, and pitch. **2** *Physics* A sound having a definite pitch, and due to vibration of a sounding body. The pitch of a tone depends on rate of vibration and its force on amplitude of vibration; its timbre is a complex resultant of concomitant vibration. If the vibration is simple harmonic motion the tone is pure; if there are complex components, the one of lowest pitch is the **fundamental tone** and the other components, in a simple ratio to the lowest, are **partial tones** or *overtones.* The combined result of all the partial tones gives the quality or *timbre* of the tone. **3** *Music* **a** The timbre, or peculiar characteristic sound, as of a voice or instrument. **b** The interval corresponding to one degree of the scale or staff; two semitones: sometimes called a **major tone** or **whole tone,** in distinction from a *semitone.* **4** A predominating disposition; especially, a frame or condition of mind; mood. **5 a** Characteristic style or tendency; tenor; quality: a want of moral *tone.* **b** Style or distinction; elegance: The party had *tone.* **6** Vocal inflection as expressive of feeling: a *tone* of pity. **7** *Ling.* A musical intonation or modulation of the voice by which a word or phrase may be changed in meaning or function: Peking Chinese distinguishes four *tones.* **8** *Phonet.* **a** The acoustical pitch, or change in pitch, of a phrase or sentence: In English, a questioning is indicated by a rising *tone.* **b** Special stress or accent given to one syllable of a word, or to one of the words in a sentence or phrase. **9** The prevailing effect of a picture, due to the management of chiaroscuro and to the effect of light upon the quality of color. **10** A shade, hue, tint, or degree of a particular color, or some slight modification of it: a deep *tone* of yellow; red with a purplish *tone.* **11** *Phot.* The shade or color of a photographic positive picture; also, the color of a negative film. **12** *Physiol.* The general condition of the body with reference to the vigorous and healthy discharge of its functions. See synonyms under SOUND[1]. — *v.* **toned, ton·ing** *v.t.* **1** To give tone to; modify in tone. **2** To tune or modify with reference to musical quality, as an instrument. **3** To intone in monotonous recitative; intone. **4** To alter the color or increase the brilliancy of (a photographic print) by a chemical bath. — *v.i.* **5** To assume a certain tone or hue. **6** To blend or harmonize, as in tone or shade. — **to tone down 1** To subdue the tone of (a painting). **2** To moderate in quality or tone. — **to tone up 1** To raise in quality or strength. **2** To elevate in pitch. **3** To gain in vitality. [<OF *ton* <L *tonus* <Gk. *tonos* a pitch of voice, a stretching < *teinein* stretch] — **ton'er** *n.*

Tone (tōn), **Wolfe,** 1763–98, Irish revolutionist and author.

tone color Timbre.

tone·less (tōn'lis) *adj.* Having no tone; without tone. — **tone'less·ly** *adv.* — **tone'less·ness** *n.*

tone poem A symphonic poem.

to·net·ic (tō·net'ik) *adj. Ling.* Tonic. [<TONE + (PHON)ETIC]

tong[1] (tông, tong) *v.t.* To gather, collect, or seize with tongs. — *v.i.* To use or fish with tongs. [<TONGS]

tong[2] (tông, tong) *n.* A Chinese closed society; in the United States, a secret society composed of Chinese. [<Chinese *t'ang* a hall, meeting place]

ton·ga (tong'gə) *n. Anglo-Indian* A light two-wheeled cart for four persons, in use in the country districts of India. [<Hind. *tāngā*]

Ton·ga (tong'gə) *n.* A Polynesian language spoken in the Tonga Islands.

Ton·ga Islands (tong'gə) An island group SE of the Fiji Islands in the South Pacific, comprising an independent Polynesian kingdom under British protection; total, 270 square miles; capital, Nukualofa: also *Friendly Islands.*

Ton·ga·land (tong'gə·land) A region of Zululand on the Mozambique border.

Ton·ga·re·va (tông'ä·rā'vä) See PENRHYN.

tongs (tôngz, tongz) *n. pl. (sometimes construed as singular)* **1** An implement for grasping, holding, or lifting objects, consisting usually of a pair of pivoted levers: also called **pair of tongs. 2** One of various grasping mechanisms. [OE *tang, tange*]

tongue (tung) *n.* **1** A protrusile, freely moving organ situated in the mouth of most vertebrates and supported by the hyoid bone: most completely developed in mammals, where it is important in taking in and masticating food, as one of the organs of taste, and in man as an organ of speech. ◆ Collateral adjective: *lingual.* **2** An organ or part of the mouth of various insects and fishes, having a similar shape or function. **3** An animal's tongue, as of beef, prepared as food. **4** The power of speech or articulation: to lose one's *tongue.* **5** Manner or style of speaking: a smooth *tongue.* **6** Mere speech, as contrasted with fact or deed. **7** Utterance; talk; discourse. **8** A language, vernacular, or dialect. **9** *Archaic* A people or race, regarded as having its own language: a Biblical use. **10** Anything resembling an animal tongue in appearance, shape, or function. **11** A slender projection of land, as a cape or small promontory. **12** A long narrow bay or inlet of water. **13** A jet of flame. **14** A strip of leather for closing the gap in the front of a laced shoe. **15** The fastening pin of a brooch or buckle. **16** *Music* The free or vibrating end of a reed in a wind instrument. **17** The clapper of a bell. **18** The harnessing pole of a horse-drawn vehicle. **19** The pointed, movable rail in a street railway switch. **20** *Mech.* Any flange or projecting part of a machine or mechanical device. **21** A projecting edge or tenon of a board for insertion into a corresponding groove of another board, thus forming a **tongue-and-groove joint. 22** A spike on a sword blade on which the hilt is secured. **23** The movable arm of a bevel. **24** A small, young sole. See synonyms under LANGUAGE. — **gift of tongues** See under GIFT. — **to hold one's tongue** To keep silent. — **with tongue in cheek** With mental reservations; facetiously; insincerely. — *v.* **tongued, tongu·ing** *v.t.* **1** To use the tongue in playing (a wind instrument) so as to produce marcato or staccato effects; also, to modify the sound of (a flute, cornet, etc.) by the use of the tongue. **2** To touch or lap with the tongue. **3 a** To cut a tongue on (a board). **b** To join or fit by a tongue-and-groove joint. **4** *Poetic* To utter; articulate. **5** *Archaic* To reproach; chide. — *v.i.* **6** To use the tongue in playing a wind instrument. **7** To talk or prattle. **8** To extend as a tongue. [OE *tunge.* Akin to LANGUAGE.]

TONGUE AND GROOVE

tongued (tungd) *adj.* Having a tongue: chiefly in compounds: four-*tongued.*

tongue·grass (tung'gras', -gräs') *n.* Peppergrass.

tongue·less (tung'lis) *adj.* Having no tongue; hence, speechless.

tongue-tie (tung'tī') *n.* Abnormal shortness of the frenum of the tongue, whereby its motion is impeded or confined. — *v.t.* **1** To deprive of speech or the power of speech, or of distinct articulation. **2** To bewilder or amaze so as to render speechless. — **tongue'-tied'** *adj.*

tongue-twist·er (tung'twis'tər) *n.* A word or phrase difficult to articulate quickly: "Miss Smith's fish-sauce shop" is a *tongue-twister.*

tongue worm A hemichordate animal.

ton·ic (ton'ik) *adj.* **1** Having power to invigorate or build up; bracing. **2** Pertaining to tone or tones; specifically, in music, pertaining to the keynote. **3** In art, denoting the general color effect and the light and shade in a picture or scene. **4** *Physiol.* **a** Of or pertaining to tension, especially muscular tension. **b** Rigid; unrelaxing: *tonic* spasm. **5** *Ling.* **a** Of or pertaining to musical intonations or modulations of words, sentences, etc. **b** Designating languages which distinguish words of identical or very similar form by variations in tone or pitch, as Chinese. **6** *Phonet.* **a** Stressed, as a syllable. **b** *Obs.* Voiced. — *n.* **1** *Med.* A drug that gradually restores the normal tone of organs from a condition of debility. **2** Whatever imparts vigor or tone. **3** The basic note of a key; keynote. [<Gk. *tonikos* < *tonos* sound, tone]

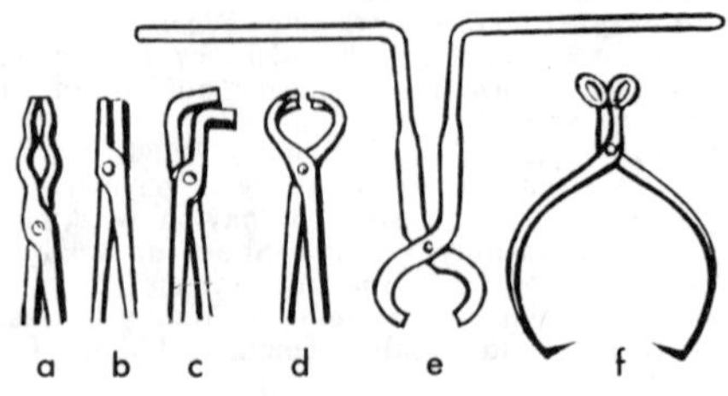

TONGS
a, b, c, d. Blacksmith's tongs.
e. Rail tongs. *f.* Ice tongs.

tonic accent 1 An accent that is spoken or pronounced rather than written. **2** *Phonet.* Emphasis placed on a syllable or sound by raising or changing the pitch of the voice.

to·nic·i·ty (tō·nis'ə·tē) *n.* **1** The state of being tonic; tone. **2** *Physiol.* The peculiar elastic condition of healthy tissue; tonus. **3** Health and vigor generally.

tonic sol-fa A system of teaching, writing, and reading music, especially vocal music, that lays particular stress on the tonal relations of the various elements of the key. The initials of the syllables used in solmization are employed to write its scale. [<TONIC + SOL[1] + FA]

to·night (tə·nīt') *adv.* **1** In or during the present or coming night. **2** *Obs.* Last night. — *n.* The night that follows this day; also, the present night. Also **to-night'.** [OE *tō niht* < *tō* to + *niht* night]

Ton·ite (tōn'īt) *n.* A blasting explosive of the guncotton class, with addition of barium nitrate and dinitrobenzene: a trade name.

Tonk (tongk) **1** A former princely state of the Rajputana States, India; merged with Rajasthan, 1948; 2,543 square miles. **2** A city of SE Rajasthan, India, formerly the capital of Tonk state.

Ton·ka bean (tong'kə) **1** An odoriferous seed obtained from a tropical American tree *(Dipteryx odorata),* and used for the adulteration of vanilla, flavoring of tobacco, snuff, etc. **2** The tree from which it is obtained. [Prob. <Negro name for the bean in Guiana]

Ton·kin (ton'kin, tong'-) A former name for northern North Vietnam, once a powerful independent kingdom, later a French protectorate; 44,670 square miles; capital, Hanoi. Also **Tong'king, Ton'king.** — **Ton'kin·ese'** *adj.* & *n.*

Tonkin, Gulf of An arm of the South China Sea between North Vietnam and the southernmost Chinese areas of Hainan island and the Luichow Peninsula.

Ton·le Sap (ton'lā sap) A lake in central Cambodia; 1,000 square miles: French *Grand Lac.*

ton·nage (tun'ij) *n.* **1** The cubic capacity of a merchant vessel expressed in tons of 100 cubic feet each. **2** The freight-carrying capacity of a vessel. **3** The aggregate freightage of a collection of vessels, especially of a country's merchant marine, as represented by their registered cubic capacity. **4** A tax levied on vessels at a given rate per ton. **5** The total weight of materials produced, mined, or transported. [<OF < *tonne* a ton, tun]

ton·neau (tu·nō') *n. pl.* **·neaus** (-nōz') or **·neaux** (-nōz') The rear part of an early type of automobile or vehicle, with low sides enclosing the seats, and a door at the rear or the side; also, the whole body of an automobile having such a rear part. [<F, lit., a barrel]

tono- *combining form* **1** Tension; pressure: *tonoplast.* **2** *Music* Tone; pitch: *tonometer* (def. 2). Also, before vowels, *ton-.* [<Gk. *tonos* tension < *teinein* stretch]

ton·o·graph (ton'ə·graf, -gräf, tō'nə-) *n.* A recording tonometer. [<TONO- + GRAPH]

to·nom·e·ter (tō·nom'ə·tər) *n.* **1** An instrument to measure strains within a liquid that tend to pull the particles asunder. **2** An accurately pitched tuning fork or set of forks; any instrument for determining the pitch of a tone. **3** An instrument for measuring tension in the eyeball or varying pressure of the blood.

to·nom·e·try (tō·nom'ə·trē) *n.* The art of using a tonometer. — **ton·o·met·ric** (ton'ə·met'rik, tō'nə-) *adj.*

ton·o·plast (ton'ə·plast) *n. Biol.* An inner plasmic membrane lining the vacuole of a cell and controlling the osmotic pressure. [<TONO- + -PLAST]

ton·o·scope (ton'ə·skōp, tō'nə-) *n.* An instrument by which a player or singer can observe departures from pitch or tone.

ton·sil (ton'səl) *n. Anat.* One of two oval lymphoid organs situated on either side of the passage from the mouth to the pharynx. [<L *tonsillae* the tonsils] — **ton'sil·lar, ton'sil·ar** *adj.*

ton·sil·lec·to·my (ton′sə·lek′tə·mē) *n. Surg.* Removal of a tonsil. [<TONSIL + -ECTOMY]

ton·sil·li·tis (ton′sə·lī′tis) *n. Pathol.* Inflammation of the tonsils. —**ton′sil·lit′ic** (-lit′ik) *adj.*

ton·sil·lo·tome (ton·sil′ə·tōm) *n.* An instrument used for cutting away a portion of the tonsils. [< *tonsillo-* (<TONSIL) + -TOME]

ton·sil·lot·o·my (ton′sə·lot′ə·mē) *n. Surg.* The operation of cutting away the tonsils or a part of them. [< *tonsillo-* (<TONSIL) + -TOMY]

ton·so·ri·al (ton·sôr′ē·əl, -sō′rē-) *adj.* Pertaining to a barber or to barbering: chiefly used in the humorous phrase, *tonsorial* artist. [<L *tonsorius* < *tonsor, -oris* a barber < *tonsus,* pp. of *tondere* shear, clip]

ton·sure (ton′shər) *n.* **1** The shaving of the head, or of the crown of the head, as of a priest or monk, or the state of being thus shaven; hence, the priestly office. **2** That part of a priest's or monk's head left bare by shaving. —*v.t.* **·sured, ·sur·ing** To shave the head of. [<OF <L *tonsura* a shearing < *tonsus.* See TONSORIAL.] —**ton′sured** *adj.*

ton·tine (ton′tēn, ton·tēn′) *n.* **1** A form of collective life annuity, the individual profits of which increase as the number of survivors diminishes, the final survivor taking the whole. **2** The subscribers to such an annuity, collectively. **3** The share of a single subscriber. [<F, after Lorenzo *Tonti,* a Neapolitan banker who introduced it into France in about 1653]

to·nus (tō′nəs) *n.* **1** Tonicity. **2** *Physiol.* **a** The ability of a muscle to contract in response to a stimulus. **b** A condition of prolonged muscular spasm. [<L, TONE]

ton·y (tō′nē) *adj.* **ton·i·er, ton·i·est** *Colloq.* Aristocratic; high-toned; fashionable; stylish; swell. [<TONE (def. 5b)]

too (to͞o) *adv.* **1** In addition; likewise; also: beautiful and good *too.* **2** In excessive quantity or degree; more than sufficiently: *too* long and *too* technical. **3** In a degree beyond expression or endurance; extremely: I am *too* happy for you. **4** *Colloq.* Indeed: an intensive, often used to reiterate a contradicted statement: You are *too* going! [Stressed var. of OE *tō* to]

took (to͝ok) Past tense of TAKE.

Tooke (to͝ok), **(John) Horne,** 1736–1812, English politician and philologist.

tool (to͞ol) *n.* **1** A simple mechanism or implement, as a hammer, saw, spade, or chisel, used chiefly in the direct manual working, moving, shaping, or transforming of material. **2** A power-driven apparatus, as a lathe, used for cutting and shaping the parts of a machine. **3** The cutting or shaping part of such an apparatus. **4** A bookbinder's hand stamp used in lettering or ornamenting book covers. **5** A person used to carry out the designs of others or another; a dupe. **6** *Law* Any instrument or apparatus necessary to the efficient prosecution of one's profession or trade. —*v.t.* **1** To shape, mark, or ornament with a tool. **2** To provide with tools. **3** *Colloq.* To drive, as an automobile, or convey (a person) by driving. **4** In bookbinding, to ornament or impress designs upon with a roller bearing a pattern. —*v.i.* **5** To work with a tool or tools. **6** *Colloq.* To drive or travel in a vehicle. [OE *tōl*]

Synonyms (noun): apparatus, appliance, implement, instrument, machine, mechanism, utensil. A *tool* is both contrived and used for extending the force of an intelligent agent to something that is to be operated upon. An *instrument* is anything through which power is applied and a result produced; in general usage, the word is of considerably wider meaning than *tool*; as, a piano is a musical *instrument. Instruments* is the word usually applied to *tools* used in scientific pursuits; as, we speak of a surgeon's or an optician's *instruments.* An *implement* is a mechanical agency considered with reference to some specific purpose to which it is adapted; as, an agricultural *implement, implements* of war. *Implement* is a less technical term than *tool.* A *utensil* is that which may be used for some special purpose; the word is especially applied to articles used for domestic or agricultural purposes; as, kitchen *utensils,* farming *utensils. Mechanism* is a word of wide meaning, denoting any combination of mechanical devices for united action. A *machine* in the most general sense is any mechanical *instrument* for the conversion of motion; in this sense a lever is a *machine*; but in more commonly accepted usage a *machine* is distinguished from a *tool* by its complexity, and by the combination and coordination of powers and movements to produce results.

tool·ing (to͞o′ling) *n.* **1** The ornamentation or work done with tools. **2** The application of a tool or tools to any work.

tool·mak·er (to͞ol′mā′kər) *n.* A maker of tools.

toom (to͞om) *adj. Scot. & Brit. Dial.* Empty; void; futile. [OE *tōm*]

Toombs (to͞omz), **Robert Augustus,** 1810–85, American Confederate general.

toon[1] (to͞on) *n.* **1** The fine, close-grained red wood of an East Indian tree *(Toona ciliata)* of the mahogany family, used for furniture, boxes, and construction. **2** The tree itself. [<Hind. *tun, tūn* <Skt. *tunna*]

toon[2] (to͞on) *n. Scot.* Hamlet; town.

toot (to͞ot) *v.i.* **1** To blow a horn, whistle, etc., especially with short blasts. **2** To give forth a blast or toot, as a horn. **3** To make a similar sound. —*v.t.* **4** To sound (a horn, etc.) with short blasts. **5** To sound (a blast, etc.). —*n.* **1** A short note or blast on a horn. **2** *Slang* A spree; especially, a drinking spree. [? <MLG *tūten*; prob. orig. imit.] —**toot′er** *n.*

tooth (to͞oth) *n. pl.* **teeth** (tēth) **1** One of the hard, dense structures in the mouth of a vertebrate, used for seizing and chewing food, as offensive and defensive weapons, etc. It consists chiefly of dentine or ivory, invested on the outer surface and crown with enamel, and a root embedded in the gum, with a small opening leading into a pulp cavity richly supplied with blood vessels and nerves. ◆ Collateral adjective: *dental.* **2** One of various hard calcareous or chitinous bodies of the oral or gastric regions of invertebrates. **3** Any one of various small toothlike projections.

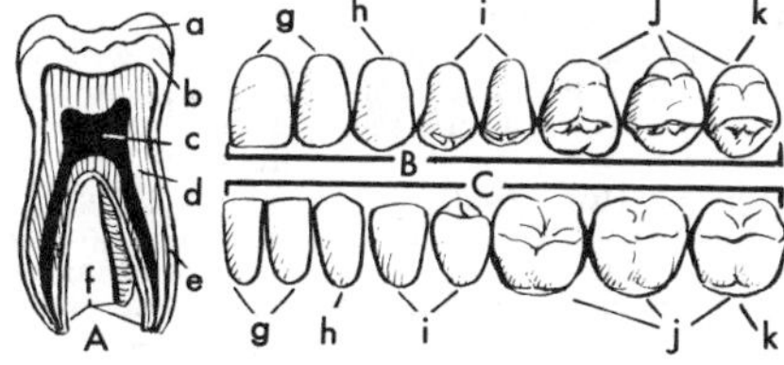

TEETH OF HUMAN ADULT
A. Cross-section of a molar.
B. Left upper jaw. *C.* Left lower jaw.
A. a. Crown. *b.* Enamel. *c.* Pulp cavity. *d.* Dentine. *e.* Cement. *f.* Roots.
B. & C. g. Incisors. *h.* Canines. *i.* Bicuspids. *j.* Molars. *k.* Wisdom teeth.

4 *Zool.* A process near the hinge of a bivalve shell. **5** *Bot.* One of the processes in the peristome of a moss. **6** Something resembling a tooth in form or use; specifically, a projecting point, pin, tine, or cog, as on a saw, comb, fork, rake, or gearwheel. **7** Appetite, liking, or taste (for something): She has a sweet *tooth.* **8** *pl.* That part which opposes, as in the gnawing, biting, or piercing manner of a tooth; the face of opposition, especially when involving resistance or risk: the *teeth* of the wind; He disobeyed them in their *teeth.* **9** *pl.* Means of enforcement: to put *teeth* into a law. **10** In paper or painting grounds, coarseness; irregularity of surface. —**armed to the teeth** Completely or heavily armed. —**by the skin of one's teeth** Barely; by the narrowest possible margin. —**in the teeth of** Directly against, counter to, or in defiance of. —**to put teeth into** To provide (something) with strength or power. —**to show one's teeth** To display a disposition to fight; threaten. —**to throw** (or **cast**) **in one's teeth** To fling at one, as a challenge or taunt. —*v.t.* **1** To supply with teeth, as a rake or saw. **2** To give a serrated edge to; indent. —*v.i.* **3** To become interlocked, as gearwheels; to gear. [<ON *tōth, tōdh*]

tooth·ache (to͞oth′āk′) *n.* **1** Pain in a tooth or the teeth, generally due to caries exposing the nerve. **2** Neuralgia of the teeth or of the jaw bone.

tooth and nail By biting and scratching; hence, fiercely; with all possible strength and effort: to fight *tooth and nail.*

tooth·brush (to͞oth′brush′) *n.* A small brush used for cleaning the teeth.

toothed (to͞otht, to͞othd) *adj.* **1** Having teeth, notches, cogs, or jags. **2** *Bot.* Dentate. **3** Coarse; irregular of surface: said of paper or painting grounds.

tooth·less (to͞oth′lis) *adj.* **1** Being without teeth. **2** Incapable of biting; harmless.

tooth·paste (to͞oth′pāst′) *n.* A paste used in cleaning the teeth.

tooth·pick (to͞oth′pik′) *n.* **1** A small sliver of wood or metal, used for removing particles of food from between the teeth. **2** *U.S. Slang* A bowie knife: sometimes **Arkansas toothpick.**

tooth·pow·der (to͞oth′pou′dər) *n.* A powder used in cleaning the teeth.

tooth rash Strophulus.

tooth·shell (to͞oth′shel′) *n.* A burrowing mollusk (genus *Dentalium*), having a long, very slender tubular shell.

tooth·some (to͞oth′səm) *adj.* Having a pleasant taste. —**tooth′some·ly** *adv.* —**tooth′some·ness** *n.*

tooth·wort (to͞oth′wûrt′) *n.* **1** Any of a genus *(Dentaria)* of spring-blooming herbs of the mustard family, with compound toothed leaves and terminal clusters of white or purplish flowers. **2** Any of a genus *(Lathraea)* of small, parasitic plants having rootstocks covered with white scales instead of leaves.

tooth·y (to͞o′thē) *adj.* **tooth·i·er, tooth·i·est** Having large or prominent teeth.

too·tle (to͞ot′l) *v.i.* **·tled, ·tling** To toot lightly or continuously, especially on the flute, as in double-tonguing. —*n.* The act of, or sound produced by, tootling. [Freq. of TOOT]

toot·sy (to͞ot′sē) *n. pl.* **·sies** *Slang* The foot of a child or woman: an endearing or humorous term. Also **toot′sy-woot′sy** (-wo͞ot′sē). [Child's term for a foot]

too·zie (to͞o′zē) See TOWZIE.

top[1] (top) *n.* **1** The uppermost or highest part, end, side, or surface of anything. **2** That end or part of anything, regarded as the higher or upper extremity: the *top* of the street. **3** A lid or cover: a bottle *top.* **4** The roof of a vehicle, as an automobile. **5** The crown of the head: from *top* to toe. **6** *pl.* The aboveground part of a plant producing root vegetables. **7** The highest degree or reach: at the *top* of one's voice; the *top* of one's ambition. **8** The highest or most prominent place or rank: at the *top* of one's profession. **9** One who is highest in rank or position: the *top* of one's class. **10** The choicest or best part: the *top* of the crop. **11** In bridge, the highest card in a suit. **12** In billiards, tennis, golf, etc.: **a** A stroke in which the player hits the ball above the center or on the upper half. **b** The forward spinning motion imparted to the ball by such a stroke. **13** *Naut.* A platform at the head of the lower section of a ship's mast, used as a place to stand and for extending the topmast rigging. **14** *Chem.* The most volatile part of a substance in distillation. **15** *Scot.* **a** The hair on one's head. **b** A bird's crest. **c** A horse's forelock. **d** A bunch of hair, wool, flax, etc. See synonyms under SUMMIT. —**to blow one's top** *Slang* **1** To break out in a rage; flare up. **2** To go insane. —*adj.* **1** Of or pertaining to the top. **2** Forming or comprising the top or upper part. **3** Highest in rank or quality; chief: *top* authors. **4** Greatest in amount or degree: *top* prices. —*v.* **topped, top·ping** *v.t.* **1** To remove the top or upper end of; prune. **2** To provide with a top, cap, etc. **3** To form the top of. **4** To reach or pass over the top of; surmount. **5** To surpass or exceed. **6** *Chem.* To take away the most volatile part of by distillation. **7** In golf, tennis, etc.: **a** To hit the upper part of (the ball) in making a stroke. **b** To make (a stroke) thus. —*v.i.* **8** To top someone or something. —**to top off** **1** To put something on the top of. **2** To complete; finish. [OE]

top[2] (top) *n.* A toy of wood or metal, with a point on which it is made to spin, as by the unwinding of a string, a spring, etc. [OE]

top– Var. of TOPO–.

to·paz (tō′paz) *n.* **1** A native fluosilicate of aluminum, often found in yellow prismatic crystals valued as gemstones. **2** The yellow sapphire, a highly prized corundum of Ceylon: also called **Oriental topaz.** **3** Citrine (def. 2). **4** Either of two large tropical American hummingbirds (*Topaza pyra* and *T. pella*) with brilliant green-and-gold plumage. **5** A brownish-gold color, the color of the mineral. [<OF *topaze, topace* <L *topazus* <Gk. *topazos*]

to·paz·o·lite (tō·paz′ə·līt) *n.* A variety of andradite, yellow or sometimes green. [<Gk. *topazos* topaz + -LITE]

top·boot (top′bōōt′) *n.* A boot with a high top, sometimes ornamented with materials different from the rest of the boot. —**top′-boot′ed** *adj.*

top buggy A buggy with a top that may be raised or folded back.

top·coat (top′kōt′) *n.* A lightweight overcoat.

top–drawer (top′drôr′) *adj. Colloq.* Of the highest standard or merit.

top–dress (top′dres′) *v.t. Agric.* To apply manure on the top of, instead of plowing it into, a field.

top dressing *Agric.* A dressing of manure not to be plowed under the surface of a field.

tope[1] (tōp) *v.t.* **toped, top·ing** To drink (alcoholic beverages) excessively and frequently. ◆ Homophone: *taupe.* [? Related to earlier *top* tilt, turn over]

tope[2] (tōp) *n. Dial.* A small European shark or dogfish (genus *Galeorhinus*). ◆ Homophone: *taupe.* [? <dial. E (Cornish); ult. origin unknown]

tope[3] (tōp) *n. Anglo-Indian* A grove, especially a mango grove. ◆ Homophone: *taupe.* [< Tamil *tōppu*]

tope[4] (tōp) *n. Anglo-Indian* A round Buddhist shrine, dome, or tower, constructed to contain relics of the Buddhas, to indicate some sacred site, or for the burial of priests: also called *stupa.* ◆ Homophone: *taupe.* [<Hind. *top,* prob. <Pali *thūpo* <Skt. *stūpa*]

to·pec·to·my (tō·pek′tə·mē, tə-) *n. Surg.* An operation in which certain prefrontal cortical areas of the brain are removed. [<TOP(O)- + -ECTOMY]

to·pee (tō·pē′, tō′pē) See TOPI.

to·pek (tō′pek) *n.* A North American Indian or Eskimo hut of weeds, twigs, and animal skins. [<Eskimo *toopik, tupek* a tent]

To·pe·ka (tə·pē′kə) The capital of Kansas, on the Kansas River in the NE part.

to·pep·o (tə·pep′ō) *n. pl.* **·pep·oes** **1** A hybrid plant obtained by crossing the Chinese pepper with a variety of tomato, cultivated for its edible fruit. **2** The fruit itself. [<TO(MAT)O + PEP(PER)]

top·er (tō′pər) *n.* A habitual drunkard; sot. [<TOPE[1]]

top·flight (top′flīt′) *adj.* Of the highest quality; outstanding; superior.

top·full (top′fŏŏl′) *adj. Rare* Brimful.

top·gal·lant (tə·gal′ənt, top′gal′ənt) *n. Naut.* **1** The mast, sail, yard, or rigging immediately above the topmast and topsail. **2** The parts of a deck that are higher than the rest. —*adj.* Pertaining to the topgallants. [<TOP[1] + GALLANT; with ref. to "making a gallant show" compared with the lower tops]

toph (tōf) *n.* Tufa. Also **tophe.** [<L *tophus, tofus*]

top·ham·per (top′ham′pər) *n. Naut.* **1** Spars and rigging usually kept aloft. **2** The light upper sails and rigging. **3** Casks, cables, rigging, etc., encumbering the deck. [<TOP[1] + HAMPER[1], *n.*] —**top′-ham′pered** *adj.*

top hat A high silk hat for men.

top·heav·y (top′hev′ē) *adj.* Having the top or upper part too heavy for the lower part; ill-proportioned; impracticable. —**top′heav′i·ness** *n.*

To·phet (tō′fet) **1** In the Old Testament, a place in the valley of Hinnom, near Jerusalem, where the Jews were said to sacrifice their children to Moloch: later used as a place for burning the city's refuse. **2** A place of endless perdition; hell. Also **To′pheth** (-fet). [<Hebrew *tōpheth,* ? an altar]

top–hole (top′hōl′) *adj. Brit. Slang* First-rate; excellent.

to·phus (tō′fəs) *n. pl.* **·phi** (-fī) **1** *Dent.* Tartar of the teeth. **2** *Pathol.* A deposit of urates around and at the surface of joints in persons affected with gout. **3** *Mineral.* Any natural calcareous tufa. [<L, tufa]

to·pi (tō·pē′, tō′pē) *n.* A hat or helmet, especially a light helmet made of pith: also spelled *topee.* [<Hind. *topī*]

to·pi·ar·y (tō′pē·er′ē) *adj.* Arranged or trimmed in, or making use of, fantastic shapes of shrubs and evergreen trees, as in gardening, etc. —*n. pl.* **·ar·ies** A topiary garden. [<L *topiarius* concerning ornamental gardening < *topia opera* ornamental gardening <Gk. *topion,* dim. of *topos* a place]

top·ic (top′ik) *n.* **1** A subject of discourse or of a treatise; any matter treated of in speech or writing; a theme for discussion. **2** *pl.* In rhetorical invention, the part that treats of the selection and arrangement of the proofs; also, the places or classes in which the various kinds of proofs are to be found. **3** A subdivision of an outline or a treatise. —*adj. Obs.* Topical. [<L *topica* <Gk. (*ta*) *topica,* lit., (matters) concerning commonplaces, title of a work by Aristotle, neut. pl. of *topikos* of a place < *topos* a place, commonplace]

Synonyms (*noun*): division, head, issue, matter, motion, point, proposition, question, subject, theme. Since a *topic* for discussion is often stated in the form of a *question, question* has come to be extensively used to denote a debatable *topic,* especially of a practical nature; as, the labor *question.* In deliberative assemblies the *motion* or other matter for consideration is known as the *question;* a member is required to speak to the *question.* In speaking or writing the general *subject* or *theme* may be termed the *topic,* but it is more usual to apply the latter term to the subordinate *divisions, points,* or *heads* of discourse; as, To enlarge on this *topic* would carry me far from my *subject.*

top·i·cal (top′i·kəl) *adj.* **1** Pertaining to a topic. **2** Of the nature of merely probable argument. **3** Belonging to a place or spot; local. **4** Pertaining to matters of present interest: a *topical* song. **5** *Med.* Local. —**top′i·cal·ly** *adv.*

top kick *Slang* A top sergeant.

top·knot (top′not′) *n.* **1** A crest, tuft, or knot on the top of the head, as of feathers on the head of a bird. **2** The hair of the human head when worn as a high knot. **3** A knot or bow worn by women, as a headdress, etc.

top·less (top′lis) *adj.* **1** Lacking a top. **2** Nude from the waist up, or characterized by such nudity. **3** Being without a covering for the breasts: a *topless* bathing suit. **4** So high that no top can be seen. —**top′less·ness** *n.*

top–loft·y (top′lôf′tē, -lof′tē) *adj.* **1** Towering very high. **2** Very proud or haughty; inflated; pompous. —**top′-loft′i·ness** *n.*

top·mast (top′məst, top′mast′, -mäst′) *n. Naut.* The mast next above the lower mast.

top minnow Any of a family (*Poeciliidae*) of small, typically viviparous fishes which feed near the surface of the water, especially *Gambusia affinis,* widely used to combat mosquitoes.

top·most (top′mōst′) *adj.* Being at the very top.

top–notch (top′noch′) *adj. Colloq.* Excellent; best. —**top′-notch′er** *n.*

topo– *combining form* A place or region; regional: *topography.* Also, before vowels, *top–.* [<Gk. *topos* a place]

to·pog·ra·pher (tə·pog′rə·fər) *n.* An expert in topography.

to·pog·ra·phy (tə·pog′rə·fē) *n.* **1** The detailed description of particular places. **2** The art of representing on a map the physical features of a place. **3** The physical features, collectively, of a region. **4** Topographic surveying. [<TOPO- + -GRAPHY] —**top·o·graph·ic** (top′ə·graf′ik) or **·i·cal** *adj.* —**top′o·graph′i·cal·ly** *adv.*

to·pol·o·gy (tə·pol′ə·jē) *n.* **1** The branch of geometry which studies those properties of figures or solid bodies which remain invariant under all continuous deformation: also called *analysis situs.* **2** *Med.* The relation between the forward part of the fetus and the birth canal. [<TOPO- + -LOGY] —**top·o·log·ic** (top′ə·loj′ik) or **·i·cal** *adj.*

top·o·nym (top′ə·nim) *n.* **1** *Anat.* The name of a region of the body, as distinguished from an organ. **2** Any name derived from the name of a place. [<TOPO- + Gk. *onoma, onyma* a name] —**top′o·nym′ic** or **·i·cal** *adj.*

to·pon·y·my (tə·pon′ə·mē) *n. pl.* **·mies** **1** The nomenclature of anatomical regions. **2** The science or study of place names, or a register of place names.

top·o·type (top′ə·tīp) *n. Biol.* A plant or animal specimen selected from the locality typical of the species. [<TOPO- + TYPE]

top·per (top′ər) *n.* **1** One who or that which cuts off the top of something. **2** *Slang* One who or that which is of supreme quality. **3** *Slang* A high silk hat.

top·ping (top′ing) *adj.* **1** Towering high above; eminent; distinguished. **2** Making great pretensions; arrogant; domineering. **3** *Brit. Colloq.* Excellent; first-rate. —*n.* **1** The act of one who tops, in any sense. **2** That which forms the top of anything.

topping lift *Naut.* A rope extending from the lower masthead to the outer end of a boom, for hoisting or supporting the boom.

top·ple (top′əl) *v.* **·pled, ·pling** *v.t.* **1** To push over and cause to totter or fall by its own weight; overturn. —*v.i.* **2** To totter and fall, as by its own weight. **3** To lean or jut out, as if about to fall. [Freq. of TOP[1], *v.*]

tops (tops) *adj. Slang* Excellent; first-rate.

top·sail (top′səl, top′sāl′) *n. Naut.* **1** In a square-rigged vessel, a square sail set next above the lowest sail of a mast. **2** In a fore-and-aft-rigged vessel, a square or triangular sail carried above the gaff of a lower sail.

top–se·cret (top′sē′krit) *adj. U.S.* Designating defense information requiring the strictest measures of secrecy and safeguard. Compare SECRET (*adj.* def. 5), CONFIDENTIAL (def. 4).

top sergeant *Colloq.* The first sergeant of a company, battery, or troop.

top·side (top′sīd′) *n. Naut.* The portion of a ship above the main deck. —*adv.* To or on the upper parts of a ship: He is going *topside.*

top·soil (top′soil′) *n.* The surface soil of land: distinguished from *subsoil.* —*v.t.* To remove the surface soil of (an area or region).

top·stone (top′stōn′) *n.* A capstone.

Top·sy (top′sē) In *Uncle Tom's Cabin,* a young Negro slave girl who, when questioned about her origins, replied that she had "just growed."

top·sy-tur·vy (top′sē·tûr′vē) *adv.* Upside-down; hind side before; in utter confusion. —*adj.* Being in an upset or disordered condition; upside-down. —*n.* A state of confusion; disorder; chaos. [Earlier *topsy-tervy, topsy-tirvy,* prob. <TOP[1] + obs. *terve, tirve* turn, overturn] —**top′sy-tur′vi·ly** *adv.* —**top′·sy-tur′vi·ness** *n.* —**top′sy-tur′vy·dom** *n.*

toque (tōk) *n.* **1** A small, close-fitting, brimless hat worn by women. **2** The tall conical headdress formerly worn by the doges of Venice. **3** A black velvet cap, ornamented with eagle's plumes and furnished with a band and brim: worn by both sexes in Europe before the Restoration. Also **to·quet** (tō·kā′). [<F, a cap <Sp. *toca* <Basque *tauka,* a kind of cap]

tor (tôr) *n.* A high, rocky hill; a jutting rock. [OE *torr* <Celtic]

to·rah (tôr′ə, tō′rə) *n.* In Hebrew literature, a law; also, counsel or instruction proceeding from a specially sacred source. Also **to′ra.** [<Hebrew *tōrāh* an instruction, law < *yārāh* throw, show, instruct]

To·rah (tôr′ə, tō′rə) *n.* The Mosaic law; the Pentateuch.

tor·bern·ite (tôr′bərn·īt) See under URANITE. [<G *torbernit, torberit* <NL *torbernus,* after *Torber* Bergmann, 18th c. Swedish chemist]

torc (tôrk) See TORQUE[2].

torch (tôrch) *n.* **1** A source of light, as from flaming pine knots, or from some material dipped in tallow or oil, and fixed at the end of a handle or pole. **2** Anything that illuminates or brightens: the *torch* of science. **3** A portable device giving off an intensely hot flame and used for burning off paint, melting solder, etc. **4** *Brit.* A flashlight. —**to carry a** (or **the**) **torch for** *Slang* To continue to love (someone), though the love is unrequited. [<OF *torche,* ult. <L *torquere* twist; so called because early torches were made of twisted tow dipped in pitch]

torch·bear·er (tôrch′bâr′ər) *n.* **1** One who carries a torch. **2** One who imparts knowledge, truth, etc. **3** *Colloq.* One loud in his praise of a friend.

torch·light (tôrch′līt′) *n.* The light of a torch or torches. —*adj.* Lighted by torches: a *torchlight* rally.

torchlight procession A parade of persons

carrying torches, usually a political demonstration.

tor·chon lace (tôr′shon, *Fr.* tôr·shôn′) **1** A coarse, durable bobbin lace in simple geometrical designs made of linen thread. **2** An imitation of this made by machine. [<F *torchon* a dishcloth < *torcher* wipe]

torch singer One who sings torch songs.

torch song A popular love song, slow and melancholy, expressing sadness and hopeless yearning. [< phrase "carry a torch for." See under TORCH.]

torch·wood (tôrch′wŏŏd′) *n.* **1** Any of a genus *(Amyris)* of tropical American shrubs and small trees, especially *A. balsamifera.* **2** Its bright-burning, fragrant wood.

Tor·de·sil·las (tôr′thā·sē′lyäs) A village in NW Spain; scene of the signing of a treaty between Spain and Portugal setting the line of demarcation for colonial expansion, 1494.

tore[1] (tôr, tōr) Past tense of TEAR[1].

tore[2] (tôr, tōr) *n.* Torus (defs. 1 and 4). [<F *tore* <L *torus* a torus]

tor·e·a·dor (tôr′ē·ə·dôr′, *Sp.* tō′rā·ä·thōr′) *n.* One who engages in a bullfight, especially on horseback; a bullfighter: also spelled *toreador.* [<Sp. < *torear* fights bulls < *toro* a bull <L *taurus*]

to·re·ro (tō·rā′rō) *n.* *pl.* **·ros** (-rōs) *Spanish* A bullfighter, usually on foot.

to·reu·tics (tə·rōō′tiks) *n. pl.* *(construed as singular)* The art of working in ornamental relief or intaglio, especially in metal. [<Gk. *toreutikos* < *toreuein* work in relief, bore] **—to·reu′tic** *adj.*

tor·ic (tôr′ik, tor′-) *adj.* Of, pertaining to, or resembling a torus; segmental.

toric lens *Optics* A lens in which one of the surfaces is a segment of a torus: used for eyeglasses because of its special refracting powers.

to·ri·i (tôr′i·ē, tō′ri·ē) *n.* The gateway of a Shinto temple or of a shrine: properly comprising two uprights with one straight crosspiece, and another above with a concave lintel. [<Japanese]

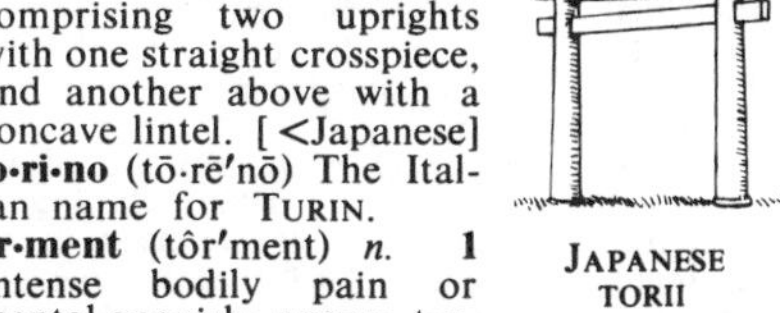

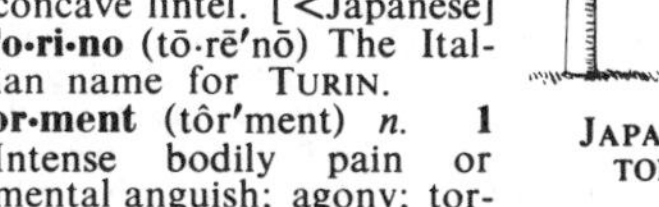

JAPANESE TORII

To·ri·no (tō·rē′nō) The Italian name for TURIN.

tor·ment (tôr′ment) *n.* **1** Intense bodily pain or mental anguish; agony; torture. **2** One who or that which torments. **3** The inflicting of torture. **4** *Archaic* Any device for inflicting torture, as the rack; also, the torture inflicted. **5** Hell. See synonyms under AGONY, PAIN. **—*v.t.*** (tôr·ment′) **1** To subject to excruciating physical or mental suffering; torture. **2** To make miserable; afflict or vex grievously. **3** To harass or tease. **4** To distort; also, to throw into violent agitation. See synonyms under PERSECUTE. [<AF *turment,* OF *torment, tourment* <L *tormentum* a rack, orig. a machine for hurling missiles by means of torsion < *torquere* twist] **—tor·ment′ing·ly** *adv.* **—tor·ment′ing·ness** *n.*

tor·men·til (tôr′men·til) *n.* A slender, trailing, Old World herb *(Potentilla erecta),* with yellow flowers. Its root, a powerful astringent, has been used in treating diarrhea and dysentery, and also in tanning. [<OF *tormentille* < Med. L *tormentilla,* dim. of L *tormentum* TORMENT; so called because used as a pain killer]

tor·men·tor (tôr·men′tər) *n.* **1** One who or that which torments. **2** A movable panel of sound-insulating material for controlling the acoustics on a sound stage outside of the field of the camera. **3** A movable piece of theater scenery at either side and back of the proscenium arch to mask sidelights and downstage entrances and exits. Also **tor·ment′er.**

torn (tôrn, tōrn) Past participle of TEAR[1].

tor·na·do (tôr·nā′dō) *n.* *pl.* **·does** or **·dos** **1** A whirling wind of exceptional violence, usually associated with thunderstorms and accompanied by a pendulous, funnel-shaped cloud marking the narrow path of greatest destruction. **2** A violent thunderstorm or squall of the west coast of Africa. **3** A hurricane or violent windstorm of the tropical Atlantic. See synonyms under CYCLONE. [Alter. of *ternado,* prob. alter. of Sp. *tronada* a thunderstorm < *tronar* thunder <L *tonare;* infl. in form by Sp. *tornar* turn, because characterized by shifting or whirling winds] **—tor·nad′ic** (-nad′ik) *adj.*

Tor·ne (tôr′nə, tōr′-) A river in northern Sweden and northern Finland, flowing 250 miles SE and south from Lake Torne to its confluence with the Muonio, and thence along the Swedish-Finnish border to the Gulf of Bothnia.

Torne, Lake A lake near the Norwegian border in extreme NW Sweden; 124 square miles; 40 miles long, 1 to 6 miles wide.

to·roid (tôr′oid, tō′roid) *n.* **1** *Geom.* **a** A surface generated by the rotation of any closed plane curve, as a circle or ellipse, about an axis lying in its plane. **b** The solid produced by such a surface. **2** *Electr.* An electromagnetic coil wound upon a ring of circular cross-section. [<TOR(US) + -OID] **—to·roi′dal** *adj.*

To·ron·to (tə·ron′tō) The capital of Ontario province, Canada, on Lake Ontario; a leading industrial center.

To·ros Dağ·la·ri (tô·rôs′ dä′lä·rē′) The Turkish name for the Taurus range.

to·rose (tôr′ōs, tō′rōs, tô·rōs′, tō-) *adj.* **1** Having protuberances; bulging. **2** *Bot.* Knobby; cylindrical and swollen at intervals. Also **to·rous** (tôr′əs, tō′rəs). [<L *torosus* < *torus* a swelling] **—to·ros·i·ty** (tô·ros′ə·tē) *n.*

tor·pe·do (tôr·pē′dō) *n.* *pl.* **·dos** or **·does** **1** A device or apparatus containing an explosive to be fired by concussion or otherwise. **2** A self-propelling, cigar-shaped projectile for carrying a powerful detonating charge under water to a hostile vessel. **3** A submarine mine. **4** A cartridge placed on a railway track and exploded by the weight of a train passing over it, the report serving as a warning signal to the train crew. **5** A cartridge exploded in an oil or gas well to start or increase the flow. **6** A toy of gravel and a fulminating powder wrapped in paper, and exploded by being dashed against some hard surface. **7** A ray fish *(Torpedo ocellata)* having an electric apparatus with which it stuns or kills its prey; a crampfish; numbfish. **8** *Colloq.* A gangster, especially an armed bodyguard prepared to attack or kill without warning. **—aerial torpedo** A torpedo projectile, moving under its own power and usually released from low-flying aircraft at fixed or floating targets. **—*v.t.*** **·doed, ·do·ing** To damage or sink (a vessel) with a torpedo or torpedos. [<L, stiffness, numbness < *torpere* be numb]

torpedo boat A small, swift, lightly armed and armored surface vessel equipped with one or more tubes for the discharge of torpedos.

tor·pe·do-boat destroyer (tôr·pē′dō·bōt′) A small, swift, lightly armed war vessel; a destroyer.

torpedo tube A tube in a torpedo boat or other war vessel, through which torpedos are launched.

tor·pid[1] (tôr′pid) *adj.* **1** Having lost sensibility or power of motion, partially or wholly, as a hibernating animal. **2** Dormant; numb. **3** Sluggish; apathetic; dull. See synonyms under LIFELESS, NUMB. [<L *torpidus* < *torpere* be numb] **—tor·pid·i·ty** (tôr·pid′ə·tē), **tor′pid·ness** *n.* **—tor′pid·ly** *adv.*

tor·pid[2] (tôr′pid) *n.* **1** An eight-oared, clinker-built racing boat for the second crew at Oxford University; also, one of its crew. **2** *pl.* The Lenten races in which such boats take part. [<TORPID[1]; so called because the second crew consisted of awkward or very young oarsmen]

tor·por (tôr′pər) *n.* **1** Complete or partial insensibility; stupor. **2** Apathy; torpidity. [<L < *torpere* be numb] **—tor·po·rif·ic** (tôr′pə·rif′ik) *adj.*

tor·quate (tôr′kwit, -kwāt) *adj. Zool.* Having a torque or ring, as of color, about the neck; collared. [<L *torquatus* having a collar < *torques.* See TORQUES.]

Tor·quay (tôr·kē′) A port and municipal borough in southern Devon, England.

torque[1] (tôrk) *n.* **1** *Mech.* **a** Anything that causes or tends to cause torsion in a body; the moment of forces that causes rotation or twisting. **b** The rotary force in a mechanism. **c** The degree of smoothness in the conversion of reciprocating into rotary motion. **2** *Optics* The rotatory effect upon the plane of polarization produced by the passage of light through certain liquids and crystals. [<L *torquere* twist]

torque[2] (tôrk) *n.* A necklace, armlet, or collar of wire, usually twisted: worn especially by ancient Gauls and Britons: also spelled *torc.* [<L *torques.* See TORQUES.]

Tor·que·ma·da (tôr′kwə·mä′də, *Sp.* tôr′kā·mä′thä), **Tomás de,** 1420–98, Dominican monk; first inquisitor general of Spain.

tor·ques (tôr′kwēz) *n. Zool.* A natural ring or collar, of feathers or hair, on the neck of a bird or other animal. [<NL <L, a twisted collar < *torquere* twist]

tor·re·a·dor (tôr′ē·ə·dôr′) See TOREADOR.

Tor·re An·nun·zia·ta (tôr′rā än′nōōn·tsyä′tä) A port on the Bay of Naples, southern Italy; destroyed by an eruption of Vesuvius, 1631, and rebuilt.

tor·re·fy (tôr′ə·fī, tor′-) *v.t.* **·fied, ·fy·ing** To dry or roast by exposure to heat, as ores or drugs. Also **tor′ri·fy.** [<MF *torréfier* <L *torrefacere* < *torrere* dry, parch + *facere* make] **—tor′re·fac′tion** (-fak′shən) *n.*

Tor·rens (tôr′ənz, tor′-), **Lake** A salt lake in SE central South Australia, often dry; 120 miles long; 2,230 square miles.

tor·rent (tôr′ənt, tor′-) *n.* **1** A stream of water flowing with great velocity or turbulence. **2** Any similar stream, as of lava. **3** Any abundant or tumultuous flow: a *torrent* of rain; a *torrent* of abuse. **—*adj.*** Like a torrent; pouring forth with violence. [<OF <L *torrens, -entis,* lit., boiling, burning, ppr. of *torrere* parch]

tor·ren·tial (tô·ren′shəl, to-) *adj.* **1** Of, pertaining to, or resulting from the action of a torrent or torrents. **2** Figuratively, suggestive of a torrent in rapidity and volume; outpouring; overpowering: *torrential* passion. **—tor·ren′tial·ly** *adv.*

Tor·re·ón (tôr′rā·ôn′) A city in Coahuila, northern Mexico; an industrial center.

Tor·res Strait (tôr′əs, -iz, tor′-) A strait between Australia and New Guinea; 95 miles wide; connects the Arafura and Coral seas.

Tor·res Ve·dras (tôr′rizh vā′thrəsh) A town north of Lisbon in western Portugal; Wellington's headquarters in the Peninsula campaign, 1810.

Tor·rey (tôr′ē, tor′ē), **John,** 1796–1873, U. S. botanist.

Tor·ri·cel·li (tôr′rē·chel′lē), **Evangelista,** 1608–1647, Italian physicist; discovered the principle of the barometer. **—Tor·ri·cel·li·an** (tôr′·i·sel′ē·ən, -chel′ē·ən) *adj.*

Torricellian tube A vertical glass tube containing mercury or other fluid, sealed at the top and having the lower end in a container of the same fluid. [after E. TORRICELLI]

Torricellian vacuum The vacuum above the fluid in a Torricellian tube or in the top of a barometer tube.

tor·rid (tôr′id, tor′-) *adj.* **1** Exposed to the full force of the sun's heat; sultry. **2** Having power to parch or burn; scorching; burning; hot and dry. [<L *torridus* < *torrere* parch] **—tor·rid·i·ty** (tô·rid′ə·tē, to-), **tor′rid·ness** *n.* **—tor′rid·ly** *adv.*

torrid zone See under ZONE.

tor·sade (tôr·säd′) *n.* **1** A molded ornament resembling a twisted cable. **2** A twisted cord for draperies. [<F <Med. L *torsus,* var. of L *tortus,* pp. of *torquere* twist]

tor·si·bil·i·ty (tôr′sə·bil′ə·tē) *n.* Capacity for undergoing torsion, measured by the amount of torsion produced.

tor·sion (tôr′shən) *n.* **1** The act of twisting, or the state of being twisted. **2** *Mech.* Deformation of a body, as a thread or rod, by twisting, one end being held fast while the other is subjected to a torque around its length as an axis. **3** The force with which a twisted cord or cable tends to return to its former position: distinguished from *tension.* [<OF <LL *torsio, -onis,* var. of L *tortio, -onis* < *tortus,* pp. of *torquere* twist] **—tor′sion·al** *adj.* **—tor′sion·al·ly** *adv.*

torsion balance An instrument for determining very minute forces by measuring the angle through which an arm turns before the resisting force of torsion acts upon the supporting wire or filament.

torsion bar A solid or laminated bar or rod, anchored on one end, which acts as a spring when subjected to torsion (def. 2). —**tor′·sion–bar′** *adj.*
torsk (tôrsk) *n.* **1** A gadoid fish; the cusk. **2** The codfish. [<Norw. <ON *thorskr,* prob. < base of *thurr* dry. Akin to THIRST.]
tor·so (tôr′sō) *n. pl.* **·sos** or **·si** (-sē) **1** The trunk of a human body. **2** In sculpture, a statue deprived of head and limbs. **3** Any fragmentary or defective thing. [<Ital., a stalk, core, trunk of a body <L *thyrsus* a stalk <Gk. *thyrsos* a thyrsus]
tort (tôrt) *n. Law* Any private or civil wrong by act or omission for which a civil suit can be brought, but not including breach of contract. [<OF <L *tortus.* See TORSION.]
torte (tôrt, *Ger.* tôr′tə) *n.* A rich cake variously made of butter, eggs, fruits, and nuts. [<G]
tort–fea·sor (tôrt′fē′zər) *n. Law* One who has committed a tort; a wrongdoer. [<OF *tortfesor, tortfaiseur* < *tort* a wrong, tort + *fesor, faiseur* a doer < *faire* do <L *facere*]
tor·ti·col·lis (tôr′tə·kol′is) *n. Pathol.* A spasmodic affection of the muscles of the neck which draws the head to one side; wryneck. [<NL <L *tortus* twisted + *collum* neck] —**tor′ti·col′lar** *adj.*
tor·tile (tôr′til) *adj.* Twisted up into a coil. [<L *tortilis* < *tortus* twisted. See TORSION.] —**tor·til·i·ty** (tôr·til′ə·tē) *n.*
tor·til·la (tôr·tē′yä) *n.* A flat cake made of coarse cornmeal and baked on a hot sheet of iron or a slab of stone: the customary substitute for bread in Mexico. [<Sp., dim. of *torta* a cake <LL, a twisted loaf <L, pp. fem. of *torquere* twist]
tor·tious (tôr′shəs) *adj. Law* Of the nature of or implying a tort; wrongful. [<AF *torcious* < *torcion, tortion,* var. of OF *torsion* torsion; infl. in meaning by TORT] —**tor′tious·ly** *adv.*
tor·tive (tôr′tiv) *adj. Obs.* Twisted. [<L *tortivus* < *tortus.* See TORSION.]
tor·toise (tôr′təs) *n.* **1** A turtle; chelonian; specifically, one of a terrestrial or fresh–water species, or a terrestrial as distinguished from an aquatic species. **2** A testudo. —**giant tortoise** Any of several species of very large herbivorous land tortoises (family *Testudinidae*), especially those found on the Galápagos Islands, which may reach a length of four feet and weigh 600 pounds. [Earlier *tortuce* < Med. L *tortuca,* ult. <L *tortus* twisted; so called from its crooked feet]

GIANT TORTOISE
(Largest specimens: up to 5 1/2 feet long by 4 1/2 feet wide)

tortoise beetle A small, iridescent beetle (family *Chrysomelidae*) having a tortoiselike form.
tortoise plant Elephant foot.
tortoise shell **1** The shell of a marine turtle, especially of the hawkbill, valuable in the arts. **2** A cat having fur mottled with black and yellow like the shell of a tortoise. —**tor′·toise–shell′** *adj.*
Tor·to·la (tôr·tō′lə) The chief island of the British Virgin Islands; 21 square miles; capital, Road Town.
tor·tri·cid (tôr′trə·sid) *n.* Any of a large family (*Tortricidae*) of small, usually bright–colored moths with rectangular fore wings, including many important pests of fruit and forest trees. —*adj.* Of or pertaining to the *Tortricidae.* [<NL <*Tortrix,* type genus <L *tortus.* See TORSION.]
Tor·tu·ga (tôr·tōō′gə) An island off the northern coast of Haiti, to which it belongs; 70 square miles; a 17th century pirate stronghold. *French* **Île de la Tor·tue** (ēl′ də lä tôr·tü′).
tor·tu·os·i·ty (tôr′chōō·os′ə·tē) *n.* **1** The quality or state of being tortuous, or an instance of it. **2** A bend or twist; winding.
tor·tu·ous (tôr′chōō·əs) *adj.* **1** Consisting of or abounding in irregular bends or turns; twisting. **2** Figuratively, morally irregular or crooked; not straightforward; devious. [<AF <L *tortuosus* < *tortus.* See TORSION.] —**tor′tu·ous·ly** *adv.* —**tor′tu·ous·ness** *n.*
tor·ture (tôr′chər) *n.* **1** Infliction of or subjection to extreme physical pain. **2** A former judicial mode of getting evidence by inflicting pain. **3** Great mental suffering; agony. **4** Something that causes severe pain. **5** A violent perversion or straining. See synonyms under AGONY, PAIN. —*v.t.* **·tured, ·tur·ing** **1** To inflict extreme pain upon; cause to suffer keenly in body or mind; specifically, to put to judicial torture. **2** To twist or turn into an abnormal form; distort; wrench. [<OF <L *tortura,* lit., a twisting < *tortus.* See TORSION.] —**tor′tur·er** *n.*
tor·u·lose (tôr′ə·lōs) *adj. Bot.* Having alternate swellings and constrictions like the vegetative growth of *Torula,* a genus of fungus. Also **tor′u·lous** (-ləs). [<NL *Torula,* dim. of *torus* a torus]
To·ruń (tô′rōōn·y′) A port on the Vistula in north central Poland: German *Thorn.*
to·rus (tôr′əs, tō′rəs) *n. pl.* **to·ri** (tôr′ī, tō′rī) **1** *Archit.* A large convex molding, nearly semicircular in cross–section: used in bases as the lowest molding, or in columns above the plinth. **2** *Anat.* A rounded ridge, as on the occipital bone of the skull. **3** *Bot.* The swollen end of a flowerstalk which bears the floral leaves; the receptacle. **4** *Geom.* The surface or solid generated by the rotation of a conic section about an axis in its own plane. [<L, lit., a swelling]
to·ry (tôr′ē, tō′rē) *n. pl.* **·ries** *Obs.* **1** A freebooter among the outlawed Irish in the 17th century. **2** Any outlaw or bandit. [<Irish *tōruidhe* a robber, a pursuer < *tōir* pursue]
To·ry (tôr′ē, tō′rē) *n. pl.* **To·ries** **1** A historical English political party, successor to the Cavaliers and opponent of the Whigs; since about 1832 called the Conservative party. **2** One who at the period of the American Revolution adhered to the cause of British sovereignty over the colonies. **3** A very conservative person: also **tory.** —**To′ry·ism** *n.*
Tos·ca·na (tôs·kä′nä) The Italian name for TUSCANY.
Tos·ca·ni·ni (tos′kə·nē′nē, tôs′-; *Ital* tôs′kä·nē′nē), **Arturo,** 1867–1957, Italian orchestra conductor active in the United States.
tosh (tosh) *n. Brit. Colloq.* Nonsense; rubbish; bosh. [? Alter of BOSH]
toss (tôs, tos) *v.t.* **1** To throw, pitch, or fling about. **2** To make restless; agitate; disturb. **3** To throw with the hand, especially with the palm of the hand upward; pitch. **4** To lift with a quick motion, as the head. **5** To bandy about, as something discussed. **6** To toss up with. See TO TOSS UP, below. —*v.i.* **7** To be moved or thrown about; be flung to and fro, as a ship in a storm. **8** To throw oneself from side to side; roll about restlessly, as in sleep. **9** To go quickly or angrily, as with a toss of the head. **10** To toss up a coin. —**to toss** (or **peak**) **oars** To raise the oars out of the rowlocks to a vertical position. —**to toss off** **1** To drink at one draft. **2** To utter, write, or do in an offhand manner. —**to toss up** To throw a coin into the air to decide a wager or choice by the way in which it falls. —*n.* **1** The act of tossing; specifically, a gentle throwing from the hand; a pitch; also, the distance over which a thing is tossed. **2** A quick upward or backward movement of the head; any quick jerk. **3** The state of being tossed about; excitement; agitation. **4** A toss–up or wager. **5** *Scot.* A belle; a toast. [Prob. <Scand. Cf. dial. Norw. *tossa* spread, strew.] —**toss′er** *n.*
toss·pot (tôs′pot′, tos′-) *n.* A toper; drunkard.
toss–up (tôs′up′, tos′-) *n. Colloq.* **1** The throwing up, as of a coin, to decide a bet, etc. **2** An even or fair chance.
tot[1] (tot) *n.* A little child; toddler; also, anything small or trifling. [Prob. <Scand. Cf. ON *tuttr* a dwarf.]
tot[2] (tot) *v.t. Colloq.* To add; total: with *up* or *together.* [Short for TOTAL]
to·tal (tōt′l) *n.* The whole sum or amount; the whole, especially when considered as an aggregate of parts or elements. See synonyms under AGGREGATE, MASS[1]. —*adj.* **1** Constituting or comprising a whole, without diminution or division; being a total: the sum *total.* **2** Extending throughout the whole; comprising everything; complete; perfect: a *total* loss. —*v.* **·taled** or **·talled, ·tal·ing** or **·tal·ling** *v.t.* **1** To ascertain the total of. **2** To come to or reach as a total; amount to. —*v.i.* **3** To amount: often with *to.* [<OF <Med. L *totalis* <L *totus* all] —**to′tal·ly** *adv.*
total abstinence See under ABSTINENCE.
total depravity The condition defined by the doctrine that human nature has no tendency to piety or spirituality, but has the opposite tendency, every faculty having an innate taint: one of the five points of Calvinism. Compare ORIGINAL SIN.
total emission *Physics* The maximum emission of electrons from the cathode of a thermionic or vacuum tube.
to·tal·i·sa·tor (tōt′l·ə·zā′tər, -ī·zā′-) *n. Brit.* A machine used at racetracks for totaling the bets, reckoning the resulting pay–off odds, and recording these on a large scoreboard visible to the grandstand; a pari–mutuel. Also **to′tal·i·za′tor.**
to·tal·i·tar·i·an (tō·tal′ə·târ′ē·ən) *adj.* Designating or characteristic of a government controlled exclusively by one party or faction, which suppresses all opposition and criticism and controls and regiments all social, cultural, and economic activity in the country to advance its political aims. —*n.* An adherent of totalitarian government. [<TOTALIT(Y) + -ARIAN] —**to·tal′i·tar′i·an·ism** *n.*
to·tal·i·ty (tō·tal′ə·tē) *n.* **1** An aggregate of parts or individuals. **2** The state of being whole or entire. **3** *Astron.* The state or period of an eclipse while it is total. Also **to′tal·ness.** See synonyms under AGGREGATE, MASS[1].
to·tal·ize (tōt′l·īz) *v.t.* **·ized, ·iz·ing** To collect into or ascertain as an aggregate; make total. —**to′tal·i·za′tion** *n.*
to·tal·iz·er (tōt′l·ī′zər) *n.* A pari–mutuel machine.
total recall *Psychol.* Hypermnesia.
total reflection *Optics* The complete reflection of a ray of light passing from a denser to a less dense medium.
to·ta·quine (tō′tə·kwin) *n.* A mixture of the alkaloids from cinchona bark, including an effective percentage of quinine: used in the treatment of malaria. [<NL *totaquina* <L *tota,* fem. of *totus* all + Quechua (*quin*)*quina* cinchona bark]
tote (tōt) *Colloq. v.t.* **tot·ed, tot·ing** **1** To carry or bear on the person, as a burden. **2** To carry, transport, or haul, as supplies. **3** In arithmetic, to carry. **4** To wear habitually: He *totes* a gun. —*n.* **1** The act of toting. **2** A load or haul. [Prob. <West African] —**tot′er** *n.*
to·tem (tō′təm) *n.* **1** Among many primitive peoples, especially the North American Indians, an animal, plant, or other natural object believed to be ancestrally related to a tribe, clan, or family group or to be its tutelar spirit. **2** The representation of such an animal, plant, or object taken as an emblem or symbol. **3** The name or symbol of a person, clan, or tribe. [<Algonquian. Cf. Ojibwa *ototeman* his relations.] —**to·tem·ic** (tō·tem′ik) *adj.*
to·tem·ism (tō′təm·iz′əm) *n.* **1** Belief in totems and the practices associated therewith. **2** The system of dividing a tribe into sibs or clans according to their totems. —**to′tem·ist** *n.* —**to′tem·is′tic** *adj.*
totem pole A post or pole, usually of cedar and sometimes as much as 50 feet high, carved or painted with totemic symbols, erected outside an Indian house or as a memorial to a deceased, especially among the Indians of the NW American coast. Also **totem post.**

TOTEM POLE
Haida Indians, Queen Charlotte Islands, B.C.

toth·er (tuth′ər) *pron. Colloq.* The other; other. Also **t'oth'er.** [ME *the tother* < *thet other* the other]
toti– *combining form* Whole; wholly: *totipalmate.* [<L *totus* whole]

to·ti·pal·mate (tō′ti·pal′māt) *adj. Ornithol.* Wholly webbed; having all four toes joined by a web, as pelicans. [<TOTI- + PALMATE] — **to′ti·pal·ma′tion** (-pal·mā′shən) *n.*

to·tip·o·tence (tō·tip′ə·təns) *n. Biol.* Power to regenerate the whole of an organism, or some one part, from a fragment. [<TOTI- + *potence,* var. of POTENCY] — **to·tip′o·tent** *adj.*

Tot·le·ben (tôt′lā·bən, tot·lā′-), **Count Franz Eduard Ivanovich,** 1818–84, Russian general and engineer. Also *Todleben.*

Tot·ten·ham (tot′n·əm) A municipal borough of SE Middlesex, and northern suburb of London, England.

tot·ter (tot′ər) *v.i.* **1** To walk feebly and unsteadily. **2** To shake or waver, as if about to fall; be unsteady. — *n.* The act of tottering. See synonyms under SHAKE. [Prob. <Scand. Cf. Norw. *totra, tutra* quiver.] — **tot′ter·er** *n.* — **tot′ter·y** *adj.*

tot·ter·ing (tot′ər·ing) *adj.* Unsteady; that totters; variable. — **tot′ter·ing·ly** *adv.*

to·tum (tō′təm) *Latin* The whole; all.

tou·can (to͞o′kan, to͞o·kän′) *n.* A large, fruit-eating bird of tropical America (family *Rhamphastidae*) with brilliant plumage and an immense thin-walled beak. [<F <Pg. *tucano* <Tupian *tucana*]

TOUCAN
(About 12 inches over-all)

touch (tuch) *v.t.* **1** To place the hand, finger, etc., in contact with. **2** To be in or come into contact with. **3** To bring into contact with something else. **4** To hit or strike lightly; tap. **5** To lay the hand or hands on. **6** To border on; adjoin. **7** To come to; reach. **8** To attain to; equal. **9** To mark or delineate lightly, as with a brush or pen. **10** To modify by adding fine strokes or lines; retouch. **11** To color slightly: The sun *touched* the clouds with gold. **12** To affect injuriously; taint: Vegetables *touched* by frost. **13** To affect by contact; act upon: The drill could not *touch* the steel. **14** To affect the emotions of; soften; move. **15** To move to anger; irritate. **16** To strike the strings or keys of (a musical instrument); play on. **17** To play (a tune). **18** To relate to; concern: This quarrel *touches* you. **19** To treat or discuss in passing; deal with. **20** To have to do with, use, or partake of: I will not *touch* this food. **21** *Slang* To borrow money from. **22** *Slang* To steal. **23** *Geom.* To be tangent to. **24** *Obs.* To test, as gold with a touchstone. — *v.i.* **25** To touch someone or something. **26** To come into or be in contact. See synonyms under REACH. — **to touch at** To stop briefly at (a port or place) in the course of a journey or voyage. — **to touch off 1** To cause to explode; detonate; fire. **2** To cause to happen or occur. — **to touch on** (or **upon**) **1** To relate to; concern. **2** To treat briefly or in passing. — **to touch up 1** To strike or prod gently; rouse. **2** To add finishing touches or corrections to. — *n.* **1** The act or process of touching or coming in contact with (something). **2** The act or state of being touched. **3** That one of the special senses that gives the impression of contact with external material objects or their impact upon the body. ◆ Collateral adjective: *tactile.* **4** The sensation conveyed by touching something: a smooth *touch.* **5** *Med.* **a** Examination by feeling; palpation. **b** Digital examination of the vagina in obstetrics. **6** A stroke; hit; blow: to give a ball a slight *touch.* **7** A stroke of wit, ridicule, etc.: He felt the *touch* of her wit. **8** In art, any slight or delicate effort or effect, as of a brush, pen, or chisel; a light stroke or mark: to apply the finishing *touches* to a painting. **9** Any slight detail or effort given to anything, as to a literary work. **10** The manner or style in which an artist, workman, or author executes his work: a master's *touch*; a freedom of *touch.* **11** A trace; tinge; hint; infusion: a *touch* of irony; a *touch* of autumn. **12** A slight attack or twinge: a *touch* of rheumatism; a *touch* of remorse. **13** A small quantity or dash: to apply a *touch* of perfume. **14** Close communication, contact, or sympathy: to keep in *touch* with; to lose *touch* with. **15** A test; trial: to put something to the *touch* of proof. **16** *Music* **a** In the pianoforte, the resistance made to the fingers by the keys. **b** The manner in which a player presses the keyboard. **17** In Rugby football and soccer, the ground just outside the touch lines. **18** An official stamp impressed upon ware made of gold, silver, or pewter, to testify to its fineness. **19** *Obs.* A touchstone, or the method of assaying by the use of a touchstone. **20** *Slang* A sum of money obtained, usually from a friend or acquaintance, by borrowing or mooching. **21** *Slang* A request for such a sum of money: to make a *touch.* **22** *Slang* A person who is an easy mark for a loan or gift of money: usually with an attributive word: a soft *touch*; an easy *touch.* [<OF *tochier, tuchier*; prob. ult. imit.] — **touch′a·ble** *adj.* — **touch′a·ble·ness** *n.* — **touch′er** *n.*

touch-and-go (tuch′ən·gō′) *adj.* **1** Risky; precarious. **2** Hasty and casual; perfunctory.

touch and go 1 An uncertain, risky, or precarious state of things; a narrow escape. **2** An instantaneous or rapid action.

touch·back (tuch′bak′) *n.* In football, the act of touching the ball to the ground behind the player's own goal line when the impetus that sent the ball over the goal line was given to it by an opponent.

touch·down (tuch′doun′) *n.* A scoring play in football in which the ball is held on or over the opponent's goal line and is there declared dead.

tou·ché (to͞o·shā′) *French adj.* In fencing, touched by the point of an opponent's foil. — *interj.* You've scored a point! That argument struck home!: an exclamation used to indicate an opponent's success.

touched (tucht) *adj.* **1** That has been subjected to contact. **2** Slightly unbalanced in mind; crack-brained.

touch·hole (tuch′hōl′) *n.* The orifice in old-fashioned cannon or firearms through which the powder was ignited.

touch·ing (tuch′ing) *adj.* Appealing to the susceptibilities; affecting; pathetic. See synonyms under PITIFUL. — *n.* **1** The act of one who touches. **2** The sense of touch. — *prep.* With regard to; concerning; with respect to. — **touch′ing·ly** *adv.* —**touch′ing·ness** *n.*

touch lines The side boundary lines of a Rugby football or soccer field.

touch-me-not (tuch′mē·not′) *n.* **1** Any plant of the genus *Impatiens,* as the garden balsam (*I. balsamina*): so called from the explosive discharge of the seeds by the ripe capsules when touched. **2** The squirting cucumber **3** *Pathol.* Lupus.

touch paper Paper made slow-burning by saturation with saltpeter: used for firing explosives, as in pyrotechny.

touch·stone (tuch′stōn′) *n.* **1** A fine-grained dark stone, as jasper, formerly used to test the fineness of gold by the color of the streak made on the stone. **2** A criterion or standard by which the qualities of something are tested.

Touch·stone (tuch′stōn) A witty clown in Shakespeare's *As You Like It.*

touch-up (tuch′up′) *n.* A finishing touch or retouch.

touch·wood (tuch′wo͝od′) *n.* **1** Wood, decayed or thoroughly dried, for use as tinder; punk. **2** Dried fungi or fungous growth; amadou.

touch·y (tuch′ē) *adj.* **touch·i·er, touch·i·est 1** Apt to take offense on very little provocation; irascible; also, apt or liable to take fire, as tinder. **2** In art, done with short, light touches of the brush or pencil instead of with firm, unbroken lines. See synonyms under FRETFUL. — **touch′i·ly** *adv.* — **touch′i·ness** *n.*

tough (tuf) *adj.* **1** Susceptible of great tension or strain without breaking; also, of a close texture. **2** Not easily separated; tenacious; viscid; ropy. **3** Possessing great physical endurance: a *tough* constitution. **4** Possessing moral or intellectual endurance; steadfast; persistent; also, stubborn. **5** Irreclaimably vicious; disreputable; vulgar. **6** Difficult to accomplish; laborious; also, severe. **7** Hard to believe; incredible. — *n.* A lawless person; a rowdy; ruffian. [OE *tōh*] — **tough′ly** *adv.* — **tough′ness** *n.*

tough·en (tuf′ən) *v.t.* & *v.i.* To make or become tough or tougher. — **tough′en·er** *n.*

Toul (to͞ol) A town in NE France; besieged and captured by the Germans in the Franco-Prussian War, 1870.

Tou·lon (to͞o·lôn′) A French port and naval base on the Mediterranean 29 miles SE of Marseille.

Tou·louse (to͞o·lo͞oz′) A city of southern France, on the Garonne, capital of the Haute-Garonne department.

Tou·louse-Lau·trec (to͞o·lo͞oz′lō·trek′), **Henri Marie Raymond de,** 1864–1901, French painter and lithographer.

toun (to͞on) *n. Scot.* A town; also, a farmhouse.

tou·pee (to͞o·pā′, -pē′) *n.* **1** A little tuft or lock of hair. **2** A curl or lock of hair worn as a false front or at the top of a wig. **3** A wig worn to cover baldness or a bald spot. [<F *toupet* <OF *toup, top* a tuft of hair, prob. <Gmc.]

tour (to͝or) *n.* **1** A round trip or journey or a rambling excursion. **2** A passing around; circuit for inspection or sightseeing. **3** A turn or shift, as of service. See synonyms under JOURNEY. — **grand tour** A tour of the principal cities of Europe, customary in the 17th and 18th centuries for young English gentlemen as a supplement to their education: chiefly used in the expression *to make the grand tour.* — *v.t.* **1** To make a tour of; travel. **2** To present on a tour: to *tour* a play. — *v.i.* **3** To go on a tour. [<MF <OF *tor, tors* <L *tornus* a lathe <Gk. *tornos;* infl. in meaning by OF *tourner* TURN]

tou·ra·co (to͝or′ə·kō) See TURACOU.

Tou·raine (to͞o·ren′) A region and former province of west central France; capital, Tours.

tour·bil·lion (to͝or·bil′yən) *n.* **1** A whirling wind or a vortex, or something resembling them. **2** A kind of rocket with a spiral flight. [<MF *tourbillon* a whirlwind <OF *torbeillon* <L *turbo, -inis*]

Tour·coing (to͝or·kwaṅ′) A city in northern France near the Belgian border in the Nord department.

tour de force (to͝or də fôrs′) *French* A feat of remarkable strength or skill.

tour·ing (to͝or′ing) *adj.* Used for touring; that tours.

touring car A large, open automobile with a capacity for five or more passengers and baggage, built especially for touring. Also *Brit.* **tour′er.** — **convertible touring car** A touring car with folding top and disappearing or removable windows.

tour·ism (to͝or′iz·əm) *n.* **1** Traveling as a recreation. **2** Touring groups; tourists. **3** The organization and guidance of tourists. — **tour·is′tic** *adj.*

tour·ist (to͝or′ist) *n.* One who makes a tour or a pleasure trip. — *adj.* Of or suitable for tourists.

tourist camp A roadside group of cabins for the accommodation of transients, usually automobilists.

tourist class A class of accommodations for steamship passengers, lower than cabin class.

tour·ma·line (to͝or′mə·lēn, -lin) *n.* A complex borosilicate of aluminum, with a vitreous to resinous luster and found commonly black or brownish or bluish-black, but sometimes blue, green, red, or colorless. The transparent variety, when cut, is esteemed as a gemstone. Also spelled *turmaline.* Also **tour′ma·lin** (-lin). [<F, ult. <Singhalese *tōramalli* carnelian]

Tour·nai (to͝or·nā′) A town in SW Belgium on the Sabeldt; a manufacturing and quarrying center. Also **Tour·nay′.**

tour·na·ment (tûr′nə·mənt, to͝or′-) *n.* **1** In medieval times, a pageant in which two opposing parties of men in armor contended on horseback, with blunted weapons, in mock combat. **2** The jousts, sports, or contests in which such combatants engaged. **3** A comparatively recent sport of skilled horsemen, who tilt at rings suspended in the air, seeking to bear them off on their lances. **4** Any contest of skill involving a number of competitors and a series of games: a chess *tournament.* **5** An encounter, as of arms: Don Quixote's *tournament* with the barber. Also *tourney.* [<OF *torneiement, tornoiement* < *torneier, tornoier* tourney, ult. <L *tornare.* See TURN.]

Tour·neur (tûr′nər), **Cyril,** 1575?–1626, English dramatist.

tour·ney (tûr′nē, tŏŏr′-) *v.i.* To take part in a tournament; tilt. —*n.* A tournament. [<OF *torneier.* See TOURNAMENT.]

tour·ni·quet (tŏŏr′nə·ket, -kā, tûr′-) *n. Surg.* A bandage, etc., for stopping the flow of blood through an artery by compression. [<F < *tourner* TURN]

tour·nure (tŏŏr·nür′) *n. French* **1** The curving shape of a figure; outline; contour. **2** A light pad or cushion formerly worn by women to give the effect of well-rounded hips; a bustle; also, the drapery at the back of a gown.

tour of duty *Mil.* The hours or period of time during which a member of the armed services is on official duty, or assigned to a particular duty: the 24-hour *tour of duty* as officer of the day.

Tours (tŏŏr) A city of west central France between the Loire and the Cher above their confluence; scene of Charles Martel's defeat of the Saracens, 732.

touse (touz) *Dial.* & *Scot. v.t.* **1** To stir up, as a row. **2** To tousle; dishevel; rumple. —*n.* Disturbance. [ME *tusen, tousen,* prob. <Gmc.] —**tous′er** *n.*

tou·sle (tou′zəl) *v.t.* **·sled, ·sling** To disarrange or disorder, as the hair or dress. —*n.* **1** *Scot.* A tussle; also, a rude dalliance. **2** A tousled mass or mop of hair. Also **tou′zle.** [Freq. of TOUSE]

tous–les–mois (tŏŏ·lā·mwä′) *n.* The edible, starchlike tubers of a perennial herb of the West Indies and South America (*Canna edulis*), used in making baby food and as a substitute for arrowroot. [<F, all the months, every month; so called because edible the year round]

Tous·saint l'Ou·ver·ture (tŏŏ·san′ lŏŏ·ver·tür′), **Dominique François,** 1743–1803, Negro general; liberator of Haiti.

tou·sy (tou′zē) See TOWSY.

tout (tout) *Colloq. v.i.* **1** To solicit patronage, customers, votes, etc. **2** To spy on a race horse so as to gain information for betting; act as a tout. —*v.t.* **3** To solicit; importune. **4 a** To spy on (a race horse) to gain information for betting. **b** To sell information concerning (a race horse). —*n.* **1** One who touts. **2** In horse-racing, a spy who sells information regarding horses entered for a race. **3** One who solicits business. **4** A spy for a robber. [OE *tōtian, tȳtan* peep, look out]

tout à fait (tŏŏ tà fe′) *French* Entirely; quite.

tout à l'heure (tŏŏ tà lœr′) *French* Instantly; just now; presently.

tout au con·traire (tŏŏ tō kôn·trâr′) *French* Quite to the contrary; quite the reverse.

tout à vous (tŏŏ tà vŏŏ′) *French* Wholly yours; sincerely yours; at your service.

tout de suite (tŏŏt swēt′) *French* Immediately; at once.

tout en·sem·ble (tŏŏ tän sän′bl′) *French* **1** All in all; everything considered. **2** The general effect.

tout·er (tou′tər) *n.* **1** One who plies or solicits customers or supporters obtrusively: a *touter* for a candidate for election. **2** *Colloq.* A runner.

tout le monde (tŏŏ lə mônd′) *French* All the world; everybody.

to·va·risch (to·vä′rish) *n. Russian* Comrade.

tow[1] (tō) *n.* A short, coarse hemp or flax fiber prepared for spinning. [Prob. OE *tōw-* for spinning, as in *tōwlic* pertaining to spinning]

tow[2] (tō) *v.t.* To pull or drag by a rope or chain; drag or pull along. See synonyms under DRAW. —*n.* **1** The act of towing, or the state of being towed. **2** That which is towed, as barges by a tugboat. **3** That which tows. **4** A rope or cable used in towing; towline. —**to take in tow** To take in charge for or as for towing; take under protection; take charge of. [OE *togian*]

tow·age (tō′ij) *n.* **1** The service of, or charge for, towing. **2** The act of towing. [<TOW[1]]

to·ward (tôrd, tōrd, tə·wôrd′) *prep.* **1** In the direction of; facing. **2** With respect to; regarding: his attitude *toward* women. **3** In anticipation of or as a contribution to; for: He is saving *toward* his education. **4** Near in point of time; approaching; about: arriving *toward* evening. **5** Tending to result in; designed or likely to achieve: a struggle *toward* mutual understanding. Also **to·wards′.** See synonyms under AT. —*adj.* (tôrd, tōrd) *Archaic* or *Rare* **1** Ready to do or learn; apt. **2** Docile. **3** In progress: used predicatively. **4** Impending or imminent. [OE *tōweard* < *tō* to + *-weard* -ward] —**to·ward′ness** *n.*

to·ward·ly (tôrd′lē, tōrd′-) *Archaic adj.* **1** Ready to do or learn; compliant; docile. **2** Favorable; promising; propitious.

tow·a·way (tō′ə·wā) *n.* The act of towing away a vehicle, especially one illegally parked. —*adj.* Of or pertaining to the towing away of such vehicles: the city *towaway* policy.

tow·boat (tō′bōt′) *n.* A tugboat.

tow·el (toul, tou′əl) *n.* **1** A cloth or paper for drying anything by wiping. **2** An altar cloth. —*v.t.* **·eled** or **·elled, ·el·ing** or **·el·ling** To wipe or dry with a towel. [<OF *toaille,* prob. < OHG *dwahila* a washcloth < *dwahan* wash]

tow·el·ing (tou′ling, tou′əl·ing) *n.* Material, as crash, for towels. Also *Brit.* **tow′el·ling.**

tow·er (tou′ər) *n.* **1** A structure very tall in proportion to its other dimensions, and frequently forming part of a large building; properly, a structure larger than a pinnacle, and less tapering than a steeple. **2** A tall, wooden, movable structure from which besiegers formerly stormed a fortress. **3** A place of security or defense; fortified place; citadel. —*v.i.* **1** To rise or stand like a tower; extend to a great height. **2** To fly directly upward, as some birds. [Fusion of OE *torr* (<L *turris*) and OE *tūr* <OF *tor, tur* <L *turris*]

tow·ered (tou′ərd) *adj.* **1** Furnished with towers for ornament or defense. **2** Rising like a tower.

tow·er·ing (tou′ər·ing) *adj.* **1** Like a tower; lofty; hence, very high or great: also **tow′er·y.** **2** Rising or increasing to a high pitch of violence or intensity; furious. See synonyms under HIGH.

Tower of London A group of buildings comprising a fortress and palace on the north bank of the Thames, built in 1078 around the original tower (the White Tower) and used as a royal residence, a political prison, and a museum.

tower of silence A circular tower with central well, having a high outer wall, and inner platform on which the Parsees expose the bodies of their dead to be eaten by vultures, so that the bodies may be dissipated without polluting the earth: also called *dakhma, dokhma.*

tow·head (tō′hed′) *n.* **1** A head of very light-colored or flaxen hair, or a person having such hair. **2** *U.S.* A wooded sandbar or newly formed island in a river. [<TOW[1] + HEAD] —**tow′–head′ed** *adj.*

tow·hee (tou′hē, tō′-) *n.* An American bird related to the buntings and the sparrows, especially the **Alabama towhee** (*Pipilo erythrophthalmus*) and the **green–tailed towhee** (*Oberholseria chlorura*) of the western United States. Also **towhee bunting.** [Imit. of one of its notes]

tow·line (tō′līn′) *n.* A line, rope, or chain used in towing.

tow·mont (tō′mənt) *n. Scot.* A twelvemonth. Also **tow′mond** (-mənd).

town (toun) *n.* **1** Any considerable collection of dwellings and other buildings larger than a village and comprising a geographical and political community unit, but not incorporated as a city. **2** The local government of such a community; also, the voters, the representatives, or the inhabitants collectively. **3** A subdivision of a county, usually rural, that may include a number of villages and towns; a township. **4** In New England, a local unit governing itself through a town meeting. **5** *Brit.* Originally, a collection of dwellings enclosed for security within some form of fortification; subsequently, any collection of dwelling houses larger than a village. ◆ Collateral adjective: *oppidan.* **6** A closely settled urban district as contrasted with the open country: *town* and country. **7** The city or town nearest to where one lives: a trip to *town*; also, the downtown or business section of a city or town. **8** A group of prairie-dog burrows. —**on the town** **1** Dependent on municipal charity. **2** *Slang* On a round of pleasure in the city. —**to go to town** *Slang* To succeed in the highest degree. —**to paint the town red** *Slang* To carouse. —*adj.* **1** Of or pertaining to, like, situated in, or for use in town: *town* clothes. **2** Supported by town funds: a *town* library. [OE *tūn, tuun* an enclosure, group of houses]

Town may appear as a combining form in hyphemes or solidemes, or as the first element in two-word phrases:

town–absorbing	**town–hating**
town–born	**town–imprisoned**
town–bound	**town jail**
town–bred	**town–keeping**
town bridge	**town life**
town car	**town lot**
town church	**town–loving**
town–dotted	**town–made**
town dweller	**town park**
town–dwelling	**town sick**
town–flanked	**townsickness**
town–frequenting	**town–tied**
town–goer	**town–trained**
town–going	**town–weary**

town clerk An official who keeps the records of a town.

town crier A person appointed to make proclamations through the streets of a town.

town farm A farm maintained by town or township funds for the poor or indigent.

town·folk (toun′fōk′) *n.* People who live in towns or in a particular town or city. Also **towns′folk′, towns′peo′ple** (-pē′pəl).

town hall The building containing the public offices of a town and used for meetings of the town council and other official business.

town house **1** A residence in a town or city. **2** A town hall. **3** *U. S. Obs.* **a** An almshouse; workhouse. **b** A town prison.

town marshal **1** An officer of a town police force. **2** In the American colonies, an officer who levied and collected taxes, fines, etc.

town meeting **1** A general assemblage of the people of a town. **2** An assembly of qualified voters for the purpose of transacting town business; also, the voters assembled.

town·ship (toun′ship) *n.* **1** *U.S.* **a** A territorial subdivision of a county with certain corporate powers of municipal government for local purposes; also, the corporation or government thereof. **b** In New England, a local political unit governed by a town meeting. **2** A unit of area in surveys of U. S. public lands, normally six miles square, subdivided into 36 sections of one square mile each. **3** *Brit.* Anciently, an organized group of families forming the political unit of early society which existed prior to the parish. [OE *tūnscipe* < *tūn* a village, group of houses]

towns·man (tounz′mən) *n. pl.* **·men** (-mən) **1** A resident of a town; also, a fellow citizen. **2** In New England, a town officer; a selectman. **3** In a school or college town, one who lives in the town as contrasted with a student or teacher in the school or college.

towns·wom·an (tounz′wŏŏm′ən) *n. pl.* **·wom·en** (-wim′in) A woman living in a town.

tow·path (tō′path′, -päth′) *n.* A path along a river or canal used by men, horses, or mules towing boats; a towing path.

tow·rope (tō′rōp′) *n.* A heavy rope or cable used in towing. Also called *towline.*

tow truck (tō) A truck equipped to tow other vehicles.

tow·y (tō′ē) *adj.* Composed of, like, or containing tow. [<TOW[1]]

tow·zie (tou′zē) *adj. Scot.* Disheveled; rumpled; shaggy: also spelled *toozie, tousy.* Also **tow′sie.**

tox·al·bu·min (tok′sal·byŏŏ′min) *n. Biochem.* Any protein substance having toxic properties, as snake venom, ricin, certain bacterial cultures, etc. [<TOX(IC) + ALBUMIN]

tox·e·mi·a (tok·sē′mē·ə) *n. Pathol.* A poisoned condition of the body caused by the absorption of bacterial toxins from a local source of infection and their distribution by the blood. Also **tox·ae′mi·a.** [<NL <Gk. *toxicon* a poison + *haima* blood] —**tox·e′mic, tox·ae′·mic** *adj.*

tox·ic (tok′sik) *adj.* **1** Pertaining to poison; poisonous. **2** Due to or caused by poison or a toxin. Also **tox′i·cal.** [<Med. L *toxicus* poisoned, poisonous <L *toxicum* a poison, orig. a poison for arrows <Gk. *toxicon* (*pharmakon*) (a poison) for arrows < *toxa* arrows < *toxon* a bow] —**tox′i·cal·ly** *adv.*

tox·i·cant (tok′sə·kənt) *adj.* **1** Possessing poisonous qualities. **2** Producing a poisonous effect. —*n.* A toxic substance; poison; also, an intoxicant. [<LL *toxicans, -antis,* ppr. of

toxicare smear with poison <L *toxicum*. See TOXIC.]

tox·i·ca·tion (tok′sə·kā′shən) *n.* 1 The act of poisoning. 2 The state of being poisoned. 3 Poisoning.

tox·ic·i·ty (tok·sis′ə·tē) *n.* 1 The quality of being toxic. 2 The degree or intensity of virulence of a poison.

toxico– *combining form* Poison; of or pertaining to poison, or to poisons: *toxicology*. Also, before vowels, **toxic–**. [<Gk. *toxicon* poison]

tox·i·co·gen·ic (tok′sə·kō·jen′ik) *adj.* 1 Producing poisons or toxins. 2 Generated or formed by toxic matter.

tox·i·col·o·gy (tok′sə·kol′ə·jē) *n.* The science that treats of the origin, nature, properties, and effects of poisons, of their detection in the organs or tissues, of their antidotes, and of the treatment of diseases due to poisoning. [<F *toxicologie*] —**tox′i·co·log′i·cal** (-kō·loj′i·kəl) *adj.* —**tox′i·co·log′i·cal·ly** *adv.* —**tox′i·col′o·gist** *n.*

tox·i·co·ma·ni·a (tok′sə·kō·mā′nē·ə, -mān′yə) *n.* A morbid desire to take poison. [<TOXICO- + -MANIA]

tox·i·co·pho·bi·a (tok′sə·kō·fō′bē·ə) *n.* A morbid fear of poison or of being poisoned: also called *iophobia, toxiphobia*. [<TOXICO- + -PHOBIA] —**tox′i·pho′bic** *adj.*

tox·i·co·sis (tok′sə·kō′sis) *n.* *pl.* **·ses** (-sēz) *Pathol.* A morbid condition due to the effect of toxins generated within the system or administered from without. [<NL <L *toxicum* poison]

tox·in (tok′sin) *n.* 1 Any of a class of more or less unstable poisonous compounds elaborated by animal, vegetable, or bacterial organisms and acting as causative agents in many diseases, usually after an incubation period. 2 Any toxic matter generated in living or dead organisms. Also **tox·ine** (tok′sēn). [<TOX(IC) + -IN]

tox·is·ter·ol (tok·sis′tər·ōl, -ol) *n. Biochem.* A toxic compound produced by the excessive irradiation of ergosterol and intermediate between calciferol and suprasterol. [<TOXI(C) + STEROL]

tox·o·phil (tok′sə·fil) *adj. Biol.* Having an affinity for or being in harmony with a toxin. Also **tox′o·phile** (-fīl, -fil). [< *toxo-* (<TOXIN) + -PHIL]

tox·o·plas·mo·sis (tok′sō·plaz·mō′sis) *n.* A diseased condition resulting from the presence of or infection by sporozoan parasites (genus *Toxoplasma*) which act principally upon the nervous system of certain animals and sometimes of man. [<NL <*Toxoplasma*, genus name]

toy (toi) *n.* 1 An article constructed for the amusement of children; a plaything; hence, any trifling or diverting object; an ornament; trinket. 2 Any diminutive object imitating a larger one and fitted for entertainment and instruction. 3 *Obs.* Wanton play; dalliance. 4 A small dog bred to extreme smallness and kept as a pet: also **toy dog.** 5 *Scot.* A head covering for women that hangs loosely over the shoulders; a toy-mutch. 6 *Obs.* A dance tune. 7 *Archaic* A quaint utterance, idle tale, or anecdote; fancy; jest. See synonyms under GAUD. —*v.i.* To trifle; play. —*adj.* Resembling a toy; of miniature size. [Prob. fusion of ME *toye* flirtation, sport + Du. *tuig* tools, stuff] —**toy′er** *n.* —**toy′ish** *adj.*

To·ya·ma (tō·yä·mä) A port of north central Honshu, Japan.

toy–mutch (toi′much) *n. Scot.* Toy (def. 5).

Toyn·bee (toin′bē), **Arnold Joseph,** born 1889, English historian.

to·yo (tō′yō) *n.* A shiny, rice–paper straw. [<Japanese]

To·yo·ha·shi (tō·yō·hä·shē) A city of southern Honshu, Japan; a manufacturing center.

to·yon (tō′yən) *n.* An evergreen shrub (*Photinia arbutifolia*) indigenous to the Pacific coast of North America, having white flowers, followed by persistent berries of a bright red color; California holly. [<Sp. *tollón* < N. Am. Ind. (Mexican)]

toy shop A shop where toys are displayed for sale.

tra·be·at·ed (trā′bē·ā′tid) *adj. Archit.* 1 Having an entablature. 2 Having beams or long stones as lintels instead of an arch. Also **tra′·be·ate** (-it, -āt). [Irregularly formed <L *trabs, trabis* a beam]

tra·be·a·tion (trā′bē·ā′shən) *n. Archit.* 1 The state of being trabeated. 2 An entablature.

tra·bec·u·la (trə·bek′yə·lə) *n.* *pl.* **·lae** (-lē) 1 A small supporting band or bar. 2 *Anat.* The interwoven bands of connective tissue that form the supporting framework of an organ, as the spleen. 3 *Bot.* A row or plate of sterile cells extending across the cavity in the sporangium of a moss. [<L, dim. of *trabs, trabis* a beam] —**tra·bec′u·lar** *adj.*

Tra·ben–Trar·bach (trä′bən·trär′bäkh) A town in Rhineland–Palatinate, West Germany, on the Mosel; a wine center.

Trab·zon (träb·zôn′) The Turkish name for TREBIZOND.

trace[1] (trās) *n.* 1 A vestige or mark left by some past event or agent, especially when regarded as a sign or clue. 2 A barely detectable quantity, quality, token, or characteristic; touch. 3 *Chem.* A proportion or ingredient too small to be weighed (often abbreviated *tr.*): a *trace* of soda. 3 An imprint or mark indicating the passage of a person or thing, as a footprint, etc. 4 A path or trail through woods or forest beaten down by men or animals. 5 A lightly drawn line; something traced. 6 The point or line on a map or on the ground indicating the position of a trench, an aircraft flight path, etc. 7 The path of a tracer bullet. 8 *Psychol.* An engram. —*v.* **traced, trac·ing** *v.t.* 1 To follow the tracks, course, or development of. 2 To follow (tracks, a course of development, etc.). 3 To discover or ascertain by examination or investigation; find out or determine. 4 To draw; sketch. 5 To copy (a drawing, etc.) on a superimposed transparent sheet. 6 To form (letters, etc.) with careful strokes. 7 To mark with an impressed design; chase. 8 To imprint (a pattern or design). 9 To mark or record by a curved or broken line. 10 To go or move over, along, or through. —*v.i.* 11 To make one's way; proceed. 12 To have its origin; go back in time. [<OF *tracier*, ult. <L *tractus* a dragging, a track < *trahere* draw] —**trace′a·ble** *adj.* —**trace′a·bil′i·ty, trace′a·ble·ness** *n.* —**trace′a·bly** *adv.* —**trace′·less** *adj.*

Synonyms (noun): footmark, footprint, footstep, mark, memorial, remains, remnant, sign, token, track, vestige. A *vestige* is always slight compared with that whose existence it recalls; as, Scattered mounds containing human implements are *vestiges* of a former civilization. A *vestige* is always a part of that which has passed away; a *trace* may be merely the *mark* it has made, or some slight evidence of its presence or of the effect it has produced; as, *Traces* of game were observed by the hunter. See CHARACTERISTIC, MARK[1].

trace[2] (trās) *n.* 1 One of two side straps or chains for connecting the collar of a harness with the swingletree. 2 *Mech.* A link or connecting bar hinged at each end to other pieces of a mechanism, to transmit motion from one part to another. —**to kick over the traces** To throw off control; become unmanageable. —*v.t.* **traced, trac·ing** To fasten, as with traces. [<OF *traiz, trais*, pl. of *trait* a dragging, a leather harness <L *tractus*. See TRACE[1].]

trac·er (trā′sər) *n.* 1 One who or that which traces. 2 One of various instruments used in tracing drawings, etc. 3 An inquiry forwarded from one point to another, to trace missing mail matter, etc. 4 *Surg.* An instrument for laying bare and tracing the course of nerves, muscles, etc. 5 One who searches for lost property, as on railroads. 6 *Mil.* **a** A chemical incorporated in certain types of ammunition used for ranging, signaling, or incendiary purposes. **b** A tracer bullet. 7 *Med.* A radioisotope introduced into the body for the purpose of following the processes of metabolism, the course or location of a disease, etc. 8 A message that describes a person or thing wanted, as by the police. [<TRACE[1]]

tracer bullet A bullet which leaves a line of smoke or fire in its wake, thus indicating its course for correction of aim.

trac·er·y (trā′sər·ē) *n.* *pl.* **·er·ies** 1 Ornamental stonework formed of ramifying lines. 2 Any work resembling this.

tra·che·a (trā′kē·ə) *n.* *pl.* **·che·ae** (-ki·ē) 1 *Anat.* The duct, composed of membrane and incomplete cartilaginous rings, by which air passes from the larynx to the bronchi and the lungs; the windpipe. 2 *Zool.* One of the passages by which air is conveyed from the exterior in air–breathing arthropods, as insects and arachnids. 3 *Bot.* A duct or vessel in plants, particularly one having spiral markings. [<Med. L <LL *trachia* <Gk. (*artēria*) *tracheia* a rough (artery), fem. of *trachys* rough] —**tra′che·al** *adj.*

tracheal tissue *Bot.* Plant tissue consisting of tracheae or tracheids: one of the chief constituents of xylem.

tra·che·id (trā′kē·id) *n. Bot.* An elongated, taper–pointed, woody plant cell, especially when marked with bordered pits and serving for support, as in the pine family. [<G *tracheïde* <Med. L *trachea* the trachea] —**tra·che·i·dal** (trə·kē′ə·dəl) *adj.*

tra·che·i·tis (trā′kē·ī′tis) *n. Pathol.* Inflammation of the trachea or windpipe. [<NL <Med. L *trachea* the trachea]

tracheo– *combining form* The trachea; of or pertaining to the trachea: *tracheotomy*. Also, before vowels, **trache–**. [<TRACHEA]

tra·che·os·co·py (trā′kē·os′kə·pē) *n. Med.* Instrumental inspection of the windpipe. —**tra′che·o·scop′ic** (-ō·skop′ik) *adj.* —**tra′che·os′co·pist** *n.*

tra·che·ot·o·my (trā′kē·ot′ə·mē) *n. Surg.* The operation of making an incision into the windpipe. —**tra′che·ot′o·mist** *n.*

trach·le (träkh′əl) *Scot. v.t.* To trail or draggle; fatigue; exhaust. —*n.* Any exercise involving or resulting in unusual fatigue; a burdensome work. Also spelled *trauchle*. [Corruption of DRAGGLE]

tra·cho·ma (trə·kō′mə) *n. Pathol.* A contagious virus disease of the eye characterized by hard papillary elevations or granular excrescences on the inner surface of the eyelids, with inflammation of the lining; granular conjunctivitis. [<NL <Gk. *trachōma, -atos* roughness < *trachys* rough] —**tra·chom·a·tous** (trə·kom′·ə·təs) *adj.*

trachy– *combining form* Rough; uneven: *trachycarpous*, bearing rough fruit. Also, before vowels, **trach–**. [<Gk. *trachys* rough]

tra·chyte (trā′kīt, trak′īt) *n.* A light–colored, rough volcanic rock having a porphyritic texture, composed essentially of alkaline feldspar and one or more secondary minerals. [<F <Gk. *trachytēs* ruggedness < *trachys* rough]

trac·ing (trā′sing) *n.* 1 The act of one who traces. 2 An ornamentation produced by etching, drawing, or tracing. 3 A copy made by tracing on transparent paper. 4 A record made by a self–registering instrument.

track (trak) *n.* 1 A mark or trail left by the passage of anything: the *track* of a storm. 2 A footprint or series of footprints. 3 Any regular path; course: the *track* of a comet round the sun. 4 Any kind of racecourse; also, sports performed on such a course; track athletics. 5 A set of rails or a rail on which something may travel; specifically, the pair of metal rails on which a railway train or tramway runs; also, the rail or pair of rails with its ties, bolts, etc.; by extension, the whole trackway. 6 A trace or vestige. 7 A sequence of events; a succession of ideas. 8 Awareness of the progress or sequence; count; record: to keep *track* of. 9 Tread (def. 2). See synonyms under MARK[1], ROAD, TRACE[1], WAY. 10 A course or trail leading to a desired goal: to be on the right *track*. 11 One of a pair of endless metal belts by means of which certain vehicles, as tanks, are capable of moving over a variety of surfaces. 12 In education, any of two or more classes covering the same course of study, segregated according to the students' preparation or ability and taught at correspondingly different levels. —**to make tracks** To hurry; run away in haste. —**in one's tracks** Right where one is; on the spot. —**to jump the track** 1 To leave the rails, as a railroad engine or car. 2 To depart from any usual course or procedure. —*v.t.* 1 To follow the tracks of; trail. 2 To discover and follow up or out, by means of marks or indications. 3 To make tracks upon or with: to *track* snow through a house. 4 To traverse, as on foot: to *track* the wild forests. 5 To furnish with rails or tracks. —*v.i.* 6 To measure a certain distance between wheels. 7 To have the wheels equal in span or gage to the wheels of another vehicle. 8 To run in the same track; be in alinement. —*adj.* Pertaining to or performed on a track. [<OF *trac,* prob. <Gmc. Cf. Du. *trek* pull.] —**track'er** *n.* —**track'a·ble** *adj.*

track·age (trak'ij) *n.* 1 Railroad tracks collectively. 2 The right of one company to use the track system of another company. 3 The charge for this right. 4 A towing, especially of a vessel in a canal, with a rope from the towpath.

track boat A boat towed from a path along the shore.

track detector *Physics* A device for showing the ionization paths of subatomic particles, as the cloud chamber.

track events The races at an athletic meet: distinguished from *field events.* Also **track athletics.**

track·less (trak'lis) *adj.* 1 Unmarked by footsteps; pathless: the *trackless* desert. 2 Leaving no traces: a *trackless* fugitive. 3 Not running on tracks or rails.

trackless trolley A trolley bus.

track·man (trak'mən) *n. pl.* **·men** (-mən) *U.S.* A person employed to inspect regularly the condition of a section of railroad track. Also **track·walk·er** (trak'wôk'ər).

track meet An athletic contest made up of track events.

track record *Colloq.* A record of achievements.

track·way (trak'wā') *n.* The permanent way of a railroad.

tract[1] (trakt) *n.* 1 An extended area, as of land or water. 2 Continued duration, as of time. 3 *Anat.* An extensive region of the body, especially one comprising a system of parts or organs: the alimentary *tract.* [<L *tractus* a drawing out, duration < *trahere* draw. Doublet of TRAIT.]

tract[2] (trakt) *n.* 1 A short treatise, as on some question of religion or morals; a propaganda leaflet. 2 An anthem sometimes substituted for the Alleluia: so styled because, instead of being treated antiphonally, it is sung *tractim* (continuously) and as a solo: also **trac'tus.** [Short for TRACTATE]

tract·a·ble (trak'tə·bəl) *adj.* 1 Easily led or controlled; manageable; docile. 2 Readily worked or handled; malleable. See synonyms under DOCILE. [<L *tractabilis* < *tractare* handle, freq. of *trahere* draw] —**tract'a·bly** *adv.* —**tract'a·ble·ness, tract'a·bil'i·ty** *n.*

Trac·tar·ian (trak·târ'ē·ən) *n.* One of the authors of the series of 90 pamphlets called *Tracts for the Times.* —*adj.* Pertaining to the Tractarians or to their teachings.

Trac·tar·i·an·ism (trak·târ'ē·ən·iz'əm) *n.* The tenets or principles expressed in *Tracts for the Times* (1833–41) by the leaders of the religious movement known as the Oxford Movement which sought to link the Anglican Church more closely to the Roman Catholic Church and opposed liberalism in theology.

trac·tate (trak'tāt) *n.* A short treatise; a tract. [<L *tractatus* a handling, treatise, pp. of *tractare.* See TRACTABLE.]

trac·tile (trak'til) *adj.* That can be drawn out; ductile. [<L *tractilis* < *tractus.* See TRACE[1].] —**trac·til'i·ty** *n.*

trac·tion (trak'shən) *n.* 1 The act of drawing, as by motive power over a surface. 2 The state of being drawn, or the power employed. 3 *Physiol.* Contraction, as of a muscle. 4 Adhesive or rolling friction, as of wheels on a track. [<Med. L *tractio, -onis* <L *tractus.* See TRACE[1].] —**trac'tion·al** *adj.*

trac·tive (trak'tiv) *adj.* Having or exerting traction.

trac·tor (trak'tər) *n.* 1 A machine or instrument for pulling or drawing. 2 A powerful, motor-driven vehicle, usually having heavy treads, used, as on farms, to draw a plow, reaper, etc. 3 An automotive vehicle with a driver's cab, used to haul trailers, etc. 4 A traction engine. 5 *Aeron.* **a** An airplane with the propeller or propellers situated in front of the supporting surface to pull it through the air: also **tractor airplane. b** The propeller of a tractor airplane. [<NL <L *tractus.* See TRACE[1].]

trad (trad) *adj. Slang* Traditional: *trad* jazz.

trade (trād) *n.* 1 A business, particularly a skilled or specialized handicraft; a craft. 2 Mercantile traffic; commerce. 3 A bargain; deal; also, an exchange; specifically, a corrupt bargain in patronage between political-party leaders. 4 The people following a particular calling. 5 The amount of business or exchange done in a particular place; a firm's customers. 6 Customary pursuit; occupation. 7 *Brit.* **a** The submarine service of the Royal Navy. **b** The liquor traffic. 8 *Obs.* A trail or track. 9 *Obs.* A course, path, passage, or way. 10 *Obs.* Custom, habit, or practice. 11 A trade wind: usually in the plural. See synonyms under BUSINESS, SALE, TRAFFIC. —*v.* **trad·ed, trad·ing** *v.t.* To dispose of by bargain and sale; now, especially, to barter; exchange. —*v.i.* To engage in commerce or in business transactions of bargain and sale. —**to trade in** To give in exchange as payment or part payment. —**to trade off** To get rid of by exchange or trading. —**to trade on** To take advantage of. [<MLG, a track. Akin to TREAD.]

trade acceptance A bill of exchange drawn by the seller of goods on the purchaser who accepts the draft by writing across the face of it when and where it is payable.

trade book An edition of a book designed for ordinary sale to the general public, as distinguished from a textbook, limited or de luxe edition, etc.

trade dollar See under DOLLAR.

trade-in (trād'in') *n.* Something given or accepted in payment or part payment for something else; an exchange.

trade journal A periodical publishing news and discussions of a particular trade or business.

trade-last (trād'last', -läst') *n. Colloq.* A favorable remark that one has heard and offers to repeat to the person complimented in return for a similar remark.

trade·mark (trād'märk') *n.* A name, symbol, design, device, or word, or any combination thereof, used by a merchant or manufacturer to identify his goods and distinguish them from those made or sold by others. A trademark may or may not be legally registered as such —*v.t.* 1 To label with a trademark. 2 To register as a trademark. —**trade'marked'** *adj.*

trade name 1 The name by which an article, process, service, or the like is designated in trade. 2 A name given by a manufacturer to designate a proprietary article, sometimes having the status of a trademark or of a copyrighted and patented proprietary name. 3 A style or a name of a business house acquired by purchase from a retiring firm or trader.

trade-off (trād'ôf', -of') *n.* 1 A giving up of something, as an objective or advantage, in exchange for something else: a *trade-off* of higher pay for longer vacations. 2 The relationship that characterizes such an exchange; a compromise or adjustment between opposing elements or positions: the *trade-off* between taxation and improved public services.

trad·er (trā'dər) *n.* 1 One who trades. 2 Any vessel employed in a particular trade. 3 A member of a stock exchange who trades for himself, and not for customers.

trade rat A pack rat.

trad·es·can·ti·a (trad'əs·kan'shē·ə, -shə) *n.* Any of a genus (*Tradescantia*) of perennial American herbs, often having grasslike leaves and showy flowers with ephemeral petals. [<NL, after John *Tradescant,* died in 1638, English traveler and naturalist]

trade school See under SCHOOL.

trades·folk (trādz'fōk') *n. pl.* People engaged in retail trade; shopkeepers or salespeople. Also **trades'peo'ple'**

trades·man (trādz'mən) *n. pl.* **·men** (-mən) 1 A retail dealer; shopkeeper. 2 *Brit.* A mechanic.

trades·wom·an (trādz'wo͝om'ən) *n. pl.* **·wom·en** (-wim'in) A woman engaged in trade or the sale of goods.

trade union An organized association of workmen formed for the protection and promotion of their common interests, especially with regard to wages, hours, and working conditions. Also **trades union.** —**trade'-un'ion·ism** *n.* —**trade'-un'ion·ist** *n.*

trade wind Either of two steady winds blowing in the same course toward the equator from about 30° N and S latitude, one from the northeast on the north, the other from the southeast on the south side of the equatorial line.

trad·ing (trā'ding) *adj.* 1 Carrying on trade. 2 Corrupt; venal: said of officials. 3 *Obs.* Pursuing a steady course.

trading post A building or small settlement in unsettled territory where a trader or trading company has set up a station for barter (usually in furs) with North American Indians or other natives.

trading stamp See under STAMP.

tra·di·tion (trə·dish'ən) *n.* 1 The transmission of knowledge, opinions, doctrines, customs, practices, etc., from generation to generation, originally by word of mouth and by example. 2 That which is so transmitted; a body of beliefs and usages handed down from generation to generation; also, any particular story, belief, or usage so handed down; hence, remembrance, or recollection existing as by transmission. 3 That body of Christian doctrine, handed down through successive generations and held by some churches to belong to the deposit of faith, even if it may not be found in the Holy Scripture. 4 Among the Jews, an unwritten code said to have been revealed to Moses on Mount Sinai at the time of the delivery of the Decalog and handed down through the oral teaching of prophets and doctors of the law. 5 The record of the acts and utterances of Mohammed, known as the *Sunna.* 6 A custom so long continued that it has almost the force of a law. 7 *Law* Delivery of possession. [<OF *tradicion* <L *traditio, -onis* a delivery, surrender < *traditus,* pp. of *tradere* deliver < *trans-* across + *dare* give. Doublet of TREASON.] —**tra·di'tion·er, tra·di'tion·ist** *n.*

tra·di·tion·al (trə·dish'ən·əl) *adj.* 1 Relating to or depending on tradition. 2 Characterizing a school of English Biblical critics who hold the Greek texts of the New Testament to be the foundation of the true text. Also **tra·di'tion·ar'y** (-er'ē). —**tra·di'tion·al·ist** *adj.* & *n.* —**tra·di'tion·al·is'tic** *adj.* —**tra·di'tion·al·ly** *adv.*

tra·di·tion·al·ism (trə·dish'ən·əl·iz'əm) *n.* 1 A system of faith founded on tradition. 2 Adherence to tradition; especially, undue reverence for tradition in religious matters.

trad·i·tive (trad'ə·tiv) *adj. Obs.* Traditional. [Appar. <MF *traditif* <L *traditus.* See TRADITION.]

trad·i·tor (trad'ə·tər) *n. pl.* **trad·i·to·res** (trad'ə·tôr'ēz, -tō'rēz) A traitor among the early Christians at the time of the Roman persecutions. [<L, a deliverer, betrayer < *tradere.* See TRADITION.]

tra·duce (trə·do͞os', -dyo͞os') *v.t.* **·duced, ·duc·ing** To misrepresent wilfully the conduct or character of; defame; slander. See synonyms under ASPERSE, REVILE. [<L *traducere* transport, bring into disgrace < *trans-* across + *ducere* lead] —**tra·duc'er** *n.* —**tra·duc'i·ble** *adj.* —**tra·duc'ing·ly** *adv.* —**tra·duc·tion** (trə·duk'shən) *n.*

tra·du·cian·ism (trə·do͞o'shən·iz'əm, -dyo͞o'-) *n.* The doctrine that the soul, equally with the body, is produced and begotten by the parent or parents: distinguished from *creationism* and *preexistence.* [<LL *traducianus* <L *tradux, -icis* a shoot for propagation < *traducere.* See TRADUCE.] —**tra·du'cian·ist** *n.* —**tra·du'cian·is'tic** *adj.*

Tra·fal·gar (trə·fal'gər, *Sp.* trä'fäl·gär'), **Cape** A headland on the Atlantic coast of SW Spain; scene of a naval battle in which Nelson, though fatally wounded, defeated the French and Spanish fleets, 1805.

traf·fic (traf'ik) *n.* 1 The exchange of goods, wares, etc.; the business of buying and selling, between individuals or communities; trade. 2 The business of transportation, as by railroad. 3 The subjects of transportation collectively; the things carried. 4 A business procedure; transaction; hence, intercourse. 5 The passing of pedestrians and vehicles along a road; the flow of telephone messages, etc. 6 Unlawful or improper trade: *traffic* in stolen goods. —*v.i.* **·ficked, ·fick·ing** 1 To engage in buying and selling; do business, especially illegally: with *in*. **2** To have dealings: with *with*. [<MF *trafic, trafique* <Ital. *traffico* < *trafficare* <L *trans-* across + Ital. *ficcare* thrust in <L *figere* fasten] —**traf′fick·er** *n.*

Synonyms (noun): business, commerce, trade. *Commerce* is the broadest and noblest term of this group. *Trade* may be local; *commerce* is always extended and is between members of distinct communities, states, or nations; as, foreign, interstate, or intrastate *commerce*; foreign, domestic, or free-port *trade*. *Traffic* is local, as between different parts of one city or between two or more cities. *Trade* may be largely by letter or telegram, etc.; *traffic* involves the actual passing to and fro of persons or commodities and may be applied directly to persons when considered as in some way a source of gain: the passenger *traffic* of a railroad. *Traffic* always suggests stir and bustle: the din of *traffic*; one may say dull *trade*, but scarcely dull *traffic*. Compare synonyms for BUSINESS.

Traffic may appear as a combining form in hyphemes or as the first element in two-word phrases, with the following meanings:

1 Of or pertaining to the flow of roadway traffic:

traffic accident **traffic congestion**
traffic artery **traffic-laden**
traffic-congested **traffic lane**

2 Of or pertaining to the laws or regulation of roadway traffic:

traffic cop **traffic signal**
traffic court **traffic violation**
traffic policeman **traffic violator**

traf·fic·a·tor (traf′ə·kā′tər) *n.* A traffic signal. [<TRAFFIC + -ATOR]

traffic circle A circular intersection, where traffic is maintained in one direction, so constructed as to allow vehicles to enter or leave it at any of the converging roads, or to change course, without interruption of the flow of traffic.

traffic light A signal light which, by changing color, directs the flow of traffic along a road or highway.

trag·a·canth (trag′ə·kanth) *n.* **1** A white or reddish gum obtained from various species of Old World leguminous herbs (genus *Astragalus*), especially *A. gummifer* of SW Asia: used in pharmacy and the arts. **2** Any of the shrubs yielding this gum. [<MF *tragacante* <L *tragacantha* <Gk. *tragakantha* a tragacanth shrub < *tragos* a male goat + *akantha* a thorn]

tra·ge·di·an (trə·jē′dē·ən) *n.* **1** An actor in tragedy. **2** A writer of tragedies.

tra·ge·di·enne (trə·jē′dē·en′) *n.* An actress of tragedy. [<F]

trag·e·dy (traj′ə·dē) *n. pl.* **·dies** **1** A form of drama in which the protagonist, having some quality of greatness (and, in Greek, Roman, and Renaissance tragedy, in high place) comes to disaster through some flaw (which may be a noble fault) in his nature that interacts with the fabric of events (the plot) to bring about his inevitable downfall or death, the action being managed in a way to produce pity and fear in the spectator and to effect a catharsis of these feelings. The failure to achieve this leads to **tragedy manquée**, which falls short of true tragedy. To the outcome of death or madness usual in ancient and Renaissance tragedy, modern tragedy adds the possibility of frustration and unfulfilment from which there seems no escape. Opposed to *comedy*. **2** A fatal event or course of events; murder, especially one involving dramatic incidents. **3** A very terrible or sorrowful fate or end. **4** The art or theory of acting or composing tragedy. [<OF *tregedie, tragedie* <L *tragoedia* <Gk. *tragōidia* appar. < *tragos* a goat + *ōidē* a song; semantic development uncertain]

Trag·e·dy (traj′ə·dē) Tragedy personified, especially as Melpomene.

trag·ic (traj′ik) *adj.* **1** Involving death or calamity; causing suffering; fatal; terrible. **2** Pertaining to or having the nature of tragedy. **3** Appropriate to or like tragedy, especially in drama. Also **trag′i·cal.** [<L *tragicus* <Gk. *tragikos* pertaining to tragedy < *tragos* a goat] —**trag′i·cal·ly, trag′ic·ly** *adv.* —**trag′i·cal·ness** *n.*

trag·i·com·e·dy (traj′i·kom′ə·dē) *n. pl.* **·dies** A drama in which tragic and comic scenes are intermingled. [<MF *tragi-comédie* <LL *tragicomoedia* <L *tragico-comoedia* < *tragicus* TRAGIC + *comoedia* COMEDY] —**trag′i·com′ic** or **·i·cal** *adj.* —**trag′i·com′i·cal·ly** *adv.*

trag·o·pan (trag′ə·pan) *n.* An Asian pheasant (genus *Tragopan*) of which the horned pheasant, having gorgeous ocellated plumage, is a variety. [<NL <L, a fabulous bird <Gk. < *tragos* a goat + *Pan* Pan]

tra·gus (trā′gəs) *n. pl.* **·gi** (-jī) *Anat.* A flattened, somewhat conical eminence of the auricle in front of the opening of the external ear. [<LL <Gk. *tragos* the hairy part of the ear, a he-goat; so called because of the hairs on it]

traik (trāk) *Scot. v.i.* **1** To wander idly or with fatigue; tramp; trudge. **2** To go astray. —*n.* **1** The flesh of sheep that have died from disease or accident. **2** A stroll or saunter; also, a wearisome tramp or journey: also spelled *trake*.

traik·et (trā′kit) *adj. Scot.* Overfatigued; tired out. Also **traik′it.**

trail (trāl) *v.t.* **1** To draw along lightly over a surface; also, to drag or draw after: to *trail* a robe. **2** To follow the trail of; trace; track. **3** *Mil.* To carry, as a rifle, by grasping it in the right hand just above the balance, with the muzzle to the front and the butt nearly touching the ground. **4** To tread or force down, as grass into a pathway. **5** *Naut.* To allow (the oars) to drift alongside the boat. —*v.i.* **6** To hang or float loosely. **7** To grow along the ground or over rocks, bushes, etc., in a loose, creeping way. **8** To follow behind loosely; stream. **9** To saunter leisurely along; move heavily. **10** To lag behind; straggle; remain in the rear. —*n.* **1** The track left by anything that has moved or been drawn or dragged over any surface. **2** The track or indications followed by a huntsman or by a dog in hunting; the scent. **3** The path worn by persons or by animals; particularly, a route made by repeated passage through a wilderness. **4** Anything drawn behind or in the wake of something; a train; specifically, the train of a dress or gown. **5** *Mil.* The inclined stock of a gun carriage, or extension of the stock that rests on the ground when the piece is not limbered up: when divided longitudinally into two parts, it is called a **split trail.** —**to hit** (or **take**) **the trail** To set out on a journey. [<AF *trailler* haul, tow a boat <L *tragula* a dragnet < *trahere* draw]

trail·er (trā′lər) *n.* **1** One who or that which trails. **2** A vehicle without automotive power designed to be coupled with a cab or tractor and used to haul freight, household goods, etc. **3** A vehicle usually drawn by an automobile or truck and equipped to serve as living quarters. **4** A preview (def. 2).

trailer truck A semitrailer (def. 2).

trailing arbutus An evergreen perennial (*Epigaea repens*) of the heath family, bearing clusters of fragrant pink flowers; the mayflower: the State flower of Massachusetts.

trailing edge *Aeron.* The rear edge of an airfoil or propeller blade.

trail rope **1** A guiderope. **2** A rope used for dragging or towing. **3** A rope attached to a horse's halter or tied around its neck, but allowed to drag while the horse grazes. **4** *Mil.* A prolonge.

train (trān) *n.* **1** Anything drawn out to a length, or any series of things drawn along. **2** A continuous line of coupled railway cars. **3** A series, succession, or set of connected things; a sequence; especially, an assemblage of people or objects drawn up processionally or in orderly disposition. **4** A retinue or body of retainers; suite. **5** Something pulled along with and in the track of another. **6** An extension of a dress skirt, trailing behind the wearer. **7** Proper order; due course. **8** *Mech.* A series of parts acting upon each other, as for transmitting motion: also called *drive train, power train.* **9** *Mil.* **a** The variation of the axis of a gun in a horizontal plane. **b** Collectively, the men, animals, and vehicles attached to a military body for the transportation of its ammunition, supplies, etc. **10** A succession or line of wagons and pack animals en route. **11** A line of gunpowder or other combustible laid to conduct fire to a charge, mine, or the like. See synonyms under PROCESSION. —*v.t.* **1** To bring to a requisite standard, as of conduct or skill, by protracted and careful instruction; specifically, to mold the character of; educate; instruct: sometimes with *up*. **2** To render skilful or proficient, as a mechanic or soldier. **3** To make obedient to orders or capable of performing tricks, as an animal. **4** To bring into a required physical condition by means of a course of diet and exercise: to *train* a man for a boat race. **5** To lead into taking a particular course; develop into a fixed shape: to *train* a plant on a trellis. **6** To put or point in an exact direction; bring to bear; aim, as a cannon. **7** *Obs.* To mislead; entice. **8** *Obs.* To draw along; trail. —*v.i.* **9** To undergo a course of training. **10** To give a course of training; drill. See synonyms under LEARN, SUBDUE, TEACH. [Fusion of OF *traïne* a dragging and *traïn* a series, procession, both < *traïner, trahiner* draw <L *trahere*] —**train′a·ble** *adj.* —**train′less** *adj.*

Train may appear as a combining form in hyphemes or solidemes, or as the first element in two-word phrases, with the meaning of definition 2:

train caller **train schedule**
train conductor **train service**
train crew **train signal**
train flagman **train staff**
train foreman **train stop**
train inspector **train ticket**
train-lighting **traintime**
train line **train trip**
train recorder **trainway**
train reporter **train whistle**
train robber **train wreck**

train·a·si·um (trā·nā′zē·əm) *n.* A structure of bars crossing and intersecting one another to form ladders, tunnels, etc.: used in developing the muscles, as in military training. [<TRAIN + (GYMN)ASIUM]

train·band (trān′band′) *n.* A militia organization, especially one in London, England, during the Stuart period (17th century). [Short for *trained band*]

train·bear·er (trān′bâr′ər) *n.* An attendant who holds the long train of a dress or robe.

trained nurse One who has been trained in and graduated from a nurses' training school.

train·ee (trā·nē′) *n.* One who undergoes training.

train·er (trā′nər) *n.* **1** One who trains. **2** One who directs and superintends a course of physical training, or who supervises the physical condition of members of an athletic team. **3** An apparatus or device used in training: a Link *trainer*. **4** One who trains a cannon; specifically, in the U. S. Navy, the member of the gun's crew who gives direction to the gun. **5** One who trains animals for shows, contests, animal acts, etc.

train·ing (trā′ning) *n.* **1** Systematic instruction and drill. **2** The condition of being physically fit for the performance of an athletic exercise or contest; also, the act or science of bringing one to such a condition. See synonyms under EDUCATION, LEARNING, NURTURE.

training school A school for practical instruction and drill; specifically, a school in which students receive special vocational or technical instruction and practice.

training ship A vessel on which apprentice seamen and cadets are educated in seamanship, navigation, etc.

train·man (trān′mən) *n. pl.* **·men** (-mən) A railway employee serving on a train; especially, a brakeman.

train·mas·ter (trān′mas′tər, -mäs′-) *n.* A railroad official supervising some division or subdivision of a rail line.

train oil Oil obtained from the fat of whales, especially from the right whale, and from cod livers, etc. [Earlier *trane* <MDu. *traen* extracted oil]

traipse (trāps) *v.i.* **traipsed, traips·ing** *Colloq.* To walk about in an idle or aimless manner; go on foot: also spelled *trapes*. [Earlier *trapass*.

prob. <OF *trapasser*, var. of *trespasser* TRESPASS]

trait (trāt) *n.* **1** A distinguishing feature or quality of mind or character. **2** A line, stroke, or touch. See synonyms under CHARACTERISTIC. [<F <MF *traict* <L *tractus*. Doublet of TRACT[1].]

trai·tor (trā′tər) *n.* **1** One who betrays a trust; especially, one who commits treason. **2** Hence, one who acts deceitfully and falsely. [<OF *traitre, traitor* <L *traditor*. See TRADITOR.] —**trai′tor·ism** *n. Obs.* —**trai′tress** (-tris) *n. fem.*

trai·tor·ous (trā′tər·əs) *adj.* **1** Inclined to treason. **2** Involving treason. See synonyms under PERFIDIOUS. —**trai′tor·ous·ly** *adv.* —**trai′tor·ous·ness** *n.*

Tra·jan (trā′jən), A.D. 56–117, Roman emperor 98–117: full name *Marcus Ulpius Trajanus*. —**Tra·jan·ic** (trā·jan′ik) *adj.*

tra·ject (trə·jekt′) *v.t.* To throw or cast over, through, or across, as a beam of light; transmit. [<L *trajectus*, pp. of *trajicere* < *trans-* over + *jacere* throw] —**tra·jec′tion** *n.*

tra·jec·to·ry (trə·jek′tər·ē) *n. pl.* **·ries** **1** The path described by an object or body moving in space. **2** The path of a projectile after leaving the muzzle of a gun. **3** *Geom.* **a** A curve which cuts a set of curves at the same angle. **b** A surface which passes through a given set of points. [<Med. L *trajectorius* <L *trajectus*. See TRAJECT.]

trake (trāk) See TRAIK (*n.* def. 2).

tral·a·ti·tion (tral′ə·tish′ən) *n. Obs.* The use of a word or expression in a figurative sense; metaphor. [<L *tralatio, -onis* < *tralatus, translatus*, pp. to *transferre* TRANSFER]

tral·a·ti·tious (tral′ə·tish′əs) *adj.* **1** Traditional; legendary. **2** Not literal; figurative; metaphorical.

Tra·lee (trə·lē′) The county town of County Kerry, Ireland, in the western part.

tram[1] (tram) *n.* **1** *Brit.* A tramway. **2** A street railway car for passengers; a tramcar. **3** A four-wheeled vehicle for conveying coals to or from a pit's mouth. —*v.t.* **trammed, tram·ming** To convey in a tramcar. [Short for TRAMROAD]

tram[2] (tram) *n.* **1** A trammel. **2** *Mech.* Accuracy or trueness of adjustment. Compare TRAMMEL. —*v.t.* **trammed, tram·ming** To use a trammel in adjusting (any part). [Short for TRAMMEL]

tram[3] (tram) *n.* A thick silk thread used for the cross threads of the best silks and velvets. Also **trame.** [<F *trame* <OF *traime* a woof, machination <L *trama* a woof]

tram·car (tram′kär′) *n. Brit.* A car or carriage that runs on a tramway; particularly, a street car; a tram. [<TRAM[1] + CAR]

tram·line (tram′līn′) *n. Brit.* A street-car line.

tram·mel (tram′əl) *n.* **1** That which limits freedom or activity; an impediment; hindrance. **2** A fetter, shackle, or bond, particularly one of such kind as is used in teaching a horse to amble. **3** An instrument whose parts slide on a rod, especially one bearing pointers, for use as a compass, or for describing ellipses. **4** A gage for adjusting machine parts. **5** A two-piece hook, adjustable for length, used to suspend cooking pots from a fireplace crane. **6** A net formed of three layers, the central one being of finer mesh in order to catch the fish which pass through either of the others: also **trammel net.** —*v.t.* **·meled** or **·melled, ·mel·ing** or **·mel·ling** **1** To hinder or obstruct; restrict. **2** To entangle in or as in a snare; imprison. Also **tram′el** or **tram′ell.** [<OF *tramail* a net <LL *tramaculum, tremaculum* <L *tri-* three + *macula* a mesh] —**tram′mel·er** or **tram′mel·ler** *n.*

tra·mon·tane (trə·mon′tān, tram′ən·tān) *adj.* **1** Situated beyond the mountains; ultramontane; hence, barbarous; foreign. **2** Coming from the other side of the mountains. —*n.* A foreigner or barbarian; originally, a resident beyond the mountains. [<Ital. *tramontana* north wind, polestar <L *transmontanus* beyond the mountains < *trans-* over + *mons, montis* a mountain]

tramp (tramp) *v.i.* **1** To walk or wander, especially as a tramp or vagabond. **2** To walk heavily or firmly. —*v.t.* **3** To walk or wander through. **4** To walk on heavily; trample. —*n.* **1** A heavy continued tread. **2** The sound produced by continuous and heavy marching or walking. **3** A long stroll on foot. **4** One who walks from place to place; a vagrant; vagabond. **5** A steam vessel that goes from port to port picking up freight wherever it can be obtained: also **tramp steamer.** **6** A metal plate on a shoe to protect it from wear or from a spade in digging. [ME *trampen* <Gmc. Cf. LG *trampen.*]

tramp·er (tram′pər) *n.* One who or that which tramps; specifically, a vagabond.

tram·ple (tram′pəl) *v.* **·pled, ·pling** *v.t.* To tread on heavily; injure, violate, or encroach upon by or as by tramping. —*v.i.* To tread heavily or ruthlessly; tramp. —*n.* The act or sound of treading under foot. [ME *trampelen*, freq. of *trampen* TRAMP] —**tram′pler** *n.*

tram·po·line (tram′pə·lin) *n.* **1** An acrobatic performance on stilts. **2** A heavy mat or net used in acrobatic exhibitions. Also **tram′po·lin.** [<Ital. *trampoli* stilts]

trampoline trainer A section of strong canvas stretched on a frame, on which a person may bound or spring: used in training for body control and acrobatics.

tram·road (tram′rōd′) *n.* A road with wheel tracks of stone, wood, or metal; especially, a railroad in a mine. [<dial. E *tram* a rail, wagon shaft (prob. <LG *traam* a beam, shaft) + ROAD]

tram·way (tram′wā′) *n. Brit.* **1** A street railroad. **2** A roadway having plates or rails on one part of it on which wheeled vehicles may run. **3** A system of cars suspended from cables, often operating in counterbalancing pairs: also called **aerial tramway.**

trance[1] (trans, träns) *n.* **1** A state in which the soul seems to have passed out of the body; an ecstasy; rapture. **2** *Psychol.* A condition between sleep and waking characterized by dissociation, involuntary movements, and automatisms of behavior, as in hypnosis and mediumistic seances. **3** A dreamlike state marked by bewilderment and an insensibility to ordinary surroundings. **4** A state of deep abstraction. See synonyms under DREAM. —*v.t.* **tranced, tranc·ing** To entrance, usually in a figurative sense; enchant. [<OF *transe* passage, dread of coming evil < *transir* pass, die, benumb <L *transire*. See TRANSIENT.]

trance[2] (trans, träns) *n. Scot.* A passage or hallway; an alley, courtyard, or close.

tran·gam (trang′gəm) *n. Obs.* A worthless person or thing; a knick-knack or trinket. Also **tran·kum** (trang′kəm). [Origin uncertain]

tran·quil (trang′kwil) *adj.* **·quil·er** or **·quil·ler, ·quil·est** or **·quil·lest** **1** Free from agitation or disturbance; calm: said of persons. **2** Quiet and motionless: said of things. See synonyms under CALM, PACIFIC, SEDATE. [<L *tranquillus* quiet] —**tran′quil·ly** *adv.* —**tran′quil·ness** *n.*

tran·quil·ize (trang′kwəl·īz) *v.t.* & *v.i.* **·ized, ·iz·ing** To make or become tranquil. Also **tran′quil·lize,** *Brit.* **tran′quil·lise.** —**tran′quil·i·za′tion** *n.*

Synonyms: allay, appease, assuage, calm, compose, hush, lull, moderate, pacify, quell, quiet, soothe, still. See ALLAY. *Antonyms*: agitate, alarm, arouse, disturb, excite, inflame, rouse, stimulate, stir.

tran·quil·iz·er (trang′kwəl·ī′zər) *n.* **1** One who or that which tranquilizes. **2** *Med.* An ataractic drug. Also **tran′quil·liz′er.**

tran·quil·li·ty (trang·kwil′ə·tē) *n.* The state of being tranquil; rest; quiet. Also **tran·quil′i·ty.** See synonyms under APATHY, REST.

trans- *prefix* **1** Across; beyond; through; on the other side of; as in:

transarctic	**transequatorial**
transborder	**transfrontier**
transchannel	**transisthmian**
transdesert	**transpolar**

In adjectives and nouns of place, the prefix may signify "on the other side of" (opposed to *cis-*) or "across; crossing." Through long usage, certain of these are written as solid words, as *transalpine, transatlantic*; otherwise, words in this class, unless by contrary official usage, are properly written with a hyphen, as in:

trans-American	**trans-Germanic**
trans-Andean	**trans-Himalayan**
trans-Arabian	**trans-Iberian**
trans-Baltic	**trans-Mediterranean**
trans-Canadian	**trans-Siberian**

2 Through and through; changing completely; as in:

transcolor	**transfashion**

3 Surpassing; transcending; beyond; as in:

transconscious	**transmundane**
transempirical	**transnational**
transhuman	**transphysical**
transmaterial	**transrational**
transmental	

4 *Anat.* Across; transversely; as in:

transcortical	**transocular**
transduodenal	**transthoracic**
transfrontal	**transuterine**

[<L <*trans* across, beyond, over]

trans·act (trans·akt′, tranz-) *v.t.* To carry through; accomplish; do. —*v.i. Rare* To do business. [<L *transactus*, pp. of *transigere* drive through, accomplish < *trans-* through + *agere* drive, do] —**trans·ac′tor** *n.*

Synonyms: accomplish, act, conduct, do, negotiate, perform, treat. There are many acts that one may *do, accomplish,* or *perform* unaided; what he *transacts* is by means of or in association with others; one may *do* a duty, *perform* a vow, *accomplish* a task, but he *transacts* business, since that always involves the agency of others. To *negotiate* and to *treat* are likewise collective acts, but *negotiate* implies deliberation with adjustment of mutual claims and interests, while *transact* implies execution. Nations may *treat* of peace without result, but when a treaty is *negotiated* peace is secured; the citizens of the two nations are then free to *transact* business with one another.

trans·ac·tion (trans·ak′shən, tranz-) *n.* **1** The management of any affair. **2** Something transacted; an affair; a business deal. **3** *pl.* Published reports, as of a society. —**trans·ac′tion·al** *adj.*

Synonyms: act, action, affair, business, deed, doing, proceeding. A man's *acts* or *deeds* may be exclusively his own; his *transactions* involve the agency or participation of others. A *transaction* is something completed; a *proceeding* is or is viewed as something in progress; but since *transaction* is often used to include the steps leading to the conclusion, while *proceedings* may result in *action*, the dividing line between the two words becomes sometimes quite faint. Both *transactions* and *proceedings* are used of the records of a deliberative body, especially when published. See ACT.

Trans-A·lai Range (trans′ä·lī′) A branch of the Pamir-Alai mountain system on the Kirgiz-Tadzhik S.S.R. border; highest point, 23,382 feet.

trans·al·pine (trans·al′pin, -pīn, tranz-) *adj.* **1** On the other side of the Alps, especially from Rome. **2** Crossing or extending across the Alps. **3** Of or pertaining to the country or the people beyond the Alps. —*n.* A native of or a resident beyond the Alps. [<L *transalpinus* < *trans-* across + *alpinus* alpine < *Alpes* the Alps]

Transalpine Gaul The section of Gaul on the northern side of the Alps.

trans·at·lan·tic (trans′ət·lan′tik, tranz′-) *adj* **1** On the other side of the Atlantic. **2** Across or crossing the Atlantic.

trans·berke·li·an (trans·bûrk′lē·ən) *adj. Physics* Of or pertaining to unstable radioactive elements beyond berkelium, atomic No. 97, as californium, einsteinium, fermium, mendelevium, and nobelium. [<TRANS- + BERKEL(IUM) + -IAN]

trans·ca·lent (trans·kā′lənt) *adj.* Permitting or facilitating the passage of heat. [<TRANS- + L *calens, -entis*, ppr. of *calere* be hot] —**trans·ca′len·cy** *n.*

Trans·cas·pi·a (trans·kas′pē·ə) A former administrative division of Russian Turkestan, roughly coextensive with the Turkmen S.S.R., in which it was incorporated in 1924; capital, Ashkhabad. Also **Trans·cas′pi·an Region.**

Trans·cau·ca·sia (trans′kô·kā′zhə, -shə) A region of southeastern U.S.S.R., between the Caucasus mountains on the north and Iran and Turkey in Asia on the south, comprising the republics of Armenia, Azerbaijan, and Georgia, and from 1922 to 1936 constituting the **Transcaucasian Socialist Federated Soviet Republic.** —**Trans′cau·ca′sian** *adj.* & *n.*

trans· cei·ver (tran·sē′vər) *n. Electronics* A radio unit, usually for portable or mobile service, containing equipment for both transmission and reception. [<TRANS(MITTER) + (RE)CEIVER]

tran·scend (tran·send′) *v.t.* **1** To rise above in excellence or degree. **2** To overstep or exceed, as a limit. —*v.i.* **3** To be surpassing; excel. See synonyms under SURPASS. [<L *transcendere* surmount <*trans-* beyond, over + *scandere* climb] —**tran·scend′i·ble** *adj.*

tran·scen·dent (tran·sen′dənt) *adj.* **1** Of very high and remarkable degree; surpassing; superexcellent. **2** *Philos.* In Kantianism, lying beyond the bounds of all possible human experience; hence, beyond knowledge. **3** *Theol.* Pertaining to God as exalted above the universe; beyond limitation; hence, perfect. See synonyms under EXCELLENT, TRANSCENDENTAL. —*n.* That which is transcendent or surpassingly great or remarkable. [<L *transcendens, -entis,* ppr. of *transcendere* TRANSCEND] —**tran·scen′dence** *n.* —**tran·scen′dent·ly** *adv.* —**tran·scen′dent·ness** *n.*

tran·scen·den·tal (tran′sen·den′təl) *adj.* **1** Of very high degree; transcendent. **2** Pertaining to or being a transcendent; not included in any of the categories. See CATEGORY. **3** *Philos.* **a** In Kant's system, of an a priori character; transcending experience but not knowledge. **b** Rising above the common notions of men; with the Cartesians, pertaining to body and spirit alike. **4** Wildly speculative; above, beyond, or contrary to common sense. **5** *Math.* That cannot be formed by the five fundamental operations of algebra, each performed a finite number of times. —**tran′scen·den′tal·ly** *adv.*

Synonyms: instinctive, intuitive, original, primordial, transcendent. *Intuitive* truths are those which are in the mind independently of all experience, not being derived from experience nor limited by it. All *intuitive* truths or beliefs are *transcendental.* But *transcendental* is a wider term than *intuitive,* including all within the limits of thought that is not derived from experience, as the ideas of space and time. *Transcendent, transcendental,* and *intuitive* are opposed to *empirical*; or, according to the philosophy of Kant, *transcendent* is opposed to *immanent,* and *transcendental* to *empirical.* See MYSTERIOUS.

tran·scen·den·tal·ism (tran′sen·den′təl·iz′əm) *n.* **1** The state or quality of being transcendental. **2** In common usage, that which, in philosophy or religion, is vague, visionary, or sublimated. **3** *Philos.* The doctrine that man can attain knowledge which goes beyond or transcends appearances or phenomena. In the Kantian sense, transcendentalism affirmed the existence of a priori principles of cognition. The New England movement, as represented by Emerson and others, has been characterized by the exaltation of the spiritual in a general sense over the material, and the immanence of the divine in all creation. —**tran′scen·den′tal·ist** *n.* & *adj.*

transcendental number See under NUMBER.

trans·con·ti·nen·tal (trans′kon·tə·nen′təl) *adj.* Extending or passing across a continent.

tran·scribe (tran·skrīb′) *v.t.* **·scribed, ·scrib·ing** **1** To write over again; copy or recopy in handwriting or typewriting from an original or from shorthand notes. **2** *Telecom.* To make an electrical recording of for use on a later radio program. **3** To adapt (a musical composition) for a change of instrument or voice. [<L *transcribere* <*trans-* over + *scribere* write] —**tran·scrib′a·ble** *adj.* —**tran·scrib′er** *n.*

tran·script (tran′skript) *n.* **1** A copy made directly from an original. **2** Any copy. **3** A copy of a student's academic record, listing courses taken and grades received. See synonyms under DUPLICATE. [Fusion of OF *transcrit* (pp. of *transcrire* transcribe <L *transcribere*) and L *transcriptus,* pp. of *transcribere* TRANSCRIBE]

tran·scrip·tion (tran·skrip′shən) *n.* **1** The act of transcribing; a copying. **2** A copy; transcript. **3** *Telecom.* An electrical recording made for the purpose of a later radio broadcast. **4** *Music* The adaptation of a composition for some instrument or voice other than that for which it was written. —**tran·scrip′tion·al, tran·scrip′tive** *adj.*

trans·cul·tu·ra·tion (trans·kul′chə·rā′shən) *n.* *Anthropol.* **1** The processes, resulting in the development of new cultural phenomena and the disappearance of old, involved in the transition of a group or a people from one culture context to another. **2** The transition itself. [<TRANS- + *culturation* development of a culture <CULTUR(E) + -ATION] —**trans·cul′tu·ra′tive** *adj.*

trans·cur·rent (trans·kûr′ənt) *adj.* Passing or extending transversely.

trans·duc·er (trans·dōō′sər, -dyōō′-, tranz-) *n.* *Physics* Any device whereby the energy of one power system may be transmitted to another system, whether of the same or a different type. [<L *transducere,* var. of *traducere.* See TRADUCE.]

tran·sect (tran·sekt′) *v.t.* To dissect transversely. [<TRANS- + L *sectus,* pp. of *secare* cut] —**tran·sec′tion** (-sek′shən) *n.*

tran·sept (tran′sept) *n.* *Archit.* One of the lateral members or projections between the nave and choir of a cruciform church: commonly distinguished as the *north* and *south transepts.* [<Med. L *transeptum,* short for L *transversum septum* <*transversus* TRANSVERSE + *septum* an enclosure] —**tran·sep′tal** *adj.*

trans·e·unt (tran′sē·ənt) *adj.* Proceeding from and operating beyond itself on another, as a physical cause: opposed to *immanent.* [<L *transiens, transeuntis.* See TRANSIENT.]

trans·fer (trans·fûr′, trans′fər) *v.* **·ferred, ·fer·ring** *v.t.* **1** To carry, or cause to pass, from one person, place, etc., to another. **2** To make over possession of to another. **3** To convey (a drawing) from one surface to another, as by specially prepared paper. —*v.i.* **4** To transfer oneself. **5** To be transferred. **6** To change from one car or line to another on a transfer. **7** To shift one's enrollment as a student from one educational institution to another. See synonyms under CONVEY. —*n.* (trans′fər) **1** The act of transferring, or the state of being transferred. **2** That which is transferred; specifically, in art, lithography, etc., a design conveyed or to be conveyed, as by copying ink or pressure, in reverse, from one surface to another. **3** A place, method, or means of transfer. **4** A ticket, entitling a passenger on one car or boat to ride on another, as on a connected line, with or without paying an additional fare; also, the place where such transfer is made. **5** A delivery of title or property from one person to another. **6** The exchange of a person from one organization to another, from one military division to another, from one school to another, etc. **7** An order transferring money or securities. [<OF *transferer* <L *transferre* <*trans-* across + *ferre* carry] —**trans·fer′a·bil′i·ty** *n.* —**trans·fer′a·ble** *adj.*

trans·fer·al (trans·fûr′əl) *n.* The act or an instance of transferring. Also **trans·fer′ral.**

trans·fer·ee (trans′fə·rē′) *n.* **1** *Law* The person to whom a transfer is made. **2** One who is transferred.

trans·fer·ence (trans·fûr′əns) *n.* **1** Transfer. **2** *Psychoanal.* **a** The reproduction of the repressed or forgotten experiences of early childhood, accompanied by a transfer of emotions from the original object or person to another. **b** Displacement (def. 7). [<NL *transferentia* <L *transferens, -entis,* ppr. of *transferre* TRANSFER] —**trans·fer·en·tial** (trans′fə·ren′shəl) *adj.*

trans·fer·or (trans·fûr′ər) *n.* The vender or conveying party in a transfer.

Trans·fig·u·ra·tion (trans′fig·yə·rā′shən) *n.* **1** The supernatural transformation of Christ on the mount as recorded in the Gospels. *Matt.* xvii 1–9. **2** A festival commemorating this: August 6.

trans·fig·ure (trans·fig′yər) *v.t.* **·ured, ·ur·ing** **1** To change the outward form or appearance of. **2** To make glorious. See synonyms under CHANGE. [<L *transfigurare* change the shape of <*trans-* across + *figura* shape] —**trans′fig·ur·a′tion, trans·fig′ure·ment** *n.*

trans·fi·nite (trans·fī′nīt) *adj.* **1** Beyond the finite. **2** *Math.* Of, pertaining to, or characterizing the properties of a set of numbers whose cardinality is not expressible by any finite number.

trans·fix (trans·fiks′) *v.t.* **1** To pierce through; impale. **2** To fix in place by impaling. **3** To make motionless, as with horror, amazement, etc. See synonyms under PIERCE. [<L *transfixus,* pp. of *transfigere* <*trans-* through, across + *figere* fasten] —**trans·fix′ion** (-fik′shən) *n.*

trans·flu·ent (trans′flōō·ənt) *adj.* **1** Flowing across or through. **2** *Her.* Flowing through the arches of a bridge. [<L *transfluens, -entis,* ppr. of *transfluere* <*trans-* across + *fluere* flow]

trans·flux (trans′fluks) *n.* A flowing or running through, across, or beyond.

trans·form (trans·fôrm′) *v.t.* **1** To give a different form to; change the character of. **2** To alter the nature of; convert. **3** *Math.* To change (one expression or operation) into another equivalent to it or having similar properties. **4** *Electr.* **a** To change the potential or the type of, as a current from higher to lower voltage, or from alternating to direct. **b** To alter the energy form of, as electrical into mechanical. **5** In alchemy, to transmute. —*v.i.* **6** To be or become changed in form or character. See synonyms under CHANGE. [<L *transformare* <*trans-* over + *formare* form <*forma* a form] —**trans·form′a·ble** *adj.*

trans·for·ma·tion (trans′fər·mā′shən) *n.* **1** A change. **2** The act of transforming or the state of being transformed. **3** A wig or partial wig worn by a woman.

trans·form·a·tive (trans·fôr′mə·tiv) *adj.* Having power or a tendency to transform.

trans·form·er (trans·fôr′mər) *n.* **1** One who or that which transforms. **2** *Electr.* A device for altering the strength and potential of a current; especially, a form of induction coil used in alternating-current systems of electrical distribution, by which a current of high voltage is transformed to one of lower voltage, or vice versa: classed accordingly either as **step-down** or **step-up transformers.**

trans·form·ism (trans·fôr′miz·əm) *n.* *Biol.* **1** The theory of the development of one species from another through gradual modifications and without the intervention of special acts of creation. **2** Any doctrine or example of evolution.

trans·fuse (trans·fyōōz′) *v.t.* **·fused, ·fus·ing** **1** To pour, as a fluid, from one vessel to another. **2** To cause to be imparted or instilled. **3** *Med.* To transfer (blood) from one person or animal to another. [<L *transfusus,* pp. of *transfundere* <*trans-* across + *fundere* pour] —**trans·fus′er** *n.* —**trans·fus′i·ble, trans·fu·sive** (trans·fyōō′siv) *adj.*

trans·fu·sion (trans·fyōō′zhən) *n.* **1** The act of pouring from one vessel into another; hence, transference; transmission. **2** *Med.* **a** The transfer of blood from one person or animal to the veins or arteries of another. **b** A similar transfer of any other fluid, as a saline solution.

trans·gress (trans·gres′, tranz-) *v.t.* **1** To break over the bounds of, as a law; violate. **2** To pass beyond or over (limits); exceed; trespass. —*v.i.* **3** To break a law; sin. See synonyms under BREAK. [Appar. <OF *transgresser* <L *transgressus,* pp. of *transgredi* <*trans-* across + *gradi* step] —**trans·gress′i·ble** *adj.* —**trans·gress′ing·ly** *adv.* —**trans·gres′sor** *n.*

trans·gres·sion (trans·gresh′ən, tranz-) *n.* **1** The act of transgressing; sin. **2** An overpassing. **3** *Geol.* An overlap. See synonyms under OFFENSE, SIN[1].

trans·gres·sive (trans·gres′iv, tranz-) *adj.* Apt to transgress; faulty; culpable. —**trans·gres′sive·ly** *adv.*

tran·shape (tran·shāp′) See TRANSSHAPE.

tran·ship (tran·ship′), **tran·ship·ment** (tran·ship′mənt) See TRANSSHIP, etc.

trans·hu·mance (trans·hyōō′məns) *n.* The moving of cattle or other animals to more suitable places as the seasons change, especially of herds to and from mountain pastures. [<F <*transhumer* <Sp. *trashumar* <L *trans-* across + *humare* cover with earth <*humus* earth] —**trans·hu′mant** *adj.*

tran·sience (tran′shəns) *n.* The quality of existing for a short time only; also, something that is transient: the *transience* of life. Also **tran′sien·cy.**

tran·sient (tran′shənt) *adj.* **1** Passing before the vision in a brief time; of short duration; brief; hasty. **2** Not permanent; temporary; casual. **3** *Obs.* Proceeding from one place or object to another; imparted. —*n.* One who or that which is transient; specifically, a lodger or boarder who remains for a short time. [<L *transiens, -euntis,* ppr. of *transire* < *trans-* across + *ire* go] —**tran′sient·ly** *adv.* —**tran′sient·ness** *n.*

Synonyms (adj.): brief, ephemeral, evanescent, fleeting, flitting, flying, fugitive, momentary, passing, short, temporary, transitory. A thing is *transient* which in fact is not lasting; a thing is *transitory* which by its very nature must soon pass away; a thing is *temporary* which is intended to last or be made use of but a little while; as, a *transient* joy; this *transitory* life; a *temporary* chairman. That which is *ephemeral,* literally lasting but for a day, is looked upon as at once slight and perishable, and the word carries often a suggestion of contempt; with no solid qualities or worthy achievement a pretender may sometimes gain an *ephemeral* popularity. That which is *fleeting* is viewed as in the act of passing swiftly by, and that which is *fugitive* as eluding attempts to detain it; that which is *evanescent* is in the act of vanishing even while we gaze, as the hues of the sunset. *Antonyms*: abiding, enduring, eternal, everlasting, immortal, imperishable, lasting, permanent, perpetual, persistent, undying, unfading.

tran·si·gent (tran′sə·jənt) *n.* A person who is willing to compromise or to be brought to terms. [<L *transigens, -entis,* ppr. of *transigere* settle. See TRANSACT.]

tran·sil·i·ent (tran·sil′ē·ənt) *adj.* Leaping or passing abruptly from one thing or condition to another; saltatory; spanning; extending over. [<L *transiliens, -entis,* ppr. of *transilire* < *trans-* across + *salire* leap] —**tran·sil′i·ence** *n.*

trans·il·lu·mi·nate (trans′i·lo͞o′mə·nāt, tranz′-) *v.t.* **·nat·ed, ·nat·ing** *Med.* To cause light to pass through (an organ or part of the body) to reveal its condition.

tran·sis·tor (tran·zis′tər, -sis′-) *n. Electronics* **1** A semiconductor device having three terminals and the property that the current between one pair of them is a function of the current between another pair. **2** A transistorized radio. [<TRANS(FER) (RES)ISTOR]

tran·sis·tor·ize (tran·zis′tər·īz, -sis′-) *v.t.* **·ized, ·iz·ing** To equip with transistors instead of vacuum tubes, as a radio, hearing aid, etc.

tran·sit (tran′sit, -zit) *n.* **1** The act of passing over or through; passage. **2** The act of carrying across or through; conveyance. **3** A specific passage or route; also, a traveler through a country. **4** *Astron.* **a** The passage of one heavenly body over the disk of another. **b** The moment of passage of a celestial body across the meridian: when in that half of the meridian containing the zenith it is *superior* or *upper* transit; when in that half containing the nadir it is *inferior* or *lower* transit. **5** A transit compass. See synonyms under JOURNEY, MOTION. [<L *transitus* < *transire* cross. See TRANSIENT.]

transit compass A surveying instrument resembling a theodolite, for measuring horizontal angles. Also **transit theodolite.**

transit instrument **1** An astronomical telescope mounted in the plane of the meridian and turning on a fixed east-and-west axis: used to determine the time of passage of an object over the meridian. **2** A transit compass.

tran·si·tion (tran·zish′ən) *n.* **1** Passage from one place, condition, or action to another; change. **2** *Music* A passing modulation, an abrupt change of key, or a passage leading from one theme to another. **3** The time, period, or place of such passage; also, its product or result. See synonyms under CHANGE, MOTION. —**tran·si′tion·al, tran·si′tion·ar′y** (-er′ē) *adj.* —**tran·si′tion·al·ly** *adv.*

transition point *Physics* A single point or temperature at which different phases of a substance can exist together.

tran·si·tive (tran′sə·tiv) *adj.* **1** *Gram.* Having, requiring, or terminating upon a direct object; also, expressing an action performed by a subject or agent, that passes over to or takes effect on some person or thing as its object. **2** Having the power of passing; effecting transition. —*n. Gram.* A transitive verb. [<LL *transitivus* <L *transitus* transit. See TRANSIT.] —**tran′si·tive·ly** *adv.* —**tran′si·tive·ness, tran′si·tiv′i·ty** *n.*

transitive verb A verb whose action, performed by a subject or agent, requires or terminates upon a direct object. The verbs in the following are transitive: *catch* the ball; he *shot* the gun; they *shot* the traitor; cats *climb* trees; we *speak* French.

tran·si·to·ry (tran′sə·tôr′ē, -tō′rē) *adj.* Existing for a short time only; transient. See synonyms under TRANSIENT. [<OF *transitoire* <L *transitorius* having, allowing passage through < *transitus.* See TRANSIT.] —**tran′si·to′ri·ly** *adv.* —**tran′si·to′ri·ness** *n.*

Trans–Jor·dan (trans·jôr′dən, tranz-) An Arab territory included in the Hashemite Kingdom of the Jordan; 34,758 square miles; capital, Amman; a former British mandate. Formerly called **Trans·jor·da·ni·a** (trans′jôr·dā′·nē·ə, tranz′-).

Trans·kei (trans·kā′) A native reserve district of Transkeian Territories; 2,504 square miles.

Trans·kei·an Territories (trans·kā′ən) A division of eastern Cape of Good Hope Province, Union of South Africa; 16,554 square miles; capital, Umtata.

trans·late (trans·lāt′, tranz-, trans′lāt, tranz′-) *v.* **·lat·ed, ·lat·ing** *v.t.* **1** To give the sense or equivalent of, as a word or an entire work, in another language; change into another language. **2** To interpret; explain in other words. **3** To remove, as an ecclesiastic, from one office to another. **4** To change into another form; transform. **5** To convey or remove from one place to another, as a human being from earth to heaven without natural death. **6** *Archaic* To transport; enrapture. **7** *Mech.* To impart to (any body) motion in which all the parts follow the same direction. **8** To retransmit, as a message, by means of a telegraphic relay. —*v.i.* **9** To act as translator; also, to admit of translation: This book *translates* easily. **10** To give form to ideas. See synonyms under INTERPRET. [? <OF *translater* <L *translatus,* pp. to *transferre* TRANSFER] —**trans·lat′a·ble** *adj.* —**trans·lat′a·ble·ness** *n.*

trans·la·tion (trans·lā′shən, tranz-) *n.* **1** The act of translating, or the state of being translated. **2** A transfer from one language to another; a turning of a foreign literary composition into the vernacular; a reproduction of a work in a language different from the original. **3** *Mech.* Motion in which all the parts of a body follow the same direction: distinguished from *rotation.* **4** Automatic resending of a telegraphic message to a more distant point. See synonyms under DEFINITION. —**trans·la′tion·al** *adj.*

trans·la·tor (trans·lā′tər, tranz-, trans′lā·tər, tranz′-) *n.* **1** One who translates; also, an interpreter. **2** A telegraph repeater. —**trans·la·to·ri·al** (trans′lə·tôr′ē·əl, -tō′rē-, tranz′-) *adj.*

Trans·lei·tha·ni·a (trans′li·thā′nē·ə, -li·tä′-) A region in Hungary east of the Leitha river.

trans·lit·er·ate (trans·lit′ə·rāt, tranz-) *v.t.* **·at·ed, ·at·ing** To represent, as a word, by the alphabetic characters of another language having the same sound: distinguished from *translate.* [<TRANS- + L *litera* a letter] —**trans·lit′er·a′tion** *n.*

trans·lo·cate (trans·lō′kāt, tranz-) *v.t.* **·cat·ed, ·cat·ing** To cause to shift from one place or position to another.

trans·lo·ca·tion (trans′lō·kā′shən, tranz′-) *n.* **1** A shift in position. **2** *Genetics* The attachment of a part of a chromosome to another chromosome, with resulting changes in the arrangement of the genes.

trans·lu·cent (trans·lo͞o′sənt, tranz-) *adj.* Allowing the passage of light, but not permitting a clear view of any object; semitransparent. See synonyms under CLEAR, TRANSPARENT. [<L *translucens, -entis,* ppr. of *translucere* < *trans-* through, across + *lucere* shine] —**trans·lu′cence, trans·lu′cen·cy** *n.* —**trans·lu′·cent·ly** *adv.*

trans·lu·nar (trans·lo͞o′nər, tranz-) *adj.* **1** Situated beyond the moon. **2** Ethereal; visionary. Also **trans·lu′na·ry** (-nər·ē). [<TRANS- + L *luna* the moon]

trans·lu·vi·al (trans·lo͞o′vē·əl, tranz-) *adj.* Pertaining to or characterized by progressive leaching, with some erosion: said of soils. [<TRANS- + (AL)LUV(IUM) + -IAL]

trans·ma·rine (trans′mə·rēn′, tranz′-) *adj.* **1** Beyond the sea. **2** Born or found overseas. **3** Crossing the sea. [<L *transmarinus* < *trans-* across + *mare* the sea]

trans·mi·grant (trans·mī′grənt, tranz-, trans′·mə-, tranz′-) *adj.* Passing from one place or condition to another. —*n.* An emigrant or an immigrant. [<L *transmigrans, -antis,* ppr. of *transmigrare* TRANSMIGRATE]

trans·mi·grate (trans·mī′grāt, tranz-, trans′·mə-, tranz′-) *v.i.* **·grat·ed, ·grat·ing** **1** To migrate, as from one place or condition to another; pass from one country or jurisdiction to another. **2** To pass into another body, as the soul at death. [<L *transmigratus,* pp. of *transmigrare* < *trans-* across + *migrare* migrate] —**trans·mi′gra·tor** *n.* —**trans·mi·gra·to·ry** (trans·mī′grə·tôr′ē, -tō′rē, tranz-) *adj.*

trans·mi·gra·tion (trans′mī·grā′shən, -mə-, tranz′-) *n.* The act of transmigrating; especially, the assumed passing of the soul from one body, after death, to another; metempsychosis. —**trans′mi·gra′tion·ism** *n.*

transmigration of souls The doctrine that souls pass into other bodies after death.

trans·mis·si·ble (trans·mis′ə·bəl, tranz-) *adj.* That may be transmitted. Also **trans·mit′ti·ble** (-mit′ə·bəl). —**trans·mis′si·bil′i·ty** *n.*

trans·mis·sion (trans·mish′ən, tranz-) *n.* **1** The act of transmitting. **2** The state of being transmitted. **3** That which is transmitted. **4** *Mech.* **a** A device that transmits power from the engine of an automobile to the driving wheels and varies the speed ratios between them. The principal types are **automatic transmission,** in which the speed ratios are automatically selected and engaged (see also FLUID DRIVE), and **manual transmission,** in which the speed ratios are selected and engaged by hand. **b** The gears for changing speed. [<L *transmissio, -onis* < *transmissus,* pp. of *transmittere* TRANSMIT]

Trans–Mis·sis·sip·pi (trans′mis′ə·sip′ē, tranz′-) *adj.* Of or pertaining to the region west of the Mississippi River.

trans·mis·sive (trans·mis′iv, tranz-) *adj.* **1** Derivable. **2** Tending to transmit; capable of sending or being sent through. **3** Derived; transmitted.

trans·mit (trans·mit′, tranz-) *v.t.* **·mit·ted, ·mit·ting** **1** To send from one place or person to another; forward or convey; dispatch. **2** To pass on by heredity; transfer. **3** To serve as a medium of passage for; conduct. **4** To send out by means of radio waves. **5** To cause (light, sound, etc.) to pass through a medium. **6** *Mech.* To convey (force, motion, etc.) from one part or mechanism to another. See synonyms under CARRY, CONVEY, SEND[1]. [<L *transmittere* < *trans-* across + *mittere* send] —**trans·mit′tal** *n.*

trans·mit·tance (trans·mit′ns, tranz-) *n.* **1** The act or process of transmitting. **2** *Physics* That proportion of radiant energy transmitted by a body upon which it is impinging. Compare OPACITY.

trans·mit·ter (trans·mit′ər, tranz-) *n.* **1** One who or that which transmits. **2** A telegraphic sending instrument. **3** That part of a telephone into which a person talks. **4** That part of a radio or television system which produces, modulates, and transmits radio-frequency waves.

trans·mog·ri·fy (trans·mog′rə·fī, tranz-) *v.t.* **·fied, ·fy·ing** To convert into a different shape; transform. [A humorous coinage; ? alter. of TRANSMIGRATE] —**trans·mog′ri·fi·ca′tion** *n.*

trans·mon·tane (trans·mon′tān, tranz-, trans′·mon·tān′, tranz′-) *adj.* Situated beyond a mountain. [Fusion of OF *transmontane,* alter. of *tramontane* polestar, north pole and L *transmontanus* TRAMONTANE]

trans·mu·ta·tion (trans′myo͞o·tā′shən, tranz′-) *n.* **1** The act of transmuting. **2** In alchemy, the supposed change of a baser metal into one of greater value, as of lead into gold. **3** *Physics* The change of one element into another through alteration of its nuclear structure, as in radioactivity or by bombardment with high-energy particles, etc. **4** *Biol.* Successive change of form; transformism. See synonyms under CHANGE. —**trans′mu·ta′tion·al, trans·mut·a·tive** (trans·myo͞o′tə·tiv, tranz-) *adj.*

trans·mute (trans·myo͞ot′, tranz-) *v.t.* **·mut·ed, ·mut·ing** To change in nature or form; alter in essence. Also **trans·mu′tate.** See synonyms under CHANGE. [<L *transmutare* < *trans-* across + *mutare* change] —**trans·mut′a·ble** *adj.* —**trans·mut′a·bil′i·ty, trans·mut′a·ble·ness** *n.* —**trans·mut′a·bly** *adv.* —**trans·mut′er** *n.*

trans·nep·tu·ni·an (trans′nep·to͞o′nē·ən, -tyo͞o′-, tranz′-) *adj. Astron.* Beyond the planet Neptune. [<TRANS- + NEPTUN(E) + -IAN]

trans·nor·mal (trans·nôr′məl, tranz-) *adj.* Supernormal.

trans·o·ce·an·ic (trans′ō·shē·an′ik, tranz′-) *adj.* 1 Lying beyond or over the ocean. 2 Crossing the ocean.

tran·som (tran′səm) *n.* 1 A horizontal piece framed across an opening; a lintel. 2 A window above such a bar, especially a small window above a door. 3 A horizontal construction dividing a window into stages. 4 A tie beam. 5 *Naut.* A beam running across and forming part of the stern frame of a ship. 6 The horizontal crossbar of a gallows or cross. [<L *transtrum* a crossbeam < *trans* across] — **tran′somed** *adj.*

transom window 1 A window divided into stages by transoms. 2 A window over a door transom and often hinged to it.

tran·son·ic (tran·son′ik) *adj. Aeron.* Of, pertaining to, or characterized by speeds between the subsonic and supersonic.

transonic barrier *Aeron.* A barrier to flight encountered by aircraft not designed to exceed subsonic speed: caused by turbulence of the airflow around different parts of the plane. Also called *sonic barrier, sound barrier.*

Trans·ox·i·an·a (trans·ok′sē·an′ə) See SOGDIANA.

trans·pa·cif·ic (trans′pə·sif′ik) *adj.* 1 Crossing the Pacific Ocean. 2 Situated across or beyond the Pacific.

trans·pa·dane (trans′pə·dān) *adj.* Being beyond the river Po, from Rome as a standpoint. [<L *transpadanus* < *trans-* across + *padanus* of the Po <*Padus* the river Po]

Transpadane Gaul The section of Gaul in Italy north of the river Po.

trans·par·en·cy (trans·pâr′ən·sē, -par′-) *n. pl.* **·cies** 1 The quality of being transparent. 2 Something, as a picture on glass, intended to be viewed by shining a light through it. 3 *Phot.* The light–transmitting power of a sensitized negative. 4 Simplicity. Also **trans·par′ence.**

trans·par·ent (trans·pâr′ənt, -par′-) *adj.* 1 Admitting the passage of light, and of clear views of objects beyond; pervious to light: *transparent* glass: distinguished from *translucent.* 2 Figuratively, easy to see through or understand; hence, without guile; frank. 3 Diaphanous. 4 Luminous; bright. [<Med. L *transparens, -entis* <L *trans-* across + *parere* appear, be visible] — **trans·par′ent·ly** *adv.* — **trans·par′ent·ness** *n.*

Synonyms: clear, diaphanous, limpid, lucid, pellucid, translucent. Whatever offers no obstruction to the vision is *clear*; *limpid, lucid,* and *pellucid* refer to a shining, sparkling clearness. A *transparent* body allows the forms and colors of objects beyond to be seen through it; a *translucent* body allows light to pass through, but may not permit forms and colors to be distinguished; plate glass is *transparent,* ground glass is *translucent. Limpid* refers to a liquid clearness, or that which suggests it; as, *limpid* streams. See CANDID, CLEAR, EVIDENT, MANIFEST, PLAIN[1]. *Antonyms*: cloudy, dark, dim, obscure, opaque, turbid.

transparent velvet A soft, lightweight velvet suitable for draping, having a silk or rayon back and a rayon pile.

tran·spic·u·ous (tran·spik′yo͞o·əs) *adj.* Transparent. [<Med. L *transpicuus* <L *transpicere* look, see through < *trans-* through + *specere* look]

trans·pierce (trans·pirs′) *v.t.* **·pierced, ·pierc·ing** To pierce through; penetrate completely. [<MF *transpercer* < *trans-* (<L, across, through) + *percer* pierce]

tran·spi·ra·tion (tran′spə·rā′shən) *n.* A transpiring or exhalation, as through a porous substance or through the tissues of a plant.

tran·spire (tran·spīr′) *v.* **·spired, ·spir·ing** *v.t.* 1 *Physiol.* To send off through the excretory organs, as of the skin and lungs; exhale. — *v.i.* 2 *Physiol.* To be emitted, as through the skin; be exhaled, as moisture or odors. 3 To become known. 4 *Colloq.* To happen; occur. [<F *transpirer* <L *trans-* across, through + *spirare* breathe]

trans·plant (trans·plant′, -plänt′) *v.t.* 1 To remove and plant in another place. 2 To remove and settle or establish for residence in another place. 3 *Surg.* To transfer (an organ or tissue) from its original site to another part of the body or to another individual. — *n.* (trans′plant′, -plänt′) 1 That which is transplanted, as a seedling or an organ of the body. 2 A transplanting. [<LL *transplantare* <L *trans-* across + *plantare* plant] — **trans′plan·ta′tion** *n.* — **trans·plant′er** *n.*

trans·pond·er (trans·pon′dər) *n. Electronics* A device that receives a signal from one telecommunication circuit and transmits the corresponding signal to another circuit: used in conjunction with an interrogator. Also called *pulse repeater.* [<TRANS(MITTER) + (RES)PONDER]

trans·po·ni·ble (trans·pō′nə·bəl) *adj.* Transposable. [<L *transponere* transpose (< *trans-* across + *ponere* put) + -IBLE] — **trans·po′ni·bil′i·ty** *n.*

trans·pon·tine (trans·pon′tin, -tīn) *adj.* Situated on the other side of a bridge: said of London south of the Thames. [<TRANS- + L *pons, pontis* a bridge]

trans·port (trans·pôrt′, -pōrt′) *v.t.* 1 To carry or convey from one place to another. 2 To carry into banishment, especially beyond the sea. 3 To carry away with emotion. 4 *Obs.* To take out of the world; kill. See synonyms under CARRY, CONVEY, RAVISH. — *n.* (trans′·pôrt, -pōrt) 1 The state of being transported, as with rapture. 2 *pl.* The varied and recurrent emotions that characterize such a state. 3 Transportation. 4 A vessel, rolling stock, or other means of conveyance used by a government to transport troops, military supplies, etc. 5 The act of transporting convicts. 6 A deported convict. 7 *Aeron.* An airplane used to transport passengers, mail, etc. See synonyms under ENTHUSIASM, RAPTURE. [<MF *transporter* <L *transportare* < *trans-* across + *portare* carry] — **trans·port′er** *n.*

trans·port·a·ble (trans·pôr′tə·bəl, -pōr′-) *adj.* 1 That may be transported. 2 Rendering liable to transportation (def. 2). — **trans·port′a·bil′i·ty** *n.*

trans·por·ta·tion (trans′pər·tā′shən) *n.* 1 The act of transporting; conveyance. 2 The sending away of a convict to a remote place. 3 Vehicles used in transporting; also, charge for conveyance. 4 A ticket, pass, or other printed matter entitling a passenger to travel on a railroad train, street car, etc.

trans·port·ing (trans·pôr′ting, -pōr′-) *adj.* Enrapturing; ravishing; ecstatic. — **trans·port′·ing·ly** *adv.*

trans·pose (trans·pōz′) *v.t.* **·posed, ·pos·ing** 1 To reverse the order or change the place of; interchange. 2 *Math.* To transfer (a term) with a changed sign from one side of an algebraic equation to the other, so as not to destroy the equality of the members. 3 To change in place or order, as a word in a sentence. 4 *Music* To write or play in a different key. 5 To transport. 6 *Obs.* To transform. [<OF *transposer* <L *trans-* over + OF *poser.* See POSE[1].] — **trans·pos′a·ble** *adj.* — **trans·pos′er** *n.*

trans·po·si·tion (trans′pə·zish′ən) *n.* 1 The act of transposing, or the state of being transposed. 2 That which has been transposed. Also **trans·po·sal** (trans·pō′zəl). — **trans′po·si′tion·al** *adj.*

trans·sex·u·al (trans·sek′sho͞o·əl, -sek′shəl) *n.* A person who is genetically and physically of one sex but who identifies psychologically with the other and may seek treatment by surgery or with hormones to bring the physical sexual characteristics into conformity with the psychological preference. — *adj.* Of, for, or characteristic of transsexuals. — **trans·sex′u·al·ism** *n.*

trans·shape (trans·shāp′) *v.t.* **·shaped, ·shap·ing** To change the shape of: also spelled *transhape.*

trans·ship (trans·ship′) *v.t.* & *v.i.* **·shipped, ·ship·ping** To transfer from one conveyance or line to another: also spelled *tranship.* — **trans·ship′ment** *n.*

tran·sub·stan·ti·ate (tran′səb·stan′shē·āt) *v.t.* **·at·ed, ·at·ing** 1 To change from one substance into another; transmute; transform. 2 *Theol.* To change the substance of (the bread and wine of the Eucharist) into the body and blood of Christ. [<Med. L *transubstantiatus,* pp. of *transubstantiare* <L *trans-* over + *substantia* substance]

tran·sub·stan·ti·a·tion (tran′səb·stan′shē·ā′·shən) *n.* 1 *Theol.* The conversion of the substance of the eucharistic elements into that of Christ's body and blood: a doctrine of the Greek and Roman Catholic churches. Compare CONSUBSTANTIATION, IMPANATION. 2 A change of anything into something essentially different. — **tran′sub·stan′ti·a′tion·al·ist** *n.*

tran·su·date (tran′so͞o·dāt) *n.* 1 The fluid that transudes. 2 The act or process of transuding. Also **tran′su·da′tion** (-dā′shən). [<NL *transudatus,* pp. of *transudare* TRANSUDE]

tran·sude (tran·so͞od′) *v.i.* **·sud·ed, ·sud·ing** To pass through the pores or tissues, as of a membrane. [<NL *transudare* <L *trans-* across, through + *sudare* sweat] — **tran·su′·da·to′ry** (-də·tôr′ē, -tō′rē) *adj.*

trans·u·ra·ni·an (trans′yo͞o·rā′nē·ən, tranz′-) *adj. Physics* Of or pertaining to those radioactive elements having an atomic number greater than that of uranium. Also **trans′u·ran′ic** (-ran′ik), **trans′u·ra′ni·um.** [<TRANS- + URAN(IUM) + -IAN]

Trans·vaal (trans·väl′, tranz-) A province of NE Republic of South Africa; 110,450 square miles; seat of government, Pretoria.

trans·val·ue (trans·val′yo͞o, tranz-) *v.t.* **·ued, ·u·ing** 1 To appraise the value of, as conduct, morals, beliefs, and the like, in accordance with principles at variance with accepted or conventional standards. 2 *Psychoanal.* To attach to an idea or complex of ideas a disproportionate emotional value, as in dreams, schizophrenia, etc. — **trans′val·u·a′tion** *n.*

trans·ver·sal (trans·vûr′səl, tranz-) *adj.* Transverse. — *n. Geom.* A straight line intersecting a system of lines.

trans·verse (trans·vûrs′, tranz-) *adj.* 1 Lying or being across; athwart. 2 *Anat.* Placed across the long axis of a part: a *transverse* muscle. — *n.* (*also* trans′vûrs, tranz′-) 1 That which is transverse. 2 *Geom.* That axis of a conic section which passes through its foci. [<L *transversus* lying across, pp. of *transvertere* < *trans-* across + *vertere* turn] — **trans·verse′ly** *adv.*

transverse process *Anat.* A long process extending laterally from a vertebra.

transverse wave *Physics* A wave whose component particles oscillate in a direction perpendicular to the line of propagation.

trans·ves·tite (trans·ves′tīt, tranz-) *n.* One who wears the clothes of the opposite sex. [<L *trans-* over + *vestire* to clothe + -ITE] — **trans·ves′tism, trans·ves′ti·tism** (-ves′tə·tiz′·əm) *n.*

Tran·syl·va·ni·a (tran′sil·vā′nē·ə) A region and former province in central Rumania; 24,000 square miles; formerly the eastern part of Hungary. — **Tran′syl·va′ni·an** *adj.* & *n.*

trap[1] (trap) *n.* 1 A device for catching game or other animals, as a pitfall or a baited device so arranged that a slight disturbance causes it to close or fall and thus kill or capture the victim. 2 A contrivance for hurling clay pigeons or glass balls into the air for sportsmen to shoot at. 3 Any artifice by which a person may be betrayed or taken unawares. 4 *Mech.* A U– or S–bend in a pipe, etc., for stopping return flow, as of noxious gas. 5 A trap door. 6 *Colloq.* A light, two–wheeled carriage suspended by springs. 7 A rattletrap. 8 *pl.* Traps. 9 a The game of trap ball. b A pivoted piece of wood, resembling a low shoe, used in the game of trap ball to throw a ball into the air. 10 In some games, especially golf, an obstacle or hazard: a water *trap,* sand *trap.* 11 *U.S. Slang* The mouth: Shut your *trap.* — *v.* **trapped, trap·ping** *v.t.* 1 To catch in a trap; ensnare. 2 To provide with a trap. 3 To stop or hold by some obstruction: said of a liquid. — *v.i.* 4 To set traps for game; be a trapper. [OE *treppe, træppe*]

trap[2] (trap) *n.* 1 *pl. Colloq.* Personal effects, as luggage; also, household goods. 2 A trapping. — *v.t.* **trapped, trap·ping** To adorn with trappings; bedeck. [Orig. a cloth covering for a horse, alter. of OF *drap* a cloth, covering <Med. L *drappus*; ult. origin uncertain]

trap[3] (trap) *n. Geol.* A dark, fine-grained igneous rock, often of columnar structure, as basalt, dolerite, etc.: also called *traprock.* [<Sw. *trapp* < *trappa* a stair; so called from the steplike arrangement of this rock in other rock]

tra·pan (trə·pan′) See TREPAN[2].

Tra·pa·ni (trä′pä·nē) An Italian port on the NW tip of Sicily: ancient *Drepanum.*

trap ball 1 A game in which a player strikes one end of a trap with a bat and thus flips a ball into the air for other players to try to catch. 2 The ball used in this game. See TRAP[1] (*n.* def. 9).

trap door A door, hinged or sliding, to cover an opening, as in a floor or roof.

trap-door spider (trap′dôr′, -dōr′) A large spider (family *Ctenizidae*) that inhabits a vertical, tubular pit in the ground, covered by a circular trap door hinged at one side to the silken lining of the tube, especially *Bothriocyrtum californica* of the SW United States.

trapes (trāps) See TRAIPSE.

tra·peze (trə·pēz′, tra-) *n.* 1 A short swinging bar, suspended by two ropes, for various gymnastic exercises. 2 *Geom.* A trapezium. [<F *trapèze* <NL *trapezium* a trapezium]

tra·pe·zi·form (trə·pē′zə·fôrm) *adj.* Having the form of a trapezium. [<TRAPEZI(UM) + -FORM]

tra·pe·zi·um (trə·pē′zē·əm) *n. pl.* **·zi·a** (-zē·ə) 1 *Geom.* **a** A four-sided plane figure of which no two sides are parallel. **b** In England, a quadrilateral of which two sides are parallel; a trapezoid. 2 *Anat.* **a** The bone of the distal row of the carpus situated on the radial side at the base of the thumb. **b** A band of transverse fibers found in the pons Varolii of the brain. 3 *Astron.* The four brightest stars in the nebula of Orion, at the angles of a trapezium. [<NL <Gk. *trapezion,* dim. of *trapeza* a table, lit., a four-footed (bench) < *tetra-* four + *peza* foot]

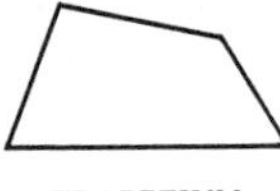
TRAPEZIUM

trap·e·zo·he·dron (trap′ə·zō·hē′drən, trə·pē′-) *n. pl.* **·dra** (-drə) A crystal figure bounded by six, eight, or twelve faces, each having unequal intercepts on all axes. [<NL < *trapezium* a trapezium + Gk. *hedra* a base]

trap·e·zoid (trap′ə·zoid) *n.* 1 *Geom.* **a** A quadrilateral of which two sides are parallel. **b** In England, a plane quadrilateral of which no two sides are parallel; a trapezium. 2 *Anat.* An irregular bone in the second row of the carpus, at the end of the forefinger. [<NL *trapezoïdes* <Gk. *trapezoeidēs* tablelike < *trapeza* a table + *eidos* a form] **—trap′e·zoi′dal** *adj.*

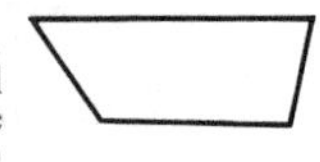
TRAPEZOID

trap·fall (trap′fôl′) *n.* A trap door yielding under pressure of feet.

trap line 1 The ensnaring filament in a spider's web. 2 A series of traps set out at approximately equal distances.

trap net A fishing net having a funnel-shaped entrance into an oblong net pen from which egress is almost impossible.

trap·pe·an (trap′ē·ən, trə·pē′ən) *adj.* Of or pertaining to traprock. Also **trap′pous, trap·pose** (trap′ōs). [<TRAP[3]]

trap·per (trap′ər) *n.* One whose occupation is the trapping of fur-bearing animals.

trap·ping (trap′ing) *n.* 1 An ornamental housing or harness for a horse. 2 *pl.* Adornments of any kind; embellishments; superficial dress. See synonyms under CAPARISON. [<TRAP[2]]

trap·pist (trap′ist) *n.* A nunbird. [<TRAPPIST]

Trap·pist (trap′ist) *n.* A member of an ascetic order of monks, a branch of the Cistercians, founded at Soligny-la-Trappe, France, and noted for silence and abstinence. [<F *Trappiste,* from *La Trappe,* name of their first abbey, established 1664]

trap·rock (trap′rok′) *n.* Trap[3].

traps (traps) *n. pl.* Percussion instruments, such as drums, cymbals, etc. [<TRAP[1] (def. 8)]

trap·shoot·ing (trap′shōō′ting) *n.* The sport of shooting pigeons, or artificial substitutes sent up from spring traps. See TRAP[1] (*n.* def. 2). **—trap′shoot′er** *n.*

trash[1] (trash) *n.* 1 Worthless or waste matter of any kind; rubbish. 2 That which is broken or lopped off, as loppings of trees. 3 The lowest grade of tobacco. 4 The dry refuse of sugarcane after the juice has been expressed. 5 A worthless person, or one of ill repute. *—v.t.* 1 To free from trash. 2 To strip of leaves; prune; lop. 3 To regard as trash; discard. [Cf. dial. Norw. *trask* lumber, trash, baggage]

trash[2] (trash) *n.* 1 Something fastened to an animal's neck to serve as a check. 2 A clog; collar; leash; any hindrance. *—v.t.* To keep in check with a leash, trash, or halter. [<OF *trachier,* var. of *tracier.* See TRACE[1].]

trash·trie (trash′trē) *n. Scot.* Trash.

trash·y (trash′ē) *adj.* **trash·i·er, trash·i·est** 1 Consisting of or like trash; worthless. 2 Cheap; inferior: said of literature. 3 Covered with underbrush or waste: said of land. **—trash′i·ly** *adv.* **—trash′i·ness** *n.*

Tra·si·me·no (trä′sē·mē′nō), **Lake** A lake in central Italy, 10 miles in diameter; 50 square miles; here Hannibal defeated the Romans, 217 B.C.: also *Lake of Perugia.* Ancient **Tras·i·me·nus** (tras′i·mē′nəs).

tras·ko (träs′kō) *n.* A Swedish dance in 4/4 time but having a polka step: also called *wooden-shoe dance.* [<Sw. < *traska* patter, trot]

trass (tras) *n.* A gray, yellow, or whitish earth, related to pozzuolana, common in volcanic districts: used in preparation of a hydraulic cement. [<G <Du. *tras* < earlier *taras.* Akin to TERRACE.]

trauch·le (troukh′lə) See TRACHLE.

trau·ma (trô′mə, trou′-) *n. pl.* **·mas** or **·ma·ta** (-mə·tə) 1 *Pathol.* Any injury to the body caused by shock, violence, etc.; a wound. 2 *Psychiatry* A severe emotional shock having a deep, often lasting effect upon the personality. 3 A traumatism. [<NL <Gk. *trauma, -atos* a wound]

trau·mat·ic (trô·mat′ik) *adj.* 1 Of or pertaining to trauma. 2 Connected with or resulting from shock, a wound, or wounds. [<LL *traumaticus* <Gk. *traumatikos* < *trauma, -atos* a wound] **—trau·mat′i·cal·ly** *adv.*

trau·ma·tism (trô′mə·tiz′əm) *n. Pathol.* 1 The general condition of the system resulting from a severe wound or external injury. 2 The injury or wound itself; a trauma. Also **trau′ma·to′sis** (-tō′sis).

trau·ma·to·pho·bi·a (trô′mə·tə·fō′bē·ə) *n.* A morbid fear of injury. [< *traumato-* (<Gk. *trauma* a wound) + -PHOBIA]

trau·mat·ro·pism (trô·mat′rə·piz′əm) *n. Biol.* The growth or involuntary movement of an organism as determined by an injury. [<TRAUMA + TROPISM]

trav·ail[1] (trav′āl, trə·vāl′) *v.t.* 1 To weary. *—v.i.* 2 To suffer the pangs of childbirth. 3 To toil; labor. *—n.* 1 Labor in childbirth. 2 Anguish or distress encountered in achievement. 3 Hard or agonizing labor. 4 Physical agony. See synonyms under TOIL[1]. [<OF < *travaillier* labor, toil, ult. <LL *trepalium* a three-pronged instrument of torture < *tres, tria* three + *palus* a stake]

tra·vail[2] (trà·và′y′) *n. pl.* **·vails** (-và′y′) *French* A travois.

Trav·an·core (trav′ən·kôr′) A former administrative division and princely state of Travancore-Cochin State, India; 7,662 square miles.

Trav·an·core-Co·chin (trav′ən·kôr′kō′chin, koch′in) A former constituent state of SW India; mostly incorporated in Kerala State, 1956; 9,144 square miles; capital, Trivandrum.

trave (trāv) *n. Obs.* 1 A frame to confine a beast of burden while being shod. 2 A crossbeam; transom. [<OF <L *trabs, trabis* a beam]

trav·el (trav′əl) *v.* **trav·eled** or **·elled, trav·el·ing** or **·el·ling** *v.i.* 1 To go from one place to another or from place to place; make a journey or tour. 2 To proceed; advance. 3 To go about from place to place as a traveling salesman. 4 *U.S. Colloq.* To move with speed. 5 To pass or be transmitted, as light, sound, etc. 6 *Mech.* To move in a fixed path, as part of a mechanism. *—v.t.* 7 To move or journey across or through; traverse. *—n.* 1 The act of traveling; a journeying: chiefly in the plural. 2 *pl.* A narration of things experienced or observed in traveling. 3 A moving or progress of any kind. 4 *Mech.* Movement or length of stroke. 5 The passage of people and vehicles to, over, or past a certain place. 6 Tourists, collectively. 7 Distance traveled; mileage. See synonyms under JOURNEY. [Var. of TRAVAIL[1]] **—trav′el·ing** or **·el·ling** *adj.* & *n.*

trav·eled (trav′əld) *adj.* 1 Having made many journeys, especially to distant lands. 2 Experienced as the result of travel. 3 Frequented or used by travelers: a *traveled* district. Also **trav′elled.**

trav·el·er (trav′əl·ər, trav′lər) *n.* 1 One who travels or journeys from place to place. 2 An animal or thing considered with reference to its mode or speed of movement. 3 A traveling salesman; specifically, a drummer: also **commercial traveler.** 4 *Naut.* **a** A metal ring or thimble running freely on a rope, rod, or spar. **b** A bar affixed to the deck, along which a ring or thimble slides. 5 A traveling crane or other moving device for transporting heavy objects. 6 In the theater, an overhead rod or pipe in the flys of the stage from which small spotlights are suspended and made available for unusual lighting effects. 7 The rings and track for drawn curtains. Also **trav′el·ler.**

traveler's tree Ravenala.

trav·el·ing (trav′əl·ing, trav′ling) *adj.* 1 Designed or used for travel: a *traveling* bag. 2 Itinerant: a *traveling* tinker. 3 Portable; movable. 4 *Mech.* **a** Running or sliding along a fixed course, as a ring or thimble. **b** Constructed with a part that travels.

traveling crane A hoisting and transporting apparatus which moves along a supporting frame or bridge, the frame itself moving on tracks. Compare illustration under GANTRY.

traveling man A commercial traveler; a traveling salesman.

trav·e·log (trav′ə·lôg, -log) *n.* A lecture or discourse on or an account of travel, usually illustrated pictorially. Also **trav′e·logue.** [< TRAVEL, on analogy with *monolog, dialog,* etc.]

trav·erse (trav′ərs, trə·vûrs′) *v.* **·ersed, ·ers·ing** *v.t.* 1 To pass over, across, or through. 2 To move back and forth over or along. 3 To examine carefully; survey or scrutinize. 4 To oppose; thwart. 5 To turn (a gun, lathe, etc.) to right or left; swivel. 6 *Law* To make denial of; in legal pleading, to deny and tender issue upon, as a matter of fact alleged by the opposite party; impeach the validity of an inquest of office. 7 *Naut.* To brace (a yard) fore and aft. *—v.i.* 8 To move back and forth. 9 To move across; cross. 10 To turn; swivel. 11 In fencing, to slide one's blade

TRAVERSE *(def. 13)*

toward the hilt of an opponent's sword while maintaining pressure on it. *—n.* (trav′ərs) 1 A part, as of a machine or structure, that traverses, as a crosspiece, crossbeam, transom, or the like. 2 *Archit.* A gallery or loft communicating with opposite sides of a building. 3 Something serving as a screen or barrier. 4 *Geom.* A transversal. 5 The act of traversing or traveling; a journey; passage. 6 *Mech.* Sidewise travel, as of the tool in a slide rest. 7 The act of traversing or denying; a denial; in legal pleading, a formal denial. 8 *Naut.* A zigzag track of a vessel while beating to windward. 9 A short line surveyed from a main line, to establish the position of a side point. 10 *Mil.* A bank of earth thrown up, as from a trench, to afford protection from gunfire. 11 Something that obstructs, vexes, or thwarts. 12 A path cut transversely in the side of a cliff or mountain; also, the cliff across which a path is cut. 13 A sled having a long board connecting two or more sleds or two or more sets of runners. *—adj.* (trav′ərs) Transverse; lying or being across. *—adv.* (trav′ərs, trə·vûrs′) Transversely; crosswise. [<OF *traverser* <LL *traversare, transversare* <L *transversus* TRANSVERSE] **—trav′ers·a·ble** *adj.* **—trav·er·sal** (trav′ər·səl, trə·vûr′səl) *n.* **—trav′ers·er** *n.*

Trav·erse (trav′ərs), **Lake** A lake on the

boundary of South Dakota and Minnesota; 26 miles long, 3 miles wide.
traverse jury A trial jury. [<TRAVERSE (*v.* def. 3) + JURY]
trav·er·tine (trav′ər·tin, -tēn, -tīn) *n.* A porous, light-yellow, crystalline calcium carbonate deposited in solution from ground or surface waters: a form of limestone used for building purposes. Also **trav′er·tin** (-tin). [<Ital. *travertino, tivertino* <L *Tiburtinus* Tiburtine < *Tiburs, -urtis* of Tibur < *Tibur* Tibur]
trav·es·ty (trav′is·tē) *n. pl.* **·ties** **1** A grotesque imitation; burlesque. **2** In literature, a burlesque treatment of a lofty subject. See synonyms under CARICATURE. —*v.t.* **·tied, ·ty·ing** To make a travesty on; burlesque; parody. [<MF *travesti,* pp. of *(se) travestir* disguise (oneself) <Ital. *travestire* disguise]
tra·vois (tra·voi′) *n. pl.* **·vois** (-voiz′) or **·vois·es** (-voi′ziz) A primitive sled constructed of two poles which serve as shafts for a dog or other draft animal and which drag on the ground, bearing a frame for the load: used by North American Indians and lumbermen in logging: also spelled *travail.* Also **tra·voise′** (-voiz′). [< dial. F (Canadian), alter. of F *travail,* a frame in which horses are held while being shod <OF]

TRAVOIS

trawl (trôl) *n.* **1** A stout line, sometimes over a mile long, anchored and buoyed, and having hanging from it many lines frequently spaced and bearing baited hooks: also called *trotline.* **2** A great net shaped like a flattened bag, for towing on the bottom of the ocean by a boat. —*v.t.* To drag, as a net to catch fish. —*v.i.* To fish with a trawl line, trawl net, or the like. [Cf. MDu. *traghel* a dragnet; prob. infl. by *trail*] —**trawl′ing** *n.*
trawl·er (trô′lər) *n.* **1** A person engaged in trawling. **2** A vessel used for trawling.
trawl·ey (trô′lē) See TROLLEY (def. 4).
tray (trā) *n.* **1** A flat shallow utensil or bowl with raised edges, for various uses. **2** A shallow box without a cover, used in trunks and otherwise. **3** A kind of flat board with a low rim, made of wood, metal, or other material, and used for carrying or holding articles; also, its contents. ◆ Homophone: *trey.* [OE *treg, trig* a wooden board]
treach·er·ous (trech′ər·əs) *adj.* **1** Traitorous; perfidious. **2** Having a good appearance, but bad in character or nature; untrustworthy; affording unsafe footing: a *treacherous* path. See synonyms under INSIDIOUS, PERFIDIOUS, ROTTEN. —**treach′er·ous·ly** *adv.* —**treach′er·ous·ness** *n.*
treach·er·y (trech′ər·ē) *n. pl.* **·er·ies** Violation of allegiance, confidence, or plighted faith; perfidy; treason. See synonyms under FRAUD. [<OF *trecherie, tricherie* < *tricher, trechier* cheat]
trea·cle (trē′kəl) *n.* **1** The sirup obtained in refining sugar. **2** Molasses. **3** A saccharine fluid of certain plants. **4** Originally, a compound used as an antidote. **5** *Obs.* A panacea. [<OF *triacle* <L *theriaca* <Gk. *thēriakē* a remedy for poisonous bites < *thērion,* dim. of *thēr* a wild beast] —**trea′cly** *adj.*
tread (tred) *v.* **trod** (*Archaic* **trode**), **trod·den** or **trod, tread·ing** *v.t.* **1** To step or walk on, over, along, etc.: to *tread* the floor. **2** To press with the feet; trample: to *tread* grass. **3** To accomplish in walking or in dancing: to *tread* a measure. **4** To copulate with: said of male birds. —*v.i.* **5** To place the foot down; walk. **6** To press the ground or anything beneath the feet: usually with *on.* —**to tread water** In swimming, to keep the body erect and the head above water by moving the feet up and down as if walking. —*n.* **1** The act or manner of treading; a walking or stepping. **2** That on which something treads or rests in moving, or which affords space for or as for treading. **3** The part of a wheel that bears upon the ground or rails. **4** The outer surface of an automobile tire, or the distance between opposite wheels. **5** The part of a rail on which the wheels bear. **6** The cicatricle or chalaza of an egg. **7** The impression made by a foot, a tire, etc. **8** The flat part of a step in stairs. [OE *tredan*] —**tread′er** *n.* —**tread′ing** *n.*
trea·dle (tred′l) *n.* A lever operated by the foot, usually to cause rotary motion. —*v.i.* **·led, ·ling** To work a treadle. Also spelled *treddle.* [OE *tredel* < *tredan* tread] —**tread′·ler** *n.*
tread·mill (tred′mil′) *n.* **1** A mechanism rotated by the walking motion of one or more persons: formerly used as a prison punishment. **2** A somewhat similar mechanism operated by a quadruped. **3** Toilsome effort; monotonous routine.
tread·way (tred′wā′) *n.* The roadway in certain types of bridges.
trea·son (trē′zən) *n.* **1** Betrayal, treachery, or breach of allegiance or of obedience toward the sovereign or government. Treason against the United States is declared by the Constitution (Article 3, section 3) to "consist only in levying war against them, or in adhering to their enemies, giving them aid and comfort." **2** A breach of faith; treachery. See synonyms under FRAUD. [<AF *treyson,* OF *traïson* <L *traditio, -onis* a betrayal, delivery. Doublet of TRADITION.]
trea·son·a·ble (trē′zən·ə·bəl) *adj.* Of, involving, or characteristic of treason. —**trea′son·a·ble·ness** *n.* —**trea′son·a·bly** *adv.*
trea·son·ous (trē′zən·əs) *adj.* Full of treason; treasonable. —**trea′son·ous·ly** *adv.*
treas·ure (trezh′ər) *n.* **1** The precious metals; money; jewels. **2** Riches accumulated or possessed; a stock or store of anything; wealth. **3** Something very precious. See synonyms under WEALTH. —*v.t.* **·ured, ·ur·ing** **1** To lay up in store; accumulate. **2** To retain carefully, as in the mind: generally with *up.* **3** To set a high value upon; prize. See synonyms under CHERISH. [<OF *tresor* <L *thesaurus.* Doublet of THESAURUS.]
Treasure Island An artificial island in San Francisco Bay, used as a naval base; 400 acres.
treas·ur·er (trezh′ər·ər) *n.* **1** One who has the care of treasure or of a treasury. **2** An officer legally authorized to receive, care for, and disburse public revenues upon lawful orders. **3** A similar custodian of the funds of a society or a corporation.
Treasure State Nickname of MONTANA.
treas·ure-trove (trezh′ər·trōv′) *n.* **1** *Law* Money, plate, or the like, found hidden in the earth, etc., the owner being unknown. **2** Any wealth-yielding discovery; loosely, treasure; riches. [<AF *tresor trové* < *tresor* TREASURE + *trové,* pp. of *trover* find]
treas·ur·y (trezh′ər·ē) *n. pl.* **·ur·ies** **1** The place of receipt and disbursement of public revenue, or of funds belonging to a corporation. **2** A repository, especially of words, as a dictionary or thesaurus. —**Department of the Treasury** An executive department of the U. S. government (established in 1789), headed by the Secretary of the Treasury, which superintends and manages the national finances, controls the coinage and printing of money, and supervises the Coast Guard (except when it is a part of the Navy, in wartime or when the president directs), the Bureau of Narcotics, and the Secret Service. Also **Treasury Department.** [<OF *tresorie* < *tresor* TREASURE]
Treasury note A demand note on which the face value is printed, issued by the Treasury: a legal tender for all debts, public and private, unless otherwise expressly stipulated.
treat (trēt) *v.t.* **1** To conduct oneself toward in a specified manner: He *treated* her shamefully. **2** To look upon or regard in a specified manner: They *treat* the matter as a joke. **3** To subject to chemical or physical action, as for altering or improving. **4** To give medical or surgical attention to. **5** To deal with in writing or speaking; handle. **6** To deal with or develop (a subject in art) in a specified manner or style. **7** To pay for the entertainment, food, or drink of. —*v.i.* **8** To handle a subject in writing or speaking: usually with *of.* **9** To carry on negotiations; negotiate. **10** To pay for another's entertainment. See synonyms under TRANSACT. —*n.* **1** Something that gives unusual pleasure. **2** Entertainment of any kind furnished gratuitously to another. **3** *Colloq.* One's turn to pay for refreshment or entertainment, especially for drinks. [<OF *tretier, traitier* <L *tractare.* See TRACTABLE.] —**treat′a·ble** *adj.* —**treat′er** *n.* —**treat′ing** *n.*
trea·tise (trē′tis) *n.* **1** An elaborate, formal, and systematic literary composition presenting a serious subject in all its parts: distinguished from an *essay* in being longer, more exhaustive, and less popular, and from a *monograph* in being less full and complete. **2** *Obs.* A story; tale. [<AF *tretiz,* OF *traitier* TREAT]
treat·ment (trēt′mənt) *n.* **1** The act, mode, or process of treating anything, as a raw material, substance, or product. **2** *Med.* The management of illness, by the use of drugs, dieting, or other means designed to bring relief or effect a cure. **3** In motion pictures and television, an expanded synopsis of a story, used in planning, writing, or marketing a play or scenario.
trea·ty (trē′tē) *n. pl.* **·ties** **1** A formal agreement or compact, duly concluded and ratified, between two or more states. **2** *Obs.* The act of negotiating for an agreement; also, the agreement so made. **3** *Obs.* An entreaty. [<AF *treté,* OF *traitié,* pp. of *traitier* TREAT]
treaty port Any of several sea and river ports, especially in China, in which foreigners were permitted to reside, purchase property, and erect business establishments: abolished by various treaties.
Treb·bia (treb′byä) A river in NW Italy, flowing 70 miles NE from the Apennines NE of Genoa to the Po river near Piacenza; on its banks Hannibal defeated the Romans, 218 B.C.
Treb·i·zond (treb′i·zond) **1** A province of NW Turkey; 1,753 square miles; an empire of Asia Minor from 1204 to 1461. **2** Its capital, a port on the Black Sea. Turkish *Trabzon.*
treb·le (treb′əl) *v.t.* & *v.i.* **·led, ·ling** To multiply by three; triple. —*adj.* **1** Threefold; triple. **2** Soprano. —*n.* **1** *Music* The soprano; the highest register of the compass of an instrument; a soprano singer. **2** High, piping sound. **3** A musical instrument of treble pitch; a violin. [<OF <L *triplus.* Doublet of TRIPLE.] —**treb′le·ness** *n.* —**treb′·ling** *n.* —**treb′ly** *adv.*
treb·u·chet (treb′yŏŏ·shet) *n.* A medieval catapultlike device for throwing heavy missiles. The missile, on the long arm of a lever, was hurled with great force by the sudden descent of a heavy weight on the short arm. Also **treb′uck·et** (-uk·it). [<OF < *trebucher* trip, fall]
tre·cen·to (trā·chen′tō) *n. Italian* The 14th century, as producing a particular style of Italian literature and art (in literature, Petrarchism); the early Italian style.
tred·dle (tred′l) See TREADLE.
tree (trē) *n.* **1** A perennial woody plant having usually a single self-supporting trunk, with branches and foliage growing at some distance above the ground, the whole ranging from about ten feet to as high as 300 feet. ◆ Collateral adjective: *arboreal.* **2** Any shrub or plant that assumes treelike shape or dimensions. **3** Something whose outline resembles that of a tree: a genealogical *tree*; a branching diagram; a treelike group of crystals. **4** A timber or heavy piece of wood, as in a framing: usually in composition: *axletree,* boot-*tree,* etc. **5** A gibbet; also, a cross. —**up a tree** *Colloq.* In a position from which there is no retreat; cornered; caught; also, in an embarrassing position. —*v.t.* **treed, tree·ing** **1** To force to climb or take refuge in a tree: to *tree* an opossum. **2** *Colloq.* To get the advantage of; corner. **3** To stretch, as a boot, on a boot-tree. [OE *trēow, trīow, trēo*]
Tree may appear as a combining form in hyphemes or solidemes, or as the first element in two-word phrases; as in:

tree-bordered	**tree-clad**	**tree-covered**
tree-boring	**tree-climbing**	**tree-crowned**

tree–dotted	**tree–hopping**	**tree protector**
tree–dwelling	**tree–inhabiting**	**tree–pruning**
tree–feeding	**tree insulator**	**tree–ripened**
tree–fringed	**tree–lined**	**tree–sawing**
tree–garnished	**tree–locked**	**tree–shaded**
tree–girt	**tree–loving**	**tree–skirted**
tree guard	**tree–marked**	**tree–spraying**
tree–haunting	**tree–planted**	**tree tag**
tree–hewing	**tree planter**	**treetop**
tree holder	**tree–planting**	**tree–trimmer**

Tree (trē), **Sir Herbert Beerbohm,** 1853–1917, English actor and impresario.

tree fern Any of various ferns (families *Cyatheaceae* and *Dicksoniaceae*) with large fronds and woody trunks that often attain a treelike size.

tree frog An arboreal amphibian (family *Hylidae*), having the toes dilated with viscous, adhesive disks. Also **tree toad.**

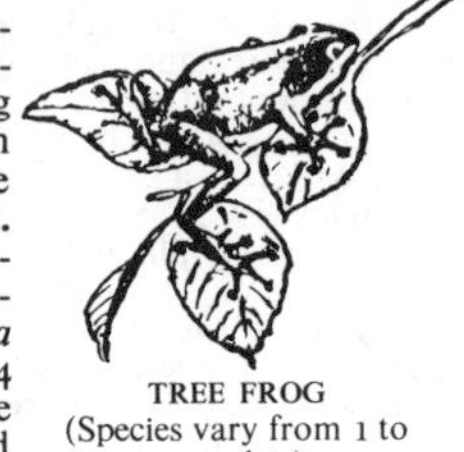

TREE FROG
(Species vary from 1 to 5 inches)

tree heath An evergreen shrub of southern Europe *(Erica arborea)* about 4 feet high, with white flowers: also called *brier.*

tree kangaroo Any of various kangaroos (genus *Dendrolagus*) of Australia and New Guinea adapted for tree–dwelling.

tree·nail (trē′nāl′, tren′əl, trun′əl) *n.* A wooden peg or nail of dry, hard wood which swells when wet, used for fastening timbers, especially in shipbuilding: also *trenail, trunnel.*

tree of heaven A large ornamental tree *(Ailanthus altissima)* of eastern Asia. It has large green flowers, those on the male trees being very ill–scented; ailanthus.

tree of knowledge of good and evil In the Bible, a tree in Eden whose fruit Adam and Eve were forbidden to eat. *Gen.* iii 3, 6. Also **tree of knowledge.**

tree of life 1 Arborvitae. 2 In the Bible: **a** A tree in the garden of Eden whose fruit conferred immortality. *Gen.* iii 22. **b** A similar tree in heaven. *Rev.* xxii 2.

Tree–Plant·er State (trē′plan′tər, -plän′-) Nickname of NEBRASKA.

tree ring A growth ring.

tree sparrow A North American sparrow *(Spizella arborea)* which nests in Canada and migrates southward in winter: also called *Canada sparrow.*

tree surgeon One skilled in tree surgery.

tree surgery The treatment of disease conditions and decay in trees by operative methods.

tref (trāf) *adj.* Unclean. See KOSHER. Also **tre·fa** (trā′fə). [<Yiddish *trēf* impure, forbidden <Hebrew *terēphāh* an animal torn by wild beasts, lit., that which is torn < *ṭāraf* tear]

tre·foil (trē′foil) *n.* 1 Any one of the clovers (genus *Trifolium*), so called from the trifoliolate leaves. 2 Certain other plants with trifoliolate leaves, as the black medic. 3 A three–lobed architectural ornamentation. [< AF *trifoil,* OF *trefeuil* <L *trifolium*]

tre·ha·la (tri·hä′lə) *n. Biochem.* A carbohydrate substance forming the pupal case of certain weevils (genus *Larixus*) and deposited upon Asian plants of the genus *Echinops.* [<NL <Turkish *tīqālah*]

tre·ha·lose (trē′hə·lōs) *n. Biochem.* A crystalline disaccharide, $C_{12}H_{22}O_{11}$, elaborated by many fungi and stored as a food reserve instead of starch. [TREHAL(A) + -OSE[2]]

treil·lage (trā′lij) *n.* A trellis. [<MF < *treille* a bower, trellis, arbor <L *trichila, tricla*]

Treitsch·ke (trīch′kə), **Heinrich von,** 1834–96, German historian and political writer.

trek (trek) *v.* **trekked, trek·king** *v.i.* 1 In South Africa, to travel by ox wagon. 2 To travel; migrate. —*v.t.* 3 In South Africa, to draw (a vehicle or load): said of an ox. —*n.* 1 An organized migration, as for the founding of a colony. 2 A journey; also, a stage in a journey. 3 The act of pulling. —**Great Trek** The migration of the Boers of Cape Colony across the Vaal, Orange, and Drakenburg rivers (1835–38) which led to the formation of the Orange Free State and the South African Republic. Also spelled *treck.* [<Du. *trekken* draw, travel <MDu. *trecken,* intensive of *trēken* <OHG *trechan* draw] —**trek′ker** *n.*

trel·lis (trel′is) *n.* 1 A crossbarred grating or lattice, used as a screen or a support for vines, etc. 2 A summerhouse or other structure of trelliswork. —*v.t.* 1 To interlace so as to form a trellis. 2 To furnish with or fasten on a trellis. [<OF *treliz, trelis* <L *trilix, trilicis* of three threads < *tri-* three + *licium* a thread]

trel·lis·work (trel′is·wûrk′) *n.* Latticework.

trem·a·tode (trem′ə·tōd) *n.* One of a class *(Trematoda)* of typically parasitic flatworms, including the liver flukes. [<NL <Gk. *trēmatōdēs* perforated < *trēma, -atos* a hole + *eidos* form] —**trem′a·toid** (-toid) *adj.*

trem·ble (trem′bəl) *v.i.* **·bled, ·bling** 1 To shake involuntarily, as with fear or weakness; be agitated. 2 To have slight, irregular vibratory motion, as from some jarring force; quiver; shake. 3 To feel anxiety or fear. 4 To quaver, as the voice. See synonyms under QUAKE, SHAKE. —*n.* 1 The act or state of trembling. 2 *pl.* A debilitating disease of cattle and sheep, possibly caused by eating certain plants, and communicated to man as the milk sickness. [<OF *trembler* <LL *tremulare* < *tremulus* tremulous < *tremere* tremble, shake] —**trem′bler** *n.* —**trem′bling** *adj.* & *n.* —**trem′bling·ly** *adv.* —**trem′bly** *adj.*

tre·men·dous (tri·men′dəs) *adj.* 1 Causing or fitted to cause astonishment by its magnitude, force, etc.: a *tremendous* blow; awe–inspiring; terrible. 2 *Colloq.* Extraordinarily big; remarkable. See synonyms under FORMIDABLE. [<L *tremendus* to be trembled at < *tremere* tremble] —**tre·men′dous·ly** *adv.* —**tre·men′dous·ness** *n.*

trem·e·tol (trem′ə·tōl, -tol) *n.* An oily, poisonous alcohol isolated from certain plants, as the white snakeroot, and believed to be the cause of trembles in sheep. [<L *tremere* tremble + -OL[1]]

trem·o·lite (trem′ə·līt) *n.* A light–colored calcium–magnesium amphibole, $CaMg_3Si_4O_{12}$. [from *Tremola,* Switzerland, where it was first found + -ITE[1]]

trem·o·lo (trem′ə·lō) *n. pl.* **·los** *Music* 1 A vibrating, beating, or throbbing sound produced vocally or instrumentally. 2 The mechanism for causing this effect in organ tones. [<Ital., trembling <L *tremulus.* See TREMBLE.]

trem·or (trem′ər, trē′mər) *n.* 1 A quick, vibratory movement caused by an external impulse; a shaking; also, a succession of such movements. 2 Any involuntary quivering or trembling of the body or limbs; a shiver. 3 *Pathol.* An involuntary and continued quivering or shaking of the whole or some part of the body: a form of paralysis. 4 Any trembling, quivering effect. See synonyms under FEAR. [<OF, fear, a trembling <L < *tremere* tremble]

trem·u·lant (trem′yə·lənt) *adj.* Trembling; tremulous: also **trem′u·lent.** —*n.* A tremolo. [<LL *tremulans, -antis,* ppr. of *tremulare* TREMBLE]

trem·u·lous (trem′yə·ləs) *adj.* 1 Characterized or affected by trembling: *tremulous* speech. 2 Showing timidity and irresolution. 3 Characterized by mental excitement. [<L *tremulus.* See TREMBLE.] —**trem′u·lous·ly** *adv.* —**trem′u·lous·ness** *n.*

tre·nail (trē′nāl, tren′əl, trun′əl) See TREENAIL.

trench (trench) *n.* 1 A long narrow excavation in the ground; ditch. 2 A long irregular ditch, lined with a parapet of the excavated earth, to protect troops: often with a descriptive word: *communication, reserve, shelter,* or *supply trench.* —*v.t.* 1 To dig a trench or trenches in. 2 *Mil.* To fortify with trenches; construct trenches against. 3 To cut deep furrows in; ditch. 4 To confine in a trench, as water; entrench. —*v.i.* 5 To cut or dig trenches. 6 To cut; carve. 7 To encroach. [<OF *trenche* a cutting, gash < *trenchier* cut, ult. <L *truncare* lop off < *truncus* a tree trunk]

Trench (trench), **Richard Chenevix,** 1807–86, English prelate, poet, and philologist.

trench·ant (tren′chənt) *adj.* 1 Cutting deeply and quickly; sharp: a *trenchant* sword. 2 Figuratively, clear, vigorous, and effective; cutting, as sarcasm. [<OF, ppr. of *trenchier.* See TRENCH.] —**trench′an·cy** *n.* —**trench′ant·ly** *adv.*

trench coat A loose–fitting overcoat of rainproof fabric with removable lining, several pockets, and a belt.

trench·er[1] (tren′chər) *n.* 1 A wooden plate formerly used at table; originally, a square piece of board used to cut food on. 2 *Archaic* The food served on trenchers; hence, the table or its pleasures. 3 *Obs.* A thick slice of bread used as a platter. [<AF *trenchour,* OF *tranchouoir* < *trenchier.* See TRENCH.]

trench·er[2] (tren′chər) *n.* 1 One who digs trenches. 2 One who carves. [<TRENCH, *v.* + -ER[1]]

trench·er·man (tren′chər·mən) *n. pl.* **·men** (-mən) 1 A feeder; eater; especially, one who enjoys food. 2 A table companion: also **trench′er·mate′** (-māt′). 3 A hanger–on; parasite.

trench fever *Pathol.* A remittent rickettsial fever transmitted by body lice and characterized by headache, nausea, high temperature, profuse sweating, muscular pains, and neuralgic pains in the legs. It attacked soldiers assigned to prolonged service in trenches during World War I.

trench foot *Pathol.* A disease of the feet caused by continued dampness and cold, and characterized by discoloration, weakness, and sometimes gangrene.

trench knife A double–edged steel knife with a long blade, used in hand–to–hand combat.

trench mortar Any of various portable, muzzleloading mortars designed for firing a projectile at a high trajectory. Also **trench gun.**

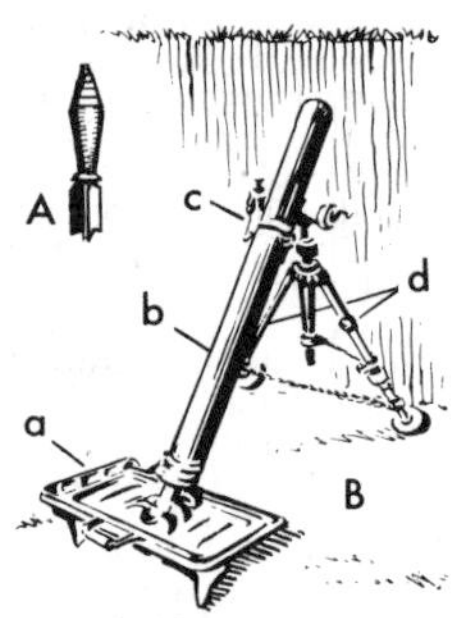

TRENCH MORTAR
A. Shell. *B.* 8 mm. mortar. *a.* Base plate. *b.* Tube. *c.* Sight. *d.* Bipod.

trench mouth *Pathol.* A mildly contagious disease of the mouth, gums, and sometimes the larynx and tonsils, caused by a soil bacillus; Vincent's angina.

trend (trend) *v.i.* To have or take a general course or direction; incline. —*n.* General course or direction; bent. [OE *trendan* roll]

trend·y (tren′dē) *adj. Slang* **trend·i·er, trend·i·est** In step with current fashion; voguish. —*n. pl.* **trend·ies** *Chiefly Brit.* A trendy person or thing. —**trend′i·ness** *n.*

Treng·ga·nu (treng·gä′nōō) A State of Malaya in the southern part on the South China Sea; 5,050 square miles; capital, Kuala Trengganu.

Trent (trent) A city in northern Italy on the Adige: ancient *Tridentum. Italian* **Tren·to** (tren′tō).

Trent (trent) The third longest river of England, flowing 170 miles SE and NE from NW Staffordshire, to a confluence with the Ouse, forming the Humber.

Trent, Council of A council of the Roman Catholic Church, held at intervals in Trent, Italy, from 1545 to 1563: it condemned the leading doctrines of the Reformation.

trente–et–qua·rante (träṅ·tā·kà·räṅt′) *n.* A gambling game played with cards laid out in two rows on a table, the top row representing "black" and the lower, "red." The players, who play against the bank, win if the row of cards they have chosen totals, in pips, nearer 31 than the other. Compare ROUGE ET NOIR. [<F, thirty and forty]

Tren·ti·no (tren·tē′nō) A district around Trent, Italy: that part of the southern Tirol under Italian control.

Tren·ton (tren′tən) The capital of New Jersey, on the Delaware River at the west central border of the State.

Trent River (trent) A river in SE Ontario, Canada, flowing 150 miles south and east to Lake Ontario.

tre·pan[1] (tri·pan′) *n.* 1 An early form of the trephine. 2 A large rock–boring tool. —*v.t.* **·panned, ·pan·ning** 1 *Mech.* To use a trepan upon. 2 *Surg.* To subject to the operation of trephining. 3 To cut a hole partly through, as the back of a brush, for the insertion of bristles. Also **trep·a·nize** (trep′ə·nīz). [<OF, a borer <Med. L *trepanum* a crown saw <Gk. *trypanon* a borer < *trypaein* bore] **—trep·a·na·tion** (trep′ə·nā′shən) *n.* **—tre·pan′ner** *n.*

tre·pan² (tri·pan′) *Obs.* & *Archaic v.t.* To ensnare. *—n.* A snare; trick; also, a trickster. Also spelled *trapan.* [<thieves' cant *trapan* <TRAP; prob. infl. in form by *trepan*¹]

tre·pang (tri·pang′) *n.* An East Indian holothurian or sea cucumber, especially *Holothuria marmorata* or a related species: a Chinese delicacy esteemed for soups: also called *bêche-de-mer.* [<Malay *trīpang*]

tre·phine (tri·fīn′, -fēn′) *n. Surg.* A cylindrical saw for removing a piece of bone from the skull, to relieve pressure, etc. *—v.t.* **·phined, ·phin·ing** To operate on with a trephine. [Earlier *trafine* <L *tres fines* three ends; infl. in form by *trepan*¹]

trep·i·da·tion (trep′ə·dā′shən) *n.* 1 A state of agitation from fear. 2 An involuntary trembling. 3 *Obs.* Confused haste. 4 *Obs.* A vibrating or vibration, as of leaves. Also **tre·pid·i·ty** (tri·pid′ə·tē). See synonyms under FEAR. [<L *trepidatio, -onis* < *trepidatus,* pp. of *trepidare* hurry, be alarmed < *trepidus* alarmed]

trep·o·neme (trep′ə·nēm) *n.* Any of a genus *(Treponema)* of corkscrew-shaped bacteria parasitic in the blood and tissues of animals. *T. pallidum* is the morbific agent of syphilis. [<NL <Gk. *trepein* turn + *nēma* thread] **—trep′o·nem′a·tous** (-nem′ə·təs) *adj.*

tres·pass (tres′pəs, -pas′) *v.i.* 1 *Law* To violate wilfully and forcibly the personal or property rights of another; commit a trespass: with *on* or *upon.* 2 To pass the bounds of propriety or rectitude, to the injury of another; intrude offensively; encroach: with *on* or *upon.* 3 To violate a positive law, rule, or custom: with *against.* *—n.* 1 Any voluntary transgression of law or rule of duty; any offense done to another. 2 *Law* Any wrongful act accompanied with force, either actual or implied, as wrongful entry on another's land, whereby another is injuriously treated; also, an action for trespass. See synonyms under AGGRESSION, ATTACK, OFFENSE. [<OF *trespasser* pass beyond, across <Med. L *transpassare* <L *trans-* across, beyond + *passare* PASS] **—tres′pass·er** *n.*

tress (tres) *n.* 1 A lock, curl, or ringlet of human hair, especially when abundant: applied also, figuratively, to adornment suggesting tresses. 2 *pl.* The hair of a woman or girl, especially when worn loose. [<OF *tresce* <LL *tricia*; ult. origin uncertain] **—tress′y** *adj.*

-tress *suffix* Used in feminine nouns corresponding to masculine nouns in *-ter, -tor*: a contracted form of *-teress, -toress.* Compare -ER¹, -ESS.

tressed (trest) *adj.* Wearing or arranged in tresses; braided; also, curled.

tres·sure (tresh′ər) *n. Her.* A bearing around the edge of a shield; modified or double orle, generally ornamented with fleurs-de-lis. Also **tres′sour.** [<OF *tresseor, tressure* < *tresce* a tress] **—tres′sured** *adj.*

tres·tle (tres′əl) *n.* 1 A beam or bar supported by four divergent legs, for bearing platforms, etc. 2 An open braced framework for supporting the horizontal stringers of a railway bridge, etc. 3 In carpentry, an intervening stud. 4 A trestletree. 5 *pl.* The props of a vessel on the ways. [<OF *trestel* <L *transtrum.* See TRANSOM.]

tres·tle·tree (tres′əl·trē′) *n. Naut.* One of a pair of pieces at right angles to a lower mast, to support the crosstrees, etc.

tres·tle·work (tres′əl·wûrk′) *n.* 1 Trestles collectively. 2 A bridge made of trestles or braced framework, especially of wood. Also **tres′tling.**

tret (tret) *n.* A former allowance to purchasers for waste due to transportation. [<AF, OF *tret,* var. of *traict.* See TRAIT.]

Tre·vel·yan (tri·vel′yən), **George Macaulay,** 1876–1962, English historian; son of the following. **—Sir George Otto,** 1838–1928, English historian and statesman.

Treves (trēvz) The English name for TRIER. *French* **Trèves** (trev).

trev·et (trev′it) See TRIVET.

trev·is (trev′is) *n.* 1 A bar or beam. 2 A crosspiece; partition. [Var. of TRAVERSE]

Tre·vi·so (trā·vē′zō) A city 16 miles NW of Venice in NE Italy: ancient *Tarvisium.*

trews (trōōz) *n. Scot.* Close-fitting tartan trousers. Also spelled *trooz.*

trey (trā) *n.* A card, domino, or die having three spots or pips. ◆ Homophone: *tray.* [<OF *trei, treis* <L *tres* three]

trez tine (trez) The royal tine. Also **tres tine, trey tine.** [Prob. <L *tres* three + TINE¹]

tri- *prefix* 1 Three; threefold; thrice: *tricycle, trisect.* 2 *Chem.* Containing three (specified) atoms, radicals, groups, etc.: *trioxide, trisulfide.* 3 Occurring every three (specified) intervals, or three times within a (specified) interval: *triweekly.* [<L *tri-* threefold < *tres* three]

tri·a·ble (trī′ə·bəl) *adj.* 1 That may be tried or tested. 2 *Law* That may undergo a judicial examination or determination. **—tri′·a·ble·ness** *n.*

tri·ac·id (trī·as′id) *n. Chem.* An acid containing three hydroxyl radicals which are replaceable by acid radicals.

tri·ad (trī′ad) *n.* 1 A group of three persons or things. 2 *Music* A chord of three tones or notes; often the common chord, consisting of a fundamental tone with its third and fifth higher. A **major triad** has a major third and a perfect fifth; a **minor triad** has a minor third and a perfect fifth. 3 *Chem.* **a** A trivalent atom or radical. **b** One of a group of three elements having similar chemical properties, as chlorine, bromine, and iodine. [<L *trias, -adis* <Gk. *trias, -ados* < *treis* three] **—tri·ad′ic** *adj.* & *n.*

tri·age (trī′ij, trē·äzh′) *n. Med.* The sorting out of a group of sick and wounded persons and classifying them according to a system of priorities for the treatment of mass casualties under conditions of limited medical resources and personnel. [<OF < *trier* pick out, sort]

tri·ag·o·nal (trī·ag′ə·nəl) *adj.* Having three angles; triangular. [Var. of TRIGONAL, on analogy with *tetragonal, pentagonal,* etc.]

tri·al (trī′əl, trīl) *n.* 1 The act of testing or proving by experience or use. 2 The state of being tried or tested by suffering: the hour of *trial.* 3 Experimental treatment or action performed to determine a result: to learn by *trial* and error. 4 An experience, person, or thing that puts strength, patience, or faith to the test. 5 An attempt or effort to do something; a try: to make a *trial.* 6 The examination, before a tribunal having assigned jurisdiction, of the facts or law involved in an issue in order to determine that issue. 7 A former method of determining guilt or innocence by subjecting the accused to physical tests of endurance, as by ordeal or by combat with his accuser. 8 *Brit.* An academic or licensing examination. See synonyms under ENDEAVOR, MISFORTUNE, PROOF. **—on trial** In the process of being tried or tested. *—adj.* 1 Of or pertaining to a trial or trials. 2 Made or performed in the course of trying or testing: a *trial* trip. 3 Used in testing: a *trial* specimen. [<AF < *trier* TRY]

trial balance In double-entry bookkeeping, a draft or statement of the debit and credit footings or balances of each account in the ledger.

trial balloon 1 A balloon released in order to test atmospheric and meteorological conditions, as wind velocities, air currents, etc. 2 Any tentative plan or scheme advanced to test public reaction.

trial jury A jury impaneled to try a civil or criminal case: also called *petit* or *petty jury.*

tri·a·morph (trī′ə·môrf) *n.* Any mineral or other substance that crystallizes in three different forms. [<L *tres, tria* three + Gk. *morphē* form] **—tri′a·mor′phous** *adj.*

tri·an·gle (trī′ang′gəl) *n.* 1 *Geom.* A figure, especially a plane figure, bounded by three sides, and having three angles. 2 Something resembling such a figure in shape or arrangement. 3 A flat drawing implement for making parallel or diagonal lines, etc. 4 A group or set of three; a triad. 5 A situation involving three persons: the eternal *triangle.* 6 *Music* A musical instrument of percussion, consisting of a resonant bar bent into a triangle and open at one corner, sounded by being struck with a small metal rod. [<OF <L *triangulum* < *triangulus* three-cornered < *tri-* three + *angulus* an angle]

TRIANGLE
a. Scalene. *b.* Isosceles. *c.* Equilateral. *d.* Right-angled. *e.* Obtuse.

tri·an·gu·lar (trī·ang′gyə·lər) *adj.* 1 Pertaining to, like, or bounded by a triangle: also **tri′an·gled.** 2 Concerned with or pertaining to three things, parties, or persons. [<LL *triangularis* <L *triangulum* a triangle] **—tri·an′gu·lar′i·ty** (-lar′ə·tē) *n.* **—tri·an′gu·lar·ly** *adv.*

triangular number See under NUMBER.

tri·an·gu·late (trī·ang′gyə·lāt) *v.t.* **·lat·ed, ·lat·ing** 1 To divide into triangles. 2 To survey by triangulation. 3 To give triangular shape to. *—adj.* Marked with triangles. [<L *triangulum* a triangle + -ATE¹]

tri·an·gu·la·tion (trī·ang′gyə·lā′shən) *n.* The laying out and accurate measurement of a network of triangles, especially on the surface of the earth, as in surveying.

Tri·an·gu·lum (trī·ang′gyə·ləm) *Astron.* A zodiacal constellation. See CONSTELLATION. [<L, a triangle]

tri·ap·si·dal (trī·ap′sə·dəl) *adj. Archit.* Distinguished by or constructed with three apses. [<TRI- + L *apsis, -idis* an apse + -AL]

tri·ar·chy (trī′är·kē) *n. pl.* **·chies** Government by three persons, or a country so governed; a triumvirate. [<Gk. *triarchia* < *tri-* three + *archein* rule]

Tri·as·sic (trī·as′ik) *adj. Geol.* Of or pertaining to the lowest of the three geological periods comprised in the Mesozoic era. *—n.* The Triassic period or rock system, following the Permian and succeeded by the Jurassic. Also **Tri·as** (trī′əs). [<LL *trias.* See TRIAD.]

tri·at·ic stay (trī·at′ik) *Naut.* A device consisting of two pendants connected by a span, and attached respectively to the foremast head and mainmast head of a ship: used principally for hoisting boats in and out of a vessel.

tri·a·tom·ic (trī′ə·tom′ik) *adj. Chem.* 1 Containing only three atoms in the molecule. 2 Containing three replaceable univalent atoms. 3 Trivalent.

tri·ax·i·al (trī·ak′sē·əl) *adj.* Having three axes.

tri·a·zine (trī′ə·zēn, -zin, trī·az′ēn, -in) *n. Chem.* 1 One of three heterocyclic compounds, $C_3H_3N_3$, each having three carbon and three nitrogen atoms in the ring. 2 Any of their derived compounds. Also **tri·a·zin** (trī′ə·zin, trī·az′in). [<TRI- + AZ(O)- + -INE²]

tri·a·zo·ic (trī′ə·zō′ik) *adj. Chem.* Hydrazoic. [<TRI- + -AZ(O)- + -IC]

tri·a·zole (trī′ə·zōl, trī·az′ōl) *n.* One of four five-membered ring compounds, $C_2H_3N_3$, in which nitrogen atoms have replaced two CH groups. [<TRI- + AZ(O)- + OLE¹]

trib·ade (trib′əd) *n.* A female homosexual, especially one who assumes the role of the male; a Lesbian. [<MF <L *tribas, -adis* <Gk. *tribas, -ados* < *tribein* rub]

trib·a·dism (trib′ə·diz′əm) *n.* Homosexual practices between females; Lesbianism.

tri·bal·ism (trī′bəl·iz′əm) *n.* Tribal organization, culture, or relations.

tri·ba·sic (trī·bā′sik) *adj. Chem.* 1 Containing three atoms of hydrogen replaceable by a base or basic radical: said of certain acids. 2 Having three hydroxyl groups in the molecule.

tribe (trīb) *n.* 1 A division, class, or group of people, varying ethnologically according to the circumstances from which their separation or distinction is supposed to originate. 2 Among primitive peoples, a group or aggregation of persons, usually consanguineous and endogamous, under one chief, characterized by its own culture, and having a name, a dialect, a government, and usually a territory of its own: Kaffir *tribes.* 3 In ancient states, an ethnic, hereditary, or political division of a united people: the *tribes* of Athens or of Israel. 4 A division of freeholders with a right to vote in certain of the ancient Roman councils. The Latins, Sabines, and Etruscans probably represented primitive clan divisions, to which Servius Tullius added a fourth when making his territorial division of Rome. Outside the city the spread of tribal organizations was coincident with the founding of new colonies. **5** A number of persons of any class or profession taken together: often derogatory or contemptuous: the theatrical *tribe.* **6** *Biol.* A group of plants or animals of indefinite rank. **7** Among stockbreeders, the descendants of a particular female bearer through females. See synonyms under PEOPLE. [Fusion of OF *tribu* (<L *tribus* a tribe) and L *tribus*] — **tri′bal** *adj.* — **tri′bal·ly** *adv.*

tribes·man (trībz′mən) *n.* *pl.* **·men** (-mən) A member of a tribe.

trib·o·e·lec·tric (trib′ō·i·lek′trik) *adj.* Of, pertaining to, or characterized by frictional electricity, as when a glass rod is rubbed with flannel. [< *tribo-* (<Gk. *tribein* rub) + ELECTRIC] — **trib′o·e·lec·tric′i·ty** (-i·lek′tris′·ə·tē) *n.*

triboelectric series A grouping of substances in such order that each one may be positively electrified by rubbing with those below it in the series.

trib·o·lu·mi·nes·cence (trib′ō·lo͞o′mə·nes′əns) *n.* Luminescence produced by crushing or grinding certain substances, as glass. [< *tribo-* (<Gk. *tribein* rub) + LUMINESCENCE] — **trib′·o·lu′mi·nes′cent** *adj.*

tri·brach (trī′brak, trib′rak) *n.* In ancient prosody, a foot composed of three short syllables, two of which belong to the thesis and one to the arsis. [<L *tribrachys* <Gk. < *tri-* three + *brachys* short]

tri·brom·eth·a·nol (trī′brom·eth′ə·nōl, -nol) *n.* *Chem.* A white crystalline compound, $C_2H_3Br_3O$, with an ethereal odor, used as a general anesthetic. Also **tri·bro′mo·eth′a·nol** (trī·brō′mō-).

tri·brom·phe·nol (trī′brom·fē′nōl, -nol) *n.* *Chem.* A colorless crystalline compound, $C_6H_3Br_3O$: used in medicine as an antiseptic.

trib·u·la·tion (trib′yə·lā′shən) *n.* A condition of affliction and distress; suffering; also, that which causes it. See synonyms under GRIEF, MISFORTUNE. [<OF *tribulacion* <LL *tribulatio, -onis* <L *tribulatus*, pp. of *tribulare* thrash < *tribulum* a threshing floor < *tri-*, root of *terere* rub, grind]

tri·bu·nal (tri·byo͞o′nəl, trī-) *n.* **1** A court of justice; any judicial body, as a board of arbitrators. **2** The seat set apart for judges, magistrates, etc. [<L < *tribunus* TRIBUNE]

trib·u·nate (trib′yə·nit, -nāt) *n.* The office or dignity of a tribune. Also **trib·une·ship** (trib′·yo͞on·ship).

trib·une[1] (trib′yo͞on, *Brit.* trī′byo͞on) *n.* **1** In Roman history, a magistrate chosen by the plebeians to protect them against patrician oppression. **2** One of various civil or military officers of later times; any champion of the people: as the title of a newspaper, often pronounced tri·byo͞on′. [<L *tribunus,* lit., head of a tribe < *tribus* a tribe] — **trib′u·nar′y** (-yə·ner′ē), **trib′u·ni′cial** (-yə·nish′əl), **trib′u·ni′cian** *adj.*

trib·une[2] (trib′yo͞on) *n.* **1** A raised floor for a Roman magistrate's chair. **2** A bishop's throne. **3** A rostrum or platform. [<MF <Ital. *tribuna* <L *tribunal* a tribunal]

trib·u·tar·y (trib′yə·ter′ē) *adj.* **1** Bringing supply; contributory; subsidiary: a *tributary* stream. **2** Offered or due as tribute; having the character of tribute: a *tributary* payment. **3** Paying tribute; hence, subordinate, as a state. — *n.* *pl.* **·tar·ies 1** A person or state paying tribute; a dependent. **2** A stream flowing into another; an affluent. [<L *tributarius* < *tributum.* See TRIBUTE.] — **trib′u·tar′i·ly** *adv.* — **trib′u·tar′i·ness** *n.*

trib·ute (trib′yo͞ot) *n.* **1** Money or other valuables paid by one state or ruler to another as an acknowledgment of submission or as the price of peace and protection, or by virtue of some treaty; also, the taxes imposed to raise money to make such payment. **2** The obligation or necessity of making such gift or payment; the state of being tributary. **3** Anything given, paid, or rendered as by a subordinate to a superior; figuratively, that which is due to worth, affection, or duty; contribution; tax; gift; offering; meed: I must render my *tribute* of praise. See synonyms under SUBSIDY, TAX. [<L *tributum,* neut. of *tributus,* pp. of *tribuere* pay, allot]

trice (trīs) *v.t.* **triced, tric·ing** To raise with a rope; also, to tie or lash: usually with *up.* — *n.* An instant: only in the phrase *in a trice.* [< MDu. *trisen* hoist]

tri·cen·ni·al (trī·sen′ē·əl) *adj.* Of or pertaining to the number thirty; taking place every thirtieth year. [<L *tricennium* a period of thirty years < *tricies* thirty times + *annus* a year]

tri·cen·ten·ni·al (trī′sen·ten′ē·əl) *adj.* & *n.* Tercentenary.

tri·ceps (trī′seps) *n.* *Anat.* A muscle having three heads; specifically, the large muscle at the back of the upper arm, of which the function is to extend the forearm. [<L *triceps, -cipitis* three-headed < *tri-* three + *caput, capitis* a head]

trich– Var. of TRICHO–.

tri·chi·a·sis (tri·kī′ə·sis) *n.* *Pathol.* **1** A condition of ingrowing hairs about an orifice, especially ingrowing eyelashes. **2** The presence of hairlike filaments in the urine. [<LL *trichiasis* <Gk. < *trichiaein* be hairy < *thrix, trichos* hair]

tri·chi·na (tri·kī′nə) *n.* *pl.* **·nae** (-nē) A small nematode parasitic worm (*Trichinella spiralis*) that in its larval stage sometimes infests the muscles of man, swine, and other mammals. [<NL <Gk. *trichinos* of hair < *thrix, trichos* hair]

trich·i·nize (trik′ə·nīz) *v.t.* **·nized, ·niz·ing** To infect with trichinae. — **trich′i·ni·za′tion** *n.*

Trich·i·nop·o·ly (trich′ə·nop′ə·lē) See TIRUCHIRAPPALI.

trich·i·no·sis (trik′ə·nō′sis) *n.* *Pathol.* The disease produced by trichinae in the intestines and muscles of the body. Also **trich′i·ni′a·sis** (-nī′ə·sis). [<TRICHINA + -OSIS] — **trich′i·nosed, trich′i·not′ic** (-not′ik), **trich′i·nous** *adj.*

trich·ite (trik′īt) *n.* **1** *Mineral.* A microscopic crystallite, curved, bent, or zigzag in form, found in volcanic rocks. **2** *Bot.* One of the needle-shaped, radial crystals occurring in starch grains. **3** *Zool.* A rodlike organ surrounding the mouth and gullet of certain ciliate protozoa. [<G *trichit* <Gk. *thrix, trichos* hair] — **tri·chit·ic** (tri·kit′ik) *adj.*

tri·chlo·ride (trī·klôr′īd, -id, -klō′rīd, -rid) *n.* *Chem.* Any compound having three chlorine atoms in its molecule. Also **tri·chlo·rid** (trī·klôr′id, -klō′rid).

tri·chlo·ro·eth·yl·ene (trī·klôr′ō·eth′əl·ēn, -klō·rō-) *n.* *Chem.* A colorless, odorless, volatile liquid, C_2HCl_3, used in organic synthesis, in chemical manufactures, and as a general anesthetic. Also **tri′chlor·eth′yl·ene** (trī′klôr-).

tricho– *combining form* Hair; of or resembling a hair or hairs: *trichocyst*: also, before vowels, *trich–* Also **trichi–.** [<Gk. *thrix, trichos* a hair]

trich·o·bac·te·ri·a (trik′ō·bak·tir′ē·ə) *n.* A group of bacteria which includes forms possessing flagella.

trich·o·cyst (trik′ə·sist) *n.* *Biol.* **1** A stinging capsule containing a protrusible hairlike body: found in various protozoans. **2** A thread cell. — **trich′o·cys′tic** *adj.*

trich·o·gyne (trik′ə·jīn, -jin) *n.* *Bot.* The slender threadlike portion of the procarp in red algae which receives the male fertilizing bodies. [<TRICHO- + Gk. *gynē* a woman, female]

trich·oid (trik′oid) *adj.* Having the form or appearance of hair. [<Gk. *trichoeidēs* < *thrix, trichos* a hair + *eidos* form]

tri·chol·o·gy (tri·kol′ə·jē) *n.* The sum of knowledge concerning the hair.

tri·cho·ma (tri·kō′mə) *n.* *pl.* **·ma·ta** (-mə·tə) **1** *Pathol.* **a** Entropion. **b** Matted and crusted hair; plica polonica. **2** *Bot.* One of the threads or filaments of filamentous algae: also spelled *trichome.* [<NL <Gk. *trichōma* growth of hair < *trichoein* cover with hair < *thrix, trichos* hair] — **tri·chom′ic** (-kom′ik) *adj.*

trich·ome (trik′ōm, trī′kōm) *n.* *Bot.* **1** Any surface appendage or epidermal outgrowth in a plant, comprising hairs, bristles, prickles, scales, root hairs, etc. **2** A trichoma (def. 2). [<Gk. *trichōma.* See TRICHOMA.]

Tri·chop·ter·a (tri·kop′tər·ə) *n. pl.* An order of insects including the caddis flies. The aquatic larvae of most species construct cases of sand or other material; the adults are mothlike, with two pairs of hairy wings and well-developed compound eyes. [<NL <Gk. *thrix, trichos* hair + *pteron* a wing]

tri·chō·sis (tri·kō′sis) *n.* *Pathol.* Any morbid condition of the hair. [<NL <Gk. *trichōsis* growth of hair < *trichoein.* See TRICHOMA.]

tri·chot·o·my (trī·kot′ə·mē) *n.* **1** Division into three parts. **2** *Logic* The threefold division of a genus or class. **3** *Theol.* The division of human nature into body, soul, and spirit. [<Gk. *tricha* threefold + -TOMY] — **trich·o·tom·ic** (trik′ə·tom′ik), **tri·chot′o·mous** *adj.* — **tri·chot′o·mous·ly** *adv.*

tri·chro·ism (trī′krō·iz′əm) *n.* The property of a crystal of transmitting light of different colors in three different directions. [<Gk. *trichroos* of three colors < *tri-* three + *chroia* color, skin] — **tri·chro·ic** (trī·krō′ik) *adj.*

tri·chro·mat·ic (trī′krō·mat′ik) *adj.* Of, pertaining to, having, or using three colors, as the normal eye, the three-color process in photography and printing, etc. Also **tri′chrome, tri·chro·mic** (trī·krō′mik). [<TRI- + CHROMATIC] — **tri·chro′ma·tism** (-mə·tiz′əm) *n.*

trick (trik) *n.* **1** A device for getting an advantage by deception; a petty artifice. **2** A malicious, injurious, or annoying act: a dirty *trick.* **3** A practical joke; prank: the *tricks* of schoolboys. **4** A particular habit or manner; characteristic; trait; also, a vicious habit. **5** A peculiar skill or knack. **6** An act of legerdemain; a feat of jugglery: conjurer's *tricks.* **7** In card games, the whole number of cards played in one round. **8** The turn of one sailor at the helm; a turn or spell of duty; a railroad or factory shift. **9** *Colloq.* A toy; trifle; plaything; a child. See synonyms under ARTIFICE, FRAUD. — **to do** (or **turn**) **the trick** *Slang* To produce the desired result. — *v.t.* **1** To deceive or cheat; delude. **2** To dress or array; adorn: with *up* or *out.* — *v.i.* **3** To practice trickery or deception. See synonyms under DECEIVE. [<AF *trique,* OF *triche* deceit < *trichier* cheat, prob. ult. <L *tricare, tricari* trifle, play tricks < *tricae* trifles, tricks] — **trick′er** *n.* — **trick′less** *adj.*

trick·er·y (trik′ər·ē) *n.* *pl.* **·er·ies 1** The practice of tricks; artifice; stratagem; wiles. **2** Dressing up; decorations. See synonyms under DECEPTION.

trick·ing (trik′ing) *n.* The act of dressing up; also, ornaments. — *adj.* *Obs.* Given to tricks; tricky.

trick·ish (trik′ish) *adj.* Apt to be tricky; partaking of trickery. — **trick′ish·ly** *adv.* — **trick′·ish·ness** *n.*

trick·le (trik′əl) *v.* **·led, ·ling** *v.i.* **1** To flow or run drop by drop or in a very thin stream. **2** To move, come, go, etc., slowly or bit by bit. — *v.t.* **3** To cause to trickle. — *n.* The act or state of trickling, or that which trickles. [ME *triklen,* prob. alter. of *striklen,* freq. of *striken* strike] — **trick′ly** *adj.*

trick·let (trik′lit) *n.* A tiny rill. [Dim. of TRICKLE]

trick·ster (trik′stər) *n.* One who plays tricks; a cheat.

trick·sy (trik′sē) *adj.* **1** Fond of tricks or pranks; mischievous; playful. **2** Given to artifice or stratagem; cunning; crafty. **3** Tending to elude or deceive; illusory. **4** Neat; trim; spruce; smartly attired. — **trick′si·ness** *n.*

trick–track (trik′trak′) *n.* A form of backgammon; specifically, an old form in which pegs as well as pieces were used. Also **tric′-trac′.** [<F *trictrac* <MF, a clicking noise; imit. of the sound of the pieces during a game]

trick·y (trik′ē) *adj.* **trick·i·er, trick·i·est 1** Disposed to or characterized by trickery; deceitful. **2** Vicious, as an animal. **3** Intricate; requiring or showing adroitness or skill in making: *tricky* clothes. See synonyms under INSIDIOUS. Also *Scot.* **trick′ie.** — **trick′i·ly** *adv.* — **trick′i·ness** *n.*

tri·clin·ic (trī·klin′ik) *adj.* Describing a crystal form having three unequal and dissimilar axes with oblique intersections. [<TRI- + Gk. *klinein* incline + -IC]

tri·clin·i·um (trī·klin′ē·əm) *n.* *pl.* **·i·a** (-ē·ə) **1** In Roman antiquity, a dining table of four sides, three sides of which were provided with low couches upon which guests could recline. **2** The Roman dining-room. [<L <Gk. *triklinion,* dim. of *triklinos* a dining-room with three couches < *tri-* three + *klinē* a couch]

tri·col·or (trī′kul′ər) *adj.* Having or characterized by three colors: also **tri′col′ored.** — *n.* **1** A flag of three colors; the French national flag of blue, white, and red vertical bands.

2 The tricolor cockade of the French Revolutionists. Also *Brit.* **tri′col′our.** [<F *tricolore* <LL *tricolor* <L *tri-* three + *color* color]

tri·corn (trī′kôrn) *n.* A hat with the brim turned up on three sides, worn during the 17th and 18th centuries by both men and women: used improperly in the form *tricorne* for the two-cornered hat of the French gendarmes. See BICORN. — *adj.* Three-horned; three-pronged; having three hornlike processes. [<F *tricorne* <L *tricornis* three-horned < *tri-* three + *cornu* a horn]

tri·cor·nered (trī′kôr′nərd) *adj.* Three-cornered.

tri·cos·tate (trī·kos′tāt) *adj. Biol.* Having three ribs or costae. [<TRI- + L *costa* a rib + -ATE[1]]

tri·cot (trē′kō, *Fr.* trē·kō′) *n.* 1 A hand-knitted or woven fabric, or a machine-made imitation thereof. 2 A soft ribbed cloth. 3 A tight-fitting garment worn by ballet dancers. [<F, knitting < *tricoter* knit, ? ult. <LG *striken* make movements]

tri·crot·ic (trī·krot′ik) *adj. Med.* Having three distinct rhythmic waves in succession, as the pulse: also **tri·cro·tous** (trī′krə·təs). [<TRI- + Gk. *kroteein* knock, beat] — **tri·crot·ism** (trī′krə·tiz′əm) *n.*

tri·cus·pid (trī·kus′pid) *adj.* 1 Having three cusps or points, as a molar tooth or a valve of the heart. 2 Of or pertaining to the tricuspid valve. Also **tri·cus′pi·dal.** [<L *tricuspis, -idis* three-pointed < *tri-* three + *cuspis, -idis* a point]

tri·cus·pi·date (trī·kus′pə·dāt) *adj.* Three-pointed: a *tricuspidate* leaf.

tricuspid valve *Anat.* A three-segmented valve which controls the flow of blood from the right atrium to the right ventricle of the heart.

tri·cy·cle (trī′sik·əl) *n.* 1 A three-wheeled vehicle of the velocipede class. 2 A motorcycle with three wheels. [<F <*tri-* three + Gk. *kyklos* a circle]

tri·cy·clic (trī·sī′klik, -sik′lik) *adj.* Having or characterized by three cycles or identical units of structure: a *tricyclic* chemical compound.

tri·dac·tyl (trī·dak′til) *adj. Anat.* Possessing three fingers or toes. [<Gk. *tridaktylos* < *tri-* three + *daktylos* a digit]

tri·dec·ane (trī·dek′ān) *n. Chem.* A light, colorless, liquid hydrocarbon, $C_{13}H_{28}$, of the methane series, having an odor like turpentine. [<TRI- + DECANE]

tri·dent (trīd′nt) *n.* 1 A three-pronged implement or weapon, the emblem of Neptune (Poseidon); hence, dominion over the sea. 2 The three-pronged spear with which the Roman retiarius was armed. 3 A fishspear with three prongs. 4 *Geom.* A plane cubic curve somewhat resembling a three-pronged spear. — *adj.* Having three teeth or prongs: also **tri·den·tate** (trī·den′tāt), **tri·den′tat·ed.** [<L *tridens, -dentis* < *tri-* three + *dens, dentis* a tooth]

Tri·den·tine (trī·den′tin, -tīn, tri-) *adj.* 1 Pertaining to Trent or to the Council of Trent. 2 Adhering to the decrees of the Council of Trent. — *n.* A Roman Catholic: from the fact that the creed (**Tridentine Creed**) of the Roman Catholic Church as now held was formulated by the Council of Trent. [<Med. L *Tridentinus* <*Tridentum* Trent]

Tri·den·tum (trī·den′təm) The ancient name for TRENT, Italy.

tri·di·men·sion·al (trī′di·men′shən·əl) *adj.* Of three dimensions; having length, breadth, and thickness. — **tri′di·men′sion·al′i·ty** *n.*

tri·di·ur·nal (trī′dī·ûr′nəl) *adj.* Occurring every three days or lasting three days.

tri·e·cious (trī·ē′shəs) See TRIOECIOUS.

tried (trīd) *adj.* 1 Tested; trustworthy, as a friend or a formula. 2 Freed of impurities, as metal or oil. 3 Rendered, as fat.

tri·en·ni·al (trī·en′ē·əl) *adj.* 1 Taking place every third year. 2 Lasting three years. — *n.* 1 A ceremony or event observed or celebrated every three years; a third anniversary. 2 A plant lasting three years. — **tri·en′ni·al·ly** *adv.*

tri·en·ni·um (trī·en′ē·əm) *n. pl.* **·en·ni·ums** or **·en·ni·a** (-en′ē·ə) A period of three years. [<L < *tri-* three + *annus* a year]

Trier (trir) A city of Rhineland-Palatinate, West Germany, on the Moselle river in the central western part near Luxembourg: English *Treves,* French *Trèves.*

tri·er·arch (trī′ər·ärk) *n.* In Greek antiquity, the captain of a trireme; also, at Athens, one who alone or with others fitted out and maintained a trireme. [<L *trierarchus* <Gk. *triērarchos* < *triērēs* a trireme + *archein* rule]

tri·er·ar·chy (trī′ər·är′kē) *n. pl.* **·chies** 1 The command of a trireme. 2 The fitting out and maintaining of a trireme. 3 The body of trierarchs collectively. [<Gk. *triērarchia* < *triērarchos* TRIERARCH]

Tri·este (trē·est′, *Ital.* trē·es′tä) An Italian port on the **Gulf of Trieste,** a NE inlet of the Gulf of Venice; formerly an Austrian port and later part of the Free Territory of Trieste.

Trieste, Free Territory of A former free territory, including the city of Trieste and adjoining portions of Istria, constituted by the Italian-Allied peace treaty of 1947; 298 square miles; in 1954 the smaller part (81 square miles, including the city of Trieste) reverted to Italy, and the larger (217 square miles) passed to Yugoslavia.

tri·e·ter·ic (trī′ə·ter′ik) *adj.* Happening every other year. [<L *trietericus* <Gk. *trietērikos* < *trietēris* a festival celebrated every other year < *tri-* three + *etos* a year]

tri·fa·cial (trī·fā′shəl) *adj.* Trigeminal (def. 2).

tri·fid (trī′fid) *adj.* Divided into three parts or sections; three-cleft. [<L *trifidus* < *tri-* three + *fid-,* stem of *findere* split]

tri·fle (trī′fəl) *v.* **·fled, ·fling** *v.i.* 1 To treat something as of no value or importance; dally: with *with.* 2 To act or speak frivolously or idly; jest. 3 To play; toy. 4 To pass time idly; idle. — *v.t.* 5 To pass (time) in an idle and purposeless way. — *n.* 1 Anything of very little value or importance. 2 A light confection, usually made of alternate layers of macaroons or ladyfingers with sugared fruit, covered with a custard and topped with meringue or whipped cream. 3 A variety of pewter. — **a trifle** Slightly; to a small extent: a *trifle* short. [<OF *truffler,* var. of *truffer* deceive, jeer at < *trufle,* dim. of *trufe* a cheating, mockery; ult. origin unknown] — **tri′fler** *n.*

tri·fling (trī′fling) *adj.* 1 Frivolous. 2 Insignificant. See synonyms under CHILDISH, IDLE, INSIGNIFICANT, LITTLE, RIDICULOUS, VAIN. — **tri′fling·ly** *adv.*

tri·fo·cal (trī·fō′kəl) *adj.* 1 Having three foci. 2 *Optics* Pertaining to or describing a lens ground in three segments, for near, intermediate, and far vision respectively.

tri·fold (trī′fōld) *adj.* Triple.

tri·fo·li·ate (trī·fō′lē·it, -āt) *adj. Bot.* Having three leaves or leaflike processes. Also **tri·fo′li·at′ed.** [<TRI- + FOLIATE]

tri·fo·li·o·late (trī·fō′lē·ə·lāt′) *adj. Bot.* Having three leaflets.

tri·fo·li·um (trī·fō′lē·əm) *n.* Any of a genus (*Trifolium*) of small plants of the bean family, the clovers, with trifoliolate leaves, and purple, red, white, or yellow flowers. [<NL <L < *tri-* three + *folium* a leaf]

tri·fo·ri·um (trī·fôr′ē·əm, -fō′rē-) *n. pl.* **·fo·ri·a** (-fôr′ē·ə, -fō′rē·ə) *Archit.* A gallery above the arches of the nave in a church. [<Med. L <L *tri-* three + *foris* a door] — **tri·fo′ri·al** *adj.*

TRIFORIUM

tri·formed (trī′fôrmd′) *adj.* 1 Having three forms or shapes. 2 Consisting of three parts or divisions. Also **tri′form.** — **tri·form′i·ty** *n.*

tri·fur·cate (trī·fûr′kāt) *adj.* Three-forked; trichotomous. Also **tri·fur′cat·ed.** — **tri·fur·ca·tion** (trī′fər·kā′shən) *n.*

trig[1] (trig) *adj.* 1 Characterized by tidiness; trim; neat. 2 Strong; sound; firm. 3 In a depreciative sense, correct; precise; prim. 4 Faithful; trustworthy; dependable. 5 Active; alert. 6 Full; inflated. — *v.t.* **trigged, trig·ging** To make trig or neat; dress finely or smartly: often with *out* or *up.* [<ON *tryggr* true, trusty] — **trig′ly** *adv.* — **trig′ness** *n.*

trig[2] (trig) *v.t.* **trigged, trig·ging** 1 To check, as with a skid; obstruct; stop. 2 To shore; prop. — *n.* A check or brake, as a skid or drag for a wheel. [? <ON *tryggja* make firm]

tri·gem·i·nal (trī·jem′ə·nəl) *adj.* 1 Being in three parts; threefold; triple. 2 Of or pertaining to the trigeminus: *trigeminal* neuralgia. — *n.* The trigeminus. [<L *trigeminus* born three at a time < *tri-* three + *geminus* a twin]

tri·gem·i·nus (trī·jem′ə·nəs) *n. pl.* **·ni** (-nī) *Anat.* The fifth cranial or trifacial nerve, the great nerve of sensation for the face and head. [<NL <L. See TRIGEMINAL.]

trig·ger[1] (trig′ər) *n.* 1 The fingerpiece of a gunlock or pistol-lock, for releasing the hammer. 2 A catch or small lever doing similar service in a trap or other mechanism. — **quick on the trigger** 1 Quick to shoot. 2 Quick to act in response to a suggestion; quick-witted; alert. — *v.t.* To cause or precipitate. [Earlier *tricker* <Du. *trekker* < *trekken* pull, tug at]

trig·ger[2] (trig′ər) *n. Dial.* A skid or trig. [< TRIG[2] + -ER]

trig·ger·fish (trig′ər·fish′) *n. pl.* **·fish** or **·fish·es** A plectognath fish (genus *Balistes*) found mainly in the tropical Pacific region, with an ovate body covered with large, rough scales: named from the triggerlike second spine of the dorsal fin.

TRIGGERFISH • (About 12 inches long)

tri·glyph (trī′glif) *n. Archit.* An ornament in a Doric frieze consisting of a tablet with three parallel vertical channels or glyphs, and standing on each side of the metopes. [<L *triglyphus* <Gk. *triglyphos* thrice grooved < *tri-* three + *glyphē* a carving < *glyphein* carve, engrave]

tri·glyph·ic (trī·glif′ik) *adj.* 1 Pertaining to or consisting of triglyphs. 2 Having three groups of characters or carvings. Also **tri′·glyph·al, tri·glyph′i·cal.**

tri·go (trē′gō) *n. Spanish* Wheat.

tri·gon (trī′gon) *n.* 1 A triangle; especially, the triangle of reference used in trilinear coördinates. 2 One of four parts of the zodiac, each consisting of three signs. 3 In Greek and Roman antiquity, a lyre or harp of triangular form. [<L *trigonum* <Gk. *trigōnon,* orig. neut. of *trigōnos* three-angled < *tri-* three + *gōnia* an angle]

trig·o·nal (trig′ə·nəl) *adj.* 1 Pertaining to or in the form of a trigon; triangular; three-cornered. 2 Characterized, in the hexagonal crystal system, by having a principal (vertical) axis of threefold symmetry. Also **trig′o·nous.** — **trig′o·nal·ly** *adv.*

trig·o·nom·e·ter (trig′ə·nom′ə·tər) *n.* 1 An instrument for solving triangles mechanically. 2 *Obs.* An expert in trigonometry.

trigonometric functions Certain functions of an angle or arc used in trigonometry. The most commonly used are: sine, cosine, tangent, cotangent, secant, cosecant. In illustration *A* the functions of the angle θ are defined as ratios or fractions. They are:

$$\text{sine } \theta = \frac{AB}{AC} \qquad \text{cosecant } \theta = \frac{AC}{AB}$$

$$\text{cosine } \theta = \frac{CB}{AC} \qquad \text{secant } \theta = \frac{AC}{CB}$$

$$\text{tangent } \theta = \frac{AB}{CB} \qquad \text{cotangent } \theta = \frac{CB}{AB}$$

The functions may be represented also as lines by constructing the reference triangle in a circle whose radius is taken as unity, and drawing additional lines as in *B.* The *sine* is then AB, the *cosine* CB, the *tangent* ED, the *cotangent* GF, the *secant* CE, and the *cosecant* CF. These are all spoken of as the sine, cosine, etc., of the arc AD as well as of the angle θ. Other, less common, trigonometric functions are: versed sine, coversed sine, exsecant, and

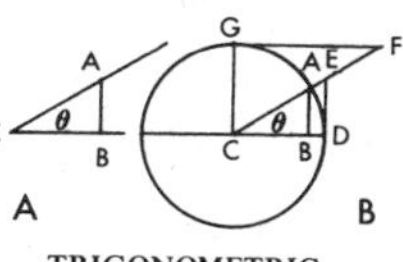

TRIGONOMETRIC FUNCTIONS

haversine. These functions are expressed as follows:

versed sine θ (or versine θ) = 1 − cosine θ
coversed sine θ (or versed cosine θ) = 1 − sine θ
exsecant θ = secant θ − 1
haversine θ = 1/2 versine θ

trig·o·nom·e·try (trig′ə·nom′ə·trē) *n.* The branch of mathematics that treats of the relations of the sides and angles of triangles and of the methods of applying these relations in the solution of problems involving triangles: widely used in navigation, surveying, etc. [<NL *trigonometria* <Gk. *trigōnon* a triangle + *metron* measure] — **trig·o·no·met·ric** (trig′ə·nō·met′rik) or **·ri·cal** *adj.* — **trig′o·no·met′ri·cal·ly** *adv.*

tri·graph (trī′graf, -gräf) *n.* A group of three letters representing one articulate sound: *eau* in *beau*; also, the sound thus represented. [<TRI- + -GRAPH] — **tri·graph′ic** *adj.*

tri·he·dron (trī·hē′drən) *n. pl.* **·dra** (-drə) *Geom.* A figure having three plane surfaces meeting at a point. [<NL <Gk. *tri-* three + *hedra* a base] — **tri·he′dral** *adj.*

tri·hy·brid (trī·hī′brid) *n. Biol.* A hybrid whose parents differ from each other in respect to three pairs of contrasting Mendelian characters.

tri·hy·dric (trī·hī′drik) *adj. Chem.* Pertaining to or designating a compound containing three hydroxyl groups. Also **tri·hy·drox·y** (trī′hī·drok′sē). [<TRI- + HYDR(OXYL) + -IC]

tri·ju·gate (trī′jo͞o·gāt, trī·jo͞o′gāt, -git) *adj. Bot.* Having three pairs of leaflets. Also **tri·ju·gous** (trī′jo͞o·gəs, trī·jo͞o′gəs). [<L *trijugus* threefold < *tri-* three + *jugum* a yoke]

tri·lat·er·al (trī·lat′ər·əl) *adj.* Having three sides. [<L *trilaterus* < *tri-* three + *latus, lateris* a side] — **tri·lat′er·al·ly** *adv.*

tril·by (tril′bē) *n.* A soft felt hat with indented crown: informal wear for men in Great Britain. [after *Trilby,* a novel (1894) by George Du Maurier, in which such hats are described]

tri·lin·e·ar (trī·lin′ē·ər) *adj.* Pertaining to, referring to, or bounded by three lines.

tri·lin·gual (trī·ling′gwəl) *adj.* Derived from, composed of, or using three languages: a *trilingual* discourse. Also **tri·lin′guar.** [<L *trilinguis* < *tri-* three + *lingua* a tongue]

tri·lit·er·al (trī·lit′ər·əl) *adj.* Consisting of three letters. — **tri·lit′er·al·ism** *n.*

trill[1] (tril) *v.t.* **1** To sing or play in a quavering or tremulous tone. **2** *Phonet.* To articulate with a trill. — *v.i.* **3** To utter, make, or give forth a quavering or tremulous sound. **4** *Music* To execute a trill or shake. — *n.* **1** A tremulous utterance of successive tones, as of certain insects or birds; a warble. **2** *Music* A quick alternation of two notes either a tone or a semitone apart; shake. **3** *Phonet.* A rapid vibration of a speech organ, as of the tip of the tongue against the alveolar ridge or the uvula against the back of the tongue, as in the articulation of *rr* in Spanish. **4** A consonant or word so uttered. Also spelled *thrill.* [<Ital. *trillare,* prob. <Gmc.]

trill[2] (tril) *v.t.* & *v.i. Archaic* **1** To flow or cause to flow in a trickle, as tears. **2** To turn or roll; also, to quiver. [ME *trillen* <Scand. Cf. Sw. & Norw. *trilla* roll.]

tril·ling (tril′ing) *n.* A compound crystal made up of three individuals. [Cf. Dan. *trilling* a triplet]

tril·lion (tril′yən) *n.* A cardinal number; in the French and United States system of numeration, 1 followed by 12 zeros; in the English and German system, 1 followed by 18 zeros. — *adj.* Numbering a trillion. [<MF < *tri-* three + *million* million] — **tril′lionth** *adj.* & *n.*

tril·li·um (tril′ē·əm) *n.* Any of a genus (*Trillium*) of North American herbs of the lily family, with a stout stem, rising from a short rootstock and bearing a whorl of three leaves and a solitary flower. The fruit is a red or purple berry. [<NL <L *tri-* three; so called because of its three leaves]

tri·lo·bate (trī·lō′bāt, trī′lə·bāt) *adj.* **1** Three-lobed. **2** *Bot.* Having three lobes, as some leaves. Also **tri·lo′bal, tri·lo′bat·ed, tri′lobed.**

tri·lo·bite (trī′lə·bīt) *n. Paleontol.* Any of a subclass or group (*Trilobita*) of early Paleozoic marine arthropods related to the crustaceans, having a flattened body divided into a variable number of segments covered by a hard dorsal shield marked in three lobes. [<NL *Trilobites* <Gk. *tri-* three + *lobos* a lobe] — **tri′lo·bit′ic** (-bit′ik) *adj.*

tri·loc·u·lar (trī·lok′yə·lər) *adj.* Having three cells or chambers. [<TRI- + L *loculus* a small receptacle, dim. of *locus* a place]

tril·o·gy (tril′ə·jē) *n. pl.* **·gies** A group of three literary or dramatic compositions, each complete in itself, but continuing the same general subject. [<Gk. *trilogia* < *tri-* three + *logos* a discourse]

trim (trim) *v.* **trimmed, trim·ming** *v.t.* **1** To put in or restore to order; make neat by clipping, pruning, etc. **2** To remove by cutting: usually with *off* or *away.* **3** To put ornaments on; decorate. **4** In carpentry, to smooth; dress. **5** *Colloq.* **a** To chide; rebuke. **b** To punish or thrash; beat. **c** To defeat. **d** To cheat; victimize. **6** *Naut.* **a** To adjust (sails or yards) for sailing. **b** To cause (a ship) to sit well in the water by adjusting cargo, ballast, etc. **7** *Aeron.* To bring (an airplane) to level or balanced flight by adjusting control surfaces. **8** *Obs.* To furnish; equip. — *v.i.* **9** *Naut.* **a** To be or remain in equilibrium: said of a ship. **b** To adjust sails or yards for sailing. **10** To act so as to appear to favor opposing sides in a controversy. — *n.* **1** State of adjustment or preparation; fitting condition; orderly disposition: All was in good *trim.* **2** Condition as to general appearance; dress; style. **3** *Naut.* Fitness for sailing: said of a vessel in reference to disposition of ballast, masts, cargo, etc. **4** *Naut.* Actual or comparative degree of immersion: said of a vessel. **5** Particular character or nature; kind; stripe. **6** The moldings, etc., as about the doors of a building; also, the hardware trimmings of a house, such as hinges, window fastenings, etc. **7** Ornament; trapping; dress. **8** Material rejected or cut out, as sections from a motion-picture film. **9** In advertising, window dressing or display. **10** The interior furnishings of an automobile body. **11** *Aeron.* The position of an aircraft relative to balanced flight. — *adj.* **trim·mer, trim·mest** **1** Adjusted to a nicety; being in perfect order; handsomely equipped or of stylish and smart appearance; spruce; precise; jaunty. **2** Excellently fit; nice; pretty; fine. See synonyms under NEAT[1], STAUNCH. — *adv.* In a trim manner: also **trim′ly.** [OE *trymman* arrange, strengthen < *trum* steadfast, strong] — **trim′ness** *n.*

tri·mer (trī′mər) *n. Chem.* A compound formed by the union of three molecules of another compound or substance, as benzene from acetylene. [<TRI- + Gk. *meros* a part]

trim·er·ous (trim′ər·əs) *adj.* **1** Composed of three similar parts. **2** *Bot.* Three-parted. **3** *Entomol.* Having three joints, as the tarsus of an insect: often written 3-*merous.* [<TRI- + Gk. *meros* a part]

tri·mes·ter (trī·mes′tər) *n.* A three-month period; quarter. [<F *trimestre* <L *trimestris* < *tri-* three + *mensis* a month] — **tri·mes′tral, tri·mes′tri·al** *adj.*

trim·e·ter (trim′ə·tər) *adj.* In prosody, consisting of three measures or of lines containing three measures. — *n.* **1** A verse consisting of three measures, as the iambic trimeter. **2** In classical prosody, a line or verse consisting of three dimeters, or six feet. [<L *trimetrus* <Gk. *trimetros* < *tri-* three + *metron* a measure]

tri·meth·yl·pen·tane (trī′meth·il·pen′tān) *n. Chem.* One of five isomers of the pentane series, C_8H_{18}, used as a solvent and high-compression motor fuel. Also called *isooctane.* Compare OCTANE NUMBER. [<TRI- + METHYL + PENTANE]

tri·met·ric (trī·met′rik) *adj.* **1** Trimeter. **2** Orthorhombic. Also **tri·met′ri·cal.**

trimetric projection *Geom.* A three-dimensional geometric projection in which each dimension is measured on a separate scale and according to arbitrarily assigned angles.

tri·met·ro·gon (trī·met′rə·gon) *n.* A high-speed system of aerial topographic photography, in which a unit of three cameras takes simultaneous pictures of one area, from three positions, one vertical and two at matching oblique angles. — *adj.* Of or pertaining to this system or camera unit. [<TRI- + METRO- + -GON]

trim·mer (trim′ər) *n.* **1** One who or that which trims. **2** A time-server. **3** *Brit.* One who keeps the balance between opposing political parties by throwing his support from one to the other. **4** A small horizontal beam, as in a floor, into which the ends of one or more joists are framed. **5** A tool or machine with which to trim; specifically, a large table with power saw used to trim lumber for buildings.

trim·ming (trim′ing) *n.* **1** Something added for ornament or to give a finished appearance or effect. **2** Material attached to a garment, etc., for ornamentation or effect. **3** *pl.* Articles or equipment; fittings, as the hardware of a house. **4** *pl.* The usual or proper accompaniments or condiments of an article or food. **5** *pl.* That which is removed by trimming, cutting, or clipping; in shearing, wool from the shanks. **6** A severe reproof or a chastisement; flogging; beating. **7** *Colloq.* A defeat. **8** The act of one who trims.

tri·mo·lec·u·lar (trī′mə·lek′yə·lər) *adj. Chem.* Having, consisting of, or pertaining to three molecules.

tri·month·ly (trī·munth′lē) *adj.* & *adv.* Done or occurring every third month.

tri·morph (trī′môrf) *n.* **1** A substance existing or occurring in three forms. **2** One of the forms in which such a substance exists. [<Gk. *trimorphos* having three forms < *tri-* three + *morphē* a form]

tri·mor·phism (trī·môr′fiz·əm) *n.* **1** *Bot.* The existence on the same plant of three distinct forms of flowers as regards the relative lengths of stamens and pistils. **2** *Mineral.* The property of crystallizing in three series of fundamentally different forms with the same ultimate chemical composition. **3** *Zool.* Difference of species in form, color, etc., characterizing three distinct types. — **tri·mor′phic, tri·mor′phous** *adj.*

Tri·mur·ti (tri·mo͝or′tē) *n.* In Hindu mythology, the triad of the Vedas, consisting of Brahma (the Creator), Vishnu (the Preserver), and Siva (the Destroyer). [<Skt. *trimūrti* < *tri-* three + *mūrti* shape]

Tri·na·cri·a (tri·nā′krē·ə, trī-) Ancient name for SICILY. — **Tri·na′cri·an** *adj.*

tri·nal (trī′nəl) *adj.* **1** Of or pertaining to three. **2** Having three parts; threefold. [<LL *trinalis* <L *trinus* three each < *tres, tria* three]

tri·na·ry (trī′nər·ē) *adj.* Made up of three parts or proceeding by threes; ternary. [<LL *trinarius* of three kinds <L *trinus.* See TRINAL.]

Trin·co·ma·lee (tring′kō·mə·lē′) **1** A port of NE Ceylon, capital of its eastern province and of Trincomalee district. **2** A district of NE Ceylon; 1,165 square miles.

trin·dle (trin′dəl) *n.* **1** One of several forked pieces of wood or metal between the cords and boards of a book to flatten its front and back edges before cutting. **2** *Brit. Dial.* A wheel, especially of a barrow. **3** A large wooden tub. — *v.t.* **1** *Brit. Dial.* To trundle; roll. — *v.i. Brit. Dial.* **2** To travel easily and rapidly. **3** To roll; advance by rolling. Also **trin′tle** (-təl). [ME *trindel,* var. of OE *trendel* a circle]

trine[1] (trīn) *adj.* **1** Threefold; triple: also *trinal.* **2** In astrology, relating to or situated in trine; auspicious. — *n.* **1** A compound in three parts or elements; a trio; triad. **2** *Her.* A charge composed of three objects. **3** In astrology, the aspect of two planets when 120° apart. — *v.t. Obs.* In astrology, to place or join in trine. [<OF *trin, trine* <L *trinus.* See TRINAL.]

trine[2] (trīn) *v.i. Obs.* To proceed; go. [< Scand. Cf. OSw. *trina* tramp.]

Trine (trīn) *n.* The Trinity.

Trin·i·dad and To·ba·go (trin′ə·dad, tō·bā′gō, *Span.* trē′nē·thäth′) An independent member of the Commonwealth of Nations, in the West Indies NE of Venezuela, comprising the islands of **Trinidad;** 1,864 square miles; and **Tobago;** 116 square miles; capital, Port-of-Spain, on Trinidad.

Tri·nil man (trē′nil) *Paleontol.* Pithecanthropus. [from *Trinil,* Java, where remains were found]

Trin·i·tar·i·an (trin′ə·târ′ē·ən) *adj.* **1** Of or pertaining to the Trinity. **2** Holding or professing belief in the Trinity: distinguished from *Unitarian.* — *n.* A believer in the doctrine of the Trinity. [<NL *trinitarius* <LL *trinitas* TRINITY] — **Trin′i·tar′i·an·ism** *n.*

tri·ni·trate (trī·nī′trāt) *n. Chem.* A nitrate containing three nitric-acid radicals in combination: bismuth *trinitrate.*

tri·ni·tro·ben·zene (trī·nī′trō·ben′zēn) *n. Chem.* A yellow crystalline compound, $C_6H_3(NO_2)_3$, occurring in three forms, one of which is highly explosive.

tri·ni·tro·cre·sol (trī·nī′trō·krē′sōl, -sol) *n. Chem.* A yellow crystalline organic compound, $C_8H_8N_3O_7$, used as an explosive. [<TRI- + NITRO- + CRESOL]

tri·ni·tro·phe·nol (trī·nī′trō·fē′nōl, -nol) *n.* Picric acid. [<TRI- + NITROPHENOL]

tri·ni·tro·tol·u·ene (trī·nī′trō·tol′yōō·ēn) *n. Chem.* A high explosive, $C_7H_5N_3O_6$, made by treating toluene with nitric acid: used for filling high explosive shells, for it melts readily and can be poured safely and rapidly: also called *TNT, trotyl.* Also **tri·ni′tro·tol′u·ol** (-yōō·ōl, -ol). [<TRI- + NITRO- + TOLUENE]

trin·i·ty (trin′ə·tē) *n. pl.* **·ties** **1** In art, a symbolic representation of the Trinity. **2** The state or character of being three; also, any union of three parts or elements in one; a trio; triad. [<OF *trinite* <LL *trinitas* <L, a triad < *trinus.* See TRINAL.]

Trin·i·ty (trin′ə·tē) *n.* **1** *Theol.* A threefold personality existing in the one divine being or substance; the union in one God of Father, Son, and Holy Spirit as three infinite persons. **2** Trinity Sunday.

Trinity, Cape A cliff on the lower Saguenay River, SE central Quebec, Canada; 1,500 feet high.

Trinity River A river in Texas, flowing 510 miles SE to **Trinity Bay,** the NE arm of Galveston Bay.

Trinity Sunday *Eccl.* The eighth Sunday after Easter, observed as a festival in honor of the Trinity. Also *Trinity.*

trin·ket (tring′kit) *n.* **1** Any small ornament, as of jewelry. **2** Any small article forming part of an outfit. **3** A trifle; a trivial object; a toy. **4** *Obs.* A knife. See synonyms under GAUD. [<AF *trenquet,* OF *trenchet* a toy knife, ornament, < *trenchier.* See TRENCH.]

trin·kums (tring′kəmz) *n. pl. Scot. & Brit. Dial.* Small ornaments; trinkets. Also **trin′·kum–tran′kums** (-trang′kəmz). [Appar. alter. of TRINKET]

tri·no·dal (trī·nōd′l) *adj. Bot.* Having three nodes or nodal points.

tri·no·mi·al (trī·nō′mē·əl) *adj.* **1** *Biol.* Of, having, or employing three terms or names—the generic, the specific, and the subspecific or varietal, as *Lynx rufus texensis,* the Texas bobcat. **2** *Math.* Consisting of three terms connected by plus or minus signs or both. —*n.* **1** An algebraic expression consisting of three terms connected by plus or minus signs or both, as $3x + y - 27z$. **2** A trinomial name. Also **tri·nom′i·nal** (-nom′ə·nəl), **tri·on′·y·mal** (-on′ə·məl). [<TRI- + (BI)NOMIAL]

tri·o (trē′ō, *for def. 1 also* trī′ō) *n. pl.* **tri·os** **1** Any three things grouped or associated together. **2** *Music* **a** A composition for three performers. **b** The second part of a minuet or scherzo, of a march, and of dance forms generally. **c** A group of three musicians who render trios. [<F <Ital. < *tre* three <L *tres, tria*]

tri·ode (trī′ōd) *n. Electronics* A three–element vacuum tube, containing an anode, cathode, and a control grid or electrode. [<TRI- + (ELECTR)ODE]

tri·oe·cious (trī·ē′shəs) *adj. Bot.* Having in different plants of the same species male, female, and hermaphrodite flowers: also spelled *triecious.* Also **tri·oi′cous** (-oi′kəs). [<NL *Trioecia,* order name <Gk. *tri-* three + *oikos* a house] —**tri·oe′cious·ly** *adv.*

tri·o·let (trī′ə·lit) *n.* A stanza of eight lines on two rimes, the first line repeated as the fourth and seventh and the second as the eighth. Its rime scheme is *abaaabab.* [<F, dim. of *trio* TRIO]

Tri·o·nal (trī′ə·nal) *n.* Proprietary name for a brand of sulfonethylmethane.

tri·ose (trī′ōs) *n. Biochem.* A monosaccharide whose molecule contains three atoms of carbon and three of oxygen. [<TRI- + -OSE[2]]

tri·ox·ide (trī·ok′sīd, -sid) *n. Chem.* An oxide containing three atoms of oxygen in combination: iron *trioxide,* Fe_2O_3. Also **tri·ox′·id** (-sid).

trip (trip) *n.* **1** A short journey; excursion; jaunt. **2** A misstep or stumble occasioned by losing the balance or striking the foot against an object. **3** An active, nimble step or movement. **4** The number of fish caught in an excursion. **5** A single tack to windward. **6** *Mech.* A pawl or similar device that trips, or the action of such a device. **7** A sudden catch, especially of the legs and feet, as of a wrestler. **8** A blunder; mistake. **9** *Slang* **a** The hallucinations and other sensations experienced by a person taking a psychedelic drug. **b** Any intense, usually personal experience. See synonyms under JOURNEY. —*v.* **tripped, trip·ping** *v.i.* **1** To stumble. **2** To move quickly with light or small steps; saunter. **3** To commit an error; make a false step; go astray. **4** *Mech.* To run past the nicks or dents in the ratchet escape wheel of a timepiece. **5** *Slang* To experience the effects of a psychedelic drug: often with *out.* —*v.t.* **6** To cause to stumble: often with *up.* **7** To detect and expose in an error; defeat the purpose of. **8** To perform (a dance) lightly. **9** *Mech.* To set free or in operation by releasing a stay, catch, trigger, etc. **10** *Naut.* **a** To loosen, as an anchor, from the bottom by a long rope or cable. **b** To hoist (the topmast) so as to prepare it for being lowered. **c** To tilt (a yard) similarly. [OF *treper, triper* leap, trample, ? <MDu. *trippen* trip, hop]

tri·pal·mi·tin (trī·pal′mə·tin) *n.* Palmitin.

tri·par·tite (trī·pär′tīt) *adj.* **1** Divided into three parts or divisions; threefold: a *tripartite* leaf: also **tri·part·ed** (trī′pär·tid). **2** *Law* Pertaining to or executed between three parties. **3** *Math.* Homogeneous in three sets of variables. [<L *tripartitus* < *tri-* three + *partitus,* pp. of *partiri* divide] —**tri·par′tite·ly** *adv.*

tri·par·ti·tion (trī′pär·tish′ən) *n.* Division into three parts, into thirds, or among three.

tripe (trīp) *n.* **1** A part of the stomach of a ruminant, as the ox, used for food. **2** *Colloq.* Contemptible or worthless stuff; an inferior, mean, or offensive thing. [<OF *tripe, trippe* <Arabic *tharb* entrails, a net]

tri·pe·dal (trī′pə·dəl, trī·pēd′l, trip′ə·dəl) *adj.* Having three feet; three–footed. [<L *tripedalis* < *tri-* three + *pes, pedis* foot]

tri·per·son·al (trī·pûr′sən·əl) *adj.* Consisting of or relating to three persons.

tri·per·son·al·i·ty (trī·pûr′sən·al′ə·tē) *n. Theol.* The state or quality of existing in three persons in one Godhead; trinity.

tri·pet·al·ous (trī·pet′l·əs) *adj. Bot.* Having three petals.

trip hammer A heavy power hammer that is raised or tilted by a cam and then allowed to drop: also called *tilt hammer.*

tri·phase (trī′fāz) *adj. Electr.* Having or employing three phases, as in an alternating current.

tri·phen·yl·meth·ane (trī·fen′əl·meth′ān) *n. Chem.* A hydrocarbon, $(C_6H_5)_3CH$, occurring in colorless leaflets: used in organic synthesis and in the manufacture of dyes. [<TRI- + PHENYL + METHANE]

tri·phib·i·an (trī·fib′ē·ən) *adj.* Describing a joint military and naval operation which utilizes terrestrial, marine, and aerial weapons.

triph·thong (trif′thông, -thong, trip′-) *n.* **1** A combination of three vowel sounds in one syllable, as in one pronunciation of *fire.* **2** A trigraph composed of vowels, as in *beau.* [<TRI- + (DI)PHTHONG] —**triph·thon′gal** *adj.*

triph·y·lite (trif′ə·līt) *n.* A greenish–gray, bluish, transparent to translucent phosphate of iron and lithium, crystallizing in the orthorhombic system. Also **triph′y·line** (-lin, -lēn). [<TRI- + Gk. *phylē* a tribe + -ITE[1]; so called because it contains three bases]

tri·pin·nate (trī·pin′āt) *adj. Bot.* Thrice pinnate, as when the pinnae of a bipinnate leaf become again pinnate in certain ferns. Also **tri·pin′nat·ed.** —**tri·pin′nate·ly** *adv.*

tri·pin·nat·i·fid (trī′pə·nat′ə·fid) *adj. Bot.* Tripinnately cleft. [<TRIPINNATE + -FID]

tri·plane (trī′plān′) *n.* An airplane having three supporting surfaces arranged one above the other.

trip·le (trip′əl) *v.* **·led, ·ling** *v.t.* **1** To make threefold in number or quantity. —*v.i.* **2** To be or become three times as many or as large. **3** In baseball, to make a triple. —*adj.* **1** Consisting of three things united or of three parts; threefold. **2** Multiplied by three; thrice said or done. **3** *Archaic* Third. —*n.* **1** A set or group of three. **2** In baseball, a three–base hit. [<MF <L *triplus* <Gk. *triploos* threefold. Doublet of TREBLE.] —**trip′ly** *adv.*

Triple Alliance **1** An alliance between England, Holland, and Sweden against Louis XIV of France, formed in 1668. **2** A league between England, France, and Holland, formed in 1717, but called **Quadruple** when joined by Austria in 1718, designed to secure the succession to the crown of England for the house of Hanover, that of France for the house of Bourbon, and to prevent the union of France and Spain under one crown. **3** An alliance formed in 1795 between Austria, Great Britain, and Russia against France. **4** A Dreibund.

Triple Entente A friendly understanding formed between Great Britain, France, and Russia prior to World War I to counteract the Dreibund.

trip·le–ex·pan·sion (trip′əl·ik·span′shən) *adj.* Designating a compound steam engine constructed with three cylinders of graduated sizes in which the steam is successively expanded.

triple measure *Music* A measure of three beats, the first accented, the second and third unaccented.

trip·le–nerved (trip′əl·nûrvd′) *adj. Bot.* Three–nerved; having three principal nerves arising from or near the base, as certain leaves.

triple play In baseball, a play during which three men are put out.

trip·let (trip′lit) *n.* **1** A group of three of a kind. **2** One of three children born at one birth. **3** A group of three rimed lines. **4** *Music* A group of three notes performed in the time of two. **5** A bicycle for three. [<TRIPLE, on analogy with *doublet*]

trip·le·tail (trip′əl·tāl′) *n.* A large edible marine fish (*Lobotes surinamensis*) of warm seas, with soft dorsal and anal fins extended backward, suggesting additional tails.

triple time See under TIME.

triple voile Ninon.

tri·plex (trī′pleks, trip′leks) *adj.* Having three parts; threefold. —*n. Music* Triple measure. [<L < *tri-* three + *plicare* fold]

trip·li·cate (trip′lə·kit) *adj.* Threefold; made in three copies. —*n.* A third thing corresponding to two others of the same kind or three similar things collectively: a document signed in *triplicate.* —*v.t.* (-kāt) **·cat·ed, ·cat·ing** To make three times as much or as many; treble. [<L *triplicatus,* pp. of *triplicare* triple < *triplex* TRIPLEX] —**trip′li·cate·ly** *adv.*

trip·li·ca·tion (trip′lə·kā′shən) *n.* **1** The act of triplicating. **2** That which is triplicated or made threefold, or is in three layers.

tri·plic·i·ty (tri·plis′ə·tē) *n. pl.* **·ties** **1** Threefold character. **2** A group or combination of three; a triad; a triplet. **3** In astrology, a combination of three of the twelve signs of the zodiac. [<LL *triplicitas, -tatis* <L *triplex, -icis* TRIPLEX]

trip·lite (trip′līt) *n.* A brown or black, translucent to opaque, fluophosphate of iron and manganese. [<G *triplit* <Gk. *triploos* triple; with ref. to its three cleavages]

trip·lo·blas·tic (trip′lə·blas′tik) *adj. Biol.* Having or characterized by three germ layers, as the embryos of the higher animals. [<Gk. *triploos* triple + BLASTIC]

trip·loid (trip′loid) *adj.* **1** Trebled. **2** *Genetics* Noting the occurrence in certain cells of three times the basic number of chromosomes. —*n.* A triploid cell or organism. [<NL *triploides* <Gk. *triploos* threefold + *eidos* form]

trip·loi·dy (trip·loi′dē) *n.* The condition of being triploid.

trip·lo·pi·a (trip·lō′pē·ə) *n. Pathol.* A defect of vision in which objects are seen tripled. [<NL <Gk. *triploos* threefold + *ōps, ōpos* eye]

tri·pod (trī′pod) *n.* **1** A utensil or article having three feet or legs. **2** A three–legged stand, as for supporting a camera, compass, or other instrument. [<L *tripus, -podis* <Gk. *tripous* < *tri-* three + *pous* foot]

trip·o·dal (trip′ə·dəl) *adj.* **1** Of the nature or form of a tripod. **2** Having three feet or legs. Also **tri·po·di·al** (tri·pō′dē·əl, trī-), **tri·pod′ic** (-pod′ik).

trip·o·dy (trip′ə·dē) *n. pl.* **·dies** A verse or meter having three feet. [<TRI- + (DI)PODY]

trip·o·li (trip′ə·lē) *n.* Rottenstone. [from *Tripoli,* Libya, where it is found]

Trip·o·li (trip′ə·lē) **1** One of the two capitals (with Bengasi) and the largest city of Libya, a port on the central Mediterranean and the capital of Tripolitania province: Phoenician *Oea.* **2** A port of NW Lebanon on the Mediterranean: ancient **Trip·o·lis** (trip′ə·lis). — **Tri·pol·i·tan** (tri·pol′ə·tən) *adj.* & *n.* — **Trip′o·line** (-lin) *adj.*

Trip·o·li·ta·ni·a (trip′ə·li·tā′nē·ə) The western province of Libya, on the Mediterranean; 82,990 square miles; capital, Tripoli; a former Barbary State. Ancient **Trip′o·lis.** — **Trip′o·li·ta′ni·an** *adj.* & *n.*

tri·pos (trī pos) *n.* **1** An honors examination held at Cambridge University, England, especially in mathematics. **2** *Obs.* A tripod. [Appar. alter. of L *tripus* TRIPOD]

trip·per (trip′ər) *n.* **1** One who trips in any sense. **2** *Brit. Colloq.* One who makes trips; a tourist or traveler. **3** *Mech.* A trip or tripping mechanism, as a device on a railroad track which operates a catch on a passing train to give a signal or alarm.

trip·pet (trip′it) *n. Mech.* A cam, toe, or projecting piece, designed to strike some other piece at fixed intervals. [<TRIP, *v.*]

trip·ping (trip′ing) *n.* **1** The act of one who or that which trips. **2** A light dance. — *adj.* Light; nimble; easy; stepping. — **trip′ping·ly** *adv.*

trip·tane (trip′tān) *n. Chem.* A hydrocarbon compound, C_7H_{16}, derived from butane and having a very high octane number. [Contraction of *tripentane* <TRI- + PENTANE]

triptane number An improved measure of the efficiency of a motor fuel, expressed in terms of a blend of normal heptane and triptane, each containing a specified amount of tetraethyl lead.

trip·ter·ous (trip′tər·əs) *adj. Bot.* Having three wings or winglike processes, as certain seeds. [<TRI- + Gk. *pteron* a wing, on analogy with *dipterous*]

Trip·tol·e·mus (trip·tol′ə·məs) In Greek mythology, a hero said to have given mankind the secret of the cultivation of grain. Also **Trip·tol′e·mos** (-mos).

trip·tote (trip′tōt) *n.* A substantive having but three cases. [<L *triptota,* pl. <Gk. *triptōta,* neut. pl of *triptōtos* having three cases]

trip·tych (trip′tik) *n.* **1** A picture, carving, or work of art on three panels side by side. **2** Three pictures associated in their subjects and placed side by side in compartments. **3** A writing tablet in three sections, made of various laminate materials. Also **trip′ty·ca** (-ti·kə), **trip′ty·chon** (-ti·kon). [<Gk. *triptychos* threefold <*tri-* three + *ptyx, ptychos* a fold <*ptyssein* fold]

tri·pu·di·ate (trī·pyōō′dē·āt) *v.i.* **·at·ed, ·at·ing** To dance, especially in a measured way [<L *tripudiatus,* pp. of *tripudiare* <*tripudium* a religious dance, prob. <*tri-* three + *pes, pedis* foot] — **tri·pu′di·a′tion** *n.*

Tri·pu·ra (tri′pōō·rä) A union territory of NE India; 4,032 square miles; capital, Agartala.

tri·quet·rous (trī·kwet′rəs, -kwē′trəs) *adj.* **1** Three-sided. **2** Having three acute or salient angles. **3** Three-cornered, as certain stems and bones. [<L *triquetrus*]

tri·ra·di·ate (trī·rā′dē·āt) *adj.* Having three rays or radiate branches: the *triradiate* sulcus of the brain. Also **tri·ra′di·al, tri·ra′di·at′ed.** — **tri·ra′di·al·ly, tri·ra′di·ate′ly** *adv.*

tri·reme (trī′rēm) *n.* An ancient Greek or Roman warship with three banks of oars. [<L *triremis* <*tri-* three + *remus* an oar]

tri·sac·cha·ride (trī·sak′ə·rīd, -rid) *n. Biochem.* Any of a class of saccharides which yield three monosaccharide molecules when subjected to hydrolysis, as raffinose. Also **tri·sac′cha·rid** (-rid).

Tris·ag·i·on (tris·ag′ē·on, -ā′gē-) *n.* A hymn, probably of Hebrew origin, in the liturgy of the Greek and Oriental churches, beginning with a threefold invocation of the Deity as Holy. Also **Tris·ag′i·um, Tris·hag′i·on.** [<Gk. *trisagion,* orig. neut. of *trisagios* thrice holy <*tris* thrice (<*treis* three) + *hagios* holy]

tri·sect (trī·sekt′) *v.t.* To divide into three parts, especially, as in geometry, into three equal parts. [<TRI- + L *sectus,* pp. of *secare* cut] — **tri·sect′ed** *adj.* — **tri·sec′tion** (-sek′·shən) *n.* — **tri·sec′tor** *n.*

tri·sec·trix of MacLaurin (trī·sek′triks) *Math.* The plane curve of the equation $x^3 + xy^2 + ay^2 - 3ax^2 = 0$. Symmetric about the x-axis, passing through the origin and asymptotic to the line $x = -a$, the trisectrix is so named because it can be employed to trisect an angle. [after Colin *MacLaurin,* 1698–1746, Scottish mathematician]

tri·seme (trī′sēm) *n.* A syllable or foot consisting of or equivalent to three morae or short syllables, as the tribrach, iambus, and trochee. — *adj.* Consisting of or equal to three morae or short syllables: also **tri·se·mic** (trī·sē′mik). [<Gk. *trisēmos* <*tri-* three + *sēma* a sign]

tri·sep·al·ous (trī·sep′əl·əs) *adj. Bot.* Having three sepals.

tri·sep·tate (trī·sep′tāt) *adj. Biol.* Having three septa.

tri·se·ri·al (trī·sir′ē·əl) *adj.* **1** Arranged in three series or rows. **2** *Bot.* Tristichous. Also **tri·se′ri·ate** (-it, -āt). — **tri·se′ri·al·ly, tri·se·ri·a·tim** (trī·sir′ē·ā′tim) *adv.*

tris·kel·i·on (tris·kel′ē·ən) *n. pl.* **·kel·i·a** (-kel′ē·ə) A symbolic figure charaterized by three lines or three human legs radiating from a common center. It is used as the arms of the Isle of Man. Also **tris·cele** (tris′sēl), **tris·kele** (tris′kēl). [<Gk. *triskelēs* of three legs <*tri-* three + *skelos* a leg]

TRISKELION

Tris·me·gis·tus (tris′mə·jis′·təs, triz′-) See HERMES TRISMEGISTUS.

tris·mus (triz′məs, tris′-) *n. Pathol.* Tetanic spasm causing rigid closure of the jaws; lockjaw. [<NL <Gk. *trismos* a gnashing of teeth, a grinding] — **tris′mic** *adj.*

tris·oc·ta·he·dron (tris·ok′tə·hē′drən) *n. pl.* **·dra** (-drə) **1** A solid having 24 equal faces corresponding by threes to the faces of an octahedron. **2** A holohedral isometric crystal included under 24 equal isosceles triangular faces with eight planes meeting at the extremities of the rectangular axes: also **trigonal trisoctahedron. 3** An isometric holohedron included under 24 similar and equal trapeziform faces; a trapezohedron: also **tetragonal trisoctahedron.** [<Gk. *tris* thrice (<*treis* three) + OCTAHEDRON.] — **tris·oc′ta·he′dral** *adj.*

tri·sper·mous (trī·spûr′məs) *adj. Bot.* Having three seeds.

tri·spo·rous (trī·spôr′əs, -spō′rəs) *adj. Bot.* Having three spores. Also **tri·spor′ic** (-spôr′ik, -spor′ik). [<TRI- + -SPOROUS]

Tris·tan (tris′tän, -tən) In medieval legend, a knight sent to Ireland to bring back the princess Iseult the Beautiful as a bride for his uncle, King Mark of Cornwall. Iseult and Tristan mistakenly drink a magic love potion, and ultimately die together. In some versions, Tristan is later married to Iseult of the White Hand, daughter of the Duke of Brittany. Also **Tris·tram** (tris′trəm).

Tris·tan da Cun·ha (tris·tän′ dä kōōn′yä) A British island group in the South Atlantic, midway between South America and the Cape of Good Hope; administered with St. Helena; 40 square miles.

triste (trēst) *adj. French* Sorrowful; sad.

tris·tesse (trēs·tes′) *n. French* Sadness; melancholy.

trist·ful (trist′fəl) *adj. Archaic* Sad; gloomy; sorrowful. [<obs. *trist* sad <OF *triste* <L *tristis*] — **trist′ful·ly** *adv.*

tris·tich (tris′tik) *n.* A strophe or system of three lines; triplet. Compare COUPLET, DISTICH. [<TRI- + (DI)STICH]

tris·ti·chous (tris′tə·kəs) *adj.* **1** Three-ranked. **2** *Bot.* Having parts, as leaves, arranged in three vertical rows. [<Gk. *tristichos* three-rowed <*tri-* three + *stichos* a row]

tri·stim·u·lus (trī·stim′yə·ləs) *adj.* **1** Having, pertaining to, or caused or characterized by three distinct stimuli. **2** In color analysis, designating an instrument or method for measuring a color stimulus in terms of three selected primary stimuli.

tri·sty·lous (trī·stī′ləs) *adj. Bot.* Having three styles.

tri·sul·fide (trī·sul′fīd, -fid) *n. Chem.* A sulfide containing three atoms of sulfur in combination. Also **tri·sul′fid** (-fid), **tri·sul′phide, tri·sul′phid.**

tri·syl·la·ble (trī·sil′ə·bəl) *n.* A word of three syllables. — **tri·syl·lab·ic** (trī′si·lab′ik) or **·i·cal** *adj.* — **tri′syl·lab′i·cal·ly** *adv.*

tri·tag·o·nist (trī·tag′ə·nist) *n.* In Greek drama, the actor who played the third part; hence, also, a third-rate actor. [<Gk. *tritagōnistēs* <*tritos* third + *agōnistēs* a contender, actor <*agōnizesthai* contend <*agōn* a contest]

trit·an·o·pi·a (trit′ən·ō′pē·ə) *n. Pathol.* Impairment of vision for blue and yellow; blue blindness. Also **trit′an·op′si·a** (-op′sē·ə). [<NL <Gk. *tritos* third + ANOPIA] — **trit′an·op′tic** (-op′tik) *adj.*

trite (trīt) *adj.* **1** Used so often as to be hackneyed; made commonplace by repetition. **2** *Archaic* Worn-out; frayed. [<L *tritus,* pp, of *terere* rub] — **trite′ly** *adv.* — **trite′ness** *n.*

Synonyms: common, commonplace, hackneyed, musty, rusty, stale, stereotyped, threadbare, worn. See COMMON. *Antonyms*: bright, brilliant, fresh, new, original, racy, striking, telling, vivid.

tri·the·ism (trī′thē·iz′əm) *n. Theol.* The doctrine of the separate existence of three Gods: sometimes opprobriously applied to belief in the distinct personality of the Father, the Son, and the Holy Spirit. [<TRI- + Gk. *theos* a god] — **tri′the·ist** *n.* — **tri′the·is′tic** or **·ti·cal** *adj.*

tri·thing (trī′thing) *n.* In English law, a riding. See RIDING[2]. [OE *thrithing* <ON *thridhungr* a third part]

Trit·i·cum (trit′ə·kəm) *n.* A widely distributed and important genus of cereal grasses, the wheats, especially *T. aestivum* and its numerous cultivated varieties. [<NL <L, wheat]

trit·i·um (trit′ē·əm, trish′ē·əm) *n.* The rare hydrogen isotope of atomic mass 3, whose nucleus contains one proton and two neutrons. [<NL <Gk. *tritos* third]

tri·ton[1] (trīt′n) *n.* A marine gastropod (genus *Triton*) with many gills and a trumpet-shaped shell. [<NL <L, Triton]

TRITON

tri·ton[2] (trī′ton) *n.* The nucleus of an atom of tritium. [<TRIT(IUM) + (ELECTR)ON]

Tri·ton (trīt′n) **1** In Greek mythology: **a** A son of Poseidon (Neptune) and Amphitrite, represented with a man's head and upper body and a dolphin's tail. **b** One of a race of attendants of the sea gods. **2** *Her.* A merman; also, a Neptune holding a trident. — **Tri′ton·ess** *n. fem.*

tri·tone (trī′tōn) *n. Music* An augmented fourth, as containing three whole tones. [<Med. L *tritonus* <Gk. *tritonos* <*tri-* three + *tonos.* See TONE.]

trit·u·rate (trich′ə·rāt) *v.t.* **·rat·ed, ·rat·ing** To reduce to a fine powder or pulp by grinding or rubbing; pulverize. — *n.* **1** That which has been triturated. **2** A trituration (def. 3). [<LL *trituratus,* pp. of *triturare* thresh <L *tritura* a rubbing, threshing <*tritus.* See TRITE.] — **trit·u·ra·ble** (trich′ər·ə·bəl) *adj.* — **trit′u·ra′tor** *n.*

trit·u·ra·tion (trich′ə·rā′shən) *n.* **1** The act of triturating; reduction to a very fine powder by grinding or rubbing, as in a mortar. **2** The process of reducing to a pulp. **3** A triturated preparation, especially one in which 10 parts of a medicinal substance are triturated with 90 parts of milk sugar: also *triturate.*

tri·umph (trī′əmf) *v.i.* **1** To win a victory; be victorious. **2** To be successful. **3** To rejoice over a victory; exult. **4** To celebrate a triumph, as a victorious Roman general. — *v.t.* **5** *Obs.* To conquer. See synonyms under REJOICE. — *n.* **1** In Roman antiquity, the religious pageant of the entry of a victorious consul, dictator, or pretor into Rome: given only for a decisive victory over a foreign enemy. **2** Exultation over victory. **3** The condition of being victorious; victory. **4** *Obs.* A trump card. **5** *Obs.* Any public spectacular display, procession, or pageant. See synonyms under HAPPINESS, VICTORY. [<OF *triumpher* <L *triumphare* <*triumphus* a triumph <Gk. *thriambos* a processional hymn to Dionysus] — **tri′umph·er** *n.*

tri·um·phal (trī·um′fəl) *adj.* 1 Of, pertaining to, or of the nature of a triumph. 2 Celebrating a victory.

triumphal arch A large monumental arch erected in ancient or modern times to commemorate any great victory or achievement.

tri·um·phant (trī·um′fənt) *adj.* 1 Exultant for or as for victory. 2 Crowned with victory; victorious. 3 *Obs.* Of supreme magnificence or beauty; glorious. 4 *Obs.* Triumphal. [<L *triumphans, -antis,* ppr. of *triumphare* TRIUMPH] — **tri·um′phant·ly** *adv.*

tri·um·vir (trī·um′vər) *n. pl.* **·virs** or **·vi·ri** (-və·rī) One of three men united in public office or authority, as in ancient Rome. [<L < *trium virorum* of three men < *tres, trium* three + *vir* a man] — **tri·um′vi·ral** *adj.*

tri·um·vi·rate (trī·um′vər·it, -və·rāt) *n.* 1 A group or coalition of three men who unitedly exercise authority or control; government by triumvirs. 2 The office of a triumvir; also, the triumvirs collectively. 3 A group of three men; a trio. [<L *triumviratus* < *triumvir* TRIUMVIR]

tri·une (trī′yōōn) *adj.* Three in one: said of the Godhead. —*n.* A group of three things united; a triad; a trinity in unity. [<TRI- + L *unus* one]

Tri·u·ni·tar·i·an (trī·yōō′nə·târ′ē·ən) *n.* A Trinitarian. [<TRIUNIT(Y) + -ARIAN]

tri·u·ni·ty (trī·yōō′nə·tē) *n.* Trinity.

tri·va·lent (trī·vā′lənt, triv′ə·lənt) *adj. Chem.* Having a valence or combining value of three. [<TRI- + L *valens, -entis,* ppr. of *valere* be strong] — **tri·va′lence, tri·va′len·cy** *n.*

tri·valve (trī′valv′) *adj.* Having three valves, as a shell. —*n.* A trivalve shell.

Tri·van·drum (tri·van′drəm) A port on the Malabar Coast, capital of Kerala State, SW India, in the SW part of the State.

triv·et (triv′it) *n.* A short, usually three-legged stand for holding cooking vessels in a fireplace, a heated iron, or a hot dish on a table: also *trevet.* [OE *trefet* <L *tripes, -pedis* three-footed < *tri-* three + *pes, pedis* a foot]

triv·i·a (triv′ē·ə) *n. pl.* Insignificant or unimportant matters; trifles. [<NL <L *trivialis* TRIVIAL]

triv·i·al (triv′ē·əl) *adj.* 1 Of little value or importance; trifling; insignificant. 2 Such as is found everywhere or every day; ordinary; commonplace. 3 Occupied with trifles; of low ability or wit; unscholarly. See synonyms under CHILDISH, INSIGNIFICANT, LITTLE, RIDICULOUS, VAIN, VENIAL. [<L *trivialis* of the crossroads, commonplace < *trivium* a crossing of three roads <*tri-* three + *via* a road] — **triv′i·al·ism** *n.* — **triv′i·al·ly** *adv.*

triv·i·al·i·ty (triv′ē·al′ə·tē) *n. pl.* **·ties** 1 The state or quality of being trivial: an age of *triviality*: also **triv′i·al·ness.** 2 A trivial matter; a trivialism.

triv·i·um (triv′ē·əm) *n.* In medieval schools, the course in the liberal arts embracing grammar, logic, and rhetoric. Compare QUADRIVIUM. [<Med. L <L. See TRIVIAL.]

tri·week·ly (trī·wēk′lē) *adj. & adv.* 1 Occurring three times a week. 2 Sometimes, done or occurring every third week.

-trix *suffix* A feminine termination of agent nouns the masculine form of which is *-tor*: *testatrix.* See -OR[1]. [<L *-trix*]

Tr·no·vo (tûr′nô·vô) See TIRNOVO.

troak (trōk) See TROKE.

Tro·as (trō′as) The region of western Asia Minor on the Aegean surrounding the ancient city of Troy: also *Teucria.* Also **the Tro′ad** (-ad).

Tro·bri·and Islands (trō′brē·änd) A volcanic island group off the eastern tip of New Guinea; a dependency of the Australian Trust Territory of Papua and New Guinea; total, 175 square miles.

tro·car (trō′kär) *n. Surg.* A sharp-pointed instrument used with a cannula to drain off internal fluids. Also **tro′char.** [<F *troquart, trois-quarts* < *trois* three + *carre* face; so called because of its triangular shape]

tro·cha (trō′chä) *n.* 1 A path; road. 2 An obstruction on a road, to hinder an enemy; a military cordon. [<Sp.]

tro·cha·ic (trō·kā′ik) *adj.* Pertaining to, containing, or composed of trochees: a *trochaic* foot or verse. —*n.* A trochaic verse or line. [<MF *trochaïque* <L *trochaicus* <Gk. *trochaikos* < *trochaios* TROCHEE]

tro·chal (trō′kəl) *adj.* 1 Shaped like a wheel; rotiform. 2 Trochilic. [<Gk. *trochos* a wheel]

tro·chan·ter (trō·kan′tər) *n.* 1 *Anat.* One of several bony processes on the upper thigh bone. 2 *Entomol.* The small second segment of an insect's leg. [<MF <Gk. *trochantēr* < *trechein* run]

tro·che (trō′kē) *n.* A medicated lozenge, usually circular. [Alter. of obs. *trochisk* <MF *trochisque* a lozenge <L *trochiscus* <Gk. *trochiskos* a small wheel, a lozenge < *trochos* a wheel < *trechein* run]

tro·chee (trō′kē) *n.* In prosody, a foot comprising a long and short syllable (—◡), or, in modern verse, an accented syllable followed by an unaccented one. [<L *trochaeus* <Gk. *trochaios (pous)* a running (foot) < *trechein* run]

Troch·el·min·thes (trok′əl·min′thēz) *n. pl.* A phylum of minute, transparent, aquatic protozoans which move by means of cilia, including the wheel animalcules. [<NL <Gk. *trochos* a wheel + *helmins, helminthos* a worm]

tro·chil·ic (trō·kil′ik) *adj.* 1 Of the nature of or pertaining to rotary motion. 2 Capable of such motion. [<Gk. *trochilos* a pulley, taken as var. of *trochos* a wheel < *trechein* run]

troch·i·lus (trok′ə·ləs) *n. pl.* **·li** (-lī) 1 The crocodile bird: also **tro·chil** (trō′kil, trok′il), **troch′i·los** (-los). 2 A hummingbird (family *Trochilidae*). 3 One of various small warblers or warblerlike birds. [<L *trochilus* a crocodile bird <Gk. *trochilos* < *trechein* run]

troch·le·a (trok′lē·ə) *n. pl.* **·le·ae** (-li·ē) *Anat.* A grooved pulleylike surface, permitting smooth motion, as between the humerus and ulna. [<L, a pulley <Gk. *trochilia, trochileia* < *trechein* run]

troch·le·ar (trok′lē·ər) *adj.* 1 *Anat.* Of, pertaining to, or situated near a trochlea. 2 Of the nature of a pulley. 3 Short, cylindrical, compressed, and contracted in the middle of its circumference like a pulley block. [<NL *trochlearis* <L *trochlea* TROCHLEA]

troch·le·ar·i·form (trok′lē·ar′ə·fôrm) *adj.* Having the form of a pulley; trochlear.

tro·choid (trō′koid) *adj.* Rotating upon its own axis; pivotal: also **tro·choi′dal.** —*n. Math.* A plane curve traced by a point on a circle or on its extended radius as the circle rolls, without slipping, on a straight line: when the point is on the circumference of the circle, the curve traced is a cycloid. [<Gk. *trochoeidēs* round, wheel-like < *trochos* a wheel + *eidos* form, shape] — **tro·choi′dal·ly** *adv.*

troch·o·phore (trok′ə·fôr, -fōr) *n. Zool.* A pear-shaped larval form of certain aquatic invertebrates, as annelids, brachiopods, and mollusks. Also **troch′o·sphere** (-sfir). [<Gk. *trochos* a wheel + -PHORE]

trock (trok) See TROKE.

trod (trod) Past tense and alternative past participle of TREAD.

trod·den (trod′n) Past participle of TREAD.

trode (trōd) Archaic past tense of TREAD.

trog·lo·dyte (trog′lə·dīt) *n.* 1 A prehistoric cave man. 2 Figuratively, a hermit; anyone of primitive or degenerate habits. 3 An anthropoid ape, as the gorilla. 4 The wren. [<L *troglodyta* <Gk. *trōglodytēs* < *trōglē* a hole + *dyein* go into] — **trog′lo·dyt′ic** (-dit′ik), **trog′lo·dyt′i·cal** *adj.*

tro·gon (trō′gon) *n.* A tropical American bird (family *Trogonidae*) noted for its resplendent plumage. [<NL <Gk. *trōgōn,* ppr. of *trōgein* gnaw]

troi·ka (troi′kə) *n.* A Russian vehicle drawn by a team of three horses driven abreast; also, the team, or both team and vehicle together. [<Russian]

Troi·lus (troi′ləs, trō′i·ləs) In Greek legend, a son of Priam killed by Achilles; in medieval legend, Chaucer's *Troilus and Criseyde,* and Shakespeare's *Troilus and Cressida,* Cressida's lover.

troilus butterfly The green-clouded or spice-bush swallowtail butterfly *(Papilio troilus)* of eastern North America. [after *Troilus*]

Trois Ri·vières (trwȧ rē·vyâr′) A city on the St. Lawrence River at the mouth of the St. Maurice River in southern Quebec, Canada: English *Three Rivers.*

Tro·jan (trō′jən) *n.* 1 A native of Troy. 2 A brave, persevering person; one who works earnestly or suffers courageously. 3 *Colloq.* A jolly fellow; boon companion. —*adj.* Of or pertaining to ancient Troy. Also called *Dardan, Dardanian.* [Earlier *Troyan, Troian* <L *Troianus* < *Troja* Troy]

Trojan horse 1 In classical legend, a large, hollow wooden horse, described in Vergil's *Aeneid,* filled with Greek soldiers and left at the Trojan gates: when it was brought within the walls the soldiers emerged at night and admitted the Greek army, who burned the city: also called *wooden horse.* 2 *Mil.* The infiltration of military men into a potentially hostile region for the purpose of nullifying resistance against attack: compare FIFTH COLUMN.

Trojan War In Greek legend, the ten years' war waged by the confederated Greeks under their king, Agamemnon, against the Trojans to recover Helen, the wife of Menelaus, who had been abducted by Paris: celebrated especially in the *Iliad* and the *Odyssey.* See APPLE OF DISCORD.

troke (trōk) *Scot. n.* 1 Exchange; also, articles of trade; small wares; truck. 2 Familiar intercourse or acquaintance. —*v.t. & v.i.* To exchange; barter. Also spelled *troak, trock.*

troll[1] (trōl) *v.t.* 1 To cause to roll; revolve. 2 To sing in succession, as in a round or catch. 3 To sing in a full, hearty manner. 4 To fish for with a moving lure, as from a moving boat. 5 To move (the line or lure) in fishing. 6 *Obs.* To pass around, as a bottle or decanter. —*v.i.* 7 To roll; turn. 8 To sing a tune, etc., in a full, hearty manner. 9 To be uttered in such a way. 10 To fish with a moving lure. 11 *Obs.* To move about; ramble. —*n.* 1 A catch or round. 2 A rolling movement or motion; hence, repetition or routine. 3 In fishing, a spoon or other lure. [? <OF *troller* quest, wander <Gmc. Cf. MHG *trollen* walk with short steps.] — **troll′er** *n.*

troll[2] (trōl) *n.* In Scandinavian folklore, a giant; later, a friendly but often mischievous dwarf. Also **trold** (trōld). [<ON]

trol·ley (trol′ē) *n. pl.* **·leys** 1 A grooved metal wheel for rolling in contact with an electric conductor (the **trolley wire**), to convey the current to an electric vehicle. 2 In a subway system, a bow or shoe adapted to the same purpose attached to a current-taker operating through a slot in the track: also **trolley wheel.** 3 A car or system so operated. 4 A small truck or car for conveying material, as in a factory, mine, etc.: also spelled *trawley.* 5 A small cart for serving food and drink: tea *trolley.* 6 *Brit. Dial.* A small hand or donkey cart. 7 A parcels carrier. 8 The mechanism of a traveling crane. 9 A small car running on tracks and worked by a lever operated by hand: used by workmen on a railway. —*v.t. & v.i.* To convey or travel by trolley. Also spelled *trolly.* [<TROLL[1]]

trolley bus A passenger conveyance operating without rails, propelled electrically by current taken from an overhead wire by means of a trolley: also called *trackless trolley.* Also **trolley coach.**

trolley car A car arranged with a trolley and motor for use on an electric railway operated by the trolley system.

trolley line A system of street cars propelled on the trolley system; also, the road itself.

trol·ley·man (trol′ē·man′) *n. pl.* **·men** (-men′) A man who operates a trolley; especially, a conductor or motorman.

trolley pole A pole on a trolley car carrying the trolley wheel.

troll·ing (trō′ling) *n.* The method or act of fishing by dragging a hook and line, as behind a boat and near the surface: usually with a spoon bait or the like. [<TROLL[1]]

trolling bait Spoon bait. Also **trolling hook, trolling spoon.**

trolling rod A strong fishing rod for trolling.

trol·lop (trol′əp) *n.* 1 A slatternly woman. 2 A prostitute. [<dial. E (Scottish) <ME

trollen roll about; prob. infl. in meaning by *trull*] — **trol′lop·ish, trol′lop·y, trol′lop·ing** *adj.*

Trol·lope (trol′əp), **Anthony,** 1815–82, English novelist.

trol·ly (trol′ē) *n. pl.* **·lies** *n.* & *v.* Trolley.

Trom·be·tas (trōnm·bā′təs) A river of NW Pará state, Brazil, flowing 470 miles south and east to the Amazon.

trom·bic·u·li·a·sis (trom·bik′yə·lī′ə·sis) *n. Pathol.* Infestation with mites of the genus *Trombicula,* the chiggers. Also **trom·bic′u·lo′·sis** (-lō′sis). [<NL *Trombicula* + -IASIS]

trom·bone (trom′bōn, trom·bōn′) *n.* A powerful brass wind instrument of the trumpet family possessing a complete chromatic scale. It consists of a cupped mouthpiece and a long tube bent twice upon itself, the outer bend being a U-shaped slide, by the motion of which the length of the vibrating air column may be so adjusted as to produce any note within its compass. [<Ital., aug. of *tromba* a trumpet] — **trom′bon·ist** *n.*

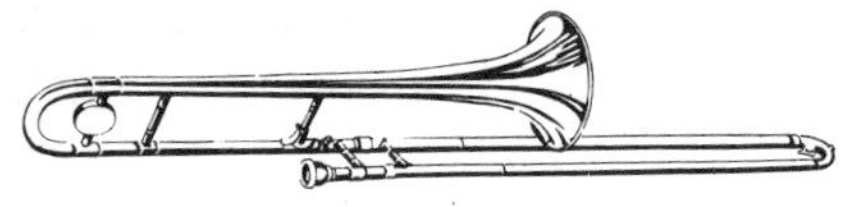

TROMBONE

trom·mel (trom′əl) *n. Metall.* A perforated steel plate, usually cylindrical in form, used for sifting or screening rock, ore, etc. [<G, a drum]

trom·o·ma·ni·a (trom′ə·mā′nē·ə, -mān′yə) *n.* Delirium tremens. [<NL <Gk. *tromos* a trembling + *mania* madness]

Tromp (trômp), **Cornelius van,** 1629–91, Dutch admiral; son of the following. — **Marten Harpertzoon,** 1597–1653, Dutch admiral.

trompe (tromp) *n.* **1** *Metall.* An apparatus that supplies a blast of air, as to a forge, by the action of a thin column of water falling through a large, long tube and thus carrying air by entanglement. **2** An arched and vaulted structure that supports a portion of a building. Also **tromp.** [<F, lit., a trumpet]

Trom·sö (trom′zō, *Norw.* trôms′œ, troŏms′œ) A port on eastern **Tromsö Island,** an islet of NW Norway (8 square miles).

tro·na (trō′nə) *n.* A vitreous, gray or white, monoclinic hydrous sodium carbonate, $Na_2CO_8HNaCO_8 \cdot 2H_2O$. [<Sw., appar. <Arabic *trōn,* short for *natrūn* NATRON]

Trond·heim (trôn′hām) A port on **Trondheim Fiord,** in Norway: formerly *Nidaros.* Formerly spelled **Trond·hjem** (trôn′yem).

troop (troōp) *n.* **1** An assembled company; gathering; a herd or flock. **2** *Usually pl.* A body of soldiers; soldiers collectively. **3** The cavalry unit of formation, corresponding to a company of infantry. **4** A body of Boy Scouts consisting of four patrols of eight scouts each. **5** Formerly, a troupe; a company of actors. See synonyms under ARMY. — *v.i.* **1** To move along or gather as a troop or as a crowd. **2** *Archaic* To associate; consort. — *v.t.* **3** To form into troops. **4** *Brit. Mil.* To carry ceremoniously before troops: to *troop* the colors. ◆ Homophone: *troupe.* [<OF *trope* <LL *troppus* a flock <Gmc.]

troop·er (troō′pər) *n.* **1** A cavalryman. **2** A mounted policeman. **3** A troop horse; charger. **4** A troopship.

troop·i·al (troō′pē·əl) *n.* Any American bird of the family *Icteridae,* including the blackbirds, orioles, bobolinks, and meadowlarks, especially *Icterus icterus* of South America and the West Indies, mostly black varied with yellow and white. Also spelled *troupial.* [<F *troupiale* <*troupe* <OF *trope* TROOP; so called because it goes in flocks]

troop·lift (troōp′lift′) *n.* **1** The troop-carrying capacity of a nation's passenger ships, merchant marine, or aviation. **2** The actual transport of troops.

troop·ship (troōp′ship′) *n.* A ship for carrying troops; a transport.

troost·ite (troōs′tīt) *n.* A variety of willemite in large reddish crystals. [after Gerhard *Troost,* 1776–1850, U.S. mineralogist]

trooz (troōz) See TREWS.

trop (trō) *adv. French* Too much; too many; too.

tro·pa·co·caine (trō′pə·kō·kān′, -kō′kān, -kō′·kə·ēn) *n. Chem.* A white crystalline compound, $C_{15}H_{19}O_2N$, obtained from Java coca leaves and also made synthetically from atropine and hyoscine: used as an anesthetic. [<(*benzoyl-pseudo*)*trop*(*eine*), its chemical name + COCAINE]

Tro·pae·o·lum (trō·pē′ə·ləm) *n.* A genus of tropical American plants with alternate leaves and bright-colored flowers supposed to resemble ancient trophies. Many species, known as *nasturtiums,* are cultivated. [<NL <Gk. *tropaion* a trophy; so called from the resemblance of the leaf and flower to a shield and helmet]

tro·pae·um (trō·pē′əm) *n.* In Greek antiquity, a monument of victory, composed of captured arms, set up by the Greeks at a place where they had defeated an enemy. Also **tro·pai·on** (trō·pā′on). [<L, TROPHY]

-tropal *combining form* -tropic.

tro·par·i·on (trō·pâr′ē·on) *n. pl.* **·par·i·a** (-pâr′·ē·ə) In the Greek Church, a stanza of, or the several stanzas constituting, a hymn. [<Gk., dim. of *tropos.* See TROPE.]

trope (trōp) *n.* **1** The figurative use of a word. **2** Loosely and less properly, a figure of speech; figurative language in general. **3** A short distinguishing cadence interpolated in Gregorian melodies. **4** An interpolated phrase that was occasionally inserted in various parts of the mass prior to the 16th century. [<F <L *tropus* a figure of speech <Gk. *tropos* a turn <*trepein* turn]

-trope *combining form* **1** One who or that which turns or changes: *allotrope.* **2** Turning; turned in a (specified) way: *hemitrope.* [<Gk. *tropos* a turning <*trepein* turn]

tro·pe·ine (trō′pē·in, -ēn) *n. Chem.* An ester of tropine, from which it is formed by the action of certain organic acids. Also **tro′pe·in** (-in). [Alter. of TROPINE]

tro·pe·o·lin (trō·pē′ə·lin) *n. Chem.* Any of several orange azo dyes formed by the action of diazosulfuric acids on phenols. Also **tro·pae′·o·lin.** [<TROPAEOL(UM) + -IN; so called because their hues resemble those of the flower]

troph·al·lax·is (trof′ə·lak′sis) *n. Biol.* The free exchange of food substances among individuals, considered as an essential factor in the life cycle of certain insects, especially army ants. [<NL <Gk. *trophē* food + *allaxis* an exchange] — **troph′al·lac′tic** (-lak′tik) *adj.*

troph·ic (trof′ik) *adj.* Pertaining to nutrition and its processes. Also **troph′i·cal.** [<Gk. *trophikos* <*trophē* nourishment <*trephein* nourish] — **troph′i·cal·ly** *adv.*

tro·phied (trō′fēd) *adj.* Adorned with trophies.

tropho- *combining form* Nutrition; nourishment; of or pertaining to food or nutrition: *trophoplasm.* Also, before vowels, **troph-.** [<Gk. *trophē* food, nourishment <*trephein* feed, nourish]

troph·o·blast (trof′ə·blast) *n. Biol.* The ectodermal layer of cells in the embryo that establishes relation with the uterus and is concerned in the nutrition of the embryo and fetus. Also **troph′o·derm** (-dûrm). [<TROPHO- + -BLAST] — **troph′o·blas′tic** *adj.*

troph·o·gen·e·sis (trof′ə·jen′ə·sis) *n. Biol.* The production of variations among plants and animals by differences in food and nutrition, as distinguished from genetic factors. Also **tro·phog·e·ny** (trō·foj′ə·nē). — **troph′o·gen′ic** *adj.*

troph·o·plasm (trof′ə·plaz′əm) *n. Biol.* **1** The nutritive or vegetative substance of the cell, as distinguished from the idioplasm. **2** Formerly, a cytoplasmic substance distinguished from the archiplasm. — **troph′o·plas′mic** *adj.*

troph·o·ther·a·py (trof′ə·ther′ə·pē) *n. Med.* The treatment of disease by diet therapy.

tro·phot·ro·pism (trō·fot′rə·piz′əm) *n. Bot.* The movement or curvature, as toward or away from nutrient substances, induced in a growing plant by the influence of the chemical nature of its surroundings. — **troph·o·trop·ic** (trof′ə·trop′ik) *adj.*

troph·o·zo·ite (trof′ə·zō′īt) *n. Zool.* A parasitic sporozoan at the stage of entering the blood cell of its host, feeding on the nutritive material in the blood. [<TROPHO- + Gk. *zōion* an animal + -ITE[1]]

tro·phy (trō′fē) *n. pl.* **·phies** **1** Anything taken from an enemy and displayed or treasured in proof of victory; hence, a memento of victory or success: *trophies* of the chase. **2** An ancient Roman memorial of victory in imitation of the Greek tropaeum, but a permanent structure, decorated with arms or beaks of ships suspended over the undecorated parts. **3** An ornamental group of objects hung together on a wall, or any collection of objects typical of some event, art, industry, or branch of knowledge. **4** A memento or memorial. **5** *Archit.* A group of arms and armor carved in marble or cast in bronze rising from a circular or quadrangular stepped base. [<MF *trophée* <L *trophaeum, tropaeum* <Gk. *tropaion* <*tropē* a defeat, turning <*trepein* turn, rout]

-trophy *combining form* A (specified) kind of nutrition or nurture: *hypertrophy.* Corresponding adjectives end in *-trophic.* [<Gk. *trophē.* See TROPHO-.]

trop·ic (trop′ik) *n.* **1** *Geog.* Either of two parallels of latitude at a distance from the equator, north and south, equal to the obliquity of the ecliptic, or 23° 27′, on which the sun is seen in the zenith on the days of its greatest declination: called respectively **tropic of Cancer** and **tropic of Capricorn.** **2** *Astron.* **a** Either of two corresponding parallels of declination in the celestial sphere similarly named, and respectively 23° 27′ north or south from the celestial equator. **b** Either of the two points in the celestial sphere where the sun reaches its maximum distance north or south of the celestial equator; a solstice. **3** *pl.* The regions of the earth's surface between the tropics of Cancer and Capricorn, where the sun crosses the zenith twice in the course of the year: with the definite article; the torrid zone. — *adj.* Of or pertaining to the tropics; tropical. [<L *tropicus* <Gk. *tropikos* (*kyklos*) the tropical (circle), pertaining to the turning of the sun at the solstice <*tropē.* See TROPHY.]

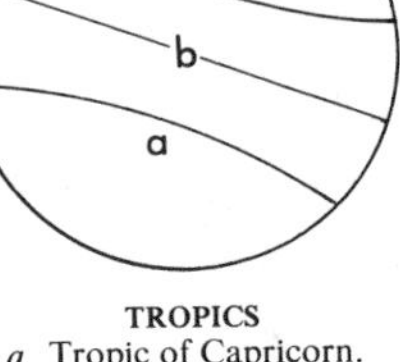

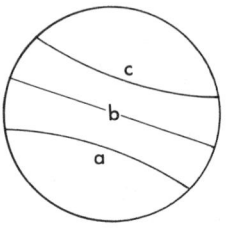

TROPICS
a. Tropic of Capricorn.
b. Equator.
c. Tropic of Cancer.

-tropic *combining form* Having a (specified) tropism; turning or changing in a (particular) way, or in response to a (given) stimulus: *chemotropic, phototropic.*

trop·i·cal (trop′i·kəl) *adj.* **1** Of, pertaining to, or characteristic of the tropics. **2** Of the nature of a trope or metaphor; changed from the original to a figurative meaning. — **trop′i·cal·ly** *adv.*

trop·i·cal·ize (trop′i·kəl·īz′) *v.t.* **·ized, ·iz·ing** To adapt, as clothing, war equipment, ships, etc., for service in tropical areas. — **trop′i·cal·i·za′tion** *n.*

tropic bird A long-winged, oceanic, tern-like bird (genus *Phaëthon*), found mostly in the tropics, having the two middle tail feathers elongated.

tro·pine (trō′pēn, -pin) *n. Chem.* A colorless crystalline alkaloid, $C_8H_{15}NO$, with a tobacco odor, formed when atropine is hydrolyzed. Also **tro′pin** (-pin). [<ATROPINE]

tro·pism (trō′piz·əm) *n. Biol.* **1** The involuntary response of an organism, or of any of its parts, to an external stimulus. **2** Any automatic reaction to a stimulus. [<Gk. *tropē* a turning] — **tro·pis·tic** (trō·pis′tik) *adj.*

-tropism *combining form* A (specified) tropism; a tendency to turn or change in response to a (given) stimulus: *chemotropism, phototropism.* Corresponding adjectives end in *-tropic.* [<TROPISM]

tro·pist (trō′pist) *n.* **1** One given to the use of tropes. **2** One who interprets and explains a text, especially Scripture, tropically or figuratively.

tro·pol·o·gy (trō·pol′ə·jē) *n.* **1** The use of tropical or figurative language. **2** Consideration or treatment of the Scriptures both literally and figuratively, or as having a double sense. **3** A treatise on figures of speech. [<LL *tropologia* <Gk. <*tropos* TROPE + *logos* discourse] — **trop·o·log·ic** (trop′ə·loj′ik) or **·i·cal** *adj.* — **trop′o·log′i·cal·ly** *adv.*

trop·o·pause (trop′ə·pôz) *n. Meteorol.* A transition zone in the atmosphere between the troposphere and the stratosphere at which the fall of temperature with increasing height abruptly ceases. [<TROPO(SPHERE) + Gk. *pausis* a ceasing]

tro·poph·i·lous (trō·pof′ə·ləs) *adj. Ecol.* Adapted to extreme conditions of moisture or of heat: said of plants. [<Gk. *tropos* a turning, change + *philos* loving; with ref. to adaptation to seasonal changes]

trop·o·phyte (trop′ə·fīt) *n. Ecol.* Any of the plants that adapt themselves to seasonal changes of dryness or cold and also of moisture: they form the highest type of temperate-zone plants, as the deciduous trees. [<Gk. *tropos* a turning, change + -PHYTE] **— trop′o·phyt′ic** (-fit′ik) *adj.*

trop·o·sphere (trop′ə·sfir) *n. Meteorol.* The region of the atmosphere from the earth's surface to the tropopause, having a height of from six to twelve miles and characterized by decreasing temperature with increasing altitude. [<F *troposphère* <Gk. *tropos* a turning + F *sphère* <L *sphaera* SPHERE]

trop·po (trop′ō, *Ital.* trôp′pō) *adv. Music* Too much: andante ma non *troppo* (andante but not too much). [<Ital.]

-tropous *combining form* Turned in a specified way: *anatropous.* Corresponding nouns end in *-tropy.*

-tropy *combining form* **1** -tropism. **2** A state of being turned. See -TROPOUS. [<Gk. *tropē* a turning < *trepein* turn]

Tros·sachs (tros′aks, -əks) A valley in Perthshire, central Scotland: scene of Scott's *The Lady of the Lake.*

trot[1] (trot) *n.* **1** A progressive motion of a quadruped, in which each diagonal pair of legs is alternately lifted, thrust forward, and placed upon the ground almost simultaneously, the body of the animal being entirely unsupported twice during each stride; the sound of this gait. **2** A race for trotters. **3** A little child; toddler: a term of endearment. **4** Steady going or movement, implying persistence and diligence: I have been on the *trot* all day. **5** *Colloq.* A literal translation of a foreign-language text, used as an aid in study or in examination; a crib; pony. **—** *v.* **trot·ted, trot·ting** *v.i.* **1** To go at a trot. **2** To go quickly; hurry. **—** *v.t.* **3** To cause to trot. **4** To ride at a trotting gait. **— to trot out** To bring forth for inspection, approval, etc. [<OF < *troter* <OHG *trottōn* tread]

trot[2] (trot) *n. Archaic* An old woman: a derogatory term. [<AF *trote*; ult. origin uncertain]

troth (trôth, trōth) *n.* **1** Good faith; fidelity; also, the act of pledging fidelity; especially, betrothal. **2** Truth; verity. **—** *v.t. Archaic* To betroth; pledge. [ME *trowthe, trouthe,* var. of OE *trēowth* truth]

troth·plight (trôth′plīt′, trōth′-) *Archaic v.t.* To betroth; affiance. **—** *n.* Betrothal. **—** *adj.* Betrothed: also **troth′-plight′ed.** [<TROTH + PLIGHT[2]]

trot·line (trot′līn′) *n.* A trawl line.

Trot·sky (trot′skē), **Leon,** 1879–1940, Russian Bolshevist leader; exiled 1929; murdered: real name *Lev Davidovitch Bronstein.*

Trot·sky·ism (trot′skē·iz′əm) *n.* The doctrines of Trotsky and his followers; especially, his belief in "permanent revolution" or the theory that Communism to succeed must be international. **— Trot′sky·ist** *n.*

Trot·sky·ite (trot′skē·īt) *n.* An adherent of any of the various factions of the Communist party originally led by Leon Trotsky, who opposed Stalinism and supported international Communism.

trot·ter (trot′ər) *n.* **1** One who or that which trots; a trotting horse; specifically, a horse trained to trot for speed. **2** *Colloq.* An animal's foot: a pig's *trotters.*

tro·tyl (trō′til) *n.* Trinitrotoluene. [<(TRINI)-TROT(OLUENE) + -YL]

trou·ba·dour (trōō′bə·dôr, -dōr, -dŏŏr) *n.* One of a class of lyric poets, sometimes including wandering minstrels and jongleurs, originating in Provence in the 11th century and flourishing in southern France, northern Italy, and eastern Spain during the 12th and 13th centuries. Compare TROUVÈRE. See synonyms under POET. [<MF <Provençal *trobador* < *trobar* compose, invent, find; ult. origin uncertain]

Trou·betz·koy (trōō·bets′koi), **Princess** See RIVES, AMÉLIE.

troub·le (trub′əl) *n.* **1** The state of being distressed, annoyed, or confused; also, grief; affliction; disturbance. **2** A person, circumstance, or event that occasions difficulty or perplexity; the vexation thus occasioned; annoyance; worry; civil unrest or agitation. **3** Toilsome exertion; pains. **4** Any serious or permanent diseased condition: lung *trouble.* See synonyms under ANXIETY, CARE, GRIEF, MISFORTUNE, PAIN. **—** *v.* **·led, ·ling** *v.t.* **1** To cause mental agitation to; distress; worry. **2** To agitate or disturb; stir up or roil, as water. **3** To inconvenience or incommode. **4** To annoy or pester; bother. **5** To cause physical pain or discomfort to; afflict. **—** *v.i.* **6** To take pains; bother. **7** To worry. See synonyms under PERPLEX. [<OF *truble, turble* < *turbler* <L *turbula* a mob, dim. of *turba* a crowd] **— troub′ler** *n.* **— troub′ling·ly** *adv.*

troub·le·mak·er (trub′əl·mā′kər) *n.* One who habitually stirs up trouble.

troub·le·shoot·er (trub′əl·shōō′tər) *n.* **1** A mechanic; a repairman. **2** One who locates difficulties and seeks to remove them. **3** A person trained to find and eliminate trouble in the operation of a machine, process, or the like; a maintenance man. **— troub′le-shoot′·ing** *n.*

troub·le·some (trub′əl·səm) *adj.* **1** Causing trouble; vexatious; burdensome; trying; afflictive: a *troublesome* business. **2** Marked by violence; tumultuous. **3** Greatly agitated or disturbed; troublous. **— troub′le·some·ly** *adv.* **— troub′le·some·ness** *n.*

Synonyms: afflictive, annoying, arduous, burdensome, difficult, galling, harassing, hard, importunate, intrusive, irksome, laborious, painful, perplexing, teasing, tiresome, trying, vexatious, wearisome. *Antonyms*: amusing, cheering, easy, entertaining, grateful, gratifying, helpful, light, pleasant.

troub·lous (trub′ləs) *adj.* **1** Marked by commotion or tumult; full of trouble: *troublous* times. **2** Uneasy; restless. **3** *Obs.* Troublesome.

trou-de-loup (trōō′də·lōō′) *n. pl.* **trous-de-loup** (trōō′də·lōō′) *Usually pl.* A conical pit having a vertical central stake with a pointed top, used as a defense against cavalry. [<F *trou* a hole + *de* of + *loup* a wolf]

trough (trôf, trof; *Dial.* trôth, troth) *n.* **1** A long, narrow, open receptacle for conveying a fluid or for holding food or water for animals. **2** A long, narrow channel or depression, as between ridges on land or waves at sea. **3** A gutter for rain water fixed under the eaves of a building. [OE *trog*]

trounce (trouns) *v.t.* **trounced, trounc·ing** **1** To beat or thrash severely; punish. **2** *Colloq.* To defeat. [<OF *tronce* a thick piece of wood <L *truncus* stem, trunk] **— trounc′ing** *n.*

troupe (trōōp) *n.* A company of actors or other performers. **—** *v.i.* **trouped, troup·ing** To travel as one of a company of actors or entertainers. ◆ Homophone: *troop.* [<MF <OF *trope* TROOP] **— troup′er** *n.*

troup·i·al (trōō′pē·əl) See TROOPIAL.

trou·sers (trou′zərz) *n. pl.* A man's garment, covering the body from the waist to the ankles or knees and divided so as to make a separate covering for each leg. Also **trow′sers.** [Blend of obs. *trouse* breeches (<Irish *triubhas*) and DRAWERS]

trousse (trōōs) *n.* **1** A collection of small implements in a sheath or case. **2** A case containing knives, tweezers, etc., fastened to the belt: a surgeon's *trousse.* [<F. See TRUSS.]

trous·seau (trōō·sō′, trōō′sō) *n. pl.* **·seaux** (-sōz′, -sōz) **1** A bride's outfit, especially of clothing. **2** *Obs.* A bundle; truss. [<F < *trousse* a packed collection of things. See TRUSS.]

trout (trout) *n.* **1** A salmonoid fish mostly found in fresh waters and highly esteemed as a game and food fish. The **brown trout** or **river trout** *(Salmo trutta),* attaining a length of 30 inches, is common in Europe; the **cut-throat trout** *(S. clarkii),* and the **rainbow trout** or steelhead *(S. gairdnerii)* are species of western North America. The **speckled trout** or **brook trout** *(Salvelinus fontinalis)* is common in eastern North America. **2** A fish resembling, or supposed to resemble, the above, as the greenling. [OE *truht* <LL *tructus, tructa* <Gk. *trōktēs* a nibbler < *trōgein* gnaw]

trou·vère (trōō·vâr′) *n.* One of a class of poets flourishing in northern France from the 11th to the 14th centuries, distinguished from the troubadours of southern France by the prevailingly narrative and epic character of their works, which include chansons de geste, fabliaux, romances, and chronicles. Also **trou·veur** (trōō·vûr′). [<F <OF *trovere* < *trover* find, compose; ult. origin uncertain]

Trou·ville (trōō·vēl′) A port and resort in northern France, 9 miles south of Le Havre. Also **Trou·ville′-sur-Mer′** (-sür·mâr′).

tro·ver (trō′vər) *n. Law* An action to recover the value of personal property of the plaintiff wrongfully withheld or converted by another to his own use: originally an action of trespass against one who found the goods of another, and refused to give them up; the finding, however, became a fiction. [<OF, find; ult. origin uncertain]

trow (trō) *v.t. & v.i.* **1** *Archaic* To suppose; think; believe. **2** *Obs.* To wonder. [Fusion of OE *truwian* < *truwa* faith and *trēowan* believe < *trēowe* true]

trow·el (trou′əl, troul) *n.* **1** A flat-bladed, sometimes pointed implement having an offset handle: used by masons, plasterers, and molders. **2** A small concave scoop with a handle: used in digging about small plants, potting them, etc. **3** A molder's smoothing tool. **—** *v.t.* **·eled** or **·elled, ·el·ing** or **·el·ling** To apply, dress, or form with a trowel. [<OF *truele* <LL *truella* <L *trulla,* dim. of *trua* a stirring spoon, ladle] **— trow′el·er** or **trow′el·ler** *n.*

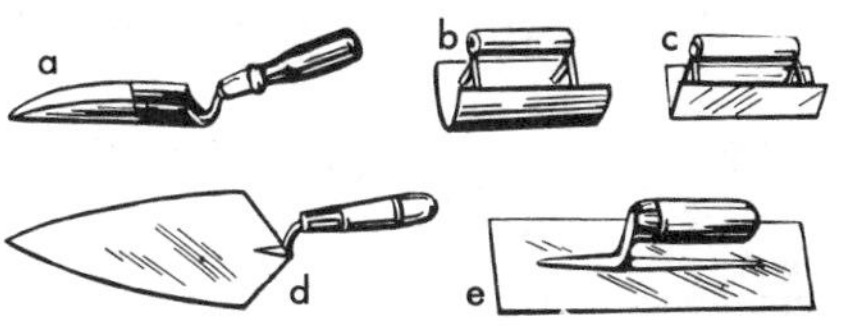

TYPES OF TROWELS
a. Garden. *b.* Circle. *c.* Corner. *d.* Brick. *e.* Plastering.

trowel bayonet A spade-shaped bayonet.

trowth (trōth) *n. Scot.* **1** Truth. **2** Troth.

troy (troi) *n.* A system of weights in which 12 troy ounces make a pound, used by jewelers in England and the United States. See under WEIGHT. Also **troy weight.** [from *Troyes*; with ref. to a weight used at a fair held there]

Troy (troi) **1** The site of nine superimposed ruined cities in NW Asia Minor: the seventh stratum, a Phrygian city of perhaps about 1200 B.C., the scene of the *Iliad,* was also called *Ilium, Ilion.* **2** A city on the Hudson River in eastern New York.

Troy coach A type of passenger coach commonly used in travel in the United States before the building of railroads, seating nine inside, having room for driver, six passengers, and baggage outside, and drawn by four to six horses. [from *Troy,* N. Y.]

Troyes (trwä) A city in NE central France, on the Seine river; a major textile center.

tru·an·cy (trōō′ən·sē) *n. pl.* **·cies** The state or habit of being truant; an act of playing truant. Also **tru′ant·ry.**

tru·ant (trōō′ənt) *n.* One who absents himself, especially from school, without leave. **—** *v.i.* To play the truant. **—** *adj.* **1** Playing the truant; idle. **2** Relating to or characterizing a truant. [<OF, a vagabond, prob. <Celtic]

truant officer *U. S.* An official who investigates truancy from school.

truce (trōōs) *n.* **1** An agreement between belligerents for a temporary suspension of hostilities; an armistice. **2** Temporary cessation or intermission. [Plural of ME *trew,* OE *truwa* faith, a promise. Akin to TRUE, TRUST.]

Tru·cial O·man (trōō′shəl ō·män′) A region on the eastern coast of the Arabian peninsula extending along the **Trucial Coast,** a nearly 400-mile section between Oman and Qatar, and consisting largely of seven **Trucial Sheikdoms** bound by treaties with Great Britain; about 32,300 square miles.

truck[1] (truk) *n.* **1** One of several forms of strong vehicles, variously constructed, for moving bulky articles, freight, etc.; a dray; a stout automotive vehicle on rubber tires able to carry heavy loads. **2** A two-wheeled barrowlike vehicle with a forward lip and no sides, for use in moving barrels, boxes, etc., by hand. **3** A two-, three-, four-, or sometimes six-wheeled vehicle used about railway stations, for moving trunks, etc.: distinguished as **baggage truck, freight truck,** or **wagon truck. 4** Any of numerous small, flat-topped cars moved by pushing or pulling and used in stores. **5** *Brit.* An open or platform freight car. **6** *Naut.* A disk at the upper extremity of a mast or flagpole through which the halyards of signals are run. **7** A wheel: the original sense, now rare, and usually implying a small tireless wheel. — *v.t.* **1** To carry on a truck. — *v.i.* **2** To carry goods on a truck. **3** To drive a truck. [Appar. <L *trochus* a hoop <Gk. *trochos* a wheel < *trechein* run]

truck[2] (truk) *v.t.* & *v.i.* To exchange or barter; also, to peddle. — *n.* **1** Commodities for sale. **2** *U.S.* Garden produce for market: often in compounds: *truck* farming, etc. **3** *Colloq.* Rubbish; worthless articles collectively. **4** Barter. **5** *Colloq.* Intercourse; dealings: I will have no *truck* with him. [<OF *troquer* barter; origin unknown]

truck·age[1] (truk'ij) *n.* **1** Money paid for conveyance of goods on trucks. **2** Such conveyance. [<TRUCK[1] + -AGE]

truck·age[2] (truk'ij) *n.* Exchange; barter. [<TRUCK[2] + -AGE]

truck·er[1] (truk'ər) *n.* One who drives or supplies trucks or moves commodities in trucks: also called *truckman.*

truck·er[2] (truk'ər) *n.* **1** *U.S.* A market gardener; a truck farmer. **2** One who barters or sells commodities; a hawker.

truck farm *U.S.* A farm on which vegetables are produced for market. [<TRUCK[2] + FARM] — **truck farming**

truck·head (truk'hed') *n.* The terminal to which supplies are brought by truck and from which they are distributed to the required points. [< TRUCK[1] + HEAD; on analogy with *railhead*]

truck house Formerly, a building used to store articles used in trading with the Indians. Also **trucking house.**

truck·ing[1] (truk'ing) *n.* The act or business of transportation by trucks.

truck·ing[2] (truk'ing) *n.* **1** Exchanging or bartering; dealings; intercourse. **2** *U.S.* Cultivation of vegetables for market; truck farming.

truck·le (truk'əl) *v.* **·led, ·ling** *v.i.* **1** To yield meanly or weakly: with *to.* **2** To roll on truckles or casters. — *v.t.* **3** To cause to roll on truckles or casters. [< *n.*] — *n.* **1** A small wheel. **2** *Dial.* A trundle bed. [<AF *trocle, trokle* <L *trochlea.* See TROCHLEA.] — **truck'ler** *n.* — **truck'ling·ly** *adv.*

truckle bed A trundle bed.

truck·man[1] (truk'mən) *n.* **1** A truck driver. **2** One engaged in the business of trucking.

truck·man[2] (truk'mən) *n.* *pl.* **·men** (-mən) A dealer in truck; one who trucks or trades.

truck system The practice of paying wages to workmen in goods instead of money.

truc·u·lence (truk'yə·ləns) *n.* Savageness of character, behavior, or aspect. Also **truc'u·len·cy.**

truc·u·lent (truk'yə·lənt) *adj.* **1** Of savage character; awakening terror; cruel; ferocious. **2** Scathing; harsh; violent: said of writing or speech. [<L *truculentus* < *trux, trucis* fierce] — **truc'u·lent·ly** *adv.*

Tru·deau (tro͞o'dō), **Edward Livingston,** 1848–1915, U.S. physician, pioneer in tuberculosis treatment. — (tro͞o·dō'), **Pierre Elliott,** born 1919, Canadian statesman; prime minister 1968–: full name *Joseph Phillippe Pierre Ives Elliotte Trudeau.*

trudge (truj) *v.i.* **trudged, trudg·ing** To walk wearily or laboriously; plod. — *n.* A tiresome walk or tramp. [Earlier *tredge, tridge*; origin uncertain] — **trudg'er** *n.*

trudg·en stroke (truj'ən) In swimming, a former racing stroke similar to the crawl stroke but performed with a frog kick or a scissors kick. Also **trudgen, trudgeon stroke.** [after John *Trudgen,* 19th c. British swimmer, who introduced the stroke into England, 1873]

Tru·dy (tro͞o'dē) Diminutive of GERTRUDE.

true (tro͞o) *adj.* **tru·er, tru·est 1** Faithful to fact or reality; not false or erroneous: a *true* judgment or proposition. **2** Being real or natural; genuine, not counterfeit: a *true* specimen, *true* gold. **3** Faithful to friends, promises, or principles; loyal; steadfast: *true* love, a *true* friend. **4** Conformable to an existing standard type or pattern; exact: a *true* copy. **5** Accurate, as in shape, dimensions, or position: a *true* fit, a *true* circle. **6** Faithful to the requirements of law or justice; legitimate: the *true* king. **7** Faithful to truth; trustful; honest: a *true* man. **8** Faithful to the promise or predicted event; correctly indicative: a *true* sign. **9** *Biol.* **a** Possessing all the attributes of a developed organ or structure of its class; complete. **b** Of pure strain or pedigree: a *true* collie dog. **c** Conformed to the structure of the type; properly so called: said of a plant or animal, as distinguished from others improperly so called: a *true* locust. **10** Exactly correspondent in pitch or key; in perfect tune: His voice is *true.* See synonyms under AUTHENTIC, CORRECT, FAITHFUL, GOOD, HONEST, JUST[1], MORAL, RIGHT, PURE. — *n.* **1** Truth; covenant; pledge. **2** *pl.* **trues** or **truce** *Obs.* An armistice or truce. — **in** (or **out of**) **true** In (or not in) line of adjustment: said of a mark or part, as in a drawing or a machine. — *adv.* **1** In truth; truly. **2** In a true and accurate manner: The wheel runs *true.* **3** Conformably to the ancestral type: in the phrase *to breed true.* — *v.t.* **trued, tru·ing** To bring to conformity with a standard or requirement; form or adjust, as with geometrical precision: to *true* a frame or a tool. [OE *trēowe.* Akin to TRUCE, TRUST.] — **true'ness** *n.*

true bill *Law* **1** The endorsement by a grand jury on a bill of indictment which they find to be sustained by the evidence. **2** A bill so endorsed.

true-blue (tro͞o'blo͞o') *n.* **1** Originally, a fast blue color or dye; hence, constancy or unchangingness. **2** In the 17th century, a Scotch Presbyterian or Covenanter, so called from the blue adopted as the distinctive color of his political party. **3** A person of uncompromising faithfulness or loyalty as to party, sect, friendship, or principle. — *adj.* Staunch; faithful; dependable; genuine.

true copy An exact, verbatim transcript of any document, report, etc.; especially, one certified as correct by a qualified authority.

true level A surface that is everywhere perpendicular to a plumb line, as that of a liquid at rest.

true·love (tro͞o'luv') *n.* **1** One truly beloved; a sweetheart: used also adjectively. **2** *Obs.* Truelovers' knot. **3** The herb-Paris, so called because its four leaves are set together in the form of a truelovers' knot.

true·lov·ers' knot (tro͞o'luv'·ərz) A complicated double knot, a symbol of fidelity in love.

TRUELOVERS' KNOT

true·pen·ny (tro͞o'pen'ē) *n.* *Archaic* **1** Originally, a coin of genuine metal. **2** A trusty or genuine person; an honest fellow.

true rib See under RIB.

true time Mean time, or mean solar time.

true toxin An endotoxin.

truf·fle (truf'əl, tro͞o'fəl) *n.* Any of various fleshy underground fungi (genus *Tuber*), regarded as a choice table delicacy. [<OF *trufe, truffe,* prob. <Ital. *truffa,* ult. <L *tuber* a tuber]

tru·ism (tro͞o'iz·əm) *n.* An obvious or self-evident truth; a platitude. See synonyms under AXIOM.

Tru·jil·lo (tro͞o·hē'yō), **Ciudad** See CIUDAD TRUJILLO.

Tru·jil·lo Mo·li·na (tro͞o·hē'yō mō·lē'nä), **Rafael,** 1891–1961, Dominican general; president of the Dominican Republic 1930–38, 1942–57; assassinated.

Truk (truk, tro͝ok) An island group in the eastern Caroline Islands; total, 40 square miles.

trull (trul) *n.* A prostitute; drab. [<G *trulle, trolle.* ? Akin to TROLL[1].]

tru·ly (tro͞o'lē) *adv.* **1** In conformity with fact. **2** With accuracy. **3** With loyalty or fidelity. **4** *Archaic* Surely; verily. **5** Lawfully; legally.

Tru·man (tro͞o'mən), **Harry S,** 1884–1972, president of the United States 1945–1953.

Trumbull (trum'bəl), **John,** 1750–1831, American poet and satirist. — **John,** 1756–1843, American painter. — **Jonathan,** 1710–85, American statesman.

trump[1] (trump) *n.* **1** In various card games, a card of the suit selected to rank above all others temporarily. **2** The suit thus determined: usually in the plural. **3** *Colloq.* A very acceptable and agreeable person; good fellow. — *v.t.* **1** To take (another card) with a trump. **2** To surpass; excel; beat. — *v.i.* **3** To play a trump. — **to trump up** To make up or invent for a fraudulent purpose. [Alter. of TRIUMPH]

trump[2] (trump) *n.* **1** *Poetic* A trumpet. **2** *Scot.* A jew's-harp. [<OF *trompe* <Gmc.]

trump·er·y (trum'pər·ē) *n.* *pl.* **·er·ies 1** Worthless finery. **2** Rubbish; nonsense. **3** Deceit; trickery. See synonyms under GAUD. — *adj.* Having a showy appearance, but valueless. [<OF *tromperie* < *tromper* TRUMP[1], *v.*]

trum·pet (trum'pit) *n.* **1** A soprano wind instrument with a flaring bell and a long metal tube. The tube was formerly always straight, but now may recurve singly or doubly. **2** A powerful reed stop in an organ. **3** Something resembling a trumpet in form. **4** A tube for collecting and conducting sounds to the ear; an ear trumpet. **5** A loud penetrating sound like that of a trumpet; trumpeting. **6** *pl.* A pitcherplant *(Sarracenia flava)* of the southern United States having trumpet-shaped leaves. **7** *Obs.* A trumpeter. — *v.t.* **1** To sound or proclaim by or as by trumpet; publish abroad. — *v.i.* **2** To blow a trumpet. **3** To give forth a sound as if from a trumpet. [<OF *trompette,* dim. of *trompe* TRUMP[2]]

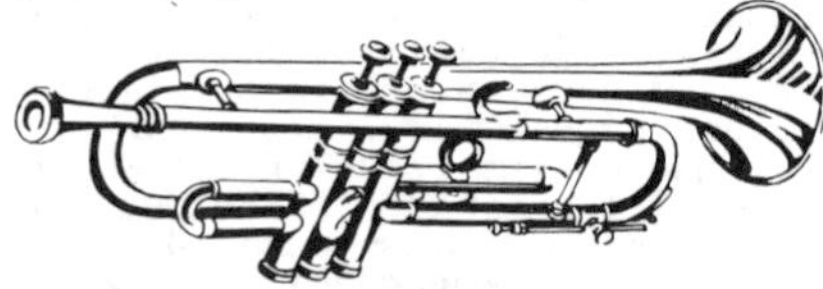

TRUMPET

trumpet creeper A woody vine *(Campsis radicans)* of the southern United States, with scarlet trumpet-shaped flowers. Also **trumpet vine.**

trum·pet·er (trum'pit·ər) *n.* **1** One who sounds a trumpet. **2** One who publishes something loudly abroad. **3** A large South American bird, related to the cranes; especially, the golden-breasted trumpeter *(Psophia crepitans),* often domesticated. **4** A large North American wild swan *(Cygnus buccinator),* having a clarionlike cry: now very scarce: also **trumpeter swan. 5** One of a breed of domestic pigeons.

trumpet flower Any of various plants having trumpet-shaped flowers, as the trumpet creeper, the trumpet honeysuckle.

trumpet honeysuckle A twining honeysuckle *(Lonicera sempervirens)* with oblong leaves and trumpet-shaped flowers, scarlet without and yellow within.

trumpet tree A West Indian and South American tree *(Cecropia peltata)* whose hollow branches are used for musical instruments. Also **trum'pet·wood'** (-wo͝od').

trum·pet·weed (trum'pit·wēd') *n.* **1** The joe-pye weed. **2** The boneset.

trun·cate (trung'kāt) *v.t.* **·cat·ed, ·cat·ing** To cut the top or end from. — *adj.* **1** Truncated. **2** *Biol.* Appearing as though cut or broken squarely off, as the end of certain leaves and shells, the tail of certain birds, the caudal fin of some fishes, etc. [<L *truncatus,* pp. of *truncare* < *truncus* TRUNK] — **trun·ca·tion** (trung·kā'shən) *n.*

trun·ca·ted (trung'kā·tid) *adj.* **1** Cut off; shortened. **2** Describing a cone or pyramid whose vertex is cut off by a plane usually parallel to the base. **3** *Mineral.* Having the edges or angles cut off, as certain crystals. **4** *Biol.* Truncate.

TRUNCATED PYRAMID

trun·cheon (trun'chən) *n.* **1** A short, heavy stick; a club; staff. **2** The baton of a military officer or marshal. **3** A tree whose branches have been lopped off to hasten growth; tree trunk: the original meaning. **4** *Obs.* A short club or cudgel; a spear shaft. **5** *Brit.* A policeman's club. — *v.t.* To beat as with a truncheon; cudgel. [<OF *trunçun, tronchon* a stump, ult. <L *truncus* TRUNK]

trun·dle (trun′dəl) *n.* **1** A small broad wheel, as of a caster. **2** The act, motion, or sound of trundling. **3** A trundle bed. **4** A lantern wheel. **5** *Obs.* A small low-wheeled vehicle; truck. — *v.t.* & *v.i.* **·dled, ·dling 1** To roll along, as a hoop. **2** To rotate. [Var. of TRINDLE] — **trun′dler** *n.*

trundle bed A bed with very low frame resting upon casters, so that it may be rolled under another bed: also called *truckle bed.*

trun·dle·tail (trun′dəl·tāl′) *n. Obs.* A curly-tailed dog; also, a curly tail.

trunk (trungk) *n.* **1** The main stem or stock of a tree, as distinguished from its branches or roots. **2** The human body, apart from the head, neck, and limbs; the torso. **3** *Entomol.* The thorax. **4** *Anat.* The main stem of a nerve, blood vessel, or lymphatic. **5** The main line of a communication or transportation system. **6** The circuit connecting two telephone exchanges. **7** The main body, line, or stem of anything, as distinct from its appendages. **8** A proboscis, as of an elephant. **9** A large box or case used for packing and carrying clothes or other articles, as for a journey. **10** A large compartment at the rear of an automobile, used for storage. **11** *pl.* A close-fitting garment covering the loins and often part of the thighs, worn by male swimmers, athletes, etc. **12** *pl. Obs.* Trunk hose. **13** *Mech.* **a** A trough, chute, or conduit. **b** A large hollow piston in which a connecting rod moves. **14** *Naut.* **a** The well for the centerboard of a vessel. **b** A casing connecting the hatchways of two or more decks and forming a shaft. **c** Any structure placed on the upper deck of a ship, as for shelter. **15** *Archit.* The shaft of a column. See synonyms under BODY. — *adj.* Being or belonging to a trunk or main body: a *trunk* railroad. [<OF *tronc* <L *truncus* stem, trunk, orig. adj., mutilated; def. 8 infl. in meaning by F *trompe* a trumpet]

trunk engine A steam engine having a trunk or open cylinder attached to the piston in place of the usual piston rod, permitting direct attachment of the connecting rod to the piston head.

trunk·fish (trungk′·fish′) *n. pl.* **·fish** or **·fish·es** A plectognath fish (family *Ostraciidae*) of warm seas, characterized by a body covering of hard, bony plates.

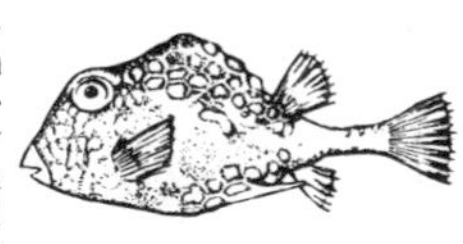

TRUNKFISH
(Rarely to 10 inches)

trunk hose Full breeches worn by gentlemen in the 16th and early 17th centuries, extending from the waist to the middle of the thigh: originally one piece with the hose. Also **trunk breeches.**

trunk line The main line of a transportation or communication system, as distinguished from a branch line.

trunk sleeve A sleeve made very full at the top after the manner of trunk hose.

trun·nel (trun′əl) *n.* A treenail. [Var. of TREENAIL]

trun·nion (trun′yən) *n.* **1** One of two opposite cylindrical projections from the sides of a cannon, forming an axis on which it is elevated or depressed. **2** A similar support on which the cylinders of some engines oscillate. [<F *trognon* the core of a fruit, a stump, trunk; ult. origin unknown]

Tru·ro (trŏŏr′ō) **1** A municipal borough in SW Cornwall, England. **2** A port of central Nova Scotia, Canada.

truss (trus) *n.* **1** *Med.* A bandage or support for a rupture. **2** A braced framework of ties, beams, or bars, usually arranged in a series of triangles, as for the support of a roof, airplane, or bridge. **3** A bundle, especially of hay or straw. In England, 56 pounds of old or 60 pounds of new hay make a *truss*; 36 pounds make a *truss* of straw. **4** *Naut.* A heavy iron piece by which a lower yard is attached to a mast. **5** *Bot.* A compact terminal cluster of flowers. **6** *Archit.* A projection from the face of a wall, used to support a cornice; a large corbel; a bracket or modillion. **7** A pack; package. — *v.t.* **1** To tie or bind; fasten: often with *up.* **2** To support by a truss; brace, as a roof. **3** To fasten the wings of (a fowl) with skewers or twine before cooking. **4** To fasten, tighten, or tie around one, as a garment or laces. **5** To hang, as a criminal: with *up.* [< OF *trusse, trousse* < *trousser, trusser* pack up, bundle, prob. <L *torca* a bundle < *torques.* See TORQUES.] — **truss′er** *n.*

trust company An incorporated institution empowered by its charter to accept and execute trusts, as provided by law, to receive deposits of money and other personal property and issue obligations therefor, and to lend money on real and personal securities.

trus·tee (trus·tē′) *n.* **1** One who holds property in trust; especially, in popular usage, one of a body of men, often elective, who hold the property and manage the affairs of a church or public institution. **2** One in whose hands property is attached by a trustee process. — *v.t.* **·teed, ·tee·ing 1** *Law* To attach by trustee process (the property of a debtor in the hands of a third person). **2** To place (property) in the care of a trustee.

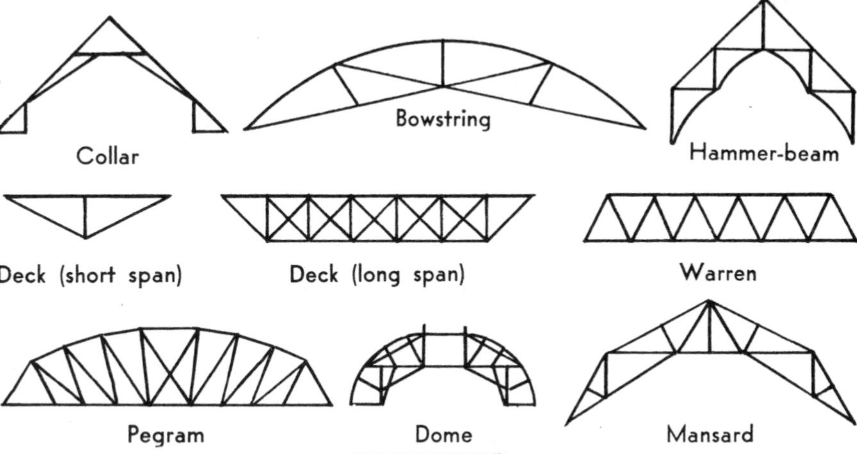

TYPES OF TRUSSES

truss bridge A bridge stiffened, supported, or formed by a truss or construction of trusses.

truss·ing (trus′ing) *n.* **1** A system of diagonal tension rods and struts for strengthening or stiffening a structure, as a railway car or a vessel's hull. **2** Trusses collectively. **3** The act of one who trusses. **4** A bracing with ties, struts, or the like.

trust (trust) *n.* **1** A confident reliance on the integrity, veracity, or justice of another; confidence; faith; also, the person or thing so trusted. **2** Something committed to one's care for use or safekeeping; a charge; responsibility. **3** The state or position of one who has received an important charge. **4** A confidence in the reliability of persons or things without careful investigation. **5** Credit, in the commercial sense. **6** *Law* The confidence, or the obligation arising from the confidence, reposed in a person (called the *trustee*) to whom the legal title to property is conveyed for the benefit of another (the *cestui que trust*), that he will faithfully apply the property according to such confidence; also, the beneficial title or ownership of property of which the legal title is in another. ◆ Collateral adjective: *fiducial.* **7** The property or thing held in trust; also, the relation subsisting between the holder and the property so held. **8** A permanent combination, now illegal, for the purpose of controlling the production, price, etc., of some commodity or the management, profits, etc., of some business; also, a trust company. Compare CARTEL, CORNER, MONOPOLY, POOL[2], SYNDICATE. **9** Confident expectation; belief; hope. **10** Custody; care; keeping. **11** *Obs.* Trustworthiness. — *v.t.* **1** To have trust in; rely upon. **2** To commit to the care of another; entrust. **3** To commit something to the care of: with *with.* **4** To allow to do something without fear of the consequences. **5** To expect with confidence or with hope. **6** To believe. **7** To allow business credit to. — *v.i.* **8** To place trust or confidence; rely: with *in.* **9** To hope: with *for.* **10** To allow business credit. — **to trust to** To depend upon; confide in. — *adj.* Held in trust: *trust* property, *trust* money. [<ON *traust,* lit., firmness. Akin to TRUCE, TRUE.] — **trust′er** *n.* — **trust′less** *adj.*

Synonyms (noun): assurance, belief, confidence, credence, expectation, faith, hope. See ASSURANCE, BELIEF, FAITH.

Synonyms (verb): believe, commit, confide, hope. See COMMIT, LEAN[1]. *Antonyms*: despair, disbelieve, discredit, distrust, doubt, mistrust, suspect.

trustee process A statutory remedy whereby a creditor may reach property or assets of his debtor in the hands of a third person.

trus·tee·ship (trus·tē′ship) *n.* **1** The post or function of a trustee. **2** Supervision and control of a trust territory by a country or countries commissioned by the United Nations; also, the territory so controlled.

trust·ful (trust′fəl) *adj.* Disposed to trust. — **trust′ful·ly** *adv.* — **trust′ful·ness** *n.*

trust fund Money, securities, or similar property held in trust.

trust·ing (trus′ting) *adj.* Having trust; trustful. — **trust′ing·ly** *adv.* — **trust′ing·ness** *n.*

trust officer An administrator of a trust company or the trust department of a bank.

Trust Territory An area, usually a former colonial possession, governed by a member state of the United Nations as an Administering Authority reporting to the United Nations Trusteeship Council functioning under the authority of the General Assembly with the exception that the trusteeships of the areas designated as strategic are supervised by the Security Council after first having approved the trust agreements. Trust Territories include former League of Nations mandates. Also **trust territory, UN Trust Territory.** The independence of the Cameroons, Somaliland, Tanganyika, and Togoland in 1960–61 and of Western Samoa in 1962 reduced the Trust Territories to:

Trust Territory	*Administered by*
Nauru	Australia on behalf of Australia, New Zealand, and the United Kingdom
(Papua and) New Guinea	Australia
Ruanda-Urundi	Belgium
Trust Territory of the Pacific Islands (a strategic territory)	United States

trust·wor·thy (trust′wûr′thē) *adj.* Worthy of confidence; reliable. See synonyms under AUTHENTIC, FAITHFUL, HONEST, RELIABLE, STAUNCH. — **trust′wor′thi·ly** (-wûr′thə·lē) *adv.* — **trust′wor′thi·ness** *n.*

trust·y (trus′tē) *adj.* **trust·i·er, trust·i·est 1** Faithful to duty or trust. **2** Staunch; firm. **3** *Obs.* Trustful. See synonyms under FAITHFUL, HONEST, JUST[1], RELIABLE, STAUNCH. — *n. pl.* **trust·ies** A trustworthy person; especially, a convict who has been found serviceable and reliable and to whom special liberties are granted. **—trust′i·ly** *adv.* **—trust′i·ness** *n.*

truth (tro͞oth) *n.* *pl.* **truths** (tro͞othz, tro͞oths) **1** The state or character of being true in relation to being, knowledge, or speech. **2** Conformity to fact or reality. **3** Conformity to rule, standard, model, pattern, or ideal. **4** Conformity to the requirements of one's being or nature; steadfastness; sincerity. **5** That which is true; a statement or belief which corresponds to the reality. **6** A fact as the object of correct belief; reality. **7** A tendency or disposition to speak or tell only what is true; veracity. **8** The quality of being true; fidelity; constancy. **9** In the fine arts, faithfulness to the facts of nature, history, or life. **10** *Obs.* Right, according to divine law. See synonyms under FIDELITY, JUSTICE, VERACITY, VIRTUE. [OE *trēowth* < *treowe* true] **—truth′less** *adj.* **—truth′less·ness** *n.*

truth·ful (tro͞oth′fəl) *adj.* Veracious, as a person; true, as a narrative; veridical. See synonyms under CANDID. **—truth′ful·ly** *adv.* **—truth′ful·ness** *n.*

try (trī) *v.* **tried, try·ing** *v.t.* **1** To make an attempt to do or accomplish; undertake; endeavor. **2** To make experimental use or application of: often with *out*: to *try* a new pen. **3** To subject to a test; put to proof. **4** To put severe strain upon; tax, as the eyes. **5** To subject to trouble or tribulation; afflict. **6** To extract by rendering or melting; refine: often with *out*: to *try* out oil. **7** *Law* **a** To determine the guilt or innocence of by judicial trial. **b** To examine or determine judicially, as a case. *—v.i.* **8** To make an attempt; put forth effort. **9** To make an examination or test. See synonyms under CHASTEN, ENDEAVOR, EXAMINE, STRUGGLE. **—to try on** To put on (a garment) to test it for fit or appearance. **—to try out** To attempt to qualify: He *tried out* for the football team. *—n.* *pl.* **tries** **1** The act of trying; trial; experiment. **2** In Rugby football, the act of touching the ball down behind an opponent's goal, which scores three points. [<OF *trier* sift, pick out, prob. <LL *tritare* thresh <L *tritus*. See TRITE.] **—tri′er** *n.*

try·ing (trī′ing) *adj.* Testing severely; hard to endure. See synonyms under ARDUOUS, DIFFICULT, TROUBLESOME.

trying plane A long plane used to true up the edges of boards to be joined; a jointer. Also **try plane.**

try·lon (trī′lon) *n.* A three-sided pylon: used as part of the main gateway to the New York World's Fair, 1939. [<TR(I)- + (P)YLON]

try·ma (trī′mə) *n.* *pl.* **·ma·ta** (-mə·tə) *Bot.* A drupelike, commonly two-celled fruit with a bony nucleus and a fleshy, leathery, or fibrous dehiscent or separating exocarp, as the hickory nut and walnut. [<NL <Gk. *tryma, trymē* a hole < *tryein* wear away]

try-out (trī′out′) *n.* *U.S. Colloq.* A test of ability, as of an actor or athlete, often in competition with others.

tryp·a·no·some (trip′ə·nə·sōm′) *n.* Any of a genus (*Trypanosoma*) of flagellate infusorians infesting the blood of man and some lower animals. They destroy the red corpuscles, and cause serious and even fatal diseases, as the sleeping sickness. Also **tryp′a·no·so′ma** (-sō′mə). [<Gk. *trypanon* a borer + -SOME[2]]

tryp·a·no·so·mi·a·sis (trip′ə·nō·sō·mī′ə·sis) *n.* *Pathol.* Any disease caused by the presence in the body of trypanosomes. Also **tryp′a·no·so′ma·to′sis** (-sō′mə·tō′sis). [<TRYPANOSOME + -IASIS]

tryp·ars·am·ide (trip′är·sam′id, -īd, trip·är′sə·mid, -mīd) *n.* *Chem.* A colorless crystalline compound, $C_8H_{10}O_4N_2AsNa$, used in the treatment of trypanosomiasis and certain forms of syphilis. [<TRYP(ANOSOME) + ARS(ENIC) + AMIDE]

tryp·sin (trip′sin) *n.* *Biochem.* A proteolytic enzyme contained in the pancreatic juice. [<G <Gk. *tripsis* a rubbing (< *tribein* rub) + (PEP)SIN] **—tryp′tic** (-tik) *adj.*

tryp·sin·o·gen (trip·sin′ə·jen) *n.* *Biochem.* The substance secreted by the pancreas and converted into trypsin by the action of intestinal enzymes. [<*trypsino-* <TRYPSIN + -GEN]

tryp·to·phan (trip′tə·fan) *n.* *Biochem.* A crystalline amino acid, $C_{11}H_{12}O_2N_2$, contained in variable amounts in most proteins and associated with the digestive functions. Also **tryp′to·phane** (-fān). [< *tryptic* (<TRYPSIN) + *-phan*, var. of -PHANE]

try·sail (trī′səl, -sāl′) *n.* *Naut.* A small sail bent to a gaff abaft the foremast and mainmast of a ship: also called *spencer.* [< nautical phrase *(at) try* lying to in a storm + SAIL]

try square A carpenter's square having usually a wooden stock and a steel blade.

tryst (trist, trīst) *v.t.* **1** To agree to meet. **2** To appoint (a time), as for meeting. **3** To arrange for in advance; engage. **4** *Obs.* To trust. *—v.i.* **5** To agree upon some place or time of meeting. *—n.* **1** An appointment to meet, or the meeting place agreed upon: also **tryst′·ing. 2** *Scot.* A market. **3** *Scot.* A journey in company. Also **tryste.** [<OF *triste, tristre* an appointed station in hunting, prob. < Scand.] **—tryst′er** *n.*

tryst·ed (tris′tid, trī′stid) *adj.* Agreed upon.

tsa·de (tsä·dā′) See SADE.

Tsa·na (tsä′nä), **Lake** See TANA, LAKE.

tsar (tsär), **tsar·e·vitch** (tsär′ə·vich), **tsa·rev·na** (tsä·rev′nä), **tsa·ri·na** (tsä·rē′nä) etc. See CZAR, etc.

Tsa·ri·tsyn (tsä·rē′tsin) A former name for STALINGRAD.

Tsar·sko·e Se·lo (tsär′skə·yə sye·lô′) Former imperial summer residence near Leningrad: modern *Pushkin.*

tset·se (tset′sē, tsē′tsē) *n.* **1** A small bloodsucking fly (*Glossina morsitans*) of southern Africa whose bite transmits disease in cattle, horses, etc. **2** A related species (*G. palpalis*), which transmits the parasite that causes sleeping sickness. For illustration see INSECTS (injurious). Also spelled *tzetze.* Also **tsetse fly.** [<Afrikaans <Bantu]

Tshi (chwē, chē) See TWI.

T-shirt (tē′shûrt′) *n.* **1** A cotton undershirt with short sleeves: so called because T-shaped. **2** A sleeveless jersey or sweater of similar cut for outer wear. Also spelled *tee shirt.* Also **T shirt.**

Tsi·nan (jē′nän′) A port in NE China, capital of Shantung province; a former treaty port: also *Chinan.*

Tsing·hai (ching′hī′) A province of NW China; 318,450 square miles; capital, Sining: also *Chinghai.*

Tsing·tao (ching′dou′) A port in eastern Shantung province, China.

Tsi·tsi·har (tsē′tsē′här′) A city in former north central Manchuria, NE China, former capital of Heilungkiang province.

Tso·ne·can (tsō·nā′kən) *n.* A linguistic stock of South American Indians, including all the Tehuelchan tribes, and, possibly, the Onas of Tierra del Fuego. By some linguists called **Cho·ne·an** (chō′nē·ən).

T-square (tē′skwâr′) *n.* An instrument by which to measure or lay out right angles or parallel lines, consisting usually of a flat strip with a shorter head at right angles to it and slightly offset so that it may be slid along the edge of a drawing board.

Tsu·ga·ru Strait (tso͞o·gä·ro͞o) The passage from the Sea of Japan to the Pacific between Honshu and southern Hokkaido, Japan; 15 to 25 miles wide.

tsu·na·mi (tso͞o·nä′mē) *n.* An extensive and often very destructive ocean wave caused by a violent submarine earthquake: erroneously called a tidal wave. [<Japanese, a storm wave < *tsu* port, harbor + *nami* wave]

Tsu·shi·ma (tso͞o·shē·mä) A Japanese island in Korea Strait; 271 square miles, including 42 offshore islets; scene of a naval battle in the Russo-Japanese War in which the Russian fleet was destroyed, 1905.

tsu·tsu·ga·mu·shi disease (tso͞o·tso͞o′gä·mo͞o′·shē) *Pathol.* A rickettsial fever endemic in Japan and the Orient, caused by a micro-organism (*Rickettsia orientalis*) transmitted to man by the infected larvae of a mite (genus *Trombicula*): also called *Japanese river fever, river fever, scrub typhus.* [<Japanese *tsutsugamush*, a small Japanese mite < *mushi* a bug]

Tu·a·mo·tu Archipelago (to͞o′ä·mō′to͞o) An island chain extending 1,300 miles south of the Marquesas Islands in eastern French Oceania; 330 square miles: also *Low Archipelago*: formerly *Paumotu Archipelago.*

Tuan (twän) *n.* Sir; mister: courteous Malayan form of address for a European. [< Malay]

Tua·reg (twä′reg) *n.* **1** A member of the nomadic Berber tribes of the central and western Sahara. **2** The Berber dialect spoken by these people.

tu·a·ta·ra (to͞o′ä·tä′rä) *n.* A sphenodon. Also **tu′a·te′ra** (-tā′rä). [<Maori < *tua* on the farther side, the back + *tara* the spine]

Tu·a·tha De Da·naan (tho͞o′ə·hə dā dä′nôn) In ancient Irish mythology, a race of gods who ruled in Ireland until their defeat by the Milesians: now conceived of as fairies. See DANU. [<OIrish, people of Danu]

tub (tub) *n.* **1** A broad, open-topped vessel, usually of wood, and formed with staves, bottom, hoops, and handles on the side. **2** A bathtub. **3** *Brit. Colloq.* A bath taken in a tub. **4** The amount that a tub contains. **5** Anything resembling a tub, as a broad, clumsy boat: contemptuous or humorous. **6** A small cask. **7** A bucket for bringing ore or coal up a shaft; also, an underground tram. **8** A keeve. **9** A sweating in a tub. *—v.t.* & *v.i.* **tubbed, tub·bing** To wash, bathe, or place in a tub. [<MDu. *tubbe*] **—tub′ba·ble** *adj.* **—tub′ber** *n.*

tu·ba (to͞o′bə, tyo͞o′-) *n.* *pl.* **·bas** or **·bae** (-bē) **1** A large bass instrument of the saxhorn family. **2** An ancient Roman war trumpet. **3** A powerful reed stop in an organ. [<L, a war trumpet]

tu·bal (to͞o′bəl, tyo͞o′-) *adj.* **1** Relating to a tube. **2** *Anat.* Pertaining to the Fallopian tube.

Tu·bal-cain (to͞o′bəl·kān, tyo͞o′-) The first artificer in brass and iron. *Gen.* iv 22.

tu·bate (to͞o′bāt, tyo͞o′-) *adj.* Of the form of or provided with a tube; tubular. [<NL *tubatus* <L *tubus* a pipe]

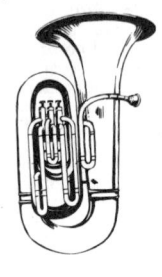

TUBA

tub·by (tub′ē) *adj.* **·bi·er, ·bi·est** **1** Resembling a tub in form; round and fat; corpulent. **2** Lacking resonance when struck; sounding dull or wooden, as a musical instrument.

tube (to͞ob, tyo͞ob) *n.* **1** A long hollow cylindrical body of metal, glass, rubber, etc., generally used for the conveyance of something through it; a pipe. **2** The principal part of a gun. **3** Any similar device having a tube or tubelike part, as a telescope. **4** *Biol.* Any elongated hollow part or organ, as the united part of a gamopetalous corolla or a gamosepalous calyx. **5** A subway or a tunnel. **6** An electron, thermionic, or vacuum tube. **7** The tubular space enclosing lines of magnetic force or induction. **8** A collapsible metal cylinder for containing paints, toothpaste, glue, and the like. *—v.t.* **tubed, tub·ing** **1** To fit or furnish with a tube. **2** To enclose in a tube or tubes. **3** To make tubular. [<F <L *tubus* a tube] **—tube′less** *adj.* **—tub′er** *n.*

Tube may appear as a combining form in hyphemes or solidemes, with the meaning of noun definition 1:

tube-drawing	**tube-rolling**
tube-drilling	**tube-scraping**
tube-fed	**tube-shaped**
tube-filling	**tubesmith**
tubemaker	**tube-straightening**
tubemaking	**tubework**

tube foot *Zool.* An ambulacral sucker; one of the small vascular locomotor processes exserted through the ambulacral pores of echinoderms.

tu·ber (to͞o′bər, tyo͞o′-) *n.* **1** *Bot.* A short, thickened portion of an underground stem, as in the potato or artichoke. **2** *Anat.* A swelling or prominence; tubercle. [<L, a swelling]

tu·ber·cle (to͞o′bər·kəl, tyo͞o′-) *n.* **1** A small rounded eminence or nodule. **2** *Bot.* A minute swelling on the roots of leguminous plants, which contains a micro-organism believed to absorb nitrogen from the air for the use of the plant. **3** *Pathol.* A small granular tumor formed within an organ from morbid or infected matter: in the lungs, the seat of pulmonary consumption. **4** *Anat.* A small knoblike excrescence, especially on the skin or on a bone. [<L *tuberculum*, dim. of *tuber* a swelling] **—tu·ber·cu·loid** (to͞o·bûr′kyə·loid, tyo͞o-) *adj.*

tubercle bacillus The rod-shaped, Gram-positive bacterium (*Mycobacterium tuberculosis*) which is the cause of tuberculosis in man.

tu·ber·cu·lar (to͞o·bûr′kyə·lər, tyo͞o-) *adj.* 1 Affected with tubercles; nodular. 2 Tuberculous. — *n.* One affected with tuberculosis.
tu·ber·cu·late (to͞o·bûr′kyə·lit, -lāt) *adj.* 1 Nodular. 2 Affected with tubercles; tuberculous. Also **tu·ber′cu·lat′ed.** [<NL *tuberculatus* <L *tuberculum* TUBERCLE] — **tu·ber′cu·la′tion** *n.*
tu·ber·cu·lin (to͞o·bûr′kyə·lin, tyo͞o-) *n. Bacteriol.* A sterile liquid prepared from attenuated cultures of the tubercle bacillus, used especially as a test for tuberculosis in children and animals. Also **tu·ber′cu·line** (-lin, -lēn). [<L *tuberculum* TUBERCLE + -IN]
tuberculo- *combining form* 1 Tuberculosis; of or pertaining to tuberculosis; tuberculous. 2 The tubercle bacillus. Also, before vowels, **tubercul-.** [<L *tuberculum,* dim. of *tuber* a swelling]
tu·ber·cu·lo·sis (to͞o·bûr′kyə·lō′sis, tyo͞o-) *n. Pathol.* A communicable disease caused by infection with the tubercle bacillus, characterized by the formation of tubercles within some organ or tissue: when affecting the lungs, known as **pulmonary tuberculosis.** [< NL <L *tuberculum* TUBERCLE + -OSIS]
tu·ber·cu·lous (to͞o·bûr′kyə·ləs, tyo͞o-) *adj.* Of, pertaining to, or affected with tuberculosis.
tu·ber·if·er·ous (to͞o′bə·rif′ər·əs, tyo͞o′-) *adj.* Bearing or producing tubers. [<TUBER + -(I)FEROUS]
tu·ber·oid (to͞o′bər·oid, tyo͞o′-) *adj.* Resembling a tuber.
tube·rose[1] (to͞ob′rōz′, tyo͞ob′-, to͞o′bə·rōs′, tyo͞o′-) *n.* A bulbous plant *(Polianthes tuberosa)* of the amaryllis family, bearing a long raceme of fragrant white flowers. [<NL *Tuberosa,* species name <L *tuberosus* knobby < *tuber* a swelling]
tu·ber·ose[2] (to͞o′bər·ōs, tyo͞o′-) *adj.* Tuberous. [<TUBER + -OSE]
tu·ber·os·i·ty (to͞o′bə·ros′ə·tē, tyo͞o′-) *n. pl.* **·ties** 1 The state of being tuberous. 2 A swelling or protuberance. 3 *Anat.* A large, rough eminence on a bone, as for the attachment of a muscle.
tu·ber·ous (to͞o′bər·əs, tyo͞o′-) *adj.* 1 Bearing projections or prominences. 2 Resembling tubers. 3 *Bot.* Bearing tubers.
tuberous root *Bot.* One of the tuberlike parts of a multiple or fascicled fleshy root, as in the dahlia.
tu·bi·form (to͞o′bə·fôrm, tyo͞o′-) *adj.* Having the form of a tube; tubular. [<*tubi-* (<TUBE) + -FORM]
tub·ing (to͞o′bing, tyo͞o′-) *n.* 1 Tubes collectively. 2 A piece of tube or material for tubes. 3 Material for pillowcases. 4 The act of making tubes.
Tü·bing·en (tü′bing·ən) A university town in the state of Baden-Württemberg, SW West Germany.
Tub·man (tub′mən), **William Vacanarat,** 1895–1971, Liberian statesman; president of Liberia 1944–1971.
tub·thump·er (tub′thum′pər) *n. U.S. Colloq.* A noisy speaker; a soapbox orator.
Tu·bu·ai Islands (to͞o′bo͞o·ī′) An island group south of the Society Islands, comprising a part of French Oceania; 115 square miles: also *Austral Islands.*
tu·bu·lar (to͞o′byə·lər, tyo͞o′-) *adj.* 1 Having the form of a tube; tube-shaped. 2 Made up of or provided with tubes. 3 Pertaining to or sounding as if produced in a tube. [<L *tubulus* TUBULE]
tu·bu·late (to͞o′byə·lāt, tyo͞o′-) *v.t.* **·lat·ed, ·lat·ing** 1 To shape or fashion into a tube. 2 To furnish with a tube. — *adj.* Shaped like or into a tube; also, provided with a tube: also **tu′bu·lat′ed.** [<L *tubulatus* tubular < *tubulus* TUBULE] — **tu′bu·la′tor** *n.*
tu·bu·la·tion (to͞o′byə·lā′shən, tyo͞o′-) *n.* 1 The formation of a tube. 2 The arrangement of a set of tubes.
tu·bule (to͞o′byo͞ol, tyo͞o′-) A minute tube. [<L *tubulus,* dim. of *tubus* a tube] — **tu′bu·li·form′** *adj.*
tu·bu·li·flo·rous (to͞o′byə·lə·flôr′əs, -flō′rəs, tyo͞o′-) *adj. Bot.* Having tubular florets: said of composite plants with all the florets tubular. [< *tubuli-* (TUBULE) + -FLOROUS]
tu·bu·lous (to͞o′byə·ləs, tyo͞o′-) *adj.* 1 Tube-shaped; tubular. 2 *Bot.* Having tubular florets. 3 Consisting of or containing small tubes. Also **tu′bu·lose** (-lōs).
tu·bu·lure (to͞o′byə·lər, tyo͞o′-) *n.* The short open tube of a retort, receiver, or bell jar. [<F <L *tubulus* TUBULE]
Tu·ca·na (to͞o·kā′nə, tyo͞o-) *Astron.* A southern constellation. See CONSTELLATION.
tu·chun (do͞o′jün′) *n. Chinese* Formerly, the military governor of a Chinese province. — **tu′chun·ate** *n.* — **tu′chun·ism** *n.*
tuck[1] (tuk) *n.* 1 A fold made in a garment, usually horizontal. 2 A flap forming a continuation of one side of a book cover, and inserted in a loop or pocket in the other side. 3 *Naut.* That part of a vessel's hull where the after planks meet. 4 *Brit. Slang* Food. 5 *U.S. Slang* Stamina; determination. [< *v.*] — *v.t.* 1 To fold under; thrust or press in the ends or edges of. 2 To wrap or cover snugly. 3 To thrust or press into a close place; cram; hide. 4 To make tucks in, by folding and stitching. — *v.i.* 5 To contract; draw together. 6 To make tucks. [Fusion of OE *tūcian* ill-treat, lit., tug and MDu. *tucken* pluck]
tuck[2] (tuk) *Scot. & Obs. n.* 1 A stroke; tap; beat, as of a drum. 2 A flourish, as of a trumpet. — *v.t. & v.i.* To beat; tap, as a drum. [<AF *toker,* OF *toucher* touch]
tuck[3] (tuk) *n. Archaic* A long narrow sword; rapier. [<AF *etoc,* OF *estoc* < *estoquier* <Du. *stocken* pierce]
Tuck (tuk), **Friar** A jovial priest, associate and confessor of Robin Hood.
tuck·a·hoe (tuk′ə·hō) *n.* An underground fungus *(Poria cocos)* with a brown edible sclerotium: found in the southern United States: also *Indian bread* or *Virginia truffle.* [<Algonquian (Virginian) *tockawhoughe*]
tuck·er[1] (tuk′ər) *n.* 1 One who or that which tucks. 2 A covering, formerly worn over the neck and shoulders by women. 3 *Austral.* Food. [<TUCK[1]]
tuck·er[2] (tuk′ər) *v.t. Colloq.* To weary completely; exhaust: usually with *out.* [Freq. of TUCK[1], *v.*]
tuck·er-bag (tuk′ər·bag) *n. Austral.* A cloth bag in which food is carried by tramps, travelers, etc.
tuck·et (tuk′it) *n. Archaic* A flourish on a trumpet. [Dim. of TUCK[2]]
Tuc·son (to͞o·son′, to͞o′son) A city in SE Arizona; a factory, rail, and mining center.
Tu·cu·mán (to͞o′ko͞o·män′) A city in NW Argentina; an agricultural and industrial center.
-tude *suffix of nouns* Condition or state of being: *gratitude.* [<F *-tude* <L *-tudo*]
Tu·dor (to͞o′dər, tyo͞o′-) *adj.* 1 Of or pertaining to the **Tudors,** an English royal family descended from Sir Owen Tudor, a Welshman who married Catherine of Valois, widow of Henry V. See the table of sovereigns under ENGLAND. 2 Designating or pertaining to the architecture, poetry, etc., developed during the reigns of the Tudors.
Tudor architecture The latest phase of the Perpendicular style, developed under the Tudors to make houses more livable. It employed large windows, many fireplaces, large bays, steep roofs, flattened arches, much carving, and paneling. The house plan was generally a quadrangle, an H or an E.
Tues·day (to͞oz′dē, -dā, tyo͞oz′-) *n.* The third day of the week; the day after Monday. [OE *tīwesdæg* day of Tiw < *Tīw,* an ancient Teutonic deity + *dæg* a day; trans. of LL *dies Martis* Mars's day]
tu·fa (to͞o′fə, tyo͞o′-) *n.* 1 A variety of calcium carbonate with cellular structure, as deposited from springs and streams. 2 Tuff. [<Ital. *tufa, tufo* <L *tofus, tophus*] — **tu·fa·ceous** (to͞o·fā′shəs, tyo͞o-) *adj.*
tuff (tuf) *n.* A volcanic rock composed of material varying in size from fine sand to coarse gravel: used for building. [<MF *tufe, tuffe* <Ital. *tufo* TUFA] — **tuff·a′ceous** *adj.*
tuft (tuft) *n.* 1 A collection or bunch of small, flexible parts, as hair, grass, or feathers, held together at the base. 2 A clump or knot; frequently, a cluster of threads drawn tightly through a quilt, mattress, or upholstery to secure the stuffing. 3 A gold tassel formerly worn by titled undergraduates at Oxford and Cambridge universities; also, a student who wears such a tuft. — *v.t.* 1 To separate or form into tufts. 2 To cover or adorn with tufts. — *v.i.* 3 To form tufts. [<OF *tuffe,* prob. <Gmc.] — **tuft′er** *n.* — **tuft′y** *adj.*
tuft·ed (tuf′tid) *adj.* 1 Having, or adorned with, a tuft; crested: the *tufted* duck. 2 Forming a tuft or dense cluster; cespitose.
tuft·hunt·er (tuft′hun′tər) *n. Archaic* 1 Originally, a student at Oxford or Cambridge who sought association with titled students distinguished by gold tufts on their hats. 2 One who seeks the acquaintance of persons of rank; a snob; sycophant; parasite. — **tuft′·hunt′ing** *n. & adj.*
tug (tug) *v.* **tugged, tug·ging** *v.t.* 1 To pull at with effort; strain at. 2 To pull, draw, or drag with effort. 3 To tow with a tugboat. — *v.i.* 4 To pull strenuously: to *tug* at an oar. 5 To strive; toil; struggle. See synonyms under DRAW. — *n.* 1 An act of tugging; a violent pull. 2 A strenuous contest; a struggle; wrestle. 3 A tugboat. 4 A trace of a harness; also, *Scot.,* rawhide: formerly used in making traces. 5 *Brit.* A colleger or member of the king's foundation at Eton College. 6 *Brit. Dial.* A high-wheeled cart for carrying logs, etc., slung beneath its axles. [ME *toggen,* intens. of OE *tēon* tow; infl. by ON *toga* draw] — **tug′ger** *n.*
tug·boat (tug′bōt′) *n.* A small, compact, ruggedly built vessel operated by steam or other power and designed for towing: also called *towboat.*
Tu·ge·la (to͞o·gā′lə) A river in Natal, Union of South Africa, flowing 300 miles east from near the Basutoland and Orange Free State borders, through the **Tugela Falls** (2,810 feet) to the Indian Ocean.
Tug·gurt (to͞o·go͝ort′) A territory of NE Southern Territories, Algeria; 52,094 square miles; capital, Tuggurt: French *Touggourt.*
tug of war 1 A contest in which a number of persons at one end of a rope pull against a like number at the other end, each side endeavoring to drag the other across a line marked between. 2 A laborious effort; supreme contest.
Tui·le·ries (twē′lər·ēz, *Fr.* twēl·rē′) A palace of the French kings in Paris; begun in 1564 and burned in 1871; site occupied by the **Tuileries Gardens,** a public park near the Louvre.
tuille (twēl) *n.* In armor, a steel protection for the thighs, attached by straps to the tassets. [<MF <OF *tieule* <L *tegula* a tile]
tu·i·tion (to͞o·ish′ən, tyo͞o-) *n.* 1 The act or business of teaching any branch of learning; instruction. 2 The charge or payment for instruction. 3 *Archaic* Guardianship; care. See synonyms under EDUCATION, LEARNING, NURTURE. [<AF *tuycioun,* OF *tuicion* <L *tuitio, -onis* a guard, guardianship < *tuitus,* pp. of *tueri* look at, watch] — **tu·i′·tion·al, tu·i′tion·ar′y** (-er′ē) *adj.*
Tu·la (to͞o′lä) 1 A city of west central European Russian S.F.S.R. 2 A city in Hidalgo state, central Mexico; site of the ancient capital of the Toltecs: officially **Tula de Al·len·de** (thä ä·yen′dā).
tu·la·re·mi·a (to͞o′lə·rē′mē·ə) *n.* A disease of rodents, especially rabbits, caused by a micro-organism *(Pasteurella tularensis)* which may be transmitted to man by flies and certain insects, producing an undulant fever; rabbit fever. Also **tu′la·rae′mi·a.** [<NL, from *Tulare* County, California + Gk. *haima* blood]
tu·le (to͞o′lē) *n.* A large bulrush *(Scirpus acutus)* of the sedge family growing on damp or flooded land in the southwestern United States. [<Sp. <Nahuatl *tullin*]
tu·lip (to͞o′lip, tyo͞o′-) *n.* 1 Any of numerous hardy bulbous herbs (genus *Tulipa*) of the lily family, bearing variously colored bell-shaped flowers. 2 A bulb or flower of this plant. [<F *tulipe* <OF *tulipan* <Turkish *tuliband* <Persian *dulband* a turban]
tu·lip·o·ma·ni·a (to͞o′lip·ə·mā′nē·ə, -mān′yə, tyo͞o′-) *n.* A craze for the acquisition or cultivation of tulips; specifically, that which arose in Holland early in the 17th century and which spread into wild speculation like

an epidemic. [< *tulipo-* (<TULIP) + -MANIA] — **tu′lip·o·ma′ni·ac** *n.*

tu·lip·tree (to͞o′lip·trē′, tyo͞o′-) *n.* **1** A large magnoliaceous tree *(Liriodendron tulipifera)* of the eastern United States, with greenish cup-shaped flowers. **2** Any of various other trees having tuliplike flowers.

tu·lip·wood (to͞o′lip·wo͝od′, tyo͞o′-) *n.* **1** The wood of the tuliptree. **2** Any of several ornamental cabinet woods yielded by various trees: so called from their color or markings. **3** Any of the trees themselves.

Tul·la·more (tul′ə·môr′, -mōr′) The county town of County Offaly, Ireland.

tulle (to͞ol, *Fr.* tül) *n.* A fine, silk, open-meshed material, used for veils, etc. [<F, from *Tulle,* a city in SW France, where first made]

Tul·ly (tul′ē) See CICERO, MARCUS TULLIUS.

Tul·sa (tul′sə) A city in NE Oklahoma, on the Arkansas River.

tum·ble (tum′bəl) *v.* **·bled, ·bling** *v.i.* **1** To roll or toss about. **2** To perform acrobatic feats, as somersaults, etc. **3** To fall violently or awkwardly. **4** To move in a careless or headlong manner; stumble. **5** *Colloq.* To understand; comprehend: with *to.* **6** *Metall.* To smooth, clean, or polish, as castings, by friction with each other or with a polishing material, in a rotating box or barrel. — *v.t.* **7** To toss carelessly; cause to fall. **8** To throw into disorder or confusion; disturb; rumple. — *n.* **1** The act of tumbling; a fall. **2** A state of disorder or confusion. [ME *tumbel,* freq. of *tumben,* OE *tumbian* fall, leap] — **tum′bling** *n.*

tum·ble·bug (tum′bəl·bug′) *n.* A scarabaeid beetle that rolls up a ball of dung to enclose its eggs.

tum·ble-down (tum′bəl·doun′) *adj.* Rickety, as if about to fall in pieces; dilapidated.

tumble gear *Mech.* A type of reversing gear comprising a rocking frame adapted to bring either of two idlers into mesh with the driving gear.

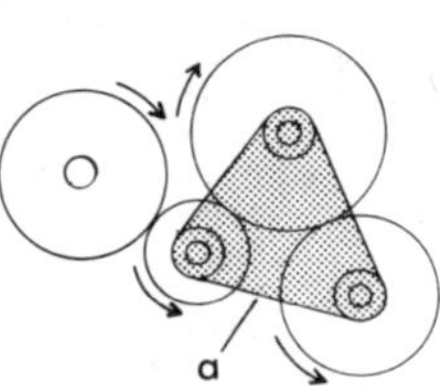

TUMBLE GEAR
a. Rocking frame.

tum·ble-home (tum′bəl·hōm′) *n. Naut.* The inward inclination of a vessel's hull above the line of extreme breadth.

tum·bler (tum′blər) *n.* **1** A drinking glass without a foot; also, its contents. The base was formerly rounded, so that the glass would not stand upright. **2** One who or that which tumbles; especially, an acrobat or contortionist. **3** One of a breed of domestic pigeons noted for the habit of turning forward somersaults during flight. **4** A greyhound used formerly in coursing. **5** In a lock, a latch that engages a bolt and prevents its being shot in either direction unless the tumbler is raised by the key bit. **6** In a firearm lock, a piece attached to the hammer and receiving the thrust of the mainspring. **7** A tumbling box. **8** *Mech.* **a** A piece of metal that projects from a revolving or rocking shaft and communicates motion to another piece. **b** The rocking frame in a tumble gear. **9** *Scot.* A light cart. **10** A child's toy, so formed and weighted as to rock at the slightest touch.

tum·ble·weed (tum′bəl·wēd′) *n.* Any of various plants which, when withered, break from the root and are driven about by the wind, widely scattering their seed.

tumbling box *Metall.* A box, usually cylindrical and mounted on a horizontal shaft, in which articles, as castings, are cleaned by friction against each other and the walls of the box. Also **tumbling barrel.**

tum·brel (tum′bril) *n.* **1** *Obs.* A two-wheeled military covered cart for carrying tools, ammunition, etc. **2** A farmer's cart; especially, a boxlike cart for carrying and dumping dung. **3** A rude cart in which prisoners were taken to the guillotine during the French Revolution. **4** Formerly, a ducking stool set on wheels. Also **tum′bril.** [<OF *tomberel* < *tomber* fall, ult. <Gmc.]

TUMBREL

tu·me·fa·cient (to͞o′mə·fā′shənt, tyo͞o′-) *adj.* Producing or tending to produce tumefaction.

tu·me·fac·tion (to͞o′mə·fak′shən, tyo͞o′-) *n.* **1** Any puffing up of a part, especially as in a tumor. **2** A swelling; puffiness. **3** The act of tumefying; state of being tumefied.

tu·me·fy (to͞o′mə·fī, tyo͞o′-) *v.t.* & *v.i.* **·fied, ·fy·ing** To swell or puff up. [<MF *tuméfier* <L *tumefacere* < *tumere* swell + *facere* make]

Tu·men (to͞o′mun′) A river on the Korea-Manchuria border, flowing 324 miles east to the Sea of Japan.

tu·mer·os·i·ty (to͞o′mə·ros′ə·tē) *n.* The state or quality of being swollen.

tu·mes·cence (to͞o·mes′əns, tyo͞o-) *n.* **1** The state or quality of being swollen. **2** The act or process of becoming tumid, as an organ or part of the body. **3** That which is swollen.

tu·mes·cent (to͞o·mes′ənt, tyo͞o-) *adj.* **1** Swelling; somewhat tumid. **2** Beginning to swell. [<L *tumescens, -entis,* ppr. of *tumescere,* inceptive of *tumere* swell]

tu·mid (to͞o′mid, tyo͞o′-) *adj.* **1** Swollen; enlarged; protuberant. **2** Inflated or pompous in style; bombastic. **3** Bursting; teeming. [<L *tumidus* < *tumere* swell] — **tu′mid·ly** *adv.*

tu·mid·i·ty (to͞o·mid′ə·tē, tyo͞o-) *n.* The state or character of being tumid. Also **tu·mid·ness** (to͞o′mid·nis, tyo͞o′-).

tu·mor (to͞o′mər, tyo͞o′-) *n.* **1** *Pathol.* A local swelling on or in any part of the body, especially from some autonomous morbid growth of tissue which may or may not become malignant; a neoplasm. **2** *Obs.* High-sounding words or style; bombast. **3** *Obs.* A swelling of any kind, as of water. Also *Brit.* **tu′mour.** — **fatty tumor** Lipoma. [<OF *tumour* <L *tumor* a swelling < *tumere* swell] — **tu′mor·ous** *adj.*

tump (tump) *n. Dial.* A little mound or hill, as about a plant; a barrow. [Cf. Welsh *twmp*] — **tump′y** *adj.*

tump·line (tump′līn′) *n. Canadian* A strap passing across the forehead and helping support a load on the back: also called *metump.* Also **tump.** [Prob. <Am. Ind.]

Tu·muc-Hu·mac Mountains (to͞o·mo͝ok′o͞o·mäk′) A range on the border between Brazil and Dutch and Surinam; highest point, 2,800 feet.

tu·mu·lar (to͞o′myə·lər, tyo͞o′-) *adj.* Having the form of a mound.

tu·mu·lose (to͞o′myə·lōs, tyo͞o′-) *adj.* Full of mounds or hills. Also **tu′mu·lous.** [<L *tumulosus* < *tumulus* a mound] — **tu′mu·los′i·ty** (-los′ə·tē) *n.*

tu·mult (to͞o′mult, tyo͞o′-) *n.* **1** The commotion, disturbance, or agitation of a multitude; an uproar; turbulence; hubbub. **2** Any violent commotion or agitation, as of the mind. [<OF *tumulte* <L *tumultus* < *tumere* swell]

Synonyms: agitation, bluster, bustle, commotion, confusion, disorder, disturbance, ferment, flurry, hubbub, hurly-burly, noise, outbreak, racket, riot, turbulence, turmoil, uproar. See NOISE, QUARREL[1], REVOLUTION. *Antonyms*: calmness, peace, quiet, repose, tranquillity.

tu·mul·tu·ous (to͞o·mul′cho͞o·əs, tyo͞o-) *adj.* **1** Characterized by tumult; disorderly. **2** Causing or affected by tumult or agitation; agitated or disturbed. Also **tu·mul′tu·ar′y** (-er′ē). See synonyms under NOISY, TURBULENT, VIOLENT. — **tu·mul′tu·ous·ly, tu·mul′tu·ar′i·ly** *adv.* — **tu·mul′tu·ous·ness, tu·mul′tu·ar′i·ness** *n.*

tu·mu·lus (to͞o′myə·ləs, tyo͞o′-) *n. pl.* **·li** (-lī) A sepulchral mound, often of great size. Compare BARROW[2], CAIRN. [<L, a mound < *tumere* swell]

tun (tun) *n.* **1** A large cask. **2** A brewers' fermenting vat. **3** The amount of malt liquor fermented at one operation; a brew. **4** A varying measure of capacity, usually equal to 252 gallons. — *v.t.* **tunned, tun·ning** **1** To put into a cask or tun. **2** To add to a liquor, as for flavoring. [OE *tunne*]

tu·na[1] (to͞o′nə) *n.* A tunny. Also **tuna fish.** [<Am. Sp., ult. <L *thunnus* TUNNY]

tu·na[2] (to͞o′nə) *n.* **1** A tropical American prickly pear *(Opuntia tuna),* or its edible fruit. **2** One of a number of other prickly pears. [<Am. Sp., prob. <Taino]

tun·a·ble (to͞o′nə·bəl, tyo͞o′-) *adj.* **1** That may be put in tune. **2** Being in tune. **3** *Obs.* Tuneful; musical. Also **tune′a·ble.** — **tun′a·ble·ness** *n.* — **tun′a·bly** *adv.*

Tun·bridge Wells (tun′brij) A municipal borough in SW Kent, England.

tun·dra (tun′drə, to͞on′-) *n.* A rolling, treeless, often marshy plain of Siberia, arctic North America, etc. [<Russian <Lapp]

tune (to͞on, tyo͞on) *n.* **1** A melodious succession of musical tones adjusted to some measure and constituting one whole; a melody or air. **2** A setting for a hymn or psalm used in worship. **3** The state or quality of being in the proper pitch or key. **4** Concord or unison. **5** Suitable temper or humor; state of mind. **6** *Obs.* A musical tone or sound. — **to change one's tune** To assume a different manner or style. — **to the tune of** To the serious or exorbitant amount of: *to the tune of* a thousand dollars. — *v.* **tuned, tun·ing** *v.t.* **1** To adjust to a musical standard; put in tune; attune. **2** To adapt to a particular tone, expression, or mood. **3** To bring into harmony or accord. **4** To utter or express musically; sing. — *v.i.* **5** To be in harmony. — **to tune in** To adjust a radio receiver to the frequency of (a station, broadcast, etc.). — **to tune out** To adjust a radio receiver to exclude (interference, a station, etc.). — **to tune up** **1** To bring (musical instruments) to a common pitch. **2** To adjust (a machine, engine, etc.) to proper working order. [Var. of TONE] — **tun′ing** *adj.* & *n.*

tune·ful (to͞on′fəl, tyo͞on′-) *adj.* Musically disposed; melodious; musical. — **tune′ful·ly** *adv.* — **tune′ful·ness** *n.*

tune·less (to͞on′lis, tyo͞on′-) *adj.* **1** Not being in tune. **2** Not employed in making music; silent. **3** Lacking in rhythm, melody, etc. — **tune′less·ly** *adv.* — **tune′less·ness** *n.*

tun·er (to͞o′nər, tyo͞o′-) *n.* **1** One who or that which tunes. **2** One who puts musical instruments, as pianos, in tune. **3** *Telecom.* A radio receiver without audio-frequency amplifiers, speaker, etc.

tune-up (to͞on′up′, tyo͞on′-) *n. Colloq.* An adjustment to bring a motor or other device into proper operating condition.

Tung (do͝ong) A river of SE China, flowing 250 miles SW and west from southern Kiangsi province to a delta in east central Kwangtung province, emptying into the Canton River.

Tung·chow (to͝ong′jō′) A former name for NANTUNG.

tung oil (tung) A yellow, ill-smelling oil extracted from the seeds of the Chinese **tung tree** *(Aleurites fordi),* now cultivated in the U. S.: used in paints, varnishes, etc., as a highly effective drying agent, and also as a waterproofing agent. [<Chinese *t'ung* the tung tree]

tung·state (tung′stāt) *n. Chem.* A salt of tungstic acid: sodium *tungstate.*

tung·sten (tung′stən) *n.* A steel-gray, brittle, heavy metallic element of the chromium group (symbol W), occurring in sheelite and in wolframite, having a high melting point and much used in the manufacture of filaments for electric lamps and tungsten-steel tools. Also called *wolfram.* See ELEMENT. [<Sw. < *tung* weighty + *sten* stone] — **tung·sten·ic** (tung·sten′ik) *adj.*

tungsten lamp An incandescent electric lamp having a filament of metallic tungsten.

tungsten steel A hard, tenacious steel that contains tungsten.

tung·stic (tung′stik) *adj. Chem.* Of, pertaining to, derived from, or containing tungsten, especially in its highest valence. [<TUNGST(EN) + -IC]

tungstic acid *Chem.* Either of two acids consisting of tungsten oxide combined with water, and uniting with bases to form salts; especially, the yellow crystalline monohydrate, H_2WO_4.

tung·stite (tung′stīt) *n.* A yellow or yellowish-green native tungsten trioxide, WO_3. Also **tungstic ocher.**

Tung·ting (do͝ong′ting′), **Lake** A lake in NE Hunan province, SE central China; one of the largest lakes in China; 1,450 square miles.

Tun·gus (to͞on·go͞oz′) *n.* **1** One of a Mongoloid people of the Tungusic group inhabiting eastern Siberia. **2** The language of the Tungus, belonging to the Manchu-Tungusic subfamily of Altaic languages: also *Tungusic.* Also **Tun·guz′.**

Tun·gus·i·an (to͞on·go͞oz′ē·ən) *adj.* Of or per-

taining to the Tungus or their language. — *n.* One of the Tungus.
Tun·gus·ic (tŏŏn·gŏŏz′ik) *adj.* **1** Of, pertaining to, or denoting a group of tribes including the Tungus and Manchus. **2** Tungusian. — *n.* The Tungus language.
Tun·gus·ka (tŏŏn·gŏŏs′kä) Any of three rivers in north central Asiatic Russian S.F.S.R., known as the **Upper Tunguska** (see ANGARA), the **Stony** (or **Middle**) **Tunguska,** flowing 975 miles NW and west to the Yenisei, and the **Lower Tunguska,** flowing 1,587 miles north and NW to the Yenisei.
tu·nic (tōō′nik, tyōō′-) *n.* **1** Among the ancient Greeks and Romans, a body garment, with or without sleeves, reaching to the knees: worn usually without a girdle. **2** A modern outer garment gathered at the waist, as a short overskirt or a blouse. **3** A surcoat worn over armor. **4** A tunica. **5** *Bot.* Any loose membranous skin enveloping an organ, as a seed coat. **6** *Brit.* The undercoat worn by soldiers, policemen, etc. **7** A bishop's tunicle; a dalmatic. [<F *tunique* <L *tunica* <Semitic]
tu·ni·ca (tōō′nə·kə, tyōō′-) *n.* *pl.* **·cae** (-sē) *Biol.* A covering or investing part; a mantle of tissue, as of the kidney, ovaries, etc.; tunic. [<NL <L, a tunic]
tu·ni·cate (tōō′nə·kit, -kāt, tyōō′-) *adj.* **1** *Bot.* Covered with a tunic, as the bulb of an onion. **2** *Zool.* Having a tunic; of or pertaining to the tunicates. Also **tu′ni·cat′ed.** — *n.* Any of a subphylum (*Tunicata* or *Urochordata*) of small marine chordates covered with a transparent tunic, as the ascidians. [<NL *tunicata* <L *tunicata (animalia)* coated (animals), neut. pl. of *tunicatus,* pp. of *tunicare* clothe with a tunic < *tunica* a tunic]
tu·ni·cle (tōō′ni·kəl, tyōō′-) *n.* **1** A light or fine tunic. **2** A slight natural covering. **3** A short ecclesiastical vestment. [<L *tunicula,* dim. of *tunica* a tunic]
tuning fork A fork-shaped piece of steel which vibrates with a definite frequency when struck: used to measure the pitch of musical tones.
Tu·nis (tōō′nis, tyōō′-) **1** A former Barbary state of northern Africa. **2** The capital and chief port of Tunisia, on the Mediterranean.
Tu·ni·sia (tōō·nish′ə, -nish′ē·ə, -nē′zhə, tyōō-) A republic in northern Africa, proclaimed July, 1957; 48,195 square miles; capital, Tunis; formerly, *Tunis.*
Tu·ni·sian (tōō·nish′ən, -nē′zhən, tyōō-) *adj.* Of or relating to Tunisia, or Tunis, or their inhabitants. — *n.* **1** An inhabitant or native of Tunisia or Tunis. **2** The speech of Tunisia, a North Arabic dialect.
tunk·et (tung′kit) *n.* *U.S. Dial.* Hell: a euphemistic expletive. [Origin unknown]
tun·nage (tun′ij) *n.* *Brit.* Tonnage.
tun·nel (tun′əl) *n.* **1** An artificial subterranean passageway or gallery, especially one under a hill, etc., as for a railway. **2** Any similar passageway under or through something. **3** A funnel. **4** The main flue or shaft of a chimney or the like. **5** An adit or level in a mine. — *v.* **·neled** or **·nelled, ·nel·ing** or **·nel·ling** *v.t.* **1** To make a tunnel through. **2** To shape or make in the form of a tunnel: to *tunnel* a passage. — *v.i.* **3** To make a tunnel. [Fusion of OF *tonnelle* a partridge net and *tonel,* dim. of *tonne* a cask] — **tun′nel·er** or **tun′nel·ler** *n.*
tunnel disease Caisson disease.
tun·ny (tun′ē) *n.* *pl.* **·nies** **1** A large, oily, marine fish (family *Thunnidae*) related to

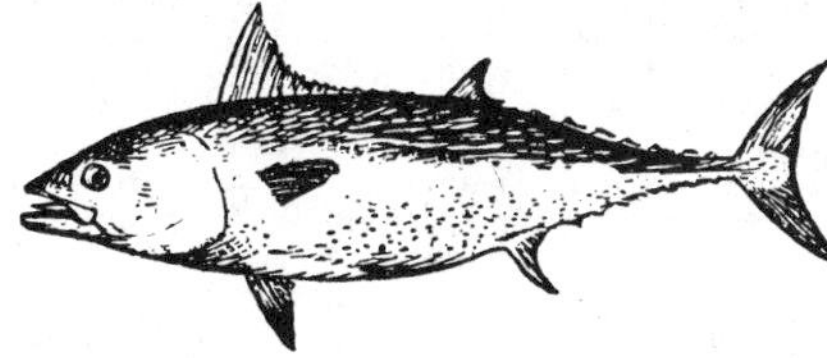

GREAT TUNNY

the mackerel, especially the **great tunny** (*Thunnus thynnus*) of warm seas, sometimes weighing 1,500 pounds. **2** One of various related fishes, as the albacore and the California horse mackerel (*Trachurus symmetricus*). [<OF *thon* <L *thunnus* <Gk. *thynnos*]
Tu·ol·um·ne River (tōō·ol′ə·mē) A river in central California, flowing 110 miles west to the San Joaquin River.
tup (tup) *n.* **1** A ram, or male sheep. **2** The striking part of a power hammer. — *v.t.* & *v.i.* **tupped, tup·ping** To copulate with (a female): said of the ram. [ME *tupe, tope,* prob. < Scand. Cf. Norw. & Sw. *tupp* a cock.]
tu·pe·lo (tōō′pə·lō) *n.* *pl.* **·los** **1** One of several trees of Asia and the southeastern United States (genus *Nyssa*), especially the sourgum or blackgum. **2** The wood of any of these trees. [<Muskhogean]
Tu·pi (tōō·pē′) *n.* *pl.* **Tu·pis** or **Tu·pi** **1** A member of any of a group of South American Indian tribes, comprising the northern branch of the Tupian stock, and occupying the Amazon, Tapajós, and Xingú valleys. **2** The language spoken by the Tupis, used as a lingua franca along the Amazon: also called *Neengatu.* [<Tupian, a comrade]
Tu·pi·an (tōō·pē′ən) *adj.* Of or pertaining to the Tupis or their language. — *n.* A large linguistic stock of South American Indians of some one hundred tribes of the Tupis and Guaranis, scattered throughout the continent (except in Venezuela): also **Tu·pi′-Gua′ra·ni′** (-gwä′rä·nē′).
Tu·pun·ga·to (tōō′pōōng·gä′tō) A peak in the Andes on the Argentine-Chile border; 21,940 feet.
tuque (tōōk, tyōōk) *n.* A Canadian cap consisting of a knitted cylindrical bag with tapered ends, worn by thrusting one end inside the other, for tobogganing, etc. [< dial. F (Canadian) <F *toque* TOQUE]
tu quo·que (tōō kwō′kwē, tyōō) *Latin* A retort in kind from a person assailed: also used attributively; literally, thou also.
tu·ra·cou (tōō′rä·kōō′) *n.* An African bird (*Turacus fischeri*) related to the cuckoo, remarkable for its red-and-green plumage: also called *touraco.* [<F *touraco* < native West African name]
Tu·ra·ni·an (tōō·rā′nē·ən, tyōō-) *adj.* Of or pertaining to a large family of agglutinative languages of Europe and northern Asia, neither Indo-European nor Semitic, specifically known as the Ural-Altaic languages, or any of the people who speak them. — *n.* **1** One whose mother tongue is a Ural-Altaic language; a person of Ural-Altaic stock. **2** The Ural-Altaic languages collectively. **3** Theoretically, one of an unknown nomadic people who antedated the Aryans in Europe and Asia. [<Persian *Tūrān,* a country north of the Oxus River]
tur·ban (tûr′bən) *n.* **1** An Oriental head covering consisting of a sash or shawl, twisted about the head or about a cap. **2** Any similar headdress. **3** A round-crowned brimless hat for women or children. [<F *turban, turbant* <Pg. *turbante* <Turkish *tülbend,* dial. alter. of *dülbend* <Persian *dulband* < *dul* a turn + *band* a band] — **tur′·baned** (-bənd) *adj.*
tur·ba·ry (tûr′bər·ē) *n.* *pl.* **·ries** **1** In English law, the liberty of digging turf or peat upon another's ground. **2** A place where turf or peat is dug. [<AF *turberie,* OF *tourberie* < *tourbe* peat <LG *turf, turv* turf]
tur·bel·lar·i·an (tûr′bə·lâr′ē·ən) *n.* Any of a class (*Turbellaria*) of motile aquatic flatworms having a ciliated epidermis and sometimes brilliantly colored: includes the planarians. [<NL <L *turbellae* a tumult, pl. dim. of *turba* a crowd]
tur·beth (tûr′bəth), **tur·bith** See TURPETH.
tur·bid (tûr′bid) *adj.* **1** Having the sediment or lees stirred up; cloudy; muddy. **2** Being in a state of confusion; disturbed. See synonyms under THICK. [<L *turbidus* < *turbare* trouble < *turba* a crowd] — **tur′bid·ly** *adv.* — **tur′bid·ness, tur·bid·i·ty** (tûr·bid′ə·tē) *n.*
tur·bi·dim·e·ter (tûr′bə·dim′ə·tər) *n.* An instrument for measuring the turbidity of a liquid. [<TURBIDI(TY) + -METER]
tur·bi·nal (tûr′bə·nəl) *adj.* Spirally coiled; turbinate; top-shaped. — *n.* A turbinate bone or cartilage. [<L *turbo, -inis* a whirlwind, top]
tur·bi·nate (tûr′bə·nit, -nāt) *adj.* **1** Top-shaped; also, spinning like a top. **2** *Zool.* Tapering from a broad base to the apex, as certain spiral shells. **3** *Anat.* Pertaining to one of the thin, curved bones on the walls of the nasal passages. Also **tur′bi·nat′ed.** [<L *turbinatus* < *turbo, -inis* a whirlwind]
tur·bi·na·tion (tûr′bə·nā′shən) *n.* **1** A cone-like formation. **2** The act, state, or condition of spinning like a top.
tur·bine (tûr′bin, -bīn) *n.* An engine consisting of one or more rotary units, mounted on a shaft and usually provided with a series of curved vanes, actuated by the reaction, impulse, or suction of steam, water, gas, or other fluid under pressure. [<F <L *turbo, -inis* a whirlwind, top]

TURBINE
Type used in an electric-light plant.

tur·bit (tûr′bit) *n.* One of a breed of domestic pigeons having a small head with the feathers at the back curled upward. [Appar. <L *turbo, -inis* a top; so called with ref. to its shape]
turbo- *combining form* A turbine; related to or operated by a turbine or turbines: *turbojet.* [<L *turbo* a top]
tur·bo·fan (tûr′bō·fan′) *n.* *Aeron.* **1** A compressor having ducted fans which supply air to a jet engine. **2** The engine using such a fan.
tur·bo-gen·er·a·tor (tûr′bō·jen′ə·rā′tər) *n.* An electric power-generating machine adapted for direct coupling to a steam turbine.
tur·bo·jet (tûr′bō·jet′) *n.* *Aeron.* **1** A gas turbine which drives the air compressor and auxiliaries of certain types of jet engines. **2** The engine itself.
tur·bo·prop (tûr′bō·prop′) *n.* *Aeron.* **1** A gas turbine connecting directly with the propeller. **2** An engine having such a turbine. [<TURBO- + PROP(ELLER)]
tur·bo·su·per·charg·er (tûr′bō·sōō′pər·chär′·jər) *n.* *Aeron.* A compact, highly efficient supercharging device utilizing exhaust gases, for use on aircraft engines operating at very high altitudes.
tur·bot (tûr′bət) *n.* *pl.* **·bot** or **·bots** **1** A large European flatfish (*Psetta maxima*) esteemed as food. **2** One of various related flatfishes. [<AF *turbut,* OF *tourbout,* ? <OSw. *törnbut* < *törn* a thorn + *but* the butt]
tur·bu·lence (tûr′byə·ləns) *n.* **1** The state or condition of being violently disturbed, restless, or confused. **2** *Physics* The irregular flow of a gas or fluid caused by an obstacle or by friction, as of a ship or airplane in rapid motion. **3** *Meteorol.* A disturbed condition of the atmosphere due to irregular wind currents. Also **tur′bu·len·cy.**
tur·bu·lent (tûr′byə·lənt) *adj.* **1** Being in violent agitation or commotion. **2** Inclined to rebel; insubordinate. **3** Having a tendency to disturb or throw into confusion. [<MF <L *turbulentus* full of disturbance < *turbare.* See TURBID.] — **tur′bu·lent·ly** *adv.*
Synonyms: agitated, blustering, boisterous, disorderly, disturbed, insurgent, mutinous, obstreperous, rebellious, refractory, riotous, seditious, tumultuous, wild. See NOISY, VIOLENT.
Tur·co (tûr′kō) *n.* *pl.* **·cos** An Algerian light-infantryman serving in the French army; an Algerian tirailleur. [<F <Sp., a Turk]
Tur·co·man (tûr′kə·mən) See TURKOMAN.
tur·di·form (tûr′də·fôrm) *adj.* Thrushlike in form or structure. [<L *turdus* a thrush + -FORM]
tur·dine (tûr′din, -dīn) *adj.* **1** Belonging or pertaining to a large and widely distributed family (*Turdidae*) of singing birds, including thrushes and bluebirds. **2** Pertaining to the subfamily (*Turdinae*) which includes the true thrushes. [<NL, subfamily name <L *turdus* a thrush]
tu·reen (tōō·rēn′, tyōō-) *n.* A deep, covered dish, as for soup. [Earlier *terrene* <F *terrine.* Doublet of TERRINE.]

Tu·renne (tü·ren′), **Viscount de,** 1611–75, Henri de la Tour d'Auvergne, French general and marshal.

turf (tûrf) *n. pl.* **turfs** (*Archaic* **turves**) **1** A mass of matted roots of grass and other fine plants filling the upper stratum of certain soils; a sod. **2** Peat. **3** Loosely, a grass plot. **4** A racecourse; horse-racing: in the phrase **the turf.** **5** *Slang* **a** A home territory, especially that of a youthful street gang, defended against invasion by rival gangs. **b** Any place regarded possessively as the center of one's activity or interest: Philadelphia is his *turf.* — *v.t.* To cover with turf; sod. [OE] — **turf′y** *adj.*

Tur·fan (to͝or′fän′) A depression in eastern Sinkiang-Uigur Autonomous Region, NW China, lowest point of the Chinese mainland (940 feet below sea level); center of an ancient Indo-Iranian civilization (A.D. 200–400) and site of the capital of a Uigur empire (about 800–1200).

turf·man (tûrf′mən) *n. pl.* **·men** (-mən) A man who is devoted to or connected with horse-racing.

Tur·ge·nev (to͝or·gā′nyef), **Ivan Sergeyevich,** 1818–83, Russian novelist. Also **Tur·ge′niev.**

tur·gent (tûr′jənt) *adj. Obs.* Turgid. [<L *turgens, -entis,* ppr. of *turgere* swell] — **tur′·gent·ly** *adv.*

tur·ges·cence (tûr·jes′əns) *n.* **1** The process of swelling up; the state of being swollen. **2** Hence, empty pompousness; inflation. Also **tur·ges′cen·cy.** [<Med. L *turgescentia* <L *turgescens, -entis,* ppr. of *turgescere,* inceptive of *turgere* swell] — **tur·ges′cent** *adj.* — **tur·ges′cent·ly** *adv.*

tur·gid (tûr′jid) *adj.* **1** Unnaturally distended, as by contained air or liquid; swollen. **2** Figuratively, inflated; bombastic; tumid: a *turgid* tale of woman wronged. [<L *turgidus* < *turgere* swell] — **tur′gid·ly** *adv.*

tur·gid·i·ty (tûr·jid′ə·tē) *n.* **1** The state or quality of being turgid. **2** *Biol.* The internal pressure of a cell against its enclosing membrane. Also **tur·gid·ness** (tûr′jid·nis).

tur·gite (tûr′jīt) *n.* A fibrous, earthy iron ore, found as a reddish-black or dark-red ferric hydroxide. [from *Turginsk,* a copper mine in the Ural Mountains]

tur·gor (tûr′gər) *n.* **1** The state of being turgid; turgidity. **2** *Physiol.* The normal condition of the blood vessels and of cells distended by their protoplasmic contents: also **vital turgor.** [<LL <L < *turgere* swell]

Tur·got (tür·gō′), **Anne Robert Jacques,** 1727–81, French statesman, financier, and economist.

Tu·rin (to͝or′in, tyo͝or′-, to͞o·rin′, tyo͞o-) A city on the Po river in NW Italy; capital of the kingdom of Sardinia until 1860 and of Italy until 1864; a major industrial and transportation center: Italian *Torino.*

Turk (tûrk) *n.* **1** A native or inhabitant of Turkey; an Ottoman. **2** One of any of the peoples speaking any of the Turkic languages, and ranging from the Adriatic to the Sea of Okhotsk: believed to be of the same ultimate extraction as the Mongols. **3** Loosely, a Moslem. **4** A Turkish horse.

Turk·cap lily (tûrk′kap′) See under LILY.

Tur·ke·stan (tûr′kə·stan′, -stän′) A region of central Asia extending from the Caspian Sea to the Gobi Desert and divided by the Pamir and Tien Shan mountain systems into **Russian** (or **Western**) **Turkestan,** comprising the Kazakh, Kirghiz, Tadzhik, Turkmen, and Uzbek S.S.R. (also called *Soviet Central Asia*); and **Chinese** (or **Eastern**) **Turkestan,** comprising the Sinkiang-Uigur Autonomous Region.

tur·key (tûr′kē) *n. pl.* **·keys** **1** A large American bird (family *Meleagridae*) related to the pheasant, having the head naked and the tail extensible upward and sideward; especially, the American domesticated turkey (*Meleagris gallopavo*): much esteemed as food. **2** A guinea fowl. **3** *U. S. Slang* A play (occasionally, a motion picture) that is a failure. [Short for *turkey cock* the guinea fowl, from *Turkey*; later applied erroneously to the American bird]

Tur·key (tûr′kē) A republic of Asia Minor and SE Europe; 296,108 square miles (Turkey in Asia, known as *Anatolia,* 287,043 square miles, Turkey in Europe, 9,065 square miles); capital, Ankara.

turkey buzzard A sooty-black vulture of tropical America (*Cathartes aura*), with a naked red head and neck.

TURKEY BUZZARD
(Length, 30 inches; wingspread, 6 feet)

Turkey carpet A handmade Turkish carpet or one having a Turkish design and texture. Also **Turkish carpet.**

turkey cock **1** A male turkey. **2** One who struts and behaves in a pompous, conceited manner.

turkey gobbler A turkey cock.

turkey red **1** A brilliant red pigment, or its color. **2** Cotton cloth dyed with this permanent bright red.

tur·key-trot (tûr′kē·trot′) *n.* A dance consisting of a stop-step, glide, and turn to syncopated music, the feet being kept well apart and a swinging motion being given to the shoulders: popular in the early 20th century.

turkey vulture The turkey buzzard.

Tur·ki (to͝or′kē) *adj.* **1** Of or pertaining to any of the languages included in the Turkic subfamily of Altaic languages. **2** Of or pertaining to any of the peoples speaking any of these languages, as the Osmanlis and Chuvashes of Turkey, NW Persia, Transcaucasia, etc., and the Asian Tatar tribes, as the Uigurs, Uzbeks, Kipchaks, Turkomans, etc., of Mongolia and Turkestan. — *n.* **1** The Turkic languages. **2** A member of any of the Turki peoples.

Turk·ic (tûr′kik) *n.* A subfamily of the Altaic family of languages, including Osmanli or Turkish, Azerbaijani, Uzbek, Chuvash, Yakut, etc. — *adj.* Pertaining to this linguistic subfamily, or to any of the peoples speaking these languages.

Turk·ish (tûr′kish) *adj.* **1** Of or pertaining to Turkey or the Turks. **2** Of or relating to the Turkic subfamily of Altaic languages, especially to Osmanli. — *n.* The Altaic language of Turkey; Osmanli.

Turkish bath A bath originating in the East in which sweating is induced by exposure to high temperature, usually in a room heated by steam, followed by washing, rubbing, kneading, or the like.

Turkish delight A sweetmeat of Turkish origin, usually consisting of cubes having a gelatinous consistency coated with powdered sugar and having any of various fruit flavors. Also **Turkish paste.**

Turkish Empire The Ottoman Empire.

Turkish pound A Turkish lira. Symbol £T.

Turkish towel A heavy, rough towel with loose, uncut pile. Also **turkish towel.**

Turk·ism (tûr′kiz·əm) *n.* **1** The religion, or the social or political system, characteristic of the Turks. **2** Any distinctive peculiarity of Turkish speech or custom.

Turk·men (tûrk′men) *n.* The Turkic language of the Turkomans.

Turk·men Soviet Socialist Republic (tûrk′·men) A constituent republic of the U. S. S. R. in Central Asia; 189,370 square miles; capital, Ashkhabad. Also **Turk·me·ni·stan** (tûrk′me·ni·stan′, -stän′; *Russian* to͝ork′mye·nyi·stän′).

tur·kois (tûr′koiz) See TURQUOISE.

Tur·ko·man (tûr′kə·mən) *n. pl.* **·mans** **1** A member of any of the Turki peoples dwelling in those parts of Turkestan comprising the Russian Turkmen, Uzbek, and Kazakh Soviet Republics. **2** Turkmen. Also spelled *Turcoman.* Also **Turk′man.** [<Persian *Turkumān* one like a Turk] — **Turk·me·ni·an** (tûrk·mē′·nē·ən) *adj.* & *n.* — **Turk·o·man·ic** (tûr′kə·man′ik) *adj.*

Turks and Cai·cos Islands (tûrks, kā′kəs) An archipelago SE of the Bahamas, comprising a dependency of Jamaica in The West Indies; 202 square miles.

Turk's-cap lily (tûrks′kap′) See under LILY.

Turk's-head (tûrks′hed′) *n.* An ornamented knot of turbanlike form.

Tur·ku (to͝or′ko͞o) A city of SW Finland, on the Gulf of Bothnia: Swedish *Åbo.*

tur·ma·line (tûr′mə·lēn) See TOURMALINE.

tur·mer·ic (tûr′mər·ik) *n.* **1** The root of an East Indian plant (*Curcuma longa*) of the ginger family, used as a condiment, aromatic stimulant, dyestuff, etc. **2** The plant. **3** Any of several plants resembling turmeric. — *adj.* Of, pertaining to, or saturated with turmeric. [Earlier *tarmaret,* ? <F *terre mérite* deserving earth <Med. L *terra merita*; ult. origin uncertain]

turmeric paper A paper, yellow from saturation with the extract of turmeric, used as a test for alkalis, turning it brown, and for boric acid, turning it red-brown: also called *curcuma paper.*

tur·moil (tûr′moil) *n.* Confused motion; disturbance; tumult. See synonyms under TUMULT. — *v.t.* & *v.i. Archaic* To be or cause to be in a state of turmoil. [? <OF *tremouille* hopper of a mill <L *tremere* tremble; prob. infl. in form by *turn* and *moil*]

turn (tûrn) *v.t.* **1** To give a rotary motion to; cause to rotate, as about an axis. **2** To change the position of, as by rotating: to *turn* a trunk on its side. **3** To move so that the upper side becomes the under: to *turn* a page. **4** To bring the subsoil of to the surface, as by plowing or spading. **5** To alter (a garment) by reversing the material: to *turn* a cuff. **6** To reverse the arrangement or order of; cause to be upside down. **7** To upset mentally; dement or distract; infatuate. **8** To revolve mentally; ponder: often with *over.* **9** To sprain or strain: to *turn* one's ankle in running. **10** To nauseate (the stomach). **11** To shape (an object revolving in a lathe, etc.) in rounded form by application of a cutting tool. **12** To give rounded or curved form to. **13** To give graceful or finished form to: to *turn* a phrase. **14** To perform by revolving: to *turn* cartwheels. **15** To bend, curve, fold, or twist. **16** To bend or blunt (the edge of a knife, etc.). **17** To change or transform; convert: to *turn* water into wine. **18** To translate: to *turn* French into English. **19** To exchange for an equivalent: to *turn* stocks into cash. **20** To adapt to some use or purpose; apply: to *turn* information to good account. **21** To cause to become as specified: The sight *turned* him sick. **22** To change the color of. **23** To make sour or rancid; ferment or curdle. **24** To change the direction of. **25** To direct or aim; point. **26** To change the direction or focus of (thought, attention, etc.). **27** To deflect or divert: to *turn* a blow. **28** To repel: to *turn* a charge. **29** To go around or to the other side of: to *turn* a corner. **30** To pass or go beyond: to *turn* twenty-one. **31** To cause or compel to go; send; drive: to *turn* a beggar from one's door. **32** To keep circulating in trade: to *turn* goods or money. **33** *Obs.* To pervert. — *v.i.* **34** To move around an axis or center; rotate; revolve. **35** To move completely or partially on or as if on an axis: He *turned* and ran. **36** To change position; also, to roll from side to side, as in bed. **37** To take a new direction: We *turned* north. **38** To reverse position; become inverted. **39** To reverse direction or flow: The tide has *turned.* **40** To change the direction or focus of one's thought, attention, etc.: Let us *turn* to the next problem. **41** To depend; hinge: with *on* or *upon.* **42** To be affected with giddiness; whirl, as the head. **43** To become upset or nauseated, as the stomach. **44** To change attitude, sympathy, or allegiance: to *turn* on one's neighbors. **45** To rebel; act in retaliation: The worm *turns*; to *turn* on one's persecutors. **46** To become transformed; change: The water *turned* into ice. **47** To become as specified: His hair *turned* gray. **48** To change color: said especially of leaves. **49** To become sour, rancid, or fermented, as milk or wine. **50** *Naut.* To tack or put about. **51** *Obs.* To vacillate. See synonyms under BEND, CHANGE, REVOLVE. — **to turn against** To become or cause to become opposed or hostile to. — **to turn an honest dollar** (or **penny**) To earn money honestly. — **to turn down** **1** To diminish the flow, volume, etc., of: *Turn down* the gas. **2** *Colloq.* **a** To reject or refuse, as a proposal, or request. **b** To refuse the request, proposal, etc., of. — **to turn in** **1** To fold or double. **2** To bend or incline inward. **3** To deliver; hand over. **4** *Colloq.* To go to bed. — **to turn off** **1** To stop the operation, flow, etc., of. **2** To leave the direct road; make a turn. **3** To deflect or divert. **4** *Brit.* To dismiss; discharge. — **to turn on** **1** To set in operation, flow, etc.: to *turn on* an engine. **2** *Slang*

To take or experience the mental and perceptual effects of taking a psychedelic drug, as marijuana, LSD, etc. 3 *Slang* To arrange for (someone) to take or be affected by such a drug. 4 *Slang* To evoke in (someone) a profound or rapt response, as though under the influence of a psychedelic drug: Baroque music really *turned* him *on*. **—to turn out** 1 To turn inside out. 2 To eject or expel; put out. 3 To dismiss or discharge. 4 To turn off (def. 1). 5 To bend or incline outward. 6 To produce by work or toil; make. 7 To come or go out, as for duty or service. 8 To prove (to be); be found. 9 To become or result. 10 To equip or fit; dress. 11 *Colloq.* To get out of bed. **—to turn over** 1 To change the position of; invert. 2 To upset; overturn. 3 To hand over; transfer or relinquish. 4 To do business to the amount of. 5 To invest and get back (capital). 6 To use in trade or exchange; buy and then sell: to *turn over* merchandise. **—to turn tail** To run away; flee. **—to turn to** 1 To set to work. 2 To seek aid from. 3 To refer or apply to. **—to turn up** 1 To bring or fold the under side upward. 2 To bend or incline upward. 3 To bring or be brought to view by plowing, digging, etc.; find or be found. 4 To increase the flow, volume, etc., of. 5 To put in an appearance; arrive. *—n.* 1 The act of turning, or the state of being turned. 2 A change to another direction, motion, or position: a *turn* of the tide. 3 A deflection or deviation from a course; a bend; a change in policy or trend: a *turn* of fortune. 4 The point at which a change takes place: a *turn* for the better in a crisis or an illness. 5 Motion about or as about a center; a rotation or revolution: the *turn* of a crank. 6 Favorable, fitting, or regular time or chance in some succession or rotation, or the work it offers; a job; also, a round; spell: one's *turn* to read, a *turn* of work. 7 Characteristic form or style; distinguishing shape; mold; cast: the *turn* of an ankle or sentence. 8 Disposition; tendency; manner: a humorous *turn*; a knack or special ability: a *turn* for study. 9 A deed performed, regarded as aiding or injuring another: an ill *turn*; also, an advantage proposed or gained: It served his *turn*. 10 A walk, drive, or trip to and fro; promenade: a *turn* in the park. 11 A trip back and forth in taking a load of anything: *turns* made to a mill; also, the load so taken. 12 A round in a skein or coil. 13 *Music* An instrumental or vocal embellishment formed by a group of four notes rapidly performed, the first a tone above and the third a tone below the principal tone, which occupies the second and fourth positions. In an **inverted turn** the tones are reversed in order. 14 *Colloq.* A spell of dizziness or faintness; a shock to the nerves, as from alarm: It gave her quite a *turn*. 15 A variation or difference in type or kind. 16 A short theatrical act of any description; also, in sport, a contest; a bout. 17 A twist, as of a rope, around a tree or post. 18 A transaction on the stock exchange, involving purchase and sale, or the reverse; also, any business transaction. 19 In infantry drill, a maneuver in which a line of troops changes the direction of its front, usually in preparation for marching. **—at every turn** On every occasion; constantly. **—by turns** 1 In alternation or sequence. 2 At intervals. **—in turn** One after another; in proper order or sequence. **—out of turn** Not in proper order or prescribed order or sequence. **—to a turn** Just right; perfectly or exactly: said especially of cooked food, in allusion to the turning of the spit in roasting. **—to take turns** To act, play, etc. in proper order. ◆ Homophones: *tern, terne*. [Fusion of OE *tyrnan* and *turnian* and OF *turner*, all <L *tornare* turn in a lathe < *turnus* a lathe <Gk. *tornos*]

turn·a·bout (tûrn′ə·bout′) *n.* 1 One who overturns things; a radical. 2 A merry-go-round. 3 A turn-about-face.

turn-a·bout-face (tûrn′ə·bout′fās′) *n.* A change from one loyalty or viewpoint to another; adoption of new opinions or policy: also *turnabout*.

turn·a·round (tûrn′ə·round′) *n.* 1 The time required for maintenance, refueling, discharging or loading cargo, etc., during a round trip of a truck, ship, aircraft, etc. 2 A space, as in a driveway, large enough for the turning around of a vehicle. 3 A shift or reversal of a trend, procedure, movement, etc.

turn·buck·le (tûrn′·buk′əl) *n. Mech.* A form of coupling so threaded that when connected lengthwise between two metal rods it may be turned so as to regulate the distance between them.

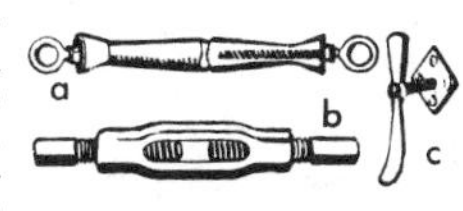

TURNBUCKLES
a. Insulated for electric wires.
b. Type for metal tie rods.
c. For window shutters.

turn·coat (tûrn′kōt′) *n.* One who goes over to the opposite side or party; a renegade.

turn-down (tûrn′doun′) *adj.* Folded down, as a collar; also, capable of being turned down.

turned comma *Printing* An inverted comma, as a single initial quotation mark.

turn·er[1] (tûr′nər) *n.* One who turns; specifically, one who fashions objects with a lathe.

turn·er[2] (tûr′nər) *n.* A gymnast; a member of a turnverein. [<G < *turnen* engage in gymnastics <F *turner* turn]

Tur·ner (tûr′nər), **Frederick Jackson,** 1861–1932, U.S. historian. **—Joseph Mallord William,** 1775–1851, English painter.

turn·er·y (tûr′nər·ē) *n. pl.* **·er·ies** 1 A place where lathework is carried on. 2 The act or process of turning, or articles and ornamentation made with a lathe.

turn·hall (tûrn′hôl′) *n.* A building in which gymnasts, especially members of a turnverein, practice; a gymnasium. Also *German* **Turn·hal·le** (tŏŏrn′häl′ə). [<G *turnhalle* < *turnen* exercise + *halle* a hall]

turn indicator In motor vehicles, any device, as a flashing light, which enables the driver to signal his intention to turn.

turn·ing (tûr′ning) *n.* 1 The act of one who turns. 2 The art of shaping wood, metal, etc., in a lathe. 3 Any deviation from a straight or customary course; a winding; bend.

turning point 1 The point of a decisive change in direction of action; a crisis. 2 The point at which the direction of a motion is reversed. 3 A marked object toward which a surveying instrument is sighted from each of two positions in the process of leveling.

tur·nip (tûr′nip) *n.* 1 The fleshy globular edible root of either of two brassicaceous biennial herbs, *Brassica rapa* and the rutabaga. 2 Either of the plants. [Earlier *turnepe*, ? <F *tour* a turn, rotation (<L *tornus* a lathe) + ME *nepe* <L *napus* a turnip; with ref. to its round shape]

tur·nix (tûr′niks) *n.* One of a genus (*Turnix*) of small three-toed birds with short tails found in warm regions of the Old World. [<NL, short for L *coturnix* a quail]

turn·key (tûrn′kē′) *n.* One who has charge of the keys of a prison; a jailer. *—adj.* Of, pertaining to, or being, by prearrangement with a buyer, a product or service in complete readiness for use when purchased: a *turnkey* housing project.

turn-off (tûrn′ôf′, -of′) *n. Colloq.* A road, path, or way branching off from a main thoroughfare.

turn·out (tûrn′out′) *n.* 1 An act of turning out or coming forth. 2 An assemblage of persons; attendance. 3 A quantity produced; output. 4 Array; equipment; outfit. 5 A railroad siding. 6 The movement of a vehicle from a line of traffic to pass other vehicles. 7 A section of narrow road widened to permit vehicles to pass one another. 8 A carriage or wagon with its horses and equipage. 9 *Brit.* A labor strike; also, a striker.

turn·o·ver (tûrn′ō′vər) *n.* 1 The act or process of turning over; an upset or overthrow, as of a vehicle. 2 A change or revolution: a *turnover* in affairs. 3 A small pie or tart made by covering half of a circular crust with fruit, jelly, or the like, and turning the other half over on top. 4 The amount of business accomplished, or of work achieved; turnout. 5 A completed commercial transaction or course of business; also, the money receipts of a business for a given period. 6 The rate at which persons hired by a given establishment within a given period are replaced by others; also, the number of persons hired. *—adj.* 1 Designed for turning over or reversing. 2 Capable of being turned over or folded down. 3 Made with a part folded down: a *turnover* collar.

turn·pike (tûrn′pīk′) *n.* 1 A road on which there are tollgates. 2 Loosely, any highway: also **turnpike road.** 3 A tollbar or tollgate. 4 *Obs.* A turnstile. See synonyms under ROAD. [ME *turnpyke* a spiked road barrier <TURN, *v.* + *pyke* PIKE[1]]

turn·sole (tûrn′sōl′) *n.* 1 Any of several plants supposed to turn their flowers toward the sun; especially, the heliotrope and the sunflower. 2 Litmus. 3 One of various other blue coloring matters obtained from certain lichens and herbs. [<OF *tournesole* <Ital. *tornasole* < *tornare* turn (<L) + *sole* the sun <L *sol*]

turn·spit (tûrn′spit′) *n.* 1 One who turns a spit; a menial. 2 A dog formerly used in a treadmill to turn a roasting spit.

turn·stile (tûrn′stīl′) *n.* 1 A kind of gate or closure consisting of a vertical post and horizontal arms which by revolving permit persons, but not cattle, to pass; also, one that permits persons to pass in one direction only. 2 A similar device for registering the number of persons entering a building or for automatically admitting passengers to subways, buses, etc., on the deposit of fares.

turn·stone (tûrn′stōn′) *n.* A ploverlike migratory bird (genus *Arenaria*) of northern regions: so called from its habit of turning over stones to obtain its food; especially, the **ruddy turnstone** (*A. interpres*) and the **black turnstone** (*A. melanocephala*) of North America.

turn·ta·ble (tûrn′tā′bəl) *n.* 1 A rotating platform arranged to turn a section of a bridge in order to open a passage for ships. 2 Such a platform to turn a locomotive, car, etc.: also *Brit.* **turn′plate′** (-plāt′). 3 A small rotating disk in a microscope. 4 A rotating table in a show window. 5 The disk which carries a phonograph record.

turn·up (tûrn′up′) *n.* 1 That which is turned up, as part of a garment. 2 A particular card or die turned up in games of chance. 3 Pure chance; a toss-up; an unexpected phenomenon. 4 *Colloq.* A boxing contest; hence, a fight or row; commotion. *—adj.* Turned up.

turn·ver·ein (tŏŏrn′fe·rīn) *n.* An association of turners or gymnasts; an athletic club. [<G < *turnen* exercise + *verein* a club]

tur·pen·tine (tûr′pən·tīn) *n.* 1 A resinous, oily mixture of various pinenes exuding from any one of several coniferous trees, especially the longleaf pine (*Pinus palustris*). 2 The semifluid resin of the terebinth: also **Chian turpentine.** **—oil of turpentine** The colorless essential oil formed when turpentine is distilled with steam and consisting of a mixture of terpenes: widely used in industry, medicine and the arts. *—v.t.* **·tined, ·tin·ing** 1 To put turpentine with or upon; saturate with turpentine. 2 To obtain crude turpentine from (a tree). [<OF *turbentine* <L *terebinthinus* of the terebinth tree < *terebinthus* the terebinth <Gk. *terebinthos*]

turpentine tree The peebeen.

tur·peth (tûr′pith) *n.* 1 The root of an East Indian plant (genus *Ipomoea*) allied to the one yielding the common jalap, similar to it in properties: also **vegetable turpeth.** 2 A lemon-yellow basic mercuric sulfate, $HgSO_4 \cdot 2HgO$, used in medicine as an emetic: also **turpeth mineral.** Also called *turbeth, turbith.* [<OF *turbit* <Med. L *turbithum* <Arabic *turbid* <Persian]

Tur·pin (tûr′pin), **Richard,** 1706–39, English highwayman: known as *Dick Turpin.*

tur·pi·tude (tûr′pə·tōōd, -tyōōd) *n.* Inherent baseness; vileness; depravity, or any action showing depravity. [<MF <L *turpitudo, -inis* < *turpis* vile]

tur·quoise (tûr′koiz, -kwoiz) *n.* 1 A blue or green hydrous aluminum phosphate, $H_5Al_2PO_8$, colored by copper: found massive, and in its highly polished blue varieties esteemed as a gemstone. 2 A light, greenish blue, the color of the turquoise: also **turquoise blue.** Also spelled *turkois.* Also *Obs.* **tur·quois** (tûr·koiz'). [<MF *(pierre) turquoise* Turkish (stone) <OF *turqueise,* fem. of *turqueis* Turkish; so called because first imported through Turkey]

tur·rel (tûr'əl) *n. Obs.* An auger used by coopers. [? Dim. of OF *tour* a turn <L *tornus* a lathe]

tur·ret (tûr'it) *n.* 1 A small tower, often merely ornamental, rising above a larger structure, as on a castle. 2 *Mil.* A rotating armed tower, large enough to contain a powerful gun or guns and gunners, forming part of a man-of-war or of a fort; a similar enclosed structure in a tank or a bombing or combat airplane. 3 The clerestory of a railway car. 4 In ancient warfare, a high wooden structure, supported on slides or wheels, intended to enable besiegers to surmount the walls against which it was pushed. 5 *Mech.* In a lathe, a cylinder fitted with sockets or chucks for the reception of various tools, any one of which may be presented in succession in the axial line of the work: also **turret head.** [<OF *torete,* dim. of *tor* TOWER]

tur·ret·ed (tûr'it·id) *adj.* 1 Provided with turrets. 2 Having the form of a turret. 3 *Zool.* Having a long spire, as certain shells.

turret lathe A power-driven metalworking machine having a rotating turret head holding various tools, each of which in turn processes the material.

tur·ri·cal (tûr'i·kəl) *adj.* Of, pertaining to, or like a turret. [<L *turris* a tower]

tur·ric·u·late (tə·rik'yə·lit, -lāt) *adj.* 1 Having or resembling a turret or turrets. 2 Turreted or having a spire: said of shells. [<L *turricula,* dim. of *turris* a tower + -ATE[1]]

tur·tle[1] (tûr'təl) *n.* 1 Any of numerous reptiles (order *Chelonia*) having a horny, toothless beak, and characterized by a short, stout body covered above and below with a bony carapace and plastron respectively, into which all the members may be drawn for protection; a tortoise; specifically, a marine species as distinguished from a terrestrial or fresh-water species. 2 The flesh of certain varieties of turtle, served as food. 3 A stout frame in the form of a segment of a cylinder, used to hold the type in a type-revolving web press. —**green turtle** An important food turtle *(Chelonia*

TURTLES
a. Wood turtle. *b.* Emyd. *c.* Trionychid.

mydas) of wide distribution in tropical and semitropical seas: so called from the greenish color of its flesh. —**to turn turtle** To overturn; capsize. —*v.i.* **·tled, ·tling** To hunt for or catch turtles. [Appar. alter. of Sp. *tortuga* <Med. L *tortuca* TORTOISE; infl. in form by TURTLE[2]]

tur·tle[2] (tûr'təl) *n. Archaic* A turtle dove. [OE <L *turtur*]

tur·tle·back (tûr'təl·bak') *n.* 1 *Naut.* An arched covering, resembling the shell of a turtle, built over the main deck of a ship as protection against heavy seas: usually at the bow or stern. Also **turtle deck.** 2 *Archeol.* A rude, chipped stone implement whose facets resemble the sculptured carapace of a turtle. [<TURTLE[1] + BACK]

turtle dove 1 An Old World dove (genus *Streptopelia*), noted for its affection for its mate and young. 2 One of other pigeons, as the mourning dove. [<TURTLE[2] + DOVE]

tur·tle·head (tûr'təl·hed') *n.* Any species of a genus *(Chelone)* of hardy American herbs of the figwort family, with large white or purple flowers.

turtle neck A high collar that fits snugly about the neck, usually rolled or turned over double: used especially on athletic sweaters. —**tur'tle-neck'** *adj.*

tur·tle·peg (tûr'təl·peg') *n.* A small, sharp, steel spike attached to a line and loosely mounted upon a shaft which is thrown like a harpoon to capture sea turtles.

tur·tle·stone (tûr'təl·stōn') *n.* Septarium.

turves (tûrvz) Archaic plural of TURF.

Tus·ca·loo·sa (tus'kə·lōō'sə) A city of west central Alabama on the Black Warrior River.

Tus·can (tus'kən) *adj.* 1 Pertaining to Tuscany. 2 Designating the Tuscan order of architecture. —*n.* 1 A native or naturalized inhabitant of Tuscany. 2 Any Italian dialect used in Tuscany; especially, the one spoken in Florence, used by Dante, who thus set the pattern for what has become the standard literary Italian language.

Tuscan Archipelago An Italian island group in the Tyrrhenian Sea between the coast of Tuscany and Corsica; total, 115 square miles.

Tuscan order A Roman order of architecture resembling Roman Doric but having bolder moldings, no decorated details, and no triglyphs.

a
b
c
d
e
f

TUSCAN ORDER
a. Cornice.
b. Frieze.
c. Architrave.
d. Capital.
e. Shaft.
f. Base.

Tus·ca·ny (tus'kə·nē) A region and former duchy of west central Italy; 8,876 square miles; chief city, Florence: Italian *Toscana.*

Tus·ca·ro·ra (tus'kə·rôr'ə, -rō'rə) *n. pl.* **·ra** or **·ras** One of a tribe of North American Indians of Iroquoian stock formerly living in North Carolina, now surviving in New York and Ontario. They joined the Five Nations in 1722.

Tus·cu·lum (tus'kyə·ləm) An ancient ruined city of Latium, SE of Rome. —**Tus'cu·lan** *adj.*

tush[1] (tush) *interj.* An exclamation expressing disapproval, impatience, etc.

tush[2] (tush) See TUSK.

tushed (tusht) *adj.* Having tushes or tusks.

tusk (tusk) *n.* 1 A long, pointed tooth, as in the boar, walrus, or elephant. 2 A sharp, projecting, toothlike point. 3 A shoulder on a tenon, to strengthen it at its base; also, a tenon having such a shoulder. —*v.t.* 1 To gore with the tusks. 2 To root up with the tusks. Also *tush.* [Metathetic var. of OE *tux*] —**tusked** (tuskt) *adj.* —**tusk'less** *adj.* —**tusk'like'** *adj.*

tusk·er (tus'kər) *n.* An elephant or wild boar with developed tusks.

tusk tenon A tenon strengthened by a step or steps, or by a shoulder. [<TUSK (def. 3) + TENON]

tus·sah (tus'ə) *n.* 1 A wild and semi-domesticated Asian silkworm *(Antheraea paphia)* which spins large cocoons of brownish or yellowish silk. 2 The silk, or the tough, durable fabric woven from it. Also **tus'sa, tus·sar** (tus'ər), **tus'seh, tus'ser, tus·sore** (tus'ôr, -ōr), **tus'sur.** [<Hind. *tasar* <Skt. *tasara, trasara,* lit., a shuttle]

tus·sis (tus'is) *n. Pathol.* A cough: bronchial *tussis.* [<NL <L] —**tus'sal, tus'sive** *adj.*

tus·sle (tus'əl) *v.t.* & *v.i.* **·sled, ·sling** To fight or struggle in a vigorous, determined way; engage in a tussle. —*n.* A disorderly struggle, as in sport; scuffle. [Var. of TOUSLE]

tus·sock (tus'ək) *n.* 1 A tuft or clump of grass or sedge. 2 A tuft, as of hair or feathers. Also **tus'suck.** [Prob. dim. of obs. *tusk* a tuft of hair, ? <TUSK] —**tus'sock·y** *adj.*

tussock moth Any of various robust, medium-sized moths (family *Lymantriidae*) whose larvae bear tufts of hairs and are very destructive of broad-leaved deciduous trees, as the gipsy moth.

tut (tut) *interj.* An exclamation to check rashness or express impatience: often repeated.

Tut-ankh-a-men (tōōt'ängk·ä'min) Egyptian pharaoh who reigned 1358–1350 B.C.

tu·te·lage (tōō'tə·lij, tyōō'-) *n.* 1 The state of being under a tutor or guardian. 2 The act or office of a guardian; guardianship. 3 The act of tutoring; instruction. [<L *tutela* a watching, guardianship < *tutus* safe < *tueri* watch, guard]

tu·te·lar (tōō'tə·lər, tyōō'-) *adj.* 1 Invested with guardianship. 2 Pertaining to a guardian. Also **tu'te·lar'y** (-ler'ē).

tu·te·nag (tōō'tə·nag, tyōō'-) *n.* 1 A white alloy, with varying proportions of copper, zinc, and nickel. 2 Zinc or spelter. Also **tu'te·nague**: sometimes spelled *teutenag.* [<Pg. *tutanaga, tutenaga* <Marathi *tuttināg* <Skt. *tuttha* copper sulphate + *nāga* tin, lead]

Tu·to·caine (tōō'tə·kān) *n.* Proprietary name for an ivory-colored, odorless, crystalline compound, $C_{14}H_{22}O_2N_2$, used as a local anesthetic.

tu·tor (tōō'tər, tyōō'-) *n.* 1 One who instructs another in one or more branches of knowledge; a private teacher. 2 A college teacher who gives individual instruction. 3 *Brit.* A college official entrusted with the tutelage and care of undergraduates assigned to him. 4 *Law* A guardian of a minor or of a woman. —*v.t.* 1 To act as tutor to; instruct; teach; train. 2 To have the guardianship of. 3 To treat severely or sternly, as a tutor might; discipline. —*v.i.* 4 To do the work of a tutor. 5 To be tutored or instructed. See synonyms under TEACH. [<AF, OF *tutour* <L *tutor* a watcher, guardian < *tutus.* See TUTELAGE.] —**tu·to·ri·al** (tōō·tôr'ē·əl, -tō'rē-, tyōō-) *adj.*

tu·tor·age (tōō'tər·ij, tyōō'-) *n.* The office of a tutor; tutorship.

tutorial system A system of education, generally collegiate, in which each student is assigned to a tutor, who directs his studies and has general supervision over his instruction.

tu·tor·ship (tōō'tər·ship, tyōō'-) *n.* 1 The office of a tutor or of a guardian. 2 Tutelage.

tu·toy·er (tü·twȧ·yā') *v.t. French* To speak to with the French singular pronoun *tu, te, toi* instead of the more formal plural pronoun *vous;* address intimately.

tut·ti (tōō'tē) *Music adj.* All: a term used to indicate that all performers are to take part: contrasted with *solo.* —*n.* A composition, piece, movement, or passage to be performed by all the voices and instruments together: contrasted with *solo.* [<Ital., pl. of *tutto* all]

tut·ti-frut·ti (tōō'tē·frōō'tē) *n.* A confection, chewing gum, ice-cream, etc., made with different fruits. —*adj.* Having fruit flavors. [<Ital., all fruits]

tut·ty (tut'ē) *n.* An impure zinc oxide obtained as a sublimate in the flues of zinc-smelting furnaces: used as a polishing powder. [<OF *tutie* <Arabic *tūtiya* oxide of zinc, ? <Persian]

tu·tu (tü·tü') *n. French* A short, full, projecting skirt consisting of many layers of sheer fabric, worn by ballet dancers.

Tu·tu·i·la (tōō'tōō·ē'lä) The chief island of the American Samoan group; 40 square miles; capital, Pago Pago.

tu·um (tōō'əm) *pron. Latin* Yours; thine: used in the phrase *meum and tuum,* mine and thine.

Tu·va Autonomous Region (tōō'və) An administrative division of southern Asiatic Russian S.F.S.R.; 66,100 square miles: formerly *Tannu-Tuva People's Republic.* Also **Tu·vin·i·an Autonomous Region** (tōō·vin'ē·ən).

tu·whit tu·whoo (tōō·hwit' tōō·hwōō') The cry of an owl. [Imit.]

tux·e·do (tuk·sē'dō) *n. pl.* **·dos** 1 A man's semi-formal dinner coat without tails. 2 The suit of which the coat is a part. Also **Tux·e'·do.** [from *Tuxedo* Park, N.Y.; so called because first worn at the country club there]

Tuxt·la (tōōst'lä) The capital of Chiapas state, southern Mexico, in the west central part of the state. Also **Tuxtla Gu·tiér·rez** (gōō·tyâr'rās).

tu·yère (twē·yâr', twir; *Fr.* tü·yâr') *n. Metall.* The pipe through which air is forced into a furnace or forge: also spelled *twyere.* [<F, a nozzle < *tuyau* a pipe]

Tver (tver) A former name for KALININ.

twa (twä, twô) *adj. Scot.* Two.

twad·dle (twod'l) *v.t.* & *v.i.* **·dled, ·dling** To talk foolishly and pretentiously. See synonyms under BABBLE. —*n.* Pretentious, silly talk; also, a twaddler. [Prob. alter. of TWATTLE] —**twad'dler** *n.*

twain (twān) *adj. Archaic* Two: rare except in poetic usage. See synonyms under BOTH. —*n.* 1 A couple; two. 2 In river navigation, two

fathoms or twelve feet. [OE *twēgen,* masculine of *twa* two]
Twain (twān), **Mark** See MARK TWAIN.
twal (twäl, twôl) *adj. Scot.* Twelve. Also **twall.**
twal·pen·nies (twäl′pen′ēz, twôl′-) *n. pl. Scot.* Twelvepence: in old Scots currency, equal to one penny sterling. — **twal′pen′nie, twal′·pen′ny** *adj.*
twang (twang) *v.t.* & *v.i.* **twanged, twang·ing** **1** To make or cause to make a sharp, vibrant sound, as a bowstring. **2** To utter or speak with a harsh, nasal sound. — *n.* **1** A sharp, vibrating sound, as of a tense string plucked. **2** A sharp, nasal sound of the voice. **3** A sound resembling either of the foregoing. Also *tang.* [Imit.] — **twang′y** *adj.*
twan·gle (twang′gəl) *v.t.* & *v.i.* **·gled, ·gling** To twang. — *n.* A twang. [Freq. of TWANG] — **twan′gler** *n.*
Twan·kay (twang′kā) *n.* A variety of green tea. Also **twan·ky** (twang′kē). [from Chinese *T'un ch'i,* a town in Anwhei province, where originally grown]
twa·some (twä′səm, twô′-) *Scot. adj.* Twosome. — *n.* Two persons in company; a pair.
twat·tle (twot′l) *v.t.* & *v.i.* **·tled, ·tling,** *n.* Twaddle. [Short for *twittle-twattle,* var. of TITTLE-TATTLE]
tway·blade (twā′blād) *n.* Any one of various hardy terrestrial orchids (genera *Listera* or *Liparis*) with two radical leaves: also spelled *twyblade.* [< archaic *tway* two, var. of TWAIN + BLADE]
tweak (twēk) *v.t.* To pinch and twist sharply; twitch. — *n.* A twisting pinch; twitch. [Var. of dial. *twick,* OE *twiccan* twitch] — **tweak′y** *adj.*
tweed (twēd) *n.* **1** A soft woolen fabric with a homespun surface: often woven in two or more colors to effect a check or plaid pattern. **2** A tweed suit or coat. — **Harris tweed** A homespun woolen cloth, usually of mixed colors, made at Harris in the Hebrides. [Alter. of dial. E (Scottish) *tweel,* var. of TWILL; prob. infl. in form by *Tweed* river, which flows through the district where it is woven]
Tweed (twēd) A river in Peeblesshire, Scotland, forming part of the boundary of England and Scotland and flowing 97 miles NE to the North Sea.
Tweed (twēd), **William Marcy,** 1823–78, U.S. politician: called "Boss Tweed."
Tweed·dale (twēd′dāl) See PEEBLES.
twee·dle[1] (twēd′l) *v.* **·dled, ·dling** *v.t.* **1** To play (a musical instrument) casually or carelessly. **2** To wheedle; cajole. — *v.i.* **3** To produce a series of shrill tones. **4** To play a musical instrument casually or carelessly. — *n.* A sound resembling the tones of a violin. [Imit. of the sound of a reed pipe]
twee·dle[2] (twēd′l) *v.* **·dled, ·dling** *v.t.* To handle carelessly. — *v.i.* To wriggle. [Var. of TWIDDLE]
twee·dle·dum and twee·dle·dee (twēd′l·dum′, twēd′l·dē′) Two things between which there is the slightest possible distinction: from John Byrom, *On the Feuds between Handel and Bononcini* (1723). [Orig. imit. of low- and high-pitched musical instruments, respectively]
Tweedledum and Tweedledee Twin brothers of almost identical appearance in Lewis Carroll's *Through the Looking-Glass.*
Tweed Ring The political group, headed by William M. ("Boss") Tweed and other Tammany Hall politicians, which controlled New York city government (1865–71) and plundered millions of dollars. — **Tweed′ism** *n.*
Tweeds·muir (twēdz′myŏŏr), **Baron** See BUCHAN, JOHN.
'tween (twēn) Contraction of BETWEEN.
tweet (twēt) *v.i.* To utter a thin, chirping note. — *n.* A twittering or chirping. Also **tweet′-tweet′.** [Imit.]
tweet·er (twē′tər) *n. Electronics* A loudspeaker used to reproduce the treble register in high-fidelity sound equipment: distinguished from *woofer.* [<TWEET]
tweeze (twēz) *v.t.* **tweezed, tweez·ing** *Colloq.* To handle, pinch, pluck, etc., with tweezers. [Back formation <TWEEZERS]
tweez·ers (twē′zərz) *n. pl.* **1** Small pincers for tiny objects: often called **a pair of tweezers.** **2** *Obs.* A set of surgeon's instruments; also, a surgeon's instrument case. [Alter. of *tweezes,* pl. of *tweeze,* earlier *etweese* a case of small instruments <F *étuis,* pl. of *étui* ÉTUI]
twelfth (twelfth) *adj.* **1** Second in order after the tenth: the ordinal of *twelve.* **2** Being one of twelve equal parts. — *n.* **1** One of twelve equal parts; the quotient obtained by dividing by twelve. **2** *Music* An interval compounded of an octave and a fifth. [OE *twelfta*]
Twelfth-cake (twelfth′kāk′) *n.* A cake prepared for a Twelfth-night festival. [Short for *Twelfth-night cake*]
Twelfth-day (twelfth′dā′) *n.* The festival of the Epiphany, the twelfth day after Christmas.
Twelfth-night (twelfth′nīt′) *n.* The eve (Jan. 5th) of Twelfth-day, or the evening before Epiphany; sometimes, the evening (Jan. 6th) of Epiphany. — *adj.* Of or pertaining to Twelfth-night.
Twelfth·tide (twelfth′tīd′) *n.* Twelfth-day; the twelfth day after Christmas; Epiphany.
twelve (twelv) *adj.* Consisting of twice six: a cardinal numeral. — *n.* The sum of ten and two, or the symbols (12, xii, XII) representing it. — **the Twelve** The twelve apostles. See APOSTLE (def. 1). [OE *twelf*]
Twelve Apostles **1** A governing body of the Mormon Church, composed of twelve high officials. **2** The twelve disciples of Jesus: more commonly *the Twelve.*
twelve·mo (twelv′mō) *adj.* & *n.* Duodecimo.
twelve·month (twelv′munth′) *n.* A year.
twelve-tone (twelv′tōn′) *adj. Music* Of, pertaining to, or composed in a system or technique developed by Arnold Schönberg, in which any particular series of twelve tones containing all twelve of the tones of the chromatic scale is used in various permutations as the basis of composition, usually without reference to a fixed tonal center; dodecaphonic.
twen·ti·eth (twen′tē·ith) *adj.* **1** Tenth in order after the tenth: the ordinal of *twenty.* **2** Being one of twenty equal parts. — *n.* One of twenty equal parts; the quotient of a unit divided by twenty. [OE *twentigotha* < *twentig* twenty]
twen·ty (twen′tē) *adj.* **1** Consisting of twice ten; vicenary. **2** *Archaic* A considerable but indefinite number. — *n. pl.* **·ties** The sum of ten and ten, or the symbols (20, xx, XX) representing it. [OE *twentig*] — **twen′ty·fold′** *adj.*
Twenty-fourth Amendment An amendment to the Constitution of the United States prohibiting the denial or abridgment of the right to vote in elections for Federal office by reason of failure to pay any poll tax or other tax: ratified in 1964.
twen·ty-one (twen′tē·wun′) *n.* Vingt-et-un: a card game.
twerp (twûrp) *n. Slang* A small, contemptible person. [Cf. obs. *twirk* twitch, var. of TWIRL]
Twi (twē) *n.* A Sudanic language spoken by African Negroes in Ghana: also called *Ashanti:* also spelled *Tshi.*
twi- *prefix* Two; double; twice: *twibil.* Also spelled *twy-.* [OE, double < *twa* two]
twi·bil (twī′bil) *n.* **1** An ax with two cutting edges. **2** A double-bladed battle-ax. **3** A garden tool like an ax; a mattock. Also **twi′·bill.** [OE < *twi-* two + *bill* an ax]
twice (twīs) *adv.* **1** Two times. **2** In double measure; doubly. [OE *twiges,* gen. of *twiga* twice]
twice-laid (twīs′lād′) *adj.* **1** Made from the yarns of old or used rope. **2** Made from remnants or refuse.
twic·er (twī′sər) *n. Brit.* A printer who is both compositor and pressman.
Twick·en·ham (twik′ən·əm) A municipal borough on the Thames, 11 miles SW of London, England; home of Alexander Pope.
twid·dle (twid′l) *v.* **·dled, ·dling** *v.t.* **1** To twirl idly; toy or play with. — *v.i.* **2** To revolve or twirl. **3** To toy with something idly. **4** To be busy about trifles. — *n.* A gentle twirling, as of the fingers. [Prob. <ON *tridla* stir; ? infl. in meaning by TWIRL and FIDDLE] — **twid′·dler** *n.*
twi·er (twī′ər) Altered form of TUYÈRE.
twig[1] (twig) *n.* A small shoot or branchlet of a tree. ◆ Collateral adjective: *viminal.* [OE *twigge*] — **twig′less** *adj.*
twig[2] (twig) *v.* **twigged, twig·ging** *Slang v.t.* **1** To observe closely; notice or watch. **2** To comprehend; understand. — *v.i.* **3** To understand. [Cf. Irish *tuigim* I understand]
twig[3] (twig) *n. Archaic* The fashion: an old fop in good *twig.* [? <obs. *twig* act vigorously; ult. origin uncertain]
twig blight **1** Any of various bacterial or fungous infections of plants which attack the twigs, resulting in extreme decay. **2** Dieback.
twig borer The larva of a lepidopterous insect (*Anarsia lineatella*) which bores into the twigs of certain fruit trees, as the peach, plum, and apricot, with destructive effect.
twigged (twigd) *adj.* Having shoots or twigs.
twig·gen (twig′ən) *adj.* Made of twigs; wicker.
twig girdler See GIRDLER (def. 3).
twig·gy (twig′ē) *adj.* Like, or abounding in, twigs.
twi·light (twī′līt′) *n.* **1** The light diffused over the sky after sunset and before sunrise (especially, in popular use, the former) which is caused by the reflection of sunlight from the higher portions of the atmosphere. **2** Any faint light; shade; obscurity: the *twilight* of the groves. **3** Indistinct apprehension or perception: the *twilight* of doubt or barbarism. **4** A hazy or obscure condition following the waning of past glory, achievements, etc.: the *twilight* of the gods. — *adj.* **1** Pertaining or peculiar to twilight; crepuscular. **2** Imperfectly or faintly lighted; shaded; dim. [ME *twyligt* <OE *twi-* (< *twa* two) + LIGHT; used in sense of "the light between the two," i.e., between day and night]
twilight arch The arch that bounds the brightest region of twilight.
twilight of the gods See RAGNARÖK.
twilight sleep *Med.* A light or partial anesthesia, induced artificially, as by injection of morphine and scopolamine, in which the patient loses the power to remember present events and sensations: sometimes used to relieve childbirth pains. [Trans. of G *dämmerschlaf*]
twill (twil) *n.* **1** One of the three foundation systems of weaves, in which the shuttle carries the woof thread over one and under two or more warp threads, producing the characteristic diagonal ribs or lines in fabrics. **2** A fabric woven with a twill; twilled cloth. — *v.t.* To weave (cloth) so as to produce diagonal lines or ribs on the surface. [Var. of ME *twile,* OE *twili* a twilled fabric < *twi-* < *twa* two, partial trans. of L *bilix* having a double thread]

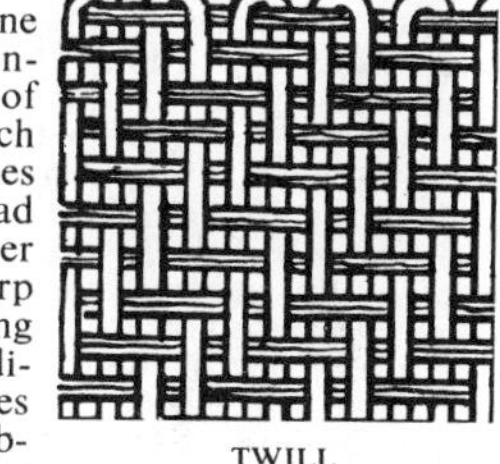
TWILL
Enlarged to show weave.

twilled (twild) *adj.* Woven so as to produce a diagonal rib or line; ribbed or ridged.
twin (twin) *n.* **1** One of two young produced at the same birth. **2** The counterpart or exact mate of another. **3** An intergrowth of two or more crystals of the same substance according to some definite law, a single plane or axis usually being common to the different individuals. — **the Twins** Castor and Pollux, the two brightest stars in the constellation Gemini; also, the constellation. — *adj.* **1** Being, or standing in the relation of, a twin or twins. **2** Consisting of, forming, or being one of a pair of similar and closely related objects; double; twofold. — **the Twin Cities** St. Paul and Minneapolis. — *v.* **twinned, twin·ning** *v.i.* **1** To bring forth twins. **2** To be matched or equal; agree. **3** *Archaic* To be born as a twin. — *v.t.* **4** To bring forth as twins. **5** To couple; match. **6** *Scot.* To separate: also **twine** (twīn). [Fusion of OE *twinn, getwinn* (< *twi-* < *twa* two) and ON *tvinnr, tvennr* double]
twin bed One of a pair of single beds.
twin·ber·ry (twin′ber′ē, -bər·ē) *n. pl.* **·ries** **1** The partridgeberry. **2** A North American shrub (*Lonicera involucrata*) with elliptic leaves, yellowish-red flowers, and shining black berries.
twin-born (twin′bôrn′) *adj.* Brought forth at the same birth; born as a twin or twins.

twine[1] (twīn) *v.* **twined, twin·ing** *v.t.* **1** To twist together, as threads. **2** To form by such twisting. **3** To coil or wrap about something. **4** To encircle by winding or wreathing. **5** To enfold; embrace. — *v.i.* **6** To interlace; become twined. **7** To proceed in a winding course; meander. See synonyms under BEND, TWIST. — *adj.* Of or like twine. — *n.* **1** A string composed of two or more strands twisted together; loosely, any small cord. **2** The act of twining or entwining. **3** A form or conformation produced by twining. **4** An interweaving or interlacing. **5** *Obs.* A twisting about rapidly; spin. [OE *twīn* a twisted double thread < *twi-* double < *twa* two] — **twin'er** *n.*

twin·flow·er (twin'flou'ər) *n.* A trailing evergreen plant (genus *Linnaea*) of the honeysuckle family, as the Old World *L. borealis,* with fragrant rose or white bell-shaped flowers growing in pairs, and its American variety, *L. borealis americana.*

twinge (twinj) *v.t.* & *v.i.* **twinged, twing·ing** To affect with or suffer a sudden pain or twinge. — *n.* A sharp, darting, local pain; twitch; also, a mental pang. See synonyms under PAIN. [OE *twengan* pinch]

twi-night (twī'nīt') *adj.* Beginning in the late afternoon and continuing, under artificial light, into the night, as baseball games or other outdoor contests. [Blend of TWILIGHT and NIGHT]

twin·kle (twing'kəl) *v.* **·kled, ·kling** *v.i.* **1** To shine with fitful, intermittent gleams, as a star. **2** To be bright, as with amusement: Her eyes *twinkled.* **3** To wink or blink; open and shut with a quick, involuntary motion. **4** To move rapidly to and fro; flicker: *twinkling* feet. — *v.t.* **5** To emit or cause to flash out, as gleams of light. **6** To move (the eyelids) quickly and repeatedly. — *n.* **1** A tremulous gleam of light; sparkle; glimmer. **2** A quick or repeated movement of the eyelids; also, a wink or sparkle of the eye. **3** An instant; a twinkling. See synonyms under LIGHT[1]. [OE *twinclian*] — **twin'kler** *n.*

twin·kling (twing'kling) *n.* **1** The act of scintillating. **2** A wink or twinkle. **3** The act of winking, or the time required for it. **4** A moment. See synonyms under LIGHT.

twin-leaf (twin'lēf') *n.* A small perennial herb (*Jeffersonia diphylla*) of the barberry family native in eastern North America, having solitary white flowers and leaves divided into kidney-shaped leaflets.

twinned (twind) *adj.* **1** Produced at one birth; twin. **2** Formed by twinning, as a crystal.

twin·ning (twin'ing) *n.* **1** The production of two young at one birth; the bearing of twins. **2** Close union or combination; coupling of two related objects. **3** The formation of twin crystals, each the counterpart of the other.

twin-screw (twin'skrōō') *adj.* Of a vessel, having two propeller shafts, one on each side of the keel, and two propellers, normally turning in opposite directions. — *n.* (twin'skrōō') Such a vessel.

twirl (twûrl) *v.t.* & *v.i.* **1** To whirl or rotate. **2** In baseball, to pitch. — *n.* **1** A whirling motion, or a quick twisting action, as of the fingers. **2** A curl; twist; coil. [Alter. of ME *tirlen,* var. of *trillen* TRILL[2]; appar. infl. by *whirl*] — **twirl'er** *n.*

twist (twist) *v.t.* **1** To wind (strands, etc.) around each other. **2** To form by such winding: to *twist* thread. **3** To give spiral, circular, or semicircular form to, as by turning at either end. **4** To force out of natural shape; distort or contort. **5** To distort the meaning of. **6** To confuse; perplex. **7** To wreathe, twine, or wrap. **8** To cause to revolve or rotate. **9** To impart spin to (a ball) so that it moves in a curve. — *v.i.* **10** To become twisted. **11** To move in a winding course; meander or bend. **12** To squirm; writhe. — *n.* **1** The act, manner, or result of twisting or turning on an axis. **2** The state of being twisted. **3** *Physics* **a** A torsional strain. **b** The angle of torsion, as of a rod or bar. **4** A curve; turn; bend; winding: This path is full of *twists* and turns. **5** A contortion or twisting of a facial or bodily feature: a smile with a certain *twist.* **6** A wrench; strain, as of a joint or limb: He fell and gave his ankle a *twist.* **7** A peculiar or perverted inclination, bent, or attitude: the *twist* of a criminal's mind. **8** A distortion; deviation; wresting: a *twist* of meaning. **9** Thread or cord made of tightly twisted or braided strands. **10** *Naut.* One of the strands of a rope. **11** A twisted roll of bread. **12** Tobacco twisted in the form of a large cord. **13** In baseball, billiards, tennis, etc.: **a** A spin or whirling motion given to a ball by a certain stroke or throw. **b** The stroke or throw producing such a spin. **c** The act or knack of imparting such a spin. [ME *twisten* divide in two, combine two, prob. <OE *-twist* a rope, as in *mæst-twist* a rope to stay a mast < *twi-* double < *twa* two]

Synonyms (verb): bend, contort, crook, encircle, entwine, twine, wreathe. To *twist* is to bend a thing somewhat spirally upon itself. To *twine* is to *bend* it around some other object. Wrestlers *twine* their arms about each other, but if a combatant's arm is *twisted* it is likely to disable him. An iron shaft may be *twisted* out of shape, but not *twined*; the groove of a rifle barrel is *twisted,* not *twined*; a wreath is *twined* around one's temples, but not *twisted.* Compare BEND, PERVERT.

twist drill *Mech.* A drill or bit whose body is cut with deep spiral grooves to carry out the chips.

twisted pine The lodge-pole pine.

twist·er (twis'tər) *n.* **1** One who or that which twists. **2** A ball, as in cricket, bowled with a twist. **3** In baseball, a curve; also, one who pitches a curve. **4** *U. S.* A tornado.

Twist·or (twis'tər) *n. Electronics* A device for increasing the storage capacity of digital computers, consisting of a grid of copper wires and segments of magnetic wire twisted to change the magnetization from longitudinal to helical: a trade name.

twit (twit) *v.t.* **twit·ted, twit·ting** To taunt, reproach, or annoy by reminding of a mistake, fault, etc. — *n.* A taunting allusion; reproach. [Aphetic var. of ME *atwite,* OE *ætwitan* taunt < *æt-* at + *witan* accuse] — **twit'ter** *n.*

twitch (twich) *v.t.* **1** To pull sharply; pluck with a jerky movement. **2** In lumbering, to drag or skid (logs) along the ground with a chain. — *v.i.* **3** To tug or move with a quick, spasmodic jerk, as a muscle. — *n.* **1** A sudden involuntary contraction of a muscle. **2** A sudden jerk or pull. [ME *twicchen.* Akin to OE *twiccian* pluck.] — **twitch'ing·ly** *adv.*

twitch·grass (twich'gras', -gräs') *n.* Couch-grass.

twit·ter[1] (twit'ər) *v.i.* **1** To utter a series of light chirping or tremulous notes, as a bird. **2** To titter. **3** *Brit. Dial.* To be excited; tremble. — *v.t.* **4** To utter or express with a twitter. — *n.* **1** A succession of light, tremulous sounds. **2** *Bot.* A disease of plants caused by insects. [Imit.]

twit·ter[2] (twit'ər) *v.t.* To taunt; upbraid. [Freq. of TWIT]

twit·ter[3] (twit'ər) *v.t.* Spin or twist unevenly. [< earlier *twit,* a fault or entanglement in thread; ult. origin uncertain]

'twixt (twikst) *prep. Poetic* Betwixt: an abbreviated form.

two (tōō) *adj.* Being one more than one, or a unit taken once again; binary: a cardinal numeral. See synonyms under BOTH. — *n.* **1** The sum of one and one: a cardinal number. **2** Any symbol or set of symbols (2, ii, II) for this number. — **in two** Bisected; bipartite; asunder; apart. [OE *twā, tū*]

two-base hit (tōō'bās') In baseball, a hit in which the batter reaches second base without benefit of an error. Also **two'-bag'ger.**

two-bit (tōō'bit') *adj. U.S. Slang* Cheap; small-time: a *two-bit* gambler.

two bits *U.S. Colloq.* Twenty-five cents.

two-by-four (tōō'bī·fôr', -fōr') *adj.* **1** Measuring two inches by four inches. **2** *U.S. Slang* Of trifling size or significance; narrow or limited. — *n.* (tōō'bī·fôr', -fōr') A piece of lumber measuring two inches by four inches before finishing: much used in building.

two-cy·cle (tōō'sī'kəl) *adj.* Designating a type of internal-combustion engine in which the piston completes its work in two strokes.

two-edged (tōō'ejd') *adj.* Having an edge on each side; cutting both ways.

two-faced (tōō'fāst') *adj.* **1** Having two faces. **2** Double-dealing; insincere; of dissimulating tendency. — **two'-fac'ed·ly** (-fā'sid·lē, -fāst'lē) *adv.*

two·fer (tōō'fər) *U.S. Slang n.* **1** An article advertised or sold at two for the price of one. **2** A free coupon which entitles the holder to two theater tickets for the price of one if presented at the box office of the designated attraction. — *adj.* Offering two of anything for the price of one: a *twofer* sale. [Alter. of *two for (one)*]

two·fold (tōō'fōld') *adj.* Double. — *adv.* In a twofold manner or degree; doubly.

two-hand·ed (tōō'han'did) *adj.* **1** Requiring both hands at once. **2** Constructed for use by two persons. **3** Ambidextrous. **4** Having two hands.

two-mast·er (tōō'mas'tər, -mäs'-) *n.* A ship with two masts.

two-name (tōō'nām') *adj.* Bearing two names or signatures.

two-name paper A negotiable paper, bearing either two signatures or one signature and one endorsement.

two·pence (tup'əns) *n. Brit.* **1** Money of account of the value of two pennies. **2** A silver coin of the same value, now issued only for alms money, distributed by order of the British sovereign on Maundy Thursday. **3** A trifle; small amount.

two·pen·ny (tup'ən·ē) *adj. Brit.* **1** Of the price or value of twopence. **2** Cheap; worthless.

two-phase (tōō'fāz') *adj. Electr.* Diphase.

two-ply (tōō'plī') *adj.* **1** Made of two united webs; woven double: a *two-ply* carpet. **2** Made of two strands or two thicknesses of material.

Two Sic·i·lies (sis'ə·lēz), **The** A kingdom formed by the union of Sicily with Naples in 1130; incorporated with Italy in 1861.

two·some (tōō'səm) *n.* **1** Two persons together. **2** A match with one player on each side. — *adj.* **1** Performed or participated in by two, as a dance. **2** Comprising two or a pair.

two-spot (tōō'spot') *n.* **1** A playing card having two pips; a deuce. **2** *U.S. Slang* An unimportant person. **3** *U.S. Slang* A two-dollar bill. **4** *U.S. Slang* A two-year prison sentence.

two-step (tōō'step') *n.* A round dance consisting of a sliding step in 2/4 time; also, the music for it.

two-time (tōō'tīm') *v.t.* **-timed, -tim·ing** *Slang* To be unfaithful to (someone), especially in love; delude; deceive. — **two'-tim'er** *n.*

two-up (tōō'up') *n. Austral.* A gambling game in which two, or sometimes three, pennies are tossed: also called *swy.*

two-way (tōō'wā') *adj.* **1** Having an arrangement that will permit a fluid to be directed in either of two channels: specifically said of cocks and valves. **2** *Math.* Having a double mode of variation. **3** Permitting traffic in either direction: a *two-way* street.

twy- See TWI-.

twy·blade (twī'blād) See TWAYBLADE.

twy·ere (twī·ir') See TUYÈRE.

-ty[1] *suffix of nouns* The state or condition of being: *sanity.* [<F *-té* <L *-tas*]

-ty[2] *suffix* Ten; ten times: used in numerals, as *thirty, forty,* etc. [OE *-tig* ten]

Tyb·alt (tib'əlt) A masculine personal name. See THEOBALD.

— **Tybalt** In Shakespeare's *Romeo and Juliet,* nephew to Lady Capulet; kills Mercutio and is killed by Romeo.

Ty·burn (tī'bərn) A former place of execution in London, England.

Ty·che (tī'kē) In Greek mythology, the goddess of chance: identified with the Roman *Fortuna.*

ty·coon (tī·kōōn') *n.* **1** *U. S. Colloq.* A wealthy and powerful industrial or business leader. **2** A shogun. [<Japanese *taikun* a mighty lord <Chinese *ta* great + *kiun* a prince]

Ty·deus (tī'dyōōs, -dē·əs) The father of Diomedes and one of the Seven against Thebes.

Ty·di·des (ti·dī'dēz) In Greek mythology, Diomedes, son of Tydeus.

ty·ing (tī'ing) *n.* The act of fastening, or a fastening, as a ribbon or cord.

tyke (tīk) *n.* **1** A tike. **2** *Brit. Dial.* A man from the county of Yorkshire. [Var. of TIKE]

Ty·ler (tī'lər), **John,** 1790–1862, president of the United States 1841–45. — **Wat,** died 1381, English rebel; opposed taxation.

ty·lo·sis (tī·lō'sis) *n. pl.* **·ses** (-sēz) **1** *Bot.* A bladderlike enlargement of a plant cell, intruding within the cavity of a vessel from the wall of a contiguous growing cell. **2** The formation of calluses, especially on the skin. **3** The callus so formed. [<Gk. *tylōsis* < *tylos* a lump, callus]

tym·bal (tim'bəl) See TIMBAL.

tymp (timp) *n. Metall.* A water-cooled block

of refractory material or of cast iron, as the top of the opening between the crucible and the forehearth of a blast furnace. [Short for TYMPAN]

tym·pan (tim′pən) *n.* **1** *Printing* A thickness (or, more usually, several thicknesses), as of paper, on the impression surface of a printing press: used to improve the quality of the presswork. **2** *Archit.* A tympanum. **3** A membrane or other thin sheet tightly stretched. **4** A drum. [<OF <L *tympanum.* See TYMPANUM.]

tym·pa·ni (tim′pə·nē) See TIMPANI.

tym·pan·ic (tim·pan′ik) *adj.* **1** Like or of the nature of a drum. **2** Of or pertaining to the middle ear.

tympanic bone *Anat.* An incomplete bony ring that surrounds the external auditory canal.

tympanic membrane *Anat.* The drumhead membrane separating the middle ear from the external ear; the eardrum. See illustration under EAR.

tym·pa·nist (tim′pə·nist) *n.* One who beats or plays upon a tympan; a drummer.

tym·pa·ni·tes (tim′pə·nī′tēz) *n. Pathol.* Swelling of the abdomen due to accumulation of gas. [<LL <Gk. *tympanitēs* < *tympanon.* See TYMPANUM.] —**tym′pa·nit′ic** (-nit′ik) *adj.*

tym·pa·ni·tis (tim′pə·nī′tis) *n. Pathol.* Inflammation of the mucous membrane lining the tympanum. [<NL <L *tympanum* a drum]

tym·pa·num (tim′pə·nəm) *n. pl.* **·na** (-nə) **1** *Anat.* The middle ear; also, the tympanic membrane. **2** *Archit.* An ornamental space, as over a doorway, bounded by an arch or within the coping of a pediment. **3** A large drum wheel fitted with buckets for raising water from a flowing stream. **4** An ancient form of drum. **5** *Electr.* The diaphragm in a telephone. Also spelled *timpanum.* [<NL <L, a drum <Gk. *tympanon* < *typtein* beat]

tym·pa·ny (tim′pə·nē) *n. pl.* **·nies** Tympanites. [<Med. L *tympanias* <Gk. < *tympanon* a drum]

Tyn·dale (tin′dəl), **William,** 1484–1536, English priest and religious reformer; translated New Testament; executed for heresy.

Tyn·dall (tin′dəl), **John,** 1820–93, English physicist born in Ireland.

Tyndall effect *Physics* The scattering of light due to its passage through a medium containing minute suspended particles in continuous rapid motion. Also **Tyndall cone.** [after John *Tyndall*]

Tyn·dal·li·za·tion (tin′dəl·ə·zā′shən, -ī·zā′-) *n. Med.* A form of sterilization in which heat is applied intermittently in order to destroy spores in their less resistant adult form. [after John *Tyndall*]

Tyn·dar·e·us (tin·dâr′ē·əs) In Greek mythology, a king of Sparta and husband of Leda.

Tyne (tīn) A river in Northumberland and Durham, England, flowing 30 miles south to the North Sea at **Tyne·mouth** (tīn′məth, tin′-), a port with a 12th century priory.

typ– Var. of TYPO–.

ty·pal (tī′pəl) *adj.* Typical.

type (tīp) *n.* **1** Something that represents or symbolizes something else; an image; emblem; symbol. **2** *Theol.* That by which something is prefigured. **3** An object representative of, or embodying the characteristics of, a class or group. **4** *Biol.* **a** The general plan of an organism, with special reference to those structural and physiological characteristics which make it representative of a group, species, class, etc. **b** An individual considered as representative of members of the next higher category in a biological system of classification: the *type* of a genus, family, order, etc. **5** A variety of some physiological substance as determined by specific differences in properties and in mode of action when compared with another variety of the same substance: a blood *type.* **6** *Printing* A piece or block of metal or of wood, bearing on its upper surface, usually in relief, a letter or character for use in printing; also, such pieces collectively. See AGATE, PICA, POINT SYSTEM. **7** A distinctive sign; stamp; mark. **8** A plan to which proposed work or action should conform, as in fine arts; a standard or model. **9** In coinage, the characteristic device on either side of a medal or coin. See synonyms under EMBLEM, EXAMPLE, LETTER, MODEL, SIGN. —*v.* **typed, typ·ing** *v.t.* **1** To assign to a particular type or role, as an actor. **2** To determine the type of; identify: to *type* a blood sample. **3** To typewrite. **4** To represent; typify. **5** To prefigure. —*v.i.* **6** To typewrite. [<MF <L *typus* <Gk. *typos* an impression, figure, type < *typtein* strike]

–type *combining form* **1** Representative form; stamp; type: *prototype.* **2** Used in or produced by printing, photography, or other duplicating processes, or by type: *Linotype, collotype.* [<Gk. *typos* stamp]

type·face (tīp′fās′) *n. Printing* **1** Face (def. 8). **2** A set of type of a particular design.

type foundry An establishment in which metal type is made. —**type founder** —**type founding**

type genus *Biol.* A genus that combines the essential characteristics of the higher group (as a family) to which it belongs; the representative genus after which a family is named.

type–high (tīp′hī′) *adj. Printing* Designating the standard height of type *(height–to–paper)* from base to the level of the printing surface; in the United States, 0.918 of an inch: also *letter–high.*

type line One of the innermost ridges that circumscribe the pattern area of a fingerprint and assist in its identification.

type metal The alloy of which type is made, usually of lead, tin, and antimony.

type·script (tīp′skript′) *n.* Matter which has been typewritten: also called *typoscript.* [< TYPE(WRITTEN) + SCRIPT]

type·set·ter (tīp′set′ər) *n.* **1** A compositor. **2** A machine for composing type. —**type′·set′ting** *n.* & *adj.*

type species *Biol.* The plant or animal species regarded as most typical of the genus to which its name is given; a genotype.

type specimen *Biol.* The individual plant or animal on whose description the distinguishing characters of a species are based.

type·write (tīp′rīt′) *v.t.* & *v.i.* **·wrote, ·writ·ten, ·writ·ing** To write with a typewriter. Also *type.*

type·writ·er (tīp′rī′tər) *n.* **1** A machine for producing printed characters as a substitute for writing: it usually has a keyboard, depression of the keys serving to impress a type upon the paper through the medium of an inked ribbon. **2** A typist.

type·writ·ing (tīp′rī′ting) *n.* **1** The act or operation of using a typewriter. **2** Work done by such process.

ty·pha (tī′fə) *n.* **1** The cat–tail. **2** A fiber resembling kapok prepared from the spikes of the cat–tail, for use in life preservers, pillows, etc. [<NL < *typhē* a cat–tail]

typh·li·tis (tif·lī′tis) *n. Pathol.* Inflammation of the cecum. [<NL <Gk. *typhlos* blind] —**typh·lit′ic** (-lit′ik) *adj.*

typhlo– *combining form* **1** Blindness; of or pertaining to blindness, or to the blind: *typhlology.* **2** *Anat.* & *Med.* The cecum; related to the cecum: *typhlotomy,* a cutting into the cecum. Also, before vowels, **typhl–.** [<Gk. *typhlos* blind]

typh·lol·o·gy (tif·lol′ə·jē) *n.* The branch of medicine and pathology that deals with blindness. [<TYPHLO- + -LOGY]

typh·lo·sis (tif·lō′sis) *n.* Blindness. [<NL <Gk. *typhlōsis* < *typhlos* blind]

typho– *combining form* Typhus; typhoid: *typhogenic.* Also, before vowels, **typh–.** [<Gk. *typhos* smoke, stupor]

Ty·pho·eus (tī·fō′yo͞os) In Greek mythology, a giant with a hundred snake heads, killed by Zeus's thunderbolt. —**Ty·pho·e·an** (tī·fō′ē·ən) *adj.*

ty·pho·gen·ic (tī′fə·jen′ik) *adj.* Producing typhus.

ty·phoid (tī′foid) *adj.* **1** Pertaining to or resembling typhoid fever: also **ty·phoi′dal, ty′·phose** (-fōs). **2** Resembling typhus. —*n.* Typhoid fever. [<TYPH(US) + -OID]

typhoid bacillus A motile, flagellated, Gram–negative bacterium *(Eberthella* or *Salmonella typhosa),* usually introduced into the body by food or drink: the bacillus that causes typhoid fever.

typhoid carrier A person who, with few or none of the clinical symptoms of infection, carries the typhoid bacillus and can communicate it to others in its active form. Also **ty·pho·phore** (tī′fə·fôr, -fōr).

typhoid fever *Pathol.* An acute, infectious fever caused by the typhoid bacillus and characterized by severe intestinal disturbances, a typical eruption of bright rose–red spots on the chest and abdomen, and great physical prostration.

ty·phoi·din (tī·foi′din) *n. Bacteriol.* A culture of the typhoid bacillus, used as a test for passive or active infection. [<TYPHOID + -IN]

ty·pho·ma·lar·i·al (tī′fō·mə·lâr′ē·əl) *adj. Pathol.* Describing a fever resembling that of typhoid but believed to be malarial in origin. [<TYPHO- + MALARIAL]

ty·pho·ma·ni·a (tī′fə·mā′nē·ə, -mān′yə) *n. Pathol.* The delirious state associated with typhoid fever or typhus. Also **ty·pho·ni·a** (tī·fō′nē·ə).

Ty·phon (tī′fon) In Greek mythology, a monster overcome and buried by Zeus under Mount Etna.

ty·phoon (tī·fo͞on′) *n.* A tropical storm of cyclonic force and peculiar violence, occurring in the western Pacific and the China Sea. See synonyms under CYCLONE. [< dial. Chinese *tai feng,* lit., big wind; infl. by obs. *typhon* a whirlwind (<Gk. *typhōn* a hurricane) and by obs. *tuphan, tufan* a typhoon <Arabic *tūfān,* ? ult. from the same Gk. source]

ty·phus (tī′fəs) *n. Pathol.* An acute, contagious, rickettsial disease caused by a micro–organism *(Rickettsia prowazeki)* and marked by high fever with eruption of red spots, cerebral disorders, and extreme prostration; typhus fever: also called *Brill's disease.* **Epidemic typhus** is transmitted by the bite of the body louse, and **endemic** or **murine typhus** by the bite of the rat flea. [<NL <Gk. *typhos* smoke, a stupor < *typhein* smoke] —**ty′·phous** *adj.*

typ·i·cal (tip′i·kəl) *adj.* **1** Having the nature or character of a type; constituting a type or pattern; symbolic. **2** Conforming to the essential features of a species, group, class, etc.; characteristic. Also **typ′ic:** also *typal.* See synonyms under NORMAL. [<Med. L *typicalis* <L *typicus* <Gk. *typikos* < *typos* TYPE] —**typ′i·cal·ly** *adv.* —**typ′i·cal·ness** *n.*

typ·i·fy (tip′ə·fī) *v.t.* **·fied, ·fy·ing** **1** To represent by a type; signify, as by an image or token. **2** To constitute a type or serve as a characteristic example of. —**typ′i·fi·ca′tion** (-fə·kā′shən) *n.* —**typ′i·fi′er** *n.*

typ·ist (tī′pist) *n.* One who uses a typewriting machine.

typo– *combining form* Type; of or related to type: *typography.* Also, before vowels, *typ–.* [<Gk. *typos* stamp, type]

ty·po·graphed (tī′pə·graft, -gräft) *adj.* Printed from type, or from plates in which the design is raised above the level of the body of the plate.

ty·pog·ra·pher (tī·pog′rə·fər) *n.* A printer.

ty·po·graph·i·cal (tī′pə·graf′i·kəl) *adj.* Pertaining to, concerned with, or effected by typography or printing. Also **ty′po·graph′ic.** —**ty′·po·graph′i·cal·ly** *adv.*

ty·pog·ra·phy (tī·pog′rə·fē) *n.* **1** The arrangement of composed type. **2** The style and appearance of printed matter. **3** The act or art of composing and printing from types. [<TYPO- + -GRAPHY]

ty·pol·o·gy (tī·pol′ə·jē) *n.* The study of types, as in systems of classification. [<TYPO- + -LOGY]

ty·po·script (tī′pō·skript) See TYPESCRIPT.

Ty·poth·e·tae (tī·poth′ə·tē, tī′pə·thē′tē) *n. pl.* An association of master printers; hence, by extension, **ty·poth′e·tae,** printers collectively: used in the names of organized groups of printers. [<NL <Gk. *typos* TYPE + *tithenai* set, put]

Tyr (tür, tir) In Norse mythology, the god of war and son of Odin: identified with the Teutonic *Tiu:* also spelled *Tyrr.*

ty·ra·mine (tī′rə·mēn′, tir′ə-) *n. Chem.* A white, crystalline, nitrogenous compound, $C_8H_{11}ON$, found in ergot, ripe cheese, and putrefying animal tissue: the hydrochloride is used in medicine. [<TYR(OSINE) + AMINE]

ty·ran·ni·cal (ti·ran′i·kəl, tī-) *adj.* Of or like a

tyrant; harsh; despotic; arbitrary. Also **ty·ran′·nic.** See synonyms under ABSOLUTE, ARBITRARY. **— ty·ran′ni·cal·ly** *adv.* **— ty·ran′ni·cal·ness** *n.*

ty·ran·ni·cide (ti·ran′ə·sīd, tī-) *n.* **1** The slayer of a tyrant. **2** The slaying of a tyrant. [<F <L *tyrannicida* < *tyrannus* a tyrant + *caedere* kill; def. 2 <L *tyrannicidium*]

tyr·an·nize (tir′ə·nīz) *v.* **·nized, ·niz·ing** *v.i.* **1** To exercise power cruelly or unjustly. **2** To rule as a tyrant; have absolute power. *—v.t.* **3** To treat tyrannically; domineer. Also *Brit.* **tyr′an·nise.** [<MF *tyranniser* <LL *tyrannizare* <Gk. *tyrannizein* < *tyrannos* a tyrant] **— tyr′·an·niz′er** *n.*

ty·ran·no·saur·us (ti·ran′ə·sôr′əs, tī-) *n.* *Paleontol.* A carnivorous dinosaur *(Tyrannosaurus rex)* inhabiting North America in the Cretaceous period: it was characterized by its huge bulk, massive jaws, and ability to walk erect on its hind legs. [<NL <Gk. *tyrannos* a tyrant + *sauros* a lizard]

tyr·an·nous (tir′ə·nəs) *adj.* Despotic, tyrannical. See synonyms under ARBITRARY. **— tyr′an·nous·ly** *adv.* **— tyr′an·nous·ness** *n.*

tyr·an·ny (tir′ə·nē) *n. pl.* **·nies** **1** Absolute power arbitrarily or unjustly administered; despotism. **2** An arbitrarily cruel exercise of power; a tyrannical act. **3** In Greek history, the office or the administration of a tyrant. **4** Severity; roughness. [<OF *tirannie* <L *tyrannia* < *tyrannus* a tyrant]

ty·rant (tī′rənt) *n.* **1** One who rules oppressively or cruelly; a despot. **2** One who exercises absolute power without legal warrant, whether ruling well or ill: the original meaning in ancient Greece. [<OF *tiran, tyran* <L *tyrannus* <Gk. *tyrannos* a master, a usurper]

tyrant flycatcher Any American flycatcher (family *Tyrannidae*), as the kingbird, pewee, etc.

Ty·ras (tī′rəs) The ancient name for BELGOROD-DNESTROVSKI.

tyre (tīr) See TIRE[2].

Tyre (tīr) A port and capital of ancient Phoenicia, on the site of modern Sur in SW Lebanon.

Tyr·i·an (tir′ē·ən) *adj.* **1** Of or pertaining to Tyre. **2** Having the color of Tyrian dye; purple. **—** *n.* A native of Tyre.

Tyrian dye **1** A purple or crimson dyestuff obtained by the ancient Greeks and Romans from certain mollusks of the genus *Murex.* **2** A violet-purple color of high saturation and low brilliance. Also **Tyrian purple.**

ty·ro (tī′rō) *n. pl.* **·ros** One who is in the rudiments of any study or the preliminary stage of any occupation; a beginner; novice: also spelled *tiro.* [<Med. L <L *tiro* a recruit]

Ty·rol (ti·rōl′, tir′ōl, tī′rōl) See TIROL.

Tyr·o·lese (tir′ə·lēz′, -lēs′) See TIROLESE.

Ty·ro·lienne (tē·rō·lyen′) *n.* A ländler. [<F, fem. of *tyrolien* Tyrolean]

Ty·rone (ti·rōn′) A county of Ulster, western Northern Ireland; 1,218 miles; county town, Omagh.

ty·ro·sin·ase (tī′rō·si·nās′, tir′ō-) *n. Biochem.* A plant and animal enzyme which converts tyrosine into dark pigments, as melanin. [< TYROSIN(E) + -ASE]

ty·ro·sine (tī′rə·sēn, -sin, tir′ə-) *n. Biochem.* A white crystalline amino acid, $C_9H_{11}O_3N$, formed by the hydrolysis of many plant and animal proteins. [<Gk. *tyros* cheese + -INE[2]]

ty·ro·sin·o·sis (tī′rō·sin·ō′sis, tir′ō-) *n. Pathol.* A disorder caused by defective metabolism of tyrosine in the body. [<TYROSIN(E) + -OSIS]

ty·ro·thri·cin (tī′rō·thrī′sin, -thris′in) *n.* An antibiotic isolated from a soil bacterium *(Bacillus brevis)*: similar to gramicidin and used therapeutically in localized infections. [<TYRO(SINE) + Gk. *thrix, trichos* a hair + -IN]

Tyrr (tür, tir) See TYR.

Tyr·rhe·ni·an Sea (ti·rē′nē·ən) The part of the Mediterranean between Italy, Sardinia, Corsica, and Sicily. [<Gk. *Tyrrhēnia* Tuscany]

Tyr·tae·us (tûr·tē′əs) Greek poet of the seventh century B.C.

Tyu·men (tyōō·men′, *Russian* tyōō·myān′y′) A city in western Asiatic Russian S.F.S.R.

Tyu·zen·zi (chōō·zen·jē) See CHUZENJI.

tzar (tsär), **tza·ri·na** (tsä·rē′nä), etc. See CZAR, etc.

tzet·ze (tset′sē) See TSETSE.

U

u, U (yōō) *n. pl.* **u's, U's** or **Us** (yōōz) **1** The twenty-first letter of the English alphabet: from Greek *upsilon.* In Roman it was written V and had both consonant and vowel value. In English U was formerly the uncial or cursive form of V; gradually V came to be preferred in initial position in writing, and, as the sound at the beginning of a word is ordinarily consonantal, U was finally restricted to vowel use. **2** Any sound of the letter *u.* See ALPHABET. *— symbol* **1** *Chem.* Uranium (symbol U). **2** Anything shaped like a U.

Uau·pés (wou·päs′) A river in SE Colombia and NW Brazil, flowing 500 miles SE to the Río Negro: also *Vaupés.*

U·ban·gi (ōō·bäng′gē) A river of central Africa, flowing 1,400 miles from NE Belgian Congo to the Congo river and forming part of the boundary between the Belgian Congo and French Equatorial Africa.

U·ban·gi-Sha·ri (ōō·bäng′gē·shä′rē) See CENTRAL AFRICAN REPUBLIC.

U·be (ōō′bē, *Japanese* ōō·be) A city of SW Honshu island, Japan.

Ü·ber·mensch (ü′bər·mensh) *n. German* The superman, in Nietzsche's terminology.

u·bi·e·ty (yōō·bī′ə·tē) *n.* The state of being in a place; local relation. [<NL *ubietas, -tatis* <L *ubi* where]

u·biq·ui·tar·i·an (yōō·bik′wə·târ′ē·ən) *n.* One who has ubiquitous existence.

U·biq·ui·tar·i·an (yōō·bik′wə·târ′ē·ən) *n.* A believer in the omnipresence of the human nature of Christ and, as a consequence, in his necessary actual bodily presence in the Eucharist. Also **U·bi·quar·i·an** (yōō′bə·kwâr′·ē·ən), **U′bi·quist, U·biq′ui·tist.**

U·biq·ui·tar·i·an·ism (yōō·bik′wə·târ′ē·ən·iz′·əm) *n.* The tenets of the Ubiquitarians. Also **U·biq·ui·tism** (yōō·bik′wə·tiz′əm).

u·biq·ui·tous (yōō·bik′wə·təs) *adj.* Existing, or seeming to exist, everywhere at once; omnipresent. Also **u·biq′ui·tar′y** (-ter′ē). **— u·biq′·ui·tous·ly** *adv.* **— u·biq′ui·tous·ness** *n.*

u·biq·ui·ty (yōō·bik′wə·tē) *n.* **1** The state of being in an indefinite number of places at once; omnipresence real or seeming. **2** The state of existing always without beginning or end. [<F *ubiquité* <L *ubique* everywhere]

u·bi su·pra (yōō′bī sōō′prə) *Latin* Where (mentioned) above.

U-boat (yōō′bōt′) *n.* A German submarine. [<G *U-boot,* contraction of *Unterseeboot,* lit., undersea boat]

U-bolt (yōō′bōlt′) *n.* A bolt bent like the letter U, and fitted with a screw and nut at each end.

U·che·an (yōō·chē′ən) *n.* A North American Indian linguistic stock, consisting only of the Yuchi tribe.

U·dai·pur (ōō·dī′pōōr, ōō′dī-) **1** A former princely state of the Rajputana States, India; since 1948 merged with the State of Rajasthan; 13,170 square miles: also *Mewar.* **2** A city of southern Rajasthan, India; formerly capital of Udaipur state.

U·dall (yōōd′l), **Nicholas,** 1506?–56, English scholar and dramatist: also *Uvedale.*

U·day Shan·kar (ōō′dī shän·kär′), born 1900, Indian dancer.

ud·der (ud′ər) *n.* A large, pendulous, milk-secreting gland having nipples or teats for the suckling of offspring, as in cows. [OE *ūder*]

U·di·ne (ōō′dē·nā) A city in NE Italy.

Ud·murt Autonomous Soviet Socialist Republic (ōōd′mōōrt, ōōd·mōōrt′) An administrative division of east central European Russian S.F.S.R.; 16,300 square miles; capital, Izhevsk.

u·do (ōō′dō) *n.* A bushy plant *(Aralia cordata)* of Japan and China which, when young, yields edible shoots. [<Japanese]

u·dom·e·ter (yōō·dom′ə·tər) *n.* A pluviometer. [<L *udus* moist + -METER] **— u·do·met·ric** (yōō′də·met′rik) *adj.* **— u·dom′e·try** *n.*

Ue·le (we′lā) A river of NE Belgian Congo, flowing 700 miles north, NW, and west to a confluence with the Bomu at the border of French Equatorial Africa, forming the Ubangi: also *Welle.*

U·fa (ōō·fä′) **1** A city on the Byelaya river in eastern European Russian S.F.S.R.; capital of Bashkir Autonomous S.S.R. **2** A river in eastern European Russian S.F.S.R., flowing 599 miles NW and SW from the southern Urals to the Byelaya river at Ufa.

UFO Unidentified flying object: an official U. S. Air Force designation. Compare FLYING SAUCER.

U·gan·da (yōō·gan′də, ōō·gän′dä) An independent member of the Commonwealth of Nations in east central Africa; 93,981 square miles; capital, Kampala.

ugh (ukh, u, ōōkh, ōō) *interj.* An exclamation of repugnance or disgust. [Imit.]

ug·li·fy (ug′lə·fī) *v.t.* **·fied, ·fy·ing** To make ugly. **— ug′li·fi·ca′tion** (-fə·kā′shən) *n.*

ug·ly (ug′lē) *adj.* **·li·er, ·li·est** **1** Displeasing to the esthetic feelings, as from lack of grace or proportion; distasteful in appearance; ill-looking; unsightly. **2** Repulsive to the moral sentiments; revolting. **3** Bad in character or consequences, as a rumor or a wound. **4** *Colloq.* Ill-tempered; quarrelsome. **5** Portending storms; threatening: said of the weather. [<ON *uggligr* dreadful < *uggr* fear] **— ug′li·ly** *adv.* **— ug′li·ness** *n.*

ugly duckling **1** In Hans Christian Andersen's story, *The Ugly Duckling,* a young swan hatched by a duck, belittled and persecuted by all the ducks for his strange appearance, until he grew into the most beautiful bird on the pond. **2** Any ill-favored or unpromising child who unexpectedly grows into a beauty or a wonder.

U·go (ōō′gō) Italian form of HUGH. Also **U′go·li′no** (-lē′nō).

U·gri·an (ōō′grē·ən, yōō′-) *n.* **1** A member of any of the Finno-Ugric peoples of Hungary and western Siberia, including the Ostyaks, Voguls, and Magyars. **2** Ugric. **—** *adj.* Of or pertaining to the Ugrians, their culture, or their languages.

U·gric (ōō′grik, yōō′-) *n.* A branch of the Finno-Ugric subfamily of Uralic languages, comprising Magyar (Hungarian), Ostyak, and Vogul. **—** *adj.* Of or pertaining to any of these languages.

U·gro-Al·ta·ic (ōō′grō·al·tā′ik, yōō′grō-) *n.* & *adj.* Ural-Altaic.

ug·some (ug′səm) *adj. Scot.* Disgusting.

uh·lan (ōō′län, ōō·län′, yōō′lən) *n.* **1** A cavalryman and lancer of a type originating in eastern Europe, formerly prominent in European armies, notably the German. **2** One of a body of Tatar militia. Also spelled *ulan.* [<G <Polish <Turkish *ōghlān* lad, servant]

Uh·land (ōō′länt), **Johann Ludwig,** 1787–1862, German poet.

Ui·gur (wē′gōōr) *n.* **1** One of a Turkic people who ruled in Mongolia and East Turkestan from the eighth to the twelfth century, now the majority of the population of the Sinkiang-Uigur Autonomous Region, NW China.

2 The Turkic language of these people. — **Ui·gu·ri·an** (wē·gŏŏr′ē·ən), **Ui·gu·ric** (wē·gŏŏr′ik) *adj.*

u·in·tah·ite (yōō·in′tə·īt) *n.* A variety of asphalt common in Utah: often called *gilsonite.* Also **u·in′ta·ite.** [from *Uinta* Mountains]

U·in·ta Mountains (yōō·in′tə) A range in NE Utah and SW Wyoming; highest point, 13,498 feet (the highest point in Utah).

uit (oit, œit) *prep. Afrikaans* Out; out of.

uit·land·er (īt′lan·dər, oit′-; *Afrikaans* œit′·län·dər) *n. Afrikaans* A foreigner; formerly, in the South African Republic, a foreign white resident.

uit·span (œit′spän) *v.* & *n. Afrikaans* Outspan.

U·ji·ji (ōō·jē′jē) A port on Lake Tanganyika in western Tanganyika, Africa.

Ú·j·pest (ōō′ē·pesht) A city on the Danube in central Hungary: German *Neupest.*

u·kase (yōō′kās, yōō·kāz′) *n.* **1** Formerly, an edict or decree of the imperial Russian government. **2** Any official decree. [<Russian *ukaz*]

U·kraine (yōō·krān′, yōō′krān, yōō·krīn′) A rich agricultural region in SW European U.S.S.R., comprised in the Ukrainian S.S.R. Also **U·krain·i·a** (yōō·krā′nē·ə, -krī′-). *Ukrainian* **U·kra·i·na** (ōō·krä·yē′nä).

U·krain·i·an (yōō·krā′nē·ən, -krī′-) *adj.* Of or pertaining to the Ukraine, its people, or their language. — *n.* **1** A native or inhabitant of the Ukraine. **2** An East Slavic language spoken in the Ukraine. See under RUSSIAN.

Ukrainian S.S.R. A constituent republic of SW European U.S.S.R.; 231,986 square miles; capital, Kiev: also *Ukraine, Ukrainia.*

u·ku·le·le (yōō′kə·lā′·lē, *Hawaiian* ōō′kōō·lā′lā) *n.* A guitar-like musical instrument having four strings. [<Hawaiian, flea <*uku* insect + *lele* jump; from the movements of the fingers in playing]

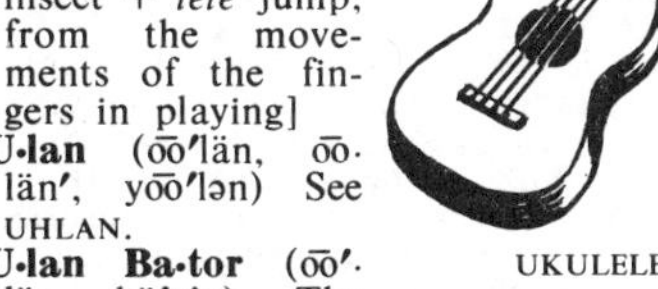

UKULELE

U·lan (ōō′län, ōō·län′, yōō′lən) See UHLAN.

U·lan Ba·tor (ōō′·län bä′tôr) The capital of the Mongolian People's Republic: formerly *Urga*: Chinese *Kulun.*

U·lan Ho·to (ōō′län khō′tō) The capital of Inner Mongolian Autonomous Region, northern China, in the NE part of the Region: Chinese *Wulanhaote*: formerly *Wangyehmiao.* Also *Khoto.*

U·lan-U·de (ōō′län·ōō′de) The capital of Buryat-Mongol Autonomous S.S.R., in SE central Asiatic Russian S.F.S.R., SE of Baikal lake.

ul·cer (ul′sər) *n.* **1** *Pathol.* An open sore on an external or internal surface of the body, usually accompanied by disintegration of tissue with the formation of pus. **2** Figuratively, a corroding fault or vice; corruption; evil. [<L *ulcus, ulceris*]

ul·cer·ate (ul′sə·rāt) *v.t.* & *v.i.* **·at·ed, ·at·ing** To make or become ulcerous. [<L *ulceratus,* pp. of *ulcerare* <*ulcus, ulceris* ulcer] — **ul′cer·a′tive** *adj.*

ul·cer·a·tion (ul′sə·rā′shən) *n.* **1** The forming of an ulcer, or the condition of being affected with ulcers. **2** An ulcer, or ulcers collectively.

ul·cer·ous (ul′sər·əs) *adj.* **1** Resembling an ulcer. **2** Affected with ulcers. — **ul′cer·ous·ly** *adv.* — **ul′cer·ous·ness** *n.*

-ule *suffix of nouns* Small; little: used to form diminutives: *granule.* [<F *-ule* <L *-ulus, -ula, -ulum,* diminutive suffix]

u·le·ma (ōō′lə·mä′) *n.* **1** In Moslem countries, a council or college of learned officials (priests, judges, or scholars) who are trained in Moslem religion and law, and interpret the Koran. **2** Hence, any Moslem scholar. [<Turkish *'ulema* <Arabic *'ulamā,* pl. of *'alim* wise <*'alama* know]

-ulent *suffix of adjectives* Abounding in; full of (what is indicated in the main element): *opulent, truculent.* Corresponding nouns are formed in **-ulence,** as in *opulence, truculence.* [<L *-ulentus*]

Ul·fi·las (ul′fi·ləs), A.D. 311?–383, bishop of the Goths; translated the Bible into Gothic: also spelled *Wulfila.* Also **Ul′fi·la** (-lə).

U·li·thi (ōō·lē′thē) An atoll of the western Caroline Islands; 19 miles long, 10 miles wide.

ul·lage (ul′ij) *n.* The quantity that a vessel, as a wine cask, lacks of being full; wantage. [<AF *ulliage,* OF *ouillage* <*ouiller* fill up (to the bunghole) <*ueil* eye, bunghole <L *oculus* eye]

Ulls·wa·ter (ulz′wô·tər, -wot·ər) The second largest English lake, in Cumberland and Westmoreland; 3 square miles.

Ulm (ōōlm) A city on the Danube River in central eastern Baden-Württemberg, SW West Germany.

ul·ma·ceous (ul·mā′shəs) *adj. Bot.* Designating or belonging to a family (*Ulmaceae*) of shrubs and trees of the order *Urticales,* the elm family, widely distributed in temperate and tropical regions, and characterized by alternate simple leaves, apetalous bisexual or unisexual flowers, and a compressed fruit. [<NL, family name <L *ulmus* elm]

ul·na (ul′nə) *n. pl.* **·nae** (-nē) or **·nas** *Anat.* In vertebrates above fishes, that one of the two long bones of the forearm or foreleg which forms a joint with the radius and is on the same side as the little finger or fifth digit. [<L, elbow] — **ul′nar** *adj.*

ULNA
A. Front view.
B. Back view.
a. Elbow joint.
b. Ulna.
c. Radius.
d. Wrist.

-ulose *suffix of adjectives* Marked by or abounding in: widely used in scientific and technical terms: *ramulose.* Compare -ULOUS (def. 2). [<L *-ulosus,* adjective suffix]

U·lot·ri·chi (yōō·lot′rə·kī) *n. pl.* In the classification of Huxley, a subdivision of the human species, characterized by woolly or crispy hair. Also **U·lot′ri·ches** (-kēz). [<NL *Ulotriches* <Gk. *oulothrix, oulotrichos* woolly-haired <*oulos* woolly + *thrix* hair] — **u·lot′ri·chous** (-kəs) *adj.*

-ulous *suffix of adjectives* **1** Tending to do or characterized by (what is indicated by the main element): *tremulous, ridiculous.* **2** Full of: *meticulous, populous.* Compare -ULOSE. [<L *-ulus* and *-ulosus,* adjective suffixes]

Ul·pi·an (ul′pē·ən), A.D. 170?–228, Roman jurist; full name *Domitius Ulpianus.*

ul·ster (ul′stər) *n.* A very long, loose overcoat, sometimes belted at the waist: made originally of frieze from Ulster, Ireland.

Ul·ster (ul′stər) A former province of northern Ireland comprising the nine counties listed below; 8,331 square miles. In 1925 six of the counties (Antrim, Armagh, Downe, Fermanagh, Londonderry, Tyrone: 5,238 square miles) became Northern Ireland and three (Cavan, Donegal, Monaghan: 3,093 square miles) the Province of Ulster of the Republic of Ireland. — **Ul′ster·man** (-mən) *n.*

Ulster cycle The older and more famous of the two cycles of Old Irish epic and romance. The manuscripts date from the seventh and eighth centuries, but celebrate the Ireland and Irish heroes of the first century, and depict a civilization of barbaric splendor that dates back centuries earlier. See FENIAN CYCLE, TAIN BO CUAILGNE.

ul·te·ri·or (ul·tir′ē·ər) *adj.* **1** More remote; not so pertinent as something else to the matter spoken of: applied to immaterial things: *ulterior* considerations; also, intentionally unrevealed; hidden: *ulterior* motives. **2** Following; succeeding; later in time, or secondary in importance. **3** Lying beyond or on the farther side of a certain bounding line. [<L, compar. of *ulter* beyond] — **ul·te′ri·or·ly** *adv.*

ul·ti·ma (ul′tə·mə) *n.* The last syllable of a word. [<L, fem. of *ultimus* last]

ul·ti·mate (ul′tə·mit) *adj.* **1** Beyond which there is no other; last of a series; final. **2** Fundamental or essential; hence, not susceptible of further analysis; elementary; primary. **3** Most distant; farthest; extreme. **4** *Mech.* Designating the maximum strength of a body, or a strain of the least intensity sufficient to cause rupture. — *n.* **1** The final result; last step; conclusion. **2** A fundamental or final fact. [<LL *ultimatus,* orig. pp. of *ultimare* come to an end <*ultimus* farthest, last, superl. of *ulter* beyond] — **ul′ti·mate·ness** *n.*

ul·ti·mate·ly (ul′tə·mit·lē) *adv.* In the end; at last; finally.

ul·ti·ma Thu·le (ul′tə·mə thōō′lē, tōō′lē) **1** Farthest Thule: in ancient geography, the northernmost habitable regions of the earth. **2** Any distant, unknown region. **3** The farthest possible point, degree, or limit.

ul·ti·ma·tum (ul′tə·mā′təm, -mä′-) *n. pl.* **·tums** or **·ta** (-tə) **1** A final statement, as concerning terms or conditions; in diplomacy, the final terms offered by one party, as during negotiations concerning a treaty, the rejection of which by the other party will result in breaking off all negotiation; loosely, a last proposal, offer, concession, or demand. **2** Anything ultimate. [<NL <LL, neut. of *ultimatus.* See ULTIMATE.]

ul·ti·mo (ul′tə·mō) *adv. Latin* In the last month: shortened to *ult.,* following a date: the 15th *ult.*: distinguished from *proximo* (*prox.*) or *instant* (*inst.*).

ul·ti·mo·gen·i·ture (ul′tə·mō·jen′ə·chər) *n.* The rule whereby the youngest son takes the inheritance: the opposite of *primogeniture.* [<L *ultimus* last + GENITURE]

ul·tra (ul′trə) *adj.* Going beyond the bounds of moderation; extreme; extravagant. — *n.* One who holds extreme opinions; a radical. [<L, beyond, on the other side]

ultra– *prefix* **1** On the other side of; beyond in space (compare TRANS-); as in:

ultra-Arctic	**ultra-Neptunian**
ultra-equinoctial	**ultra-stellar**
ultra-galactic	**ultra-terrene**
ultra-lunar	**ultra-terrestrial**
ultra-Martian	**ultra-zodiacal**

2 Going beyond the limits of; surpassing; as in:

ultra-atomic	**ultra-molecular**
ultra-centenarian	**ultra-natural**
ultra-human	**ultra-total**

3 Beyond what is usual or natural; excessively; as in:

ultra-affected	**ultra-moderate**
ultra-agnostic	**ultra-modest**
ultra-ambitious	**ultra-mulish**
ultra-Anglican	**ultra-nominalistic**
ultra-believing	**ultra-ornate**
ultra-benevolent	**ultra-orthodox**
ultra-Christian	**ultra-orthodoxy**
ultra-classical	**ultra-partisan**
ultra-confident	**ultra-physical**
ultra-conservatism	**ultra-positivistic**
ultra-conservative	**ultra-precision**
ultra-cooperative	**ultra-Protestant**
ultra-cosmopolitan	**ultra-Protestantism**
ultra-credulous	**ultra-prudent**
ultra-democratic	**ultra-purist**
ultra-despotic	**ultra-Puritan**
ultra-discipline	**ultra-radical**
ultra-educationist	**ultra-refined**
ultra-episcopal	**ultra-refinement**
ultra-evangelical	**ultrareligious**
ultra-exclusive	**ultra-revolutionary**
ultrafashionable	**ultra-revolutionist**
ultra-fastidious	**ultra-ritualism**
ultra-federalist	**ultra-romanticist**
ultra-feudal	**ultra-royalism**
ultra-filtration	**ultra-royalist**
ultra-Gallican	**ultra-scientific**
ultra-German	**ultra-sensual**
ultra-honorable	**ultra-sentimental**
ultra-intellectual	**ultra-servile**
ultra-legality	**ultra-Spartan**
ultra-liberal	**ultra-spiritual**
ultra-liberalism	**ultra-splendid**
ultra-logical	**ultra-sterile**
ultra-loyal	**ultra-strict**
ultra-manners	**ultra-theological**
ultra-maternal	**ultra-virtuous**

ul·tra·cen·tri·fuge (ul′trə·sen′trə·fyōōj) *n.* A centrifuge whose rotor, sometimes driven by blasts of hydrogen, will exert a force of about one million times gravity: used for high precision scientific and laboratory work. —**ul′tra·cen′tri·fu·ga′tion** (-fyōō·gā′shən) *n.*

ul·tra·crit·i·cal (ul′trə·krit′i·kəl) *adj.* Unduly critical.

ul·tra·fil·ter (ul′trə·fil′tər) *n. Chem.* A filter having extremely minute pores, as a living membrane or a film of gelatin on filter paper: used to sift out colloidal particles which pass through ordinary filters. —**ul′tra·fil·tra′tion** (-fil·trā′shən) *n.*

ul·tra–high frequency (ul′trə·hī′) Any wave frequency between 300 and 3,000 megahertz. Abbr. *uhf, UHF.*

ul·tra·ist (ul′trə·ist) *n.* One who in opinions or conduct goes beyond moderation; a radical; an extremist. —*adj.* Radical; extreme: also **ul′tra·is′tic.** —**ul′tra·ism** *n.*

ul·tra·ma·rine (ul′trə·mə·rēn′) *n.* **1** A deep, usually purplish–blue, permanent pigment made by treating the powdered mineral lapis lazuli. **2** A similar pigment made largely by synthesis from kaolin, silica, soda, sulfur, and charcoal: also called *new blue, French blue.* **3** The color of ultramarine. —*adj.* Being beyond or across the sea. [<Med. L *ultramarinus* <L *ultra* beyond + *marinus* marine]

ul·tra·mi·crobe (ul′trə·mī′krōb) *n.* A micro-organism that is invisible in the optical microscope.

ul·tra·mi·crom·e·ter (ul′trə·mī·krom′ə·tər) *n.* A micrometer designed for measurements requiring a high order of precision and accuracy.

ul·tra·mi·cro·scope (ul′trə·mī′krə·skōp) *n.* An optical instrument for detecting objects too small to be seen with an ordinary microscope, by means of an intense beam of light thrown from the side upon the spot to be examined.

ul·tra·mi·cro·scop·ic (ul′trə·mī′krə·skop′ik) *adj.* **1** Too minute to be seen by an ordinary microscope. **2** Relating to the ultramicroscope. Also **ul′tra·mi′cro·scop′i·cal.** —**ul′tra·mi·cros′co·py** (-mī·kros′kə·pē) *n.*

ul·tra·mod·ern (ul′trə·mod′ərn) *adj.* Excessively or inordinately new or modern; extreme in modern tendencies or ideas. —**ul′tra·mod′ern·ism** *n.* —**ul′tra·mod′ern·ist** *n.* —**ul′tra·mod′ern·is′tic** *adj.*

ul·tra·mon·tane (ul′trə·mon′tān) *adj.* **1** Situated beyond the mountains: opposed to *cismontane*; beyond or south of the Alps, i.e., Italian or papal. **2** In politics or ecclesiastical matters, supporting the policy of the papal court. —*n.* **1** One who resides beyond the Alps. **2** One who supports the papal policy in political or ecclesiastical matters. [<Med. L *ultramontanus* <L *ultra* beyond + *montanus* pertaining to a mountain <*mons, montis* mountain]

Ul·tra·mon·ta·nism (ul′trə·mon′tə·niz′əm) *n.* The policy of Roman Catholics who wish to see all power in the church in the hands of the pope, in opposition to those desiring a more independent development of the national churches; curialism: opposed to *Gallicanism.*

ul·tra·mun·dane (ul′trə·mun′dān) *adj.* Extending beyond the world, the solar system, or the present life. [<L *ultramundanus*]

ul·tra·na·tion·al·ism (ul′trə·nash′ən·əl·iz′əm) *n.* Extreme devotion to or support of national, as opposed to international, interests or considerations. —**ul′tra·na′tion·al** *adj.* —**ul′tra·na′tion·al·ist** *n.* & *adj.* —**ul′tra·na′tion·al·is′tic** *adj.*

ul·tra·pho·tic (ul′trə·fō′tik) *adj. Physics* Denoting wavelengths of radiant energy beyond the visible region of the spectrum, as ultraviolet and infrared.

ul·tra·son·ic (ul′trə·son′ik) *adj. Physics* Pertaining to or designating sound waves having a frequency above the limits of audibility, or in excess of about 15 kilocycles per second: distinguished from *supersonic*

ul·tra·son·ics (ul′trə·son′iks) *n. pl. (construed as singular)* The study of acoustic phenomena in the frequency range above that of audibility.

ul·tra·trop·i·cal (ul′trə·trop′i·kəl) *adj.* **1** Situated beyond the tropics. **2** Hotter than the tropics.

ul·tra·vi·o·let (ul′trə·vī′ə·lit) *adj. Physics* Lying beyond the violet end of the visible spectrum: said of high-frequency light waves more refrangible than the violet and having wavelengths ranging from about 3,900 angstroms to the upper limits of X–rays. Compare INFRARED.

ul·tra vi·res (ul′trə vī′rēz) *Latin* **1** *Law* Beyond the lawful capacity or powers: said especially of corporations as to acts or contracts not within the scope of the powers conferred upon them and which are *ipso facto* void: applied also to acts which although within their powers have been done without their required consent, as in the case of powers delegated to directors. **2** Figuratively, not permissible; forbidden: a colloquial use.

ul·tra·vi·rus (ul′trə·vī′rəs) *n.* A filtrable virus. [<NL]

U·lugh Muz·tagh (ōō′lōō mōōz·tä′) A peak on the east central border of the Sinkiang-Uigur and the Tibetan autonomous regions, western China; 25,340 feet.

ul·u·lant (yōōl′yə·lənt, ul′-) *adj.* Howling; hooting. [<L *ululans, -antis,* ppr. of *ululare* howl]

ul·u·late (yōōl′yə·lāt, ul′-) *v.i.* **·lat·ed, ·lat·ing** To howl, hoot, or wail. [<L *ululatus,* pp. of *ululare* howl] —**ul′u·la′tion** *n.*

Ul·ya·novsk (ōōl·yä′nôfsk) A port on the Volga in east central European Russian S.F.S.R.

U·lys·ses (yōō·lis′ēz, *Ger.* ōō·lü′ses) A masculine personal name. Also *Fr.* **U·lysse** (ü·lēs′), *Ital.* **U·lis·se** (ōō·lēs′sā). [<Gk., the hater] —**Ulysses** Odysseus.

um·bel (um′bəl) *n. Bot.* An indeterminate inflorescence in which a number of nearly equal pedicels radiate from a small area at the top of a very short axis, giving an umbrellalike appearance. [<L *umbella* a parasol, dim. of *umbra* shadow. Related to UMBRELLA.]

um·bel·late (um′bə·lit, -lāt) *adj.* Disposed in or resembling umbels. Also **um′bel·lar, um′bel·lat′ed.** [<NL *umbellatus*]

um·bel·let (um′bə·lit) *n.* An umbellule.

um·bel·lif·er·ous (um′bə·lif′ər·əs) *adj.* **1** Bearing umbels. **2** Designating or pertaining to an important and widely distributed family *(Umbelliferae)* of herbs and some shrubs, the parsley or carrot family, comprising many plants used as food, for flavoring, and in medicine. [<NL, family name <L *umbella* parasol + *ferre* bear]

um·bel·lu·late (um·bel′yə·lit, -lāt) *adj.* Having or disposed in umbellules.

um·bel·lule (um′bəl·yōōl, um·bel′-) *n. Bot.* A small or secondary umbel. [<NL *umbellula,* dim. of L *umbella* parasol]

um·ber[1] (um′bər) *n.* A chestnut– to liver–brown hydrated ferric oxide, containing some manganese oxide and clay: used as a pigment; also, the color. When in its natural state it is known as **raw umber,** and when heated, so as to produce a reddish–brown, as **burnt umber.** —*adj.* Of or pertaining to umber; of a dusky hue; brownish. —*v.t.* To color with umber; darken, as by staining. [<F *(terre d')ombre* <Ital. *ombra,* prob. <L *Umbra,* fem. of *Umber* of Umbria, where originally found; ? infl. in Ital. by *ombra* shadow, shade <L *umbra*]

um·ber[2] (um′bər) *n.* **1** Shade; hence, some indefinite dark color. **2** The grayling. [<F *ombre* <L *umbra* shade]

Um·ber·to (ōōm·ber′tō) Italian form of HUMBERT.

um·bil·i·cal (um·bil′i·kəl) *adj.* **1** Pertaining to or situated near the umbilicus. **2** Placed near the navel; central. —*n.* **1** A long, flexible tube that serves as a connecting device, conduit for air, power, communication, etc., for an astronaut or aquanaut when outside the craft. **2** A similar device used as a source of fuel, etc., for a spacecraft before launching. [<LL *umbilicalis* <L *umbilicus* navel]

umbilical cord *Anat.* The ropelike tissue connecting the navel of the fetus with the placenta.

um·bil·i·cate (um·bil′ə·kit, -kāt) *adj.* **1** Resembling a navel, as by having a central depression or mark. **2** Having an umbilicus or navel–shaped depression, as a shell. Also **um·bil′i·cat′ed.** —**um·bil′i·ca′tion** *n.*

um·bil·i·cus (um·bil′ə·kəs, um′bə·lī′kəs) *n. pl.* **·ci** (-sī) **1** *Anat.* The depression at the middle of the abdomen where the umbilical cord of the fetus was attached; the navel. **2** *Zool.* An indention or depression at the axial base of a spiral shell, as in many gastropods. **3** *Ornithol.* Either of the apertures (inferior and superior) of the calamus of a feather. **4** *Bot.* A navel–shaped depression; a hilum. [<L]

um·bil·i·form (um·bil′ə·fôrm) *adj.* Navel–shaped. [<*umbili-* (<UMBILICUS) + -FORM]

um·ble pie (um′bəl) See HUMBLE PIE.

um·bles (um′bəlz) *n. pl.* The entrails of a deer; humbles. [Var. of NUMBLES]

um·bo (um′bō) *n. pl.* **um·bo·nes** (um·bō′nēz) or **·bos** **1** The boss or projecting spike in the center of a shield. **2** *Zool.* An elevation, boss, or knob, as the prominence of a bivalve shell near the hinge, or the plate of an echinoderm. **3** *Bot.* The top of the cap of certain fungi. **4** *Anat.* The surface of the tympanic membrane at the point of attachment to the malleus. [<L] —**um′bo·nal, um·bon·ic** (um·bon′ik) *adj.*

um·bo·nate (um′bə·nit, -nāt) *adj.* Having an umbo or bosslike protuberance. Also **um′bo·nat′ed.**

um·bra (um′brə) *n. pl.* **·brae** (-brē) **1** That region of a shadow from which the direct light is entirely cut off. **2** *Astron.* **a** In an eclipse, that part of the shadow of the earth or moon within which the moon or the sun is entirely hidden. See PENUMBRA. **b** The inner dark portion of a sunspot. [<L, shadow]

um·brage (um′brij) *n.* **1** Resentment, as at being obscured by another. **2** A sense of injury; offense: now usually in **to give** (or **take) umbrage. 3** That which gives shade, as a leafy tree. **4** *Poetic* Shade or shadow cast. See synonyms under PIQUE. [<F *ombrage* <L *umbraticus* shady <*umbra* shade]

um·bra·geous (um·brā′jəs) *adj.* **1** Shady or shaded; forming or providing shade. **2** Quick to take offense; peevish; suspicious. [<F *ombrageux* <*ombrage.* See UMBRAGE.] —**um·bra′geous·ly** *adv.* —**um·bra′geous·ness** *n.*

um·brel·la (um·brel′ə) *n.* **1** A light portable canopy on a folding frame, carried as a protection against sun or rain. **2** *Zool.* The contractile, jellylike portion of the body of a medusa expanded like a bell or umbrella. **3** Something serving as a cover or shield, or as a means of linking together various things under a common designation or sponsoring agency: the expanding *umbrella* of nuclear power; various theater groups appearing under the *umbrella* of UNESCO. —*adj.* Being or serving as an umbrella (def. 3): an *umbrella* organization; an *umbrella* statement. [<Ital. *ombrella,* alter. (after *ombra* shade) of L *umbella* parasol. Related to UMBEL.]

umbrella bird Any of several South American birds (genus *Cephalopterus*), the male of which has a broad crest likened to an umbrella. *C. ornatus* has lustrous black plumage with an umbrellalike crest of blue, hairlike feathers.

umbrella leaf A smooth perennial herb *(Diphylleia cymosa)* of the barberry family, with a single large peltate leaf, one to two feet across, and a terminal cyme of white flowers. It is found in the southern United States.

umbrella palm A palm *(Hedyscepe canterburyana)* having pinnate leaves, native to Lord Howe Island in the British Solomons.

umbrella tree **1** A small magnolia *(Magnolia tripetala)* of the southern United States, with fragrant white flowers and oval leaves 16 to 30 inches long, crowded in an umbrellalike whorl at the ends of the branches. **2** Any one of several other trees with large, round cordate leaves.

um·brel·la·wort (um·brel′ə·wûrt′) *n.* A typically North American herb (genus *Allionia*) with the flowers enclosed in a three– or four–parted involucre.

Um·bri·a (um′brē·ə) An ancient and modern region of central Italy between the Tiber and the Adriatic; 3,270 square miles; capital, Perugia.

Um·bri·an (um′brē·ən) *adj.* Of Umbria, or its people. —*n.* **1** A native or inhabitant of Umbria. **2** The extinct language of ancient Umbria, belonging to the Osco–Umbrian branch of the Italic languages.

um·brif·er·ous (um·brif′ər·əs) *adj.* Affording or making a shade; umbrageous. [<L *umbrifer* <*umbra* shade + *ferre* bear] —**um·brif′er·ous·ly** *adv.*

u·mi·ak (o͞o′mē·ak) *n. Eskimo* A large, open boat, about 30 feet long and 8 feet wide, made by drawing skins over a wooden frame: also spelled *oomiak.* Also **u′mi·ack.**

um·laut (o͝om′lout) *n.* **1** *Ling.* **a** The change in quality of a vowel sound caused by its partial assimilation to a vowel or semivowel (often later lost) in the following syllable; vowel mutation: primarily a phenomenon of the Germanic languages. English plurals showing internal vowel modification, such as *feet* and *geese,* are a result of this process. **b** A vowel which has been so altered, as *ä, ö,* and *ü* in German. **2** In German, the two dots (¨) put over a vowel modified by umlaut: short for **umlaut-mark.** —*v.t.* To modify by umlaut or mutation. [<G, change of sound <*um* about + *laut* sound]

Um·nak Island (o͞om′nak) One of the Fox Islands in the Aleutian Islands; 83 miles long, 2 to 18 miles wide.

um·pir·age (um′pīr·ij, -pə·rij) *n.* The office or function of an umpire. Also **um′pire·ship.**

um·pire (um′pīr) *n.* **1** *Law* A person called upon to settle a disagreement in opinion between arbitrators. **2** In general, anything by which a question in controversy is settled. **3** In various games, as baseball, a person chosen to enforce the rules of the game, and in case of controversy to settle disputed points. See synonyms under JUDGE. —*v.t.* & *v.i.* **·pired, ·pir·ing** To decide as umpire; act as umpire (of or in). [Aphetic alter. of ME *noumpere* <OF *nonper* odd, uneven (i.e., third) <*non* not + *per* even, equal]

ump·teen (ump′tēn′) *adj. Slang* Indeterminately large in number; very many. —**ump′·teenth′** *adj.*

Um·ta·ta (o͞om·tä′tə) A city in NE Cape of Good Hope Province, Republic of South Africa.

UN See UNITED NATIONS.

un-[1] *prefix* Not; opposed to. [OE] ◆ **Un-**[1] is used to express negation, lack, incompleteness or opposition. It is freely attached to adjectives and adverbs, less often to nouns. See UN-[2].

un-[2] *prefix* Back. [OE *un-, on-, and-*] ◆ **Un-**[2] is used to express reversal of the action of verbs, or to form verbs from nouns indicating removal from the state or quality expressed by the noun, or sometimes to intensify the force of negative verbs. Beginning at the foot of this page will be found a partial list of words which are formed with **un-**[1] and **un-**[2]. Other compounds of these prefixes, with strongly positive, specific, or special meanings, will be found in vocabulary place. In the verbs in the list *un-* gives the sense of reversal: *unchain* "to loose the chains of." In the nouns and the adjectives usually it has negative or privative force. Thus, *unburdened* may be regarded as an adjective meaning "not burdened," or as a participle of the verb *unburden,* meaning "relieved of a burden." *In-* as a prefix of adjectives expresses in usage more of negation, *un-* more of mere lack or privation: a child's *unartistic* speech, a writer's *inartistic* diction. In general, *in-* is more confined to words of Latin origin.

Pronunciations may be ascertained by consulting the second element in its vocabulary place.

un·a·ble (un·ā′bəl) *adj.* **1** Lacking the necessary power or resources; not able: usually used with an infinitive: *unable* to walk. **2** Lacking mental capacity; incompetent. **3** *Obs.* Feeble; helpless. —**un·a·bil·i·ty** (un′ə·bil′ə·tē) *Obs. n.* —**un·a′bly** *Obs. adv.*

un·a·bridged (un′ə·brijd′) *adj.* Not abridged; not being a shorter or condensed version of another work; original and complete in itself: an *unabridged* dictionary.

un·ac·com·mo·dat·ed (un′ə·kom′ə·dā′tid) *adj.* **1** Not made suitable; ill-adapted or -adjusted. **2** Being without accommodations or conveniences.

un·ac·com·mo·dat·ing (un′ə·kom′ə·dā′ting) *adj.* Not disposed to accommodate; unobliging.

un·ac·com·plished (un′ə·kom′plisht) *adj.* **1** Having fallen short of accomplishment; not done or finished. **2** Lacking accomplishments.

un·ac·count·a·ble (un′ə·koun′tə·bəl) *adj.* **1** Impossible to be accounted for; inexplicable; hence, remarkable; extraordinary. **2** Exempt from supervision or control; irresponsible. —**un′ac·count′a·ble·ness** *n.* —**un′ac·count′·a·bly** *adv.*

un·ac·count·ed-for (un′ə·koun′tid·fôr′) *adj.* Unexplained; not accounted for.

un·ac·cus·tomed (un′ə·kus′təmd) *adj.* **1** Not made familiar by use or by practice: *unaccustomed* to hardship. **2** Not familiar or well known; strange: an *unaccustomed* sight. —**un′·ac·cus′tomed·ness** *n.*

un·ad·vised (un′əd·vīzd′) *adj.* **1** Not advised; not having received advice. **2** Rash or imprudent; lacking consideration. —**un′ad·vis′·ed·ly** (-vī′zid·lē) *adv.* —**un′ad·vis′ed·ness** *n.*

un·af·fect·ed (un′ə·fek′tid) *adj.* **1** Not showing affectation; natural; sincere; real. **2** Not influenced or changed. See synonyms under SIMPLE. —**un′af·fect′ed·ly** *adv.* —**un′af·fect′ed·ness** *n.*

Un·a·las·ka Island (un′ə·las′kə, o͞o′nə-) One of the SW Fox Islands of the Aleutian Islands; 30 miles long, 6 to 30 miles wide.

un·al·ien·a·ble (un·āl′yən·ə·bəl) *adj. Obs.* Inalienable.

un·al·loyed (un′ə·loid′) *adj.* Free from alloy or admixture; pure; also, figuratively, perfectly complete; absolute: *unalloyed* content.

un-A·mer·i·can (un′ə·mer′ə·kən) *adj.* Not having characteristics of persons or things native to the United States; lacking in patriotism and national feeling toward the United States; not consistent with American ideals, objectives, spirit, etc.

U·na·mu·no y Ju·go (o͞o′nä·mo͞o′nō ē ho͞o′gō), **Miguel de,** 1864–1936, Spanish philosopher and novelist.

un·a·neled (un′ə·nēld′) *adj. Obs.* Not having received extreme unction. [<UN-[1] + ANELE]

u·na·nim·i·ty (yo͞o′nə·nim′ə·tē) *n.* The state of being unanimous; complete agreement in opinion or purpose. See synonyms under HARMONY. [<OF *unanimité* <L *unanimitas, -tatis* <*unanimus.* See UNANIMOUS.]

u·nan·i·mous (yo͞o·nan′ə·məs) *adj.* **1** Sharing the same views or sentiments; consentient; harmonious. **2** Establishing or expressive of unanimity; showing or resulting from the assent of all concerned: the *unanimous* voice of the jury. [<L *unanimus, unanimis* <*unus* one + *animus* mind] —**u·nan′i·mous·ly** *adv.* —**u·nan′i·mous·ness** *n.*

un·ap·peal·a·ble (un′ə·pē′lə·bəl) *adj.* **1** Admitting no appeal to a higher court: an *unappealable* case. **2** That cannot be appealed from; conclusive; final.

un·ap·pro·pri·at·ed (un′ə·prō′prē·ā′tid) *adj.* Not set apart for special use; not taken possession of by or formally granted to a particular person or company.

un·ap·proved (un′ə·pro͞ovd′) *adj.* **1** Not regarded with approval; not approved. **2** *Obs.* Not verified by proof; not proved.

un·apt (un·apt′) *adj.* **1** Not likely or inclined. **2** Not suitable or qualified. **3** Not ready-witted. —**un·apt′ly** *adv.* —**un·apt′ness** *n.*

un·ar·gued (un·är′gyo͞od) *adj.* **1** Not argued; undebated. **2** Undisputed. **3** *Obs.* Not censured: a Latinism.

un·arm (un·ärm′) *v.t.* To disarm; deprive of weapons.

un·armed (un·ärmd′) *adj.* **1** Not armed; without weapons. **2** Having no sharp, hard projections, as spines, prickles, plates, etc.: said of plants and animals.

un·as·sum·ing (un′ə·so͞o′ming) *adj.* Unpretentious; modest. —**un′as·sum′ing·ly** *adv.*

un·at·tached (un′ə·tacht′) *adj.* **1** Not attached. **2** *Law* Not held or seized, as in satisfaction of a judgment. **3** In the armed forces, not assigned to a regiment or company.

u·nau (yo͞o·nō′, -nô′, o͞o·nou′) *n.* The common two-toed sloth of Brazil (genus *Choloepus*). [<F <Tupian]

u·na vo·ce (yo͞o′nə vō′sē) *Latin* Unanimously; with one voice.

un·a·void·a·ble (un′ə·voi′də·bəl) *adj.* **1** That cannot be avoided; inevitable. **2** That cannot be made null and void; not voidable. See synonyms under NECESSARY.

un·a·ware (un′ə·wâr′) *adj.* **1** Giving no heed; not cognizant, as of something specified. **2** *Poetic* Carelessly unmindful; inattentive; heedless. —*adv. Obs.* Unawares.

un·a·wares (un′ə·wârz′) *adv.* **1** Unexpectedly. **2** Without premeditation; unwittingly.

un·backed (un·bakt′) *adj.* **1** Never having borne a rider, as a horse; unbroken. **2** Left without backers or support; not supported financially; also, in sports, not wagered on. **3** Without a back, as a stool.

un·baked (un·bākt′) *adj.* **1** Not baked; insufficiently baked. **2** Immature; crude.

un·bal·ance (un·bal′əns) *v.t.* **·anced, ·anc·ing** **1** To deprive of balance. **2** To disturb or derange.

un·bal·anced (un·bal′ənst) *adj.* **1** Not in a state of equilibrium. **2** In bookkeeping, not adjusted so as to balance. **3** Lacking mental balance; unsound; erratic.

un·bal·last·ed (un·bal′əs·tid) *adj.* **1** Not steadied by ballast. **2** Not firm; wavering.

un·bar (un·bär′) *v.* **·barred, ·bar·ring** *v.t.* To remove the bar from. —*v.i.* To become unlocked or unbarred; open.

un·barbed (un·bärbd′) *adj.* **1** Not fitted or made with barbs. **2** *Obs.* Untrimmed; unbarbered.

un·bat·ed (un·bā′tid) *adj. Archaic* **1** Not bated or blunted by having a button on the point, as a lance or other thrusting weapon. **2** Unabated; undiminished.

un·bear (un·bâr′) *v.t.* **·beared, ·bear·ing** To free from the pressure of the checkrein, as a horse.

un·be·com·ing (un′bi·kum′ing) *adj.* **1** Not becoming; unsuited to the wearer, place, or surroundings: an *unbecoming* robe. **2** Not befitting; not worthy of. **3** Not decorous; improper. —**un′be·com′ing·ly** *adv.* —**un′be·com′·ing·ness** *n.*

un·be·known (un′bi·nōn′) *adj.* Unknown: used with *to.* Also **un′be·knownst′** (-nōnst′).

un·be·lief (un′bi·lēf′) *n.* **1** Absence of positive belief; incredulity. **2** A refusal to believe; belief in a contrary proposition; disbelief, as in religion. **3** In Scriptural use, lack of faith in God's promises. See synonyms under DOUBT.

unabashed
unabated
unabetted
unabolished
unabsolved
unacademic
unaccented
unacceptable
unaccepted
unacclimated
unacclimatized
unaccompanied
unaccredited
unacknowledged
unacquainted
unacquitted
unadaptable
unadjustable
unadjusted
unadorned
unadulterated
unadvisable
unadvisably
unaesthetic
unafraid
unaggressive
unagitated
unaided
unalleviated
unallied
unallowable
unalterable
unaltered
unaltering
unambiguous
unambitious
unamiable
unamusing
unanalytic
unanalyzable
unanimated
unannealed
unannounced
unanswerable
unanswerably
unanswered
unappalled
unapparent
unappeasable
unappeased
unappetizing
unappreciative
unapproachable
unapproachably
unapproached
unarmored
unarrested
unartful
unartistic
unashamed
unasked
unaspirated
unaspiring
unassailable
unassailably
unassailed
unassignable
unassigned
unassisted
unassoiled
unassumed
unattainable
unattained
unattempted
unattended
unattested
unattracted
unattractive
unauspicious
unauthentic
unauthentical
unauthenticated
unauthorized
unavailable
unavailably
unavailing
unavenged
unavouched
unavowed
unavowedly
unawaked
unawakened
unawed
unbaptized
unbearable
unbeaten
unbefitting
unbelievable
unbeloved
unbeneficed
unbenighted
unbenign
unbeseeming
unbesought
unbespoken

un·be·liev·er (un′bi·lē′vər) *n.* 1 One who withholds belief. 2 One who has no religious faith. 3 One having a religion different from that of the speaker or writer; specifically, a non-Christian. See synonyms under SKEPTIC.

un·be·liev·ing (un′bi·lē′ving) *adj.* 1 Doubting; skeptical; incredulous. 2 Disbelieving, particularly in regard to religious matters. —**un′·be·liev′ing·ly** *adv.* —**un′be·liev′ing·ness** *n.*

un·belt (un·belt′) *v.t.* 1 To remove the belt of. 2 To remove from the belt; ungird.

un·bend (un·bend′) *v.* **·bent, ·bend·ing** *v.t.* 1 To relax, as from exertion or formality: to *unbend* the mind. 2 To straighten (something bent or curved). 3 To relax, as a bow, from tension. 4 *Naut.* **a** To loose; untie, as a rope. **b** To detach or remove (a sail) from a spar or stay. —*v.i.* 5 To become free of restraint or formality; relax. 6 To become straight or nearly straight again.

un·bend·ing (un·ben′ding) *adj.* Not bending easily; stiff; hence, unyielding; resolute; firm, as character. —*n.* Relaxation. —**un·bend′·ing·ly** *adv.* —**un·bend′ing·ness** *n.*

un·bi·ased (un·bī′əst) *adj.* Having no bias; especially, having no mental bias; not prejudiced or warped; impartial. Also **un·bi′assed.** —**un·bi′ased·ly** *adv.* —**un·bi′ased·ness** *n.*

un·bid·den (un·bid′n) *adj.* 1 Not commanded; not invited: an *unbidden* guest. 2 Not called forth; spontaneous: *unbidden* thoughts. Also **un·bid′.**

un·bind (un·bīnd′) *v.t.* **·bound, ·bind·ing** 1 To free from bindings; undo; hence, to release. 2 To remove, as something that binds; unfasten. See synonyms under RELEASE. [OE *unbindan*]

un·bit·ted (un·bit′id) *adj.* Not furnished with or restrained by a bit or bridle; uncontrolled.

un·blenched (un·blencht′) *adj. Obs.* Not dismayed or confounded.

un·blessed (un·blest′) *adj.* 1 Not having been blessed or admitted to blessedness or divine favor. 2 Unhappy. 3 Unhallowed or unholy; evil.

un·blood·y (un·blud′ē) *adj.* 1 Not stained by blood; hence, not attended with slaughter, as a conflict. 2 Not of a bloodthirsty disposition.

un·blush·ing (un·blush′ing) *adj.* Not blushing; immodest; shameless. —**un·blush′ing·ly** *adv.*

un·bod·ied (un·bod′ēd) *adj.* 1 Having no body; immaterial. 2 Disembodied.

un·bolt (un·bōlt′) *v.t.* To release, as a door, by withdrawing a bolt; unlock; open. —*v.i. Obs.* To remove a bolt or bar; hence, to expose something to view; make explanation.

un·bolt·ed[1] (un·bōl′tid) *adj.* Not fastened by bolts; not bolted.

un·bolt·ed[2] (un·bōl′tid) *adj.* 1 Not separated by bolting; not sifted: *unbolted* flour. 2 *Obs.* Gross; coarse.

un·boned (un·bōnd′) *adj.* 1 Without bones. 2 Not having had the bones removed.

un·bon·net (un·bon′it) *v.t.* & *v.i.* To remove the bonnet or other covering from (the head); uncover. —**un·bon′net·ed** *adj.*

un·born (un·bôrn′) *adj.* 1 Not yet born; of a future time or generation; future. 2 Not in existence.

un·bos·om (un·bo͝oz′əm, -bo͞o′zəm) *v.t.* To reveal, as one's thoughts or secrets; disclose or give vent to: often used reflexively. —*v.i.* To say what is troubling one; tell one's thoughts, feelings, etc. —**un·bos′om·er** *n.*

un·bound·ed (un·boun′did) *adj.* 1 Having no bounds; of unlimited extent; very great; boundless. 2 Having no boundary, as a line that returns into itself or a closed surface. 3 Going beyond bounds; unrestrained. —**un·bound′ed·ly** *adv.* —**un·bound′ed·ness** *n.*

un·bowed (un·boud′) *adj.* Not bent; not bowed or subdued; proud in defeat or adversity.

un·brace (un·brās′) *v.t.* **·braced, ·brac·ing** 1 To free from bands or braces. 2 To free from tension; loosen. 3 To weaken; make feeble.

un·breathed (un·brētħd′) *adj.* 1 Not breathed; hence, not whispered, or spoken; not communicated to another. 2 *Obs.* Unexercised; not practiced.

un·bred (un·bred′) *adj.* 1 Devoid of good breeding; ill-bred. 2 Not taught; untrained: sometimes followed by *to*: *unbred* to spinning. 3 *Obs.* Unbegotten; not born.

un·bri·dled (un·brīd′ld) *adj.* 1 Having no bridle on: an *unbridled* horse. 2 Without restraint; unrestrained; unruly: an *unbridled* tongue; *unbridled* license. —**un·bri′dled·ly** *adv.* —**un·bri′dled·ness** *n.*

un·bro·ken (un·brō′kən) *adj.* 1 Not broken; whole; entire: an *unbroken* seal. 2 Unviolated: *unbroken* faith; an *unbroken* promise. 3 Uninterrupted; regular; smooth: *unbroken* sleep; an *unbroken* prairie. 4 Not weakened; strong; firm. 5 Not broken to harness or service, as a draft animal. 6 Not disarranged or thrown out of order. Also *Obs.* **un·broke′.** —**un·bro′ken·ly** *adv.* —**un·bro′ken·ness** *n.*

un·buck·le (un·buk′əl) *v.t.* & *v.i.* **·led, ·ling** To unfasten the buckle or buckles (of).

un·build (un·bild′) *v.t.* **·built, ·build·ing** To demolish; destroy.

un·bur·den (un·bûr′dən) *v.t.* To free from a burden; relieve. Also *Archaic* **un·bur′then** (-ħən).

un·but·ton (un·but′n) *v.t.* To unfasten the button or buttons of.

un·caged (un·kājd′) *adj.* 1 Not locked up in a cage; free. 2 Released from a cage; freed.

un·called (un·kôld′) *adj.* Not in response to a summons; without being asked or demanded.

un·called-for (un·kôld′fôr′) *adj.* Unnecessary; gratuitous; not justified by circumstances; discourteous.

un·can·ny (un·kan′ē) *adj.* 1 Exciting superstitious fear; weird; unnatural; eerie. 2 So good as to seem almost supernatural in origin: *uncanny* accuracy. 3 *Scot.* Dangerous; severe, as a wound. —**un·can′ni·ly** *adv.* —**un·can′ni·ness** *n.*

un·cap (un·kap′) *v.* **·capped, ·cap·ping** *v.t.* To take off the cap or covering of. —*v.i.* To remove the hat or cap, as in respect.

un·ca·pa·ble (un·kā′pə·bəl) *adj. Obs.* Incapable.

un·caused (un·kôzd′) *adj.* Existing without a cause; not caused; not created: an *uncaused* deity.

un·cer·e·mo·ni·ous (un′ser·ə·mō′nē·əs) *adj.* Informal; abrupt; discourteous. —**un′cer·e·mo′·ni·ous·ly** *adv.*

un·cer·tain (un·sûr′tən) *adj.* 1 Not certain; that cannot be relied upon; variable; changeful; fitful; erring: an *uncertain* friend; *uncertain* weather; an *uncertain* shot. 2 That cannot be certainly predicted; being of doubtful issue. 3 Not having certain knowledge or assured conviction. 4 Not surely or exactly known: a lady of *uncertain* age. 5 Having no exact or precise significance: *uncertain* phraseology. See synonyms under EQUIVOCAL, PRECARIOUS, VAGUE. —**un·cer′tain·ly** *adv.*

un·cer·tain·ty (un·sûr′tən·tē) *n. pl.* **·ties** 1 The state of being uncertain; doubt: also **un·cer′·tain·ness.** 2 A doubtful matter; a contingency. See synonyms under DOUBT.

uncertainty principle *Physics* A statement of the impossibility of exactly determining at any given instant or by a single operation more than one magnitude or quantity, as the velocity, position, etc., of an electron: also called *indeterminacy principle.*

un·chain (un·chān′) *v.t.* To release from a chain; set free.

un·chanc·y (un·chan′sē) *adj. Scot.* 1 Unpropitious; unlucky. 2 Ill-timed; inopportune. 3 Unsafe; dangerous.

un·charged (un·chärjd′) *adj.* 1 Not loaded. 2 Not attacked or accused. 3 Not required or asked to pay a price or meet an expense. 4 Having no electrical charge.

un·char·i·ta·ble (un·char′ə·tə·bəl) *adj.* Not charitable; harsh in judgment; censorious. —**un·char′i·ta·ble·ness** *n.* —**un·char′i·ta·bly** *adv.*

un·chris·tian (un·kris′chən) *adj.* 1 Unbecoming to a Christian. 2 Foreign to Christianity: hence, uncharitable, ungracious, rude, etc. 3 Non-Christian; pagan.

un·church (un·chûrch′) *v.t.* 1 To deprive of membership in a church; expel from a church. 2 To excommunicate. 3 To deny the validity of the sacraments and order of, as a sect.

un·cial (un′shəl, -shē·əl) *adj.* Pertaining to or consisting of a form of letters found in manuscripts from the fourth to the eighth century, and resembling modern capitals but more rounded. —*n.* 1 An uncial letter. 2 An uncial manuscript. [<L *uncialis* inch-high <*uncia* inch, ounce]

UNCIALS

a. Greek uncials — fifth century.
b. Latin uncials — circa A.D. 700.

un·ci·form (un′sə·fôrm) *adj.* Shaped like a hook; hooklike. —*n.* The unciform bone. [<L *uncus* hook + -FORM]

unciform bone *Anat.* A bone of the distal row of the wrist on the ulnar side, articulating with the fourth and fifth metacarpals.

unciform process *Anat.* 1 A projection upon the anterior surface of the unciform bone. 2 The uncinate process.

un·ci·na·ri·a·sis (un′si·nə·rī′ə·sis) *n. Pathol.* Ancylostomiasis. [<NL <*Uncinaria,* genus name <L *uncinus* a hook, barb, dim. of *uncus* hook]

un·ci·nate (un′sə·nit, -nāt) *adj. Biol.* Hooked or bent at the end; having a hooked appendage. Also **un′ci·nal, un′·ci·nat′ed.** [<L *uncinatus* <*uncinus,* dim. of *uncus* hook]

UNCINATE APPENDAGES

uncinate process *Anat.* A hooklike process on the ethmoid bone.

un·cir·cum·cised (un·sûr′kəm·sīzd) *adj.* Not circumcised; Gentile; heathen.

un·cir·cum·ci·sion (un′sûr·kəm·sizh′ən) *n.* 1 The state of being uncircumcised. 2 Those not circumcised; in Scripture, the Gentiles.

un·civ·il (un·siv′əl) *adj.* 1 Wanting in civility; discourteous; ill-bred. 2 *Obs.* Uncivilized. See synonyms under BLUFF, HAUGHTY. —**un·civ′il·ly** *adv.*

un·civ·i·lized (un·siv′ə·līzd) *adj.* Destitute of civilization; barbarous. See synonyms under BARBAROUS.

un·clad (un·klad′) *adj.* Without clothes; naked.

un·clasp (un·klasp′, -kläsp′) *v.t.* 1 To release

unbetrayed
unbetrothed
unbewailed
unbias
unblamable
unblamably
unblamed
unbleached
unblemished
unblest
unblissful
unboastful
unbookish
unborrowed
unbottomed
unbought
unbound
unboundable
unbraid
unbranched
unbranching
unbranded
unbreakable
unbreathable
unbreech
unbreeched
unbribable
unbridgeable
unbridged
unbridle
unbrotherly
unbruised
unbrushed
unburied
unburnt
unbusinesslike
unbuttoned
uncage
uncalculate
uncalculating
uncalendered
uncanceled
uncandid
uncandidly
uncanonic
uncanonical
uncarbureted
uncared-for
uncarpeted
uncastrated
uncaught
unceasing
uncensored
uncensured
uncertified
unchainable
unchained
unchallenged
unchambered
unchangeable
unchanged
unchanging
unchangingly
unchaperoned
uncharted
unchartered
unchary
unchaste
unchastened
unchastised
unchastity
unchecked
unchewed
unchilled
unchivalrous
uncholeric
unchosen
unchristened
unclaimed
unclassed
unclassic
unclassifiable
unclassified
uncleaned
uncleansed
uncleared
uncleavable
unclipped
unclog
unclogged
unclothe
unclothed
uncloud
unclouded
uncloyed
uncoated
uncocked
uncoerced
uncoffined
uncollectable, uncollectible
uncollected
uncolonized
uncolored
uncombed

from a clasp. 2 To release the clasp of. — *v.i.* 3 To become released from a clasp.

un·cle (ung′kəl) *n.* 1 The brother of one's father or mother; also, the husband of one's aunt. ◆ Collateral adjective: *avuncular.* 2 An elderly man: used in direct address. 3 *Colloq.* A pawnbroker. [<F *oncle* <L *avunculus* a mother's brother, orig. dim. of *avus* grandfather]

un·clean (un·klēn′) *adj.* 1 Not clean; foul. 2 Characterized by impure thoughts; unchaste; depraved. 3 Ceremonially impure. See synonyms under FOUL. — **un·clean′ness** *n.*

un·clean·ly[1] (un·klen′lē) *adj.* 1 Lacking cleanliness. 2 Impure; indecent; not chaste. [< UN-[1] + CLEANLY, *adj.*] — **un·clean′li·ness** *n.*

un·clean·ly[2] (un·klēn′lē) *adv.* In an unclean manner. [<UNCLEAN + -LY[2]]

un·clear (un′klir′) *adj.* 1 Not clear. 2 Not easily understandable; confused or muddled: His point was *unclear* to me.

un·clench (un·klench′) *v.t.* & *v.i.* To relax or open from a clenched condition. Also **un·clinch′** (-klinch′).

Uncle Re·mus (rē′məs) In Joel Chandler Harris's folk tales, an old southern Negro who tells the stories of Br'er Rabbit, Br'er Fox, and others to a small white boy.

Uncle Sam The personification of the government of the United States or of the people of the United States: represented as a tall, lean man with chin whiskers, wearing a plug hat, blue swallow–tailed coat, and red–and–white striped pants. See BROTHER JONATHAN.

Uncle Tom 1 The chief character in Harriet Beecher Stowe's *Uncle Tom's Cabin,* a faithful, elderly Negro slave. 2 *U.S. Slang* A Negro who toadies or truckles to white men: a contemptuous term.

un·clew (un·klōō′) *v.t.* 1 *Naut.* To unfurl. 2 *Archaic* To unroll; undo; also, to ruin.

un·cloak (un·klōk′) *v.t.* 1 To remove the cloak or covering from. 2 To unmask; expose. — *v.i.* 3 To remove one's cloak or outer garments.

un·close (un·klōz′) *v.t.* & *v.i.* **·closed, ·clos·ing** 1 To open or set open. 2 To reveal; disclose. — **un·closed′** *adj.*

un·co (ung′kō) *Scot.* & *Brit. Dial. adj.* Being out of the ordinary; strange; weird; reserved. — *n.* 1 Anything out of the common or surprising; hence, a strange person or thing. 2 *pl.* News. — *adv.* Remarkably or excessively.

un·cock (un·kok′) *v.t.* 1 To release and let down the hammer of (a firearm) without exploding the charge. 2 To restore to usual position, as a hat.

un·coft (un·koft′) *adj. Scot.* Unbought.

un·coil (un·koil′) *v.t.* & *v.i.* To unwind or become unwound.

un·coined (un·koind′) *adj.* 1 Not fabricated; natural. 2 Not minted.

un·com·fort·a·ble (un·kum′fər·tə·bəl, -kumpf′·tə·bəl) *adj.* 1 Not at ease; feeling discomfort. 2 Causing uneasiness or disquietude, physical or mental; disquieting. — **un·com′·fort·a·bly** *adv.*

un·com·mer·cial (un′kə·mûr′shəl) *adj.* 1 Not engaged or versed in commerce. 2 Conflicting with the spirit of commerce.

un·com·mit·ted (un′kə·mit′id) *adj.* 1 Not committed; specifically, not performed or done. 2 Not entrusted. 3 Not bound by a pledge.

un·com·mon (un·kom′ən) *adj.* Unusual; remarkable. See synonyms under EXTRAORDINARY, ODD, RARE. — **un·com′mon·ly** *adv.*

un·com·mu·ni·ca·tive (un′kə·myōō′nə·kə·tiv, -nə·kā′tiv) *adj.* Not communicative; not disposed to talk, either to express oneself or to give information; reserved; taciturn.

Un·com·pah·gre Peak (un′kəm·pä′grē) A mountain in SW central Colorado, the highest of the San Juan Mountains; 14,306 feet.

un·com·pro·mis·ing (un·kom′prə·mī′zing) *adj.* Making or admitting of no compromise; inflexible; strict. — **un·com′pro·mis′ing·ly** *adv.* — **un·com′pro·mis′ing·ness** *n.*

un·con·cern (un′kən·sûrn′) *n.* Absence of or freedom from concern or anxiety; indifference. See synonyms under APATHY.

un·con·cerned (un′kən·sûrnd′) *adj.* Undisturbed; not anxious; indifferent. — **un′con·cern′ed·ly** (-sûr′nid·lē) *adj.* — **un′con·cern′ed·ness** *n.*

un·con·di·tion·al (un′kən·dish′ən·əl) *adj.* Limited by no conditions; absolute. See synonyms under ABSOLUTE. — **un′con·di′tion·al·ly** *adv.*

unconditional surrender The unconditional acceptance of military defeat by a warring enemy power, subject only to terms to be subsequently imposed by the victors.

un·con·di·tioned (un′kən·dish′ənd) *adj.* 1 Not restricted; unconditional. 2 In metaphysics, not limited by conditions of space or time; free from relation; unrelated; absolute. 3 *Psychol.* Not having a reaction or reflex developed by a specified condition or conditions; not acquired; natural. 4 Admitted to a school, college, or higher class without condition.

un·con·form·a·ble (un′kən·fôr′mə·bəl) *adj.* 1 Not conforming or conformable; inconsistent. 2 *Geol.* Showing unconformity. — **un′con·form′a·bil′i·ty, un′con·form′a·ble·ness** *n.* — **un′con·form′a·bly** *adv.*

un·con·form·i·ty (un′kən·fôr′mə·tē) *n. pl.* **·ties** 1 Want of conformity; nonconformity. 2 *Geol.* **a** A lack of continuity between groups of stratified rocks in contact, indicative of a gap in the stratigraphic record. **b** The contact layer between such groups.

un·con·scion·a·ble (un·kon′shən·ə·bəl) *adj.* 1 Going beyond customary or reasonable bounds. 2 Not governed by sense or prudence; unconscientious; devoid of conscience. 3 *Law* Inequitable. — **un·con′scion·a·ble·ness** *n.* — **un·con′scion·a·bly** *adv.*

un·con·scious (un·kon′shəs) *adj.* 1 Temporarily deprived of consciousness. 2 Not cognizant; unaware: with *of*: *unconscious* of his charm. 3 Not known or felt to exist; not produced or accompanied by conscious effort: *unconscious* thought. 4 Not endowed with consciousness or a mind. — *n. Psychoanal.* That extensive area of the psyche which is not in the immediate field of awareness and whose content, when consisting of repressed material, may affect the personality through dreams, morbid fears and compulsions, forms of behavior, etc.: with *the.* — **un·con′scious·ly** *adv.* — **un·con′scious·ness** *n.*

un·con·sol·i·dat·ed (un′kən·sol′ə·dā′tid) *adj. Geol.* Not compact or solid, as rock or soil material in a form of loose aggregation.

un·con·sti·tu·tion·al (un′kon·sti·tōō′shən·əl, -tyōō′-) *adj.* Contrary to or violative of the constitution or fundamental law of a state. — **un′con·sti·tu′tion·al′i·ty** *n.* — **un·con′sti·tu′·tion·al·ly** *adv.*

un·con·trol·la·ble (un′kən·trō′lə·bəl) *adj.* Beyond control; ungovernable. See synonyms under REBELLIOUS, VIOLENT. — **un′con·trol′·la·ble·ness, un′con·trol′la·bil′i·ty** *n.* — **un′con·trol′la·bly** *adv.*

un·con·ven·tion·al (un′kən·ven′shən·əl) *adj.* Not adhering to conventional rules; informal; free. — **un′con·ven′tion·al′i·ty** *n.* — **un′con·ven′tion·al·ly** *adv.*

un·con·vert·ed (un′kən·vûr′tid) *adj.* 1 Not converted. 2 *Theol.* Impenitent; without saving faith.

un·cork (un·kôrk′) *v.t.* To draw the cork from.

un·count·ed (un·koun′tid) *adj.* 1 Not counted. 2 Beyond counting; innumerable.

un·coup·le (un·kup′əl) *v.* **·led, ·ling** *v.t.* 1 To disconnect or unfasten. 2 To set loose; unleash (dogs). — *v.i.* 3 To break loose. — **un·coup′led** (-kup′əld) *adj.*

un·couth (un·kōōth′) *adj.* 1 Marked by awkwardness or oddity; outlandish; ungainly; unrefined; rough. 2 Not common; not well–known. 3 Mysterious; alarming. See synonyms under AWKWARD, BARBAROUS, RUSTIC. [OE *uncūth* unknown < *un-* not + *cūth,* pp. of *cunnan* know] — **un·couth′ly** *adv.* — **un·couth′ness** *n.*

un·cov·e·nant·ed (un·kuv′ə·nən·tid) *adj.* 1 Not bound by a covenant or promise; not having entered into a covenant or league. 2 Not guaranteed by a covenant: used specifically to describe divine grace or mercy not promised by a covenant.

un·cov·er (un·kuv′ər) *v.t.* 1 To remove the covering from. 2 To make known; reveal; disclose. 3 In military tactics, to expose successively, as lines of formation. — *v.i.* 4 To remove a covering; raise or remove the hat, as in token of respect.

un·cov·ered (un·kuv′ərd) *adj.* 1 Not covered; devoid of covering. 2 Not covered by collateral security.

un·cre·ate (un′krē·āt′) *v.t.* **·at·ed, ·at·ing** To deprive of existence.

un·cre·at·ed (un′krē·ā′tid) *adj.* 1 Not yet created or brought into being. 2 *Philos.* Not created; self–existent.

unc·tion (ungk′shən) *n.* 1 The act of anointing, as with oil. 2 *Eccl.* **a** A ceremonial anointing with oil, as in consecration or dedication. **b** The sacramental rite of anointing the sick, reserved in the Roman Catholic Church for those in danger of death: also called **extreme unction.** 3 The act of treating medicinally by anointing. 4 A substance used in anointing, as an unguent or a salve; something that soothes or palliates. 5 The quality or characteristic of speech, especially in religious discourse, that awakens or is intended to awaken deep sympathetic feeling; sometimes, effusive or affected emotion. [<F *onction* <L *unctio, -onis* < *ungere* anoint] — **unc′·tion·less** *adj.*

unc·tu·ous (ungk′chōō·əs) *adj.* 1 Having the characteristics of an unguent; greasy. 2 Characterized by deep sympathetic feeling. 3 Characterized by affected emotion; hence, oily–tongued; unduly suave. 4 Being greasy or soapy to the touch, as certain minerals. 5 Soft; rich in organic matter, as certain soils. 6 Having plasticity, as clay. [<Med. L *unctuosus* <L *unctum* ointment, orig. neut. pp. of *ungere* anoint] — **unc′tu·ous·ly** *adv.* — **unc′·tu·ous·ness** *n.* — **unc′tu·os′i·ty** (-chōō·os′ə·tē) *n.*

un·cut (un·kut′) *adj.* 1 Not cut. 2 In bookbinding, having untrimmed margins. 3 Unground, as a gem.

un·damped (un·dampt′) *adj. Physics* Pertaining to or designating those electromagnetic oscillations which continue without change in amplitude: *undamped* radio waves.

un·daunt·ed (un·dôn′tid, -dän′-) *adj.* Not daunted; fearless; intrepid. See synonyms

uncombinable
uncombinably
uncombined
uncomely
uncomforted
uncomforting
uncommanded
uncommissioned
uncompanionable
uncomplaining
uncomplaisant
uncomplaisantly
uncompleted
uncompliable
uncomplicated
uncomplimentary
uncompounded
uncomprehended
uncomprehending
uncomprehensible
uncompressed
uncompromised
uncomputed
unconcealable
unconcealed
unconceded
unconcerted
unconciliated
uncondemned
unconfined
unconfinedly
unconfirmed
unconfused
unconfusedly
unconfuted
uncongeal
uncongealable
uncongealed
uncongenial
uncongeniality
uncongenially
unconnected
unconnectedly
unconquerable
unconquerably
unconquered
unconscientious
unconsecrated
unconsenting
unconsidered
unconsoled
unconsonant
unconstant
unconstituted
unconstrained
unconstricted
unconsumed
uncontaminated
uncontending
uncontested
uncontradictable
uncontradicted
uncontrite
uncontrolled
uncontrolledly
uncontroverted
uncontrovertible
uncontrovertibly
unconversant
unconvinced
unconvincing
uncooked
uncooperative
uncoordinated
uncorked
uncorrected
uncorroborated
uncorrupt
uncorrupted
uncorruptly
uncorruptness
uncountable
uncourteous
uncourtliness
uncourtly
uncredited
uncrippled
uncritical
uncriticizable
uncross
uncrossed
uncrowded
uncrown
uncrowned
uncrystalline
uncrystallizable
uncrystallized
uncultivable
uncultivated
uncultured
uncumbered
uncurb
uncurbable
uncurbed
uncurdled

under BRAVE. **—un·daunt′ed·ly** *adv.* **—un·daunt′ed·ness** *n.*

un·dé (un′dā) *adj. Her.* Wavy; undulating: said of an ordinary or of the lines dividing the shield. Also **un′dée, un′dy** (-dē). [<OF <L *unda* wave]

un·dec·a·gon (un·dek′ə·gon) *n.* A figure that has eleven angles and eleven sides. [<L *undecim* eleven + -GON]

un·de·ceiv·a·ble (un′di·sē′və·bəl) *adj.* **1** That cannot be deceived. **2** *Obs.* Not deceitful.

un·de·ceive (un′di·sēv′) *v.t.* **·ceived, ·ceiv·ing** To free from deception, error, or illusion.

un·de·ceived (un′di·sēvd′) *adj.* **1** Not deceived. **2** Freed from error or deception.

un·de·cen·ni·al (un′di·sen′ē·əl) *adj.* **1** Pertaining to a period of eleven years or to the eleventh year. **2** Lasting eleven years, or occurring or celebrated on the eleventh year or every eleven years. Also **un′de·cen′na·ry** (-sen′ər·ē). [<L *undecim* eleven + *annus* year]

un·de·cid·ed (un′di·sī′did) *adj.* **1** Not having the mind made up. **2** Not decided upon; not determined. See synonyms under IRRESOLUTE. **—un′de·cid′ed·ly** *adv.*

un·decked (un·dekt′) *adj.* **1** Having no ornaments; not decked out. **2** Having no deck, as a vessel.

un·dec·u·ple (un·dek′yə·pəl) *adj.* **1** Consisting of eleven. **2** Having eleven parts or members; elevenfold. **3** Taken by elevens. **—***n.* A number or sum eleven times as great as another. **—***v.t.* & *v.i.* **·pled, ·pling** To multiply by eleven; make or become eleven times as large. [<L *undecim* eleven, on analogy with *decuple*]

un·de·cu·pli·cate (un′də·kyōō′plə·kit, -kāt) *adj.* **1** Elevenfold. **2** Raised to the eleventh power. **—***v.t.* & *v.i.* (-kāt) **·cat·ed, ·cat·ing** To multiply by eleven; undecuple. **—***n.* One of eleven like things. **—un′de·cu′pli·cate·ly** *adv.* **—un′de·cu′pli·ca′tion** *n.*

un·de·mon·stra·tive (un′di·mon′strə·tiv) *adj.* Not demonstrative; not characterized by show of feeling.

un·de·ni·a·ble (un′di·nī′ə·bəl) *adj.* **1** That cannot be denied; indisputably true; obviously correct: an *undeniable* fact. **2** Unquestionably good; excellent: His reputation was *undeniable.* **—un′de·ni′a·bly** *adv.*

un·der (un′dər) *prep.* **1** Beneath, so as to have something directly above; covered by: layer *under* layer. **2** In a place lower than; at the foot or bottom of: *under* the hill. **3** Beneath the shelter of: *under* the paternal roof. **4** Beneath the concealment, guise, or assumption of: *under* a false name. **5** Less than in number, degree, age, value, or amount: *under* 10 tons. **6** Inferior to in quality, character, or rank. **7** Beneath the domination of; owing allegiance to; subordinate or subservient to: *under* the Nazi flag. **8** Subject to the guidance, tutorship, or direction of: He studied *under* Mendelssohn. **9** Subject to the moral obligation of: a statement *under* oath; subject to the sanction of; with the liability or certainty of incurring: *under* penalty of the law. **10** Subject to the influence or pressure of: *under* the circumstances; swayed or impelled by: *under* fear of death. **11** Driven or propelled by: *under* sail, *under* steam. **12** Included in the group or class of; found in the matter titled or headed: See *under* History. **13** Being the subject of: *under* medical treatment. **14** During the period of; in the reign of; pending the administration of. **15** By virtue of; authorized, substantiated, attested, or warranted by: *under* his own signature. **16** In conformity to or in accordance with; having regard to. **17** Planted or sowed with: an acre *under* wheat. See synonyms under BENEATH. **—***adv.* **1** In or into a position below something; underneath. **2** In or into an inferior or subordinate degree or rank. **3** So as to be covered or hidden; in or into concealment. **4** Less than the required or appointed amount. **—to go under** To fail or collapse, as a business venture. **—***adj.* **1** Situated or moving under something else; lower or lowermost: an *under* layer. **2** *Zool.* Ventral: the *under* side of a rattlesnake. **3** Subordinate; lower in rank or authority. **4** Insufficient; less than usual, standard, or prescribed. **5** Held in subjection or restraint: used predicatively: Hold your emotions *under.* [OE]

under– *combining form* **1** Below in position; situated or directed beneath; on the underside; as in:

underarch, **underbody**, **underbridge**, **underbud**, **undercasing**, **undercellar**, **undercurved**, **underdraw**, **undereaten**, **underfeathering**, **underfill**, **underfire**, **undergnaw**, **undergore**, **underjaw**, **underlip**, **undermark**, **undernamed**, **underpart**, **underpier**, **underprop**, **undershore**, **undersole**, **underspread**, **understroke**, **undersurface**, **undersweep**, **underthrust**

2 Below a surface or covering; lower; as in:

underbodice, **undercloth**, **undercrust**, **underdish**, **underdrawers**, **underdress**, **underearth**, **underflooring**, **undergarb**, **underglow**, **undergown**, **undergrove**, **underjacket**, **underlife**, **underpetticoat**, **underregion**

3 Inferior in rank or importance; subordinate; subsidiary; as in:

under–agent, **under–captain**, **under–chief**, **under–clerk**, **under–god**, **under–officer**, **under–secretary**, **under–secretaryship**, **under–servant**, **under–treasurer**

4 Insufficient; less than is usual or proper; as in:

underact, **underbill**, **undercapitalize**, **underclothed**, **underconsumption**, **underdeveloped**, **underexercise**, **undergrow**, **underload**, **undermanned**, **underniceness**, **underofficered**, **underpeopled**, **underpopulated**, **underpowered**, **underpraise**, **underprize**, **underproportioned**, **underripe**, **undersailed**, **undersaturated**, **underspecified**, **understaffed**, **understimulus**, **understocked**, **undertaxed**, **undertrained**

5 At a lower rate; less in degree or amount; as in:

underprice, **underspend**

6 Subdued; hidden; as in:

underbreath, **underfeeling**, **undermelody**, **undernote**, **underthought**, **undervoice**

un·der·a·chieve (un′dər·ə·chēv′) *v.i.* **·chieved, ·chiev·ing** To fail to achieve the approximate level of performance, especially in school studies, commensurate with one's abilities as indicated by testing. **—un′der·a·chieve′·ment, un′der·a·chiev′er** *n.*

under a cloud Overshadowed by reproach or distrust.

un·der–age (un′dər·āj′) *adj.* Not of a requisite age; immature.

un·der·arm (un′dər·ärm′) *adj.* Situated or placed under the arm: the *underarm* section of a blouse. **—***n.* The armpit.

un·der–arm (un′dər·ärm′) *adj.* In various sports, as tennis, baseball, etc., delivered with the hand lower than the elbow.

un·der·bel·ly (un′dər·bel′ē) *n. pl.* **·lies** **1** The lower region of the belly. **2** Any similar unprotected part: the soft *underbelly* of Europe.

un·der·bid (un′dər·bid′) *v.t.* **·bid, ·bid·ding** **1** To bid lower than, as in a competition. **2** In auction bridge, to fail to bid the full value of (a hand). **—un′der·bid′der** *n.*

un·der·bred (un′dər·bred′) *adj.* **1** Of impure breed; not thoroughbred. **2** Lacking in good breeding. See synonyms under VULGAR.

un·der·brush (un′dər·brush′) *n.* Small trees and shrubs growing beneath forest trees; undergrowth. Also **un′der·bush′** (-bŏŏsh′).

un·der·buy (un′dər·bī′) *v.t.* **·bought, ·buy·ing** **1** To buy at a price lower than that paid by (another). **2** To pay less than the value for.

un·der·car·riage (un′dər·kar′ij) *n.* **1** The framework supporting the body of a structure, as an automobile. **2** The principal landing gear of an aircraft.

un·der·charge (un′dər·chärj′) *v.t.* **·charged, ·charg·ing** **1** To make an inadequate charge for. **2** To load with an insufficient charge, as a gun. **—***n.* (un′dər·chärj′) An inadequate or insufficient charge.

un·der·class (un′dər·klas, -kläs) *n. Sociol.* The group in a society so hopelessly poverty–stricken and so unorganized as to be beneath any apparent social class structure.

un·der·class·man (un′dər·klas′mən, -kläs′-) *n. pl.* **·men** (-mən) A freshman or sophomore in a school or college.

un·der·clay (un′dər·klā′) *n.* A layer of clay underlying a coal seam, often containing the roots of ancient coal–forming plants: also called *seatstone.*

un·der·clothes (un′dər·klōz′, -klōthz′) *n. pl.* Clothes designed for underwear, or to be worn next the skin. Also **un′der·cloth′ing.**

un·der·coat (un′dər·kōt′) *n.* **1** A coat worn under another. **2** Underfur. **3** A layer of paint, varnish, etc., beneath another layer: also **un′der·coat′ing.** **—***v.t.* To provide with an undercoat (def. 3).

un·der·cool (un′dər·kōōl′) *v.t.* To supercool.

un·der·cov·er (un′dər·kuv′ər) *adj.* Secret; surreptitious; specifically, engaged in spying or secret investigation: an *undercover* man.

under cover Secretively; surreptitiously.

un·der·cov·ert (un′dər·kuv′ərt) *n. Ornithol.* A wing covert.

un·der·croft (un′dər·krôft′, -kroft′) *n.* A subterranean chamber, vault, or passage. [<UNDER- + obs. *croft* vault, ult. <L *crypta* crypt]

un·der·cur·rent (un′dər·kûr′ənt) *n.* **1** A current, as of water or air, below another or below the surface. **2** A hidden drift or tendency, as of popular sentiments.

un·der·cut (un′dər·kut′) *n.* **1** The act or result of cutting under. **2** The tenderloin. **3** A slanting cut in a sawed log. **4** A notch cut in the side of a tree so that it will fall toward that side when sawn through. **5** Any part that is cut away below: the *undercut* of a carriage. **6** In sports, a cut or backspin imparted to the ball by an underhand or downward stroke. **—***v.t.* (un′dər·kut′) **·cut, ·cut·ting** **1** To cut under. **2** To cut away a lower portion of so as to leave a part overhanging: The river *undercut* its banks. **3** To work or sell for lower

---

uncured, **uncurious**, **uncurl**, **uncurled**, **uncurrent**, **uncursed**, **uncurtained**, **uncushioned**, **undamaged**, **undangered**, **undated**, **undaughterly**, **undazzled**, **undebatable**, **undecayed**, **undecaying**, **undecipherable**, **undecipherably**, **undeciphered**, **undeclared**, **undeclinable**, **undeclined**, **undecomposable**, **undecomposed**, **undecorated**, **undefaceable**, **undefaced**, **undefacedness**, **undefeatable**, **undefeated**, **undefended**, **undefensible**, **undefiled**, **undefinable**, **undefined**, **undeformed**, **undelayable**, **undelayed**, **undelineated**, **undeliverable**, **undelivered**, **undemocratic**, **undemonstrable**, **undemonstrably**, **undenied**, **undenominational**, **undenounced**, **undependable**, **undeplored**, **undeposed**, **undepraved**, **undepreciated**, **undepressed**, **undeputed**, **underived**, **underivedness**, **underogating**, **underogatory**, **undescribed**, **undescried**, **undeserved**, **undeservedly**, **undeservedness**, **undeserving**, **undesignated**, **undesigned**, **undesignedly**, **undesignedness**, **undesirability**, **undesirable**, **undesirably**, **undesired**, **undesirous**, **undesisting**, **undespairing**, **undestroyed**, **undetachable**, **undetached**, **undetected**, **undeterminable**, **undeterred**, **undeveloped**, **undeviating**, **undevoured**, **undifferentiated**, **undiffused**, **undigested**, **undignified**, **undilated**, **undiluted**, **undiminishable**, **undiminished**, **undimmed**, **undiplomatic**, **undisbanded**, **undiscerned**, **undiscernedly**, **undiscernible**, **undiscernibly**, **undiscerning**, **undischarged**, **undisciplined**, **undisclosed**, **undisconcerted**, **undiscordant**

payment than (a rival). **4** In golf, to impart backspin to (the ball) by striking it obliquely downward. **5** In tennis, to use an underhand stroke in cutting (the ball). **6** To lessen or destroy the effectiveness or impact of; undermine. — *adj.* **1** Having the parts in relief cut under. **2** Done by undercutting.

un·der·de·vel·oped (un′dər·di·vel′əpt) *adj.* **1** Not sufficiently developed. **2** Below a normal or adequate standard in the development of industry, resources, agriculture, etc.: an *underdeveloped* country.

un·der·do (un′dər·do͞o′) *v.t.* & *v.i.* **·did, ·done, ·do·ing** To do less than is expected or needed.

un·der·dog (un′dər·dôg′, -dog′) *n.* **1** The dog that is losing, has lost, or is at a disadvantage in a dogfight. **2** The weaker or worsted person. **3** Anyone in a position of inferiority.

un·der·done (un′dər·dun′) *adj.* **1** Insufficiently done. **2** Not cooked to the full.

un·der·drive (un′dər·drīv′) *n. Mech.* A gearing device which turns a drive shaft at a speed less than that of the engine: opposed to *overdrive.*

un·der·em·ployed (un′dər·əm·ploid′) *adj.* Unable to get a full-time or regular job; employed part of the time or working too few hours. — **un′der·em·ploy′ment** *n.*

un·der·es·ti·mate (un′dər·es′tə·māt) *v.t.* **·mat·ed, ·mat·ing** To put too low an estimate or valuation upon (things or people). See synonyms under DISPARAGE. — *n.* (-mit) **1** An insufficiently high opinion. **2** An estimate below the just value or expense. — **un′der·es′ti·ma′tion** *n.*

un·der·ex·pose (un′dər·ik·spōz′) *v.t.* **·posed, ·pos·ing** *Phot.* To expose (a film) less than is required for proper development. — **un′der·ex·posed′** *adj.* — **un′der·ex·po′sure** (-spō′zhər) *n.*

un·der·feed (un′dər·fēd′) *v.t.* **·fed, ·feed·ing** **1** To feed insufficiently. **2** To supply fuel for (an engine) from beneath.

under fire Engaged in a battle; exposed to fire; being attacked: said of troops.

un·der·foot (un′dər·fo͝ot′) *adv.* **1** Beneath the feet; down on the ground; immediately below. **2** In the way.

un·der·fur (un′dər·fûr′) *n.* The coat of dense, fine hair forming the main part of a pelt.

un·der·gar·ment (un′dər·gär′mənt) *n.* A garment to be worn under the ordinary outer garments.

un·der·gird (un′dər·gûrd′) *v.t.* **·girt** or **·gird·ed, ·gird·ing** To fasten or gird, as by something that passes underneath.

un·der·glaze (un′dər·glāz′) *adj.* Used in or suitable for porcelain decoration: said of painting in vitrifiable pigment before the glaze is applied.

un·der·go (un′dər·gō′) *v.t.* **·went, ·gone, ·go·ing** **1** To be subjected to; have experience of; suffer. **2** To bear up under; endure. **3** *Obs.* To exist under. See synonyms under ENDURE.

un·der·grad·u·ate (un′dər·graj′o͞o·it) *n.* A student of a university or college who has not taken the bachelor's degree.

un·der·ground (un′dər·ground′) *adj.* **1** Situated, done, or operating beneath the surface of the ground. **2** Hence, done in secret; clandestine. — *n.* **1** That which is beneath the surface of the ground, as a passage or space. **2** A railway operated in a system of tunnels beneath the ground. **3** A group secretly organized to resist or oppose those in control of a government or country. **4** An avant-garde movement in art, cinema, journalism, etc., generally considered to be in opposition to conventional culture or society and whose works are usually experimental, erotic, or radical in style, content, or purpose: used with *the.* — *adv.* (un′dər·ground′) **1** Beneath the surface of the ground: to work *underground.* **2** Secretly.

Underground Railroad A system of cooperation among anti-slavery people, before 1861, for assisting fugitive slaves to escape to Canada and the free States.

un·der·grown (un′dər·grōn′) *adj.* Not fully grown; undersized.

un·der·growth (un′dər·grōth′) *n.* **1** A growth of smaller plants among larger ones; specifically, a thicket or coppice in or as in a forest. **2** Condition of being undergrown. **3** A close growth of hair beneath and finer than the outer growth of a pelt.

un·der·hand (un′dər·hand′) *adj.* **1** Done or acting in a treacherously secret manner; unfair; sly. **2** In baseball, cricket, etc., underarm. — *adv.* Underhandedly; slily.

un·der·hand·ed (un′dər·han′did) *adj.* Clandestinely carried on; underhand. — **un′der·hand′ed·ly** *adv.* — **un′der·hand′ed·ness** *n.*

un·der·hung (un′dər·hung′) *adj.* **1** *Anat.* Protruding from beneath, as a lower jaw: said of persons, dogs, etc., with a jaw protruding beyond the upper jaw. **2** Underslung.

un·der·laid (un′dər·lād′) *adj.* **1** Laid underneath; supporting. **2** Supported by or having something lying or placed underneath.

un·der·lay (un′dər·lā′) *v.t.* **·laid, ·lay·ing** **1** To place (one thing) under another. **2** To furnish with a base or lining. **3** *Printing* To support or raise by underlays. — *n.* (un′dər·lā′) **1** *Printing* A piece of paper, etc., placed under certain parts of a printing form, to bring them to the proper level. **2** *Mining* An inclination, as of a lode. **3** A wager made at odds unfavorable to the better: opposed to *overlay.*

un·der·lease (un′dər·lēs′) *n.* A lease of premises by a lessee; sublease.

un·der·let (un′dər·let′) *v.t.* **·let, ·let·ting** **1** To lease (premises already held on lease); sublet. **2** To lease at less than the usual rate.

un·der·lie (un′dər·lī′) *v.t.* **·lay, ·lain, ·ly·ing** **1** To lie below or under. **2** To be the ground or support of: the principle that *underlies* a scheme. **3** To constitute a first or prior claim or lien over: A first mortgage *underlies* a second. **4** To be subject, answerable, or liable to. [OE *underlicgan*]

un·der·line (un′dər·līn′) *v.t.* **·lined, ·lin·ing** **1** To mark with a line underneath; underscore. **2** To emphasize. — *n.* A line underneath, as beneath a printed or written word or syllable to indicate emphasis or stress.

un·der·lin·en (un′dər·lin′ən) *n.* Linen underwear; any underwear.

un·der·ling (un′dər·ling) *n.* A subordinate; an inferior; a servile person.

un·der·ly·ing (un′dər·lī′ing) *adj.* **1** Lying under: *underlying* strata. **2** Hence, figuratively, fundamental: *underlying* principles. **3** Prior in claim or lien. See UNDERLIE (def. 3).

un·der·men·tioned (un′dər·men′shənd) *adj.* Mentioned below in a writing.

un·der·mine (un′dər·mīn′, un′dər·mīn) *v.t.* **·mined, ·min·ing** **1** To excavate beneath; dig a mine or passage under: to *undermine* a fortress. **2** To weaken by wearing away at the base. **3** To weaken or impair secretly or by degrees: to *undermine* the influence or the health of someone. See synonyms under WEAKEN. — **un′der·min′er** *n.*

un·der·most (un′dər·mōst′) *adj.* Having the lowest place or position.

un·der·neath (un′dər·nēth′, -nēth′) *adv.* **1** In a place below. **2** On the under or lower side. See synonyms under BENEATH. — *prep.* **1** Beneath; under; below. **2** Under the form or appearance of. **3** Under the authority of; in the control of. — *adj.* Lower. — *n.* The lower or under part or side. [OE *underneothan*]

un·der·nour·ish (un′dər·nûr′ish) *v.t.* To provide with nourishment insufficient in amount or quality for proper health and growth. — **un′der·nour′ish·ment** *n.*

un·dern·song (un′dərn·sông′, -song′) *n.* Tierce (def. 5). [OE *undern* midday, midday meal + SONG]

un·der·pants (un′dər·pants′) *n. pl.* An undergarment worn over the loins and sometimes extending over the thighs or lower legs.

un·der·pass (un′dər·pas′, -päs′) *n.* A passage beneath; the section of a way or road that passes under railway tracks or under another road.

un·der·pay (un′dər·pā′) *v.t.* **·paid, ·pay·ing** To pay insufficiently.

un·der·pin (un′dər·pin′) *v.t.* **·pinned, ·pin·ning** **1** To support, as a wall or structure, from below, especially when a previous support is removed, by inserting a prop or pier. **2** To corroborate; support.

un·der·pin·ning (un′dər·pin′ing) *n.* **1** Material or framework used to support a wall or building from below. **2** *Often pl.* Something used or functioning as a basis or foundation.

un·der·pitch (un′dər·pich′) *adj. Archit.* Designating a main vault intersected by another at a lower level. [<UNDER- + PITCH[2], *n.* (def. 3)]

un·der·plant (un′dər·plant′, -plänt′) *v.t. Rare* To plant young trees under (existing trees).

un·der·plot (un′dər·plot′) *n.* **1** A subsidiary literary or dramatic plot; an episode. **2** A piece of roguery or trickery; an underhand action. — **un′der·plot′ter** *n.*

un·der·priv·i·leged (un′dər·priv′ə·lijd) *adj.* At a social or economic disadvantage; specifically, through economic cause, not privileged to enjoy certain rights theoretically possessed by all members of a community or state.

un·der·pro·duc·tion (un′dər·prə·duk′shən) *n.* Production below capacity or below requirements; abnormally low production. Compare OVERPRODUCTION.

un·der·proof (un′dər·pro͞of′) *adj.* Having less strength than proof spirit.

un·der·prop (un′dər·prop′) *v.t.* **·propped, ·prop·ping** To prop from below; support.

un·der·quote (un′dər·kwōt′) *v.t.* **·quot·ed, ·quot·ing** **1** To undersell or offer to undersell, as goods or stocks. **2** To underbid.

un·der·rate (un′dər·rāt′) *v.t.* **·rat·ed, ·rat·ing** To rate too low; underestimate. See synonyms under DISPARAGE.

un·der·run (un′dər·run′) *v.t.* **·ran, ·run, ·run·ning** **1** To run or pass beneath. **2** *Naut.* To examine (a line, hawser, etc.) from below by drawing a boat along beneath it.

un·der·score (un′dər·skôr′, -skōr′) *v.t.* **·scored, ·scor·ing** To draw a line below, as for indicating emphasis; underline. — *n.* (un′dər·skôr′, -skōr′) A line drawn beneath a word, etc., as for emphasis.

un·der·sea (un′dər·sē′) *adj.* Existing, carried on, or adapted for use beneath the surface of the sea: *undersea* exploration; an *undersea* oil well. — *adv.* Beneath the surface of the sea: also **un′der·seas′.**

un·der·sell (un′dər·sel′) *v.t.* **·sold, ·sell·ing** **1** To sell at a lower price than. **2** To sell for less than the real value. — **un′der·sell′er** *n.*

un·der·set[1] (un′dər·set′) *v.t.* **·set, ·set·ting** **1** To prop up; support. **2** *Brit.* To underlet; sublet.

---

undiscouraged
undiscoverable
undiscoverably
undiscovered
undiscredited
undiscriminating
undiscussed
undisguised
undisguisedly
undisheartened
undishonored
undisillusioned
undismantled
undismayed
undismembered
undismissed
undispatched
undispelled
undispensed
undisputable
undisputed
undissected
undissembling
undisseminated
undissolved
undissolving
undistilled
undistinguishable
undistinguished
undistinguishing
undistracted
undistraught
undistressed
undistributed
undisturbed
undisturbedly
undisturbedness
undiversified
undiverted
undivested
undivided
undivorced
undivulged
undomestic
undomesticated
undouble
undoubting
undrained
undramatic
undramatical
undramatized
undrape
undraped
undreaded
undreamed, undreamt
undreamed-of
undried
undrilled
undrinkable
undutiful
undutifully
undutifulness
undyed
uneatable
uneaten
unecclesiastic
uneclipsed
uneconomic
uneconomical
unedible
unedifying
uneducable
uneducated
uneffaced
uneliminated
unelucidated
unemancipated
unembarrassed
unembellished
unemotional
unemphatic
unemphatical
unemptied
unenclosed
unencumbered
unendangered
unendeared
unended
unending
unendorsed
unendowed
unendurable
unenduring
unenforceable
unenforced
unenfranchised
unengaged
unengaging
un-English
unenjoyable
unenjoyed
unenlightened
unenlivened
unenriched

---

un·der·set[2] (un′dər·set′) *n.* An undercurrent.

un·der·set·ter (un′dər·set′ər) *n.* **1** An underpinning prop or support. **2** *Brit.* One who sublets.

un·der·set·ting (un′dər·set′ing) *n.* Any underpinning; also, a base or pedestal.

un·der·shap·en (un′dər·shā′pən) *adj.* Below normal size; imperfectly formed.

un·der–sher·iff (un′dər·sher′if) *n.* A deputy sheriff, especially one upon whom the sheriff's duties devolve in his absence.

un·der·shirt (un′dər·shûrt′) *n.* A garment worn beneath the shirt, generally of cotton, wool and cotton, or silk.

un·der·shot (un′dər·shot′) *adj.* **1** Propelled by water that flows underneath: said of a water wheel. **2** Projecting; having a projecting lower jaw or teeth: said especially of a bulldog.

UNDERSHOT WATER WHEEL

un·der·shrub (un′dər·shrub′) *n.* A small shrub or plant, with shrubby base.

un·der·side (un′dər·sīd′) *n.* The lower or under side or surface.

un·der·sign (un′dər·sīn′) *v.t.* To sign at the foot of; subscribe: used chiefly in the past participle. **—the undersigned** The subscriber or subscribers to a document.

un·der·sized[1] (un′dər·sīzd′) *adj.* Of less than the normal or average size.

un·der·sized[2] (un′dər·sīzd′) *adj.* Insufficiently sized, as paper.

un·der·skirt (un′dər·skûrt′) *n.* **1** A skirt worn beneath another; a petticoat. **2** The foundation skirt of a draped gown.

un·der·sleeve (un′dər·slēv′) *n.* A sleeve worn beneath another, especially when of contrasting color and showing through slashes or openings.

un·der·slung (un′dər·slung′) *adj.* Having the springs fixed to the axles from below, instead of resting upon them: said of certain automobiles.

un·der·soil (un′dər·soil′) *n.* Subsoil.

un·der·song (un′dər·sông′, -song′) *n.* **1** A subordinate strain or subdued melody. **2** An underlying meaning.

un·der·sparred (un′dər·spärd′) *adj. Naut.* Having too few, too short, or too slight spars or masts.

un·der·spin (un′dər·spin′) *n.* In golf, a backward spin imparted to the ball.

un·der·stand (un′dər·stand′) *v.* **·stood, ·stand·ing** *v.t.* **1** To come to know the meaning or import of; apprehend. **2** To perceive the nature or character of: I do not *understand* her. **3** To have comprehension or mastery of: Do you *understand* German? **4** To be aware of; realize: She *understands* her position. **5** To have been told; believe: I *understand* that she went home. **6** To take or suppose to mean; infer: How am I to *understand* that remark? **7** To accept as a condition or stipulation: It is *understood* that the tenant will provide his own heat. **8** To supply in thought when unexpressed, as the subject of a sentence. *—v.i.* **9** To have understanding; comprehend. **10** To be informed; believe. See synonyms under APPREHEND, KNOW, PERCEIVE, SOLVE. **—to understand each other** To be in agreement; be privately in sympathy with each other. [OE *understandan* < *under-* under + *standan* stand] **—un′der·stand′a·ble** *adj.* **—un′·der·stand′a·bly** *adv.*

un·der·stand·ing (un′dər·stan′ding) *n.* **1** The act of one who understands, or the resulting state; intellectual apprehension; mental discernment; comprehension. **2** The power by which one understands. **3** The sum of the mental powers by which knowledge is acquired, retained, and extended; the power of apprehending relations and making inferences from them. **4** The facts or elements of a case as apprehended by any one intelligence; an individual view of a case; opinion. **5** An agreement between two or more persons; an informal or confidential compact; also, the subject of such compact; the thing agreed on; sometimes, an arrangement or settlement of differences, or of disputed points: That was not our *understanding*; They have come to an *understanding*. *—adj.* Possessing comprehension and good sense. **—un′der·stand′ing·ly** *adv.* **—un′der·stand′ing·ness** *n.*

Synonyms (noun): apprehension, comprehension, discernment, intellect, intelligence, judgment, mind, perception, reason. See INTELLECT, MIND, WISDOM.

un·der·state (un′dər·stāt′) *v.* **·stat·ed, ·stat·ing** *v.t.* **1** To state with less force than the truth warrants or allows. **2** To state, as a number or dimension, as less than the true one. *—v.i.* **3** To make an understatement.

un·der·state·ment (un′dər·stāt′mənt) *n.* A statement covering less than the truth or fact.

un·der·stood (un′dər·stŏŏd′) Past tense and past participle of UNDERSTAND. *—adj.* Taken for granted; agreed upon by all.

un·der·strap·per (un′dər·strap′ər) *n.* An underling; a subordinate agent.

un·der·strap·ping (un′dər·strap′ing) *adj.* Subordinate; inferior.

un·der·stra·tum (un′dər·strā′təm, -strat′əm) *n. pl.* **·stra·ta** (-strā′tə, -strat′ə) An underlying stratum; substratum, literal or figurative.

un·der·stud·y (un′dər·stud′ē) *v.t. & v.i.* **·stud·ied, ·stud·y·ing** **1** To study (a part) in order to be able, if necessary, to take the place of the actor playing it. **2** To act as an understudy to (another actor). *—n. pl.* **·stud·ies** **1** An actor or actress who can take the place of another actor in a given role when necessary. **2** A person prepared to perform the work or fill the position of another.

un·der·take (un′dər·tāk′) *v.* **·took, ·tak·en, ·tak·ing** *v.t.* **1** To take upon oneself; agree or attempt to do; begin. **2** To contract to do; pledge oneself to. **3** To guarantee or promise. **4** To take under charge or guidance. **5** *Obs.* To enter into combat with. *—v.i.* **6** To make oneself responsible or liable; be surety: with *for*. See synonyms under ENDEAVOR.

un·der·tak·er (un′dər·tā′kər *for def. 1*; un′dər·tā′kər *for def. 2*) *n.* **1** One who undertakes any work or enterprise; especially, a contractor. **2** One whose business it is to arrange for burying the dead and to conduct funerals.

un·der·tak·ing (un′dər·tā′king; *for def. 3* un′·dər·tā′king) *n.* **1** The act of one who undertakes any task or enterprise. **2** The thing undertaken; an enterprise; task. **3** The management of funerals; the business of an undertaker. **4** An engagement, promise, or guaranty.

under tenant A tenant of a tenant; one who holds premises by a lease from one who is himself a lessee.

under the rose Sub rosa.

under the weather *Colloq.* **1** Depressed by unpleasant weather; hence, somewhat ill; indisposed. **2** Inebriated; drunk. **3** In financial straits.

under the yoke In subjection.

un·der·thrust (un′dər·thrust′) *n. Geol.* **1** A deformation of the earth's crust in which a mass of rock is pushed beneath an overlying mass. **2** The intruded rock mass itself.

un·der·tint (un′dər·tint′) *n.* A subdued tint.

un·der·tone (un′dər·tōn′) *n.* **1** A tone of lower pitch or loudness than is usual; the tone of a subdued voice; sometimes, a whisper. **2** A subdued shade of a color, as when spread thinly on a white surface; also, a color upon which other colors have been imposed and which is seen through them, modifying their effect. **3** A meaning or suggestion implied but not expressed. **4** An underlying stability in the price level of some stocks.

un·der·took (un′dər·tŏŏk′) Past tense of UNDERTAKE.

un·der·tow (un′dər·tō′) *n.* **1** The flow of water beneath and in a direction opposite to the surface current. **2** The backward undercurrent below the surf.

un·der–trick (un′dər·trik′) *n.* In certain card games, a trick required to make the number declared, but not taken.

un·der·trump (un′dər·trump′) *v.t.* To play to (a previous card in the same trick) a trump lower than one already played by another player; also, to trump with too low a trump, and so be overtrumped.

un·der·val·ue (un′dər·val′yōō) *v.t.* **·ued, ·u·ing** **1** To value too lightly; underrate; underestimate. **2** *Obs.* To hold inferior: with *to* before the object compared. See synonyms under DISPARAGE. **—un′der·val′u·a′tion** *n.*

un·der·vest (un′dər·vest′) *n. Brit.* An undershirt.

un·der·waist (un′dər·wāst′) *n.* A waist to be worn under another waist.

un·der·wa·ter (un′dər·wô′tər, -wot′ər) *adj.* **1** Being, occurring, or used below the surface of a body of water: *underwater* research. **2** Below the water line of a ship. *—n.* The region or environment below the surface of water. *—adv.* Below the surface of water.

un·der·way (un·dər·wā′) *adv.* **1** In progress: The meeting was already *underway*. **2** Into operation or motion: to get the fund drive *underway*. Also **under way.**

un·der·wear (un′dər·wâr′) *n.* Garments worn underneath the ordinary outer garments.

un·der·weight (un′dər·wāt′) *adj.* Having less than the normal weight. *—n.* Insufficiency of weight; also, weight below normal.

un·der·went (un′dər·went′) Past tense of UNDERGO.

un·der·wing (un′dər·wing′) *n. Entomol.* One of the posterior pair of wings in an insect.

underwing moth A large noctuid moth (genus *Catocala*), whose front wings are an inconspicuous brown or gray.

un·der·wood (un′dər·wŏŏd′) *n.* Low trees and brush growing among large forest trees.

un·der·work (un′dər·wûrk′) *v.t.* **1** To work for lower wages than. **2** To exact too little work from. **3** *Obs.* To weaken or injure by underhand contrivances; undermine. *—v.i.* **4** To do too little work. *—n.* (un′dər·wûrk′) Subordinate, unimportant, or routine work.

un·der·world (un′dər·wûrld′) *n.* **1** In Greek and Roman mythology, the abode of the dead; Hades; Orcus. **2** In later folklore, sometimes a beautiful country under the earth or sea; also, fairyland, sometimes entered through a well. **3** The antipodes; also, all beneath the horizon. **4** The sublunary world; the earth. **5** The debased, criminal, or degenerate components of the social order; the world of crime and vice; gangsterdom.

un·der·write (un′dər·rīt′) *v.* **·wrote, ·writ·ten, ·writ·ing** *v.t.* **1** To write beneath; subscribe. **2** In finance, to execute and deliver (a policy of insurance on specified property, especially

---

unenrolled
unenslaved
unentangled
unentered
unenterprising
unentertaining
unenthralled
unenthusiastic
unentitled
unenviable
unenvied
unenvious
unenvying
unequipped
unerased
unescapable
unessayed
unestablished
unesthetic
unestimated
unethical
unexaggerated
unexalted
unexamined
unexcavated
unexcelled
unexchangeable
unexcited
unexciting
unexcluded
unexcused
unexecuted
unexercised
unexhausted
unexpanded
unexpectant
unexpended
unexpert
unexpiated
unexpired
unexplainable
unexplained
unexplicit
unexploded
unexploited
unexplored
unexported
unexposed
unexpressed
unexpunged
unexpurgated
unextended
unexterminated
unextinguishable
unextinguished
unfadable
unfaded
unfading
unfallen
unfaltering
unfashionable
unfashioned
unfastened
unfatherly
unfathomable
unfathomed
unfatigued
unfavored
unfeared
unfearing
unfeasible
unfed
unfederated
unfeignedly
unfeignedness
unfeigningly
unfelt
unfeminine
unfenced
unfermented
unfertile
unfertilized
unfetter
unfettered
unfilial
unfilled
unfilmed
unfiltered
unfinished
unfired
unfittingly
unfixed
unfixedness
unflagging
unflattered
unflattering
unflavored
unflickering
unfoiled
unforbearing
unforbid
unforbidden
unforced
unforcedly
unfordable

marine property); insure; assume (a risk) by way of insurance. **3** To engage to buy, at a determined price and time, all or part of the stock in (a new enterprise or company) that is not subscribed for by the public; loosely, to guarantee or assume responsibility for, as an enterprise. **4** To undertake to pay, as a subscription or written pledge of money. — *v.i.* **5** To act as an underwriter; especially, to issue a policy of insurance. [OE *underwrītan,* trans. of L *subscribere*]

un·der·writ·er (un′dər·rī′tər) *n.* **1** A body corporate or a person in the insurance business; one who sets up the premium for a risk. **2** One who underwrites (def. 3) an issue of stocks, bonds, or the like.

un·de·sign·ing (un′di·zī′ning) *adj.* Without ulterior purpose or selfish plan; artless; sincere.

un·de·ter·mined (un′di·tûr′mind) *adj.* **1** Not decided or fixed. **2** Not determined.

un·did (un·did′) Past tense of UNDO.

un·dine (un·dēn′, un′dēn, -dīn) *n. Med.* A small glass cup or flask for irrigating the eye. [<L *unda* wave + -INE[1]; from its wavy profile]

Un·dine (un·dēn′, un′dēn, -dīn) A water nymph without a soul, which she later received by marrying a mortal and bearing a child: heroine of a book (1811) by Baron de la Motte Fouqué, German author. [<G <NL *Undina* <L *unda* wave]

un·di·rect·ed (un′di·rek′tid, -dī-) *adj.* **1** Unguided, or uninformed as to direction. **2** Not addressed: said of a letter.

un·dis·posed (un′dis·pōzd′) *adj.* **1** Not sold, settled, placed, or otherwise decided: frequently with *of.* **2** *Obs.* Disinclined. — **un′·dis·pos′ed·ness** (-pō′zid·nis) *n.*

un·do (un·dōō′) *v.t.* **·did, ·done, ·do·ing 1** To cause to be as if never done; reverse, annul, or cancel. **2** To loosen or untie. **3** To unfasten and open. **4** To bring to ruin; destroy. **5** *Obs.* To solve, as a riddle. [OE *undōn*] — **un·do′er** *n.*

un·do·ing (un·dōō′ing) *n.* **1** Reversal of what has been done. **2** Destruction; ruin; cause of ruin. **3** The action of unfastening, loosening, opening, etc. **4** *Psychoanal.* The abolition of painful experiences by the unconscious, resulting in obliviousness to the unacceptable fact.

un·done[1] (un·dun′) *adj.* **1** Untied; unfastened. **2** Ruined. [Orig. pp. of UNDO]

un·done[2] (un·dun′) *adj.* Not done. [<UN-[1] + DONE]

un·doubt·ed (un·dou′tid) *adj.* **1** Assured beyond question; being beyond a doubt. **2** Not viewed with distrust; unsuspected. See synonyms under INCONTESTABLE. — **un·doubt′ed·ly** *adv.*

un·draw (un·drô′) *v.t.* & *v.i.* **·drew, ·drawn, ·draw·ing** To draw open, away, or aside.

un·dress (un·dres′) *v.t.* **1** To divest of clothes; strip. **2** To remove the dressing or bandages from, as a wound. **3** To divest of special attire; disrobe. — *v.i.* **4** To remove one's clothing. — *n.* **1** Ordinary attire; negligée, as opposed to full or evening dress; specifically, the military or naval uniform worn by officers when not on parade or at functions necessitating full dress. **2** Comfortable, informal clothing. **3** Nudity: in a state of *undress.* — *adj.* (un′dres′) Pertaining to everyday attire; hence, informal.

un·dressed (un·drest′) *adj.* **1** Not dressed. **2** Not treated or dressed: said of kid leather.

Und·set (ōōn′set), **Sigrid,** 1882–1949, Norwegian novelist.

und so wei·ter (ōōnt zō vī′tər) *German* And so forth; et cetera; abbreviated *u.s.w.*

un·due (un·dōō′, -dyōō′) *adj.* **1** Excessive; disproportionate. **2** Not justified by law; illegal. **3** Not due; in process of becoming due, but not yet demandable. **4** Not appropriate; improper.

un·du·lant (un′dyə·lənt, -də-) *adj.* Undulating; fluctuating. [<L *undul(atus)* + -ANT]

undulant fever *Pathol.* A persistent and wasting infectious disease of wide distribution, caused by a bacterium (genus *Brucella*) which is usually transmitted to man in the milk of cows and goats. The disease is marked by fluctuating or recurrent fever, with swelling of the joints, neuralgic pains, profuse perspiration, and enlargement of the spleen: also called *brucellosis, Malta fever, Mediterranean fever.*

un·du·late (un′dyə·lāt, -də-) *v.* **·lat·ed, ·lat·ing** *v.t.* **1** To cause to move like a wave or in waves. **2** To give a wavy appearance to. — *v.i.* **3** To move like a wave or waves. **4** To have a wavy form or appearance. — *adj.* (-lit, -lāt) **1** Wavy. **2** Having wavelike markings, as of color. See synonyms under FLUCTUATE. [<L *undulatus* undulated, ult. < *unda* wave]

un·du·lat·ing (un′dyə·lā′ting, -də-) *adj.* Having the appearance of waves; vibrating; wavy.

un·du·la·tion (un′dyə·lā′shən, -də-) *n.* **1** The act of undulating; a waving or sinuous motion; a wave. **2** An appearance as of waves; a gentle rise and fall. **3** *Physics* The continuous propagation of waves through a medium. — **un′du·la·to′ry** (-lə·tôr′ē, -tō′rē) *adj.*

un·du·la·tus (un′dyə·lā′təs, -də-) *n. Meteorol.* A variety of stratocumulus cloud characterized by elongated wavelike undulations, sometimes in different directions. [<NL <L. See UNDULATE.]

un·du·lous (un′dyə·ləs, -də-) *adj.* Undulatory; undulating.

un·du·ly (un·dōō′lē, -dyōō′-) *adv.* **1** Excessively. **2** In violation of a moral or of a legal standard; unjustly.

un·dy·ing (un·dī′ing) *adj.* Immortal.

un·earned (un·ûrnd′) *adj.* Not earned by labor; also, undeserved.

unearned increment See under INCREMENT.

un·earth (un·ûrth′) *v.t.* **1** To dig or root up from the earth. **2** To reveal; discover.

un·earth·ly (un·ûrth′lē) *adj.* **1** Not earthly; sublime. **2** Supernatural; terrifying; weird; terrible. **3** Ridiculously unconventional; inconvenient, or unpleasant; preposterous: at this *unearthly* hour. — **un·earth′li·ness** *n.*

un·ease (un·ēz′) *n.* Mental or emotional discomfort, dissatisfaction, anxiety, etc.

un·eas·y (un·ē′zē) *adj.* **·eas·i·er, ·eas·i·est 1** Deprived of ease; disturbed; unquiet. **2** Not affording ease or rest; uncomfortable; causing discomfort. **3** Showing embarassment or constraint; strained. **4** *Obs.* Difficult. — **un·eas′i·ly** *adv.* — **un·eas′i·ness** *n.*

un·eath (un·ēth′) *adv. Obs.* Scarcely; hardly; not easily. [OE *unēathe* not easily]

un·em·ploy·a·ble (un′əm·ploi′ə·bəl) *adj.* Not employable. — *n.* A person who, because of illness, age, mental or physical incapacity, or other reason, cannot be employed.

un·em·ployed (un′əm·ploid′) *adj.* **1** Having no occupation; out of work. **2** Not put to use or turned to account; uninvested: *unemployed* resources. See synonyms under IDLE, VACANT. — *n.* A jobless person: with *the,* unemployed persons collectively. — **un′em·ploy′ment** *n.*

un·en·cum·bered funds (un′en·kum′bərd) **1** Funds not designated for any specific use; general funds. **2** Funds not pledged in connection with present or future obligations.

un·e·qual (un·ē′kwəl) *adj.* **1** Not having equivalent or equal extension, duration, or properties; not equal in strength, ability, wealth, status, or other respects. **2** Inadequate for the purpose; insufficient: with *to.* **3** Not balanced; disproportioned; inequitable; unfair. **4** Wanting in uniformity; varying; irregular. **5** *Bot.* Unsymmetrical; *unequal* distribution. **6** Involving poorly matched competitors or contestants: an *unequal* contest. — **un·e′qual·ly** *adv.*

un·e·qualed (un·ē′kwəld) *adj.* Not equaled or matched; unrivaled; supreme. Also **un·e′qualled.**

un·e·quiv·o·cal (un′i·kwiv′ə·kəl) *adj.* Understandable in only one way; distinct; plain. See synonyms under ABSOLUTE, CLEAR, PLAIN. — **un′e·quiv′o·cal·ly** *adv.*

un·err·ing (un·ûr′ing, -er′-) *adj.* Making no mistakes; not erring: also, sure; accurate; infallible. — **un·err′ing·ly** *adv.*

UNESCO (yōō·nes′kō) The United Nations Educational, Scientific and Cultural Organization, established November, 1946, to "advance mutual knowledge and understanding of peoples," promote popular education, and assist in the diffusion of knowledge. Also **Unesco.**

un·es·sen·tial (un′ə·sen′shəl) *adj.* **1** Not absolutely required; not of prime importance. **2** Unimportant. **3** Void of essence, real or apparent. — **un′es·sen′tial·ly** *adv.*

un·e·vac·u·a·ble (un′i·vak′yōō·ə·bəl) *adj.* Not capable of being removed or evacuated, as in a military action or air raid.

un·e·ven (un·ē′vən) *adj.* **1** Not even, smooth, or level; rough. **2** Not level, parallel, or perfectly horizontal. **3** Not divisible by two without remainder; odd: said of numbers. **4** Not uniform; variable; spasmodic. **5** *Obs.* Not having correspondence; not balanced; not fair or just; also, ill-suited; not matched. See synonyms under IRREGULAR, ROUGH. — **un·e′ven·ly** *adv.* — **un·e′ven·ness** *n.*

un·e·vent·ful (un′i·vent′fəl) *adj.* Devoid of noteworthy events; quiet.

un·ex·am·pled (un′ig·zam′pəld) *adj.* So great, remarkable, or striking as to have no precedent or analogy; without a parallel example.

un·ex·cep·tion·a·ble (un′ik·sep′shən·ə·bəl) *adj.* That cannot be objected to; irreproachable. — **un′ex·cep′tion·a·ble·ness** *n.* — **un′ex·cep′·tion·a·bly** *adv.*

un·ex·cep·tion·al (un′ik·sep′shən·əl) *adj.* **1** Being no exception; ordinary. **2** Subject to no exception: *unexceptional* orders.

un·ex·pect·ed (un′ik·spek′tid) *adj.* Coming without warning; not expected: said especially of things of such a kind that one would not naturally expect them; sudden; strange and unforeseen. — **the unexpected** Unexpected things or events collectively; that which is unforeseen. — **un′ex·pect′ed·ly** *adv.* — **un′ex·pect′ed·ness** *n.*

un·ex·pe·ri·enced (un′ik·spir′ē·ənst) *adj.* **1** Not experienced; not had, undergone, possessed, or known: *unexperienced* pain. **2** Lacking experience; inexperienced.

un·ex·pres·sive (un′ik·spres′iv) *adj.* **1** Not having expression; inexpressive. **2** *Obs.* Inexpressible. — **un′ex·pres′sive·ly** *adv.*

un·fail·ing (un·fā′ling) *adj.* **1** Giving or constituting a supply that never fails; inexhaustible: an *unfailing* spring. **2** Always fulfilling

unforeboding
unforeknown
unforeseeable
unforeseeing
unforeseen
unforetold
unforfeited
unforged
unforgetful
unforgetting
unforgivable
unforgiven
unforgiving
unforgot
unforgotten
unformulated
unforsaken
unfortified
unfought
unfound
unframed
unfranchised
unfraternal
unfraught
unfree
unfreedom
unfreezable
un–French
unfrequent
unfrequently
unfrozen
unfulfilled
unfurnished
unfurrowed
ungallant
ungalled
ungarnished
ungartered
ungathered
ungenial
ungenteel
ungentle
ungentlemanly
ungently
un–get–at–able
ungird
ungirded
ungirt
ungladdened
unglazed
unglossed
unglove
ungloved
unglue
ungot
ungoverned
ungown
ungowned
ungraced
ungraceful
ungraded
ungrafted
ungrained
ungrammatical
ungrammatically
ungratified
ungrounded
ungrudging
unguided
unhackneyed
unhailed
unhalved
unhammered
unhampered
unhandicapped
unhandled
unhandsome
unhang
unhanged
unharassed
unhardened
unharmed
unharming
unharmonious
unharnessed
unharrowed
unharvested
unhasty
unhatched
unhealed
unhealthful
unheated
unheeded
unheedful
unheeding
unheedingly
unhelped
unhelpful
unheralded
unheroic
unhesitating
unhewn
unhindered
unhired
unhistoric

add, āce, câre, pälm; end, ēven; it, īce; odd, ōpen, ôrder; tŏŏk, pōōl; up, bûrn; ə = a in *above,* e in *sicken,* i in *clarity,* o in *melon,* u in *focus;* yōō = u in *fuse;* oi, oil; ou, pout; ch, check; g, go; ng, ring; th, thin; th, this; zh, vision. Foreign sounds à, œ, ü, kh, ṅ; and ◆: see page xx. < from; + plus; ? possibly.

requirements; not falling short of need, hope, or expectation. 3 Sure; infallible. —**un·fail′·ing·ly** *adv.* —**un·fail′ing·ness** *n.*

un·fair (un·fâr′) *adj.* 1 Marked by dishonesty or fraud; showing partiality or prejudice; not fair: *unfair* dealing. 2 Not compatible with law and justice; illegal: *unfair* competition. 3 *Obs.* Not pleasing or comely. See synonyms under BAD. [OE *unfæger* ugly] —**un·fair′ly** *adv.* —**un·fair′ness** *n.*

un·faith·ful (un·fāth′fəl) *adj.* 1 Manifesting lack or absence of faith; unworthy of trust; perfidious; faithless; not true to marriage vows: an *unfaithful* husband. 2 Not true to a standard or to an original; not accurate or exact: an *unfaithful* description. 3 *Obs.* Not having religious faith; unbelieving; infidel. See synonyms under PERFIDIOUS. —**un·faith′·ful·ly** *adv.* —**un·faith′ful·ness** *n.*

un·fa·mil·iar (un′fə·mil′yər) *adj.* 1 Not familiarly knowing: I am *unfamiliar* with it. 2 Not familiarly known: an *unfamiliar* face. —**un′·fa·mil′i·ar′i·ty** (-mil′ē·ar′ə·tē) *n.* —**un′fa·mil′·iar·ly** *adv.*

un·fast·en (un·fas′ən, -fäs′-) *v.t.* To untie; loosen; open. —*v.i.* To become untied.

un·fa·thered (un·fä′thərd) *adj.* 1 Having no acknowledged father; hence, illegitimate. 2 Unauthenticated.

un·fa·vor·a·ble (un·fā′vər·ə·bəl) *adj.* Not favorable; unpropitious; adverse. Also *Brit.* **un·fa′vour·a·ble.** —**un·fa′vor·a·ble·ness** *n.* —**un·fa′vor·a·bly** *adv.*

Unfederated Malay States Former collective name for the states of Perlis, Kedah, Kelantan, Trengganu, and Johore, now States of Malaya in Malaysia.

un·feel·ing (un·fē′ling) *adj.* 1 Not sympathetic; hard; cruel. 2 *Obs.* Destitute of feeling or sensation. See synonyms under HARD. —**un·feel′ing·ly** *adv.* —**un·feel′ing·ness** *n.*

un·feigned (un·fānd′) *adj.* Not feigned; not pretended; sincere; genuine.

un·fel·lowed (un·fel′ōd) *adj.* 1 Unequaled; unmatchable. 2 Alone; without a companion.

un·fit (un·fit′) *v.t* **·fit·ted** or **·fit, ·fit·ting** To deprive of requisite fitness, skill, etc.; disqualify. —*adj.* 1 Having no fitness; unsuitable. 2 Not appropriate; improper. 3 Not completely trained; not in best condition: said of race horses. —**un·fit′ly** *adv.* —**un·fit′ness** *n.*

un·fix (un·fiks′) *v.t.* 1 To unfasten; loosen; detach. 2 To unsettle.

un·flap·pa·ble (un·flap′ə·bəl) *adj.* Characterized by unshakable composure; imperturbable. —**un·flap′pa·bil′i·ty** *n.*

un·fledged (un·flejd′) *adj.* 1 Not yet fledged; immature, as a young bird. 2 Inexperienced: an *unfledged* orator.

un·flesh·ly (un·flesh′lē) *adj.* Not corporeal, worldly, or sensual; ethereal; spiritual.

un·flinch·ing (un·flin′ching) *adj.* Done without shrinking; steadfast; brave. —**un·flinch′ing·ly** *adv.* —**un·flinch′ing·ness** *n.*

un·fold[1] (un·fōld′) *v.t.* 1 To open or spread out (something folded). 2 To lay open to view. 3 To make clear by detailed explanation; explain: to *unfold* a plan. 4 To develop. —*v.i.* 5 To become opened; expand. 6 To become manifest. See synonyms under AMPLIFY, INTERPRET, SOLVE. [OE *unfealdan*]

un·fold[2] (un·fōld′) *v.t.* To free or let loose from a fold or pen.

un·for·get·ta·ble (un′fər·get′ə·bəl) *adj.* Not forgettable; memorable. —**un′for·get′ta·bly** *adv.*

un·formed (un·fôrmd′) *adj.* 1 Devoid of shape or form; not fully developed in character; crude. 2 Unorganized.

un·for·tu·nate (un·fôr′chə·nit) *adj.* 1 Having ill fortune; not prosperous; unsuccessful. 2 Causing or attended by ill fortune; disastrous. See synonyms under BAD. —*n.* 1 One who is unfortunate. 2 Specifically, one who has lapsed from virtue; a prostitute. —**un·for′·tu·nate·ly** *adv.* —**un·for′tu·nate·ness** *n.*

un·found·ed (un·foun′did) *adj.* 1 Resting on no solid foundation; groundless; baseless. 2 Not founded or established. —**un·found′·ed·ly** *adv.*

un·fre·quent·ed (un′fri·kwen′tid) *adj.* Rarely or never visited or frequented.

un·friend·ed (un·fren′did) *adj.* Without friends. —**un·friend′ed·ness** *n.*

un·friend·ly (un·frend′lē) *adj.* 1 Unkindly disposed; inimical; hostile. 2 Not favorable or propitious. See synonyms under INIMICAL. —*adv.* In an unfriendly manner. —**un·friend′·li·ness** *n.*

un·frock (un·frok′) *v.t.* 1 To divest of a frock or gown. 2 To depose, as a monk or priest, from ecclesiastical rank.

un·fruit·ful (un·frōōt′fəl) *adj.* 1 Bearing no fruit; having no offspring; barren. 2 Having no useful results; fruitless: an *unfruitful* line of thought. —**un·fruit′ful·ly** *adv.* —**un·fruit′·ful·ness** *n.*

un·fumed (un·fyōōmd′) *adj.* 1 Not fumigated. 2 *Obs.* Undistilled.

un·fund·ed (un·fun′did) *adj.* Not funded: said of a debt.

un·furl (un·fûrl′) *v.t.* & *v.i.* 1 To unroll, as a flag; spread out; expand. 2 To unfold. —**un·furled′** *adj.*

un·gain·ly (un·gān′lē) *adj.* Lacking grace or ease; clumsy. See synonyms under AWKWARD. —*adv.* In an awkward manner. —**un·gain′·li·ness** *n.*

Un·ga·va (ung·gä′və, -gā′və) A district of northern Quebec province, extending south of Ungava Bay, and including part of Labrador; 239,780 square miles: also *New Quebec.*

Ungava Bay An inlet of Hudson Strait in northern Quebec province; 200 miles long, 160 miles wide at the mouth.

Ungava Peninsula A peninsula of northern Quebec province between Ungava Bay and Hudson Bay; 400 miles long, 350 miles wide.

un·gen·er·ous (un·jen′ər·əs) *adj.* Not generous; illiberal; niggardly; unkind or harsh in judging others. —**un·gen′er·ous·ly** *adv.*

un·gift·ed (un·gif′tid) *adj.* 1 Not gifted or endowed with talent. 2 Not having received gifts.

un·god·ly (un·god′lē) *adj.* 1 Having no reverence for God; impious; wicked. 2 Unholy; sinful. 3 *Colloq.* Outrageous. —*adv.* In an ungodly manner. —**un·god′li·ness** *n.*

un·got·ten (un·got′n) *adj.* 1 Not begotten. 2 Not obtained; not acquired.

un·gov·ern·a·ble (un·guv′ər·nə·bəl) *adj.* That cannot be governed; refractory; unruly. See synonyms under PERVERSE, REBELLIOUS, VIOLENT. —**un·gov′ern·a·ble·ness** *n.* —**un·gov′·ern·a·bly** *adv.*

un·gra·cious (un·grā′shəs) *adj.* 1 Lacking in graciousness of manner; unmannerly. 2 Not pleasing; offensive; unacceptable. 3 *Obs.* Odious. —**un·gra′cious·ly** *adv.* —**un·gra′cious·ness** *n.*

un·grate·ful (un·grāt′fəl) *adj.* 1 Feeling or showing a lack of gratitude; not thankful. 2 Not pleasant; disagreeable. 3 Unrewarding; yielding no return. —**un·grate′ful·ly** *adv.* —**un·grate′ful·ness** *n.*

un·gual (ung′gwəl) *adj.* Having, resembling, or pertaining to a hoof, claw, or nail. [<L *unguis* hoof, claw, nail]

un·guard (un·gärd′) *v.t.* To deprive of a guard; expose.

un·guard·ed (un·gär′did) *adj.* 1 Having no guard; being without protection. 2 Done or spoken without proper caution; careless: *unguarded* speech. —**un·guard′ed·ly** *adv.* —**un·guard′ed·ness** *n.*

un·guent (ung′gwənt) *n.* Any ointment for local application; a salve or cerate. [<L *unguentum* < *unguere* anoint]

un·guen·tar·y (ung′gwən·ter′ē) *adj.* Of, for, like, or pertaining to unguents.

un·guic·u·late (ung·gwik′yə·lit, -lāt) *adj.* 1 *Zool.* Having claws, as a carnivorous mammal. 2 *Bot.* Having a stalklike or clawlike base, as the petals of pinks. —*n.* A mammal having claws, as distinguished from an ungulate or cetacean. [<NL *unguiculatus* <L *unguiculus* fingernail, dim. of *unguis* nail]

un·gui·form (ung′gwi·fôrm) *adj.* Claw-shaped; hooked; unciform. [<L *unguis* nail + -FORM]

un·gui·nous (ung′gwi·nəs) *adj.* Resembling, containing, or consisting of oil or fat; unctuous. [<L *unguinosus* < *unguen, -inis* ointment]

un·guis (ung′gwis) *n. pl.* **·gues** (-gwēz) 1 A nail, claw, hoof, or talon. 2 A structure resembling a nail. 3 *Bot.* A claw or lower contracted part of a petal. [<L, nail]

un·gu·la (ung′gyə·lə) *n. pl.* **·lae** (-lē) 1 *Zool.* A hoof, claw, nail, or talon. 2 *Surg.* An instrument for removing a dead fetus from the womb. 3 *Geom.* That which is left of a cone or cylinder when the top is cut off by a plane oblique to the base: so called from its resemblance to a horse's hoof. 4 *Bot.* An unguis. [<L, hoof < *unguis* nail]

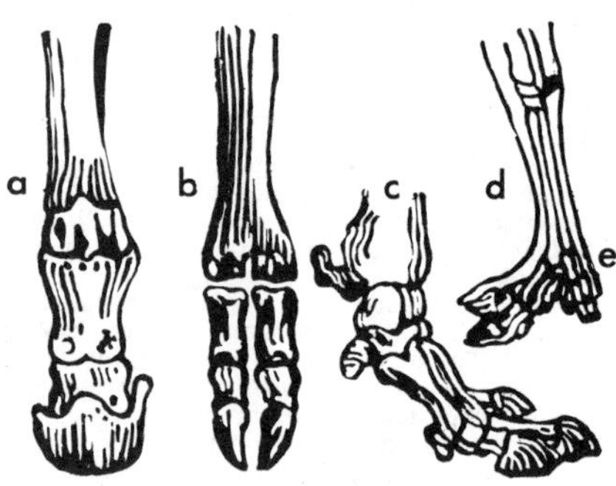

UNGULATE FEET
a. Hind foot of horse.
b. Foot of a stag.
c. Forefoot of Indian rhinoceros.
d. Side view of stag foot, showing false hoof at *e.*

un·gu·lar (ung′gyə·lər) *adj.* Of, pertaining to, or bearing a nail, hoof, or claw; ungual.

un·gu·late (ung′gyə·lit, -lāt) *adj.* 1 Having hoofs; hoof-shaped. 2 Designating, pertaining to, or belonging to a large division (*Ungulata*) of hoofed, herbivorous mammals, including the elephant, rhinoceros, horse, cony, hog, and all the ruminants. —*n.* A hoofed mammal. [<LL *ungulatus* <L *ungula* hoof]

un·gu·li·grade (ung′gyə·lə·grād′) *adj.* Walking on hoofs, as a horse or cow. [<L *ungula* hoof + -GRADE]

un·hair (un·hâr′) *v.t.* & *v.i.* To free or become free of hair, as hides by soaking and scraping.

un·hal·low (un·hal′ō) *v.t.* To profane; desecrate.

un·hal·lowed (un·hal′ōd) *adj.* 1 Left secular. 2 Not sacred. 3 Unholy; wicked.

un·halsed (un·hôlst′) *adj. Scot.* Not saluted or greeted.

un·hand (un·hand′) *v.t.* To remove one's hand from; release from the hand or hands; let go.

un·hand·y (un·han′dē) *adj.* 1 Inconvenient;

unhomogeneous
unhonored
unhood
un–Horatian
unhostile
unhoused
unhuman
unhumanize
unhung
unhurt
unhurtful
unhygienic
unhyphenated
unhyphened
unideal
unidentified
unidiomatic
unilluminated
unillumined
unillustrated
unimaginable
unimaginably
unimaginative
unimagined
unimbued
unimitated
unimpaired
unimpassioned
unimpeded
unimplored
unimportance
unimportant
unimposing
unimpressed
unimpressible
unimpressionable
unimpressive
uninaugurated
uninclosed
unincorporated
unincumbered
unindemnified
unindicated
unindorsed
uninfected
uninfested
uninflammable
uninflected
uninfluenced
uninfluential
uninformed
uninfringed
uninhabitable
uninhabited
uninhibited
uninitiated
uninjured
uninspired
uninspiring
uninstructed
uninstructive
uninsurable
uninsured
unintellectual
unintelligibility
unintelligible
unintelligibly
unintended
unintentional
unintentionally
uninteresting
uninterestingly
unintermitted
unintermittent
unintermitting
uninterpolated
uninterpreted
uninterrupted
unintimidated
unintoxicated
uninvaded
uninvented
uninventive
uninverted
uninvested
uninvited
uninviting
uninvoked
uninvolved
unissued
unjaded
unjoined
unjointed
unjoyful
unjudged
unjustifiable
unjustifiably
unkept
unkindled
unkindliness
unkingly
unkissed
unknelled
unknightly
unknit

hard to handle. 2 Clumsy; lacking in manual skill. —**un·hand′i·ly** *adv.*

un·hap·py (un·hap′ē) *adj.* **·pi·er, ·pi·est** 1 Subject to conditions that prevent or destroy happiness; sad; depressed. 2 Causing or constituting misery, unrest, or dissatisfaction: *unhappy* circumstances. 3 Characterized by or exhibiting ill fortune; unfortunate; unpropitious. 4 Exhibiting lack of tact or judgment; inappropriate; inopportune. 5 *Obs.* Evil. See synonyms under BAD, SAD. —**un·hap′pi·ly** *adv.* —**un·hap′pi·ness** *n.*

un·har·bored (un·här′bərd) *adj.* 1 Having no harbor, shelter, or cover. 2 *Obs.* Not affording shelter. Also *Brit.* **un·har′boured.**

un·har·ness (un·här′nis) *v.t.* 1 To remove the harness from; unyoke; release. 2 To remove the armor from.

un·hat (un·hat′) *v.* **·hat·ted, ·hat·ting** *v.i.* To take off one's hat, especially to show respect or in worship. —*v.t.* To remove the hat from.

un·health·y (un·hel′thē) *adj.* **·health·i·er, ·health·i·est** 1 Lacking health, vigor, or wholesomeness; sickly; unsound: *unhealthy* animals or plants; also, indicating such a condition: *unhealthy* signs. 2 Loosely, insalubrious; injurious to health. 3 Morally or spiritually unsound, defective, or pernicious: *unhealthy* fiction. —**un·health′i·ly** *adv.* —**un·health′i·ness** *n.*

un·heard (un·hûrd′) *adj.* 1 Not perceived by the ear. 2 Not granted a hearing. 3 Obscure; unknown.

un·heard-of (un·hûrd′uv′, -ov′) *adj.* Not known of before; unknown or unprecedented.

un·helm (un·helm′) *v.t.* To remove the helmet or helm of. —*v.i.* To remove one's helmet.

un·hinge (un·hinj′) *v.t.* **·hinged, ·hing·ing** 1 To take from the hinges. 2 To remove the hinges of. 3 To detach; dislodge. 4 To throw into confusion; disorder. 5 To make unstable; unsettle, as the mind.

un·hitch (un·hich′) *v.t.* To unfasten.

un·ho·ly (un·hō′lē) *adj.* **·ho·li·er, ·ho·li·est** 1 Not hallowed. 2 Lacking purity; wicked; sinful. See synonyms under PROFANE, SINFUL. [OE *unhālig*] —**un·ho′li·ly** *adv.* —**un·ho′li·ness** *n.*

un·hook (un·hŏŏk′) *v.t.* 1 To remove from a hook. 2 To unfasten the hook or hooks of. —*v.i.* 3 To become unhooked.

un·hoped (un·hōpt′) *adj.* Not hoped (for); unexpected; exceeding hope: chiefly in the compound **un·hoped′-for′.**

un·horse (un·hôrs′) *v.t.* **·horsed, ·hors·ing** 1 To throw from a horse. 2 To dislodge; overthrow. 3 To remove a horse or horses from: to *unhorse* a vehicle.

un·hou·seled (un·hou′zəld) *adj. Obs.* Not having received the last sacraments. [<UN-[1] + HOUSEL + -ED[2]]

un·hur·ried (un·hûr′ēd) *adj.* Leisurely; not hurried.

un·husk (un·husk′) *v.t.* 1 To strip the husk from. 2 To expose; lay open.

uni- *combining form* One; single; one only: *unifoliate.* [<L *unus* one]

U·ni·at (yōō′nē·at) *n.* A member of any community of Eastern Christians that acknowledges the supremacy of the pope at Rome, but retains its own liturgy, ceremonies, and rites: also called *United Armenian, United Greek.* Compare LATIN CHURCH. —*adj.* Of the Uniats or their faith. Also **U′ni·ate** (-it, -āt). [<Russian *uniyat* < *uniya* union <L *unus* one; from being in union with the Roman Catholic Church]

u·ni·ax·i·al (yōō′nē·ak′sē·əl) *adj.* 1 Having one axis. 2 Doubly refracting and having only a single optical axis, as crystals of the tetragonal and hexagonal systems. 3 *Bot.* Unbranched, as a primary stem terminating in a flower.

u·ni·cam·er·al (yōō′nə·kam′ər·əl) *adj.* Consisting of but one chamber, as a legislature.

u·ni·cel·lu·lar (yōō′nə·sel′yə·lər) *adj. Biol.* Consisting of a single cell, as a protozoan; one-celled.

u·ni·col·or (yōō′nə·kul′ər) *adj.* Of one color.

u·ni·corn (yōō′nə·kôrn) *n.* 1 A fabulous horselike animal with one horn. 2 A two-horned animal, identified with the urus, so called in the early English versions of the Bible to render the Latin and Greek mistranslations of the Hebrew *re' ēm*: translated as *wild ox* in the Revised Version. *Deut.* xxxiii 17. [<OF *unicorne* <L *unicornis* one-horned < *unus* one + *cornu* a horn]

UNICORN

u·ni·cos·tate (yōō′nə·kos′tāt) *adj.* 1 Having a single principal costa, rib, or nervure. 2 *Bot.* Having a midrib, as a leaf.

u·ni·cy·cle (yōō′nə·sī′kəl) *n.* A cycle or velocipede having a single wheel propelled by pedals.

un·i·de·aed (un′ī·dē′əd) *adj.* Not having ideas; frivolous.

u·ni·di·rec·tion·al (yōō′nə·di·rek′shən·əl, -dī-) *adj.* 1 Moving in the same direction. 2 Designed or equipped to operate best in only one direction, as a radio antenna. 3 *Electr.* Of or pertaining to a direct current.

u·ni·fi·a·ble (yōō′nə·fī′ə·bəl) *adj.* That can be unified.

u·nif·ic (yōō·nif′ik) *adj.* Unifying.

unified field theory *Physics* 1 Any mathematically rigorous generalization which will combine two or more physical theories in a form permitting accurate inclusive predictions not deducible from one theory alone, as the electromagnetic theory of Maxwell. 2 Such a generalization, as tentatively formulated by Einstein, to unify the theories of electromagnetism, gravitation, and relativity.

u·ni·fi·lar (yōō′nə·fī′lər) *adj.* 1 Possessing but a single thread. 2 Utilizing only one suspending thread.

u·ni·flo·rous (yōō′nə·flôr′əs, -flō′rəs) *adj. Bot.* One-flowered.

u·ni·fo·li·ate (yōō′nə·fō′lē·it, -āt) *adj. Bot.* Having one leaf.

u·ni·fo·li·o·late (yōō′nə·fō′lē·ə·lit, -lāt) *adj. Bot.* Having a single leaflet, as the compound leaves of the orange.

u·ni·form (yōō′nə·fôrm) *adj.* 1 Being the same or alike, as in form, appearance, quantity, quality, degree, or character; not varying: *uniform* temperature. 2 Agreeing with each other; harmonious; accordant; consonant: *uniform* tastes. See synonyms under ALIKE. —*n.* A dress or suit of uniform style and appearance worn by members of the same organization, service, etc., as soldiers, sailors, postmen, etc. See synonyms under DRESS. —**dress uniform** A military or naval uniform worn at social or ceremonial events. —*v.t.* To put into or clothe with a uniform. [<F *uniforme* <L *uniformis* < *unus* one + *forma* form] —**u′ni·form·ness** *n.* —**u′ni·form·ly** *adv.*

u·ni·for·mal·ize (yōō′nə·fôr′məl·īz) *v.t.* **·ized, ·iz·ing** To bring into a uniform system; render uniform.

Uniform Code of Military Justice The code of laws and related procedures enacted in 1951 by the U. S. Congress for the government of the personnel of the armed services: supersedes the former Army *Articles of War* and the *Articles for the Government of the Navy.*

u·ni·formed (yōō′nə·fôrmd) *adj.* Dressed in uniform.

u·ni·form·i·tar·i·an·ism (yōō′nə·fôr′mə·târ′ē·ən·iz′əm) *n. Geol.* The doctrine that essential uniformity in causes and effects, forces and phenomena, has prevailed in all ages of the world's physical history, and that the activities of the past were similar in mode and intensity to those of the present: opposed to *catastrophism.* —**u′ni·form′i·tar′i·an** *adj.* & *n.*

u·ni·form·i·ty (yōō′nə·fôr′mə·tē) *n. pl.* **·ties** 1 The state or quality of being uniform, or an instance of it; consistency throughout; lack of diversity. 2 Conformity or compliance, as in opinions or religion. 3 Monotony; sameness.

u·ni·fy (yōō′nə·fī) *v.t.* **·fied, ·fy·ing** To cause to be a unit; make uniform; unite; cause to be one. [<F *unifier* <LL *unificare* <L *unus* one + *facere* make] —**u′ni·fi·ca′tion** (-fə·kā′shən) *n.* —**u′ni·fi′er** *n.*

u·ni·gen·i·ture (yōō′nə·jen′ə·chər) *n.* The state of being an only child, or, in theology, of being the only begotten Son.

u·nij·u·gate (yōō·nij′ŏŏ·gāt, yōō′nə·jōō′git, -gāt) *adj. Bot.* Having one pair, as of leaflets: said especially of a pinnate leaf. [<UNI- + JUGATE]

u·ni·lat·er·al (yōō′nə·lat′ər·əl) *adj.* 1 One-sided; relating to one side only; made, undertaken, done, or signed by only one of two or more people or parties. 2 *Law* Binding or obligatory on one party only. 3 Arranged or growing on one side only, as a plant or animal organ. 4 *Med.* Affecting but one side of the body. 5 Relating to or tracing ancestry on one side only.

u·ni·lit·er·al (yōō′nə·lit′ər·əl) *adj.* Comprising but one letter.

u·ni·loc·u·lar (yōō′nə·lok′yə·lər) *adj. Biol.* Having or consisting of one cell or chamber, as an anther, ovary, etc.

U·ni·mak Island (yōō′nə·mak) The most northeasterly of the Fox Islands in the NE Aleutian Islands; 70 miles long.

un·im·peach·a·ble (un′im·pē′chə·bəl) *adj.* Not to be called in question as regards truth, honesty, etc.; faultless; blameless. —**un′im·peach′a·bly** *adv.*

un·im·proved (un′im·prōōvd′) *adj.* 1 Not improved; not bettered or advanced: *unimproved* health. 2 Having no improvements; not cleared, cultivated, or built upon: *unimproved* land. 3 Not made anything of; unused: *unimproved* opportunities. 4 *Obs.* Not proved or tried.

un·in·gen·ious (un′in·jēn′yəs) *adj.* 1 Lacking ingenuity; not possessed of inventiveness. 2 *Obs.* Uningenuous.

un·in·gen·u·ous (un′in·jen′yōō·əs) *adj.* Not ingenuous; sly or designing.

un·in·tel·li·gent (un′in·tel′ə·jənt) *adj.* 1 Not intelligent; characterized by lack of intelligence. 2 Unwise; ignorant. —**un′in·tel′li·gence** *n.*

un·in·ter·est·ed (un·in′tər·is·tid, -tris-) *adj.* 1 Having no interest in, as in property.

unknowable
unknowing
unlabeled,
unlabelled
unladylike
unlamented
unlash
unlashed
unlaundered
unleased
unled
unlessened
unlessoned
unlet
unletted
unlevel
unlevied
unlibidinous
unlicensed
unlifelike
unlighted
unlikable,
unlikeable
unlined
unlink
unliquefiable
unliquefied
unlit
unliveliness
unlively
unlocated
unlocked
unlovable
unloved
unloveliness
unloverlike
unloving
unlubricated
unlying
unmagnified
unmaidenly
unmailable
unmalleable
unmanageable
unmanful
unmangled
unmanifested
unmanipulated
unmannered
unmannish
unmannishly
unmanufacturable
unmanufactured
unmarketable
unmarred
unmarriageable
unmarried
unmastered
unmatched
unmated
unmaternal
unmatted
unmatured
unmeant
unmeasurable
unmeasured
unmechanical
unmedicated
unmeditated
unmelodious
unmelted
unmenaced
unmendable
unmended
unmensurable
unmentionability
unmentioned
unmercenary
unmerchantable
unmerited
unmethodical
unmilitary
unmilled
unmingle
unmingled
unmirthful
unmistaken
unmitigable
unmixed,
unmixt
unmodified
unmodish
unmoistened
unmold
unmolested
unmollified
unmolten
unmortgaged
unmotivated
unmounted
unmourned
unmovable
unmoved
unmown
unmurmuring

2 Taking no interest in; indifferent; unconcerned.

un·ion (yōōn′yən) *n.* **1** The act of uniting, or the state of being united; a joining; coalescence; junction. **2** That which is constituted as one by the combination of elements previously separate; a coalition; confederation; league. **3** A combination of co-laborers for the joint and mutual protection of their common interests. See TRADE UNION. **4** *Brit.* An amalgamation of parishes for administration of poor relief; also, a workhouse administered by such a union. **5** Agreement in sentiment or action; harmony; concord; unanimity. **6** The joining of two persons in marriage, or the resulting state of wedlock. **7** A device emblematic of union borne in the canton of a flag, as the three crosses in a British ensign; the canton itself containing such device, sometimes used separately as a flag, as the blue canton with white stars in the flag of the United States, and the Union Jack of Great Britain. **8** A coupling or connection for pipes or rods. **9** A fabric made of two or more materials, as cotton and wool. **10** *Obs.* A pearl of extraordinary worth. —*adj.* Of, pertaining to, or adhering to a union, particularly a political or trade union. [<F <LL *unio, -onis* <L *unus* one. Doublet of ONION.]

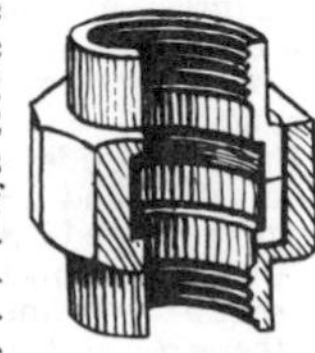
PIPE UNION

Synonyms (noun): coalition, combination, conjunction, junction, juncture, oneness, unification, unity. *Unity* is *oneness,* the state of existing as essentially one, especially of that which never has been divided or of that which cannot be conceived of as resolved into parts; as, the *unity* of the human soul. *Union* is a bringing together of things that have been distinct, so that they combine or coalesce to form a new whole, or the state or condition of things thus brought together; in a *union* the separate individuality of the things united is never lost sight of; we speak of the *union* of the parts of a fractured bone. See ALLIANCE, ASSOCIATION, ATTACHMENT, HARMONY, MARRIAGE. *Antonyms*: analysis, contrariety, decomposition, disconnection, disjunction, dissociation, disunion, division, divorce, separation, severance.

Un·ion (yōōn′yən) *n.* **1** The United States regarded as a national unit: with *the.* **2** The Union of South Africa. —*adj.* Of, pertaining to, or loyal to the United States, especially the Federal government during the Civil War: a *Union* soldier; He was *Union* to the core.

union card **1** A card certifying that the person named belongs to a certain labor union. **2** A card certifying that the shop named hires only union labor.

union catalog A library catalog combining the catalogs of more than one library, usually in a single alphabetical list.

union down Reversed, as a flag, so as to have the union or canton at the lower edge: a signal of distress.

Union Islands See TOKELAU ISLANDS.

un·ion·ism (yōōn′yən·iz′əm) *n.* **1** The principle of combination for unity of purpose and action. **2** Trade-unionism. **3** Adherence to or advocacy of political union between states, as opposed to secession. —**un′ion·is′tic** *adj.*

un·ion·ist (yōōn′yən·ist) *n.* **1** An advocate of union or unionism. **2** A member of a trade union.

Un·ion·ist (yōōn′yən·ist) *n.* **1** One who before and during the Civil War in the United States supported the Union cause and opposed secession; a Union man. **2** One of those opposed to loosening the formal ties between Great Britain and Ireland, whether belonging to the Conservatives or the branch of the Liberals (**Liberal Unionists**) that separated from their party in 1886 in opposition to the advocates of Home Rule for Ireland. From this time the term *Unionists* began to come into use, at first to signify both the Conservative and the Liberal Unionist parties, and later, as the distinction between the two wings gradually grew smaller, the Conservative Party.

un·ion·ize (yōōn′yən·īz) *v.* **·ized, ·iz·ing** *v.t.* To cause to join, or to organize into a union, especially a trade union. —*v.i.* To become a member of or organize a trade union. —**un′·ion·i·za′tion** *n.*

union jack A flag consisting of the union or canton only.

Union Jack The British national flag. It is a combination of the flags of England, Scotland, and Ireland.

Union of South Africa Former name of the Republic of South Africa.

Union of Soviet Socialist Republics A federal union of 16 constituent republics of eastern Europe and northern Asia, extending from the Arctic Ocean to the Black Sea and east to the Pacific; 8,646,400 square miles; capital, Moscow: formerly *Russia*: also *Soviet Russia, Soviet Union.* Abbr. *U.S.S.R., USSR.*

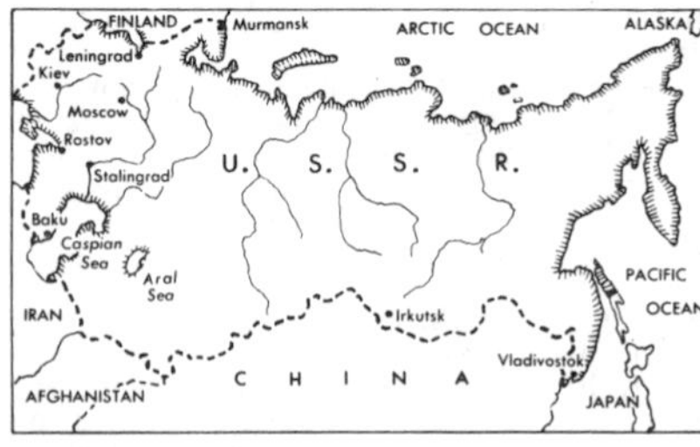

union shop An industrial establishment in which only members of a trade union are employed.

union station A railroad station or depot used by two or more railroad lines.

union suit A one-piece undergarment consisting of shirt and drawers.

Union Territory In India, under the provisions of the States Reorganization Act, which came into effect November 1, 1956, a division of India administered by the central government, rather than governing itself as a State. The six Union Territories of India are the Andaman and Nicobar Islands, Delhi, Himachal Pradesh, the Laccadive Islands, Manipura, and Tripura; Pondicherry is also temporarily administered as a Union Territory.

u·ni·pa·ren·tal (yōō′nə·pə·ren′təl) *adj.* Having or produced by one parent only; asexual.

u·nip·a·rous (yōō·nip′ər·əs) *adj.* **1** *Bot.* Having but one axis or stem. **2** Bringing forth but one offspring at a time, or not having borne more than one. [<UNI- + -PAROUS]

u·ni·per·son·al (yōō′nə·pûr′sən·əl) *adj.* **1** Manifested or existing in but one person. **2** *Gram.* Used in only one person, especially the third person singular; impersonal.

u·ni·pet·al·ous (yōō′nə·pet′l·əs) *adj. Bot.* Having only one petal.

u·ni·pla·nar (yōō′nə·plā′nər) *adj.* Lying or taking place in one plane.

u·ni·po·lar (yōō′nə·pō′lər) *adj.* **1** *Physics* Showing only one kind of polarity. **2** *Anat.* Having, or operating by means of, one pole: said especially of nerve cells having only one process.

u·nique (yōō·nēk′) *adj.* **1** Being the only one of its kind; being without equal; singular; uncommon; rare. **2** Not complicated with other things. **3** Sole. See synonyms under ODD, QUEER, RARE. [<F <L *unicus* < *unus* one] —**u·nique′ly** *adv.* —**u·nique′·ness** *n.*

u·ni·sep·tate (yōō′nə·sep′tāt) *adj.* Having a single septum or partition.

u·ni·sex (yōō′nə·seks′) *Colloq. adj.* For, appropriate to, or having characteristics of both sexes: *unisex* fashions. —*n.* The embodiment or integration of qualities, characteristics, etc., of both sexes, as in appearance, clothes, or activities.

u·ni·sex·u·al (yōō′nə·sek′shōō·əl) *adj.* **1** Of one sex: specifically said of flowers and animals having one kind of sexual organs only. **2** *Colloq.* Of or having to do with unisex.

u·ni·son (yōō′nə·sən, -zən) *n.* **1** A condition of perfect agreement and accord; harmony. **2** *Colloq.* Of or having to do with unisex. or voices perform the same part; unity of pitch; also, the interval of one or more octaves. See synonyms under HARMONY, MELODY. [<L *unisonus* having a single sound < *uni-* one + *sonus* a sound]

u·nis·o·nal (yōō·nis′ə·nəl) *adj.* Being in unison. Also **u·nis′o·nant.** —**u·nis′o·nal·ly** *adv.*

u·nit (yōō′nit) *n.* **1** A single person or thing regarded as an individual but belonging to an entire group. **2** A body or group considered as a single whole among a plurality of similars. **3** A standard quantity with which others of the same kind are compared for purposes of measurement and in terms of which their magnitude is stated. **4** *Math.* A quantity whose measure is represented by the number 1; a least whole number; specifically, in arithmetic, the number 1 itself; unity. **5** *Med.* The quantity of a drug, vaccine, serum, or antigen required to produce a given effect. **6** A fundamental quantity used in calculating how much scholastic work a student has finished. [Short for UNITY]

unit angle A radian.

u·ni·tar·i·an (yōō′nə·târ′ē·ən) *n.* One who rejects the doctrine of the Trinity; a non-Trinitarian monotheist. —*adj.* Pertaining to a unit. [<NL *unitarius* unitary]

U·ni·tar·i·an (yōō′nə·târ′ē·ən) *n.* A member of a Protestant denomination which rejects the doctrine of the Trinity, but accepts the ethical teachings of Jesus and emphasizes complete freedom of religious opinion, the importance of personal character, and the independence of each local congregation. —*adj.* Pertaining to the Unitarians, or to their teachings. —**U′ni·tar′i·an·ism** *n.*

u·ni·tar·i·an·ism (yōō′nə·târ′ē·ən·iz′əm) *n.* Any unitary system.

u·ni·tar·y (yōō′nə·ter′ē) *adj.* **1** Pertaining to a unit; characterized by, based on, or pertaining to unity. **2** Having the nature of a unit; whole.

unit cell *Crystall.* Cell (def. 6).

unit character *Genetics* One of two or more contrasting characters which is transmitted as a unit and without modification.

u·nite (yōō·nīt′) *v.* **u·nit·ed, u·nit·ing** *v.t.* **1** To join together so as to form a whole; combine; compound. **2** To bring into close connection, as by legal, physical, marital, social, or other tie; join in action, interest, etc. **3** To attach permanently or solidly; cause to

---

unmusical
unmuzzle
unmuzzled
unmystified
unnail
unnamable, unnameable
unnamed
unnaturalized
unnavigable
unnavigated
unneeded
unneedful
unnegotiable
unneighborly
unnoted
unnoticeable
unnoticed
unnurtured
unobjectionable
unobliged
unobliging
unobnoxious
unobscured
unobservant
unobserved
unobserving
unobstructed
unobtainable
unobtained
unobtruding
unobtrusive
unobtrusiveness
unoccasioned
unoffended
unoffending
unoffensive
unoffered
unofficious
unoiled
unopen
unopened
unopposed
unoppressed
unordained
unornamental
unornate
unorthodox
unorthodoxy
unostentatious
unowned
unoxidized
unpacified
unpacker
unpainful
unpalatable
unpalatably
unpardonable
unpardonably
unpardoned
unparental
unparted
unpartisan, unpartizan
unpasteurized
unpatched
unpatented
unpatriotic
unpaved
unpeaceable
unpeaceful
unpedigreed
unpen
unpenetrated
unpensioned
unperceivable
unperceived
unperceiving
unperfected
unperformed
unperplexed
unpersuadable
unpersuaded
unpersuasive
unperturbed
unperused
unphilanthropic
unphilological
unphilosophic
unphilosophical
unphonetic
unpicked
unpicturesque
unpierced
unpile
unpitying
unplaced
unplagued
unplait
unplanned
unplanted
unplayed
unpleasing
unpledged
unpliable

adhere; combine. — *v.i.* **4** To become or be merged into one; be consolidated; combine. **5** To join together for action; act in conjunction; concur. [<LL *unitus,* pp. of *unire* make one <L *unus* one]

Synonyms: amalgamate, blend, cement, cohere, combine, compound, conjoin, connect, consolidate, fuse, join, link, merge. See MIX. Compare ADD, COMPLEX. *Antonyms*: disconnect, disjoin, disrupt, dissociate, dissolve, divide, separate, sever.

u·nit·ed (yōō·nī′tid) *adj.* Incorporated into one; allied; combined; harmonious. — **u·nit′·ed·ly** *adv.* — **u·nit′ed·ness** *n.*

United Arab Republic A former republic formed in 1958 by the merger of the republics of Egypt and Syria; after the withdrawal of Syria in 1961, the official name for EGYPT.

United Arab States A federation formed in 1958 by the United Arab Republic and the Kingdom of Yemen, each of which retained its sovereignty; dissolved by the United Arab Republic in 1961.

United Armenian A Uniat.

United Church of Christ A Protestant denomination formed in 1957 by a union of the Congregational Christian Churches and the Evangelical and Reformed Church.

United Greek A Uniat.

United Kingdom **1** The kingdom of the British Isles, comprising Great Britain, Northern Ireland, the Isle of Man, and the Channel Islands; 94,284 square miles; capital, London: officially **United Kingdom of Great Britain and Northern Ireland.** **2** Formerly, Great Britain and Ireland (1801–1922).

United Nations **1** A coalition to resist the military aggression of the Axis Powers in World War II, formed of 26 national states in January, 1942. **2** An international organization of sovereign states (originally called the **United Nations Organization**) created by the United Nations Charter drafted in September–October, 1944, at Dumbarton Oaks and adopted at San Francisco in May and June, 1945: the 26 states of the United Nations coalition and 25 others form the original membership.

Original Members: Argentina, Australia, Belgium, Belorussian S.S.R., Bolivia, Brazil, Canada, Chile, China (government on Taiwan), Colombia, Costa Rica, Cuba, Czechoslovakia, Denmark, Dominican Republic, Ecuador, Egypt, El Salvador, Ethiopia, France, Greece, Guatemala, Haiti, Honduras, India, Iraq, Lebanon, Liberia, Luxembourg, Mexico, Netherlands, New Zealand, Nicaragua, Norway, Panama, Paraguay, Persia, Peru, Philippines, Poland, Saudi Arabia, Syria, Turkey, Ukrainian S.S.R., Republic of South Africa (formerly Union of South Africa), United Kingdom, United States, Uruguay, U.S.S.R., Venezuela, Yugoslavia. Nations joining later were (1946) Afghanistan, Iceland, Sweden, Thailand; (1947) Pakistan, Yemen; (1948) Burma; (1949) Israel; (1950) Indonesia; (1955) Albania, Austria, Bulgaria, Ceylon, Finland, Hungary, Ireland, Italy, Jordan, Khmer Republic (formerly Cambodia), Laos, Libya, Nepal, Portugal, Rumania, Spain; (1956) Japan, Morocco, Sudan, Tunisia; (1957) Ghana, Malaya (later merged with other territories to form Malaysia); (1958) Guinea; (1960) Cameroun, Central African Republic, Chad, Congo (People's Republic; formerly Congo, Brazzaville), Cyprus, Dahomey, Gabon, Ivory Coast, Malagasy Republic, Mali, Niger, Nigeria, Senegal, Somalia, Togo, Upper Volta, Zaire Republic (formerly Congo, Leopoldville, later Kinshasa); (1961) Mongolian People's Republic, Mauritania, Sierra Leone, Tanganyika; (1962) Algeria, Burundi, Jamaica, Rwanda, Trinidad and Tobago, Uganda; (1963) Kenya, Kuwait, Zanzibar; (1964) Malawi, Malta, Tanzania (formerly Tanganyika and Zanzibar), Zambia; (1965) Gambia, Maldive Islands, Singapore (formerly part of Malaysia); (1966) Barbados, Botswana, Guyana, Lesotho (formerly Basutoland); (1968) Equatorial Guinea, Mauritius, Swaziland; (1970) Fiji; (1971) Bahrain, Bhutan, China (People's Republic, replacing government on Taiwan), Oman, Qatar. Also called *UN.*

United Nations Trust Territory See TRUST TERRITORY.

United Presbyterian Church in the United States of America The largest U. S. Presbyterian body, formed in 1958 by the merger of two separate churches.

United Press A news-collecting and -distributing organization, merged in 1958 with the International News Service to form the **United Press International.**

United Provinces of Agra and Oudh A former British province in north central India; became the State of Uttar Pradesh, 1950.

United Society of Believers in Christ's Second Appearing See SHAKER.

United States The United States of America.

United States Army, Navy, Air Force, etc. See under ARMY, NAVY, AIR FORCE, etc.

United States of America A federal republic of North America, including 50 states, and the District of Columbia, the Canal Zone, Puerto Rico, the Virgin Islands of the United States, American Samoa, Guam, Wake, and several other scattered islands of the Pacific; total area, about 3,720,407 square miles; capital, Washington, in the District of Columbia. — **conterminous United States** The 48 contiguous States and the District of Columbia. — **continental United States** The District of Columbia and the 49 States on the continent of North America. Also *America, the States, United States*: abbr. *U.S.A., U.S., US.*

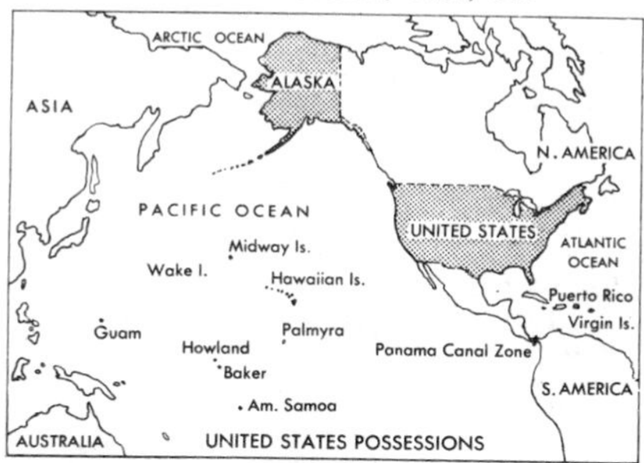

UNITED STATES POSSESSIONS

unit factor *Biol.* A gene controlling the inheritance of a unit character.

unit fraction See under FRACTION.

u·ni·tive (yōō′nə·tiv) *adj.* Productive of or promoting union; having power to unite; characterized by union.

u·ni·tize (yōō′nə·tīz) *v.t.* **·tized, ·tiz·ing** To form into a whole; unify.

unit modifier A conventional or improvised compound used adjectively before a substantive. Examples: *blue-green* algae, *bitter-sweet* chocolate, *suit-coat* pattern, *situation-comedy* plot, *storm-window* installation, *contour-plowing* method, *most-favored-nation* clause.

◆ The use of the hyphen in the unit modifier is to avoid ambiguity in a word sequence where the relationship is not immediately apparent from context: The house had faded red-brick walls (faded walls of red brick, *not* faded red walls of brick). The hyphen here is to be considered a nonce use and not as a spelling form or variant.

unit rule *U.S.* A rule in a national convention of the Democratic party, requiring that, if so instructed by a State party convention, the vote of an entire delegation shall be determined by a majority of its members.

u·ni·ty (yōō′nə·tē) *n. pl.* **·ties** **1** The state, property, or product of being united, physically, socially, or morally; oneness: opposed to *division, plurality.* **2** Union, as of constituent parts or elements: national *unity.* **3** Agreement of parts; harmonious adjustment of constituent elements; sameness of character: the *unity* of two writings. **4** The fact of something's being a whole that is more than or different from its parts or their sum. **5** Singleness of purpose or action. **6** A state of general good feeling; mutual understanding; concord: brethren dwelling together in *unity.* **7** *Math.* **a** The number one; the ratio of two equal quantities. **b** The element of a number system that leaves any number unchanged under multiplication, that is, a number e such that $ex = xe = x$ for all x. **8** In literature and the arts, combination into a homogeneous artistic whole, exhibiting oneness of purpose, thought, spirit, and style, with subordination of all parts to the general effect. **9** In the drama, observance, complete or partial, of the law of dramatic unities. **10** Identity. See synonyms under HARMONY, UNION. — **the law of dramatic unities** The law of Aristotle that in a drama there must be unity of action, unity of time, and unity of place. These unities were strictly observed by the French classical dramatists of the 17th century, but were violated by Shakespeare and certain of the German playwrights. [<F *unité* <L *unitas* <*unus* one]

U·ni·ty (yōō′nə·tē) *n.* A religious philosophy, based on the teachings of Jesus Christ, stating that man is inseparable from the spirit of God within him, and that through prayerful realization of this spirit he can obtain healing of all life's inharmonies in mind, body, etc.: founded in 1889.

Unity of the Brethren See MORAVIAN.

u·ni·va·lent (yōō′nə·vā′lənt) *adj.* **1** *Chem.* Having a valence or combining value of one; monovalent. **2** *Biol.* Pertaining to or designating a single unpaired chromosome. — **u′ni·va′lence, u′ni·va′len·cy** *n.*

u·ni·valve (yōō′nə·valv′) *adj.* Having only one valve, as a mollusk. Also **u′ni·val′vate, u′ni·valved′.** — *n.* **1** A mollusk having a univalve shell; a gastropod. **2** A shell of a single piece. — **u′ni·val′vu·lar** (-val′vyə·lər) *adj.*

u·ni·ver·sal (yōō′nə·vûr′səl) *adj.* **1** Prevalent or common everywhere or among all things or persons specified or implied: a *universal* belief; *universal* suffrage; a *universal* language. **2** Of or including everyone: a *universal* church. **3** Applicable to all cases: a *universal* law; a *universal* cure. **4** Accomplished or interested in a vast variety of subjects or activities: Leonardo da Vinci was a *universal* genius. **5** Of, pertaining to, or occurring throughout the universe: a *universal* being. **6** *Mech.* Adapted or adaptable to a great variety of uses, shapes, etc., as certain machines or machine parts. **7** *Logic* **a** Including all the

unpliant
unplighted
unplowed, unploughed
unplucked
unplugged
unpoetic
unpoetical
unpointed
unpolarized
unpolished
unpolitical
unpolluted
unpondered
unpopulated
unposted
unpractical
unpredictable
unpredictably
unpreoccupied
unprepossessing
unprescribed
unpresentable
unpreserved
unpressed
unpresumptuous
unpretending
unpretentious
unprevailing
unpreventable
unprimed
unprincely
unprinted
unprivileged
unprized
unprobed
unprocessed
unprocurable
unprofaned
unprofited
unprogressive
unprohibited
unpromising
unprompted
unpronounced
unpropitiable
unpropitiated
unpropitious
unproportionate
unproportioned
unproposed
unprosperous
unprotected
unproved
unproven
unprovoked
unprovoking
unpruned
unpublished
unpucker
unpunctual
unpunishable
unpunished
unpurchasable
unpure
unpurged
unpurified
unpurposed
unpursuing
unpuzzle
unquaffed
unquailing
unqualifying
unquelled
unquenchable
unquenched
unquestioning
unquotable
unraised
unransomed
unrated
unratified
unravaged
unrazored
unreachable
unreached
unreadable
unrealizable
unrealized
unreasoned
unreasoningly
unrebukable
unrebuked
unreceipted
unreceivable
unreceived
unreceptive
unreciprocated
unreclaimable
unreclaimed
unrecognizable
unrecognized
unrecommended
unrecompensed
unreconcilable

individuals of a class or genus; generic. **b** In a proposition, predicable of all the individuals denoted by the subject: opposed to particular: "All men are mortal" is a *universal* proposition. See synonyms under COMMON, GENERAL. — *n.* **1** *Logic* **a** A universal proposition. **b** One of the five predicables, that is, genus, species, difference, property, and accident, known collectively as the *universals.* **c** A general or abstract concept considered as having absolute reality or mental or nominal existence. **2** Any general or universal notion or idea. **3** A metaphysical being which preserves its identity in spite of the changes through which it passes, as the ego. [<OF <L *universalis* < *universus.* See UNIVERSE.] — **u′ni·ver′sal·ly** *adv.* — **u′ni·ver′sal·ness** *n.*

universal developer *Phot.* A developer adapted for use with various types of films, plates, or papers.

universal donor One whose blood belongs to group O and may be transfused with little or no danger of agglutination into a person belonging to any of the four blood groups.

U·ni·ver·sal·ism (yōō′nə·vûr′səl·iz′əm) *n. Theol.* The doctrine that all souls will finally be saved and that good will triumph universally.

U·ni·ver·sal·ist (yōō′nə·vûr′səl·ist) *adj.* Pertaining to Universalism or Universalists. — *n.* A believer in the doctrines of Universalism, or a member of the Universalist denomination.

u·ni·ver·sal·i·ty (yōō′nə·vər·sal′ə·tē) *n.* **1** The state of being all-embracing. **2** Unrestricted fitness or adaptability.

u·ni·ver·sal·ize (yōō′nə·vûr′səl·īz) *v.t.* **·ized, ·iz·ing** To make universal.

universal joint *Mech.* A joint that permits both connected parts of a machine to be turned in any direction within definite limits; specifically, a coupling for connecting two shafts, etc., so as to permit angular motion in all directions. Also **universal coupling.**

UNIVERSAL JOINT

u·ni·verse (yōō′nə·vûrs) *n.* **1** The aggregate of all existing things; the whole creation embracing all celestial bodies and all of space; the cosmos. **2** In restricted sense, the earth. **3** Human beings collectively; mankind. **4** *Logic* All objects, collectively, that are the subjects of consideration at once: also **universe of discourse.** **5** *Stat.* All the instances in a given class: contrasted with *sample.* [<F *univers* <L *universum,* neut. of *universus* turned, combined into one, all collectively < *unus* one + *versus,* pp. of *vertere* turn]

u·ni·ver·si·ty (yōō′nə·vûr′sə·tē) *n. pl.* **·ties** **1** An educational institution for higher instruction or for the examination of students already instructed. Universities arose in Europe in the Middle Ages and were first essentially ecclesiastic. Their functions gradually became specialized, some dividing into several *faculties,* each of which took charge of some one great branch of instruction, or into *colleges,* as now in the older English universities, where the relation of the university to the college is similar to that of a federal government to its component states. In the United States the word has been used loosely, chiefly to mean a collection of educational associations including a college (which offers degrees in general subjects) and several more advanced and specialized faculties, either professional, as law, medicine, etc., or academic, as history or mathematics. **2** All the students of such an institution. **3** *Brit. Colloq.* A university team or crew.

u·ni·ver·son (yōō′nə·vûr′son) *n. Physics* A hypothetical primordial entity originally containing the entire mass of the universe and whose splitting simultaneously gave rise to the cosmos and to its balanced opposite, the anticosmos. [<UNIVERSE]

u·niv·o·cal (yōō·niv′ə·kəl) *adj.* Having but one proper sense or meaning. — *n.* A word that has but one meaning. [<LL *univocus* <L *unus* one + *vox* voice]

un·just (un·just′) *adj.* **1** Not legitimate, fair, or just; wrongful. **2** Unrighteous; acting contrary to right and justice. **3** *Archaic* Faithless. **4** *Archaic* Dishonest. — **un·just′ly** *adv.* — **un·just′ness** *n.*

un·kempt (un·kempt′) *adj.* **1** Not combed; neglected; untidy. **2** Without polish; rough. [<UN-[1] + *kempt* combed, pp. of dial. *kemb,* var. of COMB] — **un·kempt′ness** *n.*

un·kenned (un·kend′) *adj. Scot.* & *Brit. Dial.* Unknown. Also **un·kend′, un·kent′** (-kent′).

un·ken·nel (un·ken′əl) *v.t.* **1** To drive or release from a kennel or lair. **2** To bring to light; disclose.

un·kind (un·kīnd′) *adj.* Showing lack of kindness; unsympathetic; harsh; cruel. [OE *uncynde* strange, unnatural] — **un·kind′ly** *adv.* — **un·kind′ness** *n.*

un·known (un·nōn′) *adj.* **1** Not known; not apprehended mentally; not recognized, as a fact or person. **2** Not ascertained; incalculable. See synonyms under MYSTERIOUS, SECRET. — *n.* An unknown person or quantity. — **the Great Unknown** Life after death; future life.

Unknown Soldier One of the unidentified dead of World War I who is honored as a symbol of all his compatriots who died in action; extended to include unknown dead of World War II and the Korean conflict.

un·la·bored (un·lā′bərd) *adj.* **1** Produced without strain or effort; seemingly free and easy; natural. **2** Uncultivated by labor; unworked; untilled. Also *Brit.* **un·la′boured.**

un·lace (un·lās′) *v.t.* **·laced, ·lac·ing** **1** To loosen or unfasten the lacing of; untie. **2** To loosen or remove (armor or clothing) in this way. **3** *Obs.* To expose to damage; disgrace.

un·lade (un·lād′) *v.t.* & *v.i.* **·lad·ed, ·lad·ing** **1** To unload the cargo of (a ship). **2** To unload or discharge (cargo, etc.).

un·laid (un·lād′) *adj.* **1** Not laid or placed; not fixed. **2** Not having parallel watermarked lines: *unlaid* paper. **3** Not allayed or pacified. **4** Not laid up; untwisted, as the strands of a rope. **5** *Obs.* Not laid out, as a corpse.

un·latch (un·lach′) *v.t.* To open or unlock by releasing the latch. — *v.i.* To come open or unlocked.

un·law·ful (un·lô′fəl) *adj.* Contrary to or in violation of law; illegal; illicit; also, illegitimate. See synonyms under CRIMINAL. — **un·law′ful·ly** *adv.* — **un·law′ful·ness** *n.*

un·lay (un·lā′) *v.t.* & *v.i.* **·laid, ·lay·ing** To untwist: said specifically of the strands of a rope. [<UN-[2] + LAY[1] (def. 21)]

un·lead (un·led′) *v.t.* **1** To strip of lead. **2** *Printing* To remove the leads from between (lines of type matter).

un·lead·ed (un·led′id) *adj.* **1** Not supplied or weighted with lead. **2** *Printing* Having no leads between the lines; not spaced with leads.

un·learn (un·lûrn′) *v.t.* **·learned** or **·learnt, ·learn·ing** To dismiss from the mind (something learned); forget.

un·learn·ed (un·lûr′nid) *adj.* **1** Not learned; not possessed of or characterized by learning; illiterate; ignorant; untaught. **2** Unworthy or unsuggestive of a scholar; not like the production of a learned man. **3** (un·lûrnd′) Not acquired by learning or study. See synonyms under IGNORANT.

un·leash (un·lēsh′) *v.t.* To set free from or as from a leash.

un·leav·ened (un·lev′ənd) *adj.* Not leavened: said specifically of the bread used at the feast of the Passover.

un·less (un·les′) *conj.* **1** If it be not a fact that; supposing that . . . not; except that: *Unless* we persevere, we shall lose. **2** *Obs.* For fear that; lest. — *prep.* Save; except; excepting: with an implied verb: *Unless* a miracle, he'll not be back in time. See synonyms under BUT. [Earlier *onlesse (that)* in a less case <ON + LESS]

un·let·tered (un·let′ərd) *adj.* Not educated; not lettered; illiterate.

un·like (un·līk′) *adj.* Having little or no resemblance; different. See synonyms under ALIEN, CONTRARY, HETEROGENEOUS. — *adv.* In another manner: with *to* expressed or implied. By the ellipsis of *to* it approaches prepositional use. [ME *unliche*] — **un·like′·ness** *n.*

un·like·ly (un·līk′lē) *adj.* **1** Improbable. **2** Not inviting or promising success. — *adv.* Improbably. — **un·like′li·ness, un·like′li·hood** *n.*

un·lim·ber (un·lim′bər) *v.t.* & *v.i.* To disconnect (a gun or caisson) from its limber; prepare for action.

un·lim·it·ed (un·lim′it·id) *adj.* **1** Having no limits in space, number, or time; unbounded; endless; unnumbered. **2** Not limited by restrictions; unconfined: *unlimited* authority. **3** Not limited by exceptions or qualifications; undefined. — **un·lim′it·ed·ly** *adv.* — **un·lim′it·ed·ness** *n.*

un·liq·ui·dat·ed (un·lik′wə·dā′tid) *adj.* **1** *Law* Unascertained as to amount; undetermined or not settled: *unliquidated* damages. **2** Not yet eliminated from the living: said of the survivors of attempted genocide.

un·list·ed (un·lis′tid) *adj.* Not listed; specifically, noting stocks quoted in the unlisted department of a stock exchange, but not admitted to dealings on the floor of the New York Stock Exchange.

un·live (un·liv′) *v.t.* **·lived, ·liv·ing** To live so as to wipe out the effects of (a former period of life); undo by living; live down.

un·load (un·lōd′) *v.t.* **1** To remove the load or cargo from. **2** To take off or discharge (cargo, etc.). **3** To relieve of something burdensome or oppressive. **4** To withdraw the charge of ammunition from. **5** *Colloq.* To dispose of, especially by selling in large quantities. — *v.i.* **6** To discharge freight, cargo, or other burden.

un·load·er (un·lō′dər) *n.* One who or that which unloads; specifically, a contrivance for unloading something, as hay or coal.

un·lock (un·lok′) *v.t.* **1** To unfasten (something locked). **2** To open or undo; release. **3** To lay open; reveal or disclose. — *v.i.* **4** To become unlocked.

un·looked-for (un·lŏŏkt′fôr′) *adj.* Not anticipated; unexpected.

un·loose (un·lōōs′) *v.t.* **·loosed, ·loos·ing** To release from fastenings; set loose or free. See synonyms under RELEASE.

un·loos·en (un·lōō′sən) *v.t.* To loose; unloose.

un·love·ly (un·luv′lē) *adj.* Unattractive; disagreeable; ugly.

un·luck·y (un·luk′ē) *adj.* **·luck·i·er, ·luck·i·est** **1** Not favored by luck; unfortunate. **2** Resulting in or attended by ill luck; causing misfortune; disastrous. **3** Ill-omened; inauspicious: an *unlucky* day. See synonyms under

---

unreconciled
unrecorded
unrecounted
unrecoverable
unrecruited
unrectified
unredeemed
unredressed
unreelable
unrefined
unreflected
unreflecting
unreformable
unreformed
unreformedness

unrefreshed
unrefreshing
unregarded
unregistered
unregretted
unregulated
unrehearsed
unrelated
unrelatedness
unrelaxed
unrelaxing
unrelievable
unrelieved
unrelished
unremarked

unremedied
unremembered
unremittable
unremitted
unremorseful
unremovable
unremoved
unremunerated
unremunerative
unrendered
unrenewed
unrenounced
unrenowned
unrent
unrented

unrepaid
unrepairable
unrepaired
unrepealed
unrepentant
unrepented
unrepenting
unrepining
unreplaced
unreplenished
unreported
unrepresentative
unrepresented
unrepressed
unreprievable

unreprieved
unreprovable
unrequested
unrequited
unresented
unresigned
unresistant
unresisted
unresisting
unresistingly
unresolved
unrespectable
unrespectful
unrested
unresting

unrestrainable
unrestraint
unrestricted
unretarded
unretentive
unretracted
unretrieved
unreturned
unrevealed
unrevenged
unreversed
unrevised
unrevoked
unrewarded
unrhetorical

unrhymed
unrhythmic
unrhythmical
unrighted
unrightful
unrimed
unripened
unrisen
unroasted
unrobe
unromantic
unromantically
unroof
unrough
unruled

BAD. —**un·luck'i·ly** *adv.* —**un·luck'i·ness** *n.*

un·make (un·māk') *v.t.* **·made, ·mak·ing** **1** To reverse the making of; reduce to the original condition or form. **2** To ruin; destroy. **3** To depose, as from a position of authority.

un·man (un·man') *v.t.* **·manned, ·man·ning** **1** To cause to lose courage or fortitude; dishearten. **2** To render unmanly or effeminate. **3** To deprive of virility; emasculate; castrate. **4** To remove the men from, as a ship or fortress.

un·man·ly (un·man'lē) *adj.* **1** Not masculine; effeminate; not virile; not courageous. **2** Not gentlemanly; not honorable. —**un·man'li·ness** *n.*

un·manned (un·mand') *adj.* **1** Not manned. **2** Deprived of virility or manhood. **3** *Obs.* Unaccustomed to men; untamed: said of hawks. **4** Uninhabited.

un·man·ner·ly (un·man'ər·lē) *adj.* Lacking manners; rude. —*adv.* Impolitely. —**un·man'·ner·li·ness** *n.*

un·marked (un·märkt') *adj.* **1** Bearing no mark; having no distinctive mark. **2** *Electr.* Denoting that pole of a magnet which points south. **3** Not noticed. **4** Not examined; hence, uncorrected; ungraded: *unmarked* test papers.

un·mask (un·mask', -mäsk') *v.t.* **1** To remove a mask from. **2** To reveal; disclose. —*v.i.* **3** To remove one's mask or disguise.

un·mean·ing (un·mē'ning) *adj.* **1** Having no meaning: an *unmeaning* speech or look. **2** Having no expression; not displaying intelligence. —**un·mean'ing·ly** *adv.* —**un·mean'·ing·ness** *n.*

un·meet (un·mēt') *adj.* Not meet, adapted, or suitable; not proper or fit; unbecoming. [OE *unmǣte*] —**un·meet'ly** *adv.* —**un·meet'·ness** *n.*

un·men·tion·a·ble (un·men'shən·ə·bəl) *adj.* Not proper to be mentioned or discussed; embarrassing; shameful; disgraceful. —**un·men'·tion·a·ble·ness** *n.* —**un·men'tion·a·bly** *adv.*

un·men·tion·a·bles (un·men'shən·ə·bəlz) *n. pl.* Things or articles not ordinarily discussed or mentioned; usually, undergarments; formerly, trousers; pants.

un·mer·ci·ful (un·mûr'sə·fəl) *adj.* **1** Showing no mercy; cruel; pitiless; unconscionable. **2** Extreme; exorbitant. —**un·mer'ci·ful·ly** *adv.* —**un·mer'ci·ful·ness** *n.*

un·mew (un·myōō') *v.t.* To release from confinement; set free.

un·mind·ful (un·mīnd'fəl) *adj.* Not keeping in mind; neglectful; inattentive. —**un·mind'ful·ly** *adv.* —**un·mind'ful·ness** *n.*

un·mis·tak·a·ble (un'mis·tā'kə·bəl) *adj.* That cannot be mistaken for something else; evident; clear; obvious. See synonyms under CLEAR, EVIDENT, MANIFEST. —**un'mis·tak'a·bly** *adv.*

un·mi·ter (un·mī'tər) *v.t.* To divest of a miter; deprive of the office of bishop. Also **un·mi'tre.**

un·mit·i·gat·ed (un·mit'ə·gā'tid) *adj.* **1** Not mitigated or lightened in effect; unabated; unassuaged: *unmitigated* sorrow. **2** As bad as can be; unconscionable: an *unmitigated* rogue. —**un·mit'i·gat'ed·ly** *adv.*

un·mod·u·lat·ed (un·moj'ōō·lā'tid) *adj.* **1** Without modulation. **2** *Telecom.* Denoting a carrier wave of constant amplitude, as during a pause in broadcasting.

un·moor (un·mōōr') *Naut. v.t.* **1** To loose the moorings of; release from moorings: to *unmoor* a ship. **2** To release all but one anchor of (a vessel formerly moored by two or more). —*v.i.* **3** To cast off moorings.

un·mor·al (un·môr'əl, -mor'-) *adj.* Having no moral sense or relation; not pertaining to morality: distinguished from *amoral* and *immoral.* —**un·mo·ral·i·ty** (un'mə·ral'ə·tē) *n.*

un·mor·tise (un·môr'tis) *v.t.* **·tised, ·tis·ing** **1** To loosen; loosen the mortised joints of. **2** To separate.

un·muf·fle (un·muf'əl) *v.* **·fled, ·fling** *v.t.* **1** To take the covering from. **2** To remove the muffling of (a drum, oar, etc.). —*v.i.* **3** To remove that which muffles.

un·nat·u·ral (un·nach'ər·əl) *adj.* **1** Contrary to the laws of nature; opposed to what is natural. **2** Contrary to the common laws of morality or decency; monstrous; inhuman: *unnatural* crimes. **3** Destitute of natural feeling. **4** Not consistent with nature; artificial: *unnatural* acting. See synonyms under FACTITIOUS, IRREGULAR. —**un·nat'u·ral·ly** *adv.* —**un·nat'u·ral·ness** *n.*

un·nec·es·sary (un·nes'ə·ser'ē) *adj.* Not required; not necessary. —**un·nec'es·sar'i·ly** *adv.* —**un·nec'es·sar'i·ness** *n.*

un·nerve (un·nûrv') *v.t.* **·nerved, ·nerv·ing** To deprive of strength, firmness, self-control, or courage; unman. See synonyms under WEAKEN.

un·num·bered (un·num'bərd) *adj.* **1** Not counted. **2** Innumerable. **3** Not assigned a number; not marked with a number.

u·no an·i·mo (yōō'nō an'ə·mō) *Latin* With one mind; unanimously; in agreement.

un·oc·cu·pied (un·ok'yə·pīd) *adj.* **1** Empty; not dwelt in; uninhabited: an *unoccupied* house. **2** Idle; unemployed; not put to use: an *unoccupied* day.

un·of·fi·cial (un'ə·fish'əl) *adj.* **1** Not of an official character. **2** Not in an official capacity. **3** Not in the regular list of the pharmacopoeia.

un·or·gan·ized (un·ôr'gən·īzd) *adj.* **1** Not organized. **2** Not living; inorganic; structureless. **3** Not unionized. Also *Brit.* **un·or'gan·ised.**

un·o·rig·i·nal (un'ə·rij'ə·nəl) *adj.* Not original.

un·pack (un·pak') *v.t.* **1** To open and take out the contents of. **2** To take out of the container, as something packed. **3** To remove a load or pack from; unload. —*v.i.* **4** To unpack a trunk, goods, etc.

un·paid (un·pād') *adj.* **1** Not met or discharged, as a debt. **2** Not receiving pay; serving without pay. **3** Having wages remaining due.

un·paired (un·pârd') *adj.* **1** Not paired; not forming one of a pair; not matched. **2** *Anat.* **a** Having no corresponding part in the opposite half of the body. **b** Situated in the median plane of the body.

un·par·al·leled (un·par'ə·leld) *adj.* Without parallel; unmatched; unprecedented.

un·par·lia·men·ta·ry (un'pär·lə·men'tər·ē) *adj.* Not parliamentary; contrary to the rules that govern deliberative or legislative bodies. —**un'par·lia·men'ta·ri·ly** *adv.* —**un'par·lia·men'·ta·ri·ness** *n.*

un·peg (un·peg') *v.t.* **·pegged, ·peg·ging** To remove the peg or pegs from; unfasten.

un·peo·ple (un·pē'pəl) *v.t.* **·pled, ·pling** To depopulate.

un·peo·pled (un·pē'pəld) *adj.* **1** Uninhabited. **2** Depopulated.

un·per·fo·rat·ed (un·pûr'fə·rā'tid) *adj.* **1** Not perforated. **2** In philately, imperforate.

un peu (œṅ pœ') *French* A little; somewhat.

un·pick (un·pik') *v.t.* **1** To undo by removing the stitches; also, to remove (stitches). **2** To open with a pick or picklock.

un·pin (un·pin') *v.t.* **·pinned, ·pin·ning** **1** To remove the pins from. **2** To unfasten by removing pins.

un·pleas·ant (un·plez'ənt) *adj.* Disagreeable; objectionable; not pleasing. —**un·pleas'ant·ly** *adv.*

un·pleas·ant·ness (un·plez'ənt·nis) *n.* **1** The quality, character, or condition of being unpleasant or disagreeable. **2** Any disagreeable experience or event; a disagreement or quarrel. —**the late unpleasantness** The American Civil War: now chiefly humorous; by extension, any recent war.

un·plumbed (un·plumd') *adj.* **1** Not sounded; not explored fully; unfathomed. **2** Not furnished with plumbing.

un·poised (un·poizd') *adj.* Not poised or balanced.

un·pol·i·cied (un·pol'ə·sēd) *adj.* **1** Having no established system of civil polity. **2** *Obs.* Unguided by reason or prudence; impolitic.

un·pol·i·tic (un·pol'ə·tik) *adj.* Impolitic.

un·polled (un·pōld') *adj.* Not registered: an *unpolled* vote or voter; not having voted at an election.

un·pop·u·lar (un·pop'yə·lər) *adj.* Having no popularity; generally disliked or condemned. —**un·pop'u·lar·ly** *adv.* —**un·pop'u·lar'i·ty** (-lar'·ə·tē) *n.*

un·prac·ticed (un·prak'tist) *adj.* **1** Being without practice; inexperienced. **2** Not carried out in practice; not used. **3** Not yet tried.

un·prec·e·dent·ed (un·pres'ə·den'tid) *adj.* Being without precedent; preceded by no similar case; unexampled. See synonyms under EXTRAORDINARY. —**un·prec'e·dent'ed·ly** *adv.*

un·prej·u·diced (un·prej'ōō·dist) *adj.* **1** Free from prejudice or bias; impartial. **2** Not impaired, as a right. See synonyms under CANDID.

un·pre·med·i·tat·ed (un'pri·med'ə·tā'tid) *adj.* **1** Not planned beforehand; undesigned: *unpremeditated* assault. **2** Not previously considered or thought of. —**un'pre·med'i·tat'ed·ly** *adv.* —**un'pre·med'i·ta'tion** *n.*

un·pre·pared (un'pri·pârd') *adj.* **1** Having made no preparations: an *unprepared* student. **2** Not brought into a state of preparation; not yet ready: Dinner is still *unprepared.* **3** Done or carried out without preparation; impromptu: an *unprepared* speech. —**un·pre·par·ed·ly** (un'pri·pâr'id·lē) *adv.* —**un'pre·par'·ed·ness** *n.*

un·priced (un·prīst') *adj.* **1** Having no fixed price. **2** Priceless.

un·prin·ci·pled (un·prin'sə·pəld) *adj.* Destitute of conscientious scruples; unscrupulous; wicked. See synonyms under BAD, IMMORAL. —**un·prin'ci·pled·ness** *n.*

un·print·a·ble (un·prin'tə·bəl) *adj.* Not fit to be printed.

un·priz·a·ble (un·prī'zə·bəl) *adj. Obs.* **1** Of worth beyond estimation; invaluable. **2** Not prized; valueless.

un·pro·duc·tive (un'prə·duk'tiv) *adj.* **1** Producing little or nothing; barren, literally or figuratively. **2** *Econ.* Not adding to exchangeable value: *unproductive* labor. —**un'pro·duc'·tive·ly** *adv.* —**un'pro·duc'tive·ness** *n.*

un·pro·fes·sion·al (un'prə·fesh'ən·əl) *adj.* **1** Having no profession; also, lay; amateur. **2** Violating the rules or ethical code of a profession; not up to the standard of a profession: *unprofessional* work. —**un'pro·fes'sion·al·ly** *adv.*

un·prof·it·a·ble (un·prof'it·ə·bəl) *adj.* Productive of no profit; serving no desirable purpose; fruitless; futile: *unprofitable* conversation; an

unsafe
unsafely
unsaintly
unsalability, unsaleability
unsalable, unsaleable
unsalaried
unsalted
unsanctified
unsanctioned
unsanitary
unsated
unsatiable
unsatiated
unsatiating
unsatisfactory
unsatisfied
unsatisfying
unsaved
unsawed
unsawn
unsayable
unscabbarded
unscaled
unscanned
unscarred
unscented
unsceptical
unscheduled
unscholarlike
unscholarly
unschooled
unscientific
unscorched
unscorned
unscoured
unscourged
unscratched
unscreened
unscriptural
unsculptured
unsealed
unseaworthiness
unseaworthy
unseconded
unsectarian
unsecured
unseeing
unsegmented
unselected
unselective
unselfish
unselfishly
unsent
unsentimental
unserved
unserviceable
unserviceably
unset
unsew
unsewn
unsexual
unshaded
unshakable
unshaken
unshamed
unshapely
unshared
unshaved
unshaven
unshed
unshelled
unsheltered
unshod
unshorn
unshrinkable
unshrinking
unshriven
unshrouded
unshrunk
unshunned
unshut
unsifted
unsigned
unsilenced
unsimilar
unsingable
unsinkable
unsisterly
unsized
unskeptical
unslacked
unslaked
unsleeping
unslumbering
unsmiling
unsmirched
unsmoked
unsoaked
unsober
unsocial
unsoiled
unsold
unsoldierlike

unprofitable transaction. **—un·prof′it·a·ble·ness** *n.* **—un·prof′it·a·bly** *adv.*

un·pro·nounce·a·ble (un′prə·noun′sə·bəl) *adj.* 1 Not easy to pronounce, especially properly. 2 Not fit to be mentioned.

un·pro·vid·ed (un′prə·vī′did) *adj.* 1 Not furnished or provided: with *with,* formerly with *of:* to be *unprovided* with suitable raiment. 2 Not fittingly prepared; not ready: *unprovided* for a sudden change. **—un′pro·vid′ed·ly** *adv.*

un·qual·i·fied (un·kwol′ə·fīd) *adj.* 1 Being without the proper qualifications; unfit. 2 Having failed to qualify; lacking legal power or authority. 3 Without limitation or restrictions; absolute; entire: *unqualified* approval. **—un·qual′i·fied′ly** *adv.* **—un·qual′i·fied′ness** *n.*

un·ques·tion·a·ble (un·kwes′chən·ə·bəl) *adj.* Too certain or sure to admit of question; being beyond a doubt; indisputable. See synonyms under INCONTESTABLE, NOTORIOUS. **—un·ques′tion·a·bly** *adv.*

un·ques·tioned (un·kwes′chənd) *adj.* 1 Not called in question; undoubted. 2 Not to be frustrated or opposed; indisputable. 3 Not interrogated.

un·qui·et (un·kwī′ət) *adj.* 1 Not at rest; disturbed; restless, in mind or physically. 2 Causing unrest or discomfort. **—un·qui′et·ly** *adv.* **—un·qui′et·ness** *n.*

un·quote (un·kwōt′) *v.t.* & *v.i.* **·quot·ed, ·quot·ing** To close (a quotation).

un·rav·el (un·rav′əl) *v.* **·eled** or **·elled, ·el·ing** or **·el·ling** *v.t.* 1 To separate the threads of, as a tangled skein or knitted article. 2 To free from entanglement; unfold; explain, as a mystery or a plot. **—***v.i.* 3 To become unraveled. See synonyms under INTERPRET.

un·read (un·red′) *adj.* 1 Not informed by reading; ignorant. 2 Not yet perused.

un·read·y (un·red′ē) *adj.* 1 Being without readiness or alertness; not apt or quick to see or appreciate. 2 Not in a condition to act effectively; unprepared. **—un·read′i·ly** *adv.* **—un·read′i·ness** *n.*

un·re·al (un·rē′əl, -rēl′) *adj.* Having no reality, actual existence, or substance; having no genuineness; insincere; artificial; also, fanciful; visionary. **—un·re·al·i·ty** (un′rē·al′ə·tē) *n.* **—un·re′al·ly** *adv.*

un·rea·son (un·rē′zən) *n.* Lack or absence of reason; irrationality; also, absurdity; nonsense.

un·rea·son·a·ble (un·rē′zən·ə·bəl) *adj.* 1 Acting without or contrary to reason. 2 Not according to reason; irrational. 3 Exceeding what is reasonable; immoderate; exorbitant. See synonyms under ABSURD, IMMODERATE. **—un·rea′son·a·ble·ness** *n.* **—un·rea′son·a·bly** *adv.*

un·rea·son·ing (un·rē′zən·ing) *adj.* So intolerant, or so unaccompanied by reason or control, as to be obstinate, blind, or wild.

un·reck·on·a·ble (un·rek′ən·ə·bəl) *adj.* That cannot be reckoned or computed; unlimited.

un·reel (un·rēl′) *v.t.* & *v.i.* To unwind, as from a reel.

un·reeve (un·rēv′) *v.* **·reeved** or **·rove** *(for pp. also* **·rov·en***),* **·reev·ing** *Naut. v.t.* 1 To take out or withdraw (a rope) from a block, thimble, deadeye, etc. **—***v.i.* 2 To become unreeved. 3 To unreeve a rope.

un·re·flec·tive (un′ri·flek′tiv) *adj.* Not given to reflection; not thoughtful.

un·re·gen·er·ate (un′ri·jen′ər·it) *adj.* Not having been changed spiritually by regeneration; remaining unreconciled to God; loosely, sinful. Also **un′re·gen′er·at′ed** (-ā′tid). **—un′re·gen′er·a·cy** (-ə·sē) *n.* **—un′re·gen′er·ate·ly** *adv.*

un·re·lent·ing (un′ri·len′ting) *adj.* 1 Continuing to be severe; pitiless; inexorable. 2 Not diminishing, or not changing, in pace, effort, speed, etc. **—un′re·lent′ing·ly** *adv.*

un·re·li·a·ble (un′ri·lī′ə·bəl) *adj.* That cannot be relied upon; not dependable. **—un′re·li′·a·bil′i·ty, un′re·li′a·ble·ness** *n.* **—un′re·li′a·bly** *adv.*

un·re·lig·ious (un′ri·lij′əs) *adj.* 1 Irreligious; hostile to religion. 2 Having no religion; not connected with religion.

un·re·mit·ting (un′ri·mit′ing) *adj.* Incessant; not relaxing. **—un′re·mit′ting·ly** *adv.* **—un′re·mit′ting·ness** *n.*

un·re·proved (un′ri·pro͞ovd′) *adj.* 1 Not censured or blamed; not reproved. 2 Not liable to reproof; above reproach.

un·re·serve (un′ri·zûrv′) *n.* Absence of reserve; freedom of style or manner.

un·re·served (un′ri·zûrvd′) *adj.* 1 Given or done without reserve. 2 Having no reserve of manner; informal; open; frank. See synonyms under CANDID, IMPLICIT. **—un·re·serv·ed·ly** (un′ri·zûr′vid·lē) *adv.* **—un′re·serv′ed·ness** *n.*

un·re·spec·tive (un′ri·spek′tiv) *adj. Obs.* 1 Undiscriminating. 2 Inattentive; heedless. 3 Common; not restricted.

un·res·pit·ed (un·res′pit·id) *adj.* 1 Not postponed; not respited, as from a sentence of the law. 2 *Obs.* Having no intermission.

un·re·spon·sive (un′ri·spon′siv) *adj.* Showing no reaction or response; unsympathetic. **—un′re·spon′sive·ly** *adv.* **—un′re·spon′sive·ness** *n.*

un·rest (un·rest′) *n.* 1 Restlessness, especially of the mind. 2 Trouble; turmoil: used with regard to public or political conditions and suggesting premonitions of revolt.

un·re·strained (un′ri·strānd′) *adj.* Not restrained; free; not controlled. **—un·re·strain·ed·ly** (un′ri·strā′nid·lē) *adv.*

un·rid·dle (un·rid′l) *v.t.* **·dled, ·dling** To solve, as a mystery.

un·ri·fled[1] (un·rī′fəld) *adj.* Smooth-bored, as a gun.

un·ri·fled[2] (un·rī′fəld) *adj.* Not rifled, seized, or plundered.

un·rig (un·rig′) *v.t.* **·rigged, ·rig·ging** *Naut.* To strip of rigging.

un·right·eous (un·rī′chəs) *adj.* 1 Not righteous; wicked; sinful. 2 Contrary to the law of right; unjust. See synonyms under SINFUL. **—un·right′eous·ly** *adv.* **—un·right′eous·ness** *n.*

un·rip (un·rip′) *v.t.* **·ripped, ·rip·ping** To separate by ripping; rip or cut open.

un·ripe (un·rīp′) *adj.* 1 Not arrived at maturity; not ripe; immature. 2 Premature. 3 Not ready; not prepared. [OE, untimely] **—un·ripe′ness** *n.*

un·ri·valed (un·rī′vəld) *adj.* Having no rival or competitor; unequaled; matchless. Also **un·ri′·valled.**

un·roll (un·rōl′) *v.t.* 1 To spread or open (something rolled up). 2 To exhibit to view. 3 *Rare* To remove from a roll or register. **—***v.i.* 4 To become unrolled.

un·root (un·ro͞ot′, -ro͝ot′) *v.t.* To uproot.

un·ruf·fled (un·ruf′əld) *adj.* 1 Not disturbed or agitated emotionally; calm. 2 Not ruffled or made rough physically.

un·ru·ly (un·ro͞o′lē) *adj.* Disposed to resist rule or discipline; intractable; ungovernable. See synonyms under RESTIVE. **—un·ru′li·ness** *n.*

un·sad·dle (un·sad′l) *v.t.* **·dled, ·dling** 1 To remove a saddle from. 2 To remove from the saddle; unhorse.

un·said (un·sed′) *adj.* Not said; not spoken.

un·sat·u·rat·ed (un·sach′ə·rā′tid) *adj.* 1 Falling short of saturation, as a solution. 2 *Chem.* Not combined to the greatest possible extent; capable of uniting with certain other elements or compounds to form additional compounds.

un·sa·vor·y (un·sā′vər·ē) *adj.* 1 Having a disagreeable taste or odor. 2 Suggesting something disagreeable, offensive, or unclean; also, morally bad: an *unsavory* reputation. 3 *Obs.* Having no savor; tasteless; odorless. Also *Brit.* **un·sa′vour·y.** **—un·sa′vor·i·ly** *adv.* **—un·sa′vor·i·ness** *n.*

un·say (un·sā′) *v.t.* **·said, ·say·ing** To retract (something said).

un·scathed (un·skāthd′) *adj.* Uninjured.

un·scram·ble (un·skram′bəl) *v.t.* **·bled, ·bling** *Colloq.* To resolve the confused, scrambled, or disordered condition of.

un·screw (un·skro͞o′) *v.t.* 1 To remove the screw or screws from. 2 To remove or detach by withdrawing screws, or by turning. **—***v.i.* 3 To permit of being unscrewed.

un·scru·pu·lous (un·skro͞o′pyə·ləs) *adj.* Not scrupulous; having no scruples; unprincipled. **—un·scru′pu·lous·ly** *adv.* **—un·scru′pu·lous·ness** *n.*

un·seal (un·sēl′) *v.t.* 1 To break or remove the seal of. 2 To open (that which has been sealed or closed).

un·seam (un·sēm′) *v.t.* To open the seam or seams of.

un·search·a·ble (un·sûr′chə·bəl) *adj.* That cannot be searched or explored; hidden; mysterious. **—un·search′a·bly** *adv.*

un·sea·son·a·ble (un·sē′zən·ə·bəl) *adj.* Not being in the proper season or not being in time; inappropriate; ill-timed. **—un·sea′son·a·ble·ness** *n.* **—un·sea′son·a·bly** *adv.*

un·sea·soned (un·sē′zənd) *adj.* 1 Not seasoned; not flavored. 2 Immature; unripe; not properly aged. 3 Not habituated. **—un·sea′soned·ness** *n.*

un·seat (un·sēt′) *v.t.* 1 To remove from a seat or fixed position. 2 To unhorse. 3 To deprive of office or rank; depose.

un·seem·ly (un·sēm′lē) *adj.* **·li·er, ·li·est** Unbecoming; indecent; not handsome. **—***adv.* In an unseemly fashion. **—un·seem′li·ness** *n.*

un·seen (un·sēn′) *adj.* Not seen; not evident; invisible; not previously seen or prepared, as a passage for translation.

un·set·tle (un·set′l) *v.* **·tled, ·tling** *v.t.* 1 To move from a fixed or settled condition. 2 To confuse; disturb. **—***v.i.* 3 To become unsteady or unfixed. See synonyms under DISPLACE.

un·sex (un·seks′) *v.t.* 1 To deprive of the distinctive qualities of a sex; especially, to render unfeminine or unwomanly. 2 To castrate.

un·shack·le (un·shak′əl) *v.t.* **·led, ·ling** To unfetter; free from shackles. **—un·shack′led** *adj.*

un·shap·en (un·shā′pən) *adj.* Not shaped; imperfectly formed; badly shaped. Also **un·shaped′.**

un·sheathe (un·shēth′) *v.t.* **·sheathed, ·sheath·ing** To take from or as from a scabbard or sheath; bare.

un·ship (un·ship′) *v.t.* **·shipped, ·ship·ping** 1 To unload from a ship or other vessel; also, to dismiss from a ship. 2 To remove from the place where it is fixed or fitted, as a rudder or oar.

un·sick·er (un·sik′ər) *adj. Scot.* Insecure; unreliable; undependable. **—un·sick′er·ly** *adv.* **—un·sick′er·ness** *n.*

un·sight·ed (un·sī′tid) *adj.* 1 Not sighted; not in view. 2 Having no sight, as a cannon. 3 Not aimed with the assistance of a sight, as a shot.

un·sight·ly (un·sīt′lē) *adj.* **·li·er, ·li·est** Offensive to the sight; ugly. **—un·sight′li·ness** *n.*

unsight unseen Sight unseen: former usage.

un·skaithed (un·skāthd′) *adj. Scot.* Unscathed.

un·skil·ful (un·skil′fəl) *adj.* 1 Lacking or not evincing skilfulness; awkward. 2 *Obs.* Lacking in discernment; ignorant. Also **un·skill′ful.** **—un·skil′ful·ly** *adv.* **—un·skil′ful·ness** *n.*

---

unsoldierly
unsolicited
unsolicitous
unsolid
unsoluble
unsolvable
unsolved
unsophistication
unsorted
unsought
unsounded
unsoured
unsowed
unsown
unspecified
unspeculative
unspelled
unspent
unspilled
unspilt
unspiritual
unspirituality
unspiritually
unspiritualness
unspoiled
unspoilt
unspoken
unsportsmanlike
unsprinkled
unsprung
unsquandered
unsquared
unstack
unstainable
unstained
unstamped
unstandardized
unstarched
unstarred
unstatesmanlike
unsteadfast
unsteadily
unsteadiness
unsteady
unstemmed
unsterilized
unstick
unstigmatized
unstinted
unstitched
unstrained
unstressed
unstripped
unstuffed
unstung
unsubdued
unsubmissive
unsubscribed
unsubstantiated
unsuccess
unsuggestive
unsuited
unsullied
unsunk
unsunned
unsupportable
unsupported
unsupportedly
unsuppressed
unsure
unsurmountable
unsurpassable
unsurpassed
unsusceptible
unsuspicious
unsustained
unswayed
unsweetened
unswept
unswerving
unsworn
unsymmetrical
unsympathetic
unsympathizing
unsystematic
unsystematized
untack
untactful
untainted
untaken
untalented
untalked-of
untamable, untameable
untame
untamed
untangled
untanned
untapped
untarnished
untasted
untaxable
untaxed
unteachable
untechnical

un·skilled (un·skild′) *adj.* 1 Destitute of skill or dexterity in artisan's work; good only for common labor: an *unskilled* workman. 2 Produced without or not requiring special skill or training; untrained. 3 Destitute of practical knowledge; unskilful.

un·sling (un·sling′) *v.t.* **·slung, ·sling·ing** 1 To remove, as a rifle, from a slung position. 2 *Naut.* To take the slings from.

un·snap (un·snap′) *v.t.* **·snapped, ·snap·ping** To undo the snap or snaps of; unfasten.

un·snarl (un·snärl′) *v.t.* To disentangle.

un·so·cia·ble (un·sō′shə·bəl) *adj.* 1 Not sociable; not inclined to seek the society of others. 2 Not congenial or in accord: an *unsociable* group. 3 Not encouraging social intercourse. — **un·so′cia·bil′i·ty, un·so′cia·ble·ness** *n.* — **un·so′cia·bly** *adv.*

un·sol·der (un·sod′ər) *v.t.* 1 To disunite or take apart (something soldered). 2 To separate; sunder.

un·son·sie (un·son′sē) *adj. Scot.* Unlucky; disagreeable. Also **un·son′cy, un·son′sy.**

un·so·phis·ti·cat·ed (un′sə·fis′tə·kā′tid) *adj.* 1 Not sophisticated; showing inexperience or naiveté; artless; simple. 2 Free from adulteration; genuine; pure. See synonyms under CANDID, RUSTIC. — **un′so·phis′ti·cat′ed·ly** *adv.* — **un′so·phis′ti·cat′ed·ness** *n.*

un·sound (un·sound′) *adj.* 1 Lacking in soundness; not having material strength and solidity; weak; rotten. 2 Not sound in health; diseased. 3 Not logically valid; erroneous; in religion, heterodox. 4 Disturbed; not profound: said of sleep. — **un·sound′ly** *adv.* — **un·sound′ness** *n.*

un·spar·ing (un·spâr′ing) *adj.* 1 Not sparing or saving; lavish; liberal. 2 Showing no mercy. — **un·spar′ing·ly** *adv.* — **un·spar′ing·ness** *n.*

un·speak (un·spēk′) *v.t.* **·spoke, ·spo·ken, ·speak·ing** To retract (something said); take back.

un·speak·a·ble (un·spē′kə·bəl) *adj.* 1 That cannot be expressed; unutterable: *unspeakable* joy. 2 Extremely bad or objectionable: an *unspeakable* crime. 3 Mute. — **un·speak′a·ble·ness** *n.* — **un·speak′a·bly** *adv.*

un·spe·cial·ized (un·spesh′əl·īzd) *adj.* 1 Not specialized. 2 *Biol.* Not set apart for a special function or purpose; generalized. Also *Brit.* **un·spe′cial·ised.**

un·sphere (un·sfir′) *v.t.* **·sphered, ·spher·ing** To take out of its sphere or place.

un·spot·ted (un·spot′id) *adj.* 1 Not marked or marred with spots. 2 Not morally tainted; immaculate; free from blemishes; perfect. 3 Ceremonially clean. See synonyms under PURE. — **un·spot′ted·ness** *n.*

un·sprung weight (un·sprung′) In automobiles, the weight of components not supported by the suspension, as the wheel assemblies: opposed to *sprung weight.*

un·sta·ble (un·stā′bəl) *adj.* 1 Lacking in stability or firmness; not stable. 2 Having no fixed purposes; easily influenced; inconstant: an *unstable* character. 3 *Chem.* Readily decomposable, as certain compounds. 4 Subject to a radical change by the application of a slight force: *unstable* equilibrium. See FICKLE, PRECARIOUS. — **un·sta′ble·ness** *n.* — **un·sta′bly** *adv.*

un·state (un·stāt′) *v.t.* **·stat·ed, ·stat·ing** 1 To divest of statehood. 2 To deprive of dignity, rank, or office.

un·steel (un·stēl′) *v.t.* To deprive of steel-like quality; disarm; soften.

un·step (un·step′) *v.t.* **·stepped, ·step·ping** To take out of a step or socket: to *unstep* a mast.

un·stop (un·stop′) *v.t.* **·stopped, ·stop·ping** 1 To remove a stop or stopper from. 2 To open by removing obstructions; clear. 3 To open the stops of (an organ).

un·stopped (un·stopt′) *adj.* 1 Not stopped; unobstructed. 2 *Phonet.* Of consonants, not stopped; capable of being prolonged: said of the continuants, as (z) and (l).

un·stowed (un·stōd′) *adj.* 1 Not stowed or filled, as a ship, with cargo. 2 Lying loose in the hold or on deck, as cargo

un·strap (un·strap′) *v.t.* **·strapped, ·strap·ping** To unfasten or loosen the strap or straps of.

un·strat·i·fied (un·strat′ə·fīd) *adj. Geol.* Not deposited in beds or strata, as igneous rocks.

un·stri·at·ed (un·strī′ā·tid) *adj.* Without striations; smooth-textured, as certain muscles.

un·string (un·string′) *v.t.* **·strung, ·string·ing** 1 To remove from a string, as pearls. 2 To take the string or strings from. 3 To loosen the string or strings of, as a bow or guitar. 4 To relax, as if by loosening; weaken: usually in the passive: Her nerves were *unstrung.*

un·striped (un·strīpt′) *adj.* 1 Not striped; unstriated. 2 *Anat.* Denoting certain muscles that act independently of the will, as the heart muscles. See under MUSCLE.

un·strung (un·strung′) *adj.* 1 Having the strings removed or relaxed. 2 Unnerved; emotionally upset; weakened; relaxed.

un·stud·ied (un·stud′ēd) *adj.* 1 Not planned; unpremeditated. 2 Not stiff or artificial; natural. 3 Not acquainted through study; unversed: with *in.* See synonyms under SIMPLE.

un·sub·stan·tial (un′səb·stan′shəl) *adj.* 1 Lacking solidity, strength, or weight. 2 Having no valid basis. 3 Having no bodily existence; fanciful. — **un′sub·stan′tial·ly** *adv.* — **un′sub·stan′ti·al′i·ty** (-shē·al′ə·tē) *n.*

un·suc·cess·ful (un′sək·ses′fəl) *adj.* Having or meeting with no success: said of persons or their acts: *unsuccessful* in business, an *unsuccessful* attempt. — **un′suc·cess′ful·ly** *adv.* — **un′suc·cess′ful·ness** *n.*

un·suit·a·ble (un·sōō′tə·bəl) *adj.* Not suitable; unfitting. — **un·suit·a·bil·i·ty** (un′sōō·tə·bil′ə·tē), **un·suit′a·ble·ness** *n.* — **un·suit′a·bly** *adv.*

un·sung (un·sung′) *adj.* 1 Not celebrated in song or poetry; obscure. 2 Not yet sung, as a song.

un·sus·pect·ed (un′sə·spek′tid) *adj.* 1 Not suspected, as of evil; not under suspicion. 2 Not imagined or known to exist.

un·sus·pect·ing (un′sə·spek′ting) *adj.* Having no suspicion; trusting.

un·swathe (un·swāth′) *v.t.* **·swathed, ·swath·ing** To remove swathings from; free from swathings.

un·swear (un·swâr′) *v.t.* **·swore, ·sworn, ·swear·ing** To revoke (an oath); retract; abjure.

un·tan·gle (un·tang′gəl) *v.t.* **·gled, ·gling** To free from entanglement or embarrassment; resolve.

un·taught (un·tôt′) *adj.* Not having been instructed; ignorant.

un·teach (un·tēch′) *v.t.* **·taught, ·teach·ing** 1 To cause to forget or to disbelieve what has been taught. 2 To cause to be forgotten or disbelieved.

un·ten·a·ble (un·ten′ə·bəl) *adj.* 1 That cannot be maintained: *untenable* theories. 2 Incapable of being defended or held, as a fortress. — **un·ten′a·ble·ness** *n.*

un·tent·ed (un·ten′tid) *adj.* 1 Having no tents. 2 *Obs.* Not kept open or dressed, as a wound.

Un·ter den Lin·den (ōōn′tər den lin′dən) A famous avenue in East Berlin; literally, under the lindens.

Un·ter·wal·den (ōōn′tər·väl′dən) A canton of central Switzerland; 296 square miles.

un·thanked (un·thangkt′) *adj.* 1 Not thanked. 2 *Obs.* Not received with thankfulness.

un·thank·ful (un·thangk′fəl) *adj.* 1 Not grateful. 2 Not received with thanks; unwelcome. — **un·thank′ful·ly** *adv.* — **un·thank′ful·ness** *n.*

un·think (un·thingk′) *v.t.* **·thought, ·think·ing** To retract in thought; change the mind concerning.

un·think·ing (un·thingk′ing) *adj.* 1 Not having the power of thought. 2 Lacking thoughtfulness, care, or attention; heedless; inconsiderate. See synonyms under IMPRUDENT. — **un·think′ing·ly** *adv.* — **un·think′ing·ness** *n.*

un·thread (un·thred′) *v.t.* 1 To remove the thread from, as a needle. 2 To find one's way out of, as a maze.

un·ti·dy (un·tī′dē) *adj.* **·di·er, ·di·est** Showing or characterized by lack of tidiness. [ME *untidi*] — **un·ti′di·ly** *adv.* — **un·ti′di·ness** *n.*

un·tie (un·tī′) *v.* **·tied, ·ty·ing** *v.t.* 1 To loosen or undo, as a knot or knotted rope. 2 To free from that which binds or restrains. — *v.i.* 3 To become untied. See synonyms under RELEASE. [OE *untīgan*] — **un·tied′** *adj.*

un·til (un·til′) *prep.* 1 Up to the time of; till: We will wait *until* midnight. 2 Before: used with a negative: The music doesn't begin *until* nine. 3 *Scot.* & *Brit. Dial.* Unto. — *conj.* 1 To the time when: *until* I die. 2 To the place or degree that: Walk east *until* you reach the river. 3 Before: with a negative: He couldn't leave *until* the car came for him. [ME *untill* < *und-* up to, as far as + TILL]

un·time·ly (un·tīm′lē) *adj.* Coming before time or not in proper time; unseasonable; ill-timed: also *Scot.* **un·time′ous.** — *adv.* Before the proper time; inopportunely.

un·ti·tled (un·tīt′ld) *adj.* 1 Having no right (to a throne). 2 Having no title, as a book. 3 Having no title of distinction: *untitled* nobility.

un·to (un′tōō) *prep.* 1 *Poetic* & *Archaic* To: used in all senses except to indicate the infinitive. 2 *Archaic* Until. — *conj. Obs.* Up to the extent or time that; until. [ME *un-, und-* up to, as far as + TO, on analogy with *until*]

un·told (un·tōld′) *adj.* 1 That cannot be told, revealed, or described; inexpressible: *untold* misery. 2 That cannot be numbered or estimated; hence, of great number or extent: *untold* numbers; *untold* treasure. 3 Not told.

un·touch·a·bil·i·ty (un′tuch·ə·bil′ə·tē) *n.* The character or state of being untouchable.

un·touch·a·ble (un·tuch′ə·bəl) *adj.* 1 Inaccessible to the touch; out of reach; intangible; unrivaled; unapproachable. 2 Forbidden to the touch. 3 Unpleasant, disgusting, vile, or dangerous to touch; that should not be touched. — *n.* In India, a member of the lowest caste; one whose touch was formerly counted as pollution by Hindus of higher station.

un·to·ward (un·tôrd′, -tōrd′) *adj.* 1 Causing annoyance or hindrance; vexatious. 2 Not yielding readily; refractory; perverse. 3 *Obs.* Uncouth; ungraceful. See synonyms under PERVERSE. — **un·to′ward·ly** *adv.* — **un·to′ward·ness** *n.*

un·trav·eled (un·trav′əld) *adj.* 1 Not passed over, as a road. 2 Not having traveled; hence, narrow in ideas; provincial. Also **un·trav′elled.**

un·tread (un·tred′) *v.t.* **·trod, ·trod·den** or **·trod, ·tread·ing** To retrace.

un·tried (un·trīd′) *adj.* 1 Not tried or tested. 2 Not tried in court.

un·trimmed (un·trimd′) *adj.* 1 Not adorned

untempered
untenanted
untended
unterrified
untested
untether
unthatched
untheatrical
unthinkable
unthoughtful
unthought-of
unthrift
unthriftiness
unthrifty
unthrone
untillable
untilled
untinged
untired
untiring
untouched
untraceable
untraced
untracked
untractable
untrained
untrammeled, untrammelled
untransferable
untransferred
untranslatable
untranslated
untransmitted
untrapped
untraversable
untraversed
untreasured
untrim
untroubled
untrustiness
untrusty
untuck
untufted
untunable
untuned
untuneful
unturned
untwilled
untwisted
untypical
un-uniformed
un-uniformly
un-united
unurged
unusable
unutilizable
unutilized
unuttered
unvaccinated
unvacillating
unvail
unvalidated
unvanquished
unvaried
unvarying
unveiled
unventilated
unveracious
unverifiable
unverified
unversed
unvexed
unvext
unvisited
unvitiated
unvitrified
unvocal
unvolatilized
unvulcanized
unwakened
unwalled
unwanted
unwarlike
unwarmed
unwarned
unwashed
unwasted
unwasting
unwatched
unwavering
unweakened
unweaned
unwearable
unweary
unwearying
unweathered
unweave
unwed
unwedded
unweeded
unwelded
unwetted
unwhetted
unwhipped
unwhipt

with trimmings: an *untrimmed* hat. **2** Not made trim or orderly; not clipped or pruned: an *untrimmed* tree. **3** *Obs.* Virgin.

un·trod·den (un·trod′n) *adj.* Not having been trodden upon; hence, unfrequented. Also **un·trod′.**

un·true (un·trōō′) *adj.* **1** Lacking truth; not true; not corresponding with fact. **2** Not conforming to rule or standard. **3** Not adhering to faith, pledge, or duty; disloyal. See synonyms under BAD, PERFIDIOUS. **— un·tru′ly** *adv.*

un·truss (un·trus′) *v.t.* **1** To loosen or free from or as from a truss; unfasten; undo. **2** *Obs.* To take off (breeches); undress.

un·trust·ful (un·trust′fəl) *adj.* **1** Not trusting or trustful. **2** Not to be trusted; untrustworthy.

un·trust·wor·thy (un·trust′wûr′thē) *adj.* Worthy of no trust; unreliable. See synonyms under BAD, PERFIDIOUS. **— un·trust′wor′thi·ness** *n.* **— un·trust′wor′thi·ly** *adv.*

un·truth (un·trōōth′) *n. pl.* **·truths** (-trōōths′, -trōōthz′) **1** The quality or character of being untrue; want of veracity. **2** *Obs.* Lack of fidelity; disloyalty. **3** Something that is not true; a falsehood; lie. See synonyms under DECEPTION, LIE. [OE *untrēowth*]

un·truth·ful (un·trōōth′fəl) *adj.* Not truthful; untrue; not veracious. **— un·truth′ful·ly** *adv.* **— un·truth′ful·ness** *n.*

un·tu·tored (un·tōō′tərd, -tyōō′-) *adj.* Having had no tutor or teacher; hence, uninstructed; raw. See synonyms under IGNORANT.

un·twine (un·twīn′) *v.* **·twined, ·twin·ing** *v.t.* To undo (something twined); unwind by disentangling. **—** *v.i.* To become untwined.

un·twist (un·twist′) *v.t.* & *v.i.* To separate or open by a movement the reverse of twisting; unwind or untwine.

U·nun·gun (ōō·nōōng′gōōn) *n. pl.* Literally, people: the collective name for two Eskimo tribes, the Unalaskans and the Atkans, inhabiting the Aleutian Islands; the Aleuts.

un·used (un·yōōzd′) *adj.* **1** Not made use of; disused; also, never having been used. **2** Not accustomed or wont: with *to.*

un·u·su·al (un·yōō′zhōō·əl) *adj.* Of a character, kind, number, or size not usually met with. See synonyms under EXTRAORDINARY, ODD, RARE. **— un·u′su·al·ly** *adv.* **— un·u′su·al·ness** *n.*

un·ut·ter·a·ble (un·ut′ər·ə·bəl) *adj.* **1** That cannot be uttered; too great or deep for verbal expression; ineffable: *unutterable* bliss. **2** Unpronounceable. **— un·ut′ter·a·ble·ness** *n.* **— un·ut′ter·a·bly** *adv.*

un·val·ued (un·val′yōōd) *adj.* **1** Not valued; neglected; unappreciated. **2** Not having a fixed value; not appraised. **3** *Obs.* Inestimable.

un·var·nished (un·vär′nisht) *adj.* **1** Having no covering of varnish. **2** Having no embellishment; plain: the *unvarnished* truth.

un·veil (un·vāl′) *v.t.* To remove the veil or covering from; disclose to view; reveal. **—** *v.i.* To remove one's veil; reveal oneself.

un·voice (un·vois′) *v.t.* **·voiced, ·voic·ing** *Phonet.* To pronounce (a voiced sound) without vibration of the vocal cords; devocalize.

un·voiced (un·voist′) *adj.* **1** Not expressed. **2** *Phonet.* Not voiced; rendered voiceless: The final (v) in "have" is often heard *unvoiced* in "have to": also *devoiced.*

un·voic·ing (un·voi′sing) *n. Phonet.* The change of a voiced consonant to its unvoiced counterpart, as of (b) to (p).

un·war·rant·a·ble (un·wôr′ən·tə·bəl, -wor′-) *adj.* That cannot be warranted; unjustifiable; indefensible. **— un·war′rant·a·bly** *adv.*

un·war·rant·ed (un·wôr′ən·tid, -wor′-) *adj.* **1** Having no warrant; unwarrantable; unjustifiable. **2** Being without warranty or guarantee.

un·war·y (un·wâr′ē) *adj.* Taking no precautions against accident or danger; especially, not realizing the necessity of such precautions; incautious. **— un·war′i·ly** *adv.* **— un·war′i·ness** *n.*

un·wea·ried (un·wir′ēd) *adj.* **1** Not tired. **2** Indefatigable.

un·wel·come (un·wel′kəm) *adj.* **1** Not welcome; not desired: an *unwelcome* guest. **2** Causing no satisfaction: *unwelcome* news. **— un·wel′come·ly** *adv.* **— un·wel′come·ness** *n.*

un·well (un·wel′) *adj.* **1** Somewhat ill; ailing. **2** Menstruating; indisposed by reason of menstruation: a euphemism. See synonyms under SICKLY. **— un·well′ness** *n.*

un·wept (un·wept′) *adj.* **1** Not lamented or wept for, as a deceased person. **2** Not shed, as tears.

un·whole·some (un·hōl′səm) *adj.* **1** Deleterious to physical or mental health. **2** Unsound in quality or condition; diseased or decayed: *unwholesome* provisions. **3** Impaired in health; sickly in appearance: an *unwholesome* look. **4** Not contributing to moral health; pernicious: *unwholesome* literature. See synonyms under BAD, NOISOME. **— un·whole′some·ly** *adv.* **— un·whole′some·ness** *n.*

un·wield·y (un·wēl′dē) *adj.* Moved or managed with difficulty, as from great size or awkward shape; bulky; clumsy. **— un·wield′i·ly** *adv.* **— un·wield′i·ness** *n.*

un·willed (un·wild′) *adj.* **1** Not willed or intended; spontaneous. **2** Being without, or deprived of, purpose or will.

un·will·ing (un·wil′ing) *adj.* **1** Not willing; reluctant; loath. **2** Done with reluctance. **3** *Obs.* Not intended; involuntary. See synonyms under RELUCTANT. **— un·will′ing·ly** *adv.* **— un·will′ing·ness** *n.*

un·wind (un·wīnd′) *v.* **·wound, ·wind·ing** *v.t.* **1** To reverse the winding of; untwist or wind off; uncoil. **2** To disentangle. **—** *v.i.* **3** To become unwound.

un·wise (un·wīz′) *adj.* Acting with, or showing, lack of wisdom; injudicious; foolish. [OE *unwīs*] **— un·wise′ly** *adv.* **— un·wis′dom** (-wiz′·dəm) *n.*

un·wish (un·wish′) *v.t.* **1** To retract (something wished); stop wishing. **2** To wish (something) not to be. **3** *Obs.* To destroy or do away with by wishing.

un·wished (un·wisht′) *adj.* **1** Not desired or wished. **2** Unwelcome.

un·wit·ting (un·wit′ing) *adj.* **1** Having no knowledge or consciousness of the thing in question; unknowing or unconscious. **2** Unintentional. [OE *unwitende*] **— un·wit′ting·ly** *adv.*

un·wont·ed (un·wun′tid, -won′-) *adj.* **1** Not according to wont or custom; unusual; uncommon. **2** *Obs.* Not accustomed; unfamiliar. See synonyms under EXTRAORDINARY. **— un·wont′ed·ly** *adv.* **— un·wont′ed·ness** *n.*

un·world·ly (un·wûrld′lē) *adj.* **1** Not motivated by worldly values or interests; spiritually minded. **2** Unearthly; spiritual; not belonging to this world. **— un·world′li·ness** *n.*

un·wor·thy (un·wûr′thē) *adj.* **1** Not worthy or deserving of something specified: usually with *of.* **2** Not befitting or becoming: often with *of*; wrong; improper: conduct *unworthy* of a gentleman. **3** Lacking worth or merit; unfit; wrong; contemptible. See synonyms under BAD, SINFUL. **— un·wor′thi·ly** *adv.* **— un·wor′thi·ness** *n.*

un·wrap (un·rap′) *v.* **·wrapped, ·wrap·ping** *v.t.* To take the wrapping from; open; undo. **—** *v.i.* To become unwrapped.

un·wrin·kle (un·ring′kəl) *v.t.* **·kled, ·kling** To free from wrinkles; smooth.

un·writ·ten (un·rit′n) *adj.* **1** Not reduced to writing; not written down; oral; traditional. **2** Having no writing upon it; blank.

unwritten law 1 A rule or custom established by general usage: an *unwritten law* of gentlemanly decorum. **2** Law which rests on custom and judicial decision, and not on a written command, decree, or statute. See COMMON LAW under LAW. **3** A custom in some communities granting a measure of immunity to those who commit criminal acts of revenge in support of personal or family honor, especially in cases of seduction, adultery, etc.

un·yoke (un·yōk′) *v.* **·yoked, ·yok·ing** *v.t.* **1** To release from a yoke. **2** To separate; part. **—** *v.i.* **3** To become unyoked. **4** To stop work; cease. [OE *ungeocian*]

un·yoked (un·yōkt′) *adj.* **1** Not subjected to or not wearing a yoke. **2** Freed from a yoke. **3** *Obs.* Unrestrained; licentious.

up (up) *adv.* **1** Toward a higher place or level: opposed to *down.* **2** In or on a higher place; above the horizon. **3** Toward that which is figuratively or conventionally higher: **a** To or at a higher price: Barley is *up.* **b** To or at a higher rank: people who have come *up* in the world. **c** To or at a greater size or larger amount: to swell *up.* **d** To or at a higher musical pitch. **e** To or at a place that is locally or arbitrarily regarded as higher: *up* north. **4** To a vertical position; standing; on one's feet. **5** Risen from bed. **6** So as to be level (to) or even (with) in space, time, degree, or amount: *up* to date; *up* to the brim. **7** In or into commotion or activity; in progress: They were stirred *up* to mutiny; to be *up* in arms. **8** Into existence: to draw *up* a document; to turn *up.* **9** In or into prominence; under consideration: The question was *up* for debate. **10** Into or in a place of safekeeping; aside: Fruits are put *up* in glass jars. **11** At an end or close: Your time is *up.* **12** Completely; wholly: Houses were burned *up*; The brooks dried *up.* **13** In baseball and cricket, at bat: He made but one hit in three times *up.* **14** In tennis and other sports: **a** In the lead; ahead: said of a player or team. **b** Apiece; alike: said of a score. **15** Bound for: said of a ship: *up* for Panama. **16** Running for as a candidate: Jones is *up* for mayor. **17** On trial before a magistrate: *up* for manslaughter. **18** *Naut.* Shifted to windward, as a tiller. **— all up with** At an end for; no further hope for. **— to be up against** *Colloq.* To meet with; be face to face with. **— to be up against it** *Colloq.* To be in difficulty; have financial trouble. **— to be up to 1** *Colloq.* To be doing or plotting; be about to do: What is he *up to*? **2** To be equal to; to be capable of: I'm not *up to* moving all this furniture today. **3** To be incumbent upon; be dependent upon: It's *up to* him to save us. **—** *adj.* **1** Moving, sloping, or directed upward or in a direction arbitrarily regarded as upward. **2** At stake, as in gambling: to have money *up* on a horse race. **3** *Colloq.* Going on; taking place: What's *up*? **4** *Colloq.* In a state acquainted (with), equal (to), or a match (for); of a kind or character capable (of): He is *up* in that subject. **5** In golf: **a** In advance of the opponent or opponents: with a number indicating the extent (in holes) of such advance: three *up* and four to play: opposed to *down.* **b** Struck so as to travel as far as or beyond the hole: said of the ball. **6** Rising, risen, overflowing, or at flood: The moon is *up*; The river is *up.* **— up and around** *Colloq.* Sufficiently recovered to walk, as following an illness or injury; on one's feet again; convalescent and ambulatory. **— up to no good** Engaged in or contemplating some mischief or improper act. **—** *prep.* **1** From a lower to a higher point or place of, on, or along; toward a higher condition or rank on or in: *up* the social ladder. **2** To or at a point farther above or along: The farm is *up* the road. **3** From the coast toward the interior of (a country, as being higher); from the mouth toward the source of (a river): to sail *up* a river. **4** At, on, or near the height or top of: said of position or situation. **—** *n.* One who or that which is up, as elevated ground, an ascent or upward movement, state of prosperity, etc.: usually plural. **— ups and downs** Changes of fortune or circumstance. **—** *v.* **upped, up·ping** *Colloq.* *v.t.* **1** To increase; make larger; cause to rise. **2** To put or take up. **—** *v.i.* **3** To rise. [OE]

up– *combining form* As an element in solidemes *up* has adverbial force with various meanings, as in the following examples:

1 To a higher place or level:

upbear	**upflow**	**upsend**
upbearer	**upgaze**	**upshoot**
upborne	**upgoing**	**upsoar**
upbuilder	**upgrow**	**upstare**
upbuilding	**upheap**	**upstep**
upclimb	**upleap**	**upsurge**
upcoil	**uppile**	**upswell**
upcurl	**upraiser**	**uptilt**
upcurve	**upreach**	**uptoss**
updart	**upreaching**	**upvomit**
updive	**uprise**	**upwaft**
upfling	**uprush**	**upwreathe**

unwifelike	**unwinning**	**unwomanlike**	**unwooed**	**unworn**	**unwounded**	**unwrung**
unwifely	**unwithered**	**unwomanly**	**unworkable**	**unworshiped, unworshipped**	**unwoven**	**unyielding**
unwincing	**unwithering**	**unwon**	**unworked**		**unwreathe**	**unyouthful**
unwinking	**unwitnessed**	**unwooded**	**unworkmanlike**	**unwound**	**unwrought**	**unzealous**

2 To a greater size or larger amount:
upbulging **upflashing** **uplight**
upflaring **upflooding** **upswell**
3 To a vertical position:
upprop **upstand** **upsticking**
4 In or into commotion or activity:
upboil **upbubbling** **upstir**
5 Completely; wholly:
upbind **upfold** **upgird**
updry **upgather** **uphoard**

up-and-coming (up′ənd·kum′ing) *adj.* Enterprising; energetic; promising.

U·pan·i·shad (o͞o·pan′ə·shad, -pä′nə·shäd) *n. Sanskrit* Literally, a philosophical treatise; one of the treatises forming the third division of the Vedas, dealing with the nature of man and the universe.

u·par·na (o͞o·pär′nə) *n.* A silk or muslin scarf, interwoven with gold or silver threads, worn as a shawl by men and as a shawl or veil by women in India. [<Hind.]

u·pas (yo͞o′pəs) *n.* **1** A tall evergreen moraceous tree *(Antiaris toxicaria)* of the island of Java, with an acrid, milky, poisonous juice. **2** The poisonous sap of this tree, used by natives in the manufacture of arrow poison; also, a similar poison from the **upas–tieute,** a climbing shrub (genus *Strychnos*) of the family *Loganiaceae.* **3** Hence, something morally deadly. [<Malay *(pohon) upas* poison (tree)]

up·beat (up′bēt′) *n. Music* An unaccented beat; the beat at which the hand is raised. —*adj.* Optimistic; confident.

up–bow (up′bō′) *n.* An upward stroke of the violin bow, indicated in score by the symbol **V**: opposed to *down–bow.*

up·braid (up·brād′) *v.t.* To reproach for some wrongdoing; scold or reprove. —*v.i.* To utter reproaches. See synonyms under REPROVE, REVILE. [OE *upbregdan* < *up-* up + *bregdan* weave, twist] —**up·braid′er** *adj.* —**up·braid′ing** *n.* —**up·braid′ing·ly** *adv.*

up·bring·ing (up′bring′ing) *n.* Rearing and training received by a person during childhood.

up·bye (up′bī) *adv. Scot.* A little farther on; up the way. Also **up′by.**

up·cast (up′kast′, -käst′) *adj.* Cast, turned, or directed upward. —*n.* **1** A casting or throwing upward; that which is so cast. **2** An air-shaft in a mine. **3** An upward current of air, as in a mine shaft. **4** *Scot.* An upset, or a reproach.

up·chuck (up′chuk′) *Colloq. v.t. & v.i.* To vomit. —*n.* Vomit.

up–coun·try (up′kun′trē) *Colloq. n.* Country somewhat distant from the seashore or from lowlands; inland country. —*adj.* Living in, from, or characteristic of inland places. —*adv.* (up′kun′trē) In, into, or toward the interior: to move *up-country.*

up·date (up·dāt′) *v.t.* **·dat·ed, ·dat·ing** To bring up to date; to revise, with corrections, additions, etc., as a textbook or manual: to *update* an encyclopedia.

up–end (up′end′) *v.t. & v.i.* To set or stand on end.

U·per·ni·vik (o͞o·pûr′nə·vēk) A Danish settlement on an islet in Baffin Bay, western Greenland. Also **U·per′na·vik.**

up·grade (up′grād′) *n.* An upward incline or slope. —*v.t.* (up·grād′) **·grad·ed, ·grad·ing** **1** To improve the breed of (animals) by the introduction of a higher strain. **2** To raise to a higher grade, rank, or responsibility, as an employee.

up·growth (up′grōth′) *n.* **1** The process of growing up. **2** That which grows or has grown up.

up·heav·al (up·hē′vəl) *n.* **1** The act of upheaving, or the state of being upheaved. **2** *Geol.* An elevation of the earth's surface due to a warping of large rock masses. **3** Overthrow or violent disturbance of the established social order.

up·heave (up·hēv′) *v.* **·heaved** or **·hove, ·heav·ing** *v.t.* To heave or raise up. —*v.i.* To be raised or lifted.

up·held (up·held′) Past tense and past participle of UPHOLD.

up·hill (up′hil′) *adv.* Up or as up a hill or an ascent; against difficulties. —*adj.* **1** Going up a hill or an ascent; sloping upward. **2** Attended with difficulty or exertion. —*n.* (up′hil′) An upward slope; rising ground.

up·hold (up·hōld′) *v.t.* **·held, ·hold·ing** **1** To hold up; raise. **2** To keep from falling or sinking. **3** To give aid or support to; encourage. **4** To regard with approval. See synonyms under ABET, AID, ASSENT, CONFIRM, HELP, JUSTIFY, PRESERVE, SUPPORT. —**up·hold′er** *n.*

up·hol·ster (up·hōl′stər) *v.t.* **1** To fit, as furniture, with coverings, cushioning, etc. **2** To provide or adorn with hangings, curtains, etc., as an apartment. **3** To furnish with a covering of any kind. [Back formation <UPHOLSTERER]

up·hol·ster·er (up·hōl′stər·ər) *n.* One who furnishes upholstery; one who upholsters. [< obs. *upholster,* alter. of ME *upholder* a tradesman + -ER[1]]

up·hol·ster·y (up·hōl′stər·ē, -strē) *n. pl.* **·ster·ies** **1** Goods used in upholstering. **2** Textile decoration of an apartment. **3** The act, art, or business of upholstering.

u·phroe (yo͞o′frō, yo͞ov′rō) See EUPHROE.

up·keep (up′kēp′) *n.* The act or state of maintenance; also, means or cost of maintenance.

up·land (up′lənd, -land′) *n.* **1** The higher portions of a region, district, farm, etc. **2** The country in the interior. —*adj.* **1** Pertaining to an upland; higher in situation. **2** Pertaining to or situated in inland districts.

upland plover See under PLOVER.

up·lift (up·lift′) *v.t.* **1** To lift up, or raise aloft; elevate. **2** To raise the tone of; put on a higher plane, mentally or morally. See synonyms under HEIGHTEN, RAISE. —*adj.* (up′lift′) Uplifted: a rare form. —*n.* (up′lift′) **1** The act of raising; the fact of being raised. **2** A movement upward. **3** *Geol.* An upheaval. **4** Mental or spiritual stimulation or elevation. **5** A social movement aiming to improve, morally or esthetically, the condition of the underprivileged. **6** A brassière designed to lift and support the breasts. —**up·lift′er** *n.*

up·most (up′mōst′) *adj.* Uppermost.

U·po·lu (o͞o·pō′lo͞o) One of the chief islands of Western Samoa; 430 square miles; capital, Apia.

up·on (ə·pon′, ə·pôn′) *prep.* **1** On, in all its meanings. **2** On, in an elevated position: *upon* the throne. **3** On, by motion upward: to get *upon* a roof. —*adv.* On: completing a verbal idea: The paper has been written *upon.* Also *Scot.* **up·o′.** See synonyms under ABOVE. [ME]
◆ *Upon* now differs little in use from *on,* the former being sometimes used for reasons of euphony and also preferably when motion into position is involved, the latter when merely rest or support is to be indicated. When *upon* has its original meaning of *up* and *on,* it is written as two words, *up* having its adverbial force: Let us go *up on* the roof.

up·per (up′ər) *adj.* **1** Higher than something else; being above. **2** Higher in place: opposed to *lower.* **3** Higher in station or dignity; superior: opposed to *inferior*: the *upper* house. —**to get the upper hand** To get the advantage. —*n.* **1** That part of a boot or shoe above the sole: the vamp. **2** *pl.* Cloth gaiters. **3** *Slang* Any of various drugs that stimulate the central nervous system, as amphetamines. —**on one's uppers** *Colloq.* **1** Having worn out the soles of one's shoes. **2** At the end of one's resources. [ME, orig. compar. of UP]

Up·per (up′ər) *adj. Geol.* Designating a later period or a later formation of a specified period: the *Upper* Cambrian.

Upper Austria A province of northern Austria; 4,624 square miles; capital, Linz. *German* **O·ber·ös·ter·reich** (ō′bər·œs′tə·rīkh).

Upper Bavaria An administrative division of southern Bavaria, West Germany; 6,308 square miles; capital, Munich. *German* **O·ber·bay·ern** (ō′bər·bī′ərn).

upper berth The top berth in a ship, railroad sleeping–car, cabin, etc., where two bunks or beds are built one above the other.

Upper Burma See BURMA, UNION OF.

Upper Canada A former British province (1791 to 1840) in the southern part of Ontario province, Canada.

upper case **1** Case[2] (def. 3). **2** Capital letters.

upper class The socially or economically superior group in society. —**up′per-class′** (-klas′, -kläs′) *adj.*

upper classman A junior or senior in a school or college.

upper crust *Colloq.* That portion of society assuming or thought of as having more social standing by reason of wealth or ancestry.

up·per·cut (up′ər·kut′) *n.* In boxing, a blow upward from the waist or hip, delivered under or inside the opponent's guard. —*v.t. & v.i.* **·cut, ·cut·ting** To strike with an uppercut.

Upper Egypt See under EGYPT.

Upper Franconia An administrative division of NE Bavaria, Germany; 2,897 square miles; capital, Bayreuth. *German* **O·ber·fran·ken** (ō′bər·fräng′kən).

upper hand The advantage.

Upper House The branch, in a bicameral legislature, where membership is more restricted, as the U. S. Senate and the English House of Lords. Also **upper house.**

up·per·most (up′ər·mōst′) *adj.* **1** Highest in place, rank, authority, or vantage ground. **2** First to come into the mind: one's *uppermost* thoughts. Also *upmost.* —*adv.* In the highest place; also, first, as in time.

Upper New York Bay An arm of the Atlantic at the junction of the Hudson and the East River, joined to Newark Bay and Long Island Sound.

Upper Peninsula The northern part of Michigan, between Lake Superior and Lake Michigan; 16,538 square miles; 320 miles long, 125 miles wide.

Upper Silesia A former province of eastern Germany, now in western Poland.

Upper Vol·ta (vol′tə), **Republic of the** An independent republic of the French Community in western Africa; 105,900 square miles; capital, Ouagadougou; formerly the French overseas territory of Upper Volta.

up·pish (up′ish) *adj. Colloq.* Inclined to be self–assertive; assuming; pretentious; snobbish. Also **up′pi·ty.** —**up′pish·ly** *adv.* —**up′·pish·ness** *n.*

up·raise (up·rāz′) *v.t.* **·raised, ·rais·ing** To lift up; elevate. Also **up·rear′** (-rir′).

up·right (up′rīt′) *adj.* **1** Being in a vertical position; erect. **2** Morally correct; especially, just and honest. See synonyms under GOOD, HONEST, INNOCENT, JUST, MORAL, PURE, VIRTUOUS. —*n.* **1** Something having a vertical position, as an upright timber or piano. **2** The state of being upright: a post out of *upright.* **3** In football, one of the goal posts. —*adv.* Vertically; honestly; sincerely; justly. [OE *upriht* < *up-* up + *riht* right] —**up′·right′ly** *adv.* —**up′right′ness** *n.*

upright piano See under PIANO.

up·rise (up·rīz′) *v.i.* **·rose, ·ris·en, ·ris·ing** **1** To get up; rise, as from a seat or from sleep. **2** To be or become erect. **3** To go upward; ascend. **4** To increase; swell. **5** To rise into view. **6** To rise in revolt. —*n.* (up′rīz′) **1** The act of rising; ascent. **2** An upward slope; upgrade.

up·ris·ing (up·rī′zing, up′rī′zing) *n.* **1** The act of rising. **2** Revolt; insurrection. **3** An ascent; a slope; acclivity.

up–riv·er (up′riv′ər) *adj. & adv.* On or toward the upper part of a river. —*n.* A region located up–river.

up·roar (up′rôr′, -rōr′) *n.* Violent disturbance and noise; tumult. See synonyms under NOISE, TUMULT. —*v.* (up·rôr′, -rōr′) *Obs. v.i.* To make an uproar. —*v.t.* To throw into uproar or confusion. [<Du. *oproer* < *op-* up + *roeren* stir]

up·roar·i·ous (up·rôr′ē·əs, -rō′rē-) *adj.* Accompanied by or making uproar. See synonyms under NOISY. —**up·roar′i·ous·ly** *adv.* —**up·roar′i·ous·ness** *n.*

up·root (up·ro͞ot′, -ro͝ot′) *v.t.* To tear up by the roots; eradicate; destroy utterly. See synonyms under EXTERMINATE. —**up·root′al** *n.* —**up·root′er** *n.*

up·rouse (up·rouz′) *v.t.* **·roused, ·rous·ing** To rouse up, as from sleep.

Up·sa·la (up·sä′lə, *Sw.* o͞op′sä·lä) A city in eastern Sweden; site of Upsala University, founded 1477, one of world's oldest universities. Also **Upp·sa′la.**

up·set (up·set′) *v.* **·set, ·set·ting** *v.t.* **1** To overturn. **2** To throw into confusion or disorder. **3** To disconcert; derange or disquiet. **4** To defeat, especially unexpectedly: Navy *upset* Army. 5 To shorten and thicken (metal) by hammering or by pressure: to *upset* a bolt to form a head or to *upset* the metal tire of a wheel. 6 To swage (the ends of the teeth of a saw). —*v.i.* 7 To become overturned. —*adj.* (*also* up′set′) Set up; required: in the phrase **upset price,** a price at which property is offered for sale, as by an auctioneer, as the lowest selling price. —*n.* (up′set′) The act of upsetting, or the state of being upset. —**up·set′ter** *n.*

up·shot (up′shot′) *n.* The final outcome. See synonyms under CONSEQUENCE.

up·side (up′sīd′) *n.* The upper side or part.

up·side–down (up′sīd′doun′) *adj.* Having the upper side down; in disorder. —*adv.* With the upper side down; in disorder. [Alter. of ME *up so down* up as if down]

up·si·lon (yōōp′sə·lon, *Brit.* yōōp·sī′lən) *n.* The twentieth letter and sixth vowel in the Greek alphabet (Υ, υ): having the sound of French *u,* Latin and Old English *y.* It is transliterated in English as *u* or *y.* See Y. [<Gk. *ypsilon* smooth y]

up·spring (up′spring′) *n.* 1 A leap up into the air. 2 *Obs.* An upstart. —*v.i.* **·sprang** or **·sprung, ·sprung, ·spring·ing** To spring up.

up·stage (up′stāj′) *n.* The half of a stage, from left to right, extending from the center to the backdrop. —*adj.* 1 Pertaining to the back half of a stage. 2 *Colloq.* Conceited; haughty; stuck–up; supercilious. —*adv.* Toward or on the back half of a stage. —*v.t.* **·staged, ·stag·ing** To steal a scene from (another actor).

up·stairs (up′stârz′) *adj.* Pertaining to an upper story. —*n.* The upper story; the part of a building above the ground floor. —*adv.* In, to, or toward an upper story. —**to kick upstairs** To promote so as to get out of the way.

up·stand·ing (up·stan′ding) *adj.* Standing up; erect; hence, honest; upright; straightforward.

up·start (up·stärt′) *v.i.* To start or spring up suddenly. —*adj.* (up′stärt′) 1 Suddenly raised to prominence, wealth, or power. 2 Characteristic of a parvenu; vulgar. —*n.* (up′·stärt′) One who has suddenly risen from a humble position to consequence; a parvenu.

up·state (up′stāt′) *U.S. adj.* Of, from, or designating that part of a State lying outside, usually north, of the principal city. —*n.* The outlying, usually northern, sections of a State. —*adv.* In or toward the outlying or northern sections of a State. —**up′stat′er** *n.*

up·stream (up′strēm′) *adv.* Toward the upper part of a stream; against the current; toward or at a place nearer the source.

up·stroke (up′strōk′) *n.* An upward stroke.

up·sweep (up′swēp′) *n.* 1 A sweeping up or upward. 2 The upturning of the lower jaw, as in the bulldog. —*v.t.* & *v.i.* (up·swēp′) **·swept, ·sweep·ing** To brush or sweep upward.

up–swept (up′swept′) *adj.* Of or pertaining to a style of hairdressing in which the hair is swept upward smoothly in the back and piled high on the top of the head.

up·swing (up′swing′) *n.* 1 A swinging upward. 2 An improvement. —*v.i.* (up·swing′) **·swung, ·swing·ing** To swing upward; improve.

up·take (up′tāk′) *n.* 1 The act of lifting or taking up. 2 A boiler flue that unites the combustion gases and carries them toward the smokestack. 3 An upward ventilating shaft in a mine. 4 Mental comprehension; understanding.

up·throw (up′thrō′) *n.* 1 A throwing upward; an upheaval. 2 *Geol.* An upward displacement of the rock on one side of a fault.

up·thrust (up′thrust′) *n.* 1 An upward thrust. 2 *Geol.* An upheaval (usually violent) of rocks in the earth's crust.

up·tight (up′tīt′) *adj. U.S. Slang* Uneasy, anxious, or tense; nervous. Also **up′–tight′, up tight.** —**up′tight′ness** *n.*

up to See under UP.

up–to–date (up′tə·dāt′) *adj.* Having the latest information, fashion, manner, or improvement: an *up–to–date* dictionary.

up to date To the present time.

up·town (up′toun′) *adv.* In or toward the upper part of a town. —*adj.* Pertaining to or resident in the upper part of a town or city, or that part which is conventionally regarded as the upper part, usually the residence section.

up·turn (up·tûrn′) *v.t.* To turn up or over, as sod with the plow; hence, to overturn; upset. —*n.* (up′tûrn′) A turning upward; an increase.

up·ward (up′wərd) *adv.* 1 In or toward a higher place; in an ascending course or direction; toward the source: to look *upward;* to trace a stream *upward.* 2 With increase or advancement; toward a higher price: Prices tended *upward.* 3 In excess; more: children five years old and *upward.* 4 Toward that which is better, nobler, or holier. 5 In the upper parts. Also **up′wards.** —**upward of** or **upwards of** Higher than or in excess of. —*adj.* Turned or directed toward a higher place. [OE *upweard* < *up-* up + *-weard* -WARD] —**up′ward·ly** *adv.*

Ur (ûr) An ancient city of Sumer, southern Mesopotamia, the site of which is on the Euphrates in SE Iraq. Old Testament **Ur of the Chal·dees** (kal·dēz′, kal′dēz).

ur–[1] Var. of URO–[1].

ur–[2] Var. of URO–[2].

u·ra·chus (yōōr′ə·kəs) *n. Anat.* A canal connecting the bladder of the fetus with the allantois. [<NL <Gk. *ourachos* urinary canal of a fetus < *ouron* urine + *echein* hold]

u·rae·mi·a (yōō·rē′mē·ə), **u·rae·mic** (yōō·rē′·mik) See UREMIA, etc.

u·rae·us (yōō·rē′əs) *n.* The emblem of the sacred serpent (haje) in the head-dress of Egyptian divinities and kings: a symbol of sovereignty. [<NL <Gk. *ouraios* of a tail < *oura* tail]

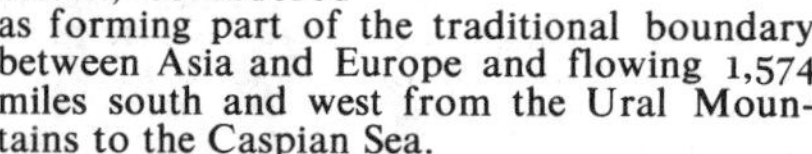
URAEUS

U·ral (yōōr′əl, *Russian* ōō·räl′) A river in SE European Russian S.F.S.R., and SW Kazakh S.S.R., considered as forming part of the traditional boundary between Asia and Europe and flowing 1,574 miles south and west from the Ural Mountains to the Caspian Sea.

U·ral–Al·ta·ic (yōōr′əl·al·tā′ik) *n.* A hypothesized family of languages embracing almost all the agglutinative languages of Europe and northern Asia, comprising the Uralic (Finno–Ugric, Samoyedic) and Altaic (Turkic, Mongolian, Manchu–Tungusic) subfamilies. —*adj.* 1 Of or pertaining to the Ural and Altai mountain ranges. 2 Of, pertaining to, or designating the Ural–Altaic languages, or any of the peoples speaking any of these languages. Also called *Turanian, Ugro–Altaic.*

U·ral·ic (yōō·ral′ik) *n.* A family of agglutinative languages comprising the Finno–Ugric and Samoyedic subfamilies: by some classified with Altaic in one great Ural–Altaic family. —adj. Of or pertaining to this linguistic family. Also **U·ra·li·an** (yōō·rā′lē·ən).

u·ral·ite (yōōr′əl·īt) *n.* A pyroxene altered to amphibole. [from *Ural* Mountains] —**u′ral·it′ic** (-it′ik) *adj.*

U·ral Mountains (yōōr′əl, *Russian* ōō·räl′) A mountain system in the Russian S.F.S.R., the traditional boundary between Asia and Europe; 1,300 miles long, from the Arctic Ocean to the Kazakh S.S.R. border; highest peak, 6,184 feet.

U·ralsk (ōō·rälsk′) A city on the Ural river in NW Kazakh S.S.R.

u·ra·nal·y·sis (yōōr′ə·nal′ə·sis) See URINALYSIS.

U·ra·ni·a (yōō·rā′nē·ə) 1 The Muse of astronomy. 2 The heavenly one: an epithet of Aphrodite. [<L <Gk. *Ourania* < *ouranios* heavenly < *ouranos* heaven] —**U·ra′ni·an** *adj.*

u·ran·ic (yōō·ran′ik) *adj. Chem.* Pertaining to or derived from uranium, especially in its higher valence. [<Gk. *ouranos* heaven]

u·ran·i·nite (yōō·ran′ə·nīt) *n.* A greenish–black, opaque uranium mineral containing also lead, nitrogen, helium, thorium, radium, and certain rare earths, occurring in octohedral crystals. In the massive form it is called *pitchblende.* [<URANIUM]

u·ran·ism (yōōr′ən·iz′əm) *n.* Homosexuality: opposed to *dionism.* [<Gk. *Ourania* URANIA (def. 2)]

u·ra·nite (yōōr′ə·nīt) *n.* Any of several uranium minerals, especially uranium phosphates, torbernite or copper uranite, autunite or lime uranite. —**u′ra·nit′ic** (-nit′ik) *adj.*

u·ra·ni·um (yōō·rā′nē·əm) *n.* A heavy, nickel–white, radioactive, metallic element (symbol U) of the actinide series, found only in combination: it is a principal source of radium, and one of its isotopes is important in the generation of atomic energy. See ELEMENT. [<URANUS]

uranium series *Physics* A series of radioactive elements beginning with uranium of mass 238 and a half–life of 4.5×10^{10} years and continuing through successive disintegrations to the stable isotope of lead of mass 206.

urano– *combining form Astron.* The heavens; of or pertaining to the heavens, or to celestial bodies: *uranography.* Also, before vowels, **uran–.** [<Gk. *ouranos* heaven]

u·ra·nog·ra·phy (yōōr′ə·nog′rə·fē) *n.* Scientific description of the celestial bodies; the making of celestial globes and maps: also spelled *ouranography.* —**u′ra·nog′ra·pher** or **·phist** *n.* —**u′ra·no·graph′ic** (-nō·graf′ik) or **·i·cal** *adj.*

u·ra·nous (yōōr′ə·nəs) *adj. Chem.* Of or pertaining to uranium, especially in its lower valence.

U·ra·nus (yōōr′ə·nəs) 1 In Greek mythology, the son and husband of Gaea (Earth) and father of the Titans, Furies, and Cyclopes: overthrown by his son Kronos: also spelled *Ouranos.* 2 *Astron.* A planet of the solar system; seventh in distance from the sun. Its mean distance from the sun is 1,781 millions of miles, its sidereal period about 84 terrestrial years, and its diameter about 29,600 miles. It has four satellites. See PLANET. [<L <Gk. *Ouranos* < *ouranos* heaven]

u·ra·nyl (yōōr′ə·nil) *n. Chem.* The bivalent radical UO_2, found in many uranium compounds. [<URANIUM + -YL]

u·ra·re (yōō·rä′rē) *n.* Curare: also called *oorali.* Also **u·ra′ri.**

U·ra·ri·coe·ra (ōō·rä′rē·kwā′rə) A river in northern Brazil, flowing 300 miles east from the Venezuela border to the Río Branco.

u·rase (yōōr′ās) See UREASE.

u·rate (yōōr′āt) *n. Chem.* A salt of uric acid.

U·ra·wa (ōō·rä·wä) A city of central Honshu island, Japan.

ur·ban (ûr′bən) *adj.* Pertaining to, characteristic of, including, or constituting a city; situated or dwelling in a city. [<L *urbanus.* See URBANE.]

Ur·ban (ûr′bən) Name of eight popes.

—**Urban II,** 1042?–99, pope 1088–99; preached the First Crusade.

urban district A subdivision, for administrative purposes, of a shire of England, Wales, or Northern Ireland.

ur·bane (ûr·bān′) *adj.* 1 Characterized by or having refinement, especially in manner; polite; courteous; suave: opposed to *rustic.* 2 *Obs.* Urban. See synonyms under POLITE. [<L *urbanus* of a city < *urbs, urbis* a city] —**ur·bane′ly** *adv.* —**ur·bane′ness** *n.*

ur·ban·ism (ûr′bən·iz′əm) *n.* 1 Life in the cities; the manner of life of urban dwellers. 2 The study of urban life, often with special attention to the physical environment. 3 The advocacy of living in a city. —**ur′ban·ist** *n.* —**ur·ban·is·tic** (ûr′bən·is′tik) *adj.*

ur·ban·ite (ûr′bən·īt) *n.* One who lives in a city.

ur·ban·i·ty (ûr·ban′ə·tē) *n. pl.* **·ties** 1 The character or quality of being urbane; refined or elegant courtesy; strictly, the city quality, from the assumption that life in the city results in superior refinement. 2 *Obs.* Polished humor or wit. [<L *urbanitas, -tatis* < *urbs, urbis* a city]

ur·ban·i·za·tion (ûr′bə·nə·zā′shən) *n.* 1 The act or process of urbanizing an area or a rural group of people. 2 The quality or state of being urbanized. Also *Brit.* **ur′ban·i·sa′tion** *n.*

ur·ban·ize (ûr′bən·īz) *v.t.* **·ized, ·iz·ing** 1 To cause (an area) to assume the characteristics of a city: to *urbanize* a suburb. 2 To cause (people) to adopt an urban life style. Also *Brit.* **ur′ban·ise.**

ur·ban·ol·o·gy (ûr′bə·nol′ə·jē) *n.* The study of problems peculiar to cities. —**ur·ban·ol′o·gist** *n.*

urban renewal The planned upgrading of a deteriorating urban area, usually using public funds and coordinated by a local government.

urban sprawl The uncontrolled spread of urban housing, shopping centers, etc., into rural or undeveloped areas close to a city.

ur·bi·cul·ture (ûr′bə·kul′chər) *n.* The study of the proper development, planning, and use of cities, especially in relation to the needs of

their inhabitants. [<L *urbs*, *urbis* a city + CULTURE]
ur·bi et or·bi (ûr′bī et ôr′bī) *Latin* To the city (Rome) and to the world: used in official announcements, as papal bulls.
Urbs Ve·tus (ûrbz vē′təs) The ancient Latin name for ORVIETO.
ur·ce·o·late (ûr′sē·ə·lit, -lāt′) *adj. Bot.* Pitcher- or urn-shaped, as a corolla. [<L *urceolus*, dim. of *urceus* pitcher]
ur·chin (ûr′chin) *n.* **1** A roguish, mischievous boy. **2** A cylinder in a carding machine. **3** A hedgehog. **4** A sea urchin. **5** *Obs.* An elf, as often assuming the form of a hedgehog. — *adj. Obs.* Elfish; mischievous. [ME *irchoun* <OF *irechon*, *ireçon* <L *ericius* hedgehog < *er* hedgehog]
Ur·du (ŏŏr′dōō, ŏŏr·dōō′, ûr′dōō) *n.* A variety of Hindustani used by the Moslems, containing many Arabic and Persian elements and written in the Arabic alphabet: the official language of Pakistan. Also spelled *Oordoo*. [<Hind. *urdū*, short for *(zaban-i-) urdū* (language of the) camp <Turkish *ordū* camp <Persian *urdū*. Related to HORDE.]
-ure *suffix of nouns* **1** The act, process, or result of: *pressure*. **2** The function, rank, or office of: *prefecture*. **3** The means or instrument of: *ligature*. [<F <L *-ura*]
u·re·a (yŏŏ·rē′ə) *n. Biochem.* A very soluble colorless crystalline compound, $CO(NH_2)_2$, formed by the oxidation of nitrogenous compounds in the body, and also made synthetically: used in medicine and in the making of plastics. Also called *carbamide*. [<NL <F *urée* <Gk. *ouron*] — **u·re′al** *adj.*
urea resin Any of a class of thermosetting resins obtained by the reaction of urea and formaldehyde in the presence of certain modifying agents.
u·re·ase (yŏŏr′ē·ās, -āz) *n. Biochem.* An enzyme which promotes the hydrolysis of urea, with the formation of ammonium carbonate. [<UREA + -ASE]
U·red·i·na·les (yŏŏ·red′ə·nā′lēz) *n. pl.* An order of fungi characterized by a branched, septate mycelium and the formation of reddish or yellow spores; the rust fungi. [<NL <L *uredo*, *-inis* blast, blight < *urere* burn]
u·re·din·i·um (yŏŏr′ə·din′ē·əm) *n. Bot.* The spore fruit of a rust fungus which produces the uredospores. Also **u·re·di·um** (yŏŏ·rē′dē·əm), **u′re·do·so′rus** (-dō·sôr′əs, -sō′rəs). [<NL <L *uredo*, *-inis* blight. See UREDO.]
u·re·do (yŏŏ·rē′dō) *n.* **1** The uredo stage. **2** Urticaria. [<L, blight < *urere* burn]
u·re·do·spore (yŏŏ·rē′də·spôr, -spōr) *n. Bot.* A unicellular thin-walled spore produced as a repeating generation in summer as part of the life cycle of a rust fungus. Also **u·re·din·i·o·spore** (yŏŏr′ə·din′ē·ə·spôr′, -spōr′).
uredo stage *Bot.* The stage in the life history of certain rust fungi during which uredospores are produced.
u·re·ide (yŏŏr′ē·īd, -id) *n. Chem.* Any of several nitrogenous compounds derived from urea and an acid or aldehyde by the removal of water.
u·re·mi·a (yŏŏ·rē′mē·ə) *n. Pathol.* An abnormal condition of the blood due to the presence of urea with other urinary constituents ordinarily excreted by the kidneys. Also *uraemia*, *urinemia*. [<NL <UR-[1] + -EMIA] — **u·re′mic** *adj.*
-uret *suffix Chem.* Used to denote a compound: now replaced by *-ide*. [<F < *-ure* -URE]
u·re·ter (yŏŏ·rē′tər) *n. Anat.* The duct by which urine passes from the kidney to the bladder or the cloaca. [<NL <Gk. *ourētēr* < *ourein* urinate] — **u·re′ter·al, u·re·ter·ic** (yŏŏr′ə·ter′ik) *adj.*
u·re·ter·ec·to·my (yŏŏ·rē′tə·rek′tə·mē) *n. Surg.* Excision of all or part of the ureter. [<URETER(O)- + -ECTOMY]
uretero- *combining form Med.* A ureter; of or related to a ureter. Also, before vowels, **ureter-**. [<Gk. *ourētēr* < *ourein* urinate]
u·re·than (yŏŏr′ə·than′, yŏŏ·reth′ən) *n. Chem.* **1** A white crystalline compound, $C_3H_7NO_2$, derived from carbamic acid by substituting ethyl for the hydrogen of the hydroxyl group: some of its derivatives are used as hypnotics and sedatives: also called *ethylurethane*. **2** Any ester of carbamic acid. Also **u·re·thane** (yŏŏr′ə·thān′, yŏŏ·reth′ān). [<UR(EA) + ETHAN(E)]
u·re·thra (yŏŏ·rē′thrə) *n. Anat.* The duct by which urine is discharged from the bladder of most mammals, and which, in males, carries the seminal discharge. [<LL <Gk. *ourēthra* < *ouron* urine] — **u·re′thral** *adj.*
u·re·thri·tis (yŏŏr′ə·thrī′tis) *n. Pathol.* Inflammation of the urethra. [<NL] — **u′re·thrit′ic** (-thrit′ik) *adj.*
urethro- *combining form Med.* The urethra; of or pertaining to the urethra: *urethroscope*. Also, before vowels, **urethr-**. [<Gk. *ourēthra* the urethra]
u·re·thro·scope (yŏŏ·rē′thrə·skōp) *n. Med.* An instrument for examining the urethra. — **u·re′thro·scop′ic** (-skop′ik) *adj.* — **u·re·thros·co·py** (yŏŏr′ə·thros′kə·pē) *n.*
u·ret·ic (yŏŏ·ret′ik) *adj. Med.* **1** Diuretic. **2** Of or pertaining to the urine; urinary. [<LL *ureticus* <Gk. *ourētikos* < *ouron* urine]
U·rey (yŏŏr′ē), **Harold Clayton,** born 1893, U. S. chemist.
Ur·fa (ŏŏr·fä′) A city in southern Turkey in Asia, near the Syrian border: ancient *Edessa*.
Ur·fé (dür·fā′), **Honoré d′,** 1568–1625, French novelist.
Ur·ga (ŏŏr′gä) The former name for ULAN BATOR.
urge (ûrj) *v.* **urged, urg·ing** *v.t.* **1** To drive or force forward; impel; push. **2** To plead with or entreat earnestly, as with arguments or explanations: He *urged* them to accept the plan. **3** To press or argue the doing, consideration, or acceptance of; advocate earnestly. **4** To move or force to some course or action; constrain. **5** To stimulate or excite; incite; intensify. **6** To ply or use vigorously, as oars. — *v.i.* **7** To present or press arguments, claims, etc. **8** To exert an impelling or prompting force. See synonyms under ACTUATE, PERSUADE, PIQUE, PLEAD, PUSH, QUICKEN. — *n.* **1** A strong impulse to perform a certain act. **2** The act of urging; the state of being urged. [<L *urgere* drive, urge]
Ur·gel (ŏŏr·hel′) A city in Lérida, NE Spain, in the Pyrenees SW of Andorra; seat of a bishop who is joint suzerain of Andorra.
ur·gen·cy (ûr′jən·sē) *n. pl.* **·cies** **1** The quality of being urgent. **2** Pressure by entreaty; pressure of necessity. **3** The act of urging. **4** Something urgent. See synonyms under NECESSITY.
ur·gent (ûr′jənt) *adj.* **1** Characterized by urging or importunity; requiring prompt attention; pressing; imperative. **2** Eagerly importunate or insistent. [<F <L *urgens*, *-entis*, ppr. of *urgere* drive] — **ur′gent·ly** *adv.*
Synonyms: importunate, pertinacious, pressing, solicitous.
-urgy *combining form* Development of or work with a (specified) material or product: *metallurgy*, *chemurgy*, *zymurgy*. [<Gk. *-ourgia* < *ergon* work]
U·ri (ŏŏr′ē) A canton in central Switzerland; 415 square miles; capital, Altdorf.
-uria *combining form Pathol.* A (specified) condition of the urine: usually used to indicate disease or abnormality: *hematuria*, *dysuria*. [<NL <Gk. *-ouria* < *ouron* urine]
U·ri·ah (yŏŏ·rī′ə) A masculine personal name. Also *Ital.* **U·ri·a** (ōō·rē′ä), **U·ri·as** (*Ger.* ōō·rē′·äs, *Lat.* yə·rī′əs), *Fr.* **U·rie** (ü·rē′). [<Hebrew, God is light]
— **Uriah** A Hittite captain in the Israelite army, husband of Bathsheba, treacherously sent to his death by David. II *Sam.* xi 15–17.
Uriah Heep An unctuous, fawning, scheming character in Dickens's *David Copperfield*; hence, an odious hypocrite.
u·ric (yŏŏr′ik) *adj.* Of, pertaining to, or derived from urine. [<F *urique*]
uric acid *Biochem.* A white, almost insoluble dibasic acid, $C_5H_4N_4O_3$, of varying crystalline forms, found in small quantity in human urine. It is a product of the incomplete oxidation of animal tissue and animal diet, and forms the nucleus of most urinary and renal calculi.
urico- *combining form* Uric acid; of or related to uric acid: *uricolysis*, the splitting up of uric acid. Also, before vowels, **uric-**. [<URIC]
U·ri·el (yŏŏr′ē·əl) A masculine personal name. [<Hebrew, light of God]
— **Uriel** One of the seven archangels of Christian legend: in Milton's *Paradise Lost*, represented as "regent of the sun."
U·rim (yŏŏr′im) *n. pl.* **1** Objects mentioned in the Old Testament (*Ex.* xxviii 30, etc.) in connection with the breastplate of the high priest: generally in the phrase **Urim and Thummim,** supposed to have been precious stones used in casting lots, one signifying an affirmative and the other a negative answer. **2** In Mormon theology, with the Thummim, the sacred objects used by seers under divine direction, especially those used by Joseph Smith in translating the *Book of Mormon*. [<Hebrew *ūrīm* fires < *ūr* shine]
u·ri·nal (yŏŏr′ə·nəl) *n.* **1** A toilet or closet convenience or fixture for men's use in urination; also, a private place containing such conveniences for public use, as in a park. **2** A receptacle for urine; a glass receptacle, as a bottle, used in the inspection of urine. [<OF <Med. L *urinale*, orig. neut. of L *urinalis* pertaining to urine < *urina* urine]
u·ri·nal·y·sis (yŏŏr′ə·nal′ə·sis) *n. pl.* **·ses** (-sēz) Chemical analysis of the urine: also spelled *uranalysis*. [<NL <URIN(O)- + (AN)ALYSIS]
u·ri·nar·y (yŏŏr′ə·ner′ē) *adj.* Of, pertaining to, or concerned in the production and excretion of urine: the *urinary* organs. — *n. pl.* **·nar·ies** **1** A reservoir for storing urine, etc., for use as manure. **2** A urinal.
urinary calculus *Pathol.* A concretion formed in the urinary passages; the stone.
u·ri·nate (yŏŏr′ə·nāt) *v.i.* **·nat·ed, ·nat·ing** To void or pass urine. [<Med. L *urinatus*, pp. of *urinare* pass urine < *urina* urine] — **u′ri·na′tion** *n.*
u·rine (yŏŏr′in) *n.* A pale-yellow fluid secreted from the blood of mammals by the kidneys, stored in the bladder, and voided through the urethra: the principal vehicle by which nitrogenous and saline matters are removed from the system. [<F <L *urina*]
u·ri·ne·mi·a (yŏŏr′ə·nē′mē·ə) *n.* Uremia. Also **u′ri·nae′mi·a.** [<URIN(O)- + -EMIA] — **u′ri·ne′mic** or **·nae′mic** *adj.*
u·ri·nif·er·ous (yŏŏr′ə·nif′ər·əs) *adj.* Concerned in the conveyance of urine.
urino- *combining form* Urine. Also, before vowels, **urin-**, as in *urinalysis*. [<L *urina* urine]
u·ri·no·gen·i·tal (yŏŏr′ə·nō·jen′ə·təl) *adj.* Urogenital.
u·ri·nos·co·py (yŏŏr′ə·nos′kə·pē) *n. pl.* **·pies** Uroscopy.
u·ri·nous (yŏŏr′ə·nəs) *adj.* Of, pertaining to, containing, or resembling urine. Also **u′ri·nose** (-nōs).
Ur·mi·a (ŏŏr′mē·ə), **Lake** The largest lake of Iran, between Tabriz and the Turkish border; in summer, 1,500 square miles; in winter, 2,300 square miles; 90 miles long, 30 miles wide: also *Rizaiyeh*. *Persian* **U·ru·mi·yeh** (ōō·rōō·mē·ye′)
urn (ûrn) *n.* **1** A rounded or angular vase having a foot, variously used in antiquity as a receptacle for the ashes of the dead, a water vessel, measure, etc. **2** A vessel for preserving the ashes of the dead; a grave. **3** In ancient Rome, a receptacle used to hold lots drawn in voting. **4** A vase-shaped receptacle having a faucet, and designed for keeping tea, coffee, etc., hot, as by means of a spirit lamp. ◆ Homophones: *earn*, *erne*. [<F *urne* <L *urna*]

URN
In park at Versailles.

uro-[1] *combining form* Urine; pertaining to urine or to the urinary tract: *urology*. Also, before vowels, *ur-*. [<Gk. *ouron* urine]
uro-[2] *combining form* A tail; of or related to the tail; caudal: *uropod*. Also, before vowels, *ur-*. [<Gk. *oura* a tail]
u·ro·bil·in (yŏŏr′ə·bil′in, -bī′lin) *n. Biochem.* A brownish, resinous bile pigment, found in urine and sometimes in the blood. [<URO-[1] + BILE + -IN]

u·ro·chord (yŏŏr′ə·kôrd) *n. Zool.* The notochord or central axis of larval ascidians and certain adult tunicates. [<URO-[2] + CHORD[2]] — **u′ro·chor′dal** *adj.*

U·ro·chor·da·ta (yŏŏr′ō·kôr·dā′tə) *n. pl.* The tunicates. [<NL <URO-[2] + CHORDATA]

u·ro·chrome (yŏŏr′ə·krōm) *n. Biochem.* The yellow pigment which gives to urine its characteristic color.

u·rochs (yŏŏr′oks) *n.* The urus. [<G]

U·ro·de·la (yŏŏr′ə·dē′lə) *n. pl.* Caudata. [<NL <URO-[2] + Gk. *dēlos* visible]

u·ro·gen·i·tal (yŏŏr′ō·jen′ə·təl) *adj.* Of or pertaining to the urinary and genital organs and their functions.

u·ro·gen·i·tals (yŏŏr′ō·jen′ə·təlz) *n. pl.* The urogenital organs.

u·rog·e·nous (yŏŏ·roj′ə·nəs) *adj.* Producing or promotive of the urinary secretion. [<URO-[1] + -GENOUS]

u·ro·lith (yŏŏr′ə·lith) *n. Pathol.* A urinary calculus. [<URO-[1] + -LITH[1]] — **u′ro·lith′ic** *adj.*

u·ro·li·thi·a·sis (yŏŏr′ō·li·thī′ə·sis) *n. Pathol.* Any diseased condition due to the formation of urinary calculi. [<NL <URO-[1] + LITHIASIS]

u·rol·o·gy (yŏŏ·rol′ə·jē) *n.* The branch of medical science that relates to the urine and to the genitourinary tract in health and in disease. — **u·ro·log·ic** (yŏŏr′ə·loj′ik) or **·i·cal** *adj.* — **u·rol′o·gist** *n.*

u·ro·pod (yŏŏr′ə·pod) *n. Zool.* An abdominal or caudal limb or appendage of an arthropod, especially one of the posterior pairs of pleopods in a crustacean. [<URO-[2] + -POD] — **u·rop·o·dal** (yŏŏ·rop′ə·dəl), **u·rop′o·dous** *adj.*

u·ro·pyg·i·al (yŏŏr′ə·pij′ē·əl) *adj.* Of or pertaining to the uropygium.

uropygial gland *Ornithol.* The gland at the base of a bird's tail, secreting an oily substance used to preen the feathers.

u·ro·pyg·i·um (yŏŏr′ə·pij′ē·əm) *n. Ornithol.* The terminal part of the body supporting the tail feathers of a bird; rump. [<NL <Gk. *ouropygion,* alter. (after *oura* tail) of *orrhopygion* < *orrhos* end of the os sacrum + *pygē* rump]

u·ros·co·py (yŏŏ·ros′kə·pē) *n. Med.* Diagnosis by examination of the urine. [<URO-[1] + -SCOPY] — **u·ro·scop·ic** (yŏŏr′ə·skop′ik) *adj.* — **u·ros′co·pist** *n.*

U·ro·tro·pin (yŏŏr′ə·trō′pin) *n.* Proprietary name for a brand of methenamine.

u·ro·xan·thin (yŏŏr′ə·zan′thin) *n.* Indican (def. 2). [<URO-[1] + XANTHIN]

Ur·qu·hart (ûr′kərt), **Sir Thomas,** 1611–60, Scottish author; translator of Rabelais.

ur·sa (ûr′sə) *n. Latin* A she-bear: used in the phrases *Ursa Major* and *Ursa Minor.*

Ursa Major *Astron.* The Great Bear, a large northern constellation containing the seven conspicuous stars called the Septentriones, including the two Pointers, Dubhe and Merak, which point to the polestar: also called *Big Dipper, the Dipper, Charles's Wain.* See CONSTELLATION.

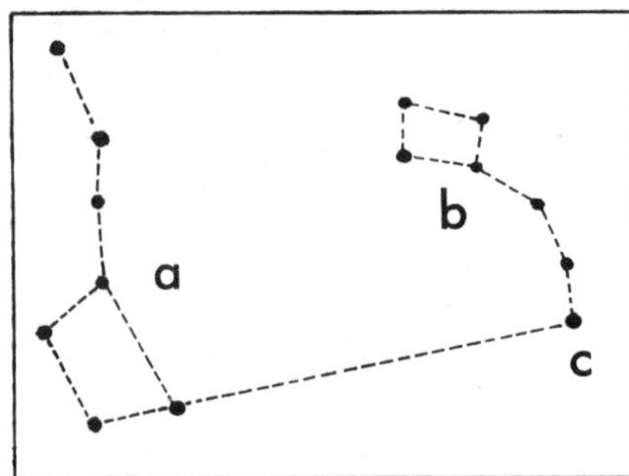

URSA MAJOR AND URSA MINOR
a. Ursa Major. *b.* Ursa Minor. *c.* Polestar.

Ursa Minor *Astron.* The Little Bear, a northern constellation including the polestar: also called *Little Dipper, Dog's Tail.* See CONSTELLATION.

ur·si·form (ûr′sə·fôrm) *adj.* Having the form of a bear. [<L *ursus* bear + -FORM]

ur·sine (ûr′sīn, -sin) *adj.* **1** Pertaining to or like a bear. **2** Clothed with dense bristles, as certain caterpillars. [<L *ursinus* < *ursus* bear]

ursine howler See HOWLER (def. 3).

Ur·spra·che (ŏŏr′shprä′khə) *n. German* A primitive, original, or parent language; particularly, a hypothetical primitive Indo-European language.

Ur·su·la (ûr′syə·lə, -sə-, *Du.* ŏŏr′sōō·lä) A feminine personal name. Also *Fr.* **Ur·sule** (ür·sül′), *Ger., Sw.* **Ur·sel** (ŏŏr′səl), *Sp.* **Ur·so·la** (ŏŏr′·sō·lä). [<L, little she-bear]

— **Ursula, Saint** A Cornish princess of the fourth or fifth century, martyred, according to legend, with eleven thousand virgins at Cologne by the Huns.

Ur·su·line (ûr′syə·lin, -sə-, -līn) *adj.* Pertaining to St. Ursula or to an order of nuns founded in 1537 by St. Angela Merici: they are engaged chiefly in the education of girls. — *n.* An Ursuline nun.

Ur·text (ŏŏr′tekst) *n. German* Earliest or primary form of a written text.

ur·ti·ca·ceous (ûr′tə·kā′shəs) *adj. Bot.* Belonging to a widely distributed family *(Urticaceae)* of trees, shrubs, or herbs, the nettle family, some of which are provided with sharp, stinging hairs. [<NL <L *urtica* nettle]

ur·ti·car·i·a (ûr′tə·kâr′ē·ə) *n. Pathol.* A disease of the skin, variously caused, characterized by evanescent, rounded elevations resembling wheals raised by a whip, and attended with intense itching; nettle rash; hives. [<NL <L *urtica* nettle] — **ur′ti·car′·i·al** or **·i·ous** *adj.*

ur·ti·cate (ûr′tə·kāt) *v.t.* & *v.i.* **·cat·ed, ·cat·ing** To sting, as with nettles. [<Med. L *urticatus,* pp. of *urticare* sting < *urtica* nettle]

ur·ti·ca·tion (ûr′tə·kā′shən) *n. Med.* **1** Formerly, the act, process, or effect of whipping with nettles as a stimulant, as in paralysis. **2** A tingling or burning sensation. **3** The development of urticaria.

U·ru·bam·ba (ōō′rōō·väm′bä) A river in southern Peru, flowing about 450 miles NW and north from the Andes of SE Peru to the Ucayali in central Peru.

U·ru·guay (yŏŏr′ə·gwā, *Sp.* ōō′rōō·gwī) **1** A republic of SE South America, on the Atlantic; 72,172 square miles; capital, Montevideo. **2** A river in SE South America, flowing 1,000 miles SW to the Río de la Plata. — **U′ru·guay′an** *adj.* & *n.*

U·rum·chi (ōō′rŏŏm′chē′) The capital of the Sinkiang-Uigur Autonomous Region, NW China. Also **U′rum′tsi′.**

U·run·di (ōō·rōōn′dē) A former district of German East Africa; since 1923, the southern county of Ruanda-Urundi; 10,658 square miles.

u·rus (yŏŏr′əs) *n.* An extinct, long-horned, wild ox of Germany *(Bos primigenius),* so named by Julius Caesar: also called *aurochs, urochs.* [<L <Gmc. Cf. OHG *ur.*]

u·ru·shi·ol (ōō′rōō·shē·ōl′, -ol′) *n.* A poisonous, irritant liquid, the active principle of poison ivy and the Japanese lac tree. [<Japanese *urushi* lacquer + -OL[2]]

us (us) *pron.* The objective case of WE. [OE *ūs*]

us·a·ble (yōō′zə·bəl) *adj.* **1** Capable of being used. **2** That can be used conveniently. Also **use′a·ble.** — **us′a·ble·ness** *n.* — **us′a·bly** *adv.*

us·age (yōō′sij, -zij) *n.* **1** The manner of using or treating a person or thing; treatment; also, the act of using. **2** Customary or habitual practice, or something permitted by it or done in accordance with it; custom or a custom: an act permitted by *usage;* ancient *usages.* **3** *Law* Uniform practice. **4** The way of using words, speech patterns, etc., that is general and established among the majority of the native speakers and writers of a language. **5** *Obs.* Conduct; behavior. See synonyms under HABIT. — **nonjurors' usages** In English and Scottish history, certain ceremonies, including mixing wine with water, prayer for the dead, trine immersion at baptism, the chrism at confirmation, anointing of the sick, etc., adopted by the nonjurors. [<OF <Med. L *usaticum* <L *usus.* See USE.]

us·ance (yōō′zəns) *n.* **1** A period of time, variable as between various countries, which, by commercial usage, is allowed, exclusive of days of grace, for payment of bills of exchange, especially foreign. **2** *Econ.* An income derived from the possession of wealth in any way it may be invested. **3** *Obs.* Employment; use. **4** *Obs.* Interest on money. **5** *Obs.* Custom. Also *Obs.* **us′aunce.** [<OF < *us* <L *usus.* See USE.]

use (yōōz) *v.* **used, us·ing** *v.t.* **1** To employ for the accomplishment of a purpose; make use of. **2** To put into practice or employ habitually; make a practice of: to *use* diligence in business. **3** To expend the whole of; consume: often with *up.* **4** To conduct oneself toward; treat: to *use* one badly. **5** To make familiar by habit or practice; accustom; inure: usually in the past participle: He is *used* to exposure. **6** To partake of; smoke or chew: He does not *use* tobacco. — *v.i.* **7** To do something customarily or habitually; be accustomed or wont: now only in the past tense as an auxiliary to form a phrase equivalent to a frequentative past tense: I *used* to go there. See synonyms under EMPLOY, OCCUPY. — *n.* (yōōs) **1** The act of using; application or employment to an end, particularly a good or useful end; the fact or condition of being employed. **2** Suitableness or adaptability to an end; serviceableness: the *uses* of adversity. **3** Way or manner of using. **4** Occasion or need to employ; necessity: I have no *use* for it; purpose; function. **5** Habitual practice or employment; the fact of being habitually used; custom; usage. **6** Any special form, ceremony, or ritual of public worship, or any individual service that arose in or was perpetuated by a church, diocese, or branch of a church: Sarum *use,* Roman *use,* York *use.* Compare LITURGY. **7** *Law* The permanent equitable right that a beneficiary has to the enjoyment of the rents and profits of lands and tenements of which the legal title and possession are vested in another in trust for the beneficiary. **8** *Obs.* Ordinary experience or occurrence. **9** Usury. See synonyms under CUSTOM, HABIT, OCCUPATION, SERVICE, UTILITY. [<OF *user* <L *usus,* pp. of *uti* use]

use·ful (yōōs′fəl) *adj.* Serviceable; serving a use or purpose, especially a valuable one; productive of good; beneficial. — **use′ful·ly** *adv.* — **use′ful·ness** *n.*

Synonyms: adapted, advantageous, available, beneficial, conducive, convenient, favorable, good, helpful, profitable, salutary, serviceable, suitable, suited. See CONVENIENT, EXPEDIENT, GOOD. Compare UTILITY. *Antonyms:* see synonyms for USELESS.

use·less (yōōs′lis) *adj.* Unserviceable; being of no use; not serving, or not capable of serving, any beneficial purpose. — **use′less·ly** *adv.* — **use′less·ness** *n.*

Synonyms: abortive, bootless, fruitless, futile, ineffectual, nugatory, null, profitless, unavailing, unprofitable, unserviceable, vain, valueless, worthless. That which is *bootless, fruitless,* or *profitless* fails to accomplish any valuable result; that which is *abortive, ineffectual,* or *unavailing* fails to accomplish a result that it was, or was supposed to be, adapted to accomplish. That which is *useless, futile,* or *vain* is inherently incapable of accomplishing a specified result. *Useless* in the widest sense signifies not of use for any valuable purpose, and is thus closely similar to *valueless* and *worthless. Fruitless* is more final than *ineffectual,* as applying to the sum or harvest of endeavor. That which is *useless* lacks fitness for a purpose; that which is *vain* lacks imaginable fitness. See VAIN, WASTE. *Antonyms:* see synonyms for USEFUL.

us·er (yōō′zər) *n.* **1** One who or that which uses. **2** *Law* The exercise or enjoyment of a right.

Ush·ant (ush′ənt) An island off NW France, comprising the westernmost point of France; 5 miles long, 2 miles wide: French *Île d'Ouessant.*

U·shas (ōō′shəs, ōō·shäs′) In Hindu mythology, the goddess of the dawn.

ush·er (ush′ər) *n.* **1** One who acts as doorkeeper, as of a court or other assemblyroom. **2** An officer whose duty it is to introduce strangers or walk before a person of rank. **3** One who conducts persons to seats, etc., as in a church or theater. **4** *Brit.* An under-teacher. — *v.t.* **1** To act as an usher to; escort; conduct. **2** To precede as a harbinger; be a forerunner of. [<OF *uissier* <L *ostiarius* doorkeeper < *ostium* door]

ush·er·ette (ush′ə·ret′) *n.* A female usher, as in a theater.

Usk (usk) A river in SW England and SE

Wales, flowing 60 miles east, SE, and south from the eastern border of Carmarthenshire to the Bristol Channel at Newport.

Üs·küb (üs·küp′) The Turkish name for SKOPLJE.

Us·ku·da·ma (o͝os′ko͞o·dä′mə) An ancient name for ADRIANOPLE.

Üs·kü·dar (üs′kü·där′) A Turkish city on the Asian side of the Bosporus opposite Istanbul: also *Scutari.*

Us·nach (o͝osh′nə) In old Irish legend, a famous warrior, father of three even more famous sons.

Us·pal·la·ta (o͞os′pä·yä′tä) A pass over the Andes between Santiago, Chile, and Mendoza, Argentina; elevation, 12,650 feet: also *La Cumbre.*

us·que·baugh (us′kwə·bô) *n.* A distilled spirit, as whisky: so called in Ireland and Scotland. Also **us′qua·bae, us′que, us′que·bae.** [<Irish and Scottish Gaelic *uisge-beatha* <*uisge* water + *beatha* life]

Ussh·er (ush′ər), **James,** 1581–1656, Irish bishop and theologian.

Us·su·ri (o͞o·so͞o′rē) A river forming part of the boundary between northeasternmost China and southeasternmost U.S.S.R., and flowing 365 miles north from the SW Sikhote–Alin Range to the Amur at Khabarovsk.

U·sta·ši (o͞o·stä′shē) A Croat fascist party in World War II supported by the German and Italian governments. Also **U·sta′chi.**

Us·ti·la·go (us′tə·lā′gō) *n.* A genus of smut fungi (order *Ustilaginales*) which attack the tissues of many plants, especially cereals, as *U. zeae,* destructive of corn, *U. tritici,* parasitic on wheat, etc. [<NL <LL <L *ustulatus* scorched. See USTULATE.]

Us·ti nad La·bem (o͞o′styē näd lä′bem) A city on the Elbe in NW Bohemia, Czechoslovakia: German *Aussig.*

us·tion (us′chən) *n.* **1** The act of burning, or the state of being burnt. **2** *Med.* Cauterization by burning. [<L *ustio, -onis* <*ustus,* pp. of *urere* burn]

us·tu·late (us′cho͞o·lit, -lāt) *adj.* Scorched, burned, or colored as if by burning or scorching. [<L *ustulatus,* pp. of *ustulare* scorch, freq. of *urere* burn]

us·tu·la·tion (us′cho͞o·lā′shən) *n.* **1** The act of burning or searing. **2** In pharmacy, the drying of substances by heat preparatory to pulverization. **3** The burning of wine.

u·su·al (yo͞o′zho͞o·əl) *adj.* Such as occurs in the ordinary course of events; frequent; common. [<OF <LL *usualis*<L *usus* use. See USE.] — **u′su·al·ly** *adv.* —**u′su·al·ness** *n.*

Synonyms: accustomed, common, customary, everyday, familiar, frequent, general, habitual, normal, ordinary, prevailing, prevalent, regular, wonted. In strictness, *common* and *general* apply to the greater number of individuals in a class; but both words are in good use as applying to the greater number of instances in a series, so that it is possible to speak of one person's *common* practice or *general* custom, but *ordinary* or *usual* would in such case be preferable. See COMMON, FREQUENT, GENERAL, HABITUAL, NORMAL. *Antonyms*: exceptional, extraordinary, infrequent, out-of-the-way, rare, singular, strange, uncommon, unusual.

u·su·fruct (yo͞o′zyo͞o·frukt, yo͞o′syo͞o-) *n. Law* The right of using the property of another and of drawing the profits it produces without wasting its substance. [<LL *usufructus* <L *ususfructus* <*usus et fructus* use and fruit]

u·su·fruc·tu·ar·y (yo͞o′zyo͞o·fruk′cho͞o·er′ē, yo͞o′·syo͞o-) *n. pl.* **·ar·ies** One who holds property for use by usufruct, as a tenant. —*adj.* Of, pertaining to, or having the nature of a usufruct. [<LL *usufructuarius* <*usufructus.* See USUFRUCT.]

u·su·rer (yo͞o′zhər·ər) *n.* **1** One who practices usury; one who lends money, especially at an exorbitant or illegal rate. **2** *Obs.* One who lends money on interest; any money-lender. [<OF *usurier* <Med. L *usurarius* <L *usura* use, usury. See USURY.]

u·su·ri·ous (yo͞o·zho͝or′ē·əs) *adj.* Practicing usury; having the nature of usury. —**u·su′ri·ous·ly** *adv.* —**u·su′ri·ous·ness** *n.*

u·surp (yo͞o·zûrp′, -sûrp′) *v.t.* **1** To seize and hold (the office, rights, or powers of another) without right or legal authority; take possession of by force. **2** To take arrogantly, as if by right. —*v.i.* **3** To practice usurpation; encroach: with *on* or *upon.* See synonyms under ASSUME. [<OF *usurper* <L *usurpare* make use of, usurp, ? <0 usususe + *rapere* seize] —**u·surp′er** *n.* —**u·surp′ing·ly** *adv.*

u·sur·pa·tion (yo͞o′zər·pā′shən, -sər-) *n.* **1** The act of usurping: said especially of unlawful or forcible seizure of kingly power. **2** *Law* The wrongful intrusion into or unjust exercise of the privileges of any office, franchise, or right of another.

u·su·ry (yo͞o′zhər·ē) *n. pl.* **·ries 1** The act or practice of exacting a rate of interest beyond what is allowed by law. **2** *Obs.* The lending of money at interest; interest in general. **3** *Law* A premium paid for the use of money beyond the rate of interest established by law. [<OF *usure* <L *usura* <*usus,* pp. of *uti* use]

u·sus lo·quen·di (yo͞o′səs lō·kwen′dī) *Latin* Usage in speaking.

ut (o͞ot) *n.* The first note in the Guido scale: now commonly *do.* [See GAMUT]

U·tah (yo͞o′tô, -tä) A State of the western United States; 84,916 square miles; capital, Salt Lake City; entered the Union Jan. 4, 1896; nickname, *Beehive State*: abbr. UT — **U′tah·an** *adj. & n.*

U·ta·ma·ro (o͞o·tä·mä·rō), **Kitagama,** 1754?–1806, Japanese engraver and designer of color prints.

ut dic·tum (ut dik′təm) *Latin* As said or directed.

Ute (yo͞ot, yo͞o′tē) *n.* One of a group of tribes of North American Indians of Shoshonean stock, including the Uncompahgre, Kaviawach, and Uinta, formerly living in Utah, Colorado, and New Mexico: now on reservations in Colorado and Utah.

u·ten·sil (yo͞o·ten′səl) *n.* A vessel, tool, implement, etc., serving a useful purpose, especially for domestic or farming use. See synonyms under TOOL. [<OF *utensile* <L *utensilis* fit for use <*utens,* ppr. of *uti* use]

u·ter·ine (yo͞o′tər·in, -īn) *adj.* **1** Pertaining to the uterus. **2** Born of the same mother, but having a different father. [<LL *uterinus* born of the same mother]

u·ter·i·tis (yo͞o′tə·rī′tis) *n. Pathol.* Metritis. [<NL]

utero– *combining form* The uterus; of or pertaining to the uterus. Also, before vowels, **uter–,** as in *uteritis.* [<L *uterus* the uterus]

u·ter·us (yo͞o′tər·əs) *n. pl.* **u·ter·i** (yo͞o′tər·ī) **1** *Anat.* The organ of a female mammal in which the young are protected and developed before birth; the womb. In the higher mammals the uterus is single, but in the lower, as marsupials and monotremes, it is double. **2** *Zool.* Any differentiated portion of an oviduct found in various animals, other than mammals, serving as a repository for the development and nourishment of the eggs or the young during the embryonic stage. [<L]

Ut·gard (o͞ot′gärd) In Norse mythology, the abode of Utgard-Loki.

Ut·gard–Lo·ki (o͞ot′gärd·lō′kē) In Norse mythology, an invulnerable giant.

U·ther (yo͞o′thər) A legendary king of Britain; father of Arthur. See ARTHUR, KING; IGRAINE; PENDRAGON.

U·ti·ca (yo͞o′tə·kə) **1** An ancient city, 20 miles NW of Carthage in northern Africa; site 18 miles north of modern Tunis. **2** A city of central New York, on the Mohawk River.

u·tile (yo͞o′til) *adj.* Useful: now rare. [<L *utilis* <*uti* use]

u·til·i·tar·i·an (yo͞o·til′ə·târ′ē·ən) *adj.* **1** Relating to utility; especially, placing utility above beauty or the amenities of life. **2** Pertaining to or advocating utilitarianism. —*n.* **1** An advocate of utilitarianism. **2** One devoted to mere material utility.

u·til·i·tar·i·an·ism (yo͞o·til′ə·târ′ē·ən·iz′əm) *n.* **1** *Philos.* A system that holds usefulness to be the end and criterion of action; specifically, the ethical doctrine that actions derive their moral quality from their usefulness as means to some end, especially as means productive of happiness or unhappiness. Jeremy Bentham, James Mill, and John Stuart Mill (who coined the word *utilitarianism*), understood by it the ethical theory which makes the pleasure or happiness of the individual or of mankind the end and criterion of the morally good and right. **2** The doctrine, in civics and politics, that the greatest happiness of the greatest number should be the sole end and criterion of all public action. **3** Devotion to mere material interests and aims.

u·til·i·ty (yo͞o·til′ə·tē) *n. pl.* **·ties 1** Fitness for some desirable, practical purpose; serviceableness; also, that which is necessary. **2** Fitness to supply the natural needs of man. **3** In philosophy, the happiness of mankind; the greatest happiness of the greatest number; the utilitarianism expounded by J. S. Mill. **4** *Obs.* Use; profit. **5** A public service, as gas, water, or other service. **6** *pl.* Shares of utility company stocks. [<F *utilité* <L *utilitas* < *utilis* useful <*uti* use]

Synonyms: advantage, advantageousness, avail, benefit, expediency, policy, profit, serviceableness, use, usefulness. *Utility* is somewhat more abstract and philosophical than *usefulness* or *use,* and is often employed to denote adaptation to produce a valuable result, while *usefulness* denotes the actual production of such result. We contrast beauty and *utility.* We say of an invention its *utility* is questionable, or, on the other hand, its *usefulness* has been proved by ample trial, or, I have found it of *use. Expediency* (literally, the getting the foot out) refers primarily to escape from or avoidance of some difficulty or trouble. *Policy* is often used in a kindred sense, more positive than *expediency,* but narrower than *utility,* as in the proverb "Honesty is the best *policy.*" See PROFIT, SERVICE. *Antonyms*: disadvantage, folly, futility, impolicy, inadequacy, inexpediency, inutility, unprofitableness, worthlessness.

utility man 1 A regular member of a theatrical company who must be prepared, on short notice, to go on in any of the less important parts. **2** In baseball, a member of a team who acts as a substitute.

u·til·ize (yo͞o′təl·īz) *v.t.* **·ized, ·iz·ing** To make useful or serviceable; turn to practical account; make use of. Also *Brit.* **u′til·ise.** — **u′til·iz′a·ble** *adj.* —**u′til·i·za′tion** *n.* —**u′til·iz′er** *n.*

ut in·fra (ut in′frə) *Latin* As below.

u·ti pos·si·de·tis (yo͞o′tī pos′ə·dē′təs) *Latin* In international law, the principle that the parties to a war retain what they possessed at its close, unless otherwise provided by treaty; literally, as you possess.

ut·most (ut′mōst) *adj.* **1** Of the highest degree or the largest amount or number; greatest; uttermost. **2** Being at the farthest limit or most distant point; most remote; last. —*n.* The greatest possible extent; the most possible. See synonyms under END. [OE *ūtmest*]

U·to–Az·tec·an (yo͞o′tō·az′tek·ən) *n.* One of the chief linguistic stocks of North American Indians, formerly occupying two large regions of the NW and SW United States, comprising three branches (Shoshonean, Piman, and Nahuatlan) and embracing about fifty tribes: still surviving in the United States and Mexico. —*adj.* Of or pertaining to this linguistic stock.

u·to·pi·a (yo͞o·tō′pē·ə) *n.* **1** Any state, condition, or place of ideal perfection. **2** A visionary, impractical scheme for social improvement. [from *Utopia*]

U·to·pi·a (yo͞o·tō′pē·ə) An imaginary island described as the seat of a perfect social and political life in a romance by Sir Thomas More, published in 1516. [<NL <Gk. *ou* not + *topos* place]

u·to·pi·an (yo͞o·tō′pē·ən) *adj.* Excellent, but existing only in fancy or theory; ideal. See synonyms under IMAGINARY. —*n.* One who advocates impractical reforms; a visionary.

U·to·pi·an (yo͞o·tō′pē·ən) *adj.* Pertaining to or like Utopia. —*n.* A dweller in Utopia.

u·to·pi·an·ism (yo͞o·tō′pē·ən·iz′əm) *n.* Highly idealistic and impractical views, especially about social problems.

U·trecht (yōō′trekt, *Du.* ü′trekht) **1** A province of central Netherlands; 511 square miles. **2** Its capital, scene of the signing of a treaty (1713) ending the War of the Spanish Succession.

u·tri·cle (yōō′tri·kəl) *n.* **1** *Anat.* A small saclike cavity, especially the larger of two found in the bony vestibule of the inner ear. **2** *Bot.* **a** A small fruit having an inflated pericarp, as in the pigweed. **b** An air cell, as in certain aquatic plants. [<L *utriculus*, dim. of *uter* skin bag]

u·tric·u·lar (yōō·trik′yə·lər) *adj.* **1** Resembling a utricle or small sac. **2** Bladderlike; bearing or provided with utricles. Also **u·tric′u·late** (-lit, -lāt).

u·tric·u·li·tis (yōō·trik′yə·lī′tis) *n. Pathol.* Inflammation of a utricle, as of the inner ear. [<NL]

u·tric·u·lus (yōō·trik′yə·ləs) *n. pl.* **·li** (-lī) Utricle. [<L]

U·tril·lo (ōō·trē′lyō, ōō·tril′ō; *Fr.* ü·trē·lō′), **Maurice**, 1883–1955, French painter.

ut su·pra (ut sōō′prə) *Latin* As above: abbreviated *ut sup.*

Ut·tar Pra·desh (ōōt′ər prə·dāsh′) A constituent State of northern India, formed in 1950; 113,409 square miles; capital, Lucknow: formerly *United Provinces of Agra and Oudh.*

ut·ter[1] (ut′ər) *v.t.* **1** To give out or send forth with audible sound; express; say. **2** *Law* To put in circulation; now, especially, to deliver or offer (something forged or counterfeit) to another. **3** *Obs.* To give vent to in any way; give forth; emit. **4** *Obs.* To issue or deliver, as merchandise, in the course of trade. See synonyms under SPEAK. [ME *outre*, freq. of obs. *out* say, speak out] —**ut′ter·a·ble** *adj.* —**ut′ter·er** *n.*

ut·ter[2] (ut′ər) *adj.* **1** Realized or developed to the last degree; absolute; total: *utter* misery. **2** Being or done without conditions or qualifications; unqualified; final; peremptory; absolute: *utter* denial. **3** *Obs.* Outer; remote. [OE *ūttra*, orig. compar. of *ūt* out]

ut·ter·ance[1] (ut′ər·əns) *n.* **1** The act of uttering; vocal expression; manner of speaking; also, the power of speech. **2** A thing uttered or expressed. See synonyms under REMARK.

ut·ter·ance[2] (ut′ər·əns) *n. Obs.* The bitter end; the uttermost; the last extremity; death: in the phrase **to the utterance.** [Var. of OUTRANCE]

ut·ter·ly (ut′ər·lē) *adv.* In a complete manner; entirely; thoroughly.

ut·ter·most (ut′ər·mōst′) *adj.* & *n.* Utmost.

U–tube (yōō′tōōb′, -tyōōb′) *n.* A tube bent into U form, especially such a tube made of glass for laboratory use.

U–turn (yōō′tûrn′) *n. Colloq.* A continuous turn which reverses the direction of a vehicle on a road.

u·va (yōō′və) *n. Bot.* A succulent fruit having a central placenta, as a grape. [<L, grape]

u·var·ov·ite (ōō·vär′ôf·īt) *n.* An emerald-green calcium–chromium garnet. [after Count S. *Uvarov*, 1785–1855, Russian nobleman]

u·va–ur·si (yōō′və·ûr′sī) *n.* A trailing plant, the bearberry (def. 1). [<L, bear's grape]

u·ve·a (yōō′vē·ə) *n. Anat.* **1** The inner, colored layer of the iris. **2** The iris, ciliary muscle, and choroid coat. [<Med. L <L *uva* grape] —**u′ve·al** *adj.*

U·vé·a (ōō·vā′ä) The largest island of the Wallis archipelago, capital of the protectorate; 7 miles long, 4 miles wide.

u·ve·i·tis (yōō′vē·ī′tis) *n. Pathol.* Inflammation of the uvea or iris. [<NL <UVEA] —**u′·ve·it′ic** (-it′ik) *adj.*

u·ve·ous (yōō′vē·əs) *adj.* **1** Resembling a grape or a cluster of grapes. **2** Uveal. [<L *uva* grape]

u·vu·la (yōō′vyə·lə) *n. pl.* **·las** or **·lae** (-lē) *Anat.* **1** The pendent fleshy portion of the soft palate. **2** Either of two other similar processes, one at the neck of the bladder and the other on the under side of the cerebellum. [<LL, dim. of *uva* grape]

u·vu·lar (yōō′vyə·lər) *adj.* **1** Pertaining to or of the uvula. **2** *Phonet.* Produced by vibration of, or with the back of the tongue near or against, the uvula. —*n. Phonet.* A uvular sound.

u·vu·li·tis (yōō′vyə·lī′tis) *n. Pathol.* Inflammation of the uvula. [<NL]

Ux·bridge (uks′brij) An urban district of Middlesex, England, NW of London.

Ux·mal (ōōz·mäl′, ōōsh-, ōōs-) An ancient Mayan city of Yucatán, SE Mexico; site, 40 miles south of Mérida.

ux·or (uk′sôr) *n. Latin* Wife: abbreviated *ux.*

ux·o·ri·al (uk·sôr′ē·əl, -sō′rē-, ug·zôr′ē·əl, -zō′·rē-) *adj.* **1** Of, pertaining to, characteristic of, or becoming to a wife. **2** Uxorious. [<L *uxorius* < *uxor* wife]

ux·o·ri·cide (uk·sôr′ə·sīd, -sō′rə-, ug·zôr′ə-, -zō′rə-) *n.* **1** The act of murdering or killing one's wife; wife-murder. **2** One who murders his wife. [<L *uxor* wife + -CIDE] —**ux·or′i·ci′dal** (-sīd′l) *adj.*

ux·o·ri·ous (uk·sôr′ē·əs, -sō′rē-, ug·zôr′ē-, -zō′rē-) *adj.* Fatuously or foolishly devoted to one's wife; showing extreme or foolish fondness for one's wife. [<L *uxorius* < *uxor* wife] —**ux·o′ri·ous·ly** *adv.* —**ux·o′ri·ous·ness** *n.*

Uz·bek (ōōz′bek, uz′-) *n.* **1** A member of a Turkic people dominant in Turkestan; a native or inhabitant of the Uzbek S.S.R. **2** The Turkic language of the Uzbeks. Also **Uz′beg.**

Uz·bek Soviet Socialist Republic (ōōz′bek, uz′-) A constituent republic of the U.S.S.R. in Central Asia; 154,014 square miles; capital, Tashkent. Also **Uz′bek·i·stan′.**

U·zhok (ōō′zhôk) A pass of the Carpathians in SW Ukrainian S.S.R. *Polish* **U·żok** (ōō′·zhôk). *Hungarian* **U·zsok** (ōō′zhôk).

V

v, V (vē) *n. pl.* **v's** or **V's, vs** or **Vs, vees** (vēz) **1** The twenty-second letter of the English alphabet; ultimately from Phoenician *vau*, vocalized by the Greeks into *upsilon*, and used by the Romans in the form V with the value of a semivowel (w) and, later, a consonant (v). In English it was used interchangeably with the character *u* until fairly modern times. Compare U, W. **2** The sound of the letter *v*, the voiced, labiodental fricative. See ALPHABET. —*n.* **1** A V-shaped piece, or two pieces at an acute angle, as part of a construction: also **vee.** **2** *Colloq.* A five-dollar bill. —*symbol* **1** The Roman numeral five. See under NUMERAL. **2** *Chem.* Vanadium (symbol V). **3** *Electr.* Volt. **4** Anything shaped like a V.

V–1 (vē′wun′) *n.* The robot bomb used against England by the Germans in World War II. See ROBOT BOMB under BOMB. [<G *vergeltungswaffe eins* retaliation weapon 1]

V–2 (vē′tōō′) *n.* A rocket bomb carrying a bomb load of one ton or more, and able to travel about 200 miles from its launching site: used against England by the Germans in World War II. [<G *vergeltungswaffe zwei* retaliation weapon 2]

Vaal (väl) A river of the Republic of South Africa, forming part of the boundary between the Orange Free State and the Transvaal and flowing 750 miles SW and west, from near the Swaziland border in SE Transvaal, to the Orange River near Kimberley.

Vaa·sa (vä′sä) A port of western Finland on the Gulf of Bothnia. *Swedish* **Va′sa.**

va·can·cy (vā′kən·sē) *n. pl.* **·cies** **1** The state of being vacant; vacuity; emptiness; specifically, emptiness of mind. **2** That which is vacant, empty, or unoccupied; empty space. **3** An interruption of continuity of thought or space; a gap; chasm. **4** An unoccupied post, place, or office; a place destitute of an incumbent. **5** *Rare* Unoccupied time; leisure.

va·cant (vā′kənt) *adj.* **1** Containing or holding nothing; being without contents or occupants; especially, devoid of occupants; empty. **2** Occupied with nothing; unemployed; unencumbered; free. **3** Being or appearing without intelligence; inane. **4** Having no incumbent; unfilled: a *vacant* office. **5** *Law* Unoccupied or unused, as land; also, abandoned; having neither claimant nor heir, as an estate. **6** Free from cares. **7** Devoid of thought; unreflecting. [<F <L *vacans, -antis*, ppr. of *vacare* be empty] —**va′cant·ly** *adv.*

Synonyms: blank, empty, unemployed, unfilled, unoccupied, vacuous, void, waste. That is *empty* which contains nothing; that is *vacant* which is without that which has filled or might be expected to fill it; *vacant* has extensive reference to rights or possibilities of occupancy. A *vacant* room may not be *empty*, and an *empty* house may not be *vacant*. *Void* and *devoid* are rarely used in the literal sense, but are for the most part confined to abstract relations, *devoid* being followed by *of*, and having with that addition the effect of a prepositional phrase: The article is *devoid of* sense; The contract is *void* for want of consideration. *Waste*, in this connection, applies to that which is made so by devastation or ruin, or gives an impression of desolation, especially as combined with vastness, probably from association of the words *waste* and vast; *waste* is applied also to uncultivated or unproductive land, if of considerable extent; we speak of a *waste* tract or region. *Vacuous* refers to the condition of being *empty* or *vacant*, regarded as continuous or characteristic. See BLANK, IDLE. *Antonyms*: brimful, brimmed, brimming, busy, crammed, crowded, full, gorged, inhabited, jammed, occupied, overflowing, packed, replete.

va·can·ti·a bo·na (vā·kan′shē·ə bō′nə) *Latin* Goods without an owner; escheated goods.

va·cate (vā′kāt) *v.* **·cat·ed, ·cat·ing** *v.t.* **1** To make vacant; surrender possession of by removal. **2** To set aside; annul. **3** To give up (a position or office); quit. —*v.i.* **4** To leave an office, position, place, etc. **5** *Colloq.* To go away; leave. See synonyms under CANCEL. [<L *vacatus*, pp. of *vacare* be empty]

va·ca·tion (vā·kā′shən) *n.* **1** An intermission of activity, employment, or stated exercises, as for recreation or rest; a holiday. **2** *Law* The period of time intervening between stated terms of court. **3** The intermission of the course of studies and exercises in an educational institution. **4** The act of vacating. **5** *Obs.* The time during which an office is vacant. —*v.i.* To take a vacation. [<F <L *vacatio, -onis* freedom from duty < *vacatus*. See VACATE.] —**va·ca′tion·er** *n.*

va·ca·tion·ist (vā·kā′shən·ist) *n.* One who is taking a vacation or staying at a resort; a tourist.

vac·ci·nal (vak′sə·nəl) *adj.* Of the nature of or relating to vaccine or vaccination.

vac·ci·nate (vak′sə·nāt) *v.* **·nat·ed, ·nat·ing** *Med. v.t.* To inoculate with a vaccine as a preventive or therapeutic measure; especially, to inoculate against smallpox. —*v.i.* To perform the act of vaccination. [<VACCIN(E) + -ATE[2]]

vac·ci·na·tion (vak′sə·nā′shən) *n. Med.* The act or process of vaccinating, especially against smallpox.

vac·ci·na·tion·ist (vak′sə·nā′shən·ist) *n. Med.* An advocate of vaccination.

vac·ci·na·tor (vak′sə·nā′tər) *n. Med.* **1** One who vaccinates. **2** An instrument used for vaccination.

vac·cine (vak′sēn, -sin) *n.* **1** The virus of cowpox, as prepared for or introduced by vaccination: usually lymph, dried or fluid, or part of the crust from a pustule. **2** Any inoculable immunizing agent; a preparation containing bacteria so treated as to give immunity from specific diseases when injected into the subject. — *adj.* **1** Pertaining to or derived from cows. **2** Pertaining to cowpox or vaccination. [<L *vaccinus* pertaining to a cow <*vacca* cow]

vaccine point *Med.* A sharp-pointed piece of bone, ivory, or the like, coated with vaccine for inoculation purposes.

vac·cin·i·a (vak·sin′ē·ə) *n. Pathol.* Cowpox. Also **vac·ci·na** (vak·sī′nə). [<NL <L *vaccinus.* See VACCINE.]

vac·cin·i·a·ceous (vak·sin′ē·ā′shəs) *adj. Bot.* Pertaining or belonging to a genus (*Vaccinium*; family *Ericaceae* or *Vacciniaceae*) of shrubs with cylindrical or globular flowers and small blue, black, or red berries, including the blueberry, huckleberry, and cranberry. [<NL <L *vaccinium* blueberry]

vac·ci·ni·za·tion (vak′sə·nə·zā′shən, -nī·zā′-) *n. Med.* Repeated inoculation with a vaccine.

vac·cin·o·ther·a·py (vak′sən·ō·ther′ə·pē) *n. Med.* Treatment by bacterial vaccines.

vac·il·late (vas′ə·lāt) *v.i.* **·lat·ed, ·lat·ing 1** To sway one way and the other; totter; waver. **2** To fluctuate. **3** To waver in mind; be irresolute. See synonyms under FLUCTUATE. [<L *vacillatus,* pp. of *vacillare* waver] — **vac′il·la′tion** *n.*

vac·il·lat·ing (vas′ə·lā′ting) *adj.* Inclined to waver; uncertain; wavering. Also **vac′il·lant, vac′il·la·to′ry** (-lə·tôr′ē, -tō′rē). — **vac′il·lat′·ing·ly** *adv.*

vac·u·a (vak′yo͞o·ə) Plural of VACUUM.

va·cu·i·ty (va·kyo͞o′ə·tē) *n. pl.* **·ties 1** The state of being a vacuum; emptiness. **2** Vacant space; a void. **3** Freedom from mental exertion; idleness. **4** Lack of intelligence; stupidity. **5** Nothingness. **6** An inane or idle thing or statement: His speech was weakened by *vacuities.* [<F *vacuité* <L *vacuitas, -tatis* <*vacuus* empty]

vac·u·o·lat·ed (vak′yo͞o·ə·lā′tid) *adj. Biol.* Having one or more vacuoles. — **vac′u·o·la′tion** *n.*

vac·u·ole (vak′yo͞o·ōl) *n. Biol.* A minute cavity containing air, a watery fluid, or a chemical secretion of the protoplasm, found in an organ, tissue, or cell. [<F <L *vacuum,* neut. of *vacuus* empty]

vac·u·ous (vak′yo͞o·əs) *adj.* **1** Having no contents; containing no matter; empty. **2** Lacking intelligence; blank. **3** Idle; unoccupied. See synonyms under VACANT. [<L *vacuus*] — **vac′u·ous·ly** *adv.* — **vac′u·ous·ness** *n.*

vac·u·um (vak′yo͞o·əm, -yo͞om) *n. pl.* **·u·ums** or **·u·a** (-yo͞o·ə) **1** *Physics* **a** A space absolutely devoid of matter. **b** A space from which air or other gas has been exhausted to a very high degree. **2** A partial diminution of the normal atmospheric pressure. **3** A void; an empty feeling. — *adj.* **1** Of, or used in the production of, a vacuum. **2** Exhausted or partly exhausted of gas, air, or vapor. **3** Operated by suction to produce a vacuum. — *v.t. & v.i. Colloq.* To clean with a vacuum cleaner. [<L, neut. of *vacuus* empty]

vacuum bottle A bottle having a double wall separated by a vacuum which permits the contents to be kept cold or hot for an appreciable period. Also **vacuum flask.**

vacuum cleaner A machine for cleaning floors, carpets, furnishings, etc., by the suction of an air current.

vacuum fan A fan producing suction or an incomplete vacuum.

vacuum gage A gage containing mercury for testing the pressure consequent on producing a vacuum, as in a condenser. Also **vacuum gauge.**

vacuum pump A pulsometer.

vacuum tube *Electronics* **1** A sealed glass tube exhausted of air to a high degree and containing electrodes between which electric discharges may be passed. **2** An electron tube.

vacuum valve *Brit.* A vacuum tube.

va·de in pa·ce (vā′dē in pā′sē) *Latin* Go in peace.

va·de me·cum (vā′dē mē′kəm) *Latin* Go with me; hence, anything carried for constant use, as a guidebook, manual, or bag. Also **va′de·me′cum, va′de–me′cum.**

Va·duz (fä·do͞ots′) The capital of the principality of Liechtenstein, near the Rhine, SE of St. Gall, Switzerland.

vae vic·tis (vē vik′təs) *Latin* Woe to the vanquished.

vag·a·bond (vag′ə·bond) *n.* **1** One who wanders from place to place without visible means of support; a tramp. **2** One without a settled home; a wanderer; nomad. **3** A worthless fellow; rascal. — *adj.* **1** Pertaining to a vagabond; nomadic. **2** Having no definite residence; wandering; irresponsible. **3** Driven to and fro; aimless. [<F <L *vagabundus* <*vagus* wandering] — **vag′a·bond′age** *n.* — **vag′a·bond′ish** *adj.* — **vag′a·bond′ism** *n.*

vagabond neurosis Dromomania.

va·gar·y (və·gâr′ē) *n. pl.* **·gar·ies** A wild fancy; extravagant notion. See synonyms under FANCY, WHIM. [<obs. *vagary, v.,* wander <L *vagari*]

va·gi·na (və·jī′nə) *n. pl.* **·nas** or **·nae** (-nē) **1** *Anat.* **a** A sheath or sheathlike covering. **b** The canal leading from the external genital orifice in female mammals to the uterus. **2** *Zool.* The terminal portion of the oviduct of various invertebrates. **3** *Bot.* A tubular part surrounding another, as the basal portion of a leaf around a stem. [<L, a sheath]

vag·i·nal (vaj′ə·nəl, və·jī′-) *adj.* **1** Pertaining to or like a sheath; thecal. **2** Pertaining to the vagina.

vag·i·nate (vaj′ə·nit, -nāt) *adj.* **1** Having a sheath. **2** Formed into a sheath; tubular. Also **vag′i·nat′ed.** [<NL *vaginatus* <L *vagina* sheath]

vag·i·nec·to·my (vaj′ə·nek′tə·mē) *n. Surg.* **1** Removal or obliteration of the vaginal canal. **2** Resection of the serous membrane of the testis: also **vag′i·na·lec′to·my** (-nə·lek′tə·mē). [<VAGIN(O)- + -ECTOMY]

vag·i·nis·mus (vaj′ə·niz′məs, -nis′-) *n. Pathol.* Spasm of the sphincter muscle of the vagina with extreme sensitivity of the adjacent parts. [<NL]

vag·i·ni·tis (vaj′ə·nī′tis) *n. Pathol.* Inflammation of the vagina. [<NL]

vagino– *combining form Med.* The vagina; of or pertaining to the vagina. Also, before vowels, **vagin–,** as in *vaginectomy.* [<L *vagina* a sheath, the vagina]

va·gi·tus (və·jī′təs) *n.* The first cry of the newborn infant. [<L, pp. of *vagire* cry, squall]

va·go·to·ni·a (vā′gə·tō′nē·ə) *n. Pathol.* Excessive or morbid excitability of the vagus nerve, characterized by vasomotor instability, involuntary spasms, sweating, and constipation. [<NL <*vagus* the vagus nerve + Gk. *tonos* tone, tension] — **va′go·ton′ic** (-ton′ik) *adj.*

va·gran·cy (vā′grən·sē) *n. pl.* **·cies** The state, condition, or action of a vagrant. Also **va′·grant·ness.**

va·grant (vā′grənt) *n.* **1** A person without a settled home; an idle wanderer; vagabond; tramp. **2** A roving person; wanderer. — *adj.* **1** Wandering about as a vagrant. **2** Pertaining to one who or that which wanders; nomadic. **3** Having a wandering course; capricious; wayward. [ME *vagaraunt,* alter. of AF *wakerant* <OF *wacrant,* ppr. of *wacrer* walk, wander <Gmc.; infl. in form by L *vagari* wander] — **va′grant·ly** *adv.*

va·grom (vā′grəm) *adj. Obs.* Vagrant. [Alter. of VAGRANT; used by Dogberry in Shakespeare's *Much Ado About Nothing*]

vague (vāg) *adj.* **1** Lacking definiteness or precision. **2** Of uncertain source or authority: a *vague* rumor. **3** Not clearly recognized, understood, stated, or felt. **4** *Obs.* Roving; vagrant. **5** Shadowy; hazy. [<F <L *vagus* wandering] — **vague′ly** *adv.* — **vague′ness** *n.*

Synonyms: ambiguous, doubtful, dreamy, indefinite, indeterminate, indistinct, lax, loose, obscure, uncertain, undetermined, unsettled.

va·gus (vā′gəs) *n. pl.* **·gi** (-jī) *Anat.* Either of the tenth pair of cranial nerves originating in the medulla oblongata and sending branches to the lungs, heart, stomach, and most of the abdominal viscera; the pneumogastric nerve. Also **vagus nerve.** [<L, wandering]

Váh (väkh) A river in western Slovakia, Czechoslovakia, flowing 245 miles SW to the Danube: German *Waag.*

vail[1] (vāl) *n. & v.t. Obs.* Veil.

vail[2] (vāl) *Obs. v.i.* To be of use; avail. — *n.* **1** *Usually pl.* A gratuity or tip; a perquisite, often corrupt. **2** A windfall; find. **3** Advantage; proceeds; profit. ◆ Homophones: *vale, veil.* [Aphetic var. of AVAIL] — **vail′a·ble** *adj.*

vail[3] (vāl) *v.t. Archaic* **1** To let fall; lower, as the topsail, in salute or submission. **2** To take off (the hat, etc.) in respect or submission. ◆ Homophones: *vale, veil.* [Aphetic form of obs. *avale* <F *avaler* lower <*à val* down <L *ad vallem,* lit., to the valley]

vain (vān) *adj.* **1** Elated with self-admiration; greedy of applause. **2** Characterized by frivolity. **3** Ostentatious; showy: said of things. **4** Unproductive; worthless; fruitless; useless. **5** Without any substantial foundation; empty; unreal. — **in vain 1** To no purpose; without effect. **2** In an irreverent or disrespectful manner: to take the Lord's name *in vain.* ◆ Homophones: *vane, vein.* [<F <L *vanus* empty] — **vain′ly** *adv.* — **vain′ness** *n.*

Synonyms: abortive, baseless, delusive, empty, fruitless, futile, idle, ineffectual, profitless, shadowy, trifling, trivial, unavailing, useless, vapid, worthless. *Vain* keeps the etymological idea through all changes of meaning; a *vain* endeavor is *empty* of result, or of adequate power to produce a result, a *vain* pretension is *empty* or destitute of support, a *vain* person has a conceit that is *empty* or destitute of adequate cause or reason. See USELESS. *Antonyms*: effective, efficient, firm, potent, powerful, real, solid, sound, substantial, valid, valuable, worthy.

vain·glo·ry (vān·glôr′ē, -glō′rē) *n.* Excessive or groundless vanity; also, vain pomp; boastfulness. See synonyms under PRIDE. [<OF *vaine gloire* <Med. L *vana gloria* empty pomp, show] — **vain·glo′ri·ous** *adj.* — **vain·glo′ri·ous·ly** *adv.* — **vain·glo′ri·ous·ness** *n.*

vair (vâr) *n.* **1** *Her.* One of the furs represented by rows of small shield-shaped figures. **2** *Obs.* A fur used for the garments of the nobility (14th century). [<F <LL *varius* ermine <L *varius* parti-colored, various]

Va·lais (và·le′) A canton in southern Switzerland, in the upper Rhône valley; 2,021 square miles; capital, Sion: German *Wallis.*

val·ance (val′əns, vā′ləns) *n.* **1** A drapery hanging from the tester of a bedstead. **2** A short, full drapery across the top of a window. **3** A damask used for upholstering. — *v.t.* **·anced, ·anc·ing** To furnish with or as with drapery, or a valance. [Prob. <OF *avalant,* ppr. of *avaler* descend] — **val′anced** *adj.*

Val·dai Hills (väl·dī′) A low plateau and group of hills in western European Russian S.F.S.R.; maximum height, 1,053 feet.

Val·de·mar (väl′də·mär) See WALDEMAR.

Val d'A·os·ta (väl dä·ôs′tä) An autonomous region of NW Italy bordering on France and Switzerland; 1,260 square miles; capital, Aosta.

Val·di·via (val·div′ē·ə, *Sp.* bäl·dē′vyä), **Pedro de,** 1500?–54, Spanish conqueror of Chile.

vale[1] (vāl) *n.* **1** A valley; a low-lying tract of land: now chiefly poetic. **2** A trough or channel. See synonyms under VALLEY. ◆ Homophones: *vail, veil.* [<OF *val* <L *vallis*]

va·le[2] (vā′lē) *interj. Latin* Farewell; literally, be in good health.

val·e·dic·tion (val′ə·dik′shən) *n.* A bidding farewell. See synonyms under FAREWELL. [<L *valedictus,* pp. of *valedicere* say farewell <*vale* farewell, orig. imperative of *valere* be well + *dicere* say]

val·e·dic·to·ri·an (val′ə·dik·tôr′ē·ən, -tō′rē-) *n.* One who delivers a valedictory; specifically, a student who delivers a valedictory at the graduating exercises of an educational institution: usually the member of the graduating class whose rank in scholarship is highest.

val·e·dic·to·ry (val′ə·dik′tər·ē) *adj.* Pertaining to a leave-taking. — *n. pl.* **·ries** A parting address, as by a member (ordinarily the first in rank) of a graduating class. See synonyms under FAREWELL.

va·lence (vā′ləns) *n. Chem.* **1** The property possessed by an element or radical of combining with or replacing other elements or radicals in definite and constant proportion. **2** The number of atoms of hydrogen (or its equivalent), taken as unity, with which an atom or radical can combine, or which it can replace. It varies with different elements, and with certain elements in different compounds. **3** *Med.* The combining power of certain substances or bodies, as serums, chromosomes, and the like. Also **va'len·cy.** [<LL *valentia* strength, orig. neut. pl. of L *valens, -entis,* ppr. of *valere* be well, be strong]

valence electron *Chem.* One of the electrons in the outermost shell of an atom, regarded as being responsible for the chemical reaction of an element.

va·len·ci·a (və·len'shē·ə, -shə) *n.* A woven fabric with wool weft and silk or cotton warp. [from VALENCIA]

Va·len·ci·a (və·len'shē·ə, -shə; *Sp.* bä·len'·thyä) **1** A region and former Moorish kingdom of eastern Spain on the Mediterranean; 8,996 square miles. **2** A province of eastern Spain, center of the Valencia region; 4,155 square miles. **3** A port of eastern Spain, the chief city of Valencia region and capital of Valencia province. **4** A city of north central Venezuela.

Va·len·ci·ennes (və·len'sē·enz', *Fr.* vȧ·läṅ·syen') *n.* A kind of bobbin lace with a floral pattern, originally made at Valenciennes. Also **Valenciennes lace, Val lace.**

Va·len·ciennes (vȧ·läṅ·syen') A city of northern France on the Escaut in Nord department.

Va·lens (vā'lenz), 328?–378, Roman emperor of the East 364–378.

val·en·tine (val'ən·tīn) *n.* **1** A letter or token of affection sent, often anonymously, to a person of the opposite sex on St. Valentine's Day (Feb. 14), the anniversary of the beheading of this martyr by the Romans. **2** A sweetheart. [<OF]

Val·en·tine (val'ən·tīn) A masculine personal name. Also **Va·len·tin** (*Russian* vä·lyen·tyin'; *Ger.* vä'len·tēn; *Sw.* vä'len·tēn'; *Fr.* vȧ·läṅ·taṅ'), *Sp.* **Va·len·tín** (bä'len·tēn'), *Pg.* **Va·len·tim** (vä'leṅ·tēṅ'), *Ital.* **Va·len·ti·no** (vä'len·tē'nō), *Lat.* **Va·len·ti·nus** (val'ən·tī'nəs), *Du.* **Va·len·tijn** (vä'len·tīn). [<L, well, healthy] — **Valentine, Saint,** Christian martyr of the third century A.D.

Val·en·tin·i·an (val'ən·tin'ē·ən) Name of three Roman emperors.
— **Valentinian I,** 321–375, reigned 364–375.
— **Valentinian II,** 372?–392, reigned 375–392.
— **Valentinian III,** 419–455, reigned 425–455: full name *Flavius Placidus Valentianus.*

Va·le·ra (və·ler'ə), **Éamon de** See under DE VALERA.

val·er·ate (val'ə·rāt) *n. Chem.* A salt of valeric acid. Also **va·le·ri·an·ate** (və·lir'ē·ən·āt').

Va·le·ri·a (və·lir'ē·ə, *Ital.* vä·ler'yä) A feminine personal name. Also *Fr.* **Va·lé·rie** (vȧ·lā·rē'), *Ger.* **Va·le·ri·e** (vä·lā'rē·ə). [<L, strong]

va·le·ri·an (və·lir'ē·ən) *n.* **1** Any of a genus *(Valeriana)* of Old World perennial herbs; especially, one species *(V. officinalis),* with small pink or white flowers and a strong odor. **2** Its root, used in medicine as a carminative and sedative. [<OF *valeriane* <Med. L *valeriana,* appar. ult. <*Valerius.* a personal name]

Va·le·ri·an (və·lir'ē·ən) Anglicized name of *Publius Licinius Valerianus,* 193?–260?, Roman emperor 254?–260?.

va·le·ri·a·na·ceous (və·lir'ē·ə·nā'shəs) *adj. Bot.* Pertaining to a family *(Valerianaceae)* of herbs, including valerian. [<NL <Med. L *valeriana* VALERIAN]

va·ler·ic (və·ler'ik, -lir'-) *adj.* **1** Of, pertaining to, or derived from valerian. **2** *Chem.* Pertaining to or designating one of four isomeric acids, $C_5H_{10}O_2$, of which two are found in valerian: all are made synthetically. Also **va·le·ri·an·ic** (və·lir'ē·an'ik).

Va·lé·ry (vȧ·lā·rē'), **Paul Ambroise,** 1871–1945, French poet and philosopher.

val·et (val'it, val'ā; *Fr.* vȧ·le') *n.* **1** A gentleman's personal servant. **2** A man servant in a hotel who performs personal services for patrons. — *v.t.* & *v.i.* To serve or act as a valet. [<F, a groom <OF *vaslet, varlet,* dim. of *vasal* vassal. Doublet of VARLET.]

va·let de cham·bre (vȧ·le' də shäṅ'br') *pl.* **va·lets de cham·bre** (vȧ·le') *French* A valet.

Va·let·ta (və·let'ə) See VALLETTA.

val·e·tu·di·nar·i·an (val'ə·to͞o'də·nâr'ē·ən, -tyo͞o'-) *n.* A chronic invalid; one unduly solicitous about his health. — *adj.* Seeking to recover health; infirm. Also **val'e·tu'di·nar'y.** [<L *valetudinarius* infirm <*valetudo, -inis* health, ill health <*valere* be well] — **val'e·tu'di·nar'·i·an·ism** *n.*

val·gus (val'gəs) *adj.* Knock-kneed or bowlegged. — *n. Pathol.* An abnormal eversion of the foot, as by a depression of the arch. [<L, bowlegged]

Val·hal·la (val·hal'ə) **1** In Norse mythology, the great hall into which the souls of heroes fallen bravely in battle were borne by the valkyries and received and feasted by Odin. **2** An edifice wherein the remains or memorials of deceased heroes of a nation are placed. Also **Val·hall** (val·hal'): also spelled *Walhalla.* [<NL <ON *valhöll,* genitive of *valhallar* hall of the slain <*valr* the slain + *höll* hall]

val·iant (val'yənt) *adj.* **1** Strong and intrepid; powerful and courageous. **2** Performed with valor; bravely conducted; heroic. See synonyms under BRAVE. [<OF *vailant,* ppr. of *valoir* be strong <L *valere*] — **val'iant·ly** *adv.* — **val'iant·ness, val'iance, val'ian·cy** *n.*

val·id (val'id) *adj.* **1** Based on evidence that can be supported; sound; just; sufficient and effective in law. **2** *Obs.* Strong. **3** *Stat.* Having a high degree of correlation with its criterion: distinguished from *reliable.* [<F *valide* <L *validus* powerful <*valere* be strong] — **val'id·ly** *adv.* — **val'id·ness** *n.*

Synonyms: cogent, conclusive, convincing, efficacious, efficient, good, incontestable, irrefragable, irrefutable, just, logical, solid, sound, substantial, sufficient, undeniable, weighty. See POWERFUL. *Antonyms:* see synonyms for VAIN.

val·i·date (val'ə·dāt) *v.t.* **·dat·ed, ·dat·ing** **1** To make valid; ratify and confirm. **2** To declare legally valid; legalize. See synonyms under RATIFY. — **val'i·da'tion** *n.*

va·lid·i·ty (və·lid'ə·tē) *n.* **1** The state or quality of being valid; soundness, as in law or reasoning; efficacy. **2** *Archaic* Health; strength. **3** *Obs.* Worth.

val·ine (val'ēn) *n. Biochem.* Either of two isomeric amino acids, $C_5H_{11}O_2N$, found in small amounts in casein and edestin. [<VAL(ERIC) + -INE[2]]

va·lise (və·lēs') *n.* A portable receptacle for clothes and toilet articles; traveling bag. [<F <Ital. *valigia;* ult. origin uncertain]

val·kyr·ie (val·kir'ē, val'kir·ē) *n.* In Norse mythology, one of the maidens who ride through the air and choose heroes from among those slain in battle, and carry them to Valhalla. Also **val'kyr, Val·kyr'ie.** [<ON *valkyrja,* lit., chooser of the slain <*valr* the slain + stem of *kjōsa* choose, select] — **val·kyr'i·an** *adj.*

Val·la·do·lid (val'ə·dō'lid, *Sp.* bä'lyä·thō'lēth) **1** A province of north central Spain; 3,221 square miles. **2** A city of central Spain, former capital of Castile and capital of Valladolid province.

val·la·tion (və·lā'shən) *n.* **1** The art of planning or erecting fortifications. **2** A rampart. [<LL *vallatio, -onis* <L *vallare* protect with a wall <*vallum* a wall] — **val·la·to·ry** (val'ə·tôr'ē, -tō'rē) *adj.*

val·lec·u·la (və·lek'yə·lə) *n. pl.* **·lae** (-lē) **1** A furrow or depression. **2** *Anat.* A deep sulcus **(vallecula cerebelli)** enclosing the median lobe on the inferior surface of the cerebellum; also, a depression on the back of the tongue on either side of the epiglottis. **3** *Bot.* A groove or furrow, as those between the ridges on the fruit of plants of the parsley family. [<NL, var. of L *vallicula,* dim. of *vallis* a valley] — **val·lec'u·lar, val·lec'u·late** (-lit, -lāt) *adj.*

Val·let·ta (və·let'ə) The capital of Malta, a port on the SE coast; site of a major British naval base: also *Valetta.*

val·ley (val'ē) *n.* **1** A depression of the earth's surface, as one through which a stream flows; level or low land between mountains, hills, or high lands; also, the people who inhabit a valley. **2** *Archit.* **a** The gutter or angle formed by the meeting of the two roof slopes. **b** An interval in a vault, or the space between vault ridges as seen from above. **3** A vallecula. [<OF *valee* <*val* <L *vallis* a valley]

Synonyms: canyon, dale, dell, dingle, glen, gorge, gulch, gully, ravine, vale.

Valley Forge A village in SE Pennsylvania, scene of Washington's winter encampment, 1777–78, in the American Revolution.

Valley of Ten Thousand Smokes A region in Katmai National Monument, southern Alaska, punctuated by thousands of small volcanoes; 72 square miles.

Val·lom·bro·sa (väl'lôm·brō'zä) A resort town near Florence, Italy, in the Apennines.

Val·my (vȧl·mē') A village in NE France, near Reims; scene of a French victory over the Prussians, 1792.

Va·lois (vȧ·lwȧ') A medieval county and former duchy of northern France.

Va·lois (vȧ·lwȧ') A French dynasty; began 1328 with Philip VI of Valois, ended with Henry III, 1589.

Va·lo·na (vä·lô'nä) An ancient port on the **Bay of Valona,** an inlet of the Strait of Otranto in SW Albania (15 miles long, 3 miles wide): formerly *Avlona:* Albanian *Vlona.*

va·lo·ni·a (və·lō'nē·ə) *n.* The dried acorn cups of the Old World **valonia oak** *(Quercus macrolepis),* used as a tanning material. [<Ital. *vallonea* <Modern Gk. *balania* an evergreen oak, pl. of *balani* an acorn <Gk. *balanos*]

val·or (val'ər) *n.* Intrepid courage, especially in warfare; personal bravery. Also *Brit.* **val'·our.** See synonyms under PROWESS. [<OF *valour* <LL *valor* worth <*valere* be strong]

val·or·i·za·tion (val'ər·ə·zā'shən, -ī·zā'-) *n.* The maintenance by governmental action of an artificial price for any product. [<Pg. *valorização* <*valor* value <LL. See VALOR.]

val·or·ize (val'ə·rīz) *v.t.* **·ized, ·iz·ing** To subject to valorization. Also *Brit.* **val'or·ise.**

val·or·ous (val'ər·əs) *adj.* Courageous; valiant. — **val'or·ous·ly** *adv.* — **val'or·ous·ness** *n.*

Val·pa·rai·so (val'pə·rā'zō, -sō, -rī'-) A port of central Chile; the most important port on the west coast of South America. *Spanish* **Val·pa·ra·í·so** (bäl'pä·rä·ē'sō).

val·u·a·ble (val'yo͞o·ə·bəl, val'yə·bəl) *adj.* **1** Having financial worth, price, or value; costly. **2** Of a nature or character capable of being valued or estimated: These goods are *valuable* by money. **3** Having moral worth, value, or importance; very serviceable; worthy; estimable: a *valuable* friend. See synonyms under EXCELLENT, GOOD, IMPORTANT. — *n. Usually pl.* An article of value, as a piece of jewelry. — **val'u·a·ble·ness** *n.* — **val'u·a·bly** *adv.*

val·u·a·tion (val'yo͞o·ā'shən) *n.* **1** The act of valuing. **2** Estimated worth or value; appraisement; price. **3** Personal estimation; judgment of merit or character: to set a high *valuation* on one's skill or power.

val·u·a·tor (val'yo͞o·ā'tər) *n.* One who makes appraisals; an appraiser.

val·ue (val'yo͞o) *n.* **1** The desirability or worth of a thing; intrinsic worth; utility. **2** *Often pl.* Something regarded as desirable, worthy, or right, as a belief, standard, or precept: the *values* of a democratic society. **3** The rate at which a commodity is potentially exchangeable for others; a fair return in service, goods, etc.; worth in money; market price; also the ratio of utility to price; a bargain. **4** Attributed or assumed valuation; esteem or regard. **5** Exact meaning; signification; import: the *value* of the words "will" and "shall." **6** *Music* The relative length of a tone as signified by a note. **7** *Math.* The quantity, magnitude, or number an algebraic symbol or expression is supposed to denote. **8** Rank in a system of classification. **9** In the graphic arts, the relation of the elements of a picture, as light and shade, to one another, especially with reference to their distribution and interdependence, apart from the idea of hue. **10** *Phonet.* The special quality of the sound represented by a written character: the *values* of the letter *e.* See synonyms under PRICE, PROFIT. — **book value** The value of property or stock as shown by the books of the company that owns it; the value of stock of a corporation based on the profit or loss shown by its books, and distinguished from the face, market, or artificially created value. — **face value** **1** The value stated on the face of a bond, coin, note, etc. **2** Seeming or apparent value: a promise taken at its *face value.* — **par value** The nominal value, or value printed on a security or stock: not necessarily the market value of the shares. — *v.t.* **·ued, ·u·ing** **1** To estimate the value or worth of; assess; appraise. **2** To regard highly; esteem; prize. **3** To place a relative estimate of value or desirability upon: to *value* honor more than life. See synonyms under APPRECIATE, CHERISH. [<OF *valu,* pp. of *valoir* be worth <L *valere*] — **val'ue·less** *adj.* — **val'u·er** *n.*

val·ue-add·ed tax (val'yo͞o·ad'id) A tax levied on each stage of a product's manufacture and marketing, from the raw material to the final retailer, the ultimate burden being placed on the consumer in the form of higher prices.

val·ued (val′yōōd) *adj.* 1 Regarded or estimated; hence, much or highly esteemed: a *valued* friend. 2 Having a value: a many-*valued* function.

valued policy An insurance policy in which the value of property or cargo is agreed on and inserted as the amount of damages in case of total loss.

val·val (val′vəl) *adj.* Of or pertaining to a valve. Also **val′var** (-vər).

val·vate (val′vāt) *adj.* 1 Serving as or like a valve; having a valve; valvular. 2 *Bot.* Touching by contiguous edges but not overlapping: applied to most dehiscent capsules in which the component parts separate like valves, to certain anthers, and to the petals or sepals of many flowers in estivation. [<L *valvatus* with folding doors <*valva.* See VALVE.]

valve (valv) *n.* 1 *Mech.* Any contrivance or arrangement that permits the flow of a liquid, gas, vapor, or loose material in either of two directions, and closes against its return. 2 *Obs.* One of a pair of folding doors. 3 *Anat.* A structure formed by one or more loose folds of the lining membrane of a vessel or other organ, preventing or retarding the flow of a fluid in one direction and allowing it in another. 4 *Zool.* **a** One of the parts of a shell, as of a mollusk. **b** A covering plate or one of two or more external pieces forming a sheath, as for an ovipositor. 5 *Bot.* **a** One of the parts into which a capsule splits in dehiscence. **b** One of the halves of an anther after its opening. 6 *Electr.* A device for controlling the direction of flow of a current, as an electrolytic cell, or a vacuum tube. 7 *Brit.* A radio tube. 8 A device in certain brass-wind instruments for lengthening the air column and lowering the pitch of the instrument's scale, by turning the air current from the main tube into an additional side tube. — *v.t.* **valved, valv·ing** To furnish with valves; control the flow of by a valve. [<L *valva* leaf of a door] — **valve′less** *adj.*

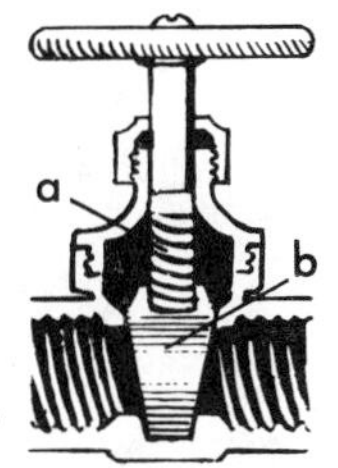

GATE VALVE
Cross-section.
a. Screw.
b. Gate closed.

valve-in-head engine (valv′in·hed′) An internal-combustion engine having overhead valves; an overhead-valve engine. See OVERHEAD VALVE.

valve·let (valv′lit) *n.* A little valve; a valvule, as of a pericarp.

val·vu·lar (val′vyə·lər) *adj.* 1 Pertaining to or of the nature of a valve, as of the heart. 2 Having valves; acting as a valve.

val·vule (val′vyōōl) *n.* A small valve; a structure like a small valve. Also **val′vu·la** (-vyə·lə). [<F <Med. L *valvula,* dim. of L *valva* a door]

val·vu·li·tis (val′vyə·lī′tis) *n. Pathol.* Inflammation of any membrane that serves as a valve in the organs or channels of circulation. [<NL < Med. L *valvula* VALVULE + -ITIS]

vam·brace (vam′brās) *n.* Armor for the forearm from the elbow to the wrist: also, *Obs., vantbrace.* [Var. of *vantbrace* <AF *vantbras,* OF *avant-bras* <*avant* in front of + *bras* arm] — **vam′braced** *adj.*

va·moose (va·mōōs′) *v.t.* & *v.i.* **·moosed, ·moos·ing** *U. S. Slang* To leave hastily or hurriedly; quit. Also **va·mose′** (-mōs′). [<Sp. *vamos* let us go]

vamp[1] (vamp) *n.* 1 The piece of leather forming the upper front part of a boot or shoe. 2 Something added to give an old thing a new appearance. 3 *Music* A simple improvised accompaniment. — *v.t.* 1 To provide with a vamp. 2 To repair or patch. 3 *Music* To improvise an accompaniment to. — *v.i.* 4 *Music* To improvise accompaniments. [<OF *avampie* forepart of the foot <*avant* before + *pied* foot] — **vamp′er** *n.*

vamp[2] (vamp) *Slang v.t.* To seduce or prey upon (a man) by utilizing one's feminine charms. — *v.i.* To play the vamp. — *n.* An unscrupulous flirt or coquette. See VAMPIRE (def. 2). [Short for VAMPIRE]

vam·pire (vam′pīr) *n.* 1 A living corpse that rises from its grave at night to feed upon the living, usually by sucking the blood: a widespread folk belief originating in primitive cannibalism but developed primarily in Slavic folklore. It is not a demon or a ghost, but the physical body of one who has died; it cannot be exorcised, but must be disinterred and either burned or fastened in the grave with a stake through its heart. Belief in vampires still exists in Slavic Europe, Hungary, Greece, and Iceland. Bram Stoker's *Dracula* is a famous treatment of the subject. 2 A man or woman who preys upon persons of the opposite sex; especially, a woman who brings her lover to a state of poverty or degradation. 3 A large bat (genera *Desmodus* and *Diphylla*) of South or Central America, which drinks the blood of horses, cattle, and, sometimes, men: more fully **true vampire.** 4 An insectivorous or frugivorous bat (genera *Phyllostomus* and *Vampyrum*) formerly supposed to suck blood: a **false vampire.** [<F <G *vampir* <Slavic] — **vam·pir′ic** (-pir′ik), **vam·pir′ish** (-pīr′ish) *adj.*

ALBINO VAMPIRE
(Bats vary from 2 to 28 inches in body length)

vam·pir·ism (vam′pī·riz′əm, -pə-) *n.* 1 Belief in vampires. See VAMPIRE (def. 1). 2 The act or practice of a vampire; bloodsucking. 3 The practice of extortion or of preying upon others.

van[1] (van) *n.* 1 A large covered wagon or vehicle, for removing furniture, household goods, etc.; a caravan. 2 *Brit.* A closed railway car for luggage, etc.; also, a vehicle, open or covered, used for carrying light goods. [Short for CARAVAN]

van[2] (van) *n.* 1 An advance guard, as of an army, or foremost division of a fleet. 2 The leaders of a movement; those at the front of any line or unit. [Short for VANGUARD]

van[3] (van) *n.* A fan or winnowing machine; hence, a wing. [Dial. var. of FAN[1]]

van[4] (vän) *prep. Dutch* Of; from: used with Dutch family names, originally designating where the family came from or received its name.

Van (vän) Singular of VANIR.

Van (vän) A town on the eastern shore of **Lake Van** (1,453 square miles) in eastern Turkey in Asia.

van·a·date (van′ə·dāt) *n. Chem.* A salt or ester of vanadic acid. Also **va·na·di·ate** (və·nā′·dē·āt).

va·nad·ic (və·nad′ik) *adj. Chem.* Of, pertaining to, or derived from vanadium, especially in its higher valence.

vanadic acid *Chem.* Any of several acids known only in their salts, as *meta*-vanadic acid, a yellow compound, HVO_3, used as a pigment and a substitute for gold bronze.

va·nad·i·nite (və·nad′ə·nīt) *n.* A native vanadate and chloride of lead, found in opaque prismatic crystals of red and yellow color. [<VANAD(IUM) + -IN + -ITE[1]]

va·na·di·um (və·nā′dē·əm) *n.* A rare, silver-white metallic element (symbol V) of the phosphorus group, difficult to extract from the vanadates and minerals in which it is found. It is useful in an alloy steel to increase tensile strength. See ELEMENT. [<NL <ON *Vanadīs,* a name of the Norse goddess Freya]

vanadium steel Steel containing from .1 to .25 percent of vanadium to increase its tensile strength.

van·a·dous (van′ə·dəs) *adj. Chem.* Of, pertaining to, or derived from vanadium, especially in its lower valence. Also **va·na·di·ous** (və·nā′dē·əs).

Van Allen radiation A high-intensity radiation consisting of charged atomic particles circling the earth in an inner and outer belt conforming to the earth's magnetic field.

Van·brugh (van·brōō′, van′brə), **Sir John,** 1664–1726, English playwright and architect.

Van Bu·ren (van byōōr′ən), **Martin,** 1782–1862, president of the United States 1837–41.

Van·cou·ver (van·kōō′vər) 1 A port of SW British Columbia opposite **Vancouver Island,** the largest island off the western coast of North America, comprising part of British Colombia; 12,408 square miles. 2 A city of SW Washington on the Columbia River.

Van·cou·ver (van·kōō′vər), **George,** 1758?–1798, English navigator.

Vancouver, Mount A peak on the Yukon-Alaska border in the St. Elias Mountains; 15,700 feet.

van·dal (van′dəl) *n.* A ruthless plunderer; wilful destroyer of what is beautiful or artistic. — *adj.* Being a vandal; barbarous. [<VANDAL] — **van·dal·ic** (van·dal′ik) *adj.*

Van·dal (van′dəl) *n.* One of a Germanic people from a region between the Vistula and Oder rivers, south of the Baltic, who invaded the western Roman Empire in the fourth century. At the beginning of the fifth century, they ravaged Gaul and overran Spain and North Africa. In 455 they pillaged the city of Rome, destroying many artistic and literary treasures. Their kingdom, established in North Africa with Carthage as its capital, was overthrown in 534 by the Romans under Belisarius. — **Van·dal·ic** (van·dal′ik) *adj.* — **Van′dal·ism** *n.*

van·dal·ism (van′dəl·iz′əm) *n.* Hostility to or wilful destruction of artistic works, or of property in general.

Van·den·berg (van′dən·bûrg), **Arthur Hendrick,** 1884–1951, U.S. statesman. — **Hoyt,** 1899–1954, U.S. Air Force general.

Van·der·bilt (van′dər·bilt), **Cornelius,** 1794–1877, U.S. capitalist: called "Commodore Vanderbilt."

Van Die·men Gulf (van dē′mən) An arm of the Timor Sea between Northern Territory and Melville Island, Australia; 90 miles long, 50 miles wide. [after Anthony *Van Diemen,* 1593–1645, Dutch admiral]

Van Die·men's Land (van dē′mənz) The former name for TASMANIA.

Van Do·ren (van dôr′ən, dō′rən), **Carl,** 1885–1950, U.S. writer and editor. — **Mark,** 1894–1972, U.S. poet, writer, and critic; brother of preceding.

Van Dyck (van dīk′), **Anthony,** 1599–1641, Flemish painter. Also **Van·dyke′.**

Van·dyke (van·dīk′) *adj.* Of or pertaining to Anthony Van Dyck (or Vandyke), or to his style; also, of or pertaining to the dress or fashions represented in the paintings of Van Dyck. — *n.* 1 A painting by Van Dyck. 2 A Vandyke cape, collar, or beard.

Van Dyke (van dīk′), **Henry,** 1852–1933, U. S. clergyman, educator, and author.

Vandyke beard A peaked or pointed beard resembling those depicted in Van Dyck's paintings.

Vandyke brown A deep-brown pigment, a kind of bog-earth or peat color used by the painter Van Dyck; any of the various brown pigments, as those resembling burnt umber.

Vandyke collar A broad, deep collar or cape of fine linen and lace resembling those represented in portraits by Van Dyck. Also **Vandyke cape.**

vane (vān) *n.* 1 A thin plate, pivoted out of center, on a vertical rod, to indicate the direction of the wind; a weathercock: also **wind vane.** 2 A slender flag or streamer used for the same purpose. 3 An arm or blade, as of a windmill, propeller, projectile, etc. 4 *Ornithol.* The web of a feather. 5 The target on a leveling rod. 6 The sight on a quadrant, compass, or similar instrument, by which the direction of the object viewed is determined. 7 One of the plates or strips of metal fixed in the tail of a bomb, guided missile, or the like, to provide stability or guidance. 8 *Obs.* A flag; pennon. ◆ Homophones: *vain, vein.* [Dial. var. of *fane* a small flag, OE *fana* a flag] — **vaned** *adj.*

WINDMILL VANES

Vane (vān), **Sir Henry,** 1613–62, English

Puritan statesman; executed on charge of treason.

Vä·ner (vā′nər), **Lake** See VENER, LAKE.

van Eyck (van īk′) See EYCK, VAN.

vang (vang) *n. Naut.* One of two guy ropes from the end of a gaff to the deck: used to steady the gaff. [<Du., a catch <*vangen* catch]

van Gogh (van gō′, gôkh′; *Du.* vän khokh′), **Vincent,** 1853–90, Dutch painter.

van·guard (van′gärd) *n.* **1** The advance guard of an army; the van. **2** Hence, one who or that which is foremost. [<OF *avangarde,* var. of *avantgarde* <*avant* before + *garde* guard]

Vanguard *n.* The second U. S. artificial satellite, launched from Cape Canaveral, Fla., on March 17, 1958, to a maximum altitude of 2,513 miles: diameter, 6.4 inches; weight, 3.25 pounds; equipment, two radio transmitters.

va·nil·la (və·nil′ə) *n.* **1** Any of a genus (*Vanilla*) of tall climbing orchids of tropical America. **2** The long dehiscent capsule of one species (*V. planifolia*) of this genus. **3** A flavoring extract made from these capsules. [<NL <Sp. *vainilla,* dim. of *vaina* sheath, pod <L *vagina* sheath; so called from the little pods that contain its seeds]

vanilla plant An erect perennial herb (*Trilisa odoratissima*) of the composite family growing in SE United States: the leaves have a vanilla odor when bruised: also called *hound's-tongue.*

va·nil·lic (və·nil′ik) *adj.* Of, pertaining to, or derived from vanilla or vanillin.

va·nil·lin (və·nil′in) *n. Chem.* A colorless crystalline compound, $C_8H_8O_3$, contained in vanilla, of which it is the odoriferous principle: also made synthetically. Also **va·nil′·line** (-in, -ēn).

Va·nir (vä′nir) *sing.* **Van** (vän) In Norse mythology, an early race of fertility deities, of whom the names Njord, Frey, and Freya survive: later combined with the Aesir.

van·ish (van′ish) *v.i.* **1** To disappear from sight; fade away; depart. **2** To pass out of existence; be annihilated. **3** *Math.* To become equal to zero. —*n. Phonet.* The slight terminal sound of certain vowels, as the faint (o͞o) heard after the (ō) in *go.* [Aphetic var. of OF *esvanniss-,* stem of *esvanir* <L *evanescere* fade away. See EVANESCE.] —**van′ish·er** *n.*

van·i·tas van·i·ta·tum (van′ə·tas van′ə·tā′təm) *Latin* Vanity of vanities.

van·i·ty (van′ə·tē) *n. pl.* **·ties 1** The condition or character of being vain; a feeling of shallow pride; conceit; ambitious display; ostentation; show. **2** The quality or state of being vain or empty, or destitute of reality, etc. **3** That which is vain or unsubstantial. **4** A vanity bag or box. **5** A dressing-table. See synonyms under ARROGANCE, EGOTISM, LEVITY, PRIDE. [<OF *vanité* <L *vanitas, -tatis* <*vanus* empty, vain]

vanity bag or **box** A bag or box containing face powder, rouge, puff, mirror, etc. Also *vanity.*

Vanity Fair 1 In Bunyan's *Pilgrim's Progress,* a fair depicting the world as a scene of vanity and folly. **2** A novel by W. M. Thackeray, satirizing the weaknesses and follies of human nature. **3** The world of fashion and frivolity.

Van Loon (van lōn), **Hendrik Willem,** 1882–1944, U. S. author and lecturer born in Holland.

van·ner (van′ər) *n. Brit.* A truck driver; one who drives a van.

van·quish (vang′kwish, van′-) *v.t.* **1** To defeat in battle; overcome; conquer. **2** To suppress or overcome (a feeling or emotion): to *vanquish* lust. **3** To defeat, as in argument; confute. See synonyms under BEAT, CONQUER, SUBDUE. [<OF *veinquiss-,* stem of *veinquir* conquer <L *vincere*] —**van′quish·a·ble** *adj.* —**van′quish·er** *n.*

Van Rens·se·laer (van ren′sə·lər, -lir), **Stephen,** 1764–1839, U. S. general and politician.

Van·sit·tart (van·sit′ərt), **Robert Gilbert,** 1881–1957, first Baron Vansittart, British diplomat.

van·tage (van′tij) *n.* **1** Superiority over a competitor, as in means of attack; advantage. **2** In lawn tennis, the state of the game when either player has scored a point after deuce. **3** An opportunity; chance. [Aphetic var. of OF *avantage* ADVANTAGE] —**van′tage·less** *adj.*

vantage ground A position or condition which gives one an advantage.

vantage point A strategic position affording perspective; point of view.

vant·brace (vant′brās) See VAMBRACE.

van't Hoff (vänt hôf), **Jacobus Henricus,** 1852–1911, Dutch physical chemist.

van't Hoff's law *Chem.* A statement that the osmotic pressure of a substance in solution approximately equals the pressure it would have in a gaseous state at the same temperature and volume as the solution. [after J. H. *van't Hoff*]

Va·nu·a Le·vu (vä′no͞o·ä lā′vo͞o) Second largest of the Fiji Islands; 2,137 square miles.

van·ward (van′wərd) *adj.* Pertaining to or situated in the van or front: *vanward* regiments.

Van·zet·ti (van·zet′ē), **Bartolomeo,** 1888–1927, Italian anarchist active in the United States. See SACCO, NIKOLA.

vap·id (vap′id) *adj.* **1** Having lost sparkling quality and flavor. **2** Flat; dull; insipid. See synonyms under FLAT, VAIN. [<L *vapidus* insipid] —**va·pid·i·ty** (və·pid′ə·tē), **vap′id·ness** *n.* —**vap′id·ly** *adv.*

va·por (vā′pər) *n.* **1** Moisture in the air; especially, visible floating moisture, as light mist. **2** Any light, cloudy substance in the air, as smoke or fumes. **3** Any substance in the gaseous state, which, under ordinary conditions, is usually a liquid or solid. **4** A gas below its critical temperature. **5** That which is fleeting and unsubstantial. **6** A remedial agent applied by inhalation; also, a substance vaporized for use in industries. **7** Boastful swagger; vaporing. **8** *pl.* Depression of spirits; hypochondria. —*v.t.* **1** To vaporize. —*v.i.* **2** To emit vapor. **3** To evaporate. **4** To make idle boasts; brag. Also *Brit.* **va′pour.** [<AF *vapour,* OF *vapeur* <L *vapor* steam] —**va′por·a·bil′i·ty** *n.* —**va′por·a·ble** *adj.* —**va′por·er** *n.*

vapor density *Physics* **1** The density of a substance in the state of vapor, reaching its maximum before the substance passes into the liquid state. **2** The density of a gas or vapor as compared with that of hydrogen at the same temperature and pressure.

va·por·es·cence (vā′pə·res′əns) *n.* The process of forming mist or vapor. —**va′por·es′cent** *adj.*

vapori– *combining form* Vapor; of or related to vapor, steam, etc.: *vaporimeter.* Also, before vowels, **vapor–.** [<L *vapor* steam]

va·por·if·ic (vā′pə·rif′ik) *adj.* Producing vapors. [<NL *vaporificus* <L *vapor, -oris* steam + *facere* make]

va·por·im·e·ter (vā′pə·rim′ə·tər) *n.* An instrument for determining vapor pressure.

va·por·ing (vā′pər·ing) *adj.* Boasting; swaggering. —*n.* The act of boasting or talking pretentiously. —**va′por·ing·ly** *adv.*

va·por·ish (vā′pər·ish) *adj.* **1** Somewhat like vapor. **2** Somewhat hypochondriac.

va·por·i·za·tion (vā′pər·ə·zā′shən, -ī·zā′-) *n.* **1** The act or process of vaporizing, or the state of being vaporized. **2** *Med.* Treatment with vapors.

va·por·ize (vā′pə·rīz) *v.t.* & *v.i.* **·ized, ·iz·ing** To convert or be converted into vapor. —**va′·por·iz′a·ble** *adj.*

va·por·iz·er (vā′pə·rī′zər) *n.* **1** One who or that which vaporizes. **2** An atomizer.

va·por·ous (vā′pər·əs) *adj.* **1** Of or like vapor; foggy; misty; ethereal. **2** Full of vapors; hypochondriac; also, producing vapors; flatulent. **3** Vainly imaginative; whimsical. Also **va′por·y.** —**va·por·os·i·ty** (vā′pə·ros′ə·tē) *n.* —**va′por·ous·ly** *adv.* —**va′por·ous·ness** *n.*

vapor pressure *Physics* The pressure of a confined vapor when it is in equilibrium with its liquid at any specific temperature. Also **vapor tension.**

va·que·ro (vä·kā′rō) *n. pl.* **·ros** (-rōz, *Sp.* -rōs) A herdsman; cowboy. [<Sp. <*vaca* cow <L *vacca*]

var (vär) *n. Electr.* The reactive volt-ampere. [<V(OLT) + A(MPERE) + R(EACTIVE)]

va·ra (vä′rä) *n.* A Spanish and Portuguese measure of length, varying from 2.7 to 3.6 feet. —**square vara** A varying measure of surface. [<Sp. and Pg., lit., a rod <L, a forked pole <*varus* bent]

Va·rang·er Fjord (vä·rang′ər) An inlet of the Barents Sea in NE Norway; 60 miles long, 3 to 35 miles wide.

Va·ran·gi·an (və·ran′jē·ən) *n.* A Norse rover; one of a group of predatory Scandinavian seamen who, in the ninth century, sailed down the Volga into the Caspian Sea and established a dynasty in Caucasia. [<Med. L *Varangus* <Med. Gk. *Barangos* <Slavic, ult. <ON *Væringi* an ally <*vārar* pledges]

va·ra·ni·an (və·rā′nē·ən) *n.* One of a family of lizards (*Varanidae*) with tongue sheathed at the root and forked at the tip; a monitor: also **var·a·nid** (var′ə·nid) —*adj.* Of or pertaining to the *Varanidae.* [<NL *Varanus* <Arabic *waran* a monitor lizard]

Var·dar (vär′där) A river of southern Yugoslavia and NE Greece, flowing 230 miles NE and SE to the Gulf of Salonika near Salonika: Greek *Axios.*

va·reuse (và·rœz′) *n. French* A loose, woolen jacket, similar to a peajacket.

Var·gas (vär′gəs), **Getulio,** 1883–1954, provisional president of Brazil 1930–34; president 1934–45 and 1951–54; forced out of office.

vari– *combining form* Various; different: *variform, varicolored.* Also *vario–.* [<L *varius* varied]

var·i·a·ble (vâr′ē·ə·bəl) *adj.* **1** Having the capacity of varying; alterable; mutable. **2** Having a tendency to change; not constant; fickle. **3** Having no definite value as regards quantity. **4** *Biol.* Prone to variation from a normal or established type: said of plants and animals. See synonyms under FICKLE, IRREGULAR, MOBILE[1]. —*n.* **1** That which is liable to change. **2** *Math.* **a** A quantity susceptible of fluctuating in value or magnitude under different conditions. **b** A symbol representing one of a group of objects. **3** *Meteorol.* A shifting wind or winds; also, in the plural, places where such winds are common. [<OF <L *variabilis* <*variare* VARY] —**var′i·a·bil′·i·ty, var′i·a·ble·ness** *n.* —**var′i·a·bly** *adv.*

variable star See under STAR.

variable zone A temperate zone.

var·i·ance (vâr′ē·əns) *n.* **1** The act of varying, or the state of being variant; difference; discrepancy; hence, dissension; discord. **2** *Law* **a** A disagreement between the allegations in the pleadings and the proof in an essential matter. **b** A material disagreement between the writ beginning an action and the declaration or complaint. **3** *Stat.* The square of the standard deviation. **4** *Chem.* Degree of freedom. See synonyms under QUARREL[1].

var·i·ant (vâr′ē·ənt) *adj.* **1** Having or showing variation; varying; differing. **2** Tending to vary; variable; changing. **3** Restless; fickle; inconstant. **4** Differing from a standard or type; discrepant. See synonyms under HETEROGENEOUS. —*n.* **1** A thing that differs from another in form only; especially, a different spelling, pronunciation, or form of the same word. **2** A variate. [<OF <L *varians, -antis,* ppr. of *variare* VARY]

var·i·ate (vâr′ē·āt) *v.t.* & *v.i. Obs.* To vary. —*n.* **1** That which varies; a variable. **2** *Stat.* The magnitude or value of a variable. [<L *variatus,* pp. of *variare* VARY]

var·i·a·tion (vâr′ē·ā′shən) *n.* **1** The act, process, state, or result of varying; modification; diversity. **2** The extent to which a thing varies. **3** Inflection, as of declensions or conjugations; also, change in certain vowel sounds. **4** A repetition of the essential features of a musical theme or melody with fanciful embellishments. **5** *Astron.* **a** An inequality in the moon's motion. **b** Any change in the elements of an orbit. **6** *Biol.* Deviation in structure or function from the type or parent form of an organism, as by heredity or in response to conditions of environment. **7** *Stat.* Dispersion. See synonyms under CHANGE, DIFFERENCE. [<F] —**var′i·a′tion·al** *adj.*

var·i·cel·la (var′ə·sel′ə) *n. Pathol.* Chicken pox. [<NL, dim. of *variola.* See VARIOLA.]

var·i·cel·late (var′ə·sel′it, -āt) *adj. Zool.* Marked with small varices, as certain shells. [<NL *varicella,* dim. of L *varix* a varicose vein]

var·i·cel·loid (var′ə·sel′oid) *adj.* Resembling varicella: *varicelloid* smallpox.

varico– *combining form Med.* A vein; of or related to veins, especially to varicose veins: *varicotomy.* Also, before vowels, **varic–.** [<L *varix, varicis* a varicose vein]

var·i·ces (var′ə·sēz) Plural of VARIX.

var·i·co·cele (var′ə·kō·sēl′) *n. Pathol.* A tumor formed by varicose veins of the spermatic cord. [<NL <L *varix, -icis* a varicose vein + Gk. *kēlē* a tumor]

var·i·col·ored (vâr′i·kul′ərd) *adj.* Variegated in color; parti-colored; diversified; of various colors. Also *Brit.* **var′i·col′oured.**

var·i·cose (var′ə·kōs) *adj. Pathol.* Abnormally dilated or contorted, as veins. [<L *varicosus* < *varix, -icis* a varicose vein]

var·i·co·sis (var′ə·kō′sis) *n. Pathol.* A condition in which there are varicose veins; varicosity. [<NL]

var·i·cos·i·ty (var′ə·kos′ə·tē) *n. pl.* **·ties** *Pathol.* **1** The condition of being varicose. **2** A varix.

var·i·cot·o·my (var′ə·kot′ə·mē) *n. Surg.* Excision of a varix or of a varicose vein. [< VARICO- + -TOMY]

var·ied (vâr′ēd) *adj.* **1** Partially or repeatedly altered. **2** Consisting of diverse sorts. **3** Differing from one another. **4** Varicolored. See VARY. — **var′ied·ly** *adv.*

varied thrush A robinlike bird of the western United States (*Ixoreus naevius*) with a plump, rust-colored body, black or gray wings, and a dark band across the breast.

var·i·e·gate (vâr′ē·ə·gāt′) *v.t.* **·gat·ed, ·gat·ing** **1** To mark with different colors or tints; dapple; spot; streak. **2** To make varied; diversify. — *adj.* Variegated. [<LL *variegatus,* pp. of *variegare* variegate < *varius* various + *agere* drive, do]

var·i·e·gat·ed (vâr′ē·ə·gā′tid) *adj.* **1** Having diverse colors; varied in color, as with streaks or blotches. **2** Having or exhibiting different forms, styles, or varieties. **3** *Bot.* Designating a type of inflorescence: see illustration under INFLORESCENCE.

var·i·e·ga·tion (vâr′ē·ə·gā′shən) *n.* **1** The act of variegating, or the state of being variegated. **2** Diversity of colors.

va·ri·e·tal (və·rī′ə·təl) *adj. Biol.* Of, pertaining to, or of the nature of a distinct variety: opposed to *specific* or *generic.* — **va·ri′e·tal·ly** *adv.*

va·ri·e·ty (və·rī′ə·tē) *n. pl.* **·ties** **1** The state or character of being various or varied; diversity. **2** A collection of diverse things; an assortment of unlike objects. **3** The possession of different characteristics by one individual. **4** A limited class of things that differ in certain common peculiarities from a larger class to which they belong; sometimes, an example of such a sort or kind. **5** *Biol.* An individual, or a group of individuals of a species, that differs from the type in certain characters capable of perpetuation, and that is usually fertile with any other member of the species; a subdivision of a species; subspecies. See synonyms under CHANGE. [<MF *variété* <L *varietas* < *varius* various]

variety shop **1** A store having a great variety of merchandise for sale, as hardware, dry-goods, notions, toys, and other small wares. **2** A general store. Also **variety store.**

variety show A theatrical show consisting of a series of short acts or numbers, including songs, dances, dramatic sketches, acrobatic feats, animal acts, etc.; a vaudeville show.

var·i·form (vâr′ə·fôrm) *adj.* Of diverse form; having different shapes.

vario– Var. of VARI–.

var·i·o–coup·ler (vâr′ē·ə·kup′lər) *n. Electr.* A tuning coil in which the secondary winding is mounted to rotate within the primary winding. It resembles the variometer.

va·ri·o·la (və·rī′ə·lə) *n. Pathol.* Smallpox. [< Med. L, a pustule <L *varius* speckled] — **va·ri′o·lar, va·ri′o·lous** *adj.*

var·i·o·late (vâr′ē·ə·lāt′) *v.t.* **·lat·ed, ·lat·ing** To vaccinate with smallpox virus. — **var′i·o·la′tion, var′i·o·li·za′tion** *n.*

var·i·ole (vâr′ē·ōl) *n.* **1** A foveola. **2** A spherulite or variolite. [<F <Med. L *variola.* See VARIOLA.]

var·i·o·lite (vâr′ē·ə·līt′) *n.* A dense, finely crystalline variety of basalt, characterized by whitish spheroid granules. [<G *variolit* < Med. L *variola.* See VARIOLA.]

var·i·o·lit·ic (vâr′ē·ə·lit′ik) *adj.* **1** Of, pertaining to, or containing variolite. **2** Spotted.

var·i·o·loid (vâr′ē·ə·loid′) *Pathol. n.* A mild form of smallpox, occurring after vaccination or in persons who have had smallpox. — *adj.* **1** Resembling smallpox. **2** Pertaining to varioloid.

var·i·om·e·ter (vâr′ē·om′ə·tər) *n. Electr.* **1** An instrument used to determine the variation of magnetic force at different times or at different places, usually by means of a needle suspended within the magnetic field. **2** A variable inductance device composed of two coils connected in series, one of which revolves within the other, and capable of controlling the strength of a current. [<VARIO- + -METER]

var·i·o·rum (vâr′ē·ôr′əm, -ō′rəm) *adj.* Having notes or comments by different critics or editors. — *n.* **1** An edition containing various versions of a text, usually with notes and commentary. **2** A text or edition, especially the complete works of a classical author, containing various notes and comments: also **variorum edition.** [<L *(cum notis) variorum* (with the notes) of various persons]

var·i·ous (vâr′ē·əs) *adj.* **1** Characteristically different from one another; diverse. **2** Being more than one and easily distinguishable; several. **3** Many-sided; variform. **4** Having a changeable or inconstant nature; unfixed. **5** Having a diversity of appearance; variegated. See synonyms under HETEROGENEOUS, MANY. [<L *varius*] — **var′i·ous·ly** *adv.* — **var′i·ous·ness** *n.*

Var·i–Typ·er (vâr′i·tī′pər) *n.* A compact, electrically operated, self-justifying composing machine for the rapid preparation of copy for all kinds of printing reproduction: a trade name.

var·ix (vâr′iks) *n. pl.* **var·i·ces** (vâr′ə·sēz) **1** *Pathol.* **a** Permanent dilatation of a vein or other vessel of circulation. **b** A vessel thus distorted, as a varicose vein. **2** *Zool.* A ridge marking the former position of the outer lip of certain univalve shells. [<L, a varicose vein]

var·let (vär′lit) *n.* **1** *Archaic* A low menial or subordinate; formerly, a page. **2** A knave or scoundrel. [<OF, a groom. Doublet of VALET.]

var·let·ry (vär′lit·rē) *n.* The rabble; the mob.

var·mint (vär′mənt) *n. Dial.* Any person or animal considered as troublesome; vermin. [Alter. of VERMIN] — **var′mint·ry** *n.*

Var·na (vär′nä) A major seaport on the Black Sea in eastern Bulgaria: formerly (1949–58) called *Stalin.*

var·nish (vär′nish) *n.* **1** A solution of certain gums or resins in alcohol, linseed oil, etc., used to produce a shining, transparent coat on a surface. **2** Any natural or artificial product resembling varnish. **3** Outward show, or any superficial polish, as of politeness. — *v.t.* **1** To cover with varnish. **2** To give a smooth or glossy appearance to. **3** To improve the appearance of; polish. **4** To hide by a deceptive covering or appearance; gloss over. [<OF *vernis* <Med. L *vernicium* sandarac <Med. Gk. *berniкē*, prob. from Gk. *Berenikē,* a city in Cyrenaica] — **var′nish·a·ble** *adj.* — **var′nish·er** *n.* — **var′nish·ing** *n.*

varnish tree **1** A tree of China and Japan (*Toxicodendron verniciflnum*) yielding a milky juice suitable for making varnish. **2** The candlenut tree.

Var·ro (var′ō), **Marcus Terentius,** 116–27? B.C., Roman scholar and author.

var·si·ty (vär′sə·tē) *n. pl.* **·ties** *Colloq.* **1** *Brit.* University. **2** The team that represents a university, college, or school in any activity, as in football, debating, etc. [Aphetic alter. of UNIVERSITY]

Var·u·na (var′ŏŏ·nə, vûr′-) In the earliest (Vedic) Hindu mythology, the god of the sky, creator and supreme god of the universe; later, in the Puranas, the god of the waters.

var·us (vâr′əs) *n. Pathol.* A malformation in which a bone or joint is turned away from its normal position. [<NL <L, growing inward, bandy-legged]

Var·us (vâr′əs), **Publius Quintilius,** died A.D. 9, Roman general, commander in Germany; defeated by Arminius.

varve (värv) *n.* One of a series of finely stratified seasonal deposits, as of clay or shale: often useful in determining the age of geological formations. [<Sw. *varv* a layer]

var·y (vâr′ē) *v.* **var·ied, var·y·ing** *v.t.* **1** To change the form, nature, substance, etc., of; modify. **2** To cause to be different from one another. **3** To impart variety to; diversify. **4** *Music* To embellish (a melody) by changes of rhythm, harmony, etc. — *v.i.* **5** To become changed in form, nature, substance, etc. **6** To be diverse or different; differ. **7** To deviate; depart: with *from.* **8** To change in succession; alternate. **9** *Math.* To be subject to continual change. **10** *Biol.* To undergo variation. See synonyms under CHANGE, FLUCTUATE. [<OF *varier* <L *variare* < *varius* various, diverse] — **var′i·er** *n.*

varying hare Any of certain hares whose coats turn white in the winter, specifically the American *Lepus americanus.*

vas (vas) *n. pl.* **va·sa** (vā′sə) *Biol.* A vessel or duct. [<L, vessel, dish]

vas– Var. of VASO–.

Va·sa·ri (vä·zä′rē), **Giorgio,** 1511–74, Italian painter, architect, and biographer of artists.

vas·cu·lar (vas′kyə·lər) *adj. Biol.* **1** Of, pertaining to, consisting of, or containing vessels or ducts, as blood vessels, etc. **2** Having vessels. **3** Richly supplied with blood vessels. Also **vas′cu·lose** (-lōs), **vas′cu·lous** (-ləs). [<L *vasculum,* dim. of *vas* vessel] — **vas′cu·lar′i·ty** (-lar′ə·tē) *n.* — **vas′cu·lar·ly** *adv.*

vascular bundle Bundle (def. 4).

vascular tissue *Bot.* Plant tissue made up of vessels or ducts through which the sap is conveyed.

vas·cu·lum (vas′kyə·ləm) *n. pl.* **·la** (-lə) **1** A small box used in plant collecting. **2** *Bot.* An ascidium. [<L, little vessel]

vas def·er·ens (vas def′ər·ənz) *Anat.* The duct by which semen is conveyed from the epididymis to the seminal vesicles. [<NL <L *vas* vessel + *deferens* leading down]

vase (vās, vāz, väz) *n.* An urnlike vessel, usually rounded and generally of greater height than width, ordinarily used as an ornament or for holding flowers. [<F <L *vas* vessel]

va·sec·to·my (və·sek′tə·mē) *n. Surg.* Removal of a portion of the vas deferens. [<VAS- + -ECTOMY]

Vas·e·line (vas′ə·lēn, -lin) *n.* Proprietary name for various semisolid hydrocarbons derived from petroleum: a brand of petrolatum.

Vash·ti (vash′tī) In the Bible, the queen of Ahasuerus, of Persia, whom he divorced because she refused to come to a royal banquet as commanded. *Esther* i 10–21.

Va·si·lev·ski (vä′sē·lyef′skē), **Alexander Mikhailovich,** born 1901, Russian marshal and chief of general staff in World War II.

vaso– *combining form* **1** *Physiol.* A vessel, especially a blood vessel: *vasomotor.* **2** *Med.* The vas deferens: *vasosection,* the severing of the vas deferens. Also, before vowels, *vas–.* [<L *vas* a vessel]

vas·o·con·stric·tor (vas′ō·kən·strik′tər) *adj. Physiol.* Causing constriction of a blood vessel when stimulated. — *n.* A nerve or drug causing such constriction.

vas·o·den·tine (vas′ō·den′tēn, -tin) *n.* Dentine in which the capillaries have remained wide enough to give passage to the blood.

vas·o·di·la·tor (vas′ō·dī·lā′tər) *adj. Physiol.* Causing dilatation of a blood vessel, as certain nerves or drugs.

vas·o·mo·tor (vas′ō·mō′tər) *adj. Physiol.* Producing movement, either of contraction or dilatation, in the walls of vessels.

vas·sal (vas′əl) *n.* **1** One who held land of a superior lord by a feudal tenure; a liegeman or feudal tenant. **2** A dependent, retainer, or servant of any kind; a slave or bondman. — *adj.* Having the character of or pertaining to a vassal; tributary; hence, servile. [<OF <Med. L *vassallus* <LL *vassus* a servant <Celtic]

vas·sal·age (vas′əl·ij) *n.* **1** The condition, duties, and obligations of a vassal; also, the feudal system. **2** Servitude in general. **3** Lands held by feudal tenure; a fief. **4** Vassals collectively.

vas·sal·ize (vas′əl·īz) *v.t.* **·ized, ·iz·ing** To reduce to vassalage; use as a vassal.

vast (vast, väst) *adj.* **1** Of great extent; immense; enormous; huge; also, very spacious. **2** Very great in number, quantity, or amount. **3** Very great in degree, intensity, or importance. **4** *Obs.* Wide and waste; desolate; desert. See synonyms under IMMENSE, LARGE. — *n.* **1** A boundless space; immensity. **2** *Brit. Dial.* A great quantity. [<L, waste, empty, vast. Related to WASTE.] — **vast′ly** *adv.*

— **vast′ness, vas·ti·tude** (vas′tə·to͞od, -tyo͞od, väs′-) *n.*
vas·ta·tion (vas·tā′shən) *n.* **1** Purification by the spiritual burning away of evil. **2** *Obs.* Devastation. [<L *vastatio, -onis* < *vastare* lay waste < *vastus* waste, empty]
Väs·ter·ås (ves·tər·ōs′) A city of east central Sweden; an industrial center: formerly *Vesterås.*
vas·ti·ty (vas′tə·tē, väs′-) *n. pl.* **·ties** Vastness; immensity. [<F *vastité* < *vaste* large]
vast·y (vas′tē, väs′-) *adj. Poetic* Vast. [<VAST]
vat (vat) *n.* A large vessel, tub, or cistern, especially for holding liquids and dyeing materials. — *v.t.* **vat·ted, vat·ting** To put into a vat; treat in a vat. [OE *fæt*]
vat dye *Chem.* A dye produced by oxidation, and resistant to sunlight and washing.
Va·té (vä′tē) See EFATE.
vat·ic (vat′ik) *adj.* Pertaining to or proceeding from a prophet or seer; oracular; prophetic; inspired: *vatic* dicta, *vatic* lips. Also **vat′i·cal.** [<L *vates* prophet]
Vat·i·can (vat′ə·kən) *n.* **1** The papal palace in Vatican City, Rome. **2** The papal government, as distinguished from the Quirinal, or Italian civil government. — **Council of the Vatican** An ecumenical council, 1869–70, at the Vatican which declared the pope's infallibility, when speaking *ex cathedra,* to be a dogma of the church. [from L *Vaticanus* Vatican Hill in Rome]
Vatican City A sovereign papal state within the city of Rome, established June 10, 1929; 108.7 acres, including the Vatican and St. Peter's Church, along with the square in front of it; twelve buildings outside this area, both in and outside Rome, enjoy extraterritorial rights: Italian *Città del Vaticano.*
Vat·i·can·ism (vat′ə·kən·iz′əm) *n.* The ecclesiastical system and the tenet based on the supremacy and infallibility of the pope.
vat·i·cide (vat′ə·sīd) *n.* The killing of a prophet; also, a prophet-slayer. [<L *vates* prophet + -CIDE]
va·tic·i·nal (və·tis′ə·nəl) *adj.* Prophetic.
va·tic·i·nate (və·tis′ə·nāt) *v.t.* & *v.i.* **·nat·ed, ·nat·ing** To prophesy; foretell. [<L *vaticinatus,* pp. of *vaticinari* prophesy < *vates* prophet] — **va·tic′i·na′tion** *n.* — **va·tic′i·na′tor** *n.* — **va·tic′i·na·to′ry** (-nə·tôr′ē, -tō′rē) *adj.*
Vät·ter (vet′ər), **Lake** The second largest lake in Sweden, in the south central part; 733 square miles: formerly *Vetter. Swedish* **Vät·tern** (vet′ərn).
Va·tu·tin (vä·to͞o′tin), **Nikolai,** 1901?–44, Russian general in World War II.
vau (väv) See VAV.
Vau·ban (vō·bäṅ′), **Marquis de,** 1633–1707, Sébastien le Prestre, French military engineer.
vau·che·ri·a·ceous (vō·kir′ē·ā′shəs) *adj. Bot.* Belonging or pertaining to a genus (*Vaucheria*) of green algae consisting of long and usually branched filaments which grow in feltlike masses in shallow water and on muddy banks: often called *green felt.* [<NL, after Jean Pierre *Vaucher,* 1763–1841, Swiss botanist]
Vau·cluse (vō·klüz′) A department in Provence, SE France; 1,381 square miles; capital, Avignon.
Vaud (vō) A canton in west central Switzerland; 1,239 square miles; capital, Lausanne: German *Waadt.*
vau·de·ville (vô′də·vil, vōd′vil) *n.* **1** A miscellaneous theatrical entertainment consisting of a slight dramatic sketch or pantomime interspersed with songs and dances; a series of short sketches, songs, dances, acrobatic feats, etc., having no dramatic connection; a variety show; also, a theater presenting such shows. **2** A street ballad; originally, a satirical or topical popular song. [<F, alter. of (*chanson de*) *Vau de Vire* (song of) the valley of the Vire river (in Normandy), where Basselin, the best-known composer of such songs, lived]
Vau·dois (vō·dwä′) *n. pl.* **·dois** (-dwä′) **1** An inhabitant, or the inhabitants collectively, of the Swiss canton of Vaud. **2** The dialect of this canton.
Vau·dois (vō·dwä′) *n. pl.* The Waldenses.
Vaughan (vôn), **Henry,** 1622–95, English poet.
Vaughan Williams, Ralph, 1872–1958, English composer.
vault[1] (vôlt) *n.* **1** An arched apartment or chamber; also, any subterranean compartment; cellar. **2** An arched structure; arched ceiling or roof. **3** Any vaultlike covering; the sky. **4** An arched roof of a cavity. **5** An underground room or compartment for storing wine, valuables, etc. **6** A burial chamber. — *v.t.* **1** To form with a vaulted roof; cover with or as with a vault. **2** To construct in the form of a vault. [<OF *volte, vaute,* ult. <L *volutus,* pp. of *volvere* turn about, roll] — **vault′ed** *adj.*

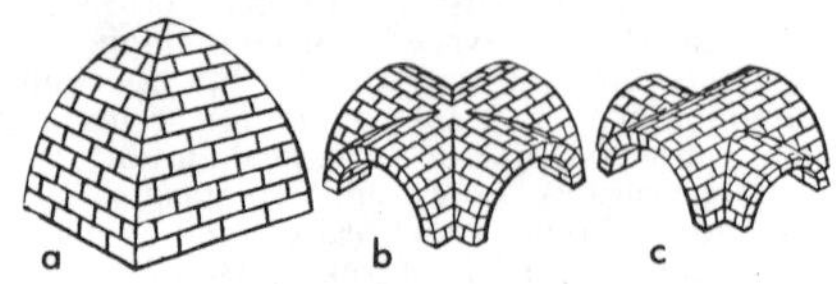

TYPES OF VAULTS
a. Cloister or cove. *b.* Groin.
c. Welsh or underpitch.

vault[2] (vôlt) *v.t.* **1** To leap over, especially with the aid of a pole or with the hands resting on something. **2** To mount with a leap, as a horse. — *v.i.* **3** To leap; spring. **4** To do a curvet. See synonyms under LEAP. — *n.* **1** A leap or bound; a springing leap, as one made with the aid of a pole. **2** The curvet of a horse. [<OF *volter* leap, gambol, ? ult. <L *volutus,* pp. of *volvere* turn about, roll] — **vault′er** *n.*
vault·ing[1] (vôl′ting) *n.* **1** Vaulted work, or vaults collectively. **2** The work or art of building a vault.
vault·ing[2] (vôl′ting) *adj.* **1** That overleaps; hence, unduly confident or presumptuous: *vaulting* ambition. **2** That can be used in vaulting, as in gymnastics.
vaunt (vônt, vänt) *v.i.* To speak boastfully. — *v.t.* To boast of. See synonyms under FLAUNT. — *n.* Boastful assertion or ostentatious display. See synonyms under OSTENTATION. [<OF *vanter* <LL *vanitare* brag <L *vanus* empty, vain] — **vaunt′er** *n.* — **vaunt′ing** *n.* — **vaunt′ing·ly** *adv.*
vaunt–cour·i·er (vänt′ko͝or′ē·ər, vônt′-) *n.* **1** *Archaic* A horseman or soldier sent in advance of an army. **2** A forerunner; precursor; herald. [<F *avant-coureur*]
vaunt·ie (vôn′tē) *adj. Scot.* Boastful. Also **vaunt′y, vawnt′ie.**
Vau·pés (vou′pās, *Sp.* bou·pās′) See UAUPÉS.
Vaux (vō) A village west of Château-Thierry in north central France; point of furthest German advance on the road to Paris in World War I, 1918.
vav (väv) *n.* The sixth Hebrew letter: also spelled *vau.* Also **vaw.** See ALPHABET.
vav·a·sor (vav′ə·sôr, -sōr) *n.* **1** The rank of a principal vassal next below a baron. **2** A vassal holding lands from a great vassal, and having other vassals under him. Also **vav′a·sour** (-so͞or). [<OF *vavassour* <LL *vassus vassorum* vassal of vassals]
va·ward (vä′wərd) *adj. Obs.* Vanward. [Alter. of obs. *avantward* <AF *avantwarde,* OF *avant-garde* vanguard]
V–day (vē′dā′) *n.* A day of victory; in World War II, **V–E Day** (vē′ē′dā′) (officially May 8, 1945), the date of victory of the United Nations in Europe, and **V–J Day** (vē′jā′dā′) (officially Sept. 2, 1945, Tokyo time), the date of their victory in the Pacific.
Ve·a·dar (vē′ä·där, vā′-) A Hebrew month. See CALENDAR (Hebrew).
veal (vēl) *n.* **1** The flesh of a calf considered as food. **2** *Obs.* A calf. — **bob veal** The flesh of a calf so young as to be unfit for food. [<OF *viel* calf <L *vitellus,* dim. of *vitulus* calf]
Veb·len (veb′lən), **Thorstein Bunde,** 1857–1929, U.S. economist and sociologist.
vec·tion (vek′shən) *n. Med.* The carrying of a disease organism from an infected to a well person. [<L *vectio, -onis* a conveyance, carrying < *vehere* carry]
vec·tor (vek′tər) *n.* **1** *Math.* **a** A line representing a physical quantity that has magnitude and direction in space, as velocity, acceleration or force: distinguished from *scalar.* **b** A radius vector. **2** *Med.* A carrier of pathogenic micro-organisms from one host to another: The anopheles mosquito is a *vector* of the malaria parasite. [<L, carrier < *vehere* carry] — **vec·to·ri·al** (vek·tôr′ē·əl, -tō′rē-) *adj.*
vectorial angle *Math.* A polar angle.
vec·tur·ism (vek′chə·riz′əm) *n. U.S.* The hobby of collecting old transportation tokens from bus and trolley lines. [<L *vecturus* fare, passage money < *vehere* carry] — **vec′tur·ist** *n.*
Ve·da (vā′də, vē′-) *n.* The body of ancient Indian sacred writings, dating from the second millennium B.C., which form the Hindu scriptures; specifically, the four major collections included in this literature: **Rigveda,** containing sacrificial hymns addressed to the gods; **Yajurveda,** containing liturgical formulas; **Samaveda,** a group of hymns chiefly in honor of Indra; and **Aharvaveda,** a large collection of charms and incantations. [<Skt., knowledge] — **Ve·da·ic** (vi·dā′ik) *adj.* — **Ve·da·ism** (vā′də·iz′əm, vē′-) *n.*
Ve·dan·ta (vi·dän′tə, -dan′-) *n.* Any of several schools of Hindu religious philosophy based on the Upanishads; especially, the monistic system of Shankara which teaches the worship of Brahma as the creator and soul of the universe. [<Skt. <*Veda* Veda + *anta* end] — **Ve·dan′tic** *adj.* — **Ve·dan′tism** *n.* — **Ve·dan′tist** *n.*
Ved·da (ved′ə) *n.* One of a primitive people of Ceylon of doubtful classification, slender, dark, small, with heavy, wavy hair, having both Caucasoid and Australoid traits, but not typically either: by some anthropologists thought to be remnants of an original Indo-Australoid race. Also **Ved′dah.** [<Singhalese, hunter]
Ved·der (ved′ər), **Elihu,** 1836–1923, U.S. painter and illustrator.
ve·dette (vi·det′) *n.* **1** A mounted sentinel placed in advance of an outpost. **2** A small vessel used to watch the movements of the enemy: also **vedette boat. 3** *Colloq.* In France, a female movie star. Also spelled *vidette.* [<F <Ital. *vedetta,* alter. (after *vedere* see) of *veletta,* dim. of Sp. *vela* vigil <L *vigilare* watch]
Ve·dic (vā′dik, vē′-) *adj.* Of or pertaining to the Vedas or the language in which they were written. — *n.* Vedic Sanskrit.
Vedic Sanskrit See under SANSKRIT.
vee (vē) *n.* **1** The sound or the shape of the letter V. **2** Anything shaped like the letter V. **3** *U.S. Slang* A five-dollar bill. — *adj.* V-shaped.
veep (vēp) *n. Slang* A vice president; specifically, the vice president of the United States. [<*V.P.,* abbr. of vice president]
veer[1] (vir) *v.i.* **1** *Naut.* To turn to another course; wear ship. **2** To change direction by a clockwise motion, as the wind. **3** To shift from one position to another; be variable or fickle. — *v.t.* **4** To change the direction of. See synonyms under CHANGE, FLUCTUATE, WANDER. — *n.* A change in direction; a swerve. [<F *virer* turn]
veer[2] (vir) *v.t.* & *v.i. Naut.* To let out or allow (a rope, anchor chain, etc.) to run out to a certain length. [<MDu. *vieren* slacken]
veer·y (vir′ē) *n. pl.* **veer·ies** A melodious tawny thrush (*Hylocichla fuscescens*) of eastern North America: also called *Wilson's thrush.* [Prob. imit.]
Ve·ga (vē′gə, vā′-) A star, Alpha in the constellation Lyra; 0.14 magnitude. [<Med. L <Arabic (*al-Nasr*) *al-Waqi* the falling (vulture)]
Ve·ga (vā′gə, *Sp.* bā′gä), **Lope de,** 1562–1635, Spanish dramatist and poet: full name Lope Felix de Vega Carpio.
veg·e·ta·ble (vej′ə·tə·bəl, vej′tə-) *n.* **1** The edible part of any herbaceous plant, raw or cooked, chiefly when served with an entree, or before the dessert. **2** Any member of the vegetable kingdom; a plant. **3** *Colloq.* A person who is mindless, apathetic, or passive. See synonyms under FRUIT. — *adj.* **1** Pertaining to plants, especially garden or farm vegetables. **2** Derived from, of the nature of, or resembling plants. **3** Made from or consisting of vegetables. **4** *Colloq.* Showing little mental activity; vacant. [<OF <LL *vegetabilis* full of life <L *vegetare* animate < *vegetus* vigorous, lively < *vegere* be lively]
vegetable butter See BUTTER[1] (def. 2).
vegetable fibers Textile fibers such as cotton, flax, kapok, jute, ramie, etc.
vegetable ivory Ivory nut.
vegetable kingdom The domain of nature that includes all organisms classified as plants. Compare ANIMAL KINGDOM, MINERAL KINGDOM.
vegetable marrow **1** A plant of the gourd family (*Cucurbita pepo*), having a tender,

edible fruit. **2** The fruit, esteemed as a vegetable: also called *marrow squash.*
vegetable oyster The salsify.
vegetable silk A cottonlike material obtained from the seed pods of a Brazilian tree *(Chorisia speciosa)* and used for stuffing cushions, etc.
vegetable sponge A luffa.
vegetable tallow Any of several fatty vegetable substances, variously derived, resembling tallow, and used locally for making candles, soap, etc.
vegetable wax Any wax derived from a plant.
veg·e·tal (vej′ə·təl) *adj.* **1** Of or pertaining to plants or vegetables; vegetative. **2** Characterizing those vital processes which are common to plants and animals, especially as distinguished from sensation and volition. [<L *vegetus* lively, vigorous. See VEGETABLE.]
veg·e·tant (vej′ə·tənt) *adj.* **1** Invigorating; vivifying; stimulating growth. **2** Vegetating; plantlike. [<L *vegetans, -antis,* ppr. of *vegere* be active, lively]
veg·e·tar·i·an (vej′ə·târ′ē·ən) *adj.* **1** Pertaining to or advocating the eating of only vegetable foods. **2** Exclusively vegetable, as a diet. —*n.* One who holds or practices vegetarianism: also **veg·e·tist** (vej′ə·tist).
veg·e·tar·i·an·ism (vej′ə·târ′ē·ən·iz′əm) *n.* The theory or practice of eating only vegetables and fruits. Also **veg′e·tism.**
veg·e·tate (vej′ə·tāt) *v.i.* **·tat·ed, ·tat·ing 1** To grow, as a plant. **2** To live in a monotonous, passive way. **3** *Pathol.* To increase in size. [<L *vegetatus,* pp. of *vegetare* animate. See VEGETABLE.]
veg·e·ta·tion (vej′ə·tā′shən) *n.* **1** The process of vegetating. **2** Plant life in the aggregate. **3** *Pathol.* An excrescence on the body; an abnormal or fibrous growth. **4** A plantlike growth. —**veg′e·ta′tion·al** *adj.*
veg·e·ta·tive (vej′ə·tā′tiv) *adj.* **1** Of, pertaining to, or exhibiting the processes of plant life. **2** Growing or capable of growing as plants; productive. **3** Having a mere physical existence; showing but little mental activity. **4** Asexual. **5** Concerned with growth and nutrition. **6** Functioning involuntarily or unconsciously: a *vegetative* process. Also **veg·e·tive** (vej′ə·tiv). —**veg′e·ta′tive·ly** *adv.* —**veg′e·ta′tive·ness** *n.*
Ve·glia (ve′lyä) The Italian name for KRK.
ve·he·ment (vē′ə·mənt) *adj.* **1** Arising from or marked by impetuosity of feeling or passion; ardent. **2** Acting with great force or energy; energetic; violent; furious. See synonyms under ARDENT, EAGER[1], HOT, VIOLENT. [<OF <L *vehemens, -entis* impetuous, rash; ult. origin uncertain] —**ve′he·mence, ve′he·men·cy** *n.* —**ve′he·ment·ly** *adv.*
ve·hi·cle (vē′ə·kəl) *n.* **1** That in or on which anything is carried; especially, a contrivance fitted with wheels or runners for carrying something; a conveyance, as a car or sled. **2** *Med.* A medium, as a liquid, with which is mixed some other substance that it may be applied or administered more easily; an excipient. **3** The medium with which pigments are mixed in painting. **4** Anything by means of which something else, as power, thought, etc., is transmitted or communicated; a device used to transmit an effect. [<F *véhicule* <L *vehiculum* < *vehere* carry, ride] —**ve·hic·u·lar** (vi·hik′yə·lər) *adj.*
Vehm·ge·richt (fām′gə·rikht) *n. pl.* **·rich·te** (-rikh′tə) An institution peculiar to Germany, especially Westphalia, from about 1150 to 1568, consisting of irregular tribunals. Civil cases were tried openly, but serious crimes, such as heresy, witchcraft, murder, etc., were tried by night in secret session. [<G < *fehm* judgment, punishment + *gericht* law, court]
Ve·ii (vē′yī) An ancient Etruscan city in central Italy, destroyed by Romans, 396 B.C.; site, 10 miles NW of Rome.
veil (vāl) *n.* **1** A piece of thin and light fabric, worn over the face or head for concealment, protection, or ornament. **2** Any piece of fabric used to conceal an object; a screen; curtain; mask. **3** Figuratively, that which conceals from inspection; a disguise; pretext. **4** A velum. **5** A caul. **6** The life of a nun; vows made by a nun. —**to take the veil** To become a nun. —*v.t.* **1** To cover with a veil. **2** To hide; disguise. See synonyms under HIDE[1], MASK[1], PALLIATE. Also, *Obs., vail.* ◆ Homophones: *vail, vale.* [<OF *veile* <L *velum* piece of cloth, sail] —**veiled** *adj.* —**veil′er** *n.*
veil·ing (vā′ling) *n.* **1** The act of covering with a veil. **2** Material for veils. **3** A veil.
vein (vān) *n.* **1** *Anat.* One of the muscular tubular vessels that convey blood to the heart; loosely, any blood vessel. ◆ Collateral adjective: *venal.* **2** *Entomol.* One of the radiating supports of an insect's wing; a rib or nerve. **3** *Bot.* One of the slender vascular bundles that form the framework of a leaf. **4** *Geol.* The filling of a fissure or fault in a rock, particularly if deposited by aqueous solutions. **5** A lode. **6** A bed or shoot of ore parallel with the fault. **7** A long, irregular, colored streak, as in wood, marble, etc. **8** A distinctive trait; a specific tendency or disposition. **9** A temporary state of mind; humor; mood. **10** A cavity; cleft; fissure. **11** A crevice or natural channel through which water trickles. —*v.t.* **1** To furnish or fill with veins. **2** To streak or ornament with veins. **3** To extend over or throughout as veins. ◆ Homophones: *vain, vane.* [<OF *veine* <L *vena* blood vessel] —**vein′less** *adj.* —**vein′y** *adj.*

VEINING OF SILVER MAPLE LEAF

veined (vānd) *adj.* **1** Having veins. **2** Marked with or abounding in veins. **3** Marked with streaks of another color.
vein·ing (vā′ning) *n.* **1** A vein or network of veins. **2** A streaked or veined surface.
vein·let (vān′lit) *n.* A small vein.
vein·stone (vān′stōn′) *n.* Gangue.
Ve·la (vē′lə) A southern constellation, formerly part of the larger one, Argo Navis. [<L, veil]
ve·la·men (və·lā′mən) *n. pl.* **·lam·i·na** (-lam′ə·nə) **1** *Anat.* Any membrane, covering, or integument. **2** *Bot.* An envelope consisting of several layers of empty cells, forming the outer covering of the aerial roots of certain orchids and arums. Also **vel·a·men·tum** (vel′ə·men′təm). [<L, covering < *velare* veil]
ve·lar (vē′lər) *adj.* **1** Of or pertaining to a velum, especially the soft palate. **2** *Phonet.* Formed with the back of the tongue touching or near the soft palate, as (k) in *cool,* (g) in *go.* —*n. Phonet.* A velar sound. [<L *velaris* < *velum* sail, curtain]
ve·lar·ize (vē′lə·rīz) *v.* **·ized, ·iz·ing** *Phonet. v.t.* To modify (a sound) by raising the back of the tongue toward the soft palate. —*v.i.* To be modified to a velar sound.
ve·lar·i·um (və·lâr′ē·əm) *n. pl.* **·lar·i·a** (-lâr′ē·ə) *Latin* The awning spread over the seats in ancient Roman theaters or amphitheaters.
Ve·lás·quez (və·las′kwiz, *Sp.* bā·läs′kāth), **Diego Rodriguez de Silva y,** 1599–1660, Spanish painter. Also **Ve·láz·quez** (bā·läth′·kāth).
ve·late (vē′lāt, -lit) *adj. Biol.* Having a velum or veil. [<L *velatus,* pp. of *velare* veil]
ve·la·tion (vē·lā′shən) *n.* **1** The forming of a velum. **2** The act of veiling, or the state of being veiled; hence, concealment; mystery.
veldt (velt, felt) *n.* In South Africa, open country or pasture land; grassland having few shrubs or trees. Low-lying wooded land is known as **bush veldt,** and the high treeless plains as **high veldt.** Also **veld.** [<Afrikaans *veld* <Du., field]
vel·i·ger (vel′ə·jər) *n. Zool.* The larva of a mollusk at the stage succeeding the trochophore and when it has a ciliated swimming membrane or membranes. [<LL *veliger* sail-bearing <L *velum* sail + *gerere* bear]
ve·lig·er·ous (və·lij′ər·əs) *adj.* Bearing a velum or membranous partition.
Ve·li·ki Kvar·ner (ve′li·kē kvär′nər) An arm of the Adriatic Sea, SE of Istria, in NW Croatia, Yugoslavia: also *Gulf of Quarnero. Italian* **Gol·fo di Quar·ne·ro** (gôl′fō dē kwär·nā′rō).
vel·i·ta·tion (vel′ə·tā′shən) *n.* A petty skirmish; a wordy controversy. [<L *velitatio, -onis* < *velitatus,* pp. of *velitari* skirmish < *veles, velitis* a foot soldier]
ve·li·tes (vē′lə·tēz) *n. pl.* Light-armed Roman soldiers used as skirmishers in ancient legions. [<L, pl. of *veles* foot soldier]
vel·le·i·ty (ve·lē′ə·tē) *n. pl.* **·ties** A very low degree of desire or volition, not leading to action; a mere wish. [<Med. L *velleitas, -tatis* <L *velle* wish]
vel·li·cate (vel′ə·kāt) *v.t.* & *v.i.* **·cat·ed, ·cat·ing** To twitch or pluck. [<L *vellicatus,* pp. of *vellicare* twitch, freq. of *vellere* pluck] —**vel′li·ca′tion** *n.* —**vel′li·ca′tive** *adj.*
vel·lum (vel′əm) *n.* **1** Fine parchment made from the skins of calves: used for expensive binding, printing, etc. **2** A manuscript written on such parchment. **3** Paper made to resemble parchment. [<OF *velin, vellin* < *veel, viel* calf. See VEAL.]
ve·lo·ce (vā·lō′chā) *adv. Music* Rapidly; in quick tempo; swiftly. [<Ital., swift]
ve·loc·i·pede (və·los′ə·pēd) *n.* **1** An early form of bicycle or tricycle; also, a child's tricycle. **2** A light handcar or vehicle propelled by hands or feet and used along railroad tracks. [<L *velox, velocis* swift + -PEDE]
ve·loc·i·ty (və·los′ə·tē) *n. pl.* **·ties 1** The state of moving swiftly; rapid motion; celerity; speed. **2** *Physics* **a** The rate of change of position in a moving object. **b** The rate of motion in a stated direction: a vector quantity: distinguished from *speed.* [<L *velocitas, -tatis* < *velox* swift]
velocity of escape *Physics* The minimum velocity at which any particle or object would permanently escape the gravitational field of a body of stated mass: on the earth this velocity is approximately 7 miles per second. See table under PLANET.
ve·lo·drome (vē′lə·drōm) *n.* A racecourse, as for bicycles. [<L *velox* speedy + -DROME]
ve·lours (və·lo͝or′) *n. pl.* **·lours** A soft, velvetlike, closely woven cotton or wool fabric having a short, thick pile. Also **ve·lour′.** [<F. See VELURE.]
ve·lou·té (və·lo͞o·tā′) *n. French* A rich white sauce made by thickening chicken or veal stock with flour and butter. Also **sauce velouté.**
ve·lum (vē′ləm) *n. pl.* **·la** (-lə) **1** *Biol.* A thin membranous covering or partition, as in certain jellyfishes, and in mushrooms. **2** *Anat.* The soft palate. See PALATE. [<L]
ve·lure (və·lo͝or′) *n.* **1** Velvet, or a fabric resembling velvet; specifically, a heavy fabric of linen, silk, or jute, used for hangings, table covers, and the like. **2** A velvet or silk pad for smoothing a silk hat. —*v.t.* **·lured, ·lur·ing** To smooth with a soft pad, as a hat. [<F *velours* <L *villosus* shaggy < *villus* shaggy hair]
ve·lu·ti·nous (və·lo͞o′tə·nəs) *adj. Bot.* Covered with close, soft hairs, like the pile of velvet; velvety. [<NL *velutinus* <Med. L *velutum,* var. of *velvetum.* See VELVET.]
vel·ver·et (vel′və·ret′) *n.* A velvet fabric with cotton backing.
vel·vet (vel′vit) *n.* **1** A fabric, properly of silk, now sometimes made of cotton or one of the synthetics, closely woven and having on one side a thick, short, smooth pile: called **pile velvet** when the pile is formed of loops, and **cut velvet** when the pile is of single threads. **2** The furry skin covering a growing antler. —**chiffon velvet** A very soft, lightweight velvet having the pile pressed flat. —*adj.* **1** Made of velvet. **2** Smooth and soft to the touch; velvety. [<Med. L *velvetum,* ult. <L *villus* shaggy hair]
velvet carpet A carpet having a pile longer than a Brussels carpet but cut in the manner of a Wilton carpet: also **tapestry velvet carpet.**
vel·vet·een (vel′və·tēn′) *n.* **1** A cotton fabric, with a short, close pile like velvet. **2** *pl.* Clothes, especially trousers, made of this material. [<VELVET] —**vel′vet·eened′** *adj.*
vel·vet·leaf (vel′vit·lēf′) *n.* **1** Any one of several plants, especially the Indian mallow. **2** A tropical climbing shrub *(Cissampelos pareira)* of the moonseed family, the bark of which yields a variety of pareira brava.
vel·vet·y (vel′vit·ē) *adj.* **1** Like velvet; smooth and soft to appearance or touch. **2**

Mild and smooth to the taste: *velvety* liqueur.

ve·na (vē′nə) *n. pl.* **·nae** (-nē) *Anat.* A vein. [<L]

ve·na ca·va (vē′nə kā′və) *n. pl.* **ve·nae ca·vae** (vē′nē kā′vē) *Anat.* Either of the two great venous trunks (called *superior* and *inferior*) emptying into the right auricle of the heart. See illustration under HEART. [<L, hollow vein]

ve·nal[1] (vē′nəl) *adj.* 1 Ready to sell honor or principle, or to accept a bribe; mercenary; purchasable: said of persons. 2 Subject to sordid bargaining or to corrupt influences; salable. 3 Characterized by corruption and venality. [<L *venalis* < *venum* sale] — **ve′nal·ly** *adv.*

Synonyms: hireling, mercenary, purchasable, salable. *Mercenary* has especial application to character or disposition; as, a *mercenary* spirit; *mercenary* motives—that is, a spirit or motives to which money is the chief consideration or the moving principle. Thus, etymologically, the *mercenary* can be hired, while the *venal* are openly or actually for sale; *hireling* signifies serving for hire or pay, or having the spirit or character of one who works or of that which is done directly for hire or pay. The *hireling*, the *mercenary*, and the *venal* are alike in making principle, conscience, and honor of less account than gold or sordid considerations; but the *mercenary* and *venal* may be simply open to the bargain and sale which the *hireling* has already consummated. A public officer who makes his office tributary to private speculation is *mercenary*; if he receives a stipulated recompense for administering his office at the behest of some leader, faction, corporation, or the like, he is both *hireling* and *venal*; if he sells essential advantages, without subjecting himself to any direct domination, his course is *venal*, but not *hireling*. *Antonyms*: disinterested, honest, honorable, incorruptible, patriotic, unpurchasable.

ve·nal[2] (vē′nəl) *adj.* Of or pertaining to the veins; venous. [<L *vena* vein]

ve·nal·i·ty (vē·nal′ə·tē) *n. pl.* **·ties** The state or character of being basely or improperly influenced by sordid considerations; prostitution, as of talents, office, etc., for gain or reward; willingness to accept bribes. [<L *venalitas, -tatis*]

ve·nat·ic (vē·nat′ik) *adj.* 1 Of, used in, or pertaining to hunting. 2 Living by or fond of hunting. Also **ven·a·to·ri·al** (ven′ə·tôr′ē·əl, -tō′rē-). [<L *venaticus* < *venatus*, pp. of *venari* hunt] — **ve·nat′i·cal** *adj.* — **ve·nat′i·cal·ly** *adv.*

ve·na·tion (vē·nā′shən) *n. Biol.* 1 The particular arrangement of veins, as in a leaf. 2 The distribution of veins in an organism or part, as an insect wing, etc. [<L *vena* a vein]

vend (vend) *v.t.* 1 To sell. 2 To utter (an opinion); publish. — *v.i.* 3 To be a vender. 4 To be sold. [<F *vendre* <L *vendere* < *venum* sale + *dare* give] — **ven·di·tion** (ven·dish′ən) *n.*

ven·dace (ven′dis) *n.* A small whitefish (*Coregonus vandesius*) of some British lakes. Also **ven′dis.** [<F *vandoise* dace]

ven·dee (ven·dē′) *n.* The person or party to whom something, especially land, is sold.

Ven·dée (vän·dā′) A region and department in western France on the Bay of Biscay; scene of a royalist revolt, 1793–95; 2,708 square miles. — **Ven·de·an** (ven·dē′ən) *adj.* & *n.*

Ven·dé·miaire (vän·dā·myâr′) See under CALENDAR (Republican).

vend·er (ven′dər) *n.* One who sells; a peddler or hawker; vendor.

ven·det·ta (ven·det′ə) *n.* Private warfare or feud, as in revenge for a murder, injury, etc.; a blood feud in which the relatives of the killed or injured person take vengeance on the offender or his relatives. It is still prevalent in Sicily, Corsica, and Montenegro, and, to some extent, in certain other districts. [<Ital. <L *vindicta* vengeance]

vend·i·ble (ven′də·bəl) *adj.* Capable of being vended or sold; marketable. — *n.* A thing exposed for sale. [<L *vendibilis* < *vendere* sell] — **vend′i·bil′i·ty, vend′i·ble·ness** *n.* — **vend′i·bly** *adv.*

Ven·dôme (vän·dôm′) A town and former duchy in north central France.

ven·dor (ven′dər) The common legal spelling of VENDER.

ven·due (ven·dōō′, -dyōō′) *n.* A public sale or auction. [<F, orig. fem. pp. of *vendre* sell]

ve·neer (və·nir′) *n.* 1 A thin layer, as of choice wood, upon a commoner surface; a layer of superior material for overlaying a cheaper one. 2 Any of the thin layers glued together to strengthen plywood. 3 Figuratively, mere outside show or elegance. — *v.t.* 1 To cover (a surface) with veneers; overlay for decoration or finer finish. 2 To glue together to form plywood. 3 To conceal, as something disagreeable or coarse, with an attractive or deceptive surface. [Earlier *fineer* <G *furnieren* inlay <F *fournir* furnish] — **ve·neer′er** *n.*

ve·neer·ing (və·nir′ing) *n.* 1 The art of applying veneer. 2 Material used for veneers. 3 A facing or surface of veneer.

ven·e·punc·ture (ven′ə·pungk′chər) See VENIPUNCTURE.

Ve·ner (ve′nər), **Lake** The largest lake of Sweden, in the SW part; 2,141 square miles; 90 miles long, 5 to 46 miles wide: also *Vaner*. *Swedish* **Vä·nern** (ve′nərn).

ven·er·a·ble (ven′ər·ə·bəl) *adj.* 1 Meriting or commanding veneration; worthy of reverence: now usually implying age. 2 Exciting reverential feelings because of sacred or elevated associations. 3 Revered: used as a title for an archdeacon in Anglican churches, and for those beatified in the Roman Catholic Church. See synonyms under ANCIENT[1]. [<OF <L *venerabilis* < *venerari* revere] — **ven′er·a·ble·ness, ven′er·a·bil′i·ty** *n.* — **ven′er·a·bly** *adv.*

ven·er·ate (ven′ə·rāt) *v.t.* **·at·ed, ·at·ing** To look upon or regard with respect and deference; revere. [<L *veneratus*, pp. of *venerari* revere]

Synonyms: adore, honor, respect, revere, reverence. In the highest sense, to *revere* or *reverence* is to hold in mingled love and honor with something of sacred fear; to *revere* is a wholly spiritual act; to *reverence* is often, but not necessarily, to give outward expression to the reverential feeling; we *revere* or *reverence* the divine majesty. *Revere* is a stronger word than *reverence* or *venerate*. To *venerate* is to hold in exalted honor without fear, and is applied to objects less removed from ourselves than those we *revere*, being said especially of aged persons, of places or objects having sacred associations, and of abstractions; we *venerate* an aged friend or some great cause, as that of civil or religious liberty; we do not *venerate* God, but *revere* or *reverence* him. We *adore* with a humble yet free outflowing of soul. See ADMIRE, DEFER. *Antonyms*: contemn, despise, disdain, dishonor, disregard, scorn, slight, spurn.

ven·er·a·tion (ven′ə·rā′shən) *n.* 1 The act of venerating; reverence; profound respect combined with awe, evoked by the high character or wisdom of a person. 2 The act of worshiping; worship.

Synonyms: adoration, awe, dread, reverence. *Awe* is inspired by that in which there is sublimity or majesty so overwhelming as to awaken a feeling akin to fear; in *awe*, considered by itself, there is no element of esteem or affection, but a sense of the vastness, power, or grandeur of the object. *Dread* is a shrinking apprehension or expectation of possible harm awakened by any one of many objects or causes; in its higher uses *dread* approaches the meaning of *awe*, but with more of chilliness and cowering, and without that subjection of soul to the grandeur and worthiness of the object that is involved in *awe*. *Reverence* and *veneration* are less overwhelming than *awe* or *dread*, and suggest something of esteem, affection, and personal nearness. We may feel *awe* of that which we cannot reverence, as a grandly terrible ocean storm; *awe* of the divine presence is more distant and less trustful than *reverence*. *Veneration* is commonly applied to things which are not subjects of *awe*. *Adoration*, in its full sense, is loftier than *veneration*, less restrained and awed than *reverence*, and with more of the spirit of direct, active, and joyful worship. See REVERENCE. Compare VENERATE. *Antonyms*: contempt, disdain, dishonor, disregard, scorn.

ve·ne·re·al (və·nir′ē·əl) *adj.* 1 Pertaining to or proceeding from sexual intercourse. 2 Communicated by sexual relations with an infected person: a *venereal* disease. 3 Pertaining to or curative of diseases so communicated. 4 Infected with venereal disease. [<L *venereus* <*Venus, -eris*, the goddess of love]

venereal disease *Pathol.* One of several diseases propagated directly or indirectly by sexual intercourse, as syphilis, gonorrhea, and chancroid.

ve·ne·re·ol·o·gy (və·nir′ē·ol′ə·jē) *n.* The study and treatment of venereal diseases. — **ve·ne′re·ol′o·gist** *n.*

ven·er·y[1] (ven′ər·ē) *n.* Sexual indulgence, especially when excessive. [<L *Venus, -eris*, the goddess of love]

ven·er·y[2] (ven′ər·ē) *n. pl.* **·er·ies** The hunting of game; the sport of hunting; the chase. [<F *venerie* < *vener* hunt <L *venari* hunt]

ven·e·sec·tion (ven′ə·sek′shən) *n. Surg.* Phlebotomy. [<Med. L *venae sectio* cutting of a vein]

Ve·ne·ti·a (və·nē′shē·ə, -shə) 1 An ancient division of the Roman Empire comprising that part of Italy between the Po river and the Alps. 2 Venezia. 3 Veneto.

Ve·ne·tian (və·nē′shən) *adj.* Pertaining to Venice, or to the medieval school of architecture developed there. — *n.* 1 A native of Venice. 2 *Colloq.* A Venetian blind. 3 A heavy braid or tape used on Venetian blinds.

Venetian blind A flexible window screen that may be raised or lowered, having overlapping horizontal slats so fastened on webbing or tape as to regulate, exclude, or admit light.

Venetian carpet A worsted carpet for stairs and hallways, commonly of a simple striped pattern.

Venetian glass A delicate and fine glassware originally made at or near Venice.

Venetian red Red ocher. See under OCHER.

Venetian school 1 A school of painting originating in and near Venice in the 15th century and distinguished by richness of coloring, as in the work of Titian, Tintoretto, Giorgione, etc. 2 A school of Italian architecture.

Ve·net·ic (və·net′ik) *n.* 1 A member of an ancient people of NE Italy. 2 Their Indo-European language, possibly related to Illyrian and Messapian. — *adj.* Of or pertaining to these people or their language.

Ve·ne·to (vā′nā·tō) A region of northern and NE Italy; 7,093 square miles; capital, Venice.

Ve·ne·zia (vā·nā′tsyä) 1 The Italian name for VENICE. 2 A province in Veneto, northern Italy; 949 square miles; capital, Venice.

Venezia Giu·lia (jōō′lyä) A former region of NE Italy including Trieste, Rijeka, and Istria; 3,370 square miles; divided 1947 between Italy (180 square miles), Yugoslavia (2,891 square miles), and the Free Territory of Trieste (298 square miles, later also divided).

Ven·e·zue·la (ven′ə·zwē′lə, -zōō·ā′lə; *Sp.* bā′·nā·swā′lä) A republic in northern South America; 352,143 square miles; capital, Caracas. — **Ven′e·zue′lan** *adj.* & *n.*

Venezuela, Gulf of See under MARACAIBO.

ven·geance (ven′jəns) *n.* 1 The infliction of a deserved penalty; retributive punishment. 2 In a bad sense, wrathful avenging of a wrong; revenge. 3 *Obs.* Mischief; evil. See synonyms under REVENGE. — **with a vengeance** With great force or violence; extremely; to an unusual extent. [<AF <OF *venger* avenge <L *vindicare* defend, avenge < *vindex, vindicis* claimant, protector]

venge·ful (venj′fəl) *adj.* Prone to inflict vengeance; vindictive. — **venge′ful·ly** *adv.* — **venge′ful·ness** *n.*

ve·ni·al (vē′nē·əl, vēn′yəl) *adj.* That may be pardoned or overlooked; excusable. [<OF <L *venialis* < *venia* forgiveness, mercy] — **ve′ni·al′i·ty** (-al′ə·tē), **ve′ni·al·ness** *n.* — **ve′ni·al·ly** *adv.*

Synonyms: excusable, pardonable, slight, trivial. Aside from its technical ecclesiastical use, *venial* is always understood as marking some fault comparatively *slight* or *trivial*. A *venial* offense is one readily overlooked; a *pardonable* offense requires more serious consideration, but on deliberation is found to be susceptible of pardon. *Excusable* is scarcely applied to offenses, but to matters open to doubt or criticism rather than direct censure; so used, it often falls little short of justifiable; as, I suppose, under those circumstances, his action was *excusable*. *Antonyms*: inexcusable, mortal, unpardonable.

venial sin *Theol.* A pardonable offense, or an unpremeditated one: opposed to *mortal* or *deadly* sin.

Ven·ice (ven′is) A port in NE Italy, built on 118 islands in the **Lagoon of Venice,** the NW part of the **Gulf of Venice,** the northern sector of the Adriatic between Istria and the Po river delta: Italian *Venezia.*

Ve·ni Cre·a·tor (vē′nī krē·ā′tər) *Latin* A hymn to the Holy Ghost: so called from its beginning, *Veni Creator Spiritus* (Come, Creator Spirit).

ven·i·punc·ture (ven′ə·pungk′chər) *n. Surg.* The operation of puncturing a vein: also spelled *venepuncture.* [<L *vena* vein + PUNCTURE]

ve·ni·re (vi·nī′rē) *n. Law* A writ issued to the sheriff for summoning persons to serve as a jury in court: from its phrase *venire facias* (that you cause to come). [<L]

ve·ni·re–man (vi·nī′rē·mən) *n. pl.* **·men** (-mən) A juryman; one summoned to be on a jury.

ven·i·son (ven′ə·zən, -sən; *Brit.* ven′zən) *n.* **1** Deer flesh used for food. **2** *Obs.* The flesh of any edible game. [<F *venaison* <L *venatio, -onis* hunting <*venatus,* pp. of *venari* hunt]

venison bird *Canadian* The Canada jay.

Ve·ni·te (vi·nī′tē) *n.* The 95th psalm, used as a canticle in various liturgies: from its first word. [<L, come, imperative of *venire* come]

ve·ni, vi·di, vi·ci (vē′nī, vī′dī, vī′sī; wā′nē, wē′dē, wē′kē) *Latin* I came, I saw, I conquered: words used by Julius Caesar to report his victory over Pharnaces, king of Pontus, to the Roman Senate.

Ve·ni·ze·los (ve′nē·ze′lôs), **Eleftherios,** 1864–1936, Greek statesman; premier 1917–20 and 1928–32.

ven·om (ven′əm) *n.* **1** The poisonous fluid that certain animals, as serpents and scorpions, secrete, and which produces toxic effects when introduced into the system by a bite or sting. **2** Something harmful; hence, malignity; spite. **3** Any poison. — *v.t.* To imbue with poison; envenom. [<OF *venim* <L *venenum* poison] —**ven′om·er** *n.*

ven·om·ous (ven′əm·əs) *adj.* **1** Having glands secreting venom. **2** Able to give a poisonous sting; virulent; noxious. **3** Working harm; baneful. **4** Malignant; spiteful. See synonyms under MALICIOUS. —**ven′om·ous·ly** *adv.* —**ven′om·ous·ness** *n.*

ve·nose (vē′nōs) *adj.* **1** Having numerous or prominent veins, as a leaf; veiny. **2** Venous. [<L *venosus*]

ve·nos·i·ty (vi·nos′ə·tē) *n.* **1** An excess of venous blood in a part. **2** A plentiful supply of blood vessels.

ve·nous (vē′nəs) *adj. Physiol.* **1** Of, pertaining to, contained, or carried in a vein or veins. **2** Designating the blood carried by the veins and distinguished from arterial blood by its darker color, absence of oxygen, and presence of carbon dioxide. **3** Marked with or having veins. [<L *venosus* <*vena* vein] —**ve′nous·ly** *adv.* —**ve′nous·ness** *n.*

vent (vent) *n.* **1** An opening, commonly small, for the passage of fluids, gases, etc.; hence, an outlet of any kind: also **vent hole.** **2** The act of giving utterance, as to passion; expression; escape; passage: now usually in the phrase **to give vent to.** **3** *Zool.* The external opening of the alimentary canal, especially of animals below mammals; the anus. **4** A touchhole of a gun. —*v.t.* **1** To give expression to: to *vent* one's rage. **2** To relieve, as by giving vent to emotion. **3** To permit to escape at a vent, as a gas. **4** To make a vent in, as a mold. [ME *fent* <OF *fente* cleft <*fendre* cleave <L *findere* split]

vent·age (ven′tij) *n.* **1** A small opening. **2** A finger hole in a musical instrument. [<VENT]

ven·tail (ven′tāl) *n.* The adjustable front of a helmet, permitting complete defense of the face in combat. [<OF *ventaile* <*vent* wind]

vent·er[1] (ven′tər) *n.* One who vents.

ven·ter[2] (ven′tər) *n.* **1** The belly or stomach. **2** Any protuberant part. **3** The womb. **4** A hollowed part, as of a bone. [<L, stomach]

ven·ti·duct (ven′tə·dukt) *n.* An air passage, especially a subterranean ventilating passage. [<L *ventus* wind + DUCT]

ven·ti·late (ven′tə·lāt) *v.t.* **·lat·ed, ·lat·ing** **1** To produce a free circulation of air in, as by means of open shafts, windows, doors, etc.; admit fresh air into. **2** To provide with a vent. **3** To make widely known; expose to examination and discussion. **4** To oxygenate, as blood. **5** *Obs.* To winnow; fan, as wheat. [<L *ventilatus,* pp. of *ventilare* fan <*ventus* wind] —**ven′ti·lat′ing, ven′ti·la′tion** *n.* —**ven′ti·la′tive** *adj.*

ven·ti·la·tor (ven′tə·lā′tər) *n.* **1** One who or that which ventilates. **2** A device or arrangement for supplying fresh air. —**ven′·ti·la·to′ry** (-lə·tôr′ē, -tō′rē) *adj.*

Ven·ti·mi·glia (ven′tē·mē′lyä) An Italian port on the Gulf of Genoa NE of Nice; an important international railroad station.

Ven·tôse (vän·tōz′) See under CALENDAR (Republican).

ven·trad (ven′trad) *adv. Biol.* Toward the belly or undersurface. [<L *venter* belly]

ven·tral (ven′trəl) *adj.* **1** *Biol.* **a** Of, pertaining to, or situated on or near the abdomen or abdominal surface of an animal. **b** On or toward the lower surface of the body: the *ventral* plates of a serpent: opposed to *dorsal.* **2** *Bot.* Pertaining to the surface of a petal, carpel, etc., that faces the center of a flower. —*n.* One of the paired fins on the underside of fishes, homologous with the hind limb of higher vertebrates: in full, **ventral fin.** [<L *ventralis* <*venter, ventris* belly] —**ven′tral·ly** *adv.*

ven·tri·cle (ven′trə·kəl) *n. Anat.* **1** Any of various cavities in the body, as of the brain, the spinal cord, or between the true and false vocal cords in the larynx. **2** One of the two lower chambers of the heart, from which blood received from the atria is forced into the arteries. [<L *ventriculus,* dim. of *venter, ventris* belly]

ven·tri·cose (ven′trə·kōs) *adj.* **1** Having a protruding belly. **2** Swelling out or inflated on one side or in the middle; bellied; distended. Also **ven′tri·cous** (-kəs). [<NL *ventricosus* <L *venter, ventris* belly] —**ven′tri·cos′i·ty** (-kos′ə·tē) *n.*

ven·tric·u·lar (ven·trik′yə·lər) *adj.* **1** Of, pertaining to, or of the nature of a ventricle. **2** Swollen and distended; ventricose.

ven·tric·u·lose (ven·trik′yə·lōs) *adj.* Slightly ventricose. [<L *ventriculosus* <*ventriculus.* See VENTRICLE.]

ven·tri·lo·qui·al (ven′trə·lō′kwē·əl) *adj.* Pertaining to, resembling, or practicing ventriloquism. Also **ven·tril·o·qual** (ven·tril′ə·kwəl), **ven·tril′o·quous.** —**ven′tri·lo′qui·al·ly** *adv.*

ven·tril·o·quism (ven·tril′ə·kwiz′əm) *n.* The art or practice of speaking in such a manner that the sounds seem to come from some source other than the person speaking. Also **ven·tril′o·quy** (-kwē). [<L *venter* belly + *loqui* speak] —**ven·tril′o·quist** *n.* —**ven·tril′o·quis′tic** *adj.*

ven·tril·o·quize (ven·tril′ə·kwīz) *v.t.* & *v.i.* **·quized, ·quiz·ing** To speak as a ventriloquist. Also *Brit.* **ven·tril′o·quise.**

ventro– *combining form Anat.* The abdomen; related to or near the abdomen; ventral. [<L *venter, ventris* the belly, abdomen]

Vents·pils (vents′pils) A port on the Baltic Sea in NW Latvia: German *Windau.*

ven·ture (ven′chər) *v.* **·tured, ·tur·ing** *v.t.* **1** To expose to chance or risk; hazard; stake. **2** To run the risk of; brave. **3** To express at the risk of denial or refutation: to *venture* a suggestion. **4** To place or send on a chance, as in a speculative business enterprise. **5** *Obs.* To trust as an agent or doer; rely on. —*v.i.* **6** To take a risk; dare. —*n.* **1** The staking of a thing upon a contingency; a risk; hazard. **2** An undertaking attended with risk; a business speculation. **3** That which is ventured; especially, property risk. **4** That which is unforeseen and hazardous; chance; fortune: a rare usage. See synonyms under HAZARD. — **at a venture** At hazard; at random; without aim or thought. [Aphetic form of ADVENTURE] —**ven′tur·er** *n.*

ven·ture·some (ven′chər·səm) *adj.* **1** Bold; daring. **2** Involving hazard; risky. See synonyms under BRAVE, IMPRUDENT. —**ven′ture·some·ly** *adv.* —**ven′ture·some·ness** *n.*

ven·tur·ous (ven′chər·əs) *adj.* **1** Adventurous; willing to take risks and brave dangers; bold. **2** Hazardous; risky; dangerous. See synonyms under IMPRUDENT. —**ven′tur·ous·ly** *adv.* —**ven′tur·ous·ness** *n.*

ven·ue (ven′yōō) *n. Law* **1** The place or neighborhood where a crime is committed or a cause of action arises; the county or political division from which the jury must be summoned and in which the trial must be held. **2** The clause, usually at the beginning of a declaration or indictment, indicating the county in which the proceeding is pending. **3** A clause in an affidavit, stating where it was made and sworn to. —**change of venue** The change of the place of trial, for good cause shown, from one county to another. [<OF, orig. fem. pp. of *venir* come <L *venire*]

ven·ule (ven′yōōl) *n.* A small vein; veinlet, as of an insect. [<L *venula,* dim. of *vena* vein] —**ven′u·lar** (-yə·lər) *adj.*

ven·u·lose (ven′yə·lōs) *adj.* Having numerous veinlets, as a leaf. Also **ven′u·lous** (-ləs). [<VENULE]

ve·nus (vē′nəs) *n.* A bivalve having three hinge teeth in each valve, as the quahaug. [<VENUS; from the resemblance of the lunula of the closed valve to the vulva]

Ve·nus (vē′nəs) **1** In Roman mythology, the goddess of spring, bloom, and beauty: identified with the Greek *Aphrodite.* **2** A statue or painting of Venus. **3** A lovely woman. **4** *Astron.* The second planet from the sun, the most brilliant object in the heavens except the sun and the moon. It moves in an orbit between those of Mercury and Earth at a mean distance from the sun of about 67,000,000 miles, completing a revolution in 224.7 days. Its diameter is about 7,700 miles and it has no satellites. **5** *Obs.* In alchemy, the metal copper. [<L]

Ve·nus·berg (vē′nəs·bûrg, *Ger.* vā′nōōs·berkh) In medieval German legend, a mountain in the dark recesses of which Venus lured men to sensuous pleasures. See TANNHÄUSER.

Venus flytrap A plant (*Dionaea muscipula*), with clustered leaves the blades of which instantly close upon insects or other objects lighting upon them: found native chiefly in the sandy bogs of eastern North and South Carolina. Also **Ve·nus's–fly·trap** (vē′nəs·iz·flī′trap′).

VENUS FLYTRAP (From 4 to 14 inches tall)

Venus of Mi·lo (mē′lō) A marble statue of Venus, nude above the thighs and with the arms missing, discovered in 1820 on the island of Milo: now in the Louvre. Also **Venus de Milo.**

Ve·nus's–comb (vē′nəs·iz·kōm′) *n.* A European plant (*Scandix pecten-veneris*) with white flowers in numerous umbels, and lobed leaves suggestive of a comb: often called *shepherd's-needle, devil's-darning-needle.*

Ve·nus's–gir·dle (vē′nəs·iz·gûr′dəl) *n.* A ctenophore of warm seas, having a transparent body that shimmers with blue, green, or violet colors.

Ve·nus's–hair (vē′nəs·iz·hâr′) *n.* A maidenhair fern (*Adiantum capillus-veneris*) having a black stipe and branches.

ver·a (ver′ə, var′ə) *adj.* & *adv. Scot.* Very.

Ve·ra (vir′ə) A feminine personal name. [<Slavic, faith]

ve·ra·cious (və·rā′shəs) *adj.* **1** Habitually disposed to speak the truth; truthful. **2** Conforming to or expressing truth; true; accurate. [<L *verax, veracis* <*verus* true] —**ve·ra′·cious·ly** *adv.* —**ve·ra′cious·ness** *n.*

ve·rac·i·ty (və·ras′ə·tē) *n. pl.* **·ties** **1** The habitual regard for truth; truthfulness; honesty. **2** Agreement with truth; accuracy, or fact; trueness. **3** That which is true; truth. [<F *véracité* <L *verax.* See VERACIOUS.]

Synonyms: candor, fact, frankness, honesty, ingenuousness, reality, truth, truthfulness, verity. *Truth* is primarily and *verity* is always a quality of thought or speech, especially of speech, as in exact conformity to *fact.* *Veracity* is properly a quality of a person, the habit of speaking and the disposition to speak the *truth. Truthfulness* is a quality that may inhere either in a person or in his statements or beliefs. *Candor, frankness, honesty,* and *ingenuousness* are closely allied with *veracity,* and *fact, reality,* and *verity* with *truth,* while *truthfulness* may accord with either. *Truth* in a secondary sense may be applied to intellectual action or moral character, in the former case becoming a close synonym of *veracity*: She knows him to be a man of *truth. Antonyms*: deceit, deception, delusion, duplicity, error, fabrication, fallacy, falsehood, falsity, fiction, guile, imposture, lie, untruth.

Ve·ra·cruz (ver'ə·kro͞oz', *Sp.* bä'rä·kro͞os', -kro͞oth') **1** A coast state in eastern Mexico; 27,752 square miles; capital, Jalapa. **2** Its chief city, a port on the Gulf of Mexico: officially **Veracruz Lla·ve** (yä'vā).

ve·ran·da (və·ran'də) *n.* An open portico, gallery, or balcony, usually roofed, along the outside of a building; a porch or stoop. Compare LOGGIA. Also **ve·ran'dah.** [<Hind. *varandā* <Pg. *varanda* railing, balustrade, prob. < *vara* rod, pole <L *vara* forked pole]

ve·ra·no (və·rä'nō) *n.* The dry midwinter season in tropical America. [<Sp., lit., summer]

ve·rat·ric acid (və·rat'rik) *Chem.* A colorless crystalline acid, $C_9H_{10}O_4$, contained in sabadilla seeds and also made synthetically. [<L *veratrum* hellebore]

ve·rat·ri·dine (və·rat'rə·dēn, -din) *n. Chem.* A yellowish, amorphous alkaloid, $C_{36}H_{51}O_{11}N$, contained in sabadilla seeds. Also **ve·rat'ri·din** (-din). [<L *veratrum* hellebore + -ID(E) + -INE[2]]

ver·a·trine (ver'ə·trēn, -trin) *n. Chem.* A white or grayish-white, amorphous (rarely crystalline), extremely poisonous mixture of alkaloids, contained in sabadilla seeds: used in medicine as an analgesic in neuralgia and rheumatism. Also **ve·ra·tri·a** (və·rā'trē·ə), **ver'a·trin** (-trin), **ver'a·tri'na** (-trī'nə). [<L *veratrum* hellebore + INE[2]]

ver·a·trize (ver'ə·trīz) *v.t.* **·trized, ·triz·ing** To treat with veratrine so as to produce its toxic effects.

ve·ra·trum (və·rā'trəm) *n.* Hellebore (def. 2). [<L]

verb (vûrb) *n. Gram.* **1** One of a class of words which assert, declare, or predicate something; that part of speech which expresses existence, action, or occurrence, as the English words *be, collide, think.* **2** Any word or construction functioning similarly. [<F *verbe* <L *verbum* word. Akin to WORD.]

ver·bal (vûr'bəl) *adj.* **1** Of, pertaining to, or connected with words; concerned with words rather than the ideas they convey: *verbal* distinctions. **2** Uttered by the mouth; expressed in words orally; not written: a *verbal* communication; a *verbal* contract or agreement. **3** Having word corresponding with word; literal: a *verbal* translation. **4** *Gram.* **a** Partaking of the nature of or derived from a verb: a *verbal* noun. **b** Used to form verbs: a *verbal* prefix. —*n. Gram.* A noun directly derived from a verb, in English often having the form of the present participle, and signifying the act or process of what is expressed in the verb root; as, there shall be *weeping* and *wailing* and *gnashing* of teeth; also, an infinitive used as a noun; as, *to err* is human: also **verbal noun.** Compare GERUND. [<F <LL *verbalis* <L *verbum* word] —**ver'bal·ly** *adv.*

Synonyms (adj.): literal, oral, vocal. These words, whose etymology would make them similar in meaning, are differentiated in usage by their applications. *Oral* (L *os* the mouth) signifies uttered through the mouth or (in common phrase) by word of mouth; *vocal* (L *vox* the voice) signifies of or pertaining to the voice, uttered or modulated by the voice, and especially uttered with or sounding with full, resonant voice; *literal* (L *litera* a letter) signifies consisting of or expressed by letters, or according to the letter in the broader sense of the exact meaning or requirement of the words used; what is called "the letter of the law" is its *literal* meaning without going behind what is expressed by the letters on the page. Thus *oral* applies to that which is given by spoken words in distinction from that which is written or printed; as, *oral* tradition; an *oral* examination. By this rule we should in strictness speak of an *oral* contract or an *oral* message, but *verbal* contract and *verbal* message, as indicating that which is spoken rather than by written word, have become fixed in the language. A *verbal* translation may be *oral* or written, so that it is word for word; a *literal* translation follows the construction and idiom of the original as well as the words; thus a *literal* translation is more than one that is merely *verbal*; both *verbal* and *literal* are opposed to *free.* In the same sense, of attending to words only, we speak of *verbal* criticism, a *verbal* change. *Vocal* has primary reference to the human voice; as, *vocal* sounds, *vocal* music; *vocal* may be applied within certain limits to inarticulate sounds given forth by other animals than man; as, The woods were *vocal* with the songs of birds; *oral* is never so applied.

ver·bal·ism (vûr'bəl·iz'əm) *n.* A verbal remark or expression; sometimes, a meaningless form of words; wordiness.

ver·bal·ist (vûr'bəl·ist) *n.* One who deals with words or is skilled in the use and meanings of words; a critic of words.

ver·bal·ize (vûr'bəl·īz) *v.* **·ized ·iz·ing** *v.t.* **1** *Gram.* To make a verb of; change into a verb. **2** To express in words. —*v.i.* **3** To speak or write verbosely. —**ver'bal·i·za'tion** *n.* —**ver'bal·iz'er** *n.*

ver·ba·tim (vər·bā'tim) *adv.* In the exact words; word for word. [<LL <L *verbum* word]

ver·ba·tim et lit·e·ra·tim (vər·bā'tim et lit'ə·rā'tim) *Latin* Word for word and letter for letter.

ver·be·na (vər·bē'nə) *n.* Any of a genus *(Verbena)* of American garden plants having dense terminal spikes of showy, often fragrant flowers. [<L, foliage, vervain. Doublet of VERVAIN.]

ver·be·na·ceous (vûr'bə·nā'shəs) *adj.* Belonging to a family *(Verbenaceae)* of herbs, shrubs, and trees, the verbena family, having opposite or whorled leaves and more or less two-lipped or irregular corollas. [<NL, family name <L *verbena* vervain]

ver·bi·age (vûr'bē·ij) *n.* Use of many words without necessity; wordiness; verbosity. See synonyms under CIRCUMLOCUTION, DICTION. [<F < *verbier* gabble < *verbe.* See VERB.]

verb·i·fy (vûr'bə·fī) *v.t.* **·fied, ·fy·ing** To form into or use as a verb.

ver·big·er·ate (vər·bij'ə·rāt) *v.i.* **·at·ed, ·at·ing** *Psychiatry* To repeat meaningless words, phrases, or sentences over and over, as in certain forms of schizophrenia. [<L *verbigerare* chatter, babble < *verbum* word + *gerere* carry on, conduct] —**ver·big'er·a'tion** *n.*

ver·bose (vər·bōs') *adj.* Using or containing a wearisome and unnecessary number of words; wordy. See synonyms under GARRULOUS. [<L *verbosus* < *verbum* word] —**ver·bose'ly** *adv.* —**ver·bose'ness** *n.*

ver·bos·i·ty (vər·bos'ə·tē) *n. pl.* **·ties** The state or quality of being verbose; wordiness.

ver·bo·ten (fər·bōt'n) *adj. German* Forbidden; authoritatively prohibited.

ver·bum sat sa·pi·en·ti (vûr'bəm sat sā'pē·en'tī) *Latin* A word to the wise is sufficient: abbr. *verbum sap.*

Ver·cin·get·o·rix (vûr'sin·jet'ər·iks) Gallic chieftain, leader of rebellion against Julius Caesar, who put him to death in 45 B.C.

Ver·dan·di (vər·dän'dē) One of the Norns.

ver·dant (vûr'dənt) *adj.* **1** Green with vegetation; covered with grass or green leaves; fresh. **2** Immature in experience; unsophisticated. See synonyms under FRESH, RUSTIC. [<F *verdoyant,* ppr. of *verdoyer* grow green, ult. <L *viridis* green] —**ver'dan·cy** *n.* —**ver'dant·ly** *adv.*

verd antique (vûrd) **1** A variety of serpentine. **2** Dark-green andesite porphyry containing crystals of feldspar: also **Oriental verd antique. 3** A green coating that forms on ancient bronzes. [<OF *verd antique* ancient green]

Verde (vûrd), **Cape** The westernmost point of Africa, in Senegal, a peninsula about 20 miles long, up to 7 miles wide: also *Cape Vert.*

ver·der·er (vûr'dər·ər) *n.* An officer in charge of the royal forests in early England. Also **ver'der·or.** [<AF *verder,* OF *verdier* <Med. L *viridarius* <L *viridis* green]

Ver·di (ver'dē), **Giuseppe,** 1813–1901, Italian composer.

ver·dict (vûr'dikt) *n.* **1** The decision of a jury in an action. **2** A conclusion expressed; an opinion. [<AF *verdit,* OF *voirdit* <L *vere dictum* truly said < *verus* true + *dictum,* pp. of *dicere* say; later refashioned after L]

ver·di·gris (vûr'də·grēs, -gris) *n.* **1** *Chem.* A green basic acetate of copper obtained by treating copper with acetic acid: used as a pigment, for dyeing and calico printing, in medicine, and in the preparation of other copper pigments. **2** The green or bluish patina formed on copper, bronze, or brass surfaces after long exposure to the air. [<OF *verd de Grice, vert de Grece,* lit., green of Greece]

ver·din (vûr'din) *n.* A small, brightly-colored titmouse *(Auriparus flaviceps)* with a yellow head, of the southwestern United States and northern Mexico. [<F, yellowhammer]

ver·di·ter (vûr'də·tər) *n.* **1** A pigment made by grinding a basic copper carbonate; bice: azurite yields **blue verditer,** malachite yields **green verditer. 2** Verdigris. [<OF *verd de terre,* lit., green of earth]

Ver·dun (vâr·dun', *Fr.* ver·dœṅ') A town on the Meuse in NE France; scene of heroic French resistance to German attack during several battles of World War I, 1916. Also **Verdun-sur-Meuse** (-sür·mœz').

ver·dure (vûr'jər) *n.* **1** The fresh greenness of growing vegetation, or such vegetation itself. **2** A tapestry representing trees and other vegetation. [<F < *verd* green <L *viridis*] —**ver'dure·less** *adj.*

ver·dur·ous (vûr'jər·əs) *adj.* Covered with verdure; verdant. —**ver'dur·ous·ness** *n.*

ver·e·cund (ver'ə·kund) *adj. Rare* Modest; bashful; coy; shy. [<L *verecundus*]

Ve·ree·ni·ging (fə·rē'nə·khing) A city in the southern Transvaal, Republic of South Africa, on the Vaal: site of the signing of the treaty concluding the Boer War, 1902.

Ver·ein (fer·īn') *n. German* A society; association: often compounded, as in *Turnverein.*

Ve·re·shcha·gin (vyi·ryish·chä'gin), **Vasili Vasilevich,** 1842–1904, Russian genre painter.

verge[1] (vûrj) *n.* **1** The extreme edge of something having defined limits; brink; margin. **2** A bounding or enclosing line; a circlet; ring; also, the space enclosed. **3** A stick or rod, or something having this shape; a wand or staff as a symbol of authority or emblem of office. **4** *Obs.* In England, a stick or wand which tenants held in the hand while swearing fealty to their lord. **5** The spindle of a balance wheel, especially in an old-fashioned vertical escapement. **6** *Archit.* **a** A column shaft. **b** The projecting edge of the tiling on a gable. **7** In old English law, the area over which the authority of an official extended. See synonyms under BOUNDARY, MARGIN. —*v.i.* **verged, verg·ing 1** To be contiguous or adjacent. **2** To form the limit or verge. [<F, rod, stick <L *virga* twig]

verge[2] (vûrj) *v.i.* **verged, verg·ing 1** To come near; approach; border: often with *on*: His speech *verges* on the chaotic. **2** To tend; slope; incline. [<L *vergere* bend, turn]

verg·er (vûr'jər) *n.* **1** An official who carries a verge before a scholastic, legal, or ecclesiastical dignitary; specifically, in English cathedrals and collegiate churches, one who carries the mace before the dean or canons. **2** *Brit.* One in charge of the interior of a cathedral or church; usher. **3** *Obs.* A master of ceremonies. [<F < *verge* rod]

Ver·gil (vûr'jil) Anglicized name of *Publius Vergilius Maro,* 70–19 B.C., Roman epic poet. Also spelled *Virgil.*

Ver·gil·i·an (vər·jil'ē·ən) *adj.* Pertaining to or in the style of Vergil: also spelled *Virgilian.*

ver·glas (vər·gläs') *n. French* A thin, slippery coating of ice on rock: a mountaineering term.

ve·rid·i·cal (və·rid'i·kəl) *adj.* Telling or expressing the truth; truthful; accurate. Also **ve·rid'ic.** [<L *veridicus* speaking the truth < *verus* true + *dicere* say] —**ve·rid'i·cal'i·ty** (-kal'ə·tē) *n.* —**ve·rid'i·cal·ly** *adv.*

ver·i·fi·ca·tion (ver'ə·fə·kā'shən) *n.* **1** The act of verifying, or the state of being verified. **2** *Law* An oath appended to an account, petition, or plea, as to the truth of the facts stated in it; also, at common law, the formal statement at the end of a plea, "and this he is ready to verify."

ver·i·fi·ca·tive (ver'ə·fə·kā'tiv) *adj.* Aiding or resulting in verification.

ver·i·fy (ver′ə·fī) *v.t.* **·fied, ·fy·ing 1** To prove to be true or accurate; substantiate; confirm. **2** To test or ascertain the accuracy or truth of. **3** *Law* **a** To affirm under oath. **b** To add a confirmation to. [<OF *verifier* <Med. L *verificare* make true <*verus* true + *facere* make] —**ver′i·fi′a·ble** *adj.* —**ver′i·fi′er** *n.*

ver·i·ly (ver′ə·lē) *adv.* **1** In truth; assuredly; certainly. **2** Sincerely and truly; really; confidently. [<VERY]

ver·i·sim·i·lar (ver′ə·sim′ə·lər) *adj.* Appearing or seeming to be true; likely; probable. [<L *verisimilis* <*verus* true + *similis* like] —**ver′i·sim′i·lar·ly** *adv.*

ver·i·si·mil·i·tude (ver′ə·si·mil′ə·to͞od, -tyo͞od) *n.* **1** Appearance of truth; likelihood. **2** That which resembles truth. See synonyms under PROBABILITY. [<L *verisimilitudo* < *verisimilis.* See VERISIMILAR.]

ver·ism (ver′iz·əm) *n.* A style in art and literature that follows the theory that reality should be rigidly represented, even when it is ugly or vulgar. [<L *verus* true] —**ver′ist** *n.* & *adj.* —**ve·ris·tic** (və·ris′tik) *adj.*

ver·i·ta·ble (ver′ə·tə·bəl) *adj.* Conforming to truth or fact; genuine; true; real. See synonyms under AUTHENTIC. [<F <*vérité.* See VERITY.] —**ver′i·ta·ble·ness** *n.* —**ver′i·ta·bly** *adv.*

ver·i·tas (ver′ə·tas) *n. Latin* Truth.

ver·i·ty (ver′ə·tē) *n. pl.* **·ties 1** The quality of being correct or true as a statement or representation of reality. **2** A true statement; a fact; truth. See synonyms under VERACITY. [<F *vérité* <L *veritas* truth <*verus* true]

ver·juice (vûr′jo͞os) *n.* **1** The sour juice of green fruit, as of unripe grapes. **2** Sharpness or sourness of disposition or manner; acidity. [<OF *verjus* <*vert* green + *jus* juice]

Ver·kho·yansk Range (vir·khō·yänsk′) A mountain system in northern Yakut Autonomous S.S.R. north of the Arctic Circle; highest point, 8,000 feet.

Ver·laine (ver·len′), **Paul,** 1844–96, French poet.

Ver·meer (vər·mâr′), **Jan,** 1632–75, Dutch painter.

ver·meil (vûr′mil) *n.* **1** Silver or bronze gilt. **2** A transparent water varnish. **3** An orange-red garnet. **4** *Poetic* Vermilion, or the color of vermilion. —*adj.* Of a bright-red color. [<OF <L *vermiculus,* dim. of *vermis* worm, the cochineal insect]

vermi– *combining form* A worm; of or related to a worm, or to worms: *vermiform.* [<L *vermis* a worm]

ver·mi·cel·li (vûr′mə·sel′ē, *Ital.* ver′mē·chel′lē) *n.* A food paste made into slender wormlike cords thinner than spaghetti or macaroni. [< Ital., lit., little worms, pl. of *vermicello* <L *vermiculus.* See VERMEIL.]

ver·mi·ci·dal (vûr′mə·sīd′l) *adj.* Destructive of intestinal worms; anthelmintic.

ver·mi·cide (vûr′mə·sīd) *n.* Any substance that kills worms; specifically, any medicine or drug destructive of intestinal worms. [<VERMI- + -CIDE]

ver·mic·u·lar (vər·mik′yə·lər) *adj.* **1** Pertaining to a worm; having the form or motion of a worm. **2** Like the tracks of a worm. [<L *vermicularis* <*vermiculus,* dim. of *vermis* worm] —**ver·mic′u·lar·ly** *adv.*

vermicular work 1 A form of rusticated masonry simulating worm tracks. **2** Ornamental work consisting of winding tracks in mosaic work. Also **vermiculated work.**

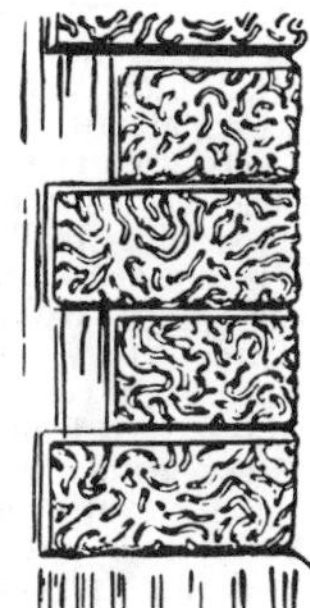
VERMICULAR WORK

ver·mic·u·late (vər·mik′yə·lāt) *v.t.* **·lat·ed, ·lat·ing 1** To adorn with tracery simulating the tracks of worms. **2** To make worm-eaten; infest with worms. —*adj.* **1** Wormlike or covered with wormlike markings. **2** Having the motions of a worm; insinuating; wavy. **3** Worm-eaten. [<L *vermiculatus,* pp. of *vermiculari* be worm-eaten <*vermiculus,* dim. of *vermis* a worm]

ver·mic·u·la·tion (vər·mik′yə·lā′shən) *n.* **1** Wormlike motion, as of the intestines. **2** Vermicular ornamentation. **3** The state of being wormy. **4** A track left by worms. **5** A fine wavy color marking, as on a bird.

ver·mic·u·lite (vər·mik′yə·līt) *n.* A laminated hydrous silicate, derived chiefly as an alteration product of biotite, phlogopite, and other micaceous minerals. [<L *vermiculus,* dim. of *vermis* worm + -ITE[1]]

ver·mic·u·lose (vər·mik′yə·lōs) *adj.* **1** Worm-eaten; wormy. **2** Worm-shaped; wormlike. Also **ver·mic′u·lous** (-ləs). [<LL *vermiculosus* <L *vermiculus,* dim. of *vermis*]

ver·mi·form (vûr′mə·fôrm) *adj.* Like a worm in shape. [<Med. L *vermiformis* <L *vermis* a worm + *forma* a form]

vermiform appendix *Anat.* A slender, wormlike diverticulum, 3 to 6 inches long, protruding from the end of the cecum in man and certain other mammals.

vermiform process *Anat.* **1** Either surface of the median lobe of the cerebellum. **2** The vermiform appendix.

ver·mi·fuge (vûr′mə·fyo͞oj) *n.* Any remedy that destroys intestinal worms. —*adj.* Anthelmintic. [<F <L *vermis* a worm + *fugare* expel]

ver·mil·ion (vər·mil′yən) *n.* **1** A brilliant, durable red pigment consisting of mercuric sulfide, obtained native by grinding the mineral cinnabar to a fine powder, or artificially, as by treating a mixture of mercury and sulfur with potassium hydroxide. **2** The color of the pigment, an intense orange red. —*adj.* Of a bright-red color. —*v.t.* To color with vermilion; dye bright red. [<OF *vermeilon, vermillon* <*vermeil* VERMEIL]

ver·min (vûr′min) *n. pl.* **·min 1** Noxious small animals or parasitic insects, as lice, fleas, worms, rats, mice, etc. **2** *Brit.* Certain animals injurious to game, as weasels, owls, etc. **3** A repulsive or noxious human being, or such persons collectively. [<OF <L *vermis* a worm]

ver·mi·nate (vûr′mə·nāt) *v.i.* **·nat·ed, ·nat·ing** To produce or breed vermin, especially parasitic vermin. —**ver′mi·na′tion** *n.*

ver·mi·nous (vûr′mə·nəs) *adj.* **1** Infested with vermin. **2** Affected with intestinal worms, or caused, as a disease, by vermin. **3** Of the nature of vermin.

Ver·mont (vər·mont′) A State in NE United States; 9,609 square miles; capital, Montpelier; entered the Union March 4, 1791; nickname, *Green Mountain State*: abbr. VT —**Ver·mont′er** *n.*

ver·mou·lu (ver·mo͞o·lü′) *adj. French* Worm-eaten.

ver·mouth (vûr′mo͞oth, vər·mo͞oth′) *n.* A liqueur made from white wine flavored with aromatic herbs. Also **ver′muth.** [<F *vermout* < G *wermuth* wormwood]

ver·nac·u·lar (vər·nak′yə·lər) *n.* **1** The native language of a locality. **2** The common daily speech of the people, as opposed to the literary language. **3** The vocabulary or jargon of a particular profession or trade: to speak the medical *vernacular.* **4** An idiomatic word or phrase. **5** The common name of a plant or animal as distinguished from its scientific designation. See synonyms under LANGUAGE. —*adj.* **1** Originating in or belonging to one's native land; indigenous: said of a language, idiom, etc. **2** Using the colloquial native tongue, rather than the literary language: *vernacular* poets. **3** Written in the language indigenous to a country or people: a *vernacular* translation of the Bible. **4** Characteristic of a specific locality or country; local: *vernacular* arts. **5** *Rare* Peculiar to a particular region; endemic: a *vernacular* disease. **6** Designating the common name of a plant or animal. [<L *vernaculus* domestic, native <*verna* a home-born slave, a native] —**ver·nac′u·lar·ly** *adv.*

ver·nac·u·lar·ism (vər·nak′yə·lə·riz′əm) *n.* **1** A vernacular term or idiom. **2** The use of the vernacular as opposed to classic or literary language.

ver·nal (vûr′nəl) *adj.* **1** Belonging to, appearing in, or appropriate to spring. **2** Pertaining to youth; having a springlike freshness. [<L *vernalis* <*vernus* belonging to spring <*ver* spring] —**ver′nal·ly** *adv.*

vernal equinox See under EQUINOX.

ver·nal·ize (vûr′nəl·īz) *v.t.* **·ized, ·iz·ing** To accelerate the growth of (a plant) by subjecting the seeds to artificial treatment, as by moistening at a low temperature. —**ver′nal·i·za′tion** *n.*

vernal point The vernal equinox. See under EQUINOX.

ver·na·tion (vər·nā′shən) *n. Bot.* The disposition of leaves within the leaf bud, as regards their folding, coiling, etc. [<NL *vernatio, -onis* <*vernare* flourish <*ver* spring]

Verne (vûrn, *Fr.* vern), **Jules,** 1828–1905, French writer of science fiction.

Ver·ner (vûr′nər), **Karl Adolph,** 1846–96, Danish philologist.

Verner's Law A law regarding certain consonant changes in Germanic languages, set forth by Karl Verner in 1876, stating that certain exceptions to Grimm's Law are due to a still wider law, namely, the position of the primary accent in the parent language. It shows that original Indo-European voiceless plosives *p, t, k,* which, according to Grimm's Law became in Germanic the voiceless fricatives *f, th* (as in *thin*), *h,* became, instead, except in specific combinations, the corresponding voiced fricatives and, ultimately, the voiced plosives, *b, d, g,* if the original Indo-European tonic stress was not on the immediately preceding syllable. This statement can be illustrated in English by the distinction in final consonant between *death* and *dead.* The same process operated for the Indo-European *s,* which became *z,* and finally *r,* as can be seen in English *was* and *were, raise* and *rear.*

ver·ni·cose (vûr′nə·kōs) *adj. Bot.* Appearing as if varnished, as some leaves. [<NL *vernicosus* <Med. L *vernicium* VARNISH]

ver·ni·er (vûr′nē·ər) *n.* **1** The small, movable, auxiliary scale for obtaining fractional parts of the subdivisions of a fixed scale on a theodolite, barometer, sextant, gage, or other measuring instrument. **2** *Mech.* An auxiliary device to insure fine adjustments in precision instruments. [after Pierre *Vernier*]

Ver·nier (ver·nyā′), **Pierre,** 1580?–1637, French mathematician.

ver·nis·sage (ver′nē·säzh′) *n.* The opening day of an exhibition of oil paintings to which critics are often invited: also called *varnishing day.* [<F <*vernir* varnish; because the painters varnish their works on this day]

Ver·no·le·ninsk (vyer′nə·lyā′nyinsk) A former name for NIKOLAEV.

Ver·non (vûr′nən), **Edward,** 1684–1757, English admiral.

Ver·nyi (vyer′nē) A former name for ALMA-ATA.

Ve·ro·na (və·rō′nə, *Ital.* vā·rō′nä) A city in Veneto, NE Italy. —**Ver·o·nese** (ver′ə·nēz′, -nēs′) *adj.* & *n.*

Ver·o·nal (ver′ə·nəl) *n.* Proprietary name for a brand of barbital.

Ve·ro·ne·se (vā′rō·nā′zā), **Paolo,** 1528–88, Venetian painter; real name *Cagliari.*

ve·ron·i·ca[1] (və·ron′i·kə) *n.* The speedwell. [< Med. L, appar. after St. *Veronica*]

ve·ron·i·ca[2] (və·ron′i·kə) *n.* A cloth said to have been miraculously impressed with the face of Christ on his way to Calvary, handed to him by a woman named Veronica to wipe the perspiration from his face; also, the representation of the face on this handkerchief; hence, a cloth or handkerchief having on it a representation of Christ's face. See SUDARIUM. [<Med. L <LL *veraiconica,* prob. <L *verus* true + Gk. *eikōn* an image, likeness]

ve·ron·i·ca[3] (və·ron′i·kə, *Sp.* bā·rō′nē·kä) *n.* In bullfighting, a maneuver in which the torero faces the bull and holds the cape directly in front of himself. [<Sp.]

Ve·ron·i·ca (və·ron′i·kə, *Ital.* vā′rō·nē′kä) A feminine personal name. Also *Fr.* **Vé·ro·nique** (vā·rō·nēk′). [See VERONICA[2]]

—**Veronica, Saint** A legendary follower of Christ, upon whose handkerchief a picture of Christ's features is said to have appeared.

Ver·ra·za·no (ver′rä·tsä′nō), **Giovanni da,** 1480?–1528?, Italian navigator.

Ver·roc·chio (ver·rôk′kyō), **Andrea del,** 1435–88, Florentine sculptor and painter.

ver·ru·ca (ve·ro͞o′kə) *n. pl.* **·cae** (-sē) **1** *Med.*

A wart. 2 *Biol.* A wart or wartlike elevation on animals or plants. [<L, a wart, orig. a steep place]

ver·ru·ca·no (ver′ə·kä′nō) *n.* A hard conglomerate of quartz cemented by various siliceous materials, usually colored. [<Ital., from Mount *Verruca* near Pisa]

ver·ru·cose (ver′ə·kōs) *adj.* Abounding in wartlike elevations; warty. Also **ver′ru·cous** (-kəs). [<L *verrucosus* < *verruca* a wart] — **ver′ru·cos′i·ty** (-kos′ə·tē) *n.*

Ver·sailles (vər·sī′, -sālz′; *Fr.* ver·sä′y′) A city of north central France, 11 miles SW of Paris; site of the palace of Louis XIV; scene of the signing of a treaty (1919) between the Allies and Germany after World War I.

ver·sant (vûr′sənt) *n. Geog.* 1 An entire area having a general slope in one direction. 2 The general aspect or slope of any portion of country; inclination. [<F, ppr. of *verser* overturn, pour <L *versare,* freq. of *vertere* turn]

ver·sa·tile (vûr′sə·til) *adj.* 1 Having an aptitude for new tasks or occupations; many-sided. 2 Subject to change; inconstant; variable. 3 Freely swinging or turning: said of an anther part so slightly attached to its support that it readily swings to and fro. 4 Capable of being turned forward or backward, as the toe of a bird; movable in every direction, as insect antennae. [<F <L *versatilis* < *versare,* freq. of *vertere* turn] — **ver′sa·tile·ly** *adv.* — **ver′sa·til′i·ty, ver′sa·tile·ness** *n.*

vers de so·cié·té (ver′ də sō·syā·tā′) *French* A form of light verse characterized by grace, elegance, and wit.

verse (vûrs) *n.* 1 A single metrical or rhythmical line made up of a number of feet, arranged according to a specific rule. 2 A group of metrical lines; a stanza. 3 Metrical composition as distinguished from prose; poetry. 4 a Composition in meter; versification. b A specified type of metrical composition; type of meter or metrical structure: iambic *verse.* 5 One of the short divisions of a chapter of the Bible; also, a short division of any composition. 6 The solo part of a song, anthem, or other piece. See synonyms under METER[2], POETRY. — *v.t.* & *v.i.* **versed, vers·ing** *Rare* To versify. [Fusion of OE *fers* and OF *vers,* both <L *versus* a turning, a verse < *vertere* turn]

versed (vûrst) *adj.* 1 Thoroughly acquainted; having ready skill; proficient. 2 Turned about; reversed. [<L *versatus,* pp. of *versari* occupy oneself]

versed sine, ver·sine (vûr′sīn) See under SINE[1]. [<NL *sinus versus* < *sinus* a sine + L *versus,* pp. of *vertere* turn]

verse·mon·ger (vûrs′mung′gər, -mong′-) *n.* A writer of inferior verses; poetaster.

ver·si·cle (vûr′si·kəl) *n.* 1 A little verse. 2 One of a series of lines said or sung alternately by minister and people. [<L *versiculus,* dim. of *versus* VERSE]

ver·si·col·or (vûr′si·kul′ər) *adj.* 1 Showing a variety of colors; variegated. 2 Changing from one color to another in different lights; iridescent. Also *Brit.* **ver′si·col′our.** [<L < *versus,* pp. of *vertere* turn + *color* color]

ver·sic·u·lar (vər·sik′yə·lər) *adj.* Relating to verses, especially Biblical verses; marking the division into verses. [<L *versiculus* VERSICLE]

ver·sie·ra (ver·syā′rä) *n. Math.* The witch of Agnesi. See WITCH OF AGNESI. [<Ital., a ghost, hobgoblin]

ver·si·fy (vûr′sə·fī) *v.* **·fied, ·fy·ing** *v.t.* 1 To change from prose into verse. 2 To narrate or treat in verse. — *v.i.* 3 To write poetry; make verses. [<OF *vercifier, versifier* <L *versificare* < *versus* VERSE + *facere* make] — **ver′si·fi·ca′tion** (-fə·kā′shən) *n.* — **ver′si·fi′er** *n.*

ver·sion (vûr′zhən, -shən) *n.* 1 That which is translated or rendered from one language into another; a translation; a translation of the original Hebrew and Greek of the Old and New Testaments, or any part of them, into some other tongue. 2 A description of something as modified by the relator. 3 *Med.* a The manual turning of a fetus in the womb so as to secure proper delivery. b Displacement of the uterus in which the organ is deflected without bending upon itself. 4 *Obs.* A transformation; conversion. [<MF <Med. L *versio, -onis* a turning <L *vertere* turn] — **ver′·sion·al** *adj.*

vers li·bre (ver lē′br′) *French* Free verse.

ver·so (vûr′sō) *n. pl.* **·sos** 1 A left-hand page of a book, piece of music, or sheet of folded paper: also called *reverso.* Compare RECTO. 2 The reverse of a coin or medal. Compare OBVERSE. [<L *verso (folio)* a turned (leaf), ablative neut. sing. pp. of *vertere* turn]

verst (vûrst) *n.* A Russian measure of distance: about two thirds of a mile, or 1.067 kilometers. [<F *verste* and G *werst* <Russian *versta,* orig. a line]

ver·sus (vûr′səs) *prep.* 1 Against: used in naming or entitling actions in courts: plaintiff *versus* defendant; in contests: Dempsey *versus* Tunney: usually contracted to *v.* or *vs.* 2 Considered as the alternative of: free trade *versus* high tariffs. [<L, toward, turned toward, orig. pp. of *vertere* turn]

vert (vûrt) *n.* 1 In English forest law, anything that grows and bears green leaves within a forest, especially thick coverts; also, the right to cut green or growing wood in a forest. 2 *Her.* The color or tincture green. [<MF *vert, verd* <L *viridis* green]

Vert (ver), **Cape** See VERDE, CAPE.

ver·te·bra (vûr′tə·brə) *n. pl.* **·brae** (-brē) or **·bras** *Anat.* One of the segmented bones of the spinal column. In man and the higher vertebrates, each vertebra, with its semicylindrical central body and attached processes, articulates with those on either side by means of elastic fibrous pads. [<L, a joint, a vertebra < *vertere* turn]

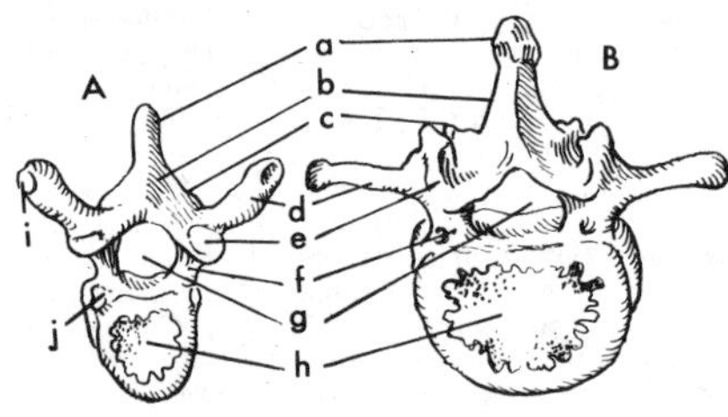

HUMAN VERTEBRAE

A. Sixth thoracic vertebra.

B. Third lumbar vertebra.

a. Spinous process.
b. Lamina.
c. Inferior articular process.
d. Transverse process.
e. Superior articular process.
f. Pedicle.
g. Vertebral foramen.
h. Body.
i. Facet for rib.
j. Demi-facet for rib.

ver·te·bral (vûr′tə·brəl) *adj.* 1 Pertaining to or of the nature of a vertebra. 2 Having, or composed of, vertebrae.

vertebral column The spinal column; the backbone.

ver·te·brate (vûr′tə·brāt, -brit) *adj.* 1 Having a backbone or spinal column. 2 Pertaining to or characteristic of vertebrates. 3 Vertebral. — *n.* Any of a primary division or subphylum *(Vertebrata)* of animals, of the phylum *Chordata,* characterized by a spinal column, as fishes, birds, mammals, and a few primitive forms in which a notochord represents the backbone. [<L *vertebratus* jointed < *vertebra* VERTEBRA]

ver·te·bra·tion (vûr′tə·brā′shən) *n.* 1 The formation of vertebrae. 2 Segmentation like that of the spinal column.

ver·tex (vûr′teks) *n. pl.* **·tex·es** or **·ti·ces** (-tə·sēz) 1 The highest point or summit of anything; apex; top. 2 *Astron.* a The zenith. b The point in the sky toward or from which a group of stars appears to be moving. 3 The top of the head; also, in craniometry, the top of the arch of the skull. 4 *Math.* a The point of intersection of the sides of an angle. b The point opposite to, and farthest from, the base. c The intersection of three or more edges of a polyhedron. [<L, the top < *vertere* turn]

ver·ti·cal (vûr′ti·kəl) *adj.* 1 Of or pertaining to the vertex. 2 Occupying a position directly above or overhead; being at the highest point. 3 Directed perpendicularly to the plane of the horizon; upright; plumb. 4 Of or pertaining to the crown of the head. 5 *Bot.* a Perpendicular to the surface or to the axis of support. b In the direction of the axis of growth; lengthwise. 6 *Econ.* Of or pertaining to a business concern that undertakes a process from raw material to consumer: a *vertical* trust. — *n.* 1 A vertical line, plane, or circle. 2 An upright beam or rod in a truss. [<MF <L *verticalis* < *vertex, -icis* VERTEX] — **ver′ti·cal′i·ty** (-kal′ə·tē), **ver′ti·cal·ness** *n.* — **ver′ti·cal·ly** *adv.*

vertical circle *Astron.* A great circle perpendicular to the plane of the horizon.

ver·ti·ces (vûr′tə·sēz) Plural of VERTEX.

ver·ti·cil (vûr′tə·sil) *n. Biol.* A set of organs, as leaves or tentacles, disposed in a circle around an axis; whorl; a volution of a spiral shell. [<L *verticillus* a whorl, dim. of *vertex, -icis* VERTEX]

ver·ti·cil·las·ter (vûr′tə·si·las′tər) *n. Bot.* An inflorescence or flower cluster with the flowers seemingly in a whorl, but composed of a pair of dense sessile cymes in the axils of opposite leaves, as in most mints. [<NL <L *verticillus* VERTICIL + -ASTER]

ver·tic·il·late (vər·tis′ə·lit, -lāt, vûr′tə·sil′it, -āt) *adj.* 1 Arranged in a verticil or whorl. 2 Having parts so arranged; whorled. Also **ver·tic′il·lat′ed.** [<NL *verticillatus* <L *verticillus* VERTICIL] — **ver·tic′il·late·ly** *adv.*

ver·tic·i·ty (vər·tis′ə·tē) *n.* Tendency to move toward the north, as manifested by a magnetic needle. [<NL *verticitas, -tatis* <L *vertex, -icis* VERTEX]

ver·tig·i·nous (vər·tij′ə·nəs) *adj.* 1 Affected by vertigo; dizzy. 2 Turning round; whirling; revolving. 3 Liable to cause giddiness. [<L *vertiginosus* < *vertigo, -inis* VERTIGO] — **ver·tig′i·nous·ly** *adv.* — **ver·tig′i·nous·ness** *n.*

ver·ti·go (vûr′tə·gō) *n. pl.* **·goes** or **ver·tig·i·nes** (vər·tij′ə·nēz) *Pathol.* Any of a group of disorders, variously caused, in which a person feels as if he or his surroundings are whirling around; dizziness. [<L, lit., a turning around < *vertere* turn]

Ver·tum·nus (vər·tum′nəs) In Roman mythology, the god of the changing seasons and growing plants; husband of Pomona: also *Vortumnus.*

Ver·u·la·mi·um (ver′yo͝o·lā′mē·əm) The ancient Roman name for ST. ALBANS.

Ve·rus (vir′əs), **Lucius Aurelius,** 130–169, Roman emperor 161–169.

ver·vain (vûr′vān) *n.* Any of various plants (genus *Verbena*), congeners of the common cultivated ornamental verbenas, as the American blue vervain *(V. hastata),* or the common European vervain *(V. officinalis).* [<OF *verveine* <L *verbena.* Doublet of VERBENA.]

verve (vûrv) *n.* 1 Enthusiasm or energy, especially as manifested in artistic production; hence, spirit; vigor. 2 *Rare* Special bent or talent. [<F, prob. <L *verba,* pl. of *verbum* a word]

ver·vet (vûr′vit) *n.* A South African monkey (genus *Cercopithecus*), grayish-green speckled with black, and with reddish-white cheeks and belly. [<F < *ver(t)* green (<L *viridis*) + *(gri)vet* a grivet; so called because of its color]

ver·y (ver′ē) *adv.* 1 In a high degree; in large measure; extremely: *very* generous. 2 Exactly: the *very* same thought. ◆ Some grammarians feel that *very* may properly be used before a participle only when the latter precedes the noun it modifies, as in *a very agitated speech*; when the participle is used after some form of the verb *to be,* another adverb is interposed, as in *He was very much* (or *greatly*) *agitated.* However, the construction without the adverb is now widely accepted with participles of emotion or feeling, and is often found, as well, with some participles describing physical condition, as in *They were very disturbed*; *His face is very changed in aspect.* — *adj.* **ver·i·er, ver·i·est** 1 Absolute; actual; simple; utter: said of truth. 2 Suitable; right: the *very* tool we need. 3 Unqualified; utter; complete: a *very* rogue. 4 Selfsame; identical: my *very* words. 5 The (thing) itself: used as an intensive equivalent to *even*: The *very* stones cry out. 6 *Obs.* True: *very* God; also, truthful; veracious. [<AF *verrai,* OF *verai* <L *verus* true]

very high frequency Any wave frequency from 30 to 300 megahertz. Abbr. *vhf, VHF.*

Ver·y light (ver′ē, vir′ē) A brilliant signal flare discharged from a special type of pistol, the **Very pistol.** [after E. W. *Very,* 1847–1910, U. S. naval officer and inventor]

Ve·sa·li·us (vi·sā′lē·əs), **Andreas,** 1514–64, Belgian physician; founder of modern anatomy.

ve·si·ca (vi·sī′kə) *n. pl.* **·cae** (-sē) A bladder. [<L]

ves·i·cal (ves′i·kəl) *adj.* Of, pertaining to, supplying, or affecting the bladder.

ves·i·cant (ves′i·kənt) *adj.* Blister-producing. — *n.* 1 That which produces blisters; a blister. **2** A chemical warfare agent which attacks the skin, as mustard gas or lewisite: also called *blister gas.* [<NL *vesicans, -antis,* ppr. of *vesicare* raise blisters <L *vesica* a blister, bladder]

ve·si·ca pis·cis (vi·sī′kə pis′is, pīsis) The pointed oval aureole used by medieval sculptors and painters to enclose the figure of Christ, the Virgin Mary, or an apostle.

ves·i·cate (ves′i·kāt) *v.* **·cat·ed, ·cat·ing** *v.t.* To raise blisters on. — *v.i.* To become blistered; blister, as the skin. [<NL *vesicatus,* pp. of *vesicare.* See VESICANT.] — **ves′i·ca′tion** *n.*

ves·i·ca·to·ry (ves′i·kə·tôr′ē, və·sik′ə·tôr′ē, -tō′rē) *adj.* Capable of producing blisters; vesicant. — *n. pl.* **·ries** Any substance, as an ointment or plaster, that causes a blister.

ves·i·cle (ves′i·kəl) *n.* **1** Any small bladderlike cavity, cell, or cyst. **2** A small sac, containing gas or fluid. **3** *Pathol.* Any small rounded elevation of the cuticle containing a clear liquid; a blister. **4** *Bot.* A small bladderlike cavity filled with air. **5** *Geol.* A small spherical cavity found commonly in volcanic rocks. [<L *vesicula,* dim. of *vesica* a bladder]

vesico– *combining form Med.* The urinary bladder; of or pertaining to the urinary bladder: *vesicotomy,* a cutting into the bladder. Also, before vowels, **vesic–.** [<L *vesica* a bladder]

ve·sic·u·la (və·sik′yə·lə) *n. pl.* **·lae** (-lē) A little bladder; vesicle. [<L, VESICLE]

ve·sic·u·lar (və·sik′yə·lər) *adj.* **1** Of, pertaining to, composed of, or resembling vesicles. **2** Bearing or containing vesicles or air bladders. [<L *vesicula* VESICLE] — **ve·sic′u·lar·ly** *adv.*

ve·sic·u·late (və·sik′yə·lāt) *v.t.* & *v.i.* **·lat·ed, ·lat·ing** To make or become vesicular or vesiculate. — *adj.* (-lit, -lāt) Full of or having vesicles; also, vesicular. [Back formation < *vesiculated* <NL *vesiculatus* <L *vesicula* VESICLE] — **ve·sic′u·la′tion** *n.*

Vesle (vel) A river in NE France, flowing 90 miles NW from the badlands of Champagne, NE of Châlons-sur-Marne, through Reims to the Aisne east of Soissons.

Ve·son·ti·o (və·son′shē·ō) The ancient name for BESANÇON.

Ve·soul (və·zōōl′) A city in eastern France, capital of Haute-Saône department.

Ves·pa·sian (ves·pā′zhən) Anglicized name of *Titus Flavius Vespasianus,* A.D. 9–79, Roman emperor 69–79.

ves·per (ves′pər) *n.* **1** A bell that calls to vespers: also **vesper bell. 2** An evening service, prayer, or song. **3** *Obs.* Evening. — *adj.* Pertaining to or suitable for evening or vespers. [<L, the evening star]

Ves·per (ves′pər) The evening star; Hesperus; the planet Venus when an evening star. [<L]

ves·per·al (ves′pər·əl) *adj.* Pertaining to evening or the service of vespers. — *n.* **1** A book of the music and office of vespers. **2** A cover for an altar cloth.

ves·pers (ves′pərz) *n. pl. Often cap.* **1** *Eccl.* The sixth in order of the canonical hours. **2** *Eccl.* A service of worship in the late afternoon or evening; specifically, in the Anglican church, Evening Prayer; in the Roman Catholic Church, a public service on Sundays or holy days at which the office of vespers is said or sung. **3** The hour of vespers, usually about sunset. [<OF *vespres* <Med. L *vesperae* <L *vespera* evening]

vesper sparrow An American sparrow (*Pooecetes gramineus*) distinguished by the partial whiteness of its outer tail feathers: so called from its evening song.

ves·per·til·i·o·nine (ves′pər·til′ē·ə·nīn′, -nin) *adj.* Belonging to a family (*Vespertilionidae*) of insectivorous bats. [<L *vespertilio, -onis* a bat + -INE[1]] — **ves′per·til′i·o·nid** *adj.* & *n.*

ves·per·tine (ves′pər·tin, -tīn) *adj.* **1** Pertaining to or occurring in the evening. **2** Flying, opening, etc., in the evening, as a bat, flower, etc. **3** Descending toward the horizon at the sunset hour. Also **ves′per·ti′nal** (-tī′nəl). [<L *vespertinus* < *vesper* VESPER]

ves·pi·ar·y (ves′pē·er′ē) *n. pl.* **·ar·ies** A nest of social wasps or its colony. [<L *vespa* a wasp + (AP)IARY]

ves·pid (ves′pid) *n.* Any of a large family (*Vespidae*) of hymenopterous insects, including social wasps and hornets. — *adj.* Of or pertaining to the *Vespidae.* [<NL <L *vespa* a wasp] — **ves′pi·form** (-pə·fôrm) *adj.*

ves·pine (ves′pīn, -pin) *adj.* Of or pertaining to wasps. [<L *vespa* a wasp + -INE[1]]

Ves·puc·ci (ves·pōōt′chē), **Amerigo,** 1451–1512, Italian navigator for whom America was named.

ves·sel (ves′əl) *n.* **1** A hollow receptacle of any form or material, especially one capable of holding a liquid. **2** A ship or craft designed to float on the water: usually one larger than a rowboat; also, an airship. **3** *Biol.* A duct or canal for containing or transporting a body fluid, as an artery, vein, etc. **4** *Bot.* A water-conducting tube in plants. **5** Figuratively, a person viewed as having capacity or fitness to receive or contain something; one who receives: chiefly in religious use: a *vessel* of mercy or of wrath. [<OF <L *vascellum,* dim. of *vas* a vessel]

vest (vest) *n.* **1** A short sleeveless jacket worn by men and sometimes by women under the coat; waistcoat; originally, a kind of cassock: in England chiefly a trade term. **2** A close jacket formerly worn by women; now, an extra piece of trimming on the front of the body or waist of a woman's dress, usually V-shaped. **3** An undervest or undershirt. **4** Clothing of any kind; vesture; array; dress. **5** *Obs.* An ecclesiastical vestment. — *v.t.* **1** To confer (ownership, authority, etc.) upon some person or persons: usually with *in.* **2** To place ownership, control, or authority with (a person or persons). **3** To clothe or robe, as with vestments. — *v.i.* **4** To clothe oneself, as in vestments. **5** To be or become vested; devolve. [<F *veste* <Ital. <L *vestis* clothing, a garment]

ves·ta (ves′tə) *n.* A friction match of wax; a short wax taper; a wooden match. [after *Vesta*]

Ves·ta (ves′tə) **1** In Roman mythology, the goddess of the hearth and the hearth fire, protectress of the state and custodian of the sacred fire tended by the vestals: identified with the Greek *Hestia.* **2** A minor planet.

ves·tal (ves′təl) *n.* **1** One of the virgin priestesses of Vesta: also **vestal virgin. 2** A woman of pure character; a virgin; nun. — *adj.* **1** Pertaining to Vesta. **2** Suitable for a vestal or a nun; hence; chaste. [<L *vestalis* <*Vesta* Vesta]

vest·ed (ves′tid) *adj.* **1** Having vestments; robed. **2** *Law* Held by a tenure subject to no contingency; complete; established by law as a permanent right: *vested* interests.

vest·ee (ves·tē′) *n.* **1** An imitation blouse-front worn in the front of a suit or dress. **2** A broadcloth garment without sleeves worn with a formal riding habit. [Dim. of VEST]

Ves·ter·å·len (ves′tər·ô′lən) A Norwegian archipelago in the Norwegian Sea north of the Lofoten Islands; total, about 1,200 square miles. Also **Ves′ter·aa′len.**

ves·ti·ar·y (ves′tē·er′ē) *adj.* Pertaining to clothes. — *n. pl.* **·ar·ies** *Obs.* A vestry; robing-room. [<OF *vestiairie* <Med. L *vestiarium.* See VESTRY.]

ves·tib·u·lar (ves·tib′yə·lər) *adj.* Pertaining to or like a vestibule. Also **ves·tib′u·late** (-lit, -lāt).

ves·ti·bule (ves′tə·byōōl) *n.* **1** A small antechamber between the outer door of a building and an interior one; an entrance hall; lobby. **2** An enclosed passage from one railway passenger car to another. **3** Formerly, a walled place before the entrance to a Roman or Greek house; later, a porch. **4** *Anat.* Any one of several chambers or channels adjoining or communicating with others: the *vestibule* of the ear. — *v.t.* **·buled, ·bul·ing 1** To provide with a vestibule or vestibules. **2** To couple (railroad cars) and connect by vestibules. [<L *vestibulum* an entrance hall] — **ves′ti·buled** *adj.*

vestibule train A passenger train with enclosed platforms connected by flexible walls and roof, forming a weatherproof passageway between connected cars, called **vestibule cars.**

ves·tige (ves′tij) *n.* **1** A visible trace, impression, or a sensible evidence or sign, of something absent, lost, or gone; trace; originally, a footprint; track. **2** *Biol.* A part or organ, small or degenerate, but well developed and functional in ancestral forms of organisms. See synonyms under MARK[1], TRACE[1]. [<F <L *vestigium* a footprint]

ves·tig·i·al (ves·tij′ē·əl) *adj.* Of, or of the nature of a vestige; surviving in small or degenerate form. — **ves·tig′i·al·ly** *adv.*

ves·tig·i·um (ves·tij′ē·əm) *n. pl.* **·tig·i·a** (-tij′·ē·ə) A vestigial part; vestige. [<L, a footprint]

vest·ment (vest′mənt) *n.* **1** An article of dress; clothing or covering; particularly, a garment or robe of state or office. **2** *Eccl.* **a** One of the ritual garments of the clergy, especially one worn at the Eucharist. **b** A chasuble. See synonyms under DRESS. [<OF *vestement* <L *vestimentum* clothes < *vestire* clothe] — **vest′ment·al** *adj.*

vest-pock·et (vest′pok′it) *adj.* **1** Small enough to fit in a vest pocket; very small; diminutive: a *vest-pocket* edition. **2** Much smaller than standard or usual size: a *vest-pocket* battleship.

vest-pock·et park A small urban park, often on a vacant lot.

ves·try (ves′trē) *n. pl.* **·tries 1** A room where vestments are put on or kept. **2** A room for altar linens, sacred vessels, etc., attached to a church and often called a *sacristy.* **3** A room in a church used for Sunday school, meetings, as a chapel, etc. **4** In the Anglican church: **a** A body administering the affairs of a parish or congregation; also, a meeting of such a body. **b** In English parishes, a business meeting of all the parishioners or their representatives. **5** A place of meeting for the parish vestry; a vestry hall. [<AF *vestrie,* OF *vestiarie* <Med. L *vestiarium* a wardrobe <L *vestis* a garment]

ves·try·man (ves′trē·mən) *n. pl.* **·men** (-mən) A member of a vestry.

ves·ture (ves′chər) *n.* **1** Something that covers; garments; clothing; a robe. **2** *Law* All that covers land, except trees. **3** A covering or envelope. See synonyms under DRESS. — *v.t.* **·tured, ·tur·ing** To cover or clothe with vesture; vest; robe; envelop: usually in the past participle. [<OF <*vestir* cloth <L *vestire* clothe]

ve·su·vi·an (və·sōō′vē·ən) *n.* **1** Vesuvianite. **2** A kind of match or fusee which burns with a spluttering flame: used for lighting cigars, etc. [from *Vesuvius*]

ve·su·vi·an·ite (və·sōō′vē·ən·īt′) *n.* A vitreous, brown to green, translucent hydrous silicate of calcium and aluminum, with traces of iron and magnesium: also called *idocrase.*

Ve·su·vi·us (və·sōō′vē·əs) The only active volcano on the European mainland, on the Bay of Naples, Italy; 3,891 feet. *Italian* **Ve·su·vio** (vā·zōō′vyō). — **Ve·su′vi·an** *adj.*

vet (vet) *Colloq. n.* A veterinary surgeon. — *v.* **vet·ted, vet·ting** *v.t.* **1** To treat as a veterinarian does. **2** *U.S. Slang* To criticize or emend: to *vet* a manuscript. — *v.i.* **3** To treat animals medically. [Short for VETERINARIAN]

vetch (vech) *n.* **1** Any of a genus (*Vicia*) of climbing herbaceous vines of the bean family, especially the common broadbean, grown for fodder. **2** A leguminous European plant (*Lathyrus sativus*) yielding edible seeds. — **bitter vetch** A species of vetch (*V. ervilia*) of which the seeds contain a bitter, poisonous alkaloid: also called *ers.* [<AF *veche, vecce* <L *vicia*]

vetch·ling (vech′ling) *n.* A plant (genus *Lathyrus*), nearly allied to the vetches; especially, a European species (*L. pratensis*), naturalized in the United States. [Dim. of VETCH]

vet·er·an (vet′ər·ən, vet′rən) *n.* **1** One who is much experienced in any service, especially a soldier or an ex-soldier. **2** A member of the armed forces who has been in active service. — *adj.* **1** Having had long experience or practice; old in service. **2** Belonging to or suggestive of a veteran. **3** Long continued; extending over a long period. [<MF <L *veteranus* < *vetus, veteris* old]

Veterans Administration An agency of the U. S. government which administers all federal laws relating to the relief of former members of the military and naval services.

Veterans Day A U. S. national holiday honoring veterans of the armed forces, held on November 11, the anniversary of the date in 1918 when the Allies granted an armistice to the Central Powers in World War I. Formerly called *Armistice Day.*

Veterans of Foreign Wars A society of ex-servicemen who have served in the United States Army, Navy, or Marine Corps in a war with and in a foreign country: founded 1899.

vet·er·i·nar·i·an (vet′ər·ə·nâr′ē·ən, vet′rə-) *n.* A practitioner of veterinary medicine or surgery. [<L *veterinarius* VETERINARY]

vet·er·i·nar·y (vet′ər·ə·ner′ē, vet′rə-) *adj.* Pertaining to the diseases or injuries of animals, and to their treatment by medical or surgical means. — *n. pl.* **·nar·ies** A veterinarian; a veterinary surgeon. [<L *veterinarius* pertaining to beasts of burden < *veterinus* < *veterina* beasts of burden, ult. < *vehere* carry]

vet·i·ver (vet′ə·vər) *n.* **1** An Asian grass (*Vetiveria zizanioides*) grown in Florida and the SE United States. **2** Its aromatic roots, used for weaving mats, fans, etc., and as a source of **vetiver oil,** an ingredient of perfumes. [<F *vétyver* <Tamil *vettivēru,* lit., a root that is dug up < *vēr* a root]

Vet·lu·ga (vet·lōō′gə) A river in central European Russian S.F.S.R., flowing 500 miles west, north, and south to the Volga.

ve·to (vē′tō) *v.t.* **·toed, ·to·ing 1** To refuse executive approval of (a bill passed by a legislative body). **2** To forbid or prohibit authoritatively; refuse consent to. — *n. pl.* **·toes 1** The prerogative in a chief executive of refusing to approve a legislative enactment by withholding his signature. **2** The act of vetoing; also, the official communication containing a refusal to approve a bill. **3** Any authoritative prohibition. [<L, I forbid] — **ve′to·er** *n.*

veto message A message giving the reasons of the chief executive for refusing his approval of a proposed law.

veto power 1 The right or power possessed by a branch of the government to forbid or refuse approval of projects proposed by another department. **2** A power vested in the chief executive to prevent the enactment of bills passed by the legislature.

Vet·ter (vet′ər), **Lake** A former spelling for VÄTTER, LAKE.

vex (veks) *v.t.* **1** To provoke to anger or displeasure by small irritations; irritate; annoy. **2** To trouble or afflict. **3** To throw into commotion; agitate. **4** To make a subject of dispute: a *vexed* question. See synonyms under PIQUE[1]. [<OF *vexer* <L *vexare* shake]

vex·a·tion (vek·sā′shən) *n.* **1** The act of vexing, or the state of being vexed; irritation. **2** That which vexes; annoyance; affliction; cause of trouble or distress. See synonyms under CHAGRIN, IMPATIENCE.

vex·a·tious (vek·sā′shəs) *adj.* **1** Being a source of vexation. **2** Full of vexation; harassing; annoying. See synonyms under TROUBLESOME, WEARISOME. —**vex·a′tious·ly** *adv.* — **vex·a′tious·ness** *n.*

vexed (vekst) *adj.* **1** Harassed; troubled; irritated; agitated; disturbed. **2** Much debated; contested: a *vexed* question. — **vex·ed·ly** (vek′sid·lē) *adv.* — **vex′ed·ness** *n.*

vex·il (vek′sil) *n.* A vexillum (def. 2). [Short for VEXILLUM]

vex·il·lar·y (vek′sə·ler′ē) *n. pl.* **·lar·ies** A standard-bearer. — *adj.* **1** Of or pertaining to a vexillum: also **vex′il·lar** (-lər). **2** Of or pertaining to a standard or ensign. [<L *vexillarius* a standard-bearer < *vexillum* VEXILLUM]

vex·il·late (vek′sə·lit, -lāt) *adj.* Having a vexillum or vexilla.

vex·il·lol·o·gy (veks′ə·lol′ə·jē) *n.* The study of flags. [<L *vexillum* flag, standard + -LOGY] — **vex′il·lo·log′ic** or **·i·cal** *adj.* — **vex′il·lol′o·gist** *n.*

vex·il·lum (vek·sil′əm) *n. pl.* **vex·il·la** (vek·sil′ə) **1** In Roman antiquity, a square flag, or standard; hence, a company or troop of soldiers serving under a separate standard. **2** *Bot.* The large upper petal of a papilionaceous flower. **3** *Ornithol.* The web of a feather. [<L < *vehere* carry]

vi·a (vī′ə, vē′ə) *prep.* By way of; by a road passing through: He went to Boston *via* New Haven. [<L, ablative sing. of *via* a way]

Vi·a Ap·pi·a (vī′ə ap′ē·ə) The ancient Latin name for the APPIAN WAY.

vi·a·ble (vī′ə·bəl) *adj.* Capable of living and developing normally, as a newborn infant, a seed, etc. [<F < *vie* life <L *vita*] — **vi′a·bil′i·ty** *n.*

Vi·a Dol·o·ro·sa (vī′ə dol′ō·rō′sə) *Latin* The road traveled by Jesus to Golgotha; literally, the sorrowful way.

vi·a·duct (vī′ə·dukt) *n.* A bridgelike structure, especially a large one of arched masonry, to carry a roadway or the like over a valley or ravine. Compare AQUEDUCT. [<L *via* a way + (AQUE)DUCT]

VIADUCT
Roman aqueduct, Nimes, France.

Vi·a Fla·min·i·a (vī′ə flə·min′ē·ə) The Latin name for the FLAMINIAN WAY.

vi·al (vī′əl) *n.* A small bottle for liquids, commonly cylindrical; also, more widely, any bottle: also spelled *phial.* — **to pour out the vials of wrath upon** To inflict retribution or vengeance on. See *Rev.* xvi. — *v.t.* **·aled** or **·alled, ·al·ing** or **·al·ling** To put or keep in or as in a vial. [<OF *viole* <L *phiala* a saucer <Gk. *phialē* a shallow cup]

vi·a me·di·a (vī′ə mē′dē·ə) *Latin* A middle way.

vi·and (vī′ənd) *n.* **1** An article of food, especially meat. **2** *pl.* Victuals; provisions; food. See synonyms under FOOD. [<AF *viaunde,* OF *viande,* ult. <L *vivenda,* neut. pl. gerundive of *vivere* live]

vi·at·ic (vī·at′ik) *adj.* Of or pertaining to a journey or to traveling. Also **vi·at′i·cal.** [<L *viaticus* < *via* a way]

vi·at·i·cum (vī·at′ə·kəm) *n. pl.* **·ca** (-kə) or **·cums 1** *Eccl.* The Eucharist, as given on the verge of death. **2** In ancient Rome, the provision of necessaries for an official journey of a magistrate; later, provisions for any journey. [<L, traveling money, neut. sing. of *viaticus* < *via* a way. Doublet of VOYAGE.]

vi·a·tor (vī·ā′tər) *n. pl.* **vi·a·to·res** (vī′ə·tôr′ēz, -tō′rēz) A traveler; wayfarer. [<L < *via* a way]

vibes (vībz) *n.pl.* (*usu. construed as sing. for def. 2*) *Slang* **1** Vibrations. See VIBRATION (def. 3). **2** A vibraphone.

Vi·borg (vē′bôr·y′) The Swedish name for VYBORG.

vi·brac·u·lum (vī·brak′yə·ləm) *n. pl.* **·la** (-lə) *Zool.* One of the slender, whiplike defensive organs of the cells of many polyzoans. [<NL < L *vibrare* shake] — **vi·brac′u·lar** *adj.* — **vi·brac′u·loid** *adj.*

vi·bran·cy (vī′brən·sē) *n. pl.* **·cies** The state or character of being vibrant; resonance.

vi·brant (vī′brənt) *adj.* **1** Having, showing, or resulting from vibration; vibrating; resonant. **2** Throbbing; pulsing: a nation *vibrant* with enthusiasm. **3** Energetic; vigorous. **4** *Phonet.* Produced with vibration of the vocal cords; voiced. — *n. Phonet.* A speech sound made with vibration of the vocal cords; a voiced sound. [<L *vibrans, -antis,* ppr. of *vibrare* shake] — **vi′brant·ly** *adv.*

vi·bra·phone (vī′brə·fōn) *n.* A type of marimba in which a pulsating sound is produced by motor-driven valves in the resonators. Also **vi′bra-harp′** (-härp′). [<VIBRA(TO) + -PHONE]

vi·brate (vī′brāt) *v.* **·brat·ed, ·brat·ing** *v.i.* **1** To move or swing back and forth, as a pendulum. **2** To move back and forth rapidly; quiver. **3** To sound: The note *vibrates* on the ear. **4** To be emotionally moved; thrill. **5** To vacillate; waver, as between choices. — *v.t.* **6** To cause to move or swing back and forth. **7** To cause to quiver or tremble. **8** To send forth (sound, etc.) by vibration. **9** To measure by each vibration: a pendulum *vibrating* seconds. See synonyms under QUAKE, SHAKE. [<L *vibratus* < *vibrare* shake]

vi·bra·tile (vī′brə·til, -tīl) *adj.* **1** Adapted to, having, or used in vibratory motion. **2** Pertaining to or resembling vibration.

vi·bra·til·i·ty (vī′brə·til′ə·tē) *n.* Capability, or quality, of being vibratile.

vi·bra·tion (vī·brā′shən) *n.* **1** The act of vibrating; oscillation. **2** *Physics* **a** A periodic, usually rapid back-and-forth motion of a particle, as of electrons in an atom, or the parts of an elastic or rigid body suddenly released from tension. **b** Any physical process characterized by cyclic variations in amplitude, intensity, or the like, as wave motion or an electric field. **c** A single complete oscillation. **3** *pl. Slang* One's emotional response to an aura felt to surround a person or thing, especially when considered in or out of harmony with oneself: good *vibrations.* — **vi·bra′tion·al** *adj.*

vi·bra·to (vē·brä′tō) *n. Music* A trembling or pulsating effect, not confined to vocal music, caused by rapid variation of emphasis on the same tone: properly distinguished from *tremolo,* where there is an alternation of tones. [<Ital., pp. of *vibrare* vibrate <L, shake]

vi·bra·tor (vī′brā·tər) *n.* **1** One who or that which vibrates. **2** An electrically operated massaging apparatus. **3** *Electronics* **a** An electromagnetic switch mechanism for converting direct into alternating current by continuously vibrating impulses. **b** An oscillator (def. 3).

vi·bra·to·ry (vī′brə·tôr′ē, -tō′rē) *adj.* Pertaining to, causing, or characterized by vibration. Also **vi′bra·tive** (-tiv).

vib·ri·o (vib′rē·ō) *n.* Any of a genus (*Vibrio*) of motile, rodlike bacteria in which the cells are but slightly sinuous and have one or more flagellae at each end; especially, the Gram-negative **comma vibrio** (*V. comma*), found in the intestines of cholera victims. [<NL <L *vibrare* shake]

vib·ri·oid (vib′rē·oid) *adj.* Resembling a vibrio. — *n.* A vibrioid body. [<VIBRI(O) + -OID]

vi·bris·sa (vī·bris′ə) *n. pl.* **·bris·sae** (-bris′ē) *Biol.* **1** One of the stiff, coarse hairs found in the nostrils of man and about the mouth of many other mammals, as the cat: they often function as tactile organs. **2** One of the vaneless, hairlike rictal feathers of many insectivorous birds, especially flycatchers. [<L *vibrissae* hairs in a man's nostrils < *vibrare* shake]

vi·bro·scope (vī′brə·skōp) *n.* A device for observing and recording vibrations, especially those of harmonic character.

vi·bro·tro·pism (vī′brə·trō′piz·əm) *n. Biol.* The involuntary response of an organism to a vibratory stimulus. [< *vibro-* (<VIBRATE) + -TROPISM] — **vi′bro·trop′ic** (-trop′ik) *adj.*

vi·bur·num (vī·bûr′nəm) *n.* Any of a large and widely distributed genus (*Viburnum*) of shrubs or small trees of the honeysuckle family, bearing small flowers and berrylike fruit; especially, the dockmackie, the sheepberry, and the hobble-bush. [<L, the wayfaring tree]

vic·ar (vik′ər) *n.* **1** In general, one who is authorized to perform functions, especially religious ones, in the stead of another; a substitute in office. **2** Hence, an agent; deputy. **3** *Brit.* The priest of a parish of which the main revenues are appropriated or impropriated by a layman, the priest himself receiving but a stipend; any incumbent of a parish who is not a rector. **4** In the Roman Catholic Church, a substitute or representative of an ecclesiastical person; in a strict sense, one whose jurisdiction is confined to the external forum. **5** In some parishes of the Protestant Episcopal Church, the clergyman who is the head of a chapel; also, a clergyman having charge of a church or mission as the bishop's deputy. [<AF *vikere, vicare,* OF *vicaire* <L *vicarius* a substitute < *vicis* a change]

vic·ar·age (vik′ər·ij) *n.* **1** The benefice, office, or duties of a vicar. **2** A vicar's residence or household.

vicar apostolic In the Roman Catholic Church, formerly, a bishop or archbishop appointed by the pope to act in his stead in a given district; more recently, a titular bishop exercising episcopal jurisdiction where there is no see canonically.

vicar fo·rane (fô·rān′, fō-) In the Roman Catholic Church, a clergyman appointed by a bishop, having a limited jurisdiction over the inferior clergy in the parishes constituting the deanery; a rural dean. [<VICAR + Med. L *foraneus* outside the episcopal city, rural <L *foras* out of doors]

vicar general 1 In the Roman Catholic Church, a functionary appointed by the bishop as assistant or representative in certain matters of jurisdiction, but without power to perform the specific function of the episcopal order. 2 In the Church of England, an official assisting the bishop or archbishop in ecclesiastical causes. 3 In English history, the ecclesiastical vicegerent of the king: a title bestowed on Thomas Cromwell by Henry VIII.

vi·car·i·al (vī·kâr′ē·əl, vi-) *adj.* 1 Vicarious; delegated. 2 Belonging to, relating to, or acting as a vicar.

vi·car·i·ate (vī·kâr′ē·it, -āt, vi-) *n.* A delegated office or power; specifically, the office or authority of a vicar. Also **vic·ar·ate** (vik′ər·it).

vi·car·i·ous (vī·kâr′ē·əs, vi-) *adj.* 1 Made or performed by substitution; suffered or done in place of another; substitutionary: a *vicarious* sacrifice; also, enjoyed or felt by a person as a result of his imagined participation in an experience that is not his own: *vicarious* gratification. 2 Filling the office of or acting for another. 3 Of, pertaining to, or belonging to a vicar or deputy; deputed; delegated. 4 *Med.* Performing, as an organ, the functions of another; substitutive; also, occurring in an abnormal situation: *vicarious* menstruation. [<L *vicarius.* See VICAR.] **— vi·car′i·ous·ly** *adv.* **— vi·car′i·ous·ness** *n.*

vic·ar·ly (vik′ər·lē) *adj.* Resembling or pertaining to a vicar.

vicar of Christ The pope, regarded as Christ's representative on earth.

vic·ar·ship (vik′ər·ship) *n.* The office or position of a vicar.

vice[1] (vīs) *n.* 1 A moral blemish or taint; an immoral habit or trait: the *vice* of intemperance. 2 Habitual indulgence in degrading or harmful appetites; deviation from moral rectitude; depravity. 3 Something that mars; a defect; blemish. 4 A physical deformity, taint, or imperfection. 5 A bad trick, as of a horse. See synonyms under SIN[1]. **— inherent vice** In insurance, a hazard arising from a preexistent condition not manifest when the commodity was insured and therefore not covered by the insurance policy: Eggs of worms were the *inherent vice* that ruined the cargo of hides. ◆ Homophone: *vise.* [<OF <L *vitium* a fault]

vice[2] (vīs) See VISE.

vice[3] (vīs) *adj.* Acting in the place of; substitute; deputy: *vice* president. **—** *n.* One who acts in the place of another; a substitute; deputy.

— vi·ce (vī′sē) *prep.* Instead of; in the place of. [<L, ablative of *vicis* change]

Vice may appear as a combining form in hyphemes or as the first element in two-word phrases:

vice-chair	**vice-ministry**
vice chairman	**vice principal**
vice-chairmanship	**vice-principalship**
vice dean	**vice rector**
vice-government	**vice-rectorship**
vice governor	**vice-reign**
vice-governorship	**vice-wardenship**

vice admiral A commissioned officer in the Navy or Coast Guard who ranks next above a rear admiral and next below an admiral. [<AF *visadmirail,* OF *visamiral* < *vis-* in place (<L *vice*) + *admirail, amiral* an admiral]

vice-ad·mir·al·ty (vīs′ad′mər·əl·tē) *n.* The area under or office of a vice admiral.

vice chancellor 1 *Law* A judge in equity courts subordinate to the chancellor. 2 A deputy chancellor in a university. [<OF *vichancelier* <Med. L *vicecancellarius* <L *vice* in place + LL *cancellarius* a chancellor] **— vice′-chan′cel·lor·ship′** *n.*

vice consul One who exercises consular authority, either as the substitute or as the subordinate of a consul. **— vice-con·su·lar** (vīs′kon′sə·lər) *adj.* **— vice-con·su·late** (vīs′·kon′sə·lit) *n.* **— vice′-con′sul·ship** *n.*

vice·ge·ren·cy (vīs·jir′ən·sē) *n. pl.* **·cies** 1 The office or authority of a vicegerent; the fact of ruling as a vicegerent or deputy. 2 A district ruled by a vicegerent.

vice·ge·rent (vīs·jir′ənt) *n.* One duly authorized to exercise the powers of another; a deputy; vicar. **—** *adj.* Acting in the place of another, usually in the place of a superior. [<Med. L *vicegerens, -entis* <L *vice* in place + *gerens, -entis,* ppr. of *gerere* carry, manage] **— vice·ge′ral** *adj.*

vic·e·nar·y (vis′ə·ner′ē) *adj.* 1 Consisting of or pertaining to twenty. 2 Relating to a system of notation based upon twenty. [<L *vicenarius* < *viceni* twenty each < *viginti* twenty]

vi·cen·ni·al (vī·sen′ē·əl) *adj.* Occurring once in twenty years; also, lasting or existing twenty years. [<L *vicennium* a twenty-year period < *vicies* twenty times + *annus* a year]

Vi·cen·te (*Pg.* vē·seṅ′tə, *Sp.* bē·then′tā) Portuguese and Spanish form of VINCENT.

Vi·cen·za (vē·chen′tsä) 1 A province in Veneto, northern Italy; 1,051 square miles. 2 A city in NE Italy, capital of Vicenza province: ancient **Vi·cen·ti·a** (vi·sen′shē·ə).

vice president An officer ranking next below a president, and acting, on occasion, in his place. The vice president of the United States is elected at the same time and in the same manner as the president, and is designated by the Constitution to be president of the Senate and to succeed the president in case of that officer's death, resignation, removal, or inability. **— vice-pres·i·den·cy** (vīs′prez′ə·dən·sē) *n.* **— vice′-pres′i·den′tial** (-prez′ə·den′shəl) *adj.*

vice·re·gal (vīs·rē′gəl) *adj.* Of or relating to a viceroy, his office, or his jurisdiction. Also **vice·roy′al** (-roi′əl). **— vice·re′gal·ly** *adv.*

vice regent A deputy regent. **— vice′-re′gent** (-rē′jənt) *adj.*

vice·roy (vīs′roi) *n.* 1 One who rules a country, colony, or province by the authority of his sovereign or king. 2 A North American nymphalid butterfly (*Basilarchia archippus*), orange-red with black markings and a row of white marginal spots. The larva feeds on the willow, poplar, and certain other trees. [<MF *viceroy, visroy* < *vice-, vis-* in place (<L *vice*) + *roy* a king, ult. <L *rex, regis*]

vice·roy·al·ty (vīs·roi′əl·tē) *n.* 1 The office or authority of a viceroy. 2 The term of office of a viceroy. 3 A district ruled or governed by a viceroy. Also **vice′roy·ship.**

vice squad A police division charged with combating illegal prostitution, perversion, gambling, and other vices.

vi·ce ver·sa (vī′sē vûr′sə, vīs′) The order being changed; the relation of terms being reversed; conversely. [<L]

Vi·cha·da (bē·chä′thä) A river in eastern Colombia, flowing 400 miles east to the Orinoco at the Venezuela border.

Vi·chy (vē·shē′) A resort city in central France; provisional capital of France during German occupation, World War II.

vi·chy·ssoise (vē′shē·swäz′) *n.* A potato cream soup flavored with leeks, celery, etc., usually served cold with a sprinkling of chives. [<F, of Vichy <*Vichy* Vichy]

Vi·chy water (vish′ē) The effervescent mineral water from the springs at Vichy, France; any mineral water resembling it. Also **Vi′chy, vi′chy.**

vic·i·nage (vis′ə·nij) *n.* 1 Neighboring places collectively; vicinity. 2 The state of being a neighbor or neighbors. See synonyms under NEIGHBORHOOD. [<OF *visenage, vicenage* <L *vicinus* nearby]

vic·i·nal (vis′ə·nəl) *adj.* 1 Neighboring; adjoining; near. 2 *Mineral.* Designating a crystal form closely approximating one of the fundamental forms. 3 *Chem.* Designating a benzene derivative in which the substituted elements or radicals are in consecutive order on the benzene ring. [<L *vicinalis* < *vicinus* a neighbor, orig. nearby]

vicinal planes In crystallography, crystal planes which may approximate or take the place of the fundamental planes.

vicinal road A local road, as distinguished from one between towns.

vic·i·nism (vis′ə·niz′əm) *n. Ecol.* Plant variation resulting from the proximity of other plants.

vi·cin·i·ty (vi·sin′ə·tē) *n. pl.* **·ties** 1 Nearness in space or relationship; proximity. 2 A region adjacent or near; neighborhood; vicinage. See synonyms under NEIGHBORHOOD. [<L *vicinitas, -tatis* < *vicinus* nearby]

vi·cious (vish′əs) *adj.* 1 Addicted to vice; corrupt in conduct or habits; wicked; depraved. 2 Partaking of what is base, low, and vile; morally injurious; evil. 3 Unruly or dangerous; refractory, as an animal. 4 Defective or faulty: *vicious* arguments. 5 Impure or incorrect; corrupted, as a text, manuscript, etc. 6 Noxious; poisonous; foul, as water, air, etc. 7 *Colloq.* Marked by malice or spite; malignant: a *vicious* lie. See synonyms under CRIMINAL, IMMORAL, IRREGULAR, RESTIVE. [<OF <L *vitiosus* < *vitium* a fault] **— vi′cious·ly** *adv.* **— vi′cious·ness** *n.*

vicious circle 1 The process or predicament that arises when the solution of a problem creates a new problem and each successive solution adds another problem. 2 *Logic* Argument in a circle. See under CIRCLE. 3 *Med.* The accelerating effect of one disease upon another when the two are coexistent.

vi·cis·si·tude (vi·sis′ə·to͞od, -tyo͞od) *n.* 1 *pl.* Irregular changes or variations, as of conditions or fortune: the *vicissitudes* of life. 2 A change; especially, a complete change; mutation or mutability. 3 Alternating change or succession, as of the seasons. See synonyms under CHANGE. [<MF <L *vicissitudo* < *vicis* a turn, change]

vi·cis·si·tu·di·nar·y (vi·sis′ə·to͞o′də·ner′ē, -tyo͞o′-) *adj.* Marked by or subject to change or alternation. Also **vi·cis′si·tu′di·nous.**

Vicks·burg (viks′bûrg) A city in western Mississippi on the Mississippi River; besieged and taken by the Union army in the Civil War, 1863.

vi·con·ti·el (vī·kon′tē·əl) *adj. Obs.* Of or pertaining to a viscount or sheriff. [<AF, OF *vicontal* < *viconte* a viscount]

vic·tim (vik′tim) *n.* 1 A living creature sacrificed to some deity or as a religious rite. 2 A person sacrificed in the pursuit of some object; one who is injured or killed, as by misfortune or calamity. 3 A sufferer from any diseased condition or morbid feeling. 4 One who is swindled; a dupe. [<L *victima* a beast for sacrifice]

vic·tim·ize (vik′tim·īz) *v.t.* **·ized, ·iz·ing** To make a victim of, especially by defrauding or swindling; dupe; cheat. See synonyms under ABUSE. **— vic′tim·i·za′tion** *n.* **— vic′tim·iz′er** *n.*

vic·tor (vik′tər) *n.* One who vanquishes an enemy; one who is successful in any struggle or contest; winner; conqueror. **—** *adj.* Pertaining to a victor; victorious; triumphant: the *victor* nation. [<AF *victor, victour,* OF *victeur* <L *victus,* pp. of *vincere* conquer]

Synonyms (noun): conqueror, master, vanquisher, winner. A *victor* wins in a single battle or contest; a *conqueror* wins by subjugating his opponents in many battles or campaigns.

Vic·tor (vik′tər, *Fr.* vēk·tôr′) A masculine personal name. [<L, a conqueror]

Vic·tor Em·man·u·el (vik′tər i·man′yo͞o·əl) Name of three Italian kings.

— Victor Emmanuel I, 1759–1824, king of Sardinia 1820–21.

— Victor Emmanuel II, 1820–78, king of Sardinia 1849–61, and first king of Italy 1861–78.

— Victor Emmanuel III, 1869–1947, king of Italy 1900–46.

vic·to·ri·a (vik·tôr′·ē·ə, -tō′rē·ə) *n.* 1 A low, light, four-wheeled carriage, with a calash top, a seat for two persons over the rear axle, and a raised driver's seat. 2 A passenger automobile with a calash top which usually covers the rear seat only. [after Queen *Victoria*]

VICTORIA

Vic·to·ri·a (vik·tôr′ē·ə, -tō′rē·ə) A feminine personal name.

— Victoria, 1819–1901, queen of Great Britain 1837–1901.

Victoria 1 A state of SE Australia; 87,884 square miles; capital, Melbourne. 2 The capital of British Columbia, a port at the southern extremity of Vancouver Island. 3 A port on Hong Kong Island, capital of Hong Kong colony, China. 4 A province of SE Southern Rhodesia; 21,028 square miles.

Victoria, Lake The largest lake in Africa

and the second largest fresh–water body in the world, in British East Africa, between Uganda and Tanganyika, with a NE portion in Kenya; 26,828 square miles. Also *Victoria Nyanza.*

Victoria, Mount 1 The highest peak of the Owen Stanley Range, SE New Guinea; 13,240 feet. **2** The highest peak of the Chin Hills, Upper Burma; 10,018 feet.

Victoria Cross See under CROSS.

Victoria Desert The southern belt of the Western Australian desert, south of the Gibson Desert: also *Great Victoria Desert.*

Victoria Falls A cataract on the Zambesi River between Northern and Southern Rhodesia; 343 ft. high; over a mile wide; discovered by Livingstone in 1855.

Victoria Island An island in SW Franklin district, Northwest Territories, Canada; 80,340 square miles.

Victoria Land A part of Antarctica south of New Zealand, east of the Ross Sea, and west of Wilkes Land, consisting of a series of snow–covered mountains; highest point, 13,350 feet.

Vic·to·ri·an (vik·tôr′ē·ən, -tō′rē-) *adj.* **1** Of or relating to Queen Victoria, or to her reign. **2** Pertaining to or characteristic of the ideals and standards of morality and taste prevalent during the reign of Queen Victoria; prudish; conventional; narrow. **3** Of or pertaining to Victoria, Australia. —*n.* **1** Anyone, especially an author, contemporary with Queen Victoria. **2** An article of furniture, dress, or the like, identified with or dating from the Victorian age.

Victoria Nile See under NILE.

Vic·to·ri·an·ism (vik·tôr′ē·ən·iz′əm, -tō′rē-) *n.* The state or quality of being Victorian, as in style or moral outlook.

Victoria Ny·an·za (nī·an′zə, nyän′zä) See VICTORIA, LAKE.

Victoria River A river in western Northern Territory, Australia, flowing 350 miles NE, north, and west to the Timor Sea.

Victoria waterlily Any of a genus *(Victoria)* of very large tropical American waterlilies, having leaves often five feet in diameter, and huge, showy, crimson–and–white flowers.

vic·to·ri·ous (vik·tôr′ē·əs, -tō′rē-) *adj.* **1** Having won victory; conquering; triumphant. **2** Bringing victory; distinguished by victory; instrumental in bringing victory. **3** Relating to victory. —**vic·to′ri·ous·ly** *adv.* —**vic·to′ri·ous·ness** *n.*

vic·to·ry (vik′tər·ē) *n. pl.* **·ries 1** The state of being a victor. **2** The overcoming of an enemy or of any difficulty. [<OF *victorie, victoire* <L *victoria* <*victor* VICTOR]

Synonyms: achievement, advantage, conquest, mastery, success, supremacy, triumph. *Victory* is the state resulting from the overcoming of an opponent or opponents in any contest, or from the overcoming of difficulties, obstacles, evils, etc., considered as opponents or enemies. In the latter sense any hard–won *achievement, advantage,* or *success* may be termed a *victory.* In *conquest* and *mastery* there is implied a permanence of state that is not implied in *victory. Triumph,* originally denoting the public rejoicing in honor of a *victory,* has come to signify also an exultant, complete, and glorious *victory.* Compare CONQUER. *Antonyms*: defeat, disappointment, disaster, failure, frustration, miscarriage, overthrow, retreat, rout.

Victory Medal Either of two bronze medals awarded to all who served in the U.S. armed forces in World War I or World War II, worn with the **Victory Ribbon,** combining six colors of the rainbow.

Vic·tro·la (vik·trō′lə) *n.* A make of phonograph: a trade name.

vict·ual (vit′l) *n.* **1** *pl.* Food for human beings, as prepared for eating: except in dialect, seldom used in any but a humorous or depreciatory sense: also spelled *vittles.* **2** *Obs.* Provisions of any kind. See synonyms under FOOD. —*v.* **·ualed** or **·ualled, ·ual·ing** or **·ual·ling** *v.t.* **1** To furnish with victuals. —*v.i.* **2** To lay in supplies of food. **3** *Rare* To eat; feed. [<OF *vitaile* <LL *victualia* provisions, neut. pl. of L *victualis* of food <*victus* food]

vict·ual·age (vit′l·ij) *n. Rare* Victuals; victualing.

vict·ual·er (vit′l·ər) *n.* **1** One who supplies or sells victuals; specifically, one engaged in supplying an army, navy, or ship with provisions; a commissary; sutler. **2** An innkeeper. **3** A victualing ship. Also **vict′ual·ler.**

vi·cu·ña (vi·kōōn′yə, -kyōō′nə, vī-) *n.* **1** A small ruminant *(Lama vicugna)* of the high Andes related to the llama and alpaca, having fine and valuable wool. **2** A fiber and textile made from this wool, or some substitute. Also **vi·cu′·gna.** [< Sp. <Quechua]

VICUÑA
(Up to 3 feet high at the shoulder)

vicuña cloth Soft cloth made of vicuña wool.

vi·de (vī′dē) See: used to make a reference or direct attention to: *vide* p. 36. [<L, imperative sing. of *videre* see]

vi·de an·te (vī′dē an′tē) *Latin* See before.

vi·de in·fra (vī′dē in′frə) *Latin* See below.

Vi·de·la (bē·thā′lä), **Gabriel González** See GONZÁLEZ–VIDELA.

vi·de·li·cet (vi·del′ə·sit) *adv.* To wit; that is to say; namely: abbr. *viz.* [<L <*videre licet* it is permitted to see]

vid·e·o (vid′ē·ō) *adj.* **1** Of or pertaining to television, especially to the picture portion of a program. Compare AUDIO. **2** Producing a signal convertible into a television picture: a *video* cassette. —*n.* A television image or the electric signal corresponding to it. [<L, I see]

vid·e·o·gen·ic (vid′ē·ō·jen′ik) *adj.* Having such characteristics, as coloration, form, etc., as appear effectively in television: also *telegenic.* [< VIDEO + -GENIC]

vid·e·o·tape (vid′ē·ō·tāp′) *n.* A recording of a television program on magnetic tape. —*v.t.* **·taped, ·tap·ing** To make such a recording.

vi·de post (vī′dē pōst′) *Latin* See after; see what follows.

vide·ruff (vīd′ruf) *n.* An old card game. Compare RUFF[2]. [<*vide,* var. of *vied,* pp. of VIE, in obs. sense of "wager money at cards" + RUFF[2]]

vi·de su·pra (vī′dē sōō′prə) *Latin* See above.

vi·dette (vi·det′) See VEDETTE.

vi·de ut su·pra (vī′dē ut sōō′prə) *Latin* See what is written above.

vid·u·age (vid′yōō·ij) *n.* Widowhood; also, widows collectively. [<L *vidua* a widow, orig. fem. of *viduus* bereft]

vie (vī) *v.* **vied, vy·ing** *v.i.* **1** To strive for superiority; put forth effort to excel or outdo others, as in a race: with *with* or *for.* —*v.t.* **2** *Obs.* To wager; bet. [<MF *envier* invite, challenge <L *invitare* invite]

Vied·ma (vyed′mä, *Sp.* byeth′mä) The capital of Río Negro province, in SE central Argentina near the Atlantic.

Vi·en·na (vē·en′ə) A city on the Danube, capital of Austria, in the NE part: German *Wien.*

Vienne (vyen) **1** A city in SE France, on the Rhône. **2** A river of west central France, flowing 230 miles west and north to the Loire. **3** A department of west central France; 2,719 square miles; capital, Poitiers.

Vi·en·nese (vē′ə·nēz′, -nēs′) *adj.* Belonging or relating to Vienna, or to its inhabitants. —*n. pl.* **·nese** A native or citizen of Vienna.

Vien·nois (vye·nwä′) An ancient county of SE France.

Vien·tiane (vyan·tyän′) A city on the Mekong river, the administrative capital of Laos, in the NW central part on the Thailand border.

Vie·ques Island (byā′kās) An island belonging to and east of Puerto Rico; 52 square miles.

Vier·wald·stät·ter See (fir′vält·shtet′ər zā) The German name for the LAKE OF LUCERNE.

vi et ar·mis (vī et är′mis) *Latin.* With force and arms.

Vi·et·cong (vē·et′kông′, vē′et-; vē·et·kong′, vē′et-) *n.* **1** The Communist guerrilla force in South Vietnam during the Vietnamese war. **2** A member of this force. —*adj.* Of or having to do with the Vietcong. Also **Viet Cong.**

Vi·et·minh (vē·et·min′, vē′et·min′) *n.* **1** The Communist party in Vietnam. **2** A member of this party. Also **Viet Minh.**

Vi·et·nam (vē·et·näm′) A country in Indochina, comprising the former **Democratic Republic of Vietnam (North Vietnam)** and the **Republic of Vietnam (South Vietnam)**; united under North Vietnamese leadership in 1975; 129,623 sq. mi.; capital Hanoi.

Vi·et·nam·ese (vē·et′nä·mēz′, -mēs′) *adj.* Of or pertaining to Vietnam. —*n.* **1** A person born or living in Vietnam. **2** The Austro–Asiatic language spoken in Vietnam.

view (vyōō) *n.* **1** The act of seeing; survey; inspection. **2** Mental examination or inspection. **3** Power of seeing, or range of vision; reach of perception or insight; range or scope of thought. **4** That which is seen; a spectacle; prospect. **5** A representation of a scene; especially, a landscape; also, a sketch; design; plan. **6** Reference to something regarded as the object of action; intention; purpose. **7** Manner of looking at things; opinion; judgment; belief: What are your *views* on this subject? **8** *Obs.* Appearance; aspect; show. See synonyms under PURPOSE, SCENE, THOUGHT[1]. —**in view of** In consideration of. —**on view** Open to the public; set up for public inspection. —**with a view to** With the aim or purpose of. —*v.t.* **1** To look at; see; behold. **2** To look at carefully; scrutinize; examine. **3** To survey mentally; consider. See synonyms under EXAMINE, LOOK. [<OF *veue,* orig. pp. of *veoir* see <L *videre*] —**view′er** *n.*

view–hal·loo (vyōō′hə·lōō′) *n.* A shout uttered by a huntsman when a fox breaks cover. Also **view′–hal·lo′** (-lō′), **view′–hal·loa′.**

view·less (vyōō′lis) *adj.* **1** Devoid of a view; that cannot be viewed. **2** Having no views or opinions. **3** Invisible; unseen. —**view′less·ly** *adv.* —**view′less·ness** *n.*

view·point (vyōō′point′) *n.* Point of view.

view·y (vyōō′ē) *adj.* **1** *Colloq.* Having visionary ideas or peculiar views; visionary. **2** Appearing good at first sight; showy.

Vi·gée–Le·brun (vē·zhā′lə·brœn′), **Marie Anne,** 1755–1842, French painter.

vi·ges·i·mal (vī·jes′ə·məl) *adj.* **1** Twentieth. **2** Of or pertaining to twenty; proceeding by twenties. [<L *vigesimus,* var. of *vicesimus* < *viceni.* See VICENARY.]

vig·il (vij′əl) *n.* **1** The act or state of keeping awake; a nightlong watch; watchfulness. **2** *Eccl.* **a** The eve of a holy day, especially the eve of a fast day. **b** *pl.* Religious devotions on such an eve. **3** *Usually pl.* Any nocturnal devotions. [<AF *vigile* <L *vigilia* <*vigil* awake]

vig·il·am·bu·lism (vij′əl·am′byə·liz′əm) *n. Psychol.* A state in which a person, while awake, is unconscious of his surroundings: a condition resembling somnambulism. [<L *vigil* awake + *ambulare* walk]

vig·i·lance (vij′ə·ləns) *n.* **1** The quality of being vigilant; alertness; watchfulness in guarding against danger or providing for safety. **2** A morbid watchfulness; insomnia. See synonyms under CARE.

vigilance committee 1 A body of men self–organized for the maintenance of order and the administration of summary justice in communities where regular authority is lacking or inefficient, especially in lawless sections of the western United States. **2** Formerly, in the southern United States, a group of white citizens organized to terrify and control Negroes and abolitionists.

vig·i·lant (vij′ə·lənt) *adj.* Characterized by vigilance; being on the alert; watchful; heedful; wary. [<MF <L *vigilans, -antis,* ppr. of *vigilare* keep awake <*vigil* awake] —**vig′i·lant·ly** *adv.* —**vig′i·lant·ness** *n.*

Synonyms: active, alert, awake, careful, cautious, circumspect, heedful, mindful, sleepless, wakeful, wary, watchful, wide–awake. *Vigilant* implies more sustained activity and more intelligent volition than *alert.* One is *vigilant* against danger; he may be *alert* or *watchful* for good as well as against evil; he is *wary* in view of suspected stratagem, trickery, or treachery. A person may be *wakeful* because of some merely physical excitement or excitability, as through insomnia; yet he may be utterly careless and negligent in his wakefulness, the reverse of *watchful*; a person who is truly *watchful* must keep himself *wakeful* while on watch, in which case *wakeful* has something of mental quality. *Watchful,* from the English, and *vigilant,* from the Latin, are almost exact equivalents; but *vigilant* has a somewhat sharper definiteness and somewhat more of a suggestion of volition; one may be habitually *watchful*; one is *vigilant* of set purpose and for direct cause. See ALERT. *Antonyms*: careless, drowsy, dull, heedless, inattentive, incautious, inconsiderate, neglectful, negligent, oblivious, thoughtless, unwary.

vig·i·lan·te (vij′ə·lan′tē) *n.* One who belongs to a vigilance committee. Also **vigilance man.** [<Sp., vigilant <L *vigilans* VIGILANT]

vi·gnette (vin·yet′) *n.* **1** Originally, a running ornament of leaves and tendrils, as in Gothic architecture. **2** A decorative or illustrative design placed on or before the title page of a book, at the end or beginning of a chapter, etc.; also, in medieval manuscript, an ornamented capital letter. **3** An engraving, photograph, or the like, having a background that shades off gradually. **4** A word-picture which delineates something subtly and delicately. — *v.t.* **·gnet·ted, ·gnet·ting 1** To make with a gradually shaded background or border, as a photograph. **2** To ornament with vignettes. [<F, dim. of *vigne* a vine]

vi·gnet·ter (vin·yet′ər) *n.* **1** A device, as a shaded paper with an oval hole in the center, used by photographers in printing vignettes. **2** One who makes vignettes: also **vi·gnet′tist.**

Vi·gno·la (vē·nyō′lä), **Giacomo da** See BAROZZI.

Vi·gny (vē·nyē′), **Comte Alfred Victor de,** 1799–1863, French poet, dramatist, and novelist.

Vi·go (vē′gō, *Sp.* bē′gō) A port of Pontevedra province, on **Vigo Bay,** an inlet of the Atlantic in NW Spain (18 miles long, 1/2 to 10 miles wide).

vig·or (vig′ər) *n.* **1** Active strength or force, physical or mental. **2** Vital or natural power, as in a healthy animal or plant. **3** Forcible exertion of strength; energy; intensity. **4** Legal force; validity. Also *Brit.* **vig′our.** — **in vigor** *Law* In operation; effective. [<AF *vigur, vigour,* OF *vigor* <L < *vigere* be lively, thrive]

vi·go·ro·so (vē′gō·rō′sō) *adj. Music* Vigorous; energetic: a direction. [<Ital.]

vig·or·ous (vig′ər·əs) *adj.* **1** Full of physical or mental vigor; robust. **2** Marked by or accompanied by vigor; performed or done with vigor; showing vigor; energetic. See synonyms under ACTIVE, FRESH, HEALTHY, POWERFUL, STRONG, VIVID. — **vig′or·ous·ly** *adv.* — **vig′or·ous·ness** *n.*

Vii·pu·ri (vē′po͝o·rē) The Finnish name for VYBORG.

Vi·ja·ya·na·gar (vij′ə·yə·nug′ər) **1** A former princely state in the Rajputana States, India; since 1949 a part of Bombay State; 135 square miles. **2** A village of northern Bombay State, India, formerly capital of Vijayanagar state.

vi·king (vī′king) *n.* One of the Scandinavian warriors who harried the coasts of Europe from the eighth to the tenth centuries; a pirate; sea rover. Also **Vi′king.** [<ON *víkingr* a pirate, ? <OE and Frisian *wicing* < *wīc* a camp <L *vicus* a village]

Vi·la (vē′lə) The capital of the New Hebrides condominium, on Efate.

vi·la·yet (vē′lä·yet′) *n.* An administrative division of Turkey. [<Turkish *vilāyet* <Arabic *wilāyat* < *wāli* a governor]

vile (vīl) *adj.* **vil·er, vil·est 1** Morally base, despicable, or loathsome; shamefully wicked; sinful; corrupt; filthy; disgusting. **2** Of little worth or account; mean. **3** Objectionable in any way; disagreeable: a general term of derogation. See synonyms under BAD[1], BASE[2], BRUTISH, COMMON, CRIMINAL, IMMORAL, INFAMOUS, SINFUL, VULGAR. [<AF, OF, fem. of *vil* <L *vilis* cheap] — **vile′ly** *adv.* — **vile′ness** *n.*

vil·i·a·co (vil′ē·ä′kō) *n. Obs.* A villain; scoundrel. [<Ital., ult. <L *vilis* cheap]

vil·i·fy (vil′ə·fī) *v.t.* **·fied, ·fy·ing 1** To speak of as vile; defame; slander; traduce. **2** To make base or vile; degrade. [<LL *vilificare* <L *vilis* cheap + *facere* make] — **vil′i·fi·ca′tion** (-fə·kā′shən) *n.* — **vil′i·fi′er** *n.*

vil·i·pend (vil′ə·pend) *v.t.* **1** To think or speak of disparagingly; depreciate. **2** To vilify; defame. [<OF *vilipender* <L *vilipendere* < *vilis* cheap + *pendere* weight]

vill (vil) *n.* In old English law, a village; hamlet; township; also, a manor. [<AF *vill,* OF *vile, ville* a country house, village <L *villa.* See VILLA.]

vil·la (vil′ə) *n.* Originally, a country house with some suggestion of opulence; now, a suburban or rural residence. See synonyms under HOUSE. [<Ital. <L, a country house, farm, dim. of *vicus* a village]

Vil·la (vē′yä, *Sp.* bē′yä), **Francisco,** 1877–1923, Mexican revolutionary leader called "Pancho": real name *Doroteo Arango.*

Vil·la Bens (bē′lyä bāns) Capital of the Southern Protectorate of Morocco, Spanish West Africa, on the SW coast; until 1940, capital of Spanish Sahara: formerly *Cabo Jubi.*

Vil·la Cis·ne·ros (bē′lyä thēs·nā′rōs) The capital of Río de Oro, Spanish West Africa, on the central western coast near the tropic of Cancer.

vil·la·dom (vil′ə·dəm) *n. Brit.* Villas collectively; also, their occupants; the world of suburban villas.

vil·lage (vil′ij) *n.* **1** A collection of houses in a rural district, smaller than a town but larger than a hamlet, and usually arranged according to a regular plan. Villages may or may not be incorporated. **2** In some States, a municipality smaller than a city. Compare TOWNSHIP. **3** A collection of habitations of animals: a gopher *village.* **4** The inhabitants of a village, collectively; the villagers. **5** An encampment or community of North American Indians or Eskimos: permanent, or sometimes temporary, during a migration or for a season. — *adj.* Of, pertaining to, or characteristic of a village. [<OF <L *villaticum,* neut. sing. of *villaticus* pertaining to a villa < *villa* a villa]

village community An agricultural community with a simple organization, such as was found in early England, Germany, Russia, India, etc.; specifically, a free, self-dependent, communal group, regarded by many writers as the political unit out of which the modern state developed.

vil·lag·er (vil′ij·ər) *n.* One who lives in a village.

vil·lage·ry (vil′ij·rē) *n. Obs.* A collection of villages.

Vil·la·her·mo·sa (bē′yä·er·mō′sä) The capital of Tabasco state, SE Mexico.

vil·lain (vil′ən) *n.* **1** One who has committed or is disposed to commit any flagitious or disgraceful crime or series of crimes; a scoundrel; rogue: often used jocosely: He's a little *villain.* **2** A character in a novel, play, etc., who represents such a person and is the opponent of the hero or protagonist; also, an actor who regularly portrays such a character. **3** A villein. **4** *Obs.* A countryman; boor; clown; rustic. — *adj.* **1** Base; vile. **2** Of low birth; occupying a low station in life. ◆ Homophone: *villein.* [<AF, OF *vilein, vilain* a farm servant <LL *villanus* <L *villa* a villa]

vil·lain·age (vil′ən·ij) See VILLEINAGE.

vil·lain·ess (vil′ən·is) *n.* A female villain.

vil·lain·ous (vil′ən·əs) *adj.* **1** Having the nature of a villain. **2** Marked by extreme depravity. **3** *Colloq.* Very bad; disgusting; abominable: said of things: *villainous* words. See synonyms under BAD[1], INFAMOUS. — **vil′lain·ous·ly** *adv.* — **vil′lain·ous·ness** *n.*

vil·lain·y (vil′ən·ē) *n. pl.* **·lain·ies 1** The quality or condition of being villainous; moral depravity. **2** Conduct befitting a villain; a villainous act; a crime. **3** *Obs.* Villeinage; servitude. **4** *Obs.* A low or miserable condition or state. See synonyms under ABOMINATION.

Vil·la-Lo·bos (vē′lə·lō′bo͝osh, -bo͞os), **Heitor,** 1887–1959, Brazilian composer and conductor.

vil·lan·age (vil′ən·ij) *n.* **1** Villeinage. **2** *Obs.* Villainy. [Var. of VILLEINAGE]

vil·la·nel·la (vil′ə·nel′ə, *Ital.* vēl′lä·nel′lä) *n. pl.* **·nel·le** (-nel′ē, *Ital.* -nel′lā) **1** A light, rustic part song, or dance accompanying it. **2** An early form of madrigal, popular in Naples during the sixteenth century. [<Ital., fem. dim. of *villano* <LL *villanus.* See VILLAIN.]

vil·la·nelle (vil′ə·nel′) *n.* A verse form, originally French, in 19 lines and 2 rimes, arranged in five tercets and a concluding quatrain. [<F <Ital. *villanella* a villanella]

Vil·lard (vi·lärd′), **Oswald Garrison,** 1872–1949, U. S. journalist.

Vil·lars (vē·làr′), **Duc Claude Louis Hector de,** 1653–1734, French marshal.

vil·lat·ic (vi·lat′ik) *adj.* Of or pertaining to a villa, farm, or village; rural. [<L *villaticus.* See VILLAGE.]

vil·lein (vil′ən) *n.* In the manorial system of feudal times, a member of any of the classes of freemen ranking below the thanes; more specifically, a free peasant ranking below a socman but above a cotter. By the 13th century the term *villein* was applied to a class of serfs who were regarded as freemen in respect to their legal relations with all persons except their lord, whose slaves they were. — *adj. Obs.* Relating to villeins; low-born. ◆ Homophone: *villain.* [<AF, OF *vilein, vilain.* See VILLAIN.]

vil·lein·age (vil′ən·ij) *n.* In feudal law, the tenure by which villeins held land; also, the status or condition of a villein: also spelled *villanage.* Also **vil′len·age.**

Ville·neuve (vēl·nœv′), **Pierre Charles Jean Baptiste Silvestre de,** 1763–1806, French admiral.

Vil·liers (vil′ərz), **George** See BUCKINGHAM.

vil·li·form (vil′ə·fôrm) *adj.* **1** Having the form of a villus. **2** Resembling nap, as of plush, as the teeth of fishes when numerous, small, and close together in velvety bands. [<NL *villiformis* <L *villus* tuft of hair + *forma* form]

Vil·lon (vē·yôṅ′), **François,** 1431–85?, French poet: real name *François de Montcorbier.*

vil·los·i·ty (vi·los′ə·tē) *n. pl.* **·ties 1** The state or condition of being villous. **2** A villous surface or coating. **3** A villus.

vil·lous (vil′əs) *adj.* **1** Covered with short, soft hairs; nappy. **2** Covered with or having villi. Also **vil′lose** (-ōs). [<L *villosus* < *villus* tuft of hair] — **vil′lous·ly** *adv.*

vil·lus (vil′əs) *n. pl.* **vil·li** (vil′ī) **1** *Anat.* One of the short, hairlike processes found on certain membranes, as of the small intestine, where they aid in the digestive process. **2** *Bot.* One of the long, close, rather soft hairs on the surface of certain plants. [<L, a tuft of hair, shaggy hair, var. of *vellus* a fleece, wool]

Vil·na (vil′nə, *Russian* vēl′nä) The capital of Lithuania, in the SE part: Polish *Wilno.* Also **Vil·ni·us** (vil′nē·əs), **Vil·nyus** (vil′nyəs).

Vi·lyui (vyē·lyo͞o′ē) A river in western Yakut Autonomous S.S.R., flowing 1,512 miles east to the Lena.

vim (vim) *n.* Force or vigor; energy; spirit. [<L, accusative of *vis* power]

vi·men (vī′mən) *n. pl.* **vim·i·na** (vim′ə·nə) *Bot.* A long, flexible shoot or branch. [<L *vimen, -inis* a twig < *viere* bend together, plait]

vim·i·nal (vim′ə·nəl) *adj. Rare* Pertaining to twigs; made of or producing twigs. [<L *vimen, -inis.* See VIMEN.]

Vim·i·nal (vim′ə·nəl) One of the seven hills on which ancient Rome was built.

vi·min·e·ous (vī·min′ē·əs) *adj.* **1** Having or resembling long, flexible shoots or branches. **2** Composed of twigs. [<L *vimineus* < *vimen, -inis.* See VIMEN.]

Vi·my (vē·mē′) A town in Pas-de-Calais department, northern France, near **Vimy Ridge,** scene of fierce fighting in World War I, 1915–1917.

vin (vaṅ) *n. French* Wine.

vin– Var. of VINI–.

vi·na (vē′nä) *n.* An East Indian musical instrument with seven steel strings stretched on a long, fretted fingerboard over two gourds. [<Hind. *vīṇā* <Skt.]

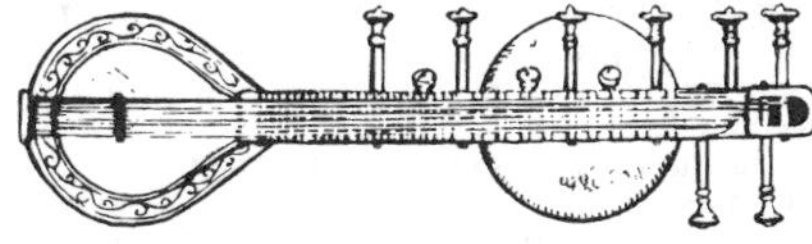

VINA OF BENARES

vi·na·ceous (vī·nā′shəs) *adj.* **1** Of or pertaining to wine or grapes. **2** Of the color of red wine. [<L *vinaceus* < *vinum* wine]

Vi·ña del Mar (bē′nyä thel mär′) A city on the Pacific in central Chile; a beach resort and industrial and agricultural center.

vin·ai·grette (vin′ə·gret′) *n.* **1** An ornamental

box or bottle, with a perforated top, for holding vinegar, smelling salts, or a pungent drug: also *vinegarette.* 2 Vinaigrette sauce. [<F, dim. of *vinaigre* vinegar]
vinaigrette sauce A vinegar and savory herb sauce served with fish and cold meats.
vi·nasse (vi·nas′) *n.* A residual product containing potassium salts, obtained from the winepress or from beets after the sugar has been extracted. [<F]
Vin·cennes (vin·senz′, *Fr.* vaṅ·sen′) 1 A city on the Wabash River in SW Indiana; site of French mission established in 1702. 2 A city just east of Paris, France.
Vin·cent (vin′sənt, *Fr.* vaṅ·säṅ′) A masculine personal name. Also *Ger.* **Vin·cenz** (vin′sents), *Ital.* **Vin·cen·zo** (vin·chen′tsō). [<L, conquering]
— **Vincent de Paul, Saint,** 1574?–1660, French Roman Catholic priest, founder of several charitable organizations.
Vin·cen·tian (vin·sen′shən) *n.* A member of a Roman Catholic order founded in 1625 by St. Vincent de Paul. See LAZARIST.
Vincent's infection *Pathol.* Trench mouth. Also **Vincent's angina, Vincent's disease.** [after J. H. *Vincent,* 1862–1950, French physician]
Vin·ci (vēn′chē), **Leonardo da** See LEONARDO DA VINCI.
vin·ci·ble (vin′sə·bəl) *adj.* That may be conquered or overcome; conquerable. [<L *vincibilis* < *vincere* conquer] — **vin′ci·bil′i·ty, vin′ci·ble·ness** *n.*
vin·cu·lum (vingk′yə·ləm) *n. pl.* **·la** (-lə) 1 A bond of union. 2 *Anat.* A confining band of fascia. 3 *Math.* A straight line drawn over several algebraic terms, or a brace uniting them to show that all are to be operated on together. [<L < *vincire* bind]
Vin·dhya Pra·desh (vind′hyə prə·däsh′) A former State of central India, incorporated in Madhya Pradesh State, 1956; 24,600 square miles; capital, Rewa.
Vin·dhya Range (vind′hyə) A chain of hills in central India; highest point, 3,400 feet.
vin·di·ca·ble (vin′də·kə·bəl) *adj.* That may be vindicated; justifiable.
vin·di·cate (vin′də·kāt) *v.t.* **·cat·ed, ·cat·ing** 1 To clear of accusation, censure, suspicion, etc. 2 To support or maintain, as a right or claim, against denial, opposition, etc. 3 To serve to justify. 4 *Rare* To lay claim to. 5 *Obs.* To avenge; punish. 6 *Obs.* To set free; rescue. See synonyms under AVENGE, JUSTIFY. [<L *vindicatus,* pp. of *vindicare* avenge, claim] — **vin′di·ca′tor** *n.*
vin·di·ca·tion (vin′də·kā′shən) *n.* The act of vindicating, or the state of being vindicated; justification; defense. See synonyms under APOLOGY, DEFENSE.
vin·di·ca·tive (vin′də·kā′tiv) *adj.* That contributes to vindication; that vindicates or serves to vindicate.
vin·di·ca·to·ry (vin′də·kə·tôr′ē, -tō′rē) *adj.* 1 Bringing to vindication; justificatory. 2 Punitive; avenging.
vin·dic·tive (vin·dik′tiv) *adj.* 1 Having a revengeful spirit; of a revengeful character. 2 *Obs.* Punitive. [<L *vindicta* a revenge] — **vin·dic′tive·ly** *adv.* — **vin·dic′tive·ness** *n.*
vine (vīn) *n.* 1 Any of a large and widely distributed group of plants having a slender, weak stem that may clasp or twine about a support by means of tendrils, leaf petioles, etc. 2 The stem itself. 3 A grapevine. [<OF *vigne, vine* <L *vinea* vineyard < *vinum* wine]
vine·dress·er (vīn′dres′ər) *n.* One who trims or prunes grapevines.
vin·e·gar (vin′ə·gər) *n.* 1 An acid liquid obtained by the acetous fermentation of alcoholic liquids, as cider, beer, wine, etc., and used as a condiment and preservative. 2 *Med.* A preparation of dilute acetic acid. 3 Anything metaphorically sour or soured, as a face; acerbity, as of speech. [<OF *vyn egre, vinaigre* < *vin* wine (<L *vinum*) + *aigre, egre* sour <L *acer* sharp] — **vin′e·gar·ish** *adj.*
vinegar eel A small nematode worm (*Anguillula aceti*) common in vinegar, sour paste, and similar fermenting liquids. Also **vinegar worm.**
vin·e·gar·ette (vin′ə·gə·ret′) See VINAIGRETTE (def. 1).
vinegar fly A fruit fly (def. 2).
vin·e·gar·roon (vin′ə·gə·rōōn′) *n.* The whip-tailed scorpion (*Mastigoproctus giganteus*) of the SW United States and Mexico, so called from its odor when alarmed: erroneously supposed to be venomous. Also **vin′e·ge·rone′** (-rōn′). [<Sp. *vinagre* vinegar < *vino* wine (<L *vinum*) + *agrio* sour <L *acer* sharp]
vin·e·gar·y (vin′ə·gər·ē) *adj.* 1 Being like or suggestive of vinegar; sour; acid. 2 Crabbed; of a sour disposition.
Vine·land (vīn′lənd) See VINLAND.
vin·er·y (vī′nər·ē) *n. pl.* **·er·ies** 1 A greenhouse for grapes; grapery. 2 Vines in general.
vine·yard (vin′yərd) *n.* 1 A large collection of cultivated grapevines. 2 Figuratively, a field for labor, especially spiritual culture or labor. [Earlier *wineyard,* OE *wīngeard*; infl. in form by VINE]
vine·yard·ist (vin′yər·dist) *n.* One who grows or cultivates grapevines.
vingt-et-un (vaṅ·tā·œṅ′) *n.* A game of cards played with a full pack, the object being to draw cards on which the aggregate number of spots shall reach as near as possible to but not exceed 21. Also called *twenty-one, blackjack.* [<F, twenty-one]
vini- *combining form* Wine; of or pertaining to wine or to wine grapes: *viniculture, viniferous*: also, before vowels, *vin-.* Also **vino-.** [<L *vinum* wine]
vi·nic (vī′nik, vin′ik) *adj.* Of, pertaining to, or derived from wine: *vinic* alcohol. [<L *vinum* wine]
vin·i·cul·ture (vin′ə·kul′chər) *n.* The cultivation of grapes for winemaking. — **vin′i·cul′tur·al** *adj.*
vin·i·cul·tur·ist (vin′ə·kul′chər·ist) *n.* One engaged in viniculture.
vi·nif·er·ous (vī·nif′ər·əs) *adj.* Producing wine. [<VINI- + -FEROUS]
vin·i·fi·ca·tor (vin′ə·fə·kā′tər) *n.* An apparatus for receiving and condensing the vapor of alcohol that rises from the fermenting must during the making of wine. [<VINI- + L *-ficator* a maker < *facere* make]
Vin·land (vin′lənd) A name given to part of the coast of North America by Norse voyagers: also *Vineland.*
Vin·ni·tsa (vin′it·sə, *Russian* vyen′nyē·tsə) A city on the Bug river in SW central Ukrainian S.S.R.
Vi·no·gra·doff (vē′nə·grä′dôf), **Sir Paul Gavrilovich,** 1854–1925, Russian jurist and medieval historian, active in England.
vi·nom·e·ter (vi·nom′ə·tər, vī-) *n.* A hydrometer for measuring the percentage of alcohol in wine. [<VINO- + -METER]
vin or·di·naire (vaṅ ôr·dē·nâr′) *French* A cheap wine; literally, ordinary wine.
vi·nos·i·ty (vī·nos′ə·tē) *n.* 1 The state or quality of being vinous. 2 The general character of a wine, including the bouquet, flavor, body, etc. 3 Addiction to or fondness for wine. [<LL *vinositas, -tatis* <L *vinosus* VINOUS]
vi·nous (vī′nəs) *adj.* 1 Pertaining to, characteristic of, or having the qualities of wine. 2 Caused by, affected by, or addicted to wine. 3 Wine-colored. [<L *vinosus* < *vinum* wine]
Vin·son (vin′sən), **Fred M.,** 1890–1953, U. S. administrator and jurist; chief justice of the United States 1946–53.
vin·tage (vin′tij) *n.* 1 The yield of a vineyard or wine-growing district for one season. 2 The visible fruit of vineyards. 3 The harvesting of a vineyard and the first steps in the making of wine. 4 Wine, especially wine of high quality. 5 The year or the region in which a particular wine is produced. 6 *Colloq.* The type or kind current or appropriate at a particular time or in a particular season of the past: a joke of ancient *vintage.* [<AF *vintage,* alter. of *vindage, vendage,* OF *vendage* <L *vindemia* < *vinum* wine + *demere* remove < *de-* off + *emere* take; infl. in form by *vintner*]
vin·tag·er (vin′tij·ər) *n.* A harvester of grapes.
vintage wine Wine of an exceptionally good year, especially a dated champagne or port.
vint·ner (vint′nər) *n.* A wine merchant, especially at wholesale. [<OF *vinetier, vinotier* < *vinot,* dim. of *vin* wine <L *vinum*]
vin·y (vī′nē) *adj.* Pertaining to, like, of, full of, or yielding vines.
vi·nyl (vī′nəl) *n. Chem.* The univalent radical, CH_2:CH, derived from ethylene, especially when used in organic synthesis. [<L *vinum* wine + -YL]
vinyl acetate *Chem.* A colorless liquid, $C_4H_6O_2$, used as a starting point in the synthesis of various resins and plastics.
vinyl alcohol *Chem.* A hypothetical unstable alcohol, C_2H_4O, derived from acetylene.
vinyl chloride *Chem.* A compound of vinyl and chlorine, C_2H_3Cl, used in the production of synthetic fibers.
vinyl polymer *Chem.* Any of a class of organic compounds obtained by the polymerization of vinyl compounds.
vi·ol (vī′əl) *n.* 1 Any member of a family of stringed musical instruments, predecessors of the violin family, originating in the later Middle Ages and passing out of use in the 18th century, having usually six strings, and played with a bow. 2 A stringed instrument of the violin class. See BASS VIOL. [Earlier *vielle* <AF, OF <Med. L *vidula, vitula* <Gmc.; infl. in form by OF *viole*]
vi·o·la (vē·ō′lə, vī-; *Ital.* vyō′lä) *n.* 1 A four-stringed musical instrument of the violin family, somewhat larger than the violin, and tuned a fifth lower, with a graver and less brilliant tone. Its four strings are tuned in fifths. 2 A medieval viol. 3 An organ stop of eight-foot length and tone, producing stringlike tones. [<Ital., orig. a viol <Med. L *vidula* <Gmc.]
Vi·o·la (vī′ō·lə, vē′-, vī·ō′lə) A feminine personal name. Also **Vi·o·lan·te** (*Pg.* vē′ō·läṅ′tə, *Sp.* bē′ō·läṅ′tā), *Ger.* **Vi·o·le** (vē·ō′lə). [<L, a violet]
— **Viola** The heroine in Shakespeare's *Twelfth Night.*
vi·o·la·ble (vī′ə·lə·bəl) *adj.* That may be violated. [<L *violabilis* < *violare* VIOLATE] — **vi′o·la·ble·ness, vi′o·la·bil′i·ty** *n.* — **vi′o·la·bly** *adv.*
vi·o·la·ceous (vī′ə·lā′shəs) *adj.* 1 Having a violet hue. 2 *Bot.* Of or pertaining to the violet or the violet family (*Violaceae*) of herbs, shrubs, and trees. [<L *violaceus* < *viola* a violet]
vio·la da gam·ba (vyō′lä dä gäm′bä) 1 The bass of the viol family, held between the legs, and having a range and tone similar to those of the violoncello: also *bass viol.* 2 An organ stop producing tones akin to those of the viola da gamba and usually having an eight-foot length and tone. [<Ital., viola of the leg]
vi·o·late (vī′ə·lāt) *v.t.* **·lat·ed, ·lat·ing** 1 To break or infringe, as a law, oath, agreement, etc. 2 To treat irreverently; profane, as a holy place. 3 To break in upon; disturb. 4 To ravish; rape. 5 To do violence to; offend grossly; outrage. 6 *Obs.* To treat roughly; abuse. [<L *violatus,* pp. of *violare* use violence < *vis* force] — **vi′o·la′tor** *n.*
Synonyms: abuse, debauch, defile, deflower, desecrate, hurt, injure, outrage, pollute, profane, rape, ravish. See ABUSE, POLLUTE.
vi·o·la·tion (vī′ə·lā′shən) *n.* The act of violating, or the state of being violated.
vi·o·la·tive (vī′ə·lā′tiv) *adj.* Having a tendency to violate; violating; involving violation.
vi·o·lence (vī′ə·ləns) *n.* 1 The quality or state of being violent; intensity; fury; also, an instance of violent action. 2 Violent or unjust exercise of power; injury; outrage; desecration; profanation. 3 *Law* Physical force unlawfully exercised; an act tending to intimidate or overawe by causing apprehension of bodily injury. 4 The perversion or distortion of the meaning of a text, word, or the like; unjustified alteration of wording. [<AF, OF <L *violentia* < *violentus* violent]
Synonyms: acuteness, boisterousness, eagerness, fierceness, force, fury, impetuosity, injury, intensity, outrage, passion, poignancy, rage, severity, sharpness, vehemence, violation, wildness, wrath. See OUTRAGE. *Antonyms*: calmness, feebleness, forbearance, gentleness, meekness, mildness, patience, self-command, self-control, self-restraint.
vi·o·lent (vī′ə·lənt) *adj.* 1 Proceeding from or marked by great physical force or roughness; sudden; forcible. 2 Caused by or exhibiting intense emotional or mental excitement; passionate; impetuous; fierce. 3 Characterized by intensity of any kind; extreme: *violent* heat. 4 Marked by unjust exercise of force; harsh; severe: to take *violent* measures. 5 Resulting from external force or injury; not in the ordinary course of nature: a *violent* death. 6 Tending to

pervert the meaning or sense: a *violent* construction. [<OF <L *violentus* <*vis* force] —**vi′o·lent·ly** *adv.*

Synonyms: acute, boisterous, fierce, forceful, frantic, frenzied, fuming, furious, immoderate, impetuous, intense, irate, mad, maniacal, outrageous, passionate, poignant, raging, raving, severe, sharp, tumultuous, turbulent, uncontrollable, ungovernable, vehement, wild. See FIERCE, HOT, IMMODERATE, TURBULENT.

violent presumption *Law* An inference based on evidence that is so strong as to be almost conclusive.

vi·o·les·cent (vī′ə·les′ənt) *adj.* Having a tinge of violet color. [<L *viola* a violet + -ESCENT]

vi·o·let (vī′ə·lit) *n.* **1** Any of a widely distributed genus *(Viola)* of herbaceous perennial herbs, bearing flowers typically of a purplish-blue color; especially, the common **garden violet** *(V. odorata).* The violet is the State flower of Illinois, New Jersey, Rhode Island, and Wisconsin. **2** Any of several similar plants: the dog's-tooth *violet.* **3** A color seen at the end of the spectrum, opposite the red and beyond the blue; also, a pigment of this color. —*adj.* Of the color of violet. [<OF *violette,* dim. of *viole* <L *viola* a violet]

violet rays High-frequency radiation from the violet end of the visible spectrum: distinguished from *ultraviolet.*

vi·o·lin (vī′ə·lin′) *n.* **1** A musical instrument having four strings and a sounding box of seasoned wood, and played by means of a bow; a fiddle. It is the treble member of the **violin family,** which includes the viola, violoncello, and double-bass, and is distinguished in its modern form by its fully molded belly and back. **2** A violinist, especially in an orchestra: He is second *violin.* [<Ital. *violino,* dim. of *viola* a viola]

VIOLIN
a. Scroll.
b. Peg box.
c. Peg.
d. Nut.
e. Fingerboard.
f. Neck plate.
g. Sound holes.
h. Bridge.
i. Tailpiece.
j. Chin rest.
k. Button.

vi·o·lin·ist (vī′ə·lin′·ist) *n.* One who plays the violin.

vi·ol·ist (vī′əl·ist) *n.* One who plays the viol or viola.

Viol·let-le-Duc (vyô·le′lə·dük′), **Eugène Emmanuel,** 1814–79, French architect and archeologist.

vi·o·lon·cel·list (vē′ə·lən·chel′ist) *n.* One who plays the violoncello: usually abbreviated to *cellist* or *'cellist.*

vi·o·lon·cel·lo (vē′ə·lən·chel′ō) *n. pl.* **·los** A bass instrument of the violin family, having four strings tuned an octave lower than the viola, and held between the performer's knees when played: commonly called *cello* or *'cello.* [<Ital., dim. of *violone* a bass viol, aug. of *viola.* See VIOLA.]

vio·lo·ne (vyō·lō′nā) *n.* **1** The double-bass of the viol family, playing an octave lower than the viola da gamba: the immediate ancestor of the modern double-bass, which replaces the true double-bass of the violin family. **2** An organ stop with stringlike tone quality, having a 16-foot length and tone. **3** A small-scaled organ stop of eight-foot length and tone. [<Ital., aug. of *viola* a viol. See VIOLA.]

vi·os·ter·ol (vī·os′tər·ōl, -ol) *n.* Irradiated ergosterol, a vitamin D preparation variously used in medicine. [<(ULTRA)VIO(LET) + (ERGO)STEROL]

vi·per (vī′pər) *n.* **1** Any of a family *(Viperidae)* of venomous Old World snakes, especially the common European viper or adder *(Vipera berus),* about two feet long and variously colored; also, the African puff adder, and the horned viper. **2** One of a family *(Crotalidae)* of typically American poisonous snakes, the **pit vipers,** including the rattlesnake, copperhead, and fer-de-lance, which are characterized by a small depression between the nostril and the eye. **3** Any poisonous or allegedly poisonous snake. **4** A venomous, malicious, treacherous, or spiteful person. **5** *U.S. Slang* A marihuana smoker. [<OF *vipere, vipre* < L *vipera,* contraction of *vivipara* <*vivus* living + *parere* bring forth] —**vi·per·ine** (vī′·pər·in, -pə·rīn) *adj.* —**vi′per·ish** *adj.*

vi·per·ous (vī′pər·əs) *adj.* **1** Snakelike; viperine. **2** Venomous. —**vi′per·ous·ly** *adv.*

vi·per's-bu·gloss (vī′pərz·byōō′glôs, -glos) *n.* Blueweed.

vir·a·gin·i·ty (vir′ə·jin′ə·tē) *n. Psychiatry* The assumption by a woman of male characteristics and reactions. [<L *virago, -inis* VIRAGO]

vi·ra·go (vi·rā′gō, vī-) *n. pl.* **·goes** or **·gos 1** A turbulent woman; vixen. **2** *Obs.* A woman of extraordinary size and courage; a female warrior; Amazon. [<L, manlike woman <*vir* a man]

vi·ral (vī′rəl) *adj. Med.* Of, pertaining to, caused by, or resembling a virus.

Vir·chow (vir′khō), **Rudolf,** 1821–1902, German pathologist.

vir·e·lay (vir′ə·lā) *n.* A form of old French verse, arranged in any of various arbitrary orders; especially, a verse form having only two rimes throughout; also, a form in which each stanza has two rimes, one repeated from the preceding stanza and a new one that will be repeated in the next. Also *French* **vire·lai** (vēr·le′). [<OF *virelai,* prob. alter. of *vireli, virli* a refrain of old dance songs]

vir·e·o (vir′ē·ō) *n. pl.* **·os** Any of various small, insectivorous birds (family *Vireonidae*), predominantly dull-green and grayish, which make slight, cup-shaped, pensile nests; a greenlet. The **red-eyed vireo** *(Vireo olivaceus),* the **yellow-throated vireo** *(V. flavifrons),* the **white-eyed vireo** *(V. griseus),* the **blue-headed** or **solitary vireo** *(V. solitarius)* and the **warbling vireo** *(V. gilvus)* are common in the United States. Many of the species are noted for their song. [<L, a kind of small bird, ? the greenfinch]

vir·e·o·nine (vir′ē·ə·nīn′, -nin) *adj.* Characteristic of or pertaining to a vireo and related birds. —*n.* A vireo or related bird. [<L *vireo, -onis.* See VIREO.]

vi·res·cence (vi·res′əns) *n.* **1** The state or condition of becoming green. **2** *Bot.* Abnormal assumption of green by the usually bright-colored organs of plants, as when petals become green like ordinary leaves.

vi·res·cent (vi·res′ənt) *adj.* Greenish or becoming green. [<L *virescens, -entis,* ppr. of *virescere* grow green <*vir* be green]

vir et ux·or (vir et uk′sôr) *Latin* Husband and wife.

vir·ga (vûr′gə) *n. Meteorol.* Drooping streamers or wisps of precipitation from clouds, usually of the altocumulus and altostratus types. [< L, twig, streak in the sky]

vir·gate[1] (vûr′git, -gāt) *adj.* **1** Long, straight, and slender like a wand. **2** *Bot.* Bearing or producing many small twigs. [<L *virga* a twig, rod]

vir·gate[2] (vûr′git, -gāt) *n.* An early English measure of land, varying greatly (15, 20, 24, 30, and sometimes 40 acres) in different parts of England. [<Med. L *virgata (terrae)* a virgate (of land) <L *virga* a rod]

Vir·gil (vûr′jəl), **Vir·gil·i·an** (vər·jil′ē·ən) See VERGIL, etc.

vir·gin (vûr′jin) *n.* **1** A person, especially a young woman, who has never had sexual intercourse; a maiden. **2** A chaste young girl or unmarried woman; a spinster. **3** *Eccl.* **a** A member of a religious community who has taken a vow of chastity; a nun. **b** A chaste, unmarried woman honored for her piety or virtue: used as an epithet of saints: St. Cecilia, *virgin* and martyr. **4** Any female animal before its first copulation. **5** *Entomol.* A female insect producing fertile eggs by parthenogenesis. —*adj.* **1** Being a virgin. **2** Consisting of virgins: a *virgin* band. **3** Pertaining or suited to a virgin; chaste; maidenly. **4** Uncorruptepure; undefiled: *virgin* whiteness. **5** Not hitherto used, touched, tilled, or worked upon by man: *virgin* soil; *virgin* forest. **6** Not previously processed, manufactured, or acted upon; new: *virgin* rubber; *virgin* wool. **7** Obtained from the first pressing (of olives, nuts, etc.) without the use of heat: said of an oil. **8** *Metall.* Produced directly from ore, or at the primary smelting: *virgin* silver. **9** *Mining* Occurring in native form; unalloyed; unmixed: *virgin* gold. **10** First: a ship's *virgin* voyage. **1** Untrained; lacking experience or contact with: waters *virgin* of ships. **12** *Zool.* Parthenogenetic. [<OF *virgine* <L *virgo, -inis* a maiden]

Vir·gin (vûr′jin) **1** Mary, the mother of Jesus: usually with *the*: also, **the Virgin Mary, the Blessed Virgin. 2** The constellation Virgo. See CONSTELLATION.

vir·gin·al[1] (vûr′jin·əl) *adj.* Related to, like, or suited to a virgin; pure; modest; maidenly. [< OF <L *virginalis* <*virgo, -inis* a virgin]

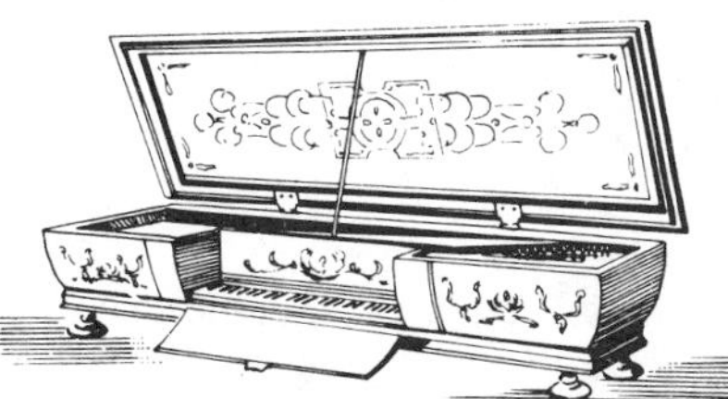

VIRGINAL — LATE 16TH CENTURY

vir·gin·al[2] (vûr′jin·əl) *n.* A legless keyboard musical instrument of the 16th and 17th centuries, predecessor of the harpsichord: often in the plural, sometimes called a **pair of virginals.** [<OF, VIRGINAL[1]; ? so called from its use by young men and girls]

virgin birth 1 *Zool.* Parthenogenesis. **2** *Usually cap. Theol.* The doctrine that Jesus Christ was conceived by divine agency and born without impairment of the virginity of his mother Mary.

vir·gin·hood (vûr′jin·hŏŏd) *n.* Virginity.

Vir·gin·ia (vər·jin′yə) A middle Atlantic State of the United States; 40,815 square miles; capital, Richmond; entered the Union June 25, 1788, one of the original thirteen States; nickname, *Old Dominion*: abbr. VA Original name: *Commonwealth of Virginia.*

Virginia cowslip A smooth perennial herb *(Mertensia virginica)* of the eastern United States, with clusters of blue or purple tubular flowers. Also **Virginia bluebell.**

Virginia creeper A common American climbing vine *(Parthenocissus* or *Ampelopsis quinquefolia)* of the grape family, with compound toothed leaves, small green flowers, and inedible blue berries: also called *American ivy, woodbine.*

Virginia deer A large, graceful, white-tailed deer *(Odocoileus virginianus),* native in the eastern United States and as far west as the Great Plains.

Virginia dogwood The flowering dogwood: State flower of Virginia. See under DOGWOOD.

Virginia Key Northernmost of the Florida Keys, one mile south of Miami Beach; about 2 miles long.

Vir·gin·ian (vər·jin′yən) *adj.* **1** Of, pertaining to, or from Virginia. **2** Of, pertaining to, or designating the language of certain Algonquian North American Indians of eastern Virginia, North Carolina, and Maryland, especially of the Powhatan confederacy, formerly dwelling on the James River, Virginia. —*n.* A native or citizen of Virginia.

Virginia nightingale The cardinal bird.

Virginia rail fence A worm fence; a stake-and-rider.

Virginia reel A country dance in which the performers stand in two parallel lines facing one another and perform various figures, usually at the direction of a caller.

Virginia truffle Tuckahoe.

Virginia trumpet flower The trumpet creeper.

Virgin Islands A group of islands in the West Indies, east of Puerto Rico; divided into the **Virgin Islands of the United States,** an unincorporated territory comprising the islands of St. Thomas, St. John, and St. Croix, and adjacent islets, purchased from Denmark in 1917; 133 square miles; capital, Charlotte Amalie, on St. Thomas: formerly *Danish West Indies*; and the BRITISH VIRGIN ISLANDS; total area, 200 square miles.

vir·gin·i·ty (vər·jin′ə·tē) *n. pl.* **·ties 1** The state of being a virgin; maidenhood; virginal chastity. **2** The state of being unsullied or unused.

vir·gin·i·um (vər·jin′ē·əm) *n.* Former name of an element now identified as francium. [from the State of Virginia]

Virgin Mary Mary, the mother of Jesus.

Virgin River A river in Utah, Arizona, and Nevada, flowing 200 miles SW to Lake Mead.

vir·gin's–bow·er (vûr′jinz·bou′ər) *n.* A species of clematis (*Clematis virginiana*) bearing white flowers in leafy panicles.

Vir·go (vûr′gō) **1** A zodiacal constellation south of Ursa Major and Boötes; the Virgin. See CONSTELLATION. **2** The sixth sign of the zodiac. See illustration under ZODIAC. [<L, a virgin]

vir·gu·late (vûr′gyə·lit, -lāt) *adj.* Diminutively virgate; like a small rod. [<L *virgula*. See VIRGULE.]

vir·gule (vûr′gyo͞ol) *n.* A slanting line (/) used to indicate a choice between two alternatives, as in the phrase *and/or.* See SOLIDUS. [<L *virgula,* dim. of *virga* a rod]

vir·i·des·cent (vir′ə·des′ənt) *adj.* Greenish, or becoming slightly green. [<LL *viridescens, -entis,* ppr. of *viridescere* become green < *viridis* green] — **vir′i·des′cence** *n.*

vi·rid·i·an (və·rid′ē·ən) *n.* A durable bluish-green pigment consisting of hydrated chromic oxide. [<L *viridis* green]

vi·rid·i·ty (və·rid′ə·tē) *n.* Fresh greenness, as of vegetation; verdure. [<L *viriditas, -tatis* greenness, verdure < *viridis* green]

vir·ile (vir′əl) *adj.* **1** Having the characteristics of manhood. **2** Having the vigor or strength of manhood; sturdy, intrepid, and forceful; masculine. **3** Capable of procreation. See synonyms under MASCULINE. [<OF <L *virilis* < *vir* a man]

vir·il·ism (vir′əl·iz′əm) *n.* **1** The appearance in a woman of secondary male sexual and physical characteristics. **2** Female hermaphroditism.

vi·ril·i·ty (və·ril′ə·tē) *n. pl.* **·ties** The state, character, or quality of being virile.

vi·rip·o·tent (və·rip′ə·tənt) *adj.* **1** Sexually mature. **2** Nubile. [<LL *viripotens, -entis* <L *vir, viri* a man + *potens, -entis* able, powerful]

virl (vûrl) *n. Scot.* A ring around a column; a band; a ferrule.

vi·rol·o·gy (və·rol′ə·jē, vī-) *n.* The study of viruses, especially in their relation to disease. [< *viro-* (<VIRUS) + -LOGY] — **vi·rol′o·gist** *n.*

Vir·ta·nen (vir′tä·nen), **Artturi Ilmari,** 1895–1973, Finnish biochemist.

vir·tu (vər·to͞o′, vûr′to͞o) *n.* **1** Rare, curious, or beautiful quality: generally in the phrase **objects** or **articles of virtu. 2** A taste for such objects. **3** Such objects collectively. [<Ital. *virtù* <L *virtus.* See VIRTUE.]

vir·tu·al (vûr′cho͞o·əl) *adj.* **1** Being in effect, but not in form or appearance; having potency, validity, or essential qualities: opposed to *apparent* or *nominal.* **2** *Obs.* Potent; effective; energizing. [<Med. L *virtualis* <L *virtus.* See VIRTUE.] — **vir′tu·al′i·ty** (-al′ə·tē) *n.* — **vir′tu·al·ly** *adv.*

virtual focus See under FOCUS.

virtual image See under IMAGE.

vir·tue (vûr′cho͞o) *n.* **1** The disposition to conform to the law of right; moral excellence; rectitude. **2** The practice of moral duties and the abstinence from immorality and vice: a life devoted to *virtue.* **3** Sexual purity; chastity, especially in women. **4** A particular moral excellence, especially one of those considered to be of special importance and classified by Plato as the four **cardinal virtues** (justice, temperance, prudence, and fortitude), to which the Christian scholastic moralists added the three **theological virtues** (faith, hope, and charity or love). The latter are sometimes called the **supernatural** or **Christian virtues** and the former the **natural virtues,** and all seven are opposed to the Seven Deadly Sins. **5** Any admirable quality, merit, or accomplishment: Patience is a *virtue.* **6** Active quality; power; efficacy; especially, medical efficacy; potency. **7** The quality of manliness; strength; valor. **8** *pl.* The fifth of the nine orders of angels in the celestial hierarchy. — **by** (or **in**) **virtue of** By or through the fact, quality, force, or authority of. [<OF *vertu* <L *virtus* strength, bravery < *vir* man]

Synonyms: chastity, duty, excellence, faithfulness, goodness, honesty, honor, integrity, justice, morality, probity, purity, rectitude, righteousness, rightness, truth, uprightness, virtuousness, worth, worthiness. *Virtue* is *goodness* that is victorious through trial, perhaps through temptation and conflict. *Goodness* may be much less than *virtue,* as lacking the strength that comes from trial and conflict, or it may be more than *virtue,* as rising above the possibility of temptation and conflict. *Virtue* is human; we do not predicate it of God. *Morality* is conformity to the moral law in action, whether in matters concerning ourselves or others, whether with or without right principle. *Honesty* and *probity* are used especially of one's relations to his fellow men, *probity* being to *honesty* much what *virtue* is to *goodness*; *probity* is *honesty* tried and proved, especially in those things that are beyond the reach of legal requirement; above the commercial sense, *honesty* may be applied to the highest truthfulness of the soul to and with itself. *Integrity,* in the full sense, is moral wholeness; when used of contracts and dealings, it has reference to inherent character and principle, and denotes more than conventional *honesty. Purity* is freedom from all admixture, especially of that which debases. *Duty,* the rendering of what is due to any person or in any relation, is the fulfilment of moral obligation. *Rectitude* and *righteousness* denote conformity to the standard of right; *righteousness* is used especially in the religious sense. *Uprightness* refers especially to conduct. Compare INNOCENCE, JUSTICE, RELIGION. *Antonyms*: evil, vice, viciousness, wrong. See synonyms for SIN.

vir·tu·os·i·ty (vûr′cho͞o·os′ə·tē) *n. pl.* **·ties 1** The state of being a virtuoso; the technical mastery of an art, as music. **2** A taste for the fine arts, especially the taste of a dilettante. **3** Virtuosi collectively.

vir·tu·o·so (vûr′cho͞o·ō′sō) *n. pl.* **·si** (-sē) or **·sos 1** A master of technique, as a skilled musician; one who displays virtuosity. **2** A connoisseur; a collector or lover of curios or works of art. **3** *Obs.* A savant; a scientist; learned person. [<Ital., skilled, learned <LL *virtuosus* full of excellence <L *virtus.* See VIRTUE.]

vir·tu·ous (vûr′cho͞o·əs) *adj.* **1** Characterized by, exhibiting, or having the nature of virtue; morally pure and good; chaste: now said especially of women. **2** Potent; efficacious. — **vir′tu·ous·ly** *adv.* — **vir′tu·ous·ness** *n.*

Synonyms: blameless, chaste, correct, dutiful, equitable, estimable, excellent, exemplary, good, honest, just, pure, right, righteous, upright, worthy. See GOOD, INNOCENT, JUST, MODEST, MORAL, PURE. *Antonyms*: see synonyms for CRIMINAL, SINFUL.

vir·tu·te of·fi·ci·i (vər·to͞o′tē ə·fish′ē·ī, vər·tyo͞o′tē) *Latin* By virtue of office.

vir·u·lence (vir′yə·ləns, vir′ə-) *n.* **1** The quality of being virulent. **2** Extreme bitterness or malignity. **3** The power of bacteria and other micro-organisms to overcome the resistance of the host.

vir·u·lent (vir′yə·lənt, vir′ə-) *adj.* **1** Manifesting or partaking of the nature of virus; exceedingly noxious. **2** Very bitter in enmity. **3** *Med.* Actively poisonous or infective; malignant. **4** Having or exhibiting virulence. See synonyms under BITTER[1], MALICIOUS. [<L *virulentus* full of poison < *virus* a poison] — **vir′u·lent·ly** *adv.*

vi·rus (vī′rəs) *n.* **1** Venom; snake poison. **2** Any virulent substance developed by morbid processes within an animal body, and capable of transmitting a specific disease, as smallpox: when inoculated in an attenuated form it is called a *vaccine.* **3** Any of a class of filter-passing, pathogenic agents, chiefly protein in composition but often reducible to crystalline form, and typically inert except when in contact with certain living cells: also **filtrable virus. 4** An illness caused by such an agent. **5** Figuratively, a moral taint; a corrupting influence. **6** Bitterness of mind; acrimony; malice. [<L, poison, slime]

vis (vis) *n. pl.* **vi·res** (vī′rēz) *Latin* Force; potency.

vi·sa (vē′zə) *n.* **1** An official endorsement, as on a passport, certifying that it has been found correct and that the bearer may proceed. **2** A signature of approval, as by an authorized inspecting officer. — *v.t.* **·saed, ·sa·ing 1** To put a visa on. **2** To give a visa to. Also spelled *visé.* [<F <L, fem. sing. pp. of *videre* see]

vis·age (viz′ij) *n.* The face or look of a person, or of an animal; distinctive aspect. [<OF < *vis* a face <L *visus* a look < *videre* see]

vis·aged (viz′ijd) *adj.* Having a visage of some character indicated.

vis·ard (viz′ərd) See VIZARD.

vis–à–vis (vē′zə·vē′, *Fr.* vē·zà·vē′) *n.* **1** One of two persons or things that face each other, as in dancing. **2** A seat having an S-shaped back so arranged that two persons can sit side by side, but facing in opposite directions. — *adj.* & *adv.* Face to face. [<F, face to face]

Vi·sa·yan (vē·sä′yən) *n.* **1** One of the native people of the Philippines, occupying the Visayan Islands and northern Mindanao. **2** The language of these people, belonging to the Indonesian subfamily of Austronesian languages. — *adj.* Of or pertaining to the Visayans or their language. Also spelled *Bisayan.*

Vi·sa·yan Islands (vē·sä′yən) A group of the central Philippines, comprising Bohol, Cebu, Leyte, Masbate, Negros, Panay, Samar, Romblon, and the islets adjacent to them; total 23,621 square miles: also *Bisayan Islands.* Also **Vi·sa′yas** (-yəs).

Visayan Sea A part of the Pacific in the central Philippines, bounded by the Visayan Islands.

Vis·by (vēs′bü) A port on western Gotland island, SE Sweden: German *Wisby.*

vis·ca·cha (vis·kä′chə) *n.* **1** A large burrowing rodent (*Lagostomus maximus*) of the South American pampas, related to the chinchilla, with three-toed hind feet. **2** An allied genus (*Lagidium*) of the Andes, resembling the gray squirrel but with large rabbitlike ears. [<Sp. <Quechuan *uiscacha*]

vis·cer·a (vis′ər·ə) *n. pl. sing.* **vis·cus** (vis′kəs) **1** *Anat.* The internal organs, especially those of the great cavities of the body, as the stomach, lungs, heart, etc. ◆ Collateral adjective: *splanchnic.* **2** Commonly, the intestines. [<L, pl. of *viscus, visceris* an internal organ]

vis·cer·al (vis′ər·əl) *adj.* **1** Pertaining to the viscera. **2** Abdominal.

Visch·er (fish′ər), **Peter,** 1455?–1529, German sculptor.

vis·cid (vis′id) *adj.* Sticky or adhesive; mucilaginous; viscous. See synonyms under ADHESIVE. [<LL *viscidus* <L *viscum* birdlime, mistletoe] — **vis′cid·ly** *adv.* — **vis′cid·ness** *n.*

vis·cid·i·ty (vi·sid′ə·tē) *n.* The quality or state of being viscid.

vis·coi·dal (vis·koid′l) *adj.* Somewhat viscid.

Vis·con·ti (vēs·kôn′tē) A Lombard family which ruled Milan from 1277 to 1447.

vis·cose (vis′kōs) *n.* A thick, honeylike substance produced by the action of caustic soda and carbon disulfide upon cellulose: an important source of rayon. — *adj.* **1** Viscous. **2** Of, pertaining to, containing, or made from viscose. [<LL *viscosus* VISCOUS]

viscose rayon Rayon formed from fibers composed of regenerated cotton or wood-pulp cellulose which has been coagulated or solidified from a solution of cellulose xanthate.

vis·co·sim·e·ter (vis′kə·sim′ə·tər) *n.* An apparatus for determining the viscosity of liquids. Also **vis·com·e·ter** (vis·kom′ə·tər). [<VISCOSI(TY) + -METER]

vis·cos·i·ty (vis·kos′ə·tē) *n. pl.* **·ties 1** The state, quality, property, or degree of being viscous. **2** *Physics* That property of fluids by virtue of which they offer resistance to flow or to any change in the arrangement of their molecules. Compare POISE[2].

vis·count (vī′kount) *n.* **1** In England, a title of nobility between earl and baron. **2** In continental Europe, a title next below that of count; also, the son or younger brother of a count. **3** Formerly, a representative or deputy of a count or earl in the government of a district; specifically, in English use, a sheriff. [<AF *viscounte*, OF *visconte* < *vis-* in place (<L *vice*) + *counte*, *conte* COUNT[2]]

vis·count·cy (vī′kount·sē) *n. pl.* **·cies** The rank, title, or dignity of a viscount. Also **vis′count·ship, vis′count·y.**

vis·count·ess (vī′koun·tis) *n.* The wife of a viscount, or a peeress holding the title in her own right.

vis·cous (vis′kəs) *adj.* **1** Glutinous; semifluid; sticky. **2** Imperfectly fluid, as warm tar. See synonyms under ADHESIVE. [<LL *viscosus* <L *viscum* birdlime, mistletoe] — **vis′cous·ly** *adv.* — **vis′cous·ness** *n.*

vis·cus (vis′kəs) Singular of VISCERA.

vise (vīs) *n.* A clamping device, usually of two jaws made to be closed together with a screw, lever, or the like, for grasping and holding a piece of work. — *v.t.* **vised, vis·ing** To hold, force, or squeeze in or as in a vise. ◆ Homophone: *vice.* Also spelled *vice.* [<OF *vis* a screw <L *vitis* vine; with ref. to the spiral growth of vine tendrils]

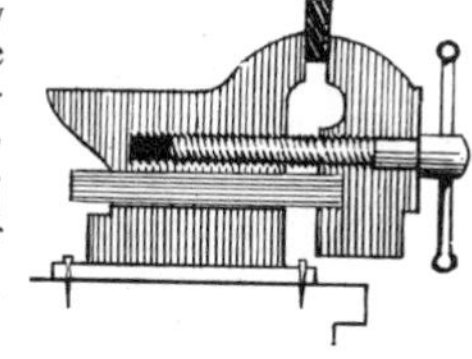
MACHINIST'S VISE
Cross-section.

vi·sé (vē′zā) See VISA.

Vish·nu (vish′nōō) In Hindu theology, the second god of the trinity (Brahma, Vishnu, and Siva), known as "the Preserver"; of his many incarnations the most famous is as Krishna.

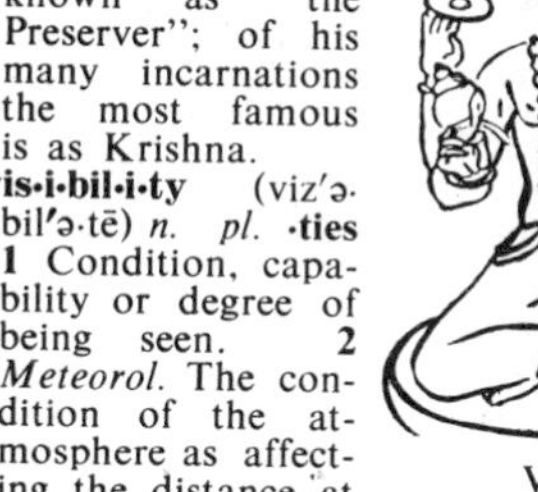

VISHNU

vis·i·bil·i·ty (viz′ə·bil′ə·tē) *n. pl.* **·ties** **1** Condition, capability or degree of being seen. **2** *Meteorol.* The condition of the atmosphere as affecting the distance at which objects can be seen and identified. **3** *Physics* The ratio of the luminous flux of a given wavelength to the radiant energy producing it.

vis·i·ble (viz′ə·bəl) *adj.* **1** Perceivable by the eye; capable of being seen. **2** Apparent at sight; evident. **3** At hand; available; manifest. See VISIBLE SUPPLY. **4** Accessible to visitors; prepared or disposed to be seen or visited. **5** Constructed so that certain parts can be seen by the operator: a *visible* typewriter. See synonyms under EVIDENT, MANIFEST. [<OF <L *visibilis* < *visus*, pp. of *videre* see] — **vis′i·ble·ness** *n.* — **vis′i·bly** *adv.*

visible speech Phonetic symbols devised by Alexander Melville Bell to represent every possible utterance of the organs of speech.

visible supply The total of the known available supply of any commodity, as wheat in elevators and in shipment.

Vis·i·goth (viz′ə·goth) *n.* One of the western Goths, a Teutonic people that invaded the Roman Empire in the third and fourth centuries and settled in France and Spain. See OSTROGOTH. [<LL *Visigothus* <Gmc.; ? lit., the western Goths] — **Vis′i·goth′ic** *adj.*

vi·sion (vizh′ən) *n.* **1** The faculty or sense of sight, localized in the eye, which, with its receptors and associated organs, is normally adapted to receive the stimulus of radiant energy within a certain range of wavelengths. **2** That which is or has been seen; also, something or someone beautiful or delightful: She is a *vision* of loveliness. **3** A mental representation of or as of external objects or scenes, as in sleep; an apparition; dream; fantasy; specifically, an inspired revelation. **4** Some product of the fancy or imagination; an imaginary or unreal thing: *visions* of sugarplums. **5** The ability to anticipate and make provision for future events; foresight. **6** Insight; imagination. See synonyms under DREAM. — *v.t.* To see in or as in a vision. [<OF <L *visio*, *-onis* < *visus*, pp. of *videre* see]

vi·sion·al (vizh′ən·əl) *adj.* Of, pertaining to, or consisting of vision or a vision. — **vi′sion·al·ly** *adv.*

vi·sion·ar·y (vizh′ən·er′ē) *adj.* **1** Not founded on fact; imaginary; impracticable. **2** Affected by fantasies; dreamy; impractical. **3** Associated with apparitions, dreams, etc. See synonyms under FANCIFUL, IDEAL, IMAGINARY, ROMANTIC. — *n. pl.* **·ar·ies** **1** One who has visions. **2** A dreamer; an impractical schemer. — **vi′sion·ar′i·ness** *n.*

vis·it (viz′it) *v.t.* **1** To go or come to see (a person) from friendship, courtesy, on business, etc.; make a call on. **2** To go or come to (a place, etc.), as for transacting business or for touring: to *visit* the Louvre. **3** To be a guest of; stay with temporarily: I *visited* them for several days. **4** To go or come to so as to make official inspection or inquiry: to *visit* a military school. **5** To come upon or afflict. **6** To inflict punishment upon or for. **7** To comfort or bless: The Lord hath *visited* His people. — *v.i.* **8** To make a visit; pay a call or calls. **9** To inflict punishment or vengeance. See synonyms under AVENGE. — *n.* **1** The act of going or coming to see a person or thing, especially with some formality and with the intention of staying some time; a sojourn in a place or with a person; a call or stay. **2** *Colloq.* A talk or friendly chat. **3** An authoritative personal call for inspection and examination or discharge of an official or professional duty. — **right of visit** See RIGHT OF SEARCH. [<OF *visiter* <L *visitare* go to see, freq. of *visare* < *visus*, pp. of *videre* see]

vis·it·a·ble (viz′it·ə·bəl) *adj.* **1** Subject to visitation or punishment. **2** Agreeable to visitors, as a country or region. **3** Having a social position.

vis·i·tant (viz′ə·tənt) *n.* **1** A visitor; that which comes and goes or makes a transient appearance. **2** A migratory animal or bird at a particular region. **3** A visitor as if from another sphere; a supernatural being. — *adj.* Acting as a visitor; paying visits. [<MF <L *visitans*, *-antis*, ppr. of *visitare* VISIT]

vis·i·ta·tion (viz′ə·tā′shən) *n.* **1** The act or fact of visiting; a visit; also, the state or circumstance of being visited. **2** The visit of a bishop to his diocese; an official or authoritative inspection and examination of a foundation, institution, or establishment to set affairs to rights, correct abuses, enforce laws or rules, etc. **3** In Biblical and religious use, a visit of blessing or affliction: a blessed *visitation* from on high; a dreadful *visitation* of famine. **4** *Obs.* The purpose or object of a visit. **5** The resorting of birds or animals to unusual places. See synonyms under MISFORTUNE. — **vis′i·ta′tion·al** *adj.*

Vis·i·ta·tion (viz′ə·tā′shən) *n.* A religious festival held on July 2 in honor of the visit of the Virgin Mary to Elizabeth. *Luke* i 40.

vis·i·ta·to·ri·al (viz′ə·tə·tôr′ē·əl, -tō′rē-) *adj.* Of or pertaining to visitation; done under an official right of visitation. Also **vis′i·to′ri·al.**

visiting card A calling card.

vis·i·tor (viz′ə·tər) *n.* One who visits. Also **vis′it·er.**

Vis·la (vēs′lə) The Russian name for the VISTULA.

vis ma·jor (vis mā′jər) *Latin* **1** Irresistible or uncontrollable force; inevitable accident. **2** *Law* An unavoidable accident: in civil law, nearly the same as, but broader than, an act of God.

vis med·i·ca·trix na·tu·rae (vis med′ə·kā′triks nə·chōōr′ē) *Latin* The curative power of nature.

vi·sor (vī′zər, viz′ər) *n.* **1** A projecting piece on a cap shielding the eyes. **2** In ancient armor, the front piece of a helmet which protected the upper part of the face and could be raised. — *v.t.* To mask; cover with a visor. Also spelled *vizor.* [<AF *viser*, OF *visiere* < *vis* face. See VISAGE.]

vis·ta (vis′tə) *n.* **1** A view or prospect, as along an avenue; an outlook. **2** A mental view embracing a series of events. [<Ital. <L *visus*, pp. of *videre* see]

Vis·tu·la (vis′chōō·lə) The longest river in Poland, flowing 678 miles north from the Carpathian Mountains to the **Vistula Lagoon** (German *Frisches Haff*), a coastal inlet (332 square miles; about 60 miles long, 7 to 11 miles wide) of the Gulf of Danzig: German *Weichsel*, Russian *Visla.*

vis·u·al (vizh′ōō·əl) *adj.* **1** Pertaining to, resulting from, or serving the sense of sight; ocular. **2** Perceptible by sight; visible. **3** Optical: the *visual* focus of a lens. **4** Produced or induced by mental images: a *visual* conception. [<MF <LL *visualis* <L *visus* a sight < *videre* see]

visual field The total area visible to the unmoving eye or eyes at any given moment.

vis·u·al·i·ty (vizh′ōō·al′ə·tē) *n. pl.* **·ties** **1** The quality or condition of being visual; mental visibility. **2** That which is or may be perceived by or as by vision.

vis·u·al·ize (vizh′ōō·əl·īz′) *v.* **·ized, ·iz·ing** *v.t.* To form a mental image of; picture in the mind. — *v.i.* To form mental images. Also *Brit.* **vis′u·al·ise′.** — **vis′u·al·ism** *n.* — **vis′u·al·i·za′tion** *n.*

vis·u·al·iz·er (vizh′ōō·əl·ī′zər) *n.* **1** One who visualizes. **2** One whose mental images are formed chiefly by visualization: also **vis′u·al·ist** (-ist).

visual purple *Biochem.* A complex reddish-purple protein present in the rods of the vertebrate retina: it is an important factor in the process of vision, especially at night: also called *rhodopsin.*

visual yellow *Biochem.* The pigmented protein into which visual purple is changed by the action of light: heat acts upon it to produce vitamin A: also called *retinene.*

vis vi·tae (vis vī′tē) *Latin* The force of life; vitality. Also **vis vi·ta·lis** (vī·tā′lis).

vi·ta·ceous (vī·tā′shəs) *adj. Bot.* Designating or belonging to a family *(Vitaceae)* of mostly woody and climbing vines, the grape family, having alternate leaves, inconspicuous greenish flowers in clusters, and berry-like fruit. [<NL, family name <L *vitis* a vine]

vi·tal (vīt′l) *adj.* **1** Pertaining to life. **2** Essential to or supporting life. **3** Affecting life; fatal to life: a *vital* error or wound. **4** Necessary to existence or continuance; necessary; essential; life-sustaining. **5** Relating to the facts of life, as births, deaths, etc.: *vital* statistics. [<OF <L *vitalis* < *vita* life] — **vi′tal·ly** *adv.*

vital force A form of energy regarded as acting independently of all physical and chemical forces in the causation of life and in the development of living phenomena. Also **vital principle.**

vi·tal·ism (vīt′l·iz′əm) *n.* **1** The doctrine that life had its origin and support in some principle that is neither material nor organic. **2** *Philos.* A movement represented by Henri Bergson, which upholds the principles of freedom and self-determination and the creative power of the human consciousness. It places intuition above intellect, and considers the universe as living and self-evolving without predestined development or end. Compare BERGSONISM, ÉLAN VITAL. **3** *Biol.* The theory that organic growth is due to forces that operate only in living organisms and differ in kind from the chemical and physical forces at work in the inorganic world: opposed to *mechanism.* — **vi′tal·ist** *n.* — **vi′tal·is′tic** *adj.*

vi·tal·i·ty (vī·tal′ə·tē) *n.* **1** The state of being vital; vital force; the principle of life; animation; life. **2** Power of continuing in force or effect. See synonyms under LIFE.

vi·tal·ize (vīt′l·īz) *v.t.* **·ized, ·iz·ing** To make vital; endow with life or energy; animate. — **vi′tal·i·za′tion** *n.* — **vi′tal·iz′er** *n.*

vi·tals (vīt′lz) *n. pl.* **1** The parts necessary to life, as the heart and brain: used also figuratively. **2** The parts essential to the health, maintenance, etc., of anything.

vital statistics Quantitative data relating to certain aspects and conditions of human life, especially in relation to large population groups.

vi·ta·mer (vī′tə·mər) *n. Biochem.* Any dietary factor or other substance that possesses the activity of a given vitamin or acts to counteract a vitamin deficiency, as carotenoid in human subjects. [<VITA(MIN) + Gk. *meros* a part]

vi·ta·min (vī′tə·min) *n. Biochem.* Any of a group of complex organic substances found in minute quantities in most natural foodstuffs, and closely associated with the maintenance of normal physiological functions in man and animals. Numerous forms have been isolated and described under special names. Also **vi′ta·mine** (-mēn, -min). [<L *vita* life + AMINE] — **vi′ta·min′ic** *adj.*

vitamin A The fat-soluble vitamin occurring in green and yellow vegetables, dairy products, liver oil, and fish oil: it prevents atrophy of epithelial tissue and protects against night blindness.

vitamin B complex A group of water-soluble vitamins widely distributed in plants and animals, most members of which have special names.

vitamin B$_1$ Thiamine.

vitamin B$_2$ Riboflavin.

vitamin B$_6$ Pyridoxine.

vitamin B$_{12}$ A vitamin extracted from liver and believed to be protective against pernicious anemia.

vitamin C Ascorbic acid.

vitamin D The anti-rachitic vitamin occurring chiefly in fish-liver oils. Many closely related forms are known.

vitamin D$_1$ An impure mixture of calciferol and lumisterol.

vitamin D$_2$ Calciferol.

vitamin D$_3$ A form of vitamin D$_2$ found principally in fish-liver oils.

vitamin E The anti-sterility vitamin, found in whole grain cereals, seeds of legumes, corn and cottonseed oils, egg yolks, meat, and milk: known to be a mixture of alpha-, beta-, and gamma-tocopherols.

vitamin G Riboflavin.

vitamin H Biotin.

vitamin K$_1$ A vitamin, found in green leafy vegetables, which promotes the clotting of blood: also called *phylloquinone.*

vitamin K$_2$ A form of vitamin K$_1$ prepared from fishmeal.

vi·ta·min·ol·o·gy (vī′tə·min·ol′ə·jē) *n.* The scientific study of vitamins. [<VITAMIN + -(O)LOGY]

vitamin P The factor present in citrus juices along with vitamin C; citrin. It promotes the normal permeability of capillary walls.

vi·ta·scope (vī′tə·skōp) *n.* A device by which pictures taken by the kinetoscope are enlarged and exhibited on a screen. [<L *vita* life + -SCOPE]

Vi·tebsk (vē′tepsk) A city on the Western Dvina river in NE Belorussian S.S.R.

vi·tel·lin (vi·tel′in, vī-) *n. Biochem.* A phosphoprotein occurring in the yolk of eggs. [<VITELL(US) + -IN]

vi·tel·line (vi·tel′in, vī-) *adj.* **1** Of or pertaining to the food yolk of an egg. **2** Of a dull yellow, approaching red; of the color of the yolk of eggs. — *n.* The yolk of an egg. [<Med. L *vitellinus* <L *vitellus* VITELLUS]

vi·tel·lus (vi·tel′əs, vī-) *n.* The egg yolk. [<L, orig. dim. of *vitulus* a calf]

vi·tesse (vē·tes′) *n. French* Speed: used especially in the phrases **grande vitesse** (grän̂d), fast express, and **pe·tite vitesse** (pə·tēt′), ordinary express, or freight, etc.

vi·ti·ate (vish′ē·āt) *v.t.* **·at·ed, ·at·ing** **1** To impair the use or value of; spoil. **2** To debase or corrupt. **3** To render legally ineffective: Fraud *vitiates* a contract. See synonyms under CORRUPT, DEFILE[1], POLLUTE. [<L *vitiatus,* pp. of *vitiare* < *vitium* a fault] — **vi·ti·a·ble** (vish′ē·ə·bəl) *adj.* — **vi′ti·a′tion** *n.* — **vi′ti·a′·tor** *n.*

vi·ti·at·ed (vish′ē·ā′tid) *adj.* Contaminated; rendered defective; invalidated.

vit·i·cul·ture (vit′ə·kul′chər, vī′tə-) *n.* **1** The science and art of grape-growing. **2** The culture of the vine. [<L *vitis* a vine + CULTURE] — **vit′i·cul′tur·al** *adj.* — **vit′i·cul′tur·er, vit′i·cul′·tur·ist** *n.*

Vi·ti Le·vu (vē′tē lā′vōō) The largest of the Fiji Islands; 4,010 square miles; capital, Suva.

vit·i·li·go (vit′ə·lī′gō) *n. Pathol.* A skin disease characterized by a partial privation of color in spots, with a tendency to increase in size; piebald skin; leukoderma. [<L *vitiligo* tetter < *vitium* a fault]

Vi·tim (vi·tēm′, *Russian* vē·tyēm′) A river in NE Buryat-Mongol Autonomous S.S.R., flowing 1,132 miles to the Lena.

Vi·to·ri·a (vē·tôr′ē·ə, *Sp.* bē·tō′ryä) A city in north central Spain, capital of a Basque province.

Vi·tó·ria (vē·tô′ryə) The capital of Espírito Santo state, SE central Brazil; a port on the Altantic coast.

vit·rain (vit′rān) *n.* A variety of bituminous coal having a vitreous appearance and a structure characterized by narrow, compact, crystalline bands. [<L *vitrum* glass, on analogy with *fusain* (def. 2)]

vit·re·ous (vit′rē·əs) *adj.* **1** Pertaining to glass; glassy. **2** Obtained from glass. **3** Resembling glass in some property or properties; vitriform. **4** Pertaining to the vitreous humor. [<L *vitreus* < *vitrum* glass] — **vit′re·os′i·ty** (-os′ə·tē), **vit′re·ous·ness** *n.*

vitreous electricity Electricity generated by rubbing glass with silk: regarded as positive.

vitreous humor *Anat.* The transparent jellylike tissue that fills the ball of the eye and is enclosed by the hyaloid membrane. Also **vitreous body.**

vi·tres·cence (vi·tres′əns) *n.* The state of becoming vitreous.

vi·tres·cent (vi·tres′ənt) *adj.* **1** Capable of being turned into glass. **2** Tending to become glass. [<L *vitrum* glass + -ESCENT]

vi·tres·ci·ble (vi·tres′ə·bəl) *adj.* Capable of forming a viscous, glasslike layer under the action of great heat, as certain crushed minerals. [<VITRESC(ENT) + -IBLE]

vitri- *combining form* Glass; of or pertaining to glass; crystalline: *vitriform.* Also, before vowels, **vitr-.** [<L *vitrum* glass]

vit·ric (vit′rik) *adj.* Pertaining to or like glass.

vit·ri·fac·ture (vit′rə·fak′chər) *n.* The manufacture of vitreous or vitrified wares, as glass. [<VITRI- + (MANU)FACTURE]

vit·ri·fi·ca·tion (vit′rə·fə·kā′shən) *n.* **1** The process of vitrifying. **2** The state of being vitrified. **3** A vitrified object. Also **vit′ri·fac′tion** (-fak′shən).

vit·ri·form (vit′rə·fôrm) *adj.* Having a glassy appearance; glasslike.

vit·ri·fy (vit′rə·fī) *v.t.* & *v.i.* **·fied, ·fy·ing** To change into glass or a vitreous substance; make or become vitreous. [<MF *vitrifier* <L *vitrum* glass + *facere* make] — **vit′ri·fi′a·ble** *adj.*

vit·rine (vit′rin) *n.* A glass showcase for art objects. [<F < *vitre* glass <L *vitrum*]

vit·ri·ol (vit′rē·ōl, -əl) *n.* **1** *Chem.* **a** Sulfuric acid, originally made from green vitriol: more commonly called **oil of vitriol. b** Any sulfate of a heavy metal, as **green vitriol,** from iron; **blue vitriol,** from copper; **white vitriol,** from zinc. **2** Anything sharp or caustic, as sarcasm. — *v.t.* **·oled** or **·olled, ·ol·ing** or **·ol·ling** **1** To injure (a person) with vitriol. **2** To subject (anything) to the agency of vitriol. [<OF <Med. L *vitriolum* <L *vitrum* glass; so called because of its glassy appearance]

vit·ri·ol·ic (vit′rē·ol′ik) *adj.* **1** Derived from a vitriol. **2** Corrosive, burning, or caustic.

vit·ri·ol·ize (vit′rē·əl·īz′) *v.t.* **·ized, ·iz·ing** **1** To corrode, injure, or burn with sulfuric acid. **2** To convert into or impregnate with vitriol. — **vit′ri·ol·i·za′tion** *n.*

Vi·tru·vi·us (vi·trōō′vē·əs) Roman architect, military engineer, and writer of the first century B.C.; full name, *Marcus Vitruvius Pollio.* — **Vi·tru′vi·an** *adj.*

vit·ta (vit′ə) *n. pl.* **vit·tae** (vit′ē) **1** A fillet or band for the head; specifically, a sacred or sacrificial headband or chaplet worn by brides, vestals, priests, poets, and sacrificial victims. **2** *Bot.* An oil tube; a tube or canal in the fruit of plants of the parsley family, containing an aromatic oil. **3** *Zool.* A band or stripe, as of color. [<L < *viere* plait]

vit·tate (vit′āt) *adj.* **1** Having or bearing vittae or a vitta. **2** Striped.

vit·tles (vit′lz) See VICTUAL.

Vit·to·rio (vit·tô′ryō) Italian form of VICTOR.

Vit·to·rio E·ma·nue·le (vit·tô′ryō ā·mä·nwā′lā) See VICTOR EMMANUEL.

Vit·to·rio Ve·ne·to (vit·tô′ryō ve′nā·tō) A city in NE Italy: scene of an Italian victory and armistice in World War I, November 3, 1918.

vit·u·line (vich′ōō·līn, -lin) *adj.* Pertaining to, of, or like a calf or veal. [<L *vitulinus* < *vitulus* a calf]

vi·tu·per·ate (vī·tōō′pə·rāt, -tyōō′-, vi-) *v.t.* **·at·ed, ·at·ing** To find fault with abusively; rail at; berate; scold. See synonyms under ABUSE. [<L *vituperatus,* pp. of *vituperare* blame, scold < *vitium* a fault + *parare* prepare] — **vi·tu′per·a′tion** *n.* — **vi·tu′per·a′tive** *adj.* — **vi·tu′per·a′tive·ly** *adv.* — **vi·tu′per·a′·tor** *n.*

vi·va (vē′vä) *interj.* Live! Long live!: a shout of applause; an acclamation or salute. [<Ital., 3rd person sing. present subjunctive of *vivere* live <L]

vi·va·ce (vē·vä′chā) *adv. Music* Lively; quickly; briskly. Also **vi·va′ce·men′te** (-mān′tā). [<Ital. <L *vivax.* See VIVACIOUS.]

vi·va·cious (vi·vā′shəs, vī-) *adj.* **1** Full of life and spirits; lively; active. **2** *Obs.* Tenacious of life. [<L *vivax, vivacis* < *vivere* live] — **vi·va′cious·ly** *adv.* — **vi·va′cious·ness** *n.*

Synonyms: animated, brisk, cheerful, frolicsome, gay, jocose, jocund, lively, merry, mirthful, pleasant, sparkling, spirited, sportive. See ALIVE, SPRIGHTLY. *Antonyms:* dead, dreary, dull, heavy, inanimate, lifeless, monotonous, moody, spiritless, stolid, stupid.

vi·vac·i·ty (vi·vas′ə·tē, vī-) *n. pl.* **·ties** **1** The state or quality of being vivacious. **2** Sprightliness, as of temper or behavior; liveliness. **3** A vivacious act, expression, etc.

Vi·val·di (vē·väl′dē), **Antonio,** 1675?–1743, Italian violinist and composer.

vi·van·dière (vē·vän·dyâr′) *n.* Formerly, a woman who supplied provisions and liquors to troops in the field, as in the French army. [<F, fem. of *vivandier* a sutler, ult. <L *vivenda.* See VIAND.]

vi·var·i·um (vī·vâr′ē·əm) *n. pl.* **·var·i·a** (-vâr′·ē·ə) or **·var·i·ums** A place for keeping or raising live animals, fish, or plants, as a park, pond, aquarium, cage, etc. Also **viv·a·ry** (viv′·ər·ē). [<L, orig. neut. of *vivarius* concerning live things < *vivus* alive < *vivere* live]

vi·va vo·ce (vī′və vō′sē) *Latin* By spoken word; orally: used both as an adverb and adjective.

vive (vēv) *French interj.* Live! Long live!: used in acclamation: opposed to *à bas.*

vive la ré·pu·blique (vēv lȧ rā·pü·blēk′) *French* Long live the republic!

vive le roi (vēv lə rwȧ′) *French* Long live the king!

vi·ver·rine (vī·ver′īn, -in, vi-) *adj.* Belonging or pertaining to a family *(Viverridae)* of small carnivores including civets and mongooses. — *n.* A civet. [<NL *viverrinus* <L *viverra* a ferret]

vi·vers (vī′vərz) *n. pl. Scot.* Food; provisions.

vives (vīvz) *n. pl.* A morbid enlargement of the submaxillary glands of the horse: also called *fives.* [Earlier *avives* <OF <Sp. *avivas* <Arabic *addhība* < *al* the + *dhība* a she-wolf]

Viv·i·an (viv′ē·ən, *Ger.* vē′vē·än) A personal name. Also **Viv·i·en** (viv′ē·ən, *Fr.* vē·vyan̂′), *Fr. fem.* **Vi·vienne** (vē·vyen′), *Ital. fem.* **Vi·via·na** (vē·vyä′nä). [<L, lively]
— **Vivian** In Arthurian romance, the wily mistress of Merlin, who imprisons him by his own magic: also known as *the Lady of the Lake, Nimue.* Also **Vivien, Viviane.**

viv·id (viv′id) *adj.* **1** Having an appearance of vigorous life; intense: said of colors having intense luminosity. **2** Producing or fitted to evoke lifelike imagery or suggestion. **3** Acting or exercised with lively interest; keen; clearly felt; strongly expressed. [<L *vividus* lively < *vivere* live] — **viv′id·ly** *adv.* — **viv′id·ness** *n.*

Synonyms: animated, bright, brilliant, clear, graphic, intense, keen, lively, luminous, quick, sprightly, stirring, telling, vigorous. See GRAPHIC. *Antonyms:* dim, dreary, dull, gloomy, heavy, lifeless, prosy, spiritless, stupid.

viv·i·fy (viv′ə·fī) *v.t.* **·fied, ·fy·ing** **1** To give life to; animate; vitalize. **2** To make more vivid or striking. [<OF *vivifier* <LL *vivificare* <L *vivus* alive + *facere* make] — **viv′i·fi·ca′tion** (-fə·kā′shən) *n.* — **viv′i·fi′er** *n.*

vi·vip·a·rous (vī·vip′ər·əs) *adj.* **1** *Zool.* Bringing forth living young, as most mammals: contrasted with *oviparous.* **2** *Bot.* Producing bulbs or seeds that germinate while still attached to the parent plant; proliferous. [<L *viviparus* < *vivus* alive + *parere* bring forth] — **vi·vip′a·rous·ly** *adv.* — **vi·vip′a·rous·ness, viv·i·par·i·ty** (viv′ə·par′ə·tē) *n.*

viv·i·sect (viv′ə·sekt) *v.t.* To dissect or operate upon (a living animal), with a view to exposing its physiological processes. —*v.i.* To practice vivisection. [Back formation <VIVISECTION] —**viv′i·sec′tor** *n.*

viv·i·sec·tion (viv′ə·sek′shən) *n.* **1** The dissection of a living animal. **2** Experimentation on living animals by means of operations designed to promote knowledge of physiological and pathological processes. [<L *vivus* living, alive + *sectio, -onis* a cutting. See SECTION.] —**viv′i·sec′tion·al** *adj.* —**viv′i·sec′tion·ist** *n.* & *adj.*

vix·en (vik′sən) *n.* **1** A turbulent, quarrelsome woman; shrew. **2** A female fox. [ME *fixen* a she–fox, fem. of OE *fox*] —**vix′en·ish** *adj.* —**vix′en·ly** *adj.* & *adv.*

viz·ard (viz′ərd) *n.* A mask; visor: also spelled *visard.* [Alter. of VISOR]

viz·ard·ed (viz′ərd·id) *adj.* Masked; disguised or protected by a vizard.

Viz·ca·ya (vēs·kä′yä, *Sp.* bēth·kä′yä) The Spanish name for BISCAY.

Viz·e·tel·ly (viz′ə·tel′ē), **Frank Horace,** 1864–1938, U. S. lexicographer and encyclopedist born in England.

vi·zier (vi·zir′, viz′yər) *n.* A high official of a Moslem country, especially of the old Turkish Empire; a minister of state. Also **vi·zir′.** —**grand vizier** The highest dignitary in Moslem countries; the prime minister. [<Turkish *vezīr* <Arabic *wazīr* a counselor, orig. a porter < *wazara* carry]

vi·zier·ate (vi·zir′it, -āt, viz′yər·it, -yə·rāt) *n.* The office or dignity of a vizier. Also **vi·zier′·al·ty, vi·zier′ship, vi·zir′ate, vi·zir′ship.**

vi·zor (vī′zər, viz′ər) *n.* The movable upper front piece of a helmet protecting the eyes. See VISOR.

VIZOR
15th century.

Vlad·i·mir (vlad′ə·mir, *Russian* vlä·dyē′mir), 956?–1015, first Christian Russian ruler.

Vlad·i·mir (vlad′ə·mir, *Russian* vlä·dyē′mir) A city in central European Russian S.F.S.R., NE of Moscow.

Vla·di·vos·tok (vlad′ə·vos·tok′, -vos′tok; *Russian* vlä′·dyē·vos·tôk′) A port on the Sea of Japan in extreme SE Asiatic Russian S.F.S.R.

Vla·minck (vlà·mank′), **Maurice de,** 1876–1958, French painter.

Vlis·sing·en (vlis′ing·ən) The Dutch name for FLUSHING.

Vlo·na (vlō′nä) The Albanian name for VALONA.

Vl·ta·va (vul′tä·vä) A river in central Bohemia, Czechoslovakia, flowing 267 miles north from the Bohemian Forest, through Prague, to the Elbe: German *Moldau.*

V–mail (vē′māl′) *n.* Mail written on special forms, transmitted overseas in World War II on microfilm, and enlarged at point of reception for final delivery. [<V(ICTORY) + MAIL¹]

vo·ca·ble (vō′kə·bəl) *n.* **1** A word, chiefly as regarded in relation to its sound or combination of sounds instead of its meaning. **2** A vocal sound. —*adj.* Utterable. [<F <L *vocabulum* a name < *vocare* call < *vox* voice]

vo·cab·u·lar·y (vō·kab′yə·ler′ē) *n. pl.* **·lar·ies** **1** A list of words or of words and phrases, especially one arranged in alphabetical order and defined or translated; a lexicon; glossary. **2** All the words of a language. **3** A sum or aggregate of the words used or understood by a particular person, class, etc., or employed in some specialized field of knowledge. **4** The range of expression at a person's disposal, especially in art. [<LL *vocabularius* <L *vocabulum.* See VOCABLE.]

vocabulary entry **1** A word or term given in a vocabulary. **2** A word, term, or phrase entered in a dictionary, in some readily distinguishable type, for purposes of definition or identification. Vocabulary entries may be listed in alphabetical place (main entries), run in within a main entry (additional parts of speech, inflected forms, idioms, etc.), run on at the end of an entry (derivatives and related words), listed under a word, prefix, or combining form (self–explanatory compounds and two–word phrases), or entered in a special section of the book. In this dictionary, all vocabulary entries are shown in boldface type or preceded by a boldface em–dash.

vo·cal (vō′kəl) *adj.* **1** Of or pertaining to the voice; uttered by the voice; oral: *vocal* protests. **2** Having voice; endowed with the power of utterance: *vocal* creatures. **3** Composed for or performed by the voice: a *vocal* score. **4** Concerned in the production of voice: the *vocal* organs. **5** Full of voices or sounds; resounding: The air was *vocal* with their cries. **6** Eloquent without need of speech: the *vocal* beauty of the Parthenon. **7** Freely expressing oneself in speech; readily given to voicing opinions: the *vocal* segment of the populace. **8** *Phonet.* **a** Voiced; sonant, as *b, d, g,* distinguished from *p, t, k.* **b** Pertaining to or like a vowel; vocalic. See synonyms under VERBAL. —*n. Phonet.* **1** A vowel. **2** A voiced consonant. [<L *vocalis* speaking, sounding < *vox, vocis* a voice. Doublet of VOWEL.] —**vo′cal·ly** *adv.*

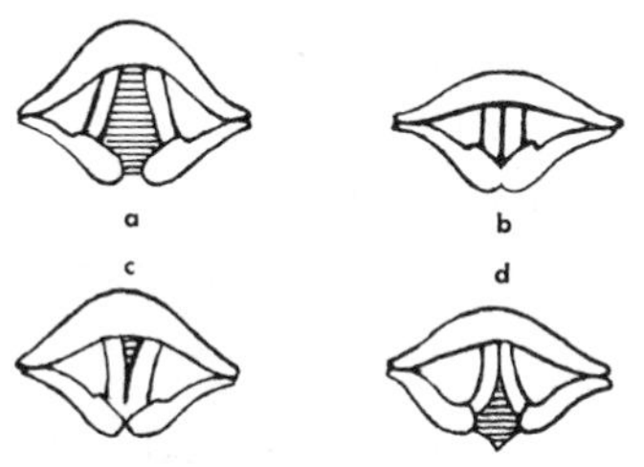

VOCAL CORDS
a. Open. *b.* Closed. *c.* Voice. *d.* Whisper.

vocal cords Two membranous bands extending from the thyroid cartilage of the larynx. The edges of these bands, when drawn tense, are caused to vibrate by the passage of air from the lungs, thereby producing voice; the degree of tension of the cords controls the pitch of the voice.

vo·cal·ic (vō·kal′ik) *adj.* Consisting of, like, or relating to vowel sounds.

vo·ca·lise (vō·kä·lēz′) *n. Music* A practice exercise for singers designed to develop flexibility and control of pitch and tonal beauty, usually employing vowels or Italian syllables. [<F]

vo·cal·ism (vō′kəl·iz′əm) *n.* **1** Vocalization. **2** A vocalic sound; also, a vowel system. **3** Singing; also, the technique of singing.

vo·cal·ist (vō′kəl·ist) *n.* A singer, especially one who has a cultivated voice.

vo·cal·ize (vō′kəl·īz) *v.* **·ized, ·iz·ing** *v.t.* **1** To make vocal; utter, say, or sing; make sonant. **2** To provide a voice for; render articulate. **3** To mark with vowel points, as a Hebrew text. **4** *Phonet.* **a** To change to or use as a vowel: to *vocalize* y. **b** To voice. —*v.i.* **5** To produce sounds with the voice, as in speaking or singing. **6** *Phonet.* To be changed to a vowel. —**vo′cal·i·za′tion** *n.* —**vo′cal·iz′er** *n.*

vo·ca·tion (vō·kā′shən) *n.* **1** A stated or regular occupation; a calling. **2** A call to, or fitness for, a certain career, especially a religious position. **3** The work or profession for which one has a sense of special fitness. See synonyms under BUSINESS. [<L *vocatio, -onis* < *vocatus,* pp. of *vocare* call] —**vo·ca′·tion·al** *adj.* —**vo·ca′tion·al·ly** *adv.*

vocational adviser One who diagnoses the personal characteristics of people with the view of suggesting suitable vocations for them; a specialist in vocational guidance. Also **vocational expert.**

vocational school See under SCHOOL.

voc·a·tive (vok′ə·tiv) *adj.* **1** Pertaining to or used in the act of calling. **2** *Gram.* In some inflected languages, denoting the case of a noun, pronoun, or adjective used in direct address: The name "Brutus" is in the *vocative* case in "Et tu, Brute." —*n. Gram.* **1** The vocative case. **2** A word in this case. [<F, fem. of *vocatif* <L *vocativus* < *vocare* call]

vo·ces (vō′sēz) Plural of VOX.

vo·cif·er·ant (vō·sif′ər·ənt) *adj.* Vociferous; clamorous; uttering loud cries. —*n.* A vociferous person. [<L *vociferans, -antis,* ppr. of *vociferari.* See VOCIFERATE.] —**vo·cif′er·ance** *n.*

vo·cif·er·ate (vō·sif′ə·rāt) *v.t.* & *v.i.* **·at·ed, ·at·ing** To cry out with a loud voice; exclaim noisily; shout; bawl. See synonyms under CALL. [<L *vociferatus,* pp. of *vociferari* cry out < *vox, vocis* a voice + *ferre* carry] —**vo·cif′er·a′tion** *n.* —**vo·cif′er·a′tor** *n.*

vo·cif·er·ous (vō·sif′ər·əs) *adj.* Making a loud outcry; clamorous. See synonyms under NOISY. —**vo·cif′er·ous·ly** *adv.* —**vo·cif′er·ous·ness** *n.*

vod·ka (vod′kə, *Russian* vôd′kä) *n.* A colorless alcoholic liquor, originally made in Poland and Russia, usually made from fermented wheat mash. [<Russian, dim. of *voda* water]

voe (vō) *n. Scot.* A small bay, creek, or inlet.

Vo·gel·kop (vō′gəl·kôp′) A peninsula of NW Netherlands New Guinea, connected to the mainland by an isthmus 20 miles wide; about 225 miles east to west, about 135 miles north to south.

vogue (vōg) *n.* **1** The prevalent way or fashion; popular temporary usage: often preceded by *in.* **2** Popular favor; popularity. [<F, fashion, orig. rowing < *voguer* row <Ital. *vogare* <MHG *wogen* sail < *woge* a wave]

Vo·gul (vō′gŏŏl) *n.* **1** One of a Finno–Ugric people of the Ural Mountains. **2** The Ugric language of these people.

voice (vois) *n.* **1** The sound produced by the vocal organs of a person or animal; also, the quality or character of such sound: a melodious *voice.* **2** The power or faculty of vocal utterance; speech. **3** A sound suggesting vocal utterance or speech: the *voice* of the wind. **4** Opinion or choice expressed; also, the right of expressing a preference or judgment: to have a *voice* in the affair. **5** Instruction; admonition; teaching: the *voice* of nature. **6** A speaker; also, a person or agency by which the thought, wish, or purpose of another is expressed: This journal is the *voice* of the teaching profession. **7** Expression of thought, opinion, feeling, etc.: to give *voice* to one's ideals. **8** *Phonet.* The sound produced by vibration of the vocal cords, as heard in the utterance of vowels and certain consonants, as (g), (m),(v): distinguished from *whisper,* and also from *breath,* as heard in (k), (sh), (f). **9** Musical tone produced by vibration of the vocal cords and resonating in the cavities of the throat and head; also, the ability to sing, or the state of the vocal organs with regard to this ability: to be in poor *voice.* **10** *Gram.* The relation of the action expressed by the verb to the subject, or the form of the verb indicating this relationship. In English, as in most Indo–European languages, a distinction between an *active* and a *passive* voice is made, indicating, respectively, that the subject of the sentence is either performing the action or is being acted upon. (Active: *He wrote the letter.* Passive: *The letter was written by him.*) In Greek and Sanskrit verbs, there is, in addition, a *middle* voice, representing the subject as acting upon himself directly, or in his own interest. **11** *Obs.* Report; rumor; fame. —**with one voice** With one accord; unitedly; unanimously. —*v.t.* **voiced, voic·ing** **1** To put into speech; give expression to; utter. **2** *Music* To regulate the tones of; tune, as the pipes of an organ. **3** *Phonet.* To utter with voice or sonance. [<OF *vois* <L *vox, vocis*]

voiced (voist) *adj.* **1** Having a voice; expressed by voice. **2** *Phonet.* Uttered with vibration of the vocal cords, as (b), (d), (z): sonant: opposed to *surd, voiceless.*

voice·ful (vois′fəl) *adj.* Having vocal quality.

voice·less (vois′lis) *adj.* **1** Having no voice, speech, or suffrage. **2** *Phonet.* Produced without voiced breath, as (p), (t), (s); surd: opposed to *sonant, voiced.* —**voice′less·ly** *adv.*

voice–o·ver (vois′ō′vər) *n.* In motion pictures and television programs, the voice of a narrator or announcer speaking off camera.

voice part A single part, as a melody written for the voice and either sung, or played by a solo instrument, in a concerted composition.

voice·print (vois′print′) *n.* A record of a speech sound, consisting of a complex pattern of wavy lines corresponding to the various pitches used in the utterance.

void (void) *adj.* **1** Not occupied by matter or by visible matter; empty. **2** Destitute; clear or free: with *of: void* of reason, *void* of offense.

3 Unoccupied, as a house or room; having no incumbent. **4** Having no legal force or validity; incapable of confirmation or ratification; invalid; null. **5** Producing no effect; useless. See synonyms under VACANT. — *n.* **1** An empty space; a vacuum. **2** A breach of surface or matter; a disconnecting space. **3** Empty condition or feeling; a blank. — *v.t.* **1** To make void or of no effect; annul. **2** To empty or remove (contents); evacuate, as urine. **3** *Archaic* To leave empty or vacant. [<OF *voide,* fem. of *voit,* ult. <LL *vocuus* empty <L *vacuus*] — **void'er** *n.*

void·a·ble (voi'də·bəl) *adj.* **1** Capable of being made void: A *voidable* contract is valid unless annulled. **2** That may be evacuated. — **void'·a·ble·ness** *n.*

void·ance (void'ns) *n.* **1** The act of voiding, evacuating, ejecting, or emptying. **2** The state or condition of being void; vacancy: *voidance* of a benefice. [<AF *voidaunce,* OF *vuidance* < *voider* empty < *voit* VOID]

void·ed (voi'did) *adj.* **1** Made empty or void; cleared of contents; having a vacant space. **2** *Her.* Having the central area removed, so as to leave only an outline through which the field is visible: said of a charge, as a cross.

voi·là (vwà·là') *interj. French* There! behold! literally, see there.

voi·là tout (vwà·là tōō') *French* That is all; there is the whole matter.

voile (voil, *Fr.* vwàl) *n.* A fine, sheer cotton, silk, wool, or rayon fabric like heavy veiling: used for summer dresses and curtains. [<F, a veil <OF *veile* VEIL]

voir dire (vwàr dēr') *Law* A legal oath administered to a witness to be examined, to make true answers to the questions to be asked him regarding his competency. [<OF *voir* truth + *dire* say]

voix (vwà) *n. French* The voice.

voix cé·leste (vwà sā·lest') *French* An organ stop consisting of two ranks of soft flue stops which produce a waving effect; literally, heavenly voice.

Voj·vo·di·na (voi'vô·di·nä) An autonomous province of NE Yugoslavia, included in Serbia as its northern part and bordering on Hungary and Rumania; 8,683 square miles; capital, Novi Sad. Also **Voy'vo·di·na, Voi'vo·di·na.**

vo·lant (vō'lənt) *adj.* **1** Passing through the air; flying, or able to fly. **2** Characterized by lightness and quickness; nimble. **3** *Her.* Flying, as a bird or bee. [<OF, ppr. of *voler* fly <L *volare*]

vo·lan·te (vō·län'tā) *adj. Music* Swift and light. [<Ital., ppr. of *volare* fly <L]

Vo·la·pük (vō'lə·pük') *n.* A proposed universal language, invented in 1879 by Johann M. Schleyer, a German priest. [<Volapük *vol* world + *pük* speech] — **Vo'la·pük'ist** *n.*

vo·lar[1] (vō'lər) *adj.* Used in flying; pertaining to flight. [<L *volare* fly]

vo·lar[2] (vō'lər) *adj.* Pertaining to the sole of the foot or palm of the hand. [<L *vola* sole, palm]

vol·a·tile (vol'ə·til) *adj.* **1** Evaporating rapidly at ordinary temperatures on exposure to the air; capable of being vaporized. **2** Easily influenced; fickle; changeable. **3** Transient; fleeting; ephemeral. **4** *Obs.* Flying, or able to fly. See synonyms under MOBILE[1]. [<OF *volatil* <L *volatilis* < *volare* fly]

volatile oil Any oil that may be readily vaporized, especially one distilled from plants: distinguished from *fixed oil.*

volatile salts Salts that volatilize without residue; sal volatile.

vol·a·til·i·ty (vol'ə·til'ə·tē) *n.* **1** The state or quality of being volatile. **2** The property of being freely or rapidly diffused in the atmosphere. Also **vol'a·tile·ness.**

vol·a·til·ize (vol'ə·til·īz') *v.t.* & *v.i.* **·ized, ·iz·ing** **1** To make or become volatile. **2** To pass off or cause to pass off in vapor; evaporate. — **vol'a·til·iz'a·ble** *adj.* — **vol'a·til·i·za'tion** *n.* — **vol'a·til·iz'er** *n.*

vol-au-vent (vôl·ō·vän') *n. French* A patty shell of light puff paste filled with a ragout of meat, fowl, or fish.

vol·can·ic (vol·kan'ik) *adj.* **1** Of, pertaining to, or characteristic of a volcano or volcanoes. **2** Produced by a volcano or by igneous action: distinguished from *plutonic.* — **vol·can·ic·i·ty** (vol'kə·nis'ə·tē) *n.* — **vol·can'·i·cal·ly** *adv.*

volcanic glass An igneous rock of volcanic origin and glassy texture having cooled too quickly to crystallize, as obsidian.

volcanic rocks Rocks formed by the consolidation of lava from volcanoes.

vol·can·ism (vol'kən·iz'əm) *n.* The conditions, phenomena, or science of volcanoes or volcanic action.

vol·can·ist (vol'kən·ist) *n.* One who studies, or is expert on volcanoes; a volcanologist.

vol·can·ize (vol'kən·īz) *v.t.* **·ized, ·iz·ing** To subject to the action and effects of volcanic heat. — **vol'can·i·za'tion** *n.*

vol·ca·no (vol·kā'nō) *n. pl.* **·noes** or **·nos** *Geol.* An opening in the earth's surface surrounded by an accumulation of ejected material, forming a hill or mountain, from which heated matter is or has been ejected: known in the former case as *active,* and in the latter as *dormant* or *extinct.* [<Ital. <L *Volcanus, Vulcanus* Vulcan]

Volcano Islands Three small islands, including Iwo Jima, in the western Pacific south of the Bonin Islands, administered by the United States; total, 11 square miles; held by Japan, 1887–1945. *Japanese* **Ka·zan Ret·to** (kä·zän ret·tō).

vol·can·ol·o·gy (vol'kən·ol'ə·jē) *n.* The scientific study of volcanoes. — **vol'can·o·log'i·cal** (-ə·loj'i·kəl) *adj.* — **vol'can·ol'o·gist** *n.*

vole[1] (vōl) *n.* Any of a genus (*Microtus*) of short-tailed, mouselike or ratlike rodents; especially, the common European field mouse or the North American meadow mouse. [Short for earlier *vole mouse* < *vole* a field (<Norw. *voll*) + MOUSE]

vole[2] (vōl) *n.* In some card games, as écarté, a winning of all the tricks in a deal; hence, the entire range; a slam. — **to go the vole** To risk all for great gains. [<F, appar. < *voler* fly <L *volare*]

vol·er·y (vol'ər·ē) *n. pl.* **·er·ies** A large bird cage; aviary; also, the birds in it. [<F *volerie* a flying < *voler.* See VOLE[2].]

Vol·ga (vol'gə, *Russian* vôl'gä) The longest river in Europe, in central European Russian S.F.S.R., flowing 2,290 miles east and south from the Valdai Hills to its delta, the **Volga Basin** (approximately 2,500 square miles), on the Caspian Sea.

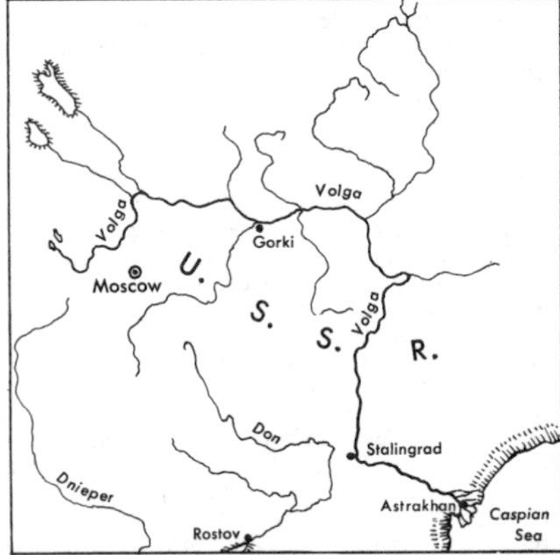

Vol·hyn·i·a (vol·hin'ē·ə, vo·lin'ē·ə) A historical region, formerly in Poland, in NW Ukrainian S.S.R.; about 27,230 square miles. *Russian* **Vo·lyn** (vo·lin'y'), *Polish* **Wo·łyń** (vô'win·y'). — **Vol·hyn'ian** *adj.*

vol·i·tant (vol'ə·tənt) *adj.* Flying, or having power to fly; volant. [<L *volitans, -antis,* ppr. of *volitare,* freq. of *volare* fly]

vol·i·ta·tion (vol'ə·tā'shən) *n.* The act or power of flying; flight. [<L *volitatus,* pp. of *volitare.* See VOLITANT.] — **vol'i·ta'tion·al** *adj.*

vo·li·tient (və·lish'ənt) *adj.* Exercising the will, or having freedom of will; willing; voluntary. [<VOLITI(ON) + -ENT] — **vo·li'tien·cy** *n.*

vo·li·tion (və·lish'ən) *n.* **1** The act or faculty of willing; exercise of the will; especially, the termination of a process of deliberation or vacillation of purpose by a decision or choice. **2** The faculty of will by which the powers are directed toward the attainment of a chosen end; willpower. **3** That which is specifically willed or determined upon. [<F <Med. L *volitio, -onis* <L *vol-,* stem of *velle* will] — **vo·li'tion·al** *adj.* — **vo·li'tion·al·ly** *adv.*

vol·i·tive (vol'ə·tiv) *adj.* **1** Of, pertaining to, or originating in the will. **2** Expressing a wish or permission.

Vol·khov (vôl'khof) A river of NW European Russian S.F.S.R., flowing 140 miles NE from Lake Ilmen, through Novgorod, to Lake Ladoga. Also **Vol'khof.**

Volks·lied (fôlks'lēt') *n. pl.* **·lied·er** (-lē'dər) *German* A folk song; popular song.

vol·ley (vol'ē) *n.* **1** A simultaneous discharge of many missiles; also, the missiles so discharged. **2** Any discharge of many things at once: a *volley* of oaths. **3** In tennis, a return of the ball before it touches the ground. **4** In soccer, a kick given the ball before its rebound. **5** In cricket, a ball bowled so that it strikes the head of the wicket before it touches the ground. — *v.t.* & *v.i.* **·leyed, ·ley·ing** **1** To discharge or be discharged in a volley; let fly together. **2** In tennis, to return (the ball) without allowing it to touch the ground. **3** In soccer, to kick (the ball) before its rebound; in cricket, to bowl (a ball) full pitch. [<MF *volée,* pp. fem. of *voler* fly <L *volare*]

volley ball A game in which a number of players on both sides of a high net endeavor to keep a large ball in motion with the hands from side to side without letting it drop; also, the ball used. Also **vol·ley·ball** (vol'ē·bôl').

Vo·log·da (vô'ləg·də) A city in north central European Russian S.F.S.R.; an industrial and dairying center; capital of a 15th century principality.

Vo·los (vō'los) A port city on the **Gulf of Volos,** an inlet of the Aegean in SE Thessaly, Greece (about 20 miles long and wide); the principal port of Thessaly and capital of Magnesia nome.

vo·lost (vō'lost) *n.* A district having one joint administrative assembly; a rural soviet; formerly, a canton. [<Russian *volost'*]

vol·plane (vol'plān) *v.i.* **·planed, ·plan·ing** To glide in an airplane. — *n.* An airplane glide. [<F *vol plané* gliding flight < *vol* flight + *plané,* pp. of *planer* glide, soar] — **vol'plan·ist** *n.*

Vol·scian (vol'shən) *adj.* Of or pertaining to the **Vol·sci** (vol'sī), a warlike people of ancient Italy, subdued by the Romans about 350 B.C. — *n.* **1** One of the Volsci. **2** Their language, belonging to the Sabellian branch of the Italic languages.

Vol·stead Act (vol'sted) An act to enforce the Eighteenth (Prohibition) Amendment to the Constitution of the United States, and defining intoxicating liquors as those containing more than one half of one percent of alcohol by volume: effective 1920–33. [after Representative Andrew J. *Volstead,* 1860–1947, of Minnesota] — **Vol'stead·ism** *n.*

Vol·sun·ga Sa·ga (vol'sŏŏng·gə sä'gə) A prose version of the Icelandic legends of the dwarf race, the Nibelungs, and Sigurd, the grandson of Volsung. See NIBELUNGENLIED. [<ON *Völsunga saga,* lit., saga of the Volsungs]

volt[1] (vōlt) *n.* The unit of electromotive force, or that difference of potential which, when steadily applied to a conductor whose resistance is one ohm, will produce a current of one ampere. Abbr. *v., V.* [after Alessandro *Volta*]

volt[2] (vōlt) *n.* **1** In horse-training, a gait in which the horse moves partially sidewise round a center with the head turned out; a circular tread. **2** In fencing, a sudden leap to avoid a thrust. [<F *volte* a turn <Ital. *volta,* orig. pp. fem. of *volvere* turn <L]

vol·ta (vol'tə, *Ital.* vôl'tä) *n. pl.* **·te** (-tā) *Music* A turning; a time: used mainly in phrases. — **prima volta** First time. — **seconda volta** Second time. — **una volta** Once. [<Ital. See VOLT[2].]

Vol·ta (vol'tä) The principal river of Ghana, formed by the confluence, in north central Ghana, of the **Black Volta** and **White Volta,** and flowing 300 miles (with Black Volta, about 800 miles) SE to the Bight of Benin.

Vol·ta (vôl'tä), **Count Alessandro,** 1745–1827, Italian physicist and pioneer in electricity.

volt·age (vōl'tij) *n.* Electromotive force expressed in volts: the *voltage* of a current.

vol·ta·ic (vol·tā'ik) *adj.* **1** Pertaining to electricity developed through chemical action or contact; galvanic: a *voltaic* battery; *voltaic* cell. **2** Of or pertaining to Alessandro Volta. [after Alessandro *Volta*]

voltaic battery An assembly of voltaic cells which operate as a unit in generating an electric current.

voltaic cell Cell (def. 5).

voltaic couple A pair of dissimilar, usually metallic, substances which will produce an electric current when immersed in an electrolyte.

voltaic pile An arrangement of dissimilar metal disks, placed alternately and having between them paper moistened with acids for the generation of an electric current. Also *galvanic pile.*

Vol·taire (vol·târ′, *Fr.* vôl·târ′), **François Marie Arouet de,** 1694–1778, French author and philosopher.

vol·ta·ism (vol′tə·iz′əm) *n.* The act of producing an electric current by the chemical action of a liquid on dissimilar metals; galvanism. [after Alessandro *Volta*]

volt·am·e·ter (vol·tam′ə·tər) *n.* A coulometer. [<VOLTA(IC) + -METER]

volt·am·me·ter (vōlt′am′mē′tər) *n.* A wattmeter. [<VOLT(AGE) + AM(PERAGE) + -METER]

volt-am·pere (vōlt′am′pir) *n.* A watt: so called because it is the rate of working in an electric circuit when the current is one ampere and the potential one volt.

volte-face (volt·fäs′, *Fr.* vôlt·fàs′) *n.* **1** A turning about so as to face in the opposite direction. **2** A complete change of attitude or reversal of opinion. [<F <Ital. *volta faccia* < *volta* a turning + *faccia* a face <L *facies*]

vol·ti (vôl′tē) *interj. Music* Turn; specifically, a direction to turn the leaf. [<Ital., imperative sing. of *voltare* turn < *volta.* See VOLT[2].]

vol·ti·geur (vôl·tē·zhœr′) *n.* One who vaults; a tumbler; formerly, in the French army, a skirmisher in a light infantry regiment. [<F < *voltiger* hover, vault <Ital. *volteggiare* < *volta.* See VOLT[2].]

volt·me·ter (vōlt′mē′tər) *n.* An instrument for determining the voltage or potential difference existing between any two points, generally consisting of a calibrated galvanometer wound with a coil of high resistance.

Vol·tur·no (vôl·to͞or′nō) The chief river of southern Italy, arising in the Apennines and flowing 109 miles to the Tyrrhenian Sea NW of Naples.

vol·u·ble (vol′yə·bəl) *adj.* **1** Having a flow of words or fluency in speaking; talkative; garrulous. **2** Turning readily or easily; revolving; apt or formed to roll. **3** Twining, as a plant. [<MF <L *volubilis* easily turned < *volutus,* pp. of *volvere* turn] **— vol′u·bil′i·ty, vol′u·ble·ness** *n.* **— vol′u·bly** *adv.*

vol·ume (vol′yo͞om, -yəm) *n.* **1** A collection of sheets of paper bound together; a book; a separately bound part of a work; anciently, a written roll, a scroll, as of papyrus or vellum. **2** Sufficient matter to fill a volume. **3** Something of a swelling form; coil; fold or turn. **4** A large quantity; a considerable amount. **5** Space occupied, as measured by cubic units, that is, cubic centimeters, cubic feet, etc. **6** The amount of space included by the bounding surfaces of a solid. **7** *Music* Fullness or quantity of sound or tone. **— to speak volumes** To be full of meaning; express a great deal. [<OF *volum* <L *volumen* a roll, scroll < *volutus.* See VOLUBLE.]

vol·umed (vol′yo͞omd, -yəmd) *adj.* **1** Rounded or swelling in form: *volumed* mists. **2** Having bulk or quantity. **3** Being in one or more volumes: a two-*volumed* history.

vo·lu·me·ter (və·lo͞o′mə·tər) *n.* An instrument for measuring the volume of a gas by the amount of liquid displaced by it in a graduated vessel, under known conditions of pressure and temperature. [<VOLU(ME) + -METER]

vol·u·met·ric (vol′yə·met′rik) *adj. Chem.* Of or pertaining to measurement of substances by comparison of volumes or by volumetric analysis. Also **vol′u·met′ri·cal.** **— vol′u·met′ri·cal·ly** *adv.* **— vo·lu·me·try** (və·lo͞o′mə·trē) *n.*

volumetric analysis *Chem.* The quantitative analysis of a substance by determining the amount of a standard solution required to effect a reaction in a known quantity of the substance.

vo·lu·mi·nos·i·ty (və·lo͞o′mə·nos′ə·tē) *n.* The state or quality of being voluminous; especially, copiousness or prolixity.

vo·lu·mi·nous (və·lo͞o′mə·nəs) *adj.* **1** Consisting of many volumes; capable of filling several volumes; also, of great bulk. **2** Writing or having written much; productive. **3** Having coils, folds, convolutions, or windings. [<LL *voluminosus* <L *volumen, -inis* a roll] **— vo·lu′mi·nous·ly** *adv.* **— vo·lu′mi·nous·ness** *n.*

vol·un·ta·rism (vol′ən·tə·riz′əm) *n.* **1** The theory that will is the ultimate principle or constituent of reality, both in experience and development of the individual, and in the constitution and evolution of the universe. **2** The theory that will is the fundamental psychic factor. Compare VITALISM. **— vol′un·ta·rist** *n.* **— vol′un·ta·ris′tic** *adj.*

vol·un·tar·y (vol′ən·ter′ē) *adj.* **1** Proceeding from the will or from one's own free choice: *voluntary* murder; specifically, unconstrained; intentional; volitional. **2** Endowed with, possessing, or exercising will or free choice: a *voluntary* donor. **3** Effected by choice or volition; acting without constraint. **4** Subject to or directed by the will, as a muscle or movement. **5** Of or relating to voluntaryism. **6** *Law* Unconstrained of will; done without compulsion; performed without legal obligation; also, done without valuable consideration; gratuitous. See synonyms under SPONTANEOUS. **—** *n. pl.* **·tar·ies 1** Any work or performance not compelled or imposed by another. **2** *Music* **a** An organ solo, often improvised, played before, during, or after a service. **b** *Rare* A piece of music, usually spontaneous, played or sung as a prelude. **3** *Obs.* A volunteer. [<OF *voluntaire* <L *voluntarius* < *voluntas* will] **— vol′un·tar′i·ly** *adv.* **— vol′un·tar′i·ness** *n.*

vol·un·tar·y·ism (vol′ən·ter′ē·iz′əm) *n.* The principle that religious and educational institutions should be supported by voluntary contributions. **— vol′un·tar′y·ist** *n.*

voluntary system A system of freely given support in distinction from state support of religious or educational institutions.

vol·un·teer (vol′ən·tir′) *n.* **1** One who enters into any service of his own free will. **2** One who voluntarily enters military service, but is then subject to the same regulations and discipline as other soldiers: opposed to *conscript.* **3** *Law* One who takes title under a deed made without valuable consideration; also, a voluntary agent or actor in a transaction. **—** *adj.* **1** Pertaining to or composed of volunteers; voluntary. **2** Springing up naturally or spontaneously, as from fallen or self-sown seed: a *volunteer* growth. **—** *v.t.* To offer to give or do. **—** *v.i.* To enter or offer to enter into some service or undertaking of one's free will; enlist. [< obs. F *voluntaire* <OF, VOLUNTARY]

Volunteers of America A religious and philanthropical organization founded in the United States in 1896 by Commander and Mrs. Ballington Booth, who resigned from the Salvation Army for that purpose.

Volunteer State Nickname of TENNESSEE.

vo·lup·tu·ar·y (və·lup′cho͞o·er′ē) *adj.* Pertaining to or promoting sensual indulgence and luxurious pleasures. **—** *n. pl.* **·ar·ies** One addicted to sensual pleasures; a sensualist. [<L *voluptuarius* < *voluptas* pleasure]

vo·lup·tu·ous (və·lup′cho͞o·əs) *adj.* **1** Belonging to, producing, exciting, or yielding sensuous gratification. **2** Pertaining to or devoted to the enjoyment of pleasures or luxuries; luxurious; sensual. **3** Having a full and beautiful form, as a woman. [<OF *voluptueux* <L *voluptuosus* full of pleasure < *voluptas* pleasure] **— vo·lup′tu·ous·ly** *adv.* **— vo·lup′tu·ous·ness** *n.*

vo·lute (və·lo͞ot′) *n.* **1** *Archit.* A spiral scroll-like ornament, as in Ionic capitals; a scroll. **2** *Zool.* One of the whorls or turns of a spiral shell. **—** *adj.* **1** Rolled up; forming spiral curves. **2** Having a spiral form, as a machine part. [<F <L *voluta* a scroll, orig. fem. pp. of *volvere* turn]

VOLUTE

vo·lut·ed (və·lo͞o′tid) *adj.* Having a volute or flat spiral scroll.

volute spring *Mech.* A flat metallic spring coiled in a spiral conical form.

vo·lu·tion (və·lo͞o′shən) *n.* **1** A spiral turn or twist; convolution. **2** A whorl of a spiral shell. **3** A revolving movement.

vol·va (vol′və) *n. Bot.* That part of the sheath enclosing certain young mushrooms which, on being ruptured in the course of growth, forms a cuplike appendage at the base of the stem. [<L < *volvere* wrap, turn]

vol·vu·lus (vol′vyə·ləs) *n. pl.* **·li** (-lī) *Pathol.* Obstruction of the intestines caused by twisting. [<NL <L *volvere* turn]

vo·mer (vō′mər) *n. Anat.* **1** A bone of the face situated between the nasal passages on the median line in vertebrates above fishes. **2** A bone of the roof of the mouth in fishes, behind the premaxillaries. [<NL <L *vomer* a plow] **— vo·mer·ine** (vō′mər·in, vom′ər-) *adj.*

vom·i·ca (vom′i·kə) *n. pl.* **·cae** (-sē) *Pathol.* **1** A collection of purulent matter within an organ. **2** An ulcerous cavity, especially in the lungs. **3** Expectoration of putrid matter. [<L, a boil, ulcer < *vomere* vomit]

vom·it (vom′it) *v.i.* **1** To throw up or eject the contents of the stomach through the mouth. **2** To issue with violence from any hollow place; be ejected. **—** *v.t.* **3** To throw up or eject from the stomach, as food. **4** To discharge or send forth copiously or forcibly: The volcano *vomited* smoke. **—** *n.* **1** Matter that is ejected, as from the stomach in vomiting. **2** A sickness which is characterized by vomiting. **3** An emetic. **4** The act of vomiting. [<L *vomitare,* freq. of *vomere* vomit] **— vom′it·er** *n.*

vomiting gas Chlorpicrin.

vom·i·tive (vom′ə·tiv) *adj.* Causing vomiting. **—** *n.* An emetic.

vom·i·to (vom′ə·tō, *Sp.* vō′mē·tō) *n. Pathol.* Yellow fever; black vomit. Also **vomito ne·gro** (nē′grō, *Sp.* nā′grō). [<Sp. *vómito* <L *vomitus,* pp. of *vomere* vomit]

vom·i·to·ry (vom′ə·tôr′ē, -tō′rē) *adj.* Efficacious in producing vomiting. **—** *n. pl.* **·ries 1** An emetic. **2** An opening or vent through which matter is discharged. **3** In a Roman amphitheater, one of the entrances from the encircling arcades to the passages leading to the seats.

vom·i·tu·ri·tion (vom′ə·cho͞o·rish′ən) *n. Pathol.* **1** Violent vomiting with the ejection of but little matter; retching. **2** Vomiting with but small effort; repeated vomiting. [<F <L *vomitus* a vomiting < *vomere* vomit]

von (von, *Ger.* fôn, *unstressed* fən) *prep. German* Of; from: used in German and Austrian family names as an attribute of nobility, corresponding to the French *de.*

voo·doo (vo͞o′do͞o) *n.* **1** A primitive religion of West African origin, found among Haitian and West Indian Negroes and the Negroes of the southern United States, characterized by belief in sorcery and the use of charms, fetishes, witchcraft, etc. **2** A witch doctor; a Negro conjurer who practices voodoo. **3** A voodoo charm or fetish. **—** *adj.* Of or pertaining to the beliefs, ceremonies, or practices of voodoo. **—** *v.t.* To put a spell upon after the manner of a voodoo; bewitch. [<Creole *voudou* <Ewe *vodu*]

voo·doo·ism (vo͞o′do͞o·iz′əm) *n.* **1** The religion of voodoo. **2** Belief in or practice of this religion. **— voo′doo·ist** *n.* **— voo′doo·is′tic** *adj.*

-vora *combining form Zool.* Used to denote orders or genera when classified according to their food: *Carnivora.* An individual member of such an order or genus is denoted by **-vore.** [<NL <L *-vorus.* See -VOROUS.]

vo·ra·cious (vô·rā′shəs, vō-, və-) *adj.* **1** Eating with greediness; ravenous. **2** Greedy; rapacious. **3** Ready to swallow up or engulf. **4** Insatiable; immoderate. See synonyms under GREEDY. [<L *vorax, -acis* < *vorare* devour] **— vo·ra′cious·ly** *adv.* **— vo·rac·i·ty** (vô·ras′ə·tē, vō-, və-), **vo·ra′cious·ness** *n.*

Vor·arl·berg (fōr′ärl·berkh) An autonomous province of western Austria, bordering on Germany, Switzerland, and Liechtenstein; 1,004 square miles; capital, Bregenz.

Vor·i·ai Spor·a·des (vô′rē·e spô·rä′thes) The Greek name for the NORTHERN SPORADES. See under SPORADES.

vor·la·ge (fōr′lä·gə) *n.* In skiing, a posture in which the body leans forward, beyond the perpendicular to the incline. [<G, lit., a lying

add,āce,câre,pälm; end,ēven; it,īce; odd,ōpen,ôrder; to͝ok,po͞ol; up,bûrn; ə = a in *above,* e in *sicken,* i in *clarity,* o in *melon,* u in *focus;* yo͞o = u in *fuse;* oi,oil; ou,pout; ch,check; g,go; ng,ring; th,thin; th,this; zh,vision. Foreign sounds à,œ,ü,kh,ṅ; and ◆: see page xx. < from; + plus; ? possibly.

forward < *vorlagern* extend forward < *vor-* forward + *lagern* lie, lay]

Vo·ro·nezh (vo·rô′nesh) A city in SW European Russian S.F.S.R.; a major industrial center.

Vo·ro·shi·lov (vo′ro·shē′lôf), **Klement Efremovich,** 1881–1969, Russian politician; marshal in World War II.

Vo·ro·shi·lov·grad (vo′ro·shē′lôf·grät) See LUGANSK.

-vorous *combining form* Consuming; eating or feeding upon: *omnivorous, carnivorous.* [<L *-vorus* < *vorare* devour]

vor·tex (vôr′teks) *n. pl.* **·tex·es** or **·ti·ces** (-tə·sēz) **1** A mass of rotating or whirling fluid, especially when sucked spirally toward the center; a whirlpool; an eddy. **2** A portion of fluid whose particles have rotary motion. [<L, var. of *vertex* top, point]

vor·ti·cal (vôr′ti·kəl) *adj.* Of, like, or causing a vortex. [<L *vortex, -icis* a vortex] — **vor′ti·cal·ly** *adv.*

vor·ti·cose (vôr′tə·kōs) *adj.* Rotating rapidly; whirling; vortical. [<L *vorticosus* < *vortex, -icis* a vortex]

vor·tig·i·nous (vôr·tij′ə·nəs) *adj.* Moving as in a vortex. [<L *vortigo, -inis,* var. of *vertigo* a spinning]

Vor·tum·nus (vôr·tum′nəs) See VERTUMNUS.

Vosges Mountains (vōzh) A mountain chain in eastern France; highest peak, 4,672 feet.

Vos·toch·no-Si·bir·sko·ye Mo·re (vos·toch′nô·sē·bir′skô·yə mô′rə) See SIBERIAN SEA, EAST.

vo·ta·ry (vō′tər·ē) *n. pl.* **·ries** **1** One devoted to some particular worship, pursuit, study, etc. **2** A worshiper, as of an idol. Also **vo′ta·rist.** — *adj.* Consecrated by a vow or promise; votive. [<L *votus,* pp. of *vovere* vow] — **vo′ta·ress, vo′tress** *n. fem.*

vote (vōt) *n.* **1** A formal expression of will or opinion in regard to some question submitted for decision, as in electing officers, passing resolutions, etc. **2** That by which such choice is expressed, as a show of hands, or ballot. **3** The result of an election; also, votes in the aggregate: the foreign *vote.* **4** The right to vote. **5** A voter. **6** *Obs.* A wish, vow, or prayer. — **casting vote** A deciding vote given by the chairman of an assembly in cases where the votes of the members tie. — *v.* **vot·ed, vot·ing** *v.t.* **1** To enact or determine by vote. **2** To cast one's vote for: to *vote* a straight ticket. **3** To elect or defeat by vote. **4** *Colloq.* To declare by general agreement: to *vote* a concert a success. — *v.i.* **5** To cast one's vote; express opinion or preference by or as by a vote. — **to vote down** To defeat or suppress by voting against. — **to vote in** To elect. [<L *votum* a vow, wish, orig. pp. neut. of *vovere* vow. Doublet of VOW.] — **vot′er** *n.*

vote-get·ter (vōt′get′ər) *n.* **1** A person with ability to win votes. **2** A campaign slogan, platform, etc., that draws votes. — **vote′-get′ting** *n.* & *adj.*

voting precinct An election district.

vo·tive (vō′tiv) *adj.* Dedicated by a vow; performed in fulfilment of a vow. [<L *votivus* < *votum.* See VOTE.] — **vo′tive·ly** *adv.* — **vo′tive·ness** *n.*

votive mass A mass not rubrically assigned to a particular day, but said at the choice of the priest.

vouch (vouch) *v.i.* **1** To give one's own assurance or guarantee; bear witness: with *for*: I will *vouch* for their honesty. **2** To serve as assurance or proof: with *for*: The evidence *vouches* for his innocence. — *v.t.* **3** To bear witness to; attest or affirm. **4** To cite as support or justification, as a precedent, authority, etc. **5** To uphold by satisfactory proof or evidence; substantiate. **6** *Law* To call upon or summon (a person) to defend a title. **7** *Obs.* To call to witness. — *n.* A declaration that attests; an assertion. [<OF *vocher, voucher* <L *vocare* call < *vox, vocis* a voice]

vouch·ee (vou·chē′) *n. Law* A person who is called into an action to warrant or defend a title.

vouch·er (vou′chər) *n.* **1** Any material thing (as a writing) that serves to vouch for the truth of something, or attest an alleged act, especially the receipt of money. **2** One who vouches for another; a witness. **3** In early English law, the calling in of a person, or the person called in, as warrantor, to defend a title.

vouch·safe (vouch′sāf′) *v.* **·safed, ·saf·ing** *v.t.* **1** To grant, as with condescension; permit; deign. **2** *Obs.* To assure or guarantee. — *v.i.* **3** To condescend; deign. [<VOUCH + SAFE] — **vouch′safe′ment** *n.*

vous·soir (vōō·swär′) *n. Archit.* A stone in an arch shaped to fit its curve. [<OF *vausoir, volsoir* curvature of a vault, ult. <L *volutus.* See VOLUBLE.]

vow (vou) *n.* **1** A solemn promise to God or to a deity or saint to perform some act or make some gift or sacrifice: generally made in a time of peril or need, and on the condition of the fulfilment of some petition or in return for special divine favor: the *vow* of Jephthah. **2** A solemn engagement to adopt a certain course of life, pursue some end, observe some moral precept, or surrender oneself to a higher life of holiness; also, a pledge of faithfulness: marriage *vows.* **3** A solemn and emphatic affirmation. See synonyms under OATH. — **to take vows** To enter a religious order. — *v.t.* **1** To promise solemnly; especially, to promise to God or to some deity. **2** To declare with assurance or solemnity. **3** To make a solemn promise or threat to do, inflict, etc. — *v.i.* **4** To make a vow. [<AF *vu,* OF *vo, vou* <L *votum.* Doublet of VOTE.] — **vow′er** *n.*

vow·el (vou′əl) *n.* **1** *Phonet.* A voiced speech sound produced by the relatively unimpeded passage of air through the mouth, altering in quality according to the shape of the resonance cavity: distinguished from *consonant.* Vowels may be characterized by the height of the tongue (high, mid, low), the place of articulation (front, central, back), the tension of the tongue muscles (tense, lax), and the presence of lip rounding; as, (ōō) is a high, back, tense, rounded vowel. **2** A letter indicating such a sound, as *a, e, i, o,* or *u.* — *adj.* Of or pertaining to a vowel; vocal. [<OF *vouele* <L *vocalis (littera)* vocal (letter) < *vox, vocis* a voice, sound. Doublet of VOCAL.]

vow·el·ize (vou′əl·īz) *v.t.* **·ized, ·iz·ing** To supply with vowel points or signs: to *vowelize* a Hebrew text. — **vow′el·i·za′tion** *n.*

vowel point One of a system of diacritical marks written above or below the consonants in Hebrew and certain other Semitic languages to indicate the vowel sound following the consonant.

vox (voks) *n. pl.* **vo·ces** (vō′sēz) Voice; especially, in music, a voice; part. [<L]

vox an·gel·i·ca (voks an·jel′i·kə) **1** An organ stop of two ranks of pipes, one of which is tuned slightly sharper than the other, so that beats are produced giving a tremulous effect; voix céleste: also **vox cae·les·tis** (si·les′tis). **2** A single-rank stop of soft, sweet quality. [<L, an angelic voice]

vox clan·des·ti·na (voks klan′des·tī′nə) *Latin* A secret voice; a whisper.

vox hu·ma·na (voks hyōō·mā′nə) A reed stop with very short pipes used for clarinet tones in an organ. [<L, a human voice]

vox po·pu·li (voks pop′yə·lī) *Latin* The voice of the people; public sentiment.

voy·age (voi′ij) *n.* **1** A journey by water, especially by sea: commonly used of a somewhat extended journey by water; formerly, any journey: a *voyage* across the sea. **2** A journey in an airship. **3** A book describing a voyage or voyaging: Hakluyt's *Voyages.* **4** Any enterprise or project; also, course. See synonyms under JOURNEY. — *v.* **·aged, ·ag·ing** *v.i.* To make a voyage; journey by water. — *v.t.* To travel over. [<OF *veiage, voiage* <L *viaticum.* Doublet of VIATICUM.] — **voy′ag·er** *n.*

voy·age·a·ble (voi′ij·ə·bəl) *adj.* Navigable.

vo·ya·geur (vwȧ·yȧ·zhœr′) *n. pl.* **·geurs** (-zhœr′) *French* An employee of Hudson's Bay Company, engaged in carrying men, supplies, etc., between remote trading posts; also, a Canadian boatman or fur trader.

vo·yeur (vwä·yûr′) *n.* One who is sexually gratified by looking at sexual objects or acts. [<F < *voir* see] — **vo·yeur′ism** *n.*

V-par·ti·cle (vē′pär′ti·kəl) *n. Physics* A hyperon.

vrai·sem·blance (vre·sän·bläns′) *n. French* A show or appearance of truth; verisimilitude. [<F < *vrai* true + *semblance* appearance]

Vry·burg (frī′bûrg) The capital of Bechuanaland, Republic of South Africa.

VT fuze A proximity fuze. [<V(ARIABLE) T(IME)]

VTOL (vē′tôl) *n. Aeron.* An aircraft that takes off and lands vertically.

Vuel·ta A·ba·jo (vwel′tä ä·bä′hō) A region including all Cuba west of Havana.

vug (vug, vōōg) *n. Mining* An opening in a mineral vein into which crystals often project. Also **vugg, vugh.** [<Cornish *vooga* a cave] — **vug′gy** *adj.*

Vuil·lard (vwē·yȧr′), **Jean Édouard,** 1868–1940, French painter.

Vul·can (vul′kən) In Roman mythology, the god of fire and of metallurgy: identified with the Greek *Hephaestus.*

vul·ca·ni·an (vul·kā′nē·ən) *adj.* **1** Volcanic: also **vul·can·ic** (vul·kan′ik). **2** Of or pertaining to Plutonism; plutonic. [<L *Vulcanius* pertaining to Vulcan < *Vulcanus* Vulcan]

Vul·ca·ni·an (vul·kā′nē·ən) *adj.* **1** Relating to Vulcan or to the art of working in metals. **2** Wrought by Vulcan or by Vulcan's art. Also **Vul·can·ic** (vul·kan′ik).

vul·can·ite (vul′kən·īt) *n.* A dark-colored hard variety of India rubber that has been subjected to vulcanization: also called *hard rubber.* — *adj.* Made of vulcanite. [after *Vulcan*]

vul·can·i·za·tion (vul′kən·ə·zā′shən, -ī·zā′-) *n.* **1** The process of treating crude India rubber with sulfur or sulfur compounds in varying proportions and at different temperatures, thereby increasing its strength and elasticity, yielding either soft rubber or vulcanite. **2** A similar process applied to other substances.

vul·can·ize (vul′kən·īz) *v.t.* & *v.i.* **·ized, ·iz·ing** To subject to or undergo the process of vulcanization. [after *Vulcan*] — **vul′can·iz′a·ble** *adj.* — **vul′can·iz′er** *n.*

vulcanized fiber A cellulose material made from cotton and linen rags passed through a solution of zinc chloride, or sometimes of sulfuric acid.

vul·can·ol·o·gy (vul′kən·ol′ə·jē) *n.* Volcanology. [<L *Vulcanus* of Vulcan + -(O)LOGY] — **vul′can·o·log′i·cal** (-ə·loj′i·kəl) *adj.* — **vul′can·ol′o·gist** *n.*

vul·gar (vul′gər) *adj.* **1** Pertaining to the common people; plebeian; general; popular. **2** Pertaining to or characteristic of the people at large, as distinguished from the privileged or educated classes; coarse; boorish; offensive to good taste or sensitive feelings; low. **3** Written in or translated into the common language or dialect; vernacular. — *n. Obs.* **1** The common people. **2** The vernacular tongue. [<L *vulgaris* < *vulgus* the common people] — **vul′gar·ly** *adv.*

Synonyms (adj.): base, broad, coarse, gross, ignoble, inelegant, inferior, loose, low, mean, obscene, obscure, offensive, rude, unauthorized, underbred, vile. See COMMON. *Antonyms*: aristocratic, chaste, choice, cultivated, cultured, dainty, elegant, high-bred, learned, literary, lofty, polite, refined, select, stylish.

vulgar fraction A common fraction. See under FRACTION.

vul·gar·i·an (vul·gâr′ē·ən) *n.* A person of vulgar tastes or manners; especially, a wealthy person with coarse ideas or low standards.

vul·gar·ism (vul′gə·riz′əm) *n.* **1** Vulgarity. **2** A word, phrase, or expression that is in common colloquial or unrefined usage, though not necessarily coarse or gross: distinguished from those in literary or standard usage.

vul·gar·i·ty (vul·gar′ə·tē) *n. pl.* **·ties** **1** The quality or character of being vulgar; low condition in life; commonness. **2** Lack of refinement in conduct or speech, or an instance of it; coarseness. Also **vul′gar·ness.**

vul·gar·ize (vul′gə·rīz) *v.t.* **·ized, ·iz·ing** To make vulgar. Also *Brit.* **vul′gar·ise.** — **vul′gar·i·za′tion** *n.* — **vul′gar·iz′er** *n.*

Vulgar Latin See under LATIN.

vul·gate (vul′gāt) *adj.* Common; popular; usual; generally accepted; in common use. — *n.* **1** The vulgar tongue; colloquial everyday speech. **2** Any commonly accepted text. [<L *vulgatus* common, orig. pp. of *vulgare* make common < *vulgus* the common people]

Vul·gate (vul′gāt) *n.* **1** St. Jerome's Latin version of the Bible, now revised and used as the authorized version by the Roman Catholics. Jerome translated the Gospels into Latin, then the vernacular or vulgar tongue, about A.D. 383, the remaining New Testament somewhat later, and the Old Testament from the Hebrew between 390 and 405. The Sistine edition of the Vulgate, published under Pope Clement VIII in 1592–93, is the source of the modern revision of the Douai version ordered by Pius X in 1908. — *adj.* Belonging

or relating to the Vulgate. [<Med. L *vulgata (editio)* the popular (edition), fem. of L *vulgatus* common]
vul·go (vul′gō) *adv. Latin* Commonly; popularly.
vul·ner·a·ble (vul′nər·ə·bəl) *adj.* **1** That may be wounded; capable of receiving injuries. **2** Liable to attack; assailable. **3** In contract bridge, having won one game of a rubber, and hence subject to doubled penalties if contract is not fulfilled. [<LL *vulnerabilis* wounding <L *vulnerare* wound < *vulnus, -eris* a wound] **— vul′ner·a·bil′i·ty, vul′ner·a·ble·ness** *n.* **— vul′·ner·a·bly** *adv.*
vul·ner·ar·y (vul′nə·rer′ē) *adj.* Tending to cure wounds. — *n. pl.* **·ries** A healing application for wounds, as a preparation of medicinal plants. [<L *vulnerarius* < *vulnus, -eris* a wound]
Vul·pec·u·la (vul·pek′yə·lə) A small northern constellation lying between Cygnus and Aquila; the Fox: sometimes called **Vulpecula cum An·se·re** (kum an′sə·rē) *(The Little Fox with the Goose).* See CONSTELLATION. [<L, dim. of *vulpes* a fox]
vul·pec·u·lar (vul·pek′yə·lər) *adj.* Of or pertaining to a fox, especially a young one; vulpine.
vul·pi·cide (vul′pə·sīd) *n.* **1** One who kills a fox otherwise than by hunting. **2** The act of killing a fox when not hunting it with hounds. [<L *vulpes, -is* a fox + -CIDE] **— vul′pi·ci′dal** (-sīd′l) *adj.*
vul·pine (vul′pin, -pīn) *adj.* **1** Pertaining to a fox; resembling foxes. **2** Like a fox; sly; crafty; cunning. [<L *vulpinus* < *vulpes* a fox]
vul·pi·nite (vul′pə·nīt) *n.* A scaly variety of anhydrite from Vulpino, Italy.
vul·ture (vul′chər) *n.* **1** Any of various large birds of prey (family *Cathartidae* or *Vulturidae*) related to the eagles, hawks, and falcons, having the head and neck naked or partly naked, and feeding mostly on carrion; especially, the common **turkey vulture,** or buzzard, and the tropical American **king vulture** *(Gypagus papa)*, strikingly colored, with black wings and tail. **2** Something or someone that preys upon a person in the manner of a vulture. [<AF *vultur,* OF *voltour* <L *vultur, vulturius*] **— vul·tur·ine** (vul′chə·rīn, -chər·in), **vul′tur·ous** *adj.*

VULTURE
(From 30 to 55 inches; wingspread from 7 to 11 feet)

vul·va (vul′və) *n. pl.* **·vae** (-vē) *Anat.* The external genital parts of the female, including the labia majora and minora, the clitoris, and the area between the clitoris and the labia minora. [<L, a covering, womb] **— vul′val, vul′var** *adj.* **— vul′vi·form** (-və·fôrm) *adj.*
Vyat·ka (vyät′kə) **1** A former name for KIROV. **2** A river in east central European Russian S.F.S.R., flowing 849 miles north, SW, and SE from the central Ural foothills to the Kama.
Vy·borg (vē′bôrg, *Russian* vi′berk) A port on the Gulf of Finland in NW Russian S.F.S.R. near the Finnish border. Swedish *Viborg,* Finnish *Viipuri.*
Vy·cheg·da (vi′chəg·də) A river in northern European Russian S.F.S.R., flowing 700 miles south and west to the Northern Dvina.
vy·ing (vī′ing) *adj.* That vies or contends. **— vy′ing·ly** *adv.*
Vy·shin·ski (vi·shin′skē), **Andrei,** 1883–1954, U.S.S.R. lawyer and politician: also *Vishinski.*

W

w, W (dub′əl·yōō, -yōō) *n. pl.* **w's, W's** or **ws, Ws** or **doub·le·yous** **1** The 23rd letter of the English alphabet; double u: a ligature of vv or uu. It first came into English writing as a substitution by Norman scribes of the 11th century for the Old English rune *wen,* which later dropped completely out of use. **2** The sound of the letter *w,* a voiced bilabial velar semivowel before vowels *(we, wage, worry),* and a *u*-glide in diphthongs *(how, allow, dew, review).* It is silent before *r (wrist, write, wrong),* and is often lost internally *(two, sword, answer).* ◆ The combination *wh-* (in Old English spelled *hw-*) is pronounced in this dictionary as (hw); many educated speakers of English, however, use simple (w) instead, and this pronunciation should be inferred as an acceptable variant in every case. Some speakers normally use still a third sound here, a voiceless allophone of (w) heard also after voiceless consonants, as in *sweet, twin,* etc. See ALPHABET. — *symbol* **1** *Chem.* Tungsten (symbol W, for *wolfram*). **2** *Electr.* Watt.
wa' (wä) *n. Scot.* Wall.
Waadt (vät) The German name for VAUD.
Waag (väkh) The German name for the VAH.
Waal (väl) The southern branch of the Rhine in the Netherlands, flowing 52 miles west from the Rhine proper to the Maas.
Waals (väls), **Johannes Diderik van der,** 1837–1923, Dutch physicist.
wab (wäb) *n. Scot.* A web.
Wa·bash (wô′bash) A river in western Ohio and north central and western Indiana, forming part of the boundary between Indiana and Illinois and flowing 475 miles NW, west, SW, and south from western Ohio to the Ohio River at the SW corner of Indiana.
wab·ble[1] (wob′əl) *n., v.t.* & *v.i.* Wobble. [Var. of WOBBLE] **— wab′bler** *n.* **— wab′bly** *adj.*
WAC (wak) *n.* A member of the Women's Army Corps. [<W(OMEN'S) A(RMY) C(ORPS)]
Wace (wäs, wās), 1100?–75, Anglo-Norman poet.
wack·e (wak′ə) *n.* A brown earthy or clayey variety of basaltic rock. [<G <MHG, a large stone <OHG *waggo* a pebble]
wack·y (wak′ē) *adj.* **wack·i·er, wack·i·est** *Slang* Extremely irrational or impractical; erratic; screwy. [Prob. <WHACK; with ref. to the mental impairment caused by repeated blows on the head]
Wa·co (wā′kō) A manufacturing city in central Texas.
wad[1] (wod) *n.* **1** A small compact mass of any soft or flexible substance, especially as used for stuffing, packing, or lining; also, a lump; mass: a *wad* of hair; also, a chew of tobacco, or a portion the right size for chewing. **2** A piece of paper, cloth, or leather used to hold in a charge of powder in a muzzleloading gun; also, a pasteboard or paper disk to hold powder and shot in place in a shotgun shell. **3** Fibrous material for stopping up breaks, leakages, etc.; wadding. **4** *Colloq.* A large amount. **5** *Colloq.* A roll of banknotes; hence, money; wealth. **6** A hydrated oxide of manganese and other metals. — *v.* **wad·ded, wad·ding** *v.t.* **1** To press (fibrous substances, as cotton) into a mass or wad. **2** To roll or fold into a tight wad, as paper. **3** To pack with wadding for protection, as valuables, or to stuff or line with wadding. **4** To place a wad in, as a gun; hold in place with a wad. — *v.i.* **5** To form into a wad. [Cf. Sw. *vadd* a wad] **— wad′dy** *adj.*
wad[2] (wod) *n. Scot.* A pledge; wager.
wad[3] (wod) *v.t.* & *v.i. Scot.* To wed.
wad[4] (wäd, wəd) *v. Scot.* Would.
Wa·dai (wä·dī′) A former independent sultanate of north central Africa; now part of central and eastern Chad; 94,225 square miles: French *Ouadï.*
wad·ding (wod′ing) *n.* **1** Wads collectively. **2** Any substance, as carded cotton, used as material for wads. **3** The act of applying a wad or wads.
Wad·ding·ton (wod′ing·tən), **Mount** The highest mountain in British Columbia, in the SW part; 13,260 feet.
wad·dle (wod′l) *v.i.* **·dled, ·dling** **1** To walk with short steps, swaying from side to side. **2** To move clumsily; totter. — *n.* The act of waddling; a clumsy rocking walk, like that of a duck. [Freq. of WADE] **— wad′dler** *n.* **— wad′dly** *adj.*
wad·dy (wod′ē) *n. pl.* **·dies** *Austral.* **1** A thick war club used by the aborigines. **2** A walking stick; piece of wood. — *v.t.* **·died, ·dy·ing** To strike with a waddy. [< native Australian pronunciation of *wood*]
wade (wād) *v.* **wad·ed, wad·ing** *v.i.* **1** To walk through water or, by extension, any substance more resistant than air, as mud, sand, etc. **2** To proceed slowly or laboriously: to *wade* through a lengthy book. **3** *Obs.* To go; proceed. — *v.t.* **4** To pass or cross, as a river, by walking on the bottom; walk through; ford. **— to wade in** (or **into**) *Colloq.* To attack or begin energetically or vigorously. — *n.* **1** The act of wading. **2** A ford. [OE *wadan* go]
wad·er (wā′dər) *n.* **1** One who wades. **2** A long-legged wading bird, as a snipe, plover, or stork. **3** *pl.* High waterproof boots, worn especially by anglers.
wa·di (wä′dē) *n. pl.* **·dies** **1** In Arabia and northern Africa, a river or valley; a ravine containing the bed of a watercourse, usually dry except in the rainy season. **2** An oasis. Also **wa′dy.** [<Arabic *wādī*]
Wa·di Hal·fa (wä′dē häl′fə) A city on the Nile in the northern Sudan near the Egyptian border; the northern gateway to the Sudan.
Wad·jak (wä′jək) A village in central Java.
Wadjak man A hominid *(Homo wadjakensis),* probably of the third interglacial period, and represented solely by two skulls found near Wadjak, Java, in 1891: of larger cranial capacity than earlier types but otherwise controversial because of the crushed condition of the remains and inadequate investigation at the site.
wad·mal (wod′məl) *n. Obs.* A thick, coarse, hairy, durable woolen cloth, used by the poor of northern Europe for garments. Also **wad′·maal, wad′mol.** [<ON *vathmāl* woolen fabric]
wad·na (wod′nə) *Scot.* Would not.
wad·set (wod′set′) *n.* In Scots law, a pledge, as of land, as security for a debt. — *v.t.* **·set·ted, ·set·ting** In Scots law, to mortgage.
wad·set·ter (wod′set′ər) *n. Scot.* One receiving a wadset.
wae (wā) *n. Scot.* Woe. **— wae′ness** *n.*
wae·ful (wā′fōōl) *adj. Scot.* Woeful; sad. Also **wae′fu** (-fōō).
wae·sucks (wā′suks) *interj. Scot.* Alas! Also **wae′suck.** [<WAE + alter. of SAKE[1]]
WAF (waf, wäf) *n.* A member of the Women in the Air Force. [<W(OMEN IN THE) A(IR) F(ORCE)]
Wafd (woft) *n.* A nationalist party in Egypt founded about 1919. [<Arabic, a deputation] **— Wafd′ist** *n.* & *adj.*
wa·fer (wā′fər) *n.* **1** A very thin crisp biscuit, cooky, or cracker; also, a small disk of candy. **2** *Eccl.* A small flat disk of unleavened bread stamped with a cross or the letters IHS, and used in the Eucharist in some churches; the sacred host. **3** A thin hardened disk of gelatin, flour, isinglass, or other suitable substance, used for sealing letters, attaching papers, or receiving the impression of a seal. **4** *Med.* **a** A thin double layer of dried paste enclosing a pill or capsule. **b** A suppository. **5** A disk of priming material used in early

artillery. —*v.t.* To attach, seal, or fasten with a wafer. [<AF *wafre* <MLG *wafel.* Akin to WAFFLE.]

waff[1] (waf, wäf) *Scot. & Brit. Dial. v.t. & v.i.* To wave. —*n.* **1** The act of waving. **2** A light ailment. **3** A gust; puff. **4** A glimpse; sight. **5** A spirit or ghost. [Var. of WAVE]

waff[2] (waf, wäf) *Scot. adj.* **1** Low-born; worthless; inferior. **2** Strayed; solitary. —*n.* A tramp; vagrant.

waff·ie (wä′fē) *n. Scot.* A tramp.

waf·fle[1] (wof′əl, wô′fəl) *n.* A batter cake, crisper than a pancake, baked in a waffle iron marked with regular indentations. [< Du. *wafel* a wafer. Akin to WAFER.]

waf·fle[2] (wof′əl, wô′fəl) *v.i.* **·fled, ·fling** *Colloq.* **1** *Chiefly Brit.* To speak or write nonsense. **2** To avoid giving a direct answer. —*n. Chiefly Brit.* Nonsense; twaddle. [<obs. *woff, waff* to yelp]

waffle iron A type of utensil for cooking waffles, consisting of two metal griddles, hinged together, and usually marked with indentations so as to give a large heating surface when closed on each other: now usually made of aluminum and heated electrically.

waft[1] (waft, wäft) *v.t.* **1** To carry or bear gently or lightly over air or water; float. **2** To convey as if on air or water. —*v.i.* **3** To float, as on the wind. —*n.* **1** The act of one who or that which wafts. **2** A breath or current of air; also, a passing odor. [Back formation < *wafter,* in obs. sense, "an escort ship" <Du. *wachter* a guard < *wachten* guard]

waft[2] (waft, wäft) *n.* **1** A signal flag or pennant, sometimes used to indicate the direction of the wind to a ship's helmsman. **2** A signal made with a flag or pennant. —*v.t. Obs.* **1** To signal or beckon to with the hand. **2** To turn; direct, as a glance. [Alter. of dial. E *waff,* var. of WAVE]

waft[3] (waft, wäft) *n. Scot.* Woof; weft.

waft·age (waf′tij, wäf′-) *n.* Conveyance by wafting.

waft·er (waf′tər, wäf′-) *n.* **1** One who or that which wafts. **2** A form of fan or revolving disk used in a blower.

waf·ture (waf′chər, wäf′-) *n.* **1** A wafting or waving motion. **2** Conveyance by wafting. **3** That which is wafted, as an odor.

wag[1] (wag) *v.* **wagged, wag·ging** *v.t.* **1** To cause to move lightly and quickly from side to side or up and down; oscillate; swing: The dog *wags* its tail. **2** To move (the tongue) in talking. —*v.i.* **3** To move lightly and quickly from side to side or up and down. **4** To move busily in animated talk or gossip: said of the tongue. **5** To proceed at a regular pace: Life *wags* on. **6** To waddle. **7** *Brit. Slang* To play truant. —*n.* The act or motion of wagging: a *wag* of the head. [ME *waggen,* prob. <Scand. Cf. Sw. *vagga* rock a cradle. Akin to OE *wagian* oscillate.]

wag[2] (wag) *n.* A droll or humorous fellow; a wit; joker. [Short for obs. *waghalter* <WAG[1] + HALTER[1]]

wage (wāj) *v.t.* **waged, wag·ing** **1** To engage in and maintain vigorously; carry on: to *wage* war. **2** *Obs.* To pledge; put down as security; hence, to wager; bet. **3** *Obs.* To attempt; risk. **4** *Brit. Dial.* To pay a salary to; hire; employ. —*n.* **1** Payment for service rendered, especially the pay of artisans or laborers receiving a fixed sum by the day, week, or month, or for a certain amount of work; hire. **2** *pl.* The remuneration received by labor as distinguished from that received by capital, including the expenses incurred for superintendence and management, called respectively **wages of superintendence** and **wages of management.** **3** Figuratively, produce; yield. **4** *Obs.* A pledge; gage; also, the state of being pledged: to lay one's fortune in *wage.* See synonyms under SALARY. See LIVING WAGE, MINIMUM WAGE. [<AF *wagier,* OF *guagier* pledge < *gage* a pledge. Doublet of GAGE[2].] ◆ The plural of *wage* is sometimes construed as a singular: The *wages* of sin *is* death.

Wage may appear as a combining form in hyphemes or solidemes, or as the first element in two-word phrases:

wage board	**wage floor**
wage ceiling	**wage–freeze**
wage–control	**wage–labor**
wage differential	**wage law**
wage–driver	**wage level**
wage–incentive	**wage–slave**
wage–increase	**wage–slavery**
wage–paying	**wage structure**
wage rate	**wagework**

wage–earn·er (wāj′ûr′nər) *n.* One who works for wages.

wa·ger (wā′jər) *v.t. & v.i.* To stake (something) on an uncertain event; bet. —*n.* **1** An agreement between persons that something, as money, shall be delivered over to one of them on the happening or not happening of an uncertain event; a bet. **2** The thing so pledged. **3** The act of giving a pledge. [<AF *wageure* < *wagier.* See WAGE.] —**wa′ger·er** *n.*

wager of law Anciently, a mode of trial whereby a defendant acquitted himself of a debt by taking his oath that he owed the plaintiff nothing, and having eleven compurgators present to swear that they believed his oath to be true.

wage scale **1** A scale or series of amounts of wages paid for similar duties. **2** The scale of wages paid by a single employer.

wage·worker (wāj′wûr′kər) *n.* An employee receiving wages.

wag·ger·y (wag′ər·ē) *n. pl.* **·ger·ies** **1** Mischievous jocularity; drollery. **2** A jest; joke. See synonyms under WIT[1]. [<WAG[2] + -ERY]

wag·gish (wag′ish) *adj.* **1** Being or acting like a wag. **2** Said or done in waggery. See synonyms under JOCOSE. —**wag′gish·ly** *adv.* —**wag′gish·ness** *n.*

wag·gle (wag′əl) *v.* **·gled, ·gling** *v.t.* To cause to move with rapid to-and-fro motions; wag; swing: The duck *waggles* its tail. —*v.i.* To totter; wobble. —*n.* The act of waggling or wagging. [Freq. of WAG[1]] —**wag′gling·ly** *adv.* —**wag′gly** *adj.*

Wag·ner (väg′nər), **(Wilhelm) Richard,** 1813–83, German composer, poet, and critical writer.

Wag·ner·esque (väg′nə·resk′) *adj.* Similar to or suggestive of the works or style of Richard Wagner.

Wag·ne·ri·an (väg·nir′ē·ən) *adj.* Relating to Richard Wagner or to his style, theory, or works. —*n.* One who advocates or accepts the theories of Richard Wagner; also, one who admires his works.

Wag·ner·ism (väg′nə·riz′əm) *n.* The theory of Richard Wagner regarding music drama, as exemplified in the construction and rendition of his own works. Its chief point, especially that in which it differs from the method of the old Italian composers of opera, is its abundant use of the leitmotif for cumulative dramatic effect and its insistence on the equal participation of music, both vocal and orchestral, poetry, scenic effect, and dramatic action, no one of these being subordinate.

Wag·ner–Jau·regg (väg′nər·you′rek), **Julius,** 1857–1940, Austrian neurologist and psychiatrist. Also **Wag′ner von Jau′regg.**

wag·on (wag′ən) *n.* **1** A strong four-wheeled vehicle used to carry heavy loads of freight. Compare DRAY, WAIN. **2** An open four-wheeled vehicle for carrying hay, corn, etc.: a farm *wagon.* **3** A light four-wheeled vehicle used for various business purposes, as a grocer's *wagon.* **4** *Brit.* A railway freight car. **5** A covered four-wheeled vehicle used as living quarters by gipsies, traveling showmen, etc. **6** *Obs.* A chariot. **7** *Colloq.* A patrol wagon. **8** A station wagon. **9** *Slang* An automobile. **10** A child's four-wheeled toy cart. **11** *Astron.* Charles's Wain. **12** A stand on wheels or casters for serving food or drink: a tea *wagon.* —**on the (water) wagon** *Colloq.* Abstaining from alcoholic beverages. —**to fix (someone's) wagon** *Slang* To even scores with; obtain revenge on: I'll *fix your wagon!* —*v.t.* To carry or transport in a wagon. Also *Brit.* **wag′gon.** [<Du. *wagen.* Akin to WAIN.]

wag·on·age (wag′ən·ij) *n.* **1** The amount paid for conveyance in a wagon. **2** Wagons collectively. Also *Brit.* **wag′gon·age.**

wagon bed The body of a wagon.

wag·on·er (wag′ən·ər) *n.* **1** One whose business is driving wagons. **2** *Obs.* A charioteer. Also *Brit.* **wag′gon·er.**

Wag·on·er (wag′ən·ər) **1** Charles's Wain. See under WAIN. **2** The constellation Auriga.

wag·on·ette (wag′ən·et′) *n.* A light wagon, with or without a cover, with lengthwise seats facing inward and a crosswise seat in front for the driver. Also **wag′on·et.** [Dim. of WAGON]

wag·on–head·ed (wag′ən·hed′id) *adj. Archit.* Having a semicylindrical head or top, resembling the top of a covered wagon; having a round-arched roof.

wa·gon–lit (và·gôṅ·lē′) *n. pl.* **–lits** (-lē′) *French* A sleeping-car on a French railway.

wag·on·load (wag′ən·lōd′) *n.* The amount that a wagon can carry.

wagon train **1** A train or line of wagons. **2** A group of wagons and families typical of those which formerly traveled together to settle new regions, especially in the western United States. **3** The equipment of a military force for the carriage of ammunition, provisions, etc.

Wa·gram (vä′gräm) A village NE of Vienna, Austria; scene of Napoleon's victory over the Austrians, 1809.

wag·some (wag′səm) *adj. Rare* Waggish.

wag·tail (wag′tāl′) *n.* **1** Any of several small singing birds (genus *Motacilla*), named from their habit of jerking the tail; especially, the **yellow wagtail** *(M. flava)* of Asia and eastern Alaska. **2** Any of certain American birds that wag the tail when walking on the ground, especially the ovenbird and the water thrush.

Wa·ha·bi (wä·hä′bē) *n.* A believer in Wahabiism. Also **Wa·ha′bee, Wah·ha′bi.**

Wa·ha·bi·ism (wä·hä′bē·iz′əm) *n.* A puristically orthodox Moslem sect of Arabia, related to the Sunnites, founded by Abdul-Wahhab; the religion of the ruling family of Saudi Arabia.

wah·con·da (wä·kon′dä) See WAKANDA.

wa·hoo[1] (wä·ho͞o′, wä′ho͞o) *n.* A deciduous North American shrub or small tree *(Euonymus atropurpureus)* with finely toothed leaves, purple flowers, and scarlet fruit: also called *burningbush.* [<Siouan (Dakota) *wanhu,* lit., arrowwood]

wa·hoo[2] (wä·ho͞o′, wä′ho͞o) *n.* **1** The American winged elm *(Ulmus alata).* **2** The white basswood *(Tilia heterophylla).* **3** The cascara buckthorn. [<Muskhogean (Creek) *uhawhu* the winged elm]

Wai·chow (wī′jō′) A former name for WAI-YEUNG.

waif (wāf) *n.* **1** A homeless, neglected wanderer; a stray. **2** *Law* Something stolen and then abandoned by the thief in his flight to avoid arrest. **3** Anything found and unclaimed, the owner being unknown. **4** A nautical signal; a waft. —*v.t.* To throw away; cast off, as a waif. —*adj.* Stray; wandering; homeless. [<AF *waif,* OF *gaif,* prob. <Scand. Cf. ON *veif* something flapping < *veifa* wave.]

Wai·ki·ki (wī′kē·kē, wī′kē·kē′) A section of Honolulu; site of a resort beach on Honolulu harbor, SE Oahu, Hawaii.

wail (wāl) *v.t. & v.i.* To grieve with mournful cries; lament; cry out in sorrow. —*n.* A prolonged, high-pitched sound of lamentation; a shrill moan of grief; also, any mournful sound, as of the wind. ◆ Homophone: *wale.* [<ON *væla* wail < *væ, vei* woe] —**wail′er** *n.*

wail·ful (wāl′fəl) *adj.* **1** Deeply sorrowing; mournful. **2** Making a mournful sound.

Wailing Wall A wall on the western side of the traditional site of Solomon's temple in Jerusalem, reputedly containing fragments of Herod's temple (20 B.C.), a place of prayer, formerly of lamentation, for Jews: also *Western Wall.*

wain (wān) *n.* An open, four-wheeled wagon for hauling heavy loads. —**Charles's Wain** Seven bright stars in Ursa Major; the Dipper: also **the Wain**: sometimes called the *Wagoner.* ◆ Homophone: *wane.* [OE *wægn, wæn.* Akin to WAGON.]

wain·scot (wān′skət, -skot) *n.* **1** A facing for inner walls, usually of wood, but sometimes of marble or other material: usually paneled and of elaborate workmanship. **2** *Brit.* A superior quality of imported oak used for paneling; also, a piece of such wood. **3** The lower part of an inner wall, when finished with material different from the rest of the wall. —*v.t.* **·scot·ed** or **·scot·ted, ·scot·ing** or **·scot·ting** To face or panel with wainscot. [<MLG *wagenschot* < *wagen* a wagon + *schot* a wooden partition]

wain·scot·ing (wān′skət·ing, -skot-) *n.* Material

for a wainscot; a wainscot; wainscots collectively. Also **wain′scot·ting.**

wain·wright (wān′rīt) *n.* A maker of wagons.

Wain·wright (wān′rīt), **Jonathan,** 1883–1953, U. S. general.

Wai·pa·hu (wī·pä′hōō) A city of southern Oahu, Hawaii, on Pearl Harbor, NW of Honolulu.

wair (wâr) See WARE³.

waist (wāst) *n.* **1** The narrow part of the body between the chest and the hips. **2** The middle part or section of any object, especially if of less diameter than the ends: the *waist* of a violin. **3** *Naut.* That section of a ship between the quarter-deck and the forecastle. **4** The central section of an airplane. **5** That part of a woman's dress or other garment covering the body from the waistline to the neck or shoulders; a bodice; also, an undergarment for children, to which other garments may be buttoned. **6** A waistband. ◆ Homophone: *waste.* [ME *wast.* Akin to OE *wæstm* growth.]

waist·band (wāst′band′, -bənd) *n.* A band encircling the waist, especially a band inside the top of a skirt or the upper part of trousers.

waist·cloth (wāst′klôth′, -kloth′) See LOINCLOTH.

waist·coat (wāst′kōt′, wes′kit) *n.* **1** A man's garment, now commonly sleeveless, buttoning in front and extending just below the waistline; a vest. **2** A similar garment worn by women. **3** A long vest formerly worn with trunk and hose under a slip doublet.

waist·coat·ing (wāst′kō′ting, wes′kit·ing) *n.* A textile fabric specially designed for men's waistcoats.

waist·er (wās′tər) *n. Rare* An apprentice or new hand on a whaling vessel, placed at work in the ship's waist to learn his duties.

waist·ing (wās′ting) *n.* Any material suitable for making waists.

waist·line (wāst′līn′) *n.* The line of the waist, between the ribs and the hips; in dressmaking, the line at which the skirt of a dress meets the waist.

wait (wāt) *v.i.* **1** To stay or remain in expectation, as of an anticipated action or event: with *for, until,* etc. **2** To be or remain in readiness. **3** To remain temporarily neglected or undone. **4** To perform duties of personal service or attendance; especially, to act as a waiter or waitress: She *waits* at table. — *v.t.* **5** To stay or remain in expectation of: to *wait* one's turn. **6** *Colloq.* To put off or postpone; defer; delay: Don't *wait* breakfast for me. **7** *Obs.* To attend; escort. **8** *Obs.* To attend as a result or consequence. See synonyms under ABIDE, LINGER. — **to wait on** (or **upon**) **1** To act as a servant or attendant to. **2** To go to see; call upon; visit. **3** To attend as a result or consequence. — **to wait up** To delay going to bed in anticipation of the arrival of someone. — *n.* **1** The act of waiting, or the time spent in waiting; delay. **2** An ambush or trap; snare: to lie in *wait* for a victim. **3** A member of a musical band organized to play and sing in the streets, at night or dawn: now applied only to those who sing carols in the streets at Christmastime. **4** *Obs.* A watchman or guard. [<AF *waitier,* OF *guaitier* <OHG *wahtēn* watch < *wahta* a guard]

wait-a-bit (wāt′ə·bit′) *n.* Any one of various plants with sharp or hooked thorns that catch and tear the clothing, and thus detain those who would pass through them, as the greenbrier or the prickly ash. [Trans. of Afrikaans *wacht-een-beetje*]

Waite (wāt), **Morrison Remick,** 1816–88, U. S. jurist; chief justice of the Supreme Court 1874–88.

wait·er (wā′tər) *n.* **1** One who waits upon others, as in a restaurant. **2** One who awaits something. **3** A tray for dishes, etc. **4** *Obs.* A watchman or keeper.

wait·ing (wā′ting) *n.* The act or business of a waiter; attendance. — **in waiting** In attendance, especially at court. — *adj.* That waits; expecting.

waiting list A list of people waiting to be admitted to some institution, as a school or club, or to some privilege or opportunity.

waiting room A room for the use of persons waiting, as for a railroad train, a doctor, dentist, or the like.

wait·ress (wā′tris) *n.* A woman or girl employed to wait on guests at table, as in a restaurant.

waive (wāv) *v.t.* **waived, waiv·ing 1** To give up or relinquish a claim to. **2** To refrain from insisting upon or taking advantage of; forgo. **3** To put off; postpone; delay. **4** *Law* To surrender, abandon, or relinquish voluntarily, either expressly or by implication, as a claim, privilege, or right. **5** *Obs.* To reject; cast off; abandon; desert. ◆ Homophone: *wave.* [<AF *weyver,* OF *gaiver* abandon <AF *weyf, waif* WAIF]

waiv·er (wā′vər) *n. Law* The voluntary relinquishment of a right, privilege, or advantage; also, the instrument which evidences such relinquishment. [<AF, var. of *weyver* abandon. See WAIF.]

Wai·yeung (wī′yŭng′) A city in eastern Kwangtung province, China; a river port on the Tung, east of Canton: formerly *Waichow.*

wa·kan·da (wä·kän′dä) *n.* Among the Sioux, the great power or supreme being behind the world: identical with Algonquian *manito*: also spelled *wahconda.* [<Siouan]

Wa·ka·ya·ma (wä·kä·yä·mä) A port of southern Honshu island, Japan.

wake¹ (wāk) *v.* **woke** or **waked, waked** (*Dial.* **wok·en), wak·ing** *v.i.* **1** To be roused from sleep or slumber. **2** To be or remain awake. **3** To become active or alert after being inactive or dormant. **4** *Dial.* To keep watch or guard at night; especially, to hold a wake (def. 1). **5** *Obs.* To feast or revel late into the night. — *v.t.* **6** To rouse from sleep or slumber; awake. **7** To rouse or stir up; excite: to *wake* evil passions. **8** *Dial.* To keep a vigil over; especially, to hold a wake over. See synonyms under STIR¹. — *n.* **1** A watch over the body of a dead person through the night, just before the burial, by the relatives and friends: common among the Irish, and often accompanied by conviviality. **2** Formerly, in the Anglican Church, a dedication festival or anniversary celebration of a parish church, preceded by a night vigil in the church. **3** The act of refraining from sleep, especially on a festive or solemn occasion. **4** *Obs.* The act of waking, or the state of being awake; vigil. [Fusion of OE *wacan* awake and *wacian* be awake. Akin to WATCH.]

◆ **awake, awaken, wake, waken** These four verbs, so similar in basic meaning, offer a confusing variety of choices in actual use. In the imperative, *Wake up!* is the familiar and homely form; the other three would be felt as poetic. *Awake* and *wake* have checkered form-histories. In the King James Bible, Shakespeare, and Milton, only the inflected forms in *-ed* are found. But *awake* and *wake* each had a strong verb as well as a weak one in its ancestry, and in the late seventeenth century the alternative inflected forms *awoke, awoken,* and *woke, woken* emerged, reinforced by analogy with *break, broke, broken,* etc. These alternative forms have led to uncertainty and confusion in usage. For the past tense of *awake, awoke* is usual; *awaked* tends to be felt as Biblical. *Awoke* as the past participle is rare, and *awaked* seems awkward to some; what happens in practice is a borrowing of the past participle from *awaken.* For *wake,* the more usual past is *woke* (or *woke up*); *waked* in the intransitive is also standard, but in the transitive sense it is dialectal, referring to holding a vigil or wake: They *waked* old Tim on Thursday night. Real uncertainty arises over the form to choose for the past participle of *wake.* In British (or dialectal American) usage, *woken,* or, for the phrasal verb, *woken up* is used: He had *woken* (or *woken up*) early. American usage here employs *waked (up),* or if this is felt as awkward, particularly in the passive, the past participle is borrowed from *waken* or *awaken*: What *woke* her? She was *awakened* (or *wakened*) by the noise of the crash.

wake² (wāk) *n.* **1** The track left by a vessel passing through the water. **2** Any course passed over. — **in the wake of 1** Following close behind. **2** In consequence of. [<ON *vök* an opening in ice]

Wake·field (wāk′fēld) **1** A county borough in southern Yorkshire, England; scene of Lancastrian victory in the Wars of the Roses, 1460. **2** The birthplace of George Washington, an estate in SE Virginia.

wake·ful (wāk′fəl) *adj.* **1** Remaining awake, especially at the ordinary time of sleep; not sleeping or sleepy. **2** Watchful; alert. **3** Unable to sleep; restless; suffering from insomnia. **4** Arousing from or as from sleep. See synonyms under VIGILANT. — **wake′ful·ly** *adv.* — **wake′ful·ness** *n.*

Wake Island (wāk) A U. S. naval and air base, comprising a coral atoll and three islands in the North Pacific, acquired by the United States in 1898; 4 square miles; about 4 1/2 miles long, 2 1/4 miles wide; occupied by Japanese forces, 1941–45.

wake·less (wāk′lis) *adj.* Uninterrupted; unbroken: a *wakeless* sleep.

wak·en (wā′kən) *v.t.* **1** To rouse from sleep; awake. **2** To rouse to alertness or activity. — *v.i.* **3** To cease sleeping; wake up. **4** *Obs.* To keep awake; also, to keep watch. [OE *waecnan, wacnian*]

wak·en·er (wā′kən·ər) *n. Archaic* One who or that which awakens.

wake·rife (wāk′rīf) *adj. Scot.* or *Obs.* Wakeful; alert. — **wake′rife·ness** *n.*

wake·rob·in (wāk′rob′in) *n.* **1** The cuckoo pint. **2** Any species of trillium; the mooseflower. **3** The jack-in-the-pulpit.

wakf (wukf) *n.* In Moslem law, the inalienable dedication of property in trust for the service of God or charitable uses; also, the property so dedicated. [<Arabic *waqf*]

wa·kif (wu′kif) *n.* One who makes a wakf.

wa·ki·ki (wä′ki·kē) *n.* Shell money of the South Sea Islands. [<Melanesian]

Waks·man (waks′mən), **Selman Abraham,** 1888–1973, U.S. microbiologist; discovered streptomycin.

Wa·la·chi·a (wo·lā′kē·ə) See WALLACHIA.

Wał·brzych (väl′bōō·bzhikh) A city in SW Poland, in former Lower Silesia; a coal-mining and manufacturing center. *German* **Wal·den·burg** (väl′dən·bŏŏrkh).

Wal·che·ren (väl′khə·rən) An island at the mouth of the Scheldt river in SW Netherlands; the westernmost island of Zeeland province; 80 square miles.

Wal·deck (väl′dek) An administrative district of Hesse; 420 square miles; formerly a principality of western Germany, a state of the German Republic (1918–29), and a Prussian province (1929–45).

Wal·de·mar (väl′də·mär) Name of four kings of Denmark: also *Valdemar.*

— **Waldemar I,** 1131–82, king 1157–82: called "Waldemar the Great."

— **Waldemar II,** 1170–1241, king 1202–41; greatly extended Danish territory: called "Waldemar the Victorious."

Wal·den·ses (wol·den′sēz) *n. pl.* A sect of religious dissenters founded about 1170 by Peter Waldo or Valdo, a rich merchant of Lyons, France. Waldo and his disciples sought to restore the church to its early purity and poverty, but were excommunicated by Pope Alexander III, and severely persecuted. [<Med. L *Waldenses* of (Peter) *Waldo*] — **Wal·den′si·an** *adj.* & *n.*

wald·grave (wôld′grāv) *n.* **1** An old German title of nobility. **2** Originally, the lord or intendant of a forest. Compare LANDGRAVE, MARGRAVE. [<G *waldgraf* < *wald* a wood + *graf* a count]

Wald·heim (vält′hīm′), **Kurt,** born 1918, Austrian statesman; secretary general of the United Nations 1972–.

Wal·do (wôl′dō), **Peter** Late 12th century French religious reformer: also *Valdo, Valdez.* See WALDENSES.

Wal·dorf salad (wôl′dôrf) A salad made of chopped celery, apples, and walnuts, and garnished with lettuce and mayonnaise. [from the first *Waldorf*-Astoria Hotel, New York City]

Wald·stät·ter, Die Vier (dē fēr vält′shtet′ər) Lucerne, Schwyz, Unterwalden and Uri, the forest cantons of Switzerland: the original cantons of the Swiss federation.

Wald·teu·fel (väl′toi·fəl), **Émile,** 1837–1915, French composer born in Alsace.

wale[1] (wāl) *n.* **1** A stripe or ridge made on living flesh by a rod, whip, or stick; a wheal. **2** *Naut.* One of certain strakes of outer planking running fore and aft on a vessel: the channel *wales.* **3** A ridge or rib on the surface of cloth; hence texture; grain. — *v.t.* **waled, wal·ing** **1** To raise wales or stripes on by striking, as with a lash; flog; beat. **2** To manufacture, as cloth, with a ridge or rib. **3** To weave, as wickerwork, with several rods together. **4** To protect, fasten, or hold with wales. ◆ Homophone: *wail.* [OE *walu*]

wale[2] (wāl) *Dial. & Scot. n.* A choice or preference of one thing from among others; also, the best; the cream. —*adj.* Well-selected; choice. —*v.t.* **waled, wal·ing** To choose; select; hence, to woo. ◆ Homophone: *wail.* [<ON *val* choice]

wal·er (wā′lər) *n. Anglo-Indian* A horse imported to India from New South Wales, Australia, for cavalry service; also, any horse from Australia.

Wales (wālz) A peninsula of SW Britain, comprising a principality of England, with which it has been politically united since 1536; 8,016 square miles.

Wal·fish Bay (wôl′fish) See WALVIS BAY.

Wal·hal·la (wal·hal′ə, -hä′lä, val-) See VALHALLA.

walk (wôk) *v.i.* **1** To advance on foot in such a manner that one part of a foot is always on the ground; of quadrupeds, to advance in such a manner that two or more feet are always on the ground. **2** To move or go on foot for exercise or amusement. **3** To proceed or advance slowly. **4** To move in a manner suggestive of walking, as a piece of masonry subjected to wind pressure. **5** To act or live in some manner: to *walk* in peace. **6** To return to earth and appear, as a ghost. **7** In baseball, to advance to first base on balls. **8** In basketball, to take more than two steps while holding the ball. **9** *Obs.* To be in continual motion. —*v.t.* **10** To pass through, over, or across at a walk: to *walk* the floor. **11** To cause to go at a walk; lead, ride, or drive at a walk: to *walk* a horse. **12** To force or help to walk. **13** To accompany on a walk. **14** To bring to a specified condition by walking. **15** To measure or survey by traversing on foot: to *walk* a boundary. **16** To cause to move with a motion resembling a walk: to *walk* a trunk on its corners. **17** In baseball, to allow to advance to first base on balls. **18** In basketball, to take more than two steps while holding (the ball). —**to walk off** **1** To depart, especially abruptly or without warning. **2** To get rid of (fat, drunkenness, etc.) by walking. —**to walk off with** **1** To win. **2** To steal. —**to walk out** *Colloq.* **1** To go out on strike. **2** To keep company: with *with* or *together.* —**to walk out on** *Colloq.* To forsake; desert. —**to walk over** **1** In certain sports, to walk over the course without a competitor so as to perform the technicality of winning; hence, to gain an easy victory. **2** To defeat easily; overwhelm. —*n.* **1** The act of walking, as for enjoyment or recreation; a stroll. **2** Manner of walking; gait; specifically, the gait of a horse in which two or more feet are always on the ground. **3** Method or way of living; behavior. **4** Chosen profession or habitual sphere of action: the different *walks* of life. **5** Distance as measured by the time taken by one who walks: It's an hour's *walk* to my house. **6** A place laid out or set apart for walking or resorted to by those who walk; a path, avenue, promenade, or sidewalk for pedestrians. **7** A ropewalk. **8** The formation of, or space between, two lines or rows of plants or trees, as in a coffee plantation. **9** A piece of ground set apart for the feeding and exercise of domestic animals; range; pasture: a *sheepwalk.* **10** A hawker's or vender's district or route; a beat. **11** A contest of speed in walking. **12** In baseball slang, a base on balls. [OE *wealcan* roll, toss] —**walk′ing** *adj. & n.*

walk·a·bout (wôk′ə·bout′) *n. Austral.* A wandering, apparently aimless journey over long distances. —**to go walkabout** To wander.

walk-a·round (wôk′ə·round′) *n.* **1** A rhythmic Negro dance performed by a group walking around in a large circle; also, the music composed for this dance. **2** A dance of this kind performed on the stage; also, the music for it.

walk-a·way (wôk′ə·wā′) *n.* A contest won without serious opposition.

walk·er (wôk′ər) *n.* **1** One who or that which walks. **2** A shoe used for walking.

Walk·er (wô′kər), **John,** 1732–1807, English lexicographer and actor. —**William,** 1824–60, U. S. filibuster in Lower California and Nicaragua.

walk·ie-talk·ie (wô′kē·tô′kē) *n. Telecom.* A portable radio set, equipped for both sending and receiving, and light enough to be carried by one man. Also spelled *walky-talky.*

walking bass An insistently reiterated bass figure, usually in eighth notes, used in boogie-woogie music.

WALKING BEAM

walking beam *Mech.* In a vertical engine, a horizontal beam that transmits power to the crankshaft through the connecting rod.

walking delegate See under DELEGATE.

walking fern A tufted evergreen fern *(Camptosorus rhizophyllus)* with fronds ending in long tapering tips which take root and thus give rise to new plants. Also **walking leaf.**

walking papers Notice of dismissal from employment, office, position, etc.

walking stick **1** A staff or cane carried in the hand. **2** Any of a family *(Phasmidae)* of insects having legs, body, and wings resembling one of the twigs among which it lives.

walk-on (wôk′on′, -ôn′) *n.* An actor who plays a bit part or merely walks on the stage; also, the part.

walk-out (wôk′out′) *n. Colloq.* **1** The act of walking out. **2** A workmen's strike.

walk-o·ver (wôk′ō′vər) *n.* **1** A horse race in which there is only one horse entered, and which can thus be won by going over the course at a mere walk. **2** An easy or unopposed success.

walk-up (wôk′up′) *Colloq. n.* An apartment house having no elevator. —*adj.* Having no elevator.

Wal·kü·re (väl·kü′rə), **Die** *German* The second music drama in Richard Wagner's tetralogy, *Der Ring des Nibelungen.* See RING OF THE NIBELUNG, VALKYRIE.

walk·way (wôk′wā′) *n.* A sidewalk; a passage; a garden path.

wal·kyr·ie (wal·kir′ē, val-) *n.* A valkyrie. [OE *wælcyrie,* lit., a chooser of the slain]

walk·y-talk·y (wô′kē·tô′kē) See WALKIE-TALKIE.

wall (wôl) *n.* **1** A continuous structure, as of stone or brick, designed to enclose an area, to provide defense or security, or to be the surrounding exterior of a house or a partition between rooms or halls; also, a fence of stone or brickwork, surrounding or separating yards, fields, etc. ◆ Collateral adjective: *mural.* **2** A barrier or rampart constructed for defense; in the plural, fortifications. **3** A sea wall; levee. **4** The side of any cavity, vessel, or receptacle; a parietal surface: the *walls* of the abdomen. **5** Something suggestive of a wall or barrier: a *wall* of bayonets. See synonyms under RAMPART. —**to drive, push,** or **thrust to the wall** To force (one) to an extremity; crush. —**to go to the wall** To be pressed or driven to an extremity; be forced to yield. —**to take the wall** To take the inner side of the walk; hence, to take a rude advantage. —*v.t.* **1** To provide, surround, protect, etc., with or as with a wall or walls. **2** To fill or block with a wall: often with *up.* —*adj.* Of or pertaining to a wall; hanging or growing on a wall [OE *weall, wall* <L *vallum* a rampart < *vallus* a stake, palisade]

Wall may appear as the first element in two-word phrases:

wall arcade	**wall bracket**	**wall crane**
wall arch	**wall case**	**wall engine**
wall berry	**wall casing**	**wall face**
wall border	**wall clock**	**wall garden**
wall box	**wall coping**	**wall map**
wall mosaic	**wall plant**	**wall tower**
wall moss	**wall plug**	**wall tree**
wall nook	**wall top**	**wall vase**

wal·la·by (wol′ə·bē) *n. pl.* **·bies** Any of various medium-sized to small kangaroos of Australia and New Guinea, ranging from the **rock wallaby** (genus *Petrogale*), to the **pademelon wallaby,** about the size of a rabbit. [<Australian *wolaba*]

Wal·lace (wol′is), **Alfred Russel,** 1823–1913, English naturalist. —**(Richard Horatio) Edgar,** 1875–1932, English novelist. —**Henry Agard,** 1888–1965, U.S. vice president 1941–1944; agriculturist, editor, and politician. —**Lewis,** 1827–1905, U. S. general, administrator, and author: known as *Lew Wallace.* —**Sir William,** 1272?–1305, Scottish national hero; executed by the English.

Wal·lach (väl′äkh), **Otto,** 1847–1931, German chemist.

Wal·la·chi·a (wo·lā′kē·ə) A historic region and former principality in southern and SE Rumania; 29,575 square miles; chief city, Bucharest: also *Walachia.* —**Wal·la′chi·an** *adj. & n.*

wal·lah (wä′lä) *n. Anglo-Indian* A person engaged in a specified occupation or activity, as a merchant, vender, agent, worker, or servant; popularly and somewhat contemptuously, a man or fellow. Also **wal′la.** —**punka-wallah** The servant whose job it is to keep the punka in motion. [<Hind. *-vālā,* suffix indicating a personal agent]

wal·la·roo (wol′ə·ro͞o′) *n.* A species of large kangaroo *(Macropus robustus).* Also **wallaroo kangaroo.** [<Australian *wolarū*]

Wal·la·sey (wol′ə·sē) A county borough in NW Cheshire, England, on the Mersey river opposite, and forming part of the port of, Liverpool.

Wal·la·wal·la (wol′ə·wol′ə) *n.* One of a small tribe of North American Indians of Shahaptian linguistic stock of the NW Pacific coast: now on a reservation in Oregon.

Wal·la Wal·la (wol′ə wol′ə) A city in SE Washington near the Oregon border on the Walla Walla River.

Walla Walla River A river in NE Oregon and SW Washington, flowing 60 miles NW to the Columbia River.

wall·board (wôl′bôrd′, -bōrd′) *n.* A material composed of several layers of compressed wood chips and pulp, molded and sized for use as a substitute for wooden boards and plaster.

wall·creep·er (wôl′krē′pər) *n.* A small, brilliantly colored Old World bird *(Tichodroma muraria)* that obtains its insect prey by creeping on cliffs and walls.

Wal·len·stein (wol′ən·stīn, *Ger.* vol′ən·shtīn), **Albrecht Wenzel Eusebius von,** 1583–1634, Duke of Friedland; Austrian general in the Thirty Years' War.

Wal·ler (wol′ər), **Edmund,** 1606–87, English poet.

wal·let (wol′it) *n.* **1** A pocketbook, usually of leather, for holding unfolded banknotes, personal papers, etc.; a billfold. **2** A leather or canvas bag for tools, etc. **3** A knapsack. **4** *Obs.* Any baggy protuberance hanging loosely. [ME *walet,* ? metathetic var. of *watel* a bag, basket <OE *watul* a wattle]

wall·eye (wôl′ī′) *n.* **1** An eye in which the iris is light-colored or white. **2** An eye in which the cornea is opaque and whitish; also, leukoma of the cornea. **3** A large staring eye, usually one showing much white, because of divergent strabismus. **4** Any of several walleyed fishes, as the walleyed pike or perch, the alewife, or the walleyed pollack. [Back formation <WALL-EYED]

wall·eyed (wôl′īd′) *adj.* **1** Affected with divergent strabismus. **2** Having a whitish or grayish eye; also, affected with leukoma of the cornea. **3** Squinting. **4** Having large, staring eyes, as a fish. **5** *Slang* Drunk. [<ON *valdeygthr,* alter. of *vagl eygr* < *vagl* a film on the eye + *eygr* having eyes < *auga* eye]

walleyed pike An American fresh-water percoid fish (genus *Stizostedion*) of the Great Lakes, having large eyes, esteemed as a game fish. Also **walleyed perch.**

walleyed pollack A coal-black North American pollack *(Pollachius fucensis)* of Pacific waters.

walleyed surf fish A sooty fish *(Hyperprosopon argenteus)* common in California waters.

wall fern The common polypody.

wall·flow·er (wôl′flou′ər) *n.* **1** Any of a genus *(Cheiranthus)* of European herbs of the mustard family, in particular the popular garden perennial *C. cheiri,* having fragrant yellow, orange, or red flowers. **2** An Australian desert shrub (genus *Gastrolobium*). **3** *Colloq.* A man or woman at a party who remains sitting or standing by the wall, presumably for want of a dancing partner.

WALL-FLOWER (Varies from 1 to 3 feet high)

wall fruit Fruit grown and ripened close to a wall or fence.

wal·lie (wol′ē) *n. Scot.* A valet.

Wal·lis and Fu·tu·na Islands (wol′is, fōō·tōō′nə) Two closely connected protectorates NE of Fiji Islands, both dependencies of New Caledonia, including the chief islands of Uvéa, Futuna, and Alofi; total, 75 square miles.

wall lizard A gecko.

Wal·lo·ni·an (wo·lō′nē·ən) *adj.* Of or pertaining to the Walloons or the dialect spoken by them. —*n.* **1** A Walloon. **2** The French dialect of the Walloons.

Wal·loon (wo·lōōn′) *n.* **1** One of a people inhabiting southern and southeastern Belgium and the adjoining regions of France, originally descended from the ancient Belgae. **2** Their language, a dialect of French. **3** One of the Huguenot colonists who came to the United States from Artois, France. —*adj.* Of or pertaining to the Walloons or their dialect.

wal·lop (wol′əp) *v.t. Colloq.* **1** To beat soundly; thrash. **2** To hit with a hard blow. **3** To defeat soundly. —*v.i. Dial.* or *Colloq.* **4** To move quickly and strenuously; gallop. **5** To move in an awkward, floundering manner; waddle. —*n.* **1** *Brit. Dial.* & *Scot.* A lively rolling motion; a gallop. **2** *Colloq.* A severe blow. [<AF *waloper,* OF *galoper.* Doublet of GALLOP.]

wal·lop·er (wol′əp·ər) *n. Colloq.* **1** One who wallops. **2** Something astounding or amazing; an extraordinary statement or act; a whopper.

wal·lop·ing (wol′əp·ing) *Colloq. adj.* Extraordinarily large; whopping: a *walloping* lie. —*n.* A beating; whipping.

wal·low (wol′ō) *v.i.* **1** To roll about, as in mud, snow, etc.; flounder: The hippopotamus *wallows* in the mud. **2** To move with a heavy, rolling motion, as a ship in a storm. **3** To live or indulge complacently or wantonly: to *wallow* in sensuality or wealth. —*n.* **1** The act of wallowing. **2** A pool, mudhole, or slough in which animals wallow; also, any depression or hollow made by or suggesting such use. [OE *wealwian*] —**wal′low·er** *n.*

wall·pa·per (wôl′pā′pər) *n.* Paper specially prepared and printed in colors and designs, for covering walls and ceilings of rooms. —*v.t.* To cover or provide with wallpaper.

wall pellitory See PELLITORY.

wall plate **1** A horizontal timber on a wall, for bearing the ends of joists, girders, etc. **2** *Mech.* A plate for attaching a bearing or the like to a wall.

wall rock *Mining* The non-metalliferous rock between two lodes.

wall rocket A British perennial *(Diplotaxis tenuifolia)* of the mustard family, with large yellow flowers.

wall rue A small delicate spleenwort *(Asplenium ruta-muraria)* growing on walls and cliffs.

Walls·end (wôlz′end) *n.* A size or grade of coal for household purposes. [from *Wallsend,* England]

Walls·end (wôlz′end) A municipal borough in SE Northumberland, England, on the Tyne just NE of Newcastle-on-Tyne.

Wall Street **1** A street in lower Manhattan, New York City: the financial center of the United States. **2** American financiers collectively, their interests, power, etc., or the American financial world.

wall tent A tent having vertical sides and peaked top.

wal·ly (wā′lē, wol′ē) See WALY[1].

wal·ly-drai·gle (wā′lē·drā′gəl, wol′ē-) *n. Scot.* **1** The youngest in a family; also, a young bird in the nest. **2** Any feeble or ill-grown creature. Also **wal′ly·drag′** (-drag′, -dräg′).

wal·nut (wôl′nut′, -nət) *n.* **1** Any of various deciduous, typically European and Asian trees (genus *Juglans*), cultivated as ornamental shade trees and valued for their timber and their edible nuts; especially, the **black walnut** *(J. nigra)* of the eastern United States, and the **English, Persian, Circassian,** or **Caucasian walnut** *(J. regia).* **2** The wood or nut of any of these trees. **3** The shagbark hickory, or its nut. **4** The color of the wood of any of these trees, especially of the black walnut, a very dark brown; also, the color of the shell of the English walnut, a dull, medium yellowish brown: also called **walnut brown.** [OE *walhhnutu, wealh hnutu* < *wealh* foreign + *hnutu* a nut]

BLACK WALNUT
a. Catkin.
b. Shuck, nut inside.
c. Nut, shuck removed.

Wal·pole (wôl′pōl, wol′-), **Horace,** 1717–97, fourth earl of Orford; English author and wit; son of Sir Robert Walpole. —**Sir Hugh Seymour,** 1884–1941, English novelist. —**Sir Robert,** 1676–1745, first earl of Orford; English statesman.

Wal·pur·gis Night (väl·pōōr′gis) The night before May 1, originally dedicated to St. Walpurga, an English nun of the eighth century who founded religious houses in Germany: associated in German folklore with a witches' Sabbath on the Brocken. Also *German* **Wal·pur′gis·nacht′** (-näkht′). [<G *Walpurgisnacht*]

wal·rus (wôl′rəs, wol′-) *n.* A large, marine, seal-like mammal (family *Odobenidae*) of arctic seas, with flexible hind limbs, tusklike canines in the upper jaw, and a thick, heavy neck; especially, the common Atlantic walrus *(Odobenus rosmarus).* —*adj.* **1** Belonging or pertaining to a walrus. **2** Designating a type of mustache suggestive of the coarse bristles on the muzzle of a walrus. [<Du. *walrus* <Scand. Cf. Dan. *hyalros,* ? <ON *hrosshalvr,* lit., a horse whale.]

WALRUS
(Body to 10 feet; weight to 3,000 pounds)

Wal·sall (wôl′sôl) A county borough in southern Staffordshire, England.

Wal·sing·ham (wôl′sing·əm), **Sir Francis,** 1530?–90, English statesman.

Wal·ter (wôl′tər, *Ger., Sw.* väl′tər) A masculine personal name. Also *Ger., Sw.* **Wal·ther** (väl′tər). [<Gmc., ruler of the army]

Wal·ter (väl′tər), **Bruno,** 1876–1962, German orchestra conductor active in the United States: real name *Bruno Schlesinger.*

Wal·ter (wôl′tər), **John,** 1739–1812, English journalist; founder of the London *Times.*

Wal·tham (wôl′thəm) An industrial city in eastern Massachusetts on the Charles River west of Boston.

Wal·tham·stow (wôl′thəm·stō, -təm-) A municipal borough of SW Essex, England, NE of London.

Wal·ther von der Vo·gel·wei·de (väl′ter fôn der fō′gəl·vī′də), 1170?–1230?, German minnesinger.

Wal·ton (wôl′tən), **Izaak,** 1593–1683, English author. —**William Turner,** born 1902, English composer.

waltz (wôlts) *n.* **1** A round dance executed to music in triple time. **2** The music for such a dance, or any composition written in the triple time characteristic of the waltz. —*v.i.* **1** To dance a waltz. **2** To move quickly: He *waltzed* out of the room. —*v.t.* **3** To cause to waltz. —*adj.* Pertaining to, or typical of, the waltz: *waltz* time. [<G *walzer* < *walzen* waltz, roll] —**waltz′er** *n.*

Wal·vis Bay (wôl′vis) **1** An inlet of the Atlantic in South-West Africa. **2** An enclave in South-West Africa, administered by that territory, but an integral part of the Cape of Good Hope Province, Union of South Africa; on Walvis Bay; 374 square miles. **3** A port in this enclave: also *Walfish Bay. Afrikaans* **Wal·vis·baai** (wôl′vis·bī′).

wa·ly[1] (wā′lē, wol′ē) *Scot. adj.* **1** Beautiful; pleasing; excellent. **2** Strong; robust; vigorous. —*n. pl.* **·lies** **1** Something pleasing to the eye; a toy; ornament. **2** Good luck. **3** *pl.* Finery. Also spelled *wally.*

wa·ly[2] (wā′lē) *interj. Dial.* & *Scot.* Alas!: an expression of sorrow or lament.

wam·ble (wom′əl, wam′-) *Dial. v.i.* **·bled, ·bling** **1** To move unsteadily; roll. **2** To twist or turn; writhe. **3** *Obs.* To feel nausea; be giddy or faint. —*n.* **1** A rolling gait. **2** A rolling or upheaving of the stomach; nausea. [ME *wamlen.* Cf. Dan. *vamle* feel nausea, Norw. *vamla* stagger.] —**wam′bling·ly** *adv.* —**wam′bly** *adj.*

wame (wām) *n. Scot.* The abdomen; belly; womb.

wame·fou (wām′fōō) *n. Scot.* A bellyful. Also **wame′fu′, wame′ful** (-fōōl).

wamp·ish (womp′ish) *v.t. Scot.* To toss or throw about; wave; brandish.

wam·pum (wom′pəm, wôm′-) *n.* **1** Beads made of the interior parts of shells, formerly used as currency among North American Indians and between the Indians and white settlers: used loose, strung on strings, and also made into belts, scarfs, etc. The strings were often worn as ornaments, necklaces, bracelets, etc. The belts, woven with symbolic designs, were used in rituals, official communications, proposals, ratification of treaties, alliances, etc. The beads were either black, dark-purple, or white, the last being specifically **wam′pum·peag** (-pēg). The dark beads were double the value of the white. See SEAWAN. **2** *Colloq.* Money. [<Algonquian *wampum(peage),* lit., a white (string of beads)]

WAMPUM
The historic Pennwampum—Iroquois Indian.

wampum snake The hoop snake: so called from its coloring.

wa·mus (wô′məs, wom′əs) *n.* A cardigan; a heavy outer jacket of strong, coarse cloth, worn in the United States. Also **wam′mus, wam′pus** (-pəs). [<Du. *wammes,* short for *wambuis* <OF *wambois* a leather doublet <OHG *wamba* the belly]

wan[1] (won) *adj.* **1** Pale, as from sickness or anxiety; pallid; livid; careworn; of a sickly hue. **2** Having a gloomy aspect; dismal; dark: said of scenes or landscapes. **3** *Obs.* Sad; mournful. **4** Faint; feeble: a *wan* smile. See synonyms under GHASTLY, PALE[2]. —*v.t.* & *v.i.* **wanned, wan·ning** To make or become wan. —*n. Rare* The quality of being wan; paleness. [OE *wann* dark, gloomy] —**wan′ly** *adv.* —**wan′ness** *n.*

wan[2] (won) Obsolete past tense of WIN.

Wan·a·mak·er (won′ə·mā′kər), **John,** 1838–1922, U.S. merchant.

wand (wond) *n.* **1** A slender, flexible rod waved by a magician, conjurer, or legerdemain artist; also, any rod indicating an office or function of the bearer, as a scepter. **2** A musician's baton. **3** A thin, flexible stick or twig; also, a willow shoot; osier. **4** In archery, a slat used as a mark and placed at varying distances for men and women.

See synonyms under STICK. [<ON *vöndr.* Akin to WIND[2].]

wan·der (won′dər) *v.i.* **1** To move or travel about without destination or purpose; roam; rove. **2** To go casually or by an indirect route; idle; stroll. **3** To extend in an irregular course; twist or meander. **4** To turn from a true or direct course; stray. **5** To deviate in conduct or opinion; go astray. **6** To think or speak deliriously or irrationally. — *v.t.* **7** *Poetic* To wander through or across. — *n.* The act of wandering; a ramble. [OE *wandrian*] — **wan′der·er** *n.* — **wan′der·ing** *adj.* — **wan′der·ing·ly** *adv.*

Synonyms (verb): deviate, digress, diverge, err, ramble, range, roam, rove, stray, swerve, veer. To *wander* is to move in an indefinite or indeterminate way which may or may not be a departure from a prescribed way; to *deviate* is to turn from a prescribed or right way, physically, mentally, or morally, usually in an unfavorable sense; to *diverge* is to turn from a course previously followed or that something else follows, and has no unfavorable implication; to *digress* is used only with reference to speaking or writing; to *err* is used of intellectual or moral action. To *swerve* or *veer* is to turn suddenly from a prescribed or previous course, and often but momentarily; *veer* is more capricious and repetitious; the horse *swerves* at the flash of a sword; the wind *veers*; the ship *veers* with the wind. To *stray* is to go in a somewhat purposeless way aside from the regular path or usual limits or abode, usually with unfavorable implication; cattle *stray* from their pastures; an author *strays* from his subject. *Stray* is in most uses a lighter word than *wander*. *Ramble* in its literal use is always a word of pleasant suggestion, but in its figurative use somewhat contemptuous; as, *rambling* talk. See RAMBLE.

wandering albatross A large, whitish, black-winged, web-footed sea bird *(Diomedea exulans)*, having extraordinary powers of flight.

wandering jew **1** A perennial trailing herb *(Tradescantia fluminensis)* of the spiderwort family, with hairy white flowers and vivid green leaves sometimes striped with yellow. **2** A related plant *(Zebrina pendula)* with red or white flowers and striped leaves.

Wandering Jew See under JEW.

wandering kidney A floating kidney.

wan·der·lust (won′dər·lust′, *Ger.* vän′dər·lo͝ost) *n.* An impulse to travel; restlessness combined with a sense of adventure. [<G < *wandern* travel + *lust* joy]

wan·der·oo (won′də·ro͞o′) *n.* **1** A large black monkey *(Macaca silenus)* of western India, having a heavy whitish mane. **2** A Ceylonese langur *(Presbytis cephalopterus)*. [<Singhalese *vanduru,* pl. of *vandurā* the Ceylonese langur <Skt. *vānara* a monkey]

wan·dle (won′dəl, -əl) *adj. Dial.* Supple; nimble. [Back formation <OE *wandlung* changeableness]

Wands·worth (wondz′wûrth) A metropolitan borough in SW London, England.

wane (wān) *v.i.* **waned, wan·ing** **1** To diminish in size and brilliance: opposed to *wax.* **2** To decline or decrease gradually; draw to an end. — *n.* **1** Decrease, as of power, prosperity, or reputation. **2** The decrease of the moon's visible illuminated surface; also, the period of such decrease. **3** The beveled edge of a board sawn from a log; also, the bark or defective portion on the edge or corner of a board. ◆ Homophone: *wain.* [OE *wanian* lessen]

wane·y (wā′nē) *adj.* Having a beveled edge, as the wane of a plank: also spelled *wany.* [<WANE, *n.* (def. 3)]

Wang·a·nu·i (wông′ə·no͞o′ē) A port of southern North Island, New Zealand.

wan·gle (wang′gəl) *v.* **·gled, ·gling** *Colloq. v.t.* **1** To obtain or make by indirect or irregular methods; contrive: to *wangle* an introduction to a celebrity. **2** To manipulate or adjust, especially dishonestly. **3** To wriggle or wag. — *v.i.* **4** To resort to indirect, irregular, or dishonest methods. **5** To wriggle. [? Alter. of WAGGLE] — **wan′gler** *n.*

Wan·hsien (wän′shyen′) A city on the Yangtze River, eastern Szechwan province, central China; a major commercial port NE of Chungking.

wan·i·gan (won′ə·gən) *n.* In American logging camps: **1** A storage chest for clothing, etc. **2** A shanty fitted with sleeping and cooking accommodations. Also **wan·gan** (won′gən), **wan′gun, wan′ni·gan.** [Earlier *wangan* <Algonquian *atawangan* < *atawan* buy, sell]

wan·ion (won′yən) *n. Archaic* Disaster, or bad luck; a curse: used only in the phrases **in a wanion, with a wanion,** etc. [Alter of dial. ME (Northern) *waniand,* ppr. of *wanien* wane]

Wan·kel engine (väng′kəl, wäng′-) A light, compact type of internal-combustion engine having combustion chambers bounded by the wall of a shallow cylinder and the sides of a triangular piston that rotates in one direction inside it. Also **Wan′kel.** [<F. *Wankel,* 1902–, German inventor]

Wan·ne-Eick·el (vän′ə·ī′kəl) A city in west central North Rhine-Westphalia NW of Bochum, West Germany.

Wan·stead and Wood·ford (won′sted, -stid, wo͝od′fərd) A municipal borough in Essex, England, NE of London.

want (wont, wônt) *v.t.* **1** To feel a desire or wish for. **2** To wish; desire: used with the infinitive: Your friends *want* to help you. **3** To be deficient in; lack; be without. **4** To be lacking to the extent of: He *wants* three inches of six feet. **5** *Brit.* To need; require. — *v.i.* **6** To have need: usually with *for.* **7** To be needy or destitute. **8** *Rare* To be lacking or absent. — *n.* **1** Lack or absence of something; scarcity; shortage. **2** Privation; indigence; destitution; need. **3** Something that is lacking or needed; a need. **4** A conscious or felt need of something; a craving. [Prob. <ON *vanta* be lacking] — **want′er** *n.*

Synonyms (noun): absence, dearth, default, defect, deficiency, lack, necessity, need, privation, scantiness, scarceness, scarcity. See NECESSITY, POVERTY. *Antonyms*: abundance, affluence, fullness, luxury, plenty, wealth.

wa'n't (wont, wônt) Was not: a dialectal contraction.

want ad *Colloq.* An advertisement in a newspaper for something wanted, as hired help, a job, a lodging, etc.

want·age (won′tij, wôn′-) *n.* Whatever is lacking; deficiency.

want column A column of want ads in a newspaper or other periodical.

want·ing (won′ting, wôn′-) *adj.* **1** Not at hand; missing; lacking: One juror is still *wanting.* **2** Marked by lack or deficiency; not coming up to need or expectation: He was found *wanting.* **3** *Colloq.* Deficient in intellect; feeble-minded. — **wanting in** Deficient in. — *prep.* With the exception of; less; save; minus.

wan·ton (won′tən) *adj.* **1** Dissolute; unchaste; licentious; lewd; lustful. **2** Recklessly inconsiderate, heartless, or unjust; evincing a malicious nature: *wanton* savagery; also, unprovoked: a *wanton* murder. **3** Of vigorous and abundant growth; rank. **4** Extravagant; running to excess; unrestrained: *wanton* speech. **5** Not bound or tied; loose: *wanton* curls; also, frolicsome; prankish. **6** *Obs.* Refractory; rebellious. — *v.i.* **1** To act wantonly or playfully; revel or sport. **2** To grow luxuriantly. — *v.t.* **3** To waste wantonly. — *n.* **1** A lewd or licentious person, especially a woman. **2** A playful or frolicsome person or animal. **3** A trifler; dallier. **4** *Obs.* A person who has been much indulged; a pet. [ME *wantoun* <OE *wan* deficient + ME *towen,* OE *togen,* pp. of *tēon* bring up, educate] — **wan′ton·ly** *adv.* — **wan′ton·ness** *n.*

Synonyms (adj.): airy, free, frisky, frolicsome, gay, loose, merry, playful, reckless, sportive, unbridled, uncurbed, unrestrained, wandering, wild. See IMMODEST. *Antonyms*: austere, demure, discreet, reserved, sedate, thoughtful.

wan·y (wā′nē) See WANEY.

wap[1] (wop, wap) *Dial.* or *Archaic v.t.* & *v.i.* **wapped, wap·ping** **1** To whip; beat; strike. **2** To flutter or flap, as wings. — *n.* **1** A stroke; blow. **2** A quarrel; fight. **3** A storm. [Prob. var. of WHOP]

wap[2] (wap, wop) *Dial. v.t.* **wapped, wap·ping** To wrap; tie; bind. — *n.* A wrapping. [? Alter. of WARP]

wap·en·shaw (wop′ən·shô, wap′-) *n. Scot.* A show of weapons; review of weapons. Also **wap′in·schaw, wap′pen·schaw′ing.**

wap·en·take (wop′ən·tāk, wap′-) *n.* An old administrative and judicial subdivision of some English counties, equivalent to the *hundred* of most counties. [OE *wǣpengetæc* <ON *vāpnatak* a (symbolical) flourish of weapons denoting confirmation of the decisions of an assembly < *vāpna,* genitive pl. of *vāpn* a weapon + *tak* a taking]

wap·i·ti (wop′ə·tē) *n.* A large North American deer *(Cervus canadensis)*: usually *elk.* [<Algonquian. Cf. Shawnee *wapiti* pale, white.]

WAPITI
(About 5 feet high at the shoulders; antler spread to 3 feet)

wap·per-jawed (wop′ər·jôd′) *adj. U. S. Dial.* **1** Having a wry or undershot jaw. **2** Out of true; askew.

war[1] (wôr) *n.* **1** A contest between or among nations or states, or between different parties in the same state, carried on by force and with arms. **2** Any act or state of hostility; enmity; strife; also, a contest or conflict. **3** *Poetic* **a** A battle. **b** The supplies and paraphernalia of war. **c** Armed troops; an army. See table MAJOR WARS OF HISTORY on page 1417. **4** The science or art of military operations; strategy. — *v.i.* **warred, war·ring** **1** To wage war; fight or take part in a war. **2** To be in any state of active opposition; contend; strive. — *adj.* Of or pertaining to, used in, or resulting from war. [OE *wyrre, werre* <AF *werre* <OHG *werra* strife, confusion]

War may appear as a combining form in hyphemes or solidemes, or as the first element in two-word phrases:

war-blasted	**war-making**
war-born	**war march**
war-breeder	**war-marked**
war-breeding	**war neurosis**
war bride	**war office**
war-broken	**war party**
war budget	**war prisoner**
war chant	**war-production**
war chief	**war-proof**
war cloud	**war-ridden**
war code	**war-risk**
warcraft	**war service**
war-debt	**war-shaken**
war-disabled	**war song**
war dog	**war-stirring**
war drum	**war-swept**
war-famed	**war talk**
war-footing	**war tax**
war gains	**wartime**
war-god	**war-torn**
war-goddess	**war-tossed**
war-hardened	**war traitor**
war-impoverished	**war vessel**
war insurance	**war-wasted**
war law	**war-wearied**
war leader	**war-weary**
war loan	**war-work**
war-loving	**war-worker**
war-machine	**war-worn**
war-made	**warworthy**
war-maimed	**war-wounded**
war-maker	**war zone**

war[2] (wär) *Dial. v.t.* To guard against; ware. — *adj.* Cautious; wary. [Var. of WARE[2]]

war[3] (wär) *adj.* & *adv. Scot.* & *Brit. Dial.* Worse.

War·beck (wôr′bek), **Perkin,** 1474–99, Walloon impostor and pretender to the English throne; hanged.

war belt Among certain North American Indians, a belt of wampum bearing symbolic figures or designs, sent by one tribe to another or passed from tribe to tribe, as a message declaring war, summoning a group of tribes to war, invoking aid in war, etc.

War between the States The United States Civil War: used especially in the former Confederate States.

war bird Among certain North American Indians, the golden eagle: so called because its feathers were worn in the war bonnet.

war·ble[1] (wôr′bəl) *v.* **·bled, ·bling** *v.t.* **1** To sing with trills and runs, or with tremulous vibrations. **2** To celebrate in song. — *v.i.* **3** To sing with trills, etc. **4** To make a liquid,

MAJOR WARS OF HISTORY

NAME	CONTESTANTS *(victor shown first)*	NOTABLE BATTLES	TREATIES
Greco–Persian Wars 499–478 B.C.	Greek states —Persia	Marathon, 490; Thermopylae, Salamis, 480; Plataea, 479	
Peloponnesian War 431–404 B.C.	Sparta —Athens	Syracuse, 415; Cyzicus, 410; Aegospotami, 405	Peace of Nicias, 421
First Punic War 264–241 B.C.; **Second Punic War** 218–201 B.C.; **Third Punic War** 149–146 B.C.	Rome —Carthage	Drepanum, 249; Aegates, 241 Lake Trasimene, 217, Cannae, 216; Zama,202	
Islamic Invasion of Europe 630–19th century	Christianity —Islam	Constantinople, 717–718; Tours, 732; Manzikert, 1071; Hattin, 187; Lepanto, 1571; Vienna, 1524, 1683; Zenta, 1697	Pruth, 1711; Kutchuk-Kanardjii, 1774; Sistova, 1791
Norman Conquest 1066	Normandy —England	Hastings, 1066	
Crusades 1096–1291	Christianity —Islam *(indecisive)*	Jerusalem, 1099; Acre, 1191	
Hundred Years' War 1338–1453	England —France	Crécy, 1346; Poitiers, 1356; Agincourt, 1415; Siege of Orléans, 1428–39	
Wars of the Roses 1455–85	Lancaster —York *(indecisive)*	St. Albans, 1455	
Thirty Years' War 1618–48	Catholics —Protestants	Leipzig, Breitenfeld, 1631; Lützen, 1632	Westphalia, 1648
Civil War (English) 1642–46	Roundheads —Cavaliers	Marston Moor, 1643; Naseby, 1645	
War of the Spanish Succession 1701–14	England, Austria, Prussia, Netherlands —France, Spain	Blenheim, 1704	Utrecht, 1713
War of the Austrian Succession 1740–48	France, Prussia, Sardinia, Spain —Austria, England	Dettingen, 1743; Fontenoy, 1745	Aix-la-Chapelle, 1748
French & Indian War 1755–63	England —France	Plains of Abraham, 1759; Montreal, 1760	
Seven Years' War 1756–63	Prussia —Austria, France, Russia	Rossbach, Leuthen, 1757	Hubertusberg, 1763
Revolutionary War 1775–83	American Colonies — England	Lexington, Concord, Bunker Hill, 1775; Saratoga, 1777; Yorktown, 1781	Paris, 1783
Napoleonic Wars 1796–1815	England, Austria, Russia, Prussia, etc. —France	Nile, 1798; Trafalgar, 1805; Jena, Auerstädt, 1806; Leipzig, 1813 Waterloo, 1815	Campoformio, 1797; Tilsit, 1807; Schönbrunn, 1809; Paris, 1814–15; Vienna, 1815
War of 1812 1812–15	United States —England	Lake Erie, 1813; New Orleans, 1815	Ghent, 1814
War of Independence (Greek) 1821–29	Greece, England, Sweden, Russia —Turkey	Navarino, 1827	London, 1827
Mexican War 1846–48	United States —Mexico	Resaca de la Palma, 1846; Chapultepec, 1847	Guadalupe Hidalgo, 1848
Crimean War 1854–56	Turkey, England, France, Sardinia —Russia	Sevastopol, 1854	Paris, 1856
Civil War (United States) 1861–65	Union (North) —Confederate States (South)	Bull Run, 1861; Antietam, 1862; Chancellorsville, Gettysburg, Vicksburg, Chattanooga, 1863; Wilderness, 1864	
Franco–Prussian War 1870–71	Prussia —France	Sedan, 1870	Versailles, 1871
Spanish–American War 1898	United States —Spain	Manila Bay, Santiago, 1898	Paris, 1898
Boer War 1899–1902	England —Transvaal Republic & Orange Free State	Ladysmith, 1899	Vereeniging, 1902
Russo–Japanese War 1904–1905	Japan —Russia	Port Arthur, Mukden, Tsushima, 1905	Portsmouth, 1905
First Balkan War 1912–13; **Second Balkan War** 1913	Bulgaria, Serbia, Greece, Montenegro —Turkey	Scutari, 1912; Salonika, 1912; Adrianople, 1912	London, 1913; Bucharest, 1913
World War I 1914–18	Allies —Central Powers	Dardanelles, 1915; Verdun, Somme, Jutland, 1916; Caporetto, 1917; Vittorio Veneto, Amiens, Marne, Ypres, 1918	Versailles, Saint-Germain, Neuilly, 1919; Trianon, Sèvres, 1920; Lausanne, 1923
Civil War (Spanish) 1936–39	Insurgents —Loyalists	Teruel, 1937; Ebro River, 1938	
World War II 1939–45	Allies —Axis 1939–45	Dunkirk 1940; Crete, 1941; El Alamein, 1942; Tunis, 1943; Stalingrad, 1942–43; Kharkov, 1943; Cassino, 1943–44; Saint-Lô, 1944; Rhine, Ruhr, Berlin, 1945	Potsdam, 1945
	Allies —Japan 1941–45	Pearl Harbor, 1941; Bataan, 1941–42; Singapore, Coral Sea, Midway Island, Guadalcanal, 1942; Bismarck Sea, Tarawa, 1943; Leyte Gulf, 1944; Philippines, 1944–45; Okinawa, 1945	San Francisco, 1951
Korean War 1950–52	United Nations —North Korea	Inchon, Pyongyang, 1950; Seoul, 1951	Panmunjom, 1953
Vietnam War 1960–73	North Vietnam — South Vietnam, United States	Tet Offensive, 1968	Paris, 1973

murmuring sound, as a stream. **5** *U. S.* To yodel. See synonyms under SING. — *n.* The act of warbling; a carol; song. [<AF *werbler,* OF *guerbler* < *werble* a warble <OHG *werbel* something that revolves. Akin to WHIRL.]

war·ble[2] (wôr′bəl) *n.* **1** A hard swelling on the back of a horse, caused by the chafing of the saddle. **2** A boil or swelling under the hide of a horse, cow, deer, or the like, caused by the maggot of a botfly or warblefly. **3** A warblefly. [Cf. obs. Sw. *varbulde* < *var* pus + *bulde* a tumor] — **war′bled** *adj.*

war·ble·fly (wôr′bəl·flī′) *n. pl.* **·flies** Any of a family *(Hypodermatidae)* of dipterous insects resembling the botflies, whose larvae produce swellings under the hides of cattle, horses, etc. [<WARBLE[2] + FLY[2]]

war·bler (wôr′blər) *n.* **1** One who or that which warbles; a songster. **2** Any of a family *(Sylviidae)* of plain-colored, mostly Old World birds allied to the kinglets and noted for their song, as the whitethroat. **3** Any of a large and varied family *(Compsothlypidae)* of small American insectivorous birds, usually brilliantly colored and with little powers of song, as the **summer** or **yellow warbler** *(Dendroica aestiva),* the redstart, ovenbird, and water thrush. Also **wood warbler.**

war bonnet The ceremonial head dress of the North American Plains Indians, consisting of a rawhide cap fitting the head and extending down the back to the heels, the crown and the extension being decorated with feathers of the golden eagle.

War·burg (vär′bŏŏrkh), **Otto Heinrich,** born 1883, German physiologist and chemist.

War College One of four colleges in the United States giving advanced instruction to experienced military, naval, and air officers; specifically, the **Army War College,** Carlisle Barracks, Pennsylvania, under the Department of the Army; the **Naval War College,** Newport, Rhode Island, under the Navy Department; and the **Air War College,** near Montgomery, Alabama, under the Department of the Air Force. The **National War College,** Washington, D.C., operating under the Joint Chiefs of Staff, prepares officers of the armed services, the State Department, and other executive departments for duties concerned with national security.

war correspondent A newspaper reporter or representative of some other periodical engaged to write up the scenes of combat from direct observation.

war cry A rallying cry used by combatants in a war, or by participants in any contest.

ward (wôrd) *n.* **1** The act of guarding; protection. **2** The state of being under a guard or guardian; custody; confinement; also, guardianship; control. **3** A guarded or protected place; a prison; jail; also, a division or subdivision of a jail or hospital: the maternity *ward.* **4** A territorial division of a city, made for convenience of government; also, in certain northern counties of England, a division equivalent to a hundred or wapentake. **5** A person who is in the charge or under the protection of a guardian. **6** An instrument or means of defense; a protection. **7** A defensive attitude or movement, as in fencing; guard. **8** A projection inside a lock, designed to obstruct the turning of any key other than the proper one; also, a corresponding notch in the bit of a key. **9** In feudal law, a minor under the care or protection of a guardian. **10** A warden; overseer. **11** A local congregation within the Mormon Church. **12** *Obs.* A company of men detailed to defend or guard; a garrison; watch. See synonyms under SHELTER. — *v.t.* **1** To repel or turn aside, as a thrust or blow: usually with *off.* **2** To put in a ward; keep in safety. **3** *Archaic* To guard; protect. [OE *weard* a watching < *weardian* watch, guard; infl. in some senses by AF *warde,* OF *garde* <Gmc.]

-ward *suffix* Toward; in the direction of: *upward, homeward.* Also **-wards.** [OE *-weard, -weardes* at, toward]

Ward (wôrd), **Artemas,** 1727–1800, American Revolutionary general. — **Artemus** Pseudonym of Charles Farrar Browne, 1834–67, U. S. humorist. — **Mary Augusta,** 1851–1920, *née* Arnold, English novelist: known as *Mrs. Humphrey Ward.*

war dance A dance of savage tribes before going to war or in celebration of a victory.

war·den[1] (wôr′dən) *n.* **1** One who keeps ward; a warder or gatekeeper. **2** A chief officer, as in a prison. **3** In England, the head of certain colleges. **4** In Connecticut, the chief executive of a borough. **5** A churchwarden. See synonyms under SUPERINTENDENT. [<AF *wardein,* OF *gardein, guarden* <Gmc. Doublet of GUARDIAN.]

war·den[2] (wôr′dən) *n.* A variety of pear used chiefly for cooking. Also **War′den.** [ME *wardon,* prob. <AF *warder,* OF *garder* keep <Gmc.]

war·den·ry (wôr′dən·rē) *n. pl.* **·ries** The office, functions, or jurisdiction of a warden. Also **war′den·ship** (-ship).

War Department A former executive department of the U. S. government (1789–1947) in charge of matters relating to the Army and (later) the Army Air Force: now absorbed into the Department of Defense.

ward·er (wôr′dər) *n.* **1** A keeper; guard; sentinel; watchman. **2** An official staff or baton; a truncheon. **3** A prison official; warden. [<AF *wardere* < *warder,* var. of OF *guarder* guard, keep]

ward-heel·er (wôrd′hē′lər) *n. U.S. Slang* A hanger-on of a political boss, who does minor tasks, canvasses votes, etc. [<WARD (def. 4) + HEELER (def. 1)]

ward-hold·ing (wôrd′hōl′ding) *n.* The holding of lands by military tenure: distinguished from *feu.*

ward·ress (wôrd′ris) *n.* A female warden.

ward·robe (wôrd′rōb′) *n.* **1** A large upright cabinet for wearing apparel; formerly, a large clothes closet or room, where clothes were also made and repaired. **2** All the garments of any one person. **3** In a noble or royal household, the department responsible for clothing, jewelry, etc. **4** The costumes of a theater or theatrical troupe. **5** The styles of a particular season taken collectively: the spring *wardrobe.* [<AF *warderobe,* OF *garderobe* < *warder* keep + *robe* a robe, dress]

ward·room (wôrd′rōōm′, -rŏŏm′) *n.* On a warship, the quarters allotted to the commissioned officers above the rank of ensign, excepting the commander, who has his own quarters; especially, the dining-room of these officers; also, these officers regarded as a group.

ward·ship (wôrd′ship) *n.* **1** The state of a ward; pupilage. **2** In feudal law, the right by which the lord had the custody of the bodies, and the custody and profits of the lands, of minor heirs of a deceased tenant.

ware[1] (wâr) *n.* **1** Articles of the same class; especially, manufactured articles: used collectively, often in composition: *tableware, glassware.* **2** *pl.* Articles of commerce; goods; merchandise; products. **3** Pottery; ceramic articles; earthenware. ◆ Homophone: *wear.* [OE *waru*]

ware[2] (wâr) *v.t.* **wared, war·ing** To beware of: used mainly in the imperative: *Ware* the dog. — *adj. Obs.* Conscious; aware; hence, on one's guard; cautious. ◆ Homophone: *wear.* [Fusion of OE *warian* beware and AF *warer,* OF *garer* <Gmc. Akin to WARN.]

ware[3] (wâr) *v.t. Scot.* To expend; lay out; also, to lavish; squander: also spelled *wair.* ◆ Homophone: *wear.*

ware·house (wâr′hous′) *n.* **1** A storehouse for goods or merchandise. **2** *Brit.* A large wholesale shop. — *v.t.* **·housed** (-houzd′), **·hous·ing** (-hou′zing) To place or store in a warehouse, especially in a bonded warehouse.

ware·house·man (wâr′hous′mən) *n. pl.* **·men** (-mən) One who makes a business of storing goods.

ware·room (wâr′rōōm′, -rŏŏm′) *n.* A room for the storage, exhibition, or sale of goods or wares.

war·fare (wôr′fâr′) *n.* **1** The waging or carrying on of war; conflict with arms; war. **2** Struggle; strife.

War·field (wôr′fēld), **David,** 1866–1951, U. S. actor.

War for Southern Independence See CIVIL WAR (AMERICAN) in table under WAR.

war game **1** Kriegspiel. **2** *pl.* Practice maneuvers imitating the conditions of actual warfare.

war hawk One who advocates war; a jingo.

war·head (wôr′hed′) *n. Mil.* **1** An ogive-shaped chamber in the nose of a torpedo, containing the charge of high explosive. **2** A similar chamber in a bomb, guided missile, or the like.

war horse **1** A heavy horse used in warfare; a charger. **2** *Colloq.* A veteran; especially, an aggressive or veteran politician.

war·i·son (war′ə·sən) *n.* **1** A signal for assault: an erroneous use. **2** Reward; healing. [<AF *warison,* OF *garison* wealth, possession]

wark[1] (wärk) *n. Scot.* Work.

wark[2] (wärk) *Scot.* & *Brit. Dial. n.* Ache; pain. — *v.i.* To suffer pain; ache; throb.

war·like (wôr′līk′) *adj.* **1** Disposed to engage in war; belligerent. **2** Relating to, used in, or suggesting war. **3** Threatening war; belligerent; hostile.

Synonyms: martial, military, soldierlike, soldierly. *Antonyms*: civil, effeminate, meek, pacific, peaceful, unmilitary, unsoldierlike, unsoldierly, unwarlike.

war·lock[1] (wôr′lok′) *n.* A wizard; sorcerer; also, a demon. [OE *wǣrloga* a traitor, foe, devil < *wǣr* a covenant + *lēogen* lie, deny]

war·lock[2] (wôr′lok′) *n.* A scalp lock worn by the warriors of certain North American Indian tribes. [<WAR + LOCK[2]]

war·lord (wôr′lôrd′) *n.* **1** A leader or high-ranking officer in a militaristic nation. **2** The warlike ruler or leader of a local region or group of bandits, especially in the Orient.

warm (wôrm) *adj.* **1** Moderately hot; having, or characterized by, heat somewhat greater than temperate: *warm* water; a *warm* climate. **2** Imparting heat: a *warm* fire. **3** Imparting, promoting, or preserving warmth; preventing loss of bodily heat: a *warm* coat. **4** Having a feeling of heat somewhat greater than ordinary: *warm* from exertion. **5** Possessing or marked by ardor, zeal, liveliness, enthusiasm, or cordiality: a *warm* argument; *warm* wishes. **6** Excited; agitated; also, vehement; passionate: a *warm* temper. **7** United by ardent affection: *warm* friends; also, amorous; loving. **8** Having predominating tones of red or yellow: opposed to *cool.* **9** Recently made; fresh: a *warm* trail; hence, near a hidden object, as in certain games of children. **10** *Colloq.* Uncomfortable by reason of annoyances or danger: They made the town *warm* for him. **11** Characterized by brisk activity: a *warm* skirmish. **12** *Colloq.* Rich; wealthy. — *v.t.* **1** To make warm; heat slightly: often with *up.* **2** To make ardent or enthusiastic; interest. **3** To fill with kindly feeling: The sight *warms* my heart. — *v.i.* **4** To become warm. **5** To become ardent or enthusiastic: often with *up* or *to.* **6** To become kindly disposed or friendly: with *to* or *toward.* — *n. Colloq.* The state or sensation of being or becoming warm; warmth; a heating. [OE *wearm*] — **warm′ly** *adv.* — **warm′ness** *n.*

warm-blood·ed (wôrm′blud′id) *adj.* **1** Having warm blood: said of animals, as mammals and birds, that preserve a nearly uniform and high body temperature, whatever the surrounding medium; homoiothermal. **2** Enthusiastic; ardent; passionate.

warm·er (wôr′mər) *n.* One who or that which warms.

warm front *Meteorol.* The irregular boundary line between an advancing mass of warm air and the underlying colder air mass.

warm-heart·ed (wôrm′här′tid) *adj.* Kind; affectionate.

warming pan A closed metal pan with a long handle, containing live coals or hot water, for warming a bed.

warm·ish (wôr′mish) *adj.* Rather warm.

war·mon·ger (wôr′mung′gər, -mong′-) *n.* One who propagates warlike ideas; a jingo. — **war′·mon′ger·ing** *adj.* & *n.*

Warm Springs A resort town in western Georgia; site of an institution for the study and treatment of poliomyelitis; here Franklin D. Roosevelt died, 1945.

warmth (wôrmth) *n.* **1** The state, quality, or sensation of being warm. **2** Ardor or fervidness of disposition or feeling; excitement of temper or mind. **3** The effect produced by warm colors. [ME *wermthe,* ult. <OE *wærm* warm]

Synonyms: animation, ardor, cordiality, eagerness, earnestness, emotion, energy, enthusiasm, excitement, fervidness, fervor, geniality, glow, heat, intensity, irascibility, life, passion, vehemence, zeal. Compare ENTHUSIASM. *Antonyms*: coldness, coolness, frigidity, iciness, indifference, insensibility, torpor.

warm-up (wôrm′up′) *n. Colloq.* The act of exercising or limbering up just before a game, contest, etc.

warn (wôrn) *v.t.* **1** To make aware of impending or possible harm; put on guard; caution. **2** To advise; admonish; counsel. **3** To inform; give notice in advance. **4** To notify (a person) to stay, go, or keep: with *off, away,* etc. See synonyms under ADMONISH. [OE *warenian, wearnian.* Akin to WARE[2].] — **warn′er** *n.*

warn·ing (wôr′ning) *n.* **1** The act of one who warns, or that which he communicates; notice of danger. **2** That which warns or admonishes. See synonyms under COUNSEL, EXAMPLE. — *adj.* Serving as a warning. — **warn′·ing·ly** *adv.*

war nose The end of a projectile or shell which carries the detonating device.

War of American Independence *Brit.* The American Revolution.

War of Independence The American Revolution.

War of Secession The Civil War in the United States.

War of the Rebellion The Civil War in the United States: used especially in the States that adhered to the Union.

War of the Spanish Succession See table under WAR.

War of 1812 See table under WAR.

warp (wôrp) *v.t.* **1** To turn or twist out of shape, as by shrinkage or heat. **2** To turn from a correct or proper course; give a twist or bias to; corrupt; pervert. **3** To stretch or arrange (yarn) so as to form a warp. **4** *Naut.* To move (a vessel) by hauling on a rope or cable, which is usually fastened to something stationary, as a pier or anchor. **5** *Aeron.* To change the curvature of (an airfoil or wing)· by twisting, so as to bring the airplane into balance. — *v.i.* **6** To become turned or twisted out of shape, as wood in drying. **7** To turn or deviate from a correct or proper course; go astray. **8** *Naut.* To move by means of ropes fastened to a pier, anchor, etc. See synonyms under BEND[1]. — *n.* **1** The state of being warped or twisted out of shape; a twist or distortion, especially in a piece of wood. **2** A mental or moral deviation or aberration; bias. **3** The threads that run the long way of a fabric, crossing the woof. **4** The heavy cords forming the carcass of a pneumatic tire. **5** *Naut.* A light cable used for warping a ship or boat; a towline or towrope. **6** A length of rope yarn or rope. [OE *weorpan* throw] — **warp′er** *n.*

war paint 1 Paint applied to faces and bodies by North American Indians and other primitive peoples in token of going to war. **2** Hence, any preparation for battle. **3** *Colloq.* Any front assumed to intimidate an adversary or increase self-confidence. **4** *Colloq.* Rouge and other cosmetics applied to the person; hence, full dress and personal adornment; finery; also, official garb or regalia.

war·path (wôr′path′, -päth′) *n.* The route taken by an attacking party of American Indians; the state of war; also, a war expedition. — **on the warpath 1** On a warlike expedition; at war. **2** Ready for a fight; thoroughly angry; ready to begin hostilities.

warp beam The roller or beam in a loom on which the warp is wound.

war·plane (wôr′plān′) *n.* An airplane equipped for fighting.

war·pow·er (wôr′pou′ər) *n.* The armed potential of a country; capacity of a nation's manpower and resources for waging war.

war powers Certain powers granted under the Constitution of the United States to the national government or to the chief executive in time of war, to prosecute war and act in all contingent emergencies.

war·rant (wôr′ənt, wor′-) *n.* **1** *Law* A judicial writ or order authorizing arrest, search, seizure, or any other designated act in aid of the administration of justice. **2** Something which assures or attests; a voucher; evidence; guarantee. **3** That which gives authority for some course or act; sanction; justification: What *warrant* have you for that statement? **4** A certificate of appointment given to army and navy officers of rank lower than commissioned officers. See under OFFICER. **5** A document giving a certain authority; specifically, a document authorizing receipt or payment of money: a dividend *warrant.* See synonyms under PRECEDENT. — *v.t.* **1** To assure or guarantee the quality, accuracy, certainty, or sufficiency of: to *warrant* a title to property. **2** To assure or guarantee the character or fidelity of; pledge oneself for. **3** To guarantee against injury, loss, etc. **4** To be sufficient grounds for; justify: The facts did not *warrant* your action. **5** To give legal authority or power to, so as to secure against harm; empower; authorize. **6** *Colloq.* To say confidently; feel sure. See synonyms under JUSTIFY. [<AF *warant,* OF *guarant* <Gmc.] — **war′rant·a·ble** *adj.* — **war′rant·a·bly** *adv.* — **war′rant·er** *n.*

war·ran·tee (wôr′ən·tē′, wor′-) *n. Law* The person to whom a warranty is given.

warrant officer See under OFFICER.

war·rant·or (wôr′ən·tôr, wor′-) *n. Law* One who makes or gives a warranty to another.

war·ran·ty (wôr′ən·tē, wor′-) *n. pl.* **·ties 1** *Law* An assurance or undertaking by the seller of property, express or implied, that the property is or shall be as it is represented or promised to be. **2** In conveyancing, a covenant in a deed whereby the grantor binds himself and his heirs to secure to the grantee the estate conveyed to him. **3** In insurance law, a stipulation or engagement on the part of the insured that the facts in relation to the risk are as stated by him. **4** Authorization; warrant. **5** *Dial.* Security; guaranty. [<AF *warantie,* OF *guarantie* <OF *guarant* a warrant. Doublet of GUARANTY.]

War·re·go River (wor′i·gō) A river in east central Australia, flowing 495 miles SW to the Darling River.

war·ren (wôr′ən, wor′-) *n.* **1** A place where rabbits live and breed in communities. **2** An enclosure for keeping small game; also, a place for keeping fish in a river. **3** An obscure crowded place of habitation. **4** In English law, a franchise, either by prescription or royal grant, to keep in an enclosure "beasts and fowls of warren," that is, animals that are by nature wild. See also FREEWARREN. [<AF *warenne* a game park, a rabbit warren < *warir* preserve <Gmc.]

War·ren (wôr′ən, wor′-), **Earl,** 1891–1974, U. S. administrator; chief justice of the U. S. Supreme Court 1953–1969. — **Joseph,** 1741–75, American physician and general. — **Robert Penn,** born 1905, U. S. poet, novelist, and educator.

war·ren·er (wôr′ən·ər, wor′-) *n.* The keeper of a warren.

Warren hoe A pointed garden hoe: used to make furrows for seeds: a trade name. See illustration under HOE.

war·ri·gal (wär′ə·gəl) *n. Austral.* **1** One who or that which is considered wild or uncivilized. **2** The dingo. Also **war′ra·gal.** [< native Australian *warregal* dog, savage]

War·ring·ton (wôr′ing·tən, wor′-) A county borough in southern Lancashire, England, on the Mersey east of Liverpool.

war·ri·or (wôr′ē·ər, -yər, wor′-) *n.* A man engaged in or experienced in warfare; one devoted to a military life. — *adj.* Military; martial. [<AF *werreieor* < *werreier* make war < *werre* WAR]

war–risk insurance (wôr′risk′) Insurance written by the government of the United States for military and naval personnel.

war·saw (wôr′sô) *n.* **1** A fish, the black grouper (*Garrupa nigrita*) of the South Atlantic and Gulf of Mexico. **2** A jewfish (*Promicrops guttatus*) of tropical American waters. [Alter. of Sp. *guasa*; prob. infl. in form by *Warsaw*]

War·saw (wôr′sô) The capital of Poland, on the Vistula, in the east central part of the country. *Polish* **War·sza·wa** (vär·shä′vä).

war·ship (wôr′ship′) *n.* Any vessel used in naval combat; especially, an armored vessel.

war·sle (wär′səl) *n., v.t.* & *v.i. Scot.* Wrestle. Also **war′stle.** — **war′sler** *n.*

Wars of the Roses See table under WAR.

wart (wôrt) *n.* **1** A small, usually hard and non-malignant excrescence formed on and rooted in the skin. **2** A spongy excrescence found on the pasterns of a horse. **3** A hard glandular protuberance on a plant. [OE *wearte*]

War·ta (vär′tä) A river in NW Poland, flowing 492 miles north and west to the Oder. *German* **War·the** (vär′tə).

Wart·burg (värt′bŏŏrkh) A castle in the former state of Thuringia, SW of Eisenach, SW East Germany, where Luther translated the New Testament (1521–22).

wart·hog (wôrt′hôg′, -hog′) *n.* An African veldt wild hog (*Phacochoerus aethiopicus*) having warty excrescences on the face and large tusks in both jaws.

WARTHOG
(From 2 to 2 1/2 feet at the shoulder)

War·ton (wôr′tən), **Thomas,** 1728–90, English literary historian, critic, and poet laureate.

wart·y (wôr′tē) *adj.* **wart·i·er, wart·i·est 1** Characterized by having warts: *warty*-flowered panic grass. **2** Of the nature of warts.

war whoop A yell made by American Indians, as a signal for attack or to terrify their opponents in battle.

War·wick (wôr′ik, wor′-) **1** A county of central England; 983 square miles. Also **War′·wick·shire** (-shir). **2** A municipal borough of central Warwick on the Avon; county town of Warwick.

War·wick (wôr′ik, wor′-), **Earl of,** 1428–71, Richard Neville, Earl of Salisbury, English statesman and soldier: called the "Kingmaker."

war·y (wâr′ē) *adj.* **war·i·er, war·i·est 1** Carefully watching and guarding. **2** Shrewd; wily. See synonyms under POLITIC, VIGILANT. [<WARE[2], *adj.*] — **war′i·ly** *adv.* — **war′i·ness** *n.*

was (woz, wuz, *unstressed* wəz) First and third person singular, past indicative of BE. [OE *wæs,* first and third person sing. of *wesan* be]

Wa·satch Plateau (wô′sach) A high tableland of central Utah at the southern end of the Wasatch Range; highest point 12,300 feet.

Wasatch Range A section of the Rocky Mountains in SE Idaho and northern Utah; highest point, 12,008 feet.

wase (wāz) *n. Obs.* or *Dial.* A wisp or bundle of hay, straw, or the like; especially, a cushion of such material for use between the head and a load borne thereon.

wash (wosh, wôsh) *v.t.* **1** To cleanse by immersing in or applying water or other liquid, often with rubbing or scrubbing. **2** To purify from pollution, defilement, or guilt. **3** To wet or cover with water or other liquid. **4** To flow against or over; lave: a beach *washed* by the ocean. **5** To carry away or remove by the action of water: with *away, off, out,* etc. **6** To form or wear by erosion: The storm *washed* gulleys in the hillside. **7** To purify, as gas, by passing through a liquid. **8** To coat with a thin or watery layer of color. **9** To cover with a thin coat of metal. **10** *Mining* **a** To subject (gravel, earth, etc.) to the action of water so as to separate the ore, etc. **b** To separate (ore, etc.) thus. **11** *Aeron.* To warp. — *v.i.* **12** To wash oneself. **13** To wash clothes, etc., in water or other liquid. **14** To withstand the effects of washing: That calico will *wash.* **15** *Brit. Colloq.* To undergo testing successfully: That story won't *wash.* **16** To flow with a lapping sound, as waves. **17** To be carried away or removed by the action of water: with *away, off, out,* etc. **18** To be eroded by the action of water. See synonyms under CLEANSE, PURIFY. — **to wash out** *Slang* **1** To fail and be dropped from a course, especially in military flight training. **2** To damage (an aircraft) irreparably, especially in landing. — *n.* **1** The act or process of washing; cleansing; ablution. **2** A number of articles, as of clothing, set apart for washing or being washed at one time; a washing; laundry. **3** Liquid or semi-liquid refuse; especially, waste food from the kitchen; swill. **4** A preparation used in washing or coating; specifically, a liquid cosmetic or a mouthwash; also, a water-color or India-ink pigment for spreading lightly and evenly on a drawing or picture. **5** The breaking of a body of water upon the shore, or the sound made by waves breaking or surging against a surface; swash. **6** Erosion of soil or earth by the action of rain or running water. **7** Backwash. **8** *Aeron.* Local air currents set up by the passing of an airplane. **9** An area washed by a sea or river; also, the shallow part of a river or an arm of the sea; a marsh; bog. **10** Material collected and deposited by water, as in the bed of a river or along its banks. **11** *U. S.* The dry bed of a stream; an arroyo. **12** Fermented liquor ready for the distillery. — *adj.* Washable; that may be washed without injury: *wash* fabrics. [OE *wæscan, wascan*]

Wash (wosh, wôsh), **The** An inlet of the North Sea on the eastern coast of England between Norfolk and Lincolnshire; 20 miles long, 15 miles wide.

wash·a·ble (wosh′ə·bəl, wôsh′-) *adj.* That may be washed without fading or injury.

wash-and-wear (wosh′ən·wâr′, wôsh′-) *adj.* Designating or pertaining to a garment or fabric so treated as to require little or no ironing after washing.

wash·board (wosh′bôrd′, -bōrd′, wôsh′-) *n.* **1** A board or frame having a corrugated surface on which to rub clothes while washing them. **2** *Naut.* A thin plank adjusted to turn the wash of the sea from a deck or port of a ship.

wash bowl A basin or bowl, either portable or stationary, used for washing the hands and face. Also **wash basin.**

wash·cloth (wosh′klôth′, -kloth′, wôsh′-) *n.* A small cloth used for washing the body.

wash·day (wosh′dā′, wôsh′-) *n.* A day of the week set aside for doing household washing.

washed-out (wosht′out′, wôsht′-) *adj.* **1** Faded; colorless; pale. **2** *Colloq.* Exhausted; worn-out; tired.

washed-up (wosht′up′, wôsht′-) *adj. Slang* Finished; done with; through.

wash·er (wosh′ər, wô′shər) *n.* **1** One who washes. **2** *Mech.* A small, flat, perforated disk of metal, leather, or wood, used for placing beneath a nut or at an axle bearing or joint, to serve as a cushion, to relieve friction, etc. **3** A machine for washing (ore or clothes). **4** A device for purifying gases; a scrubber.

wash·er·man (wosh′ər·mən, wô′shər-) *n. pl.* **·men** (-mən) A laundryman.

wash·er·wom·an (wosh′ər·wŏŏm′ən, wô′shər-) *n. pl.* **·wom·en** (-wim′in) A laundress.

wash·ing (wosh′ing, wô′shing) *n.* **1** The act of one who washes. **2** Things (as clothing) washed on one occasion, or collected during a certain time. **3** That which is retained after being washed: a *washing* of ore. **4** A thin coating of metal: The forks had received only one *washing* of silver. **5** The sale of stock or other securities at a stock exchange between parties of one interest, in order to create a fictitious activity. — *adj.* Used in or intended for washing.

washing soda Sodium carbonate.

Wash·ing·ton (wosh′ing·tən, wô′shing-) **1** A State in NW United States, adjoining Canada; 68,192 square miles; capital, Olympia; entered the Union Nov. 11, 1889; nickname, *Evergreen State*: abbr. *Wash.* **2** A city coextensive with the District of Columbia and capital of the United States. — **Wash′ing·to′·ni·an** (-tō′nē·ən) *adj.* & *n.*

Wash·ing·ton (wosh′ing·tən, wô′shing-), **Booker Taliaferro,** 1856–1915, U. S. Negro educator. — **George,** 1732–99, American patriot, soldier, and statesman; first president of the United States 1789–97. — **Martha,** 1731–1802, *née* Dandridge (Mrs. Daniel Parke Custis 1749–57), wife of George Washington.

Washington, Lake A lake in west central Washington, near Seattle; 20 miles long.

Washington, Mount The highest peak of the White Mountains of New Hampshire; 6,288 feet.

Washington palm The fan palm (*Washingtonia filifera*) of California and the Colorado desert.

Washington pie A layer cake with a filling of cream or jam.

Washington's Birthday The anniversary of George Washington's birth, February 22: a legal holiday in most States of the United States.

Wash·i·ta River (wosh′ə·tô, wô′shə-) **1** See OUACHITA RIVER. **2** A river in Texas and Oklahoma, flowing 450 miles SE and east from the Texas Panhandle near the Oklahoma border to Lake Texoma; formerly flowed 40 miles further to the Red River.

wash·out (wosh′out′, wôsh′-) *n.* **1** A considerable erosion of earth by the action of water; also, the excavation thus made; a gully or gulch. **2** *Aeron.* A decrease in the angle of incidence of an airplane wing toward the tip. **3** *Slang* A hopeless or total failure.

wash·rag (wosh′rag′, wôsh′-) *n.* A washcloth.

wash·room (wosh′rŏŏm′, -rŏŏm′, wôsh′-) *n.* A lavatory.

wash sale On a stock exchange, the buying of stock by the seller's agents, to mislead as to the real demand.

wash·stand (wosh′stand′, wôsh′-) *n.* A piece of furniture used for holding the utensils for ablutions; a stand for wash bowl, pitcher, etc.

wash·tub (wosh′tub′, wôsh′-) *n.* A tub used for washing.

wash·wom·an (wosh′wŏŏm′ən, wôsh′-) *n. pl.* **·wom·en** (-wim′in) A washerwoman.

wash·y (wosh′ē, wô′shē) *adj.* **wash·i·er, wash·i·est** **1** Overly wet; sodden; water-logged. **2** Bringing rain: said of weather or wind. **3** Wanting in substance, solidity, stamina, or force; wishy-washy; feeble. **4** Sweating: said of horses. — **wash′i·ness** *n.*

was·n't (woz′ənt, wuz′-) Was not.

wasp (wosp, wôsp) *n.* Any of numerous hymenopterous insects, chiefly of the superfamilies *Sphecoidea* and *Vespoidea*, of which the workers and females are provided with effective stings. The typical social wasps construct papery nests of masticated vegetable material; they feed on fruits, the nectar of flowers, and on insects. The solitary wasps construct nests of mud or sand. ◆ Collateral adjective: *vespine.* [OE *wæsp*]

WASP (wosp, wôsp) *n. Slang* A white Protestant American. [From the initial letters of the words "white Anglo-Saxon Protestant"]

wasp·ish (wos′pish, wôs′-) *adj.* **1** Having a nature like a wasp; irritable; irascible. **2** Having a wasplike form or slender waist. See synonyms under FRETFUL. — **wasp′ish·ly** *adv.* — **wasp′ish·ness** *n.*

wasp waist A person's waist, so slender as to suggest that of a wasp. — **wasp-waist·ed** (wosp′wās′tid, wôsp′-) *adj.*

wasp·y (wos′pē, wôs′-) *adj.* **wasp·i·er, wasp·i·est** Like a wasp; waspish.

was·sail (wos′əl, was′-, wo·sāl′) *n.* **1** An ancient salutation or toast; an expression of good will in festivities, especially when pledging someone's health. See DRINK-HAIL. **2** The liquor prepared for a wassail; especially, a mixture of ale and wine with sugar, roasted apples, spices, etc. **3** A festivity at which healths are drunk; a carousal. **4** *Brit.* A convivial song. — *v.i.* To take part in a wassail; carouse. — *v.t.* To drink the health of; toast. [ME *wæs hæil* <ON *ves heill* be whole (*i.e.,* in good health)] — **was′sail·er** *n.*

Was·ser·mann (väs′ər·män), **August von,** 1866–1925, German physician and bacteriologist. — **Jakob,** 1873–1934, German novelist.

Wasserman reaction A diagnostic test for syphilis, based on testing the serum of the blood for syphilitic antibodies. Also **Wassermann test.** [after August von *Wasserman*]

wast[1] (wost, *unstressed* wəst) Archaic second person singular, past indicative of BE: used with *thou.*

wast[2] (wast) *adj. Scot.* West.

wast·age (wās′tij) *n.* That which is lost by leakage, wear, waste, etc.

waste (wāst) *adj.* **1** Cast aside as worthless or of no practical value; used; worn out; discarded. **2** Excreted; cast out of an animal body, as food, etc. **3** Not under cultivation; untilled; hence, unproductive; unoccupied. **4** Made desolate; ruined; dismal; gloomy. **5** Containing or conveying waste products. **6** Produced in excess of consumption; superfluous: *waste* energy. **7** *Obs.* Wasteful; lavish. — **to lay waste** To destroy utterly. — *v.* **wast·ed, wast·ing** *v.t.* **1** To use or expend thoughtlessly, uselessly, or without return; be prodigal or extravagant of; squander. **2** To cause to lose strength, vigor, or bulk; make weak or feeble. **3** To use up; exhaust; consume. **4** To fail to use or take advantage of, as an opportunity. **5** To lay waste; desolate; devastate. — *v.i.* **6** To lose strength, vigor, or bulk; become weak or feeble: often with *away.* **7** To diminish or dwindle gradually. **8** To pass gradually: said of time. See synonyms under SQUANDER, WEAR[1]. — *n.* **1** The act of wasting or squandering, or the state of being wasted; useless or unnecessary expenditure. **2** A place or a region that is devastated or made desolate; wilderness; desert. **3** A continuous, gradual diminishing of strength, vigor, or substance by use or wear. **4** The act of laying waste or devastating; ravage: the *waste* of war. **5** Something rejected as worthless or unneeded; specifically, tangled spun cotton thread, the refuse of a textile factory; also, steam or other fluid that escapes without being used. **6** Garbage; rubbish; trash. **7** The waste products of the soil due to erosion by chemical or human action and carried out to sea by running water. **8** A wasting disease; specifically, consumption. ◆ Homophone: *waist.* [<AF *waster,* ult. <L *vastare* lay waste < *vastus* desert, desolate. Related to VAST.]

Synonyms (adj.): excess, extra, redundant, refuse, superfluous, useless, valueless, worthless. See BLEAK, VACANT. *Antonyms*: choice, good, precious, useful, valuable.

Synonyms (noun): chaff, debris, dregs, dross, leavings, offal, offscouring, refuse, remains, scum, sediment. See EXCESS, LOSS.

Waste may appear as a combining form in hyphemes or solidemes, or as the first element in two-word phrases, with the meaning: containing or conveying refuse or waste; as in:

waste bin	**waste sluice**
waste-collector	**waste trap**
waste gate	**waste-water**
waste heap	**wasteway**
waste pit	**wasteyard**

waste·bas·ket (wāst′bas′kit, -bäs′-) *n.* A basket for paper scraps and other waste.

waste·ful (wāst′fəl) *adj.* **1** Prone to waste; extravagant. **2** Causing waste; ruinous. — **waste′ful·ly** *adv.* — **waste′ful·ness** *n.*

waste·land (wāst′land′) *n.* A barren or desolate land.

waste paper Paper thrown away as worthless. Also **waste·pa·per** (wāst′pā′pər). — **waste′-pa′per** *adj.*

waste-paper basket A wastebasket.

waste pipe A pipe for carrying off waste-water, etc.

wast·er (wās′tər) *n.* One who wastes; a wastrel.

wast·ing (wās′ting) *adj.* **1** Producing emaciation; sapping the strength; enfeebling: a *wasting* fever. **2** Laying waste; devastating.

wast·rel (wās′trəl) *n.* **1** An abandoned child; a waif. **2** A waster; a profligate; spendthrift. [Dim. of WASTER]

wast·ry (wās′trē) *Scot.* or *Obs. adj.* Wasteful. — *n.* Wastefulness: also **waste′rie, wast′·rie, wast′rife.**

wat[1] (wat) *adj. Scot.* **1** Intemperate. **2** Wet.

wat[2] (wot) *n.* A hare. [Prob. from *Wat,* nickname for WALTER]

wa·tap (wä·täp′) *n.* Roots of the spruce, cedar, pine, etc., used by North American Indians to sew bark for canoes and other objects. Also **wa·ta·pe** (wä·tä′pe). [<Algonquian (Narraganset) *wattap* a root of a tree]

watch (woch) *v.i.* **1** To be constantly on the alert; give earnest heed; be observant, vigilant, or attentive. **2** To look attentively; observe. **3** To wait expectantly for something; be in a state of expectation: with *for.* **4** To do duty as a guard or sentinel; serve as a watchman. **5** To have in one's care or keeping; guard; tend. **6** To be awake; go without sleep; keep vigil. — *v.t.* **7** To keep under observation; look at steadily and attentively; observe. **8** To follow the course of mentally; keep informed concerning. **9** To be alert for; wait for expectantly: to *watch* one's opportunity. **10** To keep watch over; guard. See synonyms under ABIDE, LOOK. — *n.* **1** The act of watching; wakefulness with close and continuous attention; careful observation; vigil. **2** One of the divisions of the night made in ancient times: with the Hebrews, one third; with the Romans, one fourth; hence, any indefinite waking period which marks the passage of the night. **3** Position or service as a guard or sentry. **4** *Obs.* Vigilance; a vigil; wake. **5** One or more persons set to watch; a watchman or set of watchmen; sentinel; guard. **6** The place occupied by or assigned to a guard. **7** The period of time during which a guard is on duty. **8** *Naut.* **a** One of the two divisions of a ship's officers and crew, performing duty in alternation. **b** The period of time during which each division is on duty: four hours, except the dog-watches, from 4 to 6 and from 6 to 8 p.m., which are interposed daily to shift night duty from one watch to the other alternately. **9** A small, portable timepiece, actuated by a coiled spring, for keeping and indicating time. **10** *Obs.* A candle marked into equal sections, each of which burns a known length of time. **11** *Obs.* The cry of a watchman. **12** *Obs.* Wakefulness; the state of staying or being awake. See synonyms under OVERSIGHT. [OE *waeccan.* Akin to WAKE[1].]

watch cap In the U. S. Navy, a small, knitted woolen cap of navy blue worn by enlisted men during cold weather.

watch·case (woch′kās′) *n.* **1** The protecting case of a watch: usually of gold or silver. **2** *Obs.* A sentry box.

watch·cry (woch′krī′) *n. pl.* **·cries** A slogan; a watchword.

watch·dog (woch′dôg′, -dog′) *n.* A dog kept to guard a building or other property.

watch·er (woch′ər) *n.* **1** One who watches; especially, one who watches by a sickbed, deathbed, or corpse. **2** One who watches the voting at the polls on election day to detect dishonest practices.

watch·ful (woch′fəl) *adj.* **1** Vigilant. **2** *Obs.* Wakeful. See synonyms under ALERT, VIGILANT. — **watch′ful·ly** *adv.* — **watch′ful·ness** *n.*

watch·guard (woch′gärd′) *n.* A chain, cord, or ribbon attached to a watch and fastened to the clothing.

watch·mak·er (woch′mā′kər) *n.* One who makes or repairs watches.

watch·man (woch′mən) *n. pl.* **·men** (-mən) **1** Formerly, one of a group of men appointed to keep watch or patrol the streets of a town or village at night. **2** Anyone who keeps watch or guard; especially, a man employed to guard a building, etc., at night.

watch night New Year's Eve.

watch·tow·er (woch′tou′ər) *n.* A tower upon which a sentinel is stationed.

watch·word (woch′wûrd′) *n.* **1** A secret password. **2** A rallying cry or maxim.

Wa·ten·stedt–Salz·git·ter (vä′tən·shtet·zälts′·git·ər) A city in SE Lower Saxony, north central West Germany.

wa·ter (wô′tər, wot′ər) *n.* **1** A colorless limpid liquid compound of hydrogen and oxygen, H_2O, in the proportion of two volumes of hydrogen to one of oxygen, or, by weight of approximately 2 parts of hydrogen to 16 of oxygen. Water has its maximum density at 4° C. or 39° F., one cubic centimeter weighing a gram. It freezes at 0° C. or 32° F., and boils at 100° C. or 212° F. **2** Any body of water, as a lake, river, or a sea; in Scotland, a small river. **3** Any one of the aqueous or liquid secretions of animals; also, perspiration, tears, urine, etc. **4** Any preparation of water holding a gaseous or volatile substance in solution. **5** The transparency or luster of a precious stone or a pearl; hence, excellence; purity. **6** An undulating sheen given to certain fabrics, as silk, etc. **7** In commerce and finance, stock issued without increase of paid-in capital to represent it. — **above water** Out of danger; secure. — **hard water** Water containing in solution salts of calcium and magnesium, especially the sulfates or bicarbonates of these elements: so called because of the difficulty of obtaining a soap lather with such water. — **soft water** Water free from the salts of calcium and magnesium, as rain water and water found in sandstone districts. — *v.t.* **1** To pour water upon; irrigate. **2** To provide with water for drinking; give water to. **3** To dilute or weaken with water: often with *down.* **4** To give an undulating sheen to the surface of (silk, linen, etc.) by uneven pressure after damping and heating. **5** To enlarge the number of shares of (a stock company) without increasing the paid-in capital in proportion. **6** To provide with streams: used in the passive participle. — *v.i.* **7** To secrete or discharge water, tears, etc. **8** To fill with saliva, as the mouth, from desire for food. **9** To drink water. **10** To take in water, as a locomotive. [OE *wæter.* Akin to OTTER.]

Water may appear as a combining form in hyphemes or solidemes, or as the first element in two-word phrases:

water-analysis
water barge
water-bearing
water bottle
water-bound
water bucket
water-carrier
water-carrying
water cask
water channel
water content
water-deposited
water diver
water-drain
water-drawer
water-drinker
water-drinking
water flow
water-flushed
water fountain
waterfree
water-girt
water-gray
water-green
water heater
waterhole
water insect
water jar
water-laden
water-locked
water pail
waterplane
water plant
water police
water problem
water project
water pump
water-quenched
water-resistant
water resources
water-rolling
water-rot
water-rotted
water-route
water-scarcity
water-sealed
water service
water-soaked
water-sodden
water source
water tap
water trough
water turbine
water-walled
water-washed
water-wasting

water adder **1** The water moccasin. **2** The water snake.

wa·ter·age (wô′tər·ij, wot′ər-) *n. Brit.* Conveyance of merchandise by water; also, the fee paid for such transportation.

wa·ter·back (wô′tər·bak′, wot′ər-) *n.* A coil or chamber for heating water in the back of a range or other stove.

water balance *Biol.* The preservation of a nearly uniform water content in an organism, especially a plant.

water bear See under TARDIGRADE.

Wa·ter–bear·er (wô′tər·bâr′ər, wot′ər-) The constellation Aquarius.

water bearing *Mech.* A journal bearing in which water under pressure does the work of a lubricant.

wa·ter·bed (wô′tər·bed′, wot′ər-) *n.* A bed with a water-filled container serving as a mattress, adjustable in firmness and often heated.

water beetle Any of several aquatic beetles (especially of the families *Dytiscidae, Hydrophilidae* or *Gyrinidae*), having legs flattened and fringed with hairs for swimming.

water bird Any bird living on or near water.

water biscuit A plain cracker or biscuit of flour, shortening, and water.

water blink In arctic regions, a cloud or spot on the horizon arising from and indicating the presence of open water: a sign of the breaking up of winter.

water blister A blister containing limpid watery matter.

wa·ter·bloom (wô′tər·blōōm′, wot′ər-) *n.* The sudden appearance of large masses of blue-green algae in bodies of fresh water.

wa·ter–borne (wô′tər·bôrn′, -bōrn′, wot′ər-) *adj.* **1** Floating on water. **2** Transported or carried by water: *water-borne* commerce.

wa·ter·brain (wô′tər·brān′, wot′ər-) *n.* A disease of sheep characterized by staggering as from giddiness; gid.

water brake *Mech.* A brake, formerly used on steam locomotives, formed by using water pressure to provide a braking effect.

wa·ter·brash (wô′tər·brash′, wot′ər-) *n. Pathol.* Pyrosis; heartburn.

wa·ter·buck (wô′tər·buk′, wot′ər-) *n.* **1** Either of two large African antelopes (genus *Kobus*), frequenting the neighborhood of rivers and swimming with ease; especially, *K. ellipsiprymnus* of south central Africa. **2** Any of several similar antelopes. [<Du. *waterbok*]

water buffalo **1** A buffalo *(Bubalus bubalus)* of India, the largest of wild cattle, attaining a height of 6 feet at the withers and a very wide spread of horns. When domesticated it becomes a useful draft animal. **2** The carabao. Also called *Indian buffalo.*

WATER BUFFALO
(Spread of horns up to 9 feet)

water bug **1** The Croton bug. **2** Any of various hemipterous bugs (family *Belostomatidae*) which live in the water, especially the large species *(Lethocerus americanus)* common in North America. **3** The water scorpion.

Wa·ter·bu·ry (wô′tər·ber′ē, wot′ər-) A city in SW Connecticut; an industrial center, especially of the brass industry.

water chestnut **1** The hard horned edible fruit of an aquatic plant *(Trapa natans).* **2** The plant itself: also **water caltrop, wa′ter·nut′.**

water chinkapin **1** The American or yellow lotus *(Nelumbium pentapetalum).* **2** One of its edible nutlike seeds. Also **water chinquapin.**

WATER CHINKAPIN
a. Flower. *b.* Leaf. *c.* Fruit.

wa·ter·clock (wô′·tər·klok′, wot′ər-) *n.* Any device, as a clepsydra, for measuring time by the fall or flow of water.

wa·ter·clos·et (wô′tər·kloz′it, wot′ər-) *n.* A room or closet having a hopper flushed and discharged by means of water, used as a privy; also, the hopper and its trap.

wa·ter–col·or (wô′tər·kul′ər, wot′ər-) *adj.* Of, pertaining to, used with, or executed in water colors.

water color **1** A color prepared for painting with water as the medium, as distinguished from one to be used with oil, tempera, etc., as the medium, and characterized by the fact that the result may be either transparent or opaque. **2** That branch of painting in which water colors are used, or the method of using them. **3** A picture or painting done in water colors.

wa·ter–cool (wô′tər·kōōl′, wot′ər-) *v.t.* To cool by means of water, as by using a water jacket on an internal-combustion engine. — **wa′ter-cooled′** *adj.* — **wa′ter-cool′ing** *adj.* & *n.*

water cooler A vessel or apparatus for cooling and dispensing drinking water: often operated electrically.

wa·ter·course (wô′tər·kôrs′, -kōrs′, wot′ər-) *n.* **1** A stream of water; river; brook; a stream having a bed and banks. **2** The course or channel of a stream of water; a canal. See synonyms under STREAM.

wa·ter·craft (wô′tər·kraft′, -kräft′, wot′ər-) *n.* **1** Skill in sailing boats or in aquatic sports. **2** Any boat or ship; also, sailing vessels collectively.

water crake **1** The spotted crake. **2** The water ouzel. See under OUZEL.

wa·ter·cress (wô′tər·kres′, wot′ər-) *n.* A creeping perennial herb *(Rorippa nasturtium-aquaticum)* of the mustard family, having pinnate leaves and white flowers. It grows in springs and clear cool streams and is cultivated for use as salad.

water culture Hydroponics.

water cure **1** *Med.* Hydropathy. **2** *Colloq.* A kind of torture in which large quantities of water are put forcibly down the victim's throat.

water cushion A pool of water maintained to absorb the impact of water, as from the spillway of a dam.

water dog **1** A dog that takes readily to the water, as the water spaniel. **2** A dog trained to retrieve water fowl. **3** *Colloq.* An old sailor.

Wa·ter·ee (wô′tə·rē′) The lower course of the

CATAWBA RIVER, flowing about 75 miles from north central South Carolina to a junction with the Congaree, forming the Santee.

water elm The planer tree.

wa·ter·er (wô′tər·ər, wot′ər-) *n.* **1** One who waters, in any sense. **2** Any contrivance used for watering.

wa·ter·fall (wô′tər·fôl′, wot′ər-) *n.* **1** A cataract; cascade. **2** *Colloq.* A chignon suggesting a cascade. [OE *wætergefeall*]

water fence A fence built into or across a stream, or one extending into the water on the shore of a lake or the sea, to prevent cattle, horses, etc., from passing around it.

wa·ter–find·er (wô′tər·fīn′dər, wot′ər-) *n.* A dowser who tries to locate underground water with a divining rod. See RHABDOMANCY.

wa·ter·flea (wô′tər·flē′, wot′ər-) *n.* Any of numerous minute, fresh–water crustaceans (family *Daphniidae*), about the size of a flea, which swim with a jumping motion.

Wa·ter·ford (wô′tər·fərd, wot′ər-) **1** A maritime county in eastern Munster province, Ireland; 710 square miles. **2** Its county town, a port on **Waterford Harbor,** an inlet of the Atlantic in southern Ireland; 15 miles long.

water fowl 1 A bird that lives on or about the water, especially a swimming game bird. **2** Such birds collectively.

wa·ter·front (wô′tər·frunt′, wot′ər-) *n.* **1** Real property abutting on or overlooking a natural body of water. **2** That part of a town which fronts on a body of water. **3** A coil or chamber for heating water in the front of a range or other stove.

water gage A gage indicating the level of water in a boiler, etc. Also **water gauge.**

water gall 1 A hollow in the earth made by a flood, etc.; a washout. **2** A partial rainbow: also, *Scot., weather gall.* [<WATER + GALL²]

water gap A deep ravine in a mountain ridge giving passage to a stream.

water gas A highly poisonous mixture of hydrogen and carbon monoxide produced by forcing steam over white–hot carbon (as coal or coke): used for cooking and heating, and when carbureted, as an illuminant. **— wa·ter–gas** (wô′tər·gas′, wot′ər-) *adj.*

wa·ter·gate (wô′tər·gāt′, wot′ər-) *n.* Floodgate (def. 1).

wa·ter·glass (wô′tər·glas′, -gläs′, wot′ər-) *n.* **1** A waterclock; clepsydra. **2** A glass–bottomed tube or box for examining objects lying or moving under water. **3** A substance composed of sodium silicate, potassium silicate, or both, soluble in hot water: used in preserving eggs, as a facing for walls, etc. **4** A water gage on a steam boiler, etc. **5** A vessel for holding water; a drinking glass.

wa·ter·gum (wô′tər·gum′, wot′ər-) *n.* **1** The American sourgum or tupelo tree. **2** Any of several trees of the myrtle family, especially a tall, slender, ornamental shrub *(Tristania laurina)* native to Australia, with opposite leaves and yellow flowers.

water hammer 1 The concussion of confined water when its flow is suddenly arrested, as when a faucet is suddenly closed. **2** The hammering sound caused in pipes containing water when live steam is admitted. **3** A sealed tube void of air but containing water which strikes against the ends of the tube with a sharp knocking sound when shaken: used to demonstrate the equal rate of fall of solids and liquids in a vacuum.

water haul 1 In fishing, an empty haul of the net. **2** Any fruitless attempt or effort.

water hemlock Any of a genus *(Cicuta)* of poisonous, typically North American flowering herbs of the carrot family; especially, the **spotted water hemlock** *(C. maculata)* of the United States, highly injurious to livestock, and the Old World species *(C. virosa).*

water hen 1 Any of several coots or gallinules that frequent ponds and streams; especially, the moorhen. **2** The American coot *(Fulica americana).*

water hyacinth An aquatic herb of tropical America *(Eichornia crassipes)* with pendulous branched roots and a whorl of floating glossy leaves containing a cluster of bluish–purple to lilac and white flowers.

water ice 1 An ice made with water, sugar, and fruit juice. **2** Ice formed by the freezing of water as distinguished from that formed by the packing together of snow.

wa·ter–inch (wô′tər·inch′, wot′ər-) *n.* An old unit of hydraulic measure based on the discharge of water from a round hole with a diameter of one inch: reckoned at fourteen pints a minute.

wa·ter·ing (wô′tər·ing, wot′ər-) *n.* **1** The act of one who waters. **2** The process of producing a wavy ornamental effect. **—** *adj.* **1** Sprinkling; irrigating; that waters. **2** Situated near the shore or near mineral springs: a *watering* place.

watering cart A cart carrying a barrel or large tank of water: used for sprinkling streets.

watering place 1 A place where water can be obtained, as a spring; also, a place by a road where horses can be watered. **2** A health resort having mineral springs; also, a pleasure resort near the water.

watering pot A tin can having a spout fitted with a perforated nozzle: used for watering flowers, etc.

wa·ter·ish (wô′tər·ish, wot′ər-) *adj.* Resembling water; watery; hence, weak.

wa·ter–jack·et (wô′tər·jak′it, wot′ər-) *v.t.* To encase in or fit with a water jacket.

water jacket A casing containing water and surrounding a cylinder or mechanism, especially the cylinder block of an internal–combustion engine, for keeping it cool.

water jump A water barrier, as a pool, stream, or ditch, to be jumped over by the horses in a steeplechase.

water leaf Any of a genus *(Hydrophyllum)* of delicate biennial or perennial herbs with white or blue flowers, growing in the woods of North America.

wa·ter·less (wô′tər·lis, wot′ər-) *adj.* Without water; arid; dry.

wa·ter–lev·el (wô′tər·lev′əl, wot′ər-) *adj.* Following the course of a river: a *water–level* route.

water level 1 The level of still water in the sea or in any other body of water. **2** A water table. **3** *Naut.* A ship's water line. **4** A leveling instrument in which water serves to determine the horizontal line.

wa·ter·lift (wô′tər·lift′, wot′ər-) *n.* The transportation of personnel, equipment, and supplies by water, with special reference to the 1950 military campaign in Korea.

wa·ter·lil·y (wô′tər·lil′ē, wot′ər-) *n. pl.* **·lil·ies 1** Any plant of a genus *(Nymphaea)* of showy aquatic herbs of temperate and tropical regions, with large floating leaves and flowers; especially, the fragrant **white waterlily** *(N. odorata)* of the eastern United States. **2** The yellow pondlily *(Nuphar luteum)* of the same family. **3** The Victoria waterlily.

water line 1 *Naut.* That part of the hull of a ship which corresponds with the water level at various loads. **2** Water level. **3** A river or system of waterways affording transportation.

water locust A small species of the American honey locust *(Gleditsia aquatica)* growing in southern swamps and boglands: also called *swamp locust.*

wa·ter–logged (wô′tər·lôgd′, -logd′, wot′ər-) *adj.* **1** Heavy and unmanageable on account of the leakage of water into the hold, as a ship. **2** Water–soaked; saturated with water. [<WATER + LOG *v.,* in obs. sense of "to reduce to the condition of a log"]

Wa·ter·loo (wô′tər·lo͞o, wô′tər·lo͞o′) A village in central Belgium; scene of Napoleon's final defeat by Wellington and Blücher, June 18, 1815; hence, final and decisive defeat; a complete reverse.

water lot 1 A building lot fronting on a body of water, as a river, harbor, etc. **2** A lot or piece of ground wholly or partially covered by water, or a piece of marsh or swamp land designated to be filled in for use.

water main A large conduit for carrying water, especially one laid underground.

wa·ter·man (wô′tər·mən, wot′ər-) *n. pl.* **·men** (-mən) A man who plies for hire with a boat or small vessel on the water; a boatman. **— wa′ter·man·ship′** *n.*

water marigold An aquatic plant *(Bidens becki)* with terminal heads of yellow flowers.

wa·ter·mark (wô′tər·märk′, wot′ər-) *n.* **1** A mark showing the extent to which water rises; especially, the line marking the limit of the ebb and flow of the tide. **2** A series of translucent lines, letters, or designs made in paper by shaping the wires of the dandy rolls over which the paper passes while still in a pulpous state; also, the metal pattern which produces these markings. **—** *v.t.* **1** To impress (paper) with a watermark. **2** To impress as a watermark.

wa·ter·mel·on (wô′tər·mel′ən, wot′ər-) *n.* **1** The large edible fruit of a trailing plant *(Citrullus vulgaris)* of the gourd family, containing a many–seeded red or pink pulp and a refreshing sweet, watery juice. **2** The plant on which this fruit grows.

water meter An instrument for registering the amount of water flowing through a pipe, etc.

water milfoil Any of a genus *(Myriophyllum)* of aquatic herbs with graceful, feathery leaves.

water mill A mill operated by waterpower.

water moccasin The cottonmouth.

water motor 1 A turbine operated by waterpower. **2** A water wheel.

water nymph In classical mythology, any nymph or goddess living in or guarding a body of water; a naiad, Nereid, Oceanid, etc.

water oak A species of oak *(Quercus nigra)* growing near swamps and streams in the eastern United States.

water of Ayr See AYR STONE.

water of crystallization *Chem.* Water forming part of crystallized salts, from which it may be eliminated by heat, often with loss of crystalline structure. Also **water of hydration.**

water of life A rare and mysterious water that restores the dead to life. The human hope and belief that death can be overcome is expressed in the water–of–life motif in the peasant folklore of every European country, in the myths of the ancient Persians, Greeks, Romans, Hebrews, Hindus, in Japanese mythology, and in the folk tales of all primitive peoples, as the Polynesians, North and South American Indians, etc.

water ouzel See under OUZEL.

water ox A water buffalo.

wa·ter–part·ing (wô′tər·pär′ting, wot′ər-) *n.* A watershed.

wa·ter·pep·per (wô′tər·pep′ər, wot′ər-) *n.* Any of several species of knotweed, especially the common smartweed.

water pimpernel 1 The brookweed. **2** The common pimpernel.

water plantain Any of a genus *(Alsima)* of common, smooth, aquatic herbs with leaves like those of the plantain, especially the North American species *(A. plantago–aquatica).*

water polo A game played in a swimming pool by two teams of seven swimmers each, who push or throw a round, buoyant ball toward opposite goals.

wa·ter·pow·er (wô′tər·pou′ər, wot′ər-) *n.* **1** The power of water derived from its gravity or its momentum as applied to the driving of machinery. **2** A descent or fall in a stream from which motive power may be obtained.

water pox *Pathol.* Varicella.

wa·ter·proof (wô′tər·pro͞of′, wot′ər-) *adj.* **1** Proof against water. **2** Impervious to water. **3** Coated with some substance, as rubber, which resists the passage of water. **—** *n.* **1** Material or fabric rendered impervious to water. **2** *Brit.* A raincoat or other garment made of such fabric. **—** *v.t.* To render waterproof.

water purslane 1 An herb *(Isnardia* or *Ludwigia palustris)* of the evening–primrose family, procumbent and creeping in muddy places and floating in water. **2** An aquatic plant *(Didiplis* or *Peplis diandra)* growing in swampy ground in the U. S.

water ram A hydraulic ram.

water rat 1 The American muskrat. **2** The European water vole *(Microtus amphibius).* **3** Any of a subfamily *(Hydromyinae)* of aquatic rodents of New Guinea, Australia, and the Philippines. **4** *Slang* A thief or tough who frequents the waterfront.

water repellent *Chem.* Any of various chemicals, as an emulsion of aluminum acetate, used to make textiles, leather, and other porous materials resistant to wetting by water but which does not waterproof them or impair their desirable properties. **— wa·ter–re·pel·lent** (wô′tər·ri·pel′ənt, wot′ər-) *adj.*

wa·ter·right (wô′tər·rīt′, wot′ər-) *n.* **1** The right to draw upon a water supply. **2** The right to use or navigate a particular body of water. Also **water right.**

water sapphire A rich blue variety of iolite often worn as an ornament. [Trans. of F *saphir d'eau*]

wa·ter·scape (wô'tər·skāp, wot'ər-) *n.* A sea or other water view, as distinguished from a landscape. [<WATER + (LAND)SCAPE]

water scorpion Any of numerous hemipterous insects of aquatic habits (family *Nepidae*), having raptorial front legs and a long breathing tube at the end of the abdomen.

wa·ter·shed (wô'tər·shed', wot'ər-) *n.* **1** The line of separation between two contiguous drainage valleys. **2** The whole region from which a river receives its supply of water. **3** A decisive turning point profoundly affecting or altering what follows it.

wa·ter·shield (wô'tər·shēld', wot'ər-) *n.* **1** An aquatic American herb *(Brasenia schreberi)* of the waterlily family, with the stems and the under sides of the leaves covered with a viscid jelly. **2** Any plant of a kindred genus *(Cabomba)*, especially the fanwort.

wa·ter–sick (wô'tər·sik', wot'ər-) *adj.* Unproductive because of excessive irrigation: said of land.

wa·ter·side (wô'tər·sīd', wot'ər-) *n.* The shore of a body of water; the water's edge. —*adj.* **1** Of, pertaining to, or living or growing by the water's edge. **2** Working by the waterside, as a stevedore.

wa·ter–ski (wô'tər·skē', wot'ər-) *v.i.* **–skied, –ski·ing** To glide over water on water–skis, while being towed by a motorboat. —*n.* A broad, skilike runner with a fitting to hold the foot: worn in the sport of water–skiing. —**wa'ter–ski'er** *n.* —**wa'ter–ski'ing** *n.*

water snake **1** A serpent of aquatic habits. **2** Any of a genus *(Natrix)* of harmless North American snakes that live chiefly in water.

wa·ter·soak (wô'tər·sōk', wot'ər-) *v.t.* To fill the pores or crevices of with water; soak in water.

wa·ter–sol·u·ble (wô'tər·sol'yə·bəl, wot'ər-) *adj. Biochem.* Soluble in water: said especially of certain organic compounds.

water spaniel The Irish water spaniel. See under SPANIEL.

water speedwell A common plant *(Veronica anagallis–aquatica)* of the composite family, growing in damp places.

wa·ter·spout (wô'tər·spout', wot'ər-) *n.* **1** A moving, whirling column of spray and mist, with masses of water in the lower parts, accumulated because of a tornado at sea or on other large bodies of water. **2** A pipe for the free discharge of water, especially one connecting with the gutters of a roof: also called *rainspout.*

water sprite A water nymph.

water starwort Any of a widely distributed genus *(Callitriche)* of herbaceous aquatic plants, especially *C. autumnalis,* common in the United States.

water station A place beside a railroad where there is a water tank for supplying locomotives with water.

water strider Any of a family *(Gerridae)* of hemipterous insects with elongate middle and hind legs adapted for darting over the surface of water.

water supply **1** The water available for the use of a community or region. **2** The means for supplying it, as reservoirs, lakes, etc. —**wa·ter–sup·ply** (wô'tər·sə·plī', wot'ər-) *adj.*

water system **1** A river with all its tributaries, considered as a hydrologic unit. **2** Water supply.

water table **1** *Archit.* A projecting ledge, molding, or string–course, running along the sides of a building to shed the rain. **2** The surface marking the upper level of a water–saturated zone extending beneath the ground to depths determined by the thickness of the permeable strata.

water tank A large cistern of wood or metal, as upon an engine or building, for storing or supplying water.

water thrush **1** Any of certain American warblers (genus *Seiurus*), frequenting swamps and streams; especially, the common or **northern water thrush** *(S. noveboracensis)*, olive–brown above, yellowish beneath, with dusky streaks and a buffy superciliary line, or the **Louisiana water thrush** *(S. motacilla)*, with a pure–white superciliary line. **2** The water ouzel.

water tiger The larva of the diving beetle.

wa·ter·tight (wô'tər·tīt', wot'ər-) *adj.* **1** So closely made that water cannot enter or leak through. **2** Constructed so as to be impermeable; without loopholes: a *watertight* legal document.

Wa·ter·ton Lakes National Park (wô'tər·tən) A national park in SW Alberta, Canada; 204 square miles; adjoining Glacier National Park, Montana, forming with it the **Waterton–Glacier International Peace Park;** total area, 1,800 square miles; highest U. S. point, 10,448 feet; highest Canadian point, 9,600 feet; established 1932.

water tower **1** A standpipe or tower, often of considerable height, used as a reservoir for a system of water distribution. **2** A vehicular towerlike structure having an extensible vertical pipe from which water can be played on a burning building from a great height.

wa·ter–tube boiler (wô'tər·tōōb', -tyōōb', wot'·ər-) A type of boiler in which continuously heated water circulates through a series of tubes communicating with a steam chamber.

water turkey The snakebird.

water vapor The vapor of water, especially when found below the boiling point, as in the atmosphere. Compare STEAM.

water wave **1** An undulating effect of the hair, artificially produced when the hair is wet, and usually set by drying with heat. **2** A wave of water; a billow.

wa·ter·way (wô'tər·wā', wot'ər-) *n.* A river, channel, or other stream of water as a means of communication; water route.

wa·ter·weed (wô'tər·wēd', wot'ər-) *n.* **1** A submerged aquatic perennial *(Anacharis canadensis)*, having whitish flowers. **2** Any of various other aquatic plants, as the pondweed.

water wheel **1** A wheel so equipped with floats, buckets, etc., that it may be turned by flowing water. See OVERSHOT WHEEL. **2** A noria.

water wings A waterproof, wing–shaped fabric device that may be inflated with air and used as a support for the body while swimming or learning to swim.

water witch **1** One who claims to discover underground springs with the use of a divining rod or hazel wand. **2** Any of various quick–diving water birds, as certain grebes.

water witching The use of a divining rod to discover water; rhabdomancy.

wa·ter·works (wô'tər·wûrks', wot'ər-) *n. pl.* **1** A display or pageant presented on floats; a display of fountains in operation. **2** A system of machines, buildings, and appliances for furnishing a water supply, especially for a city; also, any mill or factory run by water-power. **3** *Slang* **a** Tears: usually in the phrase *to turn on the waterworks.* **b** Rain.

wa·ter·worn (wô'tər·wôrn', -wōrn', wot'ər-) *adj.* Worn smooth by running or falling water.

wa·ter·y (wô'tər·ē, wot'ər·ē) *adj.* **1** Containing or discharging water; brimming; tearful; soft and flabby. **2** Resembling water; thin or liquid. **3** Consisting of or pertaining to water. —**wa'ter·i·ness** *n.*

Wat·ford (wot'fərd) A municipal borough in Hertford, England, NW of London.

Wat·ling Island (wot'ling) See SAN SALVADOR. Also **Wat'lings Island.**

Wat·son (wot'sən), **John,** 1850–1907, Scottish minister and author: pseudonym, *Ian Maclaren.* —**John Broadus,** 1878–1958, U. S. psychologist. —**Sir William,** 1858–1935, English poet.

Wat·son–Watt (wot'sən·wot'), **Sir Robert Alexander,** born 1892, Scottish physicist.

watt (wot) *n.* The practical unit of electric power, activity, or rate of work: equivalent to 10^7 ergs or one joule per second, or approximately 1/746 of a horsepower; a volt–ampere. [after James *Watt*]

Watt (wot), **James,** 1736–1819, Scottish inventor and engineer.

wat·tage (wot'ij) *n.* **1** Amount of electric power in terms of watts. **2** The total number of watts needed to operate an appliance.

Wat·teau (wä·tō', wot'ō) *adj.* Of or pertaining to Antoine Watteau, or the costumes shown in his pictures.

Wat·teau (wä·tō', *Fr.* và·tō'), **Jean Antoine,** 1684–1721, French painter.

Watteau back A style of women's dress in which the fullness of the back is confined at the neck in plaits or gathers, and falls from there to the waistline.

Wat·ten·scheid (vät'ən·shīt) A city of east central North Rhine–Westphalia, central West Germany; a coal–mining and manufacturing center in the Ruhr.

Wat·ter·son (wot'ər·sən), **Henry,** 1840–1921, U. S. editor and journalist.

watt·hour (wot'our') *n.* Electrical energy equivalent to that represented by one watt acting for one hour.

wat·tle (wot'l) *n.* **1** A frame of rods or twigs woven together; a hurdle or other wickerwork. **2** A twig or withe, especially as used for interweaving with others; also, collectively, material for fences, hurdles, roofs, etc. **3** A naked, fleshy process, often wrinkled and brightly colored, hanging from the throat of a bird or snake. **4** A pendent fold of skin on the throat or neck of some domestic swine. **5** A barbel of a fish. **6** Any one of various acacias of Australia, Tasmania, and South Africa: so called by the early colonists, who used the branches to make hurdles. **7** *pl.* Rods for supporting thatch on a roof. —*v.t.* **·tled, ·tling** **1** To weave or twist, as twigs, into a network. **2** To form, as baskets, by intertwining flexible twigs. **3** To bind together with wattles. —*adj.* Made of or covered with wattles; formed by wattling. [OE *watul*]

wat·tle·bird (wot'l·bûrd') *n.* Any of several large Australian honey–eaters (genus *Anthochaera*), having conspicuous wattles about the head and face.

wat·tled (wot'ld) *adj.* **1** Made with wattles. **2** Having a wattle, as a bird. **3** *Her.* Having wattles, comb, or gills of a tincture different from that of the body.

watt·less (wot'lis) *adj. Electr.* Denoting an alternating current, or the component of such a current, which is neutralized by the originating electromotive force and which for that reason does not produce any power.

watt·me·ter (wot'mē'tər) *n.* An instrument for measuring in watts the rate of doing electrical work: also called *voltammeter.*

Watts (wots), **George Frederick,** 1817–1904, English painter and sculptor. —**Isaac,** 1674–1748, English theologian and hymn writer.

Watts–Dun·ton (wots'dun'tən), **Theodore,** 1832–1914, English critic and poet.

Wa·tu·si (wä·tōō'sē) *n. pl.* **·si** One of a pastoral, Bantu–speaking people of east central Africa.

Wau (wou) A town in the Territory of New Guinea, NE New Guinea; a gold–mining center reached only by air.

wauch (wôkh, wäkh) *adj. Scot.* **1** Clammy; damp; nauseous. **2** Faint; languid; weak. Also **waugh** (wôf).

waucht (wôkht, wäkht, wäft) *Scot. n.* A large draft, as of liquor. —*v.t.* & *v.i.* To drink; quaff. Also **waught** (wôft, wäft).

Waugh (wô), **Alec,** born 1898, English novelist and travel writer. —**Evelyn,** 1903–1966, English novelist and critic; brother of preceding.

wauk[1] (wôk) *v.i. Scot.* To full cloth.

wauk[2] (wôk) *v.t. Scot.* To wake; watch over.

waul (wôl) *v.i.* To give a prolonged, plaintive cry like that of a cat: also spelled *wawl.* [Imit.]

waur (wôr) *adj. Scot.* Worse.

wave (wāv) *v.* **waved, wav·ing** *v.i.* **1** To move freely back and forth or up and down, as a flag in the wind; undulate or fluctuate. **2** To be moved back and forth or up and down as a signal; also, to make a signal by moving something thus. **3** To have an undulating shape or form; be sinuous: Her hair *waves.* —*v.t.* **4** To cause to move back and forth or up and down: to *wave* a banner. **5** To form with an undulating surface, edge, or outline. **6** To give a wavy appearance to; water, as silk. **7** To form into waves or undulations: to *wave* one's hair. **8** To signal by waving something: He *waved* me aside. **9** To express by waving something: to *wave* farewell. See synonyms under FLAUNT, SHAKE. — *n.* **1** A ridge or undulation moving on the surface of a liquid, the particles composing it having an oscillatory motion usually in the form of closed or nearly closed curves in a plane at right angles to the direction of movement of the ridge itself. **2** *Physics* One of the complete vibratory impulses set up by a disturbance propagated through the particles of a body or elastic medium, as a rope, air, or water. Each impulse, as in the transmission of light or sound, has characteristics of length, frequency, duration, etc., determined by the nature of the disturbance in the medium involved. **3** One of the rising curves on an undulatory edge or surface; one of a series of curves: amber *waves* of grain. **4** Something that comes, like a wave, with great volume or power; a flood; a period of marked activity or excitement: a *wave* of enthusiasm. **5** A wavelike stripe or undulation impressed on a surface, as on watered silk; also, a wavelike tress or curl of hair. **6** *Poetic* Any body of water; the sea. **7** The act of waving; a sweeping or undulating motion, as with the hand or a flag. **8** One of a series, as of groups or events, occurring or moving with wavelike fluctuations: He went ashore with the first *wave* of Marines. **9** A progressive change in temperature or in barometrical condition passing over a large area: a heat *wave.* ◆ Homophone: *waive.* [OE *wafian*] — **wav′er** *n.*

Synonyms (noun): billow, breaker, ripple, surge, swell, undulation, vibration.

Wave (wāv) *n.* A member of the WAVES. [Back formation from WAVES (taken as a pl.)]

wave cloud *Meteorol.* A cloud consisting of parallel bands or ridges, separated by strips of clear sky, due to air currents occurring at the bounding plane between two strata of the atmosphere.

wave front The leading surface of a wave as it advances through a medium.

wave-guide (wāv′gīd′) *n.* **1** Any system of material boundaries by which the direction of waves may be controlled. **2** *Electronics* A device, typically an arrangement of hollow metal pipes of varying size and cross-section, through which high-frequency electromagnetic waves may be guided as required.

wave·length (wāv′length′) *n. Physics* The distance, measured along the line of propagation, between two points representing similar phases of two consecutive waves. It is a fundamental unit in the study of radiant energy.

wave·less (wāv′lis) *adj.* Having no waves; tranquil. See synonyms under PACIFIC.

wave·let (wāv′lit) *n.* A little wave.

Wa·vell (wā′vəl), **Sir Archibald Percival,** 1883–1950, first Earl Wavell, Viscount Wavell of Cyrenaica and Tripolitania, British field marshal and administrator in World War II.

wa·vel·lite (wā′və·līt) *n.* A vitreous, translucent, hydrous aluminum phosphate, crystallizing in the orthorhombic system. [after Dr. William *Wavell,* died 1829, English physician, its discoverer]

wave mechanics The branch of physics which investigates the wave characteristics ascribed to the atom and its associated particles, and seeks to explain physical processes in terms of these characteristics as revealed by the quantum theory of atomic structure.

wave·me·ter (wāv′mē′tər) *n.* An apparatus for determining wavelengths and wave frequencies, as in a radio circuit.

wave number *Physics* The number of electromagnetic waves in a space of 1 centimeter, equal to the frequency of the wave divided by the velocity of light: it is the reciprocal of the wavelength.

wave-off (wāv′ôf′, -of′) *n. Aeron.* The act of denying landing privileges to an approaching aircraft, usually an aircraft making a faulty approach for landing on an aircraft carrier.

wa·ver (wā′vər) *v.i.* **1** To move one way and the other; sway; flutter. **2** To be uncertain or undecided; show irresolution; vacillate. **3** To show signs of falling back or giving way; reel; falter. **4** To flicker; gleam. **5** To quaver; tremble. See synonyms under FLUCTUATE, QUAKE, SHAKE. — *n.* A wavering. ◆ Homophone: *waiver.* [<ME *waveren,* freq. of OE *wafian* wave] — **wa′ver·er** *n.* — **wa′ver·ing** *adj.* — **wa′ver·ing·ly** *adv.*

Wa·ver·ley Novels (wā′vər·lē) A series of historical novels by Sir Walter Scott, published 1814–1831.

WAVES (wāvz) *n.* A corps of women in the U. S. Navy, which includes all women except nurses; officially, *Women in the United States Navy* (1946). [<*W(omen) A(ppointed for) V(oluntary) E(mergency) S(ervice),* an earlier name]

wave train A series of waves sent out at regular intervals from a vibrating body.

wave trap **1** *Telecom.* A device, usually connected with the antenna, for improving the selectivity of a radio receiver by cutting out undesired wave frequencies. **2** A widening inward of the distance between the sides of adjoining piers to allow for the spreading of storm waves.

wa·vey (wā′vē) *n.* The snow goose. [Var. of WAVY; so called because faintly streaked on head, neck, and back with darker plumage]

wav·y (wā′vē) *adj.* **wav·i·er, wav·i·est** **1** Full of waves; ruffled by or raised into waves. **2** Undulatory; waving. **3** Unstable; wavering. — **wav′i·ly** *adv.* — **wav′i·ness** *n.*

wawl (wôl) See WAUL.

wax[1] (waks) *n.* **1** A yellow fatty solid excreted from the abdominal rings of bees and used by them to build honeycombs; beeswax. It has a honeylike odor and a balsamic taste; becomes plastic with the heat of the hand; is insoluble in water, but is almost completely dissolved by boiling alcohol. **2** Any of a class of plant and animal substances consisting of the esters of fatty acids and alcohols other than glycerol, and including spermaceti and carnauba wax; specifically, a substance derived from the fruit of the wax myrtle or bayberry. **3** A solid mineral substance resembling wax, as ozocerite or paraffin. **4** A substance used for joining surfaces, sealing documents, etc.; sealing wax. **5** A mixture of pitch and tallow or some resinous composition used by shoemakers to wax their thread. **6** Earwax; cerumen. **7** *U. S.* The sap of the sugar maple after being boiled down and cooled. **8** A substance resembling beeswax secreted by certain scale insects. — *v.t.* To coat or treat with wax. — *adj.* Made of or pertaining to wax. [OE *weax*]

wax[2] (waks) *v.i.* **waxed, waxed** (*Poetic* **wax·en**), **wax·ing** **1** To become larger gradually; increase in size or numbers; grow: said specifically of the moon as it approaches fullness: opposed to *wane.* **2** To become as specified: to *wax* angry. [OE *weaxan* grow]

wax[3] (waks) *v.t. Colloq.* To record phonographically: to *wax* a folk song. [<WAX[1]; so called because wax was formerly used in making phonograph records]

wax[4] (waks) *n. Colloq.* A tantrum; fit of bad temper. [? <phrase *wax angry*]

wax bean A variety of string bean (*Phaseolus vulgaris*) cultivated in the United States: also called *butter bean.*

wax·ber·ry (waks′ber′ē) *n. pl.* **·ries** **1** The wax myrtle, or bayberry. **2** Its wax-covered fruit. **3** The snowberry.

wax·bill (waks′bil′) *n.* **1** Any of various small Old World seed-eating birds of the weaverbird family (genus *Estrilda*), having beaks resembling sealing wax. **2** The Java sparrow.

wax·en (wak′sən) *adj.* **1** Resembling wax. **2** Consisting wholly or in part of wax; covered with wax. **3** Pale; pallid: a *waxen* complexion; also, pliable or impressible as wax.

wax end A stout thread, or the end of a thread, made stiff and pointed with shoemakers' wax, or waxed and twisted with a bristle, as for the purpose of sewing shoes. Also **waxed end.**

wax myrtle Any of a genus (*Myrica*) of North American shrubs or small trees, especially *M. cerifera,* having fragrant leaves and small berries covered with white wax, often used in making candles: also called *bayberry, candleberry.*

wax palm **1** A South American palm (*Ceroxylon andicola*) with pinnate leaves, having a lofty straight trunk covered with a waxy, whitish, resinous substance. **2** A Brazilian palm (*Copernicia cerifera*) whose young leaves yield the carnauba wax of commerce.

wax paper Paper coated or treated with wax and used to protect against moisture. Also **waxed paper.**

wax plant The Indian pipe.

wax·weed (waks′wēd′) *n.* An annual, clammy, hairy herb (*Cuphea petiolata*) of the loosestrife family with irregular purplish axillary flowers.

wax·wing (waks′wing′) *n.* Any of various crested passerine birds (family *Bombycillidae*) of America and Asia, having soft, mainly brown plumage, and the tips of the secondary wing feathers tipped with horny appendages resembling red or yellow sealing wax; especially, the two best-known North American species, the **cedar waxwing** (*Bombycilla cedrorum*), and the larger **Bohemian waxwing** (*B. garrula pallidiceps*).

CEDAR WAXWING
(About 7 inches long)

wax·work (waks′wûrk′) *n.* **1** Work produced in wax; particularly, ornaments or life-size figures of wax. **2** *pl.* A collection of such figures.

wax·work·er (waks′wûr′kər) *n.* One who works in wax; one who makes waxwork.

wax·worm (waks′wûrm′) A honeycomb moth.

wax·y (wak′sē) *adj.* **wax·i·er, wax·i·est** **1** Resembling wax in appearance, consistency, or adhesive qualities; waxen; pliable; impressionable. **2** Having the dull whitish or yellowish color of wax; pale; pallid; bloodless. **3** Made of or abounding in wax; rubbed with wax; waxed. **4** *Pathol.* Characterized by the formation of an insoluble, waxlike protein in certain organs of the body, as the kidney; amyloid. — **wax′i·ness** *n.*

way (wā) *n.* **1** Direction; turn; route; line of motion or progress: Which *way* is the city? **2** A path, course, or track leading from one place to another or along which one goes; a road, street, highway, lane, path, or the like. **3** Space or room to advance or work: Make *way* for the king. **4** Length of space passed over; hence, distance in general: a little *way* off: often, popularly or dialectally, *ways* **5** Passage from one place to another; hence, onward movement; headway; progress. **6** A customary or habitual manner or style; a manner peculiar to an individual, class, or people: the British *way* of doing things. **7** A chosen line or plan of action; a procedure; method: In what *way* will you accomplish this? **8** A point of relation; particular: He erred in two *ways.* **9** A course of life or experience: the *way* of sin. **10** *Colloq.* Vocation; line of business; profession. **11** *Colloq.* State of health: to be in a bad *way.* **12** A course wished for or resolved upon; something which one resolves to do: Have it your *way.* **13** The range of one's notice or observation: An accident threw it in his *way.* **14** *Naut.* **a** The movement of a vessel through the water; forward motion; headway. **b** *pl.* A tilted framework of timbers upon which a ship slides when launched. **15** The direction of the weave in textile goods. **16** *Law* A right of way. **17** *Mech.* A longitudinal guide for material being worked upon, or for a moving table bearing the work. **18** *Colloq.* Neighborhood, or route taken to go home: He lives out of my *way.* — **by the way** In passing; incidentally. — **by way of** **1** With the object or purpose of; to serve as: *by way of* introduction. **2** Through; via: We went home *by way of* Main Street. — **out of the way** **1** Removed, as an obstruction; unable to hinder or impede. **2** Out of the proper course; hence, remarkable; unusual; also, improper; wrong: Has he done anything *out of the way*? **3** Out of place; lost; mislaid; remote. — **under way** In motion; well along; making progress. — *adv. Colloq.* Away; very far; all the great distance: He went *way* to Denver. ◆ Homophone: *weigh.* [OE *weg*]

Synonyms (noun): alley, avenue, bridlepath, channel, course, driveway, highroad, highway, lane, pass, passage, path, pathway, road, route, street, thoroughfare, track. Wherever there is room for an object to proceed, there is a *way.* A *road* (originally a ride*way*) is a prepared way for traveling with horses or vehicles, a *way* suitable to be traversed only by foot-passengers or by animals being called a *path, bridlepath,* or *track*; as, The *roads* in that country are mere *bridlepaths.* A *road* may be private: a *highway* or *highroad* is public, *highway* being a specific name for a *road* legally set apart for the use of the public forever; a *highway* may be over water as well as over land. A *route* is a line of travel, and may be over many *roads.* A *street* is in some center of habitation, as a city, town, or village; when it passes between rows of dwellings, the country *road* becomes the village *street.* An *avenue* is a long, broad, and imposing or principal *street. Track* is a word of wide signification; we speak of a goat–*track* on a mountainside, a railroad *track,* a *racetrack,* the *track* of a comet; on a traveled *road* the line worn by regular passing of hoofs and wheels is called the *track.* A *passage* is between any two objects or lines of enclosure, a *pass* commonly between mountains. A *driveway* is within enclosed grounds, as of a private residence. A *channel* is a *waterway.* A *thoroughfare* is a *way* through. See AIR[1], DIRECTION, ROAD.

way back *Colloq.* Long ago. [Short for AWAY BACK]

way·bill (wā′bil′) *n.* A list describing or identifying goods or naming passengers carried by a common carrier, as a railroad, train, steamer, or other public vehicle.

way·far·er (wā′fâr′ər) *n.* One who journeys along a way on foot.

way·far·ing (wā′fâr′ing) *adj.* & *n.* Journeying; being on the road.

way freight Freight taken on or put off at way stations; also, a freight train stopping at way stations and handling such goods: distinguished from *through freight.*

way–go·ing (wā′gō′ing) *adj.* Pertaining to one's going away; going away; departing.

way–going crop *Law* A crop sown by a tenant during his term, but ripening after its expiration. [Short for *away–going crop*]

Way·land (wā′lənd) In Teutonic and English mythology, an invisible blacksmith with magical powers: in German folklore spelled *Wieland.* Also **Wayland (the) Smith.**

way·lay (wā′lā′) *v.t.* **·laid, ·lay·ing 1** To lie in ambush for and attack, as in order to rob. **2** To accost on the way. [<WAY + LAY[1], on analogy with MHG *wegelagen* < *wegelage* an ambush] **— way′lay′er** *n.*

Wayne (wān), **Anthony,** 1745–96, American Revolutionary general: called "Mad Anthony" Wayne.

way passenger A passenger getting on or off a public conveyance, as a train, steamship, bus, etc., at a way station; a local passenger.

-ways *suffix of adverbs* In a (specified) manner, direction, or position: *noways, sideways*: often equivalent to -WISE. Also **-way.** [<WAY + -S[3]]

ways and means Means or methods of accomplishing an end or defraying expenses; specifically, in legislation, methods of raising funds for the use of the government.

way·side (wā′sīd′) *adj.* Pertaining to the side of a road; growing or being near the wayside. — *n.* The side or edge of the road or highway.

way station Any station between principal stations, especially on a railroad; a local station.

way train A train stopping at way stations; a local train.

way·ward (wā′wərd) *adj.* **1** Wandering away; wilful; froward. **2** Without definite way or course; unsteady; vacillating; capricious. **3** Unexpected or unwished for: a *wayward* fortune. See synonyms under PERVERSE. [ME *weiward,* short for *aweiward* < *awei* away + -WARD] **— way′ward·ly** *adv.* **— way′ward·ness** *n.*

way·worn (wā′wôrn′, -wōrn′) *adj.* Fatigued by travel.

Wa·zir·i·stan (wä·zir′i·stän′) A tribal region in NW central Pakistan on the Afghanistan border; 5,214 square miles.

we (wē) *pron.* **1** The persons speaking or writing as they denote themselves, or a single person writing or speaking when referring to himself and one or more others: the nominative case. **2** A single person denoting himself, as a sovereign, editor, writer, or speaker, when wishing to give his words an impersonal character. [OE]

weak (wēk) *adj.* **1** Lacking in physical strength; wanting in energy, activity, or vigor; feeble; debilitated. **2** Insufficiently resisting stress; incapable of supporting weight: a *weak* link or bridge. **3** Lacking in strength of will or stability of character; yielding easily to temptation; pliable. **4** Ineffectual, as from deficient supply: *weak* artillery support. **5** Lacking in power or sonorousness: a *weak* voice. **6** Lacking a specified component or components in the usual or proper amount; of less than customary strength or potency: *weak* tea, a *weak* tincture. **7** Lacking the power or ability to perform properly its function: a *weak* heart. **8** Lacking in mental or moral strength; liable to err or fail through feebleness of conception or vacillation of judgment. **9** Showing or resulting from poor judgment or a want of discretion or firmness: a *weak* plan; unable to persuade or convince: a *weak* argument. **10** Lacking in influence or authority: a *weak* state. **11** Deficient in strength, durability, skill, experience, or the like. **12** *Gram.* In Germanic languages: **a** Of verbs, forming the past tense and past participle by the addition of a dental suffix to the present stem; as, English *ask, asked*; *sight, sighted*; German *leben, lebte, gelebt.* Some weak verbs in English show vowel change in the stem (as in *leave, left*), but in such cases the change is due to factors other than ablaut. Also called *regular.* **b** Of nouns and adjectives (in German and Old English), inflected in the less full manner originally restricted to stems ending in *-n.* Weak nouns and adjectives in Old English characteristically terminate in *-a* in the masculine singular (*nama* name) and *-e* in the feminine singular (*tunge* tongue). In German, a descriptive adjective appears in the weak form when preceded by a limiting word, such as the definite article, having strong inflection *(der gute Mann).* Compare STRONG (def. 28). **13** *Phonet.* Unstressed; unaccented, as a syllable or sound. **14** *Phot.* Thin; wanting in contrast: a *weak* negative. **15** In prosody, indicating a verse ending in which the accent falls on a word or syllable otherwise without stress. **16** Declining in price; without an active market: The wheat market is *weak.* **17** Wanting in impressiveness or interest: a *weak* play or book. See synonyms under FAINT, FRAGILE, PUSILLANIMOUS, SICKLY. ◆ Homophone: *week.* [<ON *veikr.* Akin to OE *wac.*] **— weak′ly** *adv.* **— weak′ness** *n.*

Weak may appear as a combining form in hyphemes or as the first element in two–word phrases; as in:

weak–backed	**weak–nerved**
weak–bodied	**weak point**
weak–built	**weak side**
weak–eyed	**weak–sighted**
weak–growing	**weak–spirited**
weak–handed	**weak–stemmed**
weak–headed	**weak–throated**
weak–headedness	**weak–toned**
weak–hearted	**weak–voiced**
weak–limbed	**weak–walled**
weak–looking	**weak–willed**
weak–made	**weak–winged**
weak–mindedness	**weak–witted**

weak·en (wē′kən) *v.t.* & *v.i.* To make or become weak or weaker. **— weak′en·er** *n.*

Synonyms: debilitate, depress, enervate, enfeeble, impair, invalidate, lower, paralyze, reduce, relax, sap, undermine, unnerve. See IMPAIR.

weak·fish (wēk′fish′) *n. pl.* **·fish** or **·fish·es** Any of various American marine food fishes (genus *Cynoscion*), especially the common variety *(C. regalis)*, frequenting coastal waters of the eastern United States.

weak–kneed (wēk′nēd′) *adj.* Weak in the knees; hence, without resolution, strong purpose, or energy; spineless.

weak·ling (wēk′ling) *n.* A feeble person or animal. — *adj.* Having no natural strength or vigor.

weak·ly (wēk′lē) *adj.* **·li·er, ·li·est** Sickly; feeble; weak. See synonyms under SICKLY.

weak–mind·ed (wēk′mīn′did) *adj.* **1** Indecisive; unable to say no. **2** Feeble–minded.

weak·ness (wēk′nis) *n.* **1** The state, condition, or quality of being weak. **2** A characteristic indicating feebleness. **3** A slight failing; a fault.

weak sister *Colloq.* **1** The weakling in any group; specifically, one who cannot be depended on to stand firm against opposition. **2** Any ineffectual person.

weak spot 1 Any spot having less strength than the contiguous area, as in a fabric, fence, etc. **2** The most vulnerable part of an argument, proposition, etc. **3** The weakest or least dependable person on a team, in a group, etc.

weal[1] (wēl) *n.* **1** A sound or healthy state, either of persons or things; prosperity; welfare. **2** *Obs.* The body politic, state, or nation: now only in the phrase, *public weal.* **3** *Obs.* Wealth; worldly store. [OE *wela.* Akin to WELL.]

weal[2] (wēl) *n.* A discolored ridge or stripe on the skin, as from the blow of a whip; a wheal. [Var. of WALE[1]; infl. in form by obs. *wheal* a pustule]

weald (wēld) *n.* An exposed forest area; waste woodland; also, an open region; down. [OE, a forest]

Weald (wēld), **The** A district of SE England between the North and South Downs in Kent, Surrey and Sussex counties; formerly forested, now primarily agricultural.

wealth (welth) *n.* **1** A large aggregate of real and personal property; an abundance of those material or worldly things that men desire to possess; riches; also, the state of being rich. **2** *Econ.* All material objects which have economic utility; also, in the private sense, all property possessing a monetary value. **3** Great abundance of anything: a *wealth* of learning. **4** *Obs.* Weal; well–being. **— personal wealth** Those faculties, energies, and habits which contribute to personal industrial efficiency. [ME *welthe* < *wele* weal, on analogy with *health*]

Synonyms: abundance, affluence, comfort, competence, competency, fortune, funds, goods, independence, lucre, mammon, money, opulence, pelf, plenty, possession, produce, property, riches, substance, treasure. See PROPERTY. *Antonyms*: see synonyms for POVERTY.

wealth·y (wel′thē) *adj.* **wealth·i·er, wealth·i·est 1** Possessing wealth; affluent. **2** More than sufficient; abounding. **— wealth′i·ly** *adv.* **— wealth′i·ness** *n.*

wean[1] (wēn) *v.t.* **1** To transfer (the young of any animal) from dependence on its mother's milk to another form of nourishment. **2** To estrange from former habits or associations; alienate the affections of: usually with *from.* [OE *wenian* accustom]

wean[2] (wēn) *n. Scot.* A baby; infant.

wean·er (wē′nər) *n.* **1** One who weans. **2** A muzzle used in weaning a calf.

wean·ling (wēn′ling) *adj.* Freshly weaned. — *n.* A child or animal newly weaned.

weap·on (wep′ən) *n.* **1** Any implement of war or combat, as a sword, gun, etc. **2** Figuratively, any means that may be used against an adversary. **3** *pl.* The thorns or prickles of plants, or the stings, claws, etc., of animals. See synonyms under ARMS. [OE *wǣpen*] **— weap′on·less** *adj.*

weap·oned (wep′ənd) *adj.* Furnished with weapons; bearing arms.

weap·on·eer (wep′ən·ir′) *n.* A person concerned with the design, improvement, production, and use of weapons, especially of the atomic and thermonuclear type.

wear[1] (wâr) *v.* **wore, worn, wear·ing** *v.t.* **1** To carry or have on the person as a garment, ornament, etc. **2** To have or bear on the person habitually or as a practice: He *wears* a derby. **3** To have in one's appearance or aspect; exhibit: He *wears* a scowl. **4** To bear habitually in a specified manner; carry: He *wears* his age well; She *wears* her hair in a chignon. **5** To display or fly: A ship *wears* its colors. **6** To impair, waste, or consume by use or constant action. **7** To cause or produce by scraping, rubbing, etc.: to *wear* a hole in a coat. **8** To bring to a specified condition by wear: to *wear* a sleeve to tatters. **9** To exhaust the strength or patience of; weary. — *v.i.* **10** To be impaired or diminished gradually by use, rubbing, etc. **11** To withstand the effects of use, wear, etc., as specified: The vest *wears* well. **12** To become as specified from use or attrition: His patience is *wearing* thin. **13** To pass gradually or tediously: with *on* or *away*. The day *wears* on. **— to wear out 1** To make or become worthless by use: The cloak is *worn out.* **2** To waste gradually; use up: He *wears out* patience. **3** To tire or exhaust. **—** *n.* **1** The act of wearing, or the state of being worn: the worse for *wear.* **2** The material or articles of dress worn or made to be worn; a fashion: silk for summer *wear*; also in compounds: *footwear, underwear.* **3** The destructive effect of use or work; impairment from use or time. **4** Capacity for resistance to use or impairment; endurance; lasting quality; durability. ◆ Homophone: *ware.* [OE *werian*] **— wear′a·ble** *adj.* **— wear′er** *n.*

Synonyms (verb): abrade, chafe, consume, deteriorate, diminish, fret, fritter, impair, rub, tire, waste.

wear[2] (wâr) *v.* **wore, worn, wear·ing** *Naut. v.t.* To change the course of (a vessel), so as to bring the wind to the other side, by turning it through an arc in which its head points momentarily directly to leeward. **—** *v.i.* To go about with the wind astern. Compare TACK[1]. ◆ Homophone: *ware.* [Prob. alter. of VEER[1]; infl. in form by *wear*[1]]

wear·a·ble (wâr′ə·bəl) *adj.* That can be worn. **—** *n. pl.* Garments.

wear and tear Loss by the service, exposure, decay, or injury incident to ordinary use.

wea·ri·ful (wir′i·fəl) *adj.* Tiresome; wearisome. **— wea′ri·ful·ly** *adv.* **— wea′ri·ful·ness** *n.*

wea·ri·less (wir′i·lis) *adj.* Unwearying; untiring.

wear·ing (wâr′ing) *adj.* **1** Fatiguing; exhausting; wasting: *wearing* trials. **2** Capable of being, or designed to be, worn. **— wear′ing·ly** *adv.*

wearing apparel Clothing; garments.

wear·ish (wâr′ish) *adj. Obs.* or *Dial.* **1** Insipid; watery. **2** Wizened; shrunk; withered. [ME *werische*; origin uncertain] **— wear′ish·ly** *adv.* **— wear′ish·ness** *n.*

wea·ri·some (wir′i·səm) *adj.* Causing fatigue; tiresome. **— wea′ri·some·ly** *adv.* **— wea′ri·some·ness** *n.*

Synonyms: annoying, fatiguing, irksome, laborious, tedious, tiresome, vexatious, wearing, weary. See TEDIOUS, TROUBLESOME. *Antonyms*: cheering, enlivening, inspiring, inspiriting, restful, reviving, rousing, soothing, stirring, thrilling.

wea·ry (wir′ē) *adj.* **·ri·er, ·ri·est 1** Worn with exertion, vexation, or suffering; tired; fatigued. **2** Discontented or vexed by continued endurance, or by something disagreeable: usually with *of*: *weary* of life. **3** Indicating or characteristic of fatigue: a *weary* sigh. **4** Causing weariness; wearisome. **—** *v.t.* & *v.i.* **·ried, ·ry·ing** To make or become weary; tire. See synonyms under TIRE[1]. [OE *wērig*] **— wea′ri·ly** *adv.* **— wea′ri·ness** *n.*

wea·sand (wē′zənd) *n. Archaic* The windpipe; in general, the throat: often spelled *wizen.* Also *Scot.* **wea′son.** [OE *wāsend*]

wea·sel (wē′zəl) *n.* Any of certain small, slender, reddish-brown, carnivorous mammals (genus *Mustela*) that prey on smaller mammals and birds. In northern regions their fur turns white in winter. [OE *wesle*]

WEASEL
(Head and body from 6 to 7 inches)

weasel word A word that weakens a statement by rendering it ambiguous or equivocal: term popularized by Theodore Roosevelt.

weath·er (weth′ər) *n.* **1** The general atmospheric condition, as regards temperature, moisture, winds, or other meteorological phenomena. **2** The common phenomena of wind, rain, cold, heat, cloudiness, or storm. **3** Bad weather; storm. **— to keep one's weather eye open** *Colloq.* To be alert. **— under the weather** *Colloq.* **1** Ailing; ill. **2** Somewhat intoxicated. **—** *v.t.* **1** To expose to the action of the weather. **2** To discolor, crumble, or otherwise affect by action of the weather. **3** To pass through and survive, as a crisis. **4** To slope, as a roof, so as to shed water. **5** *Naut.* To pass to windward of: to *weather* Cape Fear. **—** *v.i.* **6** To undergo changes resulting from exposure to the weather. **7** To resist the action of the weather. **—** *adj.* Facing the wind; windward: opposed to *lee.* ◆ Homophone: *wether.* [OE *weder*]

Weather may appear as a combining form in hyphemes or solidemes, or as the first element in two-word phrases:

weather-bitten	**weather report**
weather-bleached	**weather-reporter**
weather-blown	**weather-reporting**
weather-burnt	**weather-rotted**
weather-driven	**weather-scarred**
weather-eaten	**weathersick**
weather forecast	**weather-tanned**
weather-hardened	**weathertight**
weather-observer	**weather-tough**
weather-observing	**weather-withstanding**

weath·er-beat·en (weth′ər·bēt′n) *adj.* Bearing the effects of exposure to weather.

weath·er·board (weth′ər·bôrd′, -bōrd′) *n.* **1** A board for the outside covering of wooden buildings, usually feather-edged and nailed so as to form lap joints with the boards above and below and thus shed rain; a clapboard. **2** *Naut.* The windward side of a vessel. **—** *v.t.* To fasten weatherboards on.

weath·er·board·ing (weth′ər·bôr′ding, -bōr′-) *n.* **1** Weatherboards collectively, or material for making them. **2** The outer wooden covering of the walls and roof of a building.

weath·er-bound (weth′ər·bound′) *adj.* Detained by unfavorable weather, as a vessel in port.

Weather Bureau A bureau of the Department of Commerce in Washington, D.C., for meteorological observation, the diffusion of information concerning the weather, etc.

weath·er·cast (weth′ər·kast′, -käst′) *n.* A radio or television broadcast reporting on weather conditions. [<WEATHER + (BROAD)CAST] **— weath′er·cast′er** *n.*

weath·er·cock (weth′ər·kok′) *n.* **1** A vane, properly one in the semblance of a cock, which turns to indicate the direction of the wind; a weathervane. **2** A fickle person or variable thing.

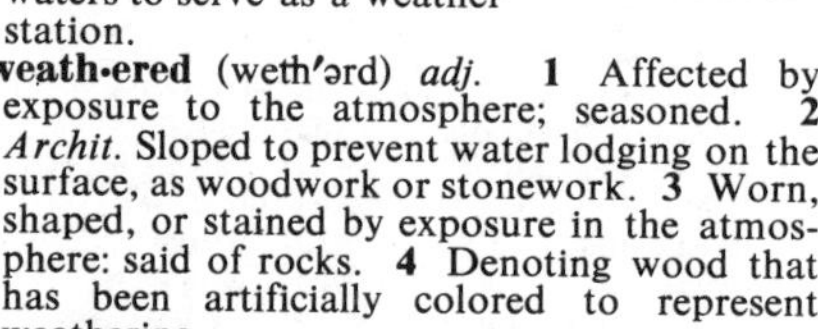

WEATHERCOCK

weath·er·drome (weth′ər·drōm′) *n. Meteorol.* A large, floating structure resembling an airdrome, permanently anchored in offshore waters to serve as a weather station.

weath·ered (weth′ərd) *adj.* **1** Affected by exposure to the atmosphere; seasoned. **2** *Archit.* Sloped to prevent water lodging on the surface, as woodwork or stonework. **3** Worn, shaped, or stained by exposure in the atmosphere: said of rocks. **4** Denoting wood that has been artificially colored to represent weathering.

weather gage 1 *Naut.* The advantage to a ship or yacht of receiving the wind first; a position to the windward. **2** Any advantage gained.

weath·er·glass (weth′ər·glas′, -gläs′) *n.* A meteorological instrument for indicating the state of the weather; especially, a common barometer.

weath·er·ize (weth′ə·rīz) *v.t.* **·ized, ·iz·ing** To process (fabrics, leather, etc.) chemically or otherwise, so as to make impervious or highly resistant to moisture or other effects of severe weather.

weath·er·ly (weth′ər·lē) *adj. Naut.* Capable of keeping close into the wind without drifting to leeward.

weath·er·man (weth′ər·man′) *n. pl.* **·men** (-men′) *n. Colloq.* A meteorologist, especially one concerned with daily weather conditions and reports.

weather map *Meteorol.* A map or chart compiled periodically from official sources and indicating, for a given region and specified time, various components of the weather, as temperature, atmospheric pressure, wind velocity, rain, snow, cloud formations, etc.

weath·er·proof (weth′ər·proo͞f′) *adj.* Capable of withstanding rough weather without appreciable deterioration. **—** *v.t.* To make weatherproof.

weather station A station or office where meteorological observations are taken and recorded.

weath·er-strip (weth′ər·strip′) *n.* A narrow strip of material to be placed over or in crevices, as at doors and windows, to exclude drafts, rain, etc.: also **weath′er-strip′ping.** **—** *v.t.* **-stripped, -strip·ping** To equip or fit with weather-strips.

weath·er·vane (weth′ər·vān′) *n.* A vane; weathercock.

weath·er·vi·sion (weth′ər·vizh′ən) *n.* A system which combines television and radar in the rapid dissemination of weather data to aircraft. [<WEATHER + (TELE)VISION]

weath·er·wise (weth′ər·wīz′) *adj.* Experienced in observing or predicting the weather.

weath·er·worn (weth′ər·wôrn′, -wōrn′) *adj.* Worn by exposure to the weather.

weave (wēv) *v.* **wove** or (*esp. for defs.* 7 *and* 10) **weaved, wo·ven** or *less frequently* **wove, weav·ing** *v.t.* **1** To form, produce, or manufacture as a textile, by interlacing threads or yarns; especially, to make by interlacing woof threads among warp threads in a loom. **2** To form by interlacing strands, strips, twigs, etc.: to *weave* a basket. **3** To produce by combining details or elements: to *weave* a story. **4** To bring together so as to form a whole: to *weave* fancies into theories. **5** To twist or introduce into, about, or through something else: to *weave* ribbons through one's hair. **6** To spin (a web). **7** To make or effect by side-to-side movements: to *weave* one's way. **—** *v.i.* **8** To make cloth, etc., by weaving. **9** To become woven or interlaced. **10** To move with a side-to-side motion. **—** *n.* A particular method or style of weaving. **— plain** or **taffeta weave** A weave in which each filling yarn passes successively over and under each warp yarn, forming an even surface. **— satin weave** An irregular weave in which the warp or filling yarns pass over a number of yarns of the other set before interweaving, thus forming a smooth, unbroken, lustrous surface. **— twill weave** A strong weave having a distinct diagonal line or rib, caused by the passage of the filling yarns over one warp yarn and under two or more. [OE *wefan.* Akin to WEB, WEFT.]

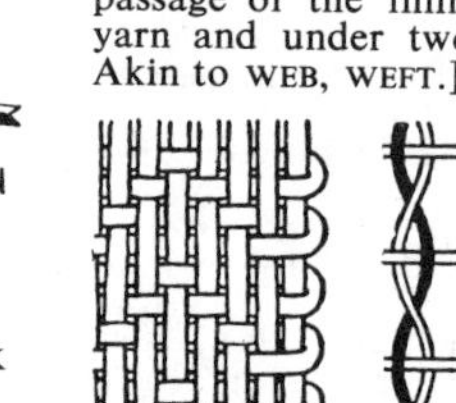
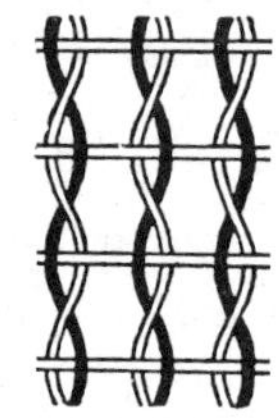
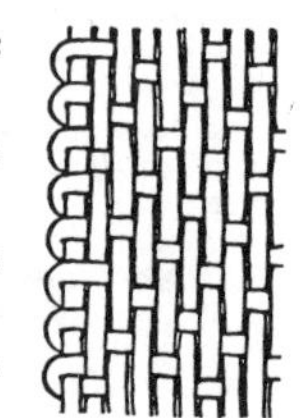
WEAVES
Simple figured. Leno. Five-shaft satin.

weav·er (wē′vər) *n.* **1** One who weaves. **2** A weaverbird.

weav·er·bird (wē′vər·bûrd′) *n.* Any of various finchlike birds (family *Ploceidae*) of the warmer parts of Asia, Africa, and Australia, that construct intricately woven nests.

weaver's bottom *Pathol.* An inflamed condition of the tissue over the ischium, or seat bone, arising from long sitting.

weaver's hitch A sheet bend. Also WEAVER'S KNOT.

web (web) *n.* **1** Textile fabric, especially as in the piece or as being woven in a loom. **2** A long sheet or roll of material formed like a web of cloth; especially, a roll of paper as it comes from the mill. **3** The network of delicate threads spun by a spider to entrap its prey; a cobweb. **4** Any complex network: a *web* of highways; anything artfully contrived or elaborated into a trap or snare: a *web* of espionage. **5** *Zool.* A membrane or fold of skin connecting the digits of an animal, as in aquatic birds, otters, bats, frogs, etc. **6** *Ornithol.* The series of barbs on either side of the shaft of a feather; the vane. **7** *Mech.* A plate or sheet, as of metal, connecting the heavier sections, ribs, frames, etc., of any tool or mechanical element. **8** The plate between the flange and head of a railroad rail. **9** *Archit.* The part of a ribbed vault between the ribs. **10** *Anat.* A membrane; tissue; tela. **11** A thin metal plate, as the blade of a saw or sword, or the bit of a key. **— pin and web** A darkening speck on the cornea, with a film spreading fanwise from the cornea. *— v.t.* **webbed, web·bing** **1** To provide with a web. **2** To cover or surround with a web; entangle. [OE. Akin to WEAVE, WEFT.]

Webb (web), **Beatrice,** 1858–1943, *née* Potter, English economist and sociologist; wife of Sidney James Webb. **— Mary,** 1881–1927, *née* Meredith, English novelist. **— Sidney James,** 1859–1947, Baron Passfield, English economist and sociologist.

webbed (webd) *adj.* **1** Having a web. **2** Having the digits united by a membrane.

web·bing (web′ing) *n.* **1** A woven strip of strong fiber, as for girths, seat bottoms, etc. **2** Any woven texture; the structure of a web.

web·by (web′ē) *adj.* **·bi·er, ·bi·est** **1** Relating to or consisting of a web or membrane. **2** Palmate.

we·ber (vā′bər, wē′bər) *n. Physics* **1** The mks unit of magnetic flux, equal to 100,000,000 maxwells. **2** *Obs.* Coulomb. **3** *Obs.* Ampere. [after Wilhelm Eduard *Weber*]

We·ber (vā′bər), **Ernst Heinrich,** 1795–1878, German physiologist. **— Baron Karl Friedrich Ernst von,** 1786–1826, German composer. **— Wilhelm Eduard,** 1804–91, German physicist; brother of Ernst Heinrich Weber.

web·foot (web′fo͝ot′) *n.* **1** A foot with webbed toes. **2** A web-footed bird or animal. **3** The condition of being web-footed.

web-foot·ed (web′fo͝ot′id) *adj.* Having the toes connected by a membrane, as many aquatic animals and birds.

web press A printing press which is fed from a continuous roll of paper instead of sheets.

web·ster (web′stər) *n. Obs.* A weaver. [OE *webbestre,* fem. of *webba* a weaver]

Web·ster (web′stər), **Daniel,** 1782–1852, U.S. statesman. **— John,** 1580?–1625, English dramatist. **— Noah,** 1758–1843, U.S. lexicographer.

Web·ste·ri·an (web·stir′ē·ən) *adj.* Of or pertaining to Daniel or Noah Webster.

web·worm (web′wûrm′) *n.* Any of various caterpillars, usually gregarious and very destructive of foliage, which build large silken webs or tents for shelter; especially, the common **garden webworm** *(Loxostege similalis).*

wecht (wekht) *n. Scot.* Weight.

wed (wed) *v.* **wed·ded, wed·ded** or **wed, wed·ding** *v.t.* **1** To take as one's husband or wife; marry. **2** To unite or give in matrimony; join in wedlock. **3** To attach as if in marriage; join securely: chiefly in the past participle, with *to*: *wedded* to his job. *— v.i.* **4** To take a husband or wife; marry. [OE *weddian* pledge]

we'd (wēd) **1** We had. **2** We would.

Wed·dell Sea (wed′l) An embayment of the South Atlantic in Antarctica, SE of the Palmer Peninsula and of South America.

wed·ding (wed′ing) *n.* **1** The ceremony of a marriage with the attendant nuptial festivities; also, the ceremony alone; originally, a betrothal. **2** The anniversary or celebration of a marriage. Such weddings are named from the character of the presents regarded as appropriate: golden *wedding* (50th); for list, see under ANNIVERSARY. See synonyms under MARRIAGE. [OE *weddung* < *weddian* pledge]

wedding cake A very rich fruit or pound cake served at a wedding reception, and also often divided among absent friends.

We·de·kind (vā′də·kint), **(Benjamin) Frank(lin),** 1864–1918, German poet and playwright.

wedge (wej) *n.* **1** One of the so-called mechanical powers, consisting of a double inclined plane; specifically, a V-shaped piece of metal, wood, etc., used for splitting substances, raising weights, and the like. **2** Anything in the form of a wedge, as a piece of pie; specifically, a formation, as of soldiers or football players, arranged like a wedge. **3** A right triangular prism, having one very acute angle. **4** Any one of the triangular characters used in cuneiform writing. **5** *Meteorol.* **a** A wedge-shaped area of high barometric pressure as shown on a weather map. **b** An air mass advancing in the form of a wedge. **6** Any action or procedure which facilitates a change in policy, entrance, intrusion, etc.: also **entering wedge.** *— v.* **wedged, wedg·ing** *v.t.* **1** To force apart or split with or as with a wedge; rend; rive. **2** To compress or fix in place with a wedge. **3** To crowd or squeeze (something). *— v.i.* **4** To force oneself or itself in like a wedge. [OE *wecg*]

wedg·ie (wej′ē) *n. Colloq.* A kind of shoe worn by women, having a wedge-shaped piece making a solid sole, flat on the ground from heel to toe.

Wedg·wood (wej′wo͝od′) *n.* Any of various fine, hard earthenwares invented by Josiah Wedgwood, characterized by an unglazed, tinted clay background bearing small, finely detailed, classical figures in cameo relief applied in white paste. It is typically tinted either light or dark blue, but **Wedgwood bamboo ware** (yellow), **Wedgwood basalt** (black), and **Wedgwood queen's** (cream-colored) are also famous. Also **Wedgwood ware.**

Wedg·wood (wej′wo͝od), **Josiah,** 1730–95, English potter; inventor of the ware bearing his name. **— Josiah Clement,** 1872–1943, first Baron Wedgwood of Barlaston, English naval architect and statesman; great-great-grandson of the preceding: called the "Father of the Labour Party."

Wedgwood blue Either of two shades of blue, a light grayish blue and a dark reddish blue: the typical blues of the Wedgwood wares.

wedg·y (wej′ē) *adj.* Having the form or uses of a wedge; cuneal.

wed·lock (wed′lok) *n.* The ceremony of marriage, or the state of being married; matrimony. See synonyms under MARRIAGE. [OE *wedlāc* < *wed* a pledge + *-lāc,* suffix of nouns of action]

Wednes·day (wenz′dē, -dā) *n.* The fourth day of the week. [OE *Wōdnes dæg* day of Woden, trans. of LL *Mercurii dies* day of Mercury]

wee (wē) *adj.* **we·er, we·est** Very small; tiny. *— n. Scot.* A short time or space; a bit: bide a *wee.* [ME *wei,* OE *wēg, wēge* a quantity]

weed[1] (wēd) *n.* **1** Any unsightly or troublesome plant that grows in abundance; especially, any coarse, herbaceous plant growing to injurious excess on cultivated or fallow ground where it is not wanted, as dock, ragweed, etc. **2** *Colloq.* Tobacco: usually with *the*; also, a cigarette or cigar. **3** Any worthless animal or thing; specifically, a horse that is unfit for racing or breeding. **4** The stem and leaves of any useful plant as distinguished from its flower and fruit: The plant runs to *weed.* **5** *Obs.* Thick, luxuriant growth, as of underbrush or shrubs. *— v.t.* **1** To pull up and remove weeds from: to *weed* a garden. **2** To remove (a weed): often with *out.* **3** To remove (anything regarded as harmful or undesirable): with *out.* **4** To rid of anything harmful or undesirable. *— v.i.* **5** To remove weeds, etc. [OE *wēod*] **— weed′less** *adj.*

weed[2] (wēd) *n.* **1** A token of mourning, as a band of crape, worn as part of the dress: He wore a *weed* on his hat; especially in the plural, a widow's mourning garb. **2** *Obs.* Any article of clothing. [OE *wǣd, wǣde* a garment]

Weed (wēd), **Thurlow,** 1797–1882, U.S. journalist and politician.

weed·er (wē′dər) *n.* **1** One who weeds. **2** An implement for removing weeds.

weeding hoe A narrow-bladed hoe for weeding: usually with prongs on the end opposite the blade. See illustration under HOE.

weed·y (wē′dē) *adj.* **weed·i·er, weed·i·est** **1** Having or containing a growth of weeds; abounding in weeds. **2** Of or pertaining to a weed or weeds. **3** Resembling a weed; weedlike, as in rapid, ready growth. **4** *Colloq.* Gawky; awkward; ungainly: *weedy* youths. **— weed′i·ly** *adv.* **— weed′i·ness** *n.*

wee folk The fairies, elves, etc.

Wee·haw·ken (wē′hô·kən) A township in NE New Jersey opposite the Hudson River from New York City; scene of the fatal wounding of Alexander Hamilton in a duel with Aaron Burr, 1804.

week (wēk) *n.* **1** A period of seven successive days; especially, such a period beginning with Sunday. **2** The period of time within a week devoted to work: The office has a 35-hour *week.* **3** A period of seven days preceding or following any given day or date: a *week* from Tuesday. ◆ Homophone: *weak.* [OE *wicu, wice*]

week·day (wēk′dā′) *n.* Any day of the week except Sunday.

week-end (wēk′end′) *n.* The end of the week; specifically, the time from Friday evening or Saturday noon to the following Monday morning. *— v.i.* To pass the week-end: We *week-ended* in the country.

week-end·er (wēk′en′dər) *n.* One who goes on week-end vacation trips.

Week·ley (wēk′lē), **Ernest,** 1865–1954, English lexicographer and etymologist.

week·ly (wēk′lē) *adv.* Once a week; especially, at regular seven-day intervals. *— adj.* **1** Of or pertaining to a week or to weekdays. **2** Done or occurring once a week; also, reckoned by the week; hebdomadal. *— n. pl.* **·lies** A publication issued once a week.

weel (wēl) *adj., adv., & interj. Scot.* Well.

Weems (wēmz), **Mason Locke,** 1759–1825, American clergyman and biographer: known as *Parson Weems.*

ween (wēn) *v.t. & v.i. Archaic* To suppose; guess; fancy. [OE *wēnan* think]

ween·di·jo (wēn′də·jō) See WINDIGO.

ween·ie (wē′nē) *n. Colloq.* A wiener.

weep[1] (wēp) *v.* **wept, weep·ing** *v.i.* **1** To manifest grief or other strong emotion by shedding tears: to *weep* for joy. **2** To mourn; lament: with *for.* **3** To give out or shed water or other liquid in drops, as the stems of some plants under pressure; bleed. *— v.t.* **4** To weep for; mourn or bewail. **5** To shed (tears, or drops of other liquid). **6** To bring to a specified condition by weeping: to *weep* oneself to sleep. *— n.* The act of weeping, or a fit of tears. [OE *wēpan*]

weep[2] (wēp) *n.* A lapwing; pewit. [Imit.]

weep·er (wē′pər) *n.* **1** One who weeps, as a hired mourner. **2** A long piece of black crape worn as a sign of mourning, customarily hanging down from the hat. **3** A pendant of moss, as from a branch. **4** A hole through which water may drip.

weep·ing (wē′ping) *adj.* **1** That weeps; crying; tearful. **2** Having slim, pendulous branches: the *weeping* ash.

weeping ash A variety of the common European ash *(Fraxinus excelsior pendula)* with drooping branches.

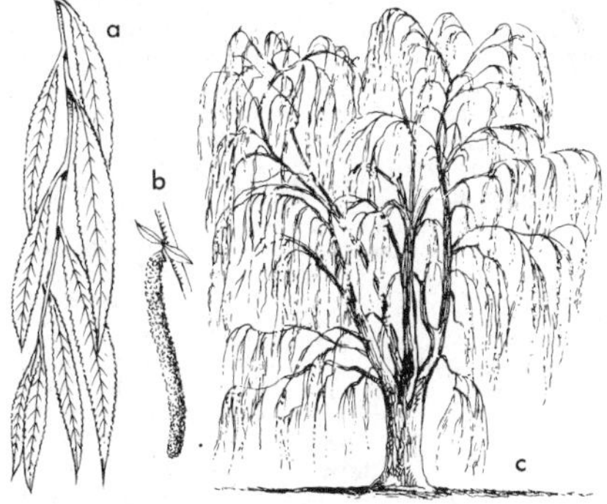

WEEPING WILLOW
a. Leaves. *b.* Catkin. *c.* Tree.

weeping willow An Old World willow *(Salix babylonica),* remarkable for its long, slender, pendulous branches.

weet (wēt) *n.* **1** The imitation of the call of various birds. **2** The peetweet, or common European sandpiper. [Imit.]

wee·ver (wē′vər) *n.* Any of various edible marine fishes (genus *Trachinus*), having upward-looking eyes and sharp dorsal and opercular spines, with which they can inflict serious wounds. [<AF *wivre,* OF *guivre,* orig. a serpent, dragon <L *vipera* a viper]

wee·vil (wē′vəl) *n.* **1** Any of numerous small beetles (family *Curculionidae*) with elongated snoutlike heads which bear the mouth parts at the end and the antennae along the sides: also called *curculio.* Weevil larvae feed on plants and plant products, especially flowers, fruits, and trees; many are serious pests. **2** Any insect injurious to stored grain. [OE *wifel* a beetle] **— wee′vil·y, wee′vil·ly** *adj.*

weft (weft) *n.* **1** The cross-threads in a web

of cloth; woof. 2 A woven fabric; web. [OE. Akin to WEAVE, WEB.]

Wehr·macht (vâr′mäkht) *n. German* The armed forces, collectively, of Germany: literally, defense force.

Wei (wā) A river in NW central China, flowing 540 miles east from SE Kansu province to the Yellow River.

Weich·sel (vīkh′səl) The German name for the Vistula.

wei·ge·la (wī·gē′lə, -jē′-, wī′jə·lə) *n.* Any of a large genus *(Weigela)* of deciduous Asian shrubs of the honeysuckle family; especially, *W. florida,* cultivated extensively in the United States for its profusion of dark rose-purple flowers. [<NL, after Dr. C. E. *Weigel,* 1748–1831, German physician]

weigh[1] (wā) *v.t.* **1** To determine the weight of, as by measuring on a scale or balance. **2** To balance or hold in the hand so as to estimate weight or heaviness. **3** To measure (a quantity or quantities of something) according to weight: with *out.* **4** To consider carefully; estimate the worth or advantages of: to *weigh* a proposal. **5** To press or force down by weight or heaviness; burden or oppress: with *down.* **6** To raise or hoist: now only in the phrase *to weigh anchor.* **7** *Obs.* To think well of; esteem; regard. — *v.i.* **8** To have weight; be heavy to a specified degree: She *weighs* ninety pounds. **9** To have influence or importance: The girl's testimony *weighed* heavily with the jury. **10** To be burdensome or oppressive: with *on* or *upon*: What *weighs* on your mind? **11** *Naut.* **a** To raise anchor. **b** To begin to sail. See synonyms under CONSIDER, DELIBERATE, EXAMINE. — **to weigh in 1** Of a prize fighter or other contestant, to be weighed before a contest. **2** In racing, to be weighed, as a jockey, after a race. — **to weigh one's words** To consider one's words carefully before speaking them. — **to weigh out** In racing, to be weighed, as a jockey, before a race. ◆ Homophone: *way.* [OE *wegan* weight, carry, lift] — **weigh′er** *n.*

weigh[2] (wā) *n.* Way: used in the phrase *under weigh* by mistaken analogy with *aweigh.* See AWEIGH. ◆ Homophone: *way.* [Var. of WAY; infl. in form by *weigh*[1], in phrase "weigh anchor"]

weight (wāt) *n.* **1** The measure of the force with which bodies tend toward the earth's center, or the quality thus measured. The weight of a body is a product of its mass and the acceleration due to gravity. **2** Any object or mass which weighs a definite or specific amount. **3** A definite mass of brass, iron, or other metal, used in weighing machines as a standard; any unit of heaviness, as a pound, ounce, etc. **4** Any mass used as a counterpoise or to exert pressure by force of gravity: a *paperweight.* **5** Burden; pressure; oppressiveness: the *weight* of care; the *weight* of an attack. **6** Any quantity of heaviness, expressed indefinitely or in terms of standard units. **7** The relative tendency of any mass toward a center of superior mass: the *weight* of a planet. **8** A scale or graduated system of standard units of weight: avoirdupois *weight.* See tables below; see also under METRIC SYSTEM. **9** Influence; importance; consequence: a man of *weight.* **10** The comparative heaviness of clothes, as appropriate to the season: summer *weight.* **11** *Stat.* **a** The relative value of an item in a statistical compilation. **b** The frequency of its occurrence among related items, or the number used to express such frequency. — *v.t.* **1** To add weight to; make heavy. **2** To oppress or burden. **3** To adulterate or treat (fabrics or other merchandise) with cheap foreign substances. **4** *Stat.* To give weight to. [OE *wiht, gewiht*]

Synonyms (noun): burden, gravity, heaviness, import, load, moment. See LOAD.

AVOIRDUPOIS WEIGHT

27.34+ grains (gr.)	=	1 dram (dr. av.)
16 drams av.	=	1 ounce (oz. av.)
16 ounces av.	=	1 pound (lb., lbs. av.)
2000 pounds av.	=	1 short ton (sh. tn.)
2240 pounds av.	=	1 long ton (l. tn.)

TROY WEIGHT

24 grains	=	1 pennyweight (dwt.)
20 pennyweight	=	1 ounce (oz. t.)
12 ounces	=	1 pound (lb., lbs. t.)

weight·less (wāt′lis) *adj.* **1** Having little or no heaviness. **2** Subject to little or no gravitational force. — **weight′less·ly** *adv.* — **weight′·less·ness** *n.*

weight·y (wā′tē) *adj.* **weight·i·er, weight·i·est 1** Having great weight; ponderous. **2** Having power to move the mind; cogent. **3** Of great importance. **4** Influential, as in public affairs. **5** Burdensome. See synonyms under HEAVY, IMPORTANT. — **weight′i·ly** *adv.* — **weight′i·ness** *n.*

Wei·hai (wā′hī′) A port and naval base in NE Shantung province, NE China; leased with the surrounding area (285 square miles) to Great Britain, 1898–1930. Formerly **Wei·hai·wei** (wā′hī′wā′).

Wei·mar (vī′mär) A city in SW East Germany, formerly capital of Thuringia.

Wei·mar·an·er (vī′mər·ä′nər) *n.* A breed of dog of the hound type, blue- or amber-eyed, gray in color, used for hunting and as a watchdog. [from *Weimar,* Germany, where the breed originated]

weir (wir) *n.* **1** An obstruction placed in a stream to raise the water, divert it into a millrace or irrigation ditches, or form a fish pond; a dam. **2** A series of wattled enclosures in a stream, to catch fish. [OE *wer* < *werian* dam up]

Weir (wir), **Robert Walter,** 1803–89, and his sons, **John Ferguson,** 1841–1926, and **Julian Alden,** 1852–1919, U. S. painters.

weird (wird) *adj.* **1** Concerned with the unnatural or with witchcraft; unearthly; uncanny. **2** Pertaining to or having to do with fate or the Fates. — **the Weird Sisters 1** The Fates. **2** The three witches in Shakespeare's *Macbeth.* — *n. Scot.* **1** One's allotted fate; fortune. **2** Destiny; fate. **3** One of the Fates. **4** A prophecy; prediction. **5** A spell; enchantment. [OE *wyrd* fate]

weird·o (wir′dō) *n. pl.* **·os** *Slang* A person who is strange or eccentric. Also **weird′ie, weird′y** (-dē).

Weis·mann (vīs′män), **August,** 1834–1914, German biologist. — **Weis·man·ni·an** (vīs·män′ē·ən) *adj.* & *n.*

Weis·mann·ism (vīs′män·iz′əm) *n.* The theory of evolution, as propounded by August Weismann, which asserts the continuity of the germ plasm within but in isolation from the soma, and denies the heritability by offspring of characters acquired by the parents during their lifetime.

weiss beer (vīs) A light, whitish beer, brewed usually from wheat. [<G *weissbier* pale Berlin beer, lit., white beer]

Weis·sen·fels (vī′sən·fels) A city in south central East Germany.

Weiss·horn (vīs′hôrn) A peak in southern Switzerland; 14,804 feet.

Weiz·mann (wīts′mən, vīts′män), **Chaim,** 1874–1952, Israeli chemist and Zionist leader; first president of Israel 1948–52; born in Russian Poland.

we·jack (wē′jak) *n.* The fisher or pekan. [<Algonquian. Cf. Cree *otchek.*]

we·ka (wē′kə, wā′-) *n.* A wingless rail (genus *Ocydroma*) of New Zealand, now nearly extinct: also called *woodhen.* [<Maori]

welch (welch, welsh) See WELSH.

Welch (welch, welsh) See WELSH.

Welch (welch), **William Henry,** 1850–1934, U.S. pathologist and sanitarian.

wel·come (wel′kəm) *adj.* **1** Admitted gladly to a place or festivity; received cordially: a *welcome* guest. **2** Producing satisfaction or pleasure; pleasing: *welcome* tidings. **3** Made free to use or enjoy: She is *welcome* to my purse. See synonyms under AGREEABLE, DELIGHTFUL. — *n.* The act of bidding or making welcome; a hearty greeting given or cordial reception accorded to a guest or visitor. — **to wear out one's welcome** To come so often or to linger so long as no longer to be welcome. — *v.t.* **·comed, ·com·ing 1** To give a welcome to; greet gladly or hospitably. **2** To receive with pleasure: to *welcome* constructive advice. [OE *wilcuma* < *will-* will, pleasure + *cuma* a guest; infl. in form by WELL[2] and COME, on analogy with OF *bien venu*] — **wel′come·ly** *adv.* — **wel′·come·ness** *n.* — **wel′com·er** *n.*

weld[1] (weld) *v.t.* **1** To unite, as two pieces of metal, with or without pressure, by the application of heat along the area of contact. **2** To bring into close association or connection. — *v.i.* **3** To admit of being welded. — *n.* The consolidation of pieces of metal by welding; also, the closed joint so formed. [Alter of WELL[1], *v.*] — **weld′a·bil′·i·ty** *n.* — **weld′a·ble** *adj.* — **weld′er** *n.*

weld[2] (weld) *n.* **1** An erect Old World annual *(Reseda luteola),* formerly cultivated for dyers' use: also called *yellowweed.* **2** The yellow pigment obtained from it: also spelled *woald.* [ME *welde.* Cf. MLG *walde,* MDu. *woude.*]

wel·fare (wel′fâr) *n.* **1** The condition of faring well; exemption from pain or discomfort; prosperity; also, condition, as regards well-being: Inquire concerning thy brethren's *welfare.* **2** Organized efforts by a community or organization to improve the social and economic condition of a group or class: also **welfare work.** **3** Money, food, clothing, etc., given to those in need; relief. — **on welfare** Receiving money, food, clothing, etc., from a local or other government because of need. [ME *wel fare* < *wel* well + *fare* a going <OE *faran* go]

Welfare Island An island in the East River, New York City; 139 acres; site of two municipal hospitals: formerly *Blackwell's Island.*

welfare state A state or polity in which the government assumes a large measure of responsibility for the social welfare of its members, as through unemployment and health insurance, etc.

wel·kin (wel′kin) *n. Archaic* or *Poetic* **1** The vault of the sky; the heavens. **2** The air. [OE *wolcn, wolcen* a cloud]

well[1] (wel) *n.* **1** A hole or shaft sunk into the earth to obtain a fluid, as water, oil, brine, or natural gas. **2** A spring of water; a place where water issues from the ground; a fountain. **3** A source of continued supply, or that which issues forth continuously; a wellspring: a *well* of learning. **4** A depression, cavity, or vessel resembling a well: an *inkwell.* **5** A cavity in the lower part of some sorts of furnaces to receive falling metal. **6** In an English law court, the railed-in space between the bench and the bar, reserved for solicitors. **7** *Archit.* **a** The vertical opening contained within a winding staircase. **b** A similar opening descending through floors, or a deep enclosed space in a building for light or ventilation: an air *well*; an elevator *well.* **8** *Naut.* The boxed-in space in a vessel's hold, enclosing the pumps. **9** A compartment admitting water, in which fish are preserved alive. — *v.i.* To pour forth or flow up, as water in a spring. — *v.t.* To gush: Her eyes *welled* tears. [OE *wielle* < *weallan* boil, bubble up]

well[2] (wel) *adv.* **bet·ter, best 1** Satisfactorily; favorably; according to one's wishes: Everything goes *well.* **2** In a good or correct manner; properly; excellently; expertly: to dance or speak *well.* **3** Suitably; befittingly; with reason or propriety: I cannot *well* remain here. **4** In a successful manner; prosperously; also, agreeably or luxuriously: He lives *well.* **5** Intimately: How *well* do you know him? **6** To a large or proper extent or degree; plentifully: a *well*-stocked larder. **7** Completely; wholly. **8** Far; at some distance: He lagged *well* behind us. — **as well 1** Also; in addition. **2** With equal effect or consequence: He might just *as well* have sold it. — **as well as 1** As satisfactorily as. **2** To the same degree as. **3** In addition to. — *adj.* **1** Satisfactory; rightly done or arranged; fortunate; suitable; gratifying: always in the predicate position: It is *well.* **2** Having physical health; free from ailment of mind or body. **3** Prosperous; comfortable. — *interj.* An exclamation used to express surprise, expectation, resignation, doubt, indignation, etc., or merely to preface a remark. [OE *wel.* Akin to WEAL.]

Synonyms (adj.): advantageous, beneficial, convenient, desirable, excellent, expedient, favorable, fortunate, good, happy, lucky, prosperous. See HEALTHY. *Antonyms*: see synonyms for BAD.

Well may appear as a combining form in hyphemes when joined to participles to form unit modifiers: thus, predicatively, His words were *well* chosen; but attributively, his *well-chosen* words. The following examples are self-explanatory:

well-accepted	**well-acquainted**
well-accustomed	**well-acted**
well-acknowledged	**well-adjusted**

well-administered
well-aimed
well-aired
well-armed
well-armored
well-arranged
well-assorted
well-assured
well-attested
well-attired
well-authenticated
well-behaved
well-beloved
well-built
well-chaperoned
well-chosen
well-considered
well-contented
well-covered
well-cultivated
well-defended
well-defined
well-deserving
well-digested
well-disciplined
well-done
well-dressed
well-earned
well-educated
well-established
well-financed
well-fitted
well-formed
well-fortified
well-fought
well-furnished
well-governed
well-handled
well-informed
well-judged
well-kept
well-knit
well-liked
well-looking
well-loved
well-made
well-managed
well-mannered
well-measured
well-ordered
well-paid
well-phrased
well-placed
well-planned
well-pleased
well-pleasing
well-poised
well-prepared
well-preserved
well-proportioned
well-recognized
well-regulated
well-remembered
well-rooted
well-seasoned
well-selected
well-skilled
well-spent
well-stocked
well-swept
well-timed
well-trained
well-trimmed
well-understood
well-used
well-versed
well-wooded
well-worded
well-worn
well-woven
well-written
well-wrought

we'll (wēl) We shall; we will: a contraction.

Wel·land (wel′ənd) A city in southern Ontario, on the **Welland Ship Canal,** a waterway (28 miles long) connecting Lake Ontario with Lake Erie.

well-ap·point·ed (wel′ə·poin′tid) *adj.* Properly equipped; excellently furnished.

well·a·way (wel′ə·wā′) *interj. Obs.* Woe is me! alas! Also **well′a·day′.** [OE *wei lā wei,* alter. of *wā lā wā* woe! lo! woe!; infl. in form by ON *vei* woe]

well-bal·anced (wel′bal′ənst) *adj.* Evenly balanced; adjusted with reference to welfare.

well-be·ing (wel′bē′ing) *n.* A condition of happiness or prosperity; welfare.

well-born (wel′bôrn′) *adj.* Of good lineage.

well-bred (wel′bred′) *adj.* **1** Well brought up; polite. **2** Of good ancestry; of good or pure stock.

well-curb (wel′kûrb′) *n.* The frame or stone ring around the mouth of a well.

well-dis·posed (wel′dis·pōzd′) *adj.* Favorably inclined.

well-do·er (wel′dōō′ər) *n.* **1** A performer of moral and social duties. **2** *Scot.* & *Brit. Dial.* One who is prosperous or well-to-do. — **well′-do′ing** *adj.* & *n.*

Wel·le (we′lā) See UELE.

well enough Tolerably good or satisfactory. — **to let well enough alone** To leave things as they are lest the result of interference be worse.

Welles (welz), **Gideon,** 1802–78, U. S. politician and writer. —**(George) Orson,** born 1915, U. S. actor and producer. —**Sumner,** 1892–1961, U. S. diplomat.

Welles·ley (welz′lē), **Richard Colley,** 1760–1842, first Marquis of Wellesley, British statesman; brother of the Duke of Wellington.

well-fa·vored (wel′fā′vərd) *adj.* Of attractive appearance; comely; handsome. Also *Brit.* **well′-fa′voured.**

well-fed (wel′fed′) *adj.* Plump; fat; sleek.

well-fixed (wel′fikst′) *adj. Colloq.* Affluent; well-to-do.

well-found (wel′found′) *adj.* **1** Found to meet expectations. **2** Well equipped.

well-found·ed (wel′foun′did) *adj.* Based on fact: *well-founded* suspicions.

well-groomed (wel′grōōmd′) *adj.* **1** Carefully curried, as a horse. **2** Carefully dressed and scrupulously neat; having a fashionable, sleek appearance.

well-ground·ed (wel′groun′did) *adj.* **1** Adequately schooled in the elements of a subject. **2** Well-founded.

well·head (wel′hed′) *n.* A natural source supplying water to a spring or well.

well-heeled (wel′hēld′) *adj. Slang* Plentifully supplied with money. [<WELL[2] + HEEL[1], *v.* (def. 6)]

Wel·ling·ton (wel′ing·tən) The capital of New Zealand, a port on southern North Island.

Wel·ling·ton (wel′ing·tən), **Duke of,** 1769–1852, Arthur Wellesley, British general; defeated Napoleon at Waterloo; prime minister; born in Ireland.

Wellington boot A high boot covering the leg as far as the knee in front but cut away behind.

well-in·ten·tioned (wel′in·ten′shənd) *adj.* Having good intentions; well-meant: often with connotation of failure or of clumsy or harmful execution.

well-known (wel′nōn′) *adj.* Widely known; famous.

well-mean·ing (wel′mē′ning) *adj.* Having good intentions. — **well′-meant′** (-ment′) *adj.*

well met Welcome.

well-nigh (wel′nī′) *adv.* Very nearly; almost.

well-off (wel′ôf′, -of′) *adj.* In comfortable circumstances; wealthy; fortunate.

well-read (wel′red′) *adj.* Having a wide knowledge of literature or books; having read much: usually with *in.*

Wells (welz) A municipal borough in east central Somerset, England; noted for its 12th century cathedral.

Wells (welz), **Henry,** 1805–78, U. S. express operator; organized Wells, Fargo & Co. in 1852. — **H(erbert) G(eorge),** 1866–1946, English author.

wells·ite (welz′īt) *n.* A vitreous hydrated silicate of barium, calcium, potassium, and aluminum, crystallizing in the monoclinic system. [after H. L. *Wells,* 1855–1924, U. S. chemist]

well-spo·ken (wel′spō′kən) *adj.* **1** Fitly or excellently said. **2** Of gentle speech and manners.

well·spring (wel′spring′) *n.* **1** An inexhaustible fountain. **2** A source of continual supply.

well sweep A long tapering pole swung on a pivot attached to a high post, and having the bucket suspended from one end, for use in drawing water.

WELL SWEEP

well-thought-of (wel′thôt′uv′, -ov′) *adj.* In good repute; esteemed; respected.

well-to-do (wel′tə·dōō′) *adj.* In prosperous circumstances; evincing a state of comfort or wealth.

well-wish·er (wel′wish′ər) *n.* One who wishes well, as to another. — **well′-wish′ing** *adj.* & *n.*

Wels·bach (welz′bak, *Ger.* vels′bäkh), **Baron Carl Auer von,** 1858–1929, Austrian chemist and inventor.

Welsbach burner A burner of the Bunsen type, having a cotton-gauze mantle impregnated with thoria and ceria, so arranged that upon ignition of a mixture of gases the mantle becomes incandescent. [after Baron Carl A. von *Welsbach*]

welsh (welsh, welch) *v.t.* & *v.i. Slang* **1** To cheat by failing to pay a bet or debt. **2** To avoid fulfilling (an obligation). Also spelled *welch.* [? Back formation < *welsher,* prob. <*Welsher* a Welshman, with ref. to supposed national traits]

Welsh (welsh, welch) *adj.* Pertaining to Wales, its people, or their language. — *n.* **1** The natives of Wales, a people of Celtic stock: with *the*: also called *Cymry.* **2** The language of Wales, belonging to the Brythonic or Cymric group of the Celtic subfamily of Indo-European languages: also called *Cymric.* Also spelled *Welch.* [OE *Welisc* < *wealh* a foreigner (one not of Saxon origin)] — **Welsh′·man** *n.*

Welsh cor·gi (kôr′gē) *n.* Either of two ancient breeds of a Welsh working dog, characterized by a long body, short legs, and erect ears: the **Cardigan Welsh corgi** has a long tail, the **Pembroke Welsh corgi** a short tail. [< Welsh < *corr* dwarf + *ci* dog]

Welsh rabbit A concoction of melted cheese cooked in cream or milk, often with ale or beer added, and served hot on toast or crackers. ◆ The form *rarebit* was a later development and is the result of mistaken etymology.

welt (welt) *n.* **1** A strip of material, covered cord, etc., applied to a seam to cover or strengthen it. **2** In shoemaking, a strip of leather set into the seam between the edges of the upper and the outer sole. **3** In carpentry, a batten or strip made fast over a flush seam. **4** A wale or stripe raised on the skin by a blow. — *v.t.* **1** To sew a welt on or in; decorate with a welt. **2** *Colloq.* To flog severely, so as to raise welts or wales. [ME *welte, walt.* Cf. OE *weltan* roll.]

Welt·an·schau·ung (velt′än·shou′ōōng) *n. German* Literally, world viewing; philosophy of life: a comprehensive philosophy regarding the cosmos; ideology.

Welt·an·sicht (velt′än·zikht) *n. German* Literally, world view; a special view or interpretation of reality, seen as a whole.

wel·ter[1] (wel′tər) *v.i.* **1** To roll about; wallow. **2** To lie or be soaked in some fluid, as blood. **3** To surge or move tumultuously, as the sea. — *n.* **1** A rolling movement, as of waves; hence, commotion. **2** That in which weltering is done; a wallow. [<MDu. *welteren*]

wel·ter[2] (wel′tər) *adj.* Designating or pertaining to a horse race in which welterweights are carried. [< *welter* a heavyweight (horseman), ? <WELT, *v.* (def. 2)]

welter race A horse race in which heavy weights are imposed on the horses, in order to permit amateur jockeys to ride.

wel·ter·weight (wel′tər·wāt′) *n.* **1** The weight (regularly 28, sometimes 40 pounds, in addition to weight for age) borne by a horse running in a welter race; hence, loosely, a heavyweight. **2** A boxer whose fighting weight is between 135 and 147 pounds. [< *welter* a heavyweight + WEIGHT]

Welt·lit·e·ra·tur (velt′lit′ə·rä·tōōr′) *n. German* World literature.

Welt·po·li·tik (velt′pō·li·tēk′) *n. German* International politics; world policy.

Welt·schmerz (velt′shmerts) *n. German* World-weariness; melancholy pessimism over the state of the world; romantic discontent.

Wem·bley (wem′blē) A municipal borough of Middlesex, England, 8 miles NW of London.

Wemyss (wēmz) A parish on the Firth of Forth, central Fifeshire, Scotland.

wen[1] (wen) *n.* **1** *Pathol.* Any encysted tumor containing a suetlike substance, occurring commonly on the scalp. **2** Any protuberance. [OE *wenn, wænn*] — **wen′nish, wen′ny** *adj.*

wen[2] (wen) *n.* The old English rune ƿ, replaced by modern English w. [OE, var. of *wynn* joy]

Wen·ces·laus (wen′səs·lôs), 1361–1419, Holy Roman Emperor 1378–1400; king of Bohemia 1378–1419. Also **Wen′ces·las** (-läs), *Ger.* **Wen·zel** (ven′tsəl), **Wen·zes·laus** (ven′tsəs·lous).

wench (wench) *n.* **1** A young peasant woman; also, a female servant; maid. **2** Any young woman; girl; maiden. **3** *Archaic* A prostitute; strumpet. — *v.i.* To keep company with strumpets. [ME *wenche,* short for *wenchel* <OE *wencel* a child, servant]

Wen·chow (wen′chou′, *Chinese* wun′jō′) A port on the Wu (def. 2) and chief city of SE Chekiang province, central eastern China.

wend (wend) *v.t.* & *v.i.* To direct (one's course); go. [OE *wendan*]

Wend (wend) *n.* One of a Slavic people now occupying the region between the Elbe and Oder rivers in Saxony and Prussia; a Sorb. [<G *Wende, Winde*]

Wen·dat (wen′dat) See WYANDOT.

Wen·dell (wen′dəl), **Barrett,** 1855–1921, U. S. scholar.

Wend·ish (wen′dish) *adj.* Of or pertaining to the Wends or their language; Sorbian. — *n.* The West Slavic language of the Wends; Sorbian. Also **Wend′ic.**

went (went) An obsolete past tense and past participle of *wend,* now used as past tense of GO.

wen·tle·trap (wen′təl·trap′) *n.* Any of a genus *(Epitonium)* or family *(Epitoniidae)* of mollusks, having a white, turreted, many-whorled shell. [<Du. *wenteltrap* a spiral staircase or shell]
wept (wept) Past tense and past participle of WEEP.
were (wûr, *unstressed* wər) Plural and second person singular past indicative, and past subjunctive singular and plural of BE. [OE *wǣre, wǣron,* pt. forms of *wesan* be]
we're (wir) We are: a contraction.
wer·en't (wûr′ənt) Were not: a contraction.
were·wolf (wir′wŏŏlf′, wûr′-) *n. pl.* **·wolves** (-wŏŏlvz′) In European folklore, a human being transformed into a wolf by bewitchment, or one having power to assume wolf form at will. Also **wer′wolf′.** [OE *werwulf* man-wolf < *wer* a man + *wulf* a wolf]
Wer·fel (ver′fəl), **Franz,** 1890–1945, German novelist, poet, and dramatist.
wer·geld (wûr′geld) *n.* In Anglo-Saxon and Teutonic law, a fine or pecuniary compensation for crime against the person, especially for homicide, paid by the kindred of the slayer to those of the slain. Also **were′gild** (-gild), **wer′gelt** (-gelt). [OE, lit., man-yield, *i.e.,* man-price <*wer* a man + *geld, gield* yield]
Wer·ner (ver′nər), **Alfred,** 1866–1919, Swiss chemist.
wer·ner·ite (wûr′nər·īt) *n.* Scapolite. [after A. G. *Werner,* 1750–1817, German mineralogist]
wert (wûrt, *unstressed* wərt) Archaic second person singular, past tense of both indicative and subjunctive of BE: used with *thou.*
Wes·cott (wes′kot), **Glenway,** born 1901, U.S. novelist and poet.
we'se (wēz) **1** *Dial.* We is: a mistake for *we are*: *We'se* going. **2** *Scot.* We shall.
We·ser (vā′zər) A river in east and north central West Germany, flowing 300 miles north to the North Sea.
Wes·ley (wes′lē, *Brit.* wez′lē), **Charles,** 1707?–1788, English clergyman and hymn writer; brother of John Wesley. **—John,** 1703–91, English clergyman; founder of Methodism.
Wes·ley·an (wes′lē·ən, *Brit.* wez′lē·ən) *adj.* Of or pertaining to the Wesleys, especially John Wesley, as the founder of Methodism. **—***n.* A disciple of John Wesley; a Methodist. **—Wes′·ley·an·ism** *n.*
Wes·sex (wes′iks) The ancient kingdom of the West Saxons, including modern Berkshire, Dorset, Hampshire, Somerset, and Wiltshire in southern England.
west (west) *n.* **1** The point of the compass at which the sun sets at the equinox, directly opposite *east.* See COMPASS CARD. **2** Any direction, region, or part of the horizon near that point. **—the West 1** The countries lying west of Asia and Turkey; the Occident. **2** The western hemisphere, discovered by explorers sailing westward from Europe. **3** The Western Roman Empire. **4** In the United States: **a** Formerly, the region west of the Allegheny Mountains. **b** The region west of the Mississippi, especially the northwestern part of this region. **—***adj.* **1** To, toward, facing, or placed in the west; western. **2** Coming from the west: the *west* wind. **3** Designating or located in that part of a church directly opposite the altar. **—***adv.* In or toward the west; in a westerly direction. **—go West, young man** Go settle in the unsettled western regions of the United States, a land of little competition and unusual opportunity: advice usually attributed to Horace Greeley. [OE]
West (west), **Benjamin,** 1738–1820, American painter. **—Rebecca** Pseudonym of Cicily Isabel Fairfield, born 1892, English novelist and critic.
West Bengal See under BENGAL.
west–bound (west′bound′) *adj.* Going westward. Also **west′bound′.**
West Brom·wich (brum′ich, -ij) A county borough in southern Stafford, England, just NW of Birmingham.
west by north One point north of west on the mariner's compass. See COMPASS CARD.
west by south One point south of west on the mariner's compass. See COMPASS CARD.
West·cott (west′kot), **Edward Noyes,** 1846–1898, U.S. banker and novelist.
West End The western part of London, England; includes parks and a fashionable shopping district and notable residential section.
west·er (wes′tər) *v.i.* To turn, trend, or shift to the west.—*n.* A wind, especially a storm, blowing from the west. [<WEST + -ER[5]]
west·er·ing (wes′tər·ing) *adj.* Moving or turning westward: the *westering* sun. **—***n.* Movement or declension toward the west.
west·er·ly (wes′tər·lē) *adj.* **1** In, toward, or of the west. **2** From the west: a *westerly* wind. **—***n. pl.* **·lies** A wind blowing from the west. **—***adv.* **1** From the west. **2** Toward the west. **—west′er·li·ness** *n.*
Wes·ter·marck (ves′tər·märk), **Edward Alexander,** 1862–1939, Finnish anthropologist.
west·ern (wes′tərn) *adj.* **1** Being in the west; of, pertaining to, or directed toward the west. **2** Coming from the west: the *western* winds. **—***n.* **1** A westerner. **2** A type of fiction or motion picture using cowboy and pioneer life in the western United States as its material.
West·ern (wes′tərn) *adj.* **1** Proceeding from or characteristic of the West; Occidental. **2** Belonging or pertaining to the Western Church: *Western* ritual. **3** Of or pertaining to the western part of the United States of America. **—***n.* A person identified with or belonging to the Western Church.
Western Australia The largest state of the Commonwealth of Australia, including all of the Australian continent west of 129° E.; about 975,920 square miles; capital, Perth.
Western Church The medieval church of the Western Roman Empire, now the Roman Catholic Church: distinguished from the church of the Eastern Empire, now the Greek or Eastern Church.
Western Dvina See DVINA (def. 2).
west·ern·er (wes′tər·nər) *n.* One who dwells in a western region, especially in the western United States.
western frontier Formerly, that part of the United States bordering on the west in still unsettled regions.
western hemisphere See under HEMISPHERE.
Western Islands The Hebrides.
west·ern·ism (wes′tər·niz′əm) *n.* An expression or practice peculiar to the West, especially the western United States.
west·ern·ize (wes′tər·nīz) *v.t.* **·ized,·iz·ing** To make western in characteristics, habits, etc. **—west′ern·i·za·tion** *n.*
Western Ocean In ancient geography, the ocean lying westward of the known world; hence, the Atlantic Ocean.
Western Reserve A region now comprising ten counties in the NE portion of Ohio, on Lake Erie from the Pennsylvania border to near Sandusky, Ohio, reserved by Connecticut for her settlers when she ceded her western lands to the Federal Government in 1786, but relinquished in 1800.
Western (Roman) Empire The part of the Roman Empire west of the Adriatic, which existed as a separate empire from 395 A.D. until the fall of Rome in 476 A.D.
Western Samoa See SAMOA.
Western Turkestan See under TURKESTAN.
Western Wall Wailing Wall.
West Flanders A province of western Belgium; 1,249 square miles; capital, Bruges.
West Germanic See under GERMANIC.
West Germany See under GERMANY.
West Ham A county borough in Essex, England; a NE suburb of London.
West Har·tle·pool (här′təl·pōōl) A county borough on the North Sea in SE Durham, England.
West Indies A series of island groups separating the North Atlantic from the Caribbean, between North and South America, divided into the *Bahamas,* the *Greater Antilles,* and the *Lesser Antilles.* **—West Indian**
West Indies, The A former federation of British colonies in the Caribbean, including Antigua, Barbados, Dominica, Grenada, Jamaica, Montserrat, St. Lucia, St. Vincent, Trinidad and Tobago, and St. Christopher, Nevis and Anguilla; formed January, 1958; dissolved May 31, 1962.
west·ing (wes′ting) *n.* **1** Distance accomplished toward the west. **2** *Naut.* The amount by which a ship has increased her west longitude from a specified meridian.
West·ing·house (wes′ting·hous), **George,** 1846–1914, U.S. inventor.
West Ir·i·an (ir′ē·ən) A province of Indonesia comprising the western part of New Guinea and several adjacent islands, the former *Netherlands New Guinea;* capital, Kotabaru: also **West New Guinea.**
West Lo·thi·an (lō′thē·ən) A county in SE Scotland on the Firth of Forth; 120 square miles; county town, Linlithgow: formerly *Linlithgowshire.*
West·meath (west′mēth) An inland county of Leinster province, Ireland; 681 square miles; county town, ingar.
West·min·ster (west′min·stər) A city and borough in the county of London, England, on the north bank of the Thames; London's largest borough; site of the Houses of Parliament and Buckingham Palace.
Westminster Abbey A Gothic church in Westminster, London, begun in A.D. 1050; burial place of English kings and notables.
West·mor·land (west′môr·lənd, -mōr-; *Brit.* west′mər·lənd) A county in the Lake District, NW England; 789 square miles; county town, Appleby.
west–north·west (west′nôrth′west′, *in nautical usage* west′nôr·west′) *adj., adv., & n.* Midway between west and northwest. See COMPASS CARD.
Wes·ton su·per Ma·re (wes′tən sōō′pər mā′rē, mâr′) A resort and municipal borough on Bristol Channel, in NE Somerset, England.
West Pakistan 1 A province of Pakistan comprising all of Pakistan west of the Republic of India with the exception of the **Federal District of Pakistan** around and including Karachi (812 square miles); formed in 1955 by the merger of the former provinces of Baluchistan, North-West Frontier Province, Punjab and Sind, along with Bahawalpur, Khairpur, and the other princely states in the area; 309,424 square miles; capital, Lahore. **2** Formerly, the region comprising all of the western portion of Pakistan, including the four former provinces, the princely states, and the present federal district; 310,236 square miles.
West·pha·li·a (west·fā′lē·ə) A former province of Prussia, since 1945 a part of North Rhine-Westphalia, West Germany; scene of the signing of a treaty by France, Sweden, and the Holy Roman Empire at the end of the Thirty Years' War, 1648; 7,806 square miles; capital, Münster. *German* **West·fa·len** (vest·fä′lən). **—West·pha′li·an** *adj. & n.*
West Point A U.S. military reservation on the Hudson River in SE New York; seat of the United States Military Academy.
West Prussia A former province of Prussia; since 1945 under Polish administration; capital, Danzig. *German* **West·preus·sen** (vest′·proi′sən).
West Quod·dy Head (kwod′ē) The easternmost point of continental United States, a promontory on the Atlantic coast of Maine near the Canadian border.
Wes·tra·li·a (wes·trā′lē·ə, -trāl′yə) A contraction of WESTERN AUSTRALIA. **—Wes·tra′li·an** *adj. & n.*
West Riding An administrative division of SW York, England; 2,936 square miles; capital, Wakefield.
West River The chief river of southern China, flowing 1,250 miles east from eastern Yünnan province (900 miles as the Hungshui to its confluence with the Yü) to the South China Sea: Chinese *Si Kiang.*
West Saxon The dialect of Old English spoken in Wessex: preserved in most of the literature of the period.
west–south·west (west′south′west′, *in nautical usage* west′sou·west′) *adj., adv., & n.* Midway between west and southwest. See COMPASS CARD.
West Spitsbergen The largest island of the Spitsbergen group, NW Svalbard; about 15,000 square miles.
West Virginia A State of the east central United States; 24,181 square miles; capital, Charleston; entered the Union June 20, 1863; nickname, *Panhandle State*: abbr. WV. **—West Virginian**
West·wall (west′wôl) See LIMES (def. 2).
west·ward (west′wərd) *adj.* Tending, moving, lying, or facing toward the west. **—***adv.* Toward the west: also **west′wards.** [OE *westweard* <*west* the west] **—west′ward·ly** *adv.*
wet (wet) *adj.* **wet·ter, wet·test 1** Moistened

or saturated with water or other liquid; consisting of or covered with moisture. 2 Marked by showers or by heavy rainfall; rainy: the *wet* season. 3 Not dry: *wet* varnish. 4 *Colloq.* Favoring or not prohibiting the manufacture and sale of alcoholic beverages: a *wet* State; also, opposed to prohibition. 5 Preserved in liquid; also, bottled in alcohol, as laboratory specimens. 6 *Chem.* Treated or separated by means of liquid reagents. **— all wet** *Slang* Quite wrong; crazy; mistaken: He's *all wet.* — *n.* 1 Water; moisture; wetness. 2 Showery or rainy weather; rain. 3 *Colloq.* One opposed to prohibition. — *v.t.* & *v.i.* **wet** or **wet·ted, wet·ting** To make or become wet. **— to wet one's whistle** *Colloq.* To take a drink. [OE *wǣt*] **— wet′ly** *adv.* **— wet′·ness** *n.* **— wet′ta·ble** *adj.* **— wet′ter** *n.*

We·tar (we′tär) One of the southern Molucca Islands, Indonesia, north of Portuguese Timor; 1,400 square miles.

wet·back (wet′bak′) *n. U.S. Colloq.* A Mexican laborer who enters the United States illegally. [So called from those who swim or wade across the Rio Grande]

wet–blank·et (wet′blang′kit) *v.t.* To discourage; depress.

wet blanket A discouragement, or one who discourages any proceedings.

weth·er (weth′ər) *n.* A castrated ram. ◆ Homophone: *weather.* [OE]

wet–nurse (wet′nûrs′) *n.* A woman who is hired to suckle the child of another woman.

wet pack *Med.* A method of reducing fever or of relieving a disturbed neurotic condition by wrapping the patient in wet sheets.

wet suit A skin-tight rubber garment worn by divers, surfers, etc., to retain body warmth in cold waters.

Wet·ter·horn (vet′ər·hôrn) A mountain of three peaks in the Bernese Alps, Switzerland; 12,153 feet.

wet·ting agent (wet′ing) *Chem.* Any of a class of substances that, by reducing surface tension, enable a liquid to spread more readily over a solid surface to which it is applied: a form of detergent.

we've (wēv) We have: a contraction.

Wex·ford (weks′fərd) 1 A maritime county of SE Leinster province, Ireland; 908 square miles. 2 Its county town, a port on **Wexford Harbor,** an inlet of St. George's Channel in SE Ireland.

Wey·den (wī′dən), **Roger van der,** 1399?–1464, Flemish painter.

Wey·gand (ve·gäṅ′), **Maxime,** 1867–1965, French general in World Wars I and II.

Wey·man (wā′mən), **Stanley,** 1855–1928, English novelist.

Wey·mouth (wā′məth) A port in southern Dorset, England; the old part of the present municipal borough of **Weymouth and Melcombe Regis.**

wha (hwä) *pron. Scot.* Who.

whack (hwak) *v.t.* & *v.i.* 1 *Colloq.* To strike sharply; beat; hit. 2 *Slang* To share: often with *up.* 3 *Slang* To drive (mules or oxen). — *n.* 1 *Colloq.* A sharp, resounding stroke or blow. 2 The noise made by such a blow. 3 *Slang* A share; portion. 3 *Slang* A turn; a chance; a try. **— to have a whack at** *Slang* 1 To give a blow to. 2 To have a chance or turn at; to have a chance to try. **— out of whack** *Slang* Out of order. [? Var. of THWACK]

whack·er (hwak′ər) *n.* 1 One who whacks. 2 The driver of a mule team. 3 *Colloq.* A whopper.

whack·ing (hwak′ing) *Colloq. adj.* Strikingly large; whopping. — *adv.* Very; extremely.

whai·sle (hwā′zəl) *v.i. Scot.* To breathe hard or roughly; wheeze. Also **whai′zle.**

whale[1] (hwāl) *n.* 1 A cetaceous mammal of fishlike form, especially one of the larger pelagic species, as distinguished from dolphins and porpoises. Whales have the fore limbs developed as broad flattened paddles, the hind limbs absent, and a thick layer of fat or blubber immediately beneath the skin. The principal types are the toothless or whalebone whales (suborder *Mysticeti*), and the toothed whales (suborder *Odontoceti*). 2 *Colloq.* Something extremely good or large: a *whale* of a party. — *v.i.* **whaled, whal·ing** To engage in the hunting of whales. [OE *hwæl*]

whale[2] (hwāl) *v.t.* **whaled, whal·ing** *Colloq.* To strike as if to produce wales or stripes; flog; wale. [Var. of WALE[1], *v.*]

whale·back (hwāl′bak′) *n.* A steamship having a convex main deck, used on the Great Lakes in passenger and freight traffic.

whale·boat (hwāl′bōt′) *n.* A long, deep rowboat, sharp at both ends, often steered with an oar: so called because first used in whaling, now carried on steamers as lifeboats.

WHALEBOAT

whale·bone (hwāl′bōn′) *n.* 1 The horny substance developed in plates from the palate of the whalebone whales; baleen. 2 A strip of whalebone, used in stiffening dress bodies, corsets, etc.

whale iron A harpoon.

whale·man (hwāl′mən) *n. pl.* **·men** (-mən) One who hunts whales; a whaler.

whal·er (hwā′lər) *n.* 1 A person or a vessel engaged in whaling. 2 A whaleboat.

Whales (hwālz), **Bay of** An inlet of the Antarctic Ocean in Ross Shelf Ice just north of Little America.

whale shark A very large pelagic shark (*Rhineodon typus*) somewhat resembling the basking shark in its habits but often reaching a length of 50 feet: it has a spotted body and very small teeth adapted for feeding on plankton.

whal·ing (hwā′ling) *n.* The industry of capturing whales. — *adj. Slang* Huge; whopping.

whaling station A place on shore to which whales are taken to be flensed and the oil tried out.

wham·my (hwam′ē) *n. pl.* **·mies** *U. S. Slang* 1 A gesture made by extending in parallel the index and little finger from the closed fist and pointing toward the person or object intended: an ancient form of hexing (*mano cornuta,* sign of the horns). If the fingers of both hands are used, the fists being in contact, it is a *double whammy.* 2 A jinx; hex: to put the *whammy* on someone. [<*wham,* colloq. interjection imit. of the sound of a hard blow]

Wham·po·a (hwäm′pō′ä′) The deep-water port for Canton in southern Kwangtung province, China, on an island in the Canton River.

whang[1] (hwang) *v.t.* & *v.i. Colloq.* To beat or sound with a resounding noise. — *n. Colloq.* A beating or banging; heavy blow; whack. [Imit.]

whang[2] (hwang) *n.* 1 A buckskin thong or one made of a deer sinew. 2 Whang leather. 3 *Scot.* A big slice, as of bread or cheese; a chunk. — *v.t.* 1 To beat as with a thong; lash. 2 To beat or strike violently. 3 *Scot.* & *Dial.* To fling; throw violently; hurl. 4 *Scot.* To slice, usually in large pieces. [Var. of OE *thwang* a thong]

whang·ee (hwang·ē′) *n.* 1 Any of a genus (*Phyllostachys*) of tall woody Asian grasses related to the bamboo. 2 A cane or stick made of the stalk of one of these plants. [<Chinese *huang* bamboo sprout]

whang leather A leather, usually of deerskin, made for lacings, thongs, etc. [<WHANG[2] + LEATHER]

Whang·poo (hwang′pōō′) See HWANGPOO.

whap (hwap), **whap·per** (hwap′ər), etc. See WHOP, etc.

wharf (hwôrf) *n. pl.* **wharves** (hwôrvz) or **wharfs** 1 A structure of masonry or timber erected on the shore of a harbor, river, or the like, alongside which vessels may lie to load or unload cargo, passengers, etc.; also, any landing place for vessels, as a pier or quay. 2 *Obs.* A river bank; also, the seashore. — *v.t.* 1 To moor to a wharf. 2 To provide or protect with a wharf or wharves. 3 To deposit or store on a wharf. [OE *hwearf, hwerf* a dam]

wharf·age (hwôr′fij) *n.* 1 Charge for the use of a wharf. 2 Wharf accommodations for shipping.

wharf boat A barge or float with a platform used as a landing stage for men and freight on rivers where the water level is changeful: usually connected with the shore or levee by a bridge.

wharf·in·ger (hwôr′fin·jər) *n.* One who keeps a wharf for landing goods and collects wharfage fees. [Earlier *wharfager* + intrusive *n*]

wharf rat 1 A rat that inhabits wharves; especially, the brown or Norway rat. 2 *U.S. Slang* A man or boy who loiters habitually about wharves, especially with thievish or other criminal intent.

Whar·ton (hwôr′tən), **Edith Newbold,** 1862–1937, *née* Jones, U. S. novelist.

wharve (hwôrv) See WHERVE.

wha's (hwäz), **whase** (hwäz) *pron. Scot.* Whose.

what (hwot, hwut) *adj.* 1 In interrogative construction, asking for information that will specify the person or thing qualified by it: Of *what* person do you speak? 2 How surprising, ridiculous, great, or the like: used in exclamation to express excess or something exceptional in the person or thing qualified: commendatory or the reverse according to circumstances: *What* genius! *What* a noise that boy is making! 3 How much: an ambiguous use: *What* cash has he? — *pron.* 1 Which circumstance, event, relation, or the like: asking for some specification concerning persons or things referred to: an interrogative pronoun used in absolute interrogation: Who and *what* is he? When used of persons, it ordinarily implies some shade of contempt. In this sense *what* is used elliptically for "What did you say?" or in surprise or indignation: *What!* did he really say that? Formerly it was used as a common introductory expletive like *well,* especially in a summons, as in the phrase *what ho!* 2 That which: a double relative, equivalent to a demonstrative followed by a simple relative: Tell me *what* it is; *What* followed occupied little time. 3 *Dial.* or *Illit.* That or which: a simple relative: a donkey *what* wouldn't go. **— what for** 1 Why: *What* did you do that *for*? 2 *Slang* Physical punishment or verbal rebuke: He took the bully outside and gave him the *what for.* — *adv.* 1 In what respect; to what extent: *What* are you profited? 2 In some measure; partly: usually followed by *with*: *What* with the heat, and *what* with the noise, it is distracting. 3 For what reason; why. 4 How extraordinarily! how!: an exclamatory or intensive use. — *conj.* 1 So far as; as well as: He did *what* he could at the time. 2 That: especially in the phrase *but what.* [OE *hwæt,* neut. of *hwa* who]

what–all (hwot′ôl′, hwut′-) *pron. Colloq.* Whatever; everything.

Whate·ly (hwāt′lē), **Richard,** 1787–1863, English prelate and logician.

what·ev·er (hwot′ev′ər, hwut′-) *pron.* 1 As a compound relative, the whole that; anything that; no matter what: often added for emphasis to a negative assertion: *whatever* makes life dear; I do not want anything *whatever.* 2 *Colloq.* What: usually interrogative: *Whatever* were you saying? Also *Poetic* **what′e′er′** (-âr′).

what–not (hwot′not′, hwut′-) *n.* 1 An ornamental set of shelves for holding bric-à-brac, etc. 2 Anything you please; something or other.

what·so·ev·er (hwot′sō·ev′ər, hwut′-) *adj.* & *pron.* Whatever: a slightly more formal usage. Also *Poetic* **what′so·e′er′** (-âr′).

whaup[1] (hwäp, hwôp) *n. Scot.* & *Brit. Dial.* A curlew. [Imit.]

whaup[2] (hwäp, hwôp) *Scot. v.i.* 1 To fuss about noisily. 2 To whine; whistle. — *n.* 1 A whistle or cry. 2 A pod; capsule. 3 A clumsy lout; also, a scamp. 4 An outcry; a fuss.

wheal (hwēl) *n.* A discolored ridge on the skin, as from hives or the stroke of a whip;

also, a whelk. ◆ Homophone: *wheel.* [Alter. of WALE[1]]

wheat (hwēt) *n.* **1** A grain yielding an edible flour, the annual product of a cereal grass (genus *Triticum*): the most important of the cereals, it is excelled only by rice in the number of people by whom it is used as a staple food. **2** The plant that produces this grain, especially *Triticum aestivum* and varieties, a tall, slender annual or biennial of cosmopolitan distribution, bearing at its summit an imbricated spike of usually four-flowered spikelets called the ear or head. **3** A wheatfield; a crop of wheat. [OE *hwǣte*]

WHEAT
a. Ear of bearded wheat.
b. Ear of beardless wheat.
c, d. Grain: front and back of *b.*

wheat·ear (hwēt′ir) *n.* A thrushlike bird *(Oenanthe oenanthe)* of the northern parts of the northern hemisphere, related to the whinchat, ash-gray above and white below, with the wings, sides of head, and tip of tail black. [Earlier *wheatears* <WHITE + *ers, eeres* rump]

wheat·en (hwēt′n) *adj.* Belonging to or made of wheat.

Wheat·ley (hwēt′lē), **Phillis,** 1753?–84, American Negro poet born in Africa.

Wheat·stone (hwēt′stōn), **Sir Charles,** 1802–1875, English physicist.

Wheat·stone bridge (hwēt′stōn) *Electr.* An instrument for the measurement of differential resistance in an electric current. Also **Wheatstone's bridge.** [after Sir Charles *Wheatstone*]

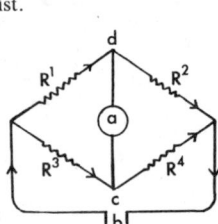

WHEATSTONE BRIDGE
a. Galvanometer.
b. Battery.
c, d. Bridge.
R^1, R^2 Resistances to be compared.
R^3, R^4 Known resistances which can be varied. When galvanometer shows no current, $R^1R^2 = R^3R^4$.

wheat·worm (hwēt′wûrm′) *n.* A threadworm *(Tylenchus tritici)* destructive of wheat. Also **wheat eelworm.**

whee·dle (hwēd′l) *v.* **·dled, ·dling** *v.t.* **1** To persuade or try to persuade by flattery, cajolery, etc.; coax. **2** To obtain by cajoling or coaxing. — *v.i.* **3** To use flattery or cajolery. [? OE *wǣdlian* beg, be poor < *wǣdl* poverty] — **whee′dler** *n.* — **whee′dling·ly** *adv.*

wheel (hwēl) *n.* **1** A circular rim and hub connected by spokes or rays in one structure, or a disk, capable of rotating on a central axis and used to reduce friction and facilitate movement or transportation, as in vehicles, or to act with a rotary motion, as in machines. **2** Anything resembling or suggestive of a wheel; a disk or a circle, or any circular object or formation. **3** An instrument or device having a wheel or wheels as its distinctive characteristic, as a bicycle, a steering wheel or steering gear, or the like. **4** An old instrument of torture or execution, consisting of a wheel to which the limbs of the victim were tied and then broken with an iron bar; also, the death so inflicted. **5** The wheel with which the goddess of fortune is represented, symbolizing the vicissitudes and uncertainty of human fate. **6** A turning; revolution; rotation. **7** Figuratively, that which imparts or directs motion or controls activity; the moving force: the *wheels* of democracy. **8** A turning of a body of troops or a swinging of a line of ships in which a change of direction is accomplished while the different units keep in alinement. **9** A rotating firework; a pinwheel or catherine wheel. **10** A refrain of a song. **11** The rotating disk used in various gambling games, especially roulette; hence, roulette. — **Pelton wheel** A device consisting of a wheel which carries on it a succession of cupshaped buckets, and is made to rotate by the impingement of high-pressure jets of water on the buckets, the form of which is such as to prevent the accumulation of dead water. — **wheels within wheels** An intricate series of motives or influences, acting and reacting on one another. — *v.t.* **1** To move or convey on wheels. **2** To cause to turn on or as on an axis; pivot or revolve. **3** To perform with a circular movement. **4** To provide with a wheel or wheels. — *v.i.* **5** To turn on or as on an axis; pivot; rotate or revolve. **6** To take a new direction or course of action; change attitudes, opinions, etc.: often with *about.* **7** To move in a circular or spiral course. **8** To roll or move on wheels. — **to wheel and deal** *Slang* To act freely, aggressively, and often unscrupulously, as in the arrangement of a business or political deal. — *adj.* **1** Pertaining to or shaped like a wheel. **2** Harnessed to a vehicle directly in front of the wheels: said of a draft animal when there is a leader or leaders in front. ◆ Homophone: *wheal.* [OE *hwēol*]

wheel and axle *Mech.* A wheel or drum mounted on an axle with a rope wound about the drum so that a slight pull on one end of the rope will raise a disproportionately heavy weight attached to the other: one of the so-called simple machines.

wheel animalcule A rotifer.

wheel·bar·row (hwēl′bar′ō) *n.* A boxlike vehicle ordinarily with one wheel and two handles, for moving small loads. — *v.t.* To convey in a wheelbarrow.

wheel·base (hwēl′bās′) *n.* The distance from the center of the back axle to the center of the front axle, as in an automobile.

wheel·bug (hwēl′bug′) *n.* A large hemipterous insect *(Arilus cristatus)* of the southern United States, which preys upon caterpillars and other soft-bodied insects: so called from a semicircular crest on the thorax resembling a cogwheel.

wheel·chair (hwēl′châr′) *n.* A mobile chair mounted between large wheels, for the use of invalids. Also **wheel chair.**

wheeled (hwēld) *adj.* **1** Having wheels; furnished with a wheel or wheels: often in compounds: a two-*wheeled* cart. **2** Effected or borne by wheels: *wheeled* transportation.

wheel·er (hwē′lər) *n.* **1** One who wheels. **2** A wheelhorse or other draft animal working next the wheel. **3** Something furnished with a wheel or wheels: a side-*wheeler.*

Wheel·er (hwē′lər), **Joseph,** 1836–1906, American Confederate general.

wheel·er-deal·er (hwē′lər·dē′lər) *n. Slang* One who wheels and deals.

wheel·horse (hwēl′hôrs′) *n.* **1** A horse harnessed to the pole or shafts when there is a leader or leaders in front; hence, one who does the heaviest work. **2** In politics, a person bearing great responsibility, or one to be greatly depended upon.

wheel·house (hwēl′hous′) *n.* **1** A small house on the deck of a vessel in which the steering wheel is located; a pilothouse. **2** A paddle box.

wheel·ing (hwē′ling) *n.* **1** The act of one who wheels, especially of one riding a bicycle. **2** The condition of the roads, as regards traveling on wheels. **3** A rotating movement; a turning.

Wheel·ing (hwē′ling) A port on the Ohio River in NW West Virginia; an industrial center.

wheel lock **1** An old form of lock for small arms, in which a small steel wheel, actuated by a spring and released by a trigger, produced sparks by rotating against a flint. **2** A lock or catch for stopping a vehicle wheel.

wheel·man (hwēl′mən) *n. pl.* **·men** (-mən) **1** The man who steers a vessel. **2** A bicyclist. Also **wheels′man.**

Whee·lock (hwē′lok), **Eleazar,** 1711–79, U.S. clergyman and educator.

wheel window See ROSE WINDOW.

wheel·work (hwēl′wûrk′) *n. Mech.* The gearing and arrangement of wheels in a machine or mechanical device.

wheel·wright (hwēl′rīt′) *n.* A man whose business is making or repairing wheels and wheeled vehicles.

wheen (hwēn) *n. Scot.* & *Dial.* A few.

wheeze (hwēz) *v.t.* & *v.i.* **wheezed, wheez·ing** To breathe or utter with a husky, whistling sound. — *n.* **1** A wheezing sound. **2** A whispering sound so exaggerated as to give rise to the sound popularly called a "stage whisper." **3** *Colloq.* A popular tale, saying, or trick, especially an ancient one. [Prob. <ON *hvæsa* hiss] — **wheez′er** *n.* — **wheez′·ing·ly** *adv.*

wheez·y (hwē′zē) *adj.* **wheez·i·er, wheez·i·est** Subject to wheezing, or making a wheezing sound. — **wheez′i·ly** *adv.* — **wheez′i·ness** *n.*

whelk[1] (hwelk) *n.* Any of various large marine mollusks (family *Buccinidae*), having whorled shells, that burrow in sand and prey on clams, etc. The common whelk *(Buccinum undatum)* is much eaten in Europe. [OE *weoloc*]

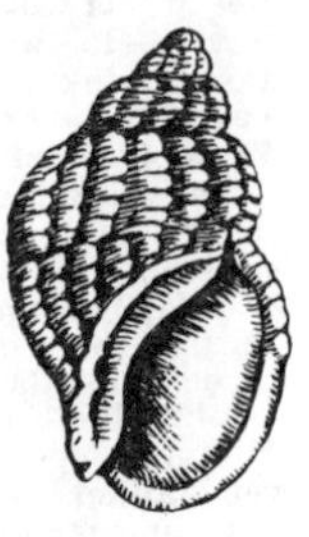

COMMON WHELK
(About 4 inches)

whelk[2] (hwelk) *n.* A swelling, protuberance, or pustule; wheal; especially, a pimple or eruption of pimples on the face. [OE *hwylca* a pustule < *hwelian* suppurate]

whelk·y[1] (hwel′kē) *adj.* **whelk·i·er, whelk·i·est** **1** Protuberant; rounded. **2** Shelly. Also spelled *welky.* [<WHELK[1]]

whelk·y[2] (hwel′kē) *adj.* **whelk·i·er, whelk·i·est** Marked with pustules or whelks. [<WHELK[2]]

whelm (hwelm) *v.t.* **1** To cover with water or other fluid; submerge; engulf. **2** To overpower; overwhelm. — *v.i.* **3** To roll with engulfing force. [Prob. blend of OE *helmian* cover and *gehwelfan* bend over]

whelp (hwelp) *n.* **1** One of the young of a dog, wolf, lion, or other beast of prey; sometimes, a dog of any age. **2** A worthless young fellow; a cub; puppy: used contemptuously. **3** *Mech.* **a** One of a series of longitudinal ridges on a windlass or capstan. **b** One of the teeth of a sprocket wheel. — *v.t.* & *v.i.* To give birth (to): said of dogs, lions, etc. [OE *hwelp*]

when (hwen) *adv.* **1** Interrogatively, at what or which time: *When* did you arrive? **2** Conjunctively: **a** At which: the time *when* we went on the picnic. **b** At which or what time: They watched till midnight *when* they fell asleep. **c** As soon as: He laughed *when* he heard it; You may play *when* you finish work. **d** Although: He walks *when* he might ride. **e** At the time that; while: *when* you were in church; *when* we were young. **f** If; considering that: *When* in doubt, ask; How can I buy it *when* I have no money? **g** After which; then: We had just awakened *when* you called. — *pron.* What or which time: since *when*; till *when.* — *n.* The time; date: I don't know the *when* or the circumstances. [OE *hwanne, hwænne*]

when·as (hwen′az′) *conj. Obs.* **1** Whereas; while. **2** When. Also **when that.**

whence (hwens) *adv.* **1** Interrogatively, from what place or source; of what origin: *Whence* and what art thou? *Whence* is the correlative of *thence.* **2** Conjunctively: **a** From what or which place, source, or cause; from which: the place *whence* these sounds arise. **b** To which place; where: Return *whence* you came. **c** For which reason; wherefore. [ME *whannes, whennes,* adverbial genitive of *whanne,* OE *hwanne* when]

whence·so·ev·er (hwens′sō·ev′ər) *adv.* & *conj.* From whatever place, cause, or source.

when·e'er (hwen′âr′) *adv.* & *conj. Poetic* Whenever.

when·ev·er (hwen′ev′ər) *adv.* & *conj.* At whatever time.

when·so·ev·er (hwen′sō·ev′ər) *adv.* & *conj.* At what time soever; whenever.

where (hwâr) *adv.* **1** Interrogatively: **a** At or in what place, relation, or situation: *Where* is my book? **b** To what place or end; whither: *Where* are you going? **c** From what place; whence: *Where* did you get that hat? **2** Conjunctively: **a** At or in which or what place; at the place in which: *where* men gather. **b** To a place or situation in or to which; whither: Let us go *where* the mountains and the trees are. ◆ *Where* is the correlative of *there.* In composition with a preposition, *where* has sometimes the force of an interrogative pronoun and sometimes that of a relative: *Wherein* was he wrong? *Wherein* he was much deceived. —*pron.* The place in which: The accident occurred 100 yards from *where* we stood. —*n.* Place; locality. [OE *hwǣr*]

where·a·bouts (hwâr′ə·bouts′) *adv.* **1** Near or at what place; about where. **2** *Obs.* About which; concerning which. Also *Rare* **where′·a·bout′.** —*n.* The place in or near which a person or thing is.

where·as (hwâr′az′) *conj.* **1** Since the facts are such as they are; seeing that: often used in the preamble of a resolution, etc. **2** The fact of the matter being that; when in truth: implying opposition to a previous statement. —*n. pl.* **·as·es** A clause or item beginning with the word "whereas."

where·at (hwâr′at′) *adv.* **1** Interrogatively, at what: *Whereat* are you angry? **2** Conjunctively, at which; for which reason; whereupon: He won the race, *whereat* we were delighted.

where·by (hwâr′bī′) *adv.* **1** Interrogatively, by what; how. **2** Conjunctively, by, near, or through which.

wher·e′er (hwâr′âr′) *adv. Poetic* Wherever.

where·fore (hwâr′fôr′, -fōr′) *adv.* **1** Interrogatively, for what reason; what for; to what end; why: *Wherefore* didst thou doubt? **2** Conjunctively, for which reason. See synonyms under THEREFORE. —*n.* The cause; reason: the whys and *wherefores.* [<WHERE + FOR]

where·from (hwâr′frum′, -from′) *conj.* From which; whence.

where·in (hwâr′in′) *adv.* **1** Interrogatively, in what; in what particular or regard: *Wherein* is the error? **2** Conjunctively, in which thing, place, circumstance, etc.: a state *wherein* there is discord.

where·in·to (hwâr′in·tōō′) *adv.* **1** Interrogatively, into what. **2** Conjunctively, into which: the gulf *whereinto* he sailed.

where·of (hwâr′uv′, -ov′) *adv.* **1** Interrogatively, of or from what: *Whereof* did you partake? **2** Conjunctively, of which or whom: the house *whereof* he is the head.

where·on (hwâr′on′, -ôn′) *adv.* **1** Interrogatively, on what or whom. **2** Conjunctively, on which: a rock *whereon* to build.

where·so·ev·er (hwâr′sō·ev′ər) *adv.* & *conj.* **1** In or to whatever place; wherever. **2** Whithersoever. **3** Whencesoever.

where·som·ev·er (hwâr′səm·ev′ər) *adv. & conj. Dial.* Wherever; wheresoever. [<WHERE + SOMEVER < *som* ever, just (<Scand.) + EVER]

where·through (hwâr′thrōō′) *adv.* & *conj.* Through which.

where·to (hwâr′tōō′) *adv.* **1** Interrogatively, to what place or end: *Whereto* serves avarice? **2** Conjunctively, to which or to whom; whither: the grave *whereto* we haste. Also *Archaic* **where′un·to′.**

where·up·on (hwâr′ə·pon′, -ə·pôn′) *adv.* **1** Interrogatively, upon what; whereon. **2** Conjunctively, upon which or whom; in consequence of which; after which: *whereupon* they took in sail.

wher·ev·er (hwâr′ev′ər) *adv.* & *conj.* In, at, or to whatever place; wheresoever.

where·with (hwâr′with′, -with′) *adv.* **1** Interrogatively, with what: *Wherewith* shall I do it? **2** Conjunctively, with which; by means of which: *wherewith* we abated hunger. —*pron.* That with or by which: with the infinitive: I have not *wherewith* to do it. —*n.* The requisites; wherewithal.

where·with·al (hwâr′with·ôl′) *n.* The necessary means or resources; especially, the necessary money: with the definite article. —*adv.* & *pron.* (hwâr′with·ôl′) Wherewith.

wher·ry (hwer′ē) *n. pl.* **·ries** **1** A light, fast rowboat used on inland waters. **2** *Brit.* A decked fishing vessel with two sails. **3** An open rowboat for racing or exercise, built for one person. **4** *Brit.* A very broad, light barge. —*v.t.* & *v.i.* **·ried, ·ry·ing** To transport in or use a wherry. [? <WHIR; with ref. to rapid movement]

wherve (hwûrv) *n.* In spinning, a pulley on the spindle: also spelled *wharve.* [OE *hweorfa*]

whet (hwet) *v.t.* **whet·ted, whet·ting** **1** To sharpen, as a knife, by friction. **2** To make more keen or eager; excite; stimulate, as the appetite. —*n.* **1** The act of whetting. **2** Something that whets. [OE *hwettan*] —**whet′ter** *n.*

wheth·er (hweth′ər) *conj.* As the first alternative; in case; if: introducing an alternative clause, followed by a correlative *or,* or *or whether*; sometimes also introducing a single alternative, the other, usually a negative, being implied: Tell us *whether* you are going (or not). —*pron.* Which: properly of two, less exactly of more than two: an archaism used interrogatively and relatively. —**whether or no** Regardless; in any case. [OE *hwæther, hwether*]

whet·slate (hwet′slāt′) *n.* A hard, fine-grained siliceous rock used for whetstones.

whet·stone (hwet′stōn′) *n.* A fine-grained stone for whetting knives, axes, etc. [OE *hwetstān* < *hwettan* whet + *stān* a stone]

whew (hwyōō) *interj.* An exclamatory sound, expressive usually of amazement, dismay, relief, admiration (real or feigned), or discomfort (from the heat). [Imit. of whistling]

Whew·ell (hyōō′əl), **William,** 1794–1866, English scientist and philosopher.

whey (hwā) *n.* A clear, straw-colored liquid that separates from the curd when milk is curdled, as in making cheese. [OE *hwæg, hweg*] —**whey′ey, whey′ish** *adj.*

whey-face (hwā′fās′) *n.* Formerly, a face or person pale as if from fear; now, one of pale, sallow complexion. —**whey′-faced′** *adj.*

which (hwich) *pron.* & *adj.* **1** Interrogatively, what individual person or thing, or group of persons or things collectively, of a certain number or class: asking for the indication or definite description. In this sense *which* is used both substantively and adjectively, singular and plural: *Which* shall I take? *Which* apple do you want? *Which* mammals are carnivorous? **2** As a relative pronoun, that particular one or ones of a certain number or class of impersonal beings or things: pointing out or definitely fixing upon that which is designated in the antecedent word, phrase, or clause to which it is related: now generally as a substantive, but sometimes as an adjective: He raised his hand, *which* gesture attracted my attention. *Which* as a relative now refers only to animals, without distinction of masculine or feminine, or to things without life; it was formerly used for persons, even in the most exalted sense, as "Our Father, *which* art in heaven." **3** Also relatively, the one that: often equivalent to the use of the interrogative in a dependent question: used substantively or adjectivally: Tell me *which* (or *which* apple) you prefer. [OE *hwelc, hwilc*]

which·ev·er (hwich′ev′ər) *pron.* & *adj.* Whether one or another (of two or of several); no matter which. Also **which′so·ev′er.**

whick·er (hwik′ər) *v.i.* & *n.* Whinny. [Imit.]

whid[1] (hwid) *Scot. n.* A brisk, nimble, scurrying movement. —*v.i.* **whid·ded, whid·ding** To move nimbly: said of small animals.

whid[2] (hwid) *Scot. n.* **1** A fib; lie. **2** A quarrel. **3** A word. —*v.i.* **whid·ded, whid·ding** To tell a lie; fib.

whid·ah bird (hwid′ə) An African weaverbird (subfamily *Viduinae*), the male of which has the tail greatly lengthened in the breeding season: formerly called *widow bird.* Also **whid′ah, whidah finch**: also spelled *whydah.* [Alter. of *widow bird*; infl. in form by *Whidah* former name of Ouidah, a seaport in French West Africa, near which this bird is commonly found]

WHIDAH BIRD
(From 12 to 14 inches over all)

whiff (hwif) *n.* **1** Any sudden or slight gust or puff of air. **2** A gust or puff of odor: a *whiff* of onions. **3** A sudden expulsion of breath or smoke from the mouth; a puff. **4** An inhalation, as of smoke. —*v.t.* **1** To drive or blow with a whiff or puff. **2** To exhale or inhale in whiffs. **3** To smoke, as a pipe. —*v.i.* **4** To blow or move in whiffs or puffs. **5** To exhale or inhale whiffs. [Alter. of ME *weffe* an offensive odor; imit.] —**whiff′er** *n.*

whif·fet (hwif′it) *n. Colloq.* **1** A trifling, useless person; whippersnapper: in slight contempt. **2** A small, snappish dog. **3** A little whiff. [? Dim. of WHIFF]

whif·fle (hwif′əl) *v.* **·fled, ·fling** *v.i.* **1** To blow with puffs or gusts; shift about, as the wind. **2** To vacillate; veer. —*v.t.* **3** To blow or dissipate with or as with a puff. [Freq. of WHIFF]

whif·fler (hwif′lər) *n.* **1** One who fluctuates or shuffles in argument; a trifler. **2** One who whiffs tobacco. **3** A piper; fifer. —**whif′·fler·y** *n.*

whif·fle·tree (hwif′əl·trē′) *n.* A swingletree: also called *whippletree.* [Var. of WHIPPLETREE]

whig[1] (hwig) *v.i. Scot.* To drive onward; move along easily; jog.

whig[2] (hwig) *n. Dial.* **1** Sour whey. **2** Buttermilk. [Var. of OE *hweg* whey]

Whig (hwig) *n.* **1** An American colonist who supported the Revolutionary War in the 18th century: opposed to *Tory*; later, a member of a party opposed to the Democratic and succeeded by the Republican party in 1856. **2** A member of the Liberal party in England in the 18th and 19th centuries, as opposed to a *Tory* or *Conservative.* **3** In earlier usage, a Presbyterian rebel of the west of Scotland in the 17th century: thus named in derision; also, after the Restoration (1660), a Roundhead, as opposed to a Cavalier. —*adj.* Consisting of or supported by Whigs. [Prob. short for WHIGGAMORE] —**Whig′gish** *adj.* —**Whig′gish·ly** *adv.* —**Whig′gish·ness** *n.*

Whig·ga·more (hwig′ə·môr, -mōr) *n.* **1** A member of a body of insurgents who in 1648 marched on Edinburgh and opposed the compromise with Charles I. **2** In the later 17th century, a Scotch Presbyterian; a Whig (def. 3). Also **Whig′a·more.** [Prob. <dial. E (Scottish) *whiggamaire* < *whig* a cry to urge on a horse + *mere* a horse]

Whig·ger·y (hwig′ər·ē) *n. pl.* **·ger·ies** The doctrines of Whigs. Also **Whig′gism.**

whig·ma·lee·rie (hwig′mə·lir′ē) *n. Scot.* A small or useless ornament; gewgaw; also, a whim. Also **whig′ma·lee′ry, whig′me·lee′rie.**

while (hwīl) *n.* **1** A short time; also, a period of time, or time in general: Stay and rest a *while.* **2** Time or pains expended on a thing; trouble; labor: only in the phrase *worth while* or *worth one's while.* —**between whiles** From time to time. —**the while** At the same time: He went about his work and sang *the while.* —*conj.* **1** During the time that; as long as. **2** At the same time that; although: *While* he found fault, he also praised. **3** *Colloq.* Whereas: This man is short, *while* that one is tall. **4** *Brit. Dial.* Until; till. —*v.t.* **whiled, whil·ing** To cause to pass lightly and pleasantly; spend; pass: usually with *away*: to *while* away the time. [OE *hwīl*]

whiles (hwīlz) *Archaic* or *Dial. adv.* Occasionally; at intervals. —*conj.* While; during the time that.

whi·lom (hwī′ləm) *Archaic adj.* Being once upon a time; former. —*adv.* **1** Formerly; at one time. **2** At times. [OE *hwīlum* at times, dative pl. of *hwīl* a while]

whilst (hwīlst) *conj.* While: an old form still widely used, especially in England. [ME *whilest* < *whiles,* genitive of WHILE + *-t*]

whim (hwim) *n.* **1** A sudden, unexpected, and unreasonable deviation of the mind from its usual or natural course; caprice; freak. **2** An old form of mine hoist, run by horsepower. [Short for earlier *whim-wham* a trifle, ? < Scand. Cf. ON *hvima* wander with the eyes.]

Synonyms: caprice, crotchet, fancy, freak, humor, kink, quirk, vagary, whimsy, wrinkle. See FANCY.

whim·brel (hwim′brəl) *n.* A small northern curlew with a white rump, especially a species (*Numenius phaeopus*) of northern portions of the eastern hemisphere. [? <obs. *whimp* whimper, prob. imit. of its cry]

whim·per (hwim′pər) *v.i.* To cry or whine with plaintive broken sounds. —*v.t.* To utter with a whimper. —*n.* A low, broken, whining cry; whine. [Imit.] —**whim′per·er** *n.* —**whim′per·ing** *n.* —**whim′per·ing·ly** *adv.*

whim·si·cal (hwim′zi·kəl) *adj.* **1** Having eccentric ideas; capricious. **2** Oddly constituted; fantastic; quaint. See synonyms under FICKLE, ODD, QUEER. **—whim′si·cal·ly** *adv.* **—whim′·si·cal·ness** *n.*

whim·si·cal·i·ty (hwim′zi·kal′ə·tē) *n. pl.* **·ties** **1** Whimsicalness. **2** A singularity. **3** A quaint, fanciful, or odd idea or its expression.

whim·sy (hwim′zē) *n. pl.* **·sies** **1** A whim; caprice; freak. **2** Tenuously fanciful humor. Also **whim′sey.** See synonyms under WHIM. [Prob. related to WHIM]

whin[1] (hwin) *n.* Furze; gorse. [Prob. <Scand. Cf. Dan. & Norw. *hvine* a kind of grass.]

whin[2] (hwin) *n.* Whinstone. [< dial. E (Scottish) *quin*; ult. origin uncertain]

whin·chat (hwin′chat) *n.* A small, Old World, thrushlike singing bird (*Saxicola rubetra*), streaked with brown above and rufous below. [< WHIN[1] + CHAT[1]]

whine (hwīn) *v.* **whined, whin·ing** *v.i.* **1** To utter a low, plaintive, nasal sound expressive of grief or distress. **2** To complain in a mean or childish way. *—v.t.* **3** To utter with a whine. *—n.* The act or sound of whining; any peevish complaint. [OE *hwīnan* whiz] **—whin′er** *n.* **—whin′ing·ly** *adv.* **—whin′y** *adj.*

whinge (hwinj) *v.i.* **whinged, whinge·ing** *Austral. Slang* To complain; whine.

whing·er (hwing′ər) *n. Brit. Dial.* A dirk, used at meals or as a weapon; a hanger. See HANGER. Also **whing′ar.** [Prob. var. of WHINYARD]

whin·ny[1] (hwin′ē) *v.* **·nied, ·ny·ing** *v.i.* To neigh, especially in a low or gentle way. *—v.t.* To express with a whinny. *—n. pl.* **·nies** The cry or call of a horse; a neigh. [<WHINE]

whin·ny[2] (hwin′ē) *adj.* **·ni·er, ·ni·est** Abounding in whin or furze. [<WHIN[1]]

whin·stone (hwin′stōn′) *n.* Any very hard, dark-colored rock, as basalt or chert. [<WHIN[2] + STONE]

whin·yard (hwin′yərd) *n. Dial.* **1** One of certain ducks, especially the pochard. **2** A hanger or sword. [Earlier *whyneherd,* ? <OE *hwīnan* whiz; the duck is so called because of the swordlike shape of its bill]

whip (hwip) *v.* **whipped** or **whipt, whip·ping** *v.t.* **1** To strike with a lash, rod, strap, etc. **2** To punish by striking thus; flog. **3** To drive or urge with lashes or blows: with *on, up, off,* etc. **4** To strike in the manner of a whip: The wind *whipped* the trees. **5** To attack with scathing criticism; berate; flay. **6** To beat, as eggs or cream, to a froth. **7** To seize, move, jerk, throw, etc., with a sudden motion: with *away, in, off, out,* etc. **8** In fishing, to make repeated casts upon the surface of (a stream, etc.). **9** To wrap (rope, cable, etc.) with light line so as to prevent chafing or wear; serve. **10** To wrap or bind about something. **11** To form, as a flat seam, by laying two selvages of a fabric together and sewing with a loose overcast or overhand stitch. **12** *U.S. Colloq.* To defeat; overcome, as in a contest. **13** *Naut.* To hoist by means of a whip (def. 5). *—v.i.* **14** To go, come, move, or turn suddenly and quickly: with *away, in, off, out,* etc. **15** To thrash about in a manner suggestive of a whip: pennants *whipping* in the wind. **16** In fishing, to make repeated casts with rod and line. **—to whip in** **1** To keep from scattering, as hounds in a hunt. **2** To keep together or united, as a political party. **—to whip up** **1** To excite; arouse. **2** *Colloq.* To prepare quickly, as a meal. *—n.* **1** An instrument consisting of a lash attached to a handle, used for driving draft animals or for administering punishment. **2** One who handles a whip expertly; a driver. **3** A stroke, blow, or cut with a whip. **4** A member of a legislative body appointed unofficially to enforce the discipline and look after the interests of his party: often called **party whip;** also, a call made upon members of a legislature by such a person to bring or keep them in their places at a given time, as when a vote or division may be expected. **5** *Mech.* A simple form of hoisting apparatus, consisting of a rope passing over an elevated single pulley, and used for lifting light objects. **6** One who operates such an apparatus. **7** A huntsman who whips in the hounds to control them; a whipper-in. **8** *Electr.* A vibrating spring that whips back and forth, closing different circuits in electrical apparatus. **9** A dish or dessert containing cream or eggs whipped to a froth: prune *whip.* **10** A thrashing motion, as of a rope or wire suddenly broken. **11** Flexibility in the shaft of a golf club. **12** An arm of a windmill. **13** *Obs.* or *Scot.* An attack of illness; also, a sudden movement; a single swift attack or blow. [ME *wippen, hwippen.* Cf. MDu. *wippen* swing, leap, dance.]

whip·cord (hwip′kôrd′) *n.* **1** A strong, hard-twisted, sometimes braided hempen cord, used in making whiplashes. **2** A cord of catgut. **3** A twill-weave fabric, similar to gabardine, but with a more pronounced diagonal rib on the right side: used for riding habits and other outdoor garments.

whip·graft (hwip′graft′, -gräft′) *v.t. Bot.* To graft by fitting a tongue cut on the cion to a slit cut slopingly in the stock. **—whip′graft′·age, whip′graft′ing** *n.*

whip·hand (hwip′hand′) *n.* **1** The hand that wields the whip; in riding or driving, the right hand. **2** An instrument or means of mastery; advantage: She, not he, has the *whiphand.*

whip·lash (hwip′lash′) *n.* The flexible striking part of a whip.

whiplash injury An injury to the upper spine or base of the brain caused by a sudden jolting of the neck, as in an automobile collision.

whip·per (hwip′ər) *n.* One who whips.

whip·per-in (hwip′ər·in′) *n.* **1** In hunting, one employed to assist the huntsman and to enforce obedience among the hounds. **2** A political or parliamentary whip.

whip·per·snap·per (hwip′ər·snap′ər) *n.* A pretentious but insignificant person. [? Extension of *whipsnapper* a cracker of whips]

whip·pet (hwip′it) *n.* **1** A swift dog resembling an English greyhound in miniature, characterized by a long, narrow head, long arched back, smooth, close coat, and a long, tapering tail. **2** A small, light, speedy tank used in World War I: also **whippet tank.** **3** Anything suggestive of a whippet, as in size, speed, etc. [Dim. of WHIP; so called with ref. to its rapid movement]

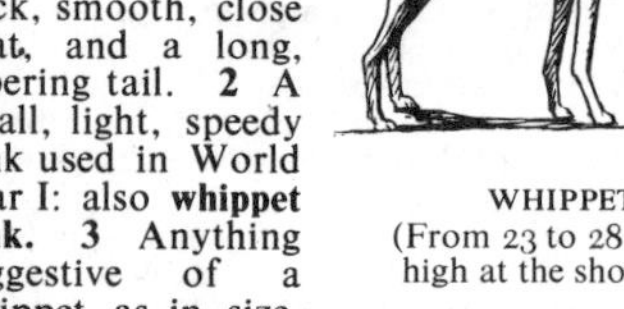

WHIPPET
(From 23 to 28 inches high at the shoulder)

whip·ping (hwip′ing) *n.* **1** The act of one who whips; castigation; state or fact of being flogged or defeated. **2** Material used to bind the head of a rope, or to bind the head to the shaft of a golf club.

whipping boy Formerly, a boy brought up as companion to a prince or other noble youth, and punished in his stead for all misdeeds; now, anyone who receives punishment deserved by another.

whipping post The fixture to which those sentenced to flogging are secured; hence, legal punishment by flogging.

Whip·ple (hwip′əl), **George Hoyt,** born 1878, U.S. pathologist. **—William,** 1730–85, American Revolutionary general; signed Declaration of Independence.

whip·ple·tree (hwip′əl·trē′) *n.* A swingletree. [Prob. <WHIP]

whip·poor·will (hwip′ər·wil) *n.* A small nocturnal bird (*Caprimulgus vociferus*), allied to the goatsuckers, common in the eastern United States. [Imit. of its reiterated cry]

whip·saw (hwip′sô′) *n.* A thin, narrow, tapering ripsaw about six feet long. *—v.t.* **·sawed, ·sawed** or **·sawn, ·saw·ing** **1** To saw with a whipsaw. **2** In faro, to beat (an opponent) in two bets, one to win and one to lose, at the same time. **3** To get the best of (an opponent) in spite of every effort he makes.

whip scorpion Any of various scorpionlike arachnids (family *Thelyphonidae*) having an abdomen terminating in a slender appendage like a whiplash, and lacking a sting; especially, the vinegarroon.

whip·stall (hwip′stôl′) *Aeron. n.* The stalled condition of a sharply climbing airplane in which the nose whips violently downward. *—v.i.* To bring about or go into a whipstall.

whip·stitch (hwip′stich′) *v.t.* To sew or gather with overcast stitches, as the turned edge of a ruffle; overcast. *—n.* **1** An overcast stitch in whipping an edge or seam. **2** A tailor.

whip·stock (hwip′stok′) *n.* That part of a whip to which the lash is attached; a whip handle.

whipt (hwipt) Alternative past tense and past participle of WHIP.

whip·worm (hwip′wûrm′) *n.* A nematode (*Trichuris trichiura*), with the posterior part of the body thickened: found in the human cecum.

whir (hwûr) *v.t.* & *v.i.* **whirred, whir·ring** To fly, move, or whirl with a buzzing sound. *—n.* **1** A whizzing, swishing sound, as that caused by the sudden rising of birds. **2** Confusion; bustle. Also **whirr.** [Prob. <Scand. Cf. Dan. *hvivre.* Akin to WHIRL.]

whirl (hwûrl) *v.i.* **1** To turn or revolve rapidly, as about a center. **2** To turn away or aside quickly. **3** To move or go swiftly. **4** To have a sensation of spinning: My head *whirls.* *—v.t.* **5** To cause to turn or revolve rapidly. **6** To carry or bear along with a revolving motion: The wind *whirled* the dust into the air. **7** *Obs.* To hurl. *—n.* **1** A swift rotating or revolving motion. **2** Something whirling, as a cloud of dust. **3** Confusion; turmoil. [Prob. <ON *hvirfla* revolve. Akin to WARBLE[1].]

whirl-a·bout (hwûrl′ə·bout′) *n.* Anything that turns swiftly around or about; a whirligig.

whirl·er (hwûr′lər) *n.* **1** One who or that which whirls. **2** A rotating hook or reel used in ropemaking.

whirl·i·gig (hwûr′lə·gig′) *n.* **1** Any toy or small device that revolves rapidly on an axis. **2** A merry-go-round. **3** Anything that performs quick revolutions or moves in a cycle: the *whirligig* of time. **4** Any of a family (*Gyrinidae*) of water beetles that frequent the surface of smooth water and move in swift circles: also **whirligig beetle.** **5** A trifling ornament, as one used by printers; also, a fanciful notion. [< *whirly* (<WHIRL) + GIG[1] (def. 4)]

whirl·pool (hwûrl′po͞ol′) *n.* **1** An eddy or vortex where water moves with a gyrating sweep, as from the meeting of two currents. **2** Any disturbance from such causes, whether accompanied by vortical motion or not.

whirl·wind (hwûrl′wind′) *n.* **1** A moving atmospheric vortex; a funnel-shaped column of air, with a rapid circular and upward spiral motion around a vertical or inclined axis, causing waterspouts, sand pillars, and dust whirls. **2** Any violent rushing or rotatory movement. See synonyms under CYCLONE. *—adj.* Extremely swift or impetuous: a *whirlwind* courtship.

whirl·y·bird (hwûr′lē·bûrd′) *n. Colloq.* A helicopter. [< *whirly* (<WHIRL) + BIRD]

whir·ry (hwûr′ē) *v.t.* & *v.i.* **·ried, ·ry·ing** *Scot.* To hurry.

whish[1] (hwish) *v.i.* To move with a sibilant, whistling sound. *—n.* A swishing sound like that made by cutting the air with a pliant rod. [Imit.]

whish[2] (hwish) *interj.* Hush! silence! Also **whisht** (hwisht). [Alter. of HUSH; infl. in form by WHISHT]

whisht (hwisht, hwist, wisht; *Scot.* hwusht) *Scot. v.t.* To hush. *—v.i.* To be silent. *—n.* The slightest sound; a whisper. **—to hold one's whisht** To be or remain silent.

whisk (hwisk) *v.t.* **1** To bear along or sweep with light movements, as of a small broom or a fan: often with *away* or *off*: to *whisk* flies away. **2** To cause to move with a quick sweeping motion. **3** To beat or mix with a quick movement, as eggs, cream, etc. *—v.i.* **4** To move quickly and lightly. *—n.* **1** A light stroke; a sudden, sweeping movement. **2** A little broom or brush. **3** A little bunch, as of straw, feathers, etc.; wisp. **4** A small culinary instrument for rapidly whipping (cream, etc.) to a froth. **5** A neckerchief of lawn or lace formerly worn by women. [Prob. <Scand. Cf. Dan. *viske* wipe, rub.]

whisk·broom (hwisk′bro͞om′, -bro͝om′) *n.* A small, short-handled broom for brushing clothing, etc.

whisk·er (hwis′kər) *n.* **1** *pl.* The hair that grows on the sides of a man's face, as distinguished from that on his lips, chin, and throat; loosely, the beard or any part of the beard; also, formerly, a mustache. **2** A hair from the whiskers or beard. **3** One of the long, bristly hairs on the sides of the mouth of some animals, as the cat, or a similar formation of bristles, as about the mouth of a bird; a vibrissa. 4 One who or that which whisks; formerly, a switch. 5 One of two small projecting spars or booms on the side of a bowsprit, to extend the jib or flying-jib guys: also **whisker boom.** —**whisk′ered, whisk′er·y** *adj.* —**whisk′er·less** *adj.*

whisk grass Zacatón.

whis·ky (hwis′kē) *n. pl.* **·kies** 1 An alcoholic liquor obtained by the distillation of a fermented starchy compound, usually a grain. Whisky is often named (sometimes improperly) from the substance from which it is made, as **corn whisky, rye whisky,** etc.; or from the place or country of production, as **Bourbon whisky, Irish whisky,** etc. 2 A drink or portion of whisky. Compare USQUEBAUGH. —*adj.* Pertaining to or made of whisky. Also **whis′·key.** [Short for *usquebaugh* <Irish *uisgebeatha,* lit., water of life < *uisge* water + *beatha* life]

whis·ky-jack (hwis′kē·jak′) *n.* The gray or Canada jay (*Perisoreus canadensis*), common in the northern forests of North America, about lumber camps, etc. [Alter. of earlier *whisky-john,* alter. of Algonquian (Cree) *wiskatjan*]

whis·per (hwis′pər) *n.* 1 A low, soft, sibilant voice; articulated but not sonant breath; also, a low, rustling sound, as of waves or leaves. See VOICE. 2 A whispered utterance; secret communication; hint; insinuation. —*v.i.* 1 To speak in a whisper. 2 To talk cautiously or furtively; plot or gossip. 3 To make a low, rustling sound, as leaves. —*v.t.* 4 To utter in a whisper. 5 To speak to in a whisper. [OE *hwisprian*] —**whis′per·er** *n.* —**whis′per·ing** *n.* & *adj.* —**whis′per·ing·ly** *adv.* —**whis′·per·y** *adj.*

whist[1] (hwist) *n.* A game of cards played by four persons with a full pack of 52 cards, opposite players being partners: all the cards are played in each hand, the highest card of the suit led played in each of the 13 tricks, or a card of the trump suit, or the highest trump played, winning such trick. Every trick above the sixth counts one point. See CONTRACT BRIDGE under BRIDGE[2]. [Alter. of earlier *whisk*; ult. origin unknown]

whist[2] (hwist) *interj.* Hush! be still! —*adj.* Silent or quiet; mute. See also WHISHT. [Prob. imit.]

whis·tle (hwis′əl) *n.* 1 A device for producing a shrill, musical sound, operated on the principle of forcing a current of air, steam, or the like, through a pipe or tube of narrowed aperture or against a thin edge. 2 A musical sound, more or less shrill, made without the use of the vocal cords, by sending the breath through a small orifice formed by contracting the lips; also, the act of making this sound. 3 The sound produced by a whistle, or any sound suggestive of it, as the sound of wind rushing by an object, or of a flying missile, or the shrill cry of some birds. 4 A summons or call made by a whistle: The dog comes at his master's *whistle.* 5 *Slang* The mouth and throat: to wet one's *whistle.* 6 The short, loud cry of a male moose or elk. —*v.* **·tled, ·tling** *v.i.* 1 To make a sound or series of sounds like a whistle. 2 To cause a sharp, shrill sound by swift passage through the air, or by passage past an edge or through an orifice: The bullets *whistled* over our heads. 3 To blow or sound a whistle. —*v.t.* 4 To produce, as a tune or melody, by whistling. 5 To call, manage, or direct by whistling. 6 To send with a whistling sound. —**to whistle for** To go without; fail to get. [OE *hwistle* a shrill pipe]

whis·tler (hwis′lər) *n.* 1 One who or that which whistles. 2 A large gray marmot (*Marmota caligata*) of NW North America. 3 One of various birds, as the American goldeneye or the English widgeon: so called from the noise of their wings in flight.

Whis·tler (hwis′lər), **James Abbott McNeill,** 1834–1903, U.S. artist and etcher. —**Whis·tle·ri·an** (hwis·lir′ē·ən) *adj.*

whistle stop *U.S. Colloq.* A small town, where a train stops only on signal. —**whis·tle-stop** (hwis′əl·stop′) *adj.*

whistling swan See under SWAN.

whit (hwit) *n.* The smallest particle; speck: usually with a negative: not a *whit* abashed. See synonyms under PARTICLE. [Var. of WIGHT[1], as used in phrases *any wight, no wight,* OE *ænig wiht, nān wiht* a little amount]

Whit·by (hwit′bē) A port on the North Sea in the North Riding, NE York, England.

white (hwīt) *adj.* **whit·er, whit·est** 1 Having the color produced by reflection of all the rays of the solar spectrum, as from a finely powdered surface; having the color of new snow: opposed to *black.* 2 Light or comparatively light in color; specifically, light-colored as opposed to *red*: *white* wine. 3 Bloodless; ashen: *white* with rage. 4 Very fair; blond. 5 Silvery, hoary, or gray, as with age. 6 Covered with snow; snowy. 7 Made of silver; also unburnished, as silverwork. 8 Habited in white clothing: *white* nuns. 9 Not intentionally wicked or evil; not malicious or harmful: a *white* lie. 10 Figuratively, free from spot or stain; innocent: a *white* soul. 11 Incandescent; being at white heat. 12 Blank; unmarked by ink: said of a space in an advertisement or the like. 13 Belonging to a racial group characterized by light-colored skin; especially, Caucasian. 14 Of, pertaining to, or controlled by white men: the *white* power structure. 15 *Colloq.* Fair and honorable; straightforward; honest. 16 Propitious; auspicious: a rare meaning. 17 In certain European countries, constitutional; conservative, as a party; opposed to the radicals or revolutionaries. See synonyms under PALE[2]. —*n.* 1 That color seen when sunlight is reflected without sensible absorption of any of the visible rays of the spectrum; the color in the scale of grays which is entirely without hue and is the opposite of *black.* 2 The state or condition of being white; whiteness; figuratively, innocence; truth. 3 The white or light-colored part of something; specifically, the albumen of an egg, or the white part of the eyeball. 4 Anything that is white or nearly white, as cloth or garments; in the plural, a white uniform or outfit: The sailor wore his summer *whites.* 5 White wine. 6 A white paint or pigment; hence, by comparison, a color approaching pure white in its effect. 7 In chess or checkers, the white or light men, or the player who has them. 8 *pl.* Flour made from the finest and whitest part of the wheat. 9 *pl. Printing* Blank spaces in a picture, plate, mold, etc. 10 In archery, the outermost ring of a target; also, a hit on that ring, scoring one point. 11 A member of the so-called white race. 12 In some European countries, a member of a party opposed to the radicals or revolutionaries; a conservative. 13 *pl. Pathol.* Leukorrhea. 14 A breed of animal, especially a swine, that is white in color. —*v.t.* **whit·ed, whit·ing** 1 To make white; whiten; bleach. 2 *Printing* To make or leave blank spaces in, as between lines or about an illustration: often with *out*: to *white* out a column. [OE *hwīt*]

White (hwīt), **Andrew,** 1832–1918, U.S. educator, historian, and diplomat. —**Byron Raymond,** born 1917, U.S. lawyer; associate justice of the Supreme Court 1962–. —**E(lwyn) B(rooks),** born 1899, U.S. writer and editor. —**Gilbert,** 1720–93, English naturalist and antiquary. —**Peregrine,** 1620–1704, first child of English parentage born in New England. —**Stanford,** 1853–1906, U.S. architect. —**William Allen,** 1868–1944, U.S. editor.

white alkali 1 The product obtained from soda ash during the manufacture of carbonate of soda, dissolved in water, clarified, and freed from moisture by evaporation. 2 Pure soda ash.

white ant A small, whitish, isopterous insect, the termite, closely resembling the true ant in general appearance and social habits: it exists in tropical and warmer temperate regions, and does much damage to wooden structures, furniture, etc., by boring. For illustration see INSECTS (injurious). —**to white ant** *Austral.* To undermine or sabotage.

white-ant·er (hwīt′ant′ər) *n. Austral.* One who undermines or sabotages.

white·bait (hwīt′bāt′) *n.* 1 The young of various clupeoid fishes, especially of sprat and herring, served as a delicacy. 2 One of various species of silversides of fresh and salt waters of the United States.

white bear The polar bear.

white·beard (hwīt′bird′) *n.* An old man with a white or gray beard.

white birch 1 The North American birch (*Betula papyrifera*) with thin, white bark resembling paper. 2 The common European birch (*Betula pendula, B. pubescens*), having an ash-colored bark; also, a related Asian species (*B. platyphylla*).

WHITE BIRCH
a. Leaf. *b.* Fruit.
(Tree 20 to 30 feet tall, rarely 40)

white book In some European countries and in Japan, a formal report issued by a government on some special subject; in England an alternate of the bluebook: so called from the colors of the bookbinding.

white brant The snow goose.

white bryony A species of bryony (*Bryonia alba*) common in Europe.

white·cap (hwīt′kap′) *n.* 1 A foam-crested wave. 2 One of several birds having white about the head.

White·cap (hwīt′kap′) *n.* Formerly, in the Middle West and southward, one of a lawless, secret organization of men, who, under the pretense of regulating public morals, imposed lynch-law rule upon individuals who incurred their ill will: so named from their white caps or hoods.

white cedar 1 An evergreen tree (*Chamaecyparis thyoides*) of the cypress family, growing in moist places along the Atlantic coast. 2 Its soft, easily worked wood. 3 The arborvitae.

White·chap·el (hwīt′chap·əl) A district in Stepney borough, eastern London, England; the older Jewish quarter.

white clover A common variety (*Trifolium repens*) of clover, with white flowers.

white coal Water considered as a source of power.

white-col·lar (hwīt′kol′ər) *adj.* Pertaining to or designating salaried workers in occupations which demand a well-dressed appearance.

white comb A contagious disease of poultry, caused by a fungus (*Lophophyton gallinae*), and marked by the formation of grayish patches on the comb and a breaking off of the feathers.

white crane The whooping crane (*Grus americana*) of North America, which is pure white when adult.

white curlew The white ibis (*Guara alba*) of the southern United States.

whit·ed sepulcher (hwī′tid) A hypocrite; a person with a pleasing outward aspect, but corrupted thoughts. *Matt* xxiii 27.

white elephant 1 A rare pale-gray variety of Asian elephant held sacred by the Burmese and Siamese. 2 Anything rare, expensive, and difficult to keep; a burdensome possession.

white-eye (hwīt′ī′) *n.* 1 The white-eyed vireo (*Vireo griseus*) of North America. 2 Any of numerous small singing birds (*Zosterops* and related genera), mostly of the Old World tropics: named from the circle of white feathers around the eye.

white-eyed (hwīt′īd′) *adj.* Having the iris of the eye white or colorless, as an albino.

white-faced (hwīt′fāst′) *adj.* 1 Pallid in countenance; pale. 2 Having a white mark or spot on the face or front of the head: the *white-faced* hornet. 3 Having a white facing or exposed surface, as a skirt.

white feather A mark of cowardice, full-blooded gamecocks being said to have no white feathers.

White·field (hwīt′fēld), **George,** 1714–70, English preacher; one of the founders of Methodism.

white·fish (hwīt′fish′) *n. pl.* **·fish** or **·fish·es** 1 A salmonoid food fish (genus *Coregonus*) of North America, living mostly in lakes and having teeth minute or absent. 2 One of various other species of fish, as the menhaden, the European whiting, or the silver salmon (*Oncorhynchus kisutch*). 3 A tropical marine food fish of California (*Caulolatilus princeps*). 4 The young of the bluefish. 5 The beluga.

white flag 1 A flag of truce. 2 A signal of surrender when hoisted over a fortified position or a body of men.

white flax Gold-of-pleasure.
white-foot·ed mouse (hwīt′fŏŏt′id) The deer mouse.
White Friar A Carmelite: so called from the color of his cloak.
White·fri·ars (hwīt′frī′ərz) The neighborhood surrounding the site of a former Carmelite monastery in Fleet Street, London.
white frost Hoar frost.
white gerfalcon The gerfalcon in the phase when its plumage is of a conspicuous, highly prized white color.
white gold An alloy of gold with a white metal, usually nickel and zinc, sometimes palladium.
white·gum (hwīt′gum′) *n.* **1** An Australian eucalyptus with a white bark. **2** The American sweetgum.
White·hall (hwīt′hôl) **1** A former royal palace near Westminster Abbey. **2** A street in Westminster, London, where a number of government offices are located. **3** The British government.
White·head (hwīt′hed), **Alfred North,** 1861–1947, English mathematician and philosopher, active in the United States.
white heat **1** The temperature at which a body becomes incandescent. **2** A condition of extreme anger or emotional strain.
White·horse (hwīt′hôrs) The capital of Yukon Territory on the upper Yukon River. Also **White Horse.**
white-hors·es (hwīt′hôr′siz) *n. pl.* Foam-crested waves; white caps (def. 1).
white-hot (hwīt′hot′) *adj.* **1** Exhibiting the condition of white heat. **2** *Colloq.* Extremely angry.
White House, The **1** The official residence of the president of the United States, at Washington, D.C.: a white building in American colonial style, officially called the *Executive Mansion.* **2** The executive branch of the United States government.
white lead **1** A poisonous white pigment composed of lead carbonate and hydrated lead oxide and prepared by several processes: also called *ceruse.* **2** Native carbonate of lead; cerusite. See LEAD.
white leather Whitleather.
white lie See under LIE.
white-liv·ered (hwīt′liv′ərd) *adj.* **1** Having a pale and feeble look. **2** Base; cowardly; envious.
white lupine A white-flowered variety *(Lupinus albus)* of lupine, grown in Europe for forage.
white·ly (hwīt′lē) *adv.* With a pale appearance; so as to look white.
white mahogany Primavera.
white man **1** A person belonging to a racial group characterized by light-colored skin: territory first settled by *white men* in 1740. **2** A male member of the so-called white race.
white man's burden The alleged duty of the white peoples to spread culture among the so-called backward peoples of the world: phrase originated by Rudyard Kipling.
white maple Any of certain maples having a whitish bark, as the silver maple *(Acer saccharinum)* and red maple *(A. rubrum),* both of North America.
white matter *Anat.* That portion of the brain and spinal cord that is composed mainly of medullated nerve fibers, giving it a white appearance: contrasted with *gray matter.*
white meat **1** The light-colored meat or flesh of animals, as veal or the breast of turkey. **2** *Obs.* Food made from milk, butter, cheese, eggs, and other animal products.
white metal See under METAL.
White Mountains **1** A range of the Appalachians in north central New Hampshire; highest peak, 6,288 feet. **2** A range of mountains in eastern Arizona; highest point, 11,590 feet. **3** A range of mountains in eastern California and SW Nevada; highest point, 14,242 feet.
whit·en (hwīt′n) *v.t.* & *v.i.* To make or become white; blanch; bleach. See synonyms under BLEACH. **— whit′en·er** *n.*
white·ness (hwīt′nis) *n.* **1** The state of being white; freedom from stains or darkness of surface. **2** Pallor from emotion or from illness. **3** Cleanness or pureness of heart; innocence.
White Nile See NILE.
white oak **1** A North American oak *(Quercus alba)* of the eastern United States, with long leaves having from five to nine entire, rounded lobes. **2** Either of two related species, the **swamp white oak** *(Q. bicolor)* and the **Oregon white oak** *(Q. garryana).* **3** The British oak *(Q. petraea).* **4** The wood of any species of white oak.

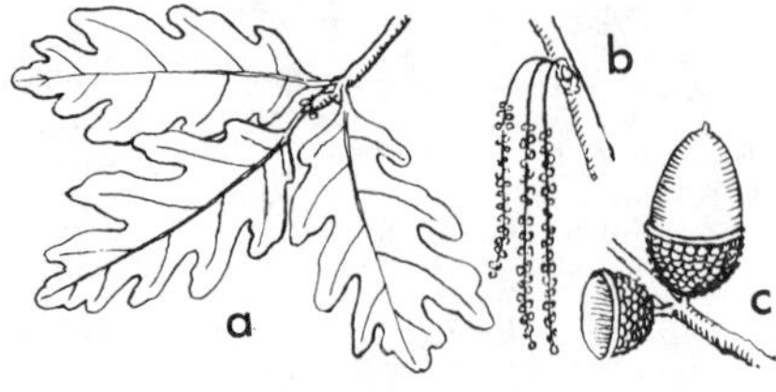

WHITE OAK
a. Leaf. *b.* Blossom. *c.* Acorn.

white of egg Egg white.
white·out (hwīt′out′) *n. Meteorol.* An atmospheric condition in arctic regions in which a blending of clouds and snow cover produces a uniform milky whiteness characterized by the absence of shadow and the invisibility of all but very dark objects.
white paper A government publication on some subject of less importance than that treated in a white book or a bluebook. See WHITE BOOK, BLUEBOOK.
White Pass A pass in the Coast Mountains, on the border between SE Alaska and NW British Columbia; elevation 2,888 feet.
white pepper See under PEPPER.
white perch A small food fish *(Morone americana)* related to the sea basses, found in Atlantic coastal waters and sometimes landlocked in streams of the United States.
white pine **1** A pine *(Pinus strobus)* widely distributed in eastern North America, with soft, bluish-green leaves in clusters of five. The cone and tassel of this tree are the State emblem of Maine. **2** The light, soft wood of this tree. **3** Any of several varieties of this pine.
white-pine weevil (hwīt′pīn′) A weevil *(Pissodes strobi)* of NE North America which feeds on the leading shoots of white pine and other conifers. For illustration see INSECTS (injurious).
white plague *Pathol.* Tuberculosis, especially of the lungs.
white poplar **1** A large, rapidly growing Old World tree *(Populus alba),* often planted in the United States for shade or for its ornamental leaves, which are green above and clothed with a silvery-white down beneath; the silver poplar. **2** The aspen.
white potato The common potato.
white rabbit The varying hare.
white race The Caucasoid ethnic division of mankind.
white rat **1** Any albino rat. **2** One of a special breed of albino Norway rats much used in biological and medical experimentation.
White River **1** A river in northern and eastern Arkansas and SW Missouri, flowing 690 miles to the Mississippi. **2** A river in Nebraska and southern South Dakota, flowing 507 miles NE to the Missouri.
White Russian See under RUSSIAN.
White Russian S.S.R. See BELORUSSIAN SOVIET SOCIALIST REPUBLIC. Also **White Russia.**
White Sands National Monument A government reservation in southern New Mexico; 219 square miles; established 1933.
white sapphire A variety of translucent, colorless corundum.
White Sea An inlet of the Barents Sea in NW European U.S.S.R.; 36,680 square miles. *Russian* **Be·lo·e Mo·re** (bye′lə·yə mô′ryə).
white slave A girl forced into or held in prostitution. **— white-slave** (hwīt′slāv′) *adj.*
White-slave Act The Mann Act.
white-slav·er (hwīt′slā′vər) *n.* One who procures for or engages in white-slavery.
white-slav·er·y (hwīt′slā′vər·ē) *n.* The business or practice of forced prostitution.
white·smith (hwīt′smith′) *n.* **1** A worker in white metals, as a tinsmith. **2** A finisher, polisher, or galvanizer of iron. Compare BLACKSMITH.
white spruce A spruce *(Picus glauca)* of Canada and the northern United States.
white squall *Meteorol.* A small whirlwind occurring in the tropics, having no accompanying cloud and often making ocean waters foam-white.
white·tail (hwīt′tāl′) *n.* **1** The white-tailed deer. **2** The wheatear.
white-tailed deer (hwīt′tāld′) The common North American deer *(Odocoileus virginianus),* having a moderately long tail white on the underside: also called *Virginia deer.*
white·throat (hwīt′thrōt′) *n.* One of various Old World warblers, especially the common or **greater whitethroat** *(Sylvia cinerea),* with gray head, white throat, and rufous wings.
white-throat·ed sparrow (hwīt′thrō′tid) A common North American sparrow *(Zonotrichia albicollis),* with a prominent white patch on the throat.
white tie **1** A white bow tie, worn with a swallowtail coat. **2** A swallowtail coat and its correct accessories: the phrase is used on invitations, etc., to indicate formal attire.
white trash Poor whites: an offensive term.
white turnip The common turnip *(Brassica rapa).*
white vitriol Hydrated zinc sulfate, $ZnSo_4 \cdot 7H_2O$, widely used in medicine as an emetic, astringent, and antiseptic.
white·wash (hwīt′wosh′, -wôsh′) *n.* **1** A mixture of slaked lime and water, sometimes with salt, whiting, and glue added, used for whitening walls, etc. **2** A toilet preparation for whitening the skin. **3** Figuratively, a report falsely ascribing virtues, suppressing adverse evidence, etc. **4** A failure to score in a game. **—** *v.t.* **1** To coat with whitewash. **2** To gloss over; hide. **3** *Colloq.* In sports, to defeat without allowing the losing side to score. See synonyms under BLEACH. **— white′wash′er** *n.*
white wax Paraffin.
white·weed (hwīt′wēd′) *n.* The oxeye daisy.
white whale The beluga.
white-wing (hwīt′wing′) *n.* **1** One of the members of the Department of Sanitation of New York City: so called because they formerly wore white uniforms. **2** Any person who wears a white uniform. **3** The surf duck.
white-winged dove (hwīt′wingd′) A dove *(Melopelia asiatica)* of the SW United States with a conspicuous white patch on the wings.
white·wood (hwīt′wŏŏd′) *n.* **1** Any of various trees yielding a whitish timber, as the basswood, the tuliptree, the cottonwood, the wild cinnamon, etc. **2** The wood of these trees.
Whi·tey (hwī′tē, wī′-) *n. pl.* **·teys** *U.S. Slang* **1** The white man, especially when considered as the oppressor or enemy of the Negro. **2** A white man: an offensive term. Also **whi′·tey.**
whith·er (hwith′ər) *adv.* **1** As a relative, to which or what: approaching a conjunctive use: the village *whither* we went. **2** As an interrogative, to which or to what place. **3** Wheresoever; whithersoever. **4** To what degree or extent. [OE *hwider*]
whith·er·so·ev·er (hwith′ər·sō·ev′ər) *adv.* To whatever place.
whit·ing[1] (hwī′ting) *n.* A pure white chalk, levigated and washed for use in making putty and whitewash, as a pigment, and for polishing.
whit·ing[2] (hwī′ting) *n.* **1** A small European gadoid food fish *(Merlangus merlangus)* without a barbel. **2** The hake (def. 1). **3** Any of several silvery sciaenoid fishes (genus *Menticirrhus*), especially the **Carolina whiting** *(M. americanus),* common on the coast of the southern United States. **4** The menhaden. [<MDu. *wijting* < *wit* white]
whit·ish (hwī′tish) *adj.* Somewhat white or, especially, very light gray. **— whit′ish·ness** *n.*
whit·leath·er (hwit′leth′ər) *n.* Leather tawed with alum to render it pliable; white leather. [<WHITE + LEATHER]
whit·low (hwit′lō) *n. Pathol.* An inflammatory tumor, especially on the terminal phalanx of a finger, seated between the epidermis and true skin; a felon. [ME *whitflaw,* appar. <WHITE + FLAW[1]]
Whit·man (hwit′mən), **Marcus,** 1802–47, U.S. missionary massacred by Indians in Oregon. **— Walt,** 1819–92, U.S. poet.

Whit-Mon·day (hwit′mun′dē, -dā) *n.* The Monday next following Whitsunday: observed in England as a holiday. Also **Whit′mon′day, Whit′sun-Mon′day.** [On analogy with WHITSUNDAY]

Whit·ney (hwit′nē), **Eli,** 1765–1825, American inventor. — **Gertrude,** 1877?–1942, *née* Vanderbilt, U. S. sculptress. — **Josiah Dwight,** 1819–96, U. S. geologist. — **William Dwight,** 1827–94, U. S. philologist; brother of Josiah Dwight.

Whit·ney (hwit′nē), **Mount** A peak of the southern Sierra Nevada Range in eastern California; 14,496 feet; highest point in the United States.

whit·rack (hwit′rak) *n. Dial. & Scot.* A weasel. [ME *whitratt* <WHITE + RAT]

Whit·sun (hwit′sən) *n.* Whitsunday: frequently used in composition: *Whitsun*-ale, *Whitsun*-week. [ME *witsonen, whitsone* < *whitsondei* WHITSUNDAY]

Whit·sun·day (hwit′sun′dē, -dā) *n.* The seventh Sunday after Easter: a church festival commemorating Pentecost. [OE *Hwīta Sunnandæg,* lit., white Sunday; so called from the white robes worn by recently baptized persons on that day]

Whit·sun-week (hwit′sən·wēk′) *n.* The week that begins with Whitsunday. Also **Whit′·sun·tide′** (-tīd′).

Whit·ta·ker (hwit′ə·kər), **Charles E(vans),** born 1901, U. S. jurist; associate justice of the U. S. Supreme Court 1957–1962.

whit·ter (hwit′ər) *n. Scot.* **1** A copious draft of liquor, etc. **2** Anything weak. **3** Chatter; loquacity. **4** A token; sign.

Whit·ti·er (hwit′ē·ər) A port of southern Alaska on Prince William Sound.

Whit·ti·er (hwit′ē·ər), **John Greenleaf,** 1807–1892, U. S. poet.

Whit·ting·ton (hwit′ing·tən), **Richard,** 1358?–1423, English tradesman; lord mayor of London, 1397, 1406, and 1419.

whit·tle[1] (hwit′l) *v.* **·tled, ·tling** *v.t.* **1** To cut or shave bits from (wood, a stick, etc.). **2** To make or shape by carving or whittling. **3** To reduce or wear away by paring a little at a time: with *down, off, away,* etc.: to *whittle* down costs. — *v.i.* **4** To whittle wood, usually as an aimless diversion. See synonyms under CUT. [< *n.*] — *n. Dial. & Scot.* A knife; especially, a sheath knife worn at the belt, or any large knife. [Alter. of ME *thwitel* <OE *thwitan* cut] — **whit′tler** *n.*

whit·tle[2] (hwit′l) *n. Dial.* **1** A blanket. **2** A shaggy mantle formerly worn by country-women. Also **whittle shawl.** [OE *hwītel* < *hwīt* white]

whit·tlings (hwit′lingz) *n. pl.* The fine chips and shavings made with a whittle or by a whittler.

Whit-Tues·day (hwit′to͞oz′dē, -dā, -tyo͞oz′-) *n.* The day after Whit-Monday. Also **Whit′sun-Tues′day.** [On analogy with WHITSUNDAY]

whiz (hwiz) *v.* **whizzed, whiz·zing** *v.i.* **1** To make a hissing and humming sound while passing rapidly through the air. **2** To move or pass with such a sound. — *v.t.* **3** To cause to whiz. — *n.* **1** A sibilant sound with some sonant character, such as is produced by a missile passing through the air. **2** *Slang* Any person or thing of extraordinary excellence or ability. **3** *Slang* A bargain. **4** *Slang* A celebration; a spree. Also **whizz.** [Imit.]

whiz-bang (hwiz′bang′) *n. Slang* A high-explosive shell; also, a firecracker that explodes with a loud noise. Also **whizz′-bang′.**

who (ho͞o) *pron. possessive case* **whose;** *objective case* **whom** **1** As an interrogative, which or what person or persons. **2** As a relative, that: pointing out or fixing upon a particular person or persons, and identifying the subject or object in a relative clause with that of the principal clause. **3** As a compound relative, he, she, or they that: *Who* steals my purse steals trash. — **as who should say** As one who should say; as if one should say. [OE *hwa, hwā*]

◆ In modern usage, *who* as a relative is applied only to persons, *which* only to animals or to inanimate objects, *that* to persons or things indifferently. *Whose* is correctly used as the possessive of *which,* as well as of *who,* especially where the phrase *of which* would seem awkward: the man *whose* house was sold; a peak *whose* (*of which* the) summit seeks the sky. The use of *whom* as an interrogative pronoun in initial position, as in *Whom* did you see?, is supported by some grammarians, but the more natural *Who* did you see? *Who* did you give the book to? are in wider use and are now considered acceptable. However, when used after a verb or preposition, *whom* is still required, as in To *whom* did you give it? You saw *whom*? See also usage note under THAT (pronoun).

whoa (hwō) *interj.* Stop! stand still! [Var. of HO]

who·dun·it (ho͞o·dun′it) *n. Colloq.* A type of mystery fiction or dramatic production which challenges the reader or auditor to detect the perpetrator of a crime. [<WHO + DONE + IT; coined by Donald Gordon in 1930 in *American News of Books*]

who·ev·er (ho͞o·ev′ər) *pron.* Any one without exception; any person who.

whole (hōl) *adj.* **1** Containing all the parts necessary to make up a total; undivided and undiminished; entire; complete. **2** Having all the essential or original parts in their proper constitution; unbroken and uninjured; sound; intact. **3** Specifically, in or having regained sound health; hale. **4** Having the same parents; full, as opposed to *half-*: a *whole* brother. **5** *Colloq.* Each one of (something); all: He ate the *whole* batch of cookies. **6** *Math.* Integral. — **on the whole** Taking one thing with another. — **out of whole cloth** Fabricated; made up, without foundation in truth or fact, as a story or lie. — *n.* **1** All the parts or elements entering into and making up a thing. **2** An organization of parts making a unity or system; an organism. See synonyms under AGGREGATE, MASS[1]. ◆ Homophone: *hole.* [OE (Northumbrian) *hol,* var. of *hāl.* Related to HALE[2].]

whole blood **1** Full blood. **2** Blood as taken direct from the body, especially that used in transfusions.

whole brother See under BROTHER.

whole gale *Meteorol.* A gale of force 10 on the Beaufort scale.

whole·heart·ed (hōl′här′tid) *adj.* Done or experienced with all earnestness; characteristically sincere, sound, generous, or kind. — **whole′heart′ed·ly** *adv.* — **whole′heart′ed·ness** *n.*

whole-hog (hōl′hôg′, -hog′) *adj. Colloq.* Thoroughgoing.

whole hog *Colloq.* **1** The whole of anything: to believe in the *whole hog,* accept the *whole hog.* **2** Reliance or approval; trust: We don't put the *whole hog* on them. — **to go the whole hog** *Colloq.* To do something thoroughly; become involved without reservation.

whole milk Milk containing all its constituents: distinguished from *skim milk.*

whole·ness (hōl′nis) *n.* Entireness; completeness.

whole note *Music* A semibreve. See NOTE *n.* (def. 12).

whole number *Math.* A unit or a number composed of units; an integral number or integer: distinguished from *fraction* and *mixed number.*

whole·sale (hōl′sāl′) *n.* The sale of goods by the piece or in large bulk or quantity: opposed to *retail.* — *adj.* **1** Selling in quantity, not at retail: a *wholesale* druggist. **2** Done in buying and selling in quantity: the *wholesale* trade. **3** Pertaining to wholesale trade: the *wholesale* price. **4** Hence, made or done on a large scale; made or done indiscriminately: *wholesale* murder. — *adv.* In bulk or quantity; hence, indiscriminately: to berate the medical profession *wholesale.* — *v.t. & v.i.* **·saled, ·sal·ing** To sell at wholesale. [ME *holesale* < *by hole sale* in large quantities] — **whole′sal′er** *n.*

whole sister See under SISTER.

whole snipe See under SNIPE.

whole·some (hōl′səm) *adj.* **1** Tending to promote health; salubrious; healthful: *wholesome* air or food. **2** Favorable to virtue and well-being; salutary; sound; beneficial. **3** Healthy; physically, mentally, and morally sound: a *wholesome* girl. **4** Indicative or characteristic of health: *wholesome* red cheeks. **5** Safe; free from danger or risk: This is not a *wholesome* situation. **6** *Obs.* Auspicious; favorable. See synonyms under HEALTHY. [ME *holsum* < *hol* WHOLE + OE *-sum* -SOME[1]] — **whole′some·ly** *adv.* — **whole′some·ness** *n.*

whole-souled (hōl′sōld′) *adj.* Feeling or acting with one's whole heart; devoted; generous.

whole-wheat (hōl′hwēt′) *adj.* Made from wheat grain and bran.

who'll (ho͞ol) Who will; who shall: a contraction.

whol·ly (hō′lē, hōl′lē) *adv.* **1** Completely; totally. **2** Exclusively; only.

whom (ho͞om) *pron.* The objective case of WHO. [OE *hwam,* dative of *hwā* who]

whom·ev·er (ho͞om′ev′ər), **whom·so** (ho͞om′·sō′), **whom·so·ev·er** (ho͞om′sō·ev′ər) Objective cases of WHOEVER, WHOSO, etc.

whoop (ho͞op, hwo͞op, hwo͝op) *v.i.* **1** To utter loud cries, as of excitement, rage, or exultation. **2** To hoot, as an owl. **3** To make a loud, gasping inspiration, as after a paroxysm of coughing. — *v.t.* **4** To utter with a whoop or whoops. **5** To call, urge, chase, etc., with whoops; hoot. — **to whoop up** **1** To arouse enthusiasm in or for; ballyhoo. **2** To raise, as a price, or sum of money. — **to whoop it** (or **things**) **up** **1** *Slang* To make noisy revelry. **2** To arouse enthusiasm. — *n.* **1** A shout of excitement, encouragement, or exultation; also, a hoot of derision. **2** A signal halloo or a guiding call, as to incite dogs or men in the chase. **3** A loud, convulsive inspiration after a paroxysm of coughing in whooping cough; a sonorous indrawing of breath. **4** An owl's hoot. — *interj.* Hurrah! halloo! [Imit.]

whoop·ee (hwo͞o′pē, hwo͞op′ē) *Slang interj.* An exclamation of joy, excitement, etc. — *n.* A hilarious, festive time. — **to make whoopee** To have a noisy, festive time. [<WHOOP]

whoop·er (ho͞o′pər, hwo͞o′pər, hwo͝op′ər) *n.* **1** One who or that which whoops. **2** A large Old World swan (*Cygnus cygnus*). **3** The white crane: so called from its loud cry.

whoop·ing cough (ho͞o′ping, ho͞op′ing) *Pathol.* A contagious respiratory disease of bacterial origin chiefly affecting children, marked in its final stage by recurrent paroxysms of violent coughing, ending with a whoop; pertussis.

whooping crane See under CRANE.

whop (hwop) *Colloq. n.* A blow or fall, or the resulting noise. — *v.* **whopped, whop·ping** *v.t.* **1** To strike or beat. **2** To defeat convincingly. — *v.i.* **3** To drop or fall suddenly; flop. Also spelled *whap.* [Var. of WAP[1]]

whop·per (hwop′ər) *n. Colloq.* **1** One who whops. **2** Something large or remarkable, especially a surprising falsehood. Also spelled *whapper.*

whop·ping (hwop′ing) *adj.* Unusually large; excessively exaggerated.

whore (hôr, hōr) *n.* A prostitute. — *v.* **whored, whor·ing** *v.i.* **1** To have illicit sexual intercourse, especially with a prostitute. **2** To be a whore. — *v.t.* **3** To make a whore of; corrupt; debauch. ◆ Homophone: *hoar.* [OE *hōre,* prob. <ON *hōra*]

whore·dom (hôr′dəm, hōr′-) *n.* **1** The practice of illicit sexual intercourse. **2** Whores collectively. **3** In the Bible, idolatry. [Prob. <ON *hōrdōmr*]

whore·house (hôr′hous′, hōr′-) *n.* A house of prostitution.

whore·mas·ter (hôr′mas′tər, -mäs′-, hōr′-) *n.* **1** A procurer; pander. **2** A whoremonger.

whore·mon·ger (hôr′mung′gər, -mong′-, hōr′-) *n.* **1** A man who has intercourse with whores. **2** A pander.

whore·son (hôr′sən, hōr′-) *n. Obs.* The son of a whore: commonly, a term of contempt. [ME *hores son,* trans. of AF *fiz a putain*]

whor·ish (hôr′ish, hōr′ish) *adj.* Addicted to unlawful sexual indulgences; unchaste; lewd. — **whor′ish·ly** *adv.* — **whor′ish·ness** *n.*

whorl (hwûrl, hwôrl) *n.* **1** The flywheel of a spindle; wherve. **2** *Bot.* A set of leaves, etc., on the same plane with one another; distributed in a circle; a verticil. **3** *Zool.* A turn or volution, as of a spiral shell. **4** Any of the convoluted ridges of a fingerprint. [ME *wharwyl,*

WHORL (*def. 2*)

whorwhil, appar. vars. of WHIRL; infl. in form by *wharve*]

whorled (hwûrld, hwôrld) *adj.* Furnished with or arranged in whorls.

whort (hwûrt) *n.* The whortleberry, or its fruit. Also **whor·tle** (hwûr'təl). [OE *horta* a whortleberry]

whor·tle·ber·ry (hwûr'təl·ber'ē) *n. pl.* **·ries** **1** A European variety of blueberry (*Vaccinium myrtillus*); the bilberry. **2** Its blue-black fruit. **3** The huckleberry. [Dial. var. of HURTLEBERRY]

whose (hōōz) The possessive case of WHO and often of WHICH. See under WHO. [OE *hwæs,* genitive of *hwā* who]

whose·so·ev·er (hōōz'sō·ev'ər) Possessive case of WHOSOEVER.

who·so (hōō'sō) *pron.* Whoever; any person who. [Reduced form of OE *swā hwā swā,* generalized form of *hwā* who]

who·so·ev·er (hōō'sō·ev'ər) *pron.* Any person whatever; who; whoever.

why (hwī) *adv.* **1** For what cause, purpose, or reason; wherefore: used interrogatively: *Why* did you go? **2** Because of which; for which; the reason or cause for which: used relatively: I don't know *why* he went; I know no reason *why* he went. — *n. pl.* **whys** **1** An explanatory cause; reason; cause. **2** A puzzling problem; riddle; enigma. — *interj.* An introductory expletive, sometimes denoting surprise. [OE *hwī, hwȳ,* instrumental case of *hwæt* what]

whyd·ah (hwid'ə), **whydah bird** See WHIDAH BIRD.

wi' (wi) *prep. Scot.* With.

wich (wich) See WITCH[2].

Wich·i·ta (wich'ə·tô) *n.* A member of a North American Indian confederacy of Caddoan linguistic stock, formerly inhabiting Oklahoma and Texas.

Wich·i·ta (wich'ə·tô) A city on the Arkansas River in south central Kansas; a center of the food and oil industries.

Wichita River A river in Texas, flowing 250 miles NE to the Red River.

wick[1] (wik) *n.* A band of loosely twisted or woven fibers, as in a candle or lamp, acting by capillary attraction to convey oil or other illuminant to a flame. [OE *wēoca*] — **wick'·ing** *n.*

wick[2] (wik) *Scot. v.t.* In curling, to strike (a stone) obliquely. — *n.* **1** In curling, an opening surrounded by stones already played. **2** A creek; inlet.

wick[3] (wik) *n.* A village or town: now mostly in composition, often as **-wich:** *Woolwich.* [OE *wīc,* appar. <L *vicus*]

wick·ed (wik'id) *adj.* **1** Evil in principle and practice; vicious; sinful; depraved. **2** Mischievous; roguish. **3** Noxious; pernicious. **4** Troublesome; painful. See synonyms under BAD, CRIMINAL, IMMORAL, INFAMOUS, PROFANE, SINFUL. [ME < *wikke, wicke,* appar. <OE *wicca* a wizard] — **wick'ed·ly** *adv.*

wick·ed·ness (wik'id·nis) *n.* **1** The quality of being wicked; moral depravity; sin; vice; crime: opposed to *goodness.* **2** A wicked thing or act; wicked conduct: to work *wickedness.*

wick·er (wik'ər) *adj.* Made of twigs, osiers, etc. — *n.* **1** A pliant young shoot or rod; twig; osier. **2** Ware made of such shoots. [Prob. <Scand. Cf. dial. Sw. *viker* < *vika* bend.]

wick·er·work (wik'ər·wûrk') *n.* A fabric or texture, as a basket, made of woven twigs, osiers, etc.; basketwork.

wick·et (wik'it) *n.* **1** A small door or gate subsidiary to or made within a larger entrance. **2** A small opening in a door. **3** A small sluicegate in a canal lock or at the end of a millrace. **4** In cricket, an arrangement of three upright rods called *stumps* set near together, with two crosspieces called *bails* laid over the top; also, the place at which the wicket is set up; the right or turn of each batsman at the wicket; the playing pitch between the wickets: a fast *wicket*; an inning that is not finished or not begun: The eleven won by three *wickets,* that is, the two men at bat and one yet to go in. **5** In croquet, an arch, usually of wire. [<AF *wiket,* OF *guichet,* prob. <Gmc.]

wick·et-keep·er (wik'it·kē'pər) *n.* In cricket, the fielder stationed immediately behind the wicket which is being bowled at.

wick·i·up (wik'ē·up) *n.* A loosely constructed hut of certain North American Indian tribes: distinguished from *tepee* or *wigwam*: also spelled *wikiup.* [<Algonquian. Cf. Sac and Fox *wikiyap* a lodge.]

Wick·liffe (wik'lif), **Wic·lif, Wic·liff·ite,** etc. See WYCLIF, etc.

Wick·low (wik'lō) A maritime county of eastern Leinster province, Ireland; 782 square miles; county town, Wicklow.

wic·o·py (wik'ə·pē) *n. pl.* **·pies** **1** The leatherwood. **2** The basswood. **3** Any of several species of willow herb. [<Algonquian. Cf. Cree *wikupiy.*]

wid·der·shins (wid'ər·shinz) See WITHERSHINS.

wid·dle (wid'l) *v.t.* & *n. Dial.* & *Scot.* Wriggle; struggle; waddle.

wid·dy[1] (wid'ē) *n. pl.* **·dies** *Scot.* A halter of withes; withy; hangman's noose; hence, the gallows. Also **wid'die.**

wid·dy[2] (wid'ē) *n. pl.* **·dies** *Dial.* Widow. [Var. of WITHY]

wide (wīd) *adj.* **wid·er, wid·est** **1** Having relatively great extent between sides; broad, as opposed to *narrow.* **2** Extended far in every direction; ample; spacious: a *wide* expanse. **3** Having a specified degree of width or breadth: an inch *wide.* **4** Distant from the desired or proper point by a great extent of space; remote; wild: *wide* of the mark. **5** Figuratively, having intellectual breadth; considering questions from all points of view; liberal: a man of *wide* views. **6** Fully open; expanded or extended: *wide* eyes. **7** *Phonet.* Lax. **8** Comprehensive; inclusive: *wide* learning. **9** Loose; ample; roomy: *wide* breeches. **10** In the stock exchange, exhibiting a considerable range between high and low, or bid and offered prices: a *wide* opening. See synonyms under LARGE. — *n.* **1** In cricket, a ball bowled too far over or on either side of the wicket to be within the batsman's reach. **2** Breadth of extent; also, a broad, open space. — *adv.* **1** To a great distance; extensively. **2** Far from the mark. **3** To the greatest extent; fully open. [OE *wīd*] — **wide'ly** *adv.* — **wide'ness** *n.*

◆ Various self-explaining compounds have *wide* as their first element: **wide'-arched', wide'-branched', wide'-brimmed',** etc.

wide-an·gle lens (wīd'ang'gəl) *Phot.* A type of camera lens designed and ground to permit an angle of view wider than that of the ordinary lens, or more than 50 degrees.

wide-a·wake (wīd'ə·wāk') *adj.* Marked by vigilance and alertness; keen. See synonyms under ALERT, VIGILANT. — *n.* A soft, broad-brimmed felt hat: also **wide'-a·wake' hat.**

wide-eyed (wīd'īd') *adj.* **1** With the eyes wide open, as if gazing intently in wonder or surprise. **2** Marked by an innocent readiness to believe or admire; uninformed or unsophisticated: *wide-eyed* trust of any stranger she happened to meet.

wid·en (wīd'n) *v.t.* & *v.i.* To make or become wide or wider. See synonyms under AMPLIFY. — **wid'en·er** *n.*

wide-o·pen (wīd'ō'pən) *adj.* **1** Opened wide: The gates are *wide-open.* **2** *Colloq.* Remiss in the enforcement of laws which regulate various forms of vice, as gambling, prostitution, etc.: a *wide-open* city.

wide-spread (wīd'spred') *adj.* Extending over a large space or territory; general: a *widespread* belief. Also **wide'spread'.**

widge·on (wij'ən) *n.* Any of a genus (*Mareca*) of river ducks with short bill and wedge-shaped tail; especially, the **American widgeon,** or baldpate (*M. americana*), esteemed as a game bird: also spelled *wigeon.* [Cf. MF *vigeon* a wild duck]

Wi·dor (vē·dôr'), **Charles Marie,** 1845–1937, French organist and composer.

wid·ow (wid'ō) *n.* **1** A woman who has lost her husband by death and has not remarried. **2** In some card games, an additional hand dealt to the table; also, a kitty. **3** *Printing* An incomplete line of type ending a paragraph; especially, a single line or less at the top of a page or column. — *v.t.* **1** To make a widow of; deprive of a husband: usually in the past participle: a woman *widowed* by war. **2** To deprive of something desirable; bereave. **3** *Rare* To survive as the widow of. **4** *Rare* To recognize as a widow; give the rights of a widow to. — *adj.* Widowed. [OE *widewe, wuduwe*]

widow bird A whidah bird. [<NL *Vidua,* genus name, trans. of Pg. *viuva,* lit., a widow]

wid·ow·er (wid'ō·ər) *n.* A man whose wife is dead, and who has not married again. [ME *widwer* < *widwe,* OE *widewe* a widow]

wid·ow·hood (wid'ō·hŏŏd) *n.* The state or condition of being a widow, or, rarely, of being a widower; also, the period during which one is a widow.

widow's cruse An endless or inexhaustible supply: in allusion to the stories in I *Kings* xvii 10–16, and II *Kings* iv 1–7.

widow's mite See MITE[2].

widow's peak See PEAK[1].

width (width) *n.* **1** Dimension or measurement of an object taken from side to side, or at right angles to the length. **2** Wideness; the state or fact of being wide. **3** Something that has width; specifically, in dressmaking, one of the several pieces of material used in making a garment. [<WIDE, on analogy with *breadth*]

width·wise (width'wīz') *adv.* In the direction of the width; from side to side. Also **width'·way'** (-wā'), **width'ways'.**

Wi·du·kind (vē'dōō·kint) See WITTEKIND.

wiel (wēl) *n. Scot.* An eddy; pool.

Wie·land (vē'länt), **Christoph Martin,** 1733–1813, German poet, novelist, and translator. — **Heinrich,** 1877–1957, German chemist.

wield (wēld) *v.t.* **1** To use or handle, as a weapon or instrument, especially with full command and effect. **2** To exercise (authority, power, influence, etc.). **3** *Obs.* To exercise authority over; command. [Fusion of OE *wealdan* cause and OE *wildan* rule] — **wield'·a·ble** *adj.* — **wield'er** *n.*

wield·y (wēl'dē) *adj.* **wield·i·er, wield·i·est** Easily handled; wieldable: opposed to *unwieldy.*

Wie·licz·ka (vye·lech'kä) A town 7 miles SE of Cracow, Poland; a salt-mining center since the 11th century.

Wien (vēn) The German name for VIENNA.

Wien (vēn), **Wilhelm,** 1864–1928, German physicist.

wie·ner (wē'nər) *n. U.S.* A kind of sausage, often shorter than a frankfurter, made of beef and pork: often called *weenie.* Also **wie·ner·wurst** (wē'nər·wûrst', *Ger.* vē'nər·vŏŏrst'). [Short for G *wiener-(wurst)* Vienna (sausage)]

Wie·ner schnit·zel (vē'nər shnit'səl) A breaded veal cutlet, seasoned or garnished in any of several ways, as with capers, anchovies, a fried egg, or the like. [<G <*Wiener* Viennese + *schnitzel* a cutlet, dim. of *schnitz* a slice < *schneiden* cut]

Wieprz (vyepsh) A river in central Poland, flowing 194 miles NW to the Vistula.

Wies·ba·den (vēs'bä·dən) The capital of Hesse, West Germany, on the Rhine west of Frankfurt: site of a famous spa.

wife (wīf) *n. pl.* **wives** (wīvz) **1** A woman joined to a man in lawful wedlock; a spouse: the correlative of *husband.* ◆ Collateral adjective: *uxorial.* **2** A grown woman; adult female: usually in composition or in certain phrases: *housewife,* old *wives'* tales. — **to take (a woman) to wife** To marry (a woman). [OE *wīf*] — **wife'dom, wife'hood** *n.* — **wife'less** *adj.* — **wife'ly** *adj.*

wife-carl (wīf'kärl) *n. Scot.* A man who meddles with household affairs, especially such as belong naturally to women.

wig (wig) *n.* An artificial covering of hair for the head, so constructed as to form an imitation of the natural growth or to act as a coiffure. — *v.t.* **wigged, wig·ging** **1** To furnish with a wig or wigs. **2** *Brit. Colloq.* To censure severely; berate or scold, especially in public. [Short for PERIWIG]

BARRISTER'S WIG

wig·an (wig'ən) *n.* A stiff, canvaslike fabric used for stiffening the borders of garments. [from *Wigan,* where originally made]

Wig·an (wig'ən) A county borough in south central Lancashire, England.

wig·eon (wij'ən) See WIDGEON.

wigged (wigd) *adj.* Furnished with or wearing a wig.

wig·ger·y (wig'ər·ē) *n. pl.* **·ger·ies** **1** A peruke;

wig; also, wigs collectively. 2 Excessive formality; red-tapism. 3 The material of a wig; false hair.
Wig·gin (wig′in), **Kate Douglas,** *née* Smith, 1856–1923, U. S. educator and novelist.
wig·ging (wig′ing) *n. Brit. Colloq.* A rebuke; a scolding.
wig·gle (wig′əl) *v.t. & v.i.* **·gled, ·gling** To move or cause to move quickly and irregularly from side to side; squirm; wriggle. — *n.* The act of wiggling. [? <MLG *wiggelen*] —**wig′gly** *adj.*
wig·gler (wig′lər) *n.* 1 One who or that which wiggles. 2 The larva of a mosquito; a wiggletail.
Wig·gles·worth (wig′əlz·wûrth), **Michael,** 1631–1705, American divine and poet.
wig·gle·tail (wig′əl·tāl′) *n.* 1 The larva of a mosquito. 2 A tadpole.
wight[1] (wīt) *n.* A person; creature: usually an archaic or humorous term. [OE *wiht* a creature]
wight[2] (wīt) *adj. Obs.* Full of prowess; strong and valiant; active; swift. [<ON *vigt,* neut. of *vigr* able to fight]
Wight (wīt), **Isle of** An island in the English Channel just off the southern coast of England, comprising an administrative county of Hampshire; 147 square miles.
Wig·man (vikh′män), **Mary,** born 1886, German dancer; leading pioneer of modern dance.
Wig·ner (wig′nər), **Eugene Paul,** born 1902, U. S. physicist born in Hungary.
Wig·town (wig′tən) A county in SW Scotland; 487 square miles; county town, Wigtown. Also **Wig′town·shire** (-shir).
wig·wag (wig′wag′) *v.t. & v.i.* **·wagged, ·wag·ging** 1 To move briskly to and fro; wag. 2 To send (a message) by hand flags, torches, etc. — *n.* The act or art of signaling with such flags, etc., or the message so sent. [< dial. E *wig* wiggle + WAG[1]] —**wig′wag′·ger** *n.*
wig·wam (wig′wom, -wôm) *n.* 1 A dwelling or lodge of the North American Indians of Algonquian stock, used in the area from Canada to North Carolina and in the Great Lakes regions: commonly an arbor-shaped or conical framework of poles covered with bark, rush matting, or hides. 2 By extension, a family of Indians. 3 A dwelling or lodge of North American Indians of other than Algonquian stock: a misuse by early travelers. 4 *Slang* A public building used for political gatherings, mass meetings, etc. — **the Wigwam** Tammany Hall. [<Algonquian (Ojibwa) *wigwaum,* lit., their dwelling]

WIGWAM
Eastern North American Indian.

wik·i·up (wik′ē·up) See WICKIUP.
Wil·ber·force (wil′bər·fôrs, -fōrs), **William,** 1759–1833, English abolitionist and philanthropist.
Wil·bur (wil′bər) A masculine personal name. [<Gmc., ? resolute protection]
Wil·cox (wil′koks), **Ella,** *née* Wheeler, 1855?–1919, U. S. poet and author.
wild (wīld) *adj.* 1 Inhabiting the forest or open field; not domesticated or tamed; living in a state of nature: a *wild* horse; shy and easily startled: The deer are *wild.* 2 Growing or produced without care or culture; not cultivated: *wild* flowers. 3 Being in the natural state: being without civilized inhabitants or cultivation; desert; waste: *wild* prairies. 4 Living without any civilization and in a rude, savage way; uncivilized: the *wild* men of Borneo. 5 Boisterous; in a bad sense, dissolute; prodigal; in a milder sense, frolicsome and gay. 6 Affected with or originating violent disturbances, as of the elements or of human passions; stormy; turbulent: a *wild* night, a *wild* crowd. 7 Showing reckless want of judgment; rashly imprudent; extravagant: a *wild* speculation. 8 Fantastically irregular or disordered; odd in arrangement or effect; strange or weird: a *wild* imagination, *wild* dress. 9 Eager and excited, as by reason of joy, fear, desire, etc.: She was *wild* with delight. 10 Excited to frenzy or distraction; roused to fury or desperation; crazed or crazy: The mosquitoes are driving me *wild.* 11 Being or going far from the proper course or from the mark aimed at; erratic; wide of the mark: a *wild* ball, a *wild* guess. 12 In some card games, having its value arbitrarily determined by the dealer or holder: to play poker with fours *wild.* 13 *Slang* **a** Terrific; great: a *wild* party. **b** Showy; jazzy: a *wild* necktie. See synonyms under ABSURD, BLEAK[1], FIERCE, INSANE, ROMANTIC, TURBULENT, VIOLENT, WANTON. — *n.* An uninhabited or uncultivated place; a waste; wilderness. — **the wild** The wilderness; also, the free, natural, wild life: the call of *the wild.* — *adv.* 1 Wildly. 2 Without control; unrestrainedly: The locomotive is running *wild.* [OE *wilde*] — **wild′ly** *adv.* — **wild′ness** *n.*
wild allspice The spicebush.
wild boar The native hog *(Sus scrofa)* of continental Europe, southern Asia, and North Africa, and formerly of Great Britain.
wild brier 1 Any species of rose in the wild state. 2 The dog rose. 3 The sweetbrier.
wild carrot An umbelliferous herb *(Daucus carota)* from which the cultivated carrot is derived; Queen Anne's lace.
wild·cat (wīld′kat′) *n.* 1 A small, undomesticated feline carnivore *(Felis sylvestris)* of Europe, resembling the domestic cat, but larger and stronger. 2 The North American bobcat (genus *Lynx*). 3 One of several other small felines, as the ocelot and serval. 4 Figuratively, an aggressive, quick-tempered person. 5 An unattached locomotive and its tender, used on special work, as when sent out to haul a train, etc. 6 A successful oil well drilled in an area previously unproductive. 7 A tricky or unsound business venture; specifically, a worthless mine. Also **wild cat.** — *adj.* 1 Unsound; risky; especially, financially unsound or risky: a *wildcat* venture. 2 Illegal; made, produced, or carried on without official sanction or authorization. 3 Not running on schedule time; also, running wild or without control, as a railroad train or engine. — *v.t. & v.i.* **·cat·ted, ·cat·ting** To drill for oil in (an area not known to be productive). — **wild′cat′ting** *n. & adj.*
wildcat bank Prior to the passage of the National Bank Act of 1863–64, a bank operating with insufficient capital to redeem its circulating notes.
wildcat bill A note of a wildcat bank.
wildcat mine A worthless mine; especially, one represented to possible investors as being profitably productive.
wildcat strike A strike unauthorized by regular union procedure.
wild·cat·ter (wīld′kat′ər) *n.* 1 A promoter of mines of doubtful value. 2 One who develops oil wells in unproved territory. 3 One who manufactures illicit whisky.
wild cherry Any of certain species of cherry found growing wild; especially, the **wild black cherry** *(Prunus serotina)* and the chokecherry.
Wilde (wīld), **Oscar Fingall O'Flahertie Wills,** 1856–1900, Irish poet and playwright.
wilde·beest (wīld′bēst, wil′də-; *Du.* vil′də·bāst) *n.* A gnu. [<Afrikaans <Du. *wild* wild + *beeste* a beast]
wil·der (wil′dər) *Poetic v.t.* 1 To bewilder. 2 To lead astray; mislead. — *v.i.* 3 To be bewildered. 4 To wander; stray. [Prob. back formation <WILDERNESS] — **wil′der·ment** *n.*
Wil·der (wīl′dər), **Thornton Niven,** 1897–1975, U.S. novelist and playwright.
wil·der·ness (wil′dər·nis) *n.* 1 An uncultivated, uninhabited, or barren region. 2 A waste, as of an ocean. 3 A multitudinous and confusing collection: a *wilderness* of curiosities. 4 *Obs.* Wildness. [OE *wilder* a wild beast (< *wilde* wild + *deor* an animal, deer) + -NESS]
Wil·der·ness (wil′dər·nis), **The** A region in NE Virginia; scene of a Civil War battle, 1864.
wild·fire (wīld′fīr′) *n.* 1 A raging, destructive fire: now generally in phrases like *to spread like wildfire.* 2 A composition of inflammable materials, or the flame produced by it, very hard to put out; Greek fire. 3 A phosphorescent luminousness; ignis fatuus. 4 *Obs.* A spreading inflammation of the skin; erysipelas. 5 A skin disease of sheep with inflammation.
wild flax 1 Toadflax. 2 Gold-of-pleasure.
wild·flow·er (wīld′flou′ər) *n.* 1 Any uncultivated flower. 2 The plant growing it. Also **wild flower.**
wild·fowl (wīld′foul′) *n.* Wild game birds, especially wild ducks and geese. Also **wild fowl.**
wild gean (gēn) 1 A European wild cherry *(Prunus avium),* yielding a fine cabinet wood. 2 Its small dark fruit, the mazzard cherry. [<WILD + dial. E *gean* the wild cherry <OF *guine,* prob. <Gmc.]
wild goose An undomesticated goose, as the English graylag, or the Canada goose.
wild-goose chase (wīld′gōōs′) Pursuit of the unknown or unattainable; a bootless enterprise.
wild honeysuckle The pinkster flower.
wild hyacinth 1 The eastern camas *(Camassia scilloides)* of the United States. 2 The wood hyacinth.
wild indigo Any of a genus *(Baptisia)* of perennial North American herbs, especially one *(B. tinctoria)* having yellow flowers and a root which yields a purgative glycoside.
wild·ing (wīl′ding) *adj.* Growing wild; uncultivated; undomesticated. — *n.* 1 An uncultivated plant; a fruit tree on its own roots growing among grafted trees. 2 A cultivated plant that has sprung up spontaneously; an escape (def. 4). 3 A creature not conforming to type.
wild lettuce 1 A tall, yellow-flowered herb *(Lactuca virosa)* found in the northern United States. 2 The round-leaved wintergreen *(Pyrola rotundifolia).* 3 The prickly lettuce *(Lactuca serriola).*
wild·life (wīld′līf′) *n.* Wild animals, trees, and plants collectively, especially as objects of government conservation. — *adj.* Pertaining to wild animals, trees, and plants collectively.
wild·ling (wīld′ling) *n.* An uncultivated plant or flower; a wild animal. [<WILD + -LING[1]]
wild madder 1 Madder (def. 1). 2 Either of two herbs (genus *Galium*) of the madder family, the white bedstraw *(G. mollugo)* and the dye bedstraw *(G. tinctorium).*
wild mandrake The May apple.
wild mare 1 A nightmare. 2 A see-saw.
wild mustard An annual herb *(Brassica kaber)* of the mustard family, frequently growing as a weed, whose seeds are sometimes used as a substitute for mustard and its leaves cooked as greens: also called *charlock.*
wild oat 1 An uncultivated grass (genus *Avena*); especially, the common European meadow weed *(A. fatua).* 2 *pl.* Indiscretions of youth.
wild olive Any of various trees resembling the olive or bearing an olivelike fruit.
wild pansy The European heartsease *(Viola tricolor),* from which the common garden pansy is derived.
wild parsley 1 Any of a genus *(Lomatium)* of perennial herbs of the carrot family, especially the nine-leaf species *(L. simplex),* valued as a forage plant in the western United States: also called *biscuitroot.* 2 Lovage.
wild parsnip 1 The parsnip in its uncultivated, weedlike form. 2 A perennial herb *(Angelica lyalli)* of the carrot family, resembling the water hemlock but non-poisonous and useful as a forage plant.
wild pink An American catchfly *(Silene caroliniana)* with white or rose-colored flowers and long spatulate or lanceolate flowers.
wild rice 1 A tall aquatic grass of North America *(Zizania aquatica).* 2 The grain of this plant: formerly used as food by North American Indians, now esteemed as a table delicacy: also called *Indian rice.*
wild rose Any of various uncultivated roses of the north temperate zone, as the sweetbrier.
wild rubber Rubber as extracted from the rubber tree (genus *Hevea*) in its wild state.
wild rye A tall perennial grass (genus *Elymus*), widely distributed in temperate regions.
wild sage 1 The sagebrush of the western United States. 2 The Old World vervain sage *(Salvia verbeneca)* known as wild clary.
wild spinach 1 A goosefoot sometimes used as a substitute for spinach. 2 One of several other spinaceous plants.
wild turkey A large North American turkey

(Meleagris gallopavo silvestris) formerly ranging east of the Rocky Mountains from southern Canada to Florida and Mexico, and first domesticated in Mexico.

wild vanilla A smooth, erect, perennial herb *(Trilisa odoratissima)* of the composite family, found in the SE United States. Its leaves give off an odor of vanilla.

wild wall A soundproof movable wall used on motion-picture sets: also called *jockey wall.*

Wild West The western United States, especially in its early period of Indian fighting, pioneer conditions, and lawlessness.

Wild West show A circus or a feature of a circus presenting feats of Indian and cowboy horsemanship; also, a rodeo.

wild·wood (wīld′wŏŏd′) *n.* Natural forest land.

wild yam An uncultivated species of yam *(Dioscorea villosa)* of the eastern United States; the colic root.

wile (wīl) *n.* **1** An act or a means of cunning deception; also, any beguiling trick or artifice. **2** Craftiness; cunning. See synonyms under ARTIFICE. —*v.t.* **wiled, wil·ing 1** To lure, beguile, or mislead. **2** To pass divertingly, as time: usually with *away*: by confusion with *while.* [OE *wīl,* prob. <Scand. Cf. ON *vēl* an artifice.]

Wi·ley (wī′lē), **Harvey Washington,** 1844–1930, U. S. chemist.

Wil·fred (wil′frid) A masculine personal name. Also **Wil′frid.** [<Gmc., willing peace]

wil·ful (wil′fəl) *adj.* **1** Bent on having one's own way; headstrong; self-willed. **2** Resulting from the exercise of one's own will; voluntary; intentional. Also spelled *willful.* See synonyms under PERVERSE. —**wil′ful·ly** *adv.* —**wil′ful·ness** *n.*

Wil·helm (vil′helm) German form of WILLIAM. —**Wilhelm I,** 1797–1888, king of Prussia 1861–88 and emperor of Germany 1871–88. —**Wilhelm II,** 1859–1941, emperor of Germany 1888–1918.

Wil·hel·mi·na (wil′hel·mē′nə) A feminine personal name. Also **Wil·hel·mine** (wil′hel·mēn, *Fr.* vē·lel·mēn′, *Ger.* vil′hel·mē′nə). [Fem. of WILHELM]

—**Wilhelmina,** 1880–1962, queen of the Netherlands 1890–1948; abdicated in favor of her daughter Juliana: full name *Wilhelmina Helena Pauline Maria of Orange-Nassau.*

Wil·helms·ha·ven (vil′helms·hä′fən) A port on the North Sea in former Oldenburg state, Lower Saxony, NW West Germany.

Wil·helm·stras·se (vil′helm·shträ′sə) **1** A street in Berlin on which the German foreign office and government offices were formerly located. **2** Formerly, the German government, especially its foreign policies.

Wilkes (wilks), **Charles,** 1798–1877, U.S. admiral and Antarctic explorer. —**John,** 1727–97, English politician.

Wilkes-Bar·re (wilks′bar·ē) A city on the Susquehanna River in NE Pennsylvania, an industrial and coal-mining center.

Wilkes Land (wilks) Part of Antarctica on the Indian Ocean south of Australia, between Queen Mary Coast and George V Coast; site of the south magnetic pole in its eastern part.

Wil·kins (wil′kinz), **Sir George Hubert,** 1888–1958, Australian aviator and explorer. —**Mary Eleanor** See FREEMAN, MARY E. WILKINS. —**Roy,** born 1901, U. S. civil rights leader for Negroes.

Wil·kin·son (wil′kən·sən), **James,** 1757–1825, American Revolutionary general and politician.

will[1] (wil) *n.* **1** The power of conscious, deliberate action; the faculty by which the rational mind makes choice of its ends of action, and directs the energies in carrying out its determinations; in popular usage, choice, purpose, or directive effort. **2** The act or experience of exercising this faculty; a volition or a choice. **3** Strong determination; practical enthusiasm; energy of character: He works with a *will*; also, self-control. **4** That which has been resolved or determined upon; a purpose. **5** Power to dispose of a matter arbitrarily; discretion. **6** *Law* The legal declaration of a man's intentions as to his estate after his death; the written instrument by which someone declares his desires for the distribution of his property. **7** A conscious inclination toward any end or course; a wish. **8** A request or command. —**at will** As one pleases. —*v.* **willed, will·ing;** third person singular, present indicative **wills** *v.t.* **1** To decide upon; choose. **2** To resolve upon as an action or course; determine to do. **3** To give, devise, or bequeath by a will. **4** To control, as a hypnotized person, by the exercise of will. **5** *Archaic* To have a wish for; desire. —*v.i.* **6** To exercise the will. [OE *willa*] —**will′a·ble** *adj.*

Synonyms (noun): decision, desire, disposition, inclination, resolution, volition, wish. *Will* is a word of wide range of meaning, and both as faculty and act has been the subject of many and various theories; in popular language *will* is often equivalent to *desire* or *inclination,* as when we speak of doing something against our *will. Volition* is a word of scientific precision, denoting the determinative element of *will.*

will[2] (wil) *v.* Present *sing.* & *pl.*: **will** (*Archaic* **thou wilt**); past: **would** (*Archaic* **thou would·est** or **wouldst**) As an auxiliary verb *will* is used with the infinitive without *to,* or elliptically without the infinitive, to express: **1** Futurity: They *will* arrive by dark. ◆ See usage note under SHALL. **2** Willingness or disposition: Why *will* you not tell the truth? **3** Capability or capacity: The ship *will* survive any storm. **4** Custom or habit: He *will* sit for hours and brood. **5** *Colloq.* Probability or inference: I expect this *will* be the main street. —*v.t.* & *v.i.* To wish or have a wish; desire: What *wilt* thou? As you *will.* [OE *willan*]

Wil·lam·ette River (wi·lam′it) A river in NW Oregon, flowing 190 miles north to the Columbia River.

Wil·lard (wil′ərd), **Emma,** 1787–1870, *née* Hart, U. S. pioneer in education for women. —**Frances Elizabeth Caroline,** 1839–98, U. S. temperance advocate.

Will·cocks (wil′koks), **Sir William,** 1852–1932, English engineer.

willed (wild) *adj.* Having a will, especially one of a given character: mostly in composition: self-*willed.*

wil·lem·ite (wil′əm·īt) *n.* A vitreous or resinous orthosilicate of zinc, crystallizing in the hexagonal system and occurring in many colors. [<Du. *willemit,* after *Willem I* William of Orange]

Wil·lem·stad (wil′əm·stät, vil′-) A town on Curaçao, capital of Netherlands Antilles.

will·er (wil′ər) *n.* One who wills.

Willes·den (wilz′dən) A municipal borough in Middlesex, England, NW of London.

wil·let (wil′it) *n.* A large, light-colored shore bird *(Catoptrophorus semipalmatus)* of North America, related to the snipes. [Short for *pill-will-willet,* imit. of the cry of the bird]

will·ful (wil′fəl), **will·ful·ly, will·ful·ness** See WILFUL, etc.

will I, nill I or **will he, nill he** or **will ye, nill ye** Willingly or unwillingly; without choice. See WILLY-NILLY.

Wil·liam (wil′yəm) A masculine personal name. Also *Du.* **Wil·lem** (vil′əm). See also WILHELM. [<Gmc., resolute protection]

—**William I,** 1027–87, invaded England, 1066; king of England 1066–87: known as *William the Conqueror.*

—**William II,** 1056–1100, king of England 1087–1100: known as *William Rufus.*

—**William III,** 1650–1702, stadholder of Holland 1672–1702; invited to England; ruled 1689–1702 jointly with his wife Mary.

—**William IV,** 1765–1837, king of England 1830–37.

—**William of Malmesbury,** 1095?–1143? English historian.

—**William of Orange,** 1533–84, founded the Dutch republic; stadholder 1579–84: called "William the Silent."

Wil·liams (wil′yəms), **Roger,** 1603?–85, English clergyman; founded Rhode Island. —**Roger John,** born 1893, U. S. biochemist. —**Tennessee,** born 1914, U. S. playwright: original name *Thomas Lanier Williams.* —**William Carlos,** 1883–1963, U. S. poet, novelist, playwright, and physician.

Wil·liams·burg (wil′yəmz·bûrg) A town in eastern Virginia; founded in 1693; capital of Virginia (1699–1779); restored to condition of the colonial period.

wil·lies (wil′ēz) *n. pl. Slang* Nervousness; jitters; the creeps: with *the.* [? <WILLY-NILLY; with ref. to a state of indecision]

will·ie·waught (wil′ē·wäkht) *n. Scot.* A draft of liquor. Also **will′ie·waucht.**

will·ing (wil′ing) *adj.* **1** Having the mind favorably inclined or disposed. **2** Answering to demand or requirement; compliant. **3** Gladly proffered or done; hearty. **4** Of or pertaining to the faculty or power of choice; volitional. See synonyms under SPONTANEOUS. —**will′ing·ly** *adv.* —**will′ing·ness** *n.*

Wil·lis (wil′is), **Nathaniel Parker,** 1806–67, U. S. writer and editor.

wil·li·waw (wil′ē·wô) *n.* A sudden, violent blast of wind moving seaward down the slope of a mountainous coast, especially in the Strait of Magellan. [Origin unknown]

Will·kie (wil′kē), **Wendell Lewis,** 1892–1944, U. S. lawyer and political leader.

will-o'-the-wisp (wil′ə·thə·wisp′) *n.* **1** Ignis fatuus. **2** Any elusive or deceptive object. —*adj.* Deceptive; fleeting; misleading. [Earlier *Will with the wisp*]

wil·low (wil′ō) *n.* **1** Any of a large genus *(Salix)* of shrubs and trees related to the poplars, having generally smooth branches and often long, slender, pliant, and sometimes pendent branchlets. **2** The soft white wood of the willow. **3** *Colloq.* Something made of willow wood, especially a baseball or cricket bat. **4** A machine for giving a preliminary cleaning to cotton, flax, hemp, wool, etc., by means of long spikes projecting from a revolving cone or cylinder. —*v.t.* To clean, as cotton, wool, etc., with a willow. —*adj.* Of or pertaining to the willow; made of willow wood. [OE *wilige, welig*] —**wil′low·ish** *adj.*

wil·low·er (wil′ō·ər) *n.* One who or that which willows.

willow herb 1 Any of a genus *(Epilobium)* of perennial herbs of the evening-primrose family, especially the fireweed *(E. angustifolium),* having scattered, willowlike leaves and large, pink flowers. **2** The purple loosestrife *(Lythrum salicaria).*

willow oak 1 An oak *(Quercus phellos)* of the eastern United States, having long, slender, entire leaves resembling willow leaves. **2** The laurel oak *(Q. laurifolia).*

willow pattern A decorative design introduced on household china in England in 1780 and since extremely popular: so called from the willow tree, usually blue on a white background, which appears in the design.

wil·low·ware (wil′ō·wâr′) *n.* China decorated with the willow pattern.

wil·low·y (wil′ō·ē) *adj.* **1** Abounding in willows. **2** Having supple grace of form or carriage. See synonyms under SUPPLE.

will·pow·er (wil′pou′ər) *n.* Ability to control oneself; determination; firmness of mind.

Will·stät·ter (vil′shtet·ər), **Richard,** 1872–1942, German organic chemist.

will·y[1] (wil′ē) *adj. Obs.* Willing; also, propitious. [Cf. ON *viljugr*]

wil·ly[2] (wil′ē) *v.t.* **·lied, ·ly·ing** To willow, as cotton, flax, hemp, etc.

will·yard (wil′yərd) *adj. Scot.* Wilful; also, abashed; bewildered. Also **will′yart** (-yərt).

wil·ly-nil·ly (wil′ē·nil′ē) *adj.* Having no decisiveness; uncertain; irresolute. —*adv.* Willingly or unwillingly. [Earlier *will I, nill I* whether I will or not]

willy willy *Austral.* **1** A violent storm of wind and rain on the NW coast of Australia: also called *cockeye bob.* **2** A brief but violent duststorm.

Wil·ming·ton (wil′ming·tən) **1** A port of entry on the Delaware River in northern Delaware. **2** A port of entry in SE North Carolina.

Wil·no (vil′nô) The Polish name for VILNA.

Wil·son (wil′sən), **Alexander,** 1766–1813, American ornithologist born in Scotland. —**Charles Thomson Rees,** 1869–1959, Scottish physicist. —**Edmund,** 1895–1972, U. S. critic, author, and dramatist. —**Henry,** 1812–75 U. S. statesman. —**James,** 1742–98, American patriot, signed Declaration of Independence. —**John,** 1785–1854, Scottish poet: pseudonym *Christopher North.* —**(Thomas) Woodrow,** 1856–1924, U. S. educator and statesman; president of the United States 1913–21.

Wil·son (wil′sən), **Mount** A peak in SW California, near Pasadena; 5,710 feet; site of a famous observatory.

Wilson Dam A power dam in the Tennessee River at Muscle Shoals, NW Alabama; 137 feet high, 4,862 feet long; forms **Lake Wilson** (25 square miles; 15 1/2 miles long, 1 1/2 miles wide) over Muscle Shoals.

Wilson's petrel The storm petrel. [after Alexander *Wilson*]
Wilson's phalarope A shore bird *(Steganopus tricolor)* which breeds in northern North America and winters as far south as the Falkland Islands. [after Alexander *Wilson*]
Wilson's plover The ring plover *(Charadrius wilsonia)* of the southern United States and South America. [after Alexander *Wilson*]
Wilson's snipe Snipe (def. 1). [after Alexander *Wilson*]
Wilson's thrush The veery. [after Alexander *Wilson*]
Wilson's warbler A small, very active flycatcher *(Wilsonia pusilla)* of eastern North America, black-crowned with a yellow and olive-green body. [after Alexander *Wilson*]
wilt[1] (wilt) *v.i.* **1** To lose freshness; droop or become limp, as a flower that has been cut or that has not been watered. **2** To lose energy and vitality; become faint or languid: We *wilted* under the hot sun. **3** To lose courage or spirit; subside suddenly. —*v.t.* **4** To cause to droop or wither. **5** To cause to lose vitality and energy. —*n.* **1** The act of wilting; also, languor; faintness. **2** An infectious and virulent disease sometimes epidemic among certain caterpillars and insect larvae, which are reduced to a liquefied mass by its ravages: also **wilt disease.** [Prob. dial. var. of obs. *welk* wither. Cf. MDu. *welken* wither.]
wilt[2] (wilt) Archaic second person singular, present tense of WILL[2], used with *thou.*
Wil·ton (wil′tən) *n.* A kind of carpet resembling the Brussels carpet, but having the loops of the pile cut, thus giving it a velvety texture: originally made at Wilton, England. Also **Wilton carpet, Wilton rug.**
Wilt·shire (wilt′shir) *n.* One of a breed of long-horned sheep raised in Wiltshire, England.
Wilt·shire (wilt′shir) A county in southern England; 1,345 square miles; county town, Salisbury. Shortened form **Wilts.**
Wiltshire cheese A variety of Cheddar cheese.
wi·ly (wī′lē) *adj.* **·li·er, ·li·est** Full of or characterized by wiles; sly; cunning. See synonyms under INSIDIOUS, POLITIC. —**wi′li·ly** *adv.* —**wi′li·ness** *n.*
wim·ble (wim′bəl) *n.* Anything that bores a hole, especially if turned by hand, as a gimlet, auger, brace and bit, or the like. —*v.t.* **·bled, ·bling** To bore or pierce, as with a wimble. [<AF, OF *guimbel* <MLG *wiemel.* Akin to GIMLET.]
Wim·ble·don (wim′bəl·dən) A town and municipal borough SW of London in NE Surrey, England; scene of international tennis matches.
wim·ple (wim′pəl) *n.* **1** A cloth, as of linen or silk, wrapped in folds around the neck close under the chin and over the head, exposing only the face: formerly worn as a protection by women outdoors, and still by nuns. **2** *Scot.* A fold; plait; also, a curve; a winding turn, as in a river or road. —*v.* **·pled, ·pling** *v.t.* **1** To cover or clothe with a wimple; veil. **2** To make or fold into plaits, as a veil. **3** To cause to move with slight undulations; ripple. **4** *Obs.* To deceive; hoodwink. —*v.i.* **5** To lie in plaits or folds. **6** To ripple. [OE *wimpel*]

WIMPLE 14th century.

Wims·hurst machine (wimz′hûrst) A machine for the generation of static electricity by means of two insulated rotating disks carrying a number of equally spaced strips of conducting material which, by friction, build up an electrostatic charge. [after James *Wimshurst,* 1832–1903, English engineer, its inventor]
win[1] (win) *v.* **won** (*Obs.* **wan**), **won, win·ning** *v.i.* **1** To gain a victory; be victorious; prevail, as in a contest: May the best man *win.* **2** To succeed in an effort or endeavor. **3** To succeed in reaching or attaining a specified end or condition; get: often with *across, over, through,* etc.: The fleet *won* through the storm. **4** *Obs.* To fight; struggle. —*v.t.* **5** To be successful in; gain victory in: to *win* a game; to *win* an argument. **6** To gain in competition or contest: to *win* the blue ribbon. **7** To gain by effort, persistence, etc.: to *win* fame or fortune. **8** To influence so as to obtain the good will or favor of: often with *over*: His eloquence *won* the audience; We *won* him over to our side. **9** To secure the love of; gain in marriage: He wooed and *won* her. **10** To succeed in reaching; attain: to *win* the harbor. **11** To make (one's way), especially with effort. **12** To capture; take possession of. **13** To earn or procure, as a living: to *win* support from poor soil. **14** *Mining* **a** To extract, as ore or coal, or metal from ore. **b** To reach and open (a deposit, vein, etc.); prepare for mining. See synonyms under ALLURE, CONQUER, GAIN[1], GET, OBTAIN, PERSUADE, SUCCEED. —**to win out** *Colloq.* To succeed to the fullest extent or expectation. —*n.* **1** A victory; success. **2** Profit; winnings. [OE *winnan* contend, labor]
win[2] (win) *v.t. Scot. & Irish* **1** To winnow. **2** To cure, as hay.
win[3] (win) *n. Scot.* Wind.
win·cey (win′sē) *n.* A fabric woven with cotton or linen warp and woolen filling. [Short for *wincey-woolsey,* alter. of LINSEY-WOOLSEY]
wince[1] (wins) *v.i.* **winced, winc·ing** To shrink back or start aside, as from a blow or pain; flinch. —*n.* The act of wincing. [<AF *wenchier* (assumed), var. of OF *quenchier* avoid <Gmc.] —**winc′er** *n.*
wince[2] (wins) *n.* A dyer's winch or windlass. [Var. of WINCH[1]]
winch[1] (winch) *n.* **1** A windlass, particularly one used for hoisting, as on a truck or the mast of a crane, derrick, etc., having usually one or more hand cranks geared to a drum around which the rope or chain winds. **2** A crank with a handle, used to impart motion to a grindstone or the like. —*v.t.* To move, hoist, or haul with or as with a winch. [OE *wince*] —**winch′er** *n.*

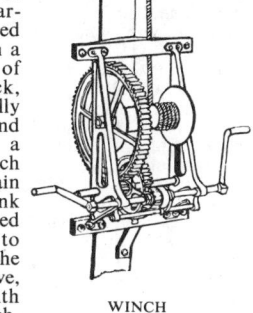

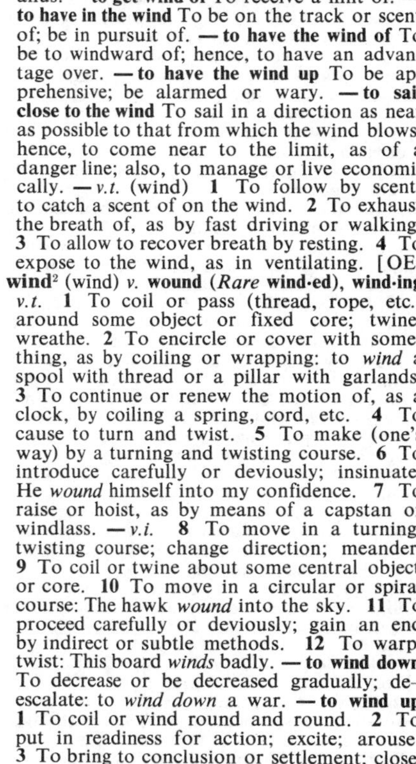
WINCH

winch[2] (winch) *v.i. Obs.* To wince; flinch. [See WINCE[1].]
Win·ches·ter (win′ches·tər) **1** The county town of Hampshire, England; known for its 11th century cathedral. **2** A city of northern Virginia near eastern West Virginia; scene of several Civil War battles, 1862 and 1864.
Winchester rifle A breechloading, lever-action, repeating rifle with a tubular magazine under the barrel, first produced in 1866: a trade name. Also **Winchester.** [after Oliver F. *Winchester,* 1810–80, U. S. industrialist]

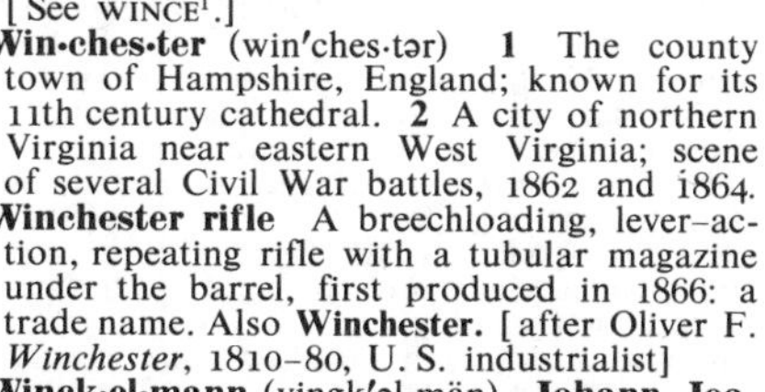

Winck·el·mann (vingk′əl·män), **Johann Joachim,** 1717–68, German archeologist and art critic.
wind[1] (wind, *Poetic* wīnd) *n.* **1** Any movement of air, especially a natural horizontal movement; air in motion naturally. See BEAUFORT SCALE. **2** Any powerful or destructive wind; a tornado; hurricane. **3** The direction from which a wind blows; one of the cardinal points of the compass: They gathered from the four *winds.* **4** Air in motion by artificial means: the *wind* of a bullet, *wind* from a bellows. **5** Air pervaded by a scent: The deer got *wind* of the hunter; hence, figuratively, a suggestion or intimation: to get *wind* of a plot. **6** The power of breathing or respiring; breath: He lost his *wind* in the race. **7** Breath as expended in words, especially as having more sound than sense; idle chatter; also, vanity; conceit. **8** *pl.* The wind instruments of an orchestra; also, the players of these instruments. See WIND INSTRUMENT. **9** The gaseous product of indigestion; flatulence. **10** In pugilism, the pit of the stomach where a blow may cause temporary stoppage of breath: He was hit in the *wind.* —**in the wind 1** Impending; astir; afoot. **2** Inebriated; drunk. —**in the wind's eye** Directly opposed to the point from which the wind blows. —**to break wind** To expel gas through the anus. —**to get wind of** To receive a hint of. —**to have in the wind** To be on the track or scent of; be in pursuit of. —**to have the wind of** To be to windward of; hence, to have an advantage over. —**to have the wind up** To be apprehensive; be alarmed or wary. —**to sail close to the wind** To sail in a direction as near as possible to that from which the wind blows; hence, to come near to the limit, as of a danger line; also, to manage or live economically. —*v.t.* (wind) **1** To follow by scent; to catch a scent of on the wind. **2** To exhaust the breath of, as by fast driving or walking. **3** To allow to recover breath by resting. **4** To expose to the wind, as in ventilating. [OE]
wind[2] (wīnd) *v.* **wound** (*Rare* **wind·ed**), **wind·ing** *v.t.* **1** To coil or pass (thread, rope, etc.) around some object or fixed core; twine; wreathe. **2** To encircle or cover with something, as by coiling or wrapping: to *wind* a spool with thread or a pillar with garlands. **3** To continue or renew the motion of, as a clock, by coiling a spring, cord, etc. **4** To cause to turn and twist. **5** To make (one's way) by a turning and twisting course. **6** To introduce carefully or deviously; insinuate: He *wound* himself into my confidence. **7** To raise or hoist, as by means of a capstan or windlass. —*v.i.* **8** To move in a turning, twisting course; change direction; meander. **9** To coil or twine about some central object or core. **10** To move in a circular or spiral course: The hawk *wound* into the sky. **11** To proceed carefully or deviously; gain an end by indirect or subtle methods. **12** To warp; twist: This board *winds* badly. —**to wind down** To decrease or be decreased gradually; de-escalate: to *wind down* a war. —**to wind up** **1** To coil or wind round and round. **2** To put in readiness for action; excite; arouse. **3** To bring to conclusion or settlement; close, as a business: He *wound up* his affairs. **4** In baseball, to swing the arm preparatory to pitching. **5** To hoist. —*n.* The act of winding, or the condition of being wound; a winding bend, turn, or twist. [OE *windan.* Akin to WAND.] —**wind′a·ble** *adj.*
wind[3] (wīnd, wind) *v.t.* **wind·ed** (*erroneously* **wound**), **wind·ing** **1** To blow, as a horn; sound. **2** To give (a call or signal), as with a horn. [<WIND[1]; infl. by *wind*[2]]
wind·age (win′dij) *n.* **1** The rush of air caused by the rapid passage of an object, as a projectile or a railway train. **2** Deflection of an object, as a bullet, from its natural course due to wind pressure. **3** In a muzzleloading rifled gun, the difference between the diameter of a projectile and the bore through which it is discharged; also, in a smoothbore gun, the space between the surface of the bore and the projectile. **4** *Mech.* The free air space between any moving piece and the socket or bore in which it travels. **5** A contusion caused by sudden compression of air due to the passing of gunshot nearby. **6** *Naut.* The surface offered to the wind by a vessel.
Win·dau (vin′dou) The German name for VENTSPILS.
wind·bag (wind′bag′) *n.* **1** A wordy talker. **2** A bellows. **3** *Slang* The chest.
wind-blown (wind′blōn′) *adj.* **1** Tossed or blown by the wind. **2** Having a permanent direction of growth as determined by prevailing winds: said of plants and trees. **3** Pertaining to an irregular hair arrangement causing the hair in front to appear as if blown forward by the wind.
wind-borne (wind′bôrn′, -bōrn′) *adj.* Carried or transported by the wind.
wind-bound (wind′bound′) *adj.* Delayed by contrary winds.
wind·break (wind′brāk′) *n.* Anything, as a hedge, fence, etc., that protects from or breaks the force of the wind.
wind·break·er (wind′brā′kər) *n.* A sports jacket for outer wear, having a close-fitting or elastic waistband and cuffs. [<*Windbreaker,* a trade name]
wind-bro·ken (wind′brō′kən) *adj.* Asthmatic; broken-winded: said of a horse.
Wind Cave National Park (wind) A region containing a large limestone cavern in the Black Hills in SW South Dakota; 41 square miles; established 1903.

wind·cone (wind′kōn′) *n.* A windsock.
wind·ed (win′did) *adj.* **1** Exposed to the wind or air, or spoiled by such exposure. **2** Breathless, as from work or exercise; out of breath.
wind·er[1] (wīn′dər) *n.* **1** One who or that which winds. **2** That upon which or from which thread, etc., may be wound. **3** A step in winding stairs. **4** A twining plant. **5** An appliance for winding up a spring.
wind·er[2] (wīn′dər, win′dər) *n.* One who winds a horn, bugle, etc.
Win·der·mere (win′dər·mir) An urban district in Westmorland, England.
Windermere, Lake The largest lake in England, in Westmorland and Lancashire; 10 1/2 miles long by 1 mile wide.
wind·fall (wind′fôl′) *n.* **1** Something, as ripening fruit, brought down by the wind; a heap of trees blown down by wind. **2** A tract of land on which trees have been felled by the wind. **3** A piece of unexpected good fortune.
wind·flaw (wind′flô) *n.* A sharp gust of wind.
wind·flow·er (wind′flou′ər) *n.* **1** The anemone. **2** The rue anemone. [Trans. of Gk. *anemōnē* the anemone < *anemos* the wind]
wind gage A scale on a gunsight to allow for windage (def. 2). Also **wind gauge.**
wind·gall (wind′gôl′) *n.* A soft swelling near the pastern joint of a horse. [<WIND + GALL[2]; so called because formerly thought to contain wind] —**wind′galled′** *adj.*
wind gap A notch or ravine in a mountain ridge, moderately deep, but not deep enough to give passage to a watercourse.
wind harp An Eolian harp.
Wind·hoek (vint′hŏŏk) The capital of South-West Africa, in the central part.
wind·hov·er (wind′huv′ər) *n. Brit.* The kestrel: so called from its habit of hovering in the face of the wind.
win·di·go (win′di·gō) *n.* In the mythology of certain Algonquian North American Indians, especially in the Labrador and Ojibwa districts, an evil demon; also, a mythical tribe of cannibals believed by the Chippewa to inhabit an island in Hudson Bay: also spelled *weendijo.* [<Algonquian (Ojibwa) *weendigo* a cannibal]
wind·ing[1] (wīn′ding) *n.* **1** The act or condition of one who or that which winds; a spiral turning or coiling. **2** A bend or turn, or a series of them. **3** A warp or twist from a plane surface. **4** *Electr.* The manner in which the wire is wound in a coil, as on the armature of a dynamo. **5** A defective gait of horses in which one leg seems to wind around the other. —*adj.* **1** Turning spirally about an axis or core. **2** Having bends or lateral turns. **3** Twisting from a plane.
wind·ing[2] (wīn′ding) *n.* A boatswain's signal.
winding frame A device or machine for winding, as a reel.
wind·ing·ly (wīn′ding·lē) *adv.* In a winding manner.
winding sheet (wīn′ding) The sheet that wraps a corpse.
wind instrument (wind) A musical instrument whose sounds are produced by vibrations of air injected by the lungs or by mechanical bellows. Those blown by air from the lungs are known as **wood-wind instruments** or **woodwinds,** consisting of the flutes, oboes, clarinets, etc., and the **brass-wind instruments** or **brasses,** consisting of the horns, trumpets, trombones, tubas, etc. Those in which the vibration of the air column is induced by bellows are the various types of organ, accordion, etc.
wind·jam·mer (wind′jam′ər) *n.* **1** *Naut.* A merchant sailing vessel, as distinguished from a steamship. **2** A member of its crew. **3** *Slang* A chatterbox; a loquacious person.
wind·lass (wind′ləs) *n.* Any of several devices for hauling or lifting, especially that form familiar in well curbs, consisting of a drum or barrel on which the hoisting rope winds, and turned by means of cranking. —**Chinese** or **differential windlass** A horizontal wheel and axle having two drums of different diameters on the same axis, one of which pays out as the other winds up, the power being increased in inverse proportion to the difference between the diameters. —*v.t.* & *v.i.* To raise or haul with a windlass. [Alter. of ME *windas* <ON *vindass* < *vinda* wind + *ass* a beam; infl. in form by WINDLE[2]]

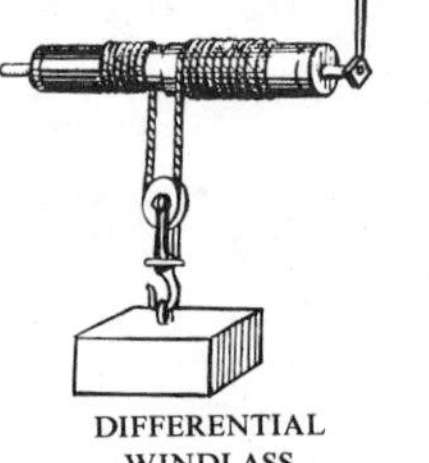
DIFFERENTIAL WINDLASS

win·dle[1] (win′dəl) *n.* A basket. [OE *windel* a basket < *windan* plait, twist]
win·dle[2] (win′dəl) *Scot. & Brit. Dial. v.t.* & *v.i.* To wind. —*n.* Something used for winding or turning. [Freq. of WIND[2]]
wind·less (wind′lis) *adj.* **1** Without wind; breezeless; calm. **2** Being out of breath.
win·dle·straw (win′dəl·strô′) *n. Scot. & Brit. Dial.* **1** A withered stalk of any one of several grasses, used in plaiting or ropemaking. **2** A feeble, unhealthy person. **3** The whitethroat warbler. Also **win′dle·strae′** (-strā′). [OE *windelstrēaw*, ? < *windel* basket + *strēaw* straw]
wind·ling (wind′ling) *n.* **1** *Dial.* That which is torn off by the wind, as a branch of a tree. **2** *Scot.* A bottle of straw. [<WIND[1] + -LING[1]]
wind·mill (wind′mil′) *n.* **1** A mill consisting of a tower within which is a shaft having at the top a horizontal axis which bears a rudder at one end and at the other a system of adjustable slats, wings, or sails which, in revolving, transmit motion to a pump, millstone, or the like. **2** Anything resembling a windmill. **3** An imaginary wrong, evil, or foe: usually in the phrase, **to fight** (or **tilt at) windmills,** in allusion to Don Quixote's combat with windmills, which he mistook for giants.
win·dow (win′dō) *n.* **1** An opening in the wall of a building, to admit light or air, capable of being opened and closed, and including, architecturally, the casement, sash, panes, etc.; in common usage, sometimes, the sash alone: Raise the *window.* **2** A windowpane. **3** Anything resembling or suggesting a window; a windowlike aperture: The eyes are the *windows* of the soul. **4** A transparent patch through which the address of an envelope can be read. —*v.t.* **1** To provide with a window or windows. **2** To fill with holes resembling windows. [<ON *vindauga* < *vindr* wind + *auga* an eye]
window box **1** One of the grooves along the sides of a window frame for the weights that counterbalance a lifting sash. **2** A box, generally long and narrow, along a window ledge or sill, for growing plants.
win·dow-dress·ing (win′dō·dres′ing) *n.* **1** The act or the art of arranging merchandise attractively in shop and store windows; also, the goods so displayed; hence, anything superficially attractive. **2** A business report that unduly stresses favorable conditions. **3** Anything added or done to make something else more attractive: The prosecution of the thieves was mere *window-dressing* for his campaign for governor. —**win′·dow-dress′er** *n.*
win·dow·pane (win′dō·pān′) *n.* A single sheet of glass for a window. Also **window pane.**
window seat A seat in the recess of a window.
window shade A flexible fabric shade, usually mounted on a spring roller, used to regulate light at a window.
win·dow-shop (win′dō·shop′) *v.i.* **-shopped, -shop·ping** To look at goods shown in store windows without buying them. —**win′dow-shop′per** *n.* —**win′dow-shop′ping** *n.* & *adj.*
wind·pipe (wind′pīp′) *n.* The duct by which the breath is carried to and from the lungs; the trachea.
Wind River Range (wind) A range of the Rocky Mountains in west central Wyoming; highest point, 13,787 feet, highest point in Wyoming.
wind rose *Meteorol.* A diagram indicating the direction and relative velocities of the wind in a given locality by means of lines of varying length radiating from a common center.
wind·row (wind′rō′) *n.* **1** A long ridge or pile of hay or grain raked together preparatory to building into cocks. **2** A row of Indian corn made by setting two rows together. **3** A wind-swept line of dust, surf, leaves, etc. **4** A deep furrow made for planting. **5** Land on which the trees have been felled by the wind; sometimes, a tornado track: also **wind slash.** —*v.t.* To rake or shape into a windrow. —**wind′row′er** *n.*
wind sail **1** *Naut.* A canvas tube or funnel with a spreading opening at one side of the top that may be stayed to face the wind: used to conduct fresh air below decks. **2** A sail on the arm of a windmill.
wind scale See BEAUFORT SCALE.
wind·shake (wind′shāk′) *n.* A defect in wood; anemosis.
wind·shield (wind′shēld′) *n.* **1** Any arrangement for breaking the force of the wind against an object. **2** A transparent screen of glass or similar material, attached in front of the occupants of an automobile, airplane, etc., as protection against wind and weather. **3** A covering for a chimney.
wind·sock (wind′sok′) *n. Meteorol.* A large, conical bag, open at both ends, mounted on a pivot, and used to indicate the direction of the wind by the current of air which blows through it; a drogue: also called *windcone.*
Wind·sor (win′zər) Name of the royal family of Great Britain since July 27, 1917, when it was officially changed from *Saxe-Coburg-Gotha.*
Wind·sor (win′zər) **1** A municipal borough in eastern Berkshire, England; site of **Windsor Castle,** a residence of the English sovereigns since the time of William the Conqueror. Officially **New Windsor.** **2** A city on the Detroit River in SE Ontario, Canada, opposite Detroit, Michigan.
Wind·sor (win′zər), **Duke of** See EDWARD VIII.
Windsor chair A wooden chair, with or without arms, common in England and America in the 18th century, typically with a spindle back, turned, slanting legs, and a flat or saddle seat.

COMB-BACKED WINDSOR CHAIR

Windsor tie A wide, soft necktie knotted loosely in a double bow, usually of black silk cut on the bias.
wind·storm (wind′·stôrm′) *n.* A violent wind, usually with little or no precipitation.
wind·suck·er (wind′suk′ər) *n.* A horse that cribs. —**wind′suck′ing** *n.* & *adj.*
wind tee (wind) A T-shaped weathervane, especially one located on or near an aircraft landing field.
wind tunnel *Aeron.* A tunnel-like structure in which the effects of artificially produced winds may be investigated, as on airplane wings and other surfaces.
wind-up (wīnd′up′) *n.* **1** The act of concluding or closing. **2** A conclusion; a final act or part. **3** In baseball, the swing of the arm preparatory to pitching the ball.
wind·ward (wind′wərd) *adj.* Being on the side exposed to the wind. —*n.* The direction from which the wind blows. —**to windward of** Advantageously placed with respect to. —*adv.* In the direction from which the wind blows: opposed to *leeward.*
Wind·ward Islands (wind′wərd) A West Indies island group north of Trinidad, comprising four British colonies, all federating units of The West Indies, on the islands of Dominica, Grenada, St. Lucia, and St. Vincent, together with the Grenadines; 820 square miles; capital, St. George's, on Grenada. The French island of Martinique; Barbados, a British colony; and three islands of the Netherlands Antilles, Aruba, Bonaire, and Curaçao, are also sometimes included in this group.
Windward Passage The strait between Cuba and Hispaniola in the West Indies; 50 miles wide.
wind·y (win′dē) *adj.* **wind·i·er, wind·i·est** **1** Pertaining to, consisting of, or abounding in wind; stormy; tempestuous: *windy* weather. **2** Exposed to the wind; wind-swept: high on a *windy* hill. **3** Suggestive of wind; boisterous;

swift: *windy* emotions. **4** Producing, due to, or troubled with gas in the stomach or intestines; producing or affected with flatulence; flatulent: *windy* food. **5** Given to or expressed in bombast; pompous, loquacious, or bragging: *windy* talk, a *windy* orator. See synonyms under BLEAK[1]. — **wind'i·ly** *adv.* — **wind'i·ness** *n.*

Windy City A nickname for CHICAGO.

wine (wīn) *n.* **1** The fermented juice of the grape, containing various percentages of alcohol by volume, commonly used as a beverage and in cooking. Wines are often classified as dry or sweet, red or white, still or sparkling. Fortified wines have brandy added, and contain alcohol of from 16 to 23 percent. **2** By extension, the fermented juice of some fruit other than the grape: elderberry *wine*; sometimes, a fermented vegetable juice: dandelion *wine*. **3** The effects of drinking too much wine; intoxication. **4** A convivial gathering at which wine and other liquors are served; a wine party. **5** A medicinal preparation in which wine is used as the menstruum: *wine* of opium. **6** Any color resembling the color of wine, especially of a red wine, usually a dark, purplish red. — **Adam's wine** Water. — **new wine in old bottles** Any dynamic new thing, as a doctrine, theory, etc., which cannot be restricted by older forms or customs: with reference to *Matt.* ix 17. — *v.* **wined, win·ing** *v.t.* To entertain or treat with wine. — *v.i.* To drink wine. [OE *wīn* <L *vinum*]

wine·bib·bing (wīn'bib'ing) *adj.* Addicted to excessive drinking of wine. — *n.* The habitual, excessive drinking of wine. — **wine'bib'ber** *n.*

wine card The list of alcoholic drinks for sale at a hotel or restaurant.

wine cellar A storage space for wines; also, the wines stored.

wine-col·ored (wīn'kul'ərd) *adj.* Having the color of red wine.

wine fly Any fly (as of the genus *Piophila*) whose larva lives in wine or other fermented liquor.

wine gallon See under GALLON.

wine·glass (wīn'glas', -gläs') *n.* A small goblet from which to drink wine.

wine·glass·ful (wīn'glas·fōōl', -gläs-) *n. pl.* **·fuls** The amount a wineglass will hold, approximately equivalent to two fluid ounces or four tablespoonfuls.

wine·grow·er (wīn'grō'ər) *n.* One who cultivates a vineyard and makes wine; a viticulturist. — **wine'grow'ing** *adj.* & *n.*

wine measure A system of liquid measures formerly used for wines and spirits in which the gallon was equal to the present U. S. gallon.

wine palm Any palm from which palm wine is obtained.

wine·press (wīn'pres') *n.* An apparatus or a place where the juice of grapes is expressed. — **wine'press'er** *n.*

wine purple A hue of purple consisting of 50 percent red, 33 percent black, and 17 percent blue.

win·er·y (wī'nər·ē) *n. pl.* **·er·ies** **1** An establishment for making wine. **2** A room for fining and storing wines.

Wine·sap (wīn'sap) *n.* An American variety of red winter apple.

wine-skin (wīn'skin') *n.* The skin of some domestic quadruped kept as entire as possible and made into a tight bag for containing wine: much used in the Orient.

wine·sop (wīn'sop') *n.* Any farinaceous foodstuff steeped or sopped in wine, as bread or cake.

wine steward An attendant in a restaurant or hotel who takes orders for wines, and who is in charge of the wine cellar.

wine·tast·er (wīn'tās'tər) *n.* A person who tastes wine to judge its quality.

wine vinegar A vinegar made from wine.

wine whey *Brit.* A beverage made of wine and curdled milk.

Win·fre·da (win·frā'də) Latin form of WINIFRED. Also *Du.* **Win·fried** (vin'frēt), *Sw.* **Win·frid** (vin'frid).

wing (wing) *n.* **1** An organ of flight; specifically, one of the anterior movable pair of appendages of a bird or bat, homologous with the forelimbs of vertebrates but adapted for flight. **2** An analogous organ in insects and some other animals. **3** One of the pectoral fins of a flying fish. **4** *Slang* An arm; specifically, in baseball, the arm used for throwing or pitching. **5** Something regarded as conferring the power of swift motion or performing some function of a wing: on *wings* of song. **6** Flight or passage by or as by wings; also, the means or act of flying: to take *wing*. **7** Anything resembling or suggestive of a wing in form, function, or appearance; specifically, one of a pair of pneumatic devices for aid in swimming; a shoulder ornament. **8** The flare of a moldboard plowshare; also, the curved mudguard or fender of an automobile. **9** Something moved by or moving in the wind, as the vane of a windmill or a winnowing fan. **10** *Mil.* Either division of a military force on either side of the center. **11** An analogous formation in certain outdoor games, as hockey or football. **12** Either of two extremist groups or factions in a political or other organization: the left *wing*. **13** *Archit.* A part attached to a side; especially, a projection or extension of a building on the side of the main portion. **14** A sidepiece at the top of an armchair. **15** A side section of something that shuts or folds, as a double door, a screen, etc. **16** In fortifications, one of the sides connecting an outwork with the main fort. **17** *Anat.* An ala: a *wing* of the nose. **18** *Bot.* Any thin membranous or foliaceous expansion of an organ, as of certain stems, seeds, samaras, etc. **19** *Zool.* One of the lateral finlike expansions of the foot of a pteropod. **20** One of the sides of a stage; a small platform at either side of the stage; also, a piece of scenery for the side. **21** *Aeron.* One of the sustaining surfaces of an airplane. **22** A tactical and administrative unit of the U. S. Air Force, under the direction of a wing commander, larger than a group and smaller than a command. **23** A shore dam or jetty for narrowing a channel; also, an extension of a dam at either end, usually built at an angle. — **on** (or **upon**) **the wing** In flight; as, a bird *on the wing*; hence, just about to go; departing; also, journeying. — **to take wing** To fly away. — **under one's wing** Under one's protection. — *v.t.* **1** To pass over or through in flight. **2** To accomplish by flying: the eagle *winged* its way. **3** To enable to fly. **4** To cause to go swiftly; speed: Hope *winged* his steps. **5** To transport by flight. **6** To provide with wings for flight; also, to feather (an arrow). **7** To supply with a side body or part: The house was *winged* on both sides. **8** To wound (a bird) in a wing; hence, to disable by a minor wound: I *winged* him in the arm. — *v.i.* **9** To fly; soar. [<ON *vængr*]

wing and wing *Naut.* With sails spread or boomed out on each side like wings: said of a fore-and-aft vessel running downwind.

wing·back (wing'bak') *n.* In football, the position taken by one (**single wingback**) or two (**double wingback**) of the backs behind or beyond the ends; also, the back so posted.

wing·bow (wing'bō') *n.* A distinctive mark of color on the bend of the wing in a domestic fowl.

wing chair A large armchair, upholstered throughout, with high back and side pieces designed as protection from drafts.

WING CHAIR

wing cover The elytron of an insect. Also **wing case.**

wing covert *Ornithol.* One of the small close feathers clothing the bend of a bird's wing and covering the insertion of the flight feathers. Those of the lining of the wing are called *undercoverts*.

winged (wingd, *Poetic* wing'id) *adj.* **1** Having wings. **2** Passing swiftly; soaring; lofty; rapt. **3** Alive with creatures having wings. **4** (wingd) *Colloq.* Wounded or disabled in or as in the wing.

winged wolf A harpy (def. 2).

wing flap *Aeron.* A control surface hinged to an airplane wing, used primarily to increase lift and to retard the speed.

wing-foot·ed (wing'fōōt'id) *adj.* Rapid; swift.

wing·less (wing'lis) *adj.* Having no wings, or having aborted wings.

wing·let (wing'lit) *n.* An alula.

wing loading *Aeron.* The over-all weight of a fully loaded airplane divided by the area of the supporting surface, exclusive of the stabilizer and elevators. Also **wing load.**

wing-nut (wing'nut') *n.* A thumbnut.

wing·o·ver (wing'ō'vər) *n.* *Aeron.* A flight maneuver in which an airplane at the top of a climbing turn and just before stalling is put into a dive before resuming normal flight in the direction from which it started.

wing rail A guardrail, as at a railway switch.

wing skid *Aeron.* A device set beneath the wing tip of an airplane to guard the tip against contact with the ground.

wing·spread (wing'spred') *n.* The distance between the tips of the fully extended wings of a bird, insect, or airplane.

wing walk *Aeron.* A reinforced section of an airplane wing, used as a walking strip.

wing-wea·ry (wing'wir'ē) *adj.* Fatigued from flight or travel.

wing·y (wing'ē) *adj.* Winged; swift.

Win·i·fred (win'ə·frid) A feminine personal name. Also **Win'e·fred, Win'i·frid.** [<Welsh *Gwenfrewi* a white wave]

wink (wingk) *v.i.* **1** To close and open the eye or eyelids quickly. **2** To draw the eyelids of one eye together, as in conveying a hint or making a sign. **3** To shut one's eyes, especially in ignoring; pretend not to see: usually with *at*. **4** To emit fitful gleams; twinkle. — *v.t.* **5** To close and open (the eye or eyelids) quickly. **6** To move, force, etc., by winking: with *away, off,* etc. **7** To signify or express by winking. — *n.* **1** The act of winking. **2** The time necessary for a wink. **3** A twinkle. **4** A hint conveyed by winking. **5** A short nap: especially in the phrase **forty winks.** [OE *wincian* close the eyes]

Win·kel·ried (ving'kəl·rēt), **Arnold von** A 14th century Swiss patriot.

wink·er (wing'kər) *n.* **1** One who winks. **2** A blinder for a horse. **3** *Slang* An eyelash. **4** A small secondary bellows for use with an organ. **5** The nictitating membrane, as of a bird. **6** The muscle by which winking is done. **7** *pl. Slang* Spectacles.

win·kle (wing'kəl) *n.* A periwinkle[1]. [Short for PERIWINKLE[1]]

win·na (win'ə) *Scot.* Will not.

Win·ne·ba·go (win'ə·bā'gō) *n. pl.* **·gos** or **·goes** One of a tribe of North American Indians of Siouan linguistic stock, formerly occupying what is now eastern Wisconsin, south of Green Bay, where many still survive.

Win·ne·ba·go (win'ə·bā'gō), **Lake** The largest lake in Wisconsin, in the eastern part; 215 square miles; 30 miles long.

Win·ne·pe·sau·kee (win'ə·pə·sô'kē), **Lake** The largest lake in New Hampshire, in the east central part; 25 miles long, 12 miles wide. Also **Win'ni·pe·sau'kee.**

win·ner (win'ər) *n.* One who or that which wins.

Win·nie (win'ē) Diminutive of WINIFRED, WINSTON.

win·ning (win'ing) *adj.* **1** Successful in achievement, especially in competition. **2** Capable of winning or charming; attractive; winsome. — *n.* **1** The act of one who wins. **2** That which is won: usually in the plural. **3** A new opening in a mine; also, a section of a mine prepared for working. — **win'ning·ly** *adv.* — **win'ning·ness** *n.*

winning gallery In court tennis, the grille or square opening in the penthouse in the rear of the hazard court: so named because a ball played into it counts as a win.

winning hazard See HAZARD *n.* (def. 6).

winning post The post or goal at the end of a racecourse.

Win·ni·peg (win'ə·peg) The capital of Manitoba, Canada, on the Red River in the SE part.

Winnipeg, Lake A lake in south central Manitoba, Canada; 240 miles long, 55 miles wide; 9,398 square miles.

Winnipeg goldeye *Canadian* The goldeye.

Win·ni·pe·go·sis (win'ə·pə·gō'sis), **Lake** A lake in western Manitoba, Canada, west of Lake Winnipeg; 125 miles long, 25 miles wide; 2,086 square miles.

Winnipeg River A river in NW Ontario and

SE Manitoba, flowing 200 miles NW from Lake of the Woods to Lake Winnipeg.
win·nock (win′ək) *n. Scot.* A window.
win·now (win′ō) *v.t.* **1** To separate (grain, etc.) from the chaff by means of wind or a current of air. **2** To blow away (the chaff) thus. **3** To examine so as to separate good from bad; analyze minutely; sift. **4** To separate (what is valuable) from what is valueless, or to eliminate (what is valueless) from what is valuable; distinguish; sort: often with *out.* **5** To blow upon; cause to flutter. **6** To beat or fan (the air) with the wings. **7** To scatter by blowing; disperse. **8** *Rare* To proceed along (a course) by flapping the wings. —*v.i.* **9** To separate grain from chaff. **10** To fly; flap. —*n.* **1** Any device used in winnowing grain. **2** The act of winnowing; also, a vibrating motion caused by a current of air. [OE *windwian* < *wind* the wind] —**win′now·er** *n.*
win·o (wī′nō) *n. pl.* **·noes** or **·nos** *U.S. Slang* A drunkard who habitually drinks sweet, fortified wines. [<WINE]
Wins·low (winz′lō), **Edward,** 1595–1655, English Puritan, governor of Plymouth Colony.
win·some (win′səm) *adj.* Having a winning appearance or manner; pleasing; attractive; rarely, joyous. See synonyms under AMIABLE, LOVELY. [OE *wynsum* < *wyn* joy] —**win′·some·ly** *adv.* —**win′some·ness** *n.*
Win·sor (win′zər), **Justin,** 1831–97, U.S. historian and librarian.
Win·ston (win′stən) A masculine personal name. [Orig. from *Winston,* a hamlet near Circencester, England]
Win·ston-Sa·lem (win′stən·sā′ləm) A city in NW central North Carolina; one of the world's chief tobacco centers.
win·ter (win′tər) *n.* **1** The coldest season of the year, extending from the end of autumn to the beginning of spring: in the northern hemisphere, astronomically from the winter solstice, December 21, to the vernal equinox, March 21, but popularly regarded as including December, January, and February. ◆ Collateral adjectives: *hibernal, hiemal.* **2** Any time compared to winter, as being marked by lack of life, warmth, and cheer. **3** A year as including the winter season: used in reckoning the age of elderly persons: a man of ninety *winters.* —*v.i.* To pass the winter: We *wintered* in Bermuda. —*v.t.* To care for, feed, or protect during the winter: to *winter* animals or plants. —*adj.* **1** Pertaining to or taking place in winter; hibernal. **2** Suitable to or characteristic of winter. [OE] —**win′ter·er** *n.* —**win′ter·ish** *adj.* —**win′·ter·less** *adj.*
winter aconite A European tuberous-rooted, hardy, flowering garden herb (*Eranthis hyemalis*) of the crowfoot family, 5 to 8 inches high, with bright-yellow sessile flowers and oblong anthers.
win·ter·ber·ry (win′tər·ber′ē) *n. pl.* **·ries** Any of several North American shrubs (genus *Ilex*) of the holly family, bearing bright-red berrylike drupes about the size of a pea; especially, the smooth winterberry (*I. laevigata*) of the eastern United States.
win·ter·bourne (win′tər·bôrn′, -bōrn′, -bo͝orn′) *n.* A stream flowing only during excessive rainfall, as in winter, when water at the source rises above a certain level. [OE *winter burna* < *winter* + *burna* a stream]
win·ter-feed (win′tər·fēd′) *v.t.* **-fed, -feed·ing** To feed (stock) during the time when grazing is impossible.
win·ter·green (win′tər·grēn) *n.* **1** A small evergreen plant (*Gaultheria procumbens*) of eastern North America, bearing a cluster of aromatic oval leaves and white, bell-shaped flowers surrounded by red berries (often called *teaberries* or *checkerberries*). **2** Oil of wintergreen: a colorless, volatile oil extracted from the leaves of the true wintergreen, used as a flavor and in medicine: often called *Gaultheria oil.* **3** Any of various English low evergreen herbs (genus *Pyrola*). In the United States they are sometimes called *shinleaf* or **English** or **false wintergreen.** [On analogy with Du. *wintergroen*; so called because it is an evergreen]
winter itch Frost itch.
win·ter·ize (win′tə·rīz) *v.t.* **·ized, ·iz·ing** To prepare or equip for winter.
win·ter·kill (win′tər·kil′) *v.t.* & *v.i.* To die or kill by exposure to extreme cold: said of plants and grains. —**win′ter·kill′ing** *adj.* & *n.*
win·ter·ly (win′tər·lē) *adj.* Wintry; cheerless.
winter melon A hardy, cold-resistant muskmelon (*Cucumis melo,* variety *inodorus*).
Win·ter·thur (vin′tər·to͞or) A city of northern Switzerland NE of Zurich; a rail and industrial center.
win·ter·tide (win′tər·tīd′) *n. Poetic* Winter. Also **win′ter·time′** (-tīm′).
winter wheat Wheat planted before snowfall and harvested the following summer.
Win·throp (win′thrəp), **John,** 1588–1649, English Puritan; governor of Massachusetts Colony. —**John,** 1606–76, governor of Connecticut Colony; son of the preceding.
win·try (win′trē) *adj.* **·tri·er, ·tri·est** Belonging to winter; cold; frosty; brumal. Also **win′·ter·y** (-tər·ē). —**win′tri·ly** *adv.* —**win′tri·ness** *n.*
win·y (wī′nē) *adj.* **win·i·er, win·i·est** Having the taste or qualities of wine.
Win·yah Bay (win′yô) An estuary of the Pee Dee and other rivers in South Carolina NE of Charleston; 14 miles long.
winze[1] (winz) *n. Mining* A small inclined shaft from one level of a mine to another. [Earlier *winds,* ? < obs. *wind* a windlass, fusion of MDu. *winde* a windlass and WIND[2]]
winze[2] (winz) *n. Scot.* An oath.
wipe (wīp) *v.t.* **wiped, wip·ing** **1** To subject to slight friction or rubbing, usually with some soft, absorbent material. **2** To remove by rubbing lightly; brush: usually with *away* or *off.* **3** To move, apply, or draw for the purpose of wiping: He *wiped* his hand across his brow. **4** To apply solder to with a piece of greased cloth or leather; solder with a wiper or pad: to *wipe* a joint. See synonyms under CLEANSE. —**to wipe out** To remove or destroy utterly; annihilate. —*n.* **1** The act of wiping or rubbing. **2** *Slang* A sweeping blow or stroke; a swipe. **3** *Mech.* A wiper or cam. **4** *Slang* A handkerchief. **5** *Slang* A jeer; jibe. [OE *wīpian.* Akin to WISP.]
wip·er (wī′pər) *n.* **1** One who wipes. **2** An article designed or used for wiping. **3** *Mech.* A cam having one or more slightly curved projections serving, when mounted on a rock shaft or rotating shaft, to give a reciprocating (usually vertical) motion to another part. **4** *Electr.* A moving member of an electrical device which makes contact with the terminals. **5** One who cleans locomotives in a roundhouse.
wire (wīr) *n.* **1** A slender rod, strand, or thread of ductile metal, usually formed by drawing through dies or holes. **2** Something made of wire, as a fence, a bar of a cage, or a snare made for catching small animals. **3** A telegraph cable. **4** The telegraph system as a means of communication. **5** A telegram. **6** The screen of a papermaking machine. **7** A fine metallic thread, a cobweb, or one of a set of ruled lines, in the focus of a telescope. **8** *Ornithol.* A long slender filament of the plumage of various birds. **9** *pl.* A secret means of exerting influence: to pull the *wires*: from the analogy with the system of hidden wires by which puppets are operated. **10** An imaginary line marking the finish of a racecourse. —**to lay wires for** To prepare for. —**under wire** Fenced. —*v.* **wired, wir·ing** *v.t.* **1** To fasten with wire. **2** To furnish or equip with wiring: The studio was *wired* for sound. **3** In croquet, to place (a ball) so that the wire of an arch will be between it and another ball. **4** To catch, as a rabbit, with a snare of wire. **5** *Colloq.* To transmit or send by electric telegraph: to *wire* an order. **6** *Colloq.* To send a telegram to: Will you *wire* John? **7** To place on wire, as beads. —*v.i.* **8** *Colloq.* To telegraph. [OE *wīr*]
wire cloth A fabric of woven wire, as for strainers, window screens, etc.
wire coat An outer coat, as of some dogs, of dense stiff hair.
wire-danc·er (wīr′dan′sər, -dän′-) *n.* One who performs feats of balancing, etc., upon a wire stretched in mid-air: also called *wirewalker.* —**wire′-danc′ing** *n.*
wire-draw (wīr′drô′) *v.t.* **-drew, -drawn, -draw·ing** **1** To draw, as a metal rod, through a series of holes of diminishing diameter to produce a wire. **2** To treat (a subject) with excessive subtlety or overrefinement. —**wire′-draw′er** *n.* —**wire′-draw′ing** *n.*
wire gage **1** A gage for measuring the diameter of round wire, usually a round plate with slots on its periphery numbered according to an arbitrary standard, or a long graduated plate with a slot of diminishing width. **2** A standard system of sizes for wire. Also **wire gauge.**
wire gauze A material of a gauzelike texture made of interwoven strands of wire.
wire glass See under GLASS.
wire·grass (wīr′gras′, -gräs′) *n.* **1** A European grass (*Poa compressa*) having slender, compressed stems, cultivated in the United States and Canada: also called *Canada bluegrass.* **2** Any one of several similar grasses.
wire-haired griffon (wīr′hârd′) A griffon (def. 2).
wire·less (wīr′lis) *adj.* **1** Without wire or wires; having no wires. **2** *Brit.* Radio. —*n.* **1** The wireless telegraph or telephone system, or a message transmitted by either. **2** *Brit.* Radio. —*v.t.* & *v.i.* *Brit.* To communicate (with) by wireless telegraphy; radio.
wireless telegraphy or **telephony** Telegraphy or telephony without wires connecting the points of transmission and reception, the message being transmitted through space by electromagnetic waves; radio communication.
wire·man (wīr′mən) *n. pl.* **·men** (-mən) **1** A man who has to do with wire. **2** One who handles wire for telegraph lines, etc.; a wirer.
wire mark The faint impression left on paper by the wires of the mold during manufacture.
wire netting Netting made of wire, as window screens, fences, etc.
Wire·pho·to (wīr′fō′tō) *n. pl.* **·tos** An apparatus and method for transmitting and receiving photographs by wire: a trade name.
wire·pull·er (wīr′po͝ol′ər) *n.* One who pulls wires, as of a puppet; hence, one who uses secret means to control others or gain his own ends; an intriguer.
wire·pull·ing (wīr′po͝ol′ing) *n.* **1** The pulling of wires, as in a puppet show. **2** The use of secret influence to obtain an end.
wir·er (wīr′ər) *n.* **1** A trapper who snares with wire contrivances. **2** A wireman.
wire recorder A device for recording sounds on an uncoiling fine wire by magnetic registration of variations in the flow of electrical current from a microphone: these sounds are reproduced as the magnetized wire is passed back between the poles of the electromagnet.
wire rope A rope of wires firmly wound together.
wire·sonde (wīr′sond′) *n. Meteorol.* A type of radiosonde for use at low altitudes, the required data being transmitted by wire to ground stations. [<WIRE + (RADIO)SONDE]
wire-spun (wīr′spun′) *adj.* Wire-drawn; spun or drawn out too fine; overrefined.
wire·tap (wīr′tap′) *n.* **1** A device used to make a connection with a telephone or telegraph wire to listen to or record the message transmitted. **2** The act of wiretapping. —*v.t.* **·tapped, ·tap·ping** **1** To connect a wiretap to. **2** To monitor by the use of a wiretap. —**wire′tap′per** *n.*
wire·walk·er (wīr′wô′kər) *n.* A wire-dancer.
wire wheel In automobiles, a wheel in which slender metal spokes, usually in a criss-cross pattern, connect the hub and rim.
wire·work (wīr′wûrk′) *n.* **1** Small articles made of wire cloth. **2** Wire fabrics in general. —**wire′work′er** *n.*
wire·works (wīr′wûrks′) *n. pl.* **·works** **1** A factory where wire or articles of wire are made. **2** A shop where wire is woven and manufactured into protective screens, filters, or the like.
wire·worm (wīr′wûrm′) *n.* **1** The cylindrical brown to whitish larva of a click beetle, with a stiff, wiry texture: some species are common in fields, where they damage the roots of plants. For illustration see INSECTS (injurious). **2** A millipede.
wire-wove (wīr′wōv′) *adj.* **1** Denoting a high grade of paper with a smooth writing surface. **2** Woven of wire.
wir·ing (wīr′ing) *n.* An entire system of wire installed for the distribution of electric power, as for lighting, heating, radio, engine ignition, or the like.

wir·ra (wir′ə) *interj.* An exclamation of sorrow or despair. [Earlier O *wirra,* partial trans. of Irish *a Muire* O Mary]

wir·y (wīr′ē) *adj.* **wir·i·er, wir·i·est 1** Having great resisting power; thin, but tough and sinewy: said of persons. **2** Like wire; stiff. —**wir′i·ly** *adv.* —**wir′i·ness** *n.*

wis (wis) *v.t. Obs.* To suppose; think. [<IWIS]

Wis·by (wiz′bē, *Ger.* viz′bē) The German name for VISBY.

Wis·con·sin (wis·kon′sən) A State of the Great Lakes region of the United States; 56,154 square miles; capital, Madison; entered the Union May 29, 1848; nickname, *Badger State*: abbr. WI —**Wis·con′sin·ite** (-īt) *n.*

Wisconsin River A river in central Wisconsin, flowing 430 miles south and SW to the Mississippi.

wis·dom (wiz′dəm) *n.* **1** The power of true and right discernment; conformity to the course of action dictated by such discernment. **2** Good practical judgment; common sense. **3** A high degree of knowledge; learning. **4** A wise saying. [OE *wīsdōm* <*wīs* wise]

Synonyms: attainment, depth, discernment, discretion, enlightenment, erudition, foresight, information, insight, judgment, judiciousness, knowledge, learning, lore, prescience, profoundity, prudence, reason, reasonableness, sagacity, sense, skill, understanding. *Enlightenment, erudition, information, knowledge, learning,* and *skill* are acquired, as by study or practice. *Insight, judgment, profundity* or *depth, reason, sagacity, sense,* and *understanding* are native qualities of mind, but are capable of increase by cultivation. *Wisdom* is mental power acting upon the materials that fullest *knowledge* gives in the most effective way. There may be what is termed "practical *wisdom*" that looks only to material results; but in its full sense *wisdom* implies the highest exercise of all the faculties. *Prudence* is a more negative form of the same virtue and largely with a view of avoiding loss and injury. *Judgment,* the power of forming decisions, is broader and more positive than *prudence,* leading one to do, as readily as to refrain from doing; but *judgment* is more limited in range and less exalted in character than *wisdom. Skill* is far inferior to *wisdom,* consisting largely in the practical application of acquired *knowledge,* power, and habitual processes, or in the ingenious contrivance that makes such application possible. In the making of something perfectly useless there may be great *skill,* but no *wisdom.* Compare KNOWLEDGE, PRUDENCE. *Antonyms*: absurdity, error, fatuity, folly, foolishness, idiocy, imbecility, imprudence, indiscretion, miscalculation, misjudgment, nonsense, shallowness, silliness, stupidity.

wisdom literature The didactic books of the Old Testament, comprising Proverbs and Ecclesiastes, and the book of Wisdom and Ecclesiasticus in the Apocrypha.

Wisdom of Jesus, the Son of Si·rach (sī′rak) Ecclesiasticus.

Wisdom of Solomon A book of the Old Testament Apocrypha, consisting of a hymn in praise of wisdom: ascribed by tradition to Solomon, but probably dating from the first or second century B.C.

wisdom tooth The last molar tooth on either side of the upper and lower jaws in man, appearing between the 17th and 22d year. —**to cut one's wisdom teeth** To acquire mature judgment by age and experience.

wise[1] (wīz) *adj.* **wis·er, wis·est 1** Possessed of wisdom; seeing clearly what is right and just; having sound judgment concerning one's highest interests, and in one's own conduct choosing the best end and the best means for reaching that end; in a lower sense, sagacious; also, shrewd or calculating. **2** Marked by wisdom; prudent; sensible. **3** Having great learning; erudite. **4** Suited to a man of wisdom; sage. **5** Having practical knowledge of the arts or sciences. **6** Versed in mysterious things. **7** *Colloq.* Aware of; onto: *wise* to his motives. —**to get wise** *Slang* To know the true facts. —*v.t. Slang* To make cognizant of; inform. —**to wise up** *Slang* To make or become aware, informed, or sophisticated. [OE *wīs*] —**wise′ly** *adv.* —**wise′ness** *n.*

Synonyms: deep, discerning, enlightened, erudite, intellectual, intelligent, judicious, knowing, profound, rational, reasonable, sagacious, sage, sapient, solid, sound, thoughtful. See EXPEDIENT, POLITIC, SAGACIOUS. *Antonyms*: see synonyms for ABSURD, IGNORANT.

wise[2] (wīz) *n.* Way of doing; manner; method: chiefly in phrases: **in any wise, in no wise,** etc. [OE *wīse* manner. Akin to GUISE.]

wise[3] (wīz) *v.t. & v.i. Dial. & Scot.* or *Obs.* To incline; turn. [OE *wīsian*]

-wise *suffix of adverbs & nouns* **1** In a (specified) way or manner: *no wise, likewise.* **2** In a (specified) direction or position: *lengthwise, clockwise*: often equivalent to *-ways.* **3** *Colloq.* With reference to: *Moneywise,* the job is worth considering. [OE *wise* manner, fashion]

Wise (wīz), **Stephen Samuel,** 1872–1949, U.S. rabbi born in Hungary.

wise·a·cre (wīz′ā′kər) *n.* **1** One who affects great wisdom. **2** A wise man; sage. [< MDu. *wijsseggher* a soothsayer; infl. in form by ACRE]

wise·crack (wīz′krak′) *Slang n.* A smart or supercilious remark. —*v.i.* To utter a smart remark. —**wise′crack′er** *n.* —**wise′crack′ing** *adj. & n.*

wise·ling (wīz′ling) *n. Rare* One who pretends to or affects wisdom.

Wise·man (wīz′mən), **Nicholas Patrick Stephen,** 1802–65, English cardinal and author born in Spain.

wis·er·ite (wis′ər·īt) *n. Mineral.* A hydrous carbonate of manganese, yellowish-white to gray in color, found in Switzerland. [after D. F. *Wiser,* 19th c. Swiss mineralogist]

wise woman A woman skilled in magic; a soothsayer; sorceress; a witch, usually benevolent, who deals in charms against disease, misfortune, etc.

wish (wish) *n.* **1** A desire or longing, usually for some definite thing. **2** An expression of such a desire; petition. **3** Something wished for. **4** *Psychoanal.* An impulse, tendency, or striving toward the satisfaction of some need, especially when originating in or generated by the unconscious. See synonyms under WILL[1]. [<*v.*] —*v.t.* **1** To have a desire or longing for; crave; want: usually with a clause or infinitive as object: We *wish* to be sure. **2** To desire a specified condition or state for (a person or thing): I *wish* this day were over. **3** To invoke upon or for someone: I *wished* him good luck. **4** To bid: to *wish* someone good morning. **5** To request or entreat: I *wish* you would tell me what you are whispering about; also, to command. —*v.i.* **6** To have or feel a desire; yearn; long: usually with *for*: to *wish* for a friend's return. **7** To make or express a wish. —**to wish on** To impose (something or someone) on a person. [OE *wȳscan*]

wish·bone (wish′bōn′) *n.* The forked bone formed by the united clavicles of a carinate bird; the furcula: so called from the old belief that when pulled apart by two persons, each making a wish, the one who gets the longer part will have his wish fulfilled. See MERRYTHOUGHT.

wish·ful (wish′fəl) *adj.* Having a wish or desire; full of longing. —**wish′ful·ly** *adv.* —**wish′·ful·ness** *n.*

wish fulfilment 1 The satisfaction of a wish. **2** *Psychoanal.* The illusory realization of a strongly motivated, often unconscious and repressed aim by mental processes divorced from or not in accord with reality.

wish·ton·wish (wish′tən·wish) *n.* **1** The prairie dog. **2** The whippoorwill: incorrect use by James Fenimore Cooper. [<Caddoan; orig. prob. imit.]

wish-wash (wish′wosh′, -wôsh′) *n.* Any thin, weak, insipid drink; slops. [Varied reduplication of WASH]

wish·y-wash·y (wish′ē·wosh′ē, -wôsh′ē) *adj. Colloq.* **1** Thin; diluted, as liquor. **2** Lacking in solidity, consistence, or vigor; unsubstantial.

Wis·mar (vis′mär) A port on the Baltic in NW East Germany, in the former state of Mecklenburg.

wisp (wisp) *n.* **1** A small bunch, as of hay, straw, or hair. **2** A small bit; a mere indication: a *wisp* of vapor. **3** A whiskbroom. **4** A will-o'-the-wisp. —*v.t.* **1** To dress, brush, or groom with a wisp or whisk. **2** To fold and lightly twist into a wisp or wisplike form; rumple; crumple. [ME *wisp, wips.* Akin to WIPE.] —**wisp′y** *adj.*

wisp·ish (wis′pish) *adj.* Like or having the nature of a wisp.

wist (wist) Past tense and past participle of WIT[2].

wis·tar·i·a (wis·târ′ē·ə) *n.* **1** Any of a genus *(Wistaria)* of woody twining shrubs of the bean family, with pinnate leaves, elongated pods, and handsome clusters of blue, purple, or white flowers. The two best-known species are the **Chinese wistaria** *(W. sinensis)* and the later blossoming **Japanese wistaria** *(W. floribunda).* The common spelling **wis·te·ri·a** (wis·tir′ē·ə, -târ′-) was the one originally given by the botanist Nuttall. **2** A shade of dull, purplish blue. [after Caspar *Wistar,* 1761–1818, U.S. anatomist]

WISTARIA

Wis·ter (wis′tər), **Owen,** 1860–1938, U.S. novelist.

wist·ful (wist′fəl) *adj.* **1** Wishful; longing. **2** Musing; pensive. [Appar. <obs. *wistly* intently; infl. in form by *wishful*] —**wist′·ful·ly** *adv.* —**wist′ful·ness** *n.*

wist·less (wist′lis) *adj. Obs.* Inattentive; unobservant.

wit[1] (wit) *n.* **1** The power of knowing or perceiving; intelligence; ingenuity; sagacity; keen or good sense. **2** The power or faculty of rapid and accurate observation; the power of comprehending and judging. **3** *pl.* The mental faculties, as of perception and understanding: to use one's *wits*; also, the mental faculties with regard to their state of balance: out of her *wits.* **4** The ready perception and happy expression of unexpected or amusing analogies or other relations between apparently incongruous ideas; sudden and ingenious association of ideas or words causing delight and surprise; loosely, any form of humor which expresses irony or satire by a happy association of words. **5** One who has a keen perception of the incongruous or ludicrous and makes skilful use of it in writing or speaking; also, a clever conversationalist; one gifted in repartee or clever sayings. **6** Significance; meaning; import. **7** *Obs.* Mental activity. —**at one's wits' end** At the limit of one's devices and resources; not knowing what to do. —**to live by one's wits** To make a living by using one's practical intelligence and resourcefulness, often in unscrupulous or fraudulent ways. [OE]

Synonyms: banter, drollery, facetiousness, fun, humor, jest, jocularity, joke, playfulness, pleasantry, raillery, waggery, waggishness. *Wit* is the quick perception of unusual or commonly unperceived analogies or relations between things apparently unrelated; it depends on the production of a diverting, entertaining, or merrymaking surprise. The analogies with which *wit* plays are often superficial or artificial; *humor* deals with real analogies of an amusing or entertaining kind, or with traits of character that are seen to have a comical side. *Wit* is keen, sudden, brief, and sometimes severe; *humor* is deep, thoughtful, sustained, and kindly. *Pleasantry* is lighter and less vivid than *wit. Fun* denotes the merry results produced by any fortuitous occasion of mirth, and is pronounced and often hilarious. *Antonyms*: gravity, seriousness, sobriety, solemnity, stolidity.

wit[2] (wit) *v.t. & v.i.* Present indicative: I **wot,** thou **wost,** he **wot,** *pl.* **wite(n)**; *pt.* and *pp.* **wist**; *ppr.* **wit·ting** *Archaic* To be or become aware (of); learn; know. —**to wit** That is to say; namely; scilicet: used, especially in legal documents, to introduce a detailed statement or an explanation. [OE *witan* know]

wit·an (wit′ən) *n. pl.* **1** Members of the national council in Saxon England. **2** The council itself. [OE, councilors, pl. of *wita* a wise man, witness]

witch[1] (wich) *n.* **1** A person who practices

sorcery; a sorcerer or sorceress; one having supernatural powers in the natural world, especially to work evil, and usually by association with evil spirits or the devil: formerly applied to men, women, and children, now generally restricted to women. **2** An ugly, malignant old woman; a hag. **3** A bewitching or fascinating woman or girl. — *v.t.* **1** To overcome by witchcraft; work an evil spell upon. **2** To effect by witchcraft or sorcery. **3** To fascinate or bewitch; enchant. [OE *wicce* a witch, fem. of *wicca* a wizard < *wiccian* bewitch]

witch[2] (wich) *n.* The wych-elm: also spelled *wich, wych.* [OE *wice* < *wican* bend]

witch alder A shrub (*Fothergilla gardeni*) resembling the witch hazel in its fruit and the alder in its leaves. It is found along shady swamps from Virginia to Florida. [<WITCH[2] + ALDER]

witch broom Leaf curl. [<WITCH[1] + BROOM]

witch·craft (wich′kraft′, -kräft′) *n.* **1** The practices or powers of witches or wizards, especially when regarded as due to dealings with evil spirits or the devil; black magic; sorcery; also, an instance of such practices. **2** Extraordinary influence or fascination; witchery. See synonyms under SORCERY.

witch doctor **1** Among certain primitive peoples of Africa, especially the Kaffirs, a medicine man skilled in detecting witches and counteracting evil spells; hence, any medicine man or magician. **2** One who professes to heal or cure by sorcery; a hex.

witch·dom (wich′dəm) *n. Rare* Witchcraft.

witch-elm (wich′elm′) *n.* The wych-elm. [<WITCH[2] + ELM]

witch·er·y (wich′ər·ē) *n. pl.* **·er·ies** **1** Witchcraft. **2** Power to charm; fascination.

witch·es′-broom (wich′iz·brōōm′, -brŏŏm′) *n.* A compact broomlike growth of portions of various trees and shrubs, characterized by excessive multiplication of branches, and due in some cases to the presence of parasitic fungi: also called *hexenbesen.* Also **witch′·broom′.**

witches′ Sabbath In medieval folklore, a midnight orgy of demons and witches, which in German folklore is believed to occur on May Day eve or Walpurgis Night: also called *sabbat.*

witch·et·ty (wich′it·ē) *n.* The grub of a longicorn beetle, living in the roots of shrubs, in decayed timber, or in the earth, which is roasted and eaten by Australian aborigines. [<Australian]

witch-find·er (wich′fīn′dər) *n.* Formerly, one employed to seek and obtain information against witches.

witch·grass (wich′gras′, -gräs′) *n.* **1** The panic grass, common in sandy soils and cultivated fields, with a very loose, pyramidal, compound hairy panicle. **2** The couchgrass. [Alter. of QUITCHGRASS]

witch hazel **1** A shrub (*Hamamelis virginiana*) of the United States and Canada, with several branching crooked trunks and small yellow flowers. **2** An ointment and fluid extract used as a remedy for bruises, sprains, etc., derived from the bark and dried leaves of this shrub. **3** The wych-elm. Also *wych-hazel.* [<WITCH[2] + HAZEL]

witch hunt An investigation of persons ostensibly to uncover subversive activities, but intended for ulterior motives, such as harassing political opposition.

witch·ing (wich′ing) *adj.* Having power to enchant; weird; fascinating. — *n.* Witchcraft; sorcery. — **witch′ing·ly** *adv.*

witch·mon·ger (wich′mung′gər, -mong′-) *n.* One who deals with witches or believes in witchcraft.

witch moth Any of several moths (family *Noctuidae*) of nocturnal habits and typically somber appearance; especially, the large black witch moth (*Erebus odora*) of South and North America.

witch of A·gne·si (ä·nyā′zē) *Math.* The plane curve of the equation $x^2y = 4a^2(2a-y)$: it is symmetric with respect to the y-axis and asymptotic to the x-axis. Also called the *versiera.* [after Donna Maria Gaetani *Agnesi,* 1718–1799, Italian mathematician]

wite (wīt) *n. Scot. & Brit. Dial.* **1** A penalty; fine. **2** A reproach; blame. **3** A guilty action; fault. [OE *wīte*]

wit·e·na·ge·mot (wit′ə·nə·gə·mōt′) *n.* The assembly of the witan. [OE *witena gemōt* councilors' assembly]

with (with, wiŧh) *prep.* **1** In the company of; as a member or associate of. **2** Next to; beside: Walk *with* me. **3** Having; bearing: a hat *with* a feather. **4** Characterized or marked by; characteristically possessed of: the house *with* green shutters; a man *with* brains. **5** In a manner characterized by; exhibiting: to dance *with* grace. **6** Among: counted *with* the others. **7** During; in the course of: We forget *with* time. **8** From; so as to be separated from: to part *with* the past; to dispense *with* luxury. **9** Against: to struggle *with* an adversary. **10** In the opinion of: That is all right *with* me. **11** Because of; as a consequence of: faint *with* hunger. **12** In charge of; in possession of: Leave the key *with* the janitor; I have my fiddle *with* me. **13** Using; by means or aid of: to write *with* a pencil. **14** By adding or having as a material or quality: trimmed *with* lace; endowed *with* beauty. **15** Under the influence of: confused *with* drink. **16** In spite of: *With* all his money, he could not buy health. **17** At the same time as: to go to bed *with* the chickens. **18** In the same direction as: to drift *with* the crowd. **19** In regard to; in the case of: Be gentle *with* the horse; I am angry *with* them. **20** Onto; to: Join this tube *with* that one. **21** In proportion to: His fame grew *with* his achievements. **22** In support of: He voted *with* the Left. **23** Of the same opinion as: I'm *with* you there! **24** Compared to; contrasted to: Consider this picture *with* that one. **25** Immediately after; following: *With* that, he slammed the door. **26** Having received or been granted: *With* your consent I'll go now. [OE]

with- *prefix* **1** Against: *withstand.* **2** Back; away: *withhold.* [OE *with-* < *with* against]

with·al (wiŧh·ôl′, with-) *Archaic adv.* With the rest; in addition. — *prep.* With: intensive form used after its object and at the end of the clause: a bow to shoot *withal.* [ME *with alle* < *with* + *alle* all]

with·draw (wiŧh·drô′, with-) *v.* **·drew, ·drawn, ·draw·ing** *v.t.* **1** To draw or take away; remove. **2** To take back, as an assertion or a promise; recall. **3** To keep or abstract from use. — *v.i.* **4** To draw back; retire. See synonyms under ABSTRACT, SEPARATE. [<WITH- + DRAW] — **with·draw′al, with·draw′ment** *n.*

with·draw·ing (wiŧh·drô′ing, with-) *adj.* Stretching back or away; receding.

withdrawing room **1** A room behind another room for retirement. **2** A drawing room.

withe (wiŧh, with, wiŧh) *n.* **1** A willowy, supple twig. **2** A band made of twisted flexible shoots, straw, or the like. **3** An elastic handle for a tool. — *v.t.* **withed, with·ing** To bind with withes. [OE *withthe*]

with·er (wiŧh′ər) *v.i.* **1** To become limp or dry, as a plant when cut down or deprived of moisture. **2** To waste, as flesh. **3** To droop or languish. — *v.t.* **4** To cause to become limp or dry. **5** To abash, as by a scornful glance. [Appar. var. of WEATHER, *v.*]

Synonyms: blast, blight, collapse, droop, shrink, shrivel. See DIE[1]. *Antonyms*: bloom, develop, expand, flourish, freshen, grow, luxuriate, swell.

With·er (wiŧh′ər), **George,** 1588–1667, English poet. Also **With′ers.**

with·er·ite (wiŧh′ə·rīt) *n.* A white, translucent barium carbonate, $BaCO_3$, occurring massive or in orthorhombic crystals. [after Dr. Wm. *Withering,* 1741–99, English physician, who first described and analyzed it]

withe rod A shrub (*Viburnum cassinoides*) of the honeysuckle family, growing in swamps from Newfoundland to New Jersey and Minnesota.

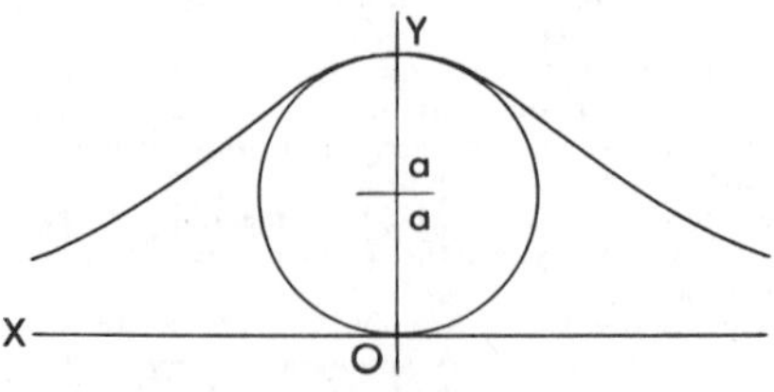

WITCH OF AGNESI

with·ers (wiŧh′ərz) *n. pl.* **1** The highest part of the back of the horse between the shoulder blades. **2** The similar part in some other animals, as the deer and ox. [OE *withre* resistance < *wither* against; so called because the horse opposes this part against the load he pulls]

with·er·shins (wiŧh′ər·shinz) *adv. Scot.* In the opposite direction; in a reversed way. Also spelled *widdershins, widershins.*

With·er·spoon (wiŧh′ər·spōōn), **John,** 1722–94, American educator born in Scotland; signed Declaration of Independence.

with·hold (with·hōld′, wiŧh-) *v.* **·held, ·hold·ing** *v.t.* **1** To hold back; restrain. **2** To keep back; decline to grant. — *v.i.* **3** To refrain; forbear. See synonyms under KEEP, RETAIN, SUSPEND. [<WITH- + HOLD] — **with·hold′er** *n.*

withholding tax That part of an employee's wages or salary which is deducted as an installment on his income tax.

with·in (wiŧh·in′, with-) *adv.* **1** In the inner part; interiorly. **2** Inside the body, heart, or mind. **3** Indoors. — *prep.* **1** In the inner or interior part or parts of; inside: *within* the house. **2** In the limits, range, or compass of (a specified time, space, or distance): *within* a mile of here; *within* ten minutes' walk. **3** Not exceeding (a specified quantity): Live *within* your means. **4** In the reach, limit, or scope of: *within* my power. See synonyms under AT. [OE *withinnan* < *with* with + *innan* in]

with·in·doors (wiŧh·in′dôrz′, -dōrz′, with-) *adv.* Inside a building.

with-it (wiŧh′it) *adj. Slang* **1** In touch with modern habits, fashions, trends, etc.; up-to-date; hip. **2** Lively and modern; swinging. Also **with it.**

with·out (wiŧh·out′, with-) *prep.* **1** Not having, as the result of loss, privation, negation, etc.; lacking: *without* money; *without* a home. **2** In the absence of: We must manage *without* help. **3** Free from: *without* fear. **4** At, on, or to the outside of. **5** Outside of or beyond the limits of: living *without* the pale of civilization. **6** With avoidance of: He listened *without* paying attention. **7** *Obs.* Besides. — *adv.* **1** In or on the outer part; externally. **2** Out of doors. — *conj. Dial.* Unless; except. [OE *withūtan* < *with* with + *ūtan* out]

without day Sine die.

with·out·doors (wiŧh·out′dôrz′, -dōrz′, with-) *adv.* Out of doors; outside.

with·stand (with·stand′, wiŧh-) *v.* **·stood, ·stand·ing** *v.t.* To oppose with any force; resist successfully. — *v.i.* To make resistance; endure. See synonyms under OPPOSE. [OE *withstandan* < *with-* against + *standan* stand] — **with·stand′er** *n.*

with·y (wiŧh′ē, with′ē) *adj.* Made of withes; flexible and tough. — *n. pl.* **with·ies** **1** A rope made of withes. **2** A withe. [<WITHE]

wit·less (wit′lis) *adj.* Lacking in wit; foolish. — **wit′less·ly** *adv.* — **wit′less·ness** *n.*

wit·ling (wit′ling) *n.* A person who has little wit or understanding. [<WIT[1] + -LING[1]]

wit·ness (wit′nis) *n.* **1** An act or fact of attestation to a fact or an event; testimony; evidence. **2** A person who has seen or knows something, and is therefore competent to give evidence concerning it; a spectator. **3** That which serves as or furnishes evidence or proof. **4** *Law* One who has knowledge of facts relating to a given cause and is subpoenaed to testify; also, a person who has signed his name to an instrument executed by another in order that he may testify to the genuineness of the maker's signature. See synonyms under SPECTATOR, TESTIMONY. — *v.t.* **1** To see or know by personal experience. **2** To furnish or serve as evidence of. **3** To give testimony to. **4** To be the site or scene of: This spot has *witnessed* many heinous crimes. **5** *Law* To see the execution of (an instrument) and subscribe to it for the purpose of establishing its authenticity. — *v.i.* **6** To give evidence; testify. See synonyms under AVOW. [OE *witnes* knowledge, testimony] — **wit′ness·er** *n.*

witness stand The platform in a courtroom from which a witness gives evidence.

wit·ney (wit′nē) *n.* A heavy woolen fabric, preshrunk and napped, used for blankets and coats. [from *Witney,* England, where it was first manufactured]

Wit·te (vit′ə), **Count Sergei Yulievitch,** 1849–1915, Russian statesman, diplomat, and financier.

wit·ted (wit′id) *adj.* Having wit: used principally in compounds with the meaning having (a specified kind of) wit: quick-*witted,* half-*witted.*

Wit·te·kind (vit′ə·kint), died in battle 807?, leader of the Saxons against Charlemagne. Also spelled *Widukind.*

Wit·ten (vit′n) A city on the Ruhr in North Rhine–Westphalia, Germany.

Wit·ten·berg (wit′n·bûrg, *Ger.* vit′n·berkh) A city on the Elbe river in central East Germany, in the former state of Saxony–Anhalt; the Protestant Reformation originated here, 1517.

Witt·gen·stein (vit′gən·shtīn), **Ludwig,** 1889–1951, Austrian philosopher active in England.

Witt·gen·stein Island (vit′gən·shtīn) A former name for FAKARAVA.

wit·ti·cism (wit′ə·siz′əm) *n.* A witty saying. [<WITTY, on analogy with *criticism*; coined by Dryden]

wit·ting[1] (wit′ing) *adj.* Aware; done consciously, with knowledge and responsibility. [<WIT[2]]

wit·ting[2] (wit′ing) *n. Obs.* Knowledge; information. [<ON *vitand* consciousness < *vita* know]

wit·ting·ly (wit′ing·lē) *adv.* With knowledge and by design; knowingly and designedly.

wit·tol (wit′l) *n. Obs.* A contented cuckold; a husband who is aware of, but indifferent to, his wife's infidelity. [ME *wetewold* < *wete* know + *(coke)wold* cuckold]

wit·ty (wit′ē) *adj.* **·ti·er, ·ti·est 1** Given to making original or clever speeches; quick at repartee; humorous. **2** Displaying or full of wit. See synonyms under HUMOROUS. [OE *wittig* wise] **—wit′ti·ly** *adv.* **—wit′ti·ness** *n.*

Wit·wa·ters·rand (wit·wä′tərs·ränt, -rand) A region of southern Transvaal on a rocky ridge near Johannesburg; 1,000 square miles; site of the world's richest gold fields: also *The Rand.*

witz·chour·a (wits·chŏŏr′ə) *n.* A mantle with large sleeves and a wide collar, worn in the early 19th century. [<F *vitchoura* <Polish *wilczura* a wolf-skin coat < *wilk* a wolf]

wive (wīv) *v.* **wived, wiv·ing** *v.t.* **1** To furnish with a wife. **2** To marry. *—v.i.* **3** To marry a woman. [OE *wīfian* < *wīf* a wife, woman]

wi·vern (wī′vərn) *n. Her.* A two-legged, winged dragon, with barbed and knotted tail: often spelled *wyvern.* Also **wi′ver.** [<AF *wivre,* OF *guivre* a dragon, serpent, var. of *vivre* <L *vipera*]

WIVERN

wives (wīvz) Plural of WIFE.

wiz (wiz) *n. Slang* A wizard (def. 2). [Short for WIZARD]

wiz·ard (wiz′ərd) *n.* **1** One supposed to be in league with the devil; a male witch; sorcerer. **2** *Colloq.* A very skilful or clever person: He's a *wizard* with machinery. **3** *Obs.* A wise man; sage. *—adj.* **1** Having magical powers. **2** Fascinating; enchanting. [ME *wysard* < *wys,* OE *wīs* wise]

wiz·ard·ry (wiz′ərd·rē) *n.* The practice or methods of a wizard.

wiz·en[1] (wiz′ən) *v.t.* & *v.i.* To become or cause to become withered; shrivel. *—adj.* Wizened; shrunken; shriveled. [OE *wisnian* dry up, wither]

wiz·en[2] (wiz′ən) *n. Dial.* or *Obs.* The weasand. Also **wiz′zen.**

wiz·ened (wiz′ənd) *adj.* Shrunken; withered; dried up.

Wło·cła·wek (vwô·tswä′vek) A city on the Vistula in central Poland; a manufacturing center. *Russian* **Vlo·tslavsk** (vlo·tsläfsk′).

woad (wōd) *n.* **1** An Old World herb *(Isatis tinctoria)* of the mustard family; dyer's-weed. **2** The blue dyestuff obtained from its leaves. [OE *wād*] **—woad′ed** *adj.*

woad·wax·en (wōd′wak′sən) *n.* Dyer's-broom: also spelled *woodwaxen.*

woald (wōld) See WELD[2].

wob·ble (wob′əl) *v.* **·bled, ·bling** *v.i.* **1** To move or sway unsteadily, as a top while rotating at a low speed. **2** To show indecision or unsteadiness; waver; vacillate. *—v.t.* **3** To cause to wobble. *—n.* An unsteady motion, as that of unevenly balanced rotating bodies. Also spelled *wabble.* [? <LG *wabbeln*] **—wob′bler** *n.* **—wob′bling** *adj.* **—wob′bling·ly** *adv.* **—wob′bly** *adj.*

wobble pump A hand pump.

wob·bly (wob′lē) *n. pl.* **·blies** *U.S. Slang* A member of the Industrial Workers of the World (I.W.W.). [Appar. mispronunciation of *w* in *I.W.W.*]

Wode·house (wŏŏd′hous, wōd′-), **Sir P(elham) G(renville),** 1881–1975, English humorous novelist.

Wo·den (wōd′n) The Old English name for Odin, the chief Norse god. Wednesday is named for Woden. Also **Wo′dan.**

woe (wō) *n.* **1** Overwhelming sorrow; grief. **2** Heavy affliction or calamity; disaster: His *woes* are many. *—interj.* Alas! used to proclaim disaster or to express sorrow, to denounce, or invoke censure. Also **wo.** [OE *wa* misery]

woe·be·gone (wō′bi·gôn′, -gon′) *adj.* Overcome with woe; mournful; sorrowful. Also **wo′be·gone′.** See synonyms under SAD.

woe·ful (wō′fəl) *adj.* **1** Accompanied by or causing woe; direful. **2** Expressive of sorrow; doleful. **3** Deserving condemnation; paltry; miserable; mean. Also **woe′some, wo′ful.** See synonyms under PITIFUL, SAD. **—woe′ful·ly** *adv.* **—woe′ful·ness** *n.*

Wo·ë·vre (vō·e′vr′) A tableland in NE France, near Verdun; scene of severe fighting in World War I, 1915 and 1918.

Wof·fing·ton (wof′ing·tən), **Margaret,** 1714?–1760; English actress born in Dublin: commonly called "Peg Woffington."

Wöh·ler (vœ′lər), **Friedrich,** 1800–82, German chemist.

wok (wok) *n.* A Chinese cooking pan, as of iron, aluminum, or copper, with handles and a rounded bottom, usually equipped with a separate metal ring to prevent tipping. [< Chinese]

wo·kas (wō′kəs) *n.* A yellow waterlily *(Nuphar polysepalum)* of western North America, having small seeds formerly roasted and eaten by the Klamath Indians. [<Klamath]

woke (wōk) Past tense of WAKE[1].

wok·en (wō′kən) Dialectal past participle of WAKE[1].

Wol·cott (wŏŏl′kət), **Oliver,** 1726–97, American statesman; signed Declaration of Independence.

wold (wōld) *n.* An undulating tract of open upland; down or moor. [OE *wald* a forest]

Wolds (wōldz), **the** A range of hills in Lincolnshire and Yorkshire, England, parallel to the coast, north and south of the Humber; highest point, 800 feet.

wolf (wŏŏlf) *n. pl.* **wolves** (wŏŏlvz) **1** Any of a genus *(Canis)* of large carnivorous mammals related to the dog, especially the common European species *(C. lupus)* or the timber wolf of North America. ◆ Collateral adjective: *lupine.* **2** Any ravenous, cruel, or rapacious person or thing; hence, popularly, a philanderer. **3** *Entomol.* The destructive larva of various beetles and moths. **4** The harsh, dissonant sound of certain chords on a keyed instrument, as an organ or piano, when tuned by a system of unequal temperament; in bowed instruments, a harsh, discordant sound caused by defective vibration of one or more notes of a scale. **—to cry wolf** To give a false alarm. **—to keep the wolf from the door** To avert want or starvation. *—v.t.* To devour ravenously; gulp down: He *wolfed* his food. [OE *wulf*]

Wolf (wŏŏlf) The constellation Lupus.

Wolf (vôlf), **Friedrich August,** 1759–1824, German classical scholar. **—Hugo,** 1860–1903, Austrian composer.

wolf·ber·ry (wŏŏlf′ber′ē) *n. pl.* **·ries** A shrub *(Symphoricarpos occidentalis)* of the honeysuckle family, with pinkish, bell-shaped flowers and white berries in spikes, growing in the western United States.

Wolf Cub A member of the division of Boy Scouts for boys between 8 and 11 years of age.

wolf dog 1 A large dog for hunting wolves. **2** A cross between a wolf and a dog.

Wolfe (wŏŏlf), **Charles,** 1791–1823, Irish poet. **—James,** 1727–59, English general; defeated the French under Montcalm at Quebec; both he and Montcalm were killed. **—Thomas Clayton,** 1900–38, U. S. novelist.

Wolff (vôlf), **Christian von,** 1679–1754, German philosopher. **—Kaspar Friedrich,** 1733–1794, German anatomist.

Wolf-Fer·ra·ri (vôlf′fer·rä′rē), **Ermanno,** 1876–1948, Italian composer.

Wolff·i·an (wŏŏl′fē·ən) *adj.* Pertaining to or named after the German anatomist Kaspar F. Wolff.

Wolffian body *Anat.* The mesonephros.

wolf fish A large fish *(Anarhichas lupus)* of the North Atlantic, with powerful teeth adapted for crushing shellfish.

Wolf·gang (vôlf′gäng) *German* A masculine personal name. [<G, a wolf's progress]

wolf·hound (wŏŏlf′hound′) *n.* Either of two breeds of large dogs, the **Russian wolfhound** or *borzoi* and the **Irish wolfhound,** a dog resembling the Great Dane, trained, or originally intended, to catch and kill wolves.

wolf·ish (wŏŏl′fish) *adj.* **1** Having the qualities of a wolf; rapacious; savage. **2** *Colloq.* Ravenously hungry. **—wolf′ish·ly** *adv.* **—wolf′ish·ness** *n.*

wolf pack A number of submarines which co-operate in making concerted attacks on enemy ships or convoys.

wolf·ram (wŏŏl′frəm) *n.* **1** Wolframite. **2** Tungsten. [<G, prob. < *wolf* a wolf + *rahm* cream, soot]

wolf·ram·ite (wŏŏl′frəm·īt) *n.* A submetallic, grayish-black or brown tungstate of iron and manganese, crystallizing in the monoclinic system. It is important commercially as a source of tungsten and its compounds. [<G *wolframit* < *wolfram* tungsten]

Wol·fram von Esch·en·bach (vôl′främ fôn esh′ən·bäkh), 1165?–1220?, German poet.

wolf's-bane (wŏŏlfs′bān′) *n.* **1** A species of aconite; monkshood. **2** A species of European arnica *(Arnica montana),* used as a lotion for bruises. **3** The silk vine. [Trans. of NL *lycoctonum* <Gk. *lykoktonon,* lit., a wolf-slayer < *lykos* a wolf + *kteinein* kill]

Wol·las·ton (wŏŏl′əs·tən), **William Hyde,** 1766–1828, English chemist and physicist.

wol·las·ton·ite (wŏŏl′əs·tən·īt′) *n.* A vitreous, white, translucent calcium silicate, crystallizing in the monoclinic system. [after Dr. W. H. *Wollaston*]

Wolse·ley (wŏŏlz′lē), **Garnet Joseph,** 1833–1913, first Viscount Wolseley, British general.

Wol·sey (wŏŏl′zē), **Thomas,** 1475?–1530, English cardinal and statesman.

wolv·er (wŏŏl′vər) *n.* One who hunts wolves.

Wol·ver·hamp·ton (wŏŏl′vər·hamp′tən) A county borough and industrial center in southern Stafford, England.

wol·ver·ine (wŏŏl′və·rēn′) *n.* A rapacious and cunning carnivore (genus *Gulo*) of northern forests, with stout body and limbs and bushy tail. Also **wol′ver·ene′.** [Dim. of WOLF]

WOLVERINE (Body to 3 feet long; tail, 1 1/2 feet)

Wolverine State Nickname of MICHIGAN.

wolves (wŏŏlvz) Plural of WOLF.

wom·an (wŏŏm′ən) *n. pl.* **wom·en** (wim′in) **1** An adult human female. **2** The female part of the human race; women collectively. **3** Womanly character; femininity: usually with *the.* **4** As applied to a man, one who is effeminate, timid, or weak. **5** A female attendant or servant. **6** A paramour or kept mistress. **7** *Colloq.* A wife. *—adj.* **1** Feminine; characteristic of women. **2** Female: when used with a plural noun, usually *women*: *women* students. **3** Affecting or pertaining to women. *—v.t. Obs.* To play the part of a woman in or in reference to. [OE *wīfmann* < *wīf* a wife + *mann* a human being]

wom·an·hood (wŏŏm′ən·hŏŏd) *n.* **1** The state of a woman or of womankind. **2** Women collectively.

wom·an·ish (wŏŏm′ən·ish) *adj.* Characteristic of a woman; effeminate. See synonyms under FEMININE. **—wom′an·ish·ly** *adv.* **—wom′an·ish·ness** *n.*

wom·an·ize (wŏŏm′ən·īz) *v.* **·ized, ·iz·ing** *v.t.*

To make effeminate or womanish. —*v.i. Colloq.* To consort with women illicitly.
wom·an·kind (wŏŏm′ən·kīnd′) *n.* Women collectively.
wom·an·ly (wŏŏm′ən·lē) *adj.* Having the qualities natural, suited, or becoming to a woman; feminine. —*adv.* In a feminine manner; like a woman. —**wom′an·li·ness** *n.*
woman suffrage See under SUFFRAGE. —**wom′an–suf′fra·gist** *n.*
womb (wōōm) *n.* **1** The organ in which the young of higher mammals are developed; the uterus. **2** The place where anything is engendered or brought into life. **3** A cavity viewed as enclosing something. **4** *Obs.* The belly or stomach. [OE *wamb, womb* the belly]
wom·bat (wom′bat) *n.* An Australian nocturnal marsupial (family *Vombatidae*) resembling a small bear. [<Australian]

WOMBAT
(From 3 to 4 feet in length)

wombed (wōōmd) *adj.* Having a womb; hence, hollow; capacious; cavernous. Also **womb′y.**
wom·en (wim′in) Plural of WOMAN.
wom·en·folk (wim′in·fōk′) *n. pl.* Women collectively. Also **wom′en·folks′.**
Women in the Air Force A corps of women in the U.S. Air Force, including all women except nurses and medical specialists. Abbr. *WAF* or *W.A.F.*
Woman's Army Corps A corps of women in the U.S. Army, composed of all women except nurses and medical specialists. Abbr. *WAC* or *W.A.C.*
women's rights The rights of women to enjoy equal legal rights and privileges with men, as of suffrage, property, and education.
wom·er·a (wom′ər·ə) *n.* A stick used by Australian aborigines for throwing javelins, spears, etc.: also *woomera.* [<Australian]
won[1] (wun) Past tense and past participle of WIN.
won[2] (wun) *v.i. Scot. & Brit. Dial.* To abide; dwell; live. [OE *wunian*]
won·der (wun′dər) *n.* **1** A feeling of mingled surprise and curiosity; astonishment. **2** That which causes wonder; a prodigy; a strange thing; a miracle. See synonyms under PRODIGY. —**nine days' wonder** Something that excites public wonder for a short time. —*v.t.* **1** To have a feeling of doubt and strong curiosity in regard to. —*v.i.* **2** To be affected or filled with wonder; marvel. **3** To be doubtful; query mentally. —*adj.* Spectacularly successful: a *wonder* drug. [OE *wundor*] —**won′der·er** *n.* —**won′der·ing** *adj.* —**won′der·ing·ly** *adv.*
won·der·ful (wun′dər·fəl) *adj.* Of a nature to excite wonder; marvelous. See synonyms under EXTRAORDINARY. —**won′der·ful·ly** *adv.* —**won′der·ful·ness** *n.*
won·der·land (wun′dər·land′) *n.* A realm of fairy romance or wonders.
won·der·ment (wun′dər·mənt) *n.* **1** The emotion of wonder; surprise. **2** Something wonderful; a marvel.
Wonder State Nickname for ARKANSAS.
won·der–strick·en (wun′dər·strik′ən) *adj.* Suddenly smitten with wonder or admiration. Also **won′der–struck′** (-struk′).
won·der–work (wun′dər·wûrk′) *n.* A work inspiring wonder; miracle. —**won′der–work′er** *n.* —**won′der–work′ing** *adj.*
won·drous (wun′drəs) *adj.* Commanding wonder; wonderful; marvelous. —*adv.* Surprisingly. [Alter. of ME *wonders,* genitive of WONDER] —**won′drous·ly** *adv.* —**won′drous·ness** *n.*
won·ky (wong′kē) *adj. Brit. Slang* Unsteady; liable to break down; shaky; feeble. [Prob. OE *wancol* shaky]
won·ner (wun′ər) *n. Scot.* A prodigy; wonder.
Won·san (wœn·sän) A port in eastern Korea: Japanese *Gensan.*
wont (wunt, wōnt) *v.* **wont, wont** or **wont·ed, wont·ing** *v.t.* **1** To accustom or habituate: used reflexively. —*v.i.* **2** To be accustomed; be used. **3** *Obs.* To dwell. [<*adj.*] —*adj.* Doing habitually; accustomed; used. —*n.* Ordinary manner of doing or acting; habit. See synonyms under HABIT. [OE *gewunod,* pp. of *gewunian* be accustomed]
won't (wōnt) Will not: a contraction of Middle English *woll not.* Also *Scot.* **won·na** (wun′nə).
wont·ed (wun′tid, wōn′-) *adj.* **1** Commonly used or done; habitual. **2** Habituated; accustomed; at ease; at home. See synonyms under HABITUAL, USUAL. —**wont′ed·ness** *n.*
woo[1] (wōō) *v.t.* **1** To make love to, especially so as to marry; court. **2** To entreat earnestly; beg. **3** To invite; solicit; seek. —*v.i.* **4** To pay court; make love. See synonyms under ADDRESS. [OE *wōgian*]
woo[2] (wōō) *n. Scot.* Wool.
wood[1] (wŏŏd) *n.* **1** A large and compact collection of trees; a forest; grove: also **woods. 2** The hard, fibrous material between the pith and bark of a tree or shrub, and also occurring in some herbaceous plants; the xylem. **3** The hard substance of a tree or shrub, whether as growing or as cut for use, for building, fuel, etc.; lumber; timber. **4** Something made of wood. **5** *pl.* A rural district; backwoods. —**to knock wood** To tap on a piece of wood or a wooden object as a charm against bad luck, especially while making an optimistic statement. —*adj.* **1** Made of wood; wooden. **2** Made for using or holding wood: a *wood* stove. **3** Living or growing in woods: the *wood* anemone. —*v.t.* **1** To furnish with wood for fuel. **2** To convert into a forest; plant with trees. —*v.i.* **3** To take on a supply of wood. [OE *widu, wiodu*]
wood[2] (wŏŏd) *Obs. v.i.* To act like a maniac; rave. —*adj.* Furious; frantic; raging; mad. [OE *wōd* insane]
Wood (wŏŏd), **Grant,** 1892–1942, U.S. painter. —**Leonard,** 1860–1927, U.S. physician, army officer, and colonial administrator.
wood alcohol Methanol.
wood anemone Any of several small plants (genus *Anemone*), growing in woodlands and blooming in the early spring, especially the common American species (*A. quinquefolia*), and the common European species (*A. nemorosa*).
wood betony **1** The common lousewort (*Pedicularis canadensis*) of the eastern United States, with yellow or reddish flowers. **2** The common betony (*Stachys officinalis*).
wood·bin (wŏŏd′bin′) *n.* A box or crib for holding firewood.
wood·bine (wŏŏd′bīn) *n.* **1** The common European honeysuckle. **2** The Virginia creeper. [OE *wudubind* < *wudu* wood + *bindan* bind]
wood·block (wŏŏd′blok′) *n.* **1** A block of wood prepared for engraving. **2** A woodcut.
wood block **1** A block of wood for paving, etc. **2** *Music* A percussion instrument consisting of a hollow block of wood struck with a drumstick.
wood·bor·er (wŏŏd′bôr′ər, -bō′rər) *n.* Any of a large family (*Buprestidae*) of brilliantly colored beetles whose larvae are very destructive of trees. For illustration see INSECTS (injurious).
wood·carv·ing (wŏŏd′kär′ving) *n.* **1** The art of carving wood, especially for decoration. **2** A carving in wood. —**wood′carv′er** *n.*
wood·chat (wŏŏd′chat) *n.* **1** A European butcherbird (*Lanius collorio*) with reddish plumage and a notched beak. **2** Any of several Asian birds (genera *Ianthia* and *Larvivora*) of the thrush family. [Prob. partial trans. of G *waldkatze* the butcherbird, lit., wood cat]
wood·chuck (wŏŏd′chuk) *n.* A marmot (*Marmota monax*) of eastern North America; a ground hog. [Prob. alter. of WEJACK; infl. in form by WOOD[1] and CHUCK[1]]

WOODCHUCK
(Head and body to 14 inches; tail, 5 inches)

wood coal **1** Charcoal made from wood: also **wood charcoal. 2** Lignite.
wood·cock (wŏŏd′kok′) *n.* **1** A small European game bird (*Scolopax rusticola*), having the thighs entirely feathered. **2** A related North American bird (*Philohela minor*). **3** *Obs.* A dolt; fool.
wood·craft (wŏŏd′kraft′, -kräft′) *n.* **1** Skill in such things as belong to woodland life, such as hunting or trapping; the faculty of finding one's way, and living comfortably in the wilderness. **2** Skill in woodwork or in constructing articles of wood. —**wood′crafts′man** (-krafts′mən, -kräfts′-) *n.*
wood·cut (wŏŏd′kut′) *n.* **1** An engraving on wood. **2** A print from such a block.
wood·cut·ter (wŏŏd′kut′ər) *n.* One who cuts or chops wood. —**wood′cut′ting** *n.*
wood·ed (wŏŏd′id) *adj.* Having a supply of wood; abounding with trees.
wood·en (wŏŏd′n) *adj.* **1** Made of wood: *wooden* tools. **2** Like a block of wood; stupid; mechanical; stiff; awkward. **3** Dull; spiritless. —**wood′en·ly** *adv.* —**wood′en·ness** *n.*
wood engraving **1** The art of cutting designs on wood for printing; the making of woodcuts. **2** A block thus engraved or a print therefrom. —**wood engraver**
wood·en·head (wŏŏd′n·hed′) *n. Colloq.* A stupid person; blockhead. —**wood′en–head′ed** *adj.*
wooden horse See TROJAN HORSE (def. 1).
wooden Indian **1** A carved and painted wooden figure of a North American Indian, usually in a standing position, formerly placed in front of cigar stores as an advertisement. **2** An inarticulate, sluggish, or dull person.
wooden nutmeg **1** An imitation nutmeg: proverbially used by New England (especially Connecticut) traders. **2** Any deceptive device.
wood·en–shoe dance (wŏŏd′n·shōō′) The trasko.
wood·en·ware (wŏŏd′n·wâr′) *n.* Dishes, vessels, bowls, etc., made of wood: said especially of household utensils.
Wood Green A municipal borough in Middlesex, England, 7 miles north of London.
wood grouse The capercaillie.
wood·hen (wŏŏd′hen′) *n.* A weka.
wood·house (wŏŏd′hous′) *n.* A house or shed for storing firewood. Also called *woodshed.*
wood hyacinth A small European squill (*Scilla nonscripta*), with clusters of bell-shaped blue, white, or pink flowers.
wood ibis A very large storklike bird (*Mycteria americana*) with a white body, glossy black tail, and naked head, common in wooded swamps of South America and the southern United States.
wood·ie (wŏŏd′ē) *n. Scot.* The gallows; a hangman's rope: used humorously.
wood·land (wŏŏd′lənd, -land′) *n.* Land occupied by or covered with wood or trees; timberland. —*adj.* (-lənd) Belonging to or dwelling in the woods. —**wood′land′er** *n.*
woodland caribou See under CARIBOU.
wood·lark (wŏŏd′lärk′) *n.* A European passerine bird (*Lullula arborea*) resembling the skylark but with a sweeter note.
Woodlark Island A Papuan island in the Territory of Papua and New Guinea SE of New Guinea; 400 square miles.
wood lot A plot of land devoted to the growing of forest trees or consisting of woodland.
wood louse Any of numerous small terrestrial flat-bodied crustaceans (genera *Oniscus, Porcellion,* and others) commonly found under old logs; a sow bug or pill bug.
wood·man (wŏŏd′mən) *n. pl.* **·men** (-mən) **1** A woodcutter; lumberman. **2** A forester; also, a dweller in forests. **3** A hunter of forest game. Also *woodsman.*
wood·note (wŏŏd′nōt′) *n.* A simple, artless, or natural song, as of a wild bird.
wood nymph **1** A goddess or nymph of the forest; a dryad. **2** Any of several South American hummingbirds (genus *Thalurania*). **3** A butterfly of the family *Satyridae,* including species usually brown in color and with eyelike spots on the wings. They occur in woods and are not attracted to flowers.
wood·peck·er (wŏŏd′pek′ər) *n.* Any of a large family (*Picidae*) of birds related to the flickers, having stiff tail feathers to aid in climbing, strong claws, and a sharp, chisel-like bill for drilling holes in wood in search of insects; especially, the **red-headed woodpecker** (*Melanerpes erythrocephalus*) of North America, which has the head

RED-HEADED WOODPECKER
(9 to 9 1/2 inches long)

and upper breast deep red and the tail black, tipped with white; and the **pileated woodpecker** of North America *(Ceophloeus pileatus)* with a scarlet crest, white throat, white wing markings, and a large yellowish bill.

wood pewee Pewee (def. 1).

wood pigeon **1** The cushat. **2** The wild band-tailed pigeon *(Columba fasciata)* of the western United States.

wood·pile (wŏŏd′pīl′) *n.* A pile of wood, especially of wood cut or split in sizes for burning in a fireplace or stove.

wood pitch The final residuum of wood tar.

wood·print (wŏŏd′print′) *n.* A woodcut.

wood pulp Wood reduced to a pulp, as by grinding to a powder and digesting with chemicals: used for making paper.

wood pussy *Colloq.* A skunk.

wood rat A pack rat.

wood·ruff (wŏŏd′ruf′) *n.* Any of several common European woodland herbs (genus *Asperula*) of the madder family, especially the **sweet-scented woodruff** *(A. odorata)*, used to flavor wine and in perfumery. [OE *wudurofe* < *wudu* wood]

woods (wŏŏdz) *n. pl.* A forest or wooded area.

Woods, Lake of the See LAKE OF THE WOODS.

wood-screw (wŏŏd′skrōō′) *n.* A screw with a thread of coarse pitch, used for fastening pieces against wood. See illustration under SCREW.

wood·shed (wŏŏd′shed′) *n.* A woodhouse.

woods·i·a (wŏŏd′zē·ə) *n.* Any of a genus *(Woodsia)* of small tufted ferns, found in rocky places. [after Joseph *Woods,* 1776–1864, English botanist]

woods·man (wŏŏdz·mən) *n.* *pl.* **·men** (-mən) **1** A woodman. **2** A man skilled in woodcraft.

wood sorrel Oxalis.

wood spirit Wood alcohol or methanol.

Wood·stock (wŏŏd′stok) A municipal borough of central Oxfordshire, England.

wood sugar Xylose.

woods·y (wŏŏd′zē) *adj. Colloq.* Of, pertaining to, or dwelling in the woods; suggesting the woods: a *woodsy* fragrance.

wood tar A tar produced by the dry distillation of wood: it contains turpentine, resins, oils, creosote, and other hydrocarbons, and yields pyroligneous acid.

wood thrush **1** A large, common woodland thrush of North America *(Hylocichla mustelina)*, noted for the vigor and sweetness of its song. **2** The missel thrush.

wood tick Any of certain ticks found in the woods, especially *Dermacentor variabilis* which transfers itself from underbrush to passing animals or human beings.

wood·turn·ing (wŏŏd′tûr′ning) *n.* The process or art of shaping blocks of wood into various forms by means of a lathe. **— wood′turn′er** *n.*

wood vinegar **1** Impure acetic acid from the distillation of wood. **2** Pyroligneous acid.

wood violet The bird's-foot violet.

wood·wax·en (wŏŏd′wak′sən) See WOADWAXEN.

wood·wind (wŏŏd′wind′) *n.* A musical wind instrument made of wood. See WIND INSTRUMENT. — *adj.* Pertaining to or characteristic of a wooden wind instrument.

wood·work (wŏŏd′wûrk′) *n.* **1** The wooden parts of any structure, especially interior wooden parts, as moldings or doors. **2** Work made of wood. **— wood′work′er** *n.* **— wood′·work′ing** *n.*

wood·worm (wŏŏd′wûrm′) *n.* A worm or larva dwelling in or that bores in wood.

wood·y (wŏŏd′ē) *adj.* **wood·i·er, wood·i·est** **1** Of the nature of wood; containing wood; ligneous. **2** Pertaining to wood; resembling wood. **3** Wooded; abounding with woods; sylvan. **— wood′i·ness** *n.*

woo·er (wōō′ər) *n.* One who woos; a lover.

woof[1] (wŏŏf) *n.* **1** The weft of a woven fabric; the threads that are carried back and forth across the fixed threads of the warp in a loom. **2** The texture of a fabric. [OE *ōwef*]

woof[2] (wŏŏf) *n.* A sound made in imitation of the growl or low suppressed bark of a dog or bear. [Imit.]

woof·er (wŏŏf′ər) *n. Electronics* A loudspeaker used to reproduce the bass register in high-fidelity sound equipment, generally in connection with a tweeter. [<WOOF[2]]

wool (wŏŏl) *n.* **1** The soft, curly or crisped hair obtained from the fleece of sheep and some allied animals, especially that from domesticated sheep, noted for its felting properties and which provides the widest range of fibers for yarns and textiles. **2** The underfur of a fur-bearing animal. **3** Short kinky or crisp human hair. **4** Material or garments made of wool. **5** Something resembling or likened to wool. **— all wool and a yard wide** Perfect in quality and quantity; hence, one hundred percent genuine. **— to pull the wool over one's eyes** To delude or deceive one. — *adj.* Made of or pertaining to wool or woolen material. [OE *wull*]

wool-clip (wŏŏl′klip′) *n.* The amount of wool clipped from the sheep in one year.

wool-dyed (wŏŏl′dīd′) *adj.* Dyed before the wool has been spun into yarn: said of fabrics.

wool·en (wŏŏl′ən) *adj.* **1** Consisting wholly or in part of wool; like wool. **2** Pertaining to wool or its manufacture. — *n.* Cloth or clothing made of wool: especially in the plural. Also **wool′len.**

Woolf (wŏŏlf), **(Adeline) Virginia,** 1882–1941, *née* Stephen, English novelist and essayist.

wool fat Lanolin. Also **wool grease.**

wool·fell (wŏŏl′fel′) *n.* The pelt of a sheep or other wool-bearing animal with the wool still on it. [<WOOL + FELL[4]]

wool·gath·er·ing (wŏŏl′gath′ər·ing) *n.* Any trivial or purposeless employment; especially, idle reverie: from gathering wool caught on bushes, which required much wandering to collect even a little. — *adj.* Idly indulging in fancies. **— wool′gath′er·er** *n.*

wool·grow·er (wŏŏl′grō′ər) *n.* A person who raises sheep for the production of wool. **— wool′grow′ing** *adj.*

Wooll·cott (wŏŏl′kət), **Alexander,** 1887–1943, U. S. journalist and critic.

Wool·ley (wŏŏl′ē), **Sir (Charles) Leonard,** 1880–1960, English archeologist.

wool·ly (wŏŏl′ē) *adj.* **·li·er, ·li·est** **1** Consisting of, covered with, or resembling wool; wool-bearing. **2** Soft and vaporous; lacking clearness; not sharply detailed; fuzzy; blurry. **3** Having a rounded and somewhat fleecy appearance, as clouds. **4** Having a growth of wool-like hairs. **5** Resembling the roughness and excitement of the West: usually in the phrase *wild and woolly.* — *n.* *pl.* **·lies** A garment made of wool; especially, woolen underwear. Also **wool′y. — wool′li·ness, wool′·i·ness** *n.*

woolly bear The larva of any of several tiger moths: so called because covered with long dense hairs.

wool·pack (wŏŏl′pak′) *n.* **1** A bag or wrapper of canvas, cotton, etc., for packing a bale of wool. **2** A bale or bundle of wool. **3** *Meteorol.* A cumulus cloud.

wool·sack (wŏŏl′sak′) *n.* **1** A sack of wool. **2** The seat of the lord chancellor in the English House of Lords, a cushion stuffed with wool. **3** The office of lord high chancellor.

wool-sta·pler (wŏŏl′stā′plər) *n.* A dealer in or sorter of wool. **— wool′-sta′pling** *adj.* & *n.*

Wool·wich (wŏŏl′ich, -ij) A metropolitan borough of London on the south bank of the Thames.

Wool·worth (wŏŏl′wûrth), **Frank Winfield,** 1852–1919, U. S. merchant; developed the five-and-ten-cent store.

woom·e·ra (wŏŏ′mər·ə) *n.* A womera.

Woon·sock·et (wŏŏn·sok′it) A city in NE Rhode Island on the Blackstone River.

woo·ra·li (wōō·rä′lē) *n.* Curare. Also **woo·ra′ri** (-rē). [Var. of CURARE]

Woo·sung (wōō′sŏŏng′) The outer port of Shanghai, China, at the mouth of the Hwangpoo, north of Shanghai.

wooz·y (wōō′zē) *adj. Slang* **1** Befuddled, especially with drink. **2** Fuzzy. [Prob. < *wooze,* var. of OOZE] **— wooz′i·ly** *adv.* **— wooz′i·ness** *n.*

wop (wop) *n. Slang* An Italian: a derogatory term. [? <dial. Ital. (Sicilian) *guapo* a dandy <Sp.]

Worces·ter (wŏŏs′tər) **1** A midland county in England; 699 square miles. Also **Worces′·ter·shire** (-shir). **2** Its county town, famous for its 14th century cathedral. **3** A city in central Massachusetts, second largest in the State; an industrial, rail, and university center.

Worces·ter (wŏŏs′tər), **Joseph Emerson,** 1784–1865, U. S. lexicographer.

Worcester china A very fine china or porcelain made in Worcester, England, from 1751: also **Worcester porcelain,** and called **Royal Worcester** by royal warrant.

Worcestershire sauce A piquant sauce made originally in Worcester, England, from vinegar and many other ingredients. Also **Worcester sauce.**

word (wûrd) *n.* **1** A speech sound or combination of sounds which has come to signify and communicate a particular idea or thought, and which functions as the smallest meaningful unit of a language when used in isolation. There are **basic** or **radical words** as *master, man,* **derivative words** as *masterful, manly,* **inflectional words** as *masters, men,* and **compound words** as *masterpiece, manpower,* etc. In terms of modern linguistics, a word may be a single morpheme (a free form, as *master*) or a union of morphemes (free and bound forms, as *masters, masterful, masterpiece*). **2** The letters or characters that stand for a significant vocal sound. **3** A vocable considered only as a sound: ideas rather than *words.* **4** *Usually pl.* Conversation; talk: a man of few *words.* **5** A brief remark; hence, a short and pithy saying. **6** A communication or message: Send him *word.* **7** A command, signal, or direction: Give the *word* to start. **8** A promise; hence, good faith: a man of his *word.* **9** A party cry; watchword. **10** *pl.* Language used in anger, rebuke, or otherwise emotionally: They had *words.* See synonyms under TERM. — *v.t.* To express in a word or words, especially in selected words; phrase. [OE. Akin to ◆ VERB.]

Word (wûrd) *n.* **1** The Logos; the Son of God. **2** Divine Wisdom, as in *John* i. **3** The Scriptures as an embodiment of divine revelation.

word·age (wûr′dij) *n.* Words collectively.

word-blind·ness (wûrd′blīnd′nis) *n.* Alexia. **— word′-blind′** *adj.*

word·book (wûrd′bŏŏk′) *n.* **1** A collection of words; vocabulary; lexicon; dictionary. **2** An opera libretto.

word-coin·er (wûrd′koi′nər) *n.* One who makes up new words; a practitioner of logotechnics.

word deafness Inability to understand speech, resulting from disease of the cortical center: a form of aphasia.

word for word In the exact words; literally; verbatim.

word·i·ly (wûr′də·lē) *adv.* In a wordy manner; verbosely. **— word′i·ness, word′ish·ness** *n.*

word·ing (wûr′ding) *n.* The act or style of expressing in words; phraseology; also, words used; expression. See synonyms under DICTION.

word·less (wûrd′lis) *adj.* Having no words; dumb; silent.

word play **1** Repartee; fencing with words. **2** Subtle discussion on words and their meaning. **3** Play on words.

word square An arrangement of a set of words in rectangular form, so that they can be read in either horizontal or vertical lines, as in the accompanying example.

FRET
REAR
EASE
TREE

Words·worth (wûrdz′wûrth), **William,** 1770–1850, English poet; laureate 1843–50.

word-watch·er (wûrd′woch′ər) *n.* A close observer of words and their ways.

word·y (wûr′dē) *adj.* **word·i·er, word·i·est** **1** Of the nature of words; verbal. **2** Expressed in many words. **3** Given to the use of words; verbose; prolix.

wore (wôr, wōr) Past tense of WEAR[1] & WEAR[2].

work (wûrk) *n.* **1** Continued exertion or activity directed to some purpose or end; especially, manual labor; hence, opportunity for labor; occupation. **2** That upon which labor is expended; an undertaking; task. **3** That which is produced by or as by labor; specifically, an engineering structure; fortification; a design produced with a needle; also, a product of mental labor, as a book or opera. **4** A manufacturing or other industrial establishment: usually in the plural. **5** *pl.* Running gear or machinery, as of a watch. **6**

Manner of working, or style of treatment; management; workmanship. **7** *pl.* Moral duties considered as external acts, especially as meritorious. **8** A froth or foam produced by fermentation in making vinegar, etc. **9** A feat or deed. **10** *Physics* A transference of energy from one body to another, resulting in the motion or displacement of the body acted upon, in the direction of the acting force: it is expressed as the product of the force and the amount of displacement in the line of its action. — *v.* **worked** (*Archaic* **wrought**), **work·ing** *v.i.* **1** To perform work; labor; toil. **2** To be employed in some trade or business. **3** To perform a function; operate: The machine *works* well. **4** To prove effective or influential; succeed: His stratagem *worked.* **5** To move or progress gradually or with difficulty: He *worked* up in his profession. **6** To become as specified, as by gradual motion: The bolts *worked* loose. **7** To have some slight improper motion in functioning: The wheel *works* on the shaft. **8** To move from nervousness or agitation: His features *worked* with passion. **9** To undergo kneading, hammering, etc.; be shaped: Copper *works* easily. **10** To ferment. **11** *Naut.* To labor in a heavy sea so as to loosen seams and fastenings: said of a ship. — *v.t.* **12** To cause or bring about; effect; accomplish: to *work* a miracle. **13** To cause to function; direct the operation of: to *work* a machine. **14** To make or shape by toil or skill. **15** To prepare, as by manipulating, hammering, etc.: to *work* dough. **16** To decorate, as with embroidery or inlaid work. **17** To cause to be productive, as by toil: to *work* a mine **18** To cause to do work: He *works* his employees too hard. **19** To cause to be as specified, usually with effort: We *worked* the timber into position. **20** To make or achieve by effort: He *worked* his way to the top of his profession; to *work* one's passage on a ship. **21** To carry on some activity in (an area, etc.); cover: to *work* a stream for trout. **22** To solve, as a problem in arithmetic. **23** To cause to move from nervousness or excitement: to *work* one's jaws. **24** To excite; provoke: He *worked* himself into a passion. **25** To influence or manage, as by insidious means; lead. **26** To cause to ferment. **27** *Colloq.* To practice trickery upon; cheat; swindle. **28** *Colloq.* To make use of for one's own purposes; use. — **to work in** To put in; insert or be inserted. — **to work off** To get rid of, as extra flesh by exercise. — **to work on** (or **upon**) **1** To try to influence or persuade. **2** To influence or affect. — **to work out 1** To make its way out or through. **2** To effect by work or effort; accomplish. **3** To exhaust, as a mineral vein or a subject of inquiry. **4** To discharge, as a debt, by labor rather than by payment of money. **5** To develop; form, as a plan. **6** To solve. **7 a** To prove effective or successful. **b** To result as specified. — **to work up 1** To excite; rouse, as rage or a person to rage. **2** To form or shape by working; develop. **3** To make one's or its way. [OE *weorc*]

Synonyms (noun): achievement, action, business, deed, doing, drudgery, employment, exertion, labor, occupation, performance, product, production, toil. *Work* is the generic term for any continuous application of energy toward an end; *work* may be hard or easy. *Labor* is hard and wearying *work*; *toil* is straining and exhausting *work*. *Work* is also used for any result of working, physical or mental; as, a *work* of art; a *work* of genius. In this connection, *work* has special uses, which *labor* and *toil* do not share. *Drudgery* is plodding, irksome, and often menial *work*. See ACT, BUSINESS, PRODUCTION, TASK, TOIL[1]. *Antonyms*: ease, idleness, leisure, recreation, relaxation, repose, rest, vacation.

-work *combining form* **1** A product made from a (specified) material: *paperwork, brickwork.* **2** Work of a (given) kind: *piecework.* **3** Work performed in a (specified) place: *housework.* [<WORK]

work·a·ble (wûr′kə·bəl) *adj.* **1** Of a nature to be operated, as a machine. **2** Practicable, as a plan. **3** That can be developed, as a mine. **4** Able to work. **5** That can be worked upon or influenced. — **work′a·bil′i·ty, work′a·ble·ness** *n.*

work·a·day (wûrk′ə·dā′) *adj.* **1** Of, pertaining to, or suitable for working days; everyday. **2** Commonplace; prosaic. [Alter. of ME *werkeday* < *werke*, OE *weorca* work + DAY; infl. in form by NOWADAYS]

work·bag (wûrk′bag′) *n.* A bag for holding tools or materials, as for needlework.

work·bench (wûrk′bench′) *n.* A bench for work, as that of a carpenter, machinist, etc.

work·book (wûrk′bo͝ok′) *n.* **1** A booklet based on a course of study and containing problems and exercises which a student works out directly on the pages. **2** A manual containing operating instructions. **3** A book for recording work performed or planned.

work·box (wûrk′boks′) *n.* A small bag or box for needlework, etc.

work·day (wûrk′dā′) *n.* **1** Any day not a Sunday or holiday; a working day. **2** The part of the day or number of hours of one day spent in work. — *adj.* Workaday.

work·er (wûr′kər) *n.* **1** One who or that which performs work; specifically, a laborer as distinguished from a *capitalist.* **2** An individual female of an insect colony, as a true ant, a bee, or a white ant, with undeveloped sexual organs.

work·fel·low (wûrk′fel′ō) *n.* A companion in work.

work·folk (wûrk′fōk′) *n. pl.* Manual laborers. Also **work′folks′** (-fōks′).

work·house (wûrk′hous′) *n.* **1** *Brit.* A house for paupers able to work; an almshouse. **2** An industrial prison for petty offenders.

work·ing (wûr′king) *adj.* **1** Engaged actively in some employment. **2** That works, or performs its function: This is a *working* model. **3** Sufficient for use or action: They formed a *working* agreement. **4** Relating to or occupied by work: a *working* day. **5** Throbbing with pain; also, twitching: said especially of the face muscles. **6** Fermenting, as wine. — *n.* **1** The act or operation of any person or thing that works, in any sense. **2** That part of a mine or quarry where excavation is going on or has gone on.

working capital 1 That part of the finances of a business available for its operation. **2** The amount of quick assets which exceed current liabilities.

working day 1 A day not a legal holiday; a workday. **2** The number of hours constituting a day's work: a four-hour *working day.*

working drawing In engineering, etc., a drawing made to scale, as of a part of a machine or building, for the direction of workmen, contractors, etc.

work·ing·man (wûr′king·man′) *n. pl.* **·men** (-men′) A male worker; laborer.

working papers An age certificate and other official papers certifying that a minor may be legally employed.

working substance *Mech.* The fluid, as steam, or gasoline vapor, under pressure, that serves to operate a prime mover. Also **working fluid.**

work·ing·wom·an (wûr′king·wo͝om′ən) *n. pl.* **·wom·en** (-wim′in) A female worker; laborer.

work·less (wûrk′lis) *adj.* Jobless; unemployed.

work·load (wûrk′lōd′) *n.* The amount of work apportioned to a person, machine, or department over a given period.

work·man (wûrk′mən) *n. pl.* **·men** (-mən) One who earns his bread by manual labor; an artisan; mechanic; workingman. — **work′·man·ly** *adj.*

work·man·like (wûrk′mən·līk) *adj.* Like or befitting a skilled workman; skilfully done. — **work′man·ly** *adv.*

work·man·ship (wûrk′mən·ship) *n.* **1** The art or skill of a workman, or the quality of work. **2** The work or result produced by a worker.

work of art A product of the fine arts, especially painting and sculpture, but including artistic, literary, and musical productions.

work·out (wûrk′out′) *n.* A test, trial, practice performance, etc., to discover, maintain, or increase ability for some work or competition, as a practice boxing bout, a fast turn around a track by a horse, runner, etc.

work·peo·ple (wûrk′pē′pəl) *n. pl.* People employed in work, especially in manual labor; working people.

work·room (wûrk′ro͞om′, -ro͝om′) *n.* A room where work is performed.

works (wûrks) *n.* **1** A manufacturing establishment including buildings and equipment: a gas *works.* **2** *Slang* The whole of anything; the kit and caboodle; everything: the whole *works.* — **to give (someone) the works** *Slang* To maul; kill by shooting. — **to shoot the works** *Slang* To make a supreme effort; risk one's all in one single attempt.

works council A committee of employed workers organized by an employer to discuss company and industrial problems and relations; a company union or similar group.

work·sheet (wûrk′shēt′) *n.* **1** A sheet of paper on which practice work or rough drafts of problems are written. **2** A sheet of paper used to record work schedules and operations.

work·shop (wûrk′shop′) *n.* **1** A building or room where any work is carried on; workroom. **2** A seminar or single session for training, discussion, etc., in a specialized field: a writer's *workshop.*

work·ta·ble (wûrk′tā′bəl) *n.* A table with drawers and other conveniences for use while working, especially while sewing.

work·week (wûrk′wēk′) *n.* The total number of hours worked in a week; also, the number of working hours in a week.

world (wûrld) *n.* **1** The earth; the terraqueous globe; the universe (of which the earth was once supposed to be the center); any similar orb; a part of the earth: the Old *World.* **2** A division of existing or created things belonging to the earth; natural grand division: the mineral, vegetable, or animal *world.* **3** The human inhabitants of the earth; mankind. **4** A definite class of people having certain interests or activities in common: the scientific *world*; a sphere or domain: the *world* of letters. **5** Man regarded socially; the public; hence, public or social life and intercourse. **6** The practices, usages, and ways of men: He knows the *world.* **7** A total of things as pertaining to or affecting an individual man; a career among men; one's experience in life: to begin the *world* anew. **8** The course of events as affecting one personally; individual condition or circumstances: How goes the *world* with you? Your *world* is changed then. **9** A scene of existence or of affairs regarded from a moral or religious point of view; secular affairs; worldly aims, pleasures, or people collectively; earthly existence; mortal life. **10** Figuratively, great quantity, number, or size: a *world* of trouble. — **for all the world** In every respect. — **on top of the world** *Colloq.* Elated. — **to bring into the world** To give birth to. [OE *weorold*]

World may appear as a combining form in hyphemes or as the first element in two-word phrases; as in:

world affairs	**world love**
world–alarming	**world–minded**
world battle	**world–old**
world builder	**world order**
world–changing	**world peace**
world citizen	**world politics**
world commerce	**world price**
world conflict	**world problem**
world–conquering	**world–rejoicing**
world–conscious	**world–renounced**
world–covering	**world–renouncing**
world destroyer	**world–renowned**
world–domination	**world report**
world dominion	**world revolution**
world–embracing	**world–roving**
world empire	**world sadness**
world–encircling	**world–shaking**
world esteem	**world sorrow**
world–famed	**world state**
world–famous	**world struggle**
world hero	**world trade**
world history	**world–wandering**
world leader	**world–winning**
world–long	**world–worn**

World Court See PERMANENT COURT OF INTERNATIONAL JUSTICE under COURT.

world·ling (wûrld′ling) *n.* One who lives merely for this world; a worldly–minded person.

world·ly (wûrld′lē) *adj.* **·li·er, ·li·est 1** Pertaining to the world; mundane; earthly; not spiritual. **2** Devoted to temporal things; secular. **3** Sophisticated; worldly–wise. **4** *Obs.* Lay, as opposed to clerical. — *adv.* In a worldly manner. See synonyms under PROFANE. — **world′li·ness** *n.*

world·ly-mind·ed (wurld′lē·mīn′did) *adj.* Absorbed in the things of this world. — **world′ly–mind′ed·ly** *adv.* — **world′ly–mind′ed·ness** *n.*

world·ly-wise (wûrld′lē·wīz′) *adj.* Wise in the

ways and affairs of the world; sophisticated.

world power A state or organization whose policy and action are of world-wide influence.

world series In baseball, the games played at the finish of the regular schedule between the champion teams of the American and National Leagues, the first team to win four games being adjudged world's champions. Also **world's series.**

world's fair An international exhibit of the folk crafts and arts, agricultural and industrial products, and scientific progress of various countries.

world soul 1 The hypothetical soul of the world; the All-Soul, conceived of after the analogy of the indwelling soul of man. 2 The principle that animates and informs the physical world. Also **world spirit.**

world's people Worldly people; those not belonging to some specific religious sect or group: a term used especially by the Friends.

World War See table under WAR.

world-wea·ry (wûrld'wir'ē) *adj.* **·ri·er, ·ri·est** Dissatisfied with life and its conditions; weary and tired of this life.

world-wide (wûrld'wīd') *adj.* Extended throughout the world.

world without end Forever.

worm (wûrm) *n.* 1 A small, legless, invertebrate crawling animal, with an elongated, soft, and usually naked body, as a flatworm, roundworm, or annelid. ◆ Collateral adjective: *vermicular.* 2 A small creeping animal with short or undeveloped feet, as an insect larva, a grub, angleworm, etc. 3 Figuratively, that which suggests the action or habit of a worm as eating away or as an agent of decay or destruction, as remorse, death, etc. 4 A despicable or despised person; also, a feeble mortal. 5 Something conceived to be like a worm. 6 A screw thread. 7 A worm screw. 8 The spiral part of a corkscrew. 9 A spiral part in a still. 10 An organ or part that resembles a worm in shape, as the lytta of the dog or the vermiform process. 11 *pl.* An intestinal disorder due to the presence of parasitic worms. 12 The windings of a log road made to lessen the steepness of a grade. 13 The zigzag course of a log fence or a rail fence. — *v.t.* 1 To insinuate (oneself or itself) in a wormlike manner; effect as by crawling: with *in* or *into*: to *worm* one's way. 2 To draw forth by artful means, as a secret: with *out.* 3 To remove worms from. 4 To wind yarn, etc., along (a rope) so as to fill up the grooves between the strands. 5 To remove the lytta or worm from, as a dog. — *v.i.* 6 To move or progress slowly and stealthily. [OE *wyrm*] — **worm'er** *n.*

Worm (vōōrm), **Olaus,** 1588–1654, Danish anatomist and physician.

worm-eat·en (wûrm'ēt'n) *adj.* Eaten or bored through by worms.

worm fence See under FENCE.

worm gear 1 *Mech.* A worm wheel having teeth shaped so as to mesh with a worm screw. 2 A worm wheel.

WORM GEAR

worm·hole (wûrm'hōl') *n.* The hole made by a worm or a wormlike animal, as in plants, earth, or stone. — **worm'holed'** *adj.*

Wor·mi·an (wôr'mē·ən) *adj.* Relating to or discovered by Olaus Worm.

Wormian bones *Anat.* Small bones occasionally lying along the lines of the cranial sutures.

wor·mil (wûr'məl) *n.* A warblefly or botfly larva. [Var. of dial. *warnel,* OE *wernægel*]

worm·root (wûrm'rōōt', -rŏŏt') *n.* Pinkroot.

Worms (wûrmz, *Ger.* vôrms) A city on the Rhine in Rhenish Hesse, SW West Germany; scene of the Diet of Worms (1521) by which Martin Luther was pronounced a heretic.

worm screw *Mech.* A short threaded portion of a shaft constituting an endless screw formed to mesh with a worm wheel.

worm·seed (wûrm'sēd') *n.* 1 The seeds of any of various plants used as a vermifuge. 2 The plants themselves; especially, santonica, and a species of goosefoot (*Chenopodium ambrosioides*).

worm wheel *Mech.* A toothed wheel gearing with a worm screw.

worm·wood (wûrm'wŏŏd') *n.* 1 Any of a genus (*Artemisia*) of European herbs or small shrubs related to the sagebrush, especially a common species (*A. absinthium*), aromatic, tonic, bitter, and used in making absinthe. 2 That which embitters or makes bitter; bitterness. [Alter. of obs. *wermod* <OE; infl. in form by *worm* and *wood*[1]]

worm·y (wûr'mē) *adj.* **worm·i·er, worm·i·est** 1 Infested with or injured by worms. 2 Of or pertaining to worms; resembling a worm. 3 Earthy; groveling. — **worm'i·ness** *n.*

worn (wôrn, wōrn) Past participle of WEAR. — *adj.* 1 Affected by attrition or any similar continuous action. 2 Used, as a garment; showing the effects of anxiety, etc., as the mind; hackneyed, as phrases. 3 Exhausted or spent; used up.

worn-out (wôrn'out', wōrn'-) *adj.* 1 Used until without value for its purpose. 2 Thoroughly tired; exhausted.

wor·ri·cow (wûr'ē·kou') *n. Scot.* A hobgoblin; the devil; any hideous object or person; bugbear; a scarecrow.

wor·ri·some (wûr'i·səm) *adj.* Causing worry or anxiety.

wor·rit (wûr'it) *n. Colloq.* Worry; vexation. [Appar. alter. of WORRY]

wor·ry (wûr'ē) *v.* **·ried, ·ry·ing** *v.i.* 1 To be uneasy in the mind; feel anxiety about something; fret. 2 To pull or tear at something with the teeth: with *at.* 3 *Colloq.* To advance or manage despite trials or difficulties: with *along* or *through.* — *v.t.* 4 To cause to feel uneasy in the mind; trouble. 5 To bother; pester. 6 To mangle or kill by biting, shaking, or tearing with the teeth. 7 *Scot.* or *Obs.* To strangle; choke. See synonyms under PERSECUTE. — *n. pl.* **·ries** A state of anxiety; vexation. See synonyms under ANXIETY, CARE. [OE *wyrgan* strangle] — **wor'ri·er** *n.* — **wor'ri·ment** *n.*

worse (wûrs) Used as comparative of *bad, ill, evil,* and the like. — *adj.* 1 Bad or ill in a greater degree; more evil, unworthy, etc. 2 Physically ill in a greater degree. 3 Less favorably situated as to means and circumstances. — *n.* Something worse; disadvantage; loss. — *adv.* 1 In a manner more evil or ill. 2 With greater intensity, severity, etc. 3 Decreasingly; less. [OE *wyrsa*]

wors·en (wûr'sən) *v.t.* & *v.i.* To make or become worse.

wors·er (wûr'sər) *adj.* & *adv.* Worse: a former redundant form of the comparative, on the analogy of *lesser*: now regarded as a vulgarism.

wors·et (wûr'sit) *adj.* & *n. Scot.* Worsted.

wor·ship (wûr'ship) *n.* 1 The act or feeling of adoration or homage; the paying of religious reverence, as in prayer, praise, etc. 2 The act or feeling of deference, respect, or honor toward virtue, power, or the like. 3 Excessive or ardent admiration; also, the object of such love or admiration. 4 A title of honor in addressing persons of station. See synonyms under RELIGION, REVERENCE. — *v.* **·shiped** or **·shipped, ·ship·ing** or **·ship·ping** *v.t.* 1 To pay an act of worship to; venerate; adore. 2 To treat with intense or exaggerated admiration or affection. 3 *Obs.* To honor. — *v.i.* 4 To perform acts or have sentiments of worship. [OE *weorthscipe* < *weorth* worthy] — **wor'ship·er, wor'ship·per** *n.*

Synonyms (verb): adore, deify, exalt, honor, idolize, revere, reverence. See PRAISE. *Antonyms*: abhor, abjure, abominate, blaspheme, curse, denounce, detest, renounce, revile, scoff, scorn.

wor·ship·ful (wûr'ship·fəl) *adj.* 1 Worthy of honor; entitled to respect by reason of character or position: applied to dignitaries, as magistrates, etc. In Freemasonry, it is part of a specific official title, as of masters. 2 Esteemed; distinguished; honorable. 3 Giving reverence; adoring. — **wor'ship·ful·ly** *adv.* — **wor'ship·ful·ness** *n.*

worst (wûrst) Used as the superlative of *bad, ill,* or *evil.* — *adj.* Bad, ill, or evil in the highest degree. — **in the worst way** *Slang* Very much. — *n.* The most evil state or result. — **at worst** On the most pessimistic estimate. — **to get the worst of it** To be defeated or put at a disadvantage. — *adv.* In the worst or most extreme manner or degree. — *v.t.* To get the advantage over; defeat; vanquish. See synonyms under BEAT, CONQUER. [OE *wyrsta*]

wors·ted (wŏŏs'tid, wûr'stid) *n.* 1 Woolen yarn spun from long staple, with fibers combed parallel and twisted hard. 2 A lightly twisted woolen yarn. 3 A tightly woven or smooth fabric made from worsted yarns, as gabardine or serge. — *adj.* Consisting of or made from this yarn. [from *Worsted,* former name of a parish in Norfolk, north of Norwich, England]

wort (wûrt) *n.* 1 A plant or herb: usually in combination: *liverwort, navelwort.* 2 The sweet, unfermented infusion of malt that becomes beer when fermented. [OE *wyrt* a root, a plant]

worth[1] (wûrth) *n.* 1 That quality which renders a thing useful or desirable; value or excellence of any kind; hence, market value. 2 That quality or combination of qualities that makes one deserving of esteem; mental and moral excellence. 3 Wealth. — *adj.* 1 Having value; equal in value (to); exchangeable (for). 2 Deserving (of): in either a good or bad sense. 3 Having possessions to the value of: He is *worth* a million. — **for all it is worth** To the utmost. — **for all one is worth** With every effort possible; to the utmost of one's capacity. [OE *weorth*]

Synonyms (noun): character, desert, excellence, integrity, merit, preciousness, value. See PRICE, VIRTUE.

worth[2] (wûrth) *v.i.* To betide or befall: now only in phrases, as **woe worth the day,** etc. [OE *weorthan* come to be]

-worth *combining form* Of the value of: *pennyworth.* [OE *weorth* worth]

Wor·thing (wûr'thing) A municipal borough on the coast of southern Sussex, southern England, west of Brighton.

worth·less (wûrth'lis) *adj.* Having no worth; having no utility or value; destitute of dignity, virtue, or standing. See synonyms under BAD[1], BASE[2], USELESS, VAIN, WASTE. — **worth'less·ly** *adv.* — **worth'less·ness** *n.*

worth·while (wûrth'hwīl') *adj.* Sufficiently important to occupy the time; of enough value to repay the effort. ◆ This compound originated from the phrase *worth the while* and it is firmly established as a solideme in American usage. In British usage it is usually a hypheme: **worth-while.** — **worth'while'ness** *n.*

wor·thy (wûr'thē) *adj.* **·thi·er, ·thi·est** 1 Possessing worth; deserving of respect or honor; having valuable or useful qualities. 2 Having such qualities as to be deserving of or adapted to some specified thing; fit; suitable: followed by *of* (rarely *for*), sometimes by an infinitive and rarely by the object directly. 3 *Obs.* Well deserved; fitting. See synonyms under BECOMING, EXCELLENT, GOOD, MORAL, VIRTUOUS. — *n. pl.* **·thies** 1 A person of eminent worth. 2 Humorously, a person of local note; a character. [ME *wurthi, worthi*] — **wor'thi·ly** *adv.* — **wor'thi·ness** *n.*

-worthy *combining form* 1 Meriting or deserving: *trustworthy.* 2 Valuable as; having worth as: *newsworthy.* 3 Fit for: *seaworthy.* [OE *wyrthe* worthy]

wot (wot) Present tense, first and third person singular, of WIT[2].

Wot·ton (wot'n), **Sir Henry,** 1568–1639, English diplomat and poet.

would (wŏŏd) Past tense of WILL, expressing desire, condition, or what might be expected: used also to express determination: He *would* go, I couldn't stop him. [OE *wolde,* pt. of *willan* will]

◆ **would & should** Anybody dealing in ifs, as-ifs, promises, threats, hopes, wishes, or similar feelings and attitudes about the real or imagined future, will find himself making plentiful use of *would* and/or *should,* which do duty to express the vestigial and fast vanishing subjunctive mood. As to which one to use, the distinctions are subtle and fine-drawn and at several points British usage calls for *should* where American practice is to use *would,* although *would* has not here displaced *should* to the extent that *shall* has given way to *will* (see usage note under SHALL vs. WILL). (1) In simple factual conditions, for example, British usage calls for *should* in the first person in the conclusion: If he failed, I *should* (U.S. *would*) still support him. (2) When one of these modal auxiliaries is to be used in the first person preceding such verbs as *like, prefer, care, be glad,* etc., British usage holds firmly to *should*; but American, Scottish, and Irish usage calls for *would*: We *would* (Brit. & formal U. S. *should*) like to have you come to dinner next Tuesday. *Would* in this example represents true present time. (3) *Would* is the true past expressing an act of will mostly in negations or expressions of indifference: They asked him to wait, but he *would* not (was unwilling to comply). (4) *Would* can also convey customary or habitual action in the past: He *would* take her gifts every time he called. Except for these rare instances in which *would* is used as a true past, it is usually confined to the purposes of the subjunctive. (5) It may express an act of will under projected or imagined conditions: (I, You, He) *wouldn't* tolerate that insult even if it were offered with smiling politeness. (6) When no condition is expressed, *would* in the second and third person often lacks even a vestigial trace of any act of will: She *would* be no more than second choice in the matrimonial sweepstakes. (7) When *would* is stressed with the voice it may indicate (a) an element of malign fate or misfortune: She *would* be the one to lose her take-home fare; or (b) the notion of persistent contrariness: You *would* insist on bumping your head against a stone wall twice! (8) In conditions contrary to fact, *would* is used in conclusion without any feeling of volition involved: Had he left sooner he *would* have heard less to his discredit. If I had been able to dodge the small souls around the commission, I *would* (Brit. *should*) have got a third share in the radio station. (9) *Would* may also express probability in cases where some contingency or hypothesis is unexpressed: "He was very boastful." "He *would* be." (10) Finally, there is the matter of the idiomatic use of *would* and *should* in indirect or reported discourse. In most cases, if the direct utterance used *shall,* the reported discourse employs *should.* Similarly, if it was *will* in the direct utterance, *would* is used in the indirect discourse. If obligation is involved, *should* must be used. Except in this area of obligation, *would* is the more common form in American usage.

would-be (wŏŏd′bē′) *adj.* Desiring or professing to be: a *would-be* poet.

would·n't (wŏŏd′nt) Would not: a contraction.

wound[1] (wōōnd, *Poetic* wound) *n.* **1** A hurt or injury caused by violence; especially, a cut, bruise, stab, etc.; a trauma. **2** A breach or cut of the bark or substance of a tree or plant. **3** Hence, any injury or cause of pain or grief, as to the feelings, honor, etc. —*v.t.* & *v.i.* To inflict a wound or wounds (upon); cause injury or grief (to); hurt. See synonyms under AFFRONT, HURT, PIQUE[1]. [OE *wund*] —**wound′ed** *adj.* —**wound′less** *adj.*

wound[2] (wound) Past tense and past participle of WIND[2].

Wou·ter (wou′tər) Dutch form of WALTER.

wove (wōv) Past tense and alternative past participle of WEAVE.

wo·ven (wō′vən) Past participle of WEAVE.

wove paper Paper carrying the marks of the wire gauze on which it was laid during finishing.

wow (wou) *interj.* An exclamation of wonder, surprise, pleasure, or pain. —*n. Slang* An extraordinary success. —*v.t. Slang* To be extraordinarily successful with.

wow·ser (wou′zər) *n. Australian Slang* One who is opposed to Sunday amusements, sports, etc.; a hypocritical censor of the lesser vices; a meddlesome puritan or sanctimonious reformer. [Origin unknown]

wrack[1] (rak) *n.* **1** Marine vegetation and floating material cast ashore by the sea, as seaweed or eelgrass; kelp. **2** The state of being wrecked; ruin; destruction: chiefly in the phrase **wrack and ruin.** **3** Shipwreck; a wrecked vessel; wreckage. **4** *Scot.* & *Brit. Dial.* Weeds. —*v.t.* & *v.i.* To wreck or be wrecked. ◆ Homophone: *rack.* [Fusion of OE *wræc* punishment, revenge and MDu. *wrak* a wreck]

wrack[2] (rak) *n.* A rack of clouds; any floating vapor. Compare RACK[3]. [Var. of RACK[3]]

wraith (rāth) *n.* **1** An apparition of a person thought to be alive, seen shortly before or shortly after his death. **2** Any specter, ghost, or apparition. [< dial. E (Scottish), alter. of *warth* <ON *vörthr* a guardian < *vartha* guard]

wrang (rang) *adj.* & *n. Scot.* Wrong.

Wran·gel (vrän′gil), **Ferdinand Petrovich von,** 1794?–1870, Russian explorer. Also **Wran′gell.**

Wran·gell (rang′gəl), **Mount** An active volcano (14,005 feet) in the western **Wrangell Mountains,** a range in SE Alaska; highest peak, 16,208 feet.

Wran·gell Island (rang′gəl) **1** An island of the Alexander Archipelago, SE Alaska; 30 miles long, 5 to 14 miles wide. **2** An island in the western Chukchi Sea off NE Siberia; part of Khabarovsk territory, Asiatic Russian S.F.S.R.; 75 miles long, 45 miles wide; 1,740 square miles. Also **Wran′gel Island.** *Russian* **O·strov Vran·ge·ly** (ô′strôf vrän′gi·lyə).

wran·gle (rang′gəl) *v.* **·gled, ·gling** *v.i.* **1** To argue or dispute noisily and angrily; brawl. —*v.t.* **2** To argue; debate. **3** To herd or round up, as livestock on a range. See synonyms under CONTEND. —*n.* An angry or noisy dispute; a quarrel. See synonyms under ALTERCATION, DISPUTE, QUARREL[1]. [Cf. LG *wrangeln* quarrel, freq. of *wrangen* struggle]

wran·gler (rang′glər) *n.* **1** One who wrangles. **2** At Cambridge University, England, one who has taken the highest mathematical honors. **3** A herdsman on a range.

wrap (rap) *v.* **wrapped** or **wrapt, wrap·ping** *v.t.* **1** To surround and cover by something folded or wound about; swathe; enwrap. **2** To cover with paper, etc., folded about and secured. **3** To wind or fold (a covering) about something. **4** To surround so as to obscure; blot out or conceal; envelop. **5** To fold, wind, or draw together. —*v.i.* **6** To be or become twined or coiled: with *about, around,* etc. —*n.* **1** An article of dress drawn or folded about a person; a wrapper. **2** *pl.* Outer garments collectively, as cloaks, scarfs, etc. **3** A blanket. [ME *wrappen*; origin uncertain]

wrap·a·round windshield (rap′ə·round) In automobiles, a windshield curving back into the sides of the body, thus providing a greater field of vision.

wrap·per (rap′ər) *n.* **1** A paper enclosing a newspaper, magazine, or similar packet for mailing or otherwise. **2** A detachable paper cover to protect the binding of a book. **3** A loose flowing outer garment; a dressing gown. **4** A tobacco leaf of high quality enclosing a cigar or plug of tobacco. **5** One who wraps articles.

wrap·ping (rap′ing) *n.* A covering; something in which an object is wrapped.

wrap-ras·cal (rap′ras′kəl) *n.* A long loose overcoat fashionable during the 18th century.

wrapt (rapt) Erroneous spelling of RAPT.

wrasse (ras) *n.* Any of a group of spiny-finned food fishes (family *Labridae*) of warm tropical seas, often highly colored; especially, the tautog. [<Cornish *wrach* < *gwrach,* orig., an old woman]

wrath (rath, räth; *Brit.* rôth) *n.* **1** Determined and lasting anger; extreme or violent rage; fury; vehement indignation. **2** An act done in violent rage. See synonyms under ANGER, VIOLENCE. —*v.t.* & *v.i. Obs.* To make or become angry. —*adj. Obs.* Wroth; angry. [OE *wræththu* < *wrath* wroth]

Wrath (rath, räth), **Cape** A promontory at the NW extremity of Scotland in NW Sutherland.

wrath·ful (rath′fəl, räth′-) *adj.* **1** Full of wrath; extremely angry. **2** Springing from or expressing wrath. —**wrath′ful·ly** *adv.* —**wrath′·ful·ness** *n.*

wrath·y (rath′ē, räth′ē) *adj.* **wrath·i·er, wrath·i·est** **1** Disposed to wrath. **2** *Colloq.* Wroth. —**wrath′i·ly** *adv.* —**wrath′i·ness** *n.*

wreak (rēk) *v.t.* **1** To inflict or exact, as vengeance. **2** To satiate; give free expression to, as a feeling or passion. ◆ Homophone: *reek.* [OE *wrecan* drive, avenge]

wreath (rēth) *n.* **1** A twisted band, as of flowers, commonly circular, as for a crown or chaplet. **2** Any curled band of circular or spiral shape, as of smoke or snow. [OE *writha* <*wrīthan* writhe] —**wreath′y** *n.*

Wreath (rēth) See CORONA AUSTRALIS.

wreathe (rēth) *v.* **wreathed, wreath·ing** *v.t.* **1** To form into a wreath, as by twisting or twining. **2** To adorn or encircle with or as with wreaths. **3** To envelop; cover: His face was *wreathed* in smiles. —*v.i.* **4** To take the form of a wreath. **5** To twist, turn, or coil, as masses of cloud. See synonyms under TWIST. [Earlier *wrethe,* back formation <ME *wrethen,* var. of *writhen,* pp. of *writhen* writhe; infl. by *wreath*]

wreck (rek) *v.t.* **1** To cause the destruction or wreck of, as a vessel; shipwreck. **2** To bring ruin, damage, or destruction upon. **3** To tear down, as a building; dismantle. —*v.i.* **4** To suffer wreck; be ruined. **5** To engage in wrecking, as for plunder or salvage. See synonyms under RUIN. [< *n.*] —*n.* **1** The act of wrecking, or the state of being wrecked; the ruin of anything, especially if effected violently. **2** That which has been wrecked or ruined, as a vessel or an army; hence, an emaciated person. **3** Wreckage; shipwreck. **4** *Law* Property cast upon land by the sea, either broken portions of a wrecked vessel or cargo from it. ◆ Homophone: *reck.* [<AF *wrec, wrech,* OF *warec* <ON (assumed) *wrek* < *wrekan* drive]

wreck·age (rek′ij) *n.* **1** The act of wrecking, or the state of being wrecked; wrecked material. **2** Broken or disordered remnants or fragments from a wreck.

wreck·er (rek′ər) *n.* **1** One who causes wreck, destruction, or frustration of any sort. **2** One employed in tearing down and removing old buildings. **3** A person, train, car, or machine that clears away wrecks. **4** One employed to recover disabled vessels or wrecked cargoes for the owners; also, a vessel employed in this service; a salvager. **5** One who lures ships to destruction by false lights on the shore in order to plunder the wreck. **6** One who ruins something valuable, as a bank or a railroad, especially for his own profit.

wreck·ful (rek′fəl) *adj. Poetic* Causing wreck; involving ruin.

wrecking company **1** A business organization that salvages wrecked ships. **2** A business organization that tears down and removes old buildings.

wren (ren) *n.* **1** Any of numerous small passerine birds (family *Troglodytidae*) having short rounded wings and a short tail, including the common **house wren** (*Troglodytes aëdon*), the **Carolina wren** (*Thryothorus ludovicianus*), **Bewick's wren** (*Thryomanes bewicki*) of North America, and the European wren (*Nannus troglodytes*). **2** Any one of numerous similar birds. [OE *wrenna*]

Wren (ren), **Sir Christopher,** 1632–1723, English architect. —**Percival Christopher,** 1885–1941, English novelist.

wrench (rench) *n.* **1** A violent twist; hence, a twist causing pain or injury; sprain. **2** Any strain or sudden and violent tension; sudden and violent emotion. **3** Any perversion or distortion of an original meaning. **4** A tool for twisting or turning bolts, nuts, pipe, etc.

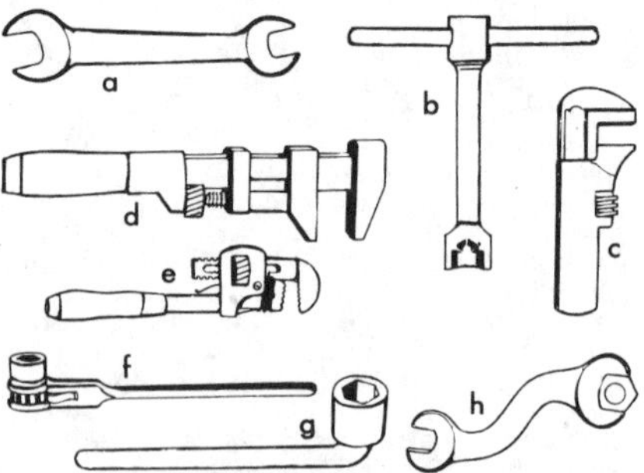

TYPES OF WRENCHES
a. Engineer's wrench. *b.* Socket wrench. *c.* Bicycle wrench. *d.* Monkey wrench. *e.* Pipe wrench. *f.* Ratchet wrench. *g.* Offset wrench. *h.* S-wrench.

—*v.t.* **1** To twist violently; turn suddenly by force; wrest. **2** To twist forcibly so as to cause strain or injury; sprain. 3 To twist from the proper meaning, intent, or use. — *v.i.* 4 To give a twist or wrench. [OE *wrenc* a trick. Akin to WRINKLE[1].]

Wrens (renz) *n. pl. Brit. Colloq.* Women's Royal Naval Service, an organization to relieve men of certain shore duties connected with the Royal Navy: so called from the initial letters *W,R,N,S,* plus *E.*

wrest (rest) *v.t.* 1 To pull or force away by violent twisting or wringing; wrench. 2 To turn from the true meaning, character, intent, or application; distort; pervert. 3 To seize forcibly by violence, extortion, or usurpation. — *n.* 1 An act of wresting; a violent twist. 2 A misapplication or perversion. 3 A crooked act; wile. 4 A key for tuning a stringed instrument, as a harp. ◆ Homophone: *rest.* [OE *wrǣstan*] — **wrest′er** *n.*

wres·tle (res′əl) *v.* **·tled, ·tling** *v.i.* 1 To engage in wrestling. 2 To struggle, as for mastery; contend. — *v.t.* 3 To engage in (a wrestling match), or wrestle with. 4 To throw (a calf) and hold it down for branding. — *n.* A wrestling match; a hard struggle. [OE *wrǣstlian,* freq. of *wrǣsten* wrest]

wres·tler (res′lər) *n.* One who wrestles; especially, a person who competes in wrestling matches.

wres·tling (res′ling) *n.* A sport or exercise in which each of two unarmed contestants endeavors to throw the other to the ground or force him into a certain fallen position.

wretch (rech) *n.* 1 A base, vile, or contemptible person; despicable character. 2 A miserable or unhappy person; also, sometimes, any person or creature viewed with pity. ◆ Homophone: *retch.* [OE *wrecca* an outcast < *wrecan* drive]

wretch·ed (rech′id) *adj.* 1 Sunk in dejection; profoundly unhappy. 2 Causing misery or grief. 3 Mean; paltry; worthless; unsatisfactory in ability or quality. 4 Despicable; contemptible. See synonyms under BAD[1], BASE[2], PITIFUL. — **wretch′ed·ly** *adv.* — **wretch′·ed·ness** *n.*

wrig·gle (rig′əl) *v.* **·gled, ·gling** *v.i.* 1 To twist in a sinuous manner; squirm; writhe. 2 To proceed as by twisting or crawling. 3 To make one's way by evasive or indirect means. — *v.t.* 4 To cause to wriggle. — *n.* The motion of one who or that which wriggles; a squirm. [<MLG *wriggeln,* freq. of *wriggen* twist] — **wrig′gly** *adj.*

wrig·gler (rig′lər) *n.* 1 Someone or something that wriggles. 2 A mosquito larva.

wright (rīt) *n.* 1 One who does mechanical or constructive work. 2 An artificer or workman: used chiefly in compounds: *shipwright.* ◆ Homophones: *right, rite, write.* [OE *wyrhta*]

Wright (rīt), **Frank Lloyd,** 1867–1959, U.S. architect. — **Harold Bell,** 1872–1944, U.S. novelist. — **Joseph,** 1855–1930, English philologist and lexicographer. — **Orville,** 1871–1948, U.S. pioneer in aviation, with his brother **Wilbur,** 1867–1912. — **Richard,** 1908–1960, U.S. novelist. — **Willard Huntington,** 1888–1939, U.S. writer and art critic: pseudonym *S. S. Van Dine.*

wring (ring) *v.* **wrung** (*Rare* **wringed**), **wring·ing** *v.t.* 1 To squeeze or compress by twisting; turn and strain with force; pass (clothes) through a wringer. 2 To squeeze or press out, as water, by twisting. 3 To extort; acquire by extortion. 4 To distress; torment. 5 To twist or wrest violently out of shape or place: to *wring* his neck. 6 *Obs.* To pervert; distort. — *v.i.* 7 To writhe or squirm, as with anguish. 8 To perform the action of wringing. ◆ Homophone: *ring.* [OE *wringan*]

wring·bolt (ring′bōlt′) A ring bolt. [Earlier *wrainbolt,* var. of *ring bolt*]

wring·er (ring′ər) *n.* 1 One who or that which wrings. 2 A contrivance used to press water out of fabrics after washing; also, the operator of such a machine.

wrin·kle[1] (ring′kəl) *n.* 1 A small ridge or prominence, as on a smooth surface; a crease; fold. 2 Specifically, a small fold or crease in the skin, usually produced by age or by excessive exposure to the elements. 3 A ripple; little wave. — *v.t. & v.i.* **·kled, ·kling** To contract or be contracted into wrinkles or ridges; pucker. [OE *wrincle.* Akin to WRENCH.] — **wrin′kly** *adj.*

wrin·kle[2] (ring′kəl) *n. Colloq.* A curious or ingenious notion or device; happy thought; a novelty, as in dress. See synonyms under WHIM. [Prob. dim. of OE *wrenc* a trick]

wrist (rist) *n.* 1 The part of the arm immediately adjoining the hand; the carpus. ◆ Collateral adjective: *carpal.* 2 The part of a glove or garment that covers the wrist. 3 A wrist pin. [OE, prob. < *wrīthan* writhe]

wrist·band (rist′band′, -bənd, riz′-) *n.* The band of a sleeve that covers the wrist or ends a shirt sleeve.

wrist-drop (rist′drop′) *n. Pathol.* Paralysis of the forearm, usually due to lead poisoning.

wrist·let (rist′lit) *n.* 1 A flexible band worn on the wrist for ornament or warmth. 2 A bracelet. 3 *Slang* A handcuff.

wrist·lock (rist′lok′) *n.* In wrestling, a hold whereby an opponent is made helpless by twisting his arm with a grip at the wrist.

wrist pin *Mech.* 1 A pin holding together the piston and connecting rod of a steam engine. 2 A similar pin in the cross-head of an internal-combustion engine.

wrist watch A watch set in a leather or metal wristlet and worn at the wrist.

writ[1] (rit) *n.* 1 *Law* A written order, under seal, issued by a court, and commanding the person to whom it is addressed to do or not to do some act. 2 That which is written: now chiefly in the phrase **Holy Writ,** meaning the Bible. [OE, a writing < *wrītan* write]

writ[2] (rit) Archaic or dialectal past tense and past participle of WRITE.

write (rīt) *v.* **wrote** (*Archaic* or *Dial.* **writ**), **writ·ten** (*Archaic* or *Dial.* **writ**), **writ·ing** *v.t.* 1 To trace or inscribe (letters, words, numbers, symbols, etc.) on a surface with pen or pencil, or by other means. 2 To describe in writing: to *write* one's impressions of a journey. 3 To communicate by letter: Be sure to *write* all the news; He *writes* that he will be home soon. 4 To communicate with by letter: He *writes* her every day. 5 To produce by writing; be the author or composer of. 6 To draw up; draft: to *write* one's will; to *write* a check. 7 To cover or fill with writing: to *write* two full pages. 8 To leave marks or evidence of: Anxiety is *written* on his face. 9 To spell or inscribe as specified: He *writes* his name with two *n's.* 10 To entitle or designate in writing: He *writes* himself "General." 11 To underwrite: to *write* an insurance policy. — *v.i.* 12 To trace or inscribe letters, etc., on a surface, as of paper. 13 To write a letter or letters; communicate in writing. 14 To be engaged in the occupation of a writer or author. 15 To produce a specified quality of writing. See synonyms under INSCRIBE. — **to write down** 1 To put into writing. 2 To injure or depreciate in writing. — **to write in** 1 To insert in writing, as in a document. 2 To cast (a vote) for one not listed on a ballot by inserting his name in writing. — **to write off** 1 To cancel or remove (claims, debts, etc.) from an open account. 2 To acknowledge the loss or failure of. — **to write out** 1 To put into writing. 2 To write in full or complete form. — **to write up** 1 To describe fully in writing; put in written form: to *write up* a report. 2 To praise fully or too fully in writing. 3 In accounting, to put an unusually high value upon. ◆ Homophones: *right, rite, wright.* [OE *wrītan*]

◆ *Writ,* the archaic or dialectal past participle of *write,* is now used chiefly in the phrase **writ large,** written or shown on a grand scale: *a name writ large in history.*

write-off (rīt′ôf′, -of′) *n.* 1 A cancellation. 2 An amount canceled or noted as a loss.

writ·er (rī′tər) *n.* 1 One who writes. 2 One who engages in literary composition. 3 That which writes or assists in writing: used in composition: *typewriter.*

writer's cramp *Pathol.* Spasmodic contraction of the muscles of the fingers and hand, caused by excessive writing. Also **writer's palsy** or **spasm.**

write-up (rīt′up′) *n. Colloq.* A written description, record, or account, usually laudatory, as of a person, theatrical performance, etc.

writhe (rīth) *v.t. & v.i.* **writhed, writh·ing** To twist with violence; wrench; distort, as the body, face, or limbs in pain. — *n.* An act of writhing; a contortion. See synonyms under STRUGGLE. [OE *wrīthan*] — **writh′er** *n.*

writh·en (rith′ən) Obsolete past participle of WRITHE. — *adj. Poetic* Twisted; distorted.

writ·ing (rī′ting) *n.* 1 The act of one who writes. 2 The characters so made; chirography; handwriting. 3 Anything written or expressed in letters, especially a literary production. 4 *Law* A written instrument: words, or characters that stand for words or ideas, traced on some substance, as paper, wood, or stone, with an implement, as a pen, pencil, or brush, or by some other device, as stamping, printing, or engraving. 5 The profession or occupation of a writer. 6 The practice, art, form, or style of literary composition.

writing machine A typewriter.

writ·ing-mas·ter (rī′ting·mas′tər, -mäs′-) *n.* A teacher of penmanship.

writing paper Paper prepared to receive ink in writing.

writ of error *Law* A commission by which the judges of one court are authorized to examine a record upon which a judgment was given in another court, and to affirm or reverse the judgment according to law.

writ of prohibition *Law* A writ issued by a superior court to an inferior court, commanding it to desist from proceeding in a matter not within its jurisdiction.

writ of right *Law* 1 Formerly, in England, a writ in an action for the purpose of establishing a title to real estate. 2 A similar common-law writ.

writ of summons *Law* The writ by which, in modern practice, a civil action is commenced; a written order to an authorized officer to notify a person to appear in court to answer a complaint.

writ·ten (rit′n) Past participle of WRITE.

Wro·claw (vrô′tswäf) A city in SW Poland, on the Oder; a German city from the 13th century; part of Prussia 1741–1945; a major industrial center: German *Breslau.*

wrong (rông, rong) *adj.* 1 Deviating from moral rectitude as prescribed by civil or divine law or by conscience; immoral. 2 Not just, proper, or equitable according to a standard, code, or convention; incongruous; improper. 3 Deviating from fact and truth; not according to reality; erroneous; mistaken: a *wrong* estimate. 4 Not in accordance with rule or appropriateness; improper; incorrect: to enter the *wrong* store. 5 Deviating from the proper design, intention, or requirement; unsuitable: the *wrong* side of cloth; the *wrong* letter in a word. 6 Unsatisfactory: a *wrong* reply. — **to go wrong** 1 To lapse from the strict path of rectitude. 2 To turn out badly; go astray. — **on the wrong side of (30, 40,** etc.) Older than (30, etc.). See synonyms under IMMORAL, SINFUL. — *adv.* In a wrong direction, place, or manner; awry or amiss; erroneously. — *n.* 1 That which is contrary to justice or rectitude; an injury; mischief. 2 Hence, some particular form of disobedience or non-conformity to lawful authority, human or divine. 3 *Law* An invasion or violation of one's legal rights; specifically, a crime; a tort. See synonyms under INJURY, INJUSTICE, SIN[1]. — *v.t.* 1 To violate the rights of; inflict injury or injustice upon. 2 To impute evil to unjustly; misrepresent: If you think so, you *wrong* him. 3 To seduce (a woman). 4 To treat dishonorably; malign. 5 *Scot.* To injure. See synonyms under ABUSE. [OE *wrang* twisted <ON *rangr* awry, unjust] — **wrong′·ness** *n.*

wrong·do·er (rông′dōō′ər, rong′-) *n.* One who commits a fault or crime. — **wrong′do′ing** *n.*

wrong·er (rông′ər, rong′-) *n.* One who commits an offense, injury, or trespass.

wrong font *Printing* The wrong font or type face: indicated by the abbreviation *w.f.* in marking printers' proofs.

wrong·ful (rông′fəl, rong′-) *adj.* 1 Characterized by wrong or injustice; injurious; unjust. 2 Unlawful; illegal. — **wrong′ful·ly** *adv.* — **wrong′ful·ness** *n.*

wrong-head·ed (rông′hed′id, rong′-) *adj.* Having perverted judgment; perverse; obstinate.

—**wrong′–head′ed·ly** *adv.* —**wrong′–head′ed·ness** *n.*
wrong·ly (rông′lē, rong′-) *adv.* In a wrong manner; erroneously; falsely.
wrote (rōt) Past tense of WRITE.
wroth (rôth) *adj.* Filled with anger; angry. —*n. Obs.* Anger. [OE *wrāth*]
wrought (rôt) Archaic past tense and past participle of WORK. —*adj.* **1** Beaten or hammered into shape by tools: *wrought* gold. **2** Worked; molded. **3** Made with delicacy; elaborated carefully. **4** Made; fashioned; formed: The cathedral was *wrought* by skilled hands. [ME *wrogt,* var. of *worht,* pp. of *wirchen* work]
wrought iron Commercially pure iron, prepared from pig iron and easily forged and welded into various shapes.
wrought up Excited.
wrung (rung) Past tense and past participle of WRING.
wry (rī) *adj.* **wri·er, wri·est 1** Bent to one side or out of position; contorted; askew; also, made by twisting or distorting the features: a *wry* smile. **2** Hence, deviating from that which is right or proper; perverted, as a course or an interpretation; warped. —*v.t.* **wried, wry·ing** To twist; contort. ◆ Homophone: *rye.* [ME *wrye* <OE *wrigian* move, tend] —**wry′ly** *adv.* —**wry′ness** *n.*

Wry may appear as a combining form in hyphemes, with the meaning of adjective definition 1:

wry–eyed	**wry–looking**	**wry–set**
wry–faced	**wry–mouthed**	**wry–toothed**

wry·neck (rī′nek′) *n.* **1** A bird (genus *Jynx*) resembling and allied to the woodpeckers, with the habit of twisting its head and neck. **2** A rheumatic affection in the muscles of the neck; torticollis. **3** One having a twisted neck; a person afflicted with torticollis.
Wu (wōō) The chief river of Kweichow province, south central China, comprising the upper course of the Kien and flowing over 5000 miles NE, north, and NW into the Kien proper in SE Szechwan province.
Wu (wōō), **C. C.,** 1886–1934, Chinese statesman and diplomat: full name *Wu Ch′ao–ch′u.*
Wu·chang (wōō′chäng′) A formerly independent city and former capital of Hupeh province, China, on the Yangtze river, now part of Wuhan.
Wuch·er·er·i·a (vukh′ə·rer′ē·ə) *n.* A genus of parasitic nematode worms, especially *W. bancrofti,* the causative agent of elephantiasis. [after Otto *Wucherer,* 1820–73, German physician]
wud (wud) *adj. Scot.* Mad; insane.
Wu·han (wōō′hän′) A city comprising the three formerly independent cities of Hankow, Hanyang, and Wuchang on the Yangtze river, capital of Hupeh province, east central China: also *Han Cities.*
Wu·hu (wōō′hōō′) A port on the Yangtze river in central Anhwei province, central eastern China.
wul·fen·ite (wōōl′fən·īt) *n.* A resinous or hard, yellow, brown, or red molybdate of lead, $PbMoO_4$, usually occurring in tabular crystals. [after F. X. von *Wulfen,* 1728–1805, Austrian mineralogist]
Wul·fi·la (wōōl′fə·lə) See ULFILAS.
wun (wun) *Scot.* Won. —*v.t. & v.i.* To win. —*n.* Wind.
Wundt (vōōnt), **Wilhelm Max,** 1832–1920, German psychologist and physiologist. —**Wundt′i·an** *adj.*
wun·na (wun′ə) *Scot.* Will not.
Wup·per·tal (vōōp′ər·täl) A city in SW central North Rhine–Westphalia, west central West Germany, formed by the union of the cities of Barmen and Elberfeld.
Würm (vürm) See GLACIAL EPOCH.
Würm·see (vürm′zā′) See STARNBERGERSEE.
Würt·tem·berg (wûr′təm·bûrg, *Ger.* vür′təm·berkh) A former state of SW Germany; 7,532 square miles; capital, Stuttgart; divided after 1945 into Württemberg–Baden and Württemberg–Hohenzollern, which merged in 1951, along with Baden, to form the state of Baden–Württemberg.
Würt·tem·berg–Ba·den (wûr′təm·bûrg·bäd′·*Ger.* vür′təm·berkh·bä′den) A former state of SW Germany in the Federal Republic (1949) formed in 1945 by the union of northern Württemberg and northern Baden; 6,062 square miles; capital, Stuttgart; in 1951 the states Baden, Württemberg–Baden and Württemberg–Hohenzollern merged to form the state of Baden–Württemberg; 13,800 square miles; capital, Stuttgart.
Würt·tem·berg–Ho·hen·zol·lern (wûr′təm·bûrg·hō′ən·zol′ərn, *Ger.* vür′təm·berkh·hō′·ən·tsôl′ərn) A state of SW Germany in the Federal Republic (1949); formed in 1945 by the union of southern Württemberg and the former Prussian province of Hohenzollern; 4,018 square miles; capital, Tübingen; merged into the state of Baden–Württemberg in 1951.
Würz·burg (wûrts′bûrg, *Ger.* vürts′bōōrkh) A city in Lower Franconia, NW Bavaria, SW central West Germany.
Wu·sih (wōō′shē′) A city of southern Kiangsu province, central eastern China.
Wu T′ing–fang (wōō′ ting′fäng′), 1841–1922, Chinese reformer and diplomat; father of C. C. Wu.
Wu·wei (wōō′wā′) A city in central Kansu province, north central China.
Wy·an·dot (wī′ən·dot) *n.* One of a tribe of North American Indians of Iroquoian stock, formerly very powerful in the Ohio valley and lake regions: descendants of a group of fugitive Hurons who called themselves *Wendat*: presently settled in Oklahoma. Also **Wy′an·dotte.**
Wy·an·dotte (wī′ən·dot) *n.* One of an American breed of domestic fowls. [after the *Wyandot* Indians]
Wy·att (wī′ət), **Sir Thomas,** 1503–42, English poet and diplomat.
wych (wich) See WITCH[2].
wych–elm (wich′elm′) *n.* **1** A wide–spreading elm *(Ulmus glabra),* with large, dull–green leaves, common in England, Ireland, and Scotland: also called *Scotch elm.* **2** Witch hazel. Also *witch.* [<*wych,* var. of WITCH[2] +ELM]
Wych·er·ley (wich′ər·lē), **William,** 1640?–1716, English dramatist and poet.
wych–ha·zel (wich′hā′zəl) *n.* **1** Witch hazel. **2** Wych–elm. [Var. of WITCH HAZEL]
Wyc·lif (wik′lif), **John,** 1324?–84, English reformer; first translator, with assistants, of the entire Bible into English. Also spelled *Wiclif, Wickliffe, Wycliffe.* —**Wyc′lif·ite** *adj. & n.*
wye (wī) *n.* The letter Y, or something Y–shaped.
Wye (wī) A river of SE Wales and SW England, flowing 130 miles SE from SW Montgomery to the Severn estuary.
Wyld (wīld), **Henry Cecil Kennedy,** 1870–1945, English philologist and lexicographer.
wyle (wīl) *v.t. Scot.* or *Obs.* To beguile; wile.
Wy·lie (wī′lē), **Elinor Morton,** 1885–1928, *née* Hoyt, U.S. poet and novelist: married name *Mrs. William Rose Benét.* —**Philip Gordon,** 1902–1971, U.S. author.
wy·lie–coat (wī′lē·kōt′, wil′ē-, wul′ē-) *n. Scot.* A boy's flannel underdress; also, a flannel petticoat.
Wy·o·ming (wī·ō′ming) A State in the NW United States; 97,914 square miles; capital, Cheyenne; entered the Union July 10, 1890; nickname, *Equality State*: abbr. WY —**Wy·o′ming·ite** *n.*
Wyoming Valley A valley along the north branch of the Susquehanna River in NE Pennsylvania; scene of a massacre of settlers by Indians and Tories, 1778; chief city, Wilkes–Barre.
Wythe (with), **George,** 1726–1806, American jurist; signer of the Declaration of Independence.
wy·vern (wī′vərn) See WIVERN.

X

x, X (eks) *n. pl.* **x's** or **X's, xs** or **Xs, ex·es** (ek′siz) **1** The 24th letter of the English alphabet: from the ancient western Greek alphabets of Chalcis, Boeotia, and Elis, and Roman *X.* **2** The sound of the letter *x*: in English variously sounded as (ks), as in *axle, box, next*; (gz), as in *executive, exert*; (ksh), as in *noxious*; (gzh), as in *luxurious*; and initially, always (z) as in *xenophobe, xylophone, Xanthippe.* See ALPHABET.—*symbol* **1** The Roman numeral ten. See under NUMERAL. **2** *Math.* The principal unknown quantity; hence, anything unknown. **3** A mark shaped like an X, representing the signature of one who cannot write. **4** A mark used in diagrams, maps, etc., to place some event or substance, or to point out something to be emphasized. **5** A symbol used to indicate a kiss. **6** Anything shaped like an X. —**X marks the spot** *Colloq.* "Here": used in diagrams, maps, or the like, to indicate a specific locality.
xan·thate (zan′thāt) *n. Chem.* A salt or ester of xanthic acid. [<XANTH(IC) + -ATE[3]]
xan·the·in (zan′thē·in) *n. Biochem.* A water–soluble yellow coloring matter found in the cell sap of some plants. [<F *xanthéine* <Gk. *xanthos* yellow]
xan·the·las·ma (zan′thə·laz′mə) *n. Pathol.* A form of xanthoma marked by the appearance of small yellowish disks on the eyelids. [<NL <Gk. *xanthos* yellow + *elasmos* a metal plate]
Xan·thi·an (zan′thē·ən) *adj.* Relating to Xanthus.
xan·thic (zan′thik) *adj.* **1** Having a yellow or yellowish color. **2** *Chem.* Of or pertaining to xanthin or xanthine. [<F *xanthique* <Gk. *xanthos* yellow]
xanthic acid *Chem.* Any of a group of unstable, colorless, liquid thio compounds made by decomposing a xanthate with a dilute acid.
xan·thin (zan′thin) *n. Biochem.* An insoluble yellow pigment found in yellow flowers. [<G <Gk. *xanthos* yellow]
xan·thine (zan′thēn, -thin) *n. Biochem.* A white, crystalline, nitrogenous compound, $C_5H_4N_4O_2$, contained in blood, urine, and other animal secretions, and in some plants. It leaves a yellow residue when evaporated with nitric acid. [<F <Gk. *xanthos* yellow]
Xan·thip·pe (zan·tip′ē) The wife of Socrates; renowned as a shrew. Also **Xan·tip′pe.**
xantho– *combining form* Yellow: *xanthophyll.* Also, before vowels, **xanth–.** [<Gk. *xanthos* yellow]
xan·tho·car·pous (zan′thō·kär′pəs) *adj. Bot.* Yellow–fruited.
xan·tho·chroid (zan′thə·kroid) *Anthropol. adj.* Characterized by a light–colored or fair complexion. —*n.* One who exhibits xanthochroid characteristics. [<XANTHO- + Gk. *chroa* color + -OID]
xan·tho·ma (zan·thō′mə) *n. Pathol.* A skin disease marked by the presence of small yellowish disks formed by the deposit of lipoids. [<XANTH- + -OMA]
xan·tho·phyll (zan′thə·fil) *n. Biochem.* A yellow pigment, $C_{40}H_{56}O_2$, contained in plants and related to carotene. Also **xan′tho·phyl.** [<F *xanthophylle* <Gk. *xanthos* yellow + *phyllon* a leaf]
xan·thop·si·a (zan·thop′sē·ə) *n. Pathol.* A disorder of vision in which all objects appear yellow. [<NL <Gk. *xanthos* yellow + *opsis* a sight]
xan·thous (zan′thəs) *adj.* **1** Yellow. **2** *Anthropol.* **a** Of or pertaining to the yellow–skinned or Mongoloid type of mankind. **b** Of or re-

lating to that variety of mankind that has yellowish, brown, or auburn hair, including the Teutons and Scandinavians; blond. Opposed to *melanous.* [<XANTH(O)- + -OUS]

Xan·thus (zan′thəs) An ancient, ruined city of Lycia, SW Turkey in Asia, near the Mediterranean.

Xa·vi·er (zā′vē·ər, zav′ē-; *Sp.* hä·vyer′), **Saint Francis,** 1506–52, Spanish Jesuit missionary in the Orient; founder, with Ignatius Loyola, of the Society of Jesus: called "the Apostle of the Indies." —**Xa·ve·ri·an** (zā·vir′ē·ən) *adj.* & *n.*

X-chro·mo·some (eks′krō′mə·sōm) *n.* A sex chromosome.

xe·bec (zē′bek) *n.* A small, three-masted Mediterranean vessel, with both square and lateen sails: formerly used by Algerine pirates: also spelled *zebec.* [Earlier *chebec* <F <Sp. *jabeque, xabeque* <Arabic *shabbāk*]

xe·ni·a (zē′nē·ə) *n. Bot.* The influence of the pollen of one species upon the maternal tissues of another species after hybrid fertilization: a phenomenon observed particularly in maize, which often shows blue kernels in a yellow-seeded variety pollinated by a blue-seeded one. [<NL <Gk. *xenia* hospitality <*xenos* a guest]

xe·ni·al (zē′nē·əl) *adj.* Of or pertaining to hospitality. [<Gk. *xenia.* See XENIA.]

xeno- *combining form* Strange; foreign; different: *xenophobia.* Also, before vowels, **xen-.** [<Gk. *xenos* a stranger]

Xe·noc·ra·tes (zi·nok′rə·tēz), 396?–314 B.C., Greek philosopher.

xe·nog·a·my (zi·nog′ə·mē) *n. Biol.* Cross-fertilization. —**xe·nog′a·mous** *adj.*

xen·o·gen·e·sis (zen′ə·jen′ə·sis) *n. Biol.* **1** Abiogenesis. **2** Metagenesis. **3** The fancied production of an organism unlike either of its parents. Also **xe·nog·e·ny** (zi·noj′ə·nē). —**xen′o·ge·net′ic** (-jə·net′ik), **zen′o·gen′ic** *adj.*

xe·no·gloss·i·a (zē′nə·glô′sē·ə, -glos′ē·ə) *n.* In psychic research, the alleged power of a person to communicate with others in a language which he has never learned. [<NL <Gk. *xenos* strange + *glōssa* a tongue]

xen·o·lith (zen′ə·lith) *n. Geol.* A rock fragment enclosed within a larger mass of igneous rock.

xen·o·mor·phic (zen′ə·môr′fik) *adj. Mineral.* Not having its own characteristic form, but having an irregular shape that is imposed by the interference of surrounding minerals: said of the constituents of a crystalline rock.

xe·non (zē′non) *n.* A heavy, inert, gaseous element (symbol Xe) occurring in extremely small quantities in the atmosphere. It solidifies at a very low temperature. See ELEMENT. [<Gk., neut. of *xenos* strange]

Xe·noph·a·nes (zi·nof′ə·nēz) Sixth century B.C. Greek philosopher and poet.

xen·o·phobe (zen′ə·fōb) *n.* A person who hates or distrusts strangers or foreigners.

xen·o·pho·bi·a (zen′ə·fō′bē·ə) *n.* Dislike of strangers or foreigners.

Xen·o·phon (zen′ə·fən), 435?–355? B.C., Greek historian and soldier.

Xe·res (hā′rās, *older* shā′rās, sher′es) The former name for JEREZ.

Xé·rez (hā′rās, -rāth), **Francisco de,** 1504–1547?, Spanish historian of the conquest of Peru.

xer·ic (zer′ik, zir′ik) *adj.* Of, pertaining to, or characterized by extreme dryness; arid.

xero- *combining form* Dry; dryness: *xerophyte.* Also, before vowels, **xer-.** [<Gk. *xēros* dry]

xe·ro·chore (zir′ə·kôr, -kōr) *n. Ecol.* A region of extreme dryness; the desert areas of the earth, collectively. —**xe′ro·chor′ic** (-kôr′ik, -kor′ik) *adj.*

xe·ro·der·ma (zir′ō·dûr′mə) *n. Pathol.* Roughness and dryness of the skin, with scaly desquamation. [<NL <Gk. *xēros* dry + *derma* skin] —**xe′ro·der·mat′ic** (-dər·mat′ik), **xe′ro·der′ma·tous** (-dûr′mə·təs) *adj.*

Xe·ro·form (zir′ə·fôrm) *n.* Proprietary name for a yellow powder containing bismuth and tribromphenol in equal quantities: used as an intestinal and surgical antiseptic.

xe·rog·ra·phy (zi·rog′rə·fē) *n.* A method of printing by electrostatic attraction in which a negatively charged ink powder is sprayed upon the positively charged copy area of a metal plate, whence it is transferred to the positively charged printing surface. —**xe·ro·graph·ic** (zir′ō·graf′ik) *adj.* —**xe·rog′raph·er** *n.*

xe·ro·mor·phy (zir′ō·môr′fē) *n. Bot.* The form or structure of the plant by which it is protected from desiccation. [<XERO- + Gk. *morphē* form] —**xe′ro·mor′phic** *adj.*

xe·roph·i·lous (zi·rof′ə·ləs) *adj. Bot.* Growing in or adapted to drought: said of plants living in dry, hot climates, as the cactus.

xe·roph·thal·mi·a (zir′əf·thal′mē·ə) *n. Pathol.* Inflammation with thickening of the lining membrane of the eye, but without liquid discharge: associated with conjunctivitis and a lack of vitamin A. [<NL <Gk. *xēros* dry + *ophthalmos* an eye]

xe·ro·phyte (zir′ə·fīt) *n. Bot.* A plant adapted to dry conditions of air and soil. —**xe′ro·phyt′ic** (-fit′ik) *adj.*

xe·ro·print·ing (zir′ō·prin′ting) *n.* A simplified variation of xerography which uses a suitably prepared plate on a rotating cylinder.

xe·ro·sere (zir′ə·sir) *n. Ecol.* The series of changes in the succession of the plant formation found upon dry soil. [<XERO- + SERE[2]]

xe·ro·sis (zi·rō′sis) *n. Pathol.* A condition of abnormal dryness of a part; specifically, a dry, thickened, and scaly condition of the skin or mucous membrane of a part. [<NL <Gk. *xēros* dry] —**xe·rot′ic** (-rot′ik) *adj.*

xe·ro·tro·pism (zir′ō·trō′piz·əm) *n. Bot.* The tendency of plants, or plant parts, to alter their position so as to protect themselves from desiccation. —**xe′ro·trop′ic** *adj.*

Xer·ox (zir′oks) *n.* A xerographic process for producing copies of printed or pictorial matter: a trade name. —*v.t.* To make or reproduce by Xerox. Also **xer′ox.**

Xerx·es (zûrk′sēz), 519?–465? B.C., Persian king 486?–465; invaded Greece, but was defeated at Salamis 480 B.C.

Xho·sa (kō′sä) *n.* The Bantu language of the Kaffirs, closely related to Zulu: also called *Kaffir*: also spelled *Xosa.*

xi (zī, sī; *Gk.* ksē) *n.* The fourteenth letter in the Greek alphabet (Ξ, ξ): equivalent to English *x* or *z.* [<Gk.]

Xin·gú (shing·gōō′) A river in northern and central Brazil, flowing 1,230 miles north from central Mato Grosso to the Amazon at the head of its delta.

-xion Var. of -TION.

xiphi- *combining form* A sword; of or pertaining to a sword: *xiphisternum.* Also, before vowels, **xiph-.** [<Gk. *xiphos* a sword]

xiph·i·ster·num (zif′ə·stûr′nəm) *n. pl.* **·na** (-nə) *Anat.* The lower segment or ensiform process of the sternum. Also *xiphoid.* [<NL <Gk. *xiphos* a sword + *sternon* the breastbone]

xiph·oid (zif′oid) *adj.* Shaped like a sword: the *xiphoid* cartilage at the lower end of the breastbone. —*n.* The xiphisternum.

xiph·o·su·ran (zif′ə·sŏŏr′ən) *n.* Any of an order *(Xiphosura)* of primitive arachnids having a horseshoe-shaped carapace and a long swordlike tail; a king crab. —*adj.* Of or pertaining to the *Xiphosura.* [<NL <Gk. *xiphos* a sword + *oura* a tail]

Xmas Christmas: popular abbreviation. [<*X*, abbr. for *Christ* <Gk. *X*, chi, the first letter of *Christos* Christ + -MAS]

Xo·chi·mil·co (sō′chi·mēl′kō) A resort city south of Mexico City in Federal District, central Mexico; famous for its "floating gardens."

Xo·sa (kō′sä) See XHOSA.

XP Chi and rho: The first two letters of ΧΡΙΣΤΟΣ, the Greek word for Christ: introduced by Constantine the Great as an emblem of Christ.

X-ray (eks′rā′) *v.t.* To examine, diagnose, or treat with X-rays. —*n.* A picture made with X-rays; roentgenogram: also **X-ray photograph.**

X-rays (eks′rāz′) *n. pl.* Electromagnetic radiations of extremely short wavelength, emitted from a substance when it is bombarded by a stream of electrons moving at a sufficiently high velocity, as in a Coolidge tube. Their great penetrating power, ionizing effect, and property of acting on photographic plates have many useful applications, especially in the detection, diagnosis, and treatment of certain organic disorders, chiefly internal. Also called *Roentgen rays.* [Trans. of G *X-strahlen,* name coined by Roentgen, their discoverer, because their nature was unknown]

X-ray therapy Medical treatment by the use of X-rays.

Xu·thus (zōō′thəs) In Greek legend, son of Hellen and ancestor of the Ionians.

xy·lan (zī′lan) *n. Biochem.* A yellow, gummy hemicellulose found in straw, oat hulls, peanut shells, and other plant wastes: it yields xylose on hydrolysis. [<Gk. *xylon* wood]

xy·lem (zī′ləm) *n. Bot.* The portion of a vascular bundle in higher plants that is made up of woody tissue, parenchyma, and associated cells, etc. Compare PHLOEM. [<G <Gk. *xylon* wood]

xy·lene (zī′lēn) *n. Chem.* Any one of three isomeric colorless hydrocarbons, $C_6H_4(CH_3)_2$, contained in coal tar and wood tar. A mixture of the three yields a colorless, inflammable liquid used as a solvent and in medicine as an antiseptic. Also **xy′lol** (-lōl, -lol). [<Gk. *xylon* wood + -ENE]

xy·lic (zī′lik) *adj.* Of, pertaining to, or derived from xylene. [<XYL(ENE) + -IC]

xylic acid *Chem.* One of six isomeric crystalline carboxyl derivatives of xylene, C_8H_9-COOH.

xy·li·dine (zī′lə·dēn, -din, zil′ə-) *n. Chem.* Any of six isomeric amino derivatives of xylene, $C_8H_{11}N$: they are homologs of aniline, and are used in the synthesis of certain dyes. Also **xy′li·din** (-din). [<XYL(ENE) + -ID(E) + -INE[2]]

xylo- *combining form* Wood; of or pertaining to wood; woody: *xylocarpous.* Also, before vowels, **xyl-.** [<Gk. *xylon* wood]

xy·lo·car·pous (zī′lō·kär′pəs) *adj. Bot.* Having a hard, woody fruit.

xy·lo·graph (zī′lə·graf, -gräf) *n.* **1** An engraving on wood, or a print from such engraving. **2** An impression obtained from the grain of wood, as used for surface decoration. —**xy′lo·graph′ic** or **·i·cal** *adj.* —**xy·log·ra·pher** (zī·log′rə·fər) *n.*

xy·log·ra·phy (zī·log′rə·fē) *n.* **1** Wood engraving, especially of the 15th century. **2** Printing with wood engravings. **3** Painting or printing on wood for decorative purposes. **4** The making of prints or impressions showing the grain of wood.

xy·loid (zī′loid) *adj.* Of, pertaining to, or resembling wood.

xy·loph·a·gous (zī·lof′ə·gəs) *adj.* Feeding on or boring in wood, as insect larvae. [<XYLO- + -PHAGOUS] —**xy·lo·phage** (zī′lə·fāj) *n.*

xy·lo·phone (zī′lə·fōn) *n.* A musical instrument consisting of a row of parallel wooden bars graduated in length to form a musical scale and struck by small mallets or sounded by rubbing. [<XYLO- + -PHONE] —**xy·loph·o·nist** (zī·lof′ə·nist) *n.*

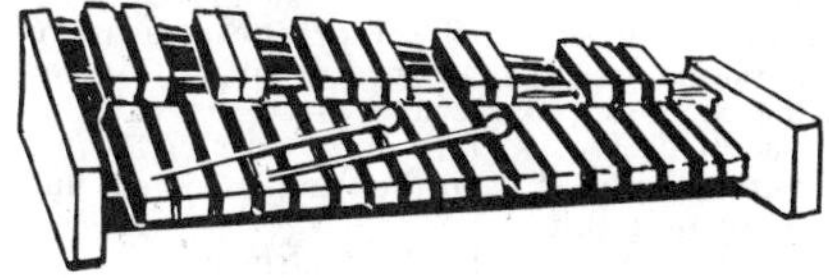

XYLOPHONE

xy·lose (zī′lōs) *n. Chem.* A pentose, $C_5H_{10}O_5$, obtained by treating xylan with sulfuric acid; wood sugar: the levorotatory form is used in the synthesis of vitamin C. [<XYL(AN) + -OSE[2]]

xy·lot·o·mous (zī·lot′ə·məs) *adj.* Adapted to cutting or boring wood, as an insect. [<XYLO- + Gk. *tomē* a cutting <*temnein* cut]

xy·lot·o·my (zī·lot′ə·mē) *n.* The preparation of wood for examination by microscope, as for scientific purposes. [<XYLO- + -TOMY] —**xy·lot′o·mist** *n.*

xy·lyl (zī′lil) *n. Chem.* The univalent radical, $(CH_3)_2C_6H_3$, derived from xylene. [<XYL(ENE) + -YL]

xy·ly·lene (zī′lə·lēn) *n. Chem.* The bivalent radical, C_8H_8, contained in xylene. [<XYLYL + -ENE]

xyst (zist) *n.* **1** In classical antiquity, a hall or covered portico used by athletes for their exercises: chiefly for use in stormy weather. **2** A garden walk or terrace. [<L *xystus* <Gk. *xystos,* orig. scraped, polished < *xyein* scrape, polish]

xys·ter (zis′tər) *n.* A surgical instrument for scraping bones. [<NL <Gk. *xystēr* a scraper, < *xyein* scrape]

Y

y, Y (wī) *n. pl.* **y's, Y's** or **ys, Ys** or **wyes** (wīz) **1** The 25th letter of the English alphabet: ultimately from Phoenician *vau,* Greek *upsilon.* The Romans took it from the Greek alphabet sometime in the first century B.C. and used it as a vowel. **2** The sound of the letter *y.* Initial *y* (introducing either a vowel or a syllable) is a voiced palatal semivowel, as in *yet, you, yonder, beyond.* Final *y* is either a vowel, pronounced (ē), as in *honey, pretty, steady*; a diphthong, pronounced (ī), as in *fly, my*; or the final glide of a diphthong, as in *gray, obey, annoy.* Internal *y* is pronounced as a vowel (i), as in *lyric, myth, syllable*; a diphthong (ī), as in *lyre, type, psychic*; an *r*–colored central vowel (ûr) or (ər), as in *myrtle, martyr.* See ALPHABET.

Y (wī) *n.* **1** Something similar to a Y in shape. **2** A branch pipe, forked pipe, or coupling in the shape of the letter Y. **3** A forked piece, often with the branches curved, usually one of a pair, serving as a rest or support, as for some part of a sighting instrument.

y– *prefix* Used in Middle English as a sign of the past participle, as an intensive, or without perceptible force: *yclad, yclept.* It survives (as *a–*) in such words as *alike, aware,* etc. Also spelled *i–,* as in *iwis.* [OE *ge-*]

–y[1] *suffix of adjectives* Being, possessing, or resembling what is expressed in the main element: *stony, rainy.* Also *–ey,* when added to words ending in *y,* as in *clayey, skyey.* [OE *-ig*]

–y[2] *suffix* The quality or state of being: *victory*: often used in abstract nouns formed from adjectives in *–ous* and *–ic.* [<F *-ie* <L *-ia*; also <Gk. *-ia, -eia*]

–y[3] *suffix* Little; small: *kitty*: often used in nicknames or to express endearment, as in *Tommy.* [Prob. < dial. E (Scottish) <OF *-i, -e,* dim. suffixes]

Ya·an (yä′än′) A city in west central Szechwan province, western China.

yab·ber (yab′ər) *n. Austral. Colloq.* Speech; talk; jabber. [<Australian *yabba* < *ya* speak]

Ya·blo·noi Range (yi·blə·noi′) Part of the watershed between the Arctic and Pacific drainage areas, in SE Asiatic Russian S.F.S.R.; highest peak, 5,280 feet. Also **Ya·blo·no·vy** (yi′blə·nô′vē).

yacht (yot) *n.* A relatively small vessel specially built or fitted for private pleasure excursions, as distinguished from war or commerce. —*v.i.* To cruise, race, or sail in a yacht. [<Du. *jaghte,* short for *jaghtschip* a pursuit ship < *jaght* hunting (< *jagen* hunt) + *schip* a ship]

yacht club A club of yachtsmen.

yacht·ing (yot′ing) *n.* The act, practice, or pastime of sailing in or managing a yacht.

yachts·man (yots′mən) *n. pl.* **·men** (-mən) One who owns or sails a yacht; a devotee of yachting. Also **yacht′er, yacht′man.** — **yachts′wom′an** (-wŏŏm′ən) *n. fem.*

yachts·man·ship (yots′mən·ship) *n.* The art of managing a yacht; skill in yachting. Also **yacht′man·ship.**

yack·er (yak′ər) *n. Austral. Slang* Work, especially hard work: also spelled *yakker.*

Yad·kin River (yad′kin) The upper course of the Pee Dee River, flowing 204 miles NE and SE from NW to south central North Carolina.

yaff (yaf) *v.i. Brit. Dial.* To bark like a dog when excited; hence, to speak sharply; scold. [Imit.]

yaf·fle (yaf′əl) *n.* The green woodpecker. [Imit. of its cry]

yag·ger (yag′ər) *n. Scot.* An itinerant peddler; wanderer; ranger.

ya·gua·run·di (yä′gwə·run′dē) See JAQUARONDI.

yah[1] (yä, ya) *interj.* An exclamation of disgust; bah.

yah[2] (yä, yâ) *interj. Colloq.* Yes. [Alter. of YES; infl. in form by G *ja* yes]

Ya·ha·ta (yä·hä·tä) See YAWATA.

ya·hoo (yä′hōō, yā′-, yä·hōō′) *n.* **1** Any person of low or vicious instincts. **2** An awkward fellow; a bumpkin. [<YAHOO]

Ya·hoo (yä′hōō, yā′-, yä·hōō′) *n.* One of an imaginary race of brutes possessing human form and vices, described by Swift in *Gulliver's Travels.* See HOUYHNHNM.

yaird (yârd) *n. Scot.* **1** A yard (36 inches). **2** A garden; courtyard; churchyard.

Yah·weh (yä′we) In the Old Testament, the national god of Israel; God: a modern transliteration of the Tetragrammaton. See JEHOVAH. Also spelled *Jahveh, Jahwe.* Also **Yah·veh** (yä′ve). [<Hebrew *YHWH*]

Yah·wism (yä′wiz·əm) *n.* **1** The ancient Hebrew religion centered on the monotheistic worship of Yahweh. **2** The use of the name Yahweh for God. Also spelled *Jahvism, Jahwism.* Also **Yah′vism** (-viz·əm).

Yah·wist (yä′wist) *n.* In Biblical criticism, the writer supposed to have written those parts of the Hexateuch in which God is mentioned as Yahweh (erroneously Jehovah). Compare ELOHIST. Also spelled *Jahvist, Jahwist.* Also **Yah′vist** (-vist).

Yah·wis·tic (yä·wis′tik) *adj.* **1** Of or relating to Yahwist or Yahwism. **2** Characterized by the use of the name Yahweh (or Jehovah) for God. Compare ELOHISTIC. Also spelled *Jahvistic, Jahwistic.* Also **Yah·vis′tic** (-vis′-).

yak (yak) *n.* A large bovine ruminant (*Bos grunniens*) of the higher regions of central Asia: it has long hair fringing the shoulders, sides, and tail, and is often domesticated. [<Tibetan *gyag*]

YAK
(From 5 to 5 1/2 feet high at the shoulder)

Yak·i·ma (yak′ə·mə) A city on the Yakima River in southern Washington.

Yakima River A river in central and southern Washington, flowing 203 miles SE from the Cascade Range to the Columbia River.

yak·ker (yak′ker) *n.* Yacker.

Ya·ko (yä′kōō) See JACO.

Ya·kof (yä′kôf) Russian form of JAMES.

Ya·kut (yä·kŏŏt′) *n.* **1** One of a people living in the Yakut Autonomous S.S.R. **2** The Turkic language of these people.

Ya·kut Autonomous Soviet Socialist Republic (y. ·kŏŏt′) An administrative division of NE Asiatic Russian S.F.S.R.; 1,181,971 square miles; capital, Yakutsk.

Ya·kutsk (yä·kŏŏtsk′) A city on the Lena river; capital of Yakut Autonomous S.S.R.

yald[1] (yäd, yôd) See YELD.

yald[2] (yäd, yôd) *adj. Scot.* Athletic; supple; active: also spelled *yauld.*

Yale (yāl), **Elihu,** 1649–1721, English merchant; benefactor of Yale College (now Yale University); born in America. — **Linus,** 1821–68, U.S. locksmith.

Yal·ta (yäl′tə, yôl′-) A port on the Black Sea in the southern Crimea, U.S.S.R.; scene of a conference of Roosevelt, Churchill, and Stalin in February, 1945.

Ya·lu (yä′lōō′) A river forming part of the boundary between Manchuria, NE China, and Korea, and flowing 500 miles SW to the Yellow Sea: Japanese *Oryokko.*

Ya·lung (yä′lŏŏng′) A river in Szechwan province, China, flowing 800 miles south from SE Tsinghai province to the Yangtze, on the border of Yünnan province.

yam (yam) *n.* **1** The fleshy, edible, tuberous root of any of a genus (*Dioscorea*) of climbing tropical plants. **2** Any of the plants growing this root. **3** A large variety of the sweet potato. **4** *Scot.* A potato. [<Pg. *inhame* <Senegal *nyami* eat]

Ya·ma·ga·ta (yä·mä·gä·tä), **Prince Aritomo,** 1838–1922, Japanese general.

Ya·mal Peninsula (ye·mäl′) A peninsula of Asiatic Russian S.F.S.R. between the Kara Sea and Ob Gulf, about 400 miles long, up to 140 miles wide.

Ya·ma·mo·to (yä·mä·mō·tō), **Isoroku,** 1884–1943, Japanese admiral.

Ya·ma·shi·ta (yä·mä·shē·tä), **Tomoyuki,** 1885–1946, Japanese general; captured Singapore (February) and Philippines (May) 1942; executed as war criminal; called "the Tiger of Malaya."

Yam·bol (yäm′bôl) A city of east central Bulgaria: also *Jambol. Turkish* **Yam·bo·li** (yäm′·bô·lē′).

yam·mer (yam′ər) *v.i. Colloq.* **1** To complain peevishly; whine; whimper. **2** To howl; roar; shout. —*v.t.* **3** To utter peevishly; complain. [OE *geōmrian* lament < *geōmor* sorrowful; infl. in form by MDu. *jammeren* complain]

ya·men (yä′mən) *n. Chinese* The office or official residence of a public functionary, as a mandarin; also, any department of the public service: the *yamen* of public justice. Also **ya′mun.**

Ya·nam (yə·num′) A city and former French settlement in NE Andhra Pradesh State, SE India. *French* **Ya·na·on** (yà·nà·ôn′).

yang (yang) *n.* In Chinese philosophy and art, the male element, source of life and heat, represented symbolically by a circular diagram bisected by an S–curve, one half red (*yang*), the other half black (*yin*): originated during the Han Dynasty: opposed to *yin.* Also **Yang.** [<Chinese]

Yang (yang), **C(hen) N(ing),** born 1922, U. S. physicist born in China.

Yang·chow (yäng′jō′) A city in central Kiangsu province, eastern China.

Yang·tze (yang′tsē′, *Chinese* yäng′tse′) The longest river of Asia and China, flowing 3,430 miles from the Tibetan highlands to the East China Sea near Shanghai; forms border between Tibetan Autonomous Region and Szechwan province. Also **Yang′tze–Ki·ang′** (-kē·ang′, *Chinese* jē·äng′), **Yangtse–Kiang.**

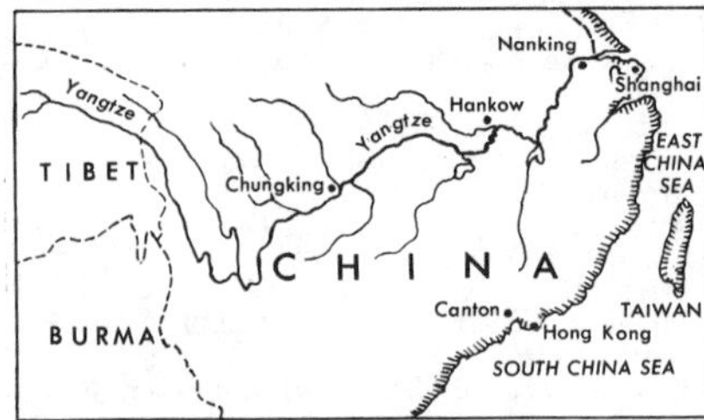

Ya·ni·na (yä′nē·nä) See IOANNINA.

yank (yangk) *v.t.* **1** To jerk or pull suddenly. —*v.i.* **2** To give a pull or jerk. **3** *Brit.* To be vigorously active. **4** *Brit.* To jabber; scold. —*n.* **1** *Colloq.* A sudden sharp pull; jerk. **2** *Scot.* A sharp blow or slap; buffet. [? < dial. E (Scottish) *yank* a sharp sudden blow]

Yank (yangk) *n. & adj. Colloq.* Yankee. [Short for YANKEE]

Yan·kee (yang′kē) *n.* **1** Originally, a native or inhabitant of New England. **2** A Northerner; especially, a Federal soldier during the Civil War: so called in the South. **3** Any citizen of the United States; an American: a foreign, chiefly British, usage. — *adj.* **1** Of or pertaining to the Yankees. **2** *Brit.* American. [Prob. back formation <*Jan Kees* (taken as a plural), John Cheese, orig. a nickname for a Hollander; later applied by Dutch colonists in New York to English settlers in Connecticut]

Yan·kee·dom (yang′kē·dəm) *n.* **1** New England or the northern States as opposed to southern. **2** The United States as a whole. **3** Yankees collectively or as a class.

Yankee Doodle A song, of many humorous verses, popular in pre-Revolutionary times and one of the national airs of the United States.

Yan·kee·ism (yang′kē·iz′əm) *n.* **1** Yankee characteristics collectively. **2** A Yankee word, trait, or idiom, especially as restricted to New England.

Yan·kee·land (yang′kē·land′) *n. Colloq.* **1** The United States. **2** New England or the northern States as opposed to the southern.

yank·ing (yang′king) *adj.* **1** Inclined to jerk or pull sharply, as a horse. **2** *Scot.* Active; enterprising.

Yan·tra (yän′trä) A river in northern Bulgaria, flowing 168 miles NE to the Danube.

Ya·oun·dé (yä·ōōn·dā′) The capital of French Cameroons, central western Africa; a trading, manufacturing, and educational center.

yap (yap) *n.* **1** *Slang* Talk; jabber. **2** *Slang* A rowdy or bumpkin. **3** A bark or yelp. **4** A worthless dog. — *v.i.* **yapped, yap·ping 1** *Slang* To prate; jabber. **2** *Colloq.* To bark or yelp, as a cur. [Imit. of a dog's bark]

Yap (yäp, yap) An island group in the western Carolines; 80 square miles: formerly *Guap.*

ya·pon (yä′pon) See YAUPON.

Ya·qui (yä′kē) *n.* One of a tribe of North American Indians belonging to the Piman branch of the Uto-Aztecan linguistic stock, now living in southern Sonora, Mexico.

Ya·qui (yä′kē) A river in NW Mexico, flowing 420 miles SW and south from the Sierra Madre Occidental to the Gulf of California; the largest river of Sonora state.

Yar·bor·ough (yär′bûr·ō, *Brit.* yär′bər·ə) *n.* A whist or bridge hand with no card above a nine. [after an earl of *Yarborough,* who bet against the occurrence of such a hand]

yard[1] (yärd) *n.* **1** The standard English and American measure of length: 3 feet, or 36 inches, or 0.914 meter. **2** A yardstick. **3** *Naut.* A long, slender, tapering spar set crosswise on a mast and used to support sails. [OE *gyrd* a rod, a measure of length]

yard[2] (yärd) *n.* **1** A tract of ground enclosed or set apart. **2** An enclosure, usually small and near a residence or other building; by extension, the grounds near a house, college, or university, whether enclosed or not. **3** An enclosure used for some specific work: often in composition: a *brickyard, shipyard.* **4** An enclosure or piece of ground adjacent to a railroad station, used for making up trains and for storing the rolling stock. **5** The winter pasturing ground of deer and moose: a moose *yard.* **6** An enclosure for animals, poultry, etc. — *v.t.* To put or collect into or as into a yard. — *v.i.* To gather into an enclosure or yard. [OE *geard* an enclosure]

yard·age[1] (yär′dij) *n.* The amount or length of something in yards, as of silk. [<YARD[1]]

yard·age[2] (yär′dij) *n.* The use of or charge for a yard in handling cattle as they are moved to and from railway cars. [<YARD[2]]

yard·arm (yärd′ärm′) *n. Naut.* Either end of a yard of a square sail.

yard·grass (yärd′gras′, -gräs′) *n.* A coarse, widely distributed, annual grass (*Eleusine indica*); goosegrass.

yard·man[1] (yärd′mən) *n. pl.* **·men** (-mən) *Naut.* A sailor who works on the yards.

yard·man[2] (yärd′mən) *n. pl.* **·men** (-mən) A man employed in a yard, especially on a railroad.

yard·mas·ter (yärd′mas′tər, -mäs′-) *n.* A railroad official having charge of a yard.

yard·stick (yärd′stik′) *n.* **1** A graduated measuring stick a yard in length. **2** A measure or standard of comparision. Also **yard′·wand′** (-wond′).

yare (yâr) *adj. Archaic & Dial.* **1** Responding quickly to the helm; manageable: said of a ship. **2** Brisk; prompt. **3** Prepared; ready. — *adv. Obs.* With dispatch; quickly; soon. [OE *gearu* ready] — **yare′ly** *adv.*

Yar·kand (yär·kand′) **1** A town and oasis of SW Sinkiang-Uigur Autonomous Region, NW China: Chinese *Soche.* **2** A river of SW Sinkiang-Uigur Autonomous Region, NW China, flowing 500 miles NE from the Karakoram range to the Tarim.

Yar·mouth (yär′məth) **1** A port at the entrance to the Bay of Fundy in SW Nova Scotia, Canada. **2** See GREAT YARMOUTH, England.

yarn (yärn) *n.* **1** Any spun material, natural or synthetic, prepared for use in weaving, knitting, or crotcheting. **2** Continuous strands of spun fiber, as wool, cotton, linen, silk, jute, or rayon. **3** A quantity of such spun material. **4** *Colloq.* A long, exciting story of adventure, often of doubtful truth: a sailor spinning a *yarn.* — *v.i. Colloq.* To tell a yarn or yarns. [OE *gearn*]

Ya·ro·slavl (yä′rō·slav′əl) A city on the Volga in north central European Russian S.F.S.R.

yar·row (yar′ō) *n.* A genus (*Achillea*) of perennial carduaceous herbs of Europe and North America; especially, the common yarrow or milfoil, with small white flowers and a pungent odor and taste. [OE *gearwe*]

yar·rup (yar′əp) *n.* Flicker[2]. [Imit. of its song]

yash·mak (yäsh·mäk′, yash′mak) *n.* The double veil or covering for the face worn by Moslem women when in public. Also **yash·mac′, yas·mak′.** [<Arabic *yashmaq*]

Yass-Can·ber·ra (yäs′kan′bər·ə) The former name for the AUSTRALIAN CAPITAL TERRITORY before it was called the FEDERAL CAPITAL TERRITORY.

yat·a·ghan (yat′ə·gan, -gən; *Turkish* yä′tä·gän′) *n.* A Turkish sword or scimitar with a double-curved blade and a handle without a guard: often called *ataghan.* Also **yat′a·gan.** [<Turkish *yātāghan*]

TURKISH YATAGHAN

yaud (yäd, yôd) *n. Scot.* An old mare. See JADE.

yauld[1] (yôd, yäd, yäld) See YALD[2].

yauld[2] (yäld) See YELD.

yaup (yôp) See YAWP.

yau·pon (yô′pən) *n.* A bushy evergreen shrub (*Ilex vomitoria*) of the holly family, found in the southern United States, where its leaves were used for tea and by the North Carolina Indians for their celebrated *black drink*: also spelled *yapon, youpon, yupon.* [<Siouan (Catawba) *yopún,* dim. of *yop* a bush]

Ya·va·ri (yä′vä·rē′) See JAVARI. Also **Ya′va·ry′.**

yaw (yô) *v.i.* **1** *Naut.* To steer wildly or out of its course, as a ship when struck by a heavy sea. **2** To move unsteadily or irregularly. **3** *Aeron.* To deviate from the flight path by angular displacement about the vertical axis; fishtail. — *v.t.* **4** To cause to yaw. — *n.* **1** A movement of a ship or aircraft by which it temporarily alters its course. **2** Irregular, unsteady, or deviating motion. [Cf. ON *jaga* move to and fro]

Ya·wa·ta (yä·wä·tä) A city of northern Kyushu island, Japan: also *Yahata.*

yawl[1] (yôl) See YOWL.

yawl[2] (yôl) *n.* **1** A fore-and-aft rigged two-masted vessel similar to a ketch but having the mizzen- or jiggermast aft of the rudder post. **2** A ship's small boat; jollyboat. **3** A small fishing boat. [Appar. <Du. *jol,* orig. a boat used in Jutland]

GAFF-RIGGED YAWL

yawl-rigged (yôl′rigd′) *adj. Naut.* Having two masts, the after one very small and stepped astern of the rudder post, and both rigged with fore-and-aft sails.

yaw·me·ter (yô′mē′tər) *n. Aeron.* An instrument for measuring the angle of yaw in an aircraft.

yawn (yôn) *v.i.* **1** To open the mouth wide, either voluntarily, as an animal seeking its prey, or involuntarily, with a long, full inspiration of the breath, usually as the result of drowsiness, fatigue, or boredom. **2** To be or stand wide open, especially as ready to engulf or receive something: A chasm *yawned* below. — *v.t.* **3** To express or utter with a yawn. — *n.* **1** A wide opening of the mouth, especially as from weariness. **2** The act of opening wide. [Prob. fusion of OE *geonian* yawn and *gānian* gape] — **yawn′er** *n.*

yawp (yôp) *v.i.* **1** To bark or yelp. **2** *Colloq.* To gape; yawn audibly. **3** *Brit. Colloq.* To shout; bawl; talk loudly. — *n.* **1** A bark or yelp. **2** A shout; noise; noisy talking; also, a loud, uncouth outcry. **3** *Scot.* The scream of a bird, especially when in distress. **4** *Scot.* A cough. Also spelled *yaup.* [Imit.] — **yawp′er** *n.*

yaws (yôz) *n. pl. Pathol.* Frambesia. [<Carib-an *yáya*]

yay (yā) *U. S. Dial. adj.* **1** This many; this much. **2** Ever so many: for *yay* years. — *adv.* **1** To this extent. **2** Ever so: *yay* big. [Cf. G *je* ever]

Yazd (yezd) See YEZD.

Yaz·oo River (yaz′ōō) A river in west central Mississippi, flowing 189 miles SW to the Mississippi at Vicksburg.

Y-car·ti·lage (wī′kär′tə·lij) *n. Anat.* A piece of cartilage shaped like the letter Y, situated at the bottom of the socket of the hip joint.

Y-chro·mo·some (wī′krō′mə·sōm) *n.* A sex chromosome.

y·clept (i·klept′) *adj. Archaic* Called; named: now a humorous term. Also **y·cleped′.** [OE *geclypod,* pp. of *clypian* call]

ye[1] (thē) The: an archaic contraction in which the *y* represents the thorn (þ) of the Old and Middle English alphabet. Often printed **y**[e].

ye[2] (yē) *pron. Archaic* The persons addressed: now confined almost exclusively to poetic or formal pulpit style. Historically *ye* is only a nominative form: "Blessed are *ye* when men shall revile *you.*" *Matt.* v 11. [OE *ge,* nominative pl.]

yea (yā) *adv.* **1** Yes: used to express affirmation or assent: in this sense now superseded by *yes.* **2** Not only so, but more so: to intensify or amplify a meaning: fifty, *yea,* a hundred: an archaic term. **3** In reality; verily: a form of introduction in a sentence. **4** So as to be realized: All the promises of God in him are *yea* and Amen; truly; really: a use of the Authorized Version of the Bible. — *n.* An expression of affirmation; an affirmative vote; by extension, one who casts such a vote. [OE *gēa*]

ye·ah (ye′ə) *adv. Slang* Yes. [<YES]

yeal·ing (yē′ling) *n. Scot.* A contemporary; an equal in age: also spelled *yeelin.*

yean (yēn) *v.t. & v.i.* To bring forth (young), as a goat or sheep. [OE (assumed) *geēanian.* Akin to OE *geēan* pregnant.]

yean·ling (yēn′ling) *n.* The young of a goat or sheep. — *adj.* Young; newly born.

year (yir) *n.* **1** The period of time in which the earth completes a revolution around the sun: about 365 days, used as a unit of time, and divided into 12 months. It is now reckoned as beginning January 1 and ending December 31. **2** Any period of 12 months. **3** The period of time during which a planet revolves around the sun. **4** *pl.* Length or time of life; age; sometimes, old age: active for his *years.* — **astronomical year** The period between two passages of the sun through the same equinox, which determines the changing seasons. Its length is 365 days, 5 hours, 48 minutes, 46 seconds. Also **equinoctial, natural, solar,** or **tropical year.** — **calendar, civil,** or **legal year** The period of time from midnight of December 31 to the same hour twelve months thereafter. Formerly, in England, the legal year began with March 25, but historic years were counted from January 1. In 1751 the English Parliament prescribed that the legal year should begin with the first of January, 1752. **— common year** That of 365 days, approaching most nearly in the number of days to the astronomical year. The leap year has 366 days. **— fiscal year** A financial year of a national treasury or of a business at the end of which accounts are balanced; any twelve-month period used as a basis of business reckoning. **— lunar year** That of thirteen months, one month being added at intervals to make the mean length of the astronomical year, as in the Hebrew calendar. **— sidereal year** The period of 365 days, 6 hours, 9 minutes, 9 seconds, in which the sun apparently returns to the same position among the stars. It is longer than the astronomical year, owing to the precession of the equinoxes. **— Sothic year** The fixed solar year of the Egyptians, consisting of 365 days and 6 hours: so called because determined by the heliacal rising of the Dog Star (Sothis). [OE *gēar*]

year·book (yir′bo͝ok′) *n.* A book published annually, presenting information about the previous year.

year·ling (yir′ling) *n.* A young animal past its first year and not yet two years old; specifically, a colt or filly a year old dating from January 1 of the year of foaling. *— adj.* Being a year old.

year·long (yir′lông′, -long′) *adj.* Continuing through a year.

year·ly (yir′lē) *adj.* **1** Included within a year's time. **2** Occurring once a year; annual. **3** Continuing or lasting for a year: a *yearly* subscription. *— adv.* Once a year; annually.

yearn (yûrn) *v.i.* **1** To desire something earnestly; long: with *for.* **2** To be deeply moved; feel sympathy. [OE *giernan, geornan.* Akin to OE *georn* eager.]

yearn·ing (yûr′ning) *n.* A strong emotion of longing or desire, especially with tenderness. **— yearn′ing·ly** *adv.*

yeast (yēst) *n.* **1** A substance consisting of minute cells of ascomycetous fungi (genus *Saccharomyces*) that clump together, forming a yellow, frothy, viscous growth which, in contact with saccharine liquids, develops or increases by germination, producing fermentation by means of enzymes, in which process alcohol and carbon dioxide are produced, as in the brewing of beer and the raising of bread. **2** Such a substance mixed with flour or meal, and sold commercially. **3** Any of a family *(Saccharomycetaceae)* of yeast-forming fungi. **4** Froth or spume. **5** Figuratively, mental or moral ferment: the *yeast* of youth. *— v.i.* To foam; froth. [OE *gist*]

yeast cake A mixture of living yeast cells and starch in compressed form suitable for use in baking or brewing.

yeast powder Dried and powdered yeast used as a leavening agent.

yeast·y (yēs′tē) *adj.* **1** Of, pertaining to, or resembling yeast. **2** Causing or characterized by fermentation. **3** Restless; unsettled; frivolous. **4** Covered with or consisting mainly of froth or foam. **5** Light or unsubstantial. **— yeast′i·ness** *n.*

Yeats (yāts), **William Butler,** 1865–1939, Irish poet, dramatist, and essayist.

Ye·do (ye·dō) A former name for TOKYO.

yeel·in (yē′lin) See YEALING.

yegg (yeg) *n. Slang* An itinerant burglar; a criminal tramp; a safe-cracker; loosely, any burglar. Also **yegg′man.** [Prob. < earlier *yekkman* a beggar in San Francisco's Chinatown < dial. Chinese *yekk* a beggar]

Ye·gor·yevsk (yə·gôr′yəfsk) A city in west central European Russian S.F.S.R.; a cotton milling center: also *Egorevsk.*

Ye·hsien (ye′shyen′) A city of NE Shantung province, NE China, near the Gulf of Chihli.

yeld (yeld) *adj. Scot.* Not giving milk; barren: also spelled *yald, yauld.* Also **yell.**

Yel·ga·va (yel′gə·və) See JELGAVA.

yelk (yelk) *n. Dial.* Yolk.

yell (yel) *v.t. & v.i.* To shout; scream; roar; also, to cheer. See synonyms under CALL, ROAR. **— *n.*** **1** A sharp, loud, inarticulate cry, as of pain, terror, anger, etc. **2** A rhythmic cheer composed of a prearranged set of words and shouted by a group in unison. [OE *gellan, giellan*] **— yell′er** *n.*

yell·och (yel′əkh) *v.i. & n. Scot.* Yell; scream.

yel·low (yel′ō) *adj.* **1** Having the color of ripe lemons, or sunflowers. **2** Changed to a sallow color by age, sickness, or the like: a paper *yellow* with age. **3** Having a sallow complexion, as a member of the Mongoloid ethnic group. **4** Jaundiced; hence, melancholy; jealous. **5** Sensational, especially offensively so: said of newspapers: *yellow* journalism. **6** *Colloq.* Cowardly; mean; dishonorable. **— *n.*** **1** The color of the spectrum between green and orange, including wavelengths centering at about 5,890 angstroms; the color of ripe lemons. **2** Any pigment or dyestuff having such a color. **3** The yolk of an egg. **4** *pl.* Any of various unrelated plant diseases in which there is stunting of growth and yellowing of the foliage; especially, an infectious virus disease of peach, nectarine, apricot, and almond trees. **5** *pl.* Jaundice, especially a variety that affects domestic animals. **6** *pl. Obs.* Jealousy; hence, a jealous frame of mind. *— v.t. & v.i.* To make or become yellow. [OE *geolu*] **— yel′low·ly** *adv.* **— yel′low·ness** *n.*

yel·low·bark (yel′ō·bärk′) *n.* Calisaya.

yel·low–bel·lied (yel′ō·bel′ēd) *adj.* **1** *Slang* Cowardly; yellow. **2** Having a yellow underside: *yellow-bellied* sapsucker.

yellow–bellied glider The fluffy glider.

yel·low·bird (yel′ō·bûrd′) *n.* **1** The goldfinch (def. 2). **2** The yellow warbler.

yellow daisy The black-eyed Susan.

yel·low–dog contract (yel′ō·dôg′, -dog′) A contract with an employer in which an employee agrees not to join a labor union.

yellow fever *Pathol.* An acute, infectious intestinal disease of tropical and semitropical regions, caused by a filtrable virus transmitted by the bite of a mosquito (genus *Aëdes*). It is characterized by hemorrhages, jaundice, vomiting, and fatty degeneration of the liver. Also *yellow jack.*

yel·low·ham·mer (yel′ō·ham′ər) *n.* **1** An Old World bunting *(Emberiza citrinella)* with the sides of the head, neck, and breast bright yellow, the back yellow and black, and the top of the head and tail feathers blackish. **2** The flicker or golden-winged woodpecker. [Alter. of earlier *yelambre,* prob. <OE *geolo* yellow + *amore,* a kind of bird]

yel·low·ish (yel′ō·ish) *adj.* Somewhat yellow. **— yel′low·ish·ness** *n.*

yellow jack **1** A carangoid fish *(Caranx bartholomaei)* of the West Indies and Florida. **2** The flag of the quarantine service. **3** Yellow fever.

yellow jacket Any of various social wasps (genus *Vespa*) with bright-yellow markings.

yellow jasmine or **jessamine** A smooth twining shrub *(Gelsemium sempervirens)* with bright-yellow flowers.

yellow journal A cheaply sensational newspaper or other publication. [So called from the use of yellow ink in printing a cartoon strip, "The Yellow Kid," in the *New York Journal,* commencing Oct. 18, 1896]

yellow lead ore Wulfenite.

yel·low·legs (yel′ō·legz′) *n.* **1** Either of two North American sandpipers (genus *Totanus*) with long yellow legs: the **greater,** or **winter, yellowlegs** *(T. melanoleucus),* or the **lesser yellowlegs** *(T. flavipes).* **2** *U.S. Colloq.* Formerly, in the U. S. Army, a cavalry soldier.

yellow metal **1** A brass consisting of 60 parts copper and 40 parts zinc. **2** Gold.

yellow perch Perch[2] (def. 1).

yellow peril The political power of the peoples of eastern Asia, conceived of as threatening white supremacy.

yellow pine **1** Any of various American pines, as the Georgia or loblolly pine. **2** Their tough, yellowish wood.

yellow poplar The tuliptree.

yellow race The Mongoloid ethnic division of mankind.

Yellow River See HWANG HO.

yel·lows (yel′ōz) See YELLOW (*n.* defs. 4 and 5).

Yellow Sea An arm of the Pacific between Korea and the eastern coast of China; 400 miles long, 400 miles wide: Chinese *Hwang Hai.*

yellow spot *Anat.* A small yellowish spot in the retina, the region of most acute vision.

Yellowstone Falls Two waterfalls of the Yellowstone River in Yellowstone National Park: **Upper Yellowstone Falls,** 109 feet; **Lower Yellowstone Falls,** 308 feet.

Yellowstone National Park The largest and oldest of the United States national parks, at the junction of Wyoming, Montana, and Idaho, largely in NW Wyoming; 3,458 square miles; established, 1872.

Yel·low·stone River (yel′ō·stōn) A river in NW Wyoming, SE Montana, and NW North Dakota, flowing 671 miles NW to the Missouri River and passing through Yellowstone National Park where it forms **Yellowstone Lake,** 20 miles long, 14 miles wide; 140 square miles.

yellow streak A personality trait combining cowardice, treachery, and meanness.

yel·low·tail (yel′ō·tāl′) *n.* **1** Any of various fishes having a yellowish tail. **2** A carangoid fish (genus *Seriola*), especially the **California yellowtail** *(S. dorsalis).* **3** A California rockfish *(Sebastodes flavidus).* **4** The menhaden.

yel·low·throat (yel′ō·thrōt′) *n.* Any of various American warblers (genus *Geothlypis*), especially the **Maryland yellowthroat** *(G. trichas),* olive-green, with yellow throat and breast.

yel·low–throat·ed warbler (yel′ō·thrō′tid) A warbler *(Dendroica petechia)* of wooded regions of the southern United States.

yellow waterlily A yellow variety of pondlily (genus *Nuphar*).

yel·low·weed (yel′ō·wēd′) *n.* **1** Any of various goldenrods; especially, the Canada goldenrod *(Solidago canadensis).* **2** The bulbous crowfoot *(Ranunculus bulbosus).* **3** The European ragwort *(Senecio jacobaea).* **4** Weld[2] (def. 1).

yel·low·wood (yel′ō·wo͝od′) *n.* **1** The yellowish wood of a tree *(Cladrastis lutea)* of the southern United States, with smooth bark and showy white flowers; gopherwood. The wood yields a yellow dye. **2** The tree. **3** Any one of several other trees with yellowish wood, as the Osage orange, buckthorn, smoketree, or the like.

yel·low·y (yel′ō·ē) *adj.* Yellowish.

yellow yel·dring (yel′drin) *Dial.* The yellowhammer. [<YELLOW + var. of dial. E *yowlring* < *yowlo* yellow + RING]

yelp (yelp) *v.i.* To utter a sharp or shrill cry; give a yelp. *— v.t.* To express by a yelp or yelps. **— *n.*** **1** A sharp, shrill cry; a sharp, crying bark, as of a dog in distress. **2** The sharp, staccato cry of the turkey hen. [OE *gielpan* boast] **— yelp′er** *n.*

yelp·ing (yel′ping) *n.* The act of one who yelps; utterance of quick, sharp cries or barks, as of a dog; also, the sounds so uttered.

Yem·en (yem′ən) A kingdom of the SW Arabian peninsula; 75,000 square miles; capitals, Sana and Ta'iz; joined United Arab States, 1958. **—Yem·e·ni** (yem′ə·nē), **Yem·e·nite** (yem′ə·nīt) *adj. & n.*

yen[1] (yen) *Slang n.* An ardent longing or desire; an intense want; an infatuation. *— v.i.* **yenned, yen·ning** To yearn; long. [<Chinese, opium, smoke]

yen[2] (yen) *n.* The monetary unit of the Japanese, containing 100 sen. [<Japanese <Chinese *yüan* round, a dollar]

Ye·nan (ye′nän′) A city in northern Shensi province, north central China; a commercial center; headquarters of the Chinese Communist party, 1937–47: formerly (1913–1948) *Fushih.*

Yen·geese (yeng′gēz) *n. pl.* White people; specifically, English settlers in New England. [Appar. N. Am. Ind. alter. of ENGLISH]

Yen·i·sei (yen′ə·sā′) A river in central Asiatic Russian S.F.S.R., flowing 2,364 miles NW through **Yenisei Bay** to **Yenisei Gulf** (90 miles wide), its estuary in the Arctic Ocean: also *Enisei.*

Yen·i·seisk (yen′ə·sāsk′) A city on the Yenisei river in central Krasnoyarsk territory, central Asiatic Russian S.F.S.R.

yen·ta (yen′tə) *n.* A female gossip or meddler. Also **yen′teh.** [<Yiddish]

Yen·tai (yen′tī′) A port on the Yellow Sea in NE Shantung province, NE China, on the northern coast of the Shantung peninsula: formerly *Chefoo.*

yeo·man (yō′mən) *n. pl.* **·men** (-mən) **1** *Brit.* A freeholder next under the rank of gentleman; in early times, one who owned a small landed estate; in modern usage, a farmer, especially one who cultivates his own farm; loosely, a man of the common people. **2** A petty officer in the U. S. Navy, Coast Guard, or Army Transport Service, who performs clerical duties. **3** *Brit.* One of the higher-class attendants in the service of a nobleman or of royalty: a *yeoman* of the crown; sometimes, a servitor of lower rank: a *yeoman* of the chamber, the buttery, etc. **4** *Brit.* A member of the yeomanry cavalry; also, a Yeoman of the (Royal) Guard. **5** *Obs.* One who acts as an assistant in a subordinate capacity; a helper; journeyman. [ME *yeman, yoman,* prob. contraction of *yengman* a young man <OE *geong* young + *mann* a man]

yeo·man·ly (yō′mən·lē) *adj.* Pertaining to or resembling a yeoman; of yeoman's rank; brave; rugged; staunch. — *adv.* Like a yeoman; bravely; staunchly.

Yeoman of the (Royal) Guard A member of the special bodyguard of the English royal household, consisting of one hundred yeomen chosen from the best rank below the gentry, and first appointed by Henry VII. See BEEFEATER.

yeo·man·ry (yō′mən·rē) *n.* **1** The collective body of yeomen; freemen; farmers. **2** *Brit.* A home guard of volunteer cavalry, created in 1761, consisting of gentlemen and gentlemen farmers, known since 1901 as the **Imperial yeomanry.** In 1907 it became a part of the Territorial Army.

yeoman's service Faithful and useful support or service; loyal assistance in need. Also **yeoman service.**

yep (yep) *adv. Colloq.* Yes. [Alter. of YES]

-yer Var. of -IER.

yer·ba (yâr′bə, yûr′-) *n.* Maté (def. 1). [<Sp. *yerba (maté)* the herb (maté)]

Yer·ba Bue·na Island (yâr′bə bwā′nə, yûr′-) An island of 300 acres in San Francisco Bay, California; mid-point of the San Francisco–Oakland Bay Bridge.

yerb tea (yûrb, yärb) *Dial.* Herb tea. [< *yerb,* dial. var. of HERB + TEA]

Ye·re·men·ko (yi·ryi·myen′kə), **Andrei Ivanovich,** born 1892, Russian general; broke the siege of Stalingrad in World War II.

Ye·re·van (ye′re·vän′) The Armenian name for ERIVAN.

yerk (yûrk) *Obs.* or *Dial. v.t.* & *v.i.* **1** To tie with a jerk; bind tightly. **2** To crack, as a whip. **3** To beat; lash; excite. **4** To jerk; to kick, as a horse. — *n.* A jerk; a smart blow.

Yer·kes (yûr′kēz), **Charles Tyson,** 1837–1905, U. S. financier. — **Robert Mearns,** 1876–1956, U. S. psychobiologist.

yes (yes) *adv.* As you say; truly; just so: a reply of affirmation or consent: opposed to *no,* and equivalent to a repetition of the words of a question or command in the form of an assertion. The word is sometimes used to enforce by repetition or addition something that precedes. — *n. pl.* **yes·es** or **yes·ses** A reply in the affirmative. — *v.t.* & *v.i.* **yessed, yes·sing** To say "yes" (to). [OE *gēse,* prob. < *gēa* yea + *sī,* third person sing. present subj. of *bēon* be]

ye'se (yēs) *Scot.* You shall; ye shall.

Ye·sil Ir·mak (ye·shēl′ ir·mäk′) A river in northern Turkey in Asia, flowing 260 miles NW to the Black Sea: ancient *Iris.*

Ye·sil·köy (ye′shēl·kœē′) The Turkish name for SAN STEFANO.

yes man *Colloq.* One who agrees without criticism; a servile, acquiescent assistant or subordinate; a toady.

yester- *prefix* Pertaining to the day before the present; by extension of the preceding, used of longer periods than a day: *yesteryear.* [<YESTER(DAY)]

yes·ter·day (yes′tər·dē, -dā′) *n.* **1** The day preceding today. **2** Loosely, the near past. — *adv.* **1** On the day last past. **2** At a recent time. [OE *geostran dæg* < *geostran* yesterday + *dæg* day]

yes·ter·eve·ning (yes′tər·ēv′ning) *n.* The evening of yesterday. Also **yes′ter·eve′, yes′ter·e′ven** (-ē′vən), **yes·treen** (yes·trēn′).

yes·ter·morn·ing (yes·tər·môr′ning) *n.* The morning of yesterday. Also **yes′ter·morn′.**

yes·tern (yes′tərn) *adj. Archaic* Of or pertaining to yesterday. [<YESTER(DAY), on analogy with *eastern, western,* etc.]

yes·ter·night (yes′tər·nīt′) *n. Archaic* & *Poetic* The night last past. — *adv.* In or during the night last past. [OE *geostran* yesterday + *niht* night]

yes·ter·noon (yes′tər·nōōn′) *n.* The noon of yesterday.

yes·ter·week (yes′tər·wēk′) *n.* Last week.

yes·ter·year (yes′tər·yir′) *n.* Last year. [Trans. of F *antan*; coined by D. G. Rossetti]

yet (yet) *adv.* **1** In addition; besides; further: often with a comparative. **2** Before or at some future time; eventually: He will *yet* succeed. **3** In continuance of a previous state or condition; still: I can hear him *yet.* **4** At the present time; now: Don't go *yet.* **5** After all the time that has or had elapsed: Are you not ready *yet*? **6** Up to the present time; heretofore: commonly with a negative: He has never *yet* lied to me. **7** Than that which has been previously affirmed: with a comparative: It was hot yesterday; today it is hotter *yet.* **8** As much as; even: He did not believe the reports, nor *yet* the evidence. — **as yet** Up to now. — *conj.* **1** Nevertheless; notwithstanding: I speak to you peaceably, *yet* you will not listen. **2** But: He is willing, *yet* unable. **3** Although: active, *yet* ill. See synonyms under BUT[1], NOTWITHSTANDING. [OE *gīet, gīeta*]

Synonyms (adverb): besides, further, hitherto, now, still. *Yet* and *still* have many closely related senses, and, with verbs of past time, are often interchangeable; we may say "while he was *still* a child." *Yet,* like *still,* often applies to past action or state extending to and including the present time, especially when joined with *as*; we can say "He is feeble *as yet,*" or "He is *still* feeble," with scarcely appreciable difference of meaning, except that the former statement implies somewhat more of expectation than the latter. *Yet* with a negative applies to completed action,, often replacing a positive statement with *still*: "He has not gone *yet*" is nearly the same as "He is here *still.*" *Yet* has a reference to the future which *still* does not share; "We may be successful *still*" implies that we may continue to enjoy in the future such success as we are winning now.

YEW

yett (yet) *n. Scot.* A gate.

yeuk (yōōk) *n.* & *v.i. Scot.* Itch. Also **yeuck, yewk.** — **yeuk′y** *adj.*

yew (yōō) *n.* **1** Any one of several evergreen trees or shrubs (genus *Taxus*), with flat, lanceolate, dark-green leaves and a red berrylike fruit; especially, the **European** or **English yew** *(T. baccata),* a medium-sized coniferous tree of slow growth and long life, with spreading horizontal branches and dense dark-green foliage. **2** The hard, fine-grained, durable wood of the common yew, of a purplish or deep-brown color. **3** A bow made from the wood of the yew tree. ◆ Homophone: *ewe.* [OE *ēow, īw*]

Yezd (yezd) A city in central Iran: also *Yazd.*

Ye·zo (ye·zō) The former name for HOKKAIDO.

Yg·dra·sil (ig′drə·sil) In Norse mythology, the huge ash tree whose roots and branches bind together heaven, earth, and hell: also spelled *Igdrasil.* Also **Yg′dra·sill, Ygg′dra·sill.**

Y·gerne (i·gûrn′) See IGRAINE.

Y-gun (wī′gun′) *n. Mil.* A gun having two barrels set at an angle, used for discharging depth bombs against enemy submarines, and mounted aft, usually on a destroyer. [So called because shaped like a Y]

YHWH Yahweh. See JEHOVAH.

Yid·dish (yid′ish) *n.* A Germanic language derived from the Middle High German spoken in the Rhineland in the thirteenth and fourteenth centuries, now spoken primarily by Jews in Poland, Lithuania, the Ukraine, and Rumania, and by Jewish immigrants from those regions in other parts of the world. It contains elements of Hebrew and the Slavic languages, and is written in slightly modified Hebrew characters. — *adj.* **1** Of or pertaining to Yiddish; written or spoken in Yiddish. **2** *Slang* Jewish. [<G *jüdisch* Jewish]

yield (yēld) *v.t.* **1** To give forth by a natural

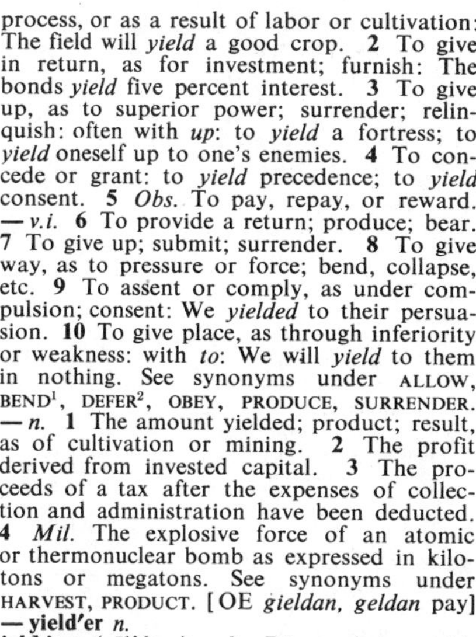

process, or as a result of labor or cultivation: The field will *yield* a good crop. **2** To give in return, as for investment; furnish: The bonds *yield* five percent interest. **3** To give up, as to superior power; surrender; relinquish: often with *up*: to *yield* a fortress; to *yield* oneself up to one's enemies. **4** To concede or grant: to *yield* precedence; to *yield* consent. **5** *Obs.* To pay, repay, or reward. — *v.i.* **6** To provide a return; produce; bear. **7** To give up; submit; surrender. **8** To give way, as to pressure or force; bend, collapse, etc. **9** To assent or comply, as under compulsion; consent: We *yielded* to their persuasion. **10** To give place, as through inferiority or weakness: with *to*: We will *yield* to them in nothing. See synonyms under ALLOW, BEND[1], DEFER[2], OBEY, PRODUCE, SURRENDER. — *n.* **1** The amount yielded; product; result, as of cultivation or mining. **2** The profit derived from invested capital. **3** The proceeds of a tax after the expenses of collection and administration have been deducted. **4** *Mil.* The explosive force of an atomic or thermonuclear bomb as expressed in kilotons or megatons. See synonyms under HARVEST, PRODUCT. [OE *gieldan, geldan* pay] — **yield′er** *n.*

yield·ing (yēl′ding) *adj.* Disposed to yield; flexible; obedient. See synonyms under DOCILE, SUPPLE. — **yield′ing·ly** *adv.* — **yield′·ing·ness** *n.*

yield point *Physics* The amount of stress, measured in unit area, under which a given material, as a rod of metal, will exhibit permanent deformation; the point at which a stress or strain just exceeds the elastic strength of the material. Also **yield strength.**

yill (yil) *n. Scot.* Ale.

yin[1] (yin) *n. Scot.* One.

yin[2] (yin) *n.* In Chinese philosophy and art, the female element, which stands for darkness, cold, and death. Compare YANG. Also **Yin.** [<Chinese]

yince (yins) *adv. Scot.* Once.

Yin·chwan (yin′chwän′) A city of NE Kansu province, NW central China; capital (1928–1954) of former Ningsia province: formerly (until 1945) *Ningsia.*

Ying·kow (ying′kō′) A port on the Gulf of Liaotung in SW Lianoing province, NE China.

yip (yip) *n.* A yelp, as of a dog. — *v.i.* **yipped, yip·ping** To yelp. [Imit.]

yird (yûrd) *n. Scot.* Earth. Also **yirth** (yûrth).

yirr (yûr) *v.i. Scot.* To snarl; yell; growl, as a dog.

yit (yit) *adv.* & *conj. Dial.* & *Obs.* Yet. [Var. of YET]

-yl *suffix Chem.* Used to denote a radical, especially a univalent one: *ethyl, butyl.* [<Gk. *hylē* wood, matter]

y·lang-y·lang (ē′läng·ē′läng) *n.* **1** A tree *(Cananga odorata)* of Malaysia; the Malayan custard apple. **2** A perfume derived from the greenish-yellow flowers of this tree. Also spelled *ilang-ilang.* [<Tagalog *álang-ílang* flower of flowers]

Y-lev·el (wī′lev′əl) *n.* A combined telescope and spirit level on a Y-shaped mounting which may be rotated: used in surveying, etc.

Y·mir (ē′mir, ü′mir) In Norse mythology, the progenitor of the giants, formed of frost and fire, out of whose body the gods created the world. Also **Y′mer.**

y·nogh (i·nuf′) *adj.* & *adv. Obs.* Enough. Also **y·nough′, y·now** (i·nou′, i·nō′). [ME, enough, OE *genōg*]

yod (yōd, *Hebrew* yōōd) *n.* The tenth Hebrew letter. Also **yodh.** See ALPHABET. [<Hebrew *yōdh,* lit., a hand]

yo·del (yōd′l) *n.* A melody or refrain sung to meaningless syllables, with abrupt changes from chest to head tones and the reverse: common among Swiss and Tyrolese mountaineers. — *v.t.* & *v.i.* **·deled** or **·delled, ·del·ing** or **·del·ling** To sing with a yodel, changing the voice quickly from its natural tone to a falsetto and back. Also **yo′dle.** [<G *jodeln,* lit., utter the syllable *jo*] — **yo′del·er, yo′del·ler, yo′dler** *n.*

yo·ga (yō′gə) *n.* A Hindu system of mystical and ascetic philosophy which involves withdrawal from the world and abstract meditation upon any object, as the Supreme Spirit, with the purpose of identifying one's consciousness with the object. [<Hind. <Skt., lit., union] **—yo'gic** *adj.*

yogh (yōkh) *n.* A Middle English letter which represented a voiced or voiceless palatal fricative, or a voiced velar fricative. It is variously spelled in Modern English as *y,* as in *lay, w,* as in *law,* and *gh,* as in *daughter* and *enough.*

yo·gi (yō'gē) *n.* A follower of the yoga philosophy; an ascetic or adept, supposed to possess magical powers. Also **yo'gee, yo'·gin.** [<Hind. *yogī* <Skt. *yogin* < *yoga* yoga]

yo·gurt (yō'gŏŏrt) *n.* A thick, curdled milk treated with cultures of bacteria regarded as beneficial to the intestines: also called *matzoon.* Also **yo'ghurt, yo'ghourt.** [<Turkish *yōghurt*]

yoicks (yoiks) *interj.* A cry formerly used in foxhunting to urge on the hounds: also *hoicks.* [Earlier *hoik,* var. of *hike*; prob. imit.]

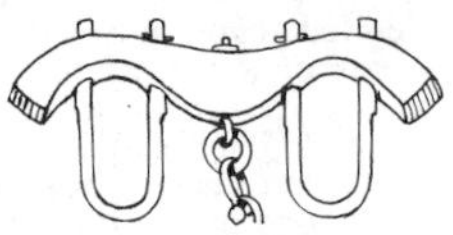
YOKE *(def. 1)*

yoke (yōk) *n.* **1** A curved timber with attachments used for coupling draft animals, as oxen, usually having a bow at each end to receive the neck of the animal. **2** Any of many similar contrivances, as a frame fitted for a person's shoulders from the ends of which are suspended burdens intended to balance, as pails of milk. **3** *Naut.* A crosspiece on a rudder head, carrying yoke lines for steering. **4** *Mech.* A strap, clamp, clip, slotted piece, or the like, serving to confine, guide, or guard the movement of a part of a machine or mechanism. **5** A crossbar suspended from the collars in double harness for supporting the tongue or pole. **6** A part of a garment designed to support a plaited or gathered part, as at the hips or shoulders, giving shape to the garment. **7** That which binds or connects; a bond: the *yoke* of love. **8** In ancient Rome, a device consisting of two upright spears with a third laid transversely across them, under which a conquered army was made to march. **9** Servitude, or some visible mark of it; bondage. **10** *sing. & pl.* A couple; pair; team: a *yoke* of oxen. **11** *Obs.* The amount of land a yoke of oxen can plow in a day. **12** *Scot.* The time required for a yoke of oxen to accomplish a specified amount of work; hence, a part of the day. **—***v.* **yoked, yok·ing** *v.t.* **1** To attach by means of a yoke, as draft animals; put a yoke upon. **2** To join with or as with a yoke; couple or link. **3** To join in marriage. **4** *Rare* To bring into bondage; enslave. **—** *v.i.* **5** To be joined or linked; unite. [OE *geoc*]

yoke·fel·low (yōk'fel'ō) *n.* A mate or companion in labor. Also **yoke'mate'** (-māt').

yo·kel (yō'kəl) *n.* A countryman; country bumpkin: a contemptuous term. [? < dial. E, a green woodpecker, a yellowhammer] **—yo'·kel·ish** *adj.*

yok·ing (yō'king) *n.* **1** The act of one who yokes. **2** *Scot.* As much work as is done by a yoke of draft animals at a time.

Yok·kai·chi (yōk·ki·chē) A city of central southern Honshu island, Japan, on Ise Bay.

Yo·ko·ha·ma (yō'kə·hä'mə) A port on Tokyo Bay in central Honshu island, Japan.

Yo·ko·su·ka (yō'kə·sōō'kə) A port at the entrance to Tokyo Bay, central Honshu island, Japan.

yol·dring (yōl'drin) *n. Scot. & Brit. Dial.* A species of bunting; the yellowhammer (def. 1). Also **yol'ding** (-ding), **yol'drin.** [Var. of earlier *yowlring* <ME *yowlow* yellow + RING]

yolk (yōk, yōlk) *n.* **1** The yellow portion of an egg. **2** *Biol.* That portion of the contents or substance of the ovum which is used for the nourishment and formation of the embryo, consisting of fat or oil drops, etc., as distinguished from the albumen or white of an egg. ◆ Collateral adjective: *vitelline.* **3** A fine yellow soapy exudation in sheep's wool. [OE *geol(o)ca,* lit., (the) yellow part < *geolu* yellow]

yolk·y (yō'kē, yōl'kē) *adj.* **yolk·i·er, yolk·i·est** **1** Of or pertaining to a yolk. **2** Affected with or containing yolk: *yolky* wool.

yom (yom, yōm) *n. Hebrew* Day: used in designating days of feast or fasting: *Yom Kippur.*

Yom Kip·pur (yom kip'ər, *Hebrew* yōm kip'·ōōr) The Jewish Day of Atonement: the 10th of Tishri (September–October). It is marked by continuous prayer and fasting for 24 hours from sundown on the evening previous. [<Hebrew *yōm kipūr* day of atonement]

yon (yon) *adj. & adv. Archaic, Dial. & Poetic* Yonder; that or those over there: *yon* fine house. [OE *geon*]

yond (yond) *adj. & adv. Archaic & Dial.* Yonder. [OE *geond* across; infl. in meaning by *yon*]

yon·der (yon'dər) *adj.* Being at a distance indicated. **—***adv.* In that place; there: Do you see that tree *yonder*? [ME, prob. extension of *yone,* OE *geon* yon]

yo·ni (yō'nē) *n.* The female organ of generation: the symbol under which Shakti is worshiped in India. [<Skt.]

yon·ker (yong'kər) See YOUNKER.

yont (yont) *prep. Scot.* Beyond.

yore (yôr, yōr) *n.* Old time; time long past: in days of *yore.* **—***adv. Obs.* Long ago; in olden times. [OE *geara* formerly, prob. orig. genitive pl. of *gear* year]

Yor·ick (yôr'ik, yor'-) A court jester to the king of Denmark, mentioned in Shakespeare's *Hamlet.*

York (yôrk) A royal house of England that reigned from 1461–85; a branch of the Plantagenet line.

York (yôrk) **1** A maritime county in NE England; the largest county in England; 6,080 square miles; divided into East, West, and North Riding: also *Yorkshire.* **2** Its county town, a city on the Ouse, famous for its Norman cathedral: capital of Roman Britain as *Eboracum.*

York (yôrk), **Alvin Cullum,** 1887–1964, U.S. soldier and hero in World War I.

York (yôrk), **Cape** **1** The northernmost point of Australia, in Queensland on Torres Strait. **2** A promontory of NW Greenland on Baffin Bay at the western end of Melville Bay; site of major meteorites, discovered by Peary.

York boat *Canadian* A type of heavy cargo canoe used by the Hudson's Bay Company. [after *York* factory on Hudson Bay]

Yorke Peninsula (yôrk) A promontory of southern South Australia; 160 miles long, 35 miles wide. Also **Yorke's Peninsula.**

York·ist (yôr'kist) *n.* An adherent of the house of York.

York River An estuary in SE Virginia, flowing into Chesapeake Bay; 40 miles long, 1 to 2 1/2 miles wide.

York·shire (yôrk'shir, -shər) See YORK (def. 1).

York·shire pudding (york'shir, -shər) A batter pudding baked in the drippings of roasting meat, often in the same pan.

York·town (yôrk'toun) A town in SE Virginia on the York River; scene of Cornwallis's surrender to Washington in 1781.

Yo·ru·ba (yō'rōō·bä) *n.* **1** A Negro belonging to an extensive linguistic family of the African Slave Coast between the lower Niger and Dahomey rivers. Many North American Negroes are of Yoruba descent. **2** The language of the Yoruba, one of the dominant tongues of the Sudanic family. **—Yo'ru·ban** *adj.*

Yo·ru·ba (yō'rōō·bä) A former native state in SW Nigeria.

Yo·sem·i·te National Park (yō·sem'ə·tē) A government reservation in east central California noted for its scenic grandeur; 1,183 square miles; highest point, 13,095 feet; established in 1890.

Yosemite Valley A gorge in the western Sierra Nevada mountains in Yosemite National Park in east central California; 7 miles long, 1 mile wide; including **Yosemite Falls,** a triple cataract (Upper Fall, 1,430 feet; Lower Fall, 320 feet; total drop, with intermediate cascades, 2,425 feet).

Yo·shi·hi·to (yō·shē·hē·tō), 1879–1926, emperor of Japan 1912–26.

Yo·su (yō·sōō) A port of southern South Korea. *Japanese* **Rei·sui** (rā·syē).

you (yōō) *pron.* **1** The person or persons, animal or animals, personified thing or things addressed, in either the nominative or objective case: as a subject, always linked with a plural verb. **2** *Colloq.* One; anyone: *You* learn by trying. [OE *ēow,* dative and accusative pl. of *ge* ye]

you'd (yōōd) You had; you would: a contraction.

you'll (yōōl) You will: a contraction.

young (yung) *adj.* **young·er** (yung'gər), **young·est** (yung'gist) **1** Being in the early period of life or growth; having existed a short or comparatively short time; not old. **2** Not having progressed far; newly formed: The day was *young.* **3** Pertaining to youth or early life. **4** Full of vigor or freshness. **5** Being without experience; immature. **6** Denoting the younger of two persons having the same name or title; junior. **7** *Geol.* Having the characteristics of an early stage in the geological cycle: said of a river or of certain land forms. **8** Radical or progressive in social or political aims: used with proper names: the *Young* Turks, *Young* Italy. See synonyms under FRESH, NEW, YOUTHFUL. **—***n.* **1** Young persons as a group; youth collectively. **2** Offspring, especially of animals. **—with young** With child; pregnant. [OE *geong*]

Young (yung), **Arthur Henry,** 1866–1943, U.S. cartoonist. **—Brigham,** 1801–77, U.S. Mormon leader. **—Edward,** 1683–1765, English poet. **—Francis Brett,** 1884–1954, English novelist. **—Mahonri Mackintosh,** 1877–1957, U.S. sculptor. **—Owen D.,** 1874–1962, U.S. lawyer and industrialist. **—Thomas,** 1773–1829, English physicist. **—Whitney Moore, Jr.,** 1921–1971, U.S. civil rights leader for Negroes.

young·ber·ry (yung'ber'ē) *n. pl.* **·ries** A type of large dark-red berry, hybridized from a trailing blackberry and a dewberry, found in the western United States. [after B. M. *Young,* U.S. horticulturist]

young blood Youth; young people.

younger hand In card games, the hand next to the leader: also called *pone*: opposed to *eldest hand.*

young-eyed (yung'īd') *adj.* Having youthful eyes or fresh vision; bright-eyed.

young·ish (yung'ish) *adj.* Rather young.

young·ling (yung'ling) *n.* **1** A young person, animal, or plant. **2** An inexperienced person. **—***adj.* Young. [OE *geongling*]

Young Plan The plan, adopted in 1929, whereby the amount of German reparations for World War I was finally determined. [after Owen D. *Young*]

Young Pretender See STUART, CHARLES EDWARD.

young·ster (yung'stər) *n.* **1** A young person; a child; youth; sometimes, also, a colt or other young animal. **2** *Colloq.* A junior military officer. [<YOUNG + -STER, infl. by *younker*]

Youngs·town (yungz'toun) A city in NE Ohio; a major steelmaking center.

youn·ker (yung'kər) *n.* **1** A German squire. **2** *Colloq.* A youngster. **3** A young gentleman; knight. Also spelled *yonker.* [<MDu. *jonckher* a young gentleman < *jonc* young + *here* a lord, master]

you·pon (yōō'pən) See YAUPON.

your (yôr, yŏŏr) *pronominal adj.* The possessive case of the pronoun *you* employed attributively; belonging or pertaining to you: *your* fate. [OE *ēower,* genitive of *gē* ye]

you're (yŏŏr, yôr) You are: a contraction.

yours (yôrz, yŏŏrz) *pron.* **1** The possessive case of *you* used predicatively; belonging or pertaining to you: This room is *yours.* **2** The things or persons belonging or pertaining to you: a home as quiet as *yours*; God bless you and *yours.* **—of yours** Belonging or relating to you; your: the double possessive. [ME *youres*]

your·self (yôr·self', yŏŏr-) *pron. pl.* **·selves** (-selvz') A reflexive and often emphatic form of the pronoun of the second person. *Yourself* is employed as a simple objective: This rests with *yourself,* or in apposition with *you*: You did it *yourself.* Its use as a subject nominative is obsolete. *Yourself* is also used reflexively: You've cut *yourself,* and, rarely, as a substantive: You're not *yourself* today. Also *Scot.* **your·sel'.**

youth (yōōth) *n. pl.* **youths** (yōōths, yōōthz) **1** The state or condition of being young. **2** The period when one is young; that part of life between childhood and manhood; adolescence. **3** The early period of being or development, as of a movement. **4** A young man: in this sense with plural: several *youths*: used, also, as a collective noun: the *youth* of the land. [OE *geoguth*]

youth·ful (yōōth′fəl) *adj.* **1** Pertaining to youth; characteristic of youth; hence, buoyant; fresh; vigorous. **2** Having youth; being still young; immature. **3** Not far advanced; early; new. **4** *Geol.* Young. — **youth′ful·ly** *adv.* — **youth′ful·ness** *n.*

Synonyms: boyish, childish, childlike, girlish, juvenile, puerile, young. *Boyish, childish,* and *girlish* are used in a good sense of those to whom they properly belong, but in a bad sense of those from whom more maturity is to be expected; *childish* eagerness or glee is pleasing in a child, but unbecoming in a man; *puerile* in modern use is distinctly contemptuous. *Juvenile* and *youthful* are commonly used in a favorable and kindly sense in their application to those still *young*; *youthful* may have a favorable import as applied to any age, as when we say the old man still retains his *youthful* ardor, vigor, or hopefulness: *juvenile* in such use would belittle the statement. See FRESH, NEW.

you've (yōōv) You have: a contraction.

yow (you) See YOWL.

yowe (yō) *n. Obs.* & *Dial.* A ewe. Also **yow** (yō). [Dial. var. of EWE]

yow·ie (yō′ē) *n. Scot.* A small ewe. [Dim. of YOWE]

yowl (youl) *v.i.* To utter a yowl; howl; yell. — *n.* A loud, prolonged, wailing cry; a howl. Also spelled *yawl, yow.* [Cf. ON *gaula* howl, yell]

yo-yo (yō′yō′) *n. pl.* **-yos** A wheel-like toy with a deep central groove around which is looped a string connecting the toy with the operator's finger. As the toy spins up and down the string it may be put through a variety of movements by manipulation of the string. [Origin unknown]

Y·pres (ē′pr′) A town in NW Belgium; site of three major battles of World War I, 1914, 1915, 1917. *Flemish* **Ie·per** (yā′pər).

Yp·si·lan·ti (ip′sə·lan′tē, *Gk.* ēp′sē·län′tē), **Alexander,** 1792–1828, Greek patriot. — **Demetrios,** 1793–1832, Greek patriot; brother of the preceding.

Y·quem (ē·kem′) *n.* A highly esteemed Sauterne wine. [from Château *Yquem,* an estate in SW France]

Y·sa·bel (ē·sä·bel′) See SANTA ISABEL.

Y·ser (ē·zer′) A river in northern France and western Belgium, flowing 48 miles NE from near St. Omer through Nord department and West Flanders to the North Sea at Nieuport.

Y·seult (i·sōōlt′) See ISEULT.

Ys·sel (ī′səl) See IJSSEL.

Ys·trad·y·fod·wg (ūs′träd·i·vod′ōōg) See RHONDDA.

Y-track (wī′trak′) *n.* A track at approximately right angles to a line of railroad, and connected with it by two switches: used in place of a turntable.

yt·ter·bi·a (i·tûr′bē·ə) *n. Chem.* White ytterbium oxide, Yb_2O_3.

yt·ter·bi·um (i·tûr′bē·əm) *n.* A rare metallic element (symbol Yb) occurring in minute amounts in gadolinite and certain other minerals which yield rare-earth elements. See ELEMENT. [<NL, from *Ytterby,* a town in Sweden where gadolinite was first found] — **yt·ter′bic** *adj.*

ytterbium metal Yttrium metal.

yt·tri·a (it′rē·ə) *n. Chem.* A white insoluble earth, yttrium sesquioxide, Y_2O_3. [<NL, from *Ytterby.* See YTTERBIUM.]

yt·tric (it′rik) *adj. Chem.* Of, pertaining to, or derived from yttrium, especially in its higher valence. [<YTTR(IUM) + -IC]

yt·trif·er·ous (i·trif′ər·əs) *adj.* Yielding or containing yttrium. [<YTTRI(UM) + -FEROUS]

yt·tri·um (it′rē·əm) *n.* A rare element (symbol Y) belonging to the lanthanide series. It is formed as a dark-gray powder upon the electrolysis of its double chloride with sodium, and occurs in gadolinite, samarskite, and other rare-earth minerals. See ELEMENT. [<NL <YTTRIA]

yttrium metal *Chem.* Any of the lanthanide series of elements related to yttrium, as dysprosium, erbium, holmium, thulium, ytterbium, and lutetium.

Yü (yü) A river of southern China, flowing 500 miles east from eastern Yünnan through southern Kwangsi to a confluence with the Hungshui, forming the West River proper: also *Siang.*

yu·an (yōō·än′, *Chinese* yü′än′) *n.* The former monetary unit of the Chinese Republic. Also **yuan dollar.** [<Chinese *yüan,* lit., a circle]

Yü·an (yü′än′) A river in NW Hunan province, SE central China, flowing 540 miles NE and east from western Kweichow province to Tungting Lake. Also **Yü·en** (yü′en′).

Yü·an Shih-k'ai (yü′än′ shē′kī′), 1859–1916, Chinese general; president of the Chinese Republic 1912–1916.

Yu·bi (yōō′bē), **Cape** See JUBY, CAPE.

Yu·ca·tán (yōō′kə·tan′, *Sp.* yōō′kä·tän′) **1** A peninsula of SE Mexico and NE Central America (including British Honduras and part of Guatemala); 70,000 square miles; separated from Cuba by **Yucatán Channel,** a strait between Yucatán and Cuba, connecting the Gulf of Mexico with the Caribbean; 135 miles wide. **2** A state in SE Mexico at the NW end of the peninsula; 13,706 square miles; capital, Mérida.

yuc·ca (yuk′ə) *n.* **1** Any of a large genus *(Yucca)* of liliaceous plants of the southern United States, Mexico, and Central America, generally found in dry, sandy places, having a woody stem, usually very short, but sometimes arborescent, which bears a large panicle of white, bell-shaped, drooping flowers emerging from a crown of sword-shaped leaves. **2** The flower of this plant, the State flower of New Mexico. [<NL <Sp. *yuca* < Taino]

YUCCA
(Plant from 2 to 10 feet tall)

yucca moth A moth *(Tegeticula* or *Pronuba yuccasella)* whose larvae feed on yucca seed pods.

Yu·chi (yōō′chē) *n.* One of a tribe of North American Indians, the one tribe comprising the Uchean linguistic stock, formerly dwelling along the Savannah River in eastern Georgia. In 1836 they migrated with the Creeks to what is now Oklahoma.

Yu·ga (yōō′gə) *n.* An age; cycle; a period of long duration according to Hindu thought. Each **Mahâ-yuga** or great age of the world, consisting of 4,320,000 years, is subdivided into four *Yugas* or ages: **Krita-yuga** (1,728,000 years), **Treta-yuga** (1,296,000 years), **Dvâpara-yuga** (864,000 years), and **Kali-yuga** (432,000 years), which began in 3094 B.C. These ages decrease successively in excellence; the life of man is supposed to last for 400 years in the first, 300 years in the second, 200 years in the third, and 100 years in the present or Kali age. Also **Yug** (yōōg). [<Skt., an age, yoke]

Yu·go·sla·vi·a (yōō′gō·slä′vē·ə), **Federal People's Republic of** A state of SE Europe on the Adriatic; the largest country of the Balkans; 98,538 square miles; capital, Belgrade; 1918–1929, the *Kingdom of the Serbs, Croats, and Slovenes,* formed by the union of Serbia and Montenegro with former Austro-Hungarian provinces; 1929–41 the *Kingdom of Yugoslavia;* 1941–45 occupied by Axis Powers; the present federal republic comprises six "people's republics": Bosnia and Herzegovina, Croatia, Macedonia, Montenegro, Serbia, and Slovenia: also *Jugoslavia.* — **Yu′·go·slav** (-släv, -slav), **Yu′go·sla′vi·an** *adj.* & *n.* — **Yu′go·slav′ic** (-slä′vik, -slav′ik) *adj.*

Yu·it (yōō′it) *n.* One of the Eskimos inhabiting northeastern Siberia. Compare INNUIT. [< Eskimo, men]

Yu·ka·wa (yōō·kä·wä), **Hideki,** born 1907, Japanese physicist.

Yu·kon (yōō′kon) A territory in NW Canada between Alaska and the Northwest Territories; 207,076 square miles; capital, Whitehorse.

Yu·kon River (yōō′kon) A river in NW Canada and central Alaska, flowing 1,979 miles to the Bering Sea.

Yule (yōōl) *n.* Christmas time, or the feast celebrating it. [OE *geōl(a)* Christmas day, Christmastide]

yule candle A large candle formerly used to light Christmas festivities.

Yule Day *Dial.* or *Scot.* Christmas Day.

yule log A large log or block of wood, brought in with much ceremony, and made the foundation of the Christmas Eve fire. Also **yule block, yule clog.**

Yule·tide (yōōl′tīd′).*n.* Christmas time.

Yu·ma (yōō′mə) *n.* One of a tribe of North American Indians, the dominant tribe of the Yuman linguistic stock, formerly living along the Gila and Colorado rivers in northern Mexico and Arizona and in SE California: now on a reservation in California.

Yu·man (yōō′mən) *n.* A North American Indian linguistic stock of the SW United States and NW Mexico, including the Mohave and Yuma tribes.

Yün·nan (yōō′nän′, *Chinese* yün′nän′) A province of SW China; 154,014 square miles; capital, Kunming.

yu·pon (yōō′pən) See YAUPON.

Yur·ev (yōōr′yəf) The Russian name for TARTU.

Yu·zov·ka (yōō′zəf·kə) The former name for STALINO.

Yve·tot (ēv·tō′) A town in northern France NW of Rouen; a monarchy in the 15th and 16th centuries; at present a textile center.

y·wis (i·wis′) See IWIS.

Z

z, Z (zē, *Brit.* zed) *n. pl.* **z's, Z's** or **zs, Zs** or **zees** (zēz) **1** The 26th letter of the English alphabet: from Phoenician *zayin,* Greek *zeta,* Roman *Z.* It was not used by the Romans until about the first century B.C. **2** The sound of the letter *z,* a voiced alveolar fricative corresponding to the voiceless *s.* See ALPHABET.

Z (zē) *n.* Something resembling a letter Z in shape: sometimes written *zee.*

Zab·rze (zäb′zhe) A city in southern Poland, formerly (1742–1945) in Upper Silesia: German *Hindenburg.*

Za·ca·te·cas (sä′kä·tā′käs) A state in central Mexico; 28,117 square miles; capital, Zacatecas.

za·ca·tón (sä′kä·tōn′, *Sp.* thä′kä·tōn′) *n.* A species of muhly grass *(Muhlenbergia macroura)* found in Mexico, the roots of which are often used in making brushes: also called *Mexican broomroot, whisk grass.* [<Sp. <*zacate* forage, grass, hay <Nahuatl *zacatl*]

Zac·chae·us (za·kē′əs) A masculine personal name. Also **Zac·che·us** (za·kē′əs), *Fr.* **Za·chée** (zà·shā′), *Ital.* **Za·che·o** (dzä·kā′ō). [< Hebrew, remembrance of the Lord]

— **Zacchaeus** A wealthy publican at whose house Jesus dined in Jericho. *Luke* xix 2.

Zach (zak) Diminutive of ZACHARIAH, ZACHARIAS.

Zach·a·ri·ah (zak′ə·rī′ə) A masculine personal

name. Also **Zach·a·ry** (zak′ər·ē), *Dan., Du., Sw.* **Za·cha·ri·as** (zä′kä·rē′äs), *Fr.* **Za·cha·rie** (zà·shà·rē′), *Ital.* **Zac·ca·ri·a** (dzäk′kä·rē′ä), *Lat.* **Zach·a·ri·as** (zak′ə·rī′əs), *Sp.* **Za·ca·ri·as** (thä′kä·rē′äs). [<Hebrew, remembrance of the Lord]
— **Zachariah** The last king of Israel of Jehu's race. II *Kings* xiv 29.
— **Zacharias** The father of John the Baptist. *Luke* i 5.
Za·cyn·thus (zə·sin′thəs) The ancient name for ZANTE.
Za·dar (zä′där) A port of western Croatia, Yugoslavia, on the Adriatic; formerly (1918–1947) in Venezia Giulia, Italy: Italian *Zara.*
Za·dok (zā′dok) A masculine personal name. Also *Fr.* **Za·doc** (zà·dôk′), *Lat.* **Za·do·cus** (zə·dō′kəs). [<Hebrew, the just]
zaf·fer (zaf′ər) *n.* A blue pigment made by roasting cobalt ores to yield an impure cobalt oxide: used for enamel and for painting on glass. Also **zaf′far, zaf′fir, zaf′fre.** [<Ital. *zaffera*, prob. <Arabic *sufr* copper]
Zag·a·zig (zag′ə·zig, zä·gä·zēg′) A city of SE Lower Egypt.
Zagh·lul Pa·sha (zag·lōōl′ pä′shä), **Saad,** 1860?–1927, Egyptian lawyer and statesman.
Za·greb (zä′greb) The capital of Croatia, in NW Yugoslavia; a major industrial center and the second largest city of Yugoslavia: German *Agram.*
Za·gre·us (zā′grē·əs, -grōōs) In Greek mythology, a son of Zeus and Persephone, slain by the Titans and revived as Dionysus. See ORPHIC MYSTERIES.
Zag·ros Mountains (zag′ros) The chief mountain system of Iran, extending from Azerbaijan to Iranian Baluchistan; highest point, over 14,900 feet.
Za·ha·roff (zä·hä′rəf), **Sir Basil,** 1850?–1936, international financier and armament manufacturer born in Turkey of Greek and Russian parents.
Zah·ran (zä′rän) See DHAHRAN.
zai·bat·su (zī·bät·sōō) *n. Japanese* The wealthy clique of Japan, representing four or five dominant families.
Zaire Republic (zâr) An independent republic in central Africa; 904,754 square miles; capital, Kinshasa: formerly *Belgian Congo, Democratic Republic of the Congo.*
Za·les·ki (zä·les′kē), **August,** born 1883, Polish statesman.
Za·ma (zā′mə) An ancient town in Numidia, northern Africa, SW of Carthage: scene of Hannibal's defeat by Scipio Africanus, 202 B.C., ending the strength of Carthage; site of a modern village of north central Tunisia.
za·mar·ra (zə·mär′ə, -mar′ə) *n.* A sheepskin coat worn by Spanish shepherds. Also **za·mar′ro** (-mär′ō, -mar′ō). [<Sp.]
Zam·be·zi (zam·bē′zē) A river in southern Africa, flowing 1,650 miles SE from northwesternmost Northern Rhodesia through Rhodesia (forming the border between Northern and Southern Rhodesia) to the Indian Ocean in Mozambique. Also **Zam·be′si.** *Portuguese* **Zam·be·ze** (zäm·bā′zə).
Zam·bi·a (zam′bē·ə) An independent member of the Commonwealth of Nations in south central Africa; 288,130 square miles; capital, Lusaka: formerly *Northern Rhodesia.*
Zam·bo·an·ga (säm′bō·äng′gä) A port of SW Mindanao, Philippines.
za·mi·a (zā′mē·ə) *n.* Any of a genus *(Zamia)* of palmlike trees and low shrubs of the cycad family, having unbranched stems terminating in a tuft of thick, pinnate, often spiny-edged leaves. [<NL <LL *zamiae*, misreading of L *(nuces) azaniae* pine (nuts)]
za·min·dar (zə·mēn′där′) See ZEMINDAR.
Za·mo·ra (thä·môr′ä) **1** An ancient city of NW Spain; capital of Zamora province. **2** A province of NW Spain, bordering on Portugal; 4,081 square miles.
Za·mo·ra y Tor·res (thä·môr′ä ē tôr′rās), **Niceto Alcalá,** 1877–1949, Spanish politician; president of Spain 1931–36.
za·na·na (zə·nä′nə) See ZENANA.
Zang·will (zang′gwil), **Israel,** 1864–1926, English novelist and dramatist.
Zan·te (zan′tē, *Ital.* dzän′tā) **1** The southernmost main island of the Ionian Islands, Greece; 157 square miles: ancient *Zacynthus. Greek* **Za·kyn·thos** (zə·kin′thəs). **2** Its capital, a port on the SE coast.
Zan·thox·y·lum (zan·thok′sə·ləm) *n.* A genus of trees of the rue family with prickly stems, of which some species have medicinal properties. [<NL <Gk. *xanthos* yellow + *xylon* wood]
za·ny (zā′nē) *adj.* **·ni·er, ·ni·est** Absurdly funny; ludicrous. — *n. pl.* **·nies 1** In old comic plays, a clown who imitates the other performers with ludicrous failure. **2** A simpleton; buffoon; fool. [<F *zani* <Ital. *zanni* servants who act as clowns in early Italian comedy < dial. Ital. *Zanni*, var. of *Giovanni* John] — **za′ni·ly** *adv.* — **za′ni·ness** *n.*
Zan·zi·bar (zan′zə·bär, zan′zə·bär′) A region of Tanzania consisting of the islands of **Zanzibar** (640 square miles) and Pemba; capital, Zanzibar.
zap (zap) *Slang v.t.* **zapped, zap·ping 1** To kill. **2** To attack; hit; clobber. **3** To confront or impress suddenly and forcefully; astound; overwhelm. — *n.* **1** Vigorous effort; punch. **2** An attack or confrontation.
Za·pa·ta (sä·pä′tä), **Emiliano,** 1877?–1919, Mexican revolutionary leader 1911–1916.
za·pa·te·o (thä′pä·tā′ō) *n.* A Spanish folk dance. [<Sp. < *zapato* a shoe, clog]
Za·po·rozh·e (zə·pə·rôzh′yə) A city on the Dnieper in southern Ukrainian S.S.R.: formerly *Aleksandrovsk, Alexandrovsk.*
Za·ra (zä′rä, *Ital.* dzä′rä) The Italian name for ZADAR.
Za·ra·go·za (thä′rä·gō′thä) The Spanish name for SARAGOSSA.
za·ra·pe (sä·rä′pā) See SERAPE.
Za·ra·thus·tra (zä′rä·thōōs′trä, zar′ə·thōōs′trə) See ZOROASTER.
za·ra·tite (zä′rə·tīt) *n.* A massive, vitreous nickel carbonate found usually as an emerald-green incrustation: also called *emerald nickel.* [<Sp. *zaratita*, after a Señor *Zarate* of Spain]
za·re·ba (zə·rē′bə) *n.* **1** In the Sudan, a stockade, thorn hedge, or other palisaded enclosure for protecting a village or camp: used also as a means of military defense. **2** A village or camp so protected; by extension, any village. Also **za·ree′ba.** [<Arabic *zarībah* a pen for cattle < *zarb* a sheepfold]
zarf (zärf) *n.* A metal cup-shaped holder, of open or ornamental filigree, for a hot coffee cup, used in the Levant. [<Arabic *ẓarf* a vessel, sheath]
zar·zue·la (thär·thwā′lä) *n. Spanish* A form of lyrical theater in which song is intermingled with spoken dialog; operetta.
za·stru·ga (zə·strōō′gə) *n. pl.* **·gi** (-jē) *Meteorol.* One of a series of long parallel snow ridges formed by the wind on the open plains of Russia: also spelled *sastruga.* [<Russian]
za·yin (zä′yin) *n.* The seventh Hebrew letter. See ALPHABET. [<Hebrew *zāyin*]
Z-bar (zē′bär′), **Z-beam** (zē′bēm′) *n.* A Z-iron.
Ze·a (zē′ə) *n.* A genus of tall annual cereal grasses which includes corn or maize. *Zea mays*, Indian corn, is the only species. [<NL <LL, *spelt* <Gk. *zeia* one-seeded wheat]
Ze·a (zē′ə) The medieval name for KEOS.
zeal (zēl) *n.* Ardor for a cause, or, less often, for a person; enthusiastic devotion; fervor. See synonyms under ENTHUSIASM, WARMTH. [<OF *zele* <L *zelus* <Gk. *zēlos* < *zēein* boil]
Zea·land (zē′lənd) A Danish island between the Kattegat and the Baltic Sea, on which Copenhagen is located; the largest island of Denmark, separated from Sweden by the Oresund; 2,709 square miles: German *Seeland*, Danish *Sjaelland.*
zeal·ot (zel′ət) *n.* One who is overzealous; a fanatic; immoderate partisan. [<LL *zelotes* <Gk. *zēlōtēs* < *zēloein* be zealous < *zēlos* zeal]
Zeal·ot (zel′ət) *n.* A member of a fanatical Jewish party (A.D. 6–70) in almost continual revolt against the Romans.
zeal·ot·ry (zel′ət·rē) *n.* The conduct or disposition of a zealot.
zeal·ous (zel′əs) *adj.* Filled with or incited by zeal; enthusiastic. See synonyms under EAGER. — **zeal′ous·ly** *adv.* — **zeal′ous·ness** *n.*
ze·a·xan·thin (zē′ə·zan′thin) *n. Biochem.* A yellow pigment, $C_{40}H_{56}O_{2}$, related to carotene and obtained in the form of golden-orange leaflets from yellow corn, egg yolk, and green leaves. [<ZEA + XANTH- + -IN]
Zeb·a·di·ah (zeb′ə·dī′ə) A masculine personal name. [<Hebrew, God has bestowed]
ze·bec (zē′bek), **ze·beck** See XEBEC.
Zeb·e·dee (zeb′ə·dē) A masculine personal name. [Contraction of ZEBADIAH]
— **Zebedee** The father of James and John, disciples of Christ. *Matt.* iv 21.
ze·bra (zē′brə) *n.* Any of various African equine mammals resembling the ass, having a white or yellowish-brown body fully marked with variously patterned, dark-brown or blackish bands; especially, the true or **mountain zebra** *(Equus zebra)* of the Cape of Good Hope Province and Grevy's zebra *(E. grevyi)* of Abyssinia and north-east Africa. [<Pg. <Bantu (Congo)] — **ze′·brine** (-brēn, -brin), **ze′broid** (-broid) *adj.*

ZEBRA
(From 10 1/2 to 13 hands high at the withers)

zebra wolf The thylacine.
ze·bra·wood (zē′brə·wŏŏd′) *n.* **1** The wood of a large tree *(Connarus guianensis)* of Guiana, light brown in color with dark stripes, used in making furniture. **2** The tree. **3** The striped or banded wood of various other trees.
ze·bu (zē′byōō) *n.* The domesticated ox *(Bos indicus)* of India, China, and East Africa, having a hump on the withers, a large dewlap, and short curved horns: there are many breeds, varying in color, some being reared for milk and flesh, and others for riding and draft. [<F *zébu* <Tibetan]

ZEBU
(From 3 to 4 1/2 feet high at the shoulder)

Zeb·u·lon (zeb′yə·lən) A son of Jacob and ancestor of the tribe of Israel bearing that name. *Gen.* xxx 20. Also **Zeb′u·lun.**
zec·chi·no (tsek·kē′nō) *n. pl.* **·ni** (-nē) A gold coin of the republic of Venice; the sequin. Also **zec·chin** (zek′in), **zech′in.** [<Ital. See SEQUIN.]
Zech·a·ri·ah (zek′ə·rī′ə) A masculine personal name. [Var. of ZACHARIAH]
— **Zechariah** Hebrew prophet of the sixth century B.C., who promoted the rebuilding of the Temple; also, the Old Testament book bearing his name. Also *Zacharias.*
zed (zed) *n. Brit.* The letter z: generally called *zee* in the United States. [<F *zède* <L *zeta* <Gk. *zēta*]
Zed·e·ki·ah (zed′ə·kī′ə) A masculine personal name. [<Hebrew, justice of the Lord]
— **Zedekiah** The last king of Judah, 597–586 B.C.; son of Josiah. II *Kings* xxiv 17.
zed·o·ar·y (zed′ō·er′ē) *n.* The root of a species of turmeric *(Curcuma zedoaria)*, used in medicine as a stomachic and as a carminative. [<Med. L *zedoarium* <Arabic *zedwār*]
zee[1] (zē, *Du.* zā) *n. Dutch* Sea: used in geographic names: Zuyder *Zee*, Tappan *Zee.*
zee[2] (zē) *n.* The letter Z, z.
Zee·brug·ge (zē′brŏŏg·ə, *Flemish* zā′brœkh·ə) A port of NW Belgium on the North Sea in West Flanders province.
Zee·land (zē′lənd, *Du.* zā′länt) A province of SE Netherlands bordering on Belgium and including Walcheren and other islands; 650 square miles.
Zee·man (zā′män), **Pieter,** 1865–1943, Dutch physicist.
Zeeman effect *Physics* The splitting of spectral lines when the source emitting them is placed in a strong magnetic field. [after Pieter *Zeeman*]
ze·in (zē′in) *n. Biochem.* A simple protein derived from corn: it is insoluble in water but soluble in 70 to 80 percent alcohol. [<ZEA + -IN]
Zeit·geist (tsīt′gīst) *n. German* The spirit of the time; the intellectual and moral tendencies that characterize any age or epoch. [<G < *zeit* time + *geist* spirit]
Zeke (zēk) Diminutive of EZEKIEL.
Ze·lin·ski (zyi·lyēn′skē), **Nikolai,** 1861–1953, Russian chemist.

ze·min·dar (zə·mēn′där′) *n.* In India, a tax farmer, required, under the Mogul rule, to pay a fixed sum for the tract of land assigned him; hence, later, especially in Bengal, a native landlord required to pay a certain land tax to the English government; an owner of the soil: also spelled *zamindar.* [<Hind. <Persian *zamīndār* < *zamīn* earth + *dār* a holder]

Zem·po·al·te·pec (säm′pō·äl′tā·pek′) A peak in Oaxaca, Mexico; 11,142 feet. Also **Zem·po·al·té·petl** (säm′pō·äl·tā′pet′l).

zemst·vo (zem′stvō, *Russian* zyem′stfô) *n.* A Russian elective district and provincial representative assembly; replaced in 1917 by the soviet system. [<Russian *zemlya* land]

Ze·mun (ze′mo͞on) The port section of Belgrade, Yugoslavia, on the Danube; formerly a separate city: German *Semlin.*

ze·na·na (zə·nä′nə) *n.* In India, the women's apartments; the East Indian harem: also spelled *zanana.* [<Hind. *zenāna* belonging to women <Persian *zanāna* < *zan* woman]

Zen Buddhism (zen) A form of meditative Buddhism whose adherents believe in and work toward abrupt enlightenment; much emphasis is placed on the identity of nirvana and samsara, and on direct transmission of the enlightened state from master to pupil, with a minimum of words; scriptures and ritual forms are minimized, while continual meditation and practical physical labor are stressed. It originated in China when late northern Indian Buddhism came into contact with Taoism around A.D. 500, whence it acquired many Taoist features; it then spread to Japan, where it greatly influenced Japanese culture in all areas, especially in the age of the Samurai, whose feudal code, bushido, derived from Zen, as did judo and jiujitsu. [<Japanese *zen* meditation <Chinese *chan* <Skt. *dhyana*]

Zend (zend) *n.* **1** The ancient translation and commentary, in a literary form of Middle Persian (Pahlavi), of the Avesta, the sacred writings of the Zoroastrian religion. **2** Erroneously, the language of the Avesta; Avestan. [<F <Persian, interpretation] **— Zend′ic** *adj.*

Zend–A·ves·ta (zend′ə·ves′tə) *n.* The Avesta, including the later translation and commentary called the Zend. [Alter. of Persian *Avestā-va-Zend* the Avesta with its interpretation <Avestan *Avestā* a sacred text + Persian *zend* interpretation] **— Zend′-A·ves·ta′ic** (-ə·ves·tā′ik) *adj.*

zen·dik (zen·dēk′) *adj.* In Eastern countries, an atheist or heretic; one who practices black magic. [<Arabic *zindīq* an atheist <Persian *zandīq* a fire worshiper]

Zeng·er (zeng′ər), **John Peter,** 1697–1746, American printer and publisher.

ze·nith (zē′nith) *n.* **1** The point in the celestial sphere that is exactly overhead: opposed to *nadir.* **2** The culminating point of prosperity, greatness, etc.; summit. [<OF *cenit* <Arabic *samt (ar-rās)* the path (over the head)]

Ze·no (zē′nō) Either of two ancient Greek philosophers:
— Zeno of Elea, 490?–430? B.C., early Greek philosopher, noted for his arguments (paradoxes) against motion and multiplicity.
— Zeno the Stoic, 342?–270? B.C., Greek philosopher; founder of the Stoic school.

Ze·no·bi·a (zi·nō′bē·ə) Queen of Palmyra in the third century; conquered and captured by the Roman emperor Aurelian.

ze·o·lite (zē′ə·līt) *n.* A secondary mineral occurring in cavities and veins in eruptive rocks, usually a hydrous silicate of aluminum and sodium: various forms are used as water softeners. [<Sw. *zeolit* <Gk. *zeein* boil + *lithos* stone] **— ze′o·lit′ic** (-lit′ik) *adj.*

Zeph·a·ni·ah (zef′ə·nī′ə) A masculine personal name. [<Hebrew, the Lord has hidden]
— Zephaniah Hebrew prophet of the seventh century B.C.; also, the book of the Old Testament bearing his name. Also *Sophonias.*

zeph·yr (zef′ər) *n.* **1** The west wind; poetically, any soft, gentle wind. **2** Worsted or woolen yarn of very light weight used for embroidery, shawls, etc.: also **zephyr worsted. 3** Figuratively, anything very light and airy. [<L *zephyrus* <Gk. *zephyros*]

zephyr cloth Thin, fine cashmere used for women's clothing.

Zeph·y·rus (zef′ər·əs) In Greek mythology, the west wind: regarded as the mildest and gentlest of all sylvan deities.

Zep·pe·lin (zep′ə·lin, *Ger.* tsep′ə·lēn′) *n.* A large dirigible having a rigid, cigar-shaped body, as originally designed and constructed by Count Ferdinand von Zeppelin.

Zep·pe·lin (zep′ə·lin, *Ger.* tsep′ə·lēn′), **Count Ferdinand von,** 1838–1917, German general; aeronaut and airship builder.

Zer·matt (tser·mät′) A resort village of SE Valais canton, SW Switzerland; elevation, 5,315 feet.

ze·ro (zir′ō, zē′rō) *n. pl.* **ze·ros** or **ze·roes 1** The numeral or symbol 0; a cipher. ◆ In nontechnical speech, this symbol is often pronounced (ō). **2** *Math.* The element of a number system that leaves any element unchanged under addition, in particular, a real number *0* such that $a + 0 = 0 + a = a$ for any real number *a.* **3** The point on a scale, as of a thermometer, from which measures are counted. **4** *Mil.* A setting for a gunsight which adjusts both for elevation and wind. **5** The lowest point in any standard of comparison; nullity. **—** *v.t.* **ze·roed, ze·ro·ing** To adjust (instruments) to an arbitrary zero point for synchronized readings. **— to zero in 1** To bring an aircraft into a desired position, as for bombing or landing. **2** To adjust the sight of (a gun) by calibrated results of firings. **— to zero in on 1** To direct gunfire, bombs, etc., toward (a specific target). **2** To concentrate or focus one's energy, attention, etc., on. **—** *adj.* Without value or appreciable change. [<F *zéro* <Ital. *zero* <Arabic *sifr.* Doublet of CIPHER.]

ze·ro-beat (zir′ō·bēt′) *adj. Electronics* Homodyne.

zero hour 1 The time set for attack or other military operations: also called *H-hour.* **2** Any critical moment.

zest (zest) *n.* **1** Agreeable excitement and keen enjoyment of the mind accompanying exercise, mental or physical. **2** That which imparts such excitement and relish. **3** Specifically, an agreeable and piquant flavor in anything tasted, especially if added to the usual flavor, as that imparted to soups or wines by the essential oil of lemon peel, or by spice; figuratively, increase of enjoyment produced by the addition of any agreeable stimulant. **4** A piece of orange or lemon peel used to flavor anything, or the aromatic oil squeezed from it: a rare usage. See synonyms under APPETITE, RELISH. **—** *v.t.* To give zest or relish to; make piquant. [<F *zeste* lemon peel (for flavoring)] **— zest′ful** *adj.*

ze·ta (zā′tə, zē′-) *n.* The sixth letter (Z,ζ) in the Greek alphabet, corresponding to English *z,* in ancient Greek sounded *zd* or *dz,* in modern Greek *z.*

Ze·thus (zē′thəs) In Greek mythology, Amphion's twin brother. Also **Ze′thos.** See AMPHION.

Zet·land (zet′lənd) See SHETLAND.

zeug·ma (zo͞og′mə) *n.* A rhetorical figure in which an adjective is made to modify, or a verb to govern, two nouns, while applying properly only to one: *She was* remembered but *they* forgotten. Compare SYLLEPSIS. [<NL <Gk., a yoking < *zeugnymi* yoke]

Zeus (zo͞os) In Greek mythology, the supreme deity, ruler of the celestial realm, son of Kronos and Rhea and husband of Hera: identified with the Roman *Jupiter.*

Zeus–Am·mon (zo͞os′am′ən) See AMMON.

Zeux·is (zo͞ok′sis) Greek painter of the late fifth century B.C.

Zhda·nov (zhdä′nôf) A port on the Sea of Azov, SE Ukrainian S.S.R.: formerly *Mariupol.*

Zhda·nov (zhdä′nôf), **Andrei,** 1896–1948, U.S.S.R. politician and general.

Zhi·to·mir (zhi·tô′mir) A city in west central Ukrainian S.S.R.

Zhu·kov (zho͞o′kôf), **Georgi,** 1895–1974, U.S.S.R. marshal and statesman.

zib·e·line (zib′ə·līn, -lin) *adj.* Pertaining to the sable; made of sable fur. **—** *n.* The fur of the sable. Also **zib′el·line.** [<F <OF *sebelin,* ult. <Slavic. Akin to SABLE.]

zib·et (zib′it) *n.* A carnivore, the Asian or Indian civet *(Viverra zibetha),* with the black markings less distinct and the tail more ringed than the common civet. It is often domesticated. Also **zib′eth.** [<Med. L *zibethum* < Arabic *zabād* a civet]

Zieg·feld (zēg′feld, zig′-), **Florenz,** 1869–1932, U. S. theatrical producer.

zig·gu·rat (zig′o͝o·rat) *n.* Among the Assyrians and Babylonians, a terraced temple tower pyramidal in form, each successive story being smaller than the one below, leaving a terrace around each of the floors. Also **zik′ku·rat** (zik′-). [<Assyrian *ziqquratu,* orig. a mountain top]

ZIGGURAT

zig·zag (zig′zag) *n.* A series of short, sharp turns or angles from one side to the other in succession, or something, as a path or pattern, characterized by such angles. **—** *adj.* Having a series of short alternating turns or angles from side to side: a *zigzag* pattern. **—** *adv.* In a zigzag manner. **—** *v.t.* & *v.i.* **·zagged, ·zag·ging** To form or move in zigzags. [<F <G *zickzack,* prob. reduplication of *zacke* a sharp point]

zig·zag·ger (zig′zag·ər) *n.* **1** One who or that which zigzags. **2** A sewing-machine attachment for stitching appliqué, joining lace and insertion to fabric, etc.

zilch (zilch) *n. Slang* Nothing; naught. [Origin unknown]

zil·lah (zil′ə) *n. Anglo-Indian* A provincial governmental district in India.

zil·lion (zil′yən) *n. Colloq.* A very large, indeterminate number: She said she had a *zillion* things to do before the plane left. [Imit. of *million, trillion,* etc.] **— zil′lionth** *adj.*

Zil·pah (zil′pə) The mother of Gad. *Gen.* xxx 10.

Zim·ba·bwe (zim·bä′bwā) The site of a ruined city (probably of a Bantu people, dating from the 15th century) of SE Southern Rhodesia; discovered about 1870.

Zim·ba·list (zim′bə·list, *Russian* zim′bə·lyēst′), **Efrem,** born 1889, U. S. violinist born in Russia.

zinc (zingk) *n.* A bluish-white metallic element (symbol Zn) occurring mostly in combination: extensively used in the arts, as in the manufacture of brass, and for roofing, etc., also as the negative electrode in electric batteries. Its salts have various applications, as the oxide in painting and the chloride and sulfate in medicine, and, like other salts of heavy metals, are poisonous. See ELEMENT. **—** *v.t.* **zinced** or **zincked, zinc·ing** or **zinck·ing** To coat or cover with zinc; galvanize. [<G *zink;* ult. origin unknown] **— zinc′ic** *adj.* **— zinck′y, zinc′y, zink′y** *adj.*

zinc·al·ism (zingk′əl·iz′əm) *n. Pathol.* Chronic zinc poisoning.

zinc·ate (zingk′āt) *n. Chem.* A salt derived from zinc hydroxide by substitution of a metal for the hydrogen. [<ZINC + -ATE[3]]

zinc blende Sphalerite.

zinc chloride *Chem.* A white deliquescent compound, $ZnCl_2$, extensively used in medicine, industry, and the arts.

zinc·if·er·ous (zingk·if′ər·əs, zin·sif′ər·əs) *adj.* Yielding zinc, as ore. Also **zink·if′er·ous.** [<ZINC + -(I)FEROUS]

zinc·i·fy (zingk′ə·fī) *v.t.* **·fied, ·fy·ing** To apply zinc to, as by coating or impregnating. [< ZINC- + -(I)FY] **— zinc′i·fi·ca′tion** (-fə·kā′shən) *n.*

zinc·ite (zingk′īt) *n.* A deep-red, translucent to subtranslucent zinc oxide, ZnO, crystallizing in the hexagonal system; zinc ore. [<ZINC + -ITE[2]]

zin·co·graph (zingk′ə·graf, -gräf) *n.* An etching on zinc; a picture obtained by zincography. Also **zin′co·type** (-tīp). [<ZINC + -(O)GRAPH] **— zin·cog·ra·pher** (zing·kog′rə·fər) *n.*

zin·cog·ra·phy (zing·kog′rə·fē) *n.* The art of etching on zinc to produce plates for printing. [<ZINC + -(O)GRAPHY] **— zinc·o·graph·ic** (zingk′ə·graf′ik) or **·i·cal** *adj.*

zinc ointment A medicated ointment containing zinc oxide.

zinc·ous (zingk′əs) *adj. Chem.* Pertaining to or derived from zinc; zincic.

zinc oxide *Chem.* White pulverulent oxide, ZnO, made by burning zinc in air. It is used as a pigment, chiefly as a substitute for white lead, and in medicine as a mild antiseptic.

zinc sulfate *Chem.* A crystalline compound, $ZnSO_4 \cdot 7H_2O$, obtained by the action of sulfuric acid on zinc; white vitriol.

zinc white Zinc oxide used as a pigment.

zin·fan·del (zin′fən·del) *n.* A dry, red or white, claret-type wine made in California. [? from a European place name]

zing (zing) *Colloq. n.* **1** A high-pitched buzzing or humming sound. **2** Energy; vitality. — *v.i.* To make a shrill, humming sound.

zin·ga·ro (tsēng′gä·rō) *n. pl.* **·ri** (-rē) *Italian* A gipsy. Also **zin′ga·no** (-nō). — **zin′ga·ra** (-rä) *n. fem.*

zin·gi·ber·a·ceous (zin′jə·bə·rā′shəs) *adj. Bot.* Of or pertaining to a family *(Zingiberaceae)* of monocotyledonous tropical plants, the ginger family, having aromatic rootstocks and including cardamon. Also **zin′zi·ber·a′ceous** (zin′zə-). [<NL, family name <LL *zingiber* GINGER]

Zin·jan·thro·pus (zin·jan′thrə·pəs) *n.* Scientific name of a supposed forerunner of modern man, the evidence consisting of the remains of a skull found in East Africa and thought to be nearly two million years old. [<NL <Arabic *Zinj* eastern Africa + Gk. *anthropos* man]

zink·en·ite (zingk′ən·īt) *n.* A metallic steel-gray mineral, $PbSb_2S_4$, crystallizing in the orthorhombic system. Also **zinck′en·ite.** [<G *zinkenit,* after J. K. L. *Zinken,* 1798–1862, German mine director]

zin·ni·a (zin′ē·ə) *n.* Any of a genus *(Zinnia)* of American, chiefly Mexican, herbs of the composite family, having opposite entire leaves and showy flowers; especially, the common zinnia *(Z. elegans),* the State flower of Indiana. [<NL, after J. G. *Zinn,* 1727–59, German professor of medicine]

Zi·nov·iev (zē·nôv′yif), **Grigori,** 1883–1936, U.S.S.R. political leader.

Zins·ser (zin′sər), **Hans,** 1878–1940, U. S. bacteriologist.

Zin·zen·dorf (tsin′tsən·dôrf), **Count Nicholas Ludwig von,** 1700–60, German theologian.

Zi·on (zī′ən) **1** A hill in Jerusalem, the site of the Temple and the royal residence of David and his successors: regarded by the Jews as a symbol for the center of Jewish national culture, government, and religion. **2** The Jewish people. **3** Any place or community considered to be especially under God's rule, as ancient Israel or the Christian church. **4** The heavenly Jerusalem; heaven. Also spelled *Sion.* [OE *Sion* <LL <Gk. *Seōn, Seiōn* <Hebrew *tsīyōn* a hill]

Zi·on·ism (zī′ən·iz′əm) *n.* A movement for a resettlement of the Jews in Palestine. The form which lays stress upon the political questions involved is sometimes called **political Zionism,** and the term **religious Zionism** is used by those Zionists who lay a special stress upon the regeneration of the Holy Land as a center of social and religious influence for Judaism. Also **Zion movement.** — **Zi′on·ist** *adj.* & *n.* — **Zi′on·is′tic** *adj.* — **Zi′on·ite** *n.*

Zion National Park A government reservation in SW Utah; 147 square miles; established in 1919; contains **Zion Canyon,** a gorge 1/2 mile deep, about 15 miles long.

Zi·on·ward (zī′ən·wərd) *adv.* Toward Zion; Godward; heavenward.

zip (zip) *n.* **1** A sharp, hissing sound, as of a bullet passing through the air. **2** *Colloq.* Energy; vitality; vim. — *v.* **zipped, zip·ping** *v.t.* **1** To fasten with a sliding fastener. — *v.i.* **2** *Colloq.* To be very energetic. **3** To move or fly with a zip. [Imit.]

Zi·pan·gu (zi·pang′gōō) Japan: name used by Marco Polo.

ZIP Code (zip) A numerical code devised by the U.S. Post Office to aid in the distribution of domestic mail. Also **Zip Code.** [< Z(ONE) I(MPROVEMENT) P(LAN)]

zip gun A home-made pistol consisting of a small pipe or other tube fastened to a block of wood and equipped with a firing pin actuated by a spring or rubber band.

zip·per (zip′ər) *n.* A slide fastener.

Zip·per (zip′ər) *n.* An overshoe or boot secured with a slide fastener: a trade name.

zip·py (zip′ē) *adj.* **·pi·er, ·pi·est** *Colloq.* Brisk; energetic; lively; snappy.

zir·con (zûr′kon) *n.* **1** An adamantine, variously colored zirconium silicate, $ZrSiO_4$. The transparent reddish variety, called *hyacinth,* is used as a gem, as are also the leaf-green, yellowish, colorless, or smoky varieties called *jargon.* **2** A variety of this mineral having an artificially produced steely-blue color of high brilliance and luster: esteemed as a gem. [<F *zircone* <Arabic *zarqūn* cinnabar <Persian *zargūn* golden < *zar* gold + *gūn* color]

zir·con·ate (zûr′kən·āt) *n. Chem.* A salt formed by replacing hydrogen in zirconium hydroxide with a metal. [<ZIRCON(IUM) + -ATE[3]]

zir·co·ni·a (zûr·kō′nē·ə) *n. Chem.* A white pulverulent zirconium dioxide, ZrO_2, obtained by heating zirconium to redness in contact with air: when strongly heated it becomes luminous, and it is hence used in certain forms of incandescent burners. [<NL <ZIRCON]

zir·co·ni·um (zûr·kō′nē·əm) *n.* A metallic element (symbol Zr) chemically resembling titanium, prepared as a black amorphous powder, as steel-gray shining scales, or as crystalline laminae: used in alloys, as an opacifier of lacquers, and as an abrasive. See ELEMENT. [<NL <ZIRCON] — **zir·con′ic** *adj.*

Z–i·ron (zē′ī′ərn) *n.* An angle iron of Z form: also called *Z-bar, Z-beam.*

Zis·ka (tsis′kä), **John,** 1360?–1424, Bohemian general; leader of the Hussites. Also **Žiž·ka** (zhish′kä).

zith·er (zith′ər) *n.* A simple form of stringed instrument, having a flat sounding board and from thirty to forty strings that are played by plucking with a plectrum. Also **zith′ern** (-ərn). [<G <L *cithara* <Gk. *kithara.* Doublet of CITHARA and GUITAR.]

zit·tern (zit′ərn) See CITHERN.

zi·zith (tsē·tsēt′, tsi′tsis) *n.* The fringe or tassel formerly worn by Jews on the outer garment (*Num.* xv 38), but now worn on the tallith during prayer. [<Hebrew *tsītsīth*]

ziz·zle (ziz′əl) *v.i.* **·zled, ·zling** *Brit. Dial.* To make a sputtering or hissing sound, as meat when cooking; sizzle. [Imit.]

Zla·to·ust (zlä′tə·ōōst′) A city of SW Asiatic Russian S.F.S.R. in the southern Urals.

zlo·ty (zlô′tē) *n. pl.* **·tys** or **·ty** The monetary unit of Poland. [<Polish, lit., golden]

zo– Var. of ZOO–.

-zoa *combining form Zool.* Used to denote the names of groups: *Protozoa, Hydrozoa.* An individual in such a group is denoted by **-zoan.** [<NL <Gk. *zōion* an animal]

Zo·an (zō′an) The Old Testament name for TANIS.

zo·an·thro·py (zō·an′thrə·pē) *n.* The obsessive delusion that one has become a beast; lycanthropy. [<NL *zoanthropia* <Gk. *zōion* animal + *anthrōpos* a man] — **zo·an·throp·ic** (zō′ən·throp′ik) *adj.*

SIGNS OF THE ZODIAC
Reading clockwise:
A. Vernal equinox: Aries, Taurus, Gemini.
B. Summer solstice: Cancer, Leo, Virgo.
C. Autumnal equinox: Libra, Scorpio, Sagittarius.
D. Winter solstice: Capricorn, Aquarius, Pisces.

zo·di·ac (zō′dē·ak) *n.* **1** An imaginary belt encircling the heavens and extending about 8° on each side of the ecliptic, within which are the orbits of the moon, sun, and larger planets. It is divided into twelve parts, called **signs of the zodiac,** which formerly corresponded to twelve constellations bearing the same names. Now, owing to the precession of the equinoxes, each constellation is in the sign that has the name next following its own. **2** Figuratively, a complete circuit; round. **3** *Rare* A circle or halo; also, a girdle. [<OF *zodiaque* <L *zodiacus* <Gk. *(kyklos) zōdiakos* (circle) of animals <*zōdion* a sculptured animal, dim. of *zōion* an animal] — **zo·di·a·cal** (zō·dī′ə·kəl) *adj.*

zodiacal light *Astron.* A cone-shaped tract of faint light lying near the plane of the ecliptic: it may be seen in the west after twilight in winter and spring, or in the east before daybreak from September till January. It is attributed to the reflection of sunlight from a cloud of fine meteoric dust.

Zo·e (zō′ē) A feminine personal name. [<Gk., life]

zo·e·trope (zō′ə·trōp) *n.* A toy having a revolving cylinder with slits through which a series of pictures inside are seen in apparent motion. Compare PHENAKISTOSCOPE. [<Gk. *zōē* life + -TROPE] — **zo′e·trop′ic** (-trop′ik) *adj.*

zo·ic (zō′ik) *adj.* Pertaining to or characterized by animals or animal life. [<Gk. *zōikos* < *zōion* an animal]

zois·ite (zoi′sīt) *n.* A vitreous, transparent to subtranslucent silicate of aluminum and calcium, in which iron sometimes replaces the aluminum. [<G *zoisit,* after Baron *Zois* von Edelstein, 1747–1819, its discoverer]

Zo·la (zō′lə, zō·lä′; *Fr.* zō·là′), **Émile,** 1840–1902, French writer. — **Zo′la·esque′** (-esk′) *adj.*

zoll·ver·ein (tsôl′fer·īn) *n.* **1** A former trade league constituted by twenty-six German states. **2** Hence, a union of states for tariff purposes. [<G < *zoll* a tax, custom + *verein* a union]

Zom·ba (zom′bə) The capital of Nyasaland, Federation of Rhodesia and Nyasaland, in the SE part.

zom·bi (zom′bē) *n.* **1** In West African voodoo cults, the python deity; also, the snake deity of the voodoo cults of Haiti and of the southern United States. **2** The supernatural power by which a dead body is believed to be reanimated; specifically, a corpse reactivated by sorcery, but still dead. **3** Loosely, a ghost. Also **zom′bie.** [<West African. Cf. Bantu (Congo) *zumbi* fetish.] — **zom′bi·ism** *n.*

Zom·bie (zom′bē) *n.* A large, strong cocktail made from several kinds of rum, fruit juices, and liqueur. [<ZOMBI]

zo·nal (zō′nəl) *adj.* Of, pertaining to, exhibiting, or marked by a zone or zones; having the form of a zone. Also **zo′na·ry** (-nər·ē).

zo·nate (zō′nāt) *adj.* **1** Marked with zones or concentric colored bands. **2** *Bot.* Disposed in a single row, as certain tetraspores. Also **zo′nat·ed.** [<ZON(E) + -ATE[1]] — **zo·na·tion** (zō·nā′shən) *n.*

zone (zōn) *n.* **1** One of five divisions of the earth's surface, enclosed between two parallels of latitude and named for the prevailing climate. These are the **torrid zone,** extending on each side of the equator 23° 27′; the **temperate** or **variable zones,** included between the parallels 23° 27′ and 66° 33′ on both sides of the equator; and the **frigid zones,** within the parallels 66° 33′ and the poles. **2** In war, a region proscribed for neutrals as being within the range of military or naval operations: a defense *zone,* combat *zone*; also, any region neutralized by agreement of combatants: a demilitarized *zone.* **3** *Ecol.* A belt or area delimited from others by the character of its plant or animal life, its climate, geological formations, etc. **4** A region of land distinguished or set off by some special characteristic: a canal *zone.* **5** *Anat.* A beltlike area distinguished from its surroundings either by structure or appearance. **6** *Mineral.* Any series of faces upon a crystal whose planes form a prismatic surface. **7** A belt, stripe, etc., distinguished by color or

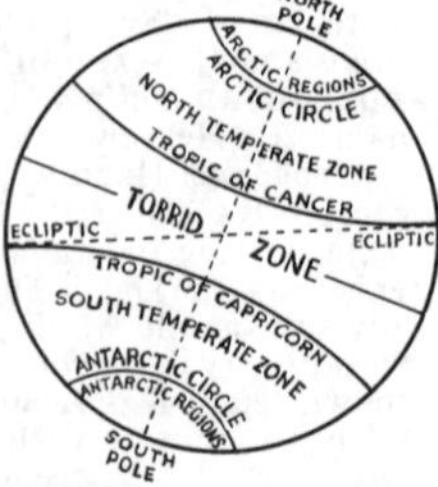

TERRESTRIAL ZONES

the like, encircling an object. 8 *Geom.* A portion of the surface of a sphere enclosed between two parallel planes. 9 Originally (now chiefly in poetry), a belt or girdle. 10 The total number of railroad stations situated in a certain area measured from a place whence traffic is shipped; also, a circular area within which a uniform fare is charged by the transportation companies. 11 In the United States parcel post system, any one of the concentric areas within each of which a uniform rate is charged. 12 A postal district in a city. —*v.t.* **zoned, zon·ing** 1 To divide into zones; especially, to divide (a city, etc.) into zones which are restricted as to types of construction and activity, as residential, industrial, etc. 2 To encircle with a zone or belt. 3 To mark with or as with zones or stripes. [<MF <L *zona* <Gk. *zōnē* a girdle] —**zoned** *adj.*

zone axis *Mineral.* The imaginary line through a crystal, to which all the faces in a given zone, and the mutual intersections of those faces, are parallel.

zone·less (zōn′lis) *adj.* Having no zone or belt.

zone time See under TIME.

Zon·gul·dak (zông′gōōl·däk′) 1 A port on the Black Sea in NW Turkey in Asia, capital of Zonguldak province; a coal-shipping center. 2 A province of NW Turkey in Asia, bordering on the Black Sea; 2,876 square miles.

zo·nule (zōn′yōōl) *n.* A small zone, belt, or ring. Also **zo′nu·la.** [<NL *zonula,* dim. of L *zona* ZONE]

zoo (zōō) *n.* A menagerie. [Short for ZOOLOGICAL GARDEN]

zoo– *combining form* Animal; of or related to animals, or to animal forms: *zoology, zoophyte.* Also, before vowels, *zo–.* [<Gk. *zōion* an animal]

zo·o·chem·is·try (zō′ə·kem′is·trē) *n.* Animal chemistry; specifically, the chemistry of the solids and fluids contained in the animal organism. —**zo′o·chem′i·cal** (-kem′i·kəl) *adj.*

zo·o·chore (zō′ə·kôr, -kōr) *n.* A plant distributed by animals.

zo·o·ge·o·graph·ic (zō′ə·jē′ə·graf′ik) *adj.* Of, pertaining to, or engaged in zoogeography. Also **zo′o·ge′o·graph′i·cal.** —**zo′o·ge′o·graph′·i·cal·ly** *adv.*

zoogeographic realm One of a series of major geographic areas characterized by the dominance of certain animal groups. The principal realms in the classification of A. R. Wallace are: the Palearctic, Nearctic, Neotropical, Ethiopian, Oriental, and Australian. The first two are often considered together as the Holarctic realm.

zo·o·ge·og·ra·phy (zō′ə·jē·og′rə·fē) *n.* 1 The systematic study of the distribution of animals and of the factors controlling it. 2 The study of the relations between special animal groups and the land or aquatic areas in which they predominate. —**zo′o·ge·og′ra·pher** *n.*

zo·o·gloe·a (zō′ə·glē′ə) *n. pl.* **·gloe·ae** (-glē′ē) A colony of bacteria forming a jellylike mass held together by a viscid sheath secreted by themselves. [<NL <Gk. *zōion* an animal + *gloios* sticky stuff]

zo·og·ra·phy (zō·og′rə·fē) *n.* The branch of zoology that describes animals; descriptive zoology. —**zo·og′ra·pher** or **·phist** *n.* —**zo·o·graph·ic** (zō′ə·graf′ik) or **·i·cal** *adj.*

zo·oid (zō′oid) *n.* 1 *Biol.* Any organism, usually very small, capable of spontaneous movement and independent existence, as a spermatozoon. 2 *Zool.* **a** One of the distinct members of a compound or colonial organism, as in a bryozoan. **b** A free-swimming organism produced as a stage in the life cycle of a jellyfish. —*adj.* Having essentially the nature of an animal: also **zo·oi·dal** (zō·oid′l). [<ZO- + -OID]

zo·ol·a·try (zō·ol′ə·trē) *n.* Animal-worship. [<ZOO- + -LATRY] —**zo·ol′at·er** *n.* —**zo·ol′a·trous** *adj.*

zo·o·log·i·cal (zō′ə·loj′i·kəl) *adj.* 1 Of, pertaining to, or occupied with zoology. 2 Relating to or characteristic of animals. Also **zo′o·log′ic.** —**zo′o·log′i·cal·ly** *adv.*

zoological garden A park or garden in which wild animals are kept for exhibition.

zo·ol·o·gy (zō·ol′ə·jē) *n.* 1 The science that treats of animals with reference to their structure, functions, development, nomenclature, and classification. 2 The animal kingdom, or local examples of it, regarded biologically. 3 A scientific treatise on animals. [<NL *zoologia* <Gk. *zōion* an animal + *logos* a word, discourse] —**zo·ol′o·gist** *n.*

zoom (zōōm) *v.i.* 1 To make a low-pitched but loud humming or buzzing sound. 2 To climb sharply in an airplane, using the energy of momentum. 3 To move a motion picture or TV camera rapidly or adjust the focus, as with a zoom lens, to make an object in view appear to come very close or become much more distant. —*v.t.* 4 To cause to zoom. —*n.* The act of zooming. [Imit.]

zo·om·e·try (zō·om′ə·trē) *n.* Measurement of the parts of animals and determination of their relative magnitude. [<ZOO- + -METRY] —**zo·o·met·ric** (zō′ə·met′rik) *adj.*

zoom lens *Photog.* A lens, used chiefly on television and motion picture cameras, that permits the size of the image to be varied continuously without loss of focus.

zo·o·mor·phism (zō′ə·môr′fiz·əm) *n.* 1 The conception, symbolization, or representation of a man or a god in the form of an animal; also, the attribution of divine or human qualities to animals. 2 The representation of animals or animal forms in art or symbolism. 3 Transformation into animals. In this sense compare BEAST MARRIAGE, SWAN MAIDEN. See also CIRCE. Also **zo′o·mor′phy.** —**zo′o·mor′·phic** *adj.*

zo·on (zō′on) *n. pl.* **zo·ons** or **zo·a** (zō′ə) *Biol.* A developed individual of a compound animal or of a simple egg. [<NL <Gk. *zōion* an animal] —**zo·on·al** (zō·on′əl) *adj.*

zo·oph·a·gous (zō·of′ə·gəs) *adj.* Feeding on animals. [<ZOO- + -PHAGOUS]

zo·o·phile (zō′ə·fīl, -fil) *n.* 1 A zoophilous plant. 2 A lover of animals; specifically, one who objects to vivisection; also, one addicted to zoophilism: also **zo·oph·i·list** (zō·of′ə·list). [<ZOO- + -PHILE] —**zo′o·phil′ic** (-fil′ik) *adj.*

zo·oph·i·lism (zō·of′ə·liz′əm) *n.* 1 Fondness for animals. 2 The obtaining of sexual gratification by the fondling of animals. Also **zo·o·phil·i·a** (zō′ə·fil′ē·ə).

zo·oph·i·lous (zō·of′ə·ləs) *adj.* 1 Animal-loving. 2 Adapted for pollination by animals, as certain plants. [<ZOO- + -PHILOUS]

zo·o·pho·bi·a (zō′ə·fō′bē·ə) *n.* A morbid fear of animals. [<ZOO- + -PHOBIA] —**zo′o·pho′·bic** *adj.*

zo·o·phyte (zō′ə·fīt) *n.* An invertebrate animal resembling a plant, as a coral or sea anemone. [<ZOO- + -PHYTE] —**zo′o·phyt′ic** (-fit′ik) or **·i·cal** *adj.*

zo·o·plas·ty (zō′ə·plas′tē) *n. Surg.* That operation by which a part of an animal body is grafted on some part of the human body. —**zo′o·plas′tic** *adj.*

zo·o·sperm (zō′ə·spûrm) *n.* 1 A zoospore. 2 A spermatozoon. —**zo′o·sper·mat′ic** (-spər·mat′ik) *adj.*

zo·o·spo·ran·gi·um (zō′ə·spə·ran′jē·əm) *n. pl.* **·gi·a** (-jē·ə) *Bot.* A sporangium producing zoospores. [<NL <Gk. *zōion* an animal + *spora* a seed + *angeion* a vessel] —**zo′o·spo·ran′gi·al** *adj.*

zo·o·spore (zō′ə·spôr, -spōr) *n.* 1 *Bot.* A motile spore destitute of any cell wall, produced particularly among some algae and fungi: they move sometimes in an ameboid manner, but more frequently they are provided with cilia, by the lashing of which the spore is propelled through the water. 2 *Zool.* A flagellate or ameboid motile cell in certain protozoa. [<ZOO- + SPORE] —**zo′o·spor′ic** (-spôr′ik, -spor′ik), **zo·os·po·rous** (zō·os′pər·əs) *adj.*

zo·ot·o·my (zō·ot′ə·mē) *n.* The anatomy or dissection of animals; comparative anatomy. [<NL *zootomia* <Gk. *zōion* an animal + *tomē* a cutting <*temnein* cut] —**zo·o·tom·ic** (zō′ə·tom′ik) or **·i·cal** *adj.* —**zo′o·tom′i·cal·ly** *adv.* —**zo·ot′o·mist** *n.*

zo·o·tox·in (zō′ə·tok′sin) *n.* A toxin derived from animals, as snake venom, the poison of bee stings, etc.

zoot suit (zōōt) *Slang* A suit having an extra-long coat and baggy trousers narrowing at the ankle. [Origin uncertain] —**zoot-suit·er** (zōōt′sōō′tər) *n.*

zor·il (zôr′il, zor′-) *n.* An African musteline carnivore *(Ictonyx striata)* which can emit a noxious odor; the Cape polecat. Also **zo·ril·la.** (zə·ril′ə). [<F *zorille* <Sp. *zorrilla* a polecat, dim. of *zorra* a fox]

Zorn (sôrn), **Anders Leonhard,** 1860–1920, Swedish painter, etcher, and sculptor.

Zo·ro·as·ter (zō′rō·as′tər) The traditional founder of the ancient Persian religion, believed to have lived about 600 B.C.: also called *Zarathustra.* —**Zo′ro·as′tri·an** *adj.* & *n.*

Zo·ro·as·tri·an·ism (zō′rō·as′trē·ən·iz′əm) *n.* The religious system founded by Zoroaster on the old Aryan folk religion and taught in the Zend-Avesta. It recognizes two creative powers, one good and the other evil, includes the belief in life after death, and teaches the final triumph of good over evil. See AHRIMAN, ORMUZD. Also **Zo′ro·as′trism.**

Zor·ril·la y Mo·ral (thôr·rē′lyä ē mō·räl′), **José,** 1817–93, Spanish poet and dramatist.

Zos·i·mus (zos′ə·məs, zō′sə-) Greek historian of the fifth century A.D.

zos·ter (zos′tər) *n.* 1 An ancient Greek belt or girdle worn especially by men. 2 *Pathol.* Shingles; herpes zoster. [<L <Gk. *zōstēr* a girdle <*zōnynai* gird]

Zou·ave (zōō·äv′, zwäv) *n.* 1 A light-armed French infantryman wearing a brilliant Oriental uniform, originally an Algerian recruit. 2 In the Civil War, a member of a volunteer regiment assuming the name and part of the dress of the French Zouaves. 3 A woman's short, gaily embroidered jacket: also **Zouave jacket.** [<F <Arabic *Zouaoua,* a Kabyle tribe; so called because orig. recruited from this tribe]

zounds (zoundz) *interj.* An exclamation denoting astonishment: also spelled *swounds.* [Short for *God's wounds*]

Zsig·mon·dy (zhig′môn·dē), **Richard,** 1865–1929, German chemist born in Austria.

zuc·chet·to (tsōōk·ket′tō) *n.* A skullcap worn by ecclesiastics in the Roman Catholic Church: black for a priest, purple for a bishop, red for a cardinal, and white for the pope. Also **zuc·chet′ta.** [Var. of Ital. *zucchetta,* orig. a small gourd, dim. of *zucca* a gourd]

zuc·chi·ni (zōō·kē′nē, *Ital.* dzōōk·kē′nē) *n.* A type of green summer squash (evolved from *Cucurbita pepo*) of a small cylindrical shape. Also called *Italian squash.* [<Ital., pl. of *zucchino,* dim. of *zucca* a gourd, squash]

Zug (tsōōkh) 1 The smallest canton of Switzerland; 92 square miles. 2 Its capital, a town on the **Lake of Zug** (15 square miles; about 9 miles long), in the north central part of the country. *French* **Zoug** (zōōg).

Zug·spit·ze (tsōōk′shpit·sə) The highest mountain in Germany, in the Bavarian Alps on the Austrian border; 9,722 feet.

Zu·lo·a·ga (thōō′lō·ä′gä), **Ignacio,** 1870–1945, Spanish painter.

Zu·lu (zōō′lōō) *n. pl.* **Zu·lus** or **Zu·lu** 1 One of a Bantu nation of Natal, South Africa, sometimes included with the Kaffirs. 2 The language of the Zulus, belonging to the Bantu family of agglutinative languages. —*adj.* Of, pertaining to, or characteristic of the Zulus or their language.

Zu·lu·land (zōō′lōō·land′) A district of NE Natal, Union of South Africa, formerly a native kingdom; 10,362 square miles.

zum Bei·spiel (tsōōm bī′shpēl) *German* For example: abbreviated *z.B.*

Zu·ñi (zōō′nyē) *n.* 1 One of a tribe of North American Indians of pueblo culture but comprising a distinct linguistic stock: still occupying the big Zuñi pueblo in New Mexico, which is now a reservation. 2 The language of this tribe. —**Zu′ñi·an** *adj.* & *n.*

Zur·ba·rán (thōōr′bä·rän′), **Francisco de,** 1598–1662, Spanish painter.

Zu·rich (zōōr′ik) 1 A canton of NE Switzerland on the border of Baden-Württemberg, West Germany; 667 square miles. 2 Its capital, a city on the northern shore of the **Lake of Zurich** (35 square miles; 25 miles long) in NE Switzerland. *German* **Zü·rich** (tsü′rikh).

Zuy·der Zee (zī′dər zē, *Du.* zœi′dər zā) A former shallow inlet of the North Sea in NW Netherlands; 80 by 34 miles; enclosed by a dike; drainage projects have reclaimed much of the land and formed Lake Ijssel. Also **Zui'·der Zee.**

Zweig (tsvīg, tsvīkh), **Arnold,** 1887–1968, German novelist. — **Stefan,** 1881–1942, Austrian dramatist and novelist.

Zwick·au (tsvik'ou) A city in the former state of Saxony, central southern East Germany.

zwie·back (zwī'bak, zwē'-, swī'-, swē'-, -bäk; *Ger.* tsvē'bäk) *n.* A biscuit of wheaten bread or rusk baked yellow in the loaf and later sliced and toasted. [<G, twice baked < *zwie-* twice (< *zwei* two) + *backen* bake]

Zwing·li (tsving'lē), **Ulrich,** 1484–1531, Swiss Protestant reformer. Also *Huldreich Zwingli.*

Zwing·li·an (zwing'lē·ən, tsving'-) *adj.* Of or pertaining to the doctrines taught by Zwingli, especially to the doctrine that the Eucharist is simply a memorial or a symbolic commemoration of the death of Christ. — *n.* A follower of Zwingli. — **Zwing'li·an·ism** *n.*

zwit·ter·i·on (tsvit'ər·ī'ən) *n. Physics* An ion which carries both a negative and a positive charge, as in certain amino acids. [<G *zwitter* hybrid, hermaphrodite, mongrel + ION] — **zwit'ter·i·on'ic** (-ī·on'ik) *adj.*

Zwol·le (zvôl'ə) The capital of Overijssel province, north central Netherlands; a manufacturing and dairy center; site of many 15th century buildings.

Zwor·y·kin (zwôr'i·kin), **Vladimir Kosma,** born 1889, U. S. research engineer in electronics; born in Russia.

zyg·a·poph·y·sis (zig'ə·pof'ə·sis) *n. pl.* **·ses** (-sēz) *Anat.* One of the processes, usually disposed in pairs, by which a vertebra articulates with another; an articular process. [<NL <Gk. *zygon* a yoke + *apophysis* a branch. See APOPHYSIS.] — **zyg'a·po·phys'e·al** (-pō·fiz'ē·əl) or **·i·al** *adj.*

zygo– *combining form* Yoke; pair; resembling a yoke, especially in shape: *zygospore.* Also, before vowels, **zyg–.** [<Gk. *zygon* a yoke]

zy·go·dac·tyl (zī'gō·dak'til) *Zool. adj.* Having paired toes, one pair directed forward and the other pair backward, as in parrots and woodpeckers. — *n.* A zygodactyl bird. [<ZYGO- + Gk. *daktylos* a finger]

zy·go·ma (zī·gō'mə) *n. pl.* **·ma·ta** (-mə·tə) *Anat.* **1** The long arch that joins the temporal and malar bones on the side of the skull. **2** The zygomatic bone. **3** The zygomatic process. [<NL <Gk. *zygōma* < *zygon* a yoke] — **zy·go·mat·ic** (zī'gō·mat'ik) *adj.*

zygomatic arch *Anat.* The zygoma.

zygomatic bone *Anat.* The malar bone or cheek bone.

zygomatic process *Anat.* That process of the temporal bone which helps to form the zygomatic arch.

zy·go·mor·phic (zī'gō·môr'fik) *adj. Biol.* Bilaterally symmetrical: said of organisms or parts of organisms divisible into similar halves in only one plane. Also **zy'go·mor'·phous.** [<ZYGO- + -MORPHIC] — **zy'go·mor'·phism** *n.*

zy·go·phyl·la·ceous (zī'gō·fi·lā'shəs) *adj. Bot.* Designating or pertaining to a family *(Zygophyllaceae)* of herbs and shrubs, the caltrop family, having jointed branches, two-foliolate or pinnate stipulate leaves, and axillary white, red, or yellow flowers: mainly tropical in distribution. [<NL <Gk. *zygon* a yoke + *phyllon* a leaf]

zy·go·phyte (zī'gō·fīt) *n. Bot.* A plant in which reproduction is by means of zygospores. [< ZYGO- + -PHYTE]

zy·go·sis (zī·gō'sis) *n. Biol.* The union of gametes or cells; conjugation. [<NL <Gk. *zygōsis* a joining < *zygon* a yoke]

zy·go·spore (zī'gō·spôr, -spōr) *n. Bot.* A spore formed by the conjugation of two similar gametes, as in algae and fungi. Also **zy'go·sperm** (-spûrm). [<ZYGO- + SPORE]

zy·gote (zī'gōt, zig'ōt) *n. Biol.* **1** The product of the union of two gametes. **2** An individual developed from such a union. [<Gk. *zygōtos* yoked < *zygoein* yoke < *zygon* a yoke] — **zy·got·ic** (zī·got'ik) *adj.*

zy·mase (zī'mās) *n. Biochem.* An enzyme, obtained principally from yeast, which induces fermentation by breaking down glucose and related carbohydrates into alcohol and carbon dioxide. [<F <Gk. *zymē* leaven]

zyme (zīm) *n.* **1** A ferment. **2** A disease germ or virus supposed to be the specific cause of a zymotic disease. [<Gk. *zymē* leaven]

zy·mic (zī'mik) *adj.* Relating to or produced by fermentation.

zymo– *combining form* Fermentation; of or related to fermentation: *zymology.* Also, before vowels, **zym–.** [<Gk. *zymē* leaven]

zy·mo·gen (zī'mə·jən) *n.* **1** *Biochem.* A substance that develops into an enzyme when suitably activated, as in the stomach or pancreas. **2** *Biol.* A bacterial organism which produces enzymes or fermentation. Compare PATHOGEN. Also **zy'mo·gene** (-jēn). [<ZYMO- + -GEN]

zy·mo·gen·e·sis (zī'mō·jen'ə·sis) *n. Biochem.* The transformation of a zymogen into an enzyme.

zy·mo·gen·ic (zī'mō·jen'ik) *adj.* **1** Of, pertaining to, or relating to zymogen. **2** Capable of producing a ferment, as yeast. Also **zy·mog·e·nous** (zī·moj'ə·nəs).

zymogenic organism Any micro-organism which causes fermentation, as yeast.

zy·mol·o·gy (zī·mol'ə·jē) *n.* The study of the principles of fermentation and the action of enzymes. [<ZYMO- + -LOGY] — **zy·mo·log·ic** (zī'mə·loj'ik) or **·i·cal** *adj.* — **zy·mol'o·gist** *n.*

zy·mol·y·sis (zī·mol'ə·sis) *n.* Fermentation or the action of enzymes. [<ZYMO- + -LYSIS] — **zy·mo·lyt·ic** (zī'mə·lit'ik) *adj.*

zy·mom·e·ter (zī·mom'ə·tər) *n.* An instrument for measuring the degree of fermentation. [<ZYMO- + -METER]

zy·mo·sis (zī·mō'sis) *n.* **1** Any form of fermentation. **2** *Med.* **a** A fermentation giving rise to a morbid or diseased condition, as by the action of bacteria. **b** Any contagious or infectious disease produced by morbific fermentation; a zymotic disease. [<NL <Gk. *zymōsis* < *zymoein* leaven, ferment < *zymē* leaven]

zy·mot·ic (zī·mot'ik) *adj.* Relating to or produced by or from fermentation, as certain epidemic or contagious diseases. [<Gk. *zymōtikos* < *zymoein.* See ZYMOSIS.]

zy·mur·gy (zī'mûr·jē) *n.* A branch of chemistry treating of processes in which fermentation is the principal feature, as brewing, making of yeast, and winemaking. [<ZYM(O)- + -URGY]

Zy·ri·an Autonomous Region (zir'ē·ən) A former name for the KOMI AUTONOMOUS S.S.R.

Zyr·ya·novsk (zir·yä'nôfsk) A city of NE Kazakh S.S.R. near the Russian S.F.S.R. border.

ABBREVIATIONS COMMONLY IN USE

The following alphabetical list of abbreviations with their meanings includes those that are commonly employed in reference works, textbooks, journals, and newspapers. Where two or more forms of an abbreviation are shown, as by capital letter or lower-case letter, or with a following period or without such period, each form is in recognized use. Where an abbreviation covers two or more meanings, each meaning is given in alphabetical sequence, and where, in such listing, a given abbreviation is sometimes used in a form which applies to one meaning only, that separate usage is shown in parentheses following the meaning to which it applies. In abbreviations of foreign words, as Latin, the meaning of the abbreviation is first given, followed by the word or phrase, in brackets, in the language of origin. Many of the abbreviations here given are not capitalized when used independently; but in combination with proper names they are properly capitalized, as *ft.* (fort) in Ft. Henry; *mt.* (mount) in Mt. Shasta; *coll.* (college) in Claverling Coll.; *dept.* (department) in Dept. of Biology.

A

a. about; alto; ampere; are (measure); area; argent; before [L *ante*]; year [L *anno*].
a., a assists (baseball).
a., A acre.
A. Absolute (temperature).
A argon.
A, A angstrom (unit).
AA, A.A. Alcoholics Anonymous; anti-aircraft.
AAA, A.A.A. American Automobile Association.
A.A.A.L. American Academy of Arts and Letters.
AAAS, A.A.A.S. American Academy of Arts and Sciences; American Association for the Advancement of Science.
AAE, A.A.E. American Association of Engineers.
AAF, A.A.F. (formerly) Army Air Forces.
A. and M. Agricultural and Mechanical (College).
Aar. Aaron.
A.A.U. Amateur Athletic Union.
a.b., ab (times) at bat.
a.b., A.B. able-bodied (seaman).
Ab alabamine.
A.B. Bachelor of Arts [L *Artium Baccalaureus*].
AB adapter booster; airborne.
ABA American Bar Association.
a & b assault and battery.
aband. abandoned.
abbr., abbrev. abbreviation.
ABC the alphabet; American Broadcasting System; Audit Bureau of Circulation.
ab ex. from without [L *ab extra*].
ab init. from the beginning [L *ab initio*].
abl. ablative.
ABM antiballistic missile.
abp. arterial blood pressure.
abr. abridged; abridgment
abs. absent; absolute (temperature); absolutely; abstract.
abstr. abstract; abstracted.
a.c., A.C. alternating current.
a/c, A/C account; account current.
Ac actinium.
AC, A.C. Air Corps.
A.C. after Christ.
a.c. before meals [L *ante cibum*].
acad. academic; academy.
acc. acceptance; accompanied; account; accountant.
acc., accus. accusative.
ACC, A.C.C. Air Coordinating Committee.
accel. accelerando; accelerate.
acct. account; accountant.
ack. acknowledge; acknowledgment.
A.C.P. American College of Physicians.
acpt. acceptance.
ACS, A.C.S. American Chemical Society.
A/cs Pay. accounts payable.
A/cs Rec. accounts receivable.
act. active.
actg. acting.
ACTH adrenocorticotropic hormone.
ad. advertisement.
a.d. before the day [L *ante diem*].
A.D. year of our Lord [L *anno domini*].
ADA, A.D.A. American Dental Association; Americans for Democratic Action.
A.D.C., a.d.c. aide-de-camp.
add. addenda; addendum; addition; additional; address.
ad fin. at the end; to one end [L *ad finem*].
ad inf. to infinity [L *ad infinitum*].
adj. adjacent; adjective; adjourned; adjunct; adjustment.
Adj., Adjt. Adjutant.
ad lib. to the amount desired [L *ad libitum*].
adm. administrative; administrator; admitted.
Adm. Admiral; Admiralty.
adv. adverb; adverbial; advertisement.
ad val. according to value [L *ad valorem*].
advt. advertisement.
ae., aet., aetat., of age [L *aetatis*].
A.E.A. Actors' Equity Association.
A.E. and P. Ambassador Extraordinary and Plenipotentiary.
AEC, A.E.C. Atomic Energy Commission.
AEF, A.E.F. American Expeditionary Force.
aeron. aeronautics.
a.f., A.F., AF, a-f audio frequency.
Af. Africa; African.
AF, A.F. Air Force.
A.F.A.M., A.F.&A.M. Ancient Free and Accepted Masons.
AFB Air Force Base.
Afg., Afgh. Afghanistan.
AFL, A.F.L., A.F. of L. American Federation of Labor.
AFL-CIO, A.F.L.-C.I.O. American Federation of Labor —Congress of Industrial Organizations.
A.F.M. American Federation of Musicians.
Afr. Africa; African.
A.F.T.R.A. American Federation of Television and Radio Artists.
A.F.T. American Federation of Teachers.
Ag. August.
Ag silver [L *argentum*].
AG, A.G. Adjutant General; Attorney General.
agcy. agency.
agr., agri., agric. agricultural; agriculture; agriculturist.
agt., Agt. agent; agreement.
AHQ, A.HQ. Army Headquarters.
A.I. in the year of the discovery [L *anno inventionis*].
AK Alaska (P.O. abbr.).
a.k.a. also known as.
A.K.C. American Kennel Club.
al. other things (persons) [L *alia, alii*].
AL, A.L. Aviation Electronicsman.
AL Alabama (P.O. abbr.).
Al aluminum.
Ala. Alabama.
ALA, A.L.A. American Library Association.
Alas. Alaska.
Alb. Albania; Albanian; Albany; Alberta.
Alba. Alberta (Canada).
Ald., Aldm. Alderman.
alg. algebra.
Alg. Algeria; Algerian.
A.L.P. American Labor Party.
alt. alteration; alternate; altitude; alto.
Alta. Alberta (Canada).
alum. aluminum.
a.m., A.M. before noon [L *ante meridiem*].
Am. America.
Am americium.
AM, am. amplitude.
am. ammeter.
AM, A.M., a-m, a.m. amplitude modulation.
Am. alabamine; America; American.
A.M. Air Mail; in the year of the world [L *anno mundi*]; Master of Arts [L *Artium Magister*].
A.M.A. American Management Association; American Medical Association.
Amb. Ambassador.
A.M.D.G., AMDG to the greater glory of God [L *ad majorem Dei gloriam*].
A.M.E. African Methodist Episcopal.
Amer. America; American.
AMG, A.M.G. Allied Military Government (of Occupied Territory).
Am. Ind. American Indian.
amp. ampere; amperage.
amp-hr. ampere-hour.
amt. amount.
amu atomic mass unit.
AMVETS American Veterans (of World War II and the Korean War).
an. anonymous; before [L *ante*].
anal. analogous; analogy; analysis; analytic(al).
anat. anatomical; anatomy.
anc. ancient; anciently.
and. moderately slow [It. *andante*].
And. Andorra.
Ang. Anglican; Angola.
Angl. Anglican; Anglicized.
anim. animated [It. *animato*].
ann. annals; annual; annuities; annuity; years [L *anni*].
anon., Anon. anonymous.
ans. answer; answered.
ant. antenna; antiquarian; antiquity; antonym.
Ant. Antarctic; Antarctica.
anthrop., anthropol. anthropological; anthropology.
antilog. antilogarithm.
antiq. antiquarian; antiquities.
a/o, A/O account of.
AOL, A.O.L., a.o.l. absent over leave.
Ap. apostle; April.
ap. apothecary.
AP, A.P., a.p. antipersonnel.
A.P., AP Associated Press.
APB all points bulletin.
apmt. appointment.
APO, A.P.O. Army Post Office.
Apoc. Apocalypse; Apocrypha; Apocryphal.
app. apparatus; apparent; appended; appendix; apprentice.
appar. apparatus; apparent.
approx. approximate; approximately.
Apr., Apr April.
APS, A.P.S. Army Postal Service.
apt(s). apartment(s).
aq., Aq. aqueous; water [L *aqua*].
AQ, A.Q. achievement quotient.
a.r. in the year of the reign [L *anno regni*].
Ar. argon; silver [L *argentum*].
ar. argent; aromatic; arrival; arrive.
Ar., Arab. Arabia; Arabian; Arabic.
AR Arkansas (P.O. abbr.).
Aram. Aramaic.
ARC, A.R.C. American Red Cross.
arch. archaic; archaism; archery; archipelago; architect.
Arch., Archbp. Archbishop.
archaeol., archeol. archaeology; archeology.
Archd. Archdeacon; Archduke.
archit. architecture.
archt. architect.
arg. argent; silver [L *argentum*].
Arg. Argentina; Argyll.
arith. arithmetic; arithmetical.
Ariz. Arizona.
Ark. Arkansas.
Arm. Armenia; Armenian.
Ar.M. Master of Architecture [L *Architecturae Magister*].
arr. arrange; arranged; arrangements; arrival; arrive; arrived.
art. article; artificial; artist.
A.R.V. American Revised (Standard) Version (of the Bible).
AS anti-submarine.
AS, AS., A.S Anglo-Saxon.
as., asym. asymmetric.
As arsenic.
ASA, A.S.A. American Standards Association.
asb. asbestos.
ASCAP, A.S.C.A.P. American Society of Composers, Authors and Publishers.
asgd. assigned.
A.S.P.C.A. American Society for the Prevention of Cruelty to Animals.
ass. assistant; association.
Ass., Assyr. Assyrian.
assd. assigned.
assn. association.
assoc. associate; association.
asst., Asst. assistant.
Assyr. Assyria; Assyrian.
astr., astron. astronomer; astronomical; astronomy.
astrol. astrologer; astrological; astrology.
AT, A.T. anti-tank.
at. atmosphere; atomic.
At astatine.
ATC, A.T.C. Air Transport Command.
athl. athlete; athletic; athletics.
Atl. Atlantic.
atm. atmosphere; atmospheric.
at. no. atomic number.
ATS, A.T.S. Army Transport Service; Auxiliary Territorial Service.
att., attn., atten. attention.
att., atty. attorney.
attrib. attribute; attributive; attributively.
Atty. Gen. Attorney General.
at. wt. atomic weight.
a.u., A.u., A.U. angstrom unit.
Au gold [L *aurum*].
A.U.C. from (the year of) the building of the city (of Rome) [L *ab urbe condita*].
aud. audible; audit; auditor.
Aug. August (**Aug**); Augustan; Augustus.
AUS, A.U.S. Army of the United States.
Aus., Aust. Austria.
Aus., Austl. Australia.
auth. authentic; author; authority; authorized.
Auth. Ver. Authorized Version (of the Bible).
auto. automatic; automotive.
aux., auxil. auxiliary.
A.V. Authorized Version (of the Bible).
a.v., a/v, A/V according to value [L *ad valorem*].
Av. avenue.
av., avdp. avoirdupois.
av., avg. average.
AVC, a.v.c. automatic volume control.
ave. avenue.
avg. average.
avn. aviation.
avoir. avoirdupois.
A/W actual weight; all water.
AWL, A.W.L., a.w.l. absent with leave.
AWOL, A.W.O.L., a.w.o.l., awol absent without leave.
AWVS, A.W.V.S. American Women's Volunteer Services.
ax. axis; axiom.
AZ Arizon (P.O. abbr.).
az. azimuth; azure.

B

b., b base; base hit; baseman.
b., B. bachelor; balboa (coin); base; bass; basso; bat; battery; bay; bench; bicuspid; bolivar (coin); boliviano; book; born; brass; breadth; brother.
B. bacillus; Bible; British; Brotherhood.
B bishop (chess); boron.
B/- bag; bale.
Ba barium.
B.A. Bachelor of Arts [L *Baccalaureus Artium*]; British Academy.
bach. bachelor.
bact., bacteriol. bacteriological; bacteriologist; bacteriology.
B.A.E. Bachelor of Aeronautical Engineering; Bachelor of Arts in Education.
B. Ag., B. Agr. Bachelor of Agriculture.
B. Ag. Sc. Bachelor of Agricultural Science.
bal. balance; balancing.
Balt. Baltic.
Bap., Bapt. Baptist.
bapt. baptized.
bar. barometer; barometric; barrel; barrister.
BAR, B.A.R. Browning automatic rifle.
B. Ar., B. Arch. Bachelor of Architecture.
barit. baritone.
Bart. Baronet.
B.A.S., B.A.Sc. Bachelor of Agricultural Science; Bachelor of Applied Science.
bat., batt. battalion; battery.
b.b., bb base(s) on balls.
B.B.A., B.Bus. Ad. Bachelor of Business Administration.
BBC, B.B.C., British Broadcasting Corporation.
bbl, bbl. barrel; barrels.
B.C. Bachelor of Chemistry; Bachelor of Commerce; before Christ; British Columbia.
B.C.E. Bachelor of Chemical Engineering; Bachelor of Civil Engineering.
bch. bunch.
B.C.L. Bachelor of Civil Law.
B.C.P. Book of Common Prayer.
B.C.S. Bachelor of Chemical Science.
bd. board; bond; bound; bundle.
B.D. Bachelor of Divinity.
b.d., B/D bank draft; bills discounted; brought down.
bd. ft. board feet.
bdg. binding.
bdl., bdle. bundle.
B.D.S. Bachelor of Dental Surgery.
bds. bundles; (bound in) boards.
BDSA Business and Defense Services Administration.
Be beryllium.
B.E. Bachelor of Education; Bachelor of Engineering; Bank of England; Board of Education.
B.E., B/E, b/e bills of exchange.
BEC Bureau of Employees' Compensation.
B.E.E. Bachelor of Electrical Engineering.
bef. before.
BEF, B.E.F. British Expeditionary Force(s).
Bel., Belg. Belgian; Belgium.
Beng. Bengal; Bengali.
B. ès L. Bachelor of Letters [F *Bachelier ès Lettres*].
B. ès S. Bachelor of Sciences [F *Bachelier ès Sciences*].
bet., betw. between.
bev, BEV billion electron volts.
BEW, B.E.W. Board of Economic Warfare.
b.f., bf. bold face.
b.f., B/F brought forward.
B.F. Bachelor of Finance; Bachelor of Forestry.
B.F.A. Bachelor of Fine Arts.
BFDC Bureau of Foreign and Domestic Commerce.
bg. bag(s).
B.G. Brigadier General.
bhp brake horsepower.
Bi bismuth.
Bib. Bible; Biblical.
bibl., Bibl. biblical; bibliographical.
bibliog. bibliography.
bicarb. bicarbonate of soda.
b.i.d. twice a day [L *bis in die*].
biochem. biochemistry.
biog. biographer; biographical; biography.
biol. biological; biologist; biology.
BIS, B.I.S. British Information Services.
B.J. Bachelor of Journalism.
Bk berkelium.
bk. bank; block; book.
bkg. banking.
bkkpg. bookkeeping.
bklr. black letter.
bkpt. bankrupt.
bks., Bks. barracks; books.
bkt. basket(s); bracket.
b.l., B/L bill of lading.
bl. bale; barrel; black; blue.
B.L., B.LL. Bachelor of Laws.
B.L.A. Bachelor of Liberal Arts.
bld bold face.
bldg., blg. building.
B.L.E. Brotherhood of Locomotive Engineers.
B. Lit., B. Litt. Bachelor of Letters (Literature) [L *Baccalaureus Litterarum*].
blk. black; block.
bln., bln balloon.
bls. bales; barrels.
BLS Bureau of Labor Statistics.
B.L.S. Bachelor of Library Science; Bachelor of Library Service.
blvd. boulevard.
b.m. board measure.
BM, B.M. Bureau of Mines.
B.M. Bachelor of Medicine [L *Baccalaureus Medicinae*]; Bachelor of Music [L *Baccalaureus Musicae*].
B.M.E. Bachelor of Mechanical Engineering; Bachelor of Mining Engineering.
B. Mech. E. Bachelor of Mechanical Engineering.
BMEWS Ballistic Missile Early Warning System.
BMR basal metabolic rate.
B. Mus. Bachelor of Music.
Bn., bn. battalion.
B.N. bank note.
B.N.A. Basel Anatomical Nomenclature [L *Basle Nomina Anatomica*]; British North

America.
b.o. back order; body odor; box office; branch office; broker's order; buyer's option.
BO, B.O. Board of Ordnance.
B/O brought over.
Boh., Bohem. Bohemia; Bohemian.
Bol. Bolivia.
bor. borough.
bot. botanical; botanist; botany; bottle.
B.O.T. Board of Trade.
bp, b.p. below proof; boiling point.
b.p. B/P bill of parcels; bills payable.
B.P. Bachelor of Pharmacy.
B.P., B.Ph., B.Phil. Bachelor of Philosophy [L *Baccalaureus Philosophiae*].
bp. birthplace; bishop.
B.Pd., B.Pe. Bachelor of Pedagogy.
B.P.E. Bachelor of Physical Education.
B.P.H. Bachelor of Public Health.
BPI, B.P.I. Bureau of Public Inquiries.
B.P.O.E. Benevolent and Protective Order of Elks.
BPPC Brussels Pact Permanent Commission.
br. branch; brand; brief; bridge; brig; bronze; brother.
Br. Breton, Britain, British.
Br bromine.
B.R., B/R Bill of Rights.
b.r., B/R bills receivable.
Braz. Brazil; Brazilian.
Brazil. Brazilian.
B.R.C.S. British Red Cross Society.
B.Rec., b.rec. bills receivable.
brev. brevet; brevetted.
Br. Hond. British Honduras.
Brig. Brigade; Brigadier.
Brig. Gen. Brigadier General.
Brit. Britain; Britannia; Britannica; British.
bro. brother.
bros. brothers.
b.s. balance sheet.
b.s., B/S bill of sale.
B.S. Bachelor of Surgery.
B/S bags; bales.
B.S., B.Sc. Bachelor of Science [L *Baccalaureus Scientiae*].
B.S.A. Bachelor of Scientific Agriculture; Bibliographical Society of America; Boy Scouts of America.
B.S.Ed. Bachelor of Science in Education.
bsh. bushel(s).
BSM Bronze Star Medal.
B.S.S., B.S.Sc. B.S. in S.S. Bachelor of (Science in) Social Sciences.
Bt. Baronet.
B.T., B.Th. Bachelor of Theology.
B.T.U., BTU, B.th.u., Btu British thermal unit.
Btry. battery.
bu. bureau.
bu., bu bushel; bushels.
buck. buckram.
bul., bull. bulletin.
Bulg. Bulgaria; Bulgarian.
B.V. Blessed Virgin [L *Beata Virgo*]; farewell [L *bene vale*].
B.V.M. Blessed Virgin Mary [L *Beata Virgo Maria*].
bvt. brevet; brevetted.
bx. box.
Bz. benzene.

C

C carbon; constant; Roman numeral for 100.
C., c. about [L *circa*]; calends; candle; capacity (electrical); cape; carton; case; catcher (baseball); cathode; cent; centime; cents; century; chapter; chief; child; church; copyright; cost; cubic; current.
c., c, C., C centigrade; centimeter.
C. Catholic; Celtic; Chancellor; Congress; Conservative; Court.
c.a., C.A. chief accountant; claim agent; commercial agent; consular agent; controller of accounts.
ca. about [L *circa*]; cathode; centiare.
Ca calcium.
C.A. Catholic Action; Central America; Coast Artillery; Confederate Army.
CA, C.A. chronological age.
CA California (P.O. abbr.).
C/A commercial account; credit account; current account.
CAA, C.A.A. Civil Aeronautics Administration (Authority).
CAB, C.A.B. Civil Aeronautics Board.
C.A.F., c.a.f. cost and freight; cost, assurance and freight.
cal. calendar; calends; caliber; calomel; small calorie **(cal).**
Cal., Cal caliber; large calorie.
Calif., Cal. California.
Cam camouflage.
can. canon; canto.
Can. Canada; Canadian.
Canad. Canadian.
canc. cancel; cancellation; canceled.
cant. canton; cantonment.
Cant. Canterbury; Canticles; Cantonese.
Cantab. Cambridge [L *Cantabrigia*].
cap. capital; capitalize; chapter [L *caput*].
CAP, C.A.P. Civil Air Patrol.
caps capital letters.
Capt. Captain.
car. carat.
CAR, C.A.R. Civil Air Regulations.
Card. Cardinal.
CARE Cooperative for American Remittances Everywhere.
cat. catalog; catechism.
cath. cathedral.
Cath. Catholic.
CATV community antenna television.
cav. cavalier; cavalry.
CAVU, C.A.V.U. ceiling and visibility unlimited.
c.b. center of buoyancy; confined to barracks.
Cb columbium; cumulonimbus.
CB Construction Battalion.
C.B. Bachelor of Surgery [L *Baccalaureus Chirurgiae*].
CBC, C.B.C. Canadian Broadcasting Corporation.
C.B.D., c.b.d. cash before delivery.
CBS, C.B.S. Columbia Broadcasting System.
c.c., C.C. carbon copy; cash credit; cashier's check; chief clerk; circuit court; city council; city councilor; civil court; common councilman; company clerk; company commander; consular clerk; contra credit; county clerk; county commissioner; county council; county court; current account [F *compte courant*].
cc. chapters.
cc, cc., c.c. cubic centimeter.
Cc cirrocumulus.
CC cyanogen chloride (poison gas).
CCA Commission for Conventional Armaments.
C.C.A. Chief Clerk of the Admiralty; Circuit Court of Appeals.
CCC, C.C.C. Civilian Conservation Corps; Commodity Credit Corporation.
CCF, C.C.F. Cooperative Commonwealth Federation (of Canada).
CCS, C.C.S. Combined Chiefs of Staff.
cd candela.
c.d. cash discount.
cd., cd cord.
Cd cadmium.
c/d, C/D carried down.
C.D. Civilian Defense.
cd. ft. cord foot (feet).
CDR, Cdr. Commander.
CE Council of Europe; Corps of Engineers.
C.E. Chemical Engineer; Chief Engineer; Church of England; Civil Engineer.
Ce cerium.
CEA Council of Economic Advisers.
CED Committee for Economic Development.
Celt. Celtic.
cen., cent. central; century.
cent. centered; centigrade; centimeter; one hundred [L *centum*].
CERN European Council for Nuclear Research [F *Centre Européen des Recherches Nucléaires*].
cert. certificate; certify.
certif. certificate; certificated.
cet. par. other things being equal [L *ceteris paribus*].
Cey. Ceylon.
c.f., cf center field(er).
c.f., C.F. cost and freight.
cf. compare [L *confer*].
Cf californium.
c/f, C/F carried forward.
c.f.i., C.F.I. cost, freight, and insurance.
cfm, c.f.m. cubic feet per minute.
CFR, C.F.R. Code of Federal Regulations.
cfs, c.f.s. cubic feet per second.
c.g., C.G. center of gravity; consul general.
cg., cg, cgm. centigram(s).
CG Commanding General.
C.G. Coast Guard.
C.G.H. Cape of Good Hope.
cgs, CGS, c.g.s. centimeter-gram-second.
c.h., C.H. clearing-house; courthouse; customhouse.
C.H. Companion of Honor.
Ch. Chaldean; Chaldee; China; Chinese.
ch. chain; champion; chargé d'affaires; check (chess); chestnut; chervonets; chief; child; children; chirurgeon; church; of surgery [L *chirurgiae*].
ch., chap. chaplain; chapter.
c.-h., c-hr. candle-hour.
Chanc. Chancelor; Chancery.
char. character; charter.
Ch.B. Bachelor of Surgery [L *Chirurgiae Baccalaureus*].
Ch. Clk. Chief Clerk.
Ch.E., Che.E. Chemical Engineer.
chem. chemical; chemist; chemistry.
chg. charge.
chgd. charged.
Chin. Chinese.
Ch.J. Chief Justice.
Ch.M. Master of Surgery [L *Chirurgiae Magister*].
chm. checkmate.
chm., chmn. chairman.
Chr. Christ; Christian.
chron., chronol. chronological; chronology.
Chron. Chronicles.
chs. chapters.
Ci cirrus.
CIA Central Intelligence Agency.
Cia., cia. company [Sp. *Compania*].
CIAA Coordinator of Inter-American Affairs.
CIC, C.I.C. Counter-Intelligence Corps.
C.I.D. Criminal Investigation Department (Brit.).
Cie., cie. company [F *compagnie*].
c.i.f., C.I.F. cost, insurance, and freight.
C. in C., C in C, CINC, Cinc Commander in Chief.
CIO, C.I.O. Congress of Industrial Organizations.
cir., circ. about [L *circa, circiter, circum*]; circular; circulation; circumference.
cit. citation; cited; citizen.
civ. civil; civilian.
C.J. body of law [L *corpus juris*]; Chief Judge; Chief Justice.
ck. cask; check; cook.
Cl chlorine.
c.l. carload; carload lots; center line; civil law; craft loss (insurance).
cl. centiliter(s); claim; class; classification; clause; clearance; clergyman; clerk; cloth.
clar. clarinet.
class. classic; classical; classification; classified; classify.
cler. clerical.
climatol. climatological; climatology.
clin. clinic; clinical.
clk. clerk; clock.
clm. column.
C.L.U. Chartered Life Underwriter.
CM court martial.
c.m. church missionary; circular mil; common meter; corresponding member.
C.M. Master of Surgery [L *Chirurgiae Magister*].
cm., cm centimeter(s)
CM curium.
Cmdr. Commander.
C.M.G. Companion (of the Order) of St. Michael and St. George.
cml. commercial.
CMTC, C.M.T.C. Citizens' Military Training Camp.
c.n., C/N circular note; credit note.
CNO Chief of Naval Operations.
Cn cumulonimbus.
CNS, C.N.S. central nervous system.
CO Colorado (P.O. abbr.).
C.O. commanding officer; conscientious objector.
co., Co. company; county.
c/o, C/O, c.o. care of; carried over; cash order.
Co cobalt.
coad. coadjutor.
c.o.d., C.O.D. cash on delivery; collect on delivery.
Cod., cod. codex.
Codd., codd. codices.
coef. coefficient.
C. of C. Chamber of Commerce.
C. of S. Chief of Staff.
cog., cogn. cognate.
col. collected; collector; college; colonial; colony; color; colored; column.
Col. Colombia; Colonel; Colorado; Columbia.
Col., Col, Coloss. Colossians.
coll. colleague; collect; collection; collective; collector; college; colloquial.
collab. collaborated; collaboration; collaborator.
collat. collateral.
colloq. colloquial; colloquialism; colloquially.
Colo., Col. Colorado.
colog cologarithm.
com. comedy; comic; comma; commentary; commerce; commercial; common; commonly; commune; communication; community.
Com. Commission; Commissioner; Committee; Commodore; Communist.
Com., Comdr. Commander; Commodore.
Com., Como., COMO, Commodore.
comb. combination.
comdg. commanding.
Comdt. Commandant.
Com. in Ch., Cominch Commander in Chief.
coml. commercial.
comm. commander; commentary; commerce; commercial; commissary; commission; committee; commonwealth; commutator.
COMO, Como Commodore.
comp. companion; compare; compilation; compiled; complete; composition; compositor; compound; comprising.
compar. comparative.
compt. compartment; comptometer.
Comr. Commissioner.
Com. Ver. Common Version (of the Bible).
con. against [L *contra*]; concerto; conclusion; condense; conduct; connection; consols; consolidate; continued; wife [L *conjunx*].
Con. Conformist; Consul.
conc. concentrate; concentrated; concentration; concerning.
Confed. Confederate; Confederation.
cong. gallon [L *congius*].
Cong. Congregational; Congress; Congressional.
conj. conjugation; conjunction; conjunctive.
Conn. Connecticut.
cons. consecrated; conserve; consigned; consignment; consolidated; consonant; construction; consulting.
cons., Cons. constable; constitution; constitutional; consul.
consol. consolidated.
const., Const. constable; constant; constitution.
constr. construction; construed.
cont. containing; contents; continent; continue; contract; contraction; contrary; control.
Cont. Continental.
contd. continued.
contemp. contemporary.
contg. containing.
contin. continued; let it be continued [L *continuetur*].
contr. contract; contralto; control.
contrib. contribution; contributor.
CONUS Continental United States.
coop., co-op. cooperative.
cop. copper; copyright; copyrighted.
Cop. Copernican; Coptic.
cor. corner; cornet; coroner; corpus; correct; corrected; correction; correlative; correspondence; correspondent; corresponding; corrupt.
Cor. Corinthians.
corol., coroll. corollary.
Corp. Corporal.
corp., corpn. corporation.
corr. correct; corrected; correspond; correspondence; correspondent; corresponding; corrupt; corrupted; corruption.
correl. correlative.
corresp. correspondence.
c.o.s., C.O.S. cash on shipment.
cos. companies; counties.
cos cosine.
cosec cosecant.
cosh hyperbolic cosine.
cot cotangent.
coth hyperbolic cotangent.
covers coversed sine.
c.p., C.P. chemically pure; court of probate.
CP command post.
cp. compare.
cp, c.p. candlepower.
C.P. Canadian Press; Cape Province; center of pressure; Chief Patriarch; Common Prayer; Communist Party.
C.P.A. Certified Public Accountant.
cpd. compound.
C.P.H. Certificate in Public Health.
Cpl. corporal.
cpm, c.p.m. cycles per minute.
CPO, C.P.O., c.p.o. Chief Petty Officer.
cps, c.p.s. cycles per second.
cpt. counterpoint.
CPTP, C.P.T.P. Civil Pilot Training Program.
CQ Charge of Quarters.
cr. created; credit; creditor; crescendo; creek; crown(s).
Cr chromium.
CR Construction Recruit.
C.R. Costa Rica.
craniol. craniological; craniology.
craniom. craniometry.
cres., cresc. crescendo.
crim.con. criminal conversation.
crit. critic; critical; criticism.
crs. credits; creditors.
CRT cathode-ray tube.
cryst. crystalline; crystallography; crystals.
Cs cesium; cirrostratus.
C.S. Christian Science; Christian Scientist; Confederate States.
C.S., c.s. capital stock; civil service.
C/S, cs. case; cases.
C.S.A. Confederate States of America.
csc cosecant.
CSC Civil Service Commission.
C.S.C. Conspicuous Service Cross.
csch hyperbolic cosecant.
csk. cask; countersink.
CSO, C.S.O. Chief Signal Officer **(CSigO)**; Chief Staff Officer.
CSS Commodity Stabilization Service.
C.S.T., CST, c.s.t. central standard time.
CT Communications Technician.
C.T., CT, c.t. central time.
ct. cent(s); certificate; county; court.
Ct. Connecticut; Count.
CTC, C.T.C. Citizens' Training Camp.
ctg. cartridge.
ctn cotangent.
ctnh hyperbolic cotangent.
ctr. center.
cts. centimes; cents; certificates.
cu., cu cubic.
Cu copper [L *cuprum*]; cumulus.
cu. cm., cu cm cubic centimeter(s).
cu.ft. cubic foot; cubic feet.
cu.in. cubic inch(es).
cur. currency; current.
cu.yd. cubic yard(s).
C.V. Common Version (of the Bible).
cv., cvt. convertible.
cw, CW continuous wave.
CWA, C.W.A. Civil Works Administration.
C.W.O., c.w.o. cash with order.
CWO, C.W.O. Chief Warrant Officer; Commissioned Warrant Officer.
CWS Chemical Warfare Service.
cwt. hundredweight.
cy. capacity; currency; cycles.
cyc. cyclopedia; cyclopedic.
cyl cylinder.
CYO, C.Y.O. Catholic Youth Organization.
C.Z. Canal Zone.

D

d. date; daughter; day(s); dead; decree; degree; delete; democrat(ic); deputy; diameter; died; director; dividend; dollar; door; dose; dyne; give [L *da*].
d penny; pence [L *denarius, denarii*].
D. December; Department; Dutch; God [L *Deus*]; Lord [L *Dominus*].
D deuterium; Roman numeral for 500.
da. daughter; day(s).
D.A. District Attorney; Delayed Action.
DA Dental Apprentice.

D.A.B., DAB Dictionary of American Biography.
D.A.E., DAE Dictionary of American English.
dal., dal decaliter.
Dak. Dakota.
Dan. Daniel; Danish.
Danl. Daniel.
D.A.R., DAR Daughters of the American Revolution.
dat. dative.
dau. daughter.
DAV, D.A.V. Disabled American Veterans.
Dav. David.
D.B. Domesday Book.
d.b. daybook.
db, db. decibel; decibels.
d.b.a. doing business as.
D.B.E. Dame (Commander, Order) of the British Empire.
d.b.h. diameter at breast height (*forestry*).
D. Bib. Douai Bible.
dbl. double.
DC Dental Corps; Disarmament Commission.
d.c., d–c, dc, d c, D.C., D–C, DC, D C direct current.
D.C. District of Columbia; Doctor of Chiropractic; from the beginning [It. *da capo*].
D.C.L. Doctor of Canon Law; Doctor of Civil Law.
D.C.M. Distinguished Conduct Medal (Brit.).
D.C.S. Deputy Clerk of Sessions; Doctor of Christian Science.
dd., d/d. delivered.
DD Department of Defense.
D.D. Doctor of Divinity [L ence; Doctor of Commercial Science.
d.d., D/D demand draft.
d.d., D/d, D/D days after date; days' date.
Divinitatis Doctor].
D.D.S. Doctor of Dental Science (or Surgery).
D.D.Sc. Doctor of Dental Science.
DE Delaware (P.O. abbr.); Destroyer Escort; Doctor of Engineering; Doctor of Entomology.
deb., deben. debenture.
Deb. Deborah.
dec. deceased; declaration; declension; declination; decrease; decrescendo.
dec., decim. decimeter.
Dec., Dec December.
decd. deceased.
decl. declension.
decoct. decoction.
decresc. decrescendo.
ded., dedic. dedication.
def. defective; defendant; defense; deferred; defined; definite; definition.
deg. degree(s).
del. delegate; delete; deliver; he (she) drew it [L *delineavit*].
Del. Delaware.
deliq. deliquescent.
Dem. Democrat; Democratic.
demon. demonstrative.
Den. Denmark.
denom. denomination.
dent. dental; dentist; dentistry.
dep. departs; departure; deposed; deposit; depot.
Dep. dependency.
dep., dept. department; deponent; deputy.
der., deriv. derivation; derivative; derive; derived.
dermatol. dermatological; dermatologist; dermatology.
desc. descendant.
descr. descriptive.
D. ès L. Doctor of Letters [F *Docteur ès Lettres*].
D. ès S. Doctor of Sciences [F *Docteur ès Sciences*].
det. detach; detachment; detail.
Deu, Deut. Deuteronomy.
devel. development.
D.F. Dean of the Faculty; Defender of the Faith [L *Defensor Fidei*]; Federal District [Pg. *Districto Federal;* Sp. *Distrito Federal*].
DF, D/F, D.F. direction finding.
D.F.C., DFC Distinguished Flying Cross.
D.G. by the grace of God [L *Dei gratia*].
dg., dg decigram(s).
dh designated hitter (baseball).
d.h. deadhead; that is to say [G *das heisst*].
DHQ Division Headquarters.
di., dia. diameter.
Di didymium.
diag., diagr. diagram.
dial. dialect; dialectic; dialectical.
diam. diameter.
dict. dictation; dictator; dictionary.
diet. dietetics.
diff. difference; different; differential.
dil. dilute.
dim. dimension.
dim., dimin. diminuendo; diminutive.
din. dinar.
dioc. diocesan; diocese.
dipl. diplomat; diplomatic.
dir. director.
dis. distance; distant.
disc. discount; discover; discovered.
disch. discharged.
diss. dissertations.
dist. discount; distance; distant; distinguish; distinguished; district.
Dist. Atty. District Attorney.
distr. distribute; distributed; distribution; distributive; distributor.
div. divergence; diversion; divide; divided; dividend; divine; division; divisor; divorced.
Div. Divinity.
DK Disbursing Clerk.
dk. deck; dock.
dkg., dkg dekagram(s).
dkl., dkl dekaliter(s).
dkm., dkm dekameter(s).
dks., dks dekastere(s).
dl., dl deciliter(s).
D/L demand loan.
D.Lit., D.Litt. Doctor of Letters (Literature) [L *Doctor Lit(t)erarum*].
dlr. dealer.
D.L.S. Doctor of Library Science.
dm., dm decameter(s); decimeter(s).
D.M. Deputy Master.
DM., Dm. Deutschemark.
DM Draftsman.
DMB Defense Mobilization Board.
D.M.D. Doctor of Dental Medicine [L *Dentariae Medicinae Doctor*].
D.Mus. Doctor of Music.
D.N. our Lord [L *Dominus noster*].
DNA deoxyribonucleic acid.
DNB, D.N.B. Dictionary of National Biography (British).
do. ditto.
D.O. Doctor of Osteopathy.
D.O.A. dead on arrival.
doc. document.
dol. dolce; dollar; dollars **(dols.)**.
Dom. Dominica; Dominican.
dom. domestic; dominion.
Dor. Dorian; Doric.
Dow. Dowager.
doz., doz dozen(s).
DP, D.P. degree of polymerization; diametrical pitch; displaced person.
D.P.H. Doctor of Public Health.
D.P.Hy. Doctor of Public Hygiene.
D.Ph., D.Phil. Doctor of Philosophy.
dpt. department; deponent.
D.P.W. Department of Public Works.
D.R., D/R, d.r. dead reckoning; deposit receipt.
dr. debtor; dram(s).
Dr. doctor; drive.
dram. pers. dramatis personae.
d.s. daylight saving; days after sight; document signed.
ds., ds decistere(s).
Ds dysprosium.
D.S., d.s. (repeat) from this sign [It. *dal segno*].
D.S., D.Sc. Doctor of Science.
D.S.C. Distinguished Service Cross.
D.S.M., DSM Distinguished Service Medal.
D.S.O. Brit. Distinguished Service Order; District Staff Officer.
d.s.p. died without issue [L *decessit sine prole*].
DSRD, D.S.R.D. Department of Scientific Research and Development.
DST, D.S.T. Daylight Saving Time.
D.S.T. Doctor of Sacred Theology.
DT Dental Technician.
d.t. delirium tremens **(d.t's)**; double time.
D.T., D.Th., D.Theol. Doctor of Theology.
Du. Duke; Dutch.
dup., dupl. duplicate.
D.V. Douay Version (of the Bible).
D.v., D.V. God willing [L *Deo volente*].
D.V.M. Doctor of Veterinary Medicine.
D.V.M.S. Doctor of Veterinary Medicine and Surgery.
D/W dock warrant.
D.W.S. Department of Water Supply.
d.w.t. dead weight tons.
dwt. pennyweight [L *denarius* weight].
DX, D.X. distance; distant.
Dy dysprosium.
dyn., dynam. dynamics.
dz. dozen.

E

e., E., E English.
e., e error(s).
e., E., E east, eastern.
e, e. erg.
E., E English.
E. Earl; Earth.
ea. each.
e. and o.e. errors and omissions excepted.
Eb erbium.
EbN east by north.
EbS east by south.
E.C. Engineering Corps; Established Church.
ECA Economic Cooperation Administration.
ECAFE Economic Commission for Asia and the Far East.
eccl., eccles. ecclesiastical.
Ecc, Eccl., Eccles. Ecclesiastes.
Ecclus. Ecclesiasticus.
ECE Economic Commission for Europe.
ECLA Economic Commission for Latin America.
ECME Economic Commission for the Middle East.
ecol. ecological; ecology.
econ. economic; economics; economy.
ECOSOC Economic and Social Council (of the United Nations).
ECSC European Coal and Steel Community.
Ecua. Ecuador.
ed. edited; edition; editor.
Ed.B. Bachelor of Education.
EDC European Defense Community.
Ed.D. Doctor of Education.
edit. edited; edition; editor.
Ed.M. Master of Education.
E.D.T., e.d.t. eastern daylight time.
educ. education; educational.
E.E. Early English; Electrical Engineer; Electrical Engineering; Envoy Extraordinary.
e.e. errors excepted.
E.E.C. European Economic Community.
E.E. & M.P. Envoy Extraordinary & Minister Plenipotentiary.
EEDC Economic Employment and Development Commission.
EEG electroencephalogram.
eff. efficiency.
efflor. efflorescent.
e.g. for example [L *exempli gratia*].
Eg. Egypt; Egyptian.
Egyptol. Egyptology.
EHF, E.H.F., ehf, e.h.f. extremely high frequency.
EHFA, E.H.F.A. Electric Home and Farm Authority.
E.I., E.Ind. East Indian; East Indies.
EIB, E.I.B. Export-Import Bank.
EKG electrocardiogram.
el., elev. elevation.
elec., elect. electric; electrical; electrician.
elem. elementary; elements.
elev. elevation.
ellipt. elliptical.
elong. elongation.
e. long. east longitude.
E.M. Engineer of Mines.
EM Electrician's Mate; enlisted man (men).
Em., eman. emanation (chemistry).
emb., embryol. embryology.
e.m.f., emf, E.M.F., EMF electromotive force.
Emp. Empire; Emperor; Empress.
emph. emphasis; emphatic.
e.m.u., emu, E.M.U. electromagnetic units.
emul. emulsion.
enc., encl. enclosed; enclosure.
ency., encyc., encycl. encyclopedia.
ENE, E.N.E., ene, e.n.e. east-northeast.
eng. engine; engineer; engineering; engraved; engraver; engraving.
Eng. England; English.
Eng.D. Doctor of Engineering.
engin. engineering.
engr. engineer; engraved; engraver; engraving.
enl. enlarged; enlisted.
Ens. Ensign.
entom., entomol. entomological; entomology.
env. envelope.
e.o. from office [L *ex officio*].
e.p. en passant (chess).
EP extended play.
Ep., Epis., Epist. Epistle(s).
Eph., Eph, Ephes. Ephesians.
epil. epilogue.
Epiph. Epiphany.
Epis., Episc. Episcopal.
epit. epitaph; epitome.
EPU European Payments Union.
E.Q., EQ educational quotient.
eq. equal; equalizer; equation; equator; equivalent **(equiv.)**.
e.r., er earned runs.
E.R. King Edward [L *Eduardus Rex*]; Queen Elizabeth [L *Elizabeth Regina*].
Er erbium.
E.R.A. Educational Research Association; Emergency Relief Administration **(ERA)**.
ERP, E.R.P. European Recovery Program.
erron. erroneous; erroneously.
E.R.V. English Revised Version (of the Bible).
Es einsteinium.
ESA Economic Stabilization Administration.
ESC Economic and Social Council.
eschat. eschatology.
Esd. Esdras.
ESE, E.S.E., ese, e.s.e. east-southeast.
Esk. Eskimo.
esp., espec. especially.
ESP extrasensory perception.
Esq., Esqr. Esquire.
est. estate; estimated; estuary.
EST, E.S.T., e.s.t. eastern standard time.
Est. Estonia.
estab. established.
Esth. Esther.
e.s.u., esu electrostatic unit.
ET Electronics Technician.
e.t.a., ETA estimated time of arrival.
et al. and others [L *et alii*]; and elsewhere [L *et alibi*].
etc. and so forth; and others [L *et ceteri, ceterae,* or *cetera*].
eth. ether; ethical; ethics.
Eth. Ethiopia; Ethiopian; Ethiopic.
ethnog. ethnographical; ethnography.
ethnol. ethnological; ethnology.
ETO European Theater of Operations.
et seq. and the following; and what follows [L *et sequens, et sequentes* or *sequentia*].
ety., etym., etymol. etymological; etymology.
Eu europium.
euphem. euphemism; euphemistic.
Eur. Europe; European.
E.V. English Version (of the Bible).
e.v., ev electron volt(s).
evac. evacuation.
evan., evang. evangelical; evangelist.
Evang. Evangelical.
evap. evaporation.
ex. examination; examine; examined; example; except; excepted; exception; exchange; excursion; executed; executive.
Ex., Ex, Exod. Exodus.
exam. examination; examined; examinee; examinor.
exc. excellent; except; excepted; exception; excursion.
Exc. Excellency.
exch. exchange; exchequer.
excl. exclusive.
excl., exclam. exclamation.
exec. executive; executor.
ex int. without interest.
ex lib. from the library (of) [L *ex libris*].
ex off. from office [L *ex officio*].
exp. expenses; expiration; expired; export; exportation; exported; exporter; express.
exper. experimental.
expt. experiment.
exptl. experimental.
exr. executor.
ext. extension; external; extinct; extra; extract.
Ez., Ez, Ezr. Ezra.
Eze., Eze, Ezek. Ezekiel.

F

F fluorine.
f activity coefficient.
f. farthing; fathom; feet; female; feminine; fine; fluid (ounce); folio; following; foot; formed; forte; franc; frequency; from; let it be made [L *flat*]; strong [L *forte*].
f., F function (of).
f., f, F., F farad.
f., f foul(s).
f, f/, f:, F, F/, F: F number (photography).
F. fahrenheit; February; Fellow; France; French; Friday; son [L *filius*].
FA Field Artillery
F.A. Fine Arts; Food Administration.
f.a. fire alarm; freight agent.
f.a., F.A. free alongside; freight agent.
F.A.A.A.S. Fellow of the American Association for the Advancement of Science.
fac. facsimile; factor; factory.
F.A.C.D. Fellow of the American College of Dentists.
F.A.C.P. Fellow of the American College of Physicians.
F.A.C.S. Fellow of the American College of Surgeons.
Fah., Fahr. Fahrenheit.
F.A.I.A. Fellow of the American Institute of Architects.
fam. familiar; family.
F.A.M., F. & A.M. Free and Accepted Masons.
FAO, F.A.O. Food and Agricultural Organization (of the United Nations).
F.A.P.S. Fellow of the American Physical Society.
f.a.s., F.A.S. free alongside ship.
F.A.S.A. Fellow of the Acoustical Society of America.
fasc. a bundle [L *fasciculus*].
fath. fathom.
f.b. freight bill.
f.b., fb fullback.
F.B.A. Fellow of the British Academy.
FBI, F.B.I. Federal Bureau of Investigation.
fbm feet board measure (board feet).
f.c. follow copy (printing).
Fc fractocumulus.
FCA, F.C.A. Farm Credit Administration.
F.C.C. Federal Communications Commission **(FCC)**; Federal Council of Churches; First Class Certificate; Food Control Committee.
FCDA Federal Civil Defense Administration.
FCIC, F.C.I.C. Federal Crop Insurance Corporation.
fcp. foolscap.
F.D. Defender of the Faith [L *Fidei Defensor*]; Fire Department.
FDA, F.D.A. Food and Drug Administration; Food Distribution Administration.
FDIC, F.D.I.C. Federal Deposit Insurance Corporation.
Fe iron [L *ferrum*].
FEB Fair Employment Board.
Feb., Feb February.
FEC Far Eastern Commission.
fec. he (or she) made it [L *fecit*].
fed. federal; federated; federation.
fem. female; feminine.
FEPC, F.E.P.C. Fair Employment Practices Committee.
FERA, F.E.R.A. Federal Emergency Relief Administration.
feud. feudal; feudalism.
ff. folios; following; fortissimo.
f.f. fixed focus.
f.f.a., F.F.A. free foreign agent; free from alongside.
F.F.A. Future Farmers of America.
F.F.V. First Families of Virginia.
F.G.S.A. Fellow of the Geological Society of America.
FHA Federal Housing Administration.
FHLBB Federal Home Loan Bank Board.
f.h.p. friction horsepower.
fid. fidelity; fiduciary.
fifo, FIFO first in, first out.
fig. figuratively; figure(s).
F.I.L. Fellow of the Institute of Linguists.
filo, FILO first in, last out.
fin. finance; financial; finished.
Fin. Finland; Finnish.
fl. floor; florin(s); flower; fluid; flute.
fl fluid.
Fl. Flanders; Flemish.
Fl fluorine.

FL Florida (P.O. abbr.)
Fla. Florida.
FLB Federal Land Bank.
fl. dr. fluid dram(s).
Flem. Flemish.
flex. flexible.
fl. oz. fluid ounce(s).
F.M. Field Manual; Field Marshal.
Fm fermium.
fm. fathom; from.
FM frequency modulation.
FMCS Federal Mediation and Conciliation Service.
FNMA Federal National Mortgage Association.
F.O. field officer; Foreign Office.
f.o.b., F.O.B. free on board.
F.O.E. Fraternal Order of Eagles.
fol. folio; following.
foll. following.
f.o.r., F.O.R. free on rails.
for. foreign; forestry.
fort. fortification; fortified.
f.p. fireplug; fire policy; floating policy; fully paid.
f.p., fp forward pass.
f.p., fp, fp. freezing point.
f.p., F.P., fp foot-pound(s).
fp forte piano (Ital.).
fp. foolscap.
FPA, F.P.A. Food Products Administration; Foreign Press Association.
FPC, F.P.C. Federal Power Commission.
FPHA, F.P.H.A. Federal Public Housing Administration.
fpm, f.p.m. feet per minute.
FPO fleet post office.
fps, f.p.s. feet per second; foot-pound-second (system).
f.r. right-hand page [L *folio recto*].
fr. fragment; franc; from.
Fr. Brother [L *Frater*]; Father; France; French; Friday; wife [G *Frau*].
Fr francium.
Frl. Miss [G *Fräulein*].
F.R.B., FRB Federal Reserve Bank; Federal Reserve Board.
FRC, F.R.C. Federal Radio Commission; Federal Relief Commission.
F.R.C.P. Fellow of the Royal College of Physicians.
F.R.C.S. Fellow of the Royal College of Surgeons.
freq. frequency; frequently; frequentative.
F.R.G.S. Fellow of the Royal Geographical Society.
Fr. Gui. French Guiana.
Fri. Friday.
Frl. Fräulein.
F.R.S. Federal Reserve System **(FRS)**; Fellow of the Royal Society.
F.R.S.A. Fellow of the Royal Society of Arts.
frt. freight.
F.S. Field Service; Fleet Surgeon.
f.s. foot-second.
Fs fractostratus.
FSA, F.S.A. Farm Security Administration; Federal Security Agency.
FSCC, F.S.C.C. Federal Surplus Commodities Corporation.
FSH follicle-stimulating hormone.
FSR, F.S.R. Field Service Regulations.
ft. feet; foot; fort; fortification; fortified.
FT Fire Control Technician.
FTC, F.T.C. Federal Trade Commission.
ft.-c. foot-candle.
fth., fthm. fathom.
ft.-l. foot-lambert.
ft.-lb. foot-pound.
fur. furlong.
furl. furlough.
furn. furnished; furniture.
fut. future.
f.v. on the back of the page [L *folio verso*].
FWA, F.W.A. Federal Works Agency.
fwd. forward.
FY fiscal year.
F.Z.S. Fellow of the Zoological Society.

G

g. gender; general; genitive; grand; guide.
g., G. conductance; gauge; gold; gourde **(gde.)**; grain(s); guilder(s); guinea(s); gulf.
g., g goal(s); goalie; goalkeeper.
g., g, G., G gram(s).
g general intelligence; (specific) gravity.
G gun.
G, G. German.
G. Germany; (specific) gravity.
g.a., G.A., G/A general average.
Ga. Georgia.
Ga gallium.
G.A. General Agent; General Assembly.
GA Georgia (P.O. abbr.).
Gael. Gaelic.
gal., gall. gallon(s).
Gal. Galatians; Galen.
galv. galvanic; galvanism; galvanized.
GAO General Accounting Office.
G.A.R., GAR Grand Army of the Republic.
GATT General Agreement on Tariffs and Trade.
G.A.W. guaranteed annual wage.
gaz. gazette; gazetteer.
G.B. Great Britain.
G.B.E. (Knight or Dame) Grand (Cross or Order) of the British Empire.
GCA, G.C.A. ground control approach (radar).
g-cal. gram calorie(s).
G.C.B. (Knight) Grand Cross of the Bath.
G.C.D. g.c.d., gcd, greatest common divisor.
g.c.f., gcf, G.C.F. greatest common factor.
GCI ground controlled interception (aircraft).
G.C.L.H. Grand Cross of the Legion of Honor.
GCM General Court Martial.
g.c.m., gcm, G.C.M. greatest common measure.
GCT, G.C.T., G.c.t. Greenwich civil time.
G.C.V.O. (Knight) Grand Cross of the (Royal) Victorian Order.
G.D. Grand Duchess; Grand Duchy; Grand Duke.
Gd gadolinium.
gds. goods.
Ge germanium.
geb. born [G *geboren*].
gel. gelatinous.
gen. gender; genera; general; generally; generator; generic; genitive; genus.
Gen. General; Genesis; Geneva; Genevan.
geneal. genealogical; genealogy.
genit. genitive.
genl. general.
gent. gentleman; gentlemen.
geod. geodesy; geodetic.
geog. geographer; geographic; geographical; geography.
geol. geologic; geological; geologist; geology.
geom. geometer; geometric; geometrical; geometry.
ger. gerund.
Ger., Germ. German; Germany.
gest. died [G *gestorben*].
G.F.T.U. General Federation of Trade Unions.
g.gr. great gross.
GHA Greenwich hour angle.
GHQ, G.H.Q. General Headquarters.
g.i., GI, G.I. gastrointestinal.
GI, G.I. general issue; government issue.
gi. gill(s).
Gib. Gibraltar.
Gk. Greek.
Gl glucinum.
gl. glass; gloss.
gld. guilder(s).
gloss. glossary.
gm. gram(s).
G.M. general manager; Grand Master.
GM Gunner's Mate.
G.m.a.t. Greenwich mean astronomical time.
Gmc. Germanic.
G.m.t. GMT, G.M.T. Greenwich mean time.
GNP, G.N.P. gross national product.
GO general orders.
G.O.P. Grand Old Party (Republican party).
Goth. gothic; Gothic.
gov., govt. government.
Gov. Governor.
G.P. general practitioner; Graduate in Pharmacy; general paresis.
g.p.m. gallons per minute.
GPO, G.P.O. General Post Office; Government Printing Office.
g.p.s. gallons per second.
GQ, G.Q., g.q. general quarters.
G.R. King George [L *Georgius Rex*].
gr. grade; grain(s); gram(s); grammar; great; gross; group.
Gr. Grecian; Greece; Greek.
grad. graduate; graduated.
gram. grammar; grammarian; grammatical.
Gr.Br., Gr.Brit. Great Britain.
gro. gross.
gr.wt. gross weight.
GS German silver.
G.S. General Secretary; General Staff; Girl Scouts.
GSA General Services Administration.
G.S.A. Girl Scouts of America.
GSC, G.S.C. General Staff Corps.
GSO, G.S.O. General Staff Officer.
gt. gilt; great.
g.t.c., G.T.C. good till canceled.
gtd. guaranteed.
gtt. a drop [L *gutta*].
g.u., g.-u. genitourinary.
guar. guaranteed.
Guat. Guatemala.
Guin. Guinea.
gun. gunnery.
guttat. by drops [L *guttatim*].
g.v. gravimetric volume.
gym. gymnasium; gymnastics.
gyn., gynecol. gynecological; gynecology.

H

h. harbor; hard; hardness; heavy sea; height; hence; high; horns (music); hour(s); hundred; husband.
h., h hit(s).
h, hy henry *(electr.)*.
H hydrogen; intensity of magnetic field.
h.a. this year [L *hoc anno*].
ha hectare(s).
Hab., Hab Habakkuk.
hab. corp. have the body [L *habeas corpus*].
Hag., Hag Haggai.
Hal halogen.
Hb hemoglobin.
hb., hb halfback.
H.B.M. His (Her) Britannic Majesty.
H.C. House of Commons.
hcap., hcp. handicap.
h.c.f., hcf, H.C.F. highest common factor.
hd. hand; head.
hdbk. handbook.
hdkf., hkf. handkerchief.
hdqrs. headquarters.
He helium.
H.E. His Eminence; His Excellency.
HE, H.E. high explosive.
Heb., Heb, Hebr. Hebrew; Hebrews.
her. heraldic; heraldry.
herp., herpetol. herpetology.
hex. hexachord; hexagon; hexagonal.
h.f., h-f, HF high frequency.
hf. half.
Hf hafnium.
hf.bd. half-bound (bookbinding).
hf.mor. half-morocco (bookbinding).
HG, H.G. High German.
H.G. His (Her) Grace; Home Guard.
hg hectogram(s); heliogram.
Hg mercury [L *hydrargyrum*].
hgt. height.
H.H. His (Her) Highness; His Holiness.
hhd hogshead.
HHFA Housing and Home Finance Agency.
HI Hawaii (P.O. abbr.).
H.I.H. His (Her) Imperial Highness.
H.I.M. His (Her) Imperial Majesty.
Hind. Hindi; Hindu; Hindustan; Hindustani.
hist. histology; historian; historical; history.
H.J. here lies [L *hic jacet*].
H.J.S. here lies buried [L *hic jacet sepultus*].
hkf. handkerchief.
hl, hl. hectoliter(s).
H.L. House of Lords.
HL mustard-lewisite (poison gas).
HLBB Home Loan Bank Board.
h.m. in this month [L *hoc mense*].
hm hectometer(s).
H.M. His (Her) Majesty.
H.M.S. His (Her) Majesty's Service (Ship, Steamer).
HN nitrogen mustard gas.
H.O. head office; Home Office.
ho. house.
Ho holmium.
HOLC, H.O.L.C. Home Owners' Loan Corporation.
hon. honorably; honorary.
Hon. Honorable.
Hond. Honduras.
hor. horizon; horizontal.
horol. horology.
hort., hortic. horticultural; horticulture.
Hos., Hos Hosea.
hosp. hospital.
HP, H.P. high power.
hp, HP, h.p., H.P. high pressure; horsepower.
hp.-hr. horsepower-hour.
h.q. look for this [L *hoc quaere*].
HQ, H.Q., hq, h.q. headquarters.
h.r., hr home run(s).
hr. hour(s).
Hr. Mister [G *Herr*].
H.R. Home Rule; House of Representatives.
H.R.E. Holy Roman Empire.
H.R.H. His (Her) Royal Highness.
H.R.I.P. here rests in peace [L *hic requiescat in pace*].
hrs. hours.
H.S. here is buried [L *hic sepultus*]; here lies [L *hic situ*]; High School; Home Secretary (Brit.); in this sense [L *hoc sensu*].
H.S.H. His (Her) Serene Highness.
H.S.M. His (Her) Serene Majesty.
h.t. at this time [L *hoc tempore*]; in or under this title [L *hoc titulo*].
ht. heat; height.
Hts. Heights.
HUD, H.U.D. Housing and Urban Development.
Hun., Hung. Hungarian; Hungary.
H.V., h.v., hv high voltage.
h.w. high water.
hyd., hydros. hydrostatics.
hydraul. hydraulic; hydraulics.
hyg. hygiene; hygroscopic.
hyp., hypoth. hypotenuse; hypothesis; hypothetical.

I

i. incisor; interest; intransitive; island.
I. Island(s); Isle(s).
I iodine; Roman numeral for 1.
IA Iowa (P.O. abbr.).
Ia. Iowa.
IADB Inter-American Defense Board.
IAEA International Atomic Energy Agency (of the United Nations).
IATA International Air Transport Association.
ib., ibid. in the same place [L *ibidem*].
IBRD International Bank for Reconstruction and Development.
IBT International Brotherhood of Teamsters.
ICA International Cooperation Administration.
ICAO International Civil Aviation Organization.
ICBM Intercontinental ballistic missile.
ICC Indian Claims Commission.
I.C.C. Interstate Commerce Commission.
Ice., Icel. Iceland; Icelandic.
ICES International Council for the Exploration of the Sea.
ICFTU International Confederation of Free Trade Unions.
ichth. ichthyology.
ICJ International Court of Justice.
ICNAF International Commission for Northwest Atlantic Fisheries.
i.c.w. interrupted continuous wave.
id. the same [L *idem*].
Id. Idaho.
ID, I.D., i.d. inside diameter.
I.D. identification; Infantry Division; Intelligence Department.
ID Idaho (P.O. abbr.).
Ida. Idaho.
i.e. that is [L *id est*].
I.E., IE Indo-European.
IF, I.F. i.f., i-f intermediate frequency.
IFCTU International Federation of Christian Trade Unions.
IFF Identification friend or foe (British radar device).
IG, I.G. amalgamation [G *Interessengemeinschaft*]; Indo-Germanic; Inspector General.
ign. ignites; ignition; unknown [L *ignotus*].
IHP, I.H.P. ihp, i.h.p., i.-hp. indicated horsepower.
I.H.S., IHS Jesus: often, incorrectly, Jesus Savior of Men [L *Iesus hominum salvator*] or, in this sign [L *in hoc signo*].
Il illinium.
IL Illinois (P.O. abbr.).
ILA International Longshoremen's Association.
I.L.G.W.U. International Ladies' Garment Workers' Union.
ill., illus., illust. illustrate; illustrated; illustration; illustrator.
Ill. Illinois.
illit. illiterate.
ILO, I.L.O. International Labor Organization (of the United Nations).
I.L.P. Independent Labour Party (Brit.).
ILS instrument landing system.
IMF International Monetary Fund.
imit. imitation; imitative.
immun. immunology.
IMO International Meteorological Organization.
imp. imperative; imperfect; imperial; impersonal; import; important; imported; importer; imprimatur; improper.
Imp. Imperator.
imper. imperative.
imperf. imperfect; imperforate.
impers. impersonal.
impf. imperfect.
imp. gal. imperial gallon.
impv. imperative.
in. inch(es).
In indium.
IN Indiana (P.O. abbr.).
inbd. inboard.
inc. inclosure; including; inclusive; income; incorporated; increase.
inch., incho. inchoative.
incl. inclosure; including.
incog. incognito.
incor., incorp. incorporated.
incorr. incorrect.
incr. increased; increasing.
I.N.D. in the name of God [L *in nomine Dei*].
ind. independence; independent; index; indicated; indicative; indigo; indirect; industrial.
Ind. India; Indian; Indiana; Indies.
indecl. indeclinable.
indef. indefinite.
inden., indent. indention (printing).
indic. indicating; indicative; indicator.
individ. individual.
induc. induction.
ined. not published.
in ex. at length [L *in extenso*].
in f. at the end [L *in fine*].
inf. below [L *infra*]; inferior; infinitive; information.
Inf. Infantry.
infin. infinitive.
infl. influence; influenced.
init. initial; in the beginning [L *initio*].
inj. injection.
in.-lb. inch-pound.
in lim. at the outset (on the threshold) [L *in limine*].
in loc. in its place [L *in loco*].
in loc. cit. in the place cited [L *in loco citato*].
inorg. inorganic.
I.N.R.I. Jesus of Nazareth, King of the Jews [L *Iesus Nazarenus Rex Iudaeorum*].
ins. inches; inspector; insular; insulated; insulation; insurance.
I.N.S., INS International News Service.
insc., inscr. inscribe; inscribed; inscription.
insep. inseparable.
insol. insoluble.
insp. inspected; inspector.
inst. instant; instantaneous; instrument.
Inst. Institute; Institution.
instr. instruction, instructor; instrument.
insur. insurance.
int. intelligence; interest; interior; interjection; internal; interval; intransitive.
intens. intensive.
inter. intermediate.
interj. interjection.
internat. international.
interp. interpreter.
Interpol. International Police Organization.
interrog. interrogative.
intr., intrans. intransitive.
in trans. on the way [L *in transitu*].
Int. Rev. Internal Revenue.
introd. introduction; introductory.
inv. invented; invention; inventor; invoice.
invert. invertebrate.
invt. inventory.
Io ionium.
I.O.B.B. Independent Order of B'nai B'rith.

I.O.O.F. Independent Order of Odd Fellows.
I.O.U., IOU I owe you.
i.p. in passing (chess).
i.p., ip innings pitched.
I.P.A., IPA International Phonetic Alphabet (Association).
IPI International Press Institute.
IPPC International Penal and Penitentiary Commission.
I.P.R. Institute of Pacific Relations.
ips, i.p.s. inches per second.
i.q. the same as [L *idem quod*].
IQ, I.Q. intelligence quotient.
i.q.e.d. what was to be proved [L *id quod erat demonstrandum*].
Ir. Ireland; Irish.
Ir iridium.
I.R.A. Irish Republican Army.
Iran. Iranian; Iranic.
IRBM intermediate range ballistic missile.
Ire. Ireland.
IRO International Refugee Organization.
irreg. irregularly.
IRS Internal Revenue Service.
is. island(s); isle(s).
Is., Is, Isa. Isaiah.
isl. island(s).
iso. isotropic.
isom. isometric.
isoth. isothermal.
Isr. Israel.
isth. isthmus.
it., ital. italic; italics.
It., Ital. Italian; Italy.
I.T.A., i/t/a Initial Teaching Alphabet.
itin. itinerant; itinerary.
ITO International Trade Organization.
ITU International Telecommunication Union; International Typographical Union.
IU, I.U. international unit(s).
IWW, I.W.W. Industrial Workers of the World.

J

J joule (physics).
J. Judge; Justice.
j.a., j/a, J.A., J/A joint account.
JA, J.A. Judge Advocate.
Ja., Jan., Jan January.
J.A.G. Judge Advocate General.
Jam. Jamaica.
Jap. Japan; Japanese.
Jas., Jas James.
J.C.D. Doctor of Canon Law [L *Juris Canonici Doctor*]; Doctor of Civil Law [L *Juris Civilis Doctor*].
JCS Joint Chiefs of Staff.
jct., jctn. junction.
J.D. Doctor of Laws [L *Jurum Doctor*].
Je., Je June.
Jer, Jer. Jeremiah.
j.g., jg junior grade.
Jl July.
Jn John.
Jon Jonah.
Jos. Joseph; Joshua **(Jos)**; Josiah.
jour. journal; journalist; journeyman.
J.P. Justice of the Peace.
jr., Jr. junior.
Ju, Judg. Judges.
Jul., Jul July.
Jun., Jun June.
jun., Jun. junior.
junc., junct. junction.
Jur.D. Doctor of Law [L *Juris Doctor*].
jurisp. jurisprudence.
jus., just. justice.
juv. juvenile.
j.v. junior varsity.
jwlr. jeweler.
Jy. July.

K

K potassium [L *kalium*].
k. capacity; carat; constant.
k., K. calends [L *kalendae*]; karat (carat); kilogram; king; king (chess); knot (naut.); kopeck; koruna; krone.
k kilo.
ka. kathode (cathode).
KA Kansas (P.O. abbr.).
kal. kalends (calends).
Kan., Kans., Kas. Kansas.
K.B. King's Bench; Knight Bachelor.
KB king's bishop (chess).
KBP king's bishop's pawn (chess).
kc., kc kilocycle(s).
K.C. King's Counsel; Knight Commander; Knights of Columbus.
kcal kilocalorie.
K.C.B. Knight Commander (of the Order) of the Bath.
K.C.V.O. Knight Commander of the (Royal) Victorian Order.
Ken. Kentucky.
kg., kg keg(s); kilogram(s).
K.G. Knight (of the Order) of the Garter.
KGB, K.G.B. Commission of State Security (Russian *Komitět Godsudarstvĕnnoi Bezopasnost'i*).
Ki Kings (book of the Bible).
kilo. kilogram(s); kilometer(s).
kilog. kilogram(s).
kilol. kiloliter(s).
kilom. kilometer(s).
kingd. kingdom.
K.K.K., KKK Ku Klux Klan.
kl., kl kiloliter(s).
km., km kilometer(s).
kn. kronen.
KN king's knight (chess).
KNP king's knight's pawn (chess).
KO, K.O., k.o. knockout.
K. of C. Knight (Knights) of Columbus.
K. of P. Knight (Knights) of Pythias.
kop. kopeck(s).
K.P. Knight (of the Order of St.) Patrick; Knights of Pythias.
KP king's pawn (chess).
KP, K.P. kitchen police.
kr., Kr. krona; krone.
Kr krypton.
KR king's rook (chess).
KRP king's rook's pawn (chess).
kt. karat (carat).
K.T. Knight (Knights) Templar.
kv., kv kilovolt(s).
kva, kv.-a. kilovolt-ampere.
kvar reactive kilovolt-ampere.
kw., kw kilowatt(s).
K.W.H., kw-h, kw.-hr., kw-hr kilowatt-hour(s).
Ky. Kentucky.
KY Kentucky (P.O. abbr.).

L

L., l. book [L *liber*]; lake; land; lat; latitude; law; leaf; league; left; lempira; length; leu; lev; lex; line; link; lira; lire; lit; low; place [L *locus*].
l, l. liter(s).
l., l (games) lost.
L. Latin; licentiate; Linnaeus.
L, £, l. pound (sterling) [L *libra*].
L Latin.
L length; lewisite; longitude.
L, l coefficient of inductance.
La. Louisiana.
La lanthanum.
L.A. Legislative Assembly; Library Association; Local Agent.
LA Louisiana (P.O. abbr.).
lab. laboratory.
L.A.M. Master of Liberal Arts [L *Liberalium Artium Magister*].
lam. laminated.
Lam., Lam Lamentations.
lang. language.
laryngol. laryngological; laryngology.
lat. latitude.
Lat. Latin; Latvia.
Latv. Latvia.
lb. pound [L *libra*].
L.B. Bachelor of Letters [L *Litterarum Baccalaureus*]; Local Board.
lb.ap. pound, apothecary.
lb.av. pound, avoirdupois.
lbs. pounds.
lb.t. pound, troy.
l.c. left center; lower case (printing); in the place cited [L *loco citato*].
l/c, L/C letter of credit; lower case.
L.C. Library of Congress.
L.C.D., l.c.d., lcd lowest common denominator.
l.c.m., lcm, L.C.M. lowest, or least, common multiple.
ld. lead (printing).
Ld. Lord.
L.D., LD., LD Low Dutch.
ldg. landing; leading; loading.
L.Div. Licentiate in Divinity.
ld. lmt. load limit.
ldry. laundry.
L.D.S. Licentiate in Dental Surgery.
l.e., le left end.
lea. league; leather; leave.
lect. lecture; lecturer.
led. ledger.
leg. legal; legate; legato; legislation.
legis. legislation; legislative; legislature.
LEM lunar excursion module.
L. ès S. Licentiate in Sciences [F *Licencié ès Sciences*].
Lev., Lev, Levit. Leviticus.
lex. lexicon.
l.f., lf. lightface (printing).
l.f., lf left field(er); left forward.
l.f., l-f, LF, L.F. low frequency.
l.g., lg left guard.
LG, LG., L.G. Low German.
lg., lge. large.
LGk. Late Greek.
lgth. length.
LH luteinizing hormone.
l.h., L.H., LH left hand.
l.h., lh, l.h.b., lhb left halfback.
LHA local hour angle.
L.H.D. Doctor of Humanities [L *Litterarum Humaniorum Doctor*].
Li lithium.
L.I. Long Island.
LI Lithographer.
lib. book [L *liber*]; librarian; library.
Lib. Liberal; Liberia.
Lieut. Lieutenant.
lifo, LIFO last in, first out.
lilo, LILO last in, last out.
lin. lineal; linear.
ling. linguistics.
linim. liniment.
Linn. Linnaeus; Linnean.
lino. linotype.
liq. liquid; liquor.
li.qts. liquid quarts.
lit. liter; literal; literally; literary; literature.
Lit. B., Litt. B. Bachelor of Letters (Literature) [L *Lit(t)erarum Baccalaureus*].
Lit.D., Litt.D. Doctor of Letters (Literature) [L *Lit(t)erarum Doctor*].
lith., litho., lithog. lithograph; lithography.
Lith. Lithuania; Lithuanian.
Lk Luke.
ll. leaves; lines.
LL, L.L. Late Latin; Legal Latin; Low Latin.
LL.B. Bachelor of Laws [L *Legum Baccalaureus*].
LL.D. Doctor of Laws [L *Legum Doctor*].
LL.M. Master of Laws [L *Legum Magister*].
LM Legion of Merit; lunar (excursion) module.
L.M. Licentiate in Medicine (or Midwifery).
LMT local mean time.
LNG liquefied natural gas.
loc. local; location.
local. localism.
loc. cit. in the place cited [L *loco citato*].
log, log. logarithm.
long. longitude.
loq. he (she, it) speaks [L *loquitur*].
lox liquid oxygen.
l.p. large paper; long primer.
l.p., lp, L.P., LP low pressure; long playing (phonograph record).
L.P.S. Lord Privy Seal.
L.S. Licentiate in Surgery; place of the seal [L *locus sigilli*].
l.s.c. in the place cited above [L *loco supra citato*].
LSD Landing Ship, Dock; lysergic acid diethylamide.
£.s.d. pounds, shillings, pence (British).
L.S.S., LSS Lifesaving Service (U.S.).
LST. Landing Ship, Tank.
l.t., l.tn. long ton.
l.t., lt left tackle.
Lt. Lieutenant.
ltd., Ltd. limited.
L.Th. Licentiate in Theology.
Lt. Inf. Light Infantry.
Ltjg. Lieutenant, Junior Grade.
Lu lutetium.
lubric. lubricate; lubrication.
Luth. Lutheran.
Lux. Luxemburg.
lv. leave(s).
lw lawrencium.
l.w.l. load waterline.
l.w.m. low watermark.
LXX Septuagint.
lyr. lyric; lyrical.

M

m., m meter(s); noon [L *meridies*].
m. majesty; male; manual; mark; married; masculine; mass; measure; medicine; medium; member; meridian; mile; mill; minim; minute; month; moon; morning; mountain; noon [L *meridies*].
M. handful [L *manipulus*]; Master [L *magister*]; monsieur; of medicine [L *medicinae*].
M Medieval; middle; Roman numeral for 1,000.
M.A. Master of Arts [L *Magister Artium*]; Military Academy.
MA Machine Accountant; Maritime Administration; Massachusetts (P.O. abbr.).
MA, M.A. mental age.
Ma masurium.
MAC mean aerodynamic chord.
Mac., Macc. Maccabees.
Maced. Macedonia; Macedonian.
mach., machin. machine; machinery; machinist.
Mad., Madm. Madam.
mag. magazine; magnet; magnetism; magnitude.
M. Agr., M. Agric. Master of Agriculture.
maj. majority.
Maj. Major.
Mal, Mal. Malachi; Malay; Malayan; Malta.
malac. malacology.
Man. manila (paper); Manitoba.
Manch. Manchukuo; Manchuria.
manuf. manufacture; manufactured; manufacturer; manufacturing.
mar. marine; maritime; married.
Mar., Mar March.
March. Marchioness.
marg. margin; marginal.
Marq. Marquis.
mas., masc. masculine.
Mass. Massachusetts.
mat. matinée; matins; maturity.
MATS Military Air Transport Service.
math. mathematical; mathematician; mathematics.
matr., matric. matriculate; matriculation.
Matt. Matthew.
max. maximum.
Max. Maximilian.
M.B. Bachelor of Medicine [L *Medicinae Baccalaureus*].
M.B.A. Master in (or of) Business Administration.
MBS Mutual Broadcasting System.
mc, m.c., mc. megacycle; millicurie.
M.C. Maritime Commission; Master Commandant; Master of Ceremonies; Medical Corps; Member of Congress.
M.Ch. Master of Surgery [L *Magister Chirurgiae*].
M.C.L. Master of Civil Law.
Md mendelevium.
Md. Maryland.
M.D. Doctor of Medicine [L *Medicinae Doctor*]; Medical Department; mentally deficient.
MD Maryland (P.O. abbr.).
MD, M.D. Middle Dutch.
M/D, m/d memorandum of deposit; months' date.
M.D.S. Master of Dental Surgery.
mdse. merchandise.
MDu. Middle Dutch.
m.e. marbled edges (bookbinding).
Me. Maine.
Me methyl.
M.E. Mechanical (Military, Mining) Engineer; Methodist Episcopal.
ME Maine (P.O. abbr.).
ME, ME., M.E. Middle English.
meas. measure; measurable.
mech., mechan. mechanical; mechanics; mechanism.
med. medical; medicine; medieval; medium.
M.Ed. Master of Education.
Med.Gk. Medieval Greek.
Medit. Mediterranean.
Med.L Medieval Latin.
meg. megacycle; megohm.
mem. member; memoir; memorandum; memorial.
memo. memorandum.
mensur. mensuration.
m.e.p. mean effective pressure.
mer. meridian; meridional.
merc. mercantile; mercurial; mercury.
Messrs., Messrs Messieurs.
met. metaphor; metaphysics; meteorological; metronome; metropolitan.
metal., metall. metallurgical; metallurgy.
metaph. metaphor; metaphorical; metaphysics.
metath. metathesis; metathetical.
meteor., meteorol. meteorological; meteorology.
meth. method; methylated.
Meth. Methodist.
meton. metonymy.
metrol. metrological; metrology.
metrop. metropolitan.
mev, Mev, MEV, m.e.v. million electron volts.
Mex. Mexican; Mexico.
MF, M.F., mf, m.f. medium frequency.
mf, mf. mezzoforte; millifarad.
mf, mf., mfd microfarad.
MF., MF, M.F. Middle French.
mfg. manufacturing.
M.Flem. Middle Flemish.
mfr. manufacture; manufacturer.
MG Military Government.
mg., mg, mgm milligram(s).
Mg magnesium.
Mgr. Manager; Monseigneur; Monsignor.
mgt. management.
MH Medal of Honor.
mh, mh. millihenry.
MHG, MHG., M.H.G. Middle High German.
MI Michigan (P.O. abbr.).
mi., mi mile(s).
Mic., Mic Micah.
Mich. Michigan.
micros. microscope; microscopic; microscopy.
mid. middle; midshipman.
Mid.Dan. Middle Danish.
Mid.Sw. Middle Swedish.
mil. mileage; military; militia; million.
milit. military.
mim., mimeo. mimeograph; mimeographed.
min. mineralogical; mineralogy; minim(s); minimum; mining; minor; minute(s).
mineral. mineralogy.
Minn. Minnesota.
m.i.p. marine insurance policy; mean indicated pressure.
MIr. Middle Irish.
MIRV multiple independently targetable reentry vehicle.
misc. miscellaneous; miscellany.
Miss. Mississippi.
mk. mark; markka.
Mk Mark.
mkd. marked.
m.k.s., mk., M.K.S. meter-kilogram-second (system).
mkt. market.
ml., ml milliliter(s).
M.L., ML., ML Medieval (or Middle) Latin.
ML Molder.
M.L.A. Modern Language Association; Member of the Legislative Assembly.
MLD, M.L.D., m.l.d. minimum lethal dose.
MLG, M.L.G., MLG. Middle Low German.
Mlle., Mlle Mademoiselle.
Mlles., Mlles Mesdemoiselles.
M.L.S. Master of Library Science.
m.m. with the necessary changes [L *mutatis mutandis*].
mm., mm millimeter(s); thousands [L *millia*].
MM. Messieurs.
MM Machinist's Mate.
Mme., Mme Madame.
Mmes., Mmes Mesdames.
m.m.f. magnetomotive force.
mmfd. micromicrofarad.
m.n. the name being changed [L *mutato nomine*].
MN Minnesota (P.O. abbr.).
Mn manganese.
mo. month(s); monthly.
Mo. Missouri; Monday.
Mo molybdenum.
M.O. mail order; Medical Officer; money order.
MO Missouri (P.O. abbr.).
mod. moderate; moderato; modern.
Mod.Gr. Modern Greek.
Mod. L Modern Latin.
Moham. Mohammedan.
M.O.I. Ministry of Information.
mol. molecular; molecule.
mol.wt. molecular weight.
mon. monastery; monetary.
Mon. Monday; Monsignor.
Mong. Mongolia; Mongolian.
monocl. monoclinic.
monog., monogr. monograph.
Mons. Monsieur.
Monsig. Monsignor.
Mont. Montana.
mor. morocco (bookbinding).
Mor. Morocco.
morn. morning.
morph., morphol. morphological; morphology.
mort. mortuary.
MOS military occupational specialty.
mos. months.
mot. motor, motorized.
mp, m.p., M.P. melting point.
MP, M.P. Member of Parliament; Military Police.
mp moderately soft (It. *mezzo piano*).
M.Pd. Master of Pedagogy.
M.P.E. Master of Physical

Education.

mph, m.p.h., MPH miles per hour.

M.P.P.D.A., MPPDA Motion Picture Producers and Distributors of America, Inc.

MR Machinery Repairman; motivational research.

Mr. Mister.

M.R.A. Moral Re-Armament.

MRC Metals Reserve Company.

Mrs. Mistress.

m.s., M/S months after sight.

ms., ms, MS., MS manuscript.

M.S. Master of Science [L *Magister Scientiae*]; sacred to the memory of [L *memoriae sacrum*]; mine sweeper.

MS Mississippi (P.O. abbr.).

MSA Mutual Security Agency.

M.Sc. Master of Science.

msg. message.

Msgr. Monsignor.

M.Sgt., M/Sgt Master Sergeant.

m.s.l., M.S.L. mean sea level.

mss., mss, MSS., MSS manuscripts.

MST, M.S.T., m.s.t. mountain standard time.

mt. mount; mountain.

m.t. mean time; metric ton; motor transport; mountain time.

Mt Matthew.

MT Montana (P.O. abbr.).

mtg. meeting; mortgage.

mtge. mortgage.

mtl. material.

m.t.l., M.T.L. mean tidal level.

mtn. mountain.

MTO Mediterranean Theater of Operations.

Mt. Rev. Most Reverend.

mts. mountains.

MU Musician.

mun. municipal; municipality.

mus. museum; music; musician.

Mus.B., Mus.Bac. Bachelor of Music [L *Musicae Baccalaureus*].

Mus.D., Mus.Doc., Mus.Dr. Doctor of Music [L *Musicae Doctor*].

Mus.M. Master of Music [L *Musicae Magister*].

mut. mutilated; mutual.

mv., mv millivolt(s).

m.v. softly (It. *mezzo voce*).

Mv mendelevium.

MVA, M.V.A. Missouri Valley Authority.

MVD Soviet Ministry of Internal Affairs [Russian *Ministerstvo Vnutrennikh Del*].

M.W. Most Worshipful; Most Worthy.

MY May.

mya. myriare(s).

mycol. mycological; mycology.

myg. myriagram(s).

myl. myrialiter(s).

mym. myriameter(s).

myth., mythol. mythological; mythology.

N

n. name; net; neuter; new; nominative; noon; normal; note; noun; number; born [L *natus*]; our [L *noster*].

n neutron.

N. Nationalist; Navy; Norse; November.

N., N, n. north; northern.

N knight (chess); nitrogen.

Na sodium [L *natrium*].

N.A. National Army; North America.

N.A.A. National Aeronautic Association; National Automobile Association.

N.A.A.C.P., NAACP National Association for the Advancement of Colored People.

NAC North Atlantic Council.

NACA National Advisory Committee for Aeronautics.

N.A.D. National Academy of Design.

Nah., Nah Nahum.

N.Am. North American.

N.A.M. National Association of Manufacturers.

NASA National Aeronautics and Space Administration.

nat. national; native; natural; naturalist.

nat.hist. natural history.

natl. national.

NATO North Atlantic Treaty Organization.

NATS National Air Transport Service.

naut. nautical.

nav. naval; navigable; navigation.

navig. navigation; navigator.

n.b., N.B. note well [L *nota bene*].

N.B. New Brunswick.

Nb niobium.

NBA, N.B.A. National Boxing Association.

NBC National Broadcasting Company.

NbE north by east.

NBS, N.B.S. National Bureau of Standards.

NbW north by west.

n.c., N.C. nitrocellulose.

N.C., N.Car. North Carolina.

NC North Carolina (P.O. abbr.).

NCAA, N.C.A.A. National Collegiate Athletic Association.

NCO, N.C.O., n.c.o. non-commissioned officer.

N.D., n.d. no date.

Nd neodymium.

N.D., N.Dak. North Dakota.

ND North Dakota (P.O. abbr.).

NDRC, N.D.R.C. National Defense Research Committee.

NE, N.E., ne, n.e. northeast; northeastern.

Ne neon.

N.E. New England.

NE Nebraska (P.O. abbr.).

NEA, N.E.A. National Education Association.

Neb., Nebr. Nebraska.

N.E.C., NEC National Electric Code; National Emergency Council.

n.e.c. not elsewhere classified.

NED, N.E.D. New English Dictionary (Oxford English Dictionary).

neg. negative; negatively.

Neh., Neh Nehemiah.

n.e.i. not elsewhere indicated.

neol. neologism.

NEP, Nep., nep. New Economic Policy.

n.e.s. not elsewhere specified (or stated).

Neth. Netherlands.

neur., neurol. neurological; neurology.

neut. neuter; neutral.

Nev. Nevada.

Newf. Newfoundland.

New M. New Mexico.

New Test. New Testament.

n.f. noun feminine.

N.F. National Formulary; Newfoundland; Norman French.

N.F., n/f. no funds.

n.g., N.G. no good.

NG, N.G. National Guard; New Guinea.

NGk, N.Gk., NGk. New Greek.

N.H. New Hampshire.

NH New Hampshire (P.O. abbr.).

NHA, N.H.A. National Housing Administration (Agency).

NHG, NHG., N.H.G. New High German.

NHI National Health Insurance (Brit.).

n.h.p. nominal horsepower.

Ni nickel.

N.I., N.Ire. Northern Ireland.

NIA National Intelligence Authority.

Nic., Nicar. Nicaragua.

Nig. Nigeria; Nigerian.

NIRA, N.I.R.A. National Industrial Recovery Act.

N.J. New Jersey.

NJ New Jersey (P.O. abbr.).

NKVD People's Commissariat of Internal Affairs [Russ. *Narodnyi Komissariat Vnutrennikh Del*].

n.l. new line (printing); north latitude; not clear [L *non liquet*]; not far [L *non longe*]; not lawful [<L *non licet*].

NL, NL., N.L. New Latin.

N.lat. north latitude.

NLRB, N.L.R.B. National Labor Relations Board.

n.m. nautical mile; noun masculine.

N.M., N.Mex. New Mexico.

NM New Mexico (P.O. abbr.).

N.M.U., NMU National Maritime Union.

NNE, N.N.E, nne, n.n.e. north-northeast.

NNW, N.N.W., nnw, n.n.w north-northwest.

No nobelium.

no., No. north; northern; number.

nob. for (or on) our part [L *nobis*].

nol. pros. unwilling to prosecute [L *nolle prosequi*].

nom. nomenclature; nominal; nominative.

nomin. nominative.

noncom. non-commissioned (officer).

non cul. not guilty [L *non culpabilis*].

non dest. notwithstanding [L *non destante*].

non obs., non obst. notwithstanding [<L *non obstante*].

non pros. he (or she) does not prosecute [L *non prosequitur*].

non seq. it does not follow [L *non sequitur*].

nor., Nor. north; northern.

Nor. Norman; Norway; Norwegian.

norm normal.

Norw. Norway; Norwegian.

nos., Nos. numbers.

nov. novelist.

Nov., Nov November.

n.p. net proceeds; new paragraph; no paging; no place (of publication).

Np neptunium.

N.P. no protest; Notary Public; unless before [L *nisi prius*].

NP knight's pawn (chess); neuropsychiatric.

NPN non-protein nitrogen.

n.p. or d. no place or date.

n.p.t., N.P.T. normal pressure and temperature.

nr. near.

NRA, N.R.A. National Recovery Administration.

n.s. near side (shipping); new series; new style.

N.S., n.s. not specified.

Ns nimbostratus.

N.S. New Style; Nova Scotia.

NSA National Shipping Authority.

NSC National Security Council.

NSF National Science Foundation.

N.S.F., N/S/F not sufficient funds.

N.S.P.C.A. National Society for the Prevention of Cruelty to Animals.

N.S.P.C.C. National Society for the Prevention of Cruelty to Children.

NSRB National Security Resources Board.

nt. net.

Nt niton.

NT., N.T. New Testament.

n.t.p., N.T.P. normal temperature and pressure.

nt.wt. net weight.

num. number(s); numeral(s).

Num., Num, Numb. Numbers.

NV Nevada (P.O. abbr.).

numis., numism. numismatic; numismatics.

nv. non-voting (stock).

NW, N.W., nw, n.w. northwest; northwestern.

N.W.T. Northwest Territories (Canada).

N.Y. New York.

NY New York (P.O. abbr.).

NYA, N.Y.A. National Youth Administration.

N.Y.C. New York City.

N.Z., N.Zeal. New Zealand.

O

o. off; only.

o., O. octavo; old; order; pint [L *octavius*].

o ohm.

o- ortho-.

O. Ocean; October; Ohio; Ontario; Oregon.

O Old; oxygen.

OAPC, O.A.P.C. Office of Alien Property Custodian.

OAr., O.Ar. Old Arabic.

OAS Organization of American States.

ob. he (or she) died [L *orbit*]; in passing [L *obiter*]; obstetrical; obstetrics.

Ob., Ob, Obad. Obadiah.

obb. obbligato.

obdt., obt. obedient.

O.B.E. Officer (of the Order) of the British Empire.

obit. obituary.

obj. object; objection; objective.

obl. oblique; oblong.

obs. obscure; observation; observatory; obsolete; obsolescence.

obsol., obsoles. obsolescent.

ob.s.p. died without issue [L *obiit sine prole*].

obstet. obstetrical; obstetrics.

obt. obedient.

obv. obverse.

o.c. in the work cited [L *opere citato*].

Oc., oc. ocean.

o/c old charter; overcharge.

O.C., OC Office of Censorship; Officer Commanding; original cover.

OCAS Organization of Central American States.

occ. occasion; occasionally; occident; occidental.

occult. occultism.

OCD, O.C.D. Office of Civilian Defense.

oceanog. oceanography.

OCS Office of Contract Settlement; Officer Candidate School.

oct. octavo.

Oct, Oct. October.

octupl. octuplicate.

o.d. olive drab; on demand; outside diameter.

O.D. Doctor of Optometry; Officer of the Day; Ordnance Department; overdraft; overdrawn.

ODan. Old Danish.

OD., OD, ODu. Old Dutch.

ODM Office of Defense Mobilization.

OE, OE., O.E. Old English.

O.E.D. Oxford English Dictionary.

OEEC Organization for European Economic Cooperation.

O.E.S. Office of Economic Stabilization **(OES)**; Order of the Eastern Star.

OF, OF., O.F. Old French.

off. offered; office; official; officinal.

O.G. Officer of the Guard; original gum (philately).

OH Ohio (P.O. abbr.).

OHE Office of the Housing Expediter.

OHG, OHG., O.H.G. Old High German.

O.H.M.S. On His (Her) Majesty's Service.

OIAA Office of Inter-American Affairs.

OIC Office of Information and Culture (of the State Department).

O.Ir. Old Irish.

OIT Office of International Trade.

OK Oklahoma (P.O. abbr.).

Okla. Oklahoma.

OL, O.L. Old Latin.

Old Test. Old Testament.

oleo. oleomargarine.

O.M. Order of Merit (Brit.).

ON, ON., O.N. Old Norse.

ONI Office of Naval Intelligence.

ONorm.Fr. Old Norman French.

onomat. onomatopoeia; onomatopoeic.

Ont. Ontario.

OOD, O.O.D. Officer of the Day; Officer of the Deck.

O.P., OP, o.p., op out of print; overprint; overproof.

OP observation post.

op. operation; opposite; work [L *opus*]; works [L *opera*].

OPA,' O.P.A. Office of Price Administration.

op. cit. in the work cited [L *opere citato*].

OPEC Organization of Petroleum Exporting Countries.

OPer. Old Persian.

ophthal. ophthalmology.

opp. oppose; opposed; opposite.

opt. optative; optical; optics.

OR, O.R. Operating room.

orat. oratorical; oratory.

ORC, O.R.C. Officers' Reserve Corps.

orch. orchestra; orchestral.

ord. ordained; order; ordinal; ordinance; ordinary; ordnance.

OR Oregon (P.O. abbr.).

ordn. ordnance.

Ore., Oreg. Oregon.

org. organic; organism; organized.

orig. original; originally.

Ork. Orkney (Islands).

ornith., ornithol. ornithological; ornithologist; ornithology.

Orth. Orthodox.

orth. orthopedic; orthopedics.

O.S. ordinary seaman.

O.S., o/s, O/S Old Style.

OS, OS., O.S. Old Saxon.

Os osmium.

O.S.A. Order of St. Augustine.

O.S.B. Order of St. Benedict.

OSD Office of the Secretary of Defense.

O.S.D. Order of St. Dominic.

osc. oscillating; oscillator.

OSerb. Old Serbian.

O.S.F. Order of St. Francis.

OSlav. Old Slavic.

O.Sp. Old Spanish.

OSRD, O.S.R.D. Office of Scientific Research and Development.

OSS, O.S.S. Office of Strategic Services.

osteo. osteopath; osteopathy.

O.T. Old Testament; on truck; overtime.

OTC, O.T.C. Officer's Training Corps.

otol. otology.

OTS, O.T.S. Officer Training School.

ott. octave [It. *ottava*].

OWI, O.W.I. Office of War Information.

Oxon. Oxford [L *Oxonia*].

oz, oz. ounce(s).

oz.ap. ounce, apothecary.

oz.av. ounce, avoirdupois.

ozs. ounces.

oz.t. ounce, troy.

P

p. after [L *post*]; by [L *per*]; by weight [L *pondere*]; first [L *primus*]; for [L *pro*]; in part [L *partim*]; page; part; participle; past; penny; perch (measure); period; perishable; peseta **(pta)**; peso; pint; pipe; pole (measure); population; post; power; pressure.

p, p. pitcher; softly [It. *piano*].

P. bishop [L *pontifex*]; father [F *père*; L *pater*]; pastor; pengö; people [L *populus*], peso; piaster; pope [L *papa*]; president; priest; prince; prompter (theater).

P parental; phosphorus; pressure; prisoner; pawn (chess).

p- para- (chemistry).

P- pursuit (military).

p.a. for the year [L *pro anno*]; participial adjective; particular average (insurance); public address; yearly [L *per annum*].

pa. paper.

Pa. Pennsylvania.

Pa protoactinium.

P.A. Passenger Agent; Petroleum Administration **(PA)**; Post Adjutant; Purchasing Agent.

P.A., P/A power of attorney; private account.

PA Pennsylvania (P.O. abbr.); physician's assistant; press agent; public-address (system).

PABA, paba para-aminobenzoic acid.

Pac., Pacif. Pacific.

P.A.C. Pan-American Congress; Political Action Committee **(PAC)**.

p. ae. equal parts [L *partes aequales*].

Pal. Palestine.

paleob. paleobotany.

paleog. paleography.

paleontol. paleontology.

palm. palmistry.

pam., pamph. pamphlet.

Pan. Panama.

P. and L. profit and loss.

pap. paper.

par. paragraph; parallel; parenthesis.

Par., Para. Paraguay.

paren. parenthesis.

parens. parentheses.

parl. parliamentary.

part. participle; particular.

pass. everywhere [L *passim*]; passage; passenger; passive.

pat. patent; patented; patrol; pattern.

patd. patented.

path., pathol. pathology.

Pat. Off. Patent Office.

pat.pend. patent pending.

P.A.U., PAU Pan American Union.

P.A.Y.E. pay as you earn; pay as you enter.

payt. payment.

P.B. Pharmacopoeia Britannica; prayer book.

PBA Public Buildings Administration.

PBS Public Buildings Service.

PBX, P.B.X. private branch (telephone) exchange.

p.c. after meals [L *post cibos*]; postcard.

p.c., Pc., P.C., PC. percent, percentage.

pc. piece; price.

p/c, P/C petty cash; price current.

P.C. Police Constable; Post Commander; Privy Council; professional corporation.

PCA Progressive Citizens of America.

Pcs. preconscious.

pct. percent.

p.d., P.D. by the day [L *per diem*]; potential difference.

pd. paid.

Pd palladium.

P.D. Police Department.

PD phenyl dichloride.

Pd.B. Bachelor of Pedagogy [L *Pedagogiae Baccalaureus*].

Pd.D. Doctor of Pedagogy [L *Pedagogiae Doctor*].

Pd.M. Master of Pedagogy [L *Pedagogiae Magister*].

P.E. Petroleum Engineer; Pre-

siding Elder; printer's error; probable error; Protestant Episcopal.
ped. pedal; pedestal; pedestrian.
P.E.I. Prince Edward Island.
pen. peninsula; penitent; penitentiary.
P.E.N. (International Association of) Poets, Playwrights, Editors, Essayists, and Novelists.
Penn., Penna. Pennsylvania.
penol. penology.
per. period; person.
per an., per ann. by the year [L *per annum*].
perd., perden. dying away [It. *perdendo*].
perf. perfect; perforated; performer.
perh. perhaps.
perm. permanent.
perp. perpendicular; perpetual.
pers. person; personal.
Pers. Persia; Persian.
persp. perspective.
pert. pertaining.
Peru., Peruv. Peruvian.
pet. petroleum.
petn. petition.
petrog. petrography.
petrol. petrology.
p.f. louder [It. *più forte*]; power factor.
pf. pfennig.
pg. page.
Pfc, Pfc. Private, first class.
pfd. preferred.
pfg. pfennig.
Pg. Portugal; Portuguese.
P.G. Past Grand (Master); paying guest; postgraduate.
PGA, P.G.A. Professional Golfers Association.
PH, P.H. Purple Heart.
ph. phrase.
Ph phenyl.
PHA Public Housing Administration.
phar., pharm. pharmaceutical; pharmacist; pharmacy.
Phar. B. Bachelor of Pharmacy [L *Pharmaciae Baccalaureus*].
Phar. D. Doctor of Pharmacy [L *Pharmaciae Doctor*].
Phar. M. Master of Pharmacy [L *Pharmaciae Magister*].
pharmacol. pharmacology.
Ph.B. Bachelor of Philosophy [L *Philosophiae Baccalaureus*].
Ph.C. Pharmaceutical Chemist.
Ph.D. Doctor of Philosophy [L *Philosophiae Doctor*].
phil., philos. philosopher; philosophical; philosophy.
Phil. Philippians; Philippines.
Phila. Philadelphia.
philol. philology.
philos. philosopher; philosophical; philosophy.
phon. phonetic; phonetics; phonology.
phonet. phonetic; phonetics.
phot., photog. photograph; photographic; photography.
photom. photometrical; photometry.
phr. phrase.
phren., phrenol. phrenological; phrenology.
PHS Public Health Service.
phys. physical; physician; physicist; physics.
physiol. physiological; physiology.
Pi., pias. piaster.
pict. pictorial; picture.
pil. pill [L *pilula*].
pinx. he (or she) painted [L *pinxit*].
pizz. plucked (music) [It. *pizzicato*].
pk. pack; park; peak; peck.
pkg. package(s).
pkt. packet.
pl. place; plate; plural.
plat. plateau; platform; platoon.
plen. plenipotentiary.
plf., plff. plaintiff.
plu. plural.
plup., plupf. pluperfect.
plur. plural; plurality.
p.m., P.M. after death [L *post mortem*]; afternoon [L *post meridiem*]; post-mortem.
P.M. Pacific Mail; Past Master; Paymaster; Police Magistrate; Postmaster; Prime Minister; Provost Marshal.
PM Postmaster; Provost Marshal.
Pm promethium.
PMA Production and Marketing Administration.
pmk. postmark.
pmkd. postmarked.
p.n., P/N promissory note.
pneum. pneumatic; pneumatics.
p.n.g. a person who is not acceptable [L *persona non grata*].
pnxt. he (or she) painted [L *pinxit*].
p.o., po put-out(s).
p.o., P.O. personnel officer; petty officer; postal order; post office.
Po polonium.
P.O.D. pay on delivery **(p.o.d.);** Post Office Department.
Pod.D. Doctor of Podiatry.
P.O.E. Port of Embarkation; Port of Entry.
poet. poetic; poetical; poetry.
pol., polit. political; politics.
Pol. Poland; Polish.
pol. econ., polit. econ. political economy.
POP Point of Purchase.
pop. popular; population.
p.o.r. pay on return.
port. portrait.
Port. Portugal; Portuguese.
pos., posit. position; positive.
poss. possession; possessive; possible; possibly.
post. postal.
pot. potential.
P.O.W., POW Prisoner of War.
p.p., P.P. parcel post; parish priest; postpaid.
pp., p.p. past participle.
pp. pages; privately printed.
pp pianissimo.
PP pellagra preventive (factor). *pour prendre congé*].
p.p.c., P.P.C. to take leave [F
ppd. postpaid; prepaid.
pph. pamphlet.
p.p.i. policy proof of interest.
PPI plan position indicator.
ppl. participle.
ppm., p.p.m. parts per million.
ppp. pianissimo.
ppr., p.pr. present participle.
p.p.s., P.P.S. additional postscript [L *post postscriptum*].
p.q. previous question.
P.Q. Province of Quebec.
pr. pair; pairs; paper; power; preferred; preposition; present; price; priest; prince; printing; pronoun.
PR public relations; Puerto Rico (P.O. abbr.).
Pr praseodymium.
P.R. Puerto Rico; proportional representation.
preb. prebend; prebendary.
prec. preceding.
pred. predicate; predication; predicative; prediction.
pref. preface; prefatory; preference; preferred; prefix.
prelim. preliminary.
prem. premium.
prep. preparation; preparatory; prepare; preposition.
Pres. President.
pres. present; presidency; president; presumptive.
Presb., Presbyt. Presbyter; Presbyterian.
pret. preterit.
prev. previous; previously.
prim. primary; primitive.
prin. principal; principally; principle.
print. printer; printing.
priv. private; privately; privative.
P.R.O., PRO public relations officer.
pro. professional.
prob. probable; probably; problem.
proc. proceedings; process; proclamation.
prod. produce; produced; product.
prof. professor.
prog. progress; progressive.
prom. promenade; promontory.
pron. pronoun; pronounced; pronunciation.
pronom. pronominal.
prop. proper; properly; property; proposition; proprietor; proprietary.
propr. proprietor; proprietary.
pros. prosody.
Prot. Protectorate; Protestant.
pro tem. for the time being [L *pro tempore*].
prov. proverbial; providence; provident; province; provincial; provision; provost.
Prov, Prov. Proverbs.
prox. next (month) [L *proximo*].
prs. pairs.
prtd. printed.
prtg. printing.
Prus., Pruss. Prussia; Prussian.
p.r.v., P.R.V. to return a call [F *pour rendre visite*].
p.s., P.S. passenger steamer; permanent secretary; postscript; prompt side (theater); public sale.
ps. pieces; pseudonym.
Ps., Ps, Psa. Psalms.
P.S. Police Sergeant; Privy Seal; Public School.
pseud. pseudonym.
p.s.f., psf pounds per square foot.
p.s.i., psi pounds per square inch.
P.S.R.O. Professional Standards Review Organization.
p.ss., P.SS. postscripts.
PST, P.S.T., P.s.t. Pacific standard time.
psych., psychol. psychological; psychologist; psychology.
psychoanal. psychoanalysis.
p.t. for the time being [L *pro tempore*]; post town; postal telegraph.
pt. part; payment; pint(s); point(s); port; preterit.
Pt platinum.
P.T. Physical Training.
P.T.A., PTA Parent-Teachers' Association.
pta. peseta.
ptbl. portable.
ptg. printing.
pts. parts; payments; pints.
pty. proprietary.
Pu plutonium.
pub. public; publication; published; publisher.
publ. publication; published; publisher.
pulv. pulverized.
punct. punctuation.
pur., purch. purchaser; purchasing.
p.v. par value; post village; priest vicar.
Pvt. Private.
P.W., PW Prisoner of War.
PWA, P.W.A. Public Works Administration.
pwr. power.
pwt. pennyweight.
PX post exchange.
pymt. payment.

Q

q. quart; quarter; quarterly; quarto; query; question; queen.
Q. Quebec.
Q queen (chess).
q., Q. quarto.
q.b., qb quarterback.
Q.B. Queen's Bench.
QB queen's bishop (chess).
QBP queen's bishop's pawn (chess).
Q.C. Quartermaster Corps; Queen's Counsel.
q.d. as if one should say [L *quasi dicat*]; as if said [L *quasi dictum*]; as if he had said [L *quasi dixisset*].
q.e. which is [L *quod est*].
Q.E.D. which was to be demonstrated [L *quod erat demonstrandum*].
Q.E.F. which was to be done [L *quod erat faciendum*].
Q.E.I., q.e.i. which was to be found out [L *quod erat inveniendum*].
q.l. as much as you please [L *quantum libet*].
ql. quintal.
qlty. quality.
QM, Q.M. Quartermaster.
QMC, Q.M.C. Quartermaster Corps.
QMG, Q.M.G., Q.M.Gen. Quartermaster General.
qn. question.
QN queen's knight (chess).
QNP queen's knight's pawn (chess).
QP queen's pawn (chess).
q.pl., Q.P. as much as you wish [L *quantum placeat*].
Qq. quartos.
qq.v. which see (plural) [L *quos vide*].
qr. quarter; quarterly; quire.
QR queen's rook (chess).
QRP queen's rook's pawn (chess).
qrs. farthings [L *quadrantes*]; quarters; quires.
qrtly. quarterly.
q.s. as much as suffices [L *quantum sufficit*]; quarter section.
qt., qt quart.
qt. quantity.
q.t. quiet.
qto. quarto.
qts., qts quarts.
qu. quart; queen; query; question.
quad. quadrangle; quadrant; quadrat; quadrilateral; quadruple.
quar., quart. quarter; quarterly.
Que. Quebec.
ques. question.
quin., quint. quintuple; quintuplet.
quor. quorum.
quot. quotation; quoted.
q.v. as much as you will [L *quantum vis*]; which see [L *quod vide*].
qy. query.

R

r. range; rare; received; recipe; residence; resides; retired; right; right-hand page [L *recto*]; rises; rod; rubber; ruble.
r roentgen(s).
r., r run(s).
r., R. commonwealth [L *res publica*]; king [L *rex*]; queen [L *regina*]; rabbi; railroad; railway; rector; redactor; river; road; royal; ruble; rupee; take [L *recipe*].
r, R resistance (electrical); royal; ruble.
R gas constant (chemistry); radical (chemistry); radius; ratio; Réaumur; Republican; respond or response (ecclesiastical); ring (chemistry); rook (chess).
Ra radium.
R.A. Rear Admiral; right ascension; Royal Academy.
RA, R.A. Regular Army.
rad. radical; radio; radius; root [L *radix*].
RAF, R.A.F. Royal Air Force.
ral., rall. gradually slower [It. *rallentando*].
r and d, R & D, R and D research and development.
R.A.R. radio acoustic ranging.
RB Renegotiation Board.
Rb rubidium.
r.b.i., rbi run(s) batted in.
R.C. Red Cross; Reserve Corps; Roman Catholic.
RCAF, R.C.A.F. Royal Canadian Air Force.
R.C.Ch. Roman Catholic Church.
rcd. received.
R.C.M.P. Royal Canadian Mounted Police.
RCP Royal College of Physicians.
rcpt. receipt.
RCS Royal College of Surgeons.
Rct. Recruit.
rd. rod; round.
rd., Rd. reduce; rix-dollar; road.
RD Research and Development.
R.D. Rural Delivery.
Rd radium.
r.e., re right end.
Re. rupee.
Re rhenium.
R.E. real estate; Reformed Episcopal; Right Excellent; Royal Engineers.
REA, R.E.A. Rural Electrification Administration.
react. reactance (electricity).
rec. receipt; received; recipe; record; recorded; recorder; recording.
recd. received.
recip. reciprocal; reciprocity.
recit. recitative.
rec. sec. recording secretary.
rect. receipt; rectified; rector; rectory.
rec't receipt.
red. reduced; reduction.
redisc. rediscount.
redup., redupl. reduplicated; reduplication.
ref. referee; reference; referred; refining; reformation; reformed.
Ref.Ch. Reformed Church.
refl. reflection; reflective; reflectively; reflex; reflexive.
refrig. refrigeration.
reg. regent; regiment; region; register; registered; registrar; registry; regular; regularly; regulation; regulator.
Reg. Queen [L *regina*].
regt. regent; regiment.
rel. relating; relative; relatively; released; religion; religious.
rel. pron. relative pronoun.
rem. remittance.
REM rapid eye movement.
rep. repair; repeat; report; reporter; representative; reprint; republic.
Rep. Representative; Republic; Republican.
repr. representing; reprinted.
Repub. Republic; Republican.
req. required; requisition.
res. research; reserve; residence; resides; residue; resigned; resistance; resistor; resolution.
resp. respective; respiration; respondent.
restr. restaurant.
Resurr. Resurrection.
ret. retain; retired; returned.
retd. retained; retired; returned.
retrog. retrogressive.
rev. revenue; reverse; reversed; review; revise; revised; revision; revolution; revolving.
Rev, Rev. Revelation; Reverend.
Rev. Ver. Revised Version (of the Bible).
r.f., rf right field(er); right forward.
r.f., R.F., RF radio frequency; range finder; rapid fire; right field.
R.F.A. Royal Field Artillery.
R.F.C. Reconstruction Finance Corporation **(RFC);** Royal Flying Corps.
RFD, R.F.D. Rural Free Delivery.
r.g., rg right guard.
r.h. relative humidity; right hand.
r.h., rh, r.h.b., rhb right halfback.
Rh Rhesus (blood factor); rhodium.
R.H. Royal Highness.
rhap. rhapsody.
rhbdr. rhombohedral.
rhet. rhetoric; rhetorical.
rhin., rhinol. rhinology.
rhomb. rhombic.
r.h.p. rated horsepower.
R.I. King and Emperor [L *Rex et Imperator*]; Queen and Empress [L *Regina et Imperatrix*]; Rhode Island.
RI Rhode Island (P.O. abbr.).
R.I.P. may he (she, or they) rest in peace [L *requiescat*, or *requiescant, in pace*].
rip. supplementary (music) [It. *ripieno*].
rit. retarded (music) [It. *ritardando*].
riv. river.
rkva reactive kilovolt-ampere.
rm. ream; room.
Rm., R.M., RM, r.m. Reichsmark(s).
rms. reams; rooms.
rms, r.m.s. root mean square.
Rn radon.
R.N. registered nurse; Royal Navy.
RNA ribonucleic acid.
R.N.R. Royal Naval Reserve.
R.N.W.M.P. Royal Northwest Mounted Police.
ro. recto; rood.
ROK Republic of Korea.
rom. roman (type).
Rom. Roman; Romance; Romania; Romanian; Romans **(Rom).**
R.O.P. record of production.
rot. rotating; rotation.
ROTC, R.O.T.C. Reserve Officers' Training Corps (Camp).
roul. roulette (philately).
Roum. Roumania; Roumanian.
roy. royal.
R.P. Reformed Presbyterian; Regius Professor.
R.P.D. Doctor of Political Science [L *Rerum Politicarum Doctor*].
rpm, r.p.m. revolutions per minute.
R.P.O. Railway Post Office.
rps, r.p.s. revolutions per second.
rpt. report.
R.R. railroad **(RR.);** Right Reverend.
rr. very rarely [L *rarissime*].
rs, RS. reis; rupees.
R.S. Recording Secretary; Reformed Spelling; Revised Statutes.
R.S.F.S.R., RSFSR Russian Soviet Federated Socialist Republic.
R.S.V., RSV Revised Standard Version (Bible).
r.s.v.p., R.S.V.P. please reply [F *répondez s'il vous plaît*].
r.t., rt right tackle.
rt. right.
Rt. Hon. Right Honorable.
Rt. Rev. Right Reverend.
Rts. rights.
Ru Ruth; ruthenium.
rub. ruble.
Rum. Rumania; Rumanian.
Rus., Russ. Russia; Russian.
RV recreational vehicle.
R.V. Revised Version (Bible).
rva, RVA reactive volt-ampere.
R.W. Right Worshipful; Right Worthy.
Ry., ry. railway.

S

s. sacral; second; section; see; semi-; series; set; shilling [L *solidus*]; sign; signed; silver; singular; sire; solo; son; south-

ern; stem; stock; substantive; sun; surplus.
s., S. buried [L *sepultus*]; fellow [L *socius* or *sodalis*]; lies [L *situs*]; saint; school; scribe; secondary; senate; singular; socialist; society; soprano; steel.
s stere(s).
S., S, s., s south; southern.
s– symmetrical (chemistry).
S. Sabbath; Saturday; Saxon; Senate; September; Signor; Sunday.
S., Sig. signature.
S Seaman; sulfur; knight (in chess) [G *Springer*].
S.A. Salvation Army; sex appeal; South Africa; South America.
Sa samarium; Samuel.
SA Seaman Apprentice.
Sab. Sabbath.
SAC Strategic Air Command.
S.A.E., SAE Society of Automotive Engineers.
S.Afr. South Africa; South African.
SALT, S.A.L.T. Strategic Arms Limitation Talks.
S.Am., S.Amer. South America; South American.
SAM surface-to-air missile.
Sans., Sansk. Sanskrit.
S.ap. apothecary's scruple.
SAR, S.A.R. Sons of the American Revolution.
Sask. Saskatchewan.
sat. saturated; saturation.
Sat. Saturday; Saturn.
SAT Scholastic Aptitude Test.
sav. savings.
s.b., sb stolen base(s).
S.B. Bachelor of Science [L *Scientiae Baccalaureus*]; Shipping Board.
sb. substantive.
Sb. antimony [L *stibium*].
SBA Small Business Administration.
SbE south by east.
SbW south by west.
s.c. salvage charges; sized and calendered; small capitals (printing); supercalendered.
S.C. Signal Corps; South Carolina; Supreme Court.
SC Security Council (of the United Nations).
sc. he (she) carved or engraved it [L *sculpsit*]; namely [L *scilicet*]; scale; scene; science; screw; scruple (weight).
Sc scandium; stratocumulus.
Scan., Scand. Scandinavia; Scandinavian.
s.caps small capitals (printing).
Sc.B. Bachelor of Science [L *Scientiae Baccalaureus*].
Sc.D. Doctor of Science [L *Scientiae Doctor*].
sch. school; schooner.
sched. schedule.
schol. scholar; scholastic.
sci. science; scientific.
sci. fa. show cause [L *scire facias*].
scil. namely [L *scilicet*].
Sc.M. Master of Science [L *Scientiae Magister*].
Scot. Scotland; Scots; Scottish.
scr. scrip; script; scruple (weight).
Script. Scriptural; Scriptures.
sculp., sculpt. he (or she) carved it [L *sculpsit*]; sculptor.
SD Steward.
s.d. indefinitely (without date) [L *sine die*].
s.d., S.D. standard deviation.
S.D. Doctor of Science [L *Scientiae Doctor*].
SD South Dakota (P.O. abbr.).
S.D., S.Dak. South Dakota.
SDR, S.D.R., SDRs, S.D.R.s Special Drawing Rights.
Se selenium.
SE, S.E., se, s.e. southeast; southeastern.
SEATO Southeast Asia Treaty Organization.
sec. according to [L *secundum*]; secant **(sec)**; second(s); secondary; secretary; section(s); sector.
SEC, S.E.C. Securities and Exchange Commission.
sec.–ft. second–foot.
sech hyperbolic secant.
sec.leg. according to law [L *secundum legem*].
sec.reg. according to rule [L *secundum regulam*].
secs. seconds; sections.
sect. section; sectional.
secy. secretary.
seg. segment.
seismol. seismology.
sel. selected; selection(s).
Sem. Seminary; Semitic.
sen., Sen. senate; senator; senior.
sent. sentence.
sep. sepal; separate.
Sep., Sept. September **(Sep)**; Septuagint.
seq. sequel.
seq., seqq. the following [L *sequens, sequentia*].
ser. serial; series; sermon.
serv. servant; service.
sess. session.
sf., sforz., sfz. with emphasis (music) [It. *sforzando, sforzato*].
S.F.S.R. Soviet Federated Socialist Republic.
s.g. specific gravity.
sg, s.g. senior grade.
sgd. signed.
Sgt. Sergeant.
sh. share; sheet; shilling(s); shunt.
SHAEF Supreme Headquarters, Allied Expeditionary Forces.
Shak. Shakespeare.
SHAPE Supreme Headquarters Allied Powers (Europe).
SHF, S.H.F., shf, s.h.f. superhigh frequency.
shipt., shpt. shipment.
shtg. shortage.
sh.tn. short ton.
Si silicon.
S.I. Staten Island (N.Y.).
Sib. Siberia; Siberian.
sig., Sig. signal; signature; signor; signore; signori.
sigill. seal [L *sigillum*].
sim. simile.
sin sine.
sing. singular.
sinh hyperbolic sine.
sist. sister.
s.j. under consideration [L *sub judice*].
S.J. Society of Jesus [L *Societas Jesu*].
S.J.D. Doctor of Juridical Science [L *Scientiae Juridicae Doctor*].
sk. sack.
Skr., Skt. Sanskrit.
s.l. without place (of publication) [L *sine loco*].
s.l.a.n. without place, date, or name [L *sine loco, anno, vel nomine*].
S. lat. south latitude.
Slav. Slavic; Slavonian.
sld. sailed; sealed.
SLIC, S.L.I.C. Savings and Loan Insurance Corporation.
s.l.p. without lawful issue [L *sine legitima prole*].
sm. small.
Sm samarium.
S.M. Master of Science [L *Scientiae Magister*]; Sergeant Major; State Militia.
sm.c., sm.caps small capitals.
smorz. dying away (music) [It. *smorzando*].
s.m.p. without male issue [L *sine mascula prole*].
s.n. without name [L *sine nomine*].
Sn tin [L *stannum*].
s.o., so struck out.
s.o. seller's option.
So. south; southern.
soc. socialist; society.
sociol. sociological; sociology.
sol. solicitor; soluble; solution.
Sol. Solomon.
soln. solution.
Som. Somaliland.
son. sonata.
SOP, S.O.P. standard operating procedure.
sop. soprano.
sos., sost., sosten. sustained (music) [It. *sostenuto*].
s.p. single phase; single pole; without issue [L *sine prole*].
SP shore patrol; shore police.
sp. special; species; specific; specimen; spelling; spirit(s).
Sp. Spain; Spaniard; Spanish.
S.P.A.S. Fellow of the American Philosophical Society [L *Societatis Philosophiae Americanae Socius*].
S.P.C.A. Society for the Prevention of Cruelty to Animals.
S.P.C.C. Society for the Prevention of Cruelty to Children.
spec. special; specification; speculation.
specif. specifically.
spg. spring.
sp. gr. specific gravity.
sp. ht. specific heat.
sph. spherical.
spp. species (plural).
S.P.R. Society for Psychical Research.
spt. seaport.
sq. square; sequence; the following [L *sequentia*].
Sq. Squadron; Square (street).
sq. ft. square foot; square feet.
sq. in. square inch(es).
sq. m., sq. mi. square mile(s).
sq. rd. square rod(s).
sq. yd. square yard(s).
sr steradian.
Sr. Senior; Señor; Sir; Sister.
Sr strontium.
Sra. Señora.
S.R.O. standing room only.
Srta. Señorita.
s.s., ss., ss shortstop.
ss namely (in law) [L *scilicet*].
SS. Saints.
S.S. Silver Star; Sunday School; written above [L *supra scriptum*].
SS, S.S., S/S steamship.
SS., SS Nazi guards [G *Schutzstaffeln*].
SSA, S.S.A. Social Security Act (Administration).
SSB, S.S.B. Social Security Board.
SSE, S.S.E., sse, s.s.e. south–southeast.
S.Sgt., S/Sgt Staff Sergeant.
SSR, S.S.R. Soviet Socialist Republic.
SSS Selective Service System.
SST supersonic transport.
SSW, S.S.W., ssw, s.s.w. south–southwest.
s.t. short ton.
st. stand; stanza; stere; stet; stitch; stone (weight); street; strophe.
st., St. statute(s); street.
St. Saint; Straight; Strait.
St stratus (clouds).
sta. station; stationary; stator.
Sta. Santa; Station.
stac., stacc. staccato.
stan. stanchion.
Staph. staphylococcus.
stat. immediately [L *statim*]; static; stationary; statistics; statuary; statute; statutes.
S.T.B. Bachelor of Sacred Theology [L *Sacrae Theologiae Baccalaureus*].
stbd. starboard.
std. standard.
S.T.D. Doctor of Sacred Theology [L *Sacrae Theologiae Doctor*].
Ste. Sainte.
steno., stenog. stenographer; stenography.
ster., stg. sterling.
St.Ex. Stock Exchange.
stge. storage.
stip. stipend; stipendiary; stipulation.
Stir. Stirling; Stirlingshire.
stk. stock.
STOL, S.T.O.L. short take–off and landing.
stor. storage.
S.T.P. Professor of Sacred Theology [L *Sacrae Theologiae Professor*].
stp. stamped.
STP standard temperature and pressure.
str. steamer; strait; string(s).
Strep. streptococcus.
stud. student.
sub. subaltern; submarine; subscription; substitute; suburb; suburban; understand (or supply) [L *subaudi*].
subd. subdivision.
subj. subject; subjective; subjunctive.
subs. subscription; subsidiary.
subseq. subsequent; subsequently.
subst. substantive; substitute.
succ. successor.
suf., suff. suffix.
sug., sugg. suggested; suggestion.
Sun., Sund. Sunday.
sup. above [L *supra*]; superfine; superior; superlative; supplement; supplementary; supply; supreme.
super. superfine; superintendent; superior; supernumerary.
superl. superlative.
supp., suppl. supplement; supplementary.
supr. supreme.
supt., Supt. superintendent.
sur. surcharged; surplus.
surg. surgeon; surgery; surgical.
surr. surrender; surrendered.
surv. survey; surveying; surveyor; surviving.
susp. suspended.
s.v. sailing vessel; under this word [L *sub verbo*].
S.V. Holy Virgin [L *Sancta Virgo*].
SW, S.W., sw, s.w. southwest; southwestern.
Sw., Swe., Swed. Sweden; Swedish.
S.W.A., S.W.Afr. South–West Africa.
Swit., Switz., Swtz. Switzerland.
syl., syll. syllable.
sym. symbol; symmetrical; symphony.
syn. synchronize; synonym; synonymous; synonymy.
syr. syrup (pharmacy).
Syr. Syria; Syriac; Syrian.
syst. system; systematic.

T

t. in the time of [L *tempore*]; tare; target; teaspoon(s); telephone; temperature; tempo; tenor; tense (grammar); terminal; territory; time; tome; ton(s); town; township; transit; transitive; troy (weight); volume [L *tomus*].
T. tablespoon(s); Testament; Tuesday; Trinity; Turkish.
T tantalum; Technician; temperature (absolute); tension (surface); time.
Ta tantalum.
TAB Technical Assistance Board.
tab. table(s).
TAC Tactical Air Command; Technical Assistance Committee.
tal. qual. as they come (or average quality) [L *talis qualis*].
tan tangent.
tanh hyperbolic tangent.
TAP Technical Assistance Program.
tart. tartaric.
taut. tautological; tautology.
t.b. trial balance.
TB, T.B., Tb., Tb, t.b., tb tubercle bacillus; tuberculosis.
Tb terbium.
tbs., tbsp. tablespoon(s); tablespoonful(s).
TC Trusteeship Council (of the United Nations).
Tc technetium.
tc. tierce(s).
tchr. teacher.
td., td, TD touchdown.
TD Tank Destroyer; Tradevman.
TD, T.D. Traffic Director; Treasury Department.
t.d.n. total digestible nutrients.
Te tellurium.
tech. technical; technological; technology.
technol. technology.
tel. telegram; telegraph; telegraphic; telephone.
telecom. telecommunication(s).
teleg. telegram; telegraph; telegraphic; telegraphy.
temp. in the time of [L *tempore*]; temperature; temporary.
ten. tenement; tenor; tenuto (music).
Tenn. Tennessee.
ter., terr. terrace; territorial; territory.
term. terminal; termination; terminology.
test. testamentary; testator.
Test. Testament.
tetr., tetrag. tetragonal.
Teut. Teuton; Teutonic.
Tex. Texas; Texan.
tfr. transfer.
t.g. type genus.
tgt. target.
Th., Thur., Thurs. Thursday.
Th thorium.
Th.B. Bachelor of Theology [L *Theologiae Baccalaureus*].
Th.D. Doctor of Theology [L *Theologiae Doctor*].
Th–Em thoron (thorium emanation).
theol. theologian; theological; theology.
theor. theorem.
theos. theosophical; theosophist; theosophy.
therm. thermometer.
thermochem. thermochemical; thermochemistry.
thermodynam. thermodynamics.
Thess. Thessalonians; Thessaly.
T.H.I., T.-H.-I. temperature-humidity index.
Ti titanium.
t.i.d. three times daily [L *ter in die*].
tinct. tincture.
tit. title.
Tit., Tit Titus.
tk. truck.
TKO, t.k.o., T.K.O. technical knockout.
Tl thallium.
T/L time loan.
T.L. trade–last.
t.m. true mean.
Tm thulium.
TN Tennessee (P.O. abbr.).
tn. ton; train.
Tn thoron.
tng. training.
TNT, T.N.T. trinitrotoluene; trinitrotoluol.
t.o. turnover; turn over.
tonn. tonnage.
top., topog. topographical; topography.
t.p. title page.
tp. township; troop.
t.p.r. temperature, pulse, respiration.
tps. townships.
Tr terbium.
Tr. Troop.
tr. tare; tincture; trace; train; transitive; translated; translation; translator; transpose; treasurer; trust.
trag. tragedy; tragic.
trans. transactions; transfer; transferred; transitive; translated; translation; translator; transportation; transpose; transverse.
transf. transfer; transference; transferred.
transl. translated; translation(s).
transp. transparent; transportation.
trav. traveler; travels.
treas. treasurer; treasury.
trf, t.r.f., t–r–f tuned radio frequency.
trfd. transferred.
tricl. triclinic (crystal).
trig., trigon. trigonometric; trigonometry.
trim. trimetric (crystal).
tripl. triplicate.
trit. triturate.
trop. tropic; tropical; tropics.
t.s. tensile strength.
T.Sgt., T/Sgt Technical Sergeant.
tsp. teaspoon(s); teaspoonful(s).
Tu., Tues. Tuesday.
Tu thulium.
T.U. Trade Union; Training Unit.
T.U.C., TUC Trades Union Congress.
Turk. Turkey; Turkish.
TV television; terminal velocity.
TVA, T.V.A. Tennessee Valley Authority (Administration).
twp. township.
TX Texas (P.O. abbr.).
Ty. Territory.
typ., typo., typog. typographer; typographic; typography.
typw. typewriter; typewritten.

U

u. and [G *und*].
u., U. uncle; university; upper.
U uranium.
UAW, U.A.W. United Automobile, Aircraft and Agricultural Implement Workers; United Automobile Workers of America.
u.c. upper case (printing).
UCMJ Uniform Code of Military Justice.
UFO, ufo unidentified flying object(s).
UHF, U.H.F., uhf, u.h.f. ultrahigh frequency.
U.J.D. Doctor of Civil and Canon Law [L *Utriusque Juris Doctor*].
U.K. United Kingdom.
Ukr. Ukraine.
ult. ultimate; ultimately.
ult., ulto. last month [L *ultimo*].
UMT Universal Military Training.
UMTS Universal Military Training Service (System).
UMW, U.M.W. United Mine Workers of America.
UN, U.N. United Nations.
unabr. unabridged.
unb., unbd. unbound (bookbinding).
undsgd. undersigned.
undtkr. undertaker.
UNEDA United Nations Economic Development Administration.
UNESCO, Unesco United Nations Educational, Scientific, and Cultural Organization.
ung. ointment [L *unguentum*].
UNICEF United Nations Children's Fund.
Unit. Unitarian; Unitarianism.
univ. universal; universally; university.
Univ. Universalist.
UNKRA United Nations Korean Reconstruction Agency.
unl. unlimited.
unm. unmarried.
UNO United Nations Organization.
unof. unofficial.
unp. unpaged.
unpub. unpublished.
UNREF United Nations Refu-

gee Emergency Fund.
UNRRA United Nations Relief and Rehabilitation Administration.
UNRWA United Nations Relief and Works Agency.
UNSCOB United Nations Special Committee on the Balkans.
U.P., UP Union Pacific (Railroad); United Press.
UPI, U.P.I. United Press International.
Ur uranium.
urol. urology.
Uru. Uruguay.
u.s. in the place mentioned above [L *ubi supra*]; as above. [L *ut supra*].
US, U.S. United States.
USA, U.S.A. United States of America; United States Army.
USAF, U.S.A.F. United States Air Force.
USAFI, U.S.A.F.I. United States Armed Forces Institute.
U.S.C. & G.S. United States Coast and Geodetic Survey.
USCG, U.S.C.G. United States Coast Guard.
USDA, U.S.D.A. United States Department of Agriculture.
USES, U.S.E.S. United States Employment Service.
USHA, U.S.H.A. United States Housing Authority (Administration).
USIA, U.S.I.A. United States Information Agency.
USIBA United States International Book Association.
USIS, U.S.I.S. United States Information Service.
USM, U.S.M. United States Mail; United States Marines; United States Mint.
USMA, U.S.M.A. United States Military Academy.
USMC, U.S.M.C. United States Marine Corps; United States Maritime Commission.
USN, U.S.N. United States Navy.
USNA, U.S.N.A. United States National Army; United States Naval Academy.
USNG, U.S.N.G. United States National Guard.
USNR, U.S.N.R. United States Naval Reserve.
USO, U.S.O. United Service Organizations.
USP, U.S.P. United States Patent; United States Pharmacopoeia **(U. S. Pharm.)**.
U.S.P.H.S., USPHS United States Public Health Service.
U.S.P.O. United States Post Office.
U.S.S. United States Senate; United States Ship (Steamer) **(USS)**.
U.S.S.B., USSB United States Shipping Board.
U.S.S.Ct. United States Supreme Court.
U.S.S.R., USSR Union of Soviet Socialist Republics.
usu. usual; usually.
u.s.w., usw and so forth [G *und so weiter*].
U.S.W.A. United Steel Workers of America.
u.t. universal time.
ut. utility.
Ut. Utah.
UT Utah (P.O. abbr.).
ut dict. as directed [L *ut dictum*].
ut sup. as above [L *ut supra*].
U.T.W.A. United Textile Workers of America.
ux. wife [L *uxor*].

V

v. of [G *von*]; see [L *vide*]; valve; ventral; verb; verse; version; versus; vicar; vice-; village; vision; vocative; voice; voltage; volunteer(s); von.
v., V. volt; volume.
V. Venerable; Viscount.
V vanadium; vector; velocity; victory; volume.
v.a. verb active; verbal adjective.
va volt-ampere(s).
Va. Virginia.
V.A. Veterans Administration **(VA)**; Vicar Apostolic; Vice Admiral; (Order of) Victoria and Albert.
VA Virginia (P.O. abbr.).
vac. vacuum.
val. valentine; valuation; value.
var. variant; variation; variety; various.
var reactive volt-ampere.
Vat. Vatican.
VAT value-added tax.
v. aux. verb auxiliary.
vb. verb; verbal.
vb. n. verbal noun.
V.C. Veterinary Corps; Vice Chairman; Vice Chancellor; Vice Consul; Victoria Cross.
v.d. vapor density; various dates.
Vd vanadium.
V.D., VD, v.d. venereal disease.
veg. vegetable; vegetation.
vel. vellum (bookbinding).
Ven. Venerable; Venice; Venus.
Venez. Venezuela.
vent. ventilating; ventilation; ventilator.
ver. verse(s); version.
vers versed sine, versine.
vert. vertebra; vertebrate; vertical.
ves. vessel; vestry; vesicle; vesicular.
vet. veteran; veterinarian; veterinary.
veter. veterinary.
VFW, V.F.W. Veterans of Foreign Wars.
V.G. Vicar General.
v.g. for example [L *verbi gratia*].
VHF, V.H.F., vhf, v.h.f. very high frequency.
v.i. see below [L *vide infra*]; verb intransitive.
V.I. Virgin Islands.
Vi virginium.
VI Virgin Islands (P.O. abbr.).
vic. vicar; vicarage.
Vic., Vict. Victoria; Victorian.
vid. for example (see) [L *vide*].
vil. village.
v.imp. verb impersonal.
VIP, V.I.P. very important person.
v.irr. verb irregular.
vis. visibility; visual.
Vis., Visc., Visct. Viscount; Viscountess.
viv. lively (music) [It. *vivace*].
viz., viz namely [L *videlicet*].
VL, V.L. Vulgar Latin.
VLF, V.L.F., vlf, v.l.f. very low frequency.
vm. voltmeter.
V.M.D. Doctor of Veterinary Medicine [L *Veterinariae Medicinae Doctor*].
v.n., v.neut. verb neuter.
vo. verso.
vocab. vocabulary.
vol. volcano; volume; volunteer.
volc. volcanic; volcano.
vols. volumes.
vox pop. voice of the people [L *vox populi*].
voy. voyage.
v.p. various pagings; various places; verb passive; voting pool (stocks).
V.P. Vice President.
V.R. Queen Victoria [L *Victoria Regina*].
v.r. verb reflexive.
V. Rev. Very Reverend.
v.s. see above [L *vide supra*]; vibration seconds (sound); volumetric solution.
vs. versus.
V.S. Veterinary Surgeon.
VSS versions.
VT Vermont (P.O. abbr.).
v.t. verb transitive.
Vt. Vermont.
VTOL Vertical takeoff and landing.
Vul., Vulg. Vulgate.
vulg. vulgar; vulgarity.
v.v. vice versa.
vv. verses; violins.

W

w. wanting; warden; warehousing; week(s); weight; wide; width; wife; with; word; work.
W, W., w, w. watt; west; western.
w., w won.
W. Wales; Washington; Wednesday; Welsh.
W tungsten [G *wolfram*].
WA Washington (P.O. abbr.).
WAC, W.A.C. Women's Army Corps.
w.a.e. when actually employed.
WAF, W.A.F. Women in the Air Force.
war. warrant.
Wash. Washington.
WASP, W.A.S.P. Women's Air Force Service Pilots.
watt-hr watt-hour(s).
WAVES, W.A.V.E.S. Women Appointed for Voluntary Emergency Service.
w.b. warehouse book; water ballast; westbound.
W.B., W/B, W/b, W.b. waybill.
WbN west by north.
WbS west by south.
w.c. water closet; without charge.
W.C.T.U. Women's Christian Temperance Union.
Wed. Wednesday.
w.f., wf wrong font (printing).
W.Flem. West Flemish.
WFTU, W.F.T.U. World Federation of Trade Unions.
WGmc., W.Ger. West Germanic.
wh, wh., whr, whr., w.-hr. watt-hour(s).
whf. wharf.
WHO World Health Organization.
w.i. when issued (stocks); wrought iron.
W.I. West Indies; West Indian.
WI Wisconsin (P.O. abbr.).
W.Ind. West Indies.
Wis., Wisc. Wisconsin.
wk. weak; week; work.
wkly. weekly.
wks. weeks; works.
w.l., WL water line; wavelength.
wldr. welder.
W. long. west longitude.
wm wattmeter.
wmk. watermark.
WMO World Meteorological Organization.
WNW, W.N.W., wnw, w.n.w. west-northwest.
WO, W.O. wait order; Warrant Officer.
w.p., W.P. weather permitting; wire payment.
WPA, W.P.A. Work Projects Administration; Works Progress Administration.
WRAC, W.R.A.C. Women's Royal Army Corps.
WRAF, W.R.A.F. Women's Royal Air Force.
WREN, W.R.N.S. Women's Royal Naval Service.
wrnt. warrant.
WSW, W.S.W., wsw, w.s.w. west-southwest.
wt., wt weight.
WV West Virginia (P.O. abbr.).
W.Va. West Virginia.
WVS, W.V.S. Women's Volunteer Service (Brit.).
WY Wyoming (P.O. abbr.).
Wyo. Wyoming.

X

x symbol for an unknown quantity.
X Christ; Christian; a ten-dollar bill; xenon.
x.c., X.C. ex-coupon.
x.d., X.D., x-div. ex-dividend.
Xe xenon.
xi., X.I., x-int. ex-interest.
Xmas Christmas.
Xn. Christian.
Xnty., Xty. Christianity.
x-ref. cross-reference.
X-rts. ex-rights.
Xtian. Christian.
xyl. xylograph.

Y

y. yard(s); year(s); younger; youngest.
Y. Young Men's (Women's) Christian Association.
Y yttrium.
Yb ytterbrium.
yd. yard(s).
yds. yards.
Yid. Yiddish.
Y.M., Y.M.C.A., YMCA Young Men's Christian Association.
Y.M.H.A., YMHA Young Men's Hebrew Association.
Y.P.S.C.E. Young People's Society of Christian Endeavor.
yr. year(s); younger; your.
yrs. years; yours.
Y.T. Yukon Territory.
Yt yttrium.
Y.W., Y.W.C.A., YWCA Young Women's Christian Association.
Y.W.H.A., YWHA Young Women's Hebrew Association.

Z

z., Z. zone.
Z zenith distance.
Zec, Zech. Zechariah.
Zep, Zeph. Zephaniah.
Z/F zone of fire.
Zn zinc.
zool. zoological; zoologist; zoology.
Zr zirconium.

Gazetteer

This section lists all of the more important political divisions and geographical features of the world, and all the urban localities in the United States and Canada having a population of 15,000 or more. The population figures given for places in the United States are from the census of 1980; those for Canada are from the census of 1976. All other population figures are rounded to the nearest thousand. Maps of virtually all countries and of other important geographical features may be found in the main section of this dictionary at the appropriate alphabetic place of entry.

Postal ZIP codes are included for places in the United States. These were not, however, available in all cases. The asterisk (*) following some ZIP codes indicates that the city is further divided into postal zones and that the number given does not adequately identify a post office. In such cases further information is available from local postal authorities.

In the table below the authorized post office abbreviations of U.S. states are listed.

Alabama	**AL**	**Kentucky**	**KY**	**Ohio**	**OH**
Alaska	**AK**	**Louisiana**	**LA**	**Oklahoma**	**OK**
Arizona	**AZ**	**Maine**	**ME**	**Oregon**	**OR**
Arkansas	**AR**	**Maryland**	**MD**	**Pennsylvania**	**PA**
California	**CA**	**Massachusetts**	**MA**	**Puerto Rico**	**PR**
Colorado	**CO**	**Michigan**	**MI**	**Rhode Island**	**RI**
Connecticut	**CT**	**Minnesota**	**MN**	**South Carolina**	**SC**
Delaware	**DE**	**Mississippi**	**MS**	**South Dakota**	**SD**
District of Columbia	**DC**	**Missouri**	**MO**	**Tennessee**	**TN**
		Montana	**MT**	**Texas**	**TX**
Florida	**FL**	**Nebraska**	**NE**	**Utah**	**UT**
Georgia	**GA**	**Nevada**	**NV**	**Vermont**	**VT**
Hawaii	**HI**	**New Hampshire**	**NH**	**Virginia**	**VA**
Idaho	**ID**	**New Jersey**	**NJ**	**Virgin Islands**	**VI**
Illinois	**IL**	**New Mexico**	**NM**	**Washington**	**WA**
Indiana	**IN**	**New York**	**NY**	**West Virginia**	**WV**
Iowa	**IA**	**North Carolina**	**NC**	**Wisconsin**	**WI**
Kansas	**KS**	**North Dakota**	**ND**	**Wyoming**	**WY**

The following abbreviations have been used throughout this section:

ab.	about	pop.	population
adm.	administrative	poss.	possession
ASSR	Autonomous Soviet Socialist Republic	prot.	protectorate
		prov.	province
betw.	between	reg.	region
boro.	borough	RSFSR	Russian Soviet Federated Socialist Republic
cap(s).	capital(s)		
CEN.	central		
co.	county	S	south(ern)
col.	colony	SE	southeast(ern)
ctr.	center	sq. mi.	square mile(s)
dept.	department	SSR	Soviet Socialist Republic
dist.	district		
div.	division	SW	southwest(ern)
E	east(ern)	terr.	territory
ft.	feet	twp.	township
isl(s).	island(s)	uninc.	unincorporated
mi.	mile(s)	urb.	urban
mtn(s).	mountain(s)	USSR	Union of Societ Socialist Republics
N	north(ern)		
NE	northeaster(ern)	vill.	village
NW	northwest(ern)	W	west(ern)
penin.	peninsula		

Aachen city, W West Germany; pop. 242,971.
Aarhus co., E Denmark; 310 sq. mi.; pop. 534,000.
— city, E Aarhus co.; cap.; pop. 238,000.
Aberdeen co., NE Scotland; 1,972 sq. mi.; pop. 324,574.
— city, SE Aberdeen co.; cap.; pop. 183,000.
— city, NE South Dakota 57401*; pop. 26,476.
— city, W Washington 98520; pop. 18,739.
Abidjan city, SE Ivory Coast; cap.; pop. 500,000.
Abilene city, CEN. Texas 79600; pop. 98,315.
Acapulco city, SW Mexico; pop. 456,655.
Accra city, S Ghana; cap.; pop. 564,000.
Achaea dept., N Peloponessus, Greece; 1,146 sq. mi.; pop. 229,000; cap. Patras.
Aconcagua extinct volcano, CEN. Argentina; 22,831 ft.
Acre city, NE Israel; pop. 24,000.
Addis Ababa city, CEN. Ethiopia; cap.; pop. 1,250,000.
Addison vill. NE Illinois 60101; pop. 28,836.
Adelaide city, SE South Australia; cap.; pop. 933,350.
Aden former British col.; now part of People's Democratic Republic of Yemen.
— city, People's Democratic Republic of Yemen; pop. 264,-000.
Aden, Gulf of inlet of Arabian Sea betw. People's Democratic Republic of Yemen and Somalia.
Aden Protectorate Formerly, group of Arab tribal districts comprising a British protectorate; now part of People's Democratic Republic of Yemen.
Adirondack Mountains mtn. range, NE New York.
Adrian city, SE Michigan 49221; pop. 21,186.
Adriatic Sea inlet of the Mediterranean Sea, E of Italy.
Aegean Sea inlet of the Mediterranean Sea betw. Greece and Asia Minor.
Afghanistan republic, SW Asia; 250,000 sq. mi.; pop. 16,250,000; cap. Kabul.
Africa second largest continent, S of Europe and W of Asia; 11,710,000 sq. mi.
Afton town, NE Missouri 63123; pop. 24,067.
Agaña city, W Guam 96910; cap.; pop. 1,642.
Agawam town, W Massachusetts 01001; pop. 21,717.
Agra city, N India; site of Taj Mahal; pop. 592,000.
Aguadilla town, NW Puerto Rico 00603*; pop. 15,943.
Aguascalientes state, CEN. Mexico; 2,499 sq. mi.; pop. 338,000.
— city, CEN. Aguascalientes state; cap.; pop. 238,694.
Agulhas, Cape cape, S South Africa; southernmost point of Africa.
Ahmedabad city, W India; former cap. of Gujarat; pop. 2,515,195.
Aisne river, N France; 175 mi. long.
Ajaccio city, W Corsica; cap.; birthplace of Napoleon; pop. 41,000.
Akron city, NE Ohio 44300*; pop. 237,177.
Alabama state, SE United States; 51,609 sq. mi.; pop. 3,890,061; cap. Montgomery.
Alameda city, W California 94501*; pop. 63,852.
— vill., SE Idaho 83201; pop. 40,036.
Alamogordo town, S New Mexico 88310; site of the first atom bomb test; pop. 24,024.
Alaska state of the United States, NW North America; 586,400 sq. mi.; pop. 400,481; cap. Juneau.
Alaska, Gulf of inlet of the Pacific on the S coast of Alaska.
Alaska Highway road joining Dawson Creek, British Columbia and Fairbanks, Alaska; 1,527 mi.
Alaska Peninsula promontory of SW Alaska; ab. 400 mi. long.
Alaska Range mtn. range, CEN. Alaska.
Albania Balkan republic S of Yugoslavia; 11,100 sq. mi.; pop. 2,800,000; cap. Tirana.
Albany city, SW Georgia 31701*; pop. 73,934.
— city, E New York 12200*; cap.; pop. 101,727.
— city, W Oregon 97321; pop. 26,546.
Albemarle Sound inlet of the Atlantic, NE North Carolina.
Alberta prov., W Canada; 255,285 sq. mi.; pop. 1,838,037; cap. Edmonton.
Albert Lea city, S Minnesota 56007; pop. 19,190.
Albuquerque city, NW New Mexico 87100*; pop. 331,767.
Alcan Highway Alaska Highway: *unofficial name.*
Alderney island, N Channel Islands; 3 sq. mi.
Aleppo city, NE Syria; pop. 640,000.
Aleutian Islands isl. group, SW of Alaska Peninsula.
Alexandria N Egypt; summer cap., pop. 2,318,655.
— city, CEN. Louisiana 71301*; pop. 51,379.
— city, NE Virginia 22300*; pop. 102,494.
Algeria republic, NW Africa; 919,352 sq. mi.; pop. 20,250,000; cap. Algiers.
Algiers city, N Algeria; cap.; pop. 2,500,000.
Alhambra city, SW California 91800*; pop. 64,615.
Alicante prov., E Spain; 2,264 sq. mi.; pop. 920,000.
— city, E Alicante prov.; cap.; pop. 163,000.
Alice city, S Texas 78332; pop. 20,961.
Aliquippa boro., W Pennsylvania 15001; pop. 17,094.
Alisal vill., W California 93901; pop. 16,473.
Allahabad city N India; pop. 491,000.
Allegheny Mountains mtn. range of Appalachian system; extends from Pennsylvania through Virginia.
Allegheny River river, W New York and Pennsylvania; 325 mi. long.
Allen Park vill., SE Michigan 48101*; pop. 34,196.
Allentown city, E Pennsylvania 18100*; pop. 103,758.
Alliance city, NE Ohio 44601*; pop. 24,315.
Alma city, S Quebec, Canada; pop. 22,622.
Alma Ata city, SE Kazakh SSR; cap.; pop. 910,000.
Alps mtn. system, S Europe; extends from S coast of France to W coast of Yugoslavia.
Alsace reg. and former prov., NE France.
Alsace-Lorraine oft-disputed border reg., NE France; adjoins SW Germany.
Altadena uninc. place, SW California 91001*; pop. 42,380.
Altai Mountains mtn. system, CEN. Asia.
Altamont uninc. place, S Oregon; pop. 15,746.
Alton city, SW Illinois 62002*; pop. 34,171.
Altoona city, CEN. Pennsylvania 16601*; pop. 57,078.
Altus city, SW Oklahoma 73521*; pop. 23,101.
Alum Rock uninc. place, SW California; pop. 18,355.
Amarillo city, NW Texas 79100*; pop. 149,230.
Amazon river, N South America; 3,910 mi. long; carries the largest volume of water of all rivers.
America **1** The United States of America. **2** North and South America; the western Hemisphere.
American Samoa See SAMOA.
Americus city, CEN. Georgia 31709; pop. 16,120.
Ames city, CEN. Iowa 50010*; pop. 45,775.
Amherst uninc. place, CEN. Massachusetts 01002*; pop. 33,229.
Amiens city, N France; pop. 135,992.
Amman city, CEN. Jordan; cap.; pop. 732,587.
Amoy isl. of China, Formosa Strait.
— city, Amoy isl.; pop. 224,000.
Amritsar city, W Punjab, India; pop. 407,000.
Amsterdam city, W Netherlands; cap.; pop. 957,700.
— city, CEN. New York 12010*; pop. 25,524.
Amur river, E Asia; 2,700 mi. long.
Anaheim city, SW California 92800*; pop. 221,847.
Anatolia penin. at W end of Asia; comprises most of Turkey.
Anchorage city, S Alaska 99501*; pop. 173,017.
Andalusia reg., S Spain.
Anderson city, CEN. Indiana 46010*; pop. 64,695.
— city, NW South Carolina 29621*; pop. 27,313.
Andes mtn. range, W South America; connects with the Rockies; over 4,000 mi. long.
Andorra republic betw. France and Spain; 179 sq. mi.; pop. 36,000.
— city, CEN. Andorra; cap.; pop. 2,700.
Andover town, NE Massachusetts 01810*; pop. 26,370.
Angel Falls waterfall, SE Venezuela; over 3,300 ft.
Angola republic, W Africa; 481,351 sq. mi.; pop. 7,819,000; cap. Luanda.
Anjou town, S Quebec, Canada; pop. 34,000.
Ankara city, CEN. Turkey; cap.; pop. 2,561,765.
Annandale uninc. place, NE Virginia 22003; pop. 27,428.
Annapolis city, CEN. Maryland 21400*; cap.; site of U.S. Naval Academy; pop. 31,740.
Ann Arbor city, SE Michigan 48103*; pop. 107,317.
Anniston city, NE Alabama 36201*; pop. 29,523.
Ansonia city, SW Connecticut 06401; pop. 19,039.

Antarctica continent surrounding the South Pole; over 5 million sq. mi. Also **Antarctic Continent.**
Antarctic Circle parallel of latitude at 66°33′S; the boundary of the South Frigid Zone.
Antarctic Ocean parts of Atlantic, Pacific, and Indian oceans bordering on Antarctica.
Antarctic Zone region enclosed by the Antarctic Circle.
Antiqua island group of the West Indies; 171 sq. mi.; pop. 62,000; cap. St. John's.
Antilles islands of the West Indies excluding the Bahamas; comprises Greater Antilles: Cuba, Hispaniola, Jamaica, and Puerto Rico: and Lesser Antilles: Trinidad, the Windward Islands, the Leeward Islands, and other small islands.
Antioch city, S Turkey; pop. 74,000.
— city, W California 94509; pop. 43,559.
Antwerp city, N Belgium; pop. 927,200.
Apennines mtn. range of Italy S of Po valley.
Appalachian Mountains E North America.
Appleton city, E Wisconsin 54910*; pop. 59,032.
Aquitaine reg., SW France.
Arabia penin., SW Asia, betw. the Red Sea and Persian Gulf.
Arabian Sea part of the Indian Ocean betw. Arabia and India.
Arab Republic of Egypt See EGYPT.
Aragon reg., NE Spain.
Aral Sea salt inland sea, CEN. **USSR.**
Ararat, Mount mtn., E Turkey; 17,011 ft.; traditional landing place of Noah's ark.
Arcadia dept., CEN. Peloponnesus, Greece; 1,168 sq. mi.; pop. 112,000; cap. Tripolis.
— city, SW California 91006*; pop. 45,994.
Arctic Circle parallel of latitude at 66°33′N; the boundary of the North Frigid Zone.
Arctic Ocean sea, N of Arctic Circle, surrounding North Pole.
Arden-Arcade uninc. place, CEN. California 95825; pop. 82,492.
Ardmore city, S Oklahoma 73401; pop. 23,689.
Arecibo town, N Puerto Rico 00612*; pop. 28,828.
Argentina republic, S South America; 1,084,362 sq. mi.; pop. 27,400,000; cap. Buenos Aires.
Argonne ridge, N France; site of battles in World Wars I and II.
Arizona state, SW United States; 113,909 sq. mi.; pop. 2,717,866; cap. Phoenix.
Arkansas state, CEN. United States; 53,104 sq. mi.; pop. 2,285,513; cap. Little Rock.
Arkhangelsk city, NW RSFSR; pop. 350,000.
Arlington town, E Massachusetts 02174; pop. 48,219;
— city, N Texas 76010*; pop. 160,123.
— city, NE Virginia 22201; pop. 174,284.
— urb. co., NE Virginia; site of **Arlington National Cemetery,** containing tomb of the Unknown Soldier.
Arlington Heights vill., NE Illinois 60004*; pop. 66,116
Armenia **1** former country, SW Asia. **2** the Armenian SSR.
Armenian SSR republic, S USSR; 11,500 sq. mi.; pop. 2,785,000; cap. Yerevan.
Arnhem city, E Netherlands; pop. 132,000.
Arvada town, CEN. Colorado 80002*; pop. 84,576.
Arvida city, CEN. Quebec, Canada; pop. 18,448.
Asbury Park city, E New Jersey 07712*; pop. 17,015.
Ascension isl. poss. of Great Britain, South Atlantic; 34 sq. mi.; pop. 750.
Asheville city, W North Carolina 28800*; pop. 53,281.
Ashland city, NE Kentucky 41101; pop. 27,064.
— city, CEN. Ohio 44805; pop. 20,326.
Ashtabula city, NE Ohio 44004*; pop. 23,449.
Asia E part of Eurasian land mass; largest of the continents; 16,900,000 sq. mi.
Asia Minor penin. of extreme W Asia, comprising most of Turkey.
Aspen city, NW Maryland 20015; pop. 16,799.
Astrakhan city, SE RSFSR; pop. 419,000.
Asunción city, SW Paraguay; cap.; pop. 437,000.
Aswan city, S Egypt; site of **Aswan Dam,** 1¼ mi. long; pop. 258,600.
Athens city, SE Greece; cap.; pop. 3,000,000.
— city, CEN. Georgia, 30601*; pop. 45,549.
— city, SE Ohio 45701; pop. 19,743.
Atlanta city, CEN. Georgia 30300*; cap.; pop. 425,022.
Atlantic City city, SE New Jersey 08400*; pop. 40,199.
Atlantic Ocean ocean, extending from the Arctic to the Antarctic between the Americas and Europe and Africa.
Atlas Mountains mtn. range, NW Africa.
Attleboro city, SE Massachusetts 02703; pop. 34,196.
Auburn city, CEN. Alabama 36830; pop. 28,471.
— city, SW Maine 04210; pop. 23,128.
— town, CEN. Massachusetts 01501; pop. 14,845.
— city, CEN. New York 13021*; pop. 32,548.
— city, CEN. Washington, 98002*; pop. 26,417.
Auckland city, N North Island, New Zealand; pop. 753,100.
Augsburg city, S West Germany; pop. 245,940.
Augusta city, E Georgia 30900*; pop. 47,532.
— city, S Maine 04301*; cap.; pop. 21,819.
Aurora city, CEN. Colorado 80010*; pop. 158,588.
— city, NE Illinois 60504*; pop. 81,293.
Auschwitz, German name for Oświecim, city, SW Poland; site of Nazi extermination camp in World War II; pop. 14,000.
Austin city, SE Minnesota 55912; pop. 23,020.
— city, CEN. Texas 78700*; cap.; pop. 345,496.
Austintown city, NE Ohio 44515; pop. 29,393.
Australasia isls. of the South Pacific, including Australia, New Zealand, and New Guinea.
Australia independent member of the Commonwealth of Nations, situated on an isl. continent in the South Pacific; 2,971,081 sq. mi.; pop. 14,900,000; cap. Canberra.
Australian Capital Territory reg., SE Australia; 939 sq. mi.; contains Canberra, the capital; pop. 144,000.
Austria republic, CEN. Europe; 32,375 sq. mi.; pop. 7,515,000; cap. Vienna.
Austronesia isls. of the South Pacific, including Indonesia, Melanesia, Micronesia, and Polynesia.
Avignon city, SE France; pop. 86,000.
Avon river, CEN. England; 96 mi. long.
Azerbaijan prov., NW Iran: **Eastern Azerbaijan:** 28,488 sq. mi.; pop. 2,600,000; cap. Tabriz; **Western Azerbaijan:** 13,644 sq. mi.; pop. 1 million; cap. Rizaiyeh.
Azerbaijan SSR republic, SW USSR; 33,590 sq. mi.; pop. 5,219,000; cap. Baku.
Azores three isl. groups of Portugal, E Atlantic; 922 sq. mi.; pop. 335,000.
Azov, Sea of inlet of the Black Sea, S USSR.
Azusa city, S California 91702; pop. 29,380.

Baden-Baden city, SW West Germany; site of famous mineral springs; pop. 40,000.
Bad Lands arid plateau, South Dakota and Nebraska. Also **Bad′lands.**
Baghdad city, CEN. Iraq; cap.; pop. 225,500.
Baguio city, Luzon, N Philippines; pop. 50,000.
Bahama Islands isl. republic of the Commonwealth of Nations, SE of Florida; 5,353 sq. mi.; pop. 3,205,600 ; cap. Nassau.
Bahrain isl. group, Persian Gulf near Saudi Arabia; independent emirate; 240 sq. mi.; pop. 400,000; cap. Manama.
Baikal freshwater lake, S USSR; 12,150 sq. mi.
Baker, Mount mtn., Cascade range, N Washington; 10,-750 ft.
Bakersfield city, S California 93300*; pop. 101,611.
Baku city, SE Azerbaijan SSR; cap.; pop. 1,550,000.
Balboa Heights adm. ctr. of Canal Zone, near Balboa; pop. 118.
Baldwin uninc. place, SE New York 11510*; pop. 34,525.
— boro., SW Pennsylvania; pop. 24,598.
Baldwin Park city, SW California 91706*; pop. 50,554.
Balearic Islands isl. group, W Mediterranean; prov. of Spain; 1,935 sq. mi.; pop. 558,000; cap. Palma.
Bali isl. of Indonesia, E of Java; 2,243 sq. mi.
Balkan Mountains, mtn. range, Balkan penin.
Balkan Peninsula large penin. of SE Europe.
Balkan States countries of Balkan penin.: Albania, Bulgaria, Greece, Rumania, Yugoslavia, and part of Turkey.

Baltic Sea inlet of the Atlantic in NW Europe.
Baltimore city, N Maryland 21200*; pop. 786,775.
Bamako city, CEN. Mali; cap.; pop. 170,000.
Banaras Hindu sacred city, NE India; pop. 553,000. Also **Benares.**
Bandar Sari Begawan city, N Brunei; cap.; pop. 37,-000.
Bandung city, W Java, Indonesia; pop. 1,282,000.
Bangalore city, E Mysore, India; cap.; pop. 4,835,000.
Bangkok city, SW Thailand; cap.; pop. 2,913,537.
Bangladesh republic, S Asia; 54,501 sq. mi.; pop. 90,-700,000; cap. Dacca.
Bangor city, CEN. Maine 04401*; pop. 31,643.
Bangui city, SW Central African Empire; cap.; pop. 150,-000.
Banjul city, W Gambia; cap.; pop. 39,000.
Barbados isl. republic of the Commonwealth of Nations, E Caribbean; 166 sq. mi.; pop. 250,000; cap. Bridgetown.
Barberton city, NE Ohio 44203; pop. 29,751.
Barcelona prov., NE Spain; 2,985 sq. mi.; pop. 3,929,000.
— city, S Barcelona prov.; cap.; pop. 1,759,000.
Barnstable town, SE Massachusetts 02630; pop. 30,898.
Barranquilla city, N Colombia; pop. 868,000.
Barrie city, S Ontario, Canada; pop. 27,676.
Barrington town, E Rhode Island 02806; pop. 16,174.
Barrow, Point extreme N point of Alaska.
Barstow city, S California 92310*; pop. 17,690.
Bartlesville city, NE Oklahoma 74003*; pop. 34,568.
Basel city, N Switzerland; pop. 235,000.
Bataan prov. S Luzon, Philippines; 517 sq. mi.; pop. 116,-000; cap. Balanga; occupies **Bataan Peninsula,** scene of World War II surrender of U.S. forces to the Japanese.
Batavia city, W New York 14020*; pop. 16,703.
Bath co. boro., SW England; pop. 85,000.
Bathurst town, NE New Brunswick, Canada; pop. 16.674.
— Banjul; *the former name.*
Baton Rouge city, CEN. Louisiana 70800*; cap.; pop. 219,486.
Battle Creek city, S Michigan 49014*; pop. 35,724.
Bavaria state, SE West Germany; 27,235 sq. mi.; pop. 10,-569,000; cap. Munich.
Bayamón town, N Puerto Rico; pop. 15,109.
Bay City city, CEN. Michigan 48706*; pop. 41,593.
Bayonne city, NE New Jersey 07002*; pop. 65,047.
Baytown city, S Texas 77520*; pop. 56,923.
Bay Village city, NE Ohio; pop. 17,846.
Beaconsfield town, S Quebec, Canada; pop. 19,389.
Beaumont city, SE Texas 77700*; pop. 118,102.
Beaverton city, NW Oregon 97005*; pop. 30,582.
Beckley city, S West Virginia 25801*; pop. 20,492.
Bedford city, NE Ohio 44014; pop. 15,056.
Beirut city, W Lebanon; cap.; pop. 600,000.
Belém city, N Brazil; pop. 573,000.
Belfast co. boro., and port, SE N. Ireland; cap.; pop. 360,000.
Belgium kingdom, NW Europe; 11,775 sq. mi.; pop. 9,870,000; cap. Brussels.
Belgrade city E Yugoslavia; cap.; pop. 1,000,000.
Belize republic of the Commonwealth of Nations, NE Central America; 8,867 sq. mi.; pop. 160,000; cap. Belmopan.
Bell city, S California 90201*; pop. 25,450.
Bellaire city, S Texas 77401*; pop. 14,950.
Belle Glade city, SE Florida 33430; pop. 16,535.
Belleville city, SW Illinois 62220*; pop. 42,150.
— town, NE New Jersey 07109; pop. 35,367.
— city, SE Ontario, Canada; pop. 35,128.
Bellevue city, E Nebraska 68005; pop. 21,813.
— city, CEN. Washington 98004; pop. 53,441.
Bellflower city, SW California 90706*; pop. 53,441.
Bell Gardens uninc. place, SW California 90201; pop. 34,117.
Bellingham city, NW Washington 98225; pop. 45,794.
Bellmawr boro., SW New Jersey 08030; pop. 13,721.
Bellmore uninc. place, SE New York 11710*; pop. 18,431.
Bellwood vill., NE Illinois 60104; pop. 19,811.
Belmont city, CEN. California 94002*; pop. 24,505.
— town, E Massachusetts 02178; pop. 35,207.
Beloit city, S Wisconsin 53511*; pop. 35,207.
Bengal former prov., NE British India; divided (1947) into: **East Bengal,** now part of Bangladesh, and **West Bengal,** a state of India; 33,928 sq. mi.; pop. 44,440,000; cap. Calcutta..
Benghazi city, N Libya; one of two caps.; pop. 140,000.
Benin independent state, W Africa; 43,483 sq. mi.; pop. 3,675,000.
Benton city, CEN. Arkansas 72015; pop. 17,437.
Benton Harbor city, SW Michigan 49022*; pop. 14,707.
Berea city, NE Ohio 44017; pop. 22,395.
Bergen city, SW Norway; pop. 113,000.
Bergenfield boro., NE New Jersey 07621; pop. 33,131.
Bering Sea part of the North Pacific betw. Alaska and the USSR, joined to the Arctic by **Bering Strait.**
Berkeley city, W California 94700*; pop. 103,328.
— city, CEN. Missouri 63134; pop. 16,146.
Berkley city, SE Michigan 48072; pop. 18,637.
Berlin city, CEN. Germany; cap. prior to 1945 when divided into the British, French, Soviet, and US sectors. In 1949 the Soviet sector, **East Berlin,** was designated capital of East Germany; pop. 1,129,000. The remaining sectors formed **West Berlin,** associated with West Germany; pop. 1,905,000.
— city, N New Hampshire 03570; pop. 15,256.
Bermuda isl. group, W Atlantic; British col.; 21 sq. mi. pop. 65,000, cap. Hamilton.
Bern city, CEN. Switzerland; cap.; pop. 142,800. Also **Berne.**
Berwyn city, NE Illinois 60402*; pop. 46,849.
Bessemer city, CEN. Alabama 35020*; pop. 31,729.
Bethany city, CEN. Oklahoma 73008; pop. 22,130.
Bethel boro., SW Pennsylvania 19507; pop. 34,791.
Bethesda uninc. area, W Maryland 20014; pop. 71,621.
Bethlehem ancient town, W Jordan; birthplace of Jesus; pop. 19,000.
— city, E Pennsylvania 18015*; pop. 70,419.
Bettendorf city, CEN. Iowa 52722; pop. 27,381.
Beverly city, NE Massachusetts 01915; pop. 37,655.
Beverly Hills city, SW California, 90210*; pop. 32,367.
Bhutan kingdom, S Asia, between NE India and Tibet; 18.000 sq. mi.; pop. 1,100,000; cap. Thimphu.
Biddeford city, SW Maine 04005; pop. 19,638.
Big Spring city, W Texas 79720*; pop. 24,804.
Bikini atoll, Marshall Islands; 2 sq. mi.; site of US nuclear tests, July 1946.
Billerica town, NE Massachusetts 01821; pop. 36,727.
Billings city, CEN. Montana 59101*; pop 66,798.
Biloxi city, SE Mississippi 39530*; pop. 49,311.
Binghamton city, CEN. New York 13990*; pop. 55,860.
Birkenhead co. boro., NW England; pop. 138,000.
Birmingham co. boro., CEN. England; pop. 1,034,000.
— city, CEN. Alabama 35200*; pop. 284,413.
— city, SE Michigan 48008*; pop. 21,689.
Biscay, Bay of inlet of the Atlantic betw. W and SW France and N and NW Spain.
Bismarck city, CEN. North Dakota 58501*; cap.; pop. 44,485.
Bismarck Archipelago isl. group, Trust Territory of New Guinea; 19,200 sq. mi.
Bizerta city, N Tunisia; pop. 95,000.
Black Forest wooded mtn. reg., SW West Germany.
Black Hills mtn. reg., SW South Dakota and NE Wyoming.
Black Sea inland sea betw. Europe and Asia, connects with the Aegean via the Bosporus, the Sea of Marmara, and the Dardanelles.
Blaine vill., E Minnesota; pop. 28,558.
Bloomfield town, CEN. Connecticut 06002; pop. 18,608.
— city, NE New Jersey 07003*; pop. 47,702.
Bloomington city, CEN. Illinois 61701*; pop. 49,189.
— city, CEN. Indiana 47401*; pop. 51,646.
— city, E Minnesota 56013; pop. 81,831.
Bluefield city, S West Virginia 24701*; pop. 16,060.
Blue Island city, NE Illinois 60406; pop. 21,855.
Blue Ridge Mountains, SW part of the Appalachians.
Blytheville city, NE Arkansas 72315*; pop. 24,314.
Boardman city, NE Ohio 44512; pop. 30,852.
Boca Raton city, SE Florida 33432; pop. 49,505.
Bogalusa city, SE Louisiana 70427; pop. 18,412.

Bogotá city, CEN Colombia; cap.; pop. 41,300,000.
Bohemia former prov., W Czechoslovakia.
Boise city, SW Idaho 83700*; cap.; pop. 102,451.
Bolivia republic, CEN South America; 424,162 sq. mi.; pop. 5,750,000; caps. Sucre (constitutional), La Paz (de facto).
Bologna prov., CEN Italy; 1,429 sq. mi.; pop. 837,000.
— city, cap. of Bologna prov.; pop. 493,000.
Bombay city, W India; pop. 4,152,000.
Bonn city, W German Federal Republic (West Germany); cap.; pop. 299,000.
Bophuthatswana, republic, S Africa; 15,610 sq. mi.; pop. 1,039,000; cap. Mmabatho.
Bordeaux city, SW France; pop. 267,000.
Borneo (Kalimantan) isl., betw. Java and South China seas; comprising North Borneo, Sarawak, Brunei, and Indonesian Borneo; 286,969 sq. mi.
Bosnia and Herzegovina constituent republic, CEN Yugoslavia; 19,745 sq. mi.; pop. 3,743,000; cap. Sarajevo.
Bosporus strait, betw. the Black Sea and the Sea of Marmara.
Bossier City city, NW Louisiana 71010; pop. 49,969.
Boston city, E Massachusetts 02100*; cap.; pop. 562,994.
Botany Bay inlet of the Pacific, S of Sydney, Australia.
Botswana independent member of the Commonwealth of Nations, S Africa; 222,000 sq. mi.; pop. 750,000; cap. Gaborone.
Boucherville town, S Quebec, Canada; pop. 19,997.
Boulder city, CEN Colorado 80301*; pop. 76,685.
Boulder Dam Hoover Dam: *the former name.*
Bountiful city, CEN Utah 84010; pop. 32,877.
Bowie city, SW Louisiana; pop. 35,028.
Bowling Green city, S Kentucky 42101*; pop. 40,450.
— city, NW Ohio 43402; pop. 25,728.
Boynton Beach city, SE Florida 33435; pop. 35,624.
Bozeman city, SW Montana 59715; pop. 21,645.
Bradenton city, W Florida 33505*; pop. 30,170.
Braintree town, E Massachusetts 02184; pop. 35,050.
Brampton town, SE Ontario, Canada; pop. 41,211.
Brandon city, SW Manitoba, Canada; pop. 31,150.
Branford town, CEN Connecticut 06405; pop. 20,444.
Brantford city, SE Ontario, Canada; pop. 64,421.
Brasília city, CEN Brazil; cap.; pop. 1,000,000.
Brazil republic, NE and CEN South America; 3,287,951 sq. mi.; pop. 127,000,000; cap. Brasília.
Brazzaville city, SE Republic of the Congo (Brazzaville); cap.; pop 156,000.
Brea city, SW California 92621; pop. 27,913.
Breed's Hill hill, near Bunker Hill. See BUNKER HILL.
Bremen state, NW West Germany, 156 sq. mi.
— city, major part of Bremen state; pop. 607,000.
Bremerhaven city, part of Bremen state, NW West Germany; pop. 149,000.
Bremerton city, W Washington 98310*; pop. 36,208.
Brenner Pass Alpine pass, Austrian-Italian border.
Brentwood uninc. place, SE New York 11717; pop. 27,-868.
Breslau Wroclaw: *the German name.*
Brest city, NW France; pop. 154,000.
— city, SW Byelorussian SSR; pop. 85,000.
Bridgeport city, SW Connecticut 06600*; pop. 142,546.
Bridgeton town, E Missouri 63044; pop. 18,445.
— city, SW New Jersey 08302*; pop. 18,795.
Brighton co. boro. and resort, SW England; pop. 166,000.
Brisbane city, SE Queensland, Australia; cap.; pop. 1,004,500.
Bristol co. boro., SW England; pop, 425,000.
— city, CEN Connecticut 06010*; pop. 57,370.
— urb. twp., SE Pennsylvania 19007; pop. 10,867.
— town, E Rhode Island 02809; pop. 20,128.
— city, NE Tennessee 37620*; pop. 23,986.
Bristol Channel inlet of the Atlantic betw. Wales and SW England.
Britain see GREAT BRITAIN.
British Columbia prov., W Canada; 366,255 sq. mi.; pop. 2,466,608, cap. Victoria.
British Guiana former British col., NE South America. See GUYANA.
British Virgin Islands British col., E Greater Antilles; 59 sq. mi.; pop. 10,000.; cap. Road Town.
British West Indies see WEST INDIES.
Brittany reg., W France; former prov.
Brno city, CEN Czechoslovakia; pop. 339,000.
Brockton city, E Massachusetts 02401*; pop. 95,172.
Brockville town, SE Ontario, Canada; pop. 19,765.
Bronx boro., N New York City 10400*; pop. 1,169,115. Also **the Bronx.**
Brookfield vill., NE Illinois 60513; pop. 19,395.
— city, SE Wisconsin 53005; pop. 34,035.
Brookline town, E Massachusetts 02146; pop. 55,062.
Brooklyn boro., SE New York City 11200*; pop. 31,230.
Brooklyn Center vill., SE Minnesota 55429; pop. 31,230.
Brooklyn Park vill., SE Minnesota; pop. 43,332.
Brook Park vill., N Ohio 44142; pop. 26,195.
Brossard city, S Quebec, Canada; pop. 23,452.
Browardale city, SE Florida; pop. 17,444.
Browns Village city, SE Florida 33101; pop. 23,442.
Brownsville uninc. place, NW Florida; pop. 20,294.
— city, S Texas 78520*; pop. 84,997.
Brownwood city, CEN Texas 76801*; pop. 19,203.
Brunei sultanate under British protection, NW Borneo; 2,226 sq. mi.; pop. 150,000; cap. Bandar Sari Begawan.
Brunswick city, NE West Germany; pop. 225,000.
— city, SE Georgia 31520*; pop. 17,605.
— uninc. place, S Maine 04011; pop. 17,366.
— vill., N Ohio 44212; pop. 27,689.
Brussels city, CEN Belgium; cap.; pop. 1,071,000.
Bryan city, CEN Texas 77801*; pop. 44,337.
Bucharest city, S Rumania; cap.; pop. 1,488,000.
Budapest city, CEN Hungary; cap.; pop. 2,039,000.
Buena Park city, SW California 90620*; pop. 64,165.
Buenos Aires city, E Argentina; cap.; pop. 3,500,000.
Buffalo city, W New York 14200*; pop. 357,870.
Bulgaria republic, SE Europe; 42,875 sq. mi.; pop. 8,000,-000; cap. Sofia.
Bull Run small stream, NE Virginia; site of Union defeats in the Civil War, 1861 and 1862.
Bunker Hill hill, Charlestown, Massachusetts, near which (on Breed's Hill) occurred the first organized engagement of the American Revolution, June 17, 1775.
Burbank city, SW California 91500*; pop. 84,825.
Burgundy reg., CEN France.
Burlingame city, CEN California 94010*; pop. 26,173.
Burlington city, SE Iowa 52601*; pop. 29,529.
— town, NE Massachusetts 01803; pop. 23,486.
— city, CEN North Carolina 27215*; pop. 37,266.
— city, NW Vermont 05401*; pop. 37,712.
— town, SE Ontario, Canada; pop, 87,023.
Burma republic, SE Asia, betw. India and Thailand; 261,789 sq. mi.; pop. 34,483,000; cap. Rangoon.
Burma Road road betw. N Burma and SW China; a World War II supply route.
Burnsville city, SE Minnesota 55378; pop. 35,674.
Burundi kingdom, CEN Africa; formerly part of Ruanda-Urundi; 10,747 sq. mi.; pop. 4,150,000; cap. Bujumbura.
Butler city, W Pennsylvania 16001*; pop. 17,026.
Butte city, SW Montana 59701*; pop. 37,205.
Byelorussian SSR constituent republic, USSR; 80,154 sq. mi.; pop. 9,100,000, cap. Minsk.

Cádiz city, SW Spain; pop. 138,000.
Caguas town, CEN Puerto Rico 00625*; pop. 32,015.
Cahokia vill. SW Illinois 62206; pop. 18,904.
Cairo city, NE Egypt; cap.; pop. 3,346,000.
Calais city, N France; pop. 75,000.
Calcutta city, NE India; pop. 2,927,000.
Calgary city, S Alberta, Canada; pop. 469,917.
Caticut Kozhikode: *an alternate name.*
California state, W United States; 158,693 sq. mi.; pop. 23,668,562; cap. Sacramento.
California, Gulf of inlet of the Pacific, W Mexico, betw. Lower California and the rest of Mexico.
Calumet City city, NE Illinois 60409; pop. 39,673.
Camarillo city, SW California 93010; pop. 37,732.
Cambodia See *Kampuchea.*
Cambridge city, SE England; site of Cambridge University; pop. 99,000.
— city, E Massachusetts 02138*; pop. 95,322.
Camden city, S Arkansas 71701; pop. 15,356.
— city, SW New Jersey 08100*; pop. 84,910.

Cameroon republic, W equatorial Africa; 183,376 sq. mi.; pop. 8,650,000; cap. Yaoundé. Also **Cameroun.**
Campbell city, W California 95008; pop. 27,067.
Camp Le Jeune city, SE North Carolina 28542; pop. 34,549.
Camp Springs city, SW Maryland 20031; pop. 22,776.
Canada independent member of the Commonwealth of Nations, N North America; 3,851,809 sq. mi.; pop. 22,-992,604; cap. Ottawa.
Canal Zone US leased terr., CEN Panama; extending five miles on either side of the Panama Canal; 648 sq. mi.; pop. 41,684; adm. ctr. Balboa Heights.
Canary Islands isl. group of Spain near NW coast of Africa; 2,808 sq. mi.; pop. 1,170,000.
Canaveral, Cape cape, E Florida 32920; site of the **John F. Kennedy Space Center,** a space research and missiles installation.
Canberra city, SE Australia; cap.; pop. 195,000.
Canea city, NW Crete; pop. 120,000. Also **Khania.**
Cannes city, SE France; pop. 58,000.
Canterbury co. boro., SE England; site of famous cathedral; pop. 33,000.
Canton city, S China; pop. 2,300,000.
— town, E Massachusetts 02021; pop. 18,182.
— city, NE Ohio 44700*; pop. 94,730.
Cap-de-la-Madeleine city, S Quebec, Canada; pop. 31,-463.
Cape Girardeau city, SE Missouri 63701; pop. 34,361.
Cape Town city, S South Africa; legislative cap.; pop. 892,000. Also **Capetown.**
Cape Verde Islands republic in the CEN. Atlantic Ocean, W of Cape Verde; 1,552 sq. mi.; pop. 330,000; cap. Praia.
Capri isl. near the W coast of Italy; 4 sq. mi.
Caracas city, N Venezuela; cap.; pop. 2,950,000.
Carbondale city, S Illinois 62901; pop. 27,194.
Cardiff co. boro., SE Wales; pop. 278,000.
Caribbean Sea part of the Atlantic betw. the West Indies and Central and South America.
Carlisle boro., S Pennsylvania 17013; pop. 18,314.
Carlsbad city, SE New Mexico 88220; pop. 21,297.
Carlsbad Caverns National Park area, SE New Mexico; contains **Carlsbad Caverns,** a series of limestone caves.
Carmichael uninc. place, CEN. California 95608; pop. 37,625.
Carnegie boro., SW Pennsylvania 15106; pop. 10,099.
Carol City uninc. place, SE Florida 33054; pop. 27,361.
Caroline Islands isl. group in the Pacific, E of the Philippines; 463 sq. mi.
Carpathian Mountains mtn. range, CEN. and E Europe.
Carpentersville vill., NE Illinois 60110; pop. 23,272.
Carrara City, CEN. Italy; site of white marble quarries; pop. 65,000.
Carson uninc. place, SW California 90745*; pop. 81,221.
Carson City city, W Nevada 89701*; cap.; pop. 32,022.
Carteret boro., NE New Jersey; pop. 20,598.
Casablanca city, NW Morocco; pop. 2,220,000.
Cascade Range mtn. range in Oregon, Washington, and British Columbia.
Cashmere See KASHMIR.
Casper city, CEN. Wyoming 82601; pop. 51,016.
Caspian Sea salt-water lake in the S USSR and N Iran; 163,800 sq. mi.
Castile reg., N and CEN. Spain.
Castro Valley uninc. place, W California 94546; pop. 44,760.
Catalina Island Santa Catalina: *an alternate name.*
Catalonia reg. NE Spain.
Catania prov., E Sicily; 1,377 sq. mi.; pop. 889,000.
— city, Catania prov.; cap.; pop. 415,000.
Cataño town, N Puerto Rico; pop. 25,208.
Catonsville uninc. place, CEN. Maryland 21228; pop. 54,-812.
Catskill Mountains range of the Appalachians in SE New York.
Caucasus mtn. range betw. the Black and Caspian Seas.
— reg., SW USSR, betw. the Black and Caspian Seas. Also **Caucasia.**
Cayey town, CEN. Puerto Rico 00633; pop. 38,061.
Cedar Falls city, CEN. Iowa 50613; pop. 36,322.
Cedar Grove twp., NE New Jersey 07009; pop. 12,600.
Cedar Rapids city, E Iowa 52400*; pop. 110,243.
Celebes Sulawesi: *the former name.*
Center Point city, CEN. Alabama 35215; pop. 15,675.
Central African Empire independent state of the French Community, CEN. Africa; 238,224 sq. mi.; pop. 2,939,000; cap. Bangui.
Central America S part of North America, betw. Mexico and Colombia.
Central Falls city, NE Rhode Island 02863; pop. 16,995.
Centralia city, S Illinois 62800*; pop. 15,126.
Central Islip city, SE New York 11722; pop. 36,369.
Cerritos city, S California 90701; pop. 52,756.
Ceylon See SRI LANKA.
Chad, Lake lake, CEN. Africa; 8,000 sq. mi.
Chad, Republic of independent state of the French Community, CEN. Africa; 495,752 sq. mi.; pop. 4,650,000, cap. N'djamena.
Chambersburg boro., S Pennsylvania 17201; pop. 16,174.
Champaign city, CEN. Illinois 61820; pop. 58,133.
Champlain, Lake lake, betw. New York and Vermont, extending into Canada; 600 sq. mi.
Changchun city, NE China; pop. 975,000.
Channel Islands British isl. group, English Channel near Normandy; includes Jersey, Guernsey, Alderney, and Sark; 75 sq. mi.
Chapel Hill town, CEN. North Carolina 27514*; pop. 32,-421.
Charlesbourg city, S Quebec, Canada; pop. 33,443.
Charleston city, E Illinois 61920; pop. 19,355.
— city, SE South Carolina 29400*; pop. 69,510.
— city, CEN. West Virginia 25300*; cap.; pop. 63,968.
Charlotte city, CEN. North Carolina 28200*; pop. 314,447.
Charlotte Amalie city, S St. Thomas, Virgin Islands of the United States 00801; cap.; pop. 12,740.
Charlottesville city, CEN. Virginia 22901; pop. 45,010.
Charlottetown city, CEN. Prince Edward Island, Canada; cap.; pop. 18,427.
Chateauguay town, S Quebec, Canada; pop. 15,797.
Chateauguay-Centre town, S Quebec, Canada; pop. 17,942.
Chatham city, S Ontario, Canada; pop. 35,317.
Chattanooga city, SE Tennessee 37400*; pop. 169,565.
Cheektowaga uninc. place, W New York 14225; pop. 113,844.
Chelmsford town, NE Massachusetts 01824; pop. 31,174.
Chelsea metropolitan boro., SW London, England; pop. 47,000.
— city, E Massachusetts 02150; pop. 25,431.
Cheltenham urb. twp., SE Pennsylvania 19012; pop. 40,-238.
Cherbourg city, N France; pop. 39,000.
Chesapeake city, SE Virginia 23320*; pop. 114,226.
Chesapeake Bay inlet of the Atlantic in Virginia and Maryland.
Cheshire town, CEN. Connecticut 06410; pop. 21,788.
Chester co. boro., W Cheshire, England; cap.; pop. 63,000.
— city, SE Pennsylvania 19013*; pop. 45,794.
Cheviot Hills mtn. range, on the border betw. England and Scotland.
Cheyenne city, SE Wyoming 82001*; cap.; pop. 47,283.
Chicago city, NE Illinois 60600*; second largest city in the United States; pop. 3,005,072.
Chicago Heights city, NE Illinois 60411*; pop. 37,026.
Chico city, CEN. California 95926*; pop. 26,601.
Chicopee city, SW Massachusetts 01013*; pop. 55,112.
Chicoutimi city, S Quebec, Canada; pop. 33,893.
Chihuahua state, N Mexico; 94,830 sq. mi.; pop. 1,613,-000.
Chihuahua city, Chihuahua state; cap.; pop. 364,000.
Chile republic, W South America; 292,258 sq. mi.; pop. 11,275,000; cap. Santiago.
Chillicothe city, CEN. Ohio 45601*; pop. 23,420.
Chillum city, SW Maryland 20783; pop. 35,656.

China, People's Republic of republic, E and CEN. Asia; 3,768,377 sq. mi.; pop. 970,000,000; cap. Peking.
China, Republic of republic on Taiwan and several smaller isls.; 13,890 sq. mi.; pop. 18,000,000; cap. Taipei.
China Sea part of the Pacific bordering on China. See EAST CHINA SEA, SOUTH CHINA SEA.
Chino city, SW California 91710; pop. 40,165.
Chula Vista city, SW California 92010*; pop. 83,927.
Chung King city, CEN. China; cap. during World War II; pop. 3,500,000.
Cicero city, NE Illinois 60650; pop. 61,232.
Cincinnati city, SW Ohio 45200*; pop. 385,457.
Circassia reg., NW Caucasus, RSFSR.
Citrus Heights city, NE California 95610; pop. 21,760.
Clairton city, SW Pennsylvania 15025; pop. 12,188.
Claremont city, SW California 91711*; pop. 30,950.
Clark twp., NE New Jersey 07066; pop. 16,699.
Clarksburg city, N West Virginia 26301*; pop. 22,371.
Clarksdale city, NW Mississippi 38614; pop. 21,137.
Clarksville city, N Tennessee 37040*; pop. 54,777.
Clawson city, SE Michigan 48017; pop. 15,103.
Clayton city, E Missouri 63105; pop. 14,219.
Clearwater city, W Florida 33515*; pop. 85,450.
Cleburne city, CEN. Texas 76031; pop. 19,218.
Cleveland city, N Ohio 44100*; pop. 573,822.
— city, SE Tennessee 37311*; pop. 26,415.
Cleveland Heights city, N Ohio 44118; pop. 56,438.
Clifton city, NE New Jersey 07011*; pop. 74,388.
Clinton city, E Iowa 52732; pop. 32,828.
Clovis city, E New Mexico 88101; pop. 31,194.
Cocoa city, E Florida 32922*; pop. 16,096.
Cod, Cape penin., SE Massachusetts.
Coeur d'Alene city, N Idaho 83814; pop. 20,054.
Coffeyville city, SE Kansas 67337; pop. 15,185.
Cohoes city, E New York 12047; pop. 18,144.
College Park city, W Georgia 30022; pop. 24,632.
— city, W Maryland 20740*; pop. 23,614.
College Station city, CEN. Texas 77840*; pop. 37,272.
Collingswood boro., W New Jersey 08108; pop. 15,838.
Collinsville city, SW Illinois 62234; pop. 19,613.
Cologne city, W West Germany; pop. 866,000.
Colombia republic, NW South America; 439,519 sq. mi.; pop. 26,289,000; cap. Bogotá.
Colombo city, W Sri Lanka; cap.; pop. 512,000.
Colón city, Caribbean end of the Canal Zone; an enclave of Panama; pop. 95,000.
Colonial Heights city, CEN. Virginia, 23834; pop. 16,-509.
Colorado state, CEN. United States; 104,247 sq. mi.; pop. 2,888,834, cap. Denver.
Colorado River river flowing through Colorado, Utah, Arizona, California, and Mexico to the Gulf of California; length ab. 1,400 mi.
Colorado Springs city, CEN. Colorado 80900*; site of U.S. Air Force Academy; pop. 215,150.
Colton city, S California, 92324; pop. 19,974.
Columbia city, CEN. Missouri 65201*; pop. 62,061.
— city, CEN. South Carolina 29200*; cap.; pop. 99,296.
— city, CEN. Tennessee 38401*; pop. 25,767.
Columbia Heights city, E Minnesota 55421; pop. 20,-029.
Columbia River river, SW Canada and NW United States; 1,200 mi. long.
Columbus, city, W Georgia 31900*; pop. 154,168.
— city, CEN. Indiana 47201*; pop. 30,292.
— city, E Mississippi 39701*; pop. 27,383.
— city, E Nebraska 68601; pop. 17,328.
— city, CEN. Ohio 43200*; cap.; pop. 564,871.
Commerce City town, CEN. Colorado 80022; pop. 16,-234.
Comoro Islands isl. republic in the Indian Ocean, NW of Madagascar; 838 sq. mi.; pop. 300,000; cap. Moroni.
Compton city, SW California 90220*; pop. 81,286.
Conakry city, W Guinea; cap.; pop. 525,671.
Concord city, W California 94520*; pop. 103,251.
— town, NE Massachusetts 01742; pop. 16,293.
— city, NE Missouri; pop. 21,217.
— city, CEN. New Hampshire 03300*; cap.; pop. 30,400.
— city, CEN. North Carolina 28025; pop. 16,942.
Congo (Brazzaville), Republic of the independent state of the French Community, CEN. Africa; 132,000 sq. mi.; pop. 1,580,000; cap. Brazzaville.
Congo River river, CEN. Africa; 2,720 mi. long.
Connecticut state, NE United States; 5,009 sq. mi.; pop. 3,107,576; cap. Hartford.
Connersville city, E Indiana 47331; pop. 17,023.
Continental Divide ridge of the Rockies separating west-flowing and east-flowing streams in North America.
Conway city, CEN. Arkansas 72032; pop. 20,375.
Coon Rapids vill., E Minnesota 55433; pop. 35,826.
Copenhagen city, E Denmark; cap.; pop. 660,500.
Copiague uninc. place, SE New York 11726; pop. 19,578.
Coral Gables city, SE Florida 33134; pop. 43,241.
Coral Sea part of the Pacific, E of Australia and New Guinea.
Cork co., SW Ireland; 2,880 sq. mi.; pop. 352,000.
— co. boro., CEN. Cork co.; cap.; pop. 122,000.
Corner Brook city, W Newfoundland, Canada; pop. 26,-309.
Corning city, W New York 14830*; pop. 12,953.
Cornwall city, SW Ontario, Canada; pop. 47,116.
Corona city, S California 91720; pop. 37,791.
Coronado city, S California 92118; pop. 16,859.
Corpus Christi city, S Texas 78400*; pop. 231,999.
Corsica isl., N Mediterranean; a dept. of France; 3,368 sq. mi.; pop. 270,000; cap. Ajaccio.
Corsicana city, CEN. Texas 75110*; pop. 21,712.
Cortland city, CEN. New York 13045*; pop. 20,138.
Corvallis city, W Oregon 97330*; pop. 35,135.
Costa Mesa city, SW California 92626*; pop. 82,291.
Costa Rica republic, Central America; 19,690 sq. mi.; pop. 2,300,000; cap. San José.
Côte-St.-Luc city, S Quebec, Canada; pop. 24,375.
Council Bluffs city, SW Iowa 51,501*; pop. 56,449.
Coventry city and co. boro., CEN. England; pop. 335,000.
— town, CEN. Rhode Island 02816; pop. 27,065.
Covina city, SW California 91722*; pop. 33,751.
Covington city, N Kentucky 41011*; pop. 49,013.
Cranford urb. twp., E New Jersey 07016; pop. 24,573.
Cranston city, E Rhode Island 02910; pop. 71,992.
Crestwood city, E Missouri; pop. 12,815.
Crete isl., E Mediterranean; adm. div. of Greece; 3,207 sq. mi.; pop. 456.000.
Crimea penin., SE Ukrainian SSR.
Croatia constituent republic, W Yugoslavia; 21,719 sq. mi.; pop. 4,423,000; cap. Zagreb.
Crowley city, S Louisiana 70526; pop. 16,036.
Croydon co. boro., SE England; pop. 334,000.
Crystal vill., SE Minnesota 55428; pop. 25,543.
Cuba isl. republic, Caribbean Sea; 44,217 sq. mi. (with the Isle of Pines); pop. 9,900,000; cap. Havana.
Cudahy city, SW California 90201; pop. 17,984.
— city, SE Wisconsin 53110; pop. 19,547.
Culver City city, SW California 90230*; pop. 38,134.
Cumberland city, NW Maryland 21501*; pop. 25,933.
— town, NE Rhode Island 02864; pop. 27,069.
Cumberland Gap passage through Cumberland Mountains, betw. Tennessee and Virginia.
Cumberland River river, Kentucky and Tennessee; flows to Ohio River.
Cupertino city, W California 95014; pop. 25,770.
Curaçao isl., W Netherlands Antilles; 171 sq. mi.; pop. 216,000; cap. Willemstad.
Cutler Ridge uninc. place, SE Florida 33157; pop. 17,-441.
Cuyahoga Falls city, NE Ohio 44221*; pop. 43,710.
Cyclades isl. group, S Aegean; a dept. of Greece; 1,023 sq. mi.; pop. 86,000; cap. Hermoupolis.
Cypress City city, SW California 90630; pop. 40,391.
Cyprus isl. republic, E Mediterranean; 3,572 sq. mi.; pop. 635,000; cap. Nicosia.
Czechoslovakia republic, CEN. Europe; 49,368 sq. mi.; pop. 15,400,000; cap. Prague.

Dacca city, CEN. Bangladesh; cap.; pop. 2,500,000.
Dachau town, SE West Germany; site of a Nazi concentration camp; pop. 25,000.
Dakar city, W Senegal; cap.; pop. 581,000.
Dallas city, N Texas 75200*; pop. 904,078.
Dalmatia reg., Croatia, W Yugoslavia; 4,954 sq. mi.; pop. 750,000; cap. Split.
Dalton city, NW Georgia 30720; pop. 20,743.
Daly City city, W California 94014*; pop. 78,519.
Damascus city, SW Syria; cap.; pop. 1,150,000.
Danbury city, SW Connecticut 06810*; pop. 60,470.
Danube river, CEN. and E Europe; 1,770 mi. long.
Danvers town, NE Massachusetts 01923; pop. 24,100.
Danville city, E Illinois 61832*; pop. 38,985.
— city, S Virginia 24540*; pop. 45,642.
Danzig city, N Poland; pop. 364,000.
Dardanelles strait, NW Turkey; connects Sea of Marmara with the Aegean.
Darien town, SW Connecticut 06820; pop. 18,892.
Darien, Gulf of inlet of the Caribbean, E coast of Panama.
Dartmouth town, SE Massachusetts 02714; pop. 23,966.
— city, S Nova Scotia, Canada; pop. 64,770.
Davenport city, E Iowa 52800*; pop. 103,264.
Davis city, CEN. California 95616; pop. 36,640.
Dayton city, SW Ohio 45400*; pop. 203,588.
Daytona Beach city, E Florida 32014*; pop. 54,176.
Dead Sea large salt lake on Israel-Jordan border; 1,292 ft. below sea level.
Dearborn city, SE Michigan 48120*; pop. 90,660.
Dearborn Heights city, SE Michigan 48127; pop. 67,706.
Death Valley desert basin, SE California; maximum depth 280 ft. below sea level.
Decatur city, N Alabama 35601*; pop. 42,002.
— city, CEN. Georgia 30030*; pop. 18,404.
— city, CEN. Illinois 62521*; pop. 94,081.
Deccan Plateau triangular tableland covering most of the penin. of India.
Dedham town, E Massachusetts 02026; pop. 25,298.
Deerfield vill., NE Illinois 60015; pop. 17,430.
Deerfield Beach town, SE Florida 33441; pop. 39,193.
Deer Park uninc. place, SE New York 11729; pop . 31,120.
Defiance city, NW Ohio 43512; pop. 16,810.
De Kalb city, N Illinois 60115; pop. 33,099.
Delaware state, E United States; 1,978 sq. mi.; pop. 595, 225; cap. Dover.
— city, CEN. Ohio 43015; pop. 15,008.
Delaware River river separating Pennsylvania and Delaware from New York and New Jersey; 315 mi. long.
Del City city, CEN. Oklahoma 73115; pop. 28,424.
Delhi terr., CEN. India; 573 sq. mi.; pop. 6,196,414; contains New Delhi.
— city; Delhi terr.; cap.; pop. 3,288,000.
Delray Beach city, SE Florida 33444; pop. 34,325.
Del Rio city, SW Texas 78840; pop. 30,034.
Denison city, N Texas 75020; pop. 23,884.
Denmark kingdom, NW Europe; 16,619 sq. mi.; pop. 5,161,000; cap. Copenhagen.
Denton city, N Texas 76201; pop. 48,063.
Denver city, CEN. Colorado 80200*; cap.; pop. 491,396.
Depew vill., W New York 14043; pop. 19,819.
Des Moines city, CEN. Iowa 50300*; cap.; pop. 191,003.
Des Plaines city, NE Illinois 60016*; pop. 53,568.
Detroit city, SE Michigan 48200*; pop. 1,203,339.
Devil's Island rocky isl. off the coast of French Guiana; formerly a penal colony.
District of Columbia federal dist., E United States; coextensive with Washington, the capital; pop. 637,651.
Dixon city N Illinois 61021; pop. 15,659.
Djibouti, republic, E Africa; 8,500 sq. mi.; pop. 116,000; cap. Djibouti.
Dnepropetrovsk city, SW Ukrainian SSR; pop. 1,066,000. Also **Dniepropetrovsk.**
Dnieper river, SW USSR; 1,420 mi. long. Also **Dnepr.**
Dneister river, SW USSR; 876 mi. long Also **Dnestr.**
Dodecanese isl. group, Aegean Sea; a dept. of Greece; 1,036 sq. mi.; pop. 120,000; cap. Rhodes.
Dolomite Alps E div. of the Alps, N Italy.
Dolton, vill., NE Illinois 60419; pop. 24,766.
Dominican Republic republic, E Hispaniola; 18,700 sq. mi.; pop. 5,580,000; cap. Santo Domingo.
Don river, SW RSFSR; 1,222 mi. long.
Donelson uninc. place, CEN. Tennessee 37214; pop 17,-195.
Donets river, SW USSR; 631 mi. long.
Dorval city, S Quebec, Canada; pop. 20,469.
Dothan city, SE Alabama 36301*; pop. 48,750.
Douai town, N France; pop. 49,000.
Dover municipal boro., SE England; pop. 35,000.
— city, CEN. Delaware 19901; cap.; pop. 23,512.
— city, SE New Hampshire 03820; pop. 23,377.
— town, N New Jersey 07801; pop. 14,681.
Dover, Strait of strait at the E end of the English Channel; 21 mi. wide.
Downers Grove vill., NE Illinois 60515; pop. 39,274.
Downey city, SW California 90240*; pop. 82,602.
Dracut town, NE Massachusetts 01826; pop. 21,249.
Drayton Plains city, SE Michigan 48020; pop. 16,462.
Dresden city, S East Germany; pop. 502,000.
Drummondville city, S Quebec, Canada; pop. 31,813.
Dublin city, E Ireland; cap.; pop. 566,000.
— city, CEN. Georgia 31021; pop. 16,083.
Dubuque city, E Iowa 52001*; pop. 62,321.
Duisburg city, W West Germany; pop 458,000.
Duluth city, NE Minnesota 55800*; pop. 92,811.
Dumont boro., NE New Jersey 07628; pop. 18,334.
Duncan city, S Oklahoma 73533; pop. 22,517.
Dundalk uninc. place, CEN. Maryland 21222; pop. 85,377.
Dundas town, S Ontario, Canada; pop. 17,208.
Dundee burgh, E Scotland; pop. 182,000.
Dunedin city, W Florida 32528; pop. 30,203.
Dunkirk town, N France; scene of evacuation of British forces in World War II, May–June 1940; pop. 28,000.
— city, W New York 14048; pop. 15,310.
Dunmore boro., NE Pennsylvania 18512; pop. 16,781.
Durban city, SE South Africa; pop. 683,000.
Durham city, CEN. North Carolina 27700*; pop. 100,831.
Düsseldorf city, W West Germany; pop. 681,000.
Dutch Guiana See SURINAM.

Eagle Pass city, SW Texas 78852; pop. 21,407.
East Berlin See BERLIN.
Eastchester city, SE New York 10709; pop. 21,330.
East Chicago city, NW Indiana 46312*; pop. 39,786.
East China Sea NE part of the China Sea.
East Cleveland city, NE Ohio 44112; pop. 36,957.
East Detroit city, SE Michigan 48021; pop. 38,281.
Easter Island isl. of Chile, South Pacific; known for stone monuments found there; 45 sq. mi.
East Germany See GERMANY.
East Hartford town, CEN. Connecticut 06108; pop. 52,-563.
East Haven town, S Connecticut 06512; pop. 25,028.
East Indies 1 The isls. of the Malay Archipelago. 2 SE Asia. 3 Formerly, India. Also **East India.**
Eastlake city, NE Ohio 44094; pop. 22,104.
East Lansing city, CEN. Michigan 48823*; pop. 48,309.
East Liverpool city, E Ohio 43920; pop. 16,687.
East Los Angeles uninc. place, SW California 90022; pop. 105,033.
East Massapequa city, SE New York; pop. 15,926.
East Meadow city, SE New York 11554; pop. 46,252.
East Millcreek city, NE Utah 84101; pop. 26,579.
East Moline city, NW Illinois 61244; pop. 20,907.
Easton city, S Pennsylvania 18042*; pop. 26,027.
East Orange city, NE New Jersey 07017*; pop. 77,025.
East Paterson boro., NE New Jersey 07407; pop. 22,749.
East Peoria city, CEN. Illinois 61611; pop. 22,385.
East Point city, CEN. Georgia 30044; pop. 37,486.
East Providence town, E Rhode Island 02914; pop. 50,980.
East Prussia former prov. of Prussia, NE Germany.
East Ridge town, SE Tennessee 37412; pop. 21236.
East Saint Louis city, SW Illinois 62201*; pop. 55,200.
Eastview town, SE Ontario, Canada; pop. 24,269.
Eau Claire city, CEN. Wisconsin 54701*; pop. 51.509.
Economy boro., W Pennsylvania; pop. 17,176.
Ecorse city, SE Michigan 48229; pop. 14,447.

Ecuador republic, NW South America; 109,484 sq. mi.; pop. 8,625,000; cap. Quito.
Eden city, CEN. North Carolina 27288; pop. 15,672.
Edina city, SE Minnesota 55424; pop. 46,073.
Edinburg city, S Texas 78539; pop. 24,075.
Edinburgh city, E Scotland; cap.; pop. 465,000.
Edmond city, CEN. Oklahoma 73034; pop. 34,637.
Edmonds city, NW Washington 98020; pop. 27,527.
Edmonton city, CEN. Alberta, Canada; cap.; pop. 451,635.
Egypt republic, NE Africa; 386,198 sq. mi.p pop. 43,000-000; cap. Cairo: official name **Arab Republic of Egypt.**
Eire Ireland: *the Irish Gaelic name.*
Elba isl. betw. Italy and Corsica; sovereign under the exiled Napolean Bonaparte, 1814–15.
Elbe river, CEN. Europe; 725 mi. long.
Elbrus, Mount mtn., NW Georgian SSR; 18,603 ft.
Elburz Mountains mtn. range N Iran.
El Cajon city, SW California 92020*; pop. 73,892.
El Centro city, S California 92243*; pop. 23,996.
El Cerrito city, W California 94530*; pop. 22,731.
El Dorado city, S Arkansas 71730*; pop. 26,685.
Elgin city, NE Illinois 60120*; pop. 63,798.
Elizabeth city, NE New Jersey 07200*; pop. 106,201.
Elk Grove Village vill., NE Illinois 60007; pop. 28,907.
Elkhart city, N Indiana 46514*; pop. 41,305.
Ellis Island isl., upper New York Bay; former site of US immigration station.
Elmhurst city, NE Illinois 60126*; pop. 44,251.
Elmira city, S New York 14901*; pop. 35,327.
Elmont uninc. place, SE New York 11003; pop. 28,363.
El Monte city, SW California 91731*; pop. 79,494.
Elmwood Park vill., NE Illinois 60635; pop. 24,016.
El Paso city, W Texas 79900*; pop. 425,259.
El Salvador republic, W Central America; 8,260 sq. mi.; pop. 4,750,000; cap. San Salvador.
El Segundo city, SW California 90245*; pop. 13,752.
Elwood city, SE New York 11731; pop. 15,031.
Elyria city, N Ohio 44035*; pop. 57,504.
Emporia city, CEN. Kansas 66801*; pop.25,287.
Endicott vill., S New York 13760*; pop. 14,457.
Endwell city, SW New York 13762; pop. 15,999.
Enfield town, N Connecticut 06030; pop. 42,695
England S part and largest political division of Great Britain; 50,366 sq. mi.; pop. 46,827,000; cap. London.
Englewood city, CEN. Colorado 80110; pop. 30,021
— city, NE New Jersey 07631*; pop. 23,701.
English Channel strait, betw. England and France; 20-100 mi. wide.
Enid city, N Oklahoma 73701*; pop. 50,363.
Eniwetok atoll, Marshall Islands; U.S. nuclear weapons testing area.
Enterprise city, SE Alabama 36330*; pop. 18,033.
Epsom town, SE England; site of famous racecourse; pop. 72,000.
Equatorial Guinea republic, W Africa; 10,830 sq. mi.; pop. 370,000; cap. Malabo.
Erie city, NW Pennsylvania 16500*; pop. 119,123.
Erie, Lake southernmost of the Great Lakes; 9,940 sq. mi.
Erie Canal waterway betw. Albany and Buffalo, New York; integrated with New York State Barge Canal.
Eritrea state E Africa; federated with Ethiopia; 45,000 sq. mi.; pop. 1,800,000; cap. Asmara.
Erivan see YEREVAN.
Escanaba city, NW Michigan 49829; pop. 14,355.
Escondido city, SW California 92025*; pop. 62,480.
Essen city, W West Germany; pop. 697,000.
Essex uninc. place, N Maryland 21221; pop. 38,193.
Estonian SSR constituent republic, W **USSR**; 17,400 sq. mi.; pop. 1,374,000; cap. Tallinn. Also **Estonia.**
Ethiopia country E Africa; 471,778 sq mi., pop. 32,000; cap. Addis Ababa.
Etna, Mount volcano, E Sicily; 10,868 ft.
Euboea isl. of Greece in the Aegean; 1,457 sq. mi.
Euclid city, NE Ohio 44117; pop. 59,999.
Eugene city, W Oregon 97401*; pop. 105,624.
Euphrates river, SW Asia; 1,740 mi. long.
Eurasia large land mass comprising Europe and Asia.
Eureka city, NW California 95501*; pop. 24,153.
Europe continent comprising the W part of the Eurasian land mass; about 4,063,000 sq. mi.
Evanston city, NE Illinois 60201*; pop. 73,706.
Evansville city, SW Indiana 47700*; pop. 130,496.
Everest mtn., E Nepal; highest point of the earth's surface; 29,028 ft.
Everett city, E Massachusetts 02149; pop. 37,195.
— city, W Washington 98201*; pop. 53,622.
Everglades large swampy reg., S Florida.
Evergreen Park vill., NE Illinois 60642; pop. 22,260.
Exeter co. boro., CEN. Devonshire, England; cap; pop. 96,-000.

Fairborn city, SW Ohio 45324; pop. 29,702.
Fairfax town, N Virginia 22030; pop. 19,390.
Fairfield city, CEN California 94533*; pop. 58,099.
— town, SW Connecticut 06430*; pop. 54,849.
Fairhaven town, SE Massachusetts 02719; pop. 15,759.
Fair Lawn boro., NE New Jersey 07410*; pop. 32,229.
Fairmont city, CEN. New York; pop. 15,317.
— city, N West Virginia 26550*; pop. 23,863.
Fairview Park city, NE Ohio 44126; pop. 19,311.
Falkland Islands British col., South Atlantic; 4,618 sq. mi.; pop. 2,000; cap. Stanley.
Fall River city, SE Massachusetts 02720*; pop. 92,574
Falls urb. twp., NE Pennsylvania 18615; pop. 29,082.
Falmouth town, E Massachusetts 02540; pop. 23,640.
Farbo city, SE North Dakota 58100*; pop. 61,308.
Faribault city, SE Minnesota 55021; pop. 16,595.
Farmers Branch city, N Texas 75234; pop. 24,863.
Farmington town, NW New Mexico 87401; pop. 30,729.
Faroe Islands isl. group of Denmark, North Atlantic; 540 sq. mi.; pop. 39,000; cap. Thorshain.
Fayetteville city, NW Arkansas 72701*; pop. 36,604.
— city, CEN. North Carolina 28301*; pop. 59,507.
Federal Republic of Germany See GERMANY.
Ferguson city, E Missouri 63135; pop. 24,740.
Ferndale city, SE Michigan 48220; pop. 26,227.
Fiji Independent member of the Commonwealth of Nations, South Pacific; comprises **Fiji Islands** (7,039 sq. mi.) and **Rotuma** (18 sq. mi.); pop. 625,000; cap. Suva.
Findlay city, CEN. Ohio 45840*; pop. 35,594.
Finland republic, N Europe; 130,119 sq. mi.; pop. 4,800-000; cap. Helsinki.
Finland, Gulf of part of the Baltic Sea betw. Finland and the USSR.
Fitchburg city, N Massachusetts 21420*; pop. 39,580.
Flagstaff city, CEN. Arizona 86001*; pop. 34,641.
Flanders reg., N France and S Belgium.
Flint city, CEN. Michigan 48500*; pop. 159,611.
Floral Park vill., SE New York 11001*; pop. 16,805.
Florence city, CEN. Tuscany, Italy; cap.; pop. 463,000.
— city, NW Alabama 35630*; pop. 37,029.
— city, E South Carolina 29501; pop. 30,062.
Florence-Graham uninc. place SW California 90001; pop. 42,895.
Florida state, SE United States; 58,560 sq. mi.; pop. 9,739,992; cap. Tallahassee.
Florida Keys isl. group SW of Florida.
Florissant city, E Missouri 63031*; pop. 55,372.
Fond du Lac town, N Wisconsin 54935*; pop. 35,515.
Fontainebleau town, N France; site of a former royal residence; pop. 20,000.
Fontana city, CEN. California 92335*; pop. 37,109.
Foochow city, SE China; pop. 616,000.
Forest Hill vill., S Ontario, Canada; pop. 23,135.
Forest Park town, CEN. Georgia 30050; pop. 18,782.
— vill., NE Illinois 60130; pop. 13,177.
— city, SW Ohio 45405; pop. 18,675.
Forestville city, SW Maryland 20028; pop. 16,152.
Formosa Taiwan: *a former name.*
Fort Benning city, W Georgia 31905; pop. 27,495.
Fort Bragg city, CEN. North Carolina 28307; pop. 46,-995.
Fort Carson city, CEN. Colorado 80913; pop. 19,399.
Fort Collins city, N Colorado 80521*; pop. 64,632.
Fort Dix city, CEN. New Jersey 07024; pop. 26,290.
Fort Dodge city, CEN. Iowa 50501; pop. 29,423.
Fort Gordon city, E Georgia 30905; pop. 15,589.

Forth, Firth of estuary of the Forth River; 51 mi. long.
Fort Hood city, CEN. Texas 76544; pop. 32,597.
Forth River river, SE Scotland; 65 mi. long.
Fort Knox military reservation, N Kentucky 40120*; site of the Federal gold bullion depository.
Fort-Lamy N'djamena: *the former name.*
Fort Lauderdale city, SE Florida 33300*; pop. 153,256.
Fort Lee boro., NE New Jersey 07024*; pop. 32,449.
Fort Leonard Wood city, SE Missouri 65473; pop. 33,-799.
Fort Lewis city, CEN. Washington 98433; pop. 38,054.
Fort Meade city, NW Maryland 20755; pop. 16,699.
Fort Myers city, SW Florida 33901; pop. 36,638.
Fort Pierce city, E Florida 33450*; pop. 48,802.
Fort Sill city, SW Oklahoma 73503; pop. 21,217.
Fort Smith city, W Arkansas 72901*; pop. 71,384
Fort Thomas city, N Kentucky 41075; pop. 16,012.
Fort Walton Beach city, NW Florida 32548; pop. 20,829.
Fort Wayne city, NE Indiana 46800; pop. 172,196.
Fort Worth city, N Texas 76100*; pop. 385,141.
Fostoria city, N Ohio 44830; pop. 15,743.
Fountain Valley city, SW California 92708; pop. 55,080.
Framingham town, E Massachusetts 01701; pop. 65,113.
France republic, W Europe; 212,974 sq. mi.; pop. 54,040,-000; cap. Paris.
Frankfort city, CEN. Kentucky 40601; cap.; pop. 25,973.
Frankfurt (on the Main) city, CEN. West Germany; pop. 660,000.
Frankfurt (on the Oder) city, E East Germany; pop. 59,000.
Franklin town, E Massachusetts 02038; pop. 18,217.
Franklin Park vill., NE Illinois 60131; pop. 17,507.
Franklin Square uninc. place, SE New York 11010; pop. 32,156.
Frederick city, NW Maryland 21701; pop. 27,557.
Fredericton city, CEN. New Brunswick, Canada; pop. 24,254.
Freeport city, NW Bahamas, on Grand Bahama Island; pop. 26,000.
— city, N Illinois 61032*; pop. 26,406.
— vill., SE New York 11520; pop. 40,347.
Fremont city, N California 94536; pop. 131,945.
— city, E Nebraska 68025; pop. 23,979.
— city, N Ohio 43420; pop. 17,834.
French Guiana French overseas dept. NE South America; 35,000 sq. mi.; pop. 67,000; cap. Cayenne.
French Polynesia French overseas terr., South Pacific; comprises the Society, Marquesas, Gambier, and other islands; 1,560 sq. mi.; pop. 160,000; cap. Papeete.
French Republic France, with its overseas depts. and terrs.
French West Indies isls. comprising Guadaloupe and Martinique.
Fresno city, CEN. California 93700*; pop. 218,202.
Fridley city, E Minnesota 55421; pop. 30,228.
Friesland prov., N Netherlands; 1,251 sq. mi.; pop. 528,-000; cap. Leeuwarden.
Frigid Zone See NORTH FRIGID ZONE, SOUTH FRIGID ZONE.
Frisian Islands isl. group, North Sea near Germany, Denmark, and the Netherlands.
Fuji extinct volcano, Honshu, Japan; 12,389 ft.
Fullerton city, SW California 92631*; pop. 102,034.
Fundy, Bay of inlet of the Atlantic betw. Nova Scotia and new Brunswick and NE Maine.

Gabonese Republic state of the French Community, W equatorial Africa; 102,290 sq. mi.; pop. 950,000; cap. Libreville. Also **Gabon.**
Gadsden city. NE Alabama 35901*; pop. 47,565.
Gainesville city, N Florida 32601*; pop. 81,371.
— city, CEN. Georgia 30501*; pop. 15,280.
Galápagos Islands isl. group of Ecuador, South Pacific.
Galesburg city, W Illinois 61401; pop. 35,305.
Galicia reg., SE Poland and NW Ukrainian SSR.
— reg., NW Spain.
Galilee reg., N Israel.
Galilee, Sea of freshwater lake; betw. NE Israel, SW Syria, and NW Jordan; 64 sq. mi.
Gallipoli Peninsula penin., NW Turkey.
Galt city, S Ontario, Canada; pop. 38,897.
Galveston city, SE Texas 77550*; pop. 61,902.
Gambia independent member of the Commonwealth of Nations, W Africa; 4,361 sq. mi.; pop. 578,000; cap. Banjul.
Ganges river, N India and Bangladesh, sacred to Hindus; 1,560 mi. long.
Gardena city, SW California 90247*; pop. 45,165.
Garden City city, SE Michigan 48135; pop. 35,640.
— vill., SE New York 11530; pop. 22,727.
Garden Grove city, SW California 92640*; pop. 123,351.
Gardner city, N Massachusetts 01440*; pop. 17,900.
Garfield city, NE New Jersey 07026; pop. 26,803.
Garfield Heights city, NE Ohio 44125; pop. 33,380.
Garland city, N Texas 75040*; pop. 138,857.
Gary city, NW Indiana 46400*; pop. 151,953.
Gascony reg., SW France.
Gastonia city, SW North Carolina 28052*; pop. 47,333.
Gatineau town, SW Quebec, Canada; pop. 22,321.
Gaza city, SW Palestine; adm. by the United Arab Republic with the **Gaza Strip,** the surrounding area; pop. 365,-000.
Gdańsk port city, N Poland: formerly, as **Danzig,** cap. of the territory of the Free City of Danzig; pop. 398,000.
Gdynia city, NW Poland; pop. 190,000.
Geneva city, SW Switzerland; pop. 332,000.
— city, CEN. New York 14456; pop. 16,793.
Geneva, Lake of lake, SW Switzerland; 224 sq. mi.
Genoa city, NW Italy; pop. 842,000.
Georgetown city, N Guyana; cap.; pop. 195,000.
— town, S Ontario, Canada; pop. 17,053.
Georgia state, SE United States; 58,876 sq. mi.; pop. 5,464,265; cap. Atlanta.
Georgian SSR constituent republic, SW USSR; 26,900 sq. mi.; pop. 4,730,000; cap. Tbilisi.
German Democratic Republic See GERMANY.
Germany country, CEN. Europe; divided in 1949 into the **Federal Republic of Germany** (West Germany); 95,735 sq. mi.; pop. 62,827,000; cap. Bonn; and the **German Democratic Republic** (East Germany); 41,479 sq. mi. (excluding East Berlin); pop. 16,716,000; cap. East Berlin.
Ghana republic of the Commonwealth of Nations, W Africa; 92,100 sq. mi.; pop. 11,750,000; cap. Accra.
Ghent city, NW Belgium; pop. 149,000.
Gilbraltar British col. on the Rock of Gilbraltar; 2.25 sq. mi.; pop. 33,000.
Gilbraltar, Rock of penin., S Spain; dominates the Strait of Gibraltar.
Gilbraltar, Strait of strait, betw. Spain and Africa, W Mediterranean.
Gilbert Islands See *Kiribati*
Glace Bay town, NE Nova Scotia, Canada; pop. 22,440.
Gladstone city, W Missouri 64118; pop. 24,990.
Glasgow burgh, SW Scotland; pop. 908,000.
Glastonbury city, CEN. Connecticut 06033; pop. 24,327.
Glen Burnie city, NE Maryland 21061; pop. 38,608.
Glen Cove city, SE New York 11542; pop. 24,618.
Gendale city, CEN. Arizona 85301; pop. 96,988.
— city, SW California 91200*; pop. 139,060.
Glendora city, SW California 91740; pop. 38,654.
Glen Ellyn vill., NE Illinois 60137*; pop. 23,649.
Glens Falls city, E New York 12801*; pop. 15,897.
Glenside city, SE Pennsylvania 19038; pop. 17,353.
Glenview vill., NE Illinois 60025*; pop. 30,842.
Gloucester co. boro., CEN. Gloucestershire, England; cap.; pop. 90,000.
— city, NE Massachusetts 01930*; pop. 27,768.
Gloversville city, CEN New York 12078*; pop. 17,836.
Goa former Portuguese terr., W India; annexed by India in 1961; 1,394 sq. mi., pop. 857,000; cap. New Goa.
Gobi Desert desert, CEN. Asia; 500,000 sq. mi.
Golden Gate strait betw. San Francisco Bay and the Pacific.
Golden Valley vill., SE Minnesota 55427; pop. 22,775.
Goldsboro city, CEN. North Carolina 27530; pop. 31,871.

Good Hope, Cape of promontory, SW South Africa.
Gorki city, CEN. RSFSR; pop. 1,344,000. Also **Gorkiy, Gorky.**
Goshen city, N Indiana 46526; pop. 19,665.
Göteborg city, SW Sweden; pop. 452,000.
Gotland isl. of SE Sweden, Baltic Sea; 1,167 sq. mi.
Granada city, S Spain; pop. 170,000.
Granby city, S Quebec, Canada; pop. 34,385.
Grand Banks submarine shoal, North Atlantic; near Newfoundland.
Grand Canyon gorge of the Colorado River, NW Arizona; ab. 250 mi. long.
Grand Forks city, E North Dakota 58201*; pop. 43,765.
Grand Island city, CEN. Nebraska 68801; pop. 33,180.
Grand Junction city, W Colorado; 81501*; pop. 28,144.
Grand' Mère city CEN. Quebec, Canada; pop. 17,137.
Grand Prairie city, N Texas 75050*; pop. 71,462.
Grand Rapids city, W Michigan 49500*; pop. 181,843.
Grandview city, W Missouri 64030*; pop. 24,502.
Granite City city, SW Illinois 62040*; pop. 36,815.
Great Barrier Reef coral reef off the coast of Queensland, Australia.
Great Bend city, CEN. Kansas 67530; pop. 16,608.
Great Britain principal isl. of the United Kingdom; comprises England, Scotland, and Wales; 94,251 sq. mi.; pop. 56,387,000; cap. London.
Great Divide See CONTINENTAL DIVIDE.
Greater Antilles See ANTILLES.
Great Falls city, CEN. Montana 59401*; pop. 56,725.
Great Lakes chain of five lakes, CEN. North America; on Canada-United States border; comprises Lakes Superior, Michigan, Huron, Ontario, and Erie; total 94,710 sq. mi.
Great Plains plateau, W North America; E of the Rockies.
Great Russia CEN. and NW reg. of the USSR.
Great Salt Lake salt lake, NW Utah; ab. 2,000 sq. mi.
Great Slave Lake lake, S Northwest Territories, Canada; 11,170 sq. mi.
Great Smoky Mountains mtn. range, North Carolina and Tennessee.
Greece republic, SE Europe; 50,944 sq. mi.; pop. 9,302,-000; cap. Athens.
Greeley city, N Colorado 80630*; pop. 53,006.
Green Bay city, E Wisconsin 54300*; pop. 87,899.
Greenbelt city, CEN. Maryland 20770*; pop. 16,000.
Greendale vill., SE Wisconsin 53129; pop. 16,928.
Greenfield uninc. place, NW Massachusetts 01301; pop. 18,436.
— town, SE Wisconsin 53220; pop. 31,467.
Greenfield Park town, S Quebec, Canada; pop. 15,348.
Greenland isl. of Denmark near NE North America; 840,154 sq. mi.; pop. 61,000.
Green Mountains mtn. range, CEN. Vermont.
Greensboro city, CEN. North Carolina 27400*; pop. 155,642.
Greensburg city, SW Pennsylvania 15601*; pop. 15,870.
Greenville city, W Mississippi 38701*; pop. 40,613.
— city, E North Carolina 27834*; pop. 35,740.
— city, NW South Carolina 29601*; pop. 58,242.
— city, NE Texas 75401*; pop. 22,161.
Greenwich boro., SE London; former site of the Royal Observatory; location of prime meridian; pop. 218,000.
— town, SW Connecticut 06830*; pop. 59,578.
Greenwood city, CEN. Mississippi 38930*; pop. 20,115.
— city, W South Carolina 29646*; pop. 21,613.
Grenada Independent republic, in the West Indies; 133 sq. mi.; pop. 106,000; cap. St. George's.
Gretna city, SE Louisiana 70053; pop. 24,875.
Griffin city, CEN. Georgia 30223; pop. 22,734.
Griffith town, NW Indiana 46319; pop. 18,168.
Grimsby town, S Ontario, Canada; pop. 15,770.
Grosse Pointe Park city, SE Michigan; pop. 15,585.
Grosse Pointe Woods city SE Michigan; pop. 21,878.
Groves city, SE Texas 77619; pop. 18,062.
Guadalajara city, CEN. Mexico; pop. 1,813,000.
Guadalcanal isl., British Solomons; scene of an Allied invasion in World War II, 1943.
Guadeloupe French overseas dept., Lesser Antilles; 687 sq. mi.; pop. 373,000; cap. Basse-Terre.
Guam uninc. terr. of the United States, an isl. in the Marianas; 212 sq. mi.; pop 103,000; cap. Agaña.
Guantánamo city, SE Cuba, near, **Guantánamo Bay**; pop. 125,000.
Guatemala republic, N Central America; 42,042 sq. mi.; pop. 7,470,000.
— city, CEN. Guatemala; cap.; pop. 769,000.
Guayama town, SE Puerto Rico 0065; pop. 16,913.
Guayaquil city, W Ecuador; pop. 1,100,000.
Guelph city, S Ontario, Canada; pop. 60,087.
Guernica town, N Spain; object of a German bombing, 1937.
Guernsey one of the Channel Islands; 25 sq. mi.
Guiana coastal reg., NE South America. See BRITISH GUIANA, FRENCH GUIANA, GUYANA, SURINAM.
Guinea republic, W Africa; 94,925 sq. mi.; pop. 5,115,000; cap. Conakry.
Guinea, Gulf of large bay of the Atlantic off W Africa.
Guinea-Bissau republic, W Africa; 13,948 sq. mi.; pop. 557,000; cap. Bissau.
Gulfport city, SE Mississippi 39501*; pop. 39,676.
Gulf Stream A warm ocean current flowing from the Gulf of Mexico northeastward toward Europe.
Guyana independent member of the Commonwealth of Nations, NE South America, 83,000 sq. mi.; pop 890,000; cap. Georgetown.

Haarlem city, W Netherlands; pop. 173,000.
Hacienda Heights city, S California 91745; pop. 35,969.
Hackensack city, NE New Jersey 07601*; pop. 36.039.
Haddon urb. twp., SW New Jersey; pop. 17,099.
Hagerstown city, W Maryland 21740*; pop. 35,862.
Hague, The city, W Netherlands; seat of government; pop. 6,715,000. Also **s'Gravenhage.**
Haifa city, NW Israel; pop. 227,200.
Haiti republic, W Hispaniola; 10,714 sq. mi.; pop. 5,100,000; cap. Port-au-Prince.
Halifax city, S Nova Scotia; Canada; cap.; pop. 122,035.
Hallandale city, SE Florida 33009; pop. 36,517.
Halle city, SW East Germany; pop. 257,000.
Haltom City vill., N Texas 79917; pop. 29,014.
Hamburg state and city, N West Germany; 288 sq. mi.; pop. 1,817,000.
Hamden town, S Connecticut 06514; pop. 49,357.
Hamilton city, CEN. Bermuda; cap.; pop. 3,000.
— city, SW Ohio 45010*; pop. 63,189.
— city, S Ontario, Canada; pop. 309,173.
Hammond city, NW Indiana 46320*; pop. 93,714.
Hampton city SE Virginia 23360*; pop. 122,617.
Hampton Roads channel, SE Virginia; connects several rivers with Chesapeake Bay; scene of the engagement of the "Monitor" and the "Merrimack," 1862.
Hamtramck city, SE Michigan 48212; pop. 27,245.
Hanford city, CEN. California 93230*; pop. 15,179.
Hangchow city, E China; pop. 784,000.
Hannibal city, NE Missouri 63401*; pop. 18,609.
Hannover city, CEN. West Germany; pop. 518,000.
Hanoi city, CEN. Vietnam; cap; pop 644,000.
Hanover boro., S Pennsylvania 7331; pop. 15,623.
Harbin city, NE China; pop. 1,552,000.
Harlingen city, S Texas 78550*; pop. 43,543.
Harper Woods city, SE Michigan 48236; pop. 20,186.
Harrisburg city, CEN. Pennsylvania 17101*; cap; pop. 53,264.
Hartford city, CEN. Connecticut 06100*; cap.; pop. 136,392.
Harvey city, NE Illinois 60426*; pop. 35,810.
Hastings city, S Nebraska 68901; pop. 23,580.
Hattiesburg city, SE Mississippi 39401*; pop. 40,829.
Havana city, W Cuba; cap.; pop. 2,000,000.
Haverford urb. twp., SE Pennsylvania 19041; pop. 55,-732.
Haverhill city, NE Massachusetts 01830*; pop. 46,865.
Hawaii state of the United States, North Pacific; coextensive with the Hawaiian Islands; 6,435 sq. mi.; pop. 965,000; cap. Honolulu.
— largest of the Hawaiian Islands; 4,020 sq. mi.
Hawthorne city, SW California 90250*; pop. 56,447.
— boro., NE New Jersey 07007; pop. 19,173.
Hays city, CEN. Kansas 67601*; pop. 15,396.

Hayward city, W California 94541; pop. 94,167.
Hazel Park city, SE Michigan 48030; pop. 23,784.
Hazleton city, E Pennsylvania 18201; pop. 27,318.
Hebrides isl. group off W coast of Scotland, ab. 3,000 sq. mi.
Heidelberg city, SW West Germany; pop. 122,000.
Hejaz div., W Saudi Arabia; 150,000 sq. mi.; pop 2 million; cap. Mecca.
Helena city, CEN. Montana 59601*; cap.; pop. 22,730.
Helicon mtn. range, CEN. Greece.
Helsinki city, S Finland; cap.; pop. 517,000.
Hempfield urb. twp., SW Pennsylvania; pop. 29,704.
Hempstead vill., SE New York 11550*; pop. 40,404.
Henderson city, NW Kentucky 42420; pop. 22,976.
— city, S Nevada 89015; pop. 16,395.
Hermosa Beach city, SW California 90254; pop. 17,412.
Herzegovina See BOSNIA AND HERZEGOVINA.
Hesse state, W West Germany; 8,150 sq. mi.; pop. 5,423,000; cap. Wiesbaden.
Hialeah city, SE Florida 33010; site of a famous racetrack; pop. 145,254.
Hibbing vill., NE Minnesota 55746; pop. 16,104.
Hickory city, CEN. North Carolina 28601*; pop. 20,569.
Hicksville vill., SE New York 11800*; pop. 48,075.
Highland town, NW Indiana 46322; pop. 24,935.
Highland Park city, NE Illinois 60035*; pop. 30,611.
— city, SE Michigan 48203; pop. 27,909.
High Point city, CEN. North Carolina 27260*; pop. 64,107.
Hillcrest Heights uninc. place. S Maryland; pop. 24,-037.
Hillside urb. twp., NE New Jersey 07205; pop. 21,636.
Hilo city, E Hawaii, Hawaii 96720; pop. 37,017.
Himalayas mtn. range. CEN. Asia.
Hindustan 1 loosely, the reg. of the Ganges where Hindi is spoken. **2** loosely, india.
Hingham town, E Massachusetts 02043; pop. 18,845.
Hinsdale vill., NE Illinois 60521*; pop. 15,918.
Hiroshima city, SW Honshu isl., Japan; devastated by the first atom bomb used in war, Aug. 6, 1945; pop. 542,000.
Hispaniola isl., West Indies; ab. 30,000 sq. mi.; divided into Haiti and the Dominican Republic.
Hobart city, SE Tasmania; cap; pop. 127,000.
— city, NW Indiana 46342; pop. 21,485.
Hobbs city, SE New Mexico 88240; pop. 28,794.
Hoboken city, NE New Jersey 07030*; pop. 42,460.
Ho Chi Minh City See Saigon.
Hoffman Estates city, NE Illinois 60172; pop. 38,258.
Hokkaido isl. of N Japan; ab. 29,000 sq. mi.
Holladay city, NW Utah 84117; pop. 23,014.
Holland See NETHERLANDS.
— city, SW Michigan 49422*; pop. 26,281.
Hollywood area, NW Los Angeles, California; ctr. of US motion-picture industry.
— city, SE Florida 33020*; pop. 117,188.
Holyoke city, CEN. Massachusetts 01040*; pop. 44,678.
Homewood city, CEN. Alabama 35209; pop. 21,245.
— vill., NE Illinois 60430; pop. 18.871.
Honduras republic, NE Central America; 43,277 sq. mi.; pop. 1,126,000; cap. Tegucigalpa.
Hong Kong British col., SE China; includes **Hong Kong Island** and some coastal terr.; 1,126 sq. mi.; pop. 4,727,000; cap. Victoria.
Honolulu City, SE Oahu, Hawaii 96800*; cap.; pop. 364,048.
Honshu isl. of GEN. Japan; 88,745 sq. mi.
Hood, Mount volcanic peak, Cascade Range, NW Oregon 11,245 ft.
Hoover Dam dam, Colorado River at the Arizona-Nevada border; 727 ft. high; 1,282 ft. long.
Hopewell city, SE Virginia 23860; pop. 23,471.
Hopkinsville city, SW Kentucky 42240; pop 27,318.
Horn, Cape S extremity of South America.
Hot Springs city, CEN. Arkansas 71901; pop. 35,166.
Houma city, SE Louisiana 70360*; pop. 32,602.
Houston city, SE Texas 77000*; pop. 1,594,086.
Huber city, SW Ohio 45424; pop. 18943.
Hudson uninc. place, CEN. Massachusetts 01749; pop. 16,-084.
Hudson Bay inland sea, N Canada; connected with the Atlantic by **Hudson Strait;** ab. 475,000 sq. mi.
Hudson River river, E New York; 306 mi. long.
Hull city, SW Quebec, Canada; pop. 63,580.
Hungary republic, CEN. Europe; 35,912 sq. mi.; pop. 10,725,000; cap. Budapest.
Huntington city, NE Indiana 46750; pop. 16,217.
— city, W West Virginia 25700*; pop. 63,684.
Huntington Beach city, SW California 94646*; pop. 170,505.
Huntington Park city, SW California 90255*; pop. 46,223.
Huntington Station uninc. place, SE New York 11746*; pop. 28,817.
Huntsville city, N. Alabama 35800* ; pop. 142,513.
— city, E Texas 77340*; pop. 17,610.
Huron, Lake one of the Great Lakes; betw. Michigan and Ontario; 23,010 sq. mi.
Hurst city, N Texas 76053; pop. 31,420.
Hutchinson city, CEN. Kansas 67501; pop. 36,885.
Hwang Ho river, N China; 2,900 mi. long.
Hyde Park public park, London, England.
Hyderabad city, CEN. India; pop. 1,796,000.
— city, SE Pakistan; pop. 628,310.

Iberia part of SW Europe containing Spain and Portugal.
Iceland isl., North Atlantic; a republic; 39,758 sq. mi.; pop. 235,000; cap. Reykjavik.
Idaho state, NW United States; 83,557 sq. mi.; pop. 943,935; cap. Boise.
Idaho Falls city, SE Idaho 83401*; pop. 39,590.
Ifni prov., SW Morocco; 741 sq. mi.; pop. 50,000; cap. Sidi Ifni.
Ijssel, Lake freshwater lake, CEN. Netherlands.
Illinois state, CEN. United States; 56,400 sq. mi.; pop. 11,418,461; cap. Springfield.
Imperial Beach city, SW California 92032; pop. 20,244.
Imperial Valley agricultural reg., SE California.
Independence city, W Missouri 64050*; pop. 111,806.
India republic of the Commonwealth of Nations, S Asia; 1,778,995 sq. mi.; pop. 683,810,000; cap. New Delhi.
Indiana state, CEN. United States; 36,291 sq. mi.; pop. 5,490,179; cap. Indianapolis.
— boro., CEN. Pennsylvania 15701; pop. 16,100.
Indianapolis city, CEN. Indiana 46200*; cap.; pop. 700,-807.
Indian Ocean ocean betw. Africa, Asia, Australia, and Antarctica.
Indies See EAST INDIES, WEST INDIES.
Indochina 1 SE penin. of Asia. **2** Cambodia, Laos, North and South Vietnam.
Indonesia republic, SE Asia; comprises over 100 isls. of the Malay Archipelago; 735,268 sq. mi.; pop. 155,300,000; cap. Jakarta.
Indus river, Tibet, Kashmir, and Pakistan; 1,800 mi. long.
Inglewood city, SW California 90301*; pop. 94,245.
— uninc. place, CEN. Tennessee; pop. 26,527.
Inkster vill. SE Michigan 48141; pop. 35,190.
Ionian Sea part of the Mediterranean betw. Greece and Sicily.
Iowa state, CEN. United States; 56,280 sq. mi.; pop. 2,913,387; cap. Des Moines.
Iowa City city, E Iowa 52240*; pop. 50,508.
Iraklion city, N CEN. Crete; pop. 78,000. Also **Candia, Heraklion.**
Iran republic, SW Asia; ab. 630,000 sq. mi.; pop. 37,400,000; cap. Teheran.
Iraq republic, SW Asia; 171,599 sq. mi.; pop. 13,400,000; cap. Baghdad.
Ireland westernmost of the British Isles; 31,838 sq. mi.
— republic, S Ireland; 26,600 sq. mi.; pop. 3,460,000; cap. Dublin. See NORTHERN IRELAND.
Irish Sea part of the Atlantic betw. Great Britain and Ireland.
Irkutsk city, S USSR; pop. 462,000.
Irondequoit city, W New York 14617; pop. 63,675.
Ironton city, S Ohio 45638; pop. 15,030.
Irrawaddy river, Tibet and Burma; 1,200 mi. long.
Irving city, N Texas 75060*; pop. 97,260.
Irvington town, NE New Jersey 07111; pop. 59,743.
Islamabad city, NE Pakistan; cap.; pop. 50,000.

Israel republic, E end of the Mediterranean; 7,993 sq. mi.; pop. 4,000,000; cap. Jerusalem.
Istanbul city, NE Turkey; pop. 2,990,680.
Italy republic, S Europe; 116,286 sq. mi.; pop. 57,150,000; cap. Rome.
Ithaca isl. of Greece, Ionian Sea; 36 sq. mi.
— city, CEN. New York 14850; pop. 26,226.
Ivory Coast republic, W Africa; 128,364 sq. mi.; pop. 8,500,000; cap. Abidjan.
Izmir city, W Turkey; pop. 521,000. Also **Smyrna.**

Jackson city, S Michigan 49201*; pop. 39,739.
— city, CEN. Mississippi 39200*; cap.; pop. 202,895.
— city, W Tennessee 38301*; pop. 49,131.
Jacksonville city, CEN. Arkansas 72076*; pop. 27,589.
— city, NE Florida 32200*; pop. 540,898.
— city, CEN. Illinois 62650*; pop. 20,553.
— city, E North Carolina 28540*; pop. 16,021.
Jacques-Cartier city, S Quebec, Canada; pop. 52,527.
Jakarta city, NW Java; cap. of Indonesia; pop. 4,750,000.
Jamaica independent member of the Commonwealth of Nations, isl. of the Greater Antilles; 4,411 sq. mi.; pop. 2,225,000; cap. Kingston.
Jamestown town, NW St. Helena; cap.; pop. 1,600.
— city, SW New York 14701; pop. 35,775.
— city, CEN. North Dakota 58401; pop. 15,385.
— restored vill., E Virginia 23081; site of the first English settlement in the present limits of the United States, 1607.
Jammu and Kashmir state, N India; subject of a territorial dispute with Pakistan; 85,806 sq. mi.; pop. 4,615,000; caps. Sringar and Jammu.
Janesville city, S Wisconsin 53545*; pop. 51,071.
Japan constitutional empire; E Asia; situated on a chain of isls.; 145,711 sq. mi.; pop. 117,650,000; cap. Tokyo.
Japan, Sea of part of the Pacific betw. Japan and the Asian mainland.
Java isl. of Indonesia; SE of Sumatra; 48,842 sq. mi.
Jeannette city, SW Pennsylvania 15644; pop. 15,209.
Jefferson city, NE Virginia 22303; pop. 25,432.
Jefferson City city, CEN. Missouri 65101*; cap.; pop. 33,619.
Jefferson Heights uninc. place, SE Louisiana 70121; pop. 16,489.
Jeffersonville city, SE Indiana 47130*; pop. 20,008.
Jennings city, E Missouri 63136; pop. 19,379.
Jericho vill., W Jordan; on the site of the ancient city.
Jersey one of the Channel Islands; 45 sq. mi.
Jersey City city, NE New Jersey 07300*; pop. 223,532.
Jerusalem city, E Israel; cap.; pop. 412,000.
Jidda city, W Saudi Arabia; pop. 300,000.
Johannesburg city, NE South Africa; cap.; pop. 1,500,000
Johnson City vill., S New York 13790; pop. 18,025.
— city, NE Tennessee 37601; pop. 39,753.
Johnston town, NE Rhode Island 02919; pop. 22,037.
Johnstown city, CEN. Pennsylvania 15901*; pop. 35,496.
Joliet city, NE Illinois 60431*; pop. 77,956.
Joliette city, S Quebec, Canada; pop. 20,127.
Jonesboro city, NE Arkansas 72401; pop. 31,530.
Jonquière city, CEN. Quebec, Canada; pop. 28,430.
Joplin city, SW Missouri 64801*; pop. 39,256.
Jordan constitutional monarchy, W Asia; 37,300 sq. mi.; pop. 3,300,000; cap. Amman.
Jordan River river, CEN. Palestine; over 200 mi. long.
Junction City city, CEN. Kansas 66441; pop. 19,018.
Juneau city, SE Alaska 99801; cap.; pop. 6,050.
Jungfrau mtn. peak, CEN. Switzerland; 13,653 ft.
Jura Mountains mtn. range, E France and W Switzerland.
Jutland penin., N Europe; comprises continental Denmark and part of Germany.

Kabul city, CEN. Afghanistan; cap.; pop. 597,000.
Kailua-Lanikai uninc. place, E Oahu, Hawaii 96734; pop. 33,783.
Kalamazoo city, SW Michigan 49001*; pop. 79,722.
Kalimantan Borneo: *the Indonesian name.*
Kaliningrad city, extreme, W USSR; pop. 331,000.
Kamchatka penin., E USSR, betw. the Bering and Okhotsk Seas.
Kampuchea country, SW Indochina peninsula, formerly Cambodia, Khmer Republic; 70,000 sq. mi.; pop. ab. 9,000,000; cap. Phnom Penh.
Kaneohe uninc. place, E Oahu, Hawaii 96744; pop. 29,903.
Kankakee city, NE Illinois 60901; pop. 30,141.
Kannapolis uninc. place, CEN. North Carolina 28081; pop. 36,293.
Kansas state, CEN. United States; 82,276 sq. mi.; pop. 2,363,208; cap. Topeka.
Kansas City city, NE Kansas 66100*; pop. 161,087.
— city, W Missouri 64100*; pop. 448,159.
Karachi city, S Pakistan; former cap.; pop. 3,469,000.
Karelian ASSR adm. div., NW RSFSR; 66,560 sq. mi.; pop. 711,000; cap. Petrozavodsk.
Karnak vill., S Egypt; near the site of ancient Thebes.
Kashmir See JAMMU AND KASHMIR.
Kathmandu city, CEN. Nepal; cap.; pop. 195,000.
Kauai one of the Hawaiian Islands; 551 sq. mi.
Kaunas city, CEN. Lithuanian SSR; pop. 314,000.
Kazakh SSR constituent republic, CEN. USSR; 1,064,000 sq. mi.; pop. 13,070,000; cap. Alma-Ata.
Kazan city, NW Tatar ASSR; cap.; pop. 885,000.
Kearney city, CEN. Nebraska 68847; pop. 19,181.
Kearns uninc. place, N Utah 84118; pop. 17,071.
Kearny town, NE New Jersey 07032; pop. 37,585.
Keene city, SW New Hampshire 03431; pop. 20,467.
Kelowna city, S British Columbia, Canada; pop. 19,412.
Kendall city, SE Florida 33156; pop. 35,479.
Kenmore vill., W New York 14217; pop. 20,890.
Kennedy, Cape Cape Canaveral: *the former name.*
Kenner city, SE Louisiana 70062; pop. 66,382.
Kennewick city, S Washington 99336; pop. 34,399.
Kenosha city, SE Wisconsin 53140*; pop. 77,685.
Kent city, NE Ohio 44240*; pop. 26,164.
— city, CEN. Washington 98031; pop. 21,510.
Kentucky state, CEN. United States; 40,395 sq. mi.; pop. 3,661,433. cap. Frankfort.
Kentucky River river, N Kentucky; 259 mi. long.
Kentwood city, SW Michigan 49508; pop. 30,438.
Kenwood city, SW Ohio 43606; pop. 15,789.
Kenya independent member of the Commonwealth of Nations, E Africa; 224,960 sq. mi.; pop. 16,300,000; cap. Nairobi.
Kenya, Mount extinct volcano, CEN. Kenya; 17,058 ft.
Kettering city, SW Ohio 45429; pop. 61,186.
Kewanee city, NW Illinois 61443; pop. 15,762.
Key West southwesternmost of the Florida Keys.
— city, Key West Island, Florida 33040*; pop. 27,563.
Kharkov city, NE Ukrainian SSR; pop. 1,444,000.
Khartoum city, CEN. Sudan; cap.; pop. 852,000.
Khmer Republic Cambodia: an earlier name.
Khyber Pass mtn. pass betw. Afghanistan and Pakistan; ab. 30 mi. long.
Kiel city, N West Germany; pop. 269,000.
Kiel Canal ship canal betw. Kiel and the mouth of the Elbe; ab. 61 mi. long.
Kiev city, CEN. Ukrainian SSR; cap.; pop. 2,144,000.
Kilauea active crater, Mauna Loa volcano, Hawaii.
Kilimanjaro, Mount mtn., NE Tanzania; highest in Africa; 19,565 ft.
Kileen city, CEN. Texas 76540*; pop. 61,186.
Kimberley city, CEN. South Africa; pop. 96,000.
Kingsport city, NE Tennessee 37660*; pop. 37,027.
Kingston city, SE Jamaica; cap.; pop. 123,000.
— city, SE New York 12401; pop. 25,554.
— boro., CEN. Pennsylvania 18704; pop. 18,325.
— city, SE Ontario, Canada; pop. 59,047.
Kingsville city, S Texas 78363*; pop. 28,808.
Kinshasa city, W Zaire; cap.; pop. 2,500,000.
Kinston city, CEN. North Carolina 28501; pop. 25,234.
Kirghiz SSR constituent republic, S USSR; 76,640; sq. mi.; pop. 3 million; cap. Frunze.
Kiribati, republic including 3 isl. groups SW Pacific, formerly Gilbert Islands; 264 sq. mi.; pop. 60,000; cap. Bairiki.
Kirkland city, CEN. Washington 98033; pop. 15,249.

Kirksville city, N Missouri 63501; pop. 15,560.
Kirkwood city E Missouri 63122; pop. 31,890.
Kitchener city, S Ontario, Canada; pop. 111,804.
Kitty Hawk vill., NE North Carolina; site of the first sustained airplane flight, by Wilbur and Orville Wright, 1903.
Klamath Falls city, S Oregon 97601*; pop. 15,775.
Klondike reg., NW Canada in the basin of the **Klondike River.**
Knoxville city, E Tennessee 37900*; pop. 183,139.
Kobe city, S Japan; pop. 1,366,500.
Kodiak Island isl., S Alaska.
Kokomo city, CEN. Indiana 46901*; pop. 47,808.
Königsberg Kaliningrad: *the former German name.*
Korea penin., E Asia; 85,266 sq. mi.; divided into the **Democratic People's Republic of Korea** (North Korea); 47,225 sq. mi.; pop. 18,350,000; cap. Pyongyang; and the **Republic of Korea** (South Korea); 38,452 sq. mi.; pop. 38,800,000; cap. Seoul.
Korea Strait strait, betw. the Sea of Japan and the East China Sea.
Kozhikode city, S India; pop. 193,000. Also **Calicut.**
Krakatoa isl. volcano betw. Sumatra and Java, Indonesia; site of most violent volcanic eruption of modern times, 1883.
Kraków city, S Poland; pop. 583,000.
Krasnodar city, SW USSR; pop. 475,000.
Kronstadt city, W USSR; pop. 59,000.
Kuala Lumpur city, CEN. Malaya; cap. of Malaya and Malaysia; pop. 1,000,000.
Kunming city, SW China; pop. 1,700,000.
Kurdistan reg., NW Iran, NE Iraq, and SE Turkey; peopled largely by Kurds.
Kure city, SW Japan; pop. 241,000.
Kurile Islands isl. group, SE USSR; 5,700 sq. mi.
Kuwait sheikdom, NE Arabia; 7,768 sq. mi.; pop. 440,000.
— city, E Kuwait; cap.; pop. 151,000.
Kyoto city, SW Japan; pop, 1,446,000.
Kyushu isl., S Japan; 16,247 sq. mi.

Labrador terr., Newfoundland, Canada; ab. 110,000 sq. mi.; pop. 21,157.
— the penin. of North America betw. the St. Lawrence River and Hudson Bay.
La Canada-Flintridge uninc. place, SW California 91011; pop. 20,652.
Lachine city, S Quebec, Canada; pop. 44,423.
Lackawanna city, W New York 14218; pop. 28,657.
La Crosse city, W Wisconsin 54601*; pop. 47,808.
Ladoga, Lake lake, NW RSFSR; 7,100 sq. mi.
Lafayette uninc. place, W California 94549; pop. 20,484.
— city, CEN. Indiana 47901*; pop. 43,011.
— city, S. Louisiana 70501*; pop. 81,961.
Lafleche city, S Quebec, Canada; pop. 15,113.
Lagos city, SW Nigeria; cap.; pop. 4,000,000.
La Grange city, W Georgia 30240; pop. 23,301.
— vill., NE Illinois 60525; pop. 16,773.
La Grange Park vill., NE Illinois 60525; pop. 15,626.
La Habra city, SW California 90631*; pop. 45,232.
Lahore city, E Pakistan; pop. 2,165,372.
Lake Charles city, SW Louisiana 70601*; pop. 75,051.
Lake District reg., NW England; contains 15 lakes.
Lake Forest city, NE Illinois 60045; pop. 15,642.
Lakeland city, CEN. Florida 33801; pop. 47,406.
Lakes District city, CEN. Washington; pop. 48,195.
Lakewood city, SW California 90712*; pop. 74,654.
— uninc. place, CEN. Colorado 80215; pop. 112,848.
— uninc. place, E New Jersey 08701; pop. 17,874.
— city, N Ohio 44107, pop. 61,963.
Lake Worth city, SE Florida 33460; pop. 40,986.
Lamarque city, SE Texas 77568; pop. 16,131.
La Mesa city, SW California 92041*; pop. 50,342.
La Mirada city, SW California 90638; pop. 40,986.
Lancaster uninc. place, SW California 93534*; pop. 48,027.
— city, CEN. Ohio 43130*; pop. 34,953.
— city, SE Pennsylvania 17600*; pop. 54,725.
— city, SE New Brunswick, Canada; pop. 15,836.
Lanchow city, NW China; pop. 732,000.
Lansdale boro., SE Pennsylvania 19446; pop. 18,451.
Lansdowne-Baltimore Highlands uninc. place, CEN. Maryland 21227; pop. 16,976.
Lansing vill., NE Illinois 60438; pop. 29,039.
— city, CEN. Michigan 48900*; cap.; pop. 130,414.
Laos republic, NW Indochina; 91,428 sq. mi.; pop. 3,800,000; cap. Vientiane.
La Paz city, W Bolivia; de facto cap.; pop. 700,000.
Lepland reg., N Norway, Sweden, and Finland, and the NE USSR; inhabited by Lapps.
La Plata city, E Argentina; pop. 330,000.
La Porte city, NW Indiana 46350*; pop. 22,140.
La Puente city, SW California 91743*; pop. 30,882.
Laramie city, SE Wyoming 82070*; pop. 23,143.
Laredo city, S Texas 78040*; pop. 91,449.
Largo city, W Florida 33540*; pop. 58,977.
Lasalle city, S Quebec; Canada; pop. 72,912.
Las Cruces city, S New Mexico 88001*; pop. 45,086.
Las Vegas city, SE Nevada 89100*; pop. 164,674.
Latvian SSR constituent republic, NE USSR; 24,600 sq. mi.; pop. 2,400,000; cap. Riga. Also **Latvia.**
Laurel city, SE Mississippi 39440*; pop. 24,145.
Lurentian Mountains mtn. range, E Canada.
Lausanne city, W Switzerland; pop. 137,000.
Laval town, S Quebec, Canada; pop. 228,010.
Lawndale city, SW California 90260; pop. 24,825.
Lawrence town, CEN. Indiana 46226; pop. 25,591.
— city, E Kansas 66044*; pop. 52,738.
— city, NE Massachusetts 01840*; pop. 63,175.
Lawton city, SW Oklahoma 73501*; pop. 74,470.
Leaside town, S Ontario, Canada; pop. 21,250.
Leavenworth city, NE Kansas 66048; pop. 25,147.
Lebanon republic, SW Asia; 4,015 sq. mi.; pop. 3,649,000; cap. Beirut.
— city, SE Pennsylvania 17042; pop. 28,572.
Leeds city and co. boro., CEN. England; pop. 495,000.
Lees Summit city, W Missouri 64063; pop. 28,741.
Leeward Islands N isl. group, Lesser Antilles.
Leghorn city, NW Italy; pop. 175,000. Also **Livorno.**
Le Havre city, N France; pop. 200,000.
Leicester co. boro., CEN. England; pop. 284,000.
Leiden city, W Netherlands; pop. 100,000.
Leipzig city, CEN. East Germany; pop. 584,000.
Lemay city, NE Missouri 63125; pop. 40,115.
Lemon Grove uninc. place, SW California 92045; pop. 19,690.
Leningrad city, NW RSFSR; pop. 4,002,000; formerly called St. Petersburg, Petrograd.
Leominster city, CEN. Massachusetts 01453; pop. 34,508.
Leopoldville Kinshasa: *the former name.*
Lesbos isl. of Greece off NW Turkey; 623 sq. mi.
Lesotho independent member of the Commonwealth of Nations; enclave in E South Africa; 11,716 sq. mi.; pop. 1,137,000; cap. Maseru.
Lesser Antilles See ANTILLES.
Lethbridge city, S Alberta, Canada; pop. 41,217.
Lévis city, S Quebec, Canada; pop. 16,597.
Levittown vill., SE New York 11756; pop. 65,440.
Lewiston city, W Idaho 83501; pop. 27,986.
— city, SW Maine 04240*; pop. 40,481.
Lewiston Orchards uninc. place. W Idaho; pop. 26,068.
Lexington city, CEN. Kentucky 40500*; pop. 204,165.
— town, NE Massachusetts 02173; pop. 31,886.
— city, CEN. North Carolina 27292; pop. 17,205.
Leyden See LEIDEN.
Leyte isl., E Philippines, 2,875 sq. mi.
Lhasa city, S Tibet, cap.; pop. 175,000.
Liberia republic, W Africa; ab. 43,000 sq. mi.; pop. 1,920,000; cap. Monrovia.
Libreville city, W Gabon; cap.; pop. 73,000.
Libya republic, N Africa; 679,358 sq. mi.; pop. 3,100,000; cap. Tripoli.
Liechtenstein principality, CEN. Europe; 61 sq. mi.; pop. 30,000; cap. Vaduz.
Liège city, E Belgium pop. 617,000.
Lille city, N France; pop. 191,000.
Lilongwe city, CEN. Malawi; cap.; pop. 70,000.
Lima city, W Peru; cap.; pop. 2,941,000.
— city, W Ohio; 45801*; pop. 47,381.
Limerick co. boro., W Ireland; pop. 57,000.

Limoges city, CEN. France; pop. 133,000.
Lincoln city, CEN. Illinois 62656; pop. 17,582.
— city, SE Nebraska 68500*; cap.; pop. 171,932.
— town, NE Rhode Island 02865; pop. 16,182.
Lincoln Park city, SE Michigan 48146; pop. 45,105.
Linden city, NE New Jersey 07036*; pop. 37,836.
Lindenhurst vill., SE New York 11757; pop. 26,919.
Lisbon city, W Portugal; cap; pop. 861,500.
Lithuanian SSR constituent republic, NW USSR; 25,200 sq. mi.; pop. 3,200,000; cap. Vilnius. Also **Lithuania.**
Little Farms city, SW Louisiana 70052; pop. 15,713.
Little Rock city, CEN. Arkansas 72200*; cap.; pop. 158,461.
Littleton town, CEN. Colorado 80120*; pop. 28,631.
Livermore city, W California 94550*; pop. 48,349.
Liverpool co. boro., W England; pop. 607,000.
Livingston urb. twp., NE New Jersey 07039; pop. 30,127.
Livonia city, SE Michigan 48150*; pop. 104,814.
Loch Raven uninc. place, N Maryland 21204; pop. 25,000.
Lockport city, NW New York 14094; pop. 25,399.
Lodi city, CEN. California 95240*; pop. 35,221.
— boro., NE New Jersey 07644; pop. 25,213.
Lódz city, CEN. Poland; pop. 830,800.
Logan city, N Utah 84321; pop. 26,844.
Logan, Mount peak, SW Yukon Territory, Canada; 19,850 ft.
Logansport city, CEN. Indiana 46947; pop. 19,255.
Loire river, SE France; 620 mi. long.
Lombard vill., NE Illinois 60148; pop. 37,295.
Lomé city, S Togo; cap.; pop. 135,000.
Lomita uninc. place, SW California 90717; pop. 19,784.
Lompoc city, SW California 93436*; pop. 26,267.
London city and co., SE England; cap.; 1 sq. mil.; pop. 5,000 (the city proper): 117 sq. mi.; pop. 3,195,000 (the co.): 693 sq. mi.; pop. 7,379,000 (Greater London).
— city, Ontario, Canada; pop. 223,222.
Long Beach city, SW California 90800*; pop. 361,334.
— city, SE New York 11561*; pop. 34,073.
Long Branch city, E New Jersey 07740*; pop. 29,819.
— city, NE Virginia; pop.
Long Island isl., SE New York; 1,723 sq. mi.
Long Island Sound inlet of the Atlantic betw. Long Island and Connecticut.
Longmeadow town, S Massachusetts 01106; pop 15,630.
Longmont city, N Colorado 80501; pop. 42,942.
Loungueuil city, SW Quebec, Canada; pop. 97,590.
Longview city, NE Texas 75601*; pop. 62,762.
— city, SW Washington 98632; pop. 31,052.
Lorain city, N Ohio 44051*; pop. 75,416.
Lorraine reg., E France.
Los Alamos town, CEN. New Mexico 87544; site of the development of the atom bomb; pop. 11,310.
Los Altos city, W California 94022; pop. 25,769.
Los Angeles city, SW California 90000*; pop. 2,966,763.
Los Gatos city, W California 95030*; pop. 26,593.
Louisiana state, S United States; 48,523 sq. mi.; pop. 4,203,972; cap. Baton Rouge.
Louisville city, N Kentucky 40200*; pop. 298,451.
Lourdes town, SW France; famous shrine; pop. 16,000.
Loveland city, N Colorado 80537; pop. 30,244.
Lowell city, NE Massachusetts 01850*; pop. 92,418.
Lower California penin., NW Mexico; betw. the Gulf of California and the Pacific. Also **Baja California.**
Lower Merion urb. twp., SE Pennsylvania; pop. 59,420.
Lowlands areas of low elevation, E and S Scotland.
Luanda city, NW Angola; cap.; pop. 600,000.
Lubbock city, NW Texas 79400*; pop. 173,979.
Lübeck city, NE West Germany; pop. 242,000.
Lucerne, Lake of lake, CEN. Switzerland; 44 sq. mi.
Lucknow city, CEN. Uttar Predesh, India; cap.; pop. 750,000.
Ludlow town, S Massachusetts 01056; pop. 17,580.
Lufkin city, E Texas 75901*; pop. 28,562.
Lumberton city, S North Carolina 28358; pop. 16,961.
Lusaka city, CEN Zambia; cap.; pop. 415,000.
Lü-ta city, NE China; pop. 1,508,000.
Lutherville-Timonium city, NE Maryland 21093; pop. 24,055.
Luxembourg constitutional grand duchy; betw. Beigium, France, and Germany; 998 sq. mi.; pop. 340,000.
— city, CEN. Luxembourg; cap.; pop. 76,000. Also **Luxemburg.**
Luxor city, E Egypt; near the site of ancient Thebes; pop. 30,000.
Luzon isl., N Philippines; 40,420 sq. mi.
Lvov city, W Ukrainian SSR; pop. 564,000.
Lynbrook vill., SE New York 11563; pop. 23,776.
Lynchburg city, CEN. Virginia 24501*; pop. 66,743.
Lyndhurst urb. twp., NE New Jersey 07071; pop. 22,729.
— city, N Ohio 44124; pop. 19,749.
Lynn city, NE Massachusetts 01901*; pop. 78,471.
Lynnwood city, CEN. Washington 98036; pop. 16,919.
Lynwood city, SW California 90262*; pop. 48,548.
Lyon city, CEN. France; pop. 528,000.

Macao isl., Canton river delta, China.
— Portuguese overseas prov. comprising a penin. of Macao isl. and two small isls.; 6 sq. mi.; pop. 248,000.
— city; cap of Macao; pop. 161,000.
Macedonia reg., SE Europe; divided among Bulgaria, Greece, and Yugoslavia; 25,636 sq. mi.
Mackenzie river, NW Canada; 2,640 mi. long.
Mackinac, Straits of channel betw. Lakes Michigan and Huron; ab. 5 mi. wide and 40 mi. long.
Mackinac Island isl., Straits of Mackinac.
Macomb city, W Illinois 61455; pop. 19,643.
Macon city, CEN. Georgia 31200*; pop. 116,860.
Madagascar isl. republic, Indian Ocean off SE Africa; 230,035 sq. mi.; pop. 9,000,000; cap. Antananarivo: formerly called **Malagasy Republic.**
Madeira isl. group W of Morocco; an adm. dist. of Portugal; 308 sq. mi.; pop. 267,000; cap. Funchal.
Madera city, CEN. California 93637; pop. 16,044.
Madison boro., N New Jersey 07940; pop. 16,710.
— city, CEN. Wisconsin 53700*; cap.; pop. 170,616.
Madison Heights city, SE Michigan 48071; pop. 35,375.
Madisonville city, W Kentucky 42431; pop. 15,332.
Madras city, S India; pop. 2,469,000.
Madrid city, CEN. Spain; cap.; pop. 3,520,000.
Madura isl. of Indonesia E of Java; 1,762 sq. mi.
Magdeburg city, CEN. East Germany; pop. 271,000.
Magellan, Strait of channel betw. the Atlantic and Pacific, separating the South American mainland from Tierra del Fuego.
Magnitogorsk city, S RSFSR; pop. 369,000.
Maine state, NE United States; 32,562 sq. mi.; pop. 1,124,660; cap. Augusta.
Main River river, CEN. West Germany; 305 mi. long.
Majorca largest of the Balearic Islands; 1,405 sq. mi.
Malabar coastal reg., SW India. Also **Malabar Coast.**
Malacca city, W Malaya; pop. 70,000.
Malacca, Strait of strait betw. Sumatra and the Malay Peninsula.
Málaga city, S Spain; pop. 351,000.
Malagasy Republic See **Madagascar.**
Malawi independent member of the Commonwealth of Nations, SE Africa; 45,747 sq. mi.; pop. 6,125,000; cap. Lilongwe.
Malaya federation of Malay states, SE Asia; ab. 50,700 sq. mi.; pop. 9,128,000; cap. Kuala Lumpur; part of Malaysia.
Malay Archipelago isl. group off SE Asia; includes isls. of Indonesia, Malaysia, and the Philippines.
Malay Peninsula S penin. of Asia; includes Malaya, Singapore, and part of Thailand.
Malaysia federation of Malaya, Sarawak, and Sabah (North Borneo); a member of the Commonwealth of Nations; 128,328 sq. mi.; pop. 14,000,000; cap. Kuala Lumpur.
Malden city, NE Massachusetts 02148; pop. 53,386.
Maldives isl. republic, Indian Ocean S of India; 115 sq. mi.; pop. 150,000; cap. Male.
Mali republic of the French Community, W Africa; pop. 4,700,000; 464,872 sq. mi.; cap. Bamako.
Mallorca Majorca: *the Spanish name.*
Malta independent member of the Commonwealth of Nations, CEN. Mediterranean; comprises the islands of Malta, Gozo, Comino, and two islets; 122 sq. mi.; pop. 350,000; cap. Valletta.
Mamaroneck vill., SE New York 10543*; pop. 18,909.

Man, Isle of one of the British Isles, CEN. Irish Sea; 227 sq. mi.; pop. 50,000; cap. Douglas.
Managua city, SW Nicaragua; cap.; pop. 300,000.
Managua, Lake lake, SW Nicaragua; 390 sq. mi.
Manchester co. boro. and city, SE Lancashire, England; pop. 541,000.
— town, N Connecticut 06040*; pop. 47,994.
— city, S New Hampshire 03100*; pop. 90,936.
Manchuria former div., NE China.
Mandalay city, CEN. Burma; pop. 417,000.
Manhattan city, NE Kansas 66502*; pop. 32,644.
— boro., New York City 10000*; pop. 1,427,533.
Manhattan Beach city, SW California 90266; pop. 31,-542.
Manila city, SW Luzon, Philippines; pop. 1,582,000.
Manitoba prov., CEN. Canada; 246,512 sq. mi.; pop. 988,-247; cap. Winnipeg.
Manitoba, Lake lake, SW Manitoba; 1,817 sq. mi.
Manitowoc city, E Wisconsin 54220*; pop. 32,547.
Mankato city, S Minnesota 56001*; pop. 28,651.
Mansfield city, NE Connecticut 06250; pop. 19,994.
— city, CEN. Ohio 44900*; pop. 53,927.
Maple Heights city, NE Ohio 44137; pop. 29,735.
Maple Shade urb. twp., SW New Jersey 08052; pop. 16,-464.
Maplewood vill., E Minnesota 55109; pop. 26,990.
— urb. twp. NE New Jersey 07040; pop. 24,932.
Maracaibo city, NW Venezuela; pop. 845,000.
Maracaibo, Lake lake, NW Venezuela; ab. 5,000 sq. mi.
Marblehead town, NE Massachusetts 01945*; pop. 21-, 295.
Marianas Islands isl. group, W Pacific; including Guam, Saipan, Tinian, and Rota; part of the UN Trust terr. of the Pacific Islands (excluding Guam); 246 sq. mi.
Marietta city, NW Georgia; 30060*; pop. 30,805.
— city, SE Ohio 45750; pop. 16,861.
Marion city, CEN. Indiana 46952*; pop. 35,874.
— city, E Iowa 52302; pop. 18,028.
— city, CEN Ohio 43301*; pop. 37,040.
Markham vill., NE Illinois 60426; pop. 15,987.
Marlborough city, CEN. Massachusetts 01752; pop. 30,-617.
Marmara, Sea of sea betw. Europe and Asia, connecting the Bosporus and the Dardanelles. Also **Marmora.**
Marne river, NE France; 325 mi. long.
Marple urb. twp., SE Pennsylvania; pop. 19,722.
Marquesas Islands isl. group, French Polynesia; 492 sq. mi.
Marquette city, NW Michigan 49855; pop. 21,967.
Marrakesh city, SW Morocco; a traditional cap.; pop. 333,000.
Marrero city, SW Louisiana 70072; pop. 29,015.
Marseille city, SE France; pop. 914,356. Also **Marseilles.**
Marshall city, NE Texas 75607*; pop. 22,937.
Marshall Islands isl. group in Pacific; an adm. dist. of the Trust Terr. of the Pacific Islands; 66 sq. mi.; pop. 25,000; cap. Jaluit.
Marshalltown city, CEN. Iowa 50158; pop. 26,938.
Marshfield city, E Massachusetts 02050; pop. 15,223.
Marshfield city, CEN. Wisconsin 54449; pop. 15,619.
Martinez city, W California 94553*; pop. 16,506.
Martinique isl. Lesser Antilles; French overseas dept.; 421 sq. mi.; pop. 381,000; cap. Fort-de-France.
Martinsville city, S Virginia 24112*; pop. 19,653.
Maryland state, E United States; 10,577 sq. mi.; pop. 4,216,446; cap. Annapolis.
Mason City city, N Iowa 50401*; pop. 30,144.
Mason-Dixon Line boundary betw. Pennsylvania and Maryland, surveyed by Charles Mason and Jeremiah Dixon in 1763; regarded as dividing the North from the South.
Massachusetts state, NE United States; 8,257 sq. mi.; pop. 5,737,037; cap. Boston.
Massapequa uninc. place, SE New York; 11758*; pop. 26,951.
Massapequa Park vill., SE New York 11762; pop. 22,-112.
Massillon city, NE Ohio 44646; pop. 30,557.
Matsu isl. of the Republic of China, Formosa Strait; 4 sq. mi.
Matterhorn mtn. in the Alps on the Swiss-Italian border; 14,701 ft.
Mattoon city, CEN. Illinois 61938; pop. 19,681.
Maui isl. of the Hawaiian Islands; 728 sq. mi.
Maumee city, NW Ohio 43537; pop. 15,937.
Mauna Loa active volcano, CEN. Hawaii (isl.); 13,675 ft.
Mauritania republic, W Africa; 397,956 sq. mi.; pop. 1,675,000; cap. Nouakchott.
Mauritius independent member of the Commonwealth of Nations on an island in the Indian Ocean, 790 sq. mi., pop. 975,000; cap. Port Louis.
Mayagüez city, W Puerto Rico 00708; pop. 50,147.
Mayfield Heights city, N Ohio; pop. 22,139.
Maywood city, SW California 90270; pop. 16,996.
— vill., NE Illinois 60153*; pop. 27,998.
McAlester city, CEN. Oklahoma 74501*; pop. 18,802.
McAllen city, S Texas 78501*; pop. 67,042.
McKeesport city, SW Pennsylvania; 15130*; pop. 31,-012.
McKinley, Mount peak, CEN. Alaska, highest in North America; 20,300 ft.
McKinney city N Texas 75069; pop. 15,193.
McLean city, NE Virginia 22101; pop. 17,698.
Mead, Lake reservoir formed by Hoover Dam in the Colorado River, Arizona and Nevada; 246 sq. mi.
Meadville city, NW Pennsylvania 16335; pop. 16,573.
Mecca city, W Saudi Arabia; one of the caps.; birthplace of Mohammed and holy city to which Muslims make pilgrimages; pop. 500,000.
Medford city, NE Massachusetts 02155; pop. 58,076.
— city, SW Oregon 97501*; pop. 39,603.
Medicine Hat city, SE Alberta, Canada; pop. 26,518.
Medina city, W Saudi Arabia; site of Mohammed's tomb; pop. 90,000.
Mediterranean Sea sea betw. Europe, Asia, and Africa; 965,000 sq. mi.
Mekong river, SE Asia; 2,500 mi. long.
Melanesia isls. of the W Pacific S of the Equator; ab. 60,000 sq. mi.
Melbourne city, S Victoria, Australia; cap.; pop. 2,717,-600.
— city, E Florida 32901*; pop. 46,536.
Melrose city, NE Massachusetts 02176; pop. 30,055.
Melrose Park vill., NE Illinois 60160*; pop. 22,706.
Memphis city, SW Tennessee 38100*; pop. 646,356.
Menlo Park city, W California 94025*; pop. 25,673.
Menomonee Falls vill., SE Wisconsin 53051*; pop. 27,-845.
Mentor city, NE Ohio 44060; pop. 42,065.
Merced city, CEN. California 95340*; pop. 36,499.
Mercerville-Hamilton Square city, CEN. New Jersey 08619*; pop. 24,465.
Meriden city, CEN. Connecticut 06450*; pop. 57,118.
Meridian city, E Mississippi 39301*; pop. 46,577.
Merrick uninc. place, SE New York 11566; pop. 25,904.
Merrillville city, NW Indiana 46410; pop. 27,677.
Merritt Island city, CEN. Florida 32952; pop. 29,233.
Mesa city, CEN. Arizona 85201*; pop. 152,453.
Mesabi Range range of hills, NE Minnesota; site of iron ore deposits.
Mesquite city, N Texas 75149; pop. 67,053.
Messina city, NE Sicily; pop. 275,000.
Metairie city, SW Louisiana 70001; pop. 135,816.
Methuen city, NE Massachusetts 01844; pop. 35,456.
Metuchen boro., NE New Jersey 08840*; pop. 16,031.
Meuse river, W Europe; 580 mi. long.
Mexico republic S North America; 761,600 sq. mi., pop. 74,500,000.
— city, CEN Mexico; cap.; pop. 9,224,000. Also **Mexico City.**
Mexico, Gulf of inlet of the Atlantic, betw. the United States, Mexico, and Cuba; 700,000 sq. mi.
Miami city, SE Florida 33100*; pop. 346,931.
Miami Beach city SE Florida 33139; pop. 96,298.
Michigan state, N United States; 58,216 sq. mi.; pop. 9,258,344; cap. Lansing.

Michigan, Lake one of the Great Lakes; betw. Michigan and Wisconsin; 22,400 sq. mi.
Michigan City city, N Indiana 46360*; pop. 36,850.
Micronesia isls. of the W Pacific N of the equator.
Middle River uninc. place, N Maryland 21,220; pop. 19,-935.
Middlesex boro., NE New Jersey 08846; pop. 15,038.
Middletown city, CEN Connecticut; 06457*; pop. 39,040.
— urb. twp., E New Jersey 07748*; pop. 54,623.
— city, SE New York 10940*; pop. 22,607.
— city, SW Ohio 45042*; pop. 43,719.
— urb. twp., SE Pennsylvania 17057; pop. 26,894.
— town, SE Rhode Island 02840; pop. 29,621.
Midi S reg. of France.
Midland city, CEN. Michigan 48640*; pop. 37,250.
— city, W Texas 79701*; pop. 70,525.
Midlands counties of CEN. England.
Midlothian vill., NE Illinois 60445*; pop. 15,939.
Midway Islands 2 isls. NW of Honolulu, under control of the U.S. Navy; 2 sq. mi.; scene of an important battle of World War II, June, 1942.
Midwest City city, CEN. Oklahoma 73110; pop. 49,559.
Milan city, N Italy; pop. 1,714,000.
Milford city, SW Connecticut 06460*; pop. 49,101.
— uninc. place, CEN. Massachusetts 01757; pop. 19,352.
Millbrae city, W California 94030*; pop. 20,781.
Millburn urb. twp., NE New Jersey 07041; pop. 21,307.
Millcreek boro., CEN. Pennsylvania 17060, pop. 28,441.
Millington town, SW Tennessee 38053; pop. 21,106.
Millville city, S New Jersey 08332; pop. 21,366.
Milpitas city, W California 95035; pop. 37,820.
Milton town, E Massachusetts 02186; pop. 27,190.
Milwaukee city, SE Wisconsin 53200*; pop. 636,212.
Milwaukie city, NW Oregon 97222; pop. 16,379.
Mimico town, S Ontario, Canada; pop. 19,431.
Mindanao isl. S Philippines; 36,537 sq. mi.
Mindoro isl., CEN. Philippines; 3,759 sq. mi.
Mineola vill., SE New York 11501*; pop. 21,845.
Mineral Wells city, CEN. Texas 76067; pop. 18,411.
Minneapolis city, E Minnesota 55400*; pop. 370,951.
Minnesota state, N United States; 84,068 sq. mi.; pop. 4,077,148; cap. St. Paul.
Minnetonka vill., E Minnesota 55343; pop. 38,683.
Minorca one of the Balearic islands; 271 sq. mi.
Minot city, N North Dakota 58701*; pop. 32,843.
Minsk city, CEN. Byelorussian SSR; cap.; pop. 955,000.
Mirada Hills city, SW California; pop. 22,444.
Miramar city, SE Florida 33023; pop. 32,813.
Mishawaka city, N Indiana 46544; pop. 40,224.
Mississippi state S United States; 47,716 sq. mi.; pop. 2,520,638; cap. Jackson.
Mississippi River river, CEN. United States; 2,350 mi. long.
Missoula city, W Montana 59801; pop. 33,388.
Missouri state, CEN. United States; 69,674 sq. mi.; pop. 4,917,444; cap. Jefferson City.
Missouri River river, CEN. United States; 2,470 mi. long.
Mobile city, SW Alabama 36600*; pop. 200,452.
Mobile Bay inlet of the Gulf of Mexico, SW Alabama.
Modesto city, CEN. California 95350*; pop. 106,105.
Mojave Desert arid reg. S California; ab. 15,000 sq. mi.
Moldavian SSR constituent republic, SW USSR; 13,000 sq. mi.; pop, 3,800,000; cap. Kishinev. Also **Moldavia.**
Moline city, NW Illinois 61265*; pop. 45,709.
Molokai isl., CEN. Hawaiian Islands; 259 sq. mi.
Molucca Islands isl. group of Indonesia, betw. Sulawesi and New Guines; 33,315 sq. mi.
Monaco independent principality, SE France; 368 acres: pop. 30,500.
Moncton city, SE New Brunswick, Canada; pop. 47,891.
Monessen city, SW Pennsylvania 15062; pop. 15,216.
Mongolia trh., CEN. Asia; ab. 1 million sq. mi.; divided into the **Mongolian People's Republic** (formerly Outer Mongolia) in the N and W part; 604,250 sq. mi.; pop. 1,725,000; cap. Ulan Bator; and **Inner Mongolia,** a reg., N China, most of which comprises the **Inner Mongolian Autonomous Region;** ab. 400,000 sq. mi.; pop. 6,240,000; cap. Huhehot.
Monongahela River river, West Virginia and W Pennsylvania; 128 mi. long.
Monroe city, N Louisiana 71201*; pop. 57,597.
— city, SE Michigan 48161: pop. 23,894.
Monroeville boro., SW Pennsylvania 15145; pop. 30,977.
Monrovia city, E Liberia; cap.; pop. 96,226.
— city, SW California 91016*; pop. 30,531.
Montana state, NW United States; 147,138 sq. mi.; pop. 786,690; cap. Helena.
Mont Blanc highest mountain of the Alps, on the French-Italian border; 15,781 ft.; site of tunnel, 7½ mi. long, connecting France and Italy.
Montclair city, SW California 91763; pop. 22,546.
— town, NE New Jersey 07042*; pop. 38,321.
Montebello city, SW California 90640*; pop. 52,929.
Monte Carlo city, Monaco; pop. 10,000.
Montenegro constituent republic, S Yugoslavia; 5,343 sq. mi.; pop. 565,000; cap. Titograd.
Monterey city, W California 93940*; pop. 27,558.
Monterey Park city, SW California 91754*; pop. 54,338.
Monterrey city, NE Mexico; pop. 1,054,000.
Montevideo city, S Uruguay; cap.; pop. 1,229,000.
Montgomery city, CEN. Alabama 36100*; cap.; pop. 178,157.
Monticello estate and residence of Thomas Jefferson, near Charlottesville, Virginia.
Montmartre dist., N Paris; former artists' quarter.
Montpelier city, CEN. Vermont 05601*; cap.; pop. 8,609.
Montreal city, S Quebec, Canada; pop. 1,214,352.
Montreal-Nord city, S Quebec, Canada; pop. 89,139. Also **Montreal-North.**
Mont-Royal town, S Quebec, Canada; pop. 21,561.
Mont Saint Michel isl. off NW France; site of an ancient fortress and abbey.
Montville city, SE Connecticut 06353; pop. 15,662.
Moorehead city, CEN. Oklahoma 73852; pop. 18,761.
Moorhead city, W Minnesota 56560*; pop. 29,998.
Moose Jaw city, S Saskatchewan, Canada; pop. 31,854.
Moravia reg., CEN. Czechoslovakia.
Morgan City city, S Louisiana 70380; pop. 16,586.
Morgantown city, N West Virginia 26500*; pop. 27,605.
Morocco kingdom, NW Africa; ab. 172,414 sq. mi.; pop. 20,500,000; cap. Rabat.
Morristown town, CEN. New Jersey 07960*; pop. 17,662.
— city, NE Tennessee 37813*; pop. 20,318.
Morton Grove vill., NE Illinois 60053; pop. 26,369.
Moscow city, W USSR; cap. USSR and RSFSR; pop. 7,635,000.
Moselle river, NE France, Luxembourg, and W West Germany; 320 mi. long.
Moss Point city, SE Mississippi 39563; pop. 19,321.
Mosul city, N Iraq; pop. 243,000.
Mountain Brook city, CEN. Alabama 35223; pop. 19,-474.
Mountain View city, W California 94042*; pop. 58,655.
Mount Clemens city, SE Michigan 48043*; pop. 20,476.
Mountlake Terrace city, CEN. Washington 98043; pop. 16,600.
Mount Lebanon urb. twp., SW Pennsylvania 15228; pop. 39,956.
Mount Pleasant city, CEN. Michigan 48858; pop. 20,504.
Mount Prospect vill., NE Illinois 60056*; pop. 52,634.
Mount Vernon home and burial place of George Washington, near Washington, D.C.
— city, S Illinois 62864; pop. 15,980.
— city, SE New York 10550*; pop. 66,713.
Mozambique republic SE Africa; 302,330 sq. mi.; pop. 10,750,000; cap. Maputo.
Muncie city, E Indiana 47302, pop. 77,216.
Mundelein vill., NE Illinois 60060; pop. 16,128.
Munhall boro., SW Pennsylvania 15120; pop. 16,674.
Munich city, SE West Germany; pop. 1,326,000.
Munster town, NW Indiana 46321; pop. 16,514.
Murfreesboro city, CEN. Tennessee; 37130*; pop. 32,-845.
Murmansk city, NW USSR; pop. 317,000.
Murray city, CEN. Utah 84107; pop. 25,750.
Murray River river, SE Australia; 1,600 mi. long.
Muscat and Oman: Oman: *the former name.*

Muscatine city, E Iowa 52761; pop. 22,405.
Muskegon city, W Michigan 49440*; pop. 40,823.
Muskegon Heights city, W Michigan 49444; pop. 17,-304.
Muskogee city, E Oklahoma 74401*; pop. 40,011.
Myrtle Grove city, CEN. Florida 32506; pop. 16,186.
Mysore city, S India; pop. 254,000.

Nacogdoches city E Texas 75961*; pop. 27,149.
Nagasaki city, NW Kyushu island, Japan; largely destroyed by a U.S. atomic bomb, Aug. 9, 1945; pop. 421,000.
Nagoya city, CEN. Honshu isl., Japan; pop. 2,080,000.
Nagpur city, CEN. India; pop. 866,000.
Nairobi city, SW Kenya; cap.; pop. 863,000.
Namibia See SOUTH-WEST AFRICA.
Nampa city, SW Idaho 83651; pop. 25,112.
Nanking city, E China; cap. 1928–37; pop. 2,000,000.
Nantes city, W France; pop. 259,000.
Nantucket isl. off SE Massachusetts; 57 sq. mi.
Napa city, W California 94558*; pop. 50,879.
Naperville city, NE Illinois 60540; pop. 42,330.
Naples city, SW Italy; pop. 1,278,000.
Narragansett Bay inlet of the Atlantic, SE Rhode Island.
Nashua city, S New Hampshire 03060; pop. 67,865.
Nashville city, CEN. Tennessee 37200*; cap.; pop. 455,-651.
Nassau city, New Providence, Bahamas Islands; cap.; pop. 80,000.
Natal prov., E South Africa; 33,578 sq. mi. (including Zululand); pop. 4,246,000; cap. Pietermaritzburg.
Natchez city, SW Mississippi 39120*; pop. 19,704.
Natchitoches city, CEN. Louisiana 71457; pop. 15,974.
Natick town, NE Massachusetts 01760*; pop. 31,057.
National City city, SW California 92050*; pop. 48,772.
Naugatuck town, CEN. Connecticut 06770*; pop. 26,456.
Nauru Republic, isl. W-CENT. Pacific just south of Equator; 8.2 sq. mi.; pop. 1,000; cap. Yaren.
Navarre reg. and former kingdom, N Spain and SW France.
Nazareth town, N Israel; scene of Christ's childhood; pop. 22,000.
Nebraska state, CEN. United States; 77,237 sq. mi.; pop. 1,570,006; cap. Lincoln.
Nederland city, SE Texas 77627; pop. 16,810.
Needham town, NE Massachusetts 02192; pop. 29,748.
Neenah city, CEN. Wisconsin 54956*; pop. 22,892.
Negev desert reg., S Israel; 4,700 sq. mi. Also **Negeb.**
Nejd prov., CEN. Saudi Arabia; ab. 450,000 sq. mi.; pop. 4 million; cap. Riyadh.
Nepal kingdom betw. Tibet and India; 54,362 sq. mi.; pop. 14,325,000; cap. Kathmandu.
Neptune urb. twp., E New Jersey 07753; pop. 27,863.
Netherlands kingdom, NW Europe; 15,780 sq. mi.; pop. 14,250,000; cap. Amsterdam; seat of government, The Hague.
Netherlands, Kingdom of the kingdom comprising the Netherlands, the Netherlands Antilles, and Surinam; cap. Amsterdam.
Netherlands Antilles 3 isls. N of Venezuela and 3 in the Leeward Islands group; 336 sq. mi.; pop. 216,000; cap. Willemstad.
Netherlands Guiana See SURINAM.
Nevada state, W United States; 110,540 sq. mi.; pop. 799,-184; cap. Carson city.
New Albany city, S Indiana 47150; pop. 37,103.
Newark city, W California 94560; pop. 32,126.
— city, NW Delaware 19711*; pop. 25,247.
— city, NE New Jersey 07100*; pop. 329,248.
— city, CEN. Ohio 43055*; pop. 41,200.
New Bedford city, SE Massachusetts 02740*; pop. 98,-478.
New Berlin city, SE Wisconsin 53151; pop. 30,529.
New Braunfels city, CEN. Texas 78130*; pop. 17,859.
New Brighton vill., E Minnesota 55112; pop. 19,507.
New Britain city, CEN. Connecticut 06050*; pop. 73,840.
New Brunswick city, CEN. New Jersey 08900*; pop. 41,442.
— prov., SE Canada; 27,836 sq. mi.; pop. 634,557; cap. Fredericton.
Newburgh city, SE New York 12550*; pop. 26,219.
Newburyport city, NE Massachusetts 01950*; pop. 15,-807.
New Caledonia isl. E of Australia; comprising with adjacent isls. a French overseas terr.; 7,335 sq. mi.; pop. 141,000; cap. Nouméa.
New Canaan city, SW Connecticut 06840; pop. 17,455.
New Castle city, E Indiana 47362; pop. 21,215.
— city, W Pennsylvania 16101*; pop. 33,621.
Newcastle upon Tyne city, NE England; pop. 222,000. Also **Newcastle, Newcastle on Tyne.**
New City city, SE New York, 10956; pop. 27,344.
New Delhi city, Delhi terr., India; cap. of India; pop. 302,000.
New England NE section of the United States, including Maine, New Hampshire, Vermont, Massachusetts, Rhode Island, and Connecticut.
Newfoundland prov., E Canada; comprising the island of **Newfoundland** (43,359 sq. mi.) and Labrador on the mainland; 156,185 sq. mi.; pop. 557,725; cap. St. John's.
New Georgia isl. group, British Solomon Islands; ab. 2,000 sq. mi.
New Guinea isl., N of Australia; 304,200 sq. mi. See PAPUA NEW GUINEA, WEST NEW GUINEA.
New Hampshire state, NE United States; 9,304 sq. mi.; pop. 920,610; cap. Concord.
New Haven city, S Connecticut 06500*; pop. 126,109.
New Hebtide See *Vanuatu.*
New Hope city, SE Minnesota 55428; pop. 23,180.
New Iberia city, S Louisiana 70560*; pop. 32,766.
New Ireland volcanic isl. of the Bismarck Archipelago, S Pacific; 3,340 sq. mi.; pop. 41,100; part of Papua New Guinea.
Newington city, CEN. Connecticut 06111, pop. 26,037.
New Jersey state, E United States; 7,836 sq. mi.; pop. 7,364,158; cap. Trenton.
New Kensington city, W Pennsylvania 15068*; pop. 20,312.
New London city, SE Connecticut 06301*; pop. 28,842.
Newmarket town, S Ontario, Canada; pop. 18,941.
New Mexico state, SW United States; 121,666 sq. mi.; pop. 1,299,968; cap. Santa Fé.
New Milford boro., NE New Jersey 07646; pop. 20,201.
New Orleans city, SE Louisiana 70100*; pop. 557,482.
New Philadelphia city, CEN. Ohio 44663; pop. 15,184.
Newport city, N Kentucky 41079*; pop. 25,998.
— city, SE Rhode Island 02840*; pop. 29,259.
Newport Beach city, SW California 92660*; pop. 63,-475.
Newport News city, SE Virginia 23600*; pop. 144,903.
New Rochelle city, SE New York 10800*; pop. 70,794.
New South Wales state, SE Australia; 309,433 sq. mi.; pop. 4,590,000; cap. Sydney.
Newton city, CEN. Iowa 50208; pop. 15,619.
— city, CEN. Kansas 67114; pop. 15,439.
— city, E Massachusetts 02158; pop. 83,622.
Newtown city, SW Connecticut 06470; pop. 16,942.
New Westminster city, SW British Columbia, Canada; pop. 42,835.
New York state, NE United States; 49,576 sq. mi.; pop. 17,557,288; cap. Albany.
— city, SE New York 10000*; divided into the five boroughs of the Bronx, Brooklyn, Manhattan, Queens, and Richmond (Staten Island); 365 sq. mi.; pop. 7,071,030.
New York State Barge Canal waterway system, New York; connects the Hudson River with Lakes Erie, Champlain, and Ontario, 525 mi. long.
New Zealand self-governing member of the Commonwealth of Nations, comprising a group of isle SE of Australia; 103,416 sq. mi., excluding island territories; pop. 3,328,000; cap. Wellington.
Niagara Falls city, W New York 14300*; pop. 85,615.
— city, S Ontario, Canada; pop. 71,384.

Niagara River river betw. Ontario, Canada, and New York State, connecting Lakes Erie and Ontario; in its course occurs **Niagara Falls,** a cataract divided by Goat Island into the American Falls, ab. 167 ft. high and 1,000 ft. wide, and Horseshoe Falls on the Canadian side, ab. 160 ft. high and 2,500 ft. wide.
Nicaragua republic, Central America; ab. 50,193 sq. mi.; pop. 2,750,000; cap. Managua.
Nicaragua, Lake lake, SW Nicaragua; 3,100 sq. mi.
Nice city, SE France; pop. 346,000.
Nicobar Islands isl. terr. of India; 19 isls. in the Bay of Bengal; 754 sq. mi.; pop. 22,000.
Nicosia city, CEN. Cyprus; cap.; pop. 115,000.
Niger river, W Africa; ab. 2,600 mi. long.
Niger, Republic of republic, CEN. Africa, 489,191 sq. mi. pop. 5,550,000; cap. Naimey.
Nigeria, Federation of independent member of the Commonwealth of Nations, W Africa; 356,669 sq. mi.; pop. 79,575,000; cap. Lagos.
Nile river, E Africa; 4,130 mi. long; the longest river in the world.
Niles vill., NE Illinois 60648; pop. 30,363.
— city, NE Ohio 44446; pop. 21,581.
Norfolk city, NE Nebraska 68701; pop. 16,607.
— city, SE Virginia 23500*; pop. 266,979.
Normal town, CEN. Illinois 61761; pop. 35,672.
Norman city, CEN. Oklahoma 73069*; pop. 68,020.
Normandy reg. and former prov., NW France.
Norridge vill., NE Illinois; pop. 16,880.
Norristown boro., SE Pennsylvania 19401*; pop. 34,684.
North Adams city, NW Massachusetts 01247*; pop. 19,-195.
North America N continent of the Western Hemisphere; 9,300,000 sq. mi. (including adjacent islands).
Northampton city, W Massachusetts 01060*; pop. 29,286.
North Andover town, NE Massachusetts 01845; pop. 16,284.
North Arlington boro., NE New Jersey 07032; pop, 18,-096.
North Atlanta vill., CEN. Georgia 30319; pop. 15,000.
North Attleborough town, E Massachusetts 02760*; pop. 18,665.
North Babylon city, SE New York 11703; pop. 39,556.
North Bay city, CEN. Ontario, Canada; pop. 49,187.
North Bellmore uninc. place, SE New York 11710; pop. 22,893.
North Bergen urb. twp., NE New Jersey 07047*; pop. 47,751.
North Borneo See SABAH.
Northbrook vill., NE Illinois 60062; pop. 30,735.
North Canton vill., NE Ohio 44720; pop. 15,228.
North Cape promontory, N Norway.
North Carolina state, SE United States; 52,712 sq. mi.; pop. 5,874,429; cap. Raleigh.
North Chicago city, NE Illinois 60064*; pop. 38,774.
North Dakota state, N United States; 70,665 sq. mi.; pop. 625,695; cap. Bismarck.
Northern Ireland part of the United Kingdom in N reg. of Ireland; 5,238 sq. mi.; pop. 1,528,000; cap. Belfast.
Northern Territory reg., N Australia; 523,620 sq. mi.; pop. 71,000; cap. Darwin.
North Glen city, CEN. Colorado 80201; pop. 29,847.
North Haven city, S Connecticut 06501; pop. 22,194.
North Highlands uninc. place, CEN. California 95660; pop. 31,854.
North Island isl., N New Zealand; 44,281 sq. mi.
North Kingston town, S Rhode Island 02852*; pop. 27,-673.
North Korea See KOREA.
North Las Vegas city, SE Nevada 89030*; pop. 42,739.
North Little Rock city, CEN. Arkansas 72114*; pop. 64,419.
North Massapequa city, SE New York 11758; pop. 23,-101.
North Miami city, SE Florida 33161; pop. 42,566.
North Miami Beach city, SE Florida 33160; pop. 36,481.
North Olmsted city, N Ohio 44070; pop. 36,486.
North Park city, NE Illinois 61101; pop. 15,679.
North Plainfield boro., NE New Jersey 07060; pop. 27,-796.
North Platte city, CEN. Nebraska 69101*; pop. 19,447.
North Pole N extremity of the earth's axis.
North Providence town, NE Rhode Island; pop, 24,337.
North Richland Hills town, N Texa; pop. 30,592.
North Sea part of the Atlantic betw. Great Britain and Europe.
North Tonawanda city, NW New York 14120*; pop. 35,760.
North Vancouver city, SW British Columbia, Canada; pop. 31,847.
North Wantagh city, SE New York; pop. 15,053.
Northwest Territories adm. div., N Canada; 1,304,903 sq. mi.; pop. 42,609.
Northwest Territory reg. awarded to the United States by Britain in 1783, extending from the Great Lakes S to the Ohio River and from Pennsylvania W to the Mississippi.
Norton Shores city, SW Michigan 49444; pop. 22,271.
Norwalk city, SW California 90650*; pop. 85,232.
— city, SW Connecticut 06850*; pop. 76,767.
Norway kingdom, N Europe; 125,182 sq. mi.; pop. 4,120,-000; cap. Oslo.
Norwich co. boro., E England; pop. 122,000.
— city, SE Connecticut 06360*; pop. 38,074.
Nottingham co. boro., CEN. England; pop. 300,000.
Nova Scotia prov., E Canada; 21,425 sq. mi.; pop. 828,-571; cap. Halifax.
Novato city, W California 94947; pop. 43,916.
Novaya Zemlya two isls., Arctic Ocean, NE RSFSR; ab. 35,000 sq. mi.
Novosibirsk city, SW Asian Russian SFSR, ab. 1,700 mi. E of Moscow; pop. 1,243,000.
Nuremberg city, CEN. West Germany; pop. 477,000.
Nutley town, NE New Jersey 07110; pop. 28,998.

Oahu isl., CEN. Hawaiian Islands; 589 sq. mi.
Oak Forest city, NE Illinois 60452; pop. 26,096.
Oakland city, W California 94600*; pop. 339,288.
Oakland Park city, SE Florida 33308; pop. 16,261.
Oak Lawn vill., NE Illinois 60453*; pop. 60,590.
Oak Park vill., NE Illinois 60300*; pop. 54,887.
— city, SE Michigan 48237; pop. 31,537.
Oak Ridge city, E Tennessee 37830*; pop. 27,662.
Oakville town, S Ontario, Canada; pop. 61,483.
Ocala city, CEN. Florida 32670; pop. 37,170.
Oceania isls. of Melanesia, Micronesia, and Polynesia, and sometimes the Malay Archipelago and Australasia.
Oceanside city, SW California 92045*; pop. 76,698.
— vill., SE New York 11572; pop. 35,028.
Oder river, CEN. Europe; 563 mi. long.
Odessa city, S Ukrainian SSR; pop. 1,046,000.
— city, W Texas 79760*; pop. 90,027.
Ogden city, N Utah 84400*; pop. 64,407.
Ohio state, CEN. United States; 41,222 sq. mi.; pop. 10,-797,419; cap. Columbus.
Ohio River river, CEN. United States; 981 mi. long.
Oil City city, NW Pennsylvania 16301*; pop. 15,033.
Oildale city, CEN. California 93308; pop. 20,879.
Okhotsk, Sea of inlet of the Pacific W of Kamchatka and the Kurile Islands.
Okinawa Japanese isl., largest of the Ryukyu Islands; 554 sq. mi.; pop. 945,000; cap. Naha.
Oklahoma state, CEN. United States; 69,919 sq. mi.; pop. 3,025,266; cap. Oklahoma City.
Oklahoma City city, CEN. Oklahoma 73100*; cap.; pop. 403,213.
Okmulgee city, CEN. Oklahoma 74447; pop 15,180.
Okolona city, NW Kentucky 40291; pop. 17,643.
Olathe city, E Kansas 66061; pop. 37,258.
Old Bridge city, CEN. New Jersey 08857; pop. 25,176.
Olean city, SW New York 14760*; pop. 19,169.
Olympia city, W Washington 98501*; cap.; pop. 27,447.

Olympus, Mount mtn., N Greece; regarded in Greek mythology as the home of the gods; 9,570 ft.
Omaha city, E Nebraska 68100*; pop. 311,681.
Oman independent sultanate, SE Arabia; 82,000 sq. mi.; pop. 920,000; cap. Muscat.
Omsk city, S RSFSR; pop. 850,000.
Oneonta city, CEN. New York 13820; pop. 16,030.
Ontario city, SW California 91761*; pop. 88,820.
— prov., SE Canada; 412,582 sq. mi.; pop. 8,264,465; cap. Toronto.
Ontario, Lake easternmost of the Great Lakes; 7,540 sq. mi.
Opelika city, E Alabama 36801; pop. 19,027.
Opelousas city, CEN. Louisiana 70570; pop. 20,121.
Oporto city, W Portugal; pop. 303,000.
Opportunity uninc. place E Washington 99214; pop. 16,604.
Orange former principality, now part of SE France.
— city, SW California 92666*; pop. 91,788.
— city, NE New Jersey 07050*; pop. 31,136.
— city, E Texas 77630*; pop. 24,457.
Orange River river, S Africa; 1,300 mi. long.
Orangevale city, CEN. California 95662; pop. 16,493.
Oregon state, NW United States; 96,981 sq. mi.; pop. 2,632,663; cap. Salem.
— city, N Ohio 43616; pop. 16,563.
Orem city, CEN. Utah 84057; pop. 52,399.
Orillia town, S Ontario, Canada; pop. 24,040.
Orinoco river, Venezuela; ab. 1,700 mi. long.
Orkney Islands isl. group, N of Scotland, comprising Orkney, a co. of Scotland; 376 sq. mi.; pop. 17,000; cap. Kirkwall.
Orlando city, CEN. Florida 32800*; pop. 128,394.
Orléans city, CEN. France; pop. 96,000.
Osaka city, S Honshu, Japan; pop. 2,980,000.
Oshawa city, S Ontario, Canada; pop. 91,587.
Oshkosh city, E Wisconsin 54901*; pop. 49,678.
Oslo city, SE Norway; cap.; pop. 481,000.
Ossa mtn., E Greece; 6,490 ft. See PELION.
Ossining vill., SE New York 10562*; pop. 21,659.
Ostend city, NW Belgium; pop. 56,000.
Oswego city, N New York 13126; pop. 23,844.
Otranto, Strait of strait betw. the Adriatic and Ionian seas; ab. 43 mi. wide.
Ottawa city, N Illinois 61350; pop. 18,716.
— city, SE Ontario, Canada; cap. of Canada; pop. 394,462.
Ottumwa city, SE Iowa 52501*; pop. 27,381.
Ouagadougou city, CEN. Upper Volta; cap.; pop. 125,-000.
Outremont city, S Quebec, Canada; pop. 28,552.
Overland city, E Missouri 63114; pop. 24,949.
Overland Park uninc. place, NE Kansas 66204; pop. 81,-784.
Overlook-Page Manor city, SW Ohio 45431; pop. 19,596.
Owatonna city, S Minnesota 55060; pop. 15,341.
Owensboro city, NW Kentucky 42301*; pop. 54,450.
Owen Sound city, S Ontario, Canada; pop. 18,469.
Owosso city, CEN. Michigan 48867; pop. 17,179.
Oxford co. boro., CEN. England; pop. 109,000.
— city, SW Ohio 45056; pop. 15,868.
Oxnard city, SW California 93030*; pop. 108,195.
Ozark Mountains hilly uplands, SW Missouri, NW Arkansas, and NE Oklahoma.

Pacifica city, W California 94044; pop. 36,866.
Pacific Ocean ocean betw. the American continents and Asia and Australia; extending betw. the Arctic and Antarctic regions; ab. 70 million sq. mi.
Padua city, NE Italy; pop. 229,000.
Paducah city, W Kentucky 42001*; pop. 29,315.
Pago Pago town, SE Tutuila, American Samoa 96920; pop. 1,251.
Painesville city, NE Ohio 44077; pop. 16,536.
Pakistan republic, S Asia; 342,750 sq. mi.; pop. 85,000,000; cap. Islamabad.
Palatine vill., NE Illinois 60067; pop. 32,166.
Palau Islands isl. group, W Caroline Island; 188 sq. mi.
Palermo city, NW Sicily; cap.; pop. 664,000.
Palestine terr., E Mediterranean; 10,434 sq. mi.; cap. Jerusalem; divided (1947) by the United Nations into Israel and a terr. that became part of Jordan.
Palma city, W Majorca; cap. of the Balearic Islands, pop. 208,000.
Palm Springs city, S California 92262*; pop. 32,271.
Palo Alto city, W California 94303*; pop. 55,225.
Palomar, Mount mtn., S California; 6,126 ft.; site of **Mount Palomar Observatory.**
Palos Verdes Peninsula city, SW California 90274; pop. 39,616.
Pampa city, N Texas 79065*; pop. 21,726.
Panama republic, Central America; 29,306 sq. mi. (excluding Canal Zone); pop. 2,000,000.
— city, near the Pacific end of the Panama Canal; cap. of Panama; pop. 418,000.
Panama, Isthmus of isthmus connecting North and South America.
Panama Canal ship canal connecting the Atlantic and the Pacific across Panama; completed (1914) by the United States on the leased Canal Zone; 40 mi. long.
Panama Canal Zone See CANAL ZONE.
Panama City city, NW Florida 32401*; pop. 33,346.
Panay isl., CEN. Philippines; 4,446 sq. mi.
Papal States region in CEN. and NE Italy over which the Roman Catholic Church formerly had temporal power.
Papua New Guinea independent member of the Common-wealth of Nations, S Pacific, consisting of the E half of New Guinea; the isls. of the Bismarck Archipelago; Bougainville and Buka in the Solomon Isls.; and a number of smaller isls.; 183,540 sq. mi.; pop. 3,250,000; cap. Port Moresby.
Paradise town, SE Nevada 89101; pop. 24,477.
Paraguay republic, CEN. South America; 157,047 sq. mi.; pop. 3,165,000; cap. Asunción.
Paraguay River river, CEN. South America; ab. 1,300 mi. long.
Paramaribo city, N Surinam; cap.; pop. 150,000.
Paramount city, SW California 90723*; pop. 36,407.
Paramus boro., NE New Jersey 07652*; pop. 26,474.
Paraná river, CEN. South America; ab. 1,827 mi. long.
Paris city, N France; cap.; pop. 2,591,000.
— city, NE Texas 75460*; pop. 25,498.
Parkersburg city, W West Virginia 26100*; pop. 39,967.
Park Forest vill., NE Illinois 60466; pop. 26,222.
Parkland city, CEN. Washington 98444; pop. 21,012.
Park Ridge city, NE Illinois 60068; pop. 38,704.
Parkville-Carney uninc. place N Maryland 21234; pop. 33,897.
Parma city, CEN. Italy; pop. 175,000.
— city, N Ohio 44129; pop. 92,548.
Parma Heights city, NE Ohio 44129; pop. 27,192.
Parnassus, Mount mtn., CEN. Greece; anciently regarded as sacred to Apollo and the Muses; 8,062 ft.
Parsippany urb. twp., N New Jersey 07054; pop. 55,112.
Pasadena city, SW California 91100*; pop. 119,374.
— city, SE Texas 77501*; pop. 112,560.
Pascagoula city, SE Mississippi 39567; pop. 29,318.
Passaic city, NE New Jersey 07055*; pop. 52,463.
Patagonia reg. at the S tip of South America.
Paterson city, NE New Jersey 07500*; pop. 137,970.
Pawtucket city, NE Rhode Island 02860*; pop. 71,204.
Peabody city, NE Massachusetts 01960*; pop. 45,976.
Pearl City city, S Oahu, Hawaii 96782; pop. 19,552.
Pearl Harbor inlet, S Oahu, Hawaii; site of a U.S. naval base, bombed by Japanese, December 7, 1941.
Pearl River city, SE New York 10965; pop. 17,146.
Peekskill city, SE New York 10566*; pop. 18,881.
Pekin city, CEN. Illinois 61554*; pop. 33,967.
Peking city, N China; cap.; pop. 7,570,000.
Pelion mtn. range, SE Thessaly, Greece. In Greek mythology, the Titans attempted to reach heaven by piling Pelion on Ossa and both on Olympus.
Peloponnesus penin. betw. Aegean and Ionian Seas; one of the main divisions of S Greece; 8,603 sq. mi.; pop. 986,000.

Pembroke town, SE Ontario, Canada; pop. 16,544.
Pembroke Pines city, SE Florida 33023; pop. 35,776.
Penn Hills urb. twp., SW Pennsylvania 15235; pop. 51, 512.
Pennine Alps SW div. of the Alps on the Swiss-Italian border.
Pennsauken urb. twp., W New Jersey 08110; pop. 36, 394.
Penn Square city, SE Pennsylvania; pop. 20,238.
Pennsylvania state, E United States, 45,333 sp. mi.; pop. 11,866,728; cap. Harrisburg.
Pensacola city, NW Florida 32501*; pop. 57,619.
Penticton city, S British Columbia, Canada; pop. 18,146.
Peoria city, CEN. Illinois 61600*; pop. 124,160.
Persia Iran; *the former name.*
Persian Gulf inlet of the Arabian Sea betw. Iran and Arabia.
Perth city, SW Western Australia; cap. pop. 701,000.
Perth Amboy city, E New Jersey 08861*; pop. 38,951.
Peru republic, W South America; 533,916 sq. mi,; pop. 18,300,000; cap. Lima.
Petaluma city, W California 94952*; pop. 33,834.
Peterborough City, S Ontario, Canada; pop. 58,111.
Petersburg city, SE Virginia 23801*; pop. 41.055.
Pharr city, S Texas 78577; pop. 15,829.
Phenix City city, E Alabama 36867; pop. 26,928.
Philadelphia city, SE Pennsylvania 19100*; pop. 1,688,210.
Philippines, Republic of the republic occupying the **Philippine Islands,** a Pacific archipelago SE of China; 115,707 sq. mi.; pop 49,000,000; cap. Quezon City; seat of administration, Manila.
Phillipsburg city, W New Jersey 08865*; pop. 17,849.
Phnom Penh city, S CEN. Cambodia; cap.; pop. 20,000.
Phoenix city CEN. Arizona 85000*; cap.; pop. 764,911.
Picardy reg. and former prov., N France.
Pico Rivera city, SW California 90660*; pop. 53,459.
Piedmont reg., E United States; extends from New Jersey to Alabama E of the Appalachians; ab. 80,000 sq. mi.
Pierre city, CEN. South Dakota 57501; cap.; pop 9,699.
Pierrefonds town, S Quebec, Canada; pop. 33,010.
Pike's Peak mtn., CEN. Colorado; 14,110 ft.
Pikesville uninc. place, CEN. Maryland 21208; pop. 25, 395.
Pine Bluff city, CEN. Arkansas 71601*; pop. 56,576.
Pinellas Park city, W Florida 33565; pop. 32,811.
Pinole city, W California 94564; pop. 15,850.
Piqua city, W Ohio 45356; pop. 20,741.
Piraeus city, S Greece; pop. 184,000.
Pisa city, NW Italy; noted for its leaning tower; pop. 103, 000.
Pittsburg city, W California 94565; pop. 33,034.
— city, SE Kansas 66762*; pop. 20,171.
Pittsburgh city, SW Pennsylvania 15200*; pop. 423,938.
Pittsfield city, W Massachusetts 01200*; pop. 51,974.
Placentia city, SW California 92670; pop. 35,041.
Plainfield city, NE New Joersey 07060; pop. 45,555.
Plainview vill., SE New York 11803; pop. 32,195.
— city, NW Texas 79072*; pop. 19,096.
Plainville city, CEN. Connecticut 06062; pop. 16,733.
Plano city, CEN. Texas 75074; pop. 72,331.
Plantation city, NE Florida 33314; pop. 48,501.
Plant City city W Florida 33566; pop. 15,451.
Platte River river, S Nebraska; 310 mi. long.
Plattsburgh city, NE New York 12901*; pop. 18,715. Also **Plattsburg.**
Pleasant Hill uninc. place, W California 94523; pop. 25,124.
Pleasanton city, W California 94566; pop. 35,160.
Pleasure Ridge Park uninc. place, N Kentucky 40158; pop. 28,566.
Plum boro., SW Pennsylvania 15239; pop. 25,390.
Plymouth co. boro. and port, SW England; pop. 239,000.
Plymouth town, E Massachusetts 02360*; site of the first settlement in New England; pop. 18,606.
— vill., E Minnesota; pop. 31,615.
Plymouth Colony colony on the shore of Massachusetts Bay founded by the Pilgrim Fathers in 1620.
Plymouth Rock rock at Plymouth, Massachusetts, on which the Pilgrim Fathers are said to have landed in 1620.
Pocatello city, Idaho 83201*; pop. 46,340.
Pointe-aux-Trembles city, S Quebec, Canada; pop. 35,-567.
Pointe-Claire city, S Quebec, Canada; pop. 27,303.
Point Pleasant boro., E New Jersey 08742; pop. 15,968.
Poland republic, CEN. Europe; 120,359 sq. mi.; pop. 35,-900,000; cap. Warsaw.
Polynesia isls. of Oceania, CEN. and SE Pacific; E of Melanesia and Micronesia.
Pomerania former province of Prussia, N Germany; now divided between East Germany and Poland.
Pomona city, SW California 91766*; pop.92,742.
Pompano Beach city, SE Florida 33060*; pop. 52,618.
Pompeii ancient city, S Italy; buried in the eruption of Mount Vesuvius, A.D. 79, now ab. half excavated.
Ponca City city N Oklahoma 74601*; pop. 26,238.
Ponce city, S Puerto Rico 00731; pop. 125,926.
Pontiac city, SE Michigan 48053*; pop. 76,715.
Pont-Viau city, S Quebec, Canada; pop. 16,077.
Poona city, W India; pop. 856,000.
Poplar Bluff city, SE Missouri 63901; pop. 16,653.
Popocatepetl dormant volcano, CEN. Mexico; 17,887 ft.
Po River river, N Italy; 405 mi. long.
Portage town, NW Indiana 46368; pop. 27,409.
— city, SW Michigan 49081; pop. 38,157.
Port Angeles city, NW Washington 98362; pop. 16,367.
Port Arthur city, SE Texas 77640*; pop. 61,195.
Port-au-Prince city, S Haiti; cap.; pop. 745,000.
Port Chester vill., SE New York 10573*; pop. 25,803.
Port Colborne town, S Ontario, Canada; pop. 21,420.
Port Huron city, E Michigan 48060*; pop. 33,981.
Portland city, SW Maine 04100*; pop. 61,572.
— city, NW Oregon 97200*; pop. 366,383.
Port-of-Spain city, NW Trinidad; cap. of Trinidad and Tobago; pop. 94,000. Also **Port of Spain.**
Porto-Novo city, SE Benin; cap.; pop. 75,000.
Port Said city, NE Egypt; at the Mediterranean end of the Suez Canal; pop. 349,000.
Portsmouth co. boro., S England; site of the chief British naval station; pop. 197,000.
— city, SE New Hampshire 03801*; pop. 26,254.
— city, S Ohio 45662*; pop. 25,943.
— city, SE Virginia 23700*; pop. 104,577.
Portugal republic, SW Europe; 35,419 sq. mi.; pop. 10,000,000; cap. Lisbon.
Port Washington uninc. place, SE New York 11050; pop. 15,923
Potomac River river betw. Maryland, West Virginia, and Virginia; 287 mi. long.
Potsdam city, CEN. East Germany; scene of meeting of Allied leaders, 1945; pop. 111,000.
Pottstown boro., SE Pennsylvania 19464*; pop. 25,355.
Pottsville city, CEN. Pennsylvania 17901*; pop. 19,715.
Poughkeepsie city, SE New York 12600*; pop. 29,757.
Poznan city, W Poland; pop. 469,000.
Prague city, W Czechoslovakia; cap.; pop. 1,188,600.
Prairie Village city, NE Kansas 66208; pp. 28,138.
Pretoria city, CEN. South Africa; adm. cap.; pop. 493,000.
Prichard city, SW Alabama 36610; pop. 39,541.
Prince Albert city, CEN. Saskatchewan, Canada; pop. 28,464.
Prince Edward Island prov., NE Canada; 2,184 sq. mi.; pop. 111,641; cap. Charlottetown.
Prince George city, CEN. British Columbia, Canada; pop. 33,101.
Prince Rupert city, W British Columbia, Canada; pop. 15,747.
Provence reg. and former prov., SE France.
Providence city, NE Rhode Island 02900*; cap.; pop. 156,804.
Provo city city, CEN. Utah 84601; pop. 73,907.

Prussia former state, N Germany; dissolved, 1947.
Pueblo city, CEN. Colorado 81000*; pop. 101,686.
Puerto Rico isl., Greater Antilles; a Commonwealth of the United States 3,423 sq. mi.; pop. 2,353,297; cap. San Juan.
Puget Sound inlet of the Pacific, NW Washington.
Pulaski town, SW Virginia 24301; pop. 16,279.
Pullman city, SE Washington 99163*; pop. 20,509.
Punjab reg., NW India and E Pakistan.
Pyongyang city, W North Korea; cap.; pop. 1,500,000.
Pyrenees mtn. chain betw. France and Spain.

Qatar emirate on the W coast of the Persian Gulf; ab. 4,247 sq. mi.; pop. 230,000; cap. Doha.
Quebec prov., E Canada; 594,860 sq. mi.; pop. 6,234,445.
— city, S Quebec prov.; cap.; pop. 177,082.
Queens boro., E New York; pop. 1,891,325.
Queensland state, NE Australia; 670,500 sq. mi.; pop. 2,037,000; cap. Brisbane.
Quemoy Islands 2 isls. of the Republic of China in Formosa Strait; 54 sq. mi.
Quezon City city, CEN. Philippines; cap.; pop. 960,000.
Quincy city, W Illinois 62301*; pop. 42,352.
— city, E Massachusetts 02169; pop. 84,743.
Quito city, CEN. Ecuador; cap.; pop. 597,000.

Rabat city, N Morocco; cap.; pop. 261,000.
Racine city, SE Wisconsin 53400*; pop. 85,725.
Radnor urb. twp. SE Pennsylvania 19087; pop. 21,697.
Rahway city, NE New Jersey 07065*; pop. 26,723.
Rainier, Mount extinct volcano, Cascade Range, SW Washington; 14,408 ft.
Raleigh city, CEN. North Carolina 27600*; cap.; pop. 149,771.
Rancho Cordova uninc. place, CEN. California 95670; pop. 30,451.
Randallstown city, NE Maryland 21133; pop. 33,683.
Randolph town, E Massachusetts 02368; pop. 27,035.
Rangoon city, S Burma; cap.; pop. 2,200,000.
Rantoul vill., CEN. Illinois 61866*; pop. 25,526.
Rapid City city, SW South Dakota 57701*; pop. 46,492.
Raritan twp. CEN. New Jersey 08869; pop. 15,334.
Ravenna city, N Italy, famous for its art treasures and architecture; pop. 133,128.
Rawalpindi city, N Pakistan; pop. 340,000.
Raytown city, W Missouri 64133; pop. 31,759.
Reading town, NE Massachusetts 01867; pop. 22, 539.
— city, SE Pennsylvania 19600*; pop. 78,686.
Recife city, NE Brazil; pop. 2,346,196.
Red Deer city, CEN. Alberta, Canada: pop. 27,674.
Redding city, N California 96001*; pop. 41,995.
Redlands city, SW California 92373*; pop. 43,619.
Redondo Beach city, SW California 90277*; pop. 57,102.
Red River river in Texas, Arkansas, and Louisiana; ab. 1,300 mi. long.
— river in N United States and S Canada; 540 mi. long.
Red Sea sea betw. Egypt and Arabia; 1,450 mi. long; ab. 170,000 sq. mi.
Redwood City city, W California 94061*; pop. 54,965.
Regina city, S Saskatchewan, Canada; cap.; pop. 139,469.
Reims city, NE France; site of a famous cathedral; pop. 179,000.
Reno city, W Nevada 89500*; pop. 100,756
Renton city, CEN. Washington 98055; pop. 30,612.
Repentigny town, S Quebec, Canada; pop. 19,520.
Réunion French overseas dept.; isl. E of Madagascar; 970 sq. mi.; pop. 446,000; cap. Saint-Denis.
Revere city, E Massachusetts 02151; pop. 42,423.
Reykjavik city, SW Iceland; cap.; pop. 84,000.
Rheims Reims: *an alternate name.*
Rhine river, CEN. Europe; 810 mi. long.
Rhode Island state, NE United States; 1,214 sq. mi.; pop. 947,154; cap. Providence.
Rhodes isl. of the Dodecanese groups; 545 sq. mi.
Rhodesia See **Zimbabwe Rhodesia.**
Rhône river, Switzerland and SE France; 504 mi. long. Also **Rhone.**
Rialto city, S California 92376; pop. 35,615.
Richardson city, N Texas 75080*; pop. 72,496.
Richfield vill., E Minnesota 55423; pop. 37,851.
Richland city, S Washington 99352; pop. 33,578.
Richmond city, W California 94800*; pop. 74,676.
— city, E Indiana 47374; pop. 41,349.
— city, CEN. Kentucky 40475*; pop. 16,861.
— boro., SW New York City; pop. 295,443.
— city, CEN. Virginia 23200*; cap.; cap. of the Confederacy 1861-65.
Richmond Hill town, S Ontario, Canada; pop. 32,384.
Ridgewood urb. twp., NE New Jersey 07450*; pop. 25,208.
Ridley urb. twp., SE Pennsylvania; pop. 35,738.
Rif mtn. range, N Morocco. Also **Riff.**
Riga city, CEN. Latvian **SSR**; cap.; pop. 743,000.
Rijeka City, NW Yugoslavia; including its SE suburb and officially called **Rijeka-Susak;** pop. 133,000.
Rimouski town, E Quebec, Canada; pop. 26,887.
Rio de Janeiro city, SE Brazil; former cap.; pop. 4,316,000. Also **Rio.**
Rio de la Plata estuary of the Paraná and Uruguay rivers betw. Argentina and Uruguay; 170 mi. long.
Rio de Oro terr., Spanish Sahara; 73,362 sq. mi.; pop. 157,000; cap. Villa Cisneros.
Rio Grande river betw. Texas and Mexico; 1,890 mi. long.
Riverdale vill., NE Illinois 60627; pop. 15,806.
River Rouge city, SE Michigan, 48218; pop. 15,947.
Riverside city, SW California 92501*; pop. 170,876.
Riviera coastal strip on the Mediterranean from Hyeres, France to La Spezia, Italy.
Riviera Beach town, SE Florida 33404; pop. 26,596.
Roanoke city, W Virginia 24001*; pop. 100,427.
Roanoke Island isl. off North Carolina; 12 mi. long, 3 mi. wide.
Robbinsdale city, E Minnesota 55422; pop. 16,845.
Rochester city, SE Minnesota 55901; pop. 57,855.
— city, SE New Hampshire 03867; pop. 17,938.
— city, W New York 14600*; pop. 241,741.
Rockford city, N Illinois 61100; pop. 139,712.
Rock Hill city, N South Carolina 29730*; pop. 35,344.
Rock Island city, NW Illinois 61201*; pop. 47,036.
Rockland town, E Massachusetts 02370; pop. 15,674.
Rockville city, CEN. Maryland 20850*; pop. 43,811.
Rockville Centre vill., SE New York 11570*; pop.25,405.
Rocky Mount city, CEN. North Carolina 27801*; pop. 43,811.
Rocky Mountains mtn. system, W North America; extends from the Arctic to Mexico.
Rocky River city, N Ohio 44116; pop. 22,958.
Rolling Meadows city, NE Illinois 60008; pop. 19,178.
Romania Rumania: *an alternate form.*
Rome city, W Italy; cap.; site of the Vatican City; cap. of the former Roman republic, the Roman Empire, and the States of the Church; pop. 2,900,000.
— city, NW Georgia 30161*; pop. 29,654.
— city, CEN. New York 13440*; pop. 43,826.
Roosevelt uninc. place, SE New York 11575; pop. 15,008.
Rosario city, CEN. Argentina; pop. 672,000.
Rosedale city, NW Maryland 21237; pop. 19,417.
Roselle boro., NE New Jersey 07203 pop. 22,585.
Rosemead city, SW California 91770*; pop. 42,604.
Roseville city, CEN. California 95678; pop. 17,805.
— city SE Michigan 48066; pop. 54,311.
— vill., SE Minnesota 55113; pop. 35,820.
Roslyn city, SW Pennsylvania 19001; pop. 18,317.
Ross urb twp., SW Pennsylvania; pop. 25,952.
Rostov-on-Don city, SW RSFSR; pop. 934,000.
Roswell city, SE New Mexico 88201*; pop. 39,676.
Rotterdam city, W Netherlands; pop. 1,014,800.
— uninc. place E New York 12303; pop. 25,153.
Rouen city, N France; site of a famous cathedral; scene of the burning of Joan of Arc; pop. 120,000.

Roumania Rumania: *an alternate form.*
Rouyn city, w Quebec, Canada; pop. 17,821.
Royal Oak city, SE Michigan 48067*; pop. 70,893.
Rugby municipal boro., CEN. England; site of a boys' school; pop. 57,000.
Ruhr river, w West Germany; 142 mi. long.
— reg. s of the Ruhr, an industrial and coal-mining district. 1,770 sq. mi.
Rumania republic, SE Europe; 91,671 sq. mi.; pop.22,-500,000; cap. Bucharest.
Russia before 1917, an empire, E Europe and N Asia; cap. Saint Petersburg (Petrograd); now part of the Union of Soviet Socialist Republics.
Russian Soviet Federated Socialist Republic constituent republic, N USSR; 6,592,800 sq. mi., pop. 130,-700,000; cap. Moscow.
Ruston city, N Louisiana 71270*; pop. 17,365.
Rutherford boro., NE New Jersey 07070*; pop. 20,802.
Rutland city, CEN. Vermont 05701*; pop. 19,293.
Rwanda republic, CEN. Africa; 10,160 sq. mi.; pop. 5,200,000; cap. Kigali.
Rye city, SE New York, 10580; pop. 15,869.
Ryukyu Islands isl. group betw. Kyushu and Taiwan; 1,205 sq. mi.; pop. 1,150,000; chief isl. Okinawa; adm. by Japan.

Saar river, NE France and Germany; 152 mi. long
Saar, The state, w West Germany; 991 sq. mi.; pop. 1,129,000; cap. Saarbrücken.
Sabah part of Malaysia in N Borneo; 29,388 sq. mi.; pop. 920,000; cap. Kota Kinabalu.
Sacramento city, CEN. California; 95801*; cap.; pop. 275,741.
Sacramento River river, CEN. California; 382 mi. long.
Saddle Brook urb. twp., NE New Jersey 07662; pop. 15,098.
Saginaw city, CEN. Michigan 48601*; pop. 77,508.
Sahara desert area, N Africa; ab. 3 million sq. mi. Also **Sahara Desert.**
Saigon city, s Vietnam; formerly cap. of South Vietnam; pop. 1,761,000: also called **Ho Chi Minh City.**
Saipan one of the Mariana isls.; 47 sq. mi.; captured from Japan by U.S. forces in World War II, 1944.
Saint, Sainte See entries beginning ST., STE.
Sakhalin isl. SE RSFSR; 29,700 sq. mi.; pop. 649,000; adm. ctr. Yuzhno-Sakhalinsk.
Salem city, NE Massachusetts 01970*; pop. 38,220.
— city, SE New Hampshire 03079; pop. 20,142.
— city, NW Oregon 97301*; cap.; pop. 89,233.
— town, CEN. Virginia 24153; pop. 21,982.
Salerno city, sw Italy; scene of a battle in World War II betw. Germans and Allied landing forces, 1943; pop. 157,-000.
Salina city, CEN. Kansas 67401*; pop. 41,843.
Salinas city, w California 93901*; pop. 80,479.
Salisbury city, SE Maryland 21801; pop. 15,252.
—city, CEN. North Carolina 28144; pop. 22,515.
— city, N Zimbabwe Rhodesia; cap.; pop. 557,000.
Salonika city, NE Greece; pop. 346,000.
Salt Lake City city, CEN. Utah 84100*; cap.; pop. 163,-033.
Salvador city, E Brazil; pop. 1,766,075.
— See EL SALVADOR
Salzburg city, w Austria; birthplace of Mozart; pop. 129,-000.
Samar one of the Visayan isls., Philippines; 5,050 sq. mi.
Samarkand city, E Uzbek SSR; pop. 272,000.
Samoa isl. group, sw Pacific; 1,173 sq. mi.; divided into **American** (or **Eastern**) **Samoa**, an uninc. terr. of the United States; 76 sq. mi.; pop. 28,000; cap. Pago Pago; and **Western Samoa**, an independent state; 1,097 sq. mi.; pop. 147,000; cap. Apia.
Samos isl. of Greece, E Aegean; 184 sq. mi.
Samothrace isl. of Greece, NE Aegean; 71 sq. mi.
San Angelo city, CEN. Texas 76901*; pop. 73,240.
San Antonio city, CEN. Texas 78200*; site of the Alamo; pop. 785,410.
San Benito city, s Texas 78586; pop. 15,176.
San Bernardino city, sw California 92400*; pop. 118,-057.
San Bruno city, w California 94066*; pop. 35,417.
San Carlos city, w California 94070*; pop. 25,924.
San Clemente city, s California 92672; pop. 35,417.
San Diego city, sw California 92100*; pop. 875,504.
San Dimas city, sw California 91773; pop. 15,692.
Sandusky city, N Ohio 44870*; pop. 31,360.
San Fernando city, sw California 91340*; pop. 16,751.
Sanford city, CEN. Florida 32771; pop. 17,393.
— uninc. place, sw Maine 04073; pop. 15,812.
San Francisco city, w California 94100*; pop. 678,974.
San Francisco Bay inlet of the Pacific, w California.
San Gabriel city, sw California 91775*; pop. 30,072.
San Joaquin River river, CEN. California; 317 mi. long.
San José city, CEN. Costa Rica; cap.; pop. 211,00.
San Jose city, w California 95100*; pop. 636,550.
San Juan city, NE Puerto Rico 00900*; cap.; pop. 452,749.
San Leandro city, w California 94577*; pop. 63,952.
San Lorenzo uninc. place, w California 94580; pop. 24,-633.
San Luis Obispo city, w California 93401*; pop. 34,252.
San Marcos city, CEN. Texas 78666; pop. 18,860.
San Marino republic, an enclave in NE Italy; 24 sq. mi.; pop. 21,000.
— city, San Marino; cap.; pop. 4,000.
San Mateo city, w California 94400*; pop. 77,561.
San Pablo city, w California 94806; pop. 21,461.
San Rafael city, w California 94901*; pop. 44,700.
San Salvador city, s El Salvador; cap.; pop. 379,000.
— isl. CEN. Bahamas; site of Columbus' first landing in the western hemisphere, 1492.
Santa Ana city, sw California 92700*; pop. 203,713.
Santa Barbara city, sw California 93100*; pop. 87,746.
Santa Catalina isl. off sw California; 70 sq. mi.
Santa Clara city, w California 95050*; pop. 87,746.
Santa Cruz city, w California 95060*; pop. 41,483.
Santa Fe city, N New Mexico 87501*; cap.; pop. 74,542.
Sante Fe Trail trade route, important from 1821–80, betw. Independence, Missouri, and Santa Fe, New Mexico.
Santa Maria city, sw California 93454*; pop. 39,685.
Santa Monica city, sw California 90400*; pop. 88,314.
Santa Paula city, sw California 93060; pop. 18,001.
Santa Rosa city, w California 95401*; pop. 83,205.
Santee city, sw California 92071; pop. 21,107.
Santiago city, CEN. Chile; cap; pop. 3,850,000. Also **Santiago de Chile.**
Santo Domingo city, s Dominican Republic; cap.; pop. 1,103,400.
São Paulo city, SE Brazil; pop. 5,241,000.
Sapulpa city, CEN. Oklahoma 74066; pop. 15,159.
Sarajevo city, CEN. Yugoslavia; scene of the assassination of Archduke Franz Ferdinand, June 28, 1914; pop. 244,000.
Sarasota city sw Florida 33577*; pop. 48,868.
Saratoga city, w California 95070; pop. 29,261.
Saratoga Springs city, CEN. New York 12866; pop. 18,-845.
Sarawak part of Malaysia on NW Borneo; 47,071 sq. mi.; pop. 945,000; cap. Kuching.
Sardinia isl., CEN. Mediterranean; with adjacent isls. a reg. of Italy; 9,298 sq. mi.; pop. 1,419,000; cap. Cagliari.
Sarnia city, s Ontario, Canada; pop. 57,644.
Saskatchewan prov., CEN. Canada; 251,700 sq. mi.; pop. 926,242; cap. Regina.
Saskatoon city, CEN. Saskatchewan, Canada; pop. 126,-449.
Saudi Arabia kingdom, N and CEN. Arabia; 873,000 sq. mi.; pop. 8,650,000; caps. Mecca and Riyadh.
Saugus town, NE Massachusetts 01906; pop. 25,110.
Sault Sainte Marie city, N Michigan 49783*; pop. 15,-136.
— city, CEN. Ontario, Canada; pop. 80,332. Also **Sault Ste. Marie.**
Sault Sainte Marie Canals 3 canals that circumvent the rapids in the St. Marys River betw. Lakes Superior and Huron.

Savannah city, E Georgia 31400*; pop. 141,634.
Saxony reg. and former duchy, electorate, kingdom and prov., CEN. Germany.
Sayreville boro., E New Jersey 08872; pop. 29,969.
Scandinavia reg., NW Europe; includes Sweden, Norway, and Denmark and sometimes Finland, Iceland, and the Faroe Islands.
Scapa Flow sea basin and British naval base in the Orkney Islands, Scotland; 50 sq. mi.
Scarsdale town, SE New York 10583; pop. 19,229.
Schaumburg city, NE Illinois 60172; pop. 52,319.
Scheldt river, N France, Belgium and the Netherlands; 270 mi. long.
Schenectady city, E New York 12300*; pop. 67,972.
Schleswig-Holstein state, NE West Germany; 6,052 sq. mi.; pop. 2,529,000; cap. Kiel.
Schuylkill River river, SE Pennsylvania; 130 mi. long.
Scituate city, NE Massachusetts 02066; pop. 16,973.
Scotch Plains urb. twp., NE New Jersey 07076; pop. 22,279.
Scotland a political div. and the N part of Great Britain; a separate kingdom until 1707; 30,405 sq. mi.; pop. 5,199,000; cap. Edinburgh.
Scott urb. twp., SW Pennsylvania; pop. 19,094.
Scottsdale city, CEN. Arizona 85251*; pop. 88,364.
Scranton city, NE Pennsylvania 18500*; pop. 88,117.
Seaford uninc. place, SE New York 11783; pop. 17,379.
Seal Beach city, SW California 90740; pop. 25,975.
Seaside city, W California 93955; pop. 36,567.
Seattle city, CEN. Washington 98100*; pop. 493,846.
Sebastopol See SEVASTOPOL.
Security unic. place, CEN. Colorado 80911; pop. 15,297.
Sedalia city, CEN. Missouri 65301*; pop. 22,847.
Seguin city, CEN. Texas 78155; pop. 15,934.
Seine river, NE France; 482 mi. long.
Selma city, CEN. Alabama 36701*; pop. 26,684.
Semarang city, N Java, Indonesia; pop. 690,000.
Senegal river, NW Africa; ab. 1,000 mi. long.
Senegal, Republic of republic of the French Community, NW Africa; 76,124 sq. mi.; pop. 5,800,000.; cap. Dakar.
Seoul city, NW South Korea; cap.; pop. 5,510,000.
Sept-Iles city, E Quebec, Canada; pop. 24,320.
Serbia constituent republic, E Yugoslavia; 34,107 sq. mi.; pop. 8,860,000; cap. Belgrade.
Sevastopol city, S Crimea, USSR; pop. 236,000.
Severn river, N. Wales and W England; 210 mi. long.
Severna city, NE Maryland 21146; pop. 16,358.
Seville city, SW Spain; pop. 630,000.
Sèvres city, N France; pop. 17,000.
Shaker Heights city, N Ohio 44120; pop. 32,487.
Shaler urb. twp., SW Pennsylvania; pop. 24,939.
Shanghai city, E China; pop. 10,820,000.
Shannon river, CEN. Ireland; 224 mi. long.
Sharon city, W Pennsylvania 16146*; pop. 22,653.
Shasta, Mount extinct volcano, Cascade Range, N California; 14,162 ft.
Shawinigan city, S Quebec, Canada; pop. 27,792.
Shawnee city, NE Kansas 66103; pop. 29,653.
— city, CEN. Oklahoma 74801*; pop. 26,306.
Sheboygan city, E Wisconsin 53081*; pop. 48,085.
Sheffield co. boro., CEN. England; pop. 520,000.
Shelby city, SW North Carolina 28150; pop. 16,328.
Shelbyville city, CEN. Indiana 46176; pop. 15,094.
Shelton city, SW Connecticut 06484*; pop. 31,314.
Shenandoah river, N Virginia and NE West Virginia; 170, mi. long.
Shenyang city, NE China; pop. 3,750,000: formerly called Mukden.
Sherbrooke city, S Quebec, Canada; pop. 80,711.
Sherman city, N Texas 75090*; pop. 30,413.
Sherrelwood city, CEN. Colorado; pop. 18,868.
Shetland Islands isl. group NE of the Orkney Islands, comprising **Shetland,** a co. of Scotland; 551 mi.; pop. 17,000; cap. Lerwick.
Shikoku isl., SW Japan; 7,248 sq. mi.
Shiloh national military park, SW Tennessee; scene of a Union victory in the Civil War, 1862; 6 sq. mi.
Shively city, N Kentucky 40216; pop. 19,223.
Shorewood vill., SE Wisconsin 53211; pop. 15,576.
Shreveport city, NW Louisiana 71100*; pop. 205,815.
Shrewsbury city, CEN. Massachusetts 01545; pop. 19,196.
Siam Thailand: *the former name.*
Siam, Gulf of part of the South China Sea betw. the Malay Peninsula and Indochina.
Siberia reg., E RSFSR; ab. 5 million sq. mi.
Sicily isl. of Italy, CEN. Mediterranean; comprises with neighboring islands a reg. of 9,926 sq. mi.; pop. 4,721,000; cap. Palermo.
Sidney city, W Ohio 45365; pop. 16,332.
Sierra Leone independent member of the Commonwealth of Nations, W Africa; 27,925 sq. mi.; pop. 3,560,000; cap. Freetown.
Sierra Nevada mtn. range, E California.
Silesia reg., CEN. Europe; divided betw. Czechoslovakia and Poland.
Silver Spring uninc. place, W Maryland 20900*; pop. 77,496.
Simi Valley city, SW California 93065; pop. 77,500.
Simla city, N India; pop. 43,000.
Simsbury city, CEN. Connecticut 06070; pop. 17,475.
Sinai penin., E Egypt, betw. the Mediterranean and the Red Sea.
Singapore isl. off the tip of the Malay Peninsula; comprises with adjacent isls. a republic of the Commonwealth of Nations; 238 sq. mi.; pop. 2,420,000.
— city, S Singapore; cap.; pop. 2,308,000.
Sinkiang-Uigur Autonomous Region div., W China; 635,829 sq. mi.; pop. ab. 8 million; cap. Urumchi (Tihwa). Also formerly **Sinkiang.**
Sioux City city, W Iowa 51100*; pop. 82,003.
Sioux Falls city, SE South Dakota 57100*; pop. 81,343.
Skokie vill., NE Illinois 60076*; pop. 60,278.
Slidell town, SE Louisiana 70458; pop. 26,718.
Slovakia reg. and former prov., E Czechoslovakia.
Slovenia constituent republic, NW Yugoslavia; 7,717 sq. mi.; pop. 1,792,000; cap. Ljubljana.
Smyrna town, CEN. Georgia 30080; pop. 19,517.
— Izmir: *an alternate name.*
Society Islands isl. group, French Polynesia; ab. 650 sq. mi.
Sofia city, W Bulgaria; cap.; pop. 1,000,000.
Solomon Islands isl. group, SW Pacific; ab. 16,500 sq. mi.; including the **British Solomon Islands,** a prot.; ab. 11,500 sq. mi.; pop. 225,000; cap. Honiara.
Somalia republic, E Africa; 246,201 sq. mi.; pop. 3,750,000; cap. Mogadiscio. Also **Somali Democratic Republic.**
Somerset town, SE Massachusetts 02725; pop. 18,088.
Somerville city, E Massachusetts 02143; pop. 77,372.
Somme river, N France; 150 mi. long.
Soo Canals *informal* Sault Sainte Marie Canals.
Sorel city, S Quebec, Canada; pop. 19,347.
South Africa, Republic of republic, S Africa; 472,359 sq. mi.; pop. 28,115,000; seat of government Pretoria; seat of legislature Cape Town.
South America S continent of the Western Hemisphere; ab. 6,900,000 sq. mi.
Southampton co. boro., S England; pop. 215,000.
South Australia state, S Australia; 380,070 sq. mi.; pop. 1,173,000; cap. Adelaide.
South Bakersfield city, CEN. California; pop. 30,249.
South Bend city, N Indiana 46600*; pop. 109,727.
Southbridge uninc. place S Massachusetts 01550*; pop. 17,057.
South Carolina state, SE United States; 31,055 sq. mi.; pop. 3,119,208; cap. Columbia.
South Charleston city, CEN. West Virginia 25303; pop. 16,333.
South China Sea part of the Pacific betw. SE Asia and the Malay Archipelago.
South Dakota state, CEN. United States; 77,047 sq. mi.; pop. 690,178; cap. Pierre.
Southern Yemen See YEMEN, PEOPLE'S DEMOCRATIC REPUBLIC OF.
South Euclid city, NE Ohio 44121; pop. 25,713.

South Farmingdale uninc. place, SE New York 11735; pop. 20,464.
Southfield city, SE Michigan 48075*; pop. 75,568.
South Fort Polk city, SW Louisiana; pop. 15,600.
Southgate city, SE Michigan 48192; pop. 33,909.
South Gate city, SW California 90280*; pop. 66,784.
South Hadley town, GEN. Massachusetts 01075; pop. 17,033.
South Holland vill, SE Illinois 60473; pop. 23,931.
Southington uninc. place, CEN. Connecticut 06489; pop. 30,946.
South Island one of the two main isls. of New Zealand; 58,093 sq. mi.
South Kingston town, S Rhode Island; pop. 16,913.
South Korea See KOREA.
South Miami city, SE Florida 33143; pop. 19,571.
South Milwaukee city SE Wisconsin 53172; pop. 23,-297.
South Orange vill., NE New Jersey 07079; pop. 16,971.
South Pasadena city, SW California 91030*; pop. 22,-979.
South Plainfield boro., NE New Jersey 07080; pop. 21,-142.
South Pole S extremity of the earth's axis.
South Portland city, SW Maine 04106; pop. 23,267.
South River boro., E New Jersey 08882; pop. 15,428.
South Sacramento-Frutridge uninc. place, CEN. California; pop. 28,574.
South San Francisco city, W California 94080*; pop. 49,393.
South Sea Islands isls. of the South Pacific.
South Seas waters of the Southern Hemisphere, esp. the **South Pacific Ocean.**
South Stickney city, NE Illinois 60459; pop. 29,900.
South Stony Brook City, SE New York; pop. 15,329.
South St. Paul city, E Minnesota 55075*; pop. 25,016.
South Valley city, CEN. New Mexico; pop. 29,389.
South-West Africa mandated terr., SW Africa; administered by the Republic of South Africa; 317,877 sq. mi.; pop. 746,000; cap. Windhoek. Also called **Namibia.**
South Whittier city, SW California 90605; pop. 46,641.
South Windsor city, CEN. Connecticut 06074; pop. 15,-553.
Soviet Russia 1 Russian Soviet Federated Socialist Republic. **2** Union of Soviet Socialist Republics.
Soviet Union Union of Soviet Socialist Republics: *an alternate name.*
Spain monarchy, SW Europe; 194,368 sq. mi.; pop. 37,750,000; cap. Madrid.
Spanish America parts of the W hemisphere where Spanish is the predominant language.
Spanish Lake city, NE Missouri 63101; pop. 15,647.
Sparks city, W Nevada 89431; pop. 40,780.
Sparta city-state of ancient Greece, famous for its military power: sometimes called *Lacedaemon.*
Spartanburg city, NW South Carolina 29301*; pop. 43,968.
Speedway town, S Indiana 46224; pop. 15,056.
Spenard uninc. place S Alaska 99503; pop. 18,089.
Spitsbergen See SVALBARD.
Spokane city E Washington 99200*; pop. 171,300.
Springdale city, NW Arkansas 72764; pop. 16,783.
Springfield city, CEN. Illinois 62700*; cap.; pop. 99,637.
— city, SW Massachusetts 01100*; pop. 152,319.
— city, SW Missouri 65800; pop. 133,116.
— urb. twp., NE New Jersey 07081; pop. 15,740.
— city, CEN. Ohio 45500; pop. 72,563.
— city, W Oregon 97477; pop. 41,621.
— urb. twp., SE Pennsylvania 19064 (Delaware County); pop. 26,733.
Springfield urb. twp., SE Pennsylvania (Montgomery County); pop. 20,652.
Spring Valley city, SE California 92077; pop. 29,742.
— vill., SE New York 10977; pop. 18,112.
Sri Lanka isl. S of India, an independent state of the Commonwealth of Nations, formerly called Ceylon; 25,332 sq. mi.; pop. 15,000,000; cap. Colombo.
Stalingrad Volgograd: *the former name.*
Stamford city, SW Connecticut 06901*; pop. 102,453.
St. Ann city, E Missouri 63074; pop. 18,215.
Stanton city, SW California 90680; pop. 17,947.
State College boro., CEN. Pennsylvania 16801*; pop. 36,130.
Staten Island isl., SE New York, at the entrance to New York Harbor; coextensive with Richmond boro. 10314*; 352,121.
Statesville city, CEN. North Carolina 28677; pop. 19,996.
Staunton city, CEN. Virginia 24401*; pop. 24,504.
St.-Bruno-de-Montarville town, CEN. Quebec, Canada; pop. 15,780.
St. Catharines city, S Ontario, Canada; pop. 109,722.
St. Charles city, E Missouri 63301*; pop. 37,379.
St. Clair, Lake lake betw. S Ontario and SE Michigan; 460 sq. mi.
St. Clair Shores vill., SE Michigan 48080*; pop. 76,210.
St. Cloud city, CEN. Minnesota 56301*; pop. 42,566.
St. Croix one of the Virgin Islands of the United States; 82 sq. mi.
Ste.-Foy city, S Quebec, Canada; pop. 68,385.
Sterling city, NW Illinois 61081; pop. 16,113.
Sterling Heights city, SE Michigan 48077; pop.
Ste.-Thérèse city, S Quebec, Canada; pop. 17,175.
Stettin Szczecin: *the German name.*
Steubenville city, E Ohio 43952; pop. 26,400.
Stevens Point city, CEN. Wisconsin 54481*; pop. 23,479.
St. Helena isl., South Atlantic; British colony with Ascension Island and the Tristan da Cunha group as dependencies; 133 sq. mi.; pop. 5,000; cap. Jamestown; site of Napoleon's exile, 1815-21.
St. Hubert town, S Quebec, Canada; pop. 21,741.
St. Hyacinthe city, S Quebec, Canada; pop. 24,562.
Stillwater city, CEN. Oklahoma 74074*; pop. 31,126.
St. James city, S Manitoba, Canada; pop. 71,431.
St. Jean city, S Quebec, Canada; pop. 32,863.
St. Jérôme city, S Quebec, Canada; pop. 26,524.
St. John one of the Virgin Islands of the United States; 19 sq. mi.
— city, S New Brunswick, Canada; pop. 51,567.
St. John's city, SE Newfoundland, Canada; cap.; pop. 88,102.
St. Joseph city, NW Missouri 64500*; pop. 76,691.
St. Lambert city, S Quebec, Canada; pop. 18,616.
St. Laurent city, S Quebec, Canada; pop. 62,955.
St. Lawrence, Gulf of inlet of the Atlantic E Canada.
St. Lawrence River river, SE Canada; the outlet of the Great Lakes system; 1,900 mi. long.
St. Lawrence Seaway system of ship canals extending 114 miles along the St. Lawrence River from Montreal to Lake Ontario.
St. Leonard city, CEN. Quebec, Canada; pop. 52,040.
St. Louis city, E Missouri 63100*; pop. 453,085.
St. Louis Park vill., E Minnesota 55426; pop. 42,931.
St. Michel city, S Quebec, Canada; pop. 71,446.
Stockholm city, SE Sweden; cap.; pop. 1,477,000.
Stockton city, CEN. California 95200*; pop. 149,779.
Stoneham town, NE Massachusetts 02180; pop. 20,725.
Stoneleigh-Rodgers Forge uninc. place, N Maryland; pop. 15,645.
Stonington city, NE Connecticut 06378; pop. 15,940.
Stoughton town, E Massachusetts 02072; pop. 23,459.
Stow vill., CEN. Ohio 44224; pop. 25,303.
St. Paul city, SE Minnesota 55100*; cap.; pop. 270,230.
St. Petersburg city, W Florida 33700*; pop. 236,893.
— Leningrad: *the former name.*
Strasbourg city, NE France; pop. 253,000.
Stratford town, SE Connecticut 06497; pop. 49,775.
— city, S Ontario, Canada; pop. 24,508.
Stratford-on-Avon town, CEN. England; birthplace and burial place of Shakespeare; pop. 17,000.
Streamwood city, NE Illinois 60103; pop. 18,176.
Streator city, CEN. Illinois 61364; pop. 15,600.
Strongsville vill., N Ohio 44136; pop. 28,577.
Struthers city, E Ohio 44471; pop. 15,343.
St. Thomas one of the Virgin Islands of the United States; 28 sq. mi.; pop. 16,201.
— city, S Ontario, Canada; pop. 25,545.
Stuttgart city, SW West Germany; pop. 628,000.

Sucre city, CEN. Bolivia; cap.; pop. 85,000.
Sudan reg., N Africa S of the Sahara.
Sudan, Republic of the republic, NE Africa; 967,500 sq. mi.; pop. 19,600,000; cap. Khartoum.
Sudbury city, CEN. Ontario, Canada; pop. 90,535.
Sudetenland border dists., W Czechoslovakia.
Suez city, NE Egypt; pop. 381,000.
Suez, Gulf of inlet of the Red Sea, NE Egypt.
Suez, Isthmus of strip of land joining Asia and Africa, betw. the Gulf of Suez and the Mediterranean.
Suez Canal ship canal across the Isthmus of Suez; 107 mi.
Suitland-Silver Hills uninc. place, CEN. Maryland 20023; pop. 30,355.
Sulawesi isl. of Indonesia, E of Borneo; 87,897 sq. mi.; pop. 9,315,000.
Sulu Archipelago isl. group, SW Philippines; 1,086 sq. mi.
Sumatra isl. of Indonesia S of the Malay Peninsula; 208,-948 sq. mi.; pop. 22,934,000.
Summit city, NE New Jersey 07901; pop. 23,620.
Sumter city, CEN. South Carolina 29150*; pop. 24,435.
Sunnyvale city, W California 94086*; pop. 106,618.
Superior city, NW Wisconsin 54880*; pop. 29,571.
Superior, Lake largest of the Great Lakes; 31,820 sq. mi.
Surabaya city, NE Java, Indonesia; pop. 1,660,000.
Surinam republic, former Dutch colony NE coast of S. America; 63,251 sq. mi.; pop. 384,900; cap. Paramaribo.
Susquehanna river, New York, Pennsylvania, and Maryland; 444 mi. long.
Suwannee River river, Georgia and Florida; 250 mi. long.
Svalbard isl. group of Norway, Arctic Ocean; 23,958 sq. mi.: sometimes called *Spitsbergen.*
Swaziland independent member of the Commonwealth of Nations, SE Africa; 6,704 sq. mi.; pop. 560,000; cap. Mbabane.
Sweden kingdom, NW Europe; 173,577 sq. mi.; pop. 8,330,000; cap. Stockholm.
Sweetwater Creek city, NW Florida 33601; pop. 19,-433.
Swift Current city, SW Saskatchewan, Canada; pop. 15,-415.
Switzerland republic, CEN. Europe; 15,940 sq. mi.; pop. 6,584,000; cap. Bern.
Sydney city, NE Nova Scotia, Canada; pop. 33,230.
— city, E New South Wales, Australia; cap.; pop. 3,200,000.
Syracuse city, CEN. New York 13200*; pop. 170,105.
Syria republic, SW Asia; 71,498 sq. mi.; pop. 9,325,000; cap. Damascus.
Szczecin city, NW Poland; pop. 340,000: German name *Stettin.*

Tabriz city, NW Iran; pop. 468,000.
Tacoma city, W Washington 98400*; pop. 154,581.
Tadzhik SSR constituent republic, S USSR; 55,043 sq. mi.; pop. 3 million; cap. Dushanbe.
Tahiti isl., Society group; 402 sq. mi.; pop. 85,000.
Tahoe, Lake lake E California and W Nevada; ab. 195 sq. mi.
Taipei city, N Taiwan; cap.; pop. 2,225,000.
Taiwan isl. off SE China; comprises with the Pescadores, the Republic of China; 13,890 sq. mi.; pop. 17,350,000; cap. Taipei; formerly called *Formosa.*
Takoma Park city W Maryland 20012; pop. 18,455.
Talledaga city, CEN. Alabama 35160; pop. 17,662.
Tallahassee city, N Florida 32301*; cap.; pop. 81,548.
Tallinn city, N Estonian SSR; cap.; pop. 371,000.
Tallmadge city, NE Ohio 44278; pop. 15,274.
Tampa city, W Florida 33600*; pop. 271,523.
Tampico city, E Mexico; pop. 231,000.
Tanganyika, Lake lake, CEN. Africa; 12,700 sq. mi.
Tangier city, N Morocco; pop. 166,000.
Tanzania republic of the Commonwealth of Nations, E Africa, includes *Tanganyika* and *Zanzibar;* 362,820 sq. mi.; pop. 19,000,000; cap. Dar es Salaam.
Taranto city, SE Italy; pop. 223,000.
Tashkent city, E Uzbek SSR; cap.; pop. 1,779,000.
Tasmania isl., SE Australia; comprises a state; 26,383 sq. mi.; pop. 407,000; cap. Hobart.
Taunton city, SE Massachusetts 02780*; pop. 45,001.
Taylor city, SE Michigan 48180; pop. 77,568.
Tbilisi city, SE Georgian SSR; cap.; pop. 1,066,000.
Teaneck urb. twp., NE New Jersey 07666; pop. 42,355.
Tegucigalpa city, CEN. Honduras; cap.; pop. 268,000.
Teheran city, CEN. Iran; cap.; pop. 4,716,000.
Tel Aviv city, W Israel; includes Jaffa; pop. 383,000.
Tempe city, CEN. Arizona 85281*; pop. 106,743.
Temple CEN. Texas 76501; pop. 42,483.
Tennessee state, CEN. United States; 42,246 sq. mi.; pop. 4,590,750; cap. Nashville.
Tennessee River river, flowing through E Tennessee, N Alabama, W Tennessee, and SW Kentucky; 652 mi. long.
Terre Haute city, W Indiana 47801*; pop. 61,135.
Tewksbury city, NE Massachusetts 01876; pop. 22755.
Texarkana city, SW Arkansas at the Arkansas-Texas line; pop. 21,682.
— city, NE Texas; adjacent to and integrated with Texarkana, Arkansas 75501*; pop. 31,271.
Texas n state S United States; 267,339 sq. mi.; pop. 14,-228,383; cap. Austin.
Texas City city, SE Texas 77590*; pop. 41,403.
Thailand constitutional monarchy, SE Asia; 198,404 sq. mi.; pop. 48,175,000; cap. Bangkok: formerly called *Siam.*
Thames river, S England; 209 mi. long.
Thessaly div., CEN. Greece; 5,399 sq. mi.
Thetford Mines city S Quebec, Canada; pop. 22,003.
Thomasville city, S Georgia 31792; pop. 18,155.
— city, CEN. North Carolina 27360; pop. 15,230.
Thorold town, S Ontario, Canada; pop. 15,065.
Thousand Islands group of ab. 1,500 isls. in the St. Lawrence River.
Thousand Oaks city, SE California 91360; pop. 77,797.
Thrace reg., E Balkan Peninsula.
Thunder Bay city, W Ontario, Canada; pop. 113,000.
Tiber river, CEN. Italy; 245 mi. long.
Tibet adm. div., W China; ab. 470,000 sq. mi.; pop. ab. 2 million; cap. Lhasa; formerly independent.
Tientsin city, NE China; pop. 4 million.
Tierra del Fuego isl. group, S South America, included in Chile and Argentina; 7,996 sq. mi. (Argentina), 19,480 sq. mi. (Chile).
Tiffin city, CEN. Ohio 44883; pop. 21,596.
Tigris river, SW Asia, ab. 1,150 mi. long.
Tijuana city, NW Lower California, Mexico; pop. 335,000.
Timbuktu town, CEN. Mali; pop. 9,000.
Timmins town, CEN. Ontario, Canada; pop. 28,542.
Timonium-Lutherville uninc. place, CEN. Maryland 21093; pop. 24,055.
Timor isl., SE Malay Archipelago; 11,965 sq. mi.; pop. 1,356,000; W Timor has been part of Indonesia since 1949; E Timor, formerly a Portuguese overseas province, was annexed by Indonesia in 1976.
Tirana city, CEN. Albania; cap.; pop. 175,000.
Tirol See Tyrol.
Titicaca, Lake lake betw. SE Peru and W Bolivia; 3,200 sq. mi.; elevation 12,500 ft.
Titusville city, E Florida 32789; pop. 31,910.
Tobago See TRINIDAD AND TOBAGO.
Togo republic, W Africa; ab. 21,853 sq. mi.; pop. 2,600,-000; cap. Lome.
Tokyo city, E Japan; cap.; pop. 8,841,000.
Toledo city, CEN. Spain; pop. 44,000.
— city, NW Ohio 43600*; pop. 354,635.
Tomsk city, S RSFSR; pop. 386,000.
Tonawanda city, W New York 14150*; pop. 21,898.
— uninc. place, W New York; pop. 83,771.
Tonga isl. group, SE of Fiji; a Polynesian kingdom in the Commonwealth of Nations; ab. 270 sq. mi.; pop. 100,-000; cap. Nukualofa.
Topeka city, NE Kansas 66600*; cap.; pop. 132,952.
Toronto city, S Ontario, Canada; pop. 633,318.
Torrance city, SW California 90500*; pop. 131,497.
Torrington city, SW Connecticut 06790*; pop. 30,987.
Toulon city, S France; pop. 175,000.
Toulouse city, S France; pop. 371,000.
Towson uninc. place, CEN. Maryland 21204; pop. 77,809.

Trafalgar, Cape headland, SW Spain; scene of a naval victory of Nelson over the French and Spanish, 1805.
Transcaucasia reg., SE USSR; betw. the Caucasus mountains and Iran and Turkey.
Transcona town, SE Manitoba, Canada; pop. 22,490.
Transvaal province, NE South Africa; 109,621 sq. mi.; pop. 8,765,000; cap. Pretoria.
Traverse City city, NW Michigan 49684; pop. 18,048.
Trenton city, SE Michigan 48183; pop. 24,127.
— city, W New Jersey 08600*; cap.; pop. 92,124.
Trieste city, NE Italy; pop. 277,000.
Trinidad and Tobago independent member of the Commonwealth of Nations off N Venezuela; comprises isls. of **Trinidad;** 1,864 sq. mi., and **Tobago;** 116 sq. mi.; pop. 1,145,000; cap. Port-of-Spain.
Tripoli city, NW Lebanon; pop. 150,000.
— city, NW Libya; cap.; pop. 376,000.
Trois-Rivieres city, S Quebec, Canada; pop. 55,869.
Troy city, SE Michigan 48084; pop. 67,102.
— city, E New York 12180*; pop. 56,638.
— city, W Ohio 45373; pop. 17,186.
Trumbull city, SE Connecticut 06611; pop. 31,394.
Tsingtao city, E China; pop. 1,900,000.
Tucson city, SE Arizona 85700*; pop. 330,537.
Tulare city, CEN. California 93274; pop. 16,235.
Tullahoma city, CEN. Tennessee 37388; pop. 15,311.
Tulsa city, NE Oklahoma 74100*; pop. 360,919.
Tunis city, NE Tunisia; cap.; pop. 1,000,000.
Tunisia republic, N Africa; 63,170 sq. mi.; pop. 6,500,000; cap. Tunis.
Tupelo city, NE Mississippi 38801*; pop. 20,471.
Turin city, NW Italy; pop. 1,191,000.
Turkestan reg., CEN. Asia; extends from the Caspian Sea to the Gobi Desert.
Turkey republic, SW Asia; 301,382 sq. mi.; pop. 45,500,000; cap. Ankara. See ANATOLIA.
Turkmen SSR constituent republic, S USSR; 189,370 sq. mi.; pop. 2,223,000; cap. Ashkhabad.
Tuscaloosa city, CEN. Alabama 35401*; pop. 75,143.
Tustin city, SW California 92680; pop. 32,073.
Tustin-Foothills city, SW California; pop. 26,598.
Tutuila chief isl., American Samoa; 53 sq. mi.; pop. 26,000.
Twin Falls city, S Idaho 83301*; pop. 26,209.
Tyler city, E Texas 75701*; pop. 70,508.
Tyrol reg., W Austria and N Italy.

Ubangi river, CEN. Africa; 1,400 mi. long.
Uganda independent member of the Commonwealth of Nations, CEN. Africa; 91,134 sq. mi.; pop. 14,000,000; cap. Kampala.
Ukrainian SSR constituent republic SW USSR; 233,090 sq. mi.; pop. 47,496,000; cap. Kiev. Also **Ukraine.**
Ulan Bator city, CEN. Mongolian People's Republic; cap.; pop. 282,000.
Ulster former prov., N Ireland, of which the N part became Northern Ireland, 1925.
— prov., N Republic of Ireland; comprises the part of Ulster that remained after 1925; 3,093 sq. mi.; pop. 207,000.
Union urb. twp., NE New Jersey 07083*; pop. 53,077.
Union City city, NE New Jersey 07087; pop. 55,593.
Uniondale uninc. place, SE New York 11553; pop. 22,077.
Union of Soviet Socialist Republics federal union of 15 constituent republics occupying most of N Eurasia; 8,649,500 sq. mi.; pop. 266,403,000; cap. Moscow.
Uniontown city, SW Pennsylvania 15401; pop. 16,282.
United Arab Emirates reg., E Arabian Peninsula, composed of 7 sheikdoms (formerly **Trucial States**); 32,300 sq. mi.; pop. 252,000.
United Arab Republic Egypt: *the former name.*
United Kingdom constitutional monarchy comprising Great Britain, Northern Ireland, the Isle of Man, and the Channel Islands; 94,284 sq. mi.; pop. 56,387,000; cap. London: officially **United Kingdom of Great Britain and Northern Ireland.**
United States of America federal republic,, including 50 states (49 in North America, and Hawaii, an archipelago in the Pacific Ocean), and the District of Columbia (3,615,222 sq. mi.; pop. 179,323,175), and the Canal Zone, Puerto Rico, the Virgin Islands of the United States, American Samoa, and Guam, Wake, and other Pacific isls.; total 3,720,407 sq. mi.; pop. 230,000,000; cap. Washington, coextensive with the District of Columbia.
University City city, E Missouri 63130; pop. 42,738.
University Heights city, N Ohio; pop. 17,055.
University Park city, N Texas 78227; pop. 23,498.
Upland city, SW California 91786; pop. 47,647.
Upper Arlington city, CEN. Ohio 43221; pop. 35,648.
Upper Darby urb. twp., SE Pennsylvania 19082*; pop. 95,510.
Upper Moreland urb. twp., SE Pennsylvania; pop. 21,032.
Upper Volta republic, W Africa; 105,900 sq. mi.; pop. 7,100,000; cap. Ouagadougou.
Ural Mountains mtn. system in the RSFSR, extending from the Arctic Ocian to the Kasakh SSR.
Ural River river S RSFSR and W Kazakh SSR; 1,574 mi. long.
Urbana city, E Illinois 61801*; pop. 35,978.
Uruguay republic, SE South America; 68,536 sq. mi.; pop. 2,820,000; cap. Montevideo.
Uruguay River river, SE South America; 1,000 mi. long.
Utah state, CEN. United States; 84,916 sq. mi.; pop. 1,461,037; cap. Salt Lake City.
Utica city, CEN. New York 13501*; pop. 75,632.
Utrecht city, CEN. Netherlands; pop. 278,000.
Uzbek SSR constituent republic S USSR; 173,592 sq. mi.; pop. 12,300,000; cap. Tashkent.

Vacaville city, CEN. California 95688; pop. 43,367.
Val-d'Or town, W Quebec, Canada; pop. 17,421.
Valdosta city, S Georgia 31601*; pop. 37,596.
Valencia city, E Spain; pop. 770,000.
Valinda city, SE California 91744; pop. 18,837.
Vallejo city, W California 94590*; pop. 80,188.
Valleyfield city, S Quebec, Canada; pop. 30,173. Also **Salaberry de Valleyfield.**
Valley Forge locality, SE Pennsylvania, scene of Washington's winter encampment 1777–78.
Valley Station uninc. place, N Kentucky 40172; pop. 24,471.
Valley Stream vill., SE New York 11580*; pop. 35,769.
Valparaiso city, CEN. Chile; pop. 296,000.
— city, NW Indiana 46383; pop. 20,020.
Vancouver city, SW Washington 98660*; pop. 42,834.
— city, SW British Columbia, Canada; pop. 410,188.
Vancouver Island isl., off SW British Columbia, Canada; 12,408 sq. mi.
Vanuatu republic, isl. group, SW Pacific, formerly **New Hebrides;** ab. 5,700 sq. mi.; pop. 110,000; cap. Villa.
Vatican City sovereign papal state within Rome; includes the Vatican and St. Peter's Church; established June 10, 1929; 108.7 acres; pop. 1,000.
Venezuela republic, N South America; 352,143 sq. mi.; pop. 14,300,000; cap. Caracas.
Venice city, NE Italy; pop. 368,000.
Venice, Gulf of N part of the Adriatic.
Ventura city, S California 93001; pop. 55,797.
Veracruz state, SE Mexico; 28,114 sq. mi.; pop. 3,815,000; cap. Jalapa; largest city Veracruz.
Verde, Cape westernmost point of Africa; a penin.; ab. 20 mi. long.
Verdun town, NE France; scene of several battles of World War I; pop. 19,000.
— city, S Quebec, Canada; pop. 68,013.
Vermont state, NE United States; 9,609 sq. mi.; pop. 511,456; cap. Montpelier.
Vernon city, NE Connecticut 06086; pop. 27,237.
Vernon Valley uninc. place, SE New York; pop. 17,925.
Verona city, NE Italy; pop. 231,000.
— boro., NE New Jersey 07044; pop. 15,067.
Versailles city, N France; site of the palace of Louis XIV; scene of the signing of a treaty (1919) betw. the Allies and Germany after World War I; pop. 91,000.
Vesuvius active volcano, W Italy; 3,891 ft.

Vichy city, CEN. France; provisional cap. during German occupation, World War II; pop. 32,000.
Vicksburg city, W Mississippi 39180*; pop. 25,434; besieged and taken by the Union Army in the Civil War, 1863.
Victoria state, SE Australia; 87,884 sq. mi.; pop. 3,647,000; cap. Melbourne.
— city, SW British Columbia; cap.; pop. 62,551.
— city, S Hong Kong; cap.; pop. 521,000.
— city, S Texas 77901*; pop. 30,695
Victoria, Lake lake betw. Uganda, Tanganyika, and Kenya; 26,828 sq. mi. Also **Victoria Nyanza.**
Victoria Falls cataract on the Zambesi River betw. Northern and Southern Rhodesia; 343 ft. high; over a mile wide.
Victoriaville town, S Quebec, Canada; pop. 22,047.
Vienna city, NE Austria; cap.; pop. 1,628,000.
— town, NE Virginia 22180; pop. 17,152.
Vientiane city, CEN. Laos; adm cap.; pop. 130,000.
Vietnam country, SW Indochina; 126,436 sq. mi.; pop. 53,550,000; cap. Hanoi; from 1954 to 1976 divided into **North Vietnam** and **South Vietnam,** with caps. at Hanoi and Saigon, respectively.
Villa Park vill., NE Illinois 60181; pop. 25,891.
Vilnius city, SE Lithuanian SSR; cap.; pop. 386,000. Also **Vilna, Vilnyus.**
Vincennes city, SW Indiana 47591; pop. 19,867.
Vineland boro., S New Jersey 08360; pop. 53,753.
Virginia state, E United States; 40,815 sq. mi.; pop. 5,346,279; cap. Richmond.
Virginia Beach city, SE Virginia 23450*; pop. 262,199.
Virgin Islands isl. group, West Indies E of Puerto Rico. See BRITISH VIRGIN ISLANDS.
Virgin Islands of the United States uninc. terr., Virgin Islands; 133 sq. mi.; pop. 104,000; cap. Charlotte Amalie.
Visalia city, CEN. California 93277*; pop. 49,729.
Visayan Islands isl. group, CEN. Philippines; 23,621 sq. mi.
Vista uninc. place, SW California 92083; pop. 35,834.
Vistula river, CEN. and N Poland; 678 mi. long.
Vladivostok city, SE RSFSR; pop. 456,000.
Volga river, W RSFSR; 2,290 mi. long.
Volgograd city, W RSFSR; scene of a Russian victory over German forces in World War II, Sept. 1942 to Jan. 1943; pop. 929,000: from 1925–61 **Stalingrad.**
Volta river, E Ghana; 800 mi. long.
Vosges Mountains mtn. chain, E France.

Wabash river, W Ohio and Indiana; 475 mi. long.
Waco city, CEN. Texas 76700*; pop. 101,261.
Wade-Hampton city, NW South Carolina 29607; pop. 17,152.
Wahiawa city, CEN. Oahu, Hawaii 96786; pop. 17,598.
Waikiki beach on Honolulu harbor, SE Oahu, Hawaii.
Waipio city, Oahu, Hawaii 96786; pop. 22,798.
Wakefield town, E Massachusetts 01880*; pop. 25,402.
Wake Island coral atoll in the North Pacific; 4 sq. mi.; site of a U.S. naval and air base.
Wales penin., SW Britain; a principality of England; 8,018 sq. mi.; pop 2,810,000.
Walla Walla city, SE Washington 99362; pop. 25,618.
Wallingford town, CEN. Connecticut 06492; pop. 35,714.
Walnut Creek city, W California 94596*; pop. 53,643.
Walpole town, E Massachusetts 02081; pop. 18,149.
Waltham city, E Massachusetts 02154; pop. 58,200.
Wantagh vill., SE New York 11793; pop. 21,873.
Warminster urb. twp., SE Pennsylvania 18974; pop. 15,994.
Warner Robins city, CEN. Georgia 31093*; pop. 39,893.
Warren city, SE Michigan 48089*; pop. 161,134.
— city, NE Ohio 44480*; pop. 56,629.
Warrensville Heights vill., N Ohio; pop. 18,925.
Warrington uninc. place, NW Florida 32507; pop. 15,848.
Warsaw city, CEN. Poland; cap.; pop. 1,576,602.
Warwick city, CEN. Rhode Island 02886*; pop. 87,123.
Washington state, NW United States; 68,192 sq. mi.; pop. 4,130,163; cap. Olympia.
— city, E United States; coextensive with the District of Columbia 20000*; pop. 637,651.
— city, SW Pennsylvania 15301; pop. 19,827.
Waterbury city. W Connecticut 06700*; pop. 103,266.
Waterford city, NE Connecticut 06385; pop. 17,227.
Waterloo vill., CEN. Belgium; scene of Napoleon's final defeat, June 18, 1815; pop. 10,000.
— city, CEN. Iowa 50700*; pop. 75,985.
— city, S Ontario, Canada; pop. 36,677.
Watertown city, SW Connecticut 06795; pop. 18,610.
— town, E Massachusetts 02172; pop. 39,307.
— city, N New York 13601*; pp. 27,861.
— city, SE Wisconsin 53094; pop. 15,683.
Waterville city, CEN. Maine 04900*; pop. 18,192.
Waukegan city, NE Illinois 60085*; pop. 67,653.
Waukesha city, SE Wisconsin 53186*; pop. 50,319.
Wausau city, CEN. Wisconsin 54401*; pop. 32,426.
Wauwatosa city, SE Wisconsin 53213; pop. 51,308.
Waycross city, SE Georgia 31501; pop. 18,996.
Wayland city, N Massachusetts 01778; pop. 13,461.
Wayne vill., SE Michigan 48184; pop. 21,054.
— urb. twp., N New Jersey 07470*; pop. 49,141.
Waynesboro city, CEN. Virginia 22980*; pop. 16,707.
Webster Groves city, E Missouri 63119; pop. 26,995.
Weimar city, SW East Germany; pop. 64,000.
Weirton city, NW West Virginia 26062*; pop. 27,131.
Welland city, S Ontario, Canada; pop. 44,397.
Welland Canal waterway betw. Lakes Erie and Ontario.
Wellesley town. E Massachusetts 02181; pop. 28,051.
Wellington city, CEN. New Zealand; cap.; pop. 327,000.
Wenatchee city, CEN. Washington 98801*; pop. 16,912.
Weslaco city, S Texas 78596; pop. 15,313.
West Allis city, SE Wisconsin 53214; pop. 63,982.
West Bend city, SE Wisconsin 53095*; pop. 16,555.
West Berlin See BERLIN.
Westbury vill., SE New York 11590; pop. 15,362.
West Carson city, SE California; pop. 15,501.
Westchester vill., NE Illinois 60153; pop. 2,033.
West Chester boro., SE Pennsylvania 19380; pop. 19,301.
West Covina city, SW California 91790*; pop. 80,094.
West Des Moines city, CEN. Iowa 50265; pop. 16,441.
Westerly uninc. place, SW Rhode Island 02891; pop. 17,248.
Western Australia state, W Australia; 975,920 sq. mi.; pop. 737,000; cap. Perth.
Western Sahara area on the W coast of Africa, claimed by Mauritania and Morocco; 102,703 sq. mi.; pop. 152,000.
Western Samoa See SAMOA.
Westfield city, SW Massachusetts 01085; pop. 36,465.
— town, E New Jersey 07090*; pop. 33,720.
West Germany See GERMANY.
West Hartford town, CEN. Connecticut 06107; pop. 68,031.
West Haven town, S Connecticut 06516; pop. 53,184.
West Hempstead-Lakeview uninc. place, SE New York 11552; pop. 23,375.
West Hollywood uninc. place, SW California; pop. 29,448.
West Indies series of isl. groups separating the North Atlantic from the Caribbean, including Cuba, Jamaica, Hispaniola, Puerto Rico, the Bahamas, Trinidad and Tobago, and the Leeward and Windward Islands.
West Indies, the group of British cols. in the Caribbean, including the Leeward Islands (Antigua, St. Christopher-Nevis-Anguilla, Montserrat, and the British Virgin Islands) and the Windward Islands (St. Vincent, St. Lucia and Dominica).
West Islip city, SE New York 11795; pop. 16,711.
West Lafayette city, CEN. Indiana 47906; pop. 19,157.
Westlake city, N Ohio 44091; pop. 15,689.
Westland city, SE Michigan 48185; pop. 84,603.
West Memphis city, E Arkansas 72301; pop. 28,138.
West Mifflin boro., SW Pennsylvania 15120; pop. 26,279.

Westminster city and metropolitan boro., London, England; site of the Houses of Parliament and Buckingham Palace; pop. 85,000.
— city, SW California 92863; pop. 71,133.
— city, CEN. Colorado 80030; pop. 50,211.
Westmont city, SE California; pop. 29,310.
Westmount city, S Quebec, Canada; pop. 23,606.
West New Guinea prov. of Indonesia comprising the W part of New Guinea and adjacent islands; 159,375 sq. mi. pop 716,000; cap. Kotabaru, Also **West Irian.**
West New York town, NE New Jersey 07093*; pop. 39,194.
West Orange town, NE New Jersey 07052; pop. 39,510.
West Palm Beach city, SE Florida 33401*; pop. 62,530.
West Pensacola city, SW Florida 32505; pop. 20,924.
West Point U.S. military reservation, SE New York 10996; seat of the U.S. Military Academy.
Westport city, SW Connecticut 06880; pop. 27,414.
West Puente Valley city, SE California; pop. 20,733.
West Saint Paul city, E Minnesota 55118; pop. 18,799.
West Seneca uninc. place, W New York 14224; pop. 48,404.
West Springfield town, S Massachusetts 01089; pop. 28,491.
West Virginia state, E United States; 24,181 sq. mi.; pop. 1,949,644; cap. Charleston.
West Warwick town, CEN. Rhode Island 02893; pop. 24,323.
West Whittier-Los Nietos city, SE California 90606; pop. 20,845.
Wethersfield town, CEN. Connecticut 06109; pop. 26,-662.
Weymouth town, E Massachusetts 02188; pop. 54,610.
Wheaton city, NE Illinois 60187*; pop. 43,043.
— uninc. place, CEN. Maryland 20902; pop. 66,247.
Wheat Ridge uninc. place, CEN. Colorado 80033; pop. 30,293.
Wheeling city, NW West Virginia 26000*; pop. 43,070.
Whitby Whitby town, S Ontario, Canada; pop. 25,324.
White Bear Lake city, E Minnesota 55110; pop. 23,-313.
Whitefish Bay vill., SE Wisconsin 53217; pop. 17,394.
Whitehall city, CEN. Ohio 43213; pop. 25,263.
— boro., SW Pennsylvania 18052; pop. 16,551.
Whitehaven uninc. place, SW Tennessee 38116; pop. 19,-000.
White Mountains range of the Appalachians, CEN. New Hampshire.
White Oak city, NE Maryland 29091; pop. 19,769.
White Plains city, SE New York 10600*; pop. 46,999.
White-Yardville city, CEN. New Jersey 08620; pop. 18,-680.
Whitney, Mount peak, E California; 14,496 ft.
Whittier city, SW California 90601*; pop. 68,872.
Wichita city, CEN. Kansas 67200*; pop. 279,272.
Wichita Falls city, N Texas 76301*; pop. 94,201.
Wickliffe city, NE Ohio 44092; pop. 21,354.
Wight, Isle of isl. off the S coast of England; 147 sq. mi.
Wilkes-Barre city, NE Pennsylvania 18700*; pop. 51,-551.
Wilkinsburg boro., SW Pennsylvania; 15221; pop. 26,780.
Williamsburg city, E Virginia 23185; capital of Virgina (1699-1779); restored to colonial condition; pop. 9,069.
Williamsport city, CEN. Pennsylvania 17701*; pop. 33,-401.
Willoughby city, NE Ohio 44094*; pop. 18,634.
Willowbrook city, SE California; pop. 28,706.
Willow Grove city, SE Pennsylvania 19090; pop. 16,494.
Willowick city, NE Ohio 44094; pop. 21,237.
Wilmette vill., NE Illinois 60091; pop. 28,229.
Wilmington city, N Delaware; 19800*; pop. 70,195.
— city, NE Massachusetts 01887; pop. 17,102.
— city, SE North Carolina 28401*; pop. 44,000.
Wilson town, CEN. North Carolina 14172; pop. 34,424.
Wilson, Mount peak, SW California; 5,710 ft; site of a famous observatory.
Wilson Dam power dam in the Tenessee River at Muscle Shoals, NW Alabama; 137 ft. high, 4,862 ft. long.
Wimbledon town and municipal boro., S England; scene of international tennis matches; pop. 20,000.
Winchester town, E Massachusetts 01890; pop. 22,269.
Windham city, NE Connecticut 06280; pop. 19,626.
Windsor municipal boro., S England; site of **Windsor Castle,** a residence of the English sovereigns; pop. 15,000: officially **New Windsor.**
— city, SE Ontario, Canada; pop. 203,300.
Windsor Locks city, CEN. Connecticut 06096; pop. 15,-080.
Windward Islands isl. group, S Lesser Antilles.
Winnipeg city, SE Manitoba, Canada; cap.; pop. 560,000.
Winnipeg, Lake lake, S Manitoba, Canada; 9,398 sq. mi.
Winona city, SE Minnesota 55987*; pop. 27,075.
Winston-Salem city, CEN. North Carolina 27100*; pop. 131,885.
Winter Haven city, CEN. Florida 33880*; pop. 16,136.
Winter Park city, CEN. Florida 32789*; pop. 21,895.
Winthrop town, E Massachusetts 02152; pop. 20,335.
Wisconsin state, N United States; 56,154 sq. mi.; pop. 4,705,335.
Wisconsin Rapids city, CEN. Wisconsin 54494; pop. 18,587.
Woburn city, E Massachusetts 01801*; pop. 36,626.
Woodbridge urb. twp., NE New Jersey 07095; pop. 98,-944.
Woodbridge-Marumso city, NE Virginia 22191; pop. 25,412.
Woodland city, CEN. California 95695*; pop. 30,235.
Woodlawn-Woodmoor uninc. place, N Maryland 20901; pop. 28,811.
Woodmere uninc. place, SE New York 11598; pop. 19,-831.
Woodstock city, S Ontario, Canada; pop. 26,173.
Woonsocket city, NE Rhode Island 02895; pop. 45,914.
Wooster city, CEN. Ohio 44691*; pop. 18,703.
Worcester city, CEN. Massachusetts 01600*; pop. 161,-799.
Worms city, SW West Germany; pop. 78,000.
Worthington city, CEN. Ohio 43085; pop. 15,326.
Wrocław city, SW Poland; pop. 528,000: formerly called *Breslau.*
Wuhan collective name for the cities of Hankow, Hanyang, and Wuchang, CEN. China; pop. 4,250,000.
Wuppertal city, W West Germany; pop. 414,000.
Würzburg city, CEN. West Germany; pop. 120,000.
Wyandotte city, SE Michigan 48192*; pop. 34,006.
Wyckoff urb. twp., NE New Jersey 07481; pop. 16,039.
Wyoming state, NW United States; 97,914 sq. mi.; pop. 470,816; cap. Cheyenne.
— city, W Michigan 49509; pop. 59,616.

Xenia city, CEN. Ohio 45385; pop. 25,373.

Yakima city, S Washington 98901*; pop. 49,826.
Yalta city, S Crimea; scene of a conference of Roosevelt. Churchill, and Stalin in February, 1945; pop. 63,000.
Yalu river forming part of the boundary betw. NE China and Korea; 500 mi. long.
Yangtze river flowing from Tibet to the East China Sea; 3,600 mi. long.
Yellow River Hwang Ho: *an alternate name.*
Yellow Sea inlet of the Pacific betw. Korea and China; 400 mi. long, 400 mi. wide.
Yellowstone Falls 2 waterfalls of the Yellowstone River in Yellowstone National Park: **Upper Yellowstone Falls,** 109 ft.; **Lower Yellowstone Falls,** 308 ft.
Yellowstone National Park largest and oldest of the US national parks, largely in NW Wyoming; 3,458 sq. mi.; established 1872.
Yellowstone River river, NW Wyoming, SE Montana, and NW North Dakota; 671 mi. long.
Yemen, People's Democratic Republic of republic, S coast of Arabian penin.; 128,560 sq. mi.; pop. 1,950,000; cap. Aden. Also **Southern Yemen.**
Yemen Arab Republic country, SW Arabian penin.; ab. 75,000 sq. mi.; pop. 7,476,000; cap. San'a.
Yerevan city, W Armenian SSR; cap.; pop. 791,000.
Yokohama city, CEN. Honshu, Japan; pop. 2,694,500.

Yonkers city, SE New York 10700*; pop. 195,351.
York co. boro., CEN. Yorkshire, England; cap.; pop. 105,000.
— city, S Pennsylvania 17400*; pop. 44,619.
Yosemite Valley gorge in **Yosemite National Park** (1,183 sq. mi., established 1890), CEN. California; 7 mi. long, 1 mi. wide; traversed by the Merced River that forms **Yosemite Falls:** Upper Fall, 1,430 ft.; Lower Fall, 320 ft.; with intermediate cascades, 2,425 ft.
Youngstown city, NE Ohio 44500*; pop. 115,436.
Ypres town, NW Belgium; site of three major battles of World War I, 1914, 1915, 1917; pop. 21,000.
Ypsilanti city, SE Michigan 48197; pop. 29,538.
Yucaipa city, SW California 92399; pop. 19,284.
Yucatán penin., SE Mexico and NE Central America; 70,000 sq. mi.
Yugoslavia, Federal People's Republic of republic, SE Europe; 98,538 sq. mi.; pop. 22,550; cap. Belgrade.
Yukon terr., NW Canada; 207,076 sq. mi.; pop. 22,000; cap. Whitehorse.
Yukon River river, NW Canada and CEN. Alaska; 1,770 mi. long.
Yuma city, SW Arizona 85364; pop. 42,433.

Zagreb city, CEN. Croatia, Yugoslavia; cap.; pop. 566,000.
Zaire republic, CEN. Africa; 905,063 sq. mi.; pop. 29,450,000; cap Kinshasa.
Zambezi river, S Africa; 1,700 mi. long.
Zambia independent member of the Commonwealth of Nations, CEN. Africa; 288,130 sq. mi.; pop. 6,000,000; cap. Lusaka.
Zanesville city, CEN. Ohio 43701*; pop. 28,655.
Zanzibar reg. of Tanzania off the coast of E Africa; comprises isls. of Zanzibar (640 sq. mi.) and **Pemba** (380 sq. mi.); pop. 354,000.
— city, W Zanzibar; cap.; pop. 58,000.
Zealand isl. of Denmark betw. the Kattegat and the Baltic Sea; 2,709 sq. mi.
Zimbabwe Rhodesia republic, S Africa; 150,804 sq. mi.; pop. 7,580,000; cap. Salisbury.
Zion city, NE Illinois 60099; pop. 17,268.
Zululand dist., NE Natal, South Africa; formerly a native kingdom; 10,362 sq. mi.; pop. 570,000.
Zurich city, NE Switzerland; pop. 423,000.
Zuyder Zee former shallow inlet of the North Sea, NW Netherlands; drainage projects have reclaimed much of the land and formed Lake Ijssel. Also **Zuider Zee.**

SPECIAL SIGNS AND SYMBOLS

ASTRONOMY

Astronomical Bodies

☉ **1.** the sun **2.** Sunday
☿ **1.** Mercury **2.** Wednesday
♀ **1.** Venus **2.** Friday
⊕, ♁, ⊖ the earth
☾, ☽, ◐ **1.** the moon **2.** Monday
○, ☻ full moon
☽, ◐,), ◑, ☽ the moon, first quarter
☾, ◑, (, ☾, ☾ the moon, last quarter
● new moon
♂ **1.** Mars **2.** Tuesday
①, ②, ③, etc. asteroids: in order of discovery, as ① Ceres, ② Pallas, etc.
♃ **1.** Jupiter **2.** Thursday
♄ **1.** Saturn **2.** Saturday
♅, ♅, ♅ Uranus
♆ Neptune
♇, P Pluto
☄ comet
✳, ✱ star; fixed star
α, *β*, *γ*, etc. stars (of a constellation): in order of brightness, the Greek letter followed by the Latin genitive of the name of the constellation, as *α* Centauri

Position and Notation

☌ in conjunction; having the same longitude or right ascension
⚹ sextile; 60° apart in longitude or right ascension
□ quadrature; 90° apart in longitude or right ascension
△ trine; 120° apart in longitude or right ascension
☍ opposition; 180° apart in longitude or right ascension
☊ ascending node
☋ descending node
♈ vernal equinox
♎ autumnal equinox
α right ascension
β celestial latitude
δ declination
λ celestial or geographical longitude
Δ distance
θ sidereal time
a mean distance
ϖ, ☊ longitude of ascending node
φ **1.** angle of eccentricity **2.** geographical latitude

Signs of the Zodiac

♈ Aries, the Ram; ♉ Taurus, the Bull; ♊, Π Gemini, the Twins — Spring Signs

♋, ⊗ Cancer, the Crab; ♌ Leo, the Lion; ♍ Virgo, the Virgin — Summer Signs

♎ Libra, the Balance; ♏ Scorpio, the Scorpion; ♐, ♐ Sagittarius, the Archer — Autumn Signs

♑, ♑ Capricorn, the Goat; ♒ Aquarius, the Water Bearer; ♓, ♓ Pisces, the Fishes — Winter Signs

BIOLOGY

○, ☉, ① annual plant
☉, ☉, ♂ biennial plant
♃ perennial herb
△ evergreen plant
☉ monocarpic plant
|w plant useful to wildlife
♂, ♁ **1.** male organism or cell **2.** staminate plant or flower
♀ **1.** female organism or cell **2.** pistillate plant or flower
☿ hermaphroditic or perfect plant or flower
⚲ neuter organism or cell
○ individual organism, especially female
□ individual organism, especially male
∞ indefinite number
P parental generation
F filial generation
F_1, F_2, F_3, etc. first, second, third, etc., filial generation

BOOKS

f° folio
4mo, 4° quarto
8vo, 8° octavo
12mo, 12° duodecimo
18mo, 18° octodecimo
32mo, 32° thirty-twomo

CHEMISTRY

Elements

See table of ELEMENTS.

Compounds

Compounds are represented by the symbols for their constituent elements, each element followed by a subscript numeral if the number of atoms of it appearing in the compound is greater than one, as NaCl, H_2O, H_2SO_4, etc. If a radical appears more than once in a compound, the radical is enclosed in parentheses followed by a subscript numeral, as $Ca(OCl)_2$, $Al_2(SO_4)_3$, etc. Molecules consisting entirely of one element are represented by the symbol for the element followed by a subscript numeral indicating the number of atoms in the molecule, as H_2, O_2, O_3, etc. In addition:

· denotes water of crystallization or hydration, as $CaSO_4 \cdot 5H_2O$.
α, *β*, *γ*, etc., *or* 1, 2, 3, etc. (in names of compounds), indicate different positions of substituted atoms or radicals.
+ denotes dextrorotation, as + 120°.
− denotes levorotation, as − 113°.
[ ] include parentheses if one radical contains another, as $Fe_3[Fe(CN)_6]_2$.

In structural formulas:
—, =, ≡, etc., *or* ., :, ⋮, etc., denote a single, double, or triple bond, etc.
R— denotes any alkyl radical.
⬡ *or* ⌬ denotes a benzene ring.

Ions

Ions are represented by the symbols for their respective elements or by the symbols for the elements composing them, followed by a superscript symbol indicating the electric charge, as H^+, Cl^-, SO_4^{--}, etc. Thus:

$^-$, $^{--}$, $^{---}$, etc., *or* $^{-1}$, $^{-2}$, $^{-3}$, etc., denote a single, double, triple, etc., negative charge.
$^+$, $^{++}$, $^{+++}$, etc., *or* $^{+1}$, $^{+2}$, $^{+3}$, etc., denote a single, double, triple, etc., positive charge.
′, ″, ‴, etc., denote single, double, triple, etc., valence or charge (especially negative), as S″.

Chemical Reactions

Chemical reactions are written in a form resembling equations, with reactants on the left and products on the right. If more than one equivalent of a compound appears, it is preceded by a coefficient. Conditions of temperature, pressure, catalysis, etc., are indicated above the arrow that shows direction. The following symbols are used:

→ *or* ← denotes "yields"; also indicates the direction of the reaction.
⇌ indicates a reversible reaction.
+ denotes "added to; together with."
↓ (written after a compound) denotes appearance as a precipitate.
↑ (written after a compound) denotes appearance as a gas.
△ denotes the presence of heat.
= *or* ⇌ denotes equivalence of amounts in a quantitative equation.

COMMERCE AND FINANCE

@ **1.** at: peaches @ $.39 per pound **2.** to: nails per pound $.50 @ $.60
$, $ dollar(s); peso(s): $100
¢ cent(s): 37¢
₱ peso(s) (Philippines)
/ shilling(s) (British): 3/
£ pound(s): £25
d penny, pence (British): 4d
¥, Y yen
₨, R rupee(s)
Rs rupees
℔ per: 50¢ ℔ dozen
number: #60 thread

MATHEMATICS

See table at MATHEMATICS.

MISCELLANEOUS

&, & and See AMPERSAND.
&c et cetera
7ber, 8ber, etc. September, October, etc.
† died
% percent
× by: used in expressing dimensions, as a sheet of paper 8½″ × 11″
© copyright; copyrighted
♠ spade
♥ heart
♦ diamond
♣ club

MUSIC

Music is generally written on one or more staves. The pitch of each staff is indicated by a clef. The forms of the various notes and their corresponding rests indicate relative duration. In addition the following are used:

♭ flat
♯ sharp
♭♭ double flat
𝄪 double sharp
♮ natural
𝄴 common time; 4/4 meter
𝄵 alla breve; 2/2 or 4/2 meter
~ turn
∾ inverted turn
𝆗 mordent
𝆖 inverted mordent
>, <, ∧ accent
· ' staccato
— tenuto
tr trill
⌒, ‿ slur or tie
’ phrase or breath mark
𝆔 grace note
𝆒 crescendo
𝆓 diminuendo; decrescendo
⊓ down-bow
V up-bow
8va all' ottava; at the octave (raises the pitch of a staff one octave when written above it, lowers it when written below)
𝄐, 𝄑 hold

PHYSICS

α alpha particle
β beta particle
c velocity of light
g acceleration due to gravity
h Planck's constant
λ wavelength
ν frequency
j square root of minus one
∽ cycles (of alternating current or voltage)

RELIGION

✠, + **1.** a sign of the cross used by bishops before their names **2.** in some service books, an indication that the sign of the cross is to be made
* in some service books, a mark used to divide psalm verses into two parts
℟ response
℣, V', V, versicle
☧, ☧, ☧ a monogram for Christ [Gk. Χρ(ιστός)]

METRIC SYSTEM AND EQUIVALENT UNITS

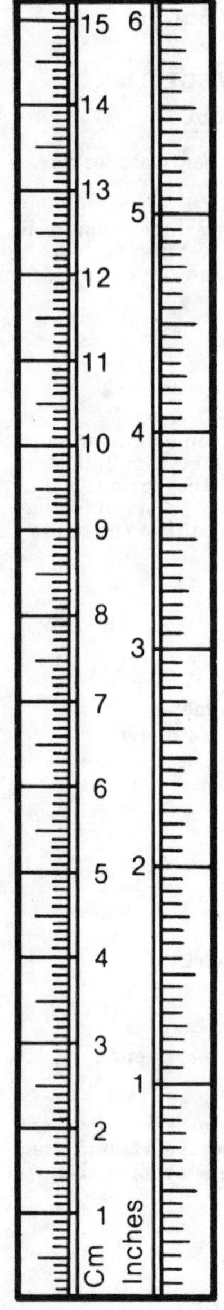

LINEAR MEASURE

10 millimeters	= 1 centimeter	= 0.3937 inch
10 centimeters	= 1 decimeter	= 3.937 inches
10 decimeters	= 1 meter	= 39.37 inches or 3.28 feet
10 meters	= 1 decameter	= 393.7 inches
10 decameters	= 1 hectometer	= 328 feet 1 inch
10 hectometers	= 1 kilometer	= 0.621 mile
10 kilometers	= 1 myriameter	= 6.21 miles

SQUARE MEASURE

100 square millimeters	= 1 square centimeter	= 0.15499 square inch
100 square centimeters	= 1 square decimeter	= 15.499 square inches
100 square decimeters	= 1 square meter	= 1,549.9 square inches or 1.196 square yards
100 square meters	= 1 square decameter	= 119.6 square yards
100 square decameters	= 1 square hectometer	= 2.471 acres
100 square hectometers	= 1 square kilometer	= 0.386 square mile

LAND MEASURE

1 square meter	= 1 centiare	= 1,549.9 square inches
100 centiares	= 1 acre	= 119.6 square yards
100 acres	= 1 hectare	= 2.471 acres
100 hectares	= 1 square kilometer	= 0.386 square mile

EQUIVALENT UNITS OF:

LENGTH																TEMP.			
Centimeters to Inches		Inches to Centimeters		Meters to Feet		Feet to Meters		Meters to Yards		Yards to Meters		Kilometers to Miles		Miles to Kilometers		Celsius to Fahrenheit		Fahrenheit to Celsius	
cm	in	in	cm	m	ft	ft	m	m	yd	yd	m	km	miles	miles	km	°C	F°	°F	°C
1	0.39	1	2.54	1	3.28	1	0.30	1	1.09	1	0.91	1	0.62	1	1.61	10	50.00	10	-12.22
2	0.79	2	5.08	2	6.56	2	0.61	2	2.19	2	1.83	2	1.24	2	3.22	20	68.00	20	-6.67
3	1.18	3	7.62	3	9.84	3	0.91	3	3.28	3	2.74	3	1.86	3	4.83	30	86.00	30	-1.11
4	1.57	4	10.16	4	13.12	4	1.22	4	4.37	4	3.66	4	2.49	4	6.44	40	104.00	40	4.44
5	1.97	5	12.70	5	16.40	5	1.52	5	5.47	5	4.57	5	3.11	5	8.05	50	122.00	50	10.00
6	2.36	6	15.24	6	19.68	6	1.83	6	6.56	6	5.49	6	3.73	6	9.66	60	140.00	60	15.56
7	2.76	7	17.78	7	22.97	7	2.13	7	7.66	7	6.40	7	4.35	7	11.27	70	158.00	70	21.11
8	3.15	8	20.32	8	26.25	8	2.44	8	8.75	8	7.32	8	4.97	8	12.87	80	176.00	80	26.67
9	3.54	9	22.86	9	29.53	9	2.74	9	9.84	9	8.23	9	5.59	9	14.48	90	194.00	90	32.22
10	3.94	10	25.40	10	32.81	10	3.05	10	10.94	10	9.14	10	6.21	10	16.09	100	212.00	100	37.78

VOLUME MEASURE

1,000 cubic millimeters = 1 cubic centimeter = .06102 cubic inch
1,000 cubic centimeters = 1 cubic decimeter = 61.02 cubic inches
1,000 cubic decimeters = 1 cubic meter = 35.314 cubic feet
(the unit is called a *stere* in measuring firewood)

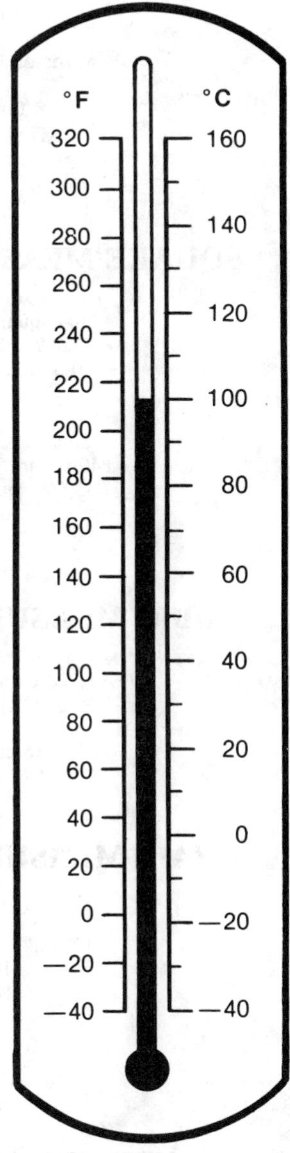

CAPACITY MEASURE

10 milliliters	= 1 centiliter	=	0.338	fluid ounce
10 centiliters	= 1 deciliter	=	3.38	fluid ounces
10 deciliters	= 1 liter	=	1.0567 0.9081	liquid quarts or dry quart
10 liters	= 1 decaliter	=	2.64 0.284	gallons or bushel
10 decaliters	= 1 hectoliter	=	26.418 2.838	gallons or bushels
10 hectoliters	= 1 kiloliter	=	264.18 35.315	gallons or cubic feet

WEIGHTS

10 milligrams	= 1 centigram	=	0.1543	grain
10 centigrams	= 1 decigram	=	1.5432	grains
10 decigrams	= 1 gram	=	15.432	grains
10 grams	= 1 decagram	=	0.3527	ounce
10 decagrams	= 1 hectogram	=	3.5274	ounces
10 hectograms	= 1 kilogram	=	2.2046	pounds
10 kilograms	= 1 myriagram	=	22.046	pounds
10 myriagrams	= 1 quintal	=	220.46	pounds
10 quintals	= 1 metric ton	=	2,204.6	pounds

EQUIVALENT UNITS OF:

VOLUME												WEIGHT							
Millileters to Ounces		Ounces to Milliliters		Liters to Quarts		Quarts to Liters		Liters to Gallons		Gallons to Liters		Grams to Ounces		Ounces to Grams		Kilograms to Pounds		Pounds to Kilograms	
ml	liq oz	liq oz	ml	l	liq qt	liq qt	l	l	gal	gal	l	g	oz	oz	g	kg	lb	lb	kg
10	0.34	1	29.57	1	1.06	1	0.95	1	0.26	1	3.79	1	0.04	1	28.3	1	2.20	1	0.45
20	0.68	2	59.15	2	2.11	2	1.89	2	0.53	2	7.57	2	0.07	2	56.7	2	4.41	2	0.91
30	1.01	3	88.72	3	3.17	3	2.84	3	0.79	3	11.36	3	0.11	3	85.0	3	6.61	3	1.36
40	1.35	4	118.29	4	4.23	4	3.79	4	1.06	4	15.14	4	0.14	4	113.4	4	8.82	4	1.81
50	1.69	5	147.87	5	5.28	5	4.73	5	1.32	5	18.93	5	0.18	5	141.7	5	11.02	5	2.27
60	2.03	6	177.44	6	6.34	6	5.68	6	1.59	6	22.71	6	0.21	6	170.1	6	13.23	6	2.72
70	2.37	7	207.01	7	7.40	7	6.62	7	1.85	7	26.50	7	0.25	7	198.4	7	15.43	7	3.18
80	2.71	8	236.59	8	8.45	8	7.57	8	2.11	8	30.28	8	0.28	8	226.8	8	17.64	8	3.63
90	3.04	9	266.16	9	9.51	9	8.52	9	2.38	9	34.07	9	0.32	9	255.1	9	19.84	9	4.08
100	3.38	10	295.74	10	10.57	10	9.46	10	2.64	10	37.85	10	0.35	10	283.5	10	22.05	10	4.54

TABLES OF WEIGHTS AND MEASURES

LINEAR MEASURE

1 inch		= 2.54 centimeters
12 inches	= 1 foot	= 0.3048 meter
3 feet	= 1 yard	= 0.9144 meter
5½ yards or 16½ feet	= 1 rod (or pole or perch)	= 5.029 meters
40 rods	= 1 furlong	= 201.17 meters
8 furlongs or 1,760 yards or 5,280 feet	= 1 (statute) mile	= 1,609.3 meters
3 miles	= 1 (land) league	= 4.83 kilometers

SQUARE MEASURE

1 square inch		= 6.452 square centimeters
144 square inches	= 1 square foot	= 929 square centimeters
9 square feet	= 1 square yard	= 0.8361 square meter
30¼ square yards	= 1 square rod (or square pole or square perch)	= 25.29 square meters
160 square rods or 4,840 square yards or 43,560 square feet	= 1 acre	= 0.4047 hectare
640 acres	= 1 square mile	= 259 hectares or 2.59 square kilometers

CUBIC MEASURE

1 cubic inch		= 16.387 cubic centimeters
1,728 cubic inches	= 1 cubic foot	= 0.0283 cubic meter
27 cubic feet	= 1 cubic yard	= 0.7646 cubic meter
	(in units for cordwood, etc.)	
16 cubic feet	= 1 cord foot	
8 cord feet	= 1 cord	= 3.625 cubic meters

CHAIN MEASURE

	(for Gunter's, or surveyor's, chain)	
7.92 inches	= 1 link	= 20.12 centimeters
100 links or 66 feet	= 1 chain	= 20.12 meters
10 chains	= 1 furlong	= 201.17 meters
80 chains	= 1 mile	= 1,609.3 meters
	(for engineer's chain)	
1 foot	= 1 link	= 0.3048 meter
100 feet	= 1 chain	= 30.48 meters
52.8 chains	= 1 mile	= 1,609.3 meters

SURVEYOR'S (SQUARE) MEASURE

625 square links	= 1 square pole	= 25.29 square meters
16 square poles	= 1 square chain	= 404.7 square meters
10 square chains	= 1 acre	= 0.4047 hectare
640 acres	= 1 square mile or 1 section	= 259 hectares or 2.59 square kilometers
36 square miles	= 1 township	= 9,324.0 hectares or 93.24 square kilometers

NAUTICAL MEASURE

6 feet	= 1 fathom	= 1.829 meters
100 fathoms	= 1 cable's length (ordinary) (In the U.S. Navy 120 fathoms or 720 feet = 1 cable's length; in the British Navy, 608 feet = 1 cable's length.)	
10 cables' lengths	= 1 nautical mile (6,076.10333 feet)	= 1.852 kilometers (by international agreement, 1954)
1 nautical mile	= 1.1508 statute miles (the length of a minute of longitude at the equator) (Also called geographical, sea, or air mile, and, in Great Britain, Admiralty mile.)	
3 nautical miles	= 1 marine league (3.45 statute miles)	= 5.56 kilometers
60 nautical miles	= 1 degree of a great circle of the earth	

DRY MEASURE

1 pint		=	33.60 cubic inches	= 0.5505 liter
2 pints	= 1 quart	=	67.20 cubic inches	= 1.1012 liters
8 quarts	= 1 peck	=	537.61 cubic inches	= 8.8096 liters
4 pecks	= 1 bushel	=	2,150.42 cubic inches	= 35.2383 liters

1 British dry quart = 1.032 U.S. dry quarts.
According to United States government standards, the following are the weights avoirdupois for single bushels of the specified grains: for wheat, 60 pounds; for barley, 48 pounds; for oats, 32 pounds; for rye, 56 pounds; for corn, 56 pounds. Some states have specifications varying from these.

LIQUID MEASURE

1 gill	= 4 fluid ounces (see next table)	=	7.219 cubic inches	= 0.1183 liter
4 gills	= 1 pint	=	28.875 cubic inches	= 0.4732 liter
2 pints	= 1 quart	=	57.75 cubic inches	= 0.9463 liter
4 quarts	= 1 gallon	=	231 cubic inches	= 3.7853 liters

The British imperial gallon (4 imperial quarts) = 277.42 cubic inches = 4.546 liters.
The barrel in Great Britain equals 36 imperial gallons, in the United States, usually 31½ gallons.

APOTHECARIES' FLUID MEASURE

1 minim		=	0.0038 cubic inch	= 0.0616 milliliter
60 minims	= 1 fluid dram	=	0.2256 cubic inch	= 3.6966 milliliters
8 fluid drams	= 1 fluid ounce	=	1.8047 cubic inches	= 0.0296 liter
16 fluid ounces	= 1 pint	=	28.875 cubic inches	= 0.4732 liter

See table immediately preceding for quart and gallon equivalents.
The British pint = 20 fluid ounces.

CIRCULAR (or ANGULAR) MEASURE

60 seconds (″)	= 1 minute (′)
60 minutes	= 1 degree (°)
90 degrees	= 1 quadrant or 1 right angle
4 quadrants or 360 degrees	= 1 circle

AVOIRDUPOIS WEIGHT

(The grain, equal to 0.0648 gram, is the same in all three tables of weight)

1 dram or 27.34 grains		=	1.772 grams
16 drams or 437.5 grains	= 1 ounce	=	28.3495 grams
16 ounces or 7,000 grains	= 1 pound	=	453.59 grams
100 pounds	= 1 hundredweight	=	45.36 kilograms
2,000 pounds	= 1 ton	=	907.18 kilograms

In Great Britain, 14 pounds (6.35 kilograms) = 1 stone, 112 pounds (50.80 kilograms) = 1 hundredweight, and 2,240 pounds (1,016.05 kilograms) = 1 long ton.

TROY WEIGHT

(The grain, equal to 0.0648 gram, is the same in all three tables of weight)

3.086 grains	= 1 carat	=	200 milligrams
24 grains	= 1 pennyweight	=	1.5552 grams
20 pennyweights or 480 grains	= 1 ounce	=	31.1035 grams
12 ounces or 5,760 grains	= 1 pound	=	373.24 grams

APOTHECARIES' WEIGHT

(The grain, equal to 0.0648 gram, is the same in all three tables of weight)

20 grains	= 1 scruple	=	1.296 grams
3 scruples	= 1 dram	=	3.888 grams
8 drams or 480 grains	= 1 ounce	=	31.1035 grams
12 ounces or 5,760 grains	= 1 pound	=	373.24 grams

ENCYCLOPEDIC SUPPLEMENTS

GRAMMAR AND USAGE HANDBOOK

by Alice Ottun

Almost everyone, no matter how well-educated, from time to time encounters problems relating to grammar and usage. It is the purpose of this Handbook to help solve these problems by presenting clear, concise statements, along with recommendations on preferred usage, about traditionally troublesome areas of language.

The author of this Handbook, Alice Ottun, was for twenty years the Administrative Dean of Pace College, and is at present the Director of Business Education of the Middle Country School District in Centereach, Long Island. Miss Ottun has served as President of the Commercial Education Association of New York City, of the Business Institutes of the State of New York, and of the Private Schools Association of New York City. She is listed in *Who's Who in American Education* and in *Who's Who of American Women.* She has for many years taught business subjects and English.

Throughout the years Funk & Wagnalls' Dictionary Department has been called upon to answer a great many inquiries about various problems relating to language. Records have been kept of these inquiries, and a report based upon them has been made available to the author of this Handbook, thus providing her with original, practical data to aid her in selecting the categories that will be most useful to those seeking advice in grammar and usage.

WORD USAGE AND WORD RELATIONSHIPS

Agreement of Subject and Verb

It may seem needless to say that a singular subject takes a singular verb, while a plural subject takes a plural verb; however, many errors occur in this respect.

The small table *was* in the hall.
The small tables *were* in the hall.

In some instances, when phrases or other elements come between the subject and the verb, the agreement may not be so clear.

The small table around which the children play *was* in the hall.
The small tables owned by the church *were* in the hall.
The men, as well as the policeman, *were* aghast at the sight.

The following words are generally considered singular and take the singular form of the verb: *each, either, neither, one, someone, anyone, everybody, nobody, somebody, much, anybody, everyone.*

The following words are plural and take the plural form of the verb: *both, few, many, several.*

The following pronouns may be singular or plural depending on the meaning intended: *all, most, some, every, none, any, half, more.*

When one is referring to two or more persons who are of different sexes, or to a group of people whose gender one has no way of determining, the pronouns *they, them,* and *their* are often used to refer to *anyone, each, everybody,* etc., in order to avoid the awkward *he or she, him or her, his or her.* Strictly speaking, one should use the masculine singular pronouns (*he, him, his*) in such cases, but in practice they are used consistently only in formal usage. Which procedure you follow will depend on how formal a style you wish to employ.

Either—Or; Neither—Nor

Neither always takes *nor*; *either* takes *or.*

When a subject is compounded with *neither . . . nor* or *either . . . or,* the verb is normally singular if the nouns joined are singular, and plural if they are plural. If, however, one noun is singular and one plural, the verb agrees with the second or nearer subject.

Either Bill or Ralph *is* lying.
Neither she nor her sisters *skate* well.

A collective noun, such as *class, company, club, crew, jury, committee,* takes a singular verb when the whole is considered as a unit, and a plural verb when part of the whole is considered separately.

The jury *has* deliberated for six hours.
The crew *were* near exhaustion after their many hours of exposure.

Some collective nouns, as *police* and *cattle,* are used only in the plural form; others, as *mankind* and *wildlife,* are generally used in the singular form.

The cattle *were* almost destroyed by the severe storm.
The New England wildlife *has* been protected.

Agreement of Pronoun with Its Antecedent

If the antecedent is singular, the pronoun is singular; if the antecedent is plural, the pronoun is likewise plural.

The *boy* did *his* best in the contest.
The *boys* in the school did *their* best.
The *boy and* the *girl* did *their* best.
Neither one of the boys did *his* best.

PUNCTUATION

For practical purposes, it is best to keep in mind that too much punctuation is as confusing as too little. The current trend is toward a minimum of punctuation, just enough to make the writer's meaning clear. This can best be accomplished by cultivating a simple, straightforward style that flows as naturally as ordinary speech.

Where a sentence is so complicated that no amount of punctuation seems adequate, a writer would be wise to reorganize his thoughts. Punctuation can help to guide a reader to the meaning of a sentence; it cannot, however, make order out of confused thinking and expression.

End Punctuation

Because the sentence is a grammatically complete and separate unit of utterance, it is necessary to show where one sentence ends and another begins. In speech, this is accomplished by falling pitch, intonation, and a full pause. In written discourse, the reader is guided by a period, a question mark, or an exclamation point, depending on the nature of the sentence.

The Period [.] The period is used at the end of a declarative sentence, an imperative sentence, an indirect question, and after a polite request that resembles a question. It is also used after initials and most abbreviations.

Mrs. Morris placed the book on the table.
The members of the committee asked when the meeting would take place.
Will you open the door for me, please.

If a sentence ends in an abbreviation, only one period is needed.

The bus will arive at 8:30 A.M.

Do not use a period and two zeros after even amounts of money, except in tabulation.

$25, not $25. or $25.00

The period should not be used in centered headings, such as manuscript and chapter headings; in the various elements in an outline; or in the items in a tabulation.

Do not use periods between the call numbers of broadcasting stations: WABC, WQXR; or between the letters indicating government agencies: FBI, CIA, FAA, IRS.

Three dots (. . .), called an *ellipsis,* are used to indicate an omission in quoted matter. When the omission comes at the end of the line, use the three dots together with the sentence period, making a total of four dots. If one or more paragraphs are omitted in the quoted matter, show the omission by using seven dots across the page.

The Question Mark [?] The question mark signifies that the sentence preceding it does not make a statement, but asks a question. This punctuation serves the same purpose in writing that rising or sustained pitch intonation of the voice does in speaking.

When may we expect to receive your check?

If a sentence consists of several questions, the question mark should appear at the close of each question within the sentence and also at the close. The separate questions within the sentence do not begin with a capital since they are part of the larger and complete question.

Who will attend the conference—the president? the vice president? or the secretary?

The Exclamation Point [!] This is used at the end of a statement denoting a strong emotional experience or a sense of urgency or excitement. If spoken, it would be gasped, shouted, groaned, or cried. Written, the exclamation point, and the reader's imagination, must suffice.

Watch out!
Oh, my head!

An interjection at the beginning of a sentence is usually followed by a comma, and the sentence is ended with an exclamation point. The interjection may, however, be immediately followed by an exclamation mark, and the following sentence punctuated without reference to it.

Oh, what a day this is!
Oh! How could you do that?

Exclamation points should be used with discretion and for particular emphasis. Excessive use tends to lessen the impact of this device.

Internal Punctuation

When sentences become more complex and deal with two or more closely related ideas, internal punctuation is necessary to show the relation between the various parts. Authorities differ in some respects on the rules applying to the use of the comma and the semicolon. Since this Handbook is a secretarial guide, however, some specific rules should be laid down, but with the understanding that research may indicate differences of opinion.

The Comma [,] The comma is used to separate the various elements in a series—either words, phrases, or clauses—when there are at least three units.

The torn, tattered, soaking flag was lowered.
The dog jumped up, barked ferociously, bared his teeth, and took off after the rabbit.

Formal punctuation requires that a comma be inserted between the last two elements of a series even when a conjunction is used; this rule is generally followed in letter writing. An informal style of writing, such as newspaper and editorial work, does not require the comma before the conjunction.

The flag is red, white and blue.

Sometimes the conjunction is used with each element in the series. When this occurs, no comma is used to separate the elements.

The banner will be red or blue or white or a combination of these colors.

When *etc.* is the concluding element in a series, it should be preceded by a comma. A comma should also follow *etc.* when it is not the last word in a sentence.

She stopped off at the supermarket to get some fruit, vegetables, etc., on the way home.

Use the comma to set off an introductory sentence element (word, phrase, clause) which is out of its natural order. Of all the comma rules, this is probably the most difficult to master. Some words, like *however*, are not always used as introductory words and would not then be followed by the comma.

Obviously, we cannot meet your request.
In order to meet the deadline, we shall have to work overtime.
When you go to see him in the hospital, bring along a few magazines.
However well you meant, it was the wrong thing to do.

When the main clause in the sentence comes first, do not use the comma between the main clause and the dependent clause.

Bring along a few magazines when you go to visit him in the hospital.

As a general rule, an introductory phrase which contains a verb should be followed with a comma.

After *making* the survey, the committee will publish the report.
To *complete* the survey, the officers worked overtime.

If the introductory phrase does not contain a verb, it should not be followed by a comma unless the phrase is parenthetical or explanatory.

After much debate the meeting was adjourned.
As an act of mercy the sick animal was killed.
Under separate cover we are sending you a catalogue.
On the contrary, I believe the President was absolutely right.

For example, consider the boy's attitude toward his parents.
In the second place, watch his behavior with his peers.

Use the comma to set off introductory *yes* or *no* or light exclamations in a sentence.

No, we shall not be ready on time.
Oh, what a wonderful day this has been!

A parenthetical expression (word, phrase, or clause) that can be omitted without changing the meaning of the sentence should be set off by commas.

The king, who was very ill, was not present at the ceremony.
Something may, of course, turn up to change what seems now to be the obvious outcome.

Note: When the information has little connection with the thought expressed in the main clause, it is usually enclosed in parentheses rather than in commas.

The strike (which began on the President's birthday) completely paralyzed the nation.

Dashes may also be used to set off any sort of nonrestrictive or parenthetical matter. Some writers feel that dashes lend a more personal dramatic effect to their writing.

The earth—all parched and dry—yearns for moisture.

Use the comma before short, direct quotations.

She asked, "Is the train on time?"

Use the comma to set off words in direct address.

We are certain, Mr. Long, that you will be satisfied with our product.

The comma or commas should be used to set off an identifying or explanatory word or phrase (called an *appositive*) which helps to make the meaning of the sentence clearer. This rule applies to a person's title or degree and to the abbreviation "Inc." when used in a company name.

Our salesman, Mr. Brown, will call on you tomorrow.
We shall write a letter to Ray Smith & Company, Inc., in New York City.
Harold Brown, Ph.D., has been appointed to the faculty.

Separate contrasting expressions—word, phrase, or clause—by using the comma.

We shall leave today, not tomorrow.

Use the comma to separate two or more parallel adjectives.

Their sleeping bags kept them warm during the long, cold nights.

Note: If the word *and* can be inserted between the two adjectives or if the two adjectives can be reversed, they are parallel and the comma should be used.

The comma is *not* used when the order of the adjectives helps to determine the meaning of the sentence.

They built the building with wide open stairways.

The comma should be used before a conjunction (*but, and, or,* etc.) that connects two independent clauses.

We have had the pleasure of counting you as one of our members for many years, but we notice that you have not yet renewed your membership.

If the clauses are short and uncomplicated, the comma may be omitted.

We were drenched but arrived safely.

The Semicolon [;] The semicolon is used to separate two independent clauses when the conjunction is omitted.

We are enclosing an envelope for your convenience; it requires no postage.

Use the semicolon to separate the members of a compound sentence when one or both members contain other punctuation marks.

If he is nominated, he will run; but his chances seem dim.

Use the semicolon to separate the members of a compound sentence when the clauses are connected by such words as *however, nevertheless, consequently,* etc.

He paid little attention to details; consequently, he failed to be promoted.

Phrases or clauses in a series are separated by the semicolon when any one or more of the phrases or clauses contain a comma.

Our profits for the three successive years were: 1960, $2,345,000; 1961, $2,070,400; 1962, $2,545,000.

The Colon [:] The colon is used most often to indicate that a list, example, strong assertion, or the like will follow to complete or fulfill some introductory statement.

The bride takes three vows: to love, honor, and obey.
We have only one goal: to win.

The colon is also used outside the sentence in certain purely conventional ways: after the salutation of a formal letter; between elements of a Biblical or bibliographical citation; after the name or other identification of the speaker in a dialogue or in a transcript of speech.

Use the colon to separate hours and minutes when time is expressed in figures. When no minutes are expressed, it is not necessary to use two zeros with the number designating the hour. When the word *o'clock* is used, do not indicate the time in figures but express the time in words.

We shall be there at 3:30 P.M.
We shall be there at 3 P.M.
We shall be there at three o'clock.

The Apostrophe [']

To Indicate Possession Apostrophes are employed most commonly to form the possessive of nouns and pronouns. In words not ending with an *s* or *z* sound, *'s* is added; in those ending with an *s* or *z* sound, the common practice is to add only an apostrophe at the end. Most singular nouns take the *'s*, and most plural forms add only '.

Words not ending in s *or* z:	*Words ending in* s *or* z:
the children's playroom	the babies' bottles
somebody's hat	for goodness' sake

Exceptions may be found in the possessive form of proper names ending in *s* or *z*. There is a growing tendency to add *'s* to a name having one syllable even though it ends with an *s* sound, thus making James *James's*, Marx *Marx's*, and Schultz *Schultz's*. With names of more than one syllable, either form may be used unless the additional *s* makes the word difficult to pronounce. Then only the apostrophe is used.

Thomas's *or* Thomas'	*but only* Genesis'
Adams's *or* Adams'	Exodus'
Titus's *or* Titus'	Moses'

Personal pronouns do not take the apostrophe in the possessive form.

my, mine	our, ours
your, yours	their, theirs
her, hers	his, its, whose

To Indicate Omission An apostrophe is also used to show that one or more letters have been omitted from a word, or that numerals have been omitted from a number.

it's—it is; can't—cannot; you're—you are;
we'll—we will; where'er—wherever; '29—1929

Plurals of Letters or Numbers The plural of a letter or a number is formed by adding 's, although it should be noted that there is a growing trend to drop the apostrophe where years are concerned. Abbreviations form the plural by adding 's.

Dot your i's and cross your t's.
There are four s's, four i's, and two p's in Mississippi.
Watch your ABC's.
6's and 7's
a company of GI's
a carload of VIP's

Quotation Marks [" "] [' ']

There are two classes of quotations: *direct* and *indirect*.

Quotation marks are required at the beginning and end of a word or words spoken in direct discourse.

Roy said, "I am reading a good book."

Indirect quotations require no quotation marks, and are commonly introduced by the word *that.*

Roy said that he was reading a good book.

If a direct quotation is interrupted by one or more words, the quotation marks are placed around the quoted matter only and not around the interrupting words.

"Hurry along," said the coach, "or we shall not make the game in time."

When quoting material, be careful to include every detail of punctuation even though you may not wholly agree with the details involved.

"Stir not up agitation! Give us peace!"

The use of slang, humor, and colloquial expressions is unsuited to formal speech or writing. If used, such words should be enclosed in quotation marks.

It was a "whale" of a story.

Translations of foreign words and phrases should be enclosed in quotations marks.

Au revoir means "till we meet again" or "good-bye."
Laissez faire means "noninterference."

In manuscripts and business correspondence, the title of a book, a booklet, a magazine, or a newspaper should be typed in capital and small letters (or all in capitals) and underlined. Enclose in quotation marks and type in capital and small letters the titles of essays, magazine articles, lectures, term papers, and the titles of chapters. The first letter of the first word and the first letter of every important word following is capitalized.

I have just finished reading Why England Slept.

The "Foreword to the Memorial Edition," written by Robert F. Kennedy, shows great depth of feeling and love for his brother, John F. Kennedy.

Did you read the article "One Man's Opinion" in this morning's New York Times?

When a lengthy quotation of two or more paragraphs is used, beginning or opening quotation marks are used at the start of each paragraph, and closing quotation marks appear only at the very end of the quoted passage.

No quotation marks are necessary in interviews, dramatic dialogues, or legal testimony where the name of the speaker or other identification precedes the speech, or where question and answer are clearly marked.

Judge: How do you plead, guilty or not guilty?
Defendant: Not guilty, Your Honor.
Q.: Where were you on the night of June 26?
A.: I don't remember.

Quotation marks are used to set off words or phrases that the writer wishes not to claim as his own. These may be the words of other persons, or they may be jargon, slang, barbarisms, figures of speech, and the like, which he "decontaminates" by using quotation marks.

Let my opponent produce his "incontrovertible evidence."
The young men apparently did it "for kicks."

A quotation within a quotation is enclosed by single quotation marks.

Jack remarked, "I believe Patrick Henry said, 'Give me liberty or give me death.' "

Note: The period within the quotation marks serves as end punctuation both for the sentence spoken by Jack and that spoken by Patrick Henry. The period is never doubled at the end of a quotation within a quotation.

The rule for punctuating quoted matter is quite simple. The period and comma are always *inside* the closing quotation marks; the colon and semicolon are always *outside* the closing quotation marks; the question mark and exclamation point will be inside or outside the closing quotation marks depending on whether they are or are not part of the quoted matter.

He said, "Call the police."
He said, "Who called the police?"
Who said, "Call the police"?
He said, "Call the police"; but the sirens were already wailing.

The Hyphen [-]

The hyphen is used primarily for end-of-line word divisions and for hyphenation of compound words.

Words may be divided *only* between syllables.

Words pronounced as one syllable may never be divided.

Words may not be divided in groups of fewer than three letters.

Abbreviations should never be carried over from one line to the next, and every attempt should be made to include the initials or first name of a person's name on the same line with his surname.

For book editing, and when preparing a manuscript, hyphens should not be used at the end of more than two successive lines. (This rule should also be followed for letter writing.) Breaking the last word of a paragraph is also considered bad form.

Do not hyphenate a word at the end of a page.

Dividing a compound word or a word already hyphenated should be avoided.

If numbers must be divided, the break should be made after a comma: There are 35,675,-
545 chickens in Nebraska.

The general rule in the hyphenation of compound words is this: When two or more words precede a noun and together form a single idea modifying the noun, they should be hyphenated; they are usually not hyphenated if they follow the noun. In many instances only the context of the sentence will determine whether a hyphenated compound is required, or whether the words should remain separate.

He said it in a very matter-of-fact way.
He knew that to be true as a matter of fact.
As a matter of fact, he knew that to be true.
Her dress was green and white.
Her green-and-white dress was pretty.

Note: Do not confuse the adverb and the adjective when they precede a noun—these are not hyphenated.

The beautifully illustrated book was enjoyed by the membership.

Hyphens are used to separate prefixes from words where the writer's meaning would otherwise be distorted.

The upholsterer re-covered the chair.
The police recovered the typewriter.

The hyphen is also used to separate a prefix from a proper noun, or to simplify a confusing combination.

anti-American, pre-Renaissance, mid-ocean

Hyphens are also used in all numbers ranging from twenty-one to ninety-nine, and in fractions: one-half, three-quarters. Hyphens are also used in designating years: nineteen-sixties, nineteen sixty-two (*not* nineteen-sixty-two).

The hyphen is used in titles when combined with *elect* or *ex*.

President-elect
ex-President

The hyphen is generally used when words are compounded with the prefix *self*.

self-satisfied, self-confident, self-possessed, self-starter

The Dash [—]

A word of caution against confusing the hyphen (-) and the dash (—). The hyphen connects, while the dash separates. The dash is formed on the typewriter with two hyphens, no space before, between, or after.

If properly used, the dash is effective to secure emphasis but has only a few legitimate uses in business letters. It may be used in place of the comma and parentheses in handling appositive and parenthetical expressions. It is also used to mark intentional repetition.

Exercise every day—*every* day—and find out for yourself how beneficial it is to your health and well being.

The dash may be used to show an abrupt change in thought.

We do not know when we shall go—here is the bus.

Parentheses [( )]

Parentheses are used to enclose words which give additional information but have little, if any, direct connection with the main thought expressed. Commas and dashes have already been discussed in this relationship. Material enclosed in commas or separated from the rest of the sentence by dashes adds something to the main thought expressed, although not something essential; material enclosed in parentheses adds nothing to the main thought and has no direct relationship to the rest of the sentence.

If we win the contest (and I feel certain we will), we shall compete in the national contest in Chicago.

Parentheses are widely used to enclose references to statements, authors, etc.

"How to Express Thoughts Properly" is outlined in full in our text (see page 124).
We are using *Effective Business English* (Jones and Smith) for reference.

The Underscore

Underscoring a word or a group of words may be done for emphasis, but this device should be used with caution. There are a few fundamental rules, however, which should be followed.

Underline the title of a book, a booklet, essay, play, magazine, or newspaper. (Full capitals are also acceptable.)

Note: This rule is discussed more fully under the subject of Quotation Marks.

When preparing copy for the printer, underline material which is to be printed in italics.

Do not use underscoring for emphasis in the body of the letter.

Do not break the underscoring when underscoring headings.

Do not break the underscoring of parts of the text unless each part or each word is intended to be emphasized separately.

Do not include the punctuation at the end of the sentence in the underscoring.

CAPITALIZATION

Conventions governing the use of capital letters are quite clear.

Capitalize the first word of every sentence.

The first person singular pronoun *I* and the vocative *O* are generally capitalized.

Unless style requires a different form, *a.m.* and *p.m.* are set in small letters without a space between them. Capital letters are used for B.C. and A.D. but, again, there is no space between them.

9:30 a.m. 10:30 p.m.
A.D. 1760 *or* 1760 A.D.
76 B.C.

Note: Although A.D. should technically precede the number of the year, popular usage permits it to follow the date. In printed matter B.C., A.D., a.m., and p.m. usually appear in small capitals (B.C., A.D., A.M., P.M.).

The first letter of a line of conventional poetry is capitalized. Much modern poetry, however, ignores this convention.

Hickory, dickory, dock
The mouse ran up the clock.

The first word after a colon should be capitalized only when it begins a complete sentence.

The candidate made only one promise: If elected, he would fight for better conditions.
The list contained these items: five pounds of flour, two dozen eggs, and a pound of butter.

Every direct quotation should begin with a capital, except where the quoted passage is grammatically woven into the text preceding it.

The announcer shouted, "There it goes, over the back wall for a home run!"
The announcer saw the ball going "over the back wall for a home run."

Capitalize the first letters of all important words in the titles of books, newspapers, magazines, chapters, poems, articles. Short conjunctions and prepositions are generally not capitalized.

How to Win Friends and Influence People

Geographical divisions and regions require capitals.

Arctic Circle	the Atlantic Seaboard
the Orient	the Great Plains

Compass points are capitalized when they are part of a generally accepted name, but not when they denote direction, or are used with common nouns.

Middle East	eastern New York
Old South	Head west for twenty-five miles.

Capitalize names of streets, parks, buildings, but not the general categories into which they fall.

General Post Office *but* We went to the *post office*.
Metropolitan Museum of Art *but* Some *museums* are open until five.
Empire State Building *but* Which is the tallest *building* in New York City?

Religions, religious leaders, the various appellations for God and the Christian Trinity require capitalization, as do all names for the Bible and its parts.

the Father, the Son, and the Holy Ghost
Virgin Mary, the Immaculate Virgin
Yahweh, Jehovah, Saviour, Messiah

Buddhism, Shintoism, Taoism
New Testament
Exodus
Sermon on the Mount
Ten Commandments

Capitalize the names of political parties, classes, clubs, organizations, movements, and their adherents. Use small letters for the terms that refer generally to ideology (bolshevism, fascism, socialism).

Democratic Party
the Right Wing
Farm Bloc
Boy Scouts of America

Political divisions are capitalized.

Holy Roman Empire	the Colonies
French Republic	Suffolk County
the Dominion	Eighth Congressional District

Government bodies, departments, bureaus, and courts are capitalized.

the Supreme Court	the Cabinet
House of Representatives	Census Bureau
Department of Labor	British Parliament

Capitalize the titles of all high-ranking government officials, and all appellations of the President of the United States. Many publishers, it should be pointed out, prefer small letters for titles that are not accompanied by the name of the official.

President	Commander-in-Chief
Secretary of State	Chief Justice
Undersecretary	Prime Minister
Ambassador to India	Minister of War

Capitalize the names of treaties, documents, and important events.

Second World War	Declaration of Independence
Treaty of Versailles	Boston Tea Party

Family designations, when used without a possessive pronoun, take a capital letter.

I sent Mother home by taxi.
I sent my mother home by taxi.

Capitalize seasons only when they are personified. All personifications require capitals.

The frosty breath of Winter settled on the land.
The voice of Envy whispered in her ear.
The mother of Invention is Necessity.
When Headquarters commands, we jump.
He saw Mother Nature's grim visage.

Names and epithets of peoples, races, and tribes are capitalized.

Caucasian	Sioux
Negro	Cliff Dwellers

Articles and prepositions are generally capitalized in the names of Englishmen and Americans, and are not capitalized in French, Italian, Spanish, German, and Dutch names, unless otherwise specified by family usage.

Thomas De Quincey	Ludwig van Beethoven
Martin Van Buren	Leonardo da Vinci
Fiorello La Guardia	San Juan de la Cruz

Capitalize the names of holidays and festivals.

Christmas Eve	Shrove Tuesday
Yom Kippur	New Year's Day

Capitalize such parts of a book as the Glossary, Contents, Index, and Preface.

Capitalize the first and last words in the salutation in business letters, and all titles.

My dear Sir	Dear Doctor Brown
My dear Reverend Lothrop	Dear Reverend Father

Capitalize only the first word of the complimentary close of a letter.

Very truly yours	Sincerely yours

SPELLING

General Suggestions

When in doubt as to the correct spelling of a word, consult the dictionary; do not take anything for granted.

Keep a list of your spelling errors and study them.

Learn the available lists of the most commonly misspelled words—there are many such lists.

Learn to spell by syllables, carefully pronouncing each syllable. Faulty spelling is often due to faulty pronunciation.

Use newly acquired words and make them part of your oral and written vocabulary.

Do not use the simplified or modern forms of spelling in business correspondence, as *thru* for *through*.

Learn some basic spelling rules such as the following.

cede, ceed, and sede endings According to the Government Style Manual, there is only one word which ends in *sede—supersede*, and three that end in *ceed—proceed* (but *procedure*), *exceed, succeed*. All other words using this combination end in *cede—precede, secede, recede*.

ie and ei a. After *c*, when the sound is long *e* (ē), the *e* usually precedes the *i*: rec*ei*ve, dec*ei*ve, c*ei*ling, rec*ei*pt.

b. After most other letters, the *i* precedes the *e* (*ie*): th*ie*f, gr*ie*f, bel*ie*ve, ach*ie*ve, l*ie*n.

The exceptions must be learned, since they follow no rule: n*ei*ther, l*ei*sure, w*ei*rd, s*ei*ze.

c. When the sound is *not* long *e* (ē), and especially if the sound is long *a* (ā), the *e* precedes the *i* (*ei*): sl*ei*gh, v*ei*l.

Beginnings and Endings of Words (Prefixes and Suffixes)

a. As a general rule, drop the final *e* in the base word when a suffix beginning with a vowel is added: decide—deciding; write—writing; type—typing. (When in doubt, use the dictionary.)

b. As a rule, retain the final *e* in the base word when a suffix beginning with a consonant is added: remote—remotely; care—carefully; adverse—adversely.

c. In applying the rule for adding *ed* or *ing*, the accent (or lack of it) may serve as a guide. Words of one syllable (and most words of more than one syllable) that end in a single consonant (except *f, h,* or *x*), preceded by a single vowel, double the final consonant *if the accent falls on the last syllable.*

plan—planned, planning; whet—whetted, whetting; bet—betting; can—canning
transfer—transferred, transferring; excel—excelled, excelling
omit—omitted, omitting; begin—beginning

d. When the word is *not* accented on the last syllable, the consonant is usually not doubled.

travel—traveled, traveling; benefit—benefited, benefiting; profit—profited, profiting; gossip—gossiped, gossiping

e. When the endings *ness* and *ly* are added to a word not ending in *y*, the base word rarely changes. In most words ending in *y*, the *y* changes to *i* when *ly* is added.

natural—naturally; similar—similarly; genuine—genuineness; blessed—blessedness; hazy—hazily; body—bodily

If the base word ends in *n* and the suffix *ness* is added, the *n* is doubled: sudden—suddenness; mean—meanness; vain—vainness.

f. In regard to the word endings *ise, ize, yze*, the most common form is *ize*, but here again the dictionary should be consulted if there is doubt.

legalize, fraternize, criticize, jeopardize
advertise, merchandise, surmise, enterprise
paralyze, analyze

◆ In British English *ise* is sometimes used for *ize*, as *realise* for *realize*. See the note under -IZE in the dictionary.

g. When the word beginnings (prefixes) *in, en, im, em, un, dis, mis, be, de, re, il,* and *over* are added to a word, the spelling of the base word is not changed.

inactive, enjoy, impending, embrace, uneasy
dismiss, mistrust, beguile, degrade, retreat, illegal, overhaul

h. When adding the suffix *ful*, the *l* is single except when *ly* is also added (*fully*): care—careful—carefully; hope—hopeful—hopefully.

Forming the Plurals of Nouns

a. Most nouns form the plural by simply adding *s*: table—tables; house—houses.

b. Some nouns, especially those ending in *s*, form the plural by adding *es*: class—classes; glass—glasses.

c. Words ending in *y* preceded by a consonant form the plural by changing the *y* to *i* and adding *es*: candy—candies; study—studies; secretary—secretaries.

d. Words ending in *y* preceded by a vowel form the plural without any change in the word: key—keys; boy—boys; money—moneys (monies when referring to "sums of money").

e. Nouns ending in *o* preceded by a vowel form the plural by adding *s*: rodeo—rodeos; radio—radios.

When the *o* is preceded by a consonant, the plural is formed by adding *es*: hero—heroes; torpedo—torpedoes.

f. Nouns referring to music which end in *o* preceded by a consonant form the plural by simply adding *s*: piano—pianos; oratorio—oratorios; contralto—contraltos; soprano—sopranos.

g. Some few nouns follow none of the above rules but form the plural in an unusual way: child—children; tooth—teeth; mouse—mice; ox—oxen.

h. Compound nouns (more than one noun) form the plural from the main word: notary public—notaries public; trade-union–trade-unions; father-in-law—fathers-in-law; court-martial—courts-martial.

i. When a solid compound ends in *ful*, the plural is formed at the end of the solid compound and not within the word: basketfuls, spoonfuls, pocketfuls.

j. Words taken from another language sometimes form the plural as they would in the original language: stratum—strata; addendum—addenda; datum—data.

k. When the words in compounds are of almost equal importance, both parts of the compound are pluralized: heads of departments; women operators.

◆ For further information, see the note under PLURAL in the body of this dictionary.

CONFUSING WORDS

[Including words that have different meanings but are pronounced the same (*homophones*) or similarly]

accept See EXCEPT.
addition, edition *addition* means the process of joining together or finding the sum of. *edition* refers to the form in which a book, magazine, or other literary work is published: first *edition*.
advice, advise *advice* is the noun: to give *advice*. *advise* is the verb: to *advise* a person.
affect See EFFECT.
all ready See ALREADY.
all right, alright *all right* is the only spelling to be used: It is *all right* to do so. The spelling *alright* is not yet considered acceptable and should not be used.
allude, elude *allude* means to make indirect or casual reference: He *alluded* to one of Shakespeare's sonnets. *elude* means to avoid or escape: The meaning *eludes* me.
already, all ready *already* means before or by this time or the time mentioned: The group has *already* gone. *all ready* (two words) means that everyone is ready to do a given thing: We are *all ready* to go.
among, between *among* is used when referring to more than two persons or things. *between* is usually preferable when referring to only two persons or things.
appraise, apprise *appraise* means to make an official valuation of. *apprise* means to notify or inform.
ascent, assent *ascent* means rising, soaring, or climbing: the *ascent* of the mountain. *assent* means to express agreement, consent, sanction: to *assent* to a course of action.
between See AMONG.
can See MAY.
capital, capitol *capital* means (*n.*) property, chief city: Albany is the *capital* of New York; and (*adj.*) of chief importance. *capitol*, always a noun, means a building in which a State legislature meets: The *capitol* is on Chamber Street.
censor, censure *censor* means (*n.*) an official examiner of manuscripts, plays, etc.; (*v.*) to act as a censor; delete; suppress. *censure* means (*v.*) to express disapproval of; condemn; (*n.*) the expression of disapproval or blame.
census See SENSES.
cite, sight, site *cite* means to quote or to summon: to *cite* an incident. *sight* means a view, a vision: a beautiful *sight*. *site* means a place or location: the *site* of the church.
compliment, complement *compliment* means praise or congratulation. *complement* means one of two parts that mutually complete each other.
consul See COUNCIL.
correspondents, correspondence *correspondents* refers to people who communicate by means of letters. *correspondence* refers to the letters written.
council, counsel, consul *council* means an assembly convened for consultation. *counsel* means guidance, advice; also, a lawyer. *consul* means an officer residing in a foreign country to protect his own country's interests.
creditable, credible *creditable* means deserving credit or esteem; praiseworthy: a *creditable* project for reducing poverty. *credible* means capable of being believed, reliable: a *credible* alibi.
decent, descent, dissent *decent* means proper; respectable. *descent* means the act of descending or going downward. *dissent* means (*v.*) to disagree; (*n.*) a disagreement.
device, devise *device* is the noun: a handy *device* for opening bottles. *devise* is the verb: He *devised* a new way to open bottles.
dissent See DECENT.
edition See ADDITION.
effect, affect *effect*, both a noun and a verb, means (*v.*) to bring about; to cause or achieve: The treatments will *effect* an early cure; and (*n.*) result, outcome. *affect*, a verb only, means to influence or act upon: Fear *affects* the mind.
effective, effectual *effective* means producing a desired result: *Effective* action averted the strike. *effectual* means having the power to produce a desired result: *effectual* legal steps.
elicit, illicit *elicit* means to bring to light: to *elicit* the truth. *illicit* means unlawful or unauthorized.
elude See ALLUDE.
eminent, imminent *eminent* means high in station; distinguished; prominent: an *eminent* statesman. *imminent* means about to happen (said especially of danger): an *imminent* calamity.
except, accept *except* means with the exclusion or omission of. *accept* means to receive or agree to; acknowledge: to *accept* an invitation.
farther, further *farther* refers to distance. *further* means to a greater degree; more; in addition.
formerly, formally *formerly* means some time ago; once: He was *formerly* a judge. *formally* means with formality or with regard to form: *formally* dressed.
further See FARTHER.
illicit See ELICIT.
imminent See EMINENT.
lay, lie See below, under CONSISTENCY OF TENSE AND PERSON OF VERBS.
learn See TEACH.
lesson, lessen *lesson* refers to instructive or corrective example. *lessen* means to make less; decrease.
loose, lose *loose* means not fastened or attached. *lose* means to part with; to be deprived of.
may, can *may* expresses permission: The child *may* play in the yard. *can* expresses ability to do: The child *can* do better than he is doing at present.
past, passed *past* means (*adj.*) ended or finished: His hopes are *past*; and (*n.*) time gone by: He dreams of the *past*. *passed*, the past tense and past participle of *pass*, means went (or gone) beyond or farther than: The car, which was going at high speed, *passed* him easily.
persecute, prosecute *persecute* means to maltreat or oppress; to harass. *prosecute* is generally used in a legal sense—to bring suit against.
personal, personnel *personal* pertains to a person: *personal* matters, *personal* opinions. *personnel* pertains to a body or group of persons: *personnel* problems, *personnel* department.
practical, practicable *practical* pertains to actual use and experience. *practicable* means feasible or usable. A *practicable* plan is a workable plan, but a *practical* plan is one based on experience rather than theory, or one that can easily be put into effect.
principal, principle *principal* means (*n.*) head or leader: The *principal* of the school will give the order; and (*adj.*) highest in rank; chief: The *principal* member of an orchestra is the concertmaster. *principle*, always a noun, means a fundamental truth or law: We cannot sacrifice the *principle* for which we stand.
prosecute See PERSECUTE.
rise, raise See below, under CONSISTENCY OF TENSE AND PERSON OF VERBS.
senses, census *senses*, the plural of *sense*, refers to the faculty of sensation, as through taste, touch, hearing, smell, or sight. *census* refers to an official count of the people of a country or district, etc.
sight See CITE.
sit, set See below, under CONSISTENCY OF TENSE AND PERSON OF VERBS.
site See CITE.
stationery, stationary *stationery* refers to writing supplies. *stationary* means remaining in one place.
sweet, suite *sweet* means agreeable to the sense of taste. *suite* refers to a set or series of things intended to be used together: *suite* of rooms, *suite* of furniture.
teach, learn The teacher *teaches*; the student *learns*.

CONSISTENCY OF TENSE AND PERSON OF VERBS

Care should be given not to change the *tense* or *form* of the verb or the *person* of a pronoun in the middle of a sentence. Such violation is generally due to carelessness.

The *tense* of a verb indicates the time when something took place; and the three main tenses are *present, past,* and *future.*

I *eat* my dinner.
I *ate* my dinner.
I *shall eat* my dinner.

The form of the verb indicates *active voice* when the subject of the verb is acting, and the *passive voice* when the subject of the verb is acted upon.

I *am helping.*
I *am being helped.*

The *person* of a pronoun denotes the speaker (*first person* I, we); the person spoken to (*second person* you); and the person spoken of (*third person* he, she, it, they). The writer of the letter should never refer to himself in the third person (as "the writer" or "the undersigned") but should use the first person.

Some verbs cause confusion in both writing and speaking because of the similarity in spelling and in principal parts.

The most common verbs in this group are: **lie—lay; rise—raise**; and **sit—set.**

The principal parts of these verbs are as follows:

lie—meaning to rest or recline
lay—meaning to place or put
Present: lie—I *lie* down to rest at ten o'clock each morning.
lay—I *lay* the wood for the fire each day.
Past: lay—I *lay* in bed too long.
laid—I *laid* the book on the table.
Past Participle: lain—She has *lain* there for an hour.
laid—She has *laid* the book on the table.

rise—meaning to move upward
raise—meaning to cause to rise up, to arouse or awaken
Present: rise—I *rise* at six o'clock in the morning.
raise—I *raise* the flag each morning.
Past: rose—I *rose* at six o'clock today.
raised—I *raised* the flag this morning.
Past Participle: risen—I shall have *risen* by six o'clock.
raised—I shall have *raised* the prices on these articles by then.

sit—meaning to seat oneself
set—meaning to fix firmly or make fast or place
Present: sit—I like to *sit* in the sun.
set—I plan to *set* the table for six persons.
Past: sat—I *sat* in the sun.
set—He *set* the alarm for four o'clock.
Past Participle: sat—I have *sat* in the sun one hour.
set—The sun has *set* in a bright glow.

shall—will ◆ See the note under SHALL in the body of this dictionary.

BUSINESS CORRESPONDENCE

Let it be stated at the outset that there are no unimportant letters. Good letters help to increase business, make friends, and influence people favorably; sloppy letters have the opposite effect.

Good letters are not written in haste. Often, they are written, revised, and rewritten until they express clearly the meaning the writer wishes to convey to his reader. As one authority puts it: "You must write not so that you can be understood but so that you cannot possibly be misunderstood."

The formalities of letter writing are definite and rigid. Brevity and clarity are the prime virtues. Carbon copies are made to give the sender an up-to-date file of his correspondence. The number of copies made will depend on the number of persons concerned with the information, but one office copy must be made of every letter or document sent out, either interoffice or through the mail.

Letter Styles The most common letter styles are the Block, Modified Block with Paragraph Indentions, Modified Block without Paragraph Indentions, and the Indented; but there are also the Inverted Paragraph style and the NOMA Simplified. (NOMA stands for National Office Management Association.)

Forms of Punctuation—Open, Closed, and Mixed

When the (Strictly) Open punctuation is used, no punctuation is used after the date line, after the inside address (unless there is an abbreviation), after the salutation, or after the complimentary close.

When Closed punctuation is used, place a period after the date line, and a comma (unless there is an abbreviation) after each line in the inside address except the last, where there is a period. Place a colon after the salutation and a comma after the complimentary close. Closed punctuation is generally used with the Indented letter style and rarely ever used with the Block style.

When Mixed punctuation is used, only two marks are involved unless abbreviations in the inside address dictate otherwise—a colon goes after the salutation and a comma after the complimentary close.

Letter Placement on the Standard-Size Letterhead

Letters are classified as short, average, and long. Short letters generally have wider side margins and are placed lower on the page than the long letters. The side (horizontal) margins should not vary by more than two or four spaces. The top and bottom (vertical) spacing should not vary by more than six lines to look well on the page.

In determining the placement of the letter on the page, the size of the typewriter type (pica or elite) must be considered. Pica type has ten spaces to the inch, whereas elite type has twelve spaces to the inch.

The following letter is in the Modified Block style. The date line is to the right and the complimentary close begins at or about the center of the letter. (The close may begin at the center of the horizontal line, five spaces to the left of center, or five spaces to the right of center, depending on the signature and title of the sender. Try to begin at the center, if possible.)

SAMPLE LETTER

(The address of the sender or merely the date line should begin eighteen or fewer spaces from the top of the page, depending on the depth of the letterhead and the length of the letter.)

811 Cedar Street (*Heading*)
San Francisco, California 94125
July 21, 1963 (*Date line*)
(leave 3 or more lines blank)

Mr. Jack Armstrong, President (*Inside Address*)
American Steel Foundation
355 Lexington Avenue
New York, New York 10017 (leave 2 spaces between State and ZIP Code)
(leave 1 line blank)
Attention: Transportation Manager
(leave 1 line blank)
Dear Mr. Armstrong: (*Salutation*)
(leave 1 line blank)
Two spaces below the Salutation begins the body of the letter, which is single-spaced, with a double space between paragraphs. Each paragraph including the first begins flush with the left-hand margin. The spacing between the Heading and the Inside Address, and also between the top of the page and the Date Line, may be expanded if the letter is short so as to improve the appearance of the page. The Attention line is used to alert a particular member of the company, as the personnel manager, the purchasing agent, etc. Where it is customary to cite the subject of the correspondence separately from the text, it may appear on the same line with the Salutation, flush against the margin on the right; or it may be centered between the Salutation and the Body of the letter; or it may be placed flush with the left-hand margin between the Salutation and the Body of the letter, depending on the style of letter used.
(leave 1 line blank between paragraphs)
Two spaces below the body of the letter, centered, or five spaces to the right or left of center (depending on the signature and title of the sender), is placed the Complimentary Close. In formal correspondence this is *Yours truly, Very truly yours*; for a person of sufficient rank, *Respectfully yours* is appropriate.
(leave 1 line blank)
Yours truly, (*Complimentary Close*)
(leave 1 line blank)
(full caps) J & B BOILER CORPORATION

(leave 3 lines blank)

(capitals and small letters) John J. Little (*Signature*)
(capitals and small letters) Chairman (*Title*) (no space between name and title)
(leave 1 line blank)
JJL: bp (*Identifying Initials*)
(leave 1 line blank)
Enclosure (*Enclosures*)
(leave 1 line blank)
cc: Mr. George Phipps (*Notation of Copies Sent*)

Elements of a Business Letter

Heading This consists of the address of the sender (often part of the letterhead) and the date of the letter. The date line ends flush with the right-hand margin except in the strictly Block and the NOMA styles.

Inside Address This identifies the recipient of the letter, and enables the sender to identify the file copy. It includes the name of the recipient, his title, if any, and the address.

Salutation For letters addressed to a company, *Gentlemen* is a suitable greeting. Where an individual is addressed, any one of the following may be appropriate: *Dear Sir, Dear Madam, Dear Mr.* (or *Mrs.* or *Miss*) (name of the person specifically addressed). When the marital status of a woman is unknown, she is addressed as *Miss* or simply by the letter *M*. The Salutation in business letters is always followed by a colon except in the Strictly Open form. The NOMA form uses no Salutation.

Complimentary Close The flowery close that was considered good form at one time, and is still used in many European countries, is a thing of the past in this country. The most-used closings are: Yours very truly, Very truly yours, Yours truly, Sincerely yours, Very sincerely yours. Except in extremely formal contexts, it is *not* considered good form to run the Body of the letter into the Complimentary Close, such as: Awaiting your decision, I remain, Very truly yours, etc. (The NOMA style letter uses no Close.)

Signature The name of the sender is usually typed in capitals and small letters, but sometimes in full capitals, four spaces below the Complimentary Close. On the line following is typed, always in capitals and small letters, the position he occupies in the firm, unless, of course, this information is included in the letterhead. When the company name is typed at the bottom of the letter, as well as the name and title of the writer, the company name is typed in full capitals two spaces below the Complimentary Close. Four spaces below this is the name of the writer in capitals and small letters; the writer's title appears on the line below the writer's name, always typed in capitals and small letters.

Identifying Initials In the lower left-hand corner of the letter, two spaces below the writer's title or name, it is customary to put the initials or name of the sender and the initials of the secretary. Full capitals or capital and small letters may be used, and the identification of the writer and secretary separated by the colon or diagonal (:/).

Enclosures Enclosures, if any, are indicated two spaces below the identification letters. If there is only one enclosure, the word "Enclosure" or merely "Enc." may be used. If more than one enclosure is being sent, the number must be indicated (Enclosures 4). Identifying the enclosure or enclosures may also be done (as Enclosure: Invoice, Number 642).

Postscript Generally, postscripts are not used in routine business correspondence. They are, however, used in sales letters for emphasis or to call attention to matters which, if placed in the body of the letter, might be overlooked. When a postscript is used, it should be prefaced by the letters P.S. (two spaces follow) and be placed two spaces below the Identification, or the Enclosure, if there is one. If the Block style is used, the letters P.S. are flush with the left-hand margin. If the Indented form of letter is used, the letters P.S. are indented five spaces from the left margin. The second and following lines are flush with the left margin, even with the lines in the body of the letter. The Postscript is not generally signed but should be initialed by the writer.

Notation of Copies Sent When a copy of a letter is sent to one or more persons, notation of this fact is usually made on the original letter and on all carbons. In this way, all parties concerned with the original letter know what other person or persons received copies. The notation is made two spaces below the Identification initials or two spaces below the last item in the letter, such as Enclosure of Postscript. The words "Copy to" or "Copies to" or the abbreviation "cc" may be used. If for some reason the writer does not wish to make known to whom copies were sent, the notation may be made only on the office file copy and is usually placed in a position other than the lower left—it may be placed in the upper left corner, which is not used for any other part of the letter. This position of the carbon notation signifies that the distribution of the carbon(s) is confidential but the notation keeps the information in the office files for future reference.

Business Envelopes The address on the envelope will coincide in all particulars with the Inside Address. Double spacing is preferred in order to expedite the mailman's task, even in the four-line address. The size of the envelope to be used (regular or legal—No. 6¾ or No. 10 being the most common with the standard 8½ by 11 inch paper) will be determined by the material to be sent. Letters of two pages or longer, or a one-page letter with an enclosure, should be sent in the larger envelope. The first line of the address should be written one or two lines below the horizontal center and five spaces to the left of the vertical center on the No. 6¾ envelope and at the center of the No. 10 envelope. If one or more of the lines in the address are particularly long or short, some adjustment should be made in placing the address properly on the envelope. The style of punctuation must agree with the inside address in the letter. The ZIP Code number is typed two spaces below the state (two spaces after the state in the inside address of the letter with no punctuation between the state and the ZIP Code number), whereas the Zone number is written between the city and state with a comma after the number (San Diego 3, California). Names of states must always be written in full on the envelope as well as in the inside address. The words *Street, Court, Boulevard, Avenue,* etc., must always be written in full. Do not use *th, st, rd* with street numbers; write the address as follows: 125 East 45 Street.

Paragraphing in Business Letters There is no one rule for paragraphing in business letters. Most letters are of the short or medium length; therefore, plan on a short opening paragraph which states the purpose of the letter, or reason for writing, in clear, concise English. Avoid trite expressions. One or two paragraphs will probably be needed to carry the message, and a short closing should suggest action. Avoid overparagraphing; on the other hand, the busy executive has to absorb the substance of the letter as quickly as possible, and the long, involved paragraph tends to lose the reader. It is better to break up one main thought into two or three paragraphs than to make it difficult for the reader to grasp your message. Enumerations and quotations should be indented at the right of the letter as well as at the left-hand margin; enumerations may be numbered as well, and each enumeration should be treated as a paragraph. If numbers are used with the enumerations, two spaces are left after the period following the number, except in the NOMA letter, where no period follows the number.

Spacing in Business Letters The single-space letter is almost invariably used, with two spaces between paragraphs. In the first place, single spacing gives a better appearance; in the second place, it saves expensive stationery, tissues, and carbon, as well as filing space, since many of the single-spaced letters would go to two or more pages if they were double-spaced. If other than the Block paragraph is used, the indention may be five or ten spaces, but most writers prefer five spaces. When the Inverted Paragraph style is used, the overhang is also five spaces.

When a letter requires two or more pages, the second and subsequent pages must be identified with the first. There are various methods of doing this, but the two neatest and quickest styles are as follows:

Acme Products -2- Date

or

Acme Products—Page 2—Date

Spacing for Rough Drafts When preparing technical or otherwise difficult and important matter for printing or mailing, the copy should be double- or triple-spaced to leave room for corrections. Single-spaced copy is very difficult to correct.

Stationery Sizes The different sizes of letterheads can be identified by name. The common terms and dimensions are as follows:

Standard	8½ x 11	inches
Half-sheet	8½ x 5½	"
Monarch	7¼ x 10½	"
Baronial	5½ x 8½	"

The Standard and Half-sheet size stationery take the No. 10 and No. 6¾ envelopes respectively.

The Monarch and Baronial, which are used for personal letters and frequently by top executives in the firm, take their own special size envelopes—7½ x 3⅞ inches and 6 x 4⅝ inches, respectively.

Having various sizes of stationery is costly and time-consuming in handling, and the pages that are smaller than the standard file-folder size are troublesome in the files.

Carbon Paper and Carbon Packs To produce good clear carbon copies, care must be given to the selection of the weight and grade of the original copy, the tissue sheets, and the carbon paper. Most typewriters have a "copy set" which makes provision for space and pressure with respect to the cylinder, and the adjustment should be made to produce the best copies.

When only one copy is required for the files and the letter will be only one page in length, many offices use the back of the incoming letter for the file copy of the reply in order to save filing space as well as time.

In offices where it is standard procedure to make many carbons, ready-made carbon packs are used. The carbon paper and tissue sheets are fastened together at the bottom and save a great deal of time because the typist does not have to collate the papers. The carbons are thrown away after one using, since an inexpensive grade of carbon paper is used. The packs may be purchased in any number of sheets.

Making Corrections by Spreading and Squeezing Letters Stenographers should learn the device for making corrections by spreading or squeezing letters instead of retyping the page containing the error. This is a difficult matter and takes a little skill. By erasing all or part of the word containing the error, and by manipulating the spacer, the word can be contracted or spread, thus concealing the insertion or deletion of a letter.

Erasing If there is a movable carriage on the machine, move the carriage to the right or to the left to prevent the erasure particles from falling into the interior of the machine. If the carriage is stationary, move the writing unit away from the place in the copy containing the error in order to avoid having the erasure particles fall into the writing unit. Use the eraser shield, which has various slots to protect the typed words not to be erased. Be careful not to smudge the paper, particularly when correcting errors on carbon copies. A softer eraser should be used on the carbon tissues than the eraser used on the original.

FORMS OF ADDRESS

President of the United States
Address: Business: The President
The White House
Washington, D.C.
Social: The President
and Mrs. Washington
The White House
Washington, D.C.
Salutation: Formal: Sir:
Informal: My dear Mr. President:
Closing: Formal: I have the honor to remain,
Most respectfully yours,
Informal: Very respectfully yours,
In Conversation: Mr. President *or* Sir
Title of Introduction: *Only the name of the person being introduced is spoken*

Vice President of the United States
Address: Business: The Vice President
United States Senate
Washington, D.C.
Social: The Vice President
and Mrs. Hope
Home Address
Salutation: Formal: Sir
Informal: My dear Mr. Vice President:
Closing: Formal: Very truly yours,
Informal: Sincerely yours, *or* Faithfully yours,
In Conversation: Mr. Vice President *or* Sir
Title of Introduction: The Vice President

Chief Justice of the United States
Address: Business: The Chief Justice
The Supreme Court
Washington, D.C.
Social: The Chief Justice
and Mrs. Page
Home Address
Salutation: Formal: Sir
Informal: My dear Mr. Chief Justice
Closing: Formal: Very truly yours,
Informal: Sincerely yours, *or* Faithfully yours,
In Conversation: Mr. Chief Justice *or* Sir
Title of Introduction: The Chief Justice

Associate Justice of the Supreme Court
Address: Business: Mr. Justice Katsaros
The Supreme Court
Washington, D.C.
Social: Mr. Justice Katsaros
and Mrs. Katsaros
Home Address
Salutation: Formal: Sir:
Informal: My dear Mr. Justice Katsaros:
Closing: Formal: Very truly yours,
Informal: Sincerely yours,
In Conversation: Mr. Justice *or* Mr. Justice Katsaros *or* Sir
Title of Introduction: Mr. Justice Katsaros

Cabinet Officer
Address: Business: The Honorable Gary George Gussin
The Secretary of the Treasury
or The Attorney General
or The Postmaster General
Washington, D.C.
Social: The Honorable
The Secretary of the Treasury
and Mrs. Gussin
Home Address
or (*for a woman cabinet member*)
Mr. and Mrs. Henry Leo Woods
Salutation: Formal: Sir: *or* Dear Sir: *or* Madam:
Informal: My dear Mr. Secretary:
or My dear Mr. Attorney General:
or My Dear Mr. Postmaster General:
or Madam Secretary:
Closing: Formal: Very truly yours,
Informal: Sincerely yours,
In Conversation: Mr. Secretary *or* Madam Secretary *or*
Mr. Attorney General *or*
Mr. Postmaster General *or* Sir
Title of Introduction: The Secretary of the Treasury *or*
The Attorney General

Former President
Address: Business: The Honorable
Alfred Edward Work
Office Address
Social: The Honorable
Alfred Edward Work
and Mrs. Work
Home Address
Salutation: Formal: Sir:
Informal: My dear Mr. Work:
Closing: Formal: Very truly yours,
Informal: Sincerely yours,
In Conversation: Mr. Work *or* Sir
Title of Introduction: The Honorable Alfred Edward Work

United States Senator
Address: Business: The Honorable
John Wandzilak
United States Senate
Washington, D.C.
Social: The Honorable
John Wandzilak
and Mrs. Wandzilak
Home Address
or (*for a woman senator*)
Mr. and Mrs. John Row Doe
Salutation: Formal: Sir: *or* Madam:
Informal: My dear Senator Wandzilak:
Closing: Formal: Very truly yours,
Informal: Sincerely yours,
In Conversation: Senator *or* Senator Wandzilak *or* Sir
Title of Introduction: Senator Wandzilak of Alaska

Speaker of the House of Representatives
Address: Business: The Honorable
Walter Grevesmuhl
The Speaker of the House of
Representatives
Washington, D.C.
Social: The Speaker
and Mrs. Grevesmuhl
Home Address
Salutation: Formal: Sir:
Informal: My dear Mr. Speaker:
Closing: Formal: Very truly yours,
Informal: Sincerely yours,
In Conversation: Mr. Speaker *or* Sir
Title of Introduction: The Speaker of the House of
Representatives

Member of the House of Representatives
Address: Business: The Honorable
Henry Cobb Wellcome
United States House of Representatives
Washington, D.C.

Social: The Honorable
Henry Cobb Wellcome
and Mrs. Wellcome
Home Address
or (for a woman member)
Mr. and Mrs. John Knox Jones
Salutation: Formal: Sir: *or* Madam:
Informal: My dear Mr. Wellcome:
Closing: Formal: Very truly yours,
Informal: Sincerely yours,
In Conversation: Mr. Wellcome *or* Mrs. Jones *or* Sir *or* Madam
Title of Introduction: Representative Wellcome from Nebraska

Ambassador of the United States
Address: Business: The Honorable
John Wilson Smith
The Ambassador of the United States
American Embassy
London, England
Social: The Honorable
John Wilson Smith
and Mrs. Smith
Home Address
or (for a woman ambassador)
Mr. and Mrs. Joseph Leeds Walker
Home Address
Salutation: Formal: Sir: *or* Madam:
Informal: My dear Mr. Ambassador: *or* My dear Madam Ambassador:
Closing: Formal: Very truly yours,
Informal: Sincerely yours,
In Conversation: Mr. Ambassador *or* Madam Ambassador *or* Sir *or* Madam
Title of Introduction: The American Ambassador *or (if necessary)* Our Ambassador to England

Minister Plenipotentiary of the United States
Address: Business: The Honorable
James Lee Row
The Minister of the United States
American Legation
Oslo, Norway
Social: The Honorable
James Lee Row
and Mrs. Row
Home Address
or (for a woman minister)
Mr. and Mrs. Arthur Johnson
Home Address
Salutation: Formal: Sir: *or* Madam:
Informal: My dear Mr. Minister *or* My dear Madam Minister:
Closing: Formal: Very truly yours,
Informal: Sincerely yours,
In Conversation: Mr. Row *or* Mrs. Johnson
Title of Introduction: Mr. Row, the American Minister *or (if necessary)* Mrs. Johnson, the American Minister to Denmark

Consul of the United States
Address: Business: Mr. John Smith
American Consul
Rue de Quelque Chose
Paris, France
Social: Mr. and Mrs. John Smith
Home Address
Salutation: Formal: Sir: *or* My dear Sir:
Informal: Dear Mr. Smith:
Closing: Formal: Sincerely yours,
Informal: Sincerely yours,
In Conversation: Mr. Smith
Title of Introduction: Mr. Smith

Ambassador of a Foreign Country
Address: Business: His Excellency
Juan Luis Ortega
The Ambassador of Mexico
Washington, D.C.
Social: His Excellency
The Ambassador of Mexico
and Señora Ortega
Home Address
Salutation: Formal: Excellency:
Informal: My dear Mr. Ambassador:
Closing: Formal: Very truly yours,
Informal: Sincerely yours, *or* Faithfully yours,
In Conversation: Mr. Ambassador *or* Excellency *or* Sir
Title of Introduction: The Ambassador of Mexico

Minister of a Foreign Country
Address: Business: The Honorable
Carluh Matti
The Minister of Kezeah
Washington, D.C.
Social: The Honorable
Carluh Matti
and Mrs. Matti
Home Address
Salutation: Formal: Sir:
Informal: My dear Mr. Minister:
Closing: Formal: Very truly yours,
Informal: Sincerely yours,
In Conversation: Mr. Minister *or* Sir
Title of Introduction: The Minister of Kezeah

Governor of a State
Address: Business: The Honorable
Joseph L. Marvin
Governor of Idaho
Boise, Idaho
Social: The Honorable
Joseph L. Marvin
and Mrs. Marvin
Home Address
Salutation: Formal: Sir:
Informal: Dear Governor Marvin:
Closing: Formal: Very truly yours,
Informal: Sincerely yours,
In Conversation: Governor Marvin *or* Sir
Title of Introduction: The Governor *or (if necessary)* The Governor of Idaho

State Senators and Representatives are addressed like U.S. Senators and Representatives, with appropriate addresses.

Mayor
Address: Business: His [or Her] Honor the Mayor
City Hall
Easton, Maryland
Social: His Honor the Mayor
and Mrs. Lake
Home Address
or (for a woman mayor)
Mr. and Mrs. L. T. Wayne
Home Address
Salutation: Formal: Sir: *or* Madam:
Informal: Dear Mayor Lake:
Closing: Formal: Very truly yours,
Informal: Sincerely yours,
In Conversation: Mr. Mayor *or* Madam Mayor
Title of Introduction: Mayor Lake

Judge
Address: Business: The Honorable
Carson Little
Justice, Appellate Division
Supreme Court of the State of New York
Albany, New York
Social: The Honorable
Carson Little
and Mrs. Little
Home Address
Salutation: Formal: Sir:
Informal: Dear Judge Little:
Closing: Formal: Very truly yours,
Informal: Sincerely yours,
In Conversation: Mr. Justice
Title of Introduction: The Honorable Carson Little, Judge of the Appellate Division of the Supreme Court

Protestant Bishop
Address: Business: The Right Reverend John S. Bowman
Bishop of Rhode Island
Providence, Rhode Island
Social: The Right Reverend John S. Bowman
and Mrs. Bowman

Salutation: Formal: Right Reverend Sir:
Informal: My dear Bishop Bowman:
Closing: Formal: Respectfully yours,
Informal: Faithfully yours, *or* Sincerely yours,
In Conversation: Bishop Bowman
Title of Introduction: Bishop Bowman

Protestant Clergyman
Address: Business: The Reverend David Dekker
Address of his church
or (*if he holds the degree*)
The Reverend David Dekker, D.D.
Address of his church
Social: The Reverend David Dekker and Mrs. Dekker
Home Address
Salutation: Formal: Sir: *or* My dear Sir:
Informal: Dear Mr. [*or* Dr.] Dekker:
Closing: Formal: Sincerely yours, *or* Faithfully yours,
Informal: Sincerely yours, *or* Faithfully yours,
In Conversation: Mr. [*or* Dr.] Dekker
Title of Introduction: Mr. [*or* Dr.] Dekker

Rabbi
Address: Business: Rabbi Paul Aaron Fine
Address of his synagogue
or (*if he holds the degree*)
Dr. Paul Aaron Fine, D.D.
Address of his synagogue
Social: Rabbi [*or* Dr.] and Mrs. Paul Aaron Fine
Home Address
Salutation: Formal: Dear Sir:
Informal: Dear Rabbi [*or* Dr.] Fine:
Closing: Formal: Sincerely yours,
Informal: Sincerely yours,
In Conversation: Rabbi [*or* Doctor] Fine
Title of Introduction: Rabbi [*or* Doctor] Fine

The Pope
Address: His Holiness Pope Paul VI
or His Holiness the Pope
Vatican City
Salutation: Your Holiness:
Closing: Your Holiness' most humble servant,
In Conversation: Your Holiness

Cardinal
Address: His Eminence Alberto Cardinal Vezzetti
Archbishop of Baltimore
Baltimore, Maryland
Salutation: Your Eminence:
Closing: I have the honor to remain,
Your Eminence's humble servant,
In Conversation: Your Eminence
Title of Introduction: *One is presented to:* His Eminence, Cardinal Vezzetti

Roman Catholic Archbishop
Address: The Most Reverend Preston Lowen
Salutation: Formal: Your Excellency: *or* Most Reverend Sir:
Informal: Most Reverend and dear Sir:
Closing: I have the honor to remain,
Your Excellency's humble servant,
In Conversation: Your Excellency
Title of Introduction: *One is presented to:* The Most Reverend The Archbishop of San Francisco

Roman Catholic Bishop
Address: The Most Reverend Matthew S. Borden
Address of his church
Salutation: Formal: Most Reverend Sir:
Informal: My dear Bishop Borden:
Closing: Formal: I have the honor to remain,
Your obedient servant,
Informal: Faithfully yours,
In Conversation: Your Excellency
Title of Introduction: Bishop Borden

Monsignor
Address: The Right Reverend Monsignor Ryan
Address of his church
Salutation: Formal: Right Reverend and dear Monsignor Ryan:
Informal: Reverend and dear Monsignor Ryan:
Closing: Respectfully yours,
In Conversation: Monsignor Ryan
Title of Introduction: Monsignor Ryan

Priest
Address: The Reverend John Matthews [and the initials of his order]
Address of his church
Salutation: Formal: Reverend Father:
Informal: Dear Father Matthews:
Closing: Formal: I remain, Reverend Father, yours faithfully,
Informal: Faithfully yours,
In Conversation: Father *or* Father Matthews *or* Your Reverence
Title of Introduction: The Reverend Father Matthews

Member of Religious Order
Address: Sister Angelica [and initials of order] *or*
Brother James [and initials]
Address
Salutation: Formal: My dear Sister: *or* My dear Brother
Informal: Dear Sister Angelica: *or* Dear Brother James
Closing: Formal: Respectfully yours,
Informal: Faithfully yours,
In Conversation: Sister Angelica *or* Brother James
Title of Introduction: Sister Angelica [*or* Brother James], may I present Mrs. Jones

University Professor
Address: Business: Professor Robert Knowles
Office Address
or (*if he holds the degree*)
Dr. Robert Knowles *or*
Mr. Robert Knowles
Office Address
Social: Professor [*or* Dr. *or* Mr.] and Mrs. Robert Knowles
Home Address
Salutation: Formal: Dear Sir:
Informal: Dear Professor [*or* Dr. *or* Mr.] Knowles:
Closing: Formal: Very truly yours,
Informal: Sincerely yours,
In Conversation: Professor [*or* Doctor] Knowles (*within the college*); Mr. Knowles (*elsewhere*)
Title of Introduction: Professor [*or* Doctor] Knowles

Physician
Address: Business: William L. Barnes, M.D.
Office Address
Social: Doctor and Mrs. William L. Barnes
Home Address
Salutation: Formal: Dear Sir:
Informal: Dear Doctor Barnes:
Closing: Formal: Very truly yours,
Informal: Sincerely yours,
In Conversation: Doctor Barnes
Title of Introduction: Doctor Barnes

CANADA

Prime Minister
Address: Business: The Right Hon. John Smith, P.C., M.P.,
Prime Minister of Canada
Parliament Building
Ottawa, Ontario
Social: The Hon. John Smith and Mrs. Smith
Home Address
Salutation: Formal: Sir: *or* Dear Sir:
Informal: Dear Mr. Prime Minister: *or*
Dear Mr. Smith:
Closing: Formal: I am, Sir,
Yours very truly,
Informal: With kind regards,
Yours very sincerely,
In Conversation: Sir *or* Mr. Smith *or* Mr. Prime Minister

Governor General—The Commonwealth
Address: Business: His Excellency
John Smith (or his personal title)
Government House
Ottawa, Ontario

Social: Their Excellencies
The Governor General and Mrs. John Smith
Home Address
Salutation: Formal: Sir:
Informal: My dear Mr. Smith:
Closing: Formal: I have the Honour to be, Sir,
Your Excellency's obedient servant,
Informal: With kind regards,
Yours very sincerely,
In Conversation: Your Excellency

Cabinet Officer
Address: Business: The Hon. John Smith, P.C., M.P.,
Minister of Forestry
Ottawa, Ontario
Social: The Hon. John Smith and Mrs. Smith
Home Address
or (for a woman cabinet member)
Mr. and Mrs. John Smith
Salutation: Formal: Sir: *or* Dear Sir: *or* Madam *or* Dear Madam:
Informal: Dear Mr. Smith: *or* Dear Mrs. Smith
Closing: Formal: I am, Sir *or* Madam,
Informal: Yours very sincerely,
In Conversation: Sir *or* Madam, formal; Mr. *or* Mrs. Smith *or* Mr. Minister; informal.

Former Prime Minister
Address: The Honourable (or Right Honourable)
John Smith
Home Address (or Office Address)

Judges
Judges of the following federal and provincial courts have the title The Honourable, and are addressed as Mr. Justice:
Supreme Court of Canada, Exchequer Court of Canada, Courts of appeal of the provinces of British Columbia, Manitoba, and Saskatchewan, Court of Chancery of the province of Prince Edward Island, Courts of Queen's Bench of the provinces of Manitoba, Quebec, and Saskatchewan, Superior Court of the province of Quebec, Supreme courts of the provinces of Alberta, British Columbia, New Brunswick, Nova Scotia, Ontario, Prince Edward Island, and Newfoundland; and the territorial courts.
Address: Business: The Hon. Mr. Justice John Smith
Social: The Hon. Mr. Justice John Smith and Mrs. Smith
Salutation: Formal: Sir:
Informal: Dear Mr. Justice Smith:
Closing: Formal: I am, Sir,
Yours sincerely,
Informal: Believe me,
Dear Mr. Justice Smith,
Yours very sincerely,
In Conversation: Sir (formal); Mr. Justice Smith (informal).

Mayor
Address: His Worship
The Mayor of St. Lazare
Salutation: Formal: Dear Sir:
Informal: Dear Mr. Mayor:
Closing: Formal: Yours sincerely,
Informal: Believe me, Dear Mr. Mayor,
Yours very sincerely,
In Conversation: Sir (formal); Mr. Mayor (informal).

Member of Parliament
Address: John Smith, Esq. M.P.
House of Commons
Ottawa, Ontario
Salutation: Formal: Dear Sir:
Informal: Dear Mr. Smith
Closing: Formal: Yours sincerely,
Informal: Believe me,
Yours very sincerely,

MANUSCRIPT PREPARATION

A writer must bear in mind that strangers will be evaluating his manuscript. It is unreasonable to assume that editors will take time out from a busy schedule to unscramble a poorly constructed manuscript when the author himself did not care sufficiently to make it presentable. A carbon copy smudged from handling and chewed around the edges is not likely to encourage an editor to read very far into it. By exerting a little effort to learn the fundamental conventions of style required by publishers and printers, a writer may save himself much time and effort later.

Before a final copy is typed, the typewriter keys should be thoroughly cleaned. A black, almost new ribbon is preferable, because the ink is too dense on a brand new ribbon. Good quality carbon paper will help to get the clearest possible impression. It is also common sense to submit the original copy to the publisher, and a carbon copy if possible. One carbon should always be retained by the author to protect against loss in transit. Radical innovations in style should be avoided, except where absolutely necessary to achieve a particular effect. More often than not, these innovations confuse the reader and distract him from the meaning of the text.

Paper Paper should be of a standard size, preferably 8½ x 11 inches, and of a good opacity, sixteen- or twenty-pound weight. Onionskin is too flimsy to serve as a printer's copy, and publishers are often put to the additional expense of retyping a manuscript for the printer.

Margins Liberal margins on both sides of the sheet are essential. The copy editor needs this space to make corrections to query the author, and to give instructions to the printer. A six-inch line (seventy-two elite spaces, or sixty pica spaces) centered on the page will insure sufficient margins. The lines should be made as even as possible, without sacrificing the rules governing word division. This will help the editor to estimate the length of the manuscript in its printed form.

Spacing Text, bibliography, and table of contents should be double-spaced. Long footnotes also require double-spacing. Shorter footnotes may be single-spaced with a double space separating them. Single-spacing is also permitted for long excerpts, thereby setting them apart from the rest of the text. The number of lines on a page should be uniform, generally twenty-five for a standard eleven-inch sheet. Some brands of carbon paper include a guide sheet which, when set in the platen behind the paper, helps to achieve the desired uniformity.

Indentation All paragraphs start seven spaces from the left-hand margin. This is true for quoted matter and footnotes. For long quotations, single-spaced, the opening line is indented the same seven spaces, but then a new margin is set four spaces from the left-hand side, and is maintained until the excerpt is concluded.

PROOFREADERS' MARKS

Mark	Meaning	Mark	Meaning
stet	Let it stand	ld>	Insert lead between lines
∧	Insert marginal addition	℈	Delete and close up
∧,	Insert comma	↻	Reverse
∨'	Insert apostrophe	⁀	Close up
∨"	Insert quotes	¶	Paragraph
;|	Insert semicolon	no ¶	Run in same paragraph
(:)	Insert colon and en quad	□	Indent one em
⊙	Insert period and en quad	=|	Hyphen
?|	Insert interrogation point	em|	Em dash
(?)	Query to author	en|	En dash
×	Broken letter	⌒	Use ligature
═	Straighten line	(sp)	Spell out
‖	Align type	tr	Transpose
⊥	Push down space	wf	Wrong font
[	Move to left	bf	Set in boldface type
]	Move to right	rom	Set in roman type
⊔	Lower	ital	Set in italic type
⊓	Elevate	lc	Set in lower case
V∧	Even space	/	Lower-case letter
#	Insert space	caps	Set in CAPITALS
hr #	Hair space between letters	sc	Set in SMALL CAPITALS

Example of Marked Proof

To every think there is a saeson, and a
time to every purpose un der the heaven,
2 a time to be born, and a tie to die;
a time to plant, and a time to Pluck up
that whichisplanted; 3 a time to kill,
and a time to heal a time to brake down
and a time to build up;
4 A time to weeep and a time to laugh;
a time to mourn, and a time to dance;
5 A timeto cast away stones, and a
time to gater stones together; a time to
emdrace and a time to refrain from embracing;
6 A time to get, and a time to lose;
a time to keep,
And a time to cast aweigh;
7 A time to rend, and a time to slew;
a time to kep silence and a time to speak
8 A time to love, and a time to hate; a
time of war, and a time of peace.

VOCABULARY AND SPELLING IMPROVEMENT

by Albert H. Marckwardt

IMPROVING YOUR VOCABULARY

Why Study Words?

The author of a recent book on the English language asks the question and then proceeds to answer it as follows: "The fact is that, if we are going to be able to talk about anything very far beyond our day-to-day, bread and butter living, if we are going to associate in an easy manner with cultivated people, if we are going to read books which such people have found to be important and significant, then we must have at our command a great many words that the man in the street and the man with the hoe neither know nor use."[1]

This is a direct and convincing answer to the question, but it is by no means the only reason for improving your vocabulary. The needs of society must be considered as well as those of the individual. If it were not for language, human society could not function; language makes it possible for human beings to cooperate and to create a social order. This is true even of the very simple, the most primitive societies. Throughout the entire twentieth century our societies have been growing more and more complex; the problems which they face both internally and externally are vastly more complicated and difficult than they were in the days of our grandparents. This places a greater burden upon the language, and thus places a greater responsibility upon every one of us to use the language as effectively as he can. Accordingly, vocabulary improvement becomes a responsibility of the man in the street as well as the man in the library.

There is, moreover, a large element of personal satisfaction in being able to use words effectively. The fluent speaker and the exact writer are widely admired for being able to express their thoughts and feelings in a manner that is both precise and direct. Precision and fluency are the qualities for which we must strive in our command of words, tempered always by a sense of what is suitable for the audience to whom our language is directed. Almost everyone of us has a dual task: to learn more words than we now know, and to use both those which we now know and the new ones that we learn as exactly as we can.

The English Lexicon

Let us set out immediately to add a new word to the total stock of many who will read this passage. *Lexicon* is often used as a term for the totality of words in a language. The few who know Greek will recognize its origin in *lexis*, the Greek for "word" or "speech." The many who know English may have encountered the words *lexical* or *lexicography.* At any rate here *lexicon* gives us a convenient alternate for *vocabulary*, although the two words do not have exactly the same range of meaning.

The point to be made, however, is that the English lexicon poses certain peculiar problems for anyone who is trying to improve his mastery of it. For one thing, it consists of two classes of words, learned and popular. As one writer has described the situation, "First, there are those words with which we become acquainted in ordinary conversation—which we learn . . . from the members of our own families and from our familiar associates, and which we should know and use even if we could not read or write. They concern the common things of life and are the stock in trade of all who speak the language. Such words may be called 'popular,' since they belong to the people at large and are not the exclusive possession of a limited class."

The author then goes on so say, "On the other hand, our language includes a multitude of words which are comparatively seldom used in ordinary conversation. Their meanings are known to every educated person, but there is little occasion to employ them at home or in the market-place. Our first acquaintance with them comes not from our mother's lips or from the talk of our schoolmates, but from the books that we read, lectures that we hear, or the more formal conversation of highly educated speakers, who are discussing some particular topic in a style appropriately elevated above the habitual level of everyday life. Such words we call 'learned' and the distinction between them and 'popular' words is of great importance to a right understanding of linguistic process."[2] He then goes on to cite the words *lively* and *vivacious* as examples of the popular and learned classes respectively.

Not all of us would necessarily agree with the author that the learned words are known to every educated person, but there can be little question over the existence in English of two sectors of the vocabulary. It is also true that these two sectors are farther apart from each other in English than in most other languages. Consequently, a manner of speaking or writing that uses learned words to the exclusion of the popular is often felt as artificial or pretentious. There is little point in saying, "There was general rejoicing over the cessation of hostilities," when we might as well say, "People were glad that the war was over." At the same time, we must recognize that the chemist who wrote, "Neuraminic acid in the form of its alkali-stable methoxy derivative was first isolated by Klenk from gangliosides and more recently from bovine sub-maxillary gland mucin," could not have expressed his ideas in the popular vocabulary.

The popular vocabulary consists of short words, native words, words which often have many meanings. The learned vocabulary for the most part contains long words, words of foreign origin, often though not always somewhat more precise in their meanings. The problem for each of us is to acquire the learned words which are necessary and useful to us in our reading, in the exercise of our professions, and in carrying on the affairs of our society, but to use them with discretion, with a feeling for our audience.

The Individual Vocabulary

Because of the very existence of the two sectors of our lexicon, the English language has a very large stock of words. The larger dictionaries generally record about 450,000, almost half a million words, and there are others, of course, that never get into the dictionary for various reasons. Some authorities on language have expressed the opinion that perhaps our language is too richly endowed, that there are too many words that almost duplicate one another in meaning. The opposing view is that a large vocabulary makes it possible to give to words a great many shades of emotion as well as of meaning, and that individual styles may thus be developed. The net result, however, is that the average individual commands a smaller proportion of the total wordstock of English than is the case with speakers of many other languages. This also creates a problem for anyone who wants to improve his vocabulary.

We must also recognize the distinction between what is called a *passive* or *recognition* vocabulary and an *active* or *use* vocabulary. The recognition vocabulary is composed of those words which you recognize when you see or hear them. The active vocabulary consists of the words which you, yourself, employ. The recognition vocabulary is by far the larger. According to some estimates, it is about three times the size of the active vocabulary.

Enlarging Your Vocabulary

We have seen that the English language contains a large number of words, divided into two fairly well-defined layers, the learned and the popular. The total lexicon of the language is vastly greater than that of any person who speaks it. Every speaker has a passive and an active vocabulary, the

[1] Thomas Pyles, *The Origins and Development of the English Language*, Harcourt, Brace, and World, Inc., New York, 1964, p. 302.

[2] J. B. Greenough and G. L. Kittredge, *Words and Their Ways in English Speech*, Macmillan, N.Y., 1901, p. 19.

former more extensive than the latter. Anyone who wants to increase his word power must do so within this context, concentrating especially upon three phases of it:

1. He must increase the range and extent of his recognition vocabulary.
2. He must transfer words from his recognition to his active or use vocabulary.
3. He must develop the ability to form new words as he needs them, particularly by using the rich supply of prefixes and suffixes in the language.

Increasing the Passive Vocabulary

How do we come to learn new words, even when we are not consciously trying to add to our stock of them? Generally we do so through reading or hearing them and then coming to some conclusion about their meaning from the context in which they appear.

Suppose, for example, you did not know what a Cape Cod lighter was, and you heard someone say that he had just bought one and luckily it was working very well. At this point you may conjecture that it is some kind of operational device, either for the purpose of illumination or kindling a fire. The next time you encountered the word was when you heard someone say that he had bought some kerosene for his Cape Cod lighter. Since illumination by kerosene is relatively rare, you eliminate the light-giving function and conclude that it must have something to do with getting a fire started. Upon your third encounter with the word you learn from the speaker that he keeps his Cape Cod lighter near the fireplace but occasionally uses it for his outdoor grill. By this time you have formed a clear idea of its function; you do not yet have an idea about its size and shape, or how it actually works. Other contextual clues will furnish this information, if you have not already seen or acquired one by that time. But this is the way that much of our adult knowledge of words comes about and, of course, all of our pre-reading knowledge.

Vocabulary enlargement through reading comes about in much the same way. Our first contact with a new word may be in a context which is not particularly suggestive or revealing. Suppose, for example, a reader's earliest encounter with *commendatory* is in the sentence, "It was a commendatory speech about our economic administration." Unless he connects this word with *commend* or *commendation*, which he may well do, he concludes, perhaps, that it refers to some quality which a speech may possess, but he gets little more out of it than just that. But when he then comes upon the sentence, "The official sent a commendatory letter to the chief of police for the excellent manner in which he quelled the riot," he is able to deduce that the kind or quality is a favorable one.

But we do have resources beyond these very general contextual clues, and we must learn to be sensitive to them. For example, words are often paired with others of similar though not identical meaning. Suppose we come upon *utilize* in a sentence such as the following: "Certainly it should be regarded as a preeminent quality of true genius to *utilize and transform to its own purposes* the rich resources of the world in which it reaches." From this we sense that *utilize* is, if not equivalent, at least not unrelated and possibly even similar to *transform to its* own *purposes*. A similar pairing, "to improve and utilize each opportunity," will give us a further notion of the positive meaning of the word, and finally when we come upon, "They must either *nullify or utilize* the mouth of the Danube," our concept of positive effort and beneficial result is strengthened by seeing the word in opposition to a strong negative. Then, when we encounter, "Let all physical exertion be utilized," and "Her services could not be utilized for missions," our sense of the meaning of the word is fairly complete.

It is also helpful to form the habit of seeing words in relation to others which are built upon the same base forms. It has already been suggested that the connection of *commendatory* with *commend, commendation*, and even *recommend* and *recommendation* would shed some light upon its meaning. *Preeminent*, in the phrase, "a preeminent quality of true genius," also quoted above, should bring to mind both *eminent* and *eminence. Utilize*, which has just been discussed, has obvious connections with *utility* and *utilitarian*. The recognition of such groups and families is bound to increase not only the knowledge of meanings but a sensitivity to the shades of feeling which they convey.

Using the Dictionary

The obvious source of information for the meanings of words that you do not know is your dictionary. Yet there are times in the course of reading even a paragraph of moderate difficulty that you will come upon a half-dozen words that are unfamiliar to you. If you were to look up every one of them, you would not only increase the reading time of the passage by five or six minutes, but you would have broken the train of thought six times. This is clearly a nuisance and tends to make reading a chore rather than a pleasure. In the long run you will profit more by reading for enjoyment and enjoying what you read. This does not mean that you should avoid what is intellectually challenging. Tackle it. Get the most out of your dictionary by using it selectively and intelligently, only after you find that contextual clues and word relationships seem not to be helpful in giving you an idea about the meaning of a word or the way in which it is being used.

When you do turn to the dictionary for the meaning of a word, it is important that you get all it has to give. Suppose, for example, that you are confronted with the following: "Precocity flames up in a brief moment, and drawing only from within, quickly burns itself out; but genius, growing with what it feeds on, its natural powers reinforced through union with congenial elements from without, glows with increasing warmth until it reaches its full potential strength." Let us assume that you are reasonably certain about the meaning of every word in the passage except the very first, *precocity*. You know that the passage is about the poet Keats, who died as a young man. You also recognize that in this passage *precocity* is somehow being contrasted with *genius*, but this is not enough for your purpose. Stupidity and mediocrity could also be contrasted with genius. You need a dictionary explanation for *precocity* if the sentence in which it occurs is to mean much of anything.

Go to the dictionary. In this dictionary you will find that *precocity* is not given a main entry. It is one of the derivatives listed under the main entry *precocious*. There are two meanings given under the main entry. One shows the word in a favorable sense: "Unusually forward or advanced, especially mentally." The other nontechnical definition is less so: "Developing before the natural season." Going back to our passage, we recognize that in it precocity is being contrasted rather unfavorably with genius, hence it is the more neutral definition that more nearly fits the case.

At the same time, we should not overlook the etymology. From it we learn that the adjective *precocious* comes from Latin *prae*, "before," combined with *coquere*, "cook." This suggests, of course, the combination *pre-cook* in our present-day speech, and if we stop to think we might also recall that the slang phrase *half-baked* makes use of virtually the same figure of speech. All of this suggests that if a single difficult word is thus carefully studied and considered, there is a far greater likelihood that it will remain in your memory than any six words hastily looked up.

To conclude, try to recognize words in their context. You will make some mistakes, as does everyone else. Look up only those words necessary to the meaning. When you do look up a word, get everything that the dictionary treatment has to offer. Interest yourself in these words. Become word conscious in a wholesome, not in a picayunish manner. When Sir Francis Bacon wrote, more than two hundred and fifty years ago, "Reading maketh a full man," this was part of what he had in mind.

From Recognition to Use

Bacon followed his statement about reading with the assertion that "conference," that is to say speaking, produces a ready man. A ready man is one who thinks clearly and swiftly, and can express his thoughts easily. He is articulate. It has already been suggested that this comes about in part by putting words to work, transferring them from the passive to the active vocabulary. "Use a word six times and it is yours," so the saying is. The number varies, all the way from three to ten, but the advice is sound on the surface. Certainly practice is necessary to bring about vocabulary increase. The question is how one goes about it.

The best suggestion is to keep reading and speaking in close relationship with each other. Talking with others about what you read is the best way to create opportunities to put into use the words you encounter in the course of your reading. It does not matter whether your reading is in connection with your occupation, your outside interests, or if it is purely recreational. The principle is valid in any event. Certainly one must avoid the difficulty which plagued Leora, the wife of Martin Arrowsmith, in Sinclair Lewis's novel. After an afternoon spent in reading about modern painting in order to impress her husband's associates, she found herself unable to maneuver the evening's conversation in that direction.

It is here that writing comes to our aid. To a degree at least, we can, when we write, choose the subject which will allow us to use our newly acquired words. Far too often we tend to shy away from opportunities to express ourselves on paper. When we sit in a meeting, we leave it to someone else to frame a resolution or a motion. If we are asked for suggestions or to frame a plan for action, we often content ourselves by making a few scattered notations instead of a well-formed and coherent statement. It is in thinking through an idea, in phrasing it in such a way that it cannot be misunderstood or misinterpreted that we call upon our vocabulary reserves and put them to use. Muscles do not develop without exercise; the same may be said of anyone's vocabulary. The third part of Bacon's statement was that "Writing maketh an exact man."

Synonyms and Antonyms

One way of achieving both precision and variety in language is to develop an awareness of the many words in English which may be used to express a particular idea, words which have nearly the same meaning. These are called synonyms, and most dictionaries will discuss the differences in shades of meaning within a group of related words, such as *postpone, adjourn, defer, delay,* and *procrastinate.* The entry in this dictionary for this group of words runs as follows: "*Adjourn* signifies literally to put off to another day, and, hence, to any future time. A deliberative assembly may *adjourn* to another day or to another hour of the same day, and resume business where it left off, as if there had been no interval; or it may *adjourn* to a definite later date or, when no day can be fixed, to meet at the call of the president or other officer. In common usage, to *adjourn* a matter is to hold it in abeyance until it may be more conveniently or suitably attended to; in such use *defer* and *postpone* are close synonyms of *adjourn*; *defer* is simply to lay or put aside temporarily; to *postpone* is strictly to lay or put aside until after something else occurs, or is done, known, obtained or the like; but *postpone* is often used without such limitation. *Adjourn, defer,* and *postpone* all imply definite expectation of later consideration or action; *delay* is much less definite, while *procrastinate* is hopelessly vague. One who *procrastinates* gives no assurance that he will ever act."

The foregoing illustration dealt with a group of words easily interchanged but which, nevertheless, are by no means identical in meaning. The problem here is to know under what circumstances they may be substituted for one another and when such a substitution would be inappropriate. Note the following examples:

1. *amateur, connoisseur, dilettante.* Etymologically, the *amateur* is the one who loves, the *connoisseur* one who knows. The *amateur* practices to some extent that in regard to which he may not be well informed; the *connoisseur* is well informed in regard to that which he may not practice at all. *Dilettante,* which had originally the sense of *amateur,* has come to denote one who is superficial, pretentious, and affected, whether in theory or practice.

2. *forgery, counterfeiting.* Imitating or altering a coin or note which passes as currency or money is *counterfeiting*; the making of a fraudulent writing, or the material alteration of a genuine writing with intent to defraud, is *forgery*. . . .

Sometimes in speaking of writing we are at a loss for words which indicate the opposite of one we have in mind. The technical term for these is *antonym.* Again the dictionary helps us here by listing these as part of the synonymy. For example, the treatment of *despair,* quoted above, is followed by the listing *hope, expectation, confidence*—words suggesting positive or healthy attitudes. Information of this kind can also be found in a thesaurus, a kind of glossary which lists and organizes words according to the classes of ideas they express. For most people, however, the dictionary is easier to use.

Prefixes and Suffixes

Many of the words in English consist of a base form or root to which prefixes and suffixes may be added. Every speaker and writer of the language forms words in this fashion, even when he has not heard them before. Let us suppose that a particular child of ten has, in his lifetime, encountered and learned the words *gladness, hardness, softness, happiness, sadness,* and *smoothness.* Out of this experience he will have learned, though he doesn't know it, that *-ness* is added to adjectives to form abstract nouns. Consequently, when he needs to form a word meaning "the quality of being rough," he merely extends the *-ness* pattern to the adjective *rough* and comes up with *roughness.* He may never have heard or read the word before, or he may have heard it and forgotten it. The process works unconsciously and automatically. In the same way, he will be able to interpret other formations with *-ness,* new to him, when he meets them in conversation or reading. This process is called word derivation. It is most useful in expanding our individual vocabularies.

In general the common prefixes and suffixes give us very little trouble, partly because they are so universally applied. Almost any verb can take the suffix *-er* to refer to the person who performs the action or undergoes the state which the meaning of the verb suggests: *work, worker; bake, baker; sit, sitter; think, thinker.* The prefix *un-* is almost equally common in its application to adjectives which suggest a state of affairs: *unwell, unhappy, unusual, unclean.* Most native speakers have a built-in set of restrictions which prevent them from concocting such unacceptable formations as *unold, smoothen,* or *coolth.* But these prefixes and suffixes are all native; they belong to the familiar part of our vocabulary.

Because of the great number of borrowed words in English and the frequency with which they are used, some foreign prefixes and suffixes have also become part of the working mechanism of the English language. Certain of these, such as *-able* (*lovable, passable*) and *-ess* (*huntress, princess*) are common and cause no difficulty. Those from Latin and Greek, however, do give trouble and will be taken up in some detail here.

Prefixes In general, prefixes tend only to modify the meanings of the words to which they are attached; they do not change the grammatical function. It is merely necessary, therefore, to associate the Latin or Greek prefix with its meaning in English. The table of prefixes on page 1534 is designed to help you make these associations. The prefixes are listed according to the meaning in English which they convey.

Suffixes It is grammatical function rather than meaning which is affected by the addition of a suffix. The meaning of the base form *coma* is still present in the combination *comatose,* but the word has changed from noun to adjective. The same would be true of *development* (noun) from *develop* (verb) or *beautify* (verb) from *beauty* (noun). Thus, suffixes serve as a means of making the language flexible. Quite often the suffix is added not to an independent word but to a base form which does not normally stand alone: *sanctify, contrary, aviatrix.* The tables of suffixes on page 1534 will give you a start toward the analysis of words, but only a start. Developing a sense for the way in which suffixes are added and what they do to the base forms is a study worth pursuing with your dictionary. This awareness will enhance your feeling for the language.

IMPROVING YOUR SPELLING

Americans have always placed a high value upon the ability to spell correctly. The blue-backed spelling book was a fixture of the colonial schoolroom and sold literally millions of copies. The spelling bee was for a long period a favorite school and even community activity, and recently newspapers, radio, and television have developed it on a national scale. Despite all this, business men constantly complain about secretaries who are unable to spell; college professors make the same charge against their students.

The very complaints bear witness to our awareness of spelling; the actual situation is not as bad as it is often painted. Recent studies have shown that the average high-school graduate spells correctly most of the words that he uses. Most of the spelling difficulties of college students are caused by no more than 250 words out of the ten thousand or so that they are likely to use. Poor spelling is seldom something that cannot be remedied if the ailing victim is determined to improve and will go about it in a systematic way.

Why We Misspell

Some of the principal reasons for our difficulties with English spelling lie in the nature of the English language and certain aspects of its history. English has always had from twelve to sixteen distinct vowel sounds, not to mention the diphthongs or vowel combinations. At the same time, there have been only five vowel characters—or seven at most, if *w* and *y* are counted—to spell them with. This is a problem which, as we shall see, has been dealt with in several ways during the twelve hundred years we have been using the Roman alphabet, but no one of them has been carried out consistently. The reduction of vowels in unstressed syllables, as in *Cuba, custom, circus, outrageous,* where *a, o, u,* and *ou* all represent the same pronunciation, has created another problem.

In addition, many of the thousands of English words which have come into English from other languages have kept the spellings which they had in those languages, sometimes a far cry from the characteristic patterns of English spelling. Finally, it was about the year 1500 when printing replaced manuscript copying, as a result of which spelling became relatively fixed. But since that time many changes in pronunciation, not only of individual words but of entire classes of words, have occurred, and this has only served to increase the distance, already great enough, between spelling and pronunciation. Therefore we have "silent" letters such as *b* in *dumb* and *gh* in *thought,* fossilized remains of sounds which are no longer pronounced. We also have various ways of spelling the same vowel sound, as in *meat* and *meet,* where the spelling once served to indicate a distinction in pronunciation no longer present.

We have discussed these matters briefly neither to excuse or justify bad spelling nor to make the task of spelling improvement seem hopelessly difficult, but rather to explain why our rules for spelling seem to have such frequent exceptions.

Ways of Indicating Vowel Length

As a background which will help us to understand some of the spelling rules, we must first notice three devices which have been developed throughout the history of our language to differentiate certain pairs of sounds. One of the earliest of these was to double the vowel letter, with a single letter indicating a short or lax sound and the doubled character signaling a long or tense sound. We still do this in pairs like *cop, coop; rot, root; met, meet; fed, feed.* Today the practice is confined to the letters *e* and *o.*

A second way of showing vowel length was to place an unpronounced final *-e* after a syllable when the vowel in it was long, but to close the syllable with a consonant when the vowel was short. Thus we have *cap* contrasting with *cape, bed* with *bede* (the Middle English form of *bead*), *bit* with *bite, hop* with *hope, us* with *use.* Notice that the *-e* has no value in and of itself; it merely signals something about the preceding vowel letter.

Finally, a doubled consonant may be used to signal a preceding short vowel, whereas a single consonant suggests the long-vowel quality usually associated with the spelling. Thus *latter* contrasts with *later, bitter* with *biter, mopping* with *moping,* and *cutter* with *cuter.* Usually this device is employed when a syllable is joined to the one in which the length of the vowel needs to be specified.

All of these devices are centuries old. Each of them has a certain logic behind it. Unfortunately no one of them has been carried out consistently. Much of our spelling difficulty arises from not knowing which device or practice to apply. But understanding just this much about them leads one to see something of a system, a kind of consistency in the use of single or double consonants and whether the final *-e* is lost or kept.

Loss of Final -e

Final *-e* is lost before a suffix beginning with a vowel. It is kept before a suffix beginning with a consonant.

We have already seen that final *-e* was used to indicate the length of a preceding vowel, as in *hope.* When a suffix like *-ful,* beginning with a consonant is added to *hope,* we still need the *-e* to show that the *o* is long; thus our spelling is *hopeful.* On the other hand, any vowel letter can serve the purpose of suggesting the long sound; hence we can spell *hoping* without it. Note the following:

	Suffix Beginning With a Vowel	*Suffix Beginning With a Consonant*
hate	hating	hateful
love	lovable	lovely
bore	boring	boredom
like	likable	likely
achieve	achievable	achievement
use	usage	useful

There are certain exceptions to this rule which a careful speller should remember:

1. After *c* or *g,* final *e* is kept before *a* and *o* in order to maintain the soft sound of the consonant: *noticeable, traceable, vengeance, outrageous.* This is not necessary when *c* or *g* is followed by *i*: *noticing, tracing.*

2. Final *e* is dropped after *g* in such combinations as *judgment, acknowledgment, abridgment.* In England the *-e* is usually retained in the spelling of these words.

3. A few other common words do not follow this pattern: *argument, awful, duly, truly, hoeing, singeing, dyeing* ("the process of coloring"), *wholly, mileage.*

Doubling of Consonants

We have already seen that our spelling system provides for such contrasts as *hop, hope, fat, fate, sit* and *site.* But when we add suffixes beginning with a vowel, the scheme is likely to break down: we need to be able to distinguish between *hop + ing* and *hope + ing.* We do it by doubling the consonant after the short vowel:

hope	hoping	hoped
hop	hopping	hopped
plane	planing	planed
plan	planning	planned
snipe	sniping	sniped
snip	snipping	snipped

Some further observations:

1. Note that when vowel length is indicated by a doubled vowel character or a combination of vowel characters, the consonant is not doubled: *stooping, reader, sleeping, boating.*

2. Thus far, we have applied the rule about doubling of consonants only to words of one syllable, when a suffix is added. In words of more than one syllable, we must notice which syllable is stressed. Compare these pairs:

adMIT	adMITTING	adMITTED
EDit	EDiting	EDited
deFER	deFERRING	deFERRED
DIFFer	DIFFering	DIFFered

Note also the position of the stress and the spelling of the following: *réference,* but *reférring; préference,* but *preférred; regrétting, fócused, prohíbitive, overlápping, devéloped.*

Spelling the Long e Sound

There is probably no sound in the English language that is spelled in quite so many ways. There are at least six that are used quite frequently, and certain others which appear from time to time. Note: *cedar, ease, agree, receive, achieve, antique, people, key, quay, Caesar.* The two spellings which are most often confused are *ie* and *ei.* A two-line jingle makes the spelling rule easy to remember:

Spell *i* before *e*
Except after *c.*

ie: *achieve, believe, chief, grief, niece, piece, relieve*
cei: *ceiling, conceit, conceive, deceive, perceive, receive, receipt*

There are two kinds of exceptions to this rule. First, certain words pronounced with a long *e* sound behave in direct opposition to the rule:

ei: *either, leisure, neither, seize, weird*
cie: *financier, species*

Moreover, there are certain *ei* spellings which are pronounced with a sound other than long *e,* usually with long *a* or with the vowel of *care*: *weigh, neighbor, veil, reign, freight, heir, their.*

Y as a Vowel

Y sometimes represents a consonant sound (*year, yet, your, youth*), usually at the beginning of a word or syllable. *Y*, in final position and preceded by a consonant, normally represents a vowel. This creates a problem when we want to spell such combinations as *dry* + *ed* or *study* + *es*, since it would be difficult at times to tell whether the *y* was indicating a vowel or consonant value. For this reason:

1. Final *y* preceded by a consonant is usually changed to *i* before all suffixes except those beginning with *i*:

cry	cried	crying
dry	drier	drying
fly	flies flier	flying
bury	burial	burying
copy	copies copied	copying
mercy	mercies merciful	
forty	fortieth	fortyish
noisy	noisier noisily	

2. Final *y* preceded by a vowel generally retains the *y* when a suffix is added.

buy	buyer	buying
delay	delays delayed	delaying
joy	joys joyful	
play	played	playing
obey	obeys	obeying
sway	swayed	swaying
valley	valleys	

Exceptions: *daily, gaily, gaiety, laid, paid, said.*

Plural of Nouns Ending in o

1. Nouns ending in *o* preceded by a consonant usually form their plurals by adding *-es*:

echo echoes	hero heroes	potato potatoes	tornado tornadoes
embargo embargoes	Negro Negroes	tomato tomatoes	veto vetoes

2. Proper names ending in *o* add *s* only:

Eskimo Eskimos	Filipino Filipinos	Romeo Romeos

3. Many nouns clearly of foreign origin and others that are seldom used in the plural or seldom used at all add only *s*: *albino, credo, crescendo, dynamo, embryo, kimono, magneto, octavo, photo, piano, silo, solo, soprano, tyro.*

4. Nouns ending in *o* preceded by a vowel add *s* only:

carabao carabaos	radio radios	zoo zoos
cameo cameos	kangaroo kangaroos	duo duos

Vowels in Unstressed Syllables

One of the characteristic features of English is the reduction of vowels in unstressed syllables to a neutral sound which is indicated in this dictionary by the symbol ə. Yet this reduced vowel may be spelled with any one of the five vowel letters: *sofa, silent, charity, kingdom, circus.* Naturally, this causes a great deal of confusion; unstressed syllables are a frequent source of misspelling. For example, *a, e,* and *i* become indistinguishable in the endings *-ate* and *-ite, -able* and *-ible, -ance* and *-ence, -ant* and *-ent.* Associating the word in question with a closely related one will sometimes be helpful in suggesting the correct spelling. If you are uncertain about *definite*, think of *finIsh* and *definItion. SeparAtion* will suggest the *a* in *separate*, as will *ultimAtum* in *ultimate.* If you know that the verb *freQUENT* is pronounced with the vowel of *let*, this will help you with the spelling of *frequent* when the stress is on the first syllable.

Unfortunately, this device will help you with only a limited number of words; for many others no such help is available. The following are particularly likely to give some trouble:

a: accept*able*, accept*ance*, attend*ance*, brilli*ant*, perform*ance*
e: consist*ent*, excell*ence*, exist*ence*, experi*ence*, independ*ent*, persist*ent*, occurr*ence*
i: irresist*ible*, plaus*ible*, poss*ible*, suscept*ible*

Confusion of Prefixes

Some spelling difficulties arise from the confusion of prefixes which look alike, are pronounced similarly, but are so different in meaning that they cannot be attached to the same roots. The following are especially troublesome:

ante, "before": *antedate*	*anti*, "against": *antidote*
de, "from, down, away": *debate*	*di*, "twice": *diploma*
dis, "separation": *disgrace*	*dys*, "hard, ill": *dystrophy*
per, "through": *perform*	*pre*, "before": *prescribe*

Pronunciation and Spelling

Some spelling errors arise from the tendency to leave out the vowels of unstressed syllables in pronunciation, or to omit one of a combination of consonants. Reasonable care in the pronunciation of the following, and words like them, may help in creating a more accurate word image:

recoGnize	liAble
quanTity	probAbly
enviroNment	sophOmore
goverNment	boundAry
diPHthong	libRary

There is always a question as to how far to go in the cultivation of pronunciations which consciously match the spelling. For example, in the case of *February*, some dictionaries recognize pronunciations with or without the first *r*. In this instance, if a pronunciaton with the *r* will help you to remember the spelling, there can be no objection to adopting it. In the case of *Wednesday*, however, where no dictionary sanctions the pronunciation of the *d*, and it is employed only by a few overzealous radio and television announcers, there is little excuse for adopting it.

There are other instances of confusion where it is difficult to say if the faulty spelling is the cause of the mispronunciation or the other way around. All that can be done is to try to straighten out both spelling and pronunciation. Words of this kind are:

cavAlry	grIEvous
irREIevant	mischIEvous
reMUNeration	heighT

Words Similar in Spelling But Different in Meaning

Some words need attention because they sound somewhat alike but differ in spelling, meaning, and origin. Here are listed some of the most troublesome pairs and triplets:

accept except	aisle isle	altogether all together
adapt adopt	alley ally	angel angle
advice advise	already all ready	ascent assent
affect effect	altar alter	bare bear

baring
barring
bearing

born
borne
bourn

breath
breathe

canvas
canvass

capital
capitol

censor
censure

cite
site
sight

clothes
cloths

compliment
complement

consul
council
counsel

corps
corpse

costume
custom

dairy
diary

decent
descent
dissent

desert
dessert

dual
duel

formally
formerly

forth
fourth

gamble
gambol

holly
holy
wholly

hoping
hopping

instance
instants

its
it's

loath
loathe

loose
lose

metal
medal

morn
mourn

passed
past

peace
piece

personal
personnel

plain
plane

planed
planned

precede
proceed
procedure

precedence
precedents

presence
presents

principal
principle

quiet
quite

rain
reign
rein

right
rite
write

serf
surf

shone
shown

sole
soul

staid
stayed

stake
steak

stationary
stationery

steal
steel

than
then

there
their
they're

to
too
two

villain
villein

wander
wonder

weak
week

weather
whether

who's
whose

your
you're

Dual Spellings

Some words have at least two acceptable spellings. In some cases there is a difference between American and British practice. With certain other words, both spellings are current in the United States. If you have already mastered one correct spelling, there is generally little point in taking the trouble to learn another. Nevertheless, it is better if you spell consistently all of the words in the same class or group: if you spell *labor* and not *labour*, then spell *humor* and not *humour*. Your dictionary will list variant spellings and often will indicate where the variants are used. The list below will give some idea of the nature and extent of the problem.

adviser
advisor

center
centre

enclose
inclose

endorse
indorse

program
programme

gipsy
gypsy

odor
odour

pretence
pretense

reflection
reflexion

enrolment
enrollment

smolder
smoulder

caliber
calibre

enquire
inquire

analog
analogue

catalog
catalogue

fledgeling
fledgling

manoeuvre
maneuver

naturalise
naturalize

gray
grey

mediaeval
medieval

theater
theatre

orthopaedic
orthopedic

practice
practise

encase
incase

Words Often Misspelled

Even though spelling seems to present a whole series of problems, studies of the words most frequently misspelled have shown that these constitute a relatively small group. The list which follows includes most of them, except for those which have been discussed previously. You will find the list useful for drills and practice. Study it carefully.

absence
abundance
acceptable
accessible
accidentally
acclaim
accommodate
accompanied
accomplish
accustom
achievement
acknowledgment
acquaintance
acquire
acquitted
across
actually
address
adequate
adolescence
aggressive
allotted
all right
analyze
anxiety
apology
apparatus
apparent
appearance
appreciate
approach
argument
arrangement
arouse
article
athletic
attended
audience
authority
balance
ballot
bargain
basically
basis
beginning
behavior
belief
beneficial
brilliance

Britain
bulletin
calendar
capitalism
career
careless
carrying
category
ceiling
cemetery
challenge
changeable
character
choose
comfortable
coming
committed
comparative
competition
completely
conceive
concentrate
condemn
conscience
conscious
consensus
considerably
consistency
continuously
controlling
controversial
convenience
cooly
counsel
courageous
courteous
criticism
curiosity
curriculum
deceive
decision
definite
despair
dependent
description
desirability
develop
difference
dilemma

disappear
disappoint
disastrous
disciple
discriminate
dissatisfied
dominant
efficient
embarrass
eminent
emphasize
entertain
entirely
entrance
environment
equipped
erroneous
escape
exaggerate
excellent
exercise
exhilarate
existence
expense
experience
explanation
extremely
fallacy
familiar
fascinate
finally
fictitious
foreign
friend
fulfill
fundamental
further
government
grammar
group
guarantee
handled
happened
happiness
height
heroine
hindrance
humorous
hundred

hungrily
hypocrisy
idea
ignorant
imagine
immediate
incidentally
independence
indispensable
inevitable
influential
ingenious
initiative
inseparable
intelligent
interest
interpretation
interrupt
involve
irrelevant
jealousy
knowledge
laboratory
laid
leisure
license
likelihood
loneliness
losing
magazine
magnificence
maintenance
marriage
mathematics
medieval

merely
mileage
miniature
mortgage
mysterious
narrative
naturally
necessity
ninety
noticeable
occasion
occurrence
operate
opinion
opportunity
oppose
optimist
origin
paid
pamphlets
parallel
paralyze
particular
performance
permanent
phenomenon
philosophy
physical
plausible
pleasant
politician
possess
possible
practical
practice

preferred
prejudice
prepare
prevalent
privilege
probably
professor
prominent
propaganda
prophecy
prove
psychology
pursue
quantity
readily
really
realistically
receive
recommend
referring
relieve
religion
repetition
response
rhythm
ridiculous
sacrifice
safety
satire
satisfied
scarcity
scene
schedule
seize
senses

sergeant
separate
shining
significance
similar
speech
sponsor
strictly
studying
substantial
subsistence
subtle
success
sufficient

summary
suppose
suppress
surprising
surround
susceptible
technique
temperament
theory
thorough
together
tragedy
transferred
tremendous

tyranny
unanimous
undoubtedly
unnecessary
unusual
useful
vacuum
valuable
variety
vengeance
warrant
weather
weird
yield

Use Your Dictionary

The dictionary is your best help. Irregular spellings of noun plurals, verb participles, and past tenses, all of which can cause trouble, are usually given in connection with the treatment of the individual word. If you are in doubt about such a spelling, look it up.

We have already seen that it is helpful to know the parts which go to make up related words. The dictionary helps you to learn these by listing all the derived forms that a word may have. Sometimes the origin of a word, its etymology, will give you useful information. Finding a Latin form such as *cura* in the etymology of *cure* will help you to understand why the English derivative is *curable* and not *curible.*

The dictionary performs another useful service in indicating whether compound words are written solid, with a hyphen, or as two words. The spelling of compounds in English is inconsistent. There are no simple rules, and no one can be expected to remember the spelling of every word combination he is likely to use. Form the habit of checking the spelling of every compound that you use in your writing.

Most experienced writers use the dictionary to check the spelling of foreign terms and of particularly difficult words. Form the dictionary habit. Looking up words when you are writing does take a little time but amply repays your efforts in the correctness it helps you to attain.

REGIONAL VARIATIONS IN AMERICAN PRONUNCIATION

by Charles K. Thomas

STANDARD SPEECH in England and France is relatively easy to determine. It is the speech used by educated persons in the political, commercial, and cultural capitals: London in England, Paris in France. Speakers in other parts of England and France who do not wish to be considered provincial adopt the speech which commands respect in the capital. The prestige of the capital sets up such strong pressures that only the ignorant and the strong-minded fail to conform.

In the United States, on the other hand, no single city combines the various sources of prestige that have developed in Paris and London. On the contrary, Boston, New York, Philadelphia, Pittsburgh, Richmond, New Orleans, Chicago, St. Louis, Salt Lake City, Seattle, and San Francisco have different traditions, including differences in speech based on the gradual settlement of the Atlantic seaboard in the seventeenth and eighteenth centuries and on the westward movements of population. Each of these cities is the center of an important regional complex. Each carries its own prestige. Nor is the story yet complete, as the growth of Los Angeles, Phoenix, and Miami attests, and as technical developments have facilitated distant communication and internal migration.

Variability must not, of course, be overemphasized. Most English words, including the unfamiliar and the technical terms for which the reader is most likely to consult a dictionary, have uniform American pronunciations, which the reader can ignore only at his own risk. But neither the reader nor the lexicographer can ignore the variations which spring from diverse backgrounds. The lexicographer must not prescribe; he must describe the regionally acceptable patterns.

At present we can recognize three main speech areas, with numerous subdivisions: the Northern, the Midland, and the Southern, each with differences in tradition and development. Because such references to points of the compass as northern, southern, eastern, and western may refer either to specific speech areas or mere geographical locations, they have been capitalized when used in this article as references to speech areas and left without capitals when used merely for geographical reference. Thus Western Pennsylvania refers to a speech area; northeastern New Jersey is purely a geographical reference.

On the Atlantic seaboard, the northernmost area is Eastern New England, with Boston as its focus. West of Eastern New England is the North Central area, which originated in the Housatonic valley of western New England and which has spread out to include the Champlain and Great Lakes basins and the northern plains as far west as the central Dakotas. Despite the size of this area, with Hartford, Syracuse, Cleveland, Detroit, Chicago, and Minneapolis serving as important regional foci, its speech is remarkably uniform. Eastern New England and the North Central area together represent the Northern type, though the speech of the Southwest Coastal area, comprising much of California, Arizona, and Nevada, is very similar.

Though geographically adjacent to both the Eastern New England and North Central areas, the New York City area does not speak the Northern type; it contains both Midland and Southern elements. Though small in extent — southern New York and parts of southwestern Connecticut and northeastern New Jersey — it is important because of its large population and the prestige of New York City. The Middle Atlantic area, extending from New Jersey to Maryland, and westward to the Pennsylvania mountains, is the easternmost of the Midland areas, with Philadelphia as its most important focus. West of the mountains the Midland areas fan out and the regional boundaries become less distinct. Western Pennsylvania, the Southern Mountain area, the Central Midland area, and the Northwest (see map) have similarities, but also

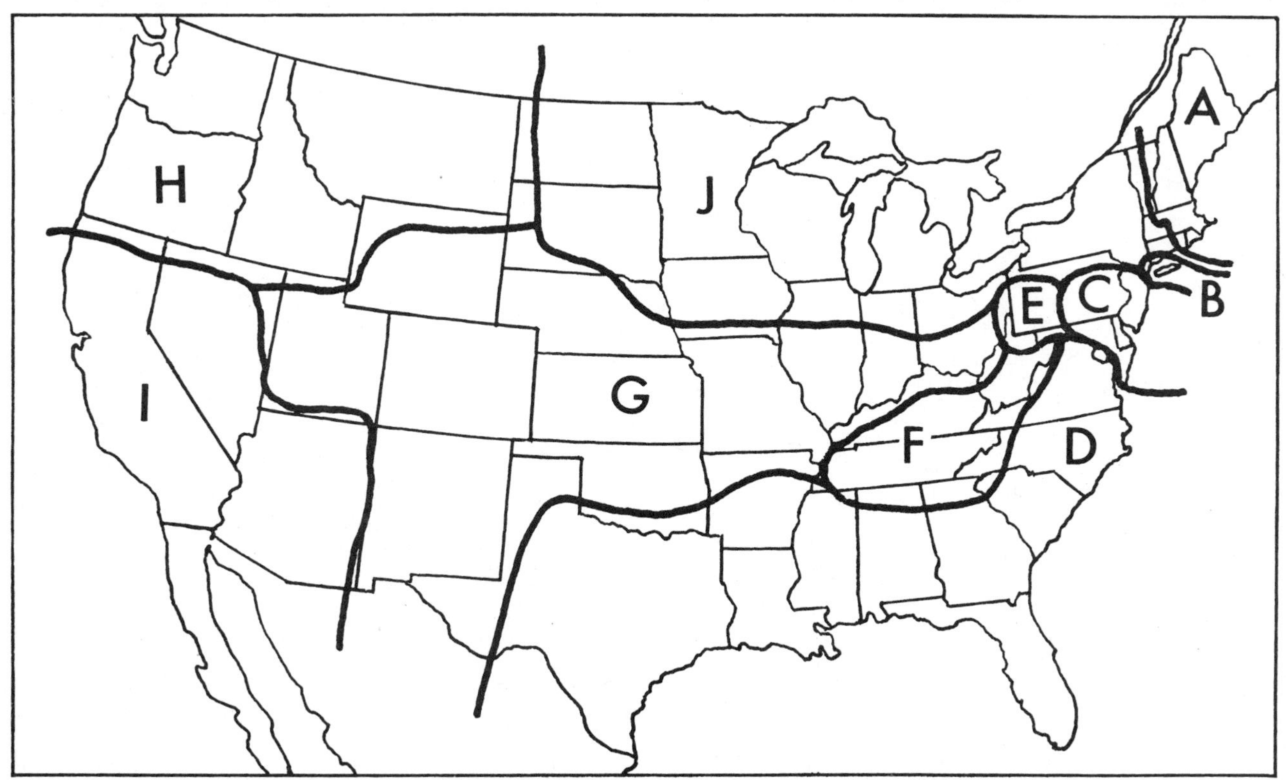

MAJOR REGIONAL SPEECH AREAS
A Eastern New England. *B* New York City. *C* Middle Atlantic. *D* Southern. *E* Western Pennsylvania. *F* Southern Mountain. *G* Central Midland. *H* Northwest. *I* Southwest. *J* North Central.

subtle differences (see table of illustrative words). Pittsburgh, St. Louis, Salt Lake City, and Seattle serve as regional foci.

The Southern area is a complex of types extending from Virginia to Georgia and westward through the Gulf states, with fringe areas in parts of Maryland, Florida, and Texas. Its diversity is represented in the speech of such regional foci as Richmond, Charleston, Montgomery, New Orleans, and Houston. Though highly varied, the speech of the South has elements of vocabulary, pronunciation, and sentence melody that unify it and mark it off from the other regions.

Before considering the pronunciations of these main areas, the reader should consult the list of symbols of the International Phonetic Alphabet in the Table of English Spellings on p. xix. In their various combinations, these symbols can be used to represent all the pronunciations with which we shall have to deal. To avoid ambiguity in this article, phonetic symbols are enclosed in square brackets; references to words and spellings are italicized; thus, there is an *h*, but no [h], in *hour*. To indicate added vowel length without change of vowel quality we add a colon to the vowel symbol; thus, *calm* [kɑ:m] has a longer vowel than *comma* [kɑmə].

Omission of the various sounds [r, ɝ, ə] represented by *r*, whenever these sounds would otherwise precede a consonant or a pause, is a feature of Eastern New England, New York City, and the South. In all three areas, however, *r* is gradually reasserting itself, and more and more of the population is gradually falling in line with the other large areas. Radio, television, and motion-picture practices encourage this trend.

Vowels associated with *r* frequently indicate regional variations. In Eastern New England the traditional vowel of such words as *far, farm, hard* and *heart* is [a:], a lengthened vowel intermediate in sound between the [æ] of *hat* and the [ɑ] of *father*. Characteristically these words are pronounced: *far* [fa:], *farm* [fa:m], *hard* [ha:d], and *heart* [ha:t]; words like *calm* [ka:m] and *father* [faðə] follow the same pattern. In all such words, [ɑ:] occurs occasionally; [æ:] occurs sporadically along the northeast coast of Maine. In the North Central area [a] also occurs frequently; here *heart* may be [hart] or [hɑrt]; *far*, [far] or [fɑr]; *calm*, [ka:m] or [kɑ:m]; and even *hot*, [hat] or [hɑt]. The use of [a] is one of the most important criteria of the Northern type.

Elsewhere such words have either [ɑ] or [ɒ], the latter a sound intermediate between the [ɑ] of *farm* and the [ɔ] of *form*. In the New York City area *heart* may be [hɑ:t], [hɒ:t], [hɑrt], or [hɒrt]; in the Middle Atlantic area, [hɑrt] or [hɒrt]. In the South, pronunciations with [ɒ:] become more frequent in all such words.

In such words as *coral, foreign, forest, horrid, moral, orange, quarrel, quarry, torrent,* and *warrant,* the predominant vowel of the stressed syllable in Eastern New England, New York City, the Middle Atlantic area, and the South is [ɑ]; elsewhere it is [ɔ]. A line extending southward through western New England, westward across the lower Hudson valley, and southwestward from the Pennsylvania mountains to Texas marks the boundary line; *forest* has [ɑ] predominantly east of the line, [ɔ] predominantly west of the line and in the country as a whole.

To the east of the same Vermont–Texas line such words as *barren, carriage, carrot, carry, marry, narrow,* and *parrot* usually have [æ]; west of the line [ɛ] is frequent. East of the line *marry* [mæri] and *merry* [mɛri] are usually audibly distinct; west of the line they may both be [mɛri].

REGIONAL PRONUNCIATIONS

The form listed first is the most frequent in the area indicated.

WORD	EASTERN NEW ENGLAND	NORTH CENTRAL	NEW YORK CITY	MIDDLE ATLANTIC	WESTERN PENNSYLVANIA
barn	[ba:n] [bɑ:n]	[bɑrn] [barn]	[bɑrn] [bɑ:n]	[bɑrn] [bɒrn]	[bɑrn] [bɒrn]
orange	[ɑrɪndʒ]	[ɔrɪndʒ]	[ɑrɪndʒ]	[ɑrɪndʒ]	[ɔrɪndʒ]
cot	[kɑt] [kɒt]	[kɑt] [kat]	[kɑt]	[kɑt]	[kɒt]
caught	[kɔt] [kɒt]	[kɔt]	[kɔt]	[kɔt]	[kɒt]
barren	[bærən]	[bɛrən] [bærən]	[bærən]	[bærən]	[bærən]
various	[vɛriəs]	[vɛriəs]	[vɛriəs] [væriəs]	[vɛriəs] [væriəs]	[vɛriəs]
ask	[æsk] [ask] [ɑsk]	[æsk]	[æsk]	[æsk]	[æsk]
greasy	[grisi]	[grisi]	[grisi]	[grisi] [grizi]	[grisi] [grizi]
hurry	[hʌri]	[hɜri]	[hʌri]	[hʌri]	[hʌri]
due	[du] [dju]	[du]	[du]	[du]	[du]
horse	[hɔ:s] [hɒ:s]	[hɔrs]	[hɔ:s] [hɔrs]	[hɔrs]	[hɔrs]
hoarse	[hoəs] [hɔ:s]	[hɔrs]	[hɔ:s] [hɔrs]	[hɔrs] [hors]	[hɔrs] [hors]
log	[lɑg]	[lɔg]	[lɑg]	[lɔg] [lɑg]	[lɔg]

WORD	SOUTHERN MOUNTAIN	SOUTHERN	CENTRAL MIDLAND	NORTH-WEST	SOUTH-WEST
barn	[bɑrn]	[bɑ:n] [bɒ:n]	[bɑrn] [bɒrn]	[bɑrn] [bɒrn]	[bɑrn]
orange	[ɔrɪndʒ]	[ɑrɪndʒ]	[ɔrɪndʒ]	[ɔrɪndʒ]	[ɔrɪndʒ]
cot	[kɑt]	[kɑt]	[kɑt] [kɒt]	[kɑt] [kɒt]	[kɑt]
caught	[kɔt]	[kɔt]	[kɔt] [kɒt]	[kɔt] [kɒt]	[kɔt]
barren	[bærən] [bɛrən]	[bærən]	[bɛrən]	[bɛrən]	[bɛrən] [bærən]
various	[vɛriəs] [veriəs]	[veriəs] [vɛriəs]	[vɛriəs]	[vɛriəs] [veriəs]	[vɛriəs]
ask	[æsk]	[æsk]	[æsk]	[æsk]	[æsk]
greasy	[grizi] [grizɪ]	[grizɪ] [grizi]	[grisi] [grizi]	[grisi] [grizi]	[grisi]
hurry	[hʌri] [hʌrɪ]	[hʌrɪ] [hʌri]	[hɜri]	[hɜri]	[hɜri]
due	[du] [dju]	[dju] [du]	[du]	[du]	[du]
horse	[hɔrs]	[hɔ:s] [hɔrs]	[hɔrs]	[hɔrs]	[hɔrs]
hoarse	[hors] [hɔrs]	[hoəs]	[hors] [hɔrs]	[hɔrs] [hors]	[hɔrs]
log	[lɔg]	[lɔg]	[lɔg]	[lɔg] [lɒg]	[lɔg]

Words like *area, dairy, fairy, Mary,* and *various* introduce an additional complication. In the South they frequently have [e]; in the Middle Atlantic and New York City areas, sometimes [æ]; in the rest of the country usually, and in all parts of the country occasionally, they have [ɛ] or a slightly lengthened [ɛ:]. Thus in the South, *Mary* [meri], *merry* [mɛri], and *marry* [mæri] may all three be audibly distinct. In the Middle Atlantic and New York City areas, *Mary* and *marry* may both be [mæri], but *merry* [mɛri] remains distinct. In Eastern New England, *Mary* and *merry* may both be [mɛri], but *marry* [mæri] is usually distinct. West of the Vermont–Texas line all three are frequently, if not always, [mɛri].

The traditional distinction between such pairs as *horse* [hɔrs] and *hoarse* [hors] survives in some areas, not in others. In the New York City area the distinction has been lost, and either word may occur as [hɔrs], [hɔəs], or [hɔ:s]. In the North Central and Southwest coastal areas both words usually occur as [hɔrs]. In the Midland areas most speakers maintain the distinction between [ɔr] and [or]; a few do not. In the South the usual pronunciations are *horse* [hɔ:s] and *hoarse* [hoəs], and much the same distinction holds in Eastern New England. Wherever the distinction survives it also survives in other pairs like *for* and *four, border* and *boarder,* and *morning* and *mourning*; and [o] survives in words like *more* and *glory.*

The most important variation not associated with a following *r* is the vowel of such words as *ask, dance, path, aunt,* and *rather.* Traditionally Eastern New England and eastern Virginia use either [a] or [ɑ] in such words, other varieties of American English use [æ], and London English uses [ɑ]. This use of [a] and [ɑ], however, seems to be rapidly declining, in both New England and Virginia, except for the two words *aunt* and *rather,* for which [a] and [ɑ] occur frequently in both areas, and occasionally in all parts of the country. Those New Englanders and Virginians who use [a] in the traditional pattern make a sharp contrast with the [æ] of *bad, land,* and *fancy.* Some speakers in other areas, especially in the New York City area, use [a], often as an acquired pronunciation, but frequently use [a] in such words as *bad, land,* and *fancy* too, thereby losing the distinction between the two categories.

Loss of the distinction between such pairs as *cot* [kɑt] and *caught* [kɔt] characterizes some of the Midland areas. In Pittsburgh, Salt Lake City, and parts of the Northwest, either word may be heard as [kɑt], [kɒt], or [kɔt], and the meaning must be determined from the context of the sentence. Such words as *loss, cough, cloth, lost, stop, hot, lock, on,* and *God* vary considerably, especially in the Midland areas west of the Pennsylvania mountains. Words of the type of *fog, frog, hog, log, gong,* and *prong* run the entire range from [ɑ] to [ɔ], but the regional patterns are too complex for inclusion in this article.

Variations between vowels and diphthongs are especially characteristic of the South, which changes some sounds heard as simple vowels elsewhere into diphthongs, and vice versa. Thus *dog* and *class,* which are usually [dɔg] and [klæs] elsewhere, are often [dɔʊg] and [klæɪs] in the South. *Time* and *oil,* which are usually [taɪm] and [ɔɪl] elsewhere, are often [ta:m] and [ɔ:l] in the South. The diphthong of such a word as *town* varies from North to South, more often [tɑʊn] in the North, [taʊn] in the Midland areas, and often [tæʊn] in the South. There is, of course, overlapping, and New York City, in particular, uses all three forms.

Except for *r,* consonantal variations are not very important. For the verb *grease* and the adjective *greasy,* but not for the noun *grease,* a line drawn westward from Philadelphia to the Ohio valley, where it joins the Vermont–Texas line, separates the territory to the north, where [s] predominates for both verb and adjective, from the territory to the south, where [z] predominates. The normal pronunciation of the noun *grease* is everywhere [gris].

Words with the so-called "long-*u*" after *t, d,* or *n,* as in *tune, due, dew, numerous,* and *new,* have retained the older [ju] of *unit* only to a limited extent, and only, in natural speech, in the South, where *due* and *dew* may be [dju] in contrast with *do* [du]. Elsewhere in the country, despite the preference of radio and television for the forms with [j], the normal pronunciations are *tune* [tun], *due* and *dew* [du], and *new* [nu].

Other variations occur, but are usually of minor importance and can be ignored. The purpose of this article has been to demonstrate not the lack of standards, but their diversity in a diversified country.

GREEK AND LATIN ELEMENTS IN ENGLISH

The following list contains a selection of English words, listed alphabetically, each of which is shown with a corresponding combining form, prefix, or suffix of Greek or Latin derivation. The list will prove of great assistance in word study and the enrichment of one's vocabulary, and will give some insight into the origins and general range of meaning of new and unfamiliar words.

COMBINING FORMS

abdomen Gk. coelo-, gastro-; L. ventro-.
agriculture Gk. agro-.
air Gk. aero-; L. aeri-. See also BREATH, WIND.
aircraft Gk. aero-.
all Gk. pan-, panto-; L. omni-. See also WHOLE.
ancient Gk. archeo-, paleo-.
angle Gk. -gon, gonio-.
animal Gk. zoo-.
appearance Gk. -opsis.
arm Gk. brachio-.
art Gk. techno-.
artery Gk. arterio-.
back Gk. noto-; L. dorsi-, dorso-.
bad Gk. caco-, dys-; L. mal-. See also DIFFICULT.
bag Gk. asco-. See also BLADDER, VESSEL.
bare Gk. gymno-; L. nudi-.
beautiful Gk. calli-.
bearing L. -fer, -ferous, -gerous, -parous. See also PRODUCING.
bent Gk. ankylo-; L. flexi-. See also CURVED.
berry L. bacci-.
berry-shaped Gk. & L. cocci-, -coccus.
big See GREAT.
bile Gk. chole-, cholo-.
bird Gk. ornitho-; L. avi-.
birth Gk. toco-; L. nati-. See also CHILD.
bitter Gk. picro-.
black Gk. melano-; L. nigri-.
bladder Gk. cysto-; L. vesico-. See also BAG, VESSEL.
blind Gk. typhlo-.
blood Gk. -emia (condition or disease), hema-, hemato-; L. sangui-.
bluish Gk. cyano-, glauco-.
body Gk. somato-, -soma, -some.
bone Gk. osteo-; L. ossi-.
book Gk. biblio-.
both Gk. amphi-; L. ambi-.
brain Gk. encephalo-, phreno-; L. cerebro-. See also MIND.
brass See COPPER.
breast Gk. masto-.
breath Gk. pneumato-; L. spiro-. See also AIR, WIND.
bristle L. seti-.
broad Gk. eury-; L. lati-. See also FLAT.
bronze See COPPER.
bud Gk. blasto-, -blast; L. gemmi-.
burning See FIRE.
carbon L. carbo-, carboni-.
carrying See BEARING.
cartilage Gk. chondro-.
carved, carving Gk. glypto-, -glyph.
cattle Gk. tauro-; L. bovi-.
cave Gk. & L. speleo-.
cavity Gk. -cele.
cell Gk. cyto-, -plast.
center Gk. centro-; L. centri-.
chemical Gk. chemo-.
chest Gk. stetho-.
chief Gk. arch-, archi-.
child Gk. pedo-, toco-.
Chinese L. Sino-.
chlorine Gk. chloro-.
circle Gk. cyclo-, gyro-, -cyclic.
class See NATION, ORDER, SPECIES, TYPE.
clear See VISIBLE.
climate Gk. climato-.
closed Gk. cleisto-.
cloud Gk. nepho-.
cold Gk. cryo-, psychro-.
colon Gk. colo-.
color Gk. chromato-, chromo-, -chrome; L. colori-.
comb Gk. cteno-.
common Gk. ceno-.
complete See FINAL.
cone Gk. cono-.
copper Gk. chalco-; L. cupro-.
cornea Gk. kerato-.
corpse Gk. necro-.
correct Gk. ortho-.
country Gk. choro-.
covered See HIDDEN.
craving Gk. -mania, -maniac.
crest Gk. lopho-.
cross Gk. stauro-; L. cruci-.
crystal Gk. crystallo-.
cup Gk. scypho-; L. scyphi-.
curly L. cirro-.
current Gk. rheo-.
curved L. curvi-.
custom Gk. nomo-.
cut Gk. tomo-, -tomy; L. -sect, -section. See also KNIFE, SPLIT.
cyanogen Gk. cyano-.
cyst Gk. cysto-.
dance Gk. choreo-, choro-.
darkness Gk. scoto-.
death Gk. thanato-. See also CORPSE.
decompose Gk. sapro-.
deep, depth Gk. batho-, bathy-.
diaphragm Gk. phreno-.
different Gk. hetero-; L. vari-, vario-. See also FOREIGN, OTHER.
difficult Gk. dys-.
disease Gk. noso-, patho-, -iasis, -osis, -pathy. See also PAIN.
dissolving Gk. lyo-, lysi-, -lysis, -lyte.
divide See CUT, SPLIT.
divining Gk. -mancy, -mantic.
double Gk. diplo-.
dream Gk. oneiro-.
drug Gk. pharmaco-.
dry Gk. xero-.
dung Gk. copro-, scato-; L. sterco-, stercori-.
duodenum L. duodeno-.
dust Gk. conio-.
ear Gk. oto-.
early, earliest Gk. eo-. See also ANCIENT, FIRST, PRIMITIVE.
earth Gk. geo-; L. terri-.
earthquake Gk. seismo-.
eat Gk. phago-, -phage, -phagous, -phagy; L. -vorous. See also FOOD, NOURISHMENT.
egg Gk. oo-; L. ovi-, ovo-.
eight Gk. & L. octa-, octo-.
electric Gk. & L. electro-. See also CURRENT.
embryo Gk. embryo-.
end See FINAL.
English L. Anglo-.
equal Gk. iso-; L. equi-, pari-. See also LIKE, SAME.
existence Gk. onto-.
external Gk. ecto-, exo-; L. extra-.
extremity See TIP.
eye Gk. ophthalmo-, -opia; L. oculo-. See also SIGHT.
eyelid Gk. blepharo-.
false Gk. pseudo-.
far Gk. tele-, telo-.
fat, fatty Gk. lipo-; L. sebi-, sebo-.
father L. patri-.
fear Gk. -phobia.
feather See WING.
feed See EAT, NOURISHMENT.
female See WOMAN.
fermentation Gk. zymo-.
fever L. febri-.
few Gk. oligo-.
fibrous L. fibro-.
field See AGRICULTURE.
fight Gk. -machy.
filament See THREAD.
fin L. pinni-.
final Gk. teleo-, telo-.
finger Gk. dactylo-; L. digiti-.
fire Gk. pyro-; L. igni-.
first Gk. proto-; L. primi-.
fish Gk. ichthyo-; L. pisci-.
five Gk. penta-; L. quinque-.
flat Gk. platy-; L. plano-.
flee L. -fugal, -fuge.
flesh Gk. sarco-.
flow Gk. -rrhea, -rrhagia, -rrhagic. See also CURRENT.
flower Gk. antho-; L. -florous.
fluorescence L. fluo-, fluoro-.
fluorine L. fluo-, fluoro-.
food Gk. sito-. See also EAT, NOURISHMENT.
foot Gk. -pod, -podous; L. pedi-, -ped, -pede.
fond of See LOVE.
force See POWER.
foreign Gk. xeno-. See also DIFFERENT, OTHER.
foretelling See DIVINING.
form Gk. morpho-, -morphic, -morphous. See also APPEARANCE, IMAGE, LIKE.
four Gk. tetra-; L. quadri-, quadru-.
French L. Gallo-.
front, frontal L. fronto-.
fruit Gk. carpo-, -carpous.
fungus Gk. myco-, -mycete; L. fungi-.
gamete Gk. gameto-.
ganglion Gk. ganglio-.
gas Gk. aero-.
genital L. genito-.
gigantic Gk. giganto-.
gills Gk. branchio-, -branch.
gland Gk. adeno-.
glass Gk. hyalo-; L. vitri-.
god Gk. theo-.
gold Gk. chryso-.
good Gk. eu-.
govern Gk. -archy, -cracy, -crat.

grain L. grani-.
gray matter Gk. polio-.
great Gk. mega-, megalo-; L. magni-. See also LARGE, LONG.
Greek L. Greco-.
green Gk. chloro-.
groin L. inguino-.
growth Gk. -plasia, -plasis. See also BUD, TUMOR.
hair Gk. chaeto-, tricho-.
half Gk. hemi-; L. demi-, semi-.
hand Gk. chiro-.
hard Gk. sclero-. See also SOLID.
hate Gk. miso-.
head Gk. cephalo-, -cephalic, -cephalous. See also SKULL.
healing See MEDICINE.
hear Gk. acous-; L. audio-.
heart Gk. cardio-.
heat Gk. thermo-. See FIRE.
the heavens Gk. urano-.
hernia Gk. -cele; L. hernio-.
hidden Gk. crypto-.
high, height Gk. hypso-; L. alti-, alto-.
hollow See CAVITY.
holy See SACRED.
horn Gk. kerato-.
horse Gk. hippo-.
hundred Gk. hecto-; L. centi-.
hysteria Gk. hystero-.
idea Gk. ideo-.
ileum L. ileo-.
image Gk. icono-.
individual Gk. idio-.
inflammation Gk. -itis.
inhabiting L. -colous.
insect Gk. entomo-.
interior Gk. endo-, ento-; L. intra-, intro-.
intestine Gk. entero-. See also COLON, DUODENUM, ILEUM, RECTUM, VISCERA.
iodine Gk. iodo-.
iris (of eye) Gk. irido-.
iron Gk. sidero-; L. ferro-, ferri-.
jaw Gk. gnatho-, -gnathous.
joint Gk. arthro-.
kidney Gk. nephro-; L. reni-.
kill L. -cidal, -cide.
knife Gk. -tome.
knowledge of Gk. -gnomy, -gnosis, -sophy.
large Gk. macro-. See also GREAT, LONG.
larynx Gk. laryngo-.
law Gk. nomo-.
lead (metal) L. plumbo-.
leading Gk. -agog, -agogue.
leaf, leafy Gk. phyllo-, -phyllous; L. -folious.
left L. levo-.
level See FLAT.
life Gk. bio-, -biosis.
light Gk. photo-; L. luci-, lumini-; Gk. actino- (light ray).
like Gk. homeo-, homoio-, -oid, -ode; L. quasi-. See also APPEARANCE, EQUAL, FORM, SAME.
lime L. calci-.
lip Gk. chilo-; L. labio-.
list Gk. -logy.
little See SMALL.
liver Gk. hepato-.
long Gk. macro-; L. longi-.
love Gk. philo-, -phile; -philia, -phily (morbid love).
lung Gk. pneumo-; L. pulmo-.
lymph L. lympho-, lymphato-.
magnet L. magneto-.
making Gk. -plastic, -poietic. See also PRODUCING.
man Gk. andro-, anthropo-, -androus.
manifestation Gk. -phany.
many Gk. poly-, myria- (very many); L. multi-.
marriage Gk. -gamy.
material, matter Gk. hylo-, -plasm.
measure Gk. metro-, -meter, -metry.
medicine Gk. iatro-, -iatrics, -iatry; L. medico-.
membrane Gk. hymeno-.
middle Gk. meso-; L. medio-.
milk Gk. galacto-; L. lacto-.
mind Gk. phreno-, psycho-. See also SPIRIT.
monster Gk. terato-.
moon Gk. seleno-; L. luni-.
mother L. matri-.
motion pictures Gk. cine-.
mountain Gk. oro-.
mouth Gk. stomato-, -stome, -stomous; L. oro-.
movement Gk. kinesi-, kineto-, -kinesis.
mucus L. muco-, muci-. See also SLIMY.
much See MANY.
muscle Gk. myo-.
myth Gk. mytho-.
naked See BARE.
narrow Gk. steno-.
nation Gk. ethno-. See also SPECIES.
nature Gk. physio-.
near Gk. para-; L. juxta-.
neck L. cervico-.
needle See POINT.
nerve Gk. neuro-.
new Gk. neo-.
night Gk. nycto-; L. nocti-.
nine Gk. ennea-.
nitrogen Gk. azo-; L. nitro-.
nose Gk. rhino-; L. naso-.
nourishment Gk. tropho-, -trophy. See also EAT, FOOD.
nucleus Gk. karyo-; L. nucleo-.
observation Gk. -scope, -scopy.
oil L. oleo-.
old age Gk. geronto-.
one Gk. mono-; L. uni-.
opening Gk. -stomy (surgical).
orchid Gk. orchido-.
order Gk. -taxis, -taxy.
organ, organic Gk. organo-.
other Gk. allo-. See also DIFFERENT, FOREIGN.
outside Gk. ecto-, exo-; L. extra-.
ovary Gk. gyno-.
oxygen Gk. oxy-.
pain Gk. -algia, -odynia. See also DISEASE, SUFFERING.
pair Gk. zygo-. See also DOUBLE, TWO.
palm L. palmi-.
paralysis Gk. -plegia.
part Gk. mero-, -mere, -merous.
path See WAY.
pelvis Gk. pyelo-; L. pelvi-.
people Gk. demo-. See also NATION.
perpendicular See UPRIGHT.
pharynx Gk. pharyngo-.
physics Gk. physico-.
pillar Gk. stylo-.
pistil See OVARY.
place Gk. topo-.
plant Gk. phyto-, -phyte.
plate See SCALE.
pleura Gk. pleuro-.
point L. acu-. See also SPINY.
poison Gk. toxico-.
position Gk. stato-.
power Gk. dyna-, dynamo-.
pressure Gk. piezo-, baro- (atmospheric pressure).
primitive Gk. archi-.
producing Gk. -gen, -genous, -geny, -gony. See also BEARING, MAKING.
pulse Gk. sphygmo-.
pus Gk. pyo-.
race See NATION, SPECIES.
radiant energy L. radio-.
radiate Gk. actino-.
radio L. radio-.
radioactive L. radio-.
rain Gk. hyeto-, ombro-; L. pluvio-.
ray See LIGHT.
recent Gk. -cene (geology and anthropology).
rectum Gk. procto-; L. recto-.
red Gk. erythro-.
region See COUNTRY, PLACE.
reproduction Gk. gono-.
rib L. costo-.
right L. dextro-.
river L. fluvio-.
rock See STONE.
root Gk. rhizo-.
rot See DECOMPOSE.
rough Gk. trachy-.
row Gk. -stichous.
rule See GOVERN.
run Gk. -drome, -dromous.
sacred Gk. hagio-, hiero-.
sacrum L. sacro-.
salt Gk. halo-.
same Gk. homo-, tauto-. See also EQUAL, LIKE.
scale Gk. lepido-; L. lamelli-.
science of Gk. -logy, -logical, -nomy.
sea Gk. halo-, thalasso-.
seaweed Gk. phyco-.
second (adj.) Gk. deutero-.
seed Gk. spermato-, -gonium, -sperm, -spermous. See also SPORE.
seizure Gk. -lepsy.
self Gk. auto-.
serum L. sero-.
seven Gk. hepta-; L. septi-.
sexual union Gk. gamo-.
sharp Gk. oxy-.
short Gk. brachy-; L. brevi-.
side Gk. pleuro-, -hedral, -hedron (geometry).
sight Gk. -opia, -opsia.
silicon L. silico-.
simple Gk. haplo-; L. simplici-.
single Gk. haplo-.
six Gk. hexa-; L. sex-.
skin Gk. dermato-, dermo-, -derm.
skull Gk. cranio-.
sleep Gk. hypno-; L. somni-.
slender Gk. lepto-.
slimy Gk. myxo-.
slope Gk. clino-, -cline (geology).
slow Gk. brady-.
small Gk. micro-. See also FEW.
snake Gk. ophio-.
society L. socio-.
soft Gk. malaco-.
solid Gk. stereo-.
sound Gk. phono-, -phone, -phony.
speech Gk. logo-, -phasia (defective).
species Gk. phylo-.
spectrum L. spectro-.
spermatozoa Gk. spermato-.
sphere Gk. -sphere.
spinal cord Gk. myelo-.
spiny Gk. acantho-, echino-; L. spini-.
spiral Gk. helico-, spiro-.
spirit Gk. pneumato-, psycho-. See also MIND.

spleen	Gk. spleno-.
split	Gk. schisto-, schizo-; L. fissi-, -fid.
spore	Gk. sporo-, -sporous.
sprout	See BUD.
stamen	Gk. andro-; L. stamini-.
star	Gk. aster-, astro-; L. sidero-, stelli-.
starch	Gk. amylo-.
stomach	Gk. gastero-, gastro-.
stone	Gk. litho-, petro-, -lith.
stop	Gk. -stat.
straight	Gk. ortho-; L. recti-.
strange	See FOREIGN.
style	Gk. stylo- (biology).
substitute	L. vice-.
suffering	Gk. patho-, -pathy.
sugar	Gk. saccharo-.
sulfur	Gk. thio-; L. sulfa-, sulfo-.
sun	Gk. helio-.
sweet	Gk. glyco-.
swift	Gk. tachy-.
sword	Gk. xiphi-.
tail	Gk. uro-.
technical	Gk. techno-.
ten	Gk. deca-.
a tenth	L. deci-.
terrible	Gk. dino-.
testicle	Gk. orchio-.
thick	Gk. pachy-.
thorax	Gk. thoraco-.
thousand, thousandth	L. milli-.
thread	Gk. nemato-.
three	L. ter-, tri-.
throat	See LARYNX, PHARYNX, TRACHEA.
thyroid	Gk. thyro-.
time	Gk. chrono-.
tip	Gk. acro-.
tissue	Gk. histo-.
toe	See FINGER.
tone	Gk. tono-.
tongue	Gk. glosso-.
tooth	Gk. odonto-, -odont; L. denti-.
top	See TIP.
torpor	Gk. narco-.
trachea	Gk. broncho-, tracheo-.
tree	Gk. dendro-, -dendron; L. arbori-.
tribe	See SPECIES.
tumor	Gk. -cele, -oma.
turned	Gk. -tropous, -tropy.
twelve	Gk. dodeca-.
two	Gk. di-; L. bi-, duo-.
type	Gk. typo-.
united	Gk. gamo-.
universe	Gk. cosmo-.
upright	Gk. ortho-.
urethra	Gk. urethro-.
urine	Gk. uro-, -uria; L. urino-.
uterus	Gk. hystero-, metro-; L. utero-.
vagina	L. vagino-.
vein	Gk. phlebo-; L. veni-.
vessel	Gk. angio-; L. vaso-. See also BAG, BLADDER, CUP.
viscera	Gk. splanchno-.
visible	Gk. phanero-.
voice	See SOUND.
walking	L. -grade.
water	Gk. hydro-; L. aqui-.
wave	Gk. cymo-.
wax	Gk. cero-.
way	Gk. hodo-, odo-, -ode.
web	L. pinni-.
wealth	Gk. pluto-.
wedge	Gk. spheno-.
weight	Gk. baro-.
wet	Gk. hygro-.
white	Gk. leuko-.
whole	Gk. holo-; L. toti-.
wide	See BROAD.
wind	Gk. anemo-. See also AIR, BREATH.
wine	L. vini-.
wing	Gk. ptero-, -pterous; L. -pennate.
woman	Gk. gyneco-, gyno-.
wood	Gk. xylo-; L. ligni-.
word	Gk. logo-.
work	Gk. ergo-.
world	See UNIVERSE.
worm	L. vermi-.
write	Gk. grapho-, -gram, -graph, -graphy.
yellow	Gk. xantho-.
yoke	Gk. zygo-.

PREFIXES

about	See AROUND.
above	Gk. hyper-; L. super-, supra-. See also ON.
across	L. trans-. See also THROUGH.
after	Gk. meta-; L. post-.
again	Gk. ana-; L. re-. See also BACK.
against	Gk. anti-; L. contra-, in- (il-, im-, ir-), ob- (oc-, of-, op-).
among	See BETWEEN, WITHIN.
apart	L. dis- (di-), se-. See also AWAY, FROM.
around	Gk. peri-; L. circum-.
at	See BESIDE, NEAR, TO.
away	Gk. apo-. See also APART, FROM.
back	L. retro-. See also AGAIN.
badly	L. mal-, mis-.
before	Gk. pro-; L. ante-, pre-.
behind	See AFTER.
beside	Gk. para-; L. juxta-.
between	L. inter-.
beyond	Gk. meta-; L. preter-, ultra-.
changed	Gk. meta-.
down	Gk. cata- (cath-); L. de-.
excessively	See ABOVE.
for	L. pro-.
forward	Gk. & L. pro-.
from	L. ab- (a-, abs-). See also DOWN.
in, into	Gk. en- (el-, em-); L. in- (il-, im-, ir-), intro-. See also WITHIN.
not	Gk. a- (an-); L. de-, in- (il-, im-, ir-), non-.
off	See APART, AWAY, FROM.
on	Gk. epi- (eph-); L. in- (il-, im-, ir-).
on that side of	L. trans-. See also BEYOND.
on this side of	L. cis-.
out	Gk. & L. ex- (e-, ec-, ef-).
outside	Gk. exo-; L. extra-. See also BEYOND.
over	See ABOVE, ON, BEYOND, VERY.
thoroughly	Gk. ana-, cata- (cath-); L. com- (co-, col-, con-, cor-), per-.
through	Gk. dia-; L. per-.
to, toward	L. ad- (ac-, af-, ag-, al-, an-, ap-, ar-, as-, at-).
under	Gk. hypo-; L. sub- (suc-, suf-, sug-, sum-, sup-, sur-, sus-), subter-.
up	Gk. ana-.
very	Gk. peri-; L. per-. See also THOROUGHLY.
with	Gk. sym- (sy-, syl-, syn-).
within	Gk. endo-; L. intra-.
without	See NOT, OUTSIDE.

SUFFIXES OF ADJECTIVES

able to, able to be	L. -able, -ile (-il).
adhering to or following	L. -an.
affected by	L. & Gk. -ac.
beginning to	L. -escent.
belonging to	L. -an (in zoology).
capable of	See ABLE TO.
causing	L. -fic.
characterized by	L. -al, -ate, -id. See also PERTAINING TO.
coming from	L. -an.
doing	L. -ant, -ent.
full of	L. -ose, -ous.
like, of the nature of	L. -ine (-in), -ive, -ory, -ose.
making	See CAUSING.
originating in	See COMING FROM.
pertaining to	Gk. & L. -ac, -ic; L. -aceous, -al, -ar, -ary, -ile (-il), -ine, -ory.
related to	See PERTAINING TO.
tending to	L. -able, -ive.
worthy of	See ABLE TO.

Many adjectives so formed are also used as nouns, as *animal, human*, etc. These nouns mean generally a person or thing related to or described by the adjective.

SUFFIXES OF NOUNS

act, action	L. -al, -ion (-cion, -sion, -tion), -ment, -ure.
advocate or adherent	Gk. -ist, -ite.
art	Gk. -ic, -ics. See also SYSTEM.
collection	L. -ana.
condition	L. -ion (-cion, -sion, -tion), -ment, -mony, -tude.
descendant of	Gk. -ite.
example	See INSTANCE.
function	See OFFICE.
instance	L. -al.
instrument	L. -ment, -ory, -ure.
methods	See SYSTEM.
native	L. -ite.
office	L. -ate, -ure
place	L. -arium, -ary, -orium, -ory.
practitioner	L. -ary, -ist, -or -aster (inferior), -trix (female).
result	L. -ate, -ion (-cion, -sion, -tion), -ment, -mony, -ure.
state	See CONDITION.
student	L. -ist.
study	See ART.
system	Gk. -ics.

SUFFIXES OF VERBS

become	Gk. -ize; L. -fy.
begin	L. -esce.
combine with	L. -ate.
make	Gk. -ize; L. -fy.
practice	Gk. -ize.
treat with	Gk. -ize; L. -ate.

GIVEN NAMES

MASCULINE NAMES

Aar·on (âr′ən, ar′ən) ? Enlightener. [< Hebrew]

A·bel (ā′bəl) Breath. [< Hebrew]

A·bi·el (ā′bē·el, ə·bī′əl) Strong father. [< Hebrew]

Ab·ner (ab′nər) Father of light. [< Hebrew]

A·bra·ham (ā′brə·ham; *Fr.* à·brà·àm′; *Ger.* ä′brä·häm) Exalted father of multitudes. [< Hebrew] Also *Sp.* **A·bra·hán** (ä′brä·än′). Dims. **Abe, A′bie.**

A·bram (ā′brəm; *Fr.* à·brän′; *Sp.* ä·bräm′) Exalted father. [< Hebrew]

Ab·sa·lom (ab′sə·ləm) The father is peace. [< Hebrew]

Ad·am (ad′əm) Red; man of red earth. [< Hebrew]

Ad·el·bert (ad′l·bûrt, ə·del′bûrt) Var. of ALBERT.

Ad·olph (ad′olf, ā′dolf) Noble wolf. [< Gmc.] Also *Dan., Du., Ger.* **A·dolf** (ä′dôlf), *Fr.* **A·dolphe** (à·dôlf′), *Ital., Sp.* **A·dol·fo** (*Ital.* ä·dôl′fō; *Sp.* ä·thôl′fō), *Lat.* **A·dol·phus** (ə·dol′fəs), *Pg.* **A·dol·pho** (ə·thôl′fo͞o).

A·dri·an (ā′drē·ən) Of Adria: from the name of two Italian cities, or the Adriatic Sea. [< L] Also *Fr.* **A·dri·en** (à·drē·aṅ′), *Ital.* **A·dri·a·no** (ä′drē·ä′nō), *Lat.* **A·dri·a·nus** (ā′drē·ā′nəs).

Af·fon·so (ə·fōn′so͞o) Pg. form of ALPHONSO.

Al·an (al′ən) Handsome. [< Celtic] Also **Al′lan, Al′len.** Dim. **Al.**

Al·a·ric (al′ə·rik) All-ruler. [< Gmc.]

Al·as·tair (al′əs·tər) Scot. contr. of ALEXANDER. Also **Al′is·ter.**

Al·ban (ôl′bən, al′-) White; of Alba: from the name of several Italian cities. [< L] Also **Al′bin.**

Al·bert (al′bûrt; *Fr.* àl·bâr′; *Ger., Sw.* äl′bert) Nobly bright. [< F < Gmc.] Also *Ital., Sp.* **Al·ber·to** (äl·ber′tō), *Lat.* **Al·ber·tus** (al·bûr′təs). Dims. **Al, Alb, Bert.**

Al·den (ôl′dən) Old friend. [OE]

Al·do (al′dō) Meaning uncertain. [< Gmc. or Hebrew]

Al·dous (ôl′dəs, al′-) From the old place. [OE] Also **Al′dis, Al′dus.**

Al·ex·an·der (al′ig·zan′dər, -zän′-; *Du., Ger.* ä′lek·sän′dər) Defender of men. [< Gk.] Also *Fr.* **A·lex·an·dre** (à·lek·säṅ′dr′), *Modern Gk.* **A·le·xan·dros** (ä·lâ′ksän·drōs), *Ital.* **A·les·san·dro** (ä′lās·sän′drō), *Pg.* **A·le·xan·dre** (ə·lē·shaṅn′drə), *Russ.* **A·le·ksandr** (ə·lyi·ksän′dər), *Sp.* **A·le·jan·dro** (ä′lā·hän′drō). Dims. **Al′ec, Al′eck, Al′ex, San′der, San′dy.**

A·lex·is (ə·lek′sis) Defender. [< Gk.]

Al·fon·so (äl·fôn′sō) Ital. and Sp. form of ALPHONSO. Also *Dan., Ger.* **Al·fons** (äl′fôns).

Al·fred (al′frid; *Ger.* äl′frāt; *Fr.* àl·fred′) Elf counselor; hence, wise. [OE] Also *Ital., Sp.* **Al·fre·do** (*Ital.* äl·frā′dō; *Sp.* äl·frā′thō), *Lat.* **Al·fre·dus** (al·frē′dəs) or **Al·u·re·dus** (al′yo͞o·rē′dəs). Dims **Al, Alf, Fred.**

Al·ger (al′jər) Noble spear. [< Gmc.]

Al·ger·non (al′jər·nən) Mustached. [< OF] Dims. **Al·gie, Al·gy** (al′jē).

Al·len (al′ən) Var. of ALAN. Also **Al′lan.**

A·lon·zo (ə·lon′zō) Var. of ALPHONSO. Also *Ital., Sp.* **A·lon·so** (ä·lôn′sō).

Al·o·y·sius (al′ō·ish′əs) Lat. form of LOUIS. Also **A·lois** (ə·lois′).

Al·phon·so (al·fon′zō, -sō) Nobly ready. [< Sp. < Gmc.] Also *Fr.* **Al·phonse** (àl·fôṅs′). Dims. **Al, Alph, Al′phy.**

Al·va (al′və; *Sp.* äl′vä) White. [< L]

Al·vin (al′vin) Noble friend. [< Gmc.] Also **Al·win** (al′win; *Ger.* äl′vēn), **Al′van,** *Fr.* **A·luin** (à·lwaṅ′), *Ital.* **Al·vi·no** (äl·vē′nō), *Sp.* **A·lui·no** (ä·lwē′nō).

Am·brose (am′brōz) Divine; immortal. [< Gk.] Also *Fr.* **Am·broise** (äṅ·brwàz′), *Lat.* **Am·bro·si·us** (am·brō′zhē·əs, -zē·əs).

A·me·ri·go (ä′mā·rē′gō) Ital. form of EMERY.

A·mos (ā′məs) Burden. [< Hebrew]

An·a·tole (an′ə·tōl; *Fr.* à·nà·tôl′) Sunrise. [< Gk.]

An·drew (an′dro͞o) Manly. [< Gk.] Also **An·dre·as** (an′drē·əs, an·drē′əs; *Dan.* än·dres′; *Du., Ger.* än·drā′äs; *Lat.* an′drē·əs), *Fr.* **An·dré** (äṅ·drā′), *Ital.* **An·dre·a** (än·drâ′ä), *Russ.* **An·drei** (än·drā′), *Sp.* **An·drés** (än·drās′). Dims. **An′dy, Drew.**

An·gus (ang′gəs) Singular. [< Celtic]

An·selm (an′selm; *Ger.* än′zelm) Divine helmet. [< Gmc.] Also **An·sel** (an′səl), *Fr.* **An·selme** (äṅ·selm′), *Ital., Sp.* **An·sel·mo** (än·sel′mō), *Lat.* **An·sel·mus** (an·sel′məs).

An·tho·ny (an′thə·nē, -tə-) Inestimable: from the name of a Roman clan. Also **An·to·ny** (an′tə·nē), *Fr.* **An·toine** (äṅ·twàn′), *Ger., Lat.* **An·to·ni·us** (*Ger.* än·tō′nē·o͝os; *Lat.* an·tō′nē·əs), *Ital., Sp.* **An·to·nio** (än·tô′nyō). Dim. **To′ny.**

An·ton (än′tōn) Dan., Du., Ger. and Sw. form of ANTHONY.

Ar·chi·bald (är′chə·bôld) Nobly bold. [< Gmc.] Dims. **Ar′chie, Ar′chy.**

Ar·mand (är′mänd; *Fr.* àr·mäṅ′) Fr. form of HERMAN.

Ar·min·i·us (är·min′ē·əs) Lat. form of HERMAN.

Ar·nold (är′nəld; *Ger.* är′nôlt) Eagle power. [< Gmc.] Also *Fr.* **Ar·naud** (àr·nō′), *Ital.* **Ar·nol·do** (är·nôl′dō), *Sp.* **Ar·nal·do** (är·näl′thō). Dims. **Arn, Ar′nie.**

Ar·te·mas (är′tə·məs) He of Artemis. [< Gk.] Also **Ar′te·mus.**

Ar·thur (är′thər; *Fr.* àr·to͞or′) He-bear: from a totemic or royal title suggesting valor, strength, and nobility. [< Celtic] Also *Ital.* **Ar·tu·ro** (är·to͞o′rō). Dims. **Art, Art′ie.**

A·sa (ā′sə) Healer. [< Hebrew]

Ash·ley (ash′lē) Dweller among ash trees: from a surname. [< Gmc.]

Ath·el·stan (ath′əl·stan) Noble stone or jewel. [OE] Also **Ath′el·stane** (-stān).

Au·brey (ô′brē) Elf ruler. [< F < Gmc.]

Au·gus·tine (ô′gəs·tēn, ô·gus′tin) Dim. of AUGUSTUS. Also **Au·gus·tin** (ô·gus′tən; *Fr.* ō·güs·tàn′; *Ger.* ou′go͞os·tēn′), *Ital.* **A·go·sti·no** (ä′gō·stē′nō), *Lat.* **Au·gus·ti·nus** (ô′gəs·tī′nəs), *Pg.* **A·gos·ti·nho** (ə·go͞osh·tē′nyo͞o), *Sp.* **A·gus·tín** (ä′go͞os·tēn′).

Au·gus·tus (ô·gus′təs) Venerable. [< L] Also **Au·gust** (ô′gəst; *Ger.* ou′go͞ost), *Fr.* **Au·guste** (ō·güst′).

Au·re·li·us (ô·rē′lē·əs, ô·rēl′yəs) The golden one. [< L]

Aus·tin (ôs′tən) Contr. of AUGUSTINE.

A·ver·y (ā′vər·ē, ā′vrē) Courageous. [< Gmc.] Also **A·ver·il, A·ver·ill** (ā′vər·əl, ā′vrəl).

Bald·win (bôld′win) Bold friend. [< Gmc.] Also *Fr.* **Bau·doin** (bō·dwaṅ′).

Bal·tha·zar (bäl·thā′zər, -thaz′ər) Bel's or Baal's prince [< Chaldean], or splendid prince [< Persian]. Also **Bal·tha′sar** (-zər).

Bap·tist (bap′tist) Baptizer. [< Gk.] Also *Fr.* **Bap·tiste** (bà·tēst′).

Bar·na·bas (bär′nə·bəs) Son of consolation [< Hebrew], or prophetic son [< Aramaic]. Also **Bar·na·by** (bär′nə·bē). Dim. **Bar′ney.**

Bar·nard (bär′nərd) Var. of BERNARD.

Bar·ney (bär′nē) Dim. of BARNABAS or BERNARD.

Bar·ry (bar′ē) Spear; hence, straightforward. [< Celtic]

Bar·thol·o·mew (bär·thol′ə·myo͞o) Son of furrows. [< Hebrew] Also *Fr.* **Bar·thé·le·my** (bàr·tāl·mē′), *Ger.* **Bar·tho·lo·mä·us** (bär′tō·lō·mā′o͝os), *Ital.* **Bar·to·lo·me·o** (bär·tō′lō·mā′ō), *Lat.* **Bar·thol·o·mae·us** (bär·tol′ə·mē′əs), *Sp.* **Bar·to·lo·mé** (bär·tō′lō·mā′). Dims. **Bart, Bat.**

Bas·il (baz′əl, bā′zəl) Kingly. [< Gk.]

Bax·ter (bak′stər) Baker. [< Gmc.]

Bay·ard (bā′ərd, bī′-, -ärd) From a surname. [< OF]

Ben·e·dict (ben′ə·dikt) Blessed. [< L] Also **Ben′e·dick,** *Fr.* **Be·noît** (bə·nwà′), *Ger.* **Be·ne·dikt** (bā′nā·dikt), *Ital.* **Be·ne·det·to** (bā′nā·dāt′tō) or **Be·ni·to** (bā·nē′tō), *Lat.* **Ben·e·dic·tus** (ben′ə·dik′təs), *Sp.* **Be·ni·to** (bā·nē′tō).

Ben·ja·min (ben′jə·mən; *Fr.* baṅ·zhà·maṅ′; *Ger.* ben′yä·mēn) Son of the right hand; hence, favorite son. [< Hebrew] Also *Ital.* **Ben·ia·mi·no** (ben′yä·mē′nō), *Sp.* **Ben·ja·mín** (ben′hä·mēn′). Dims. **Ben, Ben′jy, Ben′ny.**

Ben·net (ben′it) Var. of BENEDICT. Also **Ben′nett.**

Ber·nard (bûr′nərd, bər·närd′; *Fr.* ber·nàr′) Bear-brave: probably from a totemic title. [< Gmc.] Also *Ger.* **Bern·hard** (bern′härt), *Ital., Sp.* **Ber·nar·do** (*Ital.* bār·när′dō; *Sp.* ber·när′thō), *Lat.* **Ber·nar·dus** (bər·när′dəs). Dims. **Bar′ney, Ber′ney, Ber′nie.**

Bert (bûrt) Dim. of ALBERT, BERTRAM, GILBERT, HERBERT, and HUBERT. Also **Ber·tie** (bûr′tē).

Ber·tram (bûr′trəm) Bright raven. [< Gmc.] Also **Ber·trand** (bûr′trənd; *Fr.* ber·träṅ′). Dim. **Bert.**

Bill (bil) Dim. of WILLIAM. Also **Bil′ly.**

Bob (bob) Dim. of ROBERT. Also **Bob′bie, Bob′by.**

Bo·ris (bôr′is, bō′ris; *Russ.* bə·ryēs′) Warrior. [< Russ.]

Boyd (boid) Yellow-haired. [< Celtic]

Bri·an (brī′ən) Strong. [< Celtic] Also **Bry′an, Bry·ant** (brī′ənt).

Brice (brīs) Meaning uncertain. [? < Celtic] Also **Bryce.**

Bruce (bro͞os) From a Norman Fr. surname; orig. a place name.

Bru·no (bro͞o′nō) The brown one. [< Gmc.]

Bur·gess (bûr′jis) Citizen. [< Gmc.]

By·ron (bī′rən) From a Fr. surname; orig. a place name. Also **Bi′ron.**

Cad·wal·la·der (kad·wol′ə·dər) Battle arranger. [< Welsh] Also **Cad·wal′a·der.**

Cae·sar (sē′zər) Long-haired: ? symbolic title suggesting royalty or holiness. [< L] Also **Ce′sar,** *Fr.* **Cé·sar** (sā·zàr′), *Ital.* **Ce·sa·re** (chā′zä·rā).

Ca·leb (kā′ləb) Dog; hence, loyal. [< Hebrew]

Cal·vin (kal′vin) Bald: from a Roman name. [< L] Dim. **Cal.**

Carl (kärl) English form of KARL.

Car·ol (kar′əl) English form of CAROLUS.

Car·o·lus (kar′ə·ləs) Lat. form of CHARLES.

Car·y (kâr′ē) ? Dim. of CAROL. Also **Car′ey.**

Cas·per (kas′pər) English form of KASPAR. Also **Cas′par** (-pər).

Ce·cil (sē′səl, ses′əl) Blind: from the name of a Roman clan.

Ced·ric (sed′rik, sē′drik) War chief. [< Celtic]

Charles (chärlz; *Fr.* shàrl) Manly. [< F < Gmc.] Also *Ital.* **Car·lo** (kär′lō), *Lat.* **Car·o·lus** (kar′ə·ləs), *Sp.* **Car·los** (kär′lōs). Dims. **Char′ley, Char′lie, Chuck.**

Chaun·cey (chôn′sē, chän′-) Chancellor. [< OF]

Ches·ter (ches′tər) Dweller in camp; hence, soldier: from a surname. [< L] Dims. **Ches, Chet.**

Chris·tian (kris′chən; *Ger.* kris′tē·än) Christian. [< L < Gk.] Also *Fr.* **Chré·tien** (krā·tyaṅ′). Dim. **Chris.**

Chris·to·pher (kris′tə·fər) Bearer of Christ. [< Gk.] Also *Fr.* **Chris·tophe** (krēs·tôf′), *Ger.* **Chris·toph** (kris′tōf), *Ital.* **Chri·sto·fo·ro** (krēs·tô′fō·rō), *Sp.* **Cris·tó·bal** (krēs·tō′·väl). Dims. **Chris, Kit.**

Clar·ence (klar′əns) From the name of an English dukedom.

Claude (klôd; *Fr.* klōd) Lame: from the name of a Roman clan. Also *Ital., Sp.* **Clau·di·o** (*Ital.* klou′dyō; *Sp.* klou′·thyō), *Lat.* **Clau·di·us** (klô′dē·əs).

Clay·ton (klā′tən) From an English surname; orig. a place name.

Clem·ent (klem′ənt) Merciful. [< L] Dim. **Clem.**

Clif·ford (klif′ərd) From an English surname; orig. a place name. Dim. **Cliff.**

Clif·ton (klif′tən) From an English surname; orig. a place name.

Clin·ton (klin′tən) From an English surname; orig. a place name. Dim. **Clint.**

Clive (klīv) Cliff; cliff-dweller: from an English surname.

Clyde (klīd) From a Scot. surname; orig. the river *Clyde.*

Col·in (kol′ən, kō′lən) Dove. [< Scot. < L]

Con·rad (kon′rad) Bold counsel. [< Gmc.]

Con·stant (kon′stənt; *Fr.* kôṅ·stäṅ′) Var. of CONSTANTINE.

Con·stan·tine (kon′stən·tīn, -tēn) Constant; firm. [< L]

Cor·nel·ius (kôr·nēl′yəs; *Ger.* kôr·nā′lē·ŏŏs) ? Horn: from the name of a Roman clan. Dims. **Con, Con′nie, Neil.**

Craig (krāg) Crag; crag-dweller: from a Scot. surname.

Cris·pin (kris′pin) Curly-headed. [< L] Also *Lat.* **Cris·pi·nus** (kris·pī′nəs) or **Cris·pus** (kris′pəs).

Cur·tis (kûr′tis) Courteous. [< OF]

Cuth·bert (kuth′bərt) Notably brilliant. [OE]

Cyr·il (sir′əl) Lordly. [< Gk.]

Cy·rus (sī′rəs) The sun. [< Persian] Dim. **Cy.**

Dan (dan) Judge. [< Hebrew]

Dan·iel (dan′yəl; *Fr.* dà·nyel′; *Ger.* dä′nē·el) God is my judge. [< Hebrew] Dims. **Dan, Dan′ny.**

Da·ri·us (də·rī′əs) Wealthy. [< Persian]

Da·vid (dā′vid; *Fr.* dä·vēd′; *Ger.* dä′vēt) Beloved. [< Hebrew] Dims. **Dave, Da′vey, Da′vie, Da′vy.**

Dean (dēn) From an ancient religious or military title. [< OF < LL] Also **Deane.**

De·me·tri·us (di·mē′trē·əs) He of Demeter. [< Gk.] Also *Russ.* **Dmi·tri** (dmyē′trē).

Den·nis (den′is) Var. of DIONYSIUS. Also **Den′is,** *Fr.* **De·nis** or **De·nys** (də·nē′). Dim. **Den′ny.**

Der·ek (der′ik) Du. dim. of THEODORIC. Also **Der′rick, Dirck** (dûrk; *Du.* dirk), **Dirk.**

DeWitt (də·wit′) From a surname. Also **De Witt.**

Dex·ter (dek′stər) Right; right-handed; hence, fortunate or skillful. [< L]

Dick (dik) Dim. of RICHARD.

Dolph (dolf) Dim. of ADOLPH or RUDOLPH. Also **Dolf.**

Dom·i·nic (dom′ə·nik) Of the Lord. [< L] Also **Dom′i·nick.** Dim. **Dom.**

Don·ald (don′əld) World chief. [< Celtic] Dims. **Don, Don′nie.**

Doug·las (dug′ləs) Dark. [< Celtic] Dims. **Doug, Doug′ie.**

Drew (drōō) Skilled one [< Gmc.], or dim. of ANDREW.

Duane (dwān, dōō·ān′) Poem. [< Celtic]

Dud·ley (dud′lē) From an English surname; orig. a place name.

Duke (dōōk, dyōōk) From the title. [< OF]

Dun·can (dung′kən) Brown warrior. [< Celtic]

Dun·stan (dun′stən) From an English place name.

Dwight (dwīt) Meaning uncertain. [< Gmc.]

Earl (ûrl) From the title. [OE] Also **Earle.**

Eb·en·e·zer (eb′ə·nē′zər) Stone of help. [< Hebrew] Dim. **Eb·en** (eb′ən).

Ed·gar (ed′gər) Rich spear; hence, fortunate warrior. [OE] Dims. **Ed, Ed′die, Ned.**

Ed·mund (ed′mənd; *Ger.* et′mŏŏnt) Rich protector. [OE] Also **Ed·mond** (ed′mənd; *Fr.* ed·môṅ′). Dims. **Ed, Ed′die, Ned.**

Ed·ward (ed′wərd) Rich guardian. [OE] Also *Fr.* **É·dou·ard** (ā·dwàr′), *Ger.* **E·du·ard** (ā′dōō·ärt), *Sp.* **E·duar·do** (ā·thwär′thō). Dims. **Ed, Ed′die, Ned, Ted, Ted′dy.**

Ed·win (ed′win) Rich friend. [OE] Dims. **Ed, Ed′die.**

Eg·bert (eg′bərt) Bright sword; hence, skilled swordsman. [OE] Dims. **Bert, Bert′ie.**

El·bert (el′bərt) Var. of ALBERT.

El·dred (el′drid) Mature counsel. [OE]

El·e·a·zar (el′ē·ā′zər) God has helped. [< Hebrew] Also **El′e·a′zer.**

E·li (ē′lī) The highest one. [< Hebrew]

E·li·as (i·lī′əs) Var. of ELIJAH.

El·i·hu (el′ə·hyōō) Var. of ELIJAH.

E·li·jah (i·lī′jə) Jehovah is God. [< Hebrew]

El·i·ot (el′ē·ət) God's gift. [< Hebrew] Also **El′li·ot, El′li·ott.**

E·li·sha (i·lī′shə) God is salvation. [< Hebrew]

El·lis (el′is) Var. of ELIAS.

El·mer (el′mər) Nobly famous. [OE]

El·ton (el′tən) From an English surname; orig. a place name.

El·vin (el′vin) Of the elves. [OE] Also **El·win** (el′win).

E·man·u·el (i·man′yōō·əl) Var. of IMMANUEL. Also **Em·man′u·el.**

Em·er·y (em′ər·ē) Work ruler. [< Gmc.] Also **Em·er·ic** (em′ər·ik), **Em′o·ry.**

E·mile (ā·mēl′) From the name of a Roman clan. Also *Fr.* **É·mile** (ā·mēl′), *Ger.* **E·mil** (ā′mēl), *Ital.* **E·mi·lio** (ā·mē′lyō).

Em·mett (em′it) Ant; hence, industrious. [OE] Also **Em′met.**

E·ne·as (i·nē′əs) Praiseworthy. [< Gk.]

E·noch (ē′nək) Dedicated. [< Hebrew]

E·nos (ē′nəs) Man. [< Hebrew]

En·ri·co (än·rē′kō) Ital. form of HENRY.

E·phra·im (ē′frē·əm, ē′frəm) Doubly fruitful. [< Hebrew]

E·ras·mus (i·raz′məs) Lovable. [< Gk.]

E·ras·tus (i·ras′təs) Lovable. [< Gk.] Dim. **Ras·tus** (ras′·təs).

Er·ic (er′ik) Honorable king. [< Scand.] Also **Er′ich, Er′ik.**

Er·man·no (er·män′nō) Ital. form of HERMAN.

Er·nest (ûr′nist) Earnest. [< Gmc.] Also *Ger.* **Ernst** (ernst). Dims. **Ern, Er′nie.**

Er·win (ûr′win) Var. of IRVING.

Es·te·ban (ās·tā′bän) Sp. form of STEPHEN.

E·than (ē′thən) Firmness. [< Hebrew]

Eth·el·bert (eth′əl·bûrt) Nobly bright. [OE]

Eth·el·red (eth′əl·red) Noble council. [< Gmc.]

É·tienne (ā·tyen′) Fr. form of STEPHEN.

Eu·gene (yōō·jēn′) Well-born. [< Gk.] Dim. **Gene.**

Eus·tace (yōōs′tis) Good harvest. [< Gk.]

Ev·an (ev′ən) Welsh form of JOHN.

Ev·e·lyn (ēv′lin, ev′ə·lin) Ancestor. [< OF < Gmc.]

Ev·er·ard (ev′ər·ärd) Strong as a boar. [< Gmc.] Also **Ev·er·art** (ev′ər·ärt).

Ev·er·ett (ev′ər·it) Var. of EVERARD. Also **Ev′er·et.**

E·ze·ki·el (i·zē′kē·əl, -kyəl) God gives strength. [< Hebrew] Dim. **Zeke** (zēk).

Ez·ra (ez′rə) Helper. [< Hebrew]

Fë·dor (fyô′dər) Russ. form of THEODORE. Also **Fe·o·dor** (fyi·ô′dər).

Fe·li·pe (fā·lē′pā) Sp. form of PHILIP.

Fe·lix (fē′liks) Happy; fortunate. [< L]

Fer·di·nand (fûr′də·nand; *Fr.* fer·dē·näṅ′; *Ger.* fer′dē·nänt) Peaceful courage. [< Gmc.] Also *Sp.* **Fer·nan·do** (fer·nän′dō), **Her·nan·do** (her·nän′dō). Dim. **Fer′die.**

Floyd (floid) Var. of LLOYD.

Fran·cis (fran′sis, frän′-) Free. [< Gmc.] Also *Fr.* **Fran·çois** (fräṅ·swà′), *Ger.* **Franz** (fränts), *Ital.* **Fran·ce·sco** (frän·chā′skō), *Sp.* **Fran·cis·co** (frän·thēs′kō). Dim. **Frank, Frank′ie.**

Frank (frangk) Dim. of FRANCIS or FRANKLIN. Also **Frank′ie.**

Frank·lin (frangk′lin) Freeman. [ME] Dims. **Frank, Frank′ie.**

Fred (fred) Dim. of ALFRED, FREDERICK, or WILFRED. Also **Fred′die, Fred′dy.**

Fred·er·ick (fred′ər·ik, fred′rik) Peace ruler. [< Gmc.] Also **Fred′er·ic, Fred′ric, Fred′rick,** *Fr.* **Fré·dé·ric** (frā·dā·rēk′), *Ger.* **Frie·drich** (frē′drikh), *Sp.* **Fe·de·ri·co** (fā′dā·rē′·kō). Dims. **Fred, Fred′die, Fred′dy, Fritz.**

Fritz (frits) Ger. dim. of FREDERICK.

Ga·bri·el (gā′brē·əl; *Fr.* gà·brē·el′; *Ger.* gä′brē·el) Man of God. [< Hebrew] Dim. **Gabe** (gāb).

Ga·ma·li·el (gə·mā′lē·əl, -māl′yəl) Reward of God. [< Hebrew]

Gar·di·ner (gärd′nər, gär′də·nər) From an English surname. Also **Gar′de·ner, Gard′ner.**

Gar·ret (gar′it) Var. of GERARD. Also **Gar′rett.**

Gar·y (gâr′ē) Dim. of GARRET.

Gas·par (gas′pər) Var. of CASPER. Also *Fr.* **Gas·pard** (gàs·pär′).

Gas·ton (gas′tən; *Fr.* gàs·tôn′) Meaning uncertain.

Gau·tier (gō·tyā′) Fr. form of WALTER.

Gene (jēn) Dim. of EUGENE.

Geof·frey (jef′rē) English form of Fr. *Geoffroi*; var. of GODFREY. Dim. **Jeff.**

George (jôrj) Earthworker; farmer. [< Gk.] Also *Fr.* **Georges** (zhôrzh), *Ger.* **Ge·org** (gā·ôrkh′), *Ital.* **Gior·gio** (jôr′·jō), *Russ.* **Ge·or·gi** (gyi·ôr′gyi). Dim. **Georg′ie, Geor′die.**

Ger·ald (jer′əld) Spear ruler. [< Gmc.] Also *Fr.* **Gé·raud** (zhā·rō′) or **Gi·raud** (zhē·rō′). Dims. **Ger′ry, Jer′ry.**

Ge·rard (ji·rärd′; *Brit.* jer′ärd) Hard spear. [< Gmc.] Also *Fr.* **Gé·rard** (zhā·ràr′), *Ger.* **Ger·hard** (gār′härt). Dims. **Ger′ry, Jer′ry.**

Ge·ro·ni·mo (jā·rô′nē·mō) Ital. form of JEROME.

Gia·co·mo (jä′kō·mō) Ital. form of JAMES.

Gid·e·on (gid′ē·ən) Hewer. [< Hebrew]

Gi·e·ron·y·mus (jē′ə·ron′i·məs) Lat. form of JEROME.

Gif·ford (gif′ərd, jif′-) Meaning uncertain. [< Gmc.]

Gil·bert (gil′bərt; *Fr.* zhēl·bâr′) Bright wish. [< Gmc.] Dims. **Bert, Gil.**

Giles (jīlz) From the name of the goddess Athena's shield; hence, shield or protection. [< OF < Gk.]

Gio·van·ni (jō·vän′nē) Ital. form of JOHN.

Giu·lio (jo͞o′lyō) Ital. form of JULIUS.

Giu·sep·pe (jo͞o·zep′pā) Ital. form of JOSEPH.

Glenn (glen) From a Celtic surname; orig. a place name. Also **Glen.**

God·dard (god′ərd) Divine resoluteness. [< Gmc.]

God·frey (god′frē) Peace of God. [< Gmc.] Also *Ger.* **Gott·fried** (gôt′frēt).

God·win (god′win) Friend of God. [OE]

Gor·don (gôr′dən) From a Scot. surname.

Gra·ham (grā′əm) From an English surname; orig. a place name.

Grant (grant) From a Norman Fr. surname.

Greg·o·ry (greg′ər·ē) Vigilant. [< Gk.] Dim. **Greg.**

Grif·fin (grif′in) Var. of GRIFFITH.

Grif·fith (grif′ith) Red-haired. [< Celtic]

Gro·ver (grō′vər) Grove-dweller. [< Gmc.]

Gual·te·ri·o (gwäl·tā′rē·ō) Sp. form of WALTER.

Gu·gliel·mo (go͞o·lyel′mō) Ital. form of WILLIAM.

Guil·laume (gē·yōm′) Fr. form of WILLIAM.

Guil·ler·mo (gē·lyer′mō, gē·yer′mō) Sp. form of WILLIAM.

Gus (gus) Dim. of AUGUSTUS or GUSTAVUS.

Guy (gī; *Fr.* gē) Leader [< F < Gmc.] Also *Ital.* **Gui·do** (gwē′dō).

Hal (hal) Dim. of HAROLD or HENRY.

Ham·il·ton (ham′əl·tən) From a surname.

Hank (hangk) Dim. of HENRY.

Han·ni·bal (han′ə·bəl) Grace of Baal. [< Phoenician]

Hans (häns) Ger. dim. of JOHANNES. See JOHN.

Har·ley (här′lē) From an English surname; orig. a place name.

Har·old (har′əld) Chief of the army. [OE < Scand.] Dim. **Hal.**

Har·ry (har′ē) Dim. of HAROLD or var. of HENRY.

Har·vey (här′vē) Army battle. [< F < Gmc.]

Hec·tor (hek′tər) He who holds fast; defender. [< Gk.]

Hen·ry (hen′rē) Home ruler. [< F < Gmc.] Also *Du.* **Hen·drik** (hen′drik), *Fr.* **Hen·ri** (äṅ·rē′), *Ger.* **Hein·rich** (hīn′rikh). Dims. **Hal, Hank, Har′ry, Hen.**

Her·bert (hûr′bərt) Glory of the army. [OE] Dims. **Bert, Bert′ie, Herb.**

Her·man (hûr′mən) Man of the army. [< Gmc.] Also *Ger.* **Her·mann** (her′män).

Her·mes (hûr′mēz) Of the earth. [< Gk.]

Her·nan·do (er·nän′dō) Sp. form of FERDINAND.

Hez·e·ki·ah (hez′ə·kī′ə) God strengthens. [< Hebrew]

Hil·a·ry (hil′ər·ē) Joyful. [< L] Also *Fr.* **Hi·laire** (ē·lâr′).

Hi·ram (hī′rəm) Honored brother. [< Hebrew] Dims. **Hi, Hy.**

Ho·bart (hō′bərt, -bärt) Var. of HUBERT.

Hodge (hoj) Dim. of ROGER. Also **Hodg′kin.**

Ho·mer (hō′mər) Pledge, or blind one. [< Gk.]

Ho·no·ré (ô·nô·rā′) Honored. [< F < L]

Hor·ace (hôr′is, hor′-) Var. of HORATIO.

Ho·ra·ti·o (hə·rā′shē·ō, -shō) From the name of a Roman clan.

Ho·se·a (hō·zē′ə, -zā′ə) Salvation. [< Hebrew]

How·ard (hou′ərd) From an English surname. Dim. **How′ie.**

Hu·bert (hyo͞o′bərt) Bright spirit or mind. [< F < Gmc.]

Hugh (hyo͞o) Mind; intelligence. [< OF < Gmc.] Also **Hu·go** (hyo͞o′gō), *Fr.* **Hugues** (üg). Dim. **Hugh′ie.**

Hum·bert (hum′bərt) Bright support. [< OF < Gmc.]

Hum·phrey (hum′frē) Peaceful stake or support. [< OF < Gmc.] Also **Hum′frey, Hum′phry.**

I·an (ē′ən, ī′ən) Scot. form of JOHN.

Ich·a·bod (ik′ə·bod) ? Inglorious. [< Hebrew]

Ig·na·ti·us (ig·nā′shē·əs, -shəs) Fiery. [< Gk.] Also *Fr.* **I·gnace** (ē·nyàs′), *Ger.* **Ig·naz** (ig′näts), *Ital.* **I·gna·zio** (ē·nyä′tsyō).

Im·man·u·el (i·man′yo͞o·əl) God with us. [< Hebrew]

I·ra (ī′rə) Vigilant. [< Hebrew]

Ir·ving (ûr′ving) From a Scot. surname; orig. a place name. Also **Ir·vin** (ûr′vin).

Ir·win (ûr′win) Var. of IRVING.

I·saac (ī′zək) Laughter. [< Hebrew] Dim. **Ike** (īk).

I·sa·iah (ī·zā′ə, ī·zī′ə) Salvation of God. [< Hebrew]

Is·i·dore (iz′ə·dôr, -dōr) Gift of Isis. [< Gk.] Also **Is′a·dore, Is′a·dor, Is′i·dor.** Dim. **Iz·zy** (iz′ē).

Is·ra·el (iz′rē·əl) Contender with God. [< Hebrew]

I·van (ī′vən; *Russ.* i·vän′) Russ. form of JOHN.

Ja·bez (jā′biz) Sorrow. [< Hebrew]

Jack (jak) English form of Fr. **Jacques**; dim. of JOHN.

Ja·cob (jā′kəb) He who seizes by the heel; hence, successor. [< LL < Hebrew] Also *Ger.* **Ja·kob** (yä′kôb). Dims. **Jack, Jake** (jāk), **Jock** (jok).

Jacques (zhàk) Fr. form of JACOB. [< OF < LL]

James (jāmz) English form of Sp. *Jaime*; var. of JACOB. [< Sp. < LL] Also *Sp.* **Jai·me** (hī′mā). Dims. **Jam·ie** (jā′mē), **Jem, Jem′my, Jim, Jim′mie, Jim′my.**

Jan (yän) Du., Ger., and Pol. form of JOHN.

Já·nos (yä′nōsh) Hung. form of JOHN.

Ja·pheth (jā′fith) Enlarged; hence, powerful or honored. [< Hebrew] Also **Ja′phet** (-fit).

Jar·ed (jâr′id) Descent. [< Hebrew]

Jar·vis (jär′vis) From a Norman Fr. surname. Also **Jer·vis** (jûr′vis; *Brit.* jär′vis).

Ja·son (jā′sən) Healer. [< Gk.]

Jas·per (jas′pər) Treasury lord [< OF, ? < Persian], or from the name of the jewel.

Jay (jā) ? Jay bird. [? < OF]

Jean (jēn; *Fr.* zhäṅ) French form of JOHN.

Jef·frey (jef′rē) Var. of GEOFFREY. Dim. **Jeff.**

Je·hu (jē′hyo͞o) Jehovah is he. [< Hebrew]

Jeph·thah (jef′thə) Opposer. [< Hebrew]

Jer·e·mi·ah (jer′ə·mī′ə) God's chosen. [< Hebrew] Also **Jer·e·my** (jer′ə·mē). Dim. **Jer′ry.**

Je·rome (jə·rōm′; *Brit.* jer′əm) Holy name. [< Gk.] Also *Fr.* **Jé·rôme** (zhā·rôm′), *Sp.* **Je·ró·ni·mo** (hā·rō′nē·mō).

Jer·ry (jer′ē) Dim. of GERALD, GERARD, JEREMIAH, or JEROME.

Jes·se (jes′ē) Meaning uncertain. [< Hebrew] Also **Jess.**

Je·sus (jē′zəs) English form of Lat. *Josua*; var. of JOSHUA.

Jeth·ro (jeth′rō) Abundant or excellent. [< Hebrew]

Jim (jim) Dim. of JAMES. Also **Jim′mie, Jim′my.**

Jo·ab (jō′ab) Jehovah is father. [< Hebrew]

Jo·a·chim (jō′ə·kim) Jehovah will judge. [< Hebrew] Also *Sp.* **Joa·quín** (hwä·kēn′).

João (zhwouṅ) Pg. form of JOHN.

Job (jōb) Persecuted. [< Hebrew]

Jock (jok) Scot. form of JACK.

Joe (jō) Dim. of JOSEPH. Also **Jo′ey.**

Jo·el (jō′əl) Jehovah is God. [< Hebrew]

John (jon) God is good. [< Hebrew] Also *Ger.* **Jo·hann** (yō′hän) or **Jo·han·nes** (yō·hän′əs). Dims. **Jack, Jack′ie, Jack′y, Jock, John′nie, John′ny.**

Jon (jon) Var. of JOHN, or dim. of JONATHAN.

Jo·nah (jō′nə) Dove. [< Hebrew] Also **Jo·nas** (jō′nəs).

Jon·a·than (jon′ə·thən) God has given. [< Hebrew] Dims. **Jon, Jon′nie, Jon′ny.**

Jor·ge (*Pg.* zhôr′zhə; *Sp.* hôr′hā) Pg. and Sp. form of GEORGE.

Jo·seph (jō′zəf; *Fr.* zhō·zef′; *Ger.* yō′zef) God shall give (a son). [< Hebrew] Also *Lat.* **Jo·se·phus** (jō·sē′fəs), *Pg.*, *Sp.* **Jo·sé** (*Pg.* zho͞o·ze′; *Sp.* hō·sā′). Dims. **Jo, Joe, Jo′ey.**

Josh·u·a (josh′o͞o·ə) God is salvation. [< Hebrew] Also *Fr.* **Jo·sué** (zhō·zwā′), *Lat.* **Jos·u·a** (jos′o͞o·ə). Dim. **Josh.**

Jo·si·ah (jō·sī′ə) God supports. [< Hebrew] Also *Lat.* **Jo·si·as** (jō·sī′əs).

Jo·tham (jō′thəm) God is perfection. [< Hebrew]

Juan (hwän) Sp. form of JOHN.

Ju·dah (jo͞o′də) Praised. [< Hebrew] Also **Jude** (jo͞od; *Fr.* zhüd), *Lat.* **Ju·das** (jo͞o′dəs).

Jules (jo͞olz; *Fr.* zhül) Fr. form of JULIUS.

Jul·ian (jo͞ol′yən) Var. of JULIUS.

Jul·ius (jo͞ol′yəs) Downy-bearded; youthful: from the name of a Roman clan. Also *Sp.* **Ju·lio** (ho͞o′lyō). Dims. **Jule** (jo͞ol), **Jul·ie** (jo͞o′lē).

Jun·ius (jo͞on′yəs, jo͞o′nē·əs) Youthful: from the name of a Roman clan.

Jus·tin (jus′tin) Just. [< L] Also **Jus·tus** (jus′təs).

Karl (kärl) Ger. form of CHARLES.
Kas·par (käs′pär) Ger. form of JASPER.
Keith (kēth) From a Scot. surname; orig. a place name.
Kel·vin (kel′vin) From a Celtic surname.
Ken·neth (ken′ith) Handsome. [< Celtic] Dims. **Ken, Ken′nie, Ken′ny.**
Kent (kent) From an English surname; orig. a place name.
Kev·in (kev′ən) Handsome birth. [< Celtic]
Kit (kit) Dim. of CHRISTOPHER.
Kon·rad (kôn′rät) Ger. form of CONRAD.

La·ban (lā′bən) White. [< Hebrew]
La·fay·ette (lä′fē·et′, laf′ē·et′; *Fr.* là·fà·yet′) From a Fr. surname. Dim. **Lafe** (lāf).
Lam·bert (lam′bərt) The land's brightness. [< F < Gmc.]
Lance (lans, läns) Of the land. [< Gmc.]
Lan·ce·lot (lan′sə·lot, län′-; *Fr.* läṅ·slō′) Fr. dim. of LANCE. Also **Laun·ce·lot** (lôn′sə·lot, lan′-, län′-).
Lars (lärz; *Sw.* lärs) Sw. form of LAURENCE.
Lau·rence (lôr′əns, lor′-) Laureled; hence, prophetic or poetic. [< L] Also **Law′rence,** *Fr.* **Lau·rent** (lō·räṅ′), *Ger.* **Lo·renz** (lō′rents). Dims. **Lar·ry** (lar′ē), **Lau·rie** or **Law·rie** (lôr′ē)
Laz·a·rus (laz′ə·rəs) God has helped. [< Hebrew] Also *Fr.* **La·zare** (là·zàr′), *Ital.* **Laz·za·ro** (läd′dzä·rō).
Le·an·der (lē·an′dər) Lion man. [< Gk.]
Lee (lē) From an English surname.
Leif (lēf) Loved one. [< Scand.]
Leigh (lē) From an English surname.
Lem·u·el (lem′yo͞o·əl) Belonging to God. [< Hebrew] Dim. **Lem.**
Le·o (lē′ō) Lion. [< L < Gk.]
Le·on (lē′on, -ən) Lion. [< L < Gk.] Also *Fr.* **Lé·on** (lā·ôṅ′).
Leon·ard (len′ərd) Lion-strong. [< Gmc.] Also *Fr.* **Lé·o·nard** (lā·ō·nàr′), *Ger.* **Le·on·hard** (lā′ōn·härt), *Ital.* **Le·o·nar·do** (lā′ō·när′dō). Dims. **Len, Len′ny.**
Le·on·i·das (lē·on′ə·dəs) Lionlike. [< Gk.]
Le·o·pold (lē′ə·pōld; *Ger.* lā′ō·pōlt) The people's strong one. [< Gmc.]
Le·roy (lə·roi′, lē′roi) Royal. [< OF]
Les·lie (les′lē, lez′-) From an English surname. Dim. **Les.**
Les·ter (les′tər) From an English surname; orig. the place name *Leicester.* Dim. **Les.**
Le·vi (lē′vī) He who unites. [< Hebrew]
Lew·is (lo͞o′is) Var. of LOUIS. Dims. **Lew, Lew′ie.**
Lin·coln (ling′kən) From an English surname.
Li·nus (lī′nəs) Meaning uncertain. [< Gk.]
Li·o·nel (lī′ə·nəl, -nel) Young lion. [< F < L]
Lisle (līl) Var. of LYLE.
Llew·el·lyn (lo͞o·el′ən) Meaning uncertain. [< Welsh]
Lloyd (loid) Gray. [< Welsh]
Lo·ren·zo (lə·ren′zō; *Ital.* lō·ren′tsō; *Sp.* lō·rān′thō) Var. of LAURENCE.
Lot (lot) Veiled. [< Hebrew] Also **Lott.**
Lou·is (lo͞o′is, lo͞o′ē; *Fr.* lwē) War famous. [< OF < Gmc.] Also **Lew′is,** *Du.* **Lo·de·wijk** (lō′də·vīk), *Ger.* **Lud·wig** (lo͞ot′·vikh), *Ital.* **Lu·i·gi** (lo͞o·ē′jē), or **Lo·do·vi·co** (lō′dō·vē′kō), *Pg.* **Lu·iz** (lo͞o·ēsh′), *Sp.* **Lu·is** (lo͞o·ēs′). Dims. **Lew, Lou.**
Low·ell (lō′əl) Beloved. [OE] Also **Lov·ell** (luv′əl).
Lu·cas (lo͞o′kəs) Light. [< L]
Lu·cian (lo͞o′shən) Var. of LUCIUS. [< L *Lucianus*] Also **Lu·cien** (lo͞o′shən; *Fr.* lü·syaṅ′).
Lu·ci·fer (lo͞o′sə·fər) Light-bearer. [< L]
Lu·cius (lo͞o′shəs) Light. [< L]
Lu·cre·tius (lo͞o·krē′shəs, -shē·əs) Shining or wealthy. [< L]
Luke (lo͝ok) English form of LUCAS.
Lu·ther (lo͞o′thər) Famous warrior. [< Gmc.] Also *Fr.* **Lo·thaire** (lô·târ′), *Ital.* **Lo·ta·rio** (lo·tä′ryō).

Mac (mak) Son. [< Celtic] Also **Mack.**
Mal·a·chi (mal′ə·kī) Messenger. [< Hebrew]
Mal·colm (mal′kəm) Servant of (St.) Columba. [< Celtic]
Ma·nu·el (mä·nwel′) Sp. form of IMMANUEL.
Mar·cel·lus (mär·sel′əs) Dim. of MARCUS. Also *Fr.* **Mar·cel** (màr·sel′), *Ital.* **Mar·cel·lo** (mär·chel′lō).
Mar·cus (mär′kəs) Of Mars. [< L]
Mar·i·on (mar′ē·ən, mâr′-) Of Mary. [< F]
Mark (märk) English form of MARCUS. Also *Fr.* **Marc** (màrk), *Ital.* **Mar·co** (mär′kō).
Mar·ma·duke (mär′mə·do͞ok, -dyo͞ok) Meaning uncertain. [? < Celtic]
Mar·shal (mär′shəl) From the title. [< Gmc.] Also **Mar′shall.**
Mar·tin (mär′tən; *Fr.* màr·taṅ′; *Ger.* mär′tēn) Of Mars. [< L] Dims. **Mart, Mar′ty.**
Mar·vin (mär′vin) Sea friend. [< Gmc.]
Ma·son (mā′sən) Stoneworker. [< Gmc.]
Mat·thew (math′yo͞o) Gift of God. [< Hebrew] *Fr.* **Ma·thieu** (mà·tyœ′), *Ital.* **Mat·te·o** (mät·tā′ō), *Sp.* **Ma·te·o** (mä·tā′ō). Dims. **Mat, Matt.**
Mat·thi·as (mə·thī′əs) Var. of MATTHEW. [< Gk.]
Mau·rice (mə·rēs′, môr′is, mor′is; *Fr.* mô·rēs′) Moorish; dark. [< F < L]
Max (maks; *Ger.* mäks) Dim. of MAXIMILIAN.
Max·i·mil·ian (mak′sə·mil′yən; *Ger.* mäk′sē·mē′lē·än) Prob. coined by Frederick III from the Roman names *Maximus* and *Aemilianus.* Dim. **Max.**
May·nard (mā′nərd, -närd) Powerful strength. [< Gmc.]
Mel·vin (mel′vin) High protector. [OE] Dim. **Mel.**
Mer·e·dith (mer′ə·dith) Sea protector. [< Welsh]
Mer·vin (mûr′vin) Var. of MARVIN.
Mi·cah (mī′kə) Who is like God? [< Hebrew]
Mi·chael (mī′kəl; *Ger.* mi′khä·el) Who is like God? [< Hebrew] Also *Fr.* **Mi·chel** (mē·shel′), *Ital.* **Mi·che·le** (mē·kâ′·lā), *Sp., Pg.* **Mi·guel** (mē·gel′). Dims. **Mike** (mīk), **Mick·ey** or **Mick·y** (mik′ē), **Mik·ey** (mī′kē).
Mi·klós (mi′klōsh) Hung. form of NICHOLAS.
Miles (mīlz) Meaning uncertain. [< Gmc.] Also **Myles.**
Mi·lo (mī′lō; *Ital.* mē′lō) Ital. var. of MILES.
Mil·ton (mil′tən) From an English surname; orig. a place name. [< Gmc.] Dim. **Milt.**
Mitch·ell (mich′əl) Var. of MICHAEL. Dim. **Mitch.**
Mon·roe (mən·rō′, *Brit.* mun′rō) From a Celtic surname; orig. a place name.
Mon·ta·gue (mon′tə·gyo͞o) From a Norman Fr. surname; orig. a place name. Dim. **Mon′ty.**
Mont·gom·er·y (mont·gum′ər·ē) From a Norman Fr. surname; orig. a place name. Dim. **Mon′ty.**
Mor·gan (môr′gən) Sea-dweller. [< Welsh]
Mor·ris (môr′is, mor′-) Var. of MAURICE.
Mor·ti·mer (môr′tə·mər) From a Norman Fr. surname; orig. a place name. Dims. **Mort, Mor′ty.**
Mor·ton (môr′tən) From an English surname; orig. a place name. Dim. **Mort, Mor′ty.**
Mo·ses (mō′zis, -ziz) ? Son. [< Hebrew, ? < Egyptian] Dim. **Moe** (mō), **Moi·she** (moi′shə), **Mose** (mōz).
Moss (môs, mos) Var. of MOSES.
Mur·dock (mûr′dok) Seaman. [< Celtic] Also **Mur′doch.**
Mur·ray (mûr′ē) From a Scot. surname, or var. of MAURICE.
Myles (mīlz) Var. of MILES.

Na·hum (nā′əm) Consolation. [< Hebrew]
Na·po·le·on (nə·pō′lē·ən) Of the new city. [< F < Gk.] Also *Fr.* **Na·po·lé·on** (nà·pô·lā·ôṅ′), *Ital.* **Na·po·le·o·ne** (nä·pō′lā·ō′nā).
Na·than (nā′thən) Gift. [< Hebrew] Dims. **Nat** (nat), **Nate** (nāt).
Na·than·iel (nə·than′yəl) Gift of God. [< Hebrew] Also **Na·than′a·el.** Dims. **Nat, Nate.**
Ned (ned) Dim. of EDGAR, EDMUND, or EDWARD. Also **Ned′dy.**
Ne·he·mi·ah (nē′hə·mī′ə) Comfort of God. [< Hebrew]
Neil (nēl) Champion. [< Celtic] Also **Neal.**
Nel·son (nel′sən) Neal's son: from an English surname.
Ne·ro (nir′ō) Strong: from the name of a Roman clan.
Nev·ille (nev′il, -əl) From a Norman Fr. surname; orig. a place name. Also **Nev′il, Nev′ile, Nev′ill.**
New·ton (no͞ot′n, nyo͞ot′n) From an English surname; orig. a place name.
Nich·o·las (nik′ə·ləs) The people's victory. [< Gk.] Also **Nic′o·las,** *Fr.* **Ni·co·las** (nē·kô·lä′), *Ital.* **Nic·co·lò** (nēk′kō·lô′), *Lat.* **Ni·co·la·us** (nik′ō·lā′əs), *Russ.* **Ni·ko·lai** (nyi·kə·lī′), *Sp.* **Ni·co·lás** (nē′kō·läs′). Dims. **Nick, Nick′y.**
Ni·gel (nī′jəl) Noble. [< Celtic]
No·ah (nō′ə) Comfort. [< Hebrew]
No·el (nō′əl) Christmas. [< OF < L] Also *Fr.* **No·ël** (nō·el′).
Nor·bert (nôr′bərt) Brightness of Njord. [< Gmc.]
Nor·man (nôr′mən) Northman. [< Scand.] Dim. **Norm.**

O·ba·di·ah (ō′bə·dī′ə) Servant of God. [< Hebrew]
Oc·ta·vi·us (ok·tā′vē·əs) The eighth (born). [< L]
O·laf (ō′ləf; *Dan., Norw.* ō′läf; *Sw.* o͞o′läf) Ancestor's heirloom. Also **O′lav** [< Scand.]
Ol·i·ver (ol′ə·vər) Of the olive tree. [< F < L] Dims. **Ol′lie, Ol′ly.**
Or·lan·do (ôr·lan′dō; *Ital.* ôr·län′dō) Ital. form of ROLAND.
Os·bert (oz′bərt) Divine brilliance. [OE]
Os·car (os′kər) Divine spear. [OE]
Os·wald (oz′wəld, -wôld) Divine power. [OE] Also **Os′·wold.**
Ot·to (ot′ō; *Ger.* ôt′ō) Rich. [< Gmc.]
O·wen (ō′ən) Young warrior [< Welsh]

Pat·rick (pat′rik) Patrician; aristocratic. [< L] Dims. **Pad′dy, Pat, Pat′sy.**
Paul (pôl; *Fr.* pôl; *Ger.* poul) Little: from a given name of the Aemiliani, a Roman clan. Also *Ital.* **Pa·o·lo** (pä′ō·lō), *Lat.* **Pau·li·nus** (pô·lī′nəs) or **Pau·lus** (pô′ləs), *Pg.* **Pau·lo** (pou′lo͞o), *Sp.* **Pa·blo** (pä′vlō).

Per·ci·val (pûr′sə·vəl) Meaning uncertain. [< OF] Also **Per′ce·val.**
Per·cy (pûr′sē) From a Norman Fr. surname; orig. a place name.
Per·ry (per′ē) Of the pear tree: from an English surname.
Pe·ter (pē′tər; *Du., Ger., Norw., Sw.* pā′tər) A rock. [< Gk.] Also *Dan.* **Pe·der** (pā′thər), *Du.* **Pie·ter** (pē′tər), *Fr.* **Pierre** (pyâr), *Modern Gk.* **Pe·tros** (pâ′trôs), *Ital.* **Pie·tro** (pyâ′trō), *Pg., Sp.* **Pe·dro** (*Pg.* pā′thrōō; *Sp.* pā′thrō), *Russ.* **Pëtr** (pyô′tər). Dim. **Pete.**
Phi·lan·der (fi·lan′dər) Lover of men. [< Gk.]
Phi·le·mon (fi·lē′mən) Loving. [< Gk.]
Phil·ip (fil′ip) Lover of horses. [< Gk.] Also *Fr.* **Phi·lippe** (fē·lēp′), *Ger.* **Phi·lipp** (fē′lip). Dims. **Phil, Pip.**
Phin·e·as (fin′ē·əs) Mouth of brass: prob. an oracular priest's title. [< Hebrew]

Quen·tin (kwen′tin) The fifth (born). [< L] Also **Quin·tin** (kwin′tən).
Quin·cy (kwin′sē) ? var. of QUENTIN. [< OF]
Ralph (ralf; *Brit.* rāf) Wolf-wise. [< Gmc.] *Fr.* **Ra·oul** (rȧ·ōōl′).
Ran·dal (ran′dəl) Shield wolf. [OE] Also **Ran′dall.**
Ran·dolph (ran′dolf) Shield wolf. [OE] Dim. **Ran′dy.**
Ra·pha·el (rā′fē·əl, raf′ē·əl) God has healed. [< Hebrew]
Ray (rā) Dim. of RAYMOND.
Ray·mond (rā′mənd; *Fr.* rā·môṅ′) Wise protection. [< Gmc.] Also **Ray′mund,** *Sp.* **Rai·mun·do** (rī·mōōn′dō) or **Ra·món** (rä·mōn′). Dim. **Ray.**
Reg·i·nald (rej′ə·nəld) Judicial ruler. [< Gmc.] Also *Fr.* **Re·gnault** (rə·nyō′) or **Re·naud** (rə·nō′), *Ital.* **Ri·nal·do** (rē·näl′dō), *Sp.* **Rey·nal·do** (rā·näl′thō). Dims. **Reg** (rej), **Reg′gie, Rex.**
Re·né (rə·nā′) Reborn. [< F < L]
Reu·ben (rōō′bin) Behold, a son! [< Hebrew] Dim. **Rube.**
Rex (reks) King [< L], or dim. of REGINALD.
Rey·nard (rā′nərd, ren′ərd) Brave judgment. [< Gmc.]
Reyn·old (ren′əld) Var. of REGINALD. [< OF]
Rich·ard (rich′ərd; *Fr.* rē·shȧr′; *Ger.* rikh′ärt) Strong king. [< OF < Gmc.] Also *Ital.* **Ric·car·do** (rēk·kär′dō), *Sp.* **Ri·car·do** (rē·kär′thō). Dims. **Dick, Dick′ie, Dick′y, Rich, Rich′ie, Rick, Rick′y.**
Ro·ald (rō′äl) Famous power. [< Norw. < Gmc.]
Rob·ert (rob′ərt; *Fr.* rô·bâr′) Bright fame. [< Gmc.] Also *Ital., Sp.* **Ro·ber·to** (rō·ber′tō). Dims. **Bob, Bob′by, Dob, Dob′bin, Rob, Rob′bie, Rob′in.**
Rod·er·ick (rod′ər·ik) Famous king. [< Gmc.] Also **Rod′er·ic, Rod·rick** (rod′rik), *Fr.* **Ro·drigue** (rô·drēg′), *Ital., Sp.* **Ro·dri·go** (*Ital.* rō·drē′gō; *Sp.* rō·thrē′gō). Dims. **Rod, Rod′dy.**
Rod·ney (rod′nē) From an English surname; orig. a place name. Dim. **Rod.**
Ro·dolph (rō′dolf) Var. of RUDOLPH. Also **Ro·dol·phus** (rō·dol′fəs).
Rog·er (roj′ər; *Fr.* rô·zhā′) Famous spear. [< OF < Gmc.] Dims. **Hodge, Hodg′kin, Rodge.**
Ro·land (rō′lənd; *Fr.* rô·läṅ′) Country's fame. [< Celtic < Gmc.] Also **Row′land.**
Rolf (rolf) Dim. of RUDOLPH. Also **Rolph.**
Rol·lo (rol′ō) Dim. of RUDOLPH.
Ron·ald (ron′əld; *Norw.* rō·näl′) Old Norse form of REGINALD.
Ro·ry (rôr′ē, rō′rē) Red. [< Celtic]
Ros·coe (ros′kō) From an English surname; orig. a place name.
Ross (rôs) From an English surname; orig. a place name.
Roy (roi) King. [< OF]
Ru·dolph (rōō′dolf) Famous wolf. [< Gmc.] Also **Ru′dolf, Ru·dol·phus** (rōō·dol′fəs), *Fr.* **Ro·dolphe** (rô·dôlf′), *Ital.* **Ro·dol·pho** (rō·dôl′fō), *Sp.* **Ro·dol·fo** (rō·thôl′fō). Dims. **Rol′lo, Ru′dy.**
Ru·fus (rōō′fəs) Red-haired. [< L] Dim. **Rufe.**
Ru·pert (rōō′pərt) Var. of ROBERT. [< G] Also *Ger.* **Ru·precht** (rōō′prekht).
Rus·sell (rus′əl) Red: from an English surname. [OE < OF] Dim. **Russ.**

Sal·o·mon (sal′ə·mən) Var. of SOLOMON.
Sam·son (sam′sən) The sun. [< Hebrew] Also **Samp′son** (samp′sən, sam′-).
Sam·u·el (sam′yōō·əl) Name of God. [< Hebrew] Dims. **Sam, Sam′my.**
San·dy (san′dē) Dim. of ALEXANDER. Also **San·der** (san′dər, sän′-).
Saul (sôl) Asked (of God). [< Hebrew]
Schuy·ler (skī′lər) Shelter. [< Du.]
Scott (skot) The Scot: from an English surname.
Seam·us (shā′məs) Irish form of JAMES.
Sean (shôn, shan) Irish form of JOHN.
Se·bas·tian (si·bas′chən) Venerable. [< Gk.]
Seth (seth) Appointed. [< Hebrew]
Sew·ard (sōō′ərd) ? Sow-herder: from an English surname.
Sey·mour (sē′môr, -mōr) From an English surname; orig. a place name. Dims. **Cy, Sy.**
Shawn (shôn) Irish form of JOHN. Also **Shaun.**
Shel·don (shel′dən) From an English surname; orig. a place name.
Shir·ley (shûr′lē) From an English surname; orig. a place name.
Sid·ney (sid′nē) St. Denis: from an English surname. Dim. **Sid.**
Sieg·fried (sēg′frēd; *Ger.* zēk′frēt) Victorious peace. [< Gmc.]
Sig·is·mund (sij′əs·mənd, sig′-) Victorious protection. [< Gmc.]
Sig·mund (sig′mənd; *Ger.* zekh′mōōnt) Var. of SIGISMUND.
Si·las (sī′ləs) Meaning uncertain. [< Gk.] Dim. **Si** (sī).
Sil·va·nus (sil·vā′nəs) From the name of the Roman god of woods and crops.
Sil·ves·ter (sil·ves′tər) Of the woods; rustic. [< L]
Sim·e·on (sim′ē·ən) He who is heard (widely); hence, famous. [< Hebrew] Dim. **Sim** (sim).
Si·mon (sī′mən) Var. of SIMEON.
Sin·clair (sin·klâr′, sin′klâr) St. Clair: from a Norman Fr. surname.
Sol·o·mon (sol′ə·mən) Peaceful. [< Hebrew] Dim. **Sol.**
Stan·ley (stan′lē) From an English surname; orig. a place name. Dim. **Stan.**
Ste·phen (stē′vən) Crown. [< Gk.] Also **Ste′ven,** *Ger.* **Ste·phan** or **Ste·fan** (shte′fän), *Ital.* **Ste·fa·no** (stā′fä·nō), *Russ.* **Ste·pan** (styi·pän′). Dims. **Steve, Ste′vie.**
Stew·art (stōō′ərt, styōō′-) Steward: from an English surname. Also **Stu′art.** Dims. **Stew, Stu.**
Sum·ner (sum′nər) Summoner: from an English surname.
Syd·ney (sid′nē) Var. of SIDNEY.
Syl·va·nus (sil·vā′nəs) Var. of SILVANUS.
Syl·ves·ter (sil·ves′tər) Var. of SILVESTER.

Taf·fy (taf′ē) Welsh dim. of DAVID.
Tad (tad) Dim. of THEODORE or THADDEUS.
Ted (ted) Dim. of EDWARD or THEODORE. Also **Ted′dy.**
Ter·ence (ter′əns) From the name of a Roman clan. Also **Ter′rence.** Dim. **Ter′ry.**
Thad·de·us (thad′ē·əs) Praised. [< Aramaic] Dims. **Tad, Thad, Tha′dy, Thad′dy.**
The·o·bald (thē′ə·bôld, tib′əld) The people's brave one. [< Gmc.]
The·o·dore (thē′ə·dôr, -dōr) Gift of God. [< Gk.] Also *Fr.* **Thé·o·dore** (tā·ô·dôr′), *Ger.* **The·o·dor** (tā′ō·dôr), *Modern Gk.* **The·o·do·ros** (thâ·ô′thô·rôs), *Ital., Sp.* **Te·o·do·ro** (*Ital.* tā′ō·dô′rō; *Sp.* tā′ō·thō′rō). Dims. **Tad, Ted, Ted′dy, Dode** (dōd).
Thom·as (tom′əs; *Fr.* tô·mä′; *Ger.* tō′mäs) Twin. [< Aramaic] Also *Ital.* **Tom·ma·so** (tōm·mä′zō), *Sp.* **To·más** (tō·mäs′). Dims. **Tom, Tom′my.**
Thurs·ton (thûrs′tən) Thor's stone. [< Scand.]
Tim·o·thy (tim′ə·thē) Honor of God. [< Gk.] Also *Fr.* **Ti·mo·thée** (tē·mô·tā′), *Ital.* **Ti·mo·te·o** (tē·mô′tā·ō). Dims. **Tim, Tim′my.**
Ti·tus (tī′təs) Meaning uncertain. [< L]
To·bi·as (tō·bī′əs) God is good. [< Hebrew] Also **To·bi·ah** (tō·bī′ə). Dim. **To·by** (tō′bē).
Tod (tod) Fox: from an English surname. Also **Todd.**
To·ny (tō′nē) Dim. of ANTHONY.
Tris·tan (tris′tän; -tən) Confusion. [< Celtic] Also **Tris·tram** (tris′trəm). Dim. **Tris.**
Tyb·alt (tib′əlt) Var. of THEOBALD.

U·lys·ses (yōō·lis′ēz) ? Hater: Lat. form of Gk. *Odysseus.*
Um·ber·to (ōōm·ber′tō) Ital. form of HUMBERT.
Ur·ban (ûr′bən) Of the city. [< L]
U·ri·ah (yōō·rī′ə) God is light. [< Hebrew] Also **U·ri·as** (yōō·rī′əs).
U·ri·el (yōōr′ē·əl) Light of God. [< Hebrew]

Val·en·tine (val′ən·tīn) Strong; healthy. [< L] Dim. **Val.**
Van (van) From an English surname, or from the Ger. or Du. name element *von, van,* indicating residence or origin.
Va·si·li (və·syē′lyē) Russ. var. of BASIL.
Ver·gil (vûr′jəl) Var. of VIRGIL.
Ver·non (vûr′nən) Meaning uncertain. [< L or F] Dim. **Vern.**
Vic·tor (vik′tər; *Fr.* vēk·tôr′) Conqueror. [< L] Also *Ital.* **Vit·to·rio** (vit·tô′ryō). Dims. **Vic, Vick.**
Vin·cent (vin′sənt; *Fr.* vaṅ·säṅ′) Conquering. [< L] Also *Ger.* **Vin·cenz** (vin′tsents), *Ital.* **Vin·cen·zo** (vēn·chen′tsō), *Sp.* **Vi·cen·te** (vē·thān′tā). Dims. **Vin, Vince, Vin′ny.**
Vir·gil (vûr′jəl) Flourishing: from the name of a Roman clan. Also **Ver′gil.** Dims. **Virge, Vir′gie.**
Viv·i·an (viv′ē·ən, viv′yən) Lively. [< F] Also **Viv·i·en** (viv′ē·ən; *Fr.* vē·vyaṅ′).

Wal·do (wôl′dō, wol′-) Ruler. [< Gmc.]
Wal·lace (wol′is) Welsh(man): from a Scot. surname. Also **Wal′lis.** Dim. **Wal′ly.**
Wal·ter (wôl′tər; *Ger.* väl′tər) Ruler of the army. [< Gmc.] Also *Ger.* **Wal·ther** (väl′tər). Dims. **Walt, Wal′ly.**
Ward (wôrd) Guard: from an English surname.
War·ren (wôr′ən, wor′-) From an English surname.
Wayne (wān) From an English surname. [? < Celtic]
Wes·ley (wes′lē; *Brit.* wez′lē) From an English surname; orig. a place name. Dim. **Wes.**
Wil·bur (wil′bər) Bright will. [< Gmc.] Also **Wil′ber.**
Wil·fred (wil′frid) Resolute peace. [< Gmc.] Also **Wil′·frid.** Dim. **Fred.**
Wil·lard (wil′ərd) From an English surname.
Wil·liam (wil′yəm) Resolute protection. [< Gmc.] Also *Du.* **Wil·lem** (vil′əm), *Ger.* **Wil·helm** (vil′helm). Dims. **Bill, Bil′ly, Will, Wil′lie, Wil′ly.**
Wil·lis (wil′is) Willie's son: from an English surname.
Win·fred (win′frid) Friend of peace. [OE] Also **Win′frid.** Dims. **Win, Win′nie.**
Win·ston (win′stən) From an English surname; orig. a place name.
Wy·att (wī′ət) Dim. of GUY. [< OF]
Wys·tan (wis′tən) Battle stone. [OE]

Zach·a·ri·ah (zak′ə·rī′ə) Remembrance of God. [< Hebrew] Also **Zach·a·ri·as** (zak′ə·rī′əs). Dims. **Zach** (zak), **Zack.**
Zach·a·ry (zak′ər·ē) Var. of ZACHARIAH.
Zeb·a·di·ah (zeb′ə·dī′ə) Gift of God. [< Hebrew]
Zeb·e·dee (zeb′ə·dē) Contr. of ZEBADIAH.
Zech·a·ri·ah (zek′ə·rī′ə) Var. of ZACHARIAH.
Zeke (zēk) Dim. of EZEKIEL.
Zeph·a·ni·ah (zef′ə·nī′ə) Protected by God. [< Hebrew] Dim. **Zeph.**

FEMININE NAMES

Ab·i·gail (ab′ə·gāl) Father's joy. [< Hebrew] Dims. **Ab′·by, Ab′bie.**
A·da (ā′də) Joyful; flourishing. [< Gmc.]
A·dah (ā′də) Beauty. [< Hebrew] Also **A′da.**
Ad·e·la (ad′ə·lə; *Sp.* ä·thā′lä) Noble. [< Gmc.] Also **A·dele** (ə·del′), *Fr.* **A·dèle** (à·del′), *Ger.* **A·de·le** (ä·dā′lə).
Ad·e·laide (ad′ə·lād) Nobility. [< Gmc.] Also *Fr.* **A·dé·la·ïde** (à·dā·là·ēd′), *Ger.* **A·del·heid** (ä′dəl·hīt), *Ital.* **A·de·la·i·de** (ä′dā·lä′ē·dā). Dims. **Ad′die, Ad′dy.**
Ad·e·line (ad′ə·līn; *Fr.* àd·lēn′) Of noble birth. [< Gmc.] Also **Ad′a·line, Ad·e·li·cia** (ad′ə·lish′ə), **Ad·e·li·na** (ad′ə·lī′nə). Dims. **Ad′die, Ad′dy.**
A·dri·enne (ā′drē·en; *Fr.* à·drē·en′) Fem. of ADRIAN. [< F]
Ag·a·tha (ag′ə·thə) Good; kind. [< Gk.] Also *Fr.* **A·gathe** (à·gàt′), *Ger.* **A·ga·the** (ä·gä′tə). Dim. **Ag′gie.**
Ag·nes (ag′nis; *Ger.* äg′nes) Pure; sacred. [< Gk.] Also *Fr.* **A·gnès** (à·nyâs′). Dim. **Ag′gie.**
A·i·da (ä·ē′də, ā′də) From the heroine of Verdi's opera.
Ai·leen (ā·lēn′; *Irish* ī·lēn′) Var. of EILEEN.
Ai·mée (ā·mā′) French form of AMY.
Al·ber·ta (al·bûr′tə) Fem. of ALBERT. Also **Al·ber·ti·na** (al′bər·tē′nə), **Al·ber·tine** (al′bər·tēn).
Al·e·the·a (al′ə·thē′ə, ə·lē′thē·ə) Truth. [< Gk.]
Al·ex·an·dra (al′ig·zan′drə, -zän′-) Fem. of ALEXANDER. Also **Al·ex·an·dri·na** (al′ig·zan·drē′nə, -zän-), *Fr.* **A·lex·an·drine** (à·lek·säṅ·drēn′), *Ital.* **A·les·san·dra** (ä′läs·sän′drä), *Sp.* **A·le·jan·dra** (ä′lā·hän′drä) or **A·le·jan·dri·na** (ä′lā·hän·drē′nä). Dims. **A·lex·a** (ə·lek′sə), **Al·ex·in·a** (al′ig·zē′nə), **Al·ix** (al′iks), **San·dra** (san′drə).
A·lex·is (ə·lek′sis) Fem. of ALEX. Also **A·lex·i·a** (ə·lek′sē·ə).
Al·fre·da (al·frē′də) Fem. of ALFRED.
Al·ice (al′is; *Fr.* à·lēs′; *Ger.* ä·lē′sə; *Ital.* ä·lē′chā) Truth. [< OF < Gmc.] Also **Al′lis, Al′yce, Al′ys.** Dim. **Al′lie.**
A·li·cia (ə·lish′ə, ə·lish′ē·ə) Var. of ALICE. [< L]
A·line (ə·lēn′, al′ēn) Var. of ADELINE.
Al·i·son (al′ə·sən) Of sacred memory. [< Gmc.] Also **Al′li·son.**
Al·ix (al′iks) Dim. of ALEXANDRA.
Al·le·gra (ə·lā′grə) Spirited. [< Ital. < L]
Al·ma (al′mə) Providing; gracious. [< L]
Al·mi·ra (al·mī′rə) Lofty; princess. [< Arabic]
Al·the·a (al·thē′ə) Healer. [< Gk.]
Al·vi·na (al·vī′nə, al·vē′nə) Fem. of ALVIN.
Am·a·bel (am′ə·bel) Lovable. [< L] Also **Am′a·belle.** Dim. **Mab** (mab).
A·man·da (ə·man′də) Lovable. [< L] Also *Fr.* **A·man·dine** (à·mäṅ·dēn′). Dim. **Man′dy.**
Am·a·ran·tha (am′ə·ran′thə) Immortal. [< Gk.]
Am·a·ryl·lis (am′ə·ril′əs) Country sweetheart. [< L]
A·mel·ia (ə·mēl′yə, ə·mē′lē·ə; *Ital.* ä·mâ′lyä; *Sp.* ä·mā′lyä) Industrious. [< Gmc.] Also *Fr.* **A·mé·lie** (à·mā·lē′). Dim. **Mil′lie, Mil′ly.**
Am·i·ty (am′ə·tē) From the abstract noun.
A·my (ā′mē) Beloved. [< L]
An·as·ta·sia (an′ə·stā′zhə, -shə) Able to live again. [< L]
An·dre·a (an′drē·ə; *Ital.* än·drā′ä) Fem. of ANDREW.
An·ge·la (an′jə·lə) Angel. [< Gk.] Also **An·ge·li·na** (an′·jə·lē′nə, -lī′-), *Fr.* **An·gèle** (äṅ·zhel′).
An·gel·i·ca (an·jel′i·kə; *Ital.* än·jâ′lē·kä) Angelic. [< Gk.] Also *Fr.* **An·gé·lique** (äṅ·zhā·lēk′).
A·ni·ta (ə·nē′tə) Dim. of ANNA. [< Sp.] Also **A·ni·tra** (ə·nē′trə).
Ann (an) Grace. [< Hebrew] Also *Sp.* **A·na** (ä′nä). Dims. **An′nie, Nan, Nan′cy, Ni′na.**
An·na (an′ə; *Ger.* ä′nä) Var. of HANNAH. Dim. **An′nie.**
An·na·bel (an′ə·bel) Gracefully fair. [< Hebrew] Also **An·na·bel·la** (an′ə·bel′ə), **An′na·belle.**
Anne (an) Var. of ANN.
An·nette (ə·net′; *Fr.* à·net′) Dim. of ANNE. [< F]
An·the·a (an·thē′ə) Flowery. [< Gk.]
An·toi·nette (an′twə·net′; *Fr.* äṅ·twà·net′) Fr. form of ANTONIA. Also *Ital.* **An·to·niet·ta** (än′tō·nyet′tä). Dims. **Net′·tie, Net′ty, To′ni.**
An·to·ni·a (an·tō′nē·ə, an′tō·nē′ə) Fem. of ANTHONY. [< L] Also *Ital., Sp.* **An·to·ni·na** (än′tō·nē′nä).
A·pril (ā′prəl) From the name of the month.
Ar·i·ad·ne (ar′ē·ad′nē) Most pure. [< Gk.]
Ar·lene (är·lēn′) Meaning and origin uncertain. Also **Ar·leen** (är·lēn′), **Ar·line** (är·lēn′).
As·pa·sia (as·pā′zhə, -zhē·ə) Welcome. [< L < Gk.]
As·trid (as′trid) God's power. [< Scand.]
A·the·na (ə·thē′nə) From the name of the Greek goddess of wisdom. Also **A·the·ne** (ə·thē′nē).
Au·drey (ô′drē) Noble might. [< OF < Gmc.]
Au·gus·ta (ô·gus′tə; *Ger.* ou·go͞os′tä; *Ital.* ou·go͞os′tä) Fem. of AUGUSTUS. Also **Au·gus·ti·na** (ô′gəs·tē′nə), **Au·gus·tine** (ô′gəs·tēn). Dims. **Gus′sie, Gus′ta.**
Au·rel·ia (ô·rēl′yə) Golden. [< L]
Au·ro·ra (ô·rôr′ə, ô·rō′rə) From the name of the Roman goddess of the dawn.
A·va (ā′və) Meaning and origin uncertain.
Av·e·line (av′ə·lēn, -līn) Hazel. [< F]
A·vis (ā′vis) Bird. [< L]

Ba·bette (ba·bet′) Fr. dim. of ELIZABETH.
Bap·tis·ta (bap·tis′tə) Fem. of BAPTIST. Also *Ital.* **Bat·tis·ta** (bät·tēs′tä).
Bar·ba·ra (bär′bər·ə, -brə) Foreign; strange. [< Gk.] Dims. **Bab, Bab′bie, Babs, Barb, Bar′bie, Bob′bie.**
Bath·she·ba (bath·shē′bə, bath′shi·bə) Daughter of the promise. [< Hebrew]
Be·a·ta (bē·ā′tə) Blessed. [< L]
Be·a·trice (bē′ə·tris; *Ital.* bā′ä·trē′chā) She who makes happy. [< L] Also **Be·a·trix** (bē′ə·triks; *Ger.* bā·ä′triks), *Fr.* **Bé·a·trice** or **Bé·a·trix** (bā·à·trēs′). Dims. **Bea, Bee, Trix, Trix′ie, Trix′y.**
Beck·y (bek′ē) Dim. of REBECCA.
Be·lin·da (bə·lin′də) Serpent: title of an oracular priestess. [< Gmc.] Dim. **Lin′da.**
Bel·la (bel′ə) Dim. of ARABELLA or ISABELLA. Also **Bell.**
Belle (bel) Beautiful. [< F]
Ben·e·dic·ta (ben′ə·dik′tə) Fem. of BENEDICT. Also *Ital.* **Be·ne·det·ta** (bā′nā·dāt′tä), *Sp.* **Be·ni·ta** (bā·nē′tä).
Ber·e·ni·ce (ber′ə·nī′sē) Victorious. [< Gk.]
Ber·na·dette (bûr′nə·det′, *Fr.* ber·nà·det′) Fem. of BERNARD. [< F]
Ber·nar·dine (bûr′nər·dēn) Fem. of BERNARD. [< F] Also **Ber·nar·di·na** (bûr′nər·dē′nə).
Ber·nice (bər·nēs′, bûr′nis) Var. of BERENICE.
Ber·tha (bûr′thə; *Du., Ger., Sw.* ber′tä) Bright; famous. [< Gmc.] Also *Fr.* **Berthe** (bert), *Ital., Sp.* **Ber·ta** (ber·tä). Dims. **Ber′tie, Ber′ty.**
Ber·yl (ber′əl) From the name of the jewel.
Bess (bes) Dim. of ELIZABETH. Also **Bes′sie, Bes′sy.**
Beth (beth) Dim. of ELIZABETH.
Beth·el (beth′əl) House of God. [< Hebrew]
Bet·sy (bet′sē) Dim. of ELIZABETH.
Bet·ti·na (bə·tē′nə) Dim. of ELIZABETH. [< Ital.]
Bet·ty (bet′ē) Dim. of ELIZABETH. Also **Bet′te** (bet′ē, bet).
Beu·lah (byo͞o′lə) Married. [< Hebrew] Also **Beu′la.**
Bev·er·ly (bev′ər·lē) From an English surname; orig. a place name. Also **Bev′er·ley.** Dim. **Bev.**
Bid·dy (bid′ē) Dim. of BRIDGET.
Blanche (blanch, blänch; *Fr.* bläṅsh) White; shining. [<

F < Gmc.] Also **Blanch,** *Ital.* **Bian·ca** (byäng′kä), *Sp.* **Blan·ca** (bläng′kä).
Bon·ny (bon′ē) Good. [< F] Also **Bon′nie.**
Bren·da (bren′də) Sword or torch. [< Gmc.]
Bridg·et (brij′it) High; august. [< Celtic] Also **Brig·id** (brij′id, brē′id). Dims. **Bid′dy, Bri·die** (brī′dē).

Ca·mel·lia (kə·mēl′yə) From the name of the flower.
Ca·mil·la (kə·mil′ə; *Ital.* kä·mēl′lä) Attendant at a sacrifice. [< L] Also *Fr.* **Ca·mille** (kà·mēl′), *Sp.* **Ca·mi·la** (kä·mē′lä).
Can·dice (kan′dis) Radiant. [< L] Also **Can·da·ce** (kan′·də·sē, kan·dā′sē).
Can·di·da (kan′di·də) White; pure. [< L]
Ca·ra (kär′ə) Loved one. [< L]
Car·la (kär′lə) Fem. of CARLO.
Car·lot·ta (kär·lot′ə; *Ital.* kär·lôt′tä) Ital. form of CHARLOTTE. Also *Sp.* **Car·lo·ta** (kär·lō′tä). Dims. **Lot′ta, Lot′·tie, Lot′ty.**
Car·mel (kär′məl) Garden. [< Hebrew] Also **Car·mel·a** (kär·mel′ə). Dim. **Car·me·li·ta** (kär′mə·lē′tə).
Car·men (kär′mən) Song. [< L]
Car·ol (kar′əl) From CAROL, masc., var. of CHARLES. Also **Car·o·la** (kar′ə·lə), **Car′ole, Kar′ol.**
Car·o·line (kar′ə·līn, -lin; *Fr.* kà·rô·lēn′) Fem. of CHARLES. Also **Car·o·lyn** (kar′ə·lin), **Car·o·li·na** (kar′ə·lī′nə; *Ital., Sp.* kä′rō·lē′nä). Dim. **Car′rie.**
Cas·san·dra (kə·san′drə) From the name of the Trojan prophetess in the *Iliad.* [< Gk.] Dims. **Cass, Cas′sie.**
Cath·er·ine (kath′ər·in, kath′rin, *Fr.* kà·trēn′) Purity. [< Gk.] Also **Kath′er·ine, Cath′a·rine, Cath·a·ri·na** (kath′ə·rē′nə), *Ital., Sp.* **Ca·ta·ri·na** (kä′tä·rē′nä) or **Ca·te·ri·na** (kä′·tā·rē′nä). Dims. **Cath′y, Kate, Kath′y, Kath′ie, Ka′tie, Kay, Kit, Kit′ty.**
Cath·leen (kath′lēn, kath·lēn′) Var. of KATHLEEN.
Ce·cil·ia (si·sil′yə, -sēl′yə) Fem. of CECIL. Also **Ce·cel′ia, Ce·cile** (si·sēl′), **Cec·i·ly** (ses′ə·lē), *Fr.* **Cé·cile** (sā·sēl′). Dims. **Cis, Cis′sie, Cis′sy.**
Ce·leste (si·lest′) Heavenly. [< F < L] Also **Ce·les·tine** (si·les′tin, sel′is·tīn), *Fr.* **Cé·les·tine** (sā·les·tēn′).
Cel·ia (sēl′yə, sē′lē·ə; *Ital.* chā′lyä) From the name of a Roman clan. Also *Fr.* **Cé·lie** (sā·lē′).
Cha·ris·sa (kə·ris′ə) Love; grace. [< Gk.]
Char·i·ty (char′ə·tē) From the abstract noun. Dim. **Cher′ry.**
Char·lene (shär·lēn′) Fem. of CHARLES.
Char·lotte (shär·lət; *Fr.* shàr·lôt′; *Ger.* shär·lôt′ə) Fem. of CHARLES. [< F] Dims. **Car′ry, Lot′ta, Lot′tie, Lot′ty.**
Cher·yl (cher′əl) Meaning and origin uncertain.
Chlo·e (klō′ē) Bud; sprout. [< Gk.]
Chris·ta·bel (kris′tə·bel) The fair anointed. [< L] Also **Chris′ta·bel′la, Chris′ta·belle.**
Chris·ti·an·a (kris′tē·an′ə) Fem. of CHRISTIAN. Also *Ger.* **Chri·sti·a·ne** (kris′tē·ä′nə).
Chris·ti·na (kris·tē′nə) Var. of CHRISTIANA. Also **Chris·tine** (kris·tēn′; *Fr.* krēs·tēn′; *Ger.* kris·tē′nə). Dims. **Chris, Chris′sie, Chris′ta, Chris′tie, Ti′na.**
Cic·e·ly (sis′ə·lē) Var. of CECILIA.
Cin·dy (sin′dē) Dim. of LUCINDA.
Claire (klâr) Var. of CLARA. [< F] Also **Clare.**
Clar·a (klar′ə, klâr′ə; *Ger., Sp.* klä′rä) Bright; illustrious. [< L]
Clar·i·bel (klar′ə·bel) Brightly fair. [< L] Also **Clar′a·belle.**
Cla·rice (klə·rēs′, klar′is) Derived from CLARA. Also **Cla·ris·sa** (klə·ris′ə), **Cla·risse** (klə·rēs′).
Cla·rin·da (klə·rin′də) Derived from CLARA.
Clau·dette (klô·det′; *Fr.* klō·det′) Fem. of CLAUDE. [< F]
Clau·di·a (klô′dē·ə) Fem. of *Claudius,* Lat. form of CLAUDE.
Clem·en·tine (klem′ən·tēn, -tīn) Fem. of CLEMENT. [< F]
Cle·o·pat·ra (klē′ə·pat′rə, -pā′trə, -pä′trə) Celebrated of her country. [< Gk.] Dim. **Cle·o** (klē′ō).
Cli·o (klī′ō, klē′ō) From the name of the Greek muse of history.
Clo·til·da (klō·til′də) Famous in war. [< Gmc.] Also **Clo·thil′da, Clo·thil′de,** *Fr.* **Clo·tilde** (klô·tēld′).
Co·lette (kō·let′; *Fr.* kô·let′) Fem. dim. of NICHOLAS. [< F]
Col·leen (kol′ēn, ko·lēn′) Girl. [< Irish]
Con·stance (kon′stəns, *Fr.* kôṅ·stäṅs′) Constant; firm. [< L] Dims. **Con′nie, Con′ny.**
Con·sue·lo (kən·swā′lō; *Sp.* kōn·swā′lō) Consolation. [< Sp.]
Co·ra (kôr′ə, kō′rə) Maiden. [< Gk.]
Cor·del·ia (kôr·dēl′yə, -dē′lē·ə) Meaning uncertain. [< L]
Co·rin·na (kə·rin′ə) Maiden. [< Gk.] Also **Co·rinne** (kə·rin′, -rēn′; *Fr.* kô·rēn′).
Cor·nel·ia (kôr·nēl′yə, -nē′lē·ə) Fem. of CORNELIUS. [< L]
Cris·ti·na (krēs·tē′nä) Ital. and Sp. form of CHRISTINA.
Crys·tal (kris′təl) From the common noun.
Cyn·thi·a (sin′thē·ə) Of Mount Cynthius: an epithet of the Greek goddess Artemis; poetically, the moon.

Dag·mar (dag′mär) Bright day. [< Dan.]
Dai·sy (dā′zē) From the name of the flower.
Dale (dāl) From the common noun.
Daph·ne (daf′nē) Laurel. [< Gk.]
Dar·leen (där·lēn′) Beloved. [OE] Also **Dar·lene′, Dar·line′.**
Dawn (dôn) From the common noun.
Deb·o·rah (deb′ər·ə, deb′rə) Queen bee. [< Hebrew] Dims. **Deb, Deb′by.**
Deir·dre (dir′drə) From the name of a heroine of Irish myth.
Del·ia (dēl′yə) Of Delos: an epithet of the Greek goddess Artemis. [< Gk.]
De·li·lah (di·lī′lə) Delicate; languid. [< Hebrew]
Del·la (del′ə) Var. of ADELA.
Del·phin·i·a (del·fin′ē·ə) Of Delphi. [< Gk.] Also *Fr.* **Del·phine** (del·fēn′).
De·nise (də·nēz′, -nēs′) Fem. of *Denis,* Fr. form of DENNIS.
Des·i·ree (dez′ə·rē) Desired. [< F] Also *Fr.* **Dé·si·rée** (dā·zē·rā′).
Di·an·a (dī·an′ə) From the name of the Roman goddess of the moon. Also **Di·ane** (dī·an′; *Fr.* dyàn). Dim. **Di** (dī).
Di·nah (dī′nə) Judged. [< Hebrew]
Do·lo·res (də·lôr′is, -lō′ris; *Sp.* dō·lō′rās) Our Lady of Sorrows: a title of the Virgin Mary. [< Sp.] Dim. **Lo·la** (lō′lə).
Dom·i·nique (dom′ə·nēk; *Fr.* dô·mē·nēk′) Fr. fem. of DOMINIC. Also **Dom·i·ni·ca** (dom′ə·nē′kə, də·min′ə·kə).
Don·na (don′ə) Lady. [< Ital.]
Do·ra (dôr′ə, dō′rə) Dim. of DOROTHY, EUDORA, or THEODORA.
Dor·cas (dôr′kəs) Gazelle. [< Gk.]
Do·reen (dô·rēn′, dôr′ēn, dō-) Irish dim. of DORA.
Do·rin·da (də·rin′də) Gift. [< Gk.]
Dor·is (dôr′is, dor′-) Dorian woman. [< Gk.]
Dor·o·thy (dôr′ə·thē, dor′-) Gift of God. [< Gk.] Also **Dor·o·the·a** (dôr′ə·thē′ə, dor′-; *Ger.* dō′rō·tā′ä), *Fr.* **Do·ro·thée** (dô·rô·tā′). Dims. **Doll, Dol′lie, Dol′ly, Do′ra, Dot, Dot′ty.**
Dru·sil·la (drōō·sil′ə) She who strengthens. [< L] Also **Dru·cil′la.**

E·dith (ē′dith) Prosperous in war. [OE] Also *Lat.* **Ed·i·tha** (ed′i·thə, ē′di·thə). Dim. **E·die** or **Ea·die** (ē′dē).
Ed·na (ed′nə) Rejuvenation. [< Hebrew]
Ed·wi·na (ed·wē′nə, -win′ə) Fem. of EDWIN.
Ef·fie (ef′ē) Dim. of EUPHEMIA.
Ei·leen (ī·lēn′) Irish form of HELEN.
E·ka·te·ri·na (yə·kə·tyi·ryē′nə) Russ. form of CATHERINE.
E·laine (i·lān′, ē·lān′) Var. of HELEN. [< OF] Also **E·layne′.**
El·ber·ta (el·bûr′tə) Fem. of ELBERT.
El·ea·nor (el′ə·nər, -nôr) Var. of HELEN. [< F] Also **El′i·nor, El·ea·no·ra** (el′ə·nôr′ə, -nō′rə, el′ē·ə-), *Fr.* **É·lé·o·nore** (ā·lā·ô·nôr′), *Ger.* **E·le·o·no·re** (ā′lā·ō·nō′rə), *Ital.* **E·le·o·no·ra** (ā′lā·ō·nô′rä). Dims. **El′la, El′lie, Nell, Nel′lie, Nel′ly.**
E·lec·tra (i·lek′trə) Shining; golden-haired. [< Gk.] Also **E·lek′tra.**
El·e·na (el′ə·nə, ə·lē′nə; *Ital.* â′lā·nä) Var. of HELEN. [< Ital.]
E·li·za (i·lī′zə) Dim. of ELIZABETH. Also *Fr.* **É·lise** (ā·lēz′).
E·liz·a·beth (i·liz′ə·bəth) Consecrated to God. [< Hebrew] Also **E·lis·a·beth** (i·liz′ə·bəth; *Ger.* ā·lē′zä·bet), *Fr.* **É·li·sa·beth** (ā·lē·zà·bet′), *Ital.* **E·li·sa·bet·ta** (ā·lē′zä·bāt′tä). Dims. **Bess, Bes′sie, Beth, Bet′sy, Bet′te, Bet′ty, El′sa, El′·sie, Lib′by, Li′sa, Liz, Liz′beth, Liz′zie, Liz′zy.**
El·la (el′ə) Dim. of ELEANOR. Also **El′lie.**
El·len (el′ən) Var. of HELEN.
E·lo·i·sa (ā′lō·ē′zä) Ital. form of LOUISE.
El·o·ise (el′ō·ēz′, el′ō·ēz) Var. of LOUISE. [< F]
El·sa (el′sə; *Ger.* el′zä) Dim. of ELIZABETH. Also **El·sie** (el′·sē).
El·speth (el′spəth) Scot. form of ELIZABETH.
El·va (el′və) Elf. [< Gmc.]
El·vi·ra (el·vī′rä, -vir′ə) Elf ruler. [< Sp. < Gmc.]
Em·e·line (em′ə·līn, -lēn) Derived from EMILY. Also **Em′·me·line.**
Em·i·ly (em′ə·lē) Fem. of EMIL. Also **Em′i·lie,** *Fr.* **É·mi·lie** (ā·mē·lē′), *Ger.* **E·mi·li·e** (e·mē′lē·ə), *Ital., Sp.* **E·mi·lia** (ā·mē′lyä). Dim. **Em.**
Em·ma (em′ə) Grandmother. [< Gmc.] Dims. **Em, Em′·mie.**
E·nid (ē′nid) Chastity; purity. [< Celtic]
Er·i·ca (er′i·kə) Fem. of ERIC. Also **Er′i·ka.**
Er·ma (ûr′mə) Dim. of ERMENGARDE.
Er·men·garde (ûr′mən·gärd) Great guardian. [< Gmc.]
Er·men·trude (ûr′mən·trōōd) Great strength. [< Gmc.]
Er·nes·tine (ûr′nəs·tēn) Fem. of ERNEST.
Es·me·ral·da (ez′mə·ral′də) Emerald. [< Sp.]
Es·telle (es·tel′) Star. [< L] Also **Es·tel·la** (es·tel′ə).
Es·ther (es′tər) Star. [< Pers.] Dims. **Es′sie, Het′ty.**
Eth·el (eth′əl) Noble. [< Gmc.]

Et·ta (et′ə) Dim. of HENRIETTA.
Eu·do·ra (yo͞o·dôr′ə, -dō′rə) Good gift. [< Gk.]
Eu·ge·ni·a (yo͞o·jē′nē·ə, -jēn′yə) Fem. of EUGENE. Also **Eu·ge·nie** (yo͞o·jē′nē), *Fr.* **Eu·gé·nie** (œ·zhā·nē′). Dims. **Gene, Ge′nie.**
Eu·la·li·a (yo͞o·lā′lē·ə, -lāl′yə) Fair speech. [< Gk.] Also **Eu·la·lie** (yo͞o′lə·lē; *Fr.* œ·là·lē′).
Eu·nice (yo͞o′nis; *Lat.* yo͞o·nī′sē) Good victory. [< Gk.]
Eu·phe·mi·a (yo͞o·fē′mē·ə) Of good repute. [< Gk.] Also *Fr.* **Eu·phé·mie** (œ·fā·mē′). Dims. **Ef·fie** (ef′ē), **Phe′mie.**
E·va (ē′və; *Ger., Ital., Sp.* ā′vä) Var. of EVE. [< L]
E·van·ge·line (i·van′jə·lin, -līn, -lēn) Bearer of glad tidings. [< Gk.]
Eve (ēv; *Fr.* ev) Life. [< Hebrew]
Ev·e·lyn (ev′ə·lin; *Brit.* ēv′lin) Hazelnut. [< L] Also **Ev·e·li·na** (ev′ə·lī′nə, -lē′-).
E·vi·ta (ā·vē′tä) Sp. dim. of EVA.

Faith (fāth) From the abstract noun. Dim. **Fay.**
Fan·ny (fan′ē) Dim. of FRANCES. Also **Fan′nie.**
Faus·ti·na (fôs·tī′nə, -tē′-) Lucky. [< L] Also **Faus·tine** (fôs·tēn′; *Fr.* fōs·tēn′).
Fawn (fôn) From the name of the animal.
Fay (fā) Fairy or faith. [OF] Also **Fae, Faye.**
Fe·li·cia (fə·lish′ə, -lish′ē·ə, -lē′shə) Happy. [< L] Also **Fe·lice** (fə·lēs′), **Fe·lic′i·ty** (-lis′ə·tē).
Fern (fûrn) From the common noun.
Fer·nan·da (fer·nän′dä) Fem. of *Fernando*, Sp. form of FERDINAND.
Fi·del·ia (fi·dēl′yə, -dē′lē·ə) Faithful. [< L]
Fi·o·na (fē·ō′nə) Fair or white. [< Celtic]
Fla·vi·a (flā′vē·ə) Blonde. [< L]
Flo·ra (flôr′ə, flō′rə) Flower. [< L]
Flor·ence (flôr′əns, flor′-; *Fr.* flō·räns′) Blooming. [< L] Dims. **Flo** (flō), **Flor·rie** (flôr′ē, flor′ē), **Flos·sie** (flos′ē).
Fran·ces (fran′sis, frän′-) Fem. of FRANCIS. Also *Fr.* **Fran·çoise** (fräṅ·swȧz′) or **Fran·cisque** (fräṅ·sēsk′), *Ital.* **Fran·ces·ca** (frän·chās′kä). Dims. **Fan′nie, Fan′ny, Fran, Fran′cie, Frank, Fran′nie.**
Fran·cine (fran·sēn′) Derived from FRANCES. Also **Fran·cene′.**
Fred·er·i·ca (fred′ə·rē′kə, fred·rē′kə) Fem. of FREDERICK. Dim. **Fred′die.**
Frie·da (frē′də) Peace. [< G] Also **Fre′da.**

Ga·bri·elle (gā′brē·el′, gab′rē-; *Fr.* gȧ·brē·el′) Fem. of GABRIEL. Also **Ga·bri·el·la** (gā′brē·el′ə). Dim. **Ga·by** (gä·bē′).
Gail (gāl) Short for ABIGAIL. Also **Gale.**
Gay (gā) From the adjective.
Gen·e·vieve (jen′ə·vēv, jen′ə·vēv′) White wave. [< F < Celtic] Also *Fr.* **Ge·ne·viève** (zhen·vyev′).
Ge·nev·ra (ji·nev′rə) Var. of GUINEVERE. [< Ital.] Also **Ge·ne·va** (ji·nē′və).
Geor·gia (jôr′jə) Fem. of GEORGE.
Geor·gi·an·a (jôr′jē·an′ə) Fem. of GEORGE. Also **Geor·gi·na** (jôr·jē′nə), *Fr.* **Geor·gine** (zhôr·zhēn′) or **Geor·gette** (zhôr·zhet′).
Ger·al·dine (jer′əl·dēn) Fem. of GERALD. Dims. **Ger′ry, Jer′ry.**
Ger·maine (jər·mān′) German. [< F < L]
Ger·trude (gûr′tro͞od, *Fr.* zher·trüd′) Spear maid. [< Gmc.] Also *Ger.* **Ger·trud** (ger′tro͞ot). Dims. **Ger′tie, Ger′ty, Tru′da, Tru′dy.**
Gil·ber·ta (gil·bûr′tə) Fem. of GILBERT. Also **Gil·ber·tine** (gil′bər·tēn), *Fr.* **Gil·berte** (zhēl·bert′).
Gil·da (gil′də) Servant of God. [< Celtic]
Gil·li·an (jil′ē·ən, jil′yən) Var. of JULIANA.
Gi·nev·ra (ji·nev′rə) Var. of GUINEVERE. [< Ital.]
Gin·ger (jin′jer) From the plant name.
Gio·van·na (jō·vän′nä) Fem. of *Giovanni*, Ital. form of JOHN.
Gi·sele (zhē·zel′) Pledge or hostage. [< F < Gmc.] Also **Gi·selle′.**
Giu·lia (jo͞o′lyä) Ital. form of JULIA.
Glad·ys (glad′is) Welsh fem. form of CLAUDIUS.
Glen·na (glen′ə) Fem. of GLENN. Also **Glen·nis** (glen′is), **Glyn·is** (glin′is).
Glo·ri·a (glôr′ē·ə, glō′rē·ə) Glory. [< L]
Grace (grās) Grace; favor. [< L] Also **Gra·ci·a** or **Gra·ti·a** (grā′shē·ə, -shə).
Gret·a (gret′ə, grē′tə; *Ger.* grā′tə) Dim. of MARGARET. [< G] Also **Gre·tel** or **Gre·thel** (grā′təl).
Gretch·en (grech′ən; *Ger.* grāt′khən) Dim. of MARGARET. [< G]
Gri·sel·da (gri·zel′də) Stony or unbeatable heroine. [< Gmc.] Also **Gris·sel** (gris′əl), **Griz·el** (griz′əl).
Gus·sie (gus′ē) Dim. of AUGUSTA. Also **Gus·ta** (gus′tə).
Gwen·do·lyn (gwen′də·lin) White-browed. [< Celtic] Also **Gwen′do·len, Gwen′do·line** (-lin, -lēn). Dims. **Gwen, Gwenn, Wen·dy** (wen′dē).
Gwen·eth (gwen′ith) Fair or blessed. [< Celtic] Also **Gwen′ith, Gwyn·eth** (gwin′ith), **Gyn·eth** (gin′ith).
Gwyn (gwin) Fair or white. [< Celtic] Also **Gwynne.**

Han·nah (han′ə) Grace. [< Hebrew] Also **Han′na.**
Har·ri·et (har′ē·ət) Fem. of HARRY. Dims. **Hat′tie, Hat′ty.**
Ha·zel (hā′zəl) From the plant name.
Heath·er (heth′ər) From the plant name.
Hed·da (hed′ə) War. [< Gmc.]
Hed·wig (hed′wig) War. [< Gmc.]
Hel·en (hel′ən) Light; a torch. [< Gk.] Also *Fr.* **Hé·lène** (ā·len′). Dims. **Nell, Nel′lie, Nel′ly.**
Hel·e·na (hel′ə·nə) Var. of HELEN. Dim. **Le·na** (lē′nə).
Hel·ga (hel′gə) Holy. [< Gmc.]
Hé·lo·ïse (ā·lō·ēz′) Fr. form of ELOISE.
Hen·ri·et·ta (hen′rē·et′ə) Fem. of HENRY. Also *Fr.* **Hen·ri·ette** (äṅ·ryet′). Dims. **Et′ta, Et′tie, Hat′tie, Hat′ty, Het′ty, Net′tie, Ret′ta.**
Heph·zi·bah (hep′zə·bə) She who is my delight. [< Hebrew]
Her·mi·o·ne (hər·mī′ə·nē) Fem. of HERMES.
Hes·ter (hes′tər) Var. of ESTHER. Also **Hes′ther.** Dim. **Het′ty.**
Het·ty (het′ē) Dim. of ESTHER, HENRIETTA, or HESTER.
Hil·a·ry (hil′ər·ē) Joyful. [< L]
Hil·da (hil′də) Battle maiden. [OE]
Hil·de·garde (hil′də·gärd) Guardian battle maiden. [< Gmc.] Also **Hil′de·gard.**
Hol·ly (hol′ē) From the plant name.
Ho·no·ra (hō·nôr′ə, -nō′rə) Honor. [< L] Also **Ho·no·ri·a** (hō·nôr′ē·ə, -nō′rē·ə) Dims. **No′ra, No′rah.**
Hope (hōp) From the abstract noun.
Hor·tense (hôr′tens; *Fr.* ôr·täṅs′) Gardener: from the name of a Roman clan. [< F < L] Also *Lat.* **Hor·ten·si·a** (hôr·ten′shē·ə).

I·da (ī′də) Happy; godlike. [< Gmc.]
I·lo·na (i·lō′nə) Radiantly beautiful. [< Hung. < Gk.]
Il·se (il′sə; *Ger.* il′zə) Dim. of ELIZABETH. [< G]
Im·o·gene (im′ə·jēn) Meaning and origin uncertain. Also **Im·o·gen** (im′ə·jən).
I·na (ī′nə) From Lat. suffix for fem. names.
I·nez (ī′nez, ē′nez; *Sp.* ē·nāth′) Var. of AGNES [< Sp. & Pg.]
In·grid (ing′grid) Daughter of Ing (a god in Gmc. mythology). [< Gmc.] Also **In·ga** (ing′gə).
I·rene (ī·rēn′) Peace. [< Gk.]
I·ris (ī′ris) Rainbow [< Gk.], or from the name of the flower.
Ir·ma (ûr′mə) Var. of ERMA.
Is·a·bel (iz′ə·bel; *Sp.* ē′sä·bel′) Oath of Baal. [< Hebrew] Also **Is·a·bel·la** (iz′ə·bel′ə; *Ital.* ē′zä·bel′lä), **Is·a·belle** (iz′ə·bel; *Fr.* ē·zȧ·bel′), **Is′o·bel,** *Fr.* **I·sa·beau** (ē·zȧ·bō′). Dims. **Bell, Bel′la, Belle.**
Is·a·do·ra (iz′ə·dôr′ə, -dō′rə) Fem. of ISIDORE.
I·vy (ī′vē) From the plant name.

Jac·que·line (jak′wə·lin, -lēn, jak′ə-; *Fr.* zhä·klēn′) Fem. of *Jacques*, Fr. form of JACOB. Dim. **Jac′kie.**
Jane (jān) Var. of JOAN. [< OF]
Jan·et (jan′it, jə·net′) Dim. of JANE.
Jan·ice (jan′is) Var. of JANE.
Jas·mine (jaz′min, jas′-) From the name of the flower.
Jean (jēn) Var. of JOAN. [< F]
Jeanne (jēn, *Fr.* zhän) Fr. form of JOAN.
Jean·nette (jə·net′) Dim. of JEANNE.
Je·mi·ma (jə·mī′mə) Dove. [< Hebrew]
Jen·ni·fer (jen′ə·fər) Var of GUINEVERE. Dims. **Jen′ny, Jin′ny.**
Jer·ry (jer′ē) Dim. of GERALDINE.
Jes·si·ca (jes′i·kə) Fem. of JESSE. Dims. **Jess, Jes′sie, Jes′sy.**
Jew·el (jo͞o′əl) From the common noun.
Jill (jil) Short for JULIA.
Jo (jō) Dim. of JOSEPHINE.
Joan (jōn, jō·an′) Fem. of JOHN. Also **Jo·an·na** (jō·an′ə), **Jo·anne** (jō·an′).
Joc·e·lyn (jos′ə·lin) Playful; merry. [< L] Also **Joc′e·lin, Joc′e·line** (-lin).
Jo·han·na (jō·han′ə; *Ger.* yō·hän′ä) Ger. form of JOAN.
Jo·se·pha (jō·sē′fə) Var. of JOSEPHINE.
Jo·se·phine (jō′sə·fēn, -zə-) Fem. of JOSEPH. [< F] Dims. **Jo, Jo′sie, Jo′zy.**
Joy (joi) From the abstract noun.
Joyce (jois) Joyful. [< L]
Jua·na (wä′nə; *Sp.* hwä′nä) Fem. of *Juan*, Sp. form of JOHN.
Jua·ni·ta (wä·nē′tə; *Sp.* hwä·nē′tä) Sp. dim. of JUANA.
Ju·dith (jo͞o′dith) Praised. [< Hebrew] Dim. **Ju′dy.**
Jul·ia (jo͞ol′yə) Fem. of JULIUS. Also **Ju·lie** (jo͞o′lē; *Fr.* zhü·lē′).

Ju·li·an·a (jōō′lē·an′ə, -ä′nə) Fem. of JULIAN. Also *Fr.* **Ju·li·enne** (zhü·lyen′).
Ju·li·et (jōō′lē·et, jōō′lē·et′) Dim. of JULIA.
June (jōōn) From the name of the month.
Jus·ti·na (jus·tī′nə, -tē′-) Fem. of JUSTIN. Also **Jus·tine** (jus·tēn′; *Fr.* zhüs·tēn′).

Kar·en (kâr′ən; *Dan., Norw.* kä′rən) Var. of CATHERINE. [< Dan. & Norw.]
Kate (kāt) Dim. of CATHERINE. Also **Ka′tie.**
Kath·a·rine (kath′ə·rin, kath′rin) Var. of CATHERINE. Also **Kath′er·ine, Kath′ryn.**
Kath·leen (kath′lēn, kath·lēn′) Irish form of CATHERINE.
Kath·y (kath′ē) Dim. of CATHERINE.
Ka·tri·na (kə·trē′nə) Var. of CATHERINE. Also **Kat·rine** (kat′rin, -rēn). Dim. **Tri·na** (trē′nə).
Kay (kā) Dim. of CATHERINE.
Kir·sten (kûr′stən; *Norw.* khish′tən, khir′stən) Norw. form of CHRISTINE.
Kit·ty (kit′ē) Dim. of CATHERINE. Also **Kit.**
Kla·ra (klä′rä) Ger. form of CLARA.

Lau·ra (lôr′ə) Laurel. [< L] Also *Fr.* **Laure** (lôr). Dims. **Lau′rie, Lol′ly.**
Lau·ret·ta (lô·ret′ə) Dim. of LAURA. Also **Lau·rette′.**
Lau·rin·da (lô·rin′də) Derived from LAURA.
La·verne (lə·vûrn′) From the name of the Roman goddess of spring and grain.
La·vin·i·a (lə·vin′ē·ə) Purified. [< L]
Le·ah (lē′ə) Gazelle. [< Hebrew] Also **Le′a.**
Lei·la (lē′lä) Dark night or dark beauty. [< Arabic]
Le·na (lē′nə) Dim. of HELENA or MAGDALENE.
Le·no·ra (lə·nôr′ə, -nō′rə) Var. of ELEANOR. Also **Le·nore** (lə·nôr′).
Le·o·na (lē·ō′nə) Fem. of LEO and LEON. Also *Fr.* **Lé·o·nie** (lā·ô·nē′).
Le·or·a (lē·ôr′ə, -ō′rə) Var. of LEONORA.
Les·lie (les′lē, lez′-) From LESLIE, masc. Also **Les′ley.**
Le·ti·tia (li·tish′ə) Joy. [< L] Dim. **Let·ty** (let′ē).
Lib·by (lib′ē) Dim. of ELIZABETH.
Li·la (lī′lə, lē′-) Var. of LILIAN.
Lil·i·an (lil′ē·ən, lil′yən) Lily. [< L] Also **Lil′li·an.** Dims. **Lil, Lil′ly, Lil′y.**
Lil·y (lil′ē) From the name of the flower; also, dim. of LILIAN.
Lin·da (lin′də) Pretty [< Sp.], or short for BELINDA or MELINDA.
Li·sa (lī′zə, lē′-) Dim. of ELIZABETH. Also **Li′za,** *Ger.* **Li·se** (lē′zə).
Li·sette (lē·zet′) Fr. dim. of ELIZABETH. Also **Li·zette′.**
Liz·beth (liz′bəth) Dim. of ELIZABETH.
Liz·zie (liz′ē) Dim. of ELIZABETH. Also **Liz′zy, Liz.**
Lo·is (lō′is) Desirable. [< Gk.]
Lo·la (lō′lə; *Sp.* lō′lä) Dim. of DOLORES. [< Sp.] Dim. **Lo·li·ta** (lō·lē′tə; *Sp.* lō·lē′tä).
Lor·ene (lô·rēn′) Var. of LAURA. Also **Laur·een′, Laur·ene′, Lor·een′.**
Lor·et·ta (lô·ret′ə, lō-) Dim. of LAURA. Also **Lor·ette** (lô·ret′).
Lo·rin·da (lô·rin′də, lə-) Var. of LAURINDA.
Lor·na (lôr′nə) Lost. [OE]
Lor·raine (lə·rān′) Var. of LAURA.
Lot·tie (lot′ē) Dim. of CHARLOTTE. Also **Lot′ta, Lot′ty.**
Lou·el·la (lōō·el′ə) Var. of LUELLA.
Lou·ise (lōō·ēz′) Fem. of LOUIS. [< F] Also **Lou·i·sa** (lōō·ē′zə). Dims. **Lou, Lou′ie, Lu, Lu′lu.**
Lu·cia (lōō′shə; *Ital.* lōō·chē′ä) Fem. of LUCIUS.
Lu·cille (lōō·sēl′) Var. of LUCIA. [< F] Also **Lu·cile′.**
Lu·cin·da (lōō·sin′də) Derived from LUCY. Dim. **Cin·dy** (sin′dē).
Lu·cre·tia (lōō·krē′shə, -shē·ə) Fem. of LUCRETIUS. Also *Fr.* **Lu·crèce** (lü·kres′), *Ital.* **Lu·cre·zia** (lōō·krâ′tsyä).
Lu·cy (lōō′sē) Var. of LUCIA. Also *Fr.* **Lu·cie** (lü·sē′).
Lu·el·la (lōō·el′ə) Meaning and origin uncertain. Also **Lou·el′la.**
Lu·i·sa (lōō·ē′zä) Ital. form of LOUISA. Also *Ger.* **Lu·i·se** (lōō·ē′zə).
Lu·lu (lōō′lōō) Dim. of LOUISE.
Lyd·i·a (lid′ē·ə) She of Lydia. [< Gk.]

Ma·bel (mā′bəl) Short for AMABEL. Dim. **Mab** (mab).
Mad·e·leine (mad′ə·lin, -lān, *Fr.* må·dlen′) Var. of MAGDALENE. [< F] Also **Mad·e·line** (mad′ə·lin, -līn).
Madge (madj) Dim. of MARGARET.
Mae (mā) Var. of MAY.
Mag (mag) Dim. of MARGARET. Also **Mag′gie.**
Mag·da·lene (mag′də·lēn, mag′də·lē′nē) Woman of Magdala. [< Hebrew] Also **Mag·da·len** (mag′də·lən), **Mag·da·le·na** (mag′də·lē′nə; *Sp.* mäg′thä·lā′nä). Dims. **Le·na** (lē′nə), **Mag·da** (mag′də).
Mai·sie (mā′zē) Dim. of MARGARET. [< Scot.]
Mal·vi·na (mal·vī′nə, -vē′-) Meaning and origin uncertain.
Ma·mie (mā′mē) Dim. of MARGARET.
Man·dy (man′dē) Dim. of AMANDA.
Mar·cel·la (mär·sel′ə) Fem. of MARCELLUS. Also *Fr.* **Mar·celle** (mår·sel′).
Mar·cia (mär′shə) Fem. of *Marcius*, var. of MARCUS.
Mar·ga·ret (mär′gə·rit, mär′grit) Pearl. [< Gk.] Also *Ger.* **Mar·ga·re·te** (mär′gä·rā′tə), *Ital.* **Mar·ghe·ri·ta** (mär′·gā·rē′tä), *Ital., Sp.* **Mar·ga·ri·ta** (mär′gä·rē′tä). Dims. **Gret′a, Gretch′en, Madge, Mag, Mag′gie, Ma′mie, Meg, Me′ta, Peg, Peg′gy, Ri′ta.**
Marge (märj) Dim. of MARJORIE. Also **Mar′gie, Marj.**
Mar·ger·y (mär′jər·ē) Var. of MARGARET.
Mar·got (mär′gō; *Fr.* mår·gō′) Var. of MARGARET. [< F] Also **Mar′go.**
Mar·gue·rite (mär′gə·rēt′; *Fr.* mår·gə·rēt′) Var. of MARGARET. [< F]
Ma·ri·a (mə·rī′ə, -rē′ə; *Ger., Ital.* mä·rē′ä) Var. of MARY. [< L] Also *Sp.* **Ma·rí·a** (mä·rē′ä).
Mar·i·an (mar′ē·ən, mâr′-) Var. of MARION.
Mar·i·anne (mâr′ē·an′) From MARY and ANNE. Also **Mar·i·an·na** (mâr′ē·an′ə).
Ma·rie (mə·rē′; *Fr.* må·rē′) Var. of MARY. [< F]
Mar·i·et·ta (mâr′ē·et′ə, mar′-) Dim. of MARIA.
Mar·i·gold (mar′ə·gōld, mâr′-) From the name of the flower.
Mar·i·lyn (mar′ə·lin, mâr′-) Var. of MARY.
Mar·i·on (mar′ē·ən, mâr′-) Var. of MARY.
Mar·jo·rie (mär′jər·ē) Var. of MARGARET. Also **Mar′jo·ry.** Dims. **Marge, Mar′gie, Marj.**
Mar·lene (mär·lēn′; *Ger.* mär·lā′nə) Var. of MAGDALENE.
Mar·sha (mär′shə) Var. of MARCIA.
Mar·tha (mär′thə) Lady. [< Aramaic] Also *Fr.* **Marthe** (mårt), *Ital., Sp.* **Mar·ta** (mär′tä). Dims. **Mar′ty, Mat′tie, Mat′ty.**
Mar·y (mâr′ē) Meaning uncertain. [< Hebrew] Dims. **May, Min′nie, Mol′ly, Pol′ly.**
Ma·til·da (mə·til′də) Mighty battle maiden. [< Gmc.] Also **Ma·thil·da** (mə·til′də), *Ger.* **Ma·thil·de** (mä·til′də). Dims. **Mat′tie, Mat′ty, Pat′ty, Til′da, Til′lie, Til′ly.**
Maud (môd) Contr. of MAGDALENE. Also **Maude.**
Mau·ra (môr′ə) Irish form of MARY. Also **Maur·ya** (môr′·yə).
Mau·reen (mô·rēn′) Dim. of MAURA.
Ma·vis (mā′vis) From the name of the bird, or the Irish fairy queen Maeve or Mab.
Max·ine (mak·sēn′, mak′sēn) Fem. of MAX. [< F]
May (mā) Dim. of MARY.
Meg (meg) Dim. of MARGARET.
Mel·a·nie (mel′ə·nē) Black. [< Gk.]
Me·lin·da (mə·lin′də) Var. of BELINDA.
Me·lis·sa (mə·lis′ə) Bee. [< Gk.]
Mer·ce·des (mər·sā′dēz, -sē′-, mûr′sə·dēz; *Sp.* mer·thā′thās) Mercies. [< Sp.]
Mer·cy (mûr′sē) From the abstract noun.
Me·ta (mā′tə, mē′-) Dim. of MARGARET. [< G]
Mi·gnon (min′yon, *Fr.* mē·nyôn′) Dainty. [< F]
Mil·dred (mil′drid) Moderate power. [OE] Dims. **Mil′·lie, Mil′ly.**
Mil·li·cent (mil′ə·sənt) Power to work. [< Gmc.] Also **Mil′i·cent.**
Mi·mi (mē′mē) Fr. dim. of WILHELMINA.
Mi·na (mē′nə) Dim. of WILHELMINA.
Mi·ner·va (mi·nûr′və) From the name of the Roman goddess of wisdom.
Min·na (min′ə) Dim. of WILHELMINA.
Min·nie (min′ē) Memory or love [< Gmc.]; also, dim. of MARY.
Mi·ran·da (mi·ran′də) Admirable. [< L]
Mir·i·am (mir′ē·əm) Var. of MARY. [< Hebrew]
Moi·ra (moi′rə) Var. of MAURA.
Mol·ly (mol′ē) Dim. of MARY. Also **Moll.**
Mo·na (mō′nə) Noble. [< Irish]
Mon·i·ca (mon′ə·kə) Adviser. [< L]
Mu·ri·el (myŏŏr′ē·əl) Myrrh. [< Gk.]
Myr·na (mûr′nə) Meaning and origin uncertain.
Myr·tle (mûrt′l) From the plant name.

Na·dine (nā·dēn′, nə-; *Fr.* nå·dēn′) Hope. [< F < Russ.]
Nan (nan) Dim. of ANN.
Nan·cy (nan′sē) Dim. of ANN.
Nan·nette (na·net′) Dim. of ANN. [< F] Also **Na·nette′.**
Na·o·mi (nā·ō′mē, nā′ō·mē) Pleasant. [< Hebrew]
Nat·a·lie (nat′ə·lē) Christmas child. [< L] Also *Russ.* **Na·ta·sha** (nä·tä′shə).
Nell (nel) Dim. of ELEANOR, ELLEN, or HELEN. Also **Nel′·lie, Nel′ly.**
Net·tie (net′ē) Dim. of ANTOINETTE, HENRIETTA, or JEANNETTE. Also **Net′ty.**
Ni·cole (ni·kōl′; *Fr.* nē·kôl′) Fem. of *Nicolas*, Fr. form of NICHOLAS.
Ni·na (nī′nə, nē′-) Dim. of ANN. [< Russ.]

Ni·ta (nē′tə; *Sp.* nē′tä) Dim. of JUANITA. [< Sp.]
No·na (nō′nə) Ninth. [< L]
No·ra (nôr′ə, nō′rə) Dim. of ELEANOR, HONORA, LEONORA. Also **No′rah.**
No·reen (nôr′ēn, nô·rēn′) Irish dim. of NORA.
Nor·ma (nôr′mə) Pattern. [< L]

Oc·ta·vi·a (ok·tā′vē·ə) Fem. of OCTAVIUS.
Ol·ga (ol′gə) Holy. [< Russ. < Scand.]
O·live (ol′iv) Var. of OLIVIA.
O·liv·i·a (ō·liv′ē·ə) She of the olive tree: prob. an epithet of the goddess Athena. [< L] Dims. **Liv′i·a, Liv′ie.**
O·lym·pi·a (ō·lim′pē·ə) She of Olympus. [< L < Gk.]
O·pal (ō′pəl) From the name of the gem.
O·phel·ia (ō·fēl′yə) Help. [< Gk.]
Ot·ti·lie (ot′ə·lē) Fem. of OTTO. [< Ger.]

Pam·e·la (pam′ə·lə) ? Invented by Sir Philip Sidney. Dim. **Pam.**
Pan·sy (pan′zē) From the name of the flower.
Pa·tience (pā′shəns) From the abstract noun.
Pa·tri·cia (pə·trish′ə) Fem. of PATRICK. Dims. **Pat, Pat′sy, Pat′ty.**
Paul·a (pô′lə) Fem. of PAUL.
Pau·lette (pô·let′) Fr. fem. dim. of PAUL.
Paul·ine (pô·lēn′) Fem. of PAUL. [< F] Also *Lat.* **Pau·li·na** (pô·lī′nə).
Pearl (pûrl) From the name of the jewel.
Peg (peg) Dim. of MARGARET. Also **Peg′gy.**
Pe·nel·o·pe (pə·nel′ə·pē) Weaver. [< Gk.] Dim. **Pen′ny.**
Per·sis (pûr′sis) She of Persia. [< Gk.]
Phi·lip·pa (fi·lip′ə, fil′ə·pə) Fem. of PHILIP.
Phoe·be (fē′bē) Bright; shining: an epithet of Artemis. [< Gk.] Also **Phe′be.**
Phyl·lis (fil′is) Green bough or leaf. [< Gk.] Also **Phil′·lis.**
Pol·ly (pol′ē) Dim. of MARY.
Pop·py (pop′ē) From the name of the flower.
Por·tia (pôr′shə, pōr′-) Fem. of *Porcius*, name of a Roman clan. [< L]
Pris·cil·la (pri·sil′ə) Ancient. [< L]
Pru·dence (pro͞od′ns) From the abstract noun. Dim. **Prue.**

Queen·ie (kwē′nē) Derived from QUEEN, used as dim. of REGINA.

Ra·chel (rā′chəl; *Fr.* rȧ·shel′) Ewe or lamb. [< Hebrew] Dims. **Rae, Ray.**
Ra·mo·na (rə·mō′nə) Fem. of *Ramón*, Sp. form of RAYMOND.
Re·ba (rē′bə) Short for REBECCA.
Re·bec·ca (ri·bek′ə) Ensnarer. [< Hebrew] Dim. **Beck′y.**
Re·gi·na (ri·jē′nə, -jī′-) Queen. [< L]
Re·née (rə·nā′, rā′nē, rē′nē) Reborn. [< F]
Rhe·a (rē′ə) From the name of the Greek goddess.
Rho·da (rō′də) Rose. [< Gk.]
Ri·ta (rē′tə) Dim. of *Margarita*, Ital. and Sp. form of MARGARET.
Ro·ber·ta (rə·bûr′tə) Fem. of ROBERT. Dims. **Bert, Bob′·bie, Bob′by.**
Rob·in (rob′in) From the name of the bird, or from the masc. name.
Ro·chelle (rə·shel′) Stone or small rock. [< F]
Ron·ny (ron′ē) Dim. of VERONICA. Also **Ron′nie.**
Ro·sa (rō′zə) Var. of ROSE. [< L]
Ro·sa·bel (rō′zə·bel) Beautiful rose. [< L]
Ro·sa·lie (rō′zə·lē) Little rose. [< L] Also **Ro·sal·ia** (rō·zāl′yə, -zā′lē·ə).
Ros·a·lind (roz′ə·lind) Fair rose. [< Sp.] Also **Ros·a·lin·da** (roz′ə·lin′də).
Ros·a·line (roz′ə·lin, -līn, -lēn, rō′zə-) Var. of ROSALIND. Also **Ros′a·lyn** (-lin).
Ros·a·mond (roz′ə·mənd, rō′zə-) Famous protector. [< Gmc.] Also **Ros′a·mund, Ro·sa·mun·da** (rō′zə·mun′də).
Ros·anne (rōz·an′) From ROSE and ANNE. Also **Ros·an·na** (rōz·an′ə), **Rose·anne′, Rose·an′na.**
Rose (rōz) From the name of the flower. Also **Ro·sa** (rō′zə; *Fr.* rō·zȧ′; *Ger.* rō′zä; *Ital.* rô′zä; *Sp.* rō′sä).
Rose·mar·y (rōz′mâr′ē, -mə·rē) From the plant name. Also **Rose·ma·rie** (rōz′mə·rē).
Row·e·na (rō·ē′nə) ? From the name of an ancient Celtic goddess.
Rox·an·a (rok·san′ə) Dawn of day. [< Persian] Also **Rox·an′na,** *Fr.* **Rox·ane** (rôk·sȧn′). Dim. **Rox′y.**
Ru·by (ro͞o′bē) From the name of the jewel.
Ruth (ro͞oth) Companion. [< Hebrew]

Sa·bi·na (sə·bī′nə) A Sabine woman. [< L]
Sa·die (sā′dē) Dim. of SARAH.
Sal·ly (sal′ē) Dim. of SARAH.
Sa·lo·me (sə·lō′mē) Peace. [< Hebrew]
San·dra (san′drə, sän′-) Dim. of ALEXANDRA.
Sar·ah (sâr′ə) Princess. [< Hebrew] Also **Sar·a** (sâr′ə). Dims. **Sa′die, Sal′ly.**
Sel·ma (sel′mə) Fair [< Celtic], or a fem. dim. of ANSELM.
Se·re·na (sə·rē′nə) Serene. [< L]
Shar·on (shar′ən, shâr′-) Of Sharon. [< Hebrew]
Shei·la (shē′lə) Irish form of CECILIA.
Shir·ley (shûr′lē) From an English surname; orig. a place name.
Sib·yl (sib′əl) Prophetess. [< Gk.] Also **Syb′il.**
Sid·ney (sid′nē) From an English surname. Also **Syd′ney.**
Sig·rid (sig′rid; *Ger.* zē′grit; *Norw.* sē′grē) Conquering counsel. [< Gmc.]
Sil·vi·a (sil′vē·ə) Var. of SYLVIA.
Si·mone (sē·mōn′) Fr. fem. of SIMON.
So·fi·a (sō·fē′ä) Ger., Ital., and Sw. form of SOPHIA.
Son·ia (sōn′yə) Russ. dim. of SOPHIA. Also **Son′ya.**
So·phi·a (sō·fī′ə, -fē′ə) Wise. [< Gk.] Also **So·phie** (sō′·fē; *Fr.* sô·fē′). Dims. **So′phie, So′phy.**
So·phro·ni·a (sə·frō′nē·ə) Prudent. [< Gk.]
Sta·cie (stā′sē) Orig. dim. of ANASTASIA. Also **Sta′cy.**
Stel·la (stel′ə) Star. [< L]
Steph·a·nie (stef′ə·nē) Fem. of STEPHEN. Also **Steph·a·na** (stef′ə·nə), *Fr.* **Sté·pha·nie** (stā·fȧ·nē′).
Su·san (so͞o′zən) Var. of SUSANNAH. Dims. **Sue, Su′sie, Su′zy.**
Su·san·nah (so͞o·zan′ə) Lily. [< Hebrew] Also **Su·san′·na, Su·zanne** (so͞o·zan′; *Fr.* sü·zȧn′). Dims. **Sue, Su·ky** (so͞o′kē), **Su′sie, Su′zy.**
Syb·il (sib′əl) Var. of SIBYL.
Syl·vi·a (sil′vē·ə) Of the forest. [< L] Also **Sil′vi·a.**

Tab·i·tha (tab′ə·thə) Gazelle. [< Aramaic]
Te·re·sa (tə·rē′sə, -zə); *Ital.* tā·rā′zä; *Sp.* tā·rā′sä) Var. of THERESA. [< Ital. & Sp.] Dims. **Ter′ry, Tess, Tes′sie.**
Thal·ia (thāl′yə, thal′-) Flourishing; blooming. [< Gk.]
The·a (thē′ə) Goddess. [< Gk.]
Thel·ma (thel′mə) ? Var. of SELMA.
The·o·do·ra (thē′ə·dôr′ə, -dō′rə) Fem. of THEODORE. Dims. **Do′ra, The′da, The′o.**
The·o·do·sia (thē′ə·dō′shə) Gift of God. [< Gk.]
The·re·sa (tə·rē′sə, -zə) She who reaps. [< Gk.] Also *Fr.* **Thé·rèse** (tā·râz′) Dims. **Ter′ry, Tess, Tes′sie.**
Til·da (til′də) Dim. of MATILDA.
Til·ly (til′ē) Dim. of MATILDA. Also **Til′lie.**
Ti·na (tē′nə) Dim. of CHRISTINA.
Tri·na (trē′nə) Dim. of KATRINA.
Trix·ie (trik′sē) Dim. of BEATRICE or BEATRIX. Also **Trix, Trix′y.**
Tru·dy (tro͞o′dē) Dim. of GERTRUDE.

U·na (yo͞o′nə) One. [< L]
Un·dine (un·dēn′, un′dēn) She of the waves. [< L]
U·ra·ni·a (yo͞o·rā′nē·ə) From the name of the Greek goddess of heaven, the muse of astronomy.
Ur·su·la (ûr′syə·lə, -sə-) Little she-bear. [< L]

Va·le·ri·a (və·lir′ē·ə) Fem. of *Valerius*, name of a Roman clan. Also **Val·er·ie** or **Val·er·y** (val′ər·ē), *Fr.* **Va·lé·rie** (vȧ·lā·rē′). Dim. **Val.**
Va·nes·sa (və·nes′ə) Butterfly. [< Gk.]
Ve·ra (vir′ə) Faith [< Slavic], or truth [< L].
Ver·na (vûr′nə) Short for *Laverna*, var. of LAVERNE.
Ve·ron·i·ca (və·ron′i·kə) True image. [< LL] Also *Fr.* **Vé·ro·nique** (vā·rô·nēk′). Dim. **Ron′nie, Ron′ny.**
Vic·to·ri·a (vik·tôr′ē·ə, -tō′rē·ə) Victory. [< L] Also *Fr.* **Vic·toire** (vēk·twȧr′). Dim. **Vick′y.**
Vi·o·la (vī′ō·lə, vī·ō′lə, vē-) Violet. [< L]
Vi·o·let (vī′ə·lit) From the name of the flower.
Vir·gin·ia (vər·jin′yə) Fem. of *Virginius*, name of a Roman clan. Also *Fr.* **Vir·gi·nie** (vēr·zhē·nē′). Dim. **Gin′ny.**
Viv·i·an (viv′ē·ən, viv′yən) Lively. [< L] Also **Viv′i·en,** *Fr.* **Vi·vienne** (vē·vyen′).

Wan·da (wän′də) Shepherdess or roamer. [< Gmc.]
Wen·dy (wen′dē) Dim. of GWENDOLYN.
Wil·hel·mi·na (wil′hel·mē′nə, wil′ə-; *Ger.* vil′hel·mē′nä) Fem. of *Wilhelm*, Ger. form of WILLIAM. Dims. **Mi′na, Min′na, Wil′la, Wil′ma.**
Wil·la (wil′ə) Dim. of WILHELMINA.
Wil·ma (wil′mə) Dim. of WILHELMINA.
Win·i·fred (win′ə·frid, -fred) White wave or stream. [< Welsh] Dim. **Win′nie.**

Yo·lan·da (yō·lan′də) Meaning uncertain. [? < OF] Also **Yo·lan′de** (-də).
Y·vonne (i·von′, ē-) Meaning uncertain. [< F]

Ze·no·bi·a (zi·nō′bē·ə) She who was given life by Zeus. [< Gk.]
Zo·e (zō′ē) Life. [< Gk.]

THE LIBRARY RESEARCH PAPER

by William W. Watt

What is research? In recent years the word has filtered out of the ivory tower and spread like an epidemic in the marketplace. Loose popular usage has worn the sharp edges from its meaning and threatened to deface its value. To many people *research* refers loosely to the act of looking up or checking up on anything, anywhere, in any way. Political polls, television ratings, the detection of factual errors in unpublished magazine articles, traffic counts at intersections, questionnaires on consumer habits, comparison shopping to price silk stockings—all are called *research*. The transitive verb ("I'll research it for you") appears to be catching up with the noun in popularity, and the well-drilled team is crowding out the lonely adventurer.

Though the weakening of a noble word may be disturbing, it is a useful reminder that the natural human passion for discovering, recording, and evaluating data is not—and never was—the special province of the academic expert in the library, laboratory, museum, geological quarry, or archaeological digging. The scholar's methods may be more systematic and his conclusions more profound. He may have a more sincere faith in the freedom that lies in the pursuit of truth for its own sake—in "pure" research. But he has no monopoly on the activity of research.

Of the infinite varieties, none is more generally useful than the experience that begins as a hunting expedition in a library and ends when the last period is typed on the finished paper. The library research paper is an inevitable academic assignment. Commonly known as the *term paper*, it regularly serves as a sort of commencement exercise at the end of the course or year. For the secondary school student who goes on to college, or for the college undergraduate who proceeds to graduate professional school, there is always another commencement, another beginning of a new research paper. But though the project may become increasingly ambitious and the process more complex, the essential discipline does not change with academic advancement. The basic rules remain the same. The student who forms scholarly habits of research in school will find them invaluable later, whether under the discipline of further formal education or the self-discipline of his vocation, his avocation, or a civic activity. Because the responsible adult is a student all his life, the word *student* will have no chronological limits in this article.

The experience of writing even a single research paper pays educational dividends to any serious student. It encourages him to develop a personal interest in a subject of his own choice. It offers an opportunity for genuine independent study. It introduces him to the resources of whatever library he is privileged to use. It shows him the excitement of tracking down knowledge that is not neatly packaged in a textbook or on a blackboard. It offers him the satisfaction of completing a task more thorough than any routine writing sssignment. (The word *re-search* suggests thoroughness: a *searching again*, checking *and* double-checking.)

The task demands discriminating reading at various speeds and levels, accurate note-taking, intelligent summarizing, honest and systematic acknowledgment of intellectual indebtedness, and a more intricate organization than is ever required on a short composition. The process of separating truth from error and facts from judgments, of compiling and selecting evidence to support a credible conclusion, is a general application of *scientific* method; the problem of organizing the results on paper so that they will instruct and even intrigue a reader belongs to the province of *art*. In first-rate research the "two cultures" meet.

Ideally, then, the library research paper is the product of both critical thinking and creative writing. It should reflect the enthusiasm of an alert mind, not the methodical digging of a reluctant mole. But the most talented and enthusiastic student cannot even approach the ideal unless he is aware from the start that rigorous scholarly method (not pedantic methodology) is the foundation of success. To present an elementary understanding of that method is the purpose of this article.

FINDING AND LIMITING A SUBJECT

Unless the student has a specific assignment thrust upon him by a teacher, his first problem is to choose a subject for investigation. (He is luckier, or course, if the subject has chosen him.) Selecting a suitable subject should not be a haphazard process like rolling dice at random until the right combination pays off. As soon as the writer knows that he is faced with a research deadline—usually a comfortable number of weeks away—he should do some preliminary prowling in the library, along the open stacks if that is permitted, to see what, if anything, it contains within his spheres of general interest. If a teacher has restricted the choice to the limits of a single course, he should be on the alert for clues in the unfinished business of the required reading or class discussion. A good discussion in class is full of loose ends that need to be tied together or of questions that require more time and information to answer. A good teacher will always start more game than he can bring to earth; few mortals irritate him more than the student who, after weeks of classroom suggestions, both explicit and implicit ("This would make a good subject for a research paper") comes staggering toward the deadline still fumbling around for "something to write about."

The first rule for finding a subject is hallowed by age. Two thousand years ago the Roman poet Horace put it this way: "Choose a subject, ye who write, suited to your strength." This does not mean that a student should regard a research assignment only as another chance to ride a familiar hobby. It means that the beginner's reach should not so far exceed his grasp that he will quickly become bogged down in learned technicalities that defy translation.

The second rule is that even a subject well suited to the writer's taste and talent should be strictly limited in accordance with the proposed or required length of the paper. Overly ambitious intentions usually lead to unsuccessful research papers because the student cannot possibly treat his subject adequately within the allotted space and time.

The tentative choice of a subject may be nothing more than a general idea of the territory to be explored, but before the student has ventured far he should become aware of the boundaries so that he won't waste precious hours wandering off limits. Sometimes during the early stages of research a large, nebulous subject will rapidly assume a clearly defined shape, if only because of the limitations of a particular library. More often the reverse is true: a general topic divides and subdivides and the student, who thought he had focused on a subject, finds himself helplessly confused. It is best to limit the subject in advance and avoid this predicament, especially when there is a deadline to meet.

The problem of limiting a subject for research is no different in kind from the routine dilemma of channeling an ambitious idea into a short composition. The same writer who struggles to capture the significance of "Love" or "Ambition" or "The Beat Generation" in 500 words is just as likely to propose a research paper of 3,000 on "The Poetry of Robert Browning" or "The History of Television." Certainly "Browning's Dramatic Monologues" or "Educational Television" would be preferable. Making the necessary allowances for the experience of the writer and the resources of the library, "Browning's Dramatic Monologues on Renaissance Painters" or "Closed Circuit Television in the High School Science Class" would be even better. Nothing more quickly betrays the limitations of a writer's knowledge than his inability to limit his subject.

A more specific way of limiting is to begin with a definite *thesis*—a proposition to prove, perhaps even a side to defend in a hypothetical pro and con debate: to presume to show, for example, that Browning's failure to achieve success in the theater was largely the fault of the Victorian audience, or that classroom television costs more money than it's worth. Such a proposition gives direction to the research and provides a convenient mold for the paper. But the pre-fabricated thesis has caused many dangerous detours from the truth. When a writer has flown effortlessly to a conclusion, it is hard for him to persuade himself that he ought to go back and trudge over the land on foot. It is a human weakness, even among scholars, to warp the truth to accommodate a foregone conclusion, casually ignoring the stubborn facts that won't conform. Moreover, many useful subjects for research do not lend themselves to a thesis statement: they involve explanation, narrative, analysis, or revelation—but not necessarily proof. On the whole, unless a writer is already something of an expert on his subject at the start, he should postpone the choice of a thesis until he has done most of the digging.

He might, like a scientist, begin with a *working hypothesis*, a tentative proposition to serve as a guidepost. But he should always be careful not to mistake a hunch for a fact, or a prejudice for an opinion. Objectivity is at the heart of genuine scholarship. Any researcher would do well to remember Thomas Henry Huxley's definition of a tragedy: "the slaying of a beautiful hypothesis by an ugly fact."

Whatever the subject, there should be no misconceptions about the requirements of the job. Though no two subjects require identical treatment, *the final paper should make it clear that the writer has reflected on the material and marshaled it as evidence to support one or more convincing conclusions.* Many beginners honestly believe that research is only an exercise in genteel plagiarism: tracking down information and transferring it—in great chunks or little snippets—from print to typescript by way of hastily jotted notes—producing a result that could have been achieved more efficiently with a Gillette blade and a roll of Scotch tape. Many failing papers are little more than anthologies of unfamiliar quotations or patchwork quilts of paraphrase. To be sure, the novice is not required to aim at the goal of the ideal Ph.D. dissertation: "an original contribution to knowledge." He is not expected to be an authority on his subject and should not presume to be. Most of his material will have been carefully sifted by more experienced hands, but this does not exempt him from the duty of critical thinking. If he understands this from the start, he will not arbitrarily divide his labor into a physical act of compilation and a mental act of composition. From the first visit to the library he will be reflecting carefully upon the material, not just thoughtlessly jotting down notes. The final product will be a transfusion, not a series of transplants.

USING THE LIBRARY

Because no two libraries are identical, no general instruction on "how to use the library" is custom-tailored to the individual in Azusa or Zanesville. The best way for a reader to get familiar with the machinery of a particular library is to make himself at home there. He should not stride directly to the delivery desk and say to whoever is in charge: "Do you have any books on closed circuit television?" Though the librarian—especially a trained reference librarian—may provide indispensable help at a later stage of the investigation, the student should begin with a declaration of independence. Given the run of the stacks in a small or middle-sized library, he can get off to a good start by going at once to the general territory of his subject (he can find *English Literature* or *American History* on a chart without memorizing the Dewey Decimal System). Wandering up and down the aisles from A to Z, he can get a preliminary view of the land by merely scanning the backbones of books.

But such freedom is not usually permitted in a large library, where the student may have to spend many minutes at the delivery desk waiting to receive the books he has requested. Moreover, a good research paper is not the end-product of aimless browsing. The student will save both himself and the librarian time and trouble by learning the names of the standard reference guides, where to find them, and how to use them. To do this is to practice one of the fundamental principles of research: *Always take pains in the present to avoid panic in the future.*

Regardless of the subject, three reference guides will probably prove indispensable: (1) the card catalogue; (2) a comprehensive encyclopedia; and (3) the *Reader's Guide to Periodical Literature.*

The Card Catalogue

The proper use of a card catalogue requires both imagination and persistence. (Serendipity—the ability to discover treasures that you are not looking for—is probably more of a reward for alertness and patience than a native gift.) In a complete catalogue any book in the library may be listed alphabetically on at least three cards: by subject, author (last name first), and title. Other cards serve as cross-references.

For example, a student planning a paper on "Closed Circuit Television in the High School Science Class" might begin by looking up "Television." He should find a number of subject cards with this label at the top (probably typed in red), each alphabetically arranged by author. As he shuffles further, he should find other cards with more specific subject labels. "Television—apparatus and supplies" may interest him; "Television—law and legislation" may not. A group of books catalogued under "Television in education" certainly will. The student is on his way.

A single card, like a single dictionary entry, contains a wealth of information, some of which is essential for a bibliography. Consider the scope of the data on a typical subject card of the kind disseminated throughout the country by the Library of Congress (*below*).

A Comprehensive Encyclopedia

The reader digging for a research paper should ordinarily regard a complete encyclopedia as an indispensable guide, not an ultimate goal. The writer whose footnotes and bibliography show that he has quarried his material from a half dozen competing encyclopedias—however reputable—is easily identified as an explorer who has never left his safe home in the reference room.

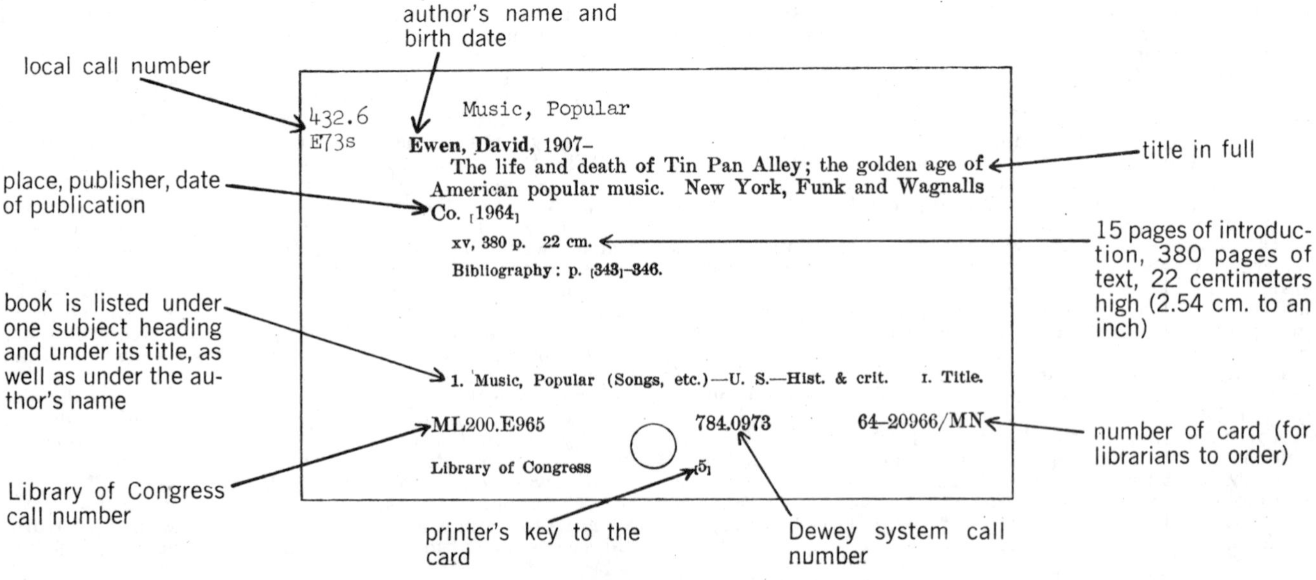

For the conscientious student a good encyclopedia article has two main virtues: (1) it provides an authoritative and comprehensive view of a general subject, probably one in which he has staked out a more restricted claim; (2) it supplies bibliographical references which the student may not have discovered in the card catalogue. Let us take one possible example. The 1963 printing of the *Encyclopaedia Britannica* has an article on "Television" that runs to 19 large double-column pages, complete with photographs and diagrams. As the key to the contributors' initials reveals in the index volume, it is an authoritative article written by the Director of the Research Division of the Philco Corporation. But less than half a column is devoted to the applications of closed circuit TV in education. On the other hand, the article is followed by a list of six more extensive treatments of the general subject, any one of which might find a place in the student's final bibliography. Moreover, if the reader turns to "television" in the index volume, he will find other references to "educational television" that do not appear in the general entry. By consulting several good encyclopedias on a subject the student may choose one which he feels will best help him construct a firm foundation for a research paper.

The *Reader's Guide*

Neither the card catalogue nor the most complete encyclopedia can pretend to give a comprehensive listing of magazine articles that have not been corralled in a book. Even in these days of prolific publishing, many interesting subjects of limited appeal have never been fully treated in book form. New developments, especially in science, are arriving and changing with such speed that even an encyclopedia publishing an annual supplement can never be completely up-to-date. On almost any subject of general interest the first place to hunt for magazine articles is the *Reader's Guide to Periodical Literature.*

The *Reader's Guide* has been indexing current contributions to the best-known American magazines since 1901 and now includes references to more than 125 publications. The semimonthly issues (monthly in July and August) are conveniently bound in volumes that cover periods of one to four years. Articles are listed by author and subject. If a student's chosen subject relates to a specific event since 1901 ("The Hamlet of John Barrymore," "The Attack on Pearl Harbor"), he can begin at that date and work toward the present. If not, especially if he has no clues to authors, he should start with the subject entries in the most recent issues and hunt backward through the bound volumes. On looking up "Television," for example, in the volume for March 1963–February 1964, he would find three articles listed under "TELEVISION, Closed circuit" and twenty-one under "TELEVISION in education." (Any abbreviations in the entries can be understood easily by referring to a key at the front of the volume.) And these would be only a selection of the articles for one year in popular magazines: a glance at the *Education Index* (see below) would uncover many more in professional journals. It is no wonder that teachers turn gray when students report that they "can't find any material" on an obvious subject in an adequate library.

The reader with limited time and facilities cannot expect to locate every one of these articles. It is one of the inevitable frustrations of research to find that the article with the most promising title of all appears in a periodical to which the library does not subscribe. The reader should not compound the frustration by vainly wandering in the stacks. On turning to the list of periodicals at the front of each volume in the *Reader's Guide,* he may find that the ones on the premises have been ticked off in ink. If not, he should have easy access to a list of periodicals in the library without riffling through the card catalogue.

After consulting the card catalogue, several encyclopedias, and the *Reader's Guide,* the student may have enough clues to books and articles—depending always on the subject and scope of his research—to keep him busy for several weeks of digging. No amateur can be expected to play the scholar's game by all the rules—traveling for months, or even years, from library to library, borrowing books and articles at long distance through interlibrary loans, examining others on photostats or microfilms, tracking down the most infinitesimal detail to its final hiding place. But any reader can vicariously experience the excitement of such sleuthing on a smaller scale. Even the beginner should be familiar with more than three guides to research. Some of these tools can prove indispensable to him for detecting clues to possible sources of information on his topic.

Of the innumerable research tools in a great library—including reference guides to reference books and bibliographies of bibliography—the following list contains only a generous sample.

Catalogues and Bibliographies

Books in Print (1948–). An annual author and title index to the *Publishers' Trade List Annual.* Lists the books still available from more than 1,100 American publishers. *Subject Guide to Books in Print* (1957–) lists them annually by subject.

Library of Congress Catalog (1942–). A complete catalogue by authors, showing facsimiles of the cards in the great library in Washington, D.C. A similar catalogue arranges books by subject.

Periodical Indexes

General

Book Review Digest (1905–). A monthly collection of excerpts from current book reviews indexed by author, subject, and title. It helps the reader to get a quick general picture of whether the first greetings were favorable, unfavorable, or lukewarm. More important, it directs him to reviews that he may want to read *in toto.*

International Index to Periodicals (1907–). A key to articles in scholarly journals that are not indexed in the *Reader's Guide,* which is limited to more popular magazines.

New York Times Index (1913–). A detailed index (now published twice a month) to a distinguished newspaper. Indispensable for a writer whose subject is related to any newsworthy event since the year before World War I. Even if the library does not have the complete file of the *Times* (now available in microfilm), he can make extensive use of the index to pin down exact dates, establish the chronological order of events, and find leads to news in any paper that may be available.

Poole's Index to Periodical Literature (1802–1906). Though much less thorough than the *Reader's Guide,* this annual subject index is a useful key to articles in English and American magazines in the nineteenth century.

Special

Agricultural Index (1916–).
Applied Science and Technology Index (1858–).
Art Index (1929–).
Dramatic Index (1909–).
Education Index (1929–).
Essay and General Literature Index (1900–).
Industrial Arts Index (1913–1957).
Public Affairs Information Service (1915–).
Short Story Index (1953–).

Dictionaries

Language (general)

Of all reference books, the general reader should be most familiar with his own desk dictionary, which to him may be "the dictionary." But if he is writing a paper on some aspect of English or American usage, or trying to pin down an accurate or comprehensive definition of a particular term at a particular time, he will find more complete or specialized information in the following works:

Dictionary of American English on Historical Principles. 4 vols. Chicago, 1936–1944. Supplemented by *A Dictionary of Americanisms,* 1951.

New "Standard" Dictionary. rev. ed. New York, 1959. A revision of an unabridged dictionary published by Funk and Wagnalls since 1913.

Oxford English Dictionary. 12 vols. and supplement. London and New York, 1933. When a writer is summoning up remembrance of things past, few records are more suggestive than the changing history of a word's meaning through the years. The great OED supplies such a record by citing the use of words in passages of prose and poetry, arranged in chronological order from the earliest occurrences. Once published as the *New English Dictionary* (NED).

Webster's Third New International Dictionary. Springfield, Mass., 1961. "Webster's Third" contains many new words and meanings not included in the second edition of 1934 and illustrates them profusely in actual contexts. Based on recent linguistic theory, it records—often without restrictive labels—many usages that are widely frowned on.

Language (special)

Evans, Bergen and Cornelia. *A Dictionary of Contemporary American Usage.* New York, 1957.
Fowler, H. W. *A Dictionary of Modern English Usage.* London, 1926.
Nicholson, Margaret. *A Dictionary of American-English Usage.* New York, 1957. Based on Fowler.
Roget's International Thesaurus. 3rd ed., New York, 1962.
Webster's Dictionary of Synonyms. Springfield, Mass., 1942.

Biography

Dictionary of American Biography. 20 vols. and supplements. New York, 1928– . The DAB contains lives of dead Americans.
Dictionary of National Biography. 22 vols. and supplements. London, 1885– . The DNB has lives of dead Britons.
International Who's Who. London, 1936– . Annual.
Kunitz, Stanley J. and Howard Haycraft. *Twentieth Century Authors.* New York, 1942. Supplement, 1945.
Webster's Biographical Dictionary. Springfield, Mass., 1943.
Who's Who. London, 1849– . An annual dictionary of living Britons.
Who's Who in America. Chicago, 1899– . A biennial dictionary of living Americans.

Encyclopedias and Surveys

General

There are many good, comprehensive encyclopedias which are following an editorial program of constant revision. Any good library should have several such encyclopedias of recent copyright. These encyclopedia publishers also supply yearbooks or supplemental material to make the most recent information promptly available to the researcher.

Special

Bailey, Liberty Hyde, ed. *Cyclopedia of American Agriculture.* 4 vols. New York, 1908–1909.
Baldwin, James M., and B. Rand, eds. *Dictionary of Philosophy and Psychology.* new ed. 3 vols. New York, 1949.
Bartlett's Familiar Quotations. 13th ed. Boston, 1955.
Blom, Eric., ed. *Grove's Dictionary of Music and Musicians.* 5th ed. 10 vols. London, 1954. Supplement, 1961.
Cambridge Ancient History. 17 vols., including plates. Cambridge, 1928–1939.
Cambridge Medieval History. 16 vols., including maps and plates. Cambridge, 1911–1936.
Cambridge Modern History. 2nd ed. 13 vols. and atlas. Cambridge, 1902–1926.
Cambridge Bibliography of English Literature. 5 vols. Cambridge, 1941. Supplement 1957.
Cambridge History of American Literature. 4 vols. New York, 1917–1921.
Cambridge History of English Literature. 15 vols. Cambridge, 1907–1927.
Catholic Encyclopedia. rev. ed. 17 vols. New York, 1936– .
Dictionary of American History. rev. ed. 5 vols. and index. New York, 1946.
Encyclopedia of World Art. New York, 1958– . In progress.
Feather, Leonard. *Encyclopedia of Jazz.* rev. ed. New York, 1960.
Fletcher, Sir Banister. *A History of Architecture.* 17th ed. New York, 1961.
Good, C. V. *Dictionary of Education.* 2nd ed. New York, 1959.
Harper's Encyclopedia of Art. 2 vols. New York, 1937. Reissued as *New Standard Encyclopedia of Art,* 1939.
Hart, James D. *Oxford Companion to American Literature.* 3rd ed. New York, 1956.
Harvey, Sir Paul, ed. *Oxford Companion to Classical Literature.* 3rd ed. New York, 1956. *Oxford Companion to English Literature.* 3rd ed. New York, 1946.
Hastings, James, ed. *Encyclopedia of Religion and Ethics.* new ed. 13 vols. New York, 1951.
Kirk, Raymond E., and Donald F. Othmer. *Encyclopedia of Chemical Technology.* 15 vols. and supplements. New York, 1947– .
Langer, William L., ed. *Encyclopedia of World History.* rev. ed. Boston, 1952.
McGraw-Hill Encyclopedia of Science and Technology. 15 vols. New York, 1960.
McLaughlin, Andrew C., and A. B. Hart, eds. *Cyclopedia of American Government.* 3 vols. New York, 1914.
Monroe, Walter S., ed. *Encyclopedia of Educational Research.* 3rd ed. by Chester Harris. New York, 1960.
Munn, Glenn G. *Encyclopedia of Banking and Finance.* rev. ed. L. Garcia. Boston, 1962.
Oxford History of English Literature. 12 vols. projected. Oxford, 1947– .
Sarton, George. *Introduction to the History of Science.* 3 vols. Baltimore, 1927–1948.
Seligman, Edwin R. A., and A. Johnson, eds. *Encyclopedia of the Social Sciences.* 15 vols. New York, 1930–1935. Reissued in 8 vols., 1948.
Singer, Charles, ed. *History of Technology.* 5 vols. New York, 1956–1958.
Smith, Horatio, ed. *Columbia Dictionary of Modern European Literature.* New York, 1947.
Spiller, Robert E., ed. *A Literary History of the United States.* 3 vols. New York, 1948. rev. ed. 1 vol. 1953. Supplement by R. M. Ludwig, 1959.
Stevenson, Burton. *The Home Book of Quotations.* 9th ed. New York, 1959. Organized by subjects.
Thompson, Oscar, and N. Slonimsky, eds. *International Cyclopedia of Music and Musicians.* new ed. 3 vols. New York, 1940.
Tweney, C. F., and L. E. C. Hughes, eds. *Chambers's Technical Dictionary.* 3rd rev. ed. New York, 1958.
Universal Jewish Encyclopedia. 10 vols. and index. New York, 1939–1944.
Van Nostrand's Scientific Encyclopedia. 3rd ed. New York, 1958.

Yearbooks

In addition to the yearbooks made available by encyclopedia publishers, the following may be found useful.

American Year Book (1910–).
The New International Year Book (1907–).
Statesman's Year Book (1864–).
World Almanac and Book of Facts (1868–).

THE WORKING BIBLIOGRAPHY

At the very beginning of his search for materials the reader should be armed with a dependable pen and a supply of 3 x 5 index cards. (Pencils may smudge and encourage illegible scribbling; items jotted in notebooks or on miscellaneous scraps of paper are harder to organize and easier to overlook.) Though the search through the reference guides will turn up some material that will later prove unavailable or useless, it will pay at this stage to make a written record of every title that may conceivably bear on the chosen subject. When arranged in alphabetical form—with no more than one title on a card—these entries will form a tentative list of sources: a working bibliography. When the actual reading of sources begins, some of the cards will be jettisoned, and—as new references turn up in the reading—others will be added. The final bibliography, compiled after the paper is written, may have only a general family resemblance to its pioneering ancestor. But it is far less trouble to tear up a card that has not proved useful than it is to remember an unrecorded title or to return repeatedly to the reference guides.

To avoid trouble later on, the student should write down *the same facts in the same form* that will be required in the final bibliography. Authorities differ about the formal details, but if every researcher were permitted to follow his own fancy, whether through careless indifference or conscious resistance to tradition, the useful shorthand of scholarship would soon degenerate into chaos. The forms illustrated here for both bibliography and footnotes (pp. 1557, 1558) are those recommended in *The MLA Style Sheet* (revised edition), compiled by William Riley Parker for the Modern Language Association after consulting with the editors of 109 journals and 34 university presses. No prudent beginner would ignore such an expert jury to accommodate his own whims. Accurate scholarly form demands *the right facts in the right order with the right punctuation.* Though the standard may seem pedantic to the novice, even the substitution of a semicolon for a colon is not acceptable.

Here are some sample entries for bibliography cards. (Other varieties appear in the specimen bibliography on page 1559.)

For a book with one author:

Galbraith, John K. *The Affluent Society.* Boston, 1958.

Notice that the entry contains four parts in the following order: (1) Author's name, last name first—for alphabetizing; (2) full title—underlined (italicized); (3) place of publication; (4) date of publication. Periods separate the parts except for the comma between place and date. A period also comes at the end of the entry. Unless a different form of an author's name is well known (Eliot, T. S., or Maugham, W. Somerset), give the first name and any initials. Nobody wants to search through a large catalogue for Brown, J.

Some authorities insist on including the name of the publisher. It comes after the place of publication and is preceded by a colon and followed by a comma:

Galbraith, John K. *The Affluent Society.* Boston: Houghton Mifflin, 1958.

For a book with more than one author:

Sledd, James H., and Gwin J. Kolb. *Dr. Johnson's Dictionary.* Chicago, 1955.

Because the second name does not determine the alphabetical placing of the entry, it follows the normal order. If a book has more than two authors, it is sufficient to give the name of the first and add "and others."

For a periodical article:

Lippmann, Walter. "Cuba and the Nuclear Risk," *Atlantic,* CCXI (February 1963), 55–58.

The standard form has five parts in this order: (1) Author's name, last name first (the title comes first if the author is not known); (2) full title of article—in quotes; (3) name of periodical—underlined (italicized); (4) volume—in Roman numerals—and date—in parentheses; (5) page numbers. Except for the period after the author's name, the parts are separated by commas. Notice that this form differs from that of the *Reader's Guide,* where the entry reads:

Cuba and the nuclear risk. Atlan 211:55–8 F '63.

Such an abbreviated form should not be copied onto bibliography cards.

For a newspaper article:

New York *Times,* December 28, 1964, p. 6.

The place of publication is not ordinarily underlined, and the page number is preceded by the standard abbreviation for *page* (lower case p.). If a newspaper has two or more sections with separate paging, the section number is included after the date:

New York *Times,* January 3, 1965, sec. 4, p. 7.

For an encyclopedia article:

Fink, Donald G. "Television," *Encyclopaedia Britannica* (1963), XXI, 910A–913.

In addition to this minimum of information, the student should allow room in the upper left-hand corner of the card for the call number. This will save unnecessary trips to the card catalogue. If the library is large and unfamiliar and the stacks are open, it is helpful to add a further note about the location:

613.84 N478s (2nd floor, north stack)	Neuberger, Maurine B. *Smoke Screen: Tobacco and the Public Welfare.* Englewood Cliffs, N.J., 1963.

EVALUATING SOURCES

As soon as the student turns from the cards of his working bibliography to the actual pages of the sources, he can begin to evaluate the material. Often a quick glance at a book or article will assure him that it is not appropriate; the card, in this case, may be torn up at once. Though other sources will require more careful attention, the researcher should always be ready to change his reading pace, slowing down when the material is complicated or difficult, and speeding up when it is readily comprehensible. The independent reading for research will give him an incomparable opportunity to practice whatever he knows about the difference between skimming and thorough reading. Bacon's proverbial wisdom will become a practical reality: "Some books are to be tasted, others to be swallowed, and some few to be chewed and digested. . . ." "A man," said Samuel Johnson, "will turn over half a library to make one book." But not, the Doctor might have added, if the man plods through all the reading at the same unchanging pace.

Only a seasoned expert in a field can know for certain what authors to respect as authorities or disregard as quacks. But even the beginner can show some intelligent discrimination. The inexperienced reader can learn to evaluate sources just as the scholar does, by asking a few questions based on *external* and *internal evidence.* For example:

External Evidence

Who wrote the book or article? What's in a name? To a conscientious scholar, a great deal. If a name turns up again and again during the investigation—especially if others explicitly refer to the owner as an authority—it is a reasonable, though not a foolproof, assumption that he is more dependable than an obscure author. If the author has a pedigree in one or more standard biographical dictionaries, so much the better, though it must not be forgotten that the elect compile their own pedigrees. A Civil War historian in a great university probably knows more about the battle of Gettysburg than a feature writer commemorating the anniversary for a small town newspaper. A professional folklorist should have a more accurate knowledge of the history of the popular ballad than an itinerant guitar strummer.

Who published it? Though it is risky to make odious comparisons in the mushrooming world of publishing, a reader with some experience will be safer in trusting a reputable imprint of long standing than a new and untested brand name. A scholarly book published by a university press is probably a safer, if duller, guide to a specialized subject than a popular best-seller concocted for the trade. A sober account in the New York *Times* should be fitter to quote than a sensational exposé in a cheap tabloid.

When was it written? Is the material first-hand, second or third? A newspaper extra printed on December 8, 1941 might capture the confused excitement of the attack on Pearl Harbor, but an unbiased study published ten years later would probably be a more reliable source for the facts. An estimate of Winston Churchill published in 1919 would lack the perspective of a book written after the Battle of Britain. A student writing on a subject that is changing as swiftly as "Space Travel" or "Jet Propulsion" will naturally look for the latest word; a scholar delving into the past will be eager to uncover the earliest. The investigator with limited time and experience will lack the scholar's opportunities for tracking down a subject to its *primary sources*—burrowing beyond the printed page to the original manuscript. But he can share the scholar's desire for getting as near as possible to the first-hand truth of an event, the actual wording of a text or document. If he is writing about Shakespeare's treatment of the theme of mercy, he doesn't have to summarize a paraphrase of Portia's speech from a student cram book when a reputable text of *The Merchant of Venice* is close at hand. Nor should he quote a critic from the *Book Review Digest* when the original review is on a nearby shelf.

Internal Evidence

What does the actual text of the book or article reveal about the reliability of the author? The experienced reader will find it easier to answer such a question than the novices but it does not take much sophistication to distinguish between critical thinking and slanted writing (is the author's manner analytical or emotional, are the words neutral or loaded?); or between a disinterested search on all sides of the truth and an argument that is mere propaganda; or between a thorough investigation leading to conclusions founded on facts and a superficial survey resulting in unsupported conjectures.

Considering the amount of piffle on paper, no experienced reader has an ingenuous faith in the sanctity of print for its own sake. But many a reader who ought to know better, eager to accumulate evidence to support a thesis, will gather material at random without the slightest attention to the quality or reliability of his sources. The true scholar does not snap up ill-considered trifles; he is a discriminating reader and a natural skeptic. He not only wants to be shown, he insists on being convinced.

TAKING NOTES

It is sometimes convenient to jot down a general note about a book or article on one of the 3 x 5 bibliography cards. "A comprehensive survey with no recent evidence on the subject." "A jazzy sketch to amuse the reader, not inform him." But more specific or extensive notes should be on separate cards. Because they will not be shuffled in the same deck with the bibliography, these note cards need not be of the same size. Most scholars recommend 4 x 6 note cards (or slips of paper); some prefer half sheets ($5\frac{1}{2}$ x 8). Here convenience is more important than tradition. Note cards should be small enough to sort handily, large enough to allow room for legible notes, but not so large as to invite wholesale transcribing.

Note-taking is a useful art, whether in routine reading, lectures, class discussions, or meetings of clubs and committees. In research it assumes some of the dimensions of an exact science. The individual may eventually derive a personal method that suits him best. The following are some hints and warnings:

Do not take too many notes. Note-taking should be an aid to discriminating reading, not an opportunity for voluminous writing. The reader who postpones all his mental sorting until he begins to go through his note cards to write the paper is making his task unnecessarily difficult.

Restrict each note to one point on one side of the card. The definition of *point* is always arbitrary. It may be a sharp point like a brief direct quotation or a broad point like a short summary of a paragraph or a whole article. But do not clutter up a note with a miscellaneous scattering of quotations and reactions scribbled at random on both sides. The careful assignment of points to cards is another step in the winnowing process that accompanies research from start to finish. Organizing a research paper is not unlike playing a hand of bridge. If aces could not be quickly distinguished from deuces, or face-up cards from face-down, the game would be impossible.

Identify each card accurately at the top with a brief caption for the note and a key to the source, including the exact page number or numbers. If the complete information on the source appears, as it should, on a bibliography card, all that is necessary on a note card is the author's name and the page —or, if he is responsible for more than one source, a short title: Muir, p. 61 or *The Present Age*, pp. 158–159. If a direct quotation extends from one page to another, carefully indicate the division with a slant line (/) at the appropriate point.

Take notes with meticulous care. Note-taking is not jotting. Even when reading rapidly, come to a full stop at any important intersection. If necessary, look back and ahead to avoid the common distortion that comes from ripping a passage hastily out of its context. Remember that a careless glance may change *psychology* to *physiology*, and a single illegible word in a key quotation may later require an emergency trip to the library to revisit a book that somebody else has since withdrawn. Get it right the first time.

Take pains to distinguish between direct quotation and paraphrase and between the author's ideas and your own reactions to them. (The word *paraphrase* is used here in its general sense to mean any rewriting of another's material in your own words, whether it expands, contracts (summarizes), or keeps to the scale of the original.)

Nothing is more confusing and annoying to the reader of a research paper than the writer's failure to make these distinctions clear. Wholesale transgressions of this kind may represent conscious plagiarism. More often they result from ignorance of the meaning of research or of the rules of literary ethics. Because the problem sometimes arises at the writing stage, it is discussed in more detail on page 1557. But often a bad research paper—like a failing examination—can be traced back to poor or carelessly taken notes. Any passage taken word-for-word from the text, even a clause or unusual phrase, should appear in the notes in bold quotation marks. The student who "forgot to put in the quotes" is either dishonest, naive, or inexcusably careless. If the note-taker temporarily abandons direct quotation for paraphrase, he should carefully close the quotes and open them again when the paraphrase is finished. If he makes an independent comment of his own

IV. 2. a "Social Balance" Galbraith, 251-269

We ignore need for balance between private production and public services. Inadequate services in cities, blighted and polluted countryside, neglected education and recreation, inadequate housing -- vs. more and more cars, T.V. sets, comic books, switchblade knives, gimmicks and gadgets. "Social balance," which would bring greater enjoyment to life, hindered by power of private advertising," the truce on inequality," tendency to inflation.
[This published in 1958. How much progress since?]

in the middle of a quotation or paraphrase, he should enclose it in square brackets [thus], not parentheses (thus). He might even go so far as to identify it with his own initials.

Take particular pains to copy quotations precisely. Any scholar will quote much more than he finally uses, but even at the note-taking stage, it is wise to limit direct quotations to short passages *precisely* transcribed. Precisely means word for word, spelling for spelling (except for obvious typographical errors), punctuation mark for punctuation mark. Any omission from a quotation should be carefully identified with three spaced periods (. . .) followed by the period at the end of the sentence where appropriate. Every theater-lover is familiar with the way a press agent can play fast and loose with a critic's review. The reviewer may write: "My final judgment is that, except for the acting, the play is brilliant." With the dots carefully omitted, the advertisement reads: "My final judgment is that the play is brilliant." The scholar's rule is not pedantry, but simple honesty.

Examine each of the sample note cards carefully. The first note, conceivably for a paper on "The Economics of American Poverty," presents a brief summary of an entire chapter in John Kenneth Galbraith's *The Affluent Society.* (The code number in the upper left-hand corner has presumably been supplied later when the cards were organized to match an outline for the paper.) Because the phrases "Social Balance" and "the truce on inequality" are, at least in this context, Galbraith's own, they are put in quotation marks. The reader's reaction is carefully segregated in square brackets.

Even the liveliest argument can't move ahead in a straight line without a well-articulated skeleton.

Though the traditional outline form can at times become a strait jacket for a writer, it has a number of virtues: (1) It tells the writer where he has been, where he is, and where he is going; (2) It reminds the writer that the reader demands the same information, suggesting the need for topic sentences (expressed or implied) and adequate transitions; (3) It avoids unnecessary repetition; (4) It emphasizes the importance of symmetry and proportion; (5) It requires the writer to coordinate his main points, subordinate his subpoints, and relegate trivia to limbo.

A formal outline should follow the accepted method of subordination:

I.
  A.
    1.
    2.
      a.
      b.
  B.

The writer should use either a *topic outline* (limited to words or phrases) or a *sentence outline* (with complete sentences). According to strict rule, the two types should not be mixed. The sentence outline has the advantage of requiring specific assertions (which may turn into topic sentences) instead of ambiguous catchall topics. But with many kinds of material, sustaining a sentence outline is an artificial struggle.

11.3.b   Services   Galbraith, pp. 258-259

Residential housing can't be limited to private sector. "It is improbable that the housing industry is greatly more incompetent or inefficient in the United States than in those countries--/Scandinavia, Holland, or (for the most part) England--where slums have been largely eliminated and where *minimum* standards of cleanliness and comfort are well above our own. As the experience of these countries shows . . . the housing industry functions well only in combination with a large, complex, and costly array of public services." Land purchase, clearance, city planning, zoning, research and architectural services, public assistance for poor.

A passage of direct quotation has been sandwiched between two short pieces of paraphrase in the second note. Notice the slant line marking the transition from page 258 to 259, the parentheses (Galbraith's, not the note-taker's), the line under *minimum* to represent Galbraith's italics, and the three spaced periods to mark an omission from the quotation. Were the omission at the end of a sentence, a fourth spaced period would follow (. . . .).

THE OUTLINE

When a student has made the last of his notes and carefully read them all through to get a bird's-eye view of the land, he is finally ready to plan the actual writing of the paper. Teachers of writing differ about the value of a formal outline for a short composition, but for a research paper of 2.000 words or more. some sort of blueprint is indispensable.

Common errors in outlining should be strictly avoided; examples of these are given below.

The meaningless category

"Introduction," "Body," and "Conclusion," for example, are often too general to be useful. Oftentimes a writer can do better by ignoring the introduction entirely and plunging his pen right into the body.

Illogical coordination

I. Athletics
  A. Football
  B. Baseball
  C. Basketball
  D. Team sports

Improper subordination

Placing a topic under the wrong heading:

I. Athletics
  A. Football
  B. Baseball
    1. Good sportsmanship

Or putting a main point in a subordinate position:

I. School life
  A. Athletics
    1. Major sports
    2. Minor sports
  B. Classroom activities
    1. Discussion
    2. Learning

Single subdivision

If *I* is divided at all, it should have at least two subheads, A and B. If A is divided, it should have at least two subheads, 1 and 2. And so forth. The temptation to use a single subhead can be resisted by following a heading with a colon and a qualifying phrase. A. Athletics: a cause of student failure.

Here is a topic outline displaying the organization of this article: (Because details can be tucked in place as the writing progresses, a practical working outline might be simpler than this. The small bones are supplied here to help the reader in studying and reviewing the article.)

The Library Research Paper

I. The meaning of research
  A. A fashionable word
  B. A popular human activity
  C. The value of the research paper

II. Choosing and limiting a subject
  A. How and where to look
  B. Over-sized subjects
  C. Ways of reducing
    1. From general to specific
    2. The thesis: use and abuse
    3. The working hypothesis
  D. Keeping the end in view

III. Using the library
  A. Browsing in the stacks
  B. Consulting reference works
    1. Three indispensable guides
      a. The card catalogue
      b. A comprehensive encyclopedia
      c. The *Reader's Guide*
    2. Other research tools
      a. Catalogues and bibliographies
      b. Periodical indexes
      c. Dictionaries
      d. Encyclopedias and surveys
      e. Yearbooks

IV. The working bibliography
  A. The value of cards and completeness
  B. The proper forms
    1. For a book
    2. For a periodical article
    3. For a newspaper article
    4. For an encyclopedia article
  C. Evaluating sources
    1. Shifting reading speed
    2. External evidence
      a. Who wrote it?
      b. Who published it?
      c. When was it written?
    3. Internal evidence: the necessity for skepticism

V. Taking notes
  A. Hints and warnings
    1. Taking too many
    2. One to a card
    3. Identifying cards
    4. Meticulous care
    5. Quotation, paraphrase, comment
    6. Precise copying
  B. Samples

VI. The outline
  A. The uses of outlining
  B. The accepted form
    1. Proper subordination
    2. Topic and sentence outlines
  C. Common errors
    1. The meaningless category
    2. Illogical coordination
    3. Improper subordination
    4. Single subdivision
  D. A sample

VII. Writing the paper
  A. Style: English vs. Acadamese
  B. Tone
  C. Quotation and paraphrase revisited
    1. Short quotation
    2. Long quotation
    3. Partial paraphrase
    4. Complete paraphrase
    5. Half-baked paraphrase
  D. Footnotes
    1. For a book
    2. For a periodical article
    3. For a newspaper article
    4. For an encyclopedia article
    5. Shortened footnotes
  E. Abbreviations
  F. The final bibliography
  G. The final draft

WRITING THE PAPER

Except for the greater complexity of organiztion and the special problems of quotation, paraphrase, and proper acknowledgment, "writing up" the results of research is not essentially different from writing any other kind of paper. Whatever laws govern grammar and diction, spelling and punctuation, sentence and paragraph structure, none of them is suspended for research. The freedom to experiment with language may be more limited; the premium on clarity and accuracy is even higher. There is less room for the infinite riches of rhetoric: the drama and poetry of narrative and description are usually replaced by the humbler virtues of clear exposition. But good writing is good writing regardless of its habitat.

Illusions about research die hard. Even students who are convinced that the paper should be composed, not compiled, often assume that the art of composition requires a special style—freighted with *Academese*—and a special tone—impersonal, stuffy, and deadly dull.

Academese is only one kind of jargon. There is also *Pedagese*, the jargon of educationists, and *Scientese*, the jargon of would-be scientists, *Legalese*, *Commercialese*, and *Officialese*. All these dialects share the traits of jargon: involved sentence structure; unnecessary repetition and interminable circumlocution; a pseudotechnical vocabulary. Such writing has been called *gobbledygook* or—suggesting that it is often contrived to impress or even confuse—*bafflegab*. It might be better to revive the old-fashioned word *crabbed*—pronounced slowly with two syllables. A crabbed style suggests an animal that can move its imposing armaments forward only by slow, sideways slithering.

An expert talking to other experts will inevitably use the technical terms of his trade. Nobody writing on a technical subject, whether the propulsion of a rocket or the scansion of a poem, can entirely avoid technical language. But the problem is to explain it, not exploit it, to understand it, not merely parrot it. Genuine technical language is concise, concrete, and clear; it serves to identify and limit a phenomenon—a *paramecium*, not a *wiggly beasty*, *iambic pentameter*, not *words with a regular beat*. Pseudotechnical language is pulpy, abstract, and cryptic—*the intellectual confrontation in an interpersonal situation* instead of *the meeting of human minds*. The proliferation of such jargon by scholars does not make it scholarly.

The style and tone appropriate to a research paper will vary, of course, with the subject, the writer, and the intended reader. A style can be formal without being involved, or informal without being casual and careless. For the general writer who does not pretent to expert knowledge, the best advice on style is simply this: Relax but don't be lax; say simple things simply in your own language; do not write anything, even a quotation or a borrowed idea, in words that you do not understand yourself; be as concrete as possible; remember that, of all the virtues of good writing, the greatest is *clarity.*

The tone of a research paper can be serious without solemnity, dignified without stuffiness. The goal is not a charming personal essay; the reader is presumably interested in the subject, not the personality of the middle man. But the studied effort to be impersonal—and therefore ostensibly disinterested—often results in writing without either personality or interest. Though practice varies, it is better for a writer to use the first person, *I*, than to get tangled in the circumlocutions—the passive voice, for example—of the impersonal manner. Humor and irony may be useful if they grow naturally out of the subject instead of being thrust upon it. Irrelevant wisecracking is taboo. Jokes will not improve stale prose. The essential rule for tone is that all good writing more nearly reflects the living sound of a human voice, than the metallic chatter of a computer.

Quotation and Paraphrase Revisited

One special writing problem—anticipated in the discussion of note-taking—requires expansion here: the proper use of quotation and paraphrase. Make a careful comparison of the following samples:

(1) Short quotation

Leo Stein once said this about composition: "Every personal letter one writes, every personal statement one makes, may be creative writing if one's interest is to make it such."

(A short quotation in a research paper, as in any other paper, is introduced by a colon, or a comma, and carefully enclosed in quotation marks.)

(2) Long quotation

Talking about how to teach the proper use of language, Leo Stein said:

> There is no difficulty in teaching them the routine of expression . . . but it is good to make them realize that there is no essential difference between them and those who write, except interest, use and purpose—that creativity in writing means nothing more than fitting words accurately and specifically to what one specifically and accurately intends. Shakespeare certainly intended more than most and had exceptional gifts, but anyone who has anything to say and wants to interest the receiver has a like object. Every personal letter one writes, every personal statement one makes, may be creative writing if one's interest is to make it such. Most people do not have this interest; what they write in ordinary communications is as dull as they can make it. They have never been taught to think of all writing as in its degree *writing* and all speaking *speaking*, and so they write in rubber stamps [clichés] and speak in the current routine of slang, as though writing and speaking were something reserved for the elect.

(Because the quotation is long—meaning, according to a common rule, five lines or more of typescript—it is set off in a separate paragraph, indented, and typed single-space without quotation marks. The student has represented Stein's italics (*writing, speaking*) by underlining. The three spaced periods in the first sentence stand for a deletion by the writer of the paper, and the bracketed word [clichés] is his addition.)

(3) Partial paraphrase

Leo Stein maintains that creative writing is "nothing more than fitting words accurately and specifically to what one specifically and accurately intends." That Shakespeare had greater intentions and gifts does not, he insists, alter the rule. "Every personal letter one writes, every personal statement one makes, may be creative writing if one's interest is to make it such." A person who has no interest in writing or speaking, who mistakenly assumes that they are "reserved for the elect," will inevitably settle for dullness couched in clichés.

(To compress Stein's passage while preserving some of the original flavor, the writer of the paper uses an acceptable blend of paraphrase and direct quotation. Restricting the paraphrase to his own words and carefully setting off Stein's exact words in quotation marks, he weaves the two into a single tapestry.)

(4) Complete paraphrase

Leo Stein argues that creativity is not a special gift awarded to writers and speakers and denied to ordinary mortals. If he has something to say and is interested in saying it well, anyone, even in a personal letter, can be a creative writer.

(The summary, entirely in the student's own words, reproduces Stein's essential meaning but loses some of the flavor. It has the advantage of brevity.)

All four techniques are acceptable, depending on the purpose and scope of the paper. One *unacceptable* technique is far too common: a confusing mixture of the words of the source and the words of the student without proper distinction between them. It has been called *half-baked paraphrase.*

(5) Half-baked paraphrase

Stein says that students ought to be taught that people in general just don't bother to take advantage of their creativity, which only means in writing fitting words accurately and specifically to what one specifically and accurately intends. Shakespeare intended more than most and had exceptional gifts, but anyone who has anything to say and wants to interest the receiver has a like object. People in general are dull with words because they couldn't care less. They don't bother to think of all writing as in its degree writing and all speaking speaking, and so they use rubber stamps and slang.

(Though they are mixed clumsily with some comment of his own, the student has appropriated appreciable amounts of Stein's own wording without identifying it in quotation marks. A footnote or a bibliographical entry does not excuse this common practice. Whether it results from carelessness, laziness, or dishonesty, it is plagiarism.)

To quote or not to quote? No sacred formula answers the question. A historian working with original documents will resort to frequent quotation. A literary scholar cannot adequately analyze the work of a poet without reproducing excerpts from the poems, line by line, exactly as they appear in the original. But many inexperienced students quote too much: their research papers are merely collections of quotes loosely tethered by incidental interruptions. Generally speaking, direct quotation is useful to clinch an important point, to preserve some of the authentic flavor of the source, or to reproduce a passage that is particularly well written or peculiarly inept. A student should never quote at length unless the passage is especially important for his purpose.

FOOTNOTES

Footnotes should be carefully supplied during the writing process, not superimposed later as an afterthought. In the first draft they can be included temporarily in the text itself. Even in the final draft, short notes may be conveniently inserted in the text in parentheses (*Hamlet* III. ii.61–64) if the source is clearly identified and they do not clutter up the page with too many interruptions. Otherwise, footnotes are usually placed at the bottom of the page, not at the end of the paper. They are keyed to the text with Arabic numerals—not asterisks or other symbols—and should be numbered consecutively throughout the paper. The number in the text should be raised slightly above the line, and placed after any mark of punctuation and at the end—not the beginning—of any quotation, long or short. The number should not be enclosed in parentheses or followed by a period, either in the text or at the bottom of the page. At the foot of the page each note should begin with a capital letter on a new line—with the number raised and indented—and end with a period.

Occasionally a footnote is useful to supply an interesting detail or incidental comment that does not fit conveniently into the text. But in a research paper most footnotes are supplied to acknowledge specific borrowings from sources. Unlike the bibliography, which is a general listing of sources, they usually provide exact page references. With that exception, a complete footnote furnishes the same essential information as a bibliographical entry, but with a different system of punctuation and in a slightly different order.

A footnote is always used to acknowledge a direct quotation unless its exact source is made clear in the text or is familiar (like the Gettysburg Address) to any educated reader. But in spite of a common illusion, the student's responsibility does not end there. He should also use a footnote (1) to acknowledge the use of another writer's idea or opinion *even if it is completely paraphrased*, and (2) as a receipt for the loan of any facts, statistics, or other illustrative material that he has not acquired by original observation.

Here is a representative group of complete footnotes: (Compare them with the corresponding bibliographical entries on page 1559, observing the differences in punctuation and order.)

For a book with one author:

[1]John K. Galbraith, *The Affluent Society* (Boston, 1958), p. 23.

For a book with more than one author:

[2]James H. Sledd and Gwin J. Kolb, *Dr. Johnson's Dictionary* (Chicago, 1955), pp. 49–50.

For a periodical article:

[3]Walter Lippmann, "Cuba and the Nuclear Risk," *Atlantic*, CCXI (February 1963), 57.

For a newspaper article:

[4]New York *Times*, December 28, 1964, p. 6.

[4]New York *Times*, January 3, 1965, sec. 4, p. 7.

For an encyclopedia article:

[5]Donald G. Fink, "Television," *Encyclopaedia Britannica* (1963), XXI, 912.

Whenever a source is used for the first time, the student should give a complete footnote even though most of the information will be repeated in the bibliography. If, however, some of the details appear in the text—the author's name, for example, or the title—it is unnecessary to repeat them at the foot of the page. After the first footnote, an abbreviated form may be used if the complete note is not buried too far back. The easiest short form is the author's last name:

[6]Galbraith, p. 29.

If previous notes refer to more than one work by the same author, a shortened title should be added:

[7]Galbraith, *Affluent Society*, p. 29.

The popularity of the following Latin abbreviations is on the wane, partly because they have led to widespread misunderstanding. Though the writer may never be required to use them, he should understand their meaning in the footnotes of others: (They are sometimes italicized because of their foreign origin.)

Ibid.	short for *ibidem*, meaning "in the same place." Refers to the same page of the same source cited in the footnote *immediately preceding*.
Ibid., p. 57.	another page of the same source cited in the footnote *immediately preceding*.
Galbraith, *op. cit.*, p. 59.	short for *opere citato*, meaning "in the work cited." Refers here to page 59 of the opus by Galbraith cited in a recent footnote. Obviously has no advantage over the use of the author's name alone or author and short title.
Op. cit., p. 59.	may be used if the author's name is made clear in the text.
Loc. cit.	short for *loco citato*, meaning "in the place cited"—that is, the same passage as in a recent footnote. Never used with a page number. Not used at all by many modern scholars.

Because documentation is intended to help the reader, not impress or confuse him, discretion is the better part of valor. If, for example, a number of short quotations from the same source appear in one paragraph of the paper, or if the writer is indebted to one authority for a tissue of small facts, it is unnecessary to present the reader with a whole flock of ibids. On occasion a single covering note may be sufficient:

[1]My main authority for the facts about the charge of the Light Brigade is Cecil Woodham-Smith, *The Reason Why* (New York, 1953), pp. 207–257.

As Frank Sullivan once observed, if you give a footnote an inch it will take a foot.

The student may find the following abbreviations useful in either footnotes or bibliography:

Abbreviations Commonly Used in Footnotes and Bibliographies

anon.—anonymous

c. or ca.—from Latin *circa*, meaning "about." Used with approximate dates (c. 1340).

cf.—compare (cf. p. 47). Should not be used interchangeably with *see* (see p. 79).

ch., chs., chap., chaps.—chapter(s)

col., cols.—column(s)

ed., eds.—editor(s), edition(s)

f., ff.—and the following page(s) or line(s). 76f. or 76ff. 76–78 and 76–87 are more exact.

l., ll.—line(s)

n., nn.—note(s). For example, p. 69, n. 3 refers to the third footnote on page 69. Also p. 69*n* (italicized without the period).

n.d.—no date. Inserted in square brackets when date of publication is not given.

no., nos.—number(s)

par., pars.—paragraph(s)

passim—here and there throughout the work

pseud.—pseudonym

rev.—review, reviewed (by), revised (by), revision

sc.—scene in a play. Unnecessary in short notes if acts are put in large Roman numerals, scenes in small Roman numerals, lines in Arabic (IV.iii.27–46).

sic—Latin for "thus" or "so." Inserted in square brackets to make a succinct comment on something in a quotation such as an error in logic or spelling [sic].

vol., vols.—volume(s)

THE FINAL BIBLIOGRAPHY

If exact indebtedness to sources is carefully acknowledged throughout the footnotes, a final bibliography may not be required. In scholarly publishing, a full-length book is usually supplied with one, an article is not. A teacher will often insist on a bibliography as an exercise in formal acknowledgment and a convenient map of the ground actually covered in preparing the paper. Ordinarily it should be no more than a *selected bibliography*. A complete inventory of all the discoverable sources may be useful to a specialist, but only an ingenuous student would expect extra credit for his ability to transcribe the card catalogue and the *Reader's Guide*. A selected bibliography contains only those items on the bibliography cards that have proved useful in writing the paper. The length of the list is roughly proportionate to the paper's scope. In a long list it may be convenient to have two or more groupings, separating books from articles, or sourses of special importance from sources of general interest. For most research papers a single alphabetical listing is sufficient. Note that each entry in the following specimen contains the same information in the same order as on a bibliography card. If a book or article does not have an author, it is usually listed alphabetically under the first important word of the title.

Selected Bibliography

Ashworth, John. "Olivier, Freud, and Hamlet," *Atlantic*, CLXXXIII (May 1949), 30–33.

Brown, John R., "Theatrical Research and the Criticism of Shakespeare and His Contemporaries," *Shakespeare Quarterly*, XIII (1962), 451–461.

Hankins, John E. "Caliban the Bestial Man," PMLA, LXII (September 1947), 793–801.

Knight, G. Wilson. "The Embassy of Death: An Essay on Hamlet," *The Wheel of Fire* (London, 1949), 17–30.

Littleton, Taylor, and Robert R. Rea, eds. *To Prove a Villain: The Case of King Richard III*. New York, 1964.

Raysor, Thomas M., ed. *Coleridge's Shakespearean Criticism*. 2 vols. Cambridge, Mass., 1930.

"Shakespeare at 400," *Life*, LVI (April 24, 1964), 58–99.

Shakespeare, William. *The Complete Works*, ed. George Lyman Kittredge. Boston, 1936.

Tillyard, E. M. W. *The Elizabethan World Picture*. London, 1943.

Traversi, D. A. *An Approach to Shakespeare*. 2nd rev. ed. New York, 1956.

THE FINAL DRAFT

The final draft of the research paper should be typed—double-spaced—on one side of heavy white paper (not onion skin) $8\frac{1}{2}$ x 11 inches and unlined. Footnotes and long indented quotations should be single-spaced. Two spaces should appear between footnotes and three between the text and the first note. The pages should be numbered with Arabic numerals, either centered at the top or in the upper right-hand corner. Whether held in a binder or merely with a paper clip, the pages should be kept flat, not folded as in a shorter composition. Margins should be at least an inch wide all around. The title should appear on both the first page (about two inches from the top) and on a separate title page, which should also include the author's name, the date, and the name of the course, if any. Corrections in the final draft should be strictly limited, preferably made by neat erasing and retyping. A sloppy paper inevitably suggests a sloppy mind. Besides, it is absurd for the writer to stumble in haste over the final barrier after he has taken so long to come so far.

MODERN PUBLIC SPEAKING

by Robert T. Oliver

Making a speech is a skill in some ways comparable to playing tennis. You should not expect to be able to make an effective speech without first learning what to do and how to do it. With instruction and conscientious effort you can master the rudiments and attain some degree of success. The amount of success you may eventually achieve will depend upon your mastery of the fundamentals, your determination to persist in overcoming difficulties, and your continuous attention to the finer points of technique. Just as in tennis, in public speaking the ultimate attainment of championship form depends upon natural abilities, but a major factor in both is the will to succeed.

Learning to be a good speaker, or tennis player, involves instruction and practice, both of which are equally important. Despite the familiar proverb, practice does *not* make perfect. Improvement comes from knowing what to do, and from careful, critical comparison of what you actually do with what you ought to be doing.

The first step is to identify the fundamentals. There are four basic elements: (1) yourself as the speaker; (2) the message you have to present; (3) the listeners; and (4) the occasion. Each element presents separate problems which must be analyzed, understood, and solved. Finally these parts must be coordinated into a single well-integrated unity, just as in playing tennis your physical coordination, your grip on the racket, your understanding of the style of your opponent, your delivery of the ball, and your placement of the shots must all be united physically, emotionally, and mentally.

When you think of the final product—assured, persuasive influence exerted upon a fascinated audience that gives willing and eager acceptance to the message you as the speaker are presenting—it seems a difficult goal to achieve. And so it is. Neither championship tennis players nor masterful speakers are developed without a combination of inherent abilities plus persistent and intensive effort. But almost anyone, with instruction and reasonable effort, can learn to play a respectable and enjoyable game of tennis. And almost everyone can attain the ability to prepare and deliver brief talks with pleasure and satisfaction to himself and to his audience. The key to good public speaking is mastery of its basic ingredients. These must be combined and assimilated simultaneously and largely unconsciously, but in the learning stage, they should be studied one by one and with careful attention to their details.

The Speaker

Your Attitude toward Speech. A good starting point for considering yourself as a speaker is to avoid or abandon any idea of becoming an admired and artistic public performer. Most of those who do a great deal of speaking and for whom success in speech is important reject the idea of public speaking as an artistic performance. Lawyers will tell you they don't want to speak well; they want to win cases. Preachers don't want to be admired for their eloquence; they want to influence beliefs and behavior. Teachers don't try to win admiration but to create new understanding and reshape attitudes. Politicians look beyond the cheers and applause of crowds to what will happen in the voting booths on election day. It matters a great deal to your eventual success as a speaker whether you set out to try to win admiration for your poise, polish, style, and wit on the platform, or whether your goal is to gain greater ability to win agreement with what you say and to present your ideas sensibly. To become an effective public speaker should not be a goal in itself but a valuable means of attaining other goals.

The value of skill in speaking was well stated by Chauncey Depew, who was highly successful in both business and politics: "There is no other accomplishment which any man can have that will so quickly make for him a career and secure recognition as the ability to speak acceptably." Most people agree with this judgment—including those who have attained success and those who have failed to reach their goals. Yet our educational practices fall far short of meeting the challenge which it propounds. We stress the importance of clear and correct writing and much effort is expended in the schools to teach students to write well—yet little effort is devoted to education in better speaking; though we speak one hundred words for every one we write. The importance of reading is stressed, and rightly so; yet the ability to listen with judgment and discrimination is even more important. The ability to speak and to listen effectively is not something that "just happens." These are highly complex (and indispensable) skills. They need to be studied with care, for their attainment is important to your success. All through your life you will have no choice as to whether or not to communicate orally with your fellow men. Your only choice is whether or not to communicate well.

Stage Fright. One of your problems as a speaker is probably stage fright. Most people feel nervous when they begin speaking to a group. For many, even the thought of getting up to address an audience is so frightening that they never surmount this initial barrier. The reason, in large part, is that public speaking for these people means doing something in public that they really don't know how to do. More than this, even skilled and experienced speakers commonly experience some stage fright because they realize that more than skill is involved: they are placing before the judgment of the public their own personalities, the quality of their minds, their worth as individuals. The essential fact is that listeners do not judge speakers merely as speakers. They form conclusions about them as human beings, conclusions involving every aspect of their characters. To give a public speech is to put on display and under examination what you are and what you aspire to. Anyone who understands all that is involved in a speaking situation will find it a challenging and frightening endeavor.

In public speaking as in much else, success is won only by courage. Analysis makes it perfectly clear that the fear of speaking is focused far less on how you may perform on the platform than on whether the audience will respect you as a person and whether they will regard your ideas, your knowledge, and your opinions with respect. The great bugaboo that frightens most speakers is the fear that they may seem ridiculous, that they will make fools of themselves in front of the group. To understand this is to reduce stage fright to a definite problem that can be dealt with reasonably.

The remedies are three-fold. First, prepare carefully what you will say, making sure your facts are right and your conclusions reasonable. After all, a speech is a message. If it is sound, it cannot at the same time be foolish. Give yourself a solid basis of confidence that what you plan to say is worth saying and worth listening to. Second, remember the earlier reminder that actually you are not trying to be a good platform performer. You may even profit from telling your audience that your aim is not to be witty or eloquent. Your aim is to present facts and ideas on a subject of importance with the hope of helping your audience to reach a right conclusion. Try to get both yourself and your listeners to think about what you are saying, rather than worry about how you are presenting it. Third, your speech fright will diminish (though it probably will never completely disappear) as you learn more about how to speak and gain the confidence that comes through experience.

Confidence through Preparation. The starting point for your improvement as a speaker is to chop away false ideas about public speaking. The greatest error commonly made is the development of anxieties about what will happen on the platform after you start speaking. Inexperienced speakers reduce their effectiveness by needless worry about whether they will forget what to say, whether their voices will sound strained, whether they will look awkward. Actually, the success or failure of a speech is very largely determined during the stage of preparation. The crucial period is the one spent at your desk, before you mount the platform. During this period, there are two separate kinds of preparation you need to make. One, concerning your subject matter, will be discussed in the following section. Prior to this, and always important, is preparing yourself. Don't worry about your voice and gestures. Do be deeply attentive to your attitudes and to your mode of thinking.

The attitude of confidence and the attitude of wanting to share ideas (the urge to communicate) are both necessary and both can be effectively supported and strengthened. Build confidence by affirmative thinking, and by psychological reinforcement. Tell yourself that you are speaking because those who invited you have confidence in you. They are convinced that you have a message worth delivering and that the audience wants to hear you. Remember your own feelings when you listen to a speech—you are hopeful the speaker will be at ease and that he will be clear, interesting, and to the point. An audience is not the enemy of the speaker. Remind yourself that you do have a good mind, that the people you talk with like to hear what you have to say, that you may not be a master of style but that you do have common sense. Tell yourself that what you have to say is important and that it deserves your best effort. Then *reinforce* your confidence by repeating and emphasizing your desire to win agreement with your message. When you feel doubts of your ability, brush them aside and concentrate instead upon the pleasing prospect of doing a good job. Your mind cannot go in two different directions at once. If you concentrate upon thoughts of success, baseless fears will not have opportunity to take root.

Rhetorical Thinking. An even more important type of self-preparation is to develop a kind of thinking that is the special province of communicative speaking. The mind of man works in four distinct ways. The *scientific* mode seeks to sheer away all personal feelings or biases and to view facts precisely as they are, letting them speak pretty much for themselves. The *logical* mode is concerned with the inevitable and inescapable kinds of relationships that exist between facts, with a completely unfeeling and objective surrender of personal desires to whatever conclusions logic may dictate. Far more prevalent than either of these modes is the *expressionistic*, which is a self-centered, highly prejudiced depiction of events and circumstances in subjective terms of personal desires and fears. This is sometimes called *egocentric* thinking, and it depicts the world *as you see it*—sometimes as you wish it were, sometimes as you are afraid it might be. You (and your associates) do these three kinds of thinking much of the time.

But the kind of thinking required for successful communication, called the *rhetorical* mode, has to be learned and practiced. Such thinking always represents the facts and their meanings in terms of: (1) your own purposes; (2) their intrinsic or probable nature; (3) the susceptibilities, needs, and wishes of the intended audience; and (4) the character of the occasion on which you will be speaking. All four need to be analyzed and kept in mind simultaneously. Whether you become an effective speaker will depend to a high degree upon how well you master the rhetorical mode of thinking. You must train your mind to operate with rhetorical effect both during the preparation of your speech and during its presentation.

Quite properly you have and should have a high regard for the integrity of the facts themselves. Communication, however, involves much more than presenting a list of facts. You may wish to speak about the need to lower taxes. A complete summary of all the facts involved would be far too complex for the average listener to absorb all at once, or for you to present in a single speech. You would have to discuss the purpose of government and present a philosophical view of what government can and should do. You would also have to consider the ability to pay taxes of vast numbers of people who live in entirely different circumstances. You would have to evaluate the efficiency with which public funds are spent and the resulting effects of such spending. Each of these separate, yet interrelated, factors involves a great many facts. Two speakers taking opposite sides of the question might both be precisely accurate in the facts they used, but neither one would have represented completely *all* the relevant facts. On this and on almost all other questions on which you might speak, factual data must be *selected* and then *interpreted.*

The interpretation involves both the relationships which you see among the facts and the relative importance you give to differing facts. The incapacity of logic to describe these relationships is indicated by the disagreements in conclusions reached by highly educated and skilled economists. Logic works best when applied to abstract symbols, as when a textbook in logic points out that "all A is A," or that "A cannot be both A and B." The events and circumstances about which people dispute are normally far too complex and ill-defined to provide opportunities for genuinely logical conclusions.

Expressionistic or egocentric thinking is often described as "bad." Prejudices that are harmful to other people are properly condemned. But your emotions, interests, enthusiasms, etc., do influence your thinking. People are incapable of the emotionless reactions of calculating machines; if they were, life would lose much of its interest. Whether or not we *should* let our thinking be affected by our likes and dislikes is a moot question. The fact is we do. As a public speaker, what you need to understand is that your own emotions and convictions are neither necessarily "true" nor universally shared by your audience. The fact that you are "certain" something is true is no proof that your listeners will feel likewise.

The rhetorician, that is the public speaker, when he undertakes to discuss a subject (taxes, for example), will ask himself first of all, "What do I wish to accomplish by speaking about this subject?" If your aim is to persuade your chosen audience to condemn the political party in power for extravagance, or inefficiency, or unfairness in spending tax receipts, then you will be interested in selecting sound and irrefutable facts which tend toward this conclusion. You will ask yourself what your listeners will feel about the subject, so that you may try to select and phrase your facts and ideas in ways that will seem sensible to them. You will have in mind the nature of the occasion, whether it is to be a meeting of a civics class, for example, or a community dinner meeting, or a partisan political rally. Every one of the four elements of rhetorical thinking will need careful attention: concentration of evidence to support your purpose; identification, selection, and vivid portrayal of undeniable facts which combine to support that purpose; adaptation of your mood and manner of expression to fit the predispositions of your audience; and conformity with the general nature of the occasion.

There is no point in giving a speech until you have a point of view you wish to support. You must have clear convictions about the matter to be discussed. Similarly, you should try to learn as much as you can about how your audience feels about the subject, and ask yourself searchingly why it holds ideas different from yours. You must try to find ways of representing your own ideas so that they will seem reasonable to others who may hold different views. This is the particular province of rhetoric. You may think as a scientist or as a logician while you are examining a subject to determine what you ought to conclude about it. You may think expressionistically or egocentrically while engaged in idle daydreams or perhaps even in carefree social conversation. But when you are preparing or presenting a public speech, the investigatory stage is behind you, and the ego-satisfying experience of simply pouring forth your own prejudices will hurt rather than help your cause. This is the communicative stage, when your efforts must all be directed toward helping a group of listeners accept the reasonableness of your conclusions.

As you accustom yourself to thinking rhetorically, you will become increasingly acute in self-analysis, so that you will see more clearly what it is that you believe, and why. You will become more sensitive to the beliefs and feelings of your associates. You will be more prone to consider facts in terms of their overall reasonableness as they relate to one another rather than how they may appear when viewed in isolation. The development of this change in yourself is the initial stage in learning to become an effective public speaker.

The Message

Your message—or your speech—needs to be viewed in two different ways: the determination of its content, and its pattern of presentation. The two elements are related but distinct. What will you say? How will you organize it? The first question is governed largely by your own convictions and by the nature of the topic. The latter is determined chiefly by your analysis of your expected audience and of the occasion.

What Will You Say? A speech, as we have said, should not be a performance. It should aim to accomplish some realistic result. The realism is attained by the relationship that exists between you as the speaker, your subject, and the audience. Your business is to speak about something you understand to listeners who need to know about it. The essential test to apply to any speech is this: Why should *this speaker* talk about *this subject* to *this audience* at *this time*?

There are several clear guidelines to keep in mind when you are searching for a subject about which to make your speech. First, talk about what you already know and about a subject on which you feel some genuine enthusiasm or deep concern. This does not mean that no special preparation is needed except to jot down some facts and ideas you already have in mind. It does mean that you should look for your subject within your own experience, rather than search through library resources to find an article or a book that looks interesting and that you might summarize. The ideal subject is one that you have been interested in for a long time, and concerning which you need further information in order to clarify your own understanding and convictions. For example, you may feel strongly that government regulations are needed to safeguard such natural resources as rivers and forest lands. But you are probably uncertain as to what manner of government action might prove effective. And undoubtedly you need many more facts concerning the nature of the problem and the partial remedies already taken. On such a subject as this you can speak with enthusiasm and even a kind of authority, for it will be natural for you to refer to your long-held interest in the subject. And you will find in your genuine interest the motivation needed to dig for the facts and test possible solutions to the problem.

Second, talk on a subject about which your listeners believe (or can be led to believe) you have something to say that merits their respectful attention. Obviously, if you live on a farm, you could speak to club members in a nearby city on how farmers in your area regard the state regulations controlling the production and sale of milk. However, if you are a young person without any great breadth of political or community experience, you may not get so respectful a hearing if you choose to speak on, say, "What is Wrong with the Milk Commission." Any topic you might think of can be *approached from the point of view of your own competence*. Examples can be multiplied. For instance, you could not address your church on how to conduct a successful fund-raising drive; but you could make a very appealing talk on what young people think about their responsibility to support the church financially. You could scarcely impress an audience by speaking on the weaknesses of the federal income tax law; but you could make a real contribution by explaining how the working habits of yourself and your associates are affected by the fact that an income tax must be paid on all your annual earnings beyond $600. If you have a hobby of raising goldfish and would like to share some of your knowledge and enthusiasm with an audience, be sure to tell them (or have the chairman who introduces you tell them) about your own experience with your hobby, so that they will know you speak from personal experience and are not merely passing along something you know superficially.

Third, talk about something that is appropriate to the interests or needs of your listeners. There is no point in trying to tell people what they don't want or don't need to hear. If they have a lively interest, your task as a speaker is easier. If you are a member of the football team and are speaking to a school rally about the problems that must be solved if you are to win the big game, you are assured of interested listeners. However, you should never feel restricted to such obviously appealing topics. Perhaps you wish to speak to an audience about religion precisely because they are *not* interested in it; or you may wish to advocate brotherhood and justice in a community that seems obsessed with selfishness and prejudice. By all means you should speak out on any and all topics on which you feel you might be able to lead your listeners out of error and into sound thinking and generous acting. The less interested people are in truth and benevolence, the greater is the need for speakers who will guide them aright. But even in instances of this kind, the principle still holds true that you should speak in terms of the interests and needs of your audience. Obviously, they *need* to be better than they are. Their interest in self-reform is another matter and will require special carefulness in your introduction and in the way in which you develop your ideas.

Fourth, whatever subject you choose, talk about it concretely and personally. Few speakers, and this especially applies to those who are young and relatively inexperienced, know enough about any complicated subject to discuss it in dogmatic terms of sweeping generalizations. You cannot tell an audience how to end poverty in America, for example. But you can discuss precisely that subject in terms of your own experience and observation. Even more importantly, you can draw upon what your listeners know, and ask them to reason with you about this kind of experience. "You and I know" is a phrase that was often used in the speeches of President Franklin D. Roosevelt. It is also an extremely valuable phrase and guideline for the speaking you yourself may do.

What you should talk about, then, is your own experience, your own knowledge, your own best ideas, reinforced by all the fresh facts you can assemble through reasonable research, and analyzed and presented in terms of the needs, interests, and experience of your audience.

How Will You Organize It? The basic requirements for the organization of any speech is that it must have a beginning, a middle, and an end. Each of these parts has its own functions to perform—and all of them must be bound together to assist one another, much as the members of a team must cooperate if there is to be success. The beginning, or introduction, must establish an effective relationship with the audience. The middle, or discussion, must develop understandably and convincingly the message you have to present. And the ending, or conclusion, must point toward what you want and expect your audience to do about your subject. All three parts must be focused to try to accomplish the purpose you have in giving the speech.

Purpose. The starting point for organizing any speech is to make a careful note of what your purpose in giving the speech will be. This is not something you may ignore or skip over lightly, for carelessness in clarifying your purpose (to yourself, and then to your listeners) is a principal cause of failure in speaking. It is excellent practice (even for skillful and experienced speakers, certainly for inexperienced ones) to begin preparing a speech by writing down the precise purpose that it should try to accomplish. This should always link the audience to the subject matter. Examples follow:

To inform: I want my audience to understand how to clean grease spots off a coat . . . what Immanuel Kant meant by "categorical imperative" . . . who is responsible for the prosperity and morality of our town . . . why even successful cheating hurts the cheater . . . where the principal trouble spots occur in our daily behavior.

To persuade: I want my audience to vote for the candidate of my choice . . . agree with my plan for improving traffic conditions . . . contribute to the Community Chest . . . stop smoking.

To entertain: I want to interest and amuse my audience by narrating my experience hunting possums . . . describing strange marriage customs of a primitive tribe . . . relating anecdotes about the Pennsylvania Dutch.

The Introduction. In spirit, if not precisely in words, the speech should begin not with the speaker or his subject but with the audience. Your aim in the introduction is to meet the listeners where they are and to engage their interest sufficiently so that they will want to go with you toward your conclusion. Thus you might say: "Everyone here has been so much interested lately in the local paper mill strike that you may not have noticed another event that has been crowded off the front page of the newspapers—I mean the destruction of the forests on which our paper industry depends, through fires caused by carelessness in the woods. Efforts are already being made to settle the strike. But I wonder what you are doing—and what we all might be able to do—to save our forests."

Sometimes in your introduction you may need to establish your own authority to speak on the subject, in which case you might say: "You may naturally wonder why a local boy like myself has undertaken to speak to you about the living conditions of an African village. Actually, I first became interested in the village when my uncle was stationed there for a year as a worker in the Peace Corps. Since then I've learned a lot about it from him and have read a number of articles about it. All of this information adds up to three main ideas that I want to pass along to you today."

Occasionally you may decide to speak in favor of an idea that is actually strongly opposed by your listeners, or to which they may be indifferent. In such instances, your opening remarks must be aimed to create a more favorable receptivity. For example, you might begin: "There's been a lot of complaint in our town recently about the amount of juvenile delinquency. As one of the high school set, I'm perhaps even more concerned about this than you adults are. I'm not sure, however, that the complaints are directed to the right source. Of course young people ought not to be causing trouble. No one denies this. What I am suggesting is that we stop complaining about the symptoms of what we might call our principal community disease, and take a good look at the probable causes. I think I can suggest what some of them are; and I think when you consider them you are going to agree with me that the fault lies not so much with our young people as with all of us—not only with the young people, not only with their parents, but with the whole community."

In every speech you will ever give, the opening remarks will always be of special importance. They establish the initial impression the listeners will have, both of your competence as a speaker, and of your fairness and your mastery of the subject. Your introduction has to get them started thinking about your topic, and your aim should be to get their thinking oriented favorably toward your conclusion.

The Discussion. The body of your speech should be organized around two or three or four "main ideas" which, if accepted by your listeners, will induce them to agree with or accept the purpose you wish to accomplish. A speech is unlikely to be any better or stronger than its skeletal outline. You should write down this outline as a guide to your own thinking in the process of preparing your speech. A sample outline might look as follows:

Title: My Plan for Saving Money

Purpose: To convince the listeners that money is "saved" when it is used for constructive and helpful purposes.

Introduction

I. Your main problem, like mine, is less what to do with money than how to get it in the first place; but this is a subject for a different speech.
II. Henry Ford, whom we would all consider an expert on both getting and saving money, used to advise young people not to save but to spend.

Transition from introduction to discussion: What he really meant was that money is more properly "saved" when it is wisely put to constructive use than it is when it is merely set aside unused.

Discussion

I. Some of your money should be "saved" from selfish or wasteful extravagance by being invested in good works—gifts to your church, Red Cross, the community charities, etc.
II. Some should be "saved" by being invested in your own future—for education, for travel, for books to be used in self-study, etc.
III. Some money should be "saved" by being set aside for emergencies and for use when your earning capacity is reduced or ended—for life insurance, medical insurance, retirement, and savings or investment in stocks or in real estate.

Conclusion

I. Saving is a virtue our ancestors taught us to value highly.
II. Saving intelligently is a complicated process that requires intelligent planning.
III. Using the three principles that have been described, you should plan your own savings program to help you achieve your own goals.

As you look at this sample outline, you may agree that if your listeners accept all three of the "main ideas" they will as a result agree with your purpose—to convince them that "saving" at its best means the wise and constructive use of money. But it is evident that the mere statement of the main ideas will not of itself win agreement with them. Each of the ideas must be supported with facts, with sound reasoning, and with examples or illustrations. In other words, along with a sound skeletal outline which every speech must have, you also need the living flesh of reasonable and convincing supporting materials; and you also will need the adornments of interest-catching humor, or specific examples, or personalized references to your own and your listeners' experience.

Sometimes you will do well to quote briefly from a well-known and accepted authority, just as in the introduction to this speech the authority of Henry Ford is drawn upon. You may find it advisable to cite statistics, such as the number of people in America who live past the normal retirement age of 65. You will need to define what you mean by "saving." Indeed, you would probably begin by giving the usual definition, that it means putting aside some money instead of spending it—and devote the rest of the speech to defining "saving" in different terms. You will need further statistics, such as the costs of education and travel or on hospitalization, and on the added income earned as a result of advanced education, whether it be in school or by self-study. And you would do well to cite specific instances to illustrate each of the major points developed to support your main ideas. All of this is the substance of your "discussion." It is most meaningful when you do have a depth of personal knowledge and experience to back up the fresh information you gather from books, magazines, and newspapers. The further enrichment you bring to the subject by referring to your own experience helps greatly to make your speech convincing. This is why you should seek your subjects from areas where you have a depth of both interest and experience. There is no substitute for really knowing what you are talking about.

The Conclusion. A sample conclusion is already illustrated in the outline above. The principal consideration is that your talk should always end with a purposive and functional conclusion, rather than merely trailing off with the comment, "This is all I have to say," or "I guess that's all." One useful method is to summarize briefly the main ideas you have presented. Another way is to embody the principal point of your speech—your purpose—in a brief anecdote, either serious or humorous. Often an even better ending consists of a practical plan of action recommended to your listeners for putting your main ideas to work. You should keep in mind that though you speak to "an audience," your listeners will react to your remarks as separate individuals. Somehow you must help them to adapt your general comments to their own particular interests and needs.

The Listeners

It has been said that in the classroom what is needed is not good teaching but good learning. The truth is, of course, that good teaching is not that which wins admiration for its cleverness, but that which actually induces good learning. So it is with speaking and listening. Your aim should never be to be admired as a good speaker, but always to help or induce your listeners to react as you think they should. If there is any one special secret to good communicative speaking, it is that it must be so definitely adapted to its audience that each listener will feel it somehow is meant particularly for him. When the widow of the Confederate President Jefferson Davis was asked to explain the secret of her husband's success in convincing his listeners, she replied: "He never forgot that his audience sat one by one."

You can learn to improve your own success in influencing audiences through attaining skill in analysis and adaptation as well as organization.

Analysis and Adaptation. Analysis of the audience should begin with an analysis of yourself. People are in many basic ways alike. You know that as you sit in an audience listening to a speaker, your principal concern is what he has to say *to you*. You observe the reactions of the others present, but you care most about whether he sounds as though he wanted to convey his message to you. Carl Sandburg, trying to explain Lincoln's success as a speaker, said that when he talked to a crowd, it was as though he had each listener sitting beside him on the seat of a buckboard, driving over the prairie, talking to him alone. When Booker T. Washington, the great Negro educator, was addressing a large audience in upstate New York, a man who sat in the third balcony said he felt as though Mr. Washington had taken him by the lapel of his coat and was speaking directly to him. The heart and core of good audience analysis is to remember that everyone in the group is a *person* and to make your speech as personalized as possible.

There are other aspects of audience analysis; if people are very much alike in basic respects, they also have many differences. Children differ from adults in interests and experience. Women have different interests from men. The educated have more knowledge and perhaps keener minds than the uneducated. Your illustrations, your anecdotes, perhaps your arguments, your selection of facts, and even your style should be selected and developed in terms of what you know about the people who will be hearing you.

How you should adapt to your audience must be determined, in part, while you are preparing your speech, long before you go to the meeting place. If you are to speak to an adult group in a Sunday school, you will want to consider their background, what lesson plan they have been following during preceding weeks, their vocations, and their level of sophistication. If your audience is to be a troop of Boy Scouts, a meeting of the Rotary Club, or a PTA, the very nature of the situation tells you a great deal about what you need to say and how you should phrase it.

Many times the occasion for the speech is also a valuable guide. If your talk is to be delivered for a celebration of Washington's birthday, or Veterans Day, or the Fourth of July, or at the annual dinner meeting of your bowling club, the occasion dictates to a large degree the tone and character of the talk you should give. Some occasions call for jocularity, some for solemnity. Some invite detailed consideration of serious topics; others call for a few carefully phrased expressions of good will. People have "patterns of expectation" associated with special events and speakers do well to conform to what is expected of them.

In part, also, both the analysis and the adaptation should occur after you arrive at the scene for the speech, and should continue while you are speaking. No matter how carefully you have prepared your talk, you should be alert to notice the special character of the immediate situation. In your opening remarks it is especially helpful to refer to others on the platform or on the program, and perhaps to events that occur immediately prior to your opening remarks. If other speakers precede you, it is often a good idea to open your own speech with some brief comment about one that has preceded yours.

While you are speaking, you normally will be best advised to follow fairly closely the outline you have prepared. But you should be alert to elements in the circumstances that may be adapted to strengthen your message. One of America's greatest speakers, Wendell Phillips, went to Faneuil Hall in Boston in 1836 prepared to speak about the murder of an abolitionist editor, Elijah Lovejoy, by a mob. When a preceding speaker said the mob reminded him of the Boston patriots who had attacked the British soldiers in 1775, Phillips abandoned his prepared introduction. Instead, he pointed dramatically at the pictures of the patriots hanging on the walls and exclaimed that he expected their "painted lips" to cry out in protest against the comparison. The audience was immensely moved by his speech—partly by the outpouring of his emotion in a storm of eloquence—partly by the extremely appropriate use he made of the portraits of their forefathers hanging on the walls about them. An audience appreciates the evidence a speaker gives that his mind is alert and alive, using the circumstances of the occasion to heighten and improve the quality of his prepared address.

Beyond the introductory remarks, as you progress in your planned address from point to point, you need to be attentive to your listeners to note and evaluate their reactions. It is of little use to go beyond your first point before your audience appears to have accepted it. You may need to add further illustrations or to restate your arguments in another way. Furthermore, if you find unexpected agreement emerging where you expected to meet opposition, you will be wise to abbreviate and condense what you had planned to say on the topic that is readily accepted. Salesmen sometimes lose sales by too much talking after the prospect has made up his mind, and speakers sometimes make the same mistake.

The analysis of your audience, then, proceeds along two lines: (1) assume your listeners are normal people, much like yourself; and (2) note and take account of their special group characteristics. Your adaptation to the audience should be accomplished in three stages: (1) while you are selecting, arranging, and phrasing your materials during the period of preparation; (2) while you are in the hall getting ready to speak; and (3) while you actually are speaking. A speech should not only be carefully and thoughtfully prepared in advance, but minor yet significant revisions of it should continually be undertaken during the course of its delivery.

Strategic Planning. Every speaker needs to remember that he is not doing all the thinking about his subject. His audience thinks, as well. A basic question to guide the preparation of the speech is: What and how much does my audience already know about the subject? At what point should the speaker begin his discussion? How much detail will he need? Will he encounter indifference, antagonism, or perhaps ignorance about basic facts?

Every speech should be planned as closely as possible to *meet the audience where it is*. If you are going to talk about a plan to organize a Little League baseball team in your community, a prior question for you to decide is whether your audience already is prepared to undertake the project and simply needs guidance on how to do it, or whether there is opposition or indifference to the idea. Perhaps you assume indifference, but when you arrive at the meeting you may discover far more enthusiasm than you had expected. In this case, you should abandon your planned opening remarks, substituting instead a compliment to the listeners for their zeal in the cause.

The planning for the body or main discussion in your speech, beyond the introduction, should follow a plan that is appropriate to your subject and also to the presumed character of your audience. For a speech on how to organize a Little League ball team, you might choose to follow chronological sequence—telling them what must be done first, what next, what after that, etc. But if the audience needs to be convinced of the need to make the sacrifices necessary to organize and support a team, you may find the problem-solution pattern more effective. For this kind of organization, you would deal first in your talk with the problem of inadequate recreation, of youngsters becoming dissatisfied and bored, of the lack of meaningful relationships between the children and adults. After the problem had been made vivid and dramatic, you would then raise the question of what to do about it and offer your solution—the establishment of a Little League team.

The philosopher John Dewey wrote a book, *How We Think*, in which he pointed out that normally in trying to deal with any problem our minds proceed through five stages. First, we become aware that a problem exists. Second, we identify or define or seek to understand the nature of the problem. Third, we cast about for all the solutions which appear to be possible or available. Fourth, we sort out the possible solutions, evaluate them, and decide which is best. Finally, we decide upon the one solution that we shall select and take steps to put it into effect. Since this pattern is normal for much of our everyday thinking, it would seem to be an excellent plan for a speech. We show the problem to the audience, making them aware that it truly and significantly affects them. We point out that there is a limited number of available solutions. Then we evaluate the possible courses of action and show the listeners why the solution advocated by the speaker is the best among them.

Another way of deciding how to adapt to your audience is to make a choice between the *deductive* and the *inductive* development of your point of view. If you are deductive, you start by telling the audience what it is that you are advocating, then build up arguments to support it. Thus you may say, "I am speaking to you this evening to advocate a rummage sale to get money with which to buy equipment for our high school basketball team." Then you go on to develop lines of argument to support your idea—that the team is worthy of support, and that your plan is the best available means of getting the needed money. If you decide on an inductive approach, you build interest by relating a number of specific incidents, which finally unite to support the idea that is withheld until the last. In this kind of speech, you might start by reminding the listeners of how proud they were when the team won the district championship. Then you might add that this pride was dampened by the derisive comments that were made about the team's poor equipment. You might interject a story about one of the players whose mother sewed up rips in a number of the shirts worn by team members. Then you would be ready to raise the question: Shouldn't we do something to remedy this situation?

Public speaking, it has aready been pointed out, calls for a special *rhetorical* kind of thinking, thinking that sees the subject of the speech in relation to the speaker's purpose and the nature of his audience. No speech is ever well prepared by simple concentration on the subject matter alone. The problem always is: What can and should be done with the subject matter of the speech to accomplish my purpose with this audience? This is a problem that calls for strategic planning based on analysis of the audience and adapted to its particular circumstances or nature.

The Occasion

Since the nature of the situation often exerts considerable influence on the type of speech that should be prepared and delivered, the occasion itself will make a difference in the style and tone of your speech, as well as governing what you might appropriately say. To a large degree, the occasion will determine your speech's content, style, and mode of delivery.

When you are invited to give a speech, you should be sure to learn whether or not it will be presented at a dinner, in a large or small hall, indoors or outdoors, before a crowd or to only a few listeners. You will also need to know whether the audience will be in a state of animated excitement, as at a political rally, or in a mood of quiet interest, as in a lecture hall. It is important to know whether the members attend because of their desire to hear you, because their attendance is required, or merely from the habit of attending that particular meeting. It will be helpful to know whether the listeners will discuss your ideas at the end of the speech or ask questions; whether they will make reports and perhaps take an examination on it; or whether they will simply expect to be entertained or casually informed. All these considerations are elements of the occasion.

The importance of the occasion in governing the kind of speaking that is (and should be) done is indicated in the following passage from a description of Puritan preaching in colonial New England:

> The length of the sermon presented special problems because of the physical discomfort suffered by the listeners. For many years, no church had either artificial light or any method of heating. Despite the icy blasts of winter, which easily penetrated the thin walls and the bare boards laid upon the ground, even foot-warmers were frowned upon during the early decades. Fireplaces were not admitted to the sanctuary until well into the eighteenth century. The preacher could keep himself warm with the ardor of his feeling and the physical activity of his speaking. But he had to warm his auditors with vivid exhortation. Since the taste of the Puritans demanded a plain style, liveliness was achieved primarily by sensational descriptions of hellfire for those not saved by predestined salvation, and, secondly, by the use of homely illustrations. Thomas Hooker, for example, compared the human body in process of resurrection to an onion, with the earthly residues being peeled off in successive layers until only the soul is left. Cotton Mather was fond of the image of the devil bound in God's chains, from which he was forever struggling to break free, and which could be kept tight only through the faith of true believers. Repetition was a frequent device to make sure no one missed the point through nursing his cold hands. And to aid further in clarity, the framework of the ideas was indicated by a succession of *firstlies, secondlies*, and so on. The style was usually not distinguished, but it was vivid, personalized, and clear. Each listener was helped to feel, "This is for me."[1]

The importance of fitting the speech to the occasion was well understood by Charles C. Nott, who in 1860 invited Abraham Lincoln to give the speech in the famous Cooper Institute hall in New York City which, far more than the Lincoln-Douglas debates, convinced the leaders of the Republican party that the gangling lawyer from Illinois should receive their nomination for the presidency of the United States. In the first place, Nott wrote to Lincoln, what was desired was not a political campaign speech, but a "political lecture." Lincoln's speech, he went on, would be the third in a series, with the first two delivered by men much better known to the audience than Lincoln would be. Nott then added: "These lectures have been *contrived* to call out our better, but busier citizens, who never attend political meetings. A large part of the audience would also consist of ladies." Lincoln was so impressed that he wrote out his speech in full, which he seldom did, and had it read over in advance by the editors of the Chicago *Tribune*, so that he might profit from their reactions.[2]

It should be evident, both from these examples and from your own observations of speakers you hear, that speaking should be fitted to the time, place, and nature of the situation in which it will be delivered. No one would wear a tuxedo to a football game, nor tennis shoes to a dance. No more should a formal address be given to a casual audience eager to be entertained, nor a colloquial or slangy talk be presented from the pulpit of a church. The nature of the occasion governs the manner of speaking as surely as etiquette guides the behavior of guests who may attend a picnic one day and a formal banquet the next. From what has been said, it is apparent that the speaker "makes his own speech" but within rather definite limitations that are imposed by the nature of his audience, the purpose and character of the meeting, the sponsorship for his talk, and the length of time assigned to him.

You Begin to Give Speeches

Part of learning to speak effectively must come from actually giving speeches. To return to the tennis analogy with which we started, you could never become a tennis player by reading about it. On the other hand, practice alone is not enough. Practice does not make perfect; it makes permanent. The things you practice become habitual. You may occasionally hear teachers or preachers (who do a vast amount of public speaking) drone, mumble, talk in tones of flat impersonality, fumble, toy with their glasses, inject a series of ah's and uh's into their talk, and in general demonstrate that boredom, clumsiness, and ineffectiveness are not necessarily eliminated through a great deal of practice in public speaking. In addition to practice, you need careful and alert study of the principles of sound oral communication; you need to be critical of what you do and how you do it in order to progress and correct or eliminate your initial mistakes. But the fact that practice alone is not enough does not detract from the fact that without practice you never can learn the skills required for platform proficiency.

In your initial stages as a public speaker you should no more seek out large and prominent audiences than you would enter a tennis tournament while you were still learning the game. Beginning tennis players match themselves against other beginners. Similarly, the best means of getting your early experience as a public speaker is to organize a small group of like-minded people and practice giving speeches to one another—with a critical analysis of each speech conducted by the group. If you find no more than three or four associates to join in these first practice sessions, that number will suffice. You need an audience; and you need one that will be attentive to the skills and insights needed for effective communicative speech, one that will have the courage and the concern required to make them courteous but thorough critics of your efforts. You, in turn, will learn the principles of effective speaking all the more thoroughly from serving as a critic of their talks.

From these practice sessions you should emerge into genuine audience situations where the purpose is not to *learn* but to *do*. Again, you will be wise not to seek large audiences nor important occasions for your first speeches, but you will also be wise to treat every audience and every speech you undertake to give as though they were of the utmost importance. Your ability to speak well will develop soundly only if you make it an unbreakable rule always to speak your best, everywhere, at all times—in your daily conversation and in casual and informal discussions, as well as in public speeches.

[1]Robert T. Oliver, *History of Public Speaking in America*, Boston: By permission, Allyn & Bacon, Inc., 1965, pp. 10–11.

[2]Nott's letter and Lincoln's reactions are taken from Andrew A. Freeman, *Abraham Lincoln Goes to New York*, New York: Coward-McCann, Inc., 1960, pp. 52 and 54.

Audiences exist all around you and are not difficult to locate if you know what to look for. Sunday schools of many denominations offer a readily accessible audience. You might volunteer to teach a class for one Sunday morning. At the very least, you can take an active part in the discussion of the lesson, which means you surely will be giving one or several brief speeches. You might suggest the formation of a committee from your class to organize a picnic or for some other purpose, and you will no doubt be appointed as one of its members. Although you might not think of two or four other committee members as an audience, they are, and they will give you the opportunity to deliver carefully prepared (though appropriately casual and informal) "speeches to convince" on your ideas as to what the committee should do.

Even the greatest speakers had to start with small audiences. Indeed, two of our greatest American orators, William Jennings Bryan and Albert J. Beveridge, gave themselves considerable experience in attaining oral fluency and variety by going out into the fields and talking to tree stumps. Both of them then entered various speech contests in their schools and developed their abilities in competition with their peers.

Russell Conwell, who was one of the most successful speakers on the Chautauqua lecture circuit, got his first experience by talking to his fellow students in a one-room country school. On Friday afternoons, and on special evening occasions, the adults were invited, to provide a larger and more demanding audience. As Conwell told one of his lecture audiences: "The ideal school of oratory in the old days was established in the country schoolhouse in the winter evenings, when some of the citizens organized an evening lyceum for the purpose of holding regular debates. I was always timid and made the most foolish blunders, and yet some tyrannical spirit within me ever pushed me forward to say something upon the question whenever an opportunity was given me to do so. It was a strange, subconscious pressure which forced me to overcome a very decided feeling of diffidence in public, and shame for my failures. . . . That debating society was the best possible training for public speaking that a boy could secure."[3]

There is an old piece of advice that used to be given to anyone who was trying to improve his ability as a speaker: "If anyone is fool enough to ask you to make a speech, you be fool enough to accept." Speakers are not born. There is not some mysterious quality of eloquence that some people have and others have not. The ability to speak well has to be learned, and it *can* be learned by anyone of reasonable intelligence who is willing to learn the principles and techniques and has the determination to persist until they are mastered.

[3]Agnes Rush Burr, *Russell H. Conwell and His Work*, Philadelphia: John C. Winston Company, 1926, p. 329. By permission, Holt, Rinehart and Winston, Inc., publishers.

HOW TO START A CLUB AND RUN ITS MEETINGS

PARLIAMENTARY PROCEDURE

by John Bradley

Every day, year in and year out, thousands of small clubs or societies, such as garden clubs, church societies, building and trade associations, may be found holding their meetings. Every day, too, new clubs are being formed. The existence of this multitude of small societies is a healthy manifestation of the democratic process in action. For in our democratic way of life even the smallest society organizes itself, and conducts its meetings in accordance with a system of rules that insures full, fair and free discussion leading to a course of action determined by the majority. This system of rules, variously called parliamentary procedure or parliamentary law or rules of order, governs every democratic assembly, from the highest legislative body to the smallest village community club. The rules used in guiding a small club are, of course, fewer and less complex than those used by Congress. Consequently this article, which aims at helping those who have a practical interest in small clubs, will not attempt a comprehensive treatment of parliamentary procedure. Rather, it will concentrate on the procedure that is necessary and sufficient to establish a small society and run its meetings in a democratic and effective manner.

ORGANIZING A CLUB

Interest in forming a club is normally shared by a few people. These people should meet and carefully discuss the kind of organization they have in mind. Attention should first be given to such things as the purpose of the club, how this purpose is to be accomplished, how the club will be financed, and who will be admitted to membership. Plans should then be made for calling the first meeting. In making these plans it is important to decide on the following details: (1) Date, time, and place of the first meeting. Who will secure the accommodations? (2) Invitations to be issued to those who would probably be interested in such a club. Invitations should announce not only the place, date and hour of the meeting, but also its purpose. How should invitations be issued? By letter, telephone, word-of-mouth, radio? Who will take care of this? (3) Who will call the first meeting to order? (4) Who will explain the purpose of the meeting to the gathering?

The First Meeting

When the people gather for the first meeting the person previously designated for this task assumes the chair, raps on the table and says, "Will the meeting please come to order." When the meeting has come to order he sets about forming a temporary organization as follows: "I nominate Mr. X for temporary chairman (alternatively he may ask for nominations from the floor). Is there a second?" When this proposal or motion has been seconded he says, "All in favor will please say, 'Aye.' All opposed will say, 'No.' " Since Mr. X was nominated because of his competence and general suitability it is unlikely that he will be defeated. The result of the vote is then announced thus: "The motion is carried, and Mr. X is elected temporary chairman. Will he please take the chair." Mr. X now takes over the chair and conducts the meeting. His first business is to call for the election of a temporary secretary. The temporary secretary, who is elected in the same manner as the temporary chairman, takes a seat at the table near the chair and records the proceedings of the meeting from the beginning.

Motion to Form a Club

The temporary chairman now calls on the person chosen for this job when the meeting was planned to explain fully the purpose of the gathering. After suitable discussion of the proposed new organization a formal motion that a club of this kind be formed should be offered: "I move that this assembly form a permanent club to be known as . . . ." If this motion is seconded and receives a majority vote, someone should move that a committee be appointed to draft bylaws. It is normal for the chairman to appoint this committee. (A word to the members of the bylaws committee: First make sure that you thoroughly understand the purposes of the proposed club. Then survey the constitutions and bylaws that have been successfully used by similar organizations. Collections of such constitutions and bylaws may be consulted in most libraries.) After the bylaws committee has been appointed the chairman asks, "Is there any other business?" When all business has been completed a motion to adjourn ("I move that we adjourn") should be made and seconded. When this motion has been carried the chairman says, "This meeting is adjourned, and will meet at (time and place of the next meeting)."

Second Meeting

The principal business of the second meeting will be a consideration of the report of the bylaws committee. The temporary chairman calls the meeting to order and instructs the secretary to read the minutes of the previous meeting. As soon as the minutes have been read, corrected, if necessary, and approved, the chairman announces the report of the bylaws committee as the next business in order. The chairman of the committee then comes forward and reads the entire list of bylaws. A second complete reading of the bylaws may be dispensed with by general consent of the assembly. Then each paragraph is read and discussed and amended. No vote is taken after each separate paragraph has been dealt with. A vote is taken at the end on the acceptance or rejection of the entire list of bylaws. For the adoption of bylaws a majority vote suffices. The next order of business is the election of permanent officers. Normally the procedures for the nomination and election of officers is prescribed in the bylaws and should be strictly observed. After the election of permanent officers, unless there is other business that requires immediate attention, the meeting should be adjourned. The club has now achieved a permanent organization, and is ready to begin its regular business at the next meeting.

Quorum

No action taken in a business meeting of any organized society is legally binding unless a certain number of its members was present. That number, usually specified in the bylaws, is called a *quorum.* It is the largest number of members that may reasonably be expected to attend meetings under ordinary circumstances, and a number that would be competent to conduct business. Bylaws frequently specify a quorum of one-third or one-quarter of the members. If the bylaws do not specify a number, a quorum is a majority of the members. It is the duty of the presiding officer to determine the presence of a quorum. When a quorum is present, decisions can be officially made whether or not all present vote. For instance, a club with a membership of 100, whose quorum is specified as one-quarter of the members, may find that though 25 members are present at a meeting only 20 vote. If the motion receives a majority vote the decision is official, even though five members did not vote. The same rule applies to decisions that require a two-thirds majority.

Order of Business

A chairman, in conducting the business of a meeting, must follow the order of business laid down in the bylaws of the club. The following order is typical:

1. Call to order.
2. Roll call. If this takes too much time, such alternatives as having the members sign their names in a roster, or having tellers check them, may be used.
3. Reading and approval of the minutes of the last meeting.
4. Reports of officers.
5. Reports of committees.
6. Unfinished business.
7. New business.
8. Announcements.
9. Adjournment.

Introducing Business

Whenever any business is brought to the attention of a meeting, the action to be taken on that business is proposed in the form of a *motion.* The member desiring to make a motion must "get the floor," i.e., he must (1) *stand,* (2) *address the chairman,* and (3) *be recognized* by him. When the member has made his motion he should take his seat. Next, the motion usually must be seconded by another member and restated by the chairman. It is then ready to be discussed by the assembly if it is a debatable motion. Any motion that is long or involved should be in writing and should be given to the secretary as soon as it has been read. Such a motion is usually called a *resolution.* A motion is proposed in the following manner:

MR. A (*standing*): Mr. (Madam) Chairman.
CHAIRMAN: Mr. A.
MR. A: I move that . . . (*or* I move to . . .)
MR. B (*seated*): I second the motion.
CHAIRMAN: It has been moved by Mr. A and seconded by Mr. B that . . . (he repeats the motion). Is there any discussion?

Discussion follows. Each person desiring to speak must first get the floor. Any person failing to observe this procedure is ruled out of order by the chairman. If two or more persons rise simultaneously and address the chairman, recognition will be given to:

1. One who has not spoken previously on the same question.
2. The one who made the motion.
3. One who is opposed to the views of the previous speaker.

Discussion

In the discussion of a question the following points should be observed:

1. No member may speak more than twice on the same question during the meeting.
2. No member may speak a second time on the same question until others who have not spoken at all have had an opportunity to speak.
3. No one may speak longer than ten minutes at one time except by general consent or a two-thirds vote.
4. Every speaker must confine his remarks to the question that is placed before the meeting by the chairman. If a speaker disregards this he is out of order.
5. Members are not allowed to address one another directly. All remarks are addressed to the chairman.
6. Any member who, in speaking from the floor, refers to another member in a discourteous manner or impugns the motives of another or uses improper language or is disorderly in any other way, should be ruled out of order. In serious cases he may be required to apologize, and if he refuses to apologize, he may be disciplined by the assembly.
7. When a speaker is ruled out of order he should take his seat immediately.
8. A person who has made a motion is not permitted to speak against it.

CLASSIFICATION AND PRECEDENCE OF MOTIONS

It should now be very clear that the device we call a "motion" has a most important role in the work of conducting a club's business. Since this is so, it follows that unless the motions themselves are governed by strict procedures, an orderly, fair, and free discussion of that business will be impossible. Consequently the various motions are governed by definite rules of precedence. In other words, there is a fixed priority or order according to which motions may be proposed, discussed and acted upon. The following four groups of motions are classified according to their purpose and precedence.

Main Motions These have the lowest rank of all motions.
Subsidiary Motions These rank immediately above main motions. They also have a fixed order of precedence among themselves.
Privileged Motions These outrank both subsidiary and main motions, and have a fixed order of precedence among themselves.
Incidental Motions As a group these rank above subsidiary motions and below privileged motions. They have no order of precedence among themselves, but take their rank from the motions to which they apply.

Order of Precedence

The following table lists the more common privileged, subsidiary, and main motions in their order of precedence.

I PRIVILEGED MOTIONS
1. Adjourn.
2. Take a recess.
3. Raise a question of privilege.
4. Call for "Orders of the Day."

II SUBSIDIARY MOTIONS
5. Lay on the table.
6. Close debate.
7. Limit or extend debate.
8. Postpone to a certain time.
9. Refer to a committee.
10. Amend.
11. Postpone indefinitely.

III MAIN MOTIONS
12. Main motions from the floor or committee.

Rules of Precedence

There are two basic rules of precedence: (1) When a motion is pending any motion that outranks it in precedence may be proposed, but no motion of lower rank may be proposed. Thus, if a motion to refer to a committee is pending (9th in order of precedence), a motion to limit or extend debate (7th in order of precedence) may be proposed. But a motion to postpone indefinitely (11th) may not be proposed. (2) Motions are considered and voted on in inverse order to their proposal. Thus, if motions ranking 12th, 10th, and 6th were proposed in that order and are all pending, the one ranking 6th is taken up and considered first, then the one ranking 10th, and finally the one ranking 12th.

Main Motions

Main motions are the most important class of motions, for they are aimed at getting some action on the primary items of business listed on the program of a business meeting. Though they are the most important, main motions are nevertheless outranked in precedence by every other motion. This shows us that precedence does not indicate importance, but simply determines the order in which the various motions are taken up and dealt with. Main motions and resolutions are identical in function, but different words are used in introducing them. A main motion begins with the form: "I move that . . ." A resolution is introduced thus: "I move the adoption of the following resolution: Resolved, that . . ." Any motion that is long or involved should be written and proposed in the form of a resolution. As soon as it has been proposed it should be given to the secretary.

Subsidiary Motions

The purpose of the various subsidiary motions is to help the assembly in considering and acting upon the main motion. Subsidiary motions outrank main motions in precedence, and have an order of precedence among themselves (see table on page 1631). Although only one main motion can be before an assembly at any given time, one or more or all of the subsidiary motions can be pending at the same time, each to be disposed of in its proper order of precedence. The subsidiary motions are outranked in precedence by the four privileged motions and are numbered accordingly in the following list.

5. **Lay on the Table** This is the highest ranking subsidiary motion. Its purpose is to lay aside, or postpone temporarily, the consideration of a motion until a later time.

Form: "I move that the motion (or amendment) be laid on the table." *or* "I move that the motion (or amendment) be postponed temporarily."

This motion requires: a second; majority vote. It is not debatable.

6. **Close Debate** This motion is also known as "Call for the Previous Question," or "Vote Immediately." Its purpose is to halt all further consideration of the questions pending and bring them to a vote.

Form: "I move that we vote immediately on the motion to . . ." *or* "I move that we vote immediately on the main motion and the motions adhering to it." *or* "I call for the 'Previous Question' on . . ."

This motion requires: a second; two-thirds vote. It is not debatable.

7. **Limit or Extend Debate** This motion is aimed at extending or restricting the time devoted to the discussion of a question. It is frequently adopted by unanimous consent.

Form: "I move that debate on . . . be limited to . . . minutes." *or* "I move that debate on . . . be limited to one five-minute speech by each speaker." *or* "I move that the discussion period be extended . . . minutes." *or* "I move that the discussion be extended to . . . o'clock."

This motion requires: a second; two-thirds vote. It is not debatable.

8. **Postpone to a Certain Time** The purpose of this motion is to suspend discussion of a question and fix a later, definite time for its further consideration. If a question is postponed to a certain time it is treated as an "order of the day" for that time and so will precede New Business.

Form: "I move to postpone consideration of the question until the next meeting (or some other specific time)."

This motion requires: a second; majority vote. Only the propriety of postponement to a certain time is debatable.

9. **Refer to a Committee** This motion may be made for various reasons. The proposer may feel that the matter requires more detailed study by a smaller group, or that it is too delicate for public airing, or that it should be held up for some time in committee. The proposer may specify such details as the type of committee, number of members, how members are to be selected, etc. If not, the chairman may ask the assembly for suggestions, which may be adopted by general consent or voted on.

Form: "I move to refer the motion to a committee." *or* "I move that the motion be referred to a committee consisting of Mrs. A, Mr. B and Mr. C." *or* "I move that the motion be referred to a committee of 5 (or 3 or 7) members appointed by the chair." *or* "I move that the motion be referred to the Committee on Membership (or some other standing committee)." *or* "I move that the chair appoint a committee of 3 (or 5 or 7) members to study the question of . . . and report suitable resolutions at our next regular meeting."

This motion requires: a second; majority vote. Only the propriety of referring the question to a committee is debatable.

10. **Amend** A motion to amend a main motion is made with the purpose of changing or modifying the main motion or resolution, so that it will more truly meet the mind of the assembly. An amendment of a main motion or resolution is called a *primary* amendment. A primary amendment may itself be amended in the same manner as a main motion. An amendment of an amendment is called a *secondary* amendment. The three common types of amendment are: (a) amendment by addition of certain words to the motion; (b) amendment by elimination of certain words from the motion; (c) amendment by the substitution of a new motion for the original motion (but the substitution must not destroy the original question).

Form: "I move to amend the motion by adding (or inserting) the words . . ." *or* "I move to amend the motion by eliminating the words . . ." *or* "I move to substitute for this motion the following motion . . ."

This motion requires: a second; majority vote. It is debatable, unless applied to an undebatable motion.

11. **Postpone Indefinitely** The name given to this motion is misleading. Its purpose is not to postpone consideration of a question but to kill it. It is often used by members who oppose a motion but fear they may not have sufficient votes to defeat it. A motion that has been postponed indefinitely may be brought up at a later meeting, but it must then be proposed as a new motion.

Form: "I move that the motion to . . . be postponed indefinitely." *or* "I move to postpone action on the main motion indefinitely."

This motion requires: a second; majority vote. It is debatable.

Privileged Motions

Privileged motions, unlike subsidiary motions, are not directly related to the main motion. They are motions dealing with matters of such urgency that they require immediate attention. Since they are emergency motions, privileged motions as a class have the highest order of precedence. They also have an order of precedence among themselves and are numbered accordingly in the following list:

1. **Adjourn (unqualified)** The purpose of this motion is to bring a meeting to an end at once. A qualified motion to adjourn ("I move we adjourn in ten minutes") is not a privileged motion; it is a main motion and as such is of the lowest rank in precedence. Although the unqualified motion to adjourn has the highest rank of any motion it is out of order when another person has the floor, or while a vote is being taken. Furthermore, the chairman should not permit the motion until announcements and important business have been disposed of, and the time and place of the next meeting settled.

Form: "I move that we adjourn."

This motion requires: a second; majority vote. It is not debatable.

2. **Take a Recess** The purpose of this motion is to provide an intermission within a meeting. After the recess the chairman calls the meeting to order, and business is resumed at the point where it was interrupted.

Form: "I move that we take a recess of . . . minutes (or hours)." *or* "I move that we take a recess until . . . o'clock."

This motion requires: a second; majority vote. It is not debatable.

3. **Raise a Question of Privilege** This motion is concerned with the rights and privileges of the assembly as a whole, or the rights and privileges of an individual member. It is used in such circumstances as the following: disorderly conduct during a meeting; unsatisfactory conditions of the meeting place; charges made against the character of a member; illness. When a member raises a question of privilege the chairman will decide whether it is such or not, and will rule accordingly. Any two

members may, of course, appeal from the chairman's ruling, thus forcing the matter to a vote.

Form: MR. A: Mr. (Madam) Chairman, (*and then, without waiting to be recognized*) I rise to a question of privilege.
CHAIRMAN: The member will please state his request.
MR. A: I request that the visitors be asked to leave this meeting before we continue.
CHAIRMAN: Your request is granted. Will the visitors please leave at once.

This motion requires: no second; no vote. It is not debatable.

4. **Call for "Orders of the Day"** This motion is concerned with deviations from the duly established order of business. If the chairman does not adhere to this order any member has the right to demand that he do so.

Form: "I call for 'orders of the day.' " *or* "I call for a return to the 'orders of the day.' "

This motion requires: no second; no vote, unless the chairman maintains there has been no deviation (majority vote needed), or contends that the deviation is justified (two-thirds vote needed). It is not debatable.

Incidental Motions

Incidental motions are so named because they arise only incidentally out of the business that is being considered by the assembly. As a group they rank in precedence above subsidiary motions and below privileged motions. Unlike all the motions discussed so far they have no fixed order of precedence among themselves. They take their rank from the motions to which they are applied. Since these motions have no precedence among themselves the order in which they are listed below is quite arbitrary.

1. **Appeal** When a decision by the chairman seems to be in error or unfair, any member may appeal from that decision. Immediately after the decision has been announced—but not later—he should rise, and without waiting to be recognized (even though another member has the floor) should make his appeal.

Form: MR. A: Mr. (Madam) Chairman, I appeal from the decision of the chair.
CHAIRMAN: The decision of the chair has been appealed from. Will the member appealing please give his grounds for appeal.
When the member has given his grounds for appeal the chairman may state the reasons for his decision (or he may postpone this until after discussion). The question is then put to vote as follows:
CHAIRMAN: Those in favor of sustaining the decision of the chair say, "Aye." Those opposed, say, "No." . . . The decision of the chair is sustained (overruled).

This motion requires: a second; majority or tie vote. It is debatable.

2. **Division of a Question** When a motion has several parts a member can request that it be divided into two or more independent propositions, and each proposition considered and voted on separately. Thus it becomes possible to adopt certain parts of the motion and reject others. The chairman will decide if a motion can be divided.

Form: MR. A: I move that the question be divided and considered in two (or more) parts as follows . . . (specifying exactly how the division is made).
CHAIRMAN: (if he decides that the question can be divided suitably) It is requested that the motion be divided into two (or more) parts. If there is no objection this will be done. The motion now before the assembly is . . .

This motion requires: no second; no vote. It is not debatable.

3. **Division of the Assembly** The purpose of this motion is to secure an accurate vote. If a vote has been taken by voice or by a show of hands and there is a reasonable doubt as to the outcome, any member may, without rising or addressing the chair, demand a standing vote.

Form: MR. A: I call for a division.
CHAIRMAN: A division has been called for. All in favor of the motion (he states the motion just voted on) please rise. The secretary will please count . . . Be seated . . . Those opposed, please rise . . . Be seated . . . The vote in favor of the motion is 10. The vote against the motion is 13. The motion, therefore, is defeated.

This motion requires: no second; no vote. It is not debatable.

4. **Objection to Consideration** The chairman may rule out of order any motion that is irrelevant, contentious, or embarrassing. If he fails to do so any member, even when another has the floor, may rise and object. Objections, however, must be made immediately after the motion to which it applies has been presented, and before debate has begun.

Form: MR. A: Mr. (Madam) Chairman, I object to the consideration of this question.
CHAIRMAN: An objection has been raised to the consideration of this question. All opposed to the consideration of this question please rise . . . Be seated . . . Those in favor, please rise . . . Be seated . . . There is a two-thirds vote opposed. The question, therefore, will not be considered.

This motion requires: no second; two-thirds vote. It is not debatable.

5. **Parliamentary Inquiry** If a member desires some information on a question of procedure he should rise and, without waiting to be recognized, put his inquiry to the chairman.

Form: MR. A: I rise to a parliamentary inquiry.
CHAIRMAN: Please state your inquiry.
MR. A: Is an amendment in order at this time?
CHAIRMAN: It is not.

Variations of a parliamentary inquiry are: (1) a request for information concerning the motion pending; (2) a request to ask the speaker a question.

Form (1): MR. A: Mr. (Madam) Chairman, I rise for information.
CHAIRMAN: What is the member's question?
MR. A: I should like to know . . .
CHAIRMAN: (will supply the information requested)
Form (2): MR. A: Mr. (Madam) Chairman, I should like to ask the speaker a question.
CHAIRMAN: Is the speaker willing to answer the question?
SPEAKER: I am willing.

This motion requires: no second; no vote. It is not debatable.

6. **Point of Order** The chairman has the duty of guarding against any breach of the rules. If he does not notice a violation of the rules or disregards it, any member may draw his attention to it and insist, if necessary, that the rules be strictly enforced. In such a case the member will rise, even though another has the floor and, without waiting to be recognized, address the chair.

Form: MR. A: Mr. (Madam) Chairman, I rise to a point of order.
CHAIRMAN: The member may state the point.

If the member is right the chairman must correct the error at once. If the chairman cannot decide whether or not there has been a violation of the rules he may: (1) ask the advice of other members he considers competent; (2) put the matter to the assembly; (3) defer a decision until he has had time to study the matter more fully.

This motion requires: no second; no vote. It is not debatable.

7. **Suspend the Rules** If an assembly finds it necessary or desirable to take some action that conflicts with the rules of order or standing rules, it may, by a two-thirds vote, suspend temporarily the rule(s) involved.

Form: MR. A: Mr. (Madam) Chairman, I move to suspend the rule(s) that interferes with . . .
CHAIRMAN: It has been moved and seconded to suspend the rule(s) that interferes with . . . All in favor please rise . . . Be seated . . . Those opposed, please rise . . . Be seated . . . There is a two-thirds vote in favor. The The rule(s) is (are), therefore suspended.

This motion requires: a second; two-thirds vote. It is not debatable.

8. **Withdraw a Motion** The author of a motion may withdraw or change his motion at any time before it is stated by the chairman. After it has been stated, however, it can be withdrawn or changed only by general consent or a vote.

Form: MR. A: Mr. (Madam) Chairman, I ask leave to withdraw (change) my motion.
CHAIRMAN: Mr. A asks leave to withdraw (change) his motion. If there is no objection, the motion is withdrawn (changed).

If anyone objects the chairman may put the question to a vote, or Mr. A or any other member may move that leave be granted to withdraw (change) the motion.

This motion requires: no second; no vote unless questioned. It is not debatable.

CONSULT STANDARD WORKS

As we observed at the beginning of this article, the foregoing explanation of parliamentary procedure is aimed at helping those who have a practical interest in starting and running a small club. It is not, nor is it meant to be, a comprehensive treatment of this complex subject. Consequently while we are confident that it will prove to be adequate for meeting its purpose in most instances, questions could arise that would require the help of a truly comprehensive treatment. In such cases the standard works on parliamentary procedure, which are readily available in most libraries, should be consulted.

QUOTATIONS

The following pages contain more than 1600 significant sayings, epigrams, and thoughts of all ages, including our own. The quotations are grouped under 178 subject headings —from *Ability* to *Youth*—and following each is the author's name, his birth and death dates, and, in most cases, the source from which the quotation was obtained.

Most of the selections come from familiar sources—Shakespeare, Emerson, Bacon, Cervantes, Cicero, La Rochefoucauld, Aristotle, Thomas Jefferson, the Old and New Testaments, etc. Many additional selections, however, have been made from the ranks of contemporary thinkers, world leaders, and authors. Among those quoted are Lyndon B. Johnson, John F. Kennedy, Pope John XXIII, Winston Churchill, Arthur Miller, Eleanor Roosevelt, Jacques Maritain, and Edith Hamilton.

ABILITY

Natural abilities are like natural plants, that need pruning by study.
— FRANCIS BACON (1561–1620) *Essays: Of Studies*

I add this also, that natural ability without education has oftener raised man to glory and virtue than education without natural ability.
— CICERO (106–43 B.C.) *Oratio Pro Licinio Archia*

Skill to do comes of doing.
— RALPH WALDO EMERSON (1803–1882) *Society and Solitude*

A man who qualifies himself well for his calling, never fails of employment.
— THOMAS JEFFERSON (1743–1826)

It is a great ability to be able to conceal one's ability.
— FRANÇOIS DE LA ROCHEFOUCAULD (1613–1680) *Maxims*

Better be proficient in one art than a smatterer in a hundred.
— JAPANESE PROVERB

So long as a man imagines that he cannot do this or that, so long is he determined not to do it; and consequently so long is it impossible to him that he should do it.
— BENEDICT SPINOZA (1632–1677) *Ethics*

They are able because they think they are able.
— VERGIL (70–19 B.C.) *Aeneid*

ABSENCE

But ay the tear comes in me ee,
To think on him that's far awa.
— ROBERT BURNS (1759–1796) *The Bonnie Lad That's Far Awa*

Our hours in love have wings; in absence crutches.
— COLLEY CIBBER (1671–1757) *Xerxes*

To him that absent is All things succeed amiss
— CERVANTES (1547–1616) *Don Quixote*

Friends, though absent, are still present.
— CICERO (106–43 B.C.) *De Amicitia*

Absence from whom we love is worse than death
And frustrate hope severer than despair
— WILLIAM COWPER (1731–1800) *Despair at his Separation*

Love reckons hours for months, and days for years;
And every little absence is an age.
— JOHN DRYDEN (1631–1700) *Amphitryon*

Out of sight, out of mind
— HOMER (*c.* 10th–8th C. B.C.) *Odyssey*

Friendship, like love, is destroyed by long absence, though it may be increased by short intermissions.
— SAMUEL JOHNSON (1709–1784) *The Idler*

But O the heavy change, now thou art gone,
Now thou art gone, and never must return!
— JOHN MILTON (1608–1674) *Lycidas*

Two evils, monstrous either one apart
Possessed me, and were long and loath at going:
A cry of Absence, Absence, in the heart,
And in the wood the furious winter blowing.
— JOHN CROWE RANSOM (1888–) *Winter Remembered*

Hast thou no care of me? shall I abide
In this dull world, which in thy absence is
No better than a sty?
— SHAKESPEARE (1564–1616) *Antony and Cleopatra*, IV, xiii, 60

The Lord watch between me and thee, when we are absent one from another.
— OLD TESTAMENT: *Genesis*, xxxi, 49

Greater things are believed of those who are absent.
— TACITUS (*c.* 55–117) *Histories*

ACTION

I am perplexed . . . whether to act or not to act.
— AESCHYLUS (525–456 B.C.) *Suppliant Maidens*

Of every noble action the intent
Is to give worth reward, vice punishment.
— FRANCIS BEAUMONT (1584–1616) and JOHN FLETCHER (1579–1625) *The Captain*

The end of man is an action, not a thought.
— THOMAS CARLYLE (1795–1881) *Sartor Resartus*

Action may not always bring happiness; but there is no happiness without action.
— BENJAMIN DISRAELI (1804–1881) *Lothair*

A man's action is only a picture book of his creed.
— RALPH WALDO EMERSON (1803–1882)

Brave actions never want a Trumpet.
— THOMAS FULLER (1608–1681) *Gnomologia*

The great end of life is not knowledge, but action.
— T. H. HUXLEY (1825–1895) *Technical Education*

We would often be ashamed of our finest actions if the world understood all the motives which produced them.
— FRANÇOIS DE LA ROCHEFOUCAULD (1613–1680) *Maxims*

Actions speak louder than words.
— PROVERB

One hour of life, crowded to the full with glorious action, and filled with noble risks, is worth whole years of those mean observances of paltry decorum.
— SIR WALTER SCOTT (1771–1832) *Count Robert of Paris*

If it were done when 'tis done, then 'twere well
It were done quickly.
— SHAKESPEARE (1564–1616) *Macbeth*, I, vii, i

Heaven n'er helps the men who will not act.
— SOPHOCLES (495–406 B.C.) *Fragment*

No sooner said than done.
— TERENCE (*c.* 190–150 B.C.) *Eunuchus*

We cannot think first and act afterwards. From the moment of birth we are immersed in action, and can only fitfully guide it by taking thought.
— ALFRED NORTH WHITEHEAD (1861–1947)

ADVERSITY

The virtue of prosperity is temperance; the virtue of adversity is fortitude . . . .
— FRANCIS BACON (1561–1620) *Essays*

Hope and patience are two sovereign remedies for all, the surest reposals, the softest cushions to lean on in adversity.
— ROBERT BURTON (1577–1640) *Anatomy of Melancholy*

Adversity is sometimes hard upon a man; but for one man who can stand prosperity there are a hundred that will stand adversity.
— THOMAS CARLYLE (1795–1881) *Heroes and Hero-Worship*

Friendship, of itself a holy tie,
Is made more sacred by adversity.
— JOHN DRYDEN (1631–1700) *The Hind and the Panther*

In time of prosperity friends will be plenty;
In time of adversity not one in twenty.
— JAMES HOWELL (1594?–1666) *Proverbs*

Mishaps are like knives, that either serve us or cut us, as we grasp them by the blade or the handle.
— HERMAN MELVILLE (1819–1891) *Cambridge Thirty Years Ago*

In adversity a man is saved by hope.
— MENANDER (342–291 B.C.) *Fragments*

It is a kingly action, believe me, to come to the help of those who are fallen.
— OVID (43 B.C.–A.D. 18?) *Epistulae ex Ponto*

Great men rejoice in adversity just as brave soldiers triumph in war.
— SENECA (4? B.C.–A.D. 65) *De Providentia*

Trial is the true test of mortal men.
— PINDAR (*c.* 522–442 B.C.) *Olympian Odes*

Of one ill comes many.
— SCOTTISH PROVERB

Sweet are the uses of adversity,
Which like the toad, ugly and venomous,
Wears yet a precious jewel in his head.
— SHAKESPEARE (1564–1616) *As You Like It,* II, i, 12

The worst is not
So long as we can say, "This is the worst."
— SHAKESPEARE (1564–1616) *King Lear,* IV, i, 28

It is the duty of all persons, when affairs are the most prosperous, then in especial to reflect within themselves in what way they are to endure adversity.
— TERENCE (*c.* 190–150 B.C.) *Phormio*

In the day of prosperity be joyful, but in the day of adversity consider.
— OLD TESTAMENT: *Ecclesiastes,* viii

A friend loveth at all times, and a brother is born for adversity.
— OLD TESTAMENT: *Proverbs,* xvii, 17

ADVICE

A fool sometimes gives weighty advice.
— NICHOLAS BOILEAU (1636–1711)

Who cannot give good counsel? 'Tis cheap, it costs them nothing.
— ROBERT BURTON (1577–1640) *Anatomy of Melancholy*

A woman's advice is not worth much, but he who doesn't heed it is a fool.
— PEDRO CALDERÓN (1600–1681) *El medico de su honra*

No one can give you better advice than yourself.
— CICERO (106–43 B.C.) *Ad Atticum*

We ask advice, but we mean approbation.
— CHARLES C. COLTON (1780?–1832) *Lacon*

When Thales was asked what was difficult, he said, "To know one's self." And what was easy, "To advise another."
— DIOGENES LAERTIUS (2nd or 3rd C.)

'Tis easier to advise the suffering than to bear suffering.
— EURIPIDES (480–406 B.C.) *Alcestis*

Don't give your advice before you are called upon.
— DESIDERIUS ERASMUS (1466–1536) *Adagia*

Whatever advice you give, be short.
— HORACE (B.C. 65–8) *Ars Poetica*

Advice is offensive, —because it shows us that we are known to others as well as to ourselves.
— SAMUEL JOHNSON (1709–1784) *The Rambler*

Advice is least heeded when most needed.
— ENGLISH PROVERB

Never advise anyone to go to war or to marry.
— SPANISH PROVERB

Many receive advice, only the wise profit by it.
— PUBLILIUS SYRUS (1st C. B.C.)

The only thing to do with good advice is to pass it on. It is never of any use to oneself.
— OSCAR WILDE (1854–1900) *An Ideal Husband*

AGE

Age appears to be the best in four things—old wood best to burn, old wine to drink, old friends to trust, and old authors to read.
— FRANCIS BACON (1561–1620) *Apothegms,* No. 97

He lives long that lives till all are weary of him.
— HENRY GEORGE BOHN (1797–1884) *Handbook of Proverbs*

Grow old along with me!
The best is yet to be,
The last of life, for which the first was made.
— ROBERT BROWNING (1812–1889) *Rabbi Ben Ezra*

Let age approve of youth, and death complete the same.
— ROBERT BROWNING (1812–1889) *Rabbi Ben Ezra*

Young men think old men are fools; but old men *know* young men are fools.
— GEORGE CHAPMAN (1559?–1634?) *All Fools,* Act V

I am ready to meet my Maker. Whether my Maker is prepared for the great ordeal of meeting me is another matter.
— WINSTON CHURCHILL (1874–1965) remark on eve of his 75th birthday

For as I like a young man in whom there is something of the old, so I like an old man in whom there is somethingof the young.
— CICERO (106–43 B.C.) *De Senectute*

No one is so old as to think he cannot live one more year.
— CICERO (106–43 B.C.) *De Senectute*

A man is as old as he's feeling
A woman as old as she looks.
— MORTIMER COLLINS (1827–1876) *How Old Are You?*

Folly in youth is sin, in age is madness.
— SAMUEL DANIEL (1562–1619)

Age is like love; it cannot be hid.
— THOMAS DEKKER (1570?–1632) *Old Fortunatus,* Act II

Youth is a blunder; Manhood a struggle;
Old Age a regret.
— BENJAMIN DISRAELI (1804–1881) *Coningsby*

A woman is as old as she looks to a man that likes to look at her.
— Finley Peter Dunne (1867–1936) *Old Age*

We do not count a man's years until he has nothing else to count.
— Ralph Waldo Emerson (1803–1882)

Forty is the old age of youth; fifty is the youth of old age.
— Victor Hugo (1802–1885)

Whenever a man's friends begin to compliment him about looking young, he may be sure that they think he is growing old.
— Washington Irving (1783–1859)

It was near a miracle to see an old man silent, since talking is the disease of age.
— Ben Jonson (1572–1637)

We hope to grow old, and we fear old age: that is to say, we love life and flee death.
— Jean de la Bruyère (1645–1696) *Caractères*

Of middle age the best that can be said is that a middle-aged person has likely learned how to have a little fun in spite of his troubles.
— Don Marquis (1878–1932) *The Almost Perfect State*

He who is of a calm and happy nature will hardly feel the pressure of Age, but to him who is of an opposite disposition, youth and age are equally a burden.
— Plato (428–347 B.C.) *The Republic*

He whom the gods favour dies in youth.
— Plautus (*c.* 254–184 B.C.) *Bacchides*

When men grow virtuous in old age, they only make a sacrifice to God of the devil's leavings.
— Alexander Pope (1664–1721) *Thoughts on Various Subjects*

To the old cat give a tender mouse.
— Italian proverb

Before old age my care was to live well; in old age, to die well.
— Seneca (4? B.C.–A.D. 65)

Age cannot wither her, nor custom stale
Her infinite variety.
— Shakespeare (1564–1616) *Antony and Cleopatra*, II, ii, 243

No wise man ever wished to be younger.
— Jonathan Swift (1667–1745)

To love is natural in a young man, a shame in an old one.
— Publilius Syrus (1st C. B.C.)

Nobody loves life like an old man.
— Sophocles (495–406 B.C.) *Acrisius*, Frag. 63

In the days of my youth I remembered my God,
And He hath not forgotten my age.
— Robert Southey (1774–1843) *The Old Man's Comforts*

We are always the same age inside.
— Gertrude Stein (1874–1946)

A fool at forty is a fool indeed.
— Edward Young (1683–1765) *Love of Fame*

AMBITION

Every eel hopes to become a whale.
— German proverb

The same ambition can destroy or save,
And makes a patriot as it makes a knave.
— Alexander Pope (1688–1744) *Essay on Man*

All ambitions are lawful except those which climb upward on the miseries or credulities of mankind.
— Joseph Conrad (1857–1924) *Personal Record*

'Tis a laudable Ambition, that aims at being better than his Neighbours.
— Ben Franklin (1706–1790) *Poor Richard's Almanack*

A man without ambition is like a woman without beauty.
— Frank Harris (1856–1931) *Montes the Matador*

Ambition is a vice, but it may be the father of virtue.
— Quintilian (40–*c.* 100)

The slave has but one master; the man of ambition has as many as there are people useful to his fortune.
— Jean de la Bruyère (1645–1696) *Caractères*

Ambition and suspicion always go together.
— Georg Christoph Lichtenberg (1742–1799)

The very substance of the ambitious is merely the shadow of a dream.
— Shakespeare (1564–1616) *Hamlet*, II, ii, 268

AMERICA

Driven from every other corner of the earth, freedom of thought and the right of private judgment in matters of conscience direct their course to this happy country as their last asylum.
— Samuel Adams (1722–1803) Speech at Philadelphia, 1776

The South! the South! God knows what will become of her.
— John C. Calhoun (1782–1850) on his deathbed.

Our country! in her intercourse with foreign nations may she always be in the right; but our country, right or wrong!
— Stephen Decatur (1779–1820) Toast at a dinner, 1816

I feel that you are justified in looking into the future with true assurance, because you have a mode of living in which we find the joy of life and the joy of work harmoniously combined. Added to this is the spirit of ambition which pervades your very being, and seems to make the day's work like a happy child at play.
— Albert Einstein (1879–1955) *New Year's Greeting*, 1931

America means opportunity, freedom, power.
— Ralph Waldo Emerson (1803–1882) *Essays, Second Series*

We must meet our duty and convince the world that we are just friends and brave enemies.
— Thomas Jefferson (1743–1826)

The citizens of America have explored the sea and air. They have given open-handed hospitality and employment to people immigrating from every land. America has continued to overcome with courage the various difficulties that have arisen from time to time and to render her legislation ever more in keeping with the dignity of the human person.
— Pope John XXIII (1881–1963), March 17, 1963

If we are to keep our system secure and our society stable, we must all begin to work where all of us work best—and that is in the communities where we all live.
— Lyndon B. Johnson (1908–) Speech, August, 1964

I am willing to love all mankind, except an American.
— Samuel Johnson (1709–1784) in Boswell's *Life*

And so, my fellow Americans: Ask not what your country can do for you—ask what you can do for your country.
— John F. Kennedy (1917–1963) Inauguration Speech, 1961

A citizen, first in war, first in peace, and first in the hearts of his countrymen.
— General Henry "Light-Horse Harry" Lee (1756–1818)

Intellectually I know that America is no better than any other country; emotionally I know she is better than every other country.
— Sinclair Lewis (1885–1951) Interview in Berlin, 1930

In the wars of the European powers in matters relating to themselves we have never taken any part, nor does it comport

with our policy so to do. It is only when our rights are invaded or seriously menaced that we resent injuries or make preparation for our defence.
— JAMES MONROE (1758–1831) Message to Congress, 1823

The United States never lost a war or won a conference.
— WILL ROGERS (1879–1935)

There is a homely adage which runs, "Speak softly and carry a big stick; you will go far." If the American nation will speak softly and yet build and keep at a pitch of the highest training the Monroe Doctrine will go far.
— THEODORE ROOSEVELT (1858–1919)

Every American takes pride in our tradition of hospitality, to men of all races and all creeds. We must be constantly vigilant against the attacks of intolerance and injustice. We must scrupulously guard the civil rights and civil liberties of all citizens, whatever their background.
— FRANKLIN D. ROOSEVELT (1882–1945)

Yesterday, December 7, 1941—a date that will live in infamy—the United States of America was suddenly and deliberately attacked by naval and air forces of the Empire of Japan.
— FRANKLIN D. ROOSEVELT, 1941

In the four quarters of the globe, who reads an American book? or goes to an American play? or looks at an American picture or statue? What does the world yet owe to American physicians or surgeons? . . . What have they done in mathematics? Who drinks out of American glasses? . . . or wears American coats and gowns? . . . Finally, under which of the old tyrannical governments of Europe is every sixth man a slave . . .?
— SIDNEY SMITH (1771–1845) in the *Edinburgh Review*, 1820

Liberty and Union, now and forever, one and inseparable!
— DANIEL WEBSTER (1782–1852) Speech, 1830

The Americans, like the English, probably make love worse than any other race.
— WALT WHITMAN (1819–1892) *An American Primer*

Our whole duty, for the present at any rate, is summed up in the motto: America first.
— WOODROW WILSON (1856–1924) Speech, 1915

America is God's crucible, the great Melting-Pot where all the races of Europe are melting and re-forming.
— ISRAEL ZANGWILL (1864–1926) *The Melting-Pot*

ANGER

I was angry with my friend:
I told my wrath, my wrath did end.
I was angry with my foe;
I told it not, my wrath did grow.
— WILLIAM BLAKE (1757–1827) *Christian Forbearance*

Anger begins with folly and ends with repentance.
— HENRY GEORGE BOHN (1796–1884) *Handbook of Proverbs*

Truly to moderate your mind and speech when you are angry, or else to hold your peace, betokens no ordinary nature.
— CICERO (106–43 B.C.) *Epistolae Quintum Fratrem*

Beware the fury of a patient man.
— JOHN DRYDEN (1631–1700) *Absalom and Achitophel*

Anger and folly walk cheek by jowl;
repentance treads on both their heels.
— BEN FRANKLIN (1706–1790) *Poor Richard's Almanack*

Two things a man should never be angry at: what he can help, and what he cannot help.
— THOMAS FULLER (1608–1681) *Historie of the Holy Warre*

Temper: a quality that, at critical moments, brings out the best in steel and the worst in people.
— OSCAR HAMMLING (1890–) *Laconics*

Let anger's fire be slow to burn.
— GEORGE HERBERT (1593–1633) *Jacula Prudentum*

When I am angry I can write, pray, and preach well, for then my whole temperament is quickened, my understanding sharpened, and all mundane vexations and temptations depart.
— MARTIN LUTHER (1483–1546) *Tablė-Talk*

The best answer to anger is silence.
— GERMAN PROVERB

A soft answer turneth away wrath; but grievous words stir up anger.
— OLD TESTAMENT: *Proverbs*, XV, i

APRIL See MONTHS

ART

It is the glory and good of Art,
That Art remains the one way possible
Of speaking truth. . . .
— ROBERT BROWNING (1812–1889) *The Ring and the Book*

Art imitates nature as well as it can, as a pupil follows his master; thus is it a sort of grandchild of God.
— DANTE (1265–1321) *Inferno*, Canto xi

In life beauty perishes, but not in art.
— LEONARDO DA VINCI (1452–1519) *Notebook*

Great art is the contempt of a great man for small art.
— F. SCOTT FITZGERALD (1896–1940) *Notebooks*

Nobody, I think, ought to read poetry, or look at pictures or statues, who cannot find a great deal more in them than the poet or artist has actually expressed.
— NATHANIEL HAWTHORNE (1804–1864) *The Marble Faun*

Rules and models destroy genius and art.
— WILLIAM HAZLITT (1778–1830) *On Taste*

Life is short, the art long, opportunity fleeting, experience treacherous, judgment difficult.
— HIPPOCRATES (460?–377? B.C.) *Aphorisms*

Art may make a suit of clothes; but Nature must produce a man.
— DAVID HUME (1711–1776) *Essays: The Epicurean*, 15

Art is nothing more than the shadow of humanity.
— HENRY JAMES (1843–1916) *Lectures*

Art hath an enemy called ignorance.
— BEN JONSON (1574–1637)

The true work of art is but a shadow of the divine perfection.
— MICHELANGELO (1475–1564)

To have faithfully studied the honorable arts, softens the manners and keeps them free from harshness.
— OVID (43 B.C.–A.D. 18?) *Epistles*

There are three arts which are concerned with all things: one which uses, another which makes, and a third which imitates them.
— PLATO (428–347 B.C.) *The Republic*

True artists are almost the only men who do their work with pleasure.
— AUGUSTE RODIN (1840–1917)

When love and skill work together expect a masterpiece.
— JOHN RUSKIN (1819–1900)

Art is not a handicraft; it is the transmission of feeling the artist has experienced.
— LEO TOLSTOY (1828–1910) *What is Art?*

A work of art is a corner of creation seen through a temperament.
— ÉMILE ZOLA (1840–1902) *Mes Haines*

An artist may visit a museum, but only a pedant can live there.
— GEORGE SANTAYANA (1853–1952) *Life of Reason*

AUGUST See MONTHS

AUTUMN

Autumn wins you best by this, its mute
Appeal to sympathy for its decay.
— ROBERT BROWNING (1812–1889) *Paracelsus*

All-cheering Plenty, with her flowing horn,
Led yellow Autumn, wreath'd with nodding corn.
— ROBERT BURNS (1759–1796) *The Brigs of Ayr*

The melancholy days are come, the saddest of the year,
Of wailing winds, and naked woods, and meadows brown
and sear.
— WILLIAM CULLEN BRYANT (1794–1878) *The Death of the Flowers*

She loves the bare, the withered tree;
She walks the sodden pasture lane.
— ROBERT FROST (1875–1963) *My November Guest*

Dread autumn, harvest-season of the Goddess of Death.
— HORACE (65–8 B.C.) *Satires*

A solemn land of long-fulfilled desires
Is this, and year by year the self-same fires
Burn in the trees.
— MARY WEBB (1881–1927) *The Plain in Autumn*

AVARICE

Be not penny-wise; riches have wings, and sometimes they fly away of themselves, sometimes they must be set flying to bring in more.
— FRANCIS BACON (1561–1620) *Essays: Of Riches*

If you would abolish avarice, you must abolish its mother, luxury.
— CICERO (106–43 B.C.) *De Oratore*

Would'st thou both eat thy cake and have it?
— GEORGE HERBERT (1593–1633) *The Size*

It is sheer madness to live in want in order to be wealthy when you die.
— JUVENAL (*c.* 60–*c.* 130) *Satires*

The beautiful eyes of my money-box!
He speaks of it as a lover of his mistress.
— MOLIÈRE (1622–1673) *L'Avare*

They are greedy dogs which can never have enough.
— OLD TESTAMENT: *Isaiah*, lvi, 11

BABY See CHILDREN

BEAUTY

Beauty is a gift of God.
— ARISTOTLE (384–322 B.C.) *Apothegm*

There is no excellent beauty that hath not some strangeness in the proportion.
— FRANCIS BACON (1561–1620) *Essays: Of Beauty*

Beauty is not caused. It is.
— EMILY DICKINSON (1830–1886) *Further Poems*

No Spring, nor Summer beauty hath such grace,
As I have seen in one Autumnal face.
— JOHN DONNE (1572–1631) *Elegies*

Beauty is in the eye of the beholder.
— MARGARET W. HUNGERFORD (1855?–1897)

A thing of beauty is a joy forever;
Its loveliness increases; it will never
Pass into nothingness . . . .
— JOHN KEATS (1795–1821) *Endymion*

"Beauty is truth, truth beauty," that is all
Ye know on earth, and all ye need to know.
— JOHN KEATS (1795–1821) *Ode on a Grecian Urn*

Euclid alone
Has looked on Beauty bare.
— EDNA ST. VINCENT MILLAY (1892–1951) *Sonnets*

Beauty and wisdom are seldom found together.
— PETRONIUS ARBITER (1st C. A.D.) *Satyricon*

It is the beautiful bird that gets caged.
— CHINESE PROVERB

Beauty provoketh thieves sooner than gold.
— SHAKESPEARE (1564–1616) *As You Like It*, I, iii, 13

O how can beautie maister the most strong!
— EDMUND SPENSER (1552?–1599) *Faerie Queene*

BOY See CHILDREN

CHILDREN

It is a great happiness to see our children rising round us, but from that good fortune spring the bitterest woes of man.
— AESCHYLUS (525–456 B.C.) *Agamemnon*

Cornelia kept her in talk till her children came from school, "And these," said she, "are my jewels."
— ROBERT BURTON (1557–1640) *Anatomy of Melancholy*

Respect the child. Be not too much his parent.
Trespass not on his solitude.
— RALPH WALDO EMERSON (1803–1882)

To a father waxing old nothing is dearer than a daughter. Sons have spirits of higher pitch, but less inclined to sweet, endearing fondness.
— EURIPIDES (480–406 B.C.)

An undutiful Daughter will prove an unmanageable Wife.
— BEN FRANKLIN (1706–1790) *Poor Richard's Almanack*

It is a wise child that knows his own father.
— HOMER (10th–8th C. B.C.) *Odyssey*

Children have more need of models than of critics.
— JOSEPH JOUBERT (1754–1824) *Pensées*, No. 261

Between the dark and the daylight,
When the night is beginning to lower,
Comes a pause in the day's occupations
That is known as the children's hour.
— HENRY W. LONGFELLOW (1807–1882) *The Children's Hour*

Suffer the little children to come unto me, and forbid them not; for such is the kingdom of God.
— NEW TESTAMENT: *Mark*, x, 14; *Luke*, xviii, 16

It were better for him that a millstone were hanged about his neck, and he cast into the sea, than that he should offend one of these little ones.
— NEW TESTAMENT: *Luke*, xvii, 2

Out of the mouths of babes and sucklings hast thou ordained strength.
— OLD TESTAMENT: *Psalms*, viii, 2

The wildest colts make the best horses.
— PLUTARCH (46–120)

A wise son maketh a glad father.
— OLD TESTAMENT: *Proverbs*, x, 1

Even a child is known by his doings.
— OLD TESTAMENT: *Proverbs*, xx, 11

Behold the child, by nature's kindly law,
Pleased with a rattle, tickled with a straw.
— ALEXANDER POPE (1688–1744) *Essay on Man*

Lacking all sense of right and wrong, a child can do nothing which is morally evil, or which merits either punishment or reproof.
— JEAN-JACQUES ROUSSEAU (1712–1778) *Emile*

At first the infant,
Mewling and puking in the nurse's arms.
And then the whining school-boy,with his satchel,
And shining morning face, creeping like snail
Unwillingly to school.
— SHAKESPEARE (1564–1616) *As You Like It*, II, viii, 143

I do not love him because he is good, but because he is my little child.
— SIR RABINDRANATH TAGORE (1861–1841) *The Crescent Moon*

A child tells in the street what its father and mother say at home.
— THE TALMUD

A babe in a house is a well-spring of pleasure.
— MARTIN FARQUHAR TUPPER (1810–1889) *Of Education*

Heaven lies about us in our infancy.
— WILLIAM WORDSWORTH (1770–1850) *Intimations of Immortality*

The child is father of the man.
— WILLIAM WORDSWORTH (1770–1850) *My Heart Leaps up When I Behold*

CIVILIZATION

Civilization degrades the many to exalt the few.
— BRONSON ALCOTT (1799–1888) *Table-Talk*

Increased means and increased leisure are the two civilizers of man.
— BENJAMIN DISRAELI (1804–1881) Speech, 1872

The true test of civilization is not the census, nor the size of cities, nor the crops, —no, but the kind of man the country turns out.
— RALPH WALDO EMERSON (1803–1882) *Essays: Society and Solitude.*

No one is so savage that he cannot become civilized, if he will lend a patient ear to culture.
— HORACE (65–8 B.C.) *Epistles*

Things have their day, and their beauties in that day. It would be preposterous to expect any one civilization to last forever.
— GEORGE SANTAYANA (1863–1952) *Character and Opinion in the United States*

A civilization which develops only on its material side, and not in corresponding measure on its mental and spiritual side, is like a vessel with a defective steering gear . . . .
— ALBERT SCHWEITZER (1875–) *The Decay and Restoration of Civilization*

COMMON SENSE

If a man can have only one kind of sense, let him have common sense. If he has that and uncommon sense too, he is not far from genius.
— HENRY WARD BEECHER (1813–1887)

Nothing astonishes men so much as common sense and plain dealing.
— RALPH WALDO EMERSON (1803–1882) *Art*

Where sense is wanting, everything is wanting.
— BEN FRANKLIN (1706–1790) *Poor Richard's Almanack*

Common sense is only a modification of talent. Genius is an exaltation of it.
— EDWARD BULWER-LYTTON (1803–1873)

Common sense is not so common.
— VOLTAIRE (1694–1778) *Philosophical Dictionary*

COMPENSATION

For every thing you have missed, you have gained something else; and for every thing you gain, you lose something.
— RALPH WALDO EMERSON (1803–1882) *Compensation*

For all our works a recompense is sure:
'Tis sweet to think on what was hard t'endure.
— ROBERT HERRICK (1591–1674) *Hesperides*

It is a comfort that the medal has two sides. There is much vice and misery in the world, I know; but more virtue and happiness, I believe.
— THOMAS JEFFERSON (1743–1826)

Whoever tries for great objects must suffer something.
— PLUTARCH (46?–120?) *Lives*

There is no evil without its compensation. Avarice promises money; luxury, pleasure; ambition, a purple robe.
— SENECA (4? B.C.–A.D. 65) *Epistulae ad Lucillium*

Give unto them beauty for ashes, the oil of joy for mourning, the garment of praise for the spirit of heaviness.
— OLD TESTAMENT: *Isaiah*, lxi, 3

CONCEIT See EGOTISM

CONSCIENCE

Conscience and reputation are two things. Conscience is due to yourself, reputation to your neighbor.
— ST. AUGUSTINE (354–430)

There is another man within me that's angry with me.
— SIR THOMAS BROWNE (1605–1682) *Religio Medici*

Conscience, good my lord,
Is but the pulse of reason.
— SAMUEL TAYLOR COLERIDGE (1772–1834) *Zapolya*

The still small voice.
— WILLIAM COWPER (1731–1800) *The Task*

A good conscience is a continual Christmas.
— BEN FRANKLIN (1706–1790) *Poor Richard's Almanack*

The man who acts never has any conscience; no one has any conscience but the man who thinks.
— GOETHE (1749–1832)

That fierce thing
They call a conscience.
— THOMAS HOOD (1799–1845) *Lamia*

The sting of conscience, like the gnawing of a dog at a bone, is mere foolishness.
— FRIEDRICH NIETZSCHE (1844–1900) *Human All-too-Human*

There is no witness so terrible, no accuser so potent, as the conscience that dwells in every man's breast.
— POLYBIUS (*c.* 204–122 B.C.) *Histories*

The worm of conscience keeps the same hours as the owl.
— SCHILLER (1759–1805) *Kabale und Liebe*

The play's the thing
Wherein I'll catch the conscience of the king.
— SHAKESPEARE (1564–1616) *Hamlet*, II, ii, 641

Trust that man in nothing who has not a conscience in everything.
— LAURENCE STERNE (1713–1768) *Tristram Shandy*

Conscience is, in most men, an anticipation of the opinion of others.
— SIR HENRY TAYLOR (1800–1886) *The Statesman*

Conscience and cowardice are really the same thing.
— OSCAR WILDE (1854–1900) *The Picture of Dorian Gray*

CONSERVATISM

The absurd man is one who never changes.
— AUGUSTE BARTHELEMY (1796–1867) *Nemesis*

Conservative: A statesman who is enamored of existing evils, as distinguished from the Liberal who wishes to replace them with others.
— AMBROSE BIERCE (1842–1914?) *The Devil's Dictionary*

A conservative government is an organized hypocrisy.
— Benjamin Disraeli (1804–1881)

A conservative is a man who is too cowardly to fight and too fat to run.
— Elbert Hubbard (1856–1915) *Epigrams*

What is conservatism? Is it not adherence to the old and tried, against the new and untried?
— Abraham Lincoln (1809–1865) *Cooper Union Address*, 1860

Be not the first by whom the new are tried,
Nor yet the last to lay the old aside.
— Alexander Pope (1688–1744) *Essay on Criticism*

The man for whom the law exists—the man of forms, the Conservative, is a tame man.
— Henry David Thoreau (1817–1862) *An Essay on Civil Disobedience*

CONSTANCY AND INCONSTANCY

Without constancy there is neither love, friendship, nor virtue in the world.
— Joseph Addison (1672–1719)

It is as absurd to say that a man can't love one woman all the time as it is to say that a violinist needs several violins to play the same piece of music.
— Honoré de Balzac (1799–1850) *Physiology of Marriage*

A good man it is not mine to see. Could I see a man possessed of constancy, that would satisfy me.
— Confucius (*c.* 551–478 B.C.) *Analects*

What is there in this vile earth that more commendeth a woman than constancy?
— John Lyly (1554?–1606) *Euphues*

There are two sorts of constancy in love—one rises from continually discovering in the loved person new subjects for love, the other arises from our making a merit of being constant.
— François de la Rochefoucauld (1613–1680) *Maxims*

But I am constant as the northern star,
Of whose true-fix'd and resting quality
There is no fellow in the firmament.
— Shakespeare (1564–1616) *Julius Caesar*, III, i, 58

There is nothing in this world constant but inconstancy.
— Jonathan Swift (1667–1745)

CONTEMPT

Familiarity breeds contempt, while rarity wins admiration.
— Apuleius (2nd C.) *De Deo Socratis*

None but the contemptible are apprehensive of contempt.
— François de la Rochefoucauld (1613–1680) *Maxims*

Here is another man with whom I cannot get angry, because I despise him.
— Benito Mussolini (1883–1945)

Man is much more sensitive to the contempt of others than to self-contempt.
— Friedrich Nietzsche (1844–1900) *Human All-too-Human*

Contempt penetrates even the shell of the tortoise.
— Persian proverb

CONTENT AND DISCONTENT

No form of society can be reasonably stable in which the majority of the people are not fairly content. People cannot be content if they feel that the foundations of their lives are wholly unstable.
— James Truslow Adams (1878–1949) *Record of America*

Be content with your lot; one cannot be first in everything.
— Aesop (6th C. B.C.) *The Peacock and Juno*

A perverse and fretful disposition makes any state of life unhappy.
— Cicero (106–43 B.C.) *De Senectute*

Who is rich? He that is content. Who is that? Nobody.
— Ben Franklin (1706–1790) *Poor Richard's Almanack*

Unhappy man! He frets at the narrow limits of the world.
— Juvenal (*c.* 60–*c.* 130 A.D.)

When we cannot find contentment in ourselves it is useless to seek it elsewhere.
— François de la Rochefoucauld (1613–1680) *Maxims*

Discontent is the first step in the progress of a man or nation.
— Oscar Wilde (1854–1900) *A Woman of No Importance*

Poor in abundance, famish'd at a feast.
— Edward Young (1683–1765) *Night Thoughts*

I have learned, in whatsoever state I am, therewith to be content.
— New Testament: *Hebrews*, iv, 11

COURAGE

Often the test of courage is not to die but to live.
— Vittorio Alfieri (1749–1903) *Oreste*

But where life is more terrible than death, it is then the truest valor to dare to live.
— Sir Thomas Browne (1663–1704) *Religio Medici*

Courage is that virtue which champions the cause of right.
— Cicero (106–43 B.C.) *De Officiis*

Every man of courage is a man of his word.
— Pierre Corneille (1606–1684) *Le Menteur*

Courage consists in equality to the problem before us.
— Ralph Waldo Emerson (1803–1882) *Society and Solitude*

Courage may be taught as a child is taught to speak.
— Euripides (480–406 B.C.) *The Suppliant Women*

A decent boldness ever meets with friends.
— Homer (*c.* 10th C.–8th C. B.C.) *Iliad*

Nothing is too high for the daring of mortals; we storm
Heaven itself in our folly.
— Horace (65–8 B.C.) *Odes*

It is better to die on your feet than to live on your knees.
— La Pasionaria (1895–) Speech at Paris, 1936

True courage is to do, without witnesses, everything that one is capable of doing before all the world.
— François de la Rochefoucauld (1613–1680) *Maxims*

What though the field be lost?
All is not lost; th'unconquerable will,
And study of revenge, immortal hate,
And courage never to submit or yield.
— John Milton (1608–1674) *Paradise Lost*

The strongest, most generous, and proudest of all virtues is true courage.
— Michel de Montaigne (1533–1592) *Essays*

Be of good cheer: it is I; be not afraid.
— New Testament: *Matthew*, xiv, 27

We shall attack and attack until we are exhausted, and then we shall attack again.
— General George S. Patton (1885–1945) Address to his troops before the invasion of North Africa, 1942

The smallest worm will turn being trodden on,
And doves will peck in safeguard of their brood.
— Shakespeare (1564–1616) *III Henry VI*, II, ii, 17

Why, courage then! What cannot be avoided
'Twere childish weakness to lament or fear.
— Shakespeare (1564–1616) *Henry VI*, V, iv, 37

COURTSHIP

Those marriages generally abound most with love and constancy that are preceded by a long courtship.
— JOSEPH ADDISON (1672–1719) *The Spectator*

He that will win his dame must do
As love does when he draws his bow;
With one hand thrust the lady from,
And with the other pull her home.
— SAMUEL BUTLER (1612–1680) *Hudibras*

Courtship to marriage is but as the music in the playhouse till the curtain's drawn.
— WILLIAM CONGREVE (1670–1729) *The Old Bachelor*

If I am not worth the wooing, I am surely not worth the winning.
— HENRY W. LONGFELLOW (1807–1882) *Courtship of Miles Standish*

Had we but world enough and time
This coyness, lady, were no crime.
— ANDREW MARVELL (1621–1678) *To His Coy Mistress*

I will now court her in the conqueror's style;
"Come, see, and overcome."
— PHILIP MASSINGER (1583–1640) *Maid of Honor*

We cannot fight for love, as men may do;
We should be woo'd and were not made to woo.
— SHAKESPEARE (1564–1616) *Midsummer Night's Dream*, II, i, 241

The weather is usually fine when people are courting.
— R. L. STEVENSON (1850–1894) *Virginibus Puerisque*

A man always chases a woman until she catches him.
— UNKNOWN

COURTESY

If a man be gracious and courteous to strangers it shows he is a citizen of the world.
— FRANCIS BACON (1561–1620) *Essays*

Politeness. The most acceptable hypocrisy.
— AMBROSE BIERCE (1842–1914?) *Devil's Dictionary*

'Tis ill talking of halters in the house of a man that was hanged.
— CERVANTES (1547–1616) *Don Quixote*, Pt. i

Politeness is the ritual of society, as prayers are of the church.
— RALPH WALDO EMERSON (1803–1882) *English Traits*

Be civil to all; sociable to many; familiar with few.
— BEN FRANKLIN (1706–1790) *Poor Richard's Almanack*

He was so generally civil, that nobody thanked him for it.
— SAMUEL JOHNSON (1709–1784) in Boswell's *Life*

Civility is a desire to receive it in turn, and to be accounted well bred.
— FRANÇOIS DE LA ROCHEFOUCAULD (1613–1680) *Maxims*

Politeness costs nothing and gains everything.
— LADY MARY WORTLEY MONTAGU (1689–1762) Letters

It is one of the greatest blessings that so many women are so full of tact. The calamity happens when a woman who has all the other riches of life just lacks that one thing.
— SIR WILLIAM OSLER (1848–1919)

True politeness consists in being easy one's self, and in making every one about one as easy as one can.
— ALEXANDER POPE (1688–1744) *Table-Talk*

To speak kindly does not hurt the tongue.
— FRENCH PROVERB

Dissembling courtesy! How fine this tyrant
Can tickle where she wounds!
— SHAKESPEARE (1564–1616) *Cymbeline*, I, i, 84

The greater man the greater courtesy.
— TENNYSON (1809–1882) *The Last Tournament*

COWARDICE

Coward. One who in a perilous emergency thinks with his legs.
— AMBROSE BIERCE (1842–1914?) *Devil's Dictionary*

To see what is right and not do it is want of courage.
— CONFUCIUS (551–478 B.C.) *Analects*

The coward never on himself relies,
But to an equal for assistance flies.
— GEORGE CRABBE (1754–1832) *The Gentleman Farmer*

Many would be cowards if they had courage enough.
— THOMAS FULLER (1608–1681) *Gnomologia*

Ever will a coward show no mercy.
— SIR THOMAS MALORY (f. 1470) *Morte d'Arthur*

It is the act of a coward to wish for death.
— OVID (43 B.C.-A.D. 18?) *Metamorphoses*

The coward calls himself cautious.
— PUBLILIUS SYRUS (1st C. B.C.) *Sententiae*

A cowardly cur barks more fiercely than it bites.
— QUINTUS CURTIUS RUFUS (*c.* 2nd C. A.D.) *De Rebus Gestis Alexandri Magni*

When all the blandishments of life are gone,
The coward sneaks to death, the brave live on.
— GEORGE SEWELL (d. 1726)

A coward, a most devout coward, religious in it.
— SHAKESPEARE (1564–1616) *Twelfth Night*, III, iv, 427

Cowards die many times before their deaths;
The valiant never taste of death but once.
— SHAKESPEARE (1564–1616) *Julius Caesar*, II, ii, 32

CRITICISM

Criticism is a disinterested endeavour to learn and propagate the best that is known and thought in the world.
— MATTHEW ARNOLD (1822–1888) *Essays in Criticism*

As the arts advance towards their perfection, the science of criticism advances with equal pace.
— EDMUND BURKE (1729–1797) *On the Sublime and Beautiful*

Let dull critics feed upon the carcasses of plays; give me the taste and the dressing.
— LORD CHESTERFIELD (1694–1773) *Letters to his Son*

Critics—murderers!
— SAMUEL TAYLOR COLERIDGE (1772–1834)

Those who write ill, and they who ne'er durst write,
Turn critics out of mere revenge and spite.
— JOHN DRYDEN (1631–1700) *Conquest of Granada*

Blame where you must, be candid where you can,
And be each critic the Good-natured Man.
— OLIVER GOLDSMITH (1728–1774) *Good-Natured Man*

Criticism is the art wherewith a critic tries to guess himself into a share of the artist's fame.
— GEORGE JEAN NATHAN (1882–1958) *House of Satan*

Damn with faint praise, assent with civil leer
And without sneering teach the rest to sneer.
— ALEXANDER POPE (1688–1744) *Epistle to Dr. Arbuthnot*

They damn what they do not understand.
— QUINTILIAN (*c.* 40–100 A.D.) *De Institutione Oratoria*

Critic: a man who writes about things he doesn't like.
— UNKNOWN

Really to stop criticism they say one must die.
— VOLTAIRE (1694–1778)

CURIOSITY

This disease of curiosity.
— ST. AUGUSTINE (354–430) *Confessions*

The first and simplest emotion which we discover in the human mind is curiosity.
— EDMUND BURKE (1729–1797) *The Sublime and Beautiful*

Shun the inquisitive person, for he is also a talker.
— HORACE (65–8 B.C.) *Epistles*

Curiosity is one of the most permanent and certain characteristics of a vigorous intellect.
— SAMUEL JOHNSON (1709–1784) *The Rambler*

Curiosity killed the cat.
— AMERICAN PROVERB

He that pryeth into every cloud may be struck by a thunderbolt.
— JOHN RAY (1627?–1705) *English Proverbs*

You know what a woman's curiosity is. Almost as great as a man's!
— OSCAR WILDE (1854–1900) *An Ideal Husband*

Curiosity. The reason why most of us haven't committed suicide long ago.
— UNKNOWN

DANGER

Dangers bring fears, and fears more dangers bring.
— RICHARD BAXTER (1615–1691) *Love Breathing Thanks*

Danger, the spur of all great minds.
— GEORGE CHAPMAN (1559?–1634?) *Bussy d'Ambois*

Moving of the earth brings harms and fears.
Men reckon what it did and meant.
But trepidation of the spheres
Though greater far, is innocent.
— JOHN DONNE (1573–1631) *Valediction Forbidding Mourning*

As soon as there is life there is danger.
— RALPH WALDO EMERSON (1803–1882) *Lectures*

Great perils have this beauty, that they bring to light the fraternity of strangers.
— VICTOR HUGO (1802–1885) *Les Misérables*

Out of this nettle, danger, we pluck this flower, safety.
— SHAKESPEARE (1564–1616) *I Henry IV*, II, iii, 10

Better face a danger once than be always in fear.
— PROVERB

DARKNESS See NIGHT

DAUGHTER See CHILDREN

DAWN See DAY

DAY

Day is a snow-white Dove of heaven
That from the East glad message brings.
— THOMAS BAILEY ALDRICH (1836–1907) *Day and Night*

Day!
O'er nights brim, day boils at last;
Boils, pure gold, o'er the cloud-cup's brim.
— ROBERT BROWNING (1812–1889) *Pippa Passes*

One day well spent is to be preferred to an eternity of error.
— CICERO (106–43 B.C.) *Tusculanarum Disputationum*

He is only rich who owns the day. There is no king, rich man, fairy, or demon who possesses such power as that. . . . The days are made on a loom whereof the warp and woof are past and future time.
— RALPH WALDO EMERSON (1803–1882) *Society and Solitude*

Rosy-fingered Dawn.
— HOMER (10th-8th? C. B.C.) *Iliad*

The day has eyes; the night has ears.
— PROVERB

Wait till it is night before saying it has been a fine day.
— FRENCH PROVERB

My days are swifter than a weaver's shuttle.
— OLD TESTAMENT: *Job*, vii, 6

Listen to the Exhortation of the Dawn!
Look to this Day! For it is Life,
The very Life of Life.
— *Salutation of the Dawn* (SANSKRIT)

The glow-worm shows the matin to be near,
And 'gins to pale his uneffectual fire.
— SHAKESPEARE (1564–1616) *Hamlet*, I, v, 89

Night's candles are burnt out, and jocund day
Stands tiptoe on the misty mountaintops.
— SHAKESPEARE (1564–1616) *Romeo and Juliet*, III, v, 9

DEATH

Death is a black camel, which kneels at the gates of all.
— ABD-EL-KADER (1807?–1883)

It is good to die before one has done anything deserving death.
— ANANANDRIDES (4th C. B.C.) *Fragment*

Men fear death as children fear to go in the dark; and as that natural fear in children is increased with tales, so is the other.
— FRANCIS BACON (1561–1620) *Essays: Of Death*

He that unburied lies wants not his hearse,
For unto him a Tomb's the Universe.
— SIR THOMAS BROWNE (1605–1682) *Religio Medici*

We all labor against our own cure, for death is the cure of all diseases.
— SIR THOMAS BROWNE (1605–1682) *Religio Medici*

The fear of death is worse than death.
— ROBERT BURTON (1577–1640) *Anatomy of Melancholy*

Ah, surely nothing dies but something mourns!
— LORD BYRON (1788–1824) *Don Juan*

Death levels all things.
— CLAUDIAN (*c.* 395) *De Raptu Proserpinae*

These have not the hope of death.
— DANTE (1265–1321) *Inferno*

Death, be not proud, though some have called thee
Mighty and dreadful, for thou art not so:
For those, whom thou think'st thou dost overthrow,
Die not, poor Death. . .
— JOHN DONNE (1572–1631) *Divine Poems: Holy Sonnet*

There were some who said that a man at the point of death was more free than all others, because death breaks every bond, and over the dead the united world has no power.
— FÉNELON (1651–1715) *Telemachus*

Death is Nature's expert advice to get plenty of Life.
— GOETHE (1749–1832)

We die ourselves a little every time we kill in others something that deserved to live.
— OSCAR HAMMLING (1890–) *Laconics*

I have been half in love with easeful death,
Call'd him soft names in many a mused rhyme.
— JOHN KEATS (1795–1821) *Ode to a Nightingale*

So now he is a legend when he would have preferred to be a man.
— MRS. JACQUELINE KENNEDY (1929–) in a tribute to her husband, Nov. 1964

Wheresoever ye be, death will overtake you, although ye be in lofty towers.
— THE KORAN

A man's dying is more the survivors' affair than his own.
— THOMAS MANN (1875–1955) *The Magic Mountain*

The grave's a fine and private place,
But none, I think, do there embrace.
— ANDREW MARVELL (1621–1678) *To His Coy Mistress*

Death has a thousand doors to let out life.
I shall find one.
— PHILIP MASSINGER (1584–1640) *A Very Woman*

Whom the gods love dies young.
— MENANDER (342–291 B.C.)

Dead men tell no tales.
— ENGLISH PROVERB

To die at the will of another is to die twice.
— PUBLILIUS SYRUS (*b.* 1st C. B.C.) *Sententiae*

Death seems to provide the minds of the Anglo-Saxon race with a greater fund of innocent amusement than any other single subject.
— DOROTHY L. SAYERS (1893–)

I have a rendezvous with Death
At some disputed barricade . . .
— ALAN SEEGER (1888–1916) *I Have a Rendezvous with Death*

Death is a punishment to some, to some a gift, and to many a favor.
— SENECA (4? B.C.–A.D. 65)

Nothing in his life became him like the leaving it . . . .
— SHAKESPEARE (1564–1616) *Macbeth*, I, iv, 7

Imperious Caesar, dead and turn'd to clay,
Might stop a hole to keep the wind away.
— SHAKESPEARE (1564–1616) *Hamlet*, V, i, 235

To die, —to sleep,
No more, and by that sleep to say we end
The heart-ache and the thousand natural shocks
That flesh is heir to . . . .
— SHAKESPEARE (1564–1616) *Hamlet*, III, i, 60

Say nothing but good of the dead.
— SOLON (638–559 B.C.)

Do not go gentle into that good night,
Old age should burn and rave at close of day;
Rage, rage against the dying of the light.
— DYLAN THOMAS (1914–1953) *Poem to My Father*

I saw him now going the way of all flesh.
— JOHN WEBSTER (1580–1625) *Westward Ho!*, Act II

O death, where is thy sting? O grave, where is thy victory?
— NEW TESTAMENT: *I Corinthians*, xv, 55

I looked and beheld a pale horse: and his name that sat on him was Death.
— NEW TESTAMENT: *Revelation*, vi, 8

Dust thou art, and unto dust shalt thou return.
— OLD TESTAMENT: *Genesis*, iii, 19

DECEIT

God is not averse to deceit in a holy cause.
— AESCHYLUS (525–456 B.C.)

We are never deceived; we deceive ourselves.
— GOETHE (1749–1832)

Hateful to me as the gates of hell,
Is he, who, hiding one thing in his heart,
Utters another.
— HOMER (*c.* 10th–8th C. B.C.) *Iliad*

It is a double pleasure to deceive the deceiver.
— JEAN DE LA FONTAINE (1621–1695) *Fables*

The surest way to be deceived is to think one's self more clever than others.
— FRANÇOIS DE LA ROCHEFOUCAULD (1613–1680) *Maxims*

You can fool some of the people all of the time, and all of the people some of the time, but you cannot fool all of the people all of the time.
— ABRAHAM LINCOLN (1809–1865)

Listen at the key-hole and you'll hear news of yourself.
— PROVERB

Oh, what a tangled web we weave,
When first we practise to deceive!
— SIR WALTER SCOTT (1771–1832) *Marmion*

Sigh no more, ladies, sigh no more,
Men were deceivers ever.
— SHAKESPEARE (1564–1616) *Much Ado About Nothing*, II, iii, 65

DECEMBER See MONTHS

DECISION AND INDECISION

There is grief in indecision.
— CICERO (106–43 B.C.) *De officiis*

The wavering mind is but a base possession.
— EURIPIDES (480–406 B.C.)

There is no more miserable human being than one in whom nothing is habitual but indecision.
— WILLIAM JAMES (1842–1910) *Psychology*

Decide not rashly. The decision made
Can never be recalled.
— HENRY W. LONGFELLOW (1807–1882) *Masque of Pandora*

Once to every man and nation comes the moment to decide . . . .
— JAMES RUSSELL LOWELL (1819–1891) *The Present Crisis*

To be or not to be, that is the question . . . .
— SHAKESPEARE (1564–1616) *Hamlet*, III, i, 56

I am at war twixt will and will not.
— SHAKESPEARE (1564–1616) *Measure for Measure*, II, ii, 32

Quick decisions are unsafe decisions.
— SOPHOCLES (495–406 B.C.) *Oedipus Tyrannus*

DEMOCRACY

If liberty and equality, as is thought by some, are chiefly to be found in democracy, they will be best attained when all persons alike share in the government to the utmost.
— ARISTOTLE (384–322 B.C.) *Politics*

The tyranny of a multitude is a multiplied tyranny.
— EDMUND BURKE (1729–1797) Letter to Thomas Mercer

Democracy means government by the uneducated, while aristocracy means government by the badly educated.
— G. K. CHESTERTON (1874–1936) Interview, 1931

The tendency of democracies is, in all things, to mediocrity.
— JAMES FENIMORE COOPER (1789–1851) *American Democrat*

Only if basically the democracy of our day satisfies the mental, moral, and physical wants of the masses living under it, can it continue to exist.
— DWIGHT D. EISENHOWER (1890–) *Crusade in Europe*

The world is weary of statesmen whom democracy has degraded into politicians.
— BENJAMIN DISRAELI (1805–1881)

Democracy has another merit. It allows criticism, and if there isn't public criticism there are bound to be hushed-up scandals.
— E. M. FORSTER (1879–) *I Believe*

Democracy is based upon the conviction that there are extraordinary possibilities in ordinary people.
— HARRY EMERSON FOSDICK (1878–) *Democracy*

The republican is the only form of government which is not eternally at open or secret war with the rights of mankind.
— THOMAS JEFFERSON (1743–1826) Reply to Address

If we fail now, then we will have forgotten in abundance what we learned in hardship: that democracy rests on faith, that freedom asks more than it gives, and the judgment of God is harshest on those who are most favored.
— LYNDON B. JOHNSON (1908–) Inaugural Address, Jan. 1965

The world is very different now. For man holds in his mortal hands the power to abolish all forms of human poverty and all forms of human life. And yet the same revolutionary beliefs for which our forebears fought are still at issue around the globe....
— JOHN F. KENNEDY (1917–1963), Inaugural Address, Jan. 1961

All creatures are members of the one family of God.
— THE KORAN

Democracy gives to every man
The right to be his own oppressor.
— JAMES RUSSELL LOWELL (1819–1891) *Bigelow Papers*

We must define democracy as that form of government and of society which is inspired above every other, with the feeling and consciousness of the dignity of man.
— THOMAS MANN (1875–1955) *The Coming Victory of Democracy*

We must be the great arsenal of democracy.
— FRANKLIN D. ROOSEVELT (1882–1945) Radio Address, 1940

Democracy is unfinished business, not fulfilment; it is a process of always advancing toward fulfilment.
— RAYMOND GRAM SWING (1887–)

Democracy is the recurrent suspicion that more than half of the people are right more than half of the time.
— E. B. WHITE (1899–)

I believe in democracy because it releases the energies of every human being.
— WOODROW WILSON(1856–1924) Address to Congress, 1917

The world must be made safe for democracy. Its peace must be planted upon the tested foundations of political liberty.
— WOODROW WILSON (1856–1924) Address to Congress, 1917

DEPENDENCE AND INDEPENDENCE

Each man for himself.
— GEOFFREY CHAUCER (1340?–1400) *Canterbury Tales*

The greatest man living may stand in need of the meanest, as much as the meanest does of him.
— THOMAS FULLER (1608–1681)

Even in the common affairs of life, in love, friendship, and marriage, how little security have we when we trust our happiness in the hands of others!
— WILLIAM HAZLITT (1778–1830) *On Living to Oneself*

The strongest man in the world is he who stands most alone.
— HENRIK IBSEN (1828–1906) *An Enemy of the People*

No degree of knowledge attainable by man is able to set him above the want of hourly assistance.
— SAMUEL JOHNSON (1709-1784)

To be independent is the business of a few only; it is the privilege of the strong.
— FRIEDRICH NIETZSCHE (1844–1900) *Beyond Good and Evil*

Independence? That's middle class blasphemy. We are all dependent on one another, every soul of us on earth.
— GEORGE BERNARD SHAW (1856–1950) *Pygmalion*

Without the help of thousands of others, any one of us would die, naked and starved.
— ALFRED E. SMITH (1873–1944)

Dependence is a perpetual call upon humanity, and a greater incitement to tenderness and pity than any other motive whatever.
— WILLIAM MAKEPEACE THACKERAY (1811–1863)

DESIRE

He begins to die that quits his desires.
— GEORGE HERBERT (1593–1633) *Outlandish Proverbs*

Naked I seek the camp of those who desire nothing.
— HORACE (65–8 B.C.) *Odes*

We live in our desires rather than in our achievements.
— GEORGE MOORE (1852–1933) *Ave*

We desire most what we ought not to have.
— PUBLILIUS SYRUS (1st C. B.C.) *Sententiae*

If wishes were horses, beggars would ride.
— SCOTTISH PROVERB

Can one desire too much of a good thing?
— SHAKESPEARE (1564–1616) *As You Like It*, IV, i, 129

The fewer desires, the more peace.
— THOMAS WILSON (1663–1755)

Desire accomplished is sweet to the soul.
— OLD TESTAMENT: *Proverbs*, xiii, 19

DESPAIR

I want to be forgotten even by God.
— ROBERT BROWNING (1812–1889) *Easter Day*

The name of the Slough was Despond.
— JOHN BUNYAN (1628–1688) *Pilgrim's Progress*

Despair is the damp of hell, as joy is the serenity of heaven.
— JOHN DONNE (1572–1631)

Despondency is not a state of humility. On the contrary, it is the vexation and despair of a cowardly pride....
— FÉNELON (1651–1715)

Then black despair,
The shadow of a starless night, was thrown
Over the world in which I moved alone.
— PERCY B. SHELLEY (1792–1822) *Revolt of Islam*

The only refuge from despair is to project one's ego into the world.
— LEO TOLSTOY (1828–1910)

When we have lost everything, including hope, life becomes a disgrace and death a duty.
— VOLTAIRE (1694–1778) *Merope*

Out of the depths have I cried unto Thee, O Lord.
— OLD TESTAMENT: *Psalms*, cxxx, 1

DESPOTISM See TYRANNY

DESTINY See FATE

DISCONTENT See CONTENT

DISCRETION AND INDISCRETION

An indiscreet man is more hurtful than an ill-natured one; for the latter will only attack his enemies, and those he wishes ill to; the other injures indifferently both friends and foes.
— JOSEPH ADDISON (1672–1719) *The Spectator*

He knows not when to be silent who knows not when to speak.
— PUBLILIUS SYRUS (1st C. B.C.)

Least said, soonest mended.
— CHARLES DICKENS (1812–1870) *David Copperfield*

For good and evil in our actions meet;
Wicked is not much worse than indiscreet.
— JOHN DONNE (1572–1631)

A demi-vierge is a woman for whom chastity, from being a temporary asset, has become a permanent liability.
— OSCAR HAMMLING (1890–)

Let your discretion be your tutor; suit the action to the word, the word to the action.
— SHAKESPEARE (1564–1616) *Hamlet*, III, ii, 18

The better part of valour is discretion; in the which better part I have saved my life.
— SHAKESPEARE (1564–1616) *I Henry IV*, V, iv, 121

Be swift to hear, slow to speak, slow to wrath.
— NEW TESTAMENT: *James*, i, 19

DOUBT

Doubt whom you will, but never doubt yourself.
— CHRISTIAN NESTELL BOVEE (1820–1904)

Doubting charms me not less than knowledge.
— DANTE (1265–1321) *Inferno*, canto xii, l. 93

Just think of the tragedy of teaching children not to doubt.
— CLARENCE DARROW (1857–1938)

Scepticism is the first step on the road to philosophy.
— DENIS DIDEROT (1713–1784)

To believe with certainty we must begin with doubting.
— STANISLAUS LESCYNSKI (1677–1766)

I respect faith, but doubt is what gets you an education.
— WILSON MIZNER (1876–1933)

Doubt makes the mountain which faith can move.
— UNKNOWN

Our doubts are traitors
And make us lose the good we oft might win
By fearing to attempt.
— SHAKESPEARE (1564–1616) *Measure for Measure*, I, iv, 77

DREAMS

The more a man dreams, the less he believes.
— H. L. MENCKEN (1990–1956) *Prejudices*

Dreams are the true interpreters of our inclinations, but art is required to sort and understand them.
— MICHEL DE MONTAIGNE (1533–1592) *Essays*

Those dreams are true which we have in the morning, as the lamp begins to flicker.
— OVID (43 B.C.–A.D. 18?) *Epistles*

All that we see or seem
Is but a dream within a dream.
— EDGAR ALLAN POE (1809–1849) *A Dream Within a Dream*

To sleep; perchance to dream: ay, there's the rub;
For in that sleep of death what dreams may come,
When we have shuffled off this mortal coil
Must give us pause.
— SHAKESPEARE (1564–1616) *Hamlet*, III, i, 65

We are such stuff
As dreams are made on, and our little life
Is rounded out with a sleep.
— SHAKESPEARE (1564–1616) *The Tempest*, IV, i, 156

We rest. A dream has power to poison sleep;
We rise. One wandering thought pollutes the day.
— PERCY B. SHELLEY (1792–1822) *Mutability*

But I, being poor, have only my dreams;
I have spread my dreams under your feet;
Tread softly, for you tread on my dreams.
— WILLIAM BUTLER YEATS (1865–1939) *The Cloths of Heaven*

Your old men shall dream dreams, your young men shall see visions.
— OLD TESTAMENT: *Joel*, II, 28

DUTY

In doing what we ought we deserve no praise, because it is our duty.
— ST. AUGUSTINE (354–430)

The fulfilment of spiritual duty in our daily life is vital to our survival.
— WINSTON CHURCHILL (1874–1965) Speech, 1949

Do your duty and leave the rest to heaven.
— PIERRE CORNEILLE (1606–1684) *Horace*

The reward of one duty is the power to fill another.
— GEORGE ELIOT (1819–1880) *Daniel Deronda*

Fear God, and keep his commandments; for this is the whole duty of man.
— OLD TESTAMENT: *Ecclesiastes*, xii, 13

Up to a certain point it is good for us to know that there are people in the world who will give us love and unquestioned loyalty to the limit of their ability. I doubt, however, if it is good for us to feel assured of this without the accompanying obligation of having to justify this devotion by our behavior.
— ELEANOR ROOSEVELT (1884–1962) *This is My Story*

There is no duty we underrate so much as the duty of being happy.
— R. L. STEVENSON (1850–1894) *Virginibus Puerisque*

He who eats the fruit should at least plant the seed.
— HENRY DAVID THOREAU (1817–1862)

Duty is what one expects from others.
— OSCAR WILDE (1854–1900) *Woman of No Importance*

EDUCATION See LEARNING

EGOTISM (See also VANITY)

Self-conceit may lead to self-destruction.
— AESOP (6th C. B.C.) *The Frog and the Ox*

Why should I be angry with a man, for loving himself better than me?
— FRANCIS BACON (1561–1620) *Essays*

Conceit is God's fit to little men.
— BRUCE BARTON (1886–) *Conceit*

I've never had any pity for conceited people, because I think they carry their comfort about with them.
— GEORGE ELIOT (1819–1880) *The Mill on the Floss*

We reproach people for talking about themselves; but it is the subject they treat best.
— ANATOLE FRANCE (1844–1924)

We would rather speak ill of ourselves than not talk of ourselves at all.
— FRANÇOIS DE LA ROCHEFOUCAULD (1613–1680) *Maxims*

There is not enough love and goodness in the world to throw any of it away on conceited people.
— FRIEDRICH NIETZSCHE (1844–1900)

If you love yourself over much, nobody else will love you at all.
— PROVERB

Every bird loves to hear himself sing.
— GERMAN PROVERB

Who loves himself need fear no rival.
— LATIN PROVERB

Conceit may puff a man up, but never prop him up.
— JOHN RUSKIN (1819–1900) *True and Beautiful*

Self-love, in nature rooted fast,
Attends us first, and leaves us last.
— JONATHAN SWIFT (1667–1745) *Cadenus and Vanessa*

We are interested in others when they are interested in us.
— PUBLILIUS SYRUS (1st C. B.C.) *Sententiae*

From his cradle to his grave a man never does a single thing which has any first and foremost object save one—to secure peace of mind, spiritual comfort, for himself.
— MARK TWAIN (1835–1910) *What is Man?*

All men think all men mortal but themselves.
— EDWARD YOUNG (1683–1765) *Night Thoughts*

ENEMY

Wise men learn much from their enemies.
— ARISTOPHANES (444–380 B.C.) *The Birds*

Every man is his own greatest enemy, and as it were his own executioner.
— SIR THOMAS BROWNE (1605–1682) *Religio Medici*

You shall judge a man by his foes as well as by his friends.
— JOSEPH CONRAD (1857–1924) *Lord Jim*

Though thy enemy seems a mouse, yet watch him like a lion.
— PROVERB

One enemy can do more hurt than ten friends can do good.
— JONATHAN SWIFT (1667–1745) Letter, 1710

He makes no friend who never made a foe.
— TENNYSON (1809–1892) *Idylls of the King*

Rejoice not over thy greatest enemy being dead, but remember that we die all.
— APOCRYPHA: *Ecclesiasticus*

A man's foes shall be they of his own household.
— NEW TESTAMENT: *Matthew* x, 36

Love your enemies, bless them that curse you, do good to them that hate you . . . .
— NEW TESTAMENT: *Matthew*, v, 44

ENJOYMENT See PLEASURE

ENVY

Those that are not envied are never wholly happy.
— AESCHYLUS (525–456 B.C.) *Agamemnon*

Envy not greatness: for thou mak'st thereby
Thyself the worse, and so the distance greater.
— GEORGE HERBERT (1593–1633) *The Church*

All the tyrants of Sicily never invented a worse torment than envy.
— HORACE (65–8 B.C.) *Epistles*

No man likes to be surpassed by those of his own level.
— LIVY (59 B.C.–A.D. 17) *Annales*

Since we cannot attain to greatness, let us revenge ourselves by railing at it.
— MICHEL DE MONTAIGNE (1533–1592) *Essays*

It is a nobler fate to be envied than to be pitied.
— PINDAR (*c.* 522–442 B.C.) *Pythian Odes*

The truest mark of being born with great qualities is being born without envy.
— FRANÇOIS DE LA ROCHEFOUCAULD (1613–1680) *Maxims*

No metal can,
No, not the hangman's axe, bear half the keenness
Of thy sharp envy.
— SHAKESPEARE (1564–1616) *Merchant of Venice*, IV, i, 123

Where envying and strife is, there is confusion, and every evil work.
— NEW TESTAMENT: *James*, iii, 16

EQUALITY AND INEQUALITY

The only stable state is the one in which all men are equal before the law.
— ARISTOTLE (384–322 B.C.) *Politics*

We hold these truths to be self-evident—that all men are created equal; that they are endowed by their Creator with certain inalienable rights; that among these are life, liberty, and the pursuit of happiness.
— DECLARATION OF INDEPENDENCE

Before God we are all equally wise—equally foolish.
— ALBERT EINSTEIN (1879–1955) *Cosmic Religion*

Men are made by nature unequal. It is vain, therefore, to treat them as if they were equal.
— JAMES ANTHONY FROUDE (1818–1894)

Though all men are made of one metal, yet they were not cast all in the same mold.
— THOMAS FULLER (1608–1681) *Gnomologia*

That all men are equal is a proposition to which at ordinary times no sane individual has ever given his assent.
— ALDOUS HUXLEY (1894–1963) *Proper Studies*

And our sorrowing gaze turns also to the other children of God everywhere, suffering because of race and economic conditions, at once complex and giving reason for anxiety, or through the limitation on the exercise of their natural and civil rights.
— POPE JOHN XXIII (1881–1963) April 17, 1960

All animals are created equal—but some animals are created more equal than others.
— GEORGE ORWELL (1903–1950) *Animal Farm*

The only real equality is in the cemetery.
— GERMAN PROVERB

Nature knows no equality; its sovereign law is subordination and dependence.
— MARQUIS DE VAUVENARGUES (1715–1747) *Reflections*

ERROR

There is many a slip
'Twixt the cup and the lip
— RICHARD HARRIS BARHAM (1788–1845) *Ingoldsby Legends*

I can pardon everybody's mistakes except my own.
— MARCUS CATO (234–149 B.C.)

Who errs and mends, to God himself commends.
— CERVANTES (1547–1616) *Don Quixote*

Mistake, error, is the discipline through which we advance.
— WILLIAM ELLERY CHANNING (1780–1842)

It is the nature of every man to err, but only the fool perseveres in error.
— CICERO (106–43 B.C.) *Philippicae*

The cautious seldom err.
— CONFUCIUS (*c.* 551–478 B.C.) *Analects*

Errors, like straws, upon the surface flow;
He who would search for pearls must dive below.
— JOHN DRYDEN (1631–1700) *All for Love*

Even a mistake may turn out to be the one thing necessary to a worthwhile achievement.
— HENRY FORD (1863–1947) Interview, 1938

Dark Error's other hidden side is truth.
— VICTOR HUGO (1802–1885) *Legend of the Centuries*

The man who makes no mistakes does not usually make anything.
— BISHOP W. C. MAGEE (1821–1891)

To err is human, to forgive divine.
— ALEXANDER POPE (1688–1744) *Essay on Criticism*

The wise course is to profit from the mistakes of others.
— TERENCE (*c.* 190–150 B.C.)

I fear our mistakes far more than the strategy of our enemies.
— THUCYDIDES (471?–400? B.C.) *Funeral Oration*

The progress of the rivers to the ocean is not so rapid as that of man to error.
— VOLTAIRE (1694–1778) *Philosophical Dictionary*

EVENING See NIGHT

EVIL

Evil events from evil causes spring.
— ARISTOPHANES (444–380 B.C.)

Better suffer a great evil than do a little one.
— HENRY GEORGE BOHN (1796–1884) *Handbook of Proverbs*

Often the fear of one evil leads us into a worse.
— NICOLAS BOILEAU (1636–1711) *The Poetic Art*

God bears with the wicked, but not forever.
— CERVANTES (1547–1616) *Don Quixote*

Evil to him who thinks evil. [Honi soit qui mal y pense.]
— EDWARD III (1327–1377) Motto of the Order of the Garter

A wicked man is his own hell.
— THOMAS FULLER (1606–1661) *Gnomologia*, No. 460

Don't let us make imaginary evils, when you know we have so many real ones to encounter.
— OLIVER GOLDSMITH (1730–1774)

The source of all wars, the source of all evil, lies in us.
— PIERRE LECOMTE DU NOÜY (1883–1947) *Human Destiny*

The evil best known is the most tolerable.
— LIVY (59 B.C.–A.D. 17) *History of Rome*

An evil life is a kind of death.
— OVID (43 B.C.–A.D. 18?) *Epistulae ex Ponto*

No evil can happen to a good man, either in life or after death.
— SOCRATES (470?–399 B.C.)

Every one that doeth evil hateth the light.
— NEW TESTAMENT: *John*, iii, 20

I have seen the wicked in great power, and spreading himself like the green bay tree. Yet he passed away, and lo, he was not.
— OLD TESTAMENT: *Isaiah*, lv, 7

Fret not thyself because of evildoers . . . for they shall soon be cut down like the grass, and wither as the green herb.
— OLD TESTAMENT: *Psalms*, xxxvii, 1–2

EXPERIENCE

All experience is an arch to build upon.
— HENRY ADAMS (1838–1918) *Education of Henry Adams*

It is costly wisdom that is bought by experience.
— ROGER ASCHAM (1515–1568) *Schoolmaster*

Thou shalt know by experience how salt the savor is of another's bread, and how sad a path it is to climb and descend another's stairs.
— DANTE (1265–1321) *Paradiso*

Experience keeps a dear school, but fools will learn in no other.
— BEN FRANKLIN (1706–1790) *Poor Richard's Almanack*

The finished man of the world must eat of every apple once.
— RALPH WALDO EMERSON (1803–1882) *Conduct of Life*

Happy is he who gains wisdom from another's mishap.
— PUBLILIUS SYRUS (1st C. B.C.) *Sententiae*

Experience is the name everyone gives to his mistakes.
— OSCAR WILDE (1854–1900) *Lady Windermere's Fan*

FAITH

Faith is a higher faculty than reason.
— PHILIP JAMES BAILEY (1816–1902)

I believe in the incomprehensibility of God.
— HONORÉ DE BALZAC (1799–1850)

To me, faith means not worrying.
— JOHN DEWEY (1859–1952)

Faith is not belief. Belief is passive. Faith is active. It is vision which passes inevitably into action.
— EDITH HAMILTON (1867–1963) *Witness to the Truth*

Faith may be defined briefly as an illogical belief in the occurrence of the improbable.
— H. L. MENCKEN (1880–1956) *Prejudices*, Series iii

Faith is like love; it cannot be forced.
— ARTHUR SCHOPENHAUER (1788–1860)

Faith is the antiseptic of the soul.
— WALT WHITMAN (1819–1892) *Leaves of Grass*, preface

We walk by faith, not by sight.
— NEW TESTAMENT: *II Corinthians*, v, 7

If ye have faith as a grain of mustard seed, ye shall say unto this mountain, Remove hence to yonder place; and it shall remove: and nothing shall be impossible unto you.
— NEW TESTAMENT: *Matthew*, xvii, 20

FALL See AUTUMN

FAMILY See MARRIAGE, FATHER, MOTHER

FATE

Nor sitting at his hearth at home doth man escape his appointed doom.
— AESCHYLUS (525–456 B.C.) *The Choephorae*

Destiny is not a matter of chance, it is a matter of choice; it is not a thing to be waited for, it is a thing to be achieved.
— WILLIAM JENNINGS BRYAN (1860–1925) Speech, 1899

'Tis fate that flings the dice, and as she flings
Of kings makes peasants, and of peasants kings.
— JOHN DRYDEN (1631–1700) *Jupiter Cannot Alter the Decrees of Fate*

The moving finger writes; and having writ
Moves on; nor all your Piety nor Wit
Shall lure it back to cancel half a Line.
— EDWARD FITZGERALD (1809–1883) tr.: *Rubáiyát of Omar Khayyám*

Man supposes that he directs his life and governs his actions, when his existence is irretrievably under the control of destiny.
— GOETHE (1749–1832)

That which God writes on thy forehead, thou wilt come to it.
— THE KORAN

Our hour is marked, and no one can claim a moment of life beyond what fate has predestined.
— NAPOLEON BONAPARTE (1811–1884)

This generation of Americans has a rendezvous with destiny.
— FRANKLIN D. ROOSEVELT (1882–1945) Address, 1936

Fate leads the willing, and drags along those who hang back.
— SENECA (4? B.C.–A.D. 65)

There is a divinity that shapes our ends,
Rough-hew them how we will.
— SHAKESPEARE (1564–1616) *Hamlet*, V, ii, 10

All things come alike to all: there is one event to the righteous, and to the wicked; to the good and to the clean, and to the unclean . . . .
— OLD TESTAMENT: *Ecclesiastes*, ix, 2

FATHER

Diogenes struck the father when the son swore.
— ROBERT BURTON (1577–1640) *Anatomy of Melancholy*

He that has his father for judge goes safe to the trial.
— CERVANTES (1547–1616) *Don Quixote*

One father is more than a hundred schoolmasters.
— GEORGE HERBERT (1593–1633) *Jacula Prudentum*

If a man strike his father his hand shall be cut off.
— *The Code of Hammurabi*

It is a wise father that knows his own child.
— SHAKESPEARE (1564–1616) *Merchant of Venice*, II, ii, 80

A wise son maketh a glad father.
— OLD TESTAMENT: *Proverbs*, x, i

He that honoureth his father shall have a long life.
— APOCRYPHA: *Ecclesiasticus*, iii, 6

FAULTS

What an absurd thing it is to pass over all the valuable parts of a man, and fix our attention on his infirmities.
— JOSEPH ADDISON (1672–1719)

The greatest of faults, I should say, is to be conscious of none.
— THOMAS CARLYLE (1795–1881) *Heroes and Hero-Worship*

Men ought to be most annoyed by the sufferings which come from their own faults.
— CICERO (106–43 B.C.) *Epistolae ad Fratrem*

The defects of great men are the consolation of dunces.
— ISAAC D'ISRAELI (1766–1848)

All his faults were such that one loved him still the better for them.
— OLIVER GOLDSMITH (1730–1774) *The Good-Natur'd Man*

A fault confessed is more than half amended.
— SIR JOHN HARINGTON (1561–1612)

If we had no faults, we should not take so much pleasure in remarking them in others.
— FRANÇOIS DE LA ROCHEFOUCAULD (1613–1680) *Maxims*

He who loves not the loved one's faults does not truly love.
— SPANISH PROVERB

The fault, dear Brutus, is not in our stars,
But in ourselves, that we are underlings.
— SHAKESPEARE (1564–1616) *Julius Caesar*, I, ii, 140

FEAR

No one loves the man whom he fears.
— ARISTOTLE (384–322 B.C.)

We listen'd and look'd sideways up!
Fear at my heart, as at a cup,
My life-blood seem'd to sip.
— SAMUEL TAYLOR COLERIDGE (1772–1834) *Ancient Mariner*

Fear always springs from ignorance.
— RALPH WALDO EMERSON (1803–1882) *The American Scholar*

Fear is the parent of cruelty.
— JAMES ANTHONY FROUDE (1818–1894)

Many may not love us, but all shall fear us.
— HEINRICH HIMMLER (1900–1945)

Let us never negotiate out of fear. But let us never fear to negotiate.
— JOHN F. KENNEDY (1917–1963), Inaugural Address, 1961

Apprehensions are greater in proportion as things are unknown.
— LIVY (B.C. 59–A.D. 17) *Annales*

Fear is a feeling that is stronger than love.
— PLINY THE YOUNGER (62–113) *Letters*

The only thing we have to fear is fear itself.
— FRANKLIN D. ROOSEVELT (1882–1945) Inaugural Address, 1933

His flight was madness; when our actions do not,
Our fears do make us traitors.
— SHAKESPEARE (1564–1616) *Macbeth*, IV, ii, 3

To him who is in fear everything rustles.
— SOPHOCLES (495–406 B.C.)

Fear, like pain, looks and sounds worse than it feels.
— REBECCA WEST (1892–)

FEBRUARY See MONTHS

FIDELITY AND INFIDELITY

Give me a man that is capable of a devotion to anything, rather than a cold, calculating average of all the virtues.
— BRET HARTE (1838–1902) *Two Men of Sandy Bar*

The fidelity of most men is merely an invention of self-love to win confidence . . . .
— FRANÇOIS DE LA ROCHEFOUCAULD (1613–1680) *Maxims*

Fidelity bought with money is overcome by money.
— SENECA (4? B.C.–A.D. 65) *Agamemnon*

Oh, where is loyalty?
If it be banish'd from the frosty head,
Where shall it find a harbour in the earth?
— SHAKESPEARE (1564–1616) *II Henry IV*, V, i, 166

To God, thy countrie, and thy friend be true.
— HENRY VAUGHAN (1622–1695) *Rules and Lessons*

Be thou faithful unto death.
— NEW TESTAMENT: *Revelation*, ii, 10

FLATTERY

A flatterer is a friend who is your inferior or pretends to be so.
— ARISTOTLE (384–322 B.C.) *Nicomachean Ethics*

We sometimes think that we hate flattery, but we only hate the manner in which it is done.
— FRANÇOIS DE LA ROCHEFOUCAULD (1613–1680) *Maxims*

'Tis hard to find a man of great estate,
That can distinguish flatterers from friends.
— HORACE (65–8 B.C.)

When flatterers meet, the Devil goes to dinner.
— JOHN RAY (1627?–1705) *English Proverbs*

But when I tell him he hates flatterers,
He says he does, being then most flattered.
— SHAKESPEARE (1564–1616) *Julius Caesar*, II, i, 208

They do abuse the king that flatter him:
For flattery is the bellows blows up sin.
— SHAKESPEARE (1564–1616) *Pericles*, I, ii, 38

A flattering mouth worketh ruin.
— OLD TESTAMENT: *Proverbs*, xxvi, 28

FLOWERS See GARDEN

FOLLY AND FOOLS

The folly of one man is the fortune of another.
— FRANCIS BACON (1561–1620) *Essays: Of Fortune*

A sucker is born every minute.
— P. T. BARNUM (1810–1891)

The hours of folly are measur'd by the clock; but of wisdom, no clock can measure.
— WILLIAM BLAKE (1757–1827) *Marriage of Heaven and Hell*

A fool always finds one still more foolish to admire him.
— NICOLAS BOILEAU (1636–1711) *The Poetic Art*

And fools cannot hold their tongue.
— GEOFFREY CHAUCER (1340?–1400) *Romaunt of the Rose*

The first degree of folly is to conceit one's self wise; the second to profess it; the third to despise counsel.
— BEN FRANKLIN (1706–1790) *Poor Richard's Almanack*

When lovely woman stoops to folly,
And finds too late that men betray,
What charm can soothe her melancholy?
What art can wash her guilt away?
— OLIVER GOLDSMITH (1730–1774) *Vicar of Wakefield*

I am always afraid of a fool. One cannot be sure that he is not a knave as well.
— WILLIAM HAZLITT (1778–1830) *Characteristics*

Folly pursues us in every period of life. If any one appears wise, it is only because his follies are proportioned to his age and fortune.
— FRANÇOIS DE LA ROCHEFOUCAULD (1613–1680) *Maxims*

There is no fool like an old fool.
— JOHN LYLY (1554?–1606)

I enjoy vast delight in the folly of mankind; and, God be praised, that is an inexhaustible source of entertainment.
— LADY MARY WORTLY MONTAGU (1689–1762) Letter

Fools rush in where angels fear to tread.
— ALEXANDER POPE (1688–1744) *An Essay on Criticism*

If every fool wore a crown, we'd all be kings.
— WELSH PROVERB

The fool doth think he is wise, but the wise man knows himself to be a fool.
— SHAKESPEARE (1564–1616) *As You Like It*, V, i, 34

Give me the young man who has brains enough to make a fool of himself.
— R. L. STEVENSON (1850–1894) *Virginibus Puerisque*

A fool and his money are soon parted.
— UNKNOWN

The best way to silence any friend of yours whom you know to be a fool is to induce him to hire a hall.
— WOODROW WILSON (1856–1924) Speech, 1916

The wise man's eyes are in his head, but the fool walketh in darkness.
— OLD TESTAMENT: *Ecclesiastes*, ii, 14

FORGETFULNESS

A man must get a thing before he can forget it.
— OLIVER WENDELL HOLMES (1809–1894) *Medical Essays*

Blessed are the forgetful; for they get the better of even their blunders.
— FRIEDRICK NIETZSCHE (1844–1900) *Beyond Good and Evil*

We have all forgotten more than we remember.
— PROVERB

We bury love,
Forgetfulness grows over it like grass;
That is a thing to weep for, not the dead.
— ALEXANDER SMITH (1830–1867) *City Poems*

If I forget thee, O Jerusalem, let my right hand forget her cunning.
— OLD TESTAMENT: *Psalms*, cxxxvii, 5

FORESIGHT See PRUDENCE

FORGIVENESS

You may pardon much to others, nothing to yourself.
— AUSONIUS (*f.* 4th C. A.D.) *Epigrams*

Those who forgive most shall be most forgiven.
— PHILIP JAMES BAILEY (1816–1902) *Festus*

He who forgives readily only invites offense.
— PIERRE CORNEILLE (1606–1684) *Cinna*

God may forgive you, but I never can.
— QUEEN ELIZABETH I (1533–1603) to the Countess of Nottingham

It is often easier to forgive those who have wronged us than those whom we have wronged.
— OSCAR HAMMLING (1890–) *Laçonics*

Know all and you will pardon all.
— THOMAS À KEMPIS (1380–1471) *Imitation of Christ*

We pardon in proportion as we love.
— FRANÇOIS DE LA ROCHEFOUCAULD (1613–1680) *Maxims*

We read that we ought to forgive our enemies; but we do not read that we ought to forgive our friends.
— COSIMO DE' MEDICI (1519–1574)

If the injured one could read your heart, you may be sure he would understand and pardon.
— R. L. STEVENSON (1850–1894) *Truth of Intercourse*

There is nothing so advantageous to a man than a forgiving disposition.
— TERENCE (*c.* 190–150 B.C.) *Adelphi*

Father, forgive them; for they know not what they do.
— NEW TESTAMENT: *Luke*, xxiii, 34

A woman may consent to forget and forgive, but she never will drop the habit of referring to the matter now and then.
— UNKNOWN

FORTUNE

Fortune is a god and rules men's lives.
— AESCHYLUS (525–456 B.C.) *The Choephorae*

Every man is the architect of his own fortune.
— APPIUS CLAUDIUS (*f.* 312 B.C.)

All fortune is to be conquered by bearing it.
— FRANCIS BACON (1561–1620) *Advancement of Learning*

I am not now in fortune's power;
He that is down can fall no lower.
— SAMUEL BUTLER (1612–1680) *Hudibras*

Fortune hath somewhat the nature of a woman; if she be too much wooed, she is the farther off.
— EMPEROR CHARLES V (1500–1588)

It is fortune, not wisdom, that rules man's life.
— CICERO (106–43 B.C.)

Ill fortune seldom comes alone.
— JOHN DRYDEN (1631–1700) *Cymon and Iphigenia*, Act I

Fortune never seems so blind as to those upon whom she confers no favors.
— FRANÇOIS DE LA ROCHEFOUCAULD (1613–1680) *Maxims*

Not many men have both good fortune and good sense.
— LIVY (59 B.C.–A.D. 17) *History of Rome*

The wheel goes round and round
And some are up and some are on the down
And still the wheel goes round.
— JOSEPHINE POLLARD (1843–1892) *Wheel of Fortune*

Fortune can take from us nothing but what she gave us.
— PUBLILIUS SYRUS (1st C. B.C.) *Sententiae*

Fear of the future is worse than one's present fortune.
— QUINTILIAN (40 –*c.* 100)

Everyone is the architect of his own fortune.
— ABBÉ REGNIER (1794–?) *Satire*

Fortune, that arrant whore
Ne'er turns the key to the poor.
— SHAKESPEARE (1564–1616) *King Lear*, II, iv, 52

FREEDOM

The cause of freedom is the cause of God.
— WILLIAM LISLE BOWLES (1762–1850) To EDMUND BURKE

A man can be free even within prison walls. Freedom is something spiritual. Whoever has once had it, can never lose it. There are some people who are never free outside a prison.
— BERTOLD BRECHT (1898–1956) *A Penny for the Poor*

Hereditary bondsmen! Know ye not
Who would be free themselves must strike the blow?
— LORD BYRON (1788–1824) *Childe Harold*

Perfect freedom is reserved for the man who lives by his own work and in that work does what he wants to do.
— ROBIN GEORGE COLLINGWOOD (1889–1943) *Speculum Mentis*

I am as free as nature first made man.
Ere the base laws of servitude began,
When wild in woods the noble savage ran.
— JOHN DRYDEN (1631–1700) *Conquest of Granada*

Freedom from fear and injustice and oppression will be ours only in the measure that men who value such freedom are ready to sustain its possession—to defend it against every thrust from within or without.
— DWIGHT D. EISENHOWER (1890–) *Crusade in Europe*

No man is free who is not master of himself.
— EPICTETUS (1st C. A.D.) *Discourses*

No man is wholly free. He is a slave to wealth, or to fortune, or the laws, or the people restrain him from acting according to his will alone.
— EURIPIDES (480–406 B.C.) *Hecuba*

The right to personal freedom comes second in importance to the duty of maintaining the race.
— ADOLF HITLER (1889–1945) *Mein Kampf*

Who then is free? the wise man who is lord over himself; Whom neither poverty nor death, nor chains alarm, strong to withstand his passions and despise honors, and who is completely finished and founded off in himself.
— HORACE (65–8 B.C.) *Satires*

Every man has a right to utter what he thinks truth, and every other man has a right to knock him down for it.
— SAMUEL JOHNSON (1709–1784) in Boswell's *Life*

The most unfree souls go west and shout of freedom. Men are freest when they are most unconscious of freedom. The shout is a rattling of chains.
— D. H. LAWRENCE (1885–1930) *Studies in Classic American Literature*

Those who deny freedom to others deserve it not for themselves, and, under a just God cannot long retain it.
— ABRAHAM LINCOLN (1809–1865) Letter, 1859

If I have freedom in my love,
And in my soul am free,
Angels alone, that soar above,
Enjoy such liberty.
— RICHARD LOVELACE (1618–1658) *To Althea from Prison*

There is only one cure for the evils which newly acquired freedom produces, and that is more freedom.
— THOMAS MACAULAY (1800–1859) *Essay on Milton*

In the modern social order, the *person* is sacrificed to the *individual*. The individual is given universal suffrage, equality of rights, freedom of opinion; while the person, isolated, naked, with no social armor to sustain and protect him, is left to the mercy of all the devouring forces which threaten the life of the soul . . . .
— JACQUES MARITAIN (1882–) *Three Reformers*

Oh, Lord, I want to be free, want to be free;
Rainbow round my shoulder, wings on my feet.
— UNKNOWN, American Negro Spiritual

Is any man free except the one who can pass his life as he pleases?
— PERSIUS (34–62) *Satires*

The people who settled in New England came here for religious freedom, but religious freedom to them meant freedom only for their kind of religion . . . . This attitude seems to be our attitude in many situations today.
— ELEANOR ROOSEVELT (1884–1962)

Man is born free—and everywhere he is in irons.
— JEAN JACQUES ROUSSEAU (1712–1778) *Social Contract*

No one can be perfectly free till all are free.
— HERBERT SPENCER (1820–1903) *Social Statics*

There are times in the lives of all people when freedom is the twin of duty, sacrifice the companion of happiness, and when courage—parent of fortitude, endurance, determination —is the first virtue.
— DOROTHY THOMPSON (1894–1961) *On the Record*

I would rather sit on a pumpkin and have it all to myself, than to be crowded on a velvet cushion.
— HENRY DAVID THOREAU (1817–1862) *Walden*

I disapprove of what you say, but I will defend to the death your right to say it.
— Attributed to VOLTAIRE by a later biographer

Freedom exists only where the people take care of the government.
— WOODROW WILSON (1856–1924) Speech, 1912

FRIENDS

One friend in a lifetime is much; two are many; three are hardly possible. Friendship needs a certain parallelism of life, a community of thought, a rivalry of aim.
— HENRY ADAMS (1838–1918) *Education of Henry Adams*

Beast knows beast; birds of a feather flock together.
— ARISTOTLE (384–322 B.C.) *Rhetoric*

Thy friendship oft has made my heart to ache:
Do be my enemy—for friendship's sake.
— WILLIAM BLAKE (1757–1827) *To H.*

Friendships multiply joys and divide griefs.
— HENRY GEORGE BOHN (1796–1884) *Handbook of Proverbs*

I have loved my friends as I do virtue, my soul, my God.
— SIR THOMAS BROWNE (1605–1682) *Religio Medici*

Tell me what company thou keepest, and I'll tell thee what thou art.
— CERVANTES (1547–1616) *Don Quixote*

Endeavor, as much as you can, to keep company with people above you.
— LORD CHESTERFIELD (1694–1773) *Letters*

Never injure a friend, even in jest.
— CICERO (106–43 B.C.) *De Amicitia*

Friendship often ends in love; but love in friendship, never.
— CHARLES C. COLTON (1780?–1832) *Lacon*

Chance makes our parents, but choice makes our friends.
— JACQUES DELILLE (1738–1813) *Pitié*

Animals are such agreeable friends—they ask no questions, they pass no criticisms.
— GEORGE ELIOT (1819–1880)

The dearest friends are separated by impassable gulfs.
— RALPH WALDO EMERSON (1803–1882) *Essays*

The only way to have a friend is to be one.
— RALPH WALDO EMERSON (1803–1882) *Essays*

Men who know the same things are not long the best company for each other.
— RALPH WALDO EMERSON (1803–1882)

In prosperity it is very easy to find a friend; in adversity, nothing is so difficult.
— EPICTETUS (1st C. A.D.) *Encheiridion*

Real friends are our greatest joy and our greatest sorrow. It were almost to be wished that all true and faithful friends should expire on the same day.
— FÉNELON (1651–1715)

If you have one true friend you have more than your share.
— THOMAS FULLER (1608–1681) *Gnomologia*

There is no better looking-glass than an old friend.
— THOMAS FULLER (1608–1681) *Gnomologia*

'Tis thus that on the choice of friends
Our good or evil name depends.
— JOHN GAY (1688–1732) *Old Woman and Her Cats*

There is no desert like being friendless.
— BALTASAR GRACIÁN (1601–1658)

To have a great man for an intimate friend seems pleasant to those who have never tried it; those who have, fear it.
— HORACE (65–8 B.C.) *Epistulae*

I never considered a difference of opinion in politics, in religion, in philosophy, as cause for withdrawing from a friend.
— THOMAS JEFFERSON (1743–1826) Letter, 1800

An injured friend is the bitterest of foes.
— THOMAS JEFFERSON (1743–1826)

I find as I grow older that I love those most whom I loved first.
— THOMAS JEFFERSON (1743–1826) Letter, 1787

I live in the crowds of jollity, not so much to enjoy company as to shun myself.
— SAMUEL JOHNSON (1709–1784) *Rasselas*

If my friends are one-eyed, I look at them in profile.
— JOSEPH JOUBERT (1754–1824) *Pensées*

In friendship, as in love, we are often more happy from the things we are ignorant of than from those we are acquainted with.
— FRANÇOIS DE LA ROCHEFOUCAULD (1613–1680) *Maxims*

If you want to make a dangerous man your friend, let him do you a favor.
— LEWIS E. LAWES (1883–1947)

The vulgar estimate friends by the advantage to be derived from them.
— OVID (43 B.C.–A.D. 18?)

It is better to be alone than in ill company.
— GEORGE PETTIE (1548–1589)

Histories are more full of examples of the fidelity of dogs than of friends.
— ALEXANDER POPE (1688–1744) Letter, 1709

A friend in need is a friend indeed.
— ENGLISH PROVERB

It is fun to be in the same decade with you.
— FRANKLIN D. ROOSEVELT (1882–1945) in a cable to WINSTON CHURCHILL

He that goeth to bed with dogs ariseth with fleas.
— JAMES SANDFORD (*f.* 1572) *Hours of Recreation*

The principal task of friendship is to foster one's friends' illusions.
— ARTHUR SCHNITZLER (1862–1931) *Anatole*

Friendship always benefits; love sometimes injures.
— SENECA (4? B.C.–A.D. 65) *Epistulae ad Lucilium*

To lose a friend is the greatest of all evils, but endeavour rather to rejoice that you possessed him than to mourn his loss.
— SENECA (4? B.C.–A.D. 65) *Epistulae ad Lucilium*

Keep thy friend under thine own life's key.
— SHAKESPEARE (1564–1616) *All's Well that Ends Well,* I, i, 74

Those friends thou hast, and their adoption tried,
Grapple them to thy soul with hoops of steel;
But do not dull thy palm with entertainment
Of each new-hatch'd, unfledg'd comrade.
— SHAKESPEARE (1564–1616) *Hamlet,* I, iii, 59

To wail friends lost
Is not by much so wholesome—profitable,
As to rejoice at friends but newly found.
— SHAKESPEARE (1564–1616) *Love's Labour Lost,* V, ii, 759

I am not of that feather to shake off
My friend when he must need me.
— SHAKESPEARE (1564–1616) *Timon of Athens,* I, i, 100

The most I can do for my friend is simply to be his friend.
— HENRY DAVID THOREAU (1817–1862) *Journal,* 1841

God save me from my friends. I can protect myself from my enemies.
— MARSHAL DE VILLARS (1653–1734)

Friendship's the wine of life.
— EDWARD YOUNG (1683–1765) *Night Thoughts*

A faithful friend is a strong defense: and he that hath found such an one hath found a treasure.
— APOCRYPHA: *Ecclesiasticus,* vi, 14

Greater love hath no man than this, that a man lay down his life for his friends.
— NEW TESTAMENT: *John,* xv, 13

Saul and Jonathan were lovely and pleasant in their lives, and in their death they were not divided.
— OLD TESTAMENT: *II Samuel,* i, 23

A friend is one who dislikes the same people that you dislike.
— UNKNOWN

FUTURE

We are always doing something for Posterity, but I would fain see Posterity do something for us.
— JOSEPH ADDISON (1672–1719) *The Spectator*

You can never plan the future by the past.
— EDMUND BURKE (1729–1797) Letter

For my part, I think that a knowledge of the future would be a disadvantage.
— CICERO (106–43 B.C.) *De Devinatione*

I never think of the future. It comes soon enough.
— ALBERT EINSTEIN (1879–1955)

The future is a convenient place for dreams.
— ANATOLE FRANCE (1844–1924)

I know of no way of judging the future but by the past.
— PATRICK HENRY (1736–1799) Speech, 1775

Trust no future, howe'er pleasant!
Let the dead Past bury its dead!
— HENRY W. LONGFELLOW (1801–1882) *Psalm of Life*

The mind that is anxious about the future is miserable.
— SENECA (4? B.C.–A.D. 65) *Epistulae ad Lucilium*

We know what we are, but know not what we may be.
— SHAKESPEARE (1564–1616) *Hamlet,* IV, v, 43

Take no thought for the morrow: for the morrow shall take thought for the things of itself.
— NEW TESTAMENT: *Matthew,* vi, 34

GARDEN AND FLOWERS

Who loves a garden still his Eden keeps . . . .
— AMOS BRONSON ALCOTT (1799–1888)

Ah, Sunflower, weary of time,
Who countest the steps of the sun;
Seeking after that sweet golden clime,
Where the traveller's journey is done . . . .
— WILLIAM BLAKE (1757–1827) *The Sunflower*

God the first garden made, and the first city Cain.
— ABRAHAM COWLEY (1618–1667) *The Garden*

Loveliest of trees, the cherry now
Is hung with bloom along the bough,
And stands about the woodland ride
Wearing white for Eastertide.
— A. E. HOUSMAN (1859–1936)

Your sacred plants, if here below,
Only among the plants will grow.
Society is all but rude,
To this delicious solitude.
— ANDREW MARVELL (1621–1678) *The Garden*

Many things grow in the garden that were never sowed there.
— PROVERB

Lilies that fester smell far worse than weeds.
— SHAKESPEARE (1564–1616) *Sonnets*, xciv

Consider the lilies of the field, how they grow; they toil not, neither do they spin: And yet I say unto you, that even Solomon in all his glory was not arrayed like one of these.
— NEW TESTAMENT: *Matthew*, vi, 28

The Lord God planted a garden eastward in Eden; and there He put the man whom He had formed.
— OLD TESTAMENT: *Genesis*, ii, 8

GENEROSITY See GIFTS AND GIVING

GENIUS

Doing easily what others find difficult is talent; doing what is impossible for talent is genius.
— HENRI-FREDERIC AMIEL (1828–1881) *Journal*

Genius is mainly an affair of energy.
— MATTHEW ARNOLD (1822–1888) *Essays in Criticism*

I have known no man of genius who had not to pay, in some affliction or defect either physical or spiritual, for what the gods had given him.
— MAX BEERBOHM (1872–1956) *The Pines*

Patience is a necessary ingredient of genius.
— BENJAMIN DISRAELI (1805–1881) *Contarini Fleming*

Genius is one percent inspiration and ninety-nine percent perspiration.
— THOMAS E. EDISON (1847–1931) Newspaper interview

Every man of genius sees the world at a different angle from his fellows, and there is his tragedy.
— HAVELOCK ELLIS (1859–1939) *Dance of Life*

Genius is the power of lighting one's own fire.
— JOHN FOSTER (1770–1843)

A man of genius makes no mistakes. His errors are volitional and are the portals of discovery.
— JAMES JOYCE (1882–1941) *Ulysses*

Gift, like genius, I often think only means an infinite capacity for taking pains.
— JANE ELLICE HOPKINS (1836–1904)

Genius is a promontory jutting out into the infinite.
— VICTOR HUGO (1802–1885) *William Shakespeare*

Genius begets great works; labor alone finished them.
— JOSEPH JOUBERT (1754–1824) *Pensées*

One science only will one genius fit;
So vast is art, so narrow human wit.
— ALEXANDER POPE (1668–1744) *Essay on Criticism*

The poets' scrolls will outlive the monuments of stone.
Genius survives; all else is claimed by death.
— EDMUND SPENSER (1552?–1599) *Shepherd's Calendar*

There is a certain characteristic common to all those whom we call geniuses. Each of them has a consciousness of being a man apart.
— MIGUEL DE UNAMUNO (1864–1936) *Essays and Soliloquies*

GIFTS AND GIVING

It is easy to become generous with other people's property.
— LATIN PROVERB

The most important thing in any relationship is not what you get but what you give. . . . In any case, the giving of love is an education in itself.
— ELEANOR ROOSEVELT (1884–1963)

You must be fit to give before you can be fit to receive.
— JAMES STEPHENS (1882–1950)

I fear the Greeks, even when they bring gifts.
— VERGIL (70–19 B.C.) *Aeneid*

It is more blessed to give than to receive.
— NEW TESTAMENT: *Acts*, xx, 35

Or what man is there of you, whom if his son ask bread, will he give him a stone?
— NEW TESTAMENT: *Matthew*, vii, 9

GIRL See CHILDREN

GOD

God's mouth knows not to utter falsehood, but he will perform each word.
— AESCHYLUS (525–456 B.C.) *Prometheus*

Nature herself has imprinted on the minds of all the idea of God.
— CICERO (106–43 B.C.) *De Natura Deorum*

Earth with her thousand voices, praises God
— SAMUEL TAYLOR COLERIDGE (1772–1834)

God moves in a mysterious way
His wonders to perform.
— WILLIAM COWPER (1731–1800) *Light Shining out of Darkness*

Father expected a great deal of God. He didn't actually accuse God of inefficiency, but when he prayed his tone was loud and angry, like that of a disatisfied guest in a carelessly managed hotel.
— CLARENCE DAY (1874–1935) *God and My Father*

God tempers the cold to the shorn lamb.
— HENRI ESTIENNE (*d.* 1520) *Premises*

There is no God but God.
— THE KORAN, Bk. iii

I live and love in God's peculiar light.
— MICHELANGELO (1475–1564)

God never shuts one door but he opens another.
— IRISH PROVERB

Had I but served my God with half the zeal
I served my king, he would not in mine age
Have left me naked to mine enemies.
— SHAKESPEARE (1564–1616) *Henry VIII*, III, ii, 456

Man proposes, but God disposes.
— THOMAS À KEMPIS (1380–1471) *Imitation of Christ*

If God didn't exist, man would have to invent Him.
— VOLTAIRE (1694–1778)

If God be for us, who can be against us?
— NEW TESTAMENT: *Romans*, viii, 31

God is our refuge and our strength, a very present help in trouble.
— OLD TESTAMENT: *Psalms*, xlvi, i

The heavens declare the glory of God; and the firmament showeth his handiwork.
— OLD TESTAMENT: *Psalms*, xix, i

GOODNESS

Goodness is easier to recognize than to define; only the greatest novelists can portray good people.
— W. H. AUDEN (1907–) *I Believe*

It is as hard for the good to suspect evil, as it is for the bad to suspect good.
— CICERO (106–43 B.C.)

Good and bad men are each less so than they seem.
— SAMUEL TAYLOR COLERIDGE (1772–1834) *Table-Talk*

True goodness springs from a man's own heart. All men are born good.
— CONFUCIUS (*c.* 551–479 B.C.) *Analects*

The ground that a good man treads is hallowed.
— GOETHE (1749–1832) *Torquato Tasso*

Let them be good that love me, though but few.
— BEN JONSON (1572–1637) *Cynthia's Revels*

The greatest pleasure I know is to do a good action by stealth, and to have it found out by accident.
— CHARLES LAMB (1775–1834)

There is no man so good, who, were he to submit all his thoughts and actions to the laws, would not deserve hanging ten times in his life.
— MICHEL DE MONTAIGNE (1533–1592) *Essays*

Goodness is a special kind of truth and beauty. It is truth and beauty in human behavior.
— HARRY ALLEN OVERSTREET (1895–)

The good die young.
— ENGLISH PROVERB

He is so good that he is good for nothing.
— ITALIAN PROVERB

The evil that men do lives after them;
The good is oft interred with their bones.
— SHAKESPEARE (1564–1616) *Julius Caesar*, III, ii, 81

The good man is his own friend.
— SOPHOCLES (495–406 B.C.) *Oedipus Coloneus*

Be good, and you will be lonesome.
— MARK TWAIN (1835–1910)

GOVERNMENT

The marvel of history is the patience with which men and women submit to burdens unnecessarily laid upon them by their governments.
— WILLIAM E. BORAH (1865–1940) Speech in U.S. Senate

And having looked to Government for bread, on the very first scarcity they will turn and bite the hand that fed them.
— EDMUND BURKE (1729–1797)

A thousand years scarce serve to form a state;
An hour may lay it in the dust.
— LORD BYRON (1788–1824) *Childe Harold*

Self-government is the natural government of man.
— HENRY CLAY (1777–1852) Speech, 1818

No man has any right to rule who is not better than the people over whom he rules.
— CYRUS THE ELDER (600?–529 B.C.)

I can retain neither respect nor affection for a Government which has been moving from wrong to wrong in order to defend its immorality.
— MOHANDAS K. GANDHI (1869–1948)

The spirit of resistance to government is so valuable on certain occasions that I wish it to be always kept alive.
— THOMAS JEFFERSON (1743–1826) to Abigail Adams

No man is good enough to govern another man without that other's consent.
— ABRAHAM LINCOLN (1809–1865) Speech, 1854

That is the best government which desires to make the people happy, and knows how to make them happy.
— THOMAS B. MACAULAY (1800–1859)

If men be good, government cannot be bad.
— WILLIAM PENN (1644–1718) *Fruits of Solitude*

Oligarchy: A government resting on a valuation of property, in which the rich have power and the poor man is deprived of it.
— PLATO (428–347 B.C.) *The Republic*

That form of government is best which includes monarchy, aristocracy, and democracy.
— POLYBIUS (205?–125 B.C.) *Histories*

Any government, like any family, can for a year spend a little more than it earns. But you and I know that a continuance of that habit means the poorhouse.
— FRANKLIN D. ROOSEVELT (1882–1945) Radio Speech, 1932

GRATITUDE AND INGRATITUDE

Gratitude is the sign of noble souls.
— AESOP (6th C. B.C.) *Androcles*

Earth produces nothing worse than an ungrateful man.
— AUSONIUS (*f.* 4th C. B.C.) *Epigrams*

Next to ingratitude, the most painful thing to bear is gratitude.
— HENRY WARD BEECHER (1813–1887)

Words are but empty thanks.
— COLLEY CIBBER (1671–1757) *Women's Wit*

When I'm not thanked at all I'm thanked enough.
— HENRY FIELDING (1707–1754)

A man is very apt to complain of the ingratitude of those who have risen far above him.
— SAMUEL JOHNSON (1709–1784) in Boswell's *Life*

A man who is ungrateful is often less to blame than his benefactor.
— FRANÇOIS DE LA ROCHEFOUCAULD (1613–1680) *Maxims*

The gratitude of most men is but a secret desire of receiving greater benefits.
— FRANÇOIS DE LA ROCHEFOUCAULD (1613–1680) *Maxims*

Gratitude is the least of virtues, but ingratitude the worst of vices.
— PROVERB

Blow, blow, thou winter wind,
Thou art not so unkind
As man's ingratitude . . . .
— SHAKESPEARE (1564–1616) *As You Like It*, II, vii, 174

How sharper than a serpent's tooth it is
To have a thankless child.
— SHAKESPEARE (1564–1616) *King Lear*, I, iv, 312

Do you like gratitude? I don't. If pity is akin to love, gratitude is akin to the other thing.
— GEORGE BERNARD SHAW (1856–1950) *Arms and the Man*

Alas! the gratitude of men
Hath often left me mourning.
— WILLIAM WORDSWORTH (1770–1850) *Simon Lee*

GREATNESS

When the dust of death has choked
A great man's voice, the common words he said
Turn oracles.
— ELIZABETH BARRETT BROWNING (1812–1861)

The price of greatness is responsibility.
— WINSTON CHURCHILL (1874–1965) Speech, 1943

The world cannot live at the level of its great men.
— SIR JAMES FRAZER (1854–1941) *The Golden Bough*

No really great man ever thought himself so.
— WILLIAM HAZLITT (1778–1830) *Table Talk*

There would be no great ones if there were no little ones.
— GEORGE HERBERT (1593–1633)

Be not afraid of greatness. Some are born great, some achieve greatness, and some have greatness thrust upon them.
— SHAKESPEARE (1564–1616) *Twelfth Night*, II, v, 156

Great men are not always wise.
— OLD TESTAMENT: *Job*, xxxii, 9

GREED See AVARICE

GRIEF

It is dangerous to abandon one's self to the luxury of grief: it deprives one of courage, and even of the wish for recovery.
— HENRI-FREDERIC AMIEL (1828–1881) *Journal*, 1871

There is no grief which time does not lessen and soften.
— CICERO (106–43 B.C.) *Epistles*

Grief is itself a medicine.
— WILLIAM COWPER (1731–1800) *Charity*

Grief is the agony of an instant: the indulgence of grief the blunder of a life.
— BENJAMIN DISRAELI (1804–1881) *Vivian Grey*

The only cure for grief is action.
— GEORGE HENRY LEWES (1817–1878)

If our inward griefs were seen written on our brow, how many would be pitied who are now envied.
— METASTASIO (1698–1782) *Guiseppe Riconosciuto*

Grief is a tree that has tears for its fruit.
— PHILEMON (361?–263? B.C.) *Fragment*

Grief fills the room up of my absent child,
Lies in his bed, walks up and down with me,
Puts on his pretty looks, repeats his words,
Remembers me of all his gracious parts,
Stuffs out his vacant garments with his form.
— SHAKESPEARE (1564–1616) *King John*, III, iv, 93

GUILT

The pot calls the kettle black.
— CERVANTES (1547–1616) *Don Quixote*

Guilt is present in the very hesitation, even though the deed be not committed.
— CICERO (106–43 B.C.) *De Officiis*

Secret guilt by silence is betrayed.
— JOHN DRYDEN (1631–1700) *The Hind and the Panther*

Men's minds are too ready to excuse guilt in themselves.
— LIVY (59 B.C.–A.D. 17) *History*

He that knows no guilt can know no fear.
— PHILIP MASSINGER (1583–1640)

He confesseth himself guilty, who refuseth to come to trial.
— PROVERB

The lady doth protest too much, methinks.
— SHAKESPEARE (1564–1616) *Hamlet*, III, ii, 242

In other words, psychoanalysts relieve their patients from feeling guilty about things of which they are not guilty, and leave them with the sense of guilt about things of which they really are guilty.
— GREGORY ZILBOORG (1890–1959) *Psychoanalysis and Religion*

HABIT

Habit is a sort of second nature.
— CICERO (106–43 B.C.) *De Finibus*

It seems, in fact, as though the second half of a man's life is made up of nothing but the habits he has accumulated during the first half.
— FËODOR DOSTOEVSKI (1821–1881) *The Possessed*

Habit is a cable; we weave a thread of it every day, and at last we cannot break it.
— HORACE MANN (1796–1859)

How use doth breed a habit in a man!
— SHAKESPEARE (1564–1616) *Two Gentlemen of Verona*, V, iv, 1

HANDS

Living from hand to mouth, soon satisfi'd.
— GUILLAUME DU BARTAS (1544–1590) *Devine Weekes*

Many hands make light work.
— PROVERB

One hand washeth the other.
— SENECA (4? B.C.–A.D. 65) *Apocolocyntosis*

All the perfumes of Arabia will not sweeten this little hand.
— SHAKESPEARE (1564–1616) *Macbeth*, V, i, 57

See, how she leans her cheek upon her hand!
O, that I were a glove upon that hand,
That I might touch that cheek!
— SHAKESPEARE (1564–1616) *Romeo and Juliet*, II, ii, 23

Let not thy left hand know what thy right hand doeth.
— NEW TESTAMENT: *Matthew*, vi, 3

His hand will be against every man and every man's hand against him.
— OLD TESTAMENT: *Genesis*, xvi, 12

HAPPINESS

Hold him alone truly fortunate who has ended his life in happy well-being.
— AESCHYLUS (525–456 B.C.) *Agamemnon*

Happiness is at once the best, the noblest and the pleasantest of things.
— ARISTOTLE (384–322 B.C.) *Nicomachean Ethics*

What is given by the gods more desirable than a happy hour?
— CATULLUS (84?–54 B.C.) *Odes*

The happiness of life is made up of minute fractions—the little soon forgotten charities of a kiss or smile, a kind look, a heartfelt compliment, and the countless infinitesimals of pleasurable and genial feeling.
— SAMUEL TAYLOR COLERIDGE (1772–1834) *Friend*

To fill the hour—that is happiness.
— RALPH WALDO EMERSON (1803–1882) *Experience*

Often the greatest enemy of present happiness is past happiness too well remembered.
— OSCAR HAMMLING (1890–)

Call no man happy till you know the nature of his death! He is at best but fortunate.
— HERODOTUS (484–424? B.C.)

And there is even a happiness
That makes the heart afraid.
— THOMAS HOOD (1799–1845) *Ode to Melancholy*

The supreme happiness of life is the conviction that we are loved.
— VICTOR HUGO (1802–1885) *Les Misérables*

He is happiest of whom the world says least, good or bad.
— THOMAS JEFFERSON (1743–1826) Letter to John Adams, 1786

The happiness or unhappiness of men depends no less upon their dispositions than on their fortunes.
— FRANÇOIS DE LA ROCHEFOUCAULD (1613–1680) *Maxims*

Oh, how bitter a thing it is to look into happiness through another man's eyes.
— SHAKESPEARE (1564–1616) *As You Like It,* V, ii, 48

Happiness is the shadow of things past,
Which fools still take for that which is to be!
— FRANCIS THOMPSON (1859–1907) *From the Night of Forebeing*

The sun and stars that float in the open air;
The apple-shaped earth, and we upon it—
surely the drift of them is something grand!
I do not know what it is, except that it is grand,
and that it is happiness.
— WALT WHITMAN (1819–1892) *Carol of Occupations*

HATRED

Now hatred is by far the greatest pleasure;
Men love in haste, but they detest at leisure.
— LORD BYRON (1788–1824) *Don Juan*

People hate those who make them feel their own inferiority.
— LORD CHESTERFIELD (1694–1773) *Letters to His Son*

There are glances of hatred that stab and raise no cry of murder.
— GEORGE ELIOT (1819–1880) *Felix Holt*

Whom men fear they hate, and whom they hate, they wish dead.
— QUINTUS ENNIUS (239–169 B.C.) *Thyestes*

How incredible it is that in this fragile existence we should hate and destroy one another. There are possibilities enough for all who will abandon mastery over others to pursue mastery over nature. There is world enough for all to seek their happiness in their own way.
— LYNDON B. JOHNSON (1908–) Inaugural Address, Jan. 1965

Men hate more steadily than they love.
— SAMUEL JOHNSON (1709–1784) Boswell's *Life of Johnson*

For never can true reconcilement grow,
Where wounds of deadly hate have pierced so deep.
— JOHN MILTON (1608–1674) *Paradise Lost*

There is no sport in hate when all the rage
Is on one side.
— PERCY B. SHELLEY (1792–1822) *Lines to a Reviewer*

It is characteristic of human nature to hate the man whom you have wronged.
— TACITUS (54–119) *Agricola*

As love, if love be perfect, casts out fear,
So hate, if hate be perfect, casts out fear.
— TENNYSON (1809–1892) *Idylls of the King*

HEALTH

In nothing do men more nearly approach the gods than in giving health to men.
— CICERO (106–43 B.C.) *Pro Ligario*

The health of the people is really the foundation upon which all their happiness and all their powers as a State depend.
— BENJAMIN DISRAELI (1804–1881)

Health is not a condition of matter, but of Mind.
— MARY BAKER G. EDDY (1821–1910) *Science and Health*

O health! health! the blessing of the rich! the riches of the poor! who can buy thee at too dear a rate, since there is no enjoying this world without thee?
— BEN JONSON (1572–1637) *Volpone*

Our prayers should be for a sound mind in a healthy body.
— JUVENAL (47–138) *Satires*

Life is not merely being alive, but being well.
— MARTIAL (*c.* A.D. 66) *Epigrams*

A man in good health is always full of advice to the sick.
— MENANDER (342–291 B.C.) *Andria*

It is part of the cure to wish to be cured.
— SENECA (8 B.C.–A.D. 65) *Hippolytus*

Measure your health by your sympathy with morning and spring. If there is no response in you to the awakening of nature, if the prospect of an early morning walk does not banish sleep, if the warble of the first bluebird does not thrill you, know that the morning and spring of your life are past, Thus may you feel your pulse.
— HENRY DAVID THOREAU (1817–1862) *Early Spring in Massachusetts*

HEART

My heart's in the Highlands, my heart is not here;
My heart's in the Highlands a-chasing the deer.
— ROBERT BURNS (1759–1796)

Maid of Athens, ere we part,
Give, oh, give me back my heart!
— LORD BYRON (1788–1824) *Maid of Athens*

Faint heart never won fair lady.
— WILLIAM CAMDEN (1551–1623) *Remains Concerning Britain*

The heart has eyes that the brain knows nothing of.
— DR. CHARLES HENRY PARKHURST (1842–1933)

And let me wring your heart; for so I shall,
If it be made of penetrable stuff.
— SHAKESPEARE (1564–1616) *Hamlet,* III, iv, 35

I will wear my heart upon my sleeve
For daws to peck at.
— SHAKESPEARE (1564–1616) *Othello,* I, i, 64

He hath a heart as sound as a bell and his tongue is the clapper, for what his heart thinks his tongue speaks.
— SHAKESPEARE (1564–1616) *Much Ado About Nothing,* III, ii, 12

My heart is a lonely hunter that hunts on a lonely hill.
— WILLIAM SHARP (1856?–1905) *The Lonely Hunter*

My true-love hath my heart, and I have his
By just exchange one for the other given
I hold his dear, and mine he cannot miss
There never was a better bargain driven.
— SIR PHILIP SIDNEY (1554–1586) *The Bargain*

Let not your heart be troubled.
— NEW TESTAMENT: *John,* xiv, 1

HEAT See WEATHER

HEAVEN

All places are distant from heaven alike.
— ROBERT BURTON (1577–1640) *Anatomy of Melancholy*

To Appreciate heaven well
'Tis good for a man to have some fifteen minutes of hell.
— WILL CARLETON (1845–1912) *Farm Ballads*

And so upon this wise I prayed,—
Great Spirit, give to me
A heaven not so large as yours
But large enough for me.
— EMILY DICKINSON (1830–1886) *A Prayer*

I sent my soul through the invisible,
Some letter of that after-life to spell:
And by and by my soul return'd to me,
And answer'd, "I myself am Heav'n and Hell."
— EDWARD FITZGERALD (1809–1883) tr.: *Rubáiyát of Omar Khayyám*

All this, and Heaven too!
— MATTHEW HENRY (1662–1714) *Life of Philip Henry*

What came from the earth returns back to the earth, and the spirit that was sent from heaven, again carried back, is received into the temple of heaven.
— LUCRETIUS (96–55 B.C.) *De Rerum Natura*

Here we may reign secure; and in my choice
To reign is worth ambition, though in Hell:
Better to reign in Hell, than serve in Heav'n.
— JOHN MILTON (1608–1674) *Paradise Lost*

Heaven-gates are not so highly arch'd
As princes' palaces; they that enter there
Must go upon their knees.
— JOHN WEBSTER (1580?–1625) *The Duchess of Malfi*

In my father's house are many mansions.
— NEW TESTAMENT: *John*, xiv, 2

HELL

Hell is full of good intentions or desires.
— ST. BERNARD OF CLAIRVAUX (1091–1153)

Here sighs, plaints, and voices of the deepest woe resounded through the starless sky. Strange languages, horrid cries, accents of grief and wrath, voices deep and hoarse, with hands clenched in despair, made a commotion which whirled forever through that air of everlasting gloom, even as sand when whirlwinds sweep the ground.
— DANTE (1265–1321) *Inferno*, Canto iii

Abandon every hope, ye who enter here.
— DANTE (1265–1321) *Inferno*, Canto iii [Inscription over the gate of Hell]

I found the original of my hell in the world which we inhabit.
— DANTE (1265–1321)

Hell is a circle about the unbelieving.
— THE KORAN

Hell hath no limits, nor is circumscrib'd
In one self-place; for where we are is hell;
And where hell is, there must we ever be;
And to conclude, when all the world dissolves,
And every creature shall be purified,
All places shall be hell that are not heaven.
— CHRISTOPHER MARLOWE (1564–1593) *Dr. Faustus*

Myself am Hell;
And, in the lowest deep, a lower deep,
Still threat'ning to devour me, opens wide;
To which the hell I suffer seems a heaven.
— JOHN MILTON (1608–1674) *Paradise Lost*

HEROISM

No man is a hero to his valet.
— MLLE. AISSE (1694?–1733) *Letters*

Heroism is the brilliant triumph of the soul over the flesh—that is to say, over fear. . . . Heroism is the dazzling and glorious concentration of courage.
— HENRI-FREDERIC AMIEL (1828–1881) *Journal*, October 1, 1849

Heroism feels and never reasons and therefore is always right.
— RALPH WALDO EMERSON (1803–1882) *Heroism*

There is nothing more touching than the sight of a Nation in search of its great men, nothing more beautiful than its readiness to accept a hero on trust.
— JAMES RUSSELL LOWELL (1819–1891) *General McClellan's Report*

HISTORY

The great object in trying to understand history is to get behind men and grasp ideas.
— LORD ACTON (1834–1902) *Letters to Mary Gladstone*

Biography is the only true history.
— THOMAS CARLYLE (1795–1881) *Journal*, January 13, 1832

All history, so far as it is not supported by contemporary evidence, is romance.
— SAMUEL JOHNSON (1709–1784) Boswell's *Tour to Hebrides*

History is the witness of the times, the torch of truth, the life of memory, the teacher of life, the messenger of antiquity.
— CICERO (106–43 B.C.) *De Oratore*

History is clarified experience.
— JAMES RUSSELL LOWELL (1819–1891) *Books and Libraries*

History repeats itself.
— THUCYDIDES (471?–400? B.C.) *History*, Bk. i

HOME

You are a King by your own Fireside, as much as any Monarch on his Throne.
— CERVANTES (1547–1616) *Don Quixote*

In love of home, the love of country has its rise.
— CHARLES DICKENS (1812–1870) *Old Curiosity Shop*

Home is the place where, when you have to go there,
They have to take you in.
— ROBERT FROST (1875–1963) *The Death of the Hired Man*

Be it ever so humble, there's no place like home.
— JOHN HOWARD PAYNE (1791–1852) *Home Sweet Home*

Home is where the heart is.
— PLINY THE ELDER (23–79)

Weep no more, my lady;
Oh, weep no more today!
We will sing one song for the old Kentucky home,
For the old Kentucky home, far away.
— STEPHEN C. FOSTER (1812–1864) *Old Folks At Home*

It takes a heap o' livin' in a house t' make it home.
— EDGAR A. GUEST (1881–1959) *Home*

To be happy at home is the ultimate result of all ambition, the end to which every enterprise and labor tends, and of which every desire prompts the prosecution.
— SAMUEL JOHNSON (1709–1784) *Rambler*

When I was at home I was in a better place.
— SHAKESPEARE (1564–1616) *As You Like It*, II, iv, 14

As a bird that wandereth from her nest, so is a man that wandereth from his place.
— OLD TESTAMENT: *Proverbs*, xxvii, 8

HONESTY

A trustee is held to something stricter than the morals of the market place. Not honesty alone, but the punctilio of an honor the most sensitive, is then the standard of behavior.
— BENJAMIN N. CARDOZO (1870–1938)

Make yourself an honest man, and then you may be sure that there is one rascal less in the world.
— THOMAS CARLYLE (1795–1881)

Honesty is the best policy.
— CERVANTES (1547–1616) *Don Quixote*

If he were
To be made honest by an act of parliament
I should not alter in my faith of him.
— BEN JONSON (1572–1637) *Devil is an Ass*

An honest man is the noblest work of God.
— ALEXANDER POPE (1688–1744) *Essay on Man*

You are underrating the President [Lincoln]. I grant that he lacks higher education and his manners are not in accord with European conceptions of the dignity of a chief magistrate. He is a well-developed child of nature and is not skilled in polite phrases and poses. But he is a man of profound feeling, correct and firm principles and incorruptible honesty. His motives are unquestionable, and he possesses to a remarkable degree the characteristic, God-given trait of this people, sound common sense.
— CARL SCHURZ (1829–1906) Letter, October, 1864

There is no terror, Cassius, in your threats,
For I am arm'd so strong in honesty
That they pass by me as the idle wind,
Which I respect not.
— SHAKESPEARE (1564–1616) *Julius Caesar*, IV, iii, 66

HONOR

The best memorial for a mighty man is to gain honour ere death.
— BEOWULF (8th C.)

Better a thousand times to die with glory than live without honor.
— LOUIS VI OF FRANCE (1081–1137)

I could not love thee, dear, so much,
Loved I not honor more.
— RICHARD LOVELACE (1618–1658) To Lucasta, On Going to Wars

Set honour in one eye and death i' the other
And I will look on both indifferently;
For let the gods so speed me as I love
The name of honour more than I fear death.
— SHAKESPEARE (1564–1616) *Julius Caesar*, I, ii, 86

Mine honour is my life; both grow in one;
Take honour from me and my life is done.
— SHAKESPEARE (1564–1616) *Richard II*, I, i, 182

HOPE

I live on hope and that I think do all
Who come into this world.
— ROBERT BRIDGES (1844–1930) *The Growth of Love*

To the sick, while there is life there is hope.
— CICERO (106–43 B.C.) *Epistolae Ad Atticum*

Hope is itself a species of happiness, and, perhaps, the chief happiness which this world affords.
— SAMUEL JOHNSON (1709–1784) in Boswell's *Life of Johnson*

The setting of a great hope is like the setting of the sun. The brightness of our life is gone.
— HENRY W. LONGFELLOW (1807–1882) *Hyperion*

Hopes are but the dreams of those who wake.
— PINDAR (*c.* 522–442 B.C.) *Fragment*

Hope springs eternal in the human breast;
Man never is, but always to be blest.
— ALEXANDER POPE (1688–1744) *Essay on Man*

Hope, dead lives nevermore,
No, not in heaven.
— CHRISTINA ROSSETTI (1830–1894) *Dead Hope*

True hope is swift, and flies with swallow's wings;
Kings it makes gods, and meaner creatures kings.
— SHAKESPEARE (1564–1616) *Richard III*, V, ii, 23

We did not dare to breathe a prayer
  Or to give our anguish scope!
Something was dead in each of us,
  And what was dead was hope.
— OSCAR WILDE (1854–1900) *The Ballad of Reading Gaol*

HOSPITALITY

People are either born hosts or born guests.
— MAX BEERBOHM (1872–)

Hospitality consists in a little fire, a little food, and an immense quiet.
— RALPH WALDO EMERSON (1803–1882) *Journal*

Then why should I sit in the scorner's seat,
  Or hurl the cynic's ban?
Let me live in my house by the side of the road,
  And be a friend to man.
— SAM WALTER FOSS (1858–1911) *House by the Side of the Road*

Hail Guest! We ask not what thou art:
If Friend, we greet thee, hand and heart;
If Stranger, such no longer be;
If Foe, our love shall conquer thee.
— ARTHUR GUITERMAN (1871–1943) *Old Welsh Door Verse*

True friendship's laws are by this rule express'd,
Welcome the coming, speed the parting guest.
— HOMER (*c.* 10th–8th C. B.C.) *The Odyssey*

Fish and guests in three days are stale.
— JOHN LYLY (1554?–1606) *Euphues*

When there is room in the heart there is room in the house.
— DANISH PROVERB

I had three chairs in my house: one for solitude, two for friendship, three for society.
— HENRY DAVID THOREAU (1817–1862) *Walden*

Be not forgetful to entertain strangers, for thereby some have entertained angels unawares.
— NEW TESTAMENT: *Hebrews*, xiii, 2

HUMILITY

Lowliness is the base of every virtue,
And he who goes the lowest builds the safest.
— PHILIP J. BAILEY (1816–1902) *Festus*

I ate umble pie with an appetite.
— CHARLES DICKENS (1812–1870) *David Copperfield*

  True humility,
The highest virtue, mother of them all.
— TENNYSON (1809–1892) *Idylls of the King*

Whosoever shall smite thee on thy right cheek, turn to him the other also.
— NEW TESTAMENT: *Matthew*, v, 39: *Luke*, vi, 29

Whosoever shall compel thee to go a mile, go with him twain.
— NEW TESTAMENT: *Matthew*, vi, 41

HUNGER

Hunger is the best sauce in the world.
— CERVANTES (1547–1616) *Don Quixote*

An empty stomach is not a good political adviser.
— ALBERT EINSTEIN (1879–1955) *Cosmic Religion*

They that die by famine die by inches.
— MATTHEW HENRY (1662–1714) *Commentaries*

Death in all its shapes is hateful to unhappy man, but the worst is death from hunger.
— HOMER (*c.* 10th–8th C. B.C.) *Odyssey*

If thine enemy be hungry, give him bread to eat.
— OLD TESTAMENT: *Lamentations*, iv, 9

HUSBAND

We wedded men live in sorrow and care.
— GEOFFREY CHAUCER (1340?–1400) *Merchant's Tale Prologue*

It is necessary to be almost a genius to make a good husband.
— HONORÉ DE BALZAC (1799–1850) *Physiology of Marriage*

Let the husband render unto the wife due benevolence: and likewise also the wife unto the husband.
— NEW TESTAMENT: *I Corinthians*, vii, 3

IDLENESS

Idleness is only the refuge of weak minds, and the holiday of fools.
— LORD CHESTERFIELD (1694–1773) *Letters*, July 20, 1749

Absence of occupation is not rest,
A mind quite vacant is a mind distress'd.
— WILLIAM COWPER (1731–1800) *Retirement*

There is no place in civilization for the idler. None of us has any right to ease.
— HENRY FORD (1863–1947)

Laziness travels so slowly that poverty soon overtakes him.
— BEN FRANKLIN (1706–1790) *Poor Richard's Almanack*

To be idle and to be poor have always been reproaches, and therefore every man endeavors with his utmost care to hide his poverty from others, and his idleness from himself.
— SAMUEL JOHNSON (1709–1784) *The Idler*

Of all our faults, the one that we excuse most easily is idleness.
— FRANÇOIS DE LA ROCHEFOUCAULD (1613–1680) *Maxims*

For Satan finds some mischief still
For idle hands to do.
— ISAAC WATTS (1674–1748) *Divine Songs*

To do nothing at all is the most difficult thing in the world, the most difficult and the most intellectual.
— OSCAR WILDE (1854–1900) *The Critic as Artist*

Go to the ant, thou sluggard; consider her ways, and be wise.
— OLD TESTAMENT: *Proverbs*, vi, 6

IGNORANCE

Ignorance is the night of the mind, but a night without moon or star.
— CONFUCIUS (*c.* 551–478 B.C.) *Analects*

To be conscious that you are ignorant is a great step to knowledge.
— BENJAMIN DISRAELI (1804–1881) *Sybil*

To the ignorant even the words of the wise seem foolishness.
— EURIPIDES (480–406 B.C.) *The Bacchae*

No more; where ignorance is bliss,
'Tis folly to be wise.
— THOMAS GRAY (1716–1771) *On a Distant Prospect of Eton College*

Ignorance of the law excuses no man: not that all can know the law, but because 'tis an excuse everyone will plead, and no man can tell how to refute him.
— JOHN SELDEN (1584–1654) *Table Talk*

There is no darkness, but ignorance.
— SHAKESPEARE (1564–1616) *Twelfth Night*, IV, ii, 44

IMAGINATION

Only in men's imagination does every truth find an effective and undeniable existence. Imagination, not invention, is the supreme master of art as of life.
— JOSEPH CONRAD (1857–1924) *A Personal Record*

To know is nothing at all; to imagine is everything.
— ANATOLE FRANCE (1844–1924) *The Crime of Sylvestre Bonnard*

Were it not for imagination a man would be as happy in the arms of a chambermaid as of a duchess.
— SAMUEL JOHNSON (1709–1784) Boswell's *Life of Johnson*

His imagination resembled the wings of an ostrich. It enabled him to run, though not to soar.
— THOMAS B. MACAULAY (1800–1859) *On John Dryden*

The human race is governed by its imagination.
— NAPOLEON BONAPARTE (1769–1821)

IMITATION

Men often applaud an imitation, and hiss the real thing.
— AESOP (6th C. B.C.) *The Buffoon and the Countryman*

Imitation is the sincerest flattery.
— CHARLES C. COLTON (1780?–1832)

He who imitates what is evil always goes beyond the example that is set; on the contrary, he who imitates what is good always falls short.
— FRANCESCO GUICCIARDINI (1483–1540) *Story of Italy*

Agesilaus, being invited once to hear a man who admirably imitated the nightingale, declined, saying he had heard the nightingale itself.
— PLUTARCH (46?–120?) *Lives: Agesilaus*

A great part of art consists in imitation. For the whole conduct of life is based on this: that what we admire in others we want to do ourselves.
— QUINTILIAN (40–*c.* 100) *De institutio Oratoria*

Go, and do thou likewise.
— NEW TESTAMENT: *Luke*, x, 37

IMMORTALITY

Let us not lament too much the passing of our friends. They are not dead, but simply gone before us along the road which all must travel.
— ANTIPHANES (*c.* 360 B.C.) *Fragment*

After the resurrection of the body shall have taken place, being set free from the condition of time, we shall enjoy eternal life, with love ineffable and steadfastness without corruption.
— ST. AUGUSTINE (354–430) *Of the Faith and of the Creed*

If I err in my belief that the souls of men are immortal, I err gladly, and I do not wish to lose so delightful an error.
— CICERO (106–43 B.C.) *De Senectute*

My humble friend, we know not how to live this life which is so short yet seek one that never ends.
— ANATOLE FRANCE (1844–1924) *The Red Lily*

Either the soul is immortal and we shall not die, or it perishes with the flesh, and we shall not know that we are dead. Live, then, as if you were eternal.
— ANDRÉ MAUROIS (1885–)

INDECISION See DECISION

INDEPENDENCE See DEPENDENCE

INDISCRETION See DISCRETION

INDIVIDUALISM

What another would have done as well as you, do not do it. What another would have said as well as you, do not say it; written as well, do not write it. Be faithful to that which exists nowhere but in yourself—and thus make yourself indispensable.
— ANDRÉ GIDE (1869–1951) *Fruits of the Earth*

Whatever crushes individuality is despotism, by whatever name it may be called.
— JOHN STUART MILL (1806–1873) *On Liberty*

An individual is as superb as a nation when he has the qualities which make a superb nation.
— WALT WHITMAN (1819–1892) *Leaves of Grass*, preface

JEALOUSY

Anger and jealousy can no more bear to lose sight of their objects than love.
— GEORGE ELIOT (1819–1880) *The Mill on the Floss*

Though jealousy be produced by love, as ashes are by fire, yet jealousy extinguishes love as ashes smother the flame.
— MARGARET OF NAVARRE (1492–1549) *Heptameron*

O! beware, my lord, of jealousy
It is the green-eyed monster which doth mock
The meat it feeds on.
— SHAKESPEARE (1564–1616) *Othello*, III, iii, 166

Love is strong as death; jealousy is cruel as the grave.
— OLD TESTAMENT: *Song of Solomon*, viii, 6

JOY

Joy rises in me like a summer's morn.
— SAMUEL TAYLOR COLERIDGE (1772–1834) *Christmas Carol*

My theory is to enjoy life, but the practice is against it.
— CHARLES LAMB (1775–1834)

My candle burns at both ends,
It will not last the night;
But ah, my foes, and oh, my friends,
It gives a lovely light!
— EDNA ST. VINCENT MILLAY (1892–1951)

Drink and dance and laugh and lie,
Love the reeling midnight through,
For tomorrow we shall die!
(But, alas, we never do.)
— DOROTHY PARKER (1893–) *The Flaw in Paganism*

A joy that's shared is a joy made double.
— JOHN RAY (1627?–1705) *English Proverbs*

Silence is the perfectest herald of joy:
I were but little happy if I could say how much.
— SHAKESPEARE (1564–1616) *Much Ado About Nothing*, II, i, 317

I have drunken deep of joy,
And I will taste no other wine to-night.
— PERCY B. SHELLEY (1792–1822) *The Cenci*

Weeping may endure for a night, but joy cometh in the morning.
— OLD TESTAMENT: *Psalms*, xxx, 5

JUSTICE

Heaven gives long life to the just and the intelligent.
— CONFUCIUS (*c.* 551–478 B.C.) *The Book of History*

Justice is truth in action.
— BENJAMIN DISRAELI (1804–1881) Speech, Feb. 11, 1851

He reminds me of the man who murdered both his parents, and then, when sentence was about to be pronounced, pleaded for mercy on the grounds that he was an orphan.
— ABRAHAM LINCOLN (1809–1865) attributed

Just as, in fact there can be no peace without order so there can be no order without justice. . . .
— POPE PIUS XII (1876–1958) Address on Easter Sunday, 1939

Only the actions of the just
Smell sweet and blossom in the dust.
— JAMES SHIRLEY (1596–1666) *The Contention of Ajax and Ulysses*

Thrice is he armed that hath his quarrel just,
And he but naked, though licked up in steel,
Whose conscience with injustice is corrupted.
— SHAKESPEARE (1564–1616) *Henry VI*, III, ii, 232

What's sauce for a goose is sauce for a gander.
— JONATHAN SWIFT (1667–1745) *Polite Conversation*

Judging from the main portions of the history of the world, so far, justice is always in jeopardy.
— WALT WHITMAN (1819–1892) *Democratic Vistas*

He that ruleth over men must be just.
— OLD TESTAMENT: *Samuel*, xxiii, 3

The spirit of just men made perfect.
— NEW TESTAMENT: *Hebrews*, xii, 23

KINDNESS

It is difficult to tell how much men's minds are conciliated by a kind manner and gentle speech.
— CICERO (106–43 B.C.) *De Officiis*

A kindness loses its grace by being noised abroad,
Who desires it to be remembered should forget it.
— PIERRE CORNEILLE (1606–1684) *Theodore*

It is a kindness to refuse gently what you intend to deny.
— PUBLILIUS SYRUS (1st C. B.C.) *Sententiae*

This was the unkindest cut of all.
— SHAKESPEARE (1564–1616) *Julius Caesar*, III, ii, 187

Yet do I fear thy nature;
It is too full o' the milk of human kindness.
— SHAKESPEARE (1564–1616) *Macbeth*, I, v, 14

KNOWLEDGE

What one knows is, in youth, of little moment; they know enough who know how to learn.
— HENRY ADAMS (1838–1918) *Education of Henry Adams*

Knowledge is, indeed, that which, next to virtue, truly and essentially raises one man above another.
— JOSEPH ADDISON (1672–1719) *The Guardian*

I assure you I had rather excel others in the knowledge of what is excellent, than in the extent of my power and dominion.
— ALEXANDER THE GREAT (356–323 B.C.)

Knowledge is power.
— FRANCIS BACON (1561–1620) *De Haeresibus*

Knowledge is a comfortable and necessary retreat and shelter for us in an advanced age; and if we do not plant it while young, it will give us no shade when we grow old.
— LORD CHESTERFIELD (1694–1773) *Letters*

No technical knowledge can outweigh knowledge of the humanities, in the gaining of which philosophy and history walk hand in hand. Our inheritance of well-founded slowly conceived codes of honor, morals and manners, the passionate convictions which so many hundreds of millions share together of the principles of freedom and justice, are far more precious to us than anything which scientific discoveries can bestow.
— WINSTON CHURCHILL (1874–1965) Speech, March 31, 1949

It is the province of knowledge to speak, and it is the privilege of wisdom to listen.
— OLIVER WENDELL HOLMES (1809–1894)

Knowledge is of two kinds. We know a subject ourselves or we know where we can find information upon it.
— SAMUEL JOHNSON (1709–1784) Boswell's *Life of Johnson*

To myself I seem to have been only like a boy playing on the sea-shore, and diverting myself in now and then finding a smoother pebble, or a prettier shell than ordinary, whilst the great ocean of truth lay all undiscovered before me.
— SIR ISAAC NEWTON (1642–1727)

Then I began to think, that it is very true which is commonly said, that the one-half of the world knoweth not how the other half liveth.
— FRANÇOIS RABELAIS (1494?–1553) *Pantagruel*

Ignorance is the curse of God,
Knowledge the wing wherewith we fly to heaven.
— SHAKESPEARE (1564–1616) *II Henry VI*, IV, vii, 78

I do not know that knowledge amounts to anything more definite than a novel and grand surprise, or a sudden revelation of the insufficiency of all that we had called knowledge before; an indefinite sense of the grandeur and glory of the universe.
— HENRY DAVID THOREAU (1817–1862) *Spring in Massachusetts*

LABOR

There is no right to strike against the public safety by anybody, anywhere, anytime.
— CALVIN COOLIDGE (1872–1933) Letter to Samuel Gompers

Each needs the other: capital cannot do without labor, nor labor without capital.
— POPE LEO XIII (1810–1903) *Rerum Novarum*

Bowed by the weight of centuries he leans
Upon his hoe and gazes on the ground,
The emptiness of the ages in his face,
And on his back the burden of the world.
— EDWIN MARKHAM (1852–1940) *Man With the Hoe*

No business which depends for existence on paying less than living wages to its workers has any right to continue in this country.
— FRANKLIN D. ROOSEVELT (1882–1945) Public statement

I am a true labourer: I earn that I eat, get that I wear, owe no man hate, envy no man's happiness, glad of other men's good.
— SHAKESPEARE (1564–1616) *As You Like It*, III, ii, 78

There is no real wealth but the labor of man. Were the mountains of gold and the valleys of silver, the world would not be one grain of corn the richer; no one comfort would be added to the human race.
— PERCY B. SHELLEY (1792–1822) *Queen Mab*, notes

The labourer is worthy of his hire.
— NEW TESTAMENT: *Luke*, x, 7

Let them be hewers of wood and drawers of water.
— OLD TESTAMENT: *Joshua*, ix, 21

LANGUAGE

You are worth as many men as you know languages.
— CHARLES V, HOLY ROMAN EMPEROR (1500–1558)

In language clearness is everything.
— CONFUCIUS (c. 551–478 B. C.) *Analects*

A man who does not know foreign languages is ignorant of his own.
— GOETHE (1749–1832) *Sprüche in Prosa*

There is no master key to the inner life of a people, but language unlocks a vast treasure house.
— EDGAR LEE HEWETT (1865–1946) *Ancient Life in Mexico*

Every language is a temple in which the soul of those who speak it is enshrined.
— OLIVER WENDELL HOLMES (1809–1894)

Language is the dress of thought.
— SAMUEL JOHNSON (1709–1784) *Lives of the Poets*

The way to learn a language is to sit down and learn it.
— WILLIAM GRAHAM SUMNER (1840–1910) *Reminiscences*

Language, as well as the faculty of speech, was the immediate gift of God.
— NOAH WEBSTER (1758–1843) *American Dictionary*, Preface

Language is not an abstract construction of the learned, or of dictionary makers, but it is something arising out of the work, needs, ties, joys, affections, tastes, of long generations of humanity, and has its bases broad and low, close to the ground.
— WALT WHITMAN (1819–1892) *Slang in America*

LAUGHTER

God hath not granted to woeful mortals even laughter without tears.
— CALLIMACHUS (*c.* 260–240 B.C.) *Fragments*

You no doubt laugh in your sleeve.
— CICERO (106–43 B.C.) *De Finibus*

The loud laugh that spoke the vacant mind.
— OLIVER GOLDSMITH (1730–1774) *The Deserted Village*

Laughter unquenchable arose among the blessed gods.
— HOMER (*c.* 10th–8th C. B.C.) *Iliad*

I laugh because I must not cry.
— ABRAHAM LINCOLN (1809–1865)

He deserves Paradise who makes his companions laugh.
— MOHAMMED (570–632) *The Koran*

Everything gives cause for either laughter or tears.
— SENECA (4? B.C.–A.D. 65) *De Ira*

The pleasantest laughter is at the expense of our enemies.
— SOPHOCLES (495–406 B.C.) *Ajax*

Laughter is not a bad beginning for a friendship, and it is the best ending for one.
— OSCAR WILDE (1854–1900) *The Picture of Dorian Gray*

Woe unto you that laugh now! for ye shall mourn and weep.
— NEW TESTAMENT: *Luke*, vi, 25

As the crackling of thorns under a pot, so is the laughter of a fool.
— OLD TESTAMENT: *Ecclesiastes*, vii, 6

LAW

Law is a pledge that the citizens of a state will do justice to one another.
— ARISTOTLE (384–322 B.C.) *Politics*

The beginning of the law is benevolence, and with benevolence it ends.
— BABYLONIAN TALMUD: *Sotah*

The laws place the safety of all before the safety of individuals.
— CICERO (106–43 B.C.) *De Finibus*

Men would be great criminals did they need as many laws as they make.
— CHARLES JOHN DARLING (1849–1936) *Scintillæ Juris*

Time is the best interpreter of every doubtful law.
— DIONYSIUS OF HALICARNASSUS (d. *c.* 7 B.C.) *Antiquities of Rome*

Possession is nine points of the law.
— THOMAS FULLER (1608–1681) *Holy War*

In law a man is guilty when he violates the rights of another. In ethics he is guilty if he only thinks of doing so.
— IMMANUEL KANT (1724–1804) *Lecture at Königsberg*, 1775

The purpose of law is to prevent the strong from always having their way.
— OVID (43 B.C.–A.D. 18?) *Fasti*

No man is above the law and no man is below it; nor do we ask any man's permission when we require him to obey it.
— THEODORE ROOSEVELT (1858–1919) Message, Jan. 1904

Ye shall have one manner of law, as well for the stranger, as for one of your own country.
— OLD TESTAMENT: *Leviticus*, xxiv, 22

Where is there any book of the law so clear to each man as that written in his heart?
— LEO TOLSTOY (1828–1910) *The Chinese Pilot*

He that pleads his own cause has a fool for his client.
— ENGLISH PROVERB

LEADERSHIP

I light my candle from their torches.
—ROBERT BURTON (1577–1640) *Anatomy of Melancholy*

And when we think we lead we most are led.
— LORD BYRON (1788–1824) *The Two Foscari*

The final test of a leader is that he leaves behind him in other men the conviction and the will to carry on.
— WALTER LIPPMANN (1889–) *Roosevelt Has Gone*

An two men ride of a horse, one must ride behind.
— SHAKESPEARE (1564–1616) *Much Ado About Nothing*, III, v, 40

Ill can he rule the great that cannot reach the small.
— EDMUND SPENSER (1552?–1599) *The Faerie Queen*

Reason and calm judgement, the qualities specially belonging to a leader.
— TACITUS (55–117) *History*

LEARNING

What one knows is, in youth, of little moment; they know enough who know how to learn.
— HENRY ADAMS (1838–1918) *Education of Henry Adams*

All men by nature desire to know.
— ARISTOTLE (384–322 B.C.)

That there should one man die ignorant who had capacity for knowledge, this I call tragedy.
— THOMAS CARLYLE (1795–1881)

Wear your learning, like your watch, in a private pocket; and do not pull it out, and strike it, merely to show that you have one.
— LORD CHESTERFIELD (1694–1773) *Letters*, February 22, 1748

A smattering of everything and a knowledge of nothing.
— CHARLES DICKENS (1812–1870) *Sketches by Boz*

Education is a controlling grace to the young, consolation to the old, wealth to the poor, and ornament to the rich.
— DIOGENES LAERTIUS (2nd or 3rd C. A.D.)

You send your child to the schoolmaster, but 'tis the schoolboys who educate him.
— RALPH WALDO EMERSON (1803–1882) *Conduct of Life*

If you have knowledge, let others light their candles at it.
— MARGARET FULLER (1810–1850)

A child's education should begin at least one hundred years before he was born.
— OLIVER WENDELL HOLMES (1809–1894)

The important thing is not so much that every child should be taught, as that every child should be given the wish to learn.
— SIR JOHN LUBBOCK (1834–1913) *Pleasures of Life*

A little learning is a dangerous thing;
Drink deep, or taste not the Pierian spring:
There shallow draughts intoxicate the brain,
And drinking largely sobers us again.
— ALEXANDER POPE (1688–1744) *An Essay On Criticism*

'Tis education forms the common mind:
Just as the twig is bent the tree's inclined.
— ALEXANDER POPE (1688–1744) *Moral Essays*

I am glad to learn, in order that I may teach.
— SENECA (4? B.C.–A.D. 65) *Ad Lucilium*

The great aim of education is not knowledge but action.
— HERBERT SPENCER (1820–1903)

There is no royal road to learning; no short cut to the acquirement of any valuable art.
— ANTHONY TROLLOPE (1815–1882) *Barchester Towers*

LEISURE

When a man's busy, why, leisure
Strikes him as wonderful pleasure;
'Faith, and at leisure once is he?
Straightway he wants to be busy.
— ROBERT BROWNING (1812–1889) *The Glove*

It is the mark of a superior man that he will take no harmful ease.
— CONFUCIUS (*c.* 551–478 B.C.) *Book of History*

A life of leisure and a life of laziness are two things.
— BEN FRANKLIN (1706–1790) *Poor Richard's Almanack*

Give time to your friends, leisure to your wife, relax your mind, give rest to your body, so that you may the better fulfil your accustomed occupation.
— PHAEDRUS (A.D. 1st C.) *Fables*

To be able to fill leisure intelligently is the last product of civilization.
— BERTRAND RUSSELL (1872–) *The Conquest of Happiness*

LIBERTY

Eternal spirit of the chainless mind!
Brightest in dungeons, Liberty! thou art.
— LORD BYRON (1788–1824) *The Prisoner of Chillon*

The condition upon which God has given liberty to man is eternal vigilance.
— JOHN PHILPOT CURRAN (1750–1817) Speech upon the Right of Election, July 10, 1790.

Those, who would give up essential liberty to purchase a little temporary safety, deserve neither liberty nor safety.
— BEN FRANKLIN (1706–1790) Historical Review of Constitution and Government of Pennsylvania

Is Life so dear or peace so sweet as to be purchased at the price of chains and slavery? Forbid it, Almighty God! I know not what course others may take, but as for me, give me liberty, or give me death.
— PATRICK HENRY (1736–1799) Speech, 1775

The God who gave us life gave us liberty at the same time.
— THOMAS JEFFERSON (1743–1826) *The Rights of British America*

It is true that liberty is precious—so precious that it must be rationed.
— NIKOLAI LENIN (1870–1924)

The inescapable price of liberty is an ability to preserve it from destruction.
— GENERAL DOUGLAS MACARTHUR (1880–1964) Speech

He that would make his own liberty secure must guard even his enemy from oppression.
— THOMAS PAINE (1737–1809) *First Principles of Government*

There is . . . no liberty but liberty under law. Law does not restrict liberty; it creates the only real liberty there is.
— WILLIAM SUMNER (1840–1910) *The Forgotten Man*

LIFE

Remember that man's life lies all within this present, as 't were but a hair's breadth of time; as for the rest, the past is gone, the future may never be. Short, therefore, is man's life, and narrow is the corner of the earth wherein he dwells.
— MARCUS AURELIUS (121–180) *Meditations*

Life is a test and this world a place of trial. Always the problems—or it may be the same problem—will be presented to every generation in different forms.
— WINSTON CHURCHILL (1874–1965) Speech 1949

I have measured out my life with coffee spoons.
— T. S. ELIOT (1888–1965) *Love Song of J. Alfred Prufrock*

The fool, with all his other faults, has this also: he is always getting ready to live.
— EPICURUS (342–270 B.C.) *Fragments*

Were it offered to my choice, I should have no objection to a repetition of the same life from its beginnings, only asking the advantages authors have in a second edition to correct some faults.
— BEN FRANKLIN (1706–1790) *Autobiography*

There is more to life than increasing its speed.
— MOHANDAS GANDHI (1869–1948)

I wish to preach, not the doctrine of ignoble ease, but the doctrine of the strenuous life.
— THEODORE ROOSEVELT (1858–1919) Speech

Life is neither a good nor an evil; it is simply the place where good and evil exist.
— SENECA (4? B.C.–A.D. 65) *Epistulae ad Lucilium*

Life is as tedious as a twice-told tale,
Vexing the dull ear of a drowsy man.
— SHAKESPEARE (1564–1616) *King John*, III, iv, 108

One man in his time plays many parts,
His acts being seven ages.
— SHAKESPEARE (1564–1616) *As You Like It*, II, vii, 142

The web of our life is of a mingled yarn, good and ill together.
— SHAKESPEARE (1564–1616) *All's Well That Ends Well*, IV, iii, 83

As for man, his days are as grass: as a flower of the field, so he flourisheth.
— OLD TESTAMENT: *Psalms*, viii, 15

The mass of men lead lives of quiet desperation.
— HENRY DAVID THOREAU (1817–1862) *Walden*

LOVE

I have never loved anyone for love's sake, except, perhaps, Josephine—a little.
— NAPOLEON BONAPARTE (1769–1821)

How do I love thee? Let me count the ways.
. . .
I love thee with a love I seemed to lose
With my lost saints, —I love thee with the breath,
Smiles, tears, of all my life!—, if God choose,
I shall but love thee better after death.
— ELIZABETH B. BROWNING (1806–1861) *Sonnets from the Portuguese*

God be thanked, the meanest of his creatures
Boasts two soul-sides, one to face the world with,
One to show a woman when he loves her.
— ROBERT BROWNING (1812–1889) *One Word More*

Oh my luve's like a red, red, rose,
  That's newly sprung in June;
Oh my luve's like the melodie
  That's sweetly played in tune.
— ROBERT BURNS (1759–1796) *Red, Red Rose*

To see her is to love her,
  And love but her forever;
For nature made her what she is,
  And never made anither!
— ROBERT BURNS (1759–1796) *Bonny Lesley*

Alas! the love of women! it is known
To be a lovely and a fearful thing.
— LORD BYRON (1788–1824) *Don Juan*

Let Time and Chance combine, combine!
Let Time and Chance combine!
The fairest love from heaven above,
  That love of yours was mine,
            My Dear!
  That love of yours was mine.
— THOMAS CARLYLE (1795–1881) *Adieu*

Love and war are the same thing, and strategems and policy are as allowable in the one as in the other.
— CERVANTES (1547–1616) *Don Quixote*

If love be good, from whennes comth my wo?
— GEOFFREY CHAUCER (1340?–1400) *Troilus and Criseyde*

The Stoics define love as the endeavor to form a friendship inspired by beauty.
— CICERO (106–43 B.C.) *Tusculanae Disputationes*

When povertie comes in at doores, love leaps out at windowes.
— JOHN CLARK (1609–1676) *Paroemiologia*

Love's but a frailty of the mind,
When 'tis not with ambition joined:
A sickly flame, which, if not fed, expires,
And feeding, wastes in self-consuming fires.
— WILLIAM CONGREVE (1670–1729) *Way of the World*

Say what you will, 'tis better to be left
Than never to have loved.
—WILLIAM CONGREVE (1670–1729) *Way of the World*

We are all born for love .... It is the principle of existence and its only end.
— BENJAMIN DISRAELI (1804–1881) *Sybil*

Men and women call one another inconstant, and accuse one another of having changed their minds, when, God knows, they have but changed the object of their eye, and seen a better white or red.
— JOHN DONNE (1572–1631) *Sermons*

Last night, ah, yesternight, betwixt her lips and mine
There fell thy shadow, Cynara! Thy breath was shed
Upon my soul between the kisses and the wine;
And I was desolate and sick of an old passion,
Yea, I was desolate and bowed my head:
I have been faithful to thee, Cynara! in my fashion.
— ERNEST DOWSON (1867–1900) *Cynara*

But you must believe me when I tell you that I have found it impossible to carry the heavy burden of responsibility and to discharge my duties as King as I would wish to do without the help and support of the woman I love.
— EDWARD VIII (1894–   ) Abdication Speech

All mankind love a lover.
— RALPH WALDO EMERSON (1803–1882) *Essays*

He is not a lover who does not love forever.
— EURIPIDES (480–406 B.C.) *Troades*

Perhaps they were right in putting love into books ...
Perhaps it could not live anywhere else.
— WILLIAM FAULKNER (1897–1962) *Light in August*

Love grants in a moment
What toil can hardly achieve in an age.
— GOETHE (1749–1832) *Torquato Tasso*

Ah! What is love? It is a pretty thing,
As sweet unto a shepherd as a king,
  And sweeter too;
For kings have cares that wait upon a crown,
And cares can make the sweetest love to frown.
— ROBERT GREENE (1560?–1592) *Shepherd's Wife*

To demand of love that it be without jealousy is to ask of light that it cast no shadows.
— OSCAR HAMMLING (1890–   ) *Laconics*

If you would be loved, love.
— HECATO (*c.* 550–476 B.C.) *Fragments*

At thy command I would change, not merely my costume, but my very soul, so entirely art thou the sole possessor of my body and my spirit. Never, God is my witness, never have I sought anything in thee but thyself; I have sought thee, and not thy gifts. I have not looked to the marriage-bond or dowry.
— HÉLOISE (1101–1164) to Abelard

Love in a hut, with water and a crust,
Is—love, forgive us!—cinders, ashes, dust.
— JOHN KEATS (1795–1821) *Lamia*

Come live with me and be my love,
And we will all the pleasures prove,
That valleys, groves, or hills, or fields,
Or woods and steepy mountains yields.
— CHRISTOPHER MARLOWE (1564–1593) *Passionate Shepherd to his Love*

If I were a king, ah love, if I were a king!
What tributary nations I would bring
To stoop before your sceptre and to swear
Allegience to your lips and eyes and hair.
— JUSTIN HUNTLY MCCARTHY (1861–1936) *If I Were King*

'Tis not love's going hurts my days,
But that it went in little ways.
— EDNA ST. VINCENT MILLAY (1892–1951) *Spring and Fall*

Take love away from life and you take away its pleasures.
— MOLIÈRE (1622–1673) *Bourgeois Gentleman*

'Tis sweet to think, that, where'er we rove,
We are sure to find something blissful and dear;
And when we're far from the lips we love,
We've but to make love to the lips we are near.
— THOMAS MOORE (1779–1852) *'Tis Sweet to Think*

But there's nothing half so sweet in life
As love's young dream.
— THOMAS MOORE (1779–1852) *Love's Young Dream*

Love that comes late oft claims a heavy toll.
— SEXTUS PROPERTIUS (50?–15 B.C.) *Elegies*

If all the world and love were young,
And truth in every shepherd's tongue,
These pretty pleasures might me move
To live with thee, and be thy love.
— SIR WALTER RALEIGH (1552?–1618)

The pleasure of love is in loving; and we are much happier in the passion we feel than in that which we inspire.
— FRANÇOIS DE LA ROCHEFOUCAULD (1613–1680) *Maxims*

If thou remember'st not the slightest folly
That ever love did make thee run into,
Thou hast not lov'd.
— SHAKESPEARE (1564–1616) *As You Like It*, II, iv, 34

No sooner met but they looked, no sooner looked but they loved, no sooner loved but they sighed, no sooner sighed but they asked one another the reason.
— SHAKESPEARE (1564–1616) *As You Like It*, V, ii, 36

Where love is great, the littlest doubts are fear;
When little fears grow great, great love grows there.
— SHAKESPEARE (1564–1616) *Hamlet*, III, ii, 188

But love is blind, and lovers cannot see
The pretty follies that themselves commit.
— SHAKESPEARE (1564–1616) *Merchant of Venice*, II, vi, 344

Ay me! for aught that I ever could read,
Could ever hear by tale or history,
The course of true love never did run smooth.
— SHAKESPEARE (1564–1616) *Midsummer Night's Dream*, I, i, 132

Speak low, if you speak love.
— SHAKESPEARE (1564–1616) *Much Ado About Nothing*, II, i, 102

There is no creature loves me,
And if I die, no soul shall pity me.
— SHAKESPEARE (1564–1616) *Richard III*, V, iii, 200

For stony limits cannot hold love out,
And what love can do that dares love attempt.
— SHAKESPEARE (1564–1616) *Romeo and Juliet*, II, ii, 67

Give me my Romeo; and, when he shall die,
Take him and cut him out in little stars,
And he will make the face of heaven so fine,
That all the world will be in love with night,
And pay no worship to the garish sun.
— SHAKESPEARE (1564–1616) *Romeo and Juliet*, III, ii, 21

Love's not Time's fool, though rosy lips and cheeks
  Within his bending sickle's compass come;
Love alters not with his brief hours and weeks,
  But bears it out even to the edge of doom.
— SHAKESPEARE (1564–1616) Sonnet CXVI.

Common as light is love,
And its familiar voice wearies not ever,
Like the wide heaven, the all-sustaining air,
It makes the reptile equal to the god.
— PERCY B. SHELLEY (1792–1822) *Prometheus Unbound*

Love is a symbol of eternity. It wipes out all sense of time, destroying all memory of a beginning and all fear of an end.
— MADAME DE STAËL (1766–1817) *Corinne*

And blessings on the falling out
That all the more endears,
When we fall out with those we love,
And kiss again with tears.
— TENNYSON (1809–1892) *The Princess*

To say that you can love one person all your life is just like saying that one candle will continue burning as long as you live.
— LEO TOLSTOY (1828–1910) *Kreutzer Sonata*

Yet each man kills the thing he loves,
By each let this be heard,
Some do it with a bitter look,
Some with a flattering word,
The coward does it with a kiss,
The brave man with a sword.
— OSCAR WILDE (1854–1900) *Ballad of Reading Gaol*

Whom the Lord loveth he chasteneth.
— NEW TESTAMENT: *Hebrews*, xii, 6

Who love too much, hate in the like extreme.
— HOMER (*c.* 10th–8th C. B.C.) *Odyssey*

Greater love hath no man than this, that a man lay down his life for his friends.
— NEW TESTAMENT: *John*, xv, 13

There is no fear in love; but perfect love casteth out fear.
— NEW TESTAMENT: *I John*, iv, 8

Whither thou goest, I will go; and where thou lodgest, I will lodge: thy people shall be my people, and thy God my God.
— OLD TESTAMENT: *Ruth*, i, 16

Many waters cannot quench love, neither can the floods drown it.
— OLD TESTAMENT: *Songs of Solomon*, viii, 7

LUXURY

Luxury and avarice—these pests have been the ruin of every state.
— CATO (234–149 B.C.) In support of the Oppian Law

Faint-hearted men are the fruit of luxurious countries. The same soil never produces both luxuries and heroes.
— HERODOTUS (484–424 B.C.) *History*

Fell luxury! more perilous to youth
Than storms or quicksands, poverty, or chains
— HANNAH MORE (1745–1833) *Belshazzar*

People have declaimed against luxury for 2000 years, in verse and in prose, and people have always delighted in it.
— VOLTAIRE (1694–1778) *Philosophical Dictionary*

On the soft beds of luxury most kingdoms have expired.
— EDWARD YOUNG (1683–1765) *Centaur*

MAJORITY AND MINORITY

The oppression of a majority is detestable and odious: the oppression of a minority is only by one degree less detestable and odious.
— WILLIAM EWART GLADSTONE (1809–1898) Speech

It is my principle that the will of the majority should always prevail.
— THOMAS JEFFERSON (1743–1826) Letter to James Madison

One, of God's side, is a majority.
— WENDELL PHILLIPS (1811–1884) Speech on John Brown

MALICE

Malice is cunning.
— CICERO (106–43 B.C.) *De Natura Deorum*

Malice hath a strong memory.
— THOMAS FULLER (1608–1681) *Pisgah Sight*

With malice toward none; with charity for all; with firmness in the right, as God gives us to see the right, let us strive on to finish the work we are in.
— ABRAHAM LINCOLN (1809–1865) *Second Inaugural Address*

MAN

This Being of mine, whatever it really is, consists of a little flesh, a little breath and the ruling Reason.
— MARCUS AURELIUS (121–180) *Meditations*

No man is an Iland, intire of it selfe; everyman is a piece of the Continent, a part of the maine, if a Clod bee washed away by the Sea, Europe is the lesse, as well as if a Promontorie were, as well as if a Mannor of thy friends or of thine owne were; any mans death diminishes me, because I am involved in Mankinde; and therefore never send to know for whom the bell tolls; it tolls for thee.
— JOHN DONNE (1572–1631) *Devotions*

Man is a fallen god who remembers the heavens.
— ALPHONSE DE LAMARTINE (1790–1869) *Meditations*

He's not the finest character that ever lived. But he's a human being, and a terrible thing is happening to him. So attention must be paid. He's not to be allowed to fall into his grave like an old dog.
— ARTHUR MILLER (1915–) *Death of a Salesman*

Man is a rope stretched between the animal and the superman—a rope over an abyss.
— FRIEDRICH W. NIETZSCHE (1844–1900) *Thus Spake Zarathustra*

What a chimera, then, is man! What a novelty! What a monster, what a chaos, what a contradiction, what a prodigy! Judge of all things, feeble worm of the earth, depositary of truth, a sink of uncertainty and error, the glory and the shame of the universe.
— BLAISE PASCAL (1623–1662) *Pensées*

Placed on this isthmus of a middle state
A being darkly wise and rudely great
Created half to rise and half to fall
Great lord of all things, yet prey to all.
Sole judge of truth in endless error hurled,
The glory, jest and riddle of the world.
— ALEXANDER POPE (1688–1744) *Essay on Man*

What a piece of work is a man! how noble in reason! how infinite in faculty! in form and moving how express and admirable! in action how like an angel! in apprehension how like a god! the beauty of the world! the paragon of animals! And, yet, to me, what is this quintessence of dust? man delights not me: no, nor woman neither, though by your smiling, you seem to say so.
— SHAKESPEARE (1564–1616) *Hamlet*, II, 2; 313

Man's capacities have never been measured; nor are we to judge of what he can do by any precedents, so little has been tried.
— HENRY DAVID THOREAU (1817–1862) *Walden*

Man is the only animal that blushes. Or needs to.
— MARK TWAIN (1835–1910) *Pudd'nhead Wilson's New Calendar*

Who shall enumerate the many ways in which that costly piece of fixed capital, a human being, may be employed! More of him is wanted everywhere! Hunt, then, for some situation in which your humanity may be used.
— ALBERT SCHWEITZER (1875–) *Civilization and Ethics*

He was a man, take him for all in all,
I shall not look upon his like again.
— SHAKESPEARE (1564–1616) *Hamlet*, I, ii, 187

How beauteous mankind is! O brave new world,
That has such people in 't!
— SHAKESPEARE (1564–1616) *The Tempest*, V, i, 183

Thou hast made him a little lower than the angels.
— OLD TESTAMENT: *Psalms*, viii, 5

MARRIAGE

He that hath a wife and children hath given hostages to fortune; for they are impediments to great enterprises, either of virtue or mischief.
— FRANCIS BACON (1561–1626) *Marriage and Single Life*

Cursed be the man, the poorest wretch in life,
The crouching vessel, to the tyrant wife,
Who has no will but her high permission;
Who has not sixpence but in her possession;
Who must to her his dear friend's secret tell;
Who dreads a curtain lecture worse than hell.
Were such the wife had fallen to my part,
I'd break her spirit or I'd break her heart.
— ROBERT BURNS (1759–1796) *Henpecked Husband*

Marriage and hanging go by destiny; matches are made in heaven.
— ROBERT BURTON (1577–1640) *Anatomy of Melancholy*

The first bond of society is marriage; the next, our children; then the whole family and all things in common.
— CICERO (106–43 B.C.) *De Officiis*

Like blood, like goods, and like age,
Make the happiest marriage.
— JOHN CLARKE (1609–1676) *Paroemiologia*

Thus grief still treads upon the heels of pleasure,
Marry'd in haste, we may repent at leisure.
— WILLIAM CONGREVE (1670–1729) *Old Bachelor*

Happy and thrice happy are they who enjoy an uninterrupted union, and whose love, unbroken by any complaints, shall not dissolve until the last day.
— HORACE (65–8 B.C.) *Carmina*

Marriages are made in heaven.
— MIDRASH: *Genesis Rabbah*, lxviii

Hail, wedded love, mysterious law; true source
Of human offspring.
— JOHN MILTON (1608–1674) *Paradise Lost*

If you would marry wisely, marry your equal.
— OVID (43 B.C.–A.D. 18?) *Heroides*

All happy families resemble one another; every unhappy family is unhappy in its own fashion.
— LEO TOLSTOY (1828–1910) *Anna Karenina*

When a man marries again it is because he adored his first wife.
— OSCAR WILDE (1854–1900) *Picture of Dorian Gray*

MEMORY

To be ignorant of what happened before you were born is to be ever a child. For what is man's lifetime unless the memory of past events is woven with those of earlier times.
— CICERO (106–43 B.C.) *De Oratore*

There is no greater sorrow than to recall, in misery, the time when we were happy.
— DANTE (1265–1321) *Inferno*

Memory is the treasure-house of the mind.
— THOMAS FULLER (1608–1681) *The Holy State: Memory*

A retentive memory is a good thing, but the ability to forget is the true token of greatness.
— ELBERT HUBBARD (1856–1915) *Epigrams*

The leaves lie thick upon the way
Of Memories.
— JAMES JOYCE (1882–1941) *Chamber Music*

To hide the fault I see:
That mercy I to others show
That mercy show to me.
— ALEXANDER POPE (1688–1744) *Universal Prayer*

Better by far you should forget and smile,
Than that you should remember and be sad.
— CHRISTINA ROSSETTI (1830–1894) *A Birthday*

Things that were hard to bear are sweet to remember.
— SENECA (4? B.C.–A.D. 65) *Hercules Furens*

Hamlet: Methinks I see my father.
Horatio: O! Where, my lord?
Hamlet: In my mind's eye, Horatio.
— SHAKESPEARE (1564–1616) *Hamlet,* I, ii, 184

Remember thee!
Ay, thou poor ghost, while memory holds a seat
In this distracted globe. Remember thee!
Yea, from the fable of my memory
I'll wipe away all trivial fond records.
— SHAKESPEARE (1564–1616) *Hamlet,* I, v, 97

When to the sessions of sweet silent thought
I summon up remembrance of things past,
I sigh the lack of many a thing I sought,
And old woes new wail my dear time's waste.
— SHAKESPEARE (1564–1616) *Sonnets,* xxx

I shall remember while the light lives yet,
And in the night-time I shall not forget.
— ALGERNON CHARLES SWINBURNE (1837–1909) *Erotion*

MERCY

The quality of mercy is not strain'd
It droppeth as the gentle rain from heaven
Upon the place beneath: it is twice blest;
It blesseth him that gives and him that takes;
'Tis mightiest in the mightiest; it becomes
The throned monarch better than his crown;
His sceptre shows the force of temporal power,
The attribute to awe and majesty,
Wherein doth sit the dread and fear of kings;
But mercy is above this sceptred sway;
It is enthroned in the hearts of kings,
It is an attribute to God himself;
And earthly power doth show likest God's
When mercy seasons justice.
— SHAKESPEARE (1564–1616) *Merchant of Venice,* IV, i, 184

Blessed are the merciful: for they shall obtain mercy.
— NEW TESTAMENT: *Matthew,* v, 7

What doth the Lord require of thee, but to do justly, and to love mercy, and to walk humbly with thy God.
— OLD TESTAMENT: *Micah,* iv, 4

Mercy and truth are met together; righteousness and peace have kissed each other.
— OLD TESTAMENT: *Psalms,* lxxxv, 10

MONTHS

Pale January lay
In its cradle day by day,
Dead or living, hard to say.
— ALFRED AUSTIN (1835–1913) *Primroses*

That blasts of January
Would blow you through and through.
— SHAKESPEARE (1564–1616) *Winter's Tale,* IV, iv, 3

Late February days; and now, at last,
Might you have thought that Winter's woe was past;
So fair the sky and so soft the air.
— WILLIAM MORRIS (1834–1896) *Earthly Paradise*

Menallo: I would chuse March, for I would come in like a Lion.
Tony: But you'd go out like a Lamb when you went to hanging.
— JOHN FLETCHER (1579–1625) *Wife for a Month*

April is the cruelest month, breeding
Lilacs out of the dead land, mixing
Memory and desire, stirring
Dull roots with spring rain.
— T. S. ELIOT (1888–1965) *The Waste Land*

Oh, to be in England
Now that April's here.
— ROBERT BROWNING (1812–1889) *Home Thoughts*

He has a hard heart who does not love in May.
— GUILLAUME DE LORRIS (d. *c.* 1235) *Roman de la Rose*

And what is so rare as a day in June?
Then, if ever, come perfect days;
Then Heaven tries earth if it be in tune,
And over it softly her warm ear lays.
— JAMES RUSSELL LOWELL (1819–1891) *Vision of Sir Launfa*

The Summer looks out from her brazen tower,
Through the flashing bars of July.
— FRANCIS THOMPSON (1859–1907) *Corymbus for Autumn*

Hot July brings cooling showers,
Apricots and gillyflowers.
— SARA COLERIDGE (1802–1852) *Pretty Lessons in Verse*

Never return in August to what you love;
Along the leaves will rust
And over the hedges dust,
And in the air vague thunder and silence burning . . .
Choose some happier time for your returning.
— BERNICE LESBIA KENYON (1897–) *Return*

I'm not a chicken; I have seen
Full many a chill September.
— OLIVER WENDELL HOLMES (1809–1894) *September Gale*

The skies they were ashen and sober;
The leaves they were crisp and sere—
The leaves they were withering and sere;
It was night in the lonesome October
Of my most immemorial year.
— EDGAR ALLAN POE (1809–1849) *Ulalume*

When chill November's surly blast
Made fields and forests bare.
— ROBERT BURNS (1759–1796) *Man Was Made to Mourn*

In a drear-nighted December,
Too happy, happy brook,
Thy bubblings ne'er remember
Apollo's summer look;
But with a sweet forgetting,
They stay their crystal fretting,
Never, never petting
About the frozen time.
— JOHN KEATS (1795–1821) *Stanzas*

When we shall hear
The rain and wind beat dark December, how
In this our pinching cave, shall we discourse
The freezing hours away.
— SHAKESPEARE (1564–1616) *Cymbeline,* III, iii, 36

MISTAKE See ERROR

MUSIC

Music, the greatest good that mortals know,
And all of heaven we have below.
— JOSEPH ADDISON (1672–1719) *Song for St. Cecilia's Day*

Music exalts each joy, allays each grief,
Expels diseases, softens every pain,
Subdues the rage of poison, and the plague.
— JOHN ARMSTRONG (1709–1779) *Preserving Health*

Who hears music, feels his solitude
Peopled at once.
— ROBERT BROWNING (1812–1889) *Balaustion's Adventure*

Music is well said to be the speech of angels.
— THOMAS CARLYLE (1795–1881) *Essays: The Opera*

Music hath charms to soothe the savage breast,
To soften rocks, or bend a knotted oak.
— WILLIAM CONGREVE (1670–1729) *The Mourning Bride*

Heard melodies are sweet, but those unheard
Are sweeter: therefore, ye soft pipes, play on;
Not to the sensual ear, but, more endear'd,
Pipe to the spirit ditties of no tone.
— JOHN KEATS (1795–1821) *Ode to a Grecian Urn*

NATION

How much more are men than nations!
— RALPH WALDO EMERSON (1803–1882) *Letters and Social Aims*

It is because nations tend to stupidity and baseness that mankind moves so slowly; it is because individuals have a capacity for better things that it moves at all.
— GEORGE GISSING (1857–1903) *Private Papers of Henry Ryecroft*

The first panacea for a mismanaged nation is inflation of the currency; the second is war. Both bring a temporary prosperity; both bring a permanent ruin. But both are the refuge of political and economic opportunists.
— ERNEST HEMINGWAY (1898–1961) *Notes on the Next War*

There is no such thing as a little country. The greatness of a people is no more determined by their number than the greatness of a man is determined by his height.
— VICTOR HUGO (1802–1885)

The political life of a nation is only the most superficial aspect of its being. In order to know its inner life, the source of its action, one must penetrate to its soul by literature, philosophy and the arts, where are reflected the ideas, the passions, the dreams of a whole people.
— ROMAIN ROLLAND (1866–1945) *Musicians of the Past*

That nation is worthless which does not joyfully stake everything in defense of her honor.
— SCHILLER (1759–1805) *Maid of Orleans*

It is a maxim founded on the universal experience of mankind that no nation is to be trusted farther than it is bound by its interest.
— GEORGE WASHINGTON (1732–1799) Letter to Congress, 1778

No nation is fit to sit in judgment upon any other nation.
— WOODROW WILSON (1856–1924)

And hath made of one blood all nations of men for to dwell on all the face of the earth.
— NEW TESTAMENT: *Acts*, xvii, 26

A little one shall be come a thousand and a small one a strong nation.
— OLD TESTAMENT: *Isaiah*, ix, 22

NATURE

The study of Nature is intercourse with the Highest Mind. You should never trifle with Nature.
— JEAN LOUIS AGASSIZ (1807–1873) *Agassiz at Penikese*

Believe one who knows: you will find something greater in woods than in books. Trees and stones will teach you that which you can never learn from masters.
— ST. BERNARD OF CLAIRVAUX (1091–1153) *Epistles*

Whatever befalls in accordance with Nature shall be accounted good.
— CICERO (106–43 B.C.) *De Senetcute*

Nor rural sounds alone, but rural sounds,
Exhilarate the spirit, and restore
The tone of languid Nature.
— WILLIAM COWPER (1731–1800) *The Task*

Hast thou named all the birds without a gun;
Loved the wood-rose, and left it on its stalk?
— RALPH WALDO EMERSON (1803–1882) *Forbearance*

Never does Nature say one thing and Wisdom another.
— JUVENAL (*c.* 60–130 A.D.) *Satires*

So Nature deals with us, and takes away
Our playthings one by one, and by the hand
Leads us to rest.
— HENRY W. LONGFELLOW (1807–1882) *Nature*

All that thy seasons, O Nature, bring is fruit for me!
All things come from thee, subsist in thee, go back to thee.
— MARCUS AURELIUS (121–180) *Meditations*

In those vernal seasons of the year, when the air is calm and pleasant, it were an injury and sullenness against Nature not to go out and see her riches and partake in her rejoicing with heaven and earth.
— JOHN MILTON (1608–1674) *Tractate of Education*

The perfections of Nature show that she is the image of God; her defects show that she is only his image.
— BLAISE PASCAL (1623–1662) *Pensées*

All Nature is but Art, unknown to thee;
All Chance, Direction, which thou canst not see.
— ALEXANDER POPE (1688–1744) *Essay on Man*

Nature abhors a vacuum.
— FRANÇOIS RABELAIS (1494?–1553) *Gargantua*

And this our life, exempt from public haunt,
Finds tongues in trees, books in the running brooks,
Sermons in stones, and good in everything.
— SHAKESPEARE (1564–1616) *As You Like It*, II, i, 15

One touch of nature makes the whole world kin.
— SHAKESPEARE (1564–1616) *Troilus and Cressida*, III, iii, 175

I inhale great draughts of space,
The east and the west are mine, and the north and the south
are mine.
I am larger than I thought,
I did not know I held so much goodness.
— WALT WHITMAN (1819–1892) *Song of the Open Road*

NEIGHBOR

Reprove thy neighbor before thou threaten.
— BEN SIRA (*c.* 190 B.C.) *Book of Wisdom*

You must ask your neighbour if you shall live in peace.
— JOHN CLARK (1609–1676) *Paroemiologia*

Good fences make good neighbors.
— ROBERT FROST (1875–1963) *Mending Wall*

Love your neighbour, yet pull not down your hedge.
— GEORGE HERBERT (1593–1633) *Jacula Prudentum*

A bad neighbor is as great a plague as a good one is a blessing; he who enjoys a good neighbor has a precious possession.
— HESIOD (*c.* 735 B.C.) *Works and Days*

There is an idea abroad among moral people that they should make their neighbors good. One person I have to make good: myself. But my duty to my neighbor is much more nearly expressed by saying that I have to make him happy—if I may.
— R. L. STEVENSON (1850–1894) *A Christmas Sermon*

Love thy neighbour as thyself.
— NEW TESTAMENT: *Matthew*, xix, 19

Better is a neighbour that is near than a brother far off.
— OLD TESTAMENT: *Proverbs*, xxvii, 10

NIGHT

I linger yet with Nature, for the night
Hath been to me a more familiar face
Than that of man; and in her starry shade
Of dim and solitary loveliness
I learn'd the language of another world.
— LORD BYRON (1788–1824) *Manfred*, III, iv

The night . . . giveth truce to all labours, and by sleeping maketh sweet all pains and travail.
— WILLIAM CAXTON (1422?–1491) *Eneydos*

Dark was the night as pich, or as the cole.
— GEOFFREY CHAUCER (1340?–1400) *Canterbury Tales*

Every evening we are poorer by a day.
— ARTHUR SCHOPENHAUER (1788–1860)

Come, seeling night,
Scarf up the tender eye of pitiful day;
And with thy bloody and invisible hand
Cancel and tear to pieces that great bond
Which keeps me pale.
— SHAKESPEARE (1564–1616) *Macbeth*, III, ii, 46

In the night there is peace for the old and hope for the young.
— GEORGE BERNARD SHAW (1856–1950) *Heartbreak House*

Press close, bare-bosom'd night—press close, magnetic
nourishing night!
Night of south winds—night of the large few stars!
Still nodding night—mad naked summernight.
— WALT WHITMAN (1819–1882) *Song of Myself*

The night cometh when no man can work.
— NEW TESTAMENT: *John*, ix, 4

Watchman, what of the night?
— OLD TESTAMENT: *Isaiah*, xxi, ii

NOBILITY

The nobleman is he whose noble mind
Is filled with inborn worth, unborrowed from his kind.
— GEOFFREY CHAUCER (1340?–1400) *Canterbury Tales*

Send your noble Blood to Market, and see what it will buy.
— THOMAS FULLER (1608–1681) *Gnomologia*

To live as one likes is plebeian; the noble man aspires to order and law.
— GOETHE (1749–1832)

Hereditary nobility is due to the presumption that we shall do well because our fathers have done well.
— JOSEPH JOUBERT (1754–1824) *Pensées*

Noblesse oblige.
— FRANÇOIS GASTON DE LÉVIS (1720–1787) *Maxims*

True nobility is exempt from fear.
— SHAKESPEARE (1564–1616) *II Henry VI*, IV, i, 129

There is
One great society alone on earth;
The Noble Living and the Noble Dead.
— WILLIAM WORDSWORTH (1770–1850) *Prelude*

OATH

An oath sworn with the clear understanding in one's mind that it should be performed must be kept.
— CICERO (106–43 B.C.) *De Officiis*

A liar is always prodigal with oaths.
— PIERRE CORNEILLE (1606–1684) *The Liar*

We mutually pledge to each other our lives, our fortunes, and our sacred honor.
— THOMAS JEFFERSON (1743–1826) *Declaration of Independence*

Ease would recant
Vows made in pain, as violent and void.
— JOHN MILTON (1608–1674) *Paradise Lost*

'Tis not the many oaths that make the truth,
But the plain single vow that is vow'd true.
— SHAKESPEARE (1564–1616) *All's Well that Ends Well*, IV, ii, 21

I write a woman's oaths in water.
— SOPHOCLES (B.C. 495–406) *Fragment*

OBEDIENCE

The fear of some divine and supreme power keeps men in obedience.
— ROBERT BURTON (1577–1640) *Anatomy of Melancholy*

All arts his own, the hungry Greekling counts;
And bid him mount the skies, the skies he mounts.
— JUVENAL (*c.* 60–130) *Satires*

Obedience,
Bane of all genius, virtue, freedom, truth,
Makes slaves of men, and, of the human frame,
A mechanized automaton.
— PERCY B. SHELLEY (1792–1822) *Queen Mab*

Learn to obey before you command.
— SOLON (638–559 B.C.)

Theirs not to make reply,
Theirs not to reason why,
Theirs but to do and die.
— TENNYSON (1809–1892) *Charge of the Light Brigade*

Obedience is the courtesy due to kings.
— TENNYSON (1809–1892) *Idylls of the King*

We ought to obey God rather than men.
— NEW TESTAMENT: *Acts*, v, 29

OPINION

The man who never alters his opinion is like standing water, and breeds reptiles of the mind.
— WILLIAM BLAKE (1757–1827) *Proverbs of Hell*

He that complies against his will
Is of his own opinion still.
— SAMUEL BUTLER (1612–1680) *Hudibras*

No well-informed person has declared a change of opinion to be inconstancy.
— CICERO (106–43 B.C.) *Ad Atticum*

The only sin which we never forgive in each other is difference of opinion.
— RALPH WALDO EMERSON (1803–1882) *Society and Solitude*

Men will die for an opinion as soon as for anything else.
— WILLIAM HAZLITT (1778–1830) *Characteristics*

With effervescing opinions, as with the not yet forgotten champagne, the quickest way to let them get flat is to let them get exposed to the air.
— JUSTICE OLIVER WENDELL HOLMES (1841–1935) *Opinion*

For a thousand heads, a thousand tastes.
— HORACE (65–8 B.C.) *Satires*

The foolish and dead alone never change their opinion.
— JAMES RUSSELL LOWELL (1819–1891) *My Study Windows*

You are young, my son, and as the years go by, time will change, and even reverse many of your present opinions. Refrain therefore, awhile from setting yourself up as a judge of the highest matters.
— PLATO (428–347 B.C.) *Laws*

Some praise at morning what they blame at night,
But always think the last opinion right.
— ALEXANDER POPE (1688–1744) *Essay on Criticism*

A plague of opinion! a man may wear it on both sides, like a leather jerkin.
— SHAKESPEARE (1564–1616) *Troilus and Cressida*, III, iii, 268

It were not best that we should all think alike; it is difference of opinion that makes horse-races.
— MARK TWAIN (1835–1910) *Pudd'nhead Wilson's Calendar*

Public opinion is stronger than the legislature, and nearly as strong as the Ten Commandments.
— CHARLES D. WARNER (1829–1900) *My Summer in a Garden*

OPPORTUNITY

A wise man makes more opportunities than he finds.
— FRANCIS BACON (1561–1620)

When one door is shut, another opens.
— CERVANTES (1547–1616) *Don Quixote*

He who seizes the (right) moment is the right man.
— GOETHE (1749–1832) *Faust*

I knock unbidden once at every gate!
If sleeping, wake; if feasting, rise before
I turn away. It is the hour of fate.
— JOHN JAMES INGALLS (1833–1900) *Opportunity*

Four things come not back:
The spoken word; The sped arrow;
Time past; The neglected opportunity.
— OMAR IBN (*c.* 581–644) *Sayings*

O Opportunity, thy guilt is great!
'Tis thou that execut'st the traitor's treason;
Thou set'st the wolf where he the lamb may get;
Whoever plots the sin, thou point'st the season.
— SHAKESPEARE (1564–1616) *The Rape of Lucrece*

OPTIMISM

Optimism. The doctrine or belief that everything is beautiful, including what is ugly.
— AMBROSE BIERCE (1842–1914?) *Devil's Dictionary*

God's in his Heaven—
All's right with the world!
— ROBERT BROWNING (1812–1889) *Pippa Passes*

A man that could look no way but downwards with a muck-rake in his hand.
— JOHN BUNYAN (1628–1688) *Pilgrim's Progress*

The optimist proclaims that we live in the best of all possible worlds; and the pessimist fears this is true.
— JAMES BRANCH CABELL (1879–1958) *Silver Stallion*

An optimist is a guy that has never had much experience.
— DON MARQUIS (1878–1937) *Maxims of Archy*

The refuge from pessimism is the good men and women existing at any time in the world—they keep faith and happiness alive.
— CHARLES E. NORTON (1827–1908)

All is for the best in the best of all possible worlds.
— VOLTAIRE (1694–1778) *Candide*

ORATORY

He can best be described as one of those orators who, before they get up, do not know what they are going to say; when they are speaking, do not know what they are saying; and, when they have sat down, do not know what they have said.
— WINSTON CHURCHILL (1874–1965)

When his words fell soft as snowflakes on a winter's day, then could no mortal man beside vie with Odysseus.
— HOMER (*c.* 10th–8th C. B.C.) *Iliad*

Oratory is the power of beating down your adversary's arguments, and putting better in their place.
— SAMUEL JOHNSON (1709–1784) Boswell's *Life of Johnson*

Fear not, my lord, I'll play the orator
As if the golden fee for which I plead
Were for myself.
— SHAKESPEARE (1564–1616) *Richard III*, III, v, 95

It is not the powerful arm,
But soft enchanting tongue that governs all.
— SOPHOCLES (495–406 B.C.) *Philoctetes*

If ever a woman feels proud of her lover, it is when she sees him as a successful public speaker.
— HARRIET BEECHER STOWE (1811–1896)

ORDER

Order means light and peace, inward liberty and free command over oneself; order is power.
— HENRI-FRÉDÉRIC AMIEL (1828–1881) *Journal*

Order is Heav'ns first law.
— ALEXANDER POPE (1688–1744) *Essay on Man*

A place for everything and everything in its place.
— SAMUEL SMILES (1812–1904) *Thrift*

Order governs the world. The Devil is the author of confusion.
— JONATHAN SWIFT (1667–1745) Letter to Stella

Have a place for everything and keep the thing somewhere else. This is not advice, it is merely custom.
— MARK TWAIN (1835–1910) *Diaries*

Let all things be done decently and in order.
— OLD TESTAMENT: *I Corinthians*, xiv, 40

PAIN

Pleasure must succeed to pleasure, else past pleasure turns to pain.
— ROBERT BROWNING (1812–1889) *La Saisiaz*

Real pain can alone cure us of imaginary ills.
— JONATHAN EDWARDS (1703–1757) *Resolutions*

He has seen but half the universe who never has been shewn the house of Pain.
— RALPH WALDO EMERSON (1803–1882)

The gods have so spun the thread for wretched mortals that they must live in pain.
— HOMER (*c.* 10th–8th C. B.C.) *Iliad*

Those who do not feel pain seldom think that it is felt.
— SAMUEL JOHNSON (1709–1784) *The Rambler*

There is a certain pleasure which is akin to pain.
— METRODORUS (*f.* 168 B.C.)

Pain is perfect misery, the worst of evils,
And excessive, overturns all patience.
— JOHN MILTON (1608–1674) *Paradise Lost*

Ay, but I fear you speak upon the rack,
Where men enforced do speak anything.
— SHAKESPEARE (1564–1616) *Merchant of Venice*, III, ii, 32

PARADISE

A book of Verses underneath the Bough,
A Jug of Wine, a Loaf of Bread—and Thou
Beside me singing in the Wilderness—
Oh, Wilderness were Paradise enow!
— EDWARD FITZGERALD (1809–1883) *Rubaiyat*

Man and Woman may only enter Paradise hand in hand. Together, the myth tells us, they left it and together must they return.
— RICHARD GARNETT (1835–1906) *De Flagello Myrteo*

Paradise is a dwelling place promised the faithful.
— MOHAMMED (570–632) *The Koran*

The loves that meet in Paradise shall cast out fear,
And Paradise hath room for you and me and all.
— CHRISTINA ROSSETTI (1830–1894) *Saints and Angels*

PARENTS

Reverence for parents—this standeth written third among the statutes of Justice to whom supreme honor is due.
— AESCHYLUS (525–456 B.C.) *Suppliants*

There are three degrees of filial piety. The highest is being a credit to our parents, the second is not disgracing them; the lowest is being able simply to support them.
— CONFUCIUS (*c.* 551–478 B.C.) *Book of Rites*

It used to be believed that the parent had unlimited claims on the child and rights over him. In a truer view of the matter, we are coming to see that the rights are on the side of the child and the duties on the side of the parent.
— WILLIAM G. SUMNER (1840–1910) *Forgotten Man's Almanac*

He argued that the principal duty which a parent owed to a child was to make him happy.
— ANTHONY TROLLOPE (1815–1882) *Doctor Thorne*

Children begin by loving their parents; as they grow older they judge them; sometimes they forgive them.
— OSCAR WILDE (1854–1900) *Dorian Gray*

Honour thy father and mother; that thy days may be long upon the land which the Lord thy God giveth thee.
— OLD TESTAMENT: *Exodus*, XX, 12

PARTING

Go from me. Yet I feel that I shall stand
Henceforward in thy shadow.
— ELIZABETH B. BROWNING (1806–1861) *Sonnets from Portuguese*

Parting is all we know of heaven,
And all we need of hell.
— EMILY DICKINSON (1830–1886) *Poems*

They who go
Feel not the pain of parting; it is they
Who stay behind that suffer.
— HENRY W. LONGFELLOW (1807–1882) *Michael Angelo*

Good night! Good night! parting is such sweet sorrow
That I shall say good night till it be morrow.
— SHAKESPEARE (1564–1616) *Romeo and Juliet*, II, ii, 185

PAST

Think only of the past as its remembrance gives you pleasure.
— JANE AUSTEN (1775–1817) *Pride and Prejudice*

I have small patience with the antiquarian habit which magnifies the past and belittles the present. . . . Change is inevitable, at once a penalty and a privilege.
— JOHN BUCHAN (1875–1940) *Memory Hold-the-Door*

He seems
To have seen better days, as who has not
Who has seen yesterday?
— LORD BYRON (1788–1824) *Age of Bronze*

Oh! leave the past to bury its own dead.
— WILLIAM S. BLUNT (1840–1922) *To One Who Would Make a Confession*

Historic continuity with the past is not a duty, it is only a necessity.
— JUSTICE OLIVER WENDELL HOLMES (1841–1935)

Tomorrow I will live, the fool does say;
Today itself's too late; the wise lived yesterday.
— MARTIAL (*c.* 66 A.D.) *Epigrams*

Those who cannot remember the past are condemned to repeat it.
— GEORGE SANTAYANA (1863–1952) *Life of Reason*

PATIENCE

There is a limit at which forbearance ceases to be a virtue.
— EDMUND BURKE (1729–1797) *Observations*

Beware the fury of a patient man.
— JOHN DRYDEN (1631–1700) *Absalom and Achitophel*

Patience, that blending of moral courage with physical timidity.
— THOMAS HARDY (1840–1928) *Tess of the D'Urbervilles*

All men commend patience, although few be willing to practise it.
— THOMAS À KEMPIS (1380–1471) *Imitation of Christ*

Forbearance is a part of justice.
— MARCUS AURELIUS (121–180) *Meditations*

They also serve who only stand and wait.
— JOHN MILTON (1608–1674) *On His Blindness*

It's a long lane that has no turning.
— SAMUEL RICHARDSON (1689–1761) *Clarissa*

'Tis all men's office to speak patience
To those who wring under the load of sorrow;
But no man's virtue nor sufficiency
To be so moral when he shall endure
The like himself.
— SHAKESPEARE (1564–1616) *Much Ado About Nothing*, V, i, 27

Ye have heard of the patience of Job.
— NEW TESTAMENT: *James*, v, ii

In your patience possess ye your souls.
— NEW TESTAMENT: *Luke*, xxi, 18

PATRIOTISM

The die was now cast; I had passed the Rubicon. Swim or sink, live or die, survive or perish with my country was my unalterable determination.
— JOHN ADAMS (1735–1826)

The country of every man is that one where he lives best.
— ARISTOPHANES (444–380 B.C.) *Plutus*

No man can be a patriot on an empty stomach.
— WILLIAM C. BRANN (1855–1898) *Iconoclast*

He who loves not his country can love nothing.
— LORD BYRON (1788–1824) *Two Foscari*

Our country! In her intercourse with foreign nations, may she always be in the right; but our country, right or wrong.
— STEPHAN DECATUR (1779–1820)

My affections are first for my own country, and then, generally, for all mankind.
— THOMAS JEFFERSON (1743–1826) Letter to Thomas Law

My country is the world, and my religion is to do good.
— THOMAS PAINE (1737–1809) *Rights of Man*

If I were an American, as I am an Englishman, while a foreign troop was landed in my country I never would lay down my arms, never! never! never!
— WILLIAM PITT (1708–1778) Speech, 1777

We should behave toward our country as women behave toward the men they love. A loving wife will do anything for her husband except stop criticizing and trying to improve him. We should cast the same affectionate but sharp glance at our country.
— J. B. PRIESTLEY (1894–)

Where is the man who owes nothing to the land in which he lives? Whatever the land may be, he owes to it the most precious thing possessed by man, the morality of his actions and the love of virtue.
— JEAN-JACQUES ROUSSEAU (1712–1778) *Émile*

Breathes there a man with soul so dead,
Who never to himself hath said,
This is my own, my native land!
— SIR WALTER SCOTT (1771–1832) *Lay of the Last Minstrel*

I do love
My country's good with a respect more tender,
More holy and profound, than my own life.
— SHAKESPEARE (1564–1616) *Coriolanus*, III, iii, 111

The proper means of increasing the love we bear our native country is to reside some time in a foreign one.
— WILLIAM SHENSTONE (1714–1763) *Of Men and Manners*

Our country, right or wrong. When right, to be kept right; when wrong, to be put right.
— CARL SCHURZ (1829–1906) Speech, 1872

The more I see of other countries, the more I love my own.
— MADAME DE STAËL (1766–1817) *Corinne*

PEACE

He makes a solitude, and calls it—peace!
— LORD BYRON (1788–1824) *Bride of Abydos*

We have preserved peace in our time.
— NEVILLE CHAMBERLAIN (1869–1940) Speech, 1938

Peace rules the day, where reason rules the mind.
— WILLIAM COLLINS (1720–1756) *Hassan*

The gentleman (Josiah Quincy) cannot have forgotten his own sentiment, uttered even on the floor of this House, "Peaceably if we can, forcibly if we must."
— HENRY CLAY (1777–1852) Speech, 1813

Peace at any price.
— ALPHONSE DE LAMARTINE (1790–1869)

Peace will come soon and come to stay, and so come as to be worth keeping in all future time. It will then have been proved that among free men there can be no successful appeal from the ballot to the bullet, and that they who take such appeal are sure to lose their cases and pay the cost.
— ABRAHAM LINCOLN (1809–1865)

We supplicate all rulers not to remain deaf to the cry of mankind. Let them do everything in their power to save peace. By so doing they will spare the world the horrors of a war that would have disastrous consequences, such as nobody can foresee.
— POPE JOHN XXIII (1881–1963) Oct. 25, 1962

We will have to want Peace, want it enough to pay for it, before it becomes an accepted rule.
— ELEANOR ROOSEVELT (1884–1964)

A peace is of the nature of a conquest;
For then both parties nobly are subdued
And neither party loser.
— SHAKESPEARE (1564–1616) *Henry IV*, IV, ii, 89

Peace be to you. [Pax vobiscum.]
— OLD TESTAMENT: *Genesis*, xliii, 23

Go in peace. [Vade in pace.]
— OLD TESTAMENT: *Exodus*, iv, 18

The peace of God, which passeth all understanding.
— NEW TESTAMENT: *Philippians*, iv, 7

Blessed are the peace-makers.
— NEW TESTAMENT: *Matthew*, v, 9

Glory to God in the highest, and on earth peace, good will toward men.
— NEW TESTAMENT: *Luke*, ii, 14

They shall beat their swords into ploughshares, and their spears into pruning-hooks; nation shall not lift up sword against nation, neither shall they learn war any more.
— OLD TESTAMENT: *Isaiah*, ii, 4

PEOPLE

A people's voice is dangerous when charged with wrath.
— AESCHYLUS (525–456 B.C.) *Agamemnon*

The individual is foolish; the multitude, for the moment is foolish, when they act without deliberation; but the species is wise, and, when time is given to it, as a species it always acts right.
— EDMUND BURKE (1729–1797)

The rabble estimate few things according to their real value, most things according to their prejudices.
— CICERO (106–43 B.C.) *Oratio Pro Quinto Roscio Comaedo*

Your people, sir, is nothing but a great beast!
— ALEXANDER HAMILTON (1757–1804) Argument with Thomas Jefferson

The Lord prefers common-looking people. That is the reason He made so many of them.
— ABRAHAM LINCOLN (1809–1865)

The people is Everyman, everybody.
Everybody is you and me and all others.
What everybody says is what we all say.
— CARL SANDBURG (1878–) *The People, Yes*

PERFECTION

There never was such beauty in another man,
Nature made him, and broke the mould.
— LODOVICO ARIOSTO (1474–1533) *Orlando Furioso*

The more a thing is perfect, the more it feels pleasure and likewise pain.
— DANTE (1265–1321) *Inferno*

In this broad earth of ours,
Amid the measureless grossness and the slag,
Enclosed and safe within its central heart,
Nestles the seed Perfection.
— WALT WHITMAN (1819–1892) *Song of the Universal*

Be ye therefore Perfect, even as your Father which is in heaven is perfect.
— NEW TESTAMENT: *Matthew*, v, 48

PHILANTHROPY

He who bestows his goods upon the poor,
Shall have as much again, and ten times more.
— JOHN BUNYAN (1628–1688) *Pilgrim's Progress*

In nothing do men more nearly approach the gods than in doing good to their fellow men.
— CICERO (106–43 B.C.) *Pro Ligario*

The most acceptable service to God is doing good to man.
— BEN FRANKLIN (1706–1790) *Autobiography*

I expect to pass through this world but once. Any good therefore that I can do, or any kindness that I can show to any fellow creature, let me do it now. Let me not defer or neglect it, for I shall not pass this way again.
— STEPHEN GRELLET (1773–1855)

The hands that help are holier than the lips that pray.
— ROBERT GREEN INGERSOLL (1833–1899)

To pity distress is but human: to relieve it is Godlike.
— HORACE MANN (1796–1859) *Lectures on Education*

Benevolence is the distinguishing characteristic of man. As embodied in man's conduct, it is called the path of duty.
— MENCIUS (372?–289 B.C.) *Discourses*

I am a man, and nothing in man's lot can be indifferent to me.
— TERENCE (*c.* 190–150 B.C.) *Heautontimoroumenos*

Myself not ignorant of adversity, I have learned to befriend the unhappy.
— VERGIL (70–19 B.C.) *Aeneid*

I was a stranger, and ye took me in.
— NEW TESTAMENT: *Matthew*, xxv, 35

PHILOSOPHY

What I have gained from philosophy is the ability to feel at ease in any society.
— ARISTIPPUS (425?–366? B.C.)

The Philosopher is he to whom the Highest has descended, and the Lowest has mounted up; who is the equal and kindly brother of all.
— THOMAS CARLYLE (1795–1881) *Sartor Resartus*

Philosophy as a fellow once said to me is only thinking. Thinking is an instrument of adjustment to the conditions of life—but it becomes an end in itself.
— JUSTICE OLIVER WENDELL HOLMES (1841–1935)

Philosophy is an attitude toward life, based on a greater or lesser, but always limited comprehension of the universe as far as we happen to know it.
— LIN YUTANG (1895–) *I Believe*

Philosophy is toleration, and it is only one step from toleration to forgiveness.
— ARTHUR W. PINERO (1855–1934) *Second Mrs. Tanqueray*

The greater the philosopher, the harder it is for him to answer the questions of common people.
— HENRYK SIENKIEWICZ (1846–1916) *Quo Vadis*

Men of Athens, I honor and love you; but I shall obey God rather than you, and while I have life and strength I shall never cease from the practise and teaching of philosophy.
— SOCRATES (470–399? B.C.) in Plato's *Apology*

Philosophers must deal with ideas, but the trouble with most nineteenth century poets is too much philosophy; they are nearer to being philosophers than poets, without being in the true sense either.
— ALLEN TATE (1899–) *Reactionary Essays*

POETRY

Poetry is simply the most beautiful, impressive and widely effective mode of saying things, and hence its importance.
— MATTHEW ARNOLD (1822–1888) *Essays*

Poetry has been to me an exceeding great reward; it has soothed my affliction; it has multiplied and refined my enjoyments; it has endeared my solitude; and it has given me the habit of wishing to discover the Good and the Beautiful in all that meets and surrounds me.
— SAMUEL TAYLOR COLERIDGE (1772–1834)

Poetry is not a turning loose of emotion, but an escape from emotion; it is not the expression of personality, but an escape from personality. But, of course, only those who have personality and emotions know what it means to want to escape from these things.
— T. S. ELIOT (1888–1965) *Tradition and the Individual Talent*

Writing free verse is like playing tennis with the net down.
— ROBERT FROST (1875–1963) Address

Do you suppose we owe nothing to Pope's deformity? —He said to himself, "If my person be crooked, my verses shall be straight."
— WILLIAM HAZLITT (1778–1830)

I have reared a monument more enduring than bronze and loftier than the royal pyramids, one that no wasting rain, no unavailing north wind can destroy; no, not even the unending years nor the flight of time itself. I shall not wholly die. The greater part of me shall escape oblivion.
— HORACE (65–8 B.C.) *Odes*

A poet is a nightingale who sits in darkness and sings to cheer its own solitude with sweet sounds.
— PERCY B. SHELLEY (1792–1822) *Defense of Poetry*

Verse without rhyme is a body without a soul.
— JONATHAN SWIFT (1667–1745) *Advice to a Young Poet*

POLITICS

Politics make strange bedfellows.
— JOHN S. BASSETT (1867–1928) *Life of Jackson*

Politics. The conduct of public affairs for private advantage.
— AMBROSE BIERCE (1842–1914?) *Devil's Dictionary*

I shall not help crucify mankind upon a cross of gold. I shall not aid in pressing down upon the bleeding brow of labor this crown of thorns.
— WILLIAM JENNINGS BRYAN (1860–1925) Speech

We are Republicans, and we don't propose to leave our party and identify ourselves with the party whose antecedents have been rum, Romanism and rebellion.
— REV. S. D. BURCHARD (1812–1891) Speech, 1884

When I was called upon to be Prime Minister, now nearly two years ago, there were not many applicants for the job. Since then perhaps the market has improved.
— WINSTON CHURCHILL (1874–1965) Speech, Jan. 1942

Damn your principles. Stick to your party.
— BENJAMIN DISRAELI (1804–1881)

Every time I bestow a vacant office I make a hundred discontented persons and one ingrate.
— LOUIS XIV OF FRANCE (1638–1715)

The various admirable movements in which I have been engaged have always developed among their members a large lunatic fringe.
— THEODORE ROOSEVELT (1858–1919)

PRAYER

"Oh, God, if I were sure I were to die tonight I would repent at once." It is the commonest prayer in all languages.
— JAMES M. BARRIE (1860–1937) *Sentimental Tommy*

He prayeth well who loveth well
Both man and bird and beast;
He prayeth best who loveth best
All things both great and small
For the dear God who loveth us,
He made and loveth all.
— SAMUEL TAYLOR COLERIDGE (1772–1834) *Ancient Mariner*

We, on our side, are praying to Him to give us victory, because we believe we are right; but those on the other side pray to Him, too, for victory, believing they are right. What must He think of us?
— ABRAHAM LINCOLN (1809–1865)

God grant me the serenity to accept the things I cannot change, courage to change things I can, and wisdom to know the difference.
— REINHOLD NIEBUHR (1892–)

More things are wrought by prayer
Than this world dreams of.
— TENNYSON (1809–1892) *Morte d'Arthur*

I have never made but one prayer to God, a very short one: "O Lord, make my enemies ridiculous." And God granted it.
— VOLTAIRE (1694–1778)

Therefore I say unto you, What things soever ye desire, when ye pray, believe that ye receive them, and ye shall receive them.
— NEW TESTAMENT: *Mark*, XI, 23, 24

Ask, and it shall be given you; seek, and ye shall find, knock, and it shall be opened unto you.
— NEW TESTAMENT: *Matthew*, vii, 7

PRIDE

Pride is the beginning of sin.
— BEN SIRA (*c.* 190 B.C.) *Book of Wisdom*

Pride, Envy, Avarice—these are the sparks
Have set on fire the hearts of all men.
— DANTE (1265–1321) *Inferno*

The readiness with which we admit a fault or acknowledge a weakness may be only our pride masquerading as humility.
— OSCAR HAMMLING (1890–)

In pride, in reas'ning pride, our error lies;
All quit their sphere, and rush into the skies!
Pride still is aiming at the bless'd abodes,
Men would be angels, Angels would be Gods.
— ALEXANDER POPE (1688–1744) *Essay on Man*

War is the child of pride, and pride the daughter of riches.
— JONATHAN SWIFT (1667–1745) *Battle of the Books*

Pride goeth before destruction, and an haughty spirit before a fall.
— OLD TESTAMENT: *Proverbs*, xvi, 18

PRUDENCE

Make haste slowly.
— AUGUSTUS CAESAR (63 B.C.–A.D. 14)

Put your trust in God, my boys, and keep your powder dry.
— OLIVER CROMWELL (1599–1658)

The greatest good is prudence; a more precious thing even than philosophy; from it spring all the other virtues.
— EPICURUS (342–270 B.C.) *Letter to Menaeceus*

That man is prudent who neither hopes nor fears anything from the uncertain events of the future.
— ANATOLE FRANCE (1844–1924) *Procurator of Judea*

Beware of rashness, but with energy and sleepless vigilance go forward and give us victories.
— ABRAHAM LINCOLN (1809–1865) Letter to Gen. Hooker

Let every man be swift to hear, slow to speak.
— NEW TESTAMENT: *James*, i, 19

READING

Reading is to the Mind, what Exercise is to the Body.
— JOSEPH ADDISON (1672–1719) *The Tatler*

To read a book for the first time is to make the acquaintance of a new friend; to read it a second time is to meet an old one.
— SELWYN G. CHAMPION (1875–1950) *Racial Proverbs*

Some read to think—these are rare; some to write—these are common; and some to talk—and these form the great majority.
— CHARLES C. COLTON (1780?–1832) *Lacon*

There is an art of reading, as well as an art of thinking, and an art of writing.
— ISAAC D'ISRAELI (1766–1848) *Literary Character*

A man ought to read just as inclination leads him; for what he reads as a task will do him little good. A young man should read five hours in a day, and so may acquire a great deal of knowledge.
— SAMUEL JOHNSON (1709–1784) Boswell's *Life*

I'm quite illiterate, but I read a lot.
— J. D. SALINGER (1919–) *Catcher in the Rye*

He hath never fed of the dainties that are bred in a book.
— SHAKESPEARE (1564–1616) *Love's Labour's Lost*, IV, ii, 25

The habit of reading is the only enjoyment in which there is no alloy; it lasts when all other pleasures fade.
— ANTHONY TROLLOPE (1815–1882)

REASON

Reason is a light that God has kindled in the soul.
— ARISTOTLE (384–322 B.C.) *Art of Rhetoric*

He who will not reason is a bigot; he who cannot is a fool; and he who dares not is a slave.
— WILLIAM DRUMMOND (1585–1649) *Academical Question*

It is wise even in adversity to listen to reason.
— EURIPIDES (480–406 B.C.) *Hecuba*

The soul of man is divided into three parts, intelligence, reason and passion. Intelligence and passion are possessed by other animals, but reason by man alone.... Reason is immortal, all else mortal.
— PYTHAGORAS (582–500 B.C.)

REGRET

Regret not that which is past; and trust not to thine own righteousness.
— ST. ANTHONY (*c.* 250–350)

O lost days of delight, that are wasted in doubting and waiting!
O lost hours and days in which we might have been happy!
— HENRY W. LONGFELLOW (1807–1882) *Tales of a Wayside Inn*

Of all sad words of tongue or pen,
The saddest are these: "It might have been."
— JOHN GREENLEAF WHITTIER (1807–1892) *Maud Muller*

RESPECT

Respect is what we owe; love, what we give.
— PHILIP JAMES BAILEY (1816–1902) *Festus*

He removes the greatest ornament of friendship, who takes away from it respect.
— CICERO (106–43 B.C.) *De Amicitia*

A man's real life is that accorded to him in the thoughts of other men by reason of respect or natural love.
— JOSEPH CONRAD (1857–1924) *Under Western Eyes*

Deference is the instinctive respect which we pay to the great and good; the unconscious acknowledgment of the superiority or excellence of others.
— TRYON EDWARDS (1809–1894)

Even a nod from a person who is esteemed is of more force than a thousand arguments or studied sentences from others.
— PLUTARCH (46?–120?) *Lives: Phocion*

There is no respect of persons with God.
— NEW TESTAMENT: *Romans*, ii, 11

RETIREMENT

Don't think of retiring from the world until the world will be sorry that you retire. I hate a fellow whom pride or cowardice or laziness drive into a corner, and who does nothing when he is there but sit and growl. Let him come out as I do, and bark.
— SAMUEL JOHNSON (1709–1784)

Let me caution persons grown old in active business, not lightly, nor without weighing their own resources, to forego their customary employment all at once, for there may be danger in it.
— CHARLES LAMB (1775–1834) *Superannuated Man*

I could be well content
To entertain the lag-end of my life
With quiet hours.
— SHAKESPEARE (1564–1616) *I Henry IV*, V, i, 23

SCIENCE

Science bestowed immense new powers on man and at the same time created conditions which were largely beyond his comprehension and still more beyond his control.
— WINSTON CHURCHILL (1874–1965) Speech, March 31, 1949

In science we must be interested in things, not in persons.
— MARIE CURIE (1867–1934)

What art was to the ancient world, science is to the modern.
— BENJAMIN DISRAELI (1804–1881) *Coningsby*

Why does this magnificient applied science, which saves work and makes life easier, bring us little happiness? The simple answer runs, because we have not yet learned to make sensible use of it.
— ALBERT EINSTEIN (1879–1955) Address, 1931

Science is the knowledge of consequences, and dependence of one fact upon another.
— THOMAS HOBBES (1588–1679) *Leviathan*

In science the credit goes to the man who convinces the world, not to the man to whom the idea first occurs.
— SIR WILLIAM OSLER (1849–1919)

SEA

Roll on, thou deep and dark blue ocean, roll.
Ten thousand fleets sweep over thee in vain:
Man marks the earth with ruin, —his control
Stops with the shore.
— LORD BYRON (1788–1824) *Childe Harold*

The sea possesses a power over one's moods that has the effect of a will. The sea can hypnotize. Nature in general can do so.
— HENDRIK IBSEN (1828–1906) *Lady from the Sea*

Comrades! now that we have established our peace on land, let us conquer the freedom of the seas.
— NAPOLEON BONAPARTE (1769–1821)

Any one can hold the helm when the sea is calm.
— PUBLILIUS SYRUS (1st C. B.C.) *Sententiae*

The sea folds away from you like a mystery. You can look and look at it and mystery never leaves it.
— CARL SANDBURG (1878–) *Remembrance Rock*

Full fathom five thy father lies;
  Of his bones are coral made;
Those are pearls that were his eyes;
  Nothing of him that doth fade
But doth suffer a sea-change
  Into something rich and strange.
— SHAKESPEARE (1564–1616) *Tempest*, I, ii, 394

All the rivers run into the sea; yet the sea is not full.
— OLD TESTAMENT: *Ecclesiastes*, i, 7

SEASON

To everything there is a season, and a time to every purpose under the heaven.
— OLD TESTAMENT: *Ecclesiastes*, iii, 1

SELF-CONTROL

One of the most important, but one of the most difficult things for a powerful mind is, to be its own master. A pond may lie quiet in a plain; but a lake wants mountains to compass and hold it in.
— JOSEPH ADDISON (1672–1719)

I count him braver who overcomes his desires than him who conquers his enemies; for the hardest victory is the victory over self.
— ARISTOTLE (384–322 B.C.) *Stobaeus: Florilegium*

Conquer thyself. Till thou hast done this, thou art but a slave for it is almost as well to be subjected to another's appetite as to thine own.
— ROBERT BURTON (1577–1640) *Anatomy of Melancholy*

Nothing gives one person so much advantage over another as to remain always cool and unruffled under all circumstances.
— THOMAS JEFFERSON (1743–1826)

No conflict is so severe as his who labors to subdue himself.
— THOMAS À KEMPIS (1380–1471) *Imitation of Christ*

He that is slow to anger is better than the mighty; and he that ruleth his spirit than he that taketh a city.
— OLD TESTAMENT: *Proverbs*, xvi, 32

SELFISHNESS

People often grudge others what they cannot enjoy themselves.
— AESOP (6th C. B.C.) *Dog in the Manger*

This is the plain truth: every one ought to keep a sharp eye for the main chance.
— PLAUTUS (*c.* 254–184 B.C.) *Asinaria*

We have always known that heedless self-interest was bad morals; we know now that it is bad economics.
— FRANKLIN D. ROOSEVELT (1882–1945) Second Inaugural

There's plenty of boys that will come hankering and gruvelling around when you've got an apple, and beg the core off you; but when *they've* got one, and you beg for the core, and remind them how you give them a core one time, they make a mouth at you, and say thank you most to death, but there ain't a-going to *be* no core.
— MARK TWAIN (1835–1910) *Tom Sawyer Abroad*

Selfishness is the only real atheism; aspiration, unselfishness, the only real religion.
— ISRAEL ZANGWILL (1864–1926) *Children of the Ghetto*

SELF-RESPECT

The reverence of a man's self is, next to religion, the chiefest bridle of all vices.
— FRANCIS BACON (1561–1620) *New Atlantis*

Few men survey themselves with so much severity as not to admit prejudices in their own favor.
— SAMUEL JOHNSON (1709–1784) *The Rambler*

I care not so much what I am in the opinion of others as what I am in my own; I would be rich of myself and not by borrowing.
— MICHEL DE MONTAIGNE (1533–1592) *Essays*

If ye would go up high, then use your own legs! Do not get yourselves *carried* aloft; do not seat yourselves on other's backs and heads!
— FRIEDRICH NIETZSCHE (1844–1900) *Thus Spake Zarathustra*

To have a respect for ourselves guides our morals; and to have a deference for others governs our manners.
— LAURENCE STERNE (1713–1768)

SERENITY

Remember to preserve an even mind in adverse circumstance and likewise in prosperity a mind free from overweening joy.
— HORACE (65–8 B.C.) *Odes*

Calm of mind, all passion spent.
— JOHN MILTON (1608–1674) *Samson Agonistes*

He who is of a calm and happy nature will hardly feel the pressure of age, but to him who is of an opposite disposition youth and age are equally a burden.
— PLATO (428–347 B.C.) *The Republic*

SILENCE

Silence gives consent.
— CANON LAW: *Decretals*

Silence is the unbearable repartee.
— G. K. CHESTERTON (1874–1936) *Dickens*

Silence is true wisdom's best reply.
— EURIPIDES (480–406 B.C.) *Fragments*

There is an eloquent silence: it serves sometimes to approve, sometimes to condemn; there is a mocking silence; there is a respectful silence.
— FRANÇOIS DE LA ROCHEFOUCAULD (1613–1680) *Reflections*

He has occasional flashes of silence, that make his conversation perfectly delightful.
— SYDNEY SMITH (1771–1845) *Speaking of Macaulay*

Even a fool, when he holdeth his peace, is counted wise.
— OLD TESTAMENT: *Proverbs*, xvii, 28

SLEEP

We sleep, but the loom of life never stops and the pattern which was weaving when the sun went down is weaving when the sun comes up tomorrow.
— HENRY WARD BEECHER (1813–1887) *Life Thoughts*

Sleep is a death; oh, make me try
By sleeping, know what it is to die,
And as gently lay my head
On my grave, as now my bed.
— THOMAS BROWNE (1605–1682) *Religio Medici*

Our life is two-fold: Sleep hath its own world,
A boundry between the things misnamed
Death and existence: Sleep hath its own world.
And a wide realm of wild reality.
— LORD BYRON (1788–1824) *The Dream*

Now blessings light on him that first invented this same sleep! It covers a man all over, thoughts and all, like a cloak; 'tis meat for the hungry, drink for the thirsty, heat for the cold, and cold for the hot. 'Tis the current coin that purchases all the pleasures of the world cheap; and the balance that sets the king and the shepherd, the fool and the wise man even.
— CERVANTES (1547–1616) *Don Quixote*

O Sleep, thou rest of all things, Sleep, gentlest of the gods, peace of the soul, who puttest care to flight.
— OVID (43 B.C.–A.D. 18?) *Metamorphoses*

Our foster-nurse of nature is repose,
The which he lacks; that to provoke in him,
Are many simples operative, whose power
Will close the eye of anguish.
— SHAKESPEARE (1564–1616) *King Lear*, IV, iv, 12

Sleep that knits up the ravell'd sleave of care,
The death of each day's life, sore labour's bath,
Balm of hurt minds, great nature's second course,
Chief nourisher in life's feast.
— SHAKESPEARE (1564–1616) *Macbeth*, II, ii, 36

Thou hast been called, O sleep! the friend of woe;
But 'tis the happy that have called thee so.
— ROBERT SOUTHEY (1774–1843) *Curse of Kehama*

Yet a little sleep, a little slumber, a little folding of the hands to sleep.
— OLD TESTAMENT: *Proverbs*, vi, 10

SMILE

What sunshine is to flowers, smiles are to humanity. They are but trifles, to be sure; but, scattered along life's pathway, the good they do is inconceivable.
— JOSEPH ADDISON (1672–1719)

There is a smile of Love,
And there is a smile of Deceit,
And there is a smile of smiles
In which these two smiles meet.
— WILLIAM BLAKE (1757–1827) *Smile and Frown*

A smile is ever the most bright and beautiful with a tear upon it. What is the dawn without the dew? The tear is rendered by the smile precious above the smile itself.
— WALTER S. LANDOR (1775–1864)

SOLDIER

It were better to be a soldier's widow than a coward's wife.
— THOMAS B. ALDRICH (1836–1907) *Mercedes*

I love a brave soldier who has undergone the baptism of fire.
— NAPOLEON BONAPARTE (1769–1821)

The army is a school in which the miser becomes generous, and the generous prodigal; miserly soldiers are like monsters, very rarely seen.
— CERVANTES (1547–1616) *Don Quixote*

How sleep the brave, who sink to rest,
By all their country's wishes blest!
— WILLIAM COLLINS (1721–1759) *Ode Written in 1746*

For it's Tommy this, an' Tommy that, an'
"Chuck 'im out, the brute!"
But it's the "Saviour of 'is country" when
the guns begin to shoot.
— RUDYARD KIPLING (1865–1936) *Tommy*

But in a larger sense, we cannot dedicate, we cannot consecrate, we cannot hallow this ground. The brave men living and dead, who struggled here, have consecrated it far above our poor power to add or detract. The world will little note, nor long remember, what we say here, but it can never forget what they did here.
— ABRAHAM LINCOLN (1809–1865) Gettysburg Address

"Companions," said he [Saturninus], "you have lost a good captain, to make of him a bad general."
— MICHEL DE MONTAIGNE (1533–1592) *Essays*

Your son, my lord, has paid a soldier's debt:
He only lived but till he was a man;
The which no sooner had his prowess confirm'd
In the unshrinking station where he fought,
But like a man he died.
—SHAKESPEARE (1564–1616) *Macbeth*, V, vii, 68

The proper qualities of a general are judgment and deliberation.
— TACITUS (*c.* 55–117) *History*

The combat infantryman should combine the arts of a successful poacher, a cat-burglar and a gunman.
— FIELD MARSHAL EARL WAVELL (1885–1950)

SON See CHILDREN

SORROW

There is no sorrow which length of time does not diminish and soften.
— CICERO (106–43 B.C.) *De Finibus*

I have had sorrows . . . but I have borne them ill.
I have broken where I should have bent.
— CHARLES DICKENS (1812–1870) *Barnaby Rudge*

When sorrows come, they come not single spies,
But in battalions.
— SHAKESPEARE (1564–1616) *Hamlet*, IV, v, 78

SUMMER

Heat, ma'am! It was so dreadful here that I found nothing left for it but to take off my flesh and sit in my bones.
— SYDNEY SMITH (1771–1845) in Lady Holland's *Memoirs*

Shall I compare thee to a summer's day?
— SHAKESPEARE (1564–1616) *Sonnets*, xviii

Today the summer has come at my window with its sighs and murmurs; and the bees are plying their minstrelsy at the court of the flowering grove.
— RABINDRANATH TAGORE (1861–1941) *Gitanjali*

SYMPATHY

The man who melts
With social sympathy, though not allied,
Is of more worth than a thousand kinsmen.
— EURIPIDES (480–406 B.C.) *Orestes*

Sympathy is a virtue much cultivated by those who are morally uplifted by the sufferings and misfortunes of others.
— OSCAR HAMMLING (1890–)

As man laughs with those that laugh, so he weeps with those that weep; if thou wish me to weep, thou must first shed tears thyself; then thy sorrows will touch me.
— HORACE (65–8 B.C.) *De Arte Poetica*

It is better to be generous than just. It is sometimes better to sympathize instead of trying to understand.
— PIERRE LECOMTE DE NOÜY (1883–1947) *Human Destiny*

TALENT

Doing easily what others find difficult is talent . . . .
— HENRI-FRÉDÉRIC AMIEL (1828–1881) *Journal*

Every man hath his proper gift of God, one after this manner and another after that.
— NEW TESTAMENT: *I Corinthians*, vii, 7

TASTE

Happy is the man possessing
The superior holy blessing
Of a judgment and a taste
Accurate, refined and chaste.
— ARISTOPHANES (444–380 B.C.) *The Frogs*

Love of beauty is Taste. . . . The creation of beauty is Art.
— RALPH WALDO EMERSON (1803–1882)

TEACHER AND TEACHING

A teacher affects eternity; he can never tell where his influence stops.
— HENRY ADAMS (1838–1918) *Education of Henry Adams*

The true teacher defends his pupils against his own personal influence.
— AMOS BRONSON ALCOTT (1799–1888) *Orphic Sayings*

To know how to suggest is the great art of teaching.
— HENRI-FRÉDÉRIC AMIEL (1828–1881) *Journal*

What nobler employment, or more valuable to the state, than that of the man who instructs the rising generation?
— CICERO (106–43 B.C.) *De Divinatione*

The secret of teaching is to appear to have known all your life what you learned this afternoon.
— UNKNOWN

THRIFT

A man's ordinary expenses ought to be but half of his receipts, and if he think to wax rich, but to the third part.
— FRANCIS BACON (1561–1620)

He will always be a slave, who does not know how to live upon a little.
— HORACE (65–8 B.C.) *Epistulae*

Resolve not to be poor; whatever you have, spend less.
— SAMUEL JOHNSON (1709–1784) Boswell's *Life*

Thrift is care and scruple in the spending of one's means. It is not a virtue, and it requires neither skill nor talent.
— IMMANUEL KANT (1724–1804) Lecture

TIME

Go, sir, gallop, and don't forget that the world was made in six days. You can ask me for anything you like except time.
— NAPOLEON BONAPARTE (1769–1821) To one of his aides

Never the time and the place
And the loved one all together!
— ROBERT BROWNING (1812–1889) *Never the Time and Place*

There is no remembrance which time does not obliterate, nor pain which death does not end.
— CERVANTES (1547–1616) *Don Quixote*

For though we sleep or wake, or roam, or ride,
Aye fleets the time, it will no man abide.
— GEOFFREY CHAUCER (1340?–1400) *Canterbury Tales*

Dost thou love life? Then do not squander time, for that is the stuff life is made of.
— BEN FRANKLIN (1706–1790) *Poor Richard's Almanack*

Gather ye rosebuds while ye may,
  Old Time is still a-flying,
And this same flower that smiles today,
  Tomorrow will be dying.
— ROBERT HERRICK (1591–1674) *To the Virgins*

Stand still, you ever moving spheres of heaven,
That time may cease, and midnight never come.
— CHRISTOPHER MARLOWE (1564–1593) *Dr. Faustus*

The time which we have at our disposal every day is elastic; the passions that we feel expand it, those that we inspire contract it; and habit fills up what remains.
— MARCEL PROUST (1871–1922) *Remembrance of Things Past*

Time flies on restless pinions—constant never.
Be constant—and thou chainest time forever.
— JOHANN SCHILLER (1759–1805) *Epigram*

Make use of time, let not advantage slip;
Beauty within itself should not be wasted:
Fair flowers that are not gather'd in their prime,
Rot and consume themselves in little time.
— SHAKESPEARE (1564–1616) *Venus and Adonis*. 129

There is . . . a time to be born, and a time to die; a time to plant, and a time to pluck up that which is planted; A time to kill, and a time to heal; a time to break down, and a time to build up; A time to weep, and a time to laugh; a time to mourn, and a time to dance; . . . A time to love and a time to hate.
— OLD TESTAMENT: *Ecclesiastes*, iii, 1

TOLERANCE AND INTOLERANCE

He knows not how to wink at human frailty,
Or pardon weakness that he never felt.
— JOSEPH ADDISON (1672–1719) *Cato*

Toleration is good for all or it is good for none.
— EDMUND BURKE (1729–1797) Speech, 1773

I have seen gross intolerance shown in support of toleration.
— SAMUEL TAYLOR COLERIDGE (1772–1834) *Biographia*

Give to every other human being every right you claim for yourself.
— ROBERT GREEN INGERSOLL (1833–1899) *Limitations of Toleration*

Shall I ask the brave soldier, who fights by my side
In the cause of mankind, if our creeds agree!
Shall I give up the friend I have valued and tried,
If he kneel not before the same altar with me.
— THOMAS MOORE (1779–1852) *Come, Send Round the Wine*

It is easy to be tolerant when you do not care.
— CLEMENT F. ROGERS (1866–) *Verify Your References*

It is now no more that toleration is spoken of, as if it were by the indulgence of one class of people that another enjoyed the exercise of their inherent rights.
— GEORGE WASHINGTON (1732–1799) Letter to Hebrew Congregation of Newport, R. I.

TRUTH

Truth is within ourselves; it takes no rise
From outward things, whate'er you may believe
There is an inmost centre in us all
Where truth abides in fulness.
— ROBERT BROWNING (1812–1889) *Paracelsus*

Truth, crushed to earth, shall rise again;
  The eternal years of God are hers;
But error, wounded, writhes in pain,
  And dies among his worshippers.
— WILLIAM CULLEN BRYANT (1794–1878) *Living Lost*

'Tis strange, but true; for truth is always strange,—
Stranger than fiction.
— LORD BYRON (1788–1824) *Don Juan*

The greatest friend of truth is Time, her greatest enemy is Prejudice, and her constant companion is Humility.
— CHARLES C. COLTON (1780?–1832) *Lacon*

God offers to every mind its choice between truth and repose. Take which you please—you can never have both.
— RALPH WALDO EMERSON (1803–1882) *Essays*

If the truth hurts most of us so badly that we don't want it told, it hurts even more grievously those who dare to tell it. It is a two-edged sword, often deadly dangerous to the user.
— JUDGE BEN LINDSEY (1869–1943) *Revolt of Modern Youth*

The smallest atom of truth represents some man's bitter toil and agony; for every ponderable chunk of it there is a brave truth-seeker's grave upon some lonely ash-dump and a soul roasting in hell.
— H. L. MENCKEN (1880–1956) *Prejudices*

Truth often suffers more by the heat of its defenders, than from the arguments of its opposers.
— WILLIAM PENN (1644–1718) *Fruits of Solitude*

'Tis not enough your counsel still be true;
Blunt truths more mischief than nice falsehoods do.
— ALEXANDER POPE (1688–1744) *Essay on Criticism*

We know the truth has been
Told over to the world a thousand times;—
But we have had no ears to listen yet
For more than fragments of it; we have heard
A murmur now and then, an echo here
And there.
— EDWIN ARLINGTON ROBINSON (1869–1935) *Captain Orsig*

A thing is not necessarily true because a man dies for it.
— OSCAR WILDE (1854–1900) *Portrait of Mr. W. H.*

That witty and eloquent old Dr. Oliver Wendell Holmes once said . . . "You needn't fear to handle the truth roughly; she is no invalid."
— WOODROW WILSON (1856–1924) Address, 1918

If you shut up truth and bury it under the ground, it will but grow, and gather to itself such explosive power that the day it bursts through, it will blow up everything in its way.
— ÈMILE ZOLA (1840–1902) *J'accuse*

Ye shall know the truth, and the truth shall make you free.
— NEW TESTAMENT: *John*, viii, 32

TYRANNY

I have sworn upon the altar of God eternal hostility against every form of tyranny over the mind of man.
— THOMAS JEFFERSON (1743–1826)

They [the people in lands with dictators] have forgotten the lessons of history that the ultimate failures of dictatorships cost humanity far more than any temporary failures of democracy.
— FRANKLIN D. ROOSEVELT (1882–1945) Address, 1937

Like the form of a seen and unheard prowler,
like a slow and cruel violence,
is the known unspoken menace:
do what we tell you or go hungry;
listen to us or you don't eat.
— CARL SANDBURG (1878–) *The People, Yes*

And the little screaming fact that sounds through all history: repression works only to strengthen and knit the repressed.
— JOHN STEINBECK (1902–) *Grapes of Wrath*

VALOR See COURAGE

VANITY

An ostentatious man will rather relate a blunder or an absurdity he has committed, than be debarred from talking of his own dear person.
— JOSEPH ADDISON (1672–1719)

One will rarely err if extreme actions be ascribed to vanity, ordinary actions to habit, and mean actions to fear.
— FRIEDRICH NIETZSCHE (1844–1900)

Vanity as an impulse has without doubt been of far more benefit to civilization than modesty has ever been.
— WILLIAM E. WOODWARD (1874–) *George Washington*

Vanity of vanities, saith the Preacher, vanity of vanities; all is vanity.
— OLD TESTAMENT: *Ecclesiastes*, i, 2

WAR

In war there are no winners.
— NEVILLE CHAMBERLAIN (1869–1940) Speech, 1938

Little did we guess that what has been called the Century of the Common Man would witness as its outstanding feature more common men killing each other with greater facilities than any other five centuries together in the history of the world.
— WINSTON CHURCHILL (1874–1965) Speech, 1949

If, however, there is to be a war of nerves let us make sure our nerves are strong and are fortified by the deepest convictions of our hearts.
— WINSTON CHURCHILL (1874–1965) Speech, Mar. 31, 1949

I wisht it cud be fixed up, so' th' men that starts th' wars could do th' fightin'.
— FINLEY PETER DUNNE (1867–1936) *War and War Makers*

So long as mankind shall continue to lavish more praise upon its destroyers than upon its benefactors war shall remain the chief pursuit of ambitious minds.
— EDWARD GIBBON (1737–1794) *Decline and Fall of the Roman Empire*

It must be thoroughly understood that the lost land will never be won back by solemn appeals to the good God, nor by hopes in any League of Nations, but only by the force of arms.
— ADOLF HITLER (1889–1945) *Mein Kampf*

If—which God prevent—a new war breaks out, nothing else will await or confront all peoples . . . but appalling destruction and ruin, and this whether they are victor or vanquished.
— POPE JOHN XXIII (1881–1963) July 2, 1959

War is the greatest plague that can afflict mankind. . . . Any scourge is preferable to it.
— MARTIN LUTHER (1483–1546) *Table-Talk*, No. 821

War ought to be the only study of a prince.
— NICCOLO MACHIAVELLI (1469–1527) *The Prince*

They shall not pass.
— MARSHAL HENRI PÉTAIN (1856–1951) Battle of Verdun, 1916

And after the strife of war begins the strife of peace.
— CARL SANDBURG (1878–) *The People, Yes*

And Caesar's spirit, ranging for revenge,
With Ate by his side come hot from hell,
Shall in these confines with a monarch's voice,
Cry "Havoc" and let slip the dogs of war.
— SHAKESPEARE (1564–1616) *Julius Caesar*, III, i, 270

In peace there's nothing so becomes a man
As modest stillness and humility;
But when the blast of war blows in our ears,
Then imitate the action of the tiger:
Stiffen the sinews, summon up the blood.
— SHAKESPEARE (1564–1616) *Henry V*, III, ii, 3

In the arts of life man invents nothing: but in the arts of death he outdoes Nature herself, and produces by chemistry and machinery all the slaughter of plague, pestilence and famine.
— GEORGE BERNARD SHAW (1856–1950) *Man and Superman*, Act III

It [War] is all hell. . . . I look upon war with horror.
— WILLIAM TECUMSEH SHERMAN (1820–1891) Address, 1880

To be prepared for war is one of the most effectual means of preserving peace.
— GEORGE WASHINGTON (1732–1799) Speech, 1790

The war to end wars.
— H. G. WELLS (1860–1946) Attributed

Wars and rumours of wars.
— NEW TESTAMENT: *Matthew*, xxiv, 6

WEATHER

For the man sound in body and serene of mind there is no such thing as bad weather! every sky has its beauty, and storms which whip the blood do but make it pulse more vigorously.
— GEORGE GISSING (1857–1903)

We may achieve climate, but weather is thrust upon us.
— O. HENRY (1862–1910) *Fog in Santone*

Climate is theory. Weather is a condition.
— OLIVER HERFORD (1865–1935)

I wonder that any human being should remain in a cold country who could find room in a warm one.
— THOMAS JEFFERSON (1743–1826) Letter

The fog comes
on little cat feet.
It sits looking
over the harbor and city
on silent haunches
and then, moves on.
— CARL SANDBURG (1878–) *Fog*

When it is evening, ye say, It will be fair weather: for the sky is red. And in the morning, It will be foul weather today: for the sky is red and lowring.
— NEW TESTAMENT: *Matthew*, xvi, 2–3

WIFE

Helmer: Before all else you are a wife and a mother.
Nora: That I no longer believe. I think that before all else I am a human being.
— HENRIK IBSEN (1828–1906) *Doll's House*

If you want peace in the house, do what your wife wants.
— AFRICAN PROVERB

A good wife should be as a looking glass to represent her husband's face and passion; if he be pleasant, she should be merry; if he laugh, she should smile; if he look sad, she should participate of his sorrow.
— PLUTARCH (46?–120?) *Moralia: Advice to a Bride*

She looketh well to the ways of her household, and eateth not the bread of idleness.
— OLD TESTAMENT: *Proverbs*, xxxi, 27

WISDOM

Wise men, though all laws were abolished, would lead the same lives.
— ARISTOPHANES (444–380 B.C.)

Make wisdom your provision for the journey from youth to old age, for it is a more certain support than all other possessions.
— BIAS (*f.* 570 B.C.)

A man doesn't begin to attain wisdom until he recognizes that he is no longer indispensable.
— ADMIRAL RICHARD E. BYRD (1888–1957) *Alone*

Wisdom is full of pity, and thereby
Men pay for too much wisdom with much pain.
— EURIPIDES (480–406 B.C.) *Electra*

Wisdom is not finally tested in the schools,
Wisdom cannot be passed from one having it to another not having it,
Wisdom is of the soul, is not susceptible of proof, is its own proof.
— WALT WHITMAN (1819–1892) *Song of the Open Road*

The fear of the Lord is the beginning of wisdom.
— OLD TESTAMENT: *Psalms*, cxi, 10

WOOING See COURTSHIP

WRITING

I don't wait for moods. You accomplish nothing if you do that. Your mind must know it has got to get down to work.
— PEARL BUCK (1892–) *Reader's Digest*

Writing a long and substantial book is like having a friend and companion at your side, to whom you can always turn for comfort and amusement, and whose society becomes more attractive as a new and widening field of interest is lighted in the mind.
— WINSTON CHURCHILL (1874–1965) *Gathering Storm*

Composition is for the most part, an effort of slow diligence and steady perseverence, to which the mind is dragged by necessity or resolution.
— SAMUEL JOHNSON (1709–1784) *The Adventurer*

The chief glory of every people arises from its authors.
— SAMUEL JOHNSON (1709–1784) *Preface to Dictionary*

The writers who have nothing to say are the ones you can buy; the others have too high a price.
— WALTER LIPPMANN (1889–) *Preface to Politics*

The impulse to create beauty is rather rare in literary men . . . Far ahead of it comes the yearning to make money. And after the yearning to make money comes the yearning to make a noise.
— H. L. MENCKEN (1880–1956) *Prejudices*

YOUTH

Young men are fitter to invent than to judge; fitter for execution than for counsel; and fitter for new projects than for settled business.
— FRANCIS BACON (1561–1626) *Of Youth and Age*

They shall not grow old, as we that are left grow old;
Age shall not weary them, nor the years condemn.
At the going down of the sun, and in the morning,
We shall remember them.
— LAURENCE BINYON (1869–1943) *For the Fallen*

Blow out, you bugles, over the rich Dead!
There's none of these so lonely and poor of old,
But dying, has made us rarer gifts than gold.
These laid the world away: poured out the red
Sweet wine of youth; gave up the years to be
Of work and joy, and that unhoped serene
That men call age, and those who would have been
Their sons, they gave their immortality.
— RUPERT BROOKE (1887–1915) *The Dead* (1914)

Ah! happy years! once more who would not be a boy!
— LORD BYRON (1788–1824) *Childe Harolde*

Youth is to all the glad season of life; but often only by what it hopes, not by what it attains, or what it escapes.
— THOMAS CARLYLE (1795–1881) *Essays*

As I approve of a youth that has something of the old man in him, so I am no less pleased with an old man that has something of the youth. He that follows this rule may be old in body, but can never be so in mind.
— CICERO (106–43 B.C.) *Cato*

There is a feeling of Eternity in youth which makes us amends for everything. To be young is to be as one of the Immortals.
— WILLIAM HAZLITT (1778–1830) *Table Talk*

When all the world is young, lad,
And all the trees are green;
And every goose a swan, lad,
And every lass a queen;
Then hey, for boot and horse, lad,
And round the world away;
Young blood must have its course, lad,
And every dog his day.
— CHARLES KINGSLEY (1819–1875) *Water Babies*

How different from the present man was the youth of earlier days!
— OVID (43 B.C.–A.D. 18) *Heroides*

We think our fathers fools, so wise we grow;
Our wiser sons, no doubt, will think us so.
— ALEXANDER POPE (1688–1744) *Essay on Criticism*

My salad days;
When I was green in judgement.
— SHAKESPEARE (1564–1616) *Antony and Cleopatra*, I, v, 73

Through all the lying days of my youth
I swayed my leaves and flowers in the sun;
Now I may wither into the truth.
— WILLIAM BUTLER YEATS (1865–1939) *The Coming of Wisdom with Time*

Youth is not rich in time; it may be poor;
Part with it as with money, sparing; pay
No moment but in purchase of its worth,
And what it's worth, ask death-beds; they can tell.
— EDWARD YOUNG (1684–1765) *Night Thoughts*

GLOSSARY OF MYTHOLOGY

The mythological terms most commonly encountered, chiefly those of Greek or Roman origin, are to be found in the main vocabulary of the dictionary. These are indicated here by cross reference.

A·a·ru (ä·a′rōō) *Egyptian* **1.** Peaceful fields in which were located Ra's throne, deities, and souls of the blessed dead. **2.** Peaceful crop-producing fields in the nether world of Osiris. Also *Yaaru.* Also **A·a′lu** (-lōō).
Aar·vak (ôr′väk) *Norse* One of the horses of the sun; the dawn.
Ach·e·ron (ak′ə·ron) See main vocabulary.
A·chil·les (ə·kil′ēz) See main vocabulary.
A·cis (ā′sis) *Greek* See GALATEA (def. 2).
Ac·tae·on (ak·tē′ən) See main vocabulary.
A·dad (ä′däd) *Babylonian* See RAMMAN.
A·da·pa (ä′dä·pä) *Babylonian* A mortal summoned to heaven for breaking the south wind's wings. There he is presented with the bread and water of life (immortality) but rejects it on Ea's advice to beware the offer.
A·di·ti (ə·dē′tē) *Hindu* Personification of the female principle in creation, variously regarded as the mother of the world, mother of the gods, supporter of the earth or sky, or the wife or mother of Vishnu.
A·dit·yas (ə·dēt′yəz) *Hindu* The seven sons of Aditi, a group of divine moral personifications.
Ad·me·tus (ad·mē′təs) See main vocabulary.
A·don·is (ə·do′nis, ə·dōn′is) See main vocabulary.
A·dras·tus (ə·dras′təs) See main vocabulary.
Æ·gir (ē′jər, ā′jər) See main vocabulary.
Ae·gis·thus (ē·jis′thəs) See main vocabulary.
Ae·ne·as (i·nē′əs) See main vocabulary.
Ae·o·lus (ē′ə·ləs) See main vocabulary.
Aes·cu·la·pi·us (es′kyə·lā′pē·əs) See main vocabulary.
A·esh·ma (ä·esh′mə) *Persian* The most malignant of the Zoroastrian demons; a fiend of lust and outrage.
Ae·sir (ā′sir, ē′-) See main vocabulary.
Ag·a·mem·non (ag′ə·mem′nən) See main vocabulary.
A·gas·tya (ə·gäs′tyə) *Hindu* A legendary holy man, son of the two gods Mitra and Varuna, and revered as the author of several Vedic hymns. He is noted for asceticism and for miracles like halting the growth of the Vindya mountains and drinking up the ocean.
Ag·dis·tis (ag·dis′tis) *Greek & Roman* A hermaphrodite whose male organs were severed by the gods in abhorrence.
A·gla·ia (ə·glā′ə) See main vocabulary.
Ag·ni (äg′nē) See main vocabulary.
A·hi (ä′hē) *Hindu* The dragon from whose body the waters, blood, and sap of life were released by Indra when he killed it with a thunderbolt: also *Vritra.*
a·him·sa (ə·him′sä) See main vocabulary.
Ah·ri·man (ä′ri·mən) See main vocabulary.
A·hu·ra Maz·da (ä′hōō·rä mäz′dä) See ORMUZD in main vocabulary.
Ai·lill mac Ma·tach (a′lil mäk·mä′täk) *Irish* The king of Connacht, husband of Medb, and father of Findabair in the Ulster Cycle. He is a henpecked husband in the *Táin Bó Cuáilgne.*
Ái·ne (ôn′yə) *Irish* A banshee of Munster, legendary mother of Gerald, Earl of Munster, and primitively a minor fertility goddess.
A·jax (ā′jaks) See main vocabulary.
Akh·tya (äk′tyə) *Persian* Chief of the sorcerers (yatus) of Zoroastrianism.
A·ku·pa·ra (a′kōō·pä′rə) *Hindu* The tortoise upon which the earth rests.
Al·ber·ich (äl′bər·ikh) See main vocabulary.
Al·burz (äl′bərz) *Persian* The sacred mountain of light, root of all other mountains.
Al·ces·tis (al·ses′tis) See main vocabulary.
al·far (äl′vär) *Germanic* The elves, some of whom dwell in their special realm (Alfheim) and some beneath the earth.
Al·la·tu (ä·lä′tōō, al′ä·tōō) *Sumerian & Babylonian* Another name for ERESHKIGAL.
A·lo·a·dae (ä·lō′ə·dē) *Greek* The giants Ephialtes and Otus, twin sons of Poseidon, who made war upon the gods, threatening to pile Mount Pelion upon Olympus and Mount Ossa upon Pelion to reach them. They were killed by Apollo.
Al·viss (äl′vis) *Norse* The earth-dwelling dwarf who sued for the hand of Thor's daughter Thrud, but was defeated in a riddling game.
A·ma·dán (ô′mə·dôn) *Irish* The fairy fool, whose touch produces incurable crippling or deformity.
A·mae·thon (ä·mī′thon) *Welsh* A son of Dôn in *Kulwch and Olwen* (see MABINOGION), a great tiller of fields. He is probably primitively an agricultural god or culture hero.
A·mal·thae·a (ə·mal′thē·ə) See main vocabulary.
A·mar·a·va·ti (ə·mär′ə·vä′tē) *Hindu* The capital of Indra's heaven, a blissful city reserved for those who do penance or sacrifice, or who die in battle.
A·ma·ter·a·su O·mi·ka·mi (ä·mä·ter·ä·sōō ô·mē·kä·mē) *Japanese* The sun goddess.
Ama-tsu-ma·ra (ä·mä·tsōō·mä·rä) *Japanese* The one-eyed blacksmith god who helped make the mirror that was used to entice Amaterasu Omikami out of a cave.
Am·a·zon (am′ə·zon, -zən) See main vocabulary.
am·bro·sia (am·brō′zhə, -zhē·ə) See main vocabulary.
A·men (ä′mən) *Egyptian* See AMON.
A·men·ti (ə·men′tē) *Egyptian* **1.** The underworld, or a hazardous stream leading to it. **2.** A goddess of the underworld.
A·me·sha Spen·tas (ə·mē′shə spen′təs) *Persian* The archangels or divine attendants of Ormuzd.
Am·mit (ä′mit) *Egyptian* A frightful hybrid monster, called the Devourer, present at the "weighing of souls" to eat all those dead whose hearts did not exactly balance the feather of truth on the scales of judgment.
A·mon (ä′mən) *Egyptian* Originally, a little-known local god of Thebes. Amon eventually merged with Ra to become the supreme deity, Amon-Ra: also *Amen.* Also **Am′mon, A′mun.**
A·mon-Ra (ä′mən-rä′) *Egyptian* The supreme deity, proclaimed king of the gods; actually a combination in which the lesser god Amon assumed the qualities of the primeval sun-god Ra. Also **A′men-Ra′, A′men-Re′** (-rā), **A′mon-Re′.**
Am·phi·a·ra·us (am′fī·ərā′yōōs) *Greek* One of the Seven Against Thebes.
am·ri·ta (äm·rē′tə) *Hindu* The water of life that confers immortality.
An (än) *Sumerian* God of heaven.
A·na·hi·ta (än′ə·hē′tə) *Persian* The great mother or fertility goddess of Zoroastrianism and earlier Iranian mythology.
A·nan ga (ə·näng′gə) *Hindu* The bodiless: an epithet of Kama, the god of love.
An·an·ta (ə·nän′tə) *Hindu* The infinite: an epithet of Vishnu and several other divinities.
An·chi·ses (an·kī′sēz) See main vocabulary.
An·drom·a·che (an·drom′ə·kē) See main vocabulary.
An·drom·e·da (an·drom′ə·də) See main vocabulary.
And·var·i (änd·vär′ē) See main vocabulary.
An·gra Main·yu (äng′grə mīn′yōō) *Persian* See AHRIMAN.
An·gur-bo·da (än′gōōr·bō′dä) *Norse* The giantess of Utgard, mother of the Fenris wolf, the Midgard serpent, and Helle.
An·gus Og (eng′gəs ōg) See main vocabulary.
An·hur (än′hər) *Egyptian* Originally a local sun-god, his identification with Shu as Anhur-Shu evoked great popularity; also thought to be Ra personified as a warrior. Also **An′her.**
An·hur-Shu (än′hər·shōō′) *Egyptian* The manifestation of the sun-god Znhur in possession of the power and influence of the higher-ranking air-god Shu.
ankh (angk) See main vocabulary.
An·kou (än′kōō) *Breton* The ghost of the last person to have died in the parish during a year, which drives a cart to the house of one about to die, along with two spectral helpers.
An·nwf·n (än·nōō′vən) *Welsh* The paradisiacal afterworld, variously described as a group of fortified islands or a great revolving castle on an island. Also **An·nwn** (än′nōōn).
An·sa (än′sə) *Hindu* One of the seven sons of Aditi, personifying bounty.
An·shar (än′shär) *Babylonian* A sky-deity born of Lahmu and Lahamu.
An·tae·us (an·tē′əs) See main vocabulary.

An·tu (än′to͞o) *Sumerian* A consort of the Babylonian sky-god Anu.
A·nu (a′no͞o) See main vocabulary.
A·nu·bis (ə·no͞o′bis, ə·nyo͞o′-) See main vocabulary.
A·nu·ket (ä·no͞o′ket) *Egyptian* Nile-goddess worshiped at Elephantine; wife of Khnum.
A·nun·na·ki (ä·no͞o·nä′kē) *Sumerian & Babylonian* Attendant gods. In Babylonian mythology they appeared most often as gods of earth, on a lower tier than the Igigi.
A·pe·pi (ä·pe′pē) *Egyptian* A night-serpent who led the underworld attack on Ra's passage each evening, but who was always overthrown. Also **Aph·o·bis** (ä′fō·bis).
Aph·ro·di·te (af′rə·dī′tē) See main vocabulary.
A·pis (ā′pis, ä′-) See main vocabulary.
A·pol·lo (ə·pol′ō) See main vocabulary.
Ap·su (ap′so͞o) *Babylonian* The primeval sweet-water abyss personified as the husband of Tiamat.
A·rach·ne (ə·rak′nē) See main vocabulary.
A·ral·lu (ä·rä′lo͞o) *Sumerian & Babylonian* The nether world.
A·ra·wn (ä·roun′) *Welsh* The lord and king of Annwfn.
Ar·ca·di·an hind (är·kā′dē·ən) *Greek* The hind that Hercules captured, after a year's chase, as his third labor.
Ar·es (âr′ēz) See main vocabulary.
Ar·go·naut (är′gə·nôt) See main vocabulary.
Ar·gus (är′gəs) *Greek* **1.** See main vocabulary. **2.** Odysseus's dog, who recognized him on his return from his wanderings.
Ar·i·ad·ne (ar′ē·ad′nē) See main vocabulary.
Ar·i·an·rhod (är′ē·än′ro͝od) *Welsh* A beautiful goddess, daughter of Dôn and mother of the twins Llew Llaw Gyffes and Dylan, to whom she was deeply inimical.
Ar·is·tae·us (ar′is·tē′əs) See main vocabulary.
Ar·ju·na (är·jo͞o′nə) *Hindu* The most prominent of the Pandavas, a great warrior and archer and favorite of Krishna.
Ar·te·mis (är′tə·mis) See main vocabulary.
A·ru·ru (ä·ro͞o′ro͞o) *Babylonian* The goddess who fashioned the ill-fated hero, Enkidu, from mud.
Ar·ya·man (är·yä′mən) *Hindu* One of the seven sons of Aditi, personifying bosom comradeship.
A·sag (ä′säg) *Sumerian* Demon of disease and sickness, dwelling in the Kur, which was attacked and destroyed by Ninurta.
As·a·pur·na (ä·sä·po͝or′nə) *Hindu* An earth or mother goddess; literally, she who fulfills desires. Also **A·sa·pur·a** (ä·sä·po͝or′ə), **A·sa·pur·i** (ä·sä·po͝or′ē).
As·can·i·us (as·kā′nē·əs) See main vocabulary.
As·cle·pi·us (as·klē′pē·əs) See main vocabulary.
As·gard (as′gärd, äs′-) See main vocabulary.
Ash·gir·bab·bar (äsh′gûr·bä′bär) *Sumerian* See NANNA.
A·shur (ä′sho͝or) See main vocabulary.
Ask (äsk) See main vocabulary.
As·tar·te (as·tär′tē) See main vocabulary.
As·vins (äs′vins) *Hindu* Twin cosmic gods, variously the deities of dawn, heaven and earth, day and night, sun and moon, morning and evening, or twilight. Also **As′wins.**
A·syn·jur (ä′sün·yo͞or) *Norse* The goddesses collectively.
At·a·lan·ta (at′ə·lan′tə) See main vocabulary.
A·tar (ä·tär′) *Persian* The fire god, a son of Ormuzd.
A·te (ā′tē) See main vocabulary.
A·tem (ä′tem) *Egyptian* See ATMU.
A·ten (ä′tən) *Egyptian* The solar disk itself, worshiped as the supreme (but not sole) deity during the reign of the so-called heretic king, Akhenaton. Also **A′ton.**
Ath·a·mas (ath′ə·mas) See main vocabulary.
A·the·na (ə·thē′nə) See main vocabulary.
At·las (at′ləs) See main vocabulary.
At·li (ät′lē) See main vocabulary.
at·man (ät′mən) See main vocabulary.
At·mu (ät′mo͞o) *Egyptian* Ra as the setting sun: also *Atem, Tem, Temu.*
A·tra·ha·sia (ä′trə·hä′sis) *Babylonian* A Noah-like mortal who survived a flood sent by the gods by building and loading a large boat.
A·tre·us (ā′trē·əs, ā′tro͞os) See main vocabulary.
At·tis (at′is) See main vocabulary.
A·tum (a′to͞om) *Egyptian* An ancient god who rose out of Nun, the primeval ocean, and masturbated to form the gods Shu and Tefnut. See also PTAH.
Aud·hum·la (oud·ho͞om′lä) *Norse* The monstrous cow, formed of the cold from Niflheim and the heat from Muspellheim, that nourished Ymir, the first giant.
Au·ge·an stables (ô·jē′ən) See main vocabulary.
Au·tol·y·cus (ô·tol′i·kəs) See main vocabulary.
A·va·lo·ki·ta (ə·vä·lō·kē′tə) *Hindu* A Buddhist god of mercy and compassion; the Bodhisattva whose face is turned in every direction in order to save everyone. Also **A·va·lo·ki·tes·va·ra** (ə·vä·lō·kē′tes·vä′rə).
av·a·tar (av′ə·tär′) See main vocabulary.

Ba (bä) See main vocabulary.
Ba·ba (bä′bə) *Sumerian* A fertility goddess and consort of Ningirsu.
Ba·ba Ya·ga (bä′bə yä·gä′) *Russian* A forest ogress that eats human flesh, preferably that of young children.
Bab·bar (bä′bär) *Sumerian* Ancient sun-god; equivalent of the Babylonian *Shamash.*
Bac·chus (bäk′əs) See main vocabulary.
Badb (bä′ib) See main vocabulary.
Bah·ram·gor (bä·räm·gôr′) *Persian* A hero-prince of many tales, both Persian and Indian. Also **Bah·ram Gur** (bä·räm′ go͝or).
Bak·ha·u (bäk′hä·o͞o) *Egyptian* The mountain that supported the sky and heaven at their eastern end. See MANU.
Bal·der (bôl′dər) See main vocabulary.
Ba·li (bä′lē) *Hindu* The king of the Daityas, favored by the gods for his goodness.
Ba·lin (bä·lēn′) *Hindu* A monkey king, said to have been born from his mother's hair.
Ba·lor (bä′lôr) See main vocabulary.
Ban·ba (ban′bə) *Irish* A queen of the Tuatha Dé Danann, wife of King Mac Cuill. She wished her name to be given to the land of Ireland by the invading Milesians.
Bast (bäst) *Egyptian* A cat-headed goddess of pleasure and protectress against disease. Mummified cats were buried in her sacred city Bubastis. Also **Bas·tet** (bäs′tit).
Battle of the Trees *Welsh* A battle between Arawn and Amaethon in which trees take part as warriors. It is described in the poem *Câd Goddeu,* and is thought to be related to the ancient Celtic tree alphabet and the druidic mysteries.
Ba·u (bä′o͞o) *Babylonian* A mother-goddess and healer.
Bau·cis (bô′sis) See main vocabulary.
Bé·find (bā′find) *Celtic* One of the three fairies present at the birth of every child, who predict its future and endow it with gifts. In Irish mythology she was a sister of Bóann.
Be·lit-se·ri (bā′lit·sâr′ē) *Sumerian & Babylonian* Wife of Namtar and scribe of the nether world.
Bel·ler·o·phon (bə·ler′ə·fon) See main vocabulary.
Bel·lo·na (bə·lō′nə) See main vocabulary.
Bel-Mer·o·dach (bāl′mer′ō·dak) *Babylonian* See MARDUK.
Bel·tane (byel′tə·nə) See main vocabulary.
Bel·tu (bāl′to͞o) *Babylonian* A mother-goddess of high rank.
ber·ser·ker (bûr′sûr′kər) See main vocabulary.
Bes (bes) See main vocabulary.
Bha·ga (bä′gə) *Hindu* One of the seven sons of Aditi, personifying good luck, wealth, and bounty.
Bhag·a·vad-Gi·ta (bä′gä·väd·gē′tə) See main vocabulary.
Bhai·ra·va (bī·rä′və) *Hindu* Any of the eight fearful forms of Siva, worshiped as a dog, drummer, or stone.
Bhai·ra·vi (bī·rä′vē) *Hindu* See DEVI.
Bhi·ma (bē′mə) *Hindu* A strong, courageous, and coarse Pandava prince, son of the wind god Vayu.
Bhu·de·vi (bo͞o·dev′ē) See DHARTI MAI.
Bi·frost (bēf′rost) See main vocabulary.
Bi·le (bil′ə) *Irish* A king of Spain, one of the Milesians.
bi·li (bil′ē) *Celtic* Sacred trees, believed to be the habitations of gods and spirits.
Bish·a·mon·ten (bēsh·ä·môn·ten) *Japanese* The god of riches.
Blod·en·wedd (blod′ən·wəd) *Welsh* The dawn goddess.
Bó·ann (bō′ən) *Irish* The queen of the Tuatha Dé Danann, wife of Dagda, and mother of Angus Og.
Bodb (bōv) *Irish* The eldest son of Dagda, and himself later chosen king of the Tuatha Dé Danann.
Bo·dhi·satt·va (bō′di·sat′wə) See main vocabulary.
Book of the Dead *Egyptian* A collection of magic formulas and incantations written on papyrus and interred with the deceased to insure his safe passage through the underworld.
Bo·re·as (bôr′ē·əs, bō′rē-) See main vocabulary.
Bo tree (bō) See main vocabulary.
Bra·gi (brä′gē) See main vocabulary.
Brah·ma (brä′mə) See main vocabulary.
Brah·ma·pur·a (brä′mä·po͝or′ə) *Hindu* The heaven and city of Brahma, situated on the summit of Mount Meru.
Bran (brän) See main vocabulary.
Bran·stock (brän′stôk′) *Germanic* An oak growing through the roof of the Volsungs' hall. Only Sigmund could withdraw the sword that Odin had thrust into its trunk.
Bres (bresh) See main vocabulary.
Bric·ri·u (brē′ə·kro͞o) *Irish* A warrior who appears in some tales as an inciter of bloodshed among the great champions of Ireland Loegaire Buadac, Conall Cearneac, and Cuchulain, but in another as an honored poet.
Brig·id (brij′id) See main vocabulary.
Bri·has·pa·ti (brē·häs·pä′tē) *Hindu* The chaplain of the gods, the lord of prayer, and wisdom incarnate. Also **Brah·man·as·pa·ti** (brä·män·äs·pä′tē).
Bri·se·is (brī·sē′is) See main vocabulary.
Bris·ing·a·men (bris′ing·gä·men′) *Germanic* The magic necklace made by the Svartalfaheim dwarfs for Freya. Loki stole it, but Heimdall recovered it after the gods had engaged in a shape-shifting contest.

Brun·hild (brōōn′hild, *Ger.* brōōn′hilt) See main vocabulary.
Brünn·hil·de (brün·hil′də) See main vocabulary.
Bryn·hild (brün′hilt) See main vocabulary.
Bu·ri (bü′rə) *Germanic* The progenitor of the gods.
Bush·yas·ta (bŏŏsh·yäs′tə) *Persian* The yellow demon of lethargy and sloth.
Bu·to (byōō′tō) *Egyptian* A protective goddess of Lower Egypt, portrayed as a cobra.

Ca·bir·i (kə·bir′ē) *Greek* Deities, perhaps Phoenician in origin, worshiped in many parts of the ancient world.
Câd Goddeu (kŏŏd god′ə) *Welsh* See BATTLE OF THE TREES.
Cad·mus (kad′məs) See main vocabulary.
Cae·ne·us (kē′nē·əs) *Greek* A Lapith who had been changed from a woman to a man, and made invulnerable to wounds. He worshiped only his own spear, and Zeus in anger caused him to be buried in fir trees by the centaurs.
Caill·e·ac (kal′yäk) *Celtic* Personification of the last sheaf as the embodiment of the field spirits; literally, old woman.
Cal·li·o·pe (kə·lī′ə·pē) See main vocabulary.
Cal·lis·to (kə·lis′tō) See main vocabulary.
Cal·y·don·i·an boar (kal′i·dō′nē·ən) See main vocabulary.
Ca·lyp·so (kə·lip′sō) See main vocabulary.
Ca·no·pic Chest (kə·nō′pik) *Egyptian* A container into which the four Canopic Jars were inserted, and which was guarded by the goddesses Isis, Nephthys, Neith and Selket.
Canopic Jars See main vocabulary.
Cap·a·neus (kap′ə·nōōs, -nyōōs, kə·pā′nē·əs) *Greek* One of the Seven Against Thebes.
Car·de·a (kär·dē′ə) *Roman* The goddess of door-hinges and protectress of children against vampire-witches.
Car·men·ta (kär·men′tə) *Roman* The goddess of prophecy and of healing. She followed her son Evander into Italy and changed the Greek alphabet into the Roman.
Car·ne·a (kär·nē′ə) **1.** *Roman* The goddess of physical health. **2.** *Greek* An important Spartan festival in honor of Apollo.
Cas·san·dra (kə·san′drə) See main vocabulary.
Cas·si·o·pe·ia (kas′ē·ə·pē′ə) See main vocabulary.
Cas·tor and Pol·lux (kas′tər, käs′-; pol′əks) See main vocabulary.
Cath·bad (käth′bŏŏd) *Irish* The chief druid of Ulster in the reign of Conchobar.
Ce·crops (sē′krops) See main vocabulary.
cen·taur (sen′tôr) See main vocabulary.
Ceph·a·lus (sē′fə·ləs) *Greek* The husband of Procris, daughter of Cecrops, with whom he became reconciled after each had been unfaithful, only to kill her by error as she jealously spied on him while he was hunting.
Ce·pheus (sē′fyōōs, -fē·əs) See main vocabulary.
Cer·ber·us (sûr′bər·əs) See main vocabulary.
Cer·co·pes (sûr·kō′pēz) *Greek* A race of apelike but human pygmies who were punished for trying to steal the weapons of Hercules and trying to trick Zeus.
Ce·res (sir′ēz) See main vocabulary.
Chan·di (chän′dē) *Hindu* See DEVI.
Chang Fei (chäng fā) *Chinese* A god of butchers, eight feet tall with a panther's head, a swallow's chin, and a voice of thunder.
Chang Hsien (chäng shē·en) *Chinese* A patron of child-bearing women.
Chang Kuo (chäng kōō·ô) *Chinese* One of the Eight Immortals of Taoism, a clever old man riding backwards on a white donkey. Also **Chang Kuo Lao** (lou).
Char·on (kâr′ən, kar′-) See main vocabulary.
Cha·ryb·dis (kə·rib′dis) See main vocabulary.
Ch'eng Huang (cheng hwäng) *Chinese* God of the ramparts, city walls, moats, and ditches, and spiritual magistrate of the people.
Cheng Wu (cheng wōō) *Chinese* The guardian of the North in Taoist lore.
Chi·me·ra (kə·mir′ə-, kī-) See main vocabulary.
Chi·ron (kī′ron) See main vocabulary.
Chit·ra·gup·ta (chēt·rä·gŏŏp′tə) *Hindu* The recorder of vices and cirtues, and the judge who sends men to heaven or hell.
Chry·se·is (krī·sē′əs) *Greek* See main vocabulary.
Churning of the Ocean *Hindu* A joint project on the part of the gods and demons to recover the amrita lost at the deluge; they churned the milk-white ocean for a thousand years, after throwing in specimens of all the plants in the world, and reproduced amrita after producing all manner of things including Parijata, Surabhi, and Varuni.
Chy·a·va·na (chē·ä·vä′nə) *Hindu* An ancient sage noted for having a faithful young wife.
Cia·ban (kē′vən) *Irish* A hero who was banished from the Fianna because of his charm for women and the jealousy of his comrades. He won Clíodna's love and carried her off, only to have her drowned by a huge wave.
Cir·ce (sûr′sē) See main vocabulary.
Cli·o (klī′ō) See main vocabulary.
Clí·od·na (klē′ə·nə) *Irish* Daughter of the chief druid of Manannán mac Lir, lord of the sea.
Cod·rus (kod′rəs) *Greek* The last king of Athens, who deliberately gave his life when the oracle said the war with the Dorians would be won by the side whose king died.
Co·mus (kō′məs) See main vocabulary.
Con·all Céar·ne·ac (kun′əl kyär′näk) *Irish* One of the three first champions of Ulster and a cousin of Cuchulain.
Con·cho·bar mac Nes·sa (krōō′khŏŏr mäk·nes′ə) *Irish* King of Ulster about the beginning of the Christian era, uncle and fosterer of Cuchulain.
Con·cor·di·a (kon·kôr′dē·ə) See main vocabulary.
Con·la (kŏŏn′lə) *Irish* Son of Cuchulain, killed by his own father in ignorance.
Con·sen·tes Di·i (kon·sen′tēz dī′ī) *Roman* The twelve major deities, six male and six female, who formed the council of Jupiter. They include Juno, Minerva, Sumanus, Vulcan, Saturn, Mars, and six others whose identities are not certain. The council was Etruscan in origin.
Con·sus (kon′səs) *Roman* An ancient god of good counsel, secret deliberation, the stored harvest, and the underworld.
Cor·mac Conn·lon·ges (kôr′môk kōn′lĭj·əz) *Irish* Son of Conchobar mac Nessa who went into hiding to protest the killing of the sons of Usnech, and was murdered on his way to assume the kingship of Ulster.
Cor·mac mac Airt (kôr′môk mäk′ärt) *Irish* A king famous for his wisdom, generosity, and good rule. He is now thought to be a historical ruler of the late third century.
cor·nu·co·pi·a (kôr′nə·kō′pē·ə) See main vocabulary.
Cor·ri·gan (kôr′i·gən) *Breton* A female fairy thought to have been an ancient druid, and hence malicious toward the Christian clergy.
Cot·yt·to (kô·tē′tō) *Greek* The great mother goddess of Thrace, whose festival was notorious for its lewdness. Her cult spread throughout Greece and Italy. Also **Cot·ys** (kô′tēs).
Cro·nus (krō′nəs) See KRONOS in main vocabulary.
Cuch·ul·ain (kŏŏ·khul′yən) See main vocabulary.
Cu·pid (kyōō′pid) See main vocabulary.
Cu·re·tes (kyōō′rə·tēz) *Greek* A group of demigods associated with the infant Zeus.
Cú Roi (kōō rē) *Irish* A great wizard of southern Ireland to whom the three champions of Ulster went for judgment.
Cwn An·nw·fn (kōōn′ ä·nōō′vən) *Welsh* The hounds that took part in raids on this world by inhabitants of Annwfn.
Cyb·e·le (sib′ə·lē) See main vocabulary.
Cy·clops (sī′klops) See main vocabulary.
Cyn·thi·a (sin′thē·ə) See main vocabulary.
Cyth·e·re·a (sith′ə·rē′ə) See main vocabulary.

Dac·tyls (dak′tilz) *Greek* The wonder-working smiths who dwelt on Mount Ida and were connected with the Phrygian cult of Rhea.
Daed·a·lus (ded′ə·ləs) See main vocabulary.
Dag·da (däg′də) See main vocabulary.
Daire mac Fiach·na (dir′ə mäk·firkh′nə) *Irish* A chief of Ulster, owner of the brown bull of Cuáilgne, and cause of the war described in the *Táin Bó Cuáilgne.*
Dak·sha (däk′shä) *Hindu* One of the seven sons of Aditi, personifying dexterity and skill.
Dam·ki·na (däm·kē′nə) *Babylonian* Consort of Ea; mother of Marduk.
Dam·o·cles (dam′ə·klēz) See main vocabulary.
Da·mon and Pyth·i·as (dā′mən; pith′ē·əs) See main vocabulary.
Dan·a·e (dan′i·ē) See main vocabulary.
Da·na·i·des (də·nā′ə·dēz) See main vocabulary.
Dan·a·us (dan′ē·əs) See main vocabulary.
Dan·u (thän′ōō) See main vocabulary.
Daph·ne (daf′nē) See main vocabulary.
Dar·da·nus (där′də·nəs) See main vocabulary.
Dech·tir·e (dekh′tə·rə) *Irish* Sister of Conchobar and mother of Cuchulain after supernatural impregnation by Lug.
De·ia·ni·ra (dē′yə·nī′rə) See main vocabulary.
Deir·dre (dir′drə) See main vocabulary.
Del·phic oracle (del′fik) See main vocabulary.
De·me·ter (di·mē′tər) See main vocabulary.
Deu·ca·li·on (dōō·kā′lē·ən, dyōō-) See main vocabulary.
de·va (dev′ə) See main vocabulary.
Dev·a·ki (dev·ä′kē) *Hindu* The mother of Krishna, who conceived him from one of Vishnu's black hairs that he placed in her womb.
Dev·i (dev′ē) See main vocabulary.
Dhar·ma (där′mə) See main vocabulary.
Dhar·ti Mai (där′tē mī) *Hindu* The earth goddess who supports human, animal, and vegetable life, and is present everywhere in the ground: also *Bhudevi.*
Di·an·a (dī·an′ə) See main vocabulary.
Di·an·cecht (dē′ən·khäkht) *Irish* A clever physician of the Tuatha Dé Danann.

Diar·muid (dir′məd) *Irish* In the Finn Cycle, the young man who eloped with Grainne, promised bride of Fionn.
Di·do (dī′dō) See main vocabulary.
Dil·mun (dil′mən) *Sumerian* A land of paradise lacking sweet water. This is supplied by Enki, the water-god.
Di·o·ne (dī·ō′nē) See main vocabulary.
Di·o·ny·sus (dī·ə·nī′səs) See main vocabulary.
Di·os·cu·ri (dī′ə·skyōō′rī) See main vocabulary.
Dis (dis) See main vocabulary.
Do·do·na (dō·dō′nə) See main vocabulary.
Don (dun) *Welsh* The mother of Arianrhod, Gwydion, and other personages in the *Mabinogion*, interpreted as a fertility goddess and identified with the Irish goddess Danu.
Do·nar (dō′när) See main vocabulary.
dry·ad (drī′əd, -ad) See main vocabulary.
Du·am·u·tef (dōō·äm′ə·tef) *Egyptian* Son of Horus whose jackal-headed image serves as a stopper for the Canopic Jar containing the mummified stomach he has been assigned to guard.
Du·at (dōō·wät′) *Egyptian* Twelve regions of the underworld, representing the hours of night, through which Ra's boat passes from west to east despite opposing demons: also *Tuat.*
Du·mu·zi (dōō′mə·zē) *Sumerian* A shepherd-god who was chosen by his wife, Inanna, to be her substitute in the nether world.
Dur·ga (dŏŏr′gə) See DEVI.
Dval·in (dväl′in) *Germanic* **1.** The dwarf who invented runes. **2.** One of the four stags who grazed on the tree Yggdrasil.
dver·gar (dver′gär) *Norse* The dwarfs, formed by the gods from maggots in the flesh of the giant Ymir.
Dy·a·us (dē·ä′əs) *Hindu* The sky god and father whose offspring included the Adityas, Agni, Asvins, Parjanya, Surya, Indra, and others.
Dy·av·a·prith·i·vi (dē·ä′vä·prēt′ə·vē) *Hindu* Heaven and earth as one deity.
Dyl·an (dil′ən) *Welsh* One of the twin sons of Arianrhod, interpreted as a sea god or the waves of the sea.

E·a (ā′ä) See main vocabulary.
E·a·ba·ni (ā′ä·bä′nē) *Babylonian* Another name for ENKIDU.
E·chid·na (ā·chid′nə) *Greek* The sister of Geryon, half woman and half serpent, and mother of many monsters like the Chimera, Cerberus, Scylla, the Nemean lion, and others.
Ech·o (ek′ō) See main vocabulary.
Ei·lei·thy·ia (ə·lē′thē·ə) *Greek* The goddess of childbirth, early an aspect of Hera and later almost identified with Artemis.
Ein·her·i·ar (īn·her′ē·är) *Germanic* The slain warriors who were Odin's guests in Valhalla.
Eir·a (ī′rä) *Germanic* The goddess of healing, an attendant of Frigga. Also **Eir** (īr), **Eyr′a.**
E·lec·tra (i·lek′trə) See main vocabulary.
El·eu·sin·i·an mysteries (el′yōō·sin′ē·ən) See main vocabulary.
E·ly·si·um (i·lizh′ē·əm, i·liz′-) See main vocabulary.
Em·bla (em′blə) *Norse* The first woman, created from an elm tree. Also **Em·la** (em′lə), **Em·o·la** (em′ō·lə).
Em·esh (em′esh) *Sumerian* Brother of Enten, created by Enlil.
En·cel·a·dus (en·sel′ə·dəs) See main vocabulary.
En·ki (en′kē) *Sumerian* Water-god and god of wisdom, the father of Uttu. A primary figure in the Sumerian pantheon who appears in many creation and culture myths, often associated with Dilmun, the locale of some of his amorous adventures.
En·ki·du (en′kē·dōō) In Babylonian myths, a savage man formed to fight the tyrant Gilgamesh. They wrestle, become boon companions and share many adventures.
En·kim·du (en·kim′dōō) *Sumerian* A farmer-god, rival of Dumuzi for the love of Inanna.
En·lil (en·lil′) *Sumerian* Air-god and supreme deity in Sumerian pantheon but lacking absolute power.
En·mer·kar (en·mûr′kär) *Sumerian* Legendary hero.
En·ten (en′ten) *Sumerian* Brother of Emesh, created by Enlil.
En·um·a el·ish (en·ōōm′ə el′ish) *Babylonian & Assyrian* Known by its first two words ("When above" or "When on high") this important myth describes the slaying of Tiamat, the organization of the universe, and the creation of man.
E·os (ē′əs) See main vocabulary.
E·phi·al·tes (i·fē′al·tēz) See main vocabulary.
E·po·na (i·pō′nə) *Celtic* The ancient goddess of horses, donkeys, mules, and all who had to do with them.
Er·a·to (er′ə·tō) See main vocabulary.
Er·e·bus (er′ə·bəs) See main vocabulary.
E·rech·theus (i·rek′thyōōs, -thē·əs) See main vocabulary.
E·resh·ki·gal (âr·esh′kē·gäl) *Sumerian & Babylonian* The goddess of death, violently hostile toward her sister (*Inanna* in Sumerian myths, *Ishtar* in Babylonian); the ruling deity of the nether world until overpowered by Nergal who, after threatening to kill her, married her: also *Allatu.*
E·rich·tho·ni·us (i·rik·thō′nē·əs) *Greek* A legendary king of Athens, son of Hephaestus and Ge.
E·rin·y·es (i·rin′i·ēz) See FURIES in main vocabulary.
E·ris (ir′is, er′is) See main vocabulary.
Er·i·u (ā′rōō) *Irish* A queen of the Tuatha Dé Danann, to whom the Milesians promised that her name would be the chief name of Ireland forever.
erl·king (ûrl′king′) See main vocabulary.
Er·os (ir′os, er′os) See main vocabulary.
Er·y·man·thi·an boar (er′ə·man′thē·ən) See main vocabulary.
E·ta·na (ā·tä′nä) *Babylonian* A childless mortal who ascended to heaven, borne aloft by an eagle.
E·te·o·cles (i·tē′ə·klēz) See main vocabulary.
Et·zel (et′sel) See main vocabulary.
Eu·phros·y·ne (yōō·fros′ə·nē) See main vocabulary.
Eu·ro·pa (yōō·rō′pə) See main vocabulary.
Eu·ryd·i·ce (yōō·rid′ə·sē) See main vocabulary.
Eu·rys·the·us (yōō·ris′thē·əs) See main vocabulary.
Eu·ter·pe (yōō·tûr′pē) See main vocabulary.
E·vad·ne (i·vad′nē) *Greek* **1.** The wife of Capaneus, who threw herself on his funeral pyre when he was killed in the siege of Thebes. **2.** A daughter of Poseidon and mother by Apollo of Iamus, whom she killed out of shame.
E·van·der (i·van′dər) *Roman* A son of Hermes and an Arcadian nymph, who came from his mother's country sixty years before the Trojan War and founded a colony at the foot of the Palatine hill.

Faf·nir (fäv′nir, fäf-) See main vocabulary.
Fates (fāts) See main vocabulary.
Fau·nus (fô′nəs) *Roman* A god of nature, patron of agriculture: identified with the Greek *Pan.*
Fen·ris wolf (fen′ris) *Norse* A huge wolf, son of Loki and Angur-boda, whom the gods attempted to fetter. He is tied by a silken cord that will hold until Ragnarök, when he will devour Odin and be torn apart by Vidar.
Fen·sa·lir (fen′sä·lir) *Norse* The mansion of Frigga in which happy married couples spend eternity together.
Fer·diad (fir′dyəd) *Irish* Sworn brother of Cuchulain, beguiled by Medb to fight against him in the war for the brown bull of Cuáilgne. See *Táin Bó Cuáilgne.*
Fer·gus mac Roich (fir′gəs mäk·rē′əkh) *Irish* A great warrior of the Red Branch and a tutor of Cuchulain.
Fi·an·na Eire·ann (fē′ə·nə er′in) See main vocabulary.
Fim·bul·win·ter (fēm′bōōl·vēn′tər) *Norse* The three uninterrupted fierce winters preceding Ragnarök.
Fin·da·bair (fin′dhŏŏr) *Irish* The beautiful daughter of Ailill and Medb, beloved of Fraech.
Finn·bear·a (fin′bûr·ə) *Irish* King of the fairies of Connacht.
Finn Cycle (fin) *Irish* A body of heroic and romantic tales dealing with the exploits of Fionn macCumhail, the Fianna, Fionn's son Oisin and grandson Oscar. Also **Fen·i·an Cycle** (fē′nē·ən).
Fionn mac·Cumal (fin′məkōōl′) See main vocabulary.
Fir·bolg (fir′bul·əg) See main vocabulary.
fire-drake (fīr′drāk′) See main vocabulary.
Fjal·ar (fyä′lär) *Norse* **1.** One of the dwarfs who killed the great teacher Kvasir. **2.** The cock who will crow to announce Ragnarök.
Fod·la (fō′lhə) *Irish* One of the three queens of the Tuatha Dé Danann encountered by the invading Milesians.
Fo·mor·i·an (fə·môr′ē·ən) See main vocabulary.
For·se·ti (fôr′se·tē) See main vocabulary.
For·tu·na (fôr·tōō′nə, -tyōō′-) See main vocabulary.
Fraech (frekh) *Irish* See FODLA.
Frag·a·rach (frä′gər·äkh) *Irish* The terrible and wonderful sword called the Answerer, which Lug brought from the other world and which could cut through any armor.
Frey (frā) See main vocabulary.
Frey·a (frā′ə) See main vocabulary.
Frigg (frig) See main vocabulary. Also **Frig·ga** (frig′ə).
Fro·di (frŏŏd′ē) *Norse* A legendary king of Denmark, supposed to be an incarnation of Frey.
Fu Hsi (fōō shē) *Chinese* A legendary emperor and culture hero who instituted the rites, laws, and customs of marriage.
Ful·la (ful′ə) *Norse* An attendant or sister of Frigga whose lovely long hair represented the golden grain.
Fur·ies (fyŏŏr′ēz) See main vocabulary.
Fur·ri·na (fŏŏr′ī·nə) *Roman* An ancient goddess whose festival survived into late Rome. She was perhaps a spirit of darkness.

Gae·a (jē′ə) See main vocabulary.
Gae Bulg (gā bul′əg) *Irish* The wonderful spear of Cuchulain, made from the bones of a sea-monster.

Ga·lar (gä′lär) *Norse* The dwarf who, along with Fjalar, killed the great teacher Kvasir.
Gal·a·te·a (gal′ə·tē′ə) **1.** See main vocabulary. **2.** *Greek* A Nereid, beloved of Polyphemus but in love with Acis, whom Polyphemus killed.
Gan·dhar·va (gän·där′və) *Hindu* **1.** The measurer of space; the sun steed. **2.** One of a group of sky-dwelling, medically skilled fertility deities. **3.** One of a group of shaggy, half-animal beings. **4.** One of a group of musicians at the banquets of the gods.
Gand·reid (gänd′rād′) *Norse* The wild hunt or spirit's ride that brings fertility to any field it passes over.
Ga·nes·a (gä·nes′ə) *Hindu* The god of wisdom, prudence, and learning, the remover of obstacles, and the leader of the troops of lesser deities; a son of Siva and Parvati. Also **Ga·nesh·a** (gä·nesh′ə), **Ga·na·pa·ti** (gä·nə·pä′tē).
Gan·y·mede (gan′ə·mēd) See main vocabulary.
Garm (gärm) *Norse* The blood-stained watchdog who guarded Hel's gate. Also **Gar·mr** (gär′mər).
Ga·ru·da (gä·ro͞o′də) *Hindu* The sun, represented as half man and half bird, with a golden body, white face, and red wings.
Gau·ri (gou′rē) *Hindu* See Devi.
Ge (jē) *Greek* Gaea. See main vocabulary.
Geb (geb) *Egyptian* God of the earth, closely united with his sister/spouse Nut, the sky-goddess, until separated from her by the air-god Shu: also *Keb, Seb.*
Gef·jon (gef′yo͞on) *Norse* The goddess of agriculture and patroness of virgins, an attendant of Frigga.
Ger·da (gûr′dä) See main vocabulary.
Gi·bil (gi′bəl) *Sumerian & Babylonian* A fire-god.
Gi·gan·tes (jə·gän′tēz) *Greek* A race of giants that sprang from Gaea when the blood of the mutilated Uranus fell upon her. They fought the gods, and were defeated with the help of Hercules.
Gil·ga·mesh (gil′gə·mesh) See main vocabulary.
Gin·nung·a·gap (yē·no͝ong′ä·gäp) *Norse* The bottomless abyss between Niflheim and Muspelheim.
Gir·ru (gir′o͞o, gir′ro͞o) *Babylonian* A fire-god.
Gish Bar (gish bär) *Babylonian* A fire-god.
Gish·zi·da (gish·zē′dä) *Babylonian* One of a pair of heavenly gatekeepers. The other was Tammuz.
Glas Gai·bleann (glas gob′lin) *Irish* A wonderful gray cow that gave an inexhaustible supply of milk.
Goib·niu (gib′no͞o) *Irish* The devine smith who made spears and arms for the Tuatha Dé Danann. His counterpart in Welsh mythology is **Go·van·non** (guv′ə·non).
golden bough In the folklore and mythology of many cultures, the mistletoe.
Golden Fleece See main vocabulary.
go·lem (gō′lem, -ləm) See main vocabulary.
Goll mac Mor·na (gul mäk·môr′nə) *Irish* Fionn macCumal's greatest rival in the Finn Cycle, usually identified with Connacht.
Gor·gon (gôr′gən) See main vocabulary.
Göt·ter·däm·mer·ung (gœt′ər·dem′ər·o͝ongk) See main vocabulary.
Gra·ces (grā′siz) See main vocabulary.
Grae·ae (grē′ē) See main vocabulary.
Gráin·ne (grän′yə) *Irish* The daughter of Cormac mac Airt and promised bride of Fionn macCumal. She eloped with Diarmuid, and after he was pursued and killed, finally married Fionn.
grif·fin (grif′ən) See main vocabulary.
Grim·hild (grim′hild) *Norse* The wife of Guiki, king of the Nibelungs, and mother of Gunnar, Gudrun, and Hogni.
Gud·run (go͝od′ro͞on) See main vocabulary.
Gu·i·ki (go͞o′ē·kē) *Norse* The king of the Nibelungs.
Gu·la (go͞o′lä] *Babylonian & Assyrian* Goddess of health; wife of Ninib.
Gung·nir (go͝ong′nir) *Norse* Odin's infallible spear.
Gun·nar (go͞on′är) See main vocabulary.
Gu·tru·ne (go͞o·tro͞o′nə) See main vocabulary.
Gwy·di·on (gwē′dē·on) *Welsh* A son of Dôn, the brother and lover of Arianrhod, and by her father of Dylan and Llew Llaw Gyffes.
Gy·ges (gī′jēz) See main vocabulary.

Ha·chi·man (hä·chē·män) *Japanese* The god of war, originally the deified Emperor Ojin of the 4th century A.D.
Ha·dad (hä′däd) *Babylonian* See Ramman.
Ha·des (hā′dēz) See main vocabulary.
Hag·en (hä′gən) See main vocabulary.
ham·a·dry·ad (ham′ə·drī′əd) See main vocabulary.
Han Chung-li (hän cho͝ong·lē) *Chinese* One of the eight immortals, a friend, teacher, and drinking companion of Lü Tung Pin.
Han·u·man (hän′o͞o·män) See main vocabulary.
Hap (häp) *Egyptian* See Apis.
Ha·pi (hä′pē) *Egyptian* A Nile-god depicted as a man with female breasts who wears a headpiece of papyrus or lotus.
Ha·py (hä′pē) *Egyptian* Son of Horus whose ape- or dog-headed image serves as a stopper for the Canopic Jar containing mummified lungs which he has been assigned to guard.
Har·akh·ti (här·äk′tē) *Egyptian* A concept of Horus as the sun, independent of his role in the Isis-Osiris myth. Later absorbed by Ra as Ra-Harakhti.
Har·pe·chru·ti (här·pə·kro͞o′tē) *Egyptian* Manifestation of the god Horus as a child.
Har·poc·ra·tes (här·pok′rə·tēz) *Greek & Roman* The god of silence; the Egyptian god Horus as a child, adopted by the Greeks and Romans in Hellenistic times.
Har·py (här′pē) See main vocabulary.
Ha·thor (hä′thôr, hath′ôr, hät′hôr) See main vocabulary.
Hav·mand (häv′mänd) *Danish* A legendary marine creature, having the head (usually bearded and handsome) and upper body of a man, and the tail of a fish.
He·be (hē′bē) See main vocabulary.
Hec·a·te (hek′ə·tē) See main vocabulary.
Hec·u·ba (hek′yo͞o·bə) See main vocabulary.
Heh (he) *Egyptian* Everlasting time personified as a god.
Heim·dall (hām′däl) See main vocabulary.
Hek·et (hek′ət) *Egyptian* Fertility goddess represented as a frog or a frog-headed woman.
Hel (hel) See main vocabulary.
Helen of Troy See main vocabulary.
He·li·o·gab·a·lus (hē′lē·ə·gab′ə·ləs) See main vocabulary.
He·li·os (hē′lē·os) See main vocabulary.
Hel·le (hel′ē) See main vocabulary.
Hel·len (hel′ən) See main vocabulary.
He·phaes·tus (hi·fes′təs) See main vocabulary.
He·ra (hir′a) See main vocabulary.
Her·cu·les (hûr′kyə·lēz) See main vocabulary. Also **Her·a·cles** or **Her·a·kles** (her′ə·klēz).
Her·maph·ro·di·tus (hûr·maf′rə·dī′təs) See main vocabulary.
Her·mes (hûr′mēz) See main vocabulary.
Her·mod (her′mōd) See main vocabulary.
He·ro (hir′ō) See main vocabulary.
He·si·o·ne (hi·sī′ə·nē) See main vocabulary.
Hes·per·i·des (hes·per′ə·dēz) See main vocabulary.
Hes·ti·a (hes′tē·ə) See main vocabulary.
Him·a·vat (hēm′ə·vät) *Hindu* The personification of the Himalayan Mountains, and father of Ganga and Devi.
Hior·dis (hyor′dis) *Norse* The third wife of Sigmund and fosterer of Sigurd.
Hip·po·crene (hip′ə·krēn, hip′ə·krē′nē) See main vocabulary.
Hip·pol·y·ta (hi·pol′i·tə) See main vocabulary.
Hip·pol·y·tus (hi·pol′i·təs) See main vocabulary.
Hip·pom·e·don (hi·pom′ə·dən) *Greek* One of the Seven Against Thebes.
Hip·pom·e·nes (hi·pom′ə·nēz) See main vocabulary.
Hi·ru·ko (hi·ro͞o·kō) *Japanese* The first child of Izanagi and Izanami, who was cast adrift in a boat.
Ho·der (hō′dər) See main vocabulary.
Hœ·nir (hœ′nir) See main vocabulary.
Hog·ni (ho͝og′nē) *Norse* The brother of Gunnar and Gudrun, whom Brynhilt asked to kill Sigurd; he hid the Nibelung gold in the Rhine.
Ho·rae (hō′rē) See main vocabulary.
Ho·rus (hō′rəs) See main vocabulary.
Ho·tei (hō·tī) *Japanese* The most popular of the Japanese gods of luck, represented as a very fat man.
Hou Chi (hō chē) *Chinese* The god of millet.
Hou T'u (hō to͞o) *Chinese* The god of earth or soil; sovereign earth.
Hrolf Kra·ki (hrolf krä′kē) The most famous Danish king of the heroic age, identified with Hrothulf of the Old English epic *Beowulf* and celebrated in several sagas.
Hrung·nir (hro͝ong′nir) *Norse* A famous giant who met Thor in single combat.
Hsi Wang Mu (shē wäng mo͞o) *Chinese* The consort of Tung Wang Kung formed from the yin principle of the purely female; the lady of the western heavens.
Huang Ti (hwäng tē) *Chinese* A legendary emperor and culture hero who was the first to unite China.
Hu·gin (ho͞o′yēn) *Norse* See Munin.
Hu·wa·wa (ho͞o·wä′wä) *Sumerian & Babylonian* Fierce monster-guardian of the cedar forest, slain by Gilgamesh and Enkidu: also *Khumbaba.* Also **Hum·ba·ba** (ho͝om·bä′bä).
Hy·ge·ia (hī·jē′ə) See main vocabulary.
Hy·las (hī′ləs) See main vocabulary.
Hy·men (hī′mən) See main vocabulary.
Hy·per·bo·re·an (hī′pər·bôr′ē·ən, -bō′rē·ən) See main vocabulary.
Hy·pe·ri·on (hī·pir′ē·ən) See main vocabulary.
Hyp·nos (hip′nos) See main vocabulary.

I·ac·chus (ī·ak′əs) *Greek* The principal god of the Eleusinian mysteries, and one of a triad with Demeter and Persephone.
I·am·be (ī·am′bē) *Greek* A daughter of Pan and Echo who with her jesting was able to make the grieving Demeter smile when she was in search of Persephone.
I·a·si·on (ī·ā′sē·ən) *Greek* The father of Pluto by Demeter.
I·car·i·us (i·kar′ē·əs) *Greek* An Attic Greek to whom Dionysus gave the secret of wine-making in return for hospitality; his neighbors, drunk on his wine, killed him.
Ic·a·rus (ik′ə·rəs, ī′kə-) See main vocabulary.
I·dom·e·neus (ī·dom′ə·nōōs, -nyōōs) See main vocabulary.
I·dun (ē′dŏŏn) *Norse* The wife of Bragi and keeper of the golden apples of youth.
I·gi·gi (i·gē′gē, i′gə·gē) *Babylonian* Attendant sky-gods who sometimes reversed roles with the Anunnaki.
Ig·nis (ig′nis) *Hindu* See AGNI.
Il·i·ad (il′ē·əd) See main vocabulary.
Im·ho·tep (im·hō′tep) *Egyptian* The human being who designed a famous pyramid, ultimately deified as a son of Ptah.
Im·se·ty (im·se′tē) *Egyptian* Son of Horus whose man-headed image served as a stopper for the Canopic Jar containing the mummified liver, which he was assigned to guard: also *Mesti.*
Im·su (im′sōō) *Egyptian* See MIN.
I·nan·na (i·nä′nä) *Sumerian* Omnipresent goddess of love and war who visited the nether world naked, having shed her garments at its seven gates. She almost succumbed but was saved, her husband, Dumuzi, dying instead.
In·a·ri (in·ä·rē) *Japanese* The rice or harvest god.
in·cu·bus (in′kyə·bəs, ing′-) See main vocabulary.
In·di·ge·tes (in·dig′ə·tēz) *Roman* The gods and heroes who had lived as mortals in Rome and were invoked and Worshiped as the protectors of the state; especially, the descendants of Aeneas.
In·dra (in′drə) See main vocabulary.
In·fer·i (in·fer′ē) *Greek & Roman* The gods of the lower world and the shades of the departed: distinguished from *Superi.*
Ing (ing) *Germanic* A mythical hero and eponymous ancestor of several Germanic tribes.
I·no (ī′nō) *Greek* The nurse of Dionysus and the cruel stepmother of Phrixus and Helle.
I·o (ī′ō) See main vocabulary.
Iph·i·cles (if′i·klēz) See main vocabulary.
Iph·i·ge·ni·a (if′ə·jə·nī′ə) See main vocabulary.
I·ris (ī′ris) See main vocabulary.
Ish·tar (ish′tär) See main vocabulary.
Is·i·mud (is′ə·mŏŏd) *Sumerian* Enki's messenger.
I·sis (ī′sis) See main vocabulary.
Ith (ē) *Irish* The first of the Milesians to visit Ireland; his death at the hands of the three kings of Ireland caused the Milesian invasion and conquest.
I·tys (ī′tis) See main vocabulary.
Ix·i·on (ik·sī′ən) See main vocabulary.
Iz·a·na·gi (i·zä·nä·gē) *Japanese* The male of the divine couple who created the eight main islands of Japan and engendered many gods.
Iz·a·na·mi (i·zä·nä·mē) *Japanese* The female of the divine couple, with Izanagi the male.

Jal·an·dhar·a (jäl·än·där′ə) *Hindu* A titan king who defeated the gods in the created spheres as a result of his extraordinary austerities, and set up a tyrannical, wicked, and selfish government.
Jam·bu·dvi·pa (jäm·bōō·dvē′pə) *Hindu* India; literally, the rose-apple island.
Ja·nus (jā′nəs) See main vocabulary.
Ja·ta·yu (jā·tä′yōō) *Hindu* The king of the vultures, a son of Garuda and the ally of Rama against Ravana.
Jim·mu Ten·no (jēm·mōō ten·nô) *Japanese* The legendary first emperor of Japan, about 660 B.C.: also *Toyomikenu.*
Ji·zo (jē·zô) *Japanese* A Bodhisattva regarded as the patron of small children travelers, pregnant women, and persons suffering from toothache.
Jo·cas·ta (jō·kas′tə) See main vocabulary.
Jord (yôrd) *Norse* A giantess, the wife of Odin and mother of Thor; a personification of the unpopulated and uncultivated earth.
Jor·mun·gan·dr (yôr′mən·gän·dər) *Norse* The Midgard serpent, son of Loki and Angur-boda, brother of the Fenris wolf and Hel.
jö·tun (yœ′tŏŏn) *n. pl.* **jöt·nar** (yœt′när) See main vocabulary.
Jö·tun·heim (yœ′tŏŏn·hām) *Norse* The home of the giants, to the northeast of Asgard.
Jove (jōv) See main vocabulary.
Jug·ger·naut (jug′ər·nôt) See main vocabulary.
Juno (jōō′nō) See main vocabulary.
Ju·pi·ter (jōō′pə·tər) See main vocabulary.
Ju·tur·na (jōō·tûr′nə) *Roman* A nymph, the personification of healing springs and wells.
Ju·ven·tas (jōō·ven′təs) *Roman* An early goddess of youth: identified with the Greek *Hebe.*

Ka (kä) *Hindu* The unknown god, an abstraction and deification of the interrogative pronoun "who."
Ka (kä) See main vocabulary.
Ka·ban·dha (kä·bän′də) *Hindu* A huge, hairy, headless Rakshasa, with a mouth in the middle of his belly and one big eye in his breast.
Kad·ru (käd′rōō) *Hindu* One of the thirteen daughters of Daksha, all of whom were married to Kasyapa.
Ka·la (kä′lə) *Hindu* The black one, the god of time, a form of Siva as the creator of the universe and its destroyer.
Ka·li (kä′lē) See main vocabulary.
Ka·li·ya (kä·lē′ə) *Hindu* The five-headed king of the serpents who lived in the river Jumna and emerged to devastate the countryside; banished by Krishna.
Kal·ki (käl′kē) *Hindu* The white horse, tenth and last incarnation of Vishnu, which will appear at the end of the present age, destroy the world, and restore purity.
Ka·ma (kä′mə) *Hindu* The god of love and desire, a beautiful young man carrying a flower bow with flower string and five flower shafts.
Kam·sa (käm′sə) *Hindu* A god and king who persecuted Krishna because it had been foretold that a child of Devaki would kill him, and was killed by Krishna.
Ka·ri (kä′rē) *Norse* A giant of tempests and lord of the storm giants.
kar·ma (kär′mə) See main vocabulary.
Kart·ti·key·a (kärt′tē·kā′ə) *Hindu* The six-faced god of war and of the planet Mars.
Ka·sy·a·pa (kä·sē·ä′pə) Hindu The old tortoise man, progenitor of all things living on the earth.
Ka·tha Sa·rit Sa·ga·ra (kä′tə sä′rēt sä·gä′rə) *Hindu* The ocean of the rivers of stories, a collection of popular fairy tales and romances written in Sanskrit about the beginning of the twelfth century.
Kau·ra·vas (kou·rä′vəs) *Hindu* The opponents of the Pandavas in the battles of the Mahabharata.
Keb (keb) *Egyptian* See GEB.
Keb·eh·se·nuf (keb′e·sə·nŏŏf′) *Egyptian* See QEBHSNUF.
kel·pie (kel′pē) See main vocabulary.
Ke·res (kē′rēz) *pl.* of **Ker** (kûr) *Greek* Malignant spirits and bringers of evil.
Khan·da·va (kän·dä′və) *Hindu* The country and forest of the Pandavas.
Khen·su (ken′sōō) *Egyptian* A healer-god identified with the moon; son of Amon and Mut: also *Khons.*
Khep·ri (kep′ri) *Egyptian* God of regeneration of life, identified with Ra, symbolized as a scarab or scarab-headed human. Also **Khep·e·ra** (kep′ə·rä).
Khnum (knŏŏm) See main vocabulary.
Khum·ba·ba (kŏŏm·bä′bä) *Babylonian & Assyrian* See HUWAWA.
Ki (kē) *Sumerian* Goddess of earth.
Kin·gu (king′gōō) *Babylonian* The consort of Tiamat, slain by Marduk. His blood was used to mold the first man.
Kin·na·ra (kēn·nä′rə) *Hindu* The heavenly musicians, followers of Kubera.
Kirt·ti·mu·kha (kirt·tē·mōō′kə) *Hindu* The face of the lion-headed monster embodying the destructive power of the universal god.
Ki·shar (kā′shär) *Babylonian* An earth deity born of Lahamu and Lahmu.
Kriem·hild (krēm′hild) See main vocabulary.
Krish·na (krish′nə) See main vocabulary.
Kro·nos (krō′nəs) See main vocabulary.
Kuan Ti (kwän tē) *Chinese* The god of war, honored because he prevents, rather than makes, war.
Kuan Yin (kwän yēn) See main vocabulary.
Ku·be·ra (kōō·ber′ə) *Hindu* The king of the Yakshas, god of wealth, and lord of the treasures of the earth.
Kuei Hsing (kwā shĕng) *Chinese* An ugly dwarf associated with Wen Ch'ang; he won first prize in the emperor's examinations, but was denied the award because of his ugliness, whereupon he threw himself into the ocean, was rescued by a dragon, and set in heaven among the stars.
Kur (kûr) *Sumerian* The nether world in some myths; in others, any inimical or foreign land.
Kur·ma (kûr′mə) *Hindu* The tortoise, second avatar of Vishnu, that helped the gods recover the amrita and other precious things lost during the deluge.
Ku·ru (kûr′ōō) *Hindu* A prince of the moon race, ancestor of the Kauravas and Pandavas.
Kva·sir (kvä′sir) *Norse* A being renowned for knowledge and goodness, who went about the earth answering all questions and thus teaching mankind.
Kwan·non (kwän·nôn) *Japanese* The goddess of mercy: identified with the Chinese *Kuan Yin.*

Lab·y·rinth (lab′ə·rinth) See main vocabulary.
La·don (lā′dən) See main vocabulary.
La·ha·mu and Lah·mu (lä·hä′mōō; lä′mōō) *Babylonian* Silt deities born of the primeval sweet-water and salt-water oceans.
Lak·shma·na (läk·shmä′nə) *Hindu* The brother and faithful companion of Lama.
Lak·shmi (läk′shmē) *Hindu* The goddess lotus, spouse of Vishnu and symbol of his creative energy, symbolized by the lotus wherever it appears in Hindu art: also called *Padma.*
La·mas·su (lä·mä′sōō, lä′mə·sōō) *Assyrian* A winged, human-headed sculptured bull, a protective genie of palaces.
La·mi·a (lā′mē·ə) See main vocabulary.
La·o·co·on (lā·ok′ə·won, -ō·won) See main vocabulary.
La·om·e·don (lā·om′ə·don) See main vocabulary.
Lap·i·thae (lap′ə·thē) See main vocabulary.
lar·es (lâr′ēz, lā′rēz) See main vocabulary.
lar·va (lär′və) *Roman* An evil spirit that frightened and worked ill against people.
La·ti·nus (lə·tī′nəs) *Roman* The father-in-law of Aeneas, and variously the son of Faunus, Odysseus, or Hercules.
La·to·na (lə·tō′nə) See main vocabulary.
La·vin·i·a (lə·vin′yə, -ē·ə) *Roman* The daughter of Latinus, won by Aeneas when he killed Turnus in a duel.
Le·an·der (lē·an′dər) See main vocabulary.
Le·da (lē′də) See main vocabulary.
Lei Kung (lā kōōng) *Chinese* The god of thunder.
Lei Tsu (lā tsōō) *Chinese* A culture hero, wife of Huang Ti, and the first to domesticate wild silkworms.
lep·re·chaun (lep′rə·kôn) See main vocabulary.
Le·the (lē′thē) See main vocabulary.
Le·to (lē′tō) See main vocabulary.
Li·a Fáil (lē′ə fôl) *Irish* The stone from the mythical city of Falias, which Lug took to Tara, and which would scream out under the foot of every rightful king of Ireland.
Li·at Ma·ca (lē′ət mäl′kä) *Irish* The gray of Macha, the wonderful gray horse of Cuchulain that died defending him in his last fight.
Li·ber and Li·be·ra (lī′bər; lī·ber′ə) *Roman* The ancient Italian deities of the vine, worshiped along with Ceres as fertility gods. Liber became identified with Bacchus, and Libera with Persephone.
Lif and Lif·tha·ser (lēf; lēf′thə·sər) *Norse* The man and woman who will sleep through Ragnarök and found a new race in the green and verdant earth after the disaster.
Lil·ith (lil′ith) See main vocabulary.
Li·nus (lī′nəs) *Greek* A youth who was exposed in infancy, raised by shepherds, and killed by dogs; he was celebrated in songs of vintagers and reapers, of Phoenician origin, and by festivals in various parts of Greece.
Lir (lir) *Irish* The personification of the sea, and father of the sea god Manannán.
Llew Llaw Gyf·fes (lōō lô jif′əs) *Welsh* One of the marvelous twin boys born to Arianrhod, twin brother of Dylan, and interpreted as a sun god.
Lludd (lōōd) *Welsh* A legendary king of Britain who freed his land of three terrible plagues, including two dragons.
Loegair·e Bua·duc (leg′rə bōōd′ok) *Irish* One of the three first champions of Ulster, along with Cuchulain and Conall Cearnac.
Lo·gi (lō′gē) *Norse* A personification of wildfire.
Lo·ki (lō′kē) See main vocabulary.
Lu·a (lōō′ə) *Roman* The ancient Italian goddess of war and calamity, the consort of Saturn in the cult.
Lu·ci·na (lōō·sī′nə) See main vocabulary.
Lug (lōōg) See main vocabulary.
Lu·gaid mac Con (lōō′ē mäk·kung′) See main vocabulary.
Lu·gal·ban·da (lōō·gal·bän′də) *Babylonian* Father of Gilgamesh; slayer of the Zu-bird.
Lu·na (lōō′nə) See main vocabulary.
Lung Wang (lōōng wäng) *Chinese* The dragon king, bringer of rain, controller of the ocean and of all storms and waters, and dweller in all lakes.
Lu Pan (lōō pän) *Chinese* The patron of carpenters.
Lü·tsu (lōō·tsōō) *Chinese* The patron of barbers, beggars, and pedicures.
Lü Tung Pin (lōō tōōng pēn) *Chinese* One of the eight immortals, a man eight feet tall with a sparse beard, renowned as a killer of devils and beloved of barbers.
Ly·ca·on (lī·kā′on) See main vocabulary.
Lyg·ni (lüg′nē) *Norse* In the *Volsunga Saga,* a suitor of Hiordis who was so angry when she married Sigmund that he killed all the Volsungs; later killed by Sigmund's son Sigurd.

Maat (mät) *Egyptian* Goddess of justice and truth, represented by the feather utilized by Anubis during the weighing of souls. See WEIGHING OF SOULS.
Mab·i·no·gi·on (mab′ə·nō′gē·ən) See main vocabulary.
Mac Cecht (mäk·kyäkht′) *Irish* A king of the Tuatha Dé Danann.
Mac Cuill (mäk·kwil′) *Irish* A king of the Tuatha Dé Danann.
Mac Greine (mäk·grān′yə) *Irish* A king of the Tuatha Dé Danann.
Mach·a (mäkh′ə) *Irish* **1.** One of the trio of war goddesses, with Morrigan and Neman being the others, who appeared on battlefields in the form of a crow. **2.** The wife of an Ulster chieftain, gifted with enormous speed. She outran the king of Ulster's horses, even when about to give birth.
mae·nad (mē′nad) See main vocabulary.
Mag Tured, Battle of (ma tōō′rid) *Irish* The great battle, according to some versions fought in two parts, in which the Tuatha Dé Danann defeated the Firbolgs and the Fomorians and came to rule all of Ireland: also *Moytura.*
Ma·ha·bhar·a·ta (mä·hä′bər·ä′tə) See main vocabulary.
Ma·ha·de·va (mä·hä·dev′ə) *Hindu* Siva.
Ma·ha·de·vi (mä·hä·dev′ē) *Hindu* See DEVI.
Mai·a (mā′yə, mī′ə) See main vocabulary.
Ma·ma (mä′mä) *Babylonian* Mother-goddess.
Ma·nan·nán (man′ə·non) *Irish* The sea god, son of Lir.
Ma·na·sa (mä·nä′sə) *Hindu* A snake goddess, depicted as yellow, with four arms, sitting on a water lily, and clothed with snakes.
ma·nes (mā′nēz) See main vocabulary.
Ma·nu (mä′nōō) **1.** *Hindu* The hero of the deluge, who built a ship and survived to repopulate the earth. **2.** *Egyptian* The mountain that supported the sky and heaven at their western end. See BAKHAU.
Mar·duk (mär′dōōk) See main vocabulary.
Mars (märz) See main vocabulary.
Mar·sy·as (mär·sī′əs) See main vocabulary.
Mart·tan·da (mär·tän′də) *Hindu* The eighth son of Aditi, by the sun.
Ma·ruts (mä·rōōts′) *Hindu* The storm gods, allies of Indra, who ride golden cars gleaming with lightning.
Ma·san (mä·sän′) *Hindu* A hideous black ghost who comes from the ashes of the funeral pyre and afflicts children with disease by throwing ashes over them.
Mat·sy·a (mät·sē′ə) *Hindu* The fish incarnation of Vishnu.
Ma Wang (mä wäng) *Chinese* The protector of horses.
Me (mē) *Sumerian* Laws that control the universe, probably in the same form as the later Babylonian Tablets of Destiny.
Medb (māb) *Irish* The wife of Ailill mac Matach, who henpecked him.
Me·de·a (mə·dē′ə) See main vocabulary.
Mef·det (mef′det) *Egyptian* A cat-goddess worshiped as a protectress against the bites of serpents.
Me·lam·pus (mə·lam′pəs) *Greek* The first person wtih prophetic powers, the first mortal physician, and the first Greek to worship Dionysus.
Mele·a·ger (mel·ē·āj′ər) See main vocabulary.
Mel·pom·e·ne (mel·pom′ə·nē) See main vocabulary.
Men·e·la·us (men′ə·lā′əs) See main vocabulary.
Men·tu (men′tōō) *Egyptian* Ancient Theban god of war, identified with Ra, depicted as a bull- or falcon-headed human: also *Mont.*
Mer·cu·ry (mûr′kyə·rē) See main vocabulary.
Mer·o·dach (mer′ō·dak) *Babylonian* See MARDUK.
Mert·seg·er (mûrt·seg′ər) *Egyptian* A snake-goddess, primarily benevolent, of the necropolis at Thebes.
Me·ru, Mount (mā′rōō) *Hindu* The mountain at the center of the earth, where the gods dwell.
Mes·khent (mes′kent) *Egyptian* Goddess of birth who eased the labor of expectant mothers and predicted the fate of newborn infants.
Mes·ti (mes′tē) *Egyptian* See IMSETY.
Mi·das (mī′dəs) See main vocabulary.
Mid·gard (mid′gärd) See main vocabulary.
Mil (mil) *Irish* The leader of the Milesians.
Mi·les·i·ans (mī·lē′zhənz) See main vocabulary.
Mi·mir (mē′mir) See main vocabulary.
Min (min) *Egyptian* Phallic god of vegetation and fertility, and patron of travelers. Also called *Imsu.*
Mi·ner·va (mi·nûr′və) See main vocabulary.
Mi·nos (mī′nəs, -nos) See main vocabulary.
Mi·no·taur (min′ə·tôr) See main vocabulary.
Mit·ra (mēt′rə) *Hindu* One of the seven sons of Aditi, personifying the light of day.
Mne·mos·y·ne (nē·mos′ə·nē, -moz′-) See main vocabulary.
Moi·rai (moi′rī) See main vocabulary.
Mon·e·ta (mon′ə·tə) *Roman* The admonisher or warner, a title of Juno. The temple of Juno Moneta later became the mint, and this event is the basis of the words "mint," "money," etc.
Mont (mont) *Egyptian* See MENTU.
Mor·phe·us (môr′fē·əs, -fyōōs) See main vocabulary.
Mor·ri·gan (môr′ə·gən) *Irish* One of a group of three war goddesses, along with Macha and Neman; sometimes used as a generic term to include all three.

Moy·tu·ra (moi·tōō′rə) *Irish* See MAG TURED.
Mu (mōō) *Egyptian* A child of Ra representing physical light personified.
Mum·mu (mōō′mōō) *Babylonian* The vizier of Apsu.
Mu·nin (mōō′nēn) *Norse* One of the two ravens, Hugin being the other, that flew about all day observing, and at nightfall perched on Odin's shoulders to tell him what they had seen and heard.
Muse (myōōz) See main vocabulary.
Mus·pell·heim (mōōs′pel·hām) *Norse* The southern abode of the fire-devils who will destroy the world at Ragnarök.
Mut (mōōt) *Egyptian* A mother-goddess whose headpiece, in the form of a vulture, symbolized maternity; wife of Amon-Ra.
My·lit·ta (mi·lit′ə) *Babylonian* Goddess in whose name every Babylonian woman was required, at least once, to submit to the embraces of a stranger in the sacred temple for a small fee.

Na·bu (nä′bōō) *Babylonian* See NEBO.
Nag·l·far (näl′fär) *Norse* A ship, made of the nail-parings of the dead, that will carry the giants to do battle against the gods at Ragnarök.
Naio·se (nē′shə) *Irish* One of the sons of Usnech, lover of Deirdre, with whom he eloped to Scotland.
Nam·mu (nä′mōō) *Sumerian* Primeval mother of heaven and earth.
Nam·tar (näm·tär′) *Sumerian & Babylonian* Messenger of Allatu, the nether-world goddess; also, a demon of disease.
Nan·di (nän′dē) *Hindu* The milk-white bull of Siva, chief of his attendants.
Nan·na (nän′nä) *Norse* The goddess of purity, blossoms, and vegetation; the wife of Balder and mother of Forseti.
Nan·na (nä′nä) *Sumerian* Moon-god and chief astral deity in the Sumerian pantheon; son of Enlil and Ninlil: also *Ashgirbabbar, Sin.*
Na·ra·da (nä·rä′də) *Hindu* A legendary sage, inventor of the lute and author of a law textbook.
Na·ra·ka (nä·rä′kə) *Hindu* A god who, in the form of an elephant, outdid the evil deeds of all other gods; he carried off 16,000 women.
Na·ra·si·nha (nä·rä·sē′nə) *Hindu* The man-lion, fourth avatar of Vishnu.
Na·ra·ya·na (nä·rä·yä′nə) *Hindu* An epithet of several gods, but especially of Brahma and Vishnu; literally, either "moving on the waters," or "son of man."
Nar·cis·sus (när·sis′əs) See main vocabulary.
Ne·bo (nā′bō) *Babylonian & Assyrian* God of wisdom: a Babylonian deity later introduced into the Assyrian pantheon, where his influence in his cult centers approached that of the great god Ashur: also *Nabu.*
Nef·er·tum (nef′r·tōōm) *Egyptian* A lotus- or lion-headed sun-god.
Ne·heb-Ka·u (ne′heb-kä′ōō) *Egyptian* A serpent-goddess symbolizing fertility and the protective mother.
Ne·ith (nē′ith) *Egyptian* Goddess of war and domestic arts; virgin-mother of Ra and other gods. Also **Net** (net).
Nekh·e·bet (nek′ə·bet) *Egyptian* Protective goddess portrayed as a vulture.
Ne·man (nem′an) *Irish* One of a group of three war goddesses, the others being Macha and Morrigan.
Ne·me·an lion (nē′mē·ən) See main vocabulary.
Neph (nef) *Egyptian* Creation-god who manifested himself also as Nun and Ptah.
Neph·e·le (nef′ə·lē) See main vocabulary.
Neph·thys (nep′this) *Egyptian* Sister-goddess of Isis and protectress of the dead: mother of Anubis.
Nep·tune (nep′tōōn, -tyōōn) See main vocabulary.
Ne·re·id (nir′ē·id) See main vocabulary.
Ner·eus (nir′ōōs, -ē·əs) See main vocabulary.
Ner·gal (nâr′gäl) *Sumerian & Babylonian* Originally a sky-god but ultimately lord of the nether world as husband of Ereshkigal.
Ner·thus (ner′tōōs) *Germanic* The ancient earth mother and goddess of fertility.
Nes·sus (nes′əs) See main vocabulary.
Nes·tor (nes′tər) See main vocabulary.
Ne·ti (ne′tē) *Sumerian* Chief gate-keeper of the seven gates to the nether world.
Ni·be·lung (nē′bə·lōōng) See main vocabulary.
Ni·be·lung·en·lied (nē′bə·lōōng′ən·lēt′) See main vocabulary.
Nif·l·heim (nif′əl·hām) See main vocabulary.
nightingale legend See main vocabulary.
Ni·na (nē′nä) *Sumerian & Assyrian* Fish-goddess, corn spirit and goddess of maternity, whose name is reflected in the Sumerian city of Nina and the Assyrian city of Nineveh.
Nin·gal (nin′gal) *Sumerian* Mother of the sun-god Utu.
Nin·gir·su (nin·gûr′sōō) *Sumerian & Babylonian* See NINURTA.
Nin·hur·sag (nin·hōōr′sag, nin′hōōr-) *Sumerian* Mother-goddess, possibly derived from earlier earth-goddess Ki. Also **Nin·mah** (nin′mä), **Nin·tu** (nin′tōō).
Nin·ib (nin′ib, ni′nib) *Babylonian & Assyrian* Benevolent god of healing, and lord of battle.
Nin·i·gi-no-Mi·ko·to (nēn·ē·gē·nô·mē·kô·tô) *Japanese* The grandson of the sun-goddess Amaterasu, who descended from heaven to Japan after receiving the three imperial jewels, married a mortal woman, and is the presumed ancestor of the Japanese sovereigns.
Nin·kur (nin·kōōr′) *Sumerian* Lover of Enki and mother of Uttu the plant goddess.
Nin·lil (nin·lil′) *Sumerian* Air-goddess, wife of Enlil.
Nin·sar (nin′sär) *Sumerian* Daughter and lover of Enki; mother of Ninkur.
Nin·shu·bur (nin·shōō′bər) *Sumerian* Inanna's messenger whose timely action rescued her from death in the nether-world realm of her sister Ereshkigal.
Ni·nur·ta (ni·nōōr′tä) *Sumerian & Babylonian* God of agriculture and war whose personified weapon, the Sharur, induced him to attack Asag, the demon of sickness: also *Ningirsu.*
Ni·o·be (nī′ə·bē) See main vocabulary.
Niord (nyôrd) *Norse* The god of the sea, especially of coastal waters, and of fishing, commerce, and prosperity.
nir·va·na (nir·vä′nə, nər·van′ə) See main vocabulary.
Nit (nit) *Egyptian* Goddess of war and hunting.
Niu Wang (nyōō wäng) *Chinese* The guardian of cattle.
nix (niks) See main vocabulary.
Norn (nôrn) See main vocabulary.
Nu·a·da (nōō′ə·də) *Irish* A king of the Tuatha Dé Danann.
Nu·dim·mud (nōō·dim′ōōd) *Babylonian* See EA.
nu·men (nōō′mən, nyōō′-) See main vocabulary.
Nun (nōōn, nōōn) *Egyptian* The primeval ocean, existing prior to creation itself, from which the gods issued. Also **Nu** (nōō, nōō).
Nus·ku (nōōs′kōō, nōōsk′ōō) *Babylonian* Fire-deity and messenger of the gods.
Nut (nōōt, nōō′it) *Egyptian* Goddess of the sky, depicted as a cow or woman held aloft by her father Shu.
nymph (nimf) See main vocabulary.

Oc·nus (ok′nəs) *Greek* The personification of delay, dwelling in the underworld where he constantly twines a rope that is constantly eaten by his donkey.
O·din (ō′din) See main vocabulary.
O·dy·seus (ō·dis′yōōs, -ē·əs) See main vocabulary.
Od·ys·sey (od′ə·sē) See main vocabulary.
Oed·i·pus (ed′ə·pəs, ē′də-) See main vocabulary.
Oe·no·ne (ē·nō′nē) See main vocabulary.
Og·ma (ō′mä) *Irish* One of the Tuatha Dé Danann, a culture god of poetry, speech, and eloquence.
Oi·sin (ä′shin) *Irish* A son of Fionn macCumal and father of Oscar. He spent many years at Tir na n'Og and returned to Ireland, not knowing that ages had passed; as a wrinkled old man he met St. Patrick and his monks, and told them the legends of the Fianna.
Om·pha·le (om′fə·lē) See main vocabulary.
om·pha·los (om′fə·ləs) See main vocabulary.
O·nu·phis (ō·nōō′fis) *Egyptian* See APIS.
O·phi·on (ō′fē·ən) *Greek* The Titan who ruled the universe before Cronus, who overthrew him.
Ops (ops) See main vocabulary.
Or·cus (ôr′kəs) See main vocabulary.
O·res·tes (ô·res′tēz, ō-) See main vocabulary.
O·ri·on (ō·rī′ən) See main vocabulary.
Or·muzd (ôr′muzd) See main vocabulary.
Or·phe·us (ôr′fē·əs) See main vocabulary.
Os·car (os′kar) *Irish* The grandson of Fionn macCumal, and a hero of the Finn Cycle.
O·si·ris (ō·sī′ris) See main vocabulary.
Os·sa (ä′sə) *Greek* See ALOADAE.
Os·ta·ra (os′tə·rä) *Germanic* The ancient goddess of spring, a development of the primitive Indo-European goddess of dawn.
O·tus (ō′təs) *Greek* One of the Aloadae.

Pad·ma (päd′mə) *Hindu* See LAKSHMI.
Pad·ma·pa·ni (päd·mä·pä′nē) *Hindu* The universal savior of Mahayana Buddhism, greatest of the Bodhisattvas, and prototype of Kuan Yin and Kwannon.
Pal·i·nu·rus (pal′i·nōōr′əs) See main vocabulary.
Pan (pan) See main vocabulary.
Pan·da·vas (pän·dä′vəs) *Hindu* One of the two families whose battles are the main subject of the *Mahabharata,* the other being the Kauravas.
Pan·di·on (pan′dē′on) *Greek* A king of Athens, son of Erichthonius and a naiad, and father of Procne and Philomela.
Pan·do·ra (pan·dôr′ə, -dō′rə) See main vocabulary.

Pap·su·kal (pap·sōō′kal) *Babylonian* Messenger of the gods whose timely action rescued Ishtar from death in the underworld realm of her sister Ereshkigal.
Pa·ra·su·ra·ma (pä′rä·sōō·rä′mə) *Hindu* The sixth incarnation of Vishnu.
Par·cae (pär′sē) See main vocabulary.
Pa·ri·ja·ta (pä·rē·jä′tə) *Hindu* The celestial coral tree that yields all desired objects; it was first planted in Indra's heaven, then removed by Krishna, and returned after Krishna's death.
Par·is (par′is) See main vocabulary.
Par·jan·ya (pär·jän′yə) *Hindu* The god of rain and personification of the rain cloud, a son of Dyaus.
Par·the·no·pae·us (pär′thə·nō′pē·əs) *Greek* One of the Seven Against Thebes.
Par·va·ti (pär·vä′tē) *Hindu* See DEVI.
Pa·ta·la (pä·tä′lə) *Hindu* Collective name for seven infernal regions.
Pa·tro·clus (pə·trō′kləs) See main vocabulary.
Peg·a·sus (peg′ə·səs) See main vocabulary.
Pe·leus (pē′lyōōs, -lē·əs) See main vocabulary.
pe·na·tes (pə·nā′tēz) See main vocabulary.
Pe·nel·o·pe (pə·nel′ə·pē) See main vocabulary.
Per·seph·o·ne (pər·sef′ə·nē) See main vocabulary.
Per·seus (pûr′syōōs, -sē·əs) See main vocabulary.
Phae·dra (fē′drə) See main vocabulary.
Pha·e·thon (fā′ə·thon) See main vocabulary.
Phe·nix (fē′niks) See main vocabulary under PHOENIX.
Phi·le·mon (fī·lē′mən) See main vocabulary.
Phil·oc·te·tes (fil′ək·tē′tēz) See main vocabulary.
Phi·lo·me·la (fī·lə·mē′lə) See main vocabulary.
Phi·neus (fī′nōōs, -nē·əs) See main vocabulary.
Phoe·be (fē′bē) See main vocabulary.
Phoe·bus (fē′bəs) See main vocabulary.
Phoe·nix (fē′niks) See main vocabulary.
Pho·lus (fō′ləs) *Greek* An Arcadian centaur, son of Silenus, who entertained Hercules in his cave during the hunt for the Erymanthian boar, and caused a battle between Hercules and other centaurs attracted by the wine.
Phor·cus (fôr′kəs) See main vocabulary.
Phrix·us (frik′səs) See main vocabulary.
Pi·rith·o·us (pī·rith′ō·əs) See main vocabulary.
Pi·sa·cha (pē·sä′chə) *Hindu* The vilest and most malevolent of demons; literally, flesh-eater.
Pi·tris (pē′trēs′) *Hindu* The sainted ancestral spirits; literally, fathers.
pix·y (piks′sē) See main vocabulary.
Plei·a·des (plē′ə·dēz, plī′-) See main vocabulary.
Plu·to (plōō′tō) See main vocabulary.
Pol·y·hym·ni·a (pol′i·him′nē·ə) See main vocabulary.
Pol·y·i·dus (pol′i·ī′dəs) *Greek* A soothsayer of Argos who was able to find the body of Minos's drowned son and eventually to restore him to life.
Pol·y·ni·ces (pol′i·nī′sēz) *Greek* A son of Oedipus, and one of the Seven Against Thebes.
Pol·y·phe·mus (pol′i·fē′məs) See main vocabulary.
Po·sei·don (pō·sī′dən) See main vocabulary.
Pra·ja·pa·ti (prä·jä·pä′tē) *Hindu* Lord of creatures, an epithet of several gods including Indra, Savitri, and Soma; in later application, Brahma, as chief and father of the gods.
Pra·kri·ti (prä·krē′tē) *Hindu* The primitive matter from which the universe is evolved, as opposed to spirit or Purusa; the creative force, prototype of the female.
Pri·am (prī′əm) See main vocabulary.
Proc·ne (prok′nē) See main vocabulary.
Proc·ris (prok′ris) *Greek* See CEPHALUS.
Pro·me·theus (prə·mē′thyōōs, -thē·əs) See main vocabulary.
Psy·che (sī′kē) See main vocabulary.
Ptah (tä) See main vocabulary.
pu·ca (pōō′kə) *Irish* A harmless but very mischievous supernatural being of Irish folklore, often appearing in animal or half-animal form. Also **poo′ka.**
Pu·ru·sa (pə·rōō′sə) *Hindu* **1.** A primeval giant sacrificed by the gods to create the world; he represents the spiritual force opposed to but working with Prakriti, the material force. **2.** Brahma as the creator and original male.
Pu·shan (pōō·shän′) *Hindu* An indistinctly defined sun god, protector and multiplier of cattle, friend and guide of travelers, guardian of paths, and patron of conjurers.
Pu·ta·na (pōō·tä′nə) *Hindu* A female demon who tried to kill the infant Krishna by suckling him with her poisonous milk.
Pyg·ma·li·on (pig·mā′lē·ən, -māl′yən) See main vocabulary.
Pyr·rha (pir′ə) See main vocabulary.
Py·thon (pī′thon) *Greek* The female dragon who dwelt at Delphi and guarded the chasm; killed by Apollo.
py·tho·ness (pī′thə·nis, pith′ə-) See main vocabulary.

Qebh·snuf (keb′snŏŏf) *Egyptian* Son of Horus whose hawk-headed image served as a stopper for the Canopic Jar containing mummified intestines, which he was assigned to guard: also *Kebehsenuf.*
Qui·ri·nus (kwi·rī′nəs) See main vocabulary.

Ra (rä) See main vocabulary.
Rag·na·rök (räg′nä·rûk) See main vocabulary.
Ra-Har·akh·ti (rä′här·äk′tē) *Egyptian* The name assumed by the sun-god Ra in absorbing the qualities and role of the sun-god Horus.
Ra·hu (rä′hōō) *Hindu* The cause of eclipses, king of meteors, and guardian of the southwest quarter; he had mischievously drunk some of the amrita produced at the Churning of the Ocean, and achieved immortality.
Rak·sha·sas (räk·shä′səs) *Hindu* Demigod demons malignantly hostile to men, capable of appearing in animal or human form, and devoted to all kinds of vileness and destruction.
Ram (räm) *Hindu* Generalized term for god or divinity.
Ra·ma (rä′mə) See main vocabulary.
Ra·ma·ya·na (rä·mä·yä′nə) See main vocabulary.
Ram·man (räm′än) *Babylonian* The storm-god, god of lightning and thunder, identified with an ancient flood myth: also *Adad, Hadad.*
Ran (rän) See main vocabulary.
Ra·va·na (rä·vä′nə) *Hindu* The king of the Rakshasas, incarnation of wickedness, breaker of laws, and ravisher of women.
Re (rā) See main vocabulary under RA.
Red Branch *Irish* The organized body of warriors around Conchobar mac Nessa, king of Ulster in the 1st century A.D.
Re·gin (rā′gin) See main vocabulary.
Ren·pet (ren′pet) *Egyptian* Goddess of youth.
Rer·et (rer′et) *Egyptian* See TAUERET.
Rhad·a·man·thus (rad′ə·man′thəs) See main vocabulary.
Rhe·a (rē·ə) See main vocabulary.
Ri·bhu (rē·bōō′) *Hindu* One of the three artisans of the gods, along with Vaja and Vibhu, who were deified because of their skill.
Rom·u·lus (rom′yə·ləs) See main vocabulary.
Ru·dra (rōō′drə) *Hindu* The god of storms who controls the cyclone, and inflicts and heals diseases.

Sa·lus (sā′ləs) See main vocabulary.
San·cus (san′kəs) *Roman* The ancient god of oaths, treaties, hospitality, marriage, and perhaps of the sown field; sometimes identified with Apollo, sometimes with Jupiter.
Sa·ra·pis (sä·rā′pis) *Egyptian* See SERAPIS.
Sa·ti (sä′tē) *Egyptian* Goddess of the Nile; wife of Khnum. Also **Sa·tet** (sä′tet).
Sa·ti (sä′tē) *Hindu* The daughter of Daksha and wife of Rudra, who killed herself by entering the fire after a quarrel between her husband and father; this act is the mythical basis of suttee.
Sat·urn (sat′ərn) See main vocabulary.
sat·yr (sat′ər, sā′tər) See main vocabulary.
Sa·vi·tri (sä·vē′trē *Hindu* **1.** A name of the sun, especially in its life-giving aspect. **2.** In the *Mahabharata,* the heroine whose devotion to her husband was so great that Yama was forced to restore her husband to life.
scar·ab (skar′əb) See main vocabulary.
scorpion-man *Babylonian* A monstrous but friendly creature met by Gilgamesh in his search for Utnapishtim.
Scyl·la (sil′ə) See main vocabulary.
Seb (seb) *Egyptian* See GEB.
Seb·ek (seb′ek) *Egyptian* Crocodile-god represented in cult centers by living, pampered crocodiles. In other areas crocodiles, identified with Set, were destroyed.
Sek·er (sek′ər) *Egyptian* Funerary deity usually depicted in the shape of a human mummy: also *Sokar.*
Sekh·et (sek′et) *Egyptian* Manifestation of Hathor sent by Ra to destroy mankind.
Se·le·ne (si·lē′nē) See main vocabulary.
Sel·ket (sel′ket) *Egyptian* Scorpion-goddess who helped guard the entrails of the deceased; depicted as a woman with a scorpion atop her head as or a human-headed scorpion. Also **Ser·ket** (sûr′ket).
Sem·e·le (sem′ə·lē) See main vocabulary.
Sem·ir·a·mis (sem·ir′ə·mis) See main vocabulary.
Se·ra·pis (si·rā′pis) See main vocabulary.
Se·sha (sesh′ə) *Hindu* The world serpent who supports the seven Patalas or hells, and the world; depicted with a thousand heads, dressed in purple, and holding a plow and a pestle.
Sesh·at (sesh′at, ses′hät) *Egyptian* Ancient goddess of learning, and most important wife of Thoth.
Set (set) See main vocabulary.
Seven Against Thebes *Greek* The seven heroes (Adrastus, Amphiaraus, Capaneus, Hippomedon, Parthenopaeus, Polynices, and Tydeus) who unsuccessfully marched on

Thebes to restore Polynices to the throne, which had been usurped by his brother, Oedipus's other son, Eteocles.
Shab·ti (shäb′tē) *Egyptian* Human figurine interred with the deceased, originally as an alternate dwelling place for the spirit but ultimately as a servant: also *Ushabti.*
Sha·la (shä′lä) *Babylonian* Wife of Ramman, the storm-god.
Sha·mash (shä′mäsh) See main vocabulary.
Shang Ti (shäng tē) *Chinese* The personification of heaven, the source of imperial power; he was worshiped only by the emperor.
Shar·ur (shar′ûr) *Sumerian* Personified weapon of Ninurta.
Shen Nung (shen nōōng) *Chinese* The great culture hero who was patron of agriculture, invented the plow, taught the people planting and the medicinal properties of herbs.
Shih Wang Mu (shû wäng mōō) *Chinese* The Taoist goddess of the western heavens.
Shu (shōō, shŏŏ) *Egyptian* God of the atmosphere who brutally separated the goddess Nut from the god Geb by thrusting her skywards and holding her there.
Sid·dha (sēd′də) *Hindu* One of the semidivine "perfect ones," 88,000 in number, dwelling between earth and sun.
Si·du·ri (sē·dōō′rē) *Babylonian* Cupbearer of the gods, encountered by Gilgamesh in his search for the immortal Utnapishtim.
Sieg·fried (sēg′frēd, *Ger.* zēkh′frēt) See main vocabulary.
Sig·mund (sig′mŏŏnd) *Norse* The father of Sigurd.
Si·gurd (sig′ŏŏrd) See main vocabulary.
Si·le·nus (sī·lē′nəs) See main vocabulary.
Sin (sin) **1.** *Sumerian* See NANNA. **2.** *Babylonian* God of wisdom and moon-god.
si·ren (sī′rən) See main vocabulary.
Si·ta (sē′tə) *Hindu* The goddess of agriculture and wife of Rama.
Sis·y·phus (sis′ə·fəs) See main vocabulary.
Si·va (sē′və) See main vocabulary.
Sleip·nir (slāp′nir) *Norse* Odin's eight-legged gray horse, son of a giant's stallion and Loki in the form of a mare.
Smin·theus (smin′thyōōs, -thē·əs) *Greek* Apollo's epithet as the mouse god.
Sol (sol) See main vocabulary.
So·ma (sô′mə) *Hindu* The god of the soma-juice, the moon, stars, plants, and Brahmans.
so·ma (sō′mə) A plant providing an astringent narcotic juice regarded as having divine power.
Som·nus (som′nəs) See main vocabulary.
Sons of Horus *Egyptian* Four gods assigned to protect mummified viscera: Imsety, Qebhsnuf, Duamutef and Hapy.
Stym·pha·li·an birds (stim·fā′lē·ən) *Greek* The huge flocks of birds chased from the Stymphalian lake by Hercules as the sixth of his labors.
suc·cu·bus (suk′yə·bəs) See main vocabulary.
Su·gri·va (sōō·grē′və) *Hindu* The monkey king who was Rama's ally in his battle with Ravana.
Su·kha·va·ti (sōō·kä·vä′tē) *Hindu* In Buddhist belief, the "happy universe of the West"; more accessible than nirvana, it is a region of universal pleasure and immeasurable life.
Su·pe·ri (sōō′pə·rē) *Greek & Roman* The Olympians, living above the earth: distinguished from *Inferi.*
Su·ra·bhi (sōō·rä′bē) *Hindu* The cow of plenty which grants all desires; created by Prajapati from his breath, or produced at the Churning of the Ocean.
Sur·tr (sür′tər) *Norse* The flame giant who presides over Muspellheim, and whose fire will destroy the world at Ragnarök
Sur·ya (sŏŏr′yə) *Hindu* One of the seven sons of Aditi, personifying the sun.
Su·sa-no-o (sōō·sä·nô·ô) *Japanese* The god of wind, who sprang from Izanagi's nose.
Svart·al·far (svärt′äl·fär) *Norse* The black elves that grew from the maggots of Ymir's flesh.
Sym·ple·ga·des (sim·plē′gə·dēz) See main vocabulary.

Tablets of Destiny *Babylonian* Symbols of authority that Marduk took from Kingu and sealed to his own breast, thereby assuming the supreme position among the gods.
Táin Bó Cuáilgne (toin bō kōōl′nä) See main vocabulary.
Tam·muz (tam′ŏŏz) See main vocabulary.
Tan·ta·lus (tan′tə·ləs) See main vocabulary.
Tash·mit (täsh′mit) *Assyrian* Wife of Nebo and intercessor with him on behalf of mortals.
Ta·uer·et (tä′wer′ət) *Egyptian* Popular goddess of childbirth depicted as a hippopotamus standing on its hind legs: also *Reret.*
Tef·nut (tef′nŏŏt) *Egyptian* Goddess of moisture; mother of Geb and Nut.
Tel·a·mon (tel′ə·mon) See main vocabulary.
Te·lem·a·chus (tə·lem′ə·kəs) See main vocabulary.
Tem (tem) *Egyptian* See ATMU.
Te·reus (tir′yōōs, tir′ē·əs) See main vocabulary.
Ter·mi·nus (tûr′mə·nəs) See main vocabulary.
Terp·sich·o·re (tûrp·sik′ə·rē) See main vocabulary.
Tha·li·a (thə·lī′ə) See main vocabulary.
The·seus (thē′syōōs, -sē·əs) See main vocabulary.
Thor (thôr) See main vocabulary.
Thoth (thōth, tōt) See main vocabulary.
Thrym (thrüm) *Norse* The frost giant who stole Thor's hammer, and demanded Freya as the price of returning it. Thor disguised himself as Freya, retrieved the hammer, and killed Thrym and his giant band.
Ti·a·mat (tē·ä′mät) *Babylonian* The primeval salt sea personified as a dragon of chaos that Marduk slew and split into two pieces, one of which he used to form the sky.
Ti·re·si·as (tī·rē′sē·əs) See main vocabulary.
Tir na nog (tir nə nōg) *Irish* The land of youth, an otherworldly paradise on an island.
Ti·tan (tīt′n) See main vocabulary.
Tri·ton (trīt′n) See main vocabulary.
Trojan War See main vocabulary.
troll (trōl) See main vocabulary.
Tsai Shen (tsī shen) *Chinese* The god of wealth.
Tsao Chün (tsou chün) *Chinese* The god of the kitchen, stove, and hearth; annually he returns to heaven to report on the misdeeds of the family.
Ts'ao Kuo-ch'iu (tsou kwō·chyōō) *Chinese* One of the eight immortals.
Tuatha Dé Danann (tōō′hə dā dä′non) See main vocabulary.
Tung Wang Kung (tŏŏng wäng kŏŏng) *Chinese* The Taoist lord of the immortals, lord of the east, and prime embodiment of the male principle, yang.
Tur·nus (tûr′nəs) *Roman* An Italian chief, the rival of Aeneas for the hand of Lavinia.
T'u Ti (tōō tē) *Chinese* The god of place or locality.
Ty·che (tī′kē) See main vocabulary.
Ty·deus (tī′dyōōs, -dē·əs) *Greek* One of the Seven Against Thebes.
Ty·phoe·us (tī′fē·əs) See main vocabulary.
Tyr (tür, tir) See main vocabulary.

Ul·ler (ōōl′lər) *Norse* The god of winter, hunting, archery, skating, and snowshoeing.
Ulster Cycle See main vocabulary.
U·ma (ōō′mə) *Hindu* See DEVI.
U·ra·ni·a (yōō·rā′nē·ə) See main vocabulary.
U·ra·nus (yŏŏr′ə·nəs) See main vocabulary.
Ur-Sha·na·bi (ûr-shə·nä′bē) *Babylonian* Utnapishtim's boatman who consented to ferry Gilgamesh over the waters of death.
U·shab·ti (ōō·shäb′tē) *Egyptian* See SHABTI.
Us·nech (ish′näkh) *Irish* Father of three sons (including Naiose) who fled to Scotland with Deirdre but were lured back to Ireland by Conchobar and beheaded.
Ut·gard (ōōt′gärd) See main vocabulary.
Ut·gard-Lo·ki (ōōt′gärd·lō′kē) See main vocabulary.
Ut·na·pish·tim (ŏŏt·nä·pish′tim) *Babylonian* The Noah-like figure of the Gilgamesh Epic who gained immortality.
Ut·tu (u′tōō) *Sumerian* Goddess of vegetation born in the paradise-like land of Dilmun; daughter of Enki and Ninkur.
U·tu (ōō′tōō) *Sumerian* Sun-god born of Nanna the moon-god and his wife Ningal.

Vai·ta·ra·ni (vī·tə·rä′nē) *Hindu* The river of death that flows between the land of the living and the kingdom of Yama.
Va·ja (vä′jə) *Hindu* One of the three artisans of the gods, along with Ribhu and Vibhu, who were deified for their great skill.
Val·hal·la (val·hal′ə) See main vocabulary.
Va·li (vä′lē) *Norse* **1.** A son of Odin, born for the purpose of avenging the death of Balder. **2.** A son of Loki.
val·kyr·ie (val·kir′ē, val′kir·ē) See main vocabulary.
Va·nir (vä′nir) See main vocabulary.
Va·ra·ha (vä·rä′hə) *Hindu* The boar avatar of Vishnu, assumed in order to deliver the world from a demon who had seized it and carried it to the bottom of the ocean.
Va·ru·na (vä·rōō′nə) See main vocabulary.
Va·ru·ni (vä·rōō′nē) *Hindu* The goddess of wine.
Va·su·ki (vä·sōō′kē) *Hindu* One of the serpent kings who ruled in Patala.
Va·yu (vä′yōō) **1.** *Hindu* The god of wind and atmosphere, and the breath of life that sprang from Purusa. **2.** *Persian* A wind god having two aspects, gentle and destructive.
Ve·da (vā′də, vē-) See main vocabulary.
Ve·dan·ta (vi·dän′tə, -dan′-) See main vocabulary.
Ve·nus (vē′nəs) See main vocabulary.
Vi·bhu (vē′bōō) *Hindu* One of the three artisans of the gods, along with Ribhu and Vaja, who were deified for their great skill.
Vi·dar (vē′där) *Norse* A son of Odin, regarded as the guardian of peace and the primeval forest, who will survive Ragnarök along with his brother Vali.

Vid·ya·dha·ra (vēd·yä·dä′rə) *Hindu* One of a group of benevolent supernatural beings who dwell in the northern mountains and can intermarry with men.
Vi·grid (vē′grid) *Norse* The battlefield of Ragnarök.
Vi·li and Ve (vē′le; vā) *Norse* Odin's two brothers, who killed Ymir and from his body created the earth.
Vi·na·ta (vē·nä′tə) *Hindu* The mother of Garuda and one of the wives of Kasyapa.
Vi·ra·bha·dra (vē·rä·bä′drə) *Hindu* An emanation of, or the son of, Siva, created as a form of his anger.
Vish·nu (vish′no͞o) See main vocabulary.
Vis·va·kar·ma (vis·vä·kär′mə) *Hindu* Originally, the epithet of a powerful god like Surya or Indra; later, the name of an independent creator-god, identified with Parjapati and having arms, face, eyes, and feet on every side.
Vis·va·va·su (vis·vä·vä′so͞o) *Hindu* The king of the Siddhas.
Vol·sun·ga Sa·ga (vol′so͝ong·gə sä′gə) See main vocabulary.
Vol·sungs (vol′so͝ongz) See main vocabulary.
Vul·can (vul′kən) See main vocabulary.

Wal·pur·gis Night (väl·po͝or′gis) See main vocabulary.
Way·land (wā′lənd) See main vocabulary.
weighing of souls *Egyptian* A ceremony conducted in the underworld before Osiris in which the heart of the deceased was placed on a balance against Maat, the feather of truth, which it was not to outweigh.
Wen Ch'ang (wen chäng) *Chinese* The god of literature.
Wyrd (wird) *Germanic* The goddess of fate, chiefly known from English sources.

Xan·thos and Ba·li·os (zän′thōs; bə·lī′ōs) *Greek* The two immortal horses given by Poseidon to Peleus as a wedding present, and used by Achilles as chariot horses.

Yak·shas (yäk′shäs) *Hindu* Supernatural beings who seceded from the demons and took over the mountain areas.
Ya·ma (yä′mə) *Hindu* The king of the dead, and later the judge of the dead.
yang (yäng) See main vocabulary.
Yang Chin (yäng chēn) *Chinese* The goat god.
Yen Lo (yen lō) *Chinese* Lord of the fifth hell and infernal jungle.
Ygg·dra·sil (ig′drə·sil) *Norse* A huge ash tree whose roots and branches bind together heaven, earth, and hell.
Yin (yin) See main vocabulary.
Y·mir (ē′mir, ü′mir) See main vocabulary.

Zar·pan·it (zär·pan′it) *Babylonian* Consort of Marduk and mother of Nebo.
Zeus (zo͞os) See main vocabulary.
Zi·u·su·dra (zē′ə·so͞o′drä) *Sumerian* A hero whose Noah-like adventures antedate those of the Babylonian Utnapishtim.
Zu-bird (zo͞o′bûrd) *Sumerian & Babylonian* Mischief-making lesser god, slain in one myth by Lugalbanda and in another by Marduk.

THE WORLD'S RELIGIONS

by John B. Noss

Primitive Religions

Hinduism

Jainism

Buddhism

Sikhism

Taoism

Confucianism

Shinto

Zoroastrianism

Judaism

Christianity

Islam

THE WORLD'S RELIGIONS

by John B. Noss

Man's religions reflect his human need to feel at home in the universe and comfortable among his neighbors. He has always sensed that he cannot stand alone; that good workable relations with his neighbors matter to him; that since mysterious powers in Nature and Society will not let him alone but affect him at every step, he must be in harmony either with them, with the great lords and kings among them, or with the one originative being that has brought the whole world into being and in some sovereign way commands all its processes.

The religions of the past (not treated in this article) have all reflected these human needs and concerns. The Neanderthal Man and his talented successors, the Cro-Magnon men of France, Spain, and Africa, very evidently sought good relations with nonhuman powers that pervaded the natural world and affected human destiny. The great national religions of the past in Egypt, Mesopotamia, Greece, Rome, and Northern Europe were constantly concerned with great lords and kings among the spirits and powers operating on earth and in the heavens, and they showed an equal concern as to the destiny of man in this life and the next.

We shall see that the living religions of man today are similarly motivated.

PRIMITIVE RELIGIONS

Religions of peoples who live close to nature, in relatively isolated societies not yet penetrated by the technology and culture of highly organized industrial societies, are said to be primitive. They include the Australian aborigines, the pygmies of Africa, the jungle tribes of India and Southeast Asia, the natives of New Guinea and of portions of the South Seas, the Indians of the Upper Amazon and of Central America, and certain Eskimo tribes.

Many primitive groups of a generation ago are now undergoing transformation through cultural, educational, and technological changes that are breaking up the established patterns of the past; but primitives are in general resistant to such changes. The traditional customs and beliefs are their means of adaptation to environment; furthermore, they unify the tribe, are comfortable for the individual in that they provide each group member with a role to play that is approved in advance, and are above all sacred, because hallowed by ancestors and divine powers, and therefore binding. Besides this, they satisfy basic biological and psychological needs. Many primitive customs and beliefs strike persons trained in scientific method as naive and supersititous, but they in fact reflect the kind of realism and common sense which follow from taking sensations at face value—a characteristic of primitives in general. Moreover the individual seldom questions what the group feels or senses to be the case. Hence, while primitives have beliefs and practices that the experimental methods of science would seem to discredit, they find them quite true and necessary. Some common features of primitive belief and practice may be discerned, as follows:

Reverence for the Sacred Events, persons, and places in any degree uncanny, mysterious, or creditable with supernatural power are sacred or holy. Included in this very large category are most rites and ceremonies and those who conduct or commandingly participate in them. The traditions of the tribe are hallowed by the ancestors who passed them on. Many places and objects are sacred, such as groves of trees or fetishes (objects thought to embody spirits or magic powers). The most common reason for considering a person, place, or action *taboo* or to be abstained from is that it is sacred and has the power to cause quick good or ill. The presence of the sacred, because it arouses anxiety, is also the chief cause of religious and magical rituals seeking reassurance and favorable outcomes.

Intermingling of Magic and Religion Religious rituals are persuasive in intent, while magical rituals seek to be coercive. But in most primitive ceremonies it is hard to disentangle the magical and religious elements; the words may be persuasive in form, but taken together they may carry the guarantee of a compulsive effect on gods and spirits, while, on the other hand, magical rites may mingle prayers with commands. This should be borne in mind when considering the topics that follow.

Veneration and Worship of Many Powers and Spirits Primitives reverence and at times worship multitudes of powers and spirits, some of which have the status of gods. Venerated or worshiped are stones, plants, trees, many kinds of animals and reptiles, fire, volcanoes, rivers and lakes, sun, moon, stars, mountains, and many other animate and inanimate things. These objects may be regarded as themselves alive with power in every part; or they may be considered the residences of separable individual spirits and powers. In the former case they may be full of *mana*, an indwelling power that causes action of an extraordinary kind; in the latter case, they are objects (bodies) containing souls capable of thought, feeling, and action of an individual kind, able to leave the body they have entered and to survive its death or destruction. Belief in the latter is called *animism*.

Recognition of High Gods There is widespread belief among primitives that there exists a great god far up in the sky, or at a distance, who has made everything—gods, men, and animals—and who is the ultimate lawgiver and overseer. But he is usually so far removed as to be beyond the reach of prayer, and certainly immune to magical coercion.

Types of Magic Magic is resorted to when danger or uncertainty attends an activity and the utterance of set words or the performance of set acts, or both, promise a favorable result. Magic rites may be variously classified. *Preventive magic* wards off happenings and *productive magic* brings them about. Thus corn or fertility dances are productive of favorable growth of grain, while a dance in which a black cloud is threatened with a spear turns aside a thunderstorm. *Sympathetic magic* presumes that like produces like or that severed portions of a body retain sympathy with the organism to which they once belonged. Thus spearing an image during a hunting dance insures success in the following hunt, and doing magic with severed hair and nails affects the person who is in the body from which they have been severed. *Black magic*, which seeks to harm, has its roots in sympathetic magic; thus, if one makes an image in wax of an enemy and pierces it to the heart with pins, the enemy will die. Another form of magic accompanies *fetishism*; it uses the powers in inanimate objects, such as distinctive stones or stuffed antelope horns. *Shamanism* makes use of the magic powers possessed by certain persons, such as medicine men and sorcerers; this is done to cure or inflict disease, to induce spirits into persons or exorcize them. Shamans are able to guide souls after death into the next world and are besought to leave their bodies temporarily in order to do so.

Attitudes to the Dead; Ancestor Worship Death is usually animistically viewed as the departure of a soul from the body that it had animated and directed. Disembodied souls are regarded with fear unless they depart to a distance; should they remain near, they are constantly appeased. If not placated, they may become demonic; this is assumed to be the case with persons killed by violence or left for any cause unburied without the customary funeral rites. Many different precautions are taken to keep the dead from harassing the living, the most common being to leave food at the grave. But not all of the dead are inimical; for ancestral spirits, if remembered, praised, and fed, may help the living in many ways, not only by warding off evil spirits, but also by bringing good fortune to their descendants.

Totemism The myths and rituals connected with this cultic practice recognize a mystical bond or relationship between various human groups and their totems—which are certain animals, plants, or objects intimately related to these groups and graphically represented by them in their religious art. The totem is sacred to the group that regards it as theirs. Sometimes a myth tells of a common ancestor of the totem and its human counterparts. The members of a totem group must marry outside of the group (a practice called exogamy); and the totem may not be eaten by members of the totem group except at a sacramental feast where the bond between them and the totem is recognized.

Other Features of primitive belief and practice are purification rites, rites of passage (i.e., rites which attend important events in an individual's life, such as birth, initiation into adulthood, marriage, and death), divination, sacrifice, war dances, and fertility rites.

In general, the primitive world abounds with ills caused by powers and spirits in the air and underground, powers immanent in every kind of natural object, beast, plant, and human being. The problem is to divine the presence of threatening powers and to take preventive action through magic, sacrifice, and prayer. Appropriate action may convert the threatened evil into productive good; but this can be achieved only by constant vigilance and care. The best course is to follow faithfully the traditional procedures of the group without deviation. But primitive life is not utterly fearful and anxious. It should be said that when all goes well, the primitive is as capable of joy and high spirits as human beings in general.

HINDUISM

The term Hinduism applies to a very complex body of traditions accumulated through at least thirty centuries. These traditions are followed today by nearly 400 million people, who, in spite of divergence in details of belief and practice, are conscious of a common heritage.

Origins The two principal contributors to early Hinduism were: (1) the light-skinned Indo-Europeans who invaded India through the Khyber Pass about 1500 B.C. and (2) the people they conquered, the dark-skinned creators of the Indus culture of western and central India. The former brought with them some forty gods and goddesses bearing names common to Indo-European cultures, such as Dyaus Pitar (Jupiter, Zeus), Prithivi Matar (Demeter), Mitra (Mithra), Varuna (Uranus), Agni (Ignis) and others. The latter supplied more earthy elements: a god presiding over reproduction (later known as Shiva), mother goddesses concerned with fertility, and (possibly) the beliefs in reincarnation and the Law of Karma.

After the invaders had established themselves in Western India, they produced an extensive oral literature, the four *Vedas* (the Rig-, Yajur-, Sama-, and Atharva-Vedas) which are still the basic scriptures of Hinduism. These were followed after 800 B.C. by a written literature in Sanskrit, the classical language of India. Based on the Vedas, the principal components of this literature were priestly treatises called the *Brahmanas* and philosophical conversations, the *Upanishads.*

One of the social effects of the Indo-European invasion was the establishment of a color barrier (*varna*) to control miscegenation between the light-skinned conquerors and their darker-skinned vassals, This resulted in the early fixed *castes*, the Brahmins (priests), the Kshatriyas (warriors and princes), the Vaishyas (artisans and peasants) and the Shudras (servants). These castes were forbidden to intermarry, sleep, or eat together. Their diets differed. In the course of centuries they subdivided further until there were 2,000 subcastes. Outside the pale were the outcastes and unclean persons, the untouchables. It is only recently, under the stress of social and economic change, that this complex system has begun to break down.

Dharma and the Way of Works What makes a Hindu feel he is a Hindu and therefore different from non-Hindus? The most comprehensive answer to this question is that it is the *Dharma*, the pattern of life which Hindus have followed for centuries as their religious and moral duty; in other words, it is the Way of Works (*Karma Marga*) laid down in tradition, the duties owing to the gods, the ancestors, priests, the family, the caste, the community, animals, and so on. Specifically, the Dharma governs the household life, The typical Hindu home begins its day with adoration of the rising sun. The household deity—Shiva, Vishnu, or some other god or perhaps goddess—is welcomed to the new day and the household with a morning ritual. In the evening another ritual puts the deity to rest for the night. At the birth of a child, and at its name giving, its first taking out to see the sun, its first feeding with boiled rice (weaning), its first hair cutting, there is a ceremony. For boys of the three highest castes, there is the rite of initiation into manhood, comparable to the bar mitzvah of Jews and the confirmation of Christians. For both sexes there are the rites of betrothal, marriage, death, and disposal of the dead (commonly by cremation). There are also the periodic *shraddha* rites for the spirits of the dead. The Dharma also includes visiting temples and going on pilgrimages to distant holy places. Nor is the subhuman world left out. The principle of *ahimsa* or noninjury to any sentient being calls for the practice of nonviolence toward the whole subhuman world, especially toward the cow. "The cow to me," said Mahatma Gandhi, "means the entire sub-human world . . . . She is the mother to millions of Indian mankind. The cow is a poem of pity."

But there is yet another dimension to the Dharma. The next life depends on how the Dharma is practiced in this. Reincarnation (*samsara*) is a universal belief in India. Hindus believe that all souls in bodies—whether of gods, men, animals, reptiles, insects, plants, or souls in hell—are subject to death and rebirth. Births are not always on the same level. If one has accumulated favorable *karma* ("deeds") by obedience to the Dharma, birth will be at a higher level; if evil has been done, the birth will be lower: one may become an insect or a being in hell. This is governed by an inflexible law, the *Law of Karma* which determines whether one rises or falls in the scale of existence.

To follow the Way of Works (i.e., to perform what is called for by the Dharma) is one of the three ways of salvation. It will not get one into Nirvana, but it will procure a better rebirth, and may even get one to heaven. Salvation through the Way of Works is not so difficult as salvation through the Way of Knowledge.

Brahmanism and the Way of Knowledge Brahmanism is a convenient term for a form of Hinduism originating in the post-Vedic period. In its first phase, beginning about 800 B.C., a vast body of sacrificial rituals honoring the various gods was created. They are contained in the ancient priestly manuals, the *Brahmanas*, and are no longer performed in their entirety. In the second and more lasting phase, Brahmanism turned to philosophy and provided a basis for the Way of Knowledge (*Jnana Marga*). Talented men and women of the Brahmin and Kshatriya castes began to speculate that the gods were symbolic of a single reality seen from various angles. All things—men, beasts, gods, all objects—had come from this One Thing or Being and would return to It. After calling It by various names, they finally settled on a neuter noun, *Brahman*. Brahman, they said, is the sole real existent; there is no second thing whatsoever. In a series of treatises called the *Upanishads* (Secret Knowledge), which were in the form of conversations, these conclusions were set forth with great subtlety.

According to the majority view, synthesized by Shankara in the eighth century A.D., That One Thing (Brahman) extrudes from itself millions of souls (each called an *atman*) and along with them a creative being called *Ishvara* ("Lord," Brahman in the form of a personal god, known to men by various names). There are thus two modes of Brahman: the unmanifested and unknowable *Nirguna Brahman* (Brahman without attributes) and the knowable personal god *Saguna Brahman* (Brahman with attributes). As for the individual soul or self, each is Brahman in the form of an individual self; consequently, full realization of this fact leads the earnest thinker to see the *identity* of himself with Brahman, an experience not fully gained without a trance of oneness (*yoga*) coming at the end of concentrated meditation, with backbone rigid, eyes gazing down the nose. The best name for the ultimate reality is therefore Brahman-Atman, and each soul must say of itself *Tat tvam asi* ("THAT is what *you* are!").

Along with this goes another realization. Ishvara, the personal god, has had from the first a magic power (*maya*) to create appearances, the millions of things in the world perceived by individual atmans. The world is therefore in every part a kind of deception of the senses, an illusion. It is only our ignorance (*avidya*, nonseeing) that causes us to consider it as real as it appears to be. Acceptance of maya entails being "bound to the ever-turning wheel" of *samsara*, i.e., it entails being reborn from one life to another endlessly. If, on the other hand, one subdues his senses by yoga exercises until he ceases to accept maya and goes into a trance of oneness with Brahman (which is what *Nirvana* means), then one has reached salvation by following the Way of Knowledge.

Bhakti and the Way of Devotion This is the third way of salvation and is distinctly religious, for *bhakti* is ardent and hopeful devotion to a particular god or goddess in gratitude for aid received or promised. Whereas the Way of Works is basically legalistic and the Way of Knowledge philosophic, the Way of Devotion involves the religious act of surrender to a deity. The first way seeks a better rebirth, the second entrance into Nirvana, the third union with a deity who may grant admission to heaven or enable one to make gigantic strides toward Nirvana in this or the next life. The classic literary expression of the way of bhakti is the *Bhagavad Gita*, an episode in the great epic, the *Mahabharata*. In the Gita the god Krishna, who is an earthly form of Vishnu, explains to a hesitant warrior, Arjuna, his duty in its cosmic setting. He tells Arjuna that if he is not able to do his caste duty (fighting) or pursue the way of knowledge, he should rely in utter faith and devotion on himself (Krishna) and enjoy the god's loving assistance and saving power.

In the lives of millions of Hindus, bhakti is of primary importance. It has led to the erection of temples to gods great and small, the proliferation of holy places, including sacred cities like Benares and Puri, the practice of going on pilgrimages to sacred shrines along the holy Ganges River, and the celebration of festivals (*utsavas*) at religious fairs to which millions throng in the hope of heavenly benefit. Bhakti also enters into the family rites centering in the patron deity of the house, whether Vishnu, Shiva, Krishna, or some other deity.

The Trimurti Although the polytheism of India embraces thousands of gods, goddesses, demons, ghosts, and powerful spirits, three manifestations of godhead are recognized as chief. They are Brahmā the Creator, Shiva the Destroyer, and Vishnu the Preserver. When Brahman manifests Itself as Ishvara, creation follows, and along with creation the eternal processes of preservation on the one hand and destruction on the other. The three gods symbolize these three phases of natural process. Each has a consort and associates. Brahmā does not have many temples erected to him, because he did his work long ago and now rides aloof on the back of a wild white goose, with his four heads attentively reading the Vedas. Shiva is a nearer presence, a name for decay and renewal, life, death, and reproduction. His feminine counterparts are called *shaktis* ("energies") and go by various names; some are benevolent like Uma and Parbati, others dour like Durga and Kali. His associates are Ganesha, his elephant-headed son, and Nandi the sacred bull. His symbol is the *lingam*, a phallic column. Vishnu is more consistently benevolent, standing as he does for conservation of the good and necessary. Although he does not himself leave his heavenly seat, in times of need he comes to earth in *avataras* ("descents"), ten being generally listed. Two of these are of prime importance, Rama, the perfect hero described in the epic, the *Ramayana*, and Krishna, the god-hero of the *Mahabharata*. They are separately worshiped. Vishnu's consort is the goddess of beauty and fortune, Lakshmi. She strokes his feet in wifely devotion as he reclines on the cosmic sea serpent, Shesha. He also uses Garuda, a great bird, as his vehicle. (This last is separately worshiped on the island of Bali.)

The Four Acceptable Ways of Life Within the general scheme of rebirth there are different qualities of existence. Hindus consider that men may justifiably follow four ways of life, that is, if they act with integrity at the level they choose. Beginning with the lowest level, these are: (1) the way of *kama* or sensuous pleasure, (2) the way of *artha* or pursuit of wealth and power, (3) the way of the *dharma* or fulfilling one's moral obligations, and (4) the way of *moksha* or salvation, with its twin aims of escape from illusion and entrance into Nirvana. It is expected that anyone who begins at either of the first two levels will find them less than fully satisfactory and will ascend to the third and fourth levels, either in this or a following life.

The Darshanas or Six Acceptable Systems of Philosophy During a period of 1500 years of unhurried philosophical discussion six systems of philosophy emerged as orthodox: (1) the *Nyaya*, concerned with logical reasoning ("things to be proved"); (2) the *Vaiseshika*, conceiving the world as a combination of atoms, souls, and an "unseen force of deity" that is the cause of the world of composite things; (3) the *Sankhya*, rejecting monism (Brahman) and accepting two ultimate principles, *prakriti* (the natural world) and *purusha* (the infinite number of selves or spirits); (4) *Yoga*, a system of mental and physical self-discipline aiming at liberation of the soul from earthly bonds; (5) the *Purva-Mimansa*, a moral philosophy derived from the four Vedas and the Brahmanas regarded as the ultimate authorities on the Dharma; and (6) the *Vedanta*, literally "the conclusion of the Vedas," a point of view including several philosophical systems of a monistic kind much like that described above as the majority view in Brahmanism. The great name here is that of Shankara (788–830 A.D. or earlier): His "unqualified nondualism" (i.e. monism) was modified by Ramanuja (died 1137) and Madhva (1199–1276) to allow greater independent reality to the universe and its souls.

Sects The two major sectarian groups are the Shaivites, devotees of Shiva, and the Vaishnavites, devotees of Vishnu. The literature of the former is contained in numerous Hindu *Tantras* ("Threads") and in six books of the *Puranas* ("Ancient Stories"), while that of the latter is found principally in the *Bhagavad Gita*, mentioned above, and in six *Puranas* other than those devoted to Shiva. From about the eighth century A.D. on, teachers of the masses began to appear trying to meet the need for images and symbols that would enable ordinary folk to understand the chief features of reality and give expression to their adoration (bhakti). In Shaivism the *lingam* became the chief symbol of the god. Groups of *shaktas* (followers of the shaktis) formed. Some were the so-called right-handed shaktas (the Dakshinacharins), who looked upon the lingam as a significant symbol of the principle of life. The left-handed shaktas (the Vamacharins) practiced secret rites, seeking to exhaust and subdue desire for meat, liquor, and sex by ritually indulging in them. The shaktas picture Shiva as half-woman on his left side and half-man on his right. The Lingayats, founded in the 12th century, carry with them at all times a soapstone lingam wrapped in a red scarf and will not be without it, They stress, however, the ascetic aspect of Shiva, remembering the time he was a *sannyasin* (holy man). The Vaishnavites are far less severe and give honor to the compassion of the kindly god who incarnates himself to save mankind from danger. Ramanuja, Madhva, and Ramananda (12th, 13th and 14th centuries) are their greatest thinkers.

Hinduism and the West The British rulers of India brought Hindus face-to-face with Western culture, science, and religion. The first result of this was a liberal movement of rapprochement with the West, started by Ram Mohun Rai and called the *Brahmo Samaj*. It welcomed insights from all religions, renounced idolatry, and proclaimed monotheism. More strictly Hindu in spirit was the *Arya Samaj* founded by Swami Dayanand. Its principles of reform come from "going back to the Vedas," the all-sufficient scriptures, in which monotheism and the basic tenets of science are found. Broad tolerance and all-inclusiveness were taught by the 19th century Hindu saint Ramakrishna, whose followers developed the world-ranging *Ramakrishna Movement.* Secularism or the acceptance of science and humanism as the sole sources of truth, with a consequent rejection of the Dharma and all religion, is widespread in India today. On the other hand, Mahatma Gandhi distrusted Western technology as threatening India's village economy and found in Hinduism an expression of religion wholly suited to his needs, although he felt all religions convey truth to their adherents in about equal measure.

JAINISM

Based in its present form on the life and presumed teachings of Mahavira or Great Hero (sixth century B.C.), this religion has rejected monistic Brahmanism on philosophical grounds. But this would not make it a heresy; its heresy consists in its rejection of the Vedas, the sacrificial system of the priests, and the caste system. "Man, you are your own friend; why do you wish for a friend beyond yourself?" Mahavira is reported to have said. In other words, a man is not saved by gods or priests but by his own efforts. Mahavira achieved *moksha* (salvation) by severe asceticism. He also zealously practiced *ahimsa* (nonviolence), never injuring any living thing because of the soul in it. He avoided stepping on or crushing any live thing and would not eat raw (i.e., live) fruit or vegetables, relying on food cooked by someone else and left over. He begged his food from strangers and wandered naked.

His followers became a new group because of their rejection of the Hindu Dharma. They believed that Mahavira had descended from heaven to enter his mother's womb, and that he was the last of 24 *Tirthankaras* ("Finders of the river ford"), all of whom are now reverenced. Historically, Mahavira did have one predecessor, Parshva, the founder of the ascetic group which Mahavira joined in his youth. Later followers divided into two main groups, the Digambaras, whose mendicants went about naked ("clad in atmosphere") and the Shvetambaras, who in public wore a single white garment. The Jains' principal influence on India has been through their practice of ahimsa. They now number about two million, most of them in the Bombay area.

BUDDHISM

Buddhists have been regarded by Hindus as a "dissenting group" (i.e., heretical). Their philosophical doctrines do not disqualify them, for Hindus allow absolute freedom of thought. But like the Jains they have renounced the Hindu Dharma and substituted one of their own; they have rejected the Vedas, the Brahmins as agents of salvation, and the Hindu caste system.

Gautama Buddha: His Life and Teachings The founder of Buddhism was born about 560 B.C. into the Kshatriya caste and was destined to be a ruling prince, but in his late twenties he left his parents, wife, and son to seek release from the misery of existence by entrance into Nirvana. His first teachers were Brahmins, but he rejected their views as unenlightening. He then turned for five years to the practice of an extreme asceticism much like that of Mahavira (who was probably unknown to him). But he found this debilitating rather than enlightening. Under a tree, later known as the Bo tree (from *bodhi,* or enlightenment, tree), at a place renamed for him Budhgaya (the place of the Enlightenment), he sat alone pondering the reasons for his failure. The ways of salvation as people practiced them were certainly all ways out of human misery; but what was the *cause* of this misery, he asked. Suddenly the answer came. It was *tanha* (desire, thirst, passion, wanting what was not possessed). Indeed the very intensity of his desire for release was a cause of his present misery. To get rid of every desire would be to get rid of every misery. Realizing that he was then utterly without desire, he went into an ecstasy, without losing "mindfulness," and experienced *bodhi,* enlightenment. Nirvana, he concluded, was exactly such a state of desirelessness and utter peace. Now he would be reborn no more; he had achieved deliverance. He was a *buddha* ("an enlightened one").

In the deer park near Benares he found five ascetics with whom he had earlier been associated, and preached to them his first sermon; it was on the Middle Way between sensuality and ascetic self-torture. He explained how control of desire would enable them to live in the world without being overcome by its passions. Together they formed the *Sangha* or Buddhist monastic order. In the 45 years remaining to him (he died about 480 B.C. at 80 years of age), the Buddha and his disciples spread the Sangha through northern India. Members of all castes and of both sexes were admitted to the order as brothers and sisters. All alike shaved their heads and wore yellow robes. They subscribed to a simple creed: "I take refuge in the Buddha, I take refuge in the Dhamma (Dharma), I take refuge in the Sangha." They used the word Dharma in a sense different from that of the Hindus, meaning by it primarily the Teaching or Doctrine. Included, of course, were such instructions concerning conduct as the Ten Precepts forbidding monks and nuns to take life, indulge in sexual intercourse, steal, tell lies, eat after noon, look on at dancing, singing, or dramatic spectacles, use garlands or perfumes, sleep on high or broad beds, accept gold or silver. But a central element in the Dharma was the *Four Noble Truths:* (1) all life is permeated with misery, (2) the cause of such misery is desire, (3) the cure of misery lies in the overcoming of desire, (4) the overcoming of desire comes from following the Noble Eightfold Path, which may be called the road leading to no-desire. It requires right beliefs, right aspirations, right speech, right conduct, right means of livelihood, right effort, right mindfulness, and right meditation. Desire for these is misery-reducing.

The philosophical context of the Buddhist ethical code is the conviction that all the constituents of any living person and the whole live world are in constant flux; nothing remains immune to change except Nirvana; the permanence of the world and the self is thus an illusion. The Wheel of Time and Rebirth is ever turning. It is set spinning by a *Chain of Causation,* beginning in a previous existence, carrying through this, and going on into the next existence. The operative causes are linked in a "dependent origination," each rising from the one before. They are: a basic ignorance of the impermanence of selves and all objects, the predispositions brought into this life as a result of such ignorance, the acceptance in infancy of the world and self as real, expression of individuality as a value, exercise of the mind and senses in such expression, making contact with other selves and with things, indulging the feelings when doing so, developing desires thereby, and at last clinging to existence and throwing oneself into the processes of becoming with its misery-producing entailments, old age, disease, and death. The Buddha taught that all selves suffer from three defects of their existence: (1) transitoriness (*anicca*), (2) the basic unreality of the self (*anatta*), and (3) consequent misery (*dukkha*). In these circumstances it is best to give up the world, to renounce love for individuals, and to seek freedom from dependence and desire, until at last one attains freedom even from the desire for no-desire; which is to be in Nirvana. At the same time one must hate no one and love all without loving any *one.*

Theravada or Hinayana Buddhism After the Buddha's death the monks of the Sangha came together to recite and give final form to his teachings. An oral tradition in the Pali language was thus formed. It is called the Theravada or Teaching of the Elders. Some years passed before it was written down. The Pali tradition was divided into three *pitakas* ("baskets"): (1) the *Vinaya Pitaka,* which contains the disciplinary rules for the Sangha; (2) the *Sutta Pitaka* or remembered discourses of the Buddha, and (3) the *Abhidamma Pitaka* or further expositions of the Doctrine. Each pitaka is subdivided into important individual treatises like the *Majjhima Nikaya* and *Digha Nikaya* of the second and the *Dhammapada* and *Jataka* of the third.

An important accession to Buddhism occurred with the conversion of the Emperor Asoka (264–223 B.C.). He sent missionaries into all parts of India and into Ceylon, Burma, and the Near East. The so-called Southern Buddhism (Theravada, or Hinayana) thus came into existence and spread farther to Thailand, Cambodia, and other areas of Southeast Asia. To this day in these areas the highest aim is becoming an *arhat* or enlightened monk intent on getting himself into Nirvana. The temples, as for example those in Rangoon and Bangkok, are elaborate and filled with gold-plated images of the Buddha, but it is understood by the informed that prayers to the Buddha, while meritorious, do not reach him, since he is in Nirvana. The layman should acquire merit by learning scripture and giving gifts to the Sangha in order that he may be reborn as a monk. The monk on his part should compassionately instruct laymen in the right path.

Mahayana Buddhism Mahayana Buddhism is self-named. *Yana* means "vehicle," e.g., a carriage or a ferry, and *maha* means "great." Hence this type of Buddhism is consciously "the great ferry," the ferry for the many, across the river between this world and Nirvana. (Because the Mahayanists named their "vehicle" the large one, the older Buddhism came to be called, not much to its adherents' liking, the Hinayana, i.e., the small or one-at-a-time ferry. No wonder they now prefer to be called Theravadins.) The Mahayana is sometimes called Northern Buddhism, for it spread into China, Korea and Japan from the south, into Mongolia by way of the passes from northwest India into central Asia, and into Tibet from Nepal.

The literature of this movement was in Sanskrit rather than Pali, and was produced not only in India but also in China and Japan. Among the hundreds of works the *Diamond-Cutter*, the *Lotus of the Good Law*, the *Prajna-Paramita Sutras*, and the *Pure Land Sutras* were especially influential.

The transition from original Buddhism to the Mahayana was made in northwest India. First it was asked whence Gautama Buddha had come. The answer: he must have been in the heavens, specifically the Tusita heaven, and came down out of compassion for suffering mankind to be born from a woman. How did he get to the Tusita heaven? He rose to it after many existences as a benevolent and self-sacrificial being, sometimes human, sometimes animal. Before his appearance on earth he was, therefore, a *bodhisattva*, a Buddha-to-be. The next steps followed swiftly. There is a bodhisattva in the heavens now, waiting for his time; because he is full of brotherly love (*maitri*), his name is Maitreya. There have also been predecessors of Gautama, buddhas who came in past ages. There must also be buddhas who never leave the heavens, although they send their holy spirits to earth; these are the buddhas who preside over special heavens to which they admit the faithful who call to them. There are thus three types of buddhas: (1) the *manushi* buddhas who have come in history and are gone to Nirvana, (2) the *bodhisattvas*, those who are preparing for future buddhahood, and (3) the *dhyani* buddhas who live in the heavens in serene contemplation (*dhyana*) yet graciously bring others to their side. The Mahayanists are prepared to name names. In addition to Maitreya there are powerful bodhisattvas who make a career of aiding persons who pray to them; among them are Avalokitesvara, who appears in China, Korea, and Japan as a mother goddess, Kwan Yin or Kannon; Manjusri, a champion of the Dharma; Samantabhadra, a bringer of happiness; and Kshitigarbha, who guides travelers and transfers souls from hell to heaven. Of the dhyani buddhas three are widely worshiped: Vairocana, the buddha of the sun; Bhaisajyaguru, the healing buddha; and Amitabha, the kindly buddha of the Pure Land, a paradise in the western sky, whom millions have adored in China and Japan by the names Omito and Amida.

The bodhisattvas are notable for one thing: they have postponed their entrance into Nirvana indefinitely in order to be helpful to all suffering and needy souls. This same unselfishness is potential in everyone; there is a Buddha-nature in all souls. Hence, anyone, man or woman, can make a vow to be a bodhisattva, to accumulate merit through many future existences for the use of others, "until the last blade of grass is saved"—a startlingly far-looking aim!

For this mythology and ethics the Buddhist philosophers and theologians supplied a cosmic setting and a profound theory of knowledge. The Madhyamika School founded by Nagarjuna in the second century A.D. held that the world and the self known to the senses are phantasmal and void (*sunya*), that is, devoid of the qualities sense and reason assign to them; but the thing-in-itself (*svabhava*) underlying the phantasms is real, although totally unknowable to a mind not yet liberated into the world of absolute truth (Nirvana). The Yogacara School, founded by the brothers Asanga and Vasubandhu, taught that the reality constituting all things is consciousness, and that there is an all-inclusive reservoir of consciousness (*alaya-vijnana*) from which all phenomena experienced by the individual mind flow as mental events. In a parallel development the ultimate consciousness was named the *Bhutatathata* ("that which is such as it is"), i.e., that which is ultimately real but which finite minds misconceive as the phenomenal world and its selves. In the *Prajna-Paramita Sutras* it is maintained that when the individual consciousness has experienced "the Wisdom gone to the Other Shore," it will cast away (as having had only provisional value) Buddhism, the Buddha, and the notion of Nirvana itself. The Alaya-Vijnana or the Bhutatathata takes on a distinctly theological dimension when it is regarded as a Buddha-essence (an Adi- or Originative-Buddha) at the heart of the universe producing Buddhas and Bodhisattvas as an essential part of its nature, which in this light becomes a love principle.

The Mahayana sects are numerous. They may conveniently be grouped as follows:

The Pure Land Sects Here the motive is getting into the heaven of Amitabha Buddha. Of prime importance is faith in the grace of Amitabha. Such faith is best shown in constant repetition of the formula "All hail to Amitabha Buddha" (in China *Namu Omito Fo*, in Japan *Nembutsu*). The chief sect in China bears the name *Ching-t'u*, while in Japan the *Jodo* and *Shin* sects both have large followings.

The Knowledge Sects The meditation (dhyana) leading to the trance of enlightenment requires, according to these sects, the preparation provided by reading, study, and discussion, as well as performance of ceremonies and rituals. In China the T'ien-t'ai and in Japan the Tendai sects have represented this view.

The Intuition Sects: Ch'an and Zen Dhyana was pronounced ch'an in China, zen in Japan. In these sects systematic study and discussion are rejected, the emphasis lying principally on the individual experience of enlightenment through an intuitive flash of insight, known in Japan as *satori*. The individual must free himself from dependence on, although he is encouraged to have some knowledge of, Buddhist literature and of Ch'an and Zen "masters." The oneness of the universe and the self is presupposed; all phenomena are alike in their Buddha-essence. The flash of insight reveals one's own Buddha-essence. Zen in particular tries to shock the seeker by presenting him with logical paradoxes (*koans*) that will make him give up logical explanations and wait for the intuition of his own Buddha-essence.

The Mystery or True-Word Sects These sects combine philosophy, the idea of a regnant deity (Buddha Vairocana) and right-handed Tantrism (see paragraph on Hindu sects, p. 1015). They emphasize a secret or true word which can be known only by immediate intuition. There is use of rituals, gestures, allegory and symbols, and these have, at least for the common man, a magical power to promote health and prosperity. In China the chief sect was the *Chen Yen*, in Japan the *Shingon*.

The Nichiren Sect This is a Japanese sect, founded in the 13th century by Nichiren, a fiery patriot who thought he had discovered original Buddhism in the *Lotus of the Good Law*. He thought the other Buddhist sects had missed the true way. The implicit patriotism of this sect is seen in its three vows: "I will be a pillar of Japan; I will be eyes to Japan; I will be a great ship for Japan." The contemporary militant *Soka Gakkai* movement is a revival of the Nichiren sect, even to the constant repetition of the *daimoku* formula: *Namu Myoho Renge Kyo*, "Hail to the Lotus of the Good Law!"

The Vajrayana of Tibet This variety of Buddhism is also called the Mantrayana, because of its heavy use of *mantras* (efficacious verses of scripture). An older but inadequate name, coined by Western scholars, was Lamaism. Vajrayana means "Vehicle of the Thunderbolt (or of the Diamond)." Coming late to Tibet (seventh century), Buddhism was slow even then in taking hold, and when it did, it came in a Tantric form. A typical theological formulation provided five celestial Buddhas, one at the zenith and the others in the four quarters of the heavens. Since, according to Tantric conceptions, natural forces are a union of male and female elements, each of these Buddhas was paired with a mate (a *prajna*, "wisdom"). All five are emanations of the Adi-Buddha, the originative Buddha-reality, and they gave rise in their turn to bodhisattvas, and these in turn to earthly incarnations. Thus, according to one view, the Adi-Buddha has produced as one of his spiritual sons Amitabha, and the latter has brought into being Avalokitesvara, who in turn has had as his earthly incarnation Gautama Buddha. These beings are said to have a magical and irresistible substance or power (*vajra*) like that of a thunderbolt and a hardness like that of a diamond, besides which all other things appear soft. If the human devotee can identify himself with any one of these heavenly beings, he will himself gain magical substance and power and will know what Nirvana is. In the meantime he can ward off evil by magical gestures and by repeating, sometimes with the aid of prayer wheels, such potent formulae as *Om mani padme hum!* ("Hail to the jewel in the lotus, hum!"), which is likely an address to Avalokitesvara.

Buddhism Today Vajrayana Buddhism is presently obscured behind the Chinese "bamboo curtain." But the Theravada and the Mahayana are experiencing a resurgence. The former is supported by a new national pride in Ceylon, Burma, Thailand, Cambodia, Laos, and Vietnam. The Mahayana is undergoing revival in Japan and Korea, although it is at an ebb in China, Mongolia, and North Vietnam. The ecumenical spirit has appeared in the Buddhist world; the Theravadins and the Mahayanists have made approaches to each other in the growing conviction that their doctrinal divergences have been logical and natural and presuppose a common heritage. A new spirit of proselytism is also in evidence, which with greater Buddhist unity would pose as its task conversion of the non-Buddhist world.

SIKHISM

One of the youngest religions of the world, Sikhism was founded in the 16th century by Nanak, a native of the Punjab. Though his parents were Hindus, he was in constant association with Muslims and felt that there must be a True Name for God differing from Allah, Brahma, Vishnu, Shiva, etc. One day while in the forest he had a vision of "the one God whose name is True" and began to preach on the theme that if men followed the True Name, they would cease to be divided into Hindus and Muslims but be one as *Sikhs* (Disciples). He dressed in a garb combining Hindu and Muslim elements and proclaimed a monotheism that owed something to both Hinduism and Islam. He subscribed to the Hindu doctrine of *maya*, accepted reincarnation and the Law of Karma, and at the same time taught that the one sovereign and omnipotent True Name predestinated all creatures, a clearly Muslim teaching. He did away with the Hindu taboo against eating meat by saying that God has ordained that man is to be served by the lower creation. He condemned idolatry and distrusted all rites and ceremonies, preferring instead the simple repetition of the True Name. His quietism and pacifism were followed by the first four *gurus* (teachers) who succeeded him as leaders of the Sikhs; but the fifth head, Guru Arjan in the 16th century, finding that the liberal emperor Akbar's successor, Jahangir, was determined to constrain the Sikhs by force, advised his son Har Govind to arm his followers. Guru Har Govind did so. His son, on his accession, named himself Guru Govind Singh ("Govind the Lion"). To change the spirit of the Sikhs, he added to the hymns of the *Granth* (the Sikh scriptures) a collection of militant chants. For his male followers he provided a Baptism of the Sword, a war cry, and an honorific title, "The Lions of the Punjab." After many battles, the Sikhs gained control of the Punjab, a control which they relinquished only to the British (1849). The British employed them widely as soldiers and police. Today their plight has worsened. In the partition of India in 1947 their home territory was divided between Pakistan and India. They have petitioned for "home rule," but so far their pleas have been denied.

TAOISM

One of the two native religions of China, Taoism is rooted, as is Confucianism, in the religious beliefs and practices of ancient China.

Beliefs of Ancient China The ancient Chinese believed that their country was centrally located under the bowl of Heaven and that it stood to benefit most from harmony between Heaven and Earth. All things and all natural processes were thought to be the result of the interaction between a masculine, positive energy mode, the *yang*, and a feminine, passive mode, the *yin*. The day, the air, the sun, the good spirits (*shen*) including ancestors, are full of yang; night, water, soil, evil spirits (*kwei*) are full of yin. Many objects exhibit yin when at rest, yang when active. Yin and yang alternate as dominant energies in events and persons, as when night alternates with day. This occurs naturally in response to a principle of order and law called the *Tao* ("way" or "proper course"). Each separate thing has its Tao and Earth and Heaven as totalities obey an all-encompassing Tao. When any animate thing conforms to its Tao, it becomes perfect in its kind. If all things in Heaven and on Earth would follow the Tao, harmony and order would be seen everywhere. In other words, when men and animals behave naturally, according to their true nature, they enjoy health and the blessing of Heaven. But, of course, evil spirits and and reckless men act contrary to the Tao, and so there are droughts, floods, famines, wars, pestilence. There is great evil in the world and it is due to the rebelliousness of multitudes of demons, devils, and dangerous spirits.

Taoism as a Philosophy The legendary Lao-tzu is usually credited with founding Taoism in the sixth century B.C. and writing the famous *Tao-Te-Ching* ("Treatise on the Tao and Its Power"). It seems certain, however, that this work was composed in the fourth rather than the sixth century B.C. According to it, the term Tao is a convenient name for a reality that has brought the universe into being out of nonbeing. All things come out of nonbeing into being and return to nonbeing. The way of the Tao is the natural way. Men should not oppose their own will to it. They should let nature take its course and not interfere. They should practice *wu-wei* or nonmeddlesomeness, and behave with instinctive spontaneity. When they do, they find themselves getting along with their neighbors and in harmony with heaven and earth; love, sincerity, and goodness will arise, and men will enjoy health and long life; wars will cease and there will be no traveling where one has no business to be and no desire to dominate others. If governments would practice noninterference, the people would spontaneously right themselves. As for the sages, they know that all things come from and blend into One and that they are themselves one with all things in the One.

In the fourth century B.C. the philosopher Chuang-tzu expounded and illustrated this point of view in a series of brilliant and witty essays that still make good reading. "In the days when natural instincts prevailed," he said, "men moved quietly and gazed steadily. . . . Their virtue could not go astray."

Taoism as Magic Both the Tao-Te-Ching and Chuang-tzu said that the Taoist sage possessed the secret of long life. In later times Taoism turned into a search for the means to prolong life magically. Pills of immortality were diligently compounded. Taoists used the alchemy furnace in order to make gold eatable, so that it might confer immortality on those who would eat it. Much speculation was spent on the whereabouts of the Three Isles of Immortality and tales multiplied about the Eight Immortals, humans who by eating the right substances had conferred immortality on themselves. Secret societies were formed to obtain immortality by meditative practices and the swallowing of potions. Some of these societies acquired great if temporary political power. To the populace, Taoist priests were diviners and doctors of thaumaturgy who were to be consulted at many critical junctures in family life.

Taoism as Religion By the second century A.D. official sacrifices were being offered to Lao-tzu in temples built in his honor. By the seventh century he was surrounded with Taoist gods and spirits gathered into a pantheon in imitation of Buddhist models. Among them were Chinese deities long known to the people, like the god of the hearth, the guardians of the door, and the city god. Heaven and hell were added to the theological scheme. Lao-tzu was elevated to a position in the Three Purities, a trinity serving the supreme deity, the Jade Emperor. But this religion, largely a patchwork, lacked real vitality and ceased to function as a living faith by the beginning of the 20th century.

CONFUCIANISM

Taoists advised a way of life away from the cities and the complexities and problems of organized social life, but this advice seemed wrong to the Confucians. They did not think that society should be decentralized; it should be better established and improved, according to its own *Tao*, i.e., its own laws of order and harmony. Their founder was Kung-fu-tzu (Confucius), who was born about 551 B.C. Left fatherless at three, Confucius was given an aristocratic training by his devoted mother and early aspired to government office. After her death he turned his home into a private school, where he taught the Six Disciplines in which he himself had been trained (history, poetry, manners, government, divination, and music). He broke with tradition by admitting poor boys to his school. He wished to train them for responsible participation in government. The feudal system established 500 years earlier by the Chou Dynasty was disintegrating, and there seemed only one way to avoid disaster and that was to reestablish *li*, the manners and morals of the sages of olden times, and to inculcate *jen*, the kindly inward disposition that led men to show "human-heartedness." Men should exhibit *shu*, mutuality, or doing as one would be done by. The higher type of man (the *chün-tzu*) was unfailingly correct in his behavior and profoundly generous and just. Confucius believed that the climate of society was set by the rulers: "the prince is like the wind and the people like grass; it is the nature of grass to bend with the wind."

Confucius encouraged ancestor worship and the domination of the family by its elders. Each member of society should know his place in it. With the ideal definition of his place and function in mind (the principle of "the rectification of names"), he should measure up: the emperor should be benevolent and just, the subject loyal; the father wise and kind, the son filially pious; the husband righteous, the wife submissive; the elder brother considerate, the younger brothers deferent; friends instilled with mutuality. This would assure justice, freedom to do easily what is required of one, and happiness arising from social cooperation and harmony.

Confucius felt that he was designated by Heaven to teach his doctrines, and to this extent he was religious, despite a skepticism about gods and spirits that allowed only a low-key recognition of supernatural influences.

After Confucius' death, his disciples formed the Confucian school. They preserved the textbook materials he used in his teaching and these became the *Five Classics*. By recording his sayings, they created the *Analects*, one of the four Confucian Books, the others being the *Great Learning*, the *Doctrine of the Mean*, and the *Essays of Mencius*. But for some time they met with strong opposition from the Taoists, the Legalists, and the followers of Mo-tzu. The last were a tightly organized group of proto-communists, who taught that universal love was superior to Confucian filial piety and hard work in the fields more necessary to social order than education. The Legalists were, on the other hand, a proto-fascist group who demanded unquestioning obedience to rulers as possessors of awesome authority (*shih*). They succeeded in motivating the Duke of Ch'in to conquer all the provinces and install himself as Shih Huang-ti ("The First Emperor"). He turned on the Confucians and burned their books; but with his death his dynasty fell, and the Han emperors who succeeded him sought to restore peace and order by a resort to Confucian principles.

Meanwhile, Confucianism had undergone development. Mencius (371–289 B.C.), the greatest writer of the Confucian school, urged that men are born with a good nature and are corrupted by their environment. Hsün-tzu (298–238 B.C.), on the other hand, maintained with the Legalists that man is born with an evil nature that must be controlled firmly; so he advocated strict Confucian training to recondition man into behaving for the general good.

The Han emperors instituted the Confucian academies to prepare students for imperial examinations in the Confucian literature, a measure designed to sift out scholars worthy to be placed in high office. Centuries later, when Buddhism and Taoism had much diminished Confucian influence, the Neo-Confucians (11th and succeeding centuries), especially Chu Hsi and Wang Yang-ming, reinterpreted Confucianism and restored its prestige. The system of examinations in the Confucian classics continued to the beginning of the 20th century, but was discontinued with the Revolution of 1912. Confucianism has been in decline for the past half-century. The present Communist regime opposes it as feudal and reactionary.

SHINTO

The Japanese native religion is centered entirely on Japan, its topography, its gods, its dead, its imperial family, and its people. Its central myth, as told in the *Kojiki*, describes how Izanagi and Izanami came down the bridge of Heaven and made an island on which they bred the great islands of Japan and their first inhabitants, who were, of course, all gods (*Kami*) in the "land of the gods." Upon Izanami's death, Izanagi followed her to the underworld; on emerging he cleansed from his right eye Amaterasu the sun goddess, from his left eye Tsukiyomi the moon god, and from his nostrils Susanowo the storm god. Amaterasu lived in the heavens and her grandson Ninigi on earth; Ninigi's great-grandson was Jimmu Tenno, the first human emperor, from whom the present emperor is lineally descended. The Japanese people have meanwhile descended from the other gods. So, according to the myth, Japan is a divine land, sprung from the womb of a goddess, and is filled with gods and their descendants.

The Shinto shrines are wooden structures of an ancient design, with unique gateways called *torii*. They honor the sun goddess and a host of other deities reflecting Japan's geography, climate, and plant and animal life. Ancestors and heroes are also venerated, and in times past the emperor also.

Shinto received its name when Japan was undergoing transformation under Chinese influences in the sixth to eighth centuries A.D. The name is derived from *shen-tao* ("the Way of the Gods"). During the period of Buddhist influence, the Shinto deities were declared to be the "appearances" of the buddhas and bodhisattvas when they came to Japan. In the 17th century, when Shinto experienced a revival, this formulation was discouraged, but with little success. In the 19th century, after the visit of U.S. Admiral Perry, the Japanese systematically brought about a second transformation of Japan to accord with their desire to become a modern world power. In the 1930's, during the Japanese Army's attempt to establish control over the Far East, the Shinto myth was invoked to intensify emperor-worship and secure unqualified obedience to the national program of war and conquest. Men of the armed forces were committed by solemn vows never to surrender to an enemy. The medieval Bushido or *samurai* code was revived, and suicide in repelled attack or hopeless defence (*hara-kiri*) was elevated to a moral principle.

Since 1945 the emperor has "descended from his divinity" and lives among the people as a fully human being. The nation has renounced war as an instrument of national policy, and the Shinto shrines formerly maintained by the government have been turned over to private control. The Shinto sects are proliferating into hundreds more, many of them seeking syncretizing solutions to religious need. It is a highly fluid situation, with an uncertain future.

ZOROASTRIANISM

Zoroastrianism was founded in ancient Iran by a prophet—its only one—probably in the seventh century B.C. His name was Zoroaster (Zarathustra), and his purpose seems to have been to reform the religion of his people, probably because it was excessively priest-ridden and demanded animal sacrifices that the agricultural economy could not afford. After experiencing a trance, during which, through the mediation of divine Good Thought (*Vohu Manah*), he was taken into the presence of God the Wise Lord (*Ahura Mazda*), the creator of the good earth and of men and cattle, he began to get revelations in the form of hymns. These became the *Gathas*, the first scripture of Zoroastrianism. He believed Ahura Mazda operated through such powerful agencies as the Good Spirit (*Spenta Mainyu*), Piety, Power, Right, Good Thought, and Immortality (all later personalized as archangels). But the good God was opposed by *Angra Mainyu*, the Evil Spirit, later known as Shaitin, and by his associates, Druj (the Lie) and many evil demons (the *daevas*). Each man, Zoroaster taught, must decide whom he will serve. After death the soul will go either to the House of Song (Paradise) or the House of the Lie (Hell). The struggle between God and Devil now convulses the world, but God will triumph in the end and there will be a Last Judgment in which the Devil and all who serve him will be finally punished.

After Zoroaster's death the reform he had instituted—a reform of the old Iranian faith, brought in by invading Indo-Europeans akin to those who invaded India—became the faith of the Achaemenian dynasty of Persia and was carried into Babylonia by Cyrus the Great. In becoming the faith of the Mesopotamian peoples it underwent significant changes. Zoroaster was transfigured into a magical personage whose birth was attended by miracle. His representative, the Saoshyant, a Messianic figure (the first in history), was to come at the end of earthly history, before the Last Judgment. Many gods and goddesses of older religions were turned into angels and divine helpers of Ahura Mazda. Thus Ishtar, the sex goddess of Mesopotamia, became Anahita, the Spotless One; and Mithra of the old Iranian religion became Ahura Mazda's right-hand agent. Attention shifted from ethics to magical cleansing from pollution by the use of *manthras* (verses of scripture). Fire was reverenced as the chief symbol of Ahura Mazda, whether in the sun or on the altar.

The Sassanian dynasty (221–651 A.D.) was overthrown by the Muslims in the seventh century, and Zoroastrians found themselves increasingly in disfavor. Thousands fled to India after the eighth century, where they became known as *Parsees* (Persians). Concentrated in the Bombay area, they maintain Fire Temples and Towers of Silence (*dakhmas*). The latter are walled-in enclosures where the dead are laid exposed to air and vultures, so that their fluids will not pollute the earth. Recent leaders of the Zoroastrian community, many of them highly educated, have started a movement "back to the Gathas," in which they see a challenge to live a good life of faith and constructive social action.

JUDAISM

Judaism arose out of a context in which there was a continuous interpenetration of the cultures of many peoples, e.g., the Canaanites, Philistines, Egyptians, Assyrians, Babylonians, Greeks and Romans. In its beginnings it was the faith of the Hebrews, a term which is derived from *Hapiru* or *Hibri*, names applied by Egyptians and Mesopotamians about 1500 B.C. to Semitic wanderers ("boundary crossers" or "desert raiders") pushing their way into Palestine. One group among these desert tribes came from the borders of Egypt and called themselves "children of Israel" because they claimed descent from the twelve sons of Israel (Jacob) whose father was Isaac and grandfather Abraham. On entering Palestine they were joined by non-Israelite Hebrews who eventually adopted their faith and national identity.

The Hebrew Faith (1250–587 B.C.) About 1250 B.C. (a much-debated date) Moses, while serving as a shepherd in Midian, had a religious experience on Mt. Sinai as a result of which he went to Egypt with a message to the Israelites, then in bondage to the Egyptians. He told them that Yahweh (or Jehovah), identified as the god of Abraham, Isaac, and Jacob, had sent him to lead the Israelites out of their bondage and take them to Canaan, their Promised Land. The Egyptians were distracted by a crisis at the time and the Israelites seized the opportunity to flee with Moses across the Sea of Reeds. The Egyptians belatedly pursued them, but their chariots sank in the mud of the lake through which the Israelites escaped. Moses led his people to Mt. Sinai, and at its base conducted a ritual of blood covenant by which the Israelites solemnly bound themselves to Yahweh. Yahweh's will for them was conveyed by Moses and his successors in the moral and ritual precepts summarized in the Ten Commandments and amplified in a growing body of law, the Torah. After forty years of wandering during which Moses died, the Israelites broke into Canaan and gradually took it over. Scholars disagree as to how historically authentic some of the events up to this point may be; succeeding events are more widely accepted as having a definite historical basis.

Called Hebrews by their neighbors, the Israelites together with their nomadic allies soon numbered enough people to become a nation. Their first king was Saul, and he was succeeded by David and Solomon. Jerusalem became the capital. A temple to Yahweh was erected there by Solomon, with many priests to perform the morning and evening sacrifices. But the Hebrews had adopted so many of the customs of the Canaanites that the Mosaic Covenant was in danger of being replaced by the native Baalism and its accompanying fertility cults. The *baals* were Canaanite farm gods operating under a Baal of Heaven, and each baal had a female consort (a *baalah*) to whom he was annually married in fertility rites. It was to protest against disloyalty to Yahweh that the prophets (*nebiim*) arose. Elijah and Elisha appeared in the ninth century and were followed in succeeding centuries by others with stern messages prefaced by the words: "Thus says the Lord." While calling the people back to Yahweh, prophets like Amos and Hosea in the eighth century issued a summons to social justice, and made it clear that failure in righteousness would arouse the wrath of Yahweh and bring on a Doomsday during which enemies would overrun the nation. When Assyria loomed as the Foe from the North who might be the instrument of Yahweh's wrath, Isaiah and Micah prophesied in Jerusalem, the former recalling the people to a faith that might save them, the latter declaring that Yahweh wanted, not sacrifices, but men who would be just and kind and walk in quiet fellowship with God. It was Isaiah who predicted that, should the Day of Doom come, a righteous remnant would survive to enjoy a new day under the benign rule of the Prince of Peace, a Messianic descendant of David. After the ten northern tribes (Israel) had been overrun by the Assyrians and transported to distant parts ("lost"), Judah survived as a remnant of ancient Israel, only to fall, in the time of King Manasseh, under the influence of Assyrian sun and star worship and erect an altar to Ishtar in the very precincts of the Temple. The good king Josiah, however, instituted a drastic reform, basing it upon a new-found farewell message of Moses (Deuteronomy). He sought by this "Deuteronomic Reform" to restore the Hebrew religion to its ancient purity, but he was killed during a gigantic clash between Egypt and the newly established Babylonian Empire, in which the Babylonians were victors. The Babylonians now demanded that Judah become a willing vassal state or suffer conquest. It fell to the prophet Jeremiah to undertake the thankless task of saying it was Yahweh's will that the nation submit, and when it refused to do so, of pronouncing its doom. His prophecy was quickly fulfilled. Nebuchadnezzar invested the city and obtained its surrender in 597 B.C. He ordered the king and court, all the men fit for war, and all craftsmen and smiths to be transported to the vicinity of Babylon. When rebellion broke out in Judah nine years later, he came back to loot and destroy every building in the city, tear down the walls, and take all but a handful of the people into exile. The city was so thoroughly laid waste that it was in ruins for over a century and a half. The religion of the Hebrews seemed to have received a mortal blow.

Post-Exile Judaism (539 B.C.–70 A.D.) The Babylonian Exile was in some sense a blessing in disguise. The Hebrew nation had been destroyed but the Jews (a term derived from Judeans) remained. Chastened by the national tragedy and fearful that their inherited faith was in jeopardy, they gathered up and pieced together the records of their past, and so produced the books of the Bible dealing with their history, their laws, the messages of their prophets and their devotional life (the Psalms). And two prophets appeared to prepare them for a return to their homeland, Ezekiel and Second-Isaiah. The former envisaged in detail the restored rites in the Temple, and the latter foresaw a day when the Jewish faith, purified in affliction, would become the whole world's way of life.

The Persians under Cyrus the Great overthrew the Babylonian Empire in 539 B.C. and shortly thereafter, honoring a Jewish plea, Cyrus issued an edict permitting the Jews to return to Judah. Only a few thousand at a time returned, but the process went on for three hundred years. The Temple was first restored, but not until a hundred years later in the time of Nehemiah was the city rebuilt. About that time Ezrah the Scribe gathered the people at the Water Gate and led them in making a binding covenant to "walk in the law of God given by Moses." It was in reality a new covenant—Israel's second. It established a theocratic state with power vested in the priests. Stress fell on tithing, offerings of the first fruits of a crop, sacrifices, and fixed festivals. The Jews pledged themselves not to marry outside their group. In their diet, they promised to distinguish between clean and unclean. Judaism, a clear-cut legalistic religion, was born; it was a way of life established in law and ritual, so laid upon Jewish consciences that it claimed them more and more. New meeting places, the scene of Sabbath services, appeared in the villages and came to be known later as synagogues. A new class of teachers arose, called rabbis, who expounded the Law and the Prophets.

In 332 B.C. Alexander the Great, after defeating the Persians, brought Judah under Greek control. His liking for the Jews won their gratitude and paved the way for powerful Hellenistic influences on their modes of thought and life. Open-air theaters, gymnasiums, libraries, and academies appeared for the first time in Palestine. The high-priest class in Jerusalem, the Sadducees, aped Greek dress, domestic architecture, and argumentation. But "the quiet in the land," the *hasidim* ("the pious"), resisted the Hellenistic influence and eventually erupted into violence against the attempt of Antiochus Epiphanes, king of Syria, to force the Jews to give up their religion and worship Greek gods. In 165 B.C. Judas Maccabeus and his Jewish rebels recaptured Jerusalem and established Jewish national independence. This Jewish nation lasted until 63 B.C., when the Romans took over.

Meanwhile, during the Maccabean period, two parties had appeared among the Jews. One was the *Pharisees*, who were anti-Hellenistic and who embraced new Messianic concepts that owed much to Zoroastrian influence. They believed that when the Messiah came the dead would rise to meet the living for a Last Judgment. The second was the *Sadducees*, who combined Hellenistic tendencies with religious conservatism, maintaining that it was best to go no further than the Torah in these and other matters; assuredly the dead would not rise. When Julius Caesar made Herod king of Judea, three other parties appeared: the *Zealots* who meant to fight for recovery of national independence and acknowledged no ruler but God; the *Herodians* who thought the Roman rule should be tolerated; and the *Essenes* who withdrew from society to live in quiet awaiting the Messiah. The recently recovered "Dead Sea Scrolls" were devotional texts of one such group of Essenes.

In 66 A.D. discontent boiled into war, and four years later the Romans captured and destroyed Jerusalem. Many thousands of Jews fled to areas outside Palestine. This scattering (*diaspora*) of the Jews was intensified after 130 when the Jews still in Palestine attempted a second war and were disastrously defeated and driven from their homeland.

Rabbinic Judaism (70–1500 A.D.) With the fall of Jerusalem in 70, the Sadducees, Essenes, and Herodians ceased to offer viable alternatives in Judaism. The Zealots struggled on to 130, but then perished. Only the Pharisees (rabbis) and and the rapidly spreading Christian "heresy" remained. The rabbis were worried. Even before the fall of Jerusalem they took measures to preserve rabbinical learning; after it, largely in secret, they produced from the *Halakah* (legal traditions) and *Haggadah* ("narratives") the *Mishnah* and the *Gemara*, which when combined became the *Talmud*. Jewish communities in Babylonia, Egypt, and cities of the Roman world found in the Talmud directives enabling them to preserve Judaism without morning and evening sacrifices. Synagogues sprang up throughout the Roman Empire to enable them to conduct Sabbath worship and perform the rituals of the festivals and fasts of the Jewish calendar. This stood them in good stead as the Roman Empire decayed and fell, followed by a time of even greater troubles.

When the Turks came from the East, the Jews in Babylonia fled to Spain (10th and 11th centuries), where they enjoyed a renaissance of literature and learning under the Moors; but with the expulsion of the Moors, those who would not turn Christian fled east again to Turkey and Syria. Their brethren in England and France had already been expelled, at least in law, in the 13th and 14th centuries, and those in Italy, Austria, and Germany were in ghettos. Northern Jews found more freedom in Poland and Russia but many perished from time to time in pogroms there. In a kind of underground fashion, they nourished their souls with the Talmud, the writings of 12th century scholars like Maimonides and Nahmanides and the esoteric mystic speculations of the *Kabbala*.

Judaism in the Modern World The Protestant Reformation only slightly eased the Jewish situation. It was not until the Napoleonic wars that the Jews began to be freed from the ghettos, and not until the social upheavals of 1848 that they won Europe-wide equality with other men before the law. Up to that time the only haven for the Jew was the New World, and so many thousands availed themselves before World War I of the opportunity to cross the Atlantic that a numerical shift of the Jewish world to the west occurred.

A momentous turn of events occurred during World War I with the issuance of the Balfour Declaration. The Zionist cause, initiated in the closing years of the 19th century by Theodore Herzl, came to fruition in the Declaration's designation of Palestine as "a national home for the Jewish people." After World War II and Hitler's annihilation of 6 million Jews, refugees poured into Palestine. In 1947 the UN General Assembly voted to partition Palestine and create Israel as an independent state, a development which the Arab states bitterly resent.

CHRISTIANITY

Christianity emerged from Judaism but in the course of centuries has absorbed substantial elements of the Greek world-view and some doctrinal and cultic elements from the Romans. It shares with Judaism indebtedness to Canaanite, Babylonian, Zoroastrian, and Egyptian sources. Its central figure, Jesus, has been regarded as an incarnation of God the Father and the source therefore of a primary revelation.

The Life and Teachings of Jesus. Jesus was born in 4 or 6 B.C. in Bethlehem of Judea, and grew up in Nazareth of Galilee. At an early age he became interested in the prophetic tradition of his people. The times were in confusion. Galilee was the scene not only of Jewish rivalries but of extensive Greek and Roman cultural penetration. The Zealots of Galilee revolted when Jesus was about ten years old and he must have witnessed their bloody suppression. At 30 years of age he went down to the Jordan River to hear John the Baptist and be baptized by him. During his immersion he experienced a call to prophecy. After a period of solitary preparation, he appeared in Galilee proclaiming that the Kingdom of Heaven was at hand. He recruited 12 disciples to accompany him while he taught in the synagogues and to large crowds in the countryside. He modified John the Baptist's proclamation of the imminent Last Judgment by making a distinction between the "end of the age" when the Kingdom would "come in power" and the indeterminate period preceding it when the Kingdom would be a reality in the lives of those who submitted to God's rule and lived in fellowship with their neighbors. The principles to govern this interim period were set forth in his ethical teaching. Although he was reared in the Pharisaic tradition, he rejected the excessively legalistic interpretation of piety, declaring that mere externalism in religion is hypocritical and that first importance must be given to justice, love, and mercy issuing from the inner self. The Sabbath was made for man, he declared, not man for the Sabbath. The "men of old were told an eye for an eye, but I say to you love your enemies." His preaching was addressed to the plain man and was notable for its parables. Miracles of healing accompanied his ministry. Great crowds attended him at first, but the Sadducees and Pharisees reduced his influence by accusing him of blasphemously claiming to supersede the Law and the Prophets and of being an instrument of the devil. He was seized in Jerusalem during the Passover of 28 A.D., accused before Pilate the Roman procurator, and crucified on Mt. Calvary along with two criminals. His disciples began to disperse, crushed by despair.

The Apostolic Age The despair of the disciples was short-lived, however, for some of Jesus' women followers reported visions of angels in his empty tomb and of the resurrected Jesus himself. After a number of appearances to the apostles and others in Judea, Jesus met them, they said, in Galilee and ascended to heaven. They were now convinced beyond doubt that he was indeed the Christ (the Messiah) and that he had come from God and had returned to God.

At Pentecost a few weeks later, the disciples were meeting in an upper room in Jerusalem and experienced the descent of the Holy Spirit. They were now empowered to spread the Gospel throughout the world. Peter and other apostles preached the new faith in the streets of Jerusalem and were arrested. The Jewish authorities, ascertaining that they adhered to the Torah, charged them not to preach their doctrine and let them go. But their Greek-speaking Jewish converts were more radical in giving up the Law and ceasing to worship in the Temple, and one of them, Stephen, was seized and stoned to death.

A witness to Stephen's death was a man from Tarsus called Saul (Paul). As an ardent Pharisee, he was active in seeking the suppression of the Christians, but while going to Damascus to pursue this cause, he had a blinding vision and heard the voice of Jesus. Converted to the Christian faith, he became a leader in missionary work among the Gentiles. In Asia Minor, Macedonia, and Greece, he established churches to which he wrote letters full of theology and admonition. He went beyond Jewish categories in describing Jesus, calling him not only the Christ but the Lord (*kurios*, a Greek term) and saying that he preexisted in heaven before taking the form of a servant and dying on the cross. Men who were in Christ, he taught, enjoyed the freedom of the Spirit and were no longer slaves of the Jewish law. Those who were baptized were mystically buried with Christ and resurrected with him to a new life in which Christ dwelt within them. To a culturally divided world he brought the good news that in Christ there was neither Jew nor Greek, barbarian, Scythian, freeman nor slave, or even male or female, for they were all one. A tinge of misogyny, however, common to Christianity's predecessors, remains in Paul—as when he recommends marriage only if a man can escape temptation and damnation in no other way. After taking a collection to the poor in the Jerusalem church, he was mobbed by the Jews, imprisoned, and sent to Rome for trial as a disturber of the peace. The verdict went against him and he became a Christian martyr.

The new churches needed a scripture of their own. The letters of Paul, and others credited to Peter, James, and John, were given scriptural rank. Four gospels were written: Mark, Matthew, Luke and John, probably in that order. To them was added Luke's Acts of the Apostles. An apocalyptic vision of the end of time, written in the manner of Daniel, became the Revelation of John. These works were ultimately gathered into the canon of the New Testament (more accurately, the New Covenant) to accompany the use of the Jewish scriptures (the Old Testament or Covenant).

In early apostolic times the Christians met in homes, but with the extension of the Church throughout the world (as far as India) special meeting places were built, elders and deacons were appointed, and leading elders became pastors (bishops). Children were given catechetic instruction. At length the bishops of large centers of population (Antioch, Alexandria, Byzantium, Rome) became archbishops and patriarchs, the bishop of Rome becoming a Holy Father (a *papa* or pope).

The Ancient Catholic Church (150–1054 A.D.) The early Church gained its name from its claim to be catholic or universal. In its struggle against opposition without and heresy within, it attained a definition of its doctrines. The Gnostics were the first group from which it had to differentiate itself. They asserted that Jesus came to earth in the masquerade of a body from a realm of spiritual powers centered in God the Father. He did this, they claimed, to save men's souls from the evil realm of matter (the physical world) created by a being of a lower order (Jehovah). Against these claims, the Church asserted Irenaeus' principle that the sign of a sound doctrine is its apostolicity and that the carefully titled *Apostles' Creed* contains what is to be believed. The Creed stresses that God created earth as well as heaven and that Jesus was physically born, died, and was buried. Also declared heretical were the fourth and fifth century views that Christ was a created being and not eternal (Arianism); that the Logos dwelt within a wholly human Jesus as in a temple, in which case Mary was not the mother of God but of "a man, the organ of deity" (Nestorianism); that Christ had, not two natures, one divine and one human, but one nature, because the Logos, as the reasoning principle, united with a human body containing an animating principle (Monophysitism). Arianism was rejected at the Council of Nicaea (325 A.D.) and the others at Chalcedon (451).

Meanwhile, monasticism had risen in Egypt and spread through the Catholic world. Orders were founded by St. Basil in Asia Minor and St. Benedict in Italy. After he became a monk, St. Augustine (354–430) gave prominence to the doctrine of original sin, the procession of the Holy Spirit from both the Father and the Son (*filioque*, a doctrine abhorrent to the East), and the distinction between the visible earthly church and the invisible heavenly one.

In the fourth century, Christianity triumphed with the accession of Constantine to the imperial throne and by the end of the century became the imperial state church. The superior dignity of the church of Rome as one founded by Peter and Paul was widely acknowledged; whereupon its heads, the Popes, began to claim that, since St. Peter was the first of the apostles, the church he founded should be accorded primacy among the churches. The pressing of this claim by the popes resulted in 1054 in the division of the Church between the Roman West and the Orthodox East.

The Medieval Church (1054–1517) During the Middle Ages, the sack of Constantinople in 1204 by an army of the Fourth Crusade and its capture in 1453 by the Turks deepened the sense of separation of East and West.

The Eastern churches arose originally in the Greek-speaking areas of the Roman Empire and spread southward into Egypt and northward into the Balkans and Russia. Many of their congregations could boast of being founded by an apostle. Hence, when the bishop of Rome claimed supremacy over them, they replied that they had equal claims to venerability. They differed—and continue to differ—with the West in other matters. They reject the *filioque* clause accepted by the West. They observe some of the seven sacraments differently: baptism is by triple immersion in infancy; confirmation comes immediately after baptism; communion (eucharist) is shared by all worshipers; the sick are anointed during life and not just at the point of death; celibacy is required only of monks and those who aspire to high office in the church. Churches are decorated with mosaics, paintings, and small pictures (*icons*) but are not allowed sculpture. The liturgy is sung, but without instrumental accompaniment. The various bodies of the Eastern Orthodox Church have been since medieval times virtually independent of each other, divided as they are into units more or less corresponding to national states, although they have always maintained full communion with each other.

In the West, the Papacy attained its greatest secular power in the 11th to 13th centuries. One pope, Gregory VII, forced the German emperor to plead for papal clemency by standing barefoot in the snow at Canossa; another, Innocent III, exercised temporal as well as spiritual power over kings and emperors. Among the monastic orders, the Dominican and Franciscan had enormous influence. Universities were founded and in them scholasticism devoted itself to exploring and corroborating the dogmas of the Church. The greatest of the scholastics, Thomas Aquinas, produced the *Summa Theologica*, which adapted Aristotle's methods to Christian revelation in a synthesis that is still honored as authoritative by Catholics today.

The Protestant Reformation and its Catholic Counterpart (1517–1700) The Middle Ages ended in a humanistic renaissance. With the rise of commercial towns independent of feudal barons, townsmen developed a new individualism and a daring demand for freedom and reform. The common man thirsted to hear the Bible in his own tongue. In Germany, Martin Luther (1483–1546) became convinced by his study of the scriptures that the Church had succumbed to unchristian pomp, worldliness, and pride, and had resorted to unscriptural devices for gain. In 1517, as a protest, he nailed his 95 Theses to the church door at Wittenberg and precipitated the Protestant Reformation. His general position was that every Christian can through faith enjoy God's favor without the necessary mediation of priest or pope, and that the true Church is a community of persons who through inward change have surrendered themselves to Christ and find their ultimate authority, not in the Pope, but in the Bible made understandable by the Holy Spirit through faith. In Switzerland, Ulrich Zwingli had independently reached the conclusion that Christians are bound by and should practice only what is commanded in the Bible; the Catholic mass should therefore be radically altered to conform to the early Christian Lord's Supper; and Christian worship should get along without organs, vestments, and images. The German and Swiss reformations spread throughout northern Europe—to France, the Netherlands, and the British Isles. Calvin in Switzerland, John Knox in Scotland, Menno Simons in the Netherlands, and George Fox in England continued and reinforced the work of the early reformers. The Church of England, while Catholic in theology, had long balked at giving primacy to the papacy in Rome; Henry VIII made this view official (though for the trivial reason of justifying his private marital whims), thus establishing the Reformation in England. And the nonconformist Puritans, in pursuit of full liberty of conscience, carried the Protestant cause to the shores of New England.

The Catholics, on their part, were incited to a reformation of their own (often called the Counter Reformation). The Council of Trent, meeting over a period of 18 years (1545–1563), instituted reforms in church discipline and management, and redefined the Catholic theological position vis-à-vis the Protestant. To revive Catholic spirit and zeal, new religious orders arose, the most famous being the Jesuit Order founded by Ignatius Loyola (1491–1566).

The Church in the Modern World (since 1700). Since the Reformation, both the Protestant and Catholic churches hardened into set positions while yet developing new and vigorous forms of mission to the world. The Deism of the 18th century cooled the religious ardor of the Church of England but also led John Wesley and his associates to organize and spread to America a religious movement (dubbed the Methodist Church) that strove to restore through "conversion" the sense of the immediacy of God's presence in human lives. The missionary movement, begun by Protestants in the 18th century, was greatly intensified in the 19th, both in Europe and America, and penetrated to every part of the world. The 19th century—which may be labeled the great Protestant century—saw the rise of a powerful educational effort resulting initially in Sunday Schools and then in the broad-gauge Christian education program of the 20th century. In the same century the long-delayed conflict between religion and science broke into the open, and led in the 20th century to Fundamentalism, Modernism, and Neo-Orthodoxy. The concern of the churches for the alleviation of poverty and injustice resulted in the early 20th century in the vigorous heralding of the Social Gospel, an attempt to reexplore and apply socially the references of Jesus to the Kingdom of God. The mid-20th century has been dominated by efforts toward concerted action by the various Protestant bodies, e.g., the World Council of Churches. This ecumenical concern is, in part, motivated by a realization that the 20th century is a post-Protestant, even a post-Christian, period, and therefore the churches need to unite for effectiveness and strength.

Meanwhile, the Roman Catnolic Church has moved along parallel lines. In hardening into set positions, it proclaimed in 1854 the Immaculate Conception of the Virgin Mary, declared in 1870 the doctrine of papal infallibility, and in 1950 added as a dogma the assumption of the uncorrupted body of the Virgin Mary to heaven after her death. But the forces of liberalism were not by any means dead. This became apparent in the pontificate of Pope John XXIII. In 1959 he issued a summons to an ecumenical council (that is, one embracing the entire Catholic world). Several sessions of the Council were held by the mid-1960's, attended by 2,500 bishops and cardinals. Official observers from the Protestant churches were given a place. The Council ordered liturgical reforms that have put large portions of the Mass into the vernacular of the countries involved, declared that the Jews are not to be held peculiarly responsible for the death of Christ, gave the bishops greater voice in the management of the Church, and put on the agenda of future meetings a resolution dealing with religious freedom.

One of the most vivid reaffirmations of Christ's teaching in the 20th century was the devotion with which U.S. Christians, both Catholic and Protestant, both clergy and laity, actively joined the Negro civil rights movement in the 1960's. Support ranged from official proclamations rejecting segregation issued by many church bodies to lobbying, picketing, and even martyrdom—as in the case of Unitarian minister James Reeb, killed in Selma, Alabama, during 1965.

ISLAM

Islam is rooted in three religions, Zoroastrianism, Judaism, and Christianity, but it has its own distinct character as befits its Arabian origin. Islam means "submission" and its adherents are Muslims (or Moslems)—"submitters" to Allah (God).

Muhammad's Life and Teaching Muhammad (or Mohammed) was born in Mecca about 570 A.D. and was an orphan at six. A ward of his grandfather and then of his uncle, Abu Talib, he took a detached and disapproving view of Arabian polytheism and social disunity. At 25 he married a rich widow, Khadijah, and had leisure to brood on religious problems. Having learned from Judaism and Christianity, he asked himself why no prophet had yet come to the Arabians to prepare them for the Last Judgment—which haunted him. When he was 40, he began to have ecstatic experiences of conversations with the Angel Gabriel, from whom he received revelations from Allah. Muhammad was astonished to find that he himself was the needed prophet to Arabia. He was accepted as such by his wife and a few converts, but when he recited his revelations in the streets, he was ridiculed by the Meccans, then threatened. Both Khadijah and Abu Talib died at about the same time and, feeling the loss of their protection, Muhammad accepted an invitation to come to Yathrib and made a *hijra* (or *hegira*, "withdrawal") with his followers to that city in 622 A.D., the year from which all Muslim dates are reckoned. He became the civil as well as religious leader of the town, which was renamed for him Medina an Nabi ("the City of the Prophet"). When the Meccans came to destroy him, he repulsed them; not long after, in 631, he took their city, making it and its central shrine, the Kabah, the holy center for Muslim pilgrimage.

In the preceding years his revelations had continued steadily. They defined his religious beliefs and prescribed the conduct of his followers. In a famous summary he warned: "Whoever disbelieves in Allah and his angels and his scriptures and his messengers and the Last Day, he truly has wandered far astray." The five chief Muslim beliefs are here listed. (1) Allah is the one true God and does not share his divinity with any associate. The Christian doctrine of the Trinity is thus a serious error. (2) Angels surround Allah's throne, Gabriel having the highest rank. There is also a fallen angel, Iblis (from the Greek *diabolos*), also called Shaitin, who with his minions, including some *jinn* (demons), are busy leading men astray. (3) The scriptures are four: the Torah of Moses, the Zabur (Psalms) of David, the Injil (Evangel) of Jesus, and the revelations to Muhammad, compiled after his death into the *Quran* (or *Koran*). The last corrects and gives final form to the truth in the others. (4) Allah's human messengers are the prophets, Muhammad himself and his honored predecessors, of whom the chief are Adam, Noah, Abraham, Moses, and Jesus. Of Jesus, Muhammad had a high opinion, incensed though he was by the doctrine that Jesus was the Son of God. He held that Jesus was virgin born, performed miracles, and ascended to heaven, but he denied that he had been crucified in his own person. (5) A Last Day is coming. It is vividly anticipated in Muhammad's earlier revelations. His descriptions of Hell are as terrifying as those of Paradise are enchanting.

Muhammad gave much attention to elevating the morals of his followers. He prohibited wine and gambling. He raised the status of women by giving them property rights and not allowing divorce from them without provision for their economic needs. Men who could afford it were allowed more than one wife, but not more than four. Orphans were not to be taken advantage of, on pain of hellfire. No man should scorn his parents. The divisive Arabian tribal organization, with its blood vengeance and violence, was to be transformed into a means of expressing inclusive brotherhood and respect for human rights. He substituted for tribal feuds the "holy war" (*jihad*) to be made on unbelievers, if the latter provided provocation.

Muhammad died of a fever in the year following his takeover of Mecca, and his successor (*caliph*) was his friend and father-in-law, Abu Bakr.

Muslim Consolidation and Expansion Shortly after Muhammad's death his revelations were gathered into the *Quran*, and the process of interpreting and supplementing it began, with a resulting accumulation of tradition (*hadith*). His recorded and remembered prescriptions concerning religious duties yielded the "Five Pillars" (*al-Arkan*), now so fixed in Muslim practice: (1) Repetition of the *Shahadah* or Creed: "There is no god but Allah and Muhammad is the prophet of Allah." (2) Prayer (*Salat*) on Friday at the mosque and five times a day facing Mecca. (3) Alms (*zakat*) for the needy. (4) Fasting during the month of Ramadan from dawn to dusk. (5) Pilgrimage (*hajj*) at least once in a lifetime to Mecca, either in person or by proxy. In addition, orthodox practice required women to go veiled in public, but men were to mingle freely without any racial or class discrimination, especially at times of prayer.

The major feasts and festivals of the Muslim year were worked out later and were also fixed at five: the "Little Feast" (*Id al-Fitr*) at the end of the month-long Ramadan fast; the "Great Feast" (*Id al-Adha*) during pilgrimage at Mecca, the New Year festival (*Muharram*), the festival of the Prophet's birthday (*Mawlid an-Nabi*), and the festival of the Prophet's Night Journey (*Lailat al-Miraj*) which commemorates Muhammad's ascension to the presence of Allah just before the Hijra.

As this process of coordination and consolidation was taking place the Arabs broke out of the desert and rapidly overran Syria, Palestine, Egypt, and Mesopotamia. Later they pushed on into Persia, India, and beyond the Himalayas. They also pressed through North Africa into Spain. Eventually they penetrated northward into Turkey and the Balkans and southward into central Africa. Muslims now number some 450 million, including those in the East Indies, the Philippines, Mongolia, and China.

Muslim Diversification The three chief traditional groupings among Muslims are: (1) the *Sunnis*, who follow the *Quran* and the hadith as closely as changing conditions permit; (2) the *Shiites* or "Partisans of Ali," who regard the son-in-law of Muhammad and his descendants as the only "legitimate" Imams (divinely designated leaders) after Muhammad; and (3) the *Sufis* or mystics, who overlap with the

Sunnis but modify the traditional accent on the transcendence of Allah by stressing his immanence and the possibilities of mystical communion with him. Within these groupings there is further diversification. Among the Sunnis, the two chief theologians are Ashari and Ghazzali, the former conservative, the latter liberal enough to see truth in the Sufi position. There are also among them Four Schools of Law. The Shiites fall into three main sects, the Zaidites, Twelvers, and Ismailis. The Aga Khan heads a sub-sect of Ismailis.

Recent Developments The impact of the West on Islam has led to a complicated attempt, on the one hand to appropriate the methods of Western science and technology, and on the other to set up defenses against Western religion and culture. At present the liberalism of half a century ago, inspired by Muhammad Abduh of Egypt and Sir Sayyid Ahmad Khan and Sir Muhammad Iqbal of India, has suffered a setback in the violent reaction against the establishment of Israel on what is regarded as Muslim soil. Attempts to destroy Israel are threatened. The drive toward a United Arab Republic astride "the crossroads of the world" has met serious setbacks but is persistently sought.

The Fruit of Islam, commonly known as the Black Muslims, purports to be an Islamic sect in the United States, composed exclusively of Negroes whose leader calls himself Elijah Muhammad. The Black Muslims stand for rigid separation of the races and for an independent black nation to be carved out of the United States as reparation for the enforced slavery of Negroes in the past. Religious leaders of orthodox Islam reject this movement's claims to authenticity and charge it with distortion of Muhammad's teachings.

On the following pages

the

Hammond Atlas of World Maps

The World

North America

Canada

United States

South America

Africa

Europe

Union of Soviet Socialist Republics

Asia

Southwest Asia

East Asia

Australia and New Zealand

Pacific Ocean

THE WORLD
MILLER CYLINDRICAL PROJECTION
(MODIFIED MERCATOR)
SCALE ALONG EQUATOR
MILES
KILOMETERS
Capitals of Countries
© Copyright HAMMOND INCORPORATED, Maplewood, N. J.
ARCTIC REGIONS
SCALE ON MERIDIANS
MILES
Steamship and Air Distances
Important Overland Air Routes
NAUTICAL MILES
Longitude West of Greenwich
Longitude East of Greenwich
ARCTIC OCEAN
NORTH PACIFIC OCEAN
NORTH ATLANTIC OCEAN
SOUTH PACIFIC OCEAN
SOUTH ATLANTIC OCEAN
INDIAN OCEAN
ANTARCTICA
NORTH AMERICA
SOUTH AMERICA
EUROPE
ASIA
AFRICA
AUSTRALIA
UNION OF SOVIET SOCIALIST REPUBLICS
UNITED STATES
CANADA
GREENLAND (KALÂTDLIT-NUNÂT) (Den.)
CHINA
INDIA
BRAZIL
WEDDELL SEA
ARCTIC OCEAN
NORTH POLE

NORTH AMERICA
LAMBERT AZIMUTHAL EQUAL-AREA PROJECTION
SCALE OF MILES
SCALE OF KILOMETRES
Capitals of Countries
International Boundaries
Other Boundaries
Canals
ARCTIC OCEAN
PACIFIC OCEAN
ATLANTIC OCEAN
Gulf of Mexico
CARIBBEAN SEA
CANADA
UNITED STATES
MEXICO
GREENLAND
SOUTH AMERICA
Longitude West of Greenwich
Copyright by C.S. HAMMOND & Co., N.Y.

CANADA
CONIC PROJECTION
SCALE OF MILES
0 50 100 200 300
SCALE OF KILOMETRES
0 50 100 200 300 400 500
Capitals of Countries
Provincial & Territorial Capitals
International Boundaries
Provincial Boundaries
Copyright by C.S. HAMMOND & Co., N.Y.
QUEEN ELIZABETH ISLANDS
Scale of Miles
ARCTIC OCEAN
SVERDRUP ISLANDS
NORTH MAGNETIC POLE
NORTHWEST TERRITORIES
DISTRICT OF MACKENZIE
DISTRICT OF KEEWATIN
DISTRICT OF FRANKLIN
YUKON TERRITORY
BRITISH COLUMBIA
ALBERTA
SASKATCHEWAN
MANITOBA
ONTARIO
QUEBEC
NEWFOUNDLAND
NEW BRUNSWICK
NOVA SCOTIA
PRINCE EDWARD ISLAND
UNITED STATES
ALASKA
GREENLAND
HUDSON BAY
BAFFIN BAY
DAVIS STRAIT
LABRADOR SEA
ATLANTIC OCEAN
PACIFIC OCEAN
BEAUFORT SEA
Hudson Str.
FOXE BASIN
BAFFIN ISLAND
Victoria Island
Banks Island
ROCKY MOUNTAINS
Ungava Peninsula
Gulf of St. Lawrence
Great Slave Lake
Great Bear Lake
L. Athabasca
L. Winnipeg
Lake Superior
Lake Huron
L. Ontario
L. Erie
L. Michigan
Ottawa
Edmonton
Regina
Winnipeg
TORONTO
Québec
MONTRÉAL
Fredericton
Halifax
Charlottetown
St. John's
Victoria
Vancouver
Whitehorse
Yellowknife
Calgary
Saskatoon
Hamilton
Saint John
NEW YORK
BOSTON
DETROIT
Buffalo
Cleveland
Seattle
Portland
Spokane
Minneapolis
St. Paul
Duluth
Milwaukee
Albany
Longitude West of Greenwich

PACIFIC OCEAN
BRITISH COLUMBIA
ALBERTA
SASKATCHEWAN
WASHINGTON
OREGON
CALIFORNIA
NEVADA
IDAHO
MONTANA
WYOMING
UTAH
COLORADO
ARIZONA
NEW MEXICO
TEXAS
NORTH DAKOTA
SOUTH DAKOTA
NEBRASKA
KANSAS
OKLAHOMA
MEXICO
SONORA
CHIHUAHUA
COAHUILA
BAJA CALIFORNIA
GULF OF CALIFORNIA
ROCKY MTS.
SANTA BARBARA IS.
Seattle
Portland
San Francisco
LOS ANGELES
San Diego
Salt Lake City
Denver
Phoenix
Spokane
Vancouver
Calgary
Edmonton
Regina
MISSOURI
ILLINOIS
St. Louis
Cincinnati
Longitude West of Greenwich
SCALE OF MILES
U.S.S.R.
BERING SEA
ALASKA
YUKON TERRITORY
CANADA
NORTHWEST TERRS.
Anchorage
Fairbanks
Juneau
Aleutian Is.
HAWAII
Honolulu
Oahu
Molokai
Maui
Kauai
Tropic of Cancer
LOS ANGELES
San Francisco
Oakland
Berkeley

UNITED STATES
POLYCONIC PROJECTION
SCALE OF MILES
0 50 100 200 300
SCALE OF KILOMETRES
0 50 100 200 300
Capitals of Countries
State and Provincial Capitals
International Boundaries
State and Provincial Boundaries
Copyright by C. S. HAMMOND & CO., N. Y.
Longitude West of Greenwich
GULF OF MEXICO
ATLANTIC OCEAN
GULF OF ST. LAWRENCE
CANADA
QUEBEC
LAKE SUPERIOR
LAKE MICHIGAN
LAKE HURON
LAKE ONTARIO
LAKE ERIE
NEW YORK
PHILADELPHIA
CHICAGO
DETROIT
BOSTON
ATLANTIC
OCEAN

CARIBBEAN SEA
ATLANTIC OCEAN
PACIFIC OCEAN
NETH. ANTILLES
WEST INDIES
BARBADOS
TRINIDAD AND TOBAGO
ST. VINC. Grenadines AND GRENS.
GRENADA
ST. LUCIA
Martinique (Fr.)
Fort de France
Bridgetown
Port of Spain
Willemstad
Aruba
Curaçao
Bonaire
NICARAGUA
COSTA RICA
San José
PANAMA
Panamá
Colón
Panama Canal
Gulf of Panamá
COLOMBIA
Bogotá
Barranquilla
Cartagena
Medellín
Cali
Cúcuta
Bucaramanga
VENEZUELA
Caracas
Maracaibo
Valencia
Barquisimeto
Ciudad Bolívar
Maturín
Cumaná
GUYANA
Georgetown
SURINAME
Paramaribo
FRENCH GUIANA
Cayenne
ECUADOR
Quito
Guayaquil
Cuenca
PERU
Lima
Callao
Trujillo
Chiclayo
Iquitos
Cusco
Arequipa
BOLIVIA
La Paz
Sucre
Cochabamba
Oruro
Potosí
PARAGUAY
Equator
RORAIMA
AMAPÁ
AMAZONAS
PARÁ
ACRE
RONDÔNIA
MATO GROSSO
MATO GROSSO DO SUL
GOIÁS
DISTRITO FEDERAL
Brasília
MARANHÃO
PIAUÍ
CEARÁ
RIO GRANDE DO NORTE
PARAÍBA
PERNAMBUCO
ALAGOAS
SERGIPE
BAHIA
MINAS GERAIS
ESPÍRITO SANTO
Manaus
Belém
São Luís
Fortaleza
Teresina
Natal
João Pessoa (Paraíba)
Recife (Pernambuco)
Maceió
Aracaju
Salvador (Bahia)
Belo Horizonte
Vitória
Goiânia
Cuiabá
Campo Grande
Macapá
Boa Vista
Pôrto Velho
Rio Branco
Santarém
Amazonas
Negro
Madeira
Tocantins
Xingu
Tapajós
Orinoco
GALÁPAGOS ISLANDS
(Archipiélago de Colón)
(To Ecuador)
I. Wolf
I. Pinta
I. Marchena
I. Genovesa
Isla Fernandina
Isla Isabela
Isla San Salvador
Isla Santa Cruz
San Cristóbal
Pto. Baquerizo
I. Santa María
I. Española
Same scale as main map

SOUTH AMERICA
LAMBERT AZIMUTHAL EQUAL-AREA PROJECTION
SCALE OF MILES
0 100 200 300 400 500
SCALE OF KILOMETRES
0 100 200 300 400 500
Capitals of Countries
Other Capitals
International Boundaries
Other Boundaries
PACIFIC OCEAN
ATLANTIC OCEAN
DRAKE PASSAGE
FALKLAND ISLANDS (Br.)
SOUTH SHETLAND IS.
SOUTH ORKNEY IS.
JUAN FERNÁNDEZ IS. (Chile)
TIERRA DEL FUEGO
ANTÁRTIDA E ISLAS DEL ATLÁNTICO SUR
URUGUAY
BUENOS AIRES
Montevideo
Santiago
Valparaíso
Asunción
Porto Alegre
RIO DE JANEIRO
Tropic of Capricorn
Longitude West of Greenwich

AFRICA
LAMBERT AZIMUTHAL EQUAL-AREA PROJECTION
SCALE OF MILES
0 100 200 400 600
SCALE OF KILOMETRES
0 100 200 400 600
Capitals of Countries
Other Capitals
International Boundaries
Internal Boundaries
Canals
Wells
NORTH ATLANTIC OCEAN
MEDITERRANEAN SEA
BLACK SEA
CASPIAN SEA
RED SEA
Persian Gulf
Gulf of Aden
Tropic of Cancer
U. S. S. R.
SAUDI ARABIA
EGYPT
LIBYA
ALGERIA
MOROCCO
TUNISIA
MAURITANIA
MALI
NIGER
CHAD
SUDAN
ETHIOPIA
NIGERIA
UPPER VOLTA
CENTRAL AFRICAN REPUBLIC
SPAIN
FRANCE
ITALY
TURKEY
IRAN
IRAQ
SYRIA

SOUTH ATLANTIC OCEAN
INDIAN OCEAN
Equator
Tropic of Capricorn
SÃO TOMÉ E PRÍNCIPE
São Tomé
Pagalu (Equat. Guinea)
Ascension (St. Helena)
St. Helena (Br.)
GABON
Libreville
Pointe-Noire
CABINDA
ZAIRE
Kinshasa (Léopoldville)
Kisangani
Mbandaka
Lubumbashi
KATANGA
Kolwezi
Likasi
Kananga
Mbuji-Mayi
Luanda
Lobito
Benguela
Moçâmedes (Mossâmedes)
Baía dos Tigres
UIGE
MALANGE
LUNDA
CUANZA SUL
HUILA
BIÉ
MOXICO
CUANDO CUBANGO
CUNENE
ZAMBIA
Lusaka
Kabwe (Broken Hill)
Ndola
Livingstone
TANZANIA
Dar es Salaam
Zanzibar
Dodoma
Tabora
Lake Tanganyika
L. Victoria
KENYA
Nairobi
Mombasa
Kampala
Entebbe
Bujumbura
BURUNDI
RWANDA
L. Nyasa
Lilongwe
Blantyre
MOZAMBIQUE
Maputo (Lourenço Marques)
Beira
Quelimane
Nampula
Moçambique
Nacala
Pemba
CABO DELGADO
NIASSA
TETE
ZAMBEZIA
SOFALA
MANICA
INHAMBANE
GAZA
MAPUTO
ZIMBABWE
Salisbury
Bulawayo
Gweru
Ft. Victoria
Umtali
Wankie
Kariba Lake
NAMIBIA (SOUTH-WEST AFRICA)
Windhoek
Swakopmund
Walvis Bay (C. of Good Hope)
Lüderitz
OVAMBOLAND
DAMARALAND
GREAT NAMALAND
Kaokoveld
Etosha Pan
Hollam's Bird I.
BOTSWANA
Gaborone
Francistown
Serowe
Kalahari Desert
L. NGAMILAND
Makgadikgadi Salt Pan
BOPHUTHATSWANA
TRANSVAAL
Pretoria
Johannesburg
ORANGE FREE STATE
Bloemfontein
Kimberley
Upington
LESOTHO
Maseru
SWAZILAND
NATAL
Pietermaritzburg
Durban
TRANSKEI
CAPE OF GOOD HOPE
Cape Town
Port Elizabeth
East London
Oudtshoorn
Mossel Bay
Worcester
Springbok
Port Nolloth
Alexander Bay
Orange
MADAGASCAR
Antananarivo
Toamasina
Majunga
Fianarantsoa
Toliary
Antsiranana (Diego-Suarez)
Faradofay (Fort-Dauphin)
Mozambique Channel
COMOROS
Moroni
Mayotte (Fr.)
Grand Comoro
Aldabra Is.
Cosmoledo Is.
Providence I.
Farquhar Is.
Assumption
Astove I.
Glorioso Is. (Réunion)
Bassas da India (Réunion)
Europa (Réunion)
Juan de Nova (Réunion)
Seychelles
Amirante Is.
SCALE OF MILES
SOUTH ATLANTIC OCEAN
Cape Town
Table Bay
Table Mtn. 3,549
Robben I.
Malmesbury
Wellington
Paarl
Stellenbosch
Worcester
Ceres
Hex River Mts.
Zonderend Mts.
Simonstown
Cape Peninsula
Cape of Good Hope
False Bay
Walker Bay
Hermanus
Caledon
Longitude East of Greenwich 19°
INDIAN OCEAN
MAURITIUS
Port Louis
Curepipe
Mahébourg
RÉUNION (Fr.)
St-Denis
St-Pierre
St-Paul
Piton des Neiges 10,069
Mascarene Islands
Longitude 56° East of Greenwich 57°
Longitude West of Greenwich
Longitude East of Greenwich
Copyright by C.S. HAMMOND & CO., N.Y.

EUROPE
LAMBERT AZIMUTHAL EQUAL AREA PROJECTION
SCALE OF MILES
0 100 200 300 400 500
SCALE OF KILOMETERS
0 100 200 300 400 500
Capitals of Countries
International Boundaries
Canals
Copyright by C.S. HAMMOND & CO., N.Y.
NORWEGIAN SEA
BARENTS SEA
ATLANTIC OCEAN
NORTH SEA
BALTIC SEA
BLACK SEA
CASPIAN SEA
MEDITERRANEAN SEA
TYRRHENIAN SEA
IONIAN SEA
Bay of Biscay
UNION OF SOVIET SOCIALIST REPUBLICS
ICELAND
NORWAY
SWEDEN
FINLAND
UNITED KINGDOM
IRELAND
DENMARK
POLAND
FRANCE
SPAIN
PORTUGAL
ITALY
HUNGARY
ROMANIA
BULGARIA
YUGOSLAVIA
TURKEY
ALGERIA
MOROCCO
Longitude West of Greenwich
Longitude East of Greenwich

UNION OF SOVIET SOCIALIST REPUBLICS
CONIC PROJECTION
SCALE OF MILES
0 100 200 300 400 500 600
SCALE OF KILOMETRES
0 100 200 300 400 500 600
Capitals
Boundaries
National
Union Republic
A.S.S.R.
Autonomous Oblast
Autonomous Okrug
ADMINISTRATIVE DIVISIONS NOT NAMED ON MAP
Division Ref.
1. Abkhaz A.S.S.R. E5
2. Adygey Aut. Oblast D5
3. Adzhar A.S.S.R. E5
4. Aginsk Autonomous Okrug M4
5. Chechen-Ingush A.S.S.R. E5
6. Chuvash A.S.S.R. E4
7. Gorno-Altay Aut. Oblast J4
8. Gorno-Badakhshan Aut. Oblast H6
9. Jewish Aut. Oblast O5
10. Kabardin-Balkar A.S.S.R. E5
11. Karachay-Cherkess Aut. Oblast E5
12. Kara-Kalpak A.S.S.R. G5
13. Khakass Aut. Oblast J4
14. Komi-Permyak Aut. Okrug F4
15. Mari A.S.S.R. E4
16. Mordvinian A.S.S.R. E4
17. Nagorno-Karabakh Aut. Oblast E5
18. Nakhichevan' A.S.S.R. E6
19. North Ossetian A.S.S.R. E5
20. South Ossetian Aut. Oblast E5
21. Tatar A.S.S.R. F4
22. Tuvinian A.S.S.R. K4
23. Udmurt A.S.S.R. F4
24. Ust'-Ordynsk Buryat Aut. Okrug L4
100° Longitude East of Greenwich 110°
© C. S. HAMMOND & Co., Maplewood, N. J.

ASIA
LAMBERT AZIMUTHAL EQUAL-AREA PROJECTION
SCALE OF MILES
0 150 300 600 900 1200
SCALE OF KILOMETRES
0 150 300 600 900 1200
Capitals of Countries
Canals
International Boundaries
Elevations in Feet
Copyright by C.S. HAMMOND & CO., N.Y.
North Pole
ARCTIC OCEAN
ATLANTIC OCEAN
GREENLAND
Iceland
UNITED STATES
ALASKA
Bering Str.
BERING SEA
Aleutian Is.
NORTH SEA
BARENTS SEA
KARA SEA
LAPTEV SEA
SEA OF OKHOTSK
PACIFIC OCEAN
UNION OF SOVIET SOCIALIST REPUBLICS
RUSSIAN SOVIET FEDERATED SOCIALIST REPUBLIC
SIBERIA
LONDON
Paris
Berlin
Leningrad
MOSCOW
Rome
BLACK SEA
CASPIAN SEA
TURKEY
SYRIA
IRAQ
IRAN (PERSIA)
Tehran
SAUDI ARABIA
Rub' al Khali
RED SEA
AFRICA
Cairo
YEMEN
HADHRAMAUT
Gulf of Aden
ARABIAN SEA
AFGHANISTAN
PAKISTAN
Karachi
KAZAKH S.S.R.
MONGOLIA
Gobi
SINKIANG
Taklamakan
Kunlun
TIBET
Trans-Himalayas
CHINA
PEKING
SHANGHAI
Chungking
MANCHURIA
JAPAN
TOKYO
SEA OF JAPAN
INDIA
Delhi
New Delhi
BOMBAY
CALCUTTA
Madras
BAY OF BENGAL
SRI LANKA (CEYLON)
Colombo
MALDIVES
BURMA
THAILAND (SIAM)
Bangkok
Gulf of Thailand
SOUTH CHINA SEA
HONG KONG
Taiwan (Formosa)
Hainan
PHILIPPINES
Manila
MALAYSIA
SINGAPORE
Borneo
KALIMANTAN
Sumatra
INDONESIA
Jakarta
JAVA SEA
Equator
INDIAN OCEAN
BRITISH INDIAN OCEAN TERRITORY
Chagos Archipelago
Diego Garcia
SEYCHELLES
COMOROS
Madagascar
Réunion (Fr.)
MAURITIUS
Cocos (Keeling) Is. (Australia)
Christmas I. (Australia)
AUSTRALIA
Great Victoria Desert
Perth
Tropic of Cancer
Tropic of Capricorn
Arctic Circle
Amsterdam I. (Fr.)
St. Paul I. (Fr.)
Longitude East of Greenwich

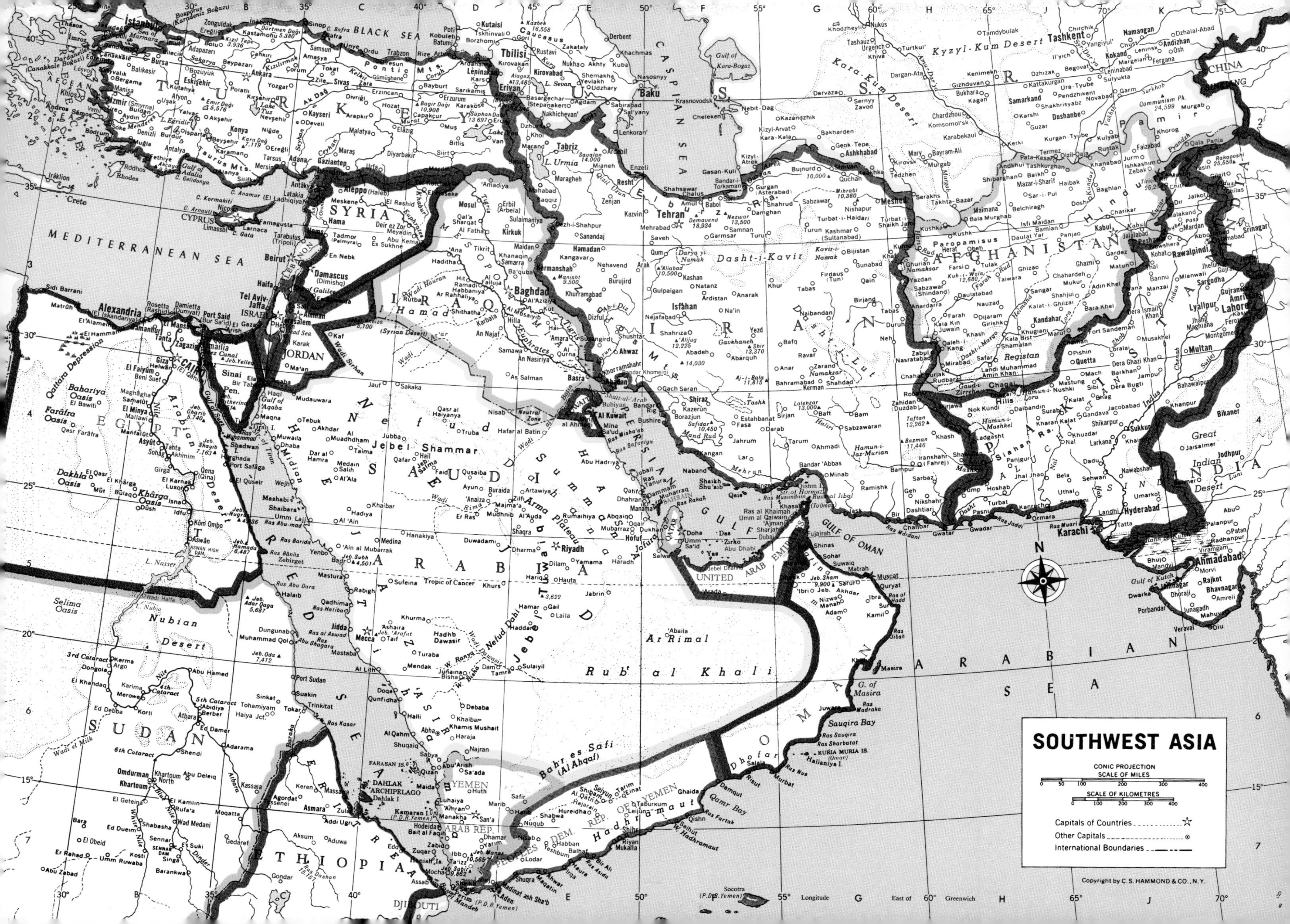
SOUTHWEST ASIA
CONIC PROJECTION
SCALE OF MILES
0 50 100 200 300 400
SCALE OF KILOMETRES
0 100 200 300 400
Capitals of Countries
Other Capitals
International Boundaries
Copyright by C. S. HAMMOND & CO., N. Y.

On this map Chinese place-names have been rendered according to the Pinyin spelling system within the area controlled by the People's Republic of China. Alphabetically listed below are selected Chinese place-names spelled in the traditional manner, followed by the equivalent Pinyin form.

Traditional	Pinyin	Traditional	Pinyin	Traditional	Pinyin
Amoy (Hsiamen)	Xiamen	Kirin	Jilin	Sian	Xi'an
Anhwei	Anhui	Kiukiang	Jiujiang	Siangtan	Xiangtan
Canton (Kwangchow)	Guangzhou	Kwangsi Chuang	Guangxi Zhuangzu	Sining	Xining
Chefoo (Yentai)	Yantai	Kwangtung	Guangdong	Sinkiang-Uighur	Xinjiang Uygur
Chekiang	Zhejiang	Kweichow	Guizhou	Soochow	Suzhou
Chengchow	Zhengzhou	Kweilin	Guilin	Süchow	Xuzhou
Chengtu	Chengdu	Kweiyang	Guiyang	Swatow	Shantou
Chinchow	Jinzhou	Lanchow	Lanzhou	Szechuan	Sichuan
Chungking	Chongqing	Liuchow	Liuzhou	Tachai	Dazhai
Foochow	Fuzhou	Loyang	Luoyang	Tatung	Datong
Fukien	Fujian	Lüta	Lüda	Tibet	Xizang
Hangchow	Hangzhou	Mutankiang	Mudanjiang	Tientsin	Tianjin
Heilungkiang	Heilongjiang	Nanking	Nanjing	Tsinan	Jinan
Hofei	Hefei	Ningpo	Ningbo	Tsinghai	Qinghai
Honan	Henan	Ningsia Hui	Ningxia Huizu	Tsingtao	Qingdao
Hopei	Hebei	Paoting	Baoding	Tsining	Jining
Huhehot	Hohhot	Paotow	Baotou	Tsitsihar	Qiqihar
Hupeh	Hubei	Penki	Benxi	Tsunyi	Zunyi
Hwainan	Huainan	Peking	Beijing	Tungchwan	Tongchuan
Inner Mongolia	Nei Monggol	Pengpu	Bengbu	Tzepo	Zibo
Kansu	Gansu	Shansi	Shanxi	Urumchi	Ürümqi
Kiangsi	Jiangxi	Shantung	Shandong	Wusih	Wuxi
Kiangsu	Jiangsu	Shensi	Shaanxi	Yenan	Yan'an
Kingtehchen	Jingdezhen	Shihkiachwang	Shijiazhuang	Yinchwan	Yinchuan

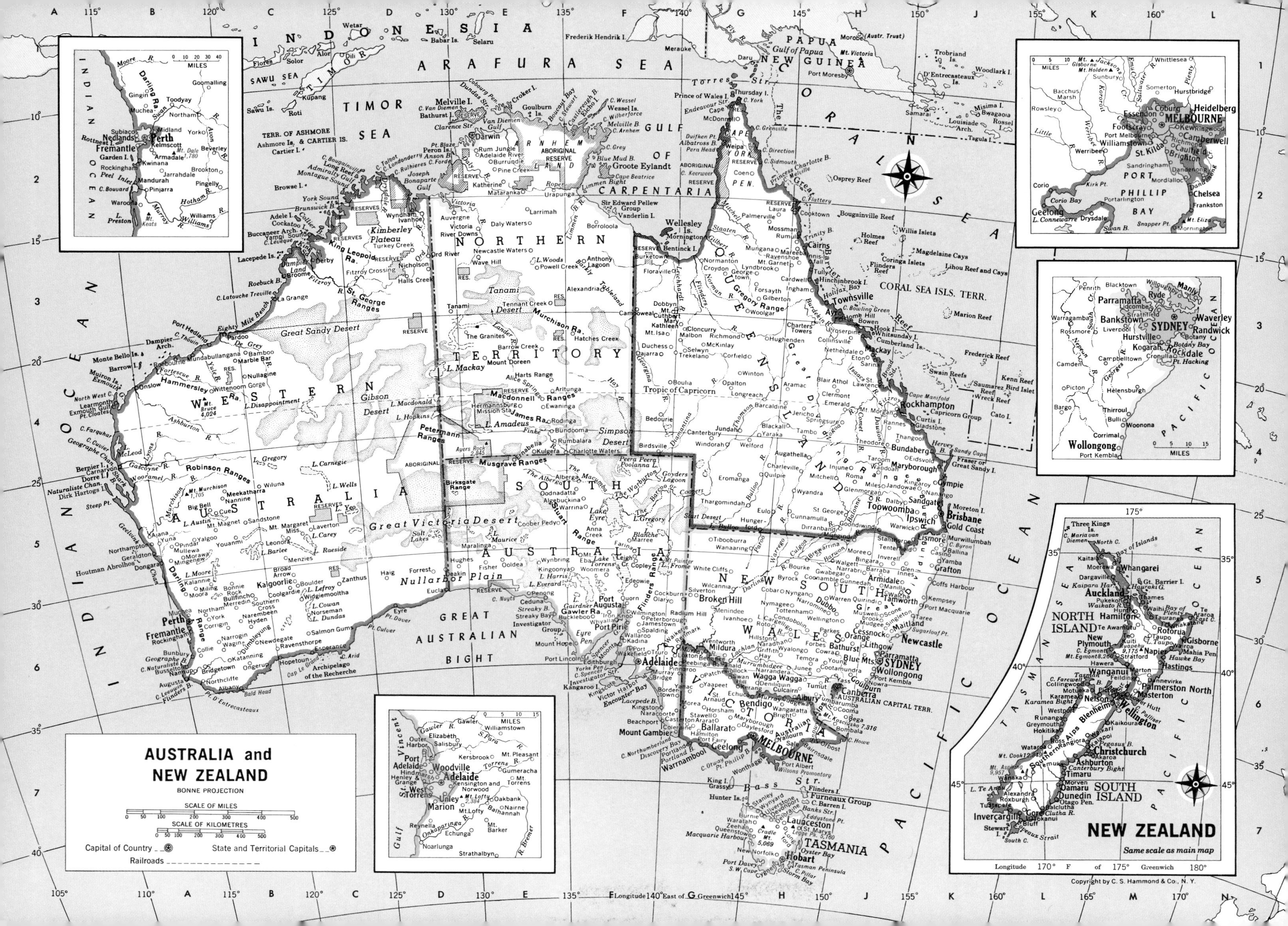
AUSTRALIA and
NEW ZEALAND
BONNE PROJECTION
SCALE OF MILES
SCALE OF KILOMETRES
Capital of Country
State and Territorial Capitals
Railroads
INDONESIA
ARAFURA SEA
TIMOR SEA
SAWU SEA
GULF OF CARPENTARIA
CORAL SEA
CORAL SEA ISLS. TERR.
PAPUA NEW GUINEA
TERR. OF ASHMORE Ashmore Is. & CARTIER IS. Cartier I.
INDIAN OCEAN
PACIFIC OCEAN
TASMAN SEA
GREAT AUSTRALIAN BIGHT
WESTERN AUSTRALIA
NORTHERN TERRITORY
SOUTH AUSTRALIA
QUEENSLAND
NEW SOUTH WALES
VICTORIA
TASMANIA
AUSTRALIAN CAPITAL TERR.
Canberra
Perth
Darwin
Adelaide
Melbourne
Sydney
Brisbane
Hobart
Great Sandy Desert
Gibson Desert
Great Victoria Desert
Simpson Desert
Nullarbor Plain
Tropic of Capricorn
Bass Str.
NEW ZEALAND
Same scale as main map
NORTH ISLAND
SOUTH ISLAND
Auckland
Wellington
Christchurch
Dunedin
Longitude 170° F of 175° Greenwich 180°
Longitude 140° East of G Greenwich 145°
Copyright by C. S. Hammond & Co., N. Y.

PACIFIC OCEAN
LAMBERT AZIMUTHAL EQUAL-AREA PROJECTION
© Copyright HAMMOND INCORPORATED, Maplewood, N. J.
NAUTICAL MILES
STATUTE MILES
KILOMETERS
Capitals of Countries
Capitals of Colonies, Dependencies, States and Territories
Administrative Centers
International Boundaries
Internal Boundaries
Railroads
Distances Between Points
5444 (nautical miles)
NORTH PACIFIC OCEAN
SOUTH PACIFIC OCEAN
INDIAN OCEAN
MICRONESIA
MELANESIA
POLYNESIA
AUSTRALIA
NEW ZEALAND
NORTH AMERICA
UNITED STATES
MEXICO
CHINA
JAPAN
PHILIPPINES
INDONESIA
PAPUA NEW GUINEA
HAWAIIAN ISLANDS
FRENCH POLYNESIA
TASMAN SEA
CORAL SEA
PHILIPPINE SEA
Tropic of Cancer
Equator
Tropic of Capricorn
International Date Line
Longitude East of Greenwich
Longitude West of Greenwich

*BUSINESS LETTER WRITING**

by Irving Rosenthal
and Harry W. Rudman

APPEARANCE AND STRUCTURE OF THE BUSINESS LETTER

In your letters, just as in your clothes, a good appearance is vital to making a favorable first impression. And the first is usually the lasting impression. Therefore it pays to take pains with the looks of your business letters. Use good paper; see that the typing is neat, well spaced and free from erasures; and let no error slip through that you can possibly catch.

PAPER

Use good stationery. A secretary, sorting her employer's mail, may put your letter into the heap for "second" instead of "first reading" if it is on recognizably cheap paper. Why run that risk?

Showy, expensive stationery should also be avoided. Certainly the reader may take notice of parchment textures, deckle edges, and other ostentation; but it may not be with the reactions you desire. Such paper may arouse suspicion or contempt. A paper stock suitable for diplomatic correspondence, ceremonial invitations, or graduation certificates is obviously out of place in business correspondence.

Moreover, the most expensive paper is not always the best for correspondence. It may take ink poorly and prevent even and legible typing.

SIZES

Use standard $8\frac{1}{2}$ by 11 inch sheets for longer letters and half sheets, $5\frac{1}{2}$ by $8\frac{1}{2}$

inches, for shorter letters. A brief message on a half sheet will look better than the same message lost on a full-size sheet.

Sometimes the so-called "Baronial" size, $10\frac{1}{2}$ by $7\frac{1}{4}$ inches, is used. But this is generally reserved for correspondence by executives, with their names and titles engraved and embossed on the letterheads.

COLOR

White will probably remain the favored color of business letters. But the trend to other colors, especially in sales correspondence, has been increasing. It has been found that the bright colors, such as yellow and red, are "attention getters." These are being used increasingly for just that purpose. Color may also be used for associative value. An air travel company may select sky blue for its stationery; a vacation resort, green.

THE LETTERHEAD

Your letterhead has two purposes. Because it is your identification, you want it to be attractive and impressive. And because it supplies the reader with essential information about your company—name, address, telephone number, etc., you want it to be clear and readable.

Fussy lettering and fancy symbols, mistakenly intended to impress the reader, unfortunately produce a different effect. Like pretentiously expensive stationery they may evoke annoyance and ill will instead. In any case, if they serve to make a letterhead hard to read at first glance, they may be considered unsatisfactory.

Below are some letterheads showing attractive lettering and symbols that are impressive and in good taste without sacrifice of clarity.

BOTTOM AND SIDE-MARGIN MESSAGES

Business stationery sometimes carries printed matter at the foot of the sheet or down the side-margins. The foot-line (it is seldom longer than a line) is usually the motto or slogan of the firm or a special sales message. Such messages may also be printed on the side margins, usually the left-hand margin. Most marginal matter, however, consists of lists of officers, sponsors, or branches of the organization.

ADDITIONAL SHEETS

Whenever a letter is longer than one page, the extra sheets should be of the same paper stock but without the letterhead imprint. A continuation line carrying the name of the addressee (the person to whom the letter is addressed), the page number, and the date should be typed at the top of each additional page. See that a minimum of three lines of text, besides the complimentary close and the signature, appear on the final page of the letter. For the sake of appearance it will be worth retyping the preceding page, if necessary, to make that possible.

FRAMING

Good typography requires proper placement of type on the page so that it sits in its margins like a well-framed picture. Since typewriting is a form of typography, accordingly it follows the same rules. The typewriting on a letter should be so arranged that, within its margins, in the spacing of dateline, salutation, and closing lines, and in its paragraphing, it resembles a well-composed and well-framed picture.

To achieve this pleasing effect the typist does not have to be an artist. She need only follow her own orderly habits of care in her margins (which should be larger in a brief letter), in her paragraph spacing, and in her indentations.

INDENTATIONS

When letters were hand-written, paragraph indentations were necessary for visual

Additional Sheets

```
Mr. John Jones -- page 2 -- January 14, 19



therefore feel that we cannot accept the return of the

merchandise at this late date.  We like to cooperate

with all our accounts. . . .
```

It was necessary, because of its length, to continue this letter on an additional sheet. The additional sheet is headed by the addressee's name, the page number, and the date. There is the requisite minimum of three lines of text, in addition to complimentary close and signature.

The "Full Block" Form

```
February 28, 19




Mr. John Jones
1492 Columbus Avenue
Louisville 3, Kentucky

Dear Mr. Jones:

I was very pleased to receive your prompt response to my
```

```
and I look forward to seeing you on your next trip to the city.

Sincerely yours,


George Sabrin
```

In the "full block" form all the letter's contents are aligned on the left hand margin.

The "Modified Block" Form

```
                                        February 28, 19




     Mr. John Jones
     1492 Columbus Avenue
     Louisville 3, Kentucky

     Dear Mr. Jones:

     I was very pleased to receive your prompt response to

     and I look forward to seeing you on your next trip to
     the city.
                              Sincerely yours,


                              George Sabrin
```

All the letter's contents, with the exception of the date, the complimentary close, the signature, are aligned on the left hand margin. This is still the most widely employed form.

Full Indention

```
                                        19 Elm Street
                                          Oswego, New York
                                            April 5, 19

     Mr. Gilbert Kahn
        67 Wren Road
          Miami, Florida

     My dear Mr. Kahn:

                    In undertaking the assignment you gave me
     when I was in your office last Thursday, I made it clear

     nevertheless intend to do the best job I can.
                              Sincerely yours,


                              Lucille Graham
```

This form is all but obsolete, and there seems little doubt that in time it will cease entirely to be used.

clarity. The universal use of the typewriter has tended to make indentations encumbrances instead of conveniences. Many business letters, today, dispense with them. It is becoming general practice to use line space separations instead. This device speeds up stenographic work and improves the appearance as well. But whichever practice is used, it should be employed uniformly throughout the letter.

Nevertheless, the change from indentations to line spaces for paragraph indications and other purposes has not been complete. Today four forms are in use: The "full block" form; a kind of transitional form called "modified block"; the old "full indentation" form; and a type used for special effects, called "hanging indentation."

THE "FULL BLOCK" FORM

The "full block" form is gaining in usage because of its simplicity. In the full block form everything under the letterhead—dateline, inside address, salutation, body of the letter, complimentary close and signature—is aligned along the left-hand margin.

THE "MODIFIED BLOCK" FORM

The "modified block" form is the style in widest use. Here certain parts of the letter, such as the date line, the complimentary close, and the signature, are aligned to the right to help balance the rest of the letter, which has a left-hand alignment.

Some companies use the full block form for short letters (where it makes a better appearance) and the modified block form for longer letters.

FULL INDENTATION

As mentioned before, the fully indented letter is a survival of the period when letters were hand-written. The typewriter has rendered this form obsolete. Today only a small proportion of business correspondence is typed in the full indentation form.

In the full indentation form not only paragraphs are indented but also the separate lines in the inside address and other sequences of lines in salutations and complimentary closings.

HANGING INDENTATION

"Hanging indentation" is seldom seen in business correspondence other than sales-promotion letters. There, it is used to focus attention or attain a repetitive, "hammering-home" effect.

PUNCTUATION AND ABBREVIATIONS

Along with the dropping of indentations there has been a tendency to do without unessential punctuation and to avoid abbreviations, especially in the inside address where these would necessitate punctuation. This economy is for improvement of appearance—lines without terminal punctuation marks look less fussy—and for speed and convenience. The typist, freed of the bother of punctuating and figuring out abbreviations, can turn out more letters a day.

A stark, attractive simplicity, characteristic of the full block form of business letter, is increasingly to be noticed in the modified block letter as well. Periods are being omitted from the end of the dateline and after ordinal numbers such as 43rd and 44th; and commas, from the ends of the inside address lines. It is now also allowable to omit the colon from the salutation and the comma from the complimentary close. Most letters, however, still retain these marks of punctuation.

Abbreviations of cities and states are being avoided. Such abbreviations as Mr. or initials for first names are being retained and are followed by periods.

The new, unpunctuated form, where all punctuation is omitted, is called "open punc-

Hanging Indention

Dear Sir:

If you've been reading COSMOS for years, I hope you'll forgive me for sending you a letter you don't need --
-- But you'll understand why I jumped at the chance
to write a special letter to a list (on which your
name appears) of successful executives who have been
appointed to even more responsible posts.

For readers of COSMOS know that the busier a man is the more
rewarding COSMOS can be. And if you haven't yet discovered
the added advantage of reading COSMOS for every week's
news, then I hope you'll look into it now.

It's a quick, reliable short-cut to information you'll use a
dozen times a day. A readable, reliable report on the

It is to be noted that this form is not appropriate for normal business correspondence, but is widely used in the sales letter for the apparent reason that it readily strikes the eye, arrests attention.

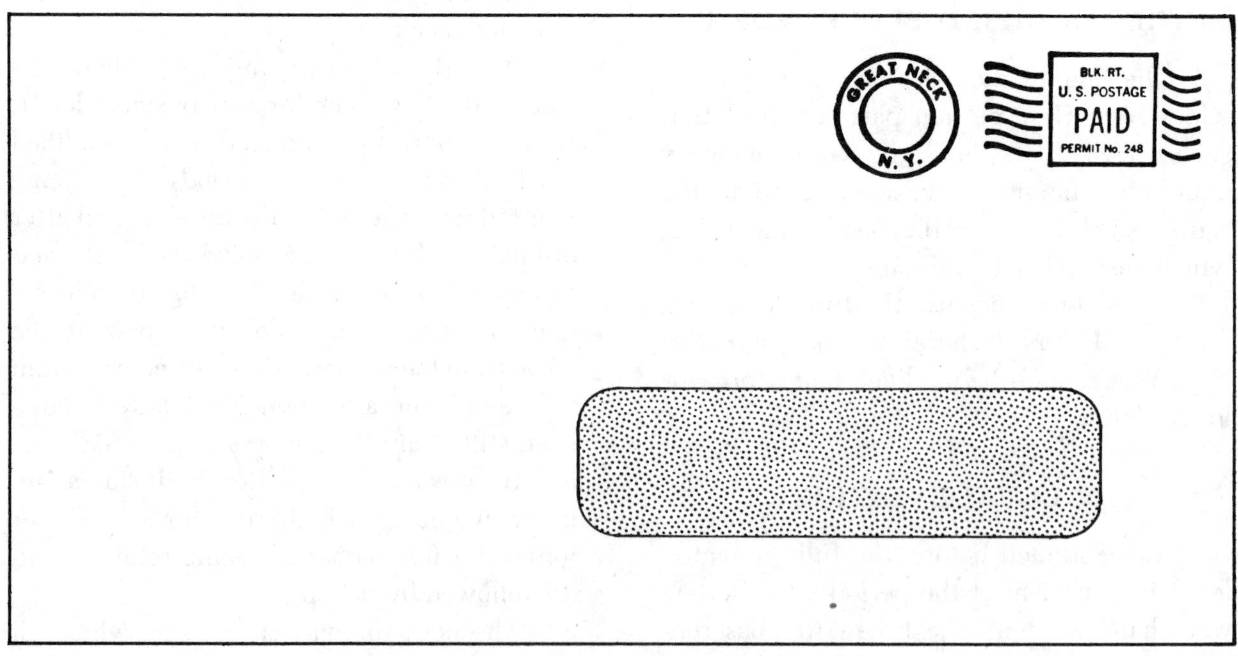

Window Envelope

tuation." The practice of using some punctuation is termed "mixed punctuation." The old form is called "closed punctuation." See the examples below:

Open Punctuation
Mr. Ferdinand L. Shorey
12 West 44 Street
New York, N. Y. 10036
Dear Mr. Shorey
Yours sincerely

Mixed Punctuation
Mr. Ferdinand L. Shorey,
12 West 44 Street,
New York, N. Y. 10036.
Dear Mr. Shorey:
Yours sincerely,

Closed Punctuation
Mr. Ferdinand L. Shorey
12 West 44 Street
New York, N. Y. 10036
Dear Mr. Shorey:
Yours sincerely,

Even in the past the use in the salutation of the semicolon or the colon and dash was incorrect. Such practices today are grossly illiterate. Do not use **Dear Mr. Shorey;** or **Dear Mr. Shorey:—**

ELEMENTS OF THE LETTER

Business letters should have at least the following elements: the letterhead, dateline, inside address, salutation, body, complimentary close, two signatures (the name of the company typed out and the written signature of the writer), and the dictator's and typist's initials, the former, usually in capitals and the latter in small letters. In addition, depending upon the operating procedure of the writer's company, there may be a file number, an order number, or a subject line for the purpose of future reference; an "attention" line where the letter is directed to a particular person or department; notice of an enclosure; and a postscript.

THE DATELINE

Usually the dateline is typed at the right. In full block letters it may be typed flush with the left margin. Sometimes it is centered under the letterhead.

The customary sequence is month, day, and year: as April 5, 1971. Some logical persons have been advocating a usage, now standard in Great Britain and in our armed forces, of a progressive time-interval sequence —the shortest interval, the day, first, followed by the month, and then the year: as 5 April 1971. Although not common, this form is acceptable.

THE INSIDE ADDRESS

Inside addresses are included in business letters for several practical purposes. The inside address serves as a ready identification since envelopes are usually thrown away; it helps in filing correspondence; and it can be used with window envelopes. It is also useful to the post office when checking misdirected letters or letters with no return address on the envelope.

The inside address usually consists of three lines: the name of the person or the firm, the street address, and the line carrying city, state, and zip code. In foreign mail a fourth line carries the name of the country. If the addressee is associated with a company, its name may appear under his as the second line.

Examples: Mr. Thomas Smith
24 West 98 Street
New York, N. Y. 10025

Mr. Alan May
16 Charing Cross
London, N.W. (Zone No.)
England

Mr. Thomas Smith
West Side Riding Academy
24 West 98 Street
New York, N. Y. 10025

THE SALUTATION

Present-day usage for the normal salutation is the word **Dear** and the title and name of the addressee: as **Dear Mr. Doe** or **Dear Mr. Roe.** In personal friendships between businessmen it is permissible for them to use first names or nicknames in salutations: as **Dear John** or **Dear Hank.** In formal address the expression, **My dear Mr. Doe,** is often used.

Sales letters addressed to regular patrons may use terms like **Dear Customer, Dear Madam, Dear Subscriber,** etc. In mass mailings any general terms such as **Dear Sir, Dear Madam, Dear Friend, Dear Fellow Citizen, Dear Reader** or any other salutation considered appropriate may be used—or none at all.

Whenever open punctuation is used, the colon may be omitted after the salutation. But, as we have mentioned before, it is more customary to retain it. The colon-dash and the semicolon, however, are never correct.

There are special forms of address for persons of high rank in government, the armed forces, the church, and the professions. These will be found in Appendix D.

BODY

The body of the letter is, of course, its most important part. In appearance it should be clearly typed, neatly spaced, and uniform in typographical construction.

Long paragraphs should be avoided. The paragraphs should not be so short, however, as to give any impression of talking down to the addressee. But in sales letters short paragraphs are almost always the rule, in order to sustain interest.

Underlining to indicate italics or to give emphasis is being displaced by capitalizing. Capitals are regarded as more readable, more emphatic, and more pleasing in appearance. Moreover, capitalizing makes for easier and more rapid typing. Titles of books and names of periodicals, however, should continue to be underlined or placed in quotation marks.

The contents of the body will be dealt with at greater length in the separate sections discussing the different types of business letters. Here we may generalize as follows:

The opening paragraph should be short and, unless there is a compelling negative reason, it should immediately introduce the subject of the letter or connect it with a previous development in the correspondence. The middle paragraphs should do the main job of the letter—expand on the subject in such a way as to persuade the addressee to act upon it in the manner you desire. Let it convince him that it will be proper for or advantageous to him to conclude the purchase or the agreement, or to make the postponement, the payment, or the adjustment you are seeking.

The closing paragraph should summarize your message and make clear the action you desire. Avoid wavering words like **hoping, wishing, trusting,** etc. Be positive. Say something like "We feel certain that you will agree that this is the most satisfactory solution." Avoid dangling participial endings, such as "Hoping we hear from you."

THE COMPLIMENTARY CLOSE

Just as you open your letter with a word of friendly greeting, so you close it with a cordial expression—what is called the complimentary close. Some people propose dispensing with both, and recommend plunging into the letter without salutation and closing abruptly with the signature. But the convention is so firmly entrenched as to render it unlikely that this suggested procedure will take hold.

The customary forms are "Yours truly," "Yours sincerely," or "Yours very truly" where the relationship is formal. The terms "Yours sincerely," "Sincerely yours," "Faithfully yours," and "Cordially yours" express rising degrees of intimacy. "Respectfully yours" has gone out of fashion and is now generally restricted to correspondence with dignitaries or official superiors in formal situations.

THE SIGNATURE

It is considered a discourtesy not to sign a letter personally. If this becomes an impossibility and a rubber stamp has to be used, it should be inked and imprinted in such a way as to resemble the true signature as closely as possible. If the writer's secretary signs for him, she should put her initials under the signature to make that fact clear.

New attitudes regarding the position of women do not seem to have penetrated into business correspondence, at least as regards their marital status. That has to be indicated in the signature. A married woman who wishes to use her maiden name in business should add her married name (Mrs. ——— ———) in parentheses. A widow retains her married name unless she takes legal steps to resume her maiden name. A divorcee retains her former husband's surname but may not use his initials or his first name.

Where the company name is included in the signature, it is typed one or two lines below the complimentary close. Four spaces should be left for the writer's signature, and his name and company position should follow:

Yours sincerely,
Thomas Smith
THE JOHN JONES COMPANY
Sales Manager

To make sure that the signature is not misread, the name is often typed above or below it.

Yours sincerely,
THE JOHN JONES COMPANY
Thomas Smith
Thomas Smith
Sales Manager

SPECIAL PARTS OF THE BUSINESS LETTER: FILE NUMBERS

In addition to the standard parts of the letter special requirements may call for additional lines or items. On traffic or mail order correspondence file or other reference numbers may appear, usually at the left of the dateline or under it.

ATTENTION LINE

When a letter is addressed to an individual in a firm but is not intended for him exclusively, or if it is intended to be routed to a certain department, a line is added to that effect. Letters are often addressed to the **attention** of an individual instead of to him directly so that, if he should be away, the letter will not be held up but will be acted upon by the person temporarily taking his place.

The attention line is usually put between the inside address and the salutation, and may be placed either at the left, as in the example below, or in the center of the line.

The John Jones Company
710 West 10 Street
New York, N. Y. 10011

Attention Mr. Thomas Smith, Sales Manager

Gentlemen:

Note that where the attention line is used, the salutation is **Gentlemen,** not **Dear Mr. Smith.**

ENCLOSURE LINE

The enclosure line in the letter is not for the addressee, who will be informed about the enclosure in the text of the letter. It is for the mailing clerk or the stenographer herself as a reminder to include the enclosure in the mailing. It should therefore be in an inconspicuous position. It is usually typed under the stenographer's initials, as an abbreviation: Encl.

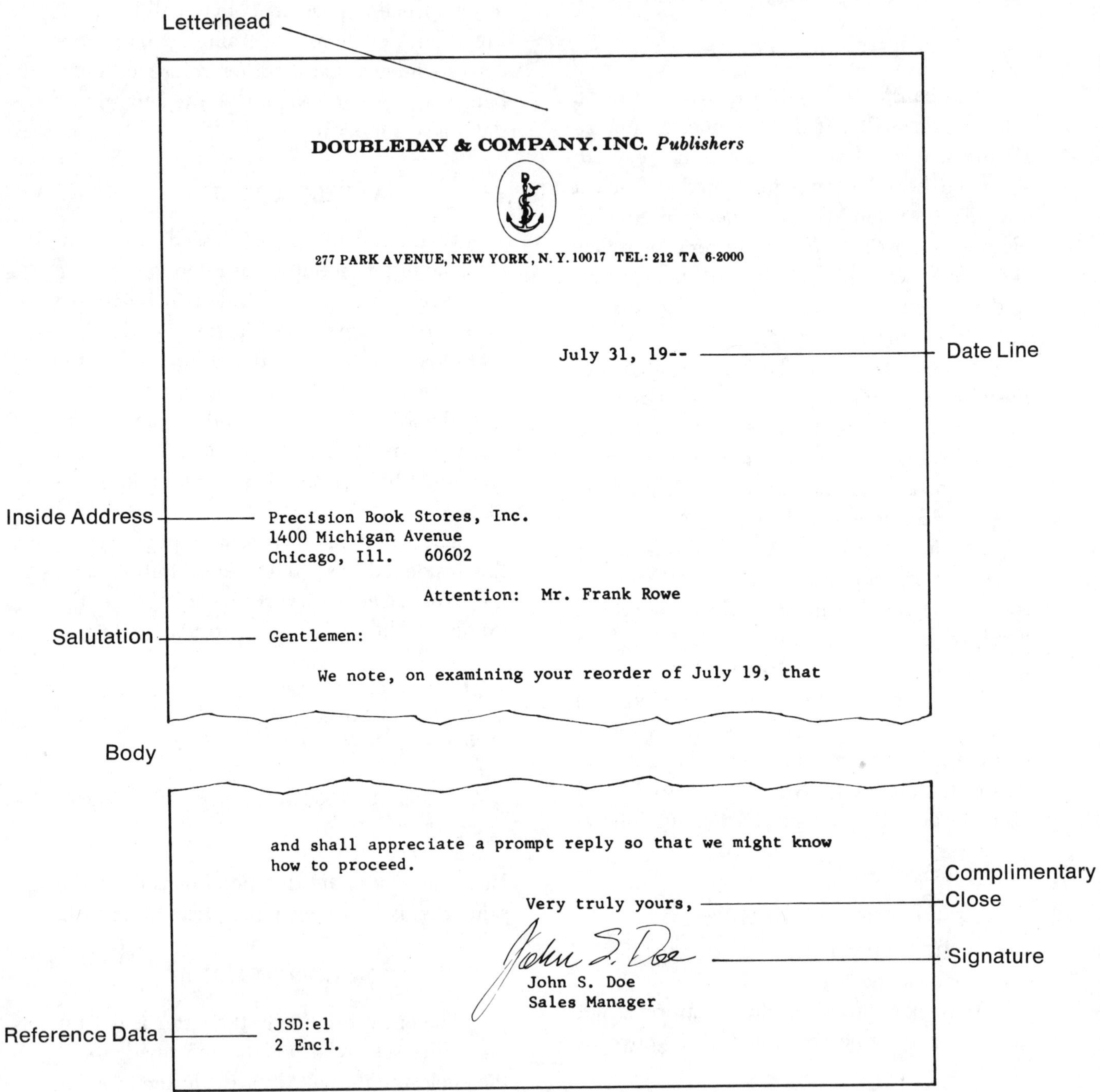

Letterhead
DOUBLEDAY & COMPANY, INC. Publishers
277 PARK AVENUE, NEW YORK, N. Y. 10017 TEL: 212 TA 6-2000
July 31, 19--
Date Line
Inside Address
Precision Book Stores, Inc.
1400 Michigan Avenue
Chicago, Ill. 60602
Attention: Mr. Frank Rowe
Salutation
Gentlemen:
We note, on examining your reorder of July 19, that
Body
and shall appreciate a prompt reply so that we might know
how to proceed.
Complimentary Close
Very truly yours,
Signature
John S. Doe
Sales Manager
Reference Data
JSD:el
2 Encl.

This model letter includes in standard form all *the elements normally employed in the business letter.*

POSTSCRIPTS

Postscripts in business letters differ from those in personal letters, which are afterthoughts set down after the letters have been finished. In business correspondence, postscripts have a definite, planned function. They may emphasize a point made elsewhere in the letter, or they may make a special offer. They are more customary in sales letters than in other business correspondence, and are designed to draw special attention. Examples will be found in the section on sales letters.

ENVELOPES

As much care should be observed with the envelope as with the letter itself. It is the first part of the letter to be seen, and, as we have already observed, the first impression is important. It should, of course, be of the same paper stock as the letter. The address should be typed in such a way as to be in pleasing balance with the imprint on the top left-hand corner, if there is such an imprint; or it should be well framed on the front of the envelope if the return address is imprinted on the flap in back.

The two standard envelope sizes are the number 6¾ and the number 10. The latter is also called the "official size" envelope. It is long enough to hold the full standard letterhead width of 8½ inches. The number 6¾ size averages that number of inches in width. Envelopes used for Baronial size stationery average 7½ inches in width, enough to permit enclosure folded the full width of the sheet.

WINDOW ENVELOPES

Window envelopes are increasingly being used, in large mailings, as a way of saving a time-taking typing operation—the addressing of the envelope. In window envelopes a space cut out of the front of the envelope is generally covered by a tough, transparent paper. The letter is folded and enclosed in the window envelope in such a way that the inside address can be seen under the transparency. Folding the letter directly below the salutation, with the writing facing you, will expose the address at the proper point for use with window envelopes.

FOLDING THE LETTER AND INSERTING ENCLOSURES

Part of the appearance of the letter depends, of course, on the way it is folded and placed in the envelope. Here the convenience of the addressee also receives consideration. The letter should be folded so that he can open it with ease and read it with comfort.

For the number 10 or the long "official size" envelope, the letter should be folded from the bottom to a little over a third of the page. Crease the fold down firmly. Then fold the top third down over the bottom fold and crease firmly again. Then slip the folded letter into the envelope.

For the number 6¾ envelope, fold the letter from the bottom to about a quarter of an inch from the top. See that the sides are even when creasing. Now fold from the sides, first from right to left about a third of the way and then from left to right, creasing firmly after each of the two folds. Then enclose the letter with the last fold toward you. This will insure that when it is received the letter can be removed with the open end on top.

Checks, receipts, or other small enclosures should be placed inside the folds. If placed outside the folds, in the envelope, such vital items may be torn or cut when the envelope is opened; or they may be overlooked by the recipient and thrown away with the discarded envelope.

Letters mailed in window envelopes must be folded in a special way, as noted in the paragraph on window envelopes.

FOLDING THE LETTER

a. 8½″ x 11″ Letter in Small Commercial Envelope

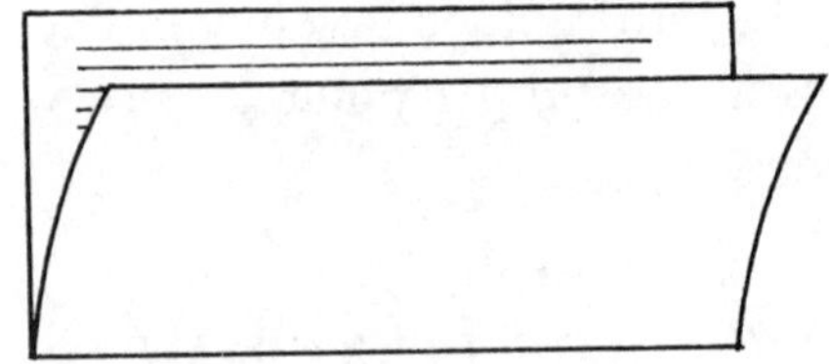
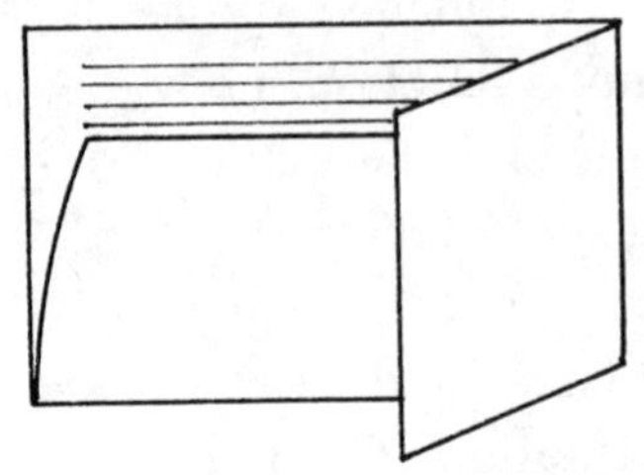
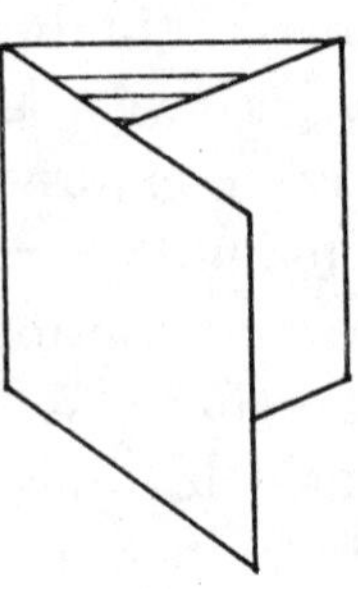

b. 8½″ x 11″ Letter in Long Commercial Envelope

c. The Four Page Leaflet

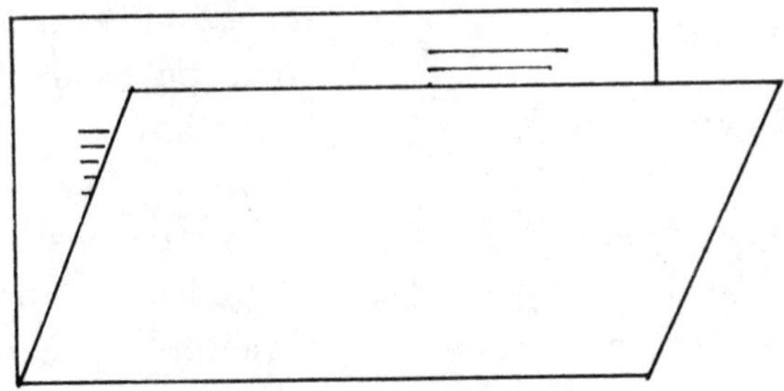

THE OUTSIDE ADDRESS

Each year, according to post office records, some thirty million pieces of mail end up in the dead letter office. The chief reason is careless addressing.

The customary address form consists of four lines: the name and title of the addressee, street address or post office box number, city, state, and zip code. On all foreign mail the name of the country will, of course, replace the state, or be added as a fifth line.

Additional lines may be required for a province or department name in a foreign address, an apartment number, a company name in addition to the name of the individual addressee, an attention line if the letter is to be routed to a department of the company or to an individual in a department, or the specification, **Personal** or **Confidential,** where the letter is intended for private reading by the addressee.

Except where they are part of the address, such additional lines are typed in the lower left-hand corners of the envelopes.

No customary position has been settled upon for postal directions like **Air Mail** or **c/o S.S. America.** These may be written, rubber-stamped, or typed anywhere on the envelope, usually above the address. They should be conspicuous, but they should not obscure the address.

For readability and appearance the following positions have been found most satisfactory. In all cases start the address slightly below the vertical center of the envelope. On a number 6¾ envelope start slightly to the left of the horizontal center when using the block style. When using the indented style on this size of envelope start about one third the width of the envelope from the left.

On the larger number 10 envelope start slightly to the right of the horizontal center when using the block style. When using the indented style, start slightly to the left of the horizontal center.

Addresses of unusual size or envelopes with the return address on the flap in back may call for variations of these positions.

Professor Michael T. Kellogg
Bernard M. Baruch School of Business and
  Civil Administration
Lexington Avenue and Twenty-third Street
New York, N. Y. 10010

THE RETURN ADDRESS

It is more convenient as well as more customary for the return address to appear on the front of the envelope than on the back flap. In any case make sure it appears somewhere on the envelope. This practice will be an additional precaution against the letter's ending up in the dead letter office.

TITLES OF RESPECT

It is customary to include certain titles of respect in the address. This courtesy extends to physicians after whose name M.D. usually appears, and to engineers (C.E., M.E., or E.E.). These abbreviations are professional as well as academic designations. Purely scholastic titles like M.A. or non-professional titles like B.S. or Ph.B., etc., are omitted. In formal correspondence, however, higher degrees like D.D., LL.D., Ph.D., etc., may be used in the address.

NUMBERS AND ABBREVIATIONS AND THEIR PUNCTUATION

It is the preferred usage to write out a numbered street or avenue—for example, **500 Fifth Avenue** or **223 East Thirty-third Street.** Where the number is above ninety-nine, it usually appears as a number: **2204 220th Street.** Do not abbreviate the name of the city, and avoid abbreviating the name of the state. The tendency is away from such abbreviations. Ordinal number-ending abbreviations like **th** and **rd** are not, today, followed by the period. Use 33rd and 34th, not 33rd. and 34th.

ZIP CODES

On July 1, 1963, a new system of mail sorting and distribution called zip code was initiated by the Post Office Department. The zip code is a 5-digit number designed to cut down the steps required to move mail from the sender to the addressee, thereby holding down postal costs. The first three digits of the code identify sectional centers, which are main points of air, highway, and rail transportation, and the last two digits identify the post office or delivery station. In cities that previously had local postal zones, the first three digits of the zip code identify the city and the last two digits (which are generally the same as the former zone number) designate the branch post office or substation.

The first numeral of the zip code, 0 to 9, identifies one of ten national service areas. The second and third digits indicate the service area subdivision and the post office, and the last two digits identify the station from which the mail is delivered.

While the use of zip codes is optional but strongly recommended for first-class mail, it is *mandatory* for second-class and third-class bulk mailers, who must also presort and bundle their mail in accordance with detailed instructions that appear in the *Postal Manual.* Large-volume mailers should familiarize themselves with the regulations regarding zip codes by consulting the *Postal Manual* or their local post office, since failure to conform to the zip coding requirements can result in refusal of the post office to handle improperly zip-coded mail at the lower bulk rates.

Placement. The zip code should appear on the last line of both the address and return address following the city and state. There should be not less than two nor more than six spaces between the last letter of the state and the zip code, and no characters of any kind should follow the zip code:

```
Mr. Harold Jones
3025 Theresa Street
Arlington, Va.    22207
```

SOME FINAL REMARKS

Some individualistic correspondents omit the salutation and the complimentary close. They may be anticipating future usage but they are violating present conventions. The practice will attract attention, certainly if that is what is desired. But the accompanying responses may not be desirable.

It is advisable that you personally look over all the letters sent from your office. If that cannot be done by you, make sure that some other responsible person examines them carefully.

It is also advisable, periodically, to make a critical reappraisal of the appearance of your letters. Perhaps you should change your style of correspondence. Even if you find nothing that, in your opinion, needs improving, it will be a pleasant reassurance to ascertain that such is really the case.

THE SALES LETTER

The concern of all business is to sell goods or services. Consequently all business letters are, directly or indirectly, sales letters.

Your best collection letter, for example, is one that does more than induce a delinquent customer to pay up. It is the one that leaves him convinced, after the payment, that he has been dealing with a fair and considerate house with which he is glad to continue doing business.

Sales letters, as such, are distinguished from other business letters by the fact that their sales objective is not indirect but direct and, more or less, immediate. The qualifying phrase, "more or less," is used because some varieties of sales letters are not intended to make an immediate sale but rather to lead **gradually** to sales. And others are intended to pave the way for sales by other means.

Certain sales letters, for example, may be written to help a salesman make the sale. Others may be written to bring customers for your products to one of your dealers.

The most common and largest variety of sales letter is used in direct mail selling. Devices employed in that type of sales letter are presented in a later section; here we shall deal with the more general aspects of sales letters, and take up types of sales correspondence that are part of regular business operations.

YOUR SATISFIED CUSTOMERS

No selling job is ever over. The alert businessman keeps analyzing his accounts. Can A's volume be increased? B's orders show a slight decline over last year's; does that mean a decline in his business? Or is he sampling the ware of a competitor? Whatever his conclusion, the alert businessman sends off the appropriate letter.

IN AN EFFORT TO INCREASE SALES

Dear Mr. Martin:

I have been very pleased to note the steady increase in the frequency and size of your orders since we started doing business together. It is gratifying to know that our product is being well received in your area and that you are making money with it.

My reason for writing is twofold—to thank you for your patronage and to offer our cooperation in any way that will build your sales of our product even further. Under separate cover I am sending you some advertising aids that can be used in window and counter displays; mats for newspaper ads; and suggested spot announcements for your local radio station. Frank Moss, our representative in your territory, will drop in on you next Thursday to help you set up these displays and to offer his assistance in every way. If there is anything special you may need, don't hesitate to get in touch with me.

I look forward to the continuance of our pleasant and, I hope, mutually profitable relationship. With all good wishes, I am,

Sincerely yours,

Robert Johns

IN AN EFFORT TO RETAIN GOOD WILL

Dear Mr. Burke:

Somewhere or other we read: "There are many good excuses for losing an order—but no excuse whatever for losing good will!"

That's why we're writing you—not to ask why you preferred to place your recent order with somebody else, but to make sure it wasn't because of something which has lost us your good will as well.

If it was the latter, we'd be most grateful if you'd write us about it.

But regardless, we sincerely hope your new equipment gives you the kind of performance you expect of it—and that you won't hesitate to make use of our nationwide service facilities should the need arise.

Next time, perhaps, it will be our good fortune to take care of your requirements.

Sincerely,
William H. Wolcott

The alert businessman never feels smug about his satisfied customers. He does not leave the initiative to them, content merely to take orders. He bears in mind those two business adages: "It costs less to keep a customer than to get one," and "Your customer is your competitor's prospect."

If he starts a new line, if he makes an improvement in one of his staples, if he has a plan for reducing the price to a customer by quantity shipping of combined orders, the alert businessman lets his satisfied customer know about it. He does not wait for the word to get around; he sees to it that it gets around. Keeping the satisfied customers posted is a good way of keeping them satisfied.

Dear Larry:

I hope this finds you well and your business booming. I think I have something that you ought to be able to go to town on.

I've just picked up a special lot of piece goods off-price that I'm going to cut tomorrow in Style 637, with which you have done so well. I plan to bring out the number at two dollars less than you have been paying, and I know it will fit in well with your January sale.

I can get a limited number of garments out of the lot, so I'd like to know how many you can use before I offer it to anyone else. We'll be able to ship within ten days.

All good wishes.

Sincerely yours,
Phil Nelson

Dear Mr. Forman:

When you were in the city several weeks ago, you mentioned the difficulties you were having in getting fast deliveries of merchandise shipped to you by us and by other manufacturers. I think I've come across something that can help you.

I have just had a conversation with Jack Bell of Vanguard Trucking, 247 Terhune Place, Jersey City, N.J., who runs a fleet of trucks through your territory. He told me that if you can work out an arrangement with a few other merchants near you to consolidate shipments, he will be glad to set aside one of his trucks to serve your group. If the amount of freight warrants it, he can provide daily overnight deliveries, and is confident he can cut your present transportation costs by forty per cent. I think its worth looking into, and I suggest you get in touch with Mr. Bell for more particulars.

Sincerely yours,
Robert Glass

FREQUENT COMMUNICATION

Keep the contacts with your customers unbroken and, so far as you can, make the contacts personal. Some firms regard communication with their customers, once a month, a minimum requirement for good customer relations. They do not limit the correspondence to invoices and routine acknowledgments of orders and payments. To the routine mail they add interesting enclosures. And they take advantage of every suitable occasion to extend the contact. They avoid formalities and try to set up a personal relationship. For signatures they do not use only the firm name but rather the name of an officer of the firm, the head of a department, or a salesman.

Some concerns go about unobtrusively getting personal items about their customers and keep the data current. Birthdays are remembered. If a buyer gets married or has an addition to the family, the event is observed.

Many service firms such as laundries and cleaning establishments find it profitable to send their customers and prospective customers blotters bearing calendars and reminders of seasonal cleaning needs.

Department stores keep in touch with their charge-customers by sending them advance notices of sales, seasonal announcements, and letters about special services. Whatever your business is, there are sure to be occasions for getting in touch with your customers other than through routine notices and acknowledgments.

YOUR EX-CUSTOMERS

Some customers die and some go bankrupt. Others move too far away or get into some other situation that makes further business with them unprofitable. So a certain calculable amount of lost business must be anticipated.

But there are other lost customers who must not be given up without prolonged and persistent effort. These are the customers who have been won away by your competitors or have been driven away by the rudeness or inefficiency of someone in your organization.

Where the customer has been lost to a competitor, your letter starts a job of reselling. Write about new lines or about improvements. Make some attractive offer.

Where the customer has been lost through rudeness or inefficiency, ask him for the whole story. Express regret in a dignified and manly way. Offer an adjustment, if it is called for, or some special inducement to bring him back into the fold.

The alert businessman keeps a regular check on his customers' buying. When one has stopped or tapered off, he does everything he can to find out why.

The point is, of course, to regain the business as soon as possible. But an important, additional reason is to discover whether the lost business signifies some weakness in the organization.

SPECIAL CUSTOMERS

In every business there are customers who rate or demand special attention. Some should get it merely because the large volume of their business calls for every possible special and even personal consideration. Special and personal letters, if feasible, will be in order.

Others may have special needs. For example, dealers located in hot, moist regions may require special packaging or other measures to keep the wares they receive in good condition. Letters dealing with such special needs are in order.

Others may be merely fussy or eccentric. These may be hard to do business with and require special sales correspondence. If you decide that the volume of their business justifies it, carry on that additional correspondence with good grace.

LETTERS TO HELP YOUR SALESMEN

The salesman may be assisted, through letters, in two general ways. One type of letter prepares the ground for him—introduces him, mentions the new line he will demonstrate, some special offer he will explain in detail, etc.

Such help to a salesman may be needed for several reasons. One is the lingering effect of the fictional presentation of the salesman as an intrusive, high-pressure man with his

Dear Mr. Watson:

I have just heard with chagrin from a mutual friend of ours that you feel you haven't been getting the same attention here that you received when we were a smaller firm. I was wondering why I hadn't seen you in our showroom lately.

I am very sorry if anyone in our organization has been remiss or negligent in taking care of you the way you deserve to be looked after as an old and loyal customer through the years. I offer my personal apology, and I hope you will give us another chance.

I shall appreciate your coming in to see me personally the next opportunity you have to drop in on us, and I shall see to it that you are taken care of to your complete satisfaction. We have had a very pleasant relationship for a number of years, and I would feel hurt -- more for personal than business reasons -- if through some fault of ours that relationship was marred in any way.

Sincerely yours,

David Redmond

This letter is written in what is obviously a difficult and delicate situation, requiring graciousness, tact, diplomacy. Ruffled feelings must be smoothed, and a disgruntled customer won back. The kind of letter to be written must be appropriate to the sort of relationship which exists between the involved parties, and the special requirements of the particular case.

Dear Miss Filene:

Thank you for your order of January 13. I have issued instructions to our shipping department to fill it exactly the way you wrote it -- without a single substitution in size or color. I have also told them to get in touch with you before shipping, if for any reason they can't fill the order as written.

I am sure you will have no more trouble with our shipments, and I shall appreciate your getting in touch with me personally if we can be of service in any way.

Very truly yours,

Ben Sloan

This letter serves the valuable purpose of assuring the customer that her order is receiving the very special and personal attention of a responsible person—who is not content merely to place the order, but who has taken pains to arrange for its smooth execution.

Dear Mr. Sanborn:

As you know, John Williams, who traveled your territory for us, is no longer with us. We have been fortunate in adding a new man, George Alexander, who I am sure will be able to look after you the way John did.

During the training period George spent with us here, he impressed me as a sincere, conscientious, straight-shooting fellow. He just came out of the service, but he has had considerable experience in our industry, so he is familiar with your needs and with our operation.

George will call on you during the week of February 14 with our new line, which looks stronger than ever. We've added a few novelty numbers that I am sure you can do well with, and I look forward to an even bigger volume with you in the future than we have enjoyed in the past. With all good wishes and regards, I am,

Sincerely yours,

Sid Frank

This letter introduces to the customer a new salesman, who is in the sometimes uncomfortable position of replacing a man whose service to the customer has been entirely satisfactory. The dual purpose is thereby served of at once reassuring the customer that he need in no way fear a deterioration of service, and assuring the new salesman of the firm's solid support in his new venture.

Dear Mr. Graves:

Thank you for your reorder of our Style 986. I am going to look after it personally and have it sent out right away.

When I visited you last month on my round through your territory, I knew the strength of this number and I am happy my recommendation worked out well for you. We've just added two more styles that I have equal confidence in; one account where we tried them out sold them out in three days. I am enclosing pictures of them, and if you'd like me to send you some, just let me know and I shall be glad to see that you get a prompt delivery.

I expect to leave for my next trip in about three weeks and look forward to seeing you around the first of the month. In the meantime, if there is anything I can do for you here, please don't hesitate to write.

Sincerely yours,

Clarence Kell

This letter serves several purposes, chiefly that of sustaining and strengthening salesman-customer relations in the period between visits. At the same time that it assures the customer of the salesman's personal attention to his needs, it also exploits the opportunity provided by the letter to advance suggestions for new sales.

toes wedged in the door sill, launched on a non-stop spiel. Even dealers who have good relations with salesmen and have found them helpful may think of those they know as exceptions and look for the obnoxious type in a new man. A letter can help the new man by presenting him in a friendly light, stressing the useful service he is to perform—the demonstration he will make or the plan he will explain, etc.

In such letters, however, take care not to tell the customer too much. Remember that the purpose is to introduce the salesman, not to substitute for his call. The letter should stimulate the customer's curiosity and leave it to the salesman to satisfy it. Similar letters can serve to bring customers to your show rooms, to exhibition booths, to dealers handling your products or services.

Letters sent between sales calls can strengthen the salesman-customer relationship. The seasonal nature of certain kinds of merchandise or the fact that salesmen will make only a few trips a year in the ordinary course, gives rise to considerable correspondence about reorders, substitutions, cancellations, returns, complaints, and the acknowledgments and adjustments these call for. As much of this correspondence as is practical should go out under the salesman's signature.

In addition it is frequently advisable to send out, also under the salesman's signature, letters advising the customer of new developments, new lines, new policies, etc. Even in business the strongest bonds are personal, and a good salesman-customer relationship means a good relationship with the customer for the firm.

TESTIMONIALS

When enough time has elapsed for a new account to have tested your products and your business procedures, it is a good plan to write to the customer and ask whether he is satisfied and whether he has any suggestions or comments to make. This kind of inquiry should be the first step in the continuous keeping-your-customer-sold campaign that was mentioned earlier.

Such letters may evoke testimonials that will prove valuable in your promotion. And the letters will probably have the additional value of providing a running check on your business methods by revealing from time to time the need for changes.

Build up a testimonial file from the favorable letters your inquiries bring you. You can draw upon such a file when approaching prospects in the same area or in the same general line as the writers of the testimonials. The signer of the testimonial can say more for you than almost anything you can say for yourself.

Dear Mr. Seaman:

It is now eight months since we first started doing business together, and I note with satisfaction that the volume each month has been increasing nicely. At first, we were skeptical about the possibility of developing sales in your territory, because our product has been sold mainly in colder sections of the country. Your experience, therefore, has been gratifying.

My purpose in writing is to find out whether you have any thoughts about how we can increase our volume to mutual advantage even further. As you can see, we're trying to work with you the best way we know how, and we'd appreciate hearing from you with any comments you may wish to make about our service and product. We like to receive brickbats as well as pats on the back. We can correct our faults—to the advantage of all concerned—only when they're pointed out.

Sincerely yours,
John Thomas

THE INQUIRY LETTER

Answers to inquiries are a major part of business correspondence, and can be the most important type of sales letter. Those that are part of a direct-mail sales campaign will be dealt with in the next section. Here we touch upon the type of inquiry that originates in other ways.

Someone in the market for your sort of goods or services has looked up your firm in a trade directory; or has had it recommended to him by one of your customers with whom he is acquainted; or has heard of you in some other way. He writes to you for information. His inquiry to you may be the only one he is making. But the chances are that he is simultaneously asking for similar information from your competitors.

It is wise to assume that that is the case, and that your answer must stand the test of competition. Do your best to make your reply a sales letter that wins the inquirer's business.

Promptness is of the first importance. Your prospect will be quite as much sold by evidence of your alertness and efficiency as by what you may say.

Directness is also important. Give specific answers to the questions. If the questions are vague, don't follow that bad example; be specific about what you have to sell and thus you will probably answer effectively the questions your prospect has not been able to express.

Being specific does not mean being detailed. Leave the details to the catalogue or the other enclosures you send. A good sales letter is organized to have a certain impact. It cannot have that impact if it interrupts itself to go into minutiae.

ENCLOSURES

Your postage outlay pays for an ounce per unit of reading matter. That ounce gives you leeway for several sheets besides your letter which—barring necessary exceptions—will usually be less than a page in length. Businessmen have found it profitable to take advantage of the full permissible weight by adding enclosures that reinforce the sales punch.

The enclosures can be particularly useful in supplying details which, if put into the body of the letter, might blunt its impact. If the prospect had to pause, while reading the letter, to take in details of measurement, construction, delivery schedules, etc., his interest would be too diffused for him to react as you would like him to.

Your letter should do two things. It should put the prospect into the buying mood and whet his interest so that he will want to look up the details. These can be furnished in an effective enclosure.

However, avoid a clutter of accompanying "literature." Some mailers believe in the more-the-better principle. But experience has shown that beyond a certain point **more** can become **too much.** Then, no matter how colorful and clever the enclosures are, they begin to clash with one another. They distract attention from the letter. They even become a nuisance to the recipient—and the letter may lose its effectiveness.

Moreover, the enclosures should not overshadow the letter. The letter itself should be attractive to look at, but above all its copy should be so carefully, sensibly, and effectively prepared that it produces the results desired.

It is generally advisable, when dealing with a small enclosure, to fold it into the letter so that it comes out along with the letter when the envelope is opened.

Dear Mr. Merton:

I am going to make this letter brief. I feel the enclosed brochure speaks for itself. But I am writing merely to let you know that the sales potential of the lamp described has been tested carefully in thirty selected stores similar to yours. Every one of them has come back with quick reorders. So we know WE HAVE SOMETHING YOU CAN DO WELL WITH.

We developed this item with a view to shooting for volume. We've brought it out at the lowest price possible, and we have complete confidence in its sales potential.

We all get a steady stream of mail across our desks, but I hope you will take a few minutes to study the brochure carefully, and to try out a sample order of the lamp. We'll let the selling talk for itself.

Sincerely yours,
Ivan Hubbell

FORM LETTERS

Whatever the special function of the sales letter you write, make it personal if possible. If the volume of the correspondence makes this impractical, use forms and methods that will make it appear like a personal letter.

There are two main kinds of form letters —**complete** and **paragraph.** The complete form, even when it is individually typed and signed, is prepared in advance to cover certain standard needs.

Usually **complete form letters** are multigraphed or mimeographed, depending on the purpose they serve. Multigraphing is useful in letters where spaces can be provided to fill in dates, individual salutations, addresses, etc. In virtually all cases, the name of an individual, even in rubber stamp or stencil reproductions, is preferable in the signature to simply the name of the firm.

Complete form letters are usually identified by some combination of letters or initials under which they can be filed. Thus there may be a series of form letters with which catalogues are to be enclosed. These are keyed with the letter C and their numbers in the series. Then the secretary can be instructed to send out Form Letter C-4.

The greater flexibility of the **paragraph form letter** makes it possible to meet a larger number of calculable special situations. Such a letter is assembled from designated prepared passages kept on file in a "paragraph book." Some firms have several paragraph books with hundreds of paragraphs in each.

For illustration let us take a paragraph book containing ninety passages. Of these, one to ten may be devoted to letter openings; eleven to forty may consist of second paragraphs; forty-one to seventy may consist of third paragraphs; and the remaining twenty entries may be closings. Thus a typist may be instructed to use 7: 24: 51: 82, and will construct the letter from the corresponding paragraphs in the paragraph book.

STRUCTURE OF THE SALES LETTER

In **sales letters** the same general principles of structure apply as in all business letters. But greater latitude is allowed in sales letters, just as greater latitude is allowed in the sales approach in general. You can be more unconventional and use more color and typographic tricks; and you will be pardoned a certain amount of puffing. Of course, if any one of these is carried to excess, it will prove self-defeating.

The salutation: One of the liberties that may be taken is with the salutation. In mass-mailings, where fill-in salutations and inside addresses are impossible, anonymous salutations such as **Dear Friend, Dear Sir** or **Dear Madame** may be used; or, if the list is a selected one permitting such specifications, **Dear Doctor, Dear Business Executive, Dear Fellow-Angler,** etc.

In some cases the salutation may be dispensed with and a flattering introductory phrase substituted for it, such as "To a Forward-Looking and Ambitious Young Businessman" or "To a Young Lady Who Keeps in Step with the Times." Or just a catchy headline like "Play Ball!" may be employed. However, these devices should be shunned in ordinary correspondence, and might be resorted to only where the multitude of identical letters is so great that individual salutations are impractical.

The opening: The opening is more crucial in a sales letter than in any other business correspondence. It is the sender's bid for attention; if it fails, the whole effort is wasted.

Some firms go to considerable trouble and expense in striving for attention-getting openings. In a conspicuous position on the letter they may have—stapled, glued on, or affixed in some other way—a small metal, cloth, or plastic object that pictorially symbolizes the opening line.

For example, one firm used a cord lasso, fastened to an upper corner of a letter so that the rope end touched the first line, to give animation to this opening: "Yes, we want to rope you in—and you'll be glad of it. . . ." Similarly a small aluminum bat glued to another letter helped to fix attention on this opening: "This is the season to go to bat for . . ."

Devices like these must be used with care for they are novelties that may appeal to some readers and by their "cuteness" irritate others. You may not be able to afford such expensive attention-getters; but still less can you afford a dull or lifeless opening. You can always attract attention with an imaginative thought and vivid words.

The question opening: One sure method is to put your opening in the form of a question. In that way you can take advantage of a quirk of human nature. We always react to a question as a challenge, and it is a rare person who does not feel the compulsion to make some response.

Of course the question should be provocative and relevant personally to the prospect, and should bring in the article or service being promoted.

This question opening was used by a home development company: "Are you over thirty, married, and a churchgoer?" Since the mailing list had been selected to concentrate on mature, married, churchgoing people, the reader was bound to answer "yes" and was thereby put in a receptive frame of mind to the rest of the proposition.

The striking statement: Another good type of opening is the **striking statement.** A good example is the one used, some twenty-five years ago, by the New York *Daily News* when it introduced itself and tabloid journalism to the metropolis. To its advertising prospects it sent a letter advising them to "Tell it to the Sweeneys" (through its pages) because "the Vanderbilts don't care." This was followed, of course, with interesting material on the advantages of the mass market and its lower sales resistance.

Another example of the striking statement as an opening was the following, used in a letter to advertisers by a large woman's magazine: "Yes, men still carry on most of the nation's business—but their wives do still more of the buying!"

A proverb, too, can provide a good opening, especially when it is given an arresting new twist: "The early bird catches the worm —but was it wise for the worm to be early?"

Body of the letter: Having gained attention by your opening, you must next sustain interest while making sales points in the body of the letter.

The anecdote: Some writers have recourse to a story or anecdote for this purpose. An organization arranging outdoor exercise and entertainment for businessmen used this anecdote in a sales letter to its prospects:

"A vigorous man in his nineties was asked the secret of his longevity. 'Wal," he replied, 'when my wife and I got married we agreed to do something to spare our nerves. If I was the grumpy one she'd go into the other room and take up her knittin'. And if she started to pick on me I'd put on my hat and go out for a walk. . . . So you see I been outdoors most of my life.'

"Being outdoors, that tried and true recipe for a long life and a healthy one, can be made easy for you by joining the ——— Outdoors Club. (And equally easy for your wife as well, who won't be so inclined to pick on you if you include her.) Drive out in your own car or one of the Club's limousines will pick you up outside your office and bring you to the club grounds. Then you can swim, golf, swing a racket, walk or do anything else you like in clear sunlight and unpolluted country air."

Enclosures gave further details.

Facts and figures: Other writers rely on facts and figures. They support tempting descriptions of the article or service they are marketing with data giving the results of laboratory tests, consumption statistics, testimonials, guarantees, and other inducements.

Incidentally, experienced sales-letter writers advise that the core of the sales message should appear about two-fifths of the way down the letter.

The closing: In earlier business correspondence, in the days when businessmen dressed in frock coats and striped trousers like diplomats, it was considered proper to close sales letters with polite wishes like "hoping" or "trusting we shall hear from you." Such expressions tend to linger on. Usually they are left in mid-air as dangling participles. If you find them in your correspondence, pull out the blue pencil!

Sales letters now end with forceful suggestions for immediate action. They ask for the order; and they enforce it with all sorts of inducements, bargain offers, samples, free examination privileges, and a wide variety of other appeals.

Here is an example of the appeal of **exclusiveness:**

"There are many more than three thousand discriminating readers who will want this book, but only three thousand copies were printed. As this letter is being mailed, the day's orders reduce the number still available to 422. Better make sure of getting **your** free-examination copy by filling out and mailing the enclosed card **today.**"

The "You" Attitude again: Among the numerous factors that contribute to effective correspondence, the "you" attitude, referred to earlier, is paramount. The seller takes care not to show his anxiety to make a sale. What he stresses is the buyer's interests. The buyer will get a bargain; he will be guaranteed against dissatisfaction by the privilege of returning the merchandise; payment will be made easy for him by special terms, etc. In sales letters as much as in any other form of business correspondence be sure to consider the reader at all times.

The postscript: In that same frock-coat-and-striped-pants business era alluded to above, the postscript was frowned upon. It was considered unkempt—allowable, perhaps, in private correspondence, but distinctly incorrect in well-dressed business correspondence.

Today, however, few sales letters are without postscripts. As a typographical device, the postscript has won general adoption because of the special services it can perform. It can remove from the body of the letter, whose unity it might impair, some special matter which should be brought to the reader's attention. Or it can give a needed emphasis to something as no other method can.

"P.S. Special discount terms can be arranged" stands out in a postscript, yet does not interfere with other persuasions as it might if set in the body of the letter. And if you have already mentioned your booth at a convention, a postscript reminder can do a lot to draw visits there: for example, "P.S. We're looking forward to seeing you at booth 16. Ask for Mr. Elkin."

"LETTERS YOU DON'T HAVE TO WRITE"

A recent speech by Maxwell C. Ross, a well known sales promotion expert, listed **sixteen** ways letters can be used to create good will—and, eventually, sales. "There's just one prerequisite," he said; "the person using them has to be a nice guy, courteous, friendly, and, above all, sincere."

Each is simply a friendly, personal letter that you send on some occasion when nobody would have thought very much about it if you hadn't sent the letter at all. They don't *have* to be written, but they create a tremendously favorable impression because they *are* written.

1. *You can use a letter to follow up a salesman's call.* You don't need to, for it isn't expected, but you'll be surprised at the reception it gets. You could start something like this: "John Smith told me today of the pleasant visit he had with you about your insurance program. I know that John will do a fine job for you." Then finish off in your own words.

2. *You can use letters to make appointments.* You say, "It's about time for me to sit down with you, Jim, and go over your insurance in the light of the new tax changes. I want to do this when you have the time for it, but it should be soon. I suggest that we get together late Friday afternoon. How would 4 o'clock be?" You don't need to say much more, but you'll be surprised at the nice reception you get.

3. *Whenever a customer or client has been promoted or changed jobs,* it's a nice gesture to send a letter like this—"Congratulations on your appointment to District Sales Manager. This is fine news, and I know you'll do a great job. If I can ever be of any help to you, please let me know."

4. *When a customer is ill,* there's no more appreciated time to get mail. All you need to say is —"I'm certainly sorry to hear that you are laid up for an operation. I hope it won't be many days before you're back at your desk." Add to that a book, or the loan of one, a magazine, or a box of candy, and the good will you build is far above the effort you take in doing it.

5. *When there is a death in the family.* If it's tactfully done a short message of sympathy can mean much.

6. *When a daughter or son gets married,* or *a new baby arrives.* These letters make no tangible effort to sell; they're simply good-will builders—the kind that some day will bring something nice to you because you went out of your way to do something nice for somebody else.

7. *When people buy a home,* write to them. Your letter doesn't need to be long or fancy. Perhaps: "I hope you are enjoying your new home, and that you have recovered from the trials of moving." If you have something to sell, go ahead and mention it. Tell these folks you'd appreciate a chance to call when things are squared away. In some cases, an inexpensive gift like a small rosebush or a young tree creates far more good will than the cost.

8. *When a customer has a birthday.* Quite a few successful salesmen make a practice of keeping birthday lists and sending cards or letters. A personal letter is best, but if you use a card, write something in longhand on it.

9. *When people move to your town* a letter of welcome is an excellent source of new business. They don't know where to go for dry cleaning, laundry, milk—what service station to trade with, where to do their banking, or the nicer places to eat. So you write: "Welcome to Omaha. We know you'll like it here. If there is any way we can help you get settled, please let us know."

10. *When people move from your town,* it may seem a futile gesture to seem sorry—but the intangible good will you create may come back to you in unsuspected ways. And sometimes people *do* return. So you write: "I am sorry you are moving away from Lincoln. We will miss you as a customer, but should you ever return we'll be waiting to serve you again."

11. *When you read about a customer in the newspaper,* send him a letter. Clip the article, send it to him, and say: "I don't know whether your children keep a scrapbook of the nice things that happen to you, but just in case they do, here's an extra copy I clipped for you to give them." And if congratulations are deserved, give them!

12. *When a customer is elected to some office,* or honored in any other way, perhaps you would say: "I've heard some nice things about the work you've done for the Chamber of Commerce, so I was not surprised to see that you have been elected vice president for the coming year."

13. *When someone has done you a favor* he will appreciate a note from you. "Those two extra tickets got me off a rough spot. I hope I can repay the favor soon."

14. *When some product or service pleases you,* take time to write about it. "Quite often people write to you only with their complaints, but I wanted you to know how pleased I am with our new floor furnace, and with the courteous and efficient way your men installed it."

15. *When a serviceman comes home write to him* or to his parents if he lives at home. That's a small way to show your appreciation of all he has done for you and his country. Never again in his life will he so much *want* to be welcomed back; or want to feel that all he went through was not in vain.

16. *You can use letters to thank new and old customers for their orders.* Perhaps you do, but many don't. In Des Moines, a filling station operator sends a post card to new customers. All the card says is, "It was nice of you to stop at our station. I hope you'll come back often." That's all it needs to say.

Talent scout, G. L. Fultz, St. Louis' best dressed credit man, and staunch enemy of Whiskers and Goozle, says of the following assembled hogwash: "I know you will want to read this letter, for it's a dandy."

"Thank you very kindly (who was kind?) for your letter of November 12th, just received. I am sorry that our bookkeeping department (mass production) erroneiously (new spelling) billed you for storage on the car that we handled for you. I am attaching corrected bill for which (?) I am sure you will find in order. Thanking you very kindly, we remain, very truly yours."

MISCELLANEOUS BUSINESS LETTERS

Inquiries and Replies; Orders and Acknowledgments; Introduction and Recommendation; Social Correspondence in Business, Inter-Office; Good Will; Payments by Mail.

ROUTINE LETTERS

In terms of quantity the largest part of business correspondence consists of routine letters—inquiries, replies to inquiries, orders and remittances, acknowledgments, bills, etc. In these letters the writer needs little art; the basic requirements are to be clear and accurate.

INQUIRY LETTERS

Inquiry letters and replies to inquiries should be concise, simple, and direct, except in cases that call for sensitivity, judgment, or tact. An inquiry about the price of an article need do no more than ask the price. But an inquiry about credit standing or about a job opportunity, and the answers to such inquiries, require care and tact. Similarly answers to inquiries in mail-order campaigns, where the objective is to produce sales, call for thought and skill.

In ordinary inquiries, however, the important thing, on the part of the inquirer, is to phrase his questions simply, precisely, and inclusively so that he can be told just what he wants to know, without extraneous matter; and also all that he wants to know so that he does not have to send further letters to fill out details. Similarly, the important thing on the part of the correspondent in answering such inquiries is to make the reply full and precise so that the inquirer does not have to come back to him to have matters cleared up or filled out.

If the information sought is adequately covered in a catalogue or booklet, enclose it in your reply and use the letter to refer to the paragraphs or pages dealing explicitly with the matter inquired about.

To facilitate quick comprehension both of the inquiry and the reply it is advisable to present them as separate items, allowing an individual paragraph for each.

If either the question or the answer is to be kept confidential, do not rely on the other person to guess it. Say so. Examples:

Gentlemen:

We are organizing a summer camp for boys and are in the market for 24 two-occupant portable tents for camping out. We are undecided whether to use conventional canvas tents, with which we are familiar, or your new nylon tents. Would you be good enough:

To send us whatever literature you have available on the construction of your nylon tents, accessory equipment, etc.

To inform us of their suitability to the summer climate of the Catskill Mountains, where the camp is located.

To furnish comparative weights and costs between canvas and nylon.

To give us an idea of the durability of

your product with estimates of how many years of service may be expected in ordinary use.

We shall appreciate your referring us to customers who have had experience with your tents in conditions approximating those of the boys' camp in the Catskills.

Sincerely yours,
Arthur Ives

Gentlemen:

We are in the market for a line of work pants. We should like to know—

What fabrics you make up.

What colors.

Minimum orders accepted per size.

Terms (including discount for cash).

Please send us a swatch catalogue with your reply.

Sincerely yours,
Bruce Samuelson

Gentlemen:

My wife and I will be in New York for the Christmas week vacation. We are people of modest means—I am an associate professor at the University here. We should like good (not lavish) hotel accommodations in Manhattan, but a little out of the immediate railroad-terminal district. We would like to take in the theater (dramas, not musicals). We enjoy good cooking, preferably without noisy entertainment.

Would your bureau book reservations such as we describe and provide information about restaurants?

Could you send us a selected list of hotels that would come within our description, listing locations and price ranges for rooms for two?

Could you list the well-reviewed plays and the price range for seats in medium locations. Fortunately our vision and hearing are good.

If you can provide such services, we will send you, by return mail, our first and alternate choices of hotel and theater reservations and a check for whatever sum you may require for deposit.

Sincerely yours,
Howard Carver

ANSWERS TO INQUIRIES

Dear Mr. Alexander:

We thank you for your letter of August 16 about our line of women's belts.

We wish to call your attention to the perforated pages in the back of the enclosed catalogue containing information on terms and convenient order forms.

Ours is a quality line. It is used for accessories by manufacturers serving exclusive shops, and is stocked by the New York Fifth Avenue stores.

We hope to have the pleasure of serving you.

Sincerely yours,
A. S. Cantor

Dear Mr. Jones:

Because of the decline in demand we have discontinued manufacture of the "union suit" type of men's underwear.

As the enclosed catalogue illustrates, we carry a full line of the currently popular types of men's underwear in a wide range of styles, colors, and prices.

We will be happy to serve you.

Sincerely yours,
V. A. Miles

Dear Mr. Hector:

Since your letter does not make clear what your speech defect is, we are unable to furnish a specific answer.

Our public speaking course has been designed to help shy people who are not sure of themselves to speak readily and effectively in public. If your defect is among those associated with shyness, we are confident that the course will help you overcome it.

But if the defect is organic, that may require surgical treatment. If it is a long-standing problem, such as chronic stuttering, that may call for psychiatric treatment. We recommend that you try to determine the cause with the aid of a physician or professionally qualified person.

But common difficulties in speaking—such as inability to face an audience, lack of practice of organizing a speech, unfamiliarity with the techniques of preparing material, groping for words, difficulties over parliamentary rules, etc.,—can be overcome by our course of study.

If you do not find here the answer you require, please try us again with the questions put in more specific terms.

Sincerely yours,
Marc Rafferty

A final note: Though answers to inquiries need not be elaborate, they should avoid stuffy over-formality. For example, instead of "Acknowledging yours of the 20th requesting a copy of our booklet, *Paint It Yourself,* we wish to advise you that the booklet is being mailed to you forthwith," write something like: "We are pleased to send you our booklet, *Paint It Yourself,* which you requested on May 20. Its suggestions have been useful to people of good taste who must keep within a modest budget." Or, instead of "Yours of September 10 received and contents noted. Be advised that the matter has been put into the hands of our Sales Department from whom you should hear shortly," write something like, "Our Sales Department has your inquiry of September 10 and is assembling material which should be helpful in answering your questions."

ORDERS

Many firms use printed order forms. If for some reason a letter is needed to accompany or precede the order to add some specific instructions about the order, make the letter concise and unmistakably clear.

Where the letter itself constitutes the order, care should be taken to make it direct, clear, and accurate. To facilitate this it is advisable to arrange the items in tabular form, giving a separate line to each. Details of color, size, material, price, identifying mark or number, etc., should be precisely stated. Manner of shipment should be specified—whether by mail, express, freight, etc.

If the goods are needed by a certain date, if method of payment is, in any way, to differ from the customary procedure, if delivery is to be made to an address other than the regular mailing address, anything requiring specific instructions should be made clear, and should be given a separate paragraph to prevent its being misunderstood or ignored.

Where remittance is enclosed, attention should be drawn to it and its nature specified —whether it is by check, money-order, express-order, draft, cash, or stamps.

Even in letters transmitting orders for goods, ordinary courtesy and tact should be observed. In his book *"Effective Letters in Business,"* Robert L. Shurter gives an example of a tactless order letter that drew a deservedly caustic reply: The letter—"Gents. Please send me one of them gasoline engines you show on page 785 and if it's any good I'll send you a check for it."

The reply—"Dear Mr. . . . Please send us the check and if it's any good we'll send you the engine."

Variations from ordinary punctuation are frequently used in orders. To compress items into single lines or a minimum number of lines, customary punctuation may be omitted and every possible abbreviation used. Names of separate articles are capitalized and also words that help to distinguish them from other kinds of goods of the same order. Thus Red will be capitalized to distinguish it from other colors an article may be manufactured in; or Wool to distinguish a garment in that fabric from garments in other fabrics. The objectives are conciseness and clarity and any typographic or grammatical means that promote these ends is justified.

ORDER LETTERS— SOME EXAMPLES

Gentlemen:

Please rush to us to reach our stockroom next Thursday: 10 doz. Yo-yos, 50 checker sets, 50 anagram sets. This is for a special sales week which is going well. Our stock on these items is running out.

Our regular purchase order is being made out in the routine way and should reach you in a day or two; but please do not hold up delivery of this special order. A delay of even a few hours may mean lost sales.

Sincerely yours,
Kenneth Miller

Dear Mr. Bates:

The enclosed purchase order is in confirmation of the order we placed with you over the phone this morning. The order was phoned in to avoid delays. I must emphasize again that the shipment must reach us before October 4, when our sales will start.

Sincerely yours,
Seth Bellows

Gentlemen:

Please send us, for earliest possible delivery, the following goods selected from your latest catalogue. Charge my account.

3 doz.	Men's Nylon Hose, Black, asst. sizes @ $4.00	$ 12.00
3 doz.	Men's Nylon Hose, Blue, asst. sizes @ $4.00	12.00
3 doz.	Men's Nylon Hose, Brown, asst. sizes @ $4.00	12.00
1½ doz.	Men's Nylon Hose, Green, asst. sizes @ $4.00	6.00
4 doz.	Men's Cotton Hose, Black, Triangle Clocks @ $4.50	18.00
2 doz.	#61 Work Shirts, asst. sizes . @ $9.00	18.00
2 doz.	Men's White Broadcloth Cotton Shirts, asst. sizes @ $16.00	32.00
		$110.00

Ship freight.

Sincerely yours,
Charles Bloom

ACKNOWLEDGMENTS

Dear Mr. Thayer:

Thank you for your order of October 5. As you instructed, it will be shipped freight, via the D & W. The order is being made up today and will be at the yards tomorrow. It should reach you well within the time you specified.

Sincerely yours,
J. H. Hudson

Dear Mr. Jones:

We have just telegraphed you the following: "Cannot ship your order May 10. Goods not available." The telegram was sent to minimize any inconvenience this may cause you. We can supply the cheaper grade, #43, on the date required. The earliest we can supply the #41 grade specified in your order would be June 11. If the #43 grade is all right, please wire collect and we will ship immediately.

Sincerely yours,
Adam Pierce

Dear Mr. Poynter:

Thank you for your order of August 14.

Unfortunately your letter did not specify which color or colors, and which weight or weights, you wish. In our Queen's Taste stationery line the colors are Rose, Fern, Mauve, Beige, Robin's Egg, Canary, Russet, Shell White, and Alpine Snow. The weights are Tissue, Regular and Baronial. Probably our catalogue was not at hand when you made out your order. We are enclosing another giving samples of each color and weight.

A prompt reply will be to our mutual advantage.

Yours sincerely,
Eric Hunter

Dear Mr. Magnes:

Thank you for your order for Clover Danish Blue Cheese. It is being shipped out to you today.

We enclose a catalogue of our other products. Please note that with orders of $10.00 or more, customers may receive, free, their choice of a jar of Lingonberry or Currant preserves.

Yours sincerely,
Einar Toksvig

FOLLOW-UPS ON ORDERS

Sometimes orders are poorly attended to and it is necessary, strange as it may seem, to jog the attention of the supplier. Here, again, as emphasized in the section on **Complaints and Adjustments,** an irritable tone is inadvisable, even where loss or inconvenience has been caused by the delay. A calm letter will get quicker and more favorable attention and will enhance the writer's status as a considerate customer whose patronage is worth retaining. It is seldom necessary to write more than one reminder; but when that becomes necessary, a sharper tone is not always politic, especially where the writer has reasons of his own for maintaining business relations with the inefficient firm. Examples:

Gentlemen:

Although our order #216 was acknowledged on June 2, and it is now near the end of the month, the air conditioners have not yet arrived. We have already undergone a hot spell, and soon July will be upon us. I cannot understand the delay or your leaving us without an explanation for your delay in delivery of such a seasonal article. Up to now your deliveries have been prompt; and expecting delivery any day, I did not write to you. There is no question now that I shall lose some sales and I expect you to make up for the lost time, not to speak of the lost business, by shipping the goods by express at your expense. Please wire what you plan to do in the matter.

Sincerely yours,
Edward Hines

Answers to follow-ups on orders should be prompt, and they should be tactful even where the tone of the complaining letter is disagreeable. Give the reason for the delay, assure the customer that care will be taken to avoid such delays in the future, and specify the date and the manner of the planned shipment.

Dear Mr. Osgood:

We regret the delay in shipping out your order #644, dated February 10.

You probably have read of the recent labor troubles in the lumber industry. These made it difficult for us to secure proper crating materials for the goods. Rather than risk damage in transit we held up the shipment until satisfactory crates were available. We have now managed to get some from another source of supply. Even though our shipping costs have risen, we feel the added expense, like the delay, is preferable to having the machinery arrive in poor condition.

Your order was shipped out today, express. We hope it reaches you in good time as, we are confident now, it will reach you in good order.

Sincerely yours,
Mark Lyons

LETTERS WITH ENCLOSURES

When remittances such as checks, etc., or when invoices or special notices are enclosed, the number of enclosures should be stated in the letter. This is customarily done in a separate line, at the left margin, under the signature.

Gentlemen:

The enclosed check for $146.00 is in settlement of our account to date. We also enclose your bill. Please receipt and return it.

Sincerely yours,
Joseph Evans

2 enclosures

Gentlemen:

Thank you for your order #324 for a dozen Pop-Up Toasters. They were shipped today. The invoice is enclosed. We also enclose the catalogue on waffle irons requested in your letter.

Sincerely yours,
Morton James

2 enclosures

LETTERS OF INTRODUCTION

Letters of introduction should not be given thoughtlessly. Avoid them unless you can feel that it would actually be in the interest of both parties to get acquainted. Good-natured people often do harm when they mean to do good, by writing letters of introduction indiscriminately. The tenth "promising" young chap sent to glean advice in the field of his ambition from a busy executive is likely to get a discouraging brushoff.

Therefore, the first consideration in writing a letter of introduction is whether to write it at all. Having decided that the letter should be written, you might well consider several other elements. Since the best way to present letters of introduction is in person, the envelope containing the introduction should be unsealed and should bear the name of the person to whom it is addressed and, in the lower left-hand corner, the line "Introducing Mr. . . ." This enables the recipient to welcome the caller by name and facilitates the relationship.

The letter should be brief and restrained. A long letter might impose an embarrassingly long wait on the caller while the letter is read. And extravagant statements about the caller, if they do not predispose the reader to skepticism, may evoke embarrassing comments of other sorts.

Sometimes there is a reason to mail the letter to the person addressed; for example, to allow him to appoint a time for the meeting. In that case a copy should be sent to the person being introduced so that he will be familiar with what has been said about him. Examples:

Dear Mr. Clements:

I hope you will have the time to see Mr. Wilbur, who was a student in my class this semester. You have several times expressed an interest in seeing "the cream of the crop" in each graduating class. It is because I can unreservedly place Mr. Wilbur in that category that I have suggested that he call on you.

Yours sincerely,
Roger Hessian

Dear Mr. Canning:

It gives me great pleasure to introduce to you Mr. Harvey Wright, who operates a large bottling plant in our city.

Mr. Wright is contemplating opening a branch in your city, and I could think of no one better for him to see than you for a quick survey of local conditions and prospects. My business association with Mr. Wright is now in its twelfth year and has led to a friendship which has enabled me to discover and appreciate his personal qualities.

I feel certain that any association this introduction may result in will be valued on both sides.

Yours sincerely,
Hiram Godkin

LETTERS OF RECOMMENDATION

There are two main types of recommendation—the general recommendation "to whom it may concern," and the individual recommendation addressed to a specific person. The latter obviously is preferable, since the writer's personal acquaintance with the person addressed generally means that the letter will be given more attention than might otherwise be the case.

The best kind of recommendation is the one that performs a mutual service to the recommended person and the one to whom he is sent. So far as possible, therefore, it is well to find out beforehand whether and how the person about whom you are writing can be of service to the individual you are addressing.

Vital to any letter of recommendation is truthfulness and restraint. False statements are almost inevitably found out. In time they create handicaps that outweigh any temporary advantage that they gain for the person recommended. And exaggerated claims usually predispose the reader to skepticism and suspicion, and thus are often more injurious than helpful. Examples:

To Whom It May Concern:

Mr. Clarence Loman has been on our sales staff for the past eight years and has compiled an excellent sales record. He is a friendly person by nature and has won the friendship as well as the business patronage of his customers. We have convincing evidence of that from the letters we have received in response to the announcement of his retirement from traveling.

For reasons of health he cannot continue traveling, but he can serve in an inside position. We regret there is nothing of this kind available in our organization. He would make a crackerjack inside salesman and we can unreservedly recommend him to anyone in need of a person with real selling talents. It would take him no time to get a feeling of your stock and your methods; and to establish really friendly relations with customers. We are confident that he would be an asset to any firm that can use his services.

Very truly yours,
Martin Ullmann

Dear Mr. Carter:

I am taking the liberty of writing to you because I know that you sometimes give out manuscripts for first readings, and accepted manuscripts for preparations for the printer, to qualified young people, on a free-lance basis. I have heard that you do this, as a means of testing or training candidates for anticipated future openings on your editorial staff.

If that is the case, I feel that you will appreciate my sending Miss Ethel Willison to you. You have already become acquainted with her work and have even complimented her, without knowing it, when you complimented me on the excellent shape of the manuscript I turned in, and again, when I sent back corrected proofs. Miss Willison assisted me through all the stages of my book, and it is to her that I owe the smoothness and ease with which it went through all its stages.

Miss Willison has taken all the courses given here in preparation for a career in publishing and has applied what she learned, first on the college paper and, later, in helping other faculty members, as she has helped me, in preparing articles and books.

I am confident that she is just the kind of person you will look for when you are considering taking on a new editorial assistant. I take great pleasure in recommending her to you.

Sincerely yours,
David Proctor

SOCIAL CORRESPONDENCE IN BUSINESS

Though the phrase "strictly business" symbolizes freedom from emotional involvements in or out of business, the words connote an attitude or a goal, rather than the reality of business itself. It would be unnatural to expect that human beings, who spend most of their waking hours in business, would not form personal relationships of varying degrees of closeness in the course of their business. The truth is that most of the friendships men form in their mature years arise out of business contacts. And friendly qualities are recognized as assets in business.

This is so generally understood that trade associations of businessmen have the fostering of friendly cooperation as their major aim. Generally, too, a business relationship would hardly be accounted good or secure if it failed to develop some measure of personal regard between heads or representatives of the two firms.

Consequently, there are many occasions for letters that should not be "strictly business," although they are essential to the conduct of business. Examples are given in the following pages:

LETTERS OF CONGRATULATIONS

Dear Mr. Leonard:

What a pleasure it was to see the item in *The Times* business section this morning about your promotion to the position of Sales-Manager. Actually I think I ought to write to the President of your concern, Mr. Tate, to congratulate him. He had the good sense to recognize a good man. From what I know about people in the field he couldn't have picked a better man. Congratulations on a well-deserved promotion.

Cordially yours,
Robert Mackinder

Dear Mr. Slocum:

I don't know how others are reacting to the news in this morning's real-estate section, but I want to congratulate you on taking such a far-sighted and enterprising step. I have already heard some say that the site is too remote for such a development, but I put them with those who once thought Forty-second Street was too far outside the city. I think you have judged correctly that the site is directly in the path of the city's future growth.

Again, my congratulations and my best wishes for the success of a project which should serve the community as well as bring you well-deserved returns.

Admiringly yours,
Edmund Gates

LETTERS OF SYMPATHY AND CONDOLENCE

Dear Walter:

When your secretary called this morning to tell me that you wouldn't be able to keep our appointment because of your sudden illness, I was deeply disturbed. She told me that you were to spend some days in the hospital, under observation, to determine whether an operation will be necessary. I hope the tests indicate no such necessity and that you will be back in your office very soon and in condition to renew our postponed engagement.

Cordially yours,
Arthur Reinhardt

Dear Mrs. Rodd:

It was a hard blow to us, too, to hear of your husband's death. We missed him here, very much, two years ago, when he retired. During our association with him over the twelve years that he was with us, all of us developed the highest regard for his wonderful qualities. We can fully understand how deeply you must feel his loss. But it must be a consolation to you that his last years were serene. We and his other friends feel grateful to you for having contributed so much to making him so happy.

Sincerely yours,
Charles U. Clifford

Dear George:

I was very sorry to receive the sad news of your great loss. I know that nothing anyone may say at a time like this can assuage your deep grief, but I hope that you will soon find abiding comfort in the high regard everyone had for your father's accomplishments, and in the good health, happiness, and achievements of those dear to you. I hope you will have no more sorrow for many years to come.

Sincerely yours,
Frank

Dear Mr. Cass:

I have just learned of the emergency appendicitis operation you have had to undergo. I had Miss Hale phone the hospital immediately and was reassured to hear that there were no complications and that you are getting along nicely.

That's fine and we want to keep it so. Therefore, I want it understood that no matter how good your recovery is, you are not to come back to the office until the doctor, on his most conservative estimate, tells you you may. And don't think of the office. This is an order!

In the meanwhile, to help you pass the time, there will be a package of books at the hospital. The well-read Miss Hale did the choosing and I think she has a good idea of your taste.

With all best wishes,
Robert E. Griffin

ACCEPTING INVITATIONS

Dear Mr. Canby:

It will be a pleasure to see you when I visit New York next month. Thank you for suggesting it. Indeed one of the prospects that made the trip so pleasing to me was the opportunity it might give me to become acquainted with you personally.

Sincerely yours,
Elmer Robinson

Dear Sir:

I consider it a great honor to be asked to speak at the Credit Men's Luncheon next month. Thank you very much.

I hope the enclosed data are what you need for the newspaper release. And I will be on hand an hour before the start of the luncheon, as you suggest, to talk over the details of the program.

Yours very truly,
Leon Hart

DECLINING INVITATIONS

Dear Mr. Hopkins:

Unfortunately I will be out of town during the week of March 10 and will not be able, therefore, to be present at the reception celebrating the opening of your new store. Since I will not be there to offer my congratulations to you in person, permit me to do so here. And I wish to add my sincere best wishes for the success of the new store and the continued growth of your business.

Sincerely yours,
Anthony Asch

Dear Mr. Mann:

It is with deep regret that I must decline the great honor of organizing and heading the committee to arrange a reception for the Vice-President, who is to be one of the speakers at our coming convention. As you may have heard, Mr. Bixby, head of our Foreign Department, died suddenly last week. I have had to take over his duties temporarily, which for the present rules out any other activities for me. I will let you know as soon as I am free again for any service to the organization.

Sincerely yours,
Horace Seton

RESIGNATIONS

Dear Sir:

I have just been appointed Coordinator of Sales for our firm. This will mean extensive traveling in order to keep in continual contact with our stores throughout the country. It will, therefore, be impossible for me to continue to serve as secretary of the club. And, so, with deep regret, I must tender my resignation from that office.

It has been a pleasure to serve the club during the past four years, and I have enjoyed and profited from the association with its able officers and members. Needless to say, I will be on hand for every get-together my new duties will permit.

Sincerely yours,
Edwin Robbins

Dear Sir:

I have agreed to serve on the Mayor's Committee for Emergency Housing. Since it may prejudice the value of the work I can do for the committee, if I continue as a member of the firm, I am submitting my resignation to take effect immediately.

This is a step I take not without regret, for the years I have been privileged to spend with the firm have been happy ones. But I feel that the opportunity afforded me by the Mayor to serve the community in so important a sphere of activity is one that I cannot pass up.

Sincerely yours,
Alan W. Furness

INTER-OFFICE CORRESPONDENCE

In concerns of any size a good many memos pass between departments, between the management and the staff, between individuals in different departments, etc. Thus the Stock Department may inform the Sales Department of the arrival of certain needed goods; or the management will send memoranda to department heads about certain changes of policy; or it may send a memo to the entire staff about price changes, the announcement of a special holiday, etc.; or a salesman may send a note to Shipping giving special instructions regarding the shipment of an order; or Promotion may send a memo to Sales and other departments concerned, reminding them of the start of a national advertising campaign so that they can prepare for the anticipated inquiries and orders.

Most firms provide printed forms and restrict inter-office correspondence to one subject only in order to encourage conciseness and clarity and to facilitate filing and reference. The printed forms also assure that the date, the department, the person, and the subject are clearly indicated. This makes salutations and signatures superfluous and they are omitted except in memoranda with a deliberately personal touch.

Although such notes are "stripped for action," the tone should nevertheless always be courteous. Inter-departmental feuds have often begun over tactless expression in such memoranda. And office morale has sometimes been damaged by an unintended curt note by management. Certain indispensable formalities of respect should be observed in inter-office correspondence as in other forms. Examples:

Form G-14	One Subject Only
Inter-Office Memorandum	Made Simple Books, Inc.
To:	From:
Department:	Department:
Subject:	Date:

• • •

To: Staffs	From: J. B. Wolcott
Department: Sales, Correspondence	Department: Management
Subject: New Price List	Date: April 10, 1954

On May 1, our new price-list goes into effect. Copies should be in the hands of all our salesmen before the end of the week and in the hands of our dealers by April 28. Copies can be obtained from Miss Andrews.

• • •

To: Staffs	From: G. E. Anderson
Department: All departments	Department: Personnel
Subject: July 4 Holiday	Date: July 1, 1954

Since July 4, this year, falls on a Sunday, the office will be closed Monday, July 5, to allow a full holiday weekend.

• • •

To: Mr. Taylor, Mr. Green, Mr. Johns, Mr. Maxfield	From: Edward Earnshaw
Department: Sales, Shipping, Personnel, Accounting	Department: Promotion
Subject: Advertising campaign	Date: February 10, 1954

This weekend our special advertising campaign on our new Infra-Red cooker opens with full pages in the magazine supplements of metropolitan newspapers. There will be page ads in leading national magazines, along with other promotion. Most of the advertising will carry keyed coupons. Your departments should be prepared for the special load of mail that will come in. Just a reminder.

• • •

To: E. Dirksen	From: J. Myers
Department: Shipping	Department: Sales
Subject: Johnson Brothers order	Date: January 11, 1954

CONTINENTAL TOOLING SERVICE, INC.

19 WEST FOURTH ST., DAYTON, OHIO 45402

H. E. FOLKERTH, MGR. TELEPHONE HE 9737

Formerly Continental Design Service

WE OUGHT TO GET TOGETHER

DOG-gone it!

I want to put in another PLUG for Continental Tooling Service.

I'd like to do it in person. I'd like to tell you all about Continental ... about the long, nine years on the average, experience of our men ... about all the DIVERSIFIED work we've been doing ... about our efforts to keep up to and a little ahead of date with our designs ... about the way we can work WITH your own tool department ... about the tools we've designed to cut down production costs for dozens of companies ... about our constant effort to see that every single tool we make is ...

Cheap ... Simple ... Good.

But, as long as I'm doing it in a letter -- and a letter that starts out with a dog and his unofficial headquarters at that -- I'd better just say:

When it comes to tool design, we want you to consider us as stable and dependable as a fire-plug and as eager and enthusiastic as a pup ... we'd like to TELL you the whole story. In short, DOG-gone it....

We ought to get together,

H. E. Fokerth

In offering the services of his firm to prospective customers, the writer of this letter has employed a device more often associated with the sales letter—using both pictorial illustration and a variety of verbal references in the text of the letter which sustain the pictorial idea. Again, we urge discretion and call attention to the possible dangers of such an approach: the "cuteness" of the idea, intended to attract and sustain attention and amusement, may instead offend and revolt.

Dear Ed:

When Billing sends down the Johnson Brothers' order, please put a note on it to double wrap the shipment. Old Mr. Johnson complains that our wrapping paper isn't thick enough. The trouble is in his storeroom, which is a filthy, damp place. So it'll be best to double wrap his stuff, or he'll come back at us with claims for spoilage. Hope it's not too much bother. Thanks.

Joe

Other types of memo forms frequently used are:

From the Desk of Frank Gannon

To: ______________ Date: ______________

To: ______________ Date: ______________

From: ____________________

It might be noted, in passing, that in large corporations or organizations, intracompany mail is frequently placed in heavy-stock envelopes than can be used over and over again. These envelopes have ruled lines on the outside, and the sender need merely place on the first free line the name and department of the person to whom the communication is addressed. That person in turn can use the same envelope by doing similarly the next time he wishes to dispatch a memo or some papers to another person in the organization.

GOOD-WILL LETTERS

It should be enough, of course, to service customers promptly and efficiently. Yet it is human for them to want to be appreciated as well and to be given personal attention. If thanking a customer for his order has been overlooked, write him a special note of appreciation for his business.

Letting customers feel that they are "in" on your operations is another way of building their good will. If you are expanding your business, or promoting a man on your staff with whom your customers may have had occasion to become acquainted, or if you are making any operational change of interest to them, let your customers know about it.

If you are making gifts—calendars, personal memo-pads, initialed pencils, etc.,—to new customers, don't leave the old customers out. Give it to them, also.

There are also occasions and circumstances that might be used for the promotion of good will by drawing attention to them. We have already mentioned letters of congratulation and letters of sympathy and condolence. Watch significant dates in the lives or careers of customers, when it is possible or advisable—anniversaries of the concern, birthdays of the officers, marriages in their families, and send congratulations and appropriate gifts. Send Christmas greetings to all customers, and mail them well in advance of the rush period, so that they don't come so late as to seem like afterthoughts.

Unusual occurrences may be made the occasion for a good-will note. Thus when Lever Brothers were constructing their striking New York building, they sent letters to all in the neighborhood within range of the sounds of construction, private families in nearby residential blocks as well as business neighbors, apologizing for the noise. They gave assurance that everything was being done to finish the building as soon as possible and that all avoidable construction sounds were being eliminated.

During the recent period of rapid and successive price boosts some firms notified their customers that they were not raising their prices though raw-material costs had risen; and others explained what they were doing to absorb part of the necessary price advances in operational economies.

Good will within an organization is as important as the good will of outside customers and neighbors. Well run concerns

IT HAPPENED IN ROME

Gentlemen:

I recently flew to Europe via XYZ and also used XYZ services while in Europe. The service of your personnel throughout was excellent.

Particularly, I am writing about the personnel in your city ticket office on Via Marconi in Rome. They were of great assistance to me, and went far beyond their normal line of duty on my behalf.

I had a small handbag that needed to have the zipper repaired. The manner in which the personnel at your Rome office took care of it was very highly appreciated.

Sincerely yours,

Robert Stevens

XYZ PRESIDENT REPLIES

Dear Mr. Stevens:

Thanks very much for your letter which was forwarded to my New York Office. I certainly appreciate your nice comments about our services, and especially those for our personnel in Rome.

In training our personnel, courtesy and efficiency are repeatedly stressed, and nothing pleases me more than to learn when our people have excelled in performance of their duties. I'm sure our personnel in Rome will be happy to know of your praise, and I am passing along your nice comments -- adding my personal thanks for the fine job.

Your selection of XYZ and your interest in writing are greatly valued. We shall anticipate the opportunity of extending our services often, and I hope you will continue to receive fine treatment all along the XYZ way whenever we are privileged to serve you.

Sincerely,

Howard W. London, President

A courtesy letter from a pleased and satisfied customer; and a letter in kind from the firm, inviting the customer to make future use of the firm's services. Although not part of "routine" business letter writing, the value of such letters cannot be exaggerated. Indeed, such letters should *be regarded as a "routine" element in the conduct of business.*

make use of their inter-office correspondence to keep up office morale through informational memoranda that make the staff feel they are part of what is happening: through announcements that will please the staff; and through personal notes of congratulation from management on pleasant occasions, such as the birth of children, the graduation of sons, etc.; and condolences in bereavements. Examples:

Dear Mr. Smythe:

The enclosed is the latest issue of our house organ, *Cuttings.* I am sure you will be interested in the piece on page twelve, on the old Smythe Tool Works which, I believe, were founded by your great-grandfather.

Would you like to get *Cuttings* regularly? I'd have it sent without asking if it weren't for my own experience. I groan at the amount of unsolicited mail I get from people who send it with the best of intentions; there aren't enough hours in the day to read everything that comes through the mail. So for that reason I have made it a policy to send *Cuttings* only if customers let us know that they want it. Incidentally, I shall be happy to send you as many copies of this issue as you may require.

Sincerely yours,
Gabriel Harcourt

Dear Mr. Connor:

It occurred to me, recently, that it was just about ten years ago that I entered your first order with our company in my order book. I was not then sales manager, of course —that came as the result of the good orders you and other friendy customers favored me with.

To make sure, I had my secretary look it up, and it turned out, sure enough, that our business connections did begin ten years ago, this month! That first order, incidentally, was for an assortment of our fans. Your latest order is for air conditioners! Time does move.

If we could get together today, we'd be celebrating the glad occasion properly at Ludlow's or Keen's. But since that's not possible, here's the next best thing. Please join me in a glass of champagne of a kind I've found particularly palatable. A case of it should be in your office this morning if American Express is on its toes.

Your health and best wishes for ten more good years of business together.

Cordially,
Ed Schacht

Dear Mr. Alter:

We prepared a map for use by our office staff of the new city postal zones. It proved to be such a convenience that we decided to print up copies for our customers. Here's your copy and we hope you'll find it useful.

Sincerely yours,
Conrad Dietrichstein

Dear Mr. Freud:

As a customer of the Hooker Hat Company you will be interested to know that we have just completed negotiations which bring this fine firm into our organization. It was our desire to fill out our line of men's furnishings with a quality hat line, and Hooker was our choice.

We were glad, of course, that with so fine a product we could make the acquaintance of new customers appreciative of fine quality apparel for men.

We want to assure you that you will continue to receive the efficient service you have become accustomed to from the Hooker staff (which is being preserved intact), plus, we venture to add, special services made possible by the facilities of our larger organization.

On his next call your Hooker salesman will have our other lines of quality goods to offer you. We are mailing you our catalogue so that you may become acquainted with them. Any orders you wish to place from the catalogue will be credited to the salesman's account, and you will be billed on the same terms as in your account with Hooker.

Please let us know if there is any way that we can be of service to you. I look forward to the continuance of what I hope will be a pleasant and profitable relationship for us both.

Sincerely yours,
A. E. Handley

Dear Mr. Gates:

Thank you for your order number 112, which arrived this morning. It will be shipped today; the invoice is enclosed.

The same company is making a new line of waffle irons, and the introductory offer is so attractive we decided to call it to the attention of all our customers. We have tested the device and found it sturdy and efficient. We are enclosing a circular giving the details. Perhaps you'll want to take advantage of this offer.

Sincerely yours,
Morton James

2 enclosures

Dear Mr. Magnus:

Thank you for your order of Clover Danish Blue Cheese. It is being shipped to you today.

I think you will be interested in seeing a copy of a periodical we issue, *Good Cheer*, which contains recipes and notes about new European delicacies being introduced to American lovers of good foods. If you would like to receive it regularly, we shall be glad to put you on our mailing list.

Sincerely yours,
Gail Longinetti

1 enclosure

REQUESTS FOR CHARITY

Although the solicitation of contributions for charity is a highly specialized, professional activity these days, businessmen frequently have occasion to sell theater tickets or to ask for donations for a pet organization. In such cases make your letter brief; leave the "selling" to the professional fund-raiser. You will get a check because the person you are writing to knows you, and values your friendship or patronage. Some examples:

Dear Mr. Adams:

I am taking the liberty of sending you the enclosed advertising blank in behalf of the United Orphans League. I am very much interested in the organization and know of its good work and great need. I shall appreciate your check to the best of your ability. With many thanks and good wishes, I am,

Sincerely yours,
Sam Laury

Dear Ben:

Enclosed are a couple of tickets for "Ah, Take the Cash." The seats are not so good, and I don't know anything about the show, but the cause is good. So I'd appreciate your taking the tickets and letting me have your check for $20 made out to the Community Chest. I hope you will enjoy the show and have the double satisfaction of knowing you've aided a worthy cause.

Sincerely yours,
Norman Rich

Although it is desirable to keep letters of this type short, they can vary in tone, length, and appeal if in the judgment of the writer, the nature of his relationship with the person to whom he is writing requires more than the semi-formal approach illustrated above.

EXAMPLE OF AN ACCEPTANCE LETTER

Dear Mr. Bingham:

I am happy to send you the enclosed check for the theater tickets you sent me. I know the cause is a good one, and I hope the project is a success. Keep up the good work.

Sincerely yours,
David K. Nelson

PAYMENTS BY MAIL

In payments by mail the remittance should be such as can be convertible into cash without expense and with a minimum of trouble to the recipient. The sender should secure evidence, wherever possible, that the money was sent and that it was received.

Remittances may be made by check (personal or certified), money order (postal or express), bank drafts, stamps, or currency. (If currency has to be mailed, it is advisable to send it in a registered letter, particularly if the sum is large; in such case the sender gets a receipt that the envelope has been delivered. In no way does this serve as a receipt for the contents.)

CURRENCY AND STAMPS

Currency or stamps are used when the remittance is under a dollar. Mail order advertisers urge this because readers are more apt to respond, when such remittances are called for.

In mail order letters, coin cards are often enclosed to facilitate payment by that means. These cards are made of cardboard from which holes, the sizes of the required coins, have been cut. A paper flap is attached to fold over the coins and keep them in place.

Home made cards to fill the same purpose are easy to prepare. If the coins do not fit into the holes exactly, they can be held in place by scotch tape or rubber bands.

When the remittance is in stamps, insert them into a small envelope or fold them into waxed paper, which will prevent the gummed surfaces from sticking.

POSTAL MONEY ORDER

A safe, cheap, and convenient method for transmitting money is available at any post office. By this method the sender is assured that the money reaches the person for whom it is intended, though neither sender nor recipient is identified on the receipt.

EXPRESS MONEY ORDERS

Postal money orders may not exceed $100 per individual order. In larger amounts the rates are higher than those of the express companies. Express money orders have one big advantage over postal money orders. The form includes the name of the sender and must be endorsed by the recipient. The completed form is kept on file at the express company; thus there is a record of the complete transaction.

CHECKS

Checks are probably the most convenient form of payment. Most banks provide two types of checking service—**regular,** which generally requires maintaining a stipulated average balance during the month; and **special,** which permits the writing of checks at a set fee, usually ten cents, per check. After endorsement and clearance, the check is returned to the maker and serves as a receipt and permanent record. For a small fee banks also furnish **cashier's checks** in exchange for cash, and can be made out to anyone indicated by the purchaser; a receipt is given.

CERTIFIED CHECKS

Certified checks are used when it is necessary to assure the recipient that the check is good. A certified check is an ordinary check on whose face there is stamped or written certification by the cashier of the bank on which it is drawn. This indicates that the bank has deducted the amount of the check from the drawer's account and has assumed responsibility for payment.

BANK DRAFTS

A bank draft is a written order for money from one bank to another. It is a convenient way of paying a bill incurred in another community, is more convenient than a check, since the recipient receives cash immediately and does not have to wait until a check is cleared.

Suppose a man in New York wishes to buy certain goods in Boston. He asks his New York bank for a draft for the necessary sum. He is charged a small sum for this service, usually twenty cents per $100. Endorsing the draft by writing on the back of it, "Pay to the order of (name of Boston firm)" and signing his name underneath, he sends the draft on to Boston.

SUMMARY OF SPELLING RULES

	RULE	EXAMPLES	EXCEPTIONS
IE and EI	I before E, except after C.	ach*ie*ve, but c*ei*ling	1. Use *EI* when: a. Sounded as ā: n*ei*ghbor, w*ei*gh b. Sounded as ĭ: counterf*ei*t c. Sounded as ī: h*ei*ght 2. Use *IE* for almost all other sounds: friend, lieutenant. 3. If *i* and *e* do not form a digraph, rules do not apply: f*ie*ry, d*ei*ty.
Final Silent **E**	1. **Drop** before suffix beginning with a vowel. 2. **Retain** before suffix beginning with a consonant.	grieve—grievance absolute—absolutely	1. Retain *e* after soft *c* and soft *g* before suffixes beginning with *a* or *o*: peaceable, manageable.
Final **Y**	1. **Change** final *y* to *i* if *y* is **preceded** by a **consonant** and **followed** by any **suffix** except one beginning with *i*. 2. **Retain** final *y* if it is **preceded** by a **vowel.**	beauty—beautiful BUT carry—carrying boy—boys; valley—valleys	dry—dryness; sly—slyness. day—daily; pay—paid
Final Consonants	**Double** final consonants when: 1. Preceded by a single vowel. 2. Followed by a suffix beginning with a vowel. 3. The consonant terminates a monosyllabic word. 4. The consonant terminates a polysyllabic word accented on the last syllable.	1. drop—dropped; beg—beggar 2. quit—quitting; swim—swimmer 3. hit—hitter; run—running 4. omit—omitted; transfer—transferred	Final consonant is not doubled if: 1. Accent shifts to preceding syllable when suffix is added: con-fer′—confer′ring BUT con′fer-ence. 2. Final consonant is already doubled: sta*rt*—sta*rt*ed. 3. Final consonant is preceded by two vowels: b*ea*t—b*ea*ting; b*oi*l—b*oi*ling.
k added to words ending in **c**	**Add** *k* to words ending in *c* before a suffix beginning with *e, i, y.*	frolic—frolicking—frolicked; picnic—picnicking—picnicked	
-cede -ceed -sede	Except for super*sede,* ex*ceed,* pro*ceed,* suc*ceed,* all words having this sound end in *-cede.*	accede, precede, recede, concede	
Plurals	1. Regular noun plurals add *-s* to the singular. 2. Irregular plurals: a. Add *-es* if noun ends in *o* preceded by consonant. b. Change *y* to *i* and add *-es* if noun ends in *y* preceded by consonant. c. Add *-s* if noun ends in *y* preceded by vowel.	boy—boys; book—books a. echo—echoes; Negro—Negroes b. sky—skies; enemy—enemies c. play—plays; day—days	a. piano—pianos; zero—zeros; solo—solos.

	RULE	EXAMPLES	EXCEPTIONS
Possessives	1. Don't confuse contractions with possessive pronouns.	*Contraction* 1. it's (it is) they're (they are) — *Possessive Pronoun* its their	
	2. Use no apostrophes with possessive or relative pronouns.	2. *his, hers, ours, yours, theirs, whose*	
	3. If singular or plural noun does **not** end in *s*, add **apostrophe** and *s*.	3. prince—prince's (Sing.), princes' (Plur.); soldier—soldier's (Sing.), soldiers' (Plur.)	
	4. If singular or plural noun **does** end in *s*, add apostrophe.	4. hostess—hostess' (Sing.), hostesses' (Plur.); Jones—Jones' (Sing.), Joneses' (Plur.)	

SPELLING LISTS. List of Words Most Frequently Misspelled by High School Seniors.

The list of words below* contains 149 words most frequently misspelled by high school seniors. These words and word-groups (those which are variants of the same word, as *acquaint* and *acquaintance*), were compiled by Dean Thomas Clark Pollock of New York University from 14,651 examples of misspelling submitted by 297 teachers in the United States, Canada and Hawaii. Each of the words represented was misspelled twenty times or more, and yet these words, comprising fewer than three per cent of the original list of 3,811 words, account for thirty per cent of the total misspellings.

NOTE: The trouble spots in each word are italicized. Numbers beside the words indicate how frequently each word is misspelled.

their 179
receive 163
too 152

{writer 11, writing 81, written 13}

{describe 28, description 38}

tragedy 64

all right 91
separate 91
until 88
privilege 82
definite 78
there 78
believe 77

{study 1, studied 3, studies 3, studying 34}

{its 52, it's 22}

{occur 9, occurred 52, occurrence 10, occurring 2}

probably 33
speech 33
argument 32

* The list compiled by Dr. Pollock appears in the *Teachers Service Bulletin in English* (Macmillan, November, 1952).

{decide 48, decision 15}

{occasion 54, occasionally 8}

{succeed 25, success 22, successful 12}

interest 56
beginning 55

{immediate 3, immediately 51}

coming 53
embarrass 48
grammar 47

{humor 2, humorous 45}

{exist 3, existence 43}

{lose 28, losing 15}

disappoint 42
rhythm 41

{acquaint 17, acquaintance 9}

affect 26
accept 25
accommodate 25
excellent 25
opportunity 25

{convenience 5, convenient 33}

{difference 15, different 23}

than 38
athletic 37
to 37
business 36

{equipped 21, equipment 14}

{principal 18, principle 18}

{prophecy 35, prophesy 35}

{benefit 16, beneficial 5, benefited 11, benefiting 1}

develop 34
environment 34
recommend 34
fascinate 33
finally 33

{necessary 24, necessity 9}

{foreign 14, foreigners 9}

performance 23
together 23
descend 13
descendant 9

{image 3, imagine 7, imaginary 5, imagination 17}

quiet 32
then 32

prejudice 30
sense 30
similar 30

{your 2, you're 28}

appearance 29
conscious 29
pleasant 29

{stop 1, stopped 24, stopping 4}

surprise 29

{excite 1, excited 7, excitement 13, exciting 7}

experience 28
government 27
laboratory 27
tried 27

familiar 21
escape 21
meant 21
where 21
chief 20

m*arr*y	4	du*r*ing	22	her*o*	10
marr*ies*	6	f*o*rty	22	hero*es*	9
mar*ria*ge	15	wom*a*n	22	hero*i*ne	1
		cert*ai*n	21		
				lon*e*ly	20
char*ac*ter	24	commi*t*	4	*o*pi*n*ion	20
compl*e*t*e*	24	com*m*it*t*ed	12	parl*ia*ment	20
fr*i*end	24	com*m*it*t*ing	5	pos*s*ess	20
tr*u*ly	24	criti*c*ism	21	pro*f*essor	20
acciden*ta*lly	23	di*s*ap*p*ear	21	rest*au*rant	20
do*esn't*	23	exaggerate	21	vill*ai*n	20

List of 100 Words Most Frequently Misspelled by College Freshmen.

absence	conscientious	forth
accidentally	conscious	forty
across	coolly	fourth
aggravate	council	friend
all right	counsel	government
amateur	criticism	grammar
argument	deceive	grievance
around	definite	hadn't
athletic	desert	height
believed	dessert	indispensable
benefited	dining	interested
business	disappointed	its
busy	doesn't	it's
capital	don't	knowledge
cemetery	effect	laboratory
choose	eighth	latter
chosen	embarrassed	literature
coming	environment	loose
committee	exercise	lose
competition	February	losing

maintenance	referred
marriage	relieve
mischievous	rhythm
noticeable	schedule
occasion	seize
occurred	separate
occurrence	shining
o'clock	stationery
omitted	strength
parallel	succeed
perhaps	superintendent
principal	supersede
principles	tragedy
privilege	tries
proceed	truly
pronunciation	villain
quiet	Wednesday
quite	weird
received	whether
recommend	woman

List of Words Frequently Misspelled on Civil Service Examinations.

accident	municipal	society
all right	principal	simplified
auxiliary	principle	technicality
athletic	promotional	tendency
buoyant	president	their
catalogue		thousandth
career	precede	transferred
comptroller	proceed	transient
criticise	promissory	truly
dividend	recommend	villain
	personnel	
embarrass	purchasable	Wednesday
expedient	responsibility	writ
government	received	whether
inveigle	regrettable	yield
monetary	supersede	

WORDS AND EXPRESSIONS TO AVOID

Superfluous, Overformal, Flabby, Tacfless, Hackneyed Language

According to our records—Often superfluous and can be omitted.

Acknowledge receipt of your letter—Overformal. Better, **We thank you for your letter.**

(Please) advise—Better **inform** or **tell** unless actually soliciting advice.

Agreeable to your letter—Old fashioned.

Along these lines—Better, **the gist of his remarks** or simply **like.**

Amount of, preceded by **in the, to the, for the—** Better say **check** or **remittance for $—.**

(Please) arrange to return—Sufficient to say, **please return.**

As per your letter—**As per** is a legal term, therefore out of place in an ordinary letter. Better, **according to** or **as mentioned in.**

As stated above—Better to repeat what you stated, or **as I have mentioned.**

As yet—For **yet.**

Assuring you of—Old fashioned.

As to—Awkward.

At all times, at this time—Usually superfluous.

At hand—Usually superfluous.

Attached you will find—Overformal. Better, **we are attaching** or **we are enclosing.**

At the present time—**Now** is preferable.

At this writing—Formal. Better **now.**

At your earliest convenience, at an early date, at the earliest possible moment—Overformal. Better say **soon.**

Awaiting your favor—Better, **please let us hear from you soon.**

Beg—Relic of old-fashioned courtesy, now abandoned in business correspondence.

Claim—Avoid in the sense of **to assert** or **assertion;** might antagonize.

Communication—Formal. Better, **message, letter, report, inquiry,** etc.

Complaint—Aggressive sound. Usually better to say **request for adjustment.**

In compliance with your request—Overformal.

Contents noted—Superfluous.

(To) date—Overformal. "To date we have not received"—better, **we have not yet received.**

Deal—Improperly used for **transaction.**

It is desired that we receive—Inactive, weak, and longwinded. Better, **we want to receive** or **we'd appreciate receiving.**

We have duly investigated—**Duly** is superfluous.

Each and every—**Each** or **every** is sufficient by itself.

Early date—May mean two or three days or two or three weeks. Better be specific.

Enclosed please find—Better **here is** or **I enclose.**

Esteemed—Old-fashioned.

Even date—(meaning today). Better be specific. Say **your letter of this morning** or **of December — 19—.**

Event—Avoid "in the event that." **If** is preferable.

Favor—In sense of letter—old-fashioned, better say **your letter of ——.** Only proper, nowadays, when referring to a specific act of kindness.

For the reason that—**Because** is preferable.

Forward—**Send** or **ship** are preferable.

For your information—Superfluous. Omit.

Hand you—**Send our check** or **enclose our check** preferable.

Have for acknowledgment—Simpler to say "thanks."

Herewith—Superfluous.

Hoping—Weak and usually superfluous. Avoid, especially as dangling participle becfore complimentary close of letter.

Inasmuch as—Just say, **because.**

(We are) in receipt of—Overformal. Better, **we have received** or **thank you for.**

In order to—Just say **to.**

In reference to—Overformal, avoid. Better, **about.**

In regard to—Just say **about.**

In reply would wish to—Overformal, avoid.

Instant—Abbreviated as Inst., meaning the current month. A legal term, out of place in ordinary correspondence. Better name the month—instead of "the 5th Inst." say **October 5.**

In the nature of—Long-winded. Just say **like.**

It is the hope of the undersigned—for **I hope.**

Kindly let us know—Kindly is old fashioned. **Please let us know** is preferable.

Liberty (May we take the liberty to . . .)—Usually no liberty involved. Preferable to be direct and say **may we.**

Line—Sometimes inaccurately used in sense of a business.

(To) lineup—Vague. Better say **try to interest, try to sell,** etc.

Lot—Often inaccurately used to indicate quantity. Watch it.

Miss—Avoid using alone. Always use with a name.

Must say—Avoid. Just say it.

Oblige—Antiquated.

Our Mr. . . . —Pretentious. If name does not sufficiently identify him, describe him as **Mr. . . . , our representative,** or **our Chicago manager,** etc.

Passive constructions—Avoid them. Recast when convenient into active construction. Instead of **The goods ordered by you have been shipped,** say **We have shipped the goods you ordered.**

Permit me to say—No permission needed; just say it.

Pertaining to—**About** is better.

Pleasure (We take pleasure in)—Overformal. Better, **We are sending** or **are glad to send.**

Posted—In sense of informed, is a poor usage. Better say **informed** or **well informed.**

Prior to—**Before** is better.

Pronoun—Should not be omitted because of risk of sounding curt. Avoid, "Goods received. Sending check today." Better say, "We have received the goods and are sending you our check today."

Proposition—Avoid using the term in the sense of task. "To ship this order during the Christmas rush will be a difficult proposition" is not as good as "To ship this order during the Christmas rush will be difficult."

Proximo—(Abbreviated as prox.) Meaning next month. Legal term, out of place in ordinary business correspondence. Say **next month.**

Pursuant to your order—Overformal. Better say **following your directions.**

Recent date—your letter of—Preferable, **your letter** or **your order of . . .** (give date).

Regret—When used the following way: **we regret very deeply,** or **most sincerely,** overformal. Better, **I'm sorry,** or **I regret.**

Replying, Regarding, Referring—Weak. Avoid hanging participles. The simple straight statement is usually more direct and forceful.

Return mail—Shopworn. Better, **this week.**

Same—Stilted. Instead of "We received the goods and found same satisfactory," "We received the goods and found them satisfactory."

State—Not as good as simple word **say** or some other expression. For example: Instead of **as stated above,** use **as we have said** or merely repeat the statement.

Thanking you in advance—A trite device; may antagonize as unwarranted.

Thank you again—Once is enough.

Trust—**Hope, believe, think,** etc. preferable.

Ultimo—(Abbreviation ult.) Meaning last month. A legal term, out of place in business correspondence. Better say, **last month.**

Under separate cover—Use sparingly. Better specify means of shipment, **we are sending you by parcel post.**

(The) Undersigned—Overformal. Preferable to say **I.**

Valued—Formal word. Avoid expressions like **your valued patronage.**

We—In place of I, is right only when emphasis is on action by the firm. Otherwise it is preferable to say **I.**

Wish to say—Say it.

Would say—Say it.

(The) Writer—Overformal. Don't hesitate to say **I.**

GLOSSARY OF TERMS COMMONLY USED IN BUSINESS AND FORMAL CORRESPONDENCE

Abstract of Title—Record summarizing deeds, mortgages, and other documents and transactions affecting title to a piece of real estate.

Accessory after the Fact—One who knowingly aids the criminal after a criminal act.

Accessory before the Fact—One who instigates or aids in a crime but takes no part in its commission.

Accommodation Paper—Negotiable paper bearing the endorsement of a person who thereby lends his credit to the maker of the paper.

Account—Right to transact business in a bank by depositing money or its equivalent therein; a salesman's customers; business transacted with a firm or an individual; right to conduct business with a firm by establishing credit; record of business transactions with a firm or an individual.

Accountant—One skilled in keeping the accounts of a firm and responsible for their accuracy. Certified Public Accountant (abbrev. CPA), corresponding to a Chartered Accountant in England, is one who has qualified for a certificate from the state and is consequently engaged to check on and certify the accuracy of a firm's books.

Account Sales—Record delivered by a broker or commission merchant to the owner of a consignment of goods, showing the amount and sale prices of goods sold and deductions for commissions and freight and other expenses.

Actuary—One whose profession is to calculate insurance risks and premiums.

Adjust (in insurance)—To determine the sum to be paid in settlement of a loss covered by a policy. **Adjustor, Adjuster**—one who makes the settlement in claims arising out of losses or complaints with the purpose of avoiding possible litigation.

Administrator, Administratrix—A person appointed by a court to settle an estate.

Advertising—Promotion of business through notices in the public prints, on posters, by radio, television, or other media. **Classified Advertising**—small advertisements listed alphabetically. **Display Advertising**—large advertisements usually using illustrations and type arrangements for effect. **Poster Advertising**—advertising on large cards posted in public places. **Outdoor Advertising**—very large advertising posted on roadside structures, on top of buildings, on sides of wall, etc. **Car Card Advertising**—small poster inserted in panels on cars, busses, railroad cars, etc. **Radio Advertising**—advertising over the radio with an "advertiser" paying the cost of programs as "sponsor." **Television Advertising**—advertising over television with an "advertiser" paying the cost of programs as "sponsor." **Mail Order Advertising**—advertising by mail or periodical advertisements, leading to purchases transacted by mail.

Affiant—A signer of an affidavit.

Affidavit—An attestation of the truth of a written statement.

Affiliate—A company in financial association with another.

Agent—Person or company acting for another person or company.

Agreement—Mutual consent to terms of trade or employment, usually in written form.

Allocation—Apportionment of goods in short supply so that all companies, when the government is the allocator, or all customers, when a company is the allocator, may secure a share assigned according to their regular consumption or their comparative immediate needs.

Allowance—A customary deduction from the gross weight of goods; in law, a sum in addition to regular taxable costs awarded by the court; a reduction in cost allowed the purchaser by the seller.

Amortization—Gradual liquidation of a mortgage or other debt by periodic payments in addition to interest.

Announcer—A person hired by a radio station or commercial sponsor to introduce radio programs and performers.

Annuity (in insurance)—Annual or periodic income to the insured for life or for a specified long term.

Appeal—Resort to a higher court for review of a lower court's decision in the hope of having it reversed, or the case retried.

Appraise—To set a value on goods, land, the estate of a deceased person; to estimate loss as by fire, etc.; **Appraisal**—act of appraising or the stated result after appraising; **Appraiser**—one designated by court or appointed by agreement to set a value on property.

Appreciate—To increase in value; **Appreciation**—a rise in value.

Arbitrage—Purchase of stock in one market for profitable resale in another.

Arbitration—Submission of a dispute to judgment by a third party agreed on by both parties to the dispute.

Arraignment—Formal summoning of accused into court where indictment is read to him and he is called upon to plead "guilty" or "not guilty."

Arrival Notice—Announcement by transportation company to consignee when shipment reaches destination.

Arson—Deliberate burning of a house (in some states, of any property); a statutory crime.

Assess—To set a value for taxation; to impose a fine; to impose a contribution as a "lodge assessment." **Assessment**—a valuation of property; a fine; an imposed contribution; **Assessor**—one appointed or elected to value property for taxation.

Asset Currency (in banking)—Currency secured exclusively by the general assets of the issuing bank as distinguished from that secured by special deposit of government bonds, commercial paper, etc.

Assets (Property)—In accounting, items on balance sheet of business showing book values of its resources as at a given date; **Fixed or Permanent Assets**—land, building, machinery, capital stock of another company which can be used repeatedly; **Current, Liquid or Floating Assets**—cash or materials which can be used only at one time; **Quick Assets**—cash or goods which can be immediately disposed of without loss.

Association—Organization of a large number of people to transact business; if not incorporated, members are liable for its debts as in a partnership.

Attachment—Court order authorizing seizure of property, usually pending outcome of trial.

Auction—Public sale of property by competitive bidding of prospective buyers.

Auctioneer—A person whose job it is to conduct auction sales.

Audit—A verification of accounts; to make an audit.

Auditor—A person authorized to examine accounts.

Backlog—Amount of orders remaining to be filled.

Balance (in bookkeeping)—To prepare an accounting of assets and liabilities; the money in a bank account left after current withdrawals.

Balance Sheet—Statement of financial condition showing current assets and liabilities.

Bank—Institution where money or other property is deposited A **National Bank** is one organized under the National Bank Act; it functions as a commercial bank but may have trust and savings departments, depending on the laws of the state in which it operates. A **State Bank** is organized under state laws; it operates as a commercial bank, but may have trust and savings departments. A **Commercial Bank** does business primarily in short-term and seasonal loans to business organizations. A **Savings Bank** does business primarily in savings and their investment, but may also do commercial banking where state law permits. A **Trust Company** acts as fiduciary agent for trust funds of individuals or corporations; if part of commercial bank, trust funds are separate from bank funds. The **Federal Reserve Bank** is a banker's bank acting under the Federal Reserve Act as agent for the government in relations with other banks. The **Land Bank** lends money on real estate mortgages under terms of the Federal Farm Loan Act.

Bank Discount—Interest deducted in advance.

Banker—Officer of a bank. **Investment Banker** is one who supplies capital in securities, and finances transactions or advises on investments. **Private Banker** generally lends money to finance international projects, may also engage in commercial banking.

Bankruptcy—Condition of a company unable to meet its debts. In **Voluntary Bankruptcy,** the company petitions to be declared bankrupt; in **Involuntary Bankruptcy,** a creditor or group of creditors is the petitioner.

Bargain—Agreement or terms of a sale; purchase of material at an advantage.

Barter—Direct exchange of commodities without use of money.

Bear—One with a pessimistic attitude toward business; one who anticipates downswings in the market, as opposed to Bull.

Beneficiary—One in whose benefit a gift, trust fund income, or insurance money, is drawn.

Bequeath—To will personal property (property other than realty).

Bid—A possible offer at which goods will be supplied or work performed.

Big Board—A term for the New York Stock Exchange.

Bill—Account of or invoice for goods sold or work done. Abbreviation for "bill or exchange," now chiefly designating piece of paper money.

Bill of Lading—Certificate drawn up and signed by transportation company, enumerating articles being shipped; acts as contract and receipt for shipment.

Binder—A sum of money or other valuable consideration binding parties to a contract.

Black Market—Trading that violates legal restrictions such as price ceilings, etc.

Blanket—Covering everything, rather than a specified item, such as blanket insurance, etc.

Block (in currency)—Legal prohibition or restriction of foreign credit, currency, securities or other property, usually during war; e.g., blocked currency.

Blue Chip—A stock regarded as an especially good investment.

Board of Directors—Group of persons directing affairs of a company, corporation, or association.

Board Room—Room in which Board of Directors meets; room in brokerage office containing board on which is posted records of transactions, prices, etc.

Board of Trade—Organization for advancement of business, usually of an industry or geographical area such as a town or state.

Bourse—The Paris Stock Exchange.

Bond—An interest-bearing certificate of indebtedness; a bond differs from stock in not representing ownership. In actuality, bonds are long-term interest-bearing notes representing loans; or goods being manufactured, stored, or transported under care of bonded agencies.

Bonded Debt—Bond issue representing indebtedness.

Bonus—Extra goods shipped without charge on an order; sum given to employee in addition to contracted wages or salary.

Bookkeeper—One who keeps "books" or accounts of a company; generally distinguished from an accountant in having less formal training and lower status.

Book Value—Value given to assets on the books of owner, may be above or below current market value.

Boycott—Organized effort to prevent purchases of goods produced by a certain firm or industry and usually arising out of labor trouble.

Brand Name—Name of manufactured article registered to prevent copying.

Breach of Contract—Refual to carry out terms of a contract in whole or in part.

Brief—Lawyer's statement of his client's case, containing legal citations supporting it.

Broker—Agent; one who buys or sells for another on commission.

Bucket Shop—A dishonest brokerage house where the customer's money is gambled with, against the customer's interest.

Budget—Plan for the expenditure of income.

Building and Loan Association—Association of investors whose savings are used to finance home construction and make loans on improved real estate.

Bull—One with optimistic attitude toward business; one who anticipates upswings in the market; opposite of Bear.

Bullion—Bars of gold and silver intended for coinage.

Business—Commercial transaction; organization conducting commercial transactions.

Business cycle—Recurrent succession of business fluctuations loosely divided into prosperity, crisis, liquidation, depression, recovery.

Call—Purchased rights to demand a certain amount of goods at a fixed price or within a fixed time; demand for payment of money as on a stockholder, member of a mutual insurance company, etc., to pay installment of subscription to capital, or a contribution to meet losses.

Call Loan—One which may be terminated by either party at any time.

Call Money—Money that must be returned when demanded.

Cancel—To annul an order for goods or services.

Capacity—Calculated space of any form of container from warehouse or ship to carton.

Capital—A stock of accumulated wealth; amount of property and funds as distinguished from income.

Capitalism—An economic system in which capital plays a leading part in production and distribution.

Capitalist—One who uses capital for investment.

Capital Stock—Shares of a corporation considered as an aggregate.

Capital Surplus—Profits, such as from sale of stock above par value, other than earned surplus.

Carrier—A company transporting passengers or freight, e.g., railroad, airlines, bus or trucking company, etc.

Cartel—International combination allocating markets and supplies, and fixing prices in order to eliminate competitive buying and selling.

Catalogue—A list, usually with illustrations and textual description, of items for sale at announced prices.

Ceiling—Maximum wage, rent, etc., fixed by the government.

Certified Check—Bearing the signature or stamp of the cashier of the bank on which it is drawn. Its significance is that the sum has been withdrawn from the account of the drawer and the bank assumes responsibility for payment.

Chain Store—Branch of a large system of stores belonging to a single ownership.

Chamber of Commerce—A board of trade; an association to promote the commerce of a community, state or nation.

Charter—Certificate from the state approving the organization of a company and authorizing it to do business in the approved form.

Check—A standard form of written order to a bank to make a designated payment out of a depositor's balance.

Circulation—In a periodical, the number of purchasers by subscription or individual sales; in a store, movement of customers in and out.

Clearing House—Organization maintained by a banking group to exchange checks and adjust accounts among its members.

Closed Corporation—One in which all stock is privately held in a few hands; it usually may not be disposed of by holders without the consent of the other holders.

C.O.D.—Abbreviation for "cash on delivery." In C.O.D. transactions, goods must be paid for at the time of delivery.

Code—An arrangement of words, letters or other symbols to achieve secrecy or brevity in communication; a set of rules governing the conduct of a business.

Codicil—Addition to a will, modifying some provision in it.

Collateral—Property used as security for a loan.

Collective Bargaining—Negotiations between employers and a committee of their workers and/or representatives of the union.

Co-Maker—One who shares obligations of another by endorsing a contract.

Commercial Paper—Promissory notes of a large, reputable firm; dealt in by note brokers and sold to banks which discount them and, in that way, realize interest on them.

Commission—Percentage or allowance made to broker or agent for transacting business for another, e.g., salesman's commission.

Company—Association of persons for carrying on commercial or industrial enterprise; may be partnership, corporation or other joint enterprise.

Complaint (in law)—Statement of the cause of an

action; the person initiating the complaint is called the complainant. In commerce, customer's charge of faulty goods, delivery or other service.

Comptroller—Auditor with the rank of executive.

Consign—To send or address goods by bill of lading, etc., to an agent in another place to be stored, sold or otherwise cared for.

Consignee—One to whom good are shipped.

Consignment—Transaction in which purchase is not final; unsold goods may be returned to consignor.

Consumer—Ultimate purchaser or user of merchandise.

Contingent Order (in advertising)—Space in small circulation media to be paid for by returns from the advertisement.

Contract—Witnessed agreement, usually in writing, the terms of which are legally enforceable.

Contractor—One who specializes in a certain type of work; e.g., building contractor. **Sub-contractor**—one who performs part of a piece of work; e.g., plumbing sub-contractor.

Convenience Merchandise—Goods kept in a store for the convenience of certain customers.

Cooperative—A business enterprise or association with the object of producing, purchasing, selling, or occupying quarters at common savings to members by eliminating middle-man fees and profits.

Copy—Text of advertising; duplicate of an original letter or of an article of commerce. Ordinarily, carbon copy duplication of typing.

Copyright—Exclusive publication rights, now extended to cover plays, movie scenarios and movie films and radio and television scripts; other pieces of creative work are copyrighted **after** publication. Application must be made to Register of Copyrights, Library of Congress, Washington, D.C.

Corner—To secure such control of stock or commodities as to be able to dictate quotation prices.

Corporation—A business association operating on a state franchise and with liability limited to the amount of the investment.

Co-Sign—To assume joint responsibility in indebtedness by adding one's signature to the note of another.

Cottage Industry—One where operations are performed by workers at home.

Countermand—To reverse a personal order.

Courts—Where cases involving offenses against the law or claims protected by the law are tried. Courts where large claim cases are tried include Superior, Circuit, certain District, Chancery or County courts. Courts where small claim cases are tried are Justice courts, presided over by a Justice of the peace, and include Magistrate's court and certain District courts.

Covenant—Promise of some future action, made in contracts and other legal papers.

Coverage—The amount and type of protection against risks agreed on in an insurance policy.

Credit—Fnancial standing influencing sales to a concern on defererd payment; permission to defer payment for a certain period.

Creditor—One who extends credit; lender.

Credit Line—Amount of credit extended; e.g., "X's credit line is $2,000." Also, reproduction of signature, symbol or other acknowledgment in print to signify the originator or owner of writing, photographs or illustrations.

Credit Rating—Summary of credit line as published in Dun & Bradstreet or other credit house ratings and reports.

Cum Div—With dividend declared or pending.

Curb Market—The usual reference is to the American Stock Exchange (formerly New York Curb Exchange), formerly conducted out-of-doors but now housed in a building of its own; it is the second largest stock market in the United States.

Custom—Generally accepted practice, company practice; customer's account.

Customer—Person or concern purchasing goods.

Cut—In printing, zinc etching, or copper or zinc halftone, usually reproducing a picture or hand-lettering.

Cutback—Reduction in production schedule; reduction in salary or other compensation.

Damage—Loss in merchandise, machinery, service, productive capacity or trade standing. Compensation for such damage may be claimed depending on the circumstances, in a court of law.

Dead Spot—Store location at point of little traffic.

Dead Stock—Unsaleable merchandise.

Debenture—Synonym for debt; documentary evidence of debt.

Debit and Credit Memoranda—Issued by companies to effect necessary adjustments in the course of business transactions.

Decontrol—Removal of government restrictions on prices, rents, etc.

Deduction—Sum or money subtracted from amount to be paid for goods or services.

Deed—Contract by which real estate is conveyed by one party to another; **Warranty Deed** contains a guarantee to clear title ownership; **Quick Claim Deed** relinquishes rights of former owner without guaranteeing clear title to purchaser; **Joint Tenancy Deed** transfers property to two or more owners with the provision that the survivor will own the entire property; **Trust Deed** is given as security for a debt and is a form of mortgage; **Tax Deed** is received by purchaser at a tax sale.

Defalcation—Misappropriation of money placed in trust; the sum misappropriated.

Default—To fail in fulfilling a contract or other financial obligation.

Deficit—Amount by which expenses exceed income, liabilities exceed assets, production falls below expectation.

Deflation—Decline in prices, volume of production, etc., usually accompanied by unemployment.

Delaware Corporation—A corporation chartered in Delaware to take advantage of low incorporation fees and tax rates.

Demand—Desire to purchase commodity together with capacity to pay for it.

Demand Bill or Draft—A bill payable at sight, or on demand.

Demand Item—Article in constant demand, which must be carried in stock constantly.

Demand Loan—Loan payable on demand.

Demand Note—Note payable on demand.

Demurrage—Charge by transportation company for detention of carriers beyond allotted time.

Deposit—Money or equivalent entrusted for safekeeping with another, as in a bank; money given as partial payment in a transaction or as a binder in a contract.

Deposition—Testimony given by witness unable to appear in court.

Depreciation—Decline in value, usually as a result of loss through wear, neglect, exposure, etc. Machinery is usually calculated to suffer an annual depreciation of 10% in value through wear.

Depression—Deep and prolonged decline of industrial and general business activity.

Deteriorate—To spoil or lose quality with time, e.g., food and certain manufactured articles such as photographic film.

Detriment—Damage by intangible cause, such as injury to a firm's reputation through rumors.

Devise—To will property in real estate.

Director—Person entrusted with determining policies and decisions of a firm.

Disbursements—Payments to meet bills.

Discount—Allowance for cash or quick payment; **Trade Discounts** are discounts from wholesale prices allowed to customers and scaled according to amount of purchases and other considerations.

Distributor—Person or company through whom goods reach the consuming public; **Wholesale Distributors** supply **Retail Distributors** who serve the public directly.

Dividend—Money paid to shareholders or depositors as share of profits.

Dock Receipt—Signed by steamship company for freight delivered to dock.

Draft—Papers by which one party, usually the seller, orders another party, usually the buyer, to deliver to a third party, usually a bank, a sum to be credited to the account of the first party. Used to assure payment and to secure settlement of unpaid accounts, since rejection of a draft when presented by the bank is recorded and affects credit standing.

Drawee—Bank on which check or draft is drawn.

Drawer—Person who draws money from his bank account by check.

Dry Goods—Commodities made from fabrics.

Due Bill—In brokerage business, a type of IOU by broker, promising to deliver certain stocks not available at time of sale; also used for promised future delivery of dividends, etc.

Dummy—Sample of proposed book, magazine, or booklet to show size, format, and sample pages.

Dummy Corporation—One organized solely for intermediate purposes, and not for open business activity.

Duplicate—Copy or identical likeness, e.g., duplicate of bill.

Duty—Payment imposed by the government on goods imported, exported, or consumed, such as customs duties, excises, etc.

Earned Income—Income derived from wages, salary, or fees in return for labor, advice or management services.

Earned Surplus—Balance of profits and income remaining after deducting losses, dividends, and transfers to capital stock, etc.

Earnest Money—Deposit or binder; a sum of money paid to seal a bargain and to be deducted from purchase payment.

Economy—Organization of the production, distribution, and consumption of goods in a community.

Efficiency Engineer—A person whose profession it is to plan or change production methods to secure greater economy and efficiency.

Embezzle—To fraudulently appropriate to one's own use property entrusted to him.

Endorse (also Indorse)—To sign one's name as a payee or to indicate co-responsibility for payment on a check, bill, note, or other document.

Enterprise—In association with the word "free" or "private" has come to replace "capitalism" to differentiate the non-socialist from the socialist type of economy.

Entrepreneur—One who takes commercial risks; enterpriser.

Entry—Item in a business record.

Equity—In real estate, difference between value of property and owner's debt on it. In margin buying difference between market value of a stock and customer's indebtedness for its purchase.

Escrow—Papers or money in keeping of responsible third party such as a bank, held until certain conditions are fulfilled.

Estate—Property in lands or tenements, sometimes inaccurately used for property other than lands or tenements; total property left by a deceased person.

Estimate—Statement of amount of goods to be produced or stored or of sum for which certain work will be done.

Ex-Bonus
Ex-Coupon
Ex-Dividend
Ex-Interest
Ex-Privileges
Ex-Rights
} Earnings or privileges not included in the purchase of particular shares.

Exchange—Transfer of goods; place where business interests of a certain sort meet for transaction, e.g., stock exchange, cotton exchange, etc.

Executor (Executrix)—One designated to carry out terms of a will.

Execution—Carrying out of terms of a will or a court order.

Expedite—To accelerate production or distribution of goods or rendering of service.

Expediter—One whose job it is to expedite or facilitate business and other transactions.

Export-Import Bank of Washington—Organized by the government in 1934 to facilitate foreign trade.

Express—Shipment by fast or unobstructed transportation; via Railway Express Agency.

Facsimile—Exact copy not necessarily of same size; photostat can serve as satisfactory facsimile.

Factor—Commercial agent who sells or buys goods for others on commission; commission agent.

Factory—Building where manufacture of goods is carried on.

Fail—To become insolvent.

Fee—Compensation for professional or special services; fixed charge for services of a public officer, e.g., sheriff's fee.

Feeder—Branch line in railroad, bus, or air transport that connects with trunkline.

Fee Simple—Unrestricted title to property.

Felony—Crime whose penalty is death or prison sentence.

Fiduciary—In trust; a fiduciary is a trustee.

Finance—Management of money matters.

Financial Rating—Financial information carried in directory such as *Moody's Manual.*

Firm—Correct meaning is partnership; in common usage, any business organization.

Fiscal—Relating to finance, e.g., U.S. fiscal year, period in which annual taxes are collected.

Fixtures—Fixed equipment in business or professional premises.

Foreclosure—Transfer of property to mortgagee when mortgagor defaults on interest payment.

Franchise—Special commercial rights granted by a city to operator of a public conveyance, e.g., a bus line; special rights granted by a manufacturer to a dealer.

Freight Bill—Prepared by transportation company and rendered to receiver or sender, depending on who is paying the freight charges.

Freight Claim—Also called "Loss and Damage Claim" or "Overcharge Claim," claim on transportation company for loss, damage or overcharge.

Fund—Cash or specified assets set aside for a specific purpose.

Funded Debt—Fund set up for payment of long-term indebtedness.

Funded Reserve—A reserve for which a fund has been invested to earn income.

Futures—In commodity exchange, contracts for subsequent delivery, as of a crop not yet harvested.

Garnishee—To take over property or money to satisfy a debt or a claim. A claimant may "garnishee" a defendant's wages.

Gold Standard—Rating of currency in terms of supposed value in gold.

Good will—Intangible asset resting on a special earning power gained through advertising, reputation, good business methods, favorable location, business standing, etc.

Gray Market—Trading by undercover methods, in between black market and regular market methods.

Gross—As a number, 12 dozen or 144; as an adjective, indicating a complete sum before deductions have been made, e.g., gross income before deductions of taxes, expenses, etc.

Handbill—Printed announcement handed out to passers-by.

Handicrafts—Goods produced by hand, e.g., certain pottery, woven goods, embroidery, basket work, etc.

Hedging—Stock trading in which sales or purchases are made to offset or "hedge" against possible loss in other transactions. "Puts and calls" are a form of hedging.

Heir—Person entitled by law or terms of a will to an inheritance.

High Pressure—To make sales of goods not actually needed or desired.

Holding Company—One organized to buy and hold stock of another company.

Holographic Will—One entirely in the handwriting of the testator, not in valid in some states.

Huckster—One who prepares radio or television advertising, usually with methods of exaggerated showmanship.

Hypothecation—Pledging of collateral. Governments may "hypothecate" tax revenues as security for a loan. Property may be "hypothecated" for payment of a debt. Its earnings may be so used and the property remain with the debtor; but if payment is defaulted, the creditor may demand sale of the property to secure payment of the debt.

Identification—Driver's license, social security card or other document required as identification in check payments at stores, hotels, or other public places.

Implement—To find means to carry out an agreement.

Impulse Item—Something marketed to appeal to spontaneous decision of customer, usually novelties and luxuries as opposed to staples or necessities.

Income Group—Classification of people according to earnings.

Incorporate—To secure a charter of incorporation from a state, and to organize operations under its provisions.

Indemnify—To make secure against loss or damage; to make good a loss or damage.

Indenture—Sealed agreement of which each party concerned holds a signed copy.

Index—Stock market term referring to listed price quotations of securities traded on the market and analyzed for trends.

Indictment—Formal grand jury charge against a person accused of a major crime.

Industry—Collectively, manufacturing as contrasted to agriculture; any branch of production, e.g., shoe industry, paper industry, etc.

Inflation—Rise in prices where income advance fails to keep up with prices.

Injunction—Court order restraining certain action.

Insert—Something added in a document; an enclosure in a mailing.

Insolvency—Inability to meet current financial obligations.

Installment—Periodic payment on a time-payment purchase. The British equivalent is "hire-purchase."

Institutional Advertising—Directed not at immediate sales but at increasing prestige leading to consideration of a company as an established institution.

Instrument—Person or document useful in accomplishing a stated purpose.

Interest—Payment by borrower for use of borrowed money measured in percentages and units of time; **simple** interest is payment on principal alone; **compound** interest is payment of accrued interest added to capital; **penal** interest is payment of special interest by defaulting debtor.

Interstate Commerce—Commerce across state boundaries.

Intestate—Descriptive of a property holder who dies without leaving a will. Division of property will then be made according to state inheritance laws.

Intrastate Commerce—Commerce within a state.

Inventory—Record of merchandise on hand and in stock rooms; **perpetual** inventory is one maintained by recording every sale and receipt of goods on an inventory card. Usually inventories are made at periodic intervals.

Investment—Money or other property risked with expectation of profit.

Investment Trust—Company whose business is investment in securities and bond issue, and which markets its own securities on the basis of these investments.

Invoice—A bill itemizing goods shipped and their prices.

IOU—Document bearing the letters "IOU" and a notation of a sum of money. If signed, an IOU has legal status as a debit account.

Island Counter—Table displaying or carrying goods for sale in such a position in a store that customers may walk around it.

Joint Stock Company—Large partnership with some of the feaures of a corporation.

Journal—Bookkeeping record in which transactions are first entered.

Judgment—Court decision; in a civil trial for damages, the sum awarded to the plaintiff.

Jury—Of two kinds. The **grand** jury consists of 12 to 23 persons who serve as an investigating body and dismiss or indict a suspect, depending on the evidence at hearings. Functions only in cases involving major crimes. **Petit** jury, an ordinary jury, usually consisting of 12 persons who hear civil suits and cases of minor law-breaking.

Kickback—Unauthorized payment out of wages, prices, or fees as extortion or bribery.

Know-How—Technical skill gained through training and experience.

Kraft—Strong brown paper used in packing for shipping.

Landlord—Owner of real estate; usually reference is to owner of specified building.

Layout—Sketch of a proposed advertisement, booklet, etc., in store merchandising, arrangement of merchandise.

Lease—A contract for the temporary conveyance of property, usually in consideration of rent.

Ledger—Account book. In larger sense, accounting in general.

Legacy—Inheritance through a will.

Legal Standard—Measure of value in gold or silver established by a government for the rating of its currency.

Legal Tender—Money that may lawfully be used in settlement of debts.

Lessee—Tenant under a lease.

Lessor—One who grants a lease.

Letters Patent—Document transferring title to public lands or rights to inventions (see Patent).

Liability—Indebtedness; **current** liabilities are short term debts such as taxes, accounts payable, etc., to be met within the year; **fixed** liabilities are long term debts such as mortgages, bonds, etc.; **deferred** liabilities are advance payments such as rent or interest before they come due.

Libel—Written statement held to be damaging to person or business about which it is made. To be distinguished from **slander,** which is a damaging statement made orally.

License—Legal permission to sell certain goods, e.g., a liquor license; or to practice a profession; or to sell goods on the street, e.g., a peddler's license, etc.

Lien—Legal right to property in payment of debt; usually has priority over other claims, e.g., tax lien, mechanics lien, etc.

Limit Order—Order to buy or sell stock at or above or below a specified price.

Line—Type of merchandise offered for sale, e.g., line of pearl buttons.

Liquid—Convertible into cash, e.g., liquid assets.

Liquidate—To convert assets into cash, generally in reference to business in financial difficulty and in need of ready cash.

List Price—Selling price as listed in catalogue.

Loan—Money lent on interest.

Lockout—Shutting out of employees during a labor dispute. Now illegal.

Logotype—Trademark or symbol used by a firm in its advertising.

Long and Short—To be **long** is to hold stock in expectation of a rise; to be **short** is to sell stocks one does not own, in a falling market, in expectation of buying them in at a still lower quotation and profiting from the difference.

Lots—In real estate, specified arrangement of ground; in the stock market, number of shares traded in. **Round** lots are those taken in round numbers, such as 100 shares; **odd** lots are transactions in lots under 100.

Maintenance of Membership—Clause in labor contract making it obligatory upon workers to keep in good standing in the union in order to retain jobs.

Malfeasance—Wrongful action: To be distinguished from **nonfeasance,** failure to perform an action agreed upon; and **misfeasance,** performance of an agreed action in such a way as to violate the rights of others.

Malice Aforethought—Intentional or planned injury.

Manifest—Invoice of a ship's cargo, for evidence at customs house.

Manufacture—Conversion of raw materials into a finished product, e.g., converting iron ore into steel plate.

Margin—Money deposited with a broker as security on stock purchases; thus margin may be forfeited if stock quotations take an adverse turn.

Markdown—Lowering of prices, usually to make sales for slow-moving goods.

Market—In general, the range for buying and selling; in particular, the range for buying and selling in a particular field, e.g., the stock market, the cotton market, etc.

Market Order—Order to sell at the market price of the day on which the order is issued.

Mark-Up—Amount added, in selling price, to wholesale price to cover overhead and profit.

Marshall Plan—Plan to extend economic aid abroad, initiated by George C. Marshall as United States Secretary of State in 1947.

Mass Market—The general public considered as potential consumers.

Mass Production—Large scale, mechanized production designed to lower production costs to permit purchase by the majority of potential consumers.

Maximum Hours—Limit of time workers may be employed without overtime payment.

Mediation—Resort to third party in disputes between employer and worker; not as conclusive as arbitration.

Melon—Extra dividend on stock, distributing surplus earnings or profits.

Merger—Consolidation of two or more companies into one.

Metes and Bounds—Dimensions and boundaries of a parcel of real estate.

Mill—A machine for grinding, pressing, stamping, or almost every repetitive process; a building or group of buildings containing manufacturing machinery.

Minimum Wage—Lowest limit of wages that may be paid to workers.

Minor—Person under legal age to assume certain responsibilities. The age varies—it is different for marriage, for business transaction, or for liability to criminal charges.

Model Change-Over—Reorganization of manufacturing process for the manufacture of a new model (sometimes called **mark**) of an article.

Monopoly—Exclusive control of an industry or some form of trade.

Morris Plan Company—Makes small personal loans for repayment in installments.

Mortgage—Transfer of rights in property as security for a loan or for other considerations. **Real estate** mortgages are on land and improvements upon it; **chattel** mortgages cover other forms of property; **crop** mortgage is a chattel mortgage on crops; a **first** mortgage is one which has priority in any claims on the property over subsequent mortgages (**second** and **third** mortgages, etc.)

Mortgage Certificates—Certificates for small shares of large first mortgages or first mortgage bonds. Issued by mortgage customers to investors.

National Advertising—Advertising in periodicals or over radio and television, nationwide in scope.

Negotiable—Salable or transferable as payment for debts.

Net—Sum, after deductions have been made, e.g., net income after expenses, taxes, etc. have been taken out.

Nonfeasance—see Malfeasance.

Notary Public—A person authorized by state law to witness and certify to the authenticity of signatures affixed to documents or statements in his presence.

Number—Item of manufacture; usually refers to item in a catalogue.

O.K.—With signature, constitutes endorsement or approval of something presented in writing. According to popular belief, from Old Kinderhook, birthplace of Martin van Buren, and used by his supporters in his campaign for the presidency.

Omnibus Clause—Section in a contract covering several items not specifically covered elsewhere in the document.

One Day Order—Order for stock transaction on a certain day, and cancelled if not executed on that day.

Open Order—Order for a stock transaction to be executed at any time and to hold good until notice of withdrawal is received. Also called GTC (Good till cancelled) order.

Option—First choice or right to obtain goods or services without competition for a specified period, e.g., ten days' option.

Order—Customer's itemized description of goods desired for purchase.

Overhead—Fixed expenses, such as rent, salaries, maintenance costs, etc.

Overstock—Goods in excess of current demand.

Over-the-Counter Trading—Trading by private dealers in securities not listed on the stock exchange.

Package—Combined merchandise and/or services, offered as a unit, in a "package deal," e.g., radio or television program in which script, actors, announcer, etc., are all provided as a unit in a "package program."

Pamphlet—Paper-covered booklet used as advertising or to convey information about a business.

Panic—Sudden widespread fright over financial situation causing artificial depression through sales of securities and other property.

Paper—Documents of any sort, negotiable notes, bills, etc.

Par—Normal or face value of securities.

Parcel—Package of goods; piece of property; to apportion merchandise in small lots to provide some supply to all accounts.

Parity—Rate of exchange at which different currencies acquire equal purchasing power.

Partnership—Defined in Uniform Partnership Act: "An association of two or more persons to carry on as co-owners of a business for profit"; except in "limited partnership" in which liability of certain partners is restricted to the amount of capital contributed, partners are individually liable for debts contracted by the business.

Passbook—A book borne by customer, containing records of credit purchases; also bankbook.

Passing a Dividend—Failure to declare an expected dividend.

Patent—Right granted by the government for a term of seventeen years, for the exclusive production of an invented article or for an improvement on an article, not renewable.

Patent Attorney—One specializing in the preparation of patent applications and in the search to determine that the invention is new and does not infringe on previous patents.

Patent Office—Government bureau that registers patent applications and issues "letters patent," granting patent rights.

Patron—Customer.

Patronage—Business given by a customer.

Pattern (in industry)—A model made for duplication as in metal casting, dress manufacture, etc.

Pattern-Maker—One who makes patterns needed in industry.

Pay—To make an acceptable return, usually in money, for property delivered, or services rendered; remuneration such as wages or salaries.

Payee—Person to whom money has been, or is to be, paid.

Paymaster—One under whose management wage or salary payments are made.

Payroll—Paymaster's list of those entitled to wages or salary.

Peculation—Embezzlement.

Peg—To hold market prices at a set value by manipulating purchases or sales.

Pension—Payment made through grant, insurance, or other arrangement to person retired from employment, business, or public office.

"Percents"—Investments such as bonds or other securities, described by their interest rate, e.g., 3%.

Perpetual Trust—Trust estate with no prescribed duration.

Personal Property or Personal Estate—Property other than real estate.

Personnel—Employed staff.

Petition—Written application to a court instituting an action or requesting action upon a matter before it.

Petition in Bankruptcy—Written application by a debtor or his creditors that he be declared bankrupt.

Petty Cash—Cash fund used to make small payments.

Photo Engraving—Process of reproducing pictures through photography, where printing surface is in relief in contrast to lithography or gravure.

Photostat—Photographic process for reproducing documents, drawings, etc.; a document or drawing so reproduced.

Pica—12-point type, usually used on typewriters and in other print where readability is desired.

Picket—Person, during a strike, standing or walking back and forth before entrance of business to discourage non-striking employees or customers from entering.

Piece-Goods—Fabrics sold by pieces or fixed lengths.

Pilot Plant—A business operated to determine rates to be charged in its industry.

Pipeline—Piping over long distances used in the transportation of oil or gas.

Piracy—Infringement on copyrighted or patent property rights.

Pit—Section of Chicago Board of Trade where a specific commodity is traded; e.g., wheat pit.

Pivotal—A stock whose quotations influence the course of the market.

Planned Economy—Economical organization, usually of a state, in which production is arranged to prevent or reduce fluctuation and waste.

Plant—The building, machinery, etc., taken together that are used in a unit of industrial production.

Plantation—Large scale farming operation, carried on by hired labor; e.g., rubber plantation.

Plastics (in industry)—Synthetic materials mainly produced by molding process.

Pledge—Piece of property given as security for a loan.

Point—Unit used in quoting prices on stocks. In the United States, one point usually stands for $1 a share.

Point System—Method of wage payment by time units of work performed. Also called the "Bedaux System," from its originator.

Policy—Contract of insurance; guiding principles of a concern, usually determined or governed by a Board of Directors.

Pool—Merger of property or financial interests of a group, usually with the expectation of manipulating the market in its favor.

Portal-to-Portal Pay—Payment for time spent, as in mines, in passing to and from the entrance of the actual place of work.

Position—On produce exchanges, undertaking to make delivery in a given month; e.g., October position.

Possession—Such control of property as to give exclusive legal enjoyment of it.

Posthumous—Taking effect after death.

Power of Attorney—Legal authority to act for another, not as a lawyer, but to carry out transactions.

Practice—Professional service; e.g., legal practice; customary procedure of a firm.

Pre-Fab—A prefabricated article, usually a house or small industrial building, to facilitate speedy erection.

Preference Shop—One where, by agreement between union and management, preference is given to union members in employment, promotion, and tenure, but management may employ non-union workers if union cannot supply qualified personnel.

Preferred Stock—Issue which receives preference over common stock in dividends or distribution of assets.

Premium (in insurance)—Money or other consideration paid by the insured according to terms of contract. (In economics)—Greater value of one currency over another; additional payment for loan of money. (On the stock market)—Amount above par that securities are being quoted at; sum paid for an option.

Prepaid—Paid in advance.

Price—Value at which goods are exchanged or services rendered.

Pricing—Setting a price on goods.

Primary Markets—Markets in farm produce such as foods or fibers.

Principal—Actual party to transaction as distinguished from agent; money or other property on which interest is earned.

Priority—Precedence as in transportation, goods production, delivery of order, etc.

Privilege—Option on the sale or purchase of securities on specified terms.

Probate—Proof established by legal procedures; e.g., probate of a will.

Process—A method of manufacture or of rendering services.

Production—Creation of goods having value to purchasers; e.g., agricultural production, industrial production.

Profit—What remains after production and sales costs have been deducted.

Profit and Loss—Accounting, after a given period, to determine condition of a business.

Promissory Note—Note undertaking payment of a debt at a specied time or occasion.

Promoter—One who initiates organization of a company, floating of securities, or other business undertaking.

Property—Things owned; real property is property in real estate, while personal property or personal estate refers to all other possessions of value.

Proprietor—Owner; one with legal right to possession.

Proxy—To act for another; one whose voting rights are entrusted to another, the usual reference being to voting of stock holders.

Public Domain—The field of property rights belonging to the public at large, such as manufacturing processes or literary properties not, or no longer, covered by patents and copyrights.

Public Utility—Company servicing the general public, such as a railroad, supplier of electricity, etc.

Put and Call—To "put" is to deliver, according to agreement, specified stock at a specified price to a buyer who receives a payment for this service. The privilege of "putting" may be sold to a third party. To "call" is to receive on demand specified stock at a specified price from a seller who is paid for this service. The privilege of "calling" may be sold to a third party.

Pyramid—To engage in transactions in banking or stock market, using gains as "margin" for further purchases or sales, in order to take continuous advantage of a market trend.

Qualified—Fit to do required work.

Quantity—Used relatively, usually in references to goods in bulk, e.g., "These casting can be supplied in any reasonable quantity."

Quantity Theory of Money—Economic theory that changes in quantity of money in circulation affect price levels and currency values.

Query—To recheck a shipment, a shipper or an account; may refer to goods, invoices, personnel, etc.; e.g., "Please query Hobson, rubber tape shipment overdue at warehouse."

Quit Claim—Document in legal form relinquishing some property right.

Quotations—Statements, oral or written, of market prices of stocks, bonds or commodities.

Quotation Board—Board in brokerage office on which market quotations are displayed.

Rebate—Repayment of a percentage of sum received in payment for goods or services. Rebate may be allowed for damage, delay, or savings in shipping costs, etc.

Receipt—Signed paper in evidence that goods or money has been received.

Receipts—Earnings of a business for a given period; e.g., "today's receipts."

Receiver—Person, firm, or bank appointed by courts to conduct a business declared bankrupt.

Recession—Decline in industrial activity, not so drastic as a depression.

Redemption—Payment of outstanding loans; e.g., redemption of a bond issue.

Referee—Appointed by court to hear evidence and render decision in business disputes.

Refund—Return of entire amount paid for goods or services, usually because of their unsatisfactory nature.

Reimburse—Repay money expended by another. An agent will be reimbursed for costs incurred during his operation.

Reorganization—Reestablishment of insolvent business with the consent of creditors and under court supervision, with the aim of avoiding receivership costs and forced sale losses.

Requisition—Order for supplies, materials, etc.

Rescued—Withdrawal of order or instructions.

Restrictive—Limiting. A restrictive covenant is a clause in a document setting certain conditions, as in real estate contracts restricting residence to certain races.

Retail Trade—Trade with consumers.

Retirement—Withdrawal from circulation, e.g., retirement of a currency.

Revenue—Source of income, usually referring to government income from taxation.

Revenue Bond—Short-term issue in anticipation of revenue payments.

Rigged Market—Subject to manipulation so that it does not reflect real values.

Rollback—Price reduction to previous levels, usually by government action.

Royalty—Share of profits paid by manufacturer to inventor (or owner of an invention), author, etc. or to his heirs.

Runaway—Removal of business to a region of low labor costs as an employer measure in labor trouble.

Sabotage—Obstruction, malicious waste of materials, or spoilage of product by workers during labor trouble.

Sales Engineering—Computing and adjusting installation and production costs from plans, as a means of promoting sales of equipment and machinery to a specific industry or factory.

Salvage—Goods rescued from shipwreck or other disaster.

Sample—A representative piece of an article offered for sale; e.g., swatch of cloth.

Scab—Opprobrious term, used in labor relations for person employed in place of strikers or refusing to strike with his fellow workers.

Schedule—Systematic listing of time for production or other performance in manufacturing, transportation, distribution, etc.

Search—To verify status of a property; e.g., mortgage title search, patent search, etc.

Seat—Membership in the Stock Exchange entitling one to share in its assets and the privilege of trading there.

Security—(Chiefly used in the plural.) Stock certificates, bonds, or other documentary evidence of indebtedness giving the possessor the right to claim property secured by the document; **listed** security is one which, by meeting certain requirements, is listed for trading on the Stock Exchange.

Self-Mailer—Advertising message that can be sent by mail without enclosure in an envelope. A sticker or stamp is affixed to hold pages or folded edges together.

Shakeout—Minor decline in industrial activity in course of adjustment after inflation.

Shape-up—Hiring of dockworkers by selection of applicants at piers, usually arbitrarily, at the discretion of labor supervisor.

Shortage—Something missing from inventory or from cash, due to theft, loss, or error.

Silver Standard—Rating of currency in terms of a specified value in silver.

Sinking Fund—Fund continually added to and invested toward the payment of bonds or other maturing debts.

Sitdown Strike—One where striking employees stay in or at their places of work to prevent operation of machinery by others.

Slander—Oral statement held to be damaging to person or business about whom it is made. To be distinguished from libel, which is a damaging written statement.

Sleeper—Film, book, novel, or other property or article of trade that gains unexpected commercial success, doing better business than other items for which greater sales were anticipated.

Slowdown—Slowing down of work operations, without actual walkout, as a worker tactic in labor dispute.

Smog—Saturation of air with smoke or other industrial exhausts leading to fog conditions.

Social Security—System and fund set up, under the Social Security Act, to insure security in old age. The fund is made up of compulsory contributions by employers and employees.

Solicit—To seek business accounts.

Solvency—Capacity to meet financial obligations.

Specie—Metal (hard) money as distinguished from paper currency.

Specimen—Sample of minerals, ores, plants, or other things that are complete units of their kind.

Speculation—Buying or selling with chance of high profits and risk of considerable loss.

Spot Announcement (in radio advertising)—A commercial not part of a sponsored program.

Spot Delivery—In stock market, immediate delivery of stock.

Staple—An established product; e.g., oil is a staple of Texas.

Statement—List of unpaid items in a business account; a financial statement is a listing of assets and liabilities.

Statute of Limitations—Law setting time limit for legal action.

Stipulation—Condition specified in agreement or contract, usually something undertaken by buyer to bolster his credit.

Stock—Share of ownership in an incorporated business; supply of merchandise for sale; **common** stock is ordinary stock as distinguished from **preferred** stock, which takes precedence over it in distribution of assets or dividends; **guaranteed** stock is one whose dividends are guaranteed by another company.

Stockpile—Reserve supply of essential material.

Strike—Refusal by employees to work unless demands, generally for pay increases, vacations, and other benefits are met. Usually accompanied by picketing of the premises of the business affected.

Strike-Breaking—Coercive action with the intention of defeating strike action.

Sublease—To lease all or part of premises one has leased.

Sublet—To rent all or part of premises one has rented.

Subpoena—Court order served on witnesses summoning them to give testimony.

Subsidiary—A company, control of whose stock is held by another company.

Subsidy—Agreed sum paid, over and above market charges, to assure supply or service that would otherwise be unavailable because of lack of profit.

Substandard—Below standard quality.

Supermarket—Departmentalized branch in chain store system, where some departments may be rented as concessions, and doing a gross annual business of a specified figure, usually $100,000.

Supply—Amount of goods for sale at a given price.

Surplus—Oversupply; amount by which assets exceed liabilities and capital; amount of goods on hand above current demand.

Swindle—To defraud; dishonest business transaction.

Swindler—One who defrauds.

Swindle Sheet—Expense account, when padding or the possibility of padding is implied.

Syndicate—Group organized for special financing, such as purchase and resale of certain securities or underwriting of a stock issue, purchasing it at a discount.

Take-Home Pay—What is left of earnings after withholding tax and other deductions have been made.

Tariff—Schedule of duties imposed on importers and exporters.

Tax—To exact payment, usually payment exacted by government to provide revenue for its operations.

Tax Sale—Sale of a property to recover unpaid taxes.

Technological—Referring to technical processes or changes in industry; e.g., technological unemployment.

Tenant—Occupant of premises, generally one who pays rent for the occupancy.

Tenders—Sealed bids or offers for securities.

Terms—Terms of payment; prearranged conditions for payment of a debt; e.g., cash in 30 days, $5 down and $1 a week, etc.

Testator—One who makes a will.

Ticker—Machine in which messages are stamped on paper tape, used in reporting market quotations.

Tie-in Sale—Where additional product must be purchased to effect purchase of a certain article.

Title—All factors combined which accord right to exclusive possession of property.

Tool Engineering—New branch of engineering concerned with perfecting new machinery processes, equipment and use of raw material in preparation for production of a new product or a new model.

Tracer—Investigation designed to trace article undelivered by post office or transportation company; one who makes such an investigation.

Trade Acceptance—Bill of exchange governing purchase price, drawn by seller upon buyer whose endorsement constitutes "acceptance."

Trade Agreement—Agreement between employer and union, fixing wages, hours, working conditions.

Trade Edition or Trade Book—Edition designed for general public as distinguished from educational and professional use.

Trademark—Coined name, monogram, logotype, signature, picture, distinctively designed words or name, symbol, emblem or device, which may be registered in the Government Patent Office for exclusive use by the applicant. Registration term is 20 years and may be renewed.

Trade Name—Name or other symbol under which a firm does business and protected by common law against attempt to deceive customers by use of a similar name by a competing firm.

Trade Paper—Endorsed notes (two or more names) given in payment for merchandise; a periodical published in the interest of a certain branch of business.

Transcript—Letter-perfect copy of a document, which does not seek to reproduce exact appearance of original.

Travelers Checks—Issued by banks, travel agencies, American Express, and Western Union for the convenience of travelers.

Treasury Bills—Short-term government offerings, bearing no interest, but sold at a discount to buyers.

Treasury Certificates—Interest-bearing certificates of indebtedness issued in place of short-term bonds.

Trust—Holding of property by a responsible person or bank (trustee) for the good of another person (beneficiary).

Turnover—Number of times, within a specified period such as a year, in which a given commodity is sold out.

Upgrade—To advance an employee, a work process or a product in rank, earnings, price or quality.

Venue—Place where case is tried. A **change of venue** may be granted with the object of securing a fairer trial.

Volume—Amount of business done.

Voucher—A receipt or other proof of money paid, vouches for the accuracy of the terms of a transaction.

Wages—Payment for labor.

Waive—To voluntarily forego a right.

Warrant—Order for the payment of money or delivery of goods or documents; in banking, primarily written order for the payment of money.

Wash Sale—Fictitious trading to give an appearance of activity to inactive stocks.

Wharfage—Fee for use of piers.

Wholesale—Sale of goods to dealers for resale to retail merchants.

Will—Testament of a property-holder directing the distribution of his property after his death.

Window Dressing—Manipulations in financial statement to give it a more favorable appearance than is due.

Withholding Tax—Income tax payment deducted at source, as from wages, dividends, etc.

Without Prejudice—A contract term signifying that the agreement will not injure any prior or subsequent rights.

Zoning—Laws governing real estate, setting off special areas for special types of occupation; e.g., residence, business, hospitals, etc.

BUSINESS MATHEMATICS

Practical Arithmetic for Business Uses

BUSINESS ARITHMETIC IS, as the term implies, the arithmetic that meets the needs of business. It differs from the arithmetic used in our daily lives only in the respect that its methods have been adapted to the special requirements of business. The businessman wants to know at what price to sell an article in order to make a certain profit, how much he may deduct from a bill if he pays for an order in cash, whether it is to his advantage to invest his money in one kind of stock or another. These and other practical problems that the businessman faces constitute the bulk of our Business Arithmetic section. In addition, we present at the outset some helpful hints that will save time in performing the arithmetical computation that is required in solving the business problems later in the section.

It is suggested that the steps given here in solving problems be followed exactly, and that all information required be written down and clearly labeled. Only later, when the methods of solution can be readily applied, should short cuts be taken and steps be performed without indicating them on paper.

Easy Methods of Calculation

SHORT CUTS IN ADDITION

In adding a column of figures, speed and rapidity will be attained by following these suggestions:

1. Take a combination of numbers which adds to 10 and add them as 10.

Example. Add:

$$\begin{array}{rrrr} & 8 & 7 & 5 \\ & 2 & 8 & 6 \\ & 2 & 8 & 4 \\ & 2 & 8 & 3 \\ & 2 & 2 & 2 \\ & 8 & 9 & 5 \\ \hline 2 & 8 & 4 & 5 \end{array}$$

Add the right-hand column from the top down as follows: 5, 15, 25, carry 2.

Add the second column from the top down as follows: 2, 9, 17, 25, 35, 44, carry 4.

Add the third column from the top down as follows: 4, 14, 16, 18, 28.

2. Take any combination of numbers which total 10 or less and add them as that total. For example, add 2, 3, 4, as 9; add 2, 2, 3 as 7; add 1, 2, 3 as 6; add 2, 4, 2 as 8.

3. Add 9 as 10 and then subtract 1. For example, $65 + 9 = 75 - 1 = 74$.

SHORT CUTS IN MULTIPLICATION

1. To multiply an integer (whole number) by 10 or a power of 10.

RULE: Add one zero to the number to be multiplied for each zero in the multiplier.

Example.

65 × 10	= 650	Add 1 zero.
301 × 100	= 30,100	Add 2 zeros.
750 × 1000	= 750,000	Add 3 zeros.
236 × 10,000	= 2,360,000	Add 4 zeros.
185 × 100,000	= 18,500,000	Add 5 zeros.

2. To multiply an integer by 5.

RULE: Multiply by 10; take ½ of the answer.

Example.

650 × 5
650 × 10 = 6500
½ of 6500 = 3250, *Answer*

3. To multiply an integer by 15.

RULE: Multiply by 10: take ½ the answer and add both.

Example.

$$\begin{array}{lr} 786 \times 15 & \\ 786 \times 10 = & 7860 \\ \tfrac{1}{2} \text{ of } 7860 = & \underline{3930} \\ & 11{,}790, \textit{ Answer} \end{array}$$

4. To multiply an integer by 11.

RULE: Multiply by 10; add the original number.

Example.

295 × 11
295 × 10 = 2950
295
(original
number) 295
3245, *Answer*

5. To multiply an integer by 9.

RULE: Multiply by 10; subtract the original number.

Example.

293 × 9
293 × 10 = 2930
293
(original
number) −293
2637, *Answer*

6. To multiply an integer by 50, 25, 12½.

RULE: Multiply by 100; then multiply the answer by ½, ¼, or ⅛ as the case may be because 50, 25, and 12½ are ½, ¼, and ⅛ of 100 respectively.

Example 1.

275 × 50
275 × 100 = 27,500
½ of 27,500 = 13,750, *Answer*

Example 2.

326 × 25
326 × 100 = 32,600
¼ of 32,600 = 8150, *Answer*

SHORT CUTS IN DIVISION

1. To divide an integer by 10 or a power of 10.

RULE: Move the decimal point in the number to be divided as many places to the left as there are zeros in the divisor.

Example 1.

875 ÷ 10
875 ÷ 10 = 87.50, *Answer*

Example 2.

$975.85 ÷ 1000
$975.85 ÷ 1000 = $.97585, *Answer*

Exercise

1. 800 × 10 =
2. 900 × 50 =
3. 1756 × 100 =
4. 288 × 25 =
5. 300 × 15 =
6. 756 ÷ 10 =
7. 97.8 ÷ 100 =
8. 42.6 ÷ 1000 =
9. 285 × 5 =
10. 88 × 11 =
11. 99 × 9 =
12. 1725 × 15 =
13. 836 × 1000 =
14. 19.5 ÷ 10 =
15. 28.65 ÷ 100 =

Answers:

1. 8000
2. 45,000
3. 175,600
4. 7200
5. 4500
6. 75.6
7. .978
8. .0426
9. 1425
10. 968
11. 891
12. 25,875
13. 836,000
14. 1.95
15. .2865

DEVICES FOR CHECKING THE FOUR FUNDAMENTAL OPERATIONS

Addition

Add the column from top to bottom. Write the answer. Check by adding the column from bottom to top.

Subtraction

Add the answer or remainder to the subtrahend. The result should equal the minuend.

OPERATION	CHECK
86 minuend	68 remainder
−18 subtrahend	+18 subtrahend
68 remainder	86 minuend

Multiplication

Multiply the multiplicand by the multiplier. Then make the multiplicand the multiplier and the multiplier the multiplicand, and multiply.

OPERATION	CHECK
85 multiplicand	15 multiplicand
×15 multiplier	×85 multiplier
425	75
85	120
1275 product	1275 product

A second check is to divide the product by the multiplier. The answer should be the multiplicand. Or divide the product by the multiplicand and the answer should be the multiplier.

CHECK

85 multiplicand
multiplier 15) 1275 product
120
75

15 multiplier
multiplicand 85) 1275 product
85
425
425

Division

Multiply the answer or quotient by the divisor. The product should equal the dividend.

OPERATION

416⅔ quotient
divisor 18) 7500 dividend
72
30
18
120
108
$\frac{12}{18} = \frac{2}{3}$

CHECK

$416\frac{2}{3}$ quotient
18 divisor
3) 36
12
3328
416
7500 dividend

PERCENTAGE

The term "per cent" is derived from the Latin. It means "by the hundred." To illustrate, take the number 1 and divide it into 100 parts. Each part is $\frac{1}{100}$ of 1 and may be expressed in three ways, as follows:

1. Common fraction—$\frac{1}{100}$.
2. Decimal fraction—.01.
3. Per cent—1%.

The value of percentage lies in its use as a basis of comparison in various business transactions. It acts as a common denominator to which everything may be reduced, thus enabling the comparison to be made.

Per Cent, Fractions, and Decimals

1. To change a decimal to per cent.

RULE: Move the decimal point two places to the right and then write a per cent sign.

Example 1. Change .15 to per cent.

.15 = 15%

Example 2. Change .075 to per cent.

.075 = 7.5%

Example 3. Change 6 to per cent.

6.00 = 600%

2. To change a common fraction to per cent.

RULE: Change the common fraction to a decimal; then change the decimal to a per cent.

Example 1. Change $\frac{3}{8}$ to a per cent.

$\frac{3}{8}$ = 8) 3.000
.375

.375 = 37.5% or $37\frac{1}{2}$%

Example 2. Change $\frac{17}{19}$ to a per cent.

$.89\frac{9}{19}$
$\frac{17}{19}$ = 19) 17.00
15 2
1 80
1 71
$\frac{9}{19}$

$.89\frac{9}{19} = 89\frac{9}{19}$%

Exercise

Express the following as per cent:

1. $\frac{1}{2}$	6. .0075
2. $\frac{4}{3}$	7. $.02\frac{1}{2}$
3. $\frac{5}{6}$	8. .3
4. $\frac{11}{20}$	9. $\frac{15}{28}$
5. .08	10. .006

Answers:

1. 50%	6. .75% or $\frac{3}{4}$%
2. $133\frac{1}{3}$%	7. $2\frac{1}{2}$%
3. $83\frac{1}{3}$%	8. $\frac{3}{10}$% or .3%
4. 55%	9. $53\frac{4}{7}$%
5. 8%	10. $\frac{3}{5}$% or .6%

3. To change a per cent to a decimal.

RULE: Move the decimal point two places to the left and take away the per cent sign.

Example 1. Express 17% as a decimal.

17% = .17

Example 2. Express 8.5% as a decimal.

08.5% = .085

Example 3. Express 525% as a decimal.

525% = 5.25

Example 4. Express .75% as a decimal.

.75% = .0075

Exercise

Express the following per cents as decimals:

1. $2\frac{1}{2}$%	6. .5%
2. $37\frac{1}{2}$%	7. .05%
3. 650%	8. .25%
4. 7.5%	9. 16.75%
5. 18.8%	10. 123%

Answers:

1. .025 or $.02\frac{1}{2}$	6. .005
2. .375 or $.37\frac{1}{2}$	7. .0005
3. 6.50	8. .0025
4. .075 or $.07\frac{1}{2}$	9. .1675
5. .188	10. 1.23

4. To change a per cent to a common fraction.

RULE: Change the common fraction to a decimal; then to a per cent.

Example 1. Change 25% to a common fraction.

25 % = .25
.25 = $\frac{25}{100}$ = $\frac{1}{4}$, *Answer*

Example 2. Change 150% to a common fraction.

150% = 1.50
1.50 = $1\frac{1}{2}$ or $\frac{3}{2}$, *Answer*

Exercise

Change the following to common fractions:

1. 50%	6. 75%
2. 20%	7. 80%
3. 40%	8. $62\frac{1}{2}$%
4. $33\frac{1}{3}$%	9. $87\frac{1}{2}$%
5. $16\frac{2}{3}$%	10. $12\frac{1}{2}$%

Answers:

1. $\frac{1}{2}$	6. $\frac{3}{4}$
2. $\frac{1}{5}$	7. $\frac{4}{5}$
3. $\frac{2}{5}$	8. $\frac{5}{8}$
4. $\frac{1}{3}$	9. $\frac{7}{8}$
5. $\frac{1}{6}$	10. $\frac{1}{8}$

Problems in Percentage

In computing a problem in percentage, the number or quantity upon which the per cent is to be computed is called the *base,* the per cent is called the *rate,* and the product of the base and the rate is called the *percentage.* All problems in percentage fall into three groups or cases.

Case I. Given the base and the rate, to find the percentage.

RULE: Base × Rate = Percentage.

Example 1. Find 25% of 7800.

Change 25% to .25; then multiply:

7800 × .25 = 1950, *Answer*

Example 2. Find 250% of 19,600.

19,600 × 2½ = 49,000, *Answer*

Exercise

Find the percentage:

1. 15% of 980	6. ¾% of 1200
2. 12½% of 640	7. .75% of 1600
3. 33⅓% of 999	8. 2½% of 1640
4. 125% of 260	9. 10% of 968
5. 18% of 480	10. 19% of 200

Answers:

1. 147	6. 9
2. 80	7. 12
3. 333	8. 41
4. 325	9. 96.8
5. 86.4	10. 38

Case II. Given the base and the percentage, to find the rate.

RULE: Divide the percentage by the base.

Example. 17 is what per cent of 29?

$\frac{17}{29} = .58\frac{18}{29} = 58\frac{18}{29}\%$

Exercise

1. 25 is what per cent of 800?
2. 16 is what per cent of 280?
3. 180 is what per cent of 36,000?
4. 17.5 is what per cent of 85.6?
5. 18.4 is what per cent of 2.86?

Answers:

1. $3\frac{1}{8}\%$	3. ½% or .5%	5. $643\frac{51}{143}\%$
2. $5\frac{5}{7}\%$	4. $20\frac{95}{214}\%$	

Case III. Given the percentage and rate, to find the base. This is called the indirect case.

RULE: Percentage divided by rate equals the base.

Example. 18 is 3% of what number?

18 ÷ .03 = 600, *Answer*

Exercise

1. 25 is 20% of what number?
2. 180 is 50% of what number?
3. 27 is 75% of what number?
4. 260 is 80% of what number?
5. 1704 is 12% of what number?

Answers:

1. 125	3. 36	5. 14,200
2. 360	4. 325	

Aliquot Parts

Arithmetical calculations may be made much easier if the aliquot parts of 100% are used. By an aliquot part is meant a number which can be divided into another number so that the answer will be a whole number. Thus 25% is an aliquot part of 100% because 100% divided by 25% equals 4. It would be well to memorize the aliquot parts of 100%, and multiples of these aliquot parts for greater ease and speed in performing problems.

ALIQUOT PARTS OF 100%

50% = ½	87½% = ⅞	70% = $\frac{7}{10}$
25% = ¼	1% = $\frac{1}{100}$	80% = ⅘
75% = ¾	10% = $\frac{1}{10}$	33⅓% = ⅓
6¼% = $\frac{1}{16}$	20% = ⅕	66⅔% = ⅔
12½% = ⅛	30% = $\frac{3}{10}$	16⅔% = ⅙
37½% = ⅜	40% = ⅖	8⅓% = $\frac{1}{12}$
62½% = ⅝	60% = ⅗	83⅓% = ⅚

Example. Find 37½% of 800.

⅜ of 800 = 300, *Answer*

Exercise

Compute the following, using aliquot parts:

1. 20% of 850	9. 80% of 9000
2. 87½% of 864	10. 8⅓% of 2460
3. 12½% of 960	11. 83⅓% of 288
4. 75% of 1200	12. 62½% of 1200
5. 33⅓% of 963	13. 6¼% of 3200
6. 10% of 786	14. 5% of 870
7. 16⅔% of 282	15. 50% of 1900
8. 66⅔% of 1296	

Answers:

1. 170	9. 7200
2. 756	10. 205
3. 120	11. 240
4. 900	12. 750
5. 321	13. 200
6. 78.6	14. 43½
7. 47	15. 950
8. 864	

ALIQUOT PARTS OF $1.00

It will be noticed that the aliquot parts of $1.00 are the same as those of 100%. Therefore the same fractional equivalents may be used at all times.

Example. Find cost of 840 yards of silks @ 62½¢ per yd.

62½ = ⅝

⅝ of 840 = 525, *Answer*

Exercise

Compute the following, using aliquot parts:

1. 160 yds. @ 50¢	9. 75 yds. @ 88¢
2. 980 yds. @ 10¢	10. 40 yds. @ $2.50
3. 750 yds. @ 40¢	11. 270 lbs. @ 66⅔¢
4. 138 lbs. @ 33⅓¢	12. 726 ft. @ 16⅔¢
5. 280 lbs. @ 62½¢	13. 6480 yds. @ 62½¢
6. 1780 lbs. @ 60¢	14. 22½ lbs. @ 40¢
7. 66⅔ lbs. @ 90¢	15. 256 ft. @ 6¼¢
8. 16⅔ lbs. @ 48¢	

In problems 7 to 10, the base and the rate may be interchanged so that problem 7 will read 90 lbs. @ 66⅔¢ and will be done in the same manner as problems 1 to 6.

Answers:

1. $80	9. $66
2. $98	10. $100
3. $300	11. $180
4. $46	12. $121
5. $175	13. $4050
6. $1068	14. $9
7. $60	15. $16
8. $8	

Business Uses of Arithmetic

DISCOUNTS ON INVOICES

Invoices and Terms

After a sale is made, the seller sends an *invoice* to the buyer. On it is listed the date, terms, goods and quantity sold, the price of each item, the extensions, and the total. The terms are most important because they are the conditions of payment. Some examples of terms are:

C.O.D.—Collect or cash on delivery.
Cash—Cash is to be paid on the date of the sale.
On account—Payment to be made within a reasonable time after the end of the month.
E.O.M.—End of the month.
n/30—Net 30 days after the date of the invoice (net means no discounts).
2/10 n/30—2% discount if paid within 10 days after the date of the invoice, net after 10 days and within 30 days.
2/5 1/15 n/30—2% discount if paid within 5 days, 1% discount if paid after 5 days but within 15 days; net if paid after 15 days and within 30 days.

Trade and Cash Discounts

Discounts on invoices are of two kinds, cash discounts and trade discounts. Cash discounts are those mentioned under terms, an inducement to the customer to pay his bill ahead of time. The customer is the one who decides whether he will take advantage of the discount. Trade discounts differ from cash discounts because they are deducted, not by the customer, but by the seller.

Manufacturers and wholesalers print catalogues once or twice a year. They are expensive. In order to bring the catalogue price down to the market price, they send their customers discount sheets, on which they list discounts given on the catalogue price to bring it down to the market price. If the price drops, two or more trade discounts may be given.

Problem 1. The Rowe Co. offers to sell a dining room suite for $250 less 20%, 10%, and 10%. The Wilson Co. offers a similar suite for $260 less 40%. Which is the better offer and by how much?

ROWE CO.

$250	List Price or Catalogue Price
50	Trade Discount 20%
$200	Balance
20	Trade Discount 10%
$180	Balance
18	Trade Discount 10%
$162	Net Cost

WILSON CO.

$260	List Price
104	Trade Discount 40%
$156	Net Cost
$162	Net Cost—Rowe Co.
156	Net Cost—Wilson Co.
$6	Wilson Co. offer better.

Problem 2. The Domestic Rug Co. received an invoice on November 10 amounting to $1280 less 20%, and 5%, terms 3/10 n/60. The invoice was paid November 20. Find the amount of the payment.

$1280.00	List Price
256.00	Trade Discount 20%
$1024.00	Balance
51.20	Trade Discount 5% (½ of 10%)
$ 972.80	Balance
29.18	Cash Discount 3%
$ 943.62	Net Cost

Problem 3. A dealer purchased a bicycle for $32.40 less 33⅓%, terms 2/10, n/30, plus a freight charge of 90¢. The invoice was dated March 15 and paid March 25. Find the amount of the payment.

$32.40	List Price
10.80	Trade Discount 33⅓%
$21.60	Balance
.43	Cash Discount 2%
$21.17	Net Cost
.90	Freight Charge
$22.07	Total Cost

NOTE: The discounts are taken only on the invoice; they cannot be taken on the freight charge or any other buying expense.

Exercise

1. Find net cost of invoice of $1375 less 20% and 10%.
2. Find total cost of invoice of $45 less 20% and buying expense of $2.10.
3. Find net cost of invoice dated April 16, terms 2/10 n/30, amounting to $1500 less 20% and 10% and paid on April 26.
4. A dealer offers a rug for $60 less 30% and 10%. Another offers the same quality for $60 less 40%. Which offer is better and how much?

Answers:

1. $990
2. $38.10
3. $1058.40
4. Second offer by $1.80

Single Discount Equivalent to a Series of Trade Discounts

For ease in computation and for purposes of comparison, it is often desirable to find one discount that is equivalent to a series. The procedure is as follows: Consider the catalogue price as 100%. Multiply this by the first discount and subtract from 100%. Multiply this difference or balance by the second discount and subtract the answer from the balance. Continue this multiplication and subtraction until all the discounts have been taken. The answer will be the net cost. To find the single discount, subtract the nèt cost from 100%.

Problem. Find one discount equivalent to a series of 30%, 20%, and 10%.

100%	List Price
30	Trade Discount 30%
70%	Balance
14	Trade Discount 20% (20% of 70%)
56.0%	Balance
5.6	Trade Discount 10% (10% of 56%)
50.4	Net Cost

100% List Price — 50.4% Net Cost = 49.6%, *Ans.*
Proof: 30% + 14% + 5.6% = 49.6%, *Answer*

Exercise

Find one discount equivalent to the following series:

1. 20% and 10%
2. 30% and 10%
3. 50% and 20%
4. 25% and 20%
5. 37½% and 24%
6. 20%, 10%, and 5%
7. 20%, 10%, and 10%
8. 50%, 25%, and 20%
9. 40%, 30%, 20%, and 10%
10. 50%, 25%, and 10%

Answers:

1. 28%
2. 37%
3. 60%
4. 40%
5. 52½%
6. 31.6%
7. 35.2%
8. 70%
9. 69.76%
10. 66.25%

COMMISSIONS

Salesmen are usually paid a percentage of their sales as compensation for their work. This percentage is called *commission.* Commissions are generally paid on the amount of the sales, although in some cases they are calculated on the quantity of merchandise sold. When a salesman is paid commission only, he is on a straight commission basis. If he receives a drawing account, the amount of the drawings is deducted from his total commission at the end of the accounting period, and the balance paid him at that time.

To encourage salesmen to greater efforts, commission may be paid on a graduated basis; that is, for example, 10% commission on the first $20,000 of sales and 15% on all sales over $20,000. Inside salesmen are usually paid on a commission and salary basis. Very often, no commission is paid until a stated amount or quota has been sold; commission is then paid on sales over the quota. The problems that follow deal with each of these phases of selling.

Straight Commission

Problem 1. A salesman sells 2500 yards of silk at $2 per yard. His rate of commission is 2½%. Find his commission.

2500 × $2 = $5000, Sales
2½% of $5000 = $125, Commission

Problem 2. A salesman sells 2500 yards of silk at $2 per yard. His rate of commission is 5¢ per yard. Find his commission.

2500 yards × 5¢ = $125, Commission

Note that in the first problem the commission was based on price whereas in the second problem it was based on quantity.

Salary and Commission

Problem. A salesman is offered a salary of $50 per week and a commission of 5% on all sales. His sales for the year are $36,000. Find his yearly earnings.

TIME	SALES	5% COMMISSION	SALARY	TOTAL
1 year	$36,000	$1800	$2600 (52 × $50)	$4400 *Answer*

Salary, Commission, and Quota

Problem. A salesman is offered a salary of $110 per month and a 6% commission on all sales over $2000 per month. In April, his sales were $1950; in May, $3250; in June, $3375. Find his total earnings.

TIME	SALARY	SALES	QUOTA OVER $2000	6% COMMISSION	TOTALS
April	$110	$1950	$ 0	$ 0	$110.00
May	110	3250	1250	75.00	185.00
June	110	3375	1375	82.50	192.50
Totals	$330	$8575	$2625	$157.50	$487.50 *Answer*

To check the answer, add the vertical totals, then the horizontal totals. The grand total must be the same.

Thus, vertically, 110 + 185 + 192.50 = 487.50
horizontally, 330 + 157.50 = 487.50

Salary, Graduated Commission, and Quota

Problem. Noll, a salesman, receives a salary of $200 per month, 1% commission on all sales, and 2% commission on all monthly sales over $3000. In January his sales were $6000; in February, $4500; in March, $7400. Find his total income for the three months.

TIME	SALARY	SALES	ON ALL SALES COM. 1%	QUOTA OVER $3000	OVER $3000 COM. 2%	TOTALS
January	$200	$6000	$ 60	$3000	$ 60	$320
February	200	4500	45	1500	30	275
March	200	7400	74	4400	88	362
Totals	$600	$17,900	$179	$8900	$178	$957 *Answer*

To check the answer of the problem just solved, add the horizontal totals:

$$600+179+178=957.$$

Exercise

In doing these problems use the diagram method of the previous problems. The headings can be found very easily by reading the problem carefully and then heading each column as the problem indicates.

1. Find the commission a salesman receives if his sales are $6500 and the commission is 7%.
2. John Miller, a salesman, receives a monthly salary of $90 and 5% commission on all sales. In addition, he receives 2% on sales over $3000 in any single month. His sales in April were $3850 and in May $2700. Find his total earnings.
3. A salesman has offers of employment from two firms. Kolapep offers him a salary of $100 per month, a commission of 5% in total monthly sales and 2% additional commission on monthly sales in excess of $2000. Cocapep offers him a commission of 8% on the first $1000 of monthly sales, 10% on the next $1000 of monthly sales and 12% on all monthly sales in excess of $2000. If his average sales are $3500 a month, where would he earn more and how much more?
4. The Electric Supply Co. has an agency for the sale of vacuum cleaners. Their commission is $12.50 each for the first 50 cleaners; $15 each for the second 50 cleaners or part thereof; $17.50 each for all over 100 cleaners sold each month. In May, they sold 76 cleaners; in June, they sold 105 cleaners. Find their commission.

Answers:

1. $455
2. $524.50
3. Cocapep is better by $55
4. $2477.50

Commission Merchants

For those people who cannot do their own buying or selling, agents known as commission merchants will attend to all such transactions. They charge a commission for their services, in the same manner as do salesmen. After selling the merchandise, they submit a statement called an *account sales*. After buying the merchandise, they submit a statement called an *account purchase*.

Problem 1. Williams has 860 bushels of potatoes to sell. He can sell them at $2.10 a bushel, with no expense. However, he sends them to a commission merchant who sells 450 bushels at $2.60 and the remainder at $2.25 a bushel. The merchant charges 3¢ a bushel for storage, $36.80 for freight, 1% for insurance, and 3% commission.

a. Find the amount of the net proceeds remitted to Williams.

b. How much does Williams gain or lose by having the merchant sell the potatoes?

a. INCOME

450 bu. @ $2.60	$1170.00	
410 bu. @ $2.25	922.50	
Total Proceeds		$2092.50

CHARGES

Storage (3¢ per bu., 860 bu.)	$25.80	
Freight	36.80	
Insurance (1% of $2092.50)	20.93	
Commission (3% of $2092.50)	62.78	
Total Charges		$ 146.31
Net Proceeds		$1946.19

b. 860 bu. @ $2.10 = $1806, Total Proceeds

$1946.19, Net Proceeds—Commission Merchant
1806.00, Total Proceeds
$ 140.19, Gain by sending to commission merchant

NOTE: All charges or expenses must be subtracted on a sale.

Problem 2. Benton, a sugar broker, purchases 35,000 pounds of sugar for a candy manufacturer at 5.5¢ per pound. Benton's expenses and charges are: handling $23.40, freight 36¢ per hundredweight, commission 5%. Find the total cost of the sugar to the candy manufacturer.

35,000 lbs. sugar @ 5.5¢ per lb. = $1925, Cost

CHARGES

Handling	$ 23.40	
Freight (36¢ per cwt.—35,000 lbs.)	126.00	
Commission (5% of $1925)	96.25	
Total Charges		$ 245.65
Total Cost		$2170.65

NOTE: All charges and expenses must be added on a purchase.

Exercise

1. Wilson, a commission merchant, receives 1500 bushels of potatoes to sell. He sold 635 bushels at $1.50; 475 bushels at $1.40; and the remainder at $1.30 a bushel. He charged a commission of 5%. His expenses were: freight charges $84.50, sorting and weighing $38.40, and storage charges of 3¢ per bushel. Find the net proceeds.
2. Harris purchased 50,000 feet of lumber for a builder at $60 per 1000 feet. Freight charges were $150, insurance 1%, trucking $75 and commission 4%. Find the total cost of the lumber to the builder.
3. A fruit farm shipped 100 crates (32 boxes per crate) of strawberries to a commission merchant. He sold 1280 boxes at $.20, 960 boxes at $.15 and the remainder at $.12 per box. Freight charges were $24, storage $22.66, cartage $15.60, commission 5%. Find the net proceeds.

Answers:

1. $1850.37
2. $3375
3. $427.18

PAYROLLS

Time Basis

Employees other than salesmen are usually paid on a time basis. So-called white-collar workers such as clerks, bookkeepers, and the like are paid on an annual, monthly, or weekly salary basis. Other workers, especially those who do manual labor, are paid on an hourly basis, with forty hours per week generally regarded as regular time, and everything over forty hours as overtime. In many organizations each employee has a time card on which an accurate record of his time may be kept.

Problem 1. Below is the time card of a worker showing the time he has worked for one week. His regular wage is \$1.10 per hour for a 40 hour week.

DAY	IN	OUT	IN	OUT
Monday	7:00	12:00	1:00	4:00
Tuesday	7:00	12:00	1:00	4:00
Wednesday	7:00	12:00	1:00	4:00
Thursday	7:00	12:00	1:00	4:00
Friday	7:00	12:00	1:00	4:00

a. Find his total wages for the week.
b. His employer deducts 3% for social security and \$6.38 for withholding tax. What is his take-home pay?

a.

DAY	HOURS
Monday	8
Tuesday	8
Wednesday	8
Thursday	8
Friday	8
Total	40
	×1.10
	\$44.00, Total Wages

b. Total wages \$44.00
Deductions

Social Security (3%)... \$1.32
Withholding Tax....... 6.38 7.70
Take-home pay \$36.30

Problem 2. A mechanic is working in a factory where his regular time is 40 hours a week. He is paid time and a half (1½ times) for overtime. His regular wages are \$1.50 per hour. Deductions are 3% for social security and \$14.25 for withholding tax. Last week he worked 57 hours.

a. Find his total earnings.
b. Find his take-home pay.

a.

TOTAL TIME (HOURS)	REGULAR TIME (HOURS)	1½ OVERTIME (HOURS)
57	40	17
		×1½
		8½
		17
		25½

(One hour of overtime equals 1½ hours of regular time. Convert overtime to regular time by multiplying by the overtime rate.)

40 Regular Allowance
25½ Overtime Allowance
65½ Total Hours
×\$1.50 Rate
\$98.25, Total Wages

b.
Total wages \$98.25
Deductions
Social Security (3%)...\$ 2.95
Withholding Tax....... 14.25 17.20
Take-home pay \$81.05

Exercise

1. William Randall, a machinist, worked last week as follows: Monday 8 hours, Tuesday 10 hours, Wednesday 11 hours, Thursday 9 hours, Friday 10 hours and Saturday 5 hours. His regular time is 40 hours per week, with time and a half for overtime. His hourly rate is \$1.60 per hour. Deductions of 3% for social security taxes and \$13.81 for withholding taxes are made.
   a. Find his total wages.
   b. Find his take-home pay.
2. Hawkins, a mechanic, worked 47 hours last week. His regular time is 40 hours with time and a half for overtime. His hourly rate is \$1.40 per hour. Social security tax deduction was 3% and withholding tax was \$11.67.
   a. Find his total wages.
   b. Find his take-home pay.

Answers:
1. *a.* \$95.20 *b.* \$78.53
2. *a.* \$70.70 *b.* \$56.91

Piecework Wages

Another method of compensation depends not on the time worked but on the quantity or pieces which the worker produces. The wage is computed by multiplying the number of pieces by the rate per piece.

Problem. Harris, a dress operator, produces 108 pieces of work during the week. His rate per piece is 35¢. Find his total wages.

108 × .35 = \$37.80, Total Wages

Deductions for social security and withholding tax are computed in the same manner as in time wages.

AVERAGES

By an average is meant a figure which is typical of a group of numbers. Averages are useful in comparing groups of numbers. To find an average, add all the items and divide the total by the number of items.

Problem 1. A salesman's sales per week are \$1500, \$2000, \$3000, \$6000, and \$2500. Find his average sales for the five weeks.

\$1500
2000
3000
6000
2500
\$15,000

\$15,000 ÷ 5 = \$3000, Average Sales per Week

Problem 2. Clark's average sales for the last 8 weeks of the year were \$362.15 a week. For the first 3 weeks of the new year, his sales per week were \$415.16, \$523.25, and \$392.35. Find his average sales per week for the 11 weeks.

\$362.15 × 8 = \$2897.20, Total sales for 8 weeks
415.16
523.25
392.35
\$4227.96, Total sales for 11 weeks

\$4227.96 ÷ 11 = \$384.36 Average sales per week for 11 weeks

Exercise

1. The Acme Sales Co. had a contest for its salesmen. Potter's average sales for the last 8 weeks of the year were $340. For the first 4 weeks of the new year, his weekly sales were $376, $625, $429, and $374. Find his average weekly sales for the 12 weeks.
2. In the same contest, Wolcott's sales for the last 6 weeks averaged $425. For the first 4 weeks of the new year, his weekly sales were $500, $735, $658, and $695. Find his average weekly sales for the 10 weeks.

Answers:

1. $377 2. $513.80

SIMPLE INTEREST

Basic Method of Calculation

Interest is the charge made for the use of money for a specified time. The money used is called the *principal.* The per cent is called the *rate.* The rule for calculating interest is:

Principal × Rate × Time = Interest

Problem 1. Find the interest on $600 for 1 year at 6%.

$600 × 6/100 × 1 = $36, Interest

Problem 2. Find the interest on $1200 for 90 days at 4%.

$1200 × 4/100 × 90/360 = $12, Interest

Note that for purposes of easier and faster computation the year is considered to have 360 days, and each month, regardless of how many days it actually has, is considered to have only 30 days.

Exercise

Find the interest:

	PRINCIPAL	TIME	RATE %	RATE %	RATE %
1.	$1600	6 months	6	4	3
2.	1200	3 months	6	3	2
3.	2400	2 months	6	5	3
4.	720	60 days	6	1	4
5.	840	80 days	6	1	2
6.	480	40 days	6	5	4
7.	220	120 days	6	3	2
8.	180	9 months	6	8	4½
9.	2800	8 months	6	2	3
10.	960	30 days	6	4	3

Answers:

1.	$ 48	$32	$24
2.	18	9	6
3.	24	20	12
4.	7.20	1.20	4.80
5.	11.20	1.87	3.73
6.	3.20	2.67	2.13
7.	4.40	2.20	1.47
8.	8.10	10.80	6.08
9.	112	37.33	56
10.	4.80	3.20	2.40

The Sixty-Day Method

To find interest on sums of money when the time is less than a year, the *sixty-day method* is used. This method is based upon the fact that 60 days (2 months) are 1/6 of one year. Therefore, if the annual interest rate is 6%, the interest charge for 60 days is 1/6 of 6% or 1%.

RULE: To find the interest on any sum of money for 60 days (2 months) take 1% of that amount.

Problem 1. Find the interest on $1200 for 60 days at 6%.

1% of $1200 = $12.00, Interest for 60 days
Proof: $1200 × 6/100 × 60/360 = $12.

Finding the interest for 60 days is the basis for computing interest for other periods of time. For example, the interest for 30 days is half of that for 60 days; for 15 days, a quarter; for 10 days, a sixth, etc.

Problem 2. Find the interest on $1200 at 6% for the days shown below:

Interest on $1200 for 60 days at 6%	=	$12.00
Interest for 30 days (½ of 60)	=	6.00
Interest for 20 days (⅓ of 60)	=	4.00
Interest for 15 days (¼ of 60)	=	3.00
Interest for 12 days (1/5 of 60)	=	2.40
Interest for 10 days (1/6 of 60)	=	2.00
Interest for 6 days (1/10 of 60)	=	1.20

From this point, it is easy to find the interest for any number of days. Always find the interest for 60 days first. That is the base. Then, break up the days for which the interest is to be calculated into aliquot parts of 60 and add the interest for those days. The following illustrations will show just what is to be done:

Problem 3. Find the interest on $1800 for 90 days at 6%. 90 = 60 + 30.

Interest on $1800 for 60 days at 6% =	$18
Interest on $1800 for 30 days at 6% =	9
Interest on $1800 for 90 days at 6% =	$27

Problem 4. Find the interest on $1500 for 47 days at 6%.

a. 47 = 20 + 20 + 6 + 1.

or

b. 47 = 30 + 15 + 2.

a.

Interest on $1500 for 60 days at 6% =	$15.00	
Interest on $1500 for 20 days at 6% =		$5.00
Interest on $1500 for 20 days at 6% =		5.00
Interest on $1500 for 6 days at 6% =		1.50
Interest on $1500 for 1 day at 6% =		.25
Interest on $1500 for 47 days at 6% =		$11.75

b.

Interest on $1500 for 60 days at 6% =	$15.00	
Interest on $1500 for 30 days at 6% =		$7.50
Interest on $1500 for 15 days at 6% =		3.75
Interest on $1500 for 2 days at 6% =		.50
Interest on $1500 for 47 days at 6% =		$11.75

Problem 5. Find the interest on $270 for 56 days at 6%.

a. 56 = 30 + 20 + 6.

or

b. $56 = 20 + 20 + 12 + 4.$

or

c. $56 = 60 - 4.$

a.

Interest on $270 for 60 days at 6% = $2.70	
Interest on $270 for 30 days at 6% =	$1.35
Interest on $270 for 20 days at 6% =	.90
Interest on $270 for 6 days at 6% =	.27
Interest on $270 for 56 days at 6% =	$2.52

b.

Interest on $270 for 60 days at 6% = $2.70	
Interest on $270 for 20 days at 6% =	$ .90
Interest on $270 for 20 days at 6% =	.90
Interest on $270 for 12 days at 6% =	.54
Interest on $270 for 4 days at 6% =	.18
Interest on $270 for 56 days at 6% =	$2.52

c.

Interest on $270 for 60 days at 6% = $2.70
Interest on $270 for 4 days at 6% = .18
Interest on $270 for 56 days at 6% = $2.52

Note that it is also possible to use aliquot parts of the other numbers besides 60 as well. Thus in Problem 4*a*, 1 day is 1/6 of 6 days. Therefore 1/6 of $1.50 = $.25. In Problem 5*b*, 4 days are 1/5 of 20 days or 1/3 of 12 days. The interest can be computed by taking 1/5 of $.90 or 1/3 of $.54, the answer in each case being $.18.

Exercise

Find the interest:

	PRINCIPAL	TIME	RATE %
1.	$1600	80 days	6
2.	1800	3 months	6
3.	1200	75 days	6
4.	4000	46 days	6
5.	280	23 days	6
6.	970	38 days	6
7.	250.68	14 days	6
8.	168.95	4 months	6
9.	1280	53 days	6
10.	560.80	44 days	6

Answers:

1. $21.33
2. 27.00
3. 15.00
4. 30.67
5. $1.07
6. 6.14
7. .58
8. 3.38
9. $11.31
10. 4.11

TO FIND THE INTEREST AT 6% FOR ANY TIME IN DAYS

Frequently the number of days in an interest problem cannot easily be divided into aliquot parts of 60, such as 29 days, 71 days, etc. In such cases another method may be used, as follows:

RULE:
1. Divide the principal by 1000.
2. Multiply the result by the number of days.
3. Divide the product by 6.

Problem. Find the interest on $150 for 29 days at 6%.

$$\frac{\$150}{1000} = \$.150$$

$$\begin{array}{r} \$.150 \\ \underline{29} \\ 1350 \\ \underline{300} \\ 6\,)\,4350 \\ .725 \end{array}$$ *Answer*

The answer arrived at by this method may be checked by the first method:

Interest on $150 for 60 days at 6% = $1.50	
Interest on $150 for 30 days at 6% =	$.75
Interest on $150 for 1 day at 6% =	.025
Interest on $150 for 31 days at 6% = .725	
Interest on $150 for 29 days at 6% =	$.725 or $.73

Exercise

Do the examples in the preceding exercise, but use the above method.

TO FIND THE INTEREST AT RATES OTHER THAN 6%

RULE:
1. Find the interest at 6%.
2. Multiply the answer by the desired rate.
3. Divide by 6.

Problem. Find the interest on $800 for 37 days at 4½%.

a.

Interest on $800 for 60 days at 6% = $8.00	
Interest on $800 for 30 days at 6% =	$4.00
Interest on $800 for 6 days at 6% =	.80
Interest on $800 for 1 day at 6% =	.133
Interest on $800 for 37 days at 6% =	$4.933

b.

$$\begin{array}{r} \$4.933 \\ \underline{4\tfrac{1}{2}} \\ \$22.1985 \end{array}$$

c.

$$6\,)\,22.1985$$
$3.6997½$ or $3.70, *Answer*

Another method may also be used. For 5% take 5/6 of the answer; for 4%, 2/3 (or 4/6); for 3%, ½ (or 3/6); for 2%, 1/3 (or 2/6) and for 1%, 1/6. Whichever method is used is a matter of one's own preference.

Exercise

Find the interest.

	PRINCIPAL	TIME	RATE %	RATE %	RATE %
1.	$1836	60 days	5	4	3
2.	680	26 days	4	3	2
3.	275	3 months	3	2	1
4.	368	6 months	2	1	5
5.	212.50	72 days	1	5	4
6.	505.80	90 days	5	4	3
7.	906	36 days	4	3	2
8.	412.76	45 days	3	2	1
9.	1300	18 days	2	1	5
10.	1560	52 days	1	5	4

Answers:

1.	$15.30	$12.24	$9.18
2.	1.97	1.48	.98
3.	2.06	1.38	.69
4.	3.68	1.84	9.20
5.	.43	2.13	1.70
6.	6.32	5.06	3.79
7.	3.62	2.72	1.81

8.	1.55	1.03	.52
9.	1.30	.65	3.25
10.	2.25	11.27	9.01

BANK DISCOUNT

Discounting One's Own Notes

When a businessman needs money, he borrows it at the bank. In return he will give the bank his written promise to repay the money at a certain time. This written promise is called a *promissory note.* The bank will charge interest on the loan which it will deduct in advance, giving the borrower the difference between the value of the note at maturity and the interest. This difference is called the *net proceeds.* When interest is deducted in advance, it is called *bank discount,* and the rate is called the *rate of bank discount.*

In order to find how much a borrower will actually receive on a loan, calculate the interest and subtract the amount from the principal.

Problem. A businessman borrows $1500 from a bank on his 60-day note at a discount rate of 6%. Find the net proceeds.

Interest on $1500 for 60 days at 6% = $15, Bank Discount

$1500	Maturity Value
15	Bank Discount
$1485	Net Proceeds

Exercise

Find the net proceeds of the following notes:

	NOTE	TIME OF DISCOUNT	RATE OF DISCOUNT %
1.	$1200	90 days	6
2.	680	45 days	6
3.	420	120 days	6
4.	1100	60 days	6
5.	975	30 days	6

Answers:

1. $1182 2. 674.90 3. $ 411.60 4. 1089 5. $970.12

Discounting Others' Notes

Frequently, a businessman who is in need of money has customers' notes and acceptances on hand. He may borrow on these.

Problem 1. Harry Williams has received a note of $600 from a customer. It is dated April 15 and runs for 90 days. On May 12, he needs money. He sells it to the bank or, to use the correct business term, he *discounts* the note. What are the net proceeds?

To do this problem, four steps must be performed.

1. Find the day the note is due (date of maturity).
2. Find how long the bank must wait for payment (term of discount).
3. Find the bank discount.
4. Find the net proceeds.

DATE OF MATURITY

Apr. 30
−15
Apr. 15
May 31
June 30
July 14 Date of Maturity
90 days

TERM OF DISCOUNT

May 31
−12
May 19
June 30
July 14
63 days, Term of Discount

BANK DISCOUNT

$6.30 for 63 days (By previously indicated method)

NET PROCEEDS

$600.00	Maturity Value
6.30	Bank Discount
$593.70	Net Proceeds

Note that in finding the date of maturity and the term of discount, the actual number of days is used.

EXPLANATION OF THE SOLUTION:

1. *Date of Maturity.* The date of maturity is 90 days from April 15. There are 30 days in April; 15 days have already passed, so we have 15 days left in April. In May there are 31, in June, 30 days. This gives us 76 days, leaving 14 more to make up the 90. We reach, then, July 14.
2. *Term of Discount.* Counting from the date the note was discounted, May 12, to the date of maturity, July 14, there are 63 days.
3. *Bank Discount.* The bank discount is found by finding the interest for the term of discount, 63 days.
4. *Net Proceeds.* Net proceeds are found by deducting the bank discount from the value at maturity.

When the time of the note is not in days, but in months, the date of maturity is found by counting months, and not days.

Problem 2. Find the net proceeds of a note of $1500, dated July 16, time 3 months, and discounted August 31.

DATE OF MATURITY

July 16
Aug.
Sept.
Oct. 16 Date of Maturity
3 months

TERM OF DISCOUNT

Aug. 31
−31
Aug. 0
Sept. 30
Oct. 16
46 days, Term of Discount

BANK DISCOUNT

$11.50, for 46 days (By previously indicated method)

NET PROCEEDS

$1500.00	Maturity Value
11.50	Bank Discount
$1488.50	Net Proceeds

Exercise

Find the net proceeds:

	FACE VALUE	DATE	TIME	RATE %	DATE OF DISCOUNT
1.	$1200	Mar. 2	60 days	6	Apr. 7
2.	1800	Apr. 30	90 days	6	June 3
3.	240	Sept. 16	30 days	6	Sept. 25
4.	550	Jan. 20	1 mo.	6	Jan. 31
5.	728	Feb. 17	3 mo.	6	Apr. 12
6.	2800	May 4	2 mo.	6	June 6

Answers:

1. $1195.20
2. 1783.20
3. $239.16
4. 548.17
5. $ 723.75
6. 2786.93

Discounting Interest-Bearing Notes

The face value and the maturity value of a non-interest-bearing note are the same. In the case of an interest-bearing note, the face value and maturity value differ, because the interest must be added to the face value to arrive at the maturity value.

Problem 1. Find the maturity value of a 60-day note of $800 bearing interest at 3%.

Interest = $4

$800	Face Value
4	Interest
$804	Maturity Value

To discount an interest-bearing note, the maturity value must be found, because the bank discount is computed on the maturity value, not the face value.

Problem 2. Find the net proceeds of a 60-day note of $1200, bearing interest at 4%, dated January 18 and discounted February 13.

DATE OF MATURITY

Jan. 31
−18
Jan. 13
Feb. 28
Mar. 19, Date of Maturity
60 days

TERM OF DISCOUNT

Feb. 28
−13
Feb. 15
Mar. 19
34 days, Time of Discount

INTEREST AND MATURITY VALUE

$1200.00	Face
9.00	Interest
$1209.00	Maturity Value

BANK DISCOUNT

$6.85 for 34 days (By previously indicated method)

NET PROCEEDS

$1209.00	Maturity Value
6.85	Bank Discount
$1202.15	Net Proceeds

Note that there is a new step in this solution; namely, finding the maturity value. Otherwise the solution is the same as in the non-interest-bearing notes.

Exercise

Find the net proceeds:

	FACE VALUE	DATE	TIME	INTEREST RATE %	RATE OF DISCOUNT %	DATE OF DISCOUNT
1.	$ 900	Mar. 12	60 da.	6	6	Mar. 30
2.	1200	Dec. 28	3 mo.	6	6	Feb. 6
3.	2600	July 6	1 mo.	3	6	July 25
4.	750	Nov. 19	90 da.	4	6	Jan. 20
5.	960	Aug. 27	120 da.	2	6	Oct. 14

Answers:

1. $ 902.64
2. 1207.85
3. $2601.29
4. 753.96
5. $954.80

Borrowing Money to Pay a Bill

A firm may buy goods and the discount for cash may be so great that it will be worthwhile borrowing the money to be able to take advantage of the discount. It is important, then, to be able to figure out how much can be gained by borrowing to pay for cash, and, also, whether it is actually worthwhile to do so.

Problem. On April 3, F. B. Clark bought goods for $1500, terms 2/10, n/30. He did not have the money to pay the invoice on April 13, so that he could take advantage of the discount. He therefore borrowed sufficient money to pay the bill on his 20-day interest-bearing note. Did he gain or lose and how much?

$1500	Amount of Invoice
30	Cash Discount 2%
$1470	Net Cost
	Interest on $1470 for 20 days at 6% = $4.90
$30.00	Cash Discount
4.90	Interest
$25.10	Gain by borrowing

Note that he must borrow the amount of the ***net cost.***

Exercise

1. A merchant bought goods for $3640, terms 3/10, n/90. To take advantage of the cash discount, he borrowed the money for 80 days at 6% and paid the bill. How much was gained by borrowing the money?
2. A merchant purchased goods for $1500 less 20% and 10%, terms 2/10, n/30. To take advantage of the cash discount, he borrowed the money for 20 days at 6% and paid the bill. How much was gained by borrowing?
3. The Hudson Co. bought goods for $2480 less 25%, terms 2/10, n/60. To take advantage of the cash discount, they borrowed the money at 6% for 50 days. How much was gained by borrowing?

Answers:

1. $62.12 **2. $18.07** **3. $22.01**

Borrowing Money from Loan Companies

Small-loan companies are permitted by law to lend money, usually up to $300, and charge a stated rate per cent of interest on the unpaid balance. Payments on such loans are generally made in monthly instalments.

Problem. A man borrows $300 from a finance company. The company charges 2% interest per month on the unpaid balance. Payments of $50 are to be made monthly. The loan is for 6 months. Find the total amount of interest paid.

INTEREST PERIOD	UNPAID BALANCE	INTEREST AT 2%	PAYMENT
End of first month....	$300	$6.00	$50
End of second month..	250	5.00	50
End of third month....	200	4.00	50
End of fourth month...	150	3.00	50
End of fifth month....	100	2.00	50
End of sixth month....	50	1.00	50
Total Interest		$21.00	

Note that the interest is computed on the amount due at the end of each month. The unpaid balance at the end of the first month is $300 so the interest at 2% of $300 is $6. At the end of the next month the unpaid balance, reduced by $50, is $250, and the interest is $5, etc.

Problem. A man borrows $200 for 4 months. The interest charges are 2½% on the first $100, 2% on the balance. Find the interest charges.

INTEREST PERIOD	UNPAID BALANCE	INTEREST CHARGES	PAYMENT
End of first month....	$200	$4.50	$50
End of second month..	150	3.50	50
End of third month....	100	2.50	50
End of fourth month..	50	1.25	50
Total Interest		$11.75	

Computation:

2½% of $100 = $2.50; 2% of $100 = $2.00;
Total $4.50
2½% of $100 = $2.50; 2% of $50 = $1.00;
Total $3.50
2½% of $100 = $2.50
2½% of $50 = $1.25

Exercise

1. Gates borrows $240 from a credit union for 5 months. He repays the loan in five monthly installments of $48 each, plus interest charges of ¾% per month on the unpaid balance. Find the interest charges.
2. Brown borrows $150 from a finance company and will repay it in 5 monthly installments of $30 each. The company charges 2½% on the first $100, 2% on the balance. Find the interest charges.
3. Aarons borrows $150 from a finance company and will repay it in 6 monthly installments of $25 each. The company charges 2% on the unpaid balance. Find the interest charges.

Answers:

1. $5.40 **2. $10.90** **3. $10.50**

COMPOUND INTEREST

Compound interest is interest which has been added to the principal, to form a part of the new principal. For example, if Brown deposits $100 in a savings bank and at the end of the year he is credited with 2% interest, his new principal is $102. At the end of the next year, the bank will compute the interest upon $102. If this is done each year, the interest is compounded annually. Banks add interest at stated periods, such as at the end of a month, quarter year, half year, or year, and interest is said to be compounded monthly, quarterly, semi-annually, or annually. Banks use compound-interest tables to compute the compound interest. Below, it will be computed arithmetically. Interest is not computed on cents, but on dollars only.

Problem. On January 2, 1943, Clark deposited $500 in a savings bank. Interest at the rate of 2% per annum was compounded semi-annually. On January 2, 1944, Clark deposited an additional $400. Find how much he had on deposit July 1, 1944.

$500.00	Principal Jan. 2, 1943
5.00	Interest July 1, 1943 (2% per year, 1% for ½ year)
$505.00	Principal July 1, 1943
5.05	Interest Jan. 2, 1944
$510.05	Principal Jan. 2, 1944
400.00	Deposit Jan. 2, 1944
$910.05	Principal Jan. 2, 1944
9.10	Interest July 1, 1944
$919.15	Principal July 1, 1944

Note that interest is computed and added before deposits are added or withdrawals deducted.

Exercise

1. A savings bank pays 2% interest on its deposits and adds the interest on June 1 and December 1 of each year. On June 1, 1944 H. Williams deposits $600. If he makes no deposits or withdrawals, how much will he have on deposit December 1, 1945?
2. A savings bank pays 1½% interest on its deposits and adds the interest on January 2 and July 1 of each year. On January 2, 1943 W. Harris deposits $600. He deposits $400 on July 1, 1943 and withdraws $100 on January 2, 1944. How much will he have on deposit July 1, 1944?

Answers:

1. $618.18 **2. $918.87**

PROFITS AND PRICING

Per Cent of Profit

Businessmen, in order to stay in business, must operate at a profit. To do so, it is imperative that they have certain information on their operations. This information will be considered here.

PER CENT OF PROFIT ON COST

The selling price of goods less the cost of goods is the entire or gross profit. The gross profit less the overhead is the net profit. By overhead is meant the expenses or cost of doing business, such as rent, salaries, supplies, etc. What the businessman wants to know very often is whether he is making a big enough profit in comparison to his cost.

Problem. Goods costing $500 are sold for $800. The overhead is $100. Find *a.* rate of gross profit on cost; *b.* rate of net profit on cost.

$800	Selling Price
500	Cost
$300	Gross Profit
100	Overhead
$200	Net Profit

a. $300/500 = 60\%$, Rate of Gross Profit on Cost
b. $200/500 = 40\%$, Rate of Net Profit on Cost

PER CENT OF PROFIT ON SALES

Many businessmen prefer to base their profit on sales and not on cost. The reasons are that the sales price is known at once whereas the cost must be looked up and because expenses and profits are compared with sales.

Problem. Goods costing $500 are sold for $800. The overhead is $100. Find (*a*) rate of gross profit on sales; (*b*) rate of net profit on sales.

$800	Selling Price
500	Cost
$300	Gross Profit
100	Overhead
$200	Net Profit

a. $300/800 = 37\frac{1}{2}\%$, Rate of Gross Profit on Sales
b. $200/800 = 25\%$, Rate of Net Profit on Sales

Exercise

	SELLING PRICE	COST	GAIN	RATE OF GAIN ON COST	RATE OF GAIN ON SALES
1.	$75	$ 60			
2.	48	32			
3.	25	15			
4.	60	30			
5.	150	100			

Answers:

	GAIN	RATE OF GAIN ON COST %	RATE OF GAIN ON SALES %
1.	$15	25	20
2.	16	50	33⅓
3.	10	66⅔	40
4.	30	100	50
5.	50	50	33⅓

Selling Prices

FINDING THE SELLING PRICE, GIVEN THE COST AND PERCENT OF PROFIT ON COST

Having determined the rate of gain on cost, it will be easy to compute the selling price of similar articles with the same rate of profit or mark-up.

Problem. Goods cost $50. The rate of profit on cost is 20%. Find the sales price.

$50	Cost
10	20% Rate of Profit on Cost 20%
$60	Sales Price

Exercise

Find the sales price.

	COST	RATE OF GROSS PROFIT ON COST %
1.	$120	50
2.	264	16⅔
3.	180	33⅓
4.	290	40
5.	175	100

Answers:
1. $180 2. 308 3. $240 4. 406 5. $350

FINDING THE SELLING PRICE, GIVEN THE COST AND PER CENT OF PROFIT ON SALES

Here the rate of profit is figured on sales and not on cost. The procedure in finding the sales price differs because an indirect method is used.

Problem. A refrigerator is billed to a dealer at $75 less 20% and 10%. At what price should he sell the refrigerator to gain 20% of the sales price?

$75	List Price
15	Trade Discount 20%
$60	Balance
6	Trade Discount 10%
$54	Net Cost

Sales Price	100%	
Profit	20%	
Cost		$54

Sales Price	100%	$67.50
Profit	20%	$13.50
Cost	80%	$54.00

$\$54 \div .8 = \$67.50$ or $\$54 \div 4/5 = \$54 \times 5/4 = \$67.50$, *Answer*

To prove, take 20% of the sales, $67.50. The profit is $13.50. Sales, $67.50, minus Profit, $13.50, equal $54, Cost.

In this type of problem, the unknown is the sales price. This is 100%. The profit on sales is known to be 20% of 100%, or 20%. The cost is known to be $54. Now, subtract 20% from 100% to get the cost: 80%. The cost also equals $54. The problem now is: $54 is 80% of what number? As done in Percentage, Percentage ÷ Rate = Base or 54 ÷ .8.

FINDING THE SELLING PRICE, GIVEN THE COST, THE PER CENT OF PROFIT AND OVERHEAD BASED ON SELLING PRICE

Problem. A refrigerator is billed to a dealer at $75 less 20% and 10%. At what price should he sell the refrigerator to gain 20% on sales, if he gives his salesman a commission of 8% on sales and his overhead is 12% of sales?

\$75	List Price
15	Trade Discount 20%
\$60	Balance
6	Trade Discount 10%
\$54	Net Cost

Sales Price	100%	
Commission 8% Overhead 12% Profit 20%	40%	
Cost		\$54

Sales Price	100%	\$90
Commission 8% Overhead 12% Profit 20%	40%	\$36
Cost	60%	\$54

$\$54 \div .6 = 90$ or
$\$54 \div \frac{3}{5} = 54 \times \frac{5}{3} = \$90$, *Answer*

The procedure followed is as in the previous problem. Everything based on sales is placed in the middle of the diagram, totaled, and subtracted from the sales, 100%. The difference is the cost. The problem is the same as before: the net cost is a certain percentage of what number? Prove as before.

Exercise

1. A merchant bought rugs at \$27 less 25%. At what price must he sell them to make a profit of 16⅔% on sales?
2. A druggist buys face powder at 50¢ per box. The wholesaler offers the druggist a discount of 10% and 5%, if he will buy a carton (36 boxes). The druggist accepts. At what price must he mark each box to make a profit of 33⅓% on cost?
3. A dealer buys radios at \$150 less 20% and 10%. He has an expense of \$6 per radio for delivery and installation. (This is a selling expense and must be added to sales price to get total sales price.)
   a. At what price must he sell each radio to gain 25% on the purchase price?
   b. At what price must he sell each radio to gain 25% on the sales price?
4. A dealer buys fountain pens at \$36 per dozen less 25% and 20%. The overhead is 25% of sales. At what price must he sell each pen to gain 15% on the sales price?
5. In 1944 the Brown Rug Co. determined its sales price by basing the gross profit of 40% on cost. In 1945, the company decided to base the 40% gross profit on sales price.
   a. If a rug cost \$6, what was the sales price in 1944?
   b. If the cost of the rug was \$6 in 1945, what was the sales price in 1945?
   c. By what per cent was the gross profit decreased or increased in 1945 as compared with 1944?
6. A dealer ordered 24 thermometers at \$45 a dozen, less 20%. He found 6 defective items and returned them. The buying expenses on the purchase were \$2.16. (Add buying expenses to find total cost.) If he wished to make a profit of 30% on sales, and if the overhead was 10%, at what price was each thermometer sold?
7. A dealer purchased bicycles at \$32.50 less 20% and 5%, plus a freight charge of 90¢ on each bicycle. If his overhead is 24% of sales, at what price must he sell each bicycle to make a profit of 12% of the sales price?

Answers:

1. \$24.30
2. 57
3. *a.* 141; *b.* 150
4. \$3
5. *a.* 8.40; *b.* 10; *c.* 19 1/21% Increase
6. \$ 5.20
7. 40

FINDING THE LIST OR MARKED PRICE, GIVEN THE SELLING PRICE AND THE TRADE DISCOUNT

Wholesalers who sell their goods subject to a trade discount must be able to compute the list or catalogue price so that they will receive the market price they desire. The procedure is the same as in the preceding problem.

Problem. A radio cost \$150 and it is to be sold at a profit of 33⅓% on cost. At what price should it be listed in the catalogue, if there is a trade discount of 60% to be given?

First Step.—To Find the Sales Price:

\$150	Cost
50	Profit 33⅓% on cost
\$200	Selling Price

Second Step.—To Find the List Price:

List Price	100%	\$500
Trade Discount	60%	\$300
Selling Price	40%	\$200

$\$200 \div .40 = \$500$, List Price or
$\$200 \div \frac{2}{5} = \$200 \times \frac{5}{2} = \$500$, List Price

Problem. A shoe store owner buys shoes at \$7 a pair. He wants to make a profit of 20% on the sales price, after offering a discount of 12½% on the marked or list price. Find the marked price.

First Step.—To Find the Sales Price:

Sales Price	100%	\$8.75
Profit	20%	\$1.75
Cost	80%	\$7.00

$\$7 \div .80 = \$8.75$, Sales Price or
$\$7 \div \frac{4}{5} = \$7 \times \frac{5}{4} = \frac{35}{4} = \$8.75$, Sales Price

Second Step.—To Find the List Price:

List Price	100%	$10.00
Trade Discount	12½%	$1.25
Sales Price	87½%	$8.75

$8.75 ÷ .875 = $10, List Price or
$8.75 ÷ ⅞ = $8.75 × 8/7 = $10, List Price

Exercise

1. A haberdasher buys hats at $40 per dozen less 25% and 20%. He wants to make a profit of 25% on the cost and to offer a trade discount of 16⅔% off the list price. Find the marked or list price.
2. A merchant buys gloves at $18 per dozen pairs. He wants to make a profit of 33⅓% on cost and offer a trade discount of 20% off the list price. Find the list price.
3. A dealer pays $60 less 30%, and 10% for a rug. Selling expenses are 7½% of the selling price. He sells the rug to gain 25% on the sales price, after allowing a trade discount of 20% off the marked price. Find the marked price.
4. It cost a manufacturer $17 to make a rug. At what price should he list the rug in his catalogue to make a profit of 15% on the sales price after allowing a trade discount of 33⅓% on the catalogue price?
5. A merchant buys rugs at $28 less 25%. What is the marked price if he wishes to make a profit of 20% on the selling price after allowing a discount of 40% on the marked price?
6. A merchant buys a desk for $80. He wants to make a profit of 25% on cost. At what price must he mark it to allow a discount of 20% off the marked price?
7. A dealer buys suits at $40 less 10%. He wants to make a profit of 25% on the selling price and allow a special discount of 16⅔% off the marked price. Find the marked price.
8. A merchant buys stoves for $40 less 20% and 10%. He wants to make a profit on 33⅓% on the selling price after allowing a 10% discount on the marked price. Find the marked price.

Answers:

1. $36
2. 30
3. 70
4. $30
5. 43.75
6. 125
7. $57.60
8. 48

Comparison of Profits

Very often a merchant will have a special sale on certain goods. He then wishes to make a comparison between the profit realized on the goods sold at the old price and the profit at the sale price.

Problem. During November a hardware dealer sold 24 coal stoves at $125 each. The net cost of each stove was $87.50. The overhead expense was $17.50 per stove. In December, he ran a special sale and reduced the sales price to $117.50 per stove, and sold 32 stoves. The overhead in December was $17.25 per stove.

a. How much profit did the dealer make in November?
b. How much profit did he make in December?
c. What was the rate of increase or decrease?

This problem may be calculated by two methods: on the basis of one stove or the total number of stoves.

CALCULATION ON 1 STOVE

a. *November*

1 stove @ $125.00 each = $125.00 Sales Price
1 stove @ $ 87.50 each = 87.50 Cost
$ 37.50 Gross Profit
17.50 Overhead
$20.00 Net Profit
24 stoves @ $20.00 profit on ea. = $480, Total Profit *Answer*

b. *December*

1 stove @ $117.50 each = $117.50 Sales Price
1 stove @ $ 87.50 each = 87.50 Cost
$ 30.00 Gross Profit
17.25 Overhead
$ 12.75 Net Profit
32 stoves @ $12.75 profit on ea. = $408, Total Profit *Answer*

c.

$480 Net Profit, November
408 Net Profit, December
$ 72 Decrease in Profit

$ 72 Decrease / $480 Net Profit, November = 72/480 =
15% Rate of Decrease *Answer*

CALCULATION ON TOTAL NUMBER OF STOVES

a. *November*

24 stoves @ $125.00 each = $3000 Sales Price
24 stoves @ $ 87.50 each = 2100 Cost
$ 900 Gross Profit
24 stoves @ $ 17.50 each = 420 Overhead
$ 480 Net Profit, *Answer*

b. *December*

32 stoves @ $117.50 each = $3760 Sales Price
32 stoves @ $ 87.50 each = 2800 Cost
$ 960 Gross Profit
32 stoves @ $ 17.25 each = 552 Overhead
$ 408 Net Profit, *Answer*

c.

$480 Net Profit, November
408 Net Profit, December
$ 72 Decrease in Profit

$ 72 Decrease / $480 Net Profit, November = 72/480 =
15% Decrease, *Answer*

Exercise

1. A merchant bought chairs at $15 each. He sold them at $25 each. During October his sales were 150 chairs. In November, he ran a special sale, reducing the sales price to $20 per chair. The sales increased to 400 chairs.
   a. How much was the profit in October?

b. How much was the profit in November?
c. What was the rate of increase or decrease in the profit?

2. The Home Appliance Co. bought washing machines at $130 less 30% each. During April, 15 machines were sold at $129 each. During May, each machine was sold at $117.50 each. As a result 30 machines were sold.
a. During which month did the company make more profit and how much?
b. What was the rate of increase or decrease in the profit?

Answers:

1. *a.* $1500 2. *a.* $570
b. $2000 *b.* $795
c. 33⅓%, Increase *c.* 39+% or 40%

DISTRIBUTION OF PARTNERSHIP PROFITS

Profits are distributed among partners according to the arrangements set forth in the partnership contract. If no mention is made, the profits or losses are distributed equally.

There are three usual methods of division of profits. They are:

1. According to an agreed-upon ratio.
2. According to partnership investment ratio.
3. Allowing interest on investment, and then dividing the balance equally.

Problem. Vincent, Dugan, and Carver have invested $6000, $8000, and $12,000 respectively in their wholesale business. The first year their profit was $7800.

a. How much will each receive if they agree to divide their profits equally?
b. How much will each receive if they agree to divide their profits in proportion to their investments (capital ratio)?
c. How much will they receive if each partner is allowed 6% on his investment, and then the remaining profit is divided equally?

a. There are three partners.
⅓ of $7800 = $2600, each partner's share

b.

PARTNER	INVESTMENT	SHARE ACCORDING TO CAPITAL RATIO	COMPUTATION OF SHARE	SHARE
Vincent	$ 6000	6000/2600	3/13 of $7800	$1800
Dugan	8000	8000/26000	4/13 of $7800	2400
Carver	12000	12000/26000	6/13 of $7800	3600
Totals	$26000	26000/26000	13/13 of $7800	$7800

c.

PARTNER	INVESTMENT	6% INTEREST ON CAPITAL	⅓ OF REMAINING PROFIT	SHARE
Vincent	$6000	$360	$2080	$2440
Dugan	8000	480	2080	2560
Carver	12000	720	2080	2800
Totals	$26000	$1560	$6240	$7800 Total Profit

$7800 Total Profit
1560 Interest
3) 6240
$2080

Exercise

1. Todd invested $12,000 and Olsen $15,000 in their business. They agreed to allow interest on their investments of 8% and divide the remaining profit equally.
a. How much must the business earn in one year to cover the 8% interest?
b. If the profit at the end of the year was $5380, how much did each receive?
2. Abbot invested $12,000, Johnson $16,000, and Moore his services. Out of the first year's profit of $9675, Abbot and Johnson were allowed 12½% interest on their investments, and Moore $1600 as salary. The remaining profit was divided equally. Find each partner's income for the year.
3. Davis and Lee invested $8000 and $4000 respectively in their business. At the end of the year their sales were $18,525, cost of goods sold was $12,200 and overhead expenses were $1522. If the profit was to be divided according to their capital ratio, find each partner's share of the profit.
4. Young and Harrington invested $6000 and $12,000 respectively in their business. The sales for the year 1944 were $28,440; cost of goods sold, $15,460; overhead, $3200.
a. Find the net profit.
b. The profits are to be shared in capital ratio. Find each partner's share.
c. If each partner is allowed 6% on his investment and the profit which remains is to be shared equally, how much will each partner receive?

Answers:

1. *a.* $2160 3. Davis $3202
b. Todd $2570 Lee $1601
Olsen $2810 4. *a.* $9780
2. Abbot $3025 *b.* Young $3260
Johnson $3525 Harrington $6520
Moore $3125

CORPORATION STOCK

Definitions and Terms

Corporations issue stock as evidence of ownership in the corporation. When a corporation makes a profit, its directors distribute a part or all of this profit among the stock holders. This distribution of profit is called a *dividend.* All undistributed profit is called *surplus.*

The value imprinted on the face of the stock certificate is called its par value. The par value of the stock is usually $100, although stock may be issued at other par values, such as $50 or $25. Some corporations issue stock with no par value. The market price of stock is the price at which the stock is sold in the various stock markets.

In this section we take up some of the problems of computing dividends and buying and selling stock.

Computing Dividends on Stock

Problem. A corporation has a capital stock of $500,000, each share having a par value of $100. It declares a dividend of 9%. If the net profits for the year are $75,000, find the amount of the dividend and how much is left in surplus.

$500,000 ÷ $100 = 5000 shares
9% of $100 = $9, Dividend on 1 share
5000 shares × $9 = $45,000, Dividend declared
$75,000 — $45,000 = $30,000, Amount left in surplus

Problem. A corporation has a capital stock of $400,000, each share having par value of $100. Its net profit for the year is $60,000. The directors declare a dividend of 4%. Find (*a*) the amount of the dividend; (*b*) the amount added to surplus; (*c*) the dividend received by a stockholder who owns 60 shares of stock.

a. $400,000 ÷ 100 = 4000 shares
4% of 100 = $4, dividend on 1 share
$4000 × 4 = $16,000, amount of dividend

b. $60,000 − $16,000 = $44,000 amount added to surplus

c. 60 shares @ $4 per share = $240, dividend received by stockholder

Exercise

(Where no par value is stated, assume it is $100.)

1. A corporation declares a semi-annual dividend of 5%. Find Mr. Jones' dividend if he owns 100 shares.
2. A corporation's capital stock is $600,000. It declares a dividend of 5%. Find the amount of the dividend declared.
3. The Lincoln Radio Co. has capital stock of $500,000. Its profit is $80,000. Its directors declare an annual dividend of 6%.
   a. What does the total annual dividend amount to?
   b. How much will go to surplus?
   c. If Harry Wells has 75 shares, how much dividend will he receive?
4. The Ocean Hardware Corp. has a capital stock of $200,000. It declares semi-annual dividends of 3%.
   a. Find the total annual dividend.
   b. Find how much Max Morse, who owns 50 shares, will receive annually.
5. Anthony Lamb has 50 shares of common stock and 12 shares of 8% preferred stock in a certain corporation. A quarterly dividend of 60¢ per share is paid on the common stock and the regular 8% dividend on the preferred. How much income annually will Mr. Lamb receive from his stock holdings?

Answers:
1. $500
2. $30,000
3. *a.* $30,000
   b. $50,000
   c. $450
4. *a.* $12,000
   b. $300
5. $216

Finding the Rate of Dividend

Problem. A corporation which has a capital stock of $400,000 has a net profit of $80,000 for the year. It decides to keep $20,000 in surplus and distribute the rest of the profits as dividends. Find the annual rate of dividend.

$80,000 Total Profit
20,000 Surplus
$60,000 Dividend declared

60,000 Dividend declared / 400,000 Capital stock = 15%, Rate of dividend, *Answer*

Exercise

1. A corporation with capital stock of $300,000 has a net profit of $50,000. The directors declare a dividend of $30,000. Find the rate of dividend.
2. A corporation is capitalized at $200,000. It makes a profit of $45,000. If $15,000 is set aside for surplus, what will be the rate of dividend?
3. The Borax Corp, is capitalized at $500,000. At the end of the year it will pay $60,000 in dividends.
   a. Find the annual dividend rate.
   b. Find how much a person who has 50 shares will receive in dividends.
4. The Lastelle Corp., with capital stock of $1,000,000, earns $180,000 for the year. The directors declare a dividend of $120,000.
   a. Find the amount left in surplus.
   b. Find the annual rate of dividend on the stock.
   c. Find how much a stockholder who has 100 shares receives.

Answers:
1. 10%
2. 15%
3. *a.* 12%
   b. $600
4. *a.* $60,000
   b. 12%
   c. $1200

Buying and Selling Stock

Stock may be bought and sold at any stock exchange through the medium of a broker who is a member of that exchange. The broker charges a fee, called *brokerage,* for his services. In addition a state and a federal tax must be paid on all stock sold.

Problem. Harry Wilson bought 300 shares of stock at 56½ (i.e., $56.50) and sold it at 65. Brokerage each way was 25¢ a share and the total taxes were 4¢ per share. Find his net profit on the transaction.

SALE

300 shares @ $65 each = $19,500 Sales Price
300 shares @ 25¢ each = $75 brokerage
300 shares @ 4¢ each = $12 tax — 87
$19,413 Net Proceeds

PURCHASE

300 shares @ $56.50 each = $16,950 Cost
300 shares @ 25¢ each = 75 Brokerage
$17,025 Total Cost

$19,413 Net Proceeds of Sale
17,025 Total Cost
$ 2,388 Net Profit

Exercise

1. Stock costing $50 per share was sold for $58 per share. Brokerage each way was 24¢ per share and the taxes on the sale amounted to 4¢ per share. Find the net profit.
2. Warren bought 100 shares of stock at 90 and sold them for 105. Brokerage each way was 24¢ per share and the taxes on the sale were 4½¢ per share. Find the net profit.
3. Harris bought 300 shares of stock at 98½¢ and sold them at 112½. If brokerage is 25¢ per share each way and the taxes on the sale were 4¢ per share, find the amount of the net profit.

Answers:
1. $7.48 2. $1447.50 3. $4038

FINDING PROFIT ON SALE OF STOCK, DIVIDENDS HAVING BEEN RECEIVED

Problem. Morris bought 300 shares of stock at 98 and sold them at 110, after holding them a year. During this time, he received 2 semi-annual dividends of 4%. Brokerage was 25¢ per share each way and taxes on the sale were 4¢. Find his total profit.

SALE

300 shares @ $110 each = $33,000 Sales Price
300 shares @ 25¢ each = $75 brokerage
300 shares @ 4¢ each = $12 tax 87
$32,913 Net Proceeds

PURCHASE

300 shares @ $98 each = $29,400 Cost
300 shares @ 25¢ each = 75 Brokerage
$29,475 Total Cost

$32,913 Net Proceeds of Sale
28,475 Total Cost
$ 3,438 Net Profit on Sale

DIVIDENDS

4% of 100 = $4 per share, dividend for ½ year
300 shares @ $4 = 1200, Dividend for ½ year
1200 × 2 = 2400, Dividend for 1 year

$ 3,438 Net Profit on Sale
2,400 Dividends
$ 5,838 Total Profit, *Answer*

Exercise

1. Harvey bought 50 shares of stock at 32, brokerage 24¢ per share. The stock pays a quarterly dividend of 1%. At the end of a year, he sold the stock at 40, brokerage 25¢ per share, tax 4¢ per share. Find his total profit on the transaction.
2. On February 1, M. King bought 70 shares of stock at 98½, brokerage 22¢ a share. On April 1 and again on October 1, he received a cash dividend of $2.50 a share. On November 1 he sold the stock at 112, brokerage 24¢ a share, tax 4¢ a share. What was King's profit?
3. Mr. Carson bought 10 shares of 7% preferred stock at $140 a share. He received dividends for one year and then sold the stock at $142 per share. Brokerage was 26¢ per share on the purchase, 27¢ per share on the sale, and there was a tax of 10¢ per share on the sale. Find his total gain on the transaction.

Answers:
1. $573.50 2. $1260 3. $83.70

FINDING THE RATE OF RETURN ON INVESTMENT

Problem. A share of stock, par value $100, is bought for $81. A dividend of 9% is declared on the stock. Find the rate of return.

9% of $100 = $9, Dividend on 1 share

$$\frac{\$9 \text{ Dividend}}{\$81 \text{ Cost of Stock}} = \frac{1}{9} = 11\frac{1}{9}\%,$$ Rate of return

Exercise

1. On January 2, 1945 J. Martin invested $3400 in aircraft stock at 42½ (including brokerage). During 1945 he received 4 quarterly dividends of 60¢ each on each share of stock. (To find the number of shares, divide the investment by the cost of 1 share.) Find the rate of return on his investment.
2. An industrial stock, which yields an annual dividend of 3%, sells at $60. A public utility stock is quoted at 90 and yields a dividend of 5%. (No brokerage charges.)
   a. Find the rate of return on each.
   b. Which is the better investment and by how much?
3. H. G. Lee purchases 50 shares of American Telephone & Telegraph at 190, paying a dividend of 9% per year. (Disregard brokerage.) Find the rate of return.

Answers:
1. $5\frac{11}{17}\%$
2. *a.* Industrial 5%, utility $5\frac{5}{9}\%$
   b. Utility by $\frac{5}{9}\%$
3. $4\frac{14}{19}\%$

BONDS

Definitions and Interest

A bond is an indebtedness of a corporation. As a rule, the par value of bonds is $1000, unless otherwise stated. Bonds with a par value of less than $1000 are called baby bonds. Since bonds are evidence of debt, the corporation which issues the bonds pays interest on the bonds, usually semi-annually. The interest is called the *income* or *yield.*

Bonds are bought and sold through brokers on the stock exchanges. The price of bonds is shown in two figures, for example, 98½; however the price actually represents three figures, namely $985. Brokers charge a commission on the purchase and sale of each bond.

Bond problems, as a rule, follow the procedures set forth in the solution of stock problems, with one exception which will be shown below.

Purchase of Bonds with Accrued Interest

Since interest on bonds is usually paid semi-annually, it follows that when bonds are bought on a day which is not a day on which interest is due and payable, the buyer will have to refund to the seller the interest which has accumulated or accrued up to the date of the purchase.

Problem. Find the cost of 10 bonds, par value $1000, bought at 96 on February 1. The interest rate is 6%. Interest is payable on January 1 and July 1. Brokerage, $2.50 per bond.

Accrued interest on $1000 for 31 days from January 1 to February 1 at 6%	$ 5.17
Brokerage	2.50
Price of 1 bond	960.00
Cost of 1 bond	$ 967.67
Cost of 10 bonds—$967.67 × 10	$9676.70, *Answer*

Exercise

1. Find the cost of 4 bonds, par value $1000, bought at 110 on March 28, interest rate 4%, interest due March 1 and September 1, brokerage $2.50 per bond.
2. Find the cost of 20 bonds, par value $1000, bought at 98 on February 18, interest rate 6%, interest due January 1 and July 1, brokerage $2.50 per bond.

Answers:

1. $4422   2. $19,810

Sale of Bonds with Accrued Interest

The procedure in the sale of bonds is the opposite of that in computing the purchase of bonds. The accrued interest is given to the seller because it is his. Therefore, the accrued interest is added on to the selling price and the commission deducted.

Problem. A man sold 10 bonds, par value $1000, for 98 on November 30. Interest on the bonds was at the rate of 6%; the interest was due on April 1 and October 1. Brokerage was $2.50 per bond.

Accrued interest on $1000 at 6% from October 1 to November 30; 60 days	$ 10.00
Price of 1 bond	980.00
Gross Proceeds	$ 990.00
Brokerage, $2.50	2.50
Net Proceeds for 1 bond	$ 987.50
Net Proceeds for 10 bonds—$987.50 × 10	$9875.00, *Answer*

Exercise

1. Find the net proceeds of 5 bonds, par value $1000, sold for 105 on September 19. Interest at the rate of 6% is due on January 1 and July 1. Brokerage $2.50 per bond.
2. Find the net proceeds of 15 bonds, par value $1000, sold for 97½ on October 30. Interest at the rate of 4%, payable on February 1 and August 1. Brokerage is $2.50 per bond.

Answers:

1. $5304.15   2. $14,737.50

FIRE INSURANCE

Computation of Premiums

Insurance is the protection of the insured against any money loss arising from destruction or damage to the insured property.

Problem. Conroy's place of business, valued at $7500, was insured for 60% of its value for one year. The 1-year rate was 15¢ per C (per hundred dollars). Find the amount of the premium.

60% of $7500 = $4500, Value of Policy
$4500 @ 15¢ per C = $6.75, Premium for 1 year

Suppose that in the above problem the insurance company offers Conroy a 3-year rate which is 2½ times the annual rate. Find the premium for the 3 years and the average annual premium on a 3-year policy.

$6.75, Premium for 1 year
$6.75 × 2½ = $16.88, Premium for 3 years
$1688 ÷ 3 = $5.62⅔ or $5.63, Average annual premium

Exercise

1. George Allen owns a building valued at $18,000. He insures it for 80% of its value at $1.65 per $100 for 3 years. He has a stock of goods worth $5250. He insures the stock at its inventory value at $1.20 per $100 for 1 year.
   a. Find the premium on the building.
   b. Find the premium on the stock.
   c. Find the total yearly cost of insurance.
2. Personal property valued at $5000 was insured for 80% of its value at the 3-year rate of $5.00 per M ($1000). Find the average yearly cost of insurance.
3. On January 1 a man received a bill for insurance as follows: car insurance for 1 year, $48.50; fire insurance for $6000 on his home at a 3-year rate of $8 per M, and insurance for $3000 on the contents at the 3-year rate of 50¢ per C.
   a. Find the total cost of the premiums to be paid.
   b. Find the average yearly cost of the insurance.

Answers:

1. *a.* $237.60 *b.* $ 63.00 *c.* $142.20
2. $6.66⅔ or $6.67
3. *a.* $111.50 *b.* $ 69.50

Eighty Per Cent Co-Insurance Clause

Experience has shown that a fire will seldom destroy a piece of property completely. Consequently, many people insure themselves only for a fraction of the value of the property. To encourage people to take greater precautions, the insurance companies have a clause in the policy which states that the insured will not be paid in full for a fire loss, unless he has insured himself for at least 80% of the value of the property. If he has insured himself for less than the stipulated 80%, he becomes a co-insurer with the insurance company and bears part of the loss.

Problem. A factory building valued at $24,000 was insured for $12,800 under an 80% co-insurance clause. A fire caused a loss of $6600. How much did the insurance company pay and how much of the loss did the insured bear?

The formula for determining the loss is:

$$\frac{\text{Policy}}{80\% \text{ of value of property}} \times \text{Loss}$$

Substituting:

$$\frac{\$12{,}800}{80\% \text{ of } \$24{,}000} = \frac{\$12{,}800}{\$19{,}200} = \frac{2}{3} \times \$6600 =$$

$4400 Company pays

$6600 Loss
4400 Company pays
$2200 Loss suffered by insured

Exercise

1. A house valued at $7500 was insured for $5000. The policy contained an 80% co-insurance clause. A fire caused a loss of $4200.
   a. How much did the insurance company pay?
   b. How much loss did the insured suffer?
2. Martin's house is valued at $6000. He insures it for $4800 under a policy containing an 80% co-insurance clause. A fire caused a loss of $3000.
   a. How much did Martin receive under his policy?
   b. How much loss did he suffer?
3. A residence valued at $9000 was insured for $6000 under a policy containing an 80% clause. A fire caused a loss of $3600.
   a. How much did the insurance company pay?
   b. What per cent of the fire loss was borne by the owner?

Answers:

1. *a.* $3500 *b.* $700
2. *a.* $3000 *b.* 0
3. *a.* $3000 *b.* 16⅔%

Reinsurance and Contributing Insurance

If a policy calls for a very large amount, the insurance company may share the risk with other companies by reinsuring the property with other companies. Thus, if a policy of $600,000 is issued, the company will reinsure the property with other companies for, say, $500,000. Thus, by reinsuring the company assumes a risk of only $100,000. Another method of sharing the risk is to have the owner of the property take policies with a number of companies. Then, when a loss occurs, each company will pay a pro-rata share.

Problem. A building is insured for $50,000 as follows: Phoenix Insurance Co., $10,000; Globe Insurance Co., $20,000; World Insurance Co., $20,000. There is a loss of $20,000. How much will each company pay?

COMPANY	POLICY	PRO-RATA SHARE	CALCULATION OF SHARE	SHARE
Phoenix	$10,000	$\frac{\$10{,}000}{50{,}000} = \frac{1}{5}$	⅕ of $20,000	$ 4000
Globe	20,000	$\frac{20{,}000}{50{,}000} = \frac{2}{5}$	⅖ of 20,000	8000
World	20,000	$\frac{20{,}000}{50{,}000} = \frac{2}{5}$	⅖ of 20,000	8000
Total	$50,000	$\frac{\$50{,}000}{50{,}000} = \frac{5}{5}$	⁵⁄₅ of $20,000	$20,000

Note that this problem is solved in the same way as the partnership problem which involved pro-rata share of profits according to capital ratio.

Exercise

1. The Atlas Co. insured its building for $10,000 in three companies as follows: Star Insurance Co., $4500; Western Insurance Co., $3500, and United Insurance Co., $2000. A fire caused a partial loss of $2000. For how much is each company liable?
2. A building was insured in three companies as follows: National Co., $8000; Standard Co., $9000; Mutual Co., $3000. If a loss of $1620 occurred, for how much is each company liable?
3. A factory valued at $20,000 was insured in two companies, each policy having an 80% co-insurance clause. The policy in the Arrow Co. was for $4000 and in the Bow Co. for $10,000. There is a fire loss of $3200. How much must each company pay? (Note: The first step is to find the loss under the 80% clause; then distribute the loss between the two companies.)

Answers:

1. Star $900
   Western $700
   United $400
2. National $648
   Standard $729
   Mutual $243
3. Arrow $800
   Bow $2000

REAL ESTATE

Rent

People who wish to buy real estate are confronted by a number of problems. Among them are:

1. Is it cheaper to rent or to buy?
2. If the house is rented to a tenant, what will be the per cent of return on the investment?
3. If the house is rented to a tenant, how much rent should be charged?

RENTING VS. BUYING

Problem. Henry Clark is paying $35 a month rent for a cottage. He can buy it for $4900 by paying 10% of the purchase price in cash and giving a mortgage bearing 5% interest on the balance. His estimated annual expenses are: taxes $125, water charges $25, repairs $50, and insurance $2. If he can earn 2% interest on his cash investment in the bank, will it be cheaper to rent or to buy?

RENTAL

12 months @ $35 per mo. = $420 Rental per year

PURCHASE

$4900 Cost of House
490 Cash Payment 10%
$4410 Mortgage

Expenses

Interest on mortgage (5% of $4410)	$220.50
Taxes	125.00
Water charges	25.00
Repairs	50.00

Insurance	2.00
Interest on investment (2% of $490)	9.80
Total Expense	$432.30

$432.30 Total Expense
420.00 Rental
$ 12.30 Cheaper to Rent

RATE OF RETURN ON INVESTMENT

Problem. Vinson bought a house for $6700, giving $1200 cash as a down payment and a 5% mortgage for the balance. In addition to the mortgage interest, other annual expenses were: taxes $143, insurance $9, repairs $75, depreciation 2% of cost of house. He rented the house to a tenant for $60 per month. Find the rate of return on his cash investment.

RENTAL TO TENANT

12 months @ $60 per mo. = $720, Rental

ANNUAL EXPENSE

$6700 Cost of House
1200 Cash Payment
$5500 Mortgage

Expenses

Interest on mortgage (5% of $5500)	$275.00
Taxes	143.00
Insurance	9.00
Repairs	75.00
Depreciation (2% of $6700)	134.00
Total Expenses	$636.00

$720 Rental
636 Expenses
$ 84 Net Income

$\frac{84}{1200}$ = 7% Return, *Answer*

Note that the actual cash investment is the down payment of $1200.

HOW MUCH RENT TO CHARGE A TENANT

Problem. Harris owns a house that cost $8500. His yearly taxes are $225, repairs $100, insurance $26, and water bill $20. What monthly rental, to the nearest dollar, must he charge to realize 6% on his investment?

DESIRED INCOME

6% of $8500 = $510 Desired Annual Income

EXPENSES

Taxes	$225
Repairs	100
Insurance	26
Water bill	20
Total expenses	$371

$510 Desired Income
371 Expenses
$881 Annual Rent to be charged

$881 ÷ 12 = $73.41⅔ or $74.00
per month (to the nearest dollar)

Since the expenses must be borne by the tenant, they are added to the desired income to calculate the rental to be paid by the tenant.

Exercise

1. Brown buys a house for $5500, paying $1000 cash and giving a 5% mortgage for the balance. He insures the house for $4500 at the rate 50¢ per C. Taxes amount to $85 and depreciation and repairs are estimated at 3% of the cost. Brown desires a 6% return on his cash investment. What monthly rent, to the nearest dollar, must he charge a tenant?
2. Bernard bought a house for $10,000, paying $3500 cash and giving a 5% mortgage for the balance. Besides the interest on the mortgage, his annual expenses were: Taxes $300, water $80, oil $250, insurance $110, depreciation $490. He rented the house to a tenant for $150 per month. Find the rate of return on his cash investment.
3. Altman is paying $4800 a year rent for the first floor of a building. He can buy the building for $60,000. He would then receive $3000 yearly in rent from the other two floors. His annual expenses would amount to: taxes $950, insurance $240, repairs and janitor service $1700. If money is worth 6% to him in his business (6% of $60,000 would be lost and therefore is considered an expense), how much would he gain or lose by buying the building?

Answers:
1. $47 2. 7% 3. $1310 saved

Real Estate Taxes

FINDING THE TAX RATE

A government, to maintain itself, must impose taxes. Chief among taxes are those imposed on real estate. To levy the tax equitably and fairly, a value is given each piece of real estate. This value is called the *assessed value* and the tax is levied on the *assessed valuation.* To find out the tax rate the rule to follow is:

$$\frac{\text{Money Needed or Expenses}}{\text{Assessed Valuation}} = \text{Tax Rate}$$

The tax rate may be expressed as a per cent, or mills per dollar (a mill is .001 cent) or dollars per C ($100) or M ($1000).

Problem. Property in the city of Newcastle is assessed at $9,850,000. The expenses for the year are estimated to be: street improvements, $18,600; salaries, $46,300; schools, $102,500; sewers, $7250; buildings, $13,750; interest on bonded debt, $1300. It is estimated that $1500 will be received from special licenses and $5000 from the state as aid for schools.

a. Find the tax rate correct to the nearest hundred thousandth (5 places).
b. Express this rate per $1000.

a. MONEY NEEDED OR EXPENSES

$ 18,600	Street improvements
46,300	Salaries
102,500	Schools
7,250	Sewers
13,750	Buildings
1,300	Interest on debt
$189,700	Total expense
6,500	Total income
$183,200	Net expense to be raised by taxes

INCOME

$1500 Special licenses
5000 State school aid
$6500 Total income

$189,700 Total expense
6,500 Total income
$183,200 Net expense to be raised by taxes

$\frac{\$183{,}200}{\$9{,}850{,}000} = \$.01859$ per dollar, *Answer*

b. $\$.01859 \times 1000 = \$18.59$ per M ($1000), *Answer*

FINDING THE TAX RATE

When an owner of real estate knows his assessed valuation and the tax rate, he can find how much tax he must pay by multiplying the assessed valuation by the tax rate.

Problem. In the above problem, how much will Jones pay if his house, worth $10,000, is assessed at 80% of its value?

80% of $10,000 = $8000, Assessed valuation
$8000 × .01859 (tax rate) or
$8000 × 18.59 per M ($1000) = $148.72 Tax

Exercise

1. Taxable property in a certain town is assessed at $4,540,000. It is estimated that $2500 will be received from special licenses and $75,300 in state aid for schools. The estimated yearly expenses are: wages, $55,000; schools, $52,800; buildings, $20,000; improvements, $8000; interest on bonds, $12,000.
   a. Find the tax rate (correct to 5 places) to yield income to pay the budget (expenses).
   b. Express this rate as a tax per M ($1000).
   c. Mr. Johnson's property is valued at $7500 and is assessed at 80% of its value. How much tax will Mr. Johnson pay?
2. The assessed valuation of taxable property in a school district is $9,450,000. The gross cost of operating the schools is $300,669.21. Income from state aid and non-resident tuition fees is $126,623.97.
   a. Find the tax rate (carry the decimal to five places).
   b. Express this rate as a tax rate per M ($1000).
   c. John Sperry's house is valued at $12,000 and assessed for 75% of its value. Find the amount of Mr. Sperry's school tax.
3. In a certain city, the assessed valuation of taxable property is $63,143,000. The city's total budget to meet expenses is $1,896,190. Receipts from other sources will amount to $736,240.
   a. Find the tax rate (carry the decimal to five places).
   b. Express the rate as a tax rate per M ($1000).
   c. H. Groves' property, valued at $16,000, is assessed at 75% of its value. Find the amount of his tax.

Answers:

1. *a.* .01541	2. *a.* .01841	3. *a.* .01837
b. $15.41	*b.* $18.41	*b.* $18.37
c. $92.46	*c.* $165.69	*c.* $220.44

YOU AND THE LAW

I – What Is "The Law"?

What is the law? It represents many things to many people. To a consumer seeking compensation for a faulty product, it stands for one thing. To a corporation executive seeking patent protection for a new product, it promises something else. To the person arrested on criminal charges, it may have yet another meaning. For the lawyer representing each of these individuals, the law has still different meanings.

The law, in short, is complex, and has many facets. The phrase, "the law," simply offers a convenient way to deal with that complexity.

The law even represents something different from laws. As a concept and a reality, the law refers to the great heritage on which the rights, benefits, and privileges of Americans are based. The laws are the specific statutes and provisions that guarantee these rights and privileges.

The different facets of the law have their own characteristics. Each facet has its own origins in history, deals with certain kinds of cases or situations, and has meaning in certain kinds of courts. And, in fact, not all cases even go to a courtroom. This suggests that the law is a flexible tool.

The law's flexibility points to another quality: continuous change and growth. New laws appear all the time; old laws disappear. The new laws help citizens to deal with new needs and problems as they arise. Supreme Court decisions provide one example of how the law grows. But the decisions of other courts, bills or pieces of legislation, and many other legal developments forward the process of growth.

No matter how much the law grows and changes, it has a definite, unchanging meaning: the law stands as a set of rules or principles of conduct designed for the common good. The law specifies what behavior is desired and not desired in specific situations. It frequently spells out what remedies to apply when undesirable behavior is encountered.

Law has been described as a set of do's and don'ts. But such rules and regulations do not exist for their own sake. They are not intended to place obstacles in the way of freedom or the pursuit of happiness. Rather, they are designed to remove or at least smooth out obstacles: to make freedom a reality. The obstacles arise inevitably when people live together in a society. Some of the more obvious of these obstacles are crimes and disputes between people.

The law tries to walk the fine line between the rights of one person to act and of another person to enjoy protection. In the words of the adage, "My right to swing my fist ends where your nose begins."

Laws are thus designed to serve and protect in two ways. First, they are designed to protect the individual's interests so long as no one else is harmed. Second, the laws are designed to protect society as a whole. Society, in turn, is protected in three ways:

1. Order is maintained and progress is ensured.
2. Society is protected from harmful acts by individuals.
3. The general welfare and justice are advanced.

Laws function in accordance with at least two principles. The first centers on fairness: if a wrong has been committed, the remedy prescribed should make amends for that wrong as much as is humanly possible. The second has universal application: all individuals, without exception, are to be treated alike under the law.

Far from being just a set of do's and don'ts, the law represents a practical instrument for individual use. A citizen of the United States of America has obligations and duties; but he also has rights under the Constitution. U.S. law is vitally concerned with preserving Constitutional rights.

THE ORIGINS OF MODERN LAW

Every society has some kind of law. In any social group the law survives because people accept and believe in it. Even the most ancient and primitive of societies have been lawful societies.

The American system of law has carried forward and refined this legal approach to solving problems. Modern man's heritage of law can be traced back to ancient civilizations.

Ancient Developments

Among ancient legal developments, several have significance today. For example, the Code of Hammurabi appeared in 1900 B.C. Basically a set of criminal laws, the Code prescribed a punishment for each crime. The Ten Commandments of Moses, dating from about 1200 B.C., provide the basis for many modern laws. Here a moral element appears: rather than stress punishment and the fear of punishment, the Commandments proceed from a conviction that certain acts are wrong.

The moral precepts of the Ten Commandments have been accepted down to the present day. Laws, it is assumed, have a moral basis. Citizens may resist or rebel against a law if they feel that it is wrong, morally or otherwise.

The Greeks developed the philosophy that a country should be ruled by laws rather than by men. The American government functions according to that belief. Typically, Greek laws dealt with property and commerce, particularly contracts. They also held trials before citizens—what are now known as jury trials.

Roman Law incorporated Greek Law in a complete set of moral precepts published in 450 B.C. The Roman Emperor Justinian I, a thousand years later, published the *Corpus Juris Civilis* ("Body of Civil Law"). Roman law became the basis for canon law in the Roman Catholic Church. Napoleon carried this tradition forward in the Napoleonic Code. Louisiana, once a French possession, still uses that code as the basis of its civil law.

The civil-law tradition exemplified by the Napoleonic Code had its counterpart in areas that were historically under Spanish control. The Spanish *fuero juzgo*, or legal court, stood as a code of laws for those areas. The *fuero juzgo* was replaced by U.S. law as the Spanish possessions came under American control.

English Common Law and the Constitution

The American legal system owes much of its character to the English Common Law. Most of the earlier developments involved establishing codes of conduct. The Common Law offered a method of establishing new laws in the courtroom. The judge, or the jury, reaches decisions on the basis of previous decisions—precedents—in similar cases.

The name Common Law comes from the fact that this form of law was commonly practiced throughout England.

Common law developed when a group of king's judges began to "ride the circuit" to hear cases. When the judges could not find any known principle to apply in a given case, they created a new one. Staying at inns, these judges would share experiences and opinions with one another. Summaries of many proceedings were written into legal *Year Books.*

Sir Edward Coke (1552-1634) analyzed many of these cases and developed a set of rules or standards. Sir William Blackstone (1723-1780) carried these analyses further. His *Commentaries* formed the basis for legal training in England through the nineteenth century. Americans have carried on this tradition of commentaries. Thus, both court decisions and commentaries on them form central parts of the common law.

Growing out of the English traditions, the U.S. Bill of Rights —the first ten amendments to the Constitution—embodies ideas expressed long before Thomas Jefferson put them down in organized form. The principles to which Jefferson referred reached all the way back to ancient Greece.

Many other thinkers contributed ideas that helped form Jefferson's thinking—and thus our Bill of Rights. One was England's John Locke. Discussing human nature and natural law, Locke wrote:

> The State of Nature has a law of nature to govern it, which obliges everyone; and reason, which is that law, teaches all mankind, who will but consult it, that all begin equal and independent, no one aught harm another in his life, health, liberty or possession.

In discussing American law today, we are actually talking about two kinds of law: case law and statutory law. Case law utilizes the precedents reached by courts in similar situations. Statutory law functions on the basis of written laws, or acts of federal, state, or local legislative bodies.

THE PURPOSES OF LAWS

The law today comprises a thorough, comprehensive body of precepts and regulations. Laws deal with every aspect of a person's life. Some ways in which the individual is affected by the law include:

Marriage and rights of the marriage partners
Relations between parent and child
Buying a house
Household loans
Wills and the disposal of property
The rights of employers and employees
Injuries to one's body, property, or reputation
Civil rights
Protection against crime
Rights if arrested

The law operates in these and other areas to achieve four different goals:

1. It serves to prevent and settle disputes.
2. It enforces standards of social conduct.
3. It establishes relations between the government and the society.
4. It distributes various kinds of resources within the society.

Preventing and Settling Disputes

Preventing and settling disputes, or conflict resolution, provides a rationale for civil lawsuits between individuals. Examples of such disputes include divorce proceedings and conflicting claims over property. In many disputes, the "case" may never come to court. Both attorneys may agree that one of the parties is entitled to all or part of his claim. For example, one party may be rewarded with ownership of a property ("have title") while the other can use it under the "easement" principle.

If the lawyers disagree, the case may go to court. "Going to court" represents an effort to obtain an impartial decision, or judgment. One or both parties may later appeal the verdict of the judge or jury. The party receiving a negative verdict may *appeal* to a higher court. The legal pathway for handling a dispute is clearly marked.

Social Conduct

The law serves also as a way to enforce standards of acceptable social conduct. Society has both informal and formal means of enforcing standards of behavior. In primitive societies, informal means such as social pressure and opinion were used for the most part. Law, the formal means, became more important as society became more complex. Today's society, especially, could not live without the law.

This use of the law applies in many areas. For example, the control of crime requires enforcement of standards of acceptable behavior. The handling of disputes involves similar enforcement of rules.

Government and Society

The U.S. Constitution is concerned with establishing overarching relations between the government and society. "Society" here means individuals as well as the group. The fifth and fourteenth amendments to the Constitution established the right of the individual to "due process." This means that the government can only take legal actions toward individuals.

Two kinds of due process have been identified. The first is procedural, meaning that the methods the government uses to deal with its citizens must be acceptable. The second is concerned with the content of the laws passed by government. In the 1930s, for example, the Supreme Court rejected many New Deal laws passed by the Roosevelt administration.

Distribution of Resources

Finally, the law helps to determine how society's resources are distributed among its members. One way in which this is done is by regulating the actions of citizens. Such regulation, in turn, may be effected through control of the criminally greedy. Regulation also takes place through supervision of contractual relations. In both cases, standards of acceptable conduct are being enforced.

Another way of effecting the distribution of resources is through taxation. Here, the government (1) takes a portion of a citizen's money or (2) finds ways to spend it. People may be taxed either directly or indirectly. In the latter case, as with sales taxes, the tax is first paid to a merchant. Sometimes members of society see the ways in which resources are distributed as unfair or unjust. Individuals or groups may try to influence the government to use some of its tax money to remedy that injustice.

These four uses of the law overlap. For example, enforcing standards of conduct affects both the settlement of disputes and the relations between government and society. Poor allocation of resources can lead to social disorder and enforcement of standards. Such enforcement can prevent disputes, which maintains social order. Resolving conflicts can smooth out relations between individuals and the government.

THE TYPES OF LAW

"The law," as noted, is not a unitary thing. Laws exist at federal, state, and local levels. These, in turn, can be classified according to whether they deal with civil or criminal matters. Finally, the law may be considered with respect to its origins: whether a law was passed by a legislative body or shaped in the courtroom because of a judge's decision. Of special importance is whether a law is civil or criminal, and how it originated.

Civil and Criminal Law

Civil and criminal law differ according to the identity of the "injured" party. In civil law the injured party is another individual. In criminal law the injured party is considered to be society. Civil law may involve either common law or statutory law while criminal law usually involves only statutory law. Criminal statutes define the offenses that are considered grave enough to be regarded as crimes against society.

Civil law typically involves a plaintiff and his lawyer, and a defendant and his lawyer. Civil suits may involve any of the following:

Auto accidents
Injuries at home
Injuries on the job
Injuries to one's reputation

In a criminal trial the defendant and his lawyer face a prosecuting attorney and his "client"—the state or federal government. Federal and state statutes describe the specific crimes and the permissible punishments for each. Violations of city ordinances are not classified as crimes, but can bring fines.

Some states have more than 200 crimes on their books. The most typical crimes are:

Murder, both first and second degree
Voluntary manslaughter
Criminal negligence
Larceny
Embezzlement
Rape
Robbery
Receiving stolen goods
Forgery
Burglary
Arson
Perjury
Kidnapping
Accessory after fact
Assault

Statutory and Common Law

In each state, legislatures pass laws, acts, or statutes from time to time. Cities, counties, townships, and other local municipal units have legislative bodies that pass ordinances. Nationally, the Congress passes laws which, as in the states, are called statutes.

Governments at all three levels have administrative agencies that make rules, regulations, and resolutions. These may have the force of law, and therefore are sometimes referred to as "administrative law." In each case, however, the agency's rulings have the backing or authorization of a specific statute or ordinance. Without that specific law, the ruling would be invalid. Thus, administrative law is often viewed as a branch of statutory law.

Administrative agencies control a wide variety of areas of public life. These include public utilities, insurance, banking, motor vehicles, taxation, and the regulation and licensing of professions and occupations.

The common law is centered in the systems of courts. Every state has its own system of courts. At the top is a State Supreme Court or a Court of Appeals. Lesser courts include Criminal Courts, Civil Courts, Alderman's Courts, Justice of the Peace Courts, Mayor's Courts, and City Courts. Each court has the duty of interpreting the law and enforcing it. They do this by imposing fines and penalties in criminal cases, or by awarding damages in civil cases.

Because courts rely on decisions made in previous cases involving similar conditions, an attorney can use his research into previous cases to advise his client of the present status of the law in a particular case.

Court Systems

The federal court system is headed by the Supreme Court of the United States. Lesser courts include the Circuit Courts of Appeal, U.S. District Courts, Tax Court, and the Court of Claims. Federal law, including statutory, administrative, and common, together with comparable kinds of law at state and local levels, comprises the sum total of what is called "the law."

Clearly, "the law" cannot be a simple thing. The average citizen may hesitate even to try to understand the total U.S. legal picture. But examination a little at a time can be helpful. For those concerned with civil matters, criminal law does not apply. If one is concerned with a federal matter, state and local matters have no immediate importance. If a case involves only statutory law, precedents may be of little concern.

Federal and State Courts

Two separate systems of courts, the state and federal systems, function side by side. State courts are established by state constitutions and state legislatures. Federal courts are established by the United States Constitution and the Congress. Both the state and federal systems have different levels of courts. These levels are classified according to their geographic jurisdiction and by the kinds of cases they try.

Federal Court System

The federal court system has three principal levels: (1) District Courts, (2) the Circuit Courts of Appeal, and (3) the United States Supreme Court.

The District Courts are known as the trial courts of the federal system. Every state in the nation is served by at least one District Court. Both Maine and Ohio have two District Courts each.

District Courts hear cases involving federal laws, the U.S. Constitution, and problems between citizens of different states. All kinds of criminal cases are tried, including felonies and misdemeanors occurring under federal statutes. Civil suits include:

- Matters governed by federal law, such as bankruptcies, patent and copyright cases, and admiralty cases, which involve laws of the seas and navigable waterways
- Suits involving the Constitution or federal statutes such as civil rights
- Suits to which the federal government is a party
- Suits by one state against another

- Trials involving citizens of different states and sums greater than $10,000

In the last instance, the kind of law used may vary with the case. For example, if a car accident occurred in Ohio between a resident of Ohio and a resident of Kentucky, Ohio law would be used. The reason for this is that the federal system has no common law of its own. It has only statutory laws and these do not cover accidents.

Each Circuit Court of Appeals covers one of the eleven "circuits" into which the country is divided. Such a court hears cases which have moved upward through the court system from a District Court within its circuit.

The Supreme Court is the highest U.S. court. The Supreme Court hears appeals of important cases from Circuit Courts. In addition, it may consent to hear appeals to decisions made in state Supreme Courts.

State Court Systems

State court systems vary from state to state. In Ohio, as one typical example, the court system functions on three levels: the Ohio Supreme Court, Ohio Court of Appeals, and Ohio trial courts. The last group includes Common Pleas Courts, Municipal and County Courts, Mayor's Courts, and the Court of Claims.

Another state, Maine, has five distinct levels of courts. The Maine District Courts try traffic cases, civil cases involving less than $20,000, some adult criminal cases, and cases involving juvenile crimes. Small Claims Courts involve private disputes involving debt or damage of less than $800. Superior Courts try all state criminal and civil cases, and hear appeals of cases from District Courts and administrative agencies.

Maine has two other special courts. The Supreme Judicial Court of Maine, called the Law Court, hears appeals from Superior Courts. The Probate Court oversees the administration of estates of deceased persons.

THE ADVERSARY PROCEDURE

A court trial, in whatever court, is based on the "adversary procedure." The case may be either civil or criminal; the two "sides" contend. Each side tries to persuade a judge or jury that it is right.

In this contest the judge acts as a referee, or authority, on questions of law. The jury decides on questions of fact. A trial proceeds according to well-defined steps:

1. Selection of a jury, where there is one
2. Opening statements by the attorneys
3. Presentation of witnesses and evidence, with the plaintiff or prosecutor appearing first
4. Closing arguments by the attorneys
5. Instructions by the judge to the jury
6. Deliberation and jury decision

Parties to civil suits and defendants in criminal cases are entitled to a jury trial. A trial jury is called a petit (or petty) jury; a grand jury in Criminal Cases decides in advance whether a trial should be held on the basis of available evidence.

A party to a trial is not always entitled to a jury. Even where one is so entitled, it may not be provided unless it is demanded. Jury trials are not allowed in cases involving minor offenses calling for penalties up to $100. Felonies and major misdemeanors usually call for trials by jury. In felony cases, twelve jurors are normally used; in misdemeanor cases, eight.

RIGHTS

Under the United States Constitution, each American has certain guaranteed rights. Briefly, these rights include:

freedom of speech and freedom of the press,
freedom of assembly,
freedom of religion,
the right to vote,
the right to hold public office,
the right to keep and bear arms,
protection of individual privacy,
full enjoyment of one's property,
equal protection under the laws,
privilege against self-incrimination,
due process of law,
the right of habeas corpus,
protection against "double jeopardy" (two trials for one offense), and
the right to a jury trial.

The first ten amendments to the Constitution make up the Bill of Rights. Other amendments have a bearing on rights, however. The Fourteenth Amendment, dealing with due process, incorporates many of the features of the first ten amendments.

The Constitution grows and changes constantly. The written document itself undergoes additions; but interpretations are made repeatedly by the Supreme Court. The Fourteenth Amendment, as indicated, has been selectively absorbing the Bill of Rights over a matter of years. Essentially, it guarantees that many of the rights provided at the federal level have also to be protected at the state level.

The law has been developed to be used. Why not make it work for you?

II – Lawyers and the Law

As society becomes more complex, so does the law. As laws become more numerous, the need for lawyers grows. One can often conduct one's personal affairs without a lawyer. But it is important to know when a lawyer is needed and when one is not. Then more effective use can be made of lawyers. This chapter tells how and when to find and use a lawyer—and when not to. The nature of the legal profession is explained. Alternatives to the use of lawyers are noted, and the question of lawyers' fees receives attention. Finally, the reader learns what to do if he or she is dissatisfied with a lawyer's work.

WHAT IS A LAWYER?

In a single sentence, a lawyer is an officer of the court who is authorized to explain the law to clients and to represent them in and out of court. As an officer of the court, the lawyer swears that he will uphold the law and conduct himself according to appropriate court procedures. The court may discipline a lawyer who fails in either role.

A lawyer has expert knowledge within the field of law. Sometimes he has specialized knowledge within the many subfields of law. A nonlawyer may know some aspects of the law, and may even be able to help himself in some instances, as this book will show. But the lawyer's expert knowledge may prove to be indispensable. Because of the very complexity of the law, his intelligent guidance of his client may make the difference between great or little expense and inconvenience.

Regardless of where a lawyer represents his client—in court or out—or what kind of advice is given, the purpose is to help the client (1) safeguard his legal rights and (2) fulfill his legal obligations. A lawyer has primary loyalty, thus, to his client. However, as he is sworn to uphold the court and the law, he will never counsel a client to break the law.

There are many different kinds of lawyers. *Family lawyers* are the "general practitioners" who help with leases, wills, estate planning, contracts, real estate transactions, and divorce. Family lawyers try to practice *preventive law*, keeping clients out of court if possible. *Trial lawyers* possess special skills in courtroom procedures and the presentation of evidence. *Corporate lawyers* are salaried employees of corporations who often specialize in legal subfields important to their employers. These subfields include labor law, patents, consumer protection, and many others. The corporate lawyer may or may not become involved in court cases.

Among the many specialties in law, the most common in addition to those named are:

Negligence
Tax law
Banking and business law
Wills, estate planning, and probate
Real estate
Criminal law
Domestic relations

What Lawyers Do

Lawyers perform in many different roles to help their clients. The lawyer's principal tasks are preparing documents and agreements, negotiating out-of-court settlements of disputes, and representing clients in court and before government agencies. Lawyers have to develop various skills, including:

- *Reading.* Lawyers must read constantly to keep informed. This is essential not only for a general knowledge of the law, but to prepare a client's case.
- *Writing.* A lawyer's writing must be clear, comprehensive, and persuasive.
- *Creative thinking.* Lawyers must be able to adapt their knowledge of the law to the particular client's needs. This may mean applying old precedents or trying to shape new ones.
- *Speaking.* This vital skill comes into use when lawyers represent clients in court or before agencies, boards, councils, commissions, and other governmental bodies.
- *Counseling.* Clients receive legal advice that can prevent legal problems and disputes.
- *Dealing with disputes.* Lawyers must anticipate legal arguments once disputes have developed.
- *Negotiation.* Lawyers try to settle legal disputes with an eye to preventing court appearances (litigation).
- *Serving the public.* Many lawyers try to improve the profession and engage in civic activities.

Their Training and Qualifications

Lawyers must meet certain requirements before they are permitted to practice law. Most or all of the following are required, with some variations among states:

- Four years of college.
- Three years in an accredited law school.
- Specialization in a particular area of law (optional). In a state such as California, before lawyers can advertise themselves as specialists in specific areas, they must be certified by the state.
- Clerkship or internship in a law office. While sometimes optional, this phase of training is usually required.
- Passing a state bar examination, a rigorous test of all areas of legal knowledge, administered and graded by personnel appointed by the state Supreme Court.
- Membership in some bar association, usually the state bar association. Memberships may also include the American Bar Association, the county bar association for smaller communities, or the local bar association for larger cities. Membership is not essential to the practice of law.
- Evidence of good character, whether vouchers of character from associates or affidavits of character from practicing lawyers or both.
- Waiver of the above requirements in some states, including Kansas, if a lawyer has been practicing in another state for over five years.
- A license to practice, upon completing all other requirements, issued by the state Supreme Court.

Discipline and Ethics

Standards of conduct for lawyers are determined both ethically and legally. Standards seek to ensure prompt, adequate, and lawful assistance to clients. Key guidelines for the lawyer-client relationship appear below.

Various codes set standards for lawyers. The Supreme

Court has adopted a Code of Professional Responsibility. The American Bar Association has its Canons of Professional Ethics that govern the behavior of members. In addition, individual state Supreme Courts and legislatures may have their own codes of conduct.

Bar associations work primarily in the public interest, not in the interest of individual lawyers. Offering voluntary memberships, such organizations also try to ensure high standards of ethics among lawyers and to improve the administration of justice. Most bar associations have a committee on *legal ethics* and *professional conduct*. Such a committee can recommend to a state Supreme Court the suspension, disbarment, or reprimand of a lawyer who has violated any standards or who has committed an act of moral turpitude.

Services provided by bar associations may include any of the following:

- Lawyer referral service or lawyer directory
- Continuing legal education
- Fee dispute arbitration
- Legal Aid
- Tel-Law, "Call for Action," and other free information and counseling services for the public

The American Bar Association began in 1980 to develop Model Rules of Professional Conduct. The Rules may be a definitive statement of lawyers' responsibilities. The preamble to the Rules spells out the lawyers' responsibilities, including statements that the lawyer:

- is an officer of the legal system, a representative of clients, and a public citizen with special responsibility for the quality of justice;
- should conform to the law both as a lawyer and as a private citizen;
- should serve the client's interests, but dissuade the client from wrongful acts against others;
- should be honest with any tribunal and respectful of the interests of other parties while asserting his client's position;
- should safeguard the client's interest when negotiating while showing fairness to others;
- may serve as intermediary between clients;
- is responsible to third parties where they exist;
- should act competently, promptly, and diligently;
- should seek improvement of the law and the administration of justice;
- is ethically bound to perform at his highest level of competence, to try to improve the law and his profession, and to try to meet the profession's ideals of public service; and
- should exercise his professional and moral judgment in resolving conflicts in his responsibilities where the Rules of Professional Conduct do not provide guidelines for such resolution.

The lawyer's obligations to the client are discussed more fully in a section below.

USING A LAWYER

How and when do lawyers become necessary? This section discusses why and when a lawyer is needed and how the citizen can utilize his or her services. The decision to use a lawyer is an individual matter, but some general considerations can help in making that decision.

Why a Lawyer May Be Needed

The individual may decide to hire a lawyer for at least three reasons. The law's complexity may require it, or the services of lawyers as officers of the court may be needed. Very importantly, lawyers can prevent bigger legal problems.

The law's complexity may present too great a problem for the average citizen. Various laws may be relevant to a particular case. Moreover, as was noted in Chapter 1, the law has different sources—the Constitution, statutory law, common law, administrative law, and so on—and each kind has its own scope and effect. Certain kinds of cases may be relatively easy for a layman to handle without a lawyer—for example, small claims cases. In many situations, however, the "amateur lawyer" would be in over his head. An old adage holds that "the person who is his own lawyer has a fool for a client."

As officers of the court, lawyers understand the procedures and protocols of the courtroom. Not all cases need to go to court. When one does, however, the layman without a lawyer may needlessly delay proceedings. An "amateur lawyer" is also prohibited from representing persons in court; only an officer of the court may do that. Similarly, only a licensed lawyer can give "legal advice." So long as a person receives advice and representation from a lawyer, he has the court's protection because the lawyer remains accountable to the court. The court may protect the individual against his or her own lawyer!

Finally, lawyers serve both to prevent and to cure problems. What kinds of problems require the aid of a lawyer? Anyone faced with the following kinds of situations should absolutely hire a lawyer:

Being arrested for a crime
Facing a lawsuit
Wanting to sue someone else
Seeking a divorce
Filing for bankruptcy

Practicing preventive law can save time, trouble, and money. The ways in which early consultation with a lawyer can help include these:

- Preventing some legal problems entirely, for instance by signing an important paper
- Consuming less time on a case by consulting a lawyer beforehand
- Making information and evidence (including witnesses) more readily available when prompt action needs to be taken
- Avoiding complications by advising a client what or what not to do, say, or sign
- Having a legal matter taken care of before a "statute of limitations" blocks action
- Settling a dispute in negotiation phase, rather than letting it mushroom into a typically more expensive court case

When a Lawyer Is Needed

At many other times in a person's life he or she should at least consider seeing a lawyer. These include:

Buying a house
Selling a house
Getting an opinion on a real estate title
Making or terminating a lease
Dealing with troubles with a landlord
Choosing the right insurance

A change in legal status, such as marriage or coming of age
Adoption
Retirement planning
Preparing and revising wills and estates
Deaths
Administering estates
Calculating taxes and dealing with tax disputes
Organizing, buying, selling, or dissolving a business
Employer-employee relations
Consumer problems
Business transactions, such as collecting debts
Money problems
A significant change in financial status
Accidents, when there is damage to property or person
Taking out copyrights and patents
Signing a contract or making a verbal agreement
When arrested for a crime
Dealing with a governmental agency on an important matter
When one's rights are threatened
When one is not certain of the need for a lawyer

Lawyers cannot, of course, solve every problem. Some problems are so minor that additional legal expenses would not be warranted—for example, in a dispute with a merchant involving less than $50. The best time to see a lawyer is in a preventive situation. Often, the individual can minimize problems by engaging a lawyer in advance. Still other legal problems can be handled by alternative means. Some disputes can be removed from the jurisdiction of the legal system, for example, and "kept out of court."

What a Lawyer Can and Cannot Do

Examination of the extent of a lawyer's powers and capabilities may influence a final decision on hiring a lawyer. Such examination may also encourage more realistic expectations about the lawyer's future performance. But sometimes, clearly, only an initial consultation can provide an individual with information on whether to proceed further with a lawyer. Among the things that a lawyer can do are:

Confer with the client to pinpoint the problem
Gather and analyze all available facts and information
Interview those involved in the case
Study applicable laws and previous court decisions
Prepare legal arguments for presentation in court
Negotiate a settlement if both sides are agreeable
Present a client's arguments before the court
Appeal the decision of a court

Within that general framework, it is important to keep in mind the things a lawyer cannot do:

- Contact a client about a new case or new legal matter before the client has requested advice. Exceptions to this rule include cases in which a lawyer is specifically hired to handle all of a person's legal affairs at all times, and where a lawyer is a close relative or friend. If a lawyer who is a stranger approaches a person, that lawyer should be reported to the local bar association.
- Take action, for a client, that conflicts with a lawyer's duty to the court. A lawyer cannot introduce misleading or false evidence or assist a client in spiteful, malicious, stubborn, or obstructive actions. Nor can a lawyer represent a client where a conflict of interest exists between lawyer and client.
- Guarantee the outcome or result of a lawsuit.
- Speed up the time required by law for processing a lawsuit. A lawyer should, upon request, inform his client as to the time allotted by the court for each phase of the proceedings.

Thus, a lawyer can often achieve for a person what the person unaided could not achieve. At the same time, the lawyer is not all-powerful, since he must abide by his obligations to the court. He also has obligations to his client.

The Lawyer's Obligations to the Client

In order to do his job effectively and to ensure client satisfaction, a lawyer has certain obligations to the client. A client has a right to expect that all of the following obligations will be fulfilled:

- To keep the client's personal legal matters confidential. The lawyer can reveal only those facts that must become public knowledge when he pleads his client's case and offers evidence and testimony.
- To account promptly and completely to the client for money and other things of value that the client has entrusted to him. A lawyer cannot mix a client's funds into his own personal account. If a client asks for a return of valuables or funds, they must be returned promptly, without delay or excuses.
- To remain absolutely loyal to the client and his cause. An exception would be where such loyalty conflicts with the lawyer's ethical duties and responsibilities. The lawyer should then advise his client of the conflict and what to do about it.
- To file the client's action, or response to an action filed against the client, within the prescribed time.
- To record in timely fashion other legal documents that are intended to notify the public as protection to the client.
- To counsel the client to obey the orders of the court. If a court order is erroneous, it should be challenged on appeal and not disobeyed or ignored.
- To keep up to date on developments in law and the latest methods and models of practice.
- To investigate thoroughly the facts and laws that are relevant to the client's legal problem.
- To analyze carefully the client's problems and give a candid opinion of the probability of success or failure of the case.
- To make a thorough effort to settle a case and avoid the risks and expense of a lawsuit.
- To make adequate and timely preparation of the client's case for trial and to prepare relevant documents and papers well in advance of a settlement or a closing of a transaction.

The Client's Obligations to the Lawyer

The relationship between a lawyer and a client is not one-sided. If a lawyer is to work effectively on the client's behalf, the client must fulfill certain obligations as well. These include:

- To give full and complete disclosure of all facts, particularly regarding the client's conduct in a case. All information given is protected by the lawyer's obligation of confidentiality. A client can even confess a crime to his lawyer; such a confession is considered privileged communication.
- To consult promptly when a problem first develops.
- To adhere strictly to a lawyer's advice. Disregarding

instructions could result in loss of a case.
- To have faith in the lawyer's opinion and judgment. In short, "let the lawyer run the case."
- To give adequate time to render satisfactory service. After a client puts a matter into a lawyer's hands, he should wait for the lawyer to make return contact unless there is an important new development.
- To feel free to ask about any relevant matter in the case.
- To give prompt notice to the lawyer of any dissatisfaction with his conduct of the client's affairs.
- To pay a fair and reasonable fee.
- To compliment the lawyer and give a good recommendation when the client feels that he has received outstanding service.

How to Conduct a Relationship with a Lawyer

Guidelines such as those just listed are directed at helping the client in specific dealings with his lawyer. The following guidelines will help the client establish a good overall atmosphere that may ensure a successful working relationship with his lawyer.

- The client should view his lawyer as another human being, not a god. The lawyer is not all-powerful; like all persons, he can make mistakes. However, he remains accountable for living up to his obligations. The client need not feel intimidated. If a lawyer appears intimidating, the client should feel free to complain or find another lawyer.
- At the outset, the client should tell the lawyer what he expects of him. If any of those expectations are unreasonable, the lawyer should say so. Similarly, the client should ask what the lawyer expects of him.
- The client should ask what steps are involved in handling the case and what kind of time schedule may be expected. This can reduce or eliminate impatience.
- The fee arrangement should be discussed at the outset. It should be made clear when the fee is to be paid. The client should know if and how he will be charged for making phone calls to ask questions. Guidelines for keeping fees down are presented later in this chapter.
- The client should help in any way he can—for example, by providing papers and evidence and finding witnesses. If the lawyer has not suggested it, the client should offer such help. In this way time is saved; the lawyer's fees may be reduced.
- The client should always choose the lawyer, not the other way around. An exception may be the class-action suit for a group or category of clients.
- The client should call with any and all questions. He should make sure that making frequent calls will not result in a higher legal bill. If it will, the client should make his phone calls count, grouping questions together on a given call.

What to Expect and Do During the First Visit

On first meeting with a lawyer, and not before, an individual will usually decide whether or not he wants to hire that lawyer. If he decides to hire the lawyer, the meeting should be used to establish the relationship. The first meeting should therefore be approached with those objectives in mind. The following pointers should help the individual in the first meeting:

- Before going to the meeting, the potential client makes notes about the problem. He can then go over the important points when talking to the lawyer.
- He should bring the names, addresses, and telephone numbers of everyone connected with the case. Some lawyers may ask to see certain papers even before a meeting takes place.
- He should ask the lawyer to tell him about cases like his that he may have handled. Note: a lawyer's ability to handle a particular case may have nothing to do with his age.
- When dealing with a law firm, the potential client should ask the lawyer conducting the interview whether he will conduct the case personally. If another lawyer in the firm will handle the case, it would be advisable to talk to the other lawyer as well.
- Beware the lawyer who guarantees results. Most lawsuits are not "sure things." A lawyer should assess the chances of success or failure, however.
- If the lawyer says something that is not clear, the individual should ask for an explanation in simpler language.
- The individual should not hurry into a decision on hiring. He can decide at the first meeting or he can "think about it."
- Considerations in the hiring decision should include: feeling comfortable with that lawyer, the lawyer's experience and skill at handling a particular type of case (insofar as these can be determined), understanding of the lawyer's explanation of what the case involves, and whether the fee seems reasonable. A "no" verdict on even one of these criteria may rule out a particular lawyer.
- If an individual has decided to hire the lawyer, he should then follow the guidelines for conducting the relationship.

Most cases, it should be noted, do not end up in court. Notable exceptions are when one is being sued or when one is arrested for a crime. In a civil case, a lawyer may see a court fight as futile or expensive or both. Litigation can then be a luxury. The lawyer may therefore recommend compromise or negotiation.

How to Find a Lawyer

If an individual does not have a lawyer, he can take several routes to find one. These include:

Recommendations
Referral services
Advertisements
Lawyer directories
Public interest groups
Prepaid plans
Various free or low-cost services such as Legal Aid, public defenders, Public Interest Bar, and various special projects for the elderly and other groups

The individual should initially develop a list of candidates from which to choose a lawyer. It may turn out that the first lawyer a person finds proves to be satisfactory on the basis of the criteria listed above. On the other hand, it helps to have a list from which to select—if only to avoid feeling pressed to take the first lawyer one finds. The various sources of lawyers are described below.

Recommendations

A lawyer may be recommended by a friend or relative who has had similar legal work done. This person can provide information on the lawyer's competence, personality, and fees. Recommendations may come also from professionals such as clergy, doctors, business executives, or social workers. Such individuals may have had to deal with a similar problem in their lives or in their professional work.

Other possibilities exist. At one's place of work, co-workers and employers can also be important sources of recommendations. One lawyer may recommend another who specializes in the particular kind of legal problem. Where a person has moved, a lawyer known or used earlier may be able to provide one or more names of lawyers in the new community. A lawyer who happens to be a neighbor might be another source.

Referral Services

Lawyer referral services are operated by state, county, and local bar associations. They may also be called attorney referral services or lawyer reference services. Such services put individuals who have legal problems in touch with attorneys; the latter may charge a modest fee for a first consultation.

Consulting a referral service is usually not a complicated process. The individual who thinks he has a legal problem contacts the lawyer referral service office, most often using a toll-free number; any information given is held in strict confidence. Office personnel will then place the individual in contact with an attorney in his area. If the problem is not a legal one, either the referral office or the lawyer will say so. If the caller has a legal problem, the individual can decide for himself whether to make another appointment or authorize the lawyer to take appropriate action.

These services are found in the Yellow Pages of the telephone directory under "Attorneys," "Lawyers," "Attorney Referral Services," or some similar entry. Some referral services deal with special problems of groups such as artists, Spanish-speaking people, or the elderly.

The lawyers obtained through referral services typically charge low fees for consultations. A typical fee would be $15. If a person thinks he cannot afford that much, he has other alternatives, such as Legal Aid and other legal services.

Advertisements

The Yellow Pages and newspaper advertisements offer other sources of lawyers' names. Most lawyers, however, choose not to advertise except to be listed in the Yellow Pages. Lawyers can advertise in the Yellow Pages, in newspapers and magazines, on radio and television, on billboards, or elsewhere as desired. The single restriction that applies is that the information in an ad cannot be false or misleading.

In addition to fees, ads may specify the legal fields in which lawyers specialize. "Legal clinics," law firms that deal with typical problems, often on a high-volume basis, may advertise their services for adoptions, divorces, bankruptcies, and wills. If an ad uses phrases like "simple will" or "uncontested divorce," it is important to ask what the service includes and what additional charges are entailed for more complicated cases or for expenses.

If the ad appeared in print, it should be clipped and kept. It tells much in few words about the lawyer's practice. If the ad appeared as a radio or television commercial, it may be helpful to take notes.

Lawyer Directories

Some bar associations publish lawyer directories. These provide names and information, usually as furnished by the lawyers themselves. Included are educational background, fees (including those for initial consultations), areas of practice or specialization, office hours, and foreign languages spoken. Such directories are usually found in public libraries and bar association offices. A nationwide directory found in most public libraries is the seven-volume Martindale and Hubbell Law Directory, now in its 112th edition (Summit, N.J.: Martindale-Hubbell, Inc., 1980).

Public Interest Groups

Nonprofit public-interest organizations may either provide legal services in specific areas or refer persons to experienced lawyers specializing in those areas. The American Civil Liberties Union, for instance, can help if one's civil rights, such as freedom of speech or religion, are threatened or violated. The Women's Legal Defense Fund provides counseling and referral services for women with problems in domestic relations or sex discrimination. The National Association for the Advancement of Colored People Legal Defense Fund handles individual and class-action cases of discrimination against minorities.

In general, such groups may be divided into those that help individuals and those that only help groups in class-action cases. These organizations may be found in a variety of ways, for example by calling a city agency or contacting the "consumer action line" of a local paper, radio station, or television station. Checking the Yellow Pages under "Associations," "Consumer Protection Organizations," "Social Service and Welfare Organizations," or other similar entries may also produce lawyers' names.

Prepaid Plans

Legal services are sometimes provided under "legal insurance" plans sponsored by an employer, by a labor union or credit union, or through individual purchase. Such a plan involves a prepaid fee or premium. An employer may establish the program on behalf of all covered employees or as an employee benefit provided either voluntarily or under collective bargaining. In some companies, an individual may join the plan by authorizing a payroll deduction.

Other characteristics may be noted. The premiums may be paid to (1) a trust fund that then provides legal services, (2) an insurance company, or (3) a private entrepreneurial group. Staff lawyers may work exclusively for plan members, or one or more law firms may handle plan services. A large group of lawyers may contribute services under the plan. Some programs offer the services of any licensed lawyer anywhere. Most such plans pay for specific service to the individual beneficiary or group member; services not covered by the plan require additional fees from the individual.

The advantages of such plans are many. Members have access to lawyers, especially for preventive services, without paying high initial consultation fees. Methods of payment are easier, and sometimes painless, depending on the plan's benefits. Fee schedules are published. In general, members are assured of quality services and good treatment. The possibility that a lawyer may lose group business has been said to motivate many plan lawyers to deliver uniformly high-quality services.

THE SHREVEPORT PLAN[1]

The Shreveport Plan was established in 1971. One of the first of the prepaid legal plans, it was created in recognition of the fact that middle-income Americans have typically been deprived of adequate legal protection: the poor could get government-financed legal aid while the rich could afford to pay lawyers.

In 1969, the American Bar Association decided to use Shreveport, Louisiana, as an experimental site for creating a prepaid legal plan. The local bar association was responsive to the idea. A local group of workers, Laborers' Local 229, joined in the experiment.

Local 229 negotiated an arrangement under which two cents an hour from the salary of each worker would be paid into the plan. The American Bar Association and the Ford Foundation also provided funds. Shreveport Legal Services Corporation, a nonprofit corporation, was formed.

The members of Local 229, mostly rural blacks, did not trust strangers, especially those representing the law. The law collected bills, repossessed furniture, or put people in jail. Officials of the Local had been giving advice on legal matters for years, but could not call it "legal advice."

Seeing a demand for real legal services and hearing about the American Bar Association's interest in starting a plan, a union official had contacted the local attorney handling the project. As a result, Shreveport became the site for the experiment.

Many members of Local 229 have been aided by the plan. In one case, a man was confronted by local, state, and federal officials with another person's check, apparently endorsed with his signature. Calling an attorney, the victim received help; a handwriting expert was able to state that it was not the man's writing. A woman neighbor was identified as the culprit.

In 1974, Ford Foundation funding was terminated. The union membership voted overwhelmingly to retain the plan. Were it not for the plan, many workers would have suffered serious financial losses or invasions of personal liberties.

[1] **Adapted from Philip J. Murphy, Ralph N. Jackson, and David Chandler,** *Lawyers for Laborers* (American Bar Association, 1975).

Free or Low-Cost Services

Inexpensive legal services are available for those who need help but cannot afford ordinary attorneys' fees. Such services include Legal Aid, law school clinical programs, public defenders, the Public Interest Bar, and Pro Bono, elderly, and other special projects.

Legal Aid, also called Legal Services, offers services for the indigent under funding by the federal and state governments and by bar associations. Lawyers in Legal Aid offices can represent clients in most legal situations. However, since the demand for services usually exceeds the supply of lawyers, Legal Aid will not handle criminal cases or cases in which a person seeks a money award (*see* Contingency Fees, below). A person must also meet an eligibility requirement by proving that his income is below a certain level. The level varies from one community to another.

Law school clinical programs provide law students with practical experience with indigent clients. At any given law school, either the supervising lawyer or the program's referral individual may be contacted. Some programs make referrals to former students who are practicing in the area. Alternatively, the law school dean may provide the name of a faculty member specializing in the area of concern. That person may refer the potential client to other attorneys.

State governments make *public defenders* available to individuals accused of crimes who cannot afford attorneys' fees. The public defender can be found in the White Pages of the phone book under Public Defender. If an area or community has no public defender, a judge may appoint a private attorney to take a case without charge.

Public interest groups, as noted, sometimes provide legal services for individuals. Other special programs for particular groups may be provided by bar associations. The Lawyer Referral Service may also be a source of inexpensive, if not free, help.

AIDS AND ALTERNATIVES

The individual has some alternatives to lawyers or law offices in resolving certain legal problems. For example, the Small Claims Court makes it possible to file claims below certain levels. Some of the specific alternatives are described in later chapters.

One aid is Tel-Law, a library of tape recordings that can be heard over the telephone. Such recordings are designed to convey an understanding of the justice system and of state laws, to aid in determining whether one has a legal problem, and to help in finding assistance. These tapes are not intended as legal advice or as a substitute for a lawyer; nor do they apply to all legal problems and situations. But diverse areas of law are covered, including adoption, bankruptcy, juvenile law, criminal law, civil law, public benefits, domestic relations, legal matters related to the handicapped, credit and consumer law, and estates and probate. The number of tapes may range from 50 to over 100 depending on the particular bar association.

Another alternative to lawyers is do-it-yourself kits. These provide aid in such areas as wills, divorces, incorporation, and avoiding probate. In the case of probate, a group of lawyers sued the author of such a kit for illegally dispensing legal advice. The author successfully appealed the action, and has sold many copies of his plan along with the appropriate forms. The plan does successfully avoid the costs of probate. Even where a lawyer is used, the kit has features that are useful to both client and lawyer.

Not all alternatives may prove as useful or foolproof as the probate-avoidance plan. A kit may provide only minimum protection for the average person. But there is no average person as far as the law is concerned: each case is unique. A kit may not anticipate some kinds of legal problems. Consequently, one could end up with more cost and trouble than expected. The objective is to make an informed, thoughtful decision on whether and how to use a lawyer.

WHEN A LAWYER MAY NOT BE NEEDED[1]

- **When money is needed in an emergency; a better way is to consult a banker.**
- **Income tax problems; consult an accountant first.**
- **Routine purchase of a house from a reputable builder; use a real estate agent or title insurance company or an attorney for a lending institution (*see* Chapter 3).**
- **Problems receiving social security or unemployment compensation; see appropriate government agency officials (*see* Chapter 12).**
- **Claims for a relatively small amount of money under the limits set by the state; go to Small Claims Court (*see* Chapter 13).**
- **Traffic accident; in states with no-fault liability laws, conflict is minimized and matters are handled by the person's insurance company (*see* Chapter 17).**
- **Divorce; some states have no-fault divorce laws, making unnecessary the adversary procedure; elsewhere, do-it-yourself divorce kits may handle the problem without a hitch (*see* Chapter 8).**
- **Incorporation; in this area, do-it-yourself kits may have their pros and cons; indeed, incorporation may not even be the best way for some to organize a business (*see* Chapter 13).**
- **Consumer complaint; new consumer protection laws are being enforced by government agencies, and private consumer groups can exert pressure (*see* Chapter 14).**

[1] **Adapted from** *You and the Law*, Copyright © 1977 The Reader's Digest Association, Inc. Copyright © 1977 The Reader's Digest Association (Canada) Ltd. Copyright © 1977 The Reader's Digest Association Far East Ltd. Philippine Copyright © 1977 The Reader's Digest Association Far East Ltd.

LAWYERS' FEES

Fees vary depending on the type of service provided. They vary also from lawyer to lawyer and community to community. Lawyers determine fees according to the following criteria:

- The fee customarily charged in the area for a particular type of service.
- The amount of time and labor invested.
- The skill of the lawyer, his experience, ability, specialties, and reputation.
- Business or office expenses, which vary from 35 to 50 per cent of the fee.
- Whether a fixed or contingent fee is established. Where a fee is contingent, the lawyer receives nothing if the case is lost.
- Results, in the case of the contingent fee.
- The amount involved in the settlement, in the case of a contingent fee.
- The complexity of the case.
- The nature and length of the relationship with the client. For example, a client doing casual business with a lawyer would be charged a higher rate than an old client doing steady business.
- Time limitations imposed by the client or by the circumstances of the case. If a lawyer is prevented from taking other employment that might have been available, he may charge more.

Types of Fees

Lawyers may charge different kinds of fees. In some instances, the client can negotiate the kind of fee; in others, it is already determined. Types include:

- *Fixed fees.* This constitutes a "standard" fee, used for routine legal matters such as drafting an uncomplicated will. Law clinics typically use this kind of fee.
- *Hourly fees.* Here, time determines the final cost. But the hourly rate varies from one lawyer and area to another. The client's objective is to obtain the best combination of hourly rate and efficiency in getting the work done more quickly.
- *Retainers.* A lawyer may ask for a retainer, or advance payment, to cover the fee or expenses. Clients requiring regular service pay monthly or annual retainers to ensure continuing service.
- *Contingency fees.* In cases where the client is suing for money, the lawyer receives a percentage of the award if he wins and nothing if he loses. The lawyer may assess his percentage according to the total amount or on the award after other costs are deducted. If the latter, the client keeps more of the award. The client should determine beforehand the lawyer's method of charging.
- *Statutory fees.* The cost of probate and other kinds of legal work is set by law, hence is "statutory." A probate court has a schedule of allowable fees. These are usually based on percentages of the value of different kinds of property.
- *Fees set by a judge.* Probate may fall under this heading. Considering the size of the estate and the amount of time the lawyer puts in, the judge determines the fee to be awarded.

Keeping Legal Fees Down

Whatever the type of fee, the client can use a number of tactics to keep fees to a minimum. He can, for example:

- Write down the names, addresses, and phone numbers of all persons involved and all the relevant facts that he can recall
- Take any pertinent papers to the first interview
- Be as brief as possible in all interviews
- Keep emotion from coloring the facts
- Make a full and honest disclosure of all facts to the lawyer
- Avoid unnecessary phone calls to the lawyer
- Obtain legal advice before signing documents or taking legal action and then follow that advice
- Consider the financial pros and cons of a proposed legal action by discussing it with a lawyer

If the Fee Is Too High

If the client feels the fee is too high, he should tell his lawyer.

Asking for an explanation may prove entirely satisfactory. Some states, including California, have arbitration services that are provided by the state bar association. The services charge set fees to determine whether the lawyer did the work he was supposed to do for the amount paid. Fees set by a court or by law are not subject to arbitration, however. Such a proceeding usually takes no more than 80 days and costs a maximum of $50. Lacking arbitration, a client may sue a lawyer.

Dissatisfaction with a Lawyer's Performance

Aside from fee disputes, a client may be dissatisfied with what the lawyer has delivered. Generally, a client does not have grounds for complaint unless the lawyer has violated standards of professional responsibility.

A formal complaint can be damaging to a lawyer even if he is not at fault. For that reason, and because dissatisfaction often springs from misunderstanding or poor communication between client and lawyer, the client should thoroughly air his grievance with the lawyer. The state bar can only discipline the lawyer; it cannot remedy any loss to the client. For that, the client must sue.

Each state has its own procedures for handling client grievances. The state Supreme Court has the power to discipline lawyers. Such discipline may include disbarment as a type of sanction. It is worth remembering that losing a case does not automatically imply incompetence or malpractice.

III – Buying, Building, Selling a Home

Purchasing a home may be the largest investment that a person makes during his or her lifetime. Numerous legal questions relate to the purchase of an existing home, construction of a new home, various types of financing, the sale of a home, and similar transactions.

BUYING AN EXISTING HOME

Some persons find their "dream homes" the first time they go house hunting. Others, undoubtedly more typical, search for weeks or months before the perfect home turns up.

House hunting takes time, usually, because many factors, legal and other, enter into the purchase process. Every home buyer should make certain that he knows exactly what he is buying. That means questions and more questions—to both the seller and his real estate agent.

Finding the Right Property

Finding the home that suits your needs is vitally important. Finding the right home in a strange area or neighborhood may add up to a major challenge. When moving into a new area without prior knowledge of the neighborhood, however, the home seeker has several possible ways to find out about the new neighborhood and the types of homes there.

Some obvious options are open. A friend who lives in the new area can show a prospective buyer the various locations and perhaps take the time to make a circuit of the city or town. A telephone call or letter to the local Chamber of Commerce or Board of Realtors can produce information on the properties in the areas of interest. Nothing, however, takes the place of a personal inspection trip.

Some of the considerations that should be investigated are fairly self-evident. The size of the home; its price and how it fits with your budget; the area, especially with respect to schools, shopping, distance from work, and other such practical considerations—all have to be checked out. Often, consulting a real estate broker in the area found to be most attractive is the best method of finding property. In order to avoid wasting their own time and the time of the broker, house hunters should explain what they are looking for. Looking at photographs of various listings before making a personal inspection of the property can clarify key points.

Many persons make a very serious mistake in house hunting: they look only at the house itself. Naturally, if the house fits in with the buyer's needs, is structurally sound and of suitable size, and falls in the right price bracket, an offer to buy may be called for as promptly as possible. However, an inspection of the house alone is never enough. The owner or the broker should take the potential buyer on a "guided tour" of the property itself. An inspection trip should follow along the borders of the property. The property line should be defined at all points. The buyer should look up in the air to determine whether or not utility lines or other apparent uses or obstructions cross the air space over the property.

Most situations follow one or another pattern. Unless all utilities are underground, telephone and electric lines connect to the house from a pole or other utility installation bordering the street. But electric power lines or telephone lines may cross the property without connection to the house. That usually means that the utility company has an easement or right of way to cross the property. Such a use might be found later to constitute interference with the complete use and enjoyment of the property.

Walking over the property, the buyer should also look down to determine whether or not visible pathways or walkways indicate that people use the property as a shortcut. A path suggests a need for full investigation—possibly by an attorney. The law in most states holds that the public can gain an easement or right of way by continuous, uninterrupted use of someone else's property for shortcut purposes.

Manhole covers could indicate the existence of a sewage system across the property. The owner or broker should be asked to explain such facilities.

It is thus very important not to overlook a physical inspection, not only of the house itself but also of the surrounding property on which it sits, including the boundary lines, utility lines, both aboveground and underground, and any other easement or rights of way that may exist.

Hand Money Deposit

Assume that a piece of property fits within the buyer's means and satisfies all other needs and desires. It may be wise to prevent the seller from selling the property to someone else before a contract of sale can be signed. In this situation a *hand money deposit* is usually made. The seller then gives the would-be buyer a deposit receipt.

Because most states require that contracts for the sale of real estate be in writing, the deposit receipt that represents the amount of hand money or *earnest money* deposited by the buyer should contain some essential elements. With these, the receipt becomes a legally enforcible contract in the event that a later long-form agreement of sale is not signed.

The amount of the earnest money deposit is not set by law and is subject to negotiation between the parties. The deposit applies as part payment of the purchase price if the buyer later buys the land and completes the sale. Usually, the contract provides that the earnest money deposit may be retained by the seller if the buyer defaults and does not buy the land. Ordinarily a seller will require a sufficiently high earnest money deposit to cover the broker's commission and other expenses of the sale to the seller—including his loss of time and loss of opportunity to sell elsewhere if the buyer should default. The hand money deposit may be a percentage of the total purchase price, such as 5 per cent, 10 per cent, and so on.

The deposit receipt given by the seller to the buyer should at least identify by name the seller and the buyer. It should also describe the property so that it can be identified easily. As an exchange of promises between the seller and the buyer to purchase and sell the property, the receipt should state the full price. All parties to the deposit receipt should sign it to make certain that it stands as a legally enforcible contract.

A deposit receipt cannot substitute for an agreement of sale. The receipt only acknowledges deposit of the earnest money under all the basic terms. The deposit receipt should refer to the fact that an agreement of sale will be entered into by the parties as soon as possible after the earnest money has been paid.

THE PURCHASE AND SALE AGREEMENT: QUESTIONS THE BUYER SHOULD ASK BEFORE SIGNING[1]

The paper first given to a prospective buyer by a real estate broker is the purchase and sale agreement. Few people realize that this paper is the most important step in making the purchase of a home, for the details of this agreement determine what you buy and how you buy it. Before signing, read the agreement carefully and discuss with your family lawyer such items as the following:

1. **Exactly what land, buildings, and furnishings are included in your offer? Are stove, refrigerator, and the like included?**
2. **What details regarding payments should be stated?**
3. **When can you take possession?**
4. **Is the seller to furnish you with a good, marketable title?**
5. **What kind of deed should the seller give?**
6. **Who pays for the examination of the title to the property in the event the offer is accepted? Who pays for the abstract of title or title insurance?**
7. **Have utilities been installed and paid for?**
8. **Should a surveyor be employed to determine whether the improvements are actually located on the property? Who should pay for the cost of the survey?**
9. **If a mortgage is to be given, who will pay the intangible tax on the mortgage?**
10. **If termite, water, or other damage is found, shall the seller pay the cost of repairs?**
11. **What are the zoning regulations, or restrictions, on the use of the property?**
12. **What is the time within which the purchase should be accepted or refused? Is the date of such acceptance to be vital to the offer?**
13. **If your offer is accepted, what steps should be taken with respect to insuring the improvements to protect you, the prospective purchaser, pending the final closing?**
14. **What persons (husbands and wives) should be required to sign and accept the offer?**
15. **Are boundary lines properly specified?**
16. **Are timber, mineral, and water rights, if any, properly covered?**
17. **Who is responsible for payment of taxes?**
18. **How should the agreement be executed to make it binding?**
19. **What are the remedies if the buyer or seller defaults?**

[1] **Adapted from** *So You're Going to Buy a Home* (Tallahassee: The Florida Bar, February 1980).

The Agreement of Sale

All the essential elements in the sale and purchase of a home converge in the agreement of sale. All these elements, including full cost, description of the property, the type of title that the owner has and will convey to the buyer, and so on, must appear in the agreement. A checklist of those items that should be in the final agreement of sale would include at least the following:

- Date of the agreement. The agreement should contain the date on which it is made.
- The name and address of the seller. These should be stated clearly, and the marital status of the seller should be stated, such as "James Smith and Mary Smith, his wife, of 121 Jane Street, Center City, State X."
- The name of the buyer. "Name" should include marital status, mailing address, and so on.

If the buyers are not husband and wife, and want to take title jointly, the nature of the title that they wish to take should be stated in the agreement of sale. Many states recognize a form of title ownership known as "joint tenancy." If the two persons, not husband and wife, want to take title as "joint tenants," such should be stated in the agreement. If they want to take title as "tenants in common," also a recognized form of ownership, this should be stated.

Agreement to Sell. The agreement of sale should contain a specific agreement by the seller to sell the property and the buyer to purchase it on a specified date. In other words, the agreement should state that the seller will "on or before 90 days from the date of this agreement, sell, and the buyer will buy" the property as described in the agreement.

Type of Deed to be Delivered. The agreement should specify the type of deed that the seller will give to the buyer. A deed of *general warranty* is the highest form of deed that can be conveyed and ordinarily is utilized in the sale of a residence. Other forms of deed, such as deeds of special warranty, are used mainly in situations involving a sale from the estate of a deceased person and in other special situations.

Type of Title to be Conveyed. The agreement should provide that the seller will convey "fee simple title," the highest form of title. The statement indicates that the seller has all the elements of title to the property that he is agreeing to sell. By specific terms, the sale should be made clear of all liens and encumbrances except as noted in the agreement, thus assuring the buyer that the seller is agreeing to convey free of any liens or encumbrances except those noted in the contract itself.

Good and Marketable Title. The buyer wants to be certain that the title he is acquiring is good. He may later want to sell the property to someone else. The agreement should thus provide that the seller is conveying a good and marketable title, one that will be insurable by a title insurance company at its regular rates and that can be freely transferred in the marketplace.

Description. The agreement of sale should contain a full-length description by "metes and bounds" and by courses and distances. This means that the description is the kind that a registered engineer would prepare from a survey of the property.

It is important that the buyer insist on a perimeter survey—one that examines the boundaries of the property only. The buyer should also insist on a survey showing the existence and location of all improvements on the lot, including the house, garage, swimming pool, toolshed, or any other building. These improvements should be located precisely on the lot. The

JOINT TENANCY: PROS AND CONS[1]

Many misleading ideas about joint tenancy are passed from person to person, usually quite innocently. You have probably heard them—"Joint tenancy eliminates the necessity of a will" . . . "Joint tenancy saves probate costs" . . . "Joint tenancy reduces 'death taxes' " . . . "Jointly held property passes 'automatically' at death to the survivor" . . . "Your creditors can't reach jointly held property" . . . and so forth. To clear up misunderstandings on these and other misconceptions, read on.

What is joint tenancy? It is a way of holding title to personal property or real estate by two or more persons. There are three types of joint tenancy: "with rights of survivorship," "as tenants in common," and "as tenants by the entireties" (limited to husband and wife).

Why do many property owners favor joint tenancy? They think the "survivorship" feature will save the surviving owner probate costs and inheritance taxes. The only costs saved are the small probate court costs and not attorney fees or transfer expenses. There is no inheritance tax due on property passing to a spouse, whether in joint tenancy or otherwise, and no inheritance taxes are saved if the property is held jointly with anyone else.

Is it a substitute for a will? No. Joint tenancy with rights of survivorship will pass that particular property to the other named owner or owners, and do nothing else. A tenant in common's undivided interest, absent a will, will pass to his or her heirs-at-law. A properly drawn will covers a number of items in addition to passing property. For example, it designates who is to handle the estate, names a guardian for minor children, etc. Joint tenancy may be the right thing for you today but the wrong thing tomorrow, but you cannot change it easily—as you can a will—to fit tomorrow's situation.

Does jointly held property pass "automatically" at death to the other joint tenant? No. If the joint tenancy was "with rights of survivorship" or "as tenants by the entirety," the property does pass by operation of law (statute or contract), to the survivor, but not automatically. A Survivorship Affidavit with respect to real estate and Consents to Transfer (except for spouses), stock powers, affidavits of domicile and perhaps other documents are required to be prepared, signed and recorded or sent to banks and transfer agents to get the title placed in the name of the surviving owner.

Why is joint tenancy difficult to change? Because one co-owner may refuse.

Can a man compel his wife to give back a joint title he has conferred on her? No.

Can creditors reach jointly held property? Yes, except possibly for real estate held by a husband and wife as tenants by the entirety if only one spouse takes bankruptcy. On death, the creditors of the deceased joint tenant can reach that person's contributions into jointly held checking and savings accounts, certificates of deposit, and other accounts if necessary.

What is common danger in joint tenancy? Joint owners—even husband and wife—may disagree. After that it becomes difficult to make such necessary decisions as those concerning management, repairs, division of income from the property, public liability problems, insurance to be carried, and so forth. If tenants in common cannot agree on the sale of real estate, one party has to bring a partition suit which generally results in the court ordering the property to be sold at a time when the market may or may not be good.

What happens to a husband-wife joint tenancy in case of a divorce? If the parties cannot agree upon a split of the property between themselves, the tenancy is converted into a "tenants in common" type of joint tenancy.

Does joint tenancy reduce taxes? When one of two joint tenants dies, for federal estate taxes and many state inheritance taxes, the law presumes that the decedent was the owner of such property and taxes it in his or her estate, except to the extent that the survivor can prove his or her contribution to the cost thereof. Trouble may arise in perfecting the record title of the joint tenancy property. The real tax liability comes upon the death of the surviving spouse and often results in "double taxation" of some of the property.

Does joint tenancy save probate expense? Very seldom. If a deceased person owned other property besides that held in joint tenancy, the other property must be probated just the same. There is also expense in perfecting the record title to the property after the death of each joint owner.

If joint owners die simultaneously (as in an accident), what happens to their joint tenancy property? Without a will containing a "survivorship clause," the jointly held property is divided one-half into each joint tenant's estate, and probate proceedings are then required to pass the property on to the devisees or heirs-at-law of each joint tenant.

Does the creation of joint tenancy ever constitute a gift? Yes, if an appropriate election is made. If no election is made, the entire property will be taxed as a part of the estate of the first joint tenant to die, and then will be taxed again when the other joint tenant dies.

Is joint tenancy ever advisable? In some circumstances, and with respect to some types of property, but only after careful consideration of all the circumstances.

[1] **Adapted from** *Joint Tenancy: Does It Fit YOU?* (Indianapolis: The Indiana State Bar Association).

surveys are important for determining:

(1) whether or not there are any encroachments onto the lot by an adjoining land owner;

(2) whether or not the buildings that exist on the property encroach on someone else's property; and

(3) whether or not the buildings and other improvements are consistent with local laws dealing with provisions for setback from the roadway, side-yard restrictions, open-space restrictions, and so on.

The parties to the sale should agree between themselves, after negotiation, on who pays for the surveys. Usually, the seller will have a completed survey that can be used by the buyer. The seller simply attaches a certificate stating that no changes, additions to property, or other structures have been erected since the date of the survey.

Under any circumstances, the buyer should have a survey that conforms to local ordinances and that shows any private covenants and restrictions that may exist if the property is within a plan of lots as well as any recorded easements or rights of way.

The legal description contained in the agreement of sale should be prepared, if possible, in accordance with the survey made by the registered engineer.

Title Reference. The agreement of sale should contain the deed book volume and page record under which the seller acquired title to the property. In all counties, a register or recorder of deeds office makes a formal record after a transfer of property has taken place. To assist the buyer in a title examination, or to give him the opportunity to inspect the title to the property, the agreement of sale should contain a title reference showing where the current deed to the property can be found in the public records.

"Under and Subject." If the agreement of sale, after negotiation, indicates that the property is to be taken subject to certain restrictions, easements, or rights of way, these should be stated specifically in the agreement of sale. For example, if a right of way crosses the rear of the property, this should be stated specifically. The buyer should have an opportunity to decide whether or not he wants to buy the property with that right of way.

Many agreements are signed with a provision like this: "Under and subject to all liens and encumbrances, easements, and rights of way that may appear of record." In this case the buyer should beware. In agreeing to such a provision, the buyer is agreeing to any liens, encumbrances, rights of way, or easements that might appear on the record before he has an opportunity to do a title search. Under no circumstances should a buyer—if he can avoid it—sign an agreement with such a provision in it except on advice of counsel. The covenant that the seller will deliver a good and marketable title gives the buyer a measure of protection in such a situation. All easements and rights of way should nonetheless be specifically itemized to the extent possible.

Any other special provisions should likewise be included in the agreement of sale. For example, if the buyer is taking the property subject to an existing mortgage—if he is assuming the mortgage of the seller—the agreement should so state. The assumption clause should be specific, should identify the mortgage and the name of the financial institution involved, the place where the mortgage is recorded, and the balance at the time of signature.

Appurtenance Clause. Why does an agreement of sale mention specifically such items as plumbing, heating fixtures and systems, laundry tubs and permanent fixtures, awnings, venetian blinds, and television antennas? Unfortunately, some sellers have removed from the property such things as blinds, fixtures, storm doors, and even light bulbs after the agreement of sale has been signed. The buyer moving into the property later finds a significantly different property from what he agreed to buy.

The agreement of sale should be specific. It should state that the sale includes all the buildings, improvements, and all plumbing and heating fixtures forming a part of the property. To be mentioned also: all built-in ranges, refrigerators, laundry tubs and other permanent fixtures, storm doors, windows and awnings if any, screens, shades, blinds, drapery rods and fixtures, television antennas, and all trees, shrubbery, and plants currently on the property.

Personal Property. Personal property includes items that are not normally considered part of the real estate. If any personal property items are to be transferred with the house, they should be separately listed, not included in the purchase price. Personal property may cover such items as wall-to-wall carpeting, rugs, drapes, mirrors, chandeliers, refrigerator, deep freeze, dishwasher, window air conditioners, fireplace items, lawnmower, garden tools, workbenches, water softeners, automatic door openers, and similar items. If any of these is being sold with the property, it should be specifically listed if it is to pass as part of the purchase price.

A better alternative should be noted. Where personal property is being sold with real estate, a separate value should be given to the personal items. They can then be listed in a separate bill of sale. For example, if the wall-to-wall carpeting, drapes, chandelier, and refrigerator are included in the sale, and the parties agree that they are worth $3,000, then the agreement of sale for the house could reflect a purchase price of $27,000. A separate bill of sale ($3,000) would list the items of personal property passing to the buyer. Total price for the entire package: $30,000.

Here a distinction has been made between the real estate and the items of personal property. This becomes important later on since, in many cases, the real estate tax assessment on the land and the house is based on the price stated in the deed. If the price in the deed reflects items of personal property that are not really part of the real estate, the real estate tax assessment may be set at too high a rate—namely, on $30,000 instead of on $27,000.

Covenant to Buy. In the agreement the buyer consents to purchase the property. The price is stated. All terms of payment should also be stated, such as the amount of earnest money paid and the balance and how it is to be paid—whether in cash or certified funds or otherwise. For example, if the price of the property is $30,000 and $5,000 has already been deposited as earnest money, the agreement should provide that the buyer agrees to pay the sum of $30,000 payable as follows: $5,000 as earnest money on the signing of the agreement, receipt of which is acknowledged by the seller, and the balance of $25,000 to be payable in cash at the time of final closing.

The contract must contain other provisions on payment of the purchase price if the buyer must sell his present home first in order to secure funds to buy the home. This is also true if the buyer must secure a mortgage himself to proceed with the purchase of the property. Too often a buyer signs without specifying that he has to sell his present house first to obtain money to buy the new house. If he cannot sell the old house in time—before the closing date—he may be in breach of his agreement with the seller.

A buyer might also have difficulty in getting a mortgage to finance the purchase of the new house. When the time comes to close, he cannot produce the money. In this case he can lose his earnest money deposit.

The buyer who has to sell his present home or obtain a mortgage to finance the new home, or both, should insist that the agreement of sale protect him. He needs *conditioned liability* under the contract: he has to be allowed to sell his existing home prior to the closing on the new home.

The seller may, of course, resist such a provision. It brings an element of uncertainty into the contract because the buyer may not be able to sell his home within the time limit set in the sale agreement. The seller should then insist on a time limitation. The buyer will have to sell his old home by a specified date or the agreement will be void, and the seller can proceed to sell to someone else.

If the buyer has to obtain a mortgage to buy the new home, he should make sure that the agreement contains a provision stating that purchase is subject to securing the mortgage. If agreeable to the seller, the interest rate should be indicated and the number of years to pay off the mortgage specified.

Such a provision is, of course, to the advantage of the buyer. It gives him an opportunity to "shop" for a mortgage that suits his situation. Again, the seller may raise the legitimate objection that this injects an element of uncertainty into the contract.

The seller who agrees to such a provision usually insists on a time limit by which the buyer has to secure a mortgage commitment in writing—to be shown to the seller. The seller is then assured that the sale will go through on schedule. If the buyer cannot procure the mortgage commitment within the time specified, the seller can offer the property to others.

Contract provisions conditioning the sale in any way should be negotiated matters in which both the seller and buyer have legitimate interests. Wherc possible, however, the buyer should insist, to the extent possible, on having these protections written into the contract. If they are not there, he is breaching the agreement if he cannot buy for those reasons at the time of closing.

THE CONTRACT[1]

The contract should be simple and complete, covering such items as:

- **Legal description of the property (not just the street address)**
- **List of all items included in the sale, including removable items such as drapes and appliances**
- **Purchase price, including down payment and any special terms and provisions as to the types of financing the buyer will accept**
- **Date abstract is to be furnished to the buyer for examination by his attorney, or terms relating to title insurance**
- **Dates of payments**
- **Date possession is to be given**
- **Date deed is to be delivered**
- **Apportionment of taxes and special assessments**
- **Whether property is to be conveyed free and clear of all encumbrances (mortgages, taxes, and assessments)**
- **Who is to bear the loss if the property is damaged or destroyed before the sale is completed**
- **Damages to be paid if the contract is forfeited**
- **How the costs, legal and other, are to be apportioned between the parties**

This list is not intended to be complete. It merely illustrates the basic items that should be included. Failure to include all necessary items could result in problems for both the buyer and seller.

[1] **Adapted from** *Tips on Buying a Home* (Montgomery: Alabama State Bar Assn., January 1978).

Settlement. The agreement should provide a specific closing date. The agreement can be closed or settled any time prior to that date. But a definite terminal date should be fixed in the contract so that all parties know what the time limitations are.

Any sale agreement should state that either party may, on written notice to the other, declare *time to be of the essence* of the contract and fix a date, time, and place for final settlement. In this way the parties are assured that a closing will eventually take place. Neither party can drag his feet or postpone the sale if the contract does not provide for such a contingency.

If, after written notice is given, either party fails to proceed with the sale or purchase, that party is in default under the contract. The contract should also provide for a method of giving notice to the other party, such as certified or registered mail at the addresses set forth in the contract.

Possession. The contract should specify the date on which the buyer can take possession of the property or move into the property. The possession date is normally the same as the date of final closing. But this is not always the case.

In a typical case, a seller may need additional time to move out of the property, and may request that the buyer take possession 30 days after the date of final closing. If the buyer agrees to the provision, the contract should provide for payment of rent or other form of payment for the 30-day waiting period. Alternatively, the buyer may want to move into the property before the closing in order to make repairs, paint, or do other work. In this case the seller should insist on some form of 30-day lease or other written agreement that would give him the right to eject the buyer if the latter cannot proceed with the closing after moving into the property.

Where possession is granted before delivery of the deed, or where the seller remains in possession after delivery of the deed to the buyer, and the party in possession does not sell or buy as specified, the contract should provide for the right of ejectment by the innocent party.

Tenants. If any part of the property included in the sale is occupied by a tenant, the sale agreement should specify this fact. The lease or leases under which the tenants are holding possession should be identified. There is need also to provide for the assignment and the proration of rent.

The agreement of sale should thus provide that the leases will be assigned at the closing to the buyer and that rent for the month during which the sale takes place will be prorated between the seller and the buyer.

Prorated Items. Normally, such things as real estate taxes, water and sewer charges, rents, and interest are prorated—divided proportionately—between seller and buyer as of the date of closing. For example, if the real estate taxes for the current year have already been paid by the seller, then he is entitled to a refund of those taxes for the balance of the year following the date of settlement. If the taxes have not been paid by the seller, the buyer is entitled to a credit for the seller's portion of the taxes for the part of the year during which the seller was the owner of the property.

Realty Transfer Taxes. Many states and local municipalities impose taxes on the transfer of real estate by sale. This tax has various names; it is in fact a realty transfer tax.

The transfer tax is usually based on a percentage of the purchase price. The agreement of sale should provide how the tax is to be paid and by whom. The amounts of these taxes can be a significant factor in the purchase of real estate, and often can be prorated between the parties. If the buyer agrees to pay all the realty transfer taxes, the seller is receiving much more than the agreed purchase price for the real estate. Thus after negotiation it is usually agreed that the parties split or divide the realty tax between them.

Risk of Loss. It happens sometimes, after an agreement of sale has been signed, that the property then is destroyed by fire or some other accidental event. In many states the buyer may nevertheless be required to perform the contract and pay the purchase price even though the house is no longer in existence.

Against that possibility, a *risk of loss* clause in the contract provides that if neither title nor possession of the property has been transferred to the buyer, and if all material part of the property is destroyed without the buyer's fault or is taken by condemnation proceedings, the seller cannot then enforce the contract. The buyer at his option can ask for return of the earnest money deposit.

Such an arrangement is fair to the seller. The real estate is ordinarily insured against fire or other casualty and the seller can recover the loss. If the property is condemned, the seller receives the condemnation proceeds awarded him. The buyer, however, needs the risk of loss clause so that he can get back his earnest money and declare the agreement void in the event of major loss.

Insurance. The agreement of sale must definitely provide for insurance coverage. The arrangement between the parties is usually one of two types. In one, the buyer agrees to take out adequate fire and casualty insurance on the property to protect his own interest starting with the effective date of the agreement. In the second, the seller agrees to add an endorsement to his own insurance policy to refer to the agreement, with a loss-payable clause making the proceeds payable to the seller and to the buyer "as their interests may appear."

Why is this insurance clause necessary? A buyer, when he signs a sale contract, becomes an owner of the property—what is known as the "equitable owner." This means that the buyer can go to court to force the seller to sell the property to him and deliver a deed—if the seller otherwise refuses to do so. As an owner, the buyer has an interest in the property; he can insure it and his interest must be protected.

The buyer may therefore want to place fire and casualty insurance on the property as of the date of the agreement, usually through a "binder" with his own insurance broker. As an alternative, the parties can agree that the seller will add an endorsement to his own policy making the proceeds payable to either the seller or the buyer or both as appropriate.

Of the two types, the first arrangement is to be preferred. The insurance proceeds would go directly to the buyer. They could not become involved in a possible legal quarrel between the seller and the buyer over entitlement to the proceeds of the policy.

Maintenance and Repair. Ordinarily, the agreement of sale should contain a provision that the seller will continue to maintain and repair the property until final closing. "Fair ordinary wear and tear," casualty damages from causes insurable under a standard fire policy, or any other loss that occurs without the fault of the seller would not, however, be covered. This clause has importance because many sellers, after they have found a buyer, do not maintain the property, but let it deteriorate until final closing.

Seller's Expense. Ordinarily the seller pays to have the deed prepared, to have all matters of title clearance taken care of, including liens, and to have other restrictions taken off the property.

Statement of Zoning Classification and Uncorrected Violations of Ordinances. Many states require that an agreement of sale, especially in large cities, contain a statement on zoning classification. The buyer then knows, on reading the applicable zoning ordinance, what uses can be made of the property.

A property may also be sold while subject to uncorrected housing, fire, building, or safety violations. The agreement should provide for disclosure of such uncorrected violations. If the seller improperly indicates that there are no such violations when in reality these exist, the buyer has a cause of action or lawsuit against the seller for breach of the agreement.

It is very useful if the agreement of sale can specify the use to which the buyer wants to put the property. The seller should guarantee that the property is properly zoned for that use. For example, in a residential area a buyer may want to use one room on the first floor of the residence as an office for meeting customers or clients. The buyer should state that intention in the agreement of sale and request the seller to state that such a use is permitted under the applicable zoning laws. The buyer cannot complain if he does not indicate what use he wants to make of the property—if in fact he cannot use the property for that purpose after the purchase is completed.

Improvements by Municipality. In many cases, the municipality in which the property is situated has served notice on a seller that certain work or improvements have to be carried out on the property. An ordinance or resolution may have been passed authorizing work that will improve the property. For that work additional property assessments will be made. It comes as quite a surprise to a buyer, after he has purchased property, to receive a bill from the municipality for a sewer that was installed six months prior to his purchase.

To avoid such surprises, the buyer should insist that the seller state in the contract that he has no notice of any municipal demand that work be done on the property, or that no ordinance or other municipal resolution has been passed authorizing improvements to the property for which an assessment might be made later. The buyer can then agree that any such notices or requirements received after the signing of the agreement of sale would be the buyer's responsibility.

Inspection of Premises. The buyer should have inspected the premises both inside and out, as noted. But the agreement should provide that the buyer has in fact made such an inspection. To protect the seller, the contract should also state that the purchase is being made with reliance on the inspection and that no representations were made except as stated in the contract. The buyer should be given the right, on reasonable notice, to enter the property to view it prior to closing.

Additional Provisions. If no construction or recent remodeling has taken place, the plans and specifications for the house should be given—if available—to the buyer. The buyer should also receive any useful survey that the seller may have in his possession along with any warranties on any equipment or structural parts of the property. A termite inspection may be necessary, particularly if the buyer's financing arrangement is being insured by a government agency. If a termite inspection is to be made, provision should be made for it and for payment for it by one or both of the parties.

Default of the Buyer. The agreement should specifically protect the seller in the event that the buyer does not go through with the deal. Ordinarily the seller has certain options in the event of the buyer's breach of the agreement. He may, for example:

(1) keep the earnest money and all monies paid toward the purchase price as liquidated damages, thus rendering the agreement null and void, and go on to sell the property to someone else;

(2) apply the earnest money toward the purchase price and sue the buyer for the balance; or

(3) apply the earnest money toward the seller's loss if he resells the property, then sue the buyer for any other damages sustained.

Default by Seller. If the seller breaches the contract by refusing to deliver the deed or close the sale, the buyer has the option to:

(1) take back the earnest money from the seller and waive any claim for "loss of bargain" damages;

(2) sue for delivery of a deed to the property; or

(3) sue for damages sustained by the buyer as a result of the breach by the seller.

No Other Warranties or Agreements. In cases on record, one or both of the parties has later said that provisions were made or agreements entered into that were not included in the contract. For that reason an agreement usually specifies that the document constitutes the entire agreement between the parties and that no other oral or written understandings regarding the sale were entered into. This avoids any problems in the future concerning so-called oral agreements made with the contract.

Other provisions may, in some areas, be required in a contract of sale. These could include provisions covering mineral rights in Pennsylvania, West Virginia, and other coal-producing states; drilling rights in oil-producing states; and water rights in some of the states in the West. Such provisions are customarily inserted into agreements in those states or areas.

The above, however, constitutes a reasonably complete checklist of items that should be contained in an agreement of sale for real estate. The sheer number of these items should make it clear that the purchase of a piece of real estate is not a simple matter—that it requires considerable time and study. Negotiation and signing of an agreement of sale are only the first steps in the sale process. Some important additional steps essential to completion of the process should be noted.

Title Examination or Title Abstract. Depending on the state in which the property is located, either the seller or the buyer has to provide a title abstract, or title search, leading to the issuance of a title insurance policy. In some states, this obligation falls on the seller. The title abstract indicates the exact condition of the title, the existence of encumbrances, liens, easements and rights of way, whether or not the mineral rights on the property have been sold to others, and all other matters dealing with the quality of the title of the real estate.

In some states the buyer can decide to conduct a title search. In that case an attorney may issue a certificate of title or a title insurance company will draw a title insurance policy that preliminarily describes the quality of the title. If the title report or title abstract indicates deficiencies in the title, and if these can be corrected before the closing, the buyer has to notify the seller of the deficiencies at once. The seller then has the opportunity to correct those defects prior to closing. For example, a judgment may have been entered against the seller without his knowledge. Unless he learns of the judgment, he will not have an opportunity to do anything about it prior to closing.

Ordinarily, the copy of the preliminary title report or preliminary abstract should be delivered to the seller by the buyer sometime prior to the closing. The seller can then clear up the defects in the title.

Final Closing or Settlement of the Sale

At this point everything comes together. The deed and final evidence of good title are delivered to the buyer. The buyer pays the balance of the purchase price. The mortgages needed by the buyer to pay the purchase price are executed and the charges against the property are prorated between the parties.

Some mystery seems to surround the "closing" in the minds of people who have never bought or sold real estate. Such persons may view the whole question of a "closing" with some fear. However, if the agreement of sale has been properly prepared and executed, and if a title examination has been properly conducted, the closing merely represents the culmination of all the various steps.

The closing usually takes place in the offices of the financial institution that granted the buyer a mortgage. In some cases the closing is held in the office of the title insurance company—if title insurance is to be placed on the property—or in the offices of one of the attorneys for the seller or buyer. At the closing, a closing sheet is prepared which lists all the various items, including:

The purchase price
Earnest money paid
Various judgments paid
Taxes and other prorated items
Net balances due the seller
Proceeds received from the buyer
The method of final disbursement of all funds

At the closing the buyer should receive a signed deed for recording. Alternatively, the deed, after being shown to the buyer, is recorded on the buyer's behalf. The buyer also receives the following:

- A title report or title insurance policy or other evidence of good title
- A bill of sale on any personal property sold with the real estate
- A receipt for the purchase price of the personal property
- A survey of the property
- The insurance policies covering the property
- A statement from the mortgagee of the amount due on any existing seller's mortgage that has to be paid from

the proceeds at the closing, or a release and satisfaction of the mortgage or other liens to be paid off and released from the property

- Leases and assignments of leases
- Letters from the seller advising any tenants to pay future rents to the buyer
- Receipts for taxes for the last three years
- Receipts showing payment of all utilities to date, including water, gas, and electricity, and especially those utilities that under the law of the state are entitled to be liened against the property for nonpayment
- Keys to the home

At the closing, the seller should also receive the balance of the purchase price as adjusted in the closing statement. If the seller is taking a "purchase money mortgage" from the buyer, to be discussed later, the seller will also want evidence at the closing that the buyer has insurance naming the seller as mortgagee. This policy protects the seller in the event that a fire or other "act of God" causes loss to the dwelling.

A COST CHECKLIST[1]

You may want to use the following real estate cost checklist while discussing costs with your attorney:

Purchaser's Closing Cost

(a) Reimbursement for Disbursements for:

County search	$	
Municipal searches		
Judgment search		
Recording costs		
Survey		
Mortgage policy of title insurance		
Owner's policy of title insurance		
Other		______
Total Reimbursement for Disbursements		$

(b) Attorney's Fee ... $

(c) Funds Required by Lending Institution:

Application fee and credit report	$	
Taxes: month at $ per month interest from to		
Review of documents, lender's counsel		
Other		______
Total Funds Required by Lender		$

(d) Miscellaneous:

Premium, homeowner's insurance policy	$	
Other, such as adjustments to seller for taxes, water and sewer charges, and fuel		$
Total Miscellaneous		$
Total Purchaser's Closing Costs (a, b, c, and d)		$

Seller's Closing Costs

(a) Attorney's fee	$
(b) Realtor's commission % × price of $	$
(c) Realty transfer fee: $3.50 per $1,000.00 of price, or less if seller qualifies for exemption	$
Total Seller's Closing Costs (a, b, and c)	$

[1] **Adapted from** *New Jersey Real Estate, the Law, and You* (Trenton: New Jersey State Bar Assn., February 1977).

IN A NUTSHELL: QUESTIONS TO ASK BEFORE SIGNING A CONTRACT[1]

As a precaution, you should know the answers to the following questions before you sign anything or pay any money for a piece of real estate:

- **When should you sign a purchase contract?**
- **Is the price specified?**
- **Does the proposed contract provide for furnishing proper evidence of title?**
- **Does the seller agree to furnish possession?**
- **Does the contract provide for the property to be insured?**
- **Is there a good marketable title to the property?**
- **Does the contract specify who is to pay the real estate taxes?**
- **Have you had your own attorney check the title?**
- **Is there an "easement or restriction of record" clause in the contract?**
- **Have you checked for zoning restrictions affecting the use of the property?**
- **Have you decided whether to hold the property in one person's name or in more than one name?**
- **Are you relying on a warranty deed alone for title protection?**
- **Will you have to pay for the property even if you can't borrow the money?**
- **Can you get your down payment back?**
- **Who is to pay the escrow fees?**
- **When will the transaction be closed?**
- **Is someone else living on the property?**
- **Will you have to pay any hidden fees?**

[1] **Adapted from** *Stop, Look and Check before Buying a Home* (Topeka: Kansas Bar Assn.)

What Is a Deed?

As noted, the owner or seller of the property has to give the buyer at the closing a properly executed deed on the property. The deed is the written instrument or document by which the owner of the property conveys the land, or some interest in the land, to the buyer.

A person may make a gift of real property by deed as well as sell property by deed. A father, for example, could make a gift of a piece of real estate to his son or other person by signing it, having it notarized before a notary public, and delivering the deed to the person receiving the property.

At the time of sale the deed will identify the parties, state the price or consideration paid, and give a complete, accurate description of the property. The deed has to be signed by the seller—or sellers if there is more than one person involved—and must be acknowledged before a notary public. At the closing, the deed is delivered to the buyer for recording.

Recording the deed is very important to the buyer. That formality constitutes notice that the buyer now owns the property and that the seller no longer has an interest as of the date of recording. If the buyer does not record the deed, anyone with a claim against the seller who is unaware of the fact of the sale can put a lien on the property. The buyer may actually have paid the purchase price and may have a deed in his possession. For the buyer's protection, the deed should be recorded immediately following the settlement.

There are various types or classes of deeds. Two rank as important insofar as individual rights are concerned:

- The *warranty deed* transfers an interest in the property and guarantees to the buyer that such interest has in fact been transferred.
- The *quitclaim deed* merely transfers whatever interest, if any, the seller may have in the property.

The latter has a special purpose. For example, as a result of the title examination a third party may be found to have an interest in the property that the buyer intends to buy. The third party may have the right to use the property as a shortcut. In order to clear the title of that possible defect, the buyer would insist that the party who claims the right of way sign and deliver to the buyer a quitclaim deed. This transfers to the buyer whatever right the third party may have with respect to the property. In this way, the buyer is assured that the third party cannot later claim an interest in the property.

At the closing the buyer should make certain that the deed conforms in all respects to the agreement of sale and all its provisions. The lawyer for the buyer should inspect the deed to make certain that all promises contained in the sale agreement are fulfilled.

After the closing, and after the deed has been recorded, the buyer should change to his own name all necessary utility services and the real estate tax records. In many instances, because the next billing cycle for the real estate taxes comes along before the ownership records are changed, a statement for real estate taxes may be sent to the former owner. The buyer should make sure he is informed when this occurs. He must obtain a statement for the tax bill or the taxes may be placed as a lien against the property. The buyer may never know that the taxes were liened.

If the seller does not pay the tax or deliver the tax bill to the buyer when he receives it, the buyer may have no way of knowing that the taxes for that year have been billed.

BUILDING A HOME

Some of the problems and procedures involved in buying an existing home have been described. Methods of financing such a purchase and the types of mortgages that may be used will be discussed later.

Suppose now that a buyer wants to build a home on a particular lot. Building is a much more complicated matter, one that requires knowledge by the proposed buyer or builder of just what is involved.

First, of course, the person who wants to build a home has the problem of finding a suitable lot. He faces the same problems in connection with the title to the lot, and with making certain that the title is good, as the buyer of an existing home. Other concerns include the cost of construction, selection of a knowledgeable builder, protection against the claims of subcontractors whom he may never have met, supervision of the work as it progresses so that he "gets his money's worth," and his need for financing.

Assuming that he has found a lot on which he hopes to build a home, the buyer may proceed in several ways. If he is buying a lot from a developer, the latter may have sets of plans and specifications available for use by the buyer. The sale may proceed as a purchase of the lot only, with an agreement to build a house later. The sale may, as an alternative, be based on an agreement to purchase the lot and the house to be built upon it. The final closing would then be held when the house is completed.

Either of these two methods may be utilized depending on the circumstances of the case and the needs of the parties as regards financing.

If the buyer decides to utilize plans and specifications already prepared by the developer, certain dangers may arise. The buyer should find out the reputation of the builder or developer—and ask some questions. What other types of homes has he built? Are the homes structurally sound? Are the people who have purchased these homes satisfied with their homes and construction features?

No one who is building should hesitate to ask the developer or builder for references. Not only the people referred by the builder or developer, but other persons who have purchased a home constructed by this particular builder should be contacted.

Most persons, it seems, will discuss such matters with people who inquire, especially if the homeowners are satisfied with their homes. A lukewarm response regarding a house built by the builder should touch off suspicions and should lead to further inquiries before buying or contracting to build.

It is very important that the plans and specifications should contain as much detail as possible so as to eliminate future problems. Some things the plans should do:

- Specify the kinds of materials and the brand names of the fixtures to be put in the house
- Be specific as far as colors are concerned
- Be very clear where specifications refer to the use of a certain type of material "or its equal"

The latter clause, of course, gives the builder the right to substitute materials that he says are equal in quality to those specified, but that may not be or that the buyer would not want in the home. The buyer should for this reason investigate models of the desired types of lighting fixtures, kitchen fixtures, furnace, air-conditioning units, and even the types of faucets or commodes. The plans can be specific as to trade names and types.

The buyer should spend as much time as necessary in the review and preparation of the specifications for the building. He will be living in that home for a long time; if it is not exactly to his liking, he will always entertain some regret or some bitterness in connection with it. Such problems can be avoided by having the specifications reviewed by an attorney and by a construction adviser if the buyer has no architect.

The architect, the agreement with the general contractor, and other subjects deserve additional close attention from the buyer.

The Architect

If you are dissatisfied with the plans and specifications furnished by the builder or developer, you can utilize the services of an architect in the planning and designing phases. An architect will submit sketches, on request, of plans that will meet all requirements.

Ordinarily, a contract with an architect is based on the normal uniform architectural agreements that the American Institute of Architects distributes. These require payments based on a percentage of the total cost of the project. The agreement with the architect should be thoroughly discussed with him and with an attorney before it is signed—for one thing because it normally contains provisions for payment of architectural fees even if the buyer is not pleased with the architect's designs. The contract should specify the architect's responsibilities and the buyer's payment obligations.

The architect's services normally include drawing up the construction plans and specifications, including those relating to the architecture, structural details, all mechanical work such as electrical, heating, and plumbing installation, and all outside work on parking areas, walks, fences, landscaping, and so on.

An architect normally draws up preliminary plans for approval by the owner or buyer. If the latter approves the preliminary drawings, the architect proceeds with the final drawings or "detailed drawings." These plans may then be submitted for bids to various contractors. The preliminary plans often save unnecessary work because they make possible advance agreement on construction designs and plans.

THE PURCHASE AND SALE AGREEMENT: QUESTIONS THE BUYER SHOULD ASK BEFORE SIGNING[1]

The paper first given to a prospective buyer by a real estate broker is the purchase and sale agreement. Few people realize that this paper is the most important step in making the purchase of a home, for the details of this agreement determine what you buy and how you buy it. Before signing, read the agreement carefully and discuss with your family lawyer such items as the following:

1. **Exactly what land, buildings, and furnishings are included in your offer? Are stove, refrigerator, and the like included?**
2. **What details regarding payments should be stated?**
3. **When can you take possession?**
4. **Is the seller to furnish you with a good, marketable title?**
5. **What kind of deed should the seller give?**
6. **Who pays for the examination of the title to the property in the event the offer is accepted? Who pays for the abstract of title or title insurance?**
7. **Have utilities been installed and paid for?**
8. **Should a surveyor be employed to determine whether the improvements are actually located on the property? Who should pay for the cost of the survey?**
9. **If a mortgage is to be given, who will pay the intangible tax on the mortgage?**
10. **If termite, water, or other damage is found, shall the seller pay the cost of repairs?**
11. **What are the zoning regulations, or restrictions, on the use of the property?**
12. **What is the time within which the purchase should be accepted or refused? Is the date of such acceptance to be vital to the offer?**
13. **If your offer is accepted, what steps should be taken with respect to insuring the improvements to protect you, the prospective purchaser, pending the final closing?**
14. **What persons (husbands and wives) should be required to sign and accept the offer?**
15. **Are boundary lines properly specified?**
16. **Are timber, mineral, and water rights, if any, properly covered?**
17. **Who is responsible for payment of taxes?**
18. **How should the agreement be executed to make it binding?**
19. **What are the remedies if the buyer or seller defaults?**

[1] **Adapted from** *So You're Going to Buy a Home* (Tallahassee: The Florida Bar, February 1980).

The agreement with the architect should contain a provision that the plans and specifications belong to the buyer or person intending to build the home. Without such a provision the plans remain the property of the architect.

Depending on the size of the home and the amount of money involved, the owner may want also to retain the architect to supervise construction. Such supervision of the general contractor and all subcontractors serves often as a guarantee that the contractor will follow the plans and specifications. Normally, additional fees are required if the architect is to supervise, but it may well be worth the expense.

If no architect is used, someone with construction experience should be hired by the buyer to inspect the property from time to time and to make certain that the contractor is following the plans and specifications. Normally, the financial institution that granted the buyer a mortgage loan will have an inspector check the property before allowing any periodic payment of construction funds to the contractor. But this type of inspection is made by the financial institution primarily for its own benefit. It cannot be considered the complete type of inspection that an owner would want to ensure that high-quality materials and workmanship are going into the project.

Agreement with General Contractor

An architect can either place a project with several general contractors for bids or suggest a builder who meets the buyer's standards. In either case, the buyer is now in a position to enter into an agreement with a builder for the construction of the home.

For obvious reasons the agreement should be in writing. It will contain the basic agreement on the construction project. The contract must provide that the home and land will be free of all liens from all contractors, subcontractors, laborers, and persons supplying material to the general contractor.

Why is the latter assurance necessary? In most cases the buyer deals only with one general contractor. The contractor in turn enters into contracts with other people to supply him with materials and to do portions of the work, such as plastering, electrical, and plumbing. These are people the buyer may never meet or ever see. If, however, they perform services on the home site and are not paid, such subcontractors, suppliers of material, and workmen can, in most states, file liens against the property, called *mechanic's liens*, even though the buyer had no agreement with them.

In specific terms the building contract provides that the general contractor, on behalf of himself and all subcontractors, laborers, and suppliers of materials, will not lien the property for nonpayment. In some states a contract between the person building the home and the general contractor may specifically waive the right to file a mechanic's lien. This contract can be recorded in the courthouse so that any contractor or other "mechanic" dealing with the general contractor can know that the general contractor has waived the right to file mechanic's liens against the property. In those states where such a contract is permitted, the contract waiving the right to file mechanic's liens must be signed and filed before any work is done or any materials are supplied.

In rare cases general contractors will try to retain the right to file mechanic's liens by having supplies delivered to the project quickly, or by doing a minimal amount of work so that they can claim later that they started the work or supplied materials before the agreement waiving the mechanic's liens was filed. This is called "spiking the work."

To avoid spiking, many financial institutions, in lending money on new construction, will insist that photographs be taken on the site on the day the construction agreement is signed. The photos prove that no work has been done on the project, and that no supplies have been delivered.

Every buyer should make certain that the building contract provides that no liens can be filed. In states where they are permitted, contracts waiving the right to file a lien should be signed and filed as soon as possible—certainly before any work is done or any supplies delivered.

The construction agreement will provide for payments to the general contractor in accordance with a fixed timetable. The latter is usually based on stages of completion of the dwelling. For example, one-fifth of the total price must be paid after the foundation is completed, and so on. Normally, such agreements should provide that no payment will be made until the architect or job supervisor is satisfied that the work has been completed to that stage and issues a certificate to that effect. In such agreements, too, the architect or job supervisor should be named as the sole judge of the quality of the work, of any damages that may have been incurred because of delays, of the timeliness with which the work is proceeding, and of the degree to which the plans and specifications have been followed.

The construction contract also provides for changes in the work, normally accomplished by a "written change order." To protect the buyer, the architect, and the general contractor, the construction contract should provide only for written change orders signed by all parties. The reason: change orders may increase or decrease in number depending on the circumstances and the type of payment due.

As an example, the builder may indicate that a certain type of furnace that was specified is no longer available. He may suggest a substitute. If the different model is available at a lower price, a written change order would be prepared indicating the substitution of the new furnace and a reduction in the cost of the dwelling.

Normally, of course, change orders call for an increase in the purchase price due to a change in market conditions. At that time the parties should decide whether or not the change order should be executed. The important thing to remember here is that provisions for change orders should be included in the original construction contract.

One of the most important parts of the building or construction contract is the clause that sets a completion date. Normally, the owner's permanent financing is based on completion of the dwelling before a certain date. The date agreed upon in the contract should make some provision for the unforeseen contingencies that may arise. For example, strikes may cause certain supplies to be delivered late to the site through no fault of the general contractor. Or bad weather might delay the contract completion date. If, however, a delay occurs through the fault of the contractor, the building and construction agreement should provide for damages to be paid by the contractor at a fixed rate per day.

Finally, the construction contract should contain provisions giving the owner the right to terminate the contract for cause. That means the contractor is not doing the work properly or is not following the specifications.

These basic contract provisions and the advice of a family lawyer will protect the buyer and provide for remedies in the event the general contractor defaults. The provisions also protect the buyer if the general contractor, after receiving payment, fails to pay the subcontractors. The latter will not be able to file a lien against the property or force the buyer to pay twice for the same work.

Construction Bonds

A bond is a personal commitment by the principal, the general contractor, and the surety, usually an insurance company, that both are bound to the third party, the buyer or owner, in a certain amount. The bond is conditioned on proper performance of the contract and payment of all subcontractors and suppliers.

- In a *performance bond,* the general contractor and the insurance company guarantee that the contractor will perform properly his end of the contract. If he does not, and the owner has to find another contractor to complete the work, the insurance company will pick up the additional costs.
- The *labor and material payment bond* guarantees that the general contractor will pay all his subcontractors and material suppliers. If he does not, the insurance company will step in and pay the claims.

While these bonds are normally used on large projects, they

are available and may be required by contract in the construction of a home. While the premiums for these bonds are normally added to the contract price by the general contractor, the bonds are well worth the money because they give valuable added protection.

A word of caution regarding construction bonds: when the construction contract or the building plans and specifications are altered or modified in any way, the written consent of the insurance company must be obtained on every change. If this is not done, and if the contractor does not perform properly, the insurance company can claim that the change increased the possibility that the company would have to pay without its consent. Since the risk was increased, the company is no longer liable on the bonds.

If the change in the plans does increase the risk to the insurance company, it will be relieved of liability under the bond. Consent to the change should be secured from the insurance company when change orders are made out. Consent may be obtained by an architect, job supervisor, or lawyer. But it must be obtained!

The construction contract should also require that the general contractor provide the owner with insurance certificates, issued by his insurance company, protecting all parties against accidents. The certificates state that the contractor has liability insurance and workers' compensation insurance in sufficient amounts to protect himself and the owner in case of a construction accident, injury, or death. The buyer should be named as an insured person in these policies. Also, obviously, materials will be delivered to the property and more and more value will be added to the structure as construction goes forward. These values could be lost if fire should destroy the incomplete home.

The construction contract itself should provide for fire insurance coverage in the event of loss by fire or some other casualty. Again, the buyer should be named as an insured. A conference with an insurance counselor on the appropriate coverage is well worth the time. It will pay off in peace of mind and in dollars and cents should a loss occur. The agreement should require that the general contractor provide the buyer with the insurance certificates so the buyer will be assured of having complete protection.

Common Disputes During Construction

Disputes arising between an owner and a contractor during construction of a dwelling usually center on whether the plans and specifications are adequate. Other questions may arise: whether the land was in the condition represented by the owner, whether the contractor suffered additional costs because of stone encountered in excavating, whether extras claimed by the contractor were properly ordered and charged to the job, and whether the contractor deviated from the plans and specifications. Many of these disputes can be avoided by careful preparation of documents, a complete investigation of the contractor's reputation and prior performance, and a common-sense effort to be fair and understand the other guy's problems.

Protection in Making Payments

After the architect or job superintendent certifies that the work has been completed, the owner should make the final payment. A "retainage," a certain percentage of each periodic payment, is usually held back from earlier payments to ensure that the work will be done properly. The retainage is also paid over to the contractor on satisfactory completion of the work.

Before making final payment, the owner should obtain from the contractor statements signed by each subcontractor and supplier that he has been paid in full. No subcontractors or suppliers will then be able to file future claims. These statements, called "releases of liens," are standard documents.

The complicated process of building a home requires the owner's close attention. He will, after all, live there for many years. A little study and care can save much money, many headaches, and a great deal of heartache. To keep that dream house from becoming a nightmare, do not hesitate to insist that the construction contract include the provisions discussed here.

The best protection, however, is a solid, competent, reputable contractor who stands behind his work. Spend as much time as necessary to find the best contractor available.

FINANCING THE PURCHASE OR BUILDING OF YOUR HOME

No discussion of the purchase or construction of a home would be complete without some discussion of how one pays for it. Not everyone, unfortunately, is in a position to pay cash when purchasing a home. Most people have to give much thought to the ways in which they can pay for it.

Mortgages have traditionally been used to finance the purchase of real estate. They are not the sole means; personal loans, with or without security, can also be utilized. But in most cases, mortgages are used. With a mortgage, the owner retains the benefits of ownership while offering the property as security for a loan from the lender. While mortgages are different in the various states, the lender's interest in all cases is solely to protect his loan.

Like a deed, a mortgage must be recorded. Then the mortgagee, the party holding the mortgage, has a protected security in the real estate against third parties who might not know of the mortgage loan. The mortgage represents a lien on the real estate; it creates no personal liability on the part of the owner of the land. The mortgage follows the land from one owner to another as long as it is not paid.

The owner may become personally liable for the total amount of the mortgage loan by means of a *note* or a *bond* that can accompany the mortgage. This means that the owner signs a personal promise to pay back the entire loan. He also, of course, signs the mortgage, which creates a *security lien* in the hands of the lender. These are different documents creating different rights and obligations.

Certain types of mortgages and ancillary documents are commonly used in buying or building a home.

Purchase Money Mortgage

Because of financial problems facing a buyer, he may be unable to secure financing to purchase a home from any conventional mortgage or finance company. At the same time the seller may be willing to finance part of the purchase price. In other words, the seller says to the buyer, "Look, if you can't come up with all the money you need, give me a down payment and I will take back monthly payments, at interest, over a term of X number of years. Give me a mortgage to that effect, and we'll go ahead with the deal."

What the seller is talking about is a *purchase money mortgage,* a mortgage running back to the seller that covers the balance of the purchase price after the down payment is made. The seller takes a position similar to that of a bank or financial institution. He gives the buyer an opportunity to pay the balance in monthly installments with interest over a term of years.

Like every other mortgage, a purchase money mortgage must be recorded. However, to protect the seller, many states, by statute, give priority to a purchase money mortgage if it is recorded within a certain number of days or weeks from the date of the settlement. This is true even though there may be other liens filed on the real estate between the final closing and the date on which the purchase money mortgage is actually recorded.

The purchase money mortgage method is a very important method of financing for those buyers who cannot secure conventional mortgages. In some cases, too, buyers may obtain mortgage money from a financial institution for part of the purchase price. These buyers then need additional funds to complete their purchases. Where the seller will take back a purchase money mortgage, that becomes a "second mortgage"—second in priority to the first mortgage provided by the financial institution.

Conventional Mortgages

Savings banks, commercial banks, savings and loan associations, building and loan groups, credit unions, and other private mortgage companies may grant *conventional mortgages* if the buyer qualifies for a loan as regards occupation, income, credit history, and so on. If a buyer goes into the mortgage department of a commercial bank seeking money to buy a dwelling, he must qualify for the loan under the rules of the individual bank. These rules touch on such things as the amount of money the buyer will put down in cash, the number of years the mortgage is to run, the interest rate to be paid on the mortgage, whether or not the buyer can afford the monthly payment in view of his monthly income, and whether or not he is a good credit risk.

In brief, the financial institution looks to the property to make certain it is sufficiently valuable to support a mortgage in the amount sought. The institution looks at the individual buyer to ensure that he is qualified for a mortgage under the rules and regulations.

Conventional mortgages change from time to time. They undergo changes, for example, in the interest rates charged, the total terms of mortgages insofar as numbers of years is concerned, and in many other respects. The economy in which we live has much to do with determining interest rates. Much has been written in recent years of the so-called "prime rate," the rate of interest that financial institutions charge their most valued clients. If the prime rate of interest at Bank X is 15 per cent, then it is to be expected that the rate of interest charged to other than prime clients will be higher than that. The individual buying a home is usually "other than a prime client." The buyer seeking a conventional loan to buy a house should, thus, "shop" for his mortgage at various financial institutions to get the best deal he can as far as interest rate and number of years are concerned.

Mortgages may be deceptive. A mortgage at one bank or financial institution for a 25-year term may mean a monthly payment of principal and interest of $400 while a mortgage at a different bank for a 20-year term may cost $450 per month. While the monthly payment may be more in the latter case, the total amount paid over the life of the mortgage would be much greater on a 25-year basis than on a 20-year basis.

In "shopping" for a mortgage, the buyer should determine the exact cost of that mortgage over the entire term of the mortgage. Only then can he make an intelligent decision on the financing of the purchase.

Other factors have also to be considered. Whether or not the mortgage has a *prepayment privilege* becomes very important. Many mortgages have a penalty clause: the buyer pays a penalty if the mortgage is paid in full prior to its expiration date. This penalty is usually stated as a percentage of the total mortgage loan. Where possible, the buyer should secure a mortgage that allows prepayment without penalty.

The lender may insist, however, that the buyer both sign a bond or note, as mentioned, and allow other property to be covered by the mortgage in order to further secure the loan.

In the case of an existing dwelling, the amount of a conventional mortgage is ordinarily based on an appraisal of the property. Either by law or by its own policy, the financial institution involved will loan only up to a certain percentage of the appraised value, whether it be 75 per cent, 66⅔ per cent, 90 per cent, or whatever figure may be involved. When money is "tight," the financial institution requires a much larger percentage of the total price as a deposit from the buyer and grants a lower percentage of the balance under the mortgage. In times of "easy money," a much larger mortgage can usually be found.

Alternative Mortgage Instruments

Home mortgage loans have evolved in new directions in the 1970s and early 1980s. The new forms sought partly to adapt the traditional fixed-rate, fixed-term, level-payment mortgage to new conditions. One type, for example, the *graduated payment mortgage* (GPM), was designed to accommodate payment levels to changing patterns of family income. Where the conventional mortgage cannot take account of the fact that a young family may see its income increasing over the years, the GPM can and does. Under this plan the payments on the mortgage start at lower than average levels and increase gradually over the years.

New mortgage formats also tried to take into account some basic economic facts in prolonged periods of inflation. The *variable-rate mortgage* seeks, for example, to protect lenders. It gives the lender the right to raise interest rates on existing mortgages as nationwide trends push interest rates up. Theoretically, rates can go down if local or regional rates drop.

At least four of the more common types of new or experimental mortgages should be described.

The "Rollover" or Renegotiable Mortgage. In effect, the "rollover" or renegotiable mortgage gives both the borrower and lender a means of re-setting the mortgage interest rate. The loan rate is set for a specific period—usually three or five years. At the end of that time it can be renegotiated to conform more closely with current mortgage loan rates.

Generally, the borrower has the option to find new financing if he and the lender cannot agree on the new loan rate.

The Variable-Rate Mortgage (VRM). The most widely used of the new mortgage formats, the VRM normally has provisions that make possible adjustments in the interest rate, the length of the loan, or a combination of the two. Both can be changed as general interest rates vary. In most cases the adjustments can be made once or twice a year. A ceiling limits the extent to which the interest rate can be changed. Customarily, this ceiling keeps aggregate changes at 2.5 percent—up or down—over the life of the loan.

The borrower using a VRM may have the option of extending the payoff period while keeping monthly payments at a given level. But the VRM favors the lender; it enables the institution to increase the loan rates on existing mortgages within legally specified limits. A loan taken out initially at 9 per cent can go to 11.5 per cent before the principal has been paid off.

The Graduated Payment Mortgage (GPM). Young people starting families have provided the most receptive market for the GPM. This type of mortgage sets monthly payments that start low, become larger over a period of time, usually five years, and then level off. The buyer of a home who takes a $40,000, 30-year mortgage at 9.5 per cent would, under a typical GPM, pay about $255 a month initially. The payments would increase by 7.5 per cent a year for five years, then remain at that level.

But—a major but—the same borrower would have been making payments at first that were $80 per month less than they would have been under a conventional loan agreement of the same size.

Over the long haul of a 30-year GPM, the borrower would pay substantially more ($127,601) than he would have with a conventional mortgage ($121,083).

The Reverse Annuity Mortgage (RAM). Where the GPM serves the young, climbing, ambitious homeowner, the RAM is adapted to the needs of older men and women. The somewhat experimental RAM makes it possible for the older person with a mortgage-free home to recover some of the equity in his or her home without moving out.

The RAM works like this. The homeowner takes out a loan on the home under an RAM. The lender pays out the loan in either a lump sum or in pre-established monthly payments. The homeowner not only continues to reside in the Old Homestead; he now has money with which to take care of rising property taxes and home maintenance costs. He may have some money for that trip to Italy.

The RAM poses many legal and other questions. Among them: does the homeowner want to sacrifice part of his estate, to pay back the loan after his death, rather than leave it all to his heirs? If Aunt Jenny dies leaving the homeowner half a million, can the RAM be set aside—paid off in full?

The questions do not mean that the RAM has no real value. In specific cases it obviously can help older persons, retired or not. A plus is that it can be adapted almost entirely to the situation of the borrower.

Commitment Letter

Once the terms of the mortgage have been agreed on, the lender will ordinarily issue a commitment letter. The letter states the terms of the mortgage, such as interest rate, number of years, and other relevant facts. The commitment letter from the financial institution usually remains in effect for a specified period of time, such as 90 days or 120 days. If the sale is not completed within that period, the financial institution is no longer committed to give the mortgage, and no other terms remain in effect. The institution can refuse to proceed on the basis of its prior commitment letter. Where a conventional mortgage is secured, the sale should obviously be closed within the time limitation indicated in the commitment letter.

Financing the Construction of a Dwelling

Financing the construction of a dwelling differs from the financing of the purchase of an existing dwelling. In the typical case, financing a home to be built is divided into two stages: the construction phase and the permanent financing phase.

A short-term mortgage, for a year or 18 months, is normally written to finance the construction of a new dwelling or improvements on an existing dwelling. Some lenders cannot, by law, make short-term loans to finance construction; other lenders can do so. In other words, certain lenders can only issue commitment letters for "permanent" mortgages when the dwelling is completed.

Essentially, this distinction means that a construction mortgage involves a somewhat higher risk than a permanent mortgage obtained after the home has been completed. For example, the home may never be built; the contractor may default; the owner may run into difficulties; as a result, the financial institution may find itself with a home that is half built and a substantial investment already paid out.

Because of the higher risk, short-term construction loans are generally made at a higher interest rate than are permanent mortgages. Thus investors are attracted to this type of investment.

The buyer has his plans and specifications prepared. The next step is to approach the lender who, he feels, may give him a construction loan. The application for the loan usually requires financial information concerning the borrower, the architect, and others. Then come the appraisal of the property by the financial institution, inspection of the survey, and investigation of the credit ratings of the owner and the contractor.

The lender will also want to know where the balance of the construction money, if any, is coming from and who will be the "permanent" lender—who will provide the permanent mortgage after the home is built.

In many cases, the construction-loan lender and the permanent lender are one and the same institution. If so, the institution may simply advance funds from time to time on the basis of the mortgage. The mortgage may become permanent after completion of the entire project. The mortgage may also set forth the full amount needed at the beginning of the work, and funds may be advanced from time to time to complete the project; at final completion, a final settlement is made.

Construction-loan mortgages may differ from permanent mortgages in many details. But the principles mentioned above ordinarily govern. The builder can sometimes aid in the securing of financing, but if the builder does extensive business with the financial institution, the owner should have his own inspector or architect follow the progress of the work from beginning to end. Otherwise, the financial institution's inspector could intentionally or unintentionally favor the contractor in a dispute arising over a progress payment. The attorney, architect, or job superintendent can assist sometimes in securing financing and in determining the type of inspection and supervision of the work on a day-to-day basis.

As noted, the financing institution will usually inspect only to determine whether or not, in its judgment, the progress of the work has proceeded sufficiently far to allow the next payment to be made to the contractor. The institution is not really as concerned as the owner with the day-to-day quality of the work. The owner should take all necessary steps to make sure the work is being done properly.

A commitment letter is issued by the financial institution on the construction-loan financing as well as on the permanent financing. Such a letter will spell out all the terms and conditions of the commitment on the construction loan.

Insured Mortgages

Because the federal government issues mortgage insurance of several different types, an owner may qualify for a mortgage at a slightly lower interest rate than is normally possible. A smaller down payment may be required. Financial institutions will make loans under such circumstances because the federal government, through the Federal Housing Administration (FHA) or through the Veterans' Administration (VA), will insure mortgages. That means the lender will be paid the amount of the mortgage on default by the borrower.

An FHA-insured mortgage will usually allow a qualified borrower to receive 90 per cent financing. The borrower pays 10 per cent down and obtains 90 per cent financing at a slightly lower interest rate than that placed on the conventional mortgage. The same holds true for a veteran's mortgage.

The rules and regulations governing these types of mortgages are very precise and complicated; the advice of an attorney is essential in qualifying and proceeding with this type of mortgage. In "shopping" for his mortgage, the owner should not overlook the possibility that he may qualify for government-insured mortgages at lower interest rates and requiring smaller down payments.

Disclosure of Interest Rates

Recent federal and state laws, including the federal "truth-in-lending" and various state consumer-protection laws, require that mortgage and loan institutions disclose to the consumer all the terms of the sale insofar as financing is concerned. These terms include interest rates and annual percentage rate of interest charged. The borrower can then ascertain the exact amount and cost of securing a loan and making a purchase.

The owner-borrower may be asked to sign a "disclosure statement" at a closing on his loan. The statement indicates that he has received all the necessary disclosures required by law with respect to interest, time payment charges, and all other required information. Failure on the part of the financial institution to make proper disclosure in cases where such disclosure is required may render the entire transaction null and void. Such failure may even make the institution liable in damages or penalty to the borrower or consumer.

Because of the nature of this legislation and its importance, the advice of a lawyer is essential to anyone dealing with these problems. A detailed discussion of truth-in-lending laws follows in a later chapter.

THE SELLER'S PROBLEMS

You may at this point be asking, "Whatever happened to the seller?" Everything appearing so far in this chapter has had to do with the buyer's problems: finding the property, obtaining an agreement of sale, checking the title, closing the deal, getting a proper deed, and finding the proper financing for both the purchase of an existing home and the building of a new home. What about the seller?

The seller in most cases has much less to worry about than does a buyer. The seller owns the property, and is primarily concerned with finding a buyer who is ready, willing, and able to purchase the property on terms that are agreeable to him.

If the seller has set a realistic price on the property—and this is important because being unrealistic leads only to delays in finding a buyer—the seller can proceed to sell in two different ways. First, he can try to find a buyer himself. Second, he may make use of a real estate broker to find a buyer.

If he tries to sell the property himself, the seller may be successful in a very short period of time. He may also have to walk many prospective buyers through his house on a regular basis. Some of these persons may only be incidentally interested in the property, or just curious.

Selection of a Real Estate Broker

If the seller decides to use the services of a broker, it is important to select a broker who is totally familiar with the area, who can answer the questions of prospective buyers, and who has a good record for moving properties.

How do you find such a broker? Again, consult other persons who have recently sold property and who have had good experience with a particular broker. Consult the real estate brokers' local board for help in this regard. Don't be afraid to ask questions to find out whether or not a particular broker is sufficiently interested in your property and is sufficiently knowledgeable in the area.

In interviewing a broker, one useful method is to quote to the particular broker a price that the seller himself knows is too high for the property. If the broker readily agrees that the property is worth what is clearly an exorbitant price, chances are he is only after the *listing* of the property. He will later come back to report that the price is too high and that it has to come down.

The broker will already have the written listing agreement. He will not have to worry about losing the seller as a client for the period of time covered by the agreement.

If the broker truthfully and sincerely indicates that the asking price is too high, the chances are that he is more reliable. The seller can usually deal with him with a high degree of confidence. These are only assumptions, however. The seller's best protection is the reputation of the broker, his memberships in the professional real estate boards in the area, and his experience.

Exclusive Listing Agreements

Once the seller has found a broker, an "exclusive listing agreement" may come up for discussion. This means that the broker wants the property listed for sale with his firm exclusively for a fixed period of time, usually from 90 days to six months. The property cannot be sold through any other broker during that period.

THE JARGON OF REAL ESTATE[1]

Here, courtesy of Sylvia Porter, is a guide to the bafflegab of buying and selling real estate.

ABSTRACT. Short legal history of a property tracing ownership over the years and noting such encumbrances as unpaid taxes and liens.

AMORTIZATION. Reduction of a debt through monthly mortgage payments (or some other schedule of repayment in which the loan principal is reduced), along with payments of interest and other loan costs.

APPRAISAL. Estimate, made by the Federal Housing Administration, the Veterans Administration, a private lender, or other qualified appraiser, of the current market value of a property.

ASSESSMENT. Special charge imposed by local government on homeowners to cover costs of special projects such as street paving or new sewer systems from which the homeowners presumably benefit.

BINDER. Tentative agreement, between a buyer and seller of real estate, to the terms of the transaction—usually involving a deposit of a small amount of money.

BROKER. Professional who is licensed by the state in which he works to assist buyers and sellers of property.

CERTIFICATE OF TITLE. Legal statement to the effect that property ownership is established by public records.

CLOSING. The occasion on which the buyer and seller of a property—or their representatives—meet to exchange payment for the deed to a property.

CLOSING COSTS. Costs, other than the basic purchase price of a piece of property, which are imposed at the time a real estate deal is closed. Closing costs can include lawyers' fees, title insurance, taxes, and several other items.

COMMISSION. Fee which a seller of property pays to a real estate agent for his services—usually amounting to six to ten per cent of the sale price.

CONDOMINIUM. Individually owned real estate consisting of a dwelling unit and an undivided interest in joint facilities and areas which serve the multiunit complex.

CO-OPERATIVE. A form of real estate ownership in which each individual owns stock in a corporation, giving him the right to live in one of the units owned and administered by the corporation.

DEED. Legal, written document used to transfer ownership of property from seller to buyer.

DEFAULT. In this context, failure by a buyer to meet a mortgage payment or other requirement of the sale—which may result in forfeiture of the property itself.

DEPOSIT (or "EARNEST MONEY"). Sum of money, normally a small fraction of the sale price of the property, which a prospective buyer gives to a seller to secure a sales contract. See "Binder."

DEPRECIATION. Decrease in the value of property due to wear and tear, obsolescence, or the action of the elements. Differs from deterioration, which signifies abnormal loss of quality.

EARNEST MONEY. A deposit. *See* above.

EASEMENT. Right granted to one property owner by another to use the grantor's land for certain purposes—for example, a right of way for an access road or for power lines.

ENCUMBRANCE (or DEFECT OF RECORD). Claim against the title of a parcel of real estate by a third party, other than the buyer or seller (e.g., a lien due to unpaid taxes or a mortgage delinquency), which challenges the property's ownership and tends to reduce its value.

EQUITY. In real estate terms, value built up in a property over the years, including the down payment, repaid portion of the mortgage principal, and appreciation (or depreciation) in the property's market value. The amount of equity in a property is the total current value of the property minus debts against the property.

ESCROW. The placing of money or other items of value in the custody of a bank or other third party until the terms of a real estate transaction are fulfilled by the two parties involved. Also, amounts paid by a homeowner into an account, usually administered by the mortgage lender, to provide for recurring expenses such as real estate taxes and homeowner insurance premiums. This type of escrow usually is included in the total monthly payments to the lender.

FHA. Federal Housing Administration, which insures mortgage holders against losses from default on loans made according to the Administration's policies.

FORECLOSURE. Sale by a bank or other lender of a property on which payments are seriously in default in order to satisfy the debt at least partially.

LIEN. Claim against a property which sometimes is kept as security for the repayment of a debt.

LISTING. Registration of a property with one or more real estate brokers or agents, entitling the broker who actually sells the property to a commission. An exclusive listing gives one individual broker the exclusive right to handle the sale of a property; a multiple listing permits a special group of brokers to handle the transaction.

MORTGAGE. Legal claim on property, given as security by a borrower to the lender of the funds in case repayment of the loan is not made.

OPTION. Often sold by a seller of property to prospective buyer, giving the latter the right to buy the property at a specified price within a specified period of time.

PLAT. Pictorial plan or map of a land subdivision or housing development.

POINTS. Part of the settlement costs of exchanging real estate. One point is 1 per cent of the amount of the mortgage. Points are paid to the mortgage lender. In some cases, the term simply means a service charge imposed by the lender to cover part of the administrative costs of processing the loan. In other cases, particularly when an FHA loan is involved, the points amount to an adjustment in the interest rate to bring an artificially administered rate up to the market rate at the time. Points, in this second sense, technically are paid by the seller of the property. However, since the price of the house normally is adjusted to allow for this, points always effectively increase the interest rate on the loan to the buyer. They tend to eliminate the interest rate advantage of government-insured or guaranteed loans.

PURCHASE MONEY MORTGAGE. Mortgage granted directly by a seller to the buyer of the seller's property, in which the seller may take back the property if the buyer does not pay off the mortgage as agreed. In brief, the seller of the house lends the buyer the money with which

to buy the house.

QUITCLAIM DEED. Deed which releases any interest a seller or other individual may have in a given piece of land. *See* "Deed."

REAL ESTATE (REAL PROPERTY). Land, and any structures situated on it.

REALTOR. Real estate agent who is a member of the National Association of Realtors. A copyrighted word, always capitalized.

SETBACK. A common restriction provided under zoning ordinances specifying the distance a new house must be set back from a road or from the lot boundaries.

SURVEY. The determination, by means of examination of land records and also field measurements based on these records, of the exact boundaries and location of a property.

TITLE. Legal document containing all necessary facts to prove ownership of property.

TITLE DEFECT. Fact or circumstance which challenges such ownership.

[1] **Selections from** *Sylvia Porter's New Money Book for the 80's* by Sylvia Porter, copyright © 1975, 1979 by Sylvia Porter. Reprinted by permission of Doubleday & Company, Inc.

Often, even though an exclusive agreement has been signed with Broker X, he will place the property on a so-called "multilist," a group of brokers who work together to sell a particular piece of property on a split commission basis. The multilist is also called a Multiple Listing Service (MLS). In this case the listing broker receives a percentage of the real estate commission regardless of which multilist broker actually sells the property.

Ordinarily, an exclusive real estate listing agreement contains a special clause. It provides that if the property is sold to someone who was introduced by the broker during the term of the exclusive listing agreement, then the broker earns his commission regardless of the fact that the property was sold directly to the buyer after the listing agreement had expired.

A hypothetical case shows what this can mean. You sign a six-month exclusive real estate listing agreement with Broker Brown. After three months have gone by, Broker Brown brings Mr. Smith to look at your house. You hear nothing from Mr. Smith for another eight months. If Mr. Smith comes back after the listing agreement has expired and says he wants to buy the property, you will owe the broker a commission since Mr. Smith was introduced to the property by the broker during the exclusive listing agreement period.

From the standpoint of the broker, the special clause prevents the parties from agreeing among themselves not to deal until the exclusive listing agreement period has expired. From the seller's point of view, however, the clause creates a difficult situation. A lawsuit could result if the seller and the broker disagree as to whether or not the individual to whom the property was sold was in fact introduced to the property by the broker.

Depending on the language used in the listing agreement, it becomes very important for the seller to protect himself in such a situation. Another provision in the exclusive listing agreement should require that the broker supply the seller with the names of all persons with whom the broker has discussed the property—or to whom he has shown the property during the term of the exclusive agreement. The list should be given to the seller at the end of the term of the agreement. This provision protects the seller in dealing with third parties after the expiration of the exclusive contract.

The requirement that the broker supply a list of names is fair to both the seller and the broker. It should not be objected to.

Multilist Plans

When a piece of property is placed on a multilist, the seller in effect engages the services of many more brokers whether he deals only through one or directly through the multilist. While some of these services have come under attack because of alleged antitrust problems, they do exist. They also bring in many brokers who will work to sell a property.

How long should an exclusive listing agreement run? Caution should be exercised. The period should not be too long. Six months, for example, is usually too long.

The circumstances of each particular case should, of course, be considered. A lawyer may be able to advise the seller. But in the normal situation, 90 to 120 days should be long enough. If more time is allowed on an exclusive agency agreement, the broker may have a tendency to push off the sale of the property while trying to "move" properties on which the listing agreements are about to expire. This is only human nature. But it may leave the seller with little activity on the sale of his property for a long time.

When Does a Broker Earn His Commission?

While the law differs from one state to another on this point, many states provide that a broker earns his commission once he finds a buyer who signs an agreement of sale. Even if the sale of the property does not go through because the buyer cannot qualify for the mortgage, or because he decides he does not want to buy for whatever reason, the broker nevertheless has earned his commission once a buyer signs an agreement.

Once again the seller should protect himself. The listing agreement should specify clearly that the broker earns his commission only when and if a final closing takes place. The buyer must of course have been introduced to the property by that broker.

Where a seller decides to keep the earnest money as liquidated damages, as noted, disagreement over a broker's commission may be minimized. Many listing agreements provide that the earnest money be split between the broker and the seller where a sale falls through. Where, however, the broker's commission exceeds the amount of the earnest money paid, the seller may have to pay the commission to the broker from his own funds.

Another form of listing agreement is the "nonexclusive" type. Here, the broker is given the right to sell the property on behalf of the seller, but other brokers have the same right. The nonexclusive agreement is similar to the multilist plans. But the seller can deal with several brokers individually, and each has the right to sell the property on his behalf. All that has been said before in connection with the exclusive agency agreement applies equally to the nonexclusive agreement.

Most real estate brokers work hard and diligently to secure buyers for residential property. While the commission earned in a particular case may seem high, usually 6 or 7 per cent, the broker may show the property to many persons before finding a buyer. Thus the selection of a qualified broker to assist in the sale of property can be of great help.

How can the law work for you in the purchase and sale of a home?

If you study the principles discussed in this chapter, you will be able to speak intelligently about real estate. You will also know what questions to ask, and can save money by understanding ahead of time what you are dealing with. You will be in a much stronger bargaining position, which, after all, is the name of the game.

Good luck in your new home!

IV – Tenant, Owner, and the Law

Suppose you have no desire to purchase or build a home. You would rather find a place to live on a somewhat temporary basis. In such a case, you will probably want to rent an apartment. This is particularly true of young married couples who may not have the means to purchase a home immediately.

What is involved in renting an apartment? What should the average tenant look for in the way of space, amount of rent, and other conditions of the lease? What is a lease and how does it operate?

FINDING THE RIGHT APARTMENT

Apartment-for-rent listings appear in the classified ad columns of local newspapers. A broker or real estate agent can often help in the search for the right apartment. So can the various neighborhood or area services that exist for that purpose.

Is an entire home needed or only a part of a residence, such as the first or second floor of a duplex? Most persons know they need a certain number of rooms. Thus, in hunting for an apartment, they consider the amount of space available, the amount of rent to be paid, and whether or not the landlord is willing to renew the lease or will grant an option to renew the lease for a future term. Other lease provisions will be discussed later.

A CHECKLIST FOR APARTMENT HUNTERS[1]

	YES	NO
Is building sound, attractive, well built?		
Is it well managed and maintained?		
Are corridors and entranceways clean and well lighted?		
Is protection from burglars provided?		
Is there a doorman?		
Is landscaping pleasant?		
Is there enough outdoor space?		
Are extras you want included (such as swimming pool, steam baths, a gym for men and women)?		
Is there parking space, indoor or outdoor?		
Is there a receiving room for packages?		
Is laundry equipment available?		
Are fire escapes adequate?		
Are there fire extinguishers?		
Is trash collected or disposed of?		
Are there storage rooms or facilities?		
Are there elevators?		
Are mailboxes locked?		
Is routine maintenance—window washing, decorating, painting—provided?		
Are servicemen available for emergency repairs?		
Is the floor plan convenient?		
Is the apartment big enough?		
Are rooms light enough?		
Are wall spaces adequate for your furniture?		
Is the apartment soundproof?		
Is decorating (if any) attractive?		
Are views attractive?		
Are there enough windows, and are they well located?		
Are there screens and storm windows?		
Are major appliances you need installed?		
Are appliances in good condition?		
Is wiring sufficient?		
Is ventilation adequate?		
Will cleaning be easy?		
Are there separate heat controls for each part of the apartment?		
Are there enough electric outlets and are they well located?		
Do windows and doors, including cabinet doors, open and close easily?		
Is there air conditioning?		
Is there a fireplace? Does it work?		
Is there carpeting?		
Is there a balcony?		
Are there workable blinds or shades?		

[1] **Selections from** *Sylvia Porter's New Money Book for the 80's* by Sylvia Porter, copyright © 1975, 1979 by Sylvia Porter. Reprinted by permission of Doubleday & Company, Inc.

Having found the right apartment, the prospective tenant should understand the relationship that he or she will be entering into with the landlord. The lease establishes that relationship.

What Is a Lease?

A lease can be oral. Much more commonly, it is a written document that transfers the *right of possession* of real estate to a tenant for a specified term. The term of the lease may be a month, several months, a year, or more than one year. A lease may be *at sufferance,* meaning that it can be terminated by the landlord at any time.

The lease should set forth all the terms and conditions of the tenant's occupancy of the property for the entire term of the lease.

Provisions Usually Found in a Lease

Leases for residential uses or occupancy, not business leases, are considered here. The terms that are discussed below are limited primarily to leases for residential purposes, not those for commercial purposes.

Rental Payments. The apartment is perfect, and vacant. The first question that comes up is, typically, the amount of rent. It is important to understand that rent is the price paid for the occupancy of the space described in the lease. If the lease is to run for one year, the amount of rent is determined, normally, on a total yearly rental basis. In other words, the lease will provide that "for the total rent of X dollars, payable in monthly installments of X dollars a month, being one-twelfth of the annual rent, you, as tenant, have the right to occupy the premises." You become legally obligated for the entire year's rent, even though you pay rent on a monthly installment basis.

This becomes important if for some reason, before the year is up, the tenant wants to vacate the property or to get out of the lease. He has committed himself, however, to pay rent for the entire year. Unless the lease provides an "out," he may be required by the landlord to pay the whole amount.

It is possible to negotiate with the landlord the proper term of the lease. The recently married person who wants to have a place to live for a year should probably ask for a one-year lease. The landlord will want to know that the property will be rented for a reasonable time. The tenant usually wants a reasonable period so that he will have time to find another place—if he is looking for a permanent home. He will want a sufficiently long term to make it unnecessary to go looking for another apartment in the near future.

How likely is it that the landlord will be prepared and willing to negotiate the terms of a lease—including the period for which it will run? In practical fact, most landlords know they want tenants who will "stay for awhile." These landlords will offer the prospective tenant a one-year or two-year lease. The apartment seeker can then accept or reject.

The flat rental has just been described: a uniform monthly installment rate for the entire term of the lease. But other, less common forms of rental arrangements are available. Each of them, however, anticipates a total rent payable in some form of installment, perhaps in equal installments. The total amount of rent for the entire term is chargeable to the tenant and payable in various ways.

- A lease may provide for graduated rental payments at specified intervals. It is used normally to compensate the landlord for increasing expenses. Or it may be used where a tenant has inadequate funds in the beginning but expects to be able to pay a higher rent later.

This type of lease provides for rent increases at specified intervals. For example, $250 a month may be charged for the first three months, $275 a month for the next three months, and so on to $325 or $350.

- A lease may provide that a specified portion of the real estate taxes, insurance, or costs of repairs be added periodically to the basic rent. This type of arrangement is normally part of a business lease; but residential leases also may provide for increases in the rent if the taxes on the property go up during the term of the lease. The rent may also go up with increases in utility charges caused by the tenant's use of the property.

The language of these leases usually provides that, "as additional rental," the tenant agrees to pay proportionate amounts of the real estate taxes or utilities. These charges are called "additional rental" to give the landlord the opportunity—if needed—to evict the tenant or sue for back rent.

- In a "cost-of-living lease," the tenant's rental obligation may fluctuate as the cost of living increases. More common in the commercial or business lease, this clause also finds its way into residential leases from time to time.
- Some leases call for a discount if the rent is paid before the tenth day of the month. This is designed to induce the tenant to make his payments promptly.

Whatever the total basic rent or the amount of the installments, the lease should specify the method of payment. If it is payable monthly, the lease should state where it is to be paid—at the home of the landlord or elsewhere. The date on which the initial rent payment is due should be set forth specifically. Then the tenant and the landlord know the date on which the rent is due every month.

Security Deposit. Most landlords try to protect themselves against a tenant's abandonment of the property, failure to maintain the property, nonpayment of rent, or other default. Usually, the tenant is required to deposit extra money with the landlord in advance: this security deposit is used to reimburse the landlord for any such default. In case of default, the lease usually authorizes the landlord to re-let the premises to someone else.

Most leases provide that the security deposit, if not applied by the landlord in the event of a default, will be treated as payment of rent for the last month or months of the lease. In other words, if two months' rent is required as a security deposit, this amount, if not utilized by the landlord because of any default or to pay for damages to the premises, will be refunded to the tenant upon termination of the lease.

Many states have considered or passed legislation concerning the so-called security deposit. Some of the possible questions are whether or not the landlord should be required to pay interest on the security deposit; whether or not security deposits should be allowed at all; and whether or not the landlord should be required to refund the security deposit without suit at the end of a lease.

Any or all of these matters can be discussed with your lawyer where questions arise.

Options in Leases. An option in a lease is a right granted normally to the tenant. There are several types of options.

An *option to renew* is a right granted to the tenant to decide, within a specific period before the expiration of the original lease, whether or not he wants to renew it and, if so, to notify the landlord of that decision. For example, the original lease may provide that the tenant has the option to renew the lease for an additional term of one year. To exercise the option, the tenant has to notify the landlord of that decision at least three months before the expiration of the original one-year lease.

The renewal option is the most common type. The landlord will often require that the renewal term be at a higher rent level than the original term so as to make certain that the rental covers increased costs, taxes, and other expenses.

The lease may contain an *option to purchase.* In this case the tenant rents part of a home that he would like to purchase but cannot for financial reasons. The owner may be willing to rent the property for one year, granting an option to buy the property at a stated price at the expiration of that year or during the term of the lease. The owner may even allow all the rental that has been paid to be applied as a down payment on the purchase of the property once the tenant is ready to proceed with the purchase.

All of this can be arranged in an "option to purchase" clause. However, if the tenant wants such a clause, he should make certain that the option to buy contains all the necessary provisions of an agreement of sale because exercise of the option to purchase turns the lease into an agreement of sale of real estate; therefore, the lease must contain all the necessary provisions of an agreement of sale, including the purchase price and the closing or settlement date.

INTEREST ON SECURITY DEPOSITS? YES, SOMETIMES

Some states, including Illinois, require landlords to pay interest on security deposits under certain conditions. The landlord of some residential real estate may, for example, have to pay 5 per cent interest on any security deposit held more than six months. This rule applies generally to landlords of larger buildings—containing, say, 25 or more units.

The landlord who is obligated to pay security deposit interest will have a "grace period" in which to make payment. The period may be 30 days from the end of the rental term. The landlord can pay the interest in cash or credit the interest to rent due.

Few tenants will go to court to recover security deposit interest—in the event that the landlord does not pay—while they are still tenants. But they have that right, and can recover not only the interest but court costs and attorneys' fees. After the tenant moves, a different situation prevails.

In some states, the landlord may have to return the entire security deposit within 45 days after the tenant moves. The landlord can deduct the costs of repairing damage to the apartment. But he may have to give the tenant an itemized bill for such damages. Then the landlord has to return the balance of the security deposit.

Two types of law may be involved in these cases. One covers payment of interest on security deposits. The second applies to refunds of security deposits.

In either case the tenant—in given states—has the right to sue if the landlord defaults or if the landlord "chisels" on the amount of interest due or the extent of damage to the apartment. A solution may be to go to a Small Claims Court, where no lawyer is required. But some states, as noted, require a defaulting or chiseling landlord to pay attorneys' fees as well as court costs.

Options for additional space or for cancellation may be specified in the lease. A tenant on a long-term lease commonly faces the problem of unexpected events that may require him to vacate before the end of the term. Also, what happens if additional space is needed because of additions to the family? These situations can both be solved by provisions in the lease—if the landlord is willing to include them.

A *cancellation option* gives the tenant the right, at a designated time and with adequate notice, to either cancel his lease with the landlord or eliminate certain space that he no longer needs. The *additional space option,* on the other hand, allows the tenant to take over additional space at designated times, as necessary.

These options, like all other provisions of the lease, must be negotiated with the landlord. If they are granted, they can substantially help the tenant to deal with an unknown future.

Sublease. The right to sublease allows the tenant to give possession of the premises to a *subtenant.* A tenant decides to allow someone else to live in the premises. The subtenant then pays rental to the tenant, who is still obligated under his original lease with the landlord.

Most residence leases contain provisions restricting the right of a tenant to sublease. The reason is that the landlord does not want "unsuitable" subtenants in the premises—persons whom the landlord has not been able to investigate. Usually this restriction states that the tenant cannot sublease all or part of the premises without the prior written consent of the landlord. Where possible, however, the tenant should try to include a sublease agreement, or at least a provision that the landlord will not unreasonably withhold his consent to a sublease.

Where the lease contains a clause against subleasing, the tenant should be prepared to remain on the premises under the lease for the full term—or pay the rent for the full term.

Identify the Premises Leased. It is important that the lease be very specific about what actually is being leased. If an apartment is being leased, the number of rooms and the location of the apartment should be spelled out. If permission to use the basement washer and dryer is granted, this should be indicated. If the right to use a garage on the property is given, this should also be spelled out. If the right to use a yard or recreation area is part of the lease, this should be clearly indicated. Any other similar permitted uses should be noted.

Right to Make Alterations. This is a very important clause in the lease. If the landlord agrees to make alterations for the tenant before the tenant moves in, this should be spelled out in detail. Specifications on the type of alterations should be listed very clearly. The tenant's obligation to pay rent should be conditioned on the landlord's performance of these alterations. Then the tenant need not move into the property until the work is done.

Where the alterations are to be made by the tenant, they are usually subject to the landlord's prior approval. It is, after all, his property. The landlord should understand that the alterations will benefit the property. If that is the case, his consent will usually be given freely.

Where alterations are made, questions may arise at the expiration of the lease regarding ownership of any fixtures attached or fixed to the property by the tenant. The normal lease provision states that such fixtures belong to the landlord unless he agrees otherwise. If possible, the tenant should seek to have the clause provide that he can take the specified fixtures away when he vacates the property.

The tenant may also want to leave specified alterations of fixtures because of the expense that removal involves. The lease should indicate that.

Alterations mean substantial changes in the premises or the addition of fixtures to the premises by a tenant.

Repairs. Perhaps no other provision of the lease causes more difficulty or more lawsuits than the one indicating who is required to repair and maintain the premises.

Normally, the lease provides that at the end of the term the tenant has to return the property to the landlord in the condition in which it was originally leased. Only normal wear and tear is allowed. So-called structural repairs—repairs to parts of the building itself, such as the roof and outside walls—are the responsibility of the landlord unless the lease states otherwise. Interior repairs, having to do with the use and occupancy of the premises, such as leaking faucets, interior plumbing, and a blown fuse, are normally the tenant's responsibility. However, the usual lease form provides that the tenant is responsible for damage resulting from such causes as short circuits, leakage of water, steam, gas, odors, frost, and bursting or leaking of pipes or plumbing.

A tenant signing such a lease is assuming a great deal of responsibility, especially where he may be occupying only a part of a dwelling rather than the entire building.

IN THE TYPICAL STATE: THE LANDLORD'S OBLIGATIONS[1]

Various states have their own laws dealing with landlord-tenant rights and obligations. A typical set of state laws specifies the following obligations of the landlord:

A. The landlord is obliged at all times during the tenancy:
   1) to comply with all applicable building, housing, or health codes, or
   2) in the absence of codes, to maintain all structural components (e.g., roofs, windows, floors, exterior walls, etc.) in good repair; and to maintain the plumbing in a reasonable working condition. The landlord may alter or modify these obligations with respect to a single-family home or duplex by stating so in writing to his tenant(s).

B. Unless otherwise agreed in writing, in addition to the above requirements, the landlord of a dwelling unit, other than a single-family home or duplex, shall also make reasonable provisions for extermination of rats and bugs; supplying locks and keys; removal of garbage; heat; running water and hot water. He must also maintain the common areas in a clean and safe condition.

C. The landlord must disclose in writing to the tenant his name and address, or that of someone authorized by him to act as his agent. He shall disclose this in writing at or before commencement of the tenancy.

D. The landlord may enter the dwelling unit at any time necessary to protect or preserve the premises under the following circumstances:
   1) with the tenant's consent;
   2) in the case of an emergency;
   3) when consent has been unreasonably withheld by the tenant; or
   4) if the legal presumption for abandonment has occurred. The landlord shall not abuse his right of access nor use it to harass the tenant.

E. The landlord must observe and comply with the requirements of the rental agreement. He cannot make any agreements with the tenant which would take away any of the rights of the tenant.

[1] **Adapted from** *Landlord-Tenant: The Law* (Tallahassee: Florida Department of Agriculture and Consumer Services).

Where the tenant is in a good negotiating position, he should demand a clause providing that he is only obligated to make interior repairs of a minor nature, or only such repairs as might result from his own misuse of the property. All other repairs, structural or otherwise, will then be the responsibility of the landlord.

Destruction or Condemnation of the Premises. What happens if, during the term of the lease, the property is destroyed or is condemned for public use? Strange as it may seem, in most states the liability of the tenant to pay rent may continue. To protect himself, therefore, the tenant should insist on a clause in the lease stating that in the event of destruction, the obligation of the tenant to pay any further rent ends immediately. The landlord ordinarily will want a provision specifying that, in the event of condemnation, the entire award for the loss of the property will go to the landlord. The tenant will then not share in the award at all.

While this clause is subject to negotiation in a residential lease, the landlord would normally have the right to claim the entire condemnation award. But it is important that the tenant should have the option to terminate the lease if the premises are destroyed.

Other Provisions of Residential Leases. Some other common clauses in leases deal with these questions:

Pets
Garbage or rubbish removal
Keeping the sidewalks free of snow and ice
Obstruction of sidewalks or doorways
Noises or disturbances in or around the building

The parties may negotiate other provisions from time to time.

DEFAULTS IN LEASES

If a tenant cannot perform under a lease, what happens? What rights does the landlord have in such a case? Normally, a residential lease contains provisions dealing with defaults by the tenant. These defaults fall in two main classes: (1) failure to pay rent or any other sum provided for under the lease, and (2) removal by the tenant of any of the landlord's goods from the premises—or expression of an intention to do so.

In a third type of case, a lien may be filed against the tenant, or bankruptcy proceedings may be begun against him. The tenant may become insolvent, or a receiver may be appointed for him—someone appointed by a court to take over the tenant's business.

Should any of these defaults occur, the landlord under the typical residential lease has the right, first of all, to declare the entire balance of the rent for the remaining term of the lease immediately due and payable. The landlord also can evict the tenant in case any of these defaults should occur. In those states that still recognize it, the landlord has the right to enter a "confession of judgment" for the balance of the rent.

The confession of judgment clause gives the landlord the right to go to court to get a judgment against the tenant for the balance of the rent. The landlord files a paper; he does not have to bring a regular lawsuit. The latter would involve filing a complaint, whereupon the tenant would file an answer to the complaint. In the normal course of events a trial would take place.

The confession of judgment has for some years been under attack in the courts. In some cases it has been declared unconstitutional. The legality of such a lease provision should always be questioned.

The landlord himself may be violating the lease agreement. This occurs most often in a situation known as "constructive eviction." The landlord, failing to make repairs or provide necessary services, such as utilities, renders the premises uninhabitable. The tenant can then claim that he has been unlawfully evicted because of the landlord's breach of the lease. If the tenant can substantiate his claim, his obligation to pay rent ceases until the landlord corrects the default.

At present, state statutes are under consideration regarding the landlord's duty to make the premises habitable. Some states have even adopted, by court decision, a rule that the landlord, in leasing property, delivers a *warranty* to the tenant that the premises are habitable. In these states a tenant can sue the landlord for breach of that warranty where "constructive eviction" occurs.

The tenant may not have to pay rent where a breach of warranty takes place or during the period of a constructive eviction. But the tenant may also have a claim for additional damages if he has to leave the premises or find other housing because of the landlord's breach.

THE SALE CLAUSE

Every residential lease should contain a clause regarding the possible sale of the property while a tenant is in possession. Ordinarily, any buyer of residential real estate buys subject to all existing leases; the buyer should find out who is in possession of the property and the basis on which that person is in possession before he completes the purchase. If a tenant has possession, the buyer should find out on what basis that tenant has possession. The buyer can then buy the property subject to the tenant's rights to remain on the property.

If the landlord wants to change that situation, the lease should provide that in the event of the sale of the property, the tenant agrees to vacate after receiving a certain number of days' or months' notice of the sale. If the lease does not contain a sale clause, then the tenant is guaranteed possession of the property for the full term of the lease, regardless of whether or not the property is ever sold.

Most printed form leases contain a waiver of this protection by the tenant. These forms are usually drawn by the landlord, and a prospective tenant should understand what it means to waive the right to remain on the premises in the event of a sale. The tenant would ordinarily want the sale clause removed from the lease; the landlord may want to keep it. This again is a negotiated item.

IN THE TYPICAL STATE: THE TENANT'S OBLIGATIONS[1]

Various states have their own laws setting out the rights and obligations of the landlord and tenant. A typical body of state law specifies the following obligations of the tenant. Every tenant shall be responsible for:

A. Ensuring that he does nothing to cause the landlord to be in violation of building, housing, and health codes.

B. Keeping that part of the premises which he occupies clean and sanitary, removal of garbage, and keeping the plumbing clean and in working order. This includes not flushing anything down the toilet or washing foreign matter down the sink drain which would have a tendency to cause these units to malfunction.

C. Operating in a reasonable manner all electrical, plumbing, sanitary, heating, ventilating, air-conditioning, and other facilities and appliances, including elevators.

D. Not destroying, damaging, or removing any property belonging to the landlord.

E. Conducting himself, and requiring those who visit him to conduct themselves, in a manner which will not disturb others.

F. Allowing the landlord entrance to the premises for purposes of inspection, repairs, or to show the dwelling unit to someone else. The tenant may not unreasonably withhold access to the unit.

G. Living up to all provisions made with the landlord when the rental agreement was made, particularly paying the rent on time. The law itself does not directly address the issue of late charges; however, it is customary and common for landlords to require a late fee for delinquent rental payments.

[1] **Adapted from** *Landlord-Tenant: The Law* (Tallahassee: Florida Department of Agriculture and Consumer Services).

HOLDOVER BY TENANT

A tenant retaining possession beyond the original term of the lease is a "holdover." Depending on the law of the state, the lease may or may not be renewed automatically for another full term, whatever the original terms of the lease. In some states, the holdover status only means that the lease is renewed for another month.

Because of this difference in the laws of various states, most leases contain a provision covering tenant holdovers. The lease usually specifies that if a tenant lawfully occupies the premises after the end of the term, the lease will be enforced for another year, or month, or whatever period is agreed to by the parties. The lease continues from month to month or year to year so long as the relationship of landlord and tenant continues. Such a clause clarifies the legal relationship where the tenant holds over beyond the original term of the lease. The clause also indicates the duration of the additional term—whether a year, a month, or another period of time.

To keep the landlord away from your door, it is important to sign a lease agreement that you understand and that benefits you. In looking for an apartment, take advantage of the comments in this chapter. Study them before entering into any agreement.

V – Wills and Estate Planning

An elderly couple requested that a lawyer stop at their home to discuss the task of writing their wills. The gentleman was 85 years of age; his wife 83. They had raised 12 children, all of whom had children of their own.

The lawyer explained the processes involved in making a will and what the couple should be thinking about regarding their property. But the old gentleman had a puzzled expression on his face. When asked whether it was his wish that all his property pass to his wife, the man said, "Yes, I leave everything to Mama, but if she marry again, she get *nothing*!"

Despite the fact that his wife had borne him 12 children and had been a good wife to him for many years, the old gentleman was worried about her marrying again. The case indicates the kinds of superstitions and fears that people entertain, even today, concerning the making of a will. The feeling occurs mostly among elderly people, but many younger persons do not appreciate the need for and importance of a will.

This chapter deals with the making of a will; what happens if you die without a will; what should be included in a will; and the process known as "estate planning" that is so much discussed today. This kind of planning seeks to ensure that your loved ones receive your property with a minimum of expense and taxes.

LAWS OF INTESTACY: DESCENT AND DISTRIBUTION

Every state has laws governing the ways in which property passes on the death of the owner who dies without a will. An "estate" is the sum total of all the property of a deceased individual. That property passes to the deceased's heirs at law, if he dies without a will, or to his beneficiaries under his will.

The laws of the various states differ regarding the transfer of property from a deceased person to his *heirs,* the persons who inherit from him under state law. If a man is survived by his wife and children, they become his primary heirs. However, in some states the wife does not inherit the entire estate of her husband if there are surviving children. Rather, she receives only a portion of the estate depending on the number of children. Or a wife may not inherit the entire estate if other relatives, such as brothers and sisters, parents, aunts and uncles, or cousins survive the deceased.

No one can assume, in short, that if he dies without a will, leaving a wife and children or other relatives, the wife will inherit the entire estate. The will in fact has this advantage: it ensures that one's wishes are carried out regardless of the state law dealing with inheritance. A will may also substantially reduce tax liabilities in the handling of an estate.

Under the laws of some states, if a person dies without a will the person appointed by the court to handle the estate must post a bond to ensure faithful performance of his duties. But the person named in a will need not post a bond in some cases. Depending on the size of the estate, a bond may involve a substantial expense. That money goes to a bonding company and is thus lost to the heirs.

A will is essential to your peace of mind. It also provides your loved ones with proof of your concern for them and shows your intentions regarding the property passing to them.

WHAT IS A WILL AND HOW IS IT MADE?

A will is a written document in which the person making the will, called the "testator," specifies how and to whom his property will pass in the event of his death. It is commonly held that a will should be written, dated, and signed at the end. Some states require two or three witnesses to attest to the signing of the will by the testator. Other states do not require witnesses.

For safety, witnesses should be present when any will is signed. A will may be made out in a state not requiring witnesses; then the testator may later die in a state which does require them. Without witnesses, the will would not be valid in the second state.

WHAT ARE THE ADVANTAGES OF A WILL?[1]

- **You can choose the executor you wish to handle your estate.**
- **The expense of bond premiums, required of the person managing your estate, as well as some probate costs, can be avoided.**
- **You decide who gets your property instead of having the law decide for you. You may wish to provide a larger share for a young or sick child, leave something to charity, or give all your property to your spouse. You may take into consideration gifts that you have made.**
- **A trust may be created to keep your property intact for the benefit of your family.**
- **Minors can be cared for without the expense of guardianship proceedings.**
- **You may avoid the forced sale of your business.**
- **You can save estate and inheritance taxes. Only your will can place the burden on the right parties.**
- **Your will is the final document that completes your lifetime of planning for your family.**

[1] **Adapted from** *Legal Facts about Wills* (Jefferson City: The Missouri Bar).

Kinds of Wills

The most common type of will is the *witnessed will.* Whether handwritten or typed, this will should be signed by the testator and witnessed by at least two, and if possible three, persons. The witnesses attest that the testator signed his own will on a specified date. Other types of wills include:

- The *holographic will* that is written out by the testator in his or her own handwriting. The holographic will may or may not be witnessed. In the former case, the will would normally be held to be valid. If the will has not been witnessed, as when a trapper in fear of death scribbles his "last will and testament" while alone, proving the will may be difficult.

- The *nuncupative will* involves an oral declaration by a testator in extreme circumstances of what he wants to do with his estate. The testator may be in grave danger; he makes his declaration in the presence of witnesses; and the will may or may not be written down later. A court may decide that such a will is valid because the testator could not put down his final wishes in any other way. But all courts examine nuncupative wills closely.
- A *joint will* is the kind made out by the husband and wife together. The joint will is rarely used today because it has proved relatively inflexible.
- The *mutual* or *reciprocal will* offers much greater flexibility. The husband and wife make out separate but complementary documents. Mutual wills make it possible for the couple to provide specifically for most family needs, including unusual ones.

Any will is effective only at death. It can be changed at any time during the life of the testator. No one has any rights under the will of a living person since the will is effective only on the death of the testator.

Once death takes place, probate, the process of putting the will, in particular the witnessed will, on record, begins. The will then controls the settlement of the deceased person's estate. The will becomes a public record when it is probated.

Because the laws require that the will be signed, dated, and witnessed, it is always dangerous to put together a "home-made" will. A violation of any of the legal requirements concerning wills will render it null and void.

Can you scratch a name out of a will and just leave it in that form? No. Scratching out a name may effect what is seen as a *material alteration.* The validity of the entire document may come into question. That means no erasures, no scratching out, no adding is permitted.

A caveat: beware of the so-called "form wills," and of those who claim that anyone can write his own will without the advice of counsel. Many lawsuits have arisen because people have attempted to write their own wills.

Information Needed to Prepare a Witnessed Will and Estate Plan

In order to draft a will properly, certain information should be made available to the family lawyer. A listing of all valuable papers, including birth certificates, deeds, mortgages, insurance policies, stocks and bonds, savings passbooks, and so on marks a beginning. This information or list is vital to the proper preparation of the will and should be kept with the will in a safe place. The information necessary is listed below in more specific form:

1. Names, ages, and addresses of the testator and all relatives who might be beneficiaries under the will, including children, spouse, and others.

2. Details concerning the testator and his immediate family, with ages, financial status, and any personal facts that may bear on the estate plan. For example, where a child has a physical deformity, a larger distribution may be necessary for that child than for the others.

3. A complete list of all assets owned by the testator and spouse. The list should be complete and should include:

- Personal effects and household furnishings, with values; all real property and its value; all investments; names of corporations and denominations of stocks and bonds; bank accounts, both savings and checking; mortgages owned on other people's property; oil and gas properties owned; patents and copyrights owned; cash; and so on
- Property such as automobiles, work of art, libraries, coin or gun collections, and yachts
- All pension and profit-sharing plans to which the testator belongs, death benefits, any stock options that the testator may elect, and the Social Security benefits involved
- Life insurance payable at the time of the testator's death along with a listing of all policies by number and name of company, all annuities (monthly payment plans) and related policies
- A listing of all the testator's business interests, including any corporate, partnership, or sole proprietorship businesses, and all documents, stock certificates, profit and loss statements, and balance sheets connected with the business interests of the testator, for the purpose of determining the value of these interests
- Any interest in any estates or trusts created by others to which he is a beneficiary, and financial statements and back tax returns

This is a relatively exhaustive list. Putting it together serves a double purpose. First, the list shows all the assets that the will should cover. Second, drawing up the list necessitates a review of exactly what is owned and of the financial direction the testator is taking. The list should be complete and up to date.

All documents relating to property owned should be gathered for inspection by the family lawyer. The manner of ownership of property—by husband and wife, jointly with someone else, or otherwise—makes a big difference in planning an estate. The form of ownership of some properties may have to be changed.

To be complete, the list should include all debts and obligations of the testator, both personal and business. These would include mortgage obligations, long-term debts, short-term debts, charge accounts, and all currently payable items such as insurance premiums.

To assist the family lawyer, the listing should include the names and addresses of the testator's accountant, insurance agent or broker, bank trust officer, and stock broker. The lawyer can consult with these others as necessary in drawing up the total estate plan.

The testator should state his objectives clearly. What is the estate plan intended to do? If primary concerns are that the spouse and children remain secure, that children receive college educations, that funds be available to start them in business or buy them a home, and that their property be protected against the claims of creditors, the family lawyer should know that. He can then draft the will and estate plan with these objectives in mind.

Next some specific points should be considered:

1. *Specific instructions regarding funeral arrangements and burial.* These may be included in the will; but because the will is usually not read or probated until after the funeral arrangements have been completed, the instructions should usually be kept separate. A letter left with one's spouse and children specifying the testator's wishes regarding burial is usually a better method.

2. *Personal belongings.* Unless the testator makes specific reference to personal belongings, they will pass under the "residuary" clause of the will. This catchall section provides that anything left after specific bequests should go to the *residuary* beneficiary. An automobile, clothing, and any other specific personal property should be left to particular individuals. But if everything is left to the spouse, all personal belongings are covered. They should, however, be listed item by item.

3. *Cash gifts in the will.* A cash bequest can create problems. The executor—the person named in the will to handle the estate—may have to pay a specific amount of money despite the effect of that payment on the balance of the will. The executor may have to sell real property in order to obtain enough money to pay the specific cash bequests.

If an estate turns out to be smaller than anticipated, the cash bequests may exhaust the great bulk of the assets. Little or nothing may remain for distribution to other beneficiaries. Bequests can be made more appropriately in the form of parts or percentages of a total net estate rather than as specific dollar amounts. Thus the beneficiaries receive their percentages of whatever the total estate is when the testator dies.

4. *Real estate.* Various choices lie open to the testator in connection with real estate. He can leave it to his beneficiary outright, or direct that it be held in trust to provide income to a family member. He can have it sold, with the proceeds to go to the beneficiaries. The testator can give a *life estate,* the right of a beneficiary to live in the property or use it for life, with ownership automatically shifting to someone else after the death of the life tenant. Finally, disposition can be left to the discretion of the executor.

5. *The remainder of the estate.* Who receives the remainder of an estate after all individual bequests have been made? The testator makes that choice. But if more than one person is to receive the remaining portions, they should, again, be left shares (½ to X, ½ to Y).

6. *The guardian for minor children.* If assets are left to children under 18, on the testator's death a court has to appoint a guardian—usually a bank or trust company—for their persons and their property. As an alternative, the will can name a guardian for any minor children. The latter is often the preferred procedure.

The terms of a will should give the guardian the power to use the property for the benefit of any minor children and to provide maintenance, support, and educational assistance.

Property left to minor children is their property. But because in the eyes of the law they are "under age," they cannot handle the property themselves. The guardian is needed to handle the property for them.

Another type of guardian should be named: the guardian of the person of each minor child. The guardian of the person takes physical charge of the children and raises them in the parent's absence. Serious consideration should be given to the appointment of someone who will raise the children, love them, and provide accommodations needed to keep them together in their younger years.

No guardians are required for adult beneficiaries. A testator who fears that an adult child will dissipate the assets received under a will can place that child's share in a special trust fund. The will in this case names a trustee to handle the property and provide for the beneficiary's maintenance, support, and education. The testator can specify the amounts to be distributed to him from time to time. The will can also include a special "spendthrift" provision that protects the trust assets from the claims of the child's creditors while the assets are being held for his benefit.

7. *The executor.* The executor, sometimes called an administrator or personal representative, is the person or firm named in the will to handle an estate to its conclusion. Depending on the state in which an estate is being settled, an executor can usually complete his work within a year of the date of death—or a year from the date on which the executor is appointed by the court. Some more complex estates, however, take years to settle.

An executor should have some understanding of financial matters. But he need not be an expert or a lawyer; nor does he have to be completely familiar with accounting or the handling of an estate. The more complicated the estate, however, the more important it is to select an executor who has experience in the handling of an estate. The best choice is, often, the trust department of a bank.

Witnesses to the Will

As noted, witnesses should invariably be provided. If other conditions are met, a witnessed will is valid in all 50 states. Also, the presence of the witnesses becomes important if the "testamentary capacity" of the testator is questioned later—if anyone asks whether the testator had sufficient mental competence or other legal ability to make a will at the time it was made.

The attorney who draws up the will can appropriately act as a witness. He stands in an excellent position to know the testamentary capacity of the testator and the intent of the testator at the time he signs the will.

Importantly, three disinterested persons—three people who are not named as beneficiaries under the will—should serve as witnesses. In certain states, if a witness acts as a beneficiary under a will, he may lose his bequest to the extent that it exceeds the amount he would have received without a will. If, therefore, a will is signed and witnessed in a state which allows beneficiaries to be witnesses, but is later probated in a state which does not, problems can arise. It is much better to have disinterested persons, in all cases, as witnesses to the will.

Formalities for Signing a Will

The following is a list of protocols and formalities that should be observed in preparing and signing a will:

1. The will should first be written out.
2. The testator should sign it. If the testator cannot sign his name, he should place his "X" in the appropriate place. A witness should sign the testator's name and the words "his mark" over and below the "X". If the testator is physically incapable of even putting an "X" on the will, one of the witnesses should sign for him in his presence and at his request. The fact that a witness has signed should be noted in the clause immediately preceding the signature, sometimes called the "attestation" clause. This clause would state that the testator is unable to sign his name and that the witness signed for him.
3. The signature of the testator or the person signing for him must follow the text of the will immediately, with nothing in between.
4. The testator should expressly declare in the presence of the witnesses that he is signing his will. He should ask the witnesses to witness his signature.
5. At least three witnesses should sign their names and addresses in the presence of the testator and of each other,

stating that they saw the testator sign the will and that they are signing as witnesses at his request.

6. The will should be dated by day, month, and year so that no question can arise as to when the will was signed.

7. Only the original copy of the will should be signed by the testator and witnesses. If more than one copy is signed, the testator might later change his will but not destroy both copies of the earlier will. Also, all copies of the will should be "conformed" copies: the names of the testator and witnesses and their addresses should be typed or printed onto the copies so that the testator cannot at some future time sign a second copy.

8. The original copy of the will should be kept in a safe place, such as a home safe or strongbox. Many testators keep the executed or original copy of the will in the office of their family lawyer so that it can be referred to at any time. It may also be appropriate to give the original copy of the will to the named executor for safekeeping.

Because bank and other institutional safety deposit boxes are usually locked when a testator dies, a will should never be kept in such a box. The will could effectively be out of reach. A representative of a state tax commission might have to be called to stand by while the box is opened by bank officers. The representative would make sure that nothing is removed but the will.

Now that we have discussed the formalities of a will and some of the factors that make the preparation of a will important to you, the planning of your total estate, as it relates to your will, will be discussed.

ESTATE PLANNING AND ESTATE TAXES

The concept of total estate planning has developed in relatively recent times. It attempts to bring together all the factors relating to a man's or woman's financial status, his or her desires regarding family members, and their security. Estate planning combines these considerations by taking into account all federal and state death, inheritance, estate, and income tax laws. The purpose of estate planning, therefore, is twofold:

- To establish a plan to meet specific objectives insofar as family needs are concerned, including as parts of the plan the will and other necessary legal documents
- To take full advantage of all available tax avoidance or tax savings provisions of the various tax laws

Proper estate planning gives the family an important protective tool.

The family will need income in the future. Liabilities will have to be settled. Income will have to be shifted from one person to another or others. An estate-planning survey may indicate that additional life insurance is needed to meet tax liabilities that may arise when the head of the family dies. Provision may have to be made for additional income over and above that immediately available. That means Social Security and other pension benefits may have to be augmented for the family's protection after the breadwinner's death.

SOME QUESTIONS TO ASK—AND ANSWER—ABOUT ESTATE PLANNING[1]

You want your assets and property to go to specific persons, or to fulfill specific purposes, after your death. You want to minimize the taxes that will be paid by your estate after you die. You want to leave enough assets that are readily convertible into cash to pay your death expenses and protect your family until your estate is settled. Why not consider these questions—and have them answered—NOW, while you can make plans for the disposition of your estate.

1. **Is there any better way of holding my property to minimize my income taxes?**
2. **If I transfer some of my property to my spouse or children during my lifetime, will I be subject to gift taxes?**
3. **Are the beneficiaries properly designated in my life insurance policies?**
4. **Would my spouse be able to carry on my business in the event of my death?**
5. **In case of a partnership, do I have any arrangements for the survivor to buy my interests?**
6. **Does my estate have sufficient liquid assets to cover the costs of my death?**
7. **Have I adequately provided for the support and education of my children?**
8. **Would part of my estate pass to minor children and be subject to guardianship proceedings?**
9. **Do I have my estate arranged to minimize the death taxes?**

[1] **Adapted from** *Estate Planning* (Des Moines: The Iowa State Bar Association, September 1978).

The complicated process of estate planning is usually approached in the following ways:

1. A complete inventory of all assets, current income, and any anticipated income is drawn up. Each asset should be listed with its cost, value, and projected future value. Insurance should be listed by its cash surrender value and face value. An "educated guess" should be made regarding the value of your business interests. The planner should have all the information necessary to make an independent business survey, including balance sheets and profit and loss statements for the last three years.

2. Cash, assets that can be readily converted to cash, and assets that are to be retained in their present form, such as real estate, should be specified. These should be analyzed to see whether noncash assets can readily be converted into cash or whether additional items should be listed.

3. All debts and liabilities, including anticipated funeral and final medical expenses and the costs of handling the estate, are reviewed and deducted from the assets of the estate.

4. After deducting all liabilities from total estate assets, the estate planner estimates the federal estate tax liability that will be charged to the estate under the value and ownership conditions that presently exist. The estate planner also projects the dollar amount needed for the federal estate tax and the state

inheritance or death taxes to calculate how much cash will be needed to pay these taxes after death. The estate planner will also indicate how these taxes may be reduced through the use of the "marital deduction," available in the federal laws.

5. The total expenses of the estate, including all taxes, costs of administration, and debts and liabilities, are deducted from the assets. If additional assets would be needed to meet various obligations, a forced sale of assets, usually at a loss, might be necessary to pay all the bills. Depending on the size of the estate, this comparison of assets and liabilities will usually reveal a need to make immediate cash available to meet postdeath expenses.

6. After making this comparison, the estate planner will discuss the distribution of the estate. He will want to know about beneficiaries and what is to be provided for them. Knowing what will be available, the planner may suggest a reevaluation of either the assets or the method of disposition.

While a great part of estate planning has to do with saving taxes, that should never be the main concern. The main goal is to provide for family members and other survivors.

7. A schedule is prepared to show the assets passing to each beneficiary and how much income is generated from those assets. The assets may be analyzed to ascertain whether they will be adequate to meet the living requirements of the beneficiaries.

8. The estate planner will explain how to reduce federal estate and other death tax liabilities through the use of lifetime gifts, provision of additional insurance or additional investments, and other means of increasing the net asset value of the estate. He may show how rearrangement of some assets may increase the value of assets passing to the beneficiaries and decrease taxes.

A key device in estate planning, lifetime giving offers a way to make gifts of assets to family members before death—to reduce the size of the estate, to provide for college educations, or for other purposes. Starting in 1982, the annual gift tax exclusion was increased from $3,000 to $10,000 per donee, with an unlimited exclusion for tuition and medical expenses. Gift taxes could also be paid on an annual rather than a quarterly basis. A husband could make the same gifts to his wife without incurring gift tax liability.

Under the 1981 tax-cut law, both spouses could make the same gifts to children or other family members, doubling the basic figures. The annual exclusion of gifts for any one person could then total $20,000.

The federal gift tax rates and the federal estate tax rates remain identical under the provisions of the 1981 law. But the top estate and gift tax rate was reduced from 70 percent to 65 percent as of 1982, to 60 percent in 1983, to 55 percent in 1984, and to 50 percent—the projected maximum—in 1985. Starting in 1985 the top rate would apply to gifts and estates of more than $2.5 million. Three cases illustrate the use of estate planning devices. In each case, the husband is assumed to be the person whose estate is being planned. He wants to provide for his wife and three children, all under the age of 18.

Estate Plan No. 1: $60,000 in Joint Assets

In this plan, the husband and wife have joint assets of $60,000. Because of the limited size of the estate, there is no federal estate tax liability at all. Under the 1981 Economic Recovery Tax Act, the total amounts of estate and gift transfers that would be exempt from estate and gift taxes would be $225,000 in 1982 (from the 1981 level of $175,625); $275,000 in 1983; $325,000 in 1984; $400,000 in 1985; $500,000 in 1986, and $600,000 in 1987.

The plan for this individual includes a will providing that everything passes to his wife if she survives him for a specified period, usually 30 or 60 days. Should she fail to survive him for that period, everything passes in equal shares to his children. The reason for the 30- or 60-day survivorship requirement is to avoid a double tax if state law provides that the wife would take ownership under the husband's will if she survives him by even one moment. In this case, without a survivorship clause, state death taxes might have to be paid on both deaths. The survivorship clause eliminates that possibility by requiring the spouse to survive for the specified period of time; if he or she does not, the assets skip the estate of the spouse and go directly to the children. Only one death tax is imposed.

In Estate Plan No. 1, a witnessed will would be used to leave everything to the wife and, if she fails to survive, to the children equally. A guardian of the person must be named for the children. A guardian of the property should be named in case both parents die.

Estate Plan No. 2: Assets of $250,000

In this estate, the assets are considerably larger than those described in Plan No. 1. But basically the same strictures apply. Because of the changed "marital deduction" provisions of the federal estate tax laws, the estate would not be subject to any federal estate tax at all. The 1981 tax act simply repealed all limits on tax-free estate or gift transfers between spouses.

The plan for the individual here includes a will that leaves everything to the wife and, when she dies, to the children equally, with the same guardianship provisions mentioned in Plan No. 1. A trust may also be used for the benefit of the wife and children, or just for the children if both parents die.

In this testamentary trust, legal title to the estate assets passes to a trustee named in the will for the benefit of the spouse or children of the deceased. Unlike a guardianship, which ends when a child reaches the age of 18 or 21, depending on state law, a trust can continue beyond the age of 18 or 21 and even over the lifetime of the beneficiary if desired. The trustee generally has power to invest, sell, and handle the assets in the trust fund. He distributes the income to the beneficiaries at fixed intervals or at the trustee's discretion.

The trust provisions may also allow the trustee to distribute the principal of the fund to the beneficiaries at intervals or on termination of the trust. The trust has flexibility in other ways. For example, spendthrift protection can be built into the terms to keep the trust assets out of creditors' hands.

Under Plan No. 2, the testator may direct that the property pass to the wife. If she should fail to survive him, the assets go to a trustee for the benefit of the children. The property may be placed in trust for the wife's lifetime. On her death, the assets pass to the children.

The tax consequences of Plans 1 and 2 are basically the same. If the will in Plan 2 leaves everything outright to the wife and then in trust to the children, the property, beginning in 1983, would not be taxable at her death. If she has only a pure life estate in trust with no power to obtain any of the principal, but receives only what the trustee at his discretion may give her, and if, at her death, the trust assets are held for the benefit of the children, there would be no estate taxes to be paid at her death.

THOSE IMPORTANT PAPERS . . . WHERE TO KEEP WHAT

Where do you keep important papers? The following checklist gives a basic breakdown of types of papers, including wills, and where they should normally be kept. Circumstances can, of course, dictate variations.

SAFE DEPOSIT BOX

1. **Birth certificates**
2. **Citizenship papers**
3. **Marriage certificates**
4. **Adoption papers**
5. **Divorce decrees**
6. **Death certificates**
7. **Deeds**
8. **Automobile titles**
9. **Household inventory**
10. **Veteran's papers**
11. **Bonds and stock certificates**
12. **Important contracts**

ACTIVE FILE

1. **Tax receipts**
2. **Unpaid bills**
3. **Paid bill receipts**
4. **Current bank statements**
5. **Current canceled checks**
6. **Income tax working papers**
7. **Employment record**
8. **Health and life insurance information and policies**
9. **Credit card information**
10. **Copies of wills**
11. **Health records**
12. **Appliance manuals and warranties**
13. **Receipts of items under warranty**
14. **Education information**
15. **Inventory of safe deposit box (and key)**
16. **Loan statements**
17. **Loan payment books**
18. **Receipts of expensive items not yet paid for**

LAWYER'S OR EXECUTOR'S SAFE

Wills

DEAD FILE

All active file papers over 3 years old

WHAT TO DISCARD

1. **Salary statements (after checking on W-2 forms)**
2. **Canceled checks for cash or nondeductible expenses**
3. **Expired warranties.**
4. **Coupons after expiration date**
5. **Other records no longer needed**

The problem with using a trust for the wife's life is that, to avoid a tax at her death, she may, depending on the type of trust, lose the right to control what she receives from the trustee. This may be too harsh and restrictive. It may prevent the wife from receiving what she needs to maintain her standard of living. Again: tax considerations have never been, and should not be, the sole concern if the family does not have the freedom that the testator desires. The trust instrument should at least give the wife the latitude to obtain part or all of the principal during her lifetime.

Estate Plan No. 3: Assets of $1.5 Million

The federal estate tax resembles the federal income tax in one way: it is not a fixed percentage tax but a graduated tax. Many state death or inheritance taxes, by contrast, are based upon a percentage of the net taxable estate. For example, if a state imposes a death tax of 6 per cent of the net taxable estate, the tax is determined by multiplying .06 times the net estate. No matter how big the net estate is, the tax rate remains the same. Under federal estate tax laws, the larger the estate, the higher the tax—up to 50 percent in 1985.

The federal tax also differs from state taxes as regards the definition of taxable property or assets. Some states do not tax such things as the jointly held property of husband and wife that passes to one spouse on the death of the other, life insurance proceeds owned by the deceased, or the share of the surviving person in jointly held property not owned by husband and wife. The federal estate tax, however, includes all this property in determining the taxable estate for federal estate tax purposes. In short, any property over which the deceased had ownership, control, or any indication of ownership is included in the federal estate tax evaluation.

Because the federal estate tax is so all-inclusive, it may include much more property than is subject to probate under the will. Most states provide that jointly held property passes automatically on death to the surviving spouse. Life insurance proceeds are payable directly to the named beneficiary without going through the probate proceedings. It may, therefore, be misleading when newspapers report that Mr. Gotrocks died leaving an estate valued in the probate proceedings at $400,000. The estate was probably much greater than that, since life insurance, joint property, and other assets under Mr. Gotrocks' control would not be reported in the state proceedings.

While the estate tax includes all those assets that are not included in state probate proceedings, it does allow for exemptions and deductions that reduce the tax considerably. Beginning with the "gross value" of your estate, it permits deductions of certain debts and expenses to arrive at the "adjusted gross estate." These include the costs of settling the estate, debts and taxes owned by the decedent at death, and funeral expenses and casualty losses suffered by the estate during administration. Also, in theory, all of the estate can—effective in 1982—be transferred, untaxed, to one's spouse or to his or her control.

Plan No. 3. In Plan No. 3 the total estate of husband and wife totals $1.5 million. The wife has no property of her own purchased solely from her own funds. Assume that $50,000 of debts and expenses are allowable. The adjusted gross estate becomes $1,450,000.

If the husband in his will leaves his entire estate to his wife, he may, according to experts, be walking into a trap. The trap works this way: Assume that the year is 1987. The husband who, in taking care of his wife's future needs, leaves his entire $1,450,000 estate to his wife may in effect be leaving his children $249,000 less than if he did two things:

- Left his wife $950,000 under his will, and
- Took advantage of the full $600,000 exclusion that will be in effect in 1987 to put the rest of the estate into a marital trust.

In so doing, the husband would be avoiding all federal taxes.

If the husband fails to make a will, the estate passes under the laws of intestacy. The wife will not receive the full $1,450,000. Depending on the laws of her state of residence, she may receive only a share of the estate. The estate will have lost the advantage of the marital deduction.

When the Wife Dies. What happens when the wife dies? What effect does her death have on the estate tax? If the wife dies shortly after the husband, her estate will include all the assets she received because of the husband's death less the taxes that were paid.

The husband in planning his estate must take into account the effect on his children if the wife should die retaining substantially the same assets that he leaves her. The sensible estate plan takes into account the effects of both deaths and the possibility of reducing the total federal estate taxes to be paid. All beneficiaries can be provided for at the same time. Two basic approaches involve the *testamentary* and the *inter vivos* or *living trust.*

Two Trusts. Trusts can take many specific forms depending on their terms. But all are either testamentary or living trusts. The former, as noted, is established in a will. The living trust is usually set up in a separate document made during the lifetime of the husband. The testamentary trust goes into effect when the testator dies. The living trust can become effective at once.

Either basic kind of trust can utilize the marital deduction privilege. Whether the marital deduction is established by will or by a separate agreement, the method of distributing the property would have the following format:

- The husband directs in his will or in the inter vivos agreement that his estate or the insurance proceeds be divided into two parts, the part that qualifies for the marital deduction and the balance or residue.
- The husband then directs that the first part (Fund A) be placed in trust on his death for the benefit of his wife. The income from the property in the trust fund would be paid to the wife for life. She would have the absolute right to reach the principal of this part as well. She has the right to direct in her will how and to whom Fund A should be distributed at her death. But on the possibility that she may fail to exercise the right to direct to whom it should go at her death, the husband may direct that the property in Fund A will pass to the second trust, Fund B, on the death of his wife or later.
- The husband directs that the second part of his estate, Fund B, be established as a second trust or separate fund. The income from this second trust is likewise to be paid to the wife for life. But the Fund B property is to be distributed to the children on his wife's death or some other date. The wife has no absolute right to take any part of the principal of that part of the estate.

Fund B thus remains outside the wife's estate on her death. She has no absolute right to any part of it. The balance remaining in the first trust, Fund A, is taxable to the wife on her death since she has the right to withdraw all or any part of it during her lifetime and can also specify in her will to whom the balance of that trust fund should pass.

Net Effect. The net effect of this plan is to divide the estate into two different parts. One part, if substantial enough, is taxed at the wife's death, the other part at the husband's death. The portion that is taxable at the death of the wife, Fund A, is the marital deduction portion of the estate. This portion is entitled to the deduction, without tax, from the husband's estate and is taxed at the death of the wife. Fund B, in which the wife has no absolute right, is taxable at the husband's death and passes tax free to the children after the death of the wife.

The more varied the types of property owned, the more involved will be the estate plan chosen. Competent counsel can play an important role in the planning of an estate. So, in many cases, can an insurance advisor, accountant, broker, and bank trust officer.

Federal Income Tax

The estate planning process should include consideration of federal income taxes as they affect the administration of the estate. Because of the complexities of the income tax laws, tax advice is usually needed to handle the tax problems that the family will face after a testator dies. If the estate is sizeable, the executor will probably be required to file income tax returns on the estate, and will be faced with many of the same problems that the testator faces in the filing of his own income tax returns. A very brief summary of some of these considerations follows:

Ordinary Income and Capital Gains. Most persons are affected most directly by the two different types or categories of income, ordinary income and capital gains. Ordinary income includes such items as salary, dividends, interest, bonuses, commissions, and so on. Ordinary income is taxed on a progressive scale. Capital gains, on the other hand, receive preferential treatment.

With certain exceptions, everything one owns is a capital asset. Stock in trade for sale to customers, accounts receivable, and many other categories are included. If a capital asset is held for six months or less, its sale or exchange may result in a capital gain or loss.

Generally, any short-term (six months or less) capital gain is treated as ordinary income. Any short-term loss must first be used to offset short-term gains and then to offset long-term (more than six months) gains.

Executors' and Administrators' Tax Duties. Executors and administrators may have a number of tax-related duties. One of them is to pay any income taxes that are unpaid when the estate owner dies. Estate tax returns must be filed with both federal and state tax authorities. Heirs may have to be informed of the basis for computing capital gains on inherited property.

The Tax Reform Act of 1976 changed the regulations governing computation of the tax basis for all inherited assets. Before the Act, the value of any asset was its value on the date of the owner's death. Afterward, the tax basis for the heirs on all assets acquired by the deceased before December 31, 1976, became the value as computed on that date. Marketable stocks and bonds were excepted because their market value fluctuated and could be determined at any time. Computation of the value of all other assets followed an established procedure:

- It was assumed that the *rate of appreciation* remained

constant from the date on which the deceased acquired the asset and the date of his death.

- The proportion of gain in value or growth would be a determinable fraction of the overall growth.
- This fraction would be: the number of years and days between the purchase and December 31, 1976, divided by the number of years and days between the purchase and deceased's death.

Other regulations further complicated the problem facing executors and administrators trying to establish asset values for tax purposes. By 1980 the U.S. Congress was considering means of simplifying these laws, which placed heavy burdens on many trustees as well as executors and administrators. An executor might have hundreds of valuable items—from boats to paintings to stamp collections—on which, in effect, individual histories might have to be compiled.

In a relatively simple instance, an executor might have to inform an heir of the value of an oil painting purchased in 1966. The cost to the deceased at that time was $60,000. The deceased owned the painting for 10 years on December 31, 1976. The fraction by which the painting has appreciated in value is estimated at $20,000. The value of the painting would then be calculated at $80,000, the original purchase price plus $20,000. The trustee, executor, or administrator would use that overall figure in computing capital gains of the estate.

The Economic Recovery Tax Act of 1981 introduced basic changes in the personal and business income tax rates. The trustee or executor would also have to take those new rates into consideration. The personal income tax reductions were to total 5 percent starting October 1, 1981, 10 percent additional on July 1, 1982, and a final 10 percent on July 1, 1983.

Other Taxable Income. Executors, trustees, and administrators have to pay estate income taxes because an estate is considered a taxpayer. Thus taxes have to be paid on income from interest-yielding bonds, savings accounts, and other investments. Municipal bonds and similar securities that are tax free are usually excluded but may be taxable under state or local income tax laws.

The sale of a corporate bond may require payment of income taxes. The amount of appreciation will be taxed, for example, if the bond was held more than six months. The Internal Revenue Code contains a formula for determining the taxable gain or loss from the sale of a corporate bond where the issue price of the bond is different from its redemption value. Competent tax advice may be required where this situation obtains.

Income from securities issued by the U.S. government, such as Series E and Series H bonds, is taxable. But these securities have advantages because the owner can choose to take the interest income in a year in which he has a reduced income or losses that put him in a lower tax bracket. No one needs to pay taxes on the accrued interest on these bonds until they are redeemed or the interest actually received. One can also exchange Series E bonds for Series H bonds which pay cash interest on a regular basis.

Certain types of income are not includable in the definition of "income" under the tax laws. Social Security and veterans' benefits are not taxable. A relief provision applies to stock dividends, excluding the first $100 of corporate dividend income. If a joint return of husband and wife is filed and the stock is owned in both names, a stock dividend exclusion of up to $200 can be claimed.

Many of these provisions apply whether assets are held by the estate of a deceased person or by a living person. Extensive regulations involve the federal income tax laws as applied to estates and the filing of the "fiduciary" income tax returns by the executor.

THE ADMINISTRATION OF AN ESTATE

What happens when someone dies? What are the duties of the executor? How long does it take to settle the estate of a deceased person? What steps are taken to settle the estate?

Many persons recall that when "Uncle Joe" died, it only took the attorney six months to close the estate. When "Aunt Emma" died, it took over two years.

Obviously, the time involved in settling an estate depends on many factors:

- The size of the estate
- The identification of the beneficiaries if they are hard to find and if tracers are needed
- The presence of trust provisions that would require the services of a trustee
- The sale of assets to preserve the value of the estate (the timing of the sale is very important)
- Claims against the estate
- The filing of tax returns and payment of taxes. No two estates are alike, and the time spent in settling one estate has nothing to do with the time spent in settling another.

Some of the duties of the executor and family lawyer, who works closely with the executor, are as follows:

- To notify all the savings institutions where the decedent may have had accounts and obtain the necessary account numbers and balances as of the date of death
- To arrange for the custody of the decedent's personal property
- To maintain and see that all the decedent's property is covered by insurance, and change the "insured" in the policies to the "estate" of the deceased person
- To estimate the size of the estate to determine whether the estate has to go through formal probate and administration proceedings or whether the estate can be settled under the "small estate" (usually under $5,000) provisions that apply in many states to short-cut the more involved, full administration
- To obtain additional copies of the will for distribution to the beneficiaries and arrange a meeting with all of the beneficiaries as soon as practical and proper after the funeral of the testator
- To advise the beneficiaries of their interest and assure them of his intent to keep them advised
- To inventory the contents of any safe deposit boxes held by the decedent, usually in the presence of state taxing authorities who may be required by law to be present
- To find out whether any beneficiary wants to take any asset "in kind," that is, in its present form, rather than have it sold and the proceeds distributed
- To have the beneficiary sign an "election to take the property in kind" as soon as possible, providing a choice in the event that the property—corporate stocks, for example—drops in value before it is sold

The executor has also to find out whether any beneficiaries want to renounce any gifts or object to any provisions of the will. He must, with the help of the family lawyer, prepare the petition to probate the will and file it in court, and make copies available to all parties. Copies of the death certificate have to be obtained; beneficiaries may need help in the collection of life insurance proceeds, including provision of any necessary forms from the insurance companies. The executor will need information on salaries, wages, or commissions owed to the deceased, and will inquire about the pension or profit-sharing plans of the company employing the deceased and the amounts due the estate, if any. Other duties:

- To decide on continuing the operations of any businesses of the deceased and to arrange for collection of loans, rents, dividends, or other obligations owed to the decedent
- To follow local requirements concerning advertising the estate and asking all debtors to pay claims and all creditors to present their claims
- To collect and keep all information needed for tax returns, file for Social Security and veterans' benefits, and assemble all data on joint property, life insurance, trusts, and other assets for tax purposes
- To file any "fiduciary" bonds that may be required of him under local laws
- To obtain certified copies of his appointment for presentation to those requiring evidence of his authority to act for the estate

"DEAR ANN LANDERS" LETTER TELLS THE NO-WILL STORY[1]

A letter to columnist Ann Landers tells the poignant story of "Thorns among the widow's weeds," a wife whose husband died leaving no will. The letter, and Ann's answer:

Dear Ann Landers:

Why would a bright, loving man who showed every consideration for his wife and children during his lifetime die without leaving them protected by a will?

It's too late for your answer to help us, but please, Ann, print this letter because both my attorney and funeral director have told me that an unbelievable number of men, responsible and competent in fiscal matters, behave as if they are going to live forever. They make no preparation whatever for the eventuality of death.

I am now faced with a financial mess beyond belief. Attorney fees and inheritance taxes are horrendous. I am also having heartbreaking problems with my husband's brother over some property—the ownership of which is unclear.

I know my husband loved me and the children with all his heart. Why didn't he take care of us properly?

Thorns among the widow's weeds

Dear Thorns:

Why? Because, like so many others, he hated to think about death—as if by ignoring it, it would ignore him.

I hope every man who reads this column will ask himself, "If I died tonight would my family be protected financially?" If the answer is yes, you deserve to sleep like a baby. If not, get busy and put your affairs in order. You owe it to those you love.

Ann Landers

[1] **From** *Your Will* (Lansing: State Bar of Michigan). Letters from Ann Landers' column in the *Detroit Free Press* reprinted by permission of Ann Landers and Field Newspaper Syndicate.

An important duty of the executor is to keep the beneficiaries advised of progress in settling the estate. More misunderstandings result from lack of communication in this area than from any other cause.

After his appointment, the executor must prepare an accurate inventory of all estate assets and then make certain that the property passes to the beneficiaries named in the will. He should secure receipts from each beneficiary showing that they have in fact received the property or the cash directed to them. Eventually, the executor has to account properly to a court, to the creditors, and to the beneficiaries of the estate for all payments, receipts, disbursements, and distributions made by him in settling the estate, including payment of taxes.

The executor should work closely with the family lawyer in handling an estate. The law of the particular state may require that the executor perform many functions; he should know what these obligations are. In practice, the lawyer prepares most of the papers for the executor and guides him in this process.

Where a testamentary trustee is named in a will, his duties begin where the executor's duties end. Most of the trustee's duties are specified in the will. State law gives the trustee certain powers and duties as well. But basically, a properly drawn will notes these powers and duties specifically.

Once the estate is closed and a final distribution of assets is made to the beneficiaries, the executor transfers the assets to be held in trust to the trustee and takes back a receipt. The trustee then takes over the administration of the trust property. In the ordinary case he is required to invest for income, pay taxes and expenses of the trust fund, exercise all obligations as set forth in the will or trust agreement, and exercise his discretion for the benefit of the trust assets and the beneficiaries.

The trustee also has to render accounts to the beneficiaries periodically. At the conclusion of the trust, he distributes the trust property to the beneficiaries. He must keep the trust property separate from his own, and pays any income from the trust assets to the beneficiaries as required by the will, trust agreement, or the law. A corporate trustee, such as the trust department of a bank, has the same rights and obligations as an individual trustee.

Both the executor and trustee are entitled to compensation or commissions for handling estates and trust assets. The amount of compensation depends on the time spent and the work performed, and is subject to the approval of the court that has jurisdiction over the administration of estates and trusts.

Estate Tax Returns

As indicated, both the estate and the trust have to pay taxes. In some cases, the executor and trustee can be personally liable for taxes unpaid or improperly paid.

The returns that have to be filed may include:

Federal Estate Tax Return. The federal tax return must be filed within nine months from the date of death of a decedent who is a U.S. citizen and who leaves an estate in any given year whose gross worth exceeds the figures noted earlier. As indicated, the total amount of estate and gift transfers that would be exempt from estate and gift taxes in 1987 would be $600,000. Starting in 1985, the maximum estate and gift tax rate would be 50 percent, not the 70 percent of 1981.

Since federal estate taxes are levied on the *gross estate*, the executor or administrator has to account for all the assets and property owned by a decedent at the time of death—less, of course, debts and other obligations. The gross estate includes three main types of gifts:

- All gifts made outright after January 1, 1977
- Gifts over whose income the decedent has retained control for life, or those for which the decedent reserved the right to name the ultimate donee
- Gifts that remained revocable or amendable by the donor during his lifetime

Not included in the gross estate after 1981 are tax-free gifts of up to $10,000 a year per donee—or $20,000 if given jointly by husband and wife. Such gifts may have been made to anyone. They remain outside the gross estate under the 1981 Act.

Federal Income Tax Return. If the estate or trust during the period of administration has income in excess of $600, a federal income tax return must be filed. A taxable year for the estate or trust must be chosen and income reported accordingly. The year need not be a calendar year. The return must be filed by the fifteenth day of the fourth month following the end of the tax year. The choice of the proper fiscal year is very important and may have serious tax consequences. The federal law contains regulations concerning the proper taxable year.

Since the income tax return may show amounts that are distributable to beneficiaries, the executor or trustee should report these amounts to the beneficiaries for inclusion in their own personal income tax returns. The executor or administrator has also to report to the Internal Revenue Service all income distributed to the beneficiaries during the taxable year.

Final Federal Income Tax Return. The executor must also file the final federal income tax return of the decedent along with any returns that the decedent had not filed in prior years. It may be difficult to reconstruct the affairs of the decedent for the year of death or for prior years, but the duty nonetheless falls on the executor. If the decedent was married at the time of his death, a joint return may be filed as his final return unless the surviving spouse remarries before the close of the tax year or if some other exception applies.

The executor or trustee has the task of making sure that all taxes are paid before he makes any distribution of the assets of the estate or trust to the beneficiaries. If he fails to do so, he can be held personally liable for those taxes, plus penalty and interest. The only exceptions would be payments of allowances to the widow or widower, the funeral expenses, and some others that the law allows the executor to pay out before payment of federal taxes due.

An executor normally takes a "clearance" from the Internal Revenue Service before making final distribution to the beneficiaries. He also requests a prompt audit of the returns filed on behalf of the estate and previous years' returns filed by the decedent to ensure that no later audit will result in a claim for additional taxes after the estate is closed.

A TEN-POINT CHECKLIST OF THE DUTIES NORMALLY PERFORMED BY AN EXECUTOR[1]

- **Notify heirs and creditors of the probate proceedings.**
- **Take possession of, inventory, and preserve the probate assets of the decedent.**
- **Collect all income, such as rents, interest, and dividends, and make demand for and collect all debts, claims, and notes due the decedent.**
- **Determine the names, ages, residences, and degrees of relationship of all heirs at law and next of kin of the decedent.**
- **Complete any pending lawsuits in which the decedent has an interest and represent the estate of the decedent in any will contests.**
- **Determine, prepare returns for, and pay all state and federal inheritance, estate, and income taxes.**
- **Pay the valid claims of creditors of the decedent and, when necessary, sell property to raise funds to pay such claims as well as taxes and expenses of administration.**
- **Transfer decedent's title to real property to his or her beneficiaries through a decree of distribution (no deed or other formal document of transfer is required).**
- **Transfer decedent's title to certain personal property, such as stocks and bonds, to his or her beneficiaries.**
- **Distribute the remaining assets to the proper persons.**

[1] **Adapted from** *Why Probate?* (Portland: Oregon State Bar).

Tax Planning by Executor and Beneficiaries

Certain steps can be taken by the executor and beneficiaries to reduce the tax impact on the estate and the beneficiaries. For example, as indicated, the correct choice of a taxable year for the estate may have a significant impact on the total tax liability. In addition, decisions regarding the timing of distributions of income from the estate to the beneficiaries may be vital. Income payable to beneficiaries and distributable to them is taxable to them personally. The individual tax status of the beneficiaries must therefore be considered by them and by the executor in deciding when to make distributions.

The basic assets of the estate are not "income." No income

tax is payable on those assets by the beneficiaries or by the estate. Only the income earned from these assets is taxable under the income tax laws.

The federal estate tax law contains provisions for an alternate valuation date. Under this provision the executor can select a date different from the date of death (six months later) for determination of the value of assets in the estate. The choice of a different valuation date is the most important means of saving on estate taxes, especially if the assets are mainly stocks, bonds, or other assets whose value is subject to shifts in value.

If the assets are worth less on the alternate valuation date than they were on the date of death, the executor will choose that date for determination of value. He thus reduces the tax liability. If the assets gain in value, he will use the date-of-death value.

Another method of tax planning to save on estate and income taxes has to do with the handling of deductions. The executor has a choice of deciding whether certain deductions should be taken against the gross estate value to reduce the federal estate tax or of taking the deductions against the estate's federal income tax liability. A correct choice may save considerable money for the estate or the beneficiaries.

The deductions that may be allowed from the gross estate include the following:

- Burial expenses
- Claims against the estate, including legitimate debts
- Unpaid mortgage balances on properties owned by the decedent
- The expenses of administration of the estate, which may include commissions
- Losses resulting from casualty or theft
- Charitable bequests within the limits imposed by federal and state laws

Special rules also deal with any income earned by the decedent prior to his death, referred to as "income in respect to a decedent." Such income should be included in the estate tax return and deducted by the beneficiaries on their income tax returns.

Obviously, a testator has to use care in selecting an executor. The executor may have to work closely with the family lawyer to ensure that the beneficiaries receive the highest amount possible from an estate. Tax evasion is a crime; but tax avoidance is perfectly legal and proper.

Dozens of articles, books, and pamphlets tell the world how easy it is to write one's own will, how estate plans can be handled without help, and so on. However, the people who try to act as their own lawyers, accountants, and insurance advisors only create additional needs for professional help once they get in trouble. The legal profession has a cliché that expresses the truth neatly: "The lawyer who handles his own case has a fool for a client."

VI – Business Organizations

Everyone has read, at one time or another, that opportunities in the United States are less numerous than they used to be. Stories abound—about the small business person, his or her problems, the bankruptcies that occur with greater frequency, and other data that seem to support the basic proposition.

The Business Opportunity section in the daily newspaper nonetheless lists numbers of enterprises that appeal to the small businessman, the person who is thinking of adopting a new way of life, and others. Franchise operations offer just one example of a field that expanded rapidly, creating thousands of opportunities.

More and more professional and business people are changing their lifestyles and their occupations. Despite whatever business or financial success they may have achieved, they launch new searches for occupations with more meaning for them and their families. Not unusually, a husband or wife may decide to start a family business and to make whatever adjustments in lifestyle may be necessary.

This chapter deals with the problems of the individual seeking to operate a small business or to start out on a new line of work. What form of business enterprise will be best suited for one's family or for others who may come into the business later? How to raise capital and do all the things that have to be done in order to make a business operation succeed. Some basic answers will provide guidelines.

THREE TYPES OF BUSINESS ORGANIZATIONS

Three forms that a business may take will be considered here: the sole proprietorship, the partnership, and the corporation. Other forms will be touched on passingly.

The Sole Proprietorship

The sole proprietorship is perhaps the most simple organizational format. It may be the best way for an individual to start out on a small scale.

In a typical situation, a person wants to operate a franchise. It is likely that he will be the sole owner. Just as likely, he will not need additional capital, at least in the beginning, and the business will probably not grow to the point where the owner will need outside help.

The sole proprietorship is the answer. One person is the boss; he has only himself to answer to. He can give orders freely if he has employees, and has only his own tax situation to worry about. If the business remains small, he can keep a finger on the growth pattern and operating costs. Many of the complicated matters that arise under the corporate form of doing business, or even the partnership form, can be controlled.

Under the laws of many states, operating a business under an assumed or fictitious name requires, initially, that the necessary information be filed with county and state authorities. The information includes the name to be used and the names and addresses of all persons interested in the business. Filing is required so that individuals dealing with the business will be able to ascertain which parties actually have an interest in the business should the need ever arise. Typically, a state law might be called an Assumed Names Act.

For example, to do business under the trade name "Acme Food Market," it would be necessary in most states to register the company name and the names and addresses of all persons interested in the name. If ownership changes, an amendment to the filing will have to be made. New information would include the name of the new owner, whether a partnership is created, and the names of any new partners.

The Partnership

A partnership is composed of two or more persons working together in a business enterprise, usually on the basis of a partnership agreement. A relatively simple way to do business, the partnership is not as complicated as the corporation. Also, the partnership has advantages and disadvantages vis-à-vis both the sole proprietorship and the corporation.

As in any new business venture, in the early stages capital will be needed. The partners may have to use their personal credit. Each partner is personally responsible for the debts and credit arrangements of any other partners and of the business itself. After a partnership has accumulated assets and can show an earnings history, credit will usually be extended to the enterprise without the personal guarantees of the principal parties.

Each partner may act for all the others. The partnership form of doing business is governed in most states by statute. These laws set out, in detail, the rights and obligations of partners where no formal partnership agreement exists.

However, most partnerships do—and should—operate under the terms of a partnership agreement. The agreement spells out all the relative rights and obligations of the parties, describes the business in detail, enumerates its objectives, and indicates the investment or contributions of each partner.

Some general observations can be made regarding the typical partnership as it is ordinarily set out in a partnership agreement.

Duration. The length of time a partnership will endure depends on the terms of the agreement. Ordinarily the agreement provides that the partnership will continue for an indefinite period until it is terminated by the death of a partner, by voluntary act of the partners, by the insolvency or bankruptcy of one of the partners, by improper activity on the part of a partner, or by other means.

The partnership agreement may specify that the partnership does not terminate or will not be dissolved on the death of a partner. Such a partnership continues so long as there are two or more partners. The remaining partners have the right to purchase the share of the deceased partner from his estate. Business insurance can help to facilitate the financing of the buy-out agreement in such a case.

Unlike a corporation, the partnership is not separate and distinct from the partners. The liability of the general partners in a partnership is individual to each of them and applies to all partnership obligations throughout the life of the agreement. *Limited partners* or other special partners may, however, have their liability limited to their investment only.

THE THREE BASIC KINDS OF BUSINESS[1]

There are three basic kinds of business in our society. The first is the individual proprietorship or ownership, the second is the partnership, and the third is the corporation. Each of these types of business organization has unique characteristics that make it more or less suitable for a specific kind of operation.

The Individual Ownership

More than half the business concerns in this country are owned by a single person. This kind of business is known legally as an individual ownership or proprietorship. It may be small, like a newsstand or a candy store, or it may be a fairly large company. The individual owner has great flexibility; he is responsible only to himself and he alone reaps the rewards of a successful operation. By the same token, however, he is entirely responsible for any debts or losses his company incurs in the course of business. Many such businesses are started from scratch by the owner. Others are purchased from a previous owner. In either case, the individual owner may operate under his own name or under a company name.

The Partnership

A partnership is a more complicated form of business than an individual ownership. Any number of people may enter into a partnership (of course there must be at least two), investing their money or their services or both in the business of which they are co-owners. Usually there is a written partnership agreement between them that sets out their rights and duties under the partnership. Unless the agreement provides otherwise, the partners share equally in the profits or the losses of the company. In a general partnership all the partners are liable for any business debts, and they may be obliged to make up deficits out of their own personal property. A partnership may be for a limited or for an indefinite term.

The Corporation

While only a small percentage of American businesses are corporations, they are by far the largest and most important ones. The corporation is a group of people who have banded together to do business and who have been granted a charter by the government which gives them, as a unit, some of the legal rights and powers of an individual. In other words, the law regards a corporation as a person. A corporation may own, buy, sell and inherit property in its own name. It may even commit a crime and be tried and punished for it. Most corporations get the capital necessary for their operations by selling stock—units or shares in the ownership of the company. If the business is successful, the profits are distributed to the stockholders in the form of dividends.

[1] **From** *You and the Law*, Copyright © 1977 The Reader's Digest Association, Inc. Copyright © 1977 The Reader's Digest Association (Canada) Ltd. Copyright © 1977 Reader's Digest Association Far East Ltd. Philippine Copyright 1977 Reader's Digest Association Far East Ltd.

Changes and Limitations. If an existing partnership decides to take in a new partner, the "old" partnership should be terminated and a new one created. All of the former partners should give their consent. If one of the partners wants to retire, arrangements have to be made to protect him insofar as partnership debts are concerned. Thus no creditor can recover from the partner who has resigned or retired.

The partnership agreement must either provide for such contingencies or it must be amended. A new partnership agreement may have to be drawn up to incorporate changes.

The partnership can raise capital only in certain ways. Loans may involve the individual guarantees of all the partners. New partners may bring in additional capital. Additional contributions may be required of the present members of the partnership.

Management of the partnership ordinarily requires the unanimous agreement of all the partners. But one partner may be appointed *managing partner* under a partnership agreement, giving him responsibility for the day-to-day management decisions. Policy-making authority may thus reside in all the partners together or in the managing partner alone. Problems may, of course, arise, especially where the partners have equal management responsibility.

A partnership has a degree of flexibility in conducting business operations. But the basic agreement should specify the nature of the partnership and the work to be done. The partnership should not engage in any activity not specified in the agreement.

Taxation. Insofar as taxation is concerned, the partnership has only to file a federal *information return* for income tax purposes. The partnership itself pays no income tax, in brief. Rather, it distributes its income to the individual partners who are taxed on their own proportionate shares of the partnership income. That income may or may not be distributed to the partners during the taxable year.

Partners are taxed on distributed earnings, on accumulated earnings, and on their proportionate shares of all gains and losses of the partnership. Partners also use the same methods of determining capital gains and losses that they would use in individual sole proprietorships. The partnership return shows the amount distributable to the partners; they in turn report this income on their own individual income tax returns.

As regards charitable contributions, partners again figure in their proportionate shares of any partnership contributions when computing income. Pension and profit-sharing plans are available to partners, but only in the limited amount permitted to self-employed persons under the current federal income tax laws. An income tax deduction may be permitted for a limited pension and profit-sharing program (see Chapter 9).

Like self-employed persons, partners have to pay their own self-employment tax. If a partner wishes to sell his share, or assign income or interest in the partnership, he ordinarily has to have the consent of all the other partners. A new partnership may result.

With respect to state taxes, the same considerations usually apply. A partnership does not have to pay any state income tax. But again, income is distributable to the partners themselves, and they have to report it as income if the particular state has such a tax. Sales taxes and other business-type taxes may be chargeable to the partnership. These are paid, usually, as ordinary and necessary business expenses.

Caveats. A partnership implies a very close relationship. It should be entered into only with someone in whom you have the utmost confidence and faith, someone who gets along well with you and whose spouse gets along well with your spouse. Make no mistake: more partnerships have been dissolved for reasons of personal animosity that arises during the partnership period than through lack of business success.

Examples of partnerships that failed are numerous. Some famous show-business partnerships have been broken up because of conflicts between the spouses of the partners.

The human element is as important as the business element in the successful operation of any partnership. Before entering into such an arrangement, the potential partner should know the person he wants to enter into business with, know the spouse, and reach an affirmative conclusion after study of all the business and personal ramifications.

The Corporation

The corporate way of doing business is much more complicated than the sole proprietorship or partnership. But where the business is such that the corporate form makes sense, it can be very flexible.

Basically, a corporation is made up of its *shareholders,* who are the owners of the company; the *board of directors,* which handles the management and policy of the company; and *officers* who handle day-to-day affairs. This division between ownership and management gives the corporation its flexibility. In addition, the corporation guarantees limited liability to the shareholders: their liability is limited to their investment only. Ordinarily, the individual shareholders need not concern themselves with the possibility that they can be held personally liable for debts of the corporation over and above their investments.

Does the corporate form of doing business apply only to a large enterprise, or to a large business operation? Not at all. The laws of many states provide for so-called "close" or "closed" corporations that have few shareholders, usually five or fewer. A corporation can have one or an unlimited number of shareholders. Thus a corporation format can be utilized by one person even if he is the only shareholder. He may thus have all the benefits of the corporate form, including these:

- A corporation may continue on a perpetual basis, until dissolved by law, unless a specific state statute limits the time. Ordinarily, however, a corporation can be organized to exist "forever."
- A corporation has an existence separate and apart from its owners, the stockholders. It has the legal capacity to sue and it can be sued, and it has the capacity to own property in its name.
- As far as liability is concerned, the corporation is liable for all of its own debts and obligations. But once its assets are exhausted by creditors, each shareholder's liability is limited to his capital contribution to the corporation.

Organizing. In organizing, a corporation as a creature of state law must adhere strictly to the laws of the state. Most states require that a corporate charter be issued after application to the appropriate state official. Usually, a corporate purpose must be stated in the charter. That purpose often sets limits on the activities of the corporation. In recent years, however, states have allowed corporations to include very broad statements of purpose in their charters.

Some states require that the prospective issuance of the charter or the application for the corporate charter be publicly announced. Once the charter is issued, the corporation is legally organized. The application for the charter is accompanied by necessary filing fees, initial tax statements, and other required documentation.

Ordinarily, the first board of directors, or the first stockholders who will elect the board of directors, must also be identified in the application. Some states require that all limitations on the transfer of stock or issuance of shares of stock, or classes of stock, be set forth in the charter.

Small Corporations. If the corporation is a closed one, the creditors may attempt to look beyond the corporation and go after the personal assets of individual shareholders. The creditors may claim that the corporation is merely a sham designed to protect the shareholders who are in fact the owners and managers of the company.

In many cases, clearly, the corporate officers may be the same as the corporate directors. They may even be the same as the shareholders: the same individuals hold all positions. Unless all corporate records are maintained accurately and precisely, according to law, the creditor may be able to support such contentions. All corporate state and federal tax returns must be filed and minutes of corporate stockholders' meetings, corporate board of directors' meetings, and executive committee meetings must be maintained.

Accurate minutes must also be kept on all actions required by law of the board of directors or the stockholders. Only in this way can a small corporation protect itself against claims that it is not operating according to law and that the shareholders should therefore be responsible for company debts.

Raising Funds. The corporate form of doing business has a very practical advantage when funds are needed for capital expansion. Also, since the ownership of the corporation is represented by shares of stock, ownership can be transferred simply by selling the shares of stock. Unless the company's bylaws contain *stock transfer restrictions,* the stock is ordinarily freely saleable.

Some stock transfer restrictions are relatively common. For example, a stockholder may be required to offer stock shares for sale to the corporation before selling to a third party.

In larger corporations whose stock is traded on a national or local exchange such as the American or New York stock exchanges, transfers are made by brokers, based on the average price of the stock on the day of transfer. Where a small company is involved, however, it becomes more difficult to assess the value of stock shares. A closely held corporation whose shares are to be sold may have to rely on company records, such as earnings and other financial reports, since there is no ready market for these shares.

Where stock is sold in this way, no new agreements need be filed. A change in stock ownership does not change such factors as corporate assets, the operation of the company, or its title to real estate.

In raising additional funds for a corporate business operation, the corporation has several options. It can sell an issue of *new stock*—stock that it issues for sale to the general public in addition to that already outstanding in the hands of stockholders. It can issue *bonds,* interest-bearing certificates of corporate debt, or other forms of securities such as preferred stock and debentures. The latter also represents corporate debt. With more options open to it than an individual proprietor or a partnership, the growth business established as a corporation can often provide periodically for expansion.

Management. The management of the corporation is in the hands of its board of directors, which ordinarily acts by majority agreement. The stockholders of the corporation elect the board of directors, usually on an annual basis at the annual stockholders' meeting. The board of directors normally appoints the top officers. Minutes of all meetings of the board of directors and stockholders are maintained. In some larger corporations, minutes are kept of all meetings of the executive committee and the officers.

As the legal owners, the stockholders may vote by proxy in electing the board of directors. The stockholders in effect give the right to vote to some other party who then votes for members of the board. However, the board of directors does not have the right to delegate its duties and must exercise its obligations directly. A director cannot, by proxy, give some other person or group his right to vote at the directors' meeting.

Taxes and Tax Reports. Many more state tax reports are ordinarily required of a corporation than of a partnership or a sole proprietorship. The various states have enacted different tax laws affecting corporations. Capital stock taxes, initial excise taxes, and a corporate net profits tax are usually levied. These may require the assistance of an experienced accountant.

Unlike the partnership, the corporation pays taxes directly on its income. The stockholders pay taxes only on the dividend income they receive less the dividend tax credit. If the corporation does not distribute its dividends, and has a surplus available for payment of dividends over and above that allowed by law, a penalty or surtax may be charged for the accumulation of income beyond that permitted.

As a major advantage, the corporation under present tax laws can set up full-scale pension and profit-sharing plans. A current deduction is allowed for payments into the pension or profit-sharing fund. The members pay no taxes on the profit-sharing or pension benefits until they actually receive them—usually after retirement.

The tax laws limit the amounts that can be paid out under corporate pension and profit-sharing plans. But these benefits are much more liberal than those available to partners or other self-employed individuals. The sick-pay provisions of the tax laws typically allow regular employees a limited tax deduction on such payments. A corporation can also deduct its own charitable contributions up to a specified amount.

Officers and employees of a corporation are entitled to all the benefits enjoyed by employees. The corporation must withhold from the pay of officers and employees the necessary Social Security and other taxes, including income taxes. Even though they may also be shareholders, the officers are employees of the corporation and not self-employed individuals, and must report income as employees.

A final tax-related advantage is the ability of the corporation owner to make gifts of stock as part of an estate plan. A sole proprietor would find it very difficult to bring his children into his business in an ownership way. If he is incorporated, however, the individual can transfer shares of stock from himself to his children on a regular basis. In doing so, he reduces the size of his estate and increases each child's ownership interest in the business.

Things to Remember. Considering incorporation? Remember that the corporation is separate and apart. That remains true even if you are the sole stockholder and the president of the company. The corporation exists as an entity; it has a separate legal existence.

Remember also that even the owner-president of a small corporation has to have a working arrangement with the company. For example, he should have an *employment agreement* with the corporation that indicates his compensation and stock rights, his pension and profit-sharing rights, if any, and so on. It may seem unnecessary to have an employment agreement when there is only one stockholder. But the value of the agreement becomes clear if additional stockholders join the corporation later. The agreement protects the original owner's status as an officer of the company and his compensation level.

An employment agreement may have major impact on tax liability, particularly where a question arises involving the valuation of stock or the reasonableness of an officer's salary. In reviewing the income received by a corporate officer, and measuring it against the duties performed, the Internal Revenue Service sometimes finds that the officer is receiving a dividend, not compensation. The dividend could then be taxed twice—once while in the corporate account and again after it reaches the stockholder.

An employment agreement that specifies the total compensation to be paid to the officer and the duties required can often eliminate such problems.

Many other considerations relating to the corporate form of doing business should be kept in mind. These can depend on the nature of the business, the company's size, its growth potential, the degree of flexibility required, and so on. The need for competent legal and financial advice is ever-present. If set up properly, the corporation can serve as practical application of business principles to bring success to an enterprise.

OTHER FORMS OF BUSINESS ORGANIZATIONS

In addition to the sole proprietorship, the general partnership, and the corporation, there are other ways to go into business. These are combinations of some of the forms already noted. All should have a place in the process of determining the appropriate way to go into business.

The Limited Partnership

A limited partnership combines some of the elements of a general partnership with those of a corporation. A limited partner makes an investment in the partnership; but he ordinarily has nothing whatever to do with the management of the business and he enjoys a limitation on his liability for partnership debts. The limit is the amount of money that he has invested. The partnership form remains, but the limited partner has liability similar to that of a stockholder in a corporation.

The limited partnership is controlled by statute in the various states. The statutory requirements have to be followed very closely if each limited partner is to enjoy the advantage of limited liability. Major tax advantages can also be claimed by limited partners.

A limited partnership and a corporation may be joined in a single enterprise. Each of the entities performs a separate function. In such instances, it is important to keep all records of the two organizations separate and apart. All agreements, arrangements, and contracts between the two are treated as though the partnership and corporation were unrelated entities and totally separate business enterprises.

The limited partnership has been widely used as a vehicle for conducting long-range, risky, and costly operations of a highly technical nature. An example would be oil and gas exploration and drilling. The partners usually do not want to take a direct role in management. They have funds to invest; in making an investment, they see the risk of loss as secondary. More importantly, the investment usually gives them a *tax write-off.* The funds in many cases would have been paid to the government as income taxes.

Every limited partnership has to have at least one general partner who organizes and runs the partnership operations. One or more limited partners—up to dozens and even hundreds—join the partnership and invest in it. If the partnership makes a profit, it is distributed to the partners according to a formula set out in the limited partnership certificate that each partner receives.

The "Sub-Chapter S" Corporation

The federal tax laws permit the so-called "sub-chapter S" corporation to be treated as a partnership insofar as taxation is concerned. The requirements are that the corporation have no more than 10 stockholders to qualify. The corporation then retains all the advantages that make the corporation form advisable, such as limited liability of stockholders. At the same time the "sub-S" corporation is not taxed as a corporation.

The shareholders of a sub-S corporation are taxed as partners. They include all the distributed income in their own income tax returns, reporting it as income.

Under the income tax laws a partnership or a sole proprietorship, if qualified, can elect to be treated as a corporation. Ordinarily, the purpose would be to reduce taxes. Typically, the corporation has unreasonably high income and wants to take advantage of certain lower tax rates.

The Joint Venture

A joint venture is similar to a partnership. Two or more individuals or a combination of individuals and companies undertake to perform certain services or do a certain job. Unlike a partnership, however, the joint venture is not a continuing arrangement. A joint venture is entered into only for one specific project. On termination or completion of that project, the joint venture terminates.

The parties to a joint venture enter into an agreement that spells out all rights and obligations and the nature of the work or project to be undertaken by the joint venture. The test of a joint venture is whether it has been formed for one specific project only.

CONTROL OF THE BUSINESS ENTERPRISE

A particular field of business has been selected. A specific form of organization—sole proprietorship, partnership, or corporation—has been decided on. How about the problem of control? How can you be assured that, having set up the business, you will be able to protect it—or keep out people whom you may not want to be in it? How do you keep the management and control of the business in your hands or subject to your approval?

The question of control involves a number of considerations. The type of business, the method by which interests can be transferred to others, restrictions on the transfer of ownership, employment contracts, and other factors become important. This is why the necessary agreements, contracts, charters, by-laws, and other documents should be prepared by a lawyer. All rights and obligations of the parties have to be spelled out clearly and precisely or questions of control may arise in the future.

The nonlawyer may not be able to assess the importance of some factors. Specific questions may turn on the provisions of state law regarding restrictions on transfers of shares, what can be included in the charter of a corporation, the attitudes of the local courts toward management, and restrictions on the transfer of control of the business. The wording of some documents may affect an owner's power to control his own business.

Some possible ways of maintaining control include the following:

1. *Restrictions on transfers of interest.* As noted, an absolute restriction on the transfer of an interest in a business enterprise may be considered unreasonable. The law generally does not favor restraints on the selling or assignment of business enterprise or property rights. This legal hurdle can be overcome, however, by a *stock transfer restriction agreement* among the shareholders. The agreement gives the other partners or stockholders an option or right of first refusal before stock shares can be sold to a third party outside the business.

An example may be noted. A partnership agreement could specify that a partnership interest could not be sold unless the partner wishing to sell first offered his partnership interest to the other partners. If the others refuse to buy under a formula established in the agreement, then the partner would be free to sell to someone else.

Other agreements might provide that before a shareholder can sell his stock to the general public, he must first offer it to the corporation itself—or to the other shareholders. The latter could buy the offered stock in proportion to the total number of shares each owns. If the stock is not purchased, the shareholder would have the right to sell to the general public.

Such stock transfer restrictions are valid and enforceable. They are not considered absolute restrictions on transfer of shares. This type of restriction is often set out in a clause in the agreement among the shareholders in a by-law provision, and in a statement on every stock certificate. Anyone who buys the stock in violation of the restriction is regarded as having been put on notice by the provision on the certificate.

2. *Employment contracts.* Continued control of a business can be assured by drawing up an employment agreement between a partnership and its partners or between a corporation and its officers. The agreement can specify the rights, duties, and obligations of the corporation or partnership and of the employee or officer.

3. *Voting rights.* Most business enterprises involve a number of people. Usually, the parties want some assurance that the business will go on as originally planned. Where the possibility exists that a majority could act contrary to the wishes of the founders and forget what the business was designed to do, voting provisions can be used to maintain control. Various approaches are utilized to protect the business operation in such cases:

- Arrangements may be made for voting and nonvoting stock, for voting rules that ensure that the minority group is represented on the board of directors, and for elections of different directors in different years.

- Shareholder agreements may be written so as to require the shareholders to vote their stock in a certain way. For example, the agreements could require all shareholders to elect each other as directors of the corporation and no one else. The stockholders would then be able to prevent others from taking control of the corporation. It should be noted, however, that such restrictions on voting or on transfers of shares will naturally inhibit someone else from buying that stock. If the intent of the corporation is to create a market for its stock and to attract additional shareholders, such restrictions will adversely affect that intent.
- Where a number of shareholders want to join together to give a lesser number the right to vote all the shares, a *voting trust agreement* may be utilized. The voting trustees are designated by the agreement. They themselves can agree on how the votes will be cast.
- Depending on the law of the state, the charter and by-law provisions of the corporation may provide for the requirements as to quorums and the number of persons required to vote. Different percentages of the total number of shares may have to be represented at meetings before votes can be taken on certain acts. For example, a two-thirds vote of all shareholders may be needed to change the by-laws of the corporation. In a small corporation, the by-laws or a separate agreement among the shareholders may specify that all shareholders must agree to any change in the company by-laws.
- Arrangements may be made to provide for arbitration. Where disagreements arise, preventing the orderly operation of the business, the partnership agreement, the by-laws of the corporation, or a separate agreement among the shareholders should provide for some means of breaking any deadlock. Arbitration, dissolution of the company, or a provision allowing one party to buy out the other are all possible methods. All can be useful, especially where only a few shareholders or partners are involved.

Not uncommonly, a partnership agreement or stockholder agreement involving a few partners or stockholders will provide that one party offer his stock to another party at a certain price. The other person then decides whether to sell or buy depending on the price. One party sets the price, and the other party decides whether to sell his own stock at that price or to buy the other person's stock at the same price.

4. *Buy-sell agreements between shareholders in a corporation.* The founder of a corporation would usually want to ensure that on his death the corporation would have an opportunity to buy his interest for the benefit of his estate or beneficiaries. These *buy-sell agreements* ordinarily establish an obligation on the part of the corporation to buy. The estate of the deceased shareholder has to sell the stock.

Sometimes such agreements are called "options" to buy and sell. They may require that if the estate wants to sell the stock, the stock must first be offered to the corporation or to the other surviving shareholders before it can be offered to others.

In order to finance the purchase of the stock of a deceased shareholder, the corporation must have a *stock retirement program* providing funds for this purpose. A *cross-purchase plan,* by contrast, gives the other stockholders the right to purchase the shares of the deceased. The corporation cannot then buy the shares.

One problem faced by a corporation in retiring stock is that under the laws of most states it must have funds for such purchases in its surplus account. It may be difficult for the company to set aside such funds. A cross-purchase plan for stockholders solves the problem. Funded through an insurance program, with each shareholder owning an insurance policy on the lives of the other shareholders, the plan makes it possible to buy the stock of a deceased shareholder with the insurance proceeds. Such funds go to the estate of the deceased to purchase his stock.

If the corporation buys the stock, the ownership interest of the other stockholders remains the same. No change has taken place in the numbers of shares owned by the surviving shareholders. If those survivors buy the decedent's stock, a change in the stock interest of the surviving shareholders does result.

How do you set the price of stock for the purpose of carrying out a corporate buy-sell agreement? If the stock is traded on a regional or national stock exchange, the price can be easily determined from the quotation for the day on which the stock is offered. In a close corporation, however, where there is no ready market for the stock, the problem of evaluation becomes critical. A mandatory buy-sell agreement must outline an effective method of determining the price of the stock or the agreement is not worth the paper it is written on.

Incidentally, an effective formula may help in determination of the value of a decedent's stock for federal estate tax purposes. The price as determined according to the agreement could be used to calculate the estate tax valuation.

A buy-sell agreement in a closely held corporation may utilize any of several different ways of determining the per-share value of stock. The shareholders can set a fixed price per share, adding provisions for revising the price on an annual or some other basis. Calculations of value would be based on the performance of the company and other criteria. The controlling price would be the last stated price set before the death of the stockholder.

Where stock values have not been updated under a buy-sell agreement, problems may arise. The stock may have inflated or deflated in value since the last stated price was set. Where a fixed price has not been calculated for more than a year, an *appraisal method* of pricing the stock may be used. Other methods are also available.

The appraisal method leaves the price of the stock open pending later appraisal by a disinterested appraiser. On the death of the stockholder, the appraiser comes in and evaluates the stock. That decision is binding on the several parties.

The *book value method* of determining stock values utilizes both the last corporate balance sheet prepared before the death of the stockholder and a "net worth" adjustment to the date of death. The book value method does not take into account the value of the business as a going concern. The net worth method, however, will serve adequately:

- if inventory, for example, is determined at its actual worth rather than at cost;
- where accounts receivable are adjusted to take care of those that are not collectible;
- where the book value of machinery and equipment adequately represents their fair value and present worth;
- where real estate and buildings reflect current market values; and

- where insurance proceeds are considered as part of the evaluation.

Various other methods combine different valuation techniques that attempt to average corporate proceeds over a period of time and either *capitalize* the proceeds or *average out* the proceeds to determine a fair price for each share of stock.

Where a valuation formula is limited to book value only, the fair market value of the depreciable assets will be ignored. Only the depreciated value will be determined. The beneficiaries may receive much less for the stock than it is actually worth.

5. *Partnership buy-sell agreement.* A partnership has problems similar to those of corporations. The partnership agreement should therefore establish the circumstances under which the surviving partners can buy the interest of the deceased partner. The obligation of the decedent's estate to offer the partnership interest for sale on agreed terms should be specified.

All partners and the partners' spouses should sign the partnership agreement—or the separate buy-sell agreement if such exists.

The valuation of the partnership interest for purposes of the buy-sell agreement involves some of the same considerations as the valuation of corporate stock. A value for good will should be placed on the partnership interest in the agreement. Provisions for payment should be spelled out clearly. The income tax laws provide for different treatments of payments depending on how they are made and the nature of the agreement. Thus care should be used in preparing the agreement to take advantage of the best possible tax thinking of professional advisors.

Where life insurance is used to fund the purchase of a partner's interest, the agreement should spell out at least the following:

- Exactly how much life insurance is to be purchased
- Whether the partnership or the other partners own the policies on the lives of individual partners
- How the premium is to be paid
- How the transfer of the policy held by the deceased to the survivors is to be handled

INSURANCE UTILIZED IN BUSINESS OPERATIONS

Chapter 12, on insurance problems, noted some situations in which the insurance advice of professionals is needed. Such advice is absolutely indispensable where business insurance is concerned.

The insurance industry has recognized its obligation to provide expert advice in a professional way in recent years. Programs have been set up to train agents and brokers. Continuing education programs of the insurance industry include programs, seminars, and courses leading to the certification of an individual as a *Chartered Life Underwriter* (CLU). Other programs lead to the professional designation of *Chartered Property and Casualty Underwriter* (CPCU). Thus the business community has available top-notch experts who have the ability, the training, and the experience to apply their knowledge to current problems.

Insurance advisors can analyze risks. They can also read a partnership agreement or an agreement among shareholders to determine whether insurance protection is needed. They can give advice on the kinds of protection required and on costs.

In many cases, insurance offers the most economical and feasible method of funding programs for the purchase of stock of a deceased shareholder or the partnership interest of a deceased partner. The insurance advisor can explain how such programs work. The method to be used depends on the nature of the plan involved and the needs of the parties. If the number of shareholders or partners is large enough to require one, a trustee may be named to own the insurance policies and see to the distribution of the proceeds. The trustee becomes the designated beneficiary under the insurance policies so that he can carry out the terms of the agreement.

In other respects the trustee plan works much the same as that involving ownership of the policy by other partners, stockholders, or the corporation. The trustee can, however, be helpful where a great number of persons is involved and where distribution may be difficult.

A key factor in determining the best method of using life insurance to retire or purchase the stock of a deceased shareholder relates to the older and the younger shareholder. In a cross-purchase plan, the younger shareholder may "take a beating." This shareholder may have to pay premiums on a policy on the life of an older shareholder. These premiums, of course, can be very high. Where this situation exists, a corporation may use a stock retirement plan rather than the cross-purchase arrangement.

Premiums paid by corporations or individuals on insurance carried on the lives of stockholders are generally not deductible from income under the federal income tax laws. But in each case the insurance proceeds will be received by the beneficiaries free of tax. In most cases the corporation will receive the proceeds from the insurance and then buy up the decedent's stock. Where the stockholders own insurance on one another, the individual stockholder receives the proceeds and then purchases the stock.

Partnership insurance is treated in similar fashion. The insurance policies can be owned by the partnership, which can later purchase the partnership interest of the deceased. Or the insurance can be owned, and the premiums paid, by the partners, who insure the other partners. Again, premium payments are not deductible by the partnership or by individual partners. But the proceeds are not includable in income or subject to income tax.

The decision to go into business raises complex questions. These relate to the form of business organization, the element of control of the business operation by various lawful means, and the funding of various plans to protect the interest of the businessman and his estate in the event of his death. What emerges constitutes a complete business plan. The need for sound business planning goes hand in hand with the necessity for consultation and advice from those whose profession or business it is to provide such assistance.

Protect your "minimum investment" by reviewing this chapter and consulting your family lawyer before taking the first step.

Despite claims to the contrary, the United States offers many opportunities for small businessmen and women. Recognition of the pitfalls and problem areas ahead of time can make your venture into the business world successful and enjoyable.

Physical Fitness

One of the most important health studies of our time was started by the National Institutes of Health back in 1949. The population of an entire community was put under continuous scrutiny by a team of doctors who recorded the daily habits of thousands of men and women. For nearly a quarter of a century, the citizens of Framingham, Massachusetts, have been observed at work, at play, and in the home. They have been measured and weighed repeatedly, their food analyzed, their cigarettes counted, blood pressure checked, and so on, without interfering with the normal life styles of the individuals.

The Framingham Study

Results of the Framingham Study of a generation of a typical American community reveal certain patterns between a way of life and the most common cause of death, which is cardiovascular disease. The links between the American way of life and the American way of death were found to be too many calories, mainly in the form of saturated fats and sugar, too many cigarettes, and too little exercise. Dr. William B. Kannel, Medical Director of the Framingham Study and a member of the Harvard Medical School faculty, reported that the most sedentary, or least active, men had about three times the heart attack risk as the most physically active. The rate of risk of cardiovascular disease seemed to be generally proportional to the degree of obesity, resulting from too many calories. The use of cigarettes was found to be associated with all manifestations of cardiovascular disease. One other link, which is still being explored, is high blood pressure.

The Framingham Study of the adult lives of some 5,000 subjects confirms what most doctors had suspected for many years—that physical activity helps counteract the effects of overweight, diets rich in fats and sugar, blood pressure, and similar factors. Dr. Kannel's report added another explanation: physical exercise probably helps extend the life and health of even those people with

---

Participating in outdoor winter recreation has an energizing effect. Thousands visit the slopes of Mount Hood in northern Oregon annually—to ski, toboggan, and take photographs.
—U.S. Forest Service (Hugh Ackroyd)

cardiovascular disease by developing collateral circulation. In other words, a person who might otherwise develop heart trouble because of a diminished blood supply in his coronary arteries can forestall that threat to his life by physical exercise which promotes the increased flow of blood through alternate blood vessels.

There is a valuable lesson in the Framingham Study for every reader of this book: daily exercise, which requires no greater investment than a more efficient use of free time, can extend your life and retard certain organic diseases of the heart and blood vessels—diseases that account for more than half of the "natural" deaths in America each year.

Winter Exercise

If you are a typical American adult, the chances are that you are a "fair weather athlete." Although some men and women enjoy a hike through the freshly fallen snow to an outdoor ice skating rink, or an occasional visit to a ski run, too many individuals use the period between Indian summer and the return of spring as a time to take things easy, and indoors. That television producers save their best shows for the fall and winter months suggests that their careful surveys find most families indoors at that time. Sales of phonograph records and tape cassettes reach a peak as winter advances. And despite the let down in physical activity, the long periods of relaxed entertainment seem to stimulate tremendous appetites for high-carbohydrate goodies like potato chips, pretzels, candy, beer, and soft drinks. This seasonal irony is compounded by the fact that autumn usually is marked by an increasingly heavy schedule of cocktail parties, business or club lunches, dinner parties, and holiday feasts that may stretch through several days.

The Value of Physical Fitness

The ancient Greek physician Hippocrates may have established the first rule of physical fitness some 2,400 years ago. He outlined what he called the Law of Use which governs the living organism: "That which is used develops; that which is not used wastes away." Modern medical practice still follows that Hippocratic concept in preventive medicine as well as in the rehabilitation of surgical patients. Dr. Harry J. Johnson, Chairman of the Medical Board of the Life Extension Institute, expresses the Hippocratic Law of Use this way: "Life itself is movement. Even the developing embryo moves and stretches within the uterus by the fifth week of life — long before the mother becomes aware of it. And what does the mother say when she feels the first detectable stirring? She says she 'feels life.' "

After the birth of the baby, doctors have found that the mother recovers more quickly from the effects of childbirth if she gets out of bed and into action as soon as possible instead of lying in bed for a week or more to recuperate. The baby, during its hours of wakefulness, is in almost continuous motion—crawling, grasping, walking, running, jumping; the joy of activity continues in most normal children until adulthood.

There are exceptional people who almost literally keep moving throughout adult life. For example, Senator William Proxmire of Wisconsin is a strong advocate of jogging and regularly runs from his place of residence to his office on Capitol Hill. President Truman kept newsmen panting at his heels during his brisk morning walks. Individuals in all walks of life who spend a good deal of time in an office recognize the importance of daily exercise.

When Dr. Leonard Larson was president of the American Medical Association, he explained the importance of exercise in developing greater strength, stamina, endurance, and recuperative powers of the human body. "During exercise," said Dr. Larson, "the muscles need more oxygen and food. The blood circulates faster to meet the needs of the muscles and to carry off wastes. Body cells increase so that muscles gain strength and flexibility. There also is improved neuromuscular coordination."

Everyday Emergencies

A frequently overlooked fringe benefit of physical fitness is an improved ability to

President Harry Truman thrived from the tonic effect of his invigorating 30-minute early morning walks.
—UPI Compix

Hiking is a delightful pastime and an exhilarating experience. These hikers are enjoying nature during a leisurely, refreshing walk in the Rocky Mountains.
—National Park Service

survive everyday emergency situations that create a sudden demand for physical strength and endurance, which in turn require greater than normal performance by the heart and blood vessels, lungs, nerves, and muscles. This was illustrated during a meeting of physicians to discuss the health hazards of flying. The medical director of one of the major airlines was asked if he had any records of passengers on his airline dying of a heart attack. "Yes," the medical director replied matter-of-factly. "Last year, seven of our passengers died of heart attacks. But not while they were flying. In each case, the passenger was running down a corridor to catch a flight when he collapsed and died." Each of the victims, it must be assumed, was "out of condition," perhaps a bit paunchy and flabby from lack of exercise, and unable to meet the ultimate test of fitness: the sudden demand on the body's organs to meet a brief modern emergency of running with suitcase in hand to reach the airline counter before the gates closed.

Running for a plane, running for a bus, running for a commuter train, pushing a stalled car, carrying an air conditioner up a flight of stairs—these are civilization's equivalents of the primitive human's battles with wild animals or hand-to-hand combat with tribal rivals. But the primitive man probably had a better chance for survival in an emergency because he maintained muscle, heart, and lung strength and endurance through the daily demands of his prehistoric life style.

Vigorous Recreational Activities

The alpine lakes of the mountains of Idaho were once stocked with trout that were carried there in milk cans strapped to the backs of husky college boys. Some years out of college and softened by sedentary jobs, the same individuals, burdened only by sack lunches and fishing rods, had to stop several times for their "second wind" when they returned recently to the same lakes. There are still duck hunters who travel each autumn to a hilltop on the California-Oregon border; it is a favorite hunting ground for waterfowl that skim over the hill which separates two lakes on the Pacific Flyway. To reach the hilltop, the hunters have to scale a thousand feet of slippery lava rocks, and many drop out along the trail because of dizzy spells, painful leg cramps, and other discouraging symptoms. The peak bears the nickname of "Cardiac Ridge."

The point here is that true physical fitness involves more than a few easy or specialized exercises. A man can be a championship weight-lifter with the physique of Mr. America, but he may not be able to compete in running, swimming, or other sports activities unless he has developed and maintained strength and endurance in the heart, lungs, and muscles used for functions other than weight-lifting. Conversely, an individual who considers himself in good physical condition because he has been jogging for the past two years might be unable to lift a portable TV set. The goal for anyone seeking an exercise program should be all-around physical fitness, with good heart and lung conditioning in addition to muscular strength.

Weight Control and Exercise

While no single set of exercises will guarantee physical fitness, neither will exercise alone control an overweight problem—although the Framingham Study has suggested a complementary relationship between exercise and weight control. The catch is that it takes a lot of exercise to get rid of a pound of fat. It would require, for example, about 90 minutes of swimming to burn up the calories you gain by eating a 450-calorie piece of chocolate layer cake; for most people, it would be easier to control weight by skipping the cake.

One pound of body fat is equivalent to about 3,600 calories of food. That amount of fat is about equal to a food intake of ten calories a day over a period of a year. In other words, you can add or lose a pound of fat by altering your diet by approximately ten calories a day. A three-inch cookie averages about 120 calories, slightly more than the amount of calories in ten medium potato chips. Translated into weight-control terms: if you eat one cookie a day beyond your body's normal food requirements—or ten potato chips more—you should gain about 12 pounds in a year. Or if you regularly munch on such goodies, you should be able to reduce your weight by approximately 12 pounds a year simply by eliminating one cookie per day, or its equivalent.

Calorie Consumption During Normal Activities

An average human body needs about 1,500 calories a day just to survive; it burns about one calorie per minute in maintaining such simple body functions as breathing, keeping the body temperature at a normal level, and so on. A person who spends most of his time sleeping or watching TV doesn't need much more than a calorie per minute of food energy. A person who operates an electric typewriter for an hour requires only about 20 calories more for that period of work than a sleeping person. Driving a car for one hour might increase the body's need for calories by about 100 more than the amount needed for sleeping; one tablespoon of mayonnaise or a half-dozen saltine crackers will provide enough calories for one hour of driving.

By matching the calories in snack foods with the calorie needs of the human body for such low levels of inactivity as driving a car, watching TV, or operating an office machine, it is easy to see how pounds of

Operating an office machine burns up few calories. Sedentary workers should be careful to avoid snacks containing the extra calories that cause overweight.
—Santa Fe Railway

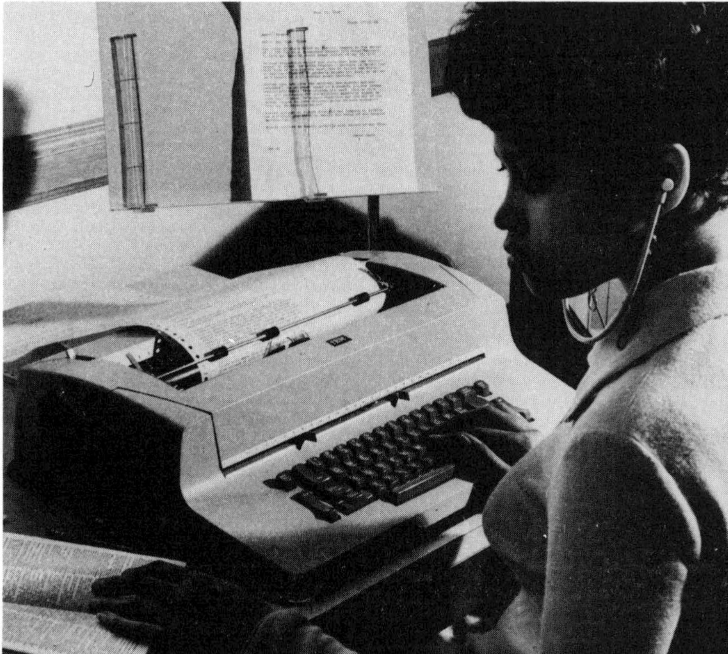

body fat can accumulate within a short period of time.

Even walking, which is considered a mildly active way of utilizing calories, burns only three calories per minute above the basic needs of the body. So you would need to walk two hours to burn an extra 360 calories—the equivalent of a slice of cherry pie. The next time a friend assures you that you can burn up the calories in a piece of fruit pie by walking back to the office after lunch, make the friend promise to walk with you because it will require six miles of walking.

Lack of Exercise and Weight Gain

Nevertheless, it is better to walk for two hours after eating a piece of pie than to remain inactive after adding hundreds of excess calories to your body's fuel supply—if you can't resist the temptation to add the calories—because there *is* a relationship between weight control and exercise. Some people apparently gain weight even though they eat no more than their friends and relatives who remain slim. Careful studies made of obese people who ate only small or average amounts of food—in some cases as few as 1,800 calories a day—showed that they were simply less active than their slim friends and relatives who consumed the same amount of calories.

In one instance involving students, motion pictures were taken of the obese youngsters working out with their classmates in physical education classes. The investigators discovered by watching the movies that the overweight students were in effect faking the exercise routines; that is, they did not play enthusiastically, but merely went through the motions.

What about the need for fat deposits in the body as a source of energy? The answer is that while fat is indeed a rich source of energy for the body, the human body chemistry is geared to convert protein to energy, if needed. But the body is not equipped to build protein molecules from fat. As for sugar in the diet, the body gets all it needs from carbohydrates in fruits, vegetables, and other food sources.

Planning Your Own Physical Fitness Program

Any weight control program in connection with physical fitness improvement should be tailored to your individual needs and directed by a physician. Only your doctor knows for sure about your individual nutrition needs, and no two individuals are precisely alike. The same rule applies to physical conditioning: you could have a hidden bodily deficiency that would not cause problems in a sedentary life style. But a sudden strenuous program of jogging, calisthenics, or other athletic activity could be enough to push you over the brink. After an examination, the doctor can recommend a tailored approach to physical conditioning—a program that will permit certain types of exercise but restrict or eliminate others. There are so many methods of exercise available today that an effective program can be built around any individual physical problems.

Exercises Keyed to Age

Age ordinarily is one factor in determining which exercises are more suitable for an individual, although everybody knows people who seem young at 60 and others who appear to be old at 30. The general rule for determining whether it is safe to begin an exercise program is this: if you are still in your 20s and have passed a standard physical examination within the past year, it should be safe to begin a progressive program of conditioning without further examination. But if you are over 30 years of age, you should have passed a complete physical examination that included an electrocardiogram within the past 90 days.

If you are over the age of 50, you can still begin a physical fitness program, but it should be a medically supervised program.

For the over 50 group, the doctor may advise that certain activities, such as jogging and competitive sports, be restricted or eliminated. Jogging can be damaging to the spine in persons beyond the age of 40 and can aggravate signs of arthritis. But walking, golf, swimming, bicycling, and exercising on a stationary cycle are alternate types of exercising for the past-middle-age set.

Fitness and Mental Health

In addition to the physical benefits gained by exercise, Dr. Ernest Simonson of the University of Minnesota Medical School found in a study of 10,000 persons that physical activity can be a definite aid to mental health. Typical comments by his subjects reflect that they "feel more alive" when they exercise. Dr. Simonson reported after analyzing the improved mental health of his subjects: "It is common logic that if one feels better, his attitude toward others will be more congenial. When one is in a cordial, happy frame of mind, he will likely make wiser decisions, and his world in general will look better."

The late Dr. William Menninger, one of the world's foremost experts on mental health, explained that

> Good mental health is directly related to the capacity and willingness of an individual to play. Regardless of his objections, resistances; or past practice, an individual will make a wise investment for himself if he will budget some of his time each day for his play—and take it seriously.

Dr. Menninger added that play provides an outlet for instinctive aggressive drives that enable a person to "blow off steam." Physical activity, he said, is a necessary supplement to daily work.

At the Beginning

Two things to remember in planning your own physical conditioning program are:

• Tailor the exercises and sports to your own needs and interests. If you have wanted

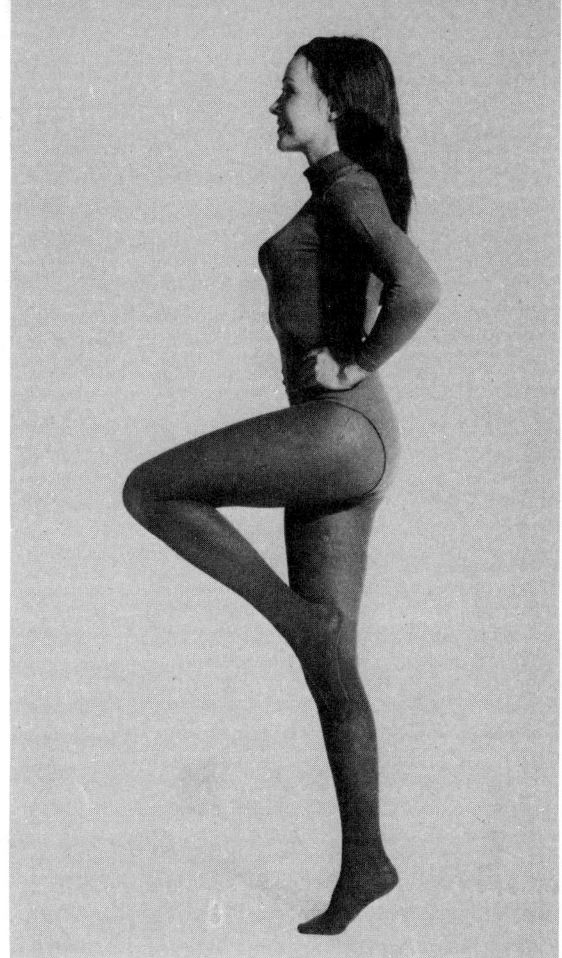

Exercise produces a healthful tone in mind and body.
—Ewing Galloway

to ride a bicycle, or learn water skiing, or take regular fishing trips, this is your opportunity to begin.

• Follow a progressive program in which you start at the bottom and improve gradually over a period of weeks or months. Don't expect overnight miracles, and be willing to cut back on the pace of your workouts if you find the going tough; you may be pushing yourself too fast. Your goal is to improve your own physical condition to the highest level feasible for your age and other possible limiting factors. Don't expect to set any new world records; just try to do the best you can—for your own health.

Warm-up exercises: The easiest place to begin your exercise program is in your own home, with the kind of warm-up exercises that you performed each day in high school. The main difference is that you will be on your own, unless you can find a friend or family member to participate in the workouts. You can do your own counting.

1 BEND AND STRETCH

Starting position: Stand erect, feet shoulder-width apart. *Action:* Count 1. Bend trunk forward and down, flexing knees. Stretch gently in attempt to touch fingers to toes or floor. Count 2. Return to starting position.

Note: Do slowly, stretch and relax at intervals rather than in rythm.

2 KNEE LIFT

Starting position: Stand erect, feet together, arms at sides. *Action:* Count 1. Raise left knee as high as possible, grasping leg with hands and pulling knee against body while keeping back straight. Count 2. Lower to starting position. Counts 3 and 4. Repeat with right knee.

3 WING STRETCHER

Starting position: Stand erect, elbows at shoulder height, fists clenched in front of chest. *Action:* Count 1. Thrust elbows backward vigorously without arching back. Keep head erect, elbows at shoulder height. Count 2. Return to starting position.

4 HALF KNEE BEND

Starting position: Stand erect, hands on hips. *Action:* Count 1. Bend knees halfway while extending arms forward, palms down. Count 2. Return to starting position.

5 ARM CIRCLES

Starting position: Stand erect, arms extended sideward at shoulder height, palms up. *Action:* Describe small circles backward with hands. Keep head erect. Do 15 backward circles. Reverse, turn palms down and do 15 small circles forward.

6 BODY BENDER

Starting position: Stand, feet shoulder-width apart, hands behind neck, fingers interlaced. *Action:* Count 1. Bend trunk sideward to left as far as possible, keeping hands behind neck. Count 2. Return to starting position. Counts 3 and 4. Repeat to the right.

7 PRONE ARCH

Starting position: Lie face down, hands tucked under thighs. *Action:* Count 1. Raise head, shoulders, and legs from floor. Count 2. Return to starting position.

8 KNEE PUSHUP

Starting position: Lie on floor, face down, legs together, knees bent with feet raised off floor, hands on floor under shoulders, palms down. *Action:* Count 1. Push upper body off floor until arms are fully extended and body is in straight line from head to knees. Count 2. Return to starting position.

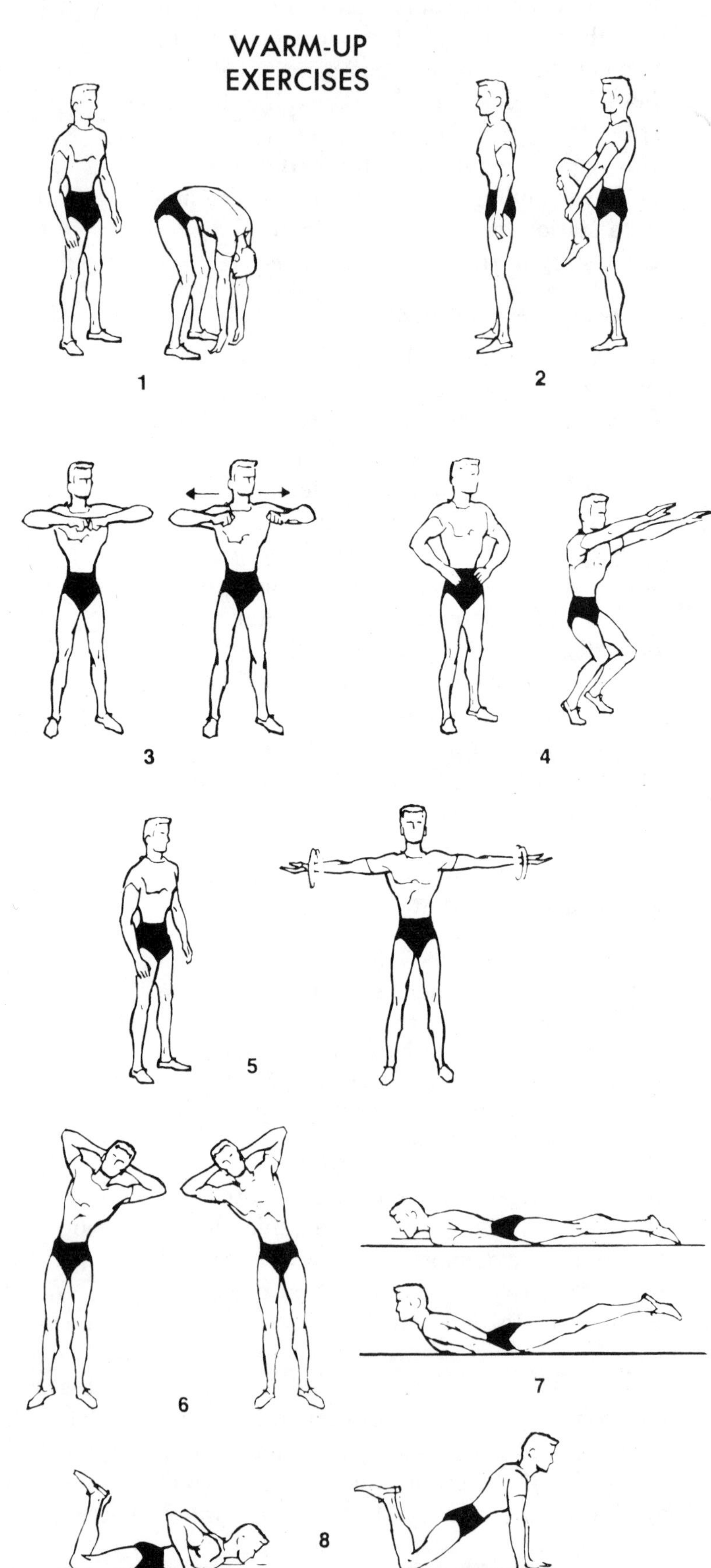

9 HEAD AND SHOULDER CURL
Starting position: Lie on back, hands tucked under small of back, palms down. *Action:* Count 1. Tighten abdominal muscles, lift head and pull shoulders and elbows up off floor. Hold for four seconds. Count 2. Return to starting position.

10 ANKLE STRETCH
Starting position: Stand on a stair, large book or block of wood, with weight on balls of feet and heels raised. *Action:* Count 1. Lower heels. Count 2. Raise heels.

11 TOE TOUCH
Starting position: Stand at attention. *Action:* Count 1. Bend trunk forward and down keeping knees straight, touching fingers to ankles. Count 2. Bounce and touch fingers to top of feet. Count 3. Bounce and touch fingers to toes. Count 4. Return to starting position.

12 SPRINTER
Starting position: Squat, hands on floor, fingers pointed forward, left leg fully extended to rear. *Action:* Count 1. Reverse position of feet in bouncing movement, bringing left foot to hands and extending right leg backward—all in one motion. Count 2. Reverse feet again, returning to starting position.

13 SITTING STRETCH
Starting position: Sit, legs spread apart, hands on knees. *Action:* Count 1. Bend forward at waist, extending arms as far forward as possible. Count 2. Return to starting position.

14 PUSHUP
Starting position: Lie on floor, face down, legs together, hands on floor under shoulders with fingers pointing straight ahead. *Action:* Count 1. Push body off floor by extending arms, so that weight rests on hands and toes. Count 2. Lower the body until chest touches floor.
Note: Body should be kept straight, buttocks should not be raised, abdomen should not sag.

15 SITUP (ARMS EXTENDED)
Starting position: Lie on back, legs straight and together, arms extended beyond head. *Action:* Count 1. Bring arms forward over head, roll up to sitting position, sliding hands along legs, grasping ankles. Count 2. Roll back to starting position.

16 LEG RAISER
Starting position: Right side of body on floor, head resting on left arm. *Action:* Lift left leg about 24″ off floor, then lower it. Do required number of repetitions. Repeat on other side.

17 FLUTTER KICK
Starting position: Lie face down, hands tucked under thighs. *Action:* Arch the back, bringing chest and head up, then flutter kick continuously, moving the legs 8″-10″ apart. Kick from hips with knees slightly bent. Count each kick as one.

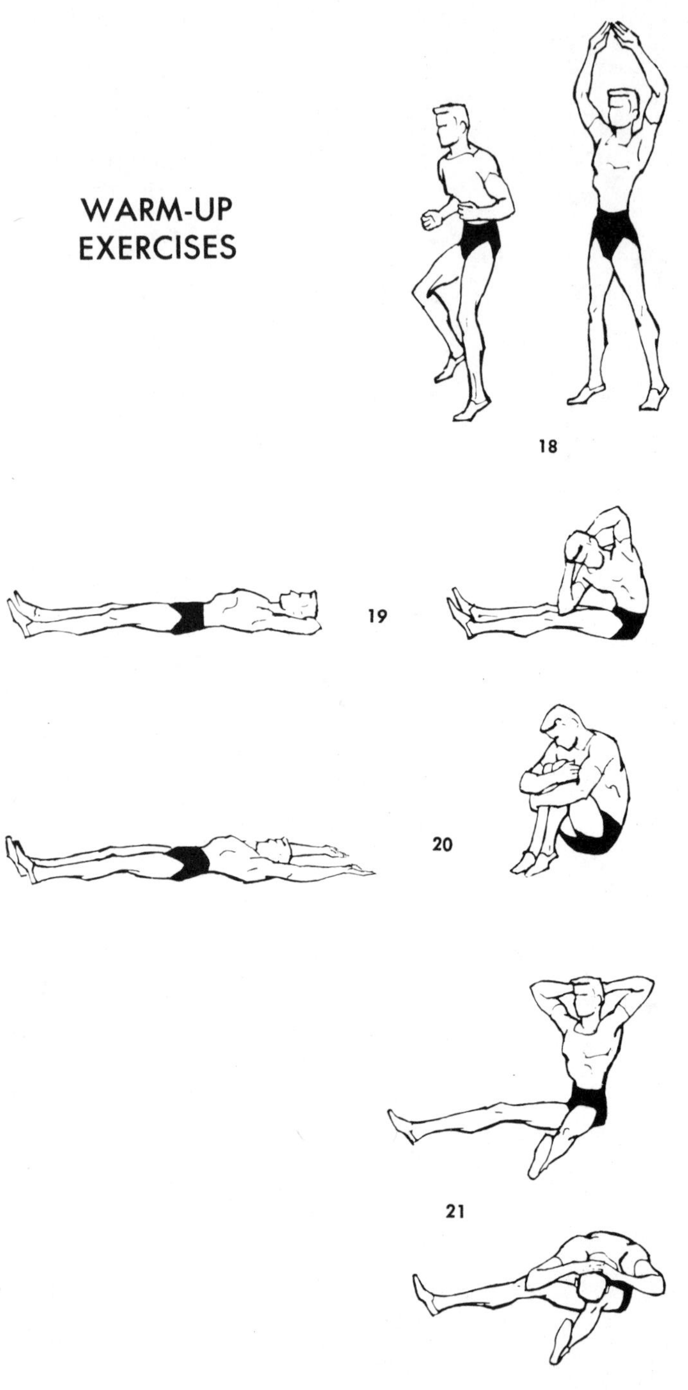

18 CIRCULATING ACTIVITIES

WALKING—Maintain a pace of 120 steps per minute for a distance of 1 mile. Swing arms and breathe deeply.

ROPE—Skip or jump rope continuously using any form for 30 seconds and then rest 30 seconds. Repeat 2 times.

RUN IN PLACE—Raise each foot at least 4″ off floor and jog in place. Count 1 each time left foot touches floor. Complete the number of running steps called for, then do specified number of straddle hops. Complete 2 cycles of alternate running and hopping.

STRADDLE HOP—Starting position: At attention. *Action:* Count 1. Swing arms sideward and upward, touching hands above head (arms straight) while simultaneously moving feet sideward and apart in a single jumping motion. Count 2. Spring back to starting position. Two counts in one hop.

19 SITUP (FINGERS LACED)

Starting position: Lie on back, legs straight and feet spread approximately 1′ apart. Fingers laced behind neck.
Action: Count 1. Curl up to sitting position and turn trunk to left. Touch the right elbow to left knee. Count 2. Return to starting position. Count 3. Curl up to sitting position and turn trunk to right. Touch left elbow to right knee. Count 4. Return to starting position. Score one situp each time you return to starting position. Knees may bend as necessary.

20 SITUP (ARMS EXTENDED, KNEES UP)

Starting position: Lie on back, legs straight, arms extended overhead.
Action: Count 1. Sit up, reaching forward with arms encircling knees while pulling them tightly to chest. Count 2. Return to starting position. Do this exercise rhythmically without breaks in the movement.

21 SITTING STRETCH (ALTERNATE)

Starting position: Sit, legs spread apart, fingers laced behind neck, elbows back.
Action: Count 1. Bend forward to left, touching forehead to left knee. Count 2. Return to starting position. Counts 3 and 4. Repeat to right. Score one repetition each time you return to starting position. Knees may be bent if necessary.

The purpose of the warm-up exercises is to increase the blood flow to the muscles and gradually limber up the body. And a warm-up period of at least 20 minutes should be used before any strenuous exercise. Otherwise, you may experience strains and sprains, or worse. It is quite possible to rupture a tendon or injure a joint by starting with certain strenuous exercises without a preliminary warm-up period. Also, remember to taper off a workout period with mild muscular activity, such as walking, until breathing and body temperature have returned to normal levels.

The warm-up exercises include body benders, situps, pushups, bend and stretch, ankle stretch, knee lifts, straddle hops, walking, running-in-place, and rope-skipping workouts, among a wide assortment of calisthenics. You can select from the assortment of warm-up exercises illustrated on pp. 778–780 those that are best suited to your own situation. If you live in a house or apartment where you are likely to irritate other occupants by running in place or skipping rope, you can find other exercises that stimulate the general body circulation. But if you have facilities, such as a basement or garage, or a ground-floor bedroom where there is room for straddle hops or rope skipping, the exercises that provide the better range of action should be followed. Most of the exercises can be done in a small area; airline personnel investigating a strange thumping in a jet aircraft at 30,000 feet altitude one morning discovered a passenger running in place in the rest room.

Although no special equipment is necessary, don't hesitate to invest in a few items of gym equipment—dumbbells, weights, a stationary cycle, or whatever you think you need to help you in your own fitness program. For the cost of one or two days in a hospital, you can buy enough exercising equipment to keep yourself out of the hospital for several years.

Muscle soreness: You can expect some muscular soreness for the first two or three weeks of the toughening stage of physical conditioning, particularly if you have shunned exercise for several years. Later on, as you progressively increase the work load on your body you may experience some stiffness or soreness. Usually this is only a warning sign that you are moving up the fitness scale too quickly. On the other hand, if the muscle soreness is relatively mild and goes away overnight, you can assume that you are not overdoing the exercise routine.

If your muscles and joints appear to suffer from the exercise load, simply slow down to an easier pace and work back up the scale again at a more gradual rate. By working at your own pace, with only the goal of improving your muscular strength and endurance, you can build a lot of flexibility into your fitness program. You don't have to compete with others; if you need an extra day or week to advance from one stage to the next, take the extra time. It's your own conditioning routine, and the suggested benchmarks or guidelines for the accompanying exercises can be adapted to your own needs.

The Indoor Exercise Program

Based on the U.S. Army's 6–12 conditioning project, the Indoor Exercise Program on pp. 782-793 includes six sets of exercise routines. Each set requires 12 minutes a day to complete. Each of the sets, from I to VI, is in turn divided into three levels of activity. They are labeled A, B, and C. The entire program, therefore, is designed to provide a progressive scale of physical conditioning for 12 minutes a day over a period of 18 weeks. You should begin at the C-level of set I and follow that routine for the first week. At the start of the second week, you progress to the B-level exercise routine of set I, and to the A-level routine at the beginning of the third week. Then, assuming that you follow the schedule according to its original design, you advance to the C-level routine of set II of the 6–12 exercises at the start of the fourth week, and so on.

The progression guides accompanying each table of 6–12 exercises represent suggested goals for healthy males. Women generally are not expected to match the suggested pace, although some may be able to do so. To follow the progression guide of Table I, read the first vertical column of numbers under the word *Exercises*. Under Exercise 1, in the age group of 17–29, are the numbers 15, 13, and 11. These numbers show the repetitions of Exercise 1 to be completed within two minutes, the number indicated at the bottom of the column. The beginner in that age group should attempt to complete 11 side straddle exercises within two minutes, or at least he should work toward that primary goal. He also should try to complete 14 of the modified pushups in 1 minute, 12 situps in 1 minute, and so on. If he can accomplish the C level goals in the first week, he progresses to the B level goal of 13 side straddle exercises within two minutes, 16 modified pushups, 13 situps, and so on. You will note that the total of the minutes suggested for the various exercises is 12 regardless of the age group or exercise level chosen. The greatest amount of time is allocated to running in place, and the number of steps ranges from a beginning level of 30, or six per minute, for men over 60 to a maximum of 250, or

TABLE I

PROGRESSION GUIDE

AGE GROUP	LEVEL	EXERCISES 1	2	3	4	5	6
17	A	15	18	14	15	15	250
to	B	13	16	13	13	13	235
29	C	11	14	12	11	11	215
30	A	13	14	12	13	13	200
to	B	11	13	11	11	11	185
39	C	9	12	10	9	9	165
40	A	11	11	10	11	11	150
to	B	9	10	9	9	9	135
44	C	7	9	8	7	7	120
45	A	9	8	8	9	9	100
to	B	7	7	7	7	7	90
49	C	5	6	6	5	5	80
50	A	7	6	6	7	7	75
to	B	5	5	5	5	5	70
59	C	3	4	4	3	3	60
60	A	4	5	4	4	4	50
and	B	3	4	3	3	3	40
over	C	2	3	2	2	2	30
Minutes for each exercise		2	1	1	1	2	5

1. Side straddle, arms overhead and straight, palms facing.

   — Turn trunk to the left and bend forward over the left thigh, attempt to touch the fingertips to the floor outside the left foot, keep the knees straight. Alternate the movement to the opposite side.

   — Down and up to one side is one repetition.

2. Kneeling front rest, hands shoulder width apart. The weight is supported on the knees and by the arms.

   — Bend elbows and lower body until chest touches the floor. Keeping knees on the floor, raise body by straightening the arms.

   — Down and up is one repetition.

3. Supine position, fingers interlaced and placed behind the head.

   — Maintaining the heels on the floor, raise the head and shoulders until the heels come into view. Lower the head and shoulders until fingers contact the floor and head rests on the hands.

   — Up and down is one repetition.

4. Body erect, feet slightly spread, fingers interlaced and placed on rear of neck at base of the head.

   — Bend the upper trunk backward, raise the chest high, pull the elbows back, and look upward. Keep the knees straight. Recover to the erect position, eyes to the front.

   — Bending backward and recovery is one repetition.

5. Body erect, feet spread less than shoulder width, hands on hips, elbows back.

   — Do a full knee bend, at the same time bend slightly forward at the waist. Touch the floor with the extended fingers, keeping the hands about six inches apart. Resume the starting position.

   — Down into the touch position and return to the starting position is one repetition.

6. Run in place, lift feet 4 to 6 inches off floor. At the completion of every 50 steps do 10 "Steam Engines." Repeat sequence until the required number of steps is completed.

   — Count a step each time left foot touches the floor.

   Steam Engines - Lace the fingers behind the neck and while standing in place raise the left knee above waist height, at the same time twist the trunk and lower the right elbow to the left knee. Lower the left leg and raise the right leg touching the knee with the left elbow thus completing the movement to that side. Continue to alternate the movement until the sequence is completed.

INDOOR EXERCISE PROGRAM

50 per minute, for a young man in good condition.

Adapting the Program to Meet Your Needs

There is considerable flexibility in adapting this program to suit your own physical abilities, whether you are a man or woman. Each individual is as different in his physical strength and endurance as his fingerprints or other traits. The important thing about these sets of exercises is that most normal adults can perform most or all of them at one of the beginning levels, and with that beginning level as a benchmark the individual can gradually follow the progression guidelines to a higher level of fitness.

Some individuals may already be in such good condition that they can work up to the A-level of Table VI at the ninth week instead of the 18th week without any of the

TABLE II

PROGRESSION GUIDE

AGE GROUP	LEVEL	EXERCISES 1	2	3	4	5	6
17 to 29	A	17	17	17	9	19	300
	B	15	15	15	8	17	270
	C	13	13	13	7	15	245
30 to 39	A	15	15	15	8	17	235
	B	13	13	13	7	15	210
	C	11	11	11	6	13	190
40 to 44	A	13	13	13	7	15	175
	B	11	11	11	6	13	155
	C	9	10	9	5	11	135
45 to 49	A	11	11	11	6	13	125
	B	9	9	9	5	11	110
	C	7	7	7	4	9	100
50 to 59	A	9	9	9	5	11	95
	B	7	7	7	4	9	85
	C	5	5	5	3	7	75
60 and over	A	6	7	7	4	9	70
	B	5	5	5	3	7	60
	C	4	4	4	2	5	50
Minutes for each exercise		1	1	1	1½	1½	6

1. Wide side straddle, arms overhead and straight, palms facing.
   - Bend at the knees and the waist, swing the arms down, and reach between the legs as far as possible. Look at the hands. The thighs are parallel to the floor during the bend. Recover to the starting position with a sharp movement.
   - Down and up is one repetition.
2. Front leaning rest position with body straight from head to heels.
   - Bending at the waist and keeping the knees locked, jump forward to a jack-knife position bringing the feet as close to the hands as possible. With the weight on the hands, thrust the legs to the rear resuming the front leaning rest position.
   - Up into the jack-knife position and return to the front leaning rest position is one repetition.
3. Supine position with arms straight overhead, palms facing.
   - With a sharp movement sit up, bringing the heels as close to the buttocks as possible and the knees to the chest. Swing the arms in an arc overhead to a position outside the knees and parallel to the floor. To recover swing the arms overhead keeping them straight. At the same time move the legs forward until they are straight.
   - Sitting up and returning to the supine position is one repetition.
4. Feet spread more than shoulder width apart, fingers laced behind the neck and elbows are back.
   - Bend forward at the waist vigorously, then twist the trunk to the left, then to the right and return to the erect position.
   - Keep the knees locked and back straight.
   - Bend forward, twist left, twist right, and return to the erect position is one repetition.
5. Bend forward at the waist, grasping the right toes with right hand, left toes with left hand, knees are slightly bent.
   - Walk forward retaining this position.
   - Count a repetition each time a foot contacts the floor.
6. Run in place, lift feet 4 to 6 inches off floor. At the completion of every 50 steps do 10 "Heel Clicks" Repeat sequence until the required number of steps is completed.
   - Count a step each time left foot touches the floor.

   Heel Clicks - Jump upward about 12 inches and bring the heels together. Before landing on the floor, separate the feet 15 to 18 inches. Immediately upon contact with the floor repeat the jump and heel click.

INDOOR EXERCISE PROGRAM

muscle stiffness or soreness that would indicate too fast a rate of advancement. Others may feel more comfortable if they spend two or three weeks at the C or B-level of Table I before moving to another level. There are no fixed rules to this program; the progression guides are merely suggestions that can be altered to fit your personal needs.

But don't go through the exercises half-heartedly. One purpose of exercising is to maintain a modest overload on the muscles and the heart and lungs, which builds up a good reserve of strength and endurance. So you have to push a bit every day to make the plan work; if some of the exercises are less demanding of your muscles and circulatory system than your daily work responsibilities, you may be wasting your time. A man who moves pianos for a living would do little to improve his strength by lifting six-pound dumbbells for exercise.

TABLE III

PROGRESSION GUIDE

AGE GROUP	LEVEL	EXERCISES 1	2	3	4	5	6
17	A	10	19	19	16	10	350
to	B	9	17	17	15	9	315
29	C	8	15	15	14	8	280
30	A	9	17	17	14	9	270
to	B	8	15	15	13	8	240
39	C	7	13	13	12	7	210
40	A	8	15	15	12	8	200
to	B	7	13	13	11	7	180
44	C	6	11	11	10	6	160
45	A	7	13	13	10	7	150
to	B	6	11	11	9	6	135
49	C	5	9	9	8	5	120
50	A	6	11	11	8	6	115
to	B	5	9	9	7	5	105
59	C	4	7	7	6	4	95
60	A	5	9	9	7	5	90
and	B	4	7	7	6	4	80
over	C	3	5	5	4	3	70
Minutes for each exercise		1½	1	1	1½	1	6

1. Feet spread less than shoulder width apart, hands on hips, elbows back.

   — Do a full knee bend, trunk erect and thrust the arms forward. Recover to the erect position, and with knees locked, bend forward at the waist and touch the toes and recover to the erect position.

   — Down into the full knee bend, recover, touch toes and recover is one repetition.

2. Front leaning rest position with body straight from head to heels.

   — Lower the body until the chest touches the floor, keep body straight. Recover by straightening the arms and raising the body.

   — Down and touch the floor and recovery to the front leaning rest position is one repetition.

3. Supine position, arms overhead, palms facing.

   — With a sharp movement sit up, thrust the arms forward and touch the toes.

   — Keep the legs straight and the heels in contact with the floor.

   — Sit up, touch toes, and resume the supine position is one repetition.

4. Supine position, arms overhead, palms upward.

   — Raise the legs and swing them backward over the head until toes touch the floor. Recover by returning legs to the starting position.

   — Touch toes overhead and recover to supine position is one repetition.

5. Erect position, feet together.

   — Bend knees and place hands on floor, shoulder width apart. Thrust legs to the rear, body straight from head to heels. Move legs forward assuming squat position, elbows inside of knees. Assume erect position.

   — Down into full squat, legs to the rear, back to full squat and return to the erect position is one repetition.

6. Run in place, lift feet 4 to 6 inches off floor. At the completion of every 50 steps do 10 "Knee Touches." Repeat sequence until the required number of steps is completed.

   — Count a step each time left foot touches the floor.

   Knee Touches - From a stride position, bend the knees and touch the knee of the rear leg to the floor, straighten legs, jump upward and change position of the feet. Again bend knees and touch the opposite knee. Continue alternately touching each knee.

INDOOR
EXERCISE
PROGRAM
EXERCISE 1
EXERCISE 2
EXERCISE 3
EXERCISE 4
EXERCISE 5
EXERCISE 6

On the other hand, there are people over the age of 45 who should be cautious about advancing beyond set IV of the Indoor Exercise Program. If they experience discomfort at the C-level of set V, they should drop back to the A-level of Table IV. This program is designed to fit all sorts of individual needs and abilities; some individuals probably should not advance beyond the Table III set of exercises. If there is any question about the level at which you should taper off your personal progressive program, discuss the matter with your doctor.

Maximum Performance Plateau

The rate of improvement in your physical condition will seem to be quite rapid at first, then increase slowly as you reach a plateau about halfway through the 18-week program. You can tell when you have reached your peak performance because you will

TABLE IV

PROGRESSION GUIDE

AGE GROUP	LEVEL	EXERCISES 1	2	3	4	5	6
17	A	12	9	12	24	25	400
to	B	11	8	11	22	23	380
29	C	10	7	10	21	21	360
30	A	11	8	11	23	23	305
to	B	10	7	10	21	21	290
39	C	9	6	9	20	20	275
40	A	10	7	10	20	21	225
to	B	9	6	9	18	18	215
44	C	8	5	8	16	16	205
45	A	8	6	8	16	16	175
to	B	7	5	7	14	14	165
49	C	6	4	6	12	12	155
50	A	6	5	6	13	13	135
to	B	5	4	5	11	11	130
59	C	4	3	4	10	10	120
60	A	5	4	5	10	10	100
and	B	4	3	4	9	9	95
over	C	3	2	3	8	8	90
Minutes for each exercise		1	2	1	1	1	6

1. Erect position, hands at sides, feet spread slightly.

   — Bend knees, incline trunk forward, and place hands on floor between legs. Straighten knees, keeping feet in place and fingers touching floor. Again bend knees and resume the first position. Recover to the erect position.

   — The above sequence is one repetition.

2. Erect position, hands at sides, feet together.

   — Bend knees, place hands on floor between legs. Thrust legs to the rear. Execute two complete push-ups and then thrust the legs forward bending the knees with arms between the knees. Recover to the erect position.

   — The completion of all eight counts is one repetition.

3. Back position with arms out to sides and legs raised to the vertical.

   — Lower legs to the left, raise legs to the vertical, lower to the right, again raise to the vertical.

   — Keep legs together and the head and hands in contact with the floor throughout the exercise.

   — The above sequence is one repetition.

4. From back position, raise legs with heels 10 to 12 inches from the floor.

   — Spread legs as far as possible, close them together. Continue to open and close legs until required repetitions have been completed.

   — Opening and closing legs in one repetition.

5. Front leaning rest position, body straight from head to heels.

   — Bend the left knee and bring the left foot as far forward as possible, return left leg to original position. Repeat movement with the right leg. Continue exercise alternating left and right legs.

   — A leg thrust forward and returned to the rear is one repetition.

6. Run in place, lift feet 4 to 6 inches off floor. At the completion of every 50 steps do 10 "Jumping Jacks." Repeat sequence until the required number of steps is completed.

   — Count a step each time left foot touches the floor.

   Jumping Jacks - Feet spread shoulder width apart, arms extended overhead. Jump upward, bring heels together and at same time squat to a full knee bend position, bring the arms downward and place hands on the floor elbows inside of knees, directly under the shoulders. Jump to the side straddle and swing the arms sideward overhead.

INDOOR
EXERCISE
PROGRAM
EXERCISE 1
1
2
3
4
5
6
7
8
EXERCISE 2
EXERCISE 3
EXERCISE 4
EXERCISE 5
EXERCISE 6

begin to experience the huffing and puffing effects of an oxygen debt when you try to push yourself beyond that particular level —even though you have learned to overcome the need to pause for a "second wind" that you may have experienced earlier in the program.

There is a practical limit to the performance of anybody—even Olympic champions —when the heart and lungs simply cannot supply oxygen fast enough to sustain the activity of the muscles. The muscle cells can "borrow" oxygen that is dissolved in the blood and other tissues in order to function temporarily, but eventually that debt of oxygen has to be repaid. That is why you may occasionally see track stars collapse in a series of agonizing gasps after they reach the finish line: they have run their oxygen debt to the point of bankruptcy.

In your own conditioning program based on the 6–12 exercise schedule, you may

TABLE V
PROGRESSION GUIDE

AGE GROUP	LEVEL	EXERCISES 1	2	3	4	5	6
17	A	14	13	28	14	30	450
to	B	13	12	27	13	28	430
29	C	12	11	26	12	26	410
30	A	12	12	25	12	26	350
to	B	11	11	24	11	24	330
39	C	10	10	23	10	22	310
40	A	11	11	23	11	23	250
to	B	10	10	21	10	21	240
44	C	9	9	19	9	19	230
45	A	9	9	20	9	20	200
to	B	8	8	18	8	18	190
49	C	7	7	16	7	16	180
50	A	7	7	16	7	16	170
to	B	6	6	14	6	14	155
59	C	5	5	12	5	12	140
60	A	6	6	12	6	12	115
and	B	5	5	11	5	10	110
over	C	4	4	9	4	9	105
Minutes for each exercise		2	1	1	2	1	5

1. Feet spread more than shoulder width, arms sideward at shoulder level, palms up.

   – Turn trunk to the left as far as possible then recover slightly, repeat to the left and recover slightly. Turn trunk to the right as far as possible, recover slightly, repeat to the right and recover slightly.

   – The head and hips remain to the front throughout the exercise.

   – The above sequence is one repetition.

2. Front leaning rest position, body straight from head to heels.

   – Bend the elbows slightly and push with the hands and toes bouncing the body upward and completely off the floor. In contact with the floor resume the front leaning rest position.

   – Propelling the body upward and the return to the floor is one repetition.

3. Back position, hands interlaced and placed under head, knees bent with feet flat on the floor.

   – Sit up bending the trunk forward and attempting to touch the chest to the thighs. Recover to the back position without moving the feet.

   – Sit up and recovery to the back position is one repetition.

4. On back, arms sideward, feet raised 12 inches from the floor, knees straight.

   – Keeping the legs together, swing legs as far to the left as possible, swing legs overhead, then to the right as far as possible and recover by swinging legs to the front.

   – Legs stop momentarily at each position and do not contact floor until all repetitions are complete.

   – One repetition is completed when legs make the complete circle.

5. From a stride position do a deep knee bend and grasp the right ankle with the right hand, left ankle with the left hand, arms outside knees.

   – Walk forward maintaining the grasp of the ankles.

   – One repetition is counted each time the left foot contacts the floor.

6. Run in place, lift feet 4 to 6 inches off floor. At the completion of every 50 steps do 10 "Hand Kicks." Repeat sequence until required number of steps is completed.

   Hand Kicks - Stand in place and kick left leg upward, at the same time extend the right arm touching the toe and hand. Repeat with right leg extending left arm.

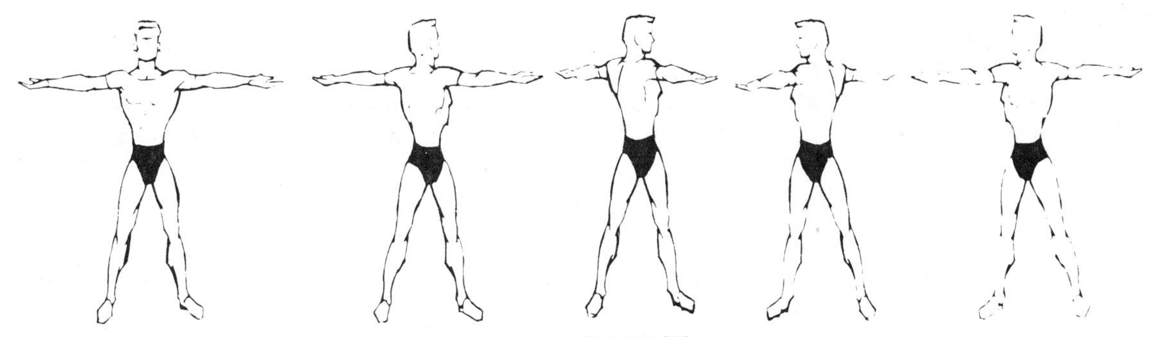

EXERCISE 1

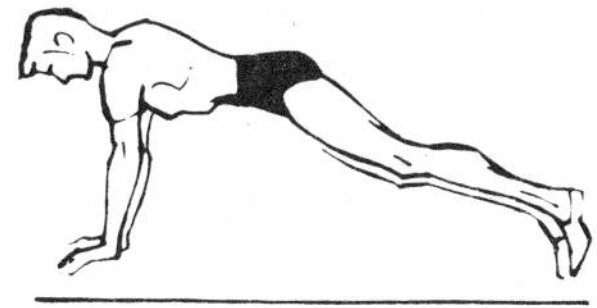
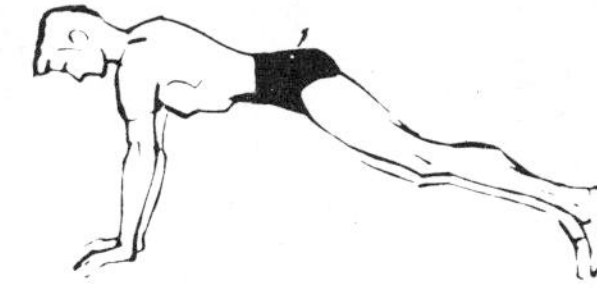

EXERCISE 2

INDOOR EXERCISE PROGRAM

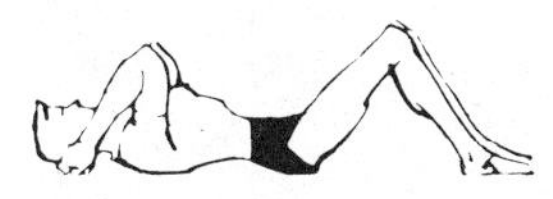

EXERCISE 3

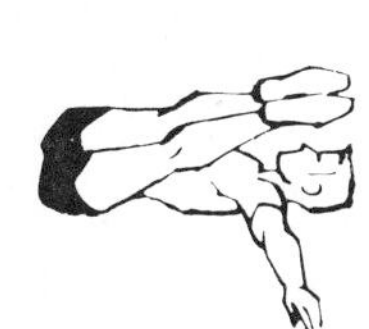

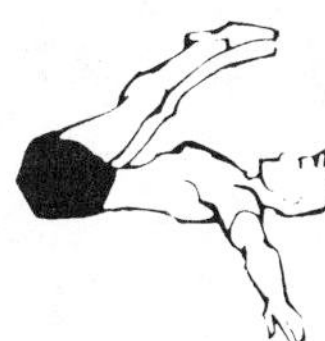

EXERCISE 4

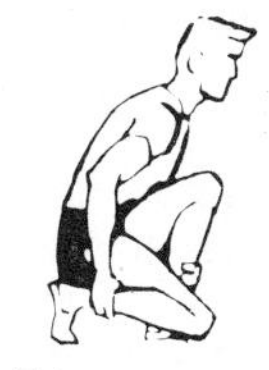

EXERCISE 5

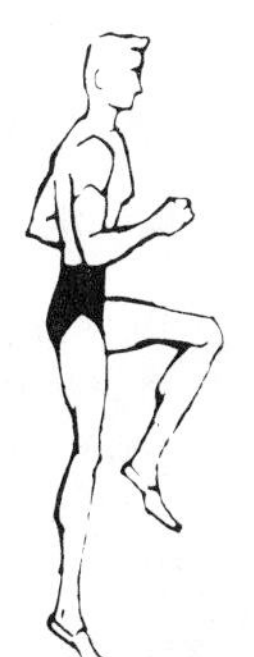

EXERCISE 6

reach a point where, for example, you can do all of the exercises at the A level of Table V without experiencing an oxygen debt, but you can't make it through the Table VI routines without huffing and puffing. Then you will know that you are at your personal plateau of maximum performance. But you don't quit exercising at that point; you simply continue working out at the highest level that is comfortable for you. If you drop out of the program after reaching the level of your maximum performance your physical condition will deteriorate within two or three weeks.

There are still goals ahead and skills to be developed after you reach your maximum performance plateau—development of strength and endurance for participation in certain sports or improvement of the function of special muscle groups used in athletic activity. Rope skipping, a traditional conditioning exercise, always a favorite of

TABLE VI

PROGRESSION GUIDE

AGE GROUP	LEVEL	EXERCISES 1	2	3	4	5	6
17	A	17	15	32	32	35	500
to	B	16	14	30	30	33	480
29	C	15	13	28	28	31	460
30	A	15	13	30	30	31	400
to	B	14	12	28	28	29	380
39	C	13	11	26	26	27	360
40	A	13	10	27	27	27	310
to	B	12	9	25	25	25	285
44	C	11	8	23	23	23	265
45	A	11	9	23	23	23	250
to	B	10	8	21	21	21	230
49	C	9	7	19	19	19	210
50	A	9	8	19	19	19	200
to	B	8	7	17	17	17	190
59	C	7	6	15	15	15	175
60	A	8	7	15	15	17	140
and	B	7	6	13	13	15	130
over	C	5	5	10	10	12	120
Minutes for each exercise		2	1	1	1	1	6

1. Feet spread shoulder width apart, left fist clenched and overhead, right fist clenched at waistline in rear of body.

   — Simultaneously thrust the left fist as far to the right as possible and the right fist as far to the left as possible. Recover and repeat. Reverse the hands with the right fist above the head and the left in rear at the waistline. Repeat the movement to the opposite side by thrusting the upper body to the left with the arm motion.

   — The above sequence is one repetition.

2. Front leaning rest position.

   — Bend elbows slightly and push with the hands and toes bouncing the body upward and completely off the floor. At the height of the bounce, clap the hands and quickly return them to a position directly under the shoulder to catch the body weight.

   — Push off the floor, clap hands, and return to the front leaning rest position is one repetition.

3. Back position, arms extended to the side at 45 degrees.

   — Raise the legs and the trunk into a V position bringing the trunk and legs as close as possible. Return to back position.

   — Raising the legs and trunk and recovery to the back position is one repetition.

4. Prone position with hands clasped in small of the back.

   — Arch the body, holding the head back and rock forward, relax and repeat the movement.

   — Arch the body, rock forward, and relax is one repetition.

5. From a sitting position lift the hips supporting the body on the hands and feet.

   — By moving the arms and legs walk on all fours either forward or backward.

   — A repetition occurs each time the left hand contacts the floor.

6. Run in place, lift feet 4 to 6 inches off floor. At the completion of every 50 steps do 10 "Pike Jumps." Repeat sequence until required number of steps is completed.

   Pike Jumps - Jump forward and upward from both feet, keeping the knees straight. Swing the legs forward and touch the toes with the hands at the top of each jump.

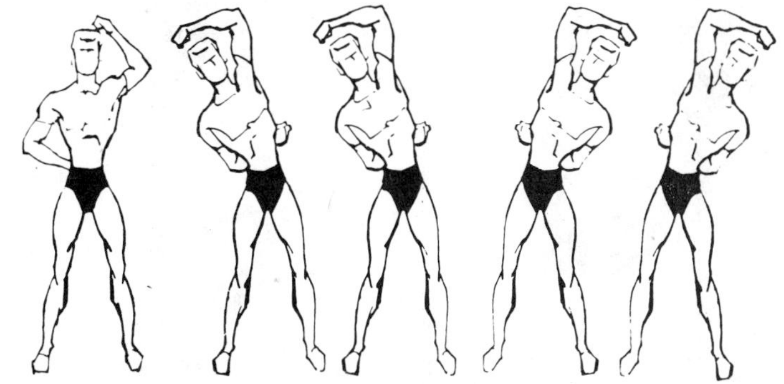

EXERCISE 1

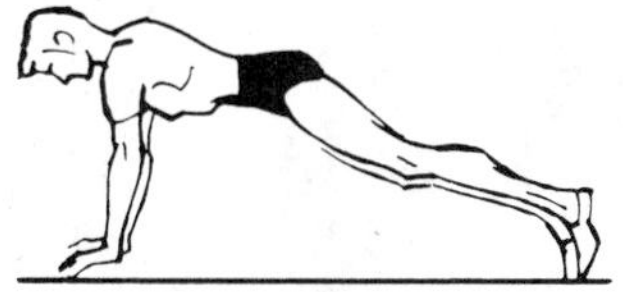

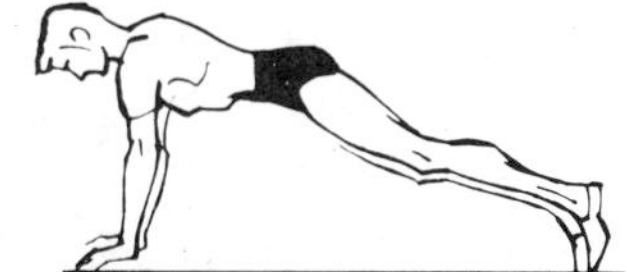

EXERCISE 2

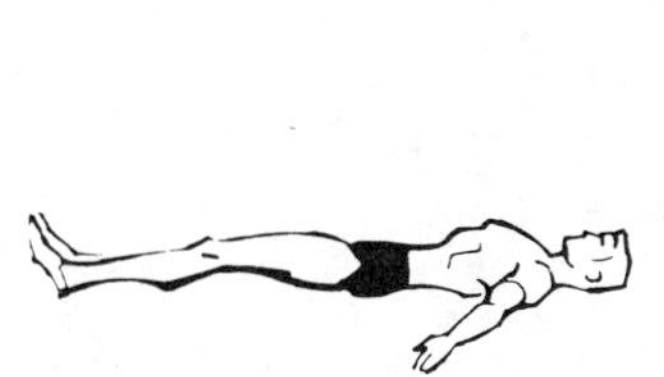

EXERCISE 3

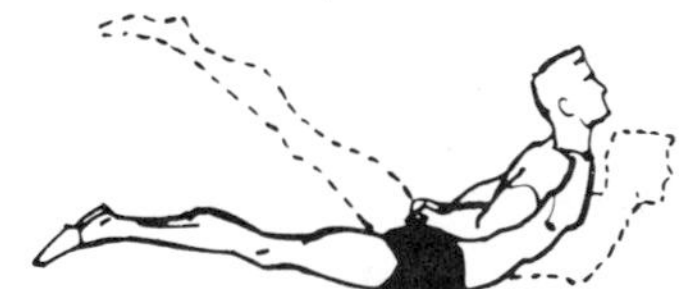

EXERCISE 4

INDOOR EXERCISE PROGRAM

EXERCISE 5

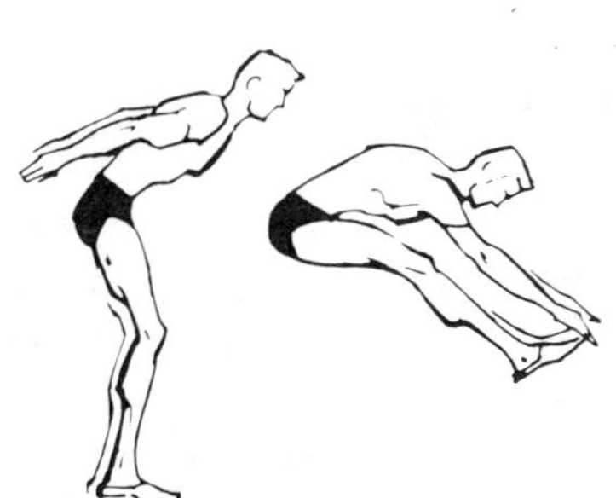

EXERCISE 6

Squash is a lively, invigorating indoor sport requiring the stamina, alertness and agility that develop physical fitness.

professional boxers in training, is an example of an athletic activity that requires a high level of coordination, muscular function, and heart-lung performance to do well. Anyone who has tried high-speed rope skipping for more than three minutes without missing a jump knows it is more than a playground game; in fact, such a test has been used by the army in training soldiers for combat duty.

Weight Lifting

Another special method of developing strength and endurance is weight lifting practice. Weight lifting may be one of the oldest known sports that utilizes equipment; youths who wanted to participate in the ancient Greek Olympics of nearly 2,750 years ago were required to lift a heavy iron weight to prove their strength before they were accepted into the ritual. Weight lifting as a formal competitive sport was popular in Europe for many generations, but it did not attract much attention in North America until the 1930s when the United States organized its first weight lifting team for Olympic competition.

Exercising With Barbells

Although competitive weight lifting generally is considered a masculine activity, there is no reason why women could not work out with barbells if they wanted to do so. Body weight is not necessarily a factor; U.S. championship weight lifting has a minimum body weight class of 114.5 pounds while A.A.U. competition is held in a 123-pound body weight class. However, most women probably are not interested in developing the muscle groups that would benefit from lifting barbells. The type of

Basic Barbell Exercises

Exercise 1: Squat. 6 repetitions, 50 pounds (commonly called the *flatfoot deep knee bend*). Place the bar upon the shoulders. Stand with feet about 18 inches apart. Keeping the feet flat, lower the body into the low squat position. Come erect and repeat. Exhale as you lower into the squat position and inhale as you come up.

Exercise 2: Waist Bender. 6 repetitions, 40 pounds. Assume the standing position with the bar across the shoulders, feet shoulder-width apart. Bend forward at the waist until the upper body is parallel to the ground; return to the starting position. • Each time you return to the upright position will constitute one repetition.

Exercise 3: Curl. 6 repetitions, 40 pounds. Grasp the barbell with the palms facing to the rear and assume the standing position, feet shoulder width apart. With the barbell held in front of the hips, flex the elbows and lift the weight until the bar touches the upper chest. Lower the barbell back to the hip level position. Inhale deeply with the upward movement and exhale on the downward movement. • Each time the bar touches the chest will constitute one repetition.

Exercise 4: Side Bender. 6 repetitions per side, 40 pounds. Assume the standing position, feet shoulder width apart, with the bar across the shoulders. Bend to the left as far as possible and return to the starting position. Repeat six times and then execute the same procedure to the right for six repetitions.

Exercise 5: Standing Press. 6 repetitions, 45 pounds. Grasp the bar with the palms facing forward and assume the starting position. Curl the weight to the upper chest position. Inhale deeply and press the bar upward to an overhead position. Exhale as you lower the bar to the chest position. • Each time the bar is pressed upward constitutes one repetition.

Exercise 6: Upward Row. 6 repetitions, 40 pounds. Grasp the bar, hands close together, palms to the rear, and assume the standing position. Starting with the bar held in front of the hips, flexing the elbows and the shoulder girdle muscles, lift the bar straight up to an overhead position. Inhale deeply as you lift the bar. Exhale as you lower the bar to the hip position. • Each time the bar returns to the hips will constitute one repetition.

Exercise 7: Shoulder Curl. 6 repetitions, 25 pounds. Grasp the bar palms down, and assume the standing position. Keeping the elbows locked, curl the bar, pivoting the arms at the shoulders until the bar is in an overhead position and as far to the rear as possible. Return the bar in the same manner to the hip position. • Each time the bar returns to hip position constitutes one repetition.

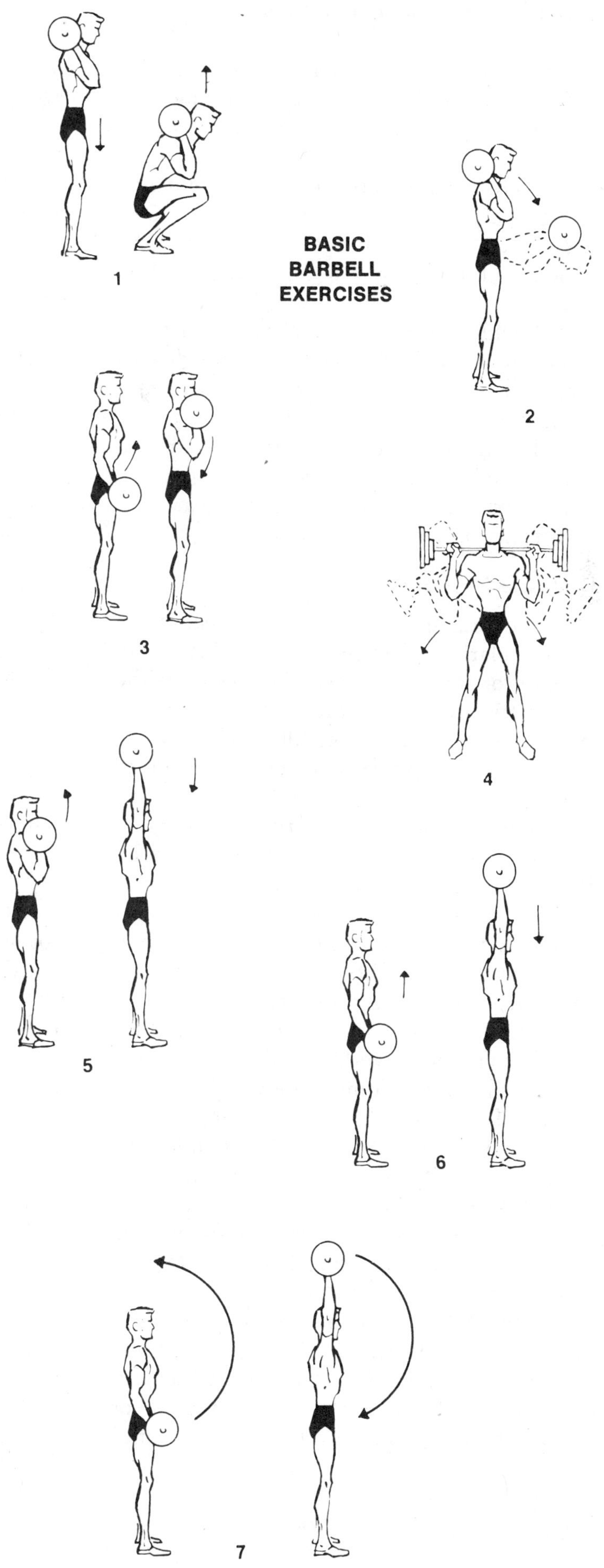

weight lifting that is more compatible with female physical fitness goals, exercising with dumbbells, is described later in this chapter.

There are two approaches to weight lifting as a part of physical conditioning. One approach is to use barbell weights in competitive lifting in which the participant lifts a tremendous amount of weight off the floor and holds it aloft for a brief period of time. The other approach is to use weights to develop the strength and tone of major muscle groups in the arms, legs, back, trunk, and shoulder girdle. The effect is to improve the blood flow to the muscles through more efficient pumping volume of the heart and distribution by the capillaries.

Muscle Overload

The principle of muscle overloading is particularly applicable in weight lifting because of the added demands made on the muscles by lifting progressively heavier weights. A person normally has no more muscular strength than he seems to need for daily work and play routines. There is, therefore, little or no reserve for emergencies unless you create an artificial need by overloading the muscles with heavy weights three or four times a week. The body responds to the extra demand by providing the extra muscle fibers.

Each time you stimulate the body to reach a certain plateau of muscle overloading, you begin working toward the next higher level by adding more weight to your barbell. You may begin, for example, with 40 to 50 pounds of weight and add five pounds when you are able. But do not overload the muscles to the point of a strain or a joint dislocation. Also, as you follow the basic barbell exercises described in this appendix, begin at the minimum number of repetitions. After you have learned to do six squats with 50 pounds of weight, continue at that rate for four or five days, then try seven squats with the same amount of weight. Do not advance to 55 pounds until you can handle 10 or 12 at the starting weight level.

Warm-up exercises: As mentioned above, you should go through a period of warm-up exercises before you begin a weight-lifting routine. Another factor to remember is that most weight-lifting exercises require postural control—which means you must hold the back straight during the lifting phase. Always squat to grasp the barbell from the floor; the bend-and-stretch technique could result in a serious back injury.

Other tips for weight lifting: Begin with the feet spread about 12 inches apart and the toes under the bar; otherwise the bar will tend to swing toward the feet when the lift movement begins. For most barbell exercises, grasp the bar overhand with the thumbs hooked under the bar; keep the arms spread apart by at least the width of the shoulders. For performing curls, reverse the hold with an underhand grip and the thumbs hooked above the bar. Breathe through the mouth and inhale as you lift; exhale on the return movement. Keep the weight evenly distributed between the hands.

Exercising With Other Weights

Another type of weight lifting is performed with dumbbells. There are at least ten different exercises that can be executed with these small, inexpensive weights to develop muscles from the waist to the shoulders and arms. Like the barbell exercises and the 6–12 program, they should be followed in a progressive order. Start with the minimum number of repetitions and advance gradually by adding one or two repetitions per week.

Dumbbells are somewhat deceptive in that they appear easy to handle when first viewed on the counter of a sporting goods store. And a pair is no heavier than a bag of groceries. But when the exercise routines with dumbbells are followed according to directions, you will discover muscles you didn't know you had.

BASIC DUMBBELL EXERCISES

1

Basic Dumbbell Exercises

Exercise 1: To develop shoulders and the back of the arm. Hold dumbbells at shoulder height. Push bells overhead to a full extension with the palms forward. Lower the bell back to the shoulder. Alternate right and left arm. Inhale as you push weight to full extension. Exhale as you lower the weight to the shoulder. • Repetitions: first week, 8; second week, 10; third week, 12.

Exercise 2: To develop the front of the upper arm. Hold dumbbells at arm's length parallel to the feet. Curl the weight to the shoulder, rotating the bell as the biceps contract. Lower the bell back to the starting position, reversing the rotation. Contract the triceps (back of the arm) to insure a full extension. This is done only after the bell has reached the starting position. Keep the bell under control as you lower it. Alternate right and left arms. Inhale as you curl the weight. Exhale as you lower the weight. • Repetitions: first week, 8; second week, 10; third week, 12.

Exercise 3: Curl weight until forearm is parallel to the floor. Return to the starting position. Repeat required number of repetitions. Curl bells to the shoulders. Lower weight until forearm is parallel to the floor. Return to the shoulder position. Repeat required number of repetitions. Lower bells to the starting position and curl required number of repetitions through full range of movement. Curl both bells at same time. • Repetitions: first week, 4 each movement; second week, 5 each movement; third week, 6 each movement.

Exercise 4: To develop the back of the upper arm. Hold dumbbells above and back of each shoulder by pointing the elbows up and holding them close to the head. Hold the elbows in place and extend the weight overhead by contracting the triceps. Lower the weight to the starting position. Alternate right and left arm. Inhale as you push weight to full extension. Exhale as you lower the weight to the shoulder. • Repetitions: first week, 8; second week, 10; third week, 12.

Exercise 5: To develop the shoulders. Use the standing position, holding the bells at arm's length in front of the thighs with the palms to the rear. Raise the bells to the shoulder, keeping the weight close to the body as the elbows go up and out. Lower the weight to the starting position, keeping the weight under control. Inhale as the weight goes up. Exhale as the weight goes down. • Repetitions: first week, 12; second week, 14; third week, 16.

Exercise 6: To develop the shoulders. Use the standing position. Place the feet at shoulder's width apart, bending the knees a little more than usual. Roll the hips back slightly. Hold the bells at arm's length in front of you. Now, raise both bells laterally rotating the arms so the back of the hands come together on completion of the contraction. Keeping the bells under control, lower them to the starting position. Elbows should be slightly bent to avoid strain. • Repetitions: first week, 6; second week, 8; third week, 10.

2

3

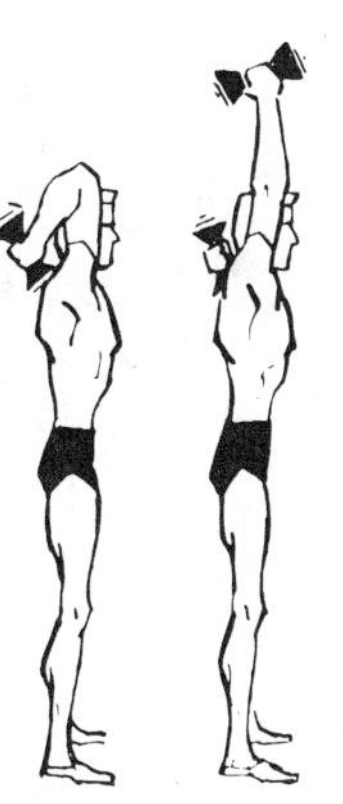

4

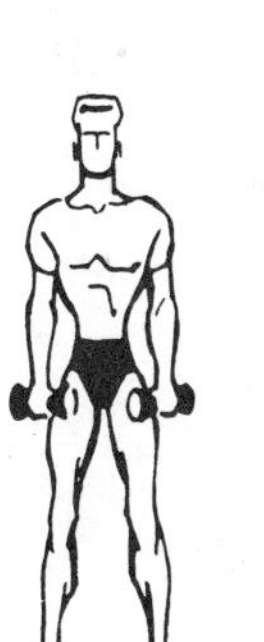

5

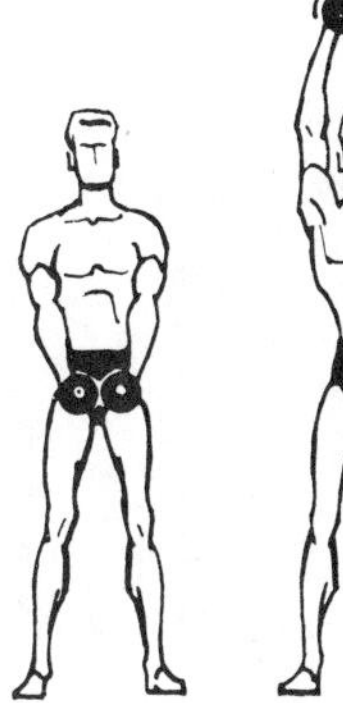

6

BASIC DUMBBELL EXERCISES

9

10

7

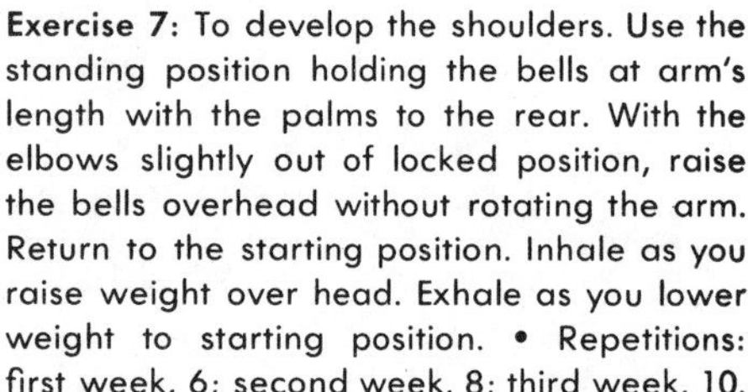

8

Exercise 7: To develop the shoulders. Use the standing position holding the bells at arm's length with the palms to the rear. With the elbows slightly out of locked position, raise the bells overhead without rotating the arm. Return to the starting position. Inhale as you raise weight over head. Exhale as you lower weight to starting position. • Repetitions: first week, 6; second week, 8; third week, 10.

Exercise 8: To develop the upper back. Stand with feet at shoulders' width apart. Bend the knees and lean forward until the trunk is parallel to the floor. Hold the bells at arm's length directly below the shoulder. Raise the bells alternately to the shoulder by driving the elbow up and to the rear. Inhale as you pull weight up. Exhale as you lower the weight to the starting position. • Repetitions: first week, 12; second week, 14; third week, 16.

Exercise 9: To develop the upper back. Stand with feet at shoulders' width apart. Bend the knees and lean forward until the trunk is parallel to the floor. Hold the bells at arm's length directly below the shoulders. Extend the arms laterally until they are parallel with the floor. Return to the starting position and repeat. Inhale as the bells are extended laterally. Exhale as the bells are lowered to the starting position. • Repetitions: first week, 6; second week, 8; third week, 10.

Exercise 10: To exercise the waist. Stand with the feet shoulder width apart. Hold one bell in the right hand at arm's length by the right thigh. Do not bend forward or backward, but lean to the right, lowering the bell below the right knee. Now, lean to the left touching the left hand below the left knee. Repeat the desired number of repetitions. Change the bell to left hand to exercise the right side of the waist. Inhale as weight rises. Exhale as weight goes down. • Repetitions: first week, 15; second week, 20; third week, 25.

TWIST GRIP

WAR CLUBS

Still other weight-lifting exercises designed to develop specific muscles are the war club swings and the twist grip. The war club weighs approximately 20 pounds and consists of a handle about 14 inches long and one inch in diameter attached to the weight. It is swung in circles with one or two hands or swung as a hatchet or a baseball bat. It is intended to improve the function of muscle groups in the trunk, back, and shoulders, but provides fringe benefits for the arms and waist also.

The twist-grip exerciser, which is used to develop muscles of the arms and hands, can be made at home from such simple objects as a foot-long piece of pipe, a length of rope, an empty container, and about 20 pounds of cement. The rope is attached to the pipe at one end and the other end is attached to the weighted container. By holding the pipe at arm's length and turning the pipe in the hands, the weight is raised and lowered, using alternately an underhand and overhand grip on the pipe.

Isometrics

Still another method of developing specific muscle groups is known as isometrics. Although isometrics was once popularized as an easy way to exercise, most physical fitness experts agree that there is no such thing as an easy exercise. This opinion applies especially to isometrics; if isometric exercises are performed according to the rules, they can be as difficult as any other kind of exercise. In fact, most isometric exercises should not be performed by an individual who has not been examined by a physician first. The effects of straining some muscle groups while holding the breath can prove dangerous for a person whose heart is not in good condition.

The term isometrics is used to describe a technique in which the muscle is contracted without moving the body part involved, and the muscle is held in contraction for about ten seconds before it is relaxed. Isometrics

This athlete is doing a neck strengthening exercise. —*IPS*

also are called static exercises, as contrasted with dynamic exercises or isotonic muscle activity in which the muscles not only contract but flex and extend extremities. Some exercise routines may include both isometrics and isotonics; in weight lifting, isometric muscle contractions are used to grasp the weight at the floor and to hold the weight in an overhead position but an isotonic contraction is involved in moving the weight through a curl or press between the isometric phases.

It should be understood that a specific isometric exercise generally is designed to develop only one specific group of muscles. To get the comparable benefits of a warm-up series of exercises and a 6–12 program you would have to perform a very large number of different isometric exercises to involve all of the body's muscles that need daily exercising. Also, they do not provide the aerobic effect of the more active exercise routines. *Aerobics* refers to the kind of physical activity that requires maximum or nearly maximum effort for at least four minutes in order to get the heart and lungs, as well as the muscles, involved in the conditioning effects. In other words, a ten-second isometric muscle contraction is not likely to require the kind of bodily effort that creates an oxygen debt.

Yet isometrics do have a place in physical conditioning, as one unit of an overall exercise effort that also includes warm-up routines and calisthenics, with perhaps a little running or jogging as well. Briefly, the best way to perform isometric exercises is to inhale deeply just before you start the muscle contraction. Hold your breath while you exert the greatest possible effort in muscle contraction. At that point the muscle should begin to quiver from the strain of the contraction. Hold the contraction for at least five seconds, longer if the exercise requires; use a watch with a sweep second hand for timing. Then relax the muscle and exhale.

Most isometric exercises can be performed with little or no equipment; although special equipment is available for some exercises, many can be performed by using a desk, wall, or door jamb as an immovable object against which you can exert the force of your muscle contractions.

Exercises for Women

Physical conditioning programs for women are essentially the same as for men, although women are more likely to be conscious of bulging muscles that seem to produce bodily proportions they may regard as unattractive. However, there are exercise routines that can have the effect of balancing proportions. Running and cycling, for example, tend to favor development of the muscles from the hips downward. Weight lifting or other exercises designed to develop the muscles from the waist up can be used to advantage by women who want to reshape that part of the body. On the other hand, exercises that tend to develop musculature where it is unwanted can be avoided. Particularly recommended for women who plan to be mothers are exercises that strengthen the abdominal and back muscles.

Basic exercises for women include running or jogging, bending and twisting at the waist, situps, and modified pushups, as well as standing on the toes while stretching the arms upward. Special exercises for enhancing the female figure can begin with a series of bustline exercises. One is an isometric press that starts with the palms of the hands facing together, fingers clasped and pointed upward, and arms close to the chest. Inhale deeply and push the hands against each other with maximum effort. Hold the breath while pressing and continue for seven seconds. Then relax, exhale, and repeat the exercise. Two other exercises are performed while lying flat on the floor with a weight in each hand; dumbbells, bricks, or books can serve as weights. Start with weights in

The bicycle exercise is beneficial to hips and thighs.
—Ewing Galloway

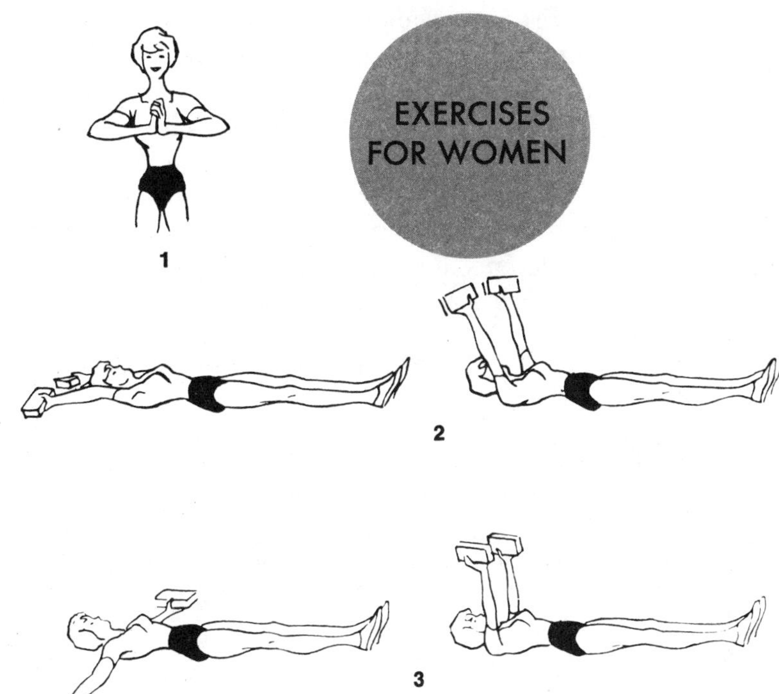

FOR THE BUSTLINE

1 The Press

Starting position: Stand or sit erect. Clasp hands, palms together, close to chest. Action: Press hands together hard and hold for 6-8 seconds. Repeat three times, resting briefly and breathing deeply between repetitions.

2 Pullover

Starting position: Lie on back with arms extended beyond head. Hold books or other objects of equal weight in hands. Action: Count 1—Lift books overhead and down to thighs, keeping arms straight. Count 2—Return slowly to starting position. Repeat 3-6 times.

3 Semaphore

Starting position: Lie on back with arms extended sideward at shoulder level. Hold books or other objects of equal weight in hands. Action: Count 1—Lift books to position over body, keeping arms straight. Count 2—Lower slowly to starting position. Repeat 3-6 times.

FOR THE WAIST

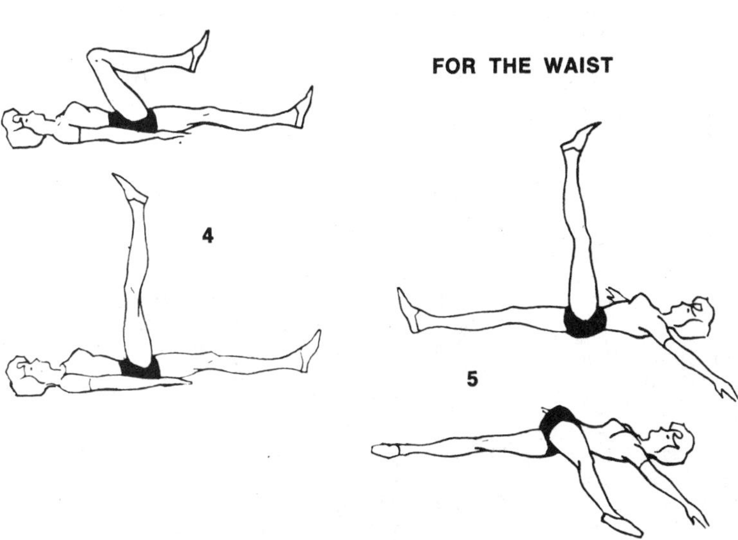

4 Knee Lifts

Starting position: Lie on back with knee slightly bent, feet on floor and arms at side. Action: Count 1—Bring one knee as close as possible to chest, keeping hands on floor. Count 2—Extend leg straight up. Count 3—Bend knee and return to chest. Count 4—Return to starting position. Repeat 5-10 times, alternating legs during exercise.

The double knee lift is done in the same manner, raising both legs at the same time. Do 5-10 repetitions.

5 Crossover

Starting position: Lie on back, arms extended sideward, palms down. Action: Count 1—Raise right leg to vertical position and move slowly to left until almost touching floor. Keep arms, head and shoulders on floor. Count 2—Return to starting position. Counts 3 and 4—Same action to other side. Do 5-10 repetitions.

hands, arm stretched back over the head with backs of the hands on the floor. Next raise both arms without bending the elbows and move the weights overhead and down to the floor at the hips. While counting to yourself for rhythm, return to the original position and repeat the exercise. The second is a variation of the previous exercise, with the weights being lifted straight overhead from a starting position of the arms extended sideward at shoulder level. But don't bend the elbows.

Cycle-type exercises and ballet stretches are recommended for hips and thighs. Ballet stretches can be performed from a standing position, with one hand on the hip and the other holding onto a steady object such as a chair. Another exercise for the hips and thighs is patterned after the "cheerleader" position. While kneeling on the floor, hands on hips and back straight, bend backward as far as is comfortable without bending the back or moving the knees. Return to the starting position and begin again.

Among the suggested exercises for calves and ankles is the rocker. With feet together and hands on hips, legs straight, rock back on your heels with toes off the floor. Then rock back with your weight on the toes and the heels off the floor. KNA

EXERCISES FOR WOMEN

FOR HIPS AND THIGHS

6

6 Cheerleader

Starting position: Kneel on floor, back straight, hands on hips. Action: Count 1—Bend backward as far as possible, keeping knees on floor and body straight. Count 2—Return to starting position. Repeat 10-15 times.

7

7 Bicycle

Starting position: Lie on back with hips and legs supported by hands. Action: Simulate bicycle pumping action with legs. Pump 50-100 times.

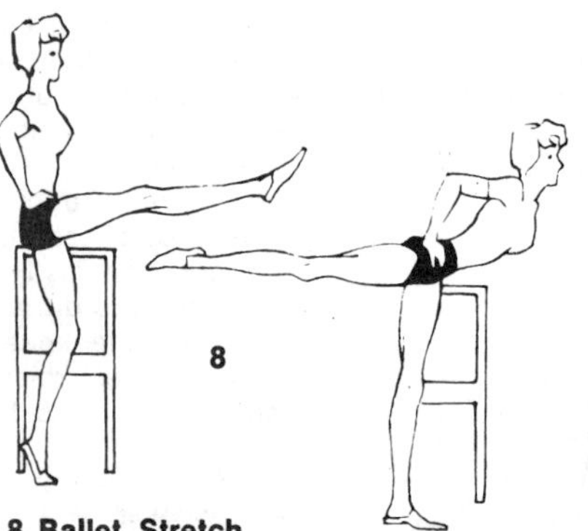

8

8 Ballet Stretch

Starting position: Stand erect with left hand resting on back of chair for support. Action: Count 1—Raise right leg sideward as high as possible. Count 2—Return to starting position. Count 3—Swing right leg forward as high as possible. Count 4—Return to starting position. Count 5—Swing right leg back as high as possible. Count 6—Return to starting position. Do 5-10 repetitions, then repeat exercise with left leg.

9

9 Two-Way Stretch

Starting position: Kneel with hands on floor, back straight. Action: Count 1—Arch back, bend head down and bring left knee as close as possible to chin. Count 2—Lift head high and extend left leg as far backward and up as possible. Repeat 6-10 times with each leg.

10

11

FOR CALVES AND ANKLES

10 Rocker

Starting position: Stand erect, feet together, hands on hips. Action: Count 1—Rock back on heels, keeping legs straight and raising toes off floor. Count 2—Rock forward on toes, lifting heels off floor. Repeat 10-20 times.

11 Hop

Starting position: Stand erect, feet close together, hands on hips. Action: Hop lightly on both feet 50 times, on the right foot 25 times, on the left foot 25 times, on both feet 50 times.

12

12 Stemwinder

Starting position: Stand erect, left foot lifted clear of floor. Action: Rotate left foot in small circles 20 times. Repeat with right foot.

THE AMERICAN PRESIDENCY

VITAL FACTS ABOUT U. S. PRESIDENTS

	Name	Born	Birthplace	Died	Age at Death
1.	George Washington	Feb. 22, 1732	Westmoreland County, Va.	Dec. 14, 1799	67
2.	John Adams	Oct. 30, 1735	Braintree, Mass.	July 4, 1826	90
3.	Thomas Jefferson	Apr. 13, 1743	Albemarle County, Va.	July 4, 1826	83
4.	James Madison	Mar. 16, 1751	Port Conway, Va.	June 28, 1836	85
5.	James Monroe	Apr. 28, 1758	Westmoreland County, Va.	July 4, 1831	73
6.	John Quincy Adams	July 11, 1767	Braintree, Mass.	Feb. 23, 1848	80
7.	Andrew Jackson	Mar. 15, 1767	Waxhaw, S. C.	June 8, 1845	78
8.	Martin Van Buren	Dec. 5, 1782	Kinderhook, N. Y.	July 24, 1862	79
9.	William H. Harrison	Feb. 9, 1773	Berkeley, Va.	Apr. 4, 1841	68
10.	John Tyler	Mar. 29, 1790	Greenway, Va.	Jan. 18, 1862	71
11.	James K. Polk	Nov. 2, 1795	Pineville, N. C.	June 15, 1849	53
12.	Zachary Taylor	Nov. 24, 1784	Orange County, Va.	July 9, 1850	65
13.	Millard Fillmore	Jan. 7, 1800	Locke, N. Y.	Mar. 8, 1874	74
14.	Franklin Pierce	Nov. 23, 1804	Hillsboro, N. H.	Oct. 8, 1869	64
15.	James Buchanan	Apr. 23, 1791	Mercersburg, Pa.	June 1, 1868	77
16.	Abraham Lincoln	Feb. 12, 1809	Hardin County, Ky.	Apr. 15, 1865	56
17.	Andrew Johnson	Dec. 29, 1808	Raleigh, N. C.	July 31, 1875	66
18.	Ulysses S. Grant	Apr. 27, 1822	Point Pleasant, O.	July 23, 1885	63
19.	Rutherford B. Hayes	Oct. 4, 1822	Delaware, O.	Jan. 17, 1893	70
20.	James A. Garfield	Nov. 19, 1831	Orange, O.	Sept. 19, 1881	49
21.	Chester A. Arthur	Oct. 5, 1830	Fairfield, Vt.	Nov. 18, 1886	56
22.	Grover Cleveland	Mar. 18, 1837	Caldwell, N. J.	June 24, 1908	71
23.	Benjamin Harrison	Aug. 20, 1833	North Bend, O.	Mar. 13, 1901	67
24.	Grover Cleveland	Mar. 18, 1837	Caldwell, N. J.	June 24, 1908	71
25.	William McKinley	Jan. 29, 1843	Niles, O.	Sept. 14, 1901	58
26.	Theodore Roosevelt	Oct. 27, 1858	New York City	Jan. 6, 1919	60
27.	William H. Taft	Sept. 15, 1857	Cincinnati, O.	Mar. 8, 1930	72
28.	Woodrow Wilson	Dec. 28, 1856	Staunton, Va.	Feb. 3, 1924	67
29.	Warren G. Harding	Nov. 2, 1865	Morrow County, O.	Aug. 2, 1923	57
30.	Calvin Coolidge	July 4, 1872	Plymouth Notch, Vt.	Jan. 5, 1933	60
31.	Herbert Hoover	Aug. 10, 1874	West Branch, Ia.	Oct. 20, 1964	90
32.	Franklin D. Roosevelt	Jan. 30, 1882	Hyde Park, N. Y.	Apr. 12, 1945	63
33.	Harry S Truman	May 8, 1884	Lamar, Mo.	Dec. 26, 1972	88
34.	Dwight D. Eisenhower	Oct. 14, 1890	Denison, Tex.	Mar. 28, 1969	78
35.	John F. Kennedy	May 29, 1917	Brookline, Mass.	Nov. 22, 1963	46
36.	Lyndon B. Johnson	Aug. 27, 1908	Gillespie County, Tex.	Jan. 22, 1973	64
37.	Richard M. Nixon	Jan. 9, 1913	Yorba Linda, Calif.		
38.	Gerald R. Ford	July 14, 1913	Omaha, Neb.		
39.	Jimmy Carter	Oct. 1, 1924	Plains, Ga.		
40.	Ronald W. Reagan	Feb. 6, 1911	Tampico, Ill.		

Burial Place	Served	Age on Taking Office	Party	Vice-President
1. Mount Vernon, Va.	1789-1797	57	Federalist	John Adams
2. Quincy, Mass.	1797-1801	61	Federalist	Thomas Jefferson
3. Monticello, Va.	1801-1809	57	Democratic-Republican	Aaron Burr George Clinton
4. Montpelier, Va.	1809-1817	57	Democratic-Republican	George Clinton Elbridge Gerry
5. Richmond, Va.	1817-1825	58	Democratic-Republican	Daniel D. Tompkins
6. Quincy, Mass.	1825-1829	57	Democratic-Republican	John C. Calhoun
7. Hermitage, Tenn.	1829-1837	61	Democratic	John C. Calhoun Martin Van Buren
8. Kinderhook, N. Y.	1837-1841	54	Democratic	Richard M. Johnson
9. North Bend, O.	1841	68	Whig	John Tyler
10. Richmond, Va.	1841-1845	51	Whig	
11. Nashville, Tenn.	1845-1849	49	Democratic	George M. Dallas
12. Louisville, Ky.	1849-1850	64	Whig	Millard Fillmore
13. Buffalo, N. Y.	1850-1853	50	Whig	
14. Concord, N. H.	1853-1857	48	Democratic	William R. King
15. Lancaster, Pa.	1857-1861	65	Democratic	John C. Breckinridge
16. Springfield, Ill.	1861-1865	52	Republican	Hannibal Hamlin Andrew Johnson
17. Greeneville, Tenn.	1865-1869	56	Democratic	
18. New York City	1869-1877	46	Republican	Schuyler Colfax Henry Wilson
19. Fremont, O.	1877-1881	54	Republican	William A. Wheeler
20. Cleveland, O.	1881	49	Republican	Chester A. Arthur
21. Albany, N. Y.	1881-1885	50	Republican	
22. Princeton, N. J.	1885-1889	47	Democratic	Thomas A. Hendricks
23. Indianapolis, Ind.	1889-1893	55	Republican	Levi P. Morton
24. Princeton, N. J.	1893-1897	55	Democratic	Adlai E. Stevenson
25. Canton, O.	1897-1901	54	Republican	Garret A. Hobart Theodore Roosevelt
26. Oyster Bay, N. Y.	1901-1909	42	Republican	Charles W. Fairbanks
27. Arlington, Va.	1909-1913	51	Republican	James S. Sherman
28. Washington, D.C.	1913-1921	56	Democratic	Thomas R. Marshall
29. Marion, O.	1921-1923	55	Republican	Calvin Coolidge
30. Plymouth, Vt.	1923-1929	51	Republican	Charles G. Dawes
31. West Branch, Ia.	1929-1933	54	Republican	Charles Curtis
32. Hyde Park, N. Y.	1933-1945	51	Democratic	John N. Garner Henry A. Wallace Harry S Truman
33. Independence, Mo.	1945-1953	60	Democratic	Alben W. Barkley
34. Abilene, Kan.	1953-1961	62	Republican	Richard M. Nixon
35. Arlington, Va.	1961-1963	43	Democratic	Lyndon B. Johnson
36. Stonewall, Tex.	1963-1969	55	Democratic	Hubert H. Humphrey
37.	1969-1974	56	Republican	Spiro Agnew
38.	1974-1977	61	Republican	Nelson A. Rockefeller
39.	1977-1981	53	Democrat	Walter F. Mondale
40.	1981-	69	Republican	George H. Bush

MAJOR CANDIDATES' POPULAR AND ELECTORAL VOTE

Year	Winner and Loser	Popular Vote and Percentage	Electoral Vote
1789	George Washington (No party)	Unknown	69
	No opposition		
1792	George Washington (F)	Unknown	132
	No opposition		
1796	John Adams (F)	Unknown	71
	Thomas Jefferson (DR)	Unknown	68
1800	Thomas Jefferson[1] (DR)	Unknown	73
	Aaron Burr (DR)	Unknown	73
1804	Thomas Jefferson (DR)	Unknown	162
	Charles C. Pinckney (F)	Unknown	14
1808	James Madison (DR)	Unknown	122
	Charles C. Pinckney (F)	Unknown	47
1812	James Madison (DR)	Unknown	128
	De Witt Clinton (F)	Unknown	89
1816	James Monroe (DR)	Unknown	183
	Rufus King (F)	Unknown	34
1820	James Monroe (DR)	Unknown	231
	John Quincy Adams (No party)	Unknown	1
1824	Andrew Jackson (No party)	153,544 — 43.1%	99
	John Quincy Adams[2] (No party)	108,740 — 30.6%	84
	William H. Crawford (No party)	46,618 — 13.1%	41
	Henry Clay (No party)	47,136 — 13.2%	37
1828	Andrew Jackson (D)	647,276 — 56.0%	178
	John Quincy Adams (NR)	508,064 — 44.0%	83
1832	Andrew Jackson (D)	687,502 — 56.5%	219
	Henry Clay (NR)	530,189 — 43.5%	49
1836	Martin Van Buren (D)	765,483 — 58.2%	170
	William H. Harrison (W)	549,567 — 41.8%	73
1840	William H. Harrison (W)	1,275,017 — 53.0%	234
	Martin Van Buren (D)	1,128,702 — 47.0%	60
1844	James K. Polk (D)	1,338,464 — 50.7%	170
	Henry Clay (W)	1,300,097 — 49.3%	105
1848	Zachary Taylor (W)	1,360,967 — 52.7%	163
	Lewis Cass (D)	1,222,342 — 47.3%	127
1852	Franklin Pierce (D)	1,601,117 — 53.6%	254
	Winfield Scott (W)	1,385,453 — 46.4%	42
1856	James C. Buchanan (D)	1,832,955 — 45.3%	174
	John C. Frémont (R)	1,339,932 — 33.1%	114
	Millard Fillmore (A)	871,731 — 21.6%	8
1860	Abraham Lincoln (R)	1,865,593 — 39.8%	180
	Stephen A. Douglas (D)	1,382,713 — 29.5%	12
	John C. Breckinridge (D)	848,356 — 18.1%	72
	John Bell (CU)	592,906 — 12.6%	39
1864	Abraham Lincoln (R)	2,206,938 — 55.0%	212
	George McClellan (D)	1,803,787 — 45.0%	21
1868	Ulysses S. Grant (R)	3,013,421 — 52.7%	214
	Horatio Seymour (D)	2,706,829 — 47.3%	80
1872	Ulysses S. Grant (R)	3,596,745 — 55.8%	286
	Horace Greeley (D)[3]	2,843,446 — 44.2%	66
1876	Rutherford B. Hayes (R)	4,033,295 — 48.5%	185
	Samuel J. Tilden (D)	4,284,265 — 51.5%	184
1880	James A. Garfield (R)	4,454,416 — 50.1%	214
	Winfield S. Hancock (D)	4,444,952 — 49.9%	155
1884	Grover Cleveland (D)	4,874,986 — 50.1%	219
	James G. Blaine (R)	4,851,981 — 49.9%	182
1888	Benjamin Harrison (R)	5,447,129 — 49.6%	233
	Grover Cleveland (D)	5,537,857 — 50.4%	168
1892	Grover Cleveland (D)	5,555,426 — 47.2%	277
	Benjamin Harrison (R)	5,182,690 — 44.0%	145
	James Weaver (P)	1,029,846 — 8.8%	22
1896	William McKinley (R)	7,102,246 — 52.2%	271
	William J. Bryan (D)	6,492,559 — 47.8%	176
1900	William McKinley (R)	7,218,491 — 53.2%	292
	William J. Bryan (D)	6,356,734 — 46.8%	155
1904	Theodore Roosevelt (R)	7,628,461 — 60.0%	336
	Alton B. Parker (D)	5,084,223 — 40.0%	140
1908	William H. Taft (R)	7,675,320 — 54.5%	321
	William J. Bryan (D)	6,412,294 — 45.5%	162
1912	Woodrow Wilson (D)	6,296,547 — 45.3%	435
	Theodore Roosevelt (Pr)	4,118,571 — 29.6%	88
	William H. Taft (R)	3,486,720 — 25.1%	8
1916	Woodrow Wilson (D)	9,127,695 — 51.7%	277
	Charles E. Hughes (R)	8,533,507 — 48.3%	254
1920	Warren G. Harding (R)	16,152,200 — 63.8%	404
	James M. Cox (D)	9,147,353 — 36.2%	127
1924	Calvin Coolidge (R)	15,718,211 — 55.9%	382
	John W. Davis (D)	8,385,283 — 29.8%	136
	Robert M. La Follette (Pr)	4,031,289 — 14.3%	13
1928	Herbert C. Hoover (R)	21,391,993 — 58.8%	444
	Alfred E. Smith (D)	15,016,169 — 41.2%	87
1932	Franklin D. Roosevelt (D)	22,809,638 — 59.1%	472
	Herbert C. Hoover (R)	15,758,901 — 40.9%	59
1936	Franklin D. Roosevelt (D)	27,752,869 — 62.5%	523
	Alfred Landon (R)	16,674,665 — 37.5%	8
1940	Franklin D. Roosevelt (D)	27,307,819 — 55.0%	449
	Wendell Willkie (R)	22,321,018 — 45.0%	82
1944	Franklin D. Roosevelt (D)	25,606,585 — 53.8%	432
	Thomas E. Dewey (R)	22,014,745 — 46.2%	99
1948	Harry S Truman (D)	24,105,812 — 49.8%	303
	Thomas E. Dewey (R)	21,970,065 — 45.4%	189
	J. Strom Thurmond (SR)	1,169,063 — 2.4%	39
	Henry A. Wallace (Pr)	1,156,103 — 2.4%	0
1952	Dwight D. Eisenhower (R)	33,936,234 — 55.4%	442
	Adlai E. Stevenson (D)	27,314,992 — 44.6%	89
1956	Dwight D. Eisenhower (R)	35,590,472 — 57.8%	457
	Adlai E. Stevenson[4] (D)	26,022,752 — 42.2%	73
1960	John F. Kennedy[5] (D)	34,227,096 — 50.1%	303
	Richard M. Nixon (R)	34,108,546 — 49.9%	219
1964	Lyndon B. Johnson (D)	43,129,484 — 61.1%	486
	Barry M. Goldwater (R)	27,178,188 — 38.5%	52
1968	Richard M. Nixon (R)	31,785,480 — 43.4%	301
	Hubert H. Humphrey (D)	31,275,165 — 42.7%	191
	George C. Wallace (AI)	9,906,473 — 13.5%	46
1972	Richard M. Nixon[6] (R)	47,169,905 — 60.7%	520
	George S. McGovern (D)	29,170,383 — 37.5%	17
	John G. Schmitz (AI)	1,098,635 — 1.4%	0
1976	Jimmy Carter (D)	40,827,292—50%	297
	Gerald R. Ford (R)	39,146,157—48%	240[7]
1980	Ronald W. Reagan (R)	43,901,812—50.7%	489
	Jimmy Carter (D)	35,483,820—41.0%	49
	John B. Anderson (Ind.)	5,719,722—6.6%	0

In those years where the percentages do not add up to 100%, votes for minor candidates have not been included in the table.

---

1. Elected by the House of Representatives due to a tie vote.
2. Elected by the House of Representatives, no candidate having polled a majority.
3. Horace Greeley died November 29, 1872. His 66 electoral votes were split as follows: Thomas A. Hendricks, 42; B. Gratz Brown, 18; Charles J. Jenkins, 2; David Davis, 1.
4. Democrats elected 74 electors but one from Alabama refused to vote for Stevenson, voted for Walter B. Jones.
5. Senator Harry F. Byrd (D-Va) received 15 electoral votes; 6 from unpledged Alabama Democrats, 8 from unpledged Mississippi Democrats, and 1 from a defecting Oklahoma Republican elector.
6. One Virginia Republican elector switched his vote from President Nixon to a minor party candidate, reducing Nixon's total from 521 to 520.
7. One Washington Republican elector switched his vote from Ford to Ronald Reagan.

Vice-Presidents of the United States

Name	*Birthplace*	*Served Under*	*Took Office*
John Adams (F) (1735–1826)	Braintree, Mass.	Washington	1789
Thomas Jefferson (R) (1743–1826)	Shadwell, Va.	J. Adams	1797
Aaron Burr (R) (1756–1836)	Newark, N.J.	Jefferson	1801
George Clinton (R) (1734–1812)	Little Britain, N.Y.	Jefferson Madison	1805
Elbridge Gerry (R) (1744–1814)	Marblehead, Mass.	Madison	1813
Daniel D. Tompkins (R) (1774–1825)	Fox Meadows, N.Y.	Monroe	1817
John C. Calhoun (R) (1782–1850)	Abbeville District, S.C.	J. Q. Adams Jackson	1825
Martin Van Buren (D) (1782–1862)	Kinderhook, N.Y.	Jackson	1833
Richard M. Johnson (D) (1780–1850)	Beargrass, Ky.	Van Buren	1837
John Tyler (W) (1790–1862)	Charles City County, Va.	W. H. Harrison	1841
George M. Dallas (D) (1792–1864)	Philadelphia, Pa.	Polk	1845
Millard Fillmore (W) (1800–74)	Cayuga County, N.Y.	Taylor	1849
William R. King (D) (1786–1853)	Sampson Co., N.C.	Pierce	1853
John C. Breckinridge (D) (1821–75)	Lexington, Ky.	Buchanan	1857
Hannibal Hamlin (R) (1809–91)	Paris, Me.	Lincoln	1861
Andrew Johnson[1] (1808–75)	Raleigh, N.C.	Lincoln	1865
Schuyler Colfax (R) (1823–85)	New York, N.Y.	Grant	1869
Henry Wilson (R) (1812–75)	Farmington, N.H.	Grant	1873
William A. Wheeler (R) (1819–87)	Malone, N.Y.	Hayes	1877
Chester A. Arthur (R) (1830–86)	Fairfield, Vt.	Garfield	1881
Thomas A. Hendricks (D) (1819–85)	Muskingum Co., Ohio	Cleveland	1885
Levi P. Morton (R) (1824–1920)	Shoreham, Vt.	B. Harrison	1889
Adlai E. Stevenson (D)[2] (1835–1914)	Christian Co., Ky.	Cleveland	1893
Garret A. Hobart (R) (1844–99)	Long Branch, N.J.	McKinley	1897
Theodore Roosevelt (R) (1858–1919)	New York, N.Y.	McKinley	1901
Charles W. Fairbanks (R) (1852–1918)	Unionville Center, Ohio	T. Roosevelt	1905
James S. Sherman (R) (1855–1912)	Utica, N.Y.	Taft	1909
Thomas R. Marshall (D) (1854–1925)	N. Manchester, Ind.	Wilson	1913
Calvin Coolidge (R) (1872–1933)	Plymouth Notch, Vt.	Harding	1921
Charles G. Dawes (R) (1865–1951)	Marietta, Ohio	Coolidge	1925
Charles Curtis (R) (1860–1936)	Topeka, Kan.	Hoover	1929
John N. Garner (D) (1868–1967)	Red River Co., Texas	F. Roosevelt	1933
Henry A. Wallace (D) (1888–1966)	Adair Co., Iowa	F. Roosevelt	1941
Harry S Truman (D) (1884–1972)	Lamar, Mo.	F. Roosevelt	1945
Alben W. Barkley (D) (1877–1956)	Graves Co., Ky.	Truman	1949
Richard M. Nixon (R) (1913–)	Yorba Linda, Calif.	Eisenhower	1953
Lyndon B. Johnson (D) (1908–73)	Near Stonewall, Texas	Kennedy	1961
Hubert H. Humphrey (D) (1911–1978)	Wallace, S.D.	Johnson	1965
Spiro Agnew (R) (1918-)	Baltimore, Md.	Nixon	1969
Gerald R. Ford (R)[3] (1913–)	Omaha, Neb.	Nixon	1973
Nelson A. Rockefeller (R)[3] (1908–1979)	Bar Harbor, Me.	Ford	1974
Walter F. Mondale (D) (1928–)	Ceylon, Minn.	Carter	1977
George H. Bush (R) (1924–)	Milton, Mass.	Reagan	1981

1. Andrew Johnson: A Democrat nominated by Republicans and elected with Lincoln on the National Union ticket.
2. Adlai E. Stevenson: 23d Vice President. Grandfather of the Democratic candidate for President, 1952 and 1956.
3. Appointed Vice-President under the 25th Amendment to the Constitution.

Aaron Burr, Vice-President under President Thomas Jefferson.

—From an engraving by E. G. Williams & Brothers

John C. Breckinridge, Vice-President under President James Buchanan.

—From an engraving by A. B. Walter

WIVES OF THE PRESIDENTS

Name	Birthplace	Married	Children
Washington, Martha (Dandridge) Custis (1731-1802)	New Kent Co., Va.	1759	—
Adams, Abigail Smith (1744-1818)	Weymouth, Mass.	1764	5
Jefferson, Martha (Wayles) Skelton (1748-1782)	Charles City Co., Va.	1772	6
Madison, Dorothea "Dolley" (Payne) Todd (1768-1849)	Guilford Co., N.C.	1794	—
Monroe, Elizabeth Kortright (1768-1830)	New York, N.Y.	1786	3
Adams, Louisa Catherine Johnson (1775-1852)	London, England	1797	4
Jackson, Rachel (Donelson) Robards (1767-1828)	Halifax Co., Va.	1791	—
Van Buren, Hannah Hoes (1783-1819)	Kinderhook, N.Y.	1807	4
Harrison, Anna Symmes (1775-1864)	Morristown, N.J.	1795	10
Tyler, Letitia Christian (1790-1842)	Cedar Grove, Va.	1813	8
Tyler, Julia Gardiner (1820-1889)	Gardiner's Is., N.Y.	1844	7
Polk, Sarah Childress (1803-1891)	Murfreesboro, Tenn.	1824	—
Taylor, Margaret Smith (1788-1852)	Calvert Co., Md.	1810	6
Fillmore, Abigail Powers (1798-1853)	Stillwater, N.Y.	1826	2
Fillmore, Caroline (Carmichael) McIntosh (1813-1881)	Morristown, N.J.	1858	—
Pierce, Jane Means Appleton (1806-1863)	Hampton, N.H.	1834	3
Lincoln, Mary Todd (1818-1882)	Lexington, Ky.	1842	4
Johnson, Eliza McCardle (1810-1876)	Leesburg, Tenn.	1827	5
Grant, Julia Dent (1826-1902)	St. Louis, Mo.	1848	4
Hayes, Lucy Ware Webb (1831-1889)	Chillicothe, Ohio	1852	8
Garfield, Lucretia Rudolph (1832-1918)	Hiram, Ohio	1858	7
Arthur, Ellen Lewis Herndon (1837-1880)	Fredericksburg, Va.	1859	3
Cleveland, Frances Folsom (1864-1947)	Buffalo, N.Y.	1886	5
Harrison, Caroline Lavinia Scott (1832-1892)	Oxford, Ohio	1853	2
Harrison, Mary Scott (Lord) Dimmick (1858-1948)	Honesdale, Pa.	1896	1
McKinley, Ida Saxton (1847-1907)	Canton, Ohio	1871	2
Roosevelt, Alice Hathaway Lee (1861-1884)	Chestnut Hill, Mass.	1880	1
Roosevelt, Edith Kermit Carow (1861-1948)	Norwich, Conn.	1886	5
Taft, Helen Herron (1861-1943)	Cincinnati, Ohio	1886	3
Wilson, Ellen Louise Axson (1860-1914)	Savannah, Ga.	1885	3
Wilson, Edith (Bolling) Galt (1872-1961)	Wytheville, Va.	1915	—
Harding, Florence (Kling) DeWolfe (1860-1924)	Marion, Ohio	1891	—
Coolidge, Grace Anna Goodhue (1879-1957)	Burlington, Vt.	1905	2
Hoover, Lou Henry (1875-1944)	Waterloo, Iowa	1899	2
Roosevelt, Anna Eleanor Roosevelt (1884-1962)	New York, N.Y.	1905	6
Truman, Elizabeth "Bess" Wallace (1885-)	Independence, Mo.	1919	1
Eisenhower, Mamie Geneva Doud (1896-1979)	Boone, Iowa	1916	2
Kennedy, Jacqueline Lee Bouvier (1929-)	Southampton, N.Y.	1953	3
Johnson, Claudia Alta Taylor (1912-)	Marshall, Texas	1934	2
Nixon, Thelma Patricia Ryan (1913-)	Ely, Nevada	1940	2
Ford, Elizabeth "Betty" Bloomer (Warren) (1918-)	Chicago, Ill.	1948	4
Carter, Rosalynn Smith (1927-)	Plains, Ga.	1946	4
Reagan, Nancy Davis (1923-)	New York, N.Y.	1952	2

Martha Washington

Names in parentheses are maiden names of formerly married women.
Children by previous marriages are not included.
Includes children who died in infancy.

SOME HIGHLIGHTS OF WHITE HOUSE HISTORY

THE WHITE HOUSE stands on eighteen landscaped, tree-shaded acres at 1600 Pennsylvania Avenue. The main building, the original President's mansion, has had two large wings added in this century to provide office space for the enlarged presidential staff. Each wing is joined to the main building by a one-story terrace. The architectural effect is one of spacious elegance, mellowed by the passing of a century and a half.

The "Palace for the President," a part of the plan for the city of Washington conceived by French engineer Pierre L'Enfant, was designed by Irish-born architect James Hoban in the taste of the Georgian country houses of the 1700s. George Washington was present at the cornerstone ceremony on October 13, 1792, but the mansion was not ready for occupancy until late in John Adams' administration. President Adams moved into what was then a gray sandstone building on November 1, 1800. Almost alone in the sparsely furnished mansion the following evening, he wrote a letter to his wife, voicing the prayer that Franklin D. Roosevelt later caused to be carved on the mantel of the State Dining Room: "I pray Heaven to bestow the best of Blessings on this House and all that shall hereafter inhabit it . . . May none but honest and wise men ever rule under this roof."

Both exterior and interior have changed under the varying influences of the long succession of Presidents and First Ladies. Three times the mansion has undergone major repair and renovation—first after the fire set by the British in 1814, a second time under Theodore Roosevelt, when it was about a hundred years old, and a third time under President Truman beginning in 1948. Nearly every First Family has left its enriching imprint on landscaping, building, furniture, or furnishings, making the house as it stands today a priceless historic museum and one of America's great national treasures.

The first additions to the still unfinished building were made by Thomas Jefferson when he assumed office in 1801. Aided by Benjamin Latrobe, his Surveyor of Public Buildings, Jefferson developed one-story East and West Terraces, which included servants' quarters, a henhouse, woodsheds, and a wine cellar. He also began to furnish the main building, importing French furniture and décor. Probably his greatest contributions to the livability of the mansion were a well and cistern. The Adamses had been forced to get their water hauled from a spring down the road.

In 1814 a British expedition, carrying out a reprisal for the burning of York, Canada, attacked the ill-defended capital and burned all the public buildings, including the presidential mansion. President and Mrs. Madison were forced to flee, Dolley Madison rescuing the silver plate and Gilbert Stuart's portrait of Washington.

James Hoban, the original architect, was commissioned to carry out reconstruction of the gutted mansion. Because the gray exterior sandstone was blackened by the flames, Hoban decided to paint it white, and at a stroke the "White House" was born.

To Madison's successor, James Monroe, fell the task of completing the refurnishing, for which he obtained a generous congressional appropriation and contributed some of his own French furniture and silver. A large suite of gilt furniture was created for the Blue Room by Paris cabinetmaker Pierre-Antoine Bellangé. Three marble busts, of Columbus, Amerigo Vespucci, and George Washington, bought for $100 each, were probably the work of the Italian sculptor Ceracchi. Monroe also commissioned Benjamin Latrobe to add the North Colonnade in 1824, the year in which the North Portico was finished.

The White House staff around 1890.

Monroe's successor, J. Q. Adams, contributed little to White House growth, owing largely to his unpopularity with Congress. But in 1829 Andrew Jackson recalled Benjamin Latrobe to work on the Porch, completed that same year. In the French tradition of Jefferson, Madison, and Monroe, Jackson furnished the spacious East Room, where Abigail Adams had hung her wash thirty years before.

Jackson's successor Van Buren added a domestically valuable though politically hazardous improvement—a water tank in the basement to supply hot bath water. Van Buren's opponents seized on the innovation as proof of the decadent luxury which they accused the President of enjoying. Polk's administration saw the installation of gas lighting, though the first time the new illumination was used it suddenly failed, plunging a presidential reception into darkness. Luckily Mrs. Polk had kept the East Room equipped with candles.

Not until 1850, when the Fillmores moved in, did the White House Kitchen receive that important nineteenth-century improvement, the stove. Until then cooking was done over an open fireplace. The new stove, made of cast iron, proved so baffling a contraption that President Fillmore had to inspect the original model in the Patent Office before he could brief his kitchen staff on its proper use. The Fillmores were responsible for another innovation—the first White House Library, established by Mrs. Fillmore in the Oval Room.

The Pierces put in the building's first central heating plant, a hot-water and hot-air system with a coal furnace which at last supplied heat to some of the corners remote from fireplaces—corners that Andrew Jackson had declared hell itself could not warm.

Both Presidents Cleveland and Harrison sought funds for office expansion, and Mrs. Harrison had an architect make several designs that would have added enormous wings virtually dwarfing the original structure. But Congress, with what was probably fortunate parsimony, rejected the proposal. President McKinley caused the plans to be scaled down, but still had no luck with Congress.

Two important improvements were nevertheless carried out in the nineties. President Harrison ordered the old gas lights replaced with Thomas Edison's new electric illumination. A young man named Ike Hoover supervised the installation, and at President Harrison's request stayed on to make sure nothing went wrong. Hoover, who recalled in his memoirs that the Harrisons "were afraid to turn the lights on and off for fear of getting a shock," stayed forty-two years, mostly as Chief Usher.

The second improvement in the nineties was not to the house itself but to its atmosphere. Since the Potomac had begun silting up in the 1840s, mud flats had formed in front of the White House, turning the area into an unwholesome swamp.

By 1901 the need for office space was so pressing that Congress could no longer procrastinate. To undertake both expansion and large-scale remodeling President Theodore Roosevelt engaged the leading architectural firm in the country, McKim, Mead and White. Under their plan a whole new building, the Executive Wing, rose on the west lawn, connecting with the main building by an open colonnade. Jefferson's west pavilion was absorbed into the new structure.

The 1902 alteration solved the major White House problems for half a century. In 1909 President Taft added an oval office for the President to the new West Wing. The first Mrs. Woodrow Wilson turned the attic—which the Theodore Roosevelt children had used as a vast playroom—into guest rooms for the growing White House list of distinguished visitors. A more unusual touch during the Wilson administration was the addition

Carriages and drivers parked outside the White House during the gaslight era, with an enormous gas fixture visible in the front hall.

of a flock of sheep grazing on the White House lawn, to free manpower from the lawn-mowing job for military service.

In 1927, under the Coolidge occupancy, the old attic on the third floor of the main building was enlarged and finished to provide additional guest rooms and servants' quarters, as well as a sun room over the rounded South Portico—a room Grace Coolidge called the "sky parlor."

The Hoovers brought a touch of the exotic when they moved in in 1929. Veteran world travelers, they had collected art objects, rugs, and bamboo furniture that brightened the second floor. Mrs. Hoover filled the fan-shaped window at the west end of the corridor with an enormous cageful of canaries.

The President's Oval Office in the West Wing of the White House during President Kennedy's administration.

Despite a fire that swept the Executive Wing and forced the Hoovers to vacate the house for a few weeks, no further extensive structural changes took place until the advent of President Franklin D. Roosevelt, whose New Deal turned the White House into a humming beehive of activity. The Executive Wing had to be enlarged to house the rapidly proliferating presidential staff. The expansion was largely concealed from the exterior by the ingenious trick of adding space underground. A noteworthy feature of the second Roosevelt renovation was the addition of a swimming pool, paid for by popular subscription so the polio-crippled

President could enjoy his favorite exercise. When the war brought demands for yet more office space, a reconstruction of the East Wing provided it.

But it was during the postwar administration of President Harry S Truman that the last truly major alteration came about. For decades the various structural changes and the addition of conduits, pipes, and wiring had weakened walls and floors of the venerable main building. The groanings of the ancient timbers gave rise to newspaper feature stories of ghosts in the White House.

Truman had already drawn considerable press attention by putting a balcony in the South Portico in 1947 to shade the windows of the Blue Room below. That teapot-tempest controversy was forgotten in 1948 when it became evident that something far more serious was wrong with the mansion. Not only did floors creak and ceilings crack, but the President's bathtub appeared to be sinking into the floor. One day Margaret Truman's piano thrust a leg down into the family dining room below. When the crystal chandelier in the Blue Room began shivering ominously during a reception a thorough study was ordered, resulting in the shocking revelation that the White House was threatened with imminent collapse. W. E. Reynolds, Commissioner of Public Buildings, said the family floor was staying in place "purely from habit." The Trumans moved bag and baggage across the street to Blair House, normally reserved for presidential guests. Then a reconstruction commission went to work.

Bulldozers rumbled in to dig a new basement and sub-basement to house the service core of what was to become a thoroughly modern, if unique, home-office building, complete with air conditioning. The entire interior of the mansion was removed from inside the shell of the outer walls, which were underpinned with concrete piers. Inside the walls a steel skeleton was erected. The whole job was carried out with the most painstaking caution. Irreplaceable chandeliers, mantelpieces and ornamental woodwork were removed and stored. Even the ornamental plasterwork was diagrammed before being removed.

When the three-year-long reconstruction job was finished in 1952, visitors discovered a subtly transformed mansion. The new décor was one of simple elegance, with many of the ornate and rococo touches of an earlier era giving way to softer, lighter, and more modern tones. Theodore Roosevelt's trophy heads vanished from the walls of the State Dining Room, no longer dark oak but soft green. The crystal chandeliers of the East Room reappeared, but in a simpler, more graceful form.

The Truman reconstruction was calculated to last. Since its completion, alterations in the mansion have been scarcely discernible. When under President Eisenhower the old need for more room for the Executive staff revived, an effective answer was found that did not touch the White House itself. A new Executive Office Building was constructed across Pennsylvania Avenue, connected to the mansion by a tunnel. Neither the Kennedys nor the Johnsons, both notably sensitive to the historic importance of their temporary residence, did more than add decorative touches. Mrs. Kennedy followed in the footsteps of Mrs. Coolidge, Mrs. Hoover, and Mrs. Eisenhower in the recovery and restoration of authentic presidential and other period pieces. She also successfully sought more appropriate art for the walls. President Kennedy followed the Fillmores and Trumans in pressing the project of a White House Library. That of Mrs. Fillmore had been replaced, in the Truman reconstruction, by a new library in the Ground Floor (originally the basement). A commission appointed by President Kennedy, under the chairmanship of James T. Babb, Librarian of Yale University, chose 2780 titles, mostly by American authors.

Today the hundred-plus-room mansion (Mrs. Eisenhower pointed out that a figure of "one hundred and two" was problematical because it is not easy to say which storerooms and other auxiliaries should be counted) is comfortable but not oversized. The scale of formal entertaining has grown steadily, and that of informal entertaining even more. Even the sightseers outside the picket fence were sometimes turned into a sort of receiving line under President Johnson, who interrupted strolls on the grounds to shake hands through the fence.

Not a palace or a fortress, but an attractive and livable dwelling, the White House stands today in cheerful contrast to the gloomy grandeur of most of the great European official residences. Yet it has its own air of majesty as America's shrine—the mansion of democracy.

The Oval Office during President Eisenhower's administration. The giant globe (*at left*) is both informative and decorative.

HOW THE PRESIDENCY WAS CREATED

THE office of President of the United States was created by the Founding Fathers during the Constitutional Convention of 1787. The delegates from the various states assembled in Philadelphia in May, planning only to revise the existing Articles of Confederation that had been written in 1777—ten years earlier—and had been ratified and became effective in 1781. Under the Articles of Confederation all the powers of the national government—including executive powers—were delegated to Congress.

There had been a president of the Congress under the Articles of Confederation, but he had been only a presiding officer with little or no power in his own right. The office was given only passing mention in the Articles of Confederation:

"The united States in congress assembled shall have authority . . . to appoint such other committees and civil officers as may be necessary for managing the general affairs of the united states under their direction—to appoint one of their number to preside, provided that no person be allowed to serve in the office of president more than one year in any term of three years . . ."

The Virginia Plan

THE first formal proposal that a chief executive be provided for the new federal government was contained in the Virginia Plan presented by Governor Edmund Randolph of Virginia on May 29, 1787:

"Resolved that a National Executive be instituted; to be chosen by the National Legislature for the term of _____ years, to receive punctually at stated times, a fixed compensation for the services rendered, in which no increase or diminution shall be made so as to affect the Magistracy, existing at the time of increase or diminution, and to be ineligible a second time; and that besides a general authority to execute the National laws, it ought to enjoy the Executive rights vested in Congress by the Confederation.

The residences of George Washington *(left)* and Robert Morris in Philadelphia.

Yale University Art Gallery.

John Rutledge
—From a painting by John Trumbull

"Resolved that the Executive and a convenient number of the National Judiciary, ought to compose a Council of revision with authority to examine every act of the National Legislature before it shall operate, and every act of a particular Legislature before a Negative thereon shall be final; and that the dissent of the said Council shall amount to a rejection, unless the Act of the National Legislature be again passed, or that of a particular Legislature be again negatived by ____ of the members of each branch."

The Pinckney Plan

On the same day Charles Pinckney of South Carolina presented his "Plan of a Federal Constitution." The Pinckney Plan did not figure in the debates during the Convention, but it was one of the documents later used by John Rutledge's committee of detail in drafting a complete constitution. Although the original of Pinckney's Plan was lost, he produced a copy of it for the national archives in 1818. Its Article VIII called for the establishment of the office of President in the following words:

"The executive power of the United States shall be vested in a President of the United States of America, which shall be his style; and his title shall be His Excellency. He shall be elected for ___ years; and shall be re-eligible.

"He shall from time give information to the Legislature, of the State of the Union, and recommend to their consideration the measures he may think necessary. He shall take care that the laws of the United States be duly executed. He shall commission all the officers of the United States; and except as to ambassadors, other ministers, and judges of the Supreme Court, he shall nominate, and, with the consent of the Senate, appoint, all other officers of the United States. He shall receive public ministers from foreign nations; and may correspond with the Executives of the different States. He shall have power to grant pardons and reprieves, except in impeachments. He shall be Commander-in-Chief of the army and navy of the United States, and of the militia of the several States; and shall reeive a compensation which shall not be increased or diminished during his continuance in office. At entering on the duties of his office, he shall take an oath faithfully to execute the duties of a President of the United States. He shall be removed from his office on impeachment by the House of Delegates, and conviction in the Supreme Court, of treason, bribery, or corruption. In case of his removal, death, resignation, or dis-

Charles Pinckney
—From a painting attributed to Gilbert Stuart
American Scenic and Historic Preservation Society Collection. Frick Art Reference Library.

ability, the President of the Senate shall exercise the duties of his office until another President be chosen. And in case of the death of the President of the Senate, the Speaker of the House of Delegates shall do so."

Madison Establishes the President's Authority

The Constitutional Convention began studying the parts of the Virginia Plan concerned with the chief executive on Friday, June 1, and continued to debate them for the next several days. On the first day of the debate the Convention adopted a motion by James Madison of Virginia to fix the extent of the chief executive's authority by changing the Resolution to read: "Resolved that a National Executive be instituted with power to carry into effect the national laws, to appoint to offices in cases not otherwise provided for . . ."

Next, the Convention began studying the question of how long the chief executive should serve. James Wilson of Pennsylvania and Roger Sherman of Connecticut proposed that the term of office be for three years. But Charles Pinckney of South Carolina and George Mason of Virginia spoke out for a term of seven years. Five states voted aye, four voted no, and one, Massachusetts, was divided. The president of the Convention, George Washington, decided that the motion for a term of seven years had carried.

The Delegates at first Reject an Electoral College

The Constitutional Convention delegates then turned their attention to deciding whether the chief executive should be elected by the people or be appointed by the Congress. James Wilson proposed the establishment of a system of presidential electors to be chosen by the people. But on June 2 this proposal was turned down by a vote of 8 to 2 and by the same number of votes it was decided that the chief executive should be elected by Congress.

Benjamin Franklin of Pennsylvania made an impassioned plea that the chief executive not be paid a salary, arguing that a higher caliber of man would be found for the office if there was no question of personal gain on his part. His motion was seconded by Alexander Hamilton of New York, but the Convention postponed debate or voting upon it, rather than hurt the old man's feelings by abruptly voting it down.

John Dickinson of Delaware, who had written the Articles of Confederation, moved "That the Executive be made removable by the National Legislature on the request of a majority of the Legislatures of individual States." He believed this would keep the states in a controlling position over the chief executive. But his moton was defeated, with all states except Delaware voting against it. The Convention then voted to make the chief executive ineligible for re-election after seven years in office.

Hugh Williamson of North Carolina moved to add that the executive "be removable on impeachment and conviction of malpractice or neglect of duty." This was approved by the delegates.

Should the Executive Be One Man or Three?

Toward the close of the session on Saturday, June 2, John Rutledge of South Carolina, who later was to be appointed Chief Justice by George Washington but be rejected by the U.S. Senate, moved that the blank for the number of persons to serve as Executive be filled with the words, "one person." Rutledge said that the reasons were so obvious and conclusive in favor of a single chief executive that he believed no one would oppose the motion.

However, Edmund Randolph, who later was to be the first Attorney General of the United States under President Washington, spoke out against the single chief executive. He said he believed the people would regard the establishment of a chief executive as resembling a monarchy. Instead, he proposed that the Executive be made up of three men on equal footing

James Madison

—From a painting by Charles Willson Peale
Thomas Gilcrease Institute of American History and Art, Tulsa, Oklahoma. Frick Art Reference Library.

An early sketch of one of the ideas for the official seal.

to be chosen from different parts of the country. The Convention adjourned that day before a vote could be taken on the matter.

After considering the matter over Sunday, the Convention resumed debate on the question of the single chief executive on Monday, June 4. James Wilson of Pennsylvania, who later was to be appointed by President Washington as one of the first associate justices of the Supreme Court, argued eloquently for a single chief executive. He said that with a triumvirate holding the executive power he foresaw "nothing but uncontrolled, continued and violent animosities." He said these quarrels would "diffuse their poison through the other branches of government, through the states, and at length through the people at large."

Finally, the delegates agreed upon a single chief executive, although three states opposed the resolution—New York, Delaware, and Maryland.

Establishment of the Veto Power

THE Convention then turned its attention to a discussion of the part of the Virginia Resolutions that called for the establishment of a "Council of revision."

Elbridge Gerry of Massachusetts, who later was to serve as Vice-President under President James Madison, moved that instead of considering the "Council of revision," the delegates should adopt a proposal "that the National Executive shall have a right to negative any legislative act, which shall not be afterwards passed by __ parts of each branch of the National Legislature."

James Wilson and Alexander Hamilton made an effort to obtain an absolute veto for the chief executive, eliminating any possibility of Congress overriding a presidential veto. Benjamin Franklin strongly opposed this, pointing out that the chief executive could use such a power to extort money from the legislature. He commented that "The Executive will be always increasing here, as elsewhere, till it ends in a monarchy."

The delegations unanimously voted down the idea of giving the chief executive an absolute veto, and agreed to fill the blank in Gerry's resolution with the word "two-thirds." In a final vote on the entire resolution giving the chief executive a limited veto that could be overridden by a two-thirds vote of each house of Congress, eight states voted for the resolution and two opposed—Connecticut and Maryland.

On Wednesday, June 6, Wilson and Madison made an effort to revive the idea of a "Council of revision" that would include representatives of the judicial branch in the exercise of veto over legislation. But their resolution was voted down, with only Connecticut, New York, and Virginia voting aye.

The question of how the chief executive was to be chosen was again brought up for debate on Saturday, June 9. Elbridge Gerry of Massachusetts proposed that the chief executive be elected by the governors of the states, instead of by Congress as had been previously agreed upon. He said he believed that the governors, being executives themselves, would be more likely to choose an able chief executive than would the legislature. However, the delegates voted down his idea.

The Revised Virginia Plan Resolutions

ON Wednesday, June 13, after the delegates had completed their initial debates on the Virginia Plan, the wording of the two resolutions concerned with the chief executive stood as follows:

> "Resolved, that a National Executive be instituted, to consist of a single person; to be chosen

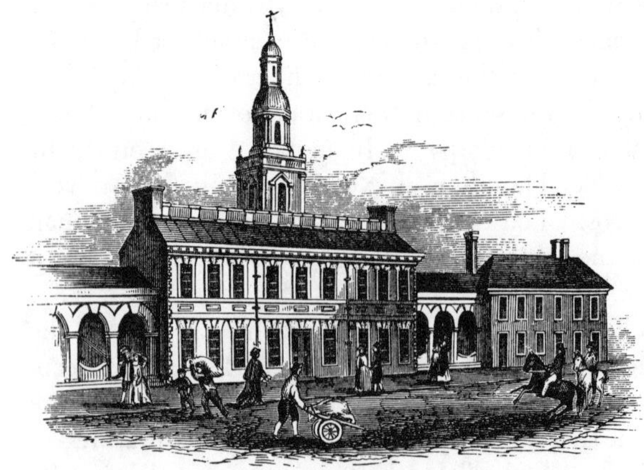

The State House of Philadelphia in 1774.

Thomas Jefferson

by the National Legislature, for the term of seven years; with power to carry into execution the national laws; to appoint to offices in cases not otherwise provided for; to be ineligible a second time; and to be removable on impeachment and conviction of malpractices or neglect of duty; to receive a fixed stipend by which he may be compensated for the devotion of his time to the public service, to be paid out of the National Treasury.

"Resolved, that the national Executive shall have a right to negative any legislative act, which shall not be afterwards passed by two-thirds of each branch of the National Legislature."

The New Jersey Plan

SEVERAL of the smaller states had been becoming increasingly concerned that the Convention was moving toward too strong a centralized government. So on Friday, June 15, William Paterson of New Jersey, who later was to serve as an associate justice of the Supreme Court, presented what became known as the "New Jersey Plan." Its provisions for the executive branch were as follows:

"Resolved, that the United States in Congress be authorized to elect a Federal Executive, to consist of__persons, to continue in office for the term of__ years; to receive punctually, at stated times, a fixed compensation for their services, in which no increase nor diminution shall be made so as to affect the persons composing the Executive at the time of such increase or diminution; to be paid out of the Federal treasury; to be incapable of holding any other office or appointment during their time of service, and for __ years thereafter: to be ineligible a second time, and removeable by Congress, on application by a majority of the Executives of the several States; that the Executive, besides their general authority to execute the Federal acts, ought to appoint all Federal officers not otherwise provided for, and to direct all military operations; provided, that none of the persons composing the Federal Executive shall, on any occasion, take command of any troops, so as personally to conduct any military enterprise, as General, or in any other capacity."

Robert Livingston

Alexander Hamilton's Plan

As the Convention began to debate the respective merits of the New Jersey Plan versus the Virginia Resolutions, Alexander Hamilton spoke out against both, saying that neither provided for a strong enough central government. In turn, he presented his own plan. In Hamilton's plan the provision for the chief executive was as follows:

"The supreme Executive authority of the United States to be vested in a Governor, to be elected to serve during good behaviour; the election to be made by Electors chosen by the people in the Election Districts aforesaid. The authorities and functions of the Executive to be as follows; to have a negative on all laws about to be passed, and the execution of all laws passed; to have the direction of war when authorized or begun; to have, with the advice and approbation of the Senate, the power of making all treaties; to have the sole appointment of the heads or chief officers of the Departments of Finance, War, and Foreign Affairs; to have the nomination of all other officers (ambassadors to foreign nations included), subject to the approbation or rejection of the Senate; to have the power of pardoning all offences except treason, which he shall not pardon without the approbation

Alexander Hamilton

Chief Justice John Jay

of the Senate.

"On the death, resignation, or removal of the Governor, his authorities to be exercised by the President of the Senate till a successor be appointed."

The delegates voted to postpone discussion of the New Jersey Plan and ignored Hamilton's Plan. For the next month the delegates devoted their consideration almost entirely to the provisions for the legislative branch of the government. It was not until Tuesday, July 17 that the resolutions concerning the executive branch again came up for discussion.

Rejection of Direct Election by the People

GOUVERNEUR Morris of Pennsylvania, who later became a U.S. Senator, moved that the chief executive be elected by the citizens of the United States, instead of by the National Legislature. He said: "If the people should elect, they will never fail to prefer some man of distinguished character, or services . . . If the Legislature elect, it will be the work of intrigue, of cabal, and of faction . . ."

The proposal for direct election by the people was opposed by Roger Sherman of Connecticut, Charles Pinckney of South Carolina, George Mason of Virginia, and Hugh Williamson of North Carolina. Mason said he believed "it would be as unnatural to refer the choice of a proper character for Chief Magistrate to the people, as it would, to refer a trial of colors to a blind man."

When Morris' resolution was put to a motion, only his own state of Pennsylvania voted for it. All the other states voted no.

By a vote of 6 to 4, the delegations voted to strike out the words "to be ineligible a second time." Gouverneur Morris in supporting the motion pointed out that if the chief executive was ineligible for re-election it would tend to "destroy the great motive to good behaviour, the hope of being rewarded by a re-appointment. It was saying to him, make hay while the sun shines."

Delegates Fear Development of a Monarchy

THE Convention next spent considerable time discussing whether or not to change the chief executive's term of office from seven years to "during good behaviour." Gouverneur Morris and James Madison were among the chief supporters of this proposed change. They saw this as a further way to free the chief executive from dependence on the national legislature. George Mason of Virginia made the main speech against the motion, declaring that "an Executive during good behaviour" was "a softer name only for an Executive for life." He said he believed the next easy step was to a hereditary monarchy. The delegates decided by a vote of 6 to 4 to retain the seven-year term for the chief executive.

Establishment of an Electoral System for Choosing the Chief Executive

ON Thursday, July 19, the Convention again took up the question of how the chief executive should be elected. James Madison made an impassioned address calling upon the delegates to free the chief executive from any dependence on the national legislature. He said, "If it be a fundamental principle of free government that the Legislative, Executive and Judiciary powers should be *separately* exercised, it is equally so that they be *independently* exercised."

Oliver Ellsworth of Connecticut, who later was to become the second Chief Justice of the United States, moved to strike out the provision for election of the chief executive by the national legislature and substitute, "to be chosen by Electors, appointed by the Legislatures of the States in the following ratio; to wit: one for each State not exceeding two hundred thousand inhabitants; two for each above that number and not exceeding three hundred thousand; and three for each State exceeding three hundred thousand." The Convention voted to accept this motion, but deferred action on the ratio of number of electors for each state.

On motion of Oliver Ellsworth, the Convention decided to reduce the length of the chief executive's term from seven years to six years.

On Friday, July 20, Elbridge Gerry moved that the Electors for the chief executive be alloted to the states in the following ratio: New Hampshire, one; Massachusetts, three; Rhode Island, one; Connecticut, two; New York, two; New Jersey, two; Pennsylvania, three; Delaware, one; Maryland, two; Virginia, three; North Carolina, two; South Carolina, two; Georgia, one. Despite opposition by the smaller states, the Convention adopted Gerry's proposal by a vote of 6 to 4. It was further agreed, "that the Electors of the Executive shall not be members of the National Legislature, nor officers of the United States, nor shall the Electors themselves be eligible to the supreme magistracy."

That same day the delegates spent a substantial amount of time discussing whether the chief executive should be made liable to impeachment and removal from office. Benjamin Franklin, James Madison, and Edmund Randolph led the arguments for preserving the right of impeachment. Franklin pointed out that without impeachment the only recourse for removal of a corrupt chief executive was assassination. The Convention retained the impeachment clause by a vote of 8 to 2, with only Massachusetts and South Carolina opposing.

Attempt to Modify the Presidential Veto

On Saturday, July 21, James Wilson of Pennsylvania revived the idea that members of the judiciary should be associated with the chief executive in exercising the veto power over legislation. James Madison supported the proposition on the basis that it would give the judicial branch "an additional opportunity of defending itself against Legislative encroachments."

Elbridge Gerry opposed Wilson's motion because he felt that it would lead to a "combining and mixing together" of the executive and judiciary. And Nathaniel Gorham, also of Massachusetts, opposed the measure, pointing out that since there would be only one chief executive and several judges the proposal would have the effect of taking the veto power "entirely out of the Executive hands, and, instead of enabling him to defend himself, would enable the Judges to sacrifice him."

John Rutledge of South Carolina also opposed the proposition saying that of all men judges were the most unfit to be given the veto power on legislation. He said, "Judges ought never to give their opinion on a law, till it comes before them."

The inclusion of the judiciary in the executive veto power narrowly missed being added to the Constitution. Four states opposed the measure—Massachusetts, Delaware, North Carolina, and South Carolina; three states voted in favor—Connecticut, Maryland, and Virginia; two states were divided—Pennsylvania and Georgia; and New Jersey was absent.

The Convention next began considering a motion by James Madison that the chief executive should nominate the members of the judiciary and that these nominations should become appointments unless two-thirds of the Senate disagreed. But several delegates objected to taking the power of appointment away from the National Legislature, so the motion went down to defeat by a vote of 3 for and 6 against.

Choosing of the President Returned to Congress

After several days debating other aspects of the Constitution, the delegates on Tuesday, July 24, again took up the question of how the chief executive was to be elected. William C. Houston of New Jersey moved that, instead of having the chief executive chosen by special electors as had already been agreed to, the National Legislature should be given the task. He said he believed the use of electors would cause extreme inconvenience and considerable expense. He also said he believed that capable men would not agree to serve as electors, particularly in the more distant states.

When the delegations were polled on the question they reversed their previous stand, and by a vote of 7 to 4 agreed to put the election of the chief executive back into the hands of the National Legislature. Then they fell to arguing about all aspects of the chief executive, the length of his term of office, and whether or not he should be eligible for re-election. After two days of wrangling, the Convention decided on Thursday, July 26, by a vote of 7 to 3 to limit the chief executive's term to seven years and make him ineligible for a second term. Later that same day the Convention turned all the resulting resolutions over to a Committee of Detail headed by John Rutledge of South Carolina to write them up into the form of a Constitution. In addition the Convention passed along to the Committee the New Jersey Plan and the Pinckney Plan and adjourned for ten days.

Draft by the Committee of Detail

When the Convention reconvened on Monday, August 6, Rutledge presented the delegates with a draft of the Constitution which had drawn heavily upon the Pinckney plan for its wording concerning the chief executive. Its Article X read as follows:

"Section 1. The Executive power of the United States shall be vested in a single person. His style shall be, "The President of the United States of America," and his title shall be, "His Excellency." He shall be elected by ballot by the Legislature. He shall hold his office during the term of seven years; but shall not be elected a second time.

"Section 2. He shall, from time to time, give information to the Legislature of the state of the Union. He may recommend to their consideration such measures as he shall judge necessary, and expedient. He may convene them on extraordinary occasions. In case of disagreement between the two Houses, with regard to the time of adjournment, he may adjourn them to such time as he thinks proper. He shall take care that the laws of the United States be duly and faithfully executed. He shall commission all the officers of the United States; and shall appoint officers in all cases not otherwise provided for by this Constitution. He shall receive Ambassadors, and may correspond with the supreme executives of the several States. He shall have power to grant reprieves and pardons, but his pardon shall not be pleadable in bar of an impeachment. He shall be Commander-in-chief of the army and navy of the United States, and of the militia of the several States. He shall, at stated times, receive for his services a compensation, which shall neither be increased nor diminished during his continuance in office. Before he shall enter on the duties of his department, he shall take the following oath or affirmation, "I ______________ solemnly swear, (or affirm) that I will faithfully execute the office of President of the United States of America." He shall be removed from his office on impeachment by the House of Representatives, and conviction in the Supreme Court, of treason, bribery, or corruption. In case of his removal, as aforesaid, death, resignation, or disability to discharge the powers and duties of his office, the President of the Senate shall exercise those powers and duties, until another President of the United States be chosen, or until the disability of the President be removed."

In the new Constitution prepared by the Committee of Detail, the provision for a presidential veto was moved to Article VI, which dealt with the procedures of the two houses of Congress.

The Convention did not take up Article X, relating to the President, until Friday, August 24, and the debate on the provisions extended until Monday, August 27. Most efforts to change the Article, whether by those trying to strengthen the office or by those trying to weaken it, were voted down. On August 31, the Convention turned over to a Committee of Eleven (with one delegate from each state) such knotty problems as how the chief executive should be elected.

Report by the Committee of Eleven

On Tuesday, September 4, the Committee of Eleven reported back to the Convention their solutions for the various problems surrounding the office of the President. They recommended creating a Vice-President and the establishment of a four-year term of office for both President and Vice-President. And the Committee solved the problem of how the President and Vice-President should be chosen by drawing up plans for an elaborate electoral system that would leave the method of choosing presidential electors up to the legislatures of the various states. The Committee established the qualifications for being President —a natural-born citizen, at least 35 years old, and a resident within the United States for at least 14 years. Another important change by the Committee gave the President the power to make treaties with the advice and consent of the Senate and to appoint judges of the Supreme Court.

For the rest of the first week of September the Convention debated the changes in the article dealing with the office of the President, making some minor but few major changes. Then on Saturday, September 8, a five-man Committee of Revision was

Rufus King

John Marshall

appointed to revise the style and arrangement of the articles that had been agreed to. The Committee included James Madison, Gouverneur Morris, Alexander Hamilton, Rufus King, and William Samuel Johnson.

Final Version in the Constitution

THE Committee of Revision submitted its report on Wednesday, September 12. In the new Constitution prepared by the Committee, the provisions concerning the President became Article II. The wording was approved with a few minor changes on Saturday, September 15. And on Monday, September 17, 1787, the delegates approved and signed the final version of the Constitution of the United States. The wording of Article II follows:

Article II

"Section 1. The executive Power shall be vested in a President of the United States of America. He shall hold his Office during the Term of four Years, and, together with the Vice President, chosen for the same Term, be elected as follows:

"Each State shall appoint, in such Manner as the Legislature thereof may direct, a Number of Electors, equal to the whole Number of Senators and Representatives to which the State may be entitled in the Congress: but no Senator or Representative, or Person holding an Office of Trust or Profit under the United States, shall be appointed an Elector.

"The Electors shall meet in their respective States, and vote by Ballot for two Persons, of whom one at least shall not be an Inhabitant of the same State with themselves. And they shall make a List of all the Persons voted for, and of the Number of Votes for each; which List they shall sign and certify, and transmit sealed to the Seat of the Government of the United States, directed to the President of the Senate. The President of the Senate shall, in the Presence of the Senate and House of Representatives, open all the Certificates, and the Votes shall then be counted. The Person having the greatest Number of Votes shall be the President, if such Number be a Majority of the whole Number of Electors appointed; and if there be more than one who have such Majority, and have an equal Number of Votes, then the House of Representatives shall immediately choose by Ballot one of them for President; and if no Person have a Majority, then from the five highest on the List the said House shall in like manner choose the President. But in choosing the President, the Votes shall be taken by States, the Representation from each State having one Vote; A quorum for this Purpose shall consist of a Member or Members from two-thirds of the States, and a Majority of all the States shall be necessary to a Choice. In every Case, after the Choice of the President, the Person having the greatest Number of Votes of the Electors shall be the Vice President. But if there should remain two or more who have equal Votes, the Senate shall choose from them by Ballot the Vice President.

"The Congress may determine the Time of choosing the Electors, and the Day on which they shall give their Votes; which Day shall be the same throughout the United States.

"No Person except a natural born Citizen, or a Citizen of the United States, at the time of the Adoption of this Constitution, shall be eligible to the Office of President; neither shall any Person be eligible to that Office who shall not have attained to the Age of thirty five Years, and been fourteen Years a Resident within the United States.

"In Case of the Removal of the President from Office, or of his Death, Resignation, or Inability to discharge the Powers and Duties of the said Office, the Same shall devolve on the Vice President, and the Congress may by Law provide for the Case of Removal, Death, Resignation or Inability, both of the President and Vice President, declaring what Officer shall then act as President, and such Officer shall act accordingly, until the Disability be removed, or a President shall be elected.

"The President shall, at stated Times, receive for his Services, a Compensation, which shall neither be increased nor diminished during the Period for which he shall have been elected, and he shall not receive within that Period any other Emolument from the United States, or any of them.

"Before he enter on the Execution of his Office, he shall take the following Oath or Affirmation:— "I do solemnly swear (or affirm) that I will faithfully execute the Office of President of the United States, and will to the best of my Ability, preserve, protect and defend the Constitution of the United States."

"Section 2. The President shall be Commander in Chief of the Army and Navy of the United States, and of the Militia of the several States, when called into the actual Service of the United States; he may require the Opinion, in writing, of the principal Officer in each of the executive Departments, upon any Subject relating to the Duties of their respective Offices, and he shall have Power to grant Reprieves and Pardons for Offences against the United States, except in Cases of Impeachment.

"He shall have Power, by and with the Advice and Consent of the Senate, to make Treaties, provided two thirds of the Senators present concur; and he shall nominate, and by and with the Advice and Consent of the Senate, shall appoint Ambassadors, other public Ministers and Consuls, Judges of the supreme Court, and all other Officers of the United States, whose Appointments are not herein otherwise provided for, and which shall be established by Law: but the Congress may by Law vest the Appointment of such inferior Officers, as they think proper, in the President alone, in the Courts of Law, or in the Heads of Departments.

"The President shall have Power to fill up all Vacancies that may happen during the Recess of the Senate, by granting Commissions which shall expire at the End of their next Session.

"Section 3. He shall from time to time give to the Congress Information of the State of the Union, and recommend to their Consideration such Measures as he shall judge necessary and expedient; he may, on extraordinary Occasions, convene both Houses, or either of them, and in Case of Disagreement between them, with Respect to the Time of Adjournment, he may adjourn them to such Time as he shall think proper; he shall receive Ambassadors and other public Ministers; he shall take Care that the Laws be faithfully executed, and shall Commission all the Officers of the United States.

"Section 4. The President, Vice President and all civil Officers of the United States, shall be removed from Office on Impeachment for, and Conviction of, Treason, Bribery, or other high Crimes and Misdemeanors."

Amendments Bearing on the Presidency

Since the Constitution went into effect in 1789, five amendments have been adopted that have modified Article II. These are as follows:

Amendment 12
(proclaimed September 25, 1804)

The Electors shall meet in their respective states, and vote by ballot for President and Vice-President, one of whom, at least, shall not be an inhabitant of the same state with themselves; they shall name in their ballots the person voted for as President, and in distinct ballots the person voted for as Vice-President, and they shall make distinct lists of all persons voted for as President, and of all persons voted for as Vice-President, and of the number of votes for each, which lists they shall sign and certify, and transmit sealed to the seat of the government of the United States, directed to the President of the Senate;—the President of the Senate shall, in the presence of the Senate and House of Representatives, open all the certificates and the votes shall then be counted;—The person having the greatest number of votes for President, shall be the President, if such number be a majority of the whole number of Electors appointed; and if no person have such majority, then from the persons having the highest numbers not exceeding three on the list of those voted for as President, the House of Representatives shall choose immediately, by ballot, the President. But in choosing the President, the votes shall be taken by states, the representation from each state having one vote; a quorum for this purpose shall consist of a member or members from two-thirds of the states, and a majority of all the states shall be necessary to a choice. And if the House of Representatives shall not choose a President whenever the right of choice shall devolve upon them, before the fourth day of March next following, then the Vice-President, as in the case of the death or other constitutional disability of the President. The person having the greatest number of votes as Vice-President, shall be the Vice-President, if such number be a majority of the whole number of Electors appointed, and if no person have a majority, then from the two highest numbers on the list, the Senate shall choose the Vice-President; a quorum for the purpose shall consist of two-thirds of the whole number of Senators, and a majority of the whole number shall be necessary to a choice. But no person constitutionally ineligible to the office of President shall be eligible to that of Vice-President of the United States.

Amendment 20
(proclaimed February 6, 1933)

Section 1. The terms of the President and Vice-President shall end at noon on the 20th day of January, and the terms of Senators and Representatives at noon on the third day of January, of the year in which such terms would have ended if this article had not been ratified; and the terms of their successors shall then begin.

Section 2. The Congress shall assemble at least once in every year, and such meeting shall begin at noon on the third day of January, unless they shall by law appoint a different day.

Section 3. If, at the time fixed for the begin-

Designs for the Great Seal of the United States as submitted by the second committee.

ning of the term of the President, the president elect shall have died, the Vice-President elect shall become President. If a President shall not have been chosen before the time fixed for the beginning of his term, or if the President elect shall have failed to qualify, then the Vice President elect shall act as President until a President shall have qualified; and the Congress may by law provide for the case wherein neither a President elect nor a Vice-President elect shall have qualified, declaring who shall then act as President, or the manner in which one who is to act shall be selected, and such person shall act accordingly until a President or Vice-President shall have qualified.

Section 4. The Congress may by law provide for the case of the death of any of the persons from whom the House of Representatives may choose a President whenever the right of choice shall have devolved upon them, and for the case of the death of any of the persons from whom the Senate may choose a Vice-President whenever the right of choice shall have devolved upon them.

Section 5. Sections 1 and 2 shall take effect on the 15th day of October following the ratification of this article.

Section 6. This article shall be inoperative unless it shall have been ratified as an amendment to the Constitution by the legislatures of three fourths of the several States within seven years from the date of its submission.

Amendment 22
(proclaimed February 27, 1951)

Section 1. No person shall be elected to the office of the President more than twice, and no person who has held the office of President, or acted as President, for more than two years of a term to which some other person was elected President shall be elected to the office of the President more than once. But this article shall not apply to any person holding the office of President, or acting as President, during the term within which this article becomes operative from holding the office of President or acting as President during the remainder of such term.

Section 2. This article shall be inoperative unless it shall have been ratified as an amendment to the Constitution by the legislatures of three fourths of the several States within seven years from the day of its submission to the States by the Congress.

Amendment 23
(proclaimed April 3, 1961)

Section 1. The District constituting the seat of Government of the United States shall appoint in such manner as the Congress may direct: A number of electors of President and Vice-President equal to the whole number of Senators and Representatives in Congress to which the District would be entitled if it were a State, but in no event more than the least populous State; they shall be in addition to those appointed by the States, but they shall be considered, for the purposes of the election of President and Vice-President, to be electors appointed by a State; and they shall meet in the District and perform such duties as provided by the twelfth article of amendment.

Section 2. The Congress shall have power to enforce this article by appropriate legislation.

Amendment 25

(proclaimed February 10, 1967)

Section 1. In case of the removal of the President from office or his death or resignation, the Vice-President shall become President.

Section 2. Whenever there is a vacancy in the office of the Vice President, the President shall nominate a Vice President who shall take the office upon confirmation by a majority vote of both houses of Congress.

Section 3. Whenever the President transmits to the President pro tempore of the Senate and the Speaker of the House of Representatives his written declaration that he is unable to discharge the powers and duties of his office, and until he transmits to them a written declaration to the contrary, such powers and duties shall be discharged by the Vice-President as Acting President.

Section 4. Whenever the Vice-President and a majority of either the principal officers of the executive departments or of such other body as Congress may by law provide, transmit to the President pro tempore of the Senate and the Speaker of the House of Representatives their written declaration that the President is unable to discharge the powers and duties of his office, the Vice-President shall immediately assume the powers and duties of the office as Acting President.

Thereafter, when the President transmits to the President pro tempore of the Senate and the Speaker of the House of Representatives his written declaration that no inability exists, he shall resume the powers and duties of his office unless the Vice-President and a majority of either the principal officers of the executive department or of such other body as Congress may by law provide, transmit within four days to the President pro tempore of the Senate and the Speaker of the House of Representatives their written declaration that the President is unable to discharge the powers and duties of his office. Thereupon Congress shall decide the issue, assembling within 48 hours for that purpose if not in session. If the Congress, within 21 days after receipt of the latter written declaration, or, if Congress is not in session, within 21 days after Congress is required to assemble, determines by two-thirds vote of both houses that the President is unable to discharge the powers and duties of his office, the Vice-President shall continue to discharge the same as Acting President; otherwise, the President shall resume the powers and duties of his office.

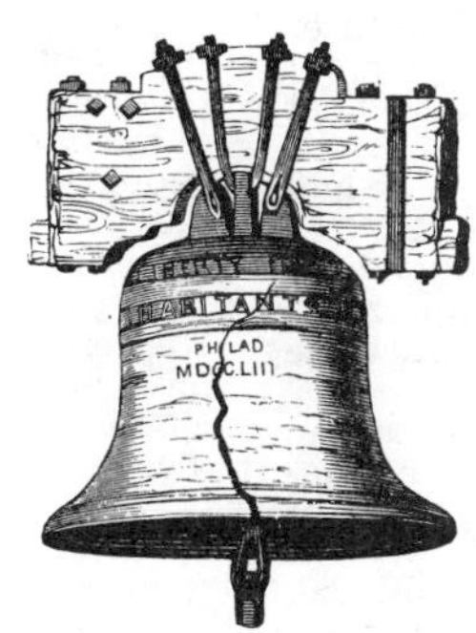

THE DECLARATION OF INDEPENDENCE

In Congress, July 4, 1776. The unanimous Declaration of the thirteen united States of America.

When in the Course of human events, it becomes necessary for one people to dissolve the political bands which have connected them with another, and to assume among the powers of the earth, the separate and equal station to which the Laws of Nature and of Nature's God entitle them, a decent respect to the opinions of mankind requires that they should declare the causes which impel them to the separation.—

We hold these truths to be self-evident, that all men are created equal, that they are endowed by their Creator with certain unalienable Rights, that among these are Life, Liberty and the pursuit of Happiness.—

That to secure these rights, Governments are instituted among Men, deriving their just powers from the consent of the governed,—

That whenever any Form of Government becomes destructive of these ends, it is the Right of the People to alter or to abolish it, and to institute new Government, laying its foundation on such principles and organizing its powers in such form, as to them shall seem most likely to effect their Safety and Happiness. Prudence, indeed, will dictate that Governments long established should not be changed for light and transient causes; and accordingly all experience hath shown, that mankind are more disposed to suffer, while evils are sufferable, than to right themselves by abolishing the forms to which they are accustomed. But when a long train of abuses and usurpations, pursuing invariably the same Object evinces a design to reduce them under absolute Despotism, it is their right, it is their duty, to throw off such Government, and to provide new Guards for their future security.—

Such has been the patient sufferance of these Colonies; and such is now the necessity which constrains them to alter their former Systems of Government. The history of the present King of Great Britain is a history of repeated injuries and usurpations, all having in direct object the establishment of an absolute Tyranny over these States. To prove this, let Facts be submitted to a candid world.—

He has refused his Assent to Laws, the most wholesome and necessary for the public good.—

He has forbidden his Governors to pass Laws of immediate and pressing importance, unless suspended in their operation till his Assent should be obtained; and when so suspended, he has utterly neglected to attend to them.—

He has refused to pass other Laws for the accommodation of large districts of people, unless those people would relinquish the right of Representation in the Legislature, a right inestimable to them and formidable to tyrants only.—

He has called together legislative bodies at places unusual, uncomfortable, and distant from the depository of their public Records, for the sole purpose of fatiguing them into compliance with his measures.—

He has dissolved Representative Houses repeatedly, for opposing with manly firmness his invasions on the rights of the people.—

He has refused for a long time, after such dissolutions, to cause others to be elected; whereby the Legislative powers, incapable of Annihilation, have returned to the People at large for their exercise; the State remaining in the mean time exposed to all the dangers of invasion from without, and convulsions within.—

He has endeavoured to prevent the population of these States; for that purpose obstructing the Laws for Naturalization of Foreigners; refusing to pass others to encourage their migrations hither, and raising the conditions of new Appropriations of Lands.—

He has obstructed the Administration of Justice, by refusing his Assent to Laws for establishing Judiciary powers.—

He has made Judges dependent on his Will alone, for the tenure of their offices, and the amount and payment of their salaries.—

He has erected a multitude of New Offices, and sent hither swarms of Officers to harrass our people, and eat out their substance.—

He has kept among us in times of peace, Standing Armies without the Consent of our legislatures.—

He has affected to render the Military independent of and superior to the Civil power.—

He has combined with others to subject us to a jurisdiction foreign to our constitution, and unacknowledged by our laws; giving his Assent to their Acts of pretended Legislation:—

For quartering large bodies of armed troops among us:—

For protecting them, by a mock Trial, from punishment for any Murders which they should commit on the Inhabitants of these States:—

For cutting off our Trade with all parts of the world:—

For imposing Taxes on us without our Consent:—

For depriving us in many cases, of the benefits of Trial by Jury:—

For transporting us beyond Seas to be tried for pretended offences:—

For abolishing the free System of English Laws in a neighbouring Province, establishing therein an Arbitrary government, and enlarging its Boundaries so as to render it at once an example and fit instrument for introducing the same absolute rule in these Colonies:—

For taking away our Charters, abolishing our most valuable Laws, and altering fundamentally the Forms of our Governments:—

For suspending our own Legislatures, and declaring themselves invested with power to legislate for us in all cases whatsoever.—

He has abdicated Government here, by declaring us out of his Protection and waging War against us.—

He has plundered our seas, ravaged our Coasts, burnt our towns, and destroyed the lives of our people.—

He is at this time transporting large Armies of foreign Mercenaries to compleat the works of death, desolation and tyranny, already begun with circumstances of Cruelty & perfidy scarcely paralleled in the most barbarous ages, and totally unworthy the Head of a civilized nation.—

He has constrained our fellow Citizens taken Captive on the high Seas to bear Arms against their Country, to become the executioners of their friends and Brethren, or to fall themselves by their Hands.—

He has excited domestic insurrections amongst us, and has endeavoured to bring on the inhabitants of our frontiers, the merciless Indian Savages, whose known rule of warfare, is an undistinguished destruction of all ages, sexes and conditions.

In every stage of these Oppressions We have Petitioned for Redress in the most humble terms: Our repeated Petitions have been answered only by repeated injury. A Prince, whose character is thus marked by every act which may define a Tyrant, is unfit to be the ruler of a free people.

Nor have We been wanting in attentions to our British brethren. We have warned them from time to time of attempts by their legislature to extend an unwarrantable jurisdiction over us. We have reminded them of the circumstances of our emigration and settlement here. We have appealed to their native justice and magnanimity, and we have conjured them by the ties of our common kindred to disavow these usurpations, which, would inevitably interrupt our connections and correspondence. They too have been deaf to the voice of justice and of consanguinity. We must, therefore acquiesce in the necessity, which denounces our Separation, and hold them, as we hold the rest of mankind, Enemies in War, in Peace Friends.—

We, therefore, the Representatives of the united States of America, in General Congress, Assembled, appealing to the Supreme Judge of the world for the rectitude of our intentions, do, in the Name, and by Authority of the good People of these Colonies, solemnly publish and declare, That these United Colonies are, and of Right ought to be, Free and Independent States; that they are Absolved from all Allegiance to the British Crown, and that all political connection between them and the State of Great Britain, is and ought to be totally dissolved; and that as Free and Independent States, they have full Power to levy War, conclude Peace, contract Alliances, establish Commerce, and to do all other Acts and Things which Independent States may of right do.—

And for the support of this Declaration, with a firm reliance on the protection of divine Providence, we mutually pledge to each other our Lives, our Fortunes and our sacred Honor.

THE SIGNERS OF THE DECLARATION OF INDEPENDENCE

Name	Born–Died	Birthplace	Age at Adoption of Declaration	Colony Represented	Profession	Later Achievements
John Adams	1735–1826	Massachusetts	40	Massachusetts	Lawyer	Vice-president of U.S. 1789–1797; President of U.S. 1797–1801
Samuel Adams	1722–1803	Massachusetts	53	Massachusetts	Businessman	Governor of Massachusetts 1794–1797
Josiah Bartlett	1729–1795	Massachusetts	46	New Hampshire	Physician	Governor of New Hampshire 1793–1794
Carter Braxton	1736–1797	Virginia	39	Virginia	Planter	Member of Virginia Council of State 1786–1791, 1794–1797
Charles Carroll	1737–1832	Maryland	38	Maryland	Lawyer-Planter	U.S. Senator from Maryland 1789–1792
Samuel Chase	1741–1811	Maryland	35	Maryland	Lawyer	Associate Justice, Supreme Court of U.S. 1796–1811
Abraham Clark	1726–1794	New Jersey	50	New Jersey	Politician	U.S. Rep. from New Jersey 1791–1794
George Clymer	1739–1813	Pennsylvania	37	Pennsylvania	Banker	Signed U.S. Constitution; U.S. Rep. from Pennsylvania 1789–1791
William Ellery	1727–1820	Rhode Island	48	Rhode Island	Lawyer	Collector of Customs, Newport, R. I. 1790–1820
William Floyd	1734–1821	New York	41	New York	Farmer	U.S. Rep. from New York 1789–1791
Benjamin Franklin	1706–1790	Massachusetts	70	Pennsylvania	Publisher	Signed U.S. Constitution
Elbridge Gerry	1744–1814	Massachusetts	31	Massachusetts	Merchant	Vice-president of U.S. 1813–1814
Button Gwinnett	1735(?)–1777	England	41	Georgia	Merchant	Acting President of Georgia 1777
Lyman Hall	1724–1790	Connecticut	52	Georgia	Physician	Governor of Georgia 1783
John Hancock	1737–1793	Massachusetts	39	Massachusetts	Merchant	Governor of Massachusetts 1780–1785, 1787–1793
Benjamin Harrison	1726–1791	Virginia	50	Virginia	Planter	Governor of Virginia 1781–1784
John Hart	1711(?)–1779	Connecticut	65	New Jersey	Farmer	Died before Independence was won
Joseph Hewes	1730–1779	New Jersey	46	North Carolina	Merchant	First executive head of American navy
Thomas Heyward, Jr.	1746–1809	South Carolina	29	South Carolina	Lawyer	Artillery officer during Revolutionary War, captured and imprisoned by British
William Hooper	1742–1790	Massachusetts	34	North Carolina	Lawyer	North Carolina State legislator 1777–1782
Stephen Hopkins	1707–1785	Rhode Island	69	Rhode Island	Merchant	Delegate to the Continental Congress 1778
Francis Hopkinson	1737–1791	Pennsylvania	38	New Jersey	Lawyer	Said to have designed U.S. Flag 1777, U.S. District Court judge 1789–1791
Samuel Huntington	1731–1796	Connecticut	45	Connecticut	Lawyer	President of Continental Congress 1779–1781 Governor of Connecticut 1786–1796

Name	Born–Died	Birthplace	Age at Adoption of Declaration	Colony Represented	Profession	Later Achievements
Thomas Jefferson	1743–1826	Virginia	33	Virginia	Planter-Lawyer	U.S. Secretary of State 1789–1793, Vice-President of U.S. 1797–1801, President of U.S. 1801–1809
Francis Lightfoot Lee	1734–1797	Virginia	41	Virginia	Planter	Delegate to Continental Congress 1775–1779
Richard Henry Lee	1732–1794	Virginia	44	Virginia	Planter	President of Continental Congress 1784, U.S. Senator from Virginia 1789–1792
Francis Lewis	1713–1802	Wales	63	New York	Merchant	Retired
Philip Livingston	1716–1778	New York	60	New York	Merchant	Died before Independence was won
Thomas Lynch, Jr.	1749–1779	South Carolina	26	South Carolina	Planter-Lawyer	Died before Independence was won
Thomas McKean	1734–1817	Pennsylvania	42	Delaware	Lawyer	Governor of Pennsylvania 1799–1808
Arthur Middleton	1742–1787	South Carolina	34	South Carolina	Lawyer-Planter	Militia officer during Revolutionary War, captured and imprisoned by British
Lewis Morris	1726–1798	New York	50	New York	Landowner	Major general in state militia during Revolutionary War
Robert Morris	1734–1806	England	42	Pennsylvania	Financier	Signed U.S. Constitution, U.S. Senator from Pennsylvania 1789–1795
John Morton	1724–1777	Pennsylvania	52	Pennsylvania	Farmer	Died before Independence was won
Thomas Nelson	1738–1789	Virginia	37	Virginia	Planter-Merchant	Commander-in-chief of state militia in Revolutionary War, Governor of Virginia 1781
William Paca	1740–1799	Maryland	35	Maryland	Lawyer	Governor of Maryland 1782–1785, U.S. District Court judge 1789–1799
Robert Treat Paine	1731–1814	Massachusetts	45	Massachusetts	Lawyer	Massachusetts Supreme Court justice 1790–1804
John Penn	1740–1788	Virginia	36	North Carolina	Lawyer	Retired by ill health
George Read	1733–1798	Maryland	42	Delaware	Lawyer	Signed U.S. Constitution, U.S. Senator 1789–1793, Chief Justice of Delaware 1793–1798
Caesar Rodney	1728–1784	Delaware	47	Delaware	Planter	Commanded state militia in Revolutionary War, President of Delaware 1778–1781
George Ross	1730–1779	Delaware	46	Pennsylvania	Lawyer	Admiralty judge of Pennsylvania 1779
Benjamin Rush	1745–1813	Pennsylvania	30	Pennsylvania	Physician	Treasurer of U.S. Mint 1797–1813
Edward Rutledge	1749–1800	South Carolina	26	South Carolina	Planter-Lawyer	Governor of South Carolina 1798–1800
Roger Sherman	1721–1793	Massachusetts	55	Connecticut	Merchant-Lawyer	Signed U.S. Constitution, U.S. Senator from Connecticut 1791–1793
James Smith	1719(?)–1806	Ireland	57	Pennsylvania	Lawyer	Pennsylvania Court of Appeals judge 1781
Richard Stockton	1730–1781	New Jersey	45	New Jersey	Lawyer	Imprisoned by British during Revolutionary War
Thomas Stone	1743–1787	Maryland	33	Maryland	Lawyer	Helped frame Articles of Confederation

Name	Born–Died	Birthplace	Age at Adoption of Declaration	Colony Represented	Profession	Later Achievements
George Taylor	1716–1781	Ireland	60	Pennsylvania	Iron-maker	Retired by ill health
Matthew Thornton	1714(?)–1803	Ireland	62	New Hampshire	Physician	Associate justice of New Hampshire Superior Court
George Walton	1741–1804	Virginia	35	Georgia	Lawyer	U.S. Senator from Georgia 1795–1796
William Whipple	1730–1785	Maine	46	New Hampshire	Merchant	Brigadier general during Revolutionary War
William Williams	1731–1811	Connecticut	45	Connecticut	Merchant	Helped frame Articles of Confederation
James Wilson	1742–1798	Scotland	33	Pennsylvania	Lawyer	Signed U.S. Constitution, Associate justice of Supreme Court of U.S. 1789–1798
John Witherspoon	1723–1794	Scotland	53	New Jersey	Clergyman	President, College of New Jersey (now Princeton)
Oliver Wolcott	1726–1797	Connecticut	49	Connecticut	Politician-Soldier	Governor of Connecticut 1796–1797
George Wythe	1726–1806	Virginia	50	Virginia	Lawyer	First professor of law in America, Chancellor of Virginia 1786–1806

THE CONSTITUTION OF THE UNITED STATES

We the People of the United States, in Order to form a more perfect Union, establish Justice, insure domestic Tranquility, provide for the common defence, promote the general Welfare, and secure the Blessings of Liberty to ourselves and our Posterity, do ordain and establish this Constitution for the United States of America.

Article I

Section 1. All legislative Powers herein granted shall be vested in a Congress of the United States, which shall consist of a Senate and House of Representatives.

Section 2. The House of Representatives shall be composed of Members chosen every second Year by the People of the several States, and the Electors in each State shall have the Qualifications requisite for Electors of the most numerous Branch of the State Legislature.

No Person shall be a Representative who shall not have attained to the Age of twenty five Years, and been seven Years a Citizen of the United States, and who shall not, when elected, be an Inhabitant of that State in which he shall be chosen.

Representatives and direct Taxes shall be apportioned among the several States which may be included within this Union, according to their respective Numbers, which shall be determined by adding to the whole Number of free Persons, including those bound to Service for a Term of Years, and excluding Indians not taxed, three fifths of all other Persons. The actual Enumeration shall be made within three Years after the first Meeting of the Congress of the United States, and within every subsequent Term of ten Years, in such Manner as they shall by Law direct. The Number of Representatives shall not exceed one for every thirty Thousand, but each State shall have at Least one Representative; and until such enumeration shall be made, the State of New Hampshire shall be entitled to chuse three, Massachusetts eight, Rhode-Island and Providence Plantations one, Connecticut five, New-York six, New Jersey four, Pennsylvania eight, Delaware one, Maryland six, Virginia ten, North Carolina five, South Carolina five, and Georgia three.

When vacancies happen in the Representation from any State, the Executive Authority thereof shall issue Writs of Election to fill such Vacancies.

The House of Representatives shall chuse their speaker and other Officers; and shall have the sole Power of Impeachment.

Section 3. The Senate of the United States shall be composed of two Senators from each State, chosen by the Legislature thereof, for six Years; and each Senator shall have one Vote.

Immediately after they shall be assembled in Consequence of the first Election, they shall be divided as equally as may be into three Classes. The Seats of the Senators of the first Class shall be vacated at the Expiration of the second Year, of the second Class at the Expiration of the fourth Year, and of the third Class at the Expiration of the sixth Year, so that one third may be chosen every second Year; and if Vacancies happen by Resignation, or otherwise, during the Recess of the Legislature of any State, the Executive thereof may make temporary Appointments until the next Meeting of the Legislature, which shall then fill such Vacancies.

No Person shall be a Senator who shall not have attained to the Age of thirty years, and been nine Years a Citizen of the United States, and who shall not, when elected, be an Inhabitant of that State for which he shall be chosen.

The Vice President of the United States shall be President of the Senate, but shall have no Vote, unless they be equally divided.

The Senate shall chuse their other Officers, and also a President pro tempore, in the Absence of the Vice President, or when he shall exercise the Office of President of the United States.

The Senate shall have the sole Power to try all Impeachments. When sitting for that Purpose, they shall be on Oath or Affirmation. When the President of the United States is tried, the Chief Justice shall preside: And no Person shall be convicted without the Concurrence of two thirds of the Members present.

Judgment in Cases of Impeachment shall not extend further than to removal from Office, and disqualification to hold and enjoy any Office of honor, Trust or Profit under the United States: but the Party convicted shall nevertheless be liable and subject to Indictment, Trial, Judgment and Punishment, according to law.

Section 4. The Times, Places and Manner of holding Elections for Senators and Representatives, shall be prescribed in each State by the Legislature thereof; but the Congress may at any time by Law make or alter such Regulations, except as to the Places of chusing Senators.

The Congress shall assemble at least once in every Year, and such Meeting shall be on the first Monday in December, unless they shall by Law appoint a different Day.

Section 5. Each House shall be the Judge of the Elections, Returns and Qualifications of its own Members, and a Majority of each shall constitute a Quorum to do Business; but a smaller Number may adjourn from day to day, and may be authorized to compel the Attendance of absent Members, in such Manner, and under such Penalties as each House may provide.

Each House may determine the Rules of its Proceedings, punish its Members for disorderly Behaviour, and, with the Concurrence of two thirds, expel a Member.

Each House shall keep a Journal of its Proceedings, and from time to time publish the same, excepting such Parts as may in their Judgment require Secrecy; and the Yeas and Nays of the Members of either House on any question shall, at the Desire of one fifth of those Present, be entered on the Journal.

Neither House, during the Session of Congress, shall, without the Consent of the other, adjourn for more than three days, nor to any other Place than that in which the two Houses shall be sitting.

Section 6. The Senators and Representatives shall receive a Compensation for their Services, to be ascertained by Law, and paid out of the Treasury of the United States. They shall in all Cases, except Treason, Felony and Breach of the Peace, be privileged from Arrest during their Attendance at the Session of their respective Houses, and in going to and returning from the same; and for any Speech or Debate in either House, they shall not be questioned in any other Place.

No Senator or Representative shall, during the Time for which he was elected, be appointed to any civil Office under the Authority of the United States, which shall have been created, or the Emoluments whereof shall have been encreased during such time; and no Person holding any Office under the United States, shall be a Member of either House during his Continuance in Office.

Section 7. All Bills for raising Revenue shall originate in the House of Representatives; but the Senate may propose or concur with Amendments as on other Bills.

Every Bill which shall have passed the House of Representatives and the Senate, shall, before it become a Law, be presented to the President of the United States; If he approve he shall sign it, but if not he shall return it, with his Objections to that House in which it shall have originated, who shall enter the Objections at large on their Journal, and proceed to reconsider it. If after such Reconsideration two thirds of that House shall agree to pass the Bill, it shall be sent, together with the Objections, to the other House, by which it shall likewise be reconsidered, and if approved by two thirds of that House, it shall become a Law. But in all such Cases the Votes of both Houses shall be determined by yeas and Nays, and the Names of the Persons voting for and against the Bill shall be entered on the Journal of each House respectively. If any Bill shall not be returned by the President within ten Days (Sundays excepted) after it shall have been presented to him, the Same shall be a Law, in like Manner as if he had signed it, unless the Congress by their Adjournment prevent its Return, in which Case it shall not be a Law.

Every Order, Resolution, or Vote to which the Concurrence of the Senate and House of Representatives may be necessary (except on a question of Adjournment) shall be presented to the President of the United States; and before the Same shall take Effect, shall be approved by him, or being disapproved by him, shall be repassed by two thirds of the Senate and House of Representatives, according to the Rules and Limitations prescribed in the Case of a Bill.

Section 8. The Congress shall have Power To lay and collect Taxes, Duties, Imposts and Excises, to pay the Debts and provide for the common Defence and general Welfare of the United States; but all Duties, Imposts and Excises shall be uniform throughout the United States;

To Borrow Money on the Credit of the United States;

To regulate Commerce with foreign Nations, and among the several States, and with the Indian Tribes;

To establish an uniform Rule of Naturalization, and uniform Laws on the subject of Bankruptcies throughout the United States;

To coin Money, regulate the Value thereof, and of foreign Coin, and fix the Standard of Weights and Measures;

To provide for the Punishment of counterfeiting the Securities and current Coin of the United States;

To establish Post Offices and post Roads;

To promote the Progress of Science and useful Arts, by securing for limited Times to Authors and Inventors the exclusive Right to their respective Writings and Discoveries;

To constitute Tribunals inferior to the supreme Court;

To define and punish Piracies and Felonies committed on the high Seas, and Offences against the Law of Nations;

To declare War, grant Letters of Marque and Reprisal, and make Rules concerning Captures on Land and Water;

To raise and support Armies, but no Appropriation of Money to that Use shall be for a longer Term than two Years;

To provide and maintain a Navy;

To make Rules for the Government and Regulation of the land and naval Forces;

To provide for calling forth the Militia to execute the Laws of the Union, suppress Insurrections and repel Invasions;

To provide for organizing, arming, and disciplining, the Militia, and for governing such Part of them as may be employed in the Service of the United States, reserving to the States respectively, the Appointment of the Officers, and the Authority of training the Militia according to the discipline prescribed by Congress;

To exercise exclusive Legislation in all Cases whatsoever, over such District (not exceeding ten Miles square) as may, by Cession of particular States, and the Acceptance of Congress, become the Seat of the Government of the United States, and to exercise like Authority over all Places purchased by the Consent of the Legislature of the State in which the Same shall be for the Erection of Forts, Magazines, Arsenals, dock-Yards, and other needful Buildings;—And

To make all Laws which shall be necessary and proper for carrying into Execution the foregoing Powers, and all other Powers vested by this Constitution in the Government of the United States, or in any Department or Officer thereof.

Section 9. The Migration or Importion of such Persons as any of the States now existing shall think proper to admit, shall not be prohibited by the Congress prior to the Year one thousand eight hundred and eight, but a Tax or duty may be imposed on such Importation, not exceeding ten dollars for each Person.

The Privilege of the Writ of Habeas Corpus shall not be suspended, unless when in Cases of Rebellion or Invasion the public Safety may require it.

No Bill of Attainder or ex post facto Law shall be passed.

No Capitation, or other direct, Tax shall be laid, unless in Proportion to the Census or Enumeration herein before directed to be taken.

No Tax or Duty shall be laid on Articles exported from any State.

No Preference shall be given by any Regulation of Commerce or Revenue to the Ports of one State over those of another: nor shall Vessels bound to, or from, one State, be obliged to enter, clear, or pay Duties in another.

No Money shall be drawn from the Treasury, but in Consequence of Appropriations made by Law; and a regular Statement and Account of the Receipts and Expenditures of all public Money shall be published from time to time.

No Title of Nobility shall be granted by the United States: And no Person holding any Office of Profit or Trust under them, shall, without the Consent of the Congress, accept of any present, Emolument, Office, or Title, of any kind whatever, from any King, Prince, or foreign State.

Section 10. No State shall enter into any Treaty, Alliance, or Confederation; grant Letters of Marque and Reprisal; coin Money; emit Bills of Credit; make any Thing but gold and silver Coin a Tender in Payment of Debts; pass any Bill of Attainder, ex post facto Law, or Law impairing the Obligation of Contracts, or grant any Title of Nobility.

No State shall, without the Consent of the Congress, lay any Imposts or Duties on Imports or Exports, except what may be absolutely necessary for executing it's inspection Laws: and the net Produce of all Duties and Imposts, laid by any State on Imports or Exports, shall be for the Use of the Treasury of the United States; and all such Laws shall be subject to the Revision and Controul of the Congress.

No State shall, without the Consent of Congress, lay any Duty of Tonnage, keep Troops, or Ships of War in time of Peace, enter into any Agreement or Compact with another State, or with a foreign Power, or engage in War, unless actually invaded, or in such imminent Danger as will not admit of delay.

Article II

Section 1. The executive Power shall be vested in a President of the United States of America. He shall hold his Office during the Term of four Years, and, together with the Vice President, chosen for the same term, be elected, as follows

Each State shall appoint, in such Manner as the Legislature thereof may direct, a Number of Electors, equal to the whole Number of Senators and Representatives to which the State may be entitled in the Congress: but no Senator or Representative, or Person holding an Office of Trust or Profit under the United States, shall be appointed an Elector.

The Electors shall meet in their respective States, and vote by Ballot for two Persons, of whom one at least shall not be an Inhabitant of the same State with themselves. And they shall make a List of all the Persons voted for, and of the Number of Votes for each; which List they shall sign and certify, and transmit sealed to the Seat of the Government of the United States, directed to the President of the Senate. The President of the Senate shall, in the Presence of the Senate and House of Representatives, open all the Certificates, and the Votes shall then be counted. The Person having the greatest Number of Votes shall be the President, if such Number be a Majority of the whole Number of Electors appointed; and if there be more than one who have such Majority, and have an equal Number of Votes, then the House of Representatives shall immediately chuse by Ballot one of them for President: and if no Person have a Majority, then from the five highest on the List the said House shall in like Manner chuse the President. But in chusing the President, the Votes shall be taken by States, the Representation from each State having one Vote; A quorum for this Purpose shall consist of a Member or Members from two thirds of the States, and a Majority of all the States shall be necessary to a Choice. In every Case, after the Choice of the President, the Person having the greatest Number of Votes of the Electors shall be the Vice President. But if there should remain two or more who have equal Votes, the Senate shall chuse from them by Ballot the Vice President.

The Congress may determine the Time of chusing the Electors, and the Day on which they shall give their Votes; which Day shall be the same throughout the United States.

No Person except a natural born Citizen, or a Citizen of the United States, at the time of the Adoption of this Constitution, shall be eligible to the Office of President; neither shall any Person be eligible to that Office who shall not have attained to the Age of thirty five Years, and been fourteen Years a Resident within the United States.

In Case of the Removal of the President from Office, or of his Death, Resignation, or Inability to discharge the Powers and Duties of the said Office, the Same shall devolve on the Vice President, and the Congress may by Law provide for the Case of Removal, Death, Resignation or Inability, both of the President and Vice President, declaring what Officer shall then act as President, and such Officer shall act accordingly, until the Disability be removed, or a President shall be elected.

The President shall, at stated Times, receive for his Services, a Compensation, which shall neither be encreased nor diminished during the Period for which he shall have been elected, and he shall not receive within that Period any other Emolument from the United States, or any of them.

Before he enter on the Execution of his Office, he shall take the following Oath or Affirmation:—"I do solemnly swear (or affirm) that I will faithfully execute the Office of President of the United States, and will to the best of my Ability, preserve, protect and defend the Constitution of the United States."

Section 2. The President shall be Commander in Chief of the Army and Navy of the United States, and of the Militia of the several States, when called into the actual Service of the United States; he may require the Opinion, in writing, of the principal Officer in each of the executive Departments, upon any Subject relating to the Duties of their respective Offices, and he shall have Power to grant Reprieves and Pardons for Offences against the United States, except in Cases of Impeachment.

He shall have Power, by and with the Advice and Consent of the Senate, to make Treaties, provided two thirds of the Senators present concur; and he shall nominate, and by and with the Advice and Consent of the Senate, shall appoint Ambassadors, other public Ministers and Consuls, Judges of the supreme Court, and all other Officers of the United States, whose Appointments are not herein otherwise provided for, and which shall be established by Law: but the Congress may by Law vest the Appointment of such inferior Officers, as they think proper, in the President alone, in the Courts of Law, or in the Heads of Departments.

The President shall have Power to fill up all Vacancies that may happen during the Recess of the Senate, by granting Commissions which shall expire at the End of their next Session.

Section 3. He shall from time to time give to the Congress Information of the State of the Union, and recommend to their Consideration such Measures as he shall judge necessary and expedient; he may, on extraordinary Occasions, convene both Houses, or either of them, and in Case of Disagreement between them, with Respect to the Time of Adjournment, he may adjourn them to such Time as he shall think proper; he shall receive Ambassadors and other public Ministers; he shall take Care that the Laws be faithfully executed, and shall Commission all the Officers of the United States.

Section 4. The President, Vice President and all civil Officers of the United States, shall be removed from Office on Impeachment for, and Conviction of, Treason, Bribery, or other High Crimes and Misdemeanors.

Article III

Section 1. The judicial Power of the United States, shall be vested in one supreme Court, and in such inferior Courts as the Congress may from time to time ordain and establish. The Judges, both of the supreme and inferior Courts, shall hold their Offices during good Behaviour, and shall, at stated Times, receive for their Services, a Compensation, which shall not be diminished during their Continuance in Office.

Section 2. The judicial Power shall extend to all Cases, in Law and Equity, arising under this Constitution, the Laws of the United States, and Treaties made, or which shall be made, under their Authority;—to all Cases affecting Ambassadors, other public Ministers and Consuls;—to all Cases of admiralty and maritime Jurisdiction;—to Controversies to which the United States shall be a Party;—to Controversies between two or more States; between a State and Citizens of another State;—between Citizens of different States; —between Citizens of the same State claiming Lands under Grants of different States, and between a State, or the Citizens thereof, and foreign States, Citizens or Subjects.

In all Cases affecting Ambassadors, other public Ministers and Consuls, and those in which a State shall be Party, the supreme Court shall have original Jurisdiction. In all the other Cases before mentioned, the supreme Court shall have appellate Jurisdiction, both as to Law and Fact, with such Exceptions, and under such Regulations as the Congress shall make.

The Trial of all Crimes, except in Cases of Impeachment, shall be by Jury; and such Trial shall be held in the State where the said Crimes shall have been committed; but when not committed within any State, the Trial shall be at such Place or Places as the Congress may by Law have directed.

Section 3. Treason against the United States, shall consist only in levying War against them, or in adhering to their Enemies, giving them Aid and Comfort. No Person shall be convicted of Treason unless on the Testimony of two Witnesses to the same overt Act, or on Confession in open Court.

The Congress shall have Power to declare the Punishment of Treason, but no Attainder of Treason shall work Corruption of Blood, or Forfeiture except during the Life of the Person attainted.

Article IV

Section 1. Full Faith and Credit shall be given in each State to the public Acts, Records, and judicial Proceedings of every other State. And the Congress may by general Laws prescribe the Manner in which such Acts, Records and Proceedings shall be proved, and the Effect thereof.

Section 2. The Citizens of each State shall be entitled to all Privileges and Immunities of Citizens in the several States.

A Person charged in any State with Treason, Felony, or other Crime, who shall flee from Justice, and be found in another State, shall on Demand of the executive Authority of the State from which he fled, be delivered up, to be removed to the State having Jurisdiction of the Crime.

No Person held to Service or Labour in one State, under the Laws thereof, escaping into another, shall, in Consequence of any Law or Regulation therein, be discharged from such Service or Labour, but shall be delivered up on Claim of the Party to whom such Service or Labour may be due.

Section 3. New States may be admitted by the Congress into this Union; but no new State shall be formed or erected within the Jurisdiction of any other State; nor any State be formed by the Junction of two or more States, or Parts of States, without the Consent of the Legislatures of the States concerned as well as of the Congress.

The Congress shall have Power to dispose of and make all needful Rules and Regulations respecting the Territory or other Property belonging to the United States; and nothing in this Constitution shall be so construed as to Prejudice any Claims of the United States, or of any particular State.

Section 4. The United States shall guarantee to every State in this Union a Republican Form of Government, and shall protect each of them against Invasion; and on Application of the Legislature, or of the Executive (when the Legislature cannot be convened) against domestic Violence.

Article V

The Congress, whenever two thirds of both Houses shall deem it necessary, shall propose Amendments to this Constitution, or, on the Application of the Legislatures of two thirds of the several States, shall call a Convention for proposing Amendments, which, in either Case, shall be valid to all Intents and Purposes, as Part of this Constitution, when ratified by the Legislatures of three fourths of the several States, or by Conventions in three fourths thereof, as the one or the other Mode of Ratification may be proposed by the Congress; Provided that no Amendment which may be made prior to the Year One thousand eight hundred and eight shall in any Manner affect the first and fourth Clauses in the Ninth Section of the first Article; and that no State, without its Consent, shall be deprived of its equal Suffrage in the Senate.

Article VI

All Debts contracted and Engagements entered into, before the Adoption of this Constitution, shall be as valid against the United States under this Constitution, as under the Confederation.

This Constitution, and the Laws of the United States which shall be made in Pursuance thereof; and all Treaties made, or which shall be made, under the Authority of the United States, shall be the supreme Law of the Land; and the Judges in every State shall be bound thereby, any Thing in the Constitution or Laws of any State to the Contrary notwithstanding.

The Senators and Representatives before mentioned, and the Members of the several State Legislatures, and all executive and judicial Officers, both of the United States and of the several States, shall be bound by Oath or Affirmation, to support this Constitution; but no religious Test shall ever be required as a Qualification to any Office or public Trust under the United States.

Article VII

The Ratification of the Conventions of nine States, shall be sufficient for the Establishment of this Constitution between the States so ratifying the Same.

DONE in Convention by the Unanimous Consent of the States present the Seventeenth Day of September in the Year of our Lord one thousand seven hundred and Eighty seven and of the Independence of the United States of America the Twelfth IN WITNESS whereof We have hereunto subscribed our Names,

G°. WASHINGTON—Presid^t^
and deputy from Virginia

AMENDMENTS

(The first 10 Amendments were ratified December 15, 1791, and form what is known as the "Bill of Rights")

Amendment 1

Congress shall make no law respecting an establishment of religion, or prohibiting the free exercise thereof; or abridging the freedom of speech, or of the press; or the right of the people peaceably to assemble, and to petition the Government for a redress of grievances.

Amendment 2

A well regulated Militia, being necessary to the security of a free State, the right of the people to keep and bear Arms, shall not be infringed.

Amendment 3

No Soldier shall, in time of peace be quartered in any house, without the consent of the Owner, nor in time of war, but in a manner to be prescribed by law.

Amendment 4

The right of the people to be secure in their persons, houses, papers, and effects, against unreasonable searches and seizures, shall not be violated, and no Warrants shall issue, but upon probable cause, supported by Oath or affirmation, and particularly describing the place to be searched, and the persons or things to be seized.

Amendment 5

No person shall be held to answer for a capital, or otherwise infamous crime, unless on a presentment or indictment of a Grand Jury, except in cases arising in the land or naval forces, or in the Militia, when in actual service in time of War or public danger; nor shall any person be subject for the same offence to be twice put in jeopardy of life or limb; nor shall be compelled in any criminal case to be a witness against himself, nor be deprived of life, liberty, or property, without due process of law; nor shall private property be taken for public use, without just compensation.

Amendment 6

In all criminal prosecutions, the accused shall enjoy the right to a speedy and public trial, by an impartial jury of the State and district wherein the crime shall have been committed, which district shall have been previously ascertained by law, and to be informed of the nature and cause of the accusation; to be confronted with the witnesses against him; to have compulsory process for obtaining witnesses in his favor, and to have the Assistance of Counsel for his defence.

Amendment 7

In Suits at common law, where the value in controversy shall exceed twenty dollars, the right of trial by jury shall be preserved, and no fact tried by a jury, shall be otherwise re-examined in any Court of the United States, than according to the rules of the common law.

Amendment 8

Excessive bail shall not be required, nor excessive fines imposed, nor cruel and unusual punishments inflicted.

Amendment 9

The enumeration in the Constitution, of certain rights, shall not be construed to deny or disparage others retained by the people.

Amendment 10

The powers not delegated to the United States by the Constitution, nor prohibited by it to the States, are reserved to the States respectively, or to the people.

Amendment 11

(Ratified February 7, 1795)

The Judicial power of the United States shall not be construed to extend to any suit in law or equity, commenced or prosecuted against one of the United States by Citizens of another State, or by Citizens or Subjects of any Foreign State.

Amendment 12

(Ratified July 27, 1804)

The Electors shall meet in their respective states and vote by ballot for President and Vice-President, one of whom, at least, shall not be an inhabitant of the same state with themselves; they shall name in their ballots the person voted for as President, and in distinct ballots the person voted for as Vice-President, and they shall make distinct lists of all persons voted for as President, and of all persons voted for as Vice-President, and of the number of votes for each, which lists they shall sign and certify, and transmit sealed to the seat of the government of the United States, directed to the President of the Senate;—The President of the Senate shall, in the presence of the Senate and House of Representatives, open all the certificates and the votes shall then be counted;—The person having the greatest number of votes for President, shall be the President, if such number be a majority of the whole number of Electors appointed; and if no person have such majority, then from the persons having the highest numbers not exceeding three on the list of those voted for as President, the House of Representatives shall choose immediately, by ballot, the President. But in choosing the President, the votes shall be taken by states, the representation from each state having one vote; a quorum for this purpose shall consist of a member or members from two-thirds of the states, and a majority of all the states shall be necessary to a choice. And if the House of Representatives shall not choose a President whenever the right of choice shall devolve upon them, before the fourth day of March next following, then the Vice-President shall act as President, as in the case of the death or other constitutional disability of the President.—The person having the greatest number of votes as Vice-President, shall be the Vice-President, if such number be a majority of the whole number of Electors appointed, and if no person have a majority, then from the two highest numbers on the list, the Senate shall choose the Vice-President; a quorum for the purpose shall consist of two-thirds of the whole number of Senators, and a majority of the whole number shall be necessary to a choice. But no person constitutionally ineligible to the office of President shall be eligible to that of Vice-President of the United States.

Amendment 13

(Ratified December 6, 1865)

Section 1. Neither slavery nor involuntary servitude, except as a punishment for crime whereof the party shall have been duly convicted, shall exist within the United States, or any place subject to their jurisdiction.

Section 2. Congress shall have power to enforce this article by appropriate legislation.

Amendment 14

(Ratified July 9, 1868)

Section 1. All persons born or naturalized in the United States, and subject to the jurisdiction thereof, are citizens of the United States and of the State wherein they reside. No State shall make or enforce any law which shall abridge the privileges or immunities of citizens of the United States; nor shall any State deprive any person of life, liberty, or property, without due process of law; nor deny to any person within its jurisdiction the equal protection of the laws.

Section 2. Representatives shall be apportioned among the several States according to their respective numbers, counting the whole number of persons in each State, excluding Indians not taxed. But when the right to vote at any election for the choice of electors for President and Vice President of the United States, Representatives in Congress, the Executive and Judicial officers of a State, or the members of the Legislature thereof, is denied to any of the male inhabitants of such State, being twenty-one years of age, and citizens of the United States, or in any way abridged, except for participation in rebellion, or other crime, the basis of representation therein shall be reduced in the proportion which the number of such male citizens shall bear to the whole number of male citizens twenty-one years of age in such State.

Section 3. No person shall be a Senator or Representative in Congress, or elector of President and Vice President, or hold any office, civil or military, under the United States, or under any State, who, having previously taken an oath, as a member of Congress, or as an officer of the United States, or as a member of any State legislature, or as an executive or judicial officer of any State, to support the Constitution of the United States, shall have engaged in insurrection or rebellion against the same, or given aid or comfort to the enemies thereof. But Congress may by a vote of two-thirds of each House, remove such disability.

Section 4. The validity of the public debt of the United States, authorized by law, including debts incurred for payment of pensions and bounties for services in suppressing insurrection or rebellion, shall not be questioned. But neither the United States nor any State shall assume or pay any debt or obligation incurred in aid of insurrection or rebellion against the United States, or any claim for the loss or emancipation of any slave; but all such debts, obligations and claims shall be held illegal and void.

Section 5. The Congress shall have power to enforce, by appropriate legislation, the provisions of this article.

Amendment 15

(Ratified February 3, 1870)

Section 1. The right of citizens of the United States to vote shall not be denied or abridged by the United States or by any State on account of race, color, or previous condition of servitude.

Section 2. The Congress shall have power to enforce this article by appropriate legislation.

Amendment 16

(Ratified February 3, 1913)

The Congress shall have power to lay and collect taxes on incomes, from whatever source derived, without apportionment among the several States, and without regard to any census or enumeration.

Amendment 17

(Ratified April 8, 1913)

The Senate of the United States shall be composed of two Senators from each State, elected by the people thereof for six years; and each Senator shall have one vote. The electors in each State shall have the qualifications requisite for electors of the most numerous branch of the State legislatures.

When vacancies happen in the representation of any State in the Senate, the executive authority of such State shall issue writs of election to fill such vacancies: *Provided*, That the legislature of any State may empower the executive thereof to make temporary appointments until the people fill the vacancies by election as the legislature may direct.

This amendment shall not be so construed as to affect the election or term of any Senator chosen before it becomes valid as part of the Constitution.

Amendment 18

(Ratified January 16, 1919)

Section 1. After one year from the ratification of this article the manufacture, sale, or transportation of intoxicating liquors within, the importation thereof into, or the exportation thereof from the United States and all territory subject to the jurisdiction thereof for beverage purposes is hereby prohibited.

Section 2. The Congress and the several States shall have concurrent power to enforce this article by appropriate legislation.

Section 3. This article shall be inoperative unless it shall have been ratified as an amendment to the Constitution by the legislatures of the several States, as provided in the Constitution, within seven years from the date of the submission hereof to the States by the Congress.

Amendment 19

(Ratified August 18, 1920)

The right of citizens of the United States to vote shall not be denied or abridged by the United States or by any State on account of sex.

Congress shall have power to enforce this article by appropriate legislation.

Amendment 20

(Ratified January 23, 1933)

Section 1. The terms of the President and Vice President shall end at noon on the 20th day of January, and the terms of Senators and Representatives at noon on the 3d day of January, of the years in which such terms would have ended if this article had not been ratified; and the terms of their successors shall then begin.

Section 2. The Congress shall assemble at least once in every year, and such meeting shall begin at noon on the 3d day of January, unless they shall by law appoint a different day.

Section 3. If, at the time fixed for the beginning of the term of the President, the President elect shall have died, the Vice President elect shall become President. If a President shall not have been chosen before the time fixed for the beginning of his term, or if the President elect shall have failed to qualify, then the Vice President elect shall act as President until a President shall have qualified; and the Congress may by law provide for the case wherein neither a President elect nor a Vice President elect shall have qualified, declaring who shall then act as President, or the manner in which one who is to act shall be selected, and such person shall act accordingly until a President or Vice President shall have qualified.

Section 4. The Congress may by law provide for the case of the death of any of the persons from whom the House of Representatives may choose a President whenever the right of choice shall have devolved upon them, and for the case of the death of any of the persons from whom the Senate may choose a Vice President whenever the right of choice shall have devolved upon them.

Section 5. Sections 1 and 2 shall take effect on the 15th day of October following the ratification of this article.

Section 6. This article shall be inoperative unless it shall have been ratified as an amendment to the Constitution by the legislatures of three-fourths of the several States within seven years from the date of its submission.

Amendment 21

(Ratified December 5, 1933)

Section 1. The eighteenth article of amendment to the Constitution of the United States is hereby repealed.

Section 2. The transportation or importation into any State, Territory, or possession of the United States for delivery or use therein of intoxicating liquors, in violation of the laws thereof, is hereby prohibited.

Section 3. This article shall be inoperative unless it shall have been ratified as an amendment to the Constitution by conventions in the several States, as provided in the Constitution, within seven years from the date of the submission hereof to the States by the Congress.

Amendment 22

(Ratified February 27, 1951)

Section 1. No person shall be elected to the office of the President more than twice, and no person who has held the office of President, or acted as President, for more than two years of a term to which some other person was elected President shall be elected to the office of the President more than once. But this Article shall not apply to any person holding the office of President when this Article was proposed by the Congress, and shall not prevent any person who may be holding the office of President, or acting as President, during the term within which this Article becomes operative from holding the office of President or acting as President during the remainder of such term.

Section 2. This article shall be inoperative unless it shall have been ratified as an amendment to the Constitution by the legislatures of three-fourths of the several States within seven years from the date of its submission to the States by the Congress.

Amendment 23

(Ratified March 29, 1961)

Section 1. The District constituting the seat of Government of the United States shall appoint in such manner as the Congress may direct:

A number of electors of President and Vice President equal to the whole number of Senators and Representatives in Congress to which the District would be entitled if it were a State, but in no event more than the least populous State; they shall be in addition to those appointed by the States, but they shall be considered, for the purposes of the election of President and Vice President, to be electors appointed by a State; and they shall meet in the District and perform such duties as provided by the twelfth article of amendment.

Section 2. The Congress shall have power to enforce this article by appropriate legislation.

Amendment 24

(Ratified January 23, 1964)

Section 1. The right of citizens of the United States to vote in any primary or other election for President or Vice President, for electors for President or Vice President, or for Senator or Representative in Congress, shall not be denied or abridged by the United States or any State by reason of failure to pay any poll tax or other tax.

Section 2. The Congress shall have power to enforce thi: article by appropriate legislation.

Amendment 25

(Ratified February 10, 1967)

Section 1. In case of the removal of the President from office or his death or resignation, the Vice President shall become President.

Section 2. Whenever there is a vacancy in the office of the Vice President, the President shall nominate a Vice President who shall take the office upon confirmation by a majority vote of both houses of Congress.

Section 3. Whenever the President transmits to the President pro tempore of the Senate and the Speaker of the House of Representatives his written declaration that he is unable to discharge the powers and duties of his office, and until he transmits to them a written declaration to the contrary, such powers and duties shall be discharged by the Vice President as Acting President.

Section 4. Whenever the Vice President and a majority of either the principal officers of the executive departments or of such other body as Congress may by law provide, transmit to the President pro tempore of the Senate and the Speaker of the House of Representatives their written declaration that the President is unable to discharge the powers and duties of his office, the Vice President shall immediately assume the powers and duties of the office as Acting President.

Thereafter, when the President transmits to the President pro tempore of the Senate and the Speaker of the House of Representatives his written declaration that no inability exists, he shall resume the powers and duties of his office unless the Vice President and a majority of either the principal officers of the executive department or of such other body as Congress may by law provide, transmit within four days to the President pro tempore of the Senate and the Speaker of the House of Representatives their written declaration that the President is unable to discharge the powers and duties of his office. Thereupon Congress shall decide the issue, assembling within 48 hours for that purpose if not in session. If the Congress, within 21 days after receipt of the latter written declaration, or, if Congress is not in session, within 21 days after Congress is required to assemble, determines by two-thirds vote of both houses that the President is unable to discharge the powers and duties of his office, the Vice President shall continue to discharge the same as Acting President; otherwise, the President shall resume the powers and duties of his office.

Amendment 26

(Ratified June 30, 1971)

Section 1. The right of citizens of the United States, who are eighteen years of age or older, to vote shall not be denied or abridged by the United States or by any State on account of age.

Section 2. The Congress shall have power to enforce this article by appropriate legislation.

THE SIGNERS OF THE UNITED STATES CONSTITUTION

Name	Born–Died	Birthplace	Age at Signing of Constitution	Colony Represented	Profession	Later Achievements
Abraham Baldwin	1754–1807	Connecticut	32	Georgia	Lawyer	U.S. Senator from Georgia 1799–1807
Richard Bassett	1745–1815	Maryland	42	Delaware	Lawyer	Governor of Delaware 1799–1800
Gunning Bedford, Jr.	1747–1812	Philadelphia	40	Delaware	Lawyer	U.S. District judge 1789–1812
John Blair	1732–1800	Virginia	55	Virginia	Lawyer	Associate justice, Supreme Court of U.S. 1789–1796
William Blount	1749–1800	North Carolina	38	North Carolina	Politician	President, Tennessee state constitutional convention 1796
David Brearley	1745–1790	New Jersey	42	New Jersey	Lawyer	U.S. District judge 1789–1790
Jacob Broom	1752–1810	Delaware	35	Delaware	Businessman	Built first cotton mill in Wilmington, Del.
Pierce Butler	1744–1822	Ireland	42	South Carolina	Soldier-Planter	U.S. Senator from South Carolina 1789–1796, 1802–1806
Daniel Carroll	1730–1796	Maryland	56	Maryland	Landowner	U.S. Representative from Maryland 1789–1791
George Clymer	1739–1813	Philadelphia	48	Pennsylvania	Banker	U.S. Representative from Pennsylvania 1789–1791
Jonathan Dayton	1760–1824	New Jersey	26	New Jersey	Lawyer	U.S. Representative from New Jersey 1791–1799; U.S. Senator 1799–1805
John Dickinson	1732–1808	Maryland	54	Delaware	Lawyer	President of Delaware 1781–1782; President of Pennsylvania 1782–1785
William Few	1748–1828	Maryland	39	Georgia	Politician	U.S. Senator from Georgia 1789–1795
Thomas FitzSimons	1741–1811	Ireland	46	Pennsylvania	Businessman	U.S. Representative from Pennsylvania 1789–1795
Benjamin Franklin	1706–1790	Massachusetts	81	Pennsylvania	Publisher	Retired
Nicholas Gilman	1755–1814	New Hampshire	32	New Hampshire	Politician	U.S. Representative 1789–1797; U.S. Senator 1805–1814
Nathaniel Gorham	1738–1796	Massachusetts	49	Massachusetts	Businessman	Became a land speculator
Alexander Hamilton	1757–1804	West Indies	30/32	New York	Lawyer	Secretary of the Treasury 1789–1795
Jared Ingersoll	1749–1822	Connecticut	38	Pennsylvania	Lawyer	Federalist candidate for Vice President of U.S. in 1812
Daniel of St. Thomas Jenifer	1723–1790	Maryland	64	Maryland	Landowner	Retired
William Samuel Johnson	1727–1819	Connecticut	59	Connecticut	Lawyer-Educator	President of Columbia College 1787–1800
Rufus King	1755–1827	Massachusetts	32	Massachusetts	Lawyer	U.S. Senator from New York 1789–1796, 1813–1825

Name	Born–Died	Birthplace	Age at Signing of Constitution	Colony Represented	Profession	Later Achievements
John Langdon	1741–1819	New Hampshire	46	New Hampshire	Shipowner	Governor of New Hampshire 1805–1809, 1810–1812
William Livingston	1723–1790	New York	63	New Jersey	Lawyer	Governor of New Jersey 1776–1790
James Madison, Jr.	1751–1836	Virginia	36	Virginia	Politician	President of U.S. 1809–1817
James McHenry	1753–1816	Ireland	33	Maryland	Physician	Secretary of War 1796–1800
Thomas Mifflin	1744–1800	Philadelphia	43	Pennsylvania	Politician	Governor of Pennsylvania 1790–1799
Gouverneur Morris	1752–1816	New York	35	Pennsylvania	Lawyer	U.S. Senator from Pennsylvania 1800–1803
Robert Morris	1734–1806	England	53	Pennsylvania	Financier	U.S. Senator from Pennsylvania 1789–1795
William Paterson	1745–1806	Ireland	42	New Jersey	Lawyer	Associate justice of Supreme Court of U.S. 1793–1806
Charles Pinckney	1757–1824	South Carolina	29	South Carolina	Lawyer	Governor of South Carolina 1789–1792; 1796–1798; 1806–1808
Charles Cotesworth Pinckney	1746–1825	South Carolina	41	South Carolina	Lawyer	Federalist candidate for President of U.S. 1804 and 1808
George Read	1733–1798	Maryland	53	Delaware	Lawyer	Chief justice of Delaware 1793–1798
John Rutledge	1739–1800	South Carolina	48	South Carolina	Lawyer	Chief justice of the United States 1795
Roger Sherman	1721–1793	Massachusetts	66	Connecticut	Merchant-Lawyer	U.S. Senator from Connecticut 1791–1793
Richard Dobbs Spaight	1758–1802	North Carolina	29	North Carolina	Politician	Governor of North Carolina 1792–1795
George Washington	1732–1799	Virginia	55	Virginia	Soldier-Planter	President of U.S. 1789–1797
Hugh Williamson	1735–1819	Pennsylvania	51	North Carolina	Physician	U.S. Representative from North Carolina 1790–1793
James Wilson	1742–1798	Scotland	44	Pennsylvania	Lawyer	Associate justice of Supreme Court of U.S. 1789–1798

THE DECADES
of the
70s and 80s

The Decade of the 70s

The Nigerian Civil War ended January 12, 1970, after 31 months of fighting with 2,000,000 killed.

On April 30 President Nixon announced that he had ordered U.S. troops into Cambodia in an effort to destroy Communist supply camps.

Four Kent State, Ohio, students were shot and killed on May 14 by National Guardsmen who had been called onto the campus after the burning of the school's ROTC building, in student protests against the Cambodian invasion.

More than 50,000 persons were reported dead and 20,000 missing May 30 following an earthquake in Peru, regarded as the worst to have been recorded in the Western Hemisphere.

Palestinian guerrillas clashed with the army of King Hussein of Jordan June 7 in and around Amman, killing and wounding hundreds.

On July 1 the nation's most liberal abortion law went into effect in New York State.

A Middle East cease-fire began along the Suez Canal zone August 7.

President Nixon signed a bill transforming the Post Office into an independent, self supporting agency on August 12. The act removed the position of Postmaster General from the Cabinet.

Salvador Allende Gossens, a Marxist-Communist, was elected President of Chile September 4.

Hostilities between the army of King Hussein of Jordan and the Palestinian guerrillas erupted into civil war September 17.

President Gamal Abdel Nasser of Egypt died September 28 of a heart attack at age 52.

Anwar Sadat was named to succeed Nasser as President of Egypt October 3.

General Charles de Gaulle, former president of France, died of a heart attack November 9 at the age of 79.

A cyclone and tidal wave struck East Pakistan November 12 killing an estimated 500,000 people.

On December 22 the U.S. Supreme Court ruled that 18-year-olds could vote in federal elections.

On January 25, 1971, the U.S. Supreme Court barred discrimination by sex in hiring.

Apollo 14 became the third successful U.S. mission to the moon on February 5.

South Vietnamese troops invaded Laos to attack Communist supply lines February 8.

Great Brltain and the Republic of Ireland adopted decimal currency February 15.

The U.S. on March 15 ended the requirement that its citizens have special passport validation for travel to Communist China.

Pakistani President Yahya Khan opened discussion in Dacca March 16 with Sheik Mujibur Rahman of East Pakistan on East's demands for self rule.

Prime Minister Chichester-Clark of Northern Ireland resigned March 20 and Brian Faulkner, a Protestant moderate, was elected March 23.

Civil War broke out March 25 in East Pakistan and rebels proclaimed the independent nation of Bangladesh.

Restrictions on trade with Communist China were eased April 14 by the U.S.

On April 17 Egypt, Syria, and Libya agreed to form an Arab Federation to be approved by plebiscite in each country.

Cuban Premier Fidel Castro welcomed President Salvador Allende Gossens of Chile after Allende's Marxist-Communist government had won the presidency in 1970. (UPI PHOTO)

Amtrak, the National Railroad Passenger Corporation, began operation May 1, partially run by the U.S. government.

A court order on June 2 halted the *New York Times* publication of a series of artlcles based on a top-secret Pentagon study of the Vietnam war. The study indicated that the Johnson administration had planned major military action even before the Tonkin Gulf incident.

On June 30 the U.S. Supreme Court upheld the right of the *Times* and other newspapers to publish the Pentagon papers.

Three Soviet cosmonauts were found dead of unknown causes when their spacecraft Soyuz 11 returned to earth June 30 after setting a 24-day endurance record in the orbital space laboratory Salyut.

The 26th Amendment to the Constitution was approved June 30, lowering the voting age in all federal, state, and local elections to 18.

The new U.S. Postal Service began operation July 1.

President Nixon on July 15 announced plans for a trip to China to visit with the Chinese Communist leaders.

On July 28 the U.S. announced an end to reconnaissance flights over China.

On August 2 the U.S. government announced in the U.N that it would no longer oppose seating of the People's Republic of China.

Apollo 15 returned to earth August 7, its crew having spent three days—July 31-August 2—on the moon.

Rioting occurred in Northern Ireland August 9 after emergency powers were invoked by the government to outlaw the Irish Republican Army (IRA).

President Nixon on August 15 announced a 90-day freeze on wages, prices, and rents, and ended convertibility of the dollar into gold. A 10 per cent surcharge was placed on imports.

A referendum September 1 endorsed the merger of Egypt, Libya, and Syria into a federation.

Associate Justice Hugo L. Black retired from the U.S. Supreme Court September 17.

Israel and Egypt exchanged fire across the Suez Canal for the first time since the cease-fire of August 1970.

Associate Justice John M. Harlan retired from the U.S. Supreme Court September 23.

The United Nations voted September 25 to admit Communist China as a member of the general body and the security council and to expel the Nationalist Chinese of Taiwan representatives who had held those seats.

The British House of Commons on September 28 approved entry of Great Britain into the Common Market.

The U.S. space probe Mariner 9 was successfully placed in orbit around Mars November 13.

The U.S. conducted its most powerful underground nuclear test in history November 6 on Amchitka in the Aleutian Islands.

Communist China tested a 20-kiloton nuclear device November 18.

Agreement between Britain and Rhodesia ending constitutional dispute was reached November 24, leading eventually to majority rule by the predominantly black population.

Premier Wasfi Tell of Jordan was assassinated November 28 by Palestinian guerrillas.

Full-scale war broke out between India and Pakistan December 3, with the Indians supporting the rebels of Bangladesh. India recognized Bangladesh on December 6.

Lewis F. Powell was confirmed as Associate Justice of the U.S. Supreme Court on December 6; William H. Rehnquist was similarly confirmed December 10.

Pakistani forces in the East on December 16 surrendered to Indian forces surrounding Dacca.

The Chinese tested a nuclear device of less than 20 kilotons on January 7, 1972.

John N. Mitchell resigned January 15 as Attorney General to head President Nixon's reelection campaign.

British troops killed 13 civilians during a protest in Northern Ireland January 30.

Barbed wire barricades marked the border of Catholic-Protestant areas in Belfast, Northern Ireland, when British troops were sent to prevent religious civil war in 1971. (UPI PHOTO)

President Richard Nixon was greeted by Chairman Mao Tse-tung, upon Nixon's historic trip to Peking in 1972. (UPI PHOTO)

On the eve of his departure for a visit to China, President Nixon announced February 17 that trade with China would be on the same basis as that with the Soviet Union.

The Irish Republican Army (IRA) on February 22 exploded a bomb at Aldershot army base, England, killing 7 and wounding 14.

President Nixon completed his China visit on February 27; he and Chou En-lai issued a statement indicating agreement on increased contact between the two nations and eventual withdrawal of U.S. troops from Taiwan.

U.S. space probe Pioneer 10 was launched March 2 on its way to a Jupiter rendezvous in December 1973.

Major league baseball players went on strike April 1 in a pension dispute with ball club owners.

Bangladesh on April 18 joined the Commonwealth of Nations.

J. Edgar Hoover, long-time head of the FBI, died in Washington, D.C., May 2.

President Nixon on May 8 ordered the mining of Haiphong harbor.

Governor George C. Wallace of Alabama was shot and seriously wounded May 18 while campaigning for the Democratic nomination for president.

On May 22 President Nixon visited Moscow to meet with leaders of the U.S.S.R.

On June 17 the Democratic National Headquarters in the Watergate Hotel in Washington was burglarized by five men who were captured in the offices.

President Nixon on August 29 declared, "I can say categorically that. . .investigation indicates that no one in this administration, presently employed, was involved in this very bizarre incident." (the Watergate Burglary)

President Nixon was elected to a second term as President November 7 in a landslide victory in which he carried 49 of the 50 states.

Eugene A. Cernan and Harrison H. Schmitt, two American astronauts, landed on the moon December 11.

Harry Truman, 33rd President of the United States, died December 26.

President Richard M. Nixon and Vice President Spiro T. Agnew were sworn in for their second terms January 20, 1973.

Lyndon B. Johnson, 36th President of the United States, died January 22.

A Vietnam peace agreement was signed in Paris January 30.

President Nixon reviewed Chinese troops with Premier Chou En-lai at his side, during his visit to China. (UPI PHOTO)

Senator Sam Ervin of South Carolina, chairman of the Watergate Committee, and co-chairman Senator Howard Baker of Tennessee, far left, studying documents with committee aides. (UPI PHOTO)

The first U.S. prisoners freed by North Vietnam were flown to the Philippines February 12.

Pablo Picasso, one of the greatest artists of the 20th century, died April 8.

Attorney General Richard Kleindienst and presidential aides John Ehrlichman, H. R. Haldeman, and John Dean were forced to resign April 30 because of the Watergate scandal.

Secretariat on June 9 became the first horse since 1948 to win thoroughbred racing's Triple Crown—the Kentucky Derby, the Preakness, and the Belmont Stakes.

Three Skylab astronauts returned to earth June 22 after spending a record 28 days in space.

The Senate Watergate committee on July 16 learned that since 1971 Nixon's conversations and telephone calls had been taped. On the same day the U.S. Department of Defense admitted that the U.S. had carried out bombing of Cambodia and Laos before 1970 and that officials falsified records of the bombings.

Chile's president Salvador Allende Gossens reportedly committed suicide when the military overthrew his government September 11.

Juan Peron and his wife Isabel were elected President and Vice President of Argentina September 23.

Egyptian and Syrian forces on October 6 attacked Israeli-held territory.

Vice President Agnew resigned October 10 pleading no contest to a charge of income tax evasion.

On October 20 Nixon ordered Watergate special prosecutor Archibald Cox fired and Attorney General Elliott L. Richardson resigned in protest in a flurry of Watergate action that became known as "the Saturday Night Massacre."

Time magazine on November 4 in its first editorial in 50 years called on President Nixon to resign.

Egypt and Israel signed a cease-fire agreement November 11.

President Nixon on November 16 signed a bill authorizing construction of the Alaskan pipeline.

Gerald R. Ford was sworn in as vice president December 6.

The Senate Watergate committee on December 18 voted to subpoena tapes and documents related to Watergate.

On January 4, 1974, Nixon refused to surrender subpoenaed tapes and documents to the Senate Watergate committee.

Israeli and Egyptian forces were separated along the Suez Canal by a signed agreement between the two countries.

President Nixon smiles despite the taunts and signs urging him to resign as he spoke during a political trip to Michigan at the height of the Watergate crisis. (UPI PHOTO)

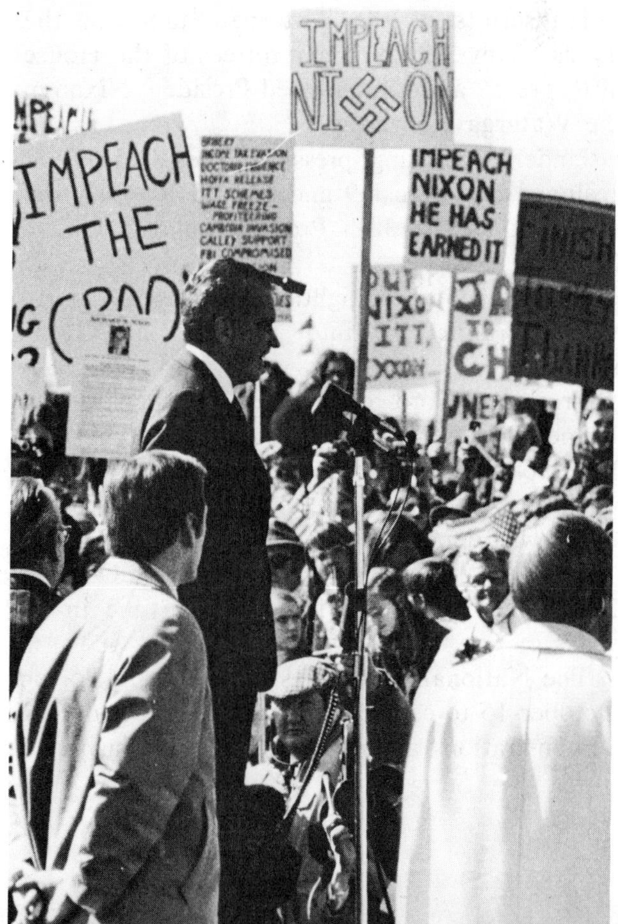

Newspaper heiress Patricia Hearst was kidnapped February 4 by radicals calling themselves the Symbionese Liberation Army.

Three astronauts splashed down February 8, having spent a record 84 days in space aboard the orbiting Skylab.

Nobel prizewinning author Aleksandr Solzhenitsyn was expelled by the Soviet Union February 13.

Hank Aaron of the Atlanta Braves broke Babe Ruth's long-standing home run record when he hit his 715th home run on April 8.

President Nixon on May 22 refused to honor a subpoena from the House Watergate committee for related materials.

Israel and Syria on May 31 signed an agreement to separate their armed forces from the combat zone.

Juan Peron died and his wife Isabel became president of Argentina May 31. She was the first woman head of state in the Americas.

The U.S. Supreme Court ruled 8-0 on July 24 that President Nixon could not use executive privilege to deny Congress and the courts access to Watergate documents.

During hearings held July 27-30 the House Judiciary committee voted three articles of impeachment against Nixon.

Transcripts of the Watergate tapes in the hands of investigating committees of the House of Representatives implicated President Nixon in the Watergate cover-up.

Under increasing pressure, President Nixon resigned on August 9 and Gerald R. Ford was sworn in as the 38th President of the United States.

After a month of fighting, Cyprus was partitioned August 16 into Turkish and Greek sections.

President Ford on September 8 pardoned former President Nixon for any crimes he may have committed as president.

Haile Selassie, emperor of Ethiopia since 1930, was deposed September 12.

The Dow Jones industrial average on October 3 dropped below 600 for the first time in 12 years.

The National Guard was called out in Boston October 15 to control violence brought about by demonstrations against court ordered busing of students to achieve integrated schools.

President Nixon is hugged by a tearful daughter Tricia after he announces his resignation from the presidency. (UPI PHOTO)

Nelson A. Rockefeller was sworn in as vice president on December 19.

On January 1, 1975, Nixon administration officials John Mitchell, H.R. Haldeman, John Ehrlichman, and Robert Mardian were convicted of Watergate cover-ups.

Construction on the Alaskan pipeline to transport oil from Prudhoe Bay south was begun March 9.

King Faisal, head of Saudi Arabia, was assassinated by a nephew March 25.

An Air Force cargo jet carrying Vietnamese orphans to the U.S. crashed March 29 killing 200.

Chiang Kai-shek, president of Nationalist China on Taiwan and the World War II leader of mainland China, died April 5.

The Cambodian government fell to communist rebels April 17.

Communist forces overran Saigon, capital of South Vietnam April 30.

U.S. forces recaptured the merchant ship *Mayaguez* and its crew from the Cambodians May 14.

The Suez Canal, closed for eight years, was reopened by Egypt June 5.

The Rockefeller Commission report on the Central Intelligence Agency released June 10 documented illegal spying on U.S. citizens.

The Soyuz and Apollo spacecrafts linked 140 miles above the earth July 17 in the first U.S.-Soviet joint spaceflight.

Thirty-five nations ratified European boundaries established at the end of World War II at the Conference on Security and Cooperation in Europe August 1 in Helsinki, Finland.

Israel and Egypt agreed September 1 to further troop disengagements.

In an apparent assassination attempt, Lynett Fromme on September 5 pointed a pistol at President Ford and attempted to pull the trigger before secret service agents wrested the gun from her.

The first American saint, Mother Elizabeth Ann Bayley Seton, was canonized by Pope Paul VI on September 14.

Missing newspaper heiress Patricia Hearst, who had been kidnapped by radical political activists and then apparently joined their cause, was captured September 18.

Sara Jane Moore fired a shot from a hand gun at President Ford September 22 as he was entering his car in San Francisco.

New York City narrowly averted default October 17 by borrowing from a union pension fund.

Angola became an independent nation on November 12 and three political factions fought a civil war for control of the government.

William O. Douglas, a member of the U.S. Supreme Court for 36 years, resigned his position because of ill health November 12.

Generalissimo Francisco Franco of Spain died November 20 and was succeeded by King Juan Carlos I, the first Spanish monarch since 1931.

John Paul Stevens, named to the Supreme Court by President Ford, was sworn in as associate justice December 19.

Chou En-lai, premier of the People's Republic of China since its founding in 1949, died in Peking January 8, 1976.

An earthquake in Guatemala on February 4 killed more than 20,000, injured nearly 75,000, and left more than a million persons homeless.

On April 25 Portugal held the first free parliamentary elections in that country in 50 years.

French and British supersonic jets on May 24 began regular flights from London and Paris to Washington, D.C., on a trial basis.

Teton Dam in Idaho burst June 5, forcing the evacuation of about 40,000 persons.

The U.S. Supreme Court on July 2 ruled 7-2 that the death penalty was not inherently cruel and unusual punishment.

North and South Vietnam on July 2 were officially reunited for the first time in 20 years.

Israeli forces raided Entebbe Airport in Uganda July 3 to free hostages held by pro-Palestinian hijackers.

The U.S. celebrated its Bicentennial July 4.

The twenty-first Olympic Games opened in Montreal, Quebec, July 17. Viking 1 landed on Mars August 2 and began transmitting color photographs of the surface back to earth.

Viking 2 landed on the Mars surface September 3.

Mao Tse-tung, founder of the People's Republic of China, died in Peking September 9.

A Yugoslavian and a British plane collided September 10 killing 176 persons, the worst midair disaster in history.

Patricia Hearst on September 24 was sentenced to seven years in prison for bank robbery and using a firearm to commit a felony.

Jimmy Carter was elected the 39th President of the United States November 2.

On January 1, 1977, the Episcopal Church ordained its first woman priest at services in Indianapolis.

Convicted murderer Gary Gilmore was executed January 17 by a Utah firing squad in the first application of the death penalty in the U.S. in almost ten years.

Jimmy Carter was inaugurated as the 39th President of the United States January 20.

President Carter on January 21 pardoned some 10,000 men who illegally evaded the U.S. military draft between August 4, 1963, and March 28, 1973.

A dramatization of Alex Haley's book *Roots* was viewed January 23-30 by about 130 million persons, the largest audience in television history.

An earthquake March 4 destroyed much of Bucharest, the capital of Rumania, and claimed more than 1,500 lives in southeastern Europe.

President Carter, in an unprecendented two-hour radio broadcast March 5, answered telephone calls and questions from ordinary citizens.

The Pakistan People's Party, headed by Prime Minister Zulfikar Ali Bhutto won a sweeping victory March 7 in the country's first general election since 1970.

President Carter, in his first address to the United Nations, on March 17 urged a world arms reduction program and called for an advance in the cause of human rights.

Prime Minister Indira Gandhi of India lost her parliamentary seat in elections held March 20, and the Congress party, in control of the government since 1947, lost to the Jenata party headed by Morarji R. Desai, who became the new prime minister.

Two Boeing 747 Jumbo jets collided at the airport of Tenerife, Canary Islands March 27, killing 582 persons in the worst air disaster in history.

Yitzhak Rabin withdrew as Labor Party candidate for prime minister of Israel April 8 after admitting violation of Israeli currency laws.

President Carter on May 23 signed a tax bill reducing federal income taxes by $34.2 billion over the next 28 months.

Officials of the United States and Vietnam met in Paris May 3 to confer on the resumption of normal diplomatic relations.

Queen Elizabeth II of England celebrated the twenty-fifth anniversary of her reign on June 5.

Leonid I. Brezhnev, general secretary of the Soviet Communist Party, was elected chief of state by the Supreme Soviet meeting on June 15.

The first oil from Alaska's North Slope began flowing June 20 through the 800-mile-long Trans-Alaska pipeline.

Menachem Begin took office as prime minister of Israel following elections June 21 that defeated the Labor Party and allowed the Likud Party to organize a coalition government.

Djibouti, formerly French Somaliland, became Africa's 49th independent country on June 27.

A massive power failure plunged New York City into darkness July ll; looters ransacked thousands of stores for food, clothing, furniture and even automobiles.

President Carter on August 4 approved the creation of the Department of Energy with cabinet status. James Schlesinger, former head of the CIA and Secretary of the Department of Defense, was named to the post.

Representatives of Panama and the U.S. on August 10 reached an agreement on a new accord that would give Panama total control over the Panama Canal and the Panama Canal Zone by the year 2000.

President Jimmy Carter, left, and Panamanian leader General Omar Torrijos, sign a Panama Canal Treaty in September 1977 while Alejandro Orfila, OAS secretary General, center, looks on. Behind them are aides and officials of both governments. (UPI PHOTO)

China detonated its 22nd nuclear device September 17.

Vietnam and Djibouti were admitted to membership at the September 20 opening of the 32nd annual session of the UN General Assembly.

Bert Lance, a long-time friend and advisor to President Carter, resigned September 21 as director of the Office of Management and Budget, amid charges of earlier financial improprieties.

Indira Gandhi, former prime minister of India, was arrested October 3 on two charges of corruption while in office.

The U.S. Supreme Court allowed the supersonic Concorde jets to begin test flights to New York City's Kennedy International Airport

A West German commando unit October 18 stormed a hijacked Lufthansa 737 at Mogadishu, Somalia, killing three hijackers but freeing all 86 hostages unharmed.

The civilian government of Thailand was ousted October 20 by the same military junta which installed it one year earlier.

The United States canceled its membership in the International Labor organization November 1. On the same day President Carter signed into law legislation that would increase the minimum wage by 45 per cent over a three-year period.

The UN Security Council on November 4 unanimously approved a resolution calling for an immediate ban on military aid to South Africa because of that country's repressive social policies.

In a dramatic and historic appearance before the Knesset (parliament) of Israel, President Anwar Sadat of Egypt called for the withdrawal of all Israeli troops from Arab lands occupied since the 1967 Arab-Israeli War. President Sadat had initiated peace moves that led the Israeli government to invite him to Jerusalem.

Jean-Bedel Bokassa, head of the Central African Republic government, on December 4 proclaimed the country to be an empire and crowned himself emperor as Bokassa I.

The government of South Africa on December 10 granted independence to Bophuthatswana, a landlocked black homeland consisting of six separate districts.

President Carter signed a new social security tax bill December 20 which would levy progressively larger contributions from employers and employees over the next three years.

Thousands of U.S. farmers demonstrated in Washington, D.C., December 10, tying up traffic with farm equipment in a protest against low prices for their products.

Israel's Prime Minister Menachem Begin and Egyptian President Anwar Sadat met in Ismailia December 26 to discuss peace in the Middle East.

Cambodia broke off diplomatic relations December 31 with neighboring Vietnam after several weeks of border clashes.

An explosion of an Air India Boeing 747 at Bombay, India, January 1, 1978, killed 213 persons.

Senator and former Vice President Hubert H. Humphrey died of cancer January 13 in Minneapolis.

A snowstorm dumped up to 31 inches of snow on the Midwestern states January 25-26.

The U.S. Department of Commerce on January 30 reported a record trade deficit of $26.72 billion for 1977.

The New England states were paralyzed by a heavy snowfall February 5-7.

Leon Spinks won the world heavyweight boxing championship by defeating Muhammad Ali February 15.

The U.S. Senate ratified the Panama Canal treaty on March 16. On the same day former Italian Prime Minister Aldo Moro was kidnapped and his five bodyguards killed by a leftist terrorist group. Moro's body was found months later in a stolen car in Rome.

The supertanker *Amoco Cadiz* spilled a record 1.6 million barrels of crude oil after striking a reef off France's Brittany coast on March 17.

Woody Allen's film *Annie Hall* won Oscars for best picture, best actress, best screenplay, and best direction at the annual film awards ceremony April 3.

The U.S. Congress passed legislation April 6 raising the mandatory retirement age in most jobs from 65 to 70.

Arkady Shevchenko, the highest ranking Russian in the United Nations, defected to the U.S. April 10.

President Mohammad Daoud of Afghanistan

President Jimmy Carter, President Anwar Sadat of Egypt, left, and Prime Minister Menachem Begin of Israel, clasp hands at conclusion of historic Mideast peace treaty hammered out by the three at Camp David, Maryland, in 1979. (UPI PHOTO)

was killed in a military coup April 27.

First class postage was raised from 13 to 15 cents per ounce by the U.S. Postal Service on May 19.

French and Belgian paratroopers May 19-20 rescued some 2,500 Europeans trapped at Kolwezi, Zaire, in an armed conflict between Zairian regulars and rebel forces.

The first legal gambling casino in Atlantic City, New Jersey, opened May 26.

Proposition 13, an initiative to reduce property taxes by 57 per cent, was approved by California voters June 6.

David R. Berkowitz, so-called "Son of Sam" killer, June 13 received maximum prison sentences for each of six murders he had been convicted of in New York.

The U.S. Supreme Court on June 28 ruled that Allan P. Bakke, a white student, must be admitted to the University of California Medical School in a reverse discrimination suit.

More than 350 fires were reported in Memphis, Tennessee, July 1-4, as the city's fire fighters went on strike.

A British couple on July 25 became the parents of the first baby conceived out of its mother's body as the result of a new medical technique.

Pope Paul VI died August 6 in the fifteenth year of his reign.

New York's three major newspapers were closed by a pressmen's strike August 9.

Three Americans landed in France August 17 to complete the first manned transatlantic ballon flight.

President Jomo Kenyatta, founder and president of Kenya since its independence from Britain, died August 22.

Albino Cardinal Luciani, patriarch of Venice, was elected pope of the Roman Catholic Church August 26; he took the name of John Paul I.

Muhammad Ali regained his world heavyweight boxing championship from Leon Spinks on September 15.

A major earthquake killed 25,000 persons in Iran September 16.

The framework for a Middle East peace treaty was signed September 17 by Israel's Prime Minister Menachem Begin, Egyptian President Anwar Sadat, and U.S. President Jimmy Carter.

President Jimmy Carter applauds while Pope John Paul II acknowledges greetings from a crowd of dignitaries at a White House reception for the Pope October 6, 1979. (UPI PHOTO)

A Pacific Airlines Boeing 727 and a small private plane collided over San Diego, California, September 25, killing 144 persons.

Pope John Paul I died September 28 in the 34th day of his reign.

Karol Cardinal Wojtyla, archbishop of Krakow, Poland, was elected pope of the Roman Catholic Church October 16. The first non-Italian pope since 1523, he took the name John Paul II.

Egyptian President Anwar Sadat and Israel's Prime Minister Menachem Begin shared the 1978 Nobel Peace Prize, announced October 27.

Soviet cosmonauts Kovalyonok and Ivanchenko set a space-flight endurance record of 139 days and 15 hours and returned safely to land on November 2.

Martial law was imposed in Iran by Shah Mohammad Reza Pahlavi November 6 in an effort to curb violent demonstrations.

The New York City newspaper strike ended November 6 after the city had been without its major papers for three months.

U.S. Representative Leo J. Ryan (D.-California) and several members of his touring group were killed in Guyana November 18 by members of the People's Temple, a religious cult headed by the Rev. Jim Jones; more than 900 members of the cult, adults and children, including Jones then committed mass suicide-murder.

Labor problems forced the *Times* of London to suspend publication on Noverber 30.

President Carter signed a bill December 1 placing 56 million acres of Alaska wilderness in the National Park System,

Golda Meir, Israel's prime minister from 1969 to 1974 died December 8 at the age of 80,

Cleveland, Ohio, defaulted December 15 on $15.5 million in short term notes, the first major U.S. city to default on its debts.

Jouari Boumediene, president of Algeria since 1965, died December 27.

The United States and the People's Republic of China on January 1, 1979, established formal diplomatic relations; at the same time the U.S. ended its ties with the Chinese Nationalist government on Taiwan.

Iran's Shah Mohammad Reza Pahlavi was

driven into exile January 16 by the civil war in his country.

Chinese Deputy Premier Teng Hsiao-ping arrived in Washington January 28 in the first official visit to the U.S. by a high ranking Chinese Communist leader.

Ayatollah Ruhollah Khomeini, an Iranian religious and political leader, returned to Iran from 15 years of exile in an attempt to seize political power and establish Iran as an Islamic republic.

Followers of the Ayatollah Khomeini overthrew the Iranian government in Teheran February 9-11 and claimed Khomeini the country's leader after bloody street fighting.

Chinese troops invaded Vietnam February 17 in retaliation for alleged Vietnamese border attacks.

President Carter visited Cairo March 8 to help negotiate an Israeli-Egyptian peace pact.

President Anwar Sadat of Egypt and Prime Minister Menachem Begin of Israel signed a formal peace treaty March 26 in Washington, D.C., thus ending the state of war that had existed between their two countries for almost 31 years.

A series of breakdowns in the cooling system of the nuclear power plant at Three Mile Island Pennsylvania, on March 28 threatened a possible core meltdown, a catastrophe that had never occurred in a western nuclear energy plant.

Ayatollah Ruhollah Khomeini, Muslim religious leader, who came to power in Iran upon the overthrow of Shah Mohammad Reza Pahlavi in 1979. (UPI PHOTO)

The Deer Hunter was voted the best picture of 1978 April 9 at the Oscar awards ceremonies by the Academy of Motion Picture Arts and Sciences.

Bishop Abel Muzorewa became Rhodesia's first black political leader April 24, winning 67.3 per cent of the ballots cast in the first universal suffrage elections in the country's history.

An accident shut down a reactor of the Three Mile Island nuclear power plant March 28, 1979, leading to the nation's most critical nuclear accident. (UPI PHOTO)

President Jimmy Carter and Defense Secretary Harold Brown plead for ratification of the Strategic Arms Limitation Treaty with the Soviet Union at a briefing in the White House October 4, 1979. (UPI PHOTO)

In national elections May 3, Great Britain's Conservative Party, headed by Margaret Thatcher, defeated the Labour government, and on May 4 Mrs. Thatcher was appointed Prime Minister, the first woman to hold that office.

An American Airlines DC-10 jet crashed shortly after take-off from Chicago's O'Hare Airport May 25, killing all 272 persons aboard, plus three men on the ground, in the worst disaster in U.S. aviation hisotory.

A black government was installed in Rhodesia May 31, and the name of the country was changed to Zimbabwe Rhodesia.

Pope John II returned to his native Poland June 2 for a 9-day visit. It was the first time a pope had visited a communist country.

Ending seven years of strategic arms limitations talks, Soviet President Leonid Brezhnev and U.S. President Jimmy Carter signed a SALT treaty in Vienna June 18.

Skylab, the 77-ton unmanned U.S. space station which had been orbiting the earth since 1973, reentered the atmosphere July 11 and disintegrated over the Indian Ocean and Australia.

A widespread insurrection in Nicaragua, which had begun May 28, ended July 17 with the resignation and flight into exile of President Anastasio Somoza Debayle.

Charan Singh became prime minister of India July 28, replacing Morarji Desai, who had resigned July 15.

Andrew Young resigned August 15 as U.S. ambassador to the United Nations following a controversy over an unauthorized meeting in July between him and a representative of the Palestine Liberation Organization.

Louis, Earl Mountbatten, a cousin of Queen Elizabeth II, a hero of World War II, and the first governor general of India, died August 27, in the explosion of a bomb placed aboard his fishing boat by members of the Provisional Irish Republican Army. On the same day 18 British soldiers were killed in an IRA ambush about 35 miles south of Belfast.

Government authorities confirmed a report August 31, that a combat force of Russian troops numbering between two and three thousand men was stationed in Cuba.

Representatives of 95 nonaligned countries gathered September 3 in Havana, Cuba, for a week-long summit meeting.

Pope John Paul II arrived in Boston October 1 at the start of a weeklong visit to the U.S. On October 2 the pope addressed the General Assembly of the United Nations. The papal itinerary also included stops in Philadelphia, Chicago, Des Moines, Washington, D.C., and a rural pastorate in Iowa.

Visiting the United States for the first time in 19 years, Cuban President Fidel Castro on October 12 addressed the United Nations.

Iranians described as "students militants" on November 4 overran the United States embassy in Tehran, taking 66 Americans hostage. The Iranian gevernment later demanded that the United States return the deposed Shah Mohammed Reza Pahlavi, in the United States for medical treatment, to Iran for trial.

In the fourth worst disaster in aviation history, the DC-10 crash (the third of 1979) took the lives of 257 persons during a November 28 sightseeing flight over the South Pole.

Soviet military forces invaded Afghanistan just before the overthrow on December 27 of Hafizullah Amin, Afghanistan's president.

The Decade of the 80s

News broke on February 2 that FBI agents posing as Arab businessmen seeking favors had been gathering evidence on U.S. Congressmen in what came to be known as the "Abscam"—short for "Arab scam"—investigation.

Liberal Pierre Elliott Trudeau scored an impressive comeback victory in Canadian elections held February 18, winning reelection as Canada's prime minister with 46.2% of the popular vote.

Israeli authorities on March 10 assumed control over part of jerusalem for construction of a housing project. The action brought under Israeli hegemony a portion of the territory taken by Israel in the 1967 Arab-Israeli war.

One hundred twenty-three persons died March 27 when a floating oil platform capsized in turbulent North Seas water.

At their 52nd annual awards ceremony on April 14, the Academy of Motion Picture Arts and Sciences voted *Kramer vs. Kramer* the best film of 1979.

The United States became the first nation to open an embassy in newly independent Zimbabwe (Rhodesia) April 17.

"Operation Blue Light," an American Armed Forces attempt to rescue the hostages still held in Iran, ended in disaster April 24 when two planes collided in an Iranian desert, killing eight Americans.

Josip Broz Tito, president of Yugoslavia and the last of the Second World War's major figures, died on May 4, three days before his 88th birthday.

Members of Great Britain's Special Air Service Commando Regiment stormed the Iranian embassy in London May 5 in a successful effort to free hostages held nearly a week by Arab Iranian terrorists. Nineteen hostages were freed. Two terrorists and one hostage were killed.

Edmund S. Muskie was sworn in as the United States' 58th secretary of state on May 7. He replaced Cyrus R. Vance, who resigned in protest of President Carter's handling of the Iranian hostage situation.

In a May 20 referendum, Quebec voters defeated by a 58.2% to 41.8% margin a proposal that the province of Quebec become independent of Canada.

Miami rioters, protesting the acquittal of four Miami police officers on murder charges, on May 14–19 caused more than $100 million in property damage. At least 14 persons died.

The first women ever to graduate from U.S. military academies, a total of 227, graduated in late May from the Coast Guard Academy, the U.S. Military Academy, the U.S. Naval Academy, and the Air Force Academy.

"Unofficial" Soviet sources were quoted June 13 as revealing that more than 250,000 workers at the Soviets' two largest auto factories staged a rare—for the Soviet Union—two-day strike in May.

Lech Walesa emerged in 1980 as Poland's foremost labor leader. He gained worldwide attention after he successfully formed Solidarity, Eastern Europe's first independent trade labor union. (BOCCON GIBO–SIPA PRESS/BLACK STAR)

Washington State authorities reported July 4 that three eruptions of the volcano Mount St. Helens had left 25 persons dead and a path of destruction across Washington and Oregon.

Mohammed Reza Pahlavi, deposed Shah of Iran and a central figure in the U.S.–Iranian hostage dispute, died in Egypt on July 27.

The first Olympic games ever held in a communist nation began July 19 in Moscow, U.S.S.R., with 81 nations participating. Some 65 other nations, including the United States, boycotted the games because of the Soviet invasion of Afghanistan.

Democratic National Convention delegates meeting in New York City August 11–14 renominated President Jimmy Carter and Vice President Walter Mondale as their canditates for second terms. In July, the Republican National Convention had nominated Ronald Reagan for president and George Bush for vice president.

After days of major strikes, representatives of more than 300,000 Polish workers on August 31 concluded agreements with Poland's communist government to pave the way for formation of Solidarity, the first independent trade union in communist Eastern Europe.

Running border disputes between Iraq and Iran erupted into open warfare September 22. The two nations attacked each other's territories with heavy artillery and planes while ground action also became intense.

Fuel in an underground Titan II missile silo exploded September 19 near Damascus, Arkansas, injuring 22 Air Force personnel, one fatally. The blast caused the 12-hour evacuation of about 1,400 persons lining within a five-mile radius. Defense Department officials reported that the missile's 10-megaton nuclear warhead was undamaged.

Soviet premier Alexei N. Kosygin resigned October 23 for health reasons. He was replaced by 75-year-old economic planner Nikolai A. Tikhonov.

Ronald Reagan won election as the 40th president of the United States in a November 4 landslide. Incumbent Jimmy Carter carried only six states and the District of Columbia.

The United States' unmanned spacecraft Voyager II flew past the planet Saturn November 12, approaching within 78,000 miles of the giant planet and sending back to earth volumes of technical and scientific information.

Border tensions between Iraq and Iran escalated into open warfare in late September, 1980. The Iraqi army occupied outposts 10 miles into Iranian territory within a week of the war's beginning. (UPI)

An earthquake that struck southern Italy November 23 took at least 2,900 lives and injured more than 7,700. Two hundred thousand persons were left homeless.

Former Beatle John Lennon was murdered by a former mental patient outside his New York City apartment December 8.

After 24 years of litigation, former workers at the defunct Darlington Manufacturing Company textile plant in Florence, South Carolina, voted December 14 to accept a $5 million settlement of their claims for back pay.

Greece joined the European Community on January 1, 1981, becoming the EC's 10th member.

Fifty-two American hostages, including three who had been held under separate guard, were released January 20, President Reagan's inauguration day. Leaving Iran after 444 days of captivity, the 52 reached the United States January 25.

Tamponas II , an Indonesian passenger liner, caught fire January 27 and sank in the Java Sea with a loss of nearly 600 lives.

An interagency U.S. government group announced on February 5 that caring for the 125,000 Cubans and 12,400 Haitians who en-

Several huge demonstrations during August, 1981, in various European cities protested the deployment of nuclear arms in NATO countries. These West German women were a part of such a demonstration in Bonn, West Germany, during a NATO nuclear planning session. (SVEN SIMON–KATHERINE YOUNG PHOTOGRAPHY)

tered the United States in 1980 had cost the American government $532 million.

Some 200 Spanish civil guards made an abortive attempt to take about 350 legislators hostage and seize power in Madrid on February 23–24.

Making his first trip outside the United States since taking office, President Ronald Reagan visited Canada March 10–11. He held talks with Canadian Prime Minister Pierre Elliott Trudeau.

A Pakistani jetliner carrying more than 100 passengers and crew members was hijacked and held for 12 days ending March 14. The hijackers surrendered to Syrian officials after the Pakistani government met their demands and freed 54 political prisoners held in Pakistani jails.

An attempt to assassinate U.S. President Ronald Reagan on March 30 failed. But the President and three others, including presidential Press Secretary James S. Brady, were wounded. The would-be assassin was identified as John W. Hinckley Jr,. 25.

Ordinary People won four Academy Awards, including best picture of 1980, at the annual film awards on March 31.

The U.S. space shuttle Columbia, the world's first reusable space vehicle, successfully completed an initial 54-hour flight on April 14.

Riots in Belfast and Londonderry, Northern Ireland, followed the death on May 5 of Irish Republican Army hunger-striker Bobby Sands in Belfast's Maze Prison.

Scoring a victory for French socialism, Francois Mitterrand defeated Valery Giscard d' Estaing in balloting held May 10. Mitterrand won about 52% of the vote, Giscard 48%.

Using a 9-mm. Browning pistol, Mehmet Ali Agca, a Turkish extremist, attempted May 13 to assassinate Pope John Paul II in St. Peter's

Square, Vatican City. The Pope was struck by two bullets, receiving multiple wounds, but recovered to make a brief public appearance June 3 after his release from Rome's Gemelli Clinic.

Two Soviet cosmonauts completed a 75-day journey in earth orbit May 26. Col. Vladimir Kovalyonok and Viktor Savinikh spent most of the 75 days in the already-orbiting Salyut 6 space station.

Flying 14 American-built planes, Israeli pilots on June 7 destroyed the Osirak nuclear reactor near Baghdad, Iraq. The Israeli government called the attack a preventive strike on an atomic weapons facility.

Major league baseball players walked out June 12, starting the longest strike in U.S. baseball history.

A black free-lance photographer, Wayne B. Williams, 23, was arrested in Atlanta, Georgia June 21 in connection with the wave of 28 murders and disappearances of blacks in the Atlanta area over a two-year period.

A bomb exploded June 28 at the Islamic Fundamentalist Party offices in Tehran, Iran, killing 72 top Iranian political leaders.

President Ronald Reagan on July 7 nominated Sandra Day O'Connor to be the United States' first woman Supreme Court justice. O'Connor, 51, became an associate justice September 25.

Rioting accompanied by attacks on police broke out in London and Liverpool, England, in early July. Over the next 10 days the disturbances spread to more than 30 cities and towns, injuring hundreds and causing millions of dollars in property damage.

A months-long battle to end a California infestation by Mediterranean fruit flies received new impetus in July as state authorities began spraying orchards and fields with malathion. Some maintained that the chemical agent would cause cancer.

As some 1,500 guests enjoyed a tea dance in the lobby of the Kansas City, Missouri, Hyatt Regency Hotel, two aerial walkways collapsed, killing 111 persons. One hundred and ninety others were injured in one of the U.S. hotels industry's worst accidents.

In glittering, formal ceremonies held at London's St. Paul's Cathedral, Great Britain's Prince Charles married Lady Diana Spencer July 29.

The United States' Alternate Representative to the United Nations vetoes a Security Council resolution condemning a South African incursion into Angola. (BRIAN F. ALPERT–KEYSTONE)

The U.S. Senate and House of Representatives on July 29 passed a new tax bill designed to spur economic recovery nationally. The vote followed earlier policy victories on the Reagan administration's budget and budget-cutting proposals.

Egyptian President Anwar Sadat and Israeli Prime Minister Menachem Begin met for the tenth time in June, 1981, near the Suez Gulf. (ALAIN KELER–SYGMA)

The 15,000-member Professional Air Traffic Controllers Organization went on strike August 3, bringing warnings from the U.S. government that the strikers would be fired if they did not return to work. Extensive litigation over the walk-out ended in October with decertification of PATCO.

United States Secretary of State Alexander Haig travelled to the People's Republic of China in June, 1981, to hold general talks with Chinese Vice Chairman Deng Xiaoping. (UPI)

U.S. government officials on August 10 announced that the United States was going into full production of the neutron bomb—the "enhanced radiation weapon"—that was designed to kill enemy forces without causing massive property damage.

In an air confrontation during U.S. maneuvers in the Mediterranean, American pilots on August 19 shot down two Soviet-built Libyan jet fighters over the Gulf of Sidra.

Mexican President Jose Lopez Portillo is greeted by his Costa Rican counterpart Rodrigo Carazo upon Portillo's arrival in San Jose, Costa Rica. (UPI)

While the Reagan administration called for further government spending cuts and asked for new taxes that would help balance the budget, an estimated 260,000 peaceful demonstrators marched September 19 in Washington, D.C. The rally was held in protest against the administration's economic policies.

About two and one-half hours after Islamic radicals jumped out of a truck and inflicted multiple gunshot injuries on him, Egyptian President Anwar Sadat died in a military hospital outside Cairo. The October 6 assault, occurring during a parade commemorating the Arab-Israeli "Yom Kippur War" of 1973, took at least eight other lives and wounded dozens of others.

The U.S. Senate, in a 52–48 vote, on October 28 approved the sale of five U.S. Airborne Warning and Control Systems (AWACS) aircraft to Saudi Arabia. The vote made it possible for the United States to close a deal that would give the Saudis $8.5 million in special military aircraft equipment as well as the surveillance planes.

The crash of a Boeing 737 Air Florida jetliner on January 13, 1982, took 78 lives. Taking off in a snowstorm from Washington, D.C., the plane smashed into a bridge jammed with evening rush-hour traffic, then sunk into the icy Potomac River. The crash was the first fatal accident since October 1979 for the nation's major airlines.

Temperatures near 100° Fahrenheit (73° Centigrade) below zero—including the wind chill factor—were recorded in the Great Lakes region January 9–17. Chicago had a record temperature January 10 of −26° F (−32°C).

Italy's biggest manhunt ever resulted on January 28 in the rescue of U.S. Brig. Gen. James L. Dozier. Kidnapped 42 days earlier, the American had been held in a Padua apartment by members of the ultraleft Red Brigades terrorist organization.

In a speech before the Organization of American States on February 24, President Reagan proposed a Caribbean aid plan that would initially cost the U.S. $350 million in economic assistance.

One of the most prolonged criminal investigations in Atlanta's history went into a new phase February 27 when a jury convicted Wayne B. Williams of 2 of 28 seemingly related murders committed over a period of two years.

The so-called *syzygy* on March 10 failed to produce the predicted "Jupiter effect" doom and disaster. *Syzygy* refers to the alignment of all nine planets on one side of the sun, a rare configuration doomsayers said meant the end of the world.

The 66th annual Pulitzer Prize awards were presented March 12 in New York City by Columbia University. Acting on the recommendations of the Pulitzer Prize advisory board, the university awarded to John Updike the fiction prize for his novel *Rabbit is Rich,* his third novel centering on the well-known character, suburban American Rabbit Angstrom. The drama award was given to Charles Fuller for *A Soldier's Play,* which was set in a military base in 1944 and concerned murder and racial conflict. William S. McFeely was awarded the Pulitzer prize in biography for his book *Grant: A Biography* and Sylvia Plath's *Collected Poems,* received, posthumously, the poetry award. The poetess committed suicide in 1963 at the age of 30.

El Salvador's reform programs seemed to be threatened when, on March 28, general election results produced a potential rightist majority. Five conservative parties gained a majority of the heavy vote.

The 54th annual awards ceremony of the Academy of Motion Picture Arts and Sciences was held March 29 in Los Angeles. Taking the Oscar for best picture of the year, as well as three other awards, was the British film *Chariots of Fire,* about two marathon runners in the 1924 Olympics. Best actor and best actress awards went to Henry Fonda and Katharine Hepburn who played husband and wife in the film *On Golden Pond.*

Billy Graham, one of the best-known of U.S. evangelists, attended a May 7–12 Church conference on disarmament in Moscow. Rev. Graham said later that he had "experienced total freedom in what I wanted to say."

Israel invaded Lebanon June 6 in an attempt to crush Palestine Liberation Organization guerrilla bases. The air and sea attack was triggered by an assassination attempt on the life of Shlomo Aagov, Israeli ambassador to London.

The Falkland Islands War ended June 14 when some 15,000 surviving Argentine troops surrendered to encircling British forces. The war had

Argentina's struggle for repossession of the Falkland Islands gives evidence of earlier military confrontations. A weathered cannon remains from a past era, while soldiers armed with more sophisticated weapons await British troops on April 12, 1982. (UPI PHOTO)

begun April 2 with Argentina's invasion of the British possession.

A jury acquitted John W. Hinckley, Jr., of murderous assault on June 21. On March 30, 1981, the defendant had shot President Reagan and three others. The acquittal was based on a finding of "insanity."

Spationaute Jean-Loup Chretien became the first Frenchman in space when a Soviet Soyuz T-6 spacecraft blasted off June 24. Chretien and two Soviet cosmonauts spent about a week aboard the orbiting Salyut 7 space station before returning to earth.

The deadline for passage of the Equal Rights Amendments expired June 30. Thirty-five state legislatures—three fewer than were needed—had approved the amendment.

The U.S. Senate unanimously confirmed George P. Shultz as Secretary of State on July 15. Shultz replaced Alexander M. Haig, who resigned June 25 over differences with the White House on foreign policy.

What was called the biggest tax increase bill in U.S. history received Congress' approval August 19. President Reagan had campaigned heavily for the measure.

Juan Corona, convicted in 1973 of murdering 25 migrant workers and burying their bodies, was convicted in a retrial September 23 in California. The retrial cost some $5 million.

Israeli Prime Minister Menachem Begin on September 29 formally requested an inquiry into the September 16–17 massacre of hundreds of Palestinian civilians. The massacre in Beirut's Sabra and Shatila refugee camps brought cries of outrage from around the world.

With Helmut Schmidt ousted by a no-confidence vote, West Germany's Bundestag, or lower house of parliament, on October 1 elected Christian Democrat Helmut Kohl to the post of Chancellor. The move presaged broader German support for U.S. policies.

Swedish author Alva Myrdal shared 1982 Nobel Peace Prize awards with Alfonso Garcia Robles of Mexico, both cited for their central roles in United Nations disarmament negotiations in Geneva, Switzerland, over the past several years. Both acted as "patient and meticulous" delegates, according to the Nobel committee of the Royal Swedish Academy in Stockholm, announcing its awards October 12–21. Americans took prizes in two fields. The Nobel Memorial Award in Economic Science was awarded to the University of Chicago Professor George Stigler, the 11th American and the 4th U of C professor to receive the economics prize. In physics, Kenneth G. Wilson, a Cornell University professor, won the Nobel Prize for the development of a mathematical system capable of explaining the changes that matter experiences at crucial points in pressure and temperature.

Women chain themselves to the White House fence to gain support for the passage of the Equal Rights Amendment. The amendment failed to pass when three state legislatures refused to approve it. (UPI PHOTO)

John Z. DeLorean, business whiz kid and former General Motors executive, was arrested October 19. His dream of building popular sports cars collapsed when he was charged with possession of 220 pounds of cocaine.

In off-year elections held November 2, the Democratic Party gained 26 seats in the U.S. House of Representatives. The Democrats also won seven additional governorships but could not change the composition of the Senate—54 Republicans, 46 Democrats.

Some 48 hours after the death on November 10 of Soviet leader Leonid I. Brezhnev, the Central Committee of the Communist Party elected Yuri V. Andropov as Brezhnev's successor as CP general secretary. Andropov pledged that he would continue Brezhnev's policies.

Following test flights in March and June, the American space shuttle *Columbia* on November 11 roared into space carrying its first four-man crew and its first payload—two commercial satellites.

Negotiators for National Football League players and owners reached tentative agreement November 16 on a new union contract. The pact ended the longest and most costly strike in sports history.

On December 2, University of Utah surgeons implanted an artificial heart, called Jarvik-7, in the chest of Washington dentist Barney Clark. A crack then appeared in the device, forcing doctors to operate again.

With fears of nuclear war at fever pitch in Europe, the Swedish government on December 8 proposed creation of a 180-mile (290 kilometers) wide nuclear-free zone on the continent.

In what police described as the biggest heist in U.S. history, two masked gunmen carried off $9.8 million on December 12. The robbery took place in the headquarters of a New York armored car company while a lone guard lay in handcuffs.

More than a year after it had been imposed, martial law was suspended by the Polish government headed by Gen. Wojciech Jaruzelski. The suspension on December 31, 1982, left in effect a number of severe restrictions.

Defense spending was to rise 14 percent and most other domestic program funding was to be frozen under the 1984 budget submitted to Congress on January 31, 1983, by President Reagan.

Klaus Barbie, head of the German Gestapo in Lyons, France, during World War II, was expelled from Bolivia February 4 and was returned to Lyons where he was charged February 5 with committing crimes against humanity. Barbie had been known as "the Butcher of Lyons" during the war.

With tests taken in Times Beach, Missouri, showing dangerously high levels of the toxic chemical dioxin in the soil there, the U.S. government offered on February 22 to buy all the town's homes and businesses. The town was later evacuated.

Soviet Communist party leader Yuri V. Andropov confers with Foreign Minister Andrei A. Gromyko during celebrations to honor Lenin's 113th birthday in April 1983. Andropov died in 1984 and was succeeded by Konstantin Cherenenkov. (WIDE WORLD PHOTOS)

Barney B. Clark died March 23, 112 days after he became the first human to have an artificial heart implanted as a permanent measure.

Heavy rains and floods took 15 lives in four Southern states April 6–12. The floods drove some 52,000 persons from their homes and did an estimated $625 million in damage in Mississippi, Tennessee, Alabama, and Louisiana.

The Academy of Motion Picture Arts and Sciences celebrated its 55th annual awards ceremony April 11 in Los Angeles. The award for best picture of 1982 went to the film *Ghandi*, a depiction of the life of Mohandas Ghandi from youth to visionary old age. The lead role was played by Englishman Ben Kingsley who was named best actor for his portrayal of Ghandi. In addition, the film received six other awards, including best original screenplay and best director. Meryl Streep was chosen best actress for her role in *Sophie's Choice.*

Chicagoans elected their first black mayor, Harold Washington, April 12, after a bitter campaign marked by racial innuendos and appeals. Washington, a Democrat, beat lawyer and former state representative Bernard Epton.

The 67th annual Pulitzer prizes were awarded in New York City April 18. On the recommendations of the Pulitzer committee, Columbia University awarded the drama prize to Marsha Norman for her play, *'Night, Mother,* about the relationship of a suicidal daughter and her mother. Russell Baker was named for his autobiography *Growing Up* and Galway Kinnell received the poetry prize for his *Selected Poems.* The fiction award went to Alice Walker for *The Color Purple,* a novel which also won the American Book Award for fiction.

A car-bomb devastated the U.S. embassy in Beirut, Lebanon, at noon, April 18, taking 47 lives and injuring more than 100. The blast, said to be the work of a pro-Iranian group, collapsed the entire central portion of the building.

The West German government announced May 6 that it had carried out chemical tests proving conclusively that the alleged "diaries" of Adolph Hitler were forgeries. The forged diaries had been appearing in the West German magazine *Stern.*

The 67th Indianapolis 500 auto race ended May 29 with Tom Sneva taking first place with an average speed of 162.117 miles (260.91 kilometers) per hour, second fastest time in the race's history.

Prime Minister Margaret Thatcher, heading the British Conservative Party, emerged victorious in June 9 elections, winning reelection with a larger majority than in her first campaign.

In a trip with immense political as well as spiritual significance, Pope John Paul II returned for a six-day visit to his native Poland. The June 16–23 tour included a visit with Solidarity Union leader Lech Walesa.

Physicist Sally K. Ride became the United States' first woman astronaut when she accompanied four male crew members on the second flight of space shuttle *Challenger.* The near-perfect mission began on June 18 and ended on June 24.

Henry Kissinger, former U.S. Secretary of State, was named July 18 as head of a bipartisan commission to study Central America. The commission was to draft recommendations that would guide the Reagan administration in the formulation of Central American policy.

A Federal nuclear weapons research center in New Mexico was among the approximately 60 computer systems "raided" by a group of Milwaukee youths. An August 21 newspaper report said the "414s"—named for the Milwaukee area code—numbered 7 to 10 young computer buffs.

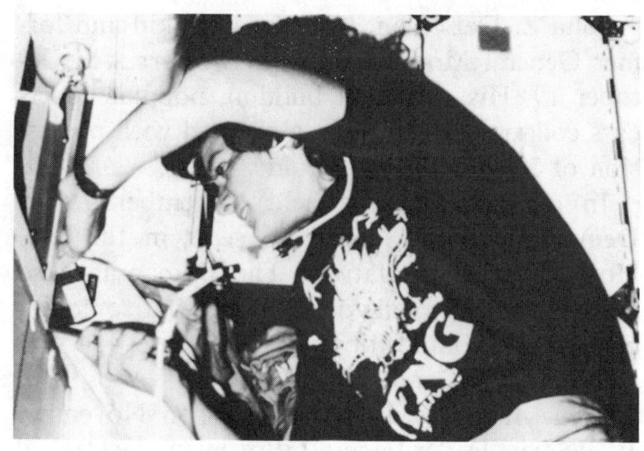

Astronaut Sally Ride, the first American woman to fly in space, cleans out an air filtering system in the Space Shuttle Challenger. During this 7th flight two communications satellites were successfully deployed. (NASA PHOTO)

After a self-imposed three-year exile in the United States, Phillipine opposition leader Benigno Aquino, Jr., was shot and killed August 21 only minutes after deplaning at Manila International Airport with three military guards. Initial reports as to the identity of the gunman were conflicting. However, in the days following the murder, the Phillipine government, headed by Aquino's foe, President Ferdinand E. Marcos, reported that it had identified the alleged assassin, describing him as a "notorious killer."

The quadrennial Pan American Games, held August 14–28 in Caracas, Venezuela, ended with the United States, Cuba, and Canada ranked first, second, and third respectively in total medals. Some 4,000 athletes took part in the ninth Pan-Am competitions.

The third 1983 flight of the space shuttle Chal-

America's first Black Astronaut, Guion S. Bluford, checks control knobs on the Space Shuttle Challenger during its 8th flight. The controls regulated the equipment that separated biological materials according to their surface electrical charge. (NASA PHOTO)

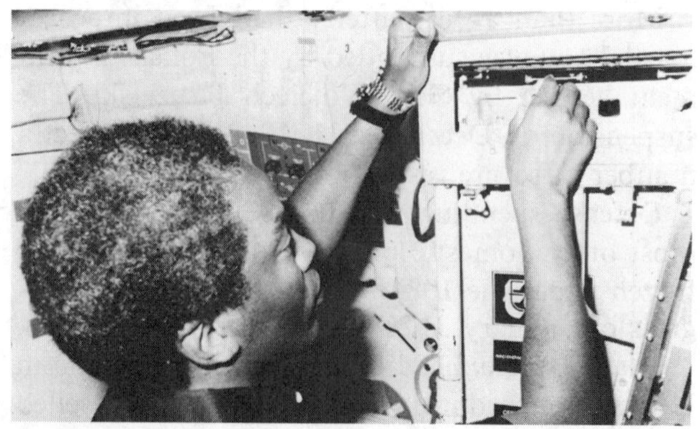

lenger on August 30 took the first U.S. black astronaut into space. Lt. Col. Guion S. Bluford, a Ph.D. in aerospace engineering, was included in the crew as a mission specialist on the week-long flight, which NASA officials referred to as "a fabulous mission" because of the shuttle's return to earth in outstanding mechanical condition.

All 240 passengers and 29 crew members aboard Korean Air Lines flight 007 perished September 1 when Soviet fighters destroyed the commercial airliner with heat-seeking missiles. Shot down over the Sea of Japan, Flight 007 had been overflying sensitive Soviet airspace.

Beating Czechoslovakia's Ivan Lendl, Jimmy Connors won his fifth men's singles title in the U.S. Open Championships at Flushing Meadows, New York. A day earlier, on September 10, Martina Navratilova had defeated Chris Evert Lloyd for her first singles title in the tournament.

Secretary of the Interior James G. Watt sparked a furor when he described a coal advisory commission as containing "a black, a woman, two Jews, and a cripple." The remark caused a rift in the Republican Party. Watt resigned October 9.

Four South Korean cabinet members and two leading advisors to South Korean President Chun Doo Hwan, died October 9 when a terrorist bomb exploded during formal ceremonies in Rangoon, Burma. The blast took 13 other lives and wounded 48. President Chun Doo Hwan, whose motorcade had been detained in traffic, arrived at the ceremonies only moments after the explosion, narrowly escaping death himself.

Following the lead of the U.S. House of Representatives, the Senate voted 78–22 on October 19 to designate the third Monday of January each year as a federal holiday in honor of civil rights leader Rev. Martin Luther King, Jr.

Shortly after dawn on October 23, a terrorist truck laden with explosives crashed into a U.S. Marine building at Beirut airport and blew up. A second truck exploded at the French paratroop barracks two miles (three kilometers) away. The death tolls: 241 Americans and 58 Frenchmen.

Accompanied by a small force representing six Caribbean nations, U.S. Marines and Rangers invaded the island of Grenada October 25. The operation marked the first significant U.S. military intervention in the Western Hemisphere since the invasion of the Dominican Republic in 1965.

The Rev. Jesse Jackson became the first black in 11 years to seek a major party's presidential nomination when he declared his candidacy November 3. Reverend Jackson said he hoped to close an existing gap between "the announced [Democratic] candidates and the masses."

Scientists from the U.S., the Soviet Union, and other countries met October 31 and November 1 in Washington, D.C., to present their findings on the effects of nuclear war. The consensus was that a "nuclear winter" could follow such a war, possibly extinguishing human life.

Few leaders of the 20th century have stirred the intellect and emotions of fellow Americans more than Martin Luther King, Jr. King's compassionate, nonviolent crusade to ensure the civil rights of America's poor is now celebrated as a national holiday. (HISTORICAL PICTURES SERVICE, INC.)

Implementation of new security measures in the U.S. Capitol was stepped up after a bomb exploded near the Senate chamber November 7. No one was injured.

American Space shuttle *Columbia* blasted off from Cape Canaveral November 28, launching a new era of space experimentation. The shuttle's six-man crew included German physicist, Ulf Merbold, the first European ever to fly in a U.S. spacecraft. The astronauts conducted more than 70 experiments before returning to earth on December 8.

AMERICA'S
CONTINUING EXPLORATION OF SPACE

Voyagers I and II

Jupiter

Saturn

The Space Shuttles

VOYAGER I

The space odyssey of the United States' Pioneer 11 culminated in September, 1979, in a Saturn flyby. Pioneer 11 became the first spacecraft to reach Saturn, a lonely planet orbiting nearly a billion miles from the sun. But the encounter proved to be little more than a warmup for the Saturn visit, 14 months later, of Voyager I, a 1,820 pound spacecraft that traveled at about 54,000 miles per hour.

On March 5, 1979, Voyager I had made its closest approach to the planet Jupiter. It came within 172,000 miles of the cloudtops which cover the giant planet. The probe transmitted back to earth a mass of data, including spectacular photographs of Jupiter and a number of its moons. The satellite was then hurled into a new space track headed for its next destination, the vicinity of Saturn.

Photographs from Voyager I revealed round spots—apparently centers of turbulence—moving at speeds of almost 200 miles an hour. The apparent storms overtake one another, move in tandem for as long as twelve days, and then finally separate. The Great Red Spot, an atmospheric landmark that astronomers have recognized ever since Jupiter was first seen by telescope and that is large enough to contain several Earths, was also studied by Voyager I, but without conclusive results.

Mission scientists announced March 7 that Voyager I had discovered a ring of dark rock particles around Jupiter. The objects composing the ring were thought to range in size from tens to hundreds of meters. The ring is apparently at least 5,400 miles wide but not more than 18 miles thick. It had not been seen from Earth because of its thinness and the angle at which it was oriented.

Perhaps the most exciting discovery of the whole Voyager mission came March 9, when scientists examined photographs of Io, the innermost of Jupiter's four Galilean satellites or moons. One of these photos showed a cloud of gas and dust rising above the moon's surface. Scientists speculated that Voyager had photographed a volcanic eruption in progress. This would make Io the only body in the solar system besides Earth known to be geologically active.

Infrared detectors on Voyager also registered on Io what the scientists interpreted as lakes of lava one of which had an area the size of the state of Hawaii. The apparent lava lakes had temperatures ranging between 100° and 200° F. in contrast with the –260° F. temperature of other parts of Io's surface.

On July 9 Voyager II made its closest pass to Jupiter. Like its counterpart Voyager I, the probe sent back spectacular photos of Jupiter's remarkable cloud cover and several of the moons including more shots of volcanic action on Io. Space mission scientists, however, were more thrilled by the brilliant photos of Jupiter's ring which Voyager I returned as it was flying by, almost, one of the scientists said, "as though the probe thought we were becoming jaded and wanted to shake us up with something new."

Voyager I soared to its rendezvous with Saturn with a full cargo of equipment. It had two television cameras on board along with ultraviolet and infrared spectrometers. The latter was designed to measure temperatures. A photopolarimeter carried by Voyager I was to conduct aerosol studies, but the instrument failed as the space vehicle was passing Jupiter on its way to Saturn. Using three charged-particle instruments, Voyager measured and monitored planetary radiation belts, cosmic rays, and the solar wind. Two 10-meter-long whip antennae had the task of "listening" for solar-satellite radio noises, plasma waves, and planetary radio emissions.

Voyager I had years of traveling ahead of it. It was scheduled to pass across the orbits of Uranus in 1985 and Pluto in 1994. It would then leave the solar system. But the data it sent back from Saturn would probably remain its crowning achievement. Scientists would be working on those data for years before they would piece together the whole story of what it all meant.

The period of discovery began in early August, when Voyager was still more than half a million miles from Saturn. The period crested on November 12, 1980, when the spacecraft made its closest approach to the planet—some 70,000 miles from Saturn's golden cloud cover. All this time Voyager's cameras recorded and sent home detailed closeups of the Saturnian rings. The pictures showed hundreds of ringlets as well, some of them elliptical, that complemented the rings. In defiance of celestial mechanics, Saturn's F ring appeared to be braided. It was also triple-stranded and kinked.

More and more pictures flowed in. Voyager's narrow-angle camera had a resolution capability 50 times greater than that of the Pioneer 11 photopolarimeter. Thus the Voyager photos showed an amazing range of heavenly phenomena. Giant beams of sunlight flooded through gaps in Saturn's rings. Distant stars twinkled in the background. In a single hour scientists learned more about the ringed planet than they had discovered in the past 370 years. Galileo had discovered the planet whirling through space in the early 1600s.

As Voyager I bored in on its hyperbolic trajectory toward the core of Saturn's environment, it examined some of the planet's 15 known moons. It also discovered two previously unknown moons that chased each other in virtually identical orbits around the planet. Spotting three additional "shepherd moons," it focused on the Saturn satellites Mimas, with its single gigantic crater, and heavily pocked Rhea. Others came into view: Tethys, showing a huge, craterlike scar that cast no shadow; Dione, a space wanderer with a terrain described as "wispy;" Iapetus, with its "day" that was six times as bright as its "night;" and Enceladus, the smooth-surfaced moonlet that followed an orbit linked to Dione's.

Titan became a center of scientific attention. Voyager I passed within 2,500 miles of this largest of Saturn's satellites on its way toward the planet's inner zones. Earlier, scientists had known that Titan had an ultraviolet spectrum showing bands of methane. With the data from Voyager I, a new picture emerged: Titan was shown as having, in all likelihood, a nitrogen atmosphere laced with perhaps 1 percent methane. Other measurements revealed the possibility that Titan may have lakes, puddles, or even oceans of liquid nitrogen.

Some mysteries about Titan did survive. Was the opaque orange smog that veiled the Saturnian moon composed of hydrocarbon aerosols? Had the moon a separate layer of liquid nitrogen clouds that perpetually hovered over its surface? The answers to such questions would have to await further study of the Voyager I data—and perhaps future space voyages.

Among the observations recorded by Voyager I, spokelike formations in the planet's rings aroused both wonderment and curiosity. Made up of clouds of particles of ice and rock, the hundreds of rings were generally only a few miles in thickness. Scientists speculated that they could have formed out of celestial debris that failed to coalesce into moons when the solar system was taking form. But the spokes appeared and disappeared. No one had an adequate explanation for them.

Voyager finally passed Saturn. More than three years from home, having traveled more than 1 billion miles, it continued on its voyage through space. From the far side of Saturn it sent back images of the planet encircled by translucent, gossamer rings. Voyager I had opened to man's awareness an icy, ethereal, breath-taking concentration of worlds while also measuring or monitoring a wide range of planetary phenomena. Radio occultation data and other evidence helped to build a profile of a Saturn that consisted largely of hydrogen and helium.

VOYAGER II

Voyager I and its mate, Voyager II, had been launched in 1977 to take advantage of an unusual celestial alignment that made it possible for an earth-launched spacecraft to visit all the more distant planets on a single journey.

Voyager II followed a special track that had taken it past Jupiter and that would swing it by Saturn, Uranus, and Neptune. The Uranus flyby was scheduled for 1986, the Neptune for 1989.

Approaching Saturn, in what scientists called its "observatory phase," the satellite transmitted images back to earth that were brighter than those sent by Voyager I. The reason: the spacecraft approached Saturn at a higher angle. The sun's rays could illuminate the pictures more effectively.

The observatory phase continued through July 31. The Far Encounter phase began. Voyager II arrived at its rendezvous with Saturn only 3.1 seconds off schedule and about 41 miles off target. One scientist compared the near-perfect space flight to an unheard-of golfing feat: sinking a 500-mile putt. With about 1 billion miles of travel behind it, the spacecraft was 63,000 miles

UPI

WIDE WORLD

(Top) *From nearly 21 million miles, Voyager II sent back to Earth this stunning photograph of Saturn. The moons Rhea and Dione appear as small dots to the lower right of Saturn.* (Bottom) *Seven of Saturn's moons are pictured in this composite photograph. The irregularly shaped satellites are not named and are referred to only by numbers.*

UPI

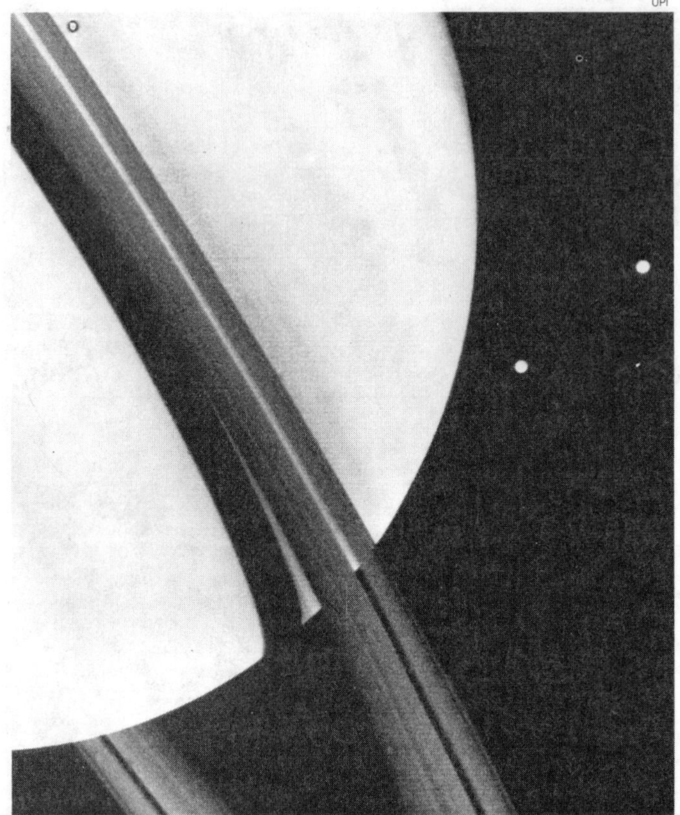

UPI

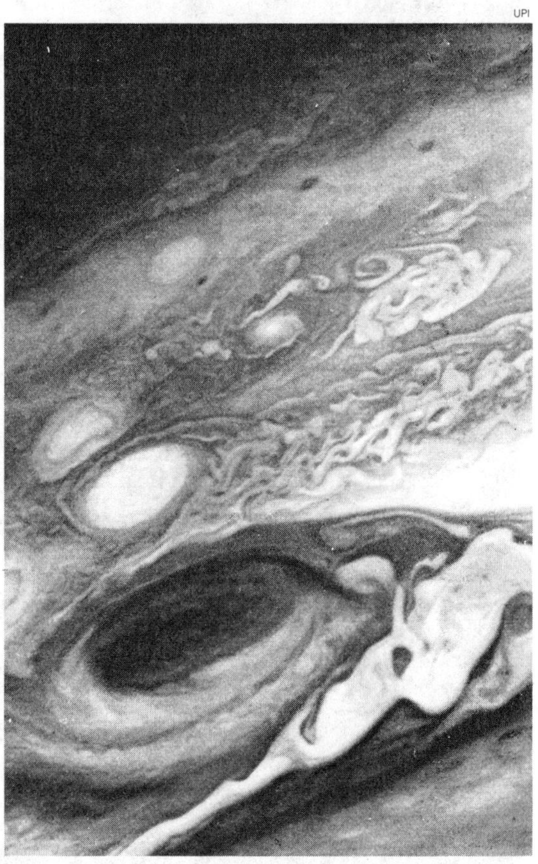

UPI

(Top, left) *Voyager I took this photo of Saturn and two of its moons, Tethys and Dione, in late 1980. The shadows of Saturn's rings can be seen cast upon the cloud tops.* (Above) *This extraordinary view of Jupiter's Great Red Spot, taken by Voyager I, shows in remarkable detail the complexity of the planet's cloud patterns.* (Bottom, left) *More than 60 bright and dark ringlets can be seen in this composite photograph of Saturn's C-ring taken by Voyager II.*

(Top, left) *Shown against a background of Jupiter, Io is the innermost of the four large satellites. Although approximately the same size as Earth's moon, Io has apparently followed a different evolutionary path.* (Top, right) *Using more than 6,000 different photographs of Jupiter, scientists are trying to better understand the small white spots in the southern hemisphere and similar dark spots in the northern hemisphere.*

UPI

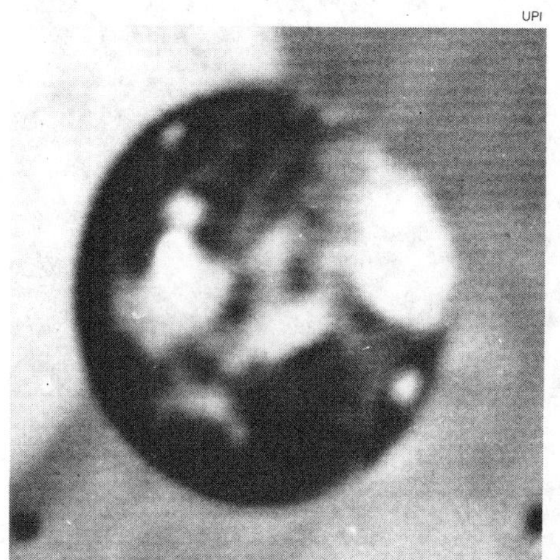

UPI

UPI

UPI

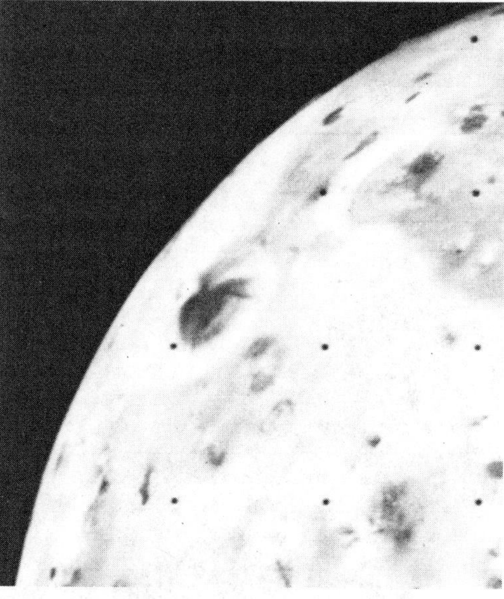

(Bottom, right) *This photo of Io, taken in 1979 by Voyager I, gave scientists their first glimpse of active volcanic eruption on another body in our solar system. At least four eruptions have been noted in Voyager I photos of Io.* (Bottom, left) *Ganymede, Jupiter's largest satellite, was photographed by Voyager I in early 1979. Its low density indicates that Ganymede is probably composed of rock and ice.*

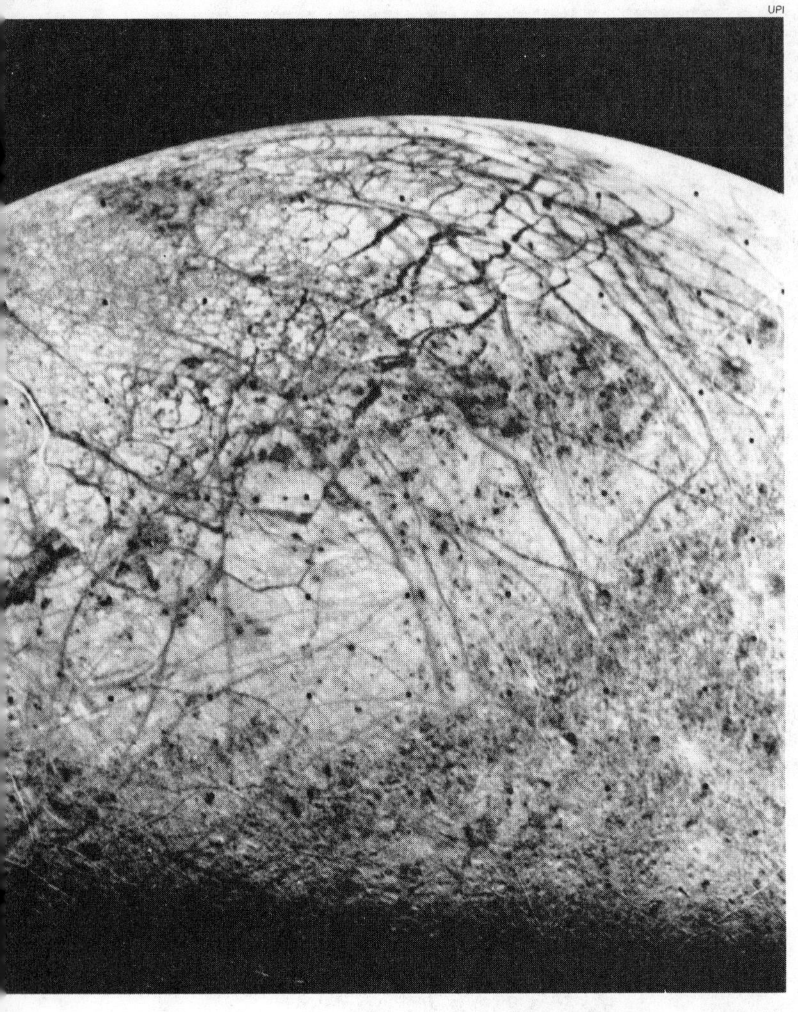
UPI

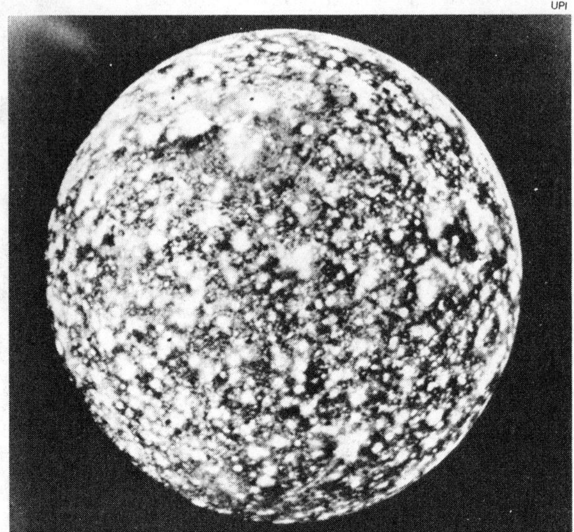
UPI

UPI

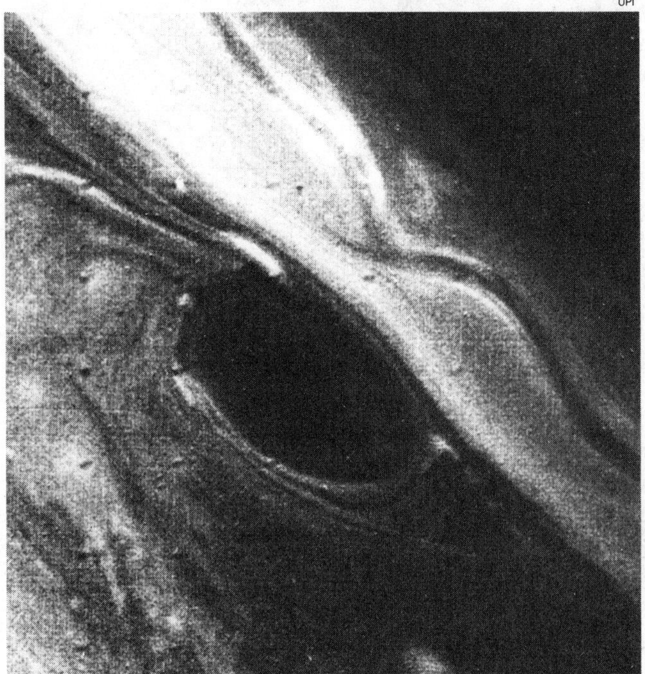
UPI

(Above, left) *Europa, the smallest and brightest of Jupiter's four Galilean satellites, is believed to have a substantial quantity of water. Scientists speculate that the complex patterned surface was formed by a fracturing of the icy surface which allows dark material from below to show through.* (Top, right) *The large Jovian moon Calliste as seen by Voyager II from a distance of nearly three-quarters of a million miles. Its icy surface is scarred with craters and fault lines.* (Bottom, right) *Impact craters on Saturn's moon Dione are a lasting record of its collision with cosmic debris.* (Bottom, left) *This large brown spot on Saturn, photographed by Voyager II, is thought to be an opening in the upper cloud deck which reveals darker underlying clouds.*

from the planet, its point of closest approach. The date: August 25, 1981.

The Far Encounter with Saturn produced more marvels of celestial photography as Voyager II's cameras busily snapped thousands of pictures. The flow was interrupted when one of the platforms on which the cameras rode jammed. When the failure occurred, Voyager II was behind Saturn and hidden from the earth. The platform was returned to service and scientists said that the malfunction would not materially reduce the mission's effectiveness.

As with Voyager I, the new findings both confirmed the earlier ones and spun new mysteries for the experts to ponder. Voyager II photographed honey-colored clouds over Saturn, an environmental mass more than 700 times the size of earth. Within its magnificent rings, some of them glowing deep blue, gold, or yellow, Saturn seemed to lie shrouded in veils of swirling ice and rock. Scientists again counted 17 Saturnian moons, with many others possibly hiding in the planet's thousands of rings.

Enceladus again merited a close look by the scientists who watched Voyager's progress from the Jet Propulsion Laboratory in Pasadena, California. The Saturnian moon appeared to be twirling in a kind of tug-of-war with other nearby moons. The pulling and tugging seemed to provide an answer to the moon's surface fissures. The activity was also cited as the cause of the glacier-like ice flows whose movements obliterated surface craters dating back thousands or millions of years.

Voyager's reexamination of Hyperion also produced some surprises. The new photos, taken at ranges as close as 300,000 miles, showed Hyperion to be just as eccentrically shaped as Voyager I had indicated. More exciting, the moon's long axis pointed away from the Saturnian core at an angle of about 45 degrees. In theory, Saturn's gravity should have pulled Hyperion's long axis directly into line with Saturn's center. The photos confirmed that Hyperion, one of the most distant of Saturn's moons, was about 220 miles across and about 130 miles thick.

Evidence of unexplained forces on and around Saturn touched off some scientific speculation. As an example, the scientists searched for new explanations for the continually shifting gaps in the Saturnian rings. They had earlier thought the gaps might be caused by the planet's shepherding moons. Whatever the real explanation, Saturn's moons and rings appeared to swirl in constant ferment. Voyager II found that the golden clouds covering the planet were hurtled along by winds traveling at 1,100 miles per hour.

Saturn's rings, moons, and curious "music" became central factors in the new image of the planet that Voyager II made possible.

The music became identifiable as scientists converted energy waves from the planet's electromagnetic field into sound. The result was a weird symphony of chirps, hums, and resounding gong noises. Bells seemed occasionally to jingle in concert.

Whirling around Saturn, Voyager II picked up speed and raced toward its programmed encounters with Uranus and Neptune. The powerful pull of Saturn's gravity helped hurl it into its new trajectory. Voyager II had written a new chapter in the history of space exploration, one that magnificently complemented the work of Voyager I. Assuming that it would experience no additional mechanical failures, Voyager II would take pictures of both Uranus and Neptune. It would thus provide the first closeups of those distant planets.

Man had learned that Earth's companions in the solar system had personalities of their own. They were no longer mere specks in a night sky. Real worlds, they boasted clouds, winds, storms, lightning, and sleet as well as canyons, cliffs, ice, quakes, mountains, and rock. Titan might have rivers or lakes of liquid methane; Mimas' massive crater, according to scientists, might have been the result of a space collision millions or billions of years ago; Iapetus, 80 percent ice and some 20 percent rock, might also be partly carbon.

What was the future of American exploration of outer space? In late 1981 no new missions were scheduled until 1985. In that year the United States planned to launch the spacecraft Galileo to orbit the planet Jupiter. Galileo would also send a probe into Jupiter's atmosphere.

THE SHUTTLE ERA

In April 1981, the United States launched a new "space truck," the shuttle Columbia. Under the command of Capt. Robert L. Crippen of the U.S. Navy, and John W. Young, a civilian, Columbia spent more than two days in earth orbit. The shuttle orbited the earth 36 times before gliding to a landing at Edwards Air Force Base in California heralding a new age in space exploration and research.

Crippen and Young brought the 80 ton vehicle to a smooth landing on California's Rogers Dry Lake at 215 miles per hour. A jetliner would have touched down at half that speed. Young, commander of the mission, was a veteran of five space flights and a walk on the moon. At 50, he ranked as the most experienced of America's spacefarers. His aide, Crippen, was making his first space flight at the age of 44.

The flight of the Columbia, the world's first reusable space vehicle, aroused awareness that man's future lies in space as well as on earth. Twenty years after Yuri Gagarin of the Soviet Union became the first human being to circle the earth in a space orbit, planners began to talk of commercial trade and travel via the shuttle or some vehicle like it. The cargoes for future flights went into the planning stage. They appeared initially to emphasize three types of payloads: Department of Defense satellites, commercial communications satellites, and scientific devices and equipment.

The 1981 success story of the Columbia encouraged the United States to continue to emphasize shuttle technology. Each new shuttle flight marked a milestone in the exploration of inner space or of man's growing knowledge of the near environment.

Of the two 1982 test flights completed by Columbia, the second and final one made the bigger headlines. The first test flight, an eight-day voyage that ended March 30, had succeeded in gathering most of the scientific data that it sought. Exposure of different parts of the craft to sunlight produced less extreme thermal stresses than expected. The shuttle's long robot arm worked even though a television camera at one joint of the arm did not. The robot made it possible to deploy a "plasma diagnostics package" to monitor magnetic and electrical charges near the shuttle.

The second, and last, test flight ended three months later when Columbia landed flawlessly at Edwards Air Force Base in California. The July 4 completion of the seven-day journey brought predictions and some contradictory statements. President Reagan voiced the U.S. intention to establish "a more permanent presence in space."

Technologically, the mission did well. Columbia carried over 22,000 pounds (10,000 kilograms) of cargo including a top-secret military payload. Specific experiments tested the possibility that biological goods could be produced in the weightless conditions of space. In electrophoresis testing, an answer was sought to the question of whether an electrical field, applied to a solution, could separate desired biological materials in higher and purer concentrations. Involved in the tests were enzymes and hormones that could have significant commercial uses.

Columbia's first operational flight in November came almost as an anticlimax. Where earlier flights had carried crews of two, four astronauts made up Columbia's November 11–16 crew. Called "operational" because it was ferrying two commercial communications satellites, the mission apparently succeeded in delivering both systems into their desired orbits.

The first operational flight for Columbia was also to be its last for sometime. The craft went into temporary "retirement" for refitting following its return to earth. The next three missions would give the shuttle Challenger its baptism in space.

While the U.S. hailed its shuttle missions, the Soviet Union pressed ahead with its own efforts in inner and outer space. Two Soviet Venus probes landed within days of each other in early March 1982. Following the March 1 and 5 landings, Venera 13 and Venera 14 survived Venus' extreme heat—estimated at 854.6° Fahrenheit (457° Celsius)—long enough to transmit radio photos of the cloud-covered planet's surface as well as information on soil-sampling experiments.

Venera 13 survived 127 minutes before heat put it out of commission. On the way to Venus the craft took chemical and isotope readings and performed other scientific tasks. Once on Venus, according to Soviet authorities, it took eight photos to add to the two already in existence—both the results of Soviet probes in 1975. For some of the new photos, filters were used to provide color. A Soviet report said, "Sharp rocks semicovered with fine dust and sand are scattered around. One can

The April 12, 1981, liftoff of the Space Shuttle Columbia ushered in a new age in spaceflight. The shuttle not only provided a launching system in space, but also could be used for more than one flight. (NASA PHOTO)

conclude that there is a little blue color on the planet's surface. The rock is mostly brownish."

Venera 14, landing on March 5, survived about an hour, long enough to carry out data-gathering experiments similar to those of Venera 13. Venera 14's landing site lay some distance from that of its sister craft. Information from both probes went first to mother ships flying past the planet, then by relay to earth. Data from the missions showed that Venus' surface had a chemical makeup similar to Earth's. "We know the chemistry is the same," said a U.S. scientist, "so we have to look for other reasons [why] the evolution is different."

Closer to Earth, the Soviets launched a space station, Salyut 7, on April 19. Salyut 7 replaced the much-used Salyut 6, home at various times to a number of cosmonauts. Putting No. 7 to work, Lt. Col. Anatoly Berezovnoy and Valentin Lebedev moved aboard for a long stay. On May 17 the two put a small communications satellite into orbit.

Salyut 7 gave the Soviets additional leverage toward space-station technology. On June 24 two Soviet cosmonauts and a French *spationaute* blasted into space to rendezous with Salyut 7. The three spent about a week aboard the orbiting space station, returning to Earth July 2 in Kazakhstan, some 2,500 miles (4,000 kilometers) east of Moscow. Jean-Loup Chretien, a French air force colonel, became the first Frenchman to soar into space.

Through the remainder of 1982, Salyut 7 remained in the news. Svetlana Savitskaya, the second Soviet woman in space, visited the station with two other crew members in August, then returned to earth in the Soyuz T-5 capsule that Berezovnoy and Lebedev had used. On November 14, with 186 days of space life behind them, Berezovnoy and Lebedev set a space endurance record, breaking the 185-day mark set by two cosmonauts in 1980. On December 12, the Salyut 7 cosmonauts vacated the space station for the journey back to earth, ending a record 211-day stay in Earth orbit.

The possibility that the Soviets might send a new, enlarged crew to man Salyut 7 opened up March 2, 1983. The Cosmos 1443 satellite sent into orbit on that date linked up with Salyut 7 eight days later, possibly doubling the space station's living space. Cosmos 1443 delivered to Salyut 7 equipment and scientific devices that could be used in further experiments. However, three cosmonauts attempting to dock with the station had to abort their mission April 22, apparently

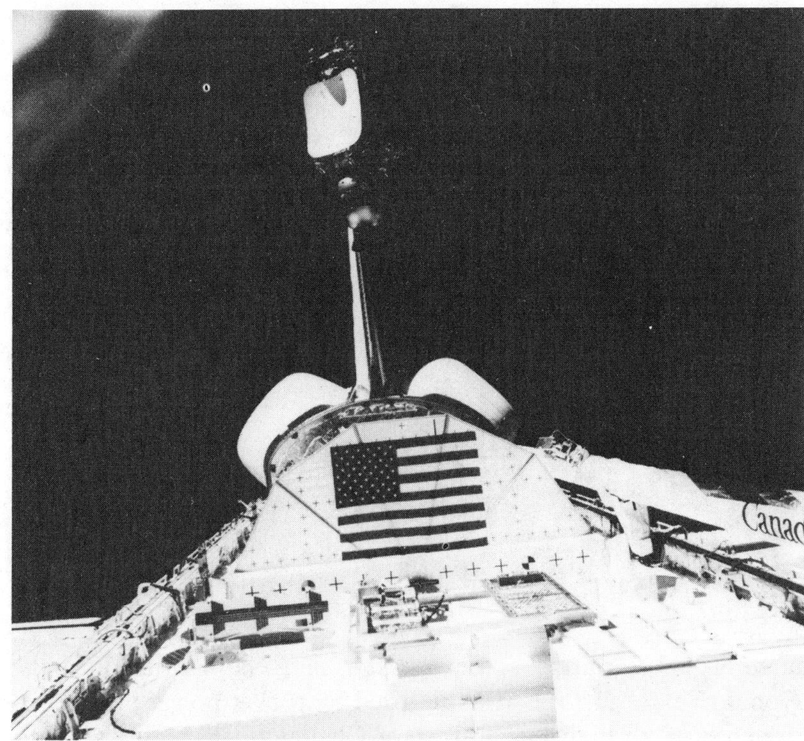

At far left, Photographed from the Columbia above the Mediterranean Sea and the Middle East, the Canadian-built remote manipulator system arm is seen in the Columbia's space hold. Center, An astronaut's camera aimed through an aft window on the flight deck captures earth's clouds and water during a test monitoring the interaction of the shuttle with its surrounding environment. Near left, The Indian National Satellite (INSAT), a shuttle payload, being prepared for launching into space to provide radio, television, and telephone communications. (NASA PHOTOS)

because of technical difficulties; but the next Soviet effort to place spacemen in Salyut 7 succeeded when, on June 28, the two-man crew of a T-9 spacecraft docked with the vacant Salyut-Cosmos complex.

The Soviets said the 40-ton space station was the largest structure ever to be linked to a manned spacecraft. Only weeks earlier, the Soviet Union had launched two new Venus probes, Venera 15 and Venera 16, in orbits that would take the craft around the planet starting in October.

With Columbia mothballed for refitting, space shuttle Challenger became the focus of the United States' efforts in space. The first of Challenger's four 1983 flights began April 4 after delays of more than two months. It ended April 9, having

The Space Shuttle Columbia touched down on a concrete runway July 4, 1982, at Edwards Air Force Base, California. The landing proved that a ship could be piloted to a precise target. (NASA PHOTO)

The crew of the Space Shuttle Challenger pose before a preset camera. In the rear (left to right) are astronauts Robert L. Crippen, Frederick H. Hauck, and John M. Fabian. In front are scientists Sally K. Ride and Norman E. Thagard. (NASA PHOTO)

scored a spectacular success. In the course of the flight, astronauts Story Musgrave and Donald Peterson took the first U. S. spacewalk in nine years. Testing their new spacesuits, the two spent four hours outside the shuttle practicing ways of maintaining and repairing orbiting satellites.

Challenger's engines produced more thrust than Columbia's, enabling the later entry in the United States' space program to carry a heavier payload. In specific terms, Columbia had gone aloft on its last flight with a payload of 32,093 pounds (14,588 kilograms); Challenger carried cargo weighing 46,615 pounds (21,189 kilograms). This payload included a $100 million Tracking and Data Relay Satellite. The 5,000 pound (2,300 kilogram) communications satellite, said to be the most sophisticated yet developed, was the first of three that would form an advanced space-based communications system.

Challenger was only warming up. On its second flight, from June 18–24, it scored a number of firsts, among them one that attracted widespread media and public attention: included in the crew as a mission specialist was the first American woman astronaut, physicist Sally K. Ride. Other members of the crew included Capt. Robert Crippen, mission commander and the first person to make a second shuttle flight. On June 18 and 19 Ride and mission specialist Col. John Fabian deployed a Canadian communications satellite, the Anik C and the Palapa B satellite for the Association of Southeast Asian Nations. Both of the latter had to be lifted by rocket power into orbits higher than that of Challenger.

The second Challenger flight blazed other trails. It was the first shuttle mission to carry a five-person crew. One crew member, Norman Thagard, a medical doctor, carried out tests designed to discover why about half the astronauts in space suffered from nausea. Ride and Fabian successfully cut free a satellite, allowing it to drift in space, then retrieved it using the shuttle's mechanical arm. The experiment involved the Shuttle Pallet Satellite, or SPAS, a space platform designed by West German scientists to carry out various experiments with different kinds of instruments. The satellite was allowed to float free, then was retrieved, five separate times.

In one respect Challenger's second jaunt into space was a disappointment. Plans had called for the shuttle to land at Cape Canaveral, the site of the launching. When bad weather over the Cape forced cancellation of that plan, mission control opted for another landing at Edwards Air Force Base.

Other June space events competed with Challenger for public attention. On June 13, the United States' unmanned Pioneer 10 deep space probe, launched in 1972, left the solar system and soared into the lonely reaches of interstellar space. On June 29, U.S. officials announced that two months of maneuvering had rectified the orbit of the

Tracking and Data Relay Satellite. Because of a rocket malfunction, the satellite had begun life in space in a skewed orbit.

August brought Challenger's third 1983 flight. Again the shuttle made space history. The first U.S. black astronaut, Guion S. Bluford, a lieutenant colonel in the Air Force and holder of a Ph.D. in aerospace engineering, went into space as a mission specialist. Challenger's third flight began August 30 and ended September 5.

Scientific and commercial business characterized the August–September flight. Challenger carried Insat-1B, a combination weather–communications satellite constructed for India. Challenger's crew launched the new satellite at night on August 31, sending it toward an orbit that was to keep it stationary 22,300 miles (35,700 kilometers) above the Indian Ocean. In a money-

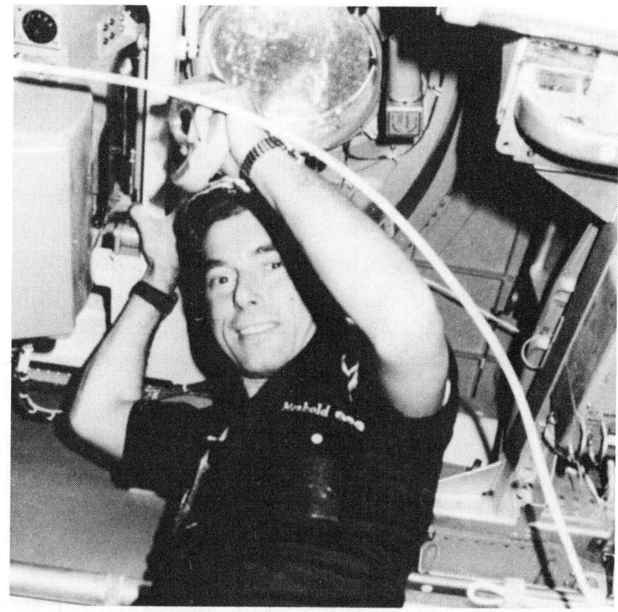

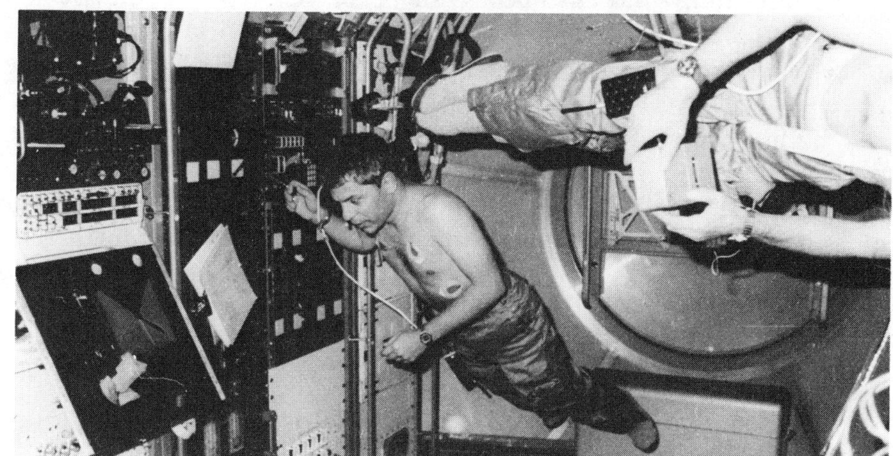

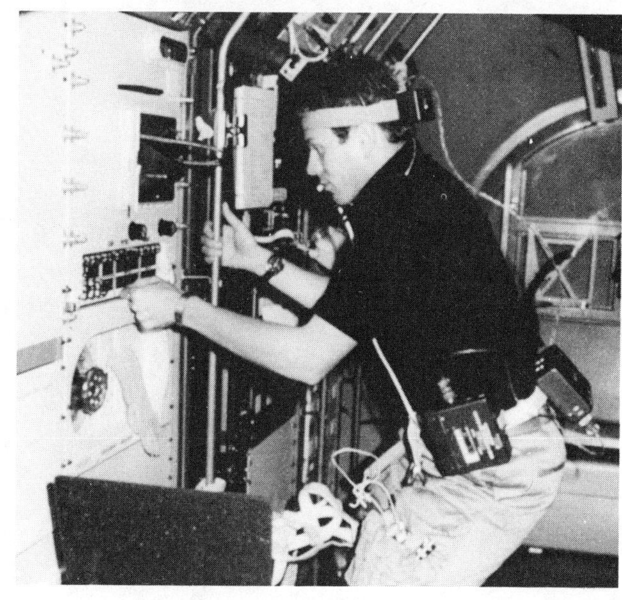

Top, German physicist Ulf Merbold, the first European to fly in a U.S. spacecraft, makes adjustments in the spacelab equipment before beginning research experiments. Center, Astronaut Robert Parker floats in the microgravity environment while participating in a Challenger biomedical test. Bottom, Payload specialist Byron Lichtenberg conducts one of the more than 30 experiments performed aboard the Challenger for investigators from nine European nations. (NASA PHOTOS)

making gimmick, the shuttle also carried into space 260,000 envelopes. Each bore the $9.35 stamp standardly used for the U.S. Postal Service's Express Mail Service. To be sold as souvenirs later, the envelopes would carry a $15.35 price tag. The Postal Service and NASA would split the profits.

Challenger began its fourth and final 1983 flight on November 28. Programmed to keep its six astronauts—the largest number yet—busy with more than 70 scientific and other experiments, the space truck encountered delays lasting a month, then blasted off perfectly. In command again was John W. Young, 53. Young, who had commanded the first shuttle flight, was making his sixth trip into space.

In addition to carrying German physicist Ulf

Merbold, the first European to fly in a U.S. spacecraft, Challenger was soaring into what was described as "a new era of research." It had on board the first laboratory designed to be used and reused in space: the $1 billion Spacelab built by the European Space Agency. Spacelab was to stay in the shuttle throughout the mission; to make optimal use of it and their other equipment, the crew was divided into two shifts, the red team and the blue team. They worked around the clock.

Challenger returned to earth on December 8, one day later than the December 7 landing originally planned. The crew's diligent—and successful—performance of the many programmed experiments had occasioned the change.

As 1983 wound down, Americans were looking more and more for ways to put high-tech development into orbit. This "commercialization of space" fell ideally into alignment with President Reagan's 1982 promise to "provide a climate [in space] conducive to expanded private sector investment. . . ." At the same time both military and commercial spinoffs from the shuttle flights were expected to proliferate. Predictions that future Columbias and Challengers would become more powerful and more sophisticated no longer raised eyebrows.

The first 1984 flight of Challenger began February 3 and ended eight days later. Descending from 170 miles out in space, Challenger landed for the first time on a new, $27 million, three-mile-long runway at the Kennedy Space Center, Cape Canaveral, Florida. The concrete landing strip was located five miles from Launch Pad 39B, from which the space shuttle had blasted off earlier.

The tenth flight by a space truck brought both successes and failures. The latter included the losses of two communications satellites whose rocket boosters misfired. The malfunctions made it impossible to put the satellites into their planned orbits. Among other problems, a target rendezvous balloon exploded during inflation and a robot arm failed to perform as programmed. In a spectacular achievement, "spacewalkers" Bruce McCandless and Robert Stewart performed the first spacewalks by astronauts who were not tethered to their spacecraft by lifelines. The two, members of Challenger's five-man crew, wore $10 million manned maneuvering units (MMUs) as they floated free as far as 300 feet from the shuttle.

While Challenger's flight was in progress, the Soviet Union sent up three cosmonauts to rendezvous with the orbiting space station Salyut-7.

MEMBERS OF THE UNITED NATIONS

Member	Year Joined
Afghanistan	1946
Albania	1955
Algeria	1962
Angola	1976
Argentina[1]	1945
Australia[1]	1945
Austria	1955
Bahamas	1973
Bahrain	1971
Bangladesh	1974
Barbados	1966
Belgium	1945
Benin[2]	1960
Bhutan	1971
Bolivia	1945
Botswana	1966
Brazil	1945
Bulgaria	1955
Burma	1948
Burundi	1962
Byelorussian SSR[1]	1945
Cambodia[3]	1955
Cameroon	1960
Canada	1945
Cape Verde Islands	1975
Central African Empire[4]	1960
Chad	1960
Chile[1]	1945
China, People's Rep.[5]	1971
Colombia[1]	1945
Comoro Islands	1975
Congo Republic[6]	1960
Costa Rica[1]	1945
Cuba[1]	1945
Cyprus	1960
Czechoslovakia[1]	1945
Denmark[1]	1945
Djibouti	1979
Dominican Republic[1]	1945
Ecuador	1945
Egypt[1, 7]	1945
El Salvador	1945
Equatorial Guinea	1968
Ethiopia[1]	1945
Fiji	1970
Finland	1955
France[1]	1945
Gabon	1960
Gambia	1965
German Dem. Rep.	1973
Germany, Federal Rep. of	1973
Ghana	1957
Greece[1]	1945
Grenada	1974
Guatemala[1]	1945
Guinea	1958
Guinea-Bissau	1974
Guyana	1966
Haiti[1]	1945
Honduras[1]	1945
Hungary	1955
Iceland	1946
India[1]	1945
Indonesia[8]	1950
Iran[1]	1945
Iraq[1]	1945
Ireland	1955
Israel	1949
Italy	1955
Ivory Coast	1960
Jamaica	1962
Japan	1956
Jordan	1955
Kenya	1963
Kuwait	1963
Laos	1955
Lebanon[1]	1945
Lesotho	1966
Liberia[1]	1945
Libya	1955
Luxembourg[1]	1945
Malagasy Republic	1960
Malawi	1964
Malaysia[9]	1957
Maldive Islands	1965
Mali	1960
Malta	1964
Mauritania	1961
Mauritius	1968
Mexico	1945
Mongolia	1961
Morocco	1956
Mozambique	1975
Nepal	1955
Netherlands[1]	1945
New Zealand[1]	1945
Nicaragua[1]	1945
Niger	1960
Nigeria	1960
Norway[1]	1945
Oman	1971
Pakistan	1947
Panama[1]	1945
Papua New Guinea	1975
Paraguay[1]	1945
Peru[1]	1945
Philippines[1]	1945
Poland[1]	1945
Portugal	1955
Qatar	1971
Rumania	1955
Rwanda	1962
São Tomé and Principe	1975
Saudi Arabia[1]	1945
Senegal	1960
Seychelles	1976
Sierra Leone	1961
Singapore	1965
Somalia	1960
South Africa[1]	1945
Spain	1955
Sri Lanka[10]	1955
Sudan	1956
Surinam	1975
Swaziland	1968
Sweden	1946
Syria[1, 7]	1945
Tanzania, United Rep.[11]	1964
Thailand	1946
Togo	1960
Trinidad and Tobago	1962
Tunisia	1956
Turkey[1]	1945
Uganda	1962
Ukranian SSR[1]	1945
Union of Soviet Socialist Republics[1]	1945
United Arab Emirates	1971
United Kingdom[1]	1945
United States[1]	1945
Upper Volta	1960
Uruguay	1945
Venezuela[1]	1945
Vietnam	1979
Western Samoa	1976
Yemen	1947
Yemen, People's Dem. Rep.[12]	1967
Yugoslavia[1]	1945
Zaire Republic[13]	1960
Zambia	1964

[1] One of the original members. [2] Admitted as Dahomey in 1960, its name was changed to Benin in 1975. [3] Admitted as Cambodia in 1955, its name was changed to Khmer Republic in 1970 and changed back to Cambodia in 1975. [4] Admitted as Central African Republic in 1960, it was renamed Central African Empire in 1976. [5] The Nationalist government of China, on the island of Taiwan, was one of the original members of the United Nations. In 1971 the Communist government of the People's Republic of China, on the mainland, was invited to join the United Nations as the sole representative of the Chinese people. [6] Formerly known as Congo (Brazzaville). [7] Syria and Egypt merged in 1958 to form the United Arab Republic, thus relinquishing one UN seat. In 1961 Syria withdrew from the federation and regained its seat. The United Arab Republic was renamed the Arab Republic of Egypt in 1971. [8] In 1965 Indonesia withdrew from the United Nations; in 1966 it was readmitted. [9] Joined under the name Malaya, later federated with other territories and renamed Malaysia. Singapore withdrew from this federation and was admitted to the United Nations as an independent state in 1965. [10] Admitted as Ceylon in 1955, its name was changed to Sri Lanka in 1972. [11] Originally Tanganyika and Zanzibar, joining the United Nations in 1961 and 1963 respectively. They merged in 1964. [12] Admitted as Southern Yemen in 1967, its name was changed to the People's Democratic Republic of Yemen in 1970. [13] Formerly known as Congo (Leopoldville). Subsequently the capital city of Leopoldville was changed in name to Kinshasa. In 1971 the nation was renamed Zaire Republic after the original name of the Congo River.

Career Guidance

THE BEST AND WORST JOBS

THE FUTURE WORLD OF WORK

HOW TO FIND A JOB

HOW AND WHERE TO LOOK UP MORE INFORMATION

The Best And Worst Job Prospects For The 1980's

WILLIAM E. HOPKE

The *Dictionary of Occupational Titles* includes definitions for more than 20,000 occupations existing in the United States. Of these thousands of occupations, which ones will be found most often in the "help wanted" ads and in openings listed by employers in job finding agencies during the 1980's? What will be the top ten best prospects for jobs in this decade? What are the top twenty occupations which will produce the most new jobs during this period? In the area of fast growing high technology jobs, which will be the top five?

The Bureau of Labor Statistics has provided answers to the above questions by counting how many people were employed in these jobs in 1980, by estimating the projected job growth for 1980 to 1990, and by predicting the percentage of growth for these occupations in the future. This information is found in the two tables below. The first table ranks the occupations according to the total number of new jobs which will be produced (projected growth). The high technology jobs are ranked according to the percentage of growth rather than the total number of new jobs which are projected.

More detailed information on each of these twenty five occupations may be found in Volumes II and III of this *Encyclopedia.* A large majority of the occupations which will produce the most new jobs are considered to be those which will require only high school education or a short period of education or on-the-job training beyond high school. This group of occupations includes nurses' aides and orderlies, janitors and sextons, sales clerks, cashiers, truck drivers, fast-food workers, general office clerks, waiters and waitresses, kitchen helpers, construction helpers, and typists. Those occupations requiring more specialized training in high school, a longer period of education, or on-the-job training beyond high school include secretaries, automotive mechanics, licensed practical nurses, carpenters, and bookkeepers. Included in the group of occupations requiring the most education and training are professional nurses, elementary school teachers, accountants and auditors and blue-collar supervisors.

The Department of Labor also offers us information on the ten worst job prospects in terms of the number of jobs which will be lost during the period 1980 to 1990. The table below indicates the number of jobs in thousands which will be lost for these ten occupations.

As indicated in the table, the jobs for farm laborers and operators as well as high school teachers are considered to have the worst job prospects with losses in the 246,000 to 173,000 range. The middle range of worst prospects include college teachers, servants and graduate assistants with losses in the range of 55,000 to

24,000. The loss of job range for compositors and typesetters, shoe machine operators, clergy, and postal clerks runs from 13,000 to 6,000 over the ten year period. More detailed information on these occupations can also be found in Volumes II and III of this *Encyclopedia.*

Among the main factors considered by young people in occupational and career choices are ability and achievement levels, fields of interest, potential income and geographical preference. The importance and use of these factors in planning a career are discussed in articles under the "You and Your Career" section of Volume I.

This article and the one entitled "The Future World of Work" supply information on another factor that needs to be considered in career decisions—that of knowledge of the opportunities that exist for employment. Further information concerning employment opportunities are found in the career field articles in Volume I.

Ten Worst Job Prospects During the Next Decade

	Number of Jobs in Thousands		
	1980	1990	
Postal clerks	316	310	−6
Clergy	296	287	−9
Shoe machine operators	65	54	−11
Compositors and typesetters	128	115	−13
Graduate assistants	132	108	−24
Servants	478	449	−29
College teachers	457	402	−55
High school teachers	1,237	1,064	−173
Farm laborers	1,175	940	−235
Farm operators	1,447	1,201	−246

Occupations Producing the Most New Jobs During the Next Decade

	1980 employment	Projected growth, 1980-90	Percent growth
1 Secretaries	2,469,000	700,000	28.3%
2 Nurses' aides, orderlies	1,175,000	508,000	43.2
3 Janitors, sextons	2,751,000	501,000	18.2
4 Sales clerks	2,880,000	479,000	16.7
5 Cashiers	1,597,000	452,000	28.4
6 Professional nurses	1,104,000	437,000	39.6
7 Truck drivers	1,696,000	415,000	24.5
8 Fast-food workers	806,000	400,000	49.6
9 General office clerks	2,395,000	377,000	15.8
10 Waiters, waitresses	1,711,000	360,000	21.1
11 Elementary teachers	1,286,000	251,000	19.5
12 Kitchen helpers	839,000	231,000	27.6
13 Accountants, auditors	833,000	221,000	26.5
14 Construction helpers	955,000	212,000	22.2
15 Automotive mechanics	846,000	206,000	24.4
16 Blue-collar supervisors	1,297,000	206,000	15.9
17 Typists	1,067,000	187,000	17.5
18 Licensed practical nurses	522,000	185,000	35.5
19 Carpenters	970,000	173,000	17.9
20 Bookkeepers	975,000	167,000	17.2

Five Fastest Growing High Technology Jobs

	1980 employment	Projected growth, 1980-90	Percent growth
1 Data processing mechanics	83,000	77,000	92.3%
2 Computer operators	185,000	133,000	71.6
3 Computer analysts	205,000	139,000	67.8
4 Office machine servicers	55,000	33,000	59.8
5 Computer programmers	228,000	112,000	48.9

Source: Bureau of Labor Statistics

The Future World of Work

WILLIAM E. HOPKE

No one knows for sure what will happen to job opportunities in the future. No one can precisely predict how an economic upswing or recession, a war or the threat of war, and social or political changes will affect employment in the next decade. Nor can we estimate exactly how the introduction of new products and changes in production methods will determine the number of new jobs or those that will disappear.

However, there is presently available much information about the future that can be used to predict what your occupational possibilities will be. We can estimate the size of the country's population, approximately how many people will be in each age group, and the kinds of goods and services they will need. We also know what the current job trends are and how these trends are likely to affect the job market in the future. What has happened in the recent past also gives us clues in predicting what the future may bring.

It is therefore possible to give you information that can be helpful as you go about the process of choosing a career. Your interests, abilities, and achievements will determine which occupational fields are attractive to you. However, the job opportunities that will be available to you in the future will be determined by economic and social conditions at the time you enter the job market.

The world of work in our nation is large and complex. There are many thousands of different jobs that exist in a variety of business, industrial, government, and agency settings. As you plan for a career, becoming more knowledgeable about current trends and predictions for the future will assist you in making better vocational choices and decisions.

This article will present information relating to population growth and changes, the nature of the labor force, and employment trends in industries and occupational fields. Also included will be a look at job prospects by regions of the United States. Sources of information include the Bureau of the Census and the Bureau of Labor Statistics.

Population and the Economy

The demand for jobs in an occupation depends on how many people seek the goods and services connected with that occupation and how many workers are available for that occupation. The Bureau of Labor Statistics has identified three types of population trends that will affect the situation in the future. They are overall growth in the population, changes in its age compositions, and patterns of population movement among regions of the country.

240 Million People

It is estimated that the population of the United States will pass 240 million people during the 1980's, and it is expected to increase to 247 million by 1990. This continued growth will increase the demands for goods and services and the needs for workers in many industries. However, changes in age groups as well as the varying rates of growth in regions of the country will affect the number and types of jobs available in the future.

Changes in Age Groups

After World War II, there was a sharp increase in the number of babies being born, a situation known as the "baby boom." This situation has caused the proportion of young people in the population to go up in recent years. During the next decade, the proportion of persons between the ages of 25 to 44 will increase. This will be the period when more and more young adults will be entering their most productive work years. Chart 1 shows the slowing in the rate of population growth since the 1960's.

Chart 1
Since 1960, the population has grown more slowly

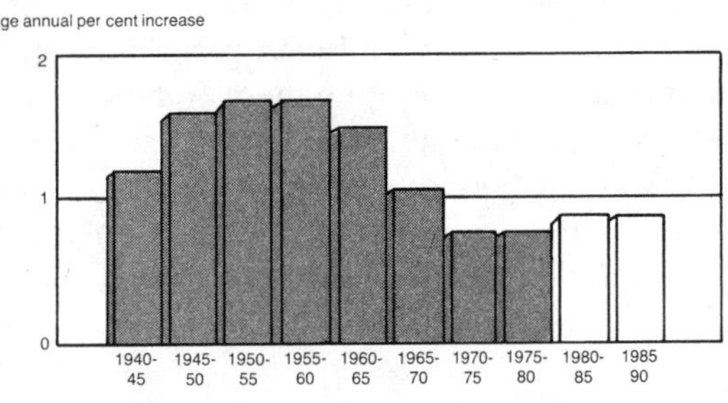

Source: Bureau of the Census

Because there was a relatively low number of births during the 1960's and early 1970's, the number of people in the 14 to 24 age group will decline during the 1980's. Older people (65 and over) will grow in numbers but more slowly than in recent years.

These changes in age groups will cause shifts in employment. As members of the "baby boom" group start their families, they will need more homes, furnishings, and appliances. The need for education services will fall as the number of young people declines.

Regional Changes

People move within states and between states for many reasons, such as finding a new job, retirement, climate, and health problems. As a result, different areas of the United States experience different growth rates. For example, during the decade 1970-80, population in the Northeast and North Central regions increased by only 0.2 per cent and 4 per cent respectively. However, in the South the increase was 20 per cent while the West increased 23.9 per cent. Chart 2 gives a picture of how the regions of the country varied in growth during the last decade.

Chart 2
Population growth varies among the States
Per cent change in State populations, 1970-80

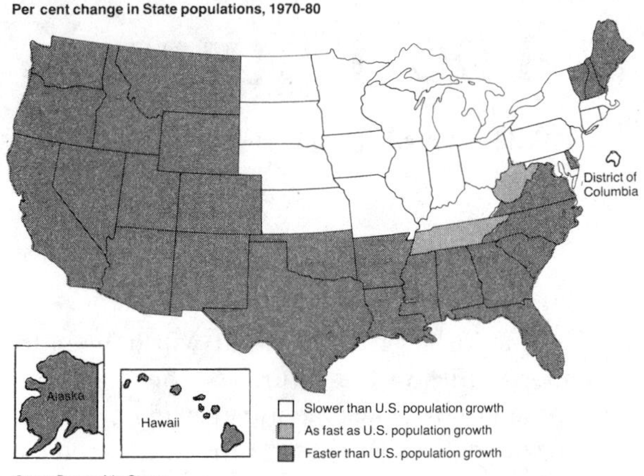

Source: Bureau of the Census

As people move and the population shifts among states, there are changes in the supply of and demand for workers in local areas or regions. Areas with growing populations need more goods and services, such as police or fire protection, water, and waste disposal. Information about regional variations in employment prospects for specific occupations is contained in articles in Volumes I, II, and III.

Chart 2 indicates that because of faster population growth, employment opportunities will probably be the greatest in parts of New England, the North Central region, and the Middle Atlantic Coast, as well as a rim around the "Sun Belt" states from the Southeast across the South to the Southwestern portion of the United States.

Changes in the Labor Force

The number and type of workers in the labor force will determine how much competition you will have for jobs when you are ready to go to work. Employment opportunities during the 1980's will be affected by the following factors: (1) growth in the size of the labor force, (2) changes in the age groups within the labor force, and (3) the rising educational level of workers.

Growth in the labor force will moderate during the early 1980's and slow even more significantly during the latter part of the decade. The growth will be caused by an increasing number of people in the working age-group and a continuing rise in the proportion of working women. However, by the late 1980's there will be fewer young people entering the world of work and a less rapid growth in the number of women in the work force. Chart 3 pictures how the total labor force and the proportion of women in it will grow.

Chart 3
The number of women workers will continue to grow faster than the total labor force

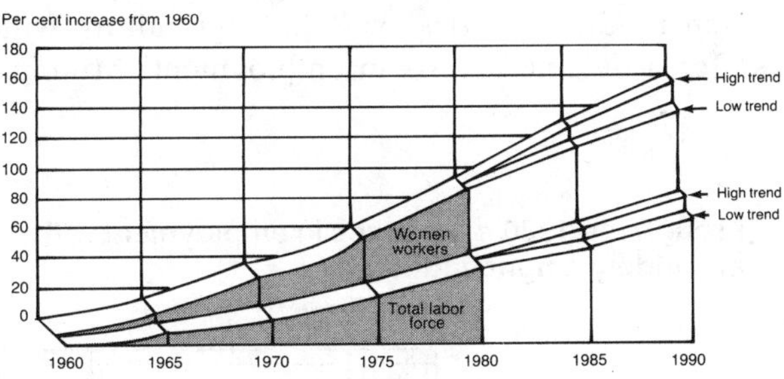

Source: Bureau of Labor Statistics

Age Shifts in the Labor Force

During recent years, competition for entry-level jobs has been strong because of the large number of young people entering the labor force. Because of this situation, many young people have found themselves in the ranks of the unemployed. However, because of the relatively low number of births during the 1960's and 1970's, there will be less competition for beginning-level jobs. People seeking entry-level positions should be able to find jobs, gain work experience, and become more productive. Chart 4 reveals how large the number of workers in this prime working age will be in comparison with other age groups.

Chart 4
Through the 1980's, the number of workers in the prime working ages will grow dramatically

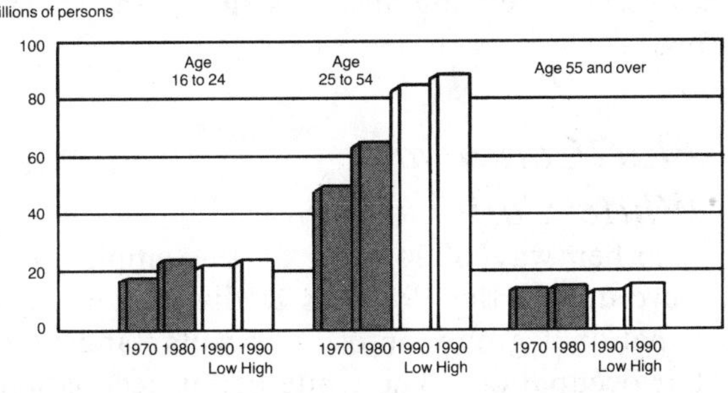

Source: Bureau of Labor Statistics

Education and Training

In 1952, the average worker had 11.1 years of school. By 1980, the number of school years had risen to 12.6, so that now a high school education has become a labor-force standard. The number of school years completed by workers will probably continue to rise slowly, and this could increase the competition for jobs in many occupations.

High school drop-outs will not be able to compete effectively for jobs offering better pay or promotion possibilities. The exception would be a person who has specific training for a job.

Many employers are now requiring education or apprenticeships beyond high school for technical, office, and craft occupations. They prefer to hire people who are already trained rather than provide costly training for new workers.

The number of college graduates in the work force more than doubled from 8 to 19 per cent of the labor force during the period from 1952 to 1980. In the past, a college education has been looked upon as a passport to better pay, more opportunities for promotion, more status, and to employment that provided more challenge and variety of duties. However, during the last decade, the supply of college graduates grew at a more rapid pace than the number of professional, managerial, and technical positions requiring a college degree. Because of this situation, approximately 25 per cent of all college graduates found it necessary to take jobs that usually had been filled by persons with less education. As a result, the proportion of college graduates in clerical, lower-level sales and managerial jobs, and blue-collar work has grown.

In the 1980's, it appears that there will continue to be a greater supply of college graduates than needed for most occupations requiring a college degree. The placement possibilities for college graduates have improved somewhat recently, but the prospect for demand catching up with supply is not considered to be good. It should also be pointed out that college graduates will continue to enjoy some advantages over those with less education. They continue to be more employable and to be able to secure the highest-paying professional and managerial jobs. Persons with interest in and abilities for occupations requiring a college education should continue to consider such career fields. However, they should also be aware of the job prospects in these fields.

Young people who develop occupational skills or acquire education up to the level of their potential will continue to have more choices in employment and better opportunities for steady and interesting work as well as good wages.

Chart 5

Industries providing services employ more people than those providing goods

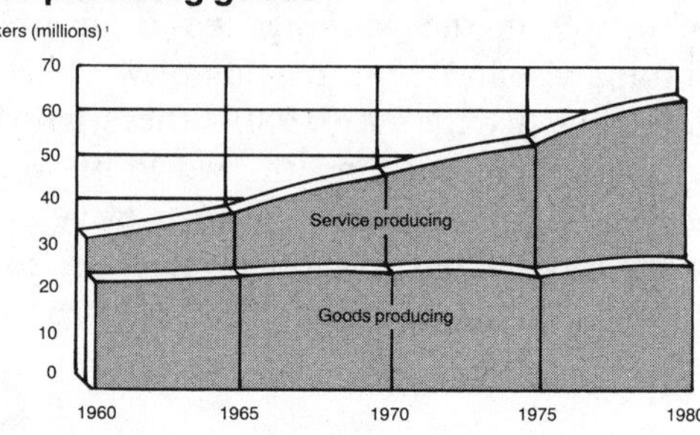

[1]Wage and salary workers, except for agriculture, which includes self-employed and unpaid family workers
Source: Bureau of Labor Statistics

The Job Market

What will the level of employment be in the year 1990 in major occupational groups and industries? To furnish answers to this important question, let us assume that, during the next years, there will be a labor force that will have a moderate increase in numbers. There will also be a relatively slow decline in inflation, and only a moderate growth in the costs of government. If these conditions fail to occur, then changes in the predictions have to be made.

The bulk of our nation's economic activity is accounted for by two large groups of industries: service-producing industries and goods-producing industries. Service industries provide services such as banking, education, government, health care, insurance, repair and maintenance, and transportation. Over two-thirds of the nation's workers are employed in these industries. The goods-producing industries include construction, farming, manufacturing, and mining. Less than one-third of the labor force is employed in these industries.

Industrial Employment Trends

Chart 5 shows how the service industries have been producing more jobs than the goods-producing industries for the past two decades. It is estimated that this faster increase in the growth of service jobs will continue during the 1980's. More specific information on how changes in employment will vary among the major industries in the United States in the next decade is given in Chart 6. It shows that agriculture will suffer a decline or loss in employment. Mining,

Chart 6

Through the 1980's, changes in employment will vary widely among industries

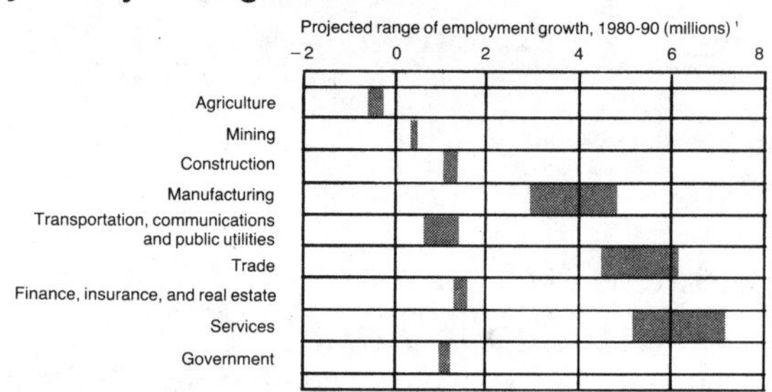

[1]Wage and salary workers, except for agriculture, which includes self-employed and unpaid family workers
Source: Bureau of Labor Statistics

government, transportation, communications, finance, insurance, real estate, public utilities, and contract construction will grow slowly. There will be a moderate to high growth rate in employment for manufacturing. The highest rate of growth will be in services and trade fields, with services leading all industries in the rate of growth.

Blue-Collar and White-Collar Jobs

Another way of looking at the employment picture during the 1980's is to divide the major occupational groups into white-collar and blue-collar occupations. The white-collar occupations are clerical, managerial, professional, sales, and technical. The blue-collar jobs include craft, farm, laborer, operative, and service occupations.

Chart 7

White-collar workers have been the largest occupational group for more than two decades

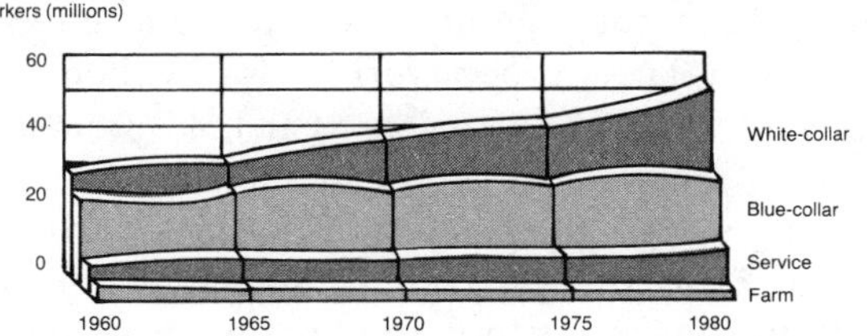

Source: Bureau of Labor Statistics

It can be seen in Chart 7 that the number of white-collar workers has been greater than blue-collar workers from the 1960's through the present. It is estimated that the difference in the numbers by which white-collar workers exceed the blue-collar group will continue through 1990. The blue-collar job field will continue to grow, but the rate will not be as high as for white-collar workers.

Varied Growth in Occupational Fields

The occupational group that has the largest potential for growth between now and 1990 is that of clerical worker. Close behind this group are service workers (except those who are employed in private households) as well as professional and technical workers. Groups that will have moderate growth include managerial and administrative, sales, craft, and operative (except transport) workers. A small amount of growth will occur in two groups: transport operatives and nonfarm laborers. One group that will suffer a loss in employment will be farm workers. Private household workers will show no growth.

Chart 8 summarizes the differences in changes in employment by occupational groups in the 1980's.

Chart 8

Through the 1980's, changes in employment will vary widely among occupational groups

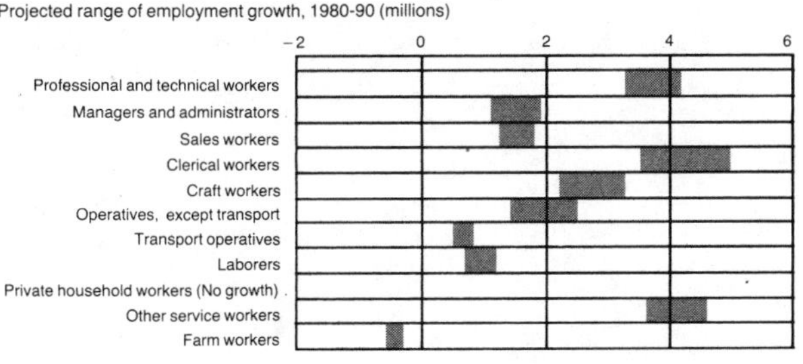

Source: Bureau of Labor Statistics

Women at Work

The percentage of women who work continues to rise. The Bureau of Labor Statistics has indicated that about forty and one-half million women were employed as of 1980. It is estimated that over eight out of ten women will work sometime during their lifetime. Employers are now hiring women for many jobs outside those once considered traditional work for females. They are also being paid salaries and attaining status not possible a decade or two ago. However, most women (about 80 per cent) continue to be employed in the lower-paying fields that have been usually considered "women's work": clerical, factory and plant work, sales, and service. Recent government data indicate the median salary for women working full-time is only 59 per cent of that of men.

Women are beginning to move into fields such as the skilled trades and technical crafts, as well as administrative and managerial jobs. Although the numbers and rates of growth have been low in most fields, there has been growth in the nontraditional fields. Chart 9 shows the percentage of growth for women in fields such as managerial/administrative, banking/finance, and buyers/purchasing agents during the past 20 years. It is estimated that this growth will increase during the 1980's in these and other fields. Gains are also expected in professional occupations such as pharmacist, engineer, mathematician, judge, lawyer, and computer programmer. Among other promising fields that women will enter in greater numbers are business, hotel and restaurant managing, information processing, insurance, and sales.

Special Groups

Concern will continue for increasing the employment prospects for special groups such as the American Indians, blacks, Hispanics, and Puerto Ricans. The youth in these groups traditionally have not been able to compete as effectively as majority group workers for beginning-level work and for those jobs that hold promise for advancement and career building.

Both government and private businesses have become involved in the training and employment of disadvantaged youth. Special efforts have been made to provide educational opportunities to young people, as well as opportunities for being hired, learning job skills, and for becoming eligible for promotions. In view of the high rate of unemployment among these young people and other disadvantaged workers, more educational and employment possibilities will have to be created during the 1980's to assist this special portion of the work force.

Finding a Job

WILLIAM E. HOPKE

How does a young person who has completed his or her training or education go about finding a job? Or how does a person who already has a job go about changing jobs?

There are some people who think that jobs are obtained mainly through contacts with friends and relatives or people they know. This approach is sometimes called the "It's not so much what you know, but who you know" method.

There are other people who believe that finding a job often takes place "by accident." That is, you have to happen to be in the right place at the right time to get the job you want.

Other methods include such activities as registering with a high school or college career planning and placement office, public employment services, private employment agencies, and civil service offices; using classified want ads and directories of employers; sending out resumes or data sheets with letters of application; calling employers on the telephone; and completing employment applications at firms in which the job seeker is interested.

William E. Hopke, M.A., Ed.D., served as a placement officer in the Office of Placement at Teachers College, Columbia University. Part of his duties as a school counselor and guidance director included placement services for secondary school students.

All of the above approaches have helped some young people secure their first jobs or new ones. Detailed descriptions of these methods will be presented in this article along with an explanation of how they can be used to help find a job.

The One Most Effective Approach

There are a growing number of placement workers who believe that the single best method of finding a job is to make personal visits to the people who do the hiring in agencies, businesses, and plants. These placement personnel have found that the one most effective approach is to have the job applicant "pound the pavement" and knock on the doors of possible employers. However, they have also found that the job seekers who use the greatest number of methods have greatest job-finding success. This article will begin therefore with the most effective approach (personal visits). This approach will be followed by the other methods most often used by those looking for jobs.

Personal Visits

Before making a personal visit to a potential employer, the job seeker should have already conducted a self-evaluation as well as a survey of potential employers. The self-evaluation should include an examination of interests and skills developed during education, training, and past experience. The first three articles in this volume (Strategies for Career Planning, Where to Go for Further Information, and Using Test Results in Vocational Planning) contain much helpful information on how to conduct a self-evaluation.

In conducting a survey of potential employers, the applicant should seek out as much information as possible about employers who may have suitable openings. Information on employers, including the products and services of the organization, and the names, addresses and telephone numbers of people to be contacted, may be obtained from libraries, school and college placement offices, private and public employment agencies, directories, want ads, civil service offices, employees of the organization, and friends and relatives. The article Where to Go for Further Information contains more specific details on these and other sources of information about potential employers.

Contacting the Employer

After job seekers have completed a self-evaluation and survey of employers, how do they go about contacting the potential employer?

The different methods of contacting an employer will vary with the source of employment information. If the information comes as the result of a referral from a private or public employment agency, the candidate may need only to telephone for an appointment. When there is competition for a job, the applicant may use other common methods of contacting employers: (1) sending letters of application, resumes, and data sheets; (2) telephone calls; (3) employment applications; and (4) personal visits to places of employment. The latter approach will be described first.

In some firms, it's possible to make an unscheduled visit to the employer or personnel office and be permitted to have an immediate interview or one within a short period of time. Other employers prefer that applicants arrange appointments in advance. Smaller firms are more likely to permit unscheduled visits. The larger, more formally organized companies and agencies are less likely to do so.

Conducting the Employment Interview

In addition to general information about the firm or agency, the candidate for a job should also learn about the employer's organization, its size and location, what types of employees work there, how the organization has been growing and developing, and its strong and weak points. This information can be obtained from annual reports, newspapers and magazine articles, employment brochures, friends who work there, and customers as well as clients of the organization. The applicant will find that potential employers are impressed by job seekers who are familiar with such information.

Following are typical questions which are asked during interviews. Candidates should be prepared to answer questions such as:

a. Why did you apply for a position with this organization? What do you know about our organization?
b. For what specific position are you applying? What makes you think you can do this job?
c. What type of work do you like best?
d. Did you enjoy your education? What are the courses you liked least and best? What kinds of grades did you get? Best subjects?
e. Do you plan to continue your education? If not, why not?
f. What do you hope to be doing at age 35? 50?
g. What are or were your mother's and father's occupations?
h. Do you get along well with people? What kinds of people do you find it difficult to work with?
i. What full or part-time jobs have you held? What did you learn from them?
j. What are your hobbies?
k. What salary do you expect?

The job applicant should also be prepared to ask three or four questions. They should be related to what you have learned or would like to learn about the employer and the field.

Arriving for the Interview

Surveys of employers and personnel workers have revealed that one of the most important factors considered in interviews is the applicant's appearance. Dress should be conservative with a good-looking suit or dress rather than sports clothes for most interviews. Men should wear a dress shirt and a businesslike tie. For some jobs, neat and clean work clothes are important. Women should apply cosmetics sparingly and avoid gaudy jewelry. Careful grooming of hair, fingernails, shoes, and clothes along with the use of deodorants are necessary. Smoking during, as well as drinking alcohol before an interview should be avoided.

If an appointment has been made for the interview, arrive five minutes before the time scheduled. Allow time for finding unfamiliar locations.

An applicant should give his or her name and the name of the persons conducting the interview to the secretary or receptionist. If not known, candidates should find out the complete name and job title of the persons they will be seeing. Applicants should sit quietly or read until they are called and not engage secretaries and receptionists in social conversations. Since employers pay for the time of these workers, they would not want to hire someone who would waste it before or after hiring.

Boy or girl friends, members of the family, or other acquaintances should not accompany the applicant into the reception area. Their appearance there suggests that the candidate needs support.

It is also a good idea for a candidate to take a pencil or pen and paper on which to take notes for keeping needed information. These notes should not be made during the interview but as soon as possible after leaving the employer.

The best advice to a young person who is going on a job interview for the first time is to be relaxed and sincere. The interviewer will recognize and appreciate enthusiasm and self-confidence.

Handling the Interviewer

Although some questions have been raised about the effectiveness of interviews for both applicants and employers, interviews are likely to remain a job-hiring requirement. They do give the employer an opportunity to get more information about whether the applicant has the qualifications needed for the opening. The job seeker also has an opportunity to find out more about the job, the firm or agency, and what the job requirements will be.

At the beginning of the interview, the employer or personnel worker will usually start off with introductions and casual or social conversation. The interviewer will then start asking questions about the applicant's qualifications and giving information about the opening. If candidates do not feel that they have been given sufficient information, it is appropriate at this point in the interview to ask questions about the employer and the opening. Likewise, if they do not believe that they have had an adequate opportunity to state their abilities, it would also be appropriate for applicants to describe them more fully. The end of the interview usually consists of a discussion about whether or not the applicant is interested in the job, salary negotiation, and information about when the candidate will be notified about the filling of the opening.

Sometimes salaries are not negotiable. Union pay scales and set salary schedules for beginning work are examples. When salaries are negotiable, the applicant should attempt to find out ranges from the personnel office or other sources before the interview. The articles on occupations in Volumes II and III of this *Encyclopedia* often contain information on salary averages, ranges, and regional differences. Fringe benefits, such as medical, dental, disability and insurance benefits, as well as vacation and retirement plans, are becoming more important as part of a salary package. They should be checked out before the interview, if possible. If not, it is appropriate to inquire about them during the interview.

After the Interview

The interview should be followed up with a thank you letter to the person seen that day. If no word is received within a week (unless other time arrangements were made), applicants should phone to check on the status of their applications.

Other actions may occur after the interview is over. The employer may wish to contact references and past employers. The applicant may be asked to take tests. (Test taking may also precede the interview.) After the first screening interview, the employer may ask candidates to return for further interviewing with potential supervisors or branch management personnel.

College graduates who are interviewed in campus placement offices may be asked to visit the organization where they may be employed. The employer often pays the expenses of these trips.

School and College Placement Offices

We indicated earlier that the best method for finding a job consists of visiting employers who have suitable job openings. However, we also indicated that a combination of job-hunting approaches pays off even better. One of the best additional avenues to explore is the world of school and college placement offices. Many high schools and nearly all colleges administer career planning and placement services. They are valuable sources of useful information and assistance.

Placement personnel contact local, state, regional, and national employers. At the post-high school level, they arrange interviews with employer representatives. In high schools, students are referred to local employers for interviews. Other services of college or university

Private employment agencies screen candidates so that those with the most suitable experience and training can be selected for specialized jobs. Fees are charged for the consultation and for all referrals to prospective employers.

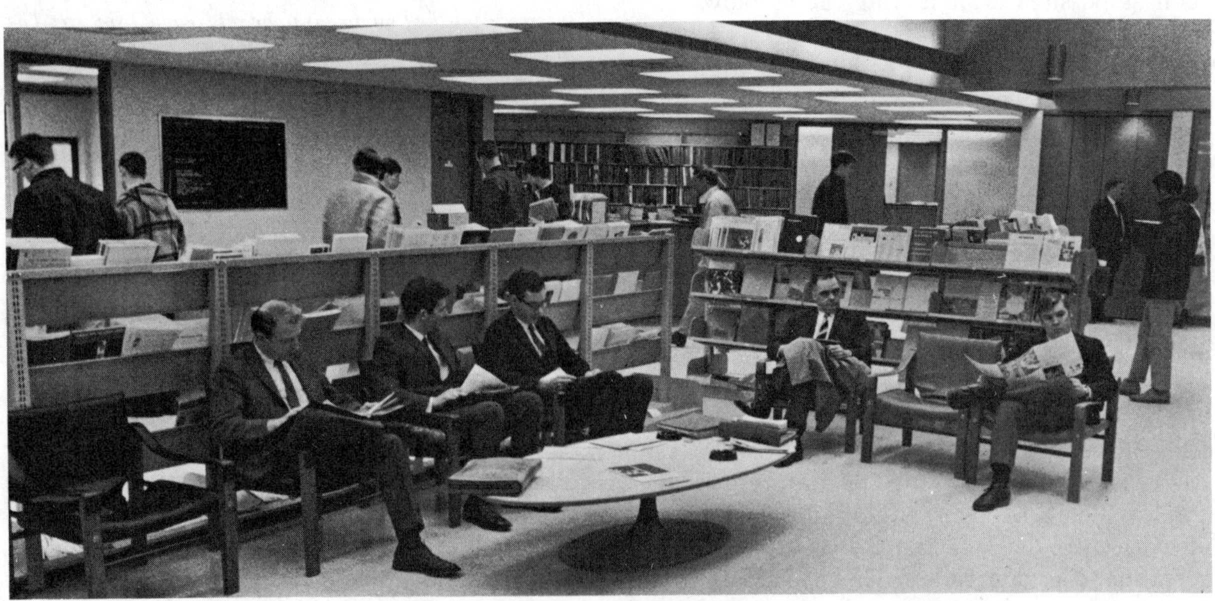

placement offices and some high schools include compiling and sending out the resumes and references of applicants as well as assistance in writing of resumes and preparing for interviews. It has been found that most employers find recommendations quite helpful in deciding whether or not to interview an applicant for an opening. Many post-high school institutions have reciprocal arrangements whereby students and graduates of one institution are elegible for assistance from a college placement office in another geographical area. This is very helpful when candidates would like to or must consider a move to a different area.

Public Employment Offices

There is a state employment service office located in most medium and large towns and cities. These public employment offices serve both job applicants and employers without charging a fee for the services. Larger offices often have specialists who work with youth and other people seeking to enter the job market. Testing by means of the General Aptitude Test Battery is made available to applicants. Descriptions of major occupations and information on employment conditions can be obtained at local offices.

In some communities, a cooperative arrangement exists between high schools and employment service offices. Representatives of the local employment service office register candidates in the school or operate the job placement program for the school. Sometimes placement personnel from the school work in the local employment office to serve high school youth in that area.

Private Employment Agencies

These agencies offer placement services for a fee that is paid by the candidate if he or she accepts a job through an agency referral. Private employment agencies receive listings from many employers, particularly small organizations. Some employers prefer to talk with a few candidates who are screened and referred by an agency than to interview much larger numbers. Many agencies specialize in areas such as advertising, finance, and publishing. Employers in such areas utilize the services of specialized agencies to secure a small number of candidates with the most suitable background, training, and experience.

When candidates register with a private employment agency, they sign a contract agreeing to pay the agency a commission if they accept a job to which they were referred by the agency. The commission is usually a percentage of the first year's salary. The percentage rate depends on the size of the salary, with a higher fee for larger salaries. Sometimes the fee is paid by the employer, but usually the candidate has to pay the charge.

Civil Service Offices

Civil service jobs are those which exist in local, county, state, and federal governments and agencies. Government jobs employ almost all types of workers in a large variety of settings. Requirements include passing one or more tests, such as a written examination to measure general or specific qualifications, an oral interview, and an evaluation of the applicant's education, military service, previous employment experience, and any other needed qualifications.

It is possible to find out about federal job announcements from state employment service offices. For more information, you can contact the Office of Personnel Management, 1900 E. Street, N.W., Washington DC 20415, or one of the seventy Federal Job Information Centers in various large cities throughout the country. These centers announce and conduct examinations, evaluate and refer applicants, and provide comprehensive information about federal job opportunities in the local area and nationwide.

To get information on state, county, or municipal positions, you should contact personnel boards or civil service commissions. Specific information may be obtained from personnel offices at the state capitol, county offices, or city hall. In smaller communities, the hiring is often handled by the mayor, city manager, or individual department heads. Many local governments are required to advertise all positions in newspapers.

Job seekers can find much information about civil service positions from the contents of position announcements: title of position, duties involved, location of the work, educational and work experience requirements, procedure for filing an application, testing to be used, and the deadline date for filing an application.

After the deadline for applications, they are evaluated and the candidates are listed in rank order. This list is called a register. The top three names on the register are interviewed for the vacancy. Persons who are not hired remain at the top of the list in the event that another vacancy occurs.

Veterans and disabled veterans often receive a special priority in hiring. For most federal positions, only United States citizens are eligible. Many state and municipal governments will hire only local residents for jobs.

Classified Want Ads

The classified advertising sections of newspapers, trade magazines, and professional journals contain ads for a large variety of job openings. Employers often advertise for inexperienced workers and trainees as well as experienced personnel. Instructions for applying by writing, telephoning, and interviewing are included in the ads. Usually brief descriptions of duties and qualifications are also included.

Employers who read "Jobs Wanted" ads are usually looking for experienced specialists. Therefore, job seekers who are just starting out their search for work may find it more profitable to read and respond to want ads than to place ads in the "Jobs Wanted" section.

Directories or Employers

Some employers seldom seek outside help from employment agencies or other sources in filling their openings. They are able to fill any available openings by reviewing the applications they already have on file and calling in people they wish to interview.

The job seeker may find helpful directories of possible employers from the following sources:

a. The Yellow Pages or classified sections of telephone directories.
b. Chamber of Commerce lists of manufacturers and other employers. There may be a small charge for large lists.
c. The membership rosters of local, state, and national trade and professional organizations.
d. General lists of employers maintained by employment services.
e. *The College Placement Annual*, available only through college placement offices, is published for college graduates seeking information about a large number of firms throughout the nation.
f. The annual reports of larger organizations contain much background information useful to applicants. Requests for free copies may be sent to the public relations office of the organization involved.

Use of Friends

Although the "it's not what you know but who you know" approach may be overrated, friends of the applicant are sometimes able to furnish leads on available openings. They may even be able to arrange for an initial interview. Young people may find the friends of their parents more helpful than personal friends. In contacting older persons, it may be useful to schedule an appointment to obtain advice or information on opportunities in a certain field. This approach is usually more fruitful than indicating "I'm looking for a job. Can you help me?"

The "who you know" avenue was probably more useful in the past when there were fewer large organizations and less competition for profits and services. It is increasingly less likely that people will be hired simply, or even primarily, on the basis of who they know. Much favoritism has been eliminated in large organizations by having several people, rather than one, approve each new person hired.

Letters of Application

One of the most useful and common methods of contacting an employer is a personally written letter of application. The letter of application should be typed on good quality, plain, white paper. It should follow standard business style. Typing mistakes should be erased along with any smudges. The applicant's name should be signed above the typed name.

The first paragraph should let the employer know of the applicant's availability and general qualifications for the job. If possible, the name of any person who referred the applicant to the employer should be included in the first paragraph.

The middle paragraph should more specifically describe qualifications for the opening. Occasionally, writers will comment on skills detailed in a resume. It is usually advisable to include a resume with a letter of application. If enclosed, that fact should be pointed out in a letter. (See description of resume or data sheet below.)

The final paragraph should ask or encourage the reader to take a positive action: (1) to send more information or an application blank or (2) to grant a request for an interview. It is seldom that an applicant receives a job through a letter of application. However, it may serve to interest the employer in giving the applicant an opportunity to present his or her qualifications more completely.

It is wise to make or keep copies of letters and resumes. They make a complete record of contacts with employers. Copies also make it easier to reuse key sections to contact other employers.

Resume or Data Sheet

The resume or data sheet is usually a one-page (rarely more than two) summary of information about the applicant's relevant background and experience. Some people who work in employment settings think that the resume is a very useful part of the application process. Others believe that the preparation of a resume is an almost worthless activity. However, many still require resumes, and applicants should be prepared to furnish them. As mentioned above, they are sometimes sent with a letter of application. They may be requested after an application has been received. Some employers like to receive resumes before an interview because they furnish a brief review of the applicant. It is a good idea to bring a copy of the resume to an interview.

The resume should be typed on plain white paper in outline form with plenty of "white space" between items in the outline. Many job hunters have the resume duplicated to save retyping time and costs. Most employers accept a neatly reproduced copy as readily as a typed original. Letters of application, by contrast, should always be typed individually.

The resume usually contains information on the following areas:

a. Identifying data: name, address, telephone number
b. Position desired: one or two objectives may be indicated
c. Educational and training background: high school and post-high school training and education
d. Work experience: usually in chronological order, beginning with last job
e. Other qualifications: areas of competence or effectiveness, hobbies, special interests, membership in organizations
f. References: names, titles, and complete addresses of three or four responsible persons who are able to comment on personal and job qualifications. Some candidates indicate that names will be supplied upon request, or state that copies of references are available in a placement office file.

A resume developed for one position may not exactly fit another position. Thus, it may be desirable to emphasize certain aspects of an applicant's background in resumes prepared for different positions.

For those applicants who may need assistance in the preparation of resumes and letters of application, there are many samples and suggestions to be found in books and pamphlets in libraries, bookstores, and counselor's offices.

Telephone Contacts

The telephone call is a handy method of finding out about an organization. A public relations or personnel office can give the caller the name and location of a department head, where branch offices may be found, and any recent changes in personnel requirements.

Under some circumstances, an applicant may inquire about an opening by telephone. A specialist, for example, may find that a telephone call is the simplest way to contact an employer who needs a person in that field. In jobs where telephone skill is important, an applicant may be able to demonstrate that skill in making a call to the employer.

Telephone solicitation has at least a couple of other advantages. The applicant can immediately find out if an opportunity is available. The employer is able to ask questions of the candidate to see if an interview would be desirable. However, some employers may resent any attempt by an applicant to apply what the employer sees as undue pressure over the telephone. They prefer to handle applications in their own way and at their own convenience. Such employers may, for instance, require that a personnel worker check the qualifications of all applicants before determining whether or not to schedule an interview. Most employers require that their organizations' application forms be completed before deciding to see a prospective employee.

Employment Applications

The employment application may be used by organizations to screen job seekers before granting an interview at a future date. Some employers permit the applicant to fill out the form on a walk-in basis and see the applicant immediately if personnel workers or interviewers are available. With either method, the employment application may be the first impression that the organization has concerning a job seeker. It is important that the application be filled out as completely, carefully, and neatly as possible so that the first impression will be a good one.

The form and content of the employment application may vary from one organization to another. However, the following areas are usually included:

a. Social Security number: If a young applicant does not have one, it should be obtained at a Social Security office. A driver's license may also be required for identification.
b. Educational background: This usually includes high school and post-high school records.
c. Employment experience: Young workers may include any part-time or summer positions. The applicant may wish to carry a written summary with all names, addresses, and the dates of employment to insure accuracy.
d. Request for references: Each applicant should have in mind the names of several people who have agreed in advance to be used as references. The business titles of references (even personal friends) should be used whenever possible. Candidates sometimes send a resume to references to remind them of the candidate's background and qualifications.
e. Reasons for interest in the position: This statement should indicate what the applicant can do for the employer rather than why the applicant wants the jobs. The applicant should find out about the company and know what he or she can do for the company.

Below are some general helpful hints to remember in filling out an employment application: (1) Complete the form as neatly as possible; print with a pen or, if possible, type answers. (2) Fill in information as completely as possible. Use "Not Applicable" ("NA") or a small dash if the question does not apply; either may be used to show that the applicant understood the question. (3) Use correct spelling; look up in the dictionary and write down difficult or key words which may be needed to answer questions to the above areas. (4) Follow all directions and re-read the application to make sure it has been completed in full.

Ending the Job Search

Applicants should end other employment contacts once a position has been accepted.

When leaving an old employer for a new one, the employee should find out how much notice must be given. Most organizations expect two weeks' notice for resignations. During this period, the worker who is leaving should assist in training a replacement and provide an orderly transfer of duties. A worker's conduct just before leaving is very important in influencing the reputation left behind. A courteous good-bye to persons with whom one has worked is appropriate—especially to persons with whom differences have existed in the past.

How and Where to Look Up More Information

JEANETTE E. MITCHELL

Today's jobs and job market are in a constant state of change: some forms of employment are being created; others are being changed; and still others are being eliminated. For this reason, and because you too may be changing, you will wish to investigate carefully the careers that interest you and that your training, ability, and achievement qualify you to enter. You will want to use the resources provided by counselors; libraries; college and scholarship guides; professional, trade, and civic organizations; city, state, and federal agencies; newspapers; and people working in the vocations and professions.

You can also obtain information by reading, visits to business and industry, work-study programs, work experience, and by formal and informal observations of people at work. This article will tell you about the many sources of information available to you.

Career Counselors

The best place to start an inventory of your abilities, aptitudes, and interests or to start a survey of materials on employment possibilities is the counseling office of your school. The counselor can aid you in planning for a broad occupational field rather than for an isolated specific job. He or she will work with you through interviews or individual or group discussions. Your school counselor is usually trained specifically for counseling and certified by the state as qualified to assist you by providing occupational information and by helping you in the decision-making process of analyzing your abilities, achievements, and interests. The counselor can give standardized tests that predict which jobs you are capable of performing and which will keep you satisfied and reasonably happy.

If you are planning to go to college, your counseling office will have the latest college catalogs for you to browse through. The catalogs will give you a general description of the courses offered, entrance requirements, approximate costs of school and housing, and other features. It is not too early to start reviewing college catalogs in junior high school. You are thus best prepared to schedule your high school program to meet the requirements of the college of your choice.

Your school counselor can also provide junior-college catalogs which explain the two-year programs preparing you for jobs in electronics, technology, engineering, design, and laboratory technology. The counseling office will also have trade school catalogs.

School counseling offices may sponsor career days or similar programs that provide you with an opportunity to listen to consultants and recruiters discuss their work, the salary ranges in their professions, and the normal requirements, advantages, and disadvantages of jobs in various fields. "College Night" meetings can give you and your family a chance to meet representatives of various colleges. National college fairs bring together representatives of hundreds of two- and four-year colleges, universities, and trade and technical schools. These fairs are held in a number of large cities each year, and your school counselor can give you information about one near you.

Local, state, and federal employment agencies provide other free counseling services. Counselors in these agencies can aid you in making contacts and can inform you about employment possibilities in specific companies in your area. In addition, community agencies, religious organizations, and college placement centers may also be able to supply information and guidance on careers. Such services are usually free to the public.

Once you have exhausted the services available through schools, government bodies, and community organizations, you may wish to turn to professional job counseling services. They can give you detailed information on specific jobs, interview you when appropriate, and make direct contact with prospective employers. Since you will probably pay a fee to a professional guidance service, you will want to make sure that you choose a good one. Your school counselor probably can give you an estimate of the usefulness of any such agency in your local area. If you cannot otherwise determine the competence of a professional agency, write the American Personnel and Guidance Association, Two Skyline Pl., Suite 400, 5203 Leesburg Pike, Falls Church, VA 22041 and ask for their *Directory of Counseling Services.* This publication, which aims to protect you from low-quality guidance services, lists places where good counseling service is available.

Libraries, Media Centers, and Resource Centers

Libraries, sometimes called media centers or resource centers, are information sources that you cannot afford to neglect because they provide so many kinds of information. These include books, magazines, brochures, pamphlets, leaflets, films, filmstrips, tapes, records, videotapes, and computer programs.

Books

A good place to start looking for comprehensive information on careers and vocations is a general encyclopedia. Look under either CAREERS or VOCATIONS or both subjects for a broad overview, and then proceed in the various encyclopedia volumes to the articles on specific careers. Current editions of *Encyclopedia Americana*, *Compton's Encyclopedia*, and *World Book Encyclopedia* are excellent sources of information. They provide not only detailed descriptions of specific careers, but also in some cases have extensive charts illustrating trends in various careers and job categories. The articles are generally authoritative because they are written by experts in the specific field or by persons experienced in areas such as guidance counseling and counseling education.

In addition, general encyclopedias often provide a list of current books for further reading at the end of the article. By checking the card catalog in your library, you can determine which books listed in the encyclopedias are available in your school and public library. Also check the catalog headings PROFESSIONS, OCCUPATIONS, and VOCATIONAL GUIDANCE for other useful books in your library.

Some helpful books on the general subject of careers and vocations that you will want to consult are:

Alexander, Sue. *Finding Your First Job.* New York, E.P. Dutton, 1980.

Barnewall, Gordon G. *Succeed as a Job Applicant.* New York, Arco, 1976.

Bolles, Richard N., and Crystal, John. *Where Do I Go from Here with My Life?* Berkeley, California, Ten Speed Press, 1980.

Bostwick, Burdette E., *Finding the Job You've Always Wanted*, 2d ed. New York, John Wiley, 1980.

Brownstone, David M., and Hawes, Gene R. *The Complete Career Guide*. New York, Simon and Schuster, 1980.

Buskirk, Richard. *Your Career: How to Plan It, Manage It, Change It*, 2d ed. Boston, CBI, 1980.

Chronicle Career Index. Moravia, N.Y., Chronicle Guidance Publishers, 1982.

The College Blue Book of Occupational Education, 5th ed. New York, Macmillan, 1981.

Cook, Paul F., et al. *Vocational Opportunities*. (Vocational Education for the Handicapped Series). Salt Lake City, Utah, Olympus, 1978.

Corwen, Leonard. *Your Job: Where to Find It—How to Get It*. New York, Arco, 1981.

DuPre, Flint O. *Your Career in Federal Civil Service*. New York, Barnes and Noble, 1981.

Evers, Dora, and Feingold, S. Norman. *Your Future in Exotic Occupations*. New York, Richards Rosen Press, 1980.

Feingold, S. Norman, and Fins, Alice. *Your Future in More Exotic Careers*. New York, Richards Rosen Press, 1982.

Feingold, S. Norman, and Miller, Norma R. *Your Future: A Guide for the Handicapped Teenager*. New York, Richards Rosen Press, 1981.

Figler, Howard. *The Complete Job-Search Handbook: All the Skills You Need to Get Any Job and Have a Good Time Doing It*. New York, Holt, Rinehart & Winston, 1980.

Fredrickson, Ronald H., *Career Information*. Englewood Cliffs, N.J., Prentice-Hall, 1982.

Gale, Barry. *The National Career Directory: An Occupational Information Handbook*. New York, Arco, 1979.

Gates, Anita. *Ninety Most Promising Careers for the Eighties*. New York, Monarch Press, 1982.

Goodman, Leonard H. *Current Career and Occupational Literature*. Bronx, N.Y., H.W. Wilson, 1982.

Greco, Ben. *How to Get the Job That's Right for You: A Career Guide for the 80's*, rev. ed. Homewood, Illinois, Dow Jones–Irwin, 1981.

Hawes, Gene R. *Careers Tomorrow*. New York, New American Library, 1979.

Heschong, Naomi H. *Get the Job You Want*, 3rd ed. Woodbury, New York, Barron, 1983.

Holland, John L. *Making Vocational Choices: A Theory of Careers*. Englewood Cliffs, New Jersey, Prentice-Hall, 1973.

Jackson, Tom, and Mayleas, Davidyne. *The Hidden Job Market for the Eighties*. New York, Quadrangle/N.Y. Times Books, 1981.

Kimbrell, Grady, and Vineyard, B. S. *Succeeding in the World of Work*. Bloomington, Illinois, McKnight, 1981.

Lederer, Muriel. *Blue-Collar Jobs for Women*. New York, E.P. Dutton, 1979.

Lobb, Charlotte. *Exploring Apprenticeship Careers*. New York, Richards Rosen Press, 1982.

__________. *Exploring Careers through Volunteerism*. New York, Richards Rosen Press, 1979.

Lovejoy, Clarence E. *Lovejoy's Career and Vocational School Guide: A Source Book, Clue Book, and Directory of Institutions Training for Job Opportunities*, 5th ed. New York, Simon and Schuster, 1978.

Manpower Research Associates. *Arco Handbook of Job and Career Opportunities*. New York, Arco, 1978.

Mitchell, Joyce Slayton. *I Can Be Anything; Careers and Colleges for Young Women*, rev. and enl. ed. New York, Bantam Books, 1978.

__________. *See Me More Clearly: Career and Life Planning for Teens with Physical Disabilities*. New York, Harcourt, Brace, Jovanovich, 1980.

__________. *The Work Book: A Guide to Skilled Jobs*. New York, Bantam, 1978.

Moldafsky, Annie. *Welcome to the Real World: A Guide to Making Your First Personal, Financial, and Career Decisions*. Garden City, N.Y., Doubleday, 1979.

Norback, Craig. *Careers Encyclopedia.* Homewood, Illinois, Dow Jones-Irwin, 1980.

Rafferty, Robert. *Careers in the Military: Good Training for Civilian Life.* New York, Lodestar, 1980.

Robinson, William C. *The Federal Employment Handbook.* New York, Monarch Press, 1982.

Shanahan, William F. *College—Yes or No.* New York, Arco, 1980.

Uleck, Ronald B. *Federal Career Guide*, rev. ed. Gaithersburg, Maryland, 1981.

U.S. Bureau of Labor Statistics. *Exploring Careers.* Washington, D.C., U.S. Department of Labor, 1979.

———. *A Guide to Job Opportunities: The Occupational Outlook for Blue-Collar Workers.* New York, Sterling, 1979.

U.S. Employment and Training Administration. *Guide for Occupational Exploration.* Washington, D.C., U.S. Department of Labor, 1979.

Yeomans, William N. *Jobs Eighty-One and Eighty-Two.* New York, G.P. Putnam's Sons, 1982.

Zehring, John W. *Careers in State and Local Government.* Garrett Park, Maryland, Garrett Park Press, 1980.

Magazines

Your library can provide you with magazines that carry more current information than books and general encyclopedias. Because magazines are published frequently (usually once a month or quarterly), they are a good source for up-to-date articles and other materials. In consulting magazines for career information, you will probably want to start your search with a review of *Reader's Guide to Periodical Literature.* This is an index listing articles in many magazines by both subject and author. Look under such subjects as VOCATIONAL-TECHNICAL EDUCATION, OCCUPATIONS, PROFESSIONS, APPRENTICES, WOMEN—OCCUPATIONS, BLACKS—OCCUPATIONS, and the names of different occupations.

Your school library or the public library will have some magazines that specialize in career information. *Career World 1* has articles, stories, games, and other activities to motivate young students to think about careers. *Career World 2* is written for the students in grades 7 through 12 and devotes each issue to the various aspects of a single career. *Occupational Outlook Quarterly*, which supplements the *Occupational Outlook Handbook* published every two years, has brief, interesting articles highlighting current employment opportunities and trends. *Occupations in Demand*, a publication of the U.S. Department of Labor, lists occupations identified as having many job opportunities. The National Student Volunteer Program publishes *Synergist* to help expose students to volunteering activities that may lead to life work in helping other people. *Equal Opportunity, Collegiate Career Woman, Forum Career Guide* and *Women's Work* are directed to college students who will be graduating soon. These magazines also contain valuable advice on job-seeking strategies, as does *Working Woman* which is addressed to the careerwoman who may also be a homemaker and a mother.

Some general-interest magazines, such as *Ebony*, *Glamour*, *Mademoiselle*, and *Seventeen*, frequently publish articles about careers, and some have a career department as a regular feature of the magazine.

Pamphlets

The school and public libraries and your school counselor have vocational pamphlets, newsletters, and other ephemeral materials. Some of these materials are kept in the vertical file, while others may be part of a kit. Ask the librarian about Science Research Associates' "Occupational Briefs." Each describes the activities, the probable earnings, and the outlook for a different job category. These briefs also provide the names of organizations to write for further information, as well as lists of articles in books and magazines. Careers, Inc. of Largo, Florida, provides information on many careers and each July publishes a list of the careers it describes. *Career Education News*, a newsletter pamphlet, is published twice a month from September through June and once in July and August by Bobit Publishing Company of Redondo Beach, California. Houghton Mifflin has an interesting kit on career opportunities linked to school subjects. One part of this series is *Subject: English; Object: Career Opportunities.* Others are *Foreign Languages*, *Science*, *Social Studies*, and *Mathematics.* The U.S. Department of Labor publishes excellent, timely pamphlets and reprints, many of which are available free.

A pamphlet you may wish to obtain for yourself is *Need a Lift?*, available from your local American Legion chapter.

Audio-Visual Sources

Your school and public library may also have vocational records, films, filmstrips, games, and videotapes. These materials are usually listed in the card catalog. Many libraries and career centers have a computer program that can help you in exploring careers. The University of Oregon Career Information System is in use in many states. Many high schools and community colleges also have computer programs that are very helpful in choosing a college or vocational school.

College Information

Your library or school counselor is likely to have a number of books on colleges, including up-to-date guides to most junior colleges, colleges, and universities in this country, as well as current catalogs of individual colleges you may be interested in attending. Generally, these guides give pertinent information on expenses, admission, enrollment, courses offered, financial aid from various sources, and opportunities for part-time work.

The following books may be useful: *Barron's Guide to the Two-Year Colleges* (in two volumes, *College Descriptions* and Occupational Program Selector); *Barron's How to Prepare for the College Entrance Examinations* by Samuel C. Brownstein and Mitchel Weiner; *Barron's Profiles of American Colleges*; James Cass and Max Birnbaum's *Comparative Guide to American Colleges*; Abraham Lass's *How to Prepare for College*; Lovejoy's *College Guide*, covering approximately 3,500 American colleges and universities; and *Lovejoy's Career and Vocational School Guide.*

Guides to Scholarships and Loans

Costs of attending college rise every year. Therefore, you need to know about scholarships and loans for which you may qualify. Don't neglect any possibility. Colleges and universities, nonprofit organizations, some industries, and the federal government are among the sources of aid that you should investigate. There are published directories and guides to sources of financial aid. Your school counselor or library will probably have *You Can Win a Scholarship*, by Samuel C. Brownstein and Mitchel Weiner; S. Norman Feingold's *Scholarships, Fellowships and Loans*; *Selected List of Postsecondary Education Opportunities for Minorities and Women*, Washington, D.C., GPO; UNESCO's *Study Abroad: International Scholarships, International Courses*; *Barron's Handbook of American College Financial Aid*, by Nicholas C. Proia and Vincent M. Di Gaspari, who are also the authors of *Barron's Handbook of Junior and Community College Financial Aid*; Donald R. Moore's *Money for College! How to Get It*; *Financing College Education: A Handbook for Students and Families*, by Kenneth A. Kohl and Irene C. Kohl; and *Five Federal Financial Aid Programs: A Student Consumer Guide*, a pamphlet that can be secured by calling, toll-free, (800) 638-6700 (residents of Maryland call (800) 492-6602) or by writing to the Bureau of Student Financial Assistance, P.O. Box 84, Washington, DC 20044. When using any of these guides, it is important to locate the latest edition.

Organizations: Professional, Trade and Civic

Professional and trade organizations, labor unions, business and industrial organizations, and civic groups keep track of careers and occupations in their field of interest. Write to them for descriptions of job groupings and specific occupations, as well as information on general and specialized education and other preparation normally required to enter the field. Some of the groups also provide counseling service. The following list gives addresses for a sample group of these organizations. See the U.S. Department of Labor's *Occupational Outlook Handbook* for a more complete listing.

Organizations with Career Information

Accounting
American Institute of Certified Public Accountants
1211 Avenue of the Americas
New York, NY 10036

Advertising
American Advertising Federation
1225 Connecticut Ave., N.W.
Washington, DC 20036

American Association of Advertising Agencies
200 Park Avenue
New York, NY 10017

Air-Conditioning
Air-Conditioning and Refrigeration Institute
1815 North Fort Meyer Drive
Arlington, VA 22209

Air Force, U.S.
Headquarters
U.S. Air Force Recruiting Service
Randolph Air Force Base, TX 78148

Anthropology
American Anthropological Association
1703 New Hampshire Avenue, N.W.
Washington, DC 20009

Archeology
Archeological Institute of America
53 Park Place, 8th Floor
New York, NY 10007

Architecture
American Institute of Architects
1735 New York Ave., N.W.
Washington, DC 20006

Army, U.S.
Commander, Headquarters
U.S. Army Recruiting Command
Fort Sheridan, IL 60037

Astronomy
Education Officer
American Astronomical Society
Sharp Laboratories
University of Delaware
Newark, DE 19711

Audiology and Speech Therapy
American Speech-Language-Hearing Association
10801 Rockville Pike
Rockville, MD 20852

Auditor
Institute of Internal Auditors, Inc.
249 Maitland Avenue
Altamonte Springs, FL 32701

Automobile Servicing
Motor Vehicle Manufacturers Association of the United States
300 New Center Building
Detroit, MI 48202

Aviation
Aviation Education Program Division
Department of Transportation
Federal Aviation Administration
800 Independence Ave., S.W.
Washington, DC 20591

Aviation Maintenance
Aviation Maintenance Foundation, Inc.
P.O. Box 739
Basin, WY 82410

Banks and Banking
American Bankers' Association
Bank Personnel Division
1120 Connecticut Ave., N.W.
Washington, DC 20036

Barbers
United Food and Commercial Workers Int'l Union
Suffridge Bldg.
1775 K St., N.W.
Washington, DC 20006

Biology
American Institute of Biological Sciences
1401 Wilson Blvd.
Arlington, VA 22209

Botany
American Society for Horticultural Science
701 N. Saint Asaph Street
Alexandria, VA 22314

Bricklaying
International Union of Bricklayers and Allied Craftsmen
International Masonry Apprenticeship Trust
815 15th Street, N.W.
Washington, DC 20005

Broadcasting
National Association of Broadcasters
1771 N Street, N.W.
Washington, DC 20036

Chemistry
American Chemical Society
Educational Activities Department
1155 16th Street, N.W.
Washington, DC 20036

Chiropractic
American Chiropractic Association
1916 Wilson Blvd.
Arlington, VA 22201

Coast Guard, U.S.
Director of Admissions
U.S. Coast Guard Academy
New London, CT 06320

Commandant (G-PMR)
U.S. Coast Guard
Washington, DC 20590

Computer Sciences
American Federation of Information Processing Societies, Inc.
1815 North Lynn St., Suite 800
Arlington, VA 22209

Construction Industry
Associated General Contractors of America
1957 E Street, N.W.
Washington, DC 20006

Dance
National Dance Association
1900 Association Drive
Reston, VA 22091

American Dance Guild
1133 Broadway, Room 1427
New York, NY 10010

Dental Hygiene
American Dental Hygienists' Association
444 North Michigan Avenue
Chicago, IL 60611

Dentistry
American Dental Association
211 East Chicago Avenue
Chicago, IL 60611

Dietetics
American Dietetic Association
430 North Michigan Avenue
Chicago, IL 60611

Drafting
American Institute for Design and Drafting
3119 Price Road
Bartlesville, OK 74003

Economics
American Economic Association
1313 21st Avenue, South
Nashville, TN 37212

Electrical Engineering
Institute of Electrical and Electronics Engineers
345 E. 47th St.
New York, NY 10017

Electronics
Electronic Industries Association
2001 Eye Street, N.W.
Washington, DC 20006

Engineering and Engineering Technician
Accreditation Board for Engineering and Technology
345 East 47th Street
New York, NY 10017

Entomology
Entomological Society of America
4603 Calvert Road
College Park, MD 20740

Federal Bureau of Investigation

Federal Bureau of Investigation
Ninth Street and Pennsylvania Avenue, N.W.
Washington, DC 20535

Fire Fighting

International Association of Fire Chiefs
1329 18th Street, N.W.
Washington, DC 20036

Flight Attendant

Air Transport Association of America
1709 New York Ave., N.W.
Washington, DC 20006

Florist

Society of American Florists and Ornamental Horticulturalists
901 North Washington Street
Alexandria, VA 22314

Forestry

Society of American Foresters
5400 Grosvenor Lane
Bethesda, MD 20814

Funeral Director

National Funeral Directors Association
135 West Wells Street
Milwaukee, WI 53203

Geology

American Geological Institute
5205 Leesburg Pike
Falls Church, VA 22041

Hairdressing

United Food and Commercial Workers Int'l Union
Suffridge Bldg.
1775 K St., N.W.
Washington, DC 20006

Home Economics

American Home Economics Association
2010 Massachusetts Ave., N.W.
Washington, DC 20036

Hotel Management

American Hotel and Motel Association
888 Seventh Avenue
New York, NY 10019

Industrial Design

Industrial Designers Society of America
6802 Poplar Pl.
McLean, VA 22101

Insurance

Insurance Information Institute
100 N. Interregional
Suite 3200
Austin, TX 78701

Interior Design

American Society of Interior Designers
730 Fifth Avenue
New York, NY 10019

Iron and Steel Industry

American Iron and Steel Institute
1000 16th Street, N.W.
Washington, DC 20036

Journalism

Society of Professional Journalists, Sigma Delta Chi
840 N. Lake Shore Dr.
Suite 801
Chicago, IL 60611

Law

American Bar Association Information Services
1155 East 60th Street
Chicago, IL 60637

Librarianship

American Library Association
50 East Huron Street
Chicago, IL 60611

Marine Corps, U.S.

Director, Personnel Procurement Division
Headquarters, U.S. Marine Corps
Washington, DC 20380

Marketing

American Marketing Association
250 S. Wacker
Suite 200
Chicago, IL 60606

Mathematics

Society for Industrial and Applied Mathematics
1405 Architect's Bldg.
117 S. 17th St.
Philadelphia, PA 19103

Medicine

American Medical Association Careers
535 North Dearborn Street
Chicago, IL 60610

Merchant Marine

Maritime Administration
Division of Maritime Academies
U.S. Department of Commerce
Washington, DC 20230

Metallurgy

American Society for Metals
Metals Park, OH 44073

Meteorology

American Meteorological Society
45 Beacon Street
Boston, MA 02108

Mining

American Institute of Mining, Metallurgical, and Petroleum Engineers
345 East 47th Street
New York, NY 10017

Music

Music Educators' National Conference
1902 Association Drive
Reston, VA 22091

Navy, U.S.

Navy Recruiting Command
Code 40
4015 Wilson Boulevard
Arlington, VA 22203

Nuclear Energy Research

U.S. Department of Energy
Office of the Assistant Secretary of Energy Technology
Washington, DC 20585

Nursing

American Nurses' Association
Committee on Nursing Careers
2420 Pershing Road
Kansas City, MO 64108

National League for Nursing
Committee on Careers
10 Columbus Circle
New York, NY 10019

Occupational Therapy

American Occupational Therapy Association
6000 Executive Boulevard, Suite 200
Rockville, MD 20852

Oceanography

Marine Technology Society
1730 M Street, N.W.
Washington, DC 20036

Optometry

American Optometric Association
243 North Lindbergh Boulevard
St. Louis, MO 63141

Osteopathy

American Osteopathic Association
Office of Osteopathic Education
212 East Ohio Street
Chicago, IL 60611

Petroleum Industry

American Petroleum Institute
2101 L Street, N.W.
Washington, DC 20037

Pharmacy

American Association of Colleges of Pharmacy
4630 Montgomery Avenue, No. 201
Bethesda, MD 20814

Photography

Professional Photographers of America
1090 Executive Way
Des Plaines, IL 60018

Physical Therapy

American Physical Therapy Association
1156 15th Street, N.W.
Washington, DC 20005

Physics

American Institute of Physics
335 East 45th Street
New York, NY 10017

Plastics

Society of Plastics Engineers
14 Fairfield Drive
Brookfield Center, CT 06805

Postal Service

Local Post Offices and State Employment Offices

Printing

Graphic Arts Technical Foundation
4615 Forbes Avenue
Pittsburgh, PA 15213

Psychiatry

American Psychiatric Association
Joint Information Service
1700 18th Street, N.W.
Washington, DC 20009

Psychology

American Psychological Association
1200 17th Street, N.W.
Washington, DC 20036

Public Relations

Public Relations Society of America
845 Third Avenue
New York, NY 10022

Railroad Operations

Association of American Railroads
American Railroads Building
1920 L Street, N.W.
Washington, DC 20036

Real Estate

National Association of Realtors
430 North Michigan Avenue
Chicago, IL 60611

Recreation

National Recreation and Park Association
1601 North Kent Street
Arlington, VA 22209

Restaurant Careers

National Institute for the Foodservice Industry
20 North Wacker Drive
Chicago, IL 60606

Retail Sales

National Retail Merchants' Association
100 West 31st Street
New York, NY 10001

Science

Scientific Manpower Commission
1776 Massachusetts Ave., N.W.
Washington, DC 20036

Social Work

National Association of Social Workers
Social Work Career Information Service
1425 H Street, N.W., Suite 600
Washington, DC 20005

Sociology

American Sociological Association
1772 N Street, N.W.
Washington, DC 20036

Speech Therapy

American Speech-Language-Hearing Association
10801 Rockville Pike
Rockville, MD 20852

Surveying and Cartography

American Congress on Surveying and Mapping
210 Little Falls Street
Falls Church, VA 22046

Teaching

National Education Association
1201 16th Street, N.W.
Washington, DC 20036

Telephone Communications

United States Independent Telephone Association
1801 K Street, N.W., Suite 1201
Washington, DC 20006

Toolmaking

National Tooling and Machining Association
9300 Livingston Road
Washington, DC 20744

Veterinary Medicine

American Veterinary Medical Association
930 North Meacham Road
Schaumburg, IL 60196

Federal, State, and Local Agencies

Recruitment offices of the Army, Air Force, Marine Corps, and the Navy are listed in the telephone directory. Each of the armed services publishes an occupational handbook which is available in your school library or the public library. The U.S. Department of Labor puts out an *Occupational Outlook Handbook* which describes more than 500 common vocations and classifies them according to occupational clusters. This handbook gives information on job requirements, working conditions, earnings for the job, and employment trends; it also predicts future opportunities and stresses preparation for change and advancement. The same federal department also produces the *Dictionary of Occupational Titles*, which describes more than 20,000 jobs and 40,000 job titles. Your counselor or librarian can advise you on how to use it. The Department of Labor provides a wealth of information, statistics, and results of research. It maintains the U.S. Employment Service, sets standards, and maintains a recruitment program. Check the Yellow Pages of your telephone directory under EMPLOYMENT AGENCIES for both governmental and private organizations that provide assistance with job finding.

State occupational-information coordinating committees have recently been established. These committees can help you find career information tailored to the situation in your state or area. The committee may provide the information directly, or refer you to other sources. In many states, it can also tell you where you can go to use the state's career information system. To find out what career materials are available, write to the director of your state occupational information coordinating committee. Following is a list of their titles and addresses, reprinted from the *Occupational Outlook Handbook*:

Alabama
Director, Alabama Occupational Information Coordinating Committee
First Southern Towers, Suite 402
100 Commerce St.
Montgomery, AL 36130
Phone: (205) 832-5737

Alaska
Coordinator, Alaska Occupational Information Coordinating Committee
Pouch F—State Office Bldg.
Juneau, AK 99811
Phone: (907) 465-2980

Arizona
Executive Director, Arizona State Occupational Information Coordinating Committee
1535 West Jefferson, Room 345
Phoenix, AZ 85007
Phone: (602) 255-3680
Arkansas
Director, Arkansas State Occupational Information Coordinating Committee
P.O. Box 2981
Little Rock, AR 72203
Phone: (501) 371-3551
California
Executive Director, California Occupational Information Coordinating Committee
1027 10th Street, No. 302
Sacramento, CA 95814
Phone: (916) 323-6544
Colorado
Director, Office of Occupational Information, Colorado Occupational Information Coordinating Committee
213 Centennial Bldg.
1313 Sherman St.
Denver, CO 80203
Phone: (303) 866-3335
Connecticut
Executive Director, Connecticut State Occupational Information Coordinating Committee
c/o Elm Hill School
569 Maple Hill Avenue
Newington, CT 06111
Phone: (203) 666-1441
Delaware
Director, State Occupational Information Coordinating Committee of Delaware
Drummond Office Plaza, Suite 3303
Building No. 3
Newark, DE 19711
Phone: (302) 368-6908
District of Columbia
Executive Director, D.C. Occupational Information Coordinating Committee
500 C St. N.W., Suite 621
Washington, DC 20001
Phone: (202) 724-3965
Florida
Director, Florida Occupational Information Coordinating Committee
325 John Knox Rd., Suite L-500
Tallahassee, FL 32303
Phone: (904) 386-6111
Georgia
Executive Director, Georgia Occupational Information Coordinating Committee
151 Ellis St. N.E., Suite 504
Atlanta, GA 30303
Phone: (404) 656-3117
Hawaii
Executive Director, Hawaii State Occupational Information Coordinating Committee
1164 Bishop St., Suite 502
Honolulu, HI 96813
Phone: (808) 548-3496
Idaho
Coordinator, Idaho Occupational Information Coordinating Committee
Len B. Jordan Bldg., Room 301
650 W. State St.
Boise, ID 83720
Phone: (208) 334-3705
Illinois
Executive Director, Illinois Occupational Information Coordinating Committee
217 E. Monroe, Suite 203
Springfield, IL 62706
Phone: (217) 785-0789
Indiana
Director, Indiana Occupational Information Coordinating Committee
17 W. Market St.
434 Illinois Bldg.
Indianapolis, IN 46204
Phone: (317) 232-3625
Iowa
Executive Director, Iowa State Occupational Information Coordinating Committee
523 E. 12th St.
Des Moines, IA 50319
Phone: (515) 281-8076
Kansas
Director, Kansas Occupational Information Coordinating Committee
320 West 7th, Suite D
Topeka, KS 66603
Phone: (913) 296-5286
Kentucky
Coordinator, Kentucky Occupational Information Coordinating Committee
275 E. Main St.
D.H.R. Bldg., 2nd Floor East
Frankfort, KY 40621
Phone: (502) 564-4258
Louisiana
Director, Louisiana State Occupational Information Coordinating Committee
P.O. Box 44094
Baton Rouge, LA 70804
Phone: (504) 925-3593
Maine
Executive Director, Maine State Occupational Information Coordinating Committee
State House Station 71
Augusta, ME 04333
Phone: (207) 289-2331
Maryland
Executive Director, Maryland Occupational Information Coordinating Committee
Jackson Towers, Suite 304
1123 N. Eutaw St.
Baltimore, MD 21201
Phone: (301) 383-6350

Massachusetts
Executive Director, Massachusetts Occupational Information Coordinating Committee
Charles F. Hurley Bldg.
Government Center
Boston, MA 02114
Phone: (617) 727-9740

Michigan
Executive Coordinator, Michigan Occupational Information Coordinating Committee
309 N. Washington
P.O. Box 30015
Lansing, MI 48909
Phone: (517) 373-0363

Minnesota
SOICC Director, Department of Economic Security
690 American Center Bldg.
150 E. Kellogg Blvd.
St. Paul, MN 55101
Phone: (612) 296-2072

Mississippi
SOICC Director, Vocational Technical Education
P.O. Box 771
Jackson, MS 39205
Phone: (601) 354-6779

Missouri
Director, Missouri Occupational Information Coordinating Committee
830d E. High St.
Jefferson City, MO 65101
Phone: (314) 751-2624

Montana
Program Manager, Montana State Occupational Information Coordinating Committee
P.O. Box 1728
Helena, MT 59624
Phone: (406) 449-2741

Nebraska
Executive Director, Nebraska Occupational Information Coordinating Committee
W. 300 Nebraska Hall
Lincoln, NB 68588
Phone: (402) 472-2062

Nevada
Director, Nevada Occupational Information Coordinating Committee
Capitol Complex
Kinkead Bldg., Room 601
505 E. King St.
Carson City, NV 89710
Phone: (702) 885-4577

New Hampshire
SOICC Director, New Hampshire Occupational Information Coordinating Committee
c/o Department of Employment and Training
155 Manchester St.
Concord, NH 03301
Phone: (603) 271-3156

New Jersey
Acting Staff Director, New Jersey Occupational Information Coordinating Committee
Department of Labor and Industry, Division of Planning and Research
P.O. Box CN056
Trenton, NJ 08625
Phone: (609) 292-2626

New Mexico
Director, New Mexico State Occupational Information Coordinating Committee
NEA Building
130 South Capitol, Suite 157
Santa Fe, NM 87501
Phone: (505) 827-3411 or 3412

New York
SOICC Director, New York Department of Labor
Labor Department Bldg. #12
State Campus, Room 559A
Albany, NY 12240
Phone: (518) 457-2930

North Carolina
SOICC Director, North Carolina Department of Administration
112 W. Lane St.
218 Howard Bldg.
Raleigh, NC 27611
Phone: (919) 733-6700

North Dakota
Director, North Dakota Occupational Information Coordinating Committee
1424 W. Century Ave.
P.O. Box 1537
Bismarck, ND 58505
Phone: (701) 224-2733

Ohio
Director, Ohio Occupational Information Coordinating Committee
State Department Bldg.
65 S. Front St., Room 904
Columbus, OH 43215
Phone: (614) 466-2095

Oklahoma
Executive Director, Oklahoma Occupational Information Coordinating Committee
School of Occupational and Adult Education
Oklahoma State University
1515 W. 6th St.
Stillwater, OK 74074
Phone: (405) 377-2000, ext. 311

Oregon
Coordinator, Oregon Occupational Information Coordinating Committee
875 Union St., N.E.
Salem, OR 97311
Phone: (503) 378-8146

Pennsylvania
Director, Pennsylvania Occupational Information Coordinating Committee
Labor and Industry Bldg.
7th and Forster Sts., Room 1008
Harrisburg, PA 17120
Phone: (717) 787-3467

Puerto Rico
Executive Director, Puerto Rico Occupational Information Coordinating Committee
Cond. El Centro II, Suite 224
Múnoz Rivera Ave.
Hato Rey, PR 00918
Phone: (809) 753-7110

Rhode Island
Executive Director, Rhode Island Occupational Information Coordinating Committee
22 Hayes St., Room 315
Providence, RI 02908
Phone: (401) 272-0830

South Carolina
Director, South Carolina Occupational Information Coordinating Committee
1550 Gladsden St.
Columbia, SC 29202
Phone: (803) 758-3165

South Dakota
Executive Director, South Dakota Occupational Information Coordinating Committee
108 E. Missouri
Pierre, SD 57501
Phone: (605) 773-3935

Tennessee
Director, Tennessee Occupational Information Coordinating Committee
512 Cordell Hull Bldg.
Nashville, TN 37219
Phone: (615) 741-6451

Texas
Executive Director, Texas Occupational Information Coordinating Committee
Texas Employment Commission Bldg.
15th and Congress, Room 526T
Austin, TX 78778
Phone: (512) 397-4970

Utah
Director, Utah Occupational Information Coordinating Committee
Elks Club Bldg., Suite 6003
139 East South Temple
Salt Lake City, UT 84111
Phone: (801) 533-2028

Vermont
Director, Vermont Occupational Information Coordinating Committee
P.O. Box 488
Montpelier, VT 05602
Phone: (802) 229-0311

Virginia
SOICC Director, Virginia Vocational and Adult Education
Department of Education
P.O. Box 6Q
Richmond, VA 23216
Phone: (804) 225-2735

Washington
SOICC Director, Washington Commission for Vocational Education
Bldg. 17, Airdustrial Park
Mail Stop LS-10
Olympia, WA 98504
Phone: (206) 754-1552

West Virginia
Executive Director, West Virginia State Occupational Information Coordinating Committee
1600½ Washington St., E.
Charleston, WV 25311
Phone: (304) 348-0061

Wisconsin
Director, Wisconsin Occupational Information Coordinating Committee
Educational Sciences Building, Room 952
1025 W. Johnson
Madison, WI 53706
Phone: (608) 263-1048

Wyoming
Director, Wyoming Occupational Information Coordinating Committee
Hathaway Bldg.—Basement
2300 Capitol Ave.
Cheyenne, WY 82002
Phone: (307) 777-7177 or 7178

American Samoa
Executive Director, American Samoa SOICC, Governor's Office
American Samoa Government
Pago Pago, American Samoa 96799

Guam
Acting Executive Director, Guam Occupational Information Coordinating Committee
P.O. Box 2817
Agana, GU 96910
Phone: (617) 477-8941

Northern Mariana Islands
Executive Director, Northern Mariana Islands Occupational Information Coordinating Committee
P.O. Box 149
Saipan, Northern Mariana Islands 96950
Phone: 7136

Trust Territory of the Pacific
Director, Trust Territory of the Pacific Islands
Occupational Information Coordinating Committee
Office of Planning and Statistics
Saipan, Mariana Islands 96950

Virgin Islands
Director, Virgin Islands Occupational Information Coordinating Committee
Department of Education
P.O. Box 630, Charlotte Amalie
St. Thomas, VI 00801
Phone: (809) 774-0100, ext. 211

CITIZENS BAND RADIO COMMUNICATIONS

TEN SIGNAL CODES

Radio communication codes vary by types of transmisson and are constantly undergoing change. Shown below are two CB ten signals codes. One is the official code of the Associated Public Safety Communications Officiers, Inc. The other code is an older variation, still used by some CBers, but generally being superseded by the newer and shorter version.

OFFICIAL APCO CODE

10-1 signal weak.
10-2 signal good.
10-3 stop transmitting.
10-4 affirmative (OK).
10-5 relay (to).
10-6 busy.
10-7 out of service.
10-8 in service.
10-9 say again.
10-10 negative.
10-11 ________ on duty.
10-12 stand by (Stop).
10-13 existing conditions.
10-14 message/information.
10-15 message delivered.
10-16 reply to message.
10-17 enroute.
10-18 urgent.
10-19 (in) contact.
10-20 location.
10-21 call (________) by phone.
10-22 disregard.
10-23 arrived at scene.
10-24 assignment completed.
10-25 report to (meet).
10-26 estimated arrival time.
10-27 license/permit information.
10-28 ownership information.
10-29 records check.
10-30 danger / caution.
10-31 pick up.
10-32 ________ units needed specify / number / type.
10-33 help me quick.
10-34 time.

TRADITIONAL TEN CODE

10-1 receiving poorly.
10-2 receiving well.
10-3 stop transmitting.
10-4 Ok, message received.
10-5 relay message.
10-6 busy, stand by.
10-7 out of service, leaving air.
10-8 in service, subject to call.
10-9 repeat message.
10-10 transmission complete, standing by.
10-11 talking too rapidly.
10-12 visitors present.
10-13 advise weather and road condition.
10-16 make pickup at ________.
10-17 urgent business.
10-18 anything for us?
10-19 nothing for you, return to base.
10-20 my location is ________.
10-21 call by telephone.
10-22 report in person to ________.
10-23 stand by.
10-24 completed last assignment.
10-25 can you contact ________.
10-26 disregard last message.
10-27 I am moving to Channel ________.
10-28 identify your station.
10-29 time is up for contact.
10-30 does not conform to FCC rules.
10-32 I will give you a radio check.
10-33 emergency traffic at this station.
10-34 trouble at this station, need help.
10-35 confidential information.
10-36 correct time is ________.
10-37 wrecker needed at ________.
10-38 ambulance needed at ________.
10-39 your message delivered.
10-41 please tune to channel ________.
10-42 traffic accident at ________.
10-43 traffic tieup at ________.
10-44 I have a message for you.
10-45 all units within range please report.
10-46 assist motorist.
10-50 break channel.
10-60 what is next message number?
10-62 unable to copy; use phone.
10-63 network directed to ________.
10-64 network clear.
10-65 awaiting your next message / assignment.
10-67 all units comply.
10-69 message received.
10-70 fire at ________.
10-71 proceed with transmission in sequence.
10-73 speed trap at ________.
10-74 negative.
10-75 you are causing interference.
10-77 negative contact.
10-81 reserve hotel room for ________.
10-82 reserve room for ________.
10-84 my telephone number is ________.
10-85 my address is ________.
10-89 radio repairman needed at ________.
10-90 I have T.V.I.
10-91 talk closer to the mike.
10-92 your transmission is out of adjustment.
10-93 check my frequency on this channel.
10-94 please give me a long count.
10-95 transmit dead carrier for five seconds.
10-97 check test signal.
10-99 mission completed, all units secure.
100-200 police needed at ________.

CB DICTIONARY

AFFIRMATIVE yes
ALLIGATOR a CBer who transmits but doesn't reply.
ANCHOR MAN a base-station operator.
BABY BUGGY school bus.
BACKGROUND interference noise heard on CB radio.
BACK OFF 1. stop transmitting. 2. slow down.
BACKSIDE return trip.
BACK TO YOU used to let whomever you're talking to know it's his turn to talk.
BANDMASTER 1. person acting as a "dispatcher" who gives others permission to talk on a channel. 2. person with a very powerful signal.
BARLEY POP beer.
BASE STATION a transceiver maintained at a fixed location.
BEAN STORE a restaurant.
BEAR police of any kind.
BEAR BAIT a speeding vehicle without CB.
BEAR BITE speeding ticket.
BEAR CAGE police station.
BEAR CAVE police or highway patrol station located on a highway.
BEAR DEN police station located off the highway.
BEAR FOOD speeding vehicle without CB.
BEAR IN THE AIR police helicopter or airplane.
BEAR IN THE SKY same as BEAR IN THE AIR.
BEAR MEAT same as BEAR FOOD.
BEAT THE BUSHES first truck in a line of two or more is said to BEAT THE BUSHES as he checks out road conditions and location of police ahead.
BELLY UP truck that's flipped over.
BENNY CHASER coffee.
BIG BROTHER police of any kind.
BIG DADDY the FCC.
BIG SLAB expressway, (also SUPER SLAB).
BIG SWITCH the on/off switch on a CB.
BIG 10-4 absolutely.
BIT ON THE SEAT OF THE BRITCHES got a speeding ticket.
BLEEDING signal from adjacent channel interrupting transmission.
BLEW MY DOORS OFF passed with great speed.
BLOCKING THE CHANNEL pressing the microphone switch without talking thereby preventing others from communicating.
BLOWING SMOKE a loud, strong signal. "You're blowing smoke tonight, good buddy."
BLOOD BANK ambulance.
BLUE AND WHITE police.
BLUE BOOK CB dictionary.
BLUE BOYS police.
BLUE SKIES AND GREEN LIGHTS TO YOU best wishes.
BOB TAILING a truck tractor traveling without a trailer.
BOONDOCK taking back roads to avoid a weight station.
BOULEVARD interstate highway.
BOX ON WHEELS hearse.
BOY SCOUTS state police.
BREAKER a CBer who wants to come in on a channel.
BREAK FOR (SPECIFIC PERSON) a call for a specific CBer on the channel.
BREAKING UP signal is erratic and difficult to comprehend.
BROWN PAPER BAG unmarked police car.
BUBBLE GUM MACHINE any vehicle with flashing lights on top, usually a police car.
BUCK ROGERS MACHINE a hand-held radar unit used by certain highway patrols.

BUCKET OF BOLTS — tractor-trailer rig, (also any truck).
BUDDY — fellow trucker or CBer.
BUG OUT — to leave a channel.
BUGS ON THE GLASS — INSECTS ON THE WINDSHIELD.
BULLDOG — Mack truck.
BUTTON PUSHER — a person who pushes his microphone button without talking, causing interference.
BUSHEL — 1000 pounds.
CALL LETTERS — official FCC letters and numbers assigned to a CB operator.
CAMERA — police radar, (also Kodak).
CANDY MAN — FCC field enforcement officer.
CATCH CAR — police car used to make speeding arrests, while another policeman is manning radar.
CATTLE CAR — bus.
CB — citizens band radio.
CHANNEL MASTER — person acting as a "dispatcher," who gives permission to talk on a channel.
CHARLIE, CHARLIE-CHARLIE or CHARLIE BROWN — yes
CHASE CAR — police car with hidden radar.
CHICKEN COOP — weight station.
CHICKEN COOP IS CLEAN — weight station is closed.
CHICKEN INSPECTOR — weight station inspector.
CHOPPER — helicopter.
CHRISTMAS CARD — speeding ticket.
CHRISTMAS TREE LIGHTS — running lights around a truck cab.
CLEAN AND GREEN — road is clear of police and obstructions.
CLEAN AS A HOUND'S TOOTH — same as above.
CLEANER CHANNEL — channel with less interference.
CLEAN SHOT — no police or road construction visible.
CLEAR — through transmitting.
CLEAR AND ROLLING — signing off and moving.
COLLECT CALL — message for a specific CBer.
COLORS GOING UP — policeman turning on lights atop patrol car.
COME BACK — answer me, also COME HERE, COME ON.
CONCRETE RIBBON — expressway.
COOKIES — cigaretts, also WEEDS.
COOKING — driving.
COOKING GOOD — driving above the legal speed limit.
COP FLOP — police-car U turn.
COPY — to understand or receive a transmission.
COUNTY MOUNTY — local police or sheriff's deputy.
COUPON — speeding ticket.
COUNTRY CADILLAC — a pick-up truck.
COUNTRY JOE — rural police.
CRANK UP THE MIKE — turn up the preamplifier.
CUB SCOUTS — sheriff's deputies
CUT LOOSE — sign off, stop transmitting.
CUT THE COAX — turn off the CB.
DADDY-O — the FCC.
DEAD PEDAL — slow driver.
DECOY — unmanned police car.
DEFINITELY — without a doubt.
DINGY WEEDS — the country.
DOG BOX — gear box.
DOG HOUSE — motor cover.
DOING THE 5-5 — driving at 55 miles per hour.
DON'T FEED THE BEARS — don't get a speeding ticket.
DOT — Department of Transport.
DOT MAN — U.S. Dept. of Transport representative.
DOUBLE NICKEL — the 55 mph speed limit.
DOUGHNUT — tire.
DOWN AND GONE — a sign off, turning off CB.
DOWN AND ON THE SIDE — through talking, but monitoring.
DOWN ONE — going to a lower channel.
DO YOU COPY? — "Do you understand?"
DRAGGIN' WAGON — a wrecker.
DROPPED IT OFF THE SHOULDER — ran off the side of the highway.
DUDLEY DO-RIGHT — a policeman.
DUMMY — unmanned police car.
DX — long distance.
EARS — antennas.
EARS ON — CB radio turned on.
EIGHTEEN WHEELER — tractor-trailer truck.
EIGHTMILER — four-wheeler who keeps you guessing for eight miles or more because he's left his turn signals on.
EIGHTS AND OTHER GOOD NUMBERS — best wishes.
EIGHTY-EIGHTS — love and kisses.
EVERYBODY MUST BE WALKING THE DOG — all channels are busy.
EVEL KNEIVEL — motorcycle rider.
EVEL KNEIVEL SMOKEY — motorcycle police.
EYE IN THE SKY — police helicopter.
FAT LOAD — overloaded.
FED INSPECTOR — DOT or FCC.
FEED THE BEARS — to get caught speeding or to pay a speeding fine.
FENDER BENDER — vehicle collision.
FINAL — end of transmission.
FIND A CLEAN ONE — switch to channel with less conversation.
FIREWORKS — police car lights.
FIVE-FIVE — 55 mph.
FLAG WAVER — highway worker.
FLATBED — tractor trailer with flatbed.
FLIP OR FLIP-FLOP — return trip.
FLIP-FLOPPING BEARS — police reversing directions.
FLUFF STUFF — snow.
FLYING KITES — material falling off back of truck.
FOR SURE — that's right.
FOUR — right, OK.
FOUR-LANE PARKING LOT — crowded expressway.
FOUR-TEN — 10-4; right on!
FOUR WHEELER — a passenger car.
FREIGHT TRAIN — tractor with two or three trailers.
FRONT DOOR — lead rig in line of two or more trucks.
FUNNY FARM — retirement home, especially for old truckers.
GANDY DANCER — road construction worker.
GBY — God Bless You.
GEARJAMMER — truck driver.
GENERATING — transmitting.
GET HORIZONTAL — go to sleep.
GET TRUCKING — make some distance.
GIRLIE BEAR — policewoman.
GIVE A SHOUT — answer back.
GLITCH — an indefinable technical defect in CB equipment.
GLORY WAGON — wildly decorated semi or truck.
GO AHEAD — answer back.
GO, BREAKER — permission for a BREAKER to speak on the channel.
GO JUICE or GO-GO JUICE — gas, fuel.
GOIN' HOME GEAR — high gear.
GOOD BUDDY — another CBer.
GOODIED UP — heavily accessorized.
GOOD SHOT — road clear of police and obstructions.
GOT A COPY — do you hear?
GRANNY GEAR — low gear.
GRAVEL BUGGY — dump truck.
GREEN LIGHT — road clear of police and obstructions.
G.S. — great signal!
GREEN STAMPS — money, dollars, used for paying tickets.
GREEN STAMP COLLECTOR — traffic court judge.
GREEN STAMP HIGHWAY — toll road.
GROUND CLOUDS — fog.
GUTTER BALLING — bowling.
HAIRCUT PALACE — bridge with low clearance.
HAMMER — accelerator.
HAMMER DOWN, ON — to accelerate.
HAMMER OFF, UP — to slow down.
HANDLE — CBer's nickname.
HANG A RIGHT (LEFT) — turn right (or left).
HANG A UEY — make a U-turn.
HANGER — garage.
HARD TO PULL OUT — difficult to understand.
HARVEY WALL BANGER — reckless driver.
HIDING IN THE BUSHES — police hiding.
HI-BALL HEAVEN — truck stop.
HIT THE HAY — go to sleep.
HOLE IN THE WALL — tunnel.
HOLDING ON TO YOUR MUD FLAPS — driving right behind another vehicle.
HOLLER — transmit.
HOME PORT — residence.
HOO-HOOER — airhorn.
HOW AM I HITTING YOU? — do you receive my signal?
HYDROPLANE — truck skidding on wet pavement.
ICE BOX — refrigerator truck.
IN A SHORT SHORT — soon.
IN THE BUSHES — off the road
IN THE GRASS — on the median divider or shoulder.
JACK IT UP — accelerate.
JACK RABBIT — speeder.
JAW JACKING — talking over.
KEEP 'EM BETWEEN THE DITCHES — drive safely.
KEYBOARD — controls on CB set.
KEYING THE MIKE — activating the mike without speaking.
KIDDIE CAR — a school bus.
KIDNEY-BUSTER — a truck.
KODAK — police radar.
KOJACK WITH A KODAK — police with radar.
KOOL AID — beer.
LADY BEAR — policewoman.
LADY BREAKER — female CB operator.
LAND LINE — telephone.
LATCH-ON — vehicle without CB following one with CB.
LAY IT OVER — stand by.
LET IT ROLL — accelerate.
LET THE HAMMER DOWN — drive full speed.
LETTUCE — money.
LET YOUR FLAPS DOWN — slow down.
LISTENING IN — monitoring.
LIT CANDLES — police-car lights turned on.
LOCAL BEARS — local police.
LOG SOME Z'S — get some sleep.
LOOKING GOOD — putting out a strong signal.
MAMA BEAR — police woman.
MANIAC — mechanic.
MAN IN BLUE — any policeman.
MAN IN WHITE — doctor.
MARKER — milepost along interstate.
MAYDAY — distress call. (10-34)
MEAT WAGON — ambulance.

MEXICAN OVERDRIVE	neutral gear.
MIDNIGHT SHOPPER	thief.
MILE POST.	marker.
MIX MASTER	highway clover leaf.
MIXING BOWL	same as above.
MOBILE PARKING LOT	auto carrier.
MONITOR	to listen, but not participate in CB conversation.
MOTOR MOUTH	constant talker.
MOTORING	traveling on.
MOUNTIES IN THE SKY	police in helicopter.
MOVABLE PARKING LOT	automobile transport.
MOVING FOREST	log-carrying truck.
M-TWENTY	meeting place.
MUD	coffee.
NAP TRAP	rest area or motel.
NATURE STOP	rest-room stop.
NEGATIVE CONTACT	station being called but not responding.
NEGATIVE COPY	no answer.
NEGATORY	no.
NIGHT CRAWLERS	unmarked police cars at night.
NINE-TO-FIVER	truck driver who only makes short runs.
OIL BURNER	car with smoking exhaust.
ON STAND BY	listening, but not transmitting.
ON THE SIDE	parked.
ONE	the original.
ONE-EYED MONSTER	a TV set
ONE HIDING IN THE GRASS	police in the median.
OUT OF IT	signing off.
OVER YOUR SHOULDER	on the road directly behind you.
PACK IT UP	finish
PAPA BEAR	state trooper with CB.
PAPER HANGER	police giving speeding tickets.
PAPER WORK	speeding ticket.
PART YOUR HAIR	be on your best behavior, police ahead.
PEAK POWER	maximum wattage.
PEDAL A LITTLE SLOWER	slow down.
PEELING OFF	getting off the expressway.
PEPPERMILL	cinder-spreading truck in winter.
PICKING PEAS	police using radar.
PICTURE BOX	police radar unit.
PIGEON	vehicle stopped by police.
PIGGY BANK	toll booth.
PIT STOP	fuel stop.
PLAY DEAD	standby.
POLAROID	radar.
PORCH LIGHTS	spot lights or fog lights.
PORKY BEAR	any police.
PORTABLE CHICKEN COOP	mobile weighing station.
PORTABLE GAS STATION	tank truck carrying gasoline.
PORTABLE PARKING LOT	auto carrier.
PORTRAIT PAINTER	police radar.
POSITIVE	yes. affirmative.
PRESS SOME SHEETS	get some sleep.
PRESSURE COOKER	sportscar.
PULL THE PLUG.	signoff.
PULL YOUR HAMMER BACK	slow down.
PUMPKIN	flat tire.
PUSHING A RIG	driving a truck.
PUT AN EYEBALL ON	look at.
PUT THE GOOD NUMBERS ON YOU	best wishes.
PUT THE HAMMER DOWN	accelerate.
RATCHET JAW	CBer who talks too much.
RATCHET JAWING	talking; idle talking.
RAT RACE	heavy traffic.
READ	to understand or receive a transmission.
READ THE MAIL	to monitor a channel.
RELOCATION CONSULTANT	moving van.
RIBBON	highway.
RIG	truck or CB transceiver.
RINGING YOUR BELL	"Someone's calling you."
ROAD JOCKEY	driver of tractor trailer.
ROGER	yes, okay.
ROGER DODGER	same as ROGER, also "Roger D."
ROGER RAMJET	driver of car going well over speed limit.
ROLLERSKATE	any small or foreign car.
ROLLING	moving, especially, on the road.
ROLLING BEARS	police on the move.
RUBBERBANDER	a new CBer who doesn't know the CB language.
RUNNING SHOTGUN	driving partner.
SAFE TRUCKIN'	good trip.
SALT MINE	place of employment.
SALT SHAKER	salt spreading truck in winter.
SANDBAGGING	monitoring, but not transmitting.
SAY WHAT	repeat.
SCALE HOUSE	truck weigh station.
SET OF DIALS	CB controls.
SET OF DOUBLES	tractor-trailer truck.
SEVEN THREE	a combination of the ten code meaning signing off.
SEVENTY-THREE(S)	best wishes.
SHAKEYSIDE	West Coast.
SHAKING IT	moving fast.
SHAKING THE WINDOWS	signal is coming in loud and clear.
SHANTY SHAKER	mobile-home driver.
SHORT SHOUT	brief CB conversation.
SHOT GUN	police radar device that looks like rifle or seat next to the driver.
SHOT OUR FIVE	to go beyond the FCC five minute limit.
SHOVELLING COAT	accelerating.
SHOW-OFF LANE	passing lane.
SIDEWINDER	single side band user.
SITTING ON THE BACK PORCH	parked near tunnel or underpass.
SITTING ON THE FRONT PORCH	located on bridge or overpass.
SIX WHEELER	small truck or car pulling trailer.
SILVER BUGLE	air horn.
SKATING RINK	slippery road.
SKIP TALK	long range conversation.
SKY BEAR	police helicopter.
SLAMMER	jail.
SLICK TOP	an unmarked police car with no light on top.
SMOKE REPORT	police location report.
SMOKE SCREEN	police radar.
SMOKE SOME DOPE	accelerate.
SMOKEY	police of any kind.
SMOKEY DOZING	police in parked car.
SMOKEY GRAZING GRASS	police in median strip
SMOKEY ON RUBBER	police moving.
SMOKEY'S THICK	police are everywhere.
SMOKEY TWO WHEELER	motorcycle cop.
SMOKEY WITH A CAMERA	police with radar.
SMOKEY WITH EARS	police with CB.
SPARKIE	electrician.
SPY IN THE SKY	police helicopter.
SQUAWK BOX	CB radio.
STAGE STOP	truck stop.
STARVE THE BEARS	don't get a ticket.
STATE BEAR	state trooper.
STEPPED ALL OVER YOU	interrupted your transmission.
STEPPING	moving.
STOP TO GET GROCERIES	stop and eat.
STRAIGHT SHOT	road clear of police and obstructions.
STREAKING	going at full speed.
STRETCHED IT OUT	picked up speed.
STUFFY	congested
SUDS	beer
SUGAR FOOT	speeder who never gets caught.
SUICIDE CARGO	dangerous cargo.
SUICIDE JOCKEY	trucker carrying explosives.
SUPER SKATE	sports car.
SUPER SLAB	expressway, interstate highway.
SUPPOSITORY	negative.
SURFER	experienced CBer.
TAGS	license plates.
TAKE IT BACK	your turn to talk.
TAKING PICTURES	police using radar.
TAKING PICTURES EACH WAY	police using radar in both directions.
TANKER	trailer carrying liquid.
TATTLETALE	police in sky
TENNIS SHOES	truck tires.
TEN ROGER	message received.
TEN-TEN, TILL WE DO IT AGAIN	signing off and see you soon.
TEN, BYE BYE	good-bye.
TEN POUNDER	excellent radio.
TENSE	congested traffic.
THERMOS BOTTLE	tank truck.
THREES AND EIGHTS (73s AND 88s)	best regards.
THREES ON YOU	best regards!
TOOLED-UP	a souped-up rig.
TRADING STAMPS	money.
TRAFFIC	CB conversation.
TRAMPOLINE	bed.
TRANSPORTER	any truck.
TRUCK STOP COMMANDO	duded-up trucker with fancy clothes.
TUCK IT IN	move into right lane.
TURN AROUND	return trip.
TURN TWENTY	location of next exit or turn.
TWENTY	location.
TWO MILES OF DITCHES FOR EVERY MILE OF ROAD	"Keep your rig in the middle of the road and drive safely."
VAN	tractor-trailer truck.
VOICE CHECK	radio check.
WALKIN'T	walkie talkie.
WALKING ON YOU	covering up your transmission.
WALKING TALL	a superpowerful CB signal.
WALL TO WALL BEARS	police all over the place.
WATCH THE PAVEMENT	drive safely.
WEST COAST MIRRORS	mirrors on both sides of cab.
WHAT ARE YOU PUSHING?	What are you driving?
WHAT'S YOUR TWENTY?	"Where are you?"
WHERE DO YOU GET YOUR GREEN STAMPS?	Where do you work?
WHO DO YOU PULL FOR?	Who do you work for?
WILLY WEAVER	drunk driver.
WINDOW WASHER	rainstorm.
WORK TWENTY	place of employment.
WORKING THE MOONLIGHT EXPRESS	running back roads at night to avoid weigh stations.
X-RAY MACHINE	police radar.
YELLOWSTONE PARK	a gathering of police.
YO	yes.
YO YO	vehicle varying speed.
ZOO	bear headquarters.